Thirty-Fourth Edition

Blue Book of Gun Values™

by S.P. Fjestad

$49.95 - Publisher's Softcover Suggested List Price

$85.00 - Publisher's Limited Edition Hardcover Suggested List Price (limited quantities)

Thirty-Fourth Edition

Blue Book of Gun Values™

Publisher's Note:

This book is the result of nonstop and continuous firearms research obtained by attending and/or participating in trade shows, gun shows, auctions, and also communicating with contributing editors, gun dealers, collectors, company historians, and other knowledgeable industry professionals worldwide each year. This book represents an analysis of prices for which collectible firearms have actually been selling during that period at an average retail level. Although every reasonable effort has been made to compile an accurate and reliable guide, gun prices may vary significantly (especially auction prices) depending on such factors as the locality of the sale, the number of sales we were able to consider, and economic conditions. Accordingly, no representation can be made that the guns listed may be bought or sold at prices indicated, nor shall the author or publisher be responsible for any error made in compiling and recording such prices and related information.

Blue Book Publications, Inc.
8009 34th Avenue South, Suite 250
Minneapolis, MN 55425 U.S.A.

Customer Service: 800-877-4867, ext. 3 (domestic only)
Phone No.: 952-854-5229
Fax No.: 952-853-1486
General Email: support@bluebookinc.com
Web site: www.bluebookofgunvalues.com

Published and printed in the United States of America

ISBN 10: 1-936120-31-3
ISBN 13: 978-1-936120-31-4

Library of Congress ISSN number - 1524-6043

Electronic Access ID Code: 31032320

Distributed in part to the book trade by Ingram Book Company and Baker & Taylor.

Distributed throughout Europe by:

Apex International
Austin Sheridan Inc.
89 Broad Street
Middleton, CT 06457
www.austinsheridanusa.com

Visier GmbH
Wipsch 1
Bad Ems, Germany D-56130
www.vsmedien.de

Deutsches Waffen Journal
Rudolf-Diesel-Strasse 46
Blaufelden, D-74572 Germany
Website: www.dwj.de

THE NRA FOUNDATION · NFM

HUNTING HERITAGE TRUST

TABLE OF CONTENTS

Title Page 1
Publisher's Note/Copyright 2
Table of Contents 3
Gun Questions/Appraisals Policy 4
Blue Book Publications, Inc. General Information 5-6
Meet the Staff 7
Acknowledgements 8-9
Fallen Comrades & Cover Credits 9
How to Use This Book 10-13
Anatomy of a Handgun 14
Anatomy of a Rifle 15
Anatomy of a Shotgun 16
Foreword by S.P. Fjestad 17-19
Jessie Duff – A Champion Who's Winning for Freedom 20-21
Grading Criteria 22
NRA Condition Standards 23
The PPGS – Firearms Grading Made Easy 24
Photo Percentage Grading System™ 25-102
34th Edition Calendar 62-63
Identifying/Buying Older Editions 103-104
Modern Firearms/Antiques Text & Pricing 105-2,208
NSSF Hunting 456
Autry National Center of the American West 770
NRA Membership Information 830
NRA Stand and Fight 1,370
Rock Island Arsenal Museum 1,890
Buffalo Bill Historical Center Information/Membership 1,966
National Firearms Museum (NFM) 2,020
Congressional Sportsmen's Foundation 2,190
Trademark Index 2,209-2,265
Glossary 2,266-2,287
Abbreviations 2,288-2,291
Museums 2,292
Firearms/Shooting Organizations 2,293-2,299
Hunting Heritage Trust 2,300
Conservation Organizations 2,301
Reference Sources 2,302-2,304
Periodicals 2,305-2,308
Store Brand Cross-Over Listings 2,309-2,315
Serialization 2,316-2,360
Proof Marks 2,361-2,367
BATFE Guide 2,368
BATFE Curios and Relics Listings 2,369-2,384
Show Time! 2,385
Index 2,386-2,407
P.S. 2,408

GUN QUESTIONS/APPRAISALS POLICY

Whether we wanted it or not, Blue Book Publications, Inc. has ended up in the driver's seat as the clearing house for gun information. Because the volume of gun questions now requires almost full-time attention, we have developed a standardized policy that will enable us to provide you with the service you have come to expect from Blue Book Publications, Inc. To that end, we have extended all of these services to our website (www.bluebookofgunvalues.com).

To ensure that the research department can answer every gun question with an equal degree of thoroughness, an extensive firearms research center has been established. It includes a massive library with well over 1,500 reference books, thousands of both new and old factory catalogs/brochures, price sheets, most major auction catalogs, and dealer inventory listings. It's a huge job, and unlike Wikipedia, we answer every question like we could go to court on it.

ONLINE SELF SERVICE

Customers can answer most of their gun questions themselves. Simply visit www.bluebookofgunvalues.com and click on Appraisals & Evaluations under the Information & Services tab for more information and pricing on these service options. It certainly is a big help to know the manufacturer/trademark and the model to use this service. To further assist you, on our website every firearms manufacturer, category, and model is listed, and a short model description is also provided free of charge. This will enable the consumer to ensure he/she selects the right make/model, or manufacturer/trademark before payment is made. There are three different levels of self service. Purchase information and current values on a single model, an entire manufacturer/trademark, or a one, two, or three-year online subscription for unlimited access to the *Blue Book of Gun Values* (best value). Color images are also available for many models and variations.

PHONE GUN QUESTIONS

The charge is $10 per gun value question, $15 per gun if the firearm's make and/or model needs to be identified first. Phone gun questions are payable with a major credit card. All phone gun questions are answered when time is permitting, on a first-come, first-serve basis. All value requests will be given within a range only, based on the accuracy of information the consumer provides – this is the most critical element of phone gun questions. Gun question telephone hours are 1:00 p.m. to 5:00 p.m., M-F, CST, no exceptions please. Phone gun questions are typically answered in 5 business days or less, unless the research staff has a production commitment or is away attending trade/gun shows.

APPRAISAL INFORMATION

Written appraisals will be performed only when time is permitting and if the following criteria are met. Research staff personnel must have good quality photos/images, a complete description(s), including manufacturer's name, model, gauge or caliber, barrel length, and other pertinent information. On some firearms, depending on the manufacturer/trademark and model, a factory letter may be necessary. Remember, since these written appraisals are done without physically inspecting the firearm(s), the appraised value(s) will only be as accurate as the information our research staff receives. High quality images are the single most important element on written appraisals. The charge for a written appraisal is 2% of the appraised value with a minimum of $30 per gun. For email appraisals, please refer to www.bluebookofgunvalues.com. Please allow 2-3 weeks response time per appraisal request.

ADDITIONAL SERVICES

Individuals requesting a photocopy of a particular page or section from any edition for insurance or reference purposes will be billed at $5 per page, up to 5 pages, and $3.50 per page thereafter. Please direct all gun questions and appraisals to:

Blue Book Publications, Inc.
Attn: Research Dept.
8009 34th Ave. S., Suite 250
Minneapolis, MN 55425 USA
Phone: 952-854-5229, ext. 16 • Fax: 952-853-1486 • www.bluebookofgunvalues.com
Email: guns@bluebookinc.com
Use "Firearm Inquiry" in the subject line or it may get deleted.

INTERESTED IN BUYING OR SELLING FIREARMS?

Over the course of many editions, we have received multiple requests for providing referrals for when buying, selling, or trading firearms. As Blue Book Publications, Inc. is a publisher, not a gun shop, this service is provided for the benefit of the buyer/seller to ensure they are treated fairly. There is no charge for this service, nor do we receive a commission (a thank you would be appreciated, however!). Our established international network of reliable dealers and collectors allows your particular buy or sell request to be referred to the most appropriate company/individual based on both your geographic location and area of collectibility. All replies are treated with strict confidentiality.

Please direct all inquiries to John Allen (see contact information above).
If this is an email request, please use "Referral" in the subject line or it may get deleted.

GENERAL INFORMATION

While many of you have probably dealt with our company for years, it may be helpful for you to know a little bit more about our operation, including information on how to contact us regarding our various titles and other informational services.

Blue Book Publications, Inc.
8009 34th Avenue South, Suite 250
Minneapolis, MN 55425 USA
GPS Coordinates: N44° 51 28.44, W93° 13.1709

Phone No.: 952-854-5229 • Orders Only (domestic and Canada): 800-877-4867
Fax No.: 952-853-1486 (available 24 hours a day)
Web site: www.bluebookofgunvalues.com

General Email: support@bluebookinc.com - we check our email at 9am, 12pm, and 4pm M - F (excluding major U.S. holidays). Please refer to individual email addresses listed below with phone extension numbers.

To find out the latest information on our products, including availability and pricing, consumer related services, and up-to-date industry information (blogs, trade show recaps with photos/captions, upcoming events, feature articles, etc.), please check our website, as it is updated on a regular basis. Surf us - you'll have fun!

Since our phone system is equipped with voice mail, you may also wish to know extension numbers, which have been provided below:

Ext. 10 - Beth Schreiber (beths@bluebookinc.com)	Ext. 16 - John Allen (johna@bluebookinc.com)
Ext. 11 - Katie Sandin (katies@bluebookinc.com)	Ext. 17 - Zach Fjestad (zachf@bluebookinc.com)
Ext. 12 – Aaron Bond (aaronb@bluebookinc.com)	Ext. 18 - Tom Stock (toms@bluebookinc.com)
Ext. 13 - S.P. Fjestad (stevef@bluebookinc.com)	Ext. 19 - Cassandra Faulkner (cassandraf@bluebookinc.com)
Ext. 14 - Kelsey Fjestad (kelseyf@bluebookinc.com)	Ext. 20 - Adam Burt (adamb@bluebookinc.com)
Ext. 15 - Clint Schmidt (clints@bluebookinc.com)	Ext. 22 – Kate Steffenson (kates@bluebookinc.com)

Office hours are: 8:30am - 5:00pm CST, Monday - Friday.

Additionally, an after-hours message service is available for ordering. All orders are processed within 24 hours of receiving them, assuming payment and order information is correct. Depending on the product, we typically ship Fed Ex, UPS, Media Mail, or Priority Mail. Expedited shipping services are also available domestically for an additional charge. Please contact us directly for an expedited shipping quotation.

All correspondence regarding technical information/values on guns or guitars is answered in a FIFO (first in, first out) system. That means that letters, faxes, and email are answered in the order in which they are received, even though some people think that their emails take preference over everything else.

GENERAL INFORMATION

Online subscriptions and informational services are available for the *Blue Book of Gun Values, Blue Book of Modern Black Powder Arms, Ammo Encyclopedia, American Gunsmiths, Blue Book of Airguns, Ammo Encyclopedia, Blue Book of Pool Cues, Blue Book of Electric Guitars, Blue Book of Acoustic Guitars,* and the *Blue Book of Guitar Amplifiers.*

As this edition goes to press, the following titles/products are currently available, unless otherwise specified:

Blue Book of Gun Values, 34th Edition by S.P. Fjestad
Blue Book of Tactical Firearms, 4th Edition by S.P. Fjestad
John Bianchi – An American Legend – 50 Years of Gunleather by Dennis Adler
3rd Edition *The Book of Colt Firearms* by R.L. Wilson
Blue Book Pocket Guide for Colt Dates of Manufacture, 2nd Edition by R.L. Wilson
Blue Book Pocket Guide for Browning/FN Firearms & Values by S.P. Fjestad
Blue Book Pocket Guide for Winchester Firearms & Values by S.P. Fjestad
Blue Book Pocket Guide for Smith & Wesson Firearms & Values by S.P. Fjestad
Blue Book Pocket Guide for Remington Firearms & Values by S.P. Fjestad
Black Powder Revolvers - Reproductions & Replicas by Dennis Adler
Black Powder Long Arms & Pistols - Reproductions & Replicas by Dennis Adler
Book of Colt Paper 1834-2011 by John Ogle
8th Edition *Blue Book of Modern Black Powder Arms* by John Allen
Ammo Encyclopedia, 4th Edition by Michael Bussard
American Engravers – The 21st Century by C. Roger Bleile
Mario Terzi – Master Engraver by Elena Micheli-Lamboy & Stephen Lamboy
Firmo & Francesca Fracassi – Master Engravers by Elena Micheli-Lamboy & Stephen Lamboy
Giancarlo & Stefano Pedretti – Master Engravers by Elena Micheli-Lamboy & Stephen Lamboy
10th Anniversary Edition *Blue Book of Airguns* by Dr. Robert D. Beeman & John B. Allen
American Gunsmiths, 2nd Edition by Frank Sellers
Parker Gun Identification & Serialization, compiled by Charlie Price and edited by S.P. Fjestad
Blue Book of Electric Guitars, 14th Edition, by Zachary R. Fjestad
Blue Book of Acoustic Guitars, 14th Edition, by Zachary R. Fjestad
Blue Book of Guitar Amplifiers, 4th Edition, by Zachary R. Fjestad
Blue Book of Guitars 14th Edition DVD-ROM
Blue Book of Guitar Amplifiers 4th Edition CD-ROM
The Gibson Flying V by Larry Meiners & Zachary R. Fjestad
Gibson Amplifiers 1933-2008 – 75 Years of the Gold Tone by Wallace Marx Jr.
The Marshall Bluesbreaker – The Story of Marshall's First Combo by John R. Wiley

If you would like to get more information about any of the above publications/products, simply check our web sites: www.bluebookofgunvalues.com and www.bluebookofguitarvalues.com

We would like to thank all of you for your business in the past – you are the reason we are successful. Our goal remains the same – to give you the best products, the most accurate and up-to-date information for the money, and the highest level of customer service available in today's marketplace. If something's right, tell the world over time. If something's wrong, please tell us immediately – we'll make it right.

MEET THE STAFF

Many of you may want to know what the person on the other end of the telephone/ fax/email looks like, so here are the faces that go with the voices and emails.

S.P. Fjestad
Author/Publisher

John B. Allen
Author & Associate Editor Arms Division

Adam Burt
Business Development Officer

Cassandra Faulkner
Executive Editor

Lisa Beuning
Manuscript Editor

David Kosowski
Copy Editor

Tom Stock
CFO

Clint H. Schmidt
Art Director

Aaron Bond
Technology Director

Zachary R. Fjestad
Author/Editor Guitar & Amp Division

Kelsey Fjestad
Web Media Manager/Proofreader

Beth Schreiber
Operations Manager

Katie Sandin
Operations

Kate Steffenson
Operations

ACKNOWLEDGEMENTS

The most often asked question I get on the *Blue Book of Gun Values* is, "How do you come up with all the values and information for the book?" My standardized answer is that on older guns, I have the best group of contributing editors that's ever been assembled for a pricing guide like this. These people are truly experts within their field(s) and deserve much of the credit on older makes/models. I can't tell you how thankful I am for all their help, support, and sharing their knowledge. Without them, this new 34th Edition would have been a lot thinner, and you wouldn't be as well informed and up-to-date.

Leonardo M. Antaris, M.D.
David Kosowski
Corey, Brian, and Bob Creamer
Rodney Herrmann
Wolf von Baumbach
Peter Horn II – The Beretta Gallery
Bill Mullins
Gary Przibilla
G. Brad Sullivan
Charles Layson
Lowell Pauli
Vic Venters
David Grant
Thomas Mintner
Randy Shuman
Glen Nilson
LeRoy Merz
Jerry Bryant
Wilmer Kellogg
Richard Machniak
Randy Davis
Dale Barnhart
Michael Kelly
Greg Martin
Glen Jensen, Cindy Jensen & Jackie Love of Browning
Beverly Haynes & Richard Churchill – Colt
Cristie Gates – Benelli USA
Jeff Swisher – H&K USA
Linda Powell – Mossberg
Alice Poluchova – CZ USA
Frank Pycha III
William Peets
Jim Supica, Phil Schreier, & Doug Wicklund from the National Firearms Museum
Rick Nahas
Larry Baer
Pat McKune
Anthony Vanderlinden
Roy Marcot
Gene Myszkowski
Doug Drummond
Michael & Karen Salisbury
Ken Blauch
Paul Pluff – Smith & Wesson
Dwight Van Brunt – Kimber
JB & Adam Blalock – Umarex USA
Stephen Wang
David Kennedy
Steve Engleson
Richard McMillan
Bill Cross
Morris Hallowell IV
Don Herigstad
John Gyde
Don Grove
Casey Nanz
Richard Desira
Mike Vertesch
Mike Finlay – Marlin
Chris Killoy & Ken Jorgensen – Sturm, Ruger & Co.
Bill Dermody & Ron Coburn – Savage Arms Co.
Eyck Pflaumer, Wulf Pflaumer, & Monika Bräutigam – Umarex Sportwaffen GmbH & Co. KG
Bruce Hart
Michael Gerulat
Richard Hummel - GGCA
Don "Duck" Combs
Gene Weicht
Ron Lough
Bill Allen
Stanley J. Ruselowski, Jr. - Glock Collector's Assoc.
Kurt House
George C. Carlson
Pat Hogan, Judy Voss & Matt Parise – Rock Island Auctions
Nick Ranzau & David Babcock – Jaqua's
Dave Trauth
Graham Greener
Jim Stubbendieck
Larry Sidener
Ian Skennerton
Dietrich Apel
John Stimson, Jr.
Axel Eichendorff
Keith Bernkrant – European American Armory
Jim Hauff
Kevin Cherry
Gurney Brown
Elena Micheli-Lamboy, Ph.D.
Stephen Lamboy
Jay Hansen
Carol and the late Don Wilkerson
Jim Ellis
Hermann Gerig, D.D.S.
Johannes Roller
Craig Gholson – Nighthawk Custom
Brian Parsons – Lion Country Supply
Tom Covault
Robert Rayburn
Bob Maze
Jean Verney-Carron
Bertram O'Neill, Jr.
Richard Spurzem
Gary Chatham
Tony Palermo
John Groenewold
Joe Gillenwater
John T. Callahan
Larry "Iron" Orr
Dave Wills
Charles Semmer
Lt. Col. Mark Rendina
David M. Rachwal
Rick Crosier
Mike Streitbeck
Dr. Joseph Eisenlauer
Brook Davis
CWO Ric Cameron
Barry Delong
Stefan Cohn
Hal Hamilton
Dan Shuck
Scott Grof
James Thynne
Brad Simpson
James A. Buelow
John Lacy
Chad Hiddleson
Glen Mattox
Jim Gentile

ACKNOWLEDGEMENTS

Joel Ziegler
Gordon Hanlan
Leon DeSpain
Richard Skeuse – Parker Reproductions
John Kopec
Orvin Olson
John Picchetti
J.B. Wood
Jack Lesher
Martin J. Lane
Jim King
Harry Klein
Rick Maples
Dieter Krieghoff
Einar Hoff & Danny Spann – Merkel USA
Rob Johansen – SKB
George Fram, Victor & Cheryl Havlin – Mossberg Collectors Association
R.L. Wilson
John Dougan
Dennis Adler
Bob Radaker
The Fausti girls!
Robert (Doc) Adelman aka, "mad" rocket scientist
Dr. Robert & Toshika Beeman (Honorary)
Doug Turnbull
Marv Adams
Jessica Kallam - Remington
Sue & Tammy – Taylor's & Co.
T. Rees Day
R.W. Elliott
Tor Karstensen
Jon W. Miller, MD, Ken Rabeneck, Maylene Rabeneck, Steve Schrott, Jerry Watson, Brad Adams, Bill Bryant & the High Standard Collectors Association
Gail Foster, Alvin Olson, Dale Peterson, Tony Schwab & the Minnesota Weapons Collectors Association
Warren Newman and crew from the Buffalo Bill Historical Center in Cody, WY
Mike Splittgerber
Lee Sundermeier
Bill Hamm
Mike Womble
Robert Livingston
Steve Adamson
Matt Olivier
Henry Bone
Sam Johnson
Vincent Carabetta
Greg Harp
Dale Dalbotten
John Fairbanks
David Noll
Dean Rinehart
A.O. Salvo
Jim Foral
Larry Wales
Edward King
Paul Warden – America Remembers
J. Purdey & Sons – Nigel Beaumont and crew
Todd Tuttle - Primary Weapons Systems
Holland & Holland - Daryl Greatrex, Roger Mitchell (ret.), Robert Pearson, David Winks (ret.), David Cruz, Guy Davies, and Russell Wilkin
Browning Collectors Association
German Gun Collectors Association
Mannlicher Collectors Association
L.C. Smith Collectors Association
Ruger Collectors Association (RCA)
Colt Collectors Association (CCA)
Remington Society of America

FALLEN COMRADES

Knox Baldwin – An old southern gentleman from Nashville, TN, Knox's inimitable style and southern drawl will be missed on the gun show circuit.

Araldo Piotti – This gifted craftsman helped start the famous firm of Piotti in 1955, located in Gardone, Italy. It remains one of the finest firearms manufacturers in the world.

CREDITS

Cover design and layout – Douglas Sandberg, Clint H. Schmidt, and S.P. Fjestad

Cover photography – courtesy Douglas Sandberg

Inside layout and design – Clint H. Schmidt

Manuscript Supervision – Lisa Beuning and Cassandra Faulkner

Proofing & Corrections – John B. Allen, Kelsey Fjestad, Cassandra Faulkner, Lisa Beuning, and S.P. Fjestad

PPGS Images – courtesy of Rock Island Auctions (RIA) with special thanks to Judy Voss and Matthew Parise, and Leonardo M. Antaris, MD

Printing – Steve Williamsen and crew from R.R. Donnelley in Crawfordsville, IN

Calculators – courtesy of Tony Martin

HOW TO USE THIS BOOK

The values listed in this 34th Edition of the *Blue Book of Gun Values* are based on national average retail prices paid for both modern and antique firearms, and some accessories/acoutrements. This is not a firearms wholesale pricing guide. More importantly, do not expect to walk into a gun/pawn shop or gun show and think that the proprietor/dealer/collector should pay you the retail values listed within this text for your gun(s). Resale offers on many models could be anywhere from near retail to 20%-50% less than the values listed, depending upon locality, desirability, dealer inventory, and profitability. In other words, if you want to receive 100% of the retail value, then you have to do 100% of the work (become the retailer, which also includes assuming 100% of the risk).

Percentages of original condition (with corresponding values) are listed between 10%-100% for most antiques (unless configuration, rarity, and age preclude upper conditions). 60%-100% condition factors are listed on most modern firearms since condition below 60% is seldom encountered (or purchased). Please consult our revised, 80-page Photo Percentage Grading System™ (PPGS) located on pages 25-102 to learn more about the condition of your firearm(s). Since condition is the overriding factor in price evaluation, study these photos and captions carefully to learn more about the condition of your specimen(s). The PPGS is also available online at no charge and contains even more examples of condition factors than those printed in this edition. Simply visit www.bluebookofgunvalues.com and click on Firearms Grading under the Information & Services tab.

Three pages (14-16) are provided (Anatomy of a Handgun, Anatomy of a Rifle, and Anatomy of a Shotgun), to help you identify various parts and firearms nomenclature used within this text. Please refer to the expanded Abbreviations section for a complete listing of abbreviations used within this text. Once again, the Glossary has been expanded in this edition, and will explain most of the firearms terminology used in the A-Z sections, especially tactical terminology. Updated BATFE regional information is also provided again, and new this year is a listing of Curios and Relics. You may also want to check out the Store Brand Cross-Over List, since hundreds of makes and models can easily be cross-referenced. A Proof Marks section will also help you identify and date many European firearms. Additionally, increased Serialization information is provided on many makes and models, enabling you to determine the year of manufacture in many cases. If you wish to contact current manufacturers, importers, and/or some distributors, please refer to the up-to-date Trademark Index for listings and contact information, which includes websites and email addresses whenever possible.

Since the 34th Edition is now 2,408 pages, it may be easier to zero in on a particular manufacturer and category (pistols, rifles, shotguns, etc.) by referring to the updated Index. For trademarks and companies with more than one configuration of firearm, individual category names are listed alphabetically. Alphabetical tabs are located on the tops of the pages next to the page number and heading, making it easier to find all the information you want quickly. Sidebar black markers are also provided, enabling you to zero in on an alphabetical section without opening the book. As in previous editions, the NRA condition standards and grading criteria have been included to make the conversion to percentages easier (see page 23). This will be especially helpful when evaluating antiques. Additionally, images for NRA condition standards are included in the PPGS.

To find a model in this text, first look under the name of the manufacturer, trademark, brand name, and in some cases, the importer (please consult the Index if necessary). Next, find the correct category name(s) (Commemoratives, Pistols, Rifles, Shotguns, etc.). When applicable, antiques will appear before modern guns, and are typically listed in chronological sequence.

Once you find the correct model or sub-model under its respective subheading, determine the specimen's percentage of original condition (see the Photo Percentage Grading System™ pages 25-102) and refer to the corresponding percentage column showing the value. Commemoratives or special/limited editions will generally appear last under a manufacturer's heading. For those of you who would like to make notes within this publication, there may be a Notes Page at the end of some alphabetical sections. For the sake of simplicity, the following organizational framework has been adopted throughout this publication.

1. Alphabetical names are located on the top of right-facing, odd-numbered pages and appear as follows:

H SECTION

2. Trademarks, manufacturers, brand names, importers, or organizations are listed alphabetically in uppercase bold typeface, like this:

ASTRA, CZ, DPMS, FRANCHI, GLOCK, WINCHESTER

3. Manufacturer/trademark information is listed directly beneath the trademark heading:

Currently manufactured by Glock GmbH in Austria beginning 1983. Sales in the U.S. began in 1986. Glock also opened a production facility for manufacturing its polymer frames and assembling complete pistols in Smyrna, GA during late 2005. Exclusively imported and distributed by Glock, Inc. USA, located in Smyrna, GA. Distributor and dealer sales.

4. Manufacturer notes may appear next under individual heading descriptions and can be differentiated by the following typeface:

All Glock pistols have a "safe action" constant operating system (double action mode) which includes trigger safety, firing pin safety, and drop safety. Glock pistols have only 35 parts for reliability and simplicity of operation. With approximately 170 or more variations, over 8 million Glock semi-auto pistols have been manufactured since 1983.

5. The next classification is the category name (normally, in alphabetical sequence) in uppercase lettering (inside a screened gray box) which primarily refers to a firearm's configuration. Category names include:

CARBINES: SEMI-AUTO, PISTOLS: SEMI-AUTO, REVOLVERS,

RIFLES: BOLT ACTION, SHOTGUNS: O/U

6. A further sub-classification may appear under a category name, as depicted below. These are sub-categories of a major category name, appear in both upper and lower case type, and typically appear in alphabetical order. Examples include:

Pistols: Semi-Auto, Model 92 & Variations – 4.9 in. barrel

7. Following a category or sub-category name, a category note may follow to help explain the category, and/or provide limited information on the models and values listed within the category. This appears as follows:

IMPORTANT NOTE: On model(s) where *N/A has replaced the normal 100% value, it indicates current market conditions are too unstable to accurately ascertain 100%-60% values. Factory retail prices (MSRs) reflect most recent updates. For more up-to-date information on current pricing trends and additional useful information, please visit www.bluebookofgunvalues.com, select "Information & Services " from the menu, and click on "Additional Book Information".

8. Model names appear flush left, are bold faced, and are in uppercase lettering either in chronological order (normally) or alphabetical order (sometimes, the previous model name and/or close sub-variation will appear at the end in parentheses) and are listed under the individual category and sub-category names. Examples include:

MODEL 27, MODEL 870 WINGMASTER, PPQ M2, MOE MID-LENGTH, MODEL 9422 LEGACY

9. Model descriptions are denoted by the following typeface and usually include the following information:

– calibers, gauges/bore, action type, barrel length(s), finish(es), weight, and other descriptive data are provided adjacent to model names in this typeface. This is where most of the information is listed for each specific model, including identifiable features and possibly some production data, including quantity, date of manufacture, and discontinuance date, if known.

10. Variations (and possible production periods) within a model appear as sub-models - they are differentiated from model names by an artistic icon * prefix, are italicized and indented, and appear in upper and lowercase type, as follows:

**** Mark II Gyro Jet, Model X7S, Model 98 Field Turkey, Challenger Gold Line, Model 700 Camo***

This is usually followed by a short description of that sub-model. These sub-model descriptions have the same typeface as the model descriptions:

– additional sub-model information could include finishes, calibers, barrel lengths, special order features, or other production data specific for that sub-model.

11. Also included is yet another layer of model/information nomenclature differentiating sub-models from variations of sub-models or a lower hierarchy of sub-model information. These items are indented from the sub-models, and have the icon graphic », for example:

    » **Model 585 Sporting Clays Set, Citori Superlight Grade I Earlier Mfg.**

    A description for this level of sub-model information may appear next to the sub-entry, and uses the same typeface as model and sub-model descriptions shown above.

12. Model notes and information appear in smaller type, generally after the price line, and should be read since they contain important, critical, and interesting facts/information. In some cases, factory recalls (some include serialization) are also provided. Examples include:

Many original 1878 barrels have "found their way" on the front end of a SAA frame since the barrels are interchangable. Because of this, many "original" Model 1878 DAs may have an incorrect and/or later SAA Colt barrel attached. Watch yourself here! Also, scarce calibers should be verified with factory.

13. Extra features/special orders which can add or subtract value are placed either under category names, model/sub-model descriptions, or pricing lines. On current models that don't have a price line, the MSR will also appear in this typeface, in addition to other pricing information regarding that model. These individual lines appear bolder than other descriptive typeface, such as the following:

Add 10% for NIB condition.
Subtract 20% for blued receiver.
Current MSR on this model is $2,384.

14. On many discontinued models/variations after 1985, the last MSR (manufacturer's suggested retail price) may appear flush right, in italics at the end of the 100%-60% pricing line. This will fall directly under the Last MSR column that appears at the end of the grading lines. Some MSRs may also appear like this:

Last MSR in 2006 was $7,500.

15. Grading lines normally appear at the top of each page, and in the middle if price lines change. If you are uncertain as to how to properly grade a particular firearm, please refer to the digital color Photo Percentage Grading System™ (PPGS) on pages 25-102 for more assistance. The most commonly encountered grading line (shown with a typical price line underneath) in this text is for 100%-60% condition factors:

GRADING - PPGS™	100%	98%	95%	90%	80%	70%	60%	*LAST MSR*
	$895	$775	$675	$575	$500	$450	$400	

Antique grading lines have additional values listed for 100%-10% and also 95%-10%. Examples (with price lines) are as follows:

100%	98%	95%	90%	80%	70%	60%	50%	40%	30%	20%	10%
$2,250	$1,850	$1,550	$1,350	$1,050	$850	$700	$600	$500	$425	$350	$300
N/A	N/A	$22,000	$18,000	$16,000	$12,000	$10,000	$6,000	$4,000	$2,500	$1,500	$1,000

When "N/A" (Not Applicable) is listed instead of a value, this indicates that this particular model is not encountered enough in those condition factors to warrant a value - especially true on antiques in upper condition factors and with commemoratives and special/limited editions under 95%.

Most commemorative/limited edition grading and price lines will appear as follows:

GRADING - PPGS™	100%	Issued Price	Qty. Made
	$1,995	$650	200

In some cases, an organization's or company's listing (i.e. Ducks Unlimited, the National Wild Turkey Federation, etc.) of guns will appear as follows:

Manufacturer/Model	Quantity	Year	Issue Price
ITHACA Model 37 Ultralight 20 ga.	750	1997	N/A

GRADING - PPGS™	100%	98%	95%	90%	80%	70%	60%	LAST MSR

16. Price line formats are as follows - when the price line shown below (with proper grading line) is encountered, it automatically indicates the gun is currently manufactured, and the MSR is shown left of the 100% column.

MSR $1,825	**$1,475**	**$1,150**	**$1,025**	**$925**	**$850**	**$750**	**$550**
No MSR	**$300**	**$250**	**$225**	**$200**	**$180**	**$160**	**$140**

Following this are the 100%-60% values. This 100% value is the national average price a consumer will typically expect to pay for that model in NIB unfired condition. 100% specimens without boxes, warranties, etc., which are currently manufactured may be discounted (5%-20%, depending on the desirability of make and model). This 100% price on currently manufactured guns also assumes not previously sold at retail. Some companies are no longer publishing MSRs, and in this case, No MSR is listed first in the pricing line.

17. When a currently manufactured or discontinued limited/special edition firearm with or without retail pricing is encountered, it typically will not have values listed from 90%-60%, but rather N/As (Not Applicable), as these lower condition factors are seldom encountered. The value lines will appear as follows in this case:

MSR $10,750	**$9,950**	**$8,750**	**$7,500**	**N/A**	**N/A**	**N/A**	**N/A**
	$995	**$850**	**$725**	**N/A**	**N/A**	**N/A**	**N/A**

18. A price line with seven values listed, as represented below, indicates a discontinued, out-of-production model with values shown for 100%-60% conditions. Because stainless steel is almost impervious to visible wear, an 80% - 60% model's value must be determined by the condition of its action and barrel (i.e., how much it has been shot/used), in addition to grip wear. Values are normally not listed for 50%-10% condition factors, since these lower conditions are seldom encountered on recently discontinued models. Examples include:

$1,900	**$1,400**	**$1,200**	**$1,100**	**$995**	**$850**	**$725**
N/A	**$10,000**	**$8,500**	**$7,000**	**$6,000**	**$5,000**	**$3,500**

Values for conditions under 60% will typically be no less than 50% (1/2) of the 60% price, unless the gun has been shot to a point where the action may be loose or questionable. Obviously, no "MSR" will appear in the left margin, but a last manufacturer's suggested retail price may appear flush right in italics within the price line, automatically indicating a discontinued gun, like this:

$300	**$225**	**$185**	**$165**	**$155**	**$145**	**$135**	***$395***

Above Average	Average	Below Average

19. Some antiques listed will not have price lines, but rather value ranges for Above Average, Average, and Below Average condition factors. These value range price lines with corresponding grading lines will appear as follows:

$80,000 - $120,000	**$35,000 - $80,000**	**$20,000 - $35,000**

An explanation of these condition factor ranges appears under the heading "Grading Explanation for Winchester Lever Actions" in the beginning of the Winchester section.

GRADING - PPGS™	100%	98%	95%	90%	80%	70%	60%	LAST MSR

20. New in this 34th edition is a special pricing line where *N/A has replaced the normal 100% values for some AR-15 makes/models that are currently too unstable to accurately ascertain 100%-60% values. MSRs reflect most recent manfacturer's suggested retail price,

MSR $1,450	***N/A**	**$1,275**	**$1,100**	**$975**	**$850**	**$725**	**$600**

the 100%-60% values may not be accurate, and a link has been provided to give more up-to-date information on this model.

Don't forget that a new section on BATFE Curios and Relics is now provided in the back of the book (page 2,369), providing a complete listing of all BATFE approved Curios and Relics.

If you're having a hard time finding a particular make/model, it might be a lot easier and faster to look it up in our expanded Index (pages 2,386-2,407). This Index not only includes all the major firearms trademarks and manufacturers, but also includes all the major categories for each one.

ANATOMY OF A HANDGUN

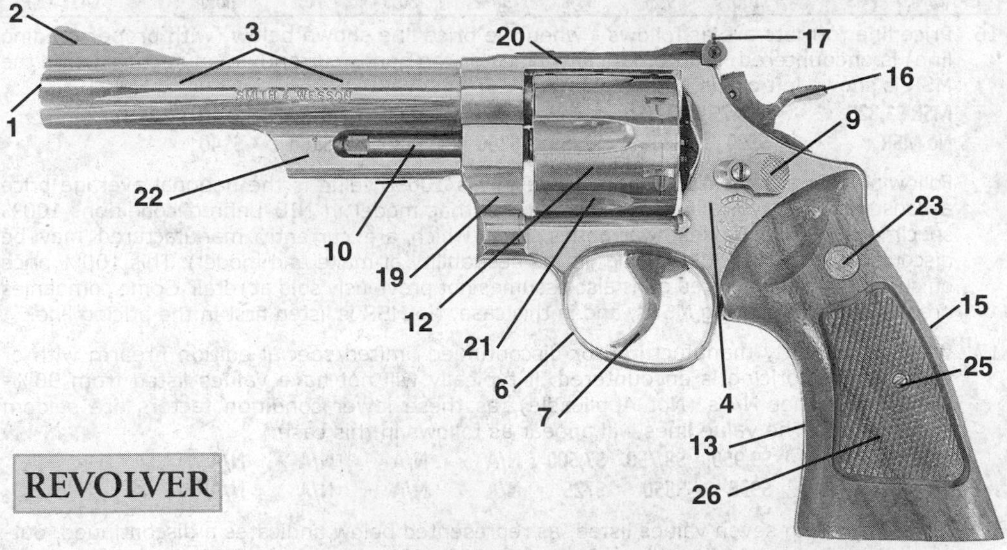

REVOLVER

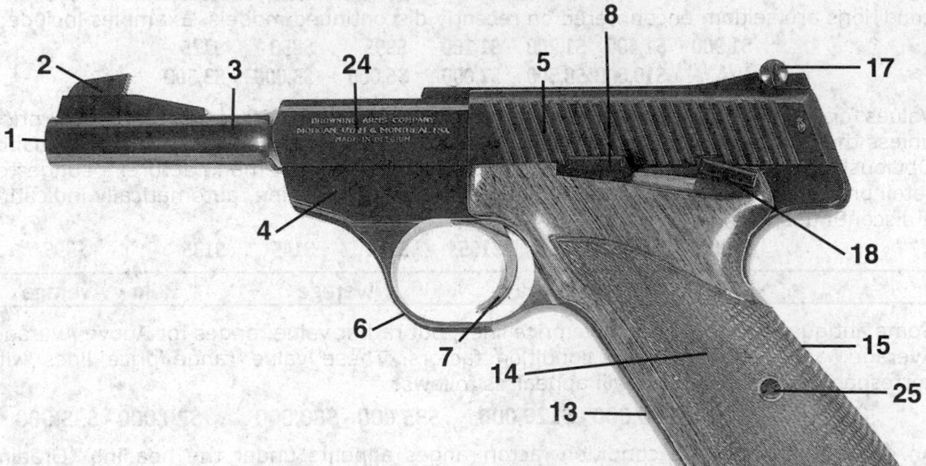

SEMI-AUTO

1. Muzzle
2. Front Sight
3. Barrel
4. Frame
5. Slide (Serrated)
6. Trigger Guard
7. Trigger
8. Slide Release Lever
9. Cylinder Release Latch
10. Cylinder Ejector Rod
11. Magazine (Hidden)
12. Cylinder
13. Front Grip Strap
14. Grip
15. Rear Grip Strap
16. Hammer
17. Rear Sight
18. Safety Lever
19. Crane
20. Top Strap
21. Cylinder Flute
22. Ejector Rod Shroud (Partial Length)
23. Grip Medallion
24. Barrel/Frame Address
25. Grip Screw
26. Grip (Square Type, Stocks On Older Mfg.)

ANATOMY OF A RIFLE

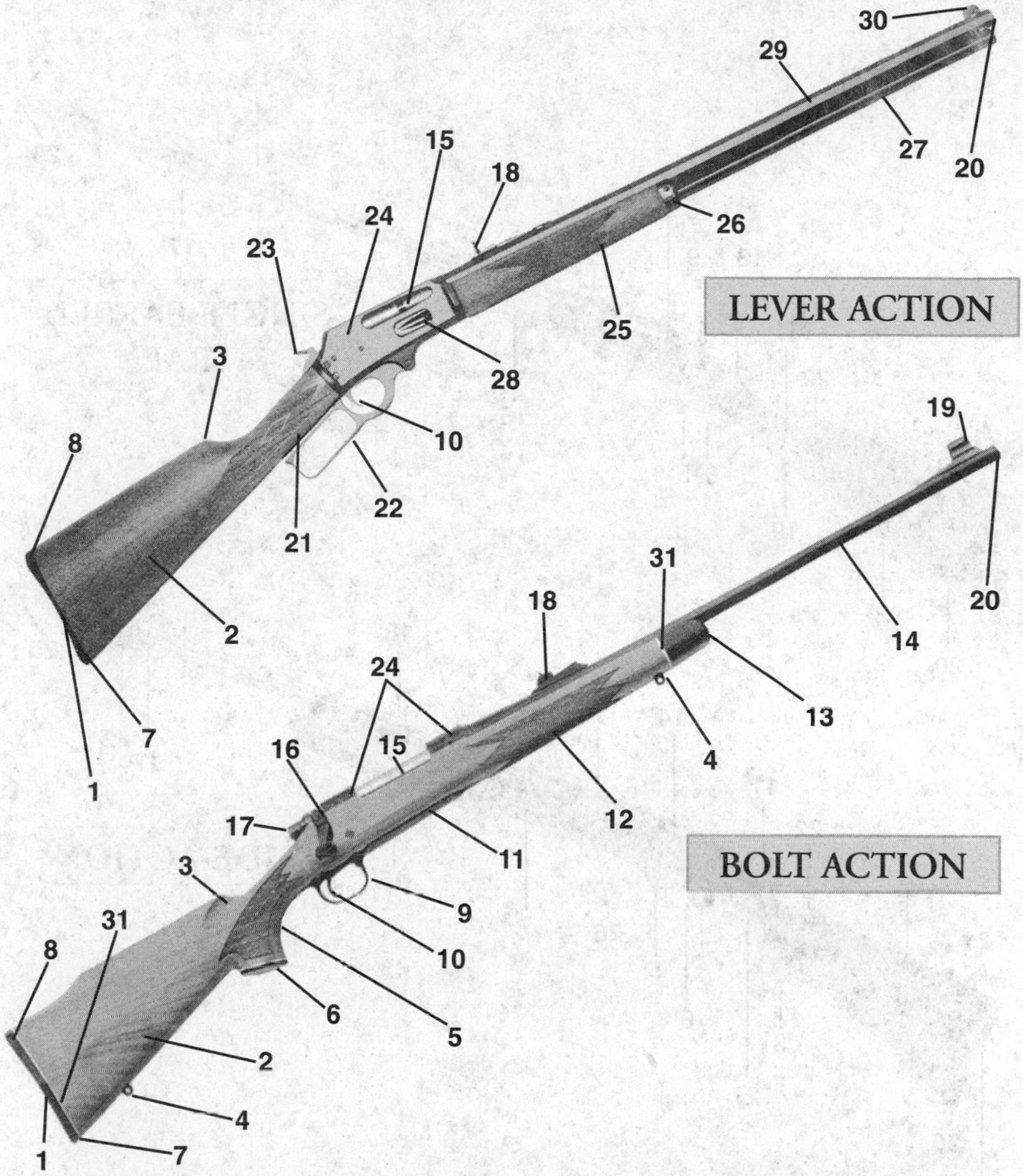

1. Buttplate
2. Buttstock
3. Comb
4. Sling Swivel Stud
5. Semi-Pistol Grip
6. Pistol Grip Cap
7. Toe
8. Heel
9. Trigger Guard
10. Trigger
11. Floor Plate
12. Forend
13. Forend Tip
14. Barrel
15. Bolt
16. Bolt Handle
17. Safety Button
18. Rear Sight
19. Hooded-Ramp Front Sight
20. Muzzle
21. Straight Grip
22. Lever
23. Hammer
24. Receiver
25. Forearm
26. Forearm Cap
27. Magazine Tube
28. Loading Port
29. Octagon Barrel
30. Blade Front Sight
31. Spacer

ANATOMY OF A SHOTGUN

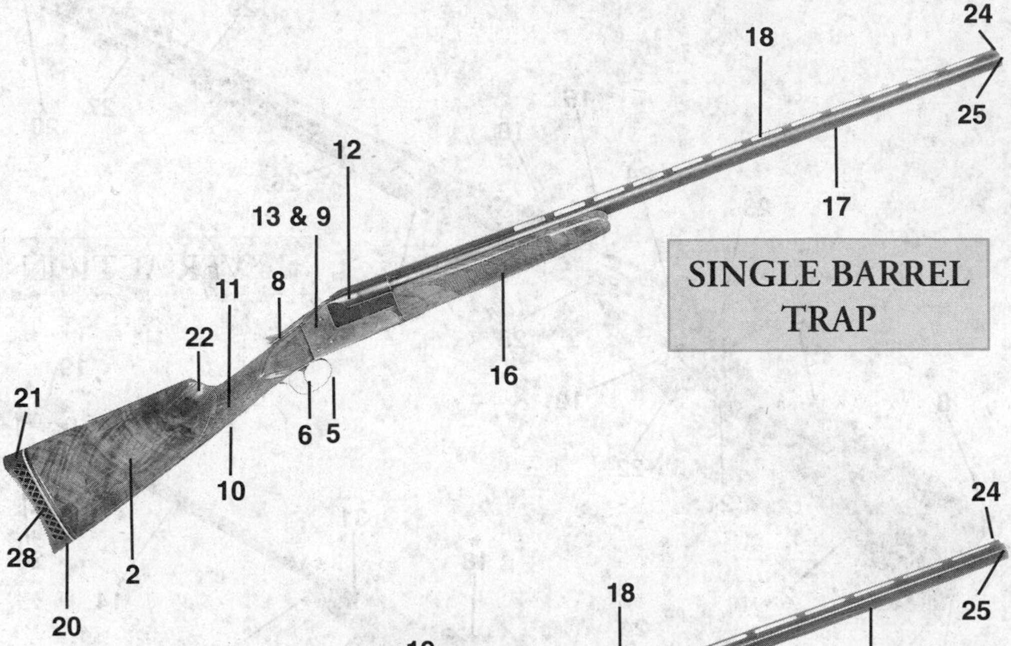

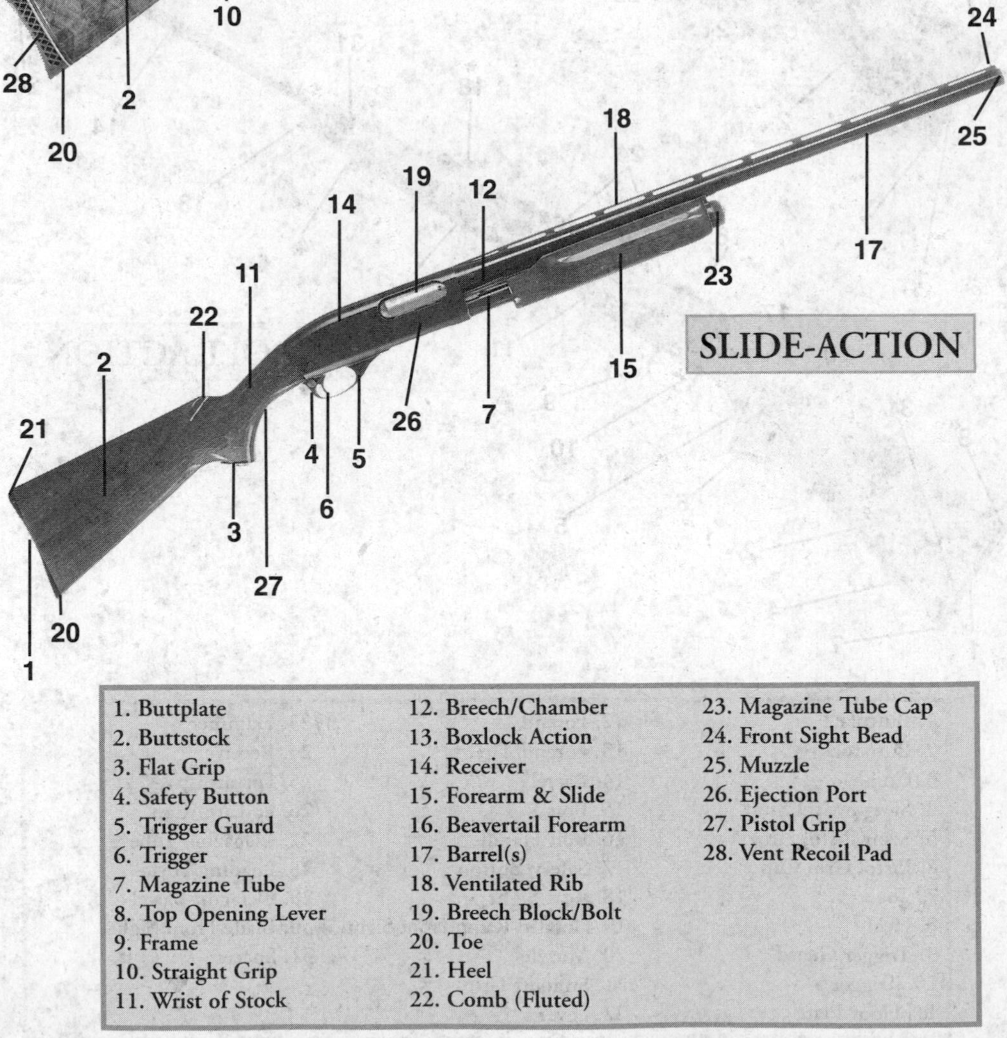

1. Buttplate
2. Buttstock
3. Flat Grip
4. Safety Button
5. Trigger Guard
6. Trigger
7. Magazine Tube
8. Top Opening Lever
9. Frame
10. Straight Grip
11. Wrist of Stock
12. Breech/Chamber
13. Boxlock Action
14. Receiver
15. Forearm & Slide
16. Beavertail Forearm
17. Barrel(s)
18. Ventilated Rib
19. Breech Block/Bolt
20. Toe
21. Heel
22. Comb (Fluted)
23. Magazine Tube Cap
24. Front Sight Bead
25. Muzzle
26. Ejection Port
27. Pistol Grip
28. Vent Recoil Pad

FOREWORD

by S.P. Fjestad

A bevy of best-selling gun writers and authors finally get together at the NRA Show in St. Louis! From left to right: Michael Bussard, C. Roger Bleile, Jim Carmichel (seated), S.P. Fjestad, John Bianchi (seated), John B. Allen, and Dennis Adler.

NAZI HQ (NÜRNBERG, GERMANY) – 03/11/13

What a difference one year can make as the final edits of this most recent Foreword are being sent from the Marienbad Hotel back to Minneapolis, following the recent European firearms trade show (IWA). Last year at this time, supply and demand factors for most high capacity semi-auto tactical carbines/rifles and pistols had almost returned to normal pre-Obama levels. After all, during his first term, the President hadn't even mentioned initiating more anti-gun laws/regulations, and the fear and speculation that had gripped the frenzied gun buyers during the last half of 2008 and 2009.

All responsible gun owners were justifiably concerned about the presidential election last fall, and I saw the results first hand in the Delta members lounge during a layover at Tokyo's Narita airport. It was so disappointing and depressing trying to accept another four years of this kind of leadership.

ONLY IN AMERICA

As expected, gun owners, speculators, and investors reacted accordingly, and once again the heat was turned up on most semi-auto high capacity tactical firearms – especially AR-15 style carbines/rifles. Yes, there was another batch of orders that went to the 150 current AR-15 manufacturers, yet the "street" price consumers were paying at gun shops or through Internet sales didn't go up that much. It certainly looked like we were going to lick our election wounds briefly, and then wait and see what might happen during the second term.

THEN ALL HELL BROKE LOOSE

On Dec. 14, 2012, the school shooting in Newtown, CT, changed everything, and very quickly. Post election gun owner jitters were already at red alert status when this tragedy occurred. What's been a game changer is how fast the gun marketplace has reacted this time. By the following Monday, the hysteria created by the Newtown aftermath had already drastically changed the sales of AR-15 style carbines/rifles, high cap. mags., and 5.56 NATO/.223 Rem. cal. ammo. This type of almost instantaneous change in a segment of the marketplace is unprecedented in America's history of commercial firearms manufacture. Social media and networking are the biggest single differences, and the public's reaction time is now measured in minutes and hours, not days and weeks like it was before.

A COUNTRY DIVIDED AND UNDECIDED

By the following Friday, not only had most gun shops already sold out of these now controversial items, but the entire country had become instantly polarized into two different factions – either pro-gun or otherwise. The devastating scar tissue created by this most recent and extremely tragic mass shooting simply could no longer be ignored. Many law-abiding citizens wanted a "sacrificial lamb" or two in an effort to try to eliminate this type of gun violence in the future.

On the altar and up for sacrifice were high capacity magazines and some configurations of "assault" rifles. A reintroduction of the Crime Bill was also bantered around by the press (demand's best friend), and organizations such as the NSSF and NRA immediately assumed a damage control position. When Wayne LaPierre finally appeared on TV a week later with his school security proposal, including armed guards, it continued to polarize the American public. In subsequent television appearances, some people

Larry and Brenda Potterfield from Midway USA (center) take a little time from their busy NRA show schedule to receive the Lifetime Sales Achievement Award from Adam Burt (l), BBP's Business Development Officer, and S.P. Fjestad.

commented that he has appeared unprepared, shrill, and petulant. And all this happened in less than a month!

FEAR, GREED, AND SPECULATION

So what's new in this 34th Edition? More than anything else, the proliferation of AR-15 manufacturers within the last fourteen years almost defies the imagination. In 1999, the 20th Anniversary Edition had approximately 32 AR-15 manufacturers. That total has escalated to approximately 150! Unfortunately, the fear and speculation of potential anti-gun legislation still remains the biggest single demand factor in today's firearms marketplace, even though not one piece of anti-gun legislation potentially affecting them has been enacted to date by Congress. Never the less, this continued additional demand factor is single handedly responsible for many AR-15 variations selling for well over the manufacturer's suggested retails. In other words, the old dog (traditional sporting longarms) is now being wagged by an energetic young tail (high cap. semi-autos) that seems to be on steroids.

As a result of this potential anti-gun legislation and speculation over re-instating the 1994 Crime Bill, this is the first edition I've ever had to put *N/As in the 100% condition column. Whenever these are found in this text, it means that prices remain so unpredictable for a particular model(s), that accurate and predictable pricing is simply not possible at this time.

To give you more information and keep you up-to-date on where AR-15 values are currently at, we have established a place on www.bluebookofgunvalues.com where you can review what selected major trademark AR-15 prices have done lately, taking into consideration both gun shop and Internet sales. Results will continue to be posted until if/when this marketplace cools down enough to return to predictable pricing.

To my knowledge, this is the first time that a publisher of a pricing guide has updated its customers with more information during a crisis by using a website to post current information.

WHEN LESS IS MORE

The other big change many of you will see immediately is that the last manufacturer's suggested retail prices that used to appear flush right on a separate line have now been incorporated at the end of the value lines. It has saved a lot of space that we can put to good use by providing additional listings. Even though this book is over 2,400 pages, we try to make every character and space count!

THE MONSTER GETS CONVERTED

One of our bigger projects last year was converting the massive *Blue Book of Gun Values* database, easily the world's largest, into an electronic format that can be quickly and easily used for a multitude of search functions. We expect it's going to take another six months to refine it into the product it needs to be, but when it's completed, it will offer consumers like yourself an almost infinite variety of ways on how to get the information more conveniently and efficiently. Please check BBP's website for more updates on this exciting new development.

WOMEN SHOOTERS RULE!

Don't forget to read the two-page article/interview entitled "Jessie Duff - A Champion Who's Winning for Freedom" on pages 20-21. At 27, Jessie Duff already holds numerous national and world championship titles in five different shooting disciplines – IPSC/USPSA, Bianchi Cup, 3-Gun, Steel Challenge, and

Cowboy Action shooting, making her one of the most accomplished American shooters of all time.

Kim Rhode is also to be congratulated for her accomplishments in London last summer, becoming the first American to win individual medals in five straight Olympic Games - her first at the tender age of only 16. She easily blew away her competition in the Skeet discipline. Along with Jessie, they are two outstanding and vibrant spokespeople for the shooting sports, as they can convey the message to this new emerging segment of the marketplace better than a bunch of older male shooters.

Women have now become a very important part of America's firearms industry, with many concerned about individual protection. This has resulted in tens of thousands of carry permits being issued throughout the country, and this new demand factor will only get bigger.

The firearms industry has certainly acknowledged both firearms and accessories tailored to the shooting needs of women, and there have never been more choices for the gals to choose from. They even have their own camo finishes now!

BUYING WHAT'S LEFT VS. WHAT YOU WANT

These are fast and furious times in the gun business. Many consumers are buying what is available, not what they want. My old friend, Bud Fini of SIG-Sauer, who has reinvented himself more times than Madonna, told me at IWA that every gun made in Exeter, NH, by 5pm gets shipped the same day. There is no inventory in stock. Several manufacturers and distributors also mentioned that business was currently "crazy, stupid, busy." Without a doubt, this situation is mostly due to Newtown and Obama, who has easily become the best gun selling politician in world history!

ANYTHING ELSE NEW & EXCITING IN THE GUN BIZ?

In terms of the collectible firearms marketplace, auctions have really taken over now as the primary source for selling better quality antiques and discontinued firearms. Gun shops and gun dealers also seem to be doing very well overall. The only real problem anybody has right now is getting enough inventory. The hardest question to answer right now is "How long is this party going to last?" Gun shows are not what they used to be, and in some cases, the gun show parking lots are busier than what's going on inside. What's truly amazing is the unprecedented shortage of .22 rimfire ammunition currently.

BBP & 2012 = EVOLUTION

If you had a chance to look at Meet the Staff, you probably already noticed there are some new faces. 2012 turned out to be an evolutionary year for the company, and these personnel changes were a major part of it. Especially hard for me was saying goodbye to my talented nephew, Zachary, who decided to pursue a new career and move back to Fergus Falls with his wife and young son, Daniel. The good news is that he will continue to update and maintain the databases for the *Blue Book of Electric Guitars, Blue Book of Acoustic Guitars*, and the *Blue Book of Guitar Amplifiers*.

The author on assignment in Hong Kong last fall.

Many of our customers have requested that a listing of BATFE-approved Curios and Relics be included, and this year we finally found enough extra space to include them – see pages 2,369-2,384.

Maybe more exciting than anything else is our new series of pocket guides, including separate titles on Browning, Remington, Smith & Wesson, and Winchester. These smaller books offer all the information from the respective sections of the *Blue Book of Gun Values* in a compact and easily portable format. The best part is the price – only $14.95 each!

IT'S A WRAP

I couldn't end this annual foreword without thanking our entire staff for its dedication, perseverance, and commitment to both quality products and services. This book is not an annuity – we have to work harder every year to continue to earn your patronage. All of the contributing editors and firearms industry personnel also deserve a large thank you for all the help and support they have provided over the years. And finally, you, the consumer/reader, are the reason this book has become the firearms industry's most recognized and accepted reference source. We will continue to expand it and make sure this publication stays the best value for your money.

Sincerely,

S.P. Fjestad

Author and Publisher – *Blue Book of Gun Values*

PS – Hope to be signing books to some of you in Tulsa within three weeks!

JESSIE DUFF

A Champion Who's Winning for Freedom

by Marshall Lewin

Very few men or women attain in their entire lives the marksmanship mastery that Jessie Duff has achieved in little over a decade of shooting experience.

Jessie now holds numerous national and world championship titles in five different shooting disciplines – IPSC/USPSA, Bianchi Cup, 3-Gun, Steel Challenge, and Cowboy Action shooting – making her one of the most accomplished female shooters, all at the age of 27.

What started her toward this remarkable record of achievement? "My dad is a World Champion Cowboy Action Shooter, and our whole family grew up around guns," Jessie says. When Jessie was 15, her father encouraged her to try her hand at Cowboy Action Shooting and "from that point forward," Jessie says, "I was hooked." So through training from her father and other accomplished shooters, she set scoring goals for herself and kept reaching ever higher.

Soon, she moved to more modern firearms and modern disciplines – where she continued to excel. "I realized that shooting was my passion, that it was what I wanted to do, and that maybe I could make a career of it," Jessie says. "So I went full-force at it and took every opportunity that came my way."

Today, Jessie puts that passion to powerful effect on shooting ranges around the world as Team Captain for Taurus International's shooting team and with her husband, Matt, with whom she co-hosts the Outdoor Channel's popular *Friends of NRA* TV show.

Q: Many readers would surely like to introduce their sons, daughters, or spouses to shooting the same way your father did for you. What advice could you offer them?

A: For parents who wish to introduce their children to the shooting sports, I encourage them to teach their children firearm safety first! Make sure they have a healthy respect for guns, and what they are capable of. Next would be to find a gun that suits them and what they are wanting to learn. To start with, a smaller caliber is ideal, so that they can control the recoil and not be intimidated. The best competition for new shooters, in my opinion, is Steel Challenge. This type of shooting requires all the fundamentals you will learn as a new shooter and gives instant feedback from steel plates. It's a very friendly sport to beginners and helps build confidence while enjoying the sport! The parents should go online and learn about the Steel Challenge Shooting Association to make sure they have a good understanding of the sport and also to help answer some of their questions.

Q: What about spouses or adults who just want to learn to shoot recreationally?

A: For someone who wishes to learn to shoot for recreational purposes, I would suggest finding someone you know that already participates in shooting who is knowledgeable on firearm safety to learn from. If you don't know anyone, then you can find certified instructors in your area, through the NRA, to take lessons from. For some women, it's very intimidating to learn to shoot, so finding the right instructor could make all the difference in the world! There are female instructors as well, which will help ease some of their fears going into it and provide them with a comfortable environment to learn in. This might be a good alternative for some spouses who are trying to teach their wives to shoot, because if she enjoys it, then that equates into more range time for the husbands too!

Q: Tell us a little bit about your *Friends of NRA* TV show.

A: With *Friends of NRA* TV, Matt and I travel the country to show off this nonprofit side of the NRA. *Friends of NRA* is a volunteer-based organization, which raises money through banquets, auctions, and special events to help support the shooting sports. Through the show, we get to meet these hard-working volunteers and the kids and families who benefit from these efforts and help spread the word about *Friends of NRA*. Since half the money pays for local projects, and half at the national level, it's a win-win for everybody. We try to tell those stories through the show and, I hope, inspire like-minded people to participate.

Q: With politicians pushing new anti-gun laws, and many in the media cheering them on, what advice could you offer readers who want to protect their rights?

A: Educate yourself and educate others about firearms, about the laws being proposed, and about why we have the Second Amendment and its importance to our freedom. If the Constitution is not respected by our leaders, and the right of the American people is infringed, then the freedoms that many of us have grown accustomed to all our lives could be lost.

I encourage those who have a platform to stand upon, to use it. Don't be afraid to stand up and speak out for what you believe in. You might change an opinion, which could make the biggest difference in our freedom. ■

At 27, Jessie Duff is already the team captain for the Taurus International Shooting Team. She also holds numerous national and world champion titles in five different shooting disciplines – IPSC/USPSA, Bianchi Cup, 3-Gun, Steel Challenge, and Cowboy Action shooting.

Jessie in action at the 2012 USPSA Open Nationals, where she claimed the Ladies Open National Championship.

GRADING CRITERIA

The older NRA modern condition descriptions relied upon adjectives such as "Excellent" or "Fair" – has served the firearms community for many years. However, many of today's dealers/collectors, especially those who deal in modern guns, have turned away from the older subjective system. There is too much variance within some of the older subjective grades, therefore making accurate grading difficult.

Most dealers and collectors are now utilizing what is essentially an objective method for deciding the condition of a gun: THE PERCENTAGE OF ORIGINAL FACTORY FINISH(ES) REMAINING ON THE GUN. After looking critically at a variety of firearms and carefully studying the Photo Percentage Grading System™ (pages 25-102), it will soon become evident if a specific gun has 98%, 90%, 70% or less finish remaining. Remember, sometimes an older unfired gun described as NIB can actually be 98% or less condition, simply because of the wear accumulated by taking it in and out of the box and excessive handling. Commemoratives are especially prone to this problem. Of course, factors such as quality of finish(es), engraving (and other embellishments), special orders/features, historical significance and/or provenance, etc. can and do affect prices immensely. Also, it seems that every year bore condition (especially on antiques) becomes more important in the overall grading factor (and price) of both collectible and desirable major trademarks such as Winchester, Remington, Sharps, Schuetzens, older Springfields, etc. Because of this, bore condition must be listed separately for those guns where it makes a difference in value. Never pay a premium for condition that isn't there. Remember, original condition still beats everything else to the bank.

Every gun's unique condition factor – and therefore the price – is best determined by the percentage of original finish(es) remaining, with the key consideration being the overall frame/receiver finish. The key word here is "original", for if anyone other than the factory has refinished the gun, its value as a collector's item has been diminished. The exceptions would be rare and historical guns that have been properly restored. Every year, top quality restorations have become more accepted, and prices have gone up proportionately with the quality of the workmanship. Also popular now are antique finishes, and a new question has come up, "What is 100% antique finish on new reproductions?" Answer – a gun that started out as new, and then has been aged to a lower condition factor to duplicate natural wear and tear.

CAREFULLY STUDY THE HIGH QUALITY DIGITAL IMAGES AND READ THE CAPTIONS ON PAGES 25-102. The PPGS is also available online at no charge and contains even more examples of condition factors than those printed in this edition. Simply visit www.bluebookofgunvalues.com and click on Firearms Grading under the Information & Services tab. Note where the finishes of a firearm typically wear off first. These are usually places where the gun accumulates wear from holster/case rubbing, and contact with the hands or body over an extended period of time. A variety of firearms have been shown in four-color to guarantee that your "sampling size" for observing finishes with their correct colors is as diversified as possible.

It should be noted that the older a collectible firearm is, the smaller the percentage of original finish one can expect to find. Some very old and/or very rare firearms are sought by collectors in almost any condition!

For your convenience, NRA Condition Standards are listed on page 23. Converting from this grading system to percentages can now be done accurately. Remember the price is wrong if the condition factor isn't right!

PHOTO PERCENTAGE GRADING SYSTEM CONVERSION GUIDELINES

New/Perfect – 100% condition with or without box. 100% on currently manufactured firearms assumes NIB (New In Box) condition and not sold previously at retail.

Mint – typically 98%-99% condition with almost no observable wear. Probably sold previously at retail, and may have been shot occasionally.

Excellent – 95%+ - 98% condition.

Very Good – 80% - 95% condition (all parts/finish should be original).

Good - 60% – 80% condition (all parts/finish should be original).

Fair – 20% - 60% condition (all parts/finish may or may not be original, but must function properly and shoot).

Poor – under 20% condition (shooting not a factor).

NRA CONDITION STANDARDS

The NRA conditions listed below have been provided as guidelines to assist the reader in converting and comparing condition factors to the Photo Percentage Grading System™ (PPGS, see pages 25-102). NRA antique and modern condition standards are now represented in the PPGS – please refer to pages 38-42; 56-61 (handguns) and 78-83; 97-102 (long guns). In order to use this book correctly, the reader is urged to examine these images of NRA condition standards. Once the gun's condition has been accurately assessed, only then can values be accurately ascertained.

NRA MODERN CONDITION DESCRIPTIONS

New – not previously sold at retail, in same condition as current factory production.

Perfect – in new condition in every respect, may have previously been sold at retail.

Excellent – near new condition, used but little, no noticeable marring of wood or metal, bluing near perfect (except at muzzle or sharp edges).

Very Good – in perfect working condition, no appreciable wear on working surfaces, no corrosion or pitting, only minor surface dents or scratches.

Good – in safe working condition, minor wear on working surfaces, no broken parts, no corrosion or pitting that will interfere with proper functioning.

Fair – in safe working condition, but well worn, perhaps requiring replacement of minor parts or adjustments which should be indicated in advertisement, no rust, but may have corrosion pits which do not render article unsafe or inoperable.

NRA ANTIQUE CONDITION DESCRIPTIONS

Factory New – all original parts; 100% original finish; in perfect condition in every respect, inside and out.

Excellent – all original parts; over 80% original finish; sharp lettering, numerals and design on metal and wood; unmarred wood; fine bore.

Fine – all original parts; over 30% original finish; sharp lettering, numerals and design on metal and wood; minor marks in wood; good bore.

Very Good – all original parts; none to 30% original finish; original metal surfaces smooth with all edges sharp; clear lettering, numerals and design on metal; wood slightly scratched or bruised; bore disregarded for collectors firearms.

Good – less than 20% original finish, some minor replacement parts; metal smoothly rusted or lightly pitted in places, cleaned or reblued; principal lettering, numerals and design on metal legible; wood refinished, scratched, bruised or minor cracks repaired; in good working order.

Fair – less than 10% original finish, some major parts replaced; minor replacement parts may be required; metal rusted, may be lightly pitted all over, vigorously cleaned or reblued; rounded edges of metal and wood; principal lettering, numerals and design on metal partly obliterated; wood scratched, bruised, cracked or repaired where broken; in fair working order or can be easily repaired and placed in working order.

Poor – little or no original finish remaining, major and minor parts replaced; major replacement parts required and extensive restoration needed; metal deeply pitted; principal lettering, numerals and design obliterated, wood badly scratched, bruised, cracked or broken; mechanically inoperative, generally undesirable as a collector's firearm.

THE PPGS

FIREARMS GRADING MADE EASY

The next 80 pages of high res color images with captions are easily the most important in this book. If you carefully study all the images, and thoroughly read the accompanying captions, the following color pages will help you accurately determine condition better than anything that's ever been published. This revised Photo Percentage Grading System™ (PPGS) includes images of both NRA new and antique condition factors, in addition to all the 100%-10% percentage conditions for revolvers, pistols, rifles, and shotguns.

More than 21 editions later, the Photo Percentage Grading System™ has now become the industry standard for visibly ascertaining various condition factors based on a percentage system. The 34th Edition also retains the "PPGS-o-meters" whenever possible, so you can get a quick fix on condition factors. Computer savvy users will be pleased to know that this revised 34th Edition PPGS™ is also included free of charge on our website at www.bluebookofgunvalues.com.

Condition factors pictured (indicated by PPGS-o-meters), unless otherwise noted, refer to the percentage of a gun's remaining finish(es), including blue, case colors, nickel, or another type of original finish remaining on the frame/receiver. On older guns, describing the receiver/frame finish accurately is absolutely critical to ascertain an accurate grade, which will determine the correct value.

Additional percentages of condition may be used to describe other specific parts of a gun (i.e. barrel, wood finish, plating, magazine tube, etc.). Percentages of patina/brown or other finish discoloration factors must also be explained separately when necessary, and likewise be interpolated accurately. **With antiques, the overall percentage within this text is NOT an average of the various condition factors, but again, refers to the overall original condition of the frame/receiver. Being able to spot original condition has never been more important, especially when the prices get into four, five, and six figures. Remember, the price is wrong if the condition factor isn't right!**

Now, more than ever, it takes well-trained senses of sight, hearing, touch, and smell, with a direct connection to the most powerful computer ever built, a trained human brain, to accurately fingerprint a gun's correct condition factor. Regardless of how much knowledge you've accumulated from books, websites, auction catalogs, dealer listings, etc., you're still in potential danger as a buyer if you can't figure out a gun's condition factor(s) accurately. More than anything else, an older gun's overall condition must "add up" (i.e., a Model 12 with visible barrel wear should not have a bright blue magazine tube, and a Model 1911 Colt with 98% frame finish should not have an 80% slide).

While the 34th Edition's Photo Percentage Grading System™ certainly isn't meant to be the Last Testament on firearms grading, it hopefully goes a lot further than anything else published on the subject. Once you've accumulated the experience necessary to grade guns accurately, a ten-second "CAT scan" is usually all the time that is needed to zero in on each gun's unique condition factor.

In closing, the publisher wishes to express his thanks and gratitude to Pat Hogan, Judy Voss, and Matt Parise at Rock Island Auctions, and Dr. Leonardo Antaris, M.D. for authorizing the use of their digital images for the Photo Percentage Grading System™ (PPGS).

Sincerely,

S.P. Fjestad
Author & Publisher - *Blue Book of Gun Values*™

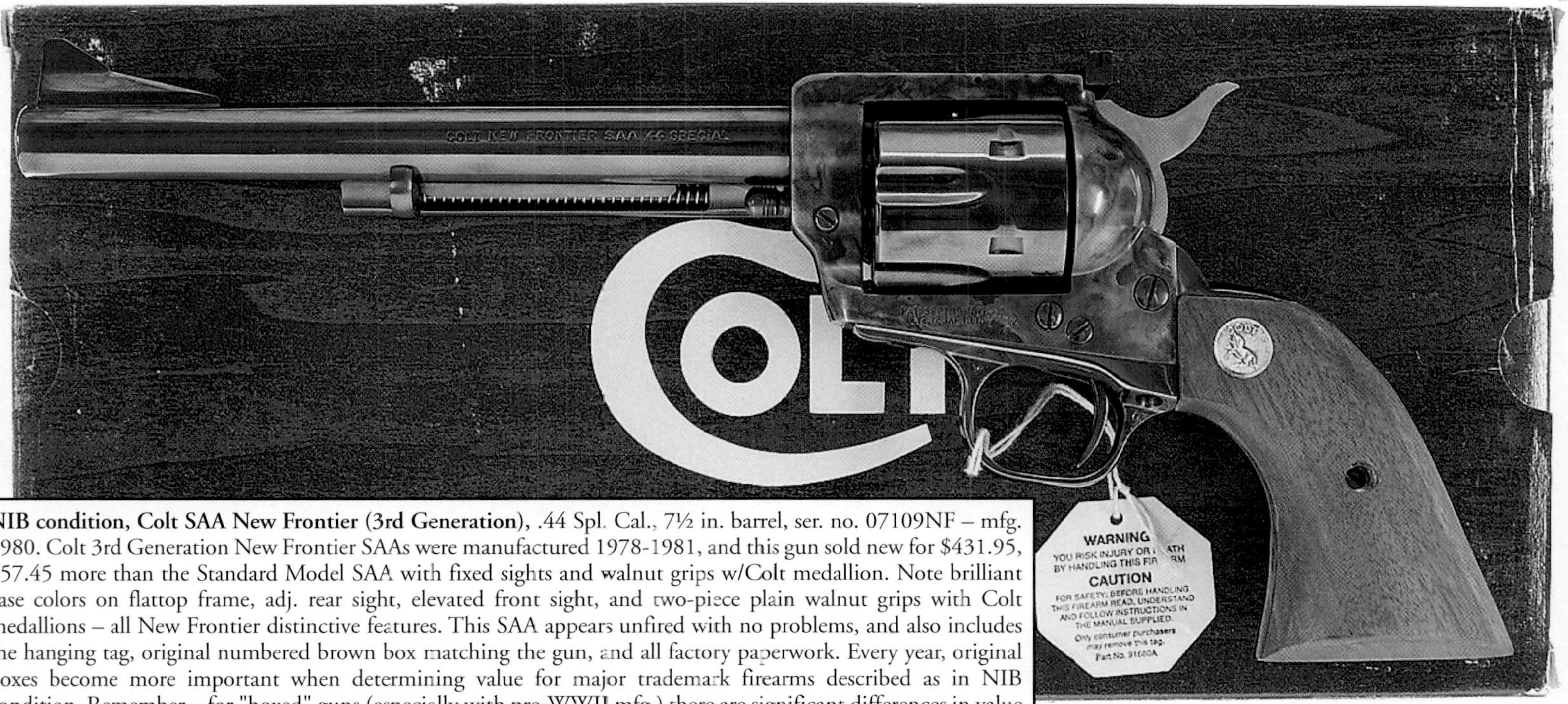

NIB condition, Colt SAA New Frontier (3rd Generation), .44 Spl. Cal., 7½ in. barrel, ser. no. 07109NF – mfg. 1980. Colt 3rd Generation New Frontier SAAs were manufactured 1978-1981, and this gun sold new for $431.95, $57.45 more than the Standard Model SAA with fixed sights and walnut grips w/Colt medallion. Note brilliant case colors on flattop frame, adj. rear sight, elevated front sight, and two-piece plain walnut grips with Colt medallions – all New Frontier distinctive features. This SAA appears unfired with no problems, and also includes the hanging tag, original numbered brown box matching the gun, and all factory paperwork. Every year, original boxes become more important when determining value for major trademark firearms described as in NIB condition. Remember – for "boxed" guns (especially with pre-WWII mfg.) there are significant differences in value between an original box numbered to the gun (most desirable), an original non-matching or unnumbered box from the same circa (less desirable), a factory box for a different model or circa (add for box only), or an outright fake (recent reproduction that adds no value). So be careful before paying a premium for a firearm advertised as "includes box," as it could mean almost anything.

This PPGS section is also available online free of charge - visit www.bluebookofgunvalues.com

REVOLVERS: PPGS CONDITION FACTORS

26

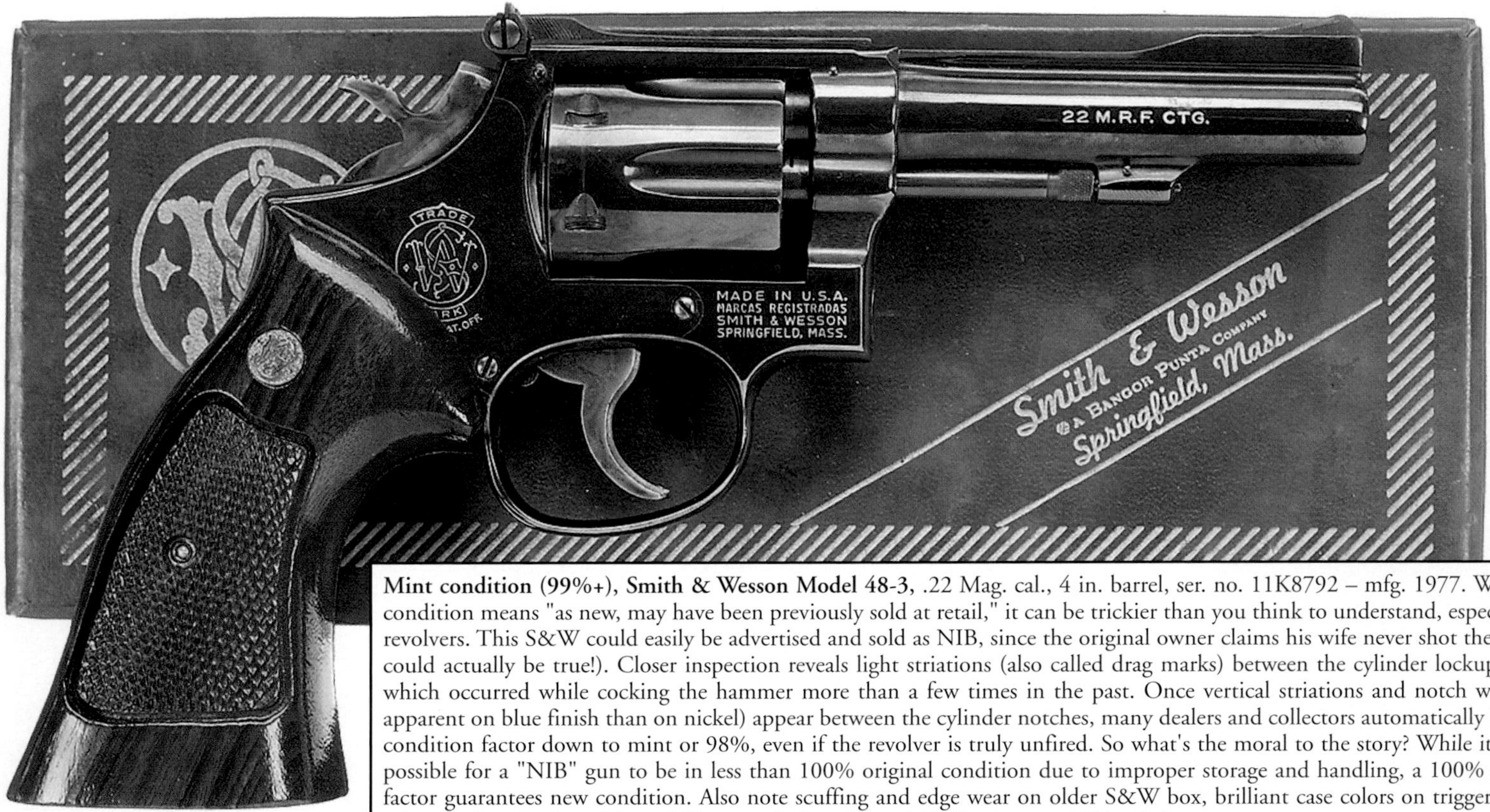

Mint condition (99%+), **Smith & Wesson Model 48-3**, .22 Mag. cal., 4 in. barrel, ser. no. 11K8792 – mfg. 1977. While mint condition means "as new, may have been previously sold at retail," it can be trickier than you think to understand, especially with revolvers. This S&W could easily be advertised and sold as NIB, since the original owner claims his wife never shot the gun (this could actually be true!). Closer inspection reveals light striations (also called drag marks) between the cylinder lockup notches, which occurred while cocking the hammer more than a few times in the past. Once vertical striations and notch wear (more apparent on blue finish than on nickel) appear between the cylinder notches, many dealers and collectors automatically knock the condition factor down to mint or 98%, even if the revolver is truly unfired. So what's the moral to the story? While it's entirely possible for a "NIB" gun to be in less than 100% original condition due to improper storage and handling, a 100% condition factor guarantees new condition. Also note scuffing and edge wear on older S&W box, brilliant case colors on trigger/hammer, mint checkered grips with medallions, and pinned barrel (indicating pre-1981 mfg.).

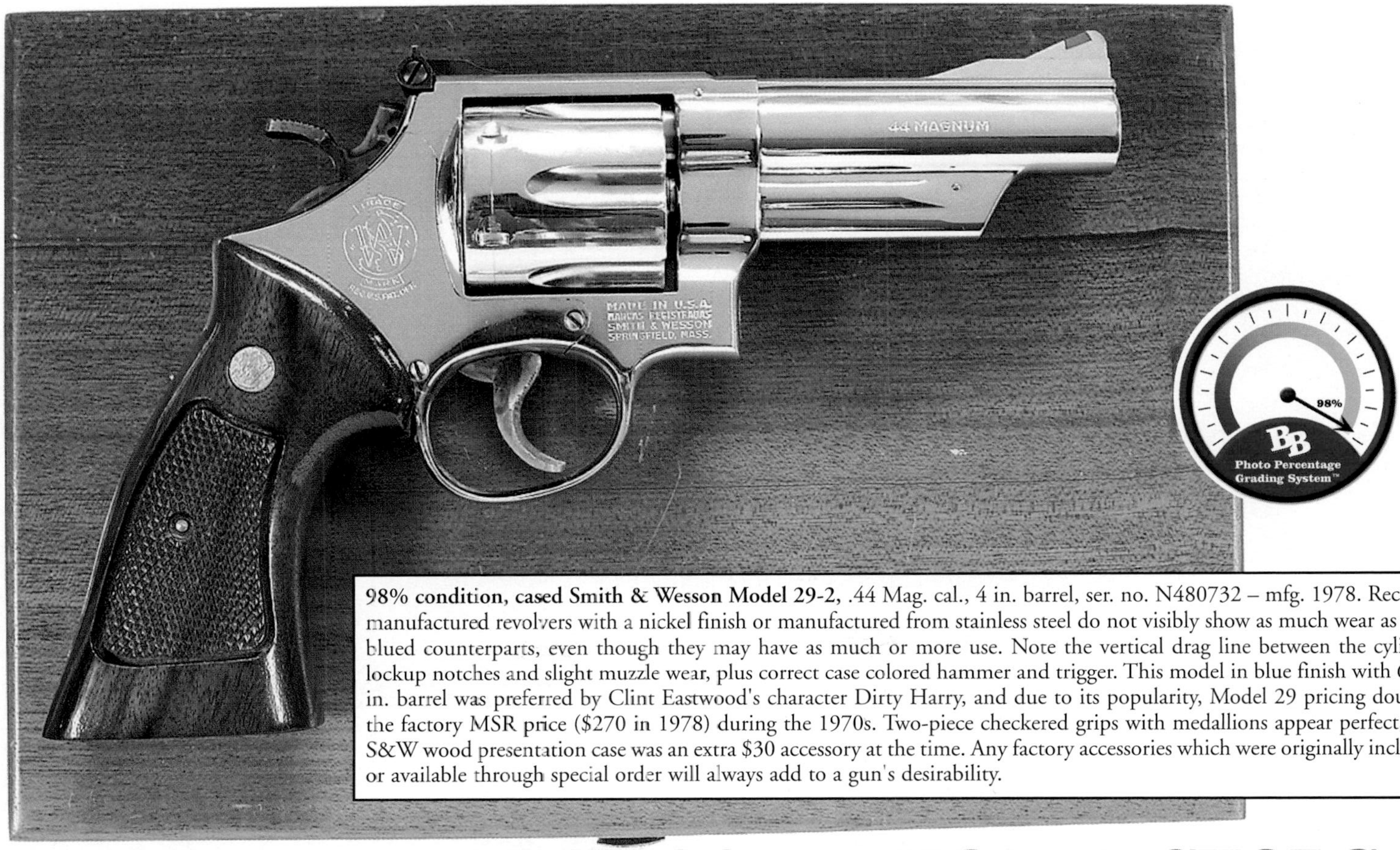

98% condition, cased Smith & Wesson Model 29-2, .44 Mag. cal., 4 in. barrel, ser. no. N480732 – mfg. 1978. Recently manufactured revolvers with a nickel finish or manufactured from stainless steel do not visibly show as much wear as their blued counterparts, even though they may have as much or more use. Note the vertical drag line between the cylinder lockup notches and slight muzzle wear, plus correct case colored hammer and trigger. This model in blue finish with 6 1/2 in. barrel was preferred by Clint Eastwood's character Dirty Harry, and due to its popularity, Model 29 pricing doubled the factory MSR price ($270 in 1978) during the 1970s. Two-piece checkered grips with medallions appear perfect, and S&W wood presentation case was an extra $30 accessory at the time. Any factory accessories which were originally included or available through special order will always add to a gun's desirability.

REVOLVERS: PPGS CONDITION FACTORS

27

REVOLVERS: PPGS CONDITION FACTORS

28

95% condition, Smith & Wesson Model 34, .22 LR cal., 4 in. barrel, ser. no. 191 – mfg. 1954. 95% on newer mfg. revolvers typically means minor barrel muzzle wear, indicating holster use, and a more noticeable wear line between the cylinder notches. Flat latch cylinder release indicates early mfg., and is worth 25% more than later mfg. Note round butt grip configuration with S&W medallions inset in slightly worn walnut grips with diamond checkering. Careful observation also reveals slight wear on frame and cylinder edges. Bluing is still bright, with several small areas of slight discoloration – case colors on hammer/trigger are near perfect. Whenever a revolver in this condition is encountered, the bore should be near perfect, and the action tight and correctly timed. Overall, a nice example of early S&W quality that can still be used and purchased for a reasonable price.

90% condition, Sturm-Ruger Single Six, .22 LR and .22 Mag. cal. cylinders, 6½ in. barrel, ser. no. 260-95611 – mfg. 1985. You might initially think that this gun's condition is actually better than the 95% S&W on the preceding page. Note that the trigger guard has been chipped and damaged, certainly not indicative of normal wear. Careful observation reveals pitting and metal discoloration on the frame (top and front), hammer, and loading gate (bad), in addition to serious drag marks between the cylinder lock-up notches, which indicates a lot of shooting. Original wood grips also show finish wear and scratching. This revolver is a good example of a 90% condition factor with problems, as opposed to a 90% revolver with normal bluing wear. The areas of pitting, freckling, finish discoloration, etc. need to be measured using the same criteria as regular wear when determining the correct condition, and are actually more detrimental to value than normal wear in the same condition factor. This shooter with problems is worth less than an 80% specimen with ordinary wear, and its only salvation is the original box.

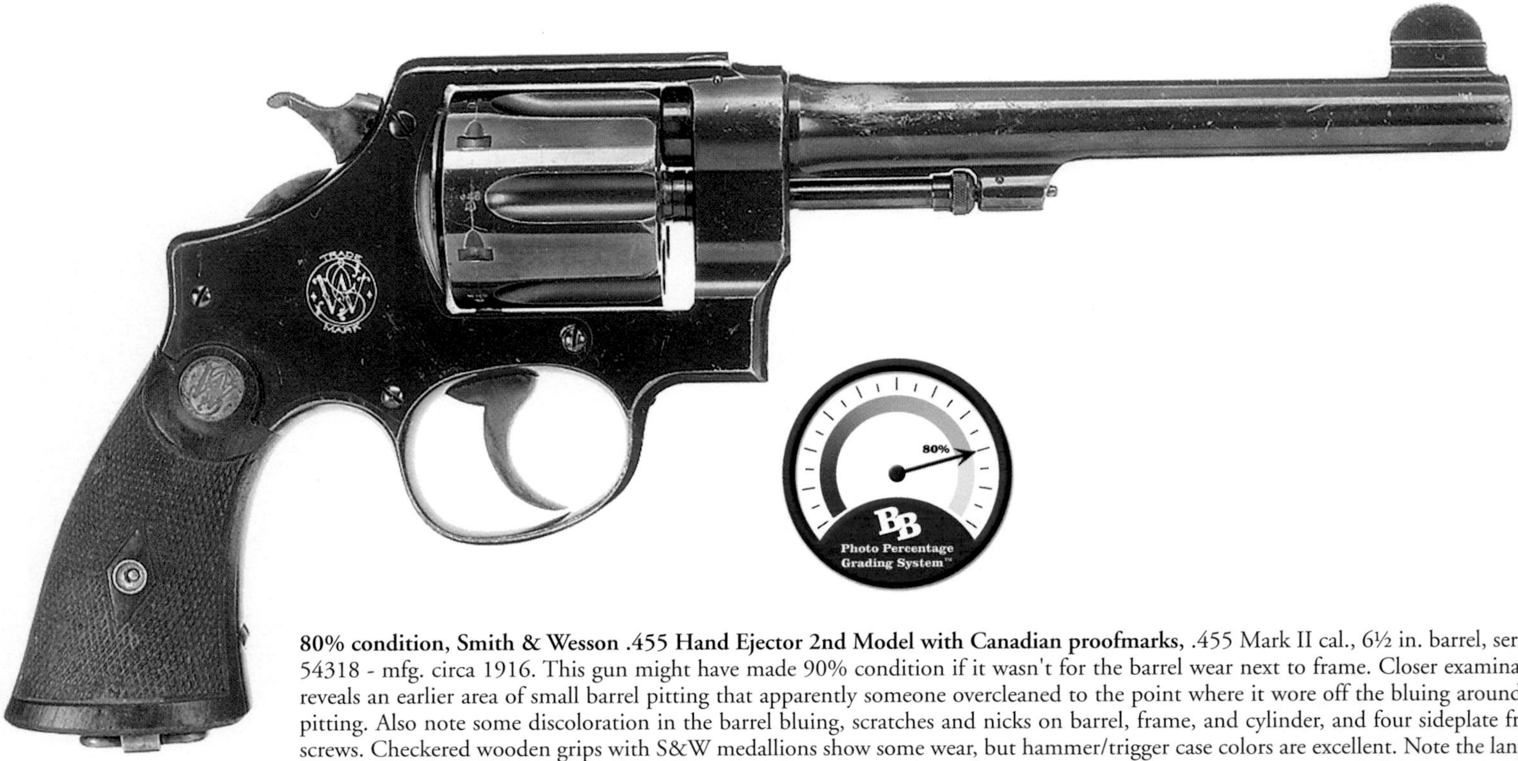

80% condition, Smith & Wesson .455 Hand Ejector 2nd Model with Canadian proofmarks, .455 Mark II cal., 6½ in. barrel, ser. no. 54318 - mfg. circa 1916. This gun might have made 90% condition if it wasn't for the barrel wear next to frame. Closer examination reveals an earlier area of small barrel pitting that apparently someone overcleaned to the point where it wore off the bluing around the pitting. Also note some discoloration in the barrel bluing, scratches and nicks on barrel, frame, and cylinder, and four sideplate frame screws. Checkered wooden grips with S&W medallions show some wear, but hammer/trigger case colors are excellent. Note the lanyard ring on the bottom of the grip frame, standard for this model. While unseen in the image, this specimen has both the Commonwealth "BNP" (British Nitro Proof), and Canadian crossed flags, indicating military usage.

70% condition, Smith & Wesson .38 Military & Police 1st Model (Model 1899 Navy), .38 Military (U.S. Service) cal., 6 in. barrel, ser. no. 5504 – mfg. circa 1900. This specimen is a good example of an older, used revolver in above average condition, even though it has barrel and cylinder discoloration and pitting (brown areas) and worn grips (the diamond pattern around the screw is barely visible). This particular revolver is one of 1,000 that were purchased by the U.S. Navy. Inset photo of bottom of grip frame reveals seven lines of marks, including the U.S. Navy anchor and "CAB" inspector initials. Considering this U.S. Navy Contract model was typically subjected to sea conditions, including salt corrosion, most specimens today are in this condition factor or worse. Even with this much finish wear, however, the action remains very tight, and the bore is still bright with very little corrosion.

REVOLVERS: PPGS CONDITION FACTORS

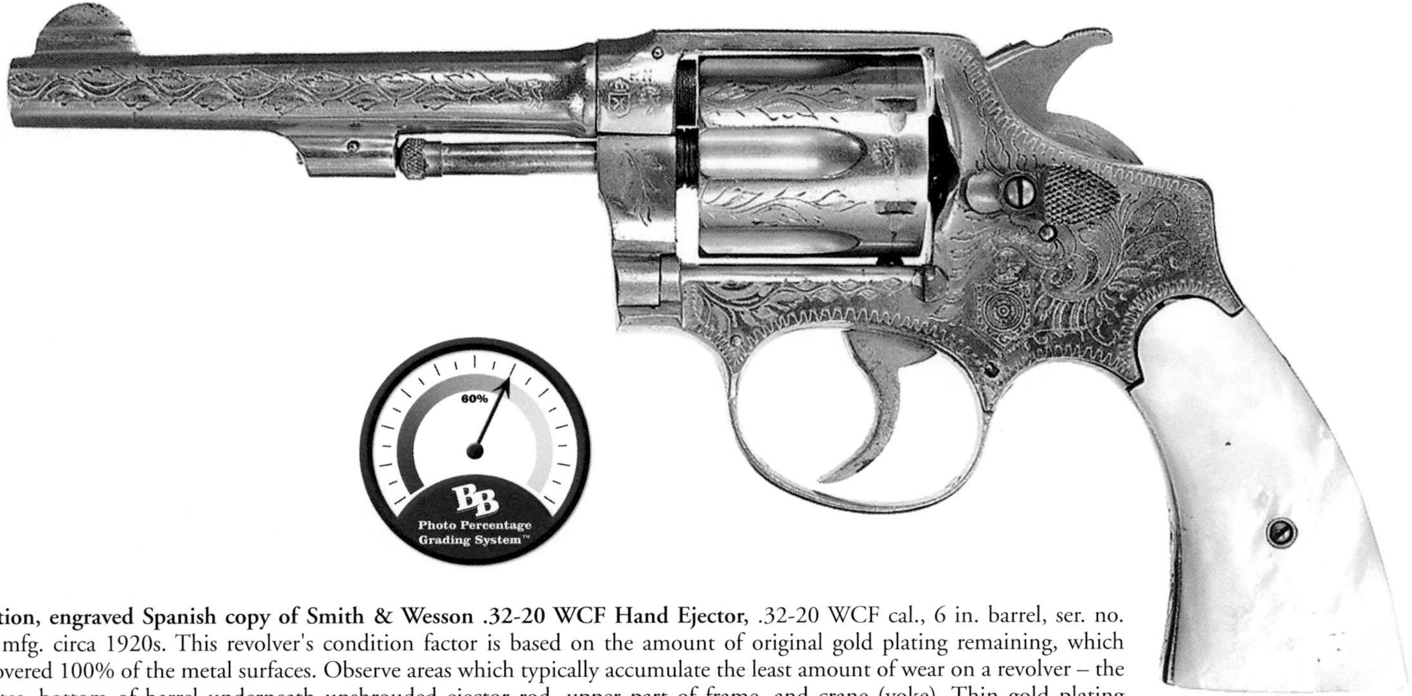

60% condition, engraved Spanish copy of Smith & Wesson .32-20 WCF Hand Ejector, .32-20 WCF cal., 6 in. barrel, ser. no. M12256 – mfg. circa 1920s. This revolver's condition factor is based on the amount of original gold plating remaining, which originally covered 100% of the metal surfaces. Observe areas which typically accumulate the least amount of wear on a revolver – the cylinder flutes, bottom of barrel underneath unshrouded ejector rod, upper part of frame, and crane (yoke). Thin gold plating explains the wear on the barrel and lower frame. Mother-of-pearl grips are probably original, but notice the gap between the arched portion of the grip and the frame. If this was an original factory engraved S&W, someone would care, and pay accordingly, but as a Spanish copy with little or no collectibility, this gun gets priced as a fancy shooter.

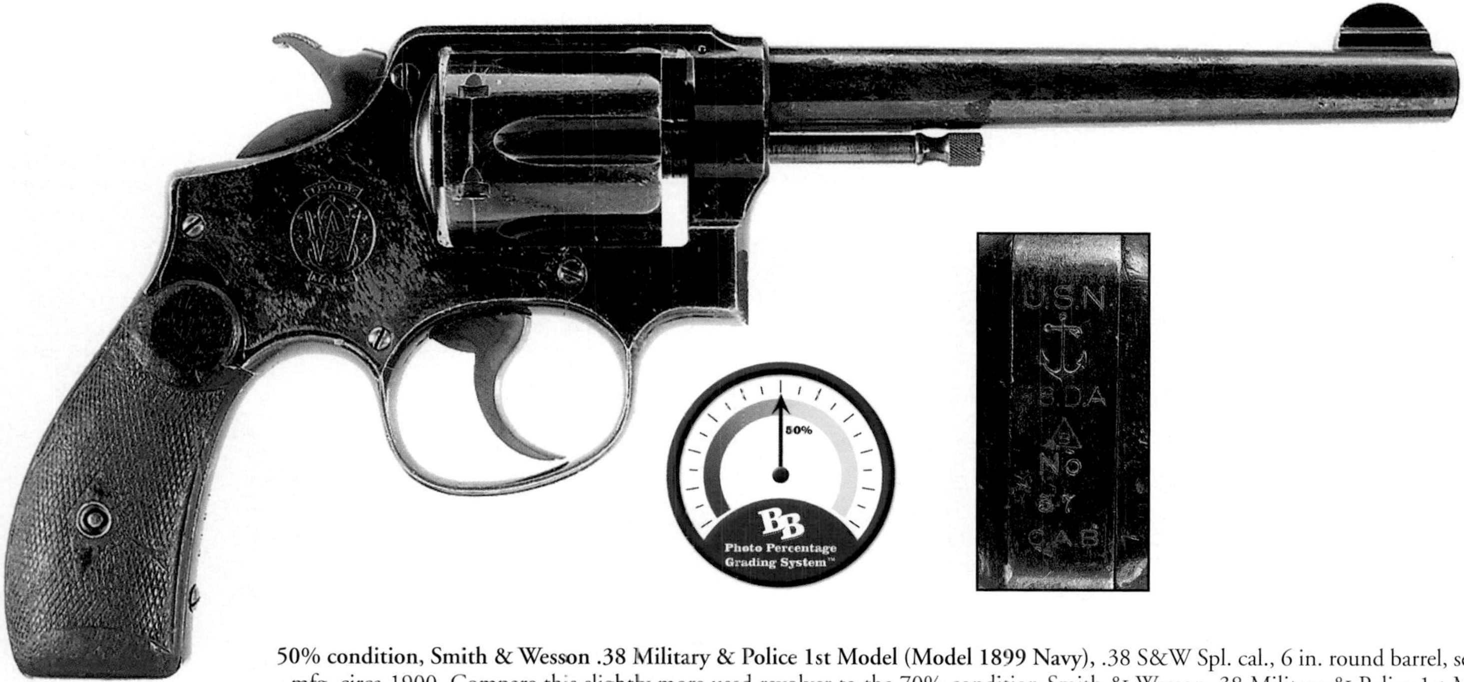

50% condition, Smith & Wesson .38 Military & Police 1st Model (**Model 1899 Navy**), .38 S&W Spl. cal., 6 in. round barrel, ser. no. 5151 - mfg. circa 1900. Compare this slightly more used revolver to the 70% condition Smith & Wesson .38 Military & Police 1st Model. Note that the overall appearance is darker, with the barrel showing more wear, and the rear frame scratching and pitting is very obvious. Even though the barrel, cylinder, and frame metal condition is less than the 60% condition engraved Spanish copy of Smith & Wesson, the case colors on the hammer and trigger are actually better on this revolver. Again, note the inset with USN and anchor markings. The checkered grips are also in worse condition. Nice, straight slots on frame screw heads on this and the previous revolver indicate that these revolvers have probably never been taken apart. Older original revolvers in this condition factor or less typically show more pitting and bluing discoloration.

REVOLVERS: PPGS CONDITION FACTORS

34

40% condition, Smith & Wesson .38 Military & Police 1st Model (**Model 1899 Navy**), .38 S&W Spl. cal., 6 in. barrel, ser. no. 5043 – mfg. circa 1900. This Model 1899 Navy would be at least 70% overall, if it wasn't for the major finish deterioration on the rear of the frame – note the brown patina and pitting in back of the S&W logo. Nicks and gouges on the barrel, frame, and cylinder are also typical of this condition factor. The ejector rod has also turned a brown patina. As you can see, each gun is unique once you get down to these lower condition factors, and each revolver component (barrel, frame, cylinder, grips, case colors, trigger/hammer) has to be taken into consideration before the overall condition factor can be accurately established. In cases where finish wear is excessive on a single part, it is usually prudent to mention/describe that lower condition factor/problem separately.

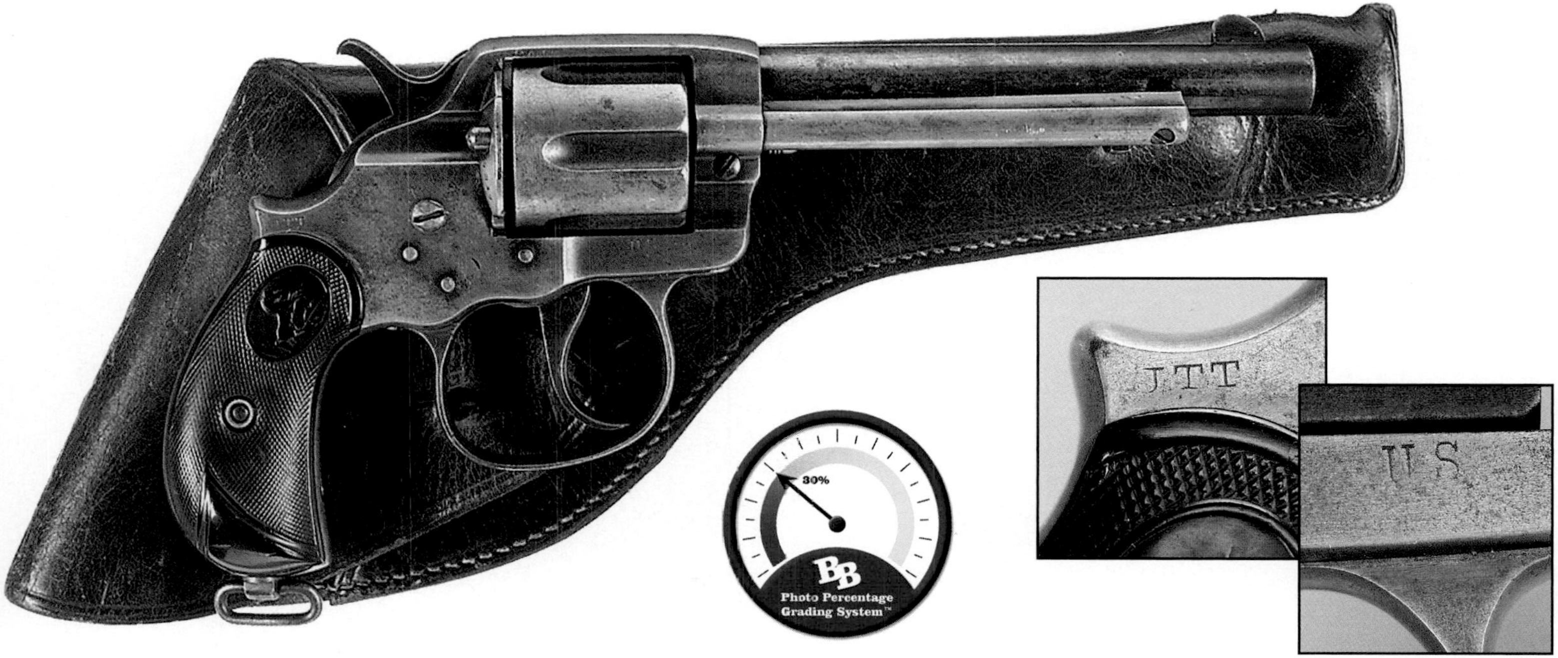

30% condition, U.S. Colt Alaskan Model 1878/1902, .45 LC cal., 6 in. round barrel, ser. no. 45317 – mfg. 1900. Notice how the overall condition of this revolver is approximately in 10% less condition than the 40% condition S&W Military & Police 1st Model. This military marked specimen, which includes "RAC" on left side and "JTT" (John T. Thompson, of Thompson sub-machine gun fame) inspector initials on right side, also has a U.S. property marking. Observe the smooth, overall brownish patina finish, while the barrel exhibits overall pitting, even though the bore is excellent. Note traces of bright barrel blue next to and in front of ejector rod assembly. Screw heads look original, and grips with rampant Colt inserts are worn proportionately with the rest of this gun's finish. Oversize trigger and trigger guard, in addition to the lanyard ring, are distinguishing features of this U.S. military contract model, allowing soldiers to fire it with mittened or gloved hands.

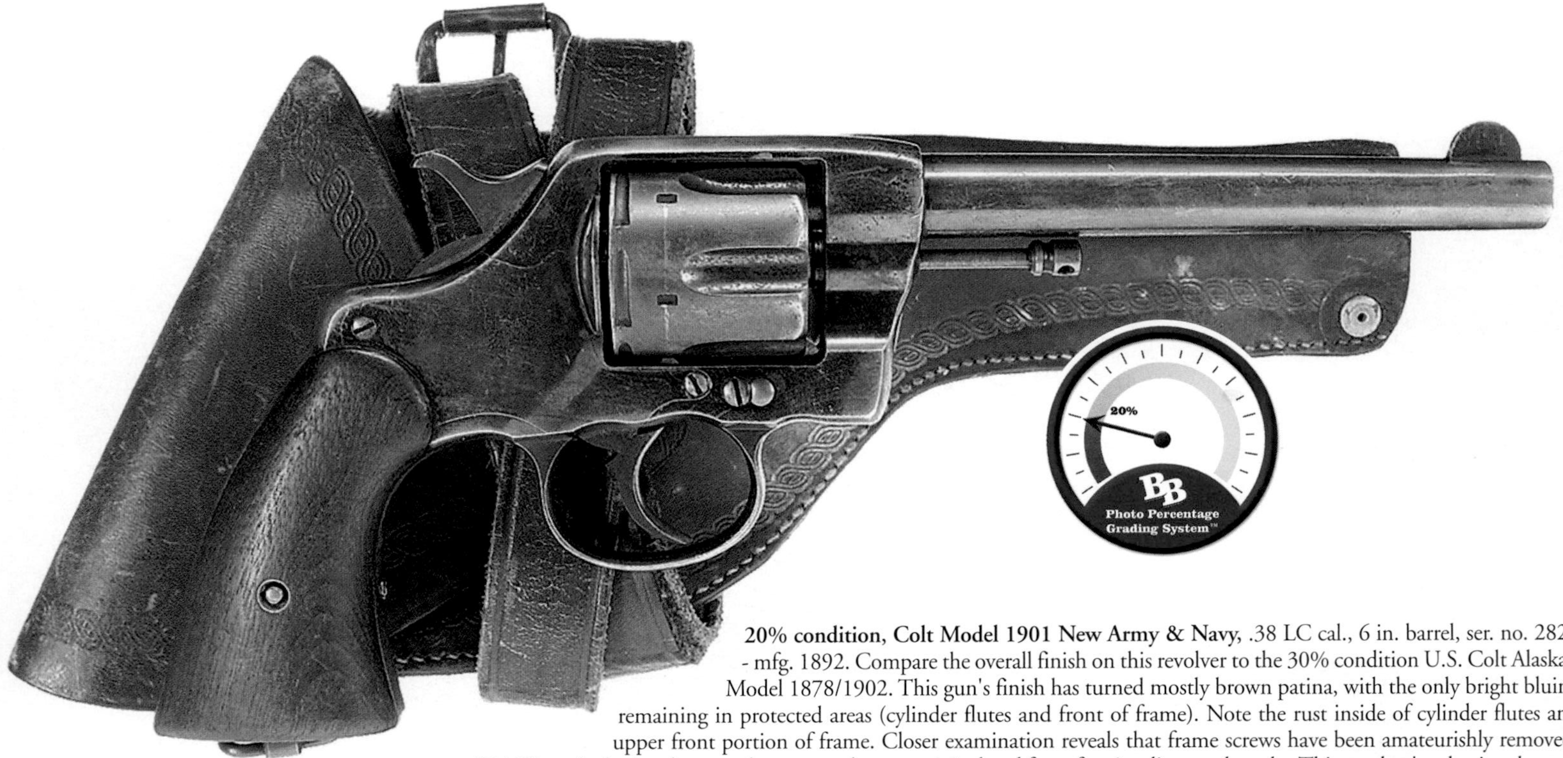

20% condition, Colt Model 1901 New Army & Navy, .38 LC cal., 6 in. barrel, ser. no. 2822 - mfg. 1892. Compare the overall finish on this revolver to the 30% condition U.S. Colt Alaskan Model 1878/1902. This gun's finish has turned mostly brown patina, with the only bright bluing remaining in protected areas (cylinder flutes and front of frame). Note the rust inside of cylinder flutes and upper front portion of frame. Closer examination reveals that frame screws have been amateurishly removed. "RAC" marked grips show moderate wear, but are original and free of major dings and cracks. This revolver's value is enhanced somewhat because it still has a very tight action and bright bore, which is very important to collectors of older revolvers. Many handgun collectors would rather have a no-problem gun in this condition than one in 50% condition, but with major pitting, a dark bore, and other problems. The original holster and belt accompany this well-worn specimen.

10%-20% condition, inscribed Colt Model 1878 DA Frontier Six Shooter, .44-40 WCF cal., 4¾ in. barrel, ser. no. 34108 - mfg. 1894. If the condition factor is less than this, it won't make much of a price difference anyway. Almost all metal surfaces have either no finish or a slight brown patina - note the exterior of the cylinder was severely rusted in the past, but cylinder flutes retain a nice brown patina finish. This particular gun's salvation is the 17 pages of documentation that are provided, proving it belonged to "G.H. Ward Sheriff Vinta Co.", the sheriff who captured Butch Cassidy and delivered him to prison - note backstrap inscription. Any gun with a documented, sterling provenance has to be appraised individually. This gun sold at auction several years ago for $3,450, the auction estimate was $1,500-$2,500, and the current Blue Book price range is $625-$850, without a famous personality premium or historically significant provenance like this.

REVOLVERS: NRA ANTIQUE CONDITIONS

38

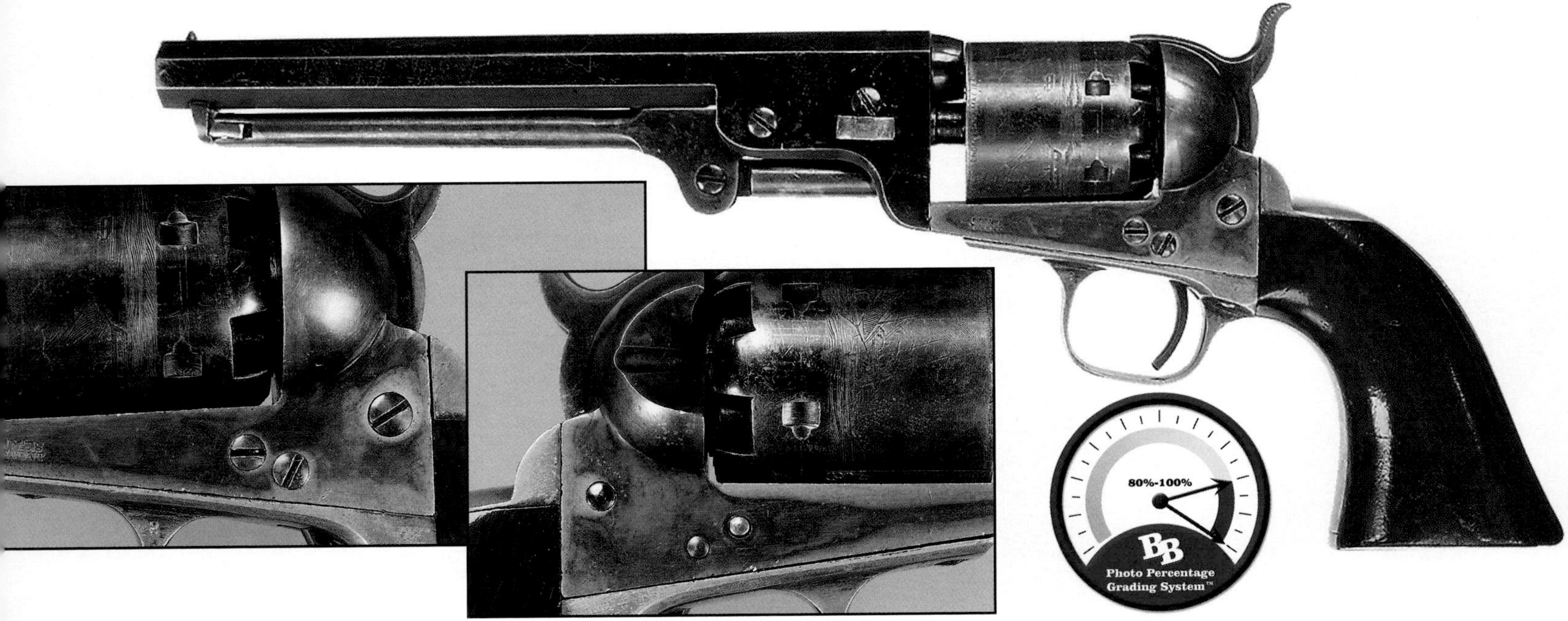

NRA Excellent (over 80% condition), inscribed Colt Model 1851 Navy Fourth Model, .36 cal. percussion, 7½ in. octagon barrel, ser. no. 127080/2 – mfg. 1862. This commercial Colt 1851 Navy was manufactured during the Civil War (1861-1865), and has the late New York barrel address. The frame, barrel, trigger guard, and backstrap all have matching 127080/2 serial numbers, indicating this gun was one of a two-gun presentation set. The backstrap is inscribed "To Major Hill, 45th Reg't OVI" (Ohio Volunteer Infantry). Also verifying this revolver's authenticity is a tintype (older photograph) of Major Hill, his saber and Colt 1851 Navy (not shown). Note the barrel and loading lever retain most of the original finish, strong frame case colors, fire blued untampered frame screws, and excellent original wood grips, all adding up to the NRA Excellent condition factor this revolver deserves. Blue Book value without provenance – approx. $5,250-$6,500. Recent auction price – $11,500.

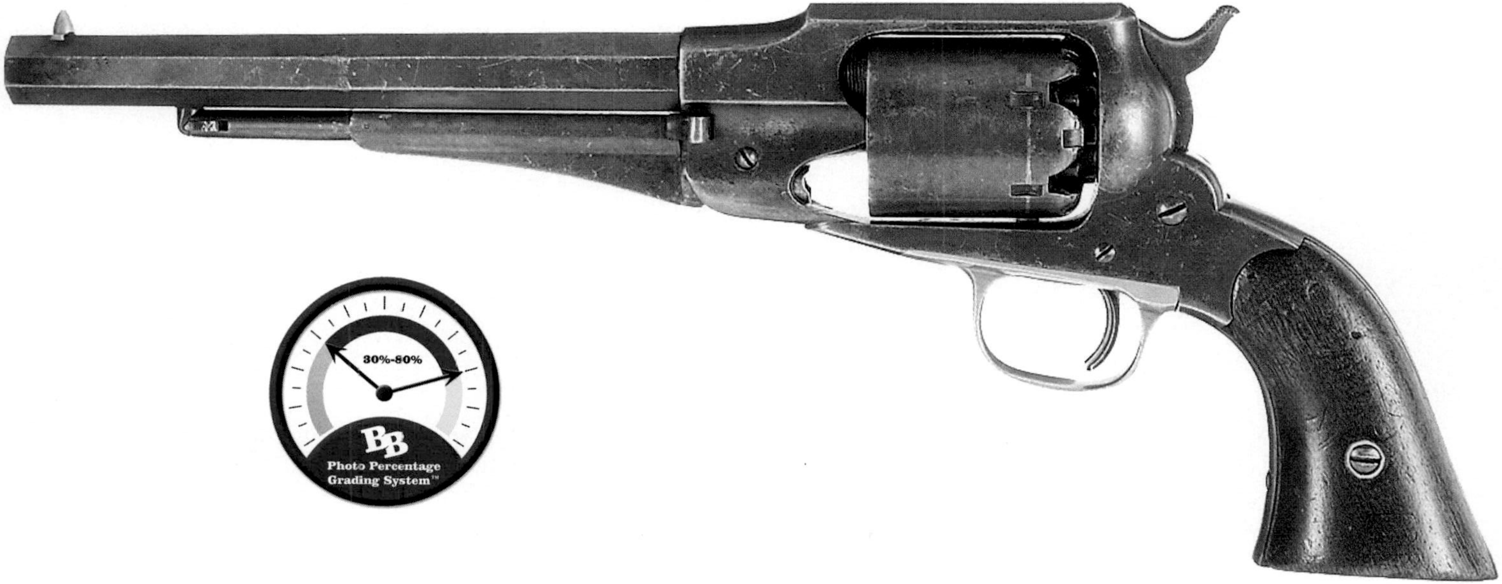

NRA Fine (30%-80% condition), Remington New Model Army, .44 cal. percussion, 8 in. octagon barrel, ser. no. 19329 – mfg. circa 1866. Overall, a nice, no problem Remington revolver retaining approx. 40%-50% original finish. Octagon barrel retains much of its bright bluing on the flats, while edges are shiny. Most of the frame and unfluted cylinder have turned a nice brown patina, while two-piece grips show normal handling marks with tiny chips. Action remains tight, and this revolver does not have the "New Model" markings used in later manufacture. While some of these guns were converted into .44 rimfire, this specimen retains its original percussion configuration. Also note the brass trigger guard and excellent condition of the screw heads. Since NRA Fine condition covers everything from 30%-80%, this revolver represents the middle of the NRA Fine condition range. Guns in better condition than this generally retain more bright blue, while guns in worse condition will have more patina.

REVOLVERS: NRA ANTIQUE CONDITIONS

40

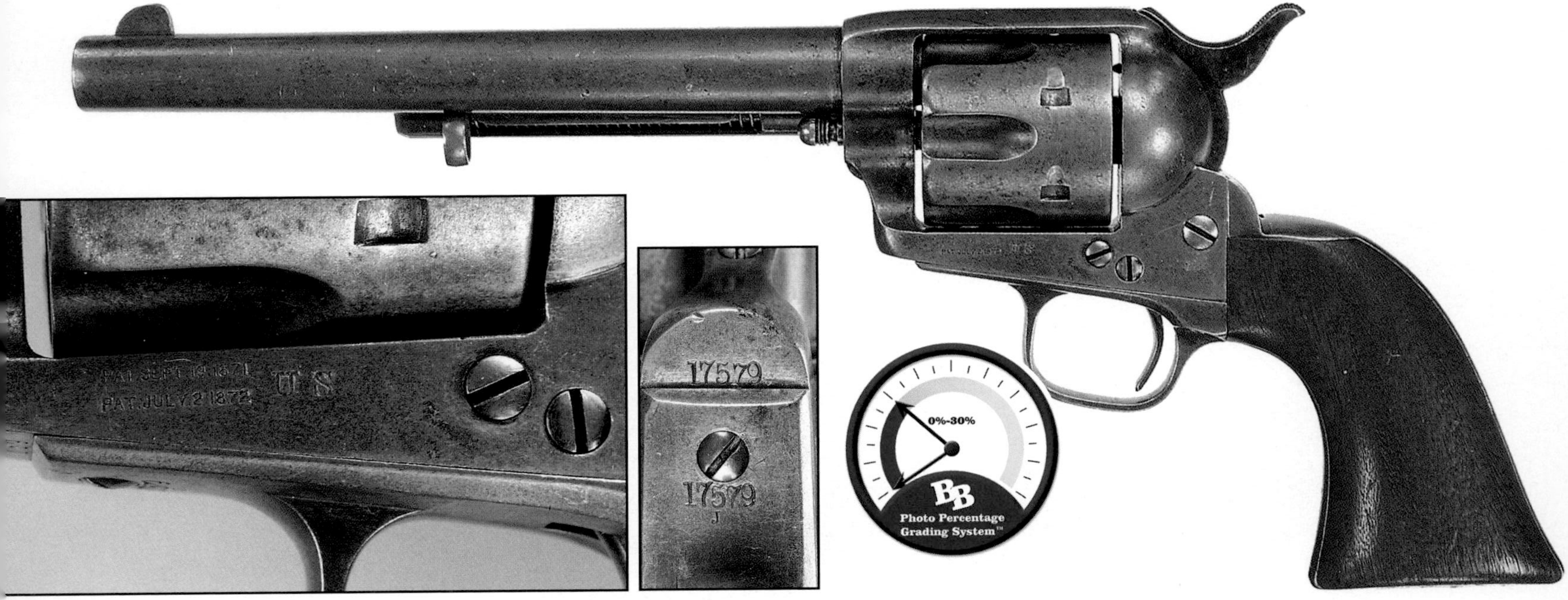

NRA Very Good (0%-30% condition), U.S. Colt SAA Cavalry Model 1873, .45 Colt cal., ser. no. 17579 - mfg. 1875. Except for protected areas, this gun's original blue and case colored finishes have turned a smooth greyish-brown patina. One-piece walnut grips are fine with only minor scratches, and matching serial numbers are on all visible components. Note how serial numbers are marked on the frame and trigger guard in the macro image. On 1st Generation SAAs, it always pays to inspect the numbers very carefully since they were stamped with a rotating roll die. Not only should all the serial numbers match and look the same, but each digit should also retain the same vertical/horizontal positioning in all three areas. The other macro image of "U.S." property stamp marking becomes very important, since revolvers in this serial range were probably issued as replacements to the 7th Cavalry after the Battle of Little Big Horn.

NRA Good (0%-20% condition), Colt Model 1849 Pocket, .31 cal. percussion, 6 in. octagon barrel, ser. no. 181985 - mfg. 1860. Note how the finish on this revolver (10%-20%) has turned an overall plum patina, as opposed to the bright bluing and case colors remaining on the NRA Excellent 1851 Navy. Dark areas on barrel and frame indicate major areas of earlier pitting. Brass trigger guard and frame, originally silver plated, indicate that this revolver is a first type, as the second type has steel grip straps. The cylinder has been filed and renumbered to match the overall serial number, while the grips have been revarnished over the dents and scratches. Screws look good, and this gun's overall condition suggests that it was never abused during its shooting career. This revolver's operating mechanism still functions smoothly, even though the bore is somewhat dark and lightly pitted.

REVOLVERS: NRA ANTIQUE CONDITIONS

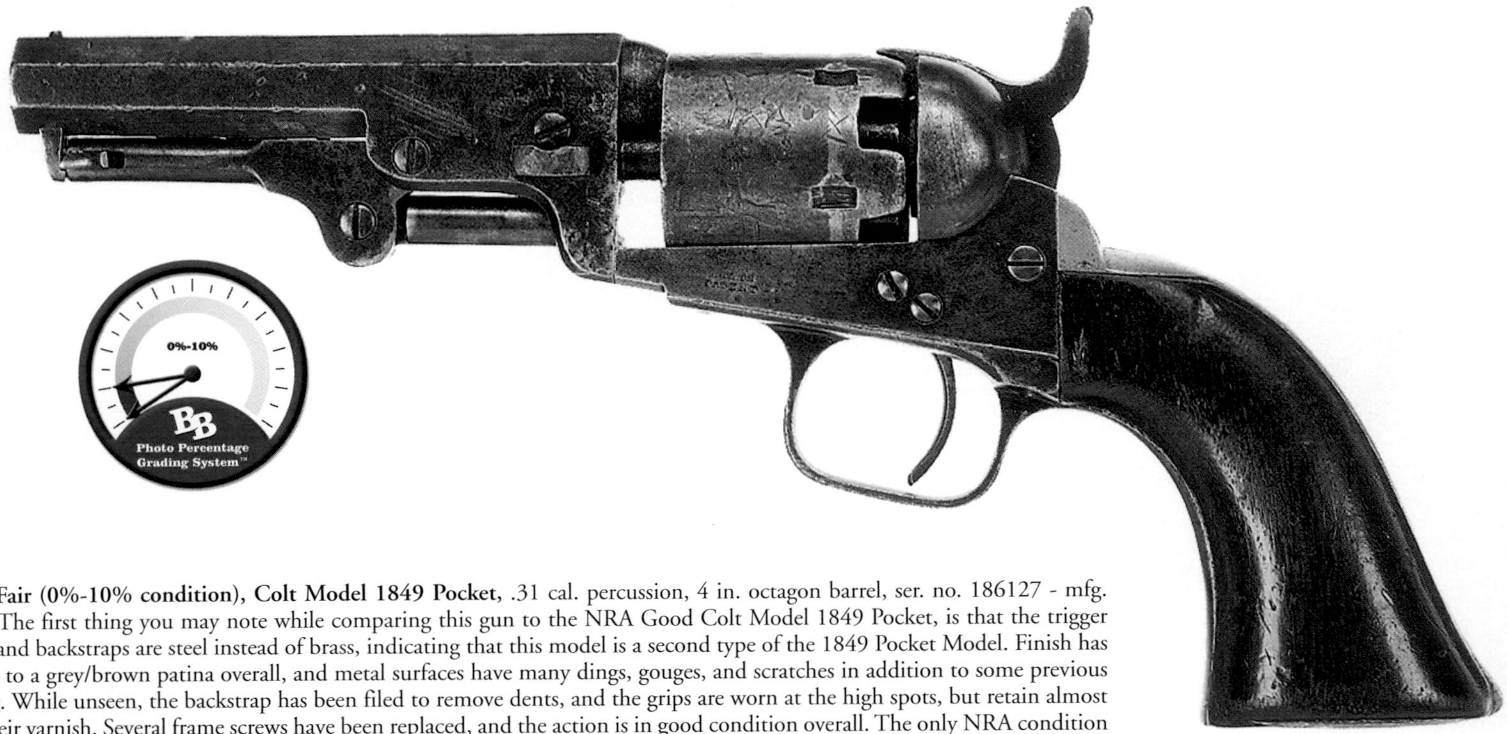

NRA Fair (0%-10% condition), Colt Model 1849 Pocket, .31 cal. percussion, 4 in. octagon barrel, ser. no. 186127 - mfg. 1861. The first thing you may note while comparing this gun to the NRA Good Colt Model 1849 Pocket, is that the trigger guard and backstraps are steel instead of brass, indicating that this model is a second type of the 1849 Pocket Model. Finish has turned to a grey/brown patina overall, and metal surfaces have many dings, gouges, and scratches in addition to some previous pitting. While unseen, the backstrap has been filed to remove dents, and the grips are worn at the high spots, but retain almost half their varnish. Several frame screws have been replaced, and the action is in good condition overall. The only NRA condition factor worse than this is Poor (not pictured), which means that both major and minor parts have been replaced, metal surfaces are deeply pitted, the mechanism is inoperative, and generally the gun is undesirable as a collector's firearm.

NIB condition, Colt MK IV Series 70 Government Model, .45 ACP cal., 5 in. barrel, ser. no. 32386B70 – mfg. 1979. When encountered in NIB condition, semi-automatic pistols, because of their design and characteristics, show less wear than revolvers. Even though a pistol may be unfired, its semi-auto action may have been racked many times, and this type of inspection use doesn't show up as wear like the revolver. This Colt Series 70 Government Model with nickel finish has never been more desirable, and NIB specimens like this one are now priced around $1,400. Note the older brown Colt box with scuff marks and edge wear, indicating that this pistol, for whatever reason, has done some traveling, even though it remains unfired. NIB condition also means that everything that was supplied with the gun originally is still in the box/case, including the instruction manual, warranty card, lock (if applicable), and other factory materials.

PISTOLS: PPGS CONDITION FACTORS

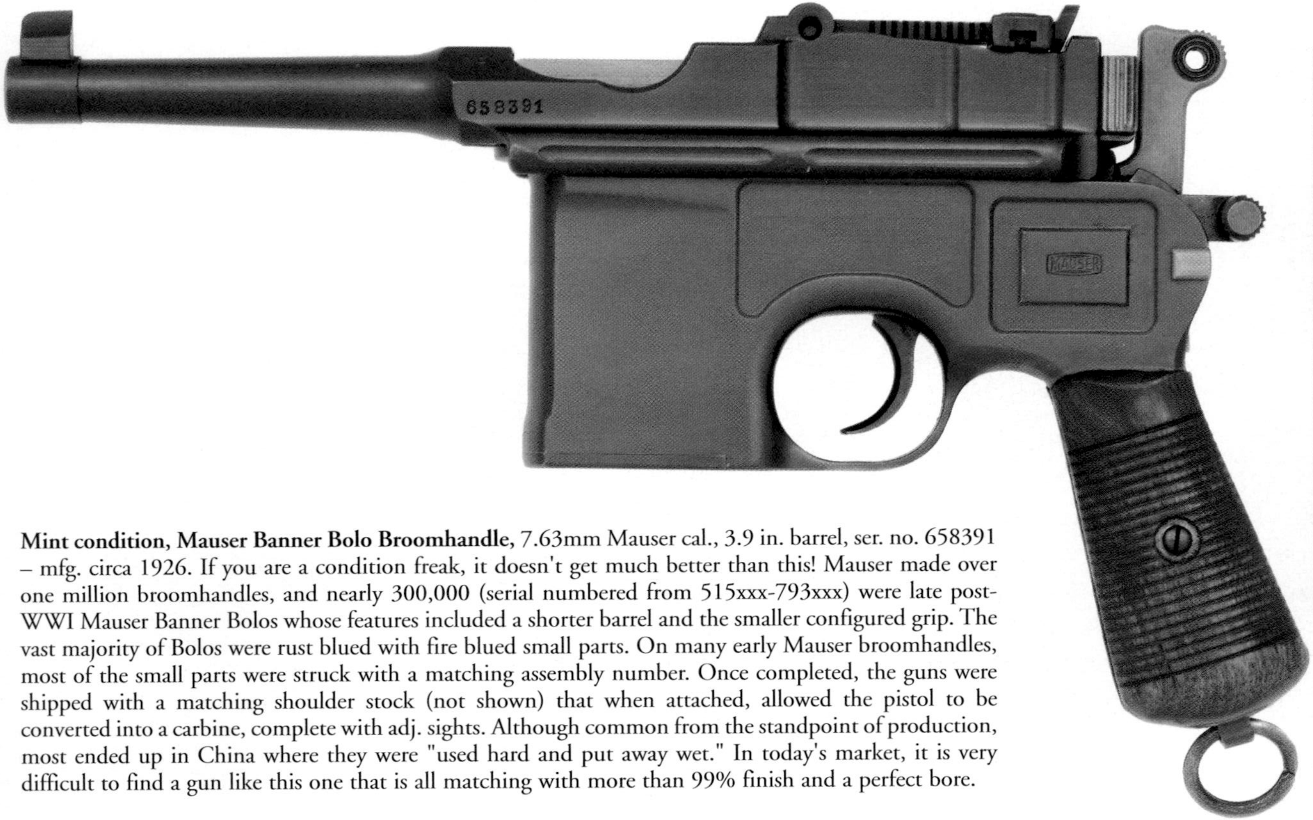

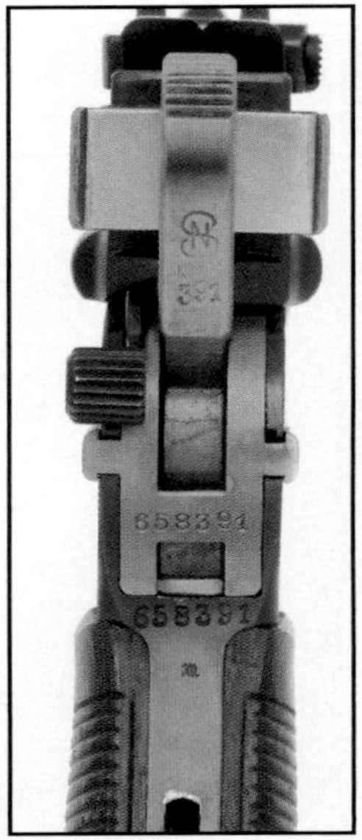

Mint condition, Mauser Banner Bolo Broomhandle, 7.63mm Mauser cal., 3.9 in. barrel, ser. no. 658391 – mfg. circa 1926. If you are a condition freak, it doesn't get much better than this! Mauser made over one million broomhandles, and nearly 300,000 (serial numbered from 515xxx-793xxx) were late post-WWI Mauser Banner Bolos whose features included a shorter barrel and the smaller configured grip. The vast majority of Bolos were rust blued with fire blued small parts. On many early Mauser broomhandles, most of the small parts were struck with a matching assembly number. Once completed, the guns were shipped with a matching shoulder stock (not shown) that when attached, allowed the pistol to be converted into a carbine, complete with adj. sights. Although common from the standpoint of production, most ended up in China where they were "used hard and put away wet." In today's market, it is very difficult to find a gun like this one that is all matching with more than 99% finish and a perfect bore.

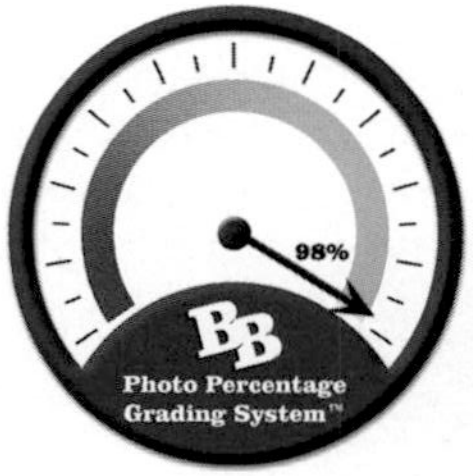

98% condition, Fabrique Nationale (F.N.) Hi-Power, 9mm Para. cal., 4 ¾ in. barrel, ser. no. 54066 – mfg. circa early 1950s. Those of you who can tell the difference in coloring between the various bluing techniques will immediately recognize this gun as being rust-blued, correct for this post-WWII F.N. pistol, as is the ring hammer. Even a little bit of additional holster wear on the front of the slide and frame would knock this specimen out of its 98% condition factor. A big plus is that the front grip strap does not show any wear or even light freckling, an indication that this pistol has spent a lot more time in its W. German police issue holster than in someone's hands. Walnut grip checkering is almost perfect, and light cleaning would probably remove the dirt/light corrosion in the slide serrations. Note definitive Belgian proofmarks on slide and frame, fixed sights, and the light metal blotching in middle of top slide legend. Original issue black leather holster also adds value to this pistol.

PISTOLS: PPGS CONDITION FACTORS

PISTOLS: PPGS CONDITION FACTORS

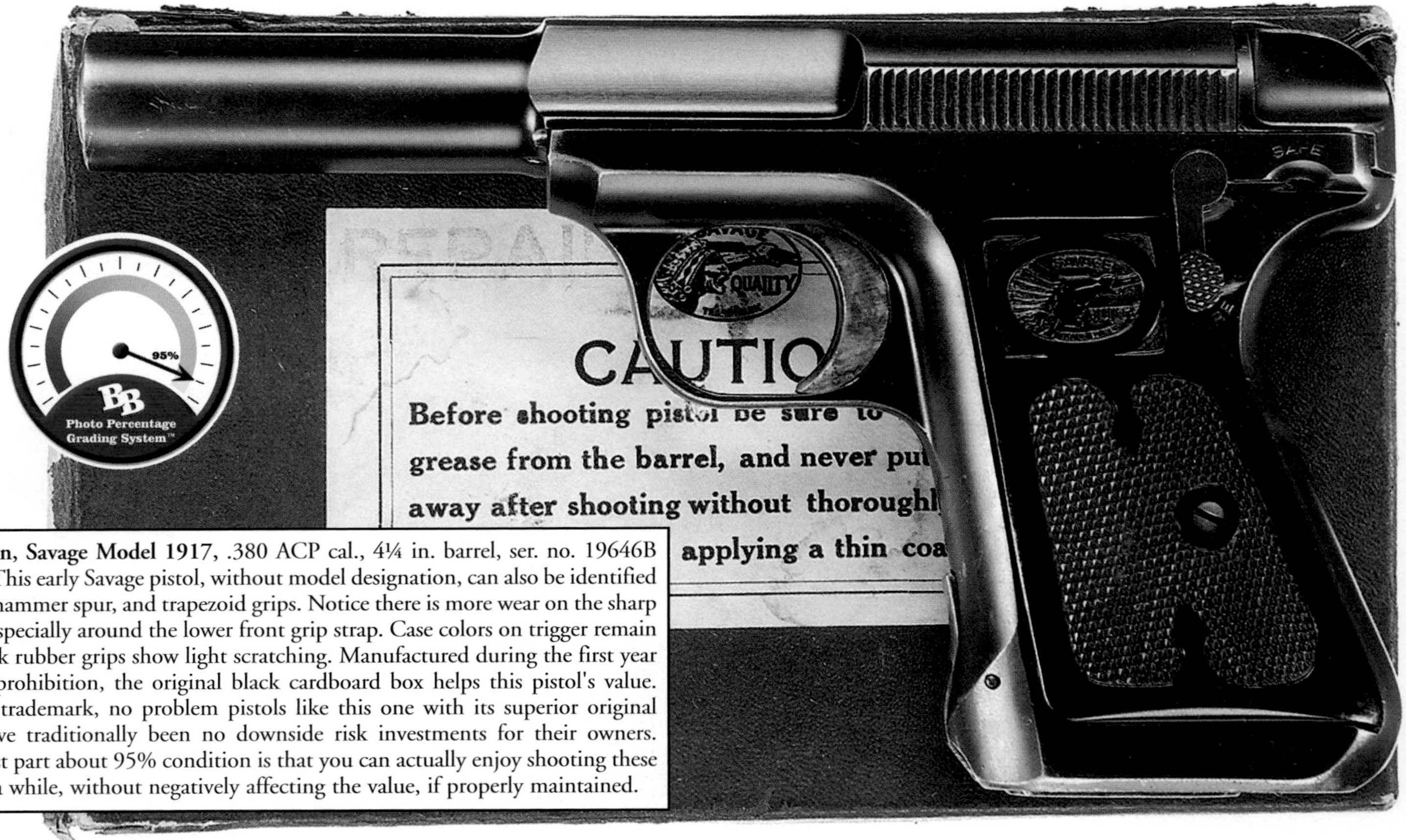

95% condition, Savage Model 1917, .380 ACP cal., 4¼ in. barrel, ser. no. 19646B – mfg. 1920. This early Savage pistol, without model designation, can also be identified by its caliber, hammer spur, and trapezoid grips. Notice there is more wear on the sharp metal edges, especially around the lower front grip strap. Case colors on trigger remain vivid and black rubber grips show light scratching. Manufactured during the first year of America's prohibition, the original black cardboard box helps this pistol's value. Clean, major trademark, no problem pistols like this one with its superior original condition, have traditionally been no downside risk investments for their owners. Maybe the best part about 95% condition is that you can actually enjoy shooting these guns once in a while, without negatively affecting the value, if properly maintained.

90% condition, Walther PP w/R.F.V. marking and holster, 7.65mm (.32 ACP) cal., 3¾ in. barrel, ser. no. 986819 – mfg. circa late 1930s. Most of the wear on this pistol has accumulated at the front of the frame and barrel, indicating a lifetime of holster storage. Metal surfaces in back of the trigger guard are an easy 95%. R.F.V. backstrap marking (see inset) indicates this pistol was made for Hitler's Reich Finance Administration. Crown N proofmarks indicate pre-April, 1940 mfg. The unmarked holster contains an extra magazine. Original black plastic grips show limited usage and are in excellent condition. Perfect action and crisp bore enhance this gun's value. The original early Walther Models PP and smaller PPK are still benchmarks for quality, reliability, and design. The Walther PP was the world's first commercially successful double action pistol, and pre-war and WWII production have become very collectible. And don't forget, the legendary James Bond carried a PPK for decades.

PISTOLS: PPGS CONDITION FACTORS

48

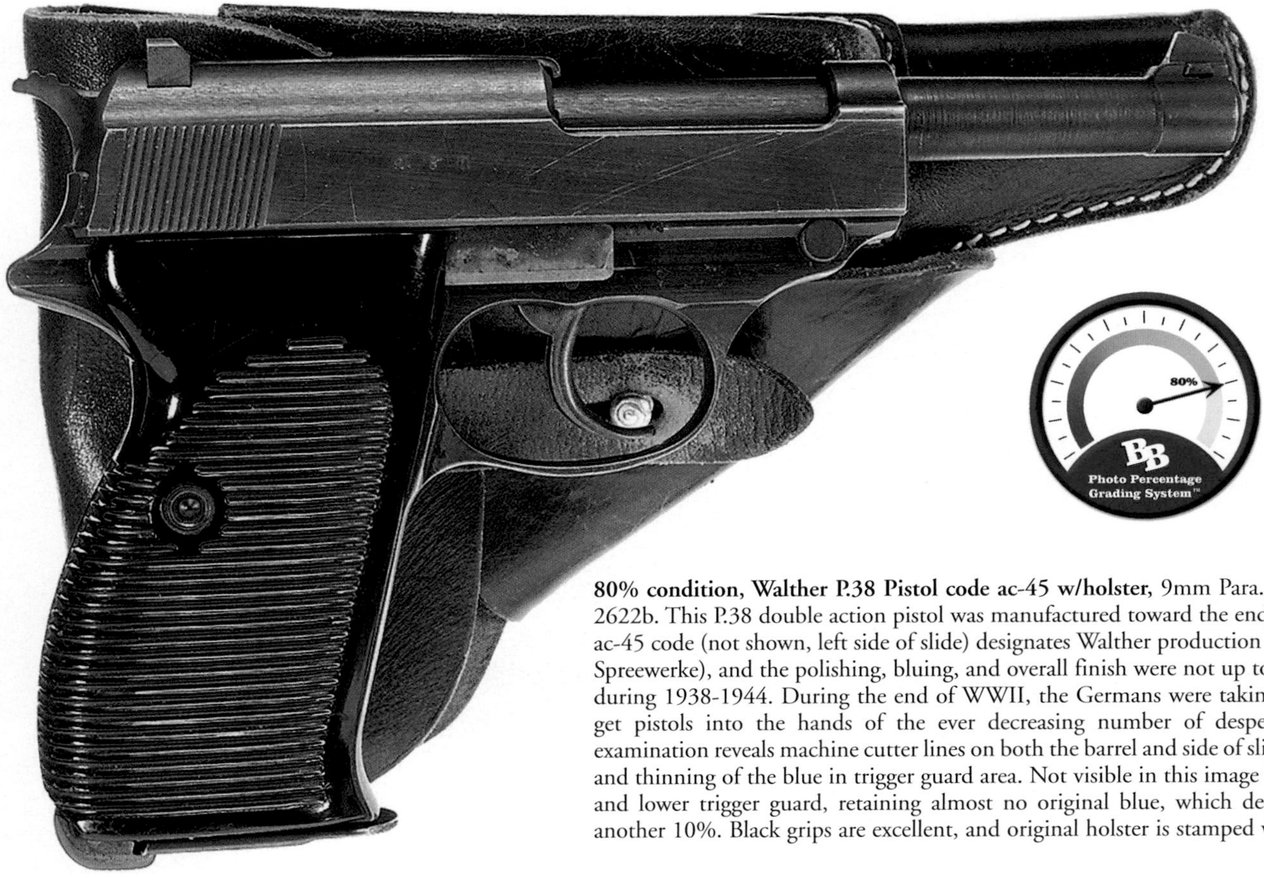

80% condition, Walther P.38 Pistol code ac-45 w/holster, 9mm Para. cal., 4 7/8 in. barrel, ser. no. 2622b. This P.38 double action pistol was manufactured toward the end of the war during 1945. The ac-45 code (not shown, left side of slide) designates Walther production (byf was Mauser, and cyq was Spreewerke), and the polishing, bluing, and overall finish were not up to par with earlier manufacture during 1938-1944. During the end of WWII, the Germans were taking quality control shortcuts to get pistols into the hands of the ever decreasing number of desperate German soldiers. Close examination reveals machine cutter lines on both the barrel and side of slide. Also note metal scratching and thinning of the blue in trigger guard area. Not visible in this image is the wear on front grip strap and lower trigger guard, retaining almost no original blue, which decreases this pistol's condition another 10%. Black grips are excellent, and original holster is stamped with the "WaA36" code.

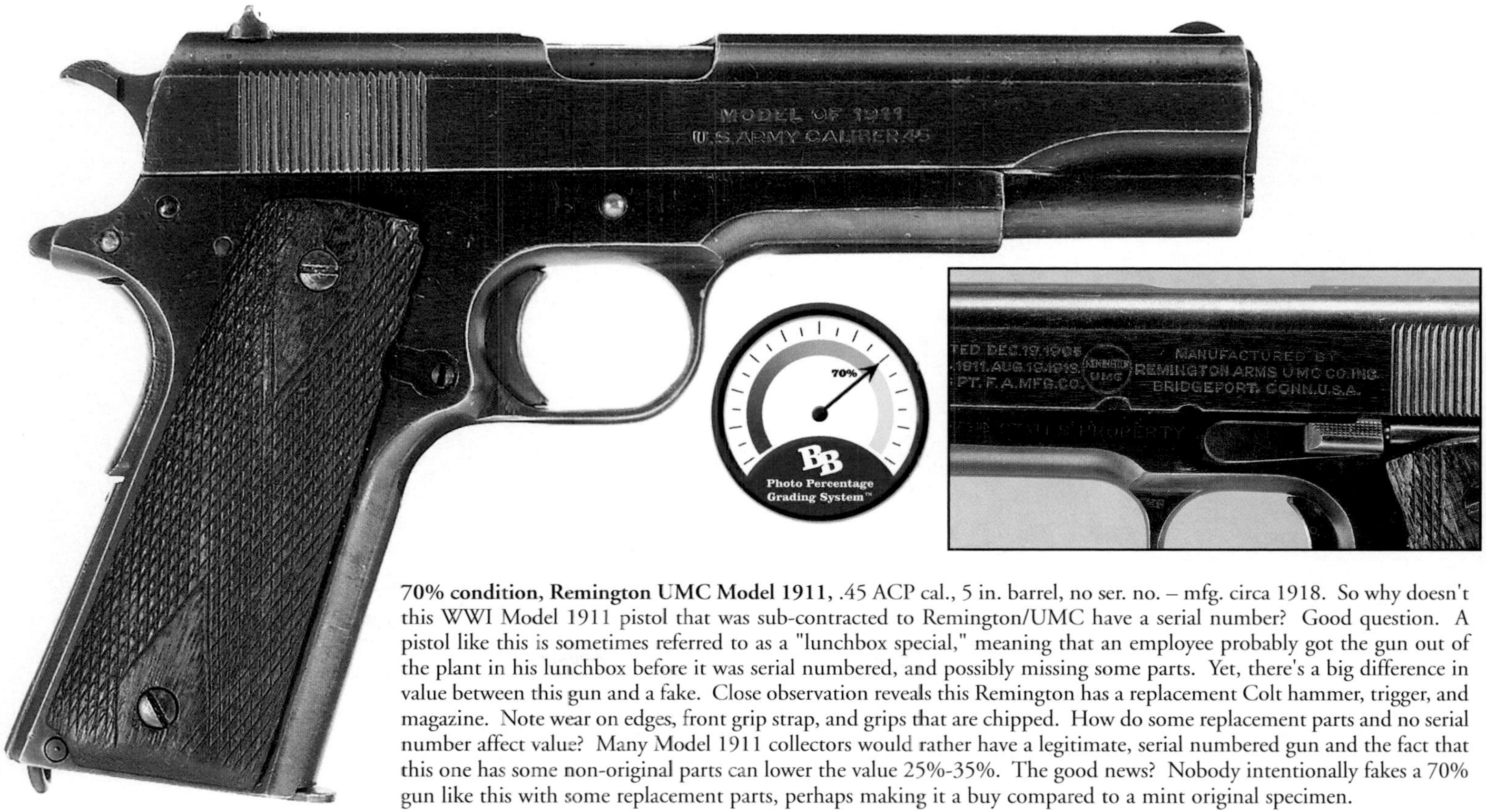

70% condition, Remington UMC Model 1911, .45 ACP cal., 5 in. barrel, no ser. no. – mfg. circa 1918. So why doesn't this WWI Model 1911 pistol that was sub-contracted to Remington/UMC have a serial number? Good question. A pistol like this is sometimes referred to as a "lunchbox special," meaning that an employee probably got the gun out of the plant in his lunchbox before it was serial numbered, and possibly missing some parts. Yet, there's a big difference in value between this gun and a fake. Close observation reveals this Remington has a replacement Colt hammer, trigger, and magazine. Note wear on edges, front grip strap, and grips that are chipped. How do some replacement parts and no serial number affect value? Many Model 1911 collectors would rather have a legitimate, serial numbered gun and the fact that this one has some non-original parts can lower the value 25%-35%. The good news? Nobody intentionally fakes a 70% gun like this with some replacement parts, perhaps making it a buy compared to a mint original specimen.

PISTOLS: PPGS CONDITION FACTORS

50

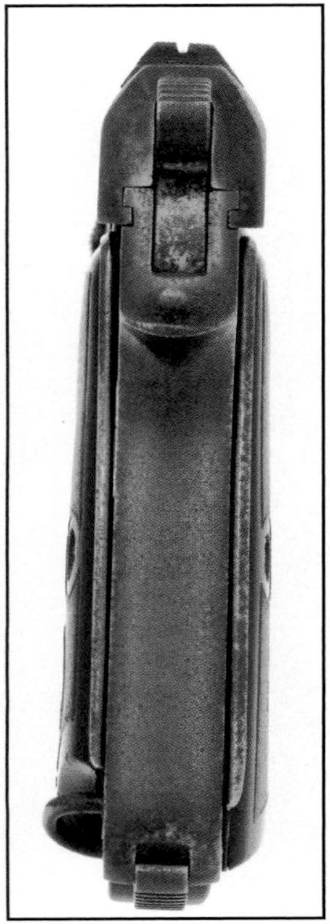

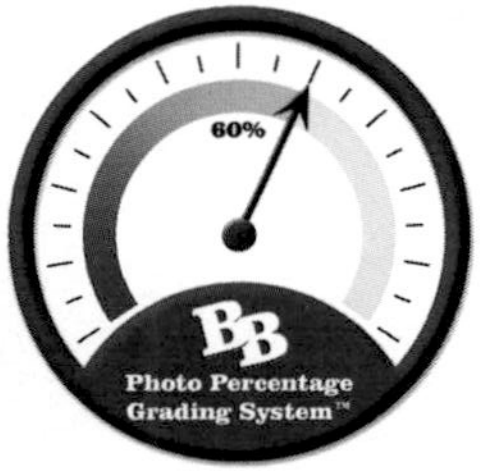

60% condition, Beretta Model 1934, .380 ACP cal., 3 3/8 in. barrel, ser. no. 666496 – mfg. 1937. One of Beretta's most popular pistols, over one million Model 1934s were manufactured between 1934-1980. Some of you may already be concerned about why the slide is a completely different color than the frame (i.e., possibly non-original finish or replaced slide). Not to worry here - this is what happens when the bluing process interacts with metal composition that differs in the carbon makeup from one part to another. In this case, even though the same bluing technique was applied to both the slide and the frame, the slide's metallurgy resulted in a plum-colored finish compared to the normal blued frame. Separate image of back of gun reveals quite a bit of wear, corrosion, and light pitting on both the rear grip strap and metal grip backing. It is especially important on handguns to carefully inspect the grip straps, because if the gun was extensively used, this is where most of the wear should accumulate.

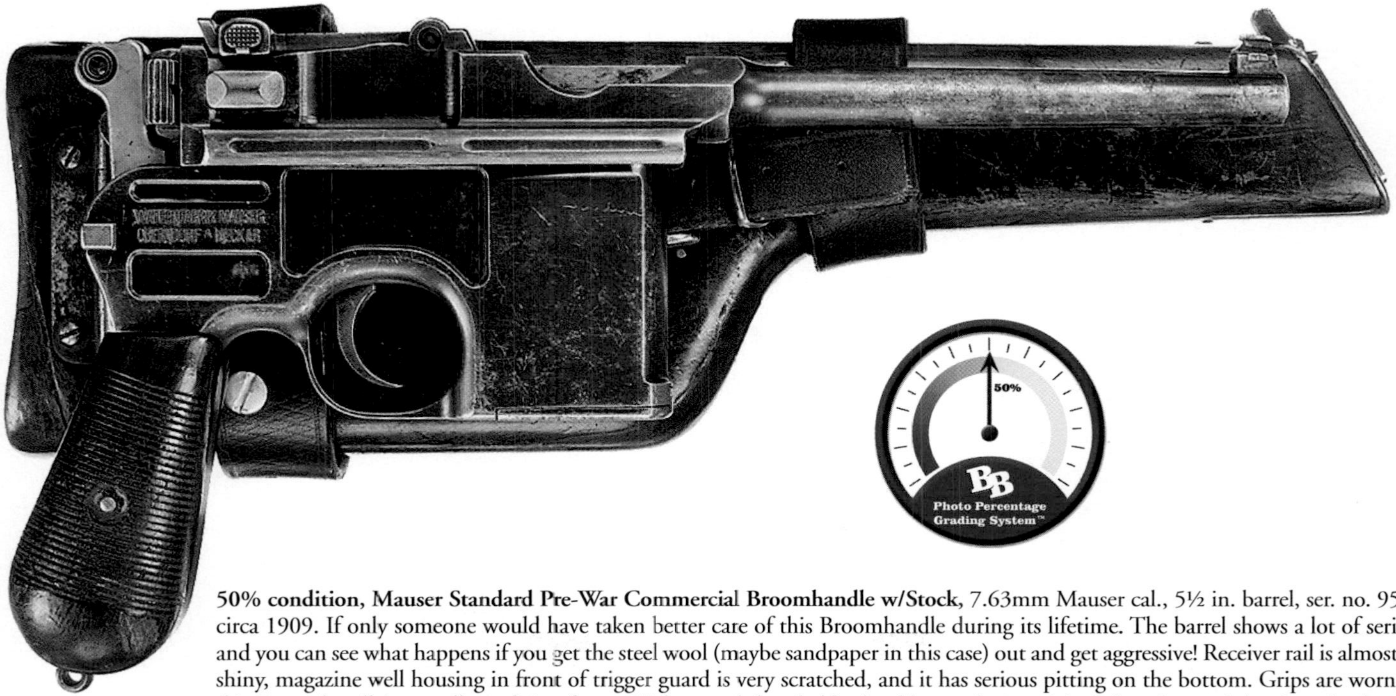

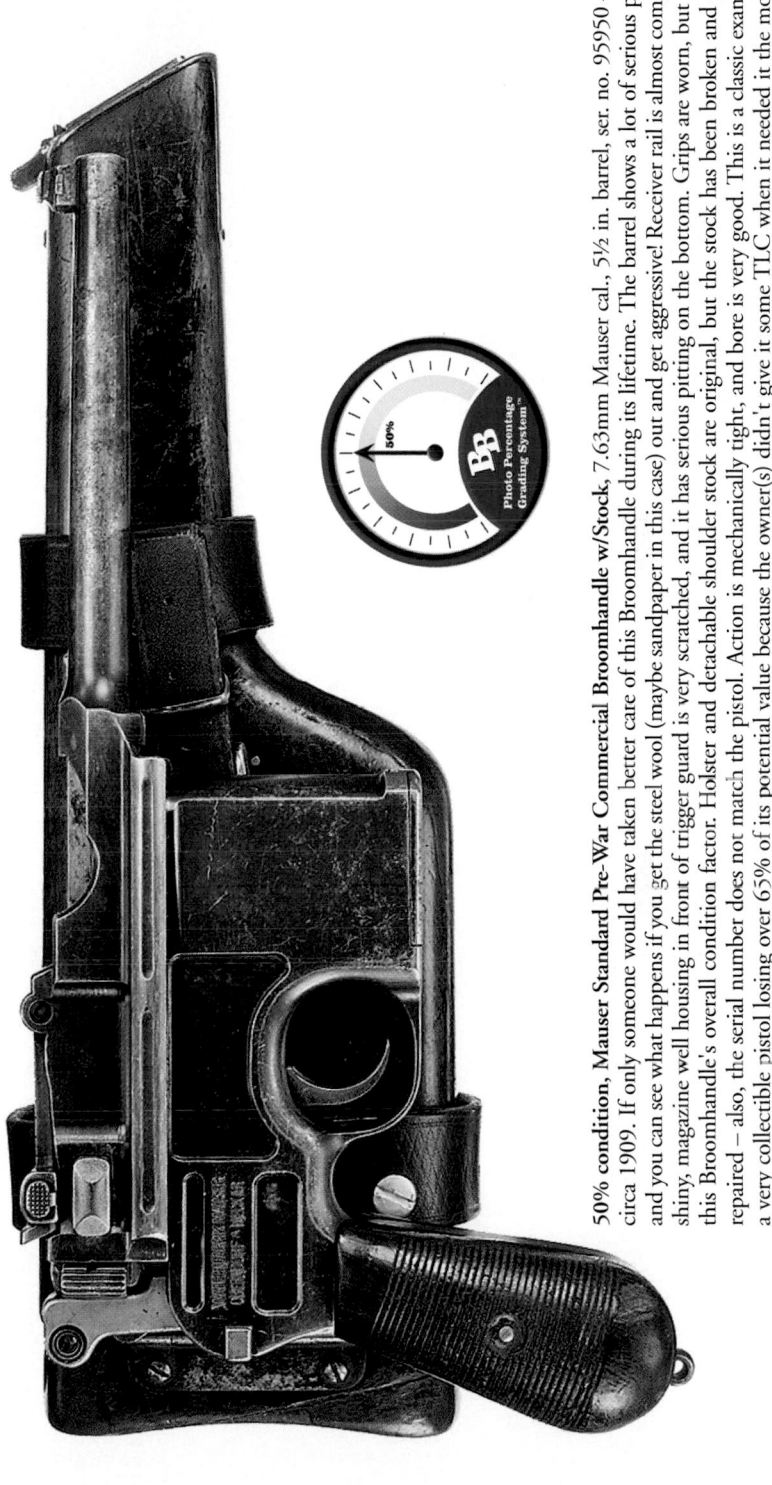

50% condition, Mauser Standard Pre-War Commercial Broomhandle w/Stock, 7.63mm Mauser cal., 5½ in. barrel, ser. no. 95950 – mfg. circa 1909. If only someone would have taken better care of this Broomhandle during its lifetime. The barrel shows a lot of serious pitting, and you can see what happens if you get the steel wool (maybe sandpaper in this case) out and get aggressive! Receiver rail is almost completely shiny, magazine well housing in front of trigger guard is very scratched, and it has serious pitting on the bottom. Grips are worn, but match this Broomhandle's overall condition factor. Holster and detachable shoulder stock are original, but the stock has been broken and poorly repaired – also, the serial number does not match the pistol. Action is mechanically tight, and bore is very good. This is a classic example of a very collectible pistol losing over 65% of its potential value because the owner(s) didn't give it some TLC when it needed it the most.

PISTOLS: PPGS CONDITION FACTORS

PISTOLS: PPGS CONDITION FACTORS

52

40% condition, Colt Model 1905, .45 ACP cal., 4 7/8 in. barrel, ser. no. 1656 – mfg. early 1907. As you can see, this gun has problems. Note the original bright bluing on frame, but overall grey finish on slide, indicating that someone acid cleaned this gun thoroughly in the past, probably trying to clean up the heavy pitting on the right side (not shown). Since the frame is one condition factor (thinning blue), and the slide is a totally different condition (grey patina), this pistol's overall condition factor had to be interpolated based on the overall appearance. Note heavy frame scratching next to grips. Grip straps are also worn and grey, and left wood grip has a crack above the top screw. Action is mechanically good, and all parts are original. This gun has lost most of its collector value because of its altered condition and poor eye appeal.

30% condition, Colt Model 1905, .45 ACP cal., 4 7/8 in. barrel, ser. no. 3730 – mfg. 1909. Most of this pistol's lifetime is behind it. Note how the original bluing has turned a dark grey patina, the front of the slide is shiny, and there is pitting throughout the slide. Frame has also turned to a mostly brown patina, and some bluing remains in protected areas. The grip straps are very worn and have turned grey, while the checkered, revarnished grips also show a lot of wear. Action is mechanically okay. This gun is a good example of when value is determined almost completely by collectibility, not shootability. 500 of this model were factory slotted for a shoulder stock (this one isn't), making it a rare configuration that automatically adds 50% to the pistol's value, regardless of condition. Most pistols in this condition factor are not very collectible, but this rare Colt is an exception.

PISTOLS: PPGS CONDITION FACTORS

20% condition, Colt Model 1905, .45 ACP cal., 4 7/8 in. barrel, ser. no. 1840 – mfg. 1907. We know what you're thinking – how did the front of this gun become so pitted? Even CSI undergraduates will quickly figure out what happened in this case. At one point (maybe several), the gun and its holster got very wet. Unfortunately, the gun was stored in the wet holster, and witness the results. Serious pitting is an understatement to describe the wear on the front and rear of this unfortunate pistol. The only thing this gun still has going for it is that it can still claim originality and functionality. Grips are well-worn, and the points are long gone on the checkering. Rampant Colt logo is still visible on rear of slide. The only original finish remaining on this gun is in the protected area on the upper frame around the radiused grips.

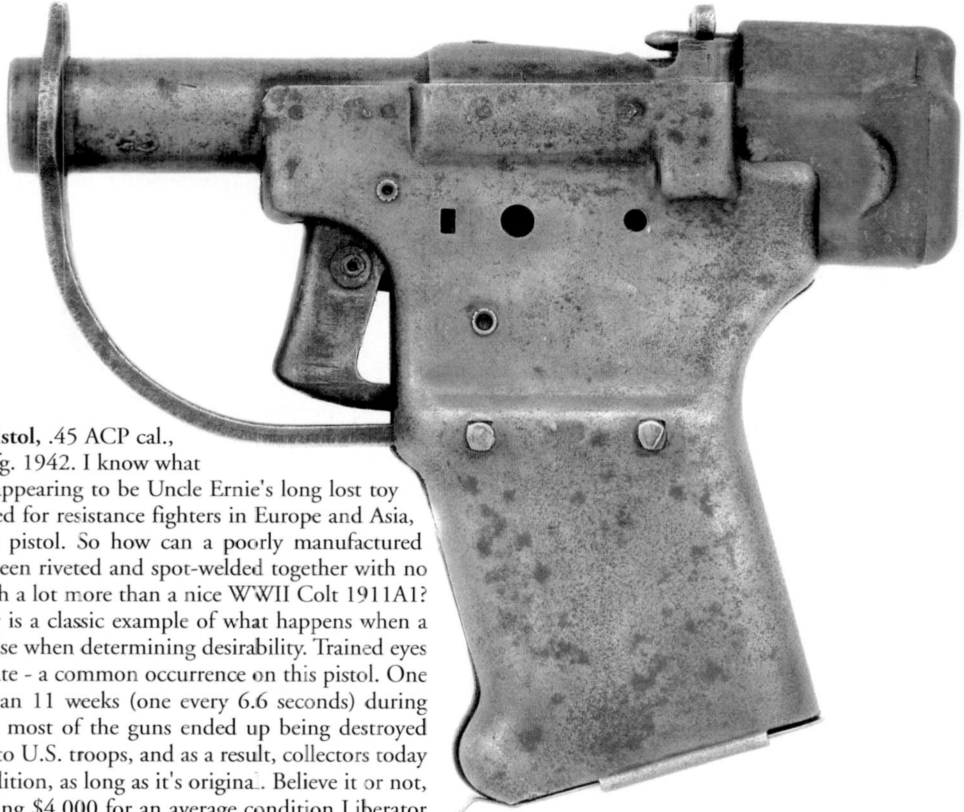

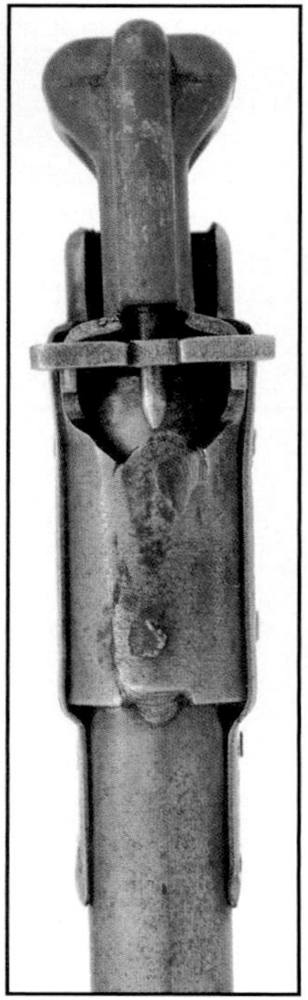

10% condition, Liberator single shot pistol, .45 ACP cal., 4 in. smoothbore barrel, no ser. no. – mfg. 1942. I know what you're thinking, and it's wrong! While appearing to be Uncle Ernie's long lost toy gun, the Liberator was originally designed for resistance fighters in Europe and Asia, and is a very desirable WWII contract pistol. So how can a poorly manufactured handgun made out of pot metal that's been riveted and spot-welded together with no condition or eye appeal possibly be worth a lot more than a nice WWII Colt 1911A1? Even though it's a weirdo, the Liberator is a classic example of what happens when a gun's rarity factor overrules everything else when determining desirability. Trained eyes may spot the shiny replacement floor plate - a common occurrence on this pistol. One million Liberators were made in less than 11 weeks (one every 6.6 seconds) during 1942 at a cost of only $1.73 each, and most of the guns ended up being destroyed overseas after the war. None were issued to U.S. troops, and as a result, collectors today will buy a Liberator in virtually any condition, as long as it's original. Believe it or not, some buyers at major auctions were paying $4,000 for an average condition Liberator like this several years ago, but no longer.

PISTOLS: NRA MODERN CONDITIONS

NRA Modern New condition (100%), Browning Hi-Power, 9mm Para. cal., 4 5/8 in. barrel, ser. no. 245NV56269 – mfg. 1995. The Hi-Power was John M. Browning's last pistol design, and production began in Belgium during 1935. It was immediately accepted, and many military contracts followed shortly. Being a venerable work horse for decades, the HP is still in action around the world today, and its design and functionality are truly ageless. This silver chrome finished HP variation with gold trigger, molded rubber grips with Browning medallions, adj. rear sight, and parkerized small parts was manufactured by F.N. in Herstal, Belgium, and shipped to Portugal for assembly and packaging. Even though NRA Modern New condition generally means not previously sold at retail on currently manufactured guns, this pistol was never fired by its original owner, nor does it show any wear. It is entirely possible for a NIB, unfired gun to accumulate wear if it has been displayed, handled, holstered, improperly stored, or over cleaned. This condition factor means NIB in every respect, with no excuses.

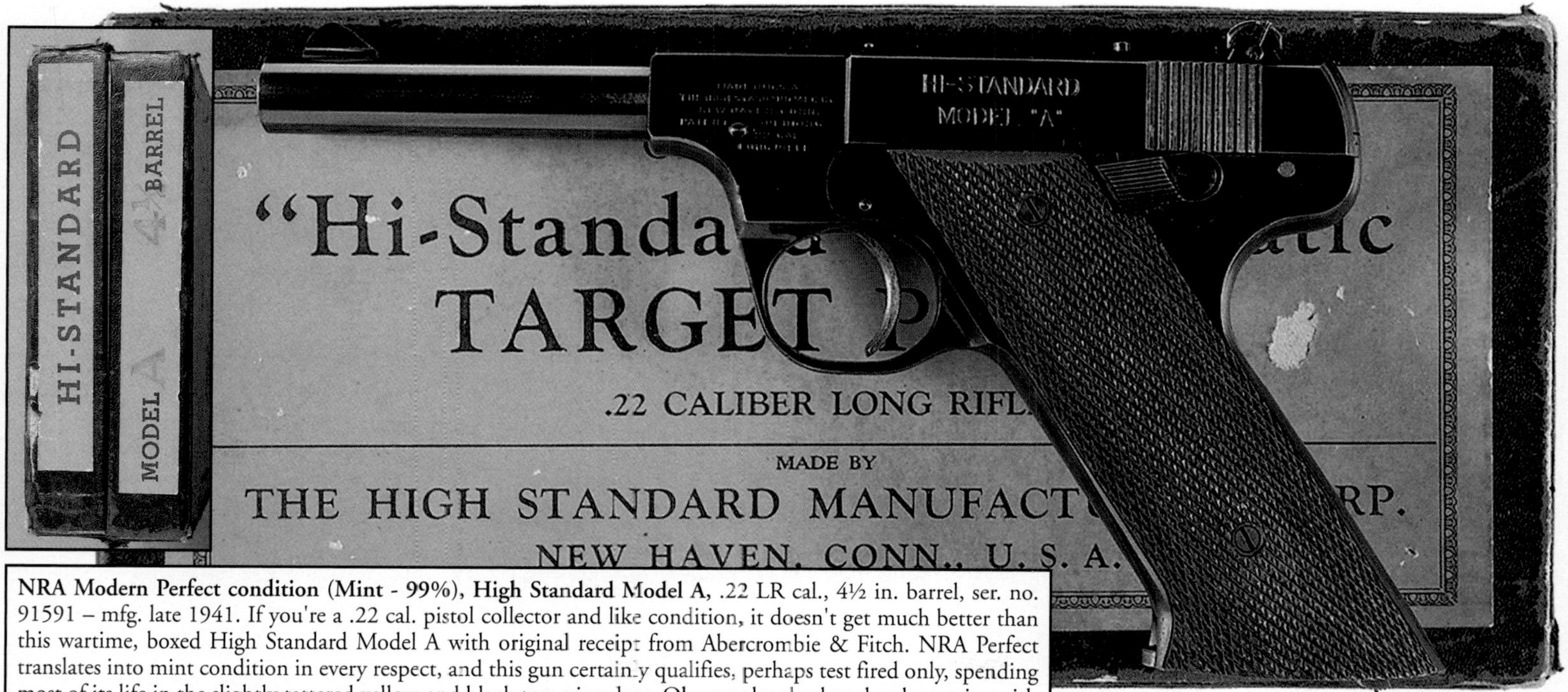

NRA Modern Perfect condition (Mint - 99%), **High Standard Model A,** .22 LR cal., 4½ in. barrel, ser. no. 91591 – mfg. late 1941. If you're a .22 cal. pistol collector and like condition, it doesn't get much better than this wartime, boxed High Standard Model A with original receipt from Abercrombie & Fitch. NRA Perfect translates into mint condition in every respect, and this gun certainly qualifies, perhaps test fired only, spending most of its life in the slightly tattered yellow and black two-piece box. Observe the checkered walnut grips with no wear on sharp points, perfect bluing with no wear on edges or end of barrel, and unturned screws still aligned. The older the gun, the harder it is to find one in this condition factor. On many older and desirable collectible firearms, values can double over NRA Excellent. Approximately 7,300 Model As were manufactured circa 1938-1942, but less than a handful may still remain in this condition with original box and bill of sale.

PISTOLS: NRA MODERN CONDITIONS

PISTOLS: NRA MODERN CONDITIONS

58

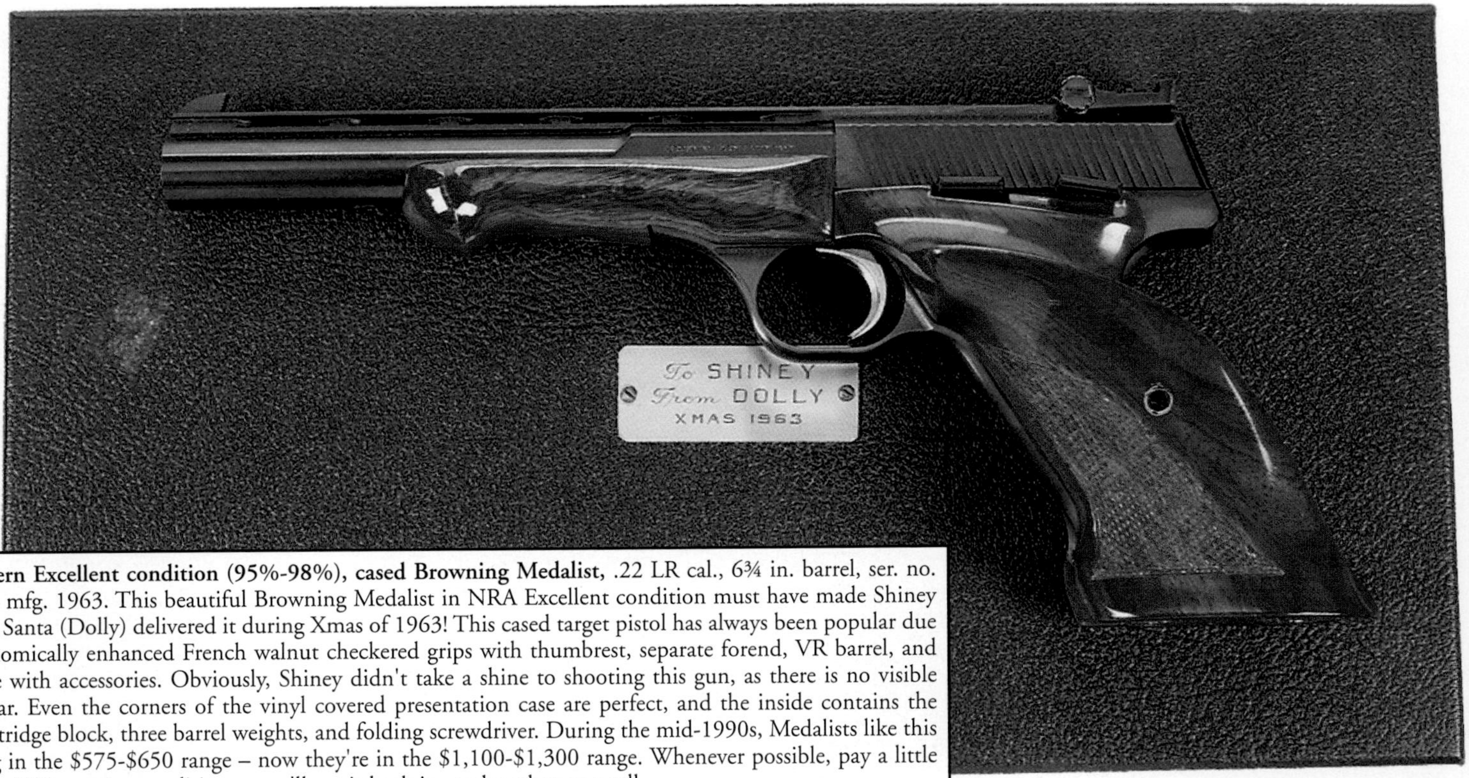

NRA Modern Excellent condition (95%-98%), cased Browning Medalist, .22 LR cal., 6¾ in. barrel, ser. no. 30491T3 – mfg. 1963. This beautiful Browning Medalist in NRA Excellent condition must have made Shiney happy after Santa (Dolly) delivered it during Xmas of 1963! This cased target pistol has always been popular due to its ergonomically enhanced French walnut checkered grips with thumbrest, separate forend, VR barrel, and unique case with accessories. Obviously, Shiney didn't take a shine to shooting this gun, as there is no visible exterior wear. Even the corners of the vinyl covered presentation case are perfect, and the inside contains the original cartridge block, three barrel weights, and folding screwdriver. During the mid-1990s, Medalists like this were selling in the $575-$650 range – now they're in the $1,100-$1,300 range. Whenever possible, pay a little bit more for NIB or mint condition – you'll get it back in spades when you sell.

NRA Modern Very Good Refinished condition (80%-95%), **Webley & Scott MK I**, .455 Webley auto cal., 5 in. barrel, ser. no. 100407 – mfg. 1913. Normally, refinished guns are not pictured in the PPGS, except when they can provide the reader information on condition which can be useful. Notice how the white marker has enhanced a soft, nearly polished off slide legend. This relatively rare, pre-WWI English pistol has been poorly reblued and polished at an earlier date. Note the previous pitting on the frame and barrel, which was poorly polished (observe horizontal slide serrations and rounded corners on slide), then cheaply refinished by hot dipping it into a bluing tank. Rubber grips also show wear, with light cracking, and the action also needs some adjustment. Unfortunately, this pistol's collector value has been virtually ruined, but will provide someone who is not concerned about originality, and is looking for a "buy," with a crude specimen. The problem is, a badly refinished gun like this very rarely goes up in value.

PISTOLS: NRA MODERN CONDITIONS

60

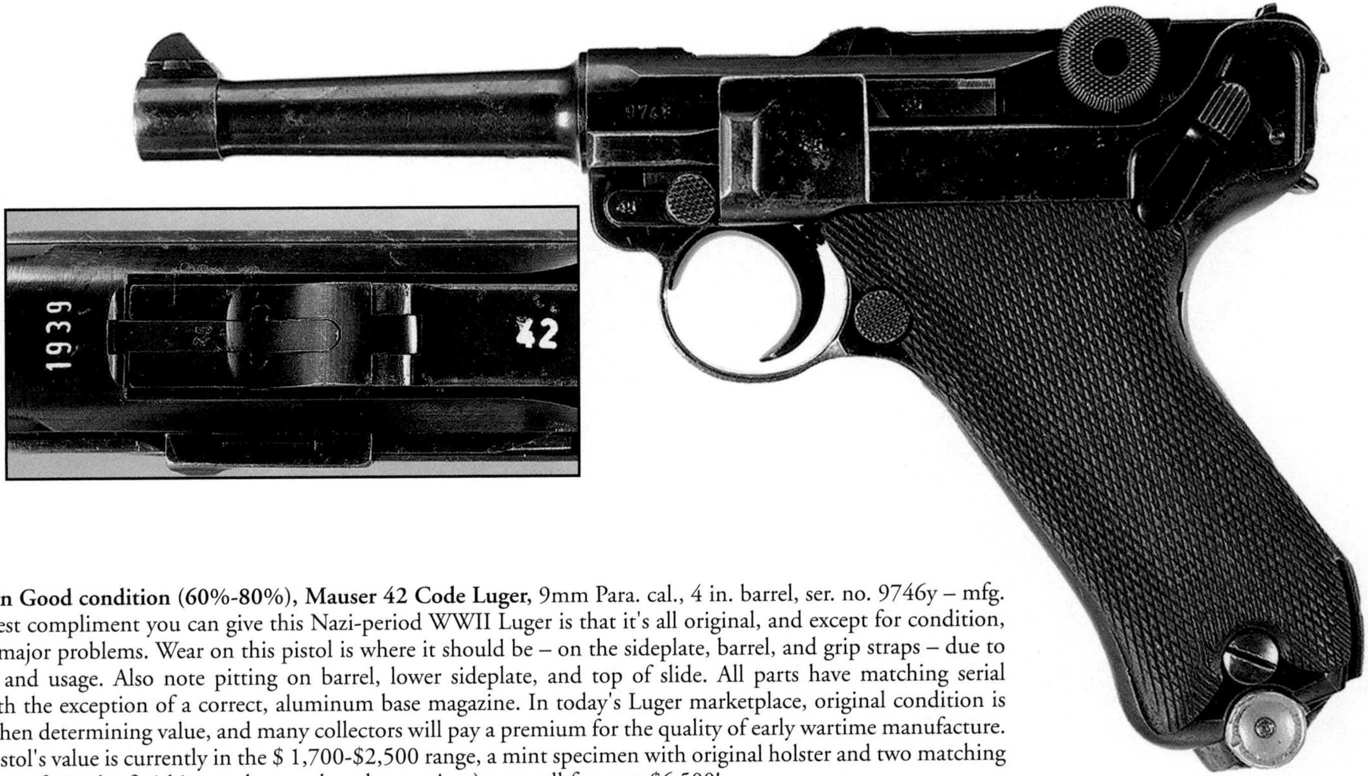

NRA Modern Good condition (60%-80%), **Mauser 42 Code Luger,** 9mm Para. cal., 4 in. barrel, ser. no. 9746y – mfg. 1939. The best compliment you can give this Nazi-period WWII Luger is that it's all original, and except for condition, there are no major problems. Wear on this pistol is where it should be – on the sideplate, barrel, and grip straps – due to holster wear and usage. Also note pitting on barrel, lower sideplate, and top of slide. All parts have matching serial numbers, with the exception of a correct, aluminum base magazine. In today's Luger marketplace, original condition is everything when determining value, and many collectors will pay a premium for the quality of early wartime manufacture. While this pistol's value is currently in the $ 1,700-$2,500 range, a mint specimen with original holster and two matching mags. (be wary of pistol refinishing and renumbered magazines) may sell for over $6,500!

NRA Modern Fair Condition (20%-60%), **CZ Model 27**, 7.65mm cal., 4 ¾ in. barrel, ser. no. 414459 – mfg. circa 1944. Manufactured in late WWII, with not a lot of time left for proper polishing and finishing (note rough horizontal machining marks on slide), this semi-auto pistol originally had a thin phosphate finish, which has turned into a greyish patina overall. Marked with the "WaA76" Waffenampt code on the frame, this Nazi-era pistol could probably tell some interesting stories about its life. Note the plastic grips with the circle CZ logo, indicating manufacture in Czechoslovakia. Observe finish discoloring on trigger and around the trigger guard. In its current condition factor, most collectors would pass on this gun, but this little WWII-era pistol has no major problems, and would still make an inexpensive, decent shooter. When condition lower than this is encountered, it won't make much difference on the price, as it's already bottomed out based on its shooting value.

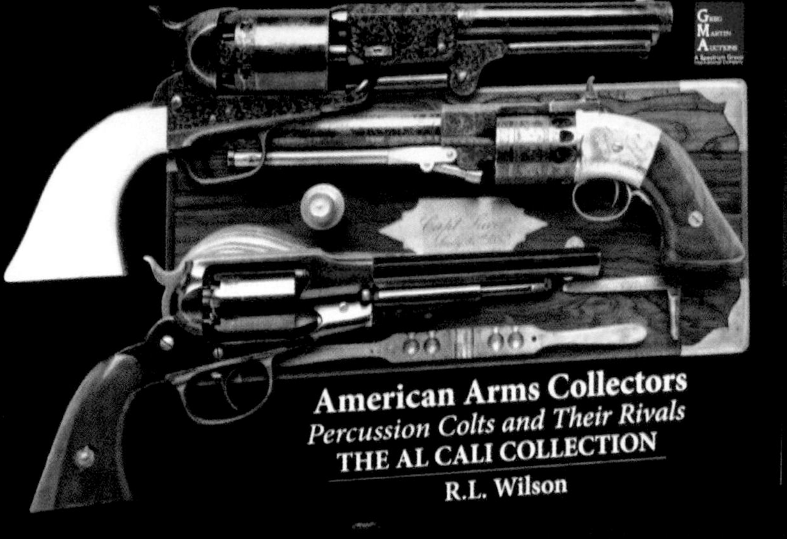

American Arms Collectors - Percussion Colts and Their Rivals - The Al Cali Collection by R. L. Wilson is arguably the finest firearms book ever published. It showcases three elements of collecting firearms that have never been combined in print before. All images depict the firearm's life size so the reader can visualize the relative sizes, and see every detail. The original condition of the guns is astonishing - some remain in virtually new condition from the mid-19th century! Furthermore, the quality of Mr. Douglas Sandberg's photography is unsurpassed.

Al Cali didn't have the biggest Colt collection ever assembled, but in terms of original condition of the specimens he chose, what he accumulated over 50 years is unequaled in the history of gun collecting. When Heritage/Greg Martin auction sold his collection on Sept. 18, 2011, the 33 Colts brought $6,690,740, averaging over $200,000 per gun, and the Texas No. 5 Paterson with 9 in. barrel gaveled for $977,500, a new world's record for a single gun!

Owning this book is the next best thing to owning Al Cali's collection. With an impressive oversized 11x17 in. format, this 194 page publication is sure to become a classic shortly!

2013 ***Thirty-Fourth Edition Blue Book of Gun Values™***

APRIL

S						S
	1	2	3	4	5	6
7	8	9	10	11	12	13
14	15	16	17	18	19	20
21	22	23	24	25	26	27
28	29	30				

MAY

S						S
			1	2	3	4
5	6	7	8	9	10	11
12	13	14	15	16	17	18
19	20	21	22	23	24	25
26	27	28	29	30	31	

JUNE

S						S
						1
2	3	4	5	6	7	8
9	10	11	12	13	14	15
16	17	18	19	20	21	22
23	24	25	26	27	28	29
30						

JULY

S						S
	1	2	3	4	5	6
7	8	9	10	11	12	13
14	15	16	17	18	19	20
21	22	23	24	25	26	27
28	29	30	31			

AUGUST

S						S
				1	2	3
4	5	6	7	8	9	10
11	12	13	14	15	16	17
18	19	20	21	22	23	24
25	26	27	28	29	30	31

SEPTEMBER

S						S
1	2	3	4	5	6	7
8	9	10	11	12	13	14
15	16	17	18	19	20	21
22	23	24	25	26	27	28
29	30					

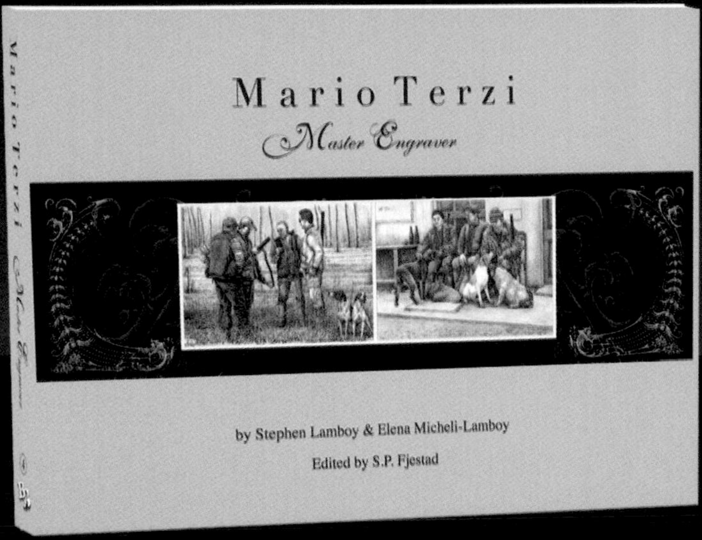

The newest engraving book featuring Mario Terzi is destined to become a classic. No other engraver in the world has his combination of engraving skills, artistic ability, and geometric interpretation of ornamentation. Terzi has also mastered the art of enamel painting on metal, enabling unprecedented realism and color in his subject matter. This new book is available as a deluxe slipcased hardcover only and has been signed by Terzi, the talented artisians in his shop, the co-authors, and the editor/publisher. *Mario Terzi – Master Engraver* has 288 pages, four pullouts, and five chapters featuring Terzi's finest works. Don't miss this limited opportunity to buy the finest engraving book ever published.

"Trying to describe Terzi's work, both ornamental and figural, in words is really beyond my ability. It must be seen and in *Mario Terzi – Master Engraver* the reader will see it in the exquisitely detailed, high resolution images that Blue Book Publications' engraving series has become renowned for. That said, the reader should be prepared for a departure from the previous three books in the Italian series. The new Terzi book is far more colorful! This is true in both the sense of the color scale and the subject matter."

- C. Roger Bleile, Author, *American Engravers - The 21st Century*

2013 ***Thirty-Fourth Edition Blue Book of Gun Values™***

OCTOBER

S						S
		1	2	3	4	5
6	7	8	9	10	11	12
13	14	15	16	17	18	19
20	21	22	23	24	25	26
27	28	29	30	31		

NOVEMBER

S						S
					1	2
3	4	5	6	7	8	9
10	11	12	13	14	15	16
17	18	19	20	21	22	23
24	25	26	27	28	29	30

DECEMBER

S						S
1	2	3	4	5	6	7
8	9	10	11	12	13	14
15	16	17	18	19	20	21
22	23	24	25	26	27	28
29	30	31				

2014 ***Thirty-Fourth Edition Blue Book of Gun Values™***

JANUARY

S						S
			1	2	3	4
5	6	7	8	9	10	11
12	13	14	15	16	17	18
19	20	21	22	23	24	25
26	27	28	29	30	31	

FEBRUARY

S						S
						1
2	3	4	5	6	7	8
9	10	11	12	13	14	15
16	17	18	19	20	21	22
23	24	25	26	27	28	

MARCH

S						S
						1
2	3	4	5	6	7	8
9	10	11	12	13	14	15
16	17	18	19	20	21	22
23	24	25	26	27	28	29
30	31					

RIFLES: PPGS CONDITION FACTORS

64

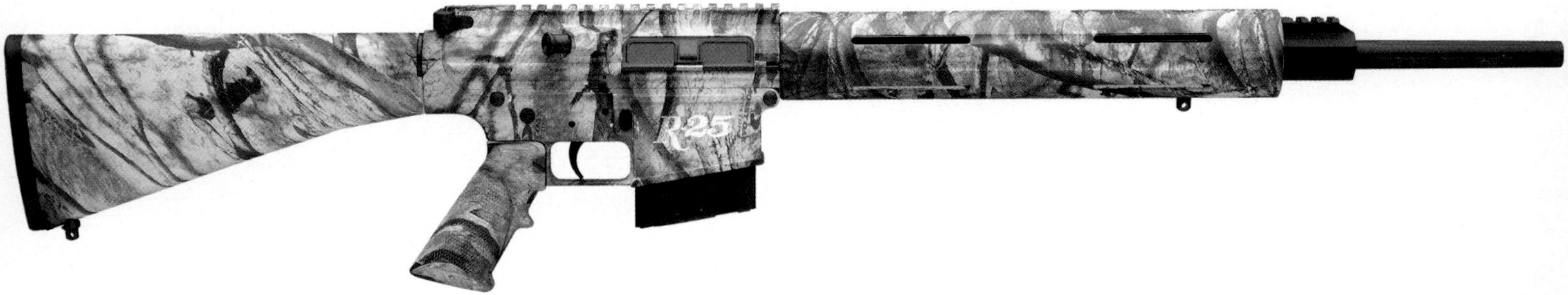

NIB Condition, Remington R-25 semi-auto rifle, .243 Win. cal., ser. no. not provided – mfg. 2009. Can you imagine Grandpa going out in the woods during the old days, trying to bag Bambi with this rifle? Welcome to the 21st century! As these camo wonders get used, observing wear in the barrel, breech block, and internal firing mechanism may be the only way to accurately determine condition as almost all of them will look 98% or better from the outside.

Initially tagged "assault rifles" or a paramilitary configuration, these "modern sporting rifles" (MSRs), now available in many hunting calibers, remain the hottest thing in the firearms industry. As this edition went to press, values for many tactical firearms, especially AR-15 style rifles and carbines, have escalated considerably following the tragedy in Newtown, CT. With a current manufacturer's suggested retail price of $1,631, and a normal 100% value of approx. $1,450, most mint R-25s for sale on websites and at gun shows are currently selling for just over $2,000! This is what happens when the demand factor created by both the fear of potential upcoming anti-gun legislation and the resulting speculation suddenly spikes. Even though most AR-15 manufacturers are working 24/7 trying to keep up, there still isn't enough additional supply to keep up with the rampant demand. Whenever this happens, accurate values are almost impossible to try and predict for the future. For the most up-to-date information available on AR-15 values and other tactical firearms, please visit www.bluebookofgunvalues.com.

Mint Condition, Russian SKS, 7.62x39mm Russian cal., 20 in. barrel, ser. no. Hh1244 (Cyrillic lettering) – mfg. date unknown. The SKS semi-auto rifle was adopted by the Soviet military in 1949, two years after the select-fire AK-47. Most of the recently imported Russian SKSs came from military stockpiles, and were refurbished at Tula Arms Works. Today, the most collectible SKS models are East German, North Korean, or North Vietnam manufacture. This particular Russian manufactured configuration with brown laminated stock, non-detachable pivoting blade bayonet, and canvas sling became very popular before the Crime Bill was enacted in September of 1994. During this time period, Chinese imports starting flooding the marketplace, reducing the prices of all SKS rifles, despite the fact that the more recent Chinese imports are typically of poor quality with thumbhole stocks. Although millions of SKSs have been imported over the years, NIB examples like this Russian manufactured specimen are actually getting harder to find and prices have gone up dramatically since Obama was re-elected. Less than five years ago, it was possible to go to almost any gun show and find an SKS in this condition factor for around $175. Not anymore - now they're averaging $500!

RIFLES: PPGS CONDITION FACTORS

66

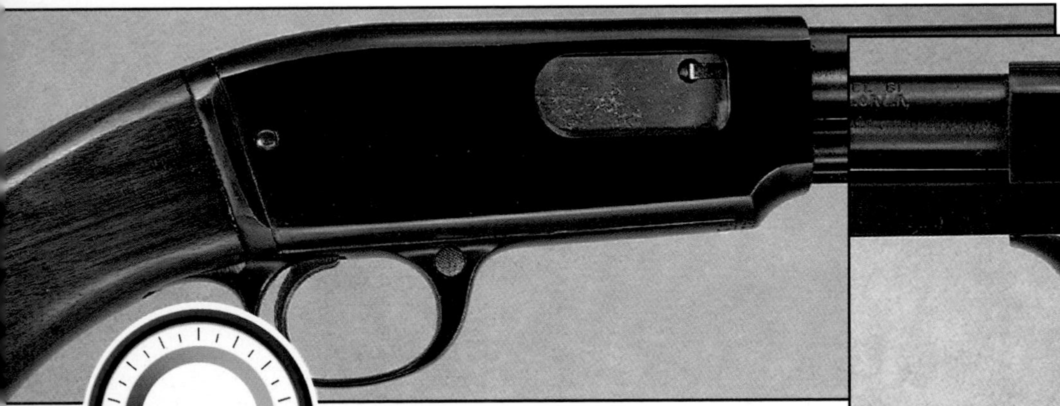

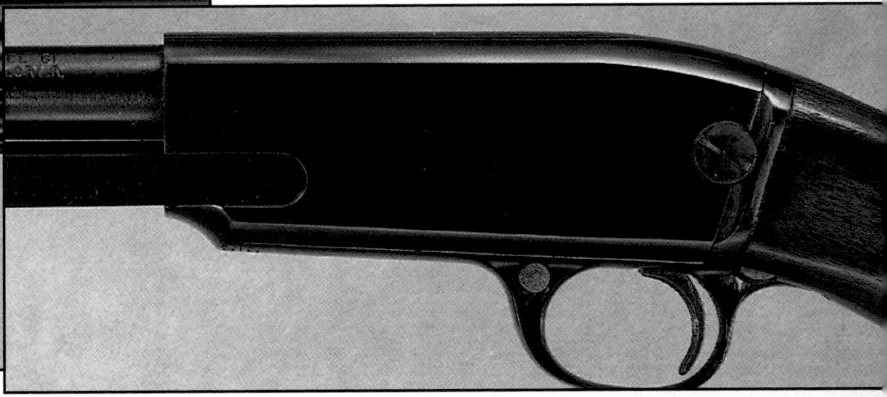

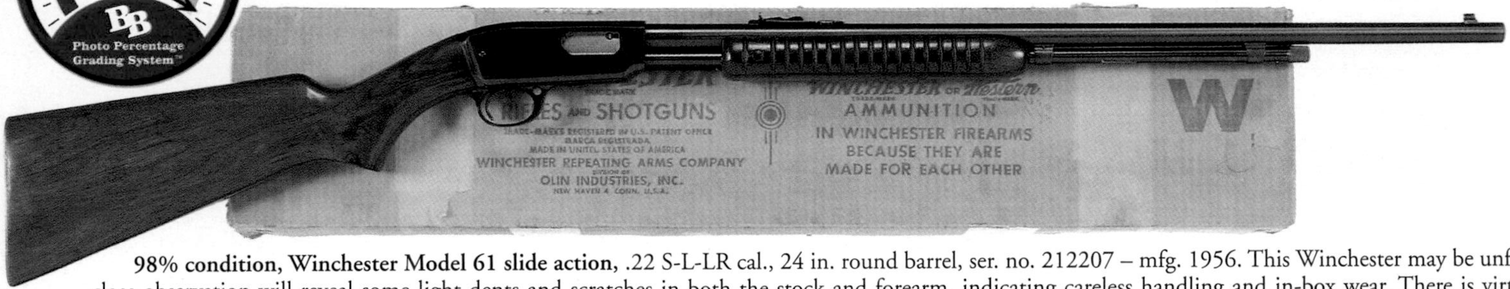

98% condition, Winchester Model 61 slide action, .22 S-L-LR cal., 24 in. round barrel, ser. no. 212207 – mfg. 1956. This Winchester may be unfired, but close observation will reveal some light dents and scratches in both the stock and forearm, indicating careless handling and in-box wear. There is virtually no bluing wear on the metal surfaces, and the grooved receiver for scope mount indicates late production, which is actually more desirable than a rifle without grooving. Even the breech block shows no vertical scratching, indicating little or no use. While the original box is somewhat tattered and has some tape marks, unfortunately, in recent years fake cardboard boxes for the Winchester Models 61, 62, and 63 have been appearing in the secondary marketplace. Since original boxes and hanging tags can add quite a bit of value to a 95%+ gun, be wary when buying these models with an "original" box.

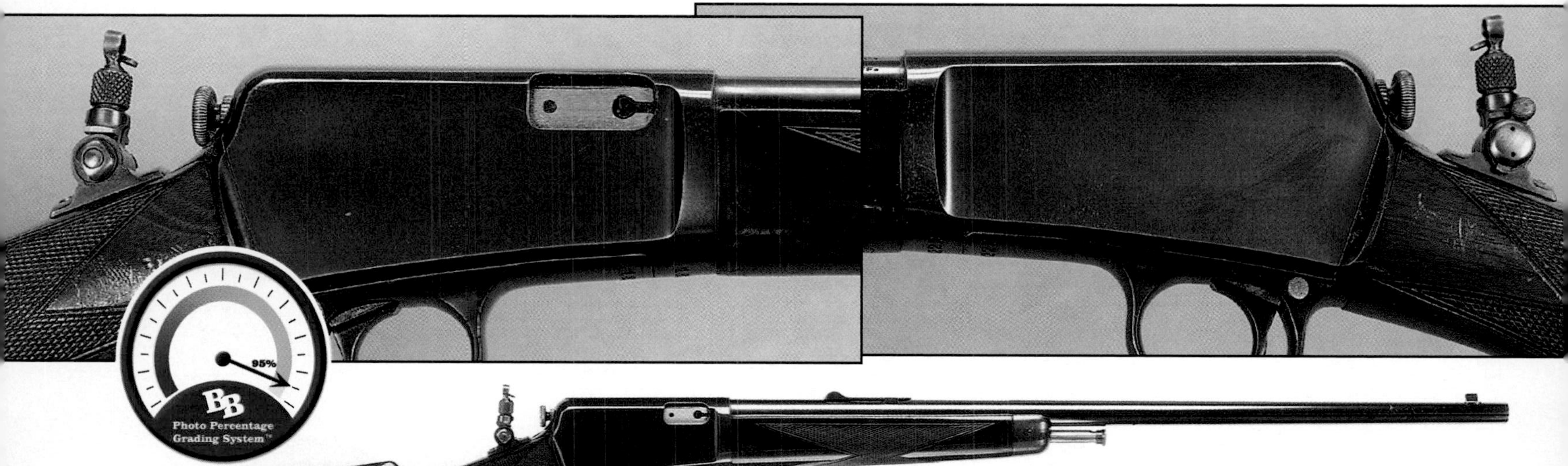

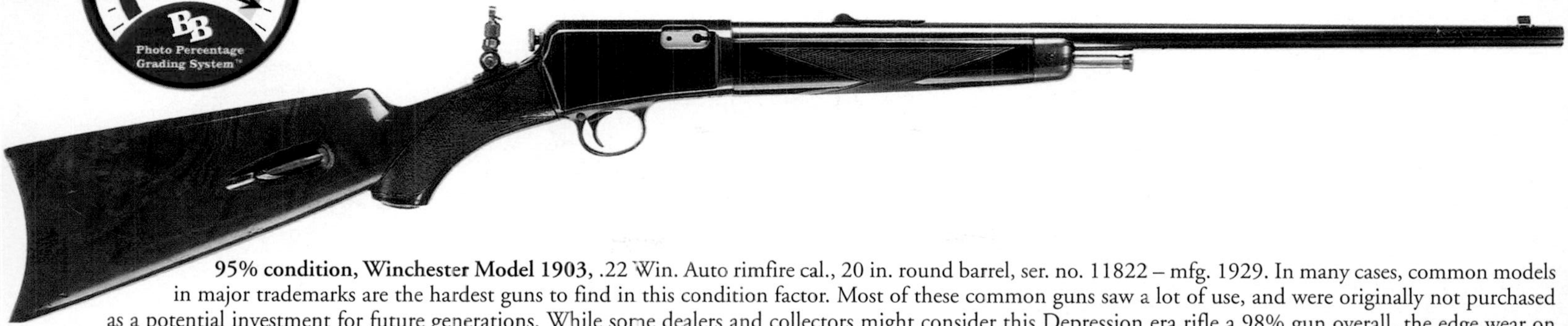

95% condition, Winchester Model 1903, .22 Win. Auto rimfire cal., 20 in. round barrel, ser. no. 11822 – mfg. 1929. In many cases, common models in major trademarks are the hardest guns to find in this condition factor. Most of these common guns saw a lot of use, and were originally not purchased as a potential investment for future generations. While some dealers and collectors might consider this Depression era rifle a 98% gun overall, the edge wear on the sharp corners of both sides of the receiver, in addition to the scratches on right side of stock, lower this rifle to 95% condition. Most experienced dealers and collectors have learned that when buying, selling, or trading, it's better to under evaluate a condition factor rather than overestimate. Deluxe checkered stock and forearm with most of the original varnish is always a big plus for Winchester collectors, especially when the condition is this good.

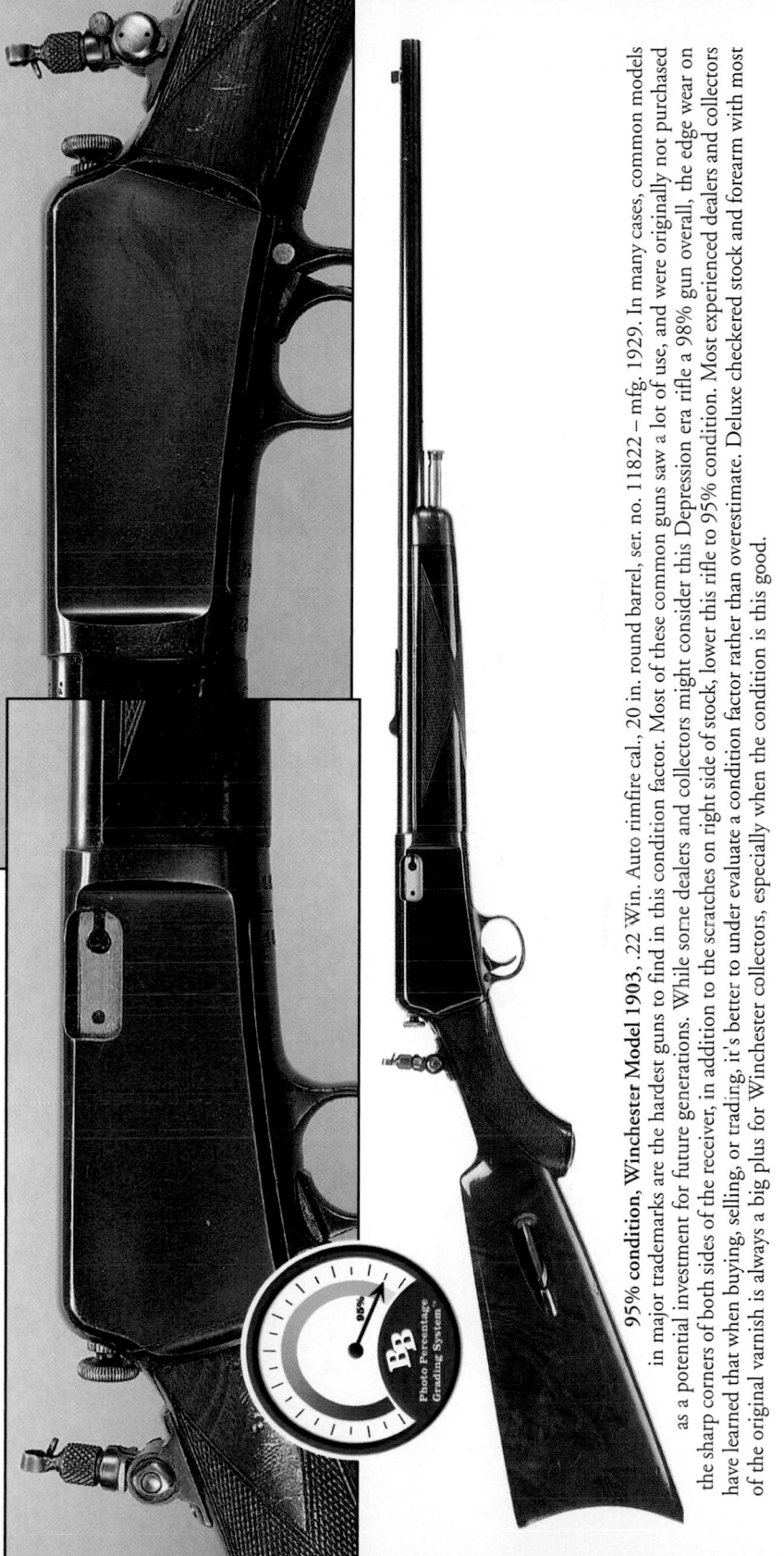

RIFLES: PPGS CONDITION FACTORS

RIFLES: PPGS CONDITION FACTORS

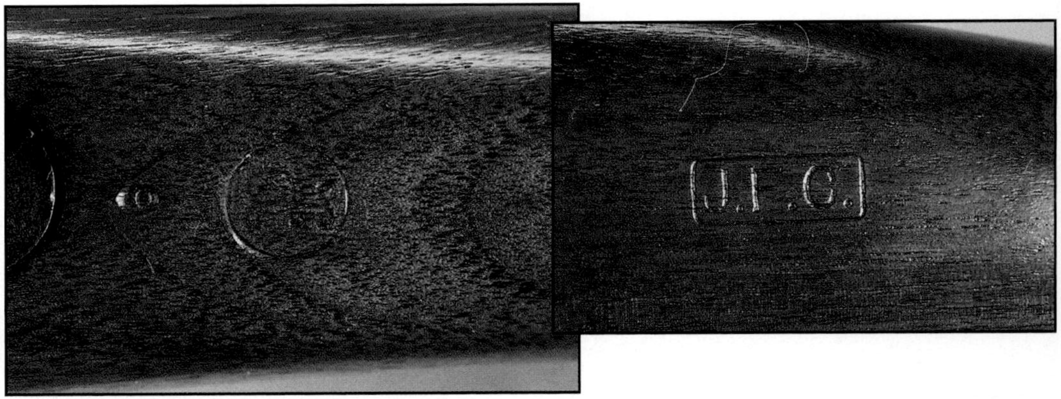

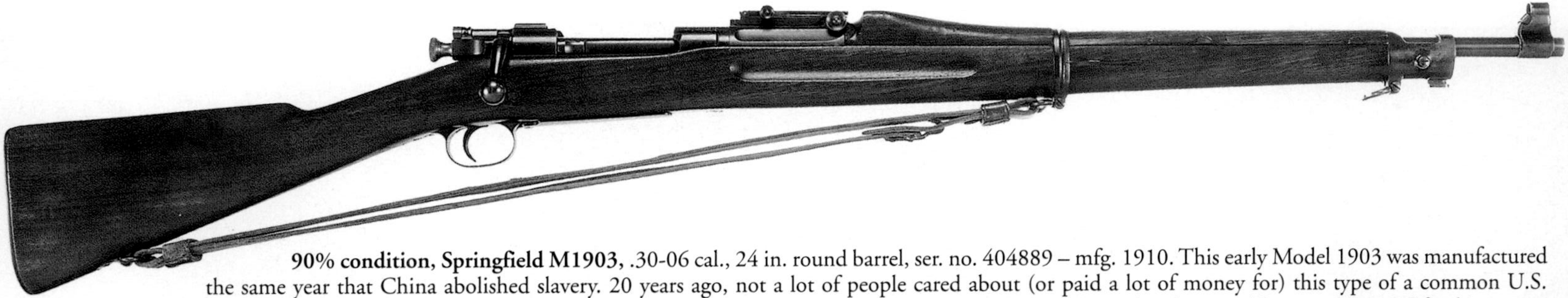

90% condition, Springfield M1903, .30-06 cal., 24 in. round barrel, ser. no. 404889 – mfg. 1910. This early Model 1903 was manufactured the same year that China abolished slavery. 20 years ago, not a lot of people cared about (or paid a lot of money for) this type of a common U.S. military rifle – that's not the case today. Note the blue and color case hardened metal finishes. It has nice original wood with no problems and "J.F.C." final inspector mark (for J.F. Coyle) in block letters inside rectangle in addition to script "P" in circle proof stamped on underside stock wrist. More than anything else, originality is the key when determining value on this type of 20th century U.S. military rifle – knowing what to look for in proofs/markings, how the original markings appear, and where to find them are absolutely critical when evaluating this rifle's value. Sling is an early RIA (Rock Island Arsenal) 1904 pattern.

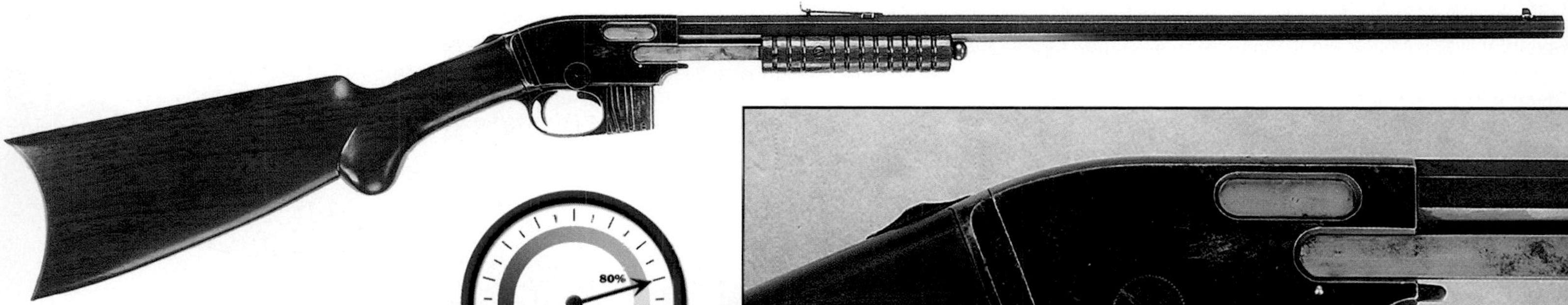

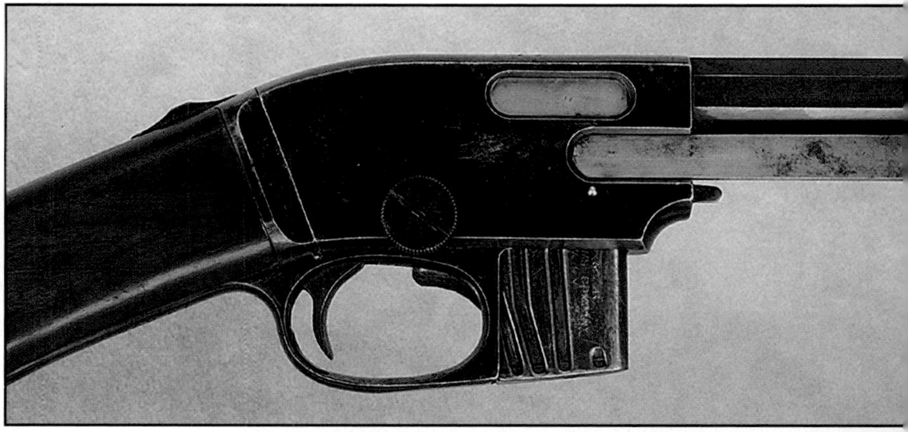

80% condition, Savage Model 1903 slide action, .22 S-L-LR cal., 24 in. octagon barrel, ser. no. 79070 - mfg. circa 1907. On most early 20th century .22 cal. slide action rifles such as this one which were inexpensively priced when new (typically $10-$15), the hardest thing to find now is superior original condition. Even at 80%, this rifle is probably still in better condition than the vast majority of original slide actions available at the time. Note wear on edges of frame that still retains most of its bright bluing, and small areas of scattered rust on the shiny slide rail and frame. The 7-shot detachable magazine with vertical indentations located in front of the trigger guard, has also faded and turned a light plum color - consistent with the rest of this gun's overall wear. Barrel bluing also shows light fading and perhaps some over aggressive cleaning. Uncheckered rounded pistol stock with crescent buttplate and eleven groove forearm retain most of the original varnish. If this rifle was in 95% condition, the value would double, and it would be easier to sell.

RIFLES: PPGS CONDITION FACTORS

RIFLES: PPGS CONDITION FACTORS

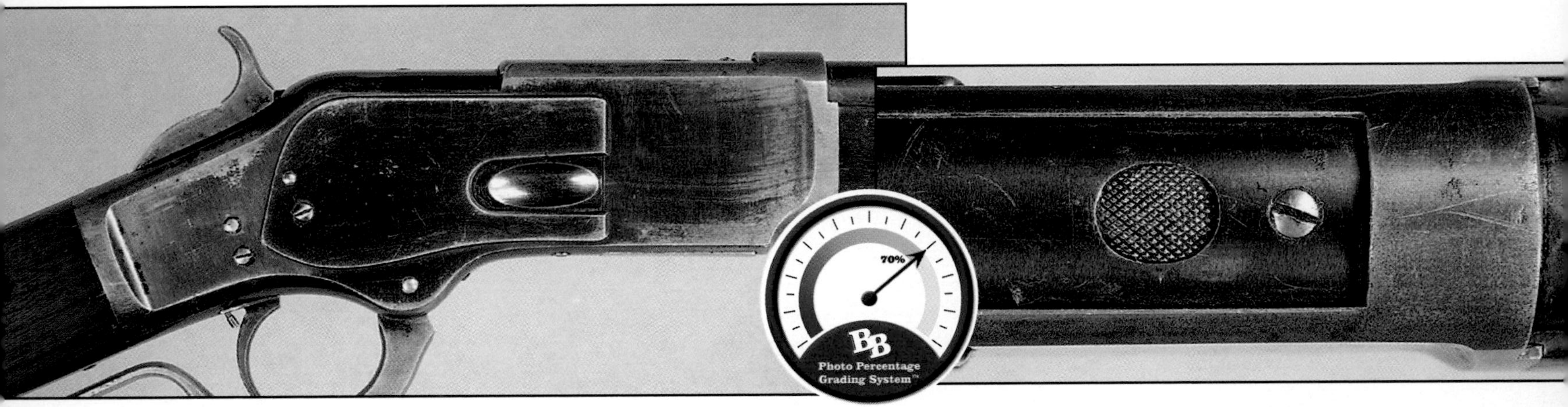

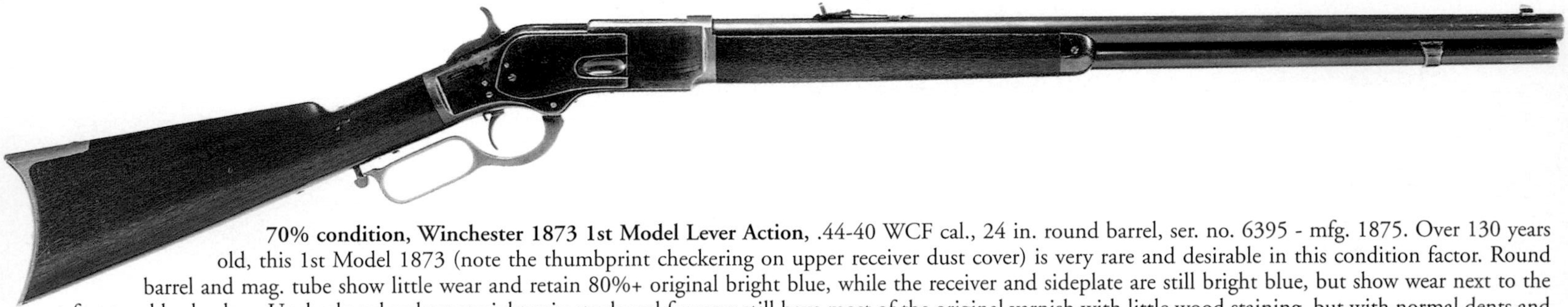

70% condition, Winchester 1873 1st Model Lever Action, .44-40 WCF cal., 24 in. round barrel, ser. no. 6395 - mfg. 1875. Over 130 years old, this 1st Model 1873 (note the thumbprint checkering on upper receiver dust cover) is very rare and desirable in this condition factor. Round barrel and mag. tube show little wear and retain 80%+ original bright blue, while the receiver and sideplate are still bright blue, but show wear next to the front and back edges. Uncheckered walnut straight grip stock and forearm still have most of the original varnish with little wood staining, but with normal dents and scratches. Case colors have mostly faded on the lever, but are still strong on the hammer. A factory letter from the Cody Firearms Museum verifies this rifle's configuration with round barrel and set trigger, and indicates that it was received in the Winchester warehouse on Sept. 1, 1875, and shipped the same day.

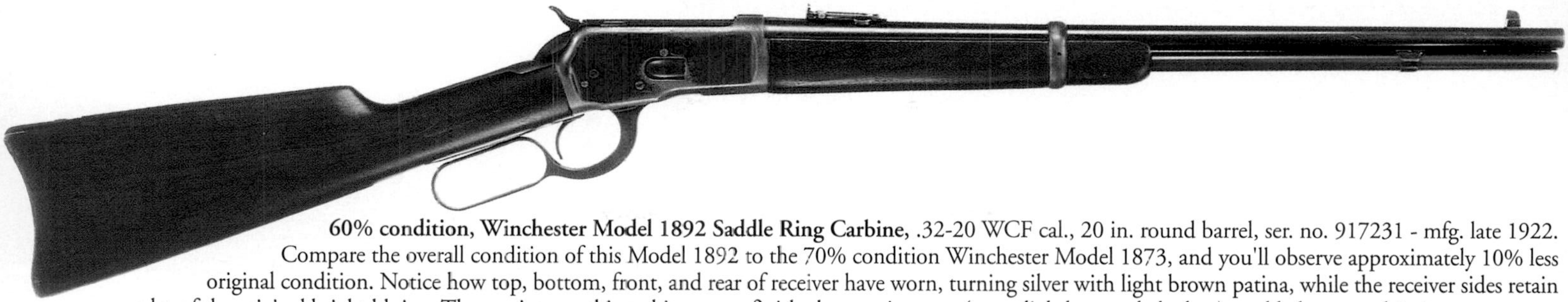

60% condition, Winchester Model 1892 Saddle Ring Carbine, .32-20 WCF cal., 20 in. round barrel, ser. no. 917231 - mfg. late 1922. Compare the overall condition of this Model 1892 to the 70% condition Winchester Model 1873, and you'll observe approximately 10% less original condition. Notice how top, bottom, front, and rear of receiver have worn, turning silver with light brown patina, while the receiver sides retain a lot of the original bright bluing. The receiver on this carbine was refinished some time ago (note slightly rounded edges), and helps to explain its current wear pattern. Saddle ring imprint on rear left side of receiver is normal, and barrel band has turned mostly grey. Uncheckered straight grip walnut stock shows signs of light cleaning, but is still flush with metal. Action remains mechanically perfect, and its overall good eye appeal help elevate its value to above that of a poor reblue.

RIFLES: PPGS CONDITION FACTORS

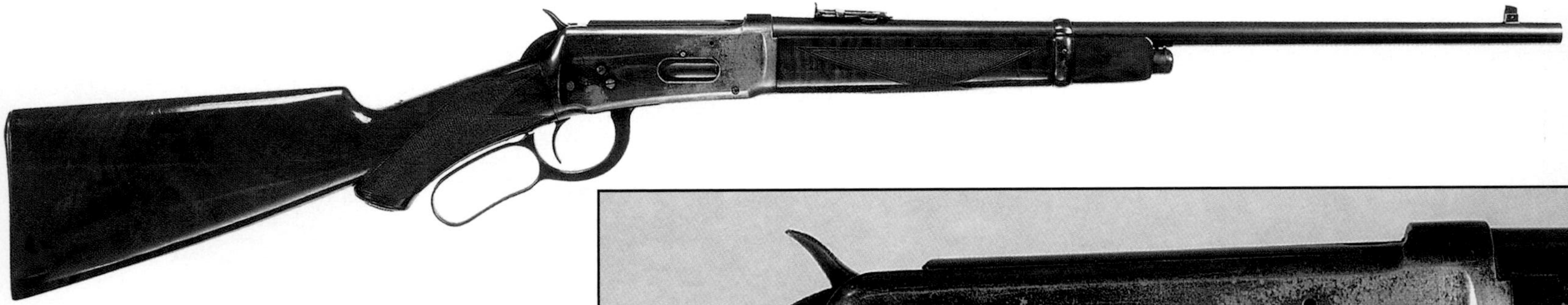

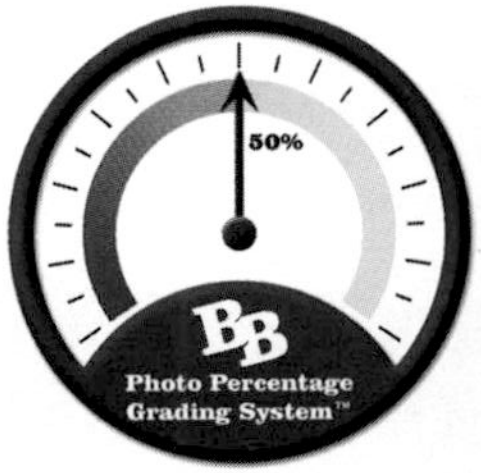

50% condition, Winchester Model 1894 Deluxe Saddle Ring Carbine, .30-30 Win. cal., 20 in. round barrel, ser. no. 582407 – mfg. 1911. Even in this condition factor, this Model 1894 deluxe saddle ring carbine is very desirable, with auction pricing now controlling the final premium paid on most major trademark firearms! Nickel steel barrel with ladder type rear sight and half magazine still has 95%+ original bluing, while the receiver has had much of its bluing flake off. Do not confuse receiver flaking with normal wear and usage – some Winchester lever action rifles can be almost unfired, but show similar frame wear as this specimen. Flaking occurred because the bluing did not adhere properly on guns with a high nickel content in the steel. Deluxe checkered walnut stock with steel shotgun buttplate may have been resprayed at a later date, but the varnish is in excellent condition, and matches the condition of the forearm.

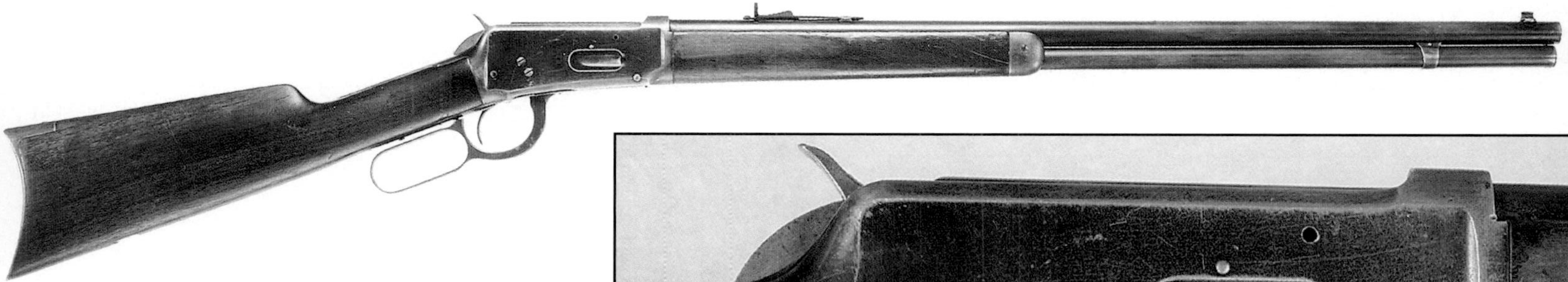

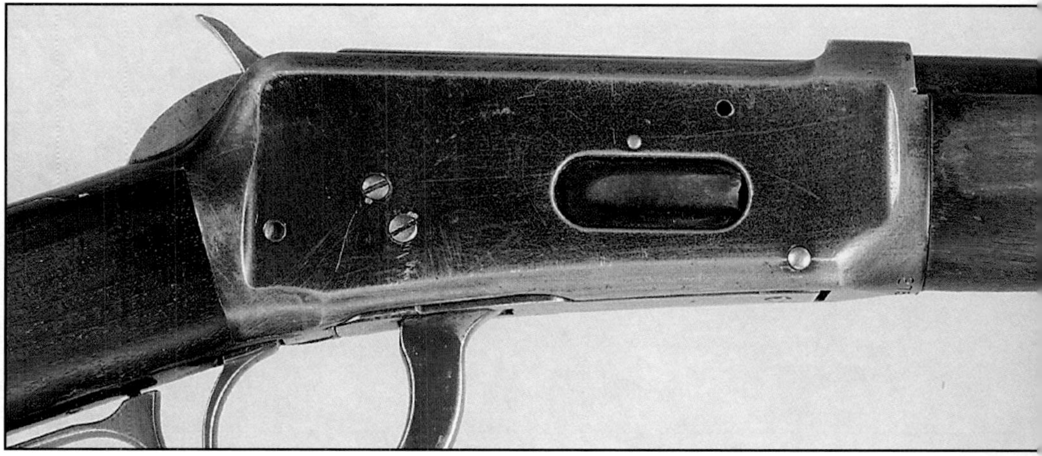

40% condition, Winchester Model 1894 Lever Action, .32 Win. Spl. cal., 26 in. round barrel, ser. no. 875560 – mfg. 1920. In the gun business, this is what you call a gun's condition factors "adding up" correctly. This plain Jane Model 1894 with 26 in. barrel is a study on what to look for when evaluating an older rifle. Note how the nickel steel barrel still has much of its bright blue, while the mag. tube has turned a brown patina overall. Metal forearm cap is mostly shiny, and matches the condition on the receiver and wood. Flat receiver sides still have a lot of bright bluing left, especially at rear – also note how the loading gate finish looks good. The original stock wood and varnish have darkened somewhat, especially next to the receiver (normal) and the forearm shows normal use in the right areas. The receiver screw heads look good, and again, this Winchester still has a lot of eye appeal.

RIFLES: PPGS CONDITION FACTORS

74

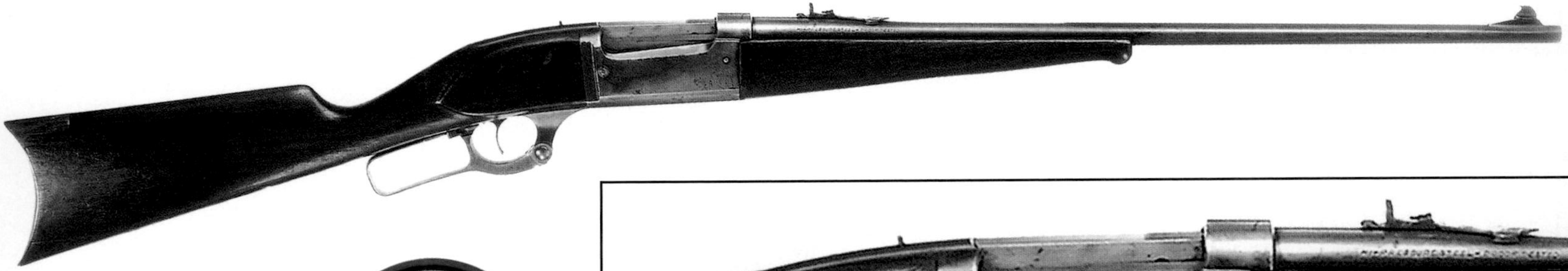

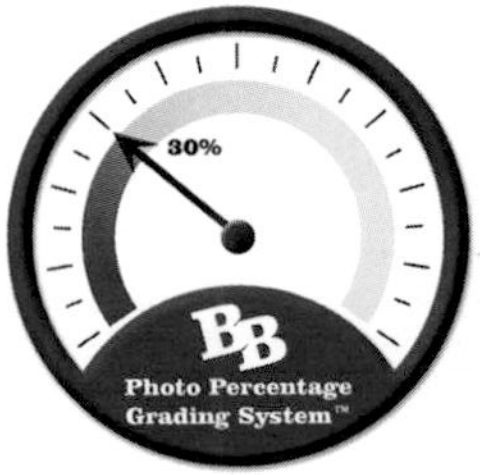

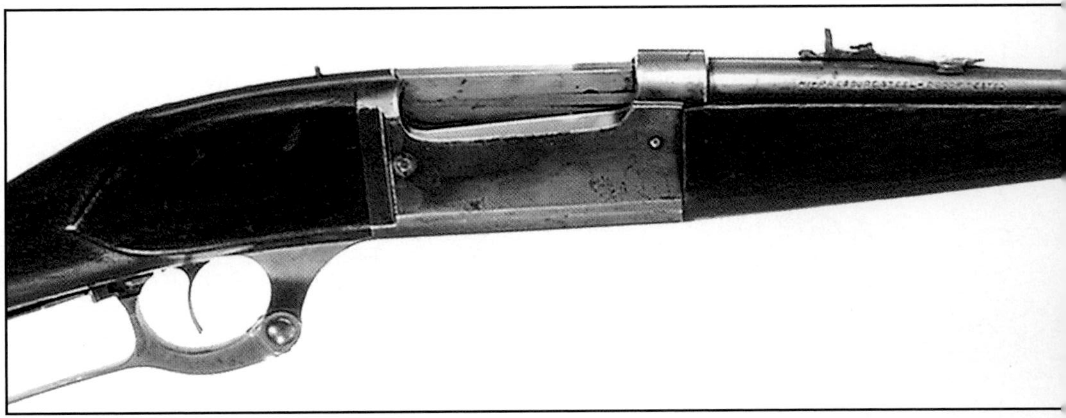

30% condition, Savage Model 1899 Lever Action, .300 Sav. cal., 24 in. round barrel, ser. no. 324301 – mfg. 1929. If this rifle could talk, you'd probably be listening to a lot of interesting older deer hunting tales. Mostly shiny receiver shows previous polishing, while thinning bluing finish on barrel indicates this lever action has been on many previous hunting trips. Uncheckered straight grip walnut stock has turned somewhat dark due to oil staining and handling, and has some dings and scratches. While unseen, serious cracks in the stock have been repaired, and some pitting is present on both the frame and the barrel. Lever is also mostly shiny, attesting to the years of use. This rifle in this condition has now reached shooter status only, since most collectors want better condition in this type of common model. In other words, figure out its price as a shooter, and don't pay a penny more.

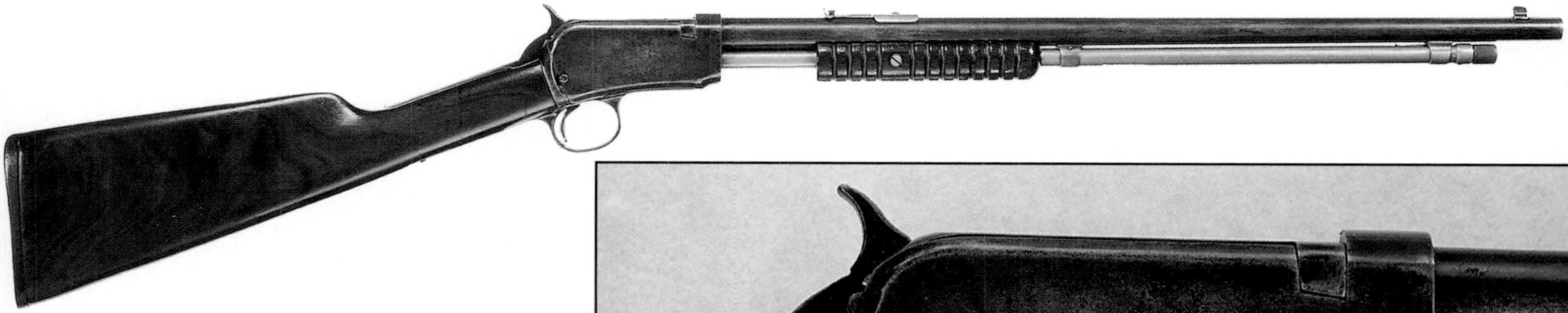

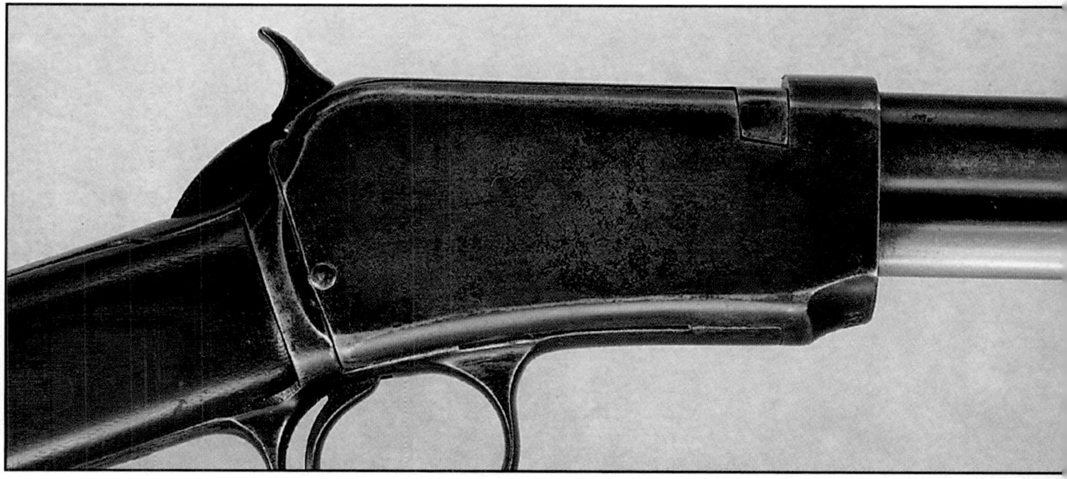

20% condition, Winchester Model 1906 Slide Action, .22 S-L-LR cal., 20 in. round barrel, ser. no. 256876 – mfg. 1926. Two of Winchester's most popular slide action .22 cal. rifles, the Models 1890 and 1906, enjoyed tremendous popularity between 1890-1932, with almost 1.7 million manufactured. Yet, a mint specimen of either model is very rare and only infrequently encountered. This Model 1906 is in below average condition, with the receiver having turned a dark brown patina, and showing major areas of pitting. Barrel has also turned an overall brown patina, while the mag. tube and action bar are nickel plated. Stock and forearm have been revarnished, and do not match the rest of this gun's condition. Action remains tight, while bore is good. This rifle's value has bottomed out in this condition factor, and has limited desirability for Winchester collectors who want better condition.

RIFLES: PPGS CONDITION FACTORS

76

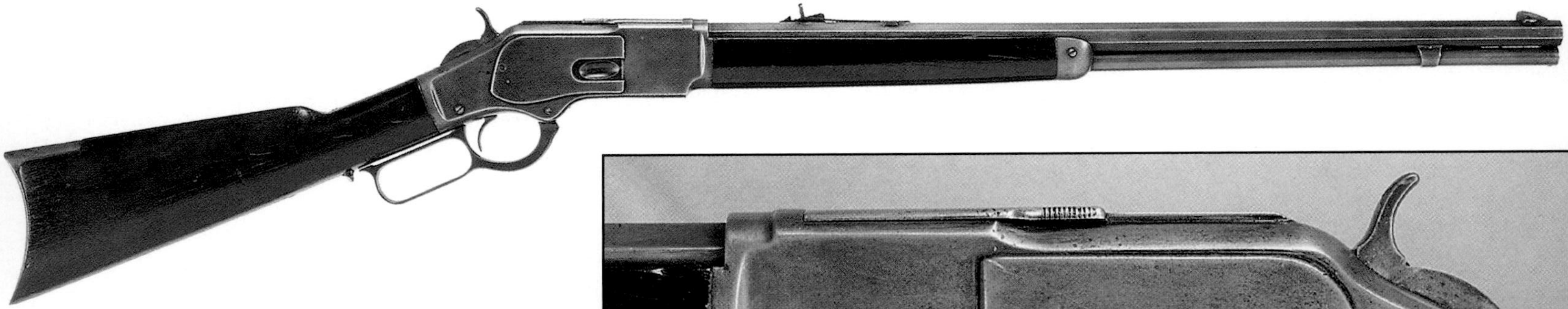

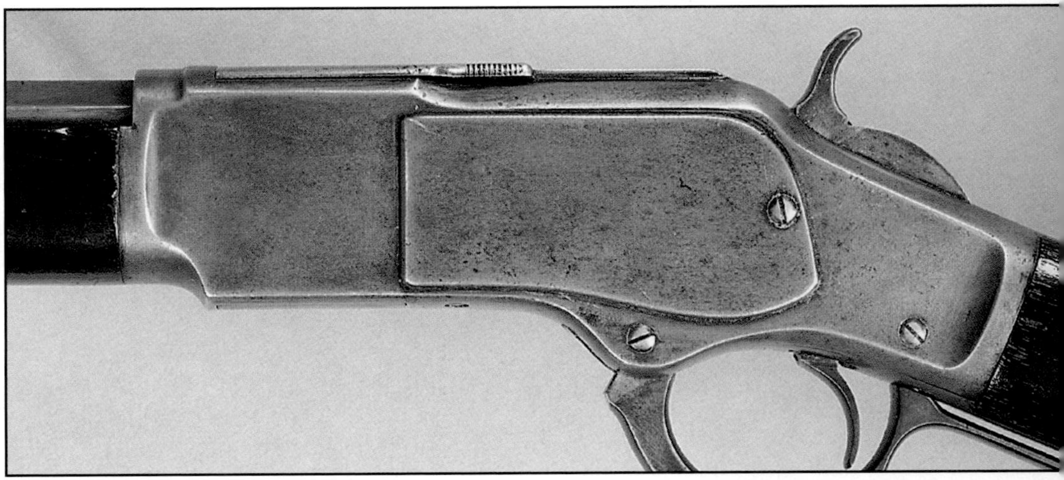

10% condition, Winchester 3rd Model 1873 Lever Action, .32-20 WCF cal., 24 in. octagon barrel, ser. no. 354761B - mfg. 1890. This Model 1873 is a good example of an antique rifle's original finish having turned a smooth grey brown patina overall (compare the finish on this gun to the 70% condition Winchester 1873 1st Model Lever Action). Even though this gun has little original finish left, it does not have major problems like severe pitting, replaced non-original parts, or damaged/cracked wood, even though the stock and forearm have been previously revarnished. All markings remain sharp, the action is mechanically okay, and the bore is fair. Many Winchester collectors would still rather have a no problem, original rifle like this than a 40% overall specimen with major finish problems and alterations. This specimen would be considered an entry-level model for collecting, based on its condition and originality.

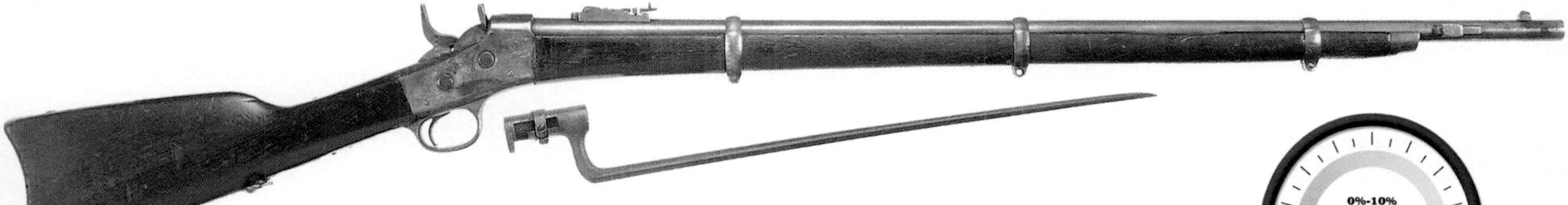

0%-10% Condition, Remington Rolling Block w/bayonet, .43 Spanish cal., 33 7/8 in. round barrel, no ser. no. – mfg. circa late 19th century. This well-worn Remington Rolling Block rifle made under contract for the Spanish government is a good example of how a gun's value can be reduced to almost nothing if there is very little original condition remaining. The metal finish has turned a greyish patina, with quite a bit of rusting and pitting on the receiver. The stock is also battered, and note that the ramrod and front sling swivel are missing. The bore is as dark as the oil-soaked wood, but at least it has the original bayonet. Remington made hundreds of thousands of rolling block rifles in various configurations and calibers for many countries, and the remaining majority now look like this. While a mint original specimen is both rare and desirable, a contract rolling block in this condition has lost most of its desirability and eye appeal. Typically priced under $250, these contract rifles, in many obsolete calibers, can no longer be considered even as shooters.

RIFLES: NRA ANTIQUE CONDITIONS

78

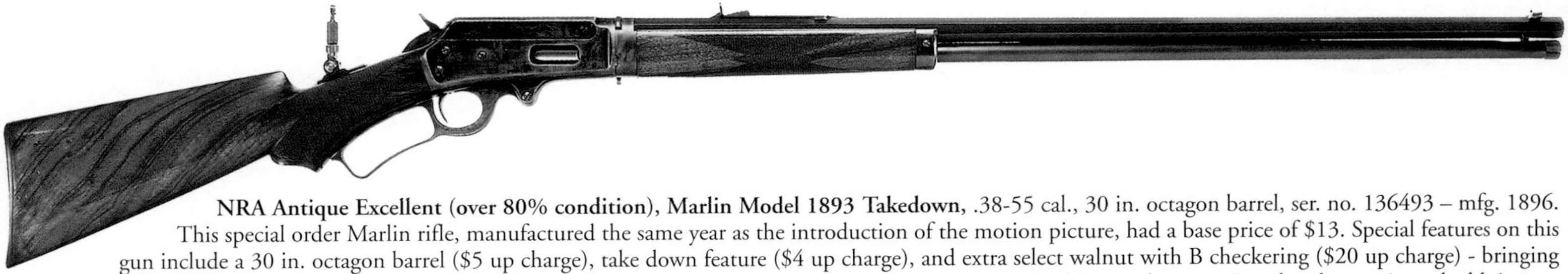

NRA Antique Excellent (over 80% condition), Marlin Model 1893 Takedown, .38-55 cal., 30 in. octagon barrel, ser. no. 136493 – mfg. 1896. This special order Marlin rifle, manufactured the same year as the introduction of the motion picture, had a base price of $13. Special features on this gun include a 30 in. octagon barrel ($5 up charge), take down feature ($4 up charge), and extra select walnut with B checkering ($20 up charge) - bringing the total up to $42! Note the vivid case colors on both sides of the receiver, featuring predominately mottled blues and greens. Barrel and magazine tube bluing are above 95%, and checkered Circassian walnut stock and forearm retain most of the original varnish. Once you start adding up what these special orders/features can do to a major trademark gun in this type of superior original condition in today's marketplace, the price tag gets turbo charged in a hurry!

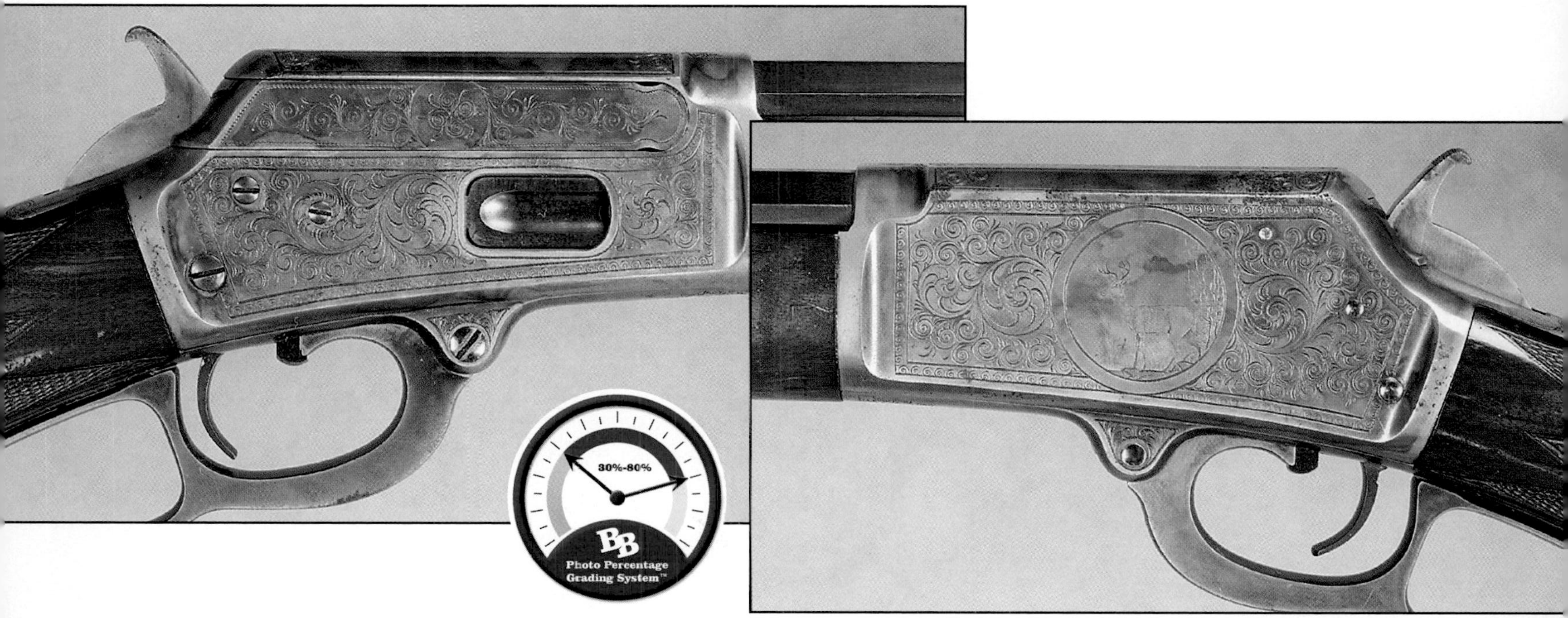

NRA Antique Fine (30%-80% condition), Engraved Marlin Model 1889 Deluxe Lever Action, .32-20 WCF cal., 24 in. octagon barrel, ser. no. 69896 – mfg. June 18, 1892. As a general rule of thumb, engraved guns appear to have less case colors than non-engraved standard models. Extensive engraving on any case colored rifle actually subdues the case colors somewhat, as the scrollwork tends to break up the overall pattern. Note how front and rear receiver edges have become shiny with light freckling, and how wood to metal fit is perfect. Also note that the case colored lever has coloration left only in the protected area where it pivots. Hammer case colors are nice, and match the overall condition factor of this fine rifle. While some dealers and collectors may refer to this condition as Very Fine, this term is not a proper NRA Antique condition factor.

RIFLES: NRA ANTIQUE CONDITIONS

80

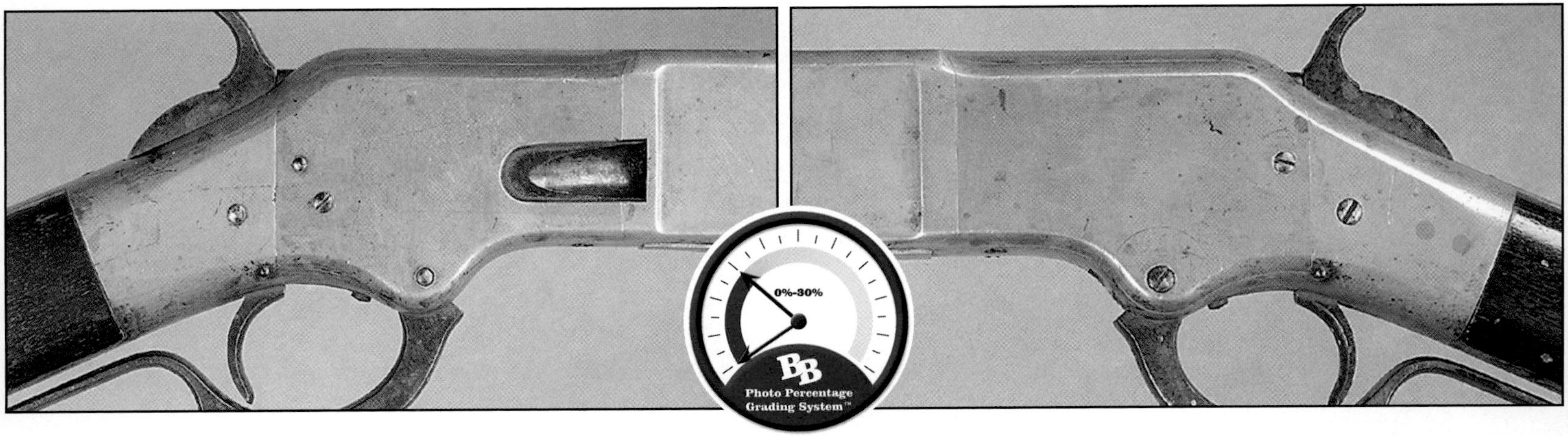

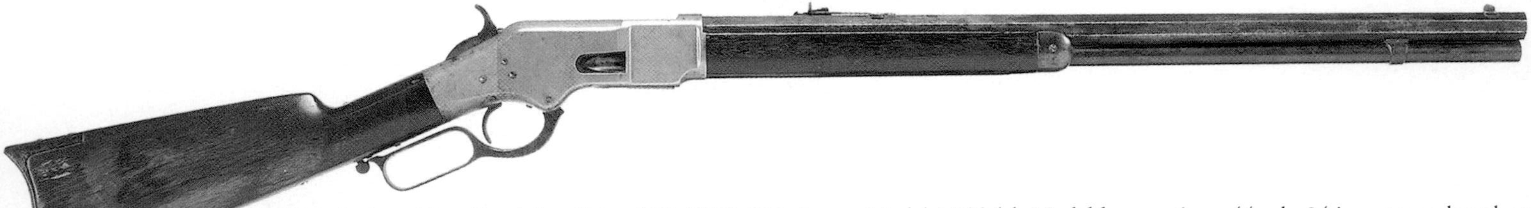

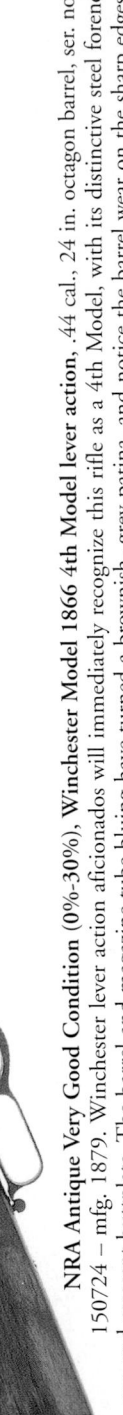

NRA Antique Very Good Condition (0%-30%), **Winchester Model 1866 4th Model lever action**, .44 cal., 24 in. octagon barrel, ser. no. 150724 – mfg. 1879. Winchester lever action aficionados will immediately recognize this rifle as a 4th Model, with its distinctive steel forend cap and crescent buttplate. The barrel and magazine tube bluing have turned a brownish- grey patina, and notice the barrel wear on the sharp edges. The condition of the brass frame is critical when evaluating this model, and note the mustard coloring and sharp edges. Many of these were sanded or polished to make them look newer. The stock may have been lightly sanded at an earlier date, but overall, this is a very nice Model 1866 4th Model. Antique Winchester lever actions like this one used to be commonly seen at most major gun shows, but in recent years, can mainly be found either at auctions or from specialized high end dealers and collectors.

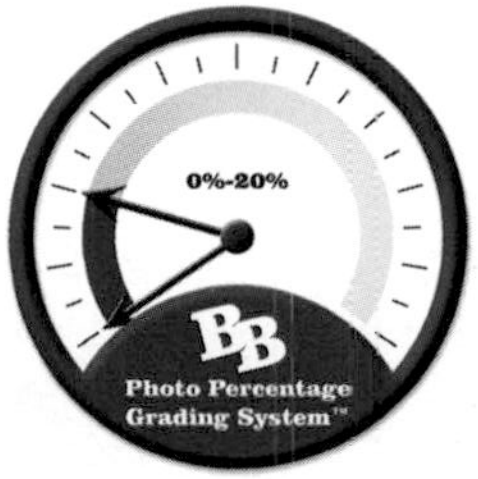

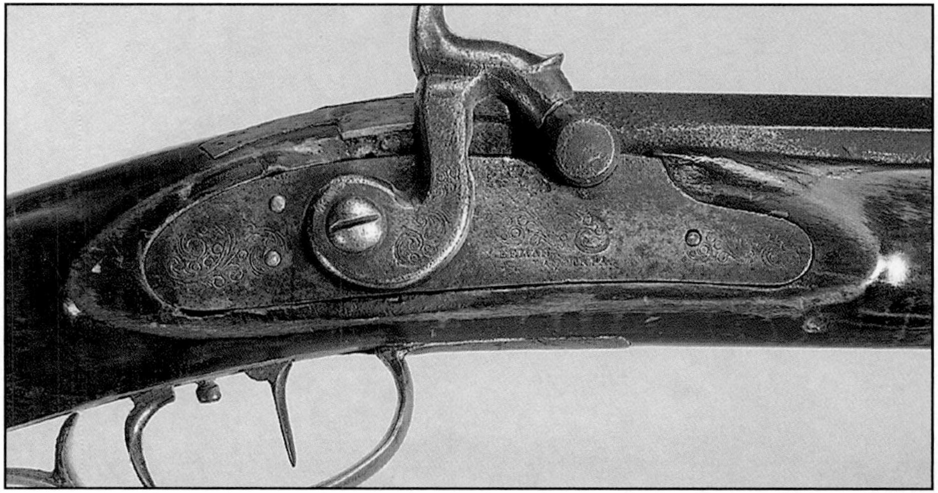

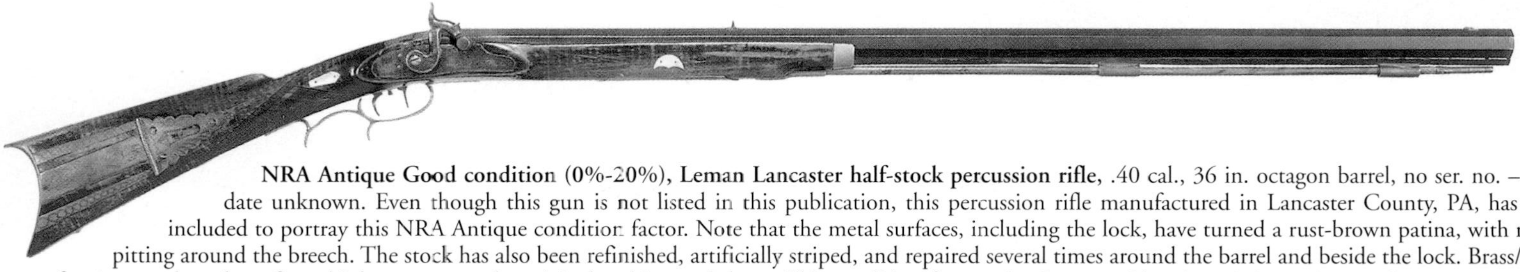

NRA Antique Good condition (0%-20%), **Leman Lancaster half-stock percussion rifle,** .40 cal., 36 in. octagon barrel, no ser. no. – mfg. date unknown. Even though this gun is not listed in this publication, this percussion rifle manufactured in Lancaster County, PA, has been included to portray this NRA Antique condition factor. Note that the metal surfaces, including the lock, have turned a rust-brown patina, with major pitting around the breech. The stock has also been refinished, artificially striped, and repaired several times around the barrel and beside the lock. Brass/silver furniture and mother-of-pearl inlays appear to be original and in good shape. This condition factor takes into consideration pitting, minor replacement parts, and wood refinishing, but in good working order. In general, the older and more common the gun, the less likely it will be found in over NRA Antique Fine condition. Collectors prefer originality over anything else once an older gun like this reaches this condition factor.

RIFLES: NRA ANTIQUE CONDITIONS

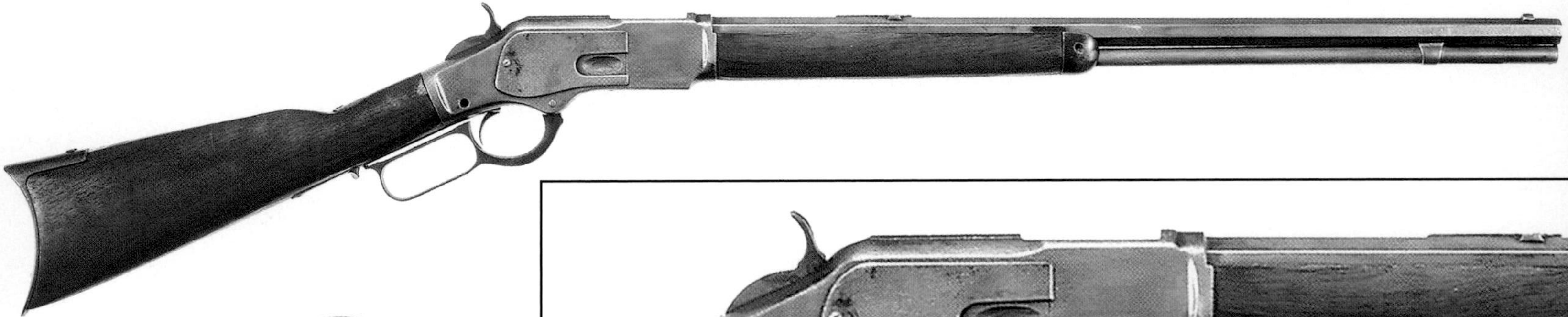

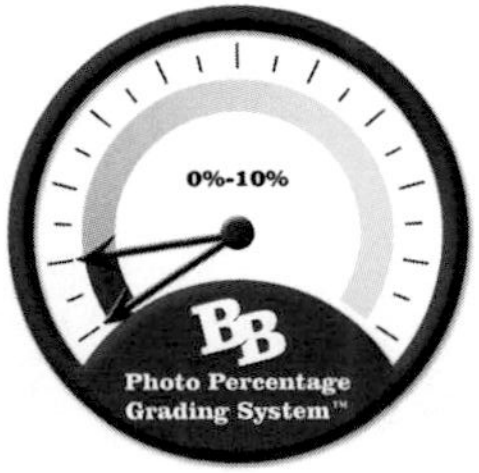

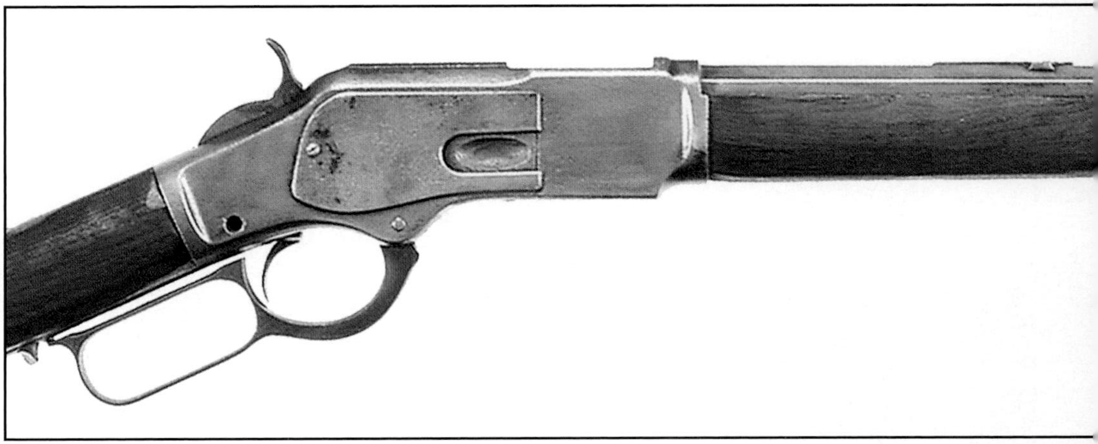

NRA Antique Fair condition (0-10%). Altered Winchester Model 1873 Lever Action, .32-20 WCF cal., 24 in. octagon barrel, ser. no. 167428 – mfg. 1884. Except for the forearm cap, there is no original finish remaining on the receiver, barrel, or magazine tube. This gun has had all its metal surfaces polished and is also missing major parts such as the dust cover, receiver screws, and rear sight. Both the stock and the forearm are crude replacements, and fit poorly to the metal. This rifle (or what's left of it) constitutes 0-10% condition (NRA Fair). So what's it worth? The answer is, add up values for the individual parts, and don't include the stock or forearm. In this case, the total is approx. $475-$550, still cheaper than a modern reproduction. Unfortunately, most guns in this condition factor never become more desirable (or expensive) as junk will always be junk, and gets priced accordingly!

NRA Antique Poor condition (no original finish remaining), Modified Sharps New Model 1863 Military parts rifle, .52 cal., 30 in. round barrel, ser. no. C1904 – mfg. circa 1863. This carbine receiver was originally rejected (or perhaps it was on a gun rejected for other reasons) and there are no inspector marks. This rifle has been put together using a rejected carbine receiver and leftover rifle parts. It was probably assembled by Schuyler Hartley & Graham, or Bannerman, using surplus spare parts from other government contracts, and finally sold cheaply in the post-Civil War consumer marketplace. This is a good example of a gun with no eye appeal. Rusted, pitted, and dark splotchy metal surfaces combined with rejected military status, non-original small parts, and an action that needs work lower this rifle's value significantly. The only way this gun can be under priced is if it can be purchased for less than the total value of its parts!

SHOTGUNS: PPGS CONDITION FACTORS

84

NIB condition, Benelli M4 tactical semi-auto, 12 ga., 3 in. chamber, 18½ in. barrel, ser. no. not provided – mfg. 2009. Without question, no other shotgun company in the past 20 years has raised the bar higher than Benelli, which has emerged from an obscure Italian trademark to a household name in America, in addition to being the world leader in semi-auto and slide action shotgun technology. This M4 tactical shotgun with pistol grip utilizes a unique auto regulating gas operated (ARGO) system, which cycles the action with only 1/2 inch movement of its dual self-cleaning gas pistons. Less than 15 years ago, most tactical shotguns like this were being sold to Europeans as a home defense gun, since handgun ownership is very restricted. With a four shot mag., ghost ring sights, and a Picatinny rail for optics, this shotgun with black synthetic tactical stock and forearm has few peers when used for close range self-defense. New technology has resulted in extremely durable and weather resistant metal finishes and in addition to the almost impervious synthetic stock and forearm, this shotgun will show almost no wear, regardless of climate conditions or how hard it has been used.

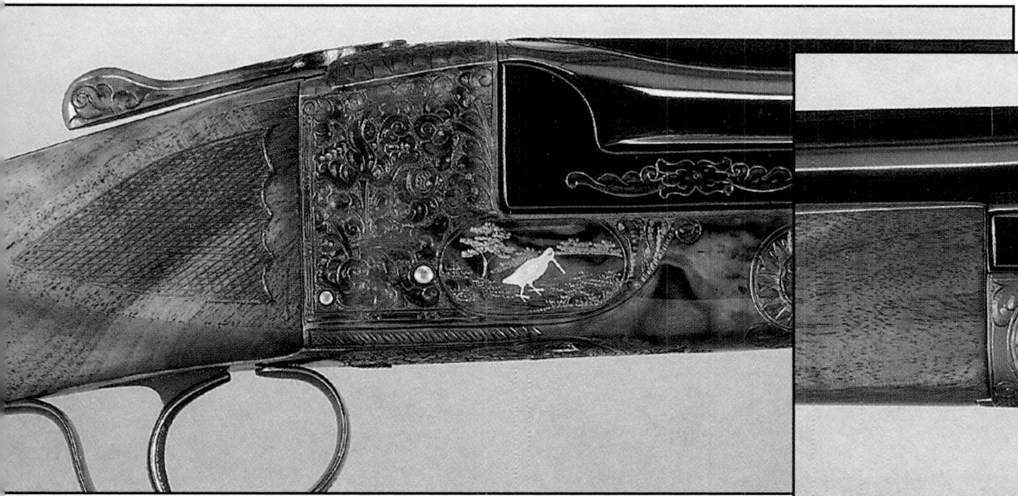

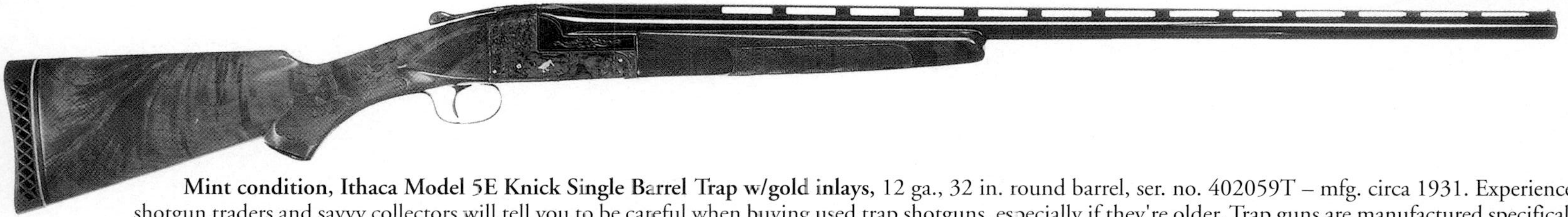

Mint condition, Ithaca Model 5E Knick Single Barrel Trap w/gold inlays, 12 ga., 32 in. round barrel, ser. no. 402059T – mfg. circa 1931. Experienced shotgun traders and savvy collectors will tell you to be careful when buying used trap shotguns, especially if they're older. Trap guns are manufactured specifically to shoot a high volume of shotshells within a relatively brief time frame. Because of this, action wear can accumulate long before wear is visible on the outside of the gun. Always focus on how tight (or loose) the action is, and if the top opening lever is still on the right side of center on upper tang. This nice Ithaca 5E Knick Model has almost no bluing or case color wear, factory engraving and gold bird inlays, definitive of the model. The uncut stock has a replacement Pachmayr recoil pad, typical on trap guns where dimensions are critical and tailored to the individual.

SHOTGUNS: PPGS CONDITION FACTORS

86

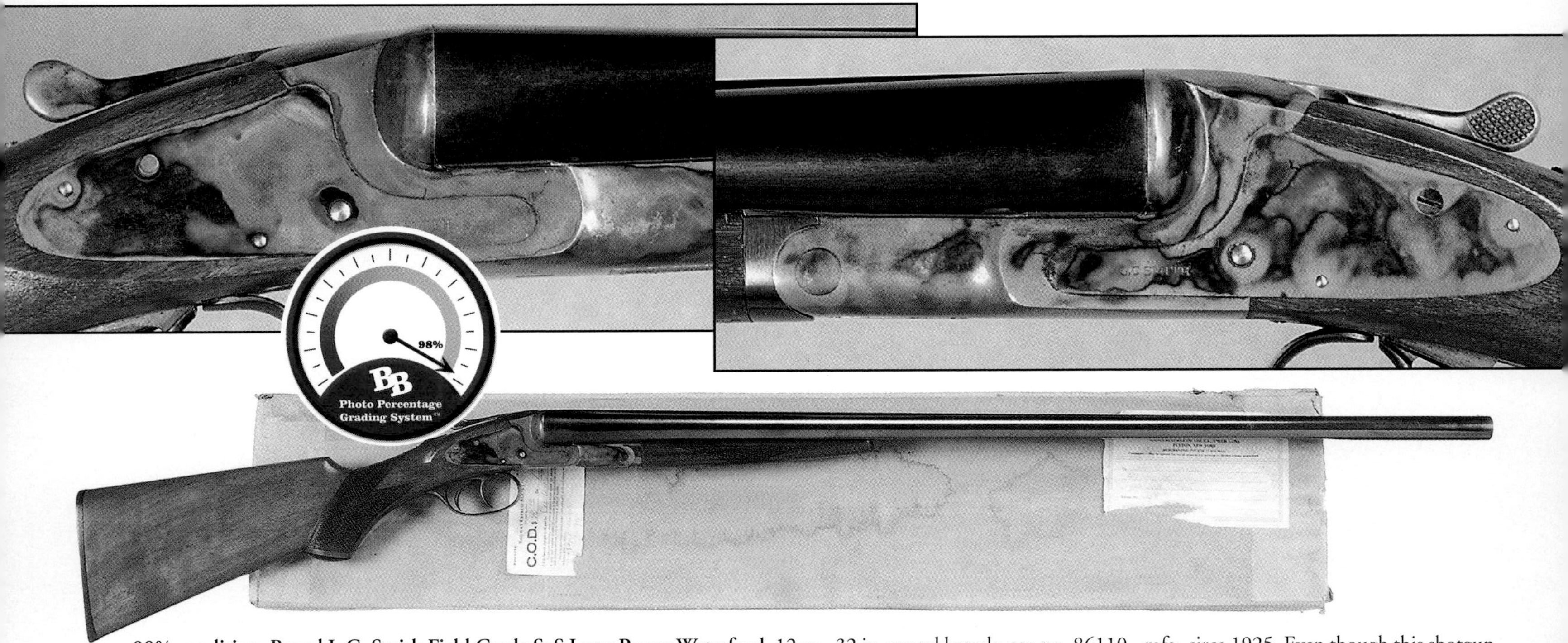

98% condition, Boxed L.C. Smith Field Grade SxS Long Range Waterfowl, 12 ga., 32 in. round barrels, ser. no. 86110 - mfg. circa 1925. Even though this shotgun is both new and unfired, normal storage wear, cleaning, and occasional assembly have all accumulated enough wear to knock this gun's condition factor down to 98%. Original L.C. Smith case colors do not get any better than this - look at the vivid blues and greens surrounded by greyish/brown swirls compared to the 40% condition L.C. Smith 00 Grade SxS and the NRA Antique Fine condition L.C. Smith Grade 2 w/ Ejectors SxS. Also note unstained, light colored, checkered standard grade walnut stock and forearm, and tight wood to metal fit around sideplates. When a desirable gun's condition factor is this good, the value may double or even triple the 90% value. L.C. Smith only had one level of quality - the best, regardless of the grade. Stock and splinter forearm show virtually no wear. In many cases, a 98%+ condition specimen of a factory's most common model is the hardest to find, since most of them were heavily used. Original box is somewhat tattered, and has water staining.

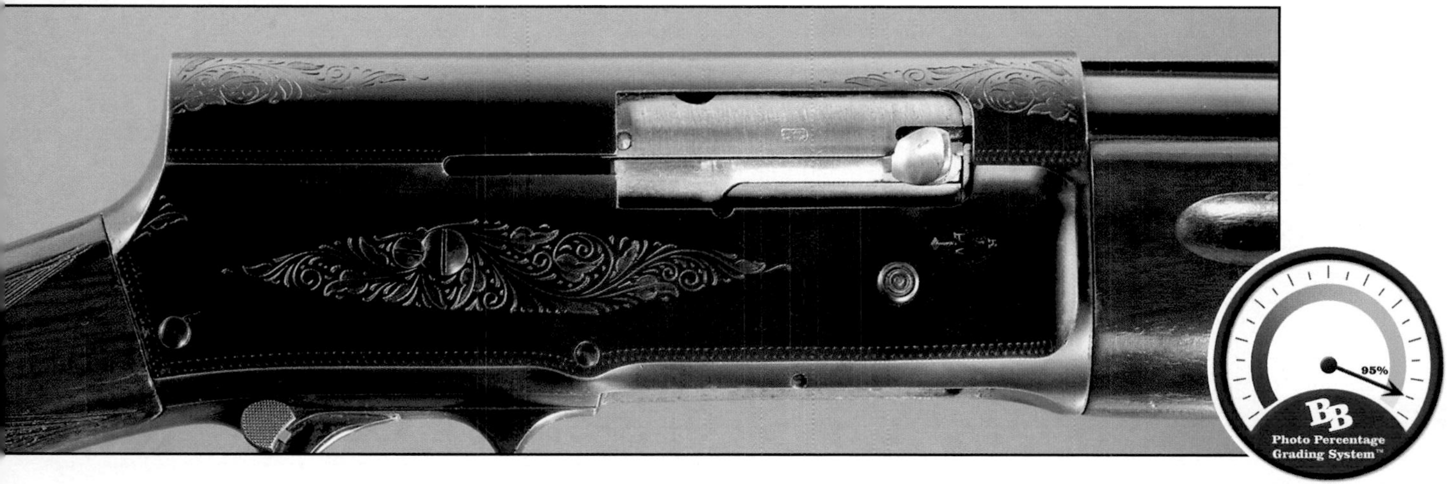

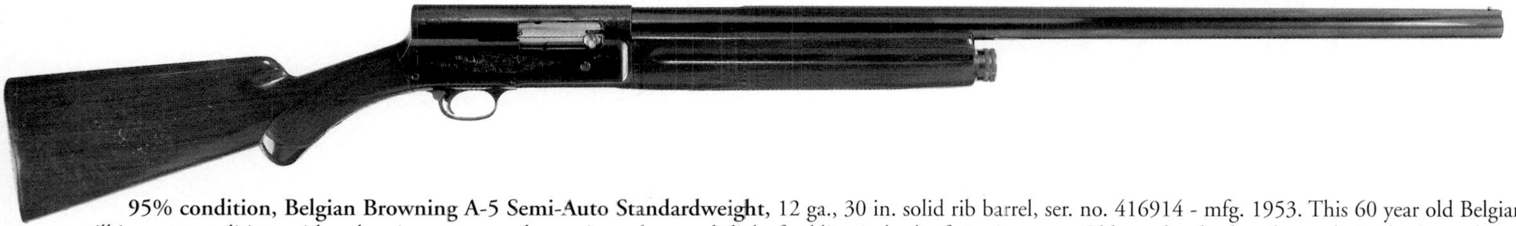

95% condition, Belgian Browning A-5 Semi-Auto Standardweight, 12 ga., 30 in. solid rib barrel, ser. no. 416914 - mfg. 1953. This 60 year old Belgian A-5 is still in great condition, with only minor wear on the receiver edges, and slight freckling in back of ejection port. Older style, checkered round pistol grip stock and 30 in. solid rib barrel also indicate earlier manufacture. Barrel is marked, "Browning Arms Co, St. Louis, MO." When A-5 condition gets lower than this, prices fall off rapidly, as most Browning collectors prefer 98% or better original condition, whenever possible. After almost 100 years of near continuous production, Browning finally discontinued the venerable Auto-5 shotgun in 1999, but reintroduced it during 2012 as a fixed barrel with the new model designated as the A5. In today's A-5 marketplace, solid rib barrels are more desirable (and expensive) than their vent. rib counterparts, as they are rarer. Also, shorter barrels (26 or 28 in.) with open field chokes are worth more than longer barrels with full chokes.

SHOTGUNS: PPGS CONDITION FACTORS

88

90% condition, Belgian Browning A-5 Sweet Sixteen, 16 ga., 28 in. solid rib barrel, ser. no. S14514 – mfg. 1954. Note the additional wear around the lower receiver edges on this Browning compared to the 95% condition Belgian Browning A-5 Semi-Auto Standardweight. This Sweet Sixteen A-5 is referred to as a round knob, long tang variation, indicating that the pistol grip is rounded (mfg. 1952-1976) instead of flat, and the lower tang is longer than recent manufacture. Note blonde French walnut stock and forearm, typical for this period of production. This is a good example of what a rarer variation of a common model can do to the price tag. While the frequently encountered 12 ga. A-5 with 30 in. solid matted rib barrel (95% condition Belgian Browning) currently has a retail value of $550, this rarer Sweet 16 in 90% condition retails in the $900-$1,000 range. This same model in 100% condition can top $1,650, even more if with the original box!

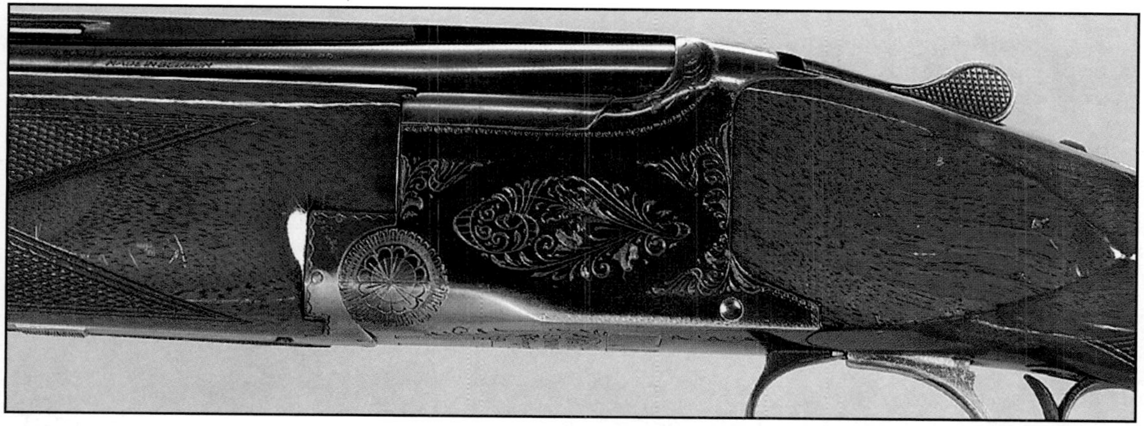

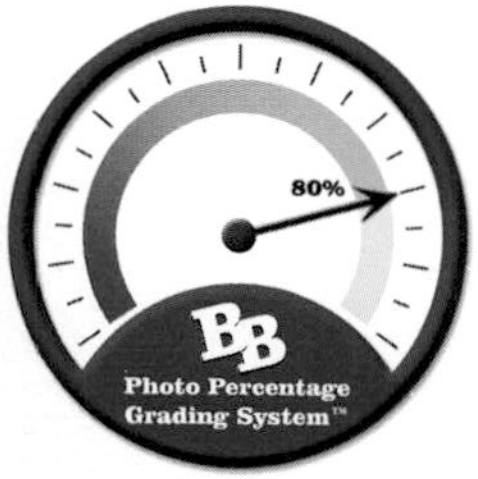

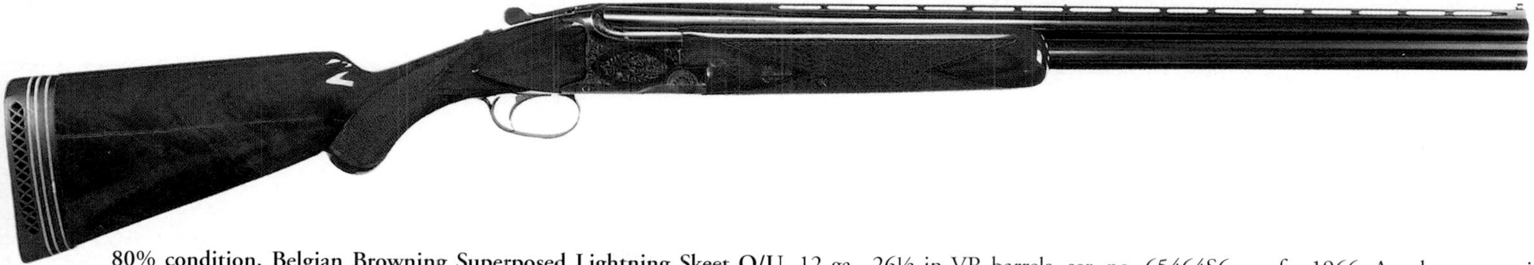

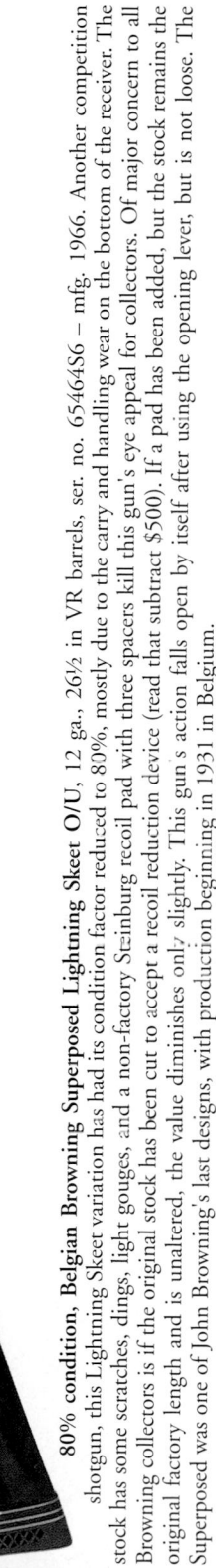

80% condition, Belgian Browning Superposed Lightning Skeet O/U, 12 ga., 26½ in VR barrels, ser. no. 65464S6 – mfg. 1966. Another competition shotgun, this Lightning Skeet variation has had its condition factor reduced to 80%, mostly due to the carry and handling wear on the bottom of the receiver. The stock has some scratches, dings, light gouges, and a non-factory Steinburg recoil pad with three spacers kill this gun's eye appeal for collectors. Of major concern to all Browning collectors is if the original stock has been cut to accept a recoil reduction device (read that subtract $500). If a pad has been added, but the stock remains the original factory length and is unaltered, the value diminishes only slightly. This gun's action falls open by itself after using the opening lever, but is not loose. The Superposed was one of John Browning's last designs, with production beginning in 1931 in Belgium.

SHOTGUNS: PPGS CONDITION FACTORS

90

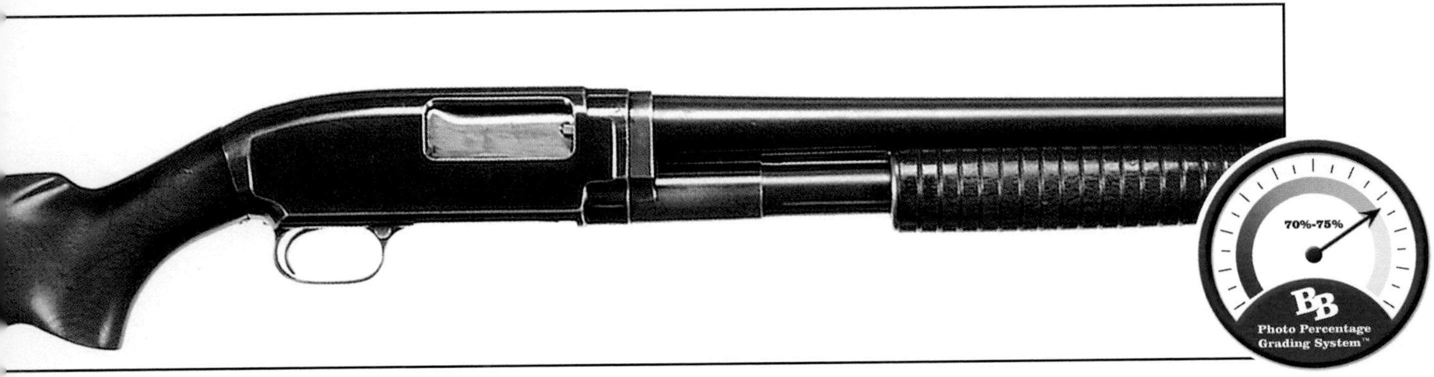

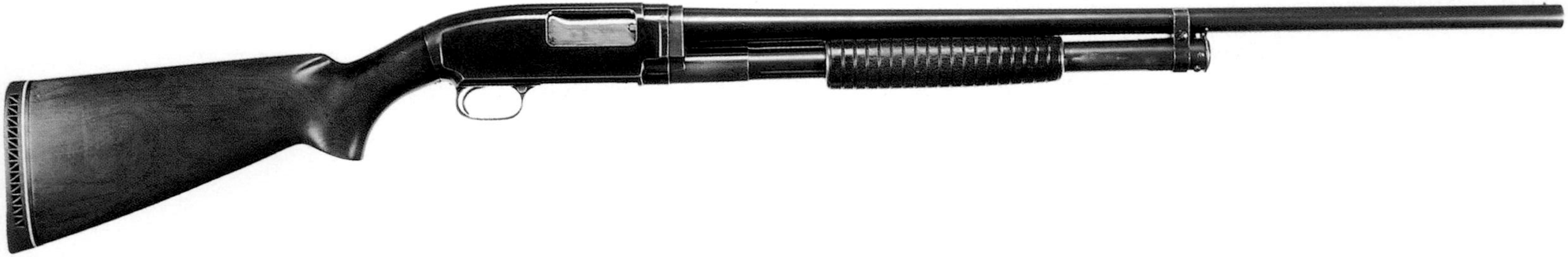

70%-75% condition, Winchester Model 12 Slide Action, 12 ga., 28 in. round barrel, ser. no. 902723 – mfg. 1941. Very few shotgun models are found in such a wide array of condition factors as the Model 12 Winchester. It's pretty hard for any shotgun enthusiast not to have a Model 12 somewhere in his/her gun vault. This particular shotgun shows normal wear, but no abuse. While some dealers and collectors might grade this gun at 80% based on the receiver and barrel bluing, the wear on the mag. tube and ring at end of barrel assembly knock this shotgun's condition down to approx. 70%-75%. Stock has a Pachmayr rubber vent. replacement recoiled pad with spacers, but it has not been cut. Horizontal striations and dulling on breech block indicate this shotgun has pumped out more than a few ounces of lead (hopefully, no steel!) in its lifetime.

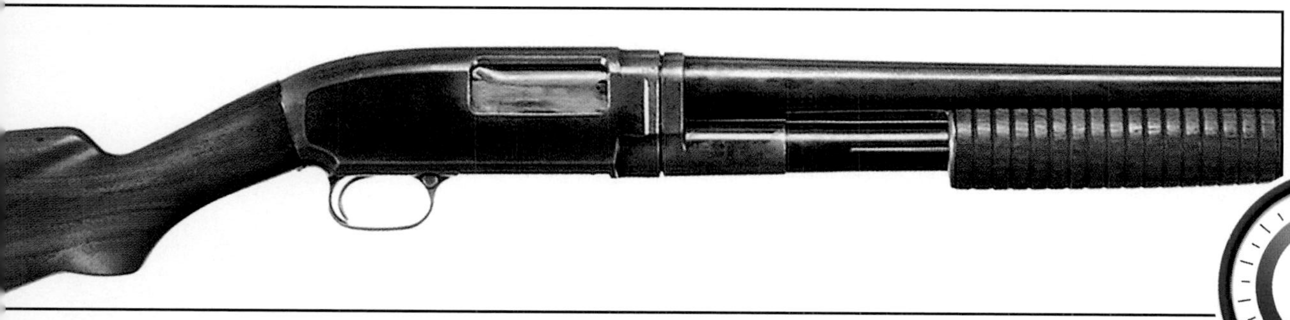

60% condition, Winchester Model 12 Slide Action, 12 ga., 30 in. round barrel, ser. no. 219576 - mfg. early Jan., 1919. When a shotgun gets down to this condition factor, normally the barrel also shows visible wear, as seen on this shotgun. Note how receiver, barrel, and mag. tube have also started to turn a brownish patina. Scuffed breech block and horizontal wear line on mag. tube tell this shotgun's shooting story. The stock has been sanded – note how light it is in the back, but gets dark where it joins the receiver (compare to the 70%-75% condition Winchester Model 12). Most of this gun's value must be determined by its worth as a reliable shooter, since the 12 ga./30 in. full choke barrel is the most common Model 12 configuration. The smaller gauges, especially the 28 ga. and .410 bore, are always more desirable than a 12 ga. in any shotgun model.

SHOTGUNS: PPGS CONDITION FACTORS

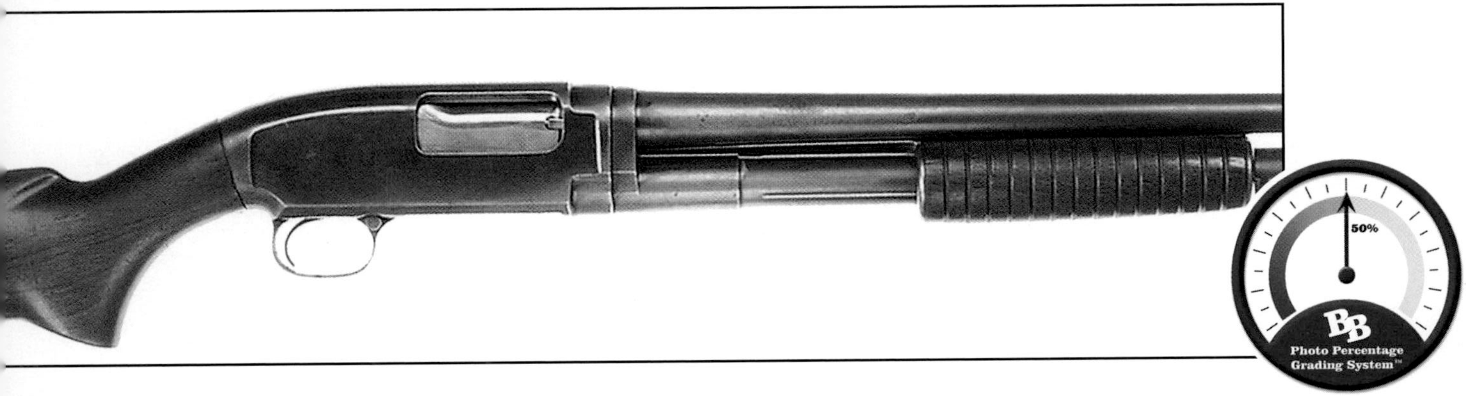

50% condition, Winchester Model 12 Slide Action, 16 ga., 28 in. round barrel, ser. no. 886875 – mfg. 1941. This is a good example of a well used, no problem Model 12. All the major components (wood, receiver, barrel, and mag. tube) are worn in all the right places, as well as not worn in all the right places. When barrel wear reaches this type of brown patina condition, the rest of the gun should look even more worn, as the barrel was normally not handled that much during usage. The mag. tube is equally worn, and the original stock and forearm reveal the right amount of original varnish to match the rest of the gun. Recently, 16 ga. guns have made a comeback in terms of collectibility, and are now priced approximately 10% higher than a 12 ga. with similar condition and features.

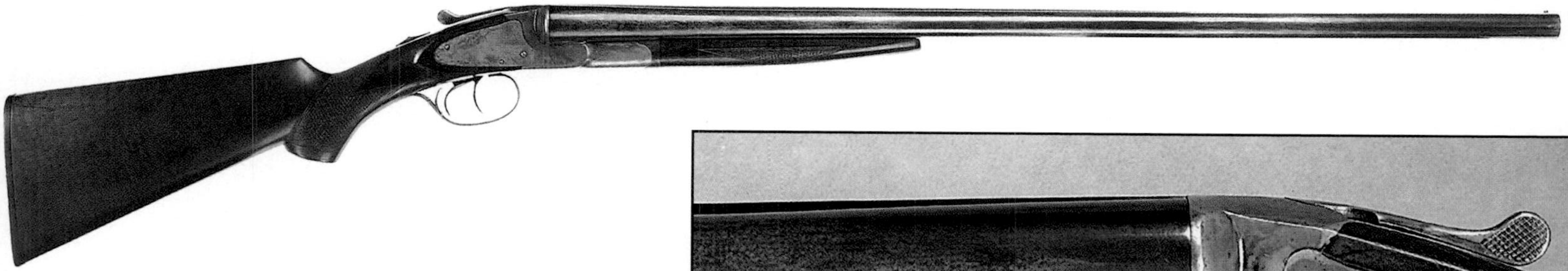

40% Condition, L.C. Smith Field Grade SxS, 12 ga., 30 in. barrels, ser. no. 125367 - mfg. circa 1905. The overall condition of this 100-year-old L.C. Smith is a good example of the individual condition factors of the wood finish, frame case colors, and barrel bluing wearing equally. This means no one or two condition factors are a lot better or a lot worse than the others - very important when evaluating older guns for originality. Compare mottled case colors on frame, mostly visible around protected areas, to the vivid patterns depicted on the 98% condition Boxed L.C. Smith Field Grade SxS Long Range Waterfowl. Checkered Field Grade stock and forearm have darkened somewhat, but do not show major cracks, nicks, or gouges. Bluing on barrels is starting to fade to a patina, but overall, this is a nice original Field Grade L.C. Smith with tight action. Often times, American major trademark Field Grade or Standard Models (including A.H. Fox, Ithaca, Lefever, Parker, Remington, and L.C. Smith) are the hardest models to find in superior original condition, since they were typically used (and possibly abused) the most.

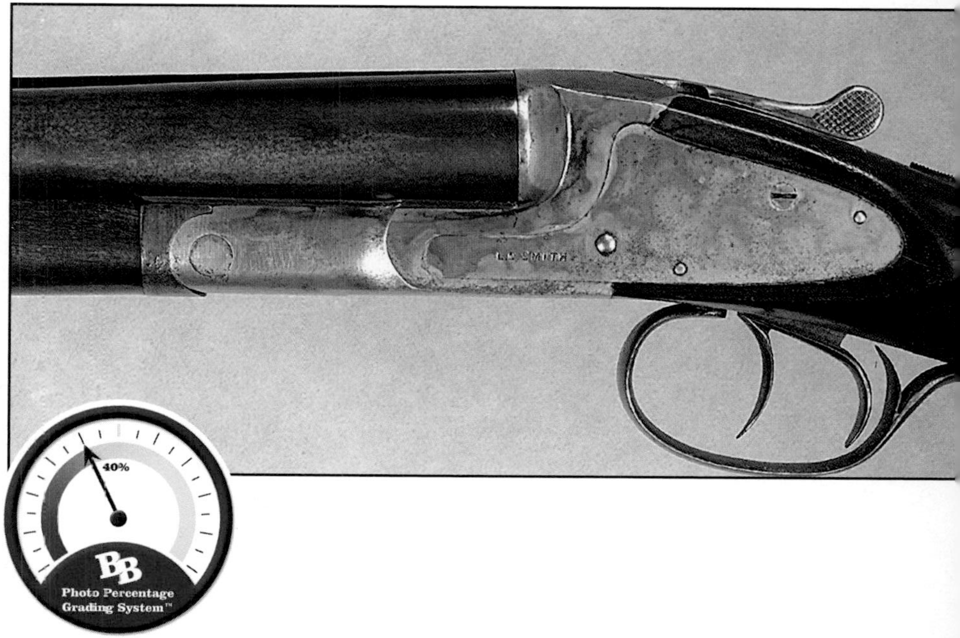

SHOTGUNS: PPGS CONDITION FACTORS

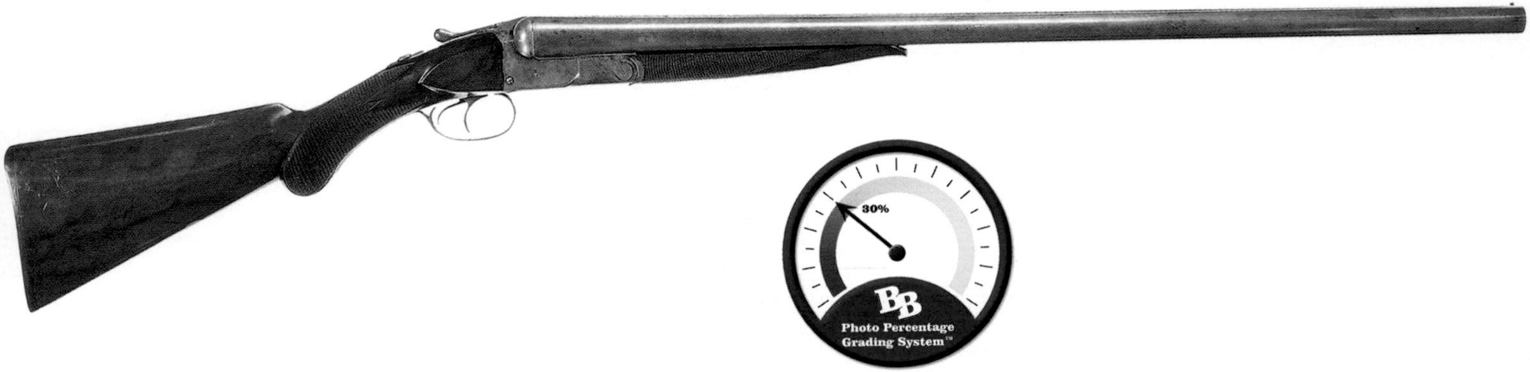

30% Condition, Colt Model 1883 hammerless, 10 ga., 30 in. barrels, ser. no. 2520 – mfg. 1887. While Colt certainly isn't known for its 19th century shotguns, they were every bit as good as the Parkers, L.C. Smiths, Lefevers, Remingtons, etc., at the time, and cost as much or more. This 10 ga. with damascus barrels is still in above average condition when compared to other remaining specimens. Less than 7,400 of this model were manufactured between 1883 and 1895, and former U.S. President Grover Cleveland shot one regularly in 8 ga., which weighed over 12 lbs! Faded case colors remain in a few protected areas, the English walnut stock and forearm have a few scratches, yet the checkering retains its entire pattern and shows little wear. The damascus barrels have turned an overall dull grey patina throughout, and the bores are still shiny. The action is tight, and because of its originality with no problems, many Colt and/or SxS shotgun collectors would be more than glad to add this gun to their collections.

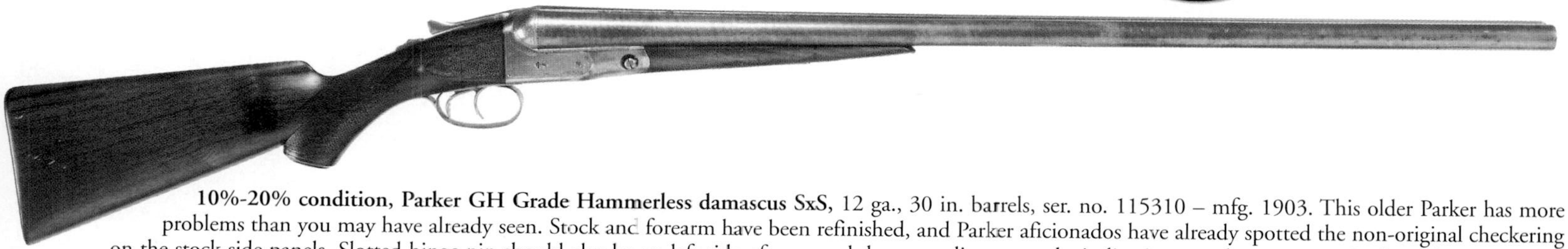

10%-20% condition, Parker GH Grade Hammerless damascus SxS, 12 ga., 30 in. barrels, ser. no. 115310 – mfg. 1903. This older Parker has more problems than you may have already seen. Stock and forearm have been refinished, and Parker aficionados have already spotted the non-original checkering on the stock side panels. Slotted hinge pin should also be on left side of gun, and does not align properly, indicating a replacement put in from the wrong side. Note that almost all the original frame case colors are gone, and this shotgun's frame may have been previously polished, as some of the engraving has thinned out in areas. The damascus hammerless barrels still show great patterning, and double triggers are to be expected on the Model GH, which retailed for approximately $80 when new, $25 more with ejectors. Parker shotguns have continued to lead the domestic SxS marketplace price appreciation, with pricing for strong, original condition guns in smaller gauges (20 ga. and less) going well above auction reserve levels. But don't forget that originality has always been Polar North for Parker shotgun collectors.

SHOTGUNS: PPGS CONDITION FACTORS

96

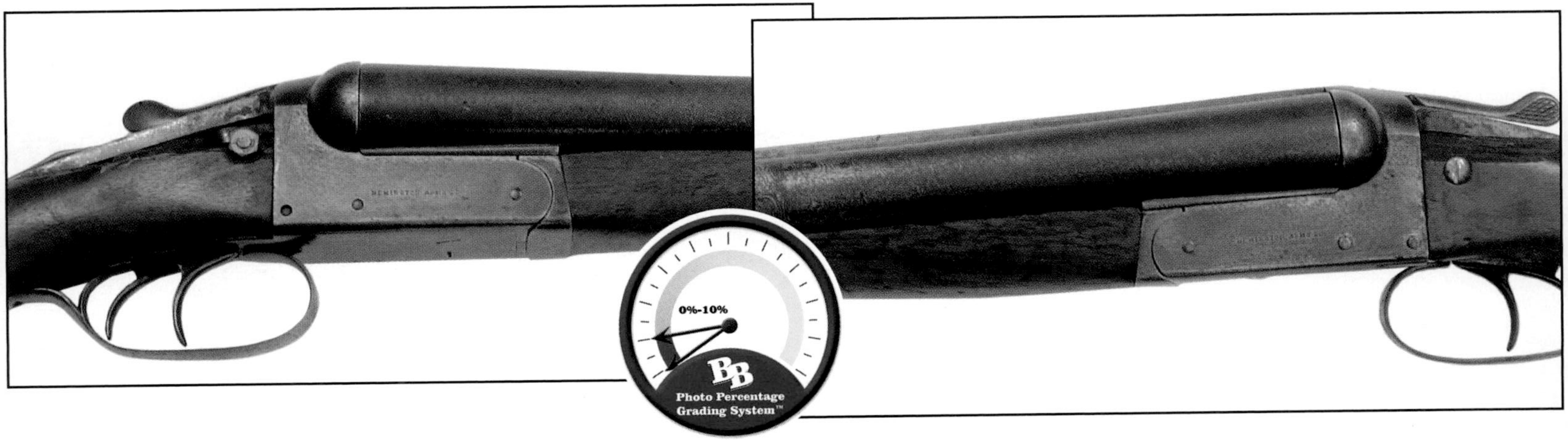

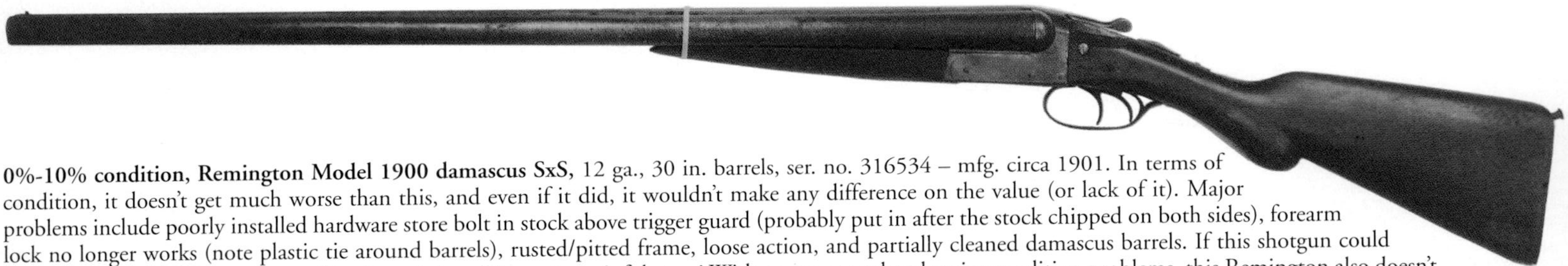

0%-10% condition, Remington Model 1900 damascus SxS, 12 ga., 30 in. barrels, ser. no. 316534 – mfg. circa 1901. In terms of condition, it doesn't get much worse than this, and even if it did, it wouldn't make any difference on the value (or lack of it). Major problems include poorly installed hardware store bolt in stock above trigger guard (probably put in after the stock chipped on both sides), forearm lock no longer works (note plastic tie around barrels), rusted/pitted frame, loose action, and partially cleaned damascus barrels. If this shotgun could talk, it would probably need a psychiatrist to help tell its entire painful story! With no eye appeal and major condition problems, this Remington also doesn't have any shooting value unless a gunsmith extensively went through it, and it wouldn't be worth it. Falling into the rusty iron/kindling category, this gun's value has been under $100 for quite some time, and the problem is, that will never change. Trash will always be trash!

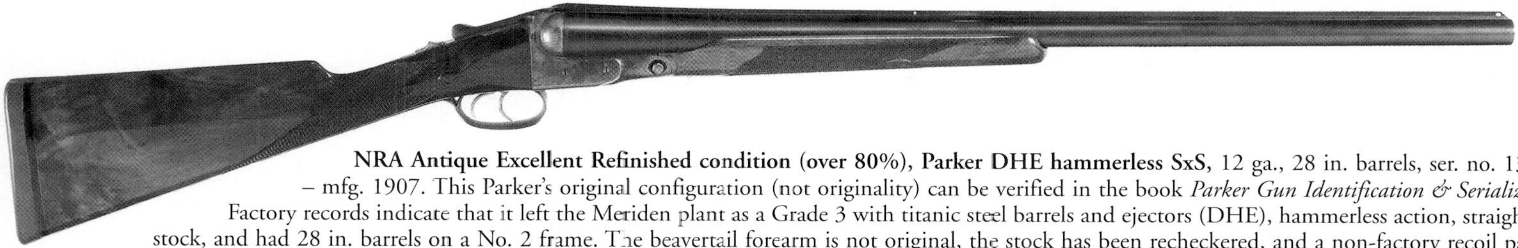

NRA Antique Excellent Refinished condition (over 80%), **Parker DHE hammerless SxS,** 12 ga., 28 in. barrels, ser. no. 139955 – mfg. 1907. This Parker's original configuration (not originality) can be verified in the book *Parker Gun Identification & Serialization.* Factory records indicate that it left the Meriden plant as a Grade 3 with titanic steel barrels and ejectors (DHE), hammerless action, straight grip stock, and had 28 in. barrels on a No. 2 frame. The beavertail forearm is not original, the stock has been recheckered, and a non-factory recoil pad has also been added. The refinished case colors resemble the factory's, and the reblued barrels also have good color. Action is still tight, and as you can see, the engraving is still very sharp. With originality being Polar North for Parker collectors, how do you determine value on a shotgun like this? If this gun was all original, and in 95% condition overall, its value would be in the $11,500-$13,500 range (and easy to sell!). This non-original DHE in this type of refurbished condition would probably be valued in the $3,250-$4,000 range, or less than half of an original.

SHOTGUNS: NRA ANTIQUE CONDITIONS

98

NRA Antique Fine condition (30%-80%), **L.C. Smith Grade 2 w/Ejectors SxS,** 12 ga., 30 in. barrels, ser. no. 210689 – mfg. early 1909. This older L.C. Smith, manufactured by Hunter Arms Company in Fulton, NY, is a typical example of the condition factor you'll find on older, pre-WWI major trademark American shotguns. The exception is the barrels, which have obviously been reblued and do not match the overall condition of this SxS. Original case colors have mottled/faded over the years, and there appears to be some surface pitting on the front part of the lower frame. Original stock appears to have no cracks around the sidelock mechanism (unusual for an L.C. Smith of this vintage), and the splinter forearm checkering has almost disappeared. This shotgun's single trigger and ejectors will raise its value approximately 65%. Overall, compare the case colors on this L.C. Smith to the 40% and 98% condition L.C. Smiths in the Shotguns: PPGS Condition Factors section. Originality and strong frame case colors are everything when determining value on America's major trademark SxS shotguns.

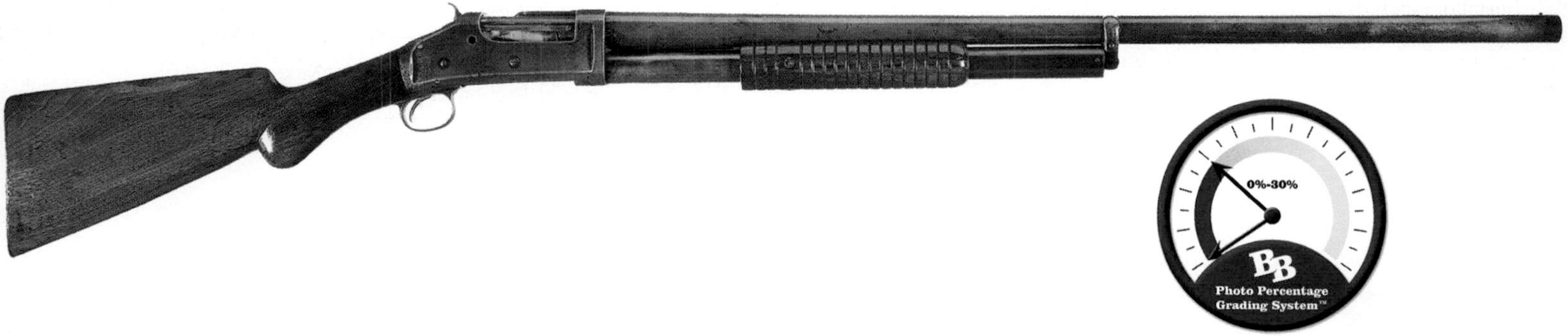

NRA Antique Very Good condition (0%-30%), **Winchester Repeating Arms Co. Model 1893 slide action,** 12 ga., 30 in. barrel, ser. no. WRACO (restamped over original ser. no.) – mfg. circa 1895. During the 1890s, Winchester Repeating Arms Co. attained many achievements with the help of design genius J.M. Browning, which have yet to be duplicated by any other firearms company in such a short time frame. Starting out with the immediately successful 1890 slide action .22 cal rifle, Winchester took the year off in 1891, but a year later, it introduced the lever action Model 1892 rifle/carbine, followed by Browning's first slide action shotgun (pictured above), then the legendary Model 1894 rifle, and finally the Model 1895 with box magazine. At the time, no other company could compete with this onslaught of major new firearms designs and innovations. This Model 1893's condition is typical of the vast majority that has survived. Note how bluing has oxidized to a warm brown patina with little pitting, and for some reason, the mag. tube has been reblued in front of the forearm. Careful observation reveals the slide release button is missing. Plain, uncheckered walnut stock and forearm also have a fresh coat of varnish, and explain the shiny appearance. Designed for black powder ammunition, only 34,050 Model 1893s were manufactured until it was replaced by the Model 1897, which was designed for smokeless powder.

SHOTGUNS: NRA ANTIQUE CONDITIONS

100

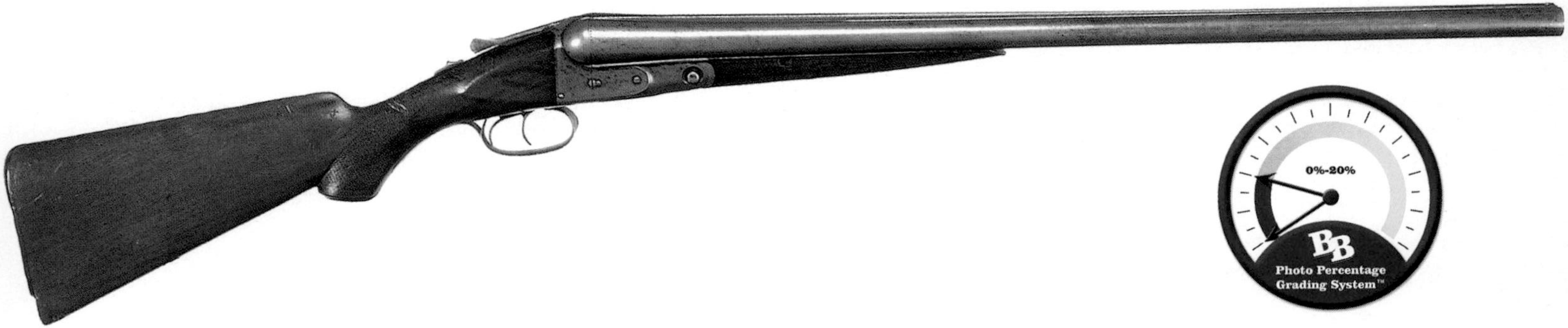

NRA Antique Good Condition (0%-20%), **Parker VH SxS hammerless,** 12 ga., 26 1/8 in. barrels, ser. no. 111718 – mfg. 1902. So what's wrong with this description? If you're a Parker collector, 26 1/8 in. barrels immediately raise a red flag, as they have been shortened from the original factory 30 in. length. Cut barrels on Parkers are a very negative alteration, seriously affecting a Parker's value, regardless of grade. Other problems include stock gouging/chipping, and only a portion of the broken buttplate remains. Original frame and barrel finish are gone and have turned an overall greyish patina. Action still remains tight (no surprise there), and this gun may still be shootable, but must be inspected carefully first. With over 242,000 Parkers manufactured between 1866 and 1938 (Remington took over production 1934-1938), this is a good example of how a lot of them look today – well used, and almost worn out. Most people, including many serious collectors, have never seen an original mint condition Parker – they are that rare!

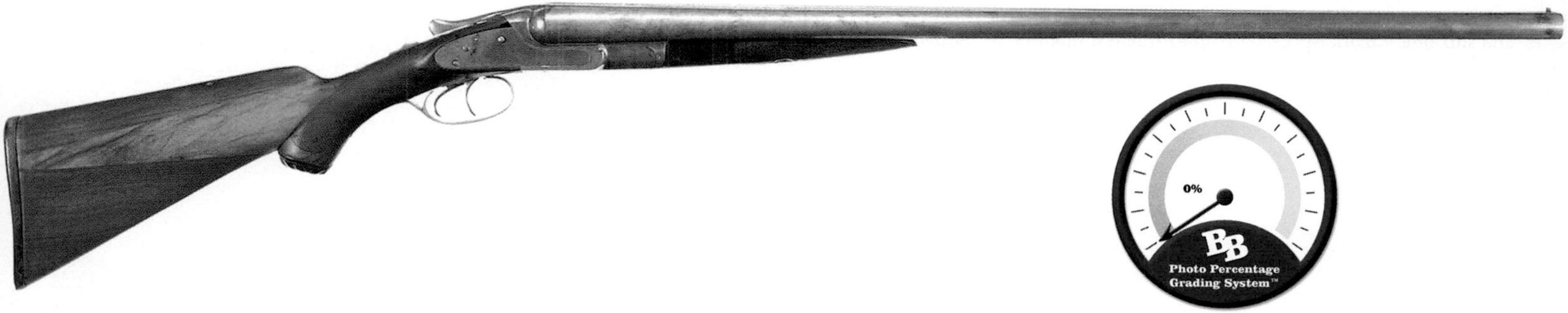

NRA Antique Fair condition (no finish, some major parts replaced), Lefever G Grade SxS, 12 ga., 30 in. barrels, ser. no. 18725 – mfg. 1893. As you can see, with NRA Antique grading factors, once you get down to Good, Fair, or Poor, there isn't a lot of difference when it comes to eye appeal, as guns in this condition are typically not that desirable. The biggest problem with this gun is that the stock was shattered at an earlier date, and a large replacement chunk with non-matching grain has been added. This gun's action is loose, and no metal finish remains on either the barrels or frame. The bores are also dark and pitted (i.e., don't shoot). Close observation will also reveal that the wood surrounding the sidelock is very thin, and appears to have been sanded. Overall, this gun's Fair condition and non-originality have bottomed out its value. Unfortunately, hundreds of similar surviving examples are in this condition factor, which explains why a really good original example is so rare (and expensive) in today's SxS marketplace.

SHOTGUNS: NRA ANTIQUE CONDITIONS

NRA Antique Poor condition (no finish w/replacement parts), French SxS, 16 ga., 28 in. barrels, ser. no. 1513 – mfg. circa 1910-1920. This is truly a no-name shotgun, as no manufacturer's name or marking appears anywhere on this gun — only the proofmarks indicate French production. Probably manufactured for a retailer's specifications, this boxlock is only chambered for 2 9/16 in. cartridges, and still has its sling swivels. There is virtually no eye appeal with this shotgun, and the crudely installed recoil pad and major dents on left barrel (not shown) further hurt this gun's overall desirability factor. So how do you determine the value of a gun like this which basically can no longer be shot, and needs to be hidden in the back of your gun cabinet when your friends come over? The answer is thousands of shotguns in this type of condition that are virtually unknown might be rare, but the only thing rarer is the person who might buy it. In other words, don't pay over $125, since in this case even the parts aren't worth anything, as virtually no one is going to have a similar make, model, and gauge.

OLDER EDITIONS

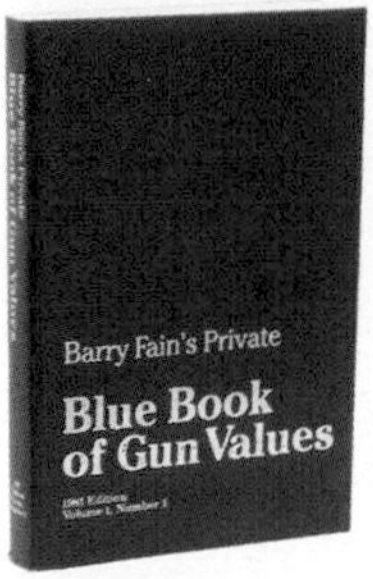

1st Edition (Vol. I, No. I)
1981

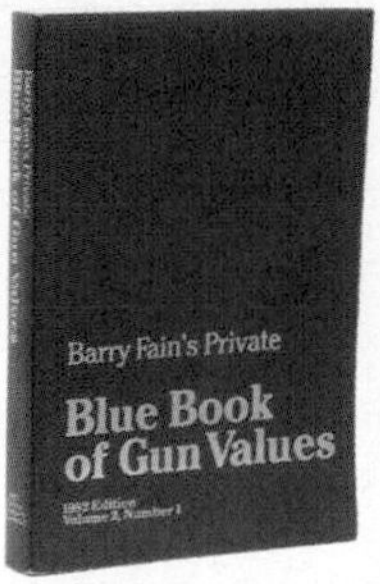

2nd Edition (Vol. II, No. I)
1982

3rd Edition (Vol. II, No. II)
1982

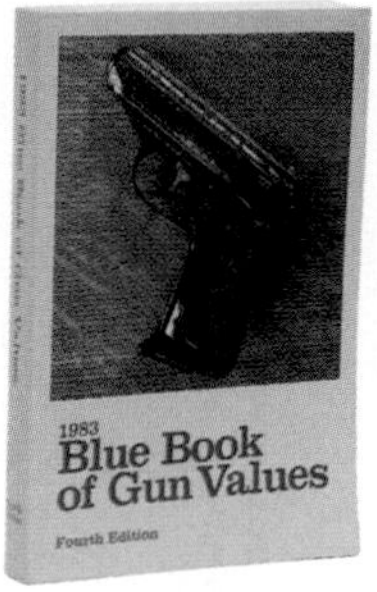

4th Edition
1983

5th Edition
1984

6th Edition
1985

7th Edition
1986

8th Edition
1987

9th Edition
1988

10th Edition
1989

11th Edition
1990

12th Edition
1991

13th Edition
1992

14th Edition
1993

15th Edition
1994

16th Edition
1995

17th Edition
1996

18th Edition
1997

19th Edition
1998

20th Edition
1999

21st Edition
2000

22nd Edition
2001

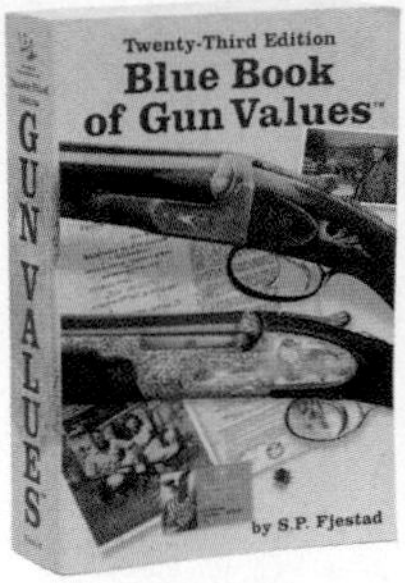

23rd Edition
2002

24th Edition
2003

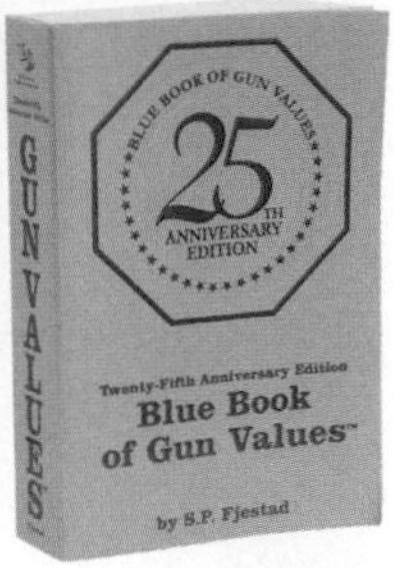

25th Edition
2004

26th Edition
2005

27th Edition
2006

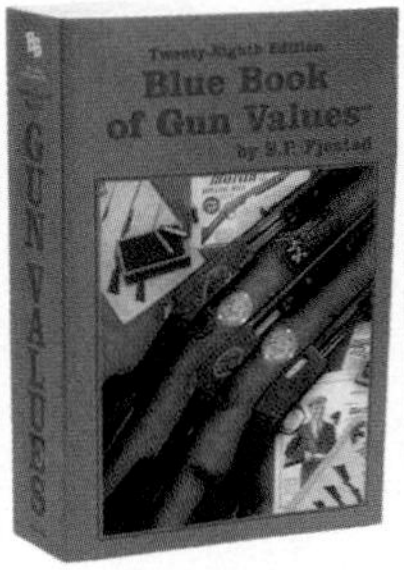

28th Edition
2007

29th Edition
2008

30th Edition
2009

31st Edition
2010

32nd Edition
2011

33rd Edition
2012

Many of you may want to pick up older editions to start or complete a collection. The rule of thumb is that the older an edition is, the harder it is to find, and the more expensive it will be. We do carry some older editions in stock, but the inventory can change daily. For more information, availability, condition, and pricing contact Kelsey at ext. 22 or email her at: support@bluebookinc.com

800.877.4867

www.BlueBookofGunValues.com

A SECTION

A.A.

Previously manufactured by Azanza & Arrizabalaga, located in Eibar, Spain.

GRADING - PPGS™	100%	98%	95%	90%	80%	70%	60%	LAST MSR

PISTOLS: SEMI-AUTO

A.A. – 7.65mm cal., semi-auto pistol, slide marked "Azanza & Arrizabalaga Model 1916, A.A." in oval on frame.

	$235	$200	$165	$135	$115	$85	$75	

REIMS – 6.35mm or 7.65mm cal., copies of M1906 Browning, marked "1914 Model".

	$185	$150	$130	$110	$90	$70	$50	

A.A.A.

Previously manufactured by Aldazabal, located in Spain.

PISTOLS: SEMI-AUTO

M1919 – 7.65mm cal., semi-auto pistol.

	$110	$100	$85	$70	$65	$60	$55	

A.A. ARMS INC.

Previous manufacturer located in Monroe, NC until 1999.

CARBINES: SEMI-AUTO

AR9 CARBINE – similar action to AP9, except has carbine length barrel and side-folding metal stock. Banned 1994.

	$750	$625	$550	$475	$400	$350	$300	

PISTOLS: SEMI-AUTO

AP9 MINI-SERIES PISTOL – 9mm Para. cal., semi-auto blowback paramilitary design, phosphate/blue or nickel finish, 2 barrel lengths, 10 (C/B 1994) or 20* shot mag. Disc. 1999, parts cleanup during 2000.

	$425	$375	$325	$275	$225	$200	$175	*$245*

Add $20 for nickel finish.
Add $200 for AP9 long barrel Target Model (banned 1994).

A & B HIGH PERFORMANCE FIREARMS

Previous competition pistol manufacturer located in Arvin, CA.

PISTOLS: SEMI-AUTO

LIMITED CLASS – 9mm Para. or .38 Super cal., single action, competition M1911-styled action, STI frame, Ultimatch bull barrel, Caspian slide, Bo-Mar adj. rear sight, blue or chrome finish.

	$1,875	$1,600	$1,375	$1,150	$925	$700	$550	*$1,875*

OPEN CLASS – 9mm Para. or .38 Super cal., single action, competition M1911-styled action, STI frame, Ultimatch or Hybrid compensated barrel, Caspian slide, C-More scope, blue or chrome finish.

	$2,800	$2,300	$1,875	$1,600	$1,375	$1,000	$750	*$2,800*

A.R. SALES

Previous manufacturer located in South El Monte, CA, circa 1968-1977.

PISTOLS: SEMI-AUTO

HANDGUN – .45 ACP cal., semi-auto patterned after Colt Model 1911 Govt., less weight than normal Colt .45.

	$295	$250	$225	$205	$175	$155	$145	

GRADING - PPGS™	100%	98%	95%	90%	80%	70%	60%	LAST MSR

RIFLES: SEMI-AUTO

MARK IV SPORTER – .308 Win. cal., semi-auto, M-14 style action, adj. sights. Approx. 200 mfg.

	$725	$650	$575	$500	$450	$400	$350	

ADC (ARMI DALLERA CUSTOM)

Current pistol and tactical semi-auto rifle manufacturer and customizer located in Concesio, Italy. Previously located in Gardone, Italy. No current U.S. importer.

ADC manufactures high quality custom pistols, mainly of M1911 design, and a tactical black rifle based on the AR-15 style. Many options and configurations are available. ADC also provides a complete range of customizing and gunsmithing services. Please contact the company directly for more information, U.S. availability, and current pricing (see Trademark Index).

AFC

Previously manufactured by Auguste Francotte located in Liege, Belgium, 1912-1914. Please refer to the Auguste Francotte listing in the F section.

A. J. ORDNANCE

Previous manufacturer located in Covina, CA.

PISTOLS: SEMI-AUTO

THOMAS – .45 ACP cal., semi-auto, double action only, 6 shot, 3 1/2 in. barrel, fixed sights, checkered plastic grips, delayed blowback action, stainless steel barrel. Disc. mid-1970s.

	$600	$525	$450	$400	$350	$300	$250	

Add 50% for chrome or stainless steel.

AK-47 DESIGN CARBINES, RIFLES, & PISTOLS

Select-fire paramilitary design rifle originally designed in Russia (initials refer to Avtomat Kalashnikova, 1947). The AK-47 was officially adopted by Russia in 1949. Russian-manufactured select fire AK-47s have not been manufactured since the mid-1950s. Semi-auto AK-47 and AKM clones are currently manufactured by several arsenals in China including Norinco and Poly Technologies, Inc. (currently illegal to import), in addition to being manufactured in other countries including the Czech Republic, Bulgaria, Russia, Egypt, and Hungary. On April 6th, 1998, recent "sporterized" variations (imported 1994-1998) with thumbhole stocks were banned by presidential order. Beginning in 2000, AK-47s were being assembled in the U.S., using both newly manufactured and older original military parts and components.

AK-47s and variations are not rare - approximately 75 million AK-47s and over 100 million AK-74 design carbine/rifles have been manufactured since 1947.

AK-47/AK-74/AKM HISTORY

Since the early 1950s, the AK-47/AK-74/AKM series of select fire rifles has been the standard issue military rifle of the former Soviet Union and its satellites. It continues to fulfill that role reliably today. The AK series of rifles, from the early variants of the AK-47 through the AKM and AK-74, is undoubtedly the most widely used military small arms design in the world. Developed by Mikhail Kalashnikov (the AK stands for Avtomat Kalashnikova) in 1946, the AK went into full production in 1947 in Izhevsk, Russia. In 1953, the milled receiver was put into mass production. Since then, variants of the original AK-47 have been manufactured by almost every former Soviet bloc country and some free world nations, including Egypt. The AK action is the basis for numerous other weapons, including the RPK (Ruchnoy Pulemyot Kalashnikova).

The AK-47 was replaced in 1959 by the AKM, and retained the same basic design. The rifle was simply updated to incorporate easier and more efficient production methods, using a stamped, sheet metal receiver that was pinned and riveted in place, rather than a milled receiver. Other changes included a beavertail forearm, muzzle compensator, and an anti-bounce device intended

to improve controllability and increase accuracy.

The AK was designed to be, and always has been, a "peasant-proof" military weapon. It is a robust firearm, both in design and function. Its record on the battlefields around the world is impressive, rivaled only by the great M1 Garand of the U.S. or bolt rifles such as the English Mark III Enfield. The original AK-47 prototypes are on display in the Red Army Museum in Moscow.

All of the current semi-auto AK "clones" are copies of the AKM's basic receiver design and internal components minus the full-auto parts. The Saiga rifle (see separate listing), manufactured by the Izhevsk Machining Plant, in Izhevsk, Russia, is the sole Russian entry into this market. It is available in the standard 7.62x39 mm, 5.45x39 mm (disc.) and 20 gauge or .410 bore. Molot (hammer) JSC also exports semi-automatic AKs to the U.S. under the trade name Vepr. (see separate listing). Saiga is imported by RWC and Vepr. is imported and distributed by Robinson Armaments. Molot was the home of the PPSh-41 sub-machine gun during WWII, and also manufactured the RPK and the RPK-74. Other AK European manufacturers include companies in the Czech Republic, Bulgaria, and the former Yugoslavia. The Egyptian-made Maahdi AK clones were also available in the U.S. market.

Interest in the Kalashnikov design is at an all-time high due to the availability of high quality military AK-74, AKS-74, AKS-74U, and RPK-74 parts kits. Some models, such as those produced by Marc Krebs, are of very high quality. Currently, it is hard to go to a gun show or page through a buy/sell firearms magazine and not see a variety of parts, accessories, and high capacity magazines available for many of the AK variants. For shooters, the value represented by these guns is undeniable for the price point.

Values for almost all of the imported AK clones are based solely on their use as sporting or target rifles. Fit and finish varies by country and importer. Most fall on the "low" side. Interest peaked prior to the passage of the 1994 Crime Bill and both AK clones and their "high capacity" magazines were bringing a premium for a short period of time in 1993 and 1994. However, interest waned during 1995-97, and the reduced demand lowered prices. In November of 1997, the Clinton Administration instituted an "administrative suspension" on all import licenses for these types of firearms in order to do a study on their use as "sporting firearms."

On April 6th, 1998, the Clinton Administration, in the political wake of the Jonesboro tragedy, banned the further import of 58 "assault-type" rifles, claiming that these semi-automatics could not be classified as sporting weapons - the AK-47 and most related configurations were included. During 1997, firearms importers obtained permits to import almost 600,000 reconfigured rifles - approximately only 20,000 had entered the country when this ban took effect. When the ban began, applications were pending to import an additional 1,000,000 guns. Previously, thumbhole-stocked AK Sporters were still legal for import, and recent exporters included the Czech Republic, Russia, and Egypt.

AK-47 DESIGN CARBINES, RIFLES, & PISTOLS: RECENT/CURRENT MFG. & IMPORTATION

The following is a listing of both current and recent manufacturers and importers that offer/have offered AK-47 design carbines, rifles, and pistols for sale domestically. Please look under each current company, importer, or brand name/trademark heading for up-to-date information and values on current makes and models that are offered.

These companies include: AKS (AK-47, AK-74, & AKM Copies), American Arms, Inc., American Tactical Imports, Armory USA LLC, Armscor, Arsenal 2000 JSCo., Arsenal Inc., Arsenal USA LLC, B-West, Baikal, Bingham, Blackheart International, Bulgaria Arsenal, Bushmaster, CZ (Ceska Zbrojovka), Century International Arms, Inc., Czechpoint Inc., E.D.M. Arms, E.M.F. Co. Inc., European American Armory Corp., Feather Industries, Inc., Federal Ordnance, FEG, German Sport Guns GmbH, Hakim, Hesse Arms, I.O., Inc., Inter Ordnance of America, LP, Interarms Arsenal, Intrac Arms International, K.B.I., K-VAR Corp., Liberty Arms International, LLC, M+M, Inc., Mitchell Arms, Inc., Molot JSCo, Navy Arms Company, Norinco, Ohio Ordnance Works, Poly Technologies, Inc., Rasheed (Rashid), Robinson Armament Co., Russian American Armory Company, SAIGA, Samco Global Arms, Inc., Sarco, Inc., Sentinel Arms, TG International, Valmet, Vector Arms Inc., Vepr, Vulcan Armament, and ZDF Import/Export.

GRADING - PPGS™	100%	98%	95%	90%	80%	70%	60%	LAST MSR

CARBINES/RIFLES: SEMI-AUTO, AK-47, AK-74, & AKM MODELS

"AK-47" stands for Automatic Kalashnikov Rifle, 1947 Model, first developed in the former Soviet Union by Mikhail Kalashnikov. This gas-operated military rifle was originally designed for select-fire operation, and quickly gained acceptance within the Soviet Union's military forces. While very early military production used stamped receivers, problems in the manufacturing process forced the adoption of milled receivers, which took more time, but solved all of the earlier production problems. The arsenals of Soviet satellite countries, as well as China also began producing AK-47s for military use, but later also began producing semi-auto variations for commercial sales. In 1959, the AKM (M designates modernized or upgraded) was developed with a stamped receiver and also featured a slanted muzzle brake - it was also approximately 33% lighter than the earlier milled AK-47s. There are far more AKMs available in the American marketplace for sale than semi-auto AK-47s. Chinese importation stopped during late 1990.

AK-47/AKM – 7.62x39mm (most common cal., former Russian M43 military), 5.45x39mm (Romanian mfg. or Saiga/MAK - recent mfg. only), or .223 Rem. cal., semi-auto Kalashnikov action, stamped (most common) or milled (pre-1959) receiver, typically 16 1/2 in. barrel, 5, 10, or 30* (C/B 1994) shot curved mag., wood or synthetic stock and forearm except on folding stock model, 1994-early 1998 importation typically had newer "sporterized" fixed stocks with thumbholes, may be supplied with bayonet, sling, cleaning kit, patterned after former military production rifle of China and Russia.

* ***AK-47/AKM Post-WWII-Pre-1994 Mfg./Importation*** – 7.62x39mm (most common cal., former Russian M43 military), 5.45x39mm (Romanian mfg. or Saiga/MAK - recent mfg. only), or .223 Rem. cal., semi-auto Kalashnikov action, stamped (most common) or milled receiver, typically 16 1/2 in. barrel, 5, 10, or 30* (C/B 1994) shot mag., wood or synthetic stock and forearm except on folding stock model, may be supplied with bayonet, sling, cleaning kit, patterned after former military production rifle of Russia and China. Check markings and/or proofs on gun for country of origin and possible importer.

Romanian mfg.	$450	$395	$350	$325	$295	$275	$250
Yugoslavian mfg.	$795	$725	$675	$575	$450	$425	$400
Hungarian mfg.	$795	$725	$675	$575	$450	$425	$400
Czech mfg.	$795	$725	$675	$575	$450	$425	$400
Bulgarian mfg.	$795	$725	$675	$575	$450	$425	$400
Egyptian mfg.	$650	$600	$550	$450	$400	$365	$335

Add 20% for milled receiver.
Add 10% for chrome-lined barrel.
Add 10% for older folding stock variations.
Add 10%-15% for 5.45x39 mm cal. on Eastern European mfg. (non-recent import).
Values are for original guns completely manufactured in the countries listed above and will have various import markings stamped on the receiver or barrel.

* ***AK-47/AKM 1994-2004 Mfg.*** – most feature "sporterized" fixed stocks with thumbholes to avoid the GCA of 1994.

$550	$450	$395	$350	$325	$295	$265

* ***AK-47/AKM Post 2004 Mfg./Importation*** – most AK-47/AKMs manufactured/imported after 1998 utilize plastic/synthetic furniture, stamped receivers, and folding/telescoping stocks which have different components and construction from those rifles/carbines produced before 1998. Recent U.S. assembly refers to an original stamped European (mostly FEG) or milled receiver with U.S. assembly, using either new parts or matched, older unused original Eastern European-manufactured parts (BATFE 922.R compliant). This newest generation of AK-47/AKMs typically have features as described above, and cannot be sold in several states. Check city and state laws regarding high capacity magazine compliance.

$450	$395	$350	$325	$295	$265	$235

The most desirable configuration of these recently assembled rifles/carbines has a folding/

GRADING - PPGS™	100%	98%	95%	90%	80%	70%	60%	LAST MSR

collapsible stock, high capacity mag., barrel compensator, and a bayonet lug.

These post-2004 AK-47/AKM variations typically do not have import markings, and indicate they have been made up as "parts guns" assembled from various manufacturers, and have usually been put together in the U.S. recently. Additional AK-47 listings can be found under current individual manufacturers and importers listed separately in this text (i.e., Arsenal Inc., Century International, Interarms, etc.).

AK-74/AKM – 5.45x39mm cal., semi-auto action based on the AKM, imported from Bulgaria and other previous Eastern bloc countries, in addition to recent assembly in the U.S., using FEG receivers, Bulgarian parts sets, and additional U.S.-made components.

Bulgarian mfg.	$700	$650	$600	$525	$450	$400	$350	
Recent U.S. assembly	$650	$575	$500	$425	$350	$300	$275	

PISTOLS: SEMI-AUTO, AK-47 VARIATIONS

AK-47 PISTOLS – 7.62x39mm, or .223 Rem. cal., patterned after the AK-47 rifle/carbine, barrel length approx. 12 1/4, but can vary according to mfg., typically wood furniture, 5 to 30 shot mag. (depends on configuration), adj. rear sight, pistol grip, parkerized finish most common, recent Romanian mfg., approx. 5 lbs.

$375	$325	$295	$275	$250	$225	$200	

A M A C

See the "Iver Johnson" section in the I section. AMAC stands for American Military Arms Corporation. Manufactured in Jacksonville, AR. AMAC ceased operations in early 1993.

A.M.S.D. (ADVANCED MILITARY SYSTEM DESIGN)

Current manufacturer located in Geneva, Switzerland. No current importation. Previously distributed 2010-2012 by Loki Weapon Systems, located in Coalgate, OK.

RIFLES: BOLT ACTION

A.M.S.D. manufactures a Tacten rifle in .338 Lapua cal., with tactical stock, bipod, two 10 shot mags., muzzle brake, two-stage trigger, cleaning kit and case. A variety of Picatinny rail options are available, as well as scopes. Prices are POR. Please contact the company directly for pricing and U.S. availability (see Trademark Index).

A.M.S.D. also manufactured the OM 50 Nemesis tactical rifle until December 2010 in a variety of configurations and options. The base rifle featured a 27 1/2 in. barrel, high performance muzzle brake, bipod, box mag., Picatinny top and side rails, adj. folding stock, adj. two-stage trigger, extended forend, adj. ground spike, scope rings, field cleaning kit, tool kit, and fitted storage case. A variety of options were available, including barrel length, stock, and finish. In 2010, AMSD sold the rights to the OM 50 Nemesis to the Swiss company San Swiss Arms AG (SAN). The model is now called the SAN 511. Rifles sold by AMSD before December 2010 are covered by AMSD's 25 year warranty. Please refer to the San Swiss section for current listings.

AMP TECHNICAL SERVICE GmbH

Previous manufacturer located in Puchheim, Germany. Previously imported and distributed 2001-2004 by CQB Products, located in Tustin, CA.

RIFLES: BOLT ACTION

DSR-1 – .300 Win. Mag., .308 Win., or .338 Lapua cal., bolt action, bull pup design with in-line stock, receiver is made from aluminum, titanium, and polymers, internal parts are stainless steel, two-stage adj. trigger, 4 or 5 shot mag., 25.6 in. Lothar Walther fluted barrel with muzzle brake and vent. shroud, includes bipod, ambidextrous 3-position safety, 13 lbs. Imported 2002-2004.

$7,295	$6,300	$5,200	$4,100	$3,000	$2,500	$2,000	*$7,795*

Add $100 for .300 Win. Mag. cal.
Add $300 for .338 Lapua cal.

GRADING - PPGS™	100%	98%	95%	90%	80%	70%	60%	LAST MSR

AMT

Current trademark manufactured beginning late 2004 by Crusader Gun Company, Inc., located in Houston, TX. Previous trademark manufactured by Galena Industries Inc. located in Sturgis, SD, 1999-Jan. 2001. Previously located in Irwindale, CA until 1998. From 1998-2001, all AMTs manufactured by Galena Industries Inc. had a lifetime warranty, which is now void. Also see Irwindale Arms, Inc. and Auto Mag for older, discontinued models.

Galena Industries phased out the use of the AMT name, but continued to use the individual model names until 2001.

During 2005, Crusader Gun Company Inc. acquired the previous tooling of AMT - Auto Mag., and reintroduced the following models: Auto Mag II, Auto Mag III, AutoMag IV, the Back Up .380, and the Back Up .45. Please contact the company directly for more information, including availability and pricing on these re-released models (see Trademark Index).

PISTOLS: SEMI-AUTO

From 1999 to 2001, AMT began using Millett sights exclusively. Between 1993 and 1998, AMT changed from white outline Millett adjustable sights to an adjustable three-dot (white) system manufactured by LPA in Italy. Early production pistols were made in El Monte, CA, and are marked "El Monte".

LIGHTNING – .22 LR cal., semi-auto, stainless steel only, 5 (bull only), 6 1/2, 8 1/2, 10 1/2, or 12 1/2 (disc. 1987) in. bull or tapered barrels, adj. sights and trigger, pistol based on semi-auto Ruger action. 23,903 were mfg. 1984-1987.

$350 $200 $150 $120 $105 $90 $80 *$289*

This model featured a frame grooved for scope mounts, Clark trigger, Millett sights, and either Pachmayr rubber or Wayland wood grips as standard equipment.

* ***Lightning Bull's Eye Regulation Target*** – similar to 6 1/2 in. Lightning with bull barrel, except has vent. rib, wood grips, extended rear sight. Mfg. 1986 only.

$425 $350 $285 $225 $175 $140 $125 *$436*

BABY AUTOMAG – .22 LR cal., semi-auto, stainless steel only, 8 1/2 in. vent. rib barrel, Millett adj. rear sight, smooth walnut grips, 1,001 mfg.

$750 $650 $550 $460 $395 $335 $285

AUTOMAG II – .22 WMR cal., stainless steel only, 3 3/8 (Compact Model, disc., limited mfg.), 4 1/2 (disc., limited mfg.), or 6 in. barrel, gas-assisted action, white outline Millett adj. rear sight, grooved Lexan grips, 7 (Compact) or 9 shot mag., 24-32 oz. Mfg. 1987-2001, reintroduced late 2004.

MSR $845 $775 $675 $575 $475 $400 $350 $300

Subtract approx. 25% for 3 3/8 or 4 1/2 in. barrel.

AUTOMAG III – .30 Carbine or 9mm Win. Mag. (mfg. 1993 only) cal., stainless steel, 6 3/8 in. barrel, patterned after Colt Govt. Model, white outline Millett adj. rear sight, grooved Lexan grips, 8 shot mag., 43 oz. Mfg. 1992-2001.

$530 $445 $335 $265 $230 $195 $170 *$549*

AUTOMAG IV – 10mm (disc. 1993) or .45 Win. Mag. cal., 6 1/2 (.45 Win. Mag. only) or 8 5/8 (disc. 1993) in. barrel, 7 or 8 shot mag., Millett adj. rear sight, stainless steel, 46 oz. Mfg. 1992-2001.

$530 $445 $325 $265 $230 $195 $170

AUTOMAG V – .50 AE cal., stainless steel, 6 1/2 in. barrel, gas venting system reduces recoil, 5 shot mag., 46 oz. Mfg. 1993-95.

$815 $700 $625 $515 $450 $375 $325 *$900*

GRADING - PPGS™	100%	98%	95%	90%	80%	70%	60%	LAST MSR

AUTOMAG 440 – .440 Cor-Bon cal., special order only. Mfg. 1999-2001.

	$775	$650	$550	$460	$395	$335	$285	*$899*

JAVELINA – 10mm cal., 7 in. barrel, 8 shot mag., Millett adj. rear sight, wraparound neoprene grips, wide adj. trigger, long grip safety, 48 oz. Mfg. 1992 only.

	$560	$460	$360	$285	$250	$215	$185	*$676*

BACKUP PISTOL SMALL FRAME – .22 LR (limited production, disc. 1987) or .380 ACP cal. (disc. 2000, reintroduced 2004), semi-auto, choice of traditional double action (disc. 1992) or double action only (new 1992), 2 1/2 in. barrel, stainless steel, Lexan grips, 5 (.380 ACP) or 8 (.22 LR) shot mag., 18 (.380 ACP only) or 23 oz. Disc. 2010.

	$450	$375	$300	$250	$200	$175	$150	*$525*

Add approx. 10% for .22 LR cal.

Older disc. walnut grip models are worth a slight premium.

In 1992, AMT reengineered this model and removed all external levers, production resumed late 2004.

BACKUP PISTOL LARGE FRAME – 9mm Para. (mfg. 1995-2006, reintroduced 2011), .357 SIG (mfg. 1996-2010), .38 Super (new 1995), .40 S&W (new 1995), .400 Cor-Bon (mfg. 1997-2010) , or .45 ACP (new 1995) cal., semi-auto, choice of traditional double action (disc. 1992) or double action only (new 1992), 3 in. barrel, stainless steel, Lexan grips, 5 (.40 S&W) or 6 shot mag., 23 oz.

MSR $525	$450	$375	$300	$250	$200	$175	$150	

Add $100 for .400 Cor-Bon cal. (disc. 2010).

Older disc. walnut grip models are worth a slight premium.

In 1992, AMT reengineered this model and removed all external levers, production resumed late 2004.

BACKUP PISTOL II – .380 ACP cal., single action, semi-auto, stainless steel, 2 1/2 in. barrel, 5 shot finger extension mag., black carbon fiber grips, 18 oz. Mfg. 1993-98.

	$295	$225	$150	$120	$105	$90	$80	*$369*

.45 ACP STANDARD GOVERNMENT MODEL – .45 ACP cal., similar to Colt semi-auto Govt. Model, stainless steel, 5 in. barrel, fixed rear sight, loaded chamber indicator, adj. trigger, wraparound neoprene grips, 38 oz. Disc. 1999.

	$450	$375	$325	$275	$225	$175	$140	*$399*

HARDBALLER II – .45 ACP cal., similar to Colt Gold Cup Model, stainless steel, 5 in. barrel, adj. Millett rear sight, serrated rib, loaded chamber indicator, adj. trigger, wraparound neoprene grips, 38 oz. Disc. 2001.

	$475	$400	$325	$250	$195	$165	$140	*$499*

Add $280 for 7 in. Hardballer conversion kit (disc. 1997).

* ***Hardballer II Longslide*** – similar to Hardballer II, except 7 in. barrel, longer slide assembly, and also available in .400 Cor-Bon (also known as .400 Accelerator, new 1998), 46 oz. Disc. 2001.

	$500	$425	$320	$250	$195	$165	$140	*$549*

Add $50 for .400 Cor-Bon (.400 Accelerator) cal.

Add $300 for 5 in. Longslide conversion kit (disc. 1997).

COMMANDO – .40 S&W cal., 4 in. barrel. Mfg. 1998-2001.

	$450	$400	$325	$250	$195	$165	$140	*$499*

SKIPPER – .45 ACP cal., re-released in 1991 with choice of .40 S&W or .45 ACP cal., similar to Hardballer, except approx. 1 in. shorter slide on pre-1984 mfg. frame, 4 1/4 in. barrel, checkered walnut grips, matte finish stainless steel, Millett adj. rear sight, 7 shot mag., 33 oz. Disc. 1991.

	$450	$400	$350	$285	$250	$195	$165	*$450*

COMBAT SKIPPER – similar to Skipper, but with fixed sights. Disc. 1984.

	$475	$450	$375	$325	$295	$240	$210	

GRADING - PPGS™	100%	98%	95%	90%	80%	70%	60%	LAST MSR

BULL'S EYE TARGET MODEL – .40 S&W cal., similar to Hardballer with 5 in. barrel, 8 shot mag., adj. Millett rear sight, wraparound neoprene grips, 38 oz. Mfg. 1991 only.

	$450	$400	$350	$295	$240	$210	$180	$500

"ON DUTY" DOUBLE ACTION – 9mm Para., .40 S&W, or .45 ACP (new late 1994) cal., stainless steel slide and barrel, 4 1/2 in. barrel, 9 (.45 ACP), 10 (C/B 1994), 11* (.40 S&W), or 15* (9mm Para.) shot mag., 3-dot sighting system, anodized aluminum frame, trigger disconnect safety, inertial firing pin, carbon fiber grips, 32 oz. Mfg. 1991-94.

	$450	$395	$295	$250	$195	$165	$140	$470

Add $60 for .45 ACP cal.

In 1992, this model became available with either traditional double action with decocking lever or double action only with safety.

RIFLES: BOLT ACTION

AMT rifles were discontinued in 1998.

BOLT ACTION STANDARD SINGLE SHOT – 11 various cals., post-1964 push-feed action, pre-1964 3-position side swing safety, cone breech, composite stock, cryogenically treated stainless steel barrel w/o sights, 8 1/2 lbs. Mfg. 1996-97.

	$825	$650	$450	$385	$335	$280	$235	$1,500

BOLT ACTION DELUXE SINGLE SHOT – 11 various cals., Mauser-type controlled feeding, short, medium, or long right-hand or left-hand action, pre-1964 3-position side swing safety and claw-type extractor, cryogenically treated stainless steel barrel w/o sights, custom Kevlar stock, approx. 8 1/2 lbs. Mfg. 1996 only.

	$995	$800	$600	$495	$430	$365	$315	$2,400

BOLT ACTION STANDARD REPEATER – 21 various cals., post-1964 push-feed action, Mauser-type mag., pre-1964 3-position side swing safety, Model 70-type trigger, composite stock, cryogenically treated stainless steel barrel w/o sights. 8 1/2 lbs. Mfg. 1996 only.

	$800	$625	$500	$430	$375	$315	$270	$1,110

BOLT ACTION DELUXE REPEATER – similar features to Bolt Action Deluxe Single Shot, except has Mauser-type mag. Mfg. 1996 only.

	$1,000	$800	$650	$540	$465	$385	$335	$1,596

RIFLES: SEMI-AUTO

LIGHTNING (25/22) – .22 LR cal., semi-auto based on Ruger 10-22 action, stainless steel, 30 shot mag., 17 1/2 in. bull or tapered barrel, nylon pistol grip handle and forearm, folding stock with recoil pad or youth stock, fixed sights, 6 lbs. Mfg. 1986-93.

	$300	$250	$225	$195	$175	$150	$125	$296

SMALL GAME HUNTER (SGH) – .22 LR cal., same mechanical action as Lightning, except has matte black nylon stock with checkered forearm and grip, 22 in. barrel, 10 shot mag., no sights. Removable recoil pad allows storage in stock. 6 lbs. Mfg. 1986-93.

	$300	$250	$225	$195	$175	$150	$125	$300

SMALL GAME HUNTER II – similar to Small Game Hunter, except has match grade 22 in. heavyweight full-floating barrel, 10 shot rotary mag., black fiberglass nylon stock, no sights, 6 lbs. Mfg. 1993 only.

	$350	$300	$250	$225	$195	$175	$150	$300

Add $70 for 17 1/2 in. stainless steel barrel.
Add $150 for 22 1/2 in. stainless steel match grade barrel.

CHALLENGE EDITION (I, II, III) – .22 LR cal., semi-auto target variation featuring McMillan fiberglass stock, 16 1/4 (choice of 6 in. barrel weight extension or 3 in. muzzle brake, new 1997), 18, 20 (mfg. 1994-96), or 22 (mfg. 1994-96) in. floating stainless steel bull barrel, custom designed or Jewell (new 1997) trigger, custom order through AMT's Custom Shop. Mfg. 1994-98.

	$800	$600	$450	$385	$335	$280	$235	$1,296

Subtract $200 if without Jewell trigger.

GRADING - PPGS™	100%	98%	95%	90%	80%	70%	60%	LAST MSR

Add $144 for 16 1/4 barrel with 3 in. muzzle brake (Challenge Edition II, new 1997).
Add $85 for 16 1/4 barrel with 6 in. barrel extension (Challenge Edition III).

* ***Challenge Edition Elite With Bloop Tube*** – features 16 1/4 in. barrel with a 6 in. bloop tube extension enabling increased bullet velocity and muzzle heavy ergonomics, McMillan fiberglass STC stock. Mfg. 1996-98.

$925	$700	$550	$460	$395	$335	$285	*$1,498*

Subtract $255 if without compensator.

SPORTER EDITION – .22 LR cal., 16 1/2, 18, 20, or 22 in. tapered sporter barrel, McMillan fiberglass sporter stock. Mfg. 1996 only.

$650	$525	$400	$335	$290	$245	$215	*$900*

HUNTER EDITION I – .22 LR cal., 18, 20, or 22 in. regular barrel with injection-molded sporter stock. Mfg. 1996 only (replaced with Hunter Edition II).

$550	$425	$300	$240	$210	$180	$155	*$800*

HUNTER EDITION II – .22 LR cal., 22 in. tapered sporter barrel with 2 lb. Jewell trigger, McMillan synthetic sporter stock. Mfg. 1997-98.

$750	$575	$425	$360	$315	$260	$225	*$1,354*

FLY SWATTER I – .22 LR cal., 16 1/2 in. regular barrel with injection molded (1996 only) or Hogue over-molded (new 1997) sporter stock. Mfg. 1996-97.

$575	$450	$325	$265	$230	$195	$170	*$822*

FLY SWATTER II – similar to Fly Swatter I, except has 3 in. muzzle brake. Mfg. 1997 only.

$675	$475	$350	$285	$250	$215	$185	*$936*

BR-50 ACCELERATOR EDITION – .22 LR cal., features 16 1/4 (new 1998) or 16 1/2 (disc. 1997) in. bull barrel with 3 in. muzzle brake (new 1998), McMillan bench rest stock, Hoehn barrel tuner (disc. 1997), and Jewell trigger. Mfg. 1997-98.

$795	$600	$450	$385	$335	$280	$235	*$1,440*

ACCULITE EDITION RIFLE – .22 LR cal., features 18 in. Magnum Research graphite barrel with muzzle brake, thumbhole sporter stock, adj. Jewell trigger, 4 3/4 lbs. Mfg. 1998 only.

$750	$575	$425	$360	$315	$260	$225	*$1,321*

INTIMIDATOR EDITION RIFLE – .22 LR cal., 16 1/4 in. Shilen select match grade barrel with 6 in. bloop tube, adj. Jewell trigger, 6 1/4 lbs. Mfg. 1998 only.

$875	$625	$475	$415	$360	$300	$255	*$1,581*

MAGNUM HUNTER – .22 WMR cal., semi-auto, 20 in. free-floating barrel, stainless steel, 10 shot single stack mag., no sights, drilled and tapped for Weaver 87-A scope base, black synthetic stock, 6 lbs. Mfg. 1995-98.

$450	$375	$295	$225	$175	$140	$125	*$459*

TARGET RIFLE SEMI-AUTO – .22 LR cal., button rifled cryogenically treated barrel with target crown, choice of Fajen laminate or Hogue composite stock, 10 shot mag., one-piece receiver with integral Weaver mount, 7 1/2 lbs. Mfg. 1997-98.

$500	$425	$350	$275	$225	$195	$165	*$549*

Add $50 for Fajen laminate stock.

AR 57 LLC (57CENTER LLC)

Current AR-15 style rifle manufacturer located in Bellevue, WA, and previously located in Redmond, WA.

CARBINES: SEMI-AUTO

AR57A1 - PDW – 5.7x28mm cal., 16 in. barrel, flash suppressor, black matte finish, ergonomic design custom grip with battery and accessory compartment, 50 shot box magazine runs horizontally over barrel and can be inserted from top or side of weapon, mil spec fire control group, M-4 carbine six position stock with forged aluminum stock tube,

GRADING - PPGS™	100%	98%	95%	90%	80%	70%	60%	LAST MSR

front and rear upper Picatinny rails between mag., lower accessory rails, includes four 50 shot mags. New 2010.

MSR $1,099 $995 $900 $825 $750 $675 $600 $550

AR57 GEN II/LEM – 5.7x28mm cal., 16 in. fluted barrel, ambidextrous mag. release and charging handle, carbine buffer, extended rear quad rail, includes two 50 shot mags. New 2013.

MSR $1,149 $1,025 $925 $825 $750 $675 $600 $550

AR-7 INDUSTRIES, LLC

Previous manufacturer 1998-2004, and located in Geneseo, IL. Previously located in Meriden, CT, from 1998 to early 2004.

In February 2004, AR-7 Industries LLC was purchased by ArmaLite, Inc., and recent manufacture was in Geneseo, IL.

RIFLES: BOLT ACTION

AR-7 TAKEDOWN – .22 LR cal., bolt action variation of the AR-7 Explorer rifle, similar takedown/storage configuration, 2 1/2 lbs. Advertised 2002 only.

While advertised during 2002, this model was never manufactured.

RIFLES: SEMI-AUTO

AR-7 EXPLORER RIFLE – .22 LR cal., takedown barrelled action stores in synthetic stock which floats, 8 shot mag., aperture rear sight, 16 in. barrel (synthetic sleeve with steel liner), black matte finish on AR-7, silvertone on AR-7S (disc. 2000), camouflage finish on AR-7C, two-tone (silver receiver with black stock and barrel) on AR-7T (disc. 2000), walnut finish on AR-W (mfg. 2001-2002), stowed length 16 1/2 in., 2 1/2 lbs. Mfg. late 1998-2004.

$175 $150 $125 $110 $100 $90 $80 *$200*

Add $15 for camouflage or walnut finish.

This model was also previously manufactured by Survival Arms, Inc. and Charter Arms - see individual listings for information.

AR-7 SPORTER (AR-20) – .22 LR cal., 16 1/2 in. steel barrel with vent. aluminum shroud, metal skeleton fixed stock with pistol grip, 8 (new 2001) or 16 shot "flip clip" (optional) mag., 3.85 lbs. Mfg. late 1998-2004.

$175 $150 $125 $110 $100 $90 $80 *$200*

Add $100 for sporter conversion kit (includes aluminum shrouded barrel, pistol grip stock, and 16 shot flip clip).

This model was also previously manufactured by Survival Arms, Inc. - see individual listing for information.

AR-7 TARGET – .22 LR cal., 16 in. bull barrel with 7/8 in. cantilever scope mount, tube stock with pistol grip, 8 shot mag., 3-9x40mm compact rubber armored scope was optional, 5.65 lbs. Mfg. 2002-2004.

$195 $175 $150 $125 $105 $95 $80 *$210*

Add $60 for compact scope.

AR-15 STYLE CARBINES, RIFLES, AND PISTOLS

AR-15 HISTORY

AR-15 refers to the model nomenclature originally given to the select-fire, gas-operated carbine/rifle featuring synthetic furniture and chambered in 5.56 NATO cal., and developed by Eugene Stoner in 1957. At the time, he was under contract by the Armalite division of the Fairchild Aircraft Corp. In 1958, this new AR-15 lost out in military competition to the select-fire M-14 manufactured by Springfield Armory. After losing this competition, Fairchild Aircraft

Corp. thought their new carbine/rifle design would never prove to be successful or obtain a military contract. As a result, during 1959 it sold the design and all future manufacturing rights to Colt. In 1962, the U.S. Department of Defense Advanced Research Projects Agency (ARPA) purchased 1,000 AR-15 rifles from Colt which were immediately sent to South Vietnam for field trials. In 1963, Colt was awarded an 85,000 rifle contract for the U.S. Army (designated XM16E1), and another 19,000 for the U.S. Armed Forces (designated M-16). This new select-fire M-16 was a direct variation of Stoner's original AR-15 design, but had U.S. ordnance markings. In 1963, a presidential order given to the U.S. Army made the M-16 its official service rifle.

In 1966, because of the U.S. involvement in the escalating war in Vietnam, the U.S. government submitted an order for 840,000 M-16s to be delivered to the U.S. Armed Forces at a cost of $92 million. The rest like they say is history.

AR-15 INFORMATION AND RECENT/CURRENT MANUFACTURERS & IMPORTERS

Because of the consumer popularity and resulting proliferation of the semi-auto AR-15 style carbines/rifles over the past twenty years, there are many companies who now offer the AR-15 style platform for sale with their brand name or trademark stamped on the guns. However, there are only four primary domestic manufacturers which currently produce the majority of lower receivers for the AR marketplace. The following listing includes those manufacturers of AR-15 lower receivers, in addition to those brand names, trademarks, and private labels for other companies.

LMT = LMT, Lauer (disc.), DS Arms, PWA, Eagle, Knights Armament, Barrett, Bushmaster (possibly).

CMT = Stag, RRA, High Standard, Noveske (disc.), Century, Global Tactical, CLE, S&W, MGI (1st variation), Wilson Tactical (not all models), Colt, Ratworx.

LAR = Grizzly, Bushmaster (L Prefix), Ameetech, DPMS (possibly), CMMG, Double Star, Fulton, Spike's Tactical, Noveske.

MMS = Mega, Gunsmoke, Dalphon, POF (forged), Alexander Arms, Singer, Spike's Tactical (disc.).

Additional smaller AR-15 lower receiver manufacturers include JP (Double Star, LRB), Olympic (Olympic, SGW, Tromix, Palmetto, Dalphon, Frankford, Century (disc.), Superior (Superior Arms, Lauer), Grenadier Precision, and Sabre Defense (disc.).

Some companies also manufacture custom cut lower receivers out of solid billets, and they include MGI, Cobb, JP, Socom, Sun Devil, POF, and S&W (Performance Center).

The following is a listing of both current and recent manufacturers and importers that offer/have offered AR-15 style carbines, rifles, and pistols for sale domestically. Please look under each current company, importer, or brand name/trademark heading for up-to-date information and values on the makes and models that are offered.

These companies include: Adams Arms, Adcor Defense, Adeq Firearms Co., Advanced Armament Corp., Alexander Arms LLC, Ambush Firearms, American Precision Arms, American Spirit Arms, American Spirit Arms Corp., American Tactical Imports, Anderson Manufacturing, AR57 LLC (57Center LLC), Ares Defense, Armalite Inc., The Arms Room, Arms Tech Ltd., Astra Arms S.A., Australian Automatic Arms Pty. Ltd., Aztek Arms, Barnes Precision Machine, Inc., Barrett Firearms Manufacturing, Inc., Blackheart International LLC, Black Rain Ordnance, Black Rifle Company, BlueGrass Armory, Bobcat Weapons Inc., Bohica, Bravo Company Mfg. Inc., Budischowsky, Bushmaster Firearms International LLC, C3 Defense, Inc., CMMG, Inc., Carbon 15, Cavalry Arms Corporation, Christensen Arms, Century International Arms, Inc., Cobb Manufacturing, Inc., Colt's Manufacturing Company, Inc., Core 15, Crossfire LLC, DPMS Firearms, LLC, DSA Inc., Daewoo, Charles Daly (1976-2010), Daniel Defense, Del-Ton Incorporated, Desert Tactical Arms, Dlask Arms Corp., Double Star Corp., E.M.F. Company, Inc., Eagle Arms, Inc., Entreprise Arms Inc., Evolution USA, Fulton Armory, G-A Precision,

GRADING - PPGS™	100%	98%	95%	90%	80%	70%	60%	LAST MSR

The Gun Room Co., LLC, Gunsmoke Enterprises, Halo Arms, LLC, Hatcher Gun Company, Head Down Products LLC, Hesse Arms, High Standard Manufacturing Co., Interarms Arsenal, Intercontinental Arms Inc., Israel Military Industries (Galil), J.B. Custom Inc., JP Enterprises, Inc., JR Carbines LLC, K.B.I. Inc., Knight's Armament Company, L.A.R. Manufacturing, Inc., LRB Arms, LWRC International, Inc., Larue Tactical, Leitner-Wise Defense, Inc., Leitner-Wise Rifle Co. Inc., Les Baer Custom, Inc., Lewis Machine & Tool Company (LMT), Liberty Arms International LLC, Loki Weapon Systems, Inc., Lone Star Armament, Inc., MBA Associates, MG Arms Incorporated, MGI, Maunz, Microtech Small Arms Research Inc. (MSAR), Mossberg, O.F. & Sons., Inc., New Evolution Military Ordnance (NEMO), Newtown Firearms, Next Generation Arms, Northern Competition, Oberland Arms, Ohio Ordnance Works, Inc., Olympic Arms, Inc., Para USA, Inc., Patriot Ordnance Factory (POF), Peace River Classics, Precision Firearms, Primary Weapons Systems (PWS), Professional Ordnance, Inc., Proof Research, Quality Parts Co., R Guns, RND Manufacturing, Red Rock Arms, Remington Arms Company, Inc., Rhino Arms, Robinson Armament Co., Rock River Arms, Inc., Rocky Mountain Arms, Inc., Russian American Armory Company, SI Defense, SOG Armory, STI International, Sabre, Sabre Defence Industries LLC, Sharps Milspec, Sig Sauer, Smith & Wesson, Spirit Gun Manufacturing Company LLC, Stag Arms, Stoner Rifle, Sturm, Ruger & Co., Inc., Superior Arms, Tactical Rifles, Thureon Defense, TNW, Inc., Tromix Corporation, VM Hy-Tech LLC, Valor Arms, Victor Arms Corporation, Volquartsen Custom, Ltd., Vulcan Armament, Inc., Wilson Combat, Windham Weaponry, Xtreme Machining, Yankee Hill Machine Co., Inc. (YHM), Z-M Weapons.

ASAI AG (ADVANCED SMALL ARMS INDUSTRIES)

Previous manufacturer located in Solothurn, Switzerland 1994-2004. Previously imported until 2000 by Magnum Research, Inc. located in Minneapolis, MN.

PISTOLS: SEMI-AUTO

ONE PRO .45 – 9mm Para. (limited mfg. in Europe, never imported into the U.S.), .40 S&W (limited mfg. in Europe, never imported into the U.S.), .400 Cor-Bon (conversion only), or .45 ACP cal., SA or DA, 3 (disc. 1998) or 3 3/4 in. barrel with polygonal rifling, steel or alloy (not imported into U.S.) frame, black contoured synthetic grips, black or two-tone (less than 10 mfg.) finish, 10 shot mag., includes plastic case, extra 10 shot mag., and cleaning kit, 25 or 31 oz. Imported mid-1997 through 2000.

$595	**$485**	**$410**	**$360**	**$330**	**$300**	**$275**	***$699***

Add $209 for .400 Cor-Bon conversion kit without compensator.
Add $249 for .45 ACP or .400 Cor-Bon conversion kit with extended barrel, compensator, and recoil spring guide.

A-SQUARE

Previous firearms manufacturer located in Glenrock, WY late 2011-2012. Ammunition and administrative offices were located in Chamberlain, SD, from late 2007-late 2011. During 2010, A-Square became a division of Sharps Rifle Company, located in Chamberlain, SD. A-Square was previously located in Jeffersonville, IN, 2003-2007, Bedford, KY until 2002, Louisville, KY until 2000, and in Madison, IN until 1991.

A-Square also offered different grades of walnut, different metal finishes, and various sights and scope rings as special orders. Custom calibers were also available by special order.

RIFLES: BOLT ACTION

Add $950 for Imperial grade walnut, $350 for A-Grade walnut (disc.), add $650 for AAA-Grade fancy walnut (disc.), add $500 for English walnut (disc.), add $100 for accent package (disc.), add $550 for black synthetic stock (disc.), add $600 for weather-impervious package (disc.), add $350 for 3-leaf steel express sights (disc.), add $300 for royal high gloss blue finish

GRADING - PPGS™	100%	98%	95%	90%	80%	70%	60%	LAST MSR

(disc. 1995), add $150 for high gloss polymer wood finish (disc. 2002), or $550 for .505 Gibbs or .577 Tyrannosaur cal.

CAESAR MODEL – most cals. available, bolt action built on a Remington M-700 receiver until 1993, Sako L-V actions were utilized beginning 1993, 22-26 in. barrel, select walnut with pistol grip and recoil pad, primarily a left-handed action with right-handed action a special order, 9-10 3/4 lbs. Mfg. 1986-2012.

	$3,500	$2,995	$2,500	$2,200	$1,825	$1,650	$1,500	*$3,750*

GENGHIS KHAN MODEL – .22-250 Rem., .243 Win., .25-06, or 6mm Rem. cal., features Winchester pre-1964 Model 70 action, heavy tapered barrel, Coil-Chek stock helps reduce recoil, designed for varmint hunting. Mfg. 1995-2012.

	$3,500	$2,995	$2,500	$2,200	$1,825	$1,650	$1,500	*$3,750*

HANNIBAL MODEL – most cals. available, bolt action built on a P-17 Enfield receiver, 22-26 in. barrel, deluxe oil finished walnut with pistol grip and recoil pad, Teflon coated metal, choice of barrel length and LOP, 9-11 1/4 lbs. Mfg. 1986-2012.

	$3,500	$2,995	$2,500	$2,200	$1,825	$1,650	$1,500	*$3,750*

HAMILCAR MODEL – various cals. available, smaller variation of the Hannibal model featuring slimmer design gained by not needing the reinforcement for heavy Mag. cals., 4, 5, 6, or 7 shot mag., cocks on opening, 8-8 1/2 lbs. Mfg. 1994-2012.

	$3,500	$2,995	$2,500	$2,200	$1,825	$1,650	$1,500	*$3,750*

ATCSA

Previously manufactured by Armas De Tiro Y Casa located in Spain.

REVOLVERS

COLT POCKET PISTOL COPY – revolver, .38 cal., 6 shot.

	$155	$140	$110	$100	$90	$75	$65	

SINGLE SHOT REVOLVER – target pistol.

	$195	$165	$145	$110	$100	$90	$75	

ATA ARMS

Current shotgun manufacturer established circa 1967, and located in Istanbul, Turkey. Select models are currently imported and private labeled beginning 2008 by Weatherby, located in Paso Robles, CA. Previously imported until 2008 (private label only) by Tristar, located in N. Kansas City, MO, and by K.B.I., located in Harrisonburg, PA.

SHOTGUNS

ATA Arms manufactures a complete line of good quality semi-automatic and O/U shotguns in various configurations. Select ATA Arms shotguns are private labeled by Weatherby - please check the Weatherby section for models and pricing.

AWA USA

Current importer established during late 2004 and located in Hialeah, FL.

AWA USA purchased the remaining assets of American Western Arms, Inc. in late 2004, and became the importer of guns manufactured by AWA International, Inc. in Brescia, Italy.

HANDGUNS

1873 CLASSIC SAA – .357 Mag. or .45 LC cal., 4 3/4 or 5 1/2 in. barrel, choice of blue or Turnbull color case hardened, nickel (disc.) or hard chrome (disc.) finish, flat main spring, walnut grips. Importation began 2007.

MSR $440	$395	$360	$330	$295	$250	$225	$195	

Add $125 for color case hardened frame or $195 for nickel (disc.) or hard chrome (disc.) finish.
Subtract $50 for kit gun configuration.

GRADING - PPGS™	100%	98%	95%	90%	80%	70%	60%	*LAST MSR*

1873 ULTIMATE SAA – .32-20 WCF, .38-40 WCF, .44 Spl., .357 Mag., .44-40 WCF, or .45 LC cal., 4 3/4, 5 1/2, or 7 1/2 in. barrel, blue, Turnbull color case hardened, nickel, or hard chrome finish, walnut grips, coil main spring. Importation began 2007.

MSR $600	$525	$450	$400	$350	$300	$250	$200	

Add $125 for color case hardened frame or $195 for nickel or hard chrome finish.
Add $115 for Jim Martin Ultimate model.
Add $150 for octagon barrel.
Subtract $50 for kit gun configuration.

Custom barrel lengths include 3 1/2, 10, and 12 in.

1884 BISLEY – .357 Mag. or .45 LC cal., 4 3/4 or 5 1/2 in. barrel, choice of blue or Turnbull color case hardened, nickel or hard chrome finish, walnut grips. Imported 2007-2008.

	$395	$360	$330	$295	$250	$225	$195	*$440*

LIGHTNINGBOLT SLIDE ACTION – .45 LC cal., 12 in. round barrel, 5 shot, walnut stock and forearm, blade front sight, available in high polish blue, color case hardened, hard chrome, or nickel finish. Importation began 2007.

MSR $1,000	$895	$750	$625	$500	$400	$300	$225	

Add $150 for color case hardened frame or $300 for White Lightningbolt with nickel or hard chrome finish.

RIFLES: SLIDE ACTION

LIGHTNING RIFLE – .32-20 WCF, .38 Spl., .38-40 WCF, .44-40 WCF, or .45 LC cal., 20 or 24 in. round or octagon barrel, patterned after the original Colt Lightning model, choice of blue, color case hardened, white (hard chrome, brushed nickel, or polished nickel) or black frame, standard or limited edition wood stock. Importation began 2007.

MSR $850	$775	$675	$600	$525	$450	$375	$300	

Add $50 for octagon barrel.
Add $100 for upgraded wood with checkering.
Add $150 for 16 in. barrel.
Add $250 for color case hardened frame.
Add $400 for White Lightning with either hard chrome or brushed/polished nickel finish.
Add $525 for Black Lightning w/black chrome finish (disc.)
Add $1,150 for limited edition model (50 each of 20 and 24 in. barrel).
Add $950 for Jerry Harper engraving.

AWC SYSTEMS TECHNOLOGY, LLC

Previous firearms and current suppressor manufacturer currently located in Phoenix, AZ and established circa 1984. AWC also private labels and distributes commercial ammunition manufactured by TTI Armory. In 2010 AWC was acquired by Strategic Armory Corps. Please contact the company directly for more information on its wide range of suppressors (see Trademark Index).

RIFLES: BOLT ACTION

AWC currently manufactures four bolt action models. They include the M91 BDR ($3,995 MSR), M92 ($3,495 MSR), the M95 ($3,495 MSR, and the M40A2 ($3,495 MSR). Please contact the factory directly for more information and special order features and options.

AYA (AGUIRRE Y ARANZABAL)

Current manufacturer established in 1917, and located in Eibar, Spain. Currently imported by AYA USA, located in Old Saybrook, CT, and New England Custom Gun Service, Ltd. (NECG), located in Claremont, NH, previously located until 2010 in Plainfield, NH. Previously imported by Anglo American Sporting Agency, located in Corona del Mar, CA, H.G. Lomas Gunmakers, located in Elkhart Lake, WI, John F. Rowe, located in Enid, OK, Fieldsport, located in Traverse City, MI, William Larkin Moore 1969-1978 (with Agoura, CA import marking), and 1978-1986 (with West Lake, CA

GRADING - PPGS™	100%	98%	95%	90%	80%	70%	60%	LAST MSR

import marking). Diarm also manufactured AYAs circa 1986-1988 in Eibar, Spain.

AYA-manufactured shotguns can be identified by serialization. Serial numbers over 600,001 with barrel flats marked "Arms de Chasse" or "Scotia Group" are post-1988 AYA manufactured while specimens numbered under 600,000 may have been manufactured by Diarm circa 1986-1989. Diarm manufacture is not covered by the AYA warranty, nor is the resale the same as values listed below.

Please refer to the AYA and Spanish year of mfg. date codes under Serialization in the back of this text for more information on AYA shotguns.

SHOTGUNS: O/U

AYA also manufactured a Coral boxlock, both in standard and deluxe configurations. The MD Series O/U models completed their European line (2007 MSR was $4,100 - $7,300).

Add 5% for gauges smaller than 12 ga.

Add 5% for 3 in. magnum chambers.

ARRATE – 12 or 20 ga., standard boxlock action or deluxe with sideplates. New 2013.

Current MSR is $6,100.

Add $1,000 for deluxe boxlock action with sideplates.

AUGUSTA – 12 ga. only, deluxe O/U sidelock, arabesque engraving in deep relief, select walnut. This model has been imported off and on over the years.

Current MSR is $21,000.

CORAL "A" – 12 or 16 ga., boxlock action with Kersten cross bolt, vent. rib, ejectors, DT. Disc. 1985.

	$1,275	$1,050	$875	$775	$695	$625	$560	*$2,195*

CORAL "B" – similar to Coral A, except for coin-washed engraved receiver. Disc. 1985.

	$1,395	$1,100	$925	$820	$720	$650	$595	*$2,450*

EXCELSIOR – 12 or 20 ga., sidelock action with elaborately engraved coin finished receiver, DTs, ejectors, fixed chokes, 28 in. VR barrels. Disc. 2010.

	$6,600	$5,750	$4,875	$4,100	$3,300	$2,600	$1,850	*$7,499*

Add $301 for SNST.

Add $1,101 for SST.

Add $1,701 for Trap configuration.

MODEL 37 SUPER – 12, 16, or 20 ga., various barrel lengths and chokes, vent. rib, sidelock, auto ejector, elaborate engraving, high grade wood. Merkel-style action. Prices below reflect older models. Disc.

12 ga.	$3,200	$2,850	$2,100	$1,900	$1,700	$1,500	$1,250	
16 ga.	$3,500	$2,750	$2,100	$1,700	$1,500	$1,350	$1,150	
20 ga.	$3,750	$2,950	$2,200	$1,900	$1,700	$1,600	$1,475	

* ***New Model 37 A/B/C*** – game scene engraved, detachable sidelock action, nickel steel receiver. This model has been imported off and on over the years.

Current MSRs are as follows: Model 37 A - $14,999, Model 37 B - $15,300, and Model 37 C - $15,900.

MODEL 77 – 12 ga. only, Merkel-style O/U sidelock with Greener crossbolt, deluxe engraving checkering. Disc. 1985.

	$3,100	$2,750	$2,500	$2,255	$2,030	$1,805	$1,600	*$4,100*

MODEL 79 "A" – 12 ga. only, boxlock with double-locking lugs, sel. trigger, ejectors. Disc. 1985.

	$1,275	$1,075	$965	$880	$790	$705	$640	*$1,595*

MODEL 79 "B" – similar to Model 79 "A," only more elaborate engraving. Disc. 1985.

	$1,395	$1,200	$1,085	$990	$890	$790	$695	*$1,795*

GRADING - PPGS™	100%	98%	95%	90%	80%	70%	60%	LAST MSR

MODEL 79 "C" – similar to Model 79 "B," only more elaborate engraving, double triggers on request. Disc. 1985.

	$2,050	$1,825	$1,605	$1,460	$1,315	$1,165	$1,000	*$2,650*

SHOTGUNS: SxS

Current retail values on the AYA shotguns listed below could vary slightly from importer to importer. For the following models, please use these guidelines for special orders and/or features.

On current models listed below, add $1,250 for SNT or approx. $1,250 for SST on recently manufactured guns.

Add $2,300 for self-opening action. Add approx. 40% for extra set of barrels.

BILL HANUS BIRDGUN – 16, 20 (disc. 2005), or 28 ga., similar wood, fit, checkering, and finish as the No. 53 sidelock, except has Anson & Deeley boxlock, patterned after the Westley Richards game gun, frames proportionate to ga., 27 (28 ga.) or 28 (16 ga.) in. barrels with fixed open chokes, case colored receiver with moderate engraving, SST (disc.) or DT, ejectors, includes leather-covered handguard, splinter forearm, straight grip. Imported 1997-2007.

	$2,650	$2,320	$1,990	$1,800	$1,460	$1,195	$930	*$2,995*

This model was available only through Bill Hanus Birdguns LLC. Stocks bent for cast-on and leather-covered decelerator pads were also available at additional cost.

BOLERO – similar to Matador, with non-selective single trigger and extractors. Disc. 1984.

	$450	$395	$340	$305	$250	$205	$160	

COUNTRYMAN GAME GUN – 12 or 20 ga. Imported 1998-2002.

	$2,050	$1,795	$1,540	$1,395	$1,130	$925	$720	*$2,295*

IBERIA – 12 or 20 ga., 3 in., boxlock, DT, plain walnut. Disc. 1984.

	$495	$435	$370	$335	$270	$225	$175	

IBERIA II – 12 or 16 ga., 28 in. barrels, 2 3/4 in. chamber only, DT, plain walnut. Mfg. 1984-85 only.

	$550	$480	$415	$375	$305	$250	$195	*$570*

MATADOR – 10, 12, 16, 20, 28 ga., or .410 bore, 26, 28, or 30 in. barrel, various chokes, Anson & Deeley boxlock, auto ejectors, beavertail forearm, SST, checkered pistol grip stock. Mfg. 1955-1963.

	$550	$480	$415	$375	$305	$250	$195	
28 ga.	$1,100	$965	$825	$750	$605	$495	$385	
.410 bore	$1,650	$1,445	$1,240	$1,120	$910	$745	$580	

Add 10% for 20 ga.

MATADOR NO. 2 – similar to Matador, with vent. rib, 12 or 20 ga. only. Disc.

	$675	$590	$505	$460	$370	$305	$235	

Add 10% for 20 ga.

MATADOR NO. 3A – 12 or 20 ga., 3 in. chamber in 20 ga. only, boxlock, vent. rib, ejectors, SST. Disc. 1985.

	$795	$695	$595	$540	$435	$360	$280	*$1,235*

Add 10% for 20 ga.

SENIOR – 12 ga. only, Beesley or Purdey-type self opener, engraved sidelock action, select walnut, top-of-the-line quality, made to special order only, lighter upland version was also available. Disc. 1987.

	$15,500	$13,565	$11,625	$10,540	$8,525	$6,975	$5,425	*$21,000*

SUPREMA – various gauges, sidelock, includes deluxe engraving, made to customer special order per individual specifications.

Current MSR is $18,695, or $18,995 with round action.

GRADING - PPGS™	100%	98%	95%	90%	80%	70%	60%	LAST MSR

IMPERIAL – 12, 16, 20, 28 ga. or .410 bore, sidelock action with DTs and hinged front trigger, chopper lump 28 in. barrels, traditional rose and scroll engraved case colored detachable sidelocks, H&H-style self-opening action, exhibition grade walnut with fine checkering, custom order only. Importation began 2008.

Current MSR on this model is $20,995.

ANNIVERSARY MODEL – 12 ga. only, forged steel action, exposed hammers with auto ejectors, 30 in. chopper lump barrels with flat hand filed rib, finest scroll engraving with gold inlays, mfg. to celebrate AYA's 50 years in the U.K. marketplace. Limited mfg.

Current MSR on this model is $24,500.

ANNIVERSARY HAMMER – similar to Anniversary Model, except has exposed hammers.

Current MSR is $24,500.

NO. 1 – 12, 16, 20, 28 ga. or .410 bore, full sidelock action, straight grip, ejectors, DT, elaborate fine scroll engraving. Importation disc. 1987, resumed in 1991.

MSR $11,600	$9,100	$7,800	$6,600	$5,800	$4,675	$3,825	$2,975	

Add $300 for rounded action.

* ***No. 1 DeLuxe*** – features bold foliate engraving.

MSR $16,600	$13,150	$11,000	$9,100	$8,200	$6,600	$5,350	$4,125	

Add $300 for rounded action.

* ***No. 1 De Luxe English*** – exhibition quality wood and engraved by Geoff Moore, English metal finish, custom order only.

This shotgun is specifically made for A.S.I., and is sold exclusively in the U.K. marketplace. Current retail is £16,995 (12 ga.) or £17,650 (16, 20, 28 ga. or .410 bore). Please contact A.S.I. for more information, including availability (see Trademark Index).

NO. 2 – 12, 16, 20, 28 ga., or .410 bore, 3 in. chambers, English-style sidelock, ejector, cocking indicators, DT. Importation disc. 1987, resumed 1991.

MSR $5,700	$4,775	$4,100	$3,500	$3,075	$2,500	$1,950	$1,600	

Add $290 for rounded action.

* ***No. 2 Bill Hanus Dreamgun Sidelock*** – features Boss rounded action, built per individual custom order, 10 month delivery. Imported 2003-2007.

	$5,500	$4,815	$4,125	$3,740	$3,025	$2,475	$1,925	*$5,950*

This model was only available from Bill Hanus Birdguns LLC.

* ***Model 2 Deluxe*** – various gauges, sidelock, includes engraving. New 2012.

Current MSR is $7,795 or $8,095 with rounded action.

NO. 3-A – 12, 16, 20, 28 ga., or .410 bore, boxlock, extractors, DT. Disc. 1985.

	$675	$590	$505	$460	$370	$305	$235	*$850*

Add 25%-35% for 28 ga. or .410 bore.

NO. 4 – 12, 16, 20, 28 ga., or .410 bore, 3 in. chambers, English-style straight stock, boxlock action, ejectors, DT, straight grip stock, standard wood. Importation disc. 1987, resumed 1991-2008.

	$2,000	$1,750	$1,500	$1,360	$1,100	$900	$700	*$2,300*

* ***No. 4/53*** – similar to No. 4, except has No. 53 wood upgrade. Importation disc. 1987, resumed 1991.

MSR $3,700	$3,100	$2,600	$2,125	$1,900	$1,550	$1,250	$975	

Add approx. $200 for No. 4/53S (includes wood upgrade, SNT, and round knob pistol grip, disc.).

Add $732 for No. 4 BL with BL engraving (disc.).

NO. 4 DELUXE – 12, 20, 28 ga. or .410 bore, English-style, boxlock, ejector, stock, forearm, trigger to order. Importation disc. 1985, resumed 1991.

MSR $6,900	$5,950	$5,275	$4,475	$3,725	$3,200	$2,850	$2,300	

GRADING - PPGS™	100%	98%	95%	90%	80%	70%	60%	LAST MSR

XXV BOXLOCK (BL) – 12, 20, 28 ga. or .410 bore, similar to No. 4 Deluxe, except 25 in. barrels, Churchill rib. Importation disc. 1986, resumed 1991-2005, reintroduced 2008-2011.

	$3,250	$2,825	$2,400	$2,175	$1,750	$1,425	$1,125	$3,895

Add approx. 40% for extra set of barrels (disc.).
Add $196 for gauges other than 12.

XXV SIDELOCK (SL) – 12, 16, 20 (disc. 1997, reintroduced 2008), 28 (disc. 1997, reintroduced 2008) ga., or .410 bore (disc. 1997, reintroduced 2008), sidelock ejector, 25 in. barrels, Churchill rib., stock, forearm, trigger to order. Importation disc. 1986, resumed 1991-2005, reintroduced 2008-2011.

	$6,100	$5,250	$4,450	$4,000	$3,300	$2,725	$2,150	$6,816

Add $600 for 28 ga. or .410 bore.

NO. 53 – 12, 16, or 20 ga., engraved sidelock ejector, sideclips, third lock. Stock, forearm, trigger to order. Importation disc. 1986, resumed 1991.

MSR $7,900	$6,850	$5,800	$4,900	$4,225	$3,700	$2,900	$2,450	

NO. 56 – 12, 16 (disc. 2010), or 20 (disc. 2010) ga., sidelock action-engraved, ejectors, SST. Importation disc. 1985, resumed 1991.

MSR $13,195	$10,400	$8,975	$7,600	$6,800	$5,500	$4,600	$3,650	

NO. 106 – 12, 16, or 20 ga., English-style boxlock, DT, pistol grip, 28 in. barrels. Disc. 1985.

	$550	$480	$415	$375	$305	$250	$195	$585

Add 20% for 16 or 20 ga.

107-LI – 12 or 16 ga., English-style boxlock, DT, straight grip, light English scroll engraving. Disc. 1985.

	$775	$680	$580	$525	$425	$350	$270	$745

MODEL 116 – 12, 16, or 20 ga., 27-30 in. barrels, any choke, hand detachable H&H sidelocks, DT, engraved, select checkered walnut pistol grip stock. Disc. 1985.

	$1,500	$1,315	$1,125	$1,020	$825	$675	$525	$1,125

MODEL 117 – 10, 12, 16, or 20 ga., 3 in. chambers, 26-30 in. barrels, any choke, hand-detachable H&H sidelocks, ejectors, SST, engraved, select checkered walnut pistol grip stock. Disc. 1986.

	$1,750	$1,530	$1,315	$1,190	$965	$790	$615	$1,075

MODEL 117 QUAIL UNLIMITED – 12 ga. only, 26 in. barrels choked IC/M with 3 in. chambers, upgraded wood and checkering, high gloss bluing, gold colored ST, engraved by Baron Technologies in PA, only 42 mfg. for Quail Unlimited of North America.

	$1,650	$1,445	$1,240	$1,120	$910	$745	$580	

This model had a retail price of $1,700 but was made available to Quail Unlimited members for approx. $1,200.

MODEL 210 – 12 or 16 ga., boxlock, exposed hammers, DT, plain walnut, light engraving. Disc. 1985.

	$795	$695	$595	$540	$435	$360	$280	$900

MODEL 711 SIDELOCK – sidelock action. Mfg. 1985 only.

	$1,450	$1,270	$1,090	$985	$800	$655	$510	$1,250

RIFLES: O/U

EXPRESS RIFLE LM – various large cals., boxlock action.

Current MSR is $6,600.

ABADIE

Previous trademark of Portuguese military revolvers manufactured by several Belgian makers.

GRADING - PPGS™	100%	98%	95%	90%	80%	70%	60%	LAST MSR

REVOLVERS

MODEL 1878 (OFFICER'S MODEL) – 9.1mm cal., solid frame revolver, 6 shot, ejector rod, officer's issue A.

	$220	$195	$165	$130	$120	$110	$100	

MODEL 1886 (TROOPER'S MODEL) – similar to 1878, but larger, trooper issue A.

	$195	$175	$160	$120	$110	$100	$90	

ABBEY, GEORGE T.

Previous manufacturer of percussion and breechloading firearms located in Utica, NY from 1845-1852, and Chicago, IL from 1852-1874.

100%	98%	95%	90%	80%	70%	60%	50%	40%	30%	20%	10%

RIFLES: PERCUSSION

PERCUSSION RIFLE

* ***Percussion Rifle .44 cal.*** – 32 in. octagon barrel.

$605	$550	$470	$415	$370	$340	$305	$275	$250	$220	$195	$165

* ***Percussion Rifle .44 cal.*** – octagon barrel, brass trimmed.

$770	$735	$695	$605	$550	$485	$450	$405	$365	$330	$275	$220

* ***Percussion Rifle .44 cal.*** – SxS, 31 in. barrels.

$1,210	$1,100	$880	$770	$715	$650	$595	$550	$515	$475	$430	$360

* ***Percussion Rifle .44 cal.*** – O/U, brass trimmed.

$1,485	$1,295	$1,130	$990	$910	$855	$770	$715	$660	$605	$495	$330

ABBEY, F.J. & COMPANY

Previous manufacturer of muzzle and breech loading shotguns and rifles located in Chicago, IL, 1858-1878.

RIFLES: PERCUSSION

PERCUSSION RIFLE – several variations.

$605	$550	$470	$415	$360	$305	$275	$250	$210	$175	$145	$110

SHOTGUNS: PERCUSSION

PERCUSSION SHOTGUN – several variations.

$800	$715	$635	$550	$470	$415	$360	$320	$285	$250	$210	$155

ABBIATICO & SALVINELLI (FAMARS)

Please refer to the Famars di Abbiatico & Salvinelli srl listing in the F section.

ACCU-MATCH INTERNATIONAL INC.

Previous handgun and pistol parts manufacturer located in Mesa, AZ circa 1996.

GRADING - PPGS™	100%	98%	95%	90%	80%	70%	60%	LAST MSR

PISTOLS: SEMI-AUTO

ACCU-MATCH PISTOL – .45 ACP cal., patterned after the Colt Govt. 1911, competition pistol features stainless steel construction with 5 1/2 in. match grade barrel with 3 ports, recoil reduction system, 8 shot mag., 3-dot sight system. Approx. 160 mfg. 1996 only.

	$795	$700	$625	$550	$450	$375	$325	*$840*

ACCU-TEK

Current trademark manufactured by Excel Industries, Inc., located in Chino, CA. Distributor and dealer direct sales.

GRADING - PPGS™	100%	98%	95%	90%	80%	70%	60%	LAST MSR

PISTOLS: SEMI-AUTO

MODEL AT-9SS – 9mm Para. cal., double action only, stainless steel, 3.2 in. barrel, 8 shot mag., firing pin block, no external safety lever, black or brushed stainless finish, 3-dot sights adj. for windage, 28 oz. Mfg. 1995-96 only.

	$260	$230	$195	$175	$145	$115	$90	*$317*

MODEL AT-25 – .25 ACP cal., single action, 2 1/2 in. barrel, 7 shot mag. with finger extension, similar to AT-32, stainless steel, aluminum, or alloy construction with choice of stainless, satin aluminum, or black finish, 11 (Model AT-25AL) or 18 (Model AT-25B, disc.) oz. Mfg. 1992-95.

	$150	$130	$115	$100	$85	$70	$55	*$182*

This model was available in satin aluminum (Model AT-25AL) or black (Model AT-25SSB) finish.

MODEL AT-32SS – .32 ACP cal., single action design, 2 1/2 in. barrel, 5 shot mag. with finger extension, alloy (disc. 1991) or stainless steel (new 1992) construction, black synthetic grips, manual safety with firing pin block and trigger disconnect, side mag. release, exposed hammer, satin aluminum (disc. 1991) finish, 1 lb. Mfg. in U.S. 1990-2003.

	$190	$165	$145	$130	$105	$85	$65	*$239*

Add $5 for black finish (Model AT-32SSB).

MODEL AT-40SS – .40 S&W cal., double action only, 3.2 in. barrel, 7 shot mag., firing pin block, no external safety lever, black or brushed stainless finish, 3-dot sights adj. for windage, 28 oz. Mfg. 1995-96 only.

	$260	$230	$195	$175	$145	$115	$90	*$317*

MODEL AT-45SS – .45 ACP cal., similar to Model AT-40SS, except has 6 shot mag., stainless only, 28 oz. Mfg. 1996 only.

	$265	$230	$200	$180	$145	$120	$95	*$327*

MODEL AT-380II (SS/SSB) – .380 ACP cal., similar to Model AT-32, except has 2 3/4 in. barrel, 6 shot mag., black synthetic grips, alloy (disc. 1991) or stainless steel construction, current mfg. includes two magazines, 23 1/2 oz. New 1990.

MSR $275	$210	$180	$155	$135	$110	$90	$70	

Add $5 for black finish (Model AT-380SSB, disc. 1999).

MODEL BL-9 – 9mm Para. cal., double action only, carbon steel, black finish, ultra compact size, includes two 5 shot mags., and lockable case. Mfg. 1997-2002.

	$195	$170	$145	$135	$105	$90	$70	*$232*

MODEL BL-380 – .380 ACP cal., double action only, carbon steel, black finish, compact size, two 5 shot mags., lockable case. Mfg. 1997-99.

	$165	$145	$125	$110	$90	$75	$60	*$199*

MODEL CP-9SS – 9mm Para. cal., double action only, stainless steel, black finish, compact size, 8 shot mag. Mfg. 1997-99.

	$220	$195	$165	$150	$120	$100	$75	*$265*

MODEL CP-40SS – .40 S&W cal., 7 shot mag., otherwise similar to CP-9SS. Mfg. 1997-99.

	$220	$195	$165	$150	$120	$100	$75	*$265*

MODEL CP-45SS – .45 ACP cal., 6 shot mag., otherwise similar to CP-40SS. Mfg. 1997-99.

	$220	$195	$165	$150	$120	$100	$75	*$265*

MODEL LT-380 – .380 ACP cal., SA/DA, 2.8 in. barrel, features blued or two-tone aluminum frame and stainless steel slide, 6 shot mag., choice of Black, OD Green, Pink or Purple grips, supplied with two mags, 15 oz. New 2012.

MSR $308	$250	$215	$185	$165	$130	$110	$85	

MODEL HC-380 (SS) – .380 ACP cal., single action semi-auto, stainless steel, 2 1/2 in. barrel, 10 (C/B 1994) or 13* shot mag., wraparound grips, manual safety with firing pin block and trigger disconnect, exposed hammer, includes two 13 shot mags., lock, and hard

GRADING - PPGS™	100%	98%	95%	90%	80%	70%	60%	LAST MSR

case, 26 oz. Mfg. 1993-2003, reintroduced 2007.

MSR $314	$250	$215	$185	$165	$130	$110	$85	

Add $5 for black finish (Model HC-380B, mfg. 1995-99).

MODEL XL-9SS – 9mm Para. cal., double action only, stainless steel, 3 in. barrel, 5 shot mag., black pebble finished grips, 3-dot adj. sights, 24 oz. Mfg. 1999-2003.

	$215	$190	$160	$145	$120	$95	$75	*$267*

ACCURACY INTERNATIONAL LTD.

Current rifle manufacturer located in Hampshire, England since 1978, with offices in Fredericksburg, VA. Currently distributed by Mile High Shooting Accessories, located in Broomfield, CO, SRT Supply, located in St. Petersburg, FL, and Tac Pro Shooting Center, located in Mingus, TX. Previously imported by Accuracy International North America, located in Orchard Park, NY until circa 2005, and 1998-2005 in Oak Ridge, TN. Also previously imported until 1998 by Gunsite Training Center, located in Paulden, AZ.

RIFLES: BOLT ACTION

In addition to the models listed, Accuracy International also makes military and law enforcement rifles, including the SR98 Australian, G22 German, and the Dutch SLA.

On Models AE, AW, AWP, and AWM listed in this section, many options and configurations are available which will add to the base prices listed.

Add $255 for Picatinny rail on all currently manufactured rifles (standard on Model AE and AW50).

AE MODEL – .243 Win., .260 Rem., .308 Win., or 6.5 Creedmoor cal., similar to AWP Model, 5 shot mag., 20 or 24 in. stainless barrel, Harris bipod attachment point, four sling attachment points, Picatinny rail, black, green, or dark earth finish, approx. 8 1/2 lbs. Importation began 2002.

MSR $3,600	$3,325	$2,775	$2,400	$2,000	$1,700	$1,425	$1,200	

Add $307 for adj. cheekpiece (disc. 2012) or $422 for folding stock.
Add $213 for standard muzzle brake.
Add $357 for butt spike.
Add $454 for 26 in. barrel.

AW MODEL – .243 Win. (new 2000), .260 Rem., .300 Win. Mag., .308 Win., .338 Lapua (disc. 2012), or 6.5 Creedmoor cal., precision bolt action featuring 20, 24, 26, or 27 (disc.) in. 1:12 twist stainless steel barrel with or w/o muzzle brake, 3-lug bolt, 10 shot detachable mag., green synthetic folding (military/LE only) thumbhole adj. stock, AI bipod, 14 lbs. Importation began 1995.

MSR $6,050	$5,500	$4,650	$4,000	$3,400	$2,850	$2,200	$1,800	

Add $203 for fluted barrel.
Add $257 for Picatinny rail or $422 for folding stock.
Add $342 for threaded barrel with muzzle brake.
Add $357 for butt spike.
Add $797 for .300 Win. Mag. cal. with 20 or 26 in. fluted and threaded barrel.
Add $376 for AW-F Model (disc. 2002).

AWP MODEL – similar to AW Model, except has 20 or 24 in. barrel w/o muzzle brake, 15 lbs. Imported 1995-2007.

	$4,250	$3,650	$3,150	$2,650	$2,150	$1,800	$1,500	*$4,600*

Add $310 for AWP-F Model (disc. 2002).

AW50 – .50 BMG, advanced ergonomic design, features built-in anti-recoil system, 5 shot mag., adj. third supporting leg, folding stock, 27 in. fluted barrel with muzzle brake, Picatinny rail, approx. 30 lbs. Mfg. 1998-2012.

	$12,500	$10,500	$8,750	$7,500	$6,250	$4,950	$3,750	*$13,096*

GRADING - PPGS™	100%	98%	95%	90%	80%	70%	60%	LAST MSR

AWM MODEL (SUPER MAGNUM) – .300 Win. Mag. or .338 Lapua cal., 6-lug bolt, 26 or 27 in. 1:9/1:10 twist stainless steel fluted barrel with muzzle brake, 5 shot mag., 15 1/2 lbs. Imported 1995-2009.

	$5,600	$5,100	$4,675	$3,800	$2,950	$2,500	$1,750	*$5,900*

Add $100 for .338 Lapua cal.
Add $324 for AWM-F Model (disc. 2002).

AX MODEL – .243 Win., .260 Rem., .308 Win., .338 Lapua, or 6.5 Creedmoor cal., 10 shot mag., 20, 24, 26, or 27 in. barrel with or w/o muzzle brake, Picatinny rail included, pistol grip with adj. cheekpiece, fixed butt pad with additional spacers, choice of green, black, or dark earth finished hardware, folding chassis.

MSR $6,500	$6,000	$5,200	$4,600	$4,000	$3,350	$2,750	$2,250	

Add $226 for muzzle brake.
Add $959 for .338 Lapua cal.

* ***AX50*** – .50 BMG cal., 27 in. stainless match grade barrel with muzzle brake, includes Picatinny rail, black folding chassis with adj. cheekpiece, butt pad, and butt spike (optional), accessory rails, choice of green, black, or dark earth finished hardware, 27 1/2 lbs.

MSR $10,610	$9,650	$8,750	$8,000	$7,250	$6,500	$5,750	$4,950	

Add $243 for butt spike.

PALMAMASTER – .308 Win. cal., available with either NRA prone or UIT style stock, 30 in. stainless steel fluted barrel, designed for competition shooting, laminated stock. Disc. 2002.

	$2,600	$2,350	$2,100	$1,900	$1,700	$1,500	$1,250	*$2,850*

CISMMASTER – .22 BR, 6mm BR, .243 Win., .308 Win., 6.5x55mm, or 7.5x55mm cal., designed for slow and rapid fire international and military shooting competition, 10 shot mag., 2-stage trigger. Disc. 2002.

	$3,175	$2,850	$2,600	$2,350	$2,100	$1,900	$1,700	*$3,480*

VARMINT RIFLE – .22 Middlested, .22 BR, .22-250 Rem., .223 Rem., 6mm BR, .243 Win., .308 Win., or 7mm-08 Rem. cal., features 26 in. fluted stainless steel barrel. Mfg. 1997-2002.

	$3,200	$2,725	$2,350	$1,950	$1,675	$1,475	$1,300	*$3,650*

ACCURATE ARMS RIFLE LLC.

Current rifle manufacturer established circa 1987 and currently located in Harrisonburg, VA.

RIFLES: BOLT ACTION

Accurate Arms currently manufactures several models, including the Raptor ($6,400 MSR), Canyon (new 2013, $8,900 MSR), Titan (new 2013, $4,200 MSR), Lonestar (new 2013, $4,200 MSR), and the Backpack (disc. 2012, last MSR was $4,900). Please contact the company directly for availability, options, and delivery time (see Trademark Index).

ACHA

Previous manufacturer located in Eibar, Spain until 1936.

PISTOLS: SEMI-AUTO

MODEL 1916 – 6.35mm cal., semi-auto pistol, 7 shot mag., 1905 Browning copy.

	$250	$185	$130	$90	$80	$70	$60	

ATLAS – 6.35mm cal., semi-auto pistol, 6 shot mag., slide marked ATLAS, 1905 Browning copy.

	$200	$165	$125	$95	$75	$65	$50	

LOOKING GLASS – 6.35mm or 7.65mm cal., 6 shot mag., blue or nickel, 1905 Browning copy, slide marked "Looking Glass", many variations.

	$235	$170	$130	$100	$85	$70	$55	

Add 50% for extended grip.

100%	98%	95%	90%	80%	70%	60%	50%	40%	30%	20%	10%

ACME

Previous trade name of Davenport Arms Company shotguns, Maltby Henley & Co. revolvers, and Merwin Hulbert & Co. "owl head" revolvers.

REVOLVERS

SEVEN SHOT REVOLVER – .22 Short rimfire cal., single action.

$360	$310	$240	$185	$165	$150	$120	$110	$100	$90	$65	$55

FIVE SHOT REVOLVER – .32 Short rimfire cal., single action.

$360	$320	$255	$200	$175	$160	$120	$110	$100	$90	$65	$55

ACME ARMS

Previous trade name for Cornwall Hardware Co., NY.

REVOLVERS

SEVEN SHOT – .22 Short rimfire cal., single action.

$275	$250	$210	$185	$165	$155	$140	$125	$110	$90	$85	$75

FIVE SHOT – .32 Short rimfire cal., single action.

$285	$255	$215	$195	$175	$165	$145	$120	$100	$90	$85	$75

SHOTGUNS: SxS

SIDE-BY-SIDE – 12 ga., damascus barrels.

$275	$240	$195	$165	$145	$125	$110	$95	$65	$60	$50	$45

ACME HAMMERLESS

Previously manufactured by Hopkins & Allen, for Hulbert Brothers, 1893.

REVOLVERS

FIVE SHOT – .32 or .38 centerfire cal., double action, top break, non-ejecting.

$145	$125	$100	$90	$80	$70	$60	$50	$40	$30	$20	$15

Also known as Forehand Model 1891, can be hammer or hammerless.

ACTION (M.S.)

Previously manufactured by Modesto Santos, located in Eibar, Spain.

GRADING - PPGS™	100%	98%	95%	90%	80%	70%	60%	LAST MSR

PISTOLS: SEMI-AUTO

MODEL 1915 – 7.65mm cal., semi-auto pistol (French Military).

	$245	$175	$140	$105	$90	$75	$65	

MODEL 1920 – 6.35mm cal., semi-auto pistol, slide marked "Action".

	$195	$150	$110	$85	$65	$45	$40	

ACTION ARMS LTD.

Previous firearms importer and distributor until 1994, located in Philadelphia, PA.

Only Action Arms Models AT-84S, AT-88S, and the Model B Sporter will be listed under this heading. Galil, Timberwolf, and Uzi trademarks can be located in their respective sections.

CARBINES: SEMI-AUTO

MODEL B SPORTER – 9mm Para. cal., patterned after the original Uzi Model B Sporter, 16.1 in. barrel, fires from closed bolt, thumbhole stock with recoil pad, 10 shot mag., adj. rear sight, 8.8 lbs. Limited importation from China 1994 only.

	$695	$625	$550	$475	$435	$385	$335	*$595*

GRADING - PPGS™	100%	98%	95%	90%	80%	70%	60%	LAST MSR

PISTOLS: SEMI-AUTO

AT-84S – 9mm Para. cal., selective SA/DA design, patterned after the CZ-75, 4.8 in. barrel, 15 shot mag., originally introduced in 1985.

$525	$450	$400	$365	$330	$275	$220	

The AT-84S Series was manufactured in Switzerland by Industrial Technology & Machines A.G. and was sold by Action Arms between June of 1987 and 1989. Serial number range is 01201-06000. No P or H models were ever mfg. in this series (2 or 3 prototypes only).

AT-88S – 9mm or .41 Action Express (available early 1990) cal., selective SA/DA design patterned after CZ-75, 4.8 in. barrel, 15 shot (9mm) or 10 shot (.41 AE) mag., can be carried "cocked and locked", fixed sights, blue metal, walnut grips, 35.3 oz. Introduced in 1987 with limited production samples imported in 1989.

$500	$450	$395	$360	$330	$275	$220	

A very small quantity of AT-88Ss (various configurations) were made by I.T.M. of Switzerland and finishes included all blue, all chrome, or two-tone. These pistols may exhibit both I.T.M. and A.A.L. markings. More recent manufacture was performed by Sphinx-Muller of Switzerland, renamed the AT-2000 Series and previously imported by Sile Distributors.

RIFLES: SLIDE ACTION

TIMBERWOLF – see separate listing in T section.

ACTION LEGENDS MFG., INC.

Previous manufacturer, importer, and distributor until circa 2006 and located in Houston, TX.

RIFLES

MODEL 888 M1 CARBINE – .22 LR or .30 Carbine cal., 18 in. barrel, mfg. from new original M1 parts and stock and unused GI parts, 10, 15, or 30 shot mag., choice of birch or walnut stock, parkerized finish, metal or wood handguard, 5 1/2 lbs.

$675	$625	$550	$495	$425	$375	$325	*$650*

Add $11 for .22 LR cal.

Add $31 for walnut/metal forearm or $47 for walnut/wood forearm.

MODEL 1903 SPRINGFIELD – .30-06 cal., 24 in. barrel, bolt action, mfg. from new and original GI parts, 5 shot mag., parkerized finish, wood stock, canvas sling.

While previously advertised at a $950 MSR, only a few prototypes were manufactured.

ADAMS

Previously manufactured by Deane, Adams, & Deane, located in London, England.

100%	98%	95%	90%	80%	70%	60%	50%	40%	30%	20%	10%

REVOLVERS: PERCUSSION

Add approx. 25% for case and accessories on the following models.

MODEL 1851 .31 CAL. – .31 cal., double action, 4 1/2 in. barrel.

N/A	N/A	$2,750	$2,500	$2,250	$2,000	$1,850	$1,600	$1,400	$1,200	$1,000	$650

MODEL 1851 .44 CAL. – .44 cal., double action, 6 in. barrel.

N/A	N/A	$2,500	$2,250	$2,000	$1,850	$1,500	$1,200	$900	$675	$475	$325

MODEL 1851 .50 CAL. – .50 cal., double action, 8 in. barrel, Dragoon frame.

N/A	N/A	$3,650	$3,250	$2,600	$2,100	$1,800	$1,400	$1,100	$700	$500	$350

ADAMS ARMS

Current rifle manufacturer located in Palm Harbor, FL. Adams Arms also manufactures a complete line of accessories for the AR-15 platform, in addition to barrels, upper assemblies, and free floating rails.

GRADING - PPGS™	100%	98%	95%	90%	80%	70%	60%	LAST MSR

RIFLES: SEMI-AUTO

Adams Arms manufactures a complete line of AR-15 platform rifles. For more information on options, availability, and delivery time, please contact the company directly (see Trademark Index).

MID TACTICAL ELITE – 5.56 NATO cal., 14 1/2 (law enforcement only) or 16 in. Government Contour melonited barrel with A2 flash hider, VLTOR IMOD collapsible stock, Ergo grip, 30 shot GI aluminum magazine, Samson free float light weight modular quad rail system, Mil-Spec forged upper and lower receiver, hard coat anodized finish, Picatinny flat top rail with dry lube internal finish and laser engraved.

MSR $1,699	$1,525	$1,325	$1,125	$925	$800	$675	$575

CARBINE TACTICAL ELITE – 5.56 NATO cal., similar to Mid Tactical Elite, except has 16 in. M4 Contour melonited barrel.

MSR $1,699	$1,525	$1,325	$1,125	$925	$800	$675	$575

MID TACTICAL EVO – 5.56 NATO cal., 14 1/2 (law enforcement only) or 16 in. Government Contour 4150 CM melonited barrel with A2 flash hider, VLTOR IMOD collapsible stock, Ergo grip, 30 shot GI aluminum magazine, Samson free float light weight modular rail system, Mil-Spec forged upper and lower receiver, hard coat anodized finish, Picatinny flat top rail with dry lube internal finish and laser engraved.

MSR $1, 550	$1,395	$1,225	$1,050	$925	$800	$675	$550

CARBINE TACTICAL EVO – 5.56 NATO cal., similar to Mid Tactical Evo model, except has 16 in. M4 Profile melonited barrel.

MSR $1, 550	$1,395	$1,225	$1,050	$925	$800	$675	$550

MID BASE – 5.56 NATO cal., 16 in. Government Contour melonited barrel with A2 flash hider, Mil Spec 6-position retractable stock, 30 shot GI aluminum magazine, Mil-Spec forged upper and lower receiver with Picatinny rail, hard coat anodized finish, ribbed mid-length M-4 style molded polymer hand guards.

MSR $1, 100	$995	$875	$750	$650	$550	$450	$350

CARBINE BASE – .223 Rem. cal., similar to Mid Base model, except has 16 in. M4 Profile 4150 CM melonited barrel, and short forearm.

MSR $1, 100	$995	$875	$750	$650	$550	$450	$350

ADAMS, JOSEPH

Previous manufacturer located in Birmingham, England.

100%	98%	95%	90%	80%	70%	60%	50%	40%	30%	20%	10%

PISTOLS: FLINTLOCK

OFFICER MODEL – .65 cal., flintlock pistol, based on Brown Bess model.

$2,850	$2,500	$2,250	$2,000	$1,800	$1,600	$1,400	$1,100	$900	$825	$725	$600

ADAMY, GEBR. JAGDWAFFEN

Current manufacturer and retailer established circa 1921 and located in Suhl, Germany. Previous limited importation by New England Custom Gun Service, located in Claremont, NH, previously located until 2010 in Plainfield, NH.

The Adamy gunmaking tradition goes back to 1820, and sixth and seventh generation descendants are currently building guns.

Adamy Jadgwaffen currently specializes in custom made, break-open rifles, drillings, and combination guns, SxS and O/U shotguns, and double rifles featuring an Anson & Deeley boxlock action or H&H type sidelocks. Since all guns are made to custom order, please contact the factory directly for information on its current models and pricing (see Trademark Index).

ADCO ARMS INC. (ADCO SALES INC.)

Adco Sales Inc. was a previous importer of Diamond shotguns circa 2007-2012 manufactured by Vega in Istanbul, Turkey. Adco Arms Inc. currently imports

GRADING - PPGS™	100%	98%	95%	90%	80%	70%	60%	LAST MSR

accessories only and is located in Woburn, MA. During 2012, the name Adco Sales Inc. was changed to Adco Arms Inc.

SHOTGUNS: O/U

DIAMOND DOUBLE FIELD GRADE – 12 or 20 ga., 3 in. chambers, DT or ST, boxlock action, extractors, includes choke tubes, checkered walnut stock and forearm. Imported 2007-2008.

	100%	98%	95%	90%	80%	70%	60%	LAST MSR
	$380	$330	$285	$250	$215	$180	$160	$449

Add $20 for single trigger.
Add $100 for Duel grade with wide VR (12 ga. only).

DIAMOND IMPERIAL – 12 or 20 ga., 3 in. chambers, boxlock action, SST, ejectors, 26 or 28 in. barrels with choke tubes, checkered fine Turkish walnut stock and forearm. Imported 2007-2008.

	100%	98%	95%	90%	80%	70%	60%	LAST MSR
	$545	$460	$415	$385	$350	$325	$300	$639

Add $20 for 20 ga.

DIAMOND FOLDING MODEL – 28 ga. or .410 bore, DT, folding boxlock action. Limited importation 2007.

	100%	98%	95%	90%	80%	70%	60%	LAST MSR
	$550	$495	$450	$400	$350	$300	$275	$629

DIAMOND DOUBLE ELITE SERIES – 12 or 20 ga., 26 or 28 in. barrels, uncheckered pistol grip walnut stock, blue receiver with light engraving, 5 choke tubes, deluxe ST, extractors. Imported 2008.

	100%	98%	95%	90%	80%	70%	60%	LAST MSR
	$495	$410	$365	$330	$295	$260	$235	$579

Add $30 for 20 ga.

SHOTGUNS: SxS

DH12 COACH GUN – 12 ga., exposed hammers, DT, 20 in. barrels with or w/o choke tubes, checkered walnut stock and splinter forearm, recent manufacture is steel shot compatible and has a top tang safety. Importation began 2006.

	100%	98%	95%	90%	80%	70%	60%	LAST MSR
	$725	$625	$550	$475	$400	$325	$250	$795

Add $20 for choke tubes or Field Gun with 28 in. barrels.

DC12 COACH GUN – 12 ga., similar to DH12 Coach Gun, except has black stock. Imported 2008.

	100%	98%	95%	90%	80%	70%	60%	LAST MSR
	$500	$415	$365	$330	$295	$260	$235	$599

DIAMOND DOUBLE FIELD GRADE – 12, 16 (2006 only), or 20 ga., exposed hammers or hammerless, 28 in. barrels with choke tubes, extractors, recent manufacture is steel shot compatible and has a top tang safety. Importation began 2006.

	100%	98%	95%	90%	80%	70%	60%	LAST MSR
	$775	$650	$575	$500	$425	$350	$275	$880

DIAMOND DOUBLE HEIRLOOM SERIES – 12 ga., exposed hammers, includes choke tubes. Limited importation 2007.

	100%	98%	95%	90%	80%	70%	60%	LAST MSR
	$775	$650	$550	$495	$450	$400	$350	$899

DIAMOND FOLDING MODEL – .410 bore, 3 in. chambers, DT, folding boxlock action. Limited importation 2007.

	100%	98%	95%	90%	80%	70%	60%	LAST MSR
	$550	$495	$450	$400	$350	$300	$275	$629

SHOTGUNS: SEMI-AUTO

All semi-auto shotguns were mfg. in Turkey.

GOLD SERIES – 12 ga., 3 in. chamber, gas operated, 24 (slug gun, non-rifled, includes open sights) or 28 in. VR barrel with 3 choke tubes, semi-humpback style, anodized alloy frame with gold etching, rotary bolt, grey trigger guard, choice of black synthetic or checkered Turkish walnut stock with recoil pad, and forearm. Imported 2001-2006.

	100%	98%	95%	90%	80%	70%	60%	LAST MSR
	$450	$375	$325	$295	$270	$235	$200	$549

Subtract $50 for black synthetic stock and forearm.

GRADING - PPGS™	100%	98%	95%	90%	80%	70%	60%	LAST MSR

DIAMOND IMPERIAL SERIES – 12 or 20 ga., 3 (20 ga.) or 3 1/2 (12 ga.) in. chamber, 24 (slug, 12 ga.), 26 (20 ga. only), or 28 in. VR barrel with 3 chokes (except slug), rotary bi-lateral bolt, deluxe checkered stock and forearm. Imported 2003-2004.

$425	$350	$300	$250	$225	$200	$175	*$499*

Subtract $20 for slug variation.

DIAMOND ELITE SERIES – 12 ga., 3 in. chamber, gas operated, similar to Gold Series, except has engraved receiver with choice of 22 (slug), 24, 26, or 28 in. VR barrel with 3 choke tubes, deluxe checkered walnut stock and forearm. Imported 2001-2006.

$375	$330	$295	$260	$230	$200	$175	*$449*

DIAMOND PANTHER SERIES – 12 ga., 3 in. chamber, gas operated, similar to Diamond Elite Series, except has black synthetic stock and forearm, 20 (slug), 20 regular, or 28 in. barrel with 3 choke tubes. Imported 2002-2006.

$335	$280	$260	$240	$225	$200	$175	*$399*

Add $20 for walnut stock and forearm (new 2003).

MARINER MODEL (SILVER SERIES) – 12 ga., 3 in. chamber, gas operated, 20 (slug, new 2003) or 22 in. VR barrel, anodized alloy frame with high strength satin silver metal finish, checkered walnut stock and forearm. Imported 2002-2006.

$425	$350	$300	$250	$225	$200	$175	*$499*

SHOTGUNS: SINGLE SHOT

DIAMOND FOLDING MODEL – 12 ga. or .410 bore, folding barrel design, folding operating lever is in front of trigger guard. Limited importation 2007.

$165	$130	$110	$95	$80	$70	$60	*$199*

Add $60 for .410 bore.

SHOTGUNS: SLIDE ACTION

All Adco slide action shotguns were manufactured in Turkey.

GOLD ELITE SERIES – 12 ga., 3 in. chamber, 24 (slug gun, non-rifled, includes open sights) or 28 in. VR barrel with 3 choke tubes, semi-humpback style, anodized alloy frame, choice of black synthetic or checkered Turkish walnut stock with recoil pad, and forearm, 7 lbs. Imported 2001-2006.

$300	$250	$205	$175	$160	$145	$120	*$379*

Subtract $60 for black synthetic stock and forearm.

DIAMOND IMPERIAL SERIES – 12 ga., 3 1/2 in. chamber, 28 in. VR barrel with 3 chokes, deluxe checkered stock and forearm. Imported 2003-2006.

$335	$280	$260	$240	$225	$200	$175	*$399*

DIAMOND ELITE SERIES – 12 ga., 3 in. chamber, similar to Gold Elite Series, except has engraved receiver with choice of 20 (slug), regular 20 (disc. 2002), 24, or 28 in. VR barrel with 3 choke tubes, deluxe checkered walnut stock and forearm. Imported 2001-2006.

$280	$240	$200	$175	$160	$145	$120	*$359*

DIAMOND PANTHER SERIES – 12 ga., 3 in. chamber, similar to Diamond Elite Series, except has black synthetic stock and forearm, 18 1/2 (slug), 20 (disc. 2002), 22 (slug, new 2003), or 28 in. barrel with 3 choke tubes. Imported 2001-2006.

$200	$165	$145	$135	$115	$105	$95	*$239*

Subtract $30 for 18 1/2 in. slug variation.

MARINER MODEL – 12 ga., 3 in. chamber, choice of 18 1/2 plain or 22 in. VR barrel with chokes, 5 shot mag., black synthetic stock and forearm. Imported 2003-2006.

$250	$225	$200	$175	$150	$135	$110	*$319*

ADCOR DEFENSE

Current manufacturer located in Baltimore, MD.

RIFLES/CARBINES

Adcor makes an Adcor Defense AR-15 style B.E.A.R. (Brown Enhanced Automatic Rifle) rifle/

100%	98%	95%	90%	80%	70%	60%	50%	40%	30%	20%	10%

carbine in 5.56 NATO cal. It is available in both semi-auto and fully auto configurations and various barrel lengths. The operating system features a gas driven piston in the upper half of the forward rail system which never touches the barrel, and therefore, allowing the barrel to free float for better accuracy. The B.E.A.R. features the quad Picatinny rail system, hammer forged barrel, Magpul MOE buttstock, forward placed charging handle, gas piston system, ejection port dust wiper, and aluminum alloy receiver and rail systems. MSRs start at $2,092 for the MB-RFPE Series with optics ready gas piston carbine, $1,849 for the MB-RFIE Series with optics ready gas impingement carbine, and $1,668 for the MB-RIE Series with optics ready gas impingement carbine.

ADEQ FIREARMS COMPANY

Current manufacturer located in Tampa, FL.

Adeq Firearms Company manufactures a variety of tactical style pistols and rifles, including the Vigilum 1911 Series semi-auto pistols and long range bolt action sniper rifles. Additionally, Adeq manufactures a line of AR-15 style semi-auto rifles, including the Paladin Patrol Series, the Venator Battle rifle, and new in 2013 the L-TAC. A wide variety of optional accessories are available and each rifle is built to customer's specifications. For pricing, available options, and delivery time, please contact the company directly (see Trademark Index).

ADIRONDACK ARMS COMPANY

Previous manufacturer located in Plattsburgh, NY, 1870-1874.

Magazine loaded repeating rifle, .44 cal., brass or iron frame, later model, may also be marked A.S. Babbitt, Plattsburgh, N.Y., absorbed by Winchester in 1874, then discontinued.

This rifle was designed in 1870 and patented by Orvill M. Robinson in Upper Jay, NY. It was available in .38 and .44 cal. rimfire versions without a wood forend and had a high cyclic rate of fire. Original models were made in Plattsburgh, NY, at which time A.S. Babbitt became one of several additional partners. In 1872, Robinson was granted a patent for a second model rifle. It was similar to the Model 1870, except a wood forend was added and the operating mechanism was changed considerably. Following these improvements, Mr. Oliver Winchester contacted Mr. Robinson and purchased the entire Robinson company, discontinuing manufacture.

RIFLES

EARLY MODEL – finger holds on hammer.

100%	98%	95%	90%	80%	70%	60%	50%	40%	30%	20%	10%
$2,400	$2,100	$1,750	$1,450	$1,325	$1,200	$1,075	$975	$875	$775	$675	$600

LATE MODEL – action worked by buttons top of receiver mid-section.

100%	98%	95%	90%	80%	70%	60%	50%	40%	30%	20%	10%
$2,200	$1,950	$1,675	$1,300	$1,200	$1,100	$975	$875	$775	$675	$550	$495

ADLER

Previously manufactured by Engelbrecht & Wolff located in Blasii, Germany, 1905-1907.

PISTOLS: SEMI-AUTO

SEMI-AUTO PISTOL – 7mm Adler cal., 8 shot mag., cocking lever on top of frame.

GRADING - PPGS™	100%	98%	95%	90%	80%	70%	60%	LAST MSR
	$5,000	$4,000	$3,000	$2,500	$2,000	$1,495	$1,100	

ADVANCED ARMAMENT CORP.

Current firearms and suppressor manufacturer located in Lawrenceville, GA. Advanced Armament Corp. is part of the Freedom Group.

Currently, Advanced Armament Corp. manufactures an AR-15 style .300 AAC Blackout model with an MSR of $1,600. It also makes a single shot .300 AAC Blackout handy rifle with an MSR of $360, and a .300 AAC Blackout Model 7 bolt action rifle with an MSR of $899.

GRADING - PPGS™	100%	98%	95%	90%	80%	70%	60%	LAST MSR

ADVANTAGE ARMS USA, INC.

Previous manufacturer located in St. Paul, MN, and distributed by Wildfire Sports, Inc. also located in St. Paul, MN. Advantage Arms USA, Inc. was sold and moved to Tucson, AZ, with the new name of New Advantage Arms, Inc. (see separate listing).

DERRINGERS

MODEL 422 - .22 LR or .22 WMR cal., 4 barrel double action derringer, rotating firing pin, patterned after the Mossberg "Brownie," 2 1/2 in. barrel, high grade alloy frame and barrel, 4 shot, available in blue, nickel, or QPQ (heat treated but appears blue) finish, 15 oz. Mfg. 1986-87 only.

100%	98%	95%	90%	80%	70%	60%	LAST MSR
$150	$135	$115	$105	$95	$85	$75	*$166*

Add 15% for .22 WMR. cal.
Add $6 for nickel finish.
Add $11 for QPQ finish.

AERON CZ s.r.o.

Current manufacturer established in 1968, and located in Brno, Czech Republic.

Aeron CZ s.r.o. was founded in 1968 by Svazarm, a Czech Army activity club. The company designed, manufactured, and serviced small airplanes. Over the years, the company changed its activities, and now manufactures sporting arms, as well as high precision air rifles and pistols. Currently, Aeron firearms are not imported into the U.S. For more information on currently imported Aeron airguns, please refer to the *Blue Book of Airguns* by Dr. Robert Beeman and John Allen.

AETNA

Previous trademark manufactured by Harrington & Richardson located in Worchester, MA.

100%	98%	95%	90%	80%	70%	60%	50%	40%	30%	20%	10%

REVOLVERS

Type: single action revolvers, all of the same general size and configuration, solid frame, spur trigger, so-called "Suicide Specials" during their day.

AETNA NO. 2 - .32 rimfire cal., 5 shot.

100%	98%	95%	90%	80%	70%	60%	50%	40%	30%	20%	10%
$330	$275	$245	$215	$190	$175	$160	$145	$120	$95	$80	$60

AETNA NO. 2 1/2 - .32 rimfire cal., 5 shot.

100%	98%	95%	90%	80%	70%	60%	50%	40%	30%	20%	10%
$330	$275	$245	$215	$190	$175	$160	$145	$120	$95	$80	$60

MODEL 1876 - .22, .32, or .38 rimfire cal., 5 (.38 or .32 cal.) or 7 shot.

100%	98%	95%	90%	80%	70%	60%	50%	40%	30%	20%	10%
$330	$275	$245	$215	$190	$175	$160	$145	$120	$95	$80	$60

AETNA ARMS COMPANY

Previous manufacturer located in New York, 1869-1883.

REVOLVERS

Single action pocket revolver, blue or nickel, birdshead grip, copy of S&W Models 1, 2, and 3, models marked "ALLING" are worth a slight premium.

SEVEN SHOT - .22 rimfire cal.

100%	98%	95%	90%	80%	70%	60%	50%	40%	30%	20%	10%
$350	$325	$275	$250	$235	$210	$195	$175	$165	$155	$130	$110

FIVE SHOT - .32 rimfire cal.

100%	98%	95%	90%	80%	70%	60%	50%	40%	30%	20%	10%
$230	$220	$205	$175	$165	$155	$145	$120	$105	$90	$75	$55

AGNER

Previous trademark manufactured by Saxhoj Products Inc. in Denmark. Imported until 1986 by Beeman Arms, Inc. located in Santa Rosa, CA.

GRADING - PPGS™	100%	98%	95%	90%	80%	70%	60%	LAST MSR

PISTOL: SEMI-AUTO

MODEL M 80 – .22 LR cal. only, stainless steel, semi-auto target pistol, novel design with unique security key safety, adj. French walnut grips, dry fire mechanism, 5.9 in. barrel, 5 shot mag., limited production, 2.4 lbs. Imported 1981-1986.

	$1,125	$995	$900	$800	$700	$600	$500	*$1,295*

Add $100 for left-hand action.

AIM SURPLUS

Current importer and distributor established during 1997 and located in Middletown, OH.

Aim Surplus currently imports a variety of military surplus rifles and pistols. The company also imports surplus European ammunition, in addition to distributing domestic accessories and ammunition. Please contact the company directly for current availability and pricing, as its inventory changes regularly (see Trademark Index).

AIR MATCH

Previously imported by Kendall International, located in Paris, KY.

PISTOLS: SINGLE SHOT

AIR MATCH 500 – .22 LR cal. match single shot pistol, target grips, adj. front counterweight, 10 1/2 in. barrel. Imported 1984-86.

	$550	$495	$450	$425	$395	$360	$330	*$788*

AJAX ARMY

Previously distributed by E.C. Meacham Co., maker unknown, circa 1880s.

100%	98%	95%	90%	80%	70%	60%	50%	40%	30%	20%	10%

REVOLVERS

SINGLE ACTION – .44 rimfire cal., spur trigger, solid frame.

$550	$440	$360	$315	$275	$255	$230	$210	$185	$170	$155	$140

AKDAL

Previous trademark of pistols and shotguns manufactured by Ücyildiz Silah Sanayi Tic Ltd. Sti. until 2012, and located in Istanbul, Turkey.

Akdal semi-auto pistols were good quality and came in a variety of configurations, including full size polymer frame 9mm cal., as well as chrome and satin finishes, and two different .25 ACP pocket pistols. Akdal also offered slide action and semi-auto shotguns, mostly in 12 ga.

Ücyildiz Silah Sanayi Tic Ltd. Sti. manufactured firearms under a variety of trademarks, including Blow, Akdal, and Voltran.

AKKAR

Current shotgun manufacturer established in 1989, and located in Istanbul, Turkey. No current U.S. importation. Previously imported during 2011 by Samco Global Arms, Inc. located in Miami, FL, and until early 2010 by K.B.I., located in Harrisburg, PA.

Akkar manufactures slide action, semi-auto, and O/U shotguns under a variety of registered trademarks, including Akkar, Altay, Apache, Karatay, M-2000, Commanchi, Maxi-Mag, Churchill, Poseidon, and Armstrong. Akkar manufactured private label slide action and semi-auto shotguns for K.B.I., Inc.

Please contact the manufacturer directly for more information on currently imported trademarks and configurations (see Trademark Index).

AKRILL, E.

Previously manufactured in France, circa mid-1800s.

RIFLES: FLINTLOCK

FLINTLOCK RIFLE – .69 cal., breech loaded, octagonal damascus barrel.

$3,300	$2,750	$2,200	$1,980	$1,460	$1,320	$1,240	$1,075	$935	$800	$745	$660

GRADING - PPGS™	100%	98%	95%	90%	80%	70%	60%	LAST MSR

ALAMO RANGER

Previous manufacturer located in Spain.

REVOLVERS

REVOLVER – .38 Spl. cal., Spanish copy of Colt Model 1929.

	$140	$120	$110	$100	$90	$85	$75	

ALASKA

Previous trademark manufactured by Hood Firearms Company, Norwich, CT, 1873-1884.

100%	98%	95%	90%	80%	70%	60%	50%	40%	30%	20%	10%

REVOLVERS

These inexpensive utilitarian revolvers were dubbed "Suicide Specials" in their day.

SINGLE ACTION – .22 rimfire cal., 7 shot, spur trigger, solid frame.

$275	$220	$195	$145	$140	$125	$110	$100	$90	$75	$70	$65

FIVE SHOT – .32 Short rimfire cal.

$220	$195	$160	$155	$150	$140	$125	$105	$95	$85	$75	$70

ALASKAN COMMEMORATIVES

Due to space considerations, individual model listings are not listed in this text, but are provided free of charge through the website. Please visit www.bluebookofgunvalues.com for a complete list of models, manufacturers, quantities, and issue pricing.

ALCHEMY ARMS COMPANY

Previous manufacturer located in Auburn, WA, 1999-circa 2006.

GRADING - PPGS™	100%	98%	95%	90%	80%	70%	60%	LAST MSR

PISTOLS: SEMI-AUTO

SPECTRE STANDARD ISSUE (SI) – 9mm Para., .40 S&W, or .45 ACP cal., single action full size design, hammerless firing mechanism, linear action trigger, keyed internal locking device, aluminum receiver with 4 1/2 in. match grade stainless steel barrel and slide, tactical rail, various silver/black finishes, lowered ejection port, 10 shot double column mag, 32 oz. Mfg. 2000-2006.

	$675	$585	$525	$465	$415	$350	$300	*$749*

SPECTRE SERVICE GRADE (SG & SGC) – similar to Spectre Standard Issue, except does not have tactical rail and rounded trigger guard, SGC is Commander style with 4 in. barrel and weighs 27 oz. Mfg. 2000-2006, SGC mfg. 2001-2006.

	$675	$585	$525	$465	$415	$350	$300	*$749*

SPECTRE TITANIUM EDITION (TI/TIC) – similar to Spectre Series, except features a titanium slide with aluminum receiver, 22 (TIC is Commander style) or 24 oz. Mfg. 2000-2006.

	$895	$775	$675	$575	$500	$450	$395	*$999*

ALDAZABAL

Previously manufactured by Aldazabal, Leturiondo & Cia., located in Spain.

PISTOLS: SEMI-AUTO

SEMI-AUTOMATIC PISTOL – 7.65mm cal., 7 shot, Eibar style.

	$195	$165	$110	$100	$90	$75	$65	

ALERT

Previous trademark manufactured by Hood Firearms Company, Norwich, CT, 1873-1881.

These revolvers were dubbed "Suicide Specials" in their day.

100%	98%	95%	90%	80%	70%	60%	50%	40%	30%	20%	10%

REVOLVERS

SINGLE ACTION – .22 rimfire cal., 7 shot, spur trigger, solid frame.

$300	$275	$250	$225	$195	$175	$145	$130	$125	$110	$100	$90

FIVE SHOT – .32 Short rimfire cal.

$250	$225	$200	$180	$160	$140	$120	$100	$85	$70	$60	$50

ALESSANDRI, LOU, AND SON

Previous custom rifle manufacturer located in Rehoboth, MA 1975-circa 1998.

Lou Alessandri and Son were noted for their top-quality custom rifles (bolt action and side-by-side). Double rifles started at $18,500, while Express bolt actions started at $5,600. All guns were custom built per individual specifications and a wide variety of special order options were available. In addition to building custom rifles, Lou Alessandri and Son also offered a complete line of high-quality cleaning kits and related accessories. To determine the used value of a Lou Alessandri & Son rifle, the configuration has to be evaluated carefully (caliber, grade of wood, embellishments, and overall desirability).

ALEXANDER ARMS LLC

Current manufacturer of AR-15 style rifles located in Radford, VA. Law enforcement, military, dealer, and consumer sales.

GRADING - PPGS™	100%	98%	95%	90%	80%	70%	60%	*LAST MSR*

RIFLES: SEMI-AUTO

IMPORTANT NOTE: On model(s) where *N/A has replaced the normal 100% value, it indicates current market conditions are too unstable to accurately ascertain 100%-60% values. Factory retail prices (MSRs) reflect most recent updates. For more up-to-date information on current pricing trends and additional useful information, please visit www.bluebookofgunvalues.com, select "Information & Services" from the menu, and click on "Additional Book Information".

Add $130 for Shilen barrel.

.50 BEOWULF – .50 Beowulf cal., AR-15 style, shoots 300-400 grain bullet at approx. 1,800 feet per second, forged upper and lower receiver, 7 shot mag., rotary locking bolt and gas delay mechanism, various configurations include Entry, Over Match kit, Over Match Plus kit, Over Match Tactical kit, Precision Entry, Precision kit, AWS, and Law Enforcement (POR). New 2002.

* ***Beowulf Overwatch .50*** – similar to .50 Beowulf, except has 24 in. stainless steel barrel, extended range model, shoots 334 grain bullet at approx. 2,000 feet per second, 9 1/4 lbs. Mfg. 2004-2005.

	*N/A	$1,355	$1,160	$1,055	$850	$695	$540	*$1,789*

* ***Beowulf Entry 16*** – .50 Beowulf cal., 16 1/2 in. chrome-moly barrel, mid length hand guard, Picatinny rail, 7 shot mag., flattop receiver, black or coyote brown stock.

MSR $1,250	*N/A	$1,045	$895	$800	$655	$540	$420	

* ***Beowulf Precision 16*** – .50 Beowulf cal., 16 1/2 in. chrome-moly barrel, composite free float hand guards, Picatinny rail, low profile gas block, 7 shot mag., black furniture standard or optional camo upgrades available.

MSR $1,350	*N/A	$1,135	$970	$880	$710	$585	$455	

* ***Beowulf AWS 16 (Advanced Weapons System)*** – .50 Beowulf cal., 16 1/2 in. chromemoly barrel, low profile gas block, four rail hand guard system, Picatinny rail, black stock, 7 shot mag., includes soft carry bag.

MSR $1,450	*N/A	$1,200	$1,025	$930	$755	$615	$480	

* ***Beowulf Overmatch Plus*** – .50 Beowulf cal., 16 1/2 in. chrome-moly barrel, flattop receiver, detachable iron sights, mid-length hand guard, Picatinny rail, 7 shot mag., rear carry handle, black stock.

MSR $1,450	*N/A	$1,200	$1,025	$930	$755	$615	$480	

GRADING - PPGS™	100%	98%	95%	90%	80%	70%	60%	LAST MSR

* ***Beowulf 24 Overwatch*** – .50 Beowulf cal., 24 in. barrel, full length free float handguard, standard trigger and buttstock, Picatinny rail. Disc. 2009.

N/A $1,555 $1,330 $1,200 $975 $800 $620 *$1,789

* ***Beowulf Piston Rifle*** – .50 Beowulf cal., gas piston operation, 10 shot mag., 16 1/2 in. threaded barrel with no standard muzzle device, Picatinny rail receiver, M4 stock, Samson EX handguard, includes soft carry bag. New 2012.

MSR $2,000 *N/A $1,600 $1,400 $1,200 $1,050 $900 $775

GENGHIS – 5.45x39mm cal., M-4 styling with 16 in. stainless steel barrel, forged upper and lower receiver, 10 shot mag., various configurations with last MSRs included Entry ($1,066 MSR), Over Match kit ($1,158 MSR), Over Match Plus kit ($1,267 MSR), and Over Match Tactical kit ($1,372 MSR). Mfg. 2002-2005.

6.5 GRENDEL – 6.5 Grendel cal., M-4 styling with 18 1/2, 19, 20, or 24 in. stainless steel barrel, 10 shot mag. New 2004.

* ***Grendel Overwatch 6.5*** – 6.5 Grendel cal., 24 in. stainless steel barrel with match chamber, extremely accurate, forged and hard anodized upper and lower receiver. Mfg. 2004-disc.

N/A $1,200 $1,030 $935 $755 $620 $480 *$1,499

* ***Grendel 20 (19.5) Entry*** – 6.5 Grendel cal., 19 1/2 (disc.) or 20 in. stainless steel fully lapped threaded barrel with A2 flash hider, A2 buttstock, Ergo grip, G10 composite free float hand guard, flat top receiver with Picatinny rail, 10 shot mag., black stock.

MSR $1,400 *N/A $1,225 $1,085 $985 $795 $650 $505

* ***Grendel 24 Overwatch*** – 6.5 Grendel cal., 24 in. stainless steel fully lapped threaded barrel with A2 flash hider, A2 buttstock, Ergo grip, compsite free float hand guard, flat top receiver with Picatinny rail, low profile gas block, black hardware.

MSR $1,480 *N/A $1,300 $1,120 $1,015 $820 $675 $525

* ***Grendel AWS*** – 6.5 Grendel cal., 20 or 24 in. stainless steel fully lapped threaded barrel with A2 flash hider, four rail hand guard, Picatinny rail, 10 shot mag., black furniture.

MSR $1,499 *N/A $1,310 $1,120 $1,015 $820 $675 $525

Add $50 for 24 in. barrel.

* ***Grendel Hunter*** – 6.5 Grendel cal., 19 1/2 in. stainless steel fully lapped threaded barrel, flat-top receiver, full length military hand guard, Picatinny rail, black or coyote brown stock, 10 shot mag., standard trigger. Disc. 2012.

N/A $1,125 $975 $875 $700 $595 $450 *$1,370

* ***Grendel Tactical 16*** – 6.5 Grendel cal., 16 in. threaded barrel with or w/o flutes, A2 flash hider, M4 style or folding stock, with or w/o rail, fixed or folding sights.

MSR $1,500 *N/A $1,325 $1,125 $1,000 $825 $700 $575

Add $100 for fluted barrel and folding stock.

Subtract approx. $175 if without mid-length rail handguard (disc. 2012).

This model is also available with a 14 1/2 in. barrel for law enforcement only (Tactical 14).

* ***Grendel Ultralight*** – 6.5 Grendel cal., 16, 18, or 20 in. unthreaded free floating 5R cut rifled barrel with six straight flutes, integral three prong flash hider (16 or 18 in. barrel only), vented composite hand guard, M4 collapsible stock, Enedine buffer. Disc. 2012.

N/A $1,730 $1,480 $1,345 $1,085 $890 $690 *$2,100

* ***GDMR*** – 6.5 Grendel cal., 10 shot mag., 16 (disc.), 20, or 24 in. barrel, Magpul PRS OD Green or black stock, Ergo grip, full tactical model, LaRue four rail hand guard, sight base, bipod mount, Magpul rail covers, tactical single stage trigger, Troy fold up front and rear back up iron sights.

MSR $3,500 *N/A $2,885 $2,470 $2,240 $1,810 $1,485 $1,155

* ***Grendel Sniper Rifle*** – 6.5 Grendel cal., 10 shot mag., 16 in. fluted barrel, side charger loading, Magpul PRS stock, SST, MK10 vented composite handguard, LaRue SPR mount and Ergo deluxe grip, includes soft carry bag. New 2012.

MSR $3,100 *N/A $2,850 $2,300 $1,900 $1,600 $1,300 $1,150

GRADING - PPGS™	100%	98%	95%	90%	80%	70%	60%	LAST MSR

* ***Grendel MK3 Gas Piston*** – 6.5 Grendel cal., gas piston operation, 16, 18, or 24 in. button rifled and fluted Lite series barrel with AAC flash hider, 10 shot mag., black or tactical dark earth furniture, includes soft carry bag. New 2012.

MSR $2,150	***N/A**	**$1,725**	**$1,525**	**$1,325**	**$1,125**	**$925**	**$750**	

* ***Grendel Lightweight Rifle*** – 6.5 Grendel cal., gas operation, lightweight 16, 18, or 20 in. button rifled stainless steel barrel with A2 flash hider, 10 shot mag., M4 folding stock, composite free floating handguard, black furniture, includes soft carry bag. New 2012.

MSR $1,400	***N/A**	**$1,100**	**$975**	**$850**	**$725**	**$600**	**$525**	

* ***GSR*** – 6.5 Grendel cal., 10 shot mag., 20, 24, or 28 (disc.) in. threaded (except 28 in.) barrel with A2 flash hider, Magpul PRS stock, Ergo deluxe pistol grip, blade style single stage tactical trigger, composite vented hand guard system, side charging handle, black or Dark Earth stock, long range precision rifle. Disc. 2012.

	***N/A**	**$2,710**	**$2,325**	**$2,110**	**$1,700**	**$1,395**	**$1,085**	***$3,100***

.17 HMR – .17 HMR cal., gas operation, 18 in. stainless steel button rifled barrel with spiral flutes, 10 shot mag., black or camo finish, flat top receiver with Picatinny rail, six vent A1 flash hider, G10 composite hand guard, non-vented mid-length free float tube, includes two mags. New 2011.

MSR $1,100	***N/A**	**$950**	**$825**	**$750**	**$600**	**$495**	**$385**	

5.56 NATO RIFLE – 5.56 NATO cal., gas operation, two 30 shot mags., 16 or 20 in. fluted barrel with A2 flash hider, flat top receiver with Picatinny rail, free-floated G10 composite handguard, M4 stock, black furniture, includes soft carry bag. New 2012.

MSR $1,600	***N/A**	**$1,325**	**$1,175**	**$1,050**	**$925**	**$775**	**$675**	

Add $80 for 20 in. barrel.

.300 AAC Rifle – .300 AAC cal., gas operation, 16 in. fluted barrel with AAC Blackout flash hider, 30 shot mag., G10 free floated composite handguard, M4 stock, black furniture, includes soft carry bag. New 2012.

MSR $1,800	***N/A**	**$1,450**	**$1,275**	**$1,100**	**$975**	**$875**	**$775**	

ALEXIA

Previous trademark manufactured by Hopkins & Allen, located in Norwich, CT, 1867-1915.

Also known as: Blue Jacket, Captain Jack, Chichester, Defender, Dictator, Monarch, Mountain Eagle, Hopkins & Allen, Towers Police Safety, and Universal.

REVOLVERS

The octagon barreled revolvers listed were single action, solid frame, spur trigger designs. They were an inexpensive vest pocket pistol marketed under numerous names by private companies.

100%	98%	95%	90%	80%	70%	60%	50%	40%	30%	20%	10%
.22 RIMFIRE – 7 shot.											
$275	**$250**	**$225**	**$200**	**$170**	**$160**	**$155**	**$145**	**$130**	**$125**	**$110**	**$100**
.32 SHORT RIMFIRE – 5 shot.											
$170	**$165**	**$160**	**$155**	**$150**	**$140**	**$125**	**$105**	**$95**	**$85**	**$75**	**$70**
SINGLE ACTION .38 SHORT RIMFIRE – 5 shot.											
$195	**$180**	**$170**	**$165**	**$160**	**$145**	**$140**	**$120**	**$110**	**$100**	**$90**	**$85**
.41 SHORT RIMFIRE – 5 shot.											
$220	**$210**	**$205**	**$195**	**$180**	**$170**	**$160**	**$145**	**$125**	**$110**	**$100**	**$90**

ALFA

Previous trademark manufactured by Armero Especialistas Reunidas, located in Eibar, Spain, circa 1920.

REVOLVERS

All revolvers are marked "Alfa" on grips.

GRADING - PPGS™	100%	98%	95%	90%	80%	70%	60%	LAST MSR

EARLY MODEL – .32, .38, or .44 cal., copies of S&W No. 2 by O. Hermanos.

	$145	$130	$120	$110	$105	$95	$75	

Add 50% for .44 cal.

LATE MODEL – .22 LR, .32 S&W, or .38 S&W cal., copies of Colt Police Positive and S&W Military and Police.

	$160	$150	$130	$120	$110	$100	$90	

ALFA PROJ

Current manufacturer established during 1993, and located in Brno, Czech Republic. Currently imported beginning 2007 by Trail Blazin' Innovations (starter guns only), located in Houston, TX. Previously imported during 2006 by GunX, LLC, located in Shelton, CT.

Alfa Proj handguns are of good quality and utilitarian manufacture, and are currently available in both double action revolver and semi-auto pistol models. Alfa Proj also manufactures blank starter revolvers, rubber bullet firing revolvers, revolver carbines and rifles. Most of these guns are not currently imported into the U.S. Please contact the importer directly for more information and U.S. availability (see Trademark Index).

ALKARTASUNA FABRICA DE ARMAS, S.A.

Previous manufacturer located in Guernica, Spain.

PISTOLS: SEMI-AUTO

ALKARTASUNA CARTRIDGE COUNTER – 6.35mm cal., 7 shot, left grip panel cartridge counter, loaded chamber indicator, grip safety.

	$450	$350	$275	$225	$175	$150	$125	

ALKARTASUNA RUBY AUTOMATIC – 7.65mm cal., 2 variations - more common is the "Ruby" type, 9 shot, 3 5/8 in. barrel, blue, fixed sights, checkered wood or hard rubber grips, used by French Army in WWI and WWII. Mfg. 1917-22.

	$325	$235	$165	$110	$65	$55	$45	

Add 25% for extended barrel.

ALLEN & THURBER

Previous manufacturer/trademark originally located in Grafton, Mass. Ethan Allen started many plants to keep up with expanding business after 1832. Listed below is a chronological order of the firms constituting the family dynasty founded by Ethan Allen.

E. Allen - Grafton, Mass. 1832-1837
Allen & Thurber - Grafton, Mass. 1837-1842
Allen & Thurber - Norwich, Conn. 1842-1847
Allen & Thurber - Worcester, Mass. 1847-1854
Allen, Thurber, & Co. - Worcester, Mass. 1854-1856
Allen & Wheelock - Worcester, Mass. 1856-1865
E. Allen & Co. - Worcester, Mass. 1865-1871
Forehand & Wadsworth - Worcester, Mass. 1871-1890
Forehand Arms Co. - Worcester, Mass. 1890-1902

No other 19th-century American firm produced a wider variety of firearms than did Ethan Allen & subsidiaries. In 1902, the Forehand Arms Co. was sold to Hopkins & Allen.

Please refer to the Hopkins & Allen section for approximate values.

ALLEN FIREARMS

Previous importer located in Santa Fe, NM importing A. Uberti firearms until early in 1987. After Allen Firearms closed, Cimarron F.A. Mfg. Co. located in Houston, TX purchased the remaining inventory (in addition to ordering new products under their name).

Allen Firearms was formerly called Western Arms and manufactured both modern and black powder reproduction firearms and accessories patterned after famous older

GRADING - PPGS™	100%	98%	95%	90%	80%	70%	60%	*LAST MSR*

models. Collectibility to date has been limited on most Allen Firearms models, and as a guideline, up-to-date values on this trademark can be established by current importation prices of Uberti firearms.

Allen Firearms' models and pricing are available free of charge on our website: www.bluebookofgunvalues.com

ALMAR

Current trademark of private label shotguns sold by S. Alamanos & Co. O.E., located in Athens, Greece.

Almar is a private label on shotguns available in various configurations. To date, these guns have had little, if any, U.S. importation. Please contact the company directly for more information, including U.S. availability and pricing (see Trademark Index).

ALPHA ARMS INC.

Previous manufacturer located in Flower Mound, TX from 1983-1987.

Retail price included custom hard case.

RIFLES: BOLT ACTION

Many special order options including an octagonal barrel, various finishes, special sights, and deluxe wood were available at extra cost on the models listed. These options, while not listed separately by price, will add value to the prices shown below. All Alpha Arms rifles were manufactured under stringent quality control.

ALPHA CUSTOM – available in most calibers from .222 Rem. through .338 Win. Mag., many other calibers available on special order, 3-position Model 70 type safety, 60 degree bolt lift, 20 to 24 in. Douglas barrel, limited production, right-hand or left-hand, deluxe checkered Claro walnut standard, approx. 6 lbs. Mfg. 1984-87.

	100%	98%	95%	90%	80%	70%	60%	Last MSR
	$1,525	$1,200	$975	$850	$725	$640	$560	*$1,735*

ALPHA GRAND SLAM – same general specifications as the Alpha Custom, except comes standard with laminated wood stock, fluted bolt and non-glare matte finished metal parts, right-hand or left-hand, approx. 6 1/2 lbs. Mfg. 1985-87.

	100%	98%	95%	90%	80%	70%	60%	Last MSR
	$1,200	$950	$875	$750	$650	$600	$525	*$1,465*

ALPHA ALASKAN – .308 Win., .350 Rem. Mag., .358 Win., or .458 Win. Mag. cal., action is similar to Alpha Grand Slam, except barrel, receiver, bolt and safety are stainless steel, right-hand or left-hand, Nitex coated small parts, approx. 6 3/4-7 1/2 lbs. Mfg. 1985-87.

	100%	98%	95%	90%	80%	70%	60%	Last MSR
	$1,525	$1,200	$975	$850	$725	$640	$560	*$1,735*

ALPHA BIG-FIVE – .300 H&H thru .375 H&H or .458 Win. Mag. cal., reinforced stock and decelerator recoil pad. Mfg. 1987 only.

	100%	98%	95%	90%	80%	70%	60%	Last MSR
	$1,575	$1,250	$1,050	$895	$750	$640	$560	*$1,795*

ALPHARMS

Current trademark of shotguns manufactured by Leader Arms Technology located in AnKara, Turkey. Please refer to listings under the Leader Arms Technology listing.

ALPINE INDUSTRIES

Previous manufacturer located in Los Angeles, CA.

Alpine Industries was a commercial M1 carbine manufacturer which produced approximately 17,000 guns between 1962-1965. Guns were made with newly manufactured cast receivers and military surplus parts, including some from England.

AMBUSH FIREARMS

Current semi-auto rifle manufacturer located in Black Creek, GA.

CARBINES: SEMI-AUTO

IMPORTANT NOTE: On model(s) where *N/A has replaced the normal 100% value, it indicates current market conditions are too unstable to accurately ascertain 100%-60% values. Factory retail prices (MSRs) reflect most recent updates. For more up-to-date information on

GRADING - PPGS™	100%	98%	95%	90%	80%	70%	60%	LAST MSR

current pricing trends and additional useful information, please visit www.bluebookofgunvalues.com, select "Information & Services" from the menu, and click on "Additional Book Information".

AMBUSH 6.8 – 5.56 NATO (new 2012), or 6.8 SPC. cal., AR-15 configuration, featuring 18 in. barrel with Magpul MOE adj. stock, free floating full length Picatinny modular rail, with two smaller rails on bottom and front, black, standard or pink (new 2013) Mossy Oak Break-Up Infinity (new 2012), or Realtree AP camo coverage, pistol grip, 5 shot mag., Geissele super semi-auto trigger, 6 lbs. New 2011.

MSR $1,789	*N/A	$1,375	$1,150	$950	$825	$700	$575

AMBUSH 300 AAC BLACKOUT – .300 AAC Blackout (7.62x35mm) cal., otherwise similar to Ambush 6.8, 6 1/2 lbs. New 2012.

MSR $1,789	*N/A	$1,375	$1,150	$950	$825	$700	$575

AMERICA REMEMBERS

Current organization located in Ashland, VA, which privately commissions historical, limited/special editions in conjunction with various manufacturers. Previously located in Mechanicsville, VA until 1999.

America Remembers is a private non-governmental organization dedicated to the remembrance of notable Americans and important historical American events. Along with its affiliates, the Armed Forces Commemorative Society, American Heroes and Legends, and the United States Society of Arms and Armour, the company produces special issue limited edition firearms. America Remembers purchased the antique arms division of the U.S. Historical Society on April 1, 1994. Older U.S.H.S. firearms can be located in the U section of this text.

Due to space considerations, individual model listings of America Remembers Special/Limited Editions are not listed in this text, but are provided free of charge through our website. Please visit www.bluebookofgunvalues.com for a complete list of models, manufacturers, quantities, and issue pricing.

AMERICAN ARMS

Previous manufacturer located in Garden Grove, CA.

PISTOLS: SEMI-AUTO

EAGLE 380 – .380 ACP cal. only, stainless steel semi-auto, copy of Walther PPK/S, 6 shot mag., 3 1/4 in. barrel, limited production, 20 oz.

$400	$250	$215	N/A	N/A	N/A	N/A	*$289*

Add $25 for case.
Add $50 for case and belt buckle.
Add $25 for black teflon finish (disc. 1985).

AMERICAN ARMS CO.

Previous manufacturer located in Boston, MA from 1870-1901 and Milwaukee, WI from 1893-1904. American Arms Co. was acquired by Marlin in 1901.

100%	98%	95%	90%	80%	70%	60%	50%	40%	30%	20%	10%

DERRINGERS

O/U DESIGN – .22 Short RF, .32 Short RF, or .41 Short RF cal., Wheeler Pat. action, brass frame, spur trigger.

$850	$800	$750	$700	$650	$600	$550	$525	$450	$395	$325	$250

SHOTGUNS: SxS

HAMMERLESS MODEL – 12 ga., semi-hammerless.

$600	$550	$500	$450	$350	$275	$225	$175	$150	$125	$100	$75

WHITMORE PATENT – 10 or 12 ga., hammerless, checkering.

$685	$625	$575	$520	$460	$400	$340	$270	$200	$150	$125	$100

Add 10% for 10 ga. (2 7/8 in. chambers).

100%	98%	95%	90%	80%	70%	60%	50%	40%	30%	20%	10%

SINGLESHOT – 12 ga., semi-hammerless, damascus barrel.

$260	$225	$200	$175	$150	$125	$90	$70	$50	$40	$30	$20

AMERICAN ARMS, INC.

Previous importer and manufacturer located in North Kansas City, MO, until 2000. American Arms imported various Spanish shotguns (Indesal, Lanber, Norica, and Zabala Hermanos), Italian shotguns including F. Stefano, several European pistols and rifles, and Sites handguns (1990-2000) mfg. in Torino, Italy. This company also manufactured several pistols in North Kansas City, MO. For more information and pricing on Norica airguns previously imported by American Arms, please refer to the *Blue Book of Airguns* by Dr. Robert Beeman & John Allen (also available online).

In late 2000, TriStar Sporting Arms, Ltd. acquired the parts inventory for some models previously imported by American Arms, Inc. Original warranties from American Arms do not apply to TriStar Sporting Arms, Ltd.

GRADING - PPGS™	100%	98%	95%	90%	80%	70%	60%	LAST MSR

COMBINATION GUNS

RS COMBO – choice of .222 Rem. or .308 Win. rifle barrel under 12 ga. barrel, engraved boxlock frame with antique silver finish, DT, 24 in. VR barrels with shotgun choke tubes, rifle sights, grooved for scope mounting, Monte Carlo stock, 7 lbs. 14 oz. Imported 1989 only.

$675	$595	$550	$495	$450	$420	$385	*$749*

PISTOLS: SEMI-AUTO

MODEL TT-9MM TOKAREV – 9mm Para. cal., semi-auto single action, 4 1/2 in. barrel, 9 shot mag., hammer block external safety, 31 oz. Imported 1988-89 only.

$395	$325	$275	$225	$200	$180	$160	*$289*

This model is patterned after the Tokarev action and was made from machined steel parts in Yugoslavia.

MODEL EP-380 – .380 ACP cal., semi-auto double action, stainless steel, 3 1/2 in. barrel, 7 shot mag., wood checkered grips, adj. rear sight, 25 oz. Imported 1988-90 only.

$375	$325	$250	$195	$165	$140	$120	*$449*

This model was made in West Germany.

MODEL PK-22 CLASSIC – .22 LR cal., semi-auto double action, styled after Govt. .45 ACP, 3 1/3 in. barrel, 8 shot finger extension mag., black polymer grips, 22 oz. Mfg. 1988-96.

$165	$140	$115	$100	$90	$80	$70	*$199*

This model was made in North Kansas City, MO. It has patented safety features such as external hammer block and internal blocking of the firing pin until the trigger is pulled.

MODEL CX-22 CLASSIC – .22 LR cal., style patterned after Walther PPK, 3 1/3 in. barrel, 8 shot finger extension mag., 22 oz. Mfg. 1990-95.

$175	$145	$125	$110	$100	$90	$80	*$213*

This model was made in North Kansas City, MO. It had patented safety features such as an external hammer block and internal firing pin block.

* ***Model CXC-22*** – similar to CX-22 Classic, except has chrome slide. Mfg. in 1990 only.

$170	$150	$125	$110	$100	$90	$80	*$189*

MODEL PX-22/25 CLASSIC – .22 LR or .25 ACP (mfg. 1991 only) cal., compact variation of the Model CX-22, 2 3/4 in. barrel, 7 shot finger extension mag., 15 oz. New 1989, PX-25 was mfg. 1991 only, PX-22 was disc. 1995.

$175	$145	$125	$110	$100	$90	$80	*$206*

This model was made in North Kansas City, MO. It had patented safety features such as an external hammer block and internal firing pin block.

GRADING - PPGS™	100%	98%	95%	90%	80%	70%	60%	LAST MSR

MODEL P-98 CLASSIC – .22 LR cal., semi-auto double action patterned after Walther P.38, 5 in. barrel, 8 shot mag., blue/black finish, grooved wraparound grips, 26 oz. Mfg. 1990-96.

$170	$145	$125	$110	$100	$90	$80	*$209*

ESCORT – .380 ACP cal., double action only, 3 3/8 in. barrel, 7 shot mag., unique thin profile, matte stainless steel, soft polymer grips, polygonal rifling, 19 oz. Mfg. 1995-97.

$285	$230	$200	$185	$170	$160	$150	*$349*

SABRE – while this model was advertised, it was never mfg.

SPECTRE – 9mm Para., .40 S&W (mfg. 1991 only), or .45 ACP (new 1993) cal., semi-auto double action, 6 in. barrel with polygonal rifling, 30 shot mag., ambidextrous safety, decocking lever, adj. sights, 4 1/2 lbs., mfg. in Italy by Sites. Imported 1990-93.

$500	$325	$275	$240	$200	$185	$170	*$429*

Add $28 for .45 ACP cal.

This model was previously imported by F.I.E. located in Hialeah, FL (1989-1990).

AUSSIE SEMI-AUTO – 9mm Para. or .40 S&W cal., semi-auto double action, polymer frame with nickeled steel slide and 4 3/4 in. barrel, 10 shot mag., features 5 safeties, last shot slide lock, 23 oz. Limited importation from Spain 1996 only.

$375	$295	$250	$225	$200	$175	$160	*$425*

These guns are marked "FELK TF 919".

REVOLVERS: SAA

REGULATOR MODEL – .357 Mag., .44-40, or .45 LC cal., 4 3/4, 5 1/2 (new 1993), or 7 1/2 in. barrel, reproduction of the Colt Peacemaker, brass trigger guard and back strap, fixed sights, half-cock and hammer block safeties, blade front, grooved rear sights, color case hardened frame and blue barrel/cylinder or nickel finish (imported 1999 only in .45 LC cal.), walnut grips, 35 oz. Mfg. by Uberti. Imported 1992-2000.

$270	$230	$200	$185	$170	$160	$150	*$320*

Add $55 for nickel finish (disc. 1999).
Add $40 for dual cylinder set (.44-40/.44 Spl. or .45 LC/.45 ACP). Disc. 1998.

* ***Regulator Model Deluxe*** – similar to Regulator Model, except .45 LC cal. only, full charcoal blue finish (mfg. 1996-97) or color case hardened frame (new 1998), case hardened (pre-1993) or blue (post-1993) steel trigger guard and back strap. Importation disc. 1992, resumed 1994-2000.

$315	$260	$215	$190	$170	$160	$150	*$365*

Add $70 for dual cylinder set (.44-40/.44 Spl. or .45 LC/.45 ACP). Disc. 1992.

* ***Regulator Model Buckhorn*** – .44 Mag cal., 4 3/4, 6, or 7 1/2 in. barrel, otherwise similar to Regulator Model, 44 oz. Imported 1993-96.

$305	$255	$205	$185	$170	$160	$150	*$379*

Add $10 for Target variation (flattop and adj. rear sight). Imported 1994 only.

* ***Regulator Model Storekeeper*** – .44-40 WCF or .45 LC cal., 4 in. barrel, smooth walnut curved grips, nickel or B/H nickel finish, 31 oz. Imported 1999 only.

$320	$265	$215	$190	$170	$160	$150	*$375*

Add $44 for B/H nickel finish.

UBERTI BISLEY – .45 LC cal., patterned after the Colt Bisley, case hardened steel frame, 4 3/4, 5 1/2, or 7 1/2 in. barrel with fixed sights, hammer block safety. Imported 1997-98 only.

$425	$340	$275	$215	$190	$170	$160	*$475*

UBERTI .454 SAA – .454 cal., 6 SR or 7 1/2 in. top-ported barrel, hammer block safety, satin nickel finish, custom hardwood grips, wide trigger, adj. rear sight. Imported 1996-97 only.

$750	$625	$550	$495	$465	$435	$375	*$869*

SILVERADO – .357 Mag., .44 Mag., or .45 LC cal., 4 3/4, 5 1/2, or 7 1/2 in. barrel, brushed nickel finish, unfluted cylinder, laminated charcoal grips. Mfg. by Uberti, imported 1999-2000.

$345	$285	$220	$195	$170	$160	$150	*$409*

GRADING - PPGS™	100%	98%	95%	90%	80%	70%	60%	LAST MSR

RIFLES: O/U

SILVER EXPRESS – 8x57JRS or 9.3x74R cal., O/U boxlock design, gold SNT, monoblock 28 in. separated barrels, manual safety, silver finished receiver with light engraving, skipline checkered walnut stock and forearm, approx. 7 3/4 lbs. Limited importation 1999-2000.

$1,800	$1,625	$1,500	$1,375	$1,250	$1,125	$1,000	*$1,949*

RIFLES: REPRODUCTIONS

MODEL 1860 HENRY REPLICA – .44-40 WCF or .45 LC cal., 24 1/4 in. blue or in-the-white finish (new 1999) barrel, 9 1/4 lbs. Mfg. by Uberti, importation disc. 2000.

$835	$625	$525	$425	$360	$320	$260	*$940*

Add $50 for white barrel finish.

* ***Model 1860 Henry Trapper Replica*** – similar to the Henry Replica, except has 18 1/2 in. barrel, 8 lbs. Imported 1999-2000.

$835	$625	$525	$425	$360	$320	$260	*$940*

Add $50 for white barrel finish.

MODEL 1866 WINCHESTER REPLICA – .44-40 WCF or .45 LC cal., 19 (Carbine) or 24 1/4 (Rifle) in. barrel, approx. 8 lbs. Mfg. by Uberti, importation disc. 2000.

$650	$550	$460	$375	$300	$250	$200	*$730*

Subtract $20 for Carbine variation (Yellowboy).

MODEL 1873 WINCHESTER REPLICA – .44-40 WCF or .45 LC cal., 24 1/4 or 30 (new 1999) in. octagon barrel, case colored receiver, approx. 8 1/4 lbs. Mfg. by Uberti, importation disc. 2000.

$775	$625	$525	$425	$360	$320	$260	*$860*

Add $80 for 30 in. barrel.

* ***Model 1873 Deluxe Winchester Replica*** – similar to Model 1873 Winchester Replica, except has better quality checkered pistol grip stock and forearm. Disc. 1997.

$1,100	$775	$625	$500	$425	$350	$275	*$1,299*

MODEL 1885 SINGLE SHOT HIGH WALL – .45-70 Govt. cal., 28 in. round barrel, color case hardened frame, 8.82 lbs. Mfg. by Uberti, imported 1998-2000.

$700	$575	$495	$395	$350	$300	$260	*$810*

SHARPS CAVALRY CARBINE – .45-70 Govt. cal., 22 in. heavy round blue barrel, case colored action, adj. rear ladder sight, DST, uncheckered walnut stock and forearm, 8 lbs. 3 oz. Imported 1999-2000.

$625	$525	$450	$400	$360	$330	$300	*$660*

SHARPS FRONTIER CARBINE – similar to Cavalry Carbine, except has regular barrel with barrel band and single trigger, 7 lbs. 13 oz. Imported 1999-2000.

$615	$535	$450	$400	$360	$330	$300	*$675*

SHARPS 1874 SPORTING RIFLE – .45-70 Govt. or .45-120 black powder cartridge, 28 in. octagon barrel, checkered walnut stock and forearm, DST, 9 lbs. 3 oz. Imported 1999-2000.

$635	$535	$450	$400	$360	$330	$300	*$685*

* ***Sharps 1874 Deluxe Sporting Rifle*** – similar to Sharps 1874 Sporting Rifle, except has brown barrel finish. Imported 1999-2000.

$650	$545	$460	$410	$360	$330	$300	*$705*

RIFLES: SEMI-AUTO

MODEL ZCY 308 – .308 Win. cal., gas operated semi-auto AK-47 type action, Yugoslavian mfg. Imported 1988 only.

$775	$650	$550	$450	$400	$375	$350	*$825*

MODEL AKY 39 – 7.62x39mm cal., gas operated semi-auto AK-47 type action, teakwood fixed stock and grip, flip up Tritium front and rear night sights, Yugoslavian mfg. Imported 1988-1989 only.

$650	$550	$495	$440	$395	$350	$300	*$559*

This model was supplied with sling and cleaning kit.

GRADING - PPGS™	100%	98%	95%	90%	80%	70%	60%	LAST MSR

* ***Model AKF 39 Folding Stock*** – 7.62x39mm cal., folding stock variation of the Model AKY-39. Imported 1988-89 only.

	$725	$625	$550	$475	$425	$375	$325	*$589*

EXP-64 SURVIVAL RIFLE – .22 LR cal., semi-auto, takedown rifle stores in oversize synthetic stock compartment, 21 in. barrel, 10 shot mag., open sights, receiver grooved for scope mounting, cross bolt safety, 40 in. overall length, 7 lbs. Imported 1989-90 only.

	$150	$135	$125	$115	$105	$95	$85	*$169*

MINI-MAX – .22 LR cal., semi-auto, 18 3/4 in. barrel, wood or black synthetic stock, 10 shot mag., adj. rear sight, 4 1/3 lbs. Imported in 1990 only.

	$85	$75	$65	$55	$45	$40	$35	*$99*

Add $6 for wood stock.

SM 64 TD SPORTER – .22 LR cal., semi-auto, takedown barrel, 21 in. barrel, checkered walnut finished hardwood stock and forend, hooded front sight and adj. rear sight, 7 lbs. Imported 1989-90 only.

	$130	$115	$105	$95	$85	$75	$65	*$149*

SHOTGUNS: O/U

American Arms imported Spanish shotguns manufactured by Zabala Hermanos, Lanber, and Indesal. Italian shotguns were also imported and mfg. by Stefano Fausti (Models Silver, Waterfowl, and Turkey Special). American Arms also imported Franchi Black Magic semi-auto and O/U shotguns until 1998. These shotguns will appear under the Franchi section in this text. Older Diarm models have been listed below.

LINCE – 12 or 20 ga., 3 in. chambers, boxlock with Greener crossbolt, various barrel lengths and chokings, available in either blue or shiny chrome finish, SST, VR, ejectors. Imported 1986 only.

	$510	$400	$380	$360	$340	$320	$300	*$610*

Add $70 for choke tubes.

SILVER MODEL – 12 or 20 ga. only, similar to Lince Model, except has brushed aluminum receiver, no engraving. Imported 1986-1987 only.

	$495	$450	$390	$360	$330	$300	$285	*$545*

Add $50 for multi-chokes.

SILVER I – similar to Silver Model, except also available in 24 (Ellett Bros. exclusive), 28 (new 1988), 32 (Ellett Bros. exclusive) ga. or .410 bore (new 1988), single selective trigger became standard in 1988, extractors, engraved frame, fixed chokes, recoil pad. Imported 1986-2000.

	$535	$430	$350	$300	$285	$270	$255	*$649*

Add 15% for 28 ga. or .410 bore.
Add 25% for 24 or 32 ga.

Engraved frame became standard in 1987.

SILVER II – similar to Silver I, except was supplied with choke tubes, deluxe walnut, and ejectors, 16 (new 1999) ga. Imported 1987-2000.

	$660	$560	$475	$400	$360	$330	$300	*$769*

Add 15% for 28 ga. or .410 bore (fixed chokes only).
Add 25% for 24 or 32 ga.

* ***Silver II Lite (Silver Upland Lite)*** – 12, 20, or 28 ga. (disc. 1995), 3 in. chambers (except for 28 ga.), 26 in. VR barrels, with Franchoke tubes (except for 28 ga.), SST, ejectors, engraved frame with antique silver finish, checkered walnut stock and forearm, 5 3/4-6 1/4 lbs. Imported 1994-98.

	$800	$660	$550	$485	$440	$400	$360	*$925*

* ***Silver II Small Gauge Combo*** – included either 20/28 ga. (new 1997) or 28 ga./.410 bore barrels. Imported 1989-2000.

	$1,080	$925	$750	$625	$550	$495	$450	*$1,239*

GRADING - PPGS™	100%	98%	95%	90%	80%	70%	60%	LAST MSR

SILVER LITE – 12 or 20 ga., 2 3/4 in. chambers, boxlock action, 26 in. vent. barrels with VR and choke tubes, blue alloy receiver, ejectors, gold SST, checkered walnut stock and forearm, 5 lbs. 14 oz. or 6 (12 ga.) lbs. Mfg. by Lanber. Imported 1990-1992.

	$625	$535	$460	$400	$360	$330	$300	*$749*

SILVER HUNTER – 12 or 20 ga., steel boxlock action, SST, extractors, monoblock VR 26 or 28 (12 ga. only) in. barrels with 2 choke tubes, checkered walnut stock and forearm. Imported 1999 only.

	$550	$450	$375	$315	$285	$270	$255	*$629*

SILVER SPORTING – 12 ga. or 20 ga. (new 1996), Sporting Clay model, boxlock action, 28, 29 (new 1999), or 30 (new 1993) in. ported vent. barrels with channelled broadway VR, choke tubes, and elongated forcing cones, nickel finished engraved receiver, SST, ejectors, figured walnut stock and forearm with handcut checkering, 7 lbs. 6 oz. Mfg. by Lanber, imported 1990-2000. 1993 manufacture by Pedersoli.

	$835	$680	$550	$485	$440	$400	$360	*$965*

SILVER SKEET – 12 ga. only, similar appearance to Silver Sporting, 26 or 28 (new 1993) in. ported vent. barrels with raised VR, 4 choke tubes, recoil pad, 7 lbs. 6 oz. Imported 1992-93 only.

	$790	$685	$575	$495	$450	$400	$360	*$899*

SILVER TRAP – similar appearance to Silver Sporting, 30 in. ported barrels with raised VR, 4 choke tubes, recoil pad, trap stock dimensions, 7 3/4 lbs. Imported 1992-1993 only.

	$790	$685	$575	$495	$450	$400	$360	*$899*

STERLING/BRISTOL – 12 or 20 ga., 3 in. chambers, boxlock with Greener crossbolt and false side plates, various barrel lengths and choke tubes, chrome finished receiver with moderate game scene engraving, SST, VR, ejectors. Imported 1986-89.

	$695	$550	$495	$450	$400	$375	$350	*$825*

Until 1989, this model was designated the Bristol. In 1988, the engraving pattern was changed from game scene to elaborate scroll type.

SIR – 12 or 20 ga., 3 in. chambers, sidelock with Greener crossbolt, various barrel lengths and chokings, chrome finished receiver with game scene engraving, ST, VR, ejectors, deluxe checkered pistol grip stock and forearm. Imported 1986 only.

	$1,100	$900	$750	$675	$610	$565	$520	*$1,090*

Add $75 for choke tubes.

ROYAL – 12 or 20 ga., 3 in. chambers, sidelock with Greener crossbolt, various barrel lengths and chokings, chrome finished receiver with elaborate scroll engraving, ST, VR, ejectors, oil finished deluxe checkered pistol grip and forearm. Imported 1986-87 only.

	$1,595	$1,310	$1,080	$960	$850	$750	$675	*$1,730*

Add $65 for choke tubes.

EXCELSIOR – 12 or 20 ga., 3 in. chambers, sidelock with Greener crossbolt, various barrel lengths and chokings, chrome finished receiver with elaborate deep relief engraving and multiple gold inlays, ST, VR, ejectors, oil finished deluxe checkered pistol grip and forearm. Imported 1986-87 only.

	$1,775	$1,510	$1,250	$1,100	$975	$885	$780	*$1,925*

Add $70 for choke tubes.

WS/WT - O/U (SILVER) 12 WATERFOWL/TURKEY SPECIAL – 12 ga. only, Mag. chambers (3 1/2 in. was added in 1989), 24 (Turkey - disc. 1996), 26 (Turkey) or 28 (Waterfowl) in. barrels with choke tubes, SST, ejectors, parkerized metal finish, matte finished stock and forearm, Mossy Oak Breakup camo pattern began 1997 for Turkey Special, sling swivels, recoil pad, approx. 7 lbs. Imported 1987-2000.

	$650	$550	$460	$395	$360	$330	$300	*$799*

Add $86 for Camo Turkey Model (WT/OU Camo 12, Breakup camo pattern, new 1997).

GRADING - PPGS™	100%	98%	95%	90%	80%	70%	60%	LAST MSR

* ***WS/WT O/U 10 ga. Waterfowl*** – 10 ga. Mag., double triggers, extractors, matte finishes similar to 12 ga. Waterfowl, beavertail forearm. Imported 1988-89 only.

$750	$625	$550	$495	$450	$390	$360	*$829*

WT-O/U10 TURKEY SPECIAL – 10 ga., 3 1/2 in. Mag., 26 in. barrels with choke tubes, SST (became standard in 1990), extractors, recoil pad, non-glare metal finish, 9 lbs. 10 oz. Imported 1988-2000.

$865	$695	$550	$500	$450	$390	$360	*$995*

F.S. 200 – 12 ga., trap or skeet model, 26 or 32 in. separated barrels only, SST, ejectors, boxlock with Greener crossbolt, black or chromed receiver, checkered walnut stock and forearm. Imported 1986-87 only.

$690	$560	$500	$450	$410	$375	$350	*$835*

F.S. 300 – 12 ga., trap or skeet model, 26, 30, or 32 in. separated barrels only, SST, ejectors, boxlock with Greener crossbolt and false side plates lightly engraved, chromed receiver, checkered walnut stock and forearm. Imported 1986 only.

$825	$675	$610	$555	$510	$470	$440	*$995*

F.S. 400 – 12 ga., trap or skeet model, 26, 30, or 32 in. separated barrels only, ST, ejectors, sidelock with Greener crossbolt, lightly engraved chromed receiver, checkered walnut stock and forearm. Imported 1986 only.

$1,145	$945	$860	$800	$740	$680	$620	*$1,360*

F.S. 500 – same specifications as F.S. 400. Importation disc. 1985.

$1,175	$950	$860	$795	$730	$660	$595	*$1,360*

SHOTGUNS: SxS

American Arms imported Spanish shotguns manufactured by Zabala Hermanos and Grulla. Older discontinued Diarm models will also be shown in this section.

GENTRY/YORK – 12, 16 (disc. 1990), 20, 28 ga., or .410 bore, 3 in. chambers, boxlock, ejectors (extractors after 1986), DT or SST (became standard in 1992), chromed receiver features fine scroll engraving, fixed chokes, pistol grip stock with recoil pad and beavertail forearm. Imported 1986-2000.

$625	$475	$375	$300	$280	$260	$240	*$750*

Add $45 for 28 ga. or .410 bore.

Before 1988 this model was designated York (case coloring began 1988, silver finish began 1993). DT were supplied with 28 ga. or .410 bore 1990-2000.

BRITTANY – 12 or 20 ga., boxlock action, 25 (20 ga. only, disc. 1996), 26, or 27 (12 ga. only, disc. 1996) in. barrels, SST, ejectors, matted solid rib, choke tubes, engraved case colored frame, checkered walnut straight grip stock with recoil pad and semi-beavertail forearm, 6 1/2 or 7 lbs. Imported 1989-2000.

$725	$575	$485	$435	$400	$375	$350	*$885*

The wood finish was changed in this model from oil to semi-gloss in 1991.

SHOGUN – 10 ga., 3 1/2 in. chambers, boxlock, ejectors, double triggers, chromed receiver features fine scroll engraving. Imported 1986 only.

$440	$350	$325	$300	$280	$260	$240	*$525*

DERBY – 12, 20, 28 (disc. 1991) ga., or .410 bore (disc. 1991) ga., 3 in. chambers, sidelock, ejectors, double (disc. 1989) or SNT, chromed receiver with fine scroll engraving, fixed chokes, straight grip walnut stock and forearm. Imported 1986-94.

$1,150	$975	$850	$750	$625	$500	$425	*$1,039*

Add 10% for 28 ga. or .410 bore (disc. 1991).
Subtract 10% for DT.
Add approx. 50%-60% for 2-barrel set (20 and 28 ga. - approx. 300 sets mfg.) - disc. 1990.

This model featured a case-colored receiver between 1988-90 and was changed to coin finish in late 1991. At the same time, the wood finish was changed from oil to semi-gloss.

GRADING - PPGS™	100%	98%	95%	90%	80%	70%	60%	LAST MSR

GRULLA NO. 2 – 12, 20, 28 ga., or .410 bore, hand fitted sidelock action, 26 or 28 in. barrels, DT, ejectors, fixed chokes, concave rib, case colored receiver with elaborate engraving, deluxe English-style straight stock and splinter forearm (checkered and hand rubbed), between 5 3/4-6 1/4 lbs. Imported 1989-2000.

Before going to a special order basis, this model retailed for $3,099 (1994).

This model was individually handcrafted with less than 800 mfg. each year.

* ***Grulla No. 2 Small Gauge Set*** – includes choice of 20/28 ga. or 28 ga./.410 bore barrel combination (26 in. fixed choke barrels). Imported 1989-95.

	$3,600	$3,000	$2,375	$2,000	$1,650	$1,325	$1,150	

Before going to a special order basis, this combination last retailed for $4,219 (1994/5).

WS/SS 10 WATERFOWL SPECIAL – 10 ga. only, 3 1/2 in. chambers, 32 in. barrels, DT, parkerized finish, sling swivels and camouflaged sling, extractors, fixed chokes, recoil pad, 11 lbs. 3 oz. Imported 1987-93.

	$560	$500	$440	$400	$375	$350	$325	*$639*

WT/SS 10 – 10 ga. only, 3 1/2 in. chambers, similar to TS/SS 12, except had 28 in. barrels with multi-chokes. Imported 1998-2000.

	$775	$650	$550	$450	$400	$375	$350	*$860*

TS/SS 10/12 TURKEY SPECIAL – 10 (disc. 1995) or 12 ga., 3 or 3 1/2 in. chambers (3 1/2 in. 12 ga. introduced in 1989), 26 in. barrels only, double triggers, parkerized finish, dull finish stock and forearm, sling swivels, recoil pad, choke tubes, 7 lbs. 6 oz. or 10 lbs. 13 oz. (10 ga.). Imported 1987-2000.

	$665	$550	$450	$400	$375	$350	$325	*$799*

This model in 12 ga. was supplied with a SST.

SHOTGUNS: SEMI-AUTO

PHANTOM FIELD – 12 ga. only, 3 in. chamber, gas operated, 24, 26, or 28 in. VR barrel with 3 choke tubes, black synthetic or checkered walnut stock and forearm, blue finish. Imported 1999-2000.

	$395	$360	$330	$275	$250	$225	$200	*$439*

* ***Phantom HP*** – similar to Phantom Field with synthetic stock and forearm, except had 19 in. threaded barrels for external choke tubes, swivel studs, and extended mag. Imported 1999-2000.

	$400	$365	$330	$275	$250	$225	$200	*$449*

SHOTGUNS: SINGLE SHOT

SINGLE SHOT MODEL – 12, 20 ga., or .410 bore, 3 in. chamber non-exposed hammer, pistol grip stock, non-reflective finish. Imported 1988-89 only.

	$90	$80	$70	$60	$55	$50	$45	*$99*

* ***Single Shot Model Camper Special*** – 12, 20 ga., or .410 bore, 3 in. chamber folding design, 21 in. barrel, pistol grip. Imported 1988-89 only.

	$95	$80	$70	$60	$55	$50	$45	*$107*

* ***Single Shot Model Slugger*** – 12 or 20 ga., 24 in. slug barrel with adj. rear and blade front sights, recoil pad. Imported 1989 only.

	$100	$85	$75	$65	$55	$50	$45	*$115*

* ***Single Shot Model Youth*** – 20 ga. or .410 bore, 26 in. barrel, 12 1/2 in. stock dimensions, recoil pad. Imported 1989 only.

	$100	$85	$75	$65	$55	$50	$45	*$115*

* ***Single Shot Model Combo*** – interchangeable rifle and shotgun barrels, choice of .22 Hornet/12 ga. with 28 in. barrel or .22 LR/20 ga. with 26 in. barrel, includes fitted hard case. Imported 1989 only.

	$195	$165	$130	$115	$100	$90	$80	*$235*

GRADING - PPGS™	100%	98%	95%	90%	80%	70%	60%	LAST MSR

* ***Single Shot Model 10 Ga.*** – 10 ga. only, 3 1/2 in. chambers, 26 in. multi-choke or 32 in. full fixed choke barrel, non-exposed hammer, non-reflective finish. Imported 1988-89 only.

	$135	$115	$95	$80	$70	$60	$55	*$149*

Add $30 for multi-chokes (26 in. barrel).

AMERICAN BARLOCK WONDER

Previous trademark manufactured by Crescent Arms for Sears Roebuck & Co.

SHOTGUNS: SxS

SIDE-BY-SIDE – various gauges, hammerless or outside hammer, damascus or steel barrels.

	$240	$225	$200	$175	$140	$100	$75	

Add 15% for steel barrels, smaller gauges.

SINGLE SHOT – various gauges, hammer, steel barrel.

	$185	$160	$140	$125	$115	$100	$90	

Add 35% for smaller gauges.

AMERICAN CLASSIC

Current trademark of pistols imported and distributed by Eagle Imports, Inc., located in Wanamassa, NJ. Please refer to listings in the Metro Arms section.

AMERICAN CUSTOM GUNMAKERS GUILD, INC. (ACGG)

The American Custom Gunmakers Guild is an organization of craftsmen who specialize in high quality custom work on firearms. Guild members share a common bond toward the betterment of fine custom firearms and the skills needed to achieve as near perfection in the field of gunmaking as possible.

There are two basic types of membership, Regular and Associate. Each Regular Member has passed an examination of his work by his fellow members as part of the application process. The privileges of Regular membership include the right to use the ACGG logo with the word "Member", use the ACGG Hallmark, vote at the annual meeting, the quarterly *Gunmaker* magazine, a discount on Guild publications, and the option to rent a display table at the annual show in Reno, NV. Current ACGG Regular members can be found by visiting the web site (see Trademark Index).

Associate membership is open to all who have an interest in custom guns. The benefits of Associate membership include free admission to the annual exhibition, the quarterly *Gunmaker* magazine, a membership card, and a discount on Guild publications.

The Guild's bylaws stress creative ability and practicing good business ethics.

The annual Firearms Engravers and Gunmakers Exhibition is the most visible activity of the ACGG. This winter event in Reno, Nevada offers the public the unique opportunity to see America's finest firearm craftsmanship and meet the individual makers (check www.acgg.org for more information, including dates). This gathering of ACGG members provides a forum to share technical expertise, honor exemplary work and accept and induct new members, and conduct association business.

The American Custom Gunmakers Guild has created a registry for custom guns which have been built by Guild members who Hallmark their work with the Guild logo. Certificates of Hallmark are provided by the Guild's Historian which describe and document the firearm's origin.

For collectors, these documents verify the work of a gunmaker through research of photographs, records, receipts, or other documentation.

For more information about this organization, please contact them directly (see Trademark Index).

AMERICAN DERRINGER CORPORATION

Current manufacturer located in Waco, TX since 1980. Distributor and dealer sales.

GRADING - PPGS™	100%	98%	95%	90%	80%	70%	60%	LAST MSR

DERRINGERS: STAINLESS STEEL

MODEL 1 – available in over 55 cals. including .22 LR through .45-70 Govt., also 2 1/2 in. .410 shot shell, O/U stainless steel derringer, top break action, satin or high polish finish, 3 in. barrels, automatic barrel selection, hammer block safety, 15 oz., spur trigger, rosewood grips. New 1980.

* ***Model 1 Rimfire Cals.*** – .22 LR or .22 WMR cal.

MSR $635	$550	$480	$415	$375	$305	$250	$195	

Add $75 for high polish finish.

* ***Model 1 Centerfire Cals.*** – many cals. between .32 H&R Mag. - .45-70 Govt. cal.

MSR $705	$625	$545	$470	$425	$345	$280	$220	

Add $75 for high polish finish.
Add approx. $30 for most common Mag. cals.
Subtract approx. $70 for .380 ACP or .38 SPL cals.
Add $170 for .223 Rem. (disc.) or $140 for .30-30 Win. cal. (disc. 2003).
Add approx. $140 for .22 Hornet (disc. 1989).

This model can be ordered with special ser. nos. and other custom features at additional cost(s).

* ***Model 1 Engraved*** – limited mfg., mostly special ordered.

Please contact the factory regarding a price quotation for this special order model.

* ***Model 1 Millennium 2000 Series*** – .45 LC/.410 shotshell only, 3 in. barrel, 15,000 mfg. beginning 1998 in various configurations including Gambler and Cowboy.

MSR $835	$700	$615	$525	$475	$385	$315	$245	

* ***Model 1 United We Stand Commemorative*** – .45 LC/.410 shotshell only, 3 in. barrel, choice of custom grips, includes red, white and blue presentation case. Limited mfg. 2002-2003.

	$355	$310	$265	$240	$195	$160	$125	*$450*

American Derringer Corporation donated a portion of the proceeds from this commemorative to the post-9/11 recovery effort.

LADY DERRINGER – available in various cals. between .22 LR - .45 LC, and .45 LC/.410 shotshell cal., current cals include .32 H&R Mag., .357 Mag., .38 Spl., .45 LC, and .45 LC/.410 shotshell, O/U top break action, 3 in. barrel, high polish stainless steel, spur trigger, scrimshawed synthetic ivory grips, handfitted action allowing easy cocking, with French styled leatherette display case, 15 1/2 oz. New 1990.

MSR $835	$700	$615	$525	$475	$385	$315	$245	

* ***Lady Derringer Deluxe Engraved*** – similar to Deluxe Grade, except hand engraved with circa 1880 patterns. Disc. 1994.

	$650	$570	$490	$440	$360	$295	$230	*$750*

Mother-of-pearl grips and personalized engraving were available as extra cost options on this model.

* ***Lady Derringer 14Kt. Gold Engraved*** – entire Derringer manufactured out of a 14Kt. gold bar (contains approx. 20 oz. of 14Kt. gold and 3 oz. of stainless steel), custom engraved with diamond sights, special order only until late 1993.

Last MSR was $100,000

Extreme rarity precludes accurate pricing on this model.

* ***Millenium Lady Derringer*** – similar to Model 1 Millenium 2000 Series. Disc.

	$390	$340	$295	$265	$215	$175	$135	*$470*

LADY DERRINGER II – .22 LR (disc.), .32 ACP (disc.), .38 Spl., or .22 WMR (disc.) cal., O/U pivot design, double action, aluminum frame, trigger guard stops at trigger bottom, 1/2 lb. Mfg. 1999-2003.

	$395	$345	$295	$270	$215	$180	$140	*$480*

GRADING - PPGS™	100%	Issue Price	Qty. Made

MODEL 1 TEXAS COMMEMORATIVE – .38 Spl., .44-40, or .45 LC cal., similar to Model 1 except has brass frame, stainless steel barrel, and stag grips.

.44-40 cal	$575	$440	N/A
.45 cal.	$575	$470	N/A
.32 Mag	$375	$255	500+
.38 Spl.	$375	$385	N/A
.22 LR (mfg. 1991-92)	$350	$238	500
.41 Rimfire (not shootable)	$300	$295	500
Fully engraved model	$795	$750	limited

GRADING - PPGS™	100%	98%	95%	90%	80%	70%	60%	LAST MSR

* ***Model 1 Texas Commemorative (Current Mfg.)*** – .38 Spl., .44-40 WCF, or .45 LC cal.

MSR $835	$700	$615	$525	$475	$385	$315	$245	

Add $75 for special serial number on the .45 LC cal. model.

GRADING - PPGS™	100%	Issue Price	Qty. Made

125TH ANNIVERSARY – special edition 125th anniversary variation with pistol case. Disc. 1993.

.44-40 or .45 cal.	$395	$320	500
.38 Spl.	$325	$225	500
Deluxe engraved model	$795	$750	limited

GRADING - PPGS™	100%	98%	95%	90%	80%	70%	60%	LAST MSR

MODEL 3 – .32 Mag. (new 1990 - limited availability) or .38 Spl. cal., single shot, 2 1/2 in. barrel, 8 1/2 oz., spur trigger, rosewood grips. Disc. 1994.

	$95	$85	$70	$65	$50	$45	$35	*$120*

MODEL 4 – .357 Mag., .357 Max., .44 Mag. (disc. 2003), .45 ACP, .45-70 Govt. (disc. 2003), 45 LC/.410 shotshell (new 2013), or .45 LC cal. on upper barrel, 3 in. .410 shotshell lower barrel, O/U derringer combination pistol, 4 1/10 in. barrel, rosewood grips, 16 1/2 oz. New 1985.

MSR $760	$665	$580	$500	$450	$365	$300	$235	

Add $110 for oversized grips.
Add $105 for .44 Mag. cal. (oversized grips became standard 1997, disc. 2003).
Add $150 for .45-70 Govt. cal. in both barrels (disc. 2003).
This model was also available on special order in either .50-70 or .50 Saunders cal. (new 1989 - single shot only). MSR was $395.

* ***Model 4 Engraved*** – .45 LC/.410 shotshell cal., allow 12 weeks for delivery. New 1997.

Please contact the factory directly for a price quotation on this special order model.

* ***Model 4 Alaskan Survival Model*** – similar to Model 4, except .45-70 Govt. cal. top barrel, and choice of .44 Mag. (disc.), .45 LC, or .45 LC/.410 shotshell lower barrel.

MSR $870	$725	$635	$525	$475	$385	$315	$245	

Add $90 for high polish finish.

MODEL 6 – .22 WMR (disc.), .357 Mag., .45 LC, .45 ACP, or .45 LC/.410 shotshell cal., O/U, 6 in. barrel, available in high polish, satin (disc. 1994) , or grey matte finish (standard), 21 oz. New 1986.

MSR $870	$740	$650	$555	$505	$405	$335	$260	

Add $100 for high polish finish.
Add $13 for satin finish (disc. 1994).
Add $50 for oversized grips (disc. 1994, reinstated 1998-99).

* ***Model 6 Engraved*** – .45 LC/.410 shotshell cal., allow 12 weeks for delivery. New 1997.

Please contact the factory directly for a price quotation on this special order model.

GRADING - PPGS™	100%	98%	95%	90%	80%	70%	60%	LAST MSR

MODEL 7 – .22 LR (disc.), .22 WMR (mfg. 1992-2003), .32 H&R Mag. (disc.), .38 Spl., .38 S&W (disc. 1989), .380 ACP, (disc.) or .44 Spl. cal., O/U, same basic specifications as Model 1, except ultra lightweight (7 1/2 oz.). Disc. 2011.

	$575	$505	$430	$390	$315	$260	$200	*$705*

Add $105 for .44 Spl. (reintroduced 2008).

MODEL 8 – .45 LC/.410 shotshell cal., O/U, 8 in. barrel, nickel finish, grooved grips, 24 oz. New 1997.

MSR $915	$725	$625	$520	$475	$380	$315	$245	

Add $150 for high polish finish.

* ***Model 8 Engraved*** – .45 LC/.410 shotshell cal. Limited mfg. 1997-98 only.

	$1,675	$1,465	$1,255	$1,140	$920	$755	$585	*$1,917*

MODEL 10 – .38 Spl. (new 1995), .45 ACP, .45 LC, or .45 LC/.410 shotshell (disc. 1997), O/U, 3 in. barrels, aluminum grip frame and barrels, matte grey finish, 7 1/2 oz. Mfg. 1988-2011.

	$525	$460	$395	$355	$290	$235	$185	*$660*

Add $45 for .45 LC or .45 ACP cal.

MODEL 11 – .22 LR (mfg. 1995-2003), .22 WMR (mfg. 1995-2003), .32 H&R Mag. (mfg. 1995-2003), .380 ACP (mfg. 1995-2003), or .38 Spl. cal., same basic specifications as Model 1, aluminum barrel, matte grey finish, only 11 oz. Disc. 2011.

	$525	$460	$395	$355	$290	$235	$185	*$660*

RIMFIRE DOUBLE ACTION – .22 LR or .22 WMR cal., 3 1/2 in. O/U barrels, double action trigger, dual extractors, hammerless, blue finish with black synthetic grips, 11 oz. Mfg. 1990-1995.

	$145	$125	$110	$100	$80	$65	$50	*$170*

This O/U Derringer was patterned after the original High Standard design.

DS22 – .22 WMR cal., 3 in. barrel, stainless steel with blue finish, 11 oz. Special order beginning 1998.

Please contact the factory directly for a price quotation on this model.

DA 38 DOUBLE ACTION – .22 LR (mfg. 1996-2003), .357 Mag. (new 1991), .38 Spl., 9mm Para., or .40 S&W (mfg. 1993-2012) cal., 3 in. O/U barrels, satin stainless steel with aluminum grip frame, double action trigger design, hammerblock thumb safety, choice of checkered rosewood, walnut, or other hardwood grips, 14 1/2 oz. New 1990.

MSR $690	$575	$505	$430	$390	$315	$260	$200	

Add $50 for .357 Mag. or .40 S&W (disc. 2012) cal.

Add $15 for Lady Derringer Model (scrimshawed synthetic ivory grips, .38 Spl. only. Mfg. 1992-94).

MINI-COP – .22 WMR cal., 4 shot double action design, stainless steel construction, patterned after the original Mini-Cop mfg. in Torrance, CA. Mfg. 1990-94.

	$250	$220	$190	$170	$140	$115	$90	*$313*

4-BARREL DERRINGER – .22 LR, .38 Spl., or .357 Mag. cal., double action, similar design to Mini-Cop, semi-matte finish, 28 oz. While advertised beginning 1991 at $425, only a few prototypes were manufactured during 1997.

CUSTOM TARGET MODELS – .38 Spl. Wadcutter or 9mm Federal (disc.) cal., mfg. for End of Trail Derringer Match, limited production. Mfg. 1990-92.

	$695	$610	$520	$475	$380	$315	$245	*$750*

PISTOLS: PEN DESIGN

MODEL 2 PEN PISTOL – .22 LR, .25 ACP, or .32 ACP cal., unique hinged action allows pen to be converted into a legal pistol within two seconds, folding design, 2 in. barrel, cocks on opening action, firing pin block and grip safeties, brushed stainless finish, 5 oz. Mfg. 1993-1994.

	$500	$450	$425	$375	$350	$325	$300	*$203*

Add $150 for .32 ACP cal.

Add $100 for .25 ACP.

GRADING - PPGS™	100%	98%	95%	90%	80%	70%	60%	LAST MSR

PISTOLS: SEMI-AUTO

STANDARD MODEL

* ***Standard Model .25 Mag. Cal.*** – .25 Mag. cal., semi-auto single action, less than 100 manufactured in stainless steel only.

	$500	$440	$375	$340	$275	$225	$175	

* ***Standard Model .25 ACP Cal.*** – .25 ACP cal., semi-auto single action, less than 400 manufactured in stainless steel, less than 50 in blue steel.

Stainless	$400	$350	$300	$270	$220	$180	$140	
Blue	$550	$480	$415	$375	$305	$250	$195	

LM-5 – .25 ACP, .32 H&R Mag. (disc. 1997, reintroduced 2008), or .380 ACP (mfg. 1998-99) cal., compact stainless semi-auto, single action, 2 1/4 in. barrel, hammerless, wood grips, 4 (.32 Mag. or .380 ACP) or 5 (.25 ACP) shot mag., 15 oz. Limited mfg. since 1997.

MSR $710	$600	$525	$450	$410	$330	$270	$210	

* ***LM-5 .380 ACP*** – limited mfg., disc. 1999.

	$365	$320	$275	$250	$200	$165	$130	*$425*

PISTOLS: SLIDE-ACTION

LM-4 (SEMMERLING) – .45 ACP cal., 2 in. barrel, super compact, thumb activated slide mechanism, blue finish, 4 shot mag., 24 oz., very limited manufacture since 1998.

MSR $4,250	$3,800	$3,500	$3,100	$2,625	$2,375	$1,925	$1,575	

AMERICAN FIREARMS MANUFACTURING CO., INC.

Previous manufacturer located in San Antonio, TX between 1972 and 1974.

DERRINGERS

AMERICAN .38 SPL. – .38 Spl. cal., O/U configuration, approx. 3,000-4,000 mfg. 1972-74.

	$200	$165	$135	$110	$90	$75	$65	

AMERICAN .380 AUTOMATIC – .380 ACP cal., 8 shot, 3 1/2 in. barrel, stainless steel, smooth walnut grips, approx. 10 mfg. 1972-74.

	$700	$500	$300	$240	$210	$180	$155	

PISTOLS: SEMI-AUTO

AMERICAN .25 AUTOMATIC – .25 ACP cal., 8 shot, 2 1/10 in. barrel, smooth walnut grips. Mfg. 1966-74.

Stainless	$195	$180	$165	$140	$120	$110	$95	
Blue	$165	$150	$140	$120	$100	$90	$85	

AMERICAN FRONTIER FIREARMS MFG., INC.

Previous manufacturer located in Aguanga, CA 1995-2000.

American Frontier Firearms Mfg., Inc. manufactured a line of replica metallic cartridge firing revolvers (black powder or smokeless). These revolvers were manufactured in .22 LR, .32 Spl., .38 Spl., .44 Russian, or .45 LC. During 2000, AFF developed a new cartridge, the .44 A.F.F. It could be used in revolvers firing .44-40 WCF, .44 Russian, .44 Spl., and .44 Mag. It also met S.A.S.S. specifications.

REVOLVERS: CARTRIDGE CONVERSIONS & OPEN TOPS

Production on these models was mid-1997 through 2000. Revolvers were supplied with standard finish high polish blue steel parts, color case hardened hammer and/or trigger, silver plated or blue backstrap and trigger guard, and varnished walnut grips. Special orders were also available featuring simulated ivory grips, special finishes, and engraving options. Some models and variations had very limited production, due to problems procuring high quality parts.

GRADING - PPGS™	100%	98%	95%	90%	80%	70%	60%	LAST MSR

1851 NAVY RICHARDS CONVERSION – .38 Spl., .38 LC, .44 Russian, or .44-40 WCF cal., 4 3/4, 5 1/2, or 7 1/2 in. octagon barrel, roll engraved cylinder, blue finish, varnished walnut grips. No ejector rod.

	$695	$550	$375	$325	$295	$265	$235	*$795*

1851 NAVY RICHARDS & MASON CONVERSION – .38 Spl., .38 LC, .44 Russian, or .44-40 WCF cal., 4 3/4, 5 1/2, or 7 1/2 in. octagon barrel with Mason ejector assembly, roll engraved cylinder, blue finish, varnished walnut grips.

	$695	$550	$375	$325	$295	$265	$235	*$795*

1858 REMINGTON NEW ARMY CAVALRY MODEL – .38 Spl., .44-40 WCF, or .45 LC cal., 7 1/2 in. barrel with ejector assembly, blue finish, color case hardened hammer, varnished walnut grips.

	$715	$575	$475	$375	$325	$275	$225	*$795*

1858 REMINGTON NEW ARMY ARTILLERY MODEL – .38 Spl., .44-40 WCF, or .45 LC cal., 5 1/2 in. barrel with ejector assembly, blue finish, color case hardened hammer, varnished walnut grips.

	$715	$575	$475	$375	$325	$275	$225	*$795*

1858 REMINGTON ORIGINAL FACTORY-TYPE CONVERSION – .38 Spl., .44-40 WCF, or .45 LC cal., 5 1/2 or 7 1/2 in. barrels, original loading lever and no gate or ejector assembly, blue finish, color case hardened hammer, varnished walnut grips.

	$715	$575	$475	$375	$325	$275	$225	*$795*

POCKET REMINGTON – .22 LR, .32 S&W Short, or .38 Spl. cal., 3 1/2 in. barrel with or without ejector rod or gate, blue finish, color case hardened hammer, varnished walnut grips.

	$425	$375	$325	$275	$225	$185	$165	*$495*

1860 ARMY RICHARDS CONVERSION – .38 Spl., .38 LC, or .44-40 WCF cal., 4 3/4, 5 1/2, or 7 1/2 in. round barrel, with or without ejector assembly, roll engraved cylinder, blue finish, silver plated trigger guard, varnished walnut grips.

	$695	$550	$375	$325	$295	$265	$235	*$795*

1861 NAVY RICHARDS CONVERSION – .38 Spl., or .38 LC cal., 4 1/2 or 7 1/2 in. round barrel with ejector assembly, blue finish, silver plated backstrap and trigger guard, varnished walnut grips.

	$695	$550	$375	$325	$295	$265	$235	*$795*

POCKET NAVY RICHARDS & MASON CONVERSION – .32 S&W Short cal., 4 1/2 in. octagon barrel with ejector assembly, blue finish, silver plated backstrap and trigger guard, color case hardened trigger and hammer, varnished walnut grips.

	$465	$375	$325	$275	$225	$185	$165	*$495*

1871-72 OPEN-TOP FRONTIER MODEL – .38 Spl., .38 LC, or .44-40 WCF cal., 4 3/4, 5 1/2, or 7 1/2 in. round barrel with ejector assembly, blue finish, varnished walnut grips.

	$695	$550	$375	$325	$295	$265	$235	*$795*

* ***1871-72 Open-Top Tiffany Model*** – similar to 1871-72 Standard Model, except has engraved gold/silver finished Tiffany grips and also available with 4 3/4 in. barrel. Mfg. 2001.

	$995	$895	$700	$525	$450	$395	$350	*$1,200*

AMERICAN GUN CO.

Previous trademark manufactured by Crescent Firearms Co. and distributed by H. & D. Folsom Co.

REVOLVERS

REVOLVER – .32 S&W cal., 5 shot, double action, top-break frame.

	N/A	$175	$160	$140	$120	$95	$65	

GRADING - PPGS™	100%	98%	95%	90%	80%	70%	60%	*LAST MSR*

SHOTGUNS: SxS

SxS – various gauges, hammer or hammerless, damascus, or steel barrels.

	N/A	$265	$240	$225	$200	$175	$140	

Add 15% for small gauges or steel barrels.

AMERICAN GUN COMPANY, LLC

Current rifle and action manufacturer located in Kalispell, MT. Consumer direct sales through FFL.

RIFLES

American Gun Company, LLC manufactures high quality reproductions of the Model 1885 High Wall single shot in .38-55 WCF, .38-56 WCF, .45-70 Govt., .45-90 WCF, .444 Marlin, or .405 Win. cal. The High Wall is available in four variations - the Classic (2010 MSR was $1,250), the Sportsman (2010 MSR was $1,350), the Montanan (2010 MSR was $1,450), and the Pro-Hunter (2010 MSR was $1,550).

Additionally, Model 1885 barreled actions are available - 2010 starting MSR was $1,050.

American Gun Company, LLC also manufactures excellent quality bolt action rifles in calibers ranging from .17 - .375 H&H. Models include the KS 23 ($1,079 was 2010 starting MSR), the KS 57 (disc. 2010, last MSR was $1,089), and the AGC 96 (disc. 2010, last MSR was $1,150). A wide variety of options are available, including custom engraving, wood stock and checkering, barrel lengths and finishes. Barreled actions are also available - 2010 starting MSR was $989.

Since guns are made per customer specifications, please contact the company directly for a price quotation and delivery time (see Trademark Index).

AMERICAN HISTORICAL FOUNDATION, THE

Current organization which privately commissions historical commemoratives in conjunction with leading manufacturers and craftsmen around the world. The Foundation is located in Ashland, VA. Previously located in Richmond, VA. During 2005, the assets of the Foundation were acquired by America Remembers, located in Ashland, VA. Direct-to-consumer sales only. Delivery to local FFL holder.

The Foundation's limited/special edition models are not all manufactured at one time. Rather, guns are fabricated as demand dictates. Limited editions include guns by Colt, Winchester, Browning, Dan Wesson, Auto-Ordnance/Thompson, Sturm Ruger, Holland & Holland, Walther, Smith & Wesson, Mauser, and Beretta.

LIMITED/SPECIAL EDITIONS

AHF consumers include members, history buffs, veterans, museums, and other interested parties who normally keep these items for a considerable time period. Very few are sold in the secondary marketplace annually. Because of this consumer direct sales program, many non-AHF consumers and gun dealers do not have a working knowledge on current pricing for AHF firearms.

The publisher suggests that those people who want more information about American Historical Foundation's Commemorative Issue firearms contact AHF directly (see Trademark Index), or visit their website: www.ahffirearms.com. Additionally, information on most AHF offerings manufactured between 1988 and 1997 can be found in the 20th and earlier editions of the *Blue Book of Gun Values*, as well as online (free of charge) at www.bluebookofgunvalues.com.

AMERICAN HUNTING RIFLES, INC. (AHR)

Current manufacturer established in 1998 and located in Corvallis, MT since 2007. Previously located in Hamilton, MT, 1998-2006.

RIFLES: BOLT ACTION

CLASSIC 550 – standard and various Howell proprietary cals., CZ-550 double square bridge standard action, controlled feed claw extractor, 25 in. chrome-moly or stainless steel

GRADING - PPGS™	100%	98%	95%	90%	80%	70%	60%	LAST MSR

sporter barrel, blue finish, black fiberglass or optional walnut stock with Decelerator recoil pad. Mfg. 1999-2009.

	$1,725	$1,375	$1,075	$900	$775	$650	$550	$1,895

Add $75 for stainless steel barrel.
Add $220 for integral and removable muzzle brake, with protective cap.

VARMINT 550 PRO - .220 Howell, .220 Swift, .22-250 Rem., .30-06, or .308 Win. cal., CZ-550 double square bridge standard action, 26 in. stainless heavy barrel, SST, black fiberglass stock with Decelerator recoil pad. Mfg. 2001-2007.

	$1,650	$1,325	$1,050	$900	$775	$650	$550	$1,795

SAFARI 550 - various Mag. cals., similar to Classic 550, except has Magnum action with integral scope mounts, oil finished fancy walnut stock, trigger guard safety. Mfg. 2001-2011.

	$1,725	$1,375	$1,075	$900	$775	$650	$550	$1,895

SAFARI 550 DGR - various standard Mag. cals. from .375 H&H - .600 Overkill, similar to Safari 550, except has 3-position safety, AAA extra fancy wood, and banded front sling attachment. New 2001.

MSR $6,200	$5,750	$5,100	$4,500	$3,950	$3,500	$3,000	$2,500	

Pricing is for base model only.
Add $500 for cals. .50 and larger.
Add $1,000 for left-hand action.
Add $500 for center feed box magazine in select calibers.

600 OK - .600 Overkill cal., features modified CZ magnum action built by Granite Arms, bull barrel with muzzle brake, deluxe English walnut stock.

Please contact the company directly for a price quotation on this model.

.700 AHR - .700 AHR cal., Granite Mt. Arms magnum action, hand checkered AAA fancy walnut stock, African blackwood forend tip and grip cap, fixed folding sight, AHR X-brake, custom serial number, custom hand engraving, custom LOP. Limited mfg. beginning 2008.

Prices for this model start at $11,500.

AHR BIG GAME - cals. up to 9.3x62, synthetic stock, built to order on modified CZ-550 action. New 2009.

MSR $2,795	$2,450	$2,000	$1,750	$1,500	$1,250	$1,050	$900	

AMERICAN INDUSTRIES

Please refer to the Calico section in this text.

AMERICAN INTERNATIONAL CORP.

Previous manufacturer and importer located in Salt Lake City, UT, circa 1972-1984. American International was a wholly owned subsidiary of ARDCO (American Research & Development). ARDCO's previous name was American Mining & Development. American International imported firearms from Voere, located in Kufstein, Austria. American Arms International (AAI) was another subsidiary of ARDCO.

In 1979, after American International Corp. had dissolved, AAI resumed production using mostly Voere parts. After running out of Voere parts, late production featured U.S. mfg. receivers (can be recognized by not having a pivoting barrel retainer slotted on the bottom of the receiver). American Arms International declared bankruptcy in 1984.

CARBINES: SEMI-AUTO

AMERICAN 180 AUTO CARBINE (M-1) - .22 LR cal., a specialized design for paramilitary use, 177 round drum mag., 16 1/2 in. barrel, aperture sight, high impact plastic stock and forearm, aluminum alloy receiver with black finish. Semi-auto variation mfg. 1979-c.1984. Total Voere production (denoted by A prefix serial number) between 1972 and 1979 was 2,300 carbines (includes both full and semi-auto versions). Later mfg. was marked either M-1 (semi-auto) or M-2 (fully auto). "B" serial number prefix was introduced in 1980, and barrel markings were changed to "Amer Arms Intl, SLC, UT."

	$725	$600	$475	$375	$350	$325	$295	

Add $550 for Laser Lok System - first commercially available laser sighting system.
Add approx. $300 for extra drum mag. and winder (fragile and subject to breakage).

AMERICAN LEGACY FIREARMS

Current company located in Ft. Collins, CO.

American Legacy Firearms specializes in special/limited edition firearms which are based on many popular makes/models. Please contact the company directly for more information, including pricing and model availability (see Trademark Index).

AMERICAN LEGENDS

Previous trademark of some handguns manufactured by IAI. Please refer to the IAI section in this text.

AMERICAN PRECISION ARMS

Current manufacturer established in 2001, and located in Jefferson, GA.

In addition to rifles, American Precision Arms offered a shotgun modification service on customer supplied Remington 870s. Prices began at $1,395. Please contact the company directly for more information on the wide lineup of available options and configurations (see Trademark Index).

RIFLES: BOLT ACTION

Current tactical models include the Critter Get'R ($4,200 MSR), Meat stick ($4,245 MSR, new 2013), Paragon ($6,175 MSR, new 2013), and the Do it ALL APR ($4,085 MSR). Previously, the company offered the .308 Raven (disc. 2011, last MSR was $3,395), and the Revelation Tactical Rifle (disc. 2011, last MSR was $3,995), Genesis Tactical Rifle (disc. 2010, last MSR was $2,450). Hunting models are also available, and previous models included the Revelation Hunter (disc. 2010, last MSR was $3,450), and the Genesis Hunter (disc. 2010, last MSR was $2,450). All MSRs are considered base price. Many options and custom services are also available.

RIFLES: SEMI-AUTO

Previous AR-15 style models included the Lycan (disc. 2011, last MSR was $3,450), the Urban Sniper .223 (disc. 2011, last MSR was $2,450), and the Urban Sniper .308 (disc. 2011, last MSR was $3,098). All MSRs reflected base pricing. Many options and custom services were also available.

RIFLES: TARGET

American Precision Arms also builds custom target rifles per customer's specifications. All models are POR, and a wide variety of options are available.

AMERICAN SPIRIT ARMS

Current manufacturer established circa 1995, and located in Scottsdale, AZ.

PISTOLS: SEMI-AUTO

American Spirit Arms offers a 5.56 NATO cal. AR-15 style pistol in either flat-top ($1,500 MSR) or A2 fixed carry handle (disc. 2012, last MSR was $1,199) configuration. A 9mm Para. cal. pistol is also available in flat-top ($1,650 MSR) or fixed carry handle (disc. 2012, last MSR was $1,299) configuration.

RIFLES/CARBINES: SEMI-AUTO

American Spirit Arms manufactures a wide variety of AR-15 style semi-auto carbines and rifles based on the AR-15, M16, and the M4 in 5.56 NATO, .223 Rem., 9mm Para., and .308 Win. cal. A complete line of options, accessories and parts are available. Base models are listed. Additionally, ASA has a Custom Shop for custom order rifles only built to customer specifications. Please contact the company directly regarding pricing for options and accessories (see Trademark Index).

IMPORTANT NOTE: On model(s) where *N/A has replaced the normal 100% value, it indicates current market conditions are too unstable to accurately ascertain 100%-60% values. Factory retail prices (MSRs) reflect most recent updates. For more up-to-date information on current pricing trends and additional useful information, please visit www.bluebookofgunvalues.com, select "Information & Services " from the menu, and click on "Additional Book Information".

GRADING - PPGS™	100%	98%	95%	90%	80%	70%	60%	LAST MSR

ASA-A2 RIFLE – 5.56 NATO cal., 20 in. barrel, fixed carry handle, fixed (A2) buttstock.

MSR $1,125 *N/A $875 $775 $675 $575 $500 $450

ASA-A320(G) RIFLE – 5.56 NATO cal., 20 in. barrel, choice of flat top or fixed carry handle, gas rifle length handguard and A2 stock, choice of A2 sight or gas block.

MSR $1,400 *N/A $1,100 $950 $825 $725 $625 $525

ASA-M4A2 CARBINE – 5.56 NATO cal., 16 in. barrel, fixed carry handle, collapsible stock.

MSR $1,125 *N/A $875 $775 $675 $575 $500 $450

ASA-M4A3 CARBINE – 5.56 NATO cal., flat-top with 16 in. barrel, 6-position collapsible stock, with (ASA-M4A3G) or without gas block.

MSR $1,400 *N/A $1,100 $950 $825 $725 $625 $525

Add $20 for mid-length handguard.

ASA-M4CS1 CARBINE – 5.56 NATO cal., 16 in. M4 profile barrel, flat top receiver, 10 in. Samson Evo Rail, low profile gas block, Ergo grip, MagPul MOE stock and trigger guard, black or flat dark earth furniture. New 2013.

MSR $1,640 *N/A $1,350 $1,175 $1,025 $900 $800 $700

ASA-M4CS2 CARBINE – 5.56 NATO cal., 16 in. M4 profile barrel with A2 flash hider, flat top receiver, MI Gen 2 drop in rail, MagPul MOE stock, grip, and trigger guard, choice of A2 front sight or gas block, choice of FDE or OD Green furniture. New 2013.

MSR $1,640 *N/A $1,350 $1,175 $1,025 $900 $800 $700

ASA-DISSIPATOR CARBINE – 5.56 NATO cal., fixed carry handle, 16 in. barrel, with (A2) or w/o (A3G) gas block, Magpul MOE handguard and six position stock, flat top receiver, dissipator CAR length gas system.

MSR $1,500 *N/A $1,125 $1,000 $875 $775 $675 $575

ASA-SPR – 5.56 NATO cal., 18 in. stainless steel heavy profile barrel with A2 flash hider, flat top receiver, low profile gas block, 12 in. Samson Evo rail, two stage trigger, Ergo grip, MOE trigger guard, VLTOR Emod stock. New 2013.

MSR $1,950 *N/A $1,600 $1,400 $1,200 $1,000 $800 $675

ASA-9mm CARBINE – 9mm Para. cal., fixed carry handle, 16 in. barrel, collapsible stock. Disc. 2012.

*N/A $975 $850 $750 $625 $550 $500 *$1,275*

ASA-9mm A3G CARBINE – 9mm Para. cal., 16 in. barrel, flat-top, gas block, collapsible stock.

MSR $1,600 *N/A $1,275 $1,100 $995 $875 $775 $675

ASA-BULL A3 CARBINE – 5.56 NATO cal., 16 in. bull barrel, flat-top, choice of six position or A2 stock.

MSR $1,650 *N/A $1,300 $1,100 $900 $800 $70 $600

ASA-BULL A3 RIFLE – 5.56 NATO cal., 24 in. bull barrel, fixed buttstock. Disc. 2012.

*N/A $1,150 $1,000 $875 $750 $625 $500 *$1,475*

ASA-BULL SIDE CHARGER CARBINE/RIFLE – .223 Rem. cal., 16 (carbine) or 24 (rifle) in. bull stainless steel barrel, features left side charger, Magpul PRS stock with circular free floating handguard with gas block. Disc. 2012.

*N/A $1,375 $1,175 $1,000 $875 $775 $675 *$1,725*

ASA-308 SIDE CHARGER CARBINE/RIFLE – .308 Win. cal., flat-top receiver with Picatinny rail, 16 (standard-disc. 2012 or bull - new 2013), 20 (bull) or 24 (disc. 2011) in. bull barrel, full length quad rail became standard 2012, Hogue grip, two-stage trigger, MagPul CTR stock, includes two 20 shot AR-10 mags.

MSR $2,600 *N/A $2,100 $1,800 41,500 $1,250 $1,000 $850

Add $450 for 20 in. bull barrel.

Subtract approx. $600 if without full length quad rail.

GRADING - PPGS™	100%	98%	95%	90%	80%	70%	60%	LAST MSR

AMERICAN SPIRIT ARMS CORP.

Previous rifle and components manufacturer 1998-2005, and located in Tempe, AZ. Previously located in Scottsdale, AZ.

RIFLES: SEMI-AUTO

IMPORTANT NOTE: On model(s) where *N/A has replaced the normal 100% value, it indicates current market conditions are too unstable to accurately ascertain 100%-60% values. Factory retail prices (MSRs) reflect most recent updates. For more up-to-date information on current pricing trends and additional useful information, please visit www.bluebookofgunvalues.com, select "Information & Services" from the menu, and click on "Additional Book Information".

Add $25 for green furniture, $65 for black barrel finish, $75 for fluted barrel, $125 for porting, $119 for two-stage match trigger, and $55 for National Match sights on .223 cal. models listed below.

ASA 24 IN. BULL BARREL FLAT-TOP RIFLE – .223 Rem. cal., patterned after AR-15, forged steel lower receiver, forged aluminum flattop upper receiver, 24 in. stainless steel bull barrel, free floating aluminum handguard, includes Harris bipod. Mfg. 1999-2005.

*N/A	$700	$625	$550	$500	$450	$400	*$950*

ASA 24 IN. BULL BARREL A2 RIFLE – similar to ASA Bull Barrel Flat-top, except features A2 upper receiver with carrying handle and sights. Mfg. 1999-2005.

*N/A	$725	$650	$565	$500	$450	$400	*$980*

OPEN MATCH RIFLE – .223 Rem. cal., 16 in. fluted and ported stainless steel match barrel with round shroud, flattop without sights, forged upper and lower receiver, two-stage match trigger, upgraded pistol grip, individually tested, USPSA/IPSC open class legal. Mfg. 2001-2005.

*N/A	$1,100	$950	$825	$725	$650	$525	*$1,500*

LIMITED MATCH RIFLE – .223 Rem. cal., 16 in. fluted stainless steel match barrel with round shroud with staggered hand grip, National Match front and rear sights, two-stage match trigger, upgraded pistol grip, individually tested, USPSA/IPSC open class legal. Mfg. 2001-2005.

*N/A	$975	$825	$725	$650	$525	$475	*$1,300*

DCM SERVICE RIFLE – .223 Rem. cal., 20 in. stainless steel match barrel with ribbed free floating shroud, National Match front and rear sights, two-stage match trigger, pistol grip, individually tested. Mfg. 2001-2005.

*N/A	$975	$825	$725	$650	$525	$475	*$1,300*

ASA 16 IN. M4 RIFLE – .223 Rem. cal., features non-collapsible stock and M4 handguard, 16 in. barrel with muzzle brake, aluminum flat-top upper receiver. Mfg. 2002-2005.

*N/A	$700	$625	$525	$450	$400	$350	*$905*

ASA 20 IN. A2 RIFLE – .223 Rem. cal., features A2 receiver and 20 in. National Match barrel. Mfg. 1999-2005.

*N/A	$640	$565	$500	$425	$350	$300	*$820*

ASA CARBINE WITH SIDE CHARGING RECEIVER – .223 Rem. cal., features aluminum side charging flattop upper receiver, M4 handguard, 16 in. NM barrel with slotted muzzle brake. Mfg. 2002-2004.

*N/A	$750	$650	$565	$500	$450	$400	*$970*

C.A.R. POST-BAN 16 IN. CARBINE – .223 Rem. cal., non-collapsible stock, Wilson 16 in. National Match barrel. Mfg. 1999-2005.

*N/A	$650	$575	$500	$450	$400	$350	*$830*

ASA 16 IN. BULL BARREL A2 INVADER – .223 Rem. cal., similar to ASA 24 in. Bull Barrel rifle, except has 16 in. stainless steel barrel. Mfg. 1999-2005.

*N/A	$725	$630	$550	$500	$450	$400	*$955*

GRADING - PPGS™	100%	98%	95%	90%	80%	70%	60%	LAST MSR

ASA 9MM A2 CAR CARBINE – 9mm Para. cal., forged upper and lower receiver, non-collapsible CAR stock, 16 in. Wilson heavy barrel w/o muzzle brake, with birdcage flash hider (pre-ban) or muzzle brake (post-ban), includes 9mm conversion block, 25 shot modified Uzi mag. Mfg. 2002-2005.

	*N/A	$725	$630	$550	$500	$450	$400	*$950*

Add $550 per extra 25 shot mag.

ASA 9MM FLAT-TOP CAR RIFLE – 9mm Para. cal., similar to A2 CAR Rifle, except has flat-top w/o sights. Mfg. 2002-2005.

	*N/A	$725	$630	$550	$500	$450	$400	*$950*

ASA 16 IN. TACTICAL RIFLE – .308 Win. cal., 16 in. stainless steel air gauged regular or match barrel, side charging handle, Hogue pistol grip, guaranteed 1/2 in. MOA accuracy, individually tested, 8 3/4 lbs. Mfg. 2002-2005.

	*N/A	$1,200	$995	$850	$750	$650	$525	*$1,675*

Add $515 for Match Rifle (includes fluted and ported barrel, 2 stage trigger, and hard chromed bolt and carrier).

ASA 24 IN. MATCH RIFLE – .308 Win. cal., 24 in. stainless steel air gauged match barrel with or w/o fluting/porting, side charging handle, Hogue pistol grip, guaranteed 1/2 in. MOA accuracy, individually tested, approx. 12 lbs. Mfg. 2002-2005.

	*N/A	$1,200	$995	$850	$750	$650	$525	*$1,675*

Add $515 for Match Rifle (includes fluted and ported barrel, 2 stage trigger, and hard chromed bolt and carrier).

AMERICAN TACTICAL IMPORTS

Current importer located in Rochester, NY.

American Tactical Imports imports a wide variety of firearms and products, including pistols, AR-15 style and AK-47 design semi-auto rifles, and shotguns. Trademarks, imports, and private labels currently include American Tactical Imports (ATI), Cavalry O/Us (new 2013), FMK, German Sport Guns (GSG), Head Down Products (manufacturer, new 2012), Masterpiece Arms (MPA, disc. 2011), Ottoman Shotguns (disc. 2011), and Xtreme Rifles (disc. 2012). Please see individual listings for current model information and pricing (see Trademark Index).

CARBINES/RIFLES: SEMI-AUTO

IMPORTANT NOTE: On model(s) where *N/A has replaced the normal 100% value, it indicates current market conditions are too unstable to accurately ascertain 100%-60% values. Factory retail prices (MSRs) reflect most recent updates. For more up-to-date information on current pricing trends and additional useful information, please visit www.bluebookofgunvalues.com, select "Information & Services" from the menu, and click on "Additional Book Information".

AT-15 – 5.56 NATO cal., AR-15 style, 16 in. barrel with muzzle brake, flat-top receiver with mid-length barrel quad rail, post front sight, collapsible stock, 30 shot mag. Limited importation 2011 only.

	*N/A	$595	$525	$465	$435	$400	$375	*$719*

AT-47 MILLED – 7.62x39mm cal., AK-47 design, 16 1/2 in. match ER Shaw barrel, blue finish, mfg. from unissued Bulgarian parts kit, wood furniture, 30 shot mag., milled receiver, includes hard case.

MSR $790	*N/A	$575	$475	$415	$315	$300	$250

AT-47 STAMPED – 7.62x39mm cal., AK-47 design, similar to AT47 Milled, except has stamped receiver and is mfg. in the US. New 2011.

MSR $600	*N/A	$450	$395	$350	$295	$250	$225

OMNI 22 (VK22 STANDARD) – .22 LR cal., AR-15 style, 16 in. barrel, fixed or tele-stock, black finish, flat-top receiver with Picatinny rail, 10 or 28 shot mag.

MSR $470	$425	$375	$325	$275	$250	$225	$200

GRADING - PPGS™	100%	98%	95%	90%	80%	70%	60%	LAST MSR

OMNI 22 OPS (VK22 TACTICAL) – .22 LR cal., AR-15 style, 16 in. barrel, fixed or tele-stock, black finish, flat-top receiver, 10 or 28 shot mag., quad rail, vertical foregrip, tactical rear sight.

MSR $520	$465	$425	$385	$335	$295	$250	$225

OMNI 556 – 5.56 NATO cal., 10 or 30 shot mag., 16 in. M4 style barrel, fixed or telescoping stock, flat top receiver with Picatinny rail, Omni polymer lower receiver, black furniture. New 2013.

MSR $600	*N/A	$525	$475	$425	$395	$365	$335

MILSPORT M4 CARBINE – 5.56 NATO cal., 10 or 30 shot mag., 16 in. barrel, A3 flat top receiver with Picatinny rail, tubular ribbed handguard, six position stock, black hardware and finish, includes hard case. New 2012.

MSR $740	*N/A	$575	$500	$450	$400	$375	$350

HDH16 CARBINE – 5.56 NATO cal., 10 or 30 shot mag., 16 in. Hbar barrel, A3 flat top receiver with Picatinny rail, six position stock, black hardware and finish, includes hard case. New 2012.

MSR $750	*N/A	$575	$500	$450	$400	$375	$350

V916/VX916 CARBINE – 5.56 NATO cal., 10 or 30 shot mag., 16 in. heavy barrel, flat top receiver with Picatinny rail, 9 or 13 in. quad rail, six position stock, black hardware and finish, includes hard case. New 2012.

MSR $889	*N/A	$695	$625	$550	$500	$450	$400

Add $20 for 13 in. quad rail (Model VX916).

.300 AAC CARBINE – .300 AAC cal., 10 or 30 shot mag., 16 in. heavy barrel with muzzle brake, six position stock, flat top receiver with Picatinny rail, 9 in. quad rail, black hardware and finish. New 2012.

MSR $999	*N/A	$875	$800	$725	$650	$575	$500

PISTOLS: SEMI-AUTO

FX 45K – .45 ACP cal., features 5 in. threaded barrel with cap, lower front Picatinny rail, bobbed hammer, beavertail safety, extended ambidextrous safety lock, skeletonized aluminum trigger, checkered mahogany grips, low profile rear sight. New 2013.

MSR $720	$625	$550	$495	$450	$400	$350	$300

FX FAT BOY – .45 ACP cal., 3.2 in. barrel, blue finish, 10 or 12 shot double stack mag., all steel serrated grips, lightweight configuration became standard 2013, mfg. by Shooters Arms Manufacturing in the Phillipines. New mid-2010.

MSR $700	$595	$525	$450	$400	$350	$300	$250

FX G.I. – .45 ACP cal., 1911 style frame, 4 1/4 in. barrel, blue finish, 8 shot mag., double diamond checkered wood grips, military style rear slide serrations, slide stop, safety lock, matte black trigger, round hammer, beavertail grip safety, mfg. by Shooters Arms Manufacturing in the Phillipines. New mid-2010.

MSR $520	$440	$375	$325	$295	$250	$225	$195

* ***FX G.I. Enhanced*** – .45 ACP cal., similar to G.I. model, except has Novak sights. New mid-2010.

MSR $565	$475	$415	$350	$315	$260	$215	$165

FX MILITARY – .45 ACP cal., 1911 style frame, 5 in. barrel, blue finish, 8 shot mag., double diamond checkered wood grips, military style rear slide serrations, slide stop, safety lock and trigger, mfg. by Shooters Arms Manufacturing in the Phillipines. New mid-2010.

MSR $520	$440	$375	$325	$295	$250	$225	$195

FX TITAN – .45 ACP cal., 1911 style frame, 3 5/8 in. bull barrel, blue (Titan), NiBX (new 2013) finish or stainless steel (Titan SS, disc. 2012), 7 shot mag., double diamond checkered wood grips, low profile rear sights, stainless steel slide, rear slide serrations, military style slide stop, safety lock, skeletonized aluminum trigger, mfg. by Shooters Arms Manufacturing in the Phillipines. New mid-2010.

MSR $585	$495	$435	$365	$315	$275	$235	$195

GRADING - PPGS™	100%	98%	95%	90%	80%	70%	60%	LAST MSR

Add $85 for NiBX finish (new 2013).
Add $100 for Titan SS (stainless steel), disc. 2012.

* ***FX Titan Lightweight*** – .45 ACP cal., similar to Titan, except has 3 1/8 in. bull barrel. New 2013.

MSR $598	$495	$435	$365	$315	$275	$235	$195	

FX THUNDERBOLT – .45 ACP cal., 1911 style frame, 5 in. non-ported or ported (new 2012) barrel, blue finish or stainless steel (mfg. 2012 only), 8 shot mag., lower Picatinny rail standard, matte chrome round hammer and extended safety, beavertail safety grip, dovetail front sight, Champion rear sight, aluminum trigger, double diamond checkered wood grips, wide front and rear slide serrations, mfg. by Shooters Arms Manufacturing in the Phillipines. New mid-2010.

MSR $876	$750	$625	$550	$475	$400	$350	$295	

Add $24 for FX Thunderbolt E with ported slide (new 2012) or $40 for FX Thunderbolt SS with stainless construction (mfg. 2012 only).

AT CS9 SERIES – 9mm Para. cal., 4 in. barrel, double action, Picatinny rail, ported slide, 18 shot mag., blue, chrome, or two tone finish, mfg. in Turkey. Limited importation 2010-2011 only.

	$335	$295	$250	$230	$185	$150	$115	*$380*

Add $60 for chrome finish.

AT CS40 SERIES – .40 S&W cal., 4 in. barrel, double action, Picatinny rail, 12 shot mag., blue, chrome, or two tone finish, mfg. in Turkey. Limited importation 2010-2011 only.

	$360	$315	$270	$245	$200	$160	$125	*$406*

Add $15 for two tone or $40 for chrome finish.

AT C45 SERIES – .45 ACP cal., 4.6 in. barrel, double action, Picatinny rail, ported slide, 9 shot mag., blue, chrome, or two tone finish, mfg. in Turkey. Limited importation 2010-2011 only.

	$325	$285	$245	$220	$180	$145	$115	*$370*

Add $36 for chrome finish.

AT FS9 SERIES – 9mm Para. cal., 5 in. barrel, double action, Picatinny rail, ported slide, 18 shot mag., blue, chrome, or two tone finish, mfg. in Turkey. Limited importation 2010-2011 only.

	$335	$295	$250	$230	$185	$150	$115	*$380*

Add $60 for chrome finish.

AT FS40 SERIES – .40 S&W cal., 5 in. barrel, double action, Picatinny rail, 12 shot mag., blue, chrome, or two tone finish, mfg. in Turkey. Limited importation 2010-2011 only.

	$360	$315	$270	$245	$200	$160	$125	*$406*

Add $14 for two tone or $40 for chrome finish.

AT HP9 SERIES – 9mm Para. cal., 5 in. barrel, double action, 18 shot mag., blue, chrome, or two tone finish, mfg. in Turkey. Limited importation 2010-2011 only.

	$335	$295	$250	$230	$185	$150	$115	*$380*

Add $31 for chrome finish.

AT MS380 SERIES – .380 ACP cal., 3.9 in. barrel, double action, 12 shot mag., black, chrome, or two tone finish, mfg. in Turkey. Disc. 2011.

	$335	$295	$250	$230	$185	$150	$115	*$380*

Add $20 for chrome or black finish.

SHOTGUNS: SEMI-AUTO

American Tactical Imports offers a Model T14 chambered in .410 ga. with 3 in. chamber. The design is an AR-15 style, and includes a detachable 5 shot mag., with 20 in. barrel. Please contact the company directly for pricing and availability (see Trademark Index).

GRADING - PPGS™	100%	98%	95%	90%	80%	70%	60%	LAST MSR

AMERICAN WESTERN ARMS, INC.

Previous trademark and importer 1999-2004, and located in Delray Beach, FL. During late 2004, the remaining assets of this company were sold and a new company was established as AWA USA in Hialeah, FL. SAA revolver components were manufactured in the former Armi San Marco factory in Italy (now AWA International, Inc.), and assembled in the U.S.

Please refer to AWA USA listing for current information.

AWA International Inc. purchased American Western Arms, Inc. in 2000, along with Classic Old West Styles (COWS) and Millenium Leather.

Please refer to the *Blue Book of Modern Black Powder Arms* by John Allen (now online also) for more information and prices on American Western Arms' lineup of modern black powder models.

Black Powder Revolvers Reproductions & Replicas and *Black Powder Long Arms & Pistols Reproductions & Replicas* by Dennis Adler are also an invaluable source for most black powder reproductions and replicas, and includes hundreds of color images on most popular makes/models, provides manufacturer/trademark histories, and up-to-date information on related items/accessories for black powder shooting - www.bluebookofgunvalues.com

REVOLVERS: CARTRIDGE CONVERSIONS & OPEN TOP

1851 NAVY RICHARDS-TYPE CARTRIDGE CONVERSION – .38 Spl., .38 LC, or .44-40 WCF cal., 5 1/2 or 7 1/2 in. octagon barrel, color case hardened frame and hammer. Disc. 2000.

100%	98%	95%	90%	80%	70%	60%	LAST MSR
$650	$525	$450	$375	$300	$225	$200	*$750*

1860 ARMY RICHARDS-TYPE CARTRIDGE CONVERSION – .38 Spl., .38 LC, or .44-40 WCF cal., 5 1/2 or 8 in. round barrel, color case hardened frame and hammer. Disc. 2000.

100%	98%	95%	90%	80%	70%	60%	LAST MSR
$650	$525	$450	$375	$300	$225	$200	*$750*

1861 NAVY RICHARDS-TYPE CARTRIDGE CONVERSION – .38 Spl., .38 LC, or .44-40 WCF cal., 5 1/2 or 7 1/2 in. round barrel, color case hardened frame and hammer. Disc. 2000.

100%	98%	95%	90%	80%	70%	60%	LAST MSR
$650	$525	$450	$375	$300	$225	$200	*$750*

1872 OPEN TOP – .38 Spl., .38 LC, or .44-40 WCF cal., 5 1/2 or 7 1/2 in. round barrel, color case hardened frame and hammer. Disc. 2000.

100%	98%	95%	90%	80%	70%	60%	LAST MSR
$650	$525	$450	$375	$300	$225	$200	*$750*

REVOLVERS: SINGLE ACTION

PEACEKEEPER (MODEL 1) – .32-20 WCF (special order), .38-40 WCF (special order), .357 Mag., .44 Spl. (special order), .44-40 WCF, or .45 LC cal., 3, 3 1/2 (Sheriff), 4, 4 3/4, 5 1/2, 7 1/2, 10 (Buntline), or 12 (Buntline) in. barrel, charcoal case colored receiver, blue finish, black powder or cross-pin frame, beveled cylinder, original hammer design w/o transfer bar safety, 2-line patent dates, 1st Generation Colt style hard rubber grips, assembled in America. While original prototypes were developed in 2000, actual importation was late 2000-2003.

100%	98%	95%	90%	80%	70%	60%	LAST MSR
$725	$600	$550	$500	$460	$430	$400	*$835*

Add $35 for Sheriff, Thunderer, Bird's Head, or Cavalry/Artillery configurations.
Add $165 for bright nickel finish.
Add $1,450 for grade A (25% coverage), $1,750 for grade B (50% coverage), $1,920 for grade C (75% coverage), or $2,240 for grade D (100% coverage) engraving - nickel finish only.
Add $90 for dual cylinder.

LONGHORN – .357 Mag., .44-40 WCF, or .45 LC cal., 3 1/2 (Sheriff), 4 3/4, 5 1/2, or 7 1/2 in. barrel, case colored receiver, blue finish, one-piece walnut grips, 2 line address, assembled in America. Imported 2001-2003.

100%	98%	95%	90%	80%	70%	60%	LAST MSR
$435	$375	$340	$315	$285	$260	$230	*$495*

Add $30 for Sheriff or Bird's Head/Thunderer Model.
Add $100 for nickel finish.

GRADING - PPGS™	100%	98%	95%	90%	80%	70%	60%	LAST MSR

CLASSIC – .357 Mag. or .45 LC cal. only, flat main spring, 4 3/4 or 5 1/2 in. barrel, blue frame, one piece smooth walnut grips, two line patent dates, 5-5 1/2 lb. trigger pull. Imported 2003-2004.

$385	$340	$315	$285	$260	$230	$200	*$440*

Add $125 for Turnbull case colors.
Add $195 for nickel or hard chrome finish.

* ***Classic Bisley*** – similar to Classic, except has Bisley configuration frame. Imported 2004 only.

$450	$395	$350	$315	$285	$260	$230	*$520*

Add $125 for Turnbull case colors.
Add $195 for nickel or hard chrome finish.

ULTIMATE – .32-20 WCF, .38-40 WCF, .357 Mag., .44-40 WCF, .44 Spl., or .45 LC cal., coil main spring, 3, 3 1/2, 4, 4 1/2, 5 1/2, or 7 1/2 in. barrel, blue frame, one piece smooth walnut grips. Imported 2003-2004.

$525	$450	$395	$350	$315	$285	$260	*$600*

Add $125 for Turnbull case colors.
Add $195 for nickel or hard chrome finish.

RIFLES: LEVER ACTION

1892 CARBINE/RIFLE – .357 Mag., .44-40 WCF, or .45 LC cal., 20 (short rifle - octagon, carbine - round) or 24 1/2 in. octagon barrel, blue finish, uncheckered walnut stock and forearm. Limited importation from Italy late 2000 only.

$625	$525	$450	$395	$350	$300	$250	*$695*

LIGHTNING CARBINE/RIFLE – .32-20 WCF, .38 Spl., .38-40 WCF, .44-40 WCF, or .45 LC cal., patterned after the Colt Lightning rifle, firing pin block safety, blue finish, 20 (carbine) or 24 in. round or octagon barrel, engraved receiver with AWA logo, walnut stock and forearm. Imported 2003-2004.

$745	$625	$575	$500	$460	$430	$400	*$850*

Add $40 for octagon barrel.
Add $350 for White Lightning Model (polished steel receiver.)
Add $300 for case colored hardened finish.

* ***Lightning Carbine/Rifle Limited Edition*** – similar to regular Lightning Carbine/Rifle, except has engraved chrome receiver and select walnut stock, only 500 mfg. Imported 2003-2004.

$1,075	$900	$775	$650	$575	$500	$460	*$1,200*

SHOTGUNS: SXS

HAMMERLESS COACHGUN – while initially advertised during 2000, this model never went into production.

AMTEC 2000, INC.

Previous trademark incorporating Erma Werke (German) and H & R 1871 (U.S.) companies located in Gardner, MA until 1999. Amtec 2000, Inc. previously imported the Erma SR 100 rifle (see listing in Erma Suhl section).

REVOLVERS

5 SHOT REVOLVER – .38 S&W cal., 5 shot double action, swing-out cylinder, 2 or 3 in. barrel, transfer bar safety, Pachmayr composition grips, high polish blue, matte electroless nickel, or stainless steel construction, fixed sights, approx. 25 oz., 200 mfg. 1996-99, all were distributed and sold in Europe only (no U.S. pricing).

ANCIENS ETABLISSEMENTS PIEPER

Please refer to the Bayard listing in the B section for Bayard Models 1908, 1923, and 1930. In addition, Bergmann-Bayard Models 1908 and 1910 mfg. in Liege, Belgium, will appear under the Bergman heading.

GRADING - PPGS™	100%	98%	95%	90%	80%	70%	60%	LAST MSR

ANDERSON MANUFACTURING

Current rifle manufacturer established during 2010 and located in Hebron, KY. Distributor and dealer sales.

Anderson Manufacturing utilizes a proprietary metal treatment for all its rifles and carbines called RF-85. This metal treatment reduces friction on steel surfaces by 85%, and RF-85 treated weapons do not require any wet lubricants, which also result in less dirt and carbon fouling in the action.

CARBINES/RIFLES: SEMI-AUTO

Anderson Manufacturing is currently producing AR-15 style rifles and carbines in various configurations. Calibers include .223 Rem./5.56 NATO or 6.8 SPC. Previously Anderson Manufacturing also produced the following models until 2011: M15M4 6.8 SPC (last MSR was $1,519), AM15M416LE (last MSR was $1,392), AM15AORNZ (was POR), AM15M416ZE (last MSR was $1,392), AM10-BD (last MSR was $1,617), or AM10-MSR (last MSR was $1,555. The preceding models have either forged receivers (standard) made from 7075-T6 steel, or can be milled from solid billets.

AM15AOR16 (HEAVY BARREL CARBINE) – .223 Rem. cal., 16 in. heavy barrel with A2 flash hider and Picatinny rail, front mounted low profile gas block, hard anodized finish with a forged aluminum flat top receiver, ribbed oval M4 handguard, optic ready front sight, 6-position collapsible butt stock, includes two 30-shot MagPul magazines and hard case, 6.43 lbs.

MSR $1,240	$1,100	$975	$875	$775	$675	$575	$475

Add $210 for AM15AOR16-Billet model.

HEAVY BARREL VARMINTER (AM-15VS24) – .223 Rem. cal., 24 in. stainless steel fluted bull barrel, flat top receiver, free float modular forearm tube, Magpul PRS butt stock, Ergo grip, two-30 shot magazines, low profile gas block, tactical charging handle, Timney trigger, includes Harris bipod and hard black case.

MSR $2,484	$2,275	$2,050	$1,800	$1,600	$1,350	$1,100	$875

Add $210 for AM-15VS24-Billet model.

M4 CARBINE (AM15M416) – .223 Rem. or 6.8 SPC cal., 16 in. M4 heavy barrel with flash hider, front mounted low profile gas block, MagPul MOE 6-position adj. stock with pistol grip and quad-rail forend with upper and lower Picatinny rails, hard anodized finish with aluminum flat top receiver, includes two 30 shot MagPul magazines and hard black case.

MSR $1,392	$1,225	$1,100	$975	$850	$725	$600	$475

Add $127 for 6.8 SPC cal.
Add $210 for AM15M416-Billet model in .223 Rem. cal., or $337 for AM15M416-Billet model in 6.8 SPC cal.

SNIPER (AM-15HBOR16/AM-15HBOR20) – .223 Rem. cal., 16 or 20 in. heavy barrel with target crown and flash suppressor, Wilson target trigger, Magpul PRS adj. stock, Magpul MIAD grip, front mounted low profile gas block, floated hand guard with upper and lower Picatinny rails, tactical charging handle, featuring hard anodized finish and aluminum flat top receiver, includes two-30 shot magazines and hard black case, 9.44 lbs.

MSR $2,330	$2,100	$1,800	$1,675	$1,475	$1,275	$1,075	$875

Add $210 for AM-15HBOR16-Billet or AM-15HBOR20-Billet models.

ANDREAS STRANK BUCHSENMACHERMEISTER

Please refer to the Strank Jagdwaffen Buchsenmachermeister listing in the S section.

ANGEL ARMS INC.

Previous manufacturer located in Hayward, CA, 1998-2001.

PISTOLS: SEMI-AUTO

The pistols listed below were designed to shoot a unique integrated case projectile (ICP). These projectiles were hollow, contained the powder charge, and since the case was the projectile, there was no ejection.

GRADING - PPGS™	100%	98%	95%	90%	80%	70%	60%	LAST MSR

MODEL 1000 SE GUN ONE – .45 ICP (Integrated Case Projectile) cal., unique semi-auto design, mag tube is located on top of 6 in. fixed barrel.

While advertised, this model never went into production. $1,900 was the projected MSR.

MODEL QT 427 ZMR - .427 ICP (Integrated Case Projectile) cal., break open action, 5 shot tube or 10 shot staggered mag., 3 1/2 in. barrel located underneath clear mag tube, compact size, 5 oz.

While advertised, this model never went into production. $900 was the projected MSR.

ANSCHÜTZ

Current manufacturer (J. G. Anschütz, GmbH & Co. KG) established in 1856 and currently located in Ulm, Germany. Sporting rifles are currently being imported beginning 2010 by Steyr Arms, Inc. located in Trussville, AL. Merkel USA imported Anschutz from 2006-2010, until the company was purchased by Steyr Arms, Inc.

Target/competition rifles are currently being imported by Champion's Choice, Inc. located in La Vergne, TN, Champion Shooters Supply located in New Albany, OH, and Altius Handcrafted Firearms located in West Yellowstone, MT.

Sporting rifles were imported 1996-2003 by Tristar Sporting Arms. Ltd., located in N. Kansas City, MO. Previously distributed until 2000 by Go Sportsmens Supply, located in Billings, MT. Previously imported and distributed through 1995 in the U.S. by Precision Sales International Inc., located in Westfield, MA.

Anschütz was founded by Julius Gottfried Anschütz in 1856, and located in Zella-Mehlis, Germany until 1945. WWII nearly ended the company. Members of the Anschütz family were evacuated to West Germany after the war, while the company's possesions were expropriated and dismantled. Brothers Max & Rudolf Anschütz, grandsons of Julius, re-established the company in Ulm after WWII. In 1968, Max Anschütz turned over general management to his son Dieter (4th generation), who retired on March 31, 2008. The family business is now managed by Dieter's two sons, Jochen (President) and Uwe.

For more information and current pricing on both new and used Anschütz airguns, please refer to the *Blue Book of Airguns* by Dr. Robert Beeman & John Allen (now online also).

PISTOLS: BOLT ACTION

Anschütz also manufactured an MSP Pistol Series with ergonomic stock for silhouette shooters. This series was designed for target shooting. Anschütz pistols were delivered with a keyed security gun lock.

MODEL 1416P/1451P (EXEMPLAR) - .22 LR cal., bolt action, Match 64 left-hand action (for right-hand shooters), blue finish, 6.92 (original Silhouette Model, mfg. 1994-95) or 10 in. barrel, single shot (Model 1451P, new 1997) or repeater with 5 shot mag. (Model 1416P), two-stage trigger, adj. rear sight, receiver grooved for scope, stippled contoured grip and forestock, 3 1/3 lbs., also available for left-hand shooters. Mfg. 1987-1997.

$395	$345	$295	$250	$225	$200	$180	*$470*

Add $17 for single shot (Model 1451P).
Add $110 for right-hand action (for left-hand shooters).

This model was previously designated the Exemplar until 1996.

* ***Exemplar Magnum*** – while advertised in 1987, only one .22 WMR was manufactured.
* ***Exemplar XIV*** – .22 LR cal., similar to Exemplar, except has 14 in. barrel, 4.15 lbs. Imported 1988-1995.

$450	$370	$300	$250	$225	$200	$180	*$562*

* ***Exemplar Hornet*** – .22 Hornet cal., 5 shot mag., Match 54 left-hand action, 10 in. barrel, grooved receiver, drilled and tapped w/o sights, 4.35 lbs. Imported 1988-1995.

$835	$685	$575	$525	$475	$415	$365	*$995*

This model may also be marked M-1730 MSPE Field.

GRADING - PPGS™	100%	98%	95%	90%	80%	70%	60%	LAST MSR

MODEL 1416 MSPR/MSPE – .22 LR cal., silhouette variation of the Exemplar pistol, MSPR designates repeater, MSPE designates single shot. Mfg. 1997 only.

$1,100	$875	$750	$625	$525	$450	$375	*$1,260*

MODEL 64P – .22 LR or .22 WMR (disc. 2001) cal., right-hand Match 64 bolt action, 10 in. barrel, drilled and tapped (sights not included), weather proof Choate Rynite stock with stippling, 2-stage trigger, 4 (.22 WMR) or 5 shot mag., 3 1/2 lbs. Mfg. 1998-2003.

$445	$385	$335	$285	$240	$200	$180	*$509*

Add 10% for .22 WMR cal. (Model 64P Mag., disc. 2001).
Add $73 for accessory sight set.

* ***Model 64LP*** – .22 LR cal., left-hand Match 64 bolt action, 12 in. drilled and tapped barrel (sights not included), Choate Rynite stock with stippling, two-stage trigger, 5 shot mag., approx. 3 1/2 lbs. Imported 2003-2004.

$495	$400	$350	$300	$275	$235	$200	*$602*

MODEL 17LP – .17 HMR cal., 4 shot mag., otherwise similar to Model 64LP. Imported 2003-2004.

$535	$450	$400	$350	$300	$250	$225	*$651*

MODEL 1730 MSPE FIELD – .22 Hornet cal., 9.3 in. barrel, single shot, target stock with ventilated forend, ergonomic grips, left handed bolt, 54 Match action, drilled and tapped. Importation disc.

$1,140	$900	$750	$625	$525	$450	$375	

RIFLES: BOLT ACTION, DISC.

Sile Distributors located in NY acted as an import agent during the early 1960s which can be identified by Sile barrel markings. Anschütz rifles imported by Savage were available from 1963-1981 and also have Savage/Anschütz barrel markings. While some of those models might not be listed below, refer to models of similar caliber and quality which are listed to ascertain values.

During the period when Savage was importing Anschütz rifles, certain models in the Anschütz line were designated either "Savage-Anschütz" or "Anschütz-Savage" for sales by Savage in the U.S. Conversely, certain models manufactured by Savage were designated "Anschütz-Savage" for sale by Anschütz in Europe. Some of these models did not have any modifications but others were restocked, supplied with different sights, and had other different features from their original counterparts. In most cases, the original model numbers were used. Some "Anschütz-Savage" rifles have made their way into the U.S. While somewhat rare, these rifles are typically based on the Savage Model 110 action. They are not as desirable as those "Savage-Anschütz" marked rifles utilizing the superior Anschütz actions. Anschütz also manufactured between 1,000-2,000 rifles utilizing SAKO actions in .222 Rem. cal. in the late 1950s-early 1960s. These guns will approximate values shown for the discontinued centerfire models listed below.

Currently, Anschütz offers 5 different actions. The 1451 action is Anschütz's entry level action, which is lightweight in design, utilizes cam cocking, and has a lateral sliding safety. The 1451 action is currently used in the Models 1451 D KL, 1451 R Sporter Target, and 1451 Target. The Match 64 utilizes a cam cocking system with claw extractor and ejector, grooved receiver, and sliding safety on the right side behind the bolt. The Model 64 match action is used on the Model 1416 and variations, 1418, 64MP R, 1516, 1517 D Classic, 1517 D HB Classic, 1517 D Monte Carlo, 1517 M PR, and the Model 64 Target pistol. The Match 54 is Anschütz's top-of-the-line action, and features dual locking lugs on its bolt eccentrically seated in the receiver, allowing more support for improved stock bedding. It also features a cam cocking system, 2 position pivoting rear safety, and a drilled and tapped receiver. The Match 54 action is currently utilized on the 1710 series, 1712D, 1717, 1720, 1730 series, 1733, and 1740 Models. The other two actions are used on Models 1770 and 1780.

The models below have been listed in numerical sequence.

GRADING - PPGS™	100%	98%	95%	90%	80%	70%	60%	LAST MSR

MARK 10 TARGET RIFLE – .22 LR cal., single shot. 26 in. heavy barrel, adj. rear sight, globe front sight, target stock with full pistol grip, adj. palm stop. Mfg. 1963-1981.

$425 $365 $335 $295 $260 $230 $210

MODEL 54 SPORTER – .22 LR cal., Match 54 action, 5 shot mag., 24 in. round tapered barrel, Monte Carlo stock with roll-over cheekpiece, folding leaf sight, checkered pistol grip. Mfg. 1963-1981.

$750 $675 $625 $525 $450 $400 $360

MODEL 54M – similar to Model 54 Sporter, except .22 WMR cal.

$850 $750 $675 $575 $500 $435 $395

MODEL MATCH 64 – .22 LR cal., Match 64 action, single shot, 26 in. barrel, hardwood stock with stippled ergonomic pistol grip, adj. buttpad, grooved receiver, approx. 8 lbs. Disc.

$575 $500 $450 $400 $350 $295 $250

Subtract $150 if w/o correct Anschütz micrometer sights (front and rear).

MODEL 141 – .22 LR cal., 5 shot mag., 23 in. round tapered barrel, Monte Carlo stock, folding leaf sight. Disc.

$475 $400 $350 $300 $250 $200 $180

* ***Model 141M (Mag.)*** – similar to Model 141, except .22 WMR cal.

$575 $495 $425 $350 $275 $225 $200

MODEL 153 – .222 Rem. cal., 24 in. barrel, folding leaf rear sight, French walnut stock, rosewood forend tip and pistol grip cap. Mfg. 1963-1981.

$950 $850 $750 $675 $575 $475 $400

MODEL 153-S – similar to Model 153, 24 in. barrel, DST.

$1,050 $950 $850 $775 $625 $525 $425

MODEL 164 – .22 LR cal., 5 shot mag., 23 in. round tapered barrel, Monte Carlo stock, folding leaf sight. Mfg. 1963-1981.

$475 $400 $350 $300 $250 $200 $180

* ***Model 164M*** – similar to Model 164, except .22 WMR cal.

$575 $495 $425 $350 $275 $225 $200

MODEL 184 – .22 LR cal., 21 1/2 in. barrel, Monte Carlo stock with checkered pistol grip, Schnabel forend, folding leaf sight. Mfg. 1963-1981.

$495 $435 $375 $325 $275 $210 $180

MODEL 1400 – .22 LR cal., standard barrel, with sights. Disc.

$400 $350 $320 $290 $260 $230 $210

The Model 1400D Meistergrade was disc. 1987 - the last advertised retail price was $930.

MODEL 1407 I.S.U. MATCH 54 – .22 LR cal., heavy barrel, match two-stage trigger, stippled walnut stock and forearm with aluminum rail, aperture sights. Disc.

$650 $550 $475 $400 $350 $300 $260 *approx. $530*

MODEL 1408 – .22 LR cal., heavy barrel, no sights. Disc.

$450 $375 $325 $275 $235 $210 $195

Add $150 for 1408 ED Model.

MODEL 1411 MATCH 54 – .22 LR cal., prone position target model, heavy barrel, front and rear adj. micrometer sights, pivoting safety, fast lock time, adj. cheekpiece. Disc.

$650 $550 $475 $400 $350 $300 $260 *approx. $575*

Subtract $150 if w/o correct Anschütz micrometer sights (front and rear).

MODEL 1413 SUPER MATCH 54 – .22 LR cal., top-of-the-line free style international target rifle, adj. cheekpiece and curved buttplate, heavy target barrel, front and rear aperture sights. Disc.

$825 $725 $625 $525 $425 $375 $325 *approx. $875*

Subtract $150 if w/o correct Anschütz micrometer sights (front and rear).

GRADING - PPGS™	100%	98%	95%	90%	80%	70%	60%	LAST MSR

MODEL 1418 – .22 LR cal., sporter variation, previous importation by Savage Arms.

	$450	$400	$350	$300	$250	$225	$195	

MODEL 1418 MANNLICHER – .22 LR cal., hunting model, fine checkering, 5 shot mag.

	$825	$750	$650	$550	$450	$375	$325	

MODEL 1450 – .22 LR cal., sporter model, 5 shot mag.

	$525	$450	$375	$325	$275	$225	$200	

MODEL 1518 MANNLICHER – deluxe model variation of the Model 1418, full Mannlicher stock.

	$950	$850	$725	$625	$525	$450	$350	

MODEL 1574 SPORTER – .22 WMR, .222 Rem., .22-250 Rem., .223 Rem., .243 Win., or .308 Win. cal. Mfg. by Krico (Kriegeskorte, located at Stuttgart) and distributed by Anschütz, approx. 1,000 imported during 1970-1973.

	$795	$695	$595	$540	$485	$430	$375	

MODEL 1807 – .22 LR cal., replacement for the Model 1407 Match 54, for I.S.U. and NRA shooting, 26 in. barrel, Match 54 action, 10 lbs. Disc.

	$495	$425	$350	$300	$250	$225	$200	

RIFLES: BOLT ACTION SPORTER, .17 RIMFIRE - RECENT MFG.

MODEL 1502D HB CLASSIC – .17 Mach 2 cal., features Model 64 action with single stage trigger, 5 shot mag., checkered walnut stock, choice of regular or grooved beavertail forend, heavy barrel w/o sights. Imported 2005-2006.

	$695	$595	$550	$495	$450	$415	$385	*$790*

Add $46 for beavertail forend.

MODEL 1517D CLASSIC – .17 HMR cal., features Model 64 action with single stage trigger, 4 shot mag., checkered walnut stock with or w/o Monte Carlo cheekpiece, 23 in. regular or heavy barrel (disc. 2011), 5 1/2 or 6.2 (heavy barrel) lbs. Importation began 2003.

MSR $1,189	$1,000	$875	$800	$700	$600	$500	$425	

Add $60 for left-hand action (mfg. 2004-2011).
Add $60 for heavy barrel with beavertail forend (mfg. 2005-2011).
Add $21 for Monte Carlo stock (disc. 2006).

* ***Model 1517 MP R Multi-Purpose*** – .17 HMR cal., 25 1/2 in. heavy match barrel, two-stage trigger, no sights, hardwood Monte Carlo stock with beavertail forend, 9 lbs. Importation began 2003.

MSR $1,429	$1,250	$1,100	$940	$825	$725	$625	$500	

Add $20 for stainless steel barrel (mfg. 2007-2008).

* ***Model 1517 S-BR (Sporter Benchrest)*** – .17 HMR cal., 22 in. heavy target barrel w/o sights, repeater action, benchrest stock with wide forend, 4 shot mag., drilled and tapped, 6.6 lbs. Mfg. 2009-2011.

	$1,450	$1,275	$1,050	$925	$800	$700	$600	*$1,639*

MODEL 1702D HB CLASSIC – .17 Mach 2 cal., Match 54 action, 23 in. heavy barrel w/o sights, 5 shot mag., checkered walnut stock and forend, match grade single stage adj. trigger, 7.3 lbs. Imported 2005-2006.

	$1,300	$1,075	$875	$750	$650	$550	$450	*$1,512*

MODEL 1713 SILHOUETTE – .17 HMR cal., 21.6 in. barrel w/o sights, Monte Carlo stock, Meistergrade features. Limited importation 2008.

	$1,775	$1,475	$1,100	$900	$800	$700	$600	*$2,199*

MODEL 1717D KL (CUSTOM) – .17 HMR cal., Match 54 action, 23 in. barrel, no sights, Monte Carlo stock with pistol grip cap and Schnabel forend, 7.3 lbs. Imported late 2002-2011.

	$1,775	$1,575	$1,350	$1,150	$950	$800	$650	*$2,089*

Add $310 for Meistergrade (select walnut and gold etched trigger guard), disc. 2011.

GRADING - PPGS™	100%	98%	95%	90%	80%	70%	60%	LAST MSR

* ***Model 1717 S-BR*** – .17 HMR cal., 22 in. target barrel w/o sights. Limited importation 2008.

	$1,095	$950	$825	$700	$600	$500	$425	*$1,349*

MODEL 1717D CLASSIC – .17 HMR cal., Match 54 action, 4 shot mag., 23 in. regular or heavy barrel, no sights, 8 lbs. Mfg. 2002-2011.

	$1,775	$1,575	$1,350	$1,150	$950	$800	$650	*$2,089*

Add $310 for Meistergrade (select walnut and gold etched trigger guard), disc. 2011.

MODEL 1717 SILHOUETTE SPORTER – .17 HMR cal., 21.6 in. barrel w/o sights, Monte Carlo stock with adj. LOP and two-stage trigger. Imported 2008-2011. Reintroduced 2013.

MSR $2,089	$1,825	$1,550	$1,275	$1,050	$950	$825	$725	*$2,179*

Add $320 for Meistergrade (mfg.late 2008-2011).

RIFLES: BOLT ACTION SPORTER, .22 LR - RECENT MFG.

All currently produced Anschütz rifles are delivered with a keyed security gun lock. Current manufactured Anschütz rifles use the following alphabetical suffixes when describing factory features and options. D = single stage trigger, G = threaded barrel, HB = heavy barrel, KL = folding leaf sight, KV = heavy tangent signt, L = left-hand action, MP = Multi-Purpose, R = repeater, and ST = double set trigger.

KADETT – .22 LR cal., youth dimensions, 22 in. barrel, 5 shot box mag., folding leaf rear sight, single stage trigger, grooved receiver, checkered hardwood stock, 5 1/2 lbs. Mfg. 1987 only.

	$235	$200	$180	$165	$150	$135	$120	*$265*

ACHIEVER – .22 LR cal., 19 1/2 in. barrel, single shot, folding leaf rear sight, two-stage trigger, grooved receiver, stippled hardwood stock with vented forearm and adj. length of pull, 5 1/4 lbs. Mfg. 1987-1995.

	$340	$280	$230	$205	$185	$165	$150	*$399*

* ***Achiever ST*** – .22 LR cal., 2000 MK single shot action, slide safety, two-stage trigger, adj. length of pull stock, target sights, approx. 6 1/2 lbs. Mfg. 1994-1995.

	$415	$360	$315	$260	$230	$205	$185	*$485*

MODEL WOODCHUCKER – .22 LR cal., similar to Model 1449D Youth, sold exclusively by R.S.R. Wholesale.

	$210	$185	$165	$150	$135	$120	$110	

MODEL 64MP R – .22 LR cal., repeater, 5 shot mag., 21.2 regular (disc. 2002) or 25 1/2 (new 2003) in. drilled and tapped, heavy match steel or stainless steel (mfg. 2000-2003) barrel, two-stage trigger, uncheckered walnut stained stock and beavertail forend, adj. rubber buttplate, approx. 9 lbs. Importation began 1999.

MSR $1,399	$1,150	$975	$825	$700	$600	$500	$450	

Add $50 for stainless steel barrel (disc. 2003, reintroduced 2007-2009).
Add $49 for left-hand action (disc. 2006).
Subtract approx. $75 if w/o swivel rail.

* ***Model 64R Sporter Target*** – .22 LR cal., repeater, Match 64 action, two-stage match trigger, 21.4 in. match grade barrel, checkered hardwood stock, 10 shot mag., adj. buttplate and stainless steel rail, 7.7 lbs. Importation 2004-2010.

	$1,100	$950	$800	$700	$600	$500	$450	*$1,149*

This model replaced the Model 1451 Sport Target during 2004.

* ***Model 64 S BR*** – .22 LR cal., features 20 in. heavy target barrel w/o sights, 5 shot mag., two-stage match grade adj. trigger, adj. buttplate, flat beavertail hardwood stock, grooved receiver rail, drilled and tapped, 9 1/2 lbs. New 2008.

MSR $1,539	$1,350	$1,150	$975	$850	$725	$600	$500	

MODEL 1416D CUSTOM (LUXUS) – .22 LR cal., Match 64 action, 22 1/2 in. barrel, 5 or 10 shot mag., cam cocking system on recent mfg., checkered Monte Carlo walnut stock, folding leaf sight, 6 lbs. 2 oz. Disc. 2007.

	$715	$575	$475	$375	$300	$250	$225	*$819*

GRADING - PPGS™	100%	98%	95%	90%	80%	70%	60%	LAST MSR

Add $40 for left-hand action.

This model utilizes the Match 64 action, and is similar to the Anschütz Model 1413 Target.

* ***Model 1416 D KL*** – .22 LR cal., similar to Model 1416D HB Classic, except has Monte Carlo stock with pistol grip cap and Schnabel forend, right or left hand action.

MSR $1,099	$975	$850	$775	$700	$625	$525	$425	

Add $100 for left-hand action.

* ***Model 1416D Fiberglass*** – similar to Model 1416D Custom, except has McMillan fiberglass stock in hunter brown color and includes roll-over cheekpiece and checkered Wundhammer palm swell pistol grip, 5 1/4 lbs. Imported 1991 only.

	$755	$650	$575	$525	$475	$415	$365	*$842*

MODEL 1416D CLASSIC – same specifications as Model 1416D Custom, except straight hardwood stock. Disc. 2011.

	$995	$875	$775	$750	$575	$475	$375	*$1,129*

Add $70 for left-hand action (Model 1416LD).
Add $28 for iron sights (disc. 2006).

* ***1416D Classic Heavy Barrel*** – similar to Model 1416D Classic, except has heavy barrel and no sights, grooved beavertail forend became standard 2005. Mfg. 2000-2001, reintroduced 2003.

MSR $1,099	$975	$850	$775	$700	$625	$525	$425	

MODEL 1418D – .22 LR cal., Match 64 action, Mannlicher full stock, skipline checkering, 19 3/4 in. barrel, same action as Model 1416D, 5 lbs. 5 oz. Importation disc. 1995, resumed 1998-2003.

	$915	$800	$700	$575	$495	$425	$360	*$1,014*

Add $40 for set trigger (mfg. 1985-89).

MODEL 1448D – .22 LR cal., Model 1451 action, 22 1/2 in. smooth bore barrel w/o sights, repeater, 5 shot mag., checkered walnut stained stock and forend. Imported 1999-2001.

	$450	$375	$300	$265	$240	$220	$200	*$349*

MODEL 1449D YOUTH – .22 LR cal., bolt action design, youth dimensions, 16 1/4 in. tapered barrel with adj. rear sight, receiver is grooved for scope mounting, 5 shot mag. with single shot adapter available, European hardwood stock, 12 1/4 in. trigger pull, 3 1/2 lbs. Imported 1990-1991 only.

	$210	$185	$165	$150	$135	$120	$110	*$249*

MODEL 1451 E/R SPORTER/TARGET – .22 LR cal., single shot (Model 1451E) or 5 shot repeater (Model 1451R), Model 1451 action, sporter target model w/o front sight, 22 (new 1998) or 22 3/4 (disc. 1997) in. barrel w/o sights, stippled pistol grip wood stock and vent. forend (with or w/o beavertail), 6 1/2 lbs. Mfg. 1996-2001.

	$435	$395	$360	$330	$300	$280	$260	*$485*

Subtract approx. $100 for Model 1451E (single shot).
Add $110 for Model 1451 Junior Super Target (single shot only).

* ***Model 1451R Sporter Target Prisma*** – .22 LR cal., entry level, 5 shot repeater, cam cocking, claw extractor, recessed bolt face, sliding safety, fully adj. stippled hardwood stock, 22 in. target barrel, grooved receiver, optional micrometer sights, 6.3 lbs. Imported 2001-2003.

	$455	$415	$385	$350	$325	$300	$275	*$515*

This model was replaced by the Model 64R Sporter Target.

* ***Model 1451ST-R*** – .22 LR cal., repeater, 5 shot mag., drilled and tapped, 22 in. barrel w/o sights, cam cocking system, 2-stage trigger, uncheckered walnut stained hardwood stock. Imported 1999-2001.

	$435	$395	$360	$330	$300	$280	$260	*$485*

GRADING - PPGS™	100%	98%	95%	90%	80%	70%	60%	LAST MSR

* ***Model 1451D Classic (Super)*** – .22 LR cal., 5 shot, 22 3/4 in. barrel with front sights, grooved receiver, walnut finished straight hardwood stock, 5 lbs. Mfg. 1996-2001.

	$335	$280	$245	$210	$175	$160	$150	*$398*

This model was designated the 1451 Super during 1996-97.

* ***Model 1451D Custom*** – similar to Model 1451D Classic, except has walnut stock with Monte Carlo cheekpiece, Schnabel forend, and sling swivels, 5 lbs. Mfg. 1998-2001.

	$430	$395	$360	$330	$300	$280	$260	*$480*

MODEL 1466D REPEATER – .22 LR cal., 24 in. tapered barrel with open sights, grooved receiver, checkered Monte Carlo walnut stock and forend. Imported 1996 only.

	$660	$525	$435	$375	$315	$260	$235	*$766*

MODEL 1710D KL CUSTOM (1700D) – .22 LR cal., Match 54 action, 5 shot mag., 23 3/4 (new 1998) or 24 (disc. 1997) in. regular (new 1998) or heavy (disc. 1997) barrel, folding rear sight, single or two-stage trigger (Model 1710 KL, mfg. 2003, reintroduced 2007), Monte Carlo stock with roll-over cheekpiece and skipline checkering, 6 1/2 - 7 1/4 lbs.

MSR $2,089	$1,750	$1,525	$1,250	$1,050	$950	$850	$750	

Add $310 for Meistergrade (select walnut and gold etched trigger guard - disc. 1996, resumed 1998-disc. 2011 w/o gold trigger guard).

This model was designated 1422D until 1989 when it was changed to the Model 1700D with some modifications. In 1996, model nomenclature changed from Model 1700D Custom to the Model 1710D Custom.

The Model 1700D Custom employs the Anschütz Match 54 action.

* ***Model 1700D Graphite*** – similar to Model 1700D Custom, except has McMillan black graphite reinforced stock with Monte Carlo roll-over cheekpiece, includes sling and swivels, 22 in. barrel, 7 1/4 lbs. Imported 1991-95.

	$1,130	$885	$760	$650	$550	$450	$375	*$1,299*

MODEL 1710D HB CLASSIC – same general specifications as 1700D/1710D Custom, regular straight stock, choice of regular (disc. 2003), heavy (new 1999), or heavy stainless (mfg. 2000-2003) barrel, open sights (disc. 1994), 7.3-8 lbs. Disc. 1994. Importation resumed 1998.

MSR $2,089	$1,750	$1,525	$1,250	$1,050	$950	$850	$750	

Add $340 for Meistergrade (select walnut and gold etched trigger guard, disc. 1994, reintroduced 2000-2011).

This model was also available as a 2000 Signature Series - includes high polish bluing, select American black walnut, "1 of 200" and "Dieter Anschütz 2000" signature in 24Kt. gold on bottom of trigger guard, aluminum case, and dated certificate at no extra charge.

This model was designated 1422DCL Classic until 1989 when it was changed to the Model 1700D Classic with some modifications. The Model 1422DCL Classic Meistergrade was disc. 1987 - the last advertised retail price was $875. In 1998, this model was reintroduced as the Model 1710D Classic.

MODEL 1710 HB 150th ANNIVERSARY – .22 LR cal., features laser etched 150th Anniversary emblem in stock, special engraving on top of barrel, and initials ACI intertwined on bottom of trigger guard. Mfg. late 2006-2011.

	$2,050	$1,825	$1,600	$1,400	$1,200	$1,000	$800	*$2,299*

MODEL 1700D FEATHERWEIGHT (FWT) – similar to Model 1700D Custom, except has matte black McMillan fiberglass stock configured like the Custom Model, 22 in. barrel, no sights, 6 1/4 lbs. Imported 1989-1995.

	$1,075	$895	$775	$650	$550	$450	$375	*$1,230*

* ***Model 1700D Featherweight Deluxe*** – similar specification to the Model 1700D Featherweight, except has skip-line checkered Fibergrain synthetic stock with realistic wood grain. Imported 1990-95.

	$1,235	$1,050	$875	$775	$650	$550	$450	*$1,460*

GRADING - PPGS™	100%	98%	95%	90%	80%	70%	60%	LAST MSR

MODEL 1700D BAVARIAN – .22 LR cal., 24 in. barrel, 5 shot mag., checkered European style stock with European Monte Carlo cheekpiece and Schnabel forend, 7 1/2 lbs. Mfg. 1988-1995.

	$1,165	$935	$775	$650	$550	$450	$375	*$1,364*

Add $199 for Meistergrade variation (select walnut).

MODEL 1710 CLASSIC HIGH GRADE – .22 LR cal., 23 in. stainless steel heavy barrel w/o sights, 150th Anniversary model featuring Anschutz 150 year logo carved in premium walnut stock, wood bolt handle, founder's logo in gold on trigger guard, original Germania 1901 logo on barrel, two different styles of carving/checkering, 8 lbs., limited mfg. 2007-2010.

	$2,300	$1,995	$1,775	$1,525	$1,350	$1,175	$950	*$2,599*

MODEL 1712D – .22 LR cal., top-of-the-line sporter rifle with deluxe walnut. Imported 1997-1998 only.

	$1,300	$1,100	$895	$775	$650	$550	$450	*$1,495*

MODEL 1712 SILHOUETTE SPORTER – .22 LR cal., similar to Model 1712D, except has Monte Carlo stock with adj. LOP and two-stage trigger. Importation began 2003.

MSR $2,089	$1,775	$1,575	$1,350	$1,150	$950	$800	$650	

Add $310 for Meistergrade (mfg. late 2008-2011).

DIE MEISTERMACHER – .22 LR cal., Match 54 action, top-of-the-line model, limited edition of 25 guns, select wood, extra polish on metal parts, hand-lapped barrel, with numerous gold inlays including Olympic wreath. Mfg. 1985.

	$2,750	$2,000	$1,600	N/A	N/A	N/A	N/A	*$2,475*

This variation sold out in late 1988.

RIFLES: BOLT ACTION SPORTER, .22 WMR - RECENT MFG.

All currently produced Anschütz rifles are delivered with a keyed security gun lock. Current manufactured Anschütz rifles use the following alphabetical suffixes when describing factory features and options. D = single stage trigger, G = threaded barrel, HB = heavy barrel, KL = folding leaf sight, KV = heavy tangent sight, L = left-hand action, MP = Multi-Purpose, R = repeater, and ST = double set trigger.

MODEL 1516D CUSTOM (LUXUS) – similar to Model 1416D, except .22 WMR cal., 4 shot mag., 6 lbs. 2 oz. Importation disc. 2003.

	$630	$530	$465	$385	$335	$275	$250	*$717*

This model utilized the Match 64 action, similar to the Anschütz Model 1403 Target. In 1996, model nomenclature changed from the Model 1516D Custom to Model 1516D Luxus and during 1998, it changed back to Model 1516D Custom.

* ***1516D/DCL Classic*** – same specifications as Model 1516D Custom, except regular hardwood stained stock, regular or heavy (new 2000) barrel.

MSR $1,169	$950	$775	$650	$575	$500	$450	$400	

MODEL 1518D (LUXUS) – .22 WMR cal., otherwise similar to Model 1418D (Mannlicher stock), 4 shot mag., 5 1/2 lbs. Importation disc. 1995, reintroduced 1997, nomenclature was changed to Model 1518D in 1997, disc. 2001.

	$895	$795	$675	$550	$440	$375	$325	*$987*

Add $50 for set trigger (disc. 1995).

MODEL 1720D CUSTOM (1700D) – .22 WMR cal., 5 shot mag., 23 3/4 (new 1998) or 24 (disc. 1991) in. regular (new 1998) or heavy (disc. 1991) barrel, iron sights, Monte Carlo stock with skipline checkering, 6 lbs. 10 oz. to 7 1/4 lbs. Importation disc. 1991, resumed 1998, disc. 2001.

	$995	$875	$750	$650	$550	$450	$375	

Last MSR was $1,104 for the Model 1720D Custom.
Last MSR was $1,229 for the Model 1700D.

Add $174 for Meistergrade variation (select walnut).

This model was designated 1522D until 1989 and then reintroduced as the Model 1700D with

GRADING - PPGS™	100%	98%	95%	90%	80%	70%	60%	LAST MSR

some modifications. The Model 1522D Custom Meistergrade was disc. 1985 - last advertised retail price was $678. In 1998, this model was reintroduced as the 1720D Custom.

MODEL 1700D/1720D CLASSIC – same general specifications as 1700D Custom, straight regular stock, choice of heavy (new 1999), or regular diameter barrel. Importation disc. 1991, resumed 1998, disc. 2001.

$900	$795	$700	$625	$525	$425	$350	

Last MSR was $1,021 for the Model 1720D Classic.
Last MSR was $1,199 for the Model 1700D Classic.

Add $174 for Meistergrade variation (select walnut).

This model was designated 1522DCL until 1989 and then reintroduced as the Model 1700D with some modifications. In 1998, this model was reintroduced as the 1720D Classic. The Model 1522DCL Classic Meistergrade was disc. 1985 - the last advertised retail price was $660.

MODEL 1700D BAVARIAN – .22 WMR cal., 24 in. barrel, clip mag., checkered European style stock with European Monte Carlo cheekpiece and schnabel forend, 7 1/2 lbs. Mfg. 1988-1995.

$1,165	$935	$775	$650	$550	$450	$375	*$1,364*

Add $199 for Meistergrade variation (select walnut).

RIFLES: BOLT ACTION SPORTER, CENTERFIRE - RECENT MFG.

All currently produced Anschütz rifles are delivered with a keyed security gun lock. Current manufactured Anschütz rifles use the following alphabetical suffixes when describing factory features and options. D = single stage trigger, G = threaded barrel, HB = heavy barrel, KL = folding leaf sight, KV = heavy tangent sight, L = left-hand action, MP = Multi-Purpose, R = repeater, and ST = double set trigger.

MODEL 1433D – .22 Hornet cal., special order only, Match 54 target action, Mannlicher full stock, 4 shot mag. Disc. 1986.

$995	$840	$740	$640	$525	$425	$350	*$826*

Add 5% for set trigger (new 1985).

MODEL 1532 – .222 Rem. cal., similar to Model 1433, sport model with standard checkered walnut stock and forearm, 24 in. barrel, open sights. Disc.

$895	$800	$725	$660	$600	$550	$475	

MODEL 1533 – .222 Rem. cal., open sights, same action as the Model 1532, except has checkered walnut Mannlicher stock and shorter barrel. Disc. 1994.

$1,100	$975	$875	$750	$625	$500	$400	

MODEL 1730D KL CUSTOM (1700D) – .22 Hornet cal., 24 in. barrel, folding leaf sight, Monte Carlo stock with skipline checkering and rosewood grip cap, 4 shot mag., 7 3/4 lbs. Model 1432D was disc. 1987, and the Model 1700D was introduced 1989. Disc. 2008.

$1,625	$1,300	$1,100	$900	$800	$700	$600	*$2,399*

Add $220 for Meistergrade variation (select walnut).

This model was designated 1432D until 1987 and then reintroduced 1989 as the Model 1700D with some modifications. In 1996, model nomenclature changed from the Model 1700D Custom to the Model 1730D Custom. The Model 1432D Custom Meistergrade was disc. 1986 - the last advertised retail price was $770.

The 1700D Custom came standard with the Anschütz Match 54 action.

* ***Model 1700D Graphite*** – similar to Model 1700D Custom, except has McMillan black graphite reinforced stock with Monte Carlo roll-over cheekpiece, includes sling and swivels, 22 in. barrel, 7 1/4 lbs. Imported 1995 only.

$1,235	$1,025	$840	$725	$625	$525	$425	*$1,478*

MODEL 1730D CLASSIC (1700D) – .22 Hornet cal., same general specifications as 1700D Custom, except regular stock and 23 1/2 (1432DCL), 5 shot, 23 3/4 regular, heavy (new

GRADING - PPGS™	100%	98%	95%	90%	80%	70%	60%	LAST MSR

1999) - 1730D, or heavy stainless (imported 2001-2002), or 24 (1700D) in. barrel. Disc. 1994, reintroduced 1998. Disc. 2008.

	$1,575	$1,250	$975	$825	$700	$600	$500	

Last MSR was $1,395 on the Model 1700D Classic.
Last MSR was $2,269 on the Model 1730D Classic.

Add $210 for Meistergrade variation (select walnut).
Add $77 for heavy stainless barrel (disc. 2002).

This model was designated 1432D until 1987, and then reintroduced 1989 as the Model 1700D with some modifications. In 1998, this model was reintroduced as the Model 1730D Classic. This model came standard with the Anschütz Match 54 action.

MODEL 1700D BAVARIAN – .22 Hornet or .222 Rem. cal., 24 in. barrel, 5 shot mag., checkered European style stock with European Monte Carlo cheekpiece and schnabel forend, 7 1/2 lbs. Mfg. 1988-1995.

	$1,325	$1,050	$900	$775	$650	$550	$425	*$1,364*

Add approx. $200 for Meistergrade variation (select walnut).

MODEL 1733D – .22 Hornet cal., Mannlicher full stock featuring skipline checkering, European walnut, and rosewood Schnabel tip, 19 3/4 in. barrel with hooded front sight, 6 lbs. 6 oz. Imported 1993-95, reintroduced 1998-2002, limited mfg. through 2008.

	$1,595	$1,275	$975	$825	$700	$600	$500	*$2,069*

MODEL 1740D CUSTOM (1700D) – .222 Rem. cal., 3 shot, otherwise similar to Model 1700D Custom, except is also available with 23 3/4 in. barrel. Importation disc. 2006.

	$1,450	$1,175	$1,050	$850	$750	$650	$550	

Last MSR was $1,729.
Last MSR was $909 on the Model 1532D.

Add $270 for Meistergrade variation (select walnut).

This model was designated 1532D until 1987 and then reintroduced 1989 as the Model 1700D with some modifications. In 1996, model nomenclature changed from the Model 1700D Custom to the Model 1740D Custom. The Model 1532D MG Custom Meistergrade was disc. 1986 - the last advertised retail price was $770.

MODEL 1740D CLASSIC (1700D) – similar to Model 1700D Custom, except regular stock. Disc. 1994, reintroduced 1998-2006.

	$1,375	$1,125	$900	$775	$675	$575	$475	

Last MSR was $1,621.
Last MSR was $849 on the Model 1532DCL.
Last MSR was $1,395 on the Model 1700D Classic.

Add $274 for Meistergrade variation (select walnut).
Add $77 for heavy stainless barrel (disc. 2002).

This model was designated 1532DCL until 1987 and then reintroduced 1989 as the Model 1700D with some modifications. In 1998, this model was reintroduced as the 1740D Classic.

MODEL 1743D – .222 Rem. cal., Mannlicher full stock variation of the Model 1740D, 6.8 lbs. Imported 1997-2001.

	$1,225	$1,000	$850	$750	$625	$500	$400	*$1,373*

MODEL 1770 (D) SPORTER – .223 Rem. cal., 22 in. medium target weight barrel with recessed target crown, detachable 3 shot box mag., single stage trigger, large bolt handle, 11mm rail is machined to the top of the action, special hardened and polished components, available in either Classic (disc. 2011), Monte Carlo (w/Schnabel forend, disc. 2011), or European style walnut stock. Approx. 7 1/4 lbs. New 2009.

MSR $2,499	$2,175	$1,800	$1,575	$1,275	$1,050	$900	$800	

MODEL 1780 D-FL (SPORTER) – .30-06, .308 Win., 8x57mm (European only), or 9.3x62mm (European only) cal., 21 in. hammer forged barrel with 3 dot target sights, choice of checkered or thumbhole deluxe walnut stock with Monte Carlo cheekpiece, new

GRADING - PPGS™	100%	98%	95%	90%	80%	70%	60%	LAST MSR

proprietary action, 4 shot mag., wood bolt handle, single stage trigger, aluminum action bedding, Picatinny Weaver rail can be added to receiver, approx. 7.1 lbs. New 2011.

MSR $3,495	$3,100	$2,750	$2,350	$2,000	$1,750	$1,500	$1,250	

RIFLES: BOLT ACTION, SILHOUETTE

Currently imported Anschütz silhouette rifles can vary somewhat in price, depending on the importer and inventory. All currently produced Anschütz rifles are delivered with a keyed security gun lock. Certain models may be special order only. There are no MSRs on some of the following rifles.

MODEL 1808MS R – .22 LR cal., 5 shot repeater designed for metallic silhouette shooting, 19.2 in. barrel w/o sights, thumbhole Monte Carlo stock with grooved forearm featuring "ANSCHÜTZ" in panel scene, approx. 8 lbs. Importation began 1998.

MSR $1,916	$1,695	$1,450	$1,175	$1,025	$900	$800	$700	

This model is distributed by Acusport Corp., Zander's Sporting Goods, Inc., and Ellett Brothers.

MODEL 2013 SUPER-MATCH FREE RIFLE (BR-50) – .22 LR cal., single shot, 20 in. heavy barrel, no sights, black synthetic stock with adj. cheekpiece and widened forend ("ANSCHÜTZ BR-50" is stenciled on sides), 15.4 lbs. Limited importation 1994-98.

	$2,225	$1,750	$1,375	$1,050	$900	$725	$625	*$2,880*

Add $300 for colored laminated stock (mfg. 1997-98 only).

Model nomenclature changed from the BR-50 to the Model 2013 in 1997.

MODEL 64S RIFLE – .22 LR cal., single shot, 26 in. round barrel, beavertail forearm, adj. single stage trigger, aperture sights, target stock with Wundhammer swell grip and adj. buttplate, checkered pistol grip. Mfg. 1963-1981.

	$475	$425	$375	$325	$285	$240	$220	

Subtract 15% if without sights (Model 64).

This model was available in left-hand or right-hand action.

MODEL 64MS/MP R – .22 LR cal., single shot (Model 64MS, disc. 1996) or 5 shot repeater (Model 64MS R), silhouette target model, 21 1/4 in. barrel, no sights, Wundhammer swell stippled pistol grip beechwood stock, adj. trigger, 8 lbs.

MSR N/A	$925	$800	$650	$550	$450	$350	$275	

Add $50 for left-hand action (disc.).

Current 100% pricing on this model is $939 from Champion's Choice, and $1,175 for Champion Shooters Supply.

This variation employs a Match 64 action. R suffix nomenclature started 1997, S suffix began 2003.

* ***Model 64MS - FWT*** – similar to Model 64MS, except single stage trigger, 6 1/4 lbs. Disc. 1988.

	$550	$475	$425	$350	$325	$260	$230	*$596*

MODEL 54.18MS – .22 LR cal., silhouette target model, 22 in. barrel, Match 54 single shot action, walnut stock with Wundhammer swell, stippled pistol grip and forearm, no sights, 8 lbs. 6 oz. Disc. 1997.

	$1,295	$1,075	$895	$760	$650	$550	$475	*$1,579*

Add $96 for left-hand action.

This model employs the Super Match 54 action.

* ***Model 54.18MS ED*** – same action as Model 54.18MS, except has 19 1/4 in. barrel (7/8 in. diameter) with 14 1/4 in. extension tube, 3 removable muzzle weights. Disc. 1988.

	$1,075	$900	$775	$675	$575	$485	$410	*$1,215*

Add $100 for left-hand action.

MODEL 54.18MS REP – similar to Model 54.18MS, except has repeater action, 5 shot mag., regular beechwood plain stock with or w/o thumbhole, vented forend, or black, grey, or tan-green swirl synthetic stock, 7 3/4 lbs.

MSR N/A	$2,049	$1,750	$1,500	$1,250	$995	$875	$750	

Subtract approx. 10% if w/o thumbhole stock.

GRADING - PPGS™	100%	98%	95%	90%	80%	70%	60%	LAST MSR

This model was introduced in 1989 with a wood stock and a retail price of $1,650.

This model features a Super Match 54 action with detachable box mag. In 1990, the stock was changed to a synthetic McMillan fiberglass finished in grey. Currently, it is available with beechwood or synthetic stock.

* ***Model 54.18MS REP Deluxe*** – deluxe version of the Model 54.18MS REP featuring Fibergrain McMillan stock with advanced thumbhole design and checkering. Imported 1990-1997.

	$2,035	$1,600	$1,275	$1,025	$915	$785	$695	*$2,450*

RIFLES: BOLT ACTION MATCH, RECENT MFG.

All currently manufactured Anschütz match/target and biathlon rifles listed in the following sections are imported by Champion's Choice, Inc., Champions Shooter's Supply, Altius Handcrafted Firearms, and Creedmoor Sports (disc. 2011) unless otherwise noted. These match/target models will vary somewhat in price, depending on the features, options, sights, stock options, and availability. Please contact the importers directly for current model availability and pricing. Typically, there are no MSRs on match rifles. All currently produced Anschütz match rifles are delivered with a keyed security gun lock.

MODEL 2000 MK – .22 LR cal., single shot match, 26 in. barrel, aperture sights, 7 1/2 lbs. Disc. 1988.

	$340	$290	$250	$210	$180	$160	$145	*$400*

MODEL 1403D – .22 LR cal., improved Model 64S match rifle, single shot, no sights, adj. trigger, 8 lbs. 6 oz. Importation disc. in 1990.

	$600	$525	$450	$360	$300	$260	$225	*$700*

Add $50 for left-hand action (disc. 1988).

MODEL 1803D – .22 LR cal., Match 64 action, 25 1/2 in. target barrel, single stage adj. trigger, blond finished wood with dark stippling on pistol grip and forearm, adj. cheekpiece and buttplate, 8.6 lbs. Imported 1987-1993.

	$850	$725	$625	$525	$430	$365	$310	*$1,012*

Add $70 for left-hand action (disc. 1989).

MODEL 1808D RT/1808MS R (RUNNING TARGET) – .22 LR cal., single shot running target model, 19 (w/o barrel weights) - 32 1/2 in. barrel, adj. stock, cheekpiece, trigger, heavy beavertail forend, no sights, muzzle barrel weights, 9 1/4 lbs. Importation disc. 1998.

	$1,850	$1,400	$1,075	$950	$800	$695	$595	*$2,220*

Add $50 for left-hand action (disc. 1991).

Subtract 20% for earlier models (Model 1808D RT and Model 1808 ED-Super).

This model was previously designated Model 1808D RT from 1991-96, and also the Model 1808 ED-Super during 1990 and earlier mfg.

MODEL 1813 SUPER MATCH – .22 LR cal., top-of-the-line competition model with sophisticated adj. cheekpiece, buttplate, trigger, pistol grip, and palm rest, Super Match 54 action, stippled walnut stock with thumbhole grip, 15.4 lbs. Mfg. 1979-1988.

	$1,850	$1,600	$1,400	$1,200	$975	$875	$775	

This model previously held all the Olympic and world records. The model nomenclature was changed to Model 1913 Super Match in 1988.

MODEL 1903D – .22 LR cal., similar specifications to the Model 1803D, except has new improved target stock and adj. cheekpiece made from walnut finished European hardwood, color laminated stock mfg. 1995-1998, full length checkering on forend and contoured pistol grip, fully adj. new style buttplate, 9.9 lbs. New 1990.

MSR N/A	$1,040	$875	$800	$725	$625	$525	$450	

Add $130 for color laminated stock (disc. 1998).

MODEL 1907 – .22 LR cal., single shot match "I.S.U." model, 26 in. button-rifled barrel, prone and position shooting, removable cheekpiece, adj. buttplate, hand stippled stock with ventilated forearm and choice of beechwood (new 1997) walnut, blond laminated

GRADING - PPGS™	100%	98%	95%	90%	80%	70%	60%	LAST MSR

(disc.), or color laminated (mfg. 1995-96) wood stock, 10 1/2 lbs.

MSR N/A	$2,025	$1,780	$1,525	$1,325	$1,100	$900	$775	

Add $125 for left-hand action. Add $130 for stainless steel barrel. Add approx. $1,070 for aluminum stock. Add $125 for quick adj. cheekpiece (disc.). Add $125 for color laminated stock (disc.). Add approx. $290 for benchrest model (Model 1907 BR) with walnut stock. Subtract $125 for Club Model with non-adj. stock.

This model is also available with an Anschütz stock no. 2213 blue laminate (Alu Color), featuring the most recent innovations in stock technology.

This variation was designated Model 1807 before 1989.

MODEL 1909 – target variation of the Model 1910 Super Match II, limited importation 1997-98 only.

	$1,925	$1,550	$1,225	$1,025	$895	$785	$695	*$2,480*

MODEL 1910 SUPER MATCH II – .22 LR cal., single shot, 27 1/4 in. barrel, diopter sights, fully adj. thumbhole stock, 12 lbs., model down from the 1813 (or 1913), special order only - limited quantities imported until 1998.

	$2,150	$1,750	$1,475	$1,100	$900	$725	$625	*$2,967*

Add $149 for left-hand action.
Subtract 20% for Model 1810.

This variation was designated as Model 1810 before 1988.

MODEL 1911 PRONE MATCH – .22 LR cal., single shot match prone rifle, 27 1/4 in. barrel, beechwood stock with adj. cheekpiece, buttplate, no sights, 11.9 lbs.

MSR N/A	$1,865	$1,550	$1,200	$995	$925	$825	$700	

Add $99 for stainless steel barrel.
Add $100 for left-hand action (disc. 1993).
Subtract 20% for Model 1811.

This variation was designated Model 1811 before 1988.

MODEL 1912 LADIES SPORT RIFLE – .22 LR cal., designed to meet I.S.S.F. ladies competiton regulations, features 1907 barreled action w/o sights, walnut stock with shorter dimensions, 11.4 lbs. Importation began 1999.

MSR N/A	$2,690	$2,175	$1,850	$1,575	$1,350	$1,100	$975	

Add $336 for aluminum stock.
Add $135 for left-hand action.

MODEL 1913 SUPER MATCH FREE RIFLE – .22 LR cal., single shot, top-of-the-line match rifle, every possible refinement, international diopter sights, 27 1/4 in. button rifled barrel, hand stop and palm rest, wood (disc. 2007) or blue aluminum Alu Color (new 2000) stock, 15 1/2 lbs.

MSR N/A	$3,250	$2,695	$2,200	$1,800	$1,550	$1,225	$1,050	

Add $130 for stainless steel barrel.
Add approx. $200 for aluminum stock.
Subtract approx. $400 for benchrest model with non-adj. walnut stock.

This variation was designated Model 1813 before 1988 (see separate listing).

MODEL 2007 ISSF STANDARD – .22 LR cal., ISSF model, featuring 19 3/4 in. standard or heavy (new 2001) barrel with 8 in. detachable front tube allowing for different sights and counter-weights (total barrel length with tube is 27 1/4 in.), adj. cheekpiece and rubber buttplate, grooved and vented forearm, choice of blond (disc. 2000), walnut, or blue aluminum Alu Color (new 2001) stock, Match 54 action, 12 lbs. New 1992.

MSR N/A	$2,525	$2,250	$1,875	$1,550	$1,325	$1,100	$965	

Add $135 for stainless steel barrel.
Add approx. $520 for Alu Color aluminum stock, right-or left-hand.

This model underwent significant engineering changes during 1994, including a heavier receiver.

GRADING - PPGS™	100%	98%	95%	90%	80%	70%	60%	LAST MSR

MODEL 2012 LADIES SPORT RIFLE – .22 LR cal., utilizes 2007 rectangular receiver barreled action designed to meet I.S.S.F. ladies competition regulations, smaller dimensions, walnut stock, 11.4 lbs. Importation began 1999.

MSR N/A	$3,295	$2,850	$2,525	$2,100	$1,775	$1,475	$1,200	

MODEL 2013 SUPER MATCH "SPECIAL" – .22 LR cal., top-of-the-line international target rifle featuring 19 3/4 in. standard or heavy (new 2001) barrel with 8 in. detachable front tube allowing for different sights and counter-weights (total barrel length with tube is 27 1/4 in.), top grain walnut, color laminate, or Alu Color aluminum stock with adj. hand rest, palm rest, cheekpiece, and elaborate metal buttplate, Match 54 action, 15.4 lbs. New 1992.

MSR N/A	$3,495	$3,000	$2,600	$2,275	$1,900	$1,600	$1,250	

This model underwent significant engineering changes during 1994.

* ***Model 2013 BR-50 (Benchrest)*** – .22 LR cal., developed especially for benchrest competition, trigger can be adjusted for either light single or two-stage action, 19.6 in. barrel, uncheckered walnut stock with wide forend, 10.3 lbs. Importation began 1999.

MSR N/A	$2,595	$2,175	$1,825	$1,475	$1,250	$975	$850	

RIFLES: BOLT ACTION, BIATHLON

MODEL 64R BIATHLON – .22 LR cal., repeater, 5 shot mag., Match 64 action, 21.2 in. barrel, match trigger, hardwood stock with adj. cheekpiece and buttplate, right or left-hand action, 7.9 lbs. Importation began 2004.

MSR N/A	$1,695	$1,375	$1,150	$925	$825	$750	$675	

MODEL 1403B – .22 LR cal., Match 64 action, 21 1/2 in. barrel, blonde finished European hardwood stock with stippled pistol grip, Biathlon design allows 4 mags. to be stored in a housing attached to the forend on right side, entry level Biathlon gun, 8 1/2 lbs. Mfg. 1990-92.

	$850	$730	$660	$525	$450	$375	$335	*$998*

MODEL 1450B – .22 LR cal., 2000 MK action, 19 1/2 in. barrel, European hardwood with vent. forearm and adj. buttplate, aperture sights, 5 lbs. Mfg. 1993 only.

	$650	$550	$450	$375	$300	$260	$230	*$765*

MODEL 1827B – .22 LR cal., Biathlon rifle, carries four 5 shot mags. in stock, special Biathlon features, 21 1/2 in. barrel, limited mfg.

	$1,875	$1,550	$1,225	$1,025	$895	$785	$695	*$2,457*

Add $120 for left-hand action (disc. 1989).

In 1990, the stock design was changed permitting 8 mags. to be stored in two housings attached to both the stock and forend on right side.

* ***Model 1827BT Fortner*** – same general specifications as Model 1827B, except has Fortner straight pull bolt action, color laminated stock became available 1995, blue or stainless barrel, 8.8 lbs. New 1986.

MSR N/A	$2,895	$2,375	$2,100	$1,800	$1,675	$1,425	$1,175	

Subtract $200 for standard blue barrel.

In 1990, the stock design was changed permitting 8 mags. to be stored in two housings attached to the right side of the buttstock and forend.

RIFLES: SEMI-AUTO

MODEL 520/61 – .22 LR cal., semi-auto, 24 in. barrel, 10 shot mag., Monte Carlo stock, 6 1/2 lbs. Disc. 1983.

	$295	$250	$215	$175	$150	$130	$120	

MARK 525 SPORTER RIFLE – .22 LR cal., semi-auto, 24 in. barrel, 10 shot mag., adj. rear sight, Monte Carlo stock, 6 1/2 lbs. Imported 1984-1995.

	$495	$425	$365	$315	$265	$225	$185	*$547*

This model is still manufactured, but is not currently imported into the U.S.

GRADING - PPGS™	100%	98%	95%	90%	80%	70%	60%	LAST MSR

* ***Mark 525 Carbine*** – similar to Mark 525 Rifle, except has 20 in. barrel. Importation disc. 1986.

	$425	$365	$325	$265	$225	$200	$175	

RX 22 – .22 LR cal., blowback action, 16 1/2 in. plain barrel, full length Picatinny rail with integrated quad rail in forend, folding iron sights, forward cocking lever, folding adj. stock, pistol grip, 10 shot mag., choice of black or desert tan finish, ambidextrous safety, adj. trigger, approx. 7 lbs. New 2012.

MSR $895	$795	$725	$650	$575	$500	$450	$400	

RX PRECISION – .22 LR cal., blowback action, 16 1/2 in. plain barrel, full length Picatinny rail with folding iron sights, forward cocking lever, skeletonized non-folding wood buttstock painted grey, pistol grip, 8 shot mag., choice of aluminum anodized or flat black receiver, ambidextrous safety, adj. trigger, approx. 7 lbs. New 2012.

MSR $995	$875	$775	$675	$575	$500	$450	$400	

SHOTGUNS: O/U

Anschütz marked O/U shotguns were manufactured by Miroku of Japan and distributed in Germany only. Several grades of these shotguns were manufactured and while rarely seen in the U.S., values approximate other Miroku O/Us of similar quality and features ($650-$1,000 assuming 95% or better condition).

ANZIO IRONWORKS CORP.

Current manufacturer established during 2000, and located in St. Petersburg, FL. Anzio Ironworks has been making gun parts and accessories since 1994. Dealer and consumer sales.

RIFLES: BOLT ACTION

.50 BMG SINGLE SHOT TAKEDOWN MODEL – .50 BMG cal., modified bullpup configuration, tube stock with 2 in. buttpad, 17 in. barrel with match or military chambering and muzzle brake, automatic ambidextrous safety and decocking mechanism, takedown action allowing disassembly in under 25 seconds, adj. target trigger, inclined sight mounting rail, cased, 25 lbs. Mfg. 2000-2002.

	$4,200	$4,000	$3,500	$2,350	$2,000	$1,800	$1,600	*$2,500*

Add $150 for 29 in. barrel or $1,050 for 29 in. barrel assembly.

.50 BMG SINGLE SHOT TITANIUM TAKEDOWN MODEL – .50 BMG cal., modified bullpup configuration, tube stock, 16 in. barrel with match or military chambering and muzzle brake, automatic ambidextrous safety and decocking mechanism, interrupted thread lockup, takedown action allowing disassembly in under 12 seconds, adj. target trigger, Picatinny rail mount, cased, 11 lbs. Limited mfg. 2002 only.

	$5,700	$5,000	$4,000	$3,500	$3,500	$3,000	$2,500	*$3,200*

Add $250 for 29 in. barrel, $350 for custom barrel length to 45 in., or $1,050 for 29 in. barrel assembly.

.50 BMG SINGLE SHOT MODEL LTD. – .50 BMG cal., laminated wood stock, butter knife bolt handle, bolt complete with ejector and extractor, parkerized finish, inclined sight mounting rail, 17 in. barrel with match or military chambering and muzzle brake, 21 lbs. Limited mfg. 2002 only.

	$2,500	$2,200	$1,950	$1,675	$1,400	$1,200	$1,000	*$2,750*

Add $150 for 29 in. barrel or $250 for custom barrel length to 45 in.

.50 BMG SINGLE SHOT MODEL – .50 BMG cal., 29 1/2 in. Lothar Walther match grade barrel, AR-15 trigger and safety, fixed metal buttstock with shrouded barrel and optional muzzle brake, 22 lbs. Mfg. 2003-2006.

	$1,800	$1,625	$1,400	$1,200	$1,000	$900	$800	*$1,995*

SINGLE SHOT MODEL W/TAKEDOWN BARREL – .50 BMG or .338 Lapua cal., similar to single shot model, except features a 20 minute inclined sight mounting rail, heavier receiver, match grade stainless steel takedown barrel with clamshell muzzle brake, .5 MOA guaranteed. New 2005.

MSR $4,200	$3,675	$3,150	$2,750	$2,400	$2,100	$1,900	$1,700	

Add $500 for .338 Lapua cal.

GRADING - PPGS™	100%	98%	95%	90%	80%	70%	60%	LAST MSR

.50 BMG SUPER LIGHTWEIGHT REPEATER MODEL – .50 BMG cal., lightweight model with 18 in. Lothar Walther fluted target barrel with 3 (standard) or 5 shot detachable mag., titanium muzzle brake, scope rail, bipod, and sling, 13 1/2 lbs. New 2003.

MSR $4,995	$4,500	$3,950	$3,300	$2,775	$2,350	$2,125	$1,850

Add $705 for takedown model.

ANZIO .50 BMG STANDARD REPEATER – .50 BMG cal., 18 or 26 in. barrel, similar to .50 Lightweight Repeater Model, except does not have barrel/receiver fluting, and is not available with titanium muzzle brake/bolt handle. New 2004.

MSR $3,995	$3,475	$2,850	$2,400	$2,000	$1,750	$1,500	$1,350

MAG. FED RIFLE – 14.5x114mm, 20mm Vulcan (requires $200 transfer tax in states where legal), or Anzio .20-50 cal., single shot or repeater, 49 in. match grade fluted take down barrel, detachable 3 shot box mag., titanium firing pin, bipod, scope rail, customer choice of Duracoat color finish, oversized bolt handle. New 2008.

MSR $11,900	$11,900	$9,950	$8,750	$8,000	$7,250	$6,500	$5,750

Add $1,100 for handguard, freefloating barrel, and adj. bipod.
Add $3,200 for muzzle brake.
Subtract $2,100 for single shot.

APACHE

Previous trademark manufactured by Ojanguren Y Vidosa located in Eibar, Spain.

PISTOLS: SEMI-AUTO

SEMI-AUTO – 6.35mm cal., clip fed magazine.

$225	$190	$160	$140	$120	$95	$75

ARCUS CO.

Current trademark of handguns manufactured in Bulgaria and currently imported by Century International Arms, located in Boca Raton, FL. Previously imported until 2000 by Miltex, Inc., located in Waldorf, MD.

PISTOLS: SEMI-AUTO

MODEL 94/94 COMPACT – 9mm Para. cal., SA or DA (disc. 2000), 4 (compact), 4 3/4 or 5 1/4 (disc. 2000) in. barrel, 10 shot mag., choice of blue (disc.), two-tone, or silver matte (disc.) metal finish, rubber or molded synthetic (disc. 2000) grips, 32-35 oz. Imported 1998-2000, reimported 2003-2008.

$335	$285	$225	$200	$180	$160	$150

MODEL 98DA/98DAC – 9mm Para. cal., SA/DA, blue or duo-tone finish, 10, 13, or 15 shot mag., soft rubber grips with finger grooves, 32 oz. Limited importation since 2002.

No MSR	$375	$295	$265	$235	$210	$190	$175

ARDESA

Current manufacturer located in Vizcaya, Spain.

Ardesa manufactures good quality centerfire external hammer design rifles and single shot shotguns under the Outfitter name. Centerfire rifles utilize Lothar Walther barrels, and come in a variety of configurations. Currently, there is no U.S. importation of Ardesa firearms. Ardesa has manufactured muzzleloading rifles for over 30 years, and these are imported by Traditions. Please contact the factory directly for more information, including pricing and U.S. availability (see Trademark Index).

ARES DEFENSE SYSTEMS INC.

Current manufacturer established in 1997, located in Melbourne, FL.

RIFLES: SEMI-AUTO

Ares Defense manufactures an AR-15 style ARES-15 MCR (Mission Configurable Rifle) with quick change barrels and a provision for belt feed. Please contact the company directly for current pricing on this model (see Trademark Index).

GRADING - PPGS™	100%	98%	95%	90%	80%	70%	60%	LAST MSR

ARISAKA

Please refer to Japanese Military section.

ARLINGTON ORDNANCE

Previous importer located in Westport, CT until 1996. Formerly located in Weston, CT.

CARBINES & RIFLES: SEMI-AUTO

M1 GARAND RIFLE – .30-06 cal., imported from Korea in used condition, various manufacturers, with import stamp. Imported 1991-96.

	$825	$750	$675	$550	$500	$475	$450	

Add $40 for stock upgrade (better wood).

* ***Arsenal Restored M1 Garand Rifle*** – .30-06 or .308 Win. cal., featured new barrel, rebuilt gas system, and reinspected components. Imported 1994-1996.

	$850	$700	$650	$600	$575	$550	$500	

Add 5% for .308 Win. cal.

TROPHY GARAND – .308 Win. cal. only, action was original mil spec., included new barrel and checkered walnut stock and forend, recoil pad. Imported 1994-1996.

	$925	$825	$725	$675	$575	$525	$475	*$695*

T26 TANKER – .30-06 or .308 Win. cal., included new barrel and other key components, updated stock finish. Imported 1994-1996.

	$850	$700	$650	$600	$575	$550	$500	

.30 CAL. CARBINE – .30 Carbine cal., 18 in. barrel, imported from Korea in used condition, various manufacturers, with import stamp. Imported 1991-1996.

	$725	$650	$575	$525	$475	$425	$400	

Add approximately $55 for stock upgrade (better wood).

MODEL FIVE CARBINE – while advertised, this model never went into production.

ARMALITE

Previous manufacturer located in Costa Mesa, CA, approx. 1959-1973.

RIFLES: SEMI-AUTO

AR-7 EXPLORER – .22 LR cal., 16 in. aluminum barrel with steel liner, aperture rear sight, take down action and barrel store in hollow plastic stock in either brown (rare), black, or multi-color, gun will float, designed by Gene Stoner, mfg. 1959-73 by Armalite, 1973-90 by Charter Arms, 1990-97 by Survival Arms located in Cocoa, FL, and by AR-7 Industries, LLC, located in Meriden, CT, 1998-2004. Current mfg. beginning 1997 by Henry Repeating Arms Co. located in NJ.

Black/Multi-color stock	$400	$375	$325	$275	$250	$215	$190	
Brown stock	$550	$500	$450	$375	$325	$260	$220	

Some unusual early Costa Mesa AR-7 variations have been observed with ported barrels, extendable wire stock, hooded front sight, and hollow pistol grip containing a cleaning kit, perhaps indicating a special military contract survival weapon.

AR-7 CUSTOM – similar to AR-7 Explorer, only with custom walnut stock including cheekpiece, pistol grip. Mfg. 1964-70.

	$325	$300	$265	$235	$200	$190	$180	

AR-180 – .223 Rem. cal., semi-auto, gas operated, 18 1/4 in. barrel, folding stock. Manufactured by Armalite in Costa Mesa, CA, 1969-1972, Howa Machinery Ltd., Nagoya, Japan, 1972 and 1973, and by Sterling Armament Co. Ltd., Dagenham, Essex, England.

Sterling Mfg.	$1,750	$1,600	$1,450	$1,300	$1,225	$1,125	$1,050	
Howa Mfg.	$2,100	$1,900	$1,800	$1,650	$1,500	$1,300	$1,150	
Costa Mesa Mfg.	$2,100	$1,900	$1,800	$1,650	$1,500	$1,300	$1,150	

GRADING - PPGS™	100%	98%	95%	90%	80%	70%	60%	LAST MSR

SHOTGUNS: SEMI-AUTO

AR-17 – 12 ga., semi-auto, 24 in. barrel, interchangeable choke tubes, recoil operated, high strength aluminum barrel and receiver, plastic stock and forearm, either gold anodized or black finish. Only 2,000 mfg. 1964-65.

	100%	98%	95%	90%	80%	70%	60%	LAST MSR
	$975	$895	$795	$725	$650	$550	$475	

ARMALITE, INC.

Current manufacturer located in Geneseo, IL. New manufacture began in 1995 after Eagle Arms, Inc. purchased the ArmaLite trademarks. The ArmaLite trademark was originally used by Armalite (no relation to ArmaLite, Inc.) during mfg. in Costa Mesa, CA, approx. 1959-1973 (see Armalite listing above). Dealer and distributor sales.

PISTOLS: SEMI-AUTO

MODEL AR-24 (ULTIMATE) – 9mm Para. cal., full size (AR-24-15 w/4.67 in. barrel) or compact (AR-24K-13 w/3.89 in. barrel) frame, blowback action, 10, 13 (compact only), or 15 shot mag., 3-dot sights with fixed or adj. rear sight, black parkerized finish, checkered polymer grips, includes case and two magazines, 35 oz. Mfg. by Sarzsilmaz in Turkey. Importation began 2007.

	100%	98%	95%	90%	80%	70%	60%
MSR $550	$475	$425	$375	$325	$275	$250	$225

Add $81 for Model AR-24-10C/15C Combat/Tactical Custom pistol with C-suffix (full or compact size), adj. rear sight and checkered grip straps.

MODEL AR-24-15 – 9mm Para. cal., SA/DA, full size frame, 4.67 in. barrel, blowback action, all steel construction, 15 shot mag., 3-dot sights with fixed or adj. rear sight, black parkerized finish, checkered polymer grips, serrated front and back strap, includes case and two magazines, 35 oz. Mfg. by Sarzsilmaz in Turkey. Importation began 2007.

	100%	98%	95%	90%	80%	70%	60%
MSR $550	$475	$425	$375	$325	$275	$250	$225

* ***Model AR-24-15C Combat Custom*** – 9mm Para. cal., similar to AR-24-15, except has fully adj. rear sight, checkered front and back strap. Mfg. by Sarzsilmaz in Turkey. Importation began 2007.

	100%	98%	95%	90%	80%	70%	60%
MSR $631	$550	$475	$425	$350	$300	$275	$250

MODEL AR-24K-13 COMPACT – 9mm Para. cal., similar to AR-24-15, except has 3.89 in. barrel and 13 shot mag., approx. 31 oz. Mfg. by Sarzsilmaz in Turkey. Importation began 2007.

	100%	98%	95%	90%	80%	70%	60%
MSR $550	$475	$425	$375	$325	$275	$250	$225

Add $81 for Model AR-24-10C/15C Combat/Tactical Custom pistol with C-suffix (full or compact size), adj. rear sight and checkered grip straps.

* ***Model AR-24K-13C Combat Custom Compact*** – 9mm Para. cal., similar to AR-24K-13, except has fully adj. rear sight, checkered front and back strap, 13 shot mag., 32 oz. Mfg. by Sarzsilmaz in Turkey. Importation began 2007.

	100%	98%	95%	90%	80%	70%	60%
MSR $631	$550	$475	$425	$350	$300	$275	$250

RIFLES: BOLT ACTION

AR-30(M) – .300 Win. Mag., .308 Win., or .338 Lapua cal., scaled down AR-50, repeater, Shilen modified single stage trigger, w/o muzzle brake, 5 shot detachable mag., 26 in. chromemoly barrel, 12 lbs. New 2003.

	100%	98%	95%	90%	80%	70%	60%
MSR $2,021	$1,850	$1,575	$1,350	$1,125	$1,000	$900	$800

Add $140 for .338 Lapua cal.

AR-50A1 (AR-50) – .50 BMG cal., single shot bolt action with octagonal receiver integrated into a skeletonized aluminum stock with adj. cheekpiece and recoil pad, 30 in. tapered barrel w/o sights and sophisticated muzzle brake (reduces felt recoil to approx. .243 Win.

GRADING - PPGS™	100%	98%	95%	90%	80%	70%	60%	LAST MSR

cal.), removable buttstock, right or left-hand action, single stage trigger, approx. 34 lbs. New 1999.

MSR $3,359	$3,195	$2,925	$2,600	$2,400	$2,175	$2,000	$1,875	

Add $336 for left-hand action (disc. 2009).

During 2004, this model was produced with a special commemorative stamp notation on the left side of the receiver.

RIFLES: SEMI-AUTO

IMPORTANT NOTE: On model(s) where *N/A has replaced the normal 100% value, it indicates current market conditions are too unstable to accurately ascertain 100%-60% values. Factory retail prices (MSRs) reflect most recent updates. For more up-to-date information on current pricing trends and additional useful information, please visit www.bluebookofgunvalues.com, select "Information & Services" from the menu, and click on "Additional Book Information".

All ArmaLite AR-15 style semi-auto rifles have a limited lifetime warranty. Some previously manufactured models had stainless steel barrels and NM triggers at an additional charge. Descriptions and pricing are for currently manufactured models.

Beginning 2009, a forward bolt assist became standard on all AR-10A4 upper receivers.

Add $99-$228 for A4 carry handle assembly.

Add $150 for 100% Realtree Hardwoods or Advantage Classic camo finish (disc.).

AR-10 SERIES – semi-auto paramilitary design, various configurations, with or w/o sights and carry handle, choice of standard green, black (new 1999), or camo finish, supplied with two 10 shot mags. (until 2004), current mfg. typically ships with one 10 round and one 20 round mag., two-stage NM trigger became standard during 2008. New late 1995.

* ***AR-10B Rifle*** – .308 Win. cal., patterned after the early Armalite AR-10 rifle, featuring tapered M16 handguards, pistol grip, distinctive charging bolt on top inside of carry handle (cannot be used to mount sighting devices), original brown color, 20 in. barrel, 9 1/2 lbs. Mfg. 1999-2008.

	*N/A	$1,225	$1,075	$975	$875	$750	$675	*$1,698*

* ***AR-10T Rifle*** – .243 Win. (mfg. 1995-2003, and 2009-2010), .260 Rem. (new 2009), .300 RSUM (mfg. 2004-2008, Ultra Mag Model), 7mm-08 Rem. (mfg. 2009-2010), .308 Win., or .338 Federal (new 2009) cal., features 20 (.308 Win.), 22 (.338 Federal), or 24 (disc. 2008) in. stainless heavy barrel, two-stage NM trigger, smooth green or black finish, black fiberglass (disc. 2008) or aluminum handguard tube, stock, and pistol grip, flat-top receiver with Picatinny rail, w/o sights or carry handle, forward bolt assist became standard in 2009, includes two 10 shot mags. and hard case, 9 1/2 - 10 1/2 lbs.

MSR $1,914	*N/A	$1,475	$1,200	$995	$875	$750	$675	

Add $80 for .338 Federal cal.

Add $214 for .300 RSUM cal. (disc. 2008).

Add $250 for Lothar Walther barrel (disc.).

* ***AR-10T Carbine (Navy Model)*** – .308 Win. cal., similar to AR-10T Rifle, except has 16 in. stainless barrel and match trigger, current mfg. has flat top receiver and Picatinny rail and round mid-lenght free floating handguard, A2 flash suppressor, black finish, 8 1/2 lbs. New 2004.

MSR $1,892	*N/A	$1,450	$1,200	$1,000	$875	$750	$650	

* ***AR-10 National Match*** – .308 Win. cal., 20 in. stainless steel barrel, forged flat-top receiver with Picatinny rail and forward assist, stainless steel flash supressor, two-stage NM trigger, 10 shot mag., Mil Std. 1913 rail handguard, extended elevation NM sights, 10.4 lbs. New 2009.

MSR $2,365	*N/A	$1,850	$1,600	$1,425	$1,200	$1,000	$775	

* ***AR-10A4 Rifle SPR - Special Purpose Rifle*** – .243 Win. (disc. 2003) or .308 Win. cal., features 20 in. chrome-lined 1:10 twist barrel, removable front sight, green or black

GRADING - PPGS™	100%	98%	95%	90%	80%	70%	60%	LAST MSR

furniture, flash suppressor, Picatinny rail, w/o carry handle, includes one 10 shot mag., one 20 shot mag., sling, and hard case, approx. 9 lbs.

MSR $1,557 *N/A $1,075 $900 $800 $700 $600 $525

* ***AR-10A4 Carbine*** - .243 Win. (new 2011), .308 Win. cal., similar to AR-10A4 Rifle, except has 16 or 20 (.243 Win. cal only) in. barrel, 8.4-9 lbs.

MSR $1,557 *N/A $1,075 $900 $800 $700 $600 $525

Add $414 for SIR System (Selective Integrated Rail System, mfg. 2004-2006).

* ***AR-10A2 Rifle (Infantry)*** - .243 Win. (disc. 2003) or .308 Win. cal., features 20 in. chrome-lined 1:10 barrel, green or black finish, includes fixed stock, A2 front sight, flash suppressor, tactical two-stage trigger, forged lower receiver, carry handle, includes one 10 shot mag., one 20 shot mag., sling, and hard case, 9.8 lbs.

MSR $1,561 *N/A $1,100 $925 $800 $700 $600 $525

* ***AR-10A2 Carbine*** - .308 Win. cal., similar to AR-10A2 Rifle, except has 16 in. barrel and six-position collapsible stock with extended tube, includes one 10 shot mag., one 20 shot mag., sling, and hard case, 9 lbs.

MSR $1,561 *N/A $1,100 $925 $800 $700 $600 $525

Add $74 for 4-way quad rail on front of forearm (mfg. 2004-2008).

AR-10A4 MOD 1 - .308 Win. cal., gas operated, 16 in. barrel with flash suppressor, forged one-piece upper receiver/rail system with detachable side and bottom rails, two-stage tactical trigger, collapsible tube stock with pistol grip, black finish and furniture. New 2012.

More research is underway on this model.

* ***AR-10SOF (Special Operation Forces) Carbine*** - .308 Win. cal., available in either A2 or A4 configurations, fixed tube stock, 16 in. barrel, black finish only. Mfg. 2003-2004.

N/A $1,075 $900 $800 $700 $600 $525** ***$1,503

Add $52 for A2 configuration (includes Picatinny rail).

* ***AR-10 Super SASS Rifle*** - .308 Win. cal., adj. gas system, AAC suppressor (military or law enforcement), mock AAC (disc.) or A2 flash suppressor, 20 in. ceramic coated stainless steel barrel, floating quad rail system with rail covers, Magpul adj. buttstock, 20 shot mag., black finish, two-stage NM trigger, available with various accessories, includes one 10 shot mag., one 20 shot mag., USMC quick adjust sling, and sling swivel mount, 12 lbs.

MSR $3,078 *N/A $2,225 $1,950 $1,600 $1,300 $1,100 $995

AR-A10A4 CARBINE - .308 cal., 16 in. barrel with flash suppressor, gas operated, two-stage tactical trigger, anodized aluminum receiver, forged aluminum flat-top receiver with Picatinny rail, 20 shot Magpul PMAG, aluminum handgaurd tube, adj. or collapsible stock, 7 3/4 lbs. New 2012.

MSR $1,557 *N/A $1,100 $925 $800 $700 $600 $525

This model has magazine interchangeability with the AR-10B.

AR-10A SUPER SASS RIFLE - .308 Win., similar to AR-10 Super SASS, except is shipped with Magpul 20 shot PMAG, 11.8 lbs. New 2012.

MSR $3,078 *N/A $2,225 $1,950 $1,600 $1,300 $1,100 $995

This model has magazine interchangeability with the AR-10B.

M4A1C CARBINE - features 16 in. chrome-lined 1:9 twist heavy barrel with National Match sights and detachable carrying handle, grooved barrel shroud, 7 lbs. Disc. 1997.

N/A $825 $750 $635 $500 $450 $415** ***$935

M4C CARBINE - similar to M4A1C Carbine, except has non-removable carrying handle and fixed sights, 7 lbs. Disc. 1997.

N/A $750 $700 $550 $500 $450 $415** ***$870

M15 RIFLE/CARBINE VARIATIONS - .223 Rem. cal. standard unless otherwise noted, various configurations, barrel lengths, sights, and other features.

GRADING - PPGS™	100%	98%	95%	90%	80%	70%	60%	LAST MSR

* ***M15 22 LR Carbine*** – .22 LR cal., 16 in. barrel with A2 flash suppressor, standard .223 lower with .22 LR upper receiver, forward assist, six inch handguard, Picatinny gas block. New 2011.

MSR $749 *N/A $575 $500 $425 $350 $325 $295

* ***M15 SPR Mod 1*** – 5.56 NATO, 6.8 SPC (new 2012), or 7.62x39mm (new 2012) cal., 16 in. barrel with flash hider, forged one-piece upper receiver/rail system with detachable side and bottom rails, two stage tactical trigger, collapsible stock, black furniture, includes one 30 shot mag. New 2011.

MSR $1,529 *N/A $1,075 $900 $800 $700 $600 $525

Add $25 for mid-length free floating quad rail.

* ***M15A2/A4 National Match Rifle*** – .223 Rem. cal. w/Wylde chamber, features 20 in. stainless steel NM sleeved 1:8 twist barrel with NM sights and NM two-stage trigger, grooved barrel shroud, black or green furniture, flash suppressor, with or w/o detachable carrying handle, includes one 30 shot mag., USMC quick adjust sling, and hard case, 9 lbs.

MSR $1,388 *N/A $1,025 $875 $775 $675 $595 $525

* ***M15A4 National Match SPR*** – .223 Rem. cal. w/Wylde chamber, similar to M15A2 National Match, except has forged flat-top receiver with Picatinny rail and NM detachable carry handle, includes one 30 shot mag., USMC quick adjust sling, and hard case, approx. 9 lbs.

MSR $1,413 *N/A $1,035 $875 $775 $675 $595 $525

* ***M15A2 Golden Eagle*** – similiar to M15A2 National Match Rifle, except has 20 in. heavy barrel, 9.4 lbs. Limited mfg. 1998 only.

N/A $975 $850 $750 $675 $595 $525** ***$1,350

* ***M15A2 Service Rifle*** – 5.56 NATO cal., includes 20 in. chrome-lined 1:9 twist barrel, green or black furniture, forged A2 receiver, fixed stock, A2 front sight, tactical two-stage trigger, flash suppressor, carrying handle, includes one 30 shot mag., sling, and hard case, 8.2 lbs.

MSR $1,150 *N/A $800 $700 $600 $500 $450 $415

* ***M15A2 Carbine*** – similar to M15A2 Service Rifle, except has six-position collapsible stock with G.I. diameter extension tube, and 16 in. barrel, includes one 30 shot mag., sling, and hard case, 7 lbs.

MSR $1,150 *N/A $800 $700 $600 $500 $450 $415

* ***M15A4 SPR (Special Purpose Rifle)*** – 5.56 NATO cal., includes 20 in. chrome-lined H-Bar 1:9 twist barrel, green or black finish, gas block with rail, forged flat-top receiver with Picatinny rail, tactical two-stage trigger, flash suppressor, includes one 30 shot mag., sling, and hard case, 7.8 lbs.

MSR $1,060 *N/A $775 $675 $575 $500 $450 $415

* ***M15 SPR Mod 1*** – 5.56 NATO, 6.8 SPL (new 2012), or 7.62x39mm (new 2012) cal., includes 16 in. chrome-lined threaded barrel, black finish, gas block with rail, forged flat-top receiver with Picatinny rail and laser engraved rail numbering, three extra detachable rails, collapsible stock, tactical two-stage trigger, flash suppressor, aluminum lower receiver, ARMS polymer sights, includes one 30 shot mag., sling, and hard case, 6 1/2 lbs. New mid-2010.

MSR $1,554 *N/A $1,225 $1,075 $950 $825 $700 $575

* ***M15A4 Carbine*** – .223 Rem., 6.8 SPC (new 2009), or 7.62x39mm (new 2009) cal., similar to M15A4 Special Purpose Rifle, except has 16 in. barrel and six-position collapsible stock with G.I. diameter extension tube, includes one 10 shot mag., one 20 shot mag., sling, and hard case, 7 lbs.

MSR $1,060 *N/A $775 $675 $575 $500 $450 $415

Add $47 for 6.8 SPC or 7.62x39mm cal.

Subtract $60 for fixed front sight w/detachable carry handle (disc.).

GRADING - PPGS™	100%	98%	95%	90%	80%	70%	60%	LAST MSR

* ***M15A4 CBA2K*** – 5.56 NATO cal., features 16 in. double lapped chrome lined barrel, flash suppressor, two-stage tactical trigger, forged flat-top receiver with Picatinny rail, A2 front sight, 8 in. mid-length handguard, forged lower receiver, six-position collapsible stock with G.I. diameter extension tube, includes one 30 shot mag., sling, and hard case, 7 lbs. New 2008.

MSR $1,017 *N/A $900 $800 $700 $600 $500 $450

* ***M15A4 SPR II National Match (Special Purpose Rifle)*** – similar to M15A4 SPR, except has triple lapped rifled barrel, strengthened free floating barrel sleeve and two-stage match trigger, green or black furniture. Mfg. 2003-2005.

N/A $1,050 $875 $800 $700 $600 $500 *$1,472

* ***M15SOF (Special Operation Forces) Carbine*** – .223 Rem. cal., available in either A2 or A4 configurations, fixed tube stock, 16 in. barrel, black finish only. Mfg. 2003-2004.

N/A $775 $675 $600 $525 $475 $450 *$1,084

Add $69 for A2 configuration (includes Picatinny rail).

* ***M15ARTN*** – .223 Rem. cal., 20 in. stainless steel barrel, National Match trigger, green or black finish. Mfg. 2004-2007.

N/A $925 $825 $700 $600 $500 $450 *$1,322

* ***M-15T (M15A4T Rifle Eagle Eye)*** – .223 Rem. cal. w/Wylde chamber, 20 or 24 (disc. 2009) in. stainless steel 1:8 twist heavy barrel, two-stage NM trigger, smooth green or black fiberglass (disc. 2008) or lightweight aluminum hand guard, Picatinny front sight rail but w/o sights and carrying handle, black or green furniture, includes one 10 shot mag. and hard case, 8.6 lbs. Disc. 2005, reintroduced 2007.

MSR $1,296 *N/A $900 $800 $700 $600 $525 $500

* ***M15A4T Carbine (Eagle Eye)*** – features 16 in. stainless steel 1:9 twist heavy barrel, picatinny rail, smooth fiberglass handguard tube, two-stage trigger, 7.1 lbs. Mfg. 1997-2004.

N/A $995 $850 $775 $675 $595 $525 *$1,383

* ***M15A4 Predator*** – similar to M15A4T Eagle Eye, except has 1:12 twist barrel. Disc. 1996.

N/A $985 $850 $750 $675 $595 $525 *$1,350

* ***M15A4 Action Master*** – includes 20 in. stainless steel 1:9 twist barrel, two-stage trigger, muzzle brake, Picatinny flat-top design w/o sights or carrying handle, 9 lbs. Disc. 1997.

N/A $975 $850 $750 $650 $550 $495 *$1,175

LEC15A4CBK (LAW ENFORCEMENT CARBINE) – 5.56 NATO cal., 16 in. double lapped chrome lined threaded barrel, forged flat-top receiver with Picatinny rail, flash suppressor, A2 front sight, 6 in. handguard, tactical two-stage trigger, six position collapsible stock with G.I. diameter extension tube, includes one 30 shot mag., sling, and hard case, 6 1/2 lbs. New 2009.

MSR $975 *N/A $825 $725 $650 $575 $525 $475

AR-180B – .223 Rem. cal., polymer lower receiver with formed sheet metal upper, standard AR-15 trigger group/magazine, incorporates the best features of the M15 (lower group with trigger and mag. well) and early AR-180 (gas system, which keeps propellant gas outside of the receiver) rifles, 19.8 in. barrel with integral muzzle brake, 6 lbs. Mfg. 2003-2007.

N/A $675 $600 $525 $475 $425 $400 *$750

For more information on the original ArmaLite AR-180 and variations, please refer to the previous ArmaLite listing.

ARMAMENT TECHNOLOGY

Previous firearms manufacturer located in Halifax, Nova Scotia, Canada 1988-2003.

Armament Technology discontinued making bolt action rifles in 2003. Currently, the company is distributing optical rifle sights only.

GRADING - PPGS™	100%	98%	95%	90%	80%	70%	60%	LAST MSR

RIFLES: BOLT-ACTION

AT1-C24 TACTICAL RIFLE – .308 Win. or .300 Win. Mag. (disc. 2000) cal., similar to AT1-M24, except has detachable mag., adj. cheekpiece, and buttstock adj. for LOP, includes 3.5-10x30mm tactical scope and mil spec shipping case, 1/2" MOA guaranteed, available in left-hand action, 14.9 lbs. Mfg. 1998-2003.

$4,095	$3,650	$2,775	$2,250	$1,825	$1,500	$1,275	*$4,195*

AT1-C24B TACTICAL RIFLE – .308 Win. cal., similar to AT1-C24, except is not available in left-hand, 15.9 lbs. Mfg. 2001-2003.

$4,250	$3,750	$2,850	$2,300	$1,850	$1,525	$1,300	*$4,695*

AT1-M24 TACTICAL RIFLE – .223 Rem. (new 1998), .308 Win., or .300 Win. Mag. (disc. 2000) cal., bolt action, tactical rifle with competition tuned right-hand or left-hand Rem. 700 action, stainless steel barrel, Kevlar reinforced fiberglass stock, Harris bipod, matte black finish, competition trigger, 1/2" MOA guaranteed, 14.9 lbs. Disc. 2003.

$4,350	$3,850	$2,850	$2,350	$1,900	$1,600	$1,350	*$4,495*

ARMAMENT TECHNOLOGY CORP.

Previous manufacturer located in Las Vegas, NV between 1972 and 1978.

RIFLES: SEMI-AUTO

In addition to the models listed below, ATC also manufactured the "Firefly II", a select fire pistol.

MODEL 4 POCKET RIFLE – .22 LR cal., semi-auto action (supplied by Mossberg), 5 in. barrel, shortened rifle (18 1/2 in. overall length) with cut stock, 7 shot mag., approx. 450 mfg., approx. 3 lbs.

$350	$295	$260	$230	$195	$175	$150

MODEL 6 – full length variation of the Model 4, Mossberg Model 453-T with ATC trademarks, approx. 12 mfg., approx. 5 1/2 lbs.

$125	$100	$85	$75	$65	$55	$45

M-2 FIREFLY – 9mm Para. cal., unique gas delayed blowback action, paramilitary configuration, collapsible stock, very limited mfg., 4 3/4 lbs.

$695	$625	$550	$475	$395	$350	$295

ARMAS AZOR, S.A.

Previous manufacturer of double rifles located in Eibar, Spain. Previously imported 1994-1997 by Armes De Chasse located in Hertford, NC.

RIFLES: SxS, SIDELOCK

The models listed below are English styled sidelock double rifles. Gold inlay and custom engraving prices were quoted per individual request.

AFRICA MARK I – available in most cals. between 9.3x74R and .375 H&H, nominal engraving and select grade wood.

Previous retail prices ranged between $8,000 and $10,000.

AFRICA MARK II – available in most cals. between 9.3x74R and .375 H&H, African game scene engraving and superior grade wood.

Previous retail prices ranged between $10,000 and $12,000.

AFRICA MARK III – available in most cals. between 9.3x74R and .470 NE Mag., intricate scroll engraving, cartridge trap, top tang, and superior quality grade wood.

Previous retail prices ranged between $13,000 and $18,000.

SHOTGUNS: SxS, SIDELOCK

SIDELOCK MODEL – 12 ga.-.410 bore, English-style sidelock game gun.

$3,275	$2,700	$2,200	$1,750	$1,500	$1,250	$995	*$3,500*

GRADING - PPGS™	100%	98%	95%	90%	80%	70%	60%	LAST MSR

ARMED

Current trademark manufactured by Doruk Silah, with factory located in Konya, Turkey, and administrative offices in Izmir, Turkey.

Doruk Silah Ltd. Sti. has been manufacturing guns since 1975. A wide variety of firearms are manufactured under the Armed trademark, including semi-auto, slide action, O/U, SxS, single barrel, and bolt action (disc.) shotguns. Additionally, Armed offers blank pistols and airguns. Currently, there is no U.S. importation. Please contact the company directly for more information, including pricing and U.S. availability (see Trademark Index).

ARMERIA DE MADRID, LA

Current long gun manufacturer established during 1995, and currently located in Madrid, Spain.

La Armeria manufactures high quality bolt action rifles based on the Johannsen magnum action in .270 Win., .30-06, 7mm Wby. Mag., 9.3x62mm, .375 H&H, .338 Win. Mag., .300 Win. Mag., or .416 Rigby cal. Many options are available and prices start at $16,000. Single shot rifles are POR. Express double rifles come in a variety of options and configurations, and have a base price of $32,500 w/o engraving and other special orders/features.

La Armeria also manufactures high quality SxS shotguns in 12, 16, 20, 28 ga. or .410 bore, with fine exhibition quality wood and hand engraving in a variety of styles. Prices start at $20,000 including standard engraving. Please contact the company directly for a price quotation, available options, and delivery time (see Trademark Index).

ARMES DE CHASSE LLC

Previous importer and distributor located in Norfolk, VA and in Hertford, NC.

SHOTGUNS: SxS

ALBEMARLE GAME GUN SIDELOCK – 12, 16 (special order only), 20, 28 ga., or .410 bore (new 2001), H&H style detachable sidelock action, Purdey style bolt, DT with articulated front trigger, 26, 27, or 28 in. barrels with concave solid rib, ejectors, checkered oil finished walnut English or pistol grip stock and forearm (base price includes custom stock dimensions), extensive lockplate engraving, 5 3/4 (20 ga.) or 6 7/8 (12 ga.) lbs. Spanish importation from 1999-2005.

100%	98%	95%	90%	80%	70%	60%	LAST MSR
$3,100	$2,650	$2,195	$1,800	$1,500	$1,200	$995	$3,525

Add 10% for 28 ga. or .410 bore.
Add $1,050 for extra set of barrels.
Add $1,525 for Grade A fine scroll engraving.
Add $1,330 for Grade A black and gold option (mfg. 2000-2003).
Add $1,310 for Grade B ribbon and scroll engraving.
Add $1,100 Grade C game scene engraving.
Add $135 for left-hand.

ALBEMARLE GAME GUN BOXLOCK – 12, 16 (special order only), 20, 28 ga., or .410 bore, H&H style boxlock action, DT, ejectors, old silver or case hardened receiver, beavertail or semi-beavertail forend available. Importation began 2003.

100%	98%	95%	90%	80%	70%	60%	LAST MSR
$2,350	$2,150	$1,875	$1,525	$1,200	$995	$875	$2,635

Add $135 for left-hand.
Add 10% for 28 ga.or .410 bore.

ARMES MATHELON

Please refer to Mathelon Armes in the M section.

ARMES PIERRE ARTISAN ETS. (P. CHAPUIS)

Current manufacturer located in St. Bonnet Le Chateau, France.

Pierre Chapuis is a third generation gunmaker and has been awarded the Best Craftsman of France award from the French President. Please contact the company directly regarding the purchase of these custom guns, including available options, delivery time (approx. 2 months currently) and availability (see Trademark Index).

RIFLES: CUSTOM

Armes Pierre Artisan manufactures high quality custom SxS and O/U double rifles in 8x57JRS or 9.3x74R cal. Rifles feature premium wood, forged steel barrels and actions, and engraving options. SxS models include the Fontainebleau 1st Grade (€6,665), Novelty Chambord (€7,655), Fontainebleau 2nd Grade (€7,690), Fontainebleau 3rd Grade (€9,935), Chenonceau 1st Grade (€8,525), Chenonceau 2nd Grade (€9,570), Rambouillet (€11,535), and the Exception (€35,200). O/U models include the Artisan II (€5,100), Novelty Cheverny (€5,535), Fontainebleau 2nd Grade (€7,285), Chenonceau 1st Grade (€8,525), Chenonceau 2nd Grade (€9,570), New Model 410 (POR), and the Rambouillet (€11,535).

Armes Pierre Artisan also manufactures a Kipplauf "Everest" express rifle in 6.5x57R, 7x65R, 30R Blaser, or 7x57R cal. Models include the Fontainebleau (€7,285), Chenonceau (€9,570), and the Rambouillet (€11,535).

Many custom options are available, including wood upgrades and custom engraving.

SHOTGUNS: CUSTOM

Armes Pierre Artisan manufactures high quality SxS and O/U custom shotguns in 20 and 28 ga. Models include the Fontainebleau (€7,165), Chenonceau (€9,300), and the Rambouillet (€11,535). Shotguns feature reinforced steel barrels, extractors, DT, English stype straight grip stocks and engraving.

Many custom options are available.

ARMI MAGAP

Current long gun manufacturer established during 2007, and currently located in Marcheno, Italy. No current U.S. importation.

Armi Magap was founded by Maurizio Piotti during 2007, and the company currently manufactures custom order, high quality round action boxlock SxS, boxlock O/U with detachable trigger assembly, and hammer sideplate shotguns. Please contact the company directly for more information, including pricing, availability, and delivery time (see Trademark Index).

ARMI PERUGINI-VISINI

Please refer to P section.

ARMI SALVINELLI

Current manufacturer established in 1975, and located in Marcheno, Italy. No current U.S. importation.

Armi Salvinelli manufactures high quality O/U competition and hunting shotguns, including a line specifically for the 2012 Olympics in London. Please contact the company directly for more information, including pricing and availability (see Trademark Index).

ARMI SAN PAOLO

Previous manufacturer located in Concesio, Italy.

During 2002, Armi San Paolo changed its name to Euroarms Italia. Please refer to the Euroarms Italia listing in the E section for current information.

REVOLVERS

Armi San Paolo manufactured double action .22 and .38 cal. revolvers in both 2 and 6 in. barrel lengths. These revolvers were manufactured in Concesio, Italy under license from J.P. Sauer & Sohn. Assuming 95%+ condition, these handguns are currently priced in the $150-$225 range.

ARMI SPORT di CHIAPPA SILVIA & C. Snc

Current manufacturer established in 1958, and located in Brescia, Italy. Armi Sport is a one division of the Chiappa group, which includes Armi Sport (replica firearms manufacturer established in 1958), Chiappa Firearms Ltd. (firearms manufacturer), Kimar Srl (firearms manufacturer), Costa srl (metal surface finsh treatment), ACP (laser

GRADING - PPGS™	100%	98%	95%	90%	80%	70%	60%	LAST MSR

training system), and AIM (video/target simulations). Currently distributed by various U.S. companies (please refer to Trademark Index).

See Chiappa Firearms Ltd. for current firearms listings. Armi Sport also manufactures firearms that are currently imported by Cimarron, Dixie Gun Works, Lyman, Puma, and Taylor's & Co. Please refer to the individual headings for listings on various models.

Armi Sport also manufactures a complete line of percussion and flintlock blackpowder reproductions and replicas, including both pistols and rifles. For more information on these replicas, please refer to the *Blue Book of Modern Black Powder Arms* by John Allen.

RIFLES: REPRODUCTIONS

Please refer to the distributors listings for current information on these models, including U.S. pricing and availability (see Trademark Index).

ARMINEX LTD.

Previous manufacturer located in Scottsdale, AZ.

PISTOLS: SEMI-AUTO

TRI-FIRE – .45 ACP cal., single action, interchangeable barrels allow caliber conversion. Available in 5, 6, or 7 (disc. 1984) in. stainless barrel lengths, no grip safety, steel frame construction, ambidextrous thumb safety (on Target and Presentation only), smooth walnut grips, 38 oz. Approx. 400 mfg. between 1981 and 1985.

$875	$775	$650	$475	$400	$375	$350	*$396*

Add $50 if presentation cased.
Add approx. $130/conversion unit (9mm Para. or .38 Super cal.).

* ***Tri-Fire Target Model*** – same specifications as Tri-Fire, except has 6 or 7 (disc. 1984) in. barrel. Very limited mfg.

$850	$725	$550	$450	$400	$360	$330	*$448*

ARMINIUS

Previous trademark of revolvers manufactured by Weihrauch Sport GmbH., located in Mellrichstadt, Germany. Previously manufactured in Zella-Mehlis, Germany beginning circa 1922 through the mid-1970s.

PISTOLS: SINGLE SHOT

MODEL 1 – .22 LR cal., target model, adj. sights.

$275	$210	$195	$165	$155	$140	$110

MODEL 2 – similar to Model 1, except has set trigger.

$340	$255	$225	$190	$170	$155	$140

REVOLVERS

Recently manufactured Arminius revolvers are not individually listed, since they were not recently imported into the U.S. There are however, many models, including combat, sport, and target variations. Calibers include .22 LR., .22 WMR, .32 S&W Wadcutter, .357 Mag., and .38 Spl.

MODEL 3 – .25 ACP cal., folding trigger, hammerless.

$175	$135	$125	$105	$100	$90	$80

MODEL 8 – .320 Revolver cal., folding trigger, hammerless.

$175	$135	$125	$105	$100	$90	$80

MODEL 9 – .32 ACP cal.

$185	$140	$130	$115	$105	$95	$85

MODEL 10 – .32 ACP cal., hammerless.

$165	$125	$120	$100	$95	$85	$75

TARGET – .22 LR cal.

$90	$70	$65	$55	$50	$45	$45

GRADING - PPGS™	100%	98%	95%	90%	80%	70%	60%	LAST MSR

ARMITAGE INTERNATIONAL, LTD.

Previous manufacturer until 1990 located in Seneca, SC.

PISTOLS: SEMI-AUTO

SCARAB SKORPION – 9mm Para. cal., paramilitary design patterned after the Czech Model 61, direct blow back action, 4.63 in. barrel, matte black finish, 12 shot (standard) or 32 shot (optional) mag., 3 1/2 lbs. Mfg. in U.S. 1989-90 only.

	$695	$625	$550	$500	$425	$375	$325	*$400*

Add $45 for threaded flash hider or imitation suppressor.

Only 602 Scarab Skorpions were manufactured during 1989-90.

ARMORY USA L.L.C.

Previous manufacturer/importer until 2008, and located in Houston, TX. Previous company name was Arsenal USA LLC.

RIFLES: SEMI-AUTO

Armory USA, LLC produced a variety of AK-47/AKM/AK-74 semi-auto rifles. Early rifles used Bulgarian milled receivers, later versions were built using sheet metal receivers made in Hungary by FEG.

During 2004, Armory USA began production of 1.6 mm thick U.S. made AK receivers, which were sold as both receivers and complete rifles. Production of 1 mm thick receivers began in Jan. 2005. Models not listed here may have been assembled by other manufacturers using these receivers. During 2004, Armory USA began assembling rifles at a new factory in Kazanlak, Bulgaria. Some components were made in the U.S., in compliance with the BATFE.

Please refer to the Arsenal USA listing for pre-2004 manufactured/imported rifles.

MODEL SSR-56-2 – 7.62x39mm cal., Armory USA made 1.6mm receiver wall thickness, Poly-Tec barrel assembly, Bulgarian internal parts. Approx. 400 mfg. during 2004.

	$750	$700	$675	$650	$600	$500	$475	*$500*

MODEL AMD-63-2 UP – 7.62x39mm cal., Armory USA made 1.6mm receiver wall thickness, Hungarian parts, underfolding buttstock. Approx. 125 mfg. 2004.

	$950	$900	$850	$800	$700	$650	$600	*$600*

Add $200 for milled receiver.

MODEL SSR-85C-2 – 7.62x39mm cal., assembled in Bulgaria, marked "ISD Ltd", blonde wood and black polymer furniture. Imported 2004-2006.

	$795	$750	$700	$650	$600	$525	$475	*$550*

Add $100 for sidefolding buttstock (Model SSR-85C-2 SF).

MODEL SSR-74-2 – 5.45x39mm cal., assembled in Bulgaria, marked "ISD Ltd", blonde wood and black polymer furniture. Imported 2005-2008.

	$775	$725	$695	$625	$600	$525	$475	*$550*

ARMS CORPORATION OF THE PHILIPPINES

Please refer to the Armscor listing in this section.

ARMS MORAVIA, LTD.

Previous European importer/exporter of firearms and accessories located in Ostrava, Czech Republic. Previously imported into the United States by Anderson & Richardson Arms Co., located in Ft. Worth, TX until 2001.

Arms Moravia Ltd. exported a wide variety of European trademarks, including their own line of pistols.

ARMS RESEARCH ASSOCIATES

Previous manufacturer until 1991, located in Stone Park, IL.

GRADING - PPGS™	100%	98%	95%	90%	80%	70%	60%	LAST MSR

CARBINES: SEMI-AUTO

KF SYSTEM – 9mm Para. cal., paramilitary design carbine, 18 1/2 in. barrel, vent. barrel shroud, 20 or 36 shot mag., matte black finish, 7 1/2 lbs., select-fire NFA class III transferable only.

$395	$350	$300	$275	$250	$230	$210	$379

ARMS ROOM LLC

Current manufacturer located in Orlando, FL.

The Arms Room manufactures both pistols and an AR-15 basic rifle package (TAR-Basic) that has a current MSR of $770. Please contact the company directly for more information on its products.

ARMS TECH LTD.

Current manufacturer established in 1987, and located in Phoenix, AZ.

RIFLES: BOLT ACTION

Current models include the SMIR, TTR-50, TTR-700, SBA 2000, USR, USR-K, Voyager, and the Overwatch. Arms Tech Ltd. also offers a wide variety of options and accessories. Please contact the company directly for more information, including pricing, options, and availability (see Trademark Index).

RIFLES: SEMI-AUTO

Current models include several models available for military/law enforcement, including the Compak-16 and the Recon Rifle. Previously, the company offered the Urban Support Rifle for the civilian marketplace. Please contact the company directly for more information, including pricing and availability for law enforcement and military models (see Trademark Index).

SUPER MATCH INTERDICTION POLICE MODEL – .243 Win., .300 Win. Mag., or .308 Win. (standard) cal., features 22 in. free floating Schnieder or Douglas air gauged stainless steel barrel, gas operation, McMillan stock, updated trigger group, detachable box mag., 13 1/4 lbs. Limited mfg. 1996-98.

$3,950	$3,650	$3,300	$3,000	$2,750	$2,350	$2,000	$4,800

SHOTGUNS: SLIDE ACTION

Currently, Arms Tech Ltd. offers the Alpha Entry, utilizing the Rem. 870 action, with a folding stock. Previously, the company offered another folding stock model called the Hammer. Please contact the company directly regarding pricing and availability (see Trademark Index).

ARMSAN

Current shotgun manufacturer located in Istanbul, Turkey.

Armsan manufactures good quality O/U, SxS, slide action, and semi-auto shotguns in both sporting and tactical configurations. Armsan is currently making private label shotguns in various configurations for Mossberg, Verney-Carron, and Weatherby.

ARMSCO

Previous North American importer and distributor of Huglu shotguns located in Des Plaines, IL. Please refer to the Huglu listing for more information.

ARMSCOR

ARMSCOR

Current trademark of firearms manufactured by Arms Corporation of the Philippines (manufacturing began 1952) established in 1985 (Armscor Precision - API). Currently imported and distributed beginning 1999 by Armscor Precision International (full line), located in Pahrump, NV. Previously imported 1995-1999 by K.B.I., Inc. located in Harrisburg, PA, by Ruko located in Buffalo, NY until 1995 and by Armscorp Precision Inc. located in San Mateo, CA until 1991.

GRADING - PPGS™	100%	98%	95%	90%	80%	70%	60%	LAST MSR

In 1991, the importation of Arms Corporation of the Philippines firearms was changed to Ruko Products, Inc., located in Buffalo, NY. Barrel markings on firearms imported by Ruko Products, Inc. state "Ruko-Armscor" instead of the older "Armscorp Precision" barrel markings. All Armscorp Precision, Inc. models were discontinued in 1991.

The models listed also provide cross-referencing for older Armscorp Precision and Ruko imported models.

PISTOLS: SEMI-AUTO

All semi-auto pistols were discontinued during 2008, and currently Armscor manufactured pistols can be found under the Rock Island Armory trademark.

M-1911-A1 FS (FULL SIZE STANDARD) – .45 ACP cal., patterned after the Colt Govt. Model, 7 shot mag. (2 provided), 5 in. barrel, parkerized (disc. 2001), blue (new 2002), two-tone (new 2002), or stainless steel (new 2002), skeletonized combat hammer and trigger, front and rear slide serrations, hard rubber grips, 38 oz. Imported 1996-97, reintroduced 2001-2008.

$350	$300	$280	$260	$240	$220	$200	*$399*

Add $31 for two-tone finish.
Add $75 for stainless steel.

This model was also available in a high capacity configuration (Model 1911-A2 HC, 13 shot mag., $519 MSR).

M-1911-A1 MS (COMMANDER) – .45 ACP cal., Commander configuration with 4 in. barrel, otherwise similar to M-1911 A1 Standard, rear slide serrations only. Imported 2001-2008.

$360	$300	$280	$260	$240	$220	$200	*$408*

Add $37 for two-tone finish.
Add $90 for stainless steel.

M-1911-A1 CS (OFFICER) – .45 ACP cal., officer's configuration with 3 1/2 in. barrel, checkered hardwood grips, 2.16 lbs. Imported 2002-2008.

$370	$310	$285	$265	$245	$220	$200	*$423*

Add $52 for two-tone finish.
Add $105 for stainless steel.

M-1911-A1 MEDALLION SERIES – 9mm Para., .40 S&W, or .45 ACP cal., 5 in. barrel, customized model including many shooting enhancements, match barrel, hand fitted slide and frame, choice of checkered wood or Pachmayr grips, available in either Standard or Tactical variation, blue, two-tone or chrome finish. Imported 2002-2008.

$445	$350	$310	$285	$260	$240	$220	*$539*

Add $129 for Tactical Model, add $198 for Tactical Model two-tone, or $203 for Tactical Model chrome.

REVOLVERS

MODEL 200 (DC) REVOLVER – .38 Spl. cal., 6 shot, double action, 2 1/2 (importation disc.), 4 (new 1998) or 6 (new 1998, importation disc.) in. barrel with shroud, transfer bar safety, combat style rubber grips, blue finish only, fixed rear sight, 26 oz. Imported 1996-99, reintroduced 2001.

No MSR	$230	$185	$150	$125	$110	$100	$80

Add approx. $6 for 4 in. barrel or $16 for 6 in. barrel (disc.)

MODEL 202 REVOLVER – similar to Model 200, except does not have barrel shroud. Imported 2001-2008.

$135	$120	$100	$90	$75	$60	$45	*$156*

MODEL 206 REVOLVER – similar to Model 200, except has 2 in. barrel, 24 oz. Importation began 2001.

No MSR	$240	$190	$155	$125	$115	$100	$80

MODEL 210 REVOLVER – similar to Model 200, except has 4 in. VR barrel, and adj. rear sight, 28 oz. Imported 2001-2008.

$175	$155	$130	$120	$95	$80	$60	*$196*

GRADING - PPGS™	100%	98%	95%	90%	80%	70%	60%	LAST MSR

RIFLES: BOLT ACTION

M-12Y/12-TY – .22 LR cal., bolt action, single shot, youth model with 18 3/8 in. barrel. Imported 1997 only, reintroduced during 2001.

	$95	$80	$70	$60	$50	$40	$35	*$109*

M-14P – .22 LR cal., bolt action, 10 shot mag., 23 in. barrel, open sights, hooded bead ramp front sight and leaf type rear sight, 6 lbs. Disc. 1997.

	$95	$75	$60	$50	$45	$40	$35	*$129*

A youth model was also available with shorter dimensions at no extra charge (M-14Y).

* ***M-14-D*** – .22 LR cal., bolt action, similar to M-14P, except has adj. rear sight and checkered mahogany stock. Importation disc. 1995.

	$105	$85	$70	$60	$50	$45	$40	*$139*

M-1400LW – .22 LR cal., similar action to M-14P, except has checkered stock and Schnabel forend, 10 shot mag., hard rubber pad, 6 lbs. Imported 1990-92.

	$185	$165	$150	$135	$120	$105	$95	*$219*

* ***M-1400S*** – .22 LR cal., similar to M-1500(S), except has 10 shot mag., 6.7 lbs. Imported 1996-97.

	$175	$125	$100	$75	$65	$55	$50	*$224*

* ***M-1400 (SC-Super Classic)*** – .22 LR cal., otherwise similar to M-1500SC, except has 10 shot mag. and 23 in. barrel, 6 lbs. Imported 1990-1997 and 2001-2008.

	$200	$150	$110	$85	$70	$60	$55	*$242*

Add $18 for stainless steel construction (new 2002).

* ***M-1400E*** – .22 LR cal., 6 or 10 shot mag., similar to M-1400, except has checkered stock and Schnabel forend, hard rubber pad, fiber optic front sight and adj. rear sight. New 2004.

This model is currently not being imported into the United States.

* ***M-1400 Sportster*** – .22 LR cal., similar to M-1400E, except has competition type stock and scalloped forearm, Monte Carlo style butt with cheekpiece. New 2004.

This model is currently not being imported into the United States.

M-1500S – .22 WMR cal., deluxe bolt action, 5 shot mag., 21 1/2 or 22 5/8 in. barrel, checkered mahogany stock, open sights, 7 lbs. Disc. 1997, reintroduced 2001.

	$145	$125	$110	$95	$85	$75	$65	*$160*

* ***M-1500LW (Lightweight)*** – similar to M-1500, except has lightweight classic European styled stock made of checkered American Walnut, with buttpad. Imported 1990-92.

	$190	$170	$150	$135	$120	$105	$95	*$229*

* ***M-1500 (SC-Super Classic)*** – checkered American Walnut stock with hard rubber pad and Monte Carlo cheekpiece, hardwood forend tip, engine turned bolt, 7 lbs. Imported 1990-1997 and 2001-2008.

	$215	$165	$120	$100	$85	$70	$60	*$260*

Subtract $3 for stainless steel.

M-1800S (CLASSIC) – .22 Hornet cal., 5 shot mag., dual locking lugs, checkered hardwood stock, adj. rear sight, 6.6 lbs. Imported 1996-1997.

	$250	$225	$200	$180	$165	$150	$135	*$358*

* ***M-1800SC (Super Classic)*** – similar to M-1800S, except has checkered walnut stock with forend tip, and high polish bluing, 7 1/4 lbs. Imported 1996-1997, reintroduced during 2001.

	$285	$260	$240	$220	$200	$185	$170	*$323*

RIFLES: SEMI-AUTO

M-1600 – .22 LR cal., 10 or 15 (disc.) shot mag., 18 in. barrel, copy of the Armalite M16, ebony stock, 5 1/4 lbs.

No MSR	$180	$150	$130	$110	$100	$80	$70	

GRADING - PPGS™	100%	98%	95%	90%	80%	70%	60%	LAST MSR

* ***M-1600R*** – similar to M-1600, except has stainless steel retractable buttstock and vent. barrel hood, 7 1/4 lbs. Importation disc. 1995, reintroduced 2008-2011.

	$155	$135	$115	$105	$85	$70	$55	

M-20 – .22 LR cal., 10 shot mag., deluxe checkered hardwood stock and forend, blue or stainless steel. Imported 2002-2008.

	$200	$180	$155	$140	$115	$90	$70	*$245*

Add $15 for stainless steel construction (new 2002).

M-20P – .22 LR cal., 15 shot mag., 20 3/4 in. barrel, open sights, 5 1/2 lbs. Disc. 1997, reintroduced during 2001, again in 2010.

No MSR	$150	$125	$100	$85	$75	$70	$55	

* ***M-20C*** – similar to M-20P, except has carbine style stock, barrel band, and curved steel buttplate, 16 1/2 in. barrel, 5 1/4 lbs. Previously available from K.B.I. only, disc. 2001.

	$130	$115	$95	$90	$70	$60	$45	*$159*

* ***M-20D*** – .22 LR cal., 22 in. barrel, 10 or 15 shot mag., checkered hardwood stock and forend, 6 1/2 lbs. Imported 2002-2008.

	$200	$180	$155	$140	$115	$90	$70	*$245*

Add $15 for stainless steel construction (new 2002).

M-2000(S) – same specifications as M-20P, except has checkered mahogany stock and adj. rear sight. Disc. 1997.

	$140	$120	$105	$95	$75	$65	$50	*$213*

* ***M-2000SC (Super Classic)*** – similar to M-2000, except has checkered American Walnut stock with cheekpiece and hardwood forend tip, engine turned bolt, 6 lbs. Imported 1990-97.

	$270	$235	$200	$185	$150	$120	$95	*$340*

M-50S – .22 LR cal., semi-auto design, 16 1/2 in. shrouded barrel, 25 or 30 shot mag., uncheckered mahogany stock, 6 1/2 lbs. Disc. 1995.

	$155	$135	$115	$105	$85	$70	$55	*$209*

M-AK22(S) – .22 LR cal., copy of the famous Russian Kalashnikov AK-47 rifle, 18 1/2 in. barrel, 10 or 15 (disc.) shot mag., mahogany stock and forearm, 7 lbs.

No MSR	$185	$160	$140	$125	$100	$85	$65	

* ***M-AK22(F)*** – similar to M-AK22, except has metal folding stock, and 30 shot mag. Disc. 1995.

	$275	$240	$205	$185	$150	$125	$95	*$299*

MIG 22 STANDARD – .22 LR cal., 18 in. barrel, blowback action, 15 shot detachable box mag., matte black finish, fixed synthetic stock, top Picatinny rail. New mid-2012.

As this edition went to press, pricing was not available on this model.

MIG 22 TARGET – .22 LR cal., 18 in. heavy barrel, blowback action, 15 shot detachable box mag., matte black finish, skeletonized aluminum stock, top Picatinny rail, 8 lbs. New mid-2012.

As this edition went to press, pricing was not available on this model.

SHOTGUNS: SLIDE ACTION

M-5 – 12 ga., 3 in. chamber, 26 in. shrouded barrel, 4 shot mag., black plastic stock and forearm, parkerized or nickel (new 2011) finish.

No MSR	$240	$195	$170	$150	$125	$110	$100	

Add $40 for matte nickel finish (new 2011).

M-30 F (INTERCHANGEABLE CHOKES) – 12 ga. only, 28 in. plain barrel with 3 choke tubes, 5 shot mag., uncheckered stock and forearm. Disc. 1999.

	$225	$190	$160	$140	$120	$95	$85	*$269*

GRADING - PPGS™	100%	98%	95%	90%	80%	70%	60%	LAST MSR

* ***M-30 D/IC (Deluxe)*** – similar to Model M30 IC, except has checkered walnut stock and forearm with recoil pad. Imported 2001 only.

	$180	$155	$125	$110	$95	$85	$75	*$208*

M-30 DG (DEER GUN) – 12 ga. only, law enforcement version of M-30, 20 in. plain barrel, iron sights, 7 shot mag., approx. 7 lbs. Importation disc. 1999, resumed during 2001.

	$165	$140	$120	$100	$85	$75	$70	*$195*

M-30SAS1 – 12 ga. only, riot configuration with 20 in. barrel and vent. barrel shroud, and Speedfeed 4 shot (disc.) or 6 shot mag., regular synthetic buttstock and forearm, matte finish, 8 lbs. Imported 1996-1999 and 2001-2008.

	$180	$155	$130	$110	$95	$85	$75	*$211*

Add $56 for Speedfeed stock (new 2002).

M-30 R6/R8 (RIOT) – 12 ga. only, similar to M-30DG, except has front bead sight only, 5 or 7 shot mag., cyl. bore. Importation disc. 1999, reintroduced 2001-2008.

	$155	$135	$110	$90	$80	$75	$70	*$181*

Add $7 for 7 shot mag.

M-30BG – 12 ga. only, 18 1/2 in. barrel, 5 shot mag., polymer pistol grip and forearm. New 2004.

This model is currently not being imported into the United States.

M-30F/FS – similar to M-30BG, except has additional folding metal stock unit. Disc. 2008.

	$180	$155	$130	$110	$95	$85	$75	*$211*

M30 C (COMBO) – 12 ga., 20 in. barrel, 5 shot mag., unique detachable black synthetic buttstock which allows pistol grip only operation. Disc. 1995.

	$210	$175	$145	$120	$100	$90	$80	*$289*

M30 RP (COMBO) – 12 ga. only, same action as M-30 DG, interchangeable black pistol grip, 18 1/4 in. plain barrel w/front bead sight, 6 1/4 lbs. Disc. 1995.

	$210	$175	$145	$120	$100	$90	$80	*$289*

ARMSCORP USA, INC.

Previous manufacturer and importer located in Baltimore, MD. Currently Armscorp USA deals in parts only.

PISTOLS: SEMI-AUTO

HI POWER – 9mm Para. cal., patterned after Browning design, 4 2/3 in. barrel, military finish, 13 shot mag., synthetic checkered grips, spur hammer, 2 lbs. mfg. in Argentina, imported 1989-90 only.

	$395	$350	$295	$275	$250	$225	$200	*$450*

Add $15 for round hammer.
Add $50 for hard chrome finish w/combat grips (disc. 1989).

* ***Hi Power Compact Detective HP*** – similar to Hi Power, except has 3 1/2 in. barrel, 1.9 lbs. Mfg. 1989 only.

	$395	$350	$295	$275	$250	$225	$200	*$475*

SD-9 – 9mm Para. cal., double action only, blowback mechanism, 3.07 in. barrel, 6 shot mag., frame is fabricated mostly of heavy gauge sheet metal stampings, chamber indicator, limited Israeli mfg., 1 1/2 lbs. Imported 1989-90 only.

	$350	$250	$230	$210	$195	$180	$170	*$350*

This pistol has also been manufactured by Sirkis Industries - refer to their section.

P22 – .22 LR cal., patterned after the Colt Woodsman, 4 or 6 in. barrel, 10 shot mag., checkered wood grips, mfg. in Argentina. Imported 1989-90 only.

	$190	$150	$130	$115	$100	$95	$85	*$225*

GRADING - PPGS™	100%	98%	95%	90%	80%	70%	60%	LAST MSR

RIFLES: SEMI-AUTO

M-14 RIFLE (NORINCO PARTS) – .308 Win. cal., 20 shot mag., mfg. M-14 using Norinco parts, wood stock. Mfg. 1991-92 only.

$1,225 $1,150 $1,050 $975 $875 $775 $675 *$688*

M-14R RIFLE (USGI PARTS) – .308 Win. cal., 10 (C/B 1994) or 20* shot mag., newly manufactured M-14 using original excellent condition forged G.I. parts including USGI fiberglass stock with rubber recoil pad. Mfg. 1986-2006.

$1,925 $1,675 $1,400 $1,275 $1,125 $1,000 $850 *$1,895*

Add $80 for medium weight National Match walnut stock (M-14RNS).
Add $25 for G.I. buttplate (disc.).
Add $45 for USGI birch stock (M-14RNSB, disc.).

M-14 BEGINNING NATIONAL MATCH – .308 Win. cal., mfg. from hand selected older USGI parts, except for new receiver and new USGI air gauged premium barrel, guaranteed to shoot 1 1/4 in. group at 100 yards. Mfg. 1993-96.

$2,050 $1,650 $1,350 $1,225 $1,125 $1,025 $925 *$1,950*

M-14 NMR (NATIONAL MATCH) – .308 Win. cal., built in accordance with USAMU mil spec standards, 3 different barrel weights to choose from, NM rear sight system, calibrated mag., leather sling, guaranteed 1 MOA. Mfg. 1987-2006.

$2,675 $2,125 $1,750 $1,400 $1,200 $1,075 $950 *$2,850*

M-21 MATCH RIFLE – .308 Win. cal., NM rear lugged receiver, choice of McMillan fiberglass or laminated wood stock, guaranteed 1 MOA accuracy.

$3,475 $2,900 $2,325 $2,000 $1,650 $1,350 $1,175 *$3,595*

T-48 FAL ISRAELI PATTERN RIFLE – .308 Win. cal., mfg. in the U.S. to precise original metric dimensions (parts are interchangeable with original Belgium FAL), forged receiver, hammer forged chrome lined mil spec. 21 in. barrel (standard or heavy) with flash suppressor, adj. front sight, aperture rear sight, 10 lbs. Imported 1990-92.

$1,650 $1,475 $1,300 $1,150 $1,075 $975 $875 *$1,244*

This model was guaranteed to shoot within 2.5 MOA with match ammunition.

* ***T-48 FAL L1A1 Pattern*** – .308 Win. cal., fully enclosed forend with vents, 10 lbs. Imported 1992 only.

$1,675 $1,500 $1,325 $1,175 $1,100 $1,000 $900 *$1,181*

Add $122 for wood handguard sporter model (limited supply).

* ***T-48 Bush Model*** – similar to T-48 FAL, except has 18 in. barrel, 9 3/4 lbs. Mfg. 1990 only.

$1,625 $1,450 $1,325 $1,175 $1,025 $925 $850 *$1,250*

FRHB – .308 Win. cal., Israeli mfg. with heavy barrel and bipod. Imported 1990 only.

$2,175 $1,900 $1,600 $1,425 $1,325 $1,225 $1,175 *$1,895*

FAL – .308 Win. cal., Armscorp forged receiver, 21 in. Argentinian rebuilt barrel, manufactured to military specs., supplied with one military 20 shot mag., aperture rear sight, 10 lbs. Mfg. 1987-89.

$1,800 $1,575 $1,425 $1,250 $1,125 $1,025 $925 *$875*

Subtract $55 if without flash hider.
Add $75 for heavy barrel with bipod (14 lbs.).
Add $400 (last retail) for .22 LR conversion kit.

This model was guaranteed to shoot within 2.5 MOA with match ammunition.

* ***FAL Bush Model*** – similar to FAL, except has 18 in. barrel with flash suppressor, 9 3/4 lbs. Mfg. 1989 only.

$2,200 $2,050 $1,925 $1,825 $1,750 $1,500 $1,250 *$900*

* ***FAL Para Model*** – similar to FAL Bush Model, except has metal folding stock, leaf rear sight. Mfg. 1989 only.

$2,400 $2,150 $1,050 $1,950 $1,750 $1,650 $1,550 *$930*

GRADING - PPGS™	100%	98%	95%	90%	80%	70%	60%	LAST MSR

* ***FAL Factory Rebuilt*** – factory (Argentine) rebuilt FAL without flash suppressor in excellent condition with Armscorp forged receiver, 9 lbs. 10 oz. Disc. 1989.

	$1,675	$1,450	$1,195	$1,025	$950	$775	$695	*$675*

Add 20% for heavy barrel variation manufactured in Argentina under license from F.N.

M36 ISRAELI SNIPER RIFLE – .308 Win. cal., gas operated semi-auto, bullpup configuration, 22 in. free floating barrel, Armscorp M14 receiver, 20 shot mag., includes flash suppressor and bipod, 10 lbs. Civilian offering 1989 only.

	$3,050	$2,650	$2,425	$2,200	$2,050	$1,925	$1,750	*$3,000*

EXPERT MODEL – .22 LR cal., semi-auto, 20.9 in. barrel, 10 shot mag., wood stock with one-screw takedown, iron sights with grooved receiver, 5.1 lbs. Imported 1989-disc.

	$195	$150	$125	$115	$105	$95	$85	*$225*

ARM SPORT LLC

Previous conversion manufacturer and customizer located in Platteville, CO.

Gunsmith R.L. Millington specialized in authentic hand-built conversions of Colt and Remington black powder pistols to metallic cartridges, custom engraving, refinishing, and antique refinishing.

CARTRIDGE CONVERSIONS

Calibers included .32 S&W Short, .38 S&W, .38 LC, .38 Spl., .44-40 WCF, and .45 LC. Antiquing and period-style engraving were options. Arms Sport LLC converted the 1839 Texas Paterson, Colt Pocket Dragoon (Wells-Fargo Model), 1851 Navy, 1861 Navy, and 1862 Pocket Navy/1862 Pocket Police, the 1847 Walker/Dragoon Models and the 1860 Army, the 1858 Remington Army, the Remington Navy, and the Remington Pocket Pistol. All prices were POR.

ARMSPORT, INC.

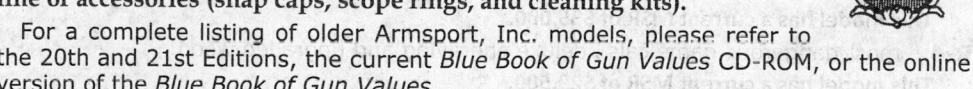

Previous importer and distributor located in Miami, FL. Armsport imported shotguns (various configurations, mfg. by Sarsilmaz of Turkey) until 2000. Armsport, Inc. imported a revolver and offered a complete line of accessories (snap caps, scope rings, and cleaning kits).

For a complete listing of older Armsport, Inc. models, please refer to the 20th and 21st Editions, the current *Blue Book of Gun Values* CD-ROM, or the online version of the *Blue Book of Gun Values*.

ARMY & NAVY

Previous department stores established in the United Kingdom circa 1871, with headquarters in London, England.

The Army & Navy trademark was originally established circa 1871 by a group of Army & Navy officers, and maintained its trademark until 2005, when it was renamed House of Fraser Victoria. In addition to selling domestic goods, the London store also sold guns using the Army & Navy trademark, manufactured by many respected English firms, including Webley & Scott, W.J. Jeffery, and others. These long guns (mostly shotguns, circa 1870s-pre WWII) were offered in a variety of both hammer and hammerless configurations, which included both plain boxlocks and special order sidelocks with elaborate engraving and deluxe wood. A few double rifles were also manufactured in various calibers. Because of the variety of guns that the Army & Navy department stores offered its customers, these guns need to be appraised individually for correct values. A general guideline is that average condition 12 ga. boxlocks sell in the $750-$2,000 range, uncased sidelocks with nice engraving and no problems typically start at $2,500 and can exceed $10,000 for best quality, cased specimens in smaller gauges.

ARNOLD ARMS CO., INC.

Previous rifle manufacturer located in Arlington, WA, 1994-2001.

In addition to making a series of accurate rifles built on their own Apollo action, Arnold Arms Co. also built rifles on Remington, Ruger, Sako, or Winchester actions. All Arnold Arms rifles had a written guarantee on accuracy (1/2 in. group or less at 100 yards with handloads), and a 5-year limited warranty. Any Arnold Arms warranty is now void. The company also made proprietary cartridges in 6mm Arnold, .257 Arnold, .270 Arnold, .300 Arnold, .338 Arnold, and .458 Arnold.

Arnold Arms Co., Inc. made a wide variety of quality bolt action rifles, including the African Trophy, Grand African Rifle, Alaskan Series, Classic Hunter Series, Neutralizer Series, Varminter Series, and the Strike Viper Series. For a complete listing of older Arnold Arms models and current values, please refer to the online or CD-ROM version of the *Blue Book of Gun Values*.

ARRIETA, S.L.

Current manufacturer established circa 1928 and located in Elgoibar, Spain. Currently imported by several importers including Wingshooting Adventures, Quality Arms, Griffin & Howe, William Larkin Moore, and Orvis (see separate listing). Previously imported by New England Arms.

More information can be obtained on the Arrieta models listed below by contacting the importers listed above.

RIFLES: SxS

Arrieta rifles have had limited U.S. importation in the past. Please contact the importers directly for more information, including availability and pricing on these models (see Trademark Index).

R-1 – 7x65R, 8x57JRS, or 9.3x74R cal., true sidelock, ejectors, quarter rib barrel with express rear sight.

MSR N/A	$19,000	$16,250	$13,250	$10,750	$9,350	$7,400	$6,200

R-2 – similar to R-1, except has more elaborate H&H style engraving, elongated tangs, and choice of English or reinforced pistol grip with metal cap, ejectors.

This model has a current MSR of $35,750 in .375 H&H, .470 NE, or .500 NE cal.

R-3 – similar to R-1, except includes .375 H&H, .470 NE, .500 NE cal.

This model has a current MSR of $35,000.

R-4 – most dangerous game cals., deluxe engraving and upgraded wood.

This model has a current MSR of $29,500.

This model is available only from Wingshooting Adventures.

R-5 – most dangerous game cals., best quality wood and engraving.

This model has a current MSR of $38,900.

This model is only available from Wingshooting Adventures.

SHOTGUNS: SxS

The models listed below are essentially custom ordered per individual specifications - delivery time is approx. 12 months.

All Arrieta shotguns have frames scaled to individual gauges. Standard gauges are 12 and 16. Most models are available with either color case hardened or coin finished frames. Many factory upgrades and custom options/special orders are available from the individual importers - please contact them directly for availability and current pricing on these special orders.

On the models listed below, there are four different types of sidelock actions. One is used on the Model 550. Another is used on Models 557, 578, and 871. A third is used on Models 590 and 595 (designed for heavy use). Finally, the best quality is used on Models 600-903, except for Model 900 (557 action), and Model 871. All Arrieta actions are assisted opening, except the Models 557, 570, 578, and 871.

MSRs may vary somewhat from importer to importer.

Add 10% for small gauges (20, 24 (disc.), 28, 32 ga., or .410 bore).

Add approx. $1,250 for single trigger depending on action.

GRADING - PPGS™	100%	98%	95%	90%	80%	70%	60%	LAST MSR

Add 10% for matched pair.
Add 5% for rounded action on standard models (except Models 871 and 872).
Extra barrels are priced from $1,500-$2,400/set depending on model.
Add $300 for pistol grip or semi-pistol grip stock or beavertail forearm.
Add $1,000-$3,000 for wood upgrade, depending on model.

06 – all gauges, elaborate engraving, assisted opening, ejectors.

MSR $17,200	$15,250	$12,000	$10,500	$9,000	$7,250	$6,000	$5,250	

557 – 12, 16, or 20 ga., Demi-Bloc steel barrels, detachable engraved sidelocks, double triggers, ejectors.

MSR $4,400	$4,225	$3,900	$3,375	$2,350	$1,750	$1,400	$1,175	

570 – 12, 16, or 20 ga., similar to 560 (non-standard model), except has non-detachable sidelocks.

MSR $5,300	$4,825	$4,275	$3,500	$2,450	$1,975	$1,500	$1,250	

578 – 12, 16, or 20 ga., similar to 570, except is fine English scrollwork engraved.

MSR $6,050	$6,225	$4,825	$3,900	$3,150	$2,450	$1,775	$1,425	

600 IMPERIAL – 12, 16, or 20 ga., top-of-the-line self-opening action, very ornate engraving throughout.

MSR $9,700	$9,100	$7,950	$6,450	$5,375	$4,250	$3,400	$2,750	

601 IMPERIAL TIRO – all gauges, sidelock action with nickel plating, ejectors, SST, self-opening action, border engraving.

MSR $9,750	$9,100	$7,750	$6,350	$5,300	$4,175	$3,300	$2,550	

801 – all gauges, Holland-style detachable sidelocks, self-opening action standard, ejectors, coin-wash finish, finest Churchill style engraving.

MSR $14,275	$12,750	$10,500	$9,300	$8,300	$7,300	$6,325	$5,275	

802 – 12, 16, or 20 ga., similar to 801 only non-detachable sidelocks, finest Holland-style engraving.

MSR $14,275	$12,750	$10,500	$9,300	$8,300	$7,300	$6,325	$5,275	

803 – all gauges, similar to 801, finest Purdey-style engraving.

MSR $11,550	$10,425	$9,100	$8,050	$7,000	$6,000	$5,000	$4,000	

871 – all gauges, rounded frame sidelock action with Demi-Bloc barrels, scroll engraved, ejectors, DTs.

MSR $7,250	$6,650	$6,000	$5,200	$4,500	$3,425	$2,750	$2,200	

872 – all gauges, rounded frame sidelock action with Demi-Bloc barrels, elaborate scroll engraving with third lever fastener.

MSR $18,250	$16,000	$12,500	$10,750	$9,000	$7,250	$6,000	$5,250	

873 – all gauges, sidelock action with Demi-Bloc barrels, game scene engraving, ejectors, SST.

MSR $18,500	$16,750	$13,000	$11,000	$9,000	$7,250	$6,000	$5,250	

874 – all gauges, sidelock action with Demi-Bloc barrels, action is gold line engraved.

MSR $14,175	$12,950	$11,500	$9,575	$8,325	$7,300	$6,325	$5,275	

875 – all gauges, top-of-the-line quality, built to individual customer specs. only, elaborate engraving with gold inlays.

MSR $21,440	$18,750	$16,250	$14,550	$11,000	$9,250	$8,100	$7,250	

931 – all gauges, self-opening action, elaborate engraving, H&H selective ejectors.

MSR $30,100	$26,450	$21,725	$19,000	$16,250	$14,550	$11,000	$9,250	

UPLANDER – small gauges only, engraved sidelock action with upgraded straight grip wood.

MSR $4,950	$4,525	$4,150	$3,850	$3,350	$2,350	$1,750	$1,250	

This model is available only from Wingshooting Adventures.

GRADING - PPGS™	100%	98%	95%	90%	80%	70%	60%	LAST MSR

ARRIETA SPECIAL – all gauges, engraved sidelock action, upgraded wood.

MSR $6,100	$5,600	$5,000	$4,475	$3,950	$3,000	$2,100	$1,525	

This model is available only from Wingshooting Adventures.

"BOSS" ROUND BODY – all gauges, Boss pattern best quality engraving, includes $1,500 wood upgrade.

MSR N/A	N/A	$8,250	$7,150	$5,950	$5,200	$4,400	$3,600	

ARRIZABALAGA, PEDRO

Current manufacturer located in Eibar, Spain since 1940. Currently imported and distributed by William Larkin Moore, located in Scottsdale, AZ and by Harry Marx Hi-Grade Imports located in Los Banos, CA. Previously imported by New England Arms Corp. located in Kittery Point, ME.

Arrizabalaga manufactures best quality guns only, carefully made to individual customer specifications. Shotguns listed below have demi-bloc chopper lump barrels and self-opening hand-detachable locks as standard features. The models listed below are essentially custom ordered per individual specifications - delivery time is approximately 12-18 months.

SHOTGUNS: SxS

Add 5% of MSRs for matched pair. Add $5,500 per extra set of same gauge barrels. Add $1,150 for 28 ga. or Add $1,900 for .410 bore. Add $2,475 for single non-selective trigger. Add $900 for beavertail forearm. Add $1,175 for pistol grip stock. Add $1,000 - $3,000 for English or Turkish wood upgrade. Add $1,650 for factory furnished fitted leather case.

HEAVY SCROLL MODEL – all gauges, sidelock action, elaborate engraving, deluxe oil finished stock and forearm.

MSR $22,800	$20,750	$18,500	$15,500	$12,750	$11,000	$8,000	$6,000	

ENGLISH SCROLL MODEL – all gauges, sidelock action, English scroll engraving, deluxe oil finished walnut stock and forearm.

MSR $23,600	$21,350	$19,000	$16,000	$13,000	$11,500	$8,000	$6,000	

MODEL DELUXE – all gauges, limited importation.

This model is POR.

BOSS STYLE ROUND ACTION MODEL – all gauges, features English Boss-style scroll engraving.

MSR $24,900	$22,250	$19,950	$16,750	$13,500	$11,750	$8,250	$6,500	

Add $700 for Luxe engraving.

SPECIAL MODEL – all gauges, sidelock top-of-the-line model, best quality wood and engraving.

This model is POR.

ARSENAL, BULGARIA

Current manufacturer located in Kazanlack, Bulgaria. Currently imported by Arsenal, Inc., located in Las Vegas, NV. Previously imported exclusively in 1994-1996 by Sentinel Arms located in Detroit, MI. For currently imported models, please refer to the Arsenal, Inc. listing.

The artillery arsenal in Rousse began operating in 1878, and was managed by Russian officers until 1884, when a Bulgarian was appointed the director. In 1891, the factory was transferred to Sofia, and was renamed the Sofia Artillery Arsenal until the entire facility was moved to Kazanlak in 1924. At that point, the name was changed to the State Military Factory. After WWII, the arsenal diversified into civilian production, and its Cold War security name was "Factory 10". In 1958, the first AK-47 design under Russian license came off the assembly line, and in 1982, the one millionth AK-47 had been manufactured.

GRADING - PPGS™	100%	98%	95%	90%	80%	70%	60%	LAST MSR

PISTOLS: SEMI-AUTO

MAKAROV MODEL – 9mm Makarov cal., 3 2/3 in. barrel, 8 shot mag., black synthetic grips, blue finish. Disc. 1996.

	100%	98%	95%	90%	80%	70%	60%	LAST MSR
	$185	$165	$125	$115	$105	$95	$85	

RIFLES: SEMI-AUTO

BULGARIAN SA-93 – 7.62x39mm cal., Kalashnikov with hardwood thumbhole stock, 16.3 in. barrel, 5 shot detachable mag., 9 lbs. Disc. 1996.

	100%	98%	95%	90%	80%	70%	60%	LAST MSR
	$800	$715	$625	$550	$600	$475	$450	

* ***Bulgarian SA-93L*** – 7.62x39mm cal., similar to Bulgarian SA-93 except has 20 in. barrel, with or without optics, 9 lbs. Disc. 1996.

	100%	98%	95%	90%	80%	70%	60%	LAST MSR
	$795	$725	$650	$595	$550	$495	$450	

Add $145 with optics.

BULGARIAN SS-94 – 7.62x39mm cal., Kalashnikov action, thumbhole hardwood stock, 5 shot detachable mag., 9 lbs. Disc. 1996.

	100%	98%	95%	90%	80%	70%	60%	LAST MSR
	$625	$550	$475	$425	$375	$350	$325	

ARSENAL FIREARMS

Current pistol manufacturer located in Gardone, Italy.

Arsenal Firearms also has plans to manufacture a Strike One semi-auto pistol, a Strike LRC conversion, and a series of bolt action rifles. Please contact the factory directly for more information and availability on these models.

PISTOLS: SEMI-AUTO

AF2011-DOUBLE BARREL PISTOL – .38 Super or .45 ACP cal., unique design allows side by side 4.92 in. barrels, double hammer with single spur, double independent or single trigger uses two single 8 shot magazines paired together with single floorplate, choice of blue steel with walnut grips and fixed sights, or stainless steel with rubber grips and adj. sights, approx. 51 oz. New 2012.

	100%	98%	95%	90%	80%	70%	60%	LAST MSR
MSR $4,400	$3,995	$3,550	$3,100	$2,750	$2,300	$2,100	$1,950	

Add $700 for stainless steel construction with rubber grips and adj. sights.

ARSENAL INC.

Current importer of non-military Arsenal 2000 JSCo (Bulgarian Arsenal), established during 2001 and located in Las Vegas, NV. Dealer and distributor sales.

RIFLES: SEMI-AUTO

Arsenal Inc. is the exclusive licensed manufacturer of various Arsenal Bulgaria AK-47 design rifles which conform 100% to Arsenal Bulgaria specifications and manufacturing procedures. Models are built on forged and milled receivers with CNC technology, and feature solid, under-folding or side-folding stock.

Additionally, Arsenal Inc. has also imported AK-47 design configurations with a thumbhole stock design (pre-2004). Values for these earlier models will be slightly less than current models with fixed or collapsible stocks.

SA M-5 SERIES – .223 Rem. cal., patterned after the AK-47, 16.3 in. barrel, black (SA M-5) or green (SA M-5G, disc. 2005) synthetic furniture with pistol grip, approx. 8.1 lbs. Mfg. 2003-2009.

	100%	98%	95%	90%	80%	70%	60%	LAST MSR
	$710	$620	$530	$480	$390	$320	$250	*$800*

Add $75 for SA M-5 R with scope rail (new 2007).
Add $10 for SA M-5G (disc. 2005).
Add $75 for SA M-5S with scope rail (limited edition, disc. 2005).
Add $80 for SA M-5SG (disc. 2005).

GRADING - PPGS™	100%	98%	95%	90%	80%	70%	60%	LAST MSR

SA M-7 S – 7.62x39mm cal., milled receiver, also available in carbine, otherwise similar to SA M-5, R Series with scope rail became standard 2009. Mfg. 2003-2011.

	$1,395	$1,295	$1,050	$850	$750	$650	$550	$1,550

Add $35 for SA M-7S with scope rail (disc.).
Add $5 for SA M-7G with OD green furniture (disc.)
Add $40 for SA M-7SG with scope rail (disc.)
Subtract approx. 15% if w/o scope rail (disc.)

SA M-7 CLASSIC – 7.62x39mm cal., features blonde wood stock, pistol grip and forearm, double stack magazine, heavy barrel and slanted gas block, Warsaw Pact buttstock, less than 200 mfg. 2001-2002, reintroduced 2007.

MSR $1,995	$1,750	$1,500	$1,250	$1,125	$900	$775	$650	

SA M-7 A1/SA M-7 A1 R – 7.62x39mm cal., milled receiver, front sight gas block w/ bayonet lug, 24mm flash hider, cleaning rod, accessory lug, black polymer furniture, NATO buttstock. Mfg. 2007-2009.

	$850	$745	$635	$580	$465	$380	$295	$960

Add $75 for SA M-7 A1 R w/scope rail.

SA M-7 R – 7.62x39mm cal., 14mm muzzle threads, muzzle nut, cleaning rod, bayonet lug, black polymer furniture, NATO buttstock, scope rail. New 2012.

MSR $2,000	$1,750	$1,500	$1,250	$1,125	$900	$775	$650	

SA M-7 SF – 7.62x39mm cal., U.S. mfg., milled receiver, front sight gas block with bayonet lug, 24mm flash hider, cleaning rod, accessory lug, black polymer furniture, right hand side folding stock, ambidextrous safety, scope rail. Mfg. 2007-2009.

	$1,025	$895	$770	$695	$565	$460	$360	$1,300

SA M-7 SFC/SA M-7 SFK – 7.62x39mm cal., U.S. mfg., milled receiver, front sight/gas block combination with 24mm thread protector, cleaning rod, black polymer furniture, right hand side folding tubular buttstock, ambidextrous safety, scope rail, SA M-7 SFK model with short gas system and laminated wood Krinkov handguards became standard 2009. Mfg. 2007-2011.

	$1,325	$1,160	$995	$900	$730	$595	$465	$1,575

SA RPK-3R – 5.45x39mm, milled receiver, RPK heavy barrel, removable flash hider, folding bipod, blonde wood furniture or black polymer, paddle style buttstock, scope rail, one 45 shot mag., sling, oil bottle, and cleaning kit. Mfg. 2011 only.

	$2,250	$1,950	$1,750	$1,500	$1,250	$1,000	$850	$2,500

SA RPK-5 (S) – .223 Rem. cal., features blonde wood stock, RPK heavy barrel, 14mm muzzle threads, pistol grip and forearm, 23 1/4 in. barrel with folding tripod, approx. 11 lbs. Limited edition 2003-2005, reintroduced 2007-2011.

	$1,750	$1,650	$1,500	$1,325	$1,150	$850	$695	$1,950

Add $75 for SA RPK-5 R model with scope rail (disc.)

SA RPK-7 – 7.62x39mm cal., paddle style buttstock, folding bipod, no scope rail, otherwise similar to SA RPK-5 (S). Limited edition 2003-2005, reintroduced 2007-2009.

	$995	$870	$745	$675	$545	$450	$350	$1,250

Add $75 for SA RPK-7 R with scope rail.

SAS M-7 – 7.62x39mm cal., U.S. mfg., authentic semi-auto version of Bulgarian model AR M1F with vertical gas block and BATFE-approved fixed metal underfolding-style stock. Mfg. 2004-2007.

	$1,075	$940	$800	$730	$590	$485	$375	$1,250

SAS M-7 CLASSIC – 7.62x39mm cal., U.S. mfg., authentic semi-auto version of Russian 1953 Model AKS-47 with slant gas block and BATFE-approved fixed metal underfolding-style stock, blonde furniture, heavy barrel. Limited edition 2001-2002, reintroduced 2007.

MSR $1,995	$1,750	$1,500	$1,250	$1,125	$900	$775	$650	

GRADING - PPGS™	100%	98%	95%	90%	80%	70%	60%	LAST MSR

SGL21 – 7.62x39mm cal., Russian made, stamped receiver, original Russian chrome lined hammer forged barrel, front sight block with bayonet lug, gas block with accessory lug, US made double stage trigger group, 5 shot mag., 4000 meter rear sight leaf, scope rail, original Warsaw, NATO or black polymer side folding buttstock with trapdoor for cleaning kit, Black, OD Green, Plum, Desert Sand (new 2012) finish. Mfg. by Arsenal, Inc. in Las Vegas, NV. New 2011.

MSR $823	$725	$625	$525	$450	$375	$325	$275	

Add $5 for OD Green, Plum, or Desert Sand (new 2012) finish.
Add $5 for NATO buttstock.
Add $30 for 40 shot mag.
Add $105 for forend rails (new 2012).
Add $422 for black polymer side folding buttstock.

SGL31 – 5.45x39mm cal., Russian made, stamped receiver, 10 shot mag., original Russian chrome lined hammer forged barrel, front sight block with bayonet lug, gas block with accessory lug, US made double stage trigger group, 1000 meter rear sight leaf, scope rail, original Warsaw or black polymer side folding buttstock with trapdoor for cleaning kit, Black, OD Green, Plum or Desert Sand (new 2012) finish. Mfg. by Arsenal, Inc. in Las Vegas, NV. New 2011.

MSR $857	$740	$635	$525	$450	$375	$325	$275	

Add $5 for Plum or Desert Sand (new 2012) finish.
Add $5 for NATO buttstock.
Add $26 for 45 shot mag.
Add $42 for OD Green finish and OD Green sling (new 2012).
Add $105 for forend rails (new 2012).
Add $316 for black polymer side folding buttstock.

SLR 101 S – 7.62x39mm cal., similar to SA M-7, except has thumbhole synthetic stock, available in black (SLR 101SB1) or OD Green (SLR 101SG1). Mfg. 2003-2005.

	$595	$550	$500	$450	$400	$350	$325	*$410*

Add $100 for SLR 101SB1.
Add $110 for SLR 101SG1.

SLR 101SB/SG – 7.62x39mm cal., double stack mag., side mount scope rail, 16 in. barrel, standard military stock configuration. Mfg. 2004-2005.

	$725	$635	$545	$495	$400	$325	$255	*$655*

Add $45 for SG Model with green polymer stock.

SLR-105 SERIES – 5.45x39.5mm cal., stamped receiver, cleaning rod, black polymer furniture, NATO buttstock. Mfg. 2007-2009.

	$695	$650	$600	$550	$475	$425	$350	*$475*

Add $50 for SLR-105 R with scope rail.
Add $150 for SLR-105 A1 model with front sight gas block, bayonet lug, and 24mm muzzle brake.
Add $200 for SLR-105 A1 R model with scope rail.

SLR-106 SERIES – 5.56 NATO cal., stamped receiver, left-side wire (disc. 2011) or solid black polymer (new 2012) folding stock, 24mm muzzle brake, gas block with bayonet lug, accessory lug (optional), stainless steel heat shield, two-stage trigger, Black or Desert Sand. New 2007.

MSR $974	$795	$695	$595	$550	$500	$450	$400	

Add $30 for Desert Sand finish and side scope rail.
Add $65 for SLR-106 CR with front sight and gas block combined (new 2012).
Add $125 for SLR-106 FR with scope and forend rails.
Subtract approx. $250 if with wire folding stock (disc. 2011).
Add $205 for SLR-106 UR Model with scope rail.
Add $199 for SLR-106 U Model with combination short-stroke gas block and front sight system and black furniture (disc.).
Add $179 for SLR-106 Model with removable muzzle attachment (disc.).

GRADING - PPGS™	100%	98%	95%	90%	80%	70%	60%	LAST MSR

SLR-107 SERIES – 7.62x39mm cal., stamped receiver, left-side wire (disc. 2011) folding solid polymer (new 2012) stock, 24mm flash hider, gas block with bayonet lug, accessory lug, stainless steel heat shield, two-stage trigger, Black or Desert Sand (disc. 2011) finish. New 2008.

MSR $989	$800	$700	$600	$550	$500	$450	$400	

Add $110 for forend rail.
Add $10 for SLR-107 CR Model with removable muzzle attachment.
Subtract $20 for wire side folding stock.
Add $6 for Desert Sand finish (disc. 2011).
Add $110 for SLR-107 FR with scope rail (disc. 2011).
Add $326 for SLR-107 UR Model with combination short-stroke gas block and front sight system and black furniture and scope rail (disc.).

ARSENAL USA LLC

Previous manufacturer/importer from 1999-2004, and located in Houston, TX. During September 2004, Arsenal USA LLC changed its name to Armory USA L.L.C. Please refer to the Armory USA L.L.C. listing for recently manufactured rifles.

RIFLES: SEMI-AUTO

MODEL SSR-99 – 7.62x39mm cal., Bulgarian milled receiver and parts, black polymer furniture. Less than 300 mfg. 1999-2000.

	$825	$750	$700	$650	$600	$550	$500	*$600*

MODEL K-101 – .223 Rem. cal., Bulgarian milled receiver and parts, black polymer furniture. Less than 200 mfg. 1999-2000.

	$875	$775	$700	$650	$600	$550	$500	*$600*

MODEL SSR-99P – 7.62x39mm cal., Bulgarian milled receiver and parts, with rare Polish grenade launching variant parts, Polish wood furniture. Less than 500 mfg. 1999-2001.

	$875	$775	$700	$650	$600	$550	$500	*$600*

MODEL SSR-85B – 7.62x39mm cal., Hungarian FEG receiver and Polish AKM parts, blond Hungarian wood furniture, small number produced using ITM U.S. made receiver. Approx. 1,200 mfg. 2000-2003.

	$875	$775	$700	$650	$600	$550	$625	*$450*

MODEL AMD-63 – 7.62x39mm cal., Hungarian FEG receiver and Polish AKM parts, unique metal lower handguard with pistol grip. 200 mfg. 2000-2003.

	$875	$775	$700	$650	$600	$550	$500	*$600*

MODEL SSR-56 – 7.62x39mm cal., Hungarian FEG receiver, Poly-Tec barrel assembly and Bulgarian internal parts. Approx. 500 mfg. 2002-2003.

	$775	$700	$650	$600	$550	$500	$450	*$450*

ART MANIFATTURA ARMI/ART ARMI

Please refer to Manifaturra Armi Art listing in the M section.

ASHBURY PRECISION ORDNANCE

Current manufacturer located in Charlottesville, VA. APO is a division of the Ashbury International Group, Inc. Consumer direct sales through FFL.

RIFLES: BOLT ACTION

Ashbury Precision Ordnance (APO) makes a high quality line of precision tactical rifles called the Asymmetric Warrior Series (ASW) and a Tactical Competition Rifle Series (TCR). Specifications, features, and options vary from model to model, so please contact the manufacturer directly for more information and current availability (see Trademark Index).

ASW50 – .50 BMG cal., McMilan bolt action repeater, Pinnacle Series 27 in. stainless steel barrel with integrated muzzle brake and suppressor system, ambidextrous paddle lever magazine release, 5 shot detachable box mag., Huber Tactical two stage trigger, Quattro

GRADING - PPGS™	100%	98%	95%	90%	80%	70%	60%	LAST MSR

carbon fiber heat/Mirage Mitigating Ergonomic forend, fully adj. PBA-H shoulder stock, Limbsaver recoil pad and grip, ErgoGrip Magpul M1AD grip set, Picatinny bottom accessory rail, Black, Flat Dark Earth, OD Green, or Nordic Gray finish, 25 3/4 lbs.

MSR $12,575 $11,250 $10,000 $9,200 $8,000 $6,750 $5,500 $4,500

ASW338 – .338 Lapua Mag. cal., Surgeon XL-II bolt action repeater, similar to ASW50 except has Pinnacle Series 20 or 27 in. stainless steel barrel, target crown with AAC Blackout muzzle brake, and detachable 5 or 10 shot box mag. 14 lbs.

MSR $8,550 $7,850 $7,100 $6,400 $5,500 $4,600 $3,700 $2,850

Add $200 for 10 shot mag.

ASW300 – .300 Win. Mag. cal., similar to ASW338, except has 24 in. stainless steel barrel.

MSR $8,500 $7,825 $7,100 $6,400 $5,500 $4,600 $3,700 $2,850

Add $250 for 10 shot detachable box mag.

ASW308 – .308 Win. Mag. cal., similar to ASW338, except has 20 in. stainless steel barrel, and 10 shot detachable box mag. only, approx. 12 1/2 lbs.

MSR $7,700 $7,000 $6,200 $5,500 $4,700 $4,000 $3,250 $2,550

ASW223 – .223 Rem. cal., otherwise similar to ASW308. New 2012.

MSR $7,700 $7,000 $6,200 $5,500 $4,700 $4,000 $3,250 $2,550

TCR338 – .338 Norma Mag. cal., Surgeon bolt action repeater, Pinnacle Series 27 in. stainless steel barrel with Badger FTE muzzle brake, ambidextrous paddle lever magazine release, 5 shot detachable box mag., Huber Tactical two stage trigger, integral scope rail, Quattro carbon fiber heat/Mirage Mitigating Ergonomic forend, hand tool adj. (HTA) shoulder stock, Limbsaver recoil pad and grip, ErgoGrip Magpul M1AD grip set, 4 in. Picatinny top and bottom accessory rail, Black, Flat Dark Earth, OD Green, or Nordic Gray finish.

MSR $7,295 $6,650 $5,750 $5,000 %4,200 $3,500 $2,850 $2,300

TCR223 – .223. Rem. cal., similar to TCR338, except has 20 in. barrel, and 10 shot detachable box mag. New 2012.

MSR $6,325 $5,650 $5,100 $4,500 $3,900 $3,300 $2,700 $2,100

TCR260 – .260 Rem. cal., similar to TCR338, except has 24 in. barrel and 10 shot detachable box mag.

MSR $6,325 $5,650 $5,100 $4,500 $3,900 $3,300 $2,700 $2,100

TCR300 – .300 Win. Mag. cal., similar to TCR338, except has a 24 in. barrel.

MSR $7,295 $6,650 $5,750 $5,000 %4,200 $3,500 $2,850 $2,300

TCR308 – .308 Win. Mag. cal., similar to TCR338, except has 20 in. barrel with muzzle target crown, and 10 shot detachable box mag.

MSR $6,325 $5,650 $5,100 $4,500 $3,900 $3,300 $2,700 $2,100

TCR6.5 – 6.5 Creedmore cal., similar to TCR338, except has 24 in. barrel, and 10 shot detachable box mag. New 2012.

MSR $6,325 $5,650 $5,100 $4,500 $3,900 $3,300 $2,700 $2,100

ASP

Previously manufactured customized variation of a S&W Model 39-2 semi-auto pistol (or related variations) manufactured by Armament Systems and Procedures located in Appleton, WI.

PISTOLS: SEMI-AUTO

ASP – 9mm Para. cal., compact double action semi-auto, see-through grips with cut-away mag. making cartridges visible, Teflon coated, re-contoured lightened slide, combat trigger guard, spurless hammer, and mostly painted Guttersnipe rear sight (no front sight), supplied with 3 mags., 24 oz. loaded. Approx. 3,000 mfg. until 1981.

$2,800 $1,500 $1,275 $1,050 $875 $775 $695

Add $200 for Tritium filled Guttersnipe sight.

This pistol is marked "ASP" on the magazine extension.

GRADING - PPGS™	100%	98%	95%	90%	80%	70%	60%	LAST MSR

* ***ASP Quest For Excellence*** – special edition, marked "Quest for Excellence". Included buffalo horn grips, presentation book case and letter opener. Approx. 100 mfg.

	$3,500	$3,150	$2,700	$2,400	$2,050	$1,775	$1,525	

REVOLVERS

ASP REVOLVER – .44 Spl. cal., conversion of a Ruger Speed or Security Six, 5 shot. Less than 100 mfg., unmarked.

	$1,275	$1,075	$950	$875	$775	$700	$650	

ASPREY

Previous long gun manufacturer located in London, England. While Asprey was established in 1781, the company manufactured high quality shotguns and rifles only from 1990-1999. During 1998, the name was changed to Asprey & Garrard. Guns are currently manufactured by William & Son, located in London, England.

Please refer to the William & Son listing for currently manufactured models.

ASTRA

Pre-1926 1926-1965 1965-1998

Previous manufacturer located in Guernica, Spain. Astra was one of the oldest and most widely recognized trademarks in Spain, with a history dating back to 1908. Though arms were manufactured for many years by Unceta y Compania, S.A., located in Guernica, Spain, corporate reorganization resulted in renaming the same firm Astra-Guernica, S.A. (1995-1997), and Astra Sport Guerniquesa de Mecanizado Tratamiento y Montaje de Armas, S.A. (1997-1998).

Although Astra had hoped to acquire Star patents and relocate to a smaller facility, these efforts were not successful. Foreclosure sealed the factory doors in July, 1998. Inventory, including the "factory collection," was released for sale in 1999.

PISTOLS: SEMI-AUTO

MODEL 1911 – .25 ACP or .32 ACP cal., semi-auto, may have external or internal hammer.

	$425	$375	$325	$250	$200	$165	$150	

Add 50% for external hammer.

MODEL 1915/1916 – .32 ACP cal., semi-auto.

	$400	$350	$300	$240	$195	$160	$125	

Note: Models 1915/1916 were later referred to as Model 100 Special.

CAMPO GIRO 1913 – 9mm Largo cal., mfg. 1913-14. Ser. No. range 1-1,300.

	$5,000	$4,375	$3,750	$3,400	$2,750	$2,250	$1,750	

Add 10% for magazine with matching ser. number.

CAMPO GIRO 1913-1916 – 9mm Largo cal., mfg. 1915-1919. Serial number range 1-13,625.

	$3,250	$2,845	$2,440	$2,210	$1,790	$1,465	$1,140	

Add 10% if fit with horn logo grips.
Add 10% for magazine with matching ser. number.
Add 150% for factory engraved with pearlite grips.

MODEL 200 FIRECAT AUTOMATIC PISTOL – .25 ACP cal., 2 1/4 in. barrel, 6 shot, blue, plastic grips. Mfg. 1920-68.

	$295	$260	$220	$200	$160	$135	$105	

100% prices assume N.I.B. condition.
Add 50% for engraved M-200.

MODEL 300 – .32 ACP or .380 ACP cal., semi-auto.

	$900	$750	$500	$400	$300	$200	$150	
lightly engraved	$2,000	$1,650	$1,200	$900	$800	$600	$500	
deeply engraved w/salesman sample grips	$3,500	$3,000	$2,500	$2,000	$1,500	$1,250	$1,000	

Add 25% for Nazi-proofed .380 ACP pistols.

GRADING - PPGS™	100%	98%	95%	90%	80%	70%	60%	LAST MSR

MODEL 400 AUTOMATIC PISTOL – 9mm Largo cal., 9 shot, 6 in. barrel, blue, fixed sights, plastic grips. Mfg. 1921-1945.

	$700	$550	$400	$300	$250	$200	$150
Nazi range specimens	$1,400	$1,100	$800	$600	$500	$400	$300
Navy variation	$2,100	$1,650	$1,200	$900	$750	$600	$450

Serial range of Nazi specimens (no special markings) is S/N 92,851-98,850.

This particular model in reworked configuration has recently been imported in large quantities.

* ***Model 400 Copies Marked "F. Ascaso"*** – close copy of the Astra Model 400, produced by the Spanish Republican forces during the later part of the Spanish Civil War, F. Ascaso marked (un-numbered) mags., salt blue, estimated production is approx. 8,000, has identifying logo on slide and grip panels, and base of magazine.

$1,250	$950	$750	$600	$500	$400	$300

* ***Model 400 Copies Marked R.E. (Republica Espagnola)*** – serial number range to approx. 15,000, has identifying logo on forward slide and grip panels.

$900	$800	$700	$600	$500	$400	$300

Add $200 for wood serrated grips with brass "RE" medallion.

MODEL 600 MOD. AUTOMATIC – 9mm Para. cal., 8 shot, 5 1/4 in. barrel, blue, fixed sights, wood or plastic grips. Mfg. 1944-1945.

	$500	$425	$325	$250	$200	$175	$150
Nazi Waffenamt proofing	$1,100	$850	$650	$500	$400	$350	$300

Add 100% for Chilean Air Force (450 mfg.), or 50% for Portuguese Navy MRP (800 mfg.).

Serial number range for Nazi Waffenamt proofing is 1-10,500.

MODEL 700 SPECIAL – .32 ACP cal., semi-auto.

$1,500	$1,315	$1,125	$1,020	$825	$675	$525

MODEL 800 CONDOR AUTOMATIC – 9mm Para. cal., similar to Model 600, except has exposed hammer. Mfg. 1958-65.

$1,850	$1,620	$1,390	$1,260	$1,020	$835	$650

Add 20% if NIB with accessories.

MODEL 900 – 7.63 Mauser cal., Broomhandle copy, parts non-interchangeable with Mauser C96. Mfg. from 1928-1936.

$3,250	$2,845	$2,440	$2,210	$1,790	$1,465	$1,140

Add $1,000 for non-matching shoulder stock.
Add $1,500 for matching stock.
Add 50% for early Bolo grip variation.
Add 20% for specimens with Chinese characters.

MODEL 902 – 7.63 Mauser cal., semi-auto, similar to Model 900 except 20 shot mag. Beware of fakes - usually created by welding up selective fire pistols.

$20,000	$17,500	$15,000	$13,600	$11,000	$9,000	$7,000

Add $1,500 for original "booted" stock.
Subtract 60% for selective fire version.

MACHINE PISTOLS – class III, transferrable only, 10 or 20 shot detachable mag., several variations.

$10,000	$8,750	$7,500	$6,800	$5,500	$4,500	$3,500

MODEL 3000 POCKET AUTOMATIC – .32 ACP or .380 ACP cal., 4 in. barrel, fixed sights, blue, plastic grips. Mfg. 1947-1956.

	$850	$750	$700	$550	$400	$200	$150
deeply engraved M3003	$2,125	$1,875	$1,750	$1,375	$1,000	$500	$375

Add 75% for lightly engraved M3002.
Add $1,000 for metallic cherub grips.

GRADING - PPGS™	100%	98%	95%	90%	80%	70%	60%	LAST MSR

MODEL 1000 OR 1000 SPECIAL – .32 ACP cal., semi-auto, extended frame to hold 12 shot mag.

	$950	$830	$715	$645	$525	$430	$335	

MODEL 2000 CUB – .22 Short or .25 ACP cal., 2 1/4 in. barrel, fixed sights, blue, plastic grips, also chrome finish, mfg. 1954-1998, U.S. importation stopped by GCA 68. Astra also made 2000 Model 2000 Cubs for Colt known as the Jr. Model (see Colt section).

	$300	$265	$225	$205	$165	$135	$105	

Add 25% for chrome finish.
Add 50% for engraved M-2000.

MODEL 2000 CAMPER – .22 Short cal. only, similar to Model 2000 Cub, with 4 in. barrel. Mfg. 1955-1960.

	$350	$305	$265	$240	$195	$160	$125	

Add 10% if in original box.

CONSTABLE – .22 LR (10 shot, disc. 1990), .32 ACP (8 shot, disc. 1984), or .380 ACP (7 shot) cal., double action, exposed hammer, 3 1/2 in. barrel, fixed sights, blue or chrome (disc.) finish, plastic grips. Imported 1965-1991.

	$325	$285	$245	$220	$180	$145	$115	*$380*

Add $10 for chrome finish or wood grips (disc. in 1990).
Add 10% for .22 LR cal.

* ***Constable Stainless*** – .380 ACP cal. only, stainless version of the Constable. Mfg. 1986 only.

	$650	$570	$490	$440	$360	$295	$230	*$345*

* ***Constable Sport*** – similar to Constable, except has 6 in. barrel, blue finish only, 35 oz. Mfg. 1986-87 only.

	$450	$395	$340	$305	$250	$205	$160	*$330*

* ***Constable Blue Engraved*** – blue engraved. Importation disc. 1987.

	$550	$480	$415	$375	$305	$250	$195	*$375*

Add $20 for .22 LR or checkered wood grips.

* ***Constable Chrome Engraved*** – chrome engraved. Importation disc. 1987.

	$500	$440	$375	$340	$275	$225	$175	*$390*

Add $20 for .22 LR or checkered wood grips.

CONSTABLE A-60 – .380 ACP cal., double action, 3 1/2 in. barrel, 13 shot mag., ambidextrous safety, adj. rear sight, blue finish only. Imported 1986-91.

	$395	$345	$295	$270	$215	$180	$140	*$475*

MODEL A-70 – 9mm Para. or .40 S&W cal., single action, 3 1/2 in. barrel, steel frame and slide, 7- (.40 S&W) or 8- (9mm Para.) shot mag., compact design, ambidextrous safety, 3-dot sights, matte blue or nickel (new 1993) finish, 25 3/4 oz. Imported 1991-1996.

	$350	$300	$250	$220	$180	$145	$115	*$358*

Add $29 for nickel finish.

* ***Model A-70 Stainless*** – stainless steel variation of the Model A-70. Mfg. 1994 only.

	$500	$440	$375	$340	$275	$225	$175	*$435*

MODEL A-75 – 9mm Para., .40 S&W, or .45 ACP (new 1994) cal., action similar to Model A-70, except has selective double action with a decocking lever, steel or aluminum (9mm Para. only) frame. Imported 1993-1998.

* ***Model A-75 9mm Para or .40 S&W*** – choice of blue or nickel steel frame or lightweight aluminum frame (23 1/2 oz.), 7 (.40 S&W) or 8 (9mm Para.) shot mag. Disc. 1998.

	$350	$305	$265	$240	$195	$160	$125	*$303*

Add $17 for nickel finish.
Add $25 for lightweight model (aluminum frame).

GRADING - PPGS™	100%	98%	95%	90%	80%	70%	60%	LAST MSR

* ***Model A-75 .45 ACP*** – blue or nickel finish, 7 shot mag. Disc. 1998.

	$350	$305	$265	$240	$195	$160	$125	*$358*

Add $23 for nickel finish.

* ***Model A-75 Stainless*** – stainless steel variation of the Model A-75. Mfg. 1994 only.

	$375	$330	$280	$255	$205	$170	$130	*$485*

MODEL A-80 – 9mm Para, .38 Super (disc.), or .45 ACP cal., double action, semi-auto, 15 shot mag. (9 for .45 ACP), 3 3/4 in. barrel. Imported 1982-89.

	$395	$350	$305	$265	$240	$195	$160	*$425*

Add $35 for chrome finish (disc.).
Add 20% for .38 Super cal. in chrome finish.

MODEL A-90 – 9mm Para. or .45 ACP cal., 1986 designation for Model A-80 with updated slide mounted safety and pushbutton mag. release, 3 3/4 in. barrel, 14 shot mag. (9mm), or 8 shot (.45 ACP), blue only, approx. 48 oz. Imported 1986-90, replaced by Model A-100.

	$450	$395	$340	$305	$250	$205	$160	*$500*

MODEL A-100 – 9mm Para., .40 S&W, or .45 ACP cal., replaced the Model A-90 in 1990, with similar specifications, blue or nickel finish, re-engineered 1993 incorporating increased mag. capacity, 10 (C/B 1994), 17*/9mm, 12*/.40 S&W, or 9 shot/.45 ACP, approx. 29 oz. Imported 1990-97.

	$400	$350	$300	$270	$220	$180	$140	*$351*

Add $22 for nickel finish.
A small number of pistols with an extended slide were made for the Turkish police - add 50%.

MODEL 4000 FALCON – .22 LR, .32 ACP, or .380 ACP cal., 4 in. barrel, fixed sights, blue, plastic grips, exposed hammer. Mfg. 1956-1986.

	$600	$475	$325	$260	$235	$200	$150	*$340*

Add 50% for .22 cal.
Add 10% for .380 ACP.

* ***Model 4000 Tri-cal. Kit*** – includes frame and 3 barrels (.22 LR, .32 ACP, and .380 ACP cals.), may have rust blue, salt blue, or chromed (rare) finish, less than 200 mfg.

	$2,250	$1,950	$1,650	$1,225	$990	$810	$630	

Subtract 15% if not in factory box.

MODEL 4002 FALCON – similar to Model 4000, except lightly engraved.

	$1,200	$950	$650	$525	$475	$400	$300	

MODEL 4003 FALCON – similar to Model 4002, except deeply engraved.

	$2,400	$1,900	$1,300	$1,000	$800	$625	$500	

REVOLVERS

CADIX DOUBLE ACTION REVOLVER – .22 LR cal., 9 shot, .38 Spl., 5 shot, 4 or 6 in. barrel, adj. sights, blue, plastic grips. Mfg. 1960-68.

	$250	$200	$150	$125	$110	$85	$75	

Add 25% for early variation with single piece grip.

.357 D/A REVOLVER – .357 Mag. cal., 6 shot, 3, 4, 6, or 8 1/2 in. barrel, adj. sights, blue, checkered wood grips. Mfg. 1972-88.

	$325	$275	$225	$195	$180	$175	$170	*$295*

Add 50% for 8 1/2 in. barrel.

* ***.357 D/A Revolver Stainless Steel*** – 4 in. barrel only. Disc. 1987.

	$350	$300	$275	$250	$225	$200	$175	*$330*

LARGE CAL. D/A REVOLVER – .41 Mag. (disc. 1985), .44 Mag., or .45 LC (disc. 1987) cal., 6 shot, 6 or 8 1/2 in. (.44 Mag. only) barrels. Mfg. 1980-87.

	$350	$300	$250	$200	$180	$175	$170	*$315*

GRADING - PPGS™	100%	98%	95%	90%	80%	70%	60%	LAST MSR

* ***Large Cal. D/A Revolver Stainless Steel*** – .44 Mag. cal. only, 6 in. barrel only, 2 1/2 lbs. Importation disc. 1993.

	$375	$325	$275	$235	$200	$185	$175	*$450*

CONVERTIBLE REVOLVER – 9mm Para. cal. with extra .357 Mag. cal. cylinder, 6 shot, 3 in. barrel, blue only, checkered walnut grips, 2 1/4 lbs. Imported 1986-1993.

	$595	$495	$425	$375	$325	$275	$225	*$395*

TERMINATOR – .44 Mag. or .44 Spl. (disc.) cal., 6 shot, adj. rear sight, Roberts rubber grips, 2 3/4 in. shrouded barrel only. Inventories were depleted in 1989.

Blue finish	$425	$350	$300	$250	$200	$175	$150	*$250*
Stainless steel	$500	$450	$400	$350	$300	$250	$200	*$275*

These models were distributed by John Jovino, located in Yonkers, NY.

ASTRA ARMS S.A.

Current manufacturer established in 2008 and located in Sion, Switzerland. No current U.S. importation.

Astra Arms manufactures a line of AR-15 style tactical rifles called the Sturmgewher 4 Series. Current models include the Carbine and Commando. These models are not currently imported into the U.S. Please contact the company directly for more information, including availability and pricing (see Trademark Index).

ATKIN, GRANT & LANG LTD.

Current gunmaker established in 1960, and located in Hertfordshire, England. Atkin, Grant & Lang is the parent company which owns the trademarks of Henry Atkin, Stephen Grant and Joseph Lang. Please refer to these individual trademarks listed separately.

ATKIN, HENRY

Current trademark established in 1877 and currently manufactured by Atkin Grant & Lang, Ltd. located in Hertfordshire, England. Henry Atkin Ltd. joined with Grant & Lang during 1960, forming Atkin Grant & Lang Ltd. No current U.S. importation.

Henry Atkin was apprenticed to his father at James Purdey & Sons in the mid-19th century. By 1890, he was considered a master craftsman of the gun trade. Atkin is best known for modified Beesley/Purdey action self-openers and modified Southgate type ejectors. Henry Atkin died in 1907, but the firm survived through various family members and later the Hodges family of gunmakers. By 1960, the firm merged with Stephen Grant and Joseph Lang.

Atkin Grant & Lang Ltd. provide a useful historical research service on older Henry Atkin shotguns and rifles. The charge for this service is £25 per gun, and the company will give you all pertinent factory information regarding its history.

Some company information courtesy of David Grant and Vic Venters.

SHOTGUNS: SxS

Prices on Henry Atkin shotguns do not include VAT or importation costs. Please contact the company directly (see Trademark Index) for more information, including availability, delivery time, and a price quotation.

Add 10% for matched pairs.

BOXLOCK MODEL – 28 (2 mfg.) or 20 (3 mfg.) ga., very limited millenium edition.

This model is POR from the factory, based on an individual custom order.

SIDELOCK MODEL – 12, 20 ga., or .410 bore, best quality sidelock ejector model with opening assist.

This model is POR from the factory, based on an individual custom order.

GRADING - PPGS™	100%	98%	95%	90%	80%	70%	60%	LAST MSR

AUSTRIAN SPORTING ARMS

Previous importer located in Ware, MA circa 2010-2011.

Austrian Sporting Arms imported the M22 pistol manufactured by ISSC Handelsgesellschaft, located in Ried, Austria. Litigation brought about by Glock regarding patent and design infringement forced them to cease operations.

AUSTRALIAN AUTOMATIC ARMS PTY. LTD.

Previous manufacturer located in Tasmania, Australia. Previously imported and distributed by California Armory, Inc. located in San Bruno, CA.

PISTOLS: SEMI-AUTO

SAP – .223 Rem. cal., semi-auto paramilitary design pistol, 10 1/2 in. barrel, 20 shot mag., fiberglass stock and forearm, 5.9 lbs. Imported 1986-93.

	100%	98%	95%	90%	80%	70%	60%	LAST MSR
	$795	$700	$600	$550	$500	$475	$450	*$799*

RIFLES: SEMI-AUTO

SAR – .223 Rem. cal., semi-auto paramilitary design rifle, 16 1/4 or 20 in. (new 1989) barrel, 5 or 20 shot M-16 style mag., fiberglass stock and forearm, 7 1/2 lbs. Imported 1986-89.

	100%	98%	95%	90%	80%	70%	60%	LAST MSR
	$1,250	$1,000	$900	$800	$775	$750	$700	*$663*

Add $25 for 20 in. barrel.

This model was also available in a fully automatic version (AR).

SAC – .223 Rem. cal., semi-auto paramilitary design carbine, 10 1/2 in. barrel, 20 shot mag., fiberglass stock and forearm, 6.9 lbs. New 1986.

This model was available to NFA class III dealers and law enforcement agencies only.

SP – .223 Rem. cal., semi-auto, sporting configuration, 16 1/4 or 20 in. barrel, wood stock and forearm, 5 or 20 shot M-16 style mag., 7 1/4 lbs. Imported late 1991-93.

	100%	98%	95%	90%	80%	70%	60%	LAST MSR
	$850	$750	$650	$600	$550	$500	$475	*$879*

Add $40 for wood stock.

AUSTRALIAN INTERNATIONAL ARMS

Previous manufacturer and exporter located in Brisbane, Australia until circa 2009. Previously, Australian International Arms worked in cooperation with ADI Limited Lithgow, formerly Small Arms Factory, known for its SMLE No. I MKIII and L1A1 rifles. AIA outsourced the manufacture of its designs and specifications. Previously imported in North America by Marstar Canada, located in Ontario, Canada, and imported and distributed until 2004 by Tristar Sporting Arms, Ltd., located in N. Kansas City, MO.

RIFLES: BOLT ACTION, ENFIELD SERIES

M10-A1 – 7.62x39mm cal., redesigned and improved No. 4 MK2 action, parkerized finish, all new components, teak furniture with No. 5 Jungle Carbine style stock with steel or brass buttplate, 20 in. chrome lined barrel with muzzle brake, adj. front sight, 10 shot mag., Picatinny rail, 8.3 lbs.

While advertised in 2007, this model never went into production.

* ***M10-A2*** – 7.62x39mm cal., similar to M10A2, except has No. 8 style forend, Monte Carlo stock, and 16.1 in. chrome lined barrel. Limited importation 2003-2004 by Tristar.

	100%	98%	95%	90%	80%	70%	60%	LAST MSR
	$750	$700	$600	$525	$450	$375	$300	*$659*

M10-B1 – .308 Win. cal., redesigned and improved No. 4 MK2 action, matte blue finish, all new components, teak furniture with sporter carbine style stock and steel buttplate, 22 in. barrel, adj. front sight, 10 shot mag., Picatinny rail, 8.3 lbs. Imported 2006-disc.

	100%	98%	95%	90%	80%	70%	60%	LAST MSR
	$575	$500	$425	$350	$300	$275	$250	*$675*

* ***M10-B2*** – .308 Win. cal., similar to M10-B1, except has brass buttplate, gloss blue finish, 25 in. chrome lined bull barrel, and bipod stud, 10 1/2 lbs. Imported 2006-disc.

	100%	98%	95%	90%	80%	70%	60%	LAST MSR
	$650	$525	$425	$350	$300	$275	$225	*$760*

GRADING - PPGS™	100%	98%	95%	90%	80%	70%	60%	LAST MSR

* ***M10-B3*** – .308 Win. cal., similar to M10-B1, except has chrome steel buttplate, gloss blue finish, and 22 in. lightweight barrel, 7 1/2 lbs. Limited importation 2006-disc.

	$900	$800	$700	$600	$500	$425	$350	*$1,000*

NO.4 MK IV – .308 Win. cal., parkerized finish, 25.2 in. chrome lined medium weight barrel, teak furniture with steel buttplate, 9.1 lbs. Prototype only imported by Tristar. Limited importation beginning 2006.

	$575	$500	$425	$350	$300	$275	$250	*$675*

Add $440 for walnut stock, glass bedding, target barrel, elevated Picatinny rail, and accessories (disc.).

M 42 – .308 Win. cal., 27.6 in. barrel with mahogany stock and extra cheekpiece, blue printed action, bright metal/barrel finish, includes Picatinny rail, 8.2 lbs. Imported 2003-2004.

	$1,125	$950	$800	$650	$550	$450	$350	*$1,295*

SHOTGUNS: LEVER ACTION

MODEL 1887 – 12 ga., 2 3/4 in. chamber, uncheckered oil finished walnut stock and forearm, blue finish, steel buttplate, 5 shot, exposed hammer with half cock, 22 in. barrel, 8 3/4 lbs. Approx. 100 units mfg. by ADI Lithgow before discontinuance due to ADI technical and quality control problems. Dealer sample importation only 2003-2004.

	$995	$850	$750	$650	$600	$550	$500	*$1,195*

AUTAUGA RIFLES, INC.

Previous manufacturer located in Prattville, AL 1996-2002. In 2000, Autauga Arms, Inc. changed their name to Autauga Rifles, Inc.

PISTOLS: SEMI-AUTO

AUTAUGA MKII 32 – .32 ACP cal., double action only, 2 in. barrel, hammerless, blowback action, 6 shot mag., stainless steel, black polymer grips, 3/4 lb. 3,200 mfg. 1996-2000.

	$325	$225	$185	$140	$120	$100	$85	*$399*

Early guns did not have the MKII designation.

RIFLES: BOLT ACTION

Autauga Rifles, Inc. manufactured a complete line of precision bolt action rifles which were special ordered per individual customer specifications. Configurations included hunting, long range competition, law enforcement, and military tactical rifles. Complete packages included rifle, optics, hardware, and cleaning equipment. Standard rifle prices varied from $2,500-$3,500, depending on options. Rifles were supplied with a Pelican 1750 case.

AUTO MAG

Previously manufactured (circa 1971-1982) by Auto Mag. Corp. and TDE Corp. Recent manufacture (Harry Sanford Commemorative) was produced by Galena Industries, located in Sturgis, SD.

Less than 9,000 Auto Mags were produced by all manufacturers. All pistols originally had all stainless steel mags., and a short recoil rotary bolt system made entirely of stainless steel. Most pistols were sold in .44 AMP cal., although .357 AMP was also a popular factory option.

A unique handgun, the Auto Mag was never a commercial success due to high manufacturing costs and initial functioning problems (mostly attributed to hand loading all the ammo - once factory ammo became available, reliability improved significantly). Initial reaction to Dirty Harry's use of this firearm in the movie "Sudden Impact" (1983), as well as Burt Reynolds in "Malone" (1987) made prices escalate considerably, but most values appear to have stabilized since 1989. Be aware of fakes - especially of the XP variety (re-serialized, re-stamped, location of markings, etc.). Also, the ease of barrel swapping should be considered when deciding on a potential purchase. Auto Mags

GRADING - PPGS™	100%	98%	95%	90%	80%	70%	60%	LAST MSR

were never Mag-Na-Ported from the factory (only The Custom 100 Series). Non-original Mag-Na-Porting actually detracts from the values listed below, since it is a non-factory alteration.

Serial number ranges for the various models are as follows: Pasadena mfg. - A0000 through A03700. TDE North Hollywood - mostly A02500 through A05015, although some were marked with very low serial numbers. TDE El Monte mfg. - A05016 through A08300. (Note: these numbers should only be used as a guideline - as the company name changed, serial numbers overlapped.)

Although High Standard claimed to be the national sales distributor in 1974 and 1975 and had flyers indicating this, Lee E. Jurras and Associates, Inc. was actually the exclusive world wide distributor. Despite this, High Standard records show sales of 1045 Auto Mags.

High Standard catalog numbers are: 9346 for .44 AMP, and 9347 for .357 AMP. High Standard sold 134 Auto Mags with an "H" prefix. Serial numbers between H1 and H198, with one at H1566 and three between H17,219-H17,222. 108 of these were .44 AMP and 26 were .357 AMP. High Standard also sold 911 Auto Mags between serial numbers A05278-A07637. 777 of these were .44 AMP and 108 were .357 AMP. The "H" prefix guns remain a collectors' item and command a 25% premium over values listed below. It is estimated that an additional 300 barrels were marked High Standard.

DE/OMC marked pistols - B00001 through B00370 are known as the "B" series or solid bolt models (only 370 manufactured). This "B" series also commands collector premiums.

AMT manufactured the last two lots of Auto Mags; the first was the "C" series and was basically the same as the "B" except that only 50 guns were fabricated. The "B" Series was manufactured in 1979. Serial numbered C00001-C00050 "C" Series was manufactured in 1979, and the "Last" Series was manufactured in 1982. The last Auto Mags made by AMT were appropriately serial numbered LAST 1 through LAST 50. These guns had the reputation of being the poorest quality, and do carry collector premiums. One interesting variation is the North Hollywood "two-line" model. Also, the first .357 cal. pistols manufactured did not have the words AUTO MAG appearing on the gun. These are also collectors' items.

In addition to the above calibers, a very few non-factory .22, .25 and .30 LMP (Lomont Magnum Pistols) cal. prototypes were fabricated by Kent Lomont. These specimens will usually demand a premium over the values listed below. Also, some barrels and pistols were made in Covina, CA.

PISTOLS: SEMI-AUTO

ORIGINAL PASADENA – .44 AMP cal. only, 6 1/2 in. VR barrel, ser. no. A0001 - A3,300.

$2,500 $2,300 $1,995 $1,735 $1,495 $1,215 $1,000

This model is generally regarded as having the most quality, as all components were milled from Carpenter 455 stainless steel stock.

TDE NORTH HOLLYWOOD – ser. no. range A3,400 - A05015.

* ***TDE North Hollywood .44 AMP*** – 6 1/2 in. VR barrel, initial guns were mfg. from existing Pasadena parts, later mfg. required new components made by TDE.

$2,275 $1,850 $1,700 $1,500 $1,235 $1,030 $855

Quality on this model goes down in later mfg. (some small parts are not stainless). Because of this, higher serial numbered guns in this model are less desirable.

* ***TDE North Hollywood .357 AMP*** – two line address, there are no factory records verifying this caliber, and most were assembled with spare barrels.

$1,850 $1,600 $1,450 $1,275 $1,040 $900 $725

TDE EL MONTE – ser. no. range A05016-A08300.

* ***TDE El Monte .44 AMP*** – 6 1/2 VR, 8 1/2, or 10 1/2 in. tapered barrel.

$2,000 $1,700 $1,600 $1,410 $1,160 $980 $800

GRADING - PPGS™	100%	98%	95%	90%	80%	70%	60%	LAST MSR

* ***TDE El Monte .357 AMP*** – 6 1/2 VR, 8 1/2, or 10 1/2 in. tapered barrel.

	$1,750	$1,600	$1,450	$1,275	$1,040	$900	$855	

HIGH STANDARD – "H" prefixed serial numbers, approx. 132 mfg. by TDE with High Standard markings.

	$2,250	$2,100	$1,850	$1,620	$1,335	$1,115	$930	

LEE JURRAS STANDARD MODELS – see listings below, custom features would vary from presentation grade polishing of barrel and frame to exotic wood or micarta grips.

* ***LEJ Standard Automag*** – .357 AMP or .44 AMP cal., 6 1/2 w/VR, 8 1/2, or 10 1/2 in. non-rib barrel, TDE markings, lion's head logo. 1,100-1,200 mfg. 1974-76 by Lee Jurras & Associates. - Lee Jurras Custom Models included the 100 (listed below), 200 International (12 mfg.), 300 Alaskan (9 mfg.), 400 Backpacker (5 mfg.), 500 Grizzly (5 mfg.), 600 Condor (2 mfg.), and Metallic Silhouette (2 mfg.). Because of the rarity factor, these models with 12 or less mfg. are difficult to price accurately, and must be evaluated and appraised individually.

	$2,225	$2,050	$1,775	$1,560	$1,280	$1,070	$885	

Lee Jurras added his Lion's head logo (1974-1976) on TDE manufactured guns. There were also a very limited quantity of original shoulder stocks (less than 12), and were available for the International and Alaskan models only - extreme rarity precludes accurate price evaluation.

Several other calibers and variations were marketed through Lee Jurras including one-of-a-kind exotics like a .30 cal. Cougar with 12 in. barrel and highly polished metal.

LEE JURRAS CUSTOM MODELS

* ***LEJ Custom Model 100*** – .357 AMP, .41 JMP (Jurras Magnum Pistol), or .44 AMP cal., 6 1/2 in. VR or 8 1/2 non-rib (only 10 mfg. in each cal.) polished Mag-Na-Ported barrel, custom laminated wood grips, special carrying case. 100 mfg. in each cal.

	$3,150	$2,850	$2,350	$2,065	$1,860	$1,430	$1,175	

TDE/OMC "B" SERIES – 6 1/2 VR or 10 in. barrel, ser. no. range B00001-B00370.

	$2,250	$2,100	$1,850	$1,620	$1,335	$1,115	$930	

AMT "C" SERIES – 6 1/2 VR or 10 in. barrel, ser. no. range C00001-C00050.

	$2,250	$2,100	$1,850	$1,620	$1,335	$1,115	$930	

Note: guns were cased (plastic attache style) with accessories. Collector caution - over the years, the foam in these plastic cases can break down, and may cause discoloration and pitting on the gun. Original Auto-Mag ammo (original mfg. only by CDM in Mexico and Norma in Sweden) is currently selling for approx. $75-$95 a box. Starline now has .44 AMP brass, and Corbon loaded .44 AMP ammo also - new 2001.

HARRY SANFORD COMMEMORATIVE AUTO MAG – .44 AMP cal., Automag, Inc. commemorative reissue, "STURGIS, SD" barrel address with Harry Sanford signature on left rear of slide, cased. 1,000 pistols were scheduled to be mfg., but only approx. 300 actually completed by Galena Industries 1999-2000.

	$2,750	$2,300	$1,995	N/A	N/A	N/A	N/A	*$2,750*

AUTO-ORDNANCE CORP.

Current manufacturer with facilities located in Worcester, MA, and corporate offices in Blauvelt, NY. Auto-Ordnance Corp. became a division of Kahr Arms in 1999. Auto-Ordnance Corp. was a division of Gun Parts Corp. until 1999. Previously located in West Hurley, NY. Consumer, dealer, and distributor sales.

CARBINES: SEMI-AUTO

AUTO-ORDNANCE M1-CARBINE (.30 CAL.) – .30 Carbine cal., birch (disc.) or walnut (standard beginning 2008) stock, 18 in. barrel, all new parts, parkerized receiver, metal handguard, aperture rear sight, and bayonet lug, 10 (new 2005) or 15 shot mag., 5.4 lbs. New 2004.

MSR $816	$700	$600	$500	$425	$375	$325	$275	

GRADING - PPGS™	100%	98%	95%	90%	80%	70%	60%	LAST MSR

* ***Auto-Ordnance M1 Carbine Paratrooper*** – .30 Carbine cal., similar to .30 cal. M1 Carbine, except has folding stock, walnut handguard, parkerized finish, 15 shot mag. New 2008.

MSR $903	$775	$675	$575	$475	$375	$325	$295	

* ***Auto-Ordnance M1 Carbine Tactical*** – .30 Carbine cal., similar to .30 cal. M1 carbine, except has black polymer folding stock, metal handguard, 15 shot mag. Mfg. 2008-2012.

	$650	$575	$475	$375	$325	$300	$275	$792

AUTO-ORDNANCE 1927 A-1 STANDARD – .45 ACP cal., 16 in. plain barrel, solid steel construction, standard military sight, walnut stock and horizontal forearm. Disc. 1986.

	$570	$490	$430	$360	$315	$290	$270	$575

PISTOLS: SEMI-AUTO

During 1997, Auto Ordnance discontinued all calibers on the pistols listed below, except for .45 ACP cal. or 9mm Para. Slide kits were available for $179. Also, conversion units (converting .45 ACP to .38 Super or 9mm Para.) were available for $195.

All current Auto Ordnance 1911 Models include a spent cartridge case, plastic carrying case, and cable lock.

1911 COMPETITION – .38 Super (1996 only) or .45 ACP cal., competition features included compensated barrel, commander hammer, flat mainspring housing, white 3-dot sighting system, beavertail grip safety, black textured wraparound grips. Mfg. 1993-1996.

	$530	$415	$375	$330	$300	$285	$270	$636

Add $10 for .38 Super cal.

1911 A1 STANDARD/COMPACT STANDARD – .38 Super (disc. 1996), 9mm Para. (disc. 1996), .40 S&W (mfg. 1991-93), 10mm (mfg. 1991-96), or .45 ACP cal., 4 1/4 (.45 ACP only, Compact Standard Model), 4 1/2 (.40 S&W cal. only) or 5 (Standard Model) in. barrel, 7 shot mag., single action, parts interchange with the original Colt Govt. Model, blue or nickel finish, checkered plastic grips, 39 oz. Disc. 2005.

	$450	$370	$295	$255	$235	$225	$215	$592

Add $28 for satin nickel (mfg. 1990-96) or $37 for duo-tone (mfg. 1992-96) finish (.45 ACP only).

* ***1911 A1 WWII Parkerized*** – .45 ACP cal., no frills variation of the 1911 A1, military parkerizing, G.I. detailing with military style roll stamp, plastic or checkered walnut (disc. 2001, reintroduced 2007) grips, and lanyard loop. New 1992.

MSR $668	$525	$425	$325	$275	$235	$225	$215	

Add $17 for wood grips with U.S. logo (new 2007).

* ***1911 A1 100th Anniversary*** – .45 ACP cal., 5 in. barrel, parkerized finish, based on the original military design, diamond checkered wood grips, anniversary laser engraving. Mfg. began 2011.

MSR $658	$525	$425	$325	$295	$250	$225	$215	

* ***1911 A1 Standard 80*** – .45 ACP cal., features firing pin block safety, 5 in. barrel, otherwise similar to 1911 A1 Standard. Mfg. 2004-2007.

	$465	$375	$310	$255	$235	$225	$215	$609

* ***1911 A1 Deluxe 80*** – .38 Super (disc. 1996), 9mm Para. (disc. 1996), or .45 ACP cal., 5 in. barrel, 3-dot sights, wraparound grips, 39 oz. Mfg. 1991-2006.

	$480	$385	$315	$260	$240	$225	$215	$615

* ***1911 A1 General*** – .38 Super (mfg. 1996 only) or .45 ACP cal., 4 1/2 in. barrel with full length recoil spring guide, 7 shot mag., blue finish, 3-dot fixed Millett sights, black rubber wraparound grips, Commander styling, 37 oz. Mfg. 1992-1998.

	$385	$315	$255	$235	$225	$215	$200	$465

* ***1911 A1 Custom High Polish*** – .45 ACP cal., 8 shot mag., 5 in. barrel, custom combat hammer, beavertail grip safety, rosewood grips with medallions, 3-dot sights, flat mainspring housing, Videcki speed trigger, 39 oz. Mfg. 1997-99.

	$485	$395	$325	$265	$235	$225	$215	$585

GRADING - PPGS™	100%	98%	95%	90%	80%	70%	60%	LAST MSR

MODEL ZG-51 "PIT BULL" – .45 ACP cal. only, compact variation of the 1911 A1, 3 5/8 in. standard (disc. 1996) or 4 3/8 in. compensated (new 1997) barrel, 7 shot mag., 36 oz. Mfg. 1988-99.

$385	$310	$255	$235	$225	$215	$200	$470

AUTO-POINTER

Previous trademark manufactured by Yamamoto Co. Formerly imported by Sloans.

SHOTGUNS: SEMI-AUTO

SEMI-AUTO SHOTGUN – 12 or 20 ga., gas operated. Disc.

$275	$240	$220	$195	$180	$160	$145

AXTELL RIFLE CO.

Previous rifle manufacturer located in Sheridan, MT. Previously distributed by The Riflesmith Inc., located in Sheridan, MT.

During 2010, the company was sold to Shiloh Mfg. Co., located in Big Timber, MT.

RIFLES: REPRODUCTIONS

New Model 1877 Sharps reproductions were available for both long-range and sporting rifles listed below in the following black powder calibers: .40-50, .40-70, .40-90, .45-70 Govt., .45-90, and .45-100 cal.

NUMBER ONE CREEDMOOR – features 34 in. Rigby style barrel, choice of high-grade black or English checkered walnut stock and forearm with ebony inlays. Long range sights. 10 lbs.

$5,000	$4,250	$3,600	$3,100	$2,500	$2,000	$1,575	$5,000

CUSTOM EXPRESS – top-of-the-line model with double set triggers, 32 or 34 in. 1/2 round, 1/2 octagon barrel, select walnut checkered stock, deluxe front and rear sights, approx. 13 lbs.

$5,700	$4,550	$3,950	$3,250	$2,650	$2,100	$1,650	$5,700

NUMBER TWO LONG RANGE – choice of 30-34 in. Rigby style barrel, select black or English checkered walnut stock and forearm. Long range sights.

$4,700	$3,650	$3,150	$2,600	$2,100	$1,650	$1,300	$4,700

OVERBAUGH SCHUETZEN – features 26-30 in. octagon barrel, double-set triggers, Schuetzen buttplate with cheekpiece, palm rest, short-range sights, 11-14 lbs.

$5,700	$4,550	$3,950	$3,250	$2,650	$2,100	$1,650	$5,700

LOWER SPORTER – 28 or 30 in. octagon barrel, double-set triggers, steel buttplate with straight grip, standard rifle weight of 9 lbs.

$3,200	$2,450	$1,875	$1,425	$1,050	$825	$700	$3,200

LOWER BUSINESS – 28 in. contoured round barrel, double-set triggers, black walnut stock has steel shotgun buttplate with straight grip, hunter tang, blade front sights, approx. 8 1/2 lbs.

$3,100	$2,400	$1,825	$1,400	$1,050	$825	$700	$3,100

AZTEK ARMS

Current rifle manufacturer located in Mapleton, UT.

RIFLES

Aztek Arms currently manufactures a T/H1200 Urban Long Range Hunter bolt action model in either tactical or hunting configuration - current MSR is $4,095. A T/H1500 variation is also available in either tactical or hunting configuration - current MSR is $4,295. A T/H2000 is also available in 7mm Rem. Mag. cal. in either tactical or hunting configuration - current MSR is $4,795. Additionally, Aztek Arms makes AR-15 style rifles in various configurations. Please contact the company directly for more information on pricing, availability, and options (see Trademark Index).

B SECTION

BCM EUROPEARMS

Current manufacturer located in Torino, Italy. No current U.S. importation.

BCM Europearms manufactures high quality bolt action competiton, hunting, and tactical/Law Enforcement rifles; the Storm semi-auto pistol (in 9x21mm and .40 S&W); and customized Remington 700 rifles. The "Barrel Block" competition rifle features a monolithic stock with integrally machined bedding (no separate bedding components) which allows both action and barrel to free float. The barrel and action are held in the stock by a "cap" which clamps over the barrel's chamber and is attached to the stock, not the action, by eight screws.

Currently these models are not being imported into the U.S. Please contact the company directly for more information, U.S. availability, and pricing (see Trademark Index).

BSA GUNS LIMITED

Current manufacturer (airguns only since circa 1986) and trademark established in 1861 and located in Birmingham, England. BSA (Birmingham Small Arms) currently manufactures airguns only. No current U.S. importation. English made BSA firearms were imported until 1985 by Precision Sports from Ithaca, NY and 1986 by BSA Guns Ltd., located in Grand Prairie, TX. Imported and distributed until 1989 by Samco Global Arms, Inc., located in Miami, FL.

For more information and current pricing on both new and used BSA airguns, please refer to the *Blue Book of Airguns* by Dr. Robert Beeman & John Allen (also available online).

HISTORY OF BIRMINGHAM SMALL ARMS

In a little over a hundred years, BSA has grown from a small union of gunsmiths to become one of Britain's important industrial groups. The story is also part of Britain's history. During 1689, King William III, worried by threats of invasion, sharply criticized the practice of obtaining military weapons from Holland. He was overheard by Sir Richard Newdegate, an MP for Warwickshire, who immediately spoke up on behalf of his Birmingham constituents - many of whom were fine gunsmiths. The result was a trial order for five of the leading Birmingham smiths. It was satisfactorily carried out, and a firm contract was made between the government and the quintet for the supply of 200 snaphance muskets a month "at seventeen shillings per piece, ready money."

This practice of trading with the gunmakers as a group continued for 150 years. At the time of the Crimean War, fourteen of the master smiths formalized their position by joining together as The Birmingham Small Arms Trade Association. On June 7, 1861, a public company was formed as the The Birmingham Small Arms Company Limited.

The company adopted the sign of three crossed rifles, known as the Piled Arms trademark. The company began making small arms by machinery to meet the growing competition from the mechanized government factory at Enfield. A 25 acre site was bought at Small Heath, at that time just outside the Birmingham boundary, and two years later, the factory was in operation. By 1866, the company could record a profit of £7,000 and in a few short years - aided by the turbulent international politics of the time - it became the largest private arms manufacturer in Europe.

One order from the Prussian government, then at war with Austria, was 40 million cartridge cases. Rather than turn down the order, the directors acquired a munitions factory and changed the company name to the Birmingham Small Arms and Metal Company Limited. The early prosperity was short-lived. As wars ceased, the demand for weapons fell, and the private arms trade was the first to suffer. Towards the end of the 1870s, the Small Heath factory was completely closed for twelve months and the future looked impossibly dark. A small contract enabled the works to be opened again, however, and in 1880 fate took a hand in the shape of an inventor, a Mr. E.C.F. Otto, who had designed a strange type of bicycle with two large wheels on either side of the rider. He demonstrated it by riding on the boardroom table under the noses of the astonished directors - and so impressed them that they put the device into production immediately.

GRADING - PPGS™	100%	98%	95%	90%	80%	70%	60%	LAST MSR

This first venture into the transport field was followed by more conventional bicycles and tricycles, but a sudden increase in the demand for rifles at the end of the 1880s caused the directors to drop cycle work. During the Boer War, the company supplied many thousands of rifles to the British forces. The Birmingham Small Arms and Metal Company Limited name was used until 1897.

In the First World War, the BSA factories were turned over almost entirely to munitions work. Huge quantities of service rifles, machine guns, military motorcycles, and the world's first folding bicycles were supplied to the troops. Right through the 1930s, BSA rifle production had been confined to comparatively small quantities of sporting weapons.

Apart from the company's own factories in Birmingham, Coventry, Redditch, Sheffield and Co. Durham, many dispersal units and shadow factories were used for the purpose of arms production. The Small Heath administration alone (BSA Cycles Ltd and BSA Guns Ltd) controlled 67 factories, employing 28,000 people and containing 25,000 machine tools. This organization produced more than half the small arms supplied to Britain's forces during the war. BSA's war production included nearly half a million of the Browning machine guns with which RAF Spitfires and Hurricanes won the Battle of Britain; one and a quarter million service rifles; 400,000 Sten guns; machine guns, cannon, anti-tank rifles, and gun carriages, ten million shell fuses, over three and a half million magazines, and 750,000 anti-aircraft rockets. Several group factories were heavily bombed and at Small Heath more than 50 employees lost their lives. At this works alone, more machine tools were destroyed or damaged by enemy action than were lost in the whole of the Coventry blitz.

Although the company no longer makes military weapons, BSA Guns Ltd makes and exports air rifles, hunting rifles, and sporting guns to most parts of the world. BSA celebrated its 150th anniversary in 2011.

Company history courtesy of BSA Guns Ltd.

RIFLES: BOLT ACTION

Importation of all BSA rimfire and centerfire rifles was disc. 1987.

MAJESTIC FEATHERWEIGHT DELUXE – .243 Win., .270 Win., .308 Win., .30-06, or .458 Win. Mag. cal., 22 in. barrel, folding sight, checkered European style stock. Mfg. 1959-1965.

	$475	$425	$375	$325	$300	$275	$250	
.458 Win. Mag.	$650	$575	$495	$450	$400	$350	$295	

MAJESTIC DELUXE – .222 Rem., .22 Hornet, .243 Win., 7x57mm, .308 Win., or .30-06 cal., heavier barrel.

	$475	$425	$375	$325	$300	$275	$250	
.22 Hornet cal.	$950	$850	$750	$650	$600	$550	$500	

MONARCH DELUXE – similar to Majestic Deluxe, but American design stock. Mfg. 1965-74.

	$575	$525	$450	$400	$350	$300	$275	

MONARCH DELUXE VARMINT – similar to Monarch Deluxe, except .222 Rem. or .243 Win. cal., 24 in. heavy barrel. Disc.

	$475	$425	$375	$325	$300	$275	$250	

MARTINI ISU MATCH .22 – .22 LR cal. only, single shot, bolt action, similar to CFT Model. Disc. 1985.

	$825	$720	$620	$560	$455	$370	$290	*$1,000*

Add $100 for Mk. V.H.B. Model.

CF-2 MODELS – .222 Rem., .22-250 Rem., .243 Win., 6.5x55mm, 7x57mm, 7x64mm, 7mm Rem. Mag., .270 Win., .308 Win., .30-06, or .300 Win. Mag. cal., bolt action, barrel length 23-26 in., 7 1/2-8 lbs. CF-2 nomenclature designates an action rather than a model. The following are CF-2 actioned models.

Add $70 for double set trigger option on the following models.

GRADING - PPGS™	100%	98%	95%	90%	80%	70%	60%	LAST MSR

* ***CF-2 Action Sporter/Classic*** – same cals. as CF-2, checkered oil finished walnut stock. Imported 1986-87.

	$475	$425	$375	$325	$300	$275	$250	*$360*

Sporter Model features Monte Carlo stock, rosewood capped forearm and pistol grip stock, and swivels.

* ***CF-2 Action Classic Varminter*** – .222 Rem. - .243 Win. cals. only, heavy barrel, matte finish, with swivels. Imported 1986 only.

	$475	$425	$375	$325	$300	$275	$250	*$345*

* ***CF-2 Action Heavy Barrel Model*** – .222 Rem., .22-250 Rem., or .243 Win. cal., approx. 9 lbs., no sights.

	$475	$425	$375	$325	$300	$275	$250	*$410*

* ***CF-2 Action Carbine Model*** – 20 in. barrel. Disc. 1985.

	$550	$495	$425	$375	$325	$295	$275	*$480*

* ***CF-2 Action Stutzen Rifle*** – Mannlicher style full length stock, same general specifications as Sporter/Classic, 20 1/2 in. barrel. Not available in 7mm Rem. Mag. or .300 Win. Mag. cal.

	$695	$625	$550	$500	$450	$400	$350	*$385*

* ***CF-2 Action Regal Custom*** – similar to Sporter Model, except has slim classic European style stock with Schnabel forend, deluxe walnut with extra checkering, ebony forend cap, engraved action and floorplate. Limited importation 1986 only.

	$1,000	$925	$850	$775	$700	$625	$550	*$950*

This model was custom-made by special order only.

CFT TARGET RIFLE – 7.62mm cal., single shot, bolt action, globe front and aperture rear sights, 26 1/2 in. barrel, 11 lbs. Disc. 1987.

	$675	$590	$500	$460	$370	$300	$235	*$780*

RIFLES: SINGLE SHOT

NO. 12 MARTINI – .22 LR cal., 29 in. barrel, target sights, straight stock, pre-WWII.

	$725	$600	$500	$425	$350	$300	$275

MILITARY MARTINI HENRY (MODELS 1871 & 1885) – various cals., pre-WWII mfg. many configurations and barrel lengths. Pricing takes into consideration most commonly encountered types with no engraving or special orders.

Post-1900 mfg.	$900	$700	$500	$450	$400	$365	$335
Pre-1899 mfg.	$650	$550	$475	$400	$350	$300	$250

MARTINI CADET – various cals., mostly military issue, many thousands previously imported into the U.S. from England, many have been sporterized or modified.

	$725	$600	$500	$425	$350	$300	$275

* ***Martini Cadet Australian Junior*** – .310 cal., mfg. by BSA and W.W. Greener, Francotte patent one-piece take out action, various rear sight configurations, some have been converted to modern cartridges.

	$550	$475	$375	$325	$275	$235	$200

MODEL 15 – similar to No. 12 Martini, except has pistol grip stock, better grade target sights, pre-WWII.

	$725	$600	$500	$425	$350	$300	$275

CENTURION MATCH RIFLE – similar to Model 15, except was guaranteed to shoot a 1 1/2 in. or less group at 100 yards, 24 in. barrel, pre-WWII.

	$800	$675	$550	$475	$425	$350	$300

MATCH 12/15 – similar to Model 15, except made after WWII.

	$725	$600	$500	$425	$350	$300	$275

GRADING - PPGS™	100%	98%	95%	90%	80%	70%	60%	LAST MSR

MODEL 12/15 – heavy barrel.

	$725	$600	$500	$425	$350	$300	$275	

MODEL 13 – lighter version of No. 12 Martini.

	$725	$600	$500	$425	$350	$300	$275	

MODEL 13 SPORTER – similar to Model 13, except has sport sights.

	$725	$600	$500	$425	$350	$300	$275	
.22 Hornet	$950	$825	$725	$625	$525	$425	$325	

MARTINI INTERNATIONAL MATCH – .22 LR cal., 29 in. heavy barrel, international sights. Mfg. 1950-53.

	$825	$700	$600	$475	$400	$350	$325	

INTERNATIONAL LIGHT – 26 in. lightweight barrel.

	$775	$675	$550	$450	$400	$350	$325	

INTERNATIONAL MKII – improved trigger, ejectors, and stock design. Mfg. 1953-1959.

	$950	$825	$700	$600	$550	$500	$450	

INTERNATIONAL MKIII – longer action, floating barrel. Mfg. 1959-1967.

	$995	$875	$750	$650	$600	$550	$500	

INTERNATIONAL ISU – modeled to meet ISU standards, 28 in. barrel. Mfg. 1968-disc.

	$1,000	$875	$750	$650	$600	$550	$500	

INTERNATIONAL MARK V – similar to ISU, but heavier barrel, mfg. 1976-disc.

	$1,000	$875	$750	$650	$600	$550	$500	

SHOTGUNS

BSA Imports, located in Ft. Lauderdale, FL, imported O/U, SxS, and semi-auto shotguns from 2004-2006 which were manufactured in Turkey and utilized the BSA logo/trademark.

BSA also manufactured SxS boxlock shotguns in various grades. Normally encountered in 12 ga. with DTs and extractors, these shotguns are of good quality and are typically encountered in the secondary market in the $250-$500 range, assuming standard grade.

SILVER EAGLE O/U – 12 or 20 ga., 3 in. chambers, 26 or 28 in. barrels, multichokes, hand-checkered Turkish walnut stock, blue receiver, gold SST, extractors (Silver Eagle) or ejectors (Silver Eagle II). Imported 2004-2006.

	$395	$360	$330	$295	$260	$230	$200	*$489*

Add $100 for ejectors (Silver Eagle II).

FALCON O/U – 12 or 20 ga., 3 in. chambers, boxlock action, 26, 28, or 30 in. barrels, Beretta style multichokes, laser-checkered field grade walnut stock with Schnabel forend, ejectors, case colored engraved receiver, gold SST. Imported 2004-2006.

	$1,000	$900	$800	$700	$600	$500	$400	*$1,199*

SPORTING O/U – 12 ga., 2 3/4 in. chambers, 28 or 30 in. ported barrels, multichokes, checkered walnut target stock, ejectors, silver finished engraved receiver, trigger guard, safety, and opening lever, gold SST. Imported 2004-2006.

	$1,025	$950	$825	$725	$625	$525	$425	*$1,249*

CLASSIC SxS – 12, 16, 20, 28 ga., or .410 bore, 2 3/4 (16 or 28 ga.) or 3 in. chambers, 26 or 28 in. barrels with Beretta style choke tubes, checkered select walnut stock with Prince of Wales pistol grip, ejectors, case colored hardened receiver, gold SST, semi-beavertail forend. Imported 2004-2006.

	$1,065	$975	$850	$750	$650	$550	$450	*$1,299*

ROYAL SxS – 12 or 20 ga., 3 in. chambers, 26 or 28 in. barrels with Beretta style choke tubes, checkered select walnut stock. Imported 2005-2006.

	$1,225	$1,075	$975	$850	$750	$650	$550	*$1,499*

GRADING - PPGS™	100%	98%	95%	90%	80%	70%	60%	LAST MSR

200/300 SERIES SEMI-AUTO – 12, 16, 20, 28 ga., or .410 bore, 2 3/4 (16, 28 ga. or .410 bore), 3 or 3 1/2 (Model 312 only) in. chamber, 24 (Model 312 only), 26 or 28 in. barrels, vent. rib, multichokes, synthetic or checkered Turkish walnut stock, blue receiver, gold trigger, drilled and tapped, firing pin block. Imported 2004-2006.

$325	$285	$250	$225	$200	$175	$150	*$399*

Add $60 for wood stock.
Add $30 for 16 or 28 ga. or .410 bore.
Add $20 for 3 1/2 in. chamber.

This model was manufactured by Matsan in Turkey, and was also available in 20 ga. at no extra charge.

BWE FIREARMS

Current rifle manufacturer and customizer with gunsmithing services established during 2002, and located in Longwood, FL.

BWE Firearms is a full service custom gunsmith shop specializing in NFA (Class III) firearms. It is also a Class II manufacturer. Additionally, BWE Firearms manufactures a bolt action rifle based on the Remington Model 700 long action. It is chambered for the .300 Blackout/Whisper, .338 Thumper, or .50 Thumper caliber, and features include blue printed actions, fully adjustable Bell and Carlson tactical stock, and Picatinny rail. Finishes include bead blast, polished blue, or parkerizing. Please contact the manufacturer directly for more information about their models, availability, and pricing.

B-WEST

Previous importer/distributor located in Tucson, AZ, until 1997.

B-West previously imported AK-47 design carbines/rifles, Saiga rifles, Dragunov rifles, and others, plus the IJ series .380 ACP Makarov pistol, and the Daewoo DP-51 semi-auto pistol.

BAER, LES

Please refer to the Les Baer Custom listing.

BAFORD ARMS, INC.

Previous manufacturer located in Bristol, TN. Previously distributed by C.L. Reedy & Associates, Inc. located in Melbourne, FL.

DERRINGERS

THUNDER DERRINGER – .44 Spl. cal./.410 shotshell, single shot, tip-up action, 3 in. barrel, blue finish steel finish, spur trigger, wood grips. Introduced late 1988 with limited mfg. until 1991, when production permanently ceased.

$130	$110	$95	$90	$85	$80	$75	*$130*

Add $90 for interchangeable barrel kit.

Interchangeable pistol barrels are chambered in various calibers between .22 Short and 9mm Para. There are two types: one fits flush while the other facilitates a scope mounting.

PISTOLS: SEMI-AUTO

MODEL 35 FIRE POWER – 9mm Para. cal., semi-auto single action, patterned after the Browning Hi-Power, total stainless steel construction, 4 3/4 in. barrel, combat hammer and safety, wood (early mfg.) or Pachmayr grips, removable barrel bushing, Millett Mk. II sights, 14 shot mag., 32 oz. Introduced late 1988 with limited mfg. until 1993.

$725	$650	$525	$425	$325	$275	$225	*$550*

BAIKAL

Current trademark of products manufactured by the Russian Federal State Unitary Plant "Izhevsky Mechanichesky Zavod" (FSUP IMZ), located in Izhevsk, Russia. Currently imported by U.S. Sporting Goods, Inc. located in Rockledge, FL beginning 2011. Previously imported from late 1998 until 2004 by European American Armory Corp., located in Sharpes, FL, and from 1993-1996 by Big Bear, located in Dallas, TX.

Baikal SxS and O/U hunting guns (including air guns) were imported and distributed exclusively 2005-2009 by U.S. Sporting Goods (USSG), located in Rockledge, FL. Many

GRADING - PPGS™	100%	98%	95%	90%	80%	70%	60%	LAST MSR

Baikal shotguns and rifles were marketed domestically by Remington under the Spartan Gunworks trademark until 2008. See listings under Spartan Gunworks for more information.

Please contact the importer directly for more information and availability on Baikal firearms (see Trademark Index).

Baikal (the name of a lake in Siberia) was one of the key holding companies from the former Soviet Union, specializing in the production of firearms, and science intensive, complex electronic equipment.

The company was founded in 1942 as part of the Russian National Defense Industry. At that time, the plant produced world renowned Tokarev TT pistols. Upon conclusion of WWII, the company expanded its operation to include non-military firearms (O/U, SxS, and single barrel shotguns). FSUP IMZ is one of the world's largest manufacturers of military and non-military firearms. The total amount of guns produced by the FSUP IMZ is 680,000 units per year. The products range from various smoothbore guns, including slide action and self-loading models, rifled and combination guns, to a full array of sporting, civil, and combat pistols, including the internationally famous Makarov pistol. Since 2000, Baikal has produced a new pistol for the Russian Army which was developed by the enterprise designers and named after the group's leader - the Yarygin pistol.

FSUP IMZ features efficient manufacturing capacity and the unique intellectual potential of its qualified engineers-and-technicians staff. The FSUP IMZ is also undertaking the task of reintroducing the world to the "Russian Custom Gunsmith". There is a gunsmith school at the factory area for custom, one-of-a-kind hand engraved shotguns and rifles. The guns produced by the school feature high-quality assembly, attractive appearance, and high functional quality according to the best traditions of Russian gunmakers.

In the past, Baikal shotguns have had limited importation into the U.S. 1993 marked the first year that Baikals were officially (and legally) imported into the U.S. because of Russia's previous export restrictions. In prior years, however, a few O/Us have been seen for sale and have no doubt been imported into this country one at a time. Currently produced Baikals are noted for their good quality at low-level costs.

COMBINATION GUNS

MP94 (IZH-94) O/U – 12 or 20 (new 2001-disc.) ga. over rifle separated rifle barrel, current US cals. include .223 Rem., .30-06, .308 Win., or 7.62x39mm cal. , 3 in. chamber, boxlock action, 19.7 or 23 1/2 (disc.) in. separated barrels with express sights, DT, extractors, fixed or screw-in chokes, checkered walnut stock and forearm, approx. 7 1/4 lbs.

MSR $717	$600	$525	$450	$400	$350	$300	$250	

This model was also sold in the U.S. under the model name SPR94, and the nomenclature changed to MP94 beginning 2009.

* ***MP94 (IZH-94) .410 Bore/Rimfire*** – .410 bore with 3 in. chamber over choice of .17 HMR (disc. 2010), .22 LR, or .22 WMR cal., 19.7 or 23 1/2 (disc.) in. barrels, extractors, single trigger, open sights, walnut stock and forearm. Imported 2003-2012.

	$425	$350	$295	$265	$240	$220	$200	*$514*

This model was also sold in the U.S. under the model names IZH94 Rimfire and SPR94 Rimfire. The nomenclature changed to MP94 in 2009.

PISTOLS: SEMI-AUTO

IZH-35M – .22 LR cal., semi-auto target pistol featuring fully adj. walnut ergonomic target grip, 6 in. hammer forged barrel, adj. trigger assembly, integral grip safety, 5 shot mag., cocking indicator and detachable scope mount, 2.3 lbs. Imported 2000-disc.

	$425	$385	$335	$300	$275	$250	$225	

U.S. options on this gun include manual lever safety, side-located push-button mag. catch, slide retainer, and removable scope base (not available in standard European version).

GRADING - PPGS™	100%	98%	95%	90%	80%	70%	60%	LAST MSR

IZH-70 (IJ-70) – .380 ACP or 9x18 Makarov cal., double action, all blue steel construction, 4 in. barrel, slide mounted safety with decocking, fully adj. target sights, choice of two 8 shot (IJ- 70), two 10 shot (C/B 1994, Model IJ-70-HC), or two 12*shot mags., holster and cleaning rod, checkered plastic grips, 25 oz. Disc. 1996.

	$175	$150	$135	$120	$105	$95	$85	*$199*

Add $40 for IJ-70-HC (High Capacity).
Add $50 for .380 ACP cal.
Add $10 for nickel finish (disc.).

This model was also imported under the model name Baikal 442.

RIFLES: O/U

IZH-94 EXPRESS – .222 Rem., .223 Rem., .30-06, .308 Win., 6.5x55mm, or 7.62x39mm cal., DT, extractors, mono bloc construction, 24 in. barrels with express sights, checkered walnut stock and forearm, 8.3 lbs. Imported 2001-2004.

	$450	$395	$365	$335	$295	$280	$265	*$529*

RIFLES: SxS

MP221 – .223 Rem. (disc.), .270 Win. (disc.), .30-06, .308 Win. (disc.), or .45-70 Govt. cal., 23 1/2 in. barrel, boxlock monobloc action, DT, adj. barrel regulation, 11mm scope rail, checkered walnut stock and forearm with sling swivels, extractors, vent. recoil pad, 7 1/2 lbs. Imported 2003-2009, reintroduced 2011.

MSR $1,041	$900	$775	$650	$575	$495	$440	$365	

This model was also sold in the U.S. under the name SPR22.

RIFLES: SEMI-AUTO

MP161K – .17 HMR (disc. 2010), .22 LR, or .22 WMR (disc. 2010) cal., 19 1/2 in. accurized barrel, grey polymer thumbhole pistol grip stock with adj. LOP and cheekpiece height, 10 shot mag., integral Picatinny rail, adj. open sight, loaded chamber indicator, trigger guard mounted bottom safety, blue recoil pad and inserts in the forend. Importation began 2009.

MSR $395	$325	$275	$245	$210	$190	$160	$140	

Add 20% for .17 HMR or .22 WMR cal. (disc. 2010).

RIFLES: SINGLE BARREL

IZH-18MN – .222 Rem. (disc.), .223 Rem., .243 Win., .270 Win., 7.62x39mm, .308 Win., .30-06 or .45-70 Govt. cal., boxlock action, 23 1/2 in. barrel with extractor and precision spiral cut fluting, underlever action next to trigger guard, blue or nickel frame finish, polymer or checkered walnut (disc.) stock with vent. recoil pad, sling swivels, iron sights or scope rail, 6.8 lbs. Imported 2003-2009.

	$250	$220	$185	$170	$135	$110	$85	*$278*

Add $16 for nickel finish.

This model has also been sold in the U.S. under the names IZH018MN and SPR-18.

MP18MN – .223 Rem., .223 Win., .30-06, or 7.62x39mm cal., boxlock break open action, features 23 1/2 in. spiral fluted barrel with adj. open sights, cocking indicator, checkered walnut stock and forearm, opening lever in back of trigger guard, blue finish, 6 3/4 lbs. Limited importation 2012 only.

	$275	$240	$210	$180	$165	$150	$140	*$335*

SHOTGUNS: O/U

IZH-27 – 12, 16, 20, 28 ga., or .410 bore, 3 in. chambers (2 3/4 in. on 16 or 28 ga.) boxlock action, 26 or 28 in. VR barrels with (standard on 12 and 20 ga.) or w/o chokes, monobloc receiver, walnut checkered (with or w/o Monte Carlo) stock and forearm, extractors or ejectors, blue or nickel finish (new 2001), SST. Imported 1999-2004.

	$400	$350	$300	$270	$220	$180	$140	*$475*

Add $10 for 16 or 20 ga.
Add $34 for 28 ga. or .410 bore.
Add $224 for 20 ga. 2 barrel set.
Add $24 for nickel finish.

GRADING - PPGS™	100%	98%	95%	90%	80%	70%	60%	LAST MSR

Add $80 for nickel finish with barrel porting (12 ga. only, disc. 2003).

E nomenclature indicates ejectors. 1C indicates single trigger. This model has also been sold in the U.S. under the model names SPR310 (SST) and SPR320 (DT).

* ***IZH-27 Sporting*** – 12 or 20 ga., 3 in. chambers, SST, ejectors, ported 29 1/2 in. barrels with MC-3 chokes, wide rib, nickel finished frame. Imported 2004.

	$525	$460	$395	$355	$290	$235	$185	*$629*

MP 233 SPORTING – 12 ga. only, 3 in. chambers, 26, 28, or 29 1/2 in. unported (disc.) or ported barrels with multi-chokes and wide VR, removable trigger group, SST, ejectors, checkered walnut stock and forearm, includes carrying case, 7.2 lbs. Imported 1999-2004.

	$775	$680	$580	$525	$425	$350	$270	*$899*

MP310 – 12, 16 (disc. 2012), 20, 28 (disc. 2010) ga., or .410 bore, 26, 28, or 29 (Sporting Model) in. vent. rib hammer forged chrome lined VR barrels with choke tubes, machined steel or nickel receiver, SST, ejectors, checkered walnut stock and forearm, gold trigger, rubber buttpad, approx. 7.4 lbs. Importation began 2009.

MSR $576	$475	$425	$375	$325	$285	$240	$195	

Add $18 for nickel finished receiver.
Add $47 for 28 ga. (disc.) or $74 for .410 bore.
Add $108 for Sporting configuration (not available in .410 bore).

* ***MP310 Sporting*** – 12 or 20 ga., 28 or 30 in. vent. rib hammer forged chrome lined barrels with screw-in chokes, engraved nickel receiver, SST, selective ejectors, checkered walnut stock with right hand palm swell, competition walnut forearm, gold trigger, rubber buttpad, double sight beads. Limited importation began 2009.

$670	$550	$475	$425	$375	$330	$295	$265	

SHOTGUNS: SxS

The IZH Bounty Hunter models were available in either 12 or 20 ga., with 3 in. chambers. These models were designed for cowboy action shooting, with choice of hammers or hammerless action, SST, DT (disc.), or double selective triggers, 20 in. barrels with or w/o choke tubes, hardwood or walnut stock and forearm, engraved receiver, extractors, and weigh approx. 7 lbs.

IZH-43 FIELD MODEL – 12 or 20 ga., DT, extractors, 20, 26 (disc.), or 28 in. barrels. Disc. 1996.

	$235	$200	$175	$160	$130	$100	$80	*$299*

Add $20 for 20 in. barrels bored C/C.

IZH-43 TRADITIONAL HUNTING MODEL – 12, 16, 20, 28 ga., or .410 bore, Anson & Deeley style boxlock action with monobloc, SST, 24, 26, or 28 in. barrels with or w/o (28 ga. and .410 bore) choke tubes, checkered walnut stock and forearm, approx. 7 lbs. Imported 1999-2004.

	$340	$295	$255	$230	$185	$155	$120	*$399*

Add $30 for 16, 20, 28 ga., or .410 bore.
Add $20 for nickel finish (new 2004).

This model has been sold in the U.S. under the model names SPR210 (SST), SPR220 (DT), and Stevens Upland Sporter 411.

* ***IZH-43 2 Barrel Set*** – includes both 20 and 28 ga. barrels. Imported 2000-2004.

	$515	$450	$385	$350	$285	$230	$180	*$599*

* ***IZH-43 Traditional Bounty Hunter*** – 12, 20 ga., or .410 bore (mfg. 2001-2002), 2 3/4 in. chambers, hammerless, 20 in. barrels with choice of cyl./cyl. bore or multichokes, nickel receiver (new 2004), DT or SST, hardwood or walnut stock. Imported 2000-2004.

	$275	$240	$200	$185	$150	$125	$95	*$329*

Add $20 for nickel receiver.
Add $40-$50 for walnut stock and forearm.
Add $50-$60 for SST.
Add $159 for .45-70 cal. barrel inserts (only if shotgun is 12 ga., has 2 3/4 in. chambers, and 20 in. barrels with choke tubes).

GRADING - PPGS™	100%	98%	95%	90%	80%	70%	60%	LAST MSR

IZH-43K EXTERNAL HAMMERS – 12 or 20 (disc.) ga., similar to IZH-43 Hunting Model, except has engraved sideplates and external cocking hammers, approx. 6.3 lbs. Imported 2000-2004.

	$330	$290	$245	$225	$180	$150	$115	*$379*

Add $20 for choke tubes.
Add $20 for external firing pins.

* ***IZH-43K External Hammer 2 Barrel Set*** – includes both 20 and 28 ga. barrels. Imported 2000 only.

	$550	$480	$410	$375	$300	$245	$190	*$639*

* ***IZH-43K Bounty Hunter Traditional*** – 12 or 20 (disc. 2002) ga., 20 in. barrels with choice of cyl./cyl. bore or multichokes. Imported 2000-2004.

	$285	$250	$215	$195	$155	$130	$100	*$329*

Add $40 for multichokes or $50 for multichokes and SST.
Add $10 for external firing pins and traditional sideplates.
Add $159 for .45-70 cal. barrel inserts (only if shotgun is 12 ga., has 2 3/4 in. chambers, and 20 in. barrels with choke tubes).

* ***IZH-43KH External Hammers*** – 20 ga., 20 or 28 in. barrels with screw-in chokes, sideplates. Disc.

	$435	$380	$325	$295	$240	$195	$150	

This model has also been sold in the U.S. under the model name SPR220F.

This model has had its nomenclature changed to the MP220F (see new listing).

MP210 – 12, 16 (disc. 2010), 20, 28 (disc. 2010) ga., or .410 bore, boxlock action, 20 (disc. 2011), 26, or 28 in. chrome lined hammer forged barrels with screw-in chokes, blue steel (disc. 2011), or nickel receiver, checkered walnut stock and forearm, SST, extractors or ejectors, approx. 7.2 lbs. Importation began 2009.

MSR $491	$415	$350	$310	$275	$225	$200	$175	

Add $36 for 28 ga. (disc. 2010) or .410 bore.
Subtract 15% for extractors (disc. 2010).

MP213 – 12 ga. only, 3 in. chambers, hammerless, SST (disc. 2000) or DT, ejectors, removable trigger assembly, 20 (Coach Gun), 24, 26, or 28 in. monobloc barrels with choke tubes, checkered walnut stock and forearm, includes carrying case, approx. 7 lbs. Disc.

	$795	$695	$595	$540	$435	$360	$280	*$939*

Add $159 for .45-70 cal. barrel inserts (only if shotgun is 12 ga., has 2 3/4 in. chambers, and 20 in. barrels with choke tubes).

MP220 – 12 or 20 ga., boxlock action, 20, 26, or 28 in. chrome lined hammer forged barrels, machined steel or nickel (disc. 2010) receiver, uncheckered walnut stock and forearm, SST, hammerless, steel buttpad, 6.5-7.2 lbs. Importation began 2009.

MSR $346	$295	$260	$220	$200	$180	$150	$125	

Add $48 for choke tubes. Add $16 for nickel finish (disc. 2010).

* ***MP220F*** – 12 ga. only, similar to MP220, except has external hammers, toggle firing pin with automatic firing pin block. Importation began 2009.

MSR $527	$450	$385	$335	$295	$250	$210	$165	

SHOTGUNS: SEMI-AUTO

MP151 – 12 ga., 3 in. chamber, 26 or 28 in. plain barrel with 2 choke tubes, black synthetic or checkered walnut Monte Carlo stock, tube or detachable box (available late 1999) mag., approx. 7.8 lbs. Imported 1999 only.

	$275	$240	$200	$185	$150	$125	$95	*$310*

MP153 – 12 ga. only, 3 1/2 in. chamber, 24 (new 2001), 26 or 28 in. VR barrel with choke tubes, blue or camo (new 2011) finish, black synthetic or walnut (disc. 2004) stock and forearm, approx. 8 lbs. Imported 2000-2004, resumed 2011.

MSR $489	$395	$350	$325	$280	$250	$215	$180	

Add $114 for camo finish. Subtract 15% for black synthetic stock and forearm.

This model has also been sold in the U.S. under the model name SPR453.

GRADING - PPGS™	100%	98%	95%	90%	80%	70%	60%	LAST MSR

SHOTGUNS: SINGLE SHOT

MP18 (IZH-18M-M) – 12, 16 (disc. 2004), 20 ga., or .410 bore, hammerless, 24 (Youth), 26, 28 or 29 1/2 (disc. 2004) in. barrel with fixed or multichokes (12 or 20 ga. only, 2001-2004), ejector (IZH-18EM-M), blue or nickel (new 2001) finish, decocking/cocking lever on rear of trigger guard, cocking indicator, hardwood or walnut (new 2001) stock and forearm, trigger block safety, approx. 5 1/2 lbs. Imported 1998-2004, importation resumed 2011.

MSR $139	$110	$85	$65	$60	$50	$40	$30	

Add $13 for Youth Model (20 ga. or .410 bore only).

Add 15% for nickel finished receiver (IZH-18 Max) with MC-3 multichokes and walnut stock and forearm (disc. 2004).

This model has also been sold in the U.S. under the model name SPR100.

* ***IZH-18 Sporting*** – 12 or 20 (new 2004) ga., 28 (20 ga.) or 29 1/2 in. VR barrel with porting, rubber butt pad, wide rib, ejector, screw-in choke, nickel finish, Monte Carlo stock. Imported 2002-2004.

	$235	$200	$175	$160	$130	$100	$80	*$299*

SHOTGUNS: SLIDE ACTION

IZH-81 – 12 ga. only, 3 in. chamber, 5 shot box mag., 20, 26, or 28 in. plain or VR barrel with (26 or 28 in. barrel only) or w/o choke tubes, hardwood or walnut (disc. 1999) stock and corncob style forearm, blue finish. Imported 1999-2000.

	$235	$200	$175	$160	$130	$100	$80	*$269*

Add $17 for walnut stock (disc.1999).

Add $68 for VR barrel (walnut stock only).

MP133 – 12 ga., 3 1/2 in. chamber, 20, 24 (new 2001), 26, or 28 in. VR barrel with choke tubes (not available with 20 in. barrel), walnut stock and forearm, approx. 7 lbs. Imported 2000-2004.

	$295	$260	$220	$200	$160	$135	$100	*$359*

BAILONS GUNMAKERS LIMITED

Previous manufacturer located in Birmingham, England until 1993, when operations ceased. Inquiries regarding this trademark (including repairs) should be directed to Guthrie Consulting (see Trademark Index for listing).

RIFLES: BOLT ACTION

HUNTING RIFLE – various cals., modified Mauser bolt action, barrel length to suit from 18 to 30 in., match or set triggers, Habicht telescopic sight (magnification and reticle to suit), engraving, and types of finishes were available at additional cost, values reflect standard rifle with no options. Imported 1986-1993.

	$2,495	$2,250	$1,995	$1,775	$1,625	$1,450	$1,300	*$2,750*

BAKER, W.H. & CO.

Previous manufacturer located in Syracuse, NY circa 1878-1883.

The company was originally started by William H. and Ellis L. Baker in 1878. During this time, Leroy H. and Lyman C. Smith financed the new company, W.H. Baker & Co. In 1880, L.C. Smith bought the interest from the two Baker partners and continued production with markings reading "L.C. Smith and Co., Maker of the Baker Gun" on the rib and "Baker Pat." on the locks. Smith decided to drop the Baker name in 1883, but continued to manufacture this gun and a three-barrel shotgun/rifle combination gun in Syracuse, NY. The company was sold to the Hunter Brothers in 1888. The new company, Baker Gun & Forging Co., began making both the New Baker shotguns (see separate listing) and the Ithaca gun. The Hunter Arms Company made L.C. Smith shotguns for approximately 60 years, until the Marlin Firearms Company bought the business in 1945.

Baker guns were originally 10 or 12 ga., and unusual in that the opening mechanism was operated by pressing forward on the front trigger. While relatively rare, most original Baker guns (including the three-barrel shotgun/rifle) do not have a lot of original finish remaining.

100%	98%	95%	90%	80%	70%	60%	50%	40%	30%	20%	10%

Most specimens are priced in the $400-$950 range, assuming finish is less than 10%. If condition is better than 40%, guns should be evaluated individually for accurate pricing.

THE BAKER GUN & FORGING CO.

Previous trademark manufactured 1877-1888 by W.H. Baker & Co. and L.C. Smith Maker in Syracuse, NY. See L.C. Smith section in the L section for listings of the Baker patented three-barrel and two-barrel guns.

This section covers the popular hammer and hammerless guns manufactured 1887-1919 by the Baker Gun & Forging Company, (founded by William H. & Ellis L. Baker) in Syracuse and Batavia, NY and the H&D Folsom Arms Co. 1920-1930 in Norwich, CT. These guns sold in substantial quantities (approx. 190,000) and they attracted a strong and devoted following.

The Baker sidelock shotgun is considered an "American Best" and is recognized as one of America's Classic shotguns manufactured during that era, like the L.C. Smith, Parker, LeFever, Fox and Ithaca. Collector interest in these high quality sidelock shotguns is on the rise.

The very popular Baker Paragon grade hammerless shotguns were made to customer order and the company went to great lengths to accommodate the customer's taste in engraving, finish and specifications. Therefore, no two guns are exactly alike. Paragon guns with damascus barrels in 80% or better original condition without pitting, reboring or polishing out are of almost equal value with shotguns with Krupp steel barrels.

All 'Baker Grade' guns were available with the Extra Draw Lug and Baker's famous Firing Pin Block Safeties. The 'Batavia Grade' guns did not have these features.

The *Blue Book of Gun Values* strongly recommends an expert examination and appraisal when contemplating the purchase of a high grade Baker in 80% or better original condition.

SHOTGUNS: EXTRA VALUE FEATURES

Add 50% for 16 ga. on all grades.

Add $200-$300 for automatic ejectors.

Add $500 for single selective trigger all grades valued at $1,500 or more or 33% on guns with values less than $1,500.

SHOTGUNS: SXS, BAKER HAMMER-LONDON TWIST OR DAMASCUS, MFG. 1897-1916

MODEL "D" 1897 – sidelock twist bar London action, extra draw lug.

N/A	N/A	N/A	$1,750	$1,250	$1,100	$1,000	$900	$800	$750	$700	$650

Add $200 for damascus barrels.

NEW BAKER 1887-1896 – boxlock twist London action.

N/A	N/A	N/A	$1,200	$750	$650	$600	$550	$500	$450	$400	$350

SHOTGUNS: SXS, BATAVIA GRADE, SIDELOCK, HAMMERLESS-DAMASCUS OR FLUID STEEL, MFG. 1898-1930

BATAVIA LEADER – London twist, later guns had special steel barrels, plain wood and finish.

N/A	N/A	N/A	$1,400	$900	$700	$600	$550	$500	$450	$400	$350

Add $200 for damascus barrels (Batavia Damascus) and $200 for automatic ejectors (Batavia Ejector).

BATAVIA SPECIAL – similar to Leader model, homo-tensil steel.

N/A	N/A	N/A	$1,200	$750	$550	$500	$450	$400	$350	$300	$250

BLACK BEAUTY – similar to Batavia Special model, cockrill steel, black oxide metal finish.

N/A	N/A	N/A	$1,200	$750	$550	$500	$450	$400	$350	$300	$250

Add $200 for automatic ejectors.

BLACK BEAUTY SPECIAL – special steel, line engraving, upgraded wood, checkering and finish.

N/A	N/A	N/A	$1,500	$1,200	$1,000	$900	$800	$750	$700	$650	$600

SHOTGUNS: SXS, BAKER GRADE, SIDELOCK, HAMMERLESS-DAMASCUS OR FLUID STEEL, MFG. 1890-1923

Baker Grade hammerless guns were made in 10, 12 and 16 gauges with 26, 28, 30 and 32 in.

100%	98%	95%	90%	80%	70%	60%	50%	40%	30%	20%	10%

barrels. Guns with damascus barrels are of almost equal value if the damascus barrels are in 80%+ original condition without pitting, reboring or polishing out. The A and B grades were mfg. 1890-1910; R and S grades 1905-1915. The Paragon, Krupp, Pigeon and Deluxe grades were made in the Standard Model between 1892-1919. The Paragon, Expert and Deluxe grades were also made in the Model NN style with the L.C. Smith style rotary locking bolt 1909-1915 and the Greener style crossbolt 1915-1919.

S GRADE – fluid tempered steel, plain line and scroll engraving.

N/A	N/A	N/A	$2,000	$1,500	$1,100	$1,000	$900	$800	$700	$650	$600

Add $300 for automatic ejectors.

R GRADE – three rod damascus or Krupp steel barrels, dog and bird on locks with line and some scroll engraving, better wood and finish.

N/A	N/A	N/A	$2,800	$2,000	$1,600	$1,400	$1,200	$1,100	$1,000	$900	$800

Add $500 for Krupp barrels or $300 for automatic ejectors.

B GRADE – London twist, good line and scroll engraving with dog or bird on locks, better wood and finish than Leader model.

N/A	N/A	N/A	$2,500	$1,600	$1,300	$1,100	$1,000	$900	$800	$750	$700

Add 25% for early models with elaborate game scene engraving.

A GRADE – three rod damascus or Krupp steel barrels, same engraving as B Grade, better wood and finish.

N/A	N/A	N/A	$2,800	$2,000	$1,600	$1,350	$1,200	$1,100	$1,000	$900	$800

Add 25% for early models with elaborate game scene engraving.
Add $500 for Krupp barrels.

PARAGON GRADE – very fine damascus or Krupp barrels, fine scroll and game scene engraving, best quality wood, checkering and finish. Special order only and made to customer specifications.

N/A	N/A	N/A	$4,500	$3,500	$3,000	$2,600	$2,400	$2,200	$2,000	$1,800	$1,600

Add $300 for automatic ejectors.

KRUPP GRADE (N) – Krupp barrels, finer scroll and game scene engraving, better wood, checkering, and finish. Most had straight stocks.

N/A	N/A	N/A	$5,000	$4,000	$3,500	$3,000	$2,700	$2,500	$2,300	$2,100	$1,900

Add $300 for automatic ejectors.

PIGEON GRADE (L) – Holland special steel barrels, elaborate scroll and game scene engraving, fancy wood, checkering, and finish.

N/A	N/A	N/A	$6,000	$5,000	$4,200	$3,700	$3,400	$3,100	$2,800	$2,600	$2,400

Add $300 for automatic ejectors.

EXPERT GRADE – Holland special steel barrels, ejectors standard, finest scroll and game scene engraving, fancy checkering, wood and finish.

N/A	N/A	N/A	$7,200	$5,800	$4,700	$4,200	$3,900	$3,600	$3,300	$3,100	$2,900

DELUXE GRADE – rare in any condition. Sir Joseph Whitworth fluid compressed steel barrels, highest quality full coverage scroll and game scene engraving, checkering, wood, and finish.

N/A	N/A	N/A	$15,000	$10,000	$8,000	$7,000	$6,700	$6,400	$6,100	$5,800	$5,500

Add $600 for automatic ejectors.

SHOTGUNS: SINGLE BARREL TRAP, BOXLOCK, HAMMERLESS, FLUID STEEL, MFG. 1909-1923

The Baker SBT guns were of the highest quality. Made in 12 ga. only with 30, 32, or 34 inch barrels in three grades. They were offered with vent ribs, automatic ejectors, and Monte Carlo stocks with a cheekpiece. The two highest grades had the famous Baker firing pin block safety. The *Blue Book of Gun Values* recommends an expert appraisal when contemplating the purchase of a high grade SBT Baker in 80% or better original condition.

STERLING GRADE – line border and scroll engraving, semi-fancy wood, neatly checkered.

N/A	N/A	N/A	$1,750	$1,350	$1,200	$1,100	$1,000	$900	$800	$700	$600

100%	98%	95%	90%	80%	70%	60%	50%	40%	30%	20%	10%

ELITE GRADE – elaborate scroll engraving, fancy wood and checkering.

N/A	N/A	N/A	$3,000	$2,200	$2,000	$1,900	$1,800	$1,700	$1,600	$1,500	$1,400

SUPERBA GRADE – ornate scroll and game scene engraving, finest wood and checkering.

N/A	N/A	N/A	$4,500	$3,600	$3,400	$3,200	$3,000	$2,800	$2,600	$2,500	$2,300

BALLARD ARMS, INC.

Current rifle manufacturer located in Onsted, MI. Previously located in Cody, WY 1996-2009. Previously named Ballard Rifles LLC until 2006 and Ballard Arms LLC from 2006-2009. Dealer and consumer direct sales.

GRADING - PPGS™	100%	98%	95%	90%	80%	70%	60%	LAST MSR

RIFLES: SINGLE SHOT

All Ballard rifles feature receivers milled from solid stock, hand polished barrels, and authentic "packed" case hardening. Rifles can be chambered for calibers between .17 to .600, including Magnum and Nitro Express. Beginning 2009, all Ballard rifles are shipped with a Pelican hardshell case. Many custom features are also available - contact the factory directly for availability and pricing.

In addition to the standard models listed (up to 12 months delivery time), special order models include: (base price only) No. 4 Perfection ($3,950 MSR), No. 8 Union Hill ($4,175 MSR), No. 3 Gallery ($3,300 MSR), 1875 Traditional Custom ($3,400 MSR), and the 1885 Traditional Custom ($3,400 MSR). Allow up to 12 months for delivery.

Previous special order models include: No. 1 Silhouette ($3,275 last MSR), No. 2 Sporting ($3,450 last MSR), No. 5 1/2 Montana ($3,510 last MSR), No. 6 Schuetzen ($3,625 last MSR), Schoyen Schuetzen ($3,750 last MSR), and No. 3F Fine Gallery ($3,475 last MSR). Most of these models were discontinued during 2008.

BALLARD NO. 1 1/2 HUNTER'S RIFLE – available in 7 cals. between .22 LR - .50-70, single trigger, uncheckered stock and forearm, S style lever action, 9 3/4 - 10 1/2 lbs.

MSR $3,250	$3,100	$2,600	$2,275	$2,050	$1,875	$1,575	$1,325	

BALLARD NO. 1 3/4 FAR WEST RIFLE – available in 8 cals. between .32-40 WCF - .50-90 Sharps Straight, patterned after the original Ballard Far West Model, 30 or 32 in. standard or heavyweight octagon barrel, double set triggers, ring style lever, 9 3/4 - 10 1/2 lbs. Disc. 2008.

	$2,850	$2,500	$2,200	$2,075	$1,750	$1,425	$1,150	*$3,260*

BALLARD NO. 5 PACIFIC – available in 9 cals. between .32-40 WCF - .50-90 SS, includes under-barrel wiping rod, otherwise similar to No. 1 3/4 Far West Rifle. Disc. 2008.

	$3,125	$2,750	$2,350	$2,100	$1,775	$1,450	$1,175	*$3,510*

BALLARD NO. 4 1/2 MID RANGE – available in 5 cals. between .32-40 WCF - .45-110, configured for black powder cartridge silhouette, half-round, half-octagon 30 or 32 in. standard or heavyweight barrel, single or double set triggers, pistol grip stock, full loop lever, hard rubber Ballard buttplate, Vernier tang sight. 10 3/4 - 11 1/2 lbs. Disc. 2008.

	$2,800	$2,475	$2,200	$1,975	$1,750	$1,425	$1,150	*$3,190*

BALLARD NO. 7 LONG RANGE – available in 5 cals. between .40-65 Win. - .45-110, designed for long range shooting, half-round, half-octagon 32 or 34 in. standard or heavyweight barrel, other features similar to Ballard No. 4 1/2 Mid Range.

MSR $3,600	$3,325	$2,800	$2,475	$2,200	$1,975	$1,750	$1,425	

MODEL 1875 #3 GALLERY – available in rimfire cals., 24-28 in. octagon barrel with tulip, single trigger, "S" lever, straight grip uncheckered walnut stock and forearm, color case hardened receiver, breechblock, and lever, shotgun buttplate, blade front sights, Rocky Mountain rear sights.

MSR $3,300	$3,125	$2,600	$2,275	$2,050	$1,875	$1,575	$1,325	

GRADING - PPGS™	100%	98%	95%	90%	80%	70%	60%	LAST MSR

MODEL 1875 #4 PERFECTION – various rimfire cals., 26-30 in. #4 octagon barrel, color case hardened receiver, breechblock and lever, double set triggers, Pacific lever, classic straight grip uncheckered American wlanut stock and forearm, shotgun buttplate, blade front sight, Rocky Mountain rear sight.

MSR $3,950	$3,600	$3,300	$2,850	$2,425	$2,100	$1,725	$1,475	

MODEL 1875 #8 UNION HILL – various rimfire cals., 28-30 in. #3 round barrel, color case hardened receiver, breechblock, and buttplate, double set triggers, four finger loop lever, classic American walnut stock with pistol grip, Schuetzen cheekpiece and steel buttplate.

MSR $4,175	$3,750	$3,400	$2,925	$2,500	$2,150	$1,775	$1,500	

MODEL 1875 TRADITIONAL CUSTOM – various rimfire cals., 26-30 in. round barrel, single trigger, "S" lever, color case hardened receiver and breechblock, straight grip classic American walnut stock with shotgun buttplate.

MSR $3,400	$3,200	$2,650	$2,295	$2,050	$1,875	$1,575	$1,325	

WINCHESTER MODEL 1885 HIGH WALL – various cals., exact copy of original Winchester Model 1885 (parts interchange), 30 or 32 in. octagon barrel, ST with small lever, case colored receiver, uncheckered straight grip walnut stock and foream, approx. 9 lbs. New 2001.

MSR $3,300	$3,125	$2,600	$2,275	$2,050	$1,875	$1,575	$1,325	

Add $300 for Special Sporting Model.

Add $800 for Helm Schuetzen Model (disc. 2008).

* ***Winchester Model 1885 High Wall Deluxe*** – similar to Model 1885 High Wall, except has deluxe checkered pistol grip stock with shotgun buttplate and forearm, double set triggers, 32 in. No. 4 barrel, aperture sights, 11 lbs. Mfg. 2001-2005.

	$3,250	$2,775	$2,350	$2,100	$1,775	$1,450	$1,175	*$3,675*

Add $75 for Express Model.

* ***Winchester Model 1885 High Wall Special Sporting*** – various cals., 28-30 in. #3 octagon barrel, color case hardened receiver, breechblock, and lever, single trigger, "S" lever, select American walnut stock with pistol grip and shotgun buttplate, sporting rear sights, blade front sights.

MSR $3,600	$3,325	$2,800	$2,475	$2,200	$1,975	$1,750	$1,425	

* ***Winchester Model 1885 High Wall Traditional Custom*** – various cals., 26-30 in. round barrel, single trigger, "S" lever, color case hardened receiver and breechblock, straight grip classic American walnut stock with shotgun buttplate.

MSR $3,400	$3,200	$2,650	$2,295	$2,050	$1,875	$1,575	$1,325	

WINCHESTER 1885 LOW WALL – color case hardened receiver, 24-28 in. octagon barrel, breech block and lever, straight grip American walnut, shotgun buttplate, sporting rear sight, blade front sight. New 2009.

MSR $3,300	$3,125	$2,600	$2,275	$2,050	$1,875	$1,575	$1,325	

AFRICAN EXPRESS – #3 hand polished thick side action, color case hardened finish, single trigger, hand selected classic American walnut pistol grip stock with English style round forearm, island rear adj. sight, banded front sight, hand polished straight taper round barrel, 8-13 lbs.

MSR $4,650	$4,350	$3,850	$3,450	$2,900	$2,500	$2,000	$1,650	

THE ROOK AND RABBIT – #2 hand polished, color case hardened action, single trigger, hand selected classic American walnut pistol grip stock with English style round forearm and ebony tip, steel grip cap and buttplate, quarter rib for Talley rings, adj. rear and ramped front sight.

MSR $4,650	$4,350	$3,850	$3,450	$2,900	$2,500	$2,000	$1,650	

THE LIGHT HUNTER – #3 hand polished thin side action, hand selected classic American walnut Accu-stock with recoil pad, steel cap, English style round forearm with ebony tip, color case hardened Jeffery's Light Hunter lever, quarter rib for Talley rings, banded front and inletted rear swivels, approx. 6 1/2 lbs.

MSR $4,750	$4,500	$3,900	$3,475	$2,900	$2,500	$2,000	$1,650	

GRADING - PPGS™	100%	98%	95%	90%	80%	70%	60%	LAST MSR

CRESSWELL – #2 hand polished low wall color case hardened action, lightweight taper barrel, hand selected classic American walnut pistol grip stock with English style round forearm and ebony tip, color case hardened Jeffery's Light Hunter lever, quarter rib for Talley rings, banded front and inletted rear swivels, approx. 5 1/2 lbs.

MSR $4,750	$4,425	$3,900	$3,475	$2,900	$2,500	$2,000	$1,650

JEFFERY'S SHARPS – #3 hand polished thick side action, custom taper barrel, hand selected classic American walnut pistol grip stock with English style round forearm and ebony tip, steel grip cap, recoil pad, color case hardened Jeffery's lever with checkered thumb tab, quarter rib for adj. rear blade, banded front and inletted rear swivels, approx. 8-13 lbs.

MSR $5,250	$4,800	$4,200	$3,600	$3,000	$2,600	$2,100	$1,750

BALLESTER MOLINA/RIGAUD (HAFDASA)

Previous trademark of semi-auto pistols manufactured by Hispano Argentino Fabricade Automoviles SA (Hafdasa).

PISTOLS: SEMI-AUTO

The Ballester-Molina was an attempt to market a less expensive alternative to the Colt Model 1927, which was an Argentine-made licensed copy of the Colt Model 1911. During the first three years of production, the pistol was marked "Ballester-Rigaud", and later marked "Ballester-Molina". Although the Ballester-Molina .45 ACP is virtually the same size and shape as the Colt Model 1911, only the barrel is interchangable.

BALLESTER-MOLINA/RIGAUD – .45 ACP or .22 LR (training version) cal., 5 in. barrel, patterned after the Colt M-1911A1 except has pinned trigger, is without grip safety, has different sear mechanism, and distinctive pattern retracting grooves in slide, issued to the Argentine Military and Police (marked on slide), also sold commercially in Latin America, ser. no. stamped on hilt next to magazine floor plate, some also marked with property numbers. Approx. 90,000 - 110,000 mfg. 1937-1953.

	$625	$545	$470	$425	$345	$280	$220
.22 LR Training Model	$1,250	$1,095	$940	$850	$690	$565	$440

During WWII the British purchased between 10,000 - 15,000 Ballester-Molinas in .45 ACP cal. for both the British military and clandestine activities. These are marked with a B prefix before the serial number. Pistol marked "Ejercito" are Army issue and pistols marked "Armada" are navy issue (this would include the Marines and the Coast Guard). Slides may be marked with various federal and police agency names and issue numbers (not to be confused with the serial number).

Guns marked "Cal. .45" or "11.25mm" will shoot .45 ACP ammo.

Pistols were exported to Columbia, Bolivia, Ecuador, Peru, Uruguay, and Venezuela.

BALTIMORE ARMS COMPANY

Previous manufacturer of SxS shotguns located in Baltimore, MD circa 1895-1902.

SHOTGUNS: SxS

STYLE 1 – this variation does not have the improved Hollenbeck barrel locking mechanism characterized by the eye-shaped hole in the top rib extension. Mfg. 1895-1900.

Prices generally range from $575 to $1,500 depending on condition and grade.

There are 4 grades of Baltimore Arms Company shotguns: Field, Grade A, Grade B, and Grade C.

STYLE 2 – this variation has the improved barrel locking mechanism and is marked with a patent date "FEB. 13, 1900" on the water table. Mfg. 1900-1902.

Prices generally range from $795 to $2,000 depending on condition and grade.

There are 4 grades of Baltimore Arms Company shotguns: Field, Grade A, Grade B, and Grade C.

BANSNER'S ULTIMATE RIFLES, L.L.C.

Current custom rifle manufacturer established during 1981 and located in Adamstown, PA. In 2000, the company name changed from Bansner's Gunsmithing Specialities to Bansner's Ultimate Rifles, L.L.C. Consumer direct sales.

GRADING - PPGS™	100%	98%	95%	90%	80%	70%	60%	LAST MSR

RIFLES: BOLT ACTION

All Bansner's UR rifles up to approx. June 1, 1999 have either Remington 700 or Winchester post-64 claw extractor actions. After this approx. date, Bansner's started using its own proprietary action, and during 2005, released the Sharpshooter model with Nesika Bay action.

ULTIMATE ONE – various cals. and configurations including different metal finishes and special orders, Rem. 700 (disc. 1999), Win. post-64 Model 70 (disc. 1999), Bansner's custom action by Nesika beginning 2004, exclusive action was mfg. by McMillan Bros. Rifle Co., Inc. (steel or stainless steel, mfg. 2001-2003), Douglas premium air gauged (disc.) or Lilja fluted barrel with M-50 muzzle brake, large extractor, plunger ejector, 3 lbs. custom tuned trigger, custom color synthetic stock with Pachmayr Decelerator pad, includes Talley custom scope bases and rings, various weights.

MSR $4,595	$4,350	$3,875	$3,300	$2,750	$2,300	$1,800	$1,500	

Add $350 for 3 position Model 70 style safety or Lazzeroni calibers (disc. 2007).

ULTIMATE SAFARI HUNTER – various dangerous game cals., Lilja Precision stainless steel 24 in. barrel, scalloped action based on the M-70 Classic (disc.), or Dakota 76 CRF action, M-50 muzzle brake, synthetic stock with Pachmayr decelerator pad, matte black teflon metal finish. Mfg. 2003-2008.

	$5,700	$4,985	$4,275	$3,875	$3,135	$2,565	$1,995	*$6,195*

SAFARI HUNTER – various dangerous game cals., Bansner custom stainless steel action, Lilja Precision match grade stainless steel contour barrel, Jewell trigger, High Tech Specialities fiberglass stock, Pachmayr Decelerator pad, custom LOP, drilled and tapped.

MSR $5,595	$5,300	$4,950	$4,300	$3,650	$3,000	$2,400	$1,950	

BIG FIVE – various dangerous game cals., Dakota 76 action, straddle floorplate, Lilja Precision match grade stainless steel barrel, muzzle brake, Polymer K-cote finish, High Tech Specialties fiberglass pillar bedded and reinforced stock, Pachmayr Decelerator recoil pad, custom LOP, zeroed in at 100 yards. Mfg. 2009-2011.

	$7,150	$6,255	$5,365	$4,860	$3,935	$3,220	$2,505	*$7,465*

CLASSIC HUNTER – various cals., Bansner's stainless steel action with spiral fluted bolt body, Lilja Precision match grade stainless steel barrel, custom "Hunter" trigger with top slide safety, Talley steel bases with fixed rings, all metal coated with polymer black, silver, or Ti K-Kote finish, High Tech Specialties fiberglass pillar bedded stock, Pachmayr Decelerator recoil pad, custom LOP. Mfg. 2009-2011.

	$3,550	$3,105	$2,665	$2,415	$1,955	$1,600	$1,245	*$3,892*

SHARPSHOOTER – various cals., Nesika Bay action, Lilja Precision medium to heavy weight match grade fluted barrel (customer choice of length), with recessed crown, Jewell trigger, brown wood laminate pillar bedded and reinforced fiberglass stock with palm swell, polymer Ti K-Kote metal finish, ebony forend tip, inletted swivel studs. Mfg. 2005-2007.

	$7,900	$6,910	$5,925	$5,370	$4,345	$3,555	$2,765	*$8,495*

SHARPSHOOTER (NEW MFG.) – various cals., long range light tactical hunting rifle, features accurized and blueprinted stainless Rem. M700 action with Sako extractor, Hart stainless steel match grade barrel with fluting and muzzle brake, jewel trigger, High-Tech Specialties, Inc. pillar bedded fiberglass stock with Pachmayr decelerator recoil pad. New 2012.

MSR $5,300	$4,995	$4,400	$3,850	$3,350	$2,800	$2,300	$1,675	

ULTIMATE OVIS SHEEP HUNTER – various cals., Rem. 700 action (disc.) or Banser's custom lightweight stainless steel action (new 2007), accurized, engine turned fluted bolt, skeletonized bolt handle, alloy ADL trigger guard, Jewell trigger, Lilja Precision barrel, fiberglass stock, 5 1/4 lbs.

MSR $4,595	$4,350	$3,875	$3,300	$2,750	$2,300	$1,800	$1,500	

ULTIMATE VARMINT HUNTER – various cals., Rem. 700 action, accurized and polished, Jewell varmint trigger, Lilja Precision stainless steel barrel, polymer Ti K-Kote metal finish, fully bedded fiberglass stock, Pachmayr Decelerator pad. Disc. 2008.

	$4,550	$3,980	$3,410	$3,095	$2,500	$2,045	$1,590	*$4,995*

GRADING - PPGS™	100%	98%	95%	90%	80%	70%	60%	LAST MSR

ALPINE HUNTER – .300 WSM cal. only, Howa 1500 action, milled receiver, fluted barrel, muzzle brake, tuned trigger, fully bedded fiberglass stock, Pachmayr Decelerator pad, polymer Ti K-Kote metal finish.

MSR $2,195	$1,995	$1,750	$1,500	$1,350	$1,150	$995	$825	

ALASKAN HUNTER – various cals., Rem. 700 action, accurized, scalloped and polished receiver, fluted bolt, skeletonized handle, alloy ADL trigger guard, Lilja Precision barrel, fiberglass stock, Pachmayr Decelerator pad, approx. 5 lbs. Disc. 2004.

	$3,525	$3,085	$2,645	$2,395	$1,940	$1,585	$1,235	*$3,895*

ULTIMATE RIFLE – various cals., Rem. 700 or Win. 70 action, accurized and polished, 3 lbs. trigger pull, Lilja Precision stainless steel barrel, fully bedded fiberglass stock, Pachmayr Decelerator pad. Disc. 2004.

	$2,995	$2,620	$2,245	$2,035	$1,645	$1,350	$1,050	*$3,300*

HIGH TECH SERIES – various cals., Howa 1500 steel or stainless steel action with factory barrel and Bansner's synthetic stock with Pachmayr Decelerator pad. Mfg. 1997-2004.

	$965	$845	$725	$655	$530	$435	$340	*$1,050*

Add $100 for all stainless steel.

ULTIMATE/TRADITIONAL CLASSIC – various cals., custom Dakota 76 controlled round feed claw extractor action, custom floorplate with release inside trigger bow, Lilja Precision match grade hand lapped barrel, choice of polymer matte blue or Ti K-Kote metal finish, synthetic stock, Pachmayr Decelerator pad. Mfg. 2005-2008.

	$4,450	$3,895	$3,335	$3,025	$2,445	$2,000	$1,555	*$4,895*

LIMITED EDITION SERIES – various cals., customized Bansner's (new 2004) or Rem. 700 action with scalloped receiver, fluted bolt body, Jewell trigger, Gentry 3-position safety, synthetic stock with choice of black or silver teflon coated metal, 25-50 of each limited edition beginning 2003.

Please contact the company directly regarding pricing on these limited editions.

25TH ANNIVERSARY MODEL – customer chosen caliber and barrel contour, stainless steel action with custom engraving, sequential serial number, Lilja Precision match grade barrel, Jewell trigger, fiberglass Sheep Hunter stock, Pachmayr Decelerator pad, includes custom aluminum case and black sling. Only 25 mfg. late 2005-2008.

This model has a current MSR of $6,195.

BARNES PRECISION MACHINE, INC.

Current semi-auto rifle manufacturer located in Apex, NC. Dealer and consumer direct sales.

RIFLES: SEMI-AUTO

Barnes manufactures a complete line of AR-15 style rifles, as well as parts and accessories. Many options are available for each rifle. Please contact the company directly for a complete list and pricing (see Trademark Index).

IMPORTANT NOTE: On model(s) where *N/A has replaced the normal 100% value, it indicates current market conditions are too unstable to accurately ascertain 100%-60% values. Factory retail prices (MSRs) reflect most recent updates. For more up-to-date information on current pricing trends and additional useful information, please visit www.bluebookofgunvalues.com, select "Information & Services " from the menu, and click on "Additional Book Information".

CQB PATROLMAN'S CARBINE – 5.56 NATO cal., 16 in. BPM stainless steel match barrel, mid-length gas system with stainless steel low profile gas block, A2-style flash hider, black or tan finish, 12 inch PSFFRS hand guard with optional sling swivels, Magpul MBUS Gen2 sights, six position or MOE adj. stock, Picatinny rail.

MSR $1,275	*N/A	$995	$875	$775	$675	$575	$475	

This model is also available in 11 1/2 or 14 1/2 in. barrel configuration for law enforcement/military.

* ***CQB Patrolman's Carbine .300 Blackout*** – .300 AAC Blackout cal., 16 in. stainless steel barrel with BPMA2 style flash hider, MagPul MOE stock and pistol grip, MagPul MBUS

GRADING - PPGS™	100%	98%	95%	90%	80%	70%	60%	LAST MSR

sights, flat top Picatinny rail receiver with 12 in. quad rail, includes plastic hard case, black finish/furniture. New 2013.

MSR $1,545 *N/A $1,050 $950 $825 $725 $625 $525

TACTICAL MATCH CARBINE – 5.56 NATO cal., 16 or 18 in. BPM stainless steel match barrel, mid-length gas system with adj. gas system, Robar NP3 electroless nickel or black finish, 12 in. Ultralite PSFFRS hand guard with optional sling swivels, ACE SOCOM rifle length stock, Picatinny rail, Miculek muzzle break, JARD non-adj. trigger system.

MSR $1,538 *N/A $1,050 $950 $825 $725 $625 $525

DESIGNATED MARKSMAN RIFLE – 5.56 NATO cal., 18 in. BPM stainless steel match barrel, mid-length gas system, black finish, 12 in. Ultralite PSFFRS hand guard with optional sling swivels, A2 fixed stock, Picatinny rail, Miculek muzzle break, JARD non-adj. trigger system.

MSR $1,454 *N/A $995 $895 $775 $675 $575 $475

BARRETT FIREARMS MANUFACTURING, INC.

Current rifle manufacturer established in 1982, and located in Murfreesboro, TN. Dealer direct sales.

RIFLES: BOLT ACTION

MODEL 90 – .50 BMG cal., 29 in. match grade barrel with muzzle brake, 5 shot detachable box mag., includes extendible bipod legs, scope optional, 22 lbs. Mfg. 1990-1995.

$3,450 $2,950 $2,400 $2,150 $1,875 $1,600 $1,500 *$3,650*

Add $1,150 for Swarovski 10X scope and rings.

MODEL 95(M) – .50 BMG cal., 29 in. match grade barrel with high efficiency muzzle brake, 5 shot detachable box mag., includes extendible bipod legs, full length M1913 receiver optics rail, scope optional, includes carrying case, 22 1/2 lbs. New 1995.

MSR $6,500 $6,150 $5,600 $5,000 $4,250 $3,500 $2,750 $2,200

Add $1,370 for Leupold scope and Barrett ultra high rings (new 2012).
Add $2,769 for rifle system including Leupold scope, BORS ultra high rings, 120 rounds of XM33 ammo, Pelican case, and bipod (new 2011).

MODEL 98B – .338 Lapua cal., 20 in. heavy unfluted, 26 (new 2013), or 27 (disc. 2012) in. fluted barrel, includes two 10 shot detachable mags. with muzzle brake, adj. stock, Harris bipod, monopod, full length M1913 optics receiver rail with 3 accessory rails on shroud, two sling loops, adj. trigger, ergonomic bolt handle, black finish, air/watertight case, 13 1/2 lbs. New 2009.

MSR $4,699 $4,300 $3,925 $3,550 $3,100 $2,800 $2,500 $2,150

Add $150 for 26 in. fluted barrel (new 2013).
Add $1,300 for Leupold scope and cleaning kit (disc. 2012).
Add $1,370 for Leupold scope and Barrett ultra high rings (new 2012).
Add $2,769 for Leupold scope, BORS, and Barrett ultra high rings.

MODEL 99 – .416 Barrett (32 in. barrel only) or .50 BMG cal., single shot bolt action, 25 (disc.) or 29 in. (.50 BMG cal. only) lightweight fluted, or 32 in. heavy barrel with muzzle brake, straight through design with pistol grip and bipod, full length M1913 receiver optics rail, Black, Brown (disc.), Silver (disc.), or Flat Dark Earth (new 2012) finish, 23-25 lbs. New 1999.

MSR $3,999 $3,650 $3,275 $2,850 $2,500 $2,175 $1,775 $1,400

Add $100 for .50 BMG cal. with flat dark earth finish.
Subtract $150 for .416 Barret cal. in black finish or $150 for .50 BMG cal. with 32 in. heavy barrel.
Subtract $50 for .416 Barret cal. in flat dark earth finish.
Add $1,370 for Leupold scope and Barrett Ultra high rings (new 2012).
Add $2,789 for Leupold scope, BORS, and Barrett Ultra high rings (new 2012).
Add $251 for Bushnell Elite 10x scope (disc.).

MODEL MRAD – .338 Lapua cal., 20 (new 2012), 24 (new 2013), 24 1/2 (disc. 2013), 26 (new 2013) or 27 (mfg. 2012 only) in. fluted or heavy barrel with muzzle brake, features aluminum receiver with modular construction including user-changeable barrel system,

GRADING - PPGS™	100%	98%	95%	90%	80%	70%	60%	LAST MSR

match grade trigger, thumb operated safety, ambidextrous mag. release, 21 3/4 in. M1913 optics rail plus side rails on vent forend, folding stock with adj. cheekpiece, Barret Multi-Role Brown or black anodized (new 2013) finish, includes two 10 shot mags., two sling loops, three accessory rails, and Pelican case, 14.8 lbs. New mid-2011.

MSR $6,000	$5,750	$5,350	$4,800	$4,300	$3,750	$3,150	$2,600

Subtract $150 for 20, 24, or 26 in. heavy barrel.
Add $1,370 for Leupold scope and Barret ultra high rings (new 2012).
Add $2,769 for Leupold scope, BORS, and ultra high rings (new 2012).

RIFLES: SEMI-AUTO

IMPORTANT NOTE: On model(s) where *N/A has replaced the normal 100% value, it indicates current market conditions are too unstable to accurately ascertain 100%-60% values. Factory retail prices (MSRs) reflect most recent updates. For more up-to-date information on current pricing trends and additional useful information, please visit www.bluebookofgunvalues.com, select "Information & Services" from the menu, and click on "Additional Book Information".

MODEL 82 RIFLE - .50 BMG cal., semi-auto recoil operation, 33-37 in. barrel, 11 shot mag., 2,850 FPS muzzle velocity, scope sight only, parkerized finish, 35 lbs. Mfg. 1982-1987.

	*N/A	$4,350	$3,950	$3,450	$2,700	$2,150	$1,800

Last MSR for consumers was $3,180 in 1985.

This model underwent design changes after initial production. Only 115 were mfg. starting with ser. no. 100.

MODEL 82A1 - .416 Barrett (new 2010) or .50 BMG cal., paramilitary design w/short recoil operating system, variant of the original Model 82, back-up iron sights, fitted hard case, 20, 29 (new late 1989), or 33 (disc. 1989) in. fluted (current mfg.) or unfluted (disc.) barrel, current mfg. has muzzle brake, 10 shot detachable or fixed (.416 Barrett cal. only) mag., black anodized or multi-role brown (new 2013) finish, 32 1/2 lbs. for 1989 and older mfg., approx. 30 lbs. for 1990 mfg. and newer. Current mfg. includes elevated M1913 optics rail, watertight case, and cleaning kit.

MSR $8,900	*N/A	$7,750	$7,000	$6,250	$5,500	$5,000	$4,650

Add $200 for multi-role brown finish (new 2013).
Add $1,370 for Leupold scope, Barrett ultra high rings, and Monopod (new 2012).
Add $2,769 for Leupold scope, BORS, Barrett ultra high rings, and Monopod (new 2012).
Add $1,500 for Leupold Mark IV 4.5-14x50mm scope (disc. 2011).
Add $375 for pack-mat backpack case (new 1999).
Add $2,800 for rifle system including Leupold scope, ultra high rings, Pelican case, and detachable bipod (new 2011).
Add approx. $4,900 per upper conversion kit.
Add $275 for camo backpack carrying case (disc.).
Add $1,325 for Swarovski 10X scope and rings (disc.).

This model boasts official U.S. military rifle (M107) status following government procurement during Operation Desert Storm. In 1992, a new "arrowhead" shaped muzzle brake was introduced to reduce recoil.

MODEL 98 - .338 Lapua Mag. cal., 10 shot box mag., 24 in. match grade barrel with muzzle brake, bipod, 15 1/2 lbs.

While advertised during mid-1999, this model was never produced.

MODEL 107A1 - .50 BMG cal., 20 (new 2012) or 29 in. fluted barrel with four port titanium muzzle brake, integrated M1913 full length receiver optics rail including flip up iron sights, features new bolt carrier group and aluminum recoil buffer system, Black (new 2013) or Flat Dark Earth finish, detachable adj. lightweight bipod, monopod on buttstock, 10 shot mag., 30.9 lbs. New mid-2011.

MSR $12,000	*N/A	$10,000	$9,000	$8,000	$7,000	$6,500	$6,000

Add $1,370 for Leupold scope and Barrett ultra high rings (new 2012).
Add $2,769 for Leupold scope, BORS, and Barrett ultra high rings (new 2012).

GRADING - PPGS™	100%	98%	95%	90%	80%	70%	60%	LAST MSR

MODEL M468 – 6.8 SPC cal., aluminum upper and lower receiver, 16 in. barrel with muzzle brake, 5, 10, or 30 shot mag., dual spring extractor system, folding front and rear sight, gas block, two-stage trigger, integrated rail system, choice of full or telescoping 4-position stock, 8 lbs. Mfg. 2005-2008.

	*N/A	$2,050	$1,675	$1,375	$1,175	$995	$875	$2,700

Add $1,590 for Model M468 upper conversion kit.

MODEL REC7 – 5.56 NATO or 6.8 SPC cal., AR-15 style gas piston operated action, aluminum upper and lower receiver, 16 in. chrome lined barrel with A-2 flash hider, 30 shot mag., folding front and ARMS rear sight, single stage trigger, ARMS selective integrated rail system (disc.) or Omega X rail (current mfg.), 6-position MOE stock, includes tactical soft case and two mags., 7.62 lbs. New 2008.

MSR $1,950	*N/A	$1,525	$1,300	$1,100	$900	$775	$650	

Add $1,650 per individual upper conversion kit.
Add $676 for Aimpoint Micro T-1 optics (mfg. 2011-2012).

BAR-STO

Previous manufacturer located in Palms, CA. Bar-Sto still manufactures barrels and firearms-related accessories.

PISTOLS: SEMI-AUTO

BAR-STO .25 ACP PISTOL – .25 ACP cal., patterned after the Baby Browning, brushed stainless steel finish, walnut grips, approx. 250 manufactured circa 1974.

	$195	$165	$125	$100	$85	$70	$65	

BARTOLOT, WERNER

Please refer to Werner Bartolot listing in the W Section.

BASERRI

Current trademark established mid-2010, manufactured by Fabarm in Brescia, Italy, and imported by Baserri located in Friendswood, TX. Dealer sales.

Baserri manufactures good quality O/U shotguns. Current models include the Mari HR Field - MSR $2,395 for 12 ga., add $100 for 20 ga. and $300 for 28 ga. The Mari Elite (Hunting and Sporting Clays configuration) is 12 ga. only - MSR $3,395. Please contact the company directly for more information, including options and availability (see Trademark Index).

BATTAGLIA, MAURO

Current manufacturer established in 1992 and located in Ravenna, Italy. No current U.S. importation.

SHOTGUNS: SxS, CUSTOM

Mauro Battaglia manufactures custom order high quality SxS shotguns. He also manufactures a sidelock action with new unique design. Many options are available.

Current models include: the Angels (€18,000), Angels Lux (€20,000), Morena (€24,000), Mercedes (€26,000), Manuela (€30,000), History (€33,000), Monia Extra (€40,000), and the Timio (€45,000). All pricing is for base model in-the-white. Many engraving options are available and feature engraver Max Gobbi.

Please contact the factory directly for more information, including delivery time, options, and a price quotation (see Trademark Index).

BATTLE RIFLE COMPANY

Current rifle manufacturer located in Seabrook, TX.

RIFLES: SEMI-AUTO

Current models include BR4, BR4 Spectre, BR4 Stryker, BR15, BR16, BR177, BR308, and the BR15 LIT. As this edition went to press, MSRs on these models could not be ascertained.

GRADING - PPGS™	100%	98%	95%	90%	80%	70%	60%	LAST MSR

BAUER FIREARMS CORPORATION

Previous manufacturer located in Fraser, MI circa 1971-1984.

COMBINATION GUNS

THE RABBIT – .22 LR cal. and .410 bore, combination gun with 20 in. barrel, all metal construction, O/U configuration, 4 3/4 lbs. Mfg. 1982-1984.

	100%	98%	95%	90%	80%	70%	60%	LAST MSR
	$250	$225	$175	$150	$125	$100	$85	

PISTOLS: SEMI-AUTO

BAUER .25 ACP – .25 ACP cal., 2 1/2 in. barrel, 6 shot, fixed sights, checkered walnut or pearlite grips. Mfg. 1972-84.

	100%	98%	95%	90%	80%	70%	60%	LAST MSR
	$150	$130	$110	$95	$75	$65	$60	

Note: These guns are identical to the Baby Browning, except stainless steel.

* ***Bauer .25 ACP Bicentennial Model*** – .25 ACP cal., engraved, with buckle and display case.

	100%	98%	95%	90%	80%	70%	60%	LAST MSR
	$300	$200	$150	$120	$100	$90	$80	

BAYARD

Previously manufactured by Anciens Etablissements Pieper located in Herstal, Belgium.

Even though Bayard Models 1908, both 1923s, and 1930 were manufactured only by Anciens Etablissements Pieper of Herstal, Belgium, these pistols are listed under this heading as they are most commonly referred to by this trademark designation.

PISTOLS: SEMI-AUTO

Add 20%+ premium for .25 ACP and .380 ACP cals. (rarer than .32 ACP cal.), unless otherwise indicated.

MODEL 1908 POCKET AUTOMATIC – .25 ACP, .32 ACP, or .380 ACP cal., 6 shot, 2 1/4 in. barrel, fixed sights, blue, hard rubber grips.

	100%	98%	95%	90%	80%	70%	60%	LAST MSR
	$450	$350	$225	$195	$150	$125	$100	
factory engraved	$1,050	$850	$700	$600	$475	$375	$295	

Add 25% if marked with Imperial Eagle.
Add 10% for .380 ACP cal.

MODEL 1923 & MODEL 1930 .25 POCKET AUTOMATIC – .25 ACP cal., 2 1/2 in. barrel, blue, fixed sights, checkered hard rubber grips.

	100%	98%	95%	90%	80%	70%	60%	LAST MSR
	$375	$325	$275	$225	$175	$150	$100	

The Model 1930 is a slight improvement over the Model 1923. Both share the same physical characteristics.

BAYARD 1923 & MODEL 1930 POCKET AUTOMATIC – .32 ACP or .380 ACP cal., 6 shot, 3 5/16 in. barrel, fixed sights, blue, checkered hard rubber grips.

	100%	98%	95%	90%	80%	70%	60%	LAST MSR
.32 ACP cal.	$675	$500	$350	$275	$225	$150	$125	
.380 ACP cal.	$750	$600	$450	$350	$275	$250	$200	

The Model 1930 is a slight improvement over the Model 1923. Both share the same physical characteristics.

SHOTGUNS: SxS

Although often recognized in the U.S for their pistols, Anciens Etablissements Pieper, was primarily a fine shotgun manufacturer with roots dating back to 1866. Re-organization and renaming of the company in 1905 brought in modern manufacturing techniques combined with old-world craftsmanship. By 1910 the company was one of Belgium's largest gun manufacturers, employing 1,100 workers. The Bayard trade-name was engraved on all barrels. Often mistaken as antiques, Bayard hammer guns were made through the 1920s and remained available in the 1930s. More than 150 various hammer models and variations were offered at any one time, with most models featuring extensive and luxurious hand engraving. Pricing varies extensively

GRADING - PPGS™	100%	98%	95%	90%	80%	70%	60%	LAST MSR

depending on the engraving style and engraving coverage, barrel styles like damascus barrels, wood checkering, etc. Observed pricing for hammer guns have been from $200 to $10,000. Although many model variants exist, hammerless shotguns are outlined below.

BOXLOCK BASIC MODELS – 12 or 16 ga., Anson-Deeley system, standard checkering on walnut stock, minor and simple engraving on select few parts.

	100%	98%	95%	90%	80%	70%	60%	LAST MSR
	$500	$400	$300	$275	$200	$150	$100	

Add 20% for auto ejectors.
Add $40 for semi-pistol grip stock option.

BOXLOCK FINE GRADE MODELS – 12 or 16 ga., Anson-Deeley system, demi-block barrels marked "Tested for Smokeless Powder" in either French, German or English depending on export market, standard checkering on walnut stock, elegant floral and/or game scene engraving styles.

	100%	98%	95%	90%	80%	70%	60%	LAST MSR
	$1,800	$1,600	$1,200	$900	$750	$650	$550	

Add 20% for auto ejectors or semi-pistol grip stock option.
Subtract $400 for Model 560, marked and finished as Fine Grade Models but with almost no engraving.

BOXLOCK LUXURY GRADE MODELS – 12 or 16 ga., Anson-Deeley system, demi-block barrels marked "Tested for Smokeless Powder" in either French, German or English depending on export market, fancy wood checkering, full coverage elegant engraving on all parts.

	100%	98%	95%	90%	80%	70%	60%	LAST MSR
	$4,000	$3,600	$3,000	$2,550	$2,000	$1,300	$800	

Add 20% for auto ejectors or for semi-pistol grip stock option.
Add a minimum of $200 for gold inlay option, depending on coverage but only if 95% condition or better.

SIDELOCK FINE GRADE MODELS – 12 or 16 ga., demi-bloc barrels marked "Tested for Smokeless Powder" in either French, German or English depending on export market, standard checkering on walnut stock, oak leaf engraving or floral and/or game scene engraving styles.

	100%	98%	95%	90%	80%	70%	60%	LAST MSR
	$1,950	$1,750	$1,300	$1,000	$800	$750	$650	

Add 20% for auto ejectors or for semi-pistol grip stock option.

SIDELOCK LUXURY GRADE MODELS – 12 or 16 ga., demi-bloc barrels marked "Tested for Smokeless Powder" in either French, German or English depending on export market, fancy wood checkering, full coverage elegant engraving on all parts.

	100%	98%	95%	90%	80%	70%	60%	LAST MSR
	$4,800	$4,500	$3,900	$3,000	$2,200	$1,500	$900	

Add 20% for auto ejectors or for semi-pistol grip stock option.
Add a minimum of $200 for gold inlay option, depending on coverage but only if 95% condition or better.

BECAS

Current trademark of shotguns manufactured by Molot JSC, located in the Kirov Region, Russia.

Becas semi-automatic and slide action rifles and shotguns have had little or no importation into the U.S. Please contact the factory for more information (see Trademark Index), including U.S. model availability.

BEEMAN OUTDOOR SPORTS

Previous importer and distributor located in Santa Rosa, CA.

On April 1, 1993, Beeman Precision Arms, Inc. was split into two independent companies: Beeman Precision Airguns, a division of S/R Industries (Maryland Corp.), located in Huntington Beach, CA retains worldwide distribution of Beeman airguns and accessories. Beeman Outdoor Sports, a Division of Robert's Precision Arms, Inc., located in Santa Rosa, CA distributed Feinwerkbau firearms until 1995.

Beeman Precision Arms, Inc. was a large volume importer, primarily specializing in high quality European air rifles and pistols. Firearms trademarks previously distributed in the U.S. include the following trademarks: Agner (disc. 1986), Erma (disc. 1985), FAS (disc.

GRADING - PPGS™	100%	98%	95%	90%	80%	70%	60%	LAST MSR

1987), Fabarm (disc. 1985), Feinwerkbau, Korth (disc. 1990), Krico (disc. 1988), Unique (disc. 1991), and Weihrauch (disc.). These trademarks appear under their respective alphabetical headings.

For more information and current pricing on both new and used Beeman Precision Airguns, please refer to the *Blue Book of Airguns* by Dr. Robert Beeman & John Allen (also available online).

The following firearms were manufactured to Beeman specifications, and are therefore listed under the Beeman Outdoor Sports heading.

PISTOLS: SEMI-AUTO

BEEMAN MP-08 – .380 ACP cal., Luger type toggle action, 3 1/2 in. barrel, 6 shot mag., blue, 1.4 lbs. Mfg. 1968-90.

$395 $335 $275 $240 $185 $145 $115 ***$390***

In 1988, Beeman took over importation of these two models (MP-08 and P-08). These revised models have new Luger style checkered walnut grips and 3 1/2 in. barrel. Previous variations had plastic grips.

BEEMAN P-08 – .22 LR cal., Luger type toggle action, 8 shot mag., 3.8 in. barrel, blue, checkered walnut grips, 1.9 lbs. Mfg. 1969-1990.

$395 $335 $275 $240 $185 $145 $115 ***$390***

PISTOLS: SINGLE SHOT

MODEL SP/SPX – .22 LR cal., designed for silhouette shooting, 10 in. heavy bull barrel, blue metal parts, birchwood stocks and forearm, aperture sights, 3.9 lbs. Disc. 1994.

$625 $550 $475 $425 $375 $330 $295 ***$700***

Only a few of these models were actually delivered.

* ***Model SPX Deluxe*** – similar to Model SPX, except has matte chrome metal finish, hand stippled walnut grips, and Anschütz rear sight. Limited mfg. 1993-94.

$800 $725 $650 $575 $500 $425 $350 ***$900***

SP STANDARD – .22 LR cal., sidelever action, 8, 10, 12, or 15 in. barrel, adj. sights and walnut grips, single shot. Made in W. Germany. Imported 1985-86 only.

$250 $220 $180 $170 $160 $150 $140 ***$250***

Add $10 or $30 for 12 or 15 in. barrel respectively.

SP DELUXE – similar to SP Standard, except has forearm, about 3 1/2 lbs. Made in W. Germany. Imported 1985-86 only.

$275 $240 $200 $185 $170 $155 $145 ***$300***

Add $10 for 12 or $30 for 15 in. barrel.

BEHOLLA PISTOL

Previously manufactured by Becker & Hollander located in Suhl, Germany.

PISTOLS: SEMI-AUTO

BEHOLLA POCKET AUTOMATIC – .32 ACP cal., 7 shot, 2.9 in. barrel, blue, serrated wood or rubber grips, mfg. 1915-20, from 1920-25 the same gun was mfg. by Stenda-Werke.

$225 $170 $150 $135 $120 $100 $90

BENELLI

Current manufacturer established in 1967, and located in Urbino, Italy. Benelli USA was formed during late 1997, and is currently importing all Benelli shotguns and rifles. Benelli pistols (and air pistols) are currently imported by Larry's Guns, located in Gray, ME beginning 2003. Company headquarters are located in Accokeek, MD. Shotguns were previously imported 1983-1997 by Heckler & Koch, Inc., located in Sterling, VA. Handguns were previously imported until 1997 by European American Armory, located in Sharpes, FL, in addition to Sile Distributors, Inc., until 1995, located in New York, NY, and Saco, located in Arlington, VA.

For more information on Benelli air pistols, please refer to the *Blue Book of Airguns* by Dr. Robert Beeman and John Allen (also available online).

GRADING - PPGS™	100%	98%	95%	90%	80%	70%	60%	LAST MSR

PISTOLS: SEMI-AUTO

Models B-77, B-80, and MP3S were previously imported by Sile Distributors. Models MP90S and MP95E Atlanta were imported by Benelli USA until 2002. Beginning 2003, Benelli pistols are exclusively imported by Larry's Guns.

MODEL B-76 – 9mm Para. cal., single/double action, all steel, 4 1/4 in. barrel, 8 shot mag., 34 oz. Importation disc. in 1990.

	$400	$375	$335	$295	$245	$225	$210	*$428*

MODEL B-76S TARGET – 9mm Para. cal., similar to B-76, except has 5 1/2 in. barrel, target grips, and adj. rear sights. Importation disc. 1990.

	$650	$550	$475	$425	$395	$350	$325	*$595*

MODEL B-77 – .32 ACP cal., single/double action, all steel, 4 1/4 in. barrel, 8 shot mag. Importation disc. 1995.

	$395	$350	$295	$255	$225	$200	$180	*$385*

MODEL B-80 – .30 Luger cal., single/double action, all steel, 4 1/4 in. barrel, 8 shot mag., 34 oz. Importation disc. 1995.

	$395	$350	$295	$255	$225	$200	$180	*$385*

MODEL B-80S TARGET – similar to B-80, except has 5 1/2 in. barrel, target grips, and adj. rear sight. Importation disc. 1995.

	$500	$450	$375	$325	$295	$275	$250	*$572*

MODEL B82 – 9mm Ultra, .30 Luger, or .32 Auto cal., contract order for Italian police, ser. no. with "D" suffix, limited production.

	$750	$625	$550	$500	$450	$400	$375	

MODEL MP3S – .32 S&W Long Wadcutter or 9mm Para. cal., target variation with 5 1/2 in. barrel, high gloss bluing, target grips, and adj. rear sight. Importation disc. 1995.

	$575	$450	$375	$325	$295	$275	$250	*$785*

Add 20% for 9mm Para. cal.
Add 25% for factory leather case (rare).

MODEL MP90S (WORLD CUP) – .22 S (disc.), .22 LR, or .32 S&W Wadcutter cal., 4.4 in. barrel, blue finish, black frame finish with chrome bolt on most recent mfg., target pistol featuring forward assisted breech bolt mechanism, anatomic grips, and adj. weight, 5 (disc.), 6 or 9 (optional) shot mag., 2.4 lbs. Imported 1992-2002, and again beginning 2003.

MSR $1,549	$1,395	$1,175	$1,000	$875	$725	$625	$525	

Add $131 for .32 S&W Wadcutter cal.

Conversion kits were previously available for this model at an extra charge.

MODEL MP95E (ATLANTA) – .22 LR or .32 S&W Wadcutter (disc. 1999, reintroduced 2006) cal., 4.4 in. barrel, features inertial recoiling mass system, integral Weaver style base mount, 5 (disc.), 6 or 9 (optional) shot mag., adj. trigger assembly, fully adj. sight, modular firing system, blue or matte chrome finish, smooth laminate (chrome finish only) or choice of checkered adj. (disc.) or non-adj. walnut grips, 2 1/2 lbs. Imported late 1994-2002, and again beginning 2003.

MSR $929	$840	$725	$625	$525	$450	$425	$395	

Add $200 for chrome finish.
Add $150 for .32 S&W Wadcutter cal.

RIFLES: SEMI-AUTO

As this edition went to press, Benelli had yet to establish 2013 pricing.

R1 STANDARD CARBINE/RIFLE – .270 WSM (mfg. 2005-2010), .30-06, .308 Win. (mfg. 2002-2010), .300 WSM (mfg. 2005-2010), .300 Win. Mag., or .338 Win. Mag. (new 2011) cal., features AutoRegulating Gas Operated (ARGO) system and rotating 3 lug bolt, 20 (carbine, .30-06 or .300 Win. Mag. only, disc.), 22, or 24 (.300 Win. Mag. and WSM cals.) in. barrel with cryogenic treatment and interchangeable rear rib, detachable 3 or 4 shot

GRADING - PPGS™	100%	98%	95%	90%	80%	70%	60%	LAST MSR

mag., optional sights, forearm is fixed to the alloy receiver, drilled and tapped, Picatinny rail included, available in black or nickel plated (Europe only) receiver finish, optional Realtree APG HD camo treatment (new 2007), black ComforTech synthetic with GripTight inserts (new 2006) or checkered walnut Monte Carlo stock and forearm (current finish is satin), recoil pad is cut into the stock (adj., with shims), ambidextrous safety, approx. 7 lbs. New 2002.

MSR $1,019	$900	$800	$700	$625	$550	$475	$395	

Add $120 for ComforTech GripTight synthetic stock.

Add $230 for Realtree APG camo finish with ComforTech GripTight stock.

This model is designated the Argo in Europe. An Argo Deluxe is also available for European sales, with better grade wood and hand engraving on both sides of the frame.

* ***R1 Limited Edition Rifle*** – .30-06 cal., 22 in. barrel, 4 shot mag., highly figured AAA satin finished checkered walnut stock and forearm, coin finished receiver with detailed game scenes and gold inlays, fully adj. rear blade and front sight with red fiber optic insert, optional recoil pad, 7.1 lbs., available from World Class dealers only. New 2010.

MSR $2,900	$2,475	$2,000	$1,550	$1,250	$1,100	$925	$850	

MR1 CARBINE/RIFLE – 5.56 NATO cal., self-adjusting gas operation (similar to the Benelli M4 shotgun used by the Marines) with rotating bolt head featuring three lugs, accepts 5 shot AR-15 style mags., 12 1/2 (law enforcement only), 16, or 20 (Europe only) in. barrel, regular or pistol grip (12 1/2 or 16 in. barrel only), rifle sights, includes Picatinny rail with ghost ring sights, push button safety on trigger guard, black finish, approx. 8 lbs. New late 2009.

MSR $1,339	$1,175	$1,000	$875	$750	$650	$550	$450	

* ***MR1 ComforTech Carbine*** – 5.56 NATO, 16 in. barrel features black pistol grip ComforTech stock, otherwise similar to MR1 Carbine/Rifle. New 2011.

MSR $1,469	$1,275	$1,075	$925	$775	$675	$575	$475	

SHOTGUNS: SEMI-AUTO, 1985-OLDER

Benelli semi-auto 3rd generation (inertia recoil) shotguns were imported starting in the late 1960s. The receivers were mfg. of light aluminum alloy - the SL-80 Model 121 had a semi-gloss, anodized black finish, the Model 123 had an ornate photo-engraved receiver, the Model Special 80 had a brushed, white nickel-plated receiver, and the Model 121 M1 had a matte finish receiver, barrel, and stock. All 12 ga. SL-80 Series shotguns will accept 2 3/4 or 3 in. shells, and all SL-80 Series 12 ga. Models have interchangeable barrels (except the 121 M1) with 4 different model receivers (121, 121 M1, 123, and Special 80). All 4 models had fixed choke barrels.

The SL-80 Series shotguns were disc. during 1985, and neither H&K nor Benelli USA has parts for these guns. Some misc. parts still available for the 12 ga. from Gun Parts Corp. (see Trademark Index for more information).

Approx. 50,000 SL-80 series shotguns were mfg. before discontinuance - choke markings (located on the side or bottom of the barrel) are as follows: * full choke, ** imp. mod., * mod., **** imp. cyl. SL-80 series guns used the same action (much different than current mfg.) and all had the split receiver design. Be aware of possible wood cracking where the barrel rests on the thin area of the forend and also on the underside of the buttstock behind trigger guard.**

The marketplace for older Benelli semi-auto shotguns has changed recently, with more interest being shown on these older models as they represent a value compared to Benelli's new offerings. As a result of this additional interest and demand, values have gone up, after being dormant for many years.

100% values within this section assume NIB condition.

Subtract 5% for "SACO" importation (Saco was located in Arlington, VA).

SL-80 SERIES MODEL SL-121V – 12 ga., field grade, 26 or 28 in. fixed choke VR barrel, anodized and black semi-gloss finish on lower receiver. Disc. 1985.

	$675	$595	$525	$475	$395	$300	$250	*$397*

GRADING - PPGS™	100%	98%	95%	90%	80%	70%	60%	LAST MSR

SL-80 SERIES MODEL SL-121/SL-122 SLUG – 12 ga., features Monte Carlo stock and flat bottom Trap Grade beavertail forearm, 21 1/16 in. cyl. bore barrel, fixed open ring rear iron sights and fixed front ramp, 5 shot mag., recoil pad, 7 lbs. 3 oz. Disc. 1985.

$675	$595	$500	$400	$350	$300	$240	*$434*

SL-80 SERIES MODEL SL-123V – 12 ga., stylish field grade, Ergal special aluminum alloy receiver with photo engraving, 26 or 28 in. VR barrel with various chokes, approx. 6 lbs. 13 oz. Disc. 1985.

$675	$600	$550	$450	$375	$275	$225	*$464*

Add $20 for trap stock, $10 for beavertail forearm and $25 for skeet barrel.

The only difference between the SL-123V and SL-121V is the photo engraved receiver. The SL-123V was at times referred to as the deluxe model when compared to the SL-121V. Both models were field grade shotguns.

EX-L – 12 ga., similar in appearance to the Model SL-123V, except has hand-engraved receiver, very limited mfg. with unpredictable premiums over Model SL-123V.

SL-80 SERIES MODEL 121 M1 POLICE/MILITARY – 12 ga. only, similar in appearance to the Super 90 M1, hardwood stock, 7 shot mag., matte metal and wood finish, most stocks had adj. lateral sling attachment inside of buttstock, 18 3/4 in. barrel. Disc. 1985.

$550	$400	$350	$275	$240	$210	$185

Since many of this model were sold to the police and military, used specimens should be checked carefully for excessive wear and/or possible damage. Since these guns usually saw extensive use, they are much less desirable than other SL-80 listed in this section, It is also difficult to find commonly needed parts for these guns. These models are not rare, but fewer have been traded, most likely due to poor sales history.

MODEL 80 SPECIAL SKEET/TRAP – 12 ga. only, 28 in. VR barrel with mod. choke and phosphorescent bead sight, trap/skeet Monte Carlo grade/style wood stock with recoil pad, lower receiver was nickel plated, 7 lbs. 10 oz. Disc. 1986.

$650	$550	$475	$425	$350	$275	$195	*$531*

Trap guns should have high comb trap stock and trap grade forearm (not field grade/style wood). Trap guns should also be inspected carefully for internal wear before buying/selling. Also inspect the nickel plating carefully before considering a purchase, as it tends to flake.

SL-80 SERIES MODEL SL201 FIELD GRADE – 20 ga., 26 in. VR mod. choke barrel, black anodized lower receiver, approx. 5 lbs. 10 oz., mfg. in Spain for Benelli. Disc. 1985.

$525	$475	$410	$375	$285	$210	$185	*$399*

Parts for this gun might be hard to find. It was offered only in a Modified choke which may have limited interest in the used marketplace.

BRI-BENELLI SL-80 123 SLUG GUN – 12 ga. only, custom design, premium slug gun, SL-80 Series action with drilled and tapped rifled barrel by E. R. Shaw Barrel Co., assembled by BRI in the U.S., Monte Carlo stock with beavertail forend, barrels stamped "BRI", ser. nos. 0001-0025, approx. 25 guns total mfg. 1986-1987.

$1,895	$1,275	$1,025	$875	$750	$625	$525

Subtract 40% if w/o trap style beavertail forend and Monte Carlo stock.
Subtract 60%-70% if barrel is not stamped "BRI".
Original issue price on this model was $750-$850.

These specimens were marked "BRI-Benelli" on barrel. No warranties exist on this model.

SHOTGUNS: SEMI-AUTO, 1986-NEWER

Unless indicated otherwise, all currently manufactured Benelli shotguns utilize a red fiber optic sight, and are equipped with a patented Benelli keyed chamber lock. As of 2011, Benelli had manufactured well over 2 million shotguns in many configurations.

As this edition went to press, Benelli had yet to establish 2013 pricing.

M1 FIELD (SUPER 90) – 12 (disc. 2005) or 20 (new 2001) ga., 3 in. chamber, inertia recoil operating system, alloy receiver, 21 (mfg. 1990-2005, 12 ga. only), 24 (new 1990), 26,

GRADING - PPGS™	100%	98%	95%	90%	80%	70%	60%	LAST MSR

or 28 (disc. 2005) in. vent. rib barrel and 3 shot mag., includes 5 screw in choke tubes, satin walnut (mfg. 1994-2005) or black polymer stock, Turkey Models include SteadyGrip buttstock with integral pistol grip (mfg. 2003-2005) or regular pistol grip, red fiber optic front sight, matte finish, 100% Realtree X-tra Brown (mfg. 1997-2001) or Advantage Timber HD (new 2001) camo coverage, approx. 5.8 (20 ga.) or 7.2 (12 ga.) lbs. Disc. 2006.

$850	$725	$625	$450	$375	$335	$300	*$1,030*

Subtract $30 for 12 ga.
Add $15 for satin walnut stock (12 ga., 26 or 28 in. barrel only, disc. 2005).
Add $120 for Advantage Timber HD camo finish.
Add $195 for Turkey configuration with 24 in. barrel, steady-grip and 100% Timber HD camo coverage (disc. 2005).
Add $100 for Turkey configuration with 24 in. barrel and Timber HD camo finish (disc. 2004).
Add $95 for Realtree Xtra Brown camo finish (disc. 2001).
Add $60 for 11 oz. mercury recoil reducer (synthetic stock only).
Add $20 for left-hand action (mfg. 2000-2003, available in synthetic and camo, 12 ga. only).

During 2000, Benelli improved this model with a stepped VR and oversized safety.

This model was available with an extended magazine tube (26 or 28 in. barrel only).

M1 FIELD SLUG (SUPER 90) – 12 (disc. 2004) or 20 (new 2004) ga., 3 in. chamber, incorporated improvements on the Benelli action, including rotating Montefeltro bolt system, 19 3/4 cyl. bore (disc. 1997) or 24 (new 1998) in. rifled barrel with iron sights (disc. 1997, reintroduced 2001), drilled and tapped beginning 1998, 3 (new 1998) or 7 (disc. 1997) shot mag., Realtree Xtra Brown camo (mfg. 2000-2001), Advantage Timber HD (new 2002) camo, or black fiberglass stock and forearm, 6 1/2 - 7.6 lbs. Mfg. 1986-2006.

$895	$750	$650	$475	$375	$335	$300	*$1,105*

Add $110 for Advantage Timber HD camo finish.
Add $105 for Realtree Xtra Brown camo finish (disc. 2001).
Subtract 15% for 19 3/4 in. cyl. bore barrel with iron sights.

M1 DEFENSE (SUPER 90) – similar to Super 90 Slug, except has pistol grip stock, 7.1 lbs. Disc. 1998.

$700	$560	$425	$325	$300	$270	$250	*$851*

Add $41 for ghost-ring sighting system.

M1 PRACTICAL (SUPER 90) – 12 ga. only, 3 in. chamber, 26 in. plain barrel with muzzle brake, designed for IPSC events, extended 8 shot mag. tube, oversized safety, speed loader, larger bolt handle, mil spec adj. ghost ring sight and Picatinny rail, black regular synthetic stock and forearm, matte metal finish, includes 3 choke tubes, 7.6 lbs. Mfg. 1998-2004.

$925	$785	$675	$575	$450	$350	$300	*$1,285*

M1 TACTICAL (SUPER 90) – 12 ga. only, 3 in. chamber, 18 1/2 in. barrel, fixed rifle or ghost ring sighting system, available with synthetic pistol grip or standard buttstock, includes 3 choke tubes, 5 shot mag., 6.7 - 7 lbs. Mfg. 1993-2004.

$725	$600	$525	$425	$335	$275	$250	*$975*

Add $50 for ghost ring sighting system.
Add $50-$65 for pistol grip stock.

* ***M1 Tactical M*** – similar to M1 Tactical, except has military ghost ring sights and standard synthetic stock, 7.1 lbs. Mfg. 1999-2000.

$725	$600	$525	$425	$335	$275	$250	*$960*

Add $10 for pistol grip stock.

M1 ENTRY (SUPER 90) – 12 ga. only, 14 in. barrel, choice of synthetic pistol grip or standard stock, choice of rifle or ghost ring sights, 5 shot mag. (2 shot extension), approx. 6.7 lbs. Mfg. 1992-2006.

$810	$675	$585	$450	$395	$340	$310	

Add $15 for synthetic pistol grip stock.
Add $65 for ghost ring sighting system.

This model required special licensing (special tax stamp) for civilians, and was normally available to law enforcement/military only.

GRADING - PPGS™	100%	98%	95%	90%	80%	70%	60%	LAST MSR

M1 SPORTING SPECIAL (SUPER 90) – 12 ga., 18 1/2 in. barrel, matte black finish, ghost ring sighting system, 6 1/2 lbs. Mfg. 1993-1997.

	$750	$650	$550	$450	$395	$340	$310	*$924*

M2 FIELD – 12 or 20 (new 2007) ga., 3 in. chamber, similar operating system as the M1, redesigned receiver, trigger guard, and safety, left-hand action available on 20 ga. (new 2013), 3 shot mag., red fiber optic front sight, short forearm with large magazine cap, includes ComforTech stock system with two recoil reducing gel pads (not available w/ walnut stock), 21 (Turkey), 24 (Turkey, with SteadyGrip), 26, or 28 in. VR barrel with cryo treatment, satin walnut, synthetic, or choice of 100% coverage Advantage Max-4 HD, APG HD (new 2007), or Advantage Timber HD (disc. 2007) camo stock, M2 compact with shorter LOP (black finish only) became available during 2013, 6.9 - 7.2 lbs. New 2004.

MSR $1,269	$1,175	$1,000	$850	$725	$575	$450	$375	

Add $90 for black synthetic stock w/ComforTech and forearm.
Add $200 for 100% camo coverage.
Add $90 for M2 compact in 12 ga. (new 2013), $140 for M2 compact in 20 ga. (new 2013).
Add $250 for left-hand action (new 2013).
Add $260 for 24 in. barrel with SteadyGrip Turkey configuration (new 2005).
Add $50 for Turkey configuration with pistol grip.
Add $150 for left hand action w/black synthetic stock or $260 for left-hand action w/camo.
Add $140 for 20 ga. (not available w/walnut stock and forearm) with Griptight ComforTech stock.

* ***M2 Field Super Slug*** – 12 or 20 ga., 24 in. rifled barrel with open sights, 3 in. chamber, choice of black synthetic or 100% camo coverage (Realtree APG is current mfg.) ComforTech stock and forearm, 7.3 lbs. New 2004.

MSR $1,469	$1,295	$1,050	$895	$725	$600	$525	$450	

Add $120 for camo coverage.

M2 THREE GUN – 12 ga., 3 in. chamber, 21 in. VR barrel, black synthetic ComforTech stock, designed for 3 gun competition. New 2012.

MSR $2,669	$2,350	$2,000	$1,750	$1,500	$1,250	$1,000	$875	

M2 PRACTICAL – 12 ga. only, 3 in. chamber, 26 in. compensated barrel with ghost ring sights, designed for IPSC competition, 8 shot mag., Picatinny rail. Limited importation 2005.

	$1,135	$965	$825	$650	$550	$475	$425	*$1,335*

M2 TACTICAL – 12 ga. only, 3 in. chamber, 18 1/2 in. barrel with choice of pistol grip, regular stock, or ComforTech stock configuration, matte finish, 5 shot mag., AirTouch checkering pattern on stock and forearm, open rifle or ghost ring sights, 6.7-7 lbs. New 2005.

MSR $1,359	$1,225	$1,025	$875	$750	$600	$500	$400	

Add $110 for ghost ring sights w/ComforTech stock.
Subtract $110 for tactical open rifle sights.

M2 AMERICAN SERIES – 12 ga., 2 3/4 or 3 in. chamber, 26 or 28 in. barrel, synthetic stock with matte black or Realtree Max-4 camo finish, 3 shot mag., red bar front sight, approx. 7 lbs. Mfg. mid-2010-2011.

	$995	$875	$750	$675	$625	$550	$495	*$1,109*

Add $40 for camo.

M3 CONVERTIBLE AUTO/PUMP (SUPER 90) – 12 ga. only, 3 in. chamber, defense configuration incorporating convertible (fingertip activated) pump or semi-auto action, 19 3/4 in. cyl. bore barrel with ghost ring or rifle (disc. 2007) sights, 5 shot mag., choice of standard black polymer stock or integral pistol grip (disc. 1996, reintroduced 1999), approx. 7.3 lbs. New 1989.

MSR $1,589	$1,375	$1,175	$1,025	$900	$800	$700	$600	

Add $110 for folding stock (mfg. 1990-disc.) - only available as a complete gun.
Add $340 for Model 200 Laser Sight System with bracket (disc.).
Subtract approx. 10% for rifle sights (disc. 2007).

GRADING - PPGS™	100%	98%	95%	90%	80%	70%	60%	LAST MSR

M4 TACTICAL – 12 ga. only, 3 in. chamber, consumer version of the U.S. Military M4, includes Auto Regulating Gas Operating (ARGO) system, dual stainless self cleaning pistons, 4 shot mag., matte black phosphated metal standard, or 100% Desert camo coverage (except for pistol grip, new 2007), 18 1/2 in. barrel with ghost ring sights, pistol grip, tactical (new 2012), telescoping (new 2012), or non-collapsible (disc. 2004) stock and forearm, Picatinny rail, approx. 7.8 lbs. Importation began late 2003.

MSR $1,899	$1,675	$1,450	$1,225	$1,050	$925	$850	$750	

Add $100 for 100% desert camo coverage (new 2007).

Add $370 for tactical stock with H2O coating (new 2012) or $500 for telescoping stock with H2O coating (new 2012).

M1014 LIMITED EDITION – similar to M4, except only available with non-collapsible stock, U.S. flag engraved on receiver, 8 lbs. Limited edition of 2,500 mfg. 2003-2004.

	$1,375	$1,100	$950	$825	$725	$650	$600	*$1,575*

MONTEFELTRO STANDARD HUNTER (SUPER 90) – 12 or 20 (new 1993) ga., 3 in. chamber, aluminum alloy receiver, right or left-hand (12 ga. only) action, rotary bolt, 21 (disc. 1997), 24, 26, or 28 (12 ga. only) in. VR barrel with 5 choke tubes, matte black metal or 100% Realtree camo (20 ga. only, mfg. 1998-2000) finish, checkered walnut stock and forearm with choice of high gloss (disc. 1997) or satin finish, 4 shot mag., approx. 5 1/2 (20 ga.) or 7.1 lbs. Mfg. 1988-2011.

	$1,175	$950	$850	$725	$600	$450	$395	*$1,269*

Add $100 for 100% Realtree camo finish on 20 ga. only (disc.).

This model is also available in a Youth configuration (12 1/2 in. LOP, 20 ga.) at no extra charge.

* ***Montefeltro Grade II*** – 12 or 20 (disc. 2005) ga., 26 in. VR barrel with 5 chokes, red fiber optic front sight, includes upgraded select walnut and gold accents, 5 1/2 (20 ga.) or 6.9 (12 ga.) lbs. Mfg. 2004-2006.

	$995	$875	$775	$650	$575	$495	$450	*$1,220*

* ***Montefeltro Silver*** – 12 or 20 ga., 3 in. chamber, 4 shot mag., nickel/blue receiver with etched game scenes, 26 (20 ga.) or 28 (12 ga.) in. VR barrel with choke tubes, AA grade satin finished checkered walnut stock and forearm, 5.6 or 6.9 lbs. New 2007.

MSR $1,779	$1,585	$1,350	$1,150	$900	$750	$650	$575	

* ***Montefeltro Limited Edition (Super 90)*** – 20 ga. only, nickel plated lower receiver with etched gold highlights, 26 in. VR barrel. Limited mfg. 1995-96.

	$1,825	$1,550	$1,300	$1,050	$875	$750	$625	*$2,080*

* ***Montefeltro Turkey Gun*** – 12 ga., similar to Montefeltro Standard Hunter except has 24 in. VR barrel with 3 choke tubes, satin finish wood only, 7 lbs. Imported 1989 only.

	$650	$575	$500	$450	$415	$365	$310	*$675*

* ***Montefeltro Uplander*** – 12 ga., similar to Montefeltro Turkey Gun except has 21 or 24 in. VR barrel with 3 choke tubes, satin finish wood only, 7 lbs. Mfg. 1989-92.

	$650	$575	$500	$450	$415	$365	$310	*$799*

* ***Montefeltro Slug Gun*** – 12 ga., deer gun configuration with 19 3/4 in. slug barrel. Disc. 1992.

	$650	$500	$475	$425	$400	$350	$310	*$799*

MONTEFELTRO – 12 or 20 ga., 3 in. chamber, 24, 26, or 28 in. VR barrel, black synthetic (new 2013) or checkered satin finished walnut stock and forearm, also available with left-hand (12 ga. only) ejection or shortened LOP stock (20 ga. only). New 2012.

MSR $1,139	$1,000	$875	$750	$625	$525	$450	$395	

Add $60 for left-hand action (12 ga. only).

ULTRA LIGHT – 12 or 20 (new mid-2008), or 28 (new 2012) ga., 3 in. chamber (except for 28 ga.), 24 or 26 (12 ga. only new 2007) in. VR blue barrel, WeatherCoat stock, 2 shot mag., featherweight alloy receiver, shortened mag. tube and forearm, raised carbon fiber target rib, 6 lbs. Importation began 2006.

MSR $1,649	$1,475	$1,175	$1,000	$800	$700	$600	$550	

Add $128 for 28 ga. (new 2012).

GRADING - PPGS™	100%	98%	95%	90%	80%	70%	60%	LAST MSR

CORDOBA – 12 or 20 ga., 3 in. chamber, 28 or 30 in. 10mm ported VR cyro barrel with extended choke tubes, 4 shot mag., matte black finish, black synthetic ComforTech stock with GripTight overcoating on stock and forearm, or Max 4 HD (12 ga. only, 28 in. barrel, rifle sights, mfg. 2007-2011) camo coverage, 7.2 lbs. New 2005.

MSR $2,069	$1,795	$1,500	$1,225	$995	$875	$750	$650	

Add $30 for 20 ga. or Grip Tight ComforTech stock in 12 ga.

Add $170 for Max 4 HD camo (not available in 20 ga., mfg. 2007-2011).

Grip Tight ComforTech stock and forearm became standard in 2012.

* ***Cordoba Performance Shop Edition*** – 12 or 20 ga., 3 in. chamber, 4 shot mag., 28 in. ported barrel with lengthened forcing cone, black synthetic ComforTech stock with GripTight panels, Briley EZ Bolt release and enlarged bolt operating handle, Briley extended chokes, red bar front sight, metal bead mid-sight, 6.7-7.7 lbs. New 2010.

MSR $2,719	$2,450	$2,000	$1,750	$1,500	$1,250	$1,000	$875	

Add $110 for 12 ga.

SPORT MODEL – 12 ga., 3 in. chamber, one piece blued alloy receiver, 26 (disc. 1999, reintroduced during 2001 only) or 28 in. barrel with 5 choke tubes and 2 removable and interchangeable carbon fiber vent. ribs, 4 shot mag., adj. butt pad and buttstock, satin finished select checkered walnut stock and forearm, "Benelli" outlined in red on matte finished receiver side, approx. 7.1 lbs. Mfg. 1997-2002.

	$1,125	$895	$750	$575	$500	$450	$400	*$1,375*

SPORT II – 12 or 20 ga., 3 in. chamber, one piece satin nickel finished alloy receiver, blued upper receiver and barrel, 26 (disc. 2004), 28, or 30 (new 2005, 12 ga. only) in. cryo-treated ported barrel with 5 extra long (not flush with barrel) choke tubes, twin bead sights, 4 shot mag., gel recoil pad with stock spacer kit provided, satin finished select checkered walnut stock and forearm, "Sport II" on receiver side, approx. 7 7/8 lbs. Importation began 2003.

MSR $1,799	$1,625	$1,375	$1,250	$900	$775	$675	$575	

SUPERSPORT – 12 or 20 ga., 3 in. chamber, dimpled black carbon fiber stock and forearm with AirTouch recoil reduction system, 4 shot mag. (shell view feature in 20 ga. only), 28 or 30 in. ported VR cryo-treated barrel with extended cryo choke tubes, twin bead sights, satin nickel receiver finish with "Supersport" on right side, 7.9 lbs. New 2004.

MSR $2,199	$1,900	$1,625	$1,375	$1,200	$900	$775	$675	

* ***Supersport Performance Shop*** – 12 or 20 ga., 3 in. chamber, 28 (20 ga. only) or 30 (12 ga. only) in. ported barrel with lengthened forcing cones, 4 shot, carbon fiber stock with ComforTech, nickel/blue finish, Briley EZ bolt release and enlarged bolt operating handle, Briley screw-in chokes, red bar front sight, metal bead mid-sight, 6.7 - 7.7 lbs. New 2010.

MSR $2,839	$2,650	$2,250	$2,025	$1,725	$1,275	$1,050	$925	

Add $110 for 12 ga.

LEGACY MODEL – 12, 20 (new 1999), or 28 (new 2010) ga., 3 in. chamber, 24 (20 or 28 ga. only), 26 or 28 (12 ga. only) in. VR barrel with 5 choke tubes and red bar front sight with bead mid-sight, 4 shot mag., engraved nickel finished alloy lower or all alloy (20 ga. only) receiver, cartridge drop lever, select AA checkered walnut stock with vent. recoil pad and forearm, stock shim kit provided, mfg. to commemorate the 30th Anniversary of Benelli shotgun manufacturing, approx. 5.8 lbs. or 7 1/2 lbs. New 1998.

MSR $1,799	$1,620	$1,375	$1,250	$900	$775	$675	$575	

Add $240 for 28 ga.

* ***Legacy Limited Edition*** – 12 or 20 ga., acid etched engraving with gold filled game scenes, only 250 of each ga. mfg. for the new millennium only, deluxe checkered walnut stock and forearm. Limited mfg. 2000 only.

	$1,750	$1,475	$850	$675	$600	$500	$450	*$1,600*

Add 20% to individual prices for a 2 gun set with matching serial numbers (NIB only).

GRADING - PPGS™	100%	98%	95%	90%	80%	70%	60%	LAST MSR

* ***Legacy Sport*** – 12 ga. only, 3 in. chamber, 28 or 30 in. ported VR barrel with choke tubes, distinctive grey medallion with birds in flight engraved on both sides of receiver, AA grade satin finished walnut stock and forearm. New 2008.

MSR $2,439 $2,175 $1,850 $1,550 $1,200 $950 $800 $700

VINCI – 12 ga., 3 in. chamber, three-piece modular construction (consists of buttstock module, barrel/receiver module, and trigger group/forearm module), inline inertia operating system with rotating bolt, 3 shot mag., 24 (Turkey with SteadyGrip), 26 or 28 in. VR barrel with 5 choke tubes, push button safety integrated into trigger guard which is part of lower modular receiver, ComforTech and QuadraFit synthetic stock with vertical grooved forearm integrated into modular lower receiver, choice of black, Realtree Max-4 HD or APG HD 100% camo coverage, 6.9 lbs. New 2009.

MSR $1,359 $1,250 $1,050 $925 $775 $650 $550 $475

Add $110 for 100% camo coverage.
Add $270 for APG HD camo Steadygrip with 24 in. barrel.

VINCI SPEED BOLT – 12 ga. only, 3 in. chamber, features Speed-Bolt made from tungsten allowing for faster cycling and handling loads down to 1 oz., inline inertia driven system also has less recoil and muzzle climb, black QuadraFit buttstock, 6.7 lbs. New 2013.

MSR $1,599 $1,425 $1.200 $1,075 $950 $775 $650 $575

VINCI SUPERSPORT – 12 ga., 3 in. chamber, 28 or 30 in. ported barrel with extended choke tubes, Vinci model with Supersport features including carbon fiber finish and ComforTech recoil dampening system, approx. 7 lbs. New 2011.

MSR $2,199 $1,950 $1,625 $1,250 $1,050 $850 $775 $675

* ***Vinci Cordoba*** – 12 ga., features black synthetic, black ComforTech stock and forearm, ported barrel with choke tubes. New 2011.

MSR $2,069 $1,795 $1,475 $1,125 $1,000 $850 $750 $650

SUPER VINCI – 12 ga. only, 3 1/2 in. chamber, 26 or 28 in. VR barrel, choice of black synthetic ComforTech Plus stock, Max-4 HD, or APG Realtree camo finish, approx. 7 lbs. New 2011.

MSR $1,699 $1,525 $1,275 $1,150 $900 $725 $600 $525

Add $100 for 100% camo coverage.

RAFFAELLO SERIES – 12 ga., 3 in. chamber, 26 in. VR barrel with choke tubes, higher grade model with three different levels of embellishments and checkered select walnut stock and forearm, 4 shot mag., available through Benelli World Class dealers only, 7.4 lbs. Importation began late 2005.

* ***Raffaello Standard*** – unengraved black receiver with Raffaello marked on right side.

MSR $1,900 $1,625 $1,350 $1,050 $900 $800 $700 $600

* ***Raffaello Deluxe*** – features etched fine scroll engraving with game scenes on coin finished lower receiver, fancy walnut.

MSR $2,300 $1,995 $1,675 $1,325 $1,125 $950 $875 $750

* ***Raffaello Limited Edition Deluxe Legacy*** – features fine scroll engraved with gold inlaid birds and animals on coin finished lower receiver, deluxe walnut with wood buttplate.

MSR $2,900 $2,475 $2,000 $1,550 $1,250 $1,100 $925 $850

RAFFAELLO CRIO 28 – 28 ga., rotating bolt, 2 shot mag., black anodized Ergal receiver with matte and high polish finishes, select checkered walnut stock and forearm, 24 or 26 in. Crio barrel with carbon fiber VR and red fiber optic front sight, 5 1/4 lbs. Released in Europe during 2009, and in the U.S. during 2010.

MSR $1,900 $1,750 $1,575 $1,350 $1,125 $995 $850 $700

RAFFAELLO EXCLUSIVE LIMITED EDITION – 20 ga., 3 in. chamber, 26 in. VR barrel with choke tubes, satin finished checkered walnut stock and forearm, silver receiver with light scroll and game bird inlays, 4 shot mag., red bar sights, silver "E" inset pistol grip cap, 6 lbs. Importation began 2007, available through World Class dealers only.

MSR $2,900 $2,475 $2,000 $1,550 $1,250 $1,100 $925 $850

GRADING - PPGS™	100%	98%	95%	90%	80%	70%	60%	LAST MSR

ELITE TWO-GUN SET – 12 and 20 ga., 3 in. chamber, 26 in. VR barrel with choke tubes, oil finished checkered walnut stock and forearm, silver receiver with scroll engraving, gold borders and game bird inlays, 4 shot mag., 5.8 (20 ga.) - 7.4 lbs. Importation began 2007, available through World Class dealers only.

MSR $4,900	$4,450	$3,900	$3,375	$2,950	$2,600	$2,350	$2,100	

CURATOR LIMITED EDITION TWO-GUN SET – 12 and 20 ga., 26 in. barrel, satin finished AAA Grade checkered walnut stock and forearm, coin finished receiver with deep scrollwork, bevel cut floral engraving and gold inlays, includes sterling silver medallion that can be custom engraved and set into the pistol grip cap, matched walnut buttplate and fitted rubber recoil pad, includes hard case, 6 - 7.3 lbs., available through World Class dealers only. Limited mfg. of 250 sets beginning 2010.

MSR $5,500	$5,000	$4,600	$4,250	$3,850	$3,400	$3,000	$2,600	

BIMILLIONAIRE – 12 or 20 ga., 26 in. barrel, 4 shot mag., satin finished checkered walnut stock and forearm, coin finished two-tone receiver with floral scroll and gold game scenes by Giovanelli, walnut buttplate with or w/o recoil pad, includes sterling silver medallion that can be engraved and placed into the pistol grip cap, 6 - 7.3 lbs., limited mfg. available through World Class dealers only. New 2010.

MSR $2,900	$2,475	$2,000	$1,550	$1,250	$1,100	$925	$850	

EXECUTIVE SERIES – 12 ga. only, 3 in. chamber, features all-steel greyed lower receiver engraved by Giovanelli, mid-rib barrel bead, high polish upper receiver and barrel bluing, extra select grade walnut with standard stock dimensions, 5 choke tubes, and other accessories, choice of 21 (disc.), 24 (disc.), 26, or 28 in. VR barrel, approx. 7 3/4 lbs. Importation began 1996, available through World Class dealers only.

* ***Executive Grade I (Type I)***

MSR $7,600	$6,500	$5,250	$4,100	$3,650	$3,000	$2,500	$2,100	

* ***Executive Grade II (Type II)***

MSR $8,400	$7,350	$6,000	$4,750	$3,950	$3,350	$2,800	$2,400	

* ***Executive Grade III (Type III)***

MSR $9,800	$8,500	$7,000	$5,250	$4,450	$3,650	$3,150	$2,950	

BLACK EAGLE – 12 ga., 3 in. chamber, Montefeltro action, similar to Montefeltro Super 90 Standard Hunter except has black synthetic regular or pistol grip stock and forearm, 21 (disc. 1990), 24 (disc. 1990), 26, or 28 (new 1990) in. VR barrel with 3 choke tubes, right-hand only. Originally imported 1989-90, resumed 1997 only.

	$800	$675	$550	$450	$375	$315	$285	$992

This configuration changed in 1991 (see Black Eagle Competition Model).

* ***Black Eagle Competition Model*** – 12 ga. only, designed for competition shooting with action adj. for lighter loads, silver finished etched lower receiver, 26 or 28 in. VR barrel with 5 choke tubes and wrench, includes buttstock drop adjustment kit. Mfg. 1991-1997.

	$875	$775	$675	$550	$475	$375	$300	$1,229

* ***Black Eagle 1994 Limited Edition*** – 12 ga. only, features 26 in. VR barrel with extra fancy grade checkered walnut and gold inlays on receiver sides, 1,000 mfg. 1994-95 only with special serialization.

	$1,500	$1,300	$1,150	$995	$875	$750	$625	$2,000

* ***Black Eagle Slug Gun*** – 12 ga., 24 in. rifled barrel with integral scope mounting bases on receiver. Imported 1990-1991 only.

	$735	$625	$500	$425	$365	$315	$285	$859

SUPER BLACK EAGLE – 12 ga. only, 3 1/2 in. chamber, updated Montefeltro action accepts all 12 ga. loads, right or left-hand (new 1999) action, upper steel/lower alloy receiver, 24, 26, or 28 in. VR barrel with 5 choke tubes and wrench, 3 shot mag., choice of matte finish and satin wood stock, blue finish and high gloss wood finish (26 or 28 in. barrel only, disc. 2004), or 100% coverage Advantage Timber HD (new 2002), or Realtree X-tra Brown

GRADING - PPGS™	100%	98%	95%	90%	80%	70%	60%	LAST MSR

camo (mfg. 1997-2001) finish on polymer stock and forearm, Turkey Models include SteadyGrip buttstock with integral pistol grip (new 2003) or regular pistol grip with 24 in. barrel, red fiber optic front sight, black synthetic stock and forearm with matte metal finish was introduced in 1993, vent. recoil pad, includes buttstock drop adjustment kit, approx. 7.4 lbs. Mfg. 1991-2005.

	$1,075	$825	$725	$625	$525	$475	$425	$1,305

Add $95 for camo finish (Turkey Models).
Add $95 for 100% coverage Realtree camo wood/metal finish (disc. 2001).
Add $10 for satin walnut stock and forearm (26 or 28 in. barrel only).
Add $45 for 11 oz. mercury recoil reducer (synthetic stock only).
Add $75 for left-hand action for either black synthetic stock/forearm or full coverage camo finish (disc. 2004).
Add $180 for Turkey configuration with 24 in. barrel, steady-grip, and 100% camo coverage.

* ***Super Black Eagle Limited Edition*** – 12 ga. only, features 26 in. VR barrel with extra fancy grade checkered walnut and gold inlays on nickel plated receiver sides, 1,000 mfg. beginning 1997 with special serialization, 7.4 lbs. Disc. 1999.

	$1,825	$1,500	$1,225	$995	$875	$750	$625	$2,095

* ***Super Black Eagle Limited Edition 10th Anniversary*** – 12 ga., 3 1/2 in. chamber, 26 in. barrel, matte finish, wildlife engraving on both sides of receiver featuring two turkeys and three geese, gold inlays similar to Executive Type III with "Super Black Eagle Tenth Anniversary" on left, "1 of 500", and "SBE10XXX" special serialization on right, 500 mfg. 2002.

	$2,250	$1,950	$1,650	$1,325	$1,050	$900	$800	

* ***Super Black Eagle Slug Gun*** – 12 ga., 3 in. chamber, 24 in. rifled barrel with adj. rifle sights, drilled and tapped receiver, choice of matte or camo metal finish, choice of black polymer (new 1993), satin finished wood, or 100% Advantage Timber HD (new 2002) or Realtree X-tra Brown camo (mfg. 2000-2001), 7.6 lbs. Mfg. 1992-2003.

	$1,110	$910	$775	$650	$575	$475	$425	$1,335

Add $10 for wood stock.
Add $125 for Advantage Timber HD camo finish.
Add $100 for Realtree X-tra Brown camo finish (disc. 2001).

SUPER BLACK EAGLE I – 12 ga. only, 3 1/2 in. chamber, 24, 26, or 28 in. barrel, choice of satin walnut wood with matte metal finish, synthetic, Advantage Max-4 HD camo (100% coverage), Advantage Timber HD (100% coverage), or SteadyGrip (Turkey, 24 in. barrel only) with Advantage Timber HD, red fiber optic front sight with bead metal sight, 3 shot mag. Mfg. 2005.

	$1,100	$925	$800	$650	$550	$500	$450	$1,333

Add $67 for satin walnut stock and forearm.
Add $120 for camo finish.
Add $200 for Turkey configuration with SteadyGrip stock.

* ***Super Black Eagle I Slug*** – 12 ga. only, 24 in. smoothbore barrel, satin walnut stock and forearm, matte metal finish, 3 shot mag., adj. rifle sights. Mfg. 2005.

	$1,185	$950	$825	$700	$600	$475	$425	$1,465

SUPER BLACK EAGLE II – 12 ga. only, 3 1/2 in. chamber, action similar to Super Black Eagle, with or w/o ComforTech recoil reduction in stock with two gel pads, 3 shot mag., 24 (Turkey, with SteadyGrip), 26 or 28 in. VR barrel with cryogenic treatment, larger trigger guard, AirTouch checkering on stock and shortened forearm, choice of satin finished walnut, black synthetic, or 100% coverage of Advantage Max-4 HD, APG HD (new 2007) or Advantage Timber HD camo, approx. 7.2 lbs. New 2004.

MSR $1,659	$1,525	$1,275	$1,100	$900	$750	$650	$575	

Add $40 for ComforTech.
Add $180 for SteadyGrip (pistol grip) stock (Turkey configuration with APG HD camo).
Add $60 for left-hand (ComforTech only).
Add $100 for 100% camo treatment.
Subtract approx. 10% if w/o ComforTech stock (became standard mid-2008).

GRADING - PPGS™	100%	98%	95%	90%	80%	70%	60%	LAST MSR

* ***Super Black Eagle II Slug*** – 12 ga. only, 3 in. chamber, 24 in. barrel with rifled bore and adj. sights, includes Picatinny rail, choice of satin walnut stock and forearm or black synthetic stock, ComforTech became standard 2007, or 100% camo coverage of Timber HD (disc. 2008) or APG HD, approx. 7.4 lbs. New 2004.

MSR $1,739	$1,625	$1,375	$1,100	$900	$700	$600	$525	

Add $180 for 100% camo treatment.

Add $80 for black synthetic ComforTech stock and forearm.

* ***Super Black Eagle II Performance Shop Turkey Edition*** – 12 ga., 3 1/2 in. chamber, 3 shot mag., 24 in. ported barrel, 100% APG HD camo with ComforTech synthetic stock with black pistol grip, approx. 7 lbs. New 2010.

MSR $2,949	$2,650	$2,250	$2,025	$1,700	$1,450	$1,050	$925	

* ***Super Black Eagle II Performance Shop Waterfowl Edition*** – 12 ga. 3-1/2 in. chamber, 28 in. VR Crio barrel with Bob Roberts custom triple threat choke tubes, features 100% Realtree Max-4 camo coverage, ComforTech stock. New 2012.

MSR $2,669	$2,350	$2,000	$1,750	$1,500	$1,250	$1,000	$875	

* ***Super Black Eagle II Flyway Limited Edition*** – four variations include: the Atlantic, Mississippi, Central, and Pacific Flyways, roll engraved satin grey receiver finish with four gold duck/goose inlays (each Flyway has four different inlays), select checkered walnut stock and forearm, 7.2 lbs. 175 of each Flyway manufactured 2004.

	$1,795	$1,500	$1,275	$1,000	$875	$800	$725	*$2,130*

SHOTGUNS: SLIDE-ACTION

All currently manufactured Benelli shotguns are equipped with a patented Benelli keyed chamber lock.

NOVA – 12 or 20 (new 2001) ga., 3 (20 ga. only) or 3 1/2 in. chamber, unique design allows stock and internal metal receiver "shell" to be molded in one unit, utilizing a glass polymer matrix, Montefeltro rotating bolt, dual action bars, 24 (Turkey only), 26, or 28 in. VR barrel with 3 choke tubes and red fiber optic front sight, 3 (3 1/2 in. shells) or 4 shot mag., matte metal finish, choice of black synthetic, full coverage Realtree X-tra brown (disc. 2002), Realtree Max-4 HD, APG HD (new 2007), or Advantage Timber HD (mfg. 2001-2007, 20 ga. only until 2002) camo stock and forearm with grooved hand ribs, mag. shell stop button in bottom of forearm, approx. 6 1/2 (20 ga.) or 8 lbs. New 1999.

MSR $449	$400	$350	$300	$250	$200	$180	$170	

Add $20 for 20 ga.

Add $90 for full camo coverage.

Add $20 for 20 ga. Youth Model with 13 in. LOP.

Add $60 for 2 (12 ga.) or $45 for 4 (20 ga. only) shot magazine extension.

Add $110 for recoil reducer - 10 oz. (disc.) or 14 oz. mercury, installed in stock with reduction tube operation (12 ga.).

Add $65 for Realtree X-tra Brown full camo finish (12 ga. only, disc. 2002).

* ***Nova Tactical (Special Purpose Smooth Bore)*** – 12 ga. only, 3 1/2 in. chamber, similar action to Nova, features 18 1/2 in. cyl. bore barrel with choice of rifle or ghost ring (new 2000) sights, black synthetic stock and forearm only, 7.2 lbs. New 1999.

MSR $419	$350	$285	$260	$230	$210	$200	$190	

Add $40 for ghost ring sights.

* ***Nova H20*** – 12 ga. only, 3 1/2 in. chamber, 18 1/2 in. matte nickel finished barrel, mag. tube, trigger group, and inner metal parts, black synthetic stock and forearm, open rifle sights, 4 shot mag., 7.2 lbs. Importation began 2003.

MSR $639	$575	$475	$400	$335	$285	$250	$225	

* ***Nova Entry*** – 12 ga. only, 14 in. barrel, choice of ghost ring or open rifle sights, black synthetic stock and forearm, 4 shot mag., approx. 6.9 lbs. Importation began 2003.

This model is available to law enforcement or military only.

GRADING - PPGS™	100%	98%	95%	90%	80%	70%	60%	LAST MSR

* ***Nova Slug*** – 12 or 20 ga., 3 in. chamber, features 24 in. rifled bore drilled and tapped barrel with open rifle sights, black synthetic or 100% coverage Advantage Timber HD camo stock and forearm, 8.1 lbs. Mfg. 2000-2006.

	$445	$390	$355	$315	$285	$260	$240	*$535*

Add $90 for Advantage Timber HD camo.

» **Nova Slug & Field Combo** – 12 or 20 ga., 3 in. chamber, combo features 24 in. rifled bore drilled and tapped barrel with extra 26 in. field barrel, open rifle sights, black synthetic or 100% coverage Advantage Timber HD camo stock and forearm, 8.1 lbs. Mfg. 2000-2007.

	$460	$400	$365	$325	$290	$260	$240	*$560*

SUPERNOVA – 12 ga. only, 3 1/2 in. chamber, 24, 26, or 28 in. VR barrel with choke tubes, choice of matte synthetic, Realtree APG HD (new 2007) Advantage Max-4 HD or Advantage Timber HD (disc. 2007) 100% camo coverage, includes ComforTech stock system, approx. 8 lbs. New 2006.

MSR $549	$485	$400	$350	$275	$250	$225	$195

Add $120 for 100% camo coverage.

* ***SuperNova SteadyGrip*** – features 24 in. barrel with SteadyGrip buttstock with integral pistol grip, choice of matte finish (disc. 2009) or Realtree APG HD (new 2007) or Advantage Timber HD (disc. 2007) camo. New 2006.

MSR $669	$600	$500	$450	$400	$350	$300	$250

Subtract 20% if w/matte finish.

* ***SuperNova Tactical*** – features 18 1/2 in. barrel with choice of ComforTech or pistol grip synthetic stock, matte finish or Desert camo (new 2007, pistol grip only), choice of rifle or ghost ring sights. New 2006.

MSR $499	$450	$350	$300	$250	$225	$200	$185

Add $60 for ghost ring sights.

Add $170 for Desert camo w/pistol grip and ghost ring sights (new 2007).

* ***SuperNova Slug*** – 12 ga., 3 in. chamber, features 24 in. rifled bore drilled and tapped barrel with adj. rifle sights, black synthetic ComforTech or 100% coverage Realtree APG HD camo stock and forearm, 8.1 lbs. New 2007.

MSR $829	$700	$575	$450	$375	$325	$275	$250

Add $100 for 100% camo coverage.

Add $10 for Field & Slug combo with extra 26 in. Field barrel (mfg. 2007 only).

BENSON FIREARMS LTD.

Previous importer for guns manufactured by Aldo Uberti in Italy. Previously imported and distributed from 1987-1989 by Benson Firearms Ltd. located in Seattle, WA. Benson Firearms Ltd. combined with A. Uberti USA Inc. in early 1989 and discontinued importation.

Benson Firearms can be differentiated from other A. Uberti imports by the "Benson Firearms Seattle, WA" barrel marking.

Rather than provide a complete listing of Benson Firearms models, the following rules usually apply. Since Benson Firearms imported A. Uberti firearms, the Uberti section in this text should be referenced for current values regarding models with similar configurations. Collectibility to date has been limited on most Benson Fireams models, and as a rule, up-to-date values on this trademark are established by current importation prices of Uberti firearms.

A complete listing of older Benson Firearms models can be found online at www.bluebookofgunvalues.com free of charge, or in the 11th and 12th Editions of the *Blue Book of Gun Values.*

GRADING - PPGS™	100%	98%	95%	90%	80%	70%	60%	LAST MSR

BENTON & BROWN FIREARMS, INC.

Previous manufacturer located in Fort Worth, TX and Delhi, LA circa 1993-1996.

RIFLES: BOLT ACTION

MODEL 93 – available in 15 cals. between .243 Win. and .375 H&H Mag., patterned after the Model R-84 Blaser, takedown, free floating 22 or 24 in. barrels, right or left-hand action, checkered walnut stock and forearm, 7-8 1/2 lbs. Mfg. 1993-1996.

	$1,875	$1,550	$1,225	$1,100	$995	$875	$750	*$2,075*

Subtract $200 for fiberglass stock.
Add $450 per interchangeable barrel.

BERETTA, DR. FRANCO

Previous manufacturer located in Concesio (Brescia), Italy until 1994.

SHOTGUNS: O/U, BLACK DIAMOND SERIES

Black Diamond target guns were imported exclusively by Double M Shooting Sports until 1988.

FIELD MODEL – 12, 16, 20, 28 ga., or .410 bore, variety of chokes, coin finish receiver.

	$595	$550	$495	$450	$395	$365	$335	*$960*

GRADE ONE – 12, 16, 20, 28 ga., or .410 bore, variety of chokes, coin finish receiver with acid etched engraving, French walnut. Trap or skeet model also available, except in 16 ga.

	$1,020	$900	$810	$720	$630	$570	$525	*$1,440*

GRADE TWO – 12, 16, 20, 28 ga., or .410 bore, variety of chokes, coin finish receiver with moderate engraving, French walnut. Trap or skeet model also available, except in 16 ga.

	$1,475	$1,320	$1,200	$1,080	$930	$815	$750	*$2,040*

GRADE THREE – 12, 16, 20, 28 ga., or .410 bore, variety of chokes, coin finish receiver with scrollwork engraving, French walnut. Trap or skeet model also available, except in 16 ga.

	$2,100	$1,920	$1,775	$1,560	$1,410	$1,200	$1,035	*$3,000*

GRADE FOUR – 12, 16, 20, 28 ga., or .410 bore, variety of chokes, coin finish receiver with elaborate engraving, French walnut. Trap or skeet model also available, except in 16 ga.

	$2,500	$2,250	$1,950	$1,650	$1,375	$1,125	$995	*$3,960*

SKEET SET – includes 12, 20, 28 ga., and .410 bore barrels, available in Grades One through Four.

Multiply values on Grades One - Four by 275% for 4 ga. skeet sets.

SHOTGUNS: O/U, SxS, & SINGLE BARREL, RECENT MFG.

GAMMA STANDARD O & U – 12, 16, or 20 ga., 26 or 28 in. barrels, coin finish receiver with extensive engraving, Italian walnut. Imported 1984-88.

	$400	$360	$330	$300	$275	$260	$240	*$445*

Add $83 with single trigger and ejectors.

* ***Gamma Standard*** – with interchangeable choke tubes. Importation disc. 1993.

	$825	$695	$525	$425	$325	$250	$195	*$1,000*

Add 20% for auto ejectors.
Add $100 for single trigger.
Add 36% for Gamma Trap or Skeet variation (ST).

GAMMA DELUXE O & U – 12, 16, or 20 ga., 26 or 28 in. barrels, coin finish receiver with extensive engraving, Italian walnut. Imported 1984-88.

	$445	$405	$370	$350	$325	$300	$275	*$480*

Add $84 with single trigger and ejectors.

* ***Gamma Deluxe*** – with interchangeable choke tubes. Importation disc. 1988.

	$635	$570	$530	$490	$450	$420	$390	*$685*

GAMMA TARGET O & U – 12 ga. only, SST, ejectors, Wundhammer swell pistol grip, English walnut stock and beavertail forearm. Imported 1986-88.

	$550	$505	$455	$410	$370	$350	$325	*$595*

GRADING - PPGS™	100%	98%	95%	90%	80%	70%	60%	LAST MSR

ALPHA STANDARD O & U – 12, 16, or 20 ga., 26 or 28 in. barrels, coin finish receiver with extensive engraving, Italian walnut. Imported 1984-88, resumed 1993-1994.

	$720	$650	$525	$450	$375	$300	$250	$780

Add 18% for auto ejectors.
Add $100 for single trigger.

ALPHA DELUXE O & U – 12, 16, or 20 ga., 26 or 28 in. barrels, coin finish receiver with extensive engraving, sling swivels, Italian walnut. Imported 1984-88.

	$395	$355	$330	$300	$275	$250	$230	$435

Add $75 with single trigger and ejectors.
Add $80 for interchangeable choke tubes (disc. 1985).

AMERICA STANDARD O & U – .410 bore only, 26 or 28 in. barrels, coin finish receiver with extensive engraving, Italian walnut. Imported 1984-88.

	$305	$280	$265	$240	$215	$205	$190	$335

Add $85 for Deluxe model.

EUROPA O & U – .410 bore only, 26 in. barrels, coin finish receiver with some engraving, Italian walnut. Imported 1984-88.

	$275	$250	$235	$220	$210	$200	$185	$295

Add $95 for Deluxe model (disc. 1985).

FRANCIA STANDARD SxS – .410 bore only, double triggers, extractors, checkered walnut. Imported 1986-88.

	$235	$220	$210	$200	$185	$175	$160	$255

Add $19 for Deluxe Model.

OMEGA STANDARD SxS – 12, 16, or 20 ga., 26 or 28 in. barrels, coin finish receiver with extensive engraving, Italian walnut. Imported 1984-93.

	$780	$695	$550	$450	$375	$300	$250	$880

Add 32% for auto ejectors.
Add 10% for single trigger (disc. 1985).

MILANO O/U – 9mm Flobert, folding design. Imported 1993 only.

	$380	$330	$295	$250	$210	$180	$150	$420

VERONA/BERGAMO SxS – 9mm Flobert, folding design, Bergamo model has hammers, Verona model is hammerless. Imported 1993 only.

	$270	$225	$180	$140	$115	$95	$75	$300

BRESCIA SINGLE BARREL – 9mm Flobert, folding design. Imported 1993 only.

	$175	$150	$130	$110	$90	$70	$55	$200

BETA SINGLE BARREL – 12, 16, 20, 24, 28, 32 ga., or .410 bore, single barrel field gun, VR, chrome finish receiver, folding design. Imported 1985-93.

	$215	$185	$160	$145	$135	$125	$115	$240

Add 10% for VR.

SHOTGUNS: SEMI-AUTO

ARIETE STANDARD – 12 ga. only, gas operated, 2 3/4 or 3 in. chamber, various barrel lengths, with or without choke tubes, aluminum receiver, checkered stock and forearm, approx. 6.9 lbs. Imported 1993 only.

	$995	$795	$525	$425	$325	$250	$195	$1,180

Add $20 for 3 in. mag. variation.

SHOTGUNS: SLIDE ACTION

ARIETE – 12 ga. only, 3 in. chamber, various barrel lengths without VR, twin action bars, matte finish, recoil pad. Imported 1993 only.

	$780	$695	$550	$450	$375	$300	$250	$880

GRADING - PPGS™	100%	98%	95%	90%	80%	70%	60%	LAST MSR

BERETTA

Current manufacturer located in Brescia, Italy since 1526. The company name in Italy is Fabbrica d'Armi Pietro Beretta. Beretta U.S.A. Corp. was formed in 1977 and is located in Accokeek, MD. Beretta U.S.A. Corp. has been importing Beretta Firearms exclusively since 1980. 1970-1977 manufacture was imported exclusively by Garcia. Distributor and dealer direct sales.

Beretta is one of the world's oldest family owned industrial firms, having started business in 1526. In addition to Beretta owning Benelli, Stoeger, and Franchi, the company also purchased Sako and Tikka Companies in late 1999, Aldo Uberti & Co. in 2000, Burris Optics in 2002, and Steiner International Optics. Beretta continues to be a leader in firearms development and safety, and shooters attest to the reliability of their guns worldwide.

For more information and current pricing on both new and used Beretta precision airguns, please refer to the *Blue Book of Airguns* by Dr. Robert Beeman & John Allen (also available online).

PISTOLS: SEMI-AUTO, PRE-WWII MFG.

MODEL 1915 – .32 ACP or 9mm Glisenti cal., Beretta's first military pistol, exaggerated slide stop, safety on rear of tang, checkered wood grips, 7 shot mag., serial range 1-16,000.

	100%	98%	95%	90%	80%	70%	60%
	$1,500	$1,250	$1,000	$750	$600	$500	$400

9mm Para. cal. is not interchangeable and potentially dangerous if interchanged with 9mm Glisenti cal.

MODEL 1915-1917 – later 7.65mm cal. variation, 8 shot mag., exaggerated slide stop, wood grips, sold commercially and to the military. A few marked "RM" were issued to the Italian Navy, ser. no. range 16,000-72,000. Mfg. 1917-1921.

	100%	98%	95%	90%	80%	70%	60%
	$750	$600	$450	$350	$275	$225	$175
Navy issue	$1,500	$1,200	$900	$700	$550	$450	$350

MODEL 1922 – successor to the Model 1915-1917, mfg. with more open slide and modern slide stop, wood or pressed metal grips, ser. no. range 200,000-243,000. Mfg. 1922-1932.

	100%	98%	95%	90%	80%	70%	60%
	$700	$550	$450	$350	$275	$225	$175
Navy issue	$1,400	$1,225	$1,050	$950	$770	$625	$495

MODEL 1923 – 9mm Glisenti cal., 8 shot, 4 in. barrel, fixed sights, usually with pressed steel grips, less frequently smooth wood with PB emblem, occasionally slotted for shoulder stock. Most were purchased by the Italian Army and marked "RE," ser. no. range 300,000-310,400. Mfg. 1923-26.

	100%	98%	95%	90%	80%	70%	60%
	$2,000	$1,750	$1,500	$1,250	$1,000	$750	$500

Add 25% if slotted for shoulder stock.

MODEL 1919 – .25 ACP cal., 8 shot mag., offered in several variations, first type in serial range 100,000-156,000, subsequent improvement involved changing the disconnector and left panel in serial range 156,000-185,000.

	100%	98%	95%	90%	80%	70%	60%
	$375	$325	$275	$250	$200	$175	$125

MODEL 1926 – similar to Model 1919, except has wood panels bearing an encircled PB. Approx. 11,000 pistols were mfg. in ser. no. range 187,000-198,000.

	100%	98%	95%	90%	80%	70%	60%
	$350	$315	$275	$220	$190	$160	$130

MODEL 1931 – .32 ACP cal., similar to Model 1926, except has small modifications in the slide, two styles of grips are no longer impressed with the PB monogram, interrupted serial range from 198,000-200,000 and 600,000-601,000.

	100%	98%	95%	90%	80%	70%	60%
	$325	$285	$250	$225	$175	$150	$125

MODEL 318 – .25 ACP cal., 2 1/2 in. barrel, fixed sights, blue, modifications in the slide legend, grip configuration, and magazine floor plate. Limited production during 1936-37, in ser. no. range 609,000-615,000.

	100%	98%	95%	90%	80%	70%	60%
	$275	$250	$200	$185	$160	$140	$120

GRADING - PPGS™	100%	98%	95%	90%	80%	70%	60%	LAST MSR

Add 50%-100% for engraved and plated variations if in 98%+ original condition.

Embellished variations of the Model 318 included the Model 319 (engraved/blue), Model 320 (engraved/nickel plated) and Model 321 (engraved/gold plated).

MODEL 418 – .25 ACP cal., fixed sights, similar to Model 318, but with loaded chamber indicator and grip safety (early type is semi-circular, late type is curved), occasionally was made with an alloy frame, popular pistol mfg. 1937-1961 with minor modifications. Later guns are suffixed with the letters A, B, and C, 178,000 mfg.

	100%	98%	95%	90%	80%	70%	60%	LAST MSR
	$250	$225	$200	$175	$150	$135	$120	

Add 50%-100% for engraved and plated variations if in 98%+ original condition.

Embellished variations of the Model 418 included the Model 419 (engraved blue), Model 420 (engraved nickel), and Model 421 (engraved gold plated).

MODEL 1932 – 7.65mm (rare) or 9mm Corto (most common) cal., two variations including straight and curved rear grip strap, smooth wood grips bearing PB monogram (commercial) or RM monogram (Italian Navy). 8,000 mfg. in ser. no. range 400,000-408,000.

	100%	98%	95%	90%	80%	70%	60%	LAST MSR
	$2,750	$2,000	$1,500	$1,000	$750	$500	$400	

Add 20% for RM variation.

MODEL 1934 – 7.65mm or .380 ACP cal., (9mm Corto cal.), 3 3/8 in. barrel, fixed sights, blue, plastic grips, Italy's service weapon in WWII, one of the most common Beretta pistols - over one million manufactured between 1934-1980, many of the military pistols have a parkerized finish, usually with metal-backed grips, later guns have an alphabetical prefix. Post-war production (1946) serial numbers start with C00001.

	100%	98%	95%	90%	80%	70%	60%	LAST MSR
	$550	$425	$325	$275	$250	$225	$200	
Dlx. post-war coml.	$3,000	$2,500	$2,000	$1,750	$1,500	$1,250	$1,000	

Add 10% for high polish, unless post-war production.
Add 20% for Italian Air Force.
Add 30% for military proofed (circled 4 over UT).

Deluxe post-war commercial pistols were engraved, gold plated, and cased with a spare mag. and cleaning brush.

The model was sold to the German Army in Italy during 1944. Ser. no. ranges are: 0001AA - 10,000AA and 0001BB - 8903BB.

MODEL 1935 – 7.65mm cal., otherwise similar to the Model 1934, 3 1/2 in. barrel, fixed sights, blue, plastic grips, the wartime model had poor finish, a small number had an experimental slide safety in ser. no. range 500,xxx, military issue was often parkerized. 525,000 mfg. 1935-1967.

	100%	98%	95%	90%	80%	70%	60%	LAST MSR
	$425	$375	$325	$275	$200	$175	$150	
Dlx. post-war coml.	$3,000	$2,500	$2,000	$1,750	$1,500	$1,250	$1,000	

Add 10% for high polish, unless post-war production.
Add 30% for Axis contract production.
Add 250% for alloy frame version, usually dated 1937-1939.

Deluxe post-war commercial pistols were engraved, gold plated, and cased with a spare mag. and cleaning brush.

There are five military groupings on this model. They include: Group I (mfg. for the German Army and Mussolini government in Italy during 1943-44, with ser. no. range 500,000 - 509,000), Group II (ser. no. range 509,000 - 525,000), Group III (sold to the German Army and Imperial Japanese Army, ser. no. range 525,000 - 534,000, control stamp is 4 UT), Group IV (mfg. 1944-45, ser. no. range 534,000 - 599,000, control stamp is 4 UT), and Group V (mfg. Feb. to Arpil of 1945, ser. no. range 599,000 - 616,000).

PISTOLS: SEMI-AUTO, POST WWII MFG.

On Beretta's large frame pistols, alphabetical suffixes refer to the following: F Model - double/single action system with external safety decocking lever, G Model - double/single action system with external decocking only lever, D Model - double action only without safety lever, DS Model - double action only with external safety lever. Pistols have been manufactured in both Italy and

GRADING - PPGS™	100%	98%	95%	90%	80%	70%	60%	LAST MSR

America, and country of origin can be determined on the slide legend.

The models in this section appear in numerical sequence.

MODEL 20 – .25 ACP cal., double action, alloy frame, 9 shot, 2 1/2 in. barrel, plastic or walnut grips, 10.9 oz. Disc. 1985.

	$160	$140	$125	$115	$95	$85	$75	*$214*

MODEL 21(A)-W BOBCAT – .22 LR or .25 ACP cal., double action, alloy frame, 7 (.22 LR) or 8 (.25 ACP) shot mag., 2.4 in. barrel, plastic or walnut (EL Model, disc. 2000) grips, 11 1/2 oz.

* ***Model 21(A)-W Blue Finish***

	$240	$195	$150	$130	$115	$95	$85	*$300*

Add approx. $75 for engraving and wood grips (EL Model, disc. 2000).

* ***Model 21(A)-W Nickel Finish*** – disc. 2000.

	$255	$215	$165	$140	$130	$115	$95	*$322*

* ***Model 21(A)-W Matte Finish*** – matte finished metal, plastic grips. New 1992.

MSR $310	$250	$210	$160	$135	$115	$95	$85	

This model is manufactured by Beretta U.S.A. Corp. in Accokeek, MD.

* ***Model 21(A)-W Stainless Steel (Inox)*** – similar to Model 21 Bobcat, except is .22 LR cal. only, stainless steel with plastic grips, approx. 11 1/2 oz. New 2000.

MSR $350	$275	$225	$175	$150	$125	$110	$95	

* ***Model 21(A)-W Lady Beretta*** – .22 LR cal. only, similar to Model 21-W, except is specially serial numbered and has gold etching on top of frame and slide sides. Supplied with a blue velvet drawstring bag. 1990 issue.

	$245	$185	$160	$140	$130	$115	$100	*$285*

This model was sold exclusively by Lew Horton Distributing Co.

MODEL U22 NEOS – .22 LR cal., single action, unique design features modular construction and modern styling, matte black finish, 10 shot mag., 4 1/2 or 6 in. barrel with sights incorporated into integral full length sight rail, interchangeable colored (black, grey, aqua, red) accessory grip frames with aqua, grey, or blue (black standard) rubber inlays, 31 1/2 or 36 oz. New 2002.

MSR $280	$225	$195	$165	$145	$120	$100	$90	

A carbine kit, which includes a 16 in. barrel and skeletonized buttstock is available for $249 (website only).

* ***Model U22 Neos Inox*** – similar to Model U22 Neos, except slide and barrel are stainless steel. New 2002.

MSR $375	$300	$245	$200	$165	$130	$110	$100	

MODEL U22 NEOS DLX – .22 LR cal., similar to Model U22 Neos, except includes adj. trigger and interchangeable front and rear sights (six included), 6 or 7 1/2 in. barrel, laser engraved "U22 NEOS" on slide. Mfg. mid-2003-2007.

	$280	$230	$200	$170	$145	$125	$110	*$350*

* ***Model U22 Neos DLX Inox*** – similar to U22 Neos DLX, except is stainless steel. Mfg. mid-2003-2007.

	$310	$255	$215	$185	$145	$130	$110	*$375*

MODEL 70 (PUMA OR COUGAR) – .32 ACP or .380 ACP cal., 3 1/2 in. barrel, fixed or adj. sights, blue, plastic grips, .32 Puma alloy frame, .380 Cougar steel frame. Disc.

	$275	$245	$215	$180	$165	$150	$130	

Add 10% for .380 ACP cal.

MODEL 70S – .22 LR or .380 ACP cal., single action, 3 1/2 in. barrel, 9 shot, blue finish, plastic grips, steel frame, .22 LR has adj. rear sight on slide, 18 oz. (.22 cal.), or 23 oz.(.380 ACP cal.). Disc. 1985.

	$375	$325	$300	$250	$225	$200	$185	*$295*

GRADING - PPGS™	100%	98%	95%	90%	80%	70%	60%	LAST MSR

MODEL 70T – .32 ACP cal., similar to Model 70, target sights. Disc.

	$325	$275	$250	$220	$195	$165	$150	

MODEL 71 (JAGUAR) – .22 LR cal., single action, 8 shot, 3 1/2 in. barrel, plastic grips with thumbrest, finger extension mag. Jaguar was dropped from the model name in 1983 and used only for marketing purposes in addition to the Jaguar Plinker. Importation disc. 1987.

	$350	$315	$275	$240	$210	$175	$150	*$215*

MODEL 72 JAGUAR – similar to Model 71 Jaguar, except includes extra 6 in. barrel. Disc.

	$350	$275	$230	$200	$180	$160	$150	

MODEL 73 – similar to Model 72, except has 6 in. barrel only, longer grip frame, 10 shot mag., and fixed rear sight moved from slide to barrel.

	$295	$250	$225	$195	$175	$155	$135	

MODEL 74 – similar to Model 73, except has adj. rear sight on barrel.

	$395	$350	$325	$250	$220	$195	$165	

MODEL 75 JAGUAR – similar to Model 71 Jaguar.

	$300	$265	$225	$195	$180	$160	$150	

MODEL 76P-76W TARGET PISTOL – .22 LR cal., single action, 11 shot, steel frame, 6 in. barrel, adj. sights, blue finish, thumbrest plastic grips (76-P). Disc. 1985.

	$795	$725	$650	$575	$500	$450	$395	*$395*

Add $40 for thumbrest wood grips (Model 76-W).

MODEL 80 – .22 Short cal., target pistol, only a couple are known to exist in the U.S.

	$2,000	$1,750	$1,500	$1,250	$995	$750	$500	

MODEL 81P-81W – .32 ACP cal., double action, 13 shot, 3.8 in. barrel, fixed sights, blue finish. Imported 1976-84.

	$300	$250	$225	$195	$175	$155	$135	

Add $90 for nickel finish.
Add $20 for wood grips (W suffix).

MODEL 82W – .32 ACP cal., double action, more compact than Model 81, 10 shot, walnut grips, 17 oz. Importation disc. 1984.

	$295	$250	$225	$195	$175	$155	$135	

Add $75 for nickel finish.

MODEL 84B – .380 ACP cal., DA, 3.8 in. barrel, smooth walnut grips, 13 shot mag., blue finish, alloy frame, fixed sights, 22 1/2 oz. Mfg. 1980-approx. 1985.

	$295	$250	$225	$195	$175	$155	$135	

MODEL 84BB – .380 ACP cal., similar to Model 84B, except safety mechanism was modified beginning in 1982, first listed in Beretta catalog during 1985, plastic or walnut grips, 23 oz.

	$295	$250	$225	$195	$175	$155	$135	

MODEL 84W-EL – similar to Model 84 but specially engraved, select walnut grips. Presentation case. Disc. 1984.

	$1,025	$770	$720	$615	$565	$520	$460	

MODEL 84 (CHEETAH) – .380 ACP cal., single/double action semi-auto, 3.82 in. barrel, alloy frame, steel slide, 10 (C/B 1994) or 13* (reintroduced late 2004) shot staggered mag., firing pin block, ambidextrous manual safety (also used as a decocking lever), low-profile 3-dot sights, curved trigger guard, plastic or wood (available with nickel finish) grips, blue (disc.), Bruniton, or nickel (disc. 2001, reintroduced 2004) finish, 23.3 oz.

MSR $770	$585	$450	$365	$310	$255	$210	$190	

Add $30 for wood grips (Model 84W, disc. 2001).
Add $60 for nickel finish (Model 84FS, includes checkered wood grips).

GRADING - PPGS™	100%	98%	95%	90%	80%	70%	60%	LAST MSR

* ***Model 84F*** – similar specifications to the Model 84P-84W, except patterned after the Model 92F Govt. Model, matte black Bruniton finish, squared off trigger guard, plastic or wood grips, 23 oz. Mfg. 1990 only.

	$395	$330	$300	$270	$240	$210	$190	*$479*

MODEL 85BB – .380 ACP cal., 8 shot mag., similar to Model 84BB, except safety mechanism was modified beginning in 1982, first listed in Beretta catalog during 1985, plastic or checkered walnut grips, blue or nickel plated finish (new 1988), 21.8 oz.

	$295	$250	$225	$195	$175	$155	$135	

MODEL 85FS CHEETAH – .380 ACP cal., same general specifications as the Model 84 Cheetah, except slimmer profile because of 8 shot straight line mag., Model 85P has plastic grips, available in nickel or Bruniton finish, 21.9 oz. Disc. 2012.

	$585	$450	$365	$310	$255	$210	$190	*$770*

Add $60 for nickel finish (includes wood grips, disc. 2001, reintroduced 2004).
Add $33 for wood grips with blue finish (Model 85W - disc. 2000).

* ***Model 85F*** – similar specifications to the Model 85P-85W, except patterned after the Model 92F Govt. Model, matte black Bruniton finish, squared off trigger guard, plastic or wood grips, 21.8 oz. Mfg. in 1990 only.

	$375	$300	$270	$240	$210	$190	$175	*$440*

Add $25 for wood grips.

MODEL 86P-86W – .380 ACP cal. only, double action, tip-up 4 1/3 in. barrel, 8 shot mag., plastic or walnut grips, 23 oz. While this model was advertised, it was never released.

Advertised MSR on this model was $480 in 1986, walnut grips were $80 extra (86-W).

MODEL 86 CHEETAH – .380 ACP cal., SA/DA with 4.4 in. tip-up barrel, 8 shot mag., checkered walnut grips, matte Bruniton finish, fixed sights, 23.3 oz. Imported 1991-2004.

	$650	$575	$500	$450	$400	$350	$295	*$615*

MODEL 87BB – .22 LR cal., similar to Model 85BB, 8 shot single column mag., plastic or checkered walnut grips, blue or nickel plated finish, 20.8 oz.

	$295	$250	$225	$195	$175	$155	$135	

MODEL 87 CHEETAH – .22 LR cal., single/double action semi-auto, 7 shot mag., 3.82 or 6 in. target barrel with counterweight (disc. 1994), blue finish, wood grips, 20 oz. (3.82 in. barrel). Importation began 1986.

MSR $845	$665	$525	$425	$350	$300	$265	$230	

* ***Model 87 Target*** – .22 LR cal., single action only target variation of the Model 87 with 5.9 in. barrel, 10 shot mag., 23.3 (older mfg.) or 41 (new mfg.) oz. Disc. 1994, reintroduced 2000.

MSR $880	$695	$550	$450	$365	$325	$290	$260	

This model was reintroduced in 2000, and now features adj. rear target sight, integral scope base rail machined on the aluminum barrel sleeve, and Bruniton finish with anodized aluminum frame.

MODEL 89 GOLD STANDARD – .22 LR cal., single action target semi-auto, matte Bruniton black finish on metal parts, 6 in. barrel, 10 shot mag., anatomical wood grips, adj. sights, 41 oz. Imported 1988-2000.

	$630	$510	$410	$360	$310	$275	$250	*$802*

MODEL 90 DOUBLE ACTION AUTOMATIC – .32 ACP cal., 3 5/8 in. barrel, fixed sights, blue, plastic grips. Mfg. 1969-83.

	$275	$195	$175	$155	$130	$110	$95	

Add 25% if without external slide latch.

MODEL 100 – .32 ACP cal., fixed sights. Disc.

	$250	$220	$195	$165	$150	$140	$130	

MODEL 101 – similar to Model 70T, except in .22 LR cal. Disc.

	$250	$220	$195	$165	$150	$140	$130	

GRADING - PPGS™	100%	98%	95%	90%	80%	70%	60%	LAST MSR

MODEL 102 – .22 LR cal., target pistol, single action, steel/alloy construction, plastic grips, 10 shot mag. with finger extension, adj. rear sight. Disc.

	$325	$250	$220	$195	$165	$150	$140	

MODEL 948 – .22 LR cal., 3 1/2 or 6 in. barrel, fixed sights, hammer.

	$175	$150	$125	$100	$75	$60	$50	

MODEL 949 OLYMPIC TARGET – .22 S or LR cal., 8 3/4 in. barrel, target sights, adj. barrel weights, blue, muzzle brake, checkered wood grips with thumbrest. Limited mfg. 1959-64.

	$660	$550	$495	$385	$305	$250	$195	

MODEL 950CC MINX M2 – .22 Short cal., hinged 2 3/8 in. barrel, fixed sights, blue, plastic grips. Mfg. 1955-disc.

	$135	$115	$105	$95	$85	$75	$70	

MODEL 950CC SPECIAL MINX M4 – similar to M2, with 4 in. barrel.

	$135	$115	$105	$95	$85	$75	$70	

MODEL 950B JETFIRE – similar to M2, in .25 ACP cal.

	$150	$120	$105	$95	$85	$75	$70	

MODEL 950 JETFIRE (BS) – .22 Short (disc. 1992) or .25 ACP cal., single action, alloy frame, 8 shot (.25 cal. only) or 6 shot mag., tip-up 2 1/2 and 4 in. (.22 S only) barrel, plastic grips, thumb safety, matte (new 1992, plastic grips only), blue or nickel finish, 9.9 oz. Mfg. in America beginning circa 1978. Disc. 2002.

	$180	$140	$115	$100	$90	$80	$70	*$226*

Add $22 for blue finish (disc. 1999).
Add $80 for nickel finish (disc. 1999).

This model was manufactured by Beretta U.S.A. Corp. in Accokeek, MD.

* ***Model 950 Jetfire Stainless (Inox)*** – similar to Model 950 BS, except is stainless steel. Mfg. 2000-2002.

	$210	$150	$120	$100	$85	$70	$65	*$267*

* ***Model 950 EL*** – same general specifications as Model 950 BS, only with wood grips and gold plated parts. Disc. 1999.

	$275	$230	$200	$180	$165	$150	$135	*$337*

MODEL 951 BRIGADIER – 9mm Para. cal., 4 1/2 in. barrel, fixed sights, blue, plastic grips, former Italian service pistol and immediate predecessor to the M92 Series. Mfg. 1952-disc.

	$550	$475	$395	$350	$295	$250	$195	

Subtract approx. 10% for "Egyptian" (denoted by E prefix) or "Israeli" Model.
Add 20% for short slide (about first 1,000 mfg.).

MODEL 3032 TOMCAT – .32 ACP cal., similar to Model 21 Bobcat, except has 2.45 in. barrel, 7 shot mag., choice of matte or blue (disc. 2007) finish, plastic grips, regular or Tritium AO Big Dot Express (new 2002) sights, approx. 14 1/2 oz., mfg. by Beretta U.S.A. New 1996.

MSR $390	$300	$240	$200	$175	$150	$135	$120	

Add $25 for blue finish (disc. 2007).
Add $150 for laser grips (mfg. 2008-2009).
Add $75 for Alley Cat package - includes Tritium AO Big Dot Express sights and in-the-pants Alcantara synthetic holster (disc.).

* ***Model 3032 Tomcat Stainless (Inox)*** – .32 ACP cal., similar to Model 3032 Tomcat, except has stainless steel slide and barrel, grey anodized alloy frame, 15.8 oz. New 2000.

MSR $430	$350	$285	$225	$185	$160	$140	$120	

* ***Model 3032 Tomcat Titanium*** – similar to Model 3032 Tomcat, except has titanium frame, blue finish only, 16.9 oz. Mfg. 2001-late 2002.

	$460	$360	$310	$275	$250	$225	$200	*$589*

GRADING - PPGS™	100%	98%	95%	90%	80%	70%	60%	LAST MSR

MODEL 8000 COUGAR F/D – 9mm Para. cal., single/double (Model 8000 Cougar F) or DA (Model 8000 Cougar D, disc. 2000) only, short recoil system with 3.6 in. rotating barrel, 10 or 13 (became option late 2004) shot mag., fixed sights, anodized aluminum alloy frame, black plastic grips, Bruniton matte black finish, 32.6 oz. Mfg. 1995-2005.

$665 $575 $440 $385 $335 $300 $275 *$800*

* ***Model 8000 Mini Cougar*** – similar to Model 8000 Cougar, except overall height has been reduced to 4 1/2 in. and weight is 27.6 oz. Mfg. 1998-2003.

$600 $545 $415 $375 $330 $300 $275 *$709*

* ***Model 8000L Cougar*** – similar to Model 8000F Cougar, except has shortened grip, 10 or 13 (optional late 2004) shot double stack mag., 28.2 oz. Mfg. 2003-2005.

$665 $575 $440 $385 $335 $300 $275 *$800*

* ***Model 8000 Cougar (Inox)*** – similar to Model 8000F Cougar, except is stainless steel. Limited mfg. 2004 only.

$715 $575 $450 $385 $335 $280 $235 *$875*

MODEL 8040 COUGAR F/D – .40 S&W cal., single/double (Model 8040 Cougar F) or DA (Model 8040 Cougar D, disc. 2000) only, short recoil system with 3.6 in. rotating barrel, 10 or 11 (became optional late 2004) shot mag., fixed sights, anodized aluminum alloy frame, Bruniton matte black finish, 32.4 oz. Mfg. 1995-2005.

$665 $575 $440 $385 $335 $300 $275 *$800*

* ***Model 8040 Cougar (Inox)*** – similar to Model 8040F Cougar, except is stainless steel. Limited mfg. 2004 only.

$715 $575 $450 $385 $335 $280 $235 *$875*

* ***Model 8040 Mini Cougar*** – similar to Model 8040 Cougar, except overall height was reduced to 4 1/2 in. and weight is 27.6 oz., supplied with 8 and extended 10 shot mag. Mfg. 1998-2003.

$600 $545 $415 $375 $330 $300 $275 *$709*

MODEL 8045 COUGAR F/D – .45 ACP cal., 8 shot mag., otherwise similar to Models 8000 and 8040, 32 oz. Mfg. 1998-2004, D Model disc. 2002.

$710 $560 $450 $395 $345 $300 $275 *$860*

Subtract approx. $25 for Model 8045 Cougar D (DA only, disc. 2002).

* ***Model 8045 Mini Cougar D/F*** – similar to Model 8045 Cougar, except overall height was reduced to 4 1/2 in., and weight is 27.6 oz, supplied with 6 shot mag. Importation began 1999, D Model disc. 2002, F disc. in 2003.

$635 $515 $435 $385 $340 $300 $275 *$764*

Subtract approx. $25 for Model 8045 Mini-Cougar D (DA only, disc. 2002).

MODEL 8357 COUGAR F – .357 SIG cal., single/double action, 5 1/2 in. barrel, blue finish with plastic grips, 10 shot mag., 32.4 oz. Mfg. 2001-2004.

$665 $575 $450 $395 $350 $300 $275 *$800*

MODEL 9000S TYPE F/D – 9mm Para. or .40 S&W cal., single/double (Model 9000S Type F) or DA only (Model 9000S Type D, disc. 2003), 3 1/2 in. tilt barrel, 10 or 12 (9mm Para. only, optional late 2004) shot mag., spurless (Type D only) or external (Type F) hammer, ambidextrous safety with hammer decocking, sub-compact pistol utilizing state of the art ergonomic design by Giugiaro Design, matte black techno-polymer frame, overmolded rubber grip, cased, approx. 26 1/2 oz. Mfg. 2000-2005.

$410 $330 $285 $260 $240 $220 $200 *$485*

Add $24 for B-Lok safety system using key lock (mfg. 2003, Type F only).

MODEL PX4 STORM – 9mm Para, .40 S&W, or .45 ACP (new 2007) cal., single/double action, 3.2 (Compact model) 4 in. barrel, polymer frame, locked breech with rotating barrel system, matte black finish with plastic grips, Pronox (disc.) or Super Luminova 3-dot night sights, 9 (.45 ACP only), 10, 14, or 17 shot mag. (varies due to caliber), accessory rail on lower frame, approx. 27 1/2 oz. New mid-2005.

MSR $575 $485 $435 $380 $330 $275 $250 $225

GRADING - PPGS™	100%	98%	95%	90%	80%	70%	60%	LAST MSR

Add $75 for .45 ACP cal. (new 2007).

The trigger mechanism of this gun can be customized to four different configurations: Type F (single/double action decocker and manual safety), Type D (DAO with spurless hammer, LE only), Type G (single/double action decocker with no manual safety, LE only), or Type C (constant action, spurless hammer). Values are for Type C and Type F variations.

* ***Model PX4 Storm Inox*** – 9mm Para. or .40 S&W cal., similar to Model PX4 Storm, except has stainless steel construction, and 10, 14, or 17 shot only. New 2012.

MSR $650	$545	$485	$410	$360	$300	$275	$250	

* ***Model PX4 Storm Special Duty*** – .45 ACP cal. only, 4.6 in. extended barrel, Type F action only, dark earth polymer frame and matte black slide, includes one 9 shot flush and two 10 shot extended mags., two additional backstraps and waterproof case, 28.6 oz.

MSR $1,035	$895	$775	$675	$575	$500	$425	$350	

* ***Model PX4 Storm Compact*** – 9mm Para. or .40 S&W (new 2012) cal., similar to Model PX4 Storm, except has compact frame and 3.2 in. barrel, 10, 12 (.40 S&W only, new 2012) or 15 (9mm Para. cal. only) shot mag., 27.3 oz. New late 2010.

MSR $575	$485	$435	$380	$330	$275	$250	$225	

* ***Model PX4 Storm Sub-Compact*** – 9mm Para. or .40 S&W cal., similar to Model PX4 Storm, except has 10 or 13 (9mm Para. cal. only) shot mag., has sub-compact frame with 3 in. barrel, includes three backstraps, 26 oz. New 2007.

MSR $575	$485	$435	$380	$330	$275	$250	$225	

BU-9 NANO – 9mm Para cal., 3 in. barrel, black nitride finish, 6 shot mag., stainless/alloy steel fiberglass reinforced technopolymer frame, DAO, removable dovetailed white dot front sight and rear sight with lockscrews, black grips, 17.1 oz. New late 2011.

MSR $475	$385	$325	$275	$225	$200	$175	$150	

ARX 160 – .22 LR cal., 15 shot mag. New 2013.

MSR $540	$465	$425	$375	$325	$275	$250	$225	

Pistols: Semi-Auto, Model 92 & Variations - 5.9 in. barrel

MODEL 92 COMBAT – similar to Model 92, except has 5.9 in. target barrel, blue finish, plastic or aluminum grips, only 50 imported into the U.S. for competition.

	$2,000	$1,750	$1,500	$1,250	$1,050	$900	$775	

Pistols: Semi-Auto, Model 92 & Variations - 4.9 in. barrel

MODEL 92 (FIRST SERIES) – 9mm Para. cal., 4.9 in. barrel, early production Model 92s had a step slide, frame mounted safety, and mag. release button at base of pistol grip. Production of the M92 was approx. 5,000 pistols. Originally mfg. 1976. Disc.

	$800	$725	$625	$495	$395	$325	$275	

MODEL 92S (SECOND SERIES) – similar to Model 92, except has a slide mounted firing pin blocking safety. Disc.

	$700	$495	$375	$300	$250	$240	$220	

MODEL 92SB-P (THIRD SERIES) – 9mm Para. cal., double action, 15 shot mag., 4.9 in. barrel, fixed sights, alloy frame, high-polish blue finish, plastic grips (Model 92SB-P), conventionally located push button magazine release, ambidextrous safety, 34 1/2 oz. Mfg. 1980-1985.

	$525	$425	$395	$350	$325	$295	$270	*$600*

* ***Model 92SB-W*** – similar to above, only with wood grips. Disc. 1985.

	$550	$450	$400	$355	$330	$290	$260	*$620*

MODEL 92D – 9mm Para. cal., double action only, otherwise similar to Model 92F, except does not have a manual safety lever, includes black plastic grips, 3-dot sights, 33.8 oz. Introduced 1992 - disc. 1998.

	$475	$400	$350	$300	$250	$210	$190	*$586*

Add $90 for Tritium (new 1994) sight system.
Add 10% for Trijicon (disc.) sights and early guns with Model 92F features.

GRADING - PPGS™	100%	98%	95%	90%	80%	70%	60%	LAST MSR

MODEL 90-TWO TYPE F – 9mm Para. or .40 S&W cal., 4.9 in. barrel, single/double action, matte metal finish, removable single piece wraparound grip in two sizes, internal recoil buffer and captive recoil sping guide assembly, low profile fixed sights, 10, 12 (.40 S&W cal.), or 17 (9mm Para. cal.) shot mag., lower accessories rail with cover, 32 1/2 oz. Mfg. 2006-2009.

	$600	$525	$450	$375	$330	$300	$275	*$700*

MODEL 92FS & 92F – 9mm Para. cal., official U.S. military variation of 92 Series, 4.9 in. barrel, alloy frame, steel slide, 10 (C/B 1994), or 15* (reintroduced late 2004) shot mag., loaded chamber indicator, matte black Bruniton or olive drab (mfg. 2004 only) finish, squared off trigger guard to facilitate two-hand shooting, extended mag. base, choice of regular or 3-dot sights (new 1991), approx 34 1/2 oz. Model 92F-P has plastic grips. Model 92F-W has wood grips. New 1984, mfg. in Italy or Accokeek, MD (disc.).

MSR $700	$595	$495	$450	$395	$350	$310	$280	

Add $369 for .22 LR conversion kit (includes slide, barrel, recoil spring, and .22 LR mag., new 2002).
Add $25 for olive drab finish (mfg. 2004 only).
Add $24 for B-Lok safety system using key lock (mfg. 2003 only).
Add approx. $20 for checkered wood grips (Model 92F-W, disc. 1998).
Add approx. $80 for Tritium sight system (mfg. 1994-98).
Add 10% for Trijicon (disc.) sights.
Add approx. $175 for gold engraving/accenting (Model EL-3, 92F-W only, disc. 1998).
Add $395 for 9mm Competition Conversion Kit (mfg. 1992-98).

The Model 92FS incorporates a slide retaining pin engineering change not included in the Model 92F. The U.S. military on January 15, 1985 announced that the M9 military variation of the commercial Model 92F would replace the Colt Govt. Model .45 ACP as the standard government issue sidearm. Because of domestic political pressures, Congress requested that a new sidearm competition be conducted again in 1988. The result of this second trial was that the Department of the Army announced on May 22, 1989 that Beretta had won again. This military contract with Beretta U.S.A. Corp. initially involved over 320,000 Model M9s (military designation for the commercial Model 92F) manufactured for U.S. military consumption in the 1990s. Actual delivery of commercial Model 92s began in January of 1986, while M9 delivery to U.S. Armed Forces exceeded 430,000 units, and was completed in 1999.

During 2005, Beretta USA received 13 separate contracts to provide M9 pistols and associated spare parts to the U.S. armed forces. In Jan., 2009, Beretta announced that it had been awarded a U.S. Army contract for 450,000 Model 92FS pistols, for U.S. military customers throughout the world. This contract, if all pistol quantities and associated spare parts are ordered, is worth $220 million.

During 2009, Beretta USA Corp. received another order from the U.S. Army to provide 450,000 Beretta Model 92FS pistols to U.S. military customers worldwide. 50,000 pistols from this contract were scheduled for delivery by the end of 2010.

* ***Model 92FS & 92F Stainless (Inox)*** – similar to Model 92F/92FS, except is mfg. from stainless steel, satin finish with plastic grips, 3-dot sights, initially released to law enforcement agencies only, this model was commercially manufactured in quantity. Reintroduced 2008, disc. 2012.

	$650	$545	$450	$400	$350	$315	$285	*$795*

Add $180 for laser grips (mfg. 2004-2008).
Add $24 for B-Lok safety system using key lock (mfg. 2003 only).
Add approx. $20 for wood grips (disc. 1998).
Add approx. $90 for Trijicon (1993 only) or Tritium (mfg. 1994-98) sight system.

MODEL 92FS BRIGADIER – similar to the Model 92FS, except has heavier slide to reduce felt recoil, wraparound rubber grips, and 3-dot sights, 35.3 oz. Mfg. 1999-2005.

	$650	$525	$425	$385	$335	$300	$275	*$795*

* ***Model 92FS Brigadier Stainless (Inox)*** – similar to Model 92FS Brigadier, except is stainless steel, 35.3 oz. Mfg. 2000-2005.

	$690	$575	$475	$415	$360	$300	$255	*$845*

GRADING - PPGS™	100%	98%	95%	90%	80%	70%	60%	LAST MSR

MODEL 92FS B.A.T.S. – 9mm Para. cal., 4.9 in. barrel, features black matte Bruniton finish and textured rubber wraparound grips with finger grooves, package includes both 10 and 15 shot mags., Airlight knife, aluminum carrying case, 34.4 oz. Limited mfg. late 2000 only.

$665	$550	$465	$415	$360	$300	$275	*$785*

MODEL 92FS VERTEC – 9mm Para. cal., single/double action, straight backstrap grip, special short reach trigger, thin dual textured grip panels, and integral accessory rail on lower frame, removable front sight, beveled magwell, 10 shot mag., Bruniton finish, 32.2 oz. Mfg. 2002-2005.

$635	$495	$440	$385	$340	$300	$275	*$760*

Add $25 for B-Lok safety system using key lock (mfg. 2003).

* ***Model 92FS Vertec Stainless (Inox)*** – stainless variation of the Model 92FS Vertec. Mfg. 2002-2005.

$670	$525	$425	$360	$315	$260	$225	*$825*

Add $170 for laser grips (new 2004).
Add $25 for B-Lok safety system using key lock (mfg. 2003).

MODEL 92 BLACK INOX – 9mm Para. cal., single/double action, features black stainless slide and stippled, finger groove plastic grips. Limited mfg. 2002 only.

$610	$485	$390	$325	$280	$240	$200	*$734*

MODEL 92 BILLENIUM – 9mm Para. cal., single action only, frame mounted safety, contoured steel frame with checkered grip straps and contoured carbon fiber grips, interchangeable sights, oversize mag. release button, unique slide serrations and Billenium engraving, nickel alloy surface treatment finish, included deluxe lockable carrying case, 43.3 oz. Limited mfg. in Italy of 2,000 during 2002-2003.

$1,100	$900	$750	$650	$575	$500	$425	*$1,429*

MODEL 92 STEEL I – 9mm Para. cal., single action only or SA/DA, plastic grips, features all-steel construction, frame mounted safety, nickel alloy finish, includes two 10 shot mags., 41.1 oz. Mfg. 2004-2005.

$1,295	$1,150	$900	$825	$750	$675	$595	*$1,600*

MODEL 92FS YEAR 2000 – 9mm Para. cal., 4.9 in. barrel, matte black Bruniton finish, features rosewood laminate grips with Beretta "trident" logo on brass medallions. 2,000 mfg. during 2000 only.

$615	$500	$450	$400	$350	$300	$275	*$726*

MODEL 92F-ELS – deluxe variation of the Model 92F featuring high polish stainless steel finish with gold highlights, frame etchings, and small parts, plastic grips. Mfg. 1992-1994.

$685	$550	$425	$360	$315	$260	$225	*$790*

MODEL 92F/FS "UNITED WE STAND" LIMITED EDITION – 9mm Para. cal., features laser etched gold American flag and "United We Stand" slide lettering, Bruniton finish, black plastic grips. Mfg. limited to 2001 (Model 92F) and 3,900 (Model 92FS) pistols in late 2001 - early 2002.

$625	$560	$485	$425	$375	$300	$275	$734

Beretta USA made a donation from the proceeds of this model to the NYPD Foundation and the Survivor's Fund of the National Capitol Region.

MODEL 92FS 470th ANNIVERSARY LIMITED EDITION – features stainless steel construction with mirror polished finish, smooth select walnut grips with inlaid gold plated medallions, gold filled engraving with Dr. Ugo Gussalli-Beretta's signature, 470th Anniversary logos, only 470 mfg. (with "1 of 470" gold filled on each gun) beginning 1999, lockable walnut case. Disc. 2004.

$1,950	$1,575	$1,100	$985	$795	$675	$565	*$2,217*

MODEL 92F/FS "DESERT STORM" SPECIAL EDITION – 9mm Para. cal., features U.S. Central Command seal, marked "Official Sidearm U.S. Armed Forces" on left side of slide, right side is marked "DESERT STORM", stamped "15 January 1991 - 11 April 1991", special ser. no. Approx. 8,000 mfg. 1991-92.

$625	$560	$485	$425	$375	$300	$275	*$660*

GRADING - PPGS™	100%	98%	95%	90%	80%	70%	60%	LAST MSR

MODEL 92F DELUXE – deluxe model featuring gold or silver plating and elaborate engraving. Importation began 1993.

MSR $6,750	$5,750	$4,950	$3,750	$2,500	$2,175	$1,950	$1,625	

This model is available at the Beretta Galleries or select Beretta Premium dealers only.

MODEL 92G – 9mm Para. cal., SA/DA, identical to the Model 92F, except features a spring loaded decocking lever which safely lowers the hammer allowing fire-ready when unholstering the pistol. New 1990.

The Model 92G is sold to law enforcement agencies only and prices are slightly higher than the standard Model 92FS. This pistol has been used by French Gendarmes since 1987.

MODEL 92G-SD – 9mm Para. cal., similar to Model 92G, except has an integral accessory rail machined into frame in front of trigger guard, Bruniton finish, 10 shot mag., Tritium sights, 35.3 oz. Mfg. 2003-2005.

	$955	$745	$585	$510	$450	$400	$350	*$1,175*

MODEL 92F WITH U.S. M9 MARKED SLIDE/FRAME – 9mm Para. cal., 100 mfg. with special serial no. range, "BER" prefix, government assembly numbers on frame, slide, hammer, mag. etc., includes plastic case and cleaning brush. Mfg. for the Armed Forces Reserve shooters, identical to military M9, except for serial number.

	$1,750	$1,525	$1,350	$1,100	$950	$825	$700	

MODEL 92FS OPERATION ENDURING FREEDOM – 9mm Para. cal., M9 U.S. Army edition, two 10 shot mags., "BER" prefix, 2,500 mfg. 2003 only.

	$625	$500	$425	$360	$315	$260	$225	*$712*

M9 LIMITED STANDARD EDITION – commercial limited edition of the U.S. Govt. M9 military pistol, features gold inscribed slide legend "The First Decade 1985-1995", Air Force or Marine Corps emblems on right slide side, 10,000 mfg. during 1995-97.

	$600	$475	$425	$360	$315	$260	$225	*$643*

* ***M9 Limited Deluxe Edition*** – features checkered walnut grips, gold-plated hammer, grip screws, and mag. release button. Disc. 1997.

	$695	$525	$475	$415	$360	$300	$255	*$750*

MODEL 92A1 – 9mm Para. cal., DA/SA action, similar to Model 92FS/F, except includes three 10 or 17 shot mags., has removable front sight, frame accessory rail, internal recoil buffer, rounded trigger guard, and captive recoil spring assembly, black Bruniton finish, plastic grips, 34.4 oz, mfg. in Italy. New 2010.

MSR $725	$625	$540	$465	$415	$360	$300	$285	

M9 SPECIAL EDITION – patterned after the U.S. Armed Forces M9, special M9- XXXX ser. no. range, one 15 shot mag. (pre-1994 mfg.), dot and post sight system, M9 military packaging including Army operator's manual, Bianchi M12 holster, mag. pouch, and web pistol belt. Mfg. 1998-2000.

	$950	$700	$550	$460	$395	$335	$285	*$861*

M9 20TH ANNIVERSARY – 9mm Para. cal., special edition for 20th anniversary of the U.S. government M9, 10 or 15 shot mag. Mfg. 2006-2009.

	$540	$465	$415	$375	$330	$300	$275	*$625*

M9 (25TH ANNIVERSARY) – 9mm Para. cal., special edition for 25th Anniversary of U.S. Government M9, 10 or 15 shot mag., includes military style markings, M9 prefixed serial numbers and dot and post sighting system, limited mfg. beginning 2010.

MSR $700	$595	$495	$440	$385	$350	$310	$280	

M9A1 – 9mm Para. cal., SA/DA, features accessory rail on lower frame and checkered grip straps, 10 or 15 shot mag., 3-dot sights, beveled mag. well, 35.3 oz. New 2006.

MSR $725	$625	$525	$450	$395	$340	$315	$285	

GRADING - PPGS™	100%	98%	95%	90%	80%	70%	60%	LAST MSR

Pistols: Semi-Auto, Model 92 & Variations - 4.7 in. barrel

MODEL 92FS INOX TACTICAL – 9mm Para. cal., 4.7 in. barrel, features satin matte finished stainless steel slide and alloy frame, rubber grips, Tritium sights. Mfg. 1999-2000.

$695	$560	$480	$425	$375	$325	$295	*$822*

MODEL 92FS BORDER MARSHAL – 9mm Para. cal., commercial equivalent of the I.N.S. (Immigration & Naturalization Service) government contract, 4.7 in. barrel, heavy duty steel slide, Tritium sights, Border Marshal engraving on the slide. Mfg. 1999-2000.

$670	$560	$480	$425	$375	$325	$295	*$802*

MODEL 92G ELITE IA (BRIGADIER) – 9mm Para. cal., similar to Model 92FS Brigadier, except has 4.7 in. stainless barrel and many standard I.D.P.A. competition features including front and rear serrated slide, skeletonized hammer, and removable three-dot sighting system, plastic grips, includes Elite engraving on slide, 35.3 oz. Mfg. 1999-2005.

$725	$585	$495	$425	$360	$300	$275	*$875*

* ***Model 92G Elite II (Brigadier)*** – similar to Model 92G Elite, except has stainless steel slide with black "Elite II" markings, target barrel crown, extended mag. release, optimized trigger mechanism, front and back strap checkering, low profile Novak rear sight, 35 oz. Mfg. mid-2000-2005.

$815	$635	$530	$450	$385	$325	$295	*$985*

Pistols: Semi-Auto, Model 92 & Variations - 4.3 in. barrel

MODEL 92D CENTURION – 9mm Para. cal., compact variation with 4.3 in. barrel, plastic grips only, without safety, choice of 3 dot or Tritium sights. Mfg. 1994-98.

$460	$360	$300	$250	$210	$190	$175	*$586*

Add $90 for Tritium sights.

MODEL 92SB-P COMPACT – similar to Model 92SB, except has 4.3 in. barrel, 14 shot mag., plastic grips (Model 92SB-P), rarer when frontstrap has curved lip, 31 oz. Disc. 1985.

$500	$440	$385	$345	$310	$285	$260	*$620*

Add $60 for nickel finish.

* ***Model 92SB-W Compact*** – similar to Model 92SB-P Compact, except has wood grips. Disc. 1985.

$525	$465	$395	$355	$335	$300	$280	*$635*

MODEL 92F/92FS COMPACT – similar to Model 92F, except has 4.3 in. barrel and 13 shot mag., plastic or wood grips, 31 1/2 oz. While temporarily suspended in 1986, production was resumed 1989-1993.

$550	$450	$415	$375	$335	$300	$275	*$625*

Add $20 for checkered walnut grips (Model 92F Wood).
Add $65 for Trijicon sight system.

* ***Model 92F Compact "M"*** – similar to Model 92F Compact, except has 8 shot straight line mag., plastic grips only. Imported 1990-93.

$550	$450	$415	$375	$335	$300	$275	*$625*

Add $65 for Trijicon sight system.
Add $100 for the approx. 1,200 SBM Models that were imported in the 1980's.

MODEL 92F & 92FS CENTURION – 9mm Para. cal., similar to Model 92F, except has compact barrel slide unit with full size frame, 4.3 in. barrel, choice of plastic or wood grips, 3 dot sight system, same length as Model 92F Compact, 10 (C/B 1994) or 15* shot mag., 33.2 oz. Mfg. 1992-98.

$525	$435	$395	$365	$335	$300	$275	*$613*

Add approx. $20 for checkered walnut grips (Model 92F Wood).
Add $90 for Tritium sight system (mfg. 1994-98).
Add 10% for Trijicon sights (disc).

MODEL 92FS COMPACT – 9mm Para. cal., similar to Model 92 Compact Type M, except has 10 shot staggered mag., 35.3 oz. Mfg. 1999-2003.

$575	$465	$415	$370	$335	$300	$275	*$691*

GRADING - PPGS™	100%	98%	95%	90%	80%	70%	60%	LAST MSR

* ***Model 92FS Compact Stainless (Inox)*** – similar to Model 92FS Compact, except is stainless steel. Mfg. 2000-2003.

	$620	$490	$395	$325	$275	$235	$200	$748

* ***Model 92FS Custom Carry*** – 9mm Para. cal., 4.3 in. barrel, shortened grip, low profile control levers, left side only safety lever, blue only, 10 shot staggered mag., plastic grips. Mfg. 1999-2000.

	$550	$450	$400	$365	$335	$300	$275	$655

* ***Model 92FS Custom Carry II (Type M)*** – 9mm Para. cal., similar dimensions as Custom Carry, except is stainless steel construction with black components and black slide markings, Novak low profile 3-dot sights, 8 shot single stack mag., 30.9 oz. Mfg. 2000.

	$560	$455	$410	$345	$295	$245	$215	$669

MODEL 92 TYPE M COMPACT – same features as the Model 92FS, except has 4.3 in. barrel, overall height is 5.3 in., Bruniton matte finish, choice of single/double or double action only (disc. 1998), plastic grips, single column 8 shot mag., 30.9 oz. Mfg. 1998-2003.

	$575	$465	$415	$370	$335	$300	$275	$691

Add approx. $90 for Tritium sight system (disc. 1998).
Subtract approx. $25 for double action only (disc. 1998).

* ***Model 92 Type M Compact Stainless (Inox)*** – similar to Model 92 Type M, except is stainless steel. Mfg. 2000-2003.

	$615	$475	$395	$340	$295	$245	$215	$748

Pistols: Semi-Auto, Model 96 & Variations, Recent Mfg.

The models in this section appear in approximate chronological sequence.

MODEL 96D – .40 S&W cal., 4.9 in. barrel, double action only variation of the Model 96F, no safety, 3 dot sight system, 33.8 oz. Introduced 1992 - disc. 1998.

	$460	$360	$300	$250	$210	$190	$175	$586

Add $90 for Tritium sight system (new 1994).
Add $65 for Trijicon sights (disc.).

* ***Model 96D Centurion*** – similar to Model 96D, except is compact variation with 4.3 in. barrel, 3-dot sights. Mfg. 1994-98.

	$460	$360	$300	$250	$210	$190	$175	$586

Add $90 for Tritium sight system.

MODEL 96, 96F, & 96FS – .40 S&W cal., similar to Model 92F, 4.9 in. barrel, plastic grips only, flared grip with grip strap serrations, Bruniton matte black finish, 3 dot sight system, 10 or 11 (optional) shot mag., 34.4 oz. Mfg. 1992-2005.

	$595	$475	$420	$380	$335	$300	$275	$715

Add $24 for B-Lok safety system with key lock (mfg. 2003).
Add $91 for Tritium sight system (mfg. 1994-99).
Add 10% for Trijicon sights (disc.).

Current model nomenclature for this pistol is the Model 96.

* ***Model 96, 96FS Stainless (Inox)*** – stainless variation of the Model 96FS, rubber grips, 34.4 oz. Mfg. 1999-2005, reintroduced 2009.

	$600	$515	$435	$395	$350	$315	$285	$725

Recent model nomenclature for this pistol is the Model 96 Inox.

* ***Model 96F Compact*** – 4.3 in. barrel, 10 shot mag., 3-dot sights, plastic grips, approx. 32 oz. Mfg. 2000-2003.

	$580	$465	$415	$370	$335	$300	$275	$691

While advertised during the 1990s, this gun finally went into production during 2000.

* ***Model 96F Compact Stainless (Inox)*** – similar to Model 96F Compact, except is stainless steel. Mfg. 2000-2003.

	$620	$500	$415	$370	$335	$300	$275	$748

GRADING - PPGS™	100%	98%	95%	90%	80%	70%	60%	LAST MSR

* ***Model 96F Centurion*** – similar to Model 96F, except has 4.3 in. barrel, 33.2 oz. Mfg. 1992-99.

	$525	$435	$395	$365	$335	$300	$275	*$613*

Add $91 for Tritium sight system (new 1994).

* ***Model 96 Stainless (Inox) "United We Stand" Limited Edition*** – .40 S&W cal., features laser etched gold American flag and "United We Stand" slide lettering. Mfg. limited to 3,900 pistols in late 2001 - early 2002.

	$625	$560	$485	$425	$365	$305	$260	*$734*

Beretta USA made a donation from the proceeds of this model to the NYPD Foundation and the Survivor's Fund of the National Capitol Region.

* ***Model 96FS B.A.T.S.*** – .40 S&W cal., 4.9 in. barrel, black matte Bruniton finish and textured rubber wraparound grips with finger grooves, included both 10 and 11 shot mags., Airlight knife, aluminum carrying case, 34.4 oz. Limited mfg. mid-2000 only.

	$675	$550	$465	$415	$360	$300	$275	*$785*

* ***Model 96G Elite IA (Brigadier)*** – .40 S&W cal., similar to Model 96 Brigadier, except has 4.7 in. stainless barrel and many standard I.D.P.A. competition features including front and rear serrated slide, skeletonized hammer, and removable 3-dot sighting system, plastic grips, includes Elite engraving on slide. Mfg. 1999-2005.

	$725	$575	$480	$420	$350	$300	$275	*$875*

* ***Model 96G Elite II (Brigadier)*** – similar to Model 96G Elite, except has stainless steel slide with black "Elite II" markings, target barrel crown, extended mag. release, optimized trigger mechanism, front and back strap checkering, low profile Novak rear sight, 35.3 oz. Mfg. mid-2000-2005.

	$815	$625	$525	$450	$385	$325	$295	*$985*

MODEL 96G-SD – .40 S&W cal., similar to Model 92G, except has an integral accessory rail machined into frame in front of trigger guard, Bruniton finish, 10 shot mag., Tritium sights, 35.3 oz. Mfg. 2003-2005.

	$955	$725	$625	$525	$450	$400	$350	*$1,175*

MODEL 96 STEEL I – .40 S&W cal., single action only or SA/DA, plastic grips, features steel construction, nickel alloy frame, slim vertical grip, frame mounted safety, includes two 10 shot mags. Mfg. 2004-2005.

	$1,295	$1,140	$950	$825	$750	$675	$595	*$1,600*

MODEL 96 COMBAT – .40 S&W cal., single action only, similar to Model 96 Stock, except has factory tuned trigger, 4.9 (new 1998) or 5.9 in. barrel with weight and fully adj. rear target sight, aluminum or plastic grips. Mfg. in Italy 1997-2001.

	$1,350	$1,060	$900	$775	$625	$550	$495	*$1,735*

Add approx. $250 for 5.9 in. barrel (previously available as a Combat Combo).

MODEL 96 VERTEC – .40 S&W cal., single/double action, 4.9 in. barrel, straight backstrap grip, special short reach trigger, thin dual textured grip panels, and integral accessory rail on lower frame, removable front sight, beveled magwell, 10 shot mag., Bruniton finish, 32.2 oz. Mfg. 2002-2005.

	$635	$495	$440	$385	$340	$300	$275	*$760*

Add $25 for B-Lok safety system with key lock (mfg. 2003).

* ***Model 96 Vertec Stainless (Inox)*** – stainless variation of the Model 96 Vertec. Mfg. 2002-2005.

	$670	$530	$430	$365	$320	$260	$225	*$825*

Add $25 for B-Lok safety system with key lock (mfg. 2003).

MODEL 96 BLACK INOX – .40 S&W cal., single/double action, features black stainless slide and stippled finger groove plastic grips. Limited mfg. 2002 only.

	$610	$485	$390	$325	$285	$240	$210	*$734*

GRADING - PPGS™	100%	98%	95%	90%	80%	70%	60%	LAST MSR

MODEL 96 BORDER MARSHAL – .40 S&W cal., commercial equivalent of the I.N.S. (Immigration & Naturalization Service) government contract model, 4.7 in. barrel, heavy duty steel slide, Tritium sights, Border Marshal engraving on the slide. Mfg. 1999-2000.

	$670	$560	$480	$425	$375	$325	$295	*$802*

MODEL 96 BRIGADIER – similar to Model 96FS, except has heavier slide to reduce felt recoil, wraparound rubber grips, and 3-dot sights, 35.3 oz. Mfg. 1999-2005.

	$660	$510	$440	$385	$335	$300	$275	*$795*

* ***Model 96 Brigadier Stainless (Inox)*** – similar to Model 96 Brigadier, except is stainless steel. New 2000.

	$680	$530	$425	$360	$315	$260	$225	*$845*

MODEL 96 CUSTOM CARRY – .40 S&W cal., 4.3 in. barrel, shortened grip, low profile control levers, left side only safety lever, blue only, 10 shot staggered mag., plastic grips. Mfg. 1999-2000.

	$550	$450	$400	$365	$335	$300	$275	*$655*

MODEL 96 STOCK – .40 S&W cal., designed for practical shooting competition, includes accurized barrel bushing, 4.9 in. barrel, competition frame mounted ambidextrous safety, 3 interchangeable front sights, checkered front and back grip straps, aluminum grips, beveled magwell, cased with two mags. and tool kit, 35 oz. Mfg. 1997-1999, limited quantities remained into 2000.

	$1,200	$995	$865	$725	$600	$550	$495	*$1,407*

MODEL 96A1 – .40 S&W, DA/SA action, similar to Model 96F/FS, except includes three 10 or 12 shot mags., has removable front sight, frame accessory rail, internal recoil buffer, rounded trigger guard, and captive recoil spring assembly, black Bruniton finish, plastic grips, 34.4 oz, mfg. in Italy. New 2010.

MSR $725	$625	$525	$450	$400	$350	$300	$285	

REVOLVERS: SINGLE ACTION

Beretta's SAA revolvers were manufactured in Italy between 2005-2012 by Aldo Uberti & Co., S.r.l., which was purchased by Beretta in 2000.

LARAMIE – .38 Spl. or .45 LC cal., patterned after S&W Model 1870 Schofield, 5 or 6 1/2 in. barrel, 6 shot, blued finish with case colored hammer and trigger guard, smooth walnut grips with Beretta medallions, top-break, approx. 37-43 oz. Mfg. 2005-2008.

	$1,025	$795	$750	$650	$550	$475	$375	*$1,200*

Add $175 for nickel finish or 6 1/2 in. barrel.

STAMPEDE SAA – .357 Mag., .44-40 WCF (mfg. 2003), or .45 LC cal., patterned after the Colt SAA, transfer bar and half-cock safeties, 6 shot, 4 3/4, 5 1/2, or 7 1/2 (disc. 2010) in. barrel, various finishes, approx. 37 oz. Mfg. by Uberti beginning mid-2003.

* ***Stampede SAA Blue*** – features blue finish with case colored frame and black polymer grips. Disc. 2012.

	$495	$400	$340	$300	$270	$240	$220	*$600*

* ***Stampede SAA Brushed Nickel*** – .45 LC cal., features brushed nickel finish, smooth walnut grips with Beretta medallions, and fire blued frame screws. Disc. 2010.

	$515	$425	$350	$315	$285	$255	$230	*$625*

* ***Stampede SAA Old West*** – .357 Mag. (new 2008) or .45 LC (disc. 2010) cal., features distressed Old West finish, 4 3/4 (disc. 2010) or 5 1/2 in. barrel. Mfg. 2007-2011.

	$525	$465	$415	$365	$325	$280	$250	*$650*

* ***Stampede SAA Bisley*** – features Bisley styled grips/frame and raked hammer, blue or nickel finish. Mfg. 2005-2008.

	$515	$425	$350	$315	$285	$255	$230	*$650*

Add $50 for nickel finish.

GRADING - PPGS™	100%	98%	95%	90%	80%	70%	60%	LAST MSR

* ***Stampede Buntline Carbine*** – .45 LC cal., 18 in. blue barrel, replica of the Buntline revolver, transfer bar safety, 6 shot, hooked trigger guard, brass crescent buttplate, satin walnut stock with gold Beretta medallions. Mfg. 2007-2008.

$750	$650	$575	$500	$425	$350	$275	*$850*

* ***Stampede SAA Stainless (Inox)*** – .357 Mag. (new 2011), or .45 LC cal. only, features stainless steel construction, otherwise similar to Stampede. Mfg. 2004-2007, reintroduced 2011-2012.

$495	$400	$340	$300	$270	$240	$220	*$600*

* ***Stampede SAA Marshal*** – .357 Mag. (disc. 2010) or .45 LC cal., 3 1/2 in. barrel, bird's head grips, blue (disc. 2010) or Old West (.45 LC cal. only) finish. Mfg. 2004-2011.

$525	$465	$415	$365	$325	$280	$250	*$650*

* ***Stampede SAA Deluxe*** – features charcoal blue metal finish, case colored frame and deluxe smooth walnut grips. Disc. 2010.

$540	$465	$420	$365	$320	$275	$250	*$695*

* ***Stampede SAA Patton*** – .45 LC cal., features charcoal blue metal finish, engraved case colored frame, light gold accents, simulated ivory grips. Mfg. 2005-2006.

$925	$800	$700	$600	$525	$450	$375	*$1,095*

This model was also available as a set - MSR was $2,190.

* ***Stamped SAA Matched Pairs*** – .45 LC cal. only, 5 1/2 in. barrel, case colored frame, wood grips with Beretta medallions, Philadelphia Centennial laser engraving (Philadelphia) or German silver trigger guard and backstrap (Gemini), paired serial numbers. Mfg. 2007-2008.

» **Stampede Gemini Matched Pair**

$1,175	$1,025	$900	$800	$700	$650	$600	*$1,350*

» **Stampede Philadelphia Centennial Matched Pair**

$1,775	$1,550	$1,325	$1,100	$950	$850	$750	*$2,100*

RIFLES: BOLT ACTION, RECENT MFG.

MODEL 500 CUSTOM – .222 Rem., .223 Rem., .243 Win., .270 Win., .30-06, or .308 Win. cal., 3 action lengths, 24 in. barrel, iron sights, checkered walnut stock with recoil pad. Importation was resumed 1988 only.

$595	$530	$450	$395	$350	$315	$275	*$725*

Add 10%-15% for .223 Rem. cal.

* ***Model 500 S*** – similar to Model 500, except is equipped with iron sights. Imported 1986 only.

$615	$560	$460	$400	$350	$315	$275	*$700*

* ***Model 500 DL*** – same specifications as Model 500, only better walnut and light engraving. Disc. 1986.

$1,395	$1,260	$1,000	$875	$795	$725	$650	*$1,595*

Add 10%-15% for .223 Rem. cal.

* ***Model 500 DLS*** – similar to Model 500 DL, except is equipped with iron sights. Imported 1986 only.

$1,420	$1,285	$1,020	$875	$795	$725	$650	*$1,625*

* ***Model 500 EELL*** – same specifications as Model 500 DL, only select walnut and more engraving. Disc. 1986.

$1,550	$1,260	$1,150	$1,000	$875	$800	$725	*$1,745*

Add 10%-15% for .223 Rem. cal.

* ***Model 500 EELLS*** – similar to Model 500 EELL, except is equipped with iron sights. Imported 1986 only.

$1,575	$1,425	$1,200	$1,120	$875	$800	$725	*$1,785*

GRADING - PPGS™	100%	98%	95%	90%	80%	70%	60%	LAST MSR

MODEL 501 – .243 Win. or .308 Win. cal., medium length receiver, 6 shot, 23 in. barrel, no sights, checkered walnut stock. Disc. 1986.

$595 $530 $465 $395 $350 $315 $275 *$665*

* ***Model 501 S*** – similar to Model 501, except is equipped with iron sights. Imported 1986 only.

$615 $560 $460 $400 $350 $315 $275 *$700*

* ***Model 501 DL*** – same specifications as Model 501, only better walnut and light engraving. Disc. 1986.

$1,395 $1,260 $1,000 $875 $795 $725 $650 *$1,575*

* ***Model 501 DLS*** – similar to Model 501 DL, except is equipped with iron sights. Imported 1986 only.

$1,420 $1,285 $1,020 $875 $795 $725 $650 *$1,625*

* ***Model 501 EELL*** – same specifications as Model 501 DL, only select walnut and more engraving. Disc. 1986.

$1,550 $1,260 $1,150 $1,000 $875 $800 $725 *$1,745*

* ***Model 501 EELLS*** – similar to Model 501 EELL, except is equipped with iron sights. Imported 1986 only.

$1,575 $1,425 $1,200 $1,120 $875 $800 $725 *$1,785*

MODEL 502 – .30-06, .270, or 7mm Rem. Mag. cal., long action receiver, 5 or 6 shot, 24 in. barrel, no sights, checkered walnut stock. Disc. 1986.

$625 $565 $490 $440 $395 $360 $330 *$710*

* ***Model 502 S*** – similar to Model 502, except is equipped with iron sights. Imported 1986 only.

$650 $595 $525 $460 $395 $360 $330 *$745*

* ***Model 502 DL*** – same specifications as Model 502, only better walnut and light engraving. Also available in .375 H&H Mag. Disc. 1986.

$1,495 $1,310 $1,175 $1,025 $900 $775 $695 *$1,640*

* ***Model 502 DLS*** – similar to Model 502, except is equipped with iron sights. Imported 1986 only.

$1,410 $1,325 $1,175 $1,025 $900 $775 $695 *$1,660*

* ***Model 502 EELL*** – same specifications as Model 502 DL, only select walnut and more engraving. Also available in .375 H&H Mag. Disc. 1986.

$1,575 $1,425 $1,200 $1,120 $875 $800 $725 *$1,785*

* ***Model 502 EELLS*** – similar to Model 502 EELL, except is equipped with iron sights. Imported 1986 only.

$1,575 $1,425 $1,200 $1,120 $875 $800 $725 *$1,785*

MATO SYNTHETIC – .270 Win., .280 Rem., .30-06, .300 Win. Mag., .338 Win. Mag., .375 H&H, or 7mm Rem. Mag. cal., 23.6 in. barrel, composite black synthetic stock with integral bedding block, Mauser 98 action with controlled round feeding, 3-position safety, ergonomic bolt handle, 3 or 4 shot detachable box mag., adj. trigger, black satin metal finish, mfg. in the U.S., 8 lbs. Mfg. 1997-2002.

$975 $825 $750 $675 $575 $495 $400 *$1,117*

Add $357 for .375 H&H cal. (includes muzzle brake and iron sights).

* ***Mato Deluxe*** – same cals. as the standard model, features deluxe checkered walnut with ebony forend tip, cased, 7.9 lbs. Mfg. 1997-2002.

$2,025 $1,575 $1,150 $995 $825 $675 $600 *$2,470*

Add $325 for .375 H&H cal. (includes muzzle brake and iron sights).

* ***Mato Deluxe Safari Grade*** – .375 H&H cal. only, elaborately hand engraved with best quality wood. Available through Beretta Premium dealers only. Disc. 2002.

$14,750 $12,500 $10,250 $8,000 $6,750 $5,500 $4,350 *$16,500*

GRADING - PPGS™	100%	98%	95%	90%	80%	70%	60%	LAST MSR

RIFLES: LEVER ACTION

1873 RENEGADE SHORT RIFLE – .357 Mag. or .45 LC cal., patterned after the Winchester Model 1873 rifle, case colored frame, 20 in. octagon barrel, 10 shot full mag., uncheckered straight grip walnut stock and forearm. Mfg. 2008-2011.

	$1,150	$925	$750	$650	$525	$425	$375	*$1,350*

MODEL 1876 RIFLE – .45-75 WCF cal., 28 in. octagon barrel with full mag., case colored receiver. Ltd. mfg. 2008.

	$1,350	$1,125	$900	$775	$675	$575	$500	*$1,625*

RIFLES: SEMI-AUTO, RECENT MFG.

BM-59 M-1 GARAND – with original Beretta M1 receiver, M-14 style detachable mag., only 200 imported into the U.S.

	$3,200	$2,900	$2,400	$1,800	$1,500	$1,300	$1,175	*$2,080*

BM-62 – similar to BM-59, except has flash suppressor and is Italian marked.

	$3,200	$2,900	$2,400	$1,800	$1,500	$1,300	$1,175	

AR-70 – .222 Rem. or .223 Rem. cal., semi-auto paramilitary design rifle, 5, 8, or 30 shot mag., diopter sights, epoxy finish, 17.72 in. barrel, 8.3 lbs.

	$1,925	$1,675	$1,375	$1,150	$1,025	$850	$750	*$1,065*

1989 Federal legislation banned the importation of this model into U.S.

ARX 160 – .22 LR cal., 18 in. barrel, 14 shot mag. New 2013.

MSR $585	$495	$425	$365	$335	$315	$285	$250	

CX4 STORM CARBINE – 9mm Para. (92 Carbine), .40 S&W (96 Carbine) or .45 ACP (8045 Carbine) cal., blowback single action, Giugiaro design featuring paramilitary styling with one-piece matte black synthetic stock with thumbhole, rubber recoil pad and stock cheekpiece, quad Picatinny rails, ghost ring sights, 16.6 in. hammer forged barrel, reversible crossbolt safety, mag. button, bolt handle, and ejection port, mag. capacities vary depending on caliber, current mfg. has 8 (.45 ACP cal.), 14 (.40 S&W cal., Px4 Storm mag.), 15 (9mm Para. with high cap Model 92 mag.), or 17 (high cap PX4 Storm mag.) shot mag., (this series also accepts Models 96, 8000, 8040, and 8045 pistol mags.), 29.7 in. overall length, 5 3/4 lbs. New mid-2003.

MSR $915	$795	$625	$550	$495	$450	$395	$350	

Add $95 for 92 Carbine package (includes scope, 9mm Para. (disc. 2005) or .40 S&W cal.). Disc.
Add $50 for top rail (only available in 9mm Para. or .40 S&W cal., mfg. 2006-2007).

This model has been available in many variations - 8045 (.45 ACP), 92 Carbine (8000, 9mm Para.), 92 Carbine package (w/scope), and 96 Carbine (8040, .40 S&W).

RX4 STORM CARBINE – .223 Rem. cal., gas operating system, available in collapsible five position telescoping stock or sporter style stock with optional pistol grip, black matte finish, ghost ring sights, includes 5 and 10 shot AR-15 style magazines. Limited importation 2007-2008.

	$1,100	$925	$800	$700	$600	$525	$450	*$1,100*

While advertised, only a few samples were brought into the U.S.

RIFLES: O/U, CUSTOM

Current high grade Beretta O/U and SxS rifles are sold only by premium grade franchised Beretta dealers. For a listing of these dealers, contact a Beretta Gallery (see Trademark Index).

MODEL S686/S689 SILVER SABLE – .30-06, 9.3x74R, or .444 Marlin cal. (disc. 1995), boxlock action, single or double (special order only) triggers. Importation began 1995.

MSR $4,200	$4,000	$3,500	$3,000	$2,700	$2,200	$2,000	$1,800	

Add $500 for 9.3x74R cal.

MODEL S689 GOLD SABLE – 9.3x74R or .30-06 cal., boxlock action, nickel (disc. 1985) or case hardened (new 1986) receiver, double triggers, 23 in. barrels, auto ejectors, sling swivels, 7.7 lbs.

MSR $9,000	$7,750	$6,500	$5,250	$4,250	$3,300	$2,750	$2,500	

Add $500 for 9.3x74R cal. Add approx. $4,500 for scope and quick detachable claw mounts.

GRADING - PPGS™	100%	98%	95%	90%	80%	70%	60%	LAST MSR

MODEL S686/S689 EELL DIAMOND SABLE – .30-06, 9.3x74R, or .444 Marlin cal., moderate engraving. New 1995.

MSR $12,750	$10,500	$8,750	$7,750	$6,750	$5,975	$5,325	$4,700	

Add $1,250 for an extra set of 20 ga. barrels with forearm (disc. 2011).
Add approx. $4,500 for scope and quick detachable claw mounts.

SSO EXPRESS – .375 H&H or .458 Win. Mag. cal., sidelock action, case hardened receiver, double triggers, 23 in. barrels, auto ejectors, 11 lbs., cased. Importation disc. 1989.

	$15,750	$13,000	$10,500	$8,500	$7,250	$6,500	$6,000	*$17,533*

SSO5 EXPRESS – similar to SSO Express except has more elaborate engraving and better walnut.

	$18,500	$16,250	$14,250	$11,750	$8,750	$7,500	$6,750	*$19,600*

SSO6 EXPRESS CUSTOM SIDELOCK – 9.3x74R, .375 H&H, or .458 Win. Mag. cal., next to top-of-the-line sidelock double rifle, individually built to the customer's specifications, cased. New 1990.

The current MSR on this model is $75,000.
Add $12,000 for extra set of barrels.
Add approx. $4,000 for scope mounts for Zeiss 4x32mm scope.

* ***SS06 EELL Gold Custom*** – same cals. as SS06 Express, features multiple gold inlays and best quality wood.

The current MSR on this model is $125,000.
Add $12,000 for extra set of barrels.
Add approx. $25,000-$45,000 for upgraded master engraving.
Add approx. $4,500 for scope mounts for Zeiss 4x32mm scope.

RIFLES: SxS, CUSTOM

MODEL 455 SIDE-BY-SIDE – .375 H&H, .416 Rigby, .458 Win. Mag., .470 NE, or .500 3 in. NE cal., top of the line sidelock double rifle, individually built to the customer's specifications, color case hardened (new 2010), cased. New 1990.

The current MSR on this model ranges from $95,000 - $110,000, depending on amount of engraving and the engraver.
Add approx. $2,000 for scope mounts for Zeiss 4x32mm scope.

* ***Model 455 EELL*** – similar cals. as Model 455 SxS, top-of-the-line custom sidelock double rifle featuring every refinement of the gunmaker's art, cased.

MSR's on this model range from $125,000 - $175,000, depending on amount of engraving and the engraver.
Add approx. $2,000 for scope mounts for Zeiss 4x32mm scope.

RIFLES: SLIDE ACTION

GOLD RUSH CARBINE/RIFLE – .357 Mag. or .45 LC cal., patterned after Colt Lightning model with improved feeding system and hammer block safety, 20 (carbine), 24 1/4, or 26 (mfg. 2005) in. round or octagon barrel, 10-15 shot full mag., case colored receiver, blued barrel/mag. tube, checkered straight grip stock with Beretta medallions and forearm, adj. sights, 6 1/2 - 7 1/2 lbs. Imported 2005-2008.

	$1,195	$1,050	$925	$800	$675	$550	$475	*$1,375*

Add $475 for deluxe model with oil finished deluxe walnut stock with fish scale checking, charcoal blued barrel and mag. tube, and jeweled hammer. Add $50 for rifle configuration.

SHOTGUNS: O/U, DISC.

Beretta discontinued O/U Models/Variations 682, 685, 686, 687, Onyx Pro, Whitewing, and Blackwing can be found in the Shotguns: O/U, Field - Recent Mfg. category.

BL-1 – 12 ga., 26, 28, or 30 in. barrels with fixed chokes, blued receiver/barrel finish, boxlock, extractors, double triggers, checkered pistol grip stock, approx. 7 lbs. Mfg. 1968-73.

	$395	$350	$300	$250	$200	$150	$125	

BL-2 – similar to BL-1, except with single selective trigger, more engraving.

	$400	$375	$325	$275	$250	$200	$150	

GRADING - PPGS™	100%	98%	95%	90%	80%	70%	60%	LAST MSR

BL-2 STAKE-OUT – riot configuration with 18 in. barrels, DT, blue finish, approx. 6,000 mfg.

	$395	$350	$295	$260	$230	$200	$180	

BL-2/S – similar to BL-2, with vent. rib and speed trigger. Mfg. 1974-76.

	$475	$425	$375	$325	$275	$250	$200	

BL-3 – also available in 20 or 28 ga., blued receiver/barrel finish, similar to BL-2, with more engraving and vent. rib., 6-7 1/4 lbs. Mfg. 1968-1976.

	$600	$550	$500	$450	$400	$350	$300	

Add 100% for 28 ga., if original condition is 90%+.

BL-3 SKEET

	$600	$550	$500	$450	$400	$350	$275	

Subtract 10% for 26 in. barrels.

BL-3 TRAP

	$550	$475	$400	$350	$300	$275	$225	

BL-4 – 12, 20, or 28 ga., 3 in. chambers (12 and 20 ga. only), blued receiver/barrel finish, deluxe version of BL-3, more engraving, better wood, and ejectors, 6-7 1/4 lbs.

	$850	$700	$600	$450	$375	$325	$275	

Add 50% for 20 ga. Add 100% for 28 ga.

BL-4 SKEET

	$700	$650	$500	$400	$350	$300	$250	

Subtract 10% for 26 in. barrels.

BL-4 TRAP

	$600	$550	$500	$425	$350	$300	$250	

BL-5 – 12, 20, or 28 ga., higher grade version of BL-4 with more engraving, matte grey receiver with blued barrels, full pistol grip stock.

	$900	$775	$675	$600	$500	$450	$400	

Add 10% for 20 ga.
Add 100% for 28 ga.

BL-5 SKEET

	$875	$750	$650	$575	$475	$425	$375	

Subtract 10% for 26 in. barrels.

BL-5 TRAP

	$875	$750	$650	$575	$475	$425	$375	

BL-6 – 12, 20, or 28 ga., boxlock with coin finished scroll engraved sideplates, deluxe checkered walnut stock with full pistol grip and slender forearm, ejectors, SST.

	$1,175	$995	$850	$750	$650	$550	$450	

Add 50% for 20 ga.
Add 100% for 28 ga.

BL-6 SKEET

	$1,000	$900	$800	$700	$600	$550	$500	

Subtract 10% for 26 in. barrels.

BL-6 TRAP

	$1,000	$900	$725	$625	$525	$475	$425	

MODEL S55 B – 12 or 20 ga., 26, 28, or 30 in. barrels, various chokes, boxlock, extractors, selective trigger, checkered pistol grip stock. Disc.

	$550	$500	$475	$440	$385	$330	$300	

Add 10% for 20 ga.

MODEL S56 E – similar to S55B, with engraved receiver and auto ejectors. Disc.

	$750	$700	$675	$650	$600	$550	$500	

Add 10% for 20 ga.

GRADING - PPGS™	100%	98%	95%	90%	80%	70%	60%	LAST MSR

MODEL S58 SKEET – similar to S56E, with 26 in. Bohler steel barrels, skeet bore, wide vent. rib.

	$775	$725	$650	$550	$495	$445	$395	

Subtract 10% for 26 in. barrels.

MODEL S58 TRAP – similar to S58 Skeet, with 30 in. barrels, imp. mod. and full choke, Monte Carlo stock with pad.

	$700	$600	$500	$450	$400	$350	$300	

SILVER SNIPE – 12, 20 or 28 ga., 26, 28, or 30 in. barrels, boxlock, extractors, checkered pistol grip stock. Mfg. 1955-1967.

	$700	$650	$600	$550	$500	$425	$400	

Add 50% for 20 ga.
Add 100% for 28 ga.

* ***Silver Snipe SST*** – with vent. rib and SST.

	$700	$650	$600	$550	$500	$475	$400	

Add 50% for 20 ga.
Add 25% for ejectors.
Add 25% for 28 ga.

GOLDEN SNIPE – similar to Silver Snipe, with auto ejectors and vent. rib standard.

	$900	$800	$700	$600	$550	$500	$425	

Add 10% for 20 ga.
Add 100% for 28 ga.

* ***Golden Snipe SST*** – with SST.

	$1,075	$900	$800	$700	$600	$550	$500	

Add 10% for 20 ga.
Add 100% for 28 ga.

MODEL (S)57 E – higher quality version of Golden Snipe. Mfg. 1955-1967.

	$900	$800	$700	$600	$550	$500	$425	

Add 10% for 20 ga.
Add 100% for 28 ga.

* ***Model (S)57 E SST*** – with single selective trigger.

	$1,075	$900	$800	$700	$600	$550	$500	

Add 10% for 20 ga.
Add 100% for 28 ga.

ASE MODEL – 12 or 20 ga., light border scroll engraving, mfg. approx. 1947-1964.

12 ga.	$1,600	$1,400	$1,200	$1,050	$875	$750	$600	
20 ga.	$2,400	$2,200	$1,875	$1,600	$1,400	$1,200	$900	

ASEL MODEL – 12 or 20 ga., 26, 28, or 30 in. barrels, various chokes, single trigger, receiver moderately engraved, checkered pistol grip stock, auto ejectors. Mfg. 1947-1964.

12 ga.	$2,375	$2,000	$1,600	$1,400	$1,200	$900	$700	
20 ga.	$3,950	$3,500	$3,000	$2,500	$2,000	$1,675	$1,375	

ASEELL MODEL – 12 or 20 ga., full coverage engraving, rare, very limited mfg.

12 ga.	$4,000	$3,500	$3,000	$2,500	$2,000	$1,675	$1,325	
20 ga.	$7,400	$6,500	$5,750	$5,000	$4,250	$3,500	$2,750	

GRADE 100 – 12 ga., 26, 28, or 30 in. barrels, any choke, sidelock, double trigger, auto ejectors, checkered pistol grip or straight stock.

	$1,550	$1,300	$1,100	$900	$775	$695	$575	

MODEL 200 – similar to 100, with chrome lined bores and action parts, higher quality engraving.

	$2,000	$1,875	$1,650	$1,375	$1,100	$875	$750	

GRADING - PPGS™	100%	98%	95%	90%	80%	70%	60%	LAST MSR

MODEL 680 – 12 ga. only, competition trap and skeet model, boxlock, various chokes, mono-trap model available, silver finish receiver, hand engraved, premium walnut. Disc.

	$900	$850	$800	$700	$600	$550	$500	

Add approx. $300 for 2 barrel combo. package.

SHOTGUNS: O/U, FIELD - RECENT MFG.

All models listed in this category are field grade configuration regardless of model nomenclature. All currently manufactured Berettas in this category include hardshell cases.

BERETTA CHOKES AND THEIR CODES (ON REAR LEFT-SIDE OF BARREL)

*** designates full choke (F).**

**** designates improved modified choke (IM).**

***** designates modified choke (M).**

****** designates improved cylinder choke (IC).**

******* designates cylinder bore (CYL).**

SK designates skeet (SK).

QUICK REFERENCE GUIDE FOR CURRENT CHOKES

MC3 - includes three Mobilchokes. MC6 - includes six Mobilchokes. MCF - Mobilchoke Field. MCS - Mobilechoke Sport. MCS2 - Mobilechoke Sport 2. OBF - Optima Bore Field. OBF-HP - Optima Bore Field. OBSP - Optima Bore Sporting. OBS - Optima Bore Sport. OBSK - Optima Bore Skeet. OBTR - Optima Bore Trap. OBTS - Optima Bore Trap Single. OCF - Optima Choke Field. OBSP-HP - Optima Bore Sporting HP.

During 2003, Beretta introduced X-Tra Wood on stocks and forearms of select models. X-Tra Wood is a patented and exclusive Beretta wood enhancement finish where average wood is encapsulated with a waterproof film which resembles best quality Circassian walnut. Normal checkering is possible, and all X-Tra Wood stocks are marked clearly on the bottom of the pistol grip cap. It can also be refinished through a special refinishing program available with Beretta USA.

Note: values are for unaltered guns.

Subtract 20% on the following factory multi-choke models if w/o newer Beretta Optima-Chokes (12 ga. only, became standard 2003).

MODEL 685 – 12 or 20 ga. 2 3/4 or 3 in. chambers, matte finished chromed receiver, extractors, single trigger. Disc. 1986.

	$600	$550	$485	$440	$360	$320	$295	*$875*

MODEL 686 ONYX – please refer to Ultralight 687. The 686 Onyx model designation was changed to the Ultralight 687 circa 1997.

MODEL 686 WHITE ONYX FIELD (ONYX) – 12, 20, or 28 (new 2003) ga., 2 3/4 (28 ga. only) or 3 in. chambers, boxlock action, 26 or 28 in. barrels with MobilChokes, matte blue metal (disc. 2003) or Dura-Jewel satin nickel alloy (new 2003, became standard 2004) frame, choice of left (disc.) or right hand standard pistol grip or English straight (disc. 1999) stock with gloss (new 1999), matte (disc. 2003) or X-Tra (standard beginning 2004) wood finish, single trigger, ejectors, approx. 6.2 or 6.8 lbs. Mfg. 1988-2012.

	$1,925	$1,600	$1,400	$1,100	$900	$750	$600	*$2,240*

Add $154 for deluxe wood upgrade (mfg. 2001-2002, included case).
Subtract 10% for matte blue finish.

* ***Model 686 White Onyx Waterfowler Magnum*** – 12 ga. only, similar to Model S686 Onyx, except has 3 1/2 in. chambers, 28 in. barrels only, matte wood and metal finish. Mfg. 1993, reintroduced 1996-2003.

	$1,400	$1,200	$1,000	$800	$650	$525	$450	*$1,648*

* ***Model 686 Onyx Essential*** – 12 ga. only, 3 in. chambers, 26 or 28 in. VR separated barrels with choke tubes, checkered high-gloss walnut stock and forearm, matte finished metal, 6.7 lbs. Mfg. 1994-96.

	$835	$735	$600	$500	$400	$350	$300	*$1,186*

Subtract 10% for 26 in. barrels.

GRADING - PPGS™	100%	98%	95%	90%	80%	70%	60%	LAST MSR

* ***Model S686 Onyx Silver Essential*** – 12 ga. only, 3 in. chambers, 26 or 28 in. VR separated barrels with choke tubes, checkered matte finished walnut stock and forearm, chrome matte finished receiver, 6.7 lbs. Imported 1997-1998 only.

$835 $735 $600 $500 $400 $350 $300 *$1,070*

Subtract 10% for 26 in. barrels.

* ***Model 686 Onyx Quail Unlimited Covey Limited Edition*** – 12 (disc. 2002) 20, or 28 (new 2003) ga., similar to Model 686 Onyx, except includes 6 quail inlays in 24Kt. gold on receiver sides and Quail Unlimited logo on bottom of receiver, marked "1 of 750," deluxe checkered high gloss stock and forearm, cased with 5 choke tubes, 750 of each ga. Mfg. 2002-2004.

$1,475 $1,350 $1,150 $900 $720 $600 $475 *$2,000*

This model was available through Beretta Showcase Dealers only.

* ***Model 686 Onyx Ringneck Pheasants Forever Limited Edition*** – 12 or 20 ga., similar to Onyx Model 686 Quail Unlimited, except includes multiple ringneck pheasant inlays in 24Kt. gold on receiver sides and Pheasants Forever logo on bottom of receiver, marked "1 of 500," deluxe checkered high gloss stock and forearm, cased with 5 choke tubes, 500 of each ga. Mfg. 2003-2004.

$1,475 $1,350 $1,150 $900 $720 $600 $475 *$2,027*

ULTRALIGHT 687 (686/ONYX) – 12 ga. only, 2 3/4 in. chambers, Ergal alloy receiver reinforced with titanium plate, electroless nickel finish receiver with game scene engraving (new 1998, restyled 2002 with several gold inlays) or matte black finish on receiver (disc. 1997) and 26 (disc. 2001) or 28 in. VR barrels, choice of English (new 2001) straight or pistol grip checkered walnut stock and forearm, matte (new 2001, restyled) or gloss wood finish, choke tubes, gilded lettering and logo (disc. 1997), gold SST, ejectors, very light weight, 5 lbs. 11 oz. Imported 1992-2011.

$1,850 $1,675 $1,275 $950 $800 $700 $600 *$2,175*

Add approx. $150 for deluxe wood upgrade (includes case, mfg. 2001 only).
Subtract approx. 10%-15% if with matte black finish, depending on condition.

This model is discontinued as a 686 Series.

* ***Ultralight Deluxe (Onyx)*** – 12 ga. only, 2 3/4 in. chambers, similiar to 1998 Model 686 Ultralight, except has gold game scene engraving and select walnut stock and forearm, 28 in. barrels. Mfg. began 1998.

MSR $2,550 $2,290 $1,950 $1,750 $1,485 $1,250 $1,000 $800

ONYX PRO – 12, 20, or 28 ga., 2 3/4 (28 ga. only) or 3 in. chambers, matte blue finish with Dura-Jewel treatment on receiver, X-Tra wood finish on stock and forearm, Gel-tek recoil pad, gold trigger, TruGlo sights, includes case and 5 choke tubes, 6.8 lbs. (12 ga.). Imported 2003-2006.

$1,650 $1,300 $1,100 $950 $800 $650 $500 *$1,875*

* ***Onyx Pro 3.5*** – 12 ga., 3 1/2 in. chambers, otherwise similar to Onyx Pro, 6.9 lbs. Imported 2003-2006.

$1,650 $1,325 $1,150 $975 $825 $675 $595 *$1,975*

WHITEWING – 12 or 20 ga., 3 in. chambers, 26 or 28 in. separated VR barrels and MC3 choke tubes, similar to Model 686 Silver Essential, except has checkered gloss finish walnut stock and silver polished receiver with game scene engraving, 6.7 lbs. Mfg. 1999-2003.

$975 $825 $625 $525 $475 $425 $375 *$1,332*

BLACKWING – similar to Whitewing, except has matte black receiver finish, lower stock dimensions, and Schnabel forearm. Mfg. 2002-2003.

$1,095 $950 $875 $750 $650 $525 $400 *$1,332*

MODEL 686(L) SILVER PERDIZ – 12 (disc. 1990), 20 (disc. 1990), or 28 ga., field model, boxlock action, various barrels/ chokes, ejectors, single trigger, engraved silver finished receiver, special walnut, pistol or straight grip stock, fixed chokes disc. 1987. Importation disc. 1994.

$975 $825 $625 $525 $475 $425 $375 *$1,355*

Subtract 20% with fixed chokes (disc.). Add 20% for 20 ga., or 30% for 28 ga.

GRADING - PPGS™	100%	98%	95%	90%	80%	70%	60%	LAST MSR

MODEL 686 SILVER PIGEON S & SILVER PIGEON (SILVER PERDIZ) – 12, 20, or 28 (mfg. 1995-2001, reintroduced 2004) ga. or .410 bore (new 2005), 3 in. chambers (except for 28 ga.), 26 or 28 in. VR barrels with choke tubes, choice of polished (new 1999) or regular nickel finished receiver with scroll engraving, gold trigger, gloss finish checkered pistol grip or straight grip (disc. 1999) walnut stock and forearm, supplied with carrying case, 5 choke tubes, recoil pad and sling swivels beginning 2004, includes hardshell case, 6.8 lbs. Mfg. 1992-2008.

	$2,000	$1,550	$1,365	$1,050	$825	$700	$600	*$2,450*

Add $153 for deluxe wood upgrade (Silver Pigeon only, 12 or 20 ga. only, includes case, mfg. 2001-2002).

During 1996, the model nomenclature was changed from the Silver Perdiz to the Silver Pigeon.

* ***Model 686 Silver Pigeon S King Ranch*** – 20 or 28 ga. only, similar to Model 686 Silver Pigeon, except features special cowboy and western engraving motifs. Mfg. 2006-2010.

	$2,500	$2,200	$1,750	$1,500	$1,150	$900	$775	*$2,800*

* ***Model 686 Silver Pigeon S (Silver Perdiz) and 686 Silver Pigeon Combo*** – similar to Model 686 Onyx, except is supplied with 1 set each of 20 ga. (28 in.) and 28 ga. (26 in.) barrels, includes carrying case, 5 choke tubes, recoil pad, and sling swivels, polished receiver became standard 1999. Mfg. 1986-2008.

	$2,775	$2,415	$1,900	$1,600	$1,250	$1,000	$875	*$3,175*

Subtract 10% for 26 in. barrels.

MODEL 686 SILVER PIGEON I – 12, 20 (new 2012), 28 (new 2012) or .410 (new 2012) ga., 3 in. chambers, 26, 28, or 30 in. VR barrels with 3 MobilChokes, coin finished receiver, checkered oil-finished stock and Schnabel forearm, SST, ejectors. New 2011.

MSR $2,240	$1,925	$1,475	$1,250	$1,050	$875	$700	$550	

* ***Model S686 Silver Pigeon I Combo*** – choice of 20 and 28 ga. barrels or 28 ga/.410 bore barrels. New 2012.

MSR $3,675	$3,200	$2,600	$2,200	$1,800	$1,500	$1,300	$1,250	

MODEL S686 EL GOLD PERDIZ – 12 or 20 ga., 3 in. chambers, boxlock action with floral scroll engraved sideplates, silver receiver finish, 26 or 28 (20 ga. only beginning 1997) in. VR barrels with choke tubes, gold SST, checkered walnut stock and forearm, cased, approx. 6.8 lbs. Mfg. 1992-1997.

	$1,600	$1,425	$1,200	$1,000	$875	$800	$695	*$1,930*

Add 10% for 20 ga.

Subtract 10% for 26 in. barrels.

MODEL S687(L) SILVER PIGEON – 12 (disc. 1999) or 20 ga., 3 in. chambers, boxlock, various barrels/chokes, ejectors, game scene engraved nickel finished receiver, gloss finished select walnut stock and forearm, approx. 6.8 lbs., fitted case was optional. Disc. 2000.

	$1,600	$1,425	$1,200	$1,000	$875	$750	$695	*$2,255*

Subtract 30% without MobilChokes (disc.).

Subtract 10% for 26 in. barrels.

The "L" suffix model nomenclature was disc. 1996.

MODEL S687 SILVER PIGEON II – 12 or 20 ga., similar to Model S687 Silver Pigeon, except has deep relief engraved game scenes on receiver sides and oil finished (matte) walnut stock and forearm, 26 or 28 in. VR barrels with MC3 choke tubes. Mfg. 1999-2011.

	$2,740	$2,190	$1,975	$1,580	$1,265	$1,000	$825	*$3,050*

* ***Model S687 Silver Pigeon II Combo*** – includes 1 set each of 28 ga. and 20 ga. with 28 in. barrels, cased with 5 choke tubes. Imported 2003-2010.

	$3,400	$2,750	$2,275	$1,900	$1,600	$1,400	$1,200	*$4,050*

MODEL 687 SILVER PIGEON III – 12, 20, or 28 ga., 26 or 28 in. VR barrels, engraved boxlock action with game scenes, select checkered walnut stock and forearm, Gel-Tek recoil pad, gold SST, TruGlo front sight, 6.8 lbs. New 2004.

MSR $3,430	$2,850	$2,175	$1,850	$1,400	$1,125	$975	$875	

A left hand variation was disc. in 2007.

GRADING - PPGS™	100%	98%	95%	90%	80%	70%	60%	LAST MSR

MODEL 687 SILVER PIGEON IV – 12, 20, or 28 ga., 2 3/4 (28 ga. only) or 3 in. chambers, black metal finished receiver with full coverage scroll engraving and 4 gold bird inlays, 26 or 28 in. barrels, checkered oil finished walnut stock with Gel-Tek recoil pad, TruGlo front sight, includes molded case with 5 choke tubes, 6.8 lbs. (12 ga.). Imported 2003-2008.

	$2,700	$2,100	$1,800	$1,400	$1,100	$1,000	$900	*$3,150*

* ***Model 687 Silver Pigeon IV King Ranch*** – 20 or 28 ga., similar to Model 687 Silver Pigeon IV, except has special cowboy and western engraving motifs. Mfg. 2006-2009.

	$3,375	$2,875	$2,175	$1,800	$1,400	$1,050	$875	*$3,375*

MODEL 687 SILVER PIGEON V – 12, 20, 28 ga., or .410 bore (new 2005), 26 or 28 in. barrels, case colored finished receiver with gold bird inlays, 28 ga. is on a true "baby frame," upgraded select oil finished checkered straight grip English (not available in 12 ga.) or pistol grip walnut stock and forearm, gold SST, Gel-Tek recoil pad, Schnabel forend, 6.8 lbs., includes hardshell case. New 2004.

MSR $4,075	$3,450	$2,775	$2,225	$1,900	$1,550	$1,250	$1,125	

MODEL 687 DU – 12 (1990 release) or 20 ga., mfg. for DU dinner gun auctions and membership, prices may vary significantly from region to region.

	$1,200	$1,050	$925	$800	$700	$575	$475	

Add 10% for 20 ga.

MODEL 687 BLACK & GOLD TERCENTENNIAL – 12 ga. only, 2 3/4 in. chambers, 28 in. barrels with fixed F/M chokes, bottom of blued receiver features special 1680-1980 Tercentennial logo, inlaid (with gold) and engraved by Giovanelli (signed), ser. no. 001-300.

	$1,800	$1,675	$1,500	$1,225	$995	$900	$800	

MODEL 687 TERCENTENNIAL COMMEMORATIVE – 12 ga. only, 2 3/4 in. chambers, 28 in. barrels, engraved and signed by Giovanelli, with ducks and woodcocks on sides of grey finished frame, oil finished walnut stock and forearm, ser. no. 001-200.

	$1,800	$1,675	$1,500	N/A	N/A	N/A	N/A	

MODEL 687 L ONYX – 12 or 20 ga., 3 in. chambers, same game scene engraving as standard Model 687 L, except has Onyx blackened receiver, multi-chokes standard. Mfg. 1990 only.

	$1,150	$1,000	$900	$750	$650	$575	$525	*$1,590*

Add 15% for 20 ga.

MODEL 687 GOLDEN ONYX – 12 or 20 ga., 3 in. chambers, similar to Model 686 Onyx, except has more engraving, better walnut, and several gold inlays. Imported 1988-89 only.

	$1,375	$1,275	$995	$825	$700	$650	$575	*$1,800*

Add 15% for 20 ga.
Subtract 10% for 26 in. barrels.

MODEL S687 EL GOLD PIGEON – same general specifications as Model 687L, except also available in 28 ga. (new 1990) or .410 (new 1990) bore, 20 ga. disc. 2001, 2 3/4 or 3 in. chambers, boxlock with gold inlaid game scene on sideplates, highly figured walnut, and more engraving, oval nameplate, approx. 6.8 lbs, cased. Disc. 2002.

	$2,600	$2,200	$1,950	$1,575	$1,350	$1,150	$1,000	*$4,099*

Add $100 for 28 ga.
Subtract 10% for 26 in. barrels.

* ***Model 687 EL DU*** – 28 ga. or .410 bore, small frame, released 1992 for DU auctions and membership.

	$2,300	$2,000	$1,800	$1,550	$1,400	$1,200	$1,050	

MODEL S687 EL GOLD PIGEON II – 12, 20, 28 ga., or .410 bore, similar to EL Gold Pigeon, except features deep relief engraving on sideplates, 6.8 lbs., cased. Mfg. 2001-2006.

	$4,325	$3,525	$3,150	$2,625	$2,050	$1,800	$1,500	*$5,095*

* ***S687 Gold Pigeon II Combo*** – includes either 20 and 28 ga. barrels or 28 ga. and .410 bore barrels, cased with 5 choke tubes. Imported 2003-2007.

	$5,475	$4,375	$3,800	$3,200	$2,825	$2,475	$2,050	*$6,400*

GRADING - PPGS™	100%	98%	95%	90%	80%	70%	60%	LAST MSR

MODEL 687 EL ONYX – 12 or 20 ga., 3 in. chambers, simulated sidelock plates with classic scroll engraving. Mfg. 1990 only.

	$1,895	$1,700	$1,500	$1,350	$1,075	$950	$800	*$2,660*

Subtract 10% for 26 in. barrels.

MODEL S687 EELL DIAMOND PIGEON – 12, 20, 28 (available in combo only beginning 2012) ga. or .410 bore (new 2003), boxlock action, silver receiver with full sideplates and hand engraved game scenes (new motif began 2012, except on .410 bore), 26 or 28 in. VR barrels, 3 in. (except 28 ga.) chambers and gold plated trigger, cased, MobilChokes introduced 1988, 6.8 lbs.

MSR $7,830	$6,725	$5,100	$4,350	$3,695	$3,000	$2,500	$1,800	

Add $400 for King Ranch model with special cowboy and western engraving motifs (mfg. 2006-2011).
Add 10%-20% for earlier mfg. with hand chased engraving (non-machine engraved), depending on condition.
Subtract 20% if without MobilChokes.
Subtract 10% for 26 in. barrels.

This model is also available with a straight grip English stock at no extra charge (20 ga. only).

If hand engraved, the engraver's name will be next to the trigger guard.

* ***Model S687 EELL Combo*** – includes either 20 and 28 ga. or 28 ga. and .410 bore MobilChoke 26 or 28 in. barrels, cased. Limited importation.

MSR $9,505	$7,995	$6,750	$5,700	$4,700	$3,850	$3,200	$2,700	

Subtract 20% for fixed chokes.

MobileChokes became standard in 1991.

* ***Model S687 EELL Gallery Edition*** – 12, 20, 28 ga., or .410 bore, available as a pair (optional) or 2 barrel sets, featuring special engraving and upgraded wood with oil finish. New 2000.

Prices start at $8,250 for single guns and go up for 2 barrel sets, depending on ga. and options. Pairs start at $16,675. Available at Beretta Galleries only.

MODEL S687 EXTRA – 12, 20, 28 ga., or .410 bore, available in pairs or 2 barrel sets (special order only), features special engraving and upgraded wood with oil finish. New 2001.

Prices start at $8,250 for Field Model, and vary depending on ga. and options. Pairs start at approx. $16,675. Available at Beretta Premium dealers only.

MODEL ASE 90 PIGEON – 12 ga. only, 28 in. fixed choke (IM/F) barrels with VR, new design features nickel-chromium-molybdenum receiver with special hardening and cross bolt engaging 2 monobloc lugs, detachable trigger grouping, V-shaped main springs, cold hammered barrels, choice of silver or blue receiver with gold etching and no engraving, top quality checkered walnut stock and forearm with vent. recoil pad, choke tubes, 7 lbs. 13 oz., cased. Imported 1992-1994.

	$3,650	$3,225	$2,950	$2,650	$2,300	$2,000	$1,750	*$8,070*

SV10 PERENNIA III – 12 (disc. 2012) or 20 (new 2011) ga., boxlock action, 3 in. chamber, 26, 28, or 30 (disc. 2010) in. barrels, select matte finished checkered pistol grip walnut stock with or w/o Kick-Off recoil mechanism, titanium SST, semi-beavertail forend, Optima-Choke/s, patented Q-stock quick takedown system that features shortened stock bolt built into back of trigger system, alloy laser engraved receiver, removable trigger group, approx. 7.3 lbs. New mid-2008.

MSR $3,620	$3,050	$2,550	$2,125	$1,850	$1,550	$1,275	$1,100	

Add $325 for Kick-Off recoil system (avail. only in 20 ga. beginning 2011).
Subtract $750 for 12 ga. without Kick-Off recoil system.

SV10 PERENNIA I – 12 or 20 ga., 26 or 28 in. VR barrels with optima bore field chokes, satin finished receiver with classic floral pattern engraving, checkered walnut stock and forearm, available with standard or Kick-Off recoil pad. New 2012.

MSR $2,890	$2,475	$2,100	$1,825	$1,600	$1,400	$1,200	$975	

Add $405 for Kick-Off recoil pad.

GRADING - PPGS™	100%	98%	95%	90%	80%	70%	60%	LAST MSR

SHOTGUNS: O/U, SKEET - RECENT MFG.

Full descriptions for the following models may be found under the corresponding model numbers in the Field Shotguns category.

QUICK REFERENCE GUIDE FOR CURRENT CHOKES

MC3 - includes three MobilChokes. MC6 - includes six MobilChokes. OBSK - OptimaBore Skeet.

Note: values are for unaltered guns.

Subtract 20% on the following factory MobilChoke models if w/o newer Beretta OptimaChokes (12 ga. only, became standard 2003).

MODEL S682 GOLD SKEET – 12, 20 (disc. 1991), 28 ga. (disc. 1988), or .410 bore (disc. 1988), competition skeet model, 26 (disc.) or 28 in. barrels, boxlock, skeet chokes, silver finish (disc.) or Greystone (titanium nitrate) receiver, hand engraved, premium walnut, cased. Mfg. 1984-99.

	100%	98%	95%	90%	80%	70%	60%	LAST MSR
	$1,400	$1,300	$1,275	$1,025	$900	$800	$700	$2,850

Subtract 20% for 26 in. barrels.
Subtract 20% for fixed chokes.
Subtract 20% for silver finish.

* ***Model S682 Gold Skeet With Adj. Stock*** – similar to Model S682 Gold Skeet, except has fully adj. stock, allowing the comb, drop, and cast to be adjusted per shooter. Imported 1999-2000.

	100%	98%	95%	90%	80%	70%	60%	LAST MSR
	$1,600	$1,500	$1,450	$1,350	$1,075	$950	$825	$3,515

* ***Model S682 Gold E Skeet*** – 12 ga. only, 28 or 30 in. VR barrels with OptimaBore and OptimaChoke, adj. stock with memory system, dual color finished receiver with engraved merging circular lines and gold highlights, including trigger, deluxe wide checkered stock and Schnabel forearm with gloss wood finish, 7.6 lbs. New 2001.

	100%	98%	95%	90%	80%	70%	60%	LAST MSR
MSR $4,805	$4,000	$3,150	$2,500	$2,250	$2,000	$1,650	$1,425	

* ***Model 682 Super Skeet*** – 12 ga. only, 28 in. VR barrels bored SK/SK, factory porting, stock has separate adj. comb cheekpiece. Mfg. 1991-1995.

	100%	98%	95%	90%	80%	70%	60%	LAST MSR
	$1,500	$1,300	$1,200	$1,100	$1,050	$900	$800	$3,006

* ***Model 682 Skeet Deluxe*** – similar to Model 682, except deluxe walnut and elaborate engraving. Disc. 1986.

	100%	98%	95%	90%	80%	70%	60%	LAST MSR
	$1,850	$1,700	$1,550	$1,250	$1,050	$900	$800	$3,000

* ***Model 682 2-Barrel Skeet Set*** – 12 ga. only, two barrel set bored for skeet and sporting clays competition. Imported 1988 only.

	100%	98%	95%	90%	80%	70%	60%	LAST MSR
	$2,400	$2,150	$2,000	$1,850	$1,600	$1,400	$1,300	$6,650

Subtract 25% if w/o choke tubes.

* ***Model 682 4-Ga. Skeet Set*** – four barrel skeet set comes with interchangeable barrels (28 in.) in 12, 20, 28 gauges, and .410 bore. Imported 1985-95.

	100%	98%	95%	90%	80%	70%	60%	LAST MSR
	$3,300	$3,100	$3,000	$2,850	$2,500	$2,175	$1,900	$6,037

Subtract 10% for silver frame.

MODEL S686 SKEET SILVER PERDIZ/SILVER PIGEON – 12 ga. only, 28 in. VR barrels bored SK/SK, checkered walnut stock and forearm, Silver Perdiz was disc. 1996 and featured silver finish, while Silver Pigeon nomenclature began 1997 and features nickel finish, 7.6 lbs. Imported 1994-98.

	100%	98%	95%	90%	80%	70%	60%	LAST MSR
	$825	$775	$700	$675	$625	$550	$480	$1,795

MODEL S687 EELL SKEET DIAMOND PIGEON – 12 ga. only, fixed chokes, 28 in. barrels, elaborate game scene engraving on sideplates, cased. Disc. 2002.

	100%	98%	95%	90%	80%	70%	60%	LAST MSR
	$2,750	$2,500	$2,250	$2,000	$1,800	$1,500	$1,250	$4,984

* ***Model S687 EELL Skeet Diamond Pigeon With Adj. Stock*** – similar to Model S687 EELL Skeet Diamond Pigeon, except has fully adj. stock, allowing the comb, drop, and cast to be adjusted per shooter. Imported 1999-2004.

	100%	98%	95%	90%	80%	70%	60%	LAST MSR
	$4,600	$4,200	$3,950	$3,750	$3,250	$2,600	$2,150	$6,207

GRADING - PPGS™	100%	98%	95%	90%	80%	70%	60%	*LAST MSR*

* ***Model S687 EELL 4-Ga. Skeet Set*** – 4 ga. skeet set, cased. Imported 1988-1998.

$5,000 $4,600 $4,200 $3,750 $3,400 $2,900 $2,450 ***$8,405***

DT10 TRIDENT SKEET – 12 ga. only, 3 in. chambers, 28 or 30 in. vent. barrels with target VR, specially designed skeet gun featuring removable adj. trigger group, massive crossbolt locking system, OptimaChokes competition choke tubes, OptimaBore internal barrel configuration, specific point of impact, and unique distribution of mass that helps target acquisition and eliminate muzzle rise, adj. walnut stock with memory system, carbon reinforced frame, 7.9 lbs. Mfg. 2000-2009.

$6,650 $5,000 $4,500 $4,000 $3,600 $3,150 $2,550 ***$7,900***

MODEL ASE 90 GOLD SKEET – 12 ga. only, 28 in. fixed choke vent. barrels with VR, similar action and specifications as the Model ASE 90 Pigeon, except has more elaborate hand scroll engraving and extra fine wood, 7.6 lbs., cased. Mfg. 1992-99.

$3,600 $3,400 $3,250 $3,000 $2,750 $2,500 $2,250 ***$12,060***

SHOTGUNS: O/U, SPORTING CLAYS - RECENT MFG.

These variations have been specifically designed for sporting clay target shooting. All of the following models have 3 in. chambers, unless specified otherwise. Full descriptions for the following models may be found under the corresponding model numbers in the Field Shotguns category.

QUICK REFERENCE GUIDE FOR CURRENT CHOKES - see all current listings in the Shotguns: O/U, Field - Recent Mfg. section.

Subtract 10% for 28 in. barrels on all used Sporting models in this section.

Subtract 20% on the following factory multi-choke models if w/o newer Beretta Optima-Chokes (12 ga. only, became standard 2003).

MODEL S682 CONTINENTAL COURSE – 12 ga. only, 2 3/4 in. chambers, 28 or 30 (disc. 1995) in. VR barrels with MobilChokes, designed for English Sporting Clays courses, previously was Model Super Sport with tapered rib, cased. Mfg. 1993-97.

$1,400 $1,300 $1,200 $975 $875 $775 $675 ***$2,345***

MODEL S682 GOLD SPORTING – 12 or 20 (mfg. 1992-94) ga., similar specifications to Model 682 Skeet, 2 3/4 in. chambers, 28, 30 (new 1989), or 31 (new 1997) in. unported or ported (new 1995) VR barrels, except over-field stock dimensions and hand engraved silver (disc.) or Greystone (titanium nitrate) finished receiver, cased, 7.6 lbs. MobilChokes were standard. Disc. 2000.

$1,650 $1,500 $1,250 $1,075 $950 $875 $800 ***$3,100***

Add $500 for extra set of 12 ga. barrels (combo. package - mfg. 1990-94).

* ***Model S682 Gold E Sporting*** – 12 ga. only, 28 (disc. 2011), 30 or 32 in. VR barrels with OptimaBore and OptimaChokes, dual color finished receiver with engraved merging circular lines and gold highlights, including trigger, select wide checkered stock and Schnabel forearm with gloss wood finish, approx. 7.6 lbs. New 2001.

MSR $4,590 $3,850 $3,150 $2,475 $1,925 $1,650 $1,425 $1,200

MODEL 682 SUPER SPORTING – 12 ga. only, 2 3/4 in. chambers, 28 or 30 in. VR ported (new 1993) barrels with MobilChokes and tapered rib, otherwise similar to Model 682 Sporting, cased, 7.6 lbs. Imported 1989-1995.

$1,500 $1,375 $1,250 $1,100 $950 $875 $800 ***$3,017***

Beginning 1993, this model featured a special fully adj. stock and LOP.

MODEL 682 LTD – 12 ga. only, 30 or 32 in. barrels, limited edition mfg. 2006.

$4,100 $3,600 $3,175 $2,775 $2,300 $2,000 $1,650 ***$5,075***

MODEL 686 SPORTING/SPECIAL SPORTING – 12 ga. only, 3 in. chambers, deluxe checkered walnut stock and forearm with over-field dimensions, 28 or 30 (new 1991) in. barrels only, MobileChokes standard. Mfg. 1987-1992.

$1,200 $1,100 $925 $825 $675 $625 $550 ***$1,940***

The Model 686 Special Sporting is marked "Model S686 Special," and the barrels are marked "Sporting."

GRADING - PPGS™	100%	98%	95%	90%	80%	70%	60%	LAST MSR

* ***Model S686 Silver Pigeon (Silver Perdiz) Sporting*** – 12 or 20 (disc. 2000) ga., 28 or 30 in. VR barrels with MobilChokes, 7.7 lbs. Mfg. 1993-2002.

	$1,300	$1,175	$995	$850	$725	$650	$575	$1,931

Add $139 for deluxe wood upgrade (includes case, mfg. 2001-2002).

Until 1994, this model was named the Model 686 Hunter Sport. Between 1994-95, this model was named the S686 Silver Perdiz, and beginning 1996, this model was again renamed to the 686 Silver Pigeon Sporting.

* ***Model 686 E Sporting*** – 12, 20 or 28 ga., 3 in. chambers, 28 (20 ga. only) or 30 in. VR barrels with 5 chokes, improved styling, oil finished walnut stock and Schnabel forearm, includes accessories, 5 choke tubes, and carrying case, 7.7 lbs. Mfg. 2001-2004.

	$1,475	$1,275	$1,075	$975	$850	$750	$650	$2,008

* ***Model 686 Silver Perdiz/S686 Silver Pigeon Sporting Combo*** – 12 ga., includes extra set of 30 in. barrels. Model 686 Silver Perdiz was manufactured 1991-95, Model S686 Silver Pigeon was manufactured 1997-99.

	$1,925	$1,700	$1,475	$1,250	$1,025	$900	$800	$2,210.

Last MSR was $2,687 for the 686 Silver Perdiz Combo.

MODEL 686 COLLECTION SPORT – 12 ga. only, features multi-colored checkered wood stock and forearm, 28 in. VR barrels, 7.7 lbs. Mfg. 1996 only.

	$900	$775	$650	$550	$475	$400	$350	$1,499

MODEL 686 ONYX SPORTING – 12 ga. only, 28 or 30 in. vent. fixed choke barrels with VR, high luster blue finish with gold lettering on receiver sides. Mfg. 1992 only.

	$900	$775	$650	$550	$475	$400	$350	$1,940

* ***Model 686 Onyx Sporting w/Multi-chokes*** – 12 ga. only, 28 or 30 in. VR barrels with MultiChokes, matte wood finish, choice of semi-matte black (disc. 1998) or polished black receiver with "P. Beretta" engraved in gold, 7.7 lbs. Mfg. 1993-2002.

	$1,200	$1,050	$925	$800	$700	$600	$500	$1,639

Add approx. 15% for deluxe wood upgrade (includes case, mfg. 2001-2002).

* ***Model 686 English Course*** – 12 ga. only, features 28 in. VR barrels and special reverse tapered VR with special sighting plane designed for English courses. Mfg. 1991-92.

	$995	$895	$775	$675	$600	$500	$400	$2,015

MODEL 686 WHITE ONYX SPORTING – 12 ga. only, 30 or 32 in. VR barrels, nickel alloy finish, gold SST, oil finished checkered select walnut stock and forearm, black rubber recoil pad, Schnabel forend, 7-8 1/2 lbs. Mfg. 2004-2012.

	$2,000	$1,575	$1,425	$1,125	$875	$700	$600	$2,460

MODEL S687(L) SILVER PIGEON (SILVER PERDIZ) SPORTING – 12 or 20 ga. only, deluxe checkered walnut stock and forearm with over-field dimensions, game scene engraved, 28 or 30 (12 ga. only) in. barrels, Mobilchokes standard. Mfg. 1987-2001.

	$1,450	$1,350	$1,215	$975	$875	$775	$675	$2,363

* ***Model 687 Silver Pigeon Sporting Combo*** – 12 ga., includes set of 28 and 30 in. barrels. Mfg. 2002 only.

	$1,850	$1,725	$1,600	$1,400	$1,200	$1,000	$875	$3,151

* ***Model 687 English Course*** – 12 ga. only, features 28 in. VR barrels and special reverse tapered VR with special sighting plane designed for English courses. Mfg. 1991-92.

	$1,500	$1,400	$1,300	$1,075	$975	$895	$800	$2,630

MODEL S686 SILVER PIGEON I SPORTING – 12 ga. only, 3 in. chambers, 30 or 32 in. VR barrels with OBS chokes, otherwise similar to Model S686 Silver Pigeon 1 Field. New 2011.

MSR $2,240	$1,925	$1,575	$1,325	$1,025	$800	$650	$500	

MODEL S687 SILVER PIGEON II SPORTING – 12, 20 (new 2002), or 28 ga. (new 2002), features deep relief game scene engraving on receiver sides, matte oil finished select walnut stock and forearm, 28, 30, or 32 (12 ga. only, new 2002) in. OptimaBore barrels, OptimaChoke

GRADING - PPGS™	100%	98%	95%	90%	80%	70%	60%	LAST MSR

extended tubes became standard on 12 ga. in 2003, 7.7 lbs. Importation began 1999.

MSR $3,700	$3,100	$2,350	$1,950	$1,625	$1,375	$1,100	$875	

Subtract 20% if w/o Optima-Choke/s.

MODEL S687 SILVER PIGEON III SPORTING – 12 ga. only, 30 or 32 in. VR barrels, select checkered walnut stock and forearm, game scene engraving on receiver sides, floral and scroll engraving on bottom of receiver and trigger guard, approx. 8 lbs. Mfg. 2004-2009.

	$2,850	$2,280	$2,000	$1,600	$1,350	$1,100	$900	*$3,425*

MODEL S687 EL GOLD PIGEON SPORTING – 12 ga. only, 28 or 30 in. VR barrels with MobileChokes, 7.7 lbs. Mfg. 1993-2001.

	$2,650	$1,900	$1,675	$1,450	$1,250	$1,050	$875	*$4,182*

MODEL S687 EL GOLD PIGEON II SPORTING – 12, 20 (new 2003), 28 ga., or .410 bore (new 2003), similar to Model S687 Gold Pigeon Sporting, except features deep relief engraving on sideplates, also available in 28 ga. and 32 in. barrels beginning 2002, OptimaBore barrels with OptimaChoke flush tubes became standard on 12 ga. in 2003. Mfg. 2001-2006.

	$4,200	$3,700	$3,200	$2,850	$2,350	$2,025	$1,600	*$5,495*

* ***Model 687 EL Gold Pigeon II Sporting 20 ga./.410 Bore*** – includes set of 20 ga. and .410 bore barrels, cased. Imported 2003 only.

	$4,500	$4,000	$3,350	$2,850	$2,350	$1,975	$1,625	*$6,071*

* ***Model 687 EL Gold Pigeon II Sporting Combo*** – 28 ga. and .410 bore, includes set of 30 in. barrels. Mfg. 2002-2007.

	$5,100	$4,300	$3,700	$3,100	$2,950	$2,800	$2,375	*$6,600*

MODEL S687 EELL DIAMOND PIGEON SPORTING – 12, 20 (disc. 1992, reintroduced 2003), 28 (new 2003) ga. or .410 bore (mfg. 2003-2011), features fine scroll engraving on receiver and sideplates (new motif on 12 ga. only began 2012), deluxe checkered walnut stock and forearm with over-field dimensions, 28 (disc. 2011), 30 (new 1995), or 32 (new 2002) in. barrels only, OptimaBore barrels with OptimaChoke flush tubes became standard on 12 ga. in 2003 or with MobilChokes, cased, 7.6 lbs. New 1987.

MSR $8,400	$7,400	$6,250	$5,500	$4,650	$3,700	$2,950	$2,100	

Add $1,500 for extra set of barrels (combo. package - 1990 mfg. only).
Subtract 10% if w/o OptimaChokes.

DT10 TRIDENT SPORTING – 12 ga. only, 3 in. chambers, 28, 30, or 32 in. vent. OptimaBore barrels with target VR, specially designed sporting gun featuring removable adj. trigger group, massive crossbolt locking system, OptimaChoke competition choke tubes, specific point of impact, and unique distribution of mass which helps target acquisition and eliminate muzzle rise, deluxe checkered walnut stock and Schnabel forearm, carbon reinforced frame, cased, approx. 8 lbs. New 2000.

MSR $7,500	$6,750	$6,100	$5,125	$4,150	$3,600	$3,100	$2,500	

* ***DT10 Trident L Sporting*** – 12 ga., 30 or 32 in. barrels, floral engraved receiver and trigger guard, palm swell, adj. trigger. New 2004.

MSR $9,500	$8,100	$6,900	$5,875	$4,975	$3,950	$3,300	$2,600	

* ***DT10 Trident EELL Sporting*** – 12 ga., 30 or 32 in. barrels, hand engraved, upgraded wood. New 2004.

MSR $15,750	$14,500	$12,000	$10,250	$9,000	$8,000	$7,000	$6,000	

This model is available by special order through Beretta Galleries only.

MODEL ASE 90 GOLD SPORTING CLAYS – 12 ga. only, 28, 30, or 31 (new 1997) in. vent. barrels with VR, similar action and specifications to Model ASE 90 Pigeon, 7 1/2 lbs., cased. Mfg. 1992-99.

	$3,800	$3,600	$3,400	$3,250	$3,000	$2,850	$2,500	*$12,145*

SV10 PREVAIL I SPORTING – 12 ga., 30 or 32 in. separated VR barrels with OBSP-HP choke tubes, satin finished boxlock aluminum receiver, choice of extraction or ejection, titanium

GRADING - PPGS™	100%	98%	95%	90%	80%	70%	60%	LAST MSR

trigger, quick takedown stock allows disassembly in a few seconds, regular or Kick-Off recoil pad. New 2012.

MSR $2,900	$2,495	$2,125	$1,825	$1,600	$1,400	$1,200	$975	

Add $400 for Kick-Off recoil pad.

SV10 PREVAIL III SPORTING – 12 ga., 3 in. chamber, 26, 28, 30, or 32 in. OptimaBore barrels with five OptimaChoke High Performance tubes, vent. rib, dual locking lugs, coin finished receiver with or w/o game scene engraving, Alpacca sights, titanium SST, beavertail forend, quick take down stock with pistol grip, optional Kick-Off recoil reduction, rubber recoil pad, sling swivels, and case, approx. 7.7 lbs. New mid-2009.

MSR $3,295	$2,825	$2,250	$1,925	$1,475	$1,125	$975	$850	

Add $325 for Kick-Off recoil system.

SHOTGUNS: O/U, TRAP - RECENT MFG.

QUICK REFERENCE GUIDE FOR CURRENT CHOKES

MC3 - includes three Mobilchokes. MC6 - includes six Mobilchokes. OBTR - Optima Bore Trap. OBTS - Optima Bore Trap Single.

Note: values are for unaltered trap guns.

Subtract 20% on the following factory multi-choke models if w/o newer Beretta Optima-chokes (12 ga. only, became standard 2003).

Subtract 10% for 28 in. barrels on used Trap models.

MODEL S682 GOLD TRAP (GOLD X) – 12 ga. only, competition trap model, Greystone (titanium nitrate) or Bruniton finish (matte black, disc.), 30 or 32 in. barrels with or w/o choke tubes (became standard 1996), adj. trigger, supplied with case, 8.8 lbs. Mfg. 1985-2000.

	$1,650	$1,350	$1,200	$1,050	$900	$775	$650	*$3,100*

Subtract 15% for Bruniton finish.
Subtract 20% if w/o choke tubes.

* ***Model S682 Mono/Top Combo Trap (Gold X)*** – 12 ga. only, supplied with mono under or upper single barrel and O/U barrel sets, MobilChokes became standard 1996, otherwise same specifications as Model S682 Gold Trap, cased. Disc. 2000.

	$2,000	$1,850	$1,700	$1,600	$1,400	$1,200	$1,000	*$4,085*

Subtract 15% for Bruniton finish.

* ***Model S682 Gold Trap Adjustable Stock*** – 12 ga. only, features Monte Carlo style stock with adj. comb, 30 or 32 in. barrels, 8.8 lbs. Mfg. 1998-2000.

	$1,700	$1,600	$1,550	$1,475	$1,250	$1,050	$895	*$3,625*

Add $985 for combo package (includes extra set of 34 in. barrels).

* ***Model 682 Mono*** – single under-barrel trap model, high post vent. rib, 32 or 34 in. barrel. Imported 1985-88.

	$1,250	$1,100	$1,000	$900	$800	$700	$600	*$1,890*

Subtract if w/o choke tubes.

* ***Model S682 Gold Trap Live Bird (Pigeon Trap)*** – 12 ga. only, includes features for international style pigeon and competition shooters including international style stock, standard or flat (new 1995) VR, and mid-rib sights, Greystone (new 1991) or matte black (disc.) metal finish, semi-gloss American walnut stock, light scroll engraving, sliding trigger, includes MobilChokes, cased, 8.8 lbs. Imported 1990-1998.

	$1,700	$1,625	$1,325	$1,175	$950	$895	$800	*$2,910*

Subtract 15% for matte black.

* ***Model 682 Gold X Trap Mono (Top Single)*** – 12 ga. only, single over-barrel trap model, 32 or 34 in. barrel. Imported 1986-1995.

	$1,400	$1,275	$1,150	$925	$850	$775	$675	*$2,734*

Subtract 10% if w/o choke tubes.

MobilChokes became standard in 1989.

GRADING - PPGS™	100%	98%	95%	90%	80%	70%	60%	LAST MSR

* ***Model 682 Unsingle Trap*** – 12 ga. only, single under-barrel trap model with 32 in. high post VR, optional choke tubes. Imported 1992-94.

	$1,495	$1,350	$1,150	$925	$850	$775	$675	$2,650

Subtract 10% if w/o choke tubes.

MODEL S682 (GOLD X) SUPER TRAP – 12 ga. only, competition trap model, 30 in. barrels, step tapered rib, factory porting, LOP, and separate stock cheekpiece are adjustable, cased. Imported 1991-95.

	$1,800	$1,650	$1,375	$1,050	$900	$800	$700	$2,907

* ***Model S682 Top Mono Super Trap (Gold X)*** – 12 ga. only, single over-barrel trap model, 32 or 34 in. barrel with choice of fixed or MobilChokes. Imported 1991-1995.

	$1,550	$1,375	$1,200	$1,050	$900	$800	$700	$3,083

Subtract 10% for 32 in. barrel.
Subtract 10% for fixed choke.

* ***Model S682 Gold Super Trap Top Combo (Gold X)*** – 12 ga. only, supplied with upper single barrel and O/U barrel sets, otherwise same specifications as Model 682 Super Trap, MobilChokes became standard 1996, cased. Imported 1991-1997.

	$2,200	$1,950	$1,825	$1,650	$1,400	$1,125	$895	$4,040

MODEL S682 GOLD E TRAP – 12 ga. only, 30 or 32 in. VR OptimaBore barrel, OptimaChokes, adj. stock with memory system, dual color finished receiver with engraved merging circular lines and gold highlights, including trigger, deluxe wide checkered stock with gloss wood finish, bottom single configuration became standard 2009, 7.6 lbs. Mfg. 2001-2010.

	$3,750	$3,100	$2,775	$2,350	$2,050	$1,650	$1,425	$4,350

* ***Model S682 Gold E Trap Combo Top/Bottom*** – 12 ga. only, includes 30 (scarce, disc. 2001), 32 (disc. 2002) or 34 (new 2002) in. mono top or bottom barrel and choice of 30 or 32 in. O/U barrels, cased. New 2001.

MSR $5,185	$4,700	$3,900	$3,500	$2,800	$2,375	$2,000	$1,700	

Add $380 for bottom single combo.

* ***Model S682 Gold E Trap Bottom Single*** – 12 ga., features 34 in. bottom single barrel with OBTR chokes.

MSR $4,805	$4,000	$3,150	$2,500	$2,250	$2,000	$1,650	$1,425	

MODEL S682 LTD. – 12 ga. only, 32 or 34 in. barrel, includes adj. stock. Limited edition mfg. 2006.

	$5,400	$4,900	$4,475	$4,200	$3,850	$3,600	$3,300	$6,775

MODEL S686 SILVER PIGEON TRAP – 12 ga. only, low-profile action, 30 in. VR barrels with 3/8 in. flat rib, matte wood finish, choke tubes, nickel finished receiver with scroll engraving, 7.7 lbs. Mfg. 1997-99.

	$1,095	$925	$750	$625	$525	$460	$415	$1,795

* ***Model S686 Silver Pigeon Trap Top Mono*** – 12 ga. only, single over-barrel trap model, 32 or 34 in. barrel with MobilChokes, gloss wood finish, 8.14 lbs. Mfg. 1998-2002.

	$1,000	$900	$775	$650	$550	$475	$415	$1,869

MODEL 686 INTERNATIONAL TRAP – 12 ga. only, 30 in. VR barrels bored IM/F, checkered walnut stock and forearm. Imported 1994 only.

	$900	$800	$725	$650	$550	$500	$460	$1,300

MODEL S687 EELL DIAMOND PIGEON TRAP (X TRAP) – 12 ga. only, boxlock action with engraved black (new 1992) or silver (disc. 1991) finished side plates, Monte Carlo stock with recoil pad, 30 in. barrels with choke tubes, cased, 8.8 lbs. Disc. 1999.

	$2,750	$2,475	$2,150	$1,875	$1,650	$1,475	$1,200	$4,815

* ***Model S687 EELL Diamond Pigeon Trap Top Mono*** – 12 ga. only, single over-barrel trap model, 32 or 34 in. barrel, fixed chokes standard. Imported 1988-92, resumed 1996, disc. 1999.

	$2,500	$2,250	$2,000	$1,850	$1,700	$1,425	$1,150	$5,060

Subtract 20% if w/o OptimaChokes.

GRADING - PPGS™	100%	98%	95%	90%	80%	70%	60%	LAST MSR

* ***Model S687 EELL Diamond Pigeon X Bottom Mono Trap Combo*** – 12 ga. only, supplied with 30 or 32 in. O/U barrels and a mono trap bottom barrel. Imported 1986-1988, resumed 1994-1995.

	100%	98%	95%	90%	80%	70%	60%	LAST MSR
	$3,500	$3,150	$2,725	$2,500	$2,250	$2,000	$1,725	*$4,984*

Add 5% for MobilChokes.

* ***Model S687 EELL Diamond Pigeon X Top Mono Trap Combo*** – 12 ga. only, supplied with 30 or 32 in. O/U barrels and a mono trap upper barrel, MobilChokes became standard 1995. Mfg. 1988-1997.

	100%	98%	95%	90%	80%	70%	60%	LAST MSR
	$3,850	$3,350	$3,000	$2,800	$2,650	$2,475	$2,175	*$6,070*

MODEL ASE 90 GOLD TRAP – 12 ga. only, 30 in. vent. barrels with VR, similar action and specifications to Model ASE 90 Pigeon, 8.2 lbs., cased with extra trigger group, MobilChokes became standard 1995. Mfg. 1992-1999.

	100%	98%	95%	90%	80%	70%	60%	LAST MSR
	$4,250	$4,000	$3,750	$3,250	$2,750	$2,450	$2,250	*$12,145*

Add $1,000 for Trap Combo package.
Subtract 10% if w/o choke tubes.
Subtract $250 if w/o extra trigger assembly.

DT10 TRIDENT TRAP – 12 ga. only, 3 in. chambers, 30 or 32 in. vent. OptimaBore barrels with target VR, specially designed trap gun featuring removable adj. trigger group, massive crossbolt locking system, OptimaChoke competition choke tubes, specific point of impact, and unique distribution of mass that helps target acquisition and eliminate muzzle rise, adj. walnut stock with memory system, carbon reinforced frame, 8.8 lbs., cased. Mfg. 2000-2008.

	100%	98%	95%	90%	80%	70%	60%	LAST MSR
	$7,500	$6,000	$5,000	$3,950	$3,250	$2,500	$2,000	*$7,400*

* ***DT10 Trident Trap Top Single*** – includes 34 in. top single barrel, cased. Mfg. 2000-2008.

	100%	98%	95%	90%	80%	70%	60%	LAST MSR
	$7,500	$6,000	$5,000	$3,950	$3,250	$2,500	$2,000	*$7,400*

* ***DT10 Trident Trap Bottom Single*** – includes 34 in. bottom single barrel with adj. rib, cased. Mfg. 2004-disc.

	100%	98%	95%	90%	80%	70%	60%	LAST MSR
	$7,500	$6,000	$5,000	$3,950	$3,250	$2,500	$2,000	*$8,500*

* ***DT10 Trident Trap Combo*** – includes choice of 30 or 32 in. O/U barrels and a 34 in. top single barrel, cased. Mfg. 2000-2008.

	100%	98%	95%	90%	80%	70%	60%	LAST MSR
	$9,000	$7,550	$6,800	$6,050	$5,500	$4,500	$4,000	*$10,475*

* ***DT10 Trident Trap Bottom Single Combo*** – includes 34 in. bottom single barrel and choice of 30 or 32 in. O/U barrels, rib on bottom single barrel is adj. for point of impact, cased. New 2001.

	100%	98%	95%	90%	80%	70%	60%
MSR $11,300	$9,950	$8,450	$7,175	$5,750	$4,800	$4,000	$3,450

This model is available by special order through Beretta Galleries only.

SV10 PREVAIL I TRAP – 12 ga., 30 or 32 in. VR barrels with OBSP-HP choke tubes, satin finished boxlock aluminum receiver, choice of extraction or ejection, titanium trigger, quick takedown stock allows disassembly in a few seconds, regular or Kick-Off recoil pad. New 2012.

	100%	98%	95%	90%	80%	70%	60%
MSR $3,000	$2,650	$2,350	$2,050	$1,800	$1,550	$1,225	$1,000

Add $450 for Kick-Off recoil pad.

SHOTGUNS: O/U, CUSTOM GRADE - RECENT MFG.

Current high grade Beretta O/U and SxS shotguns are sold only by premium grade franchised Beretta dealers. For a listing of these dealers, contact a Beretta Gallery (see Trademark Index).

Where applicable, Beretta's new SST, with selector switch built into safety, is more desirable than older manufacture utilizing the disc. single, non-selective trigger.

Subtract 10%-15% for older style non-selective single trigger.

ROYAL PIGEON (GALLERY SPECIAL) – 12 or 20 ga., non-sideplated Model 600 action, hand engraved in the EELL style, upgraded wood, made especially for Beretta Galleries. 40 mfg. in each gauge beginning 2004.

	100%	98%	95%	90%	80%	70%	60%
MSR $5,950	$5,250	$4,550	$4,100	$3,550	$3,200	$2,800	$2,400

GRADING - PPGS™	100%	98%	95%	90%	80%	70%	60%	LAST MSR

ASEL – 12 or 20 ga., best SO grade boxlock with vintage 1960s action, SO grade hand finished wood, Boehler Antinit steel barrels, 28 mfg. in 20 ga. (2004-2005), 300 mfg. in 12 ga. New 2004.

MSR $15,000	$12,500	$10,500	$9,000	$7,500	$6,000	$5,000	$4,500	
20 ga.	$22,250	$18,500	$14,000	$10,500	$9,500	$8,500	$7,500	*$25,750*

Pairs on this model are available for $59,225.

ASE GOLD – see individual models with descriptions under Skeet, Sporting Clays, and Trap category names.

ASE 90 DE LUXE – 12 ga. only, specifications furnished by customer, deep scroll engraving signed by the engraver, upgraded wood, Sporting or Field Model, cased. New 1996.

MSR $24,500	$20,500	$15,000	$10,750	$8,750	$7,250	$6,000	$5,000	

JUBILEE – 12, 20, 28 ga., or .410 bore, choice of Field or Sporting Clays configuration, signed scroll or game scene engraving, upgraded wood, tru-oil finish, and hand polished details throughout, cased. New 1998.

MSR $18,000	$14,995	$12,250	$9,000	$7,250	$6,150	$5,200	$4,750	

Add $3,500 for 2-barrel set (20/28 ga., new 2010).

* ***Jubilee Matched Pair*** – available with consecutive serial numbers, made to special order, cased. New 2002.

MSR $42,500	$35,000	$29,000	$24,000	$18,750	$15,000	$13,250	$11,000	

SO-1 – 12 ga. only, entry level SO model, sidelock action with Greener crossbolt, ejectors, DT, checkered walnut stock and forearm, perimeter engraving only, various configurations. Mfg. circa 1935-disc.

	$3,250	$2,950	$2,600	$2,250	$1,850	$1,725	$1,600	

SO-2 – 12 ga., 26-30 in. barrels, sidelock, any chokes, vent. rib, auto ejectors, SST, checkered stock in various configurations (field, skeet, or trap), grades differ in wood, engraving, and finish, cased. SO series mfg. beginning 1948.

MSR $4,750	$3,995	$2,950	$2,350	$1,950	$1,675	$1,475	$1,250	

SO-3 – 2nd grade of the SO series.

MSR $6,250	$4,500	$3,550	$3,200	$2,800	$2,400	$2,100	$1,850	

SO-3 EL – grade-up from SO-3 with better wood and engraving.

MSR $7,750	$6,250	$4,250	$3,600	$3,050	$2,500	$2,200	$1,950	

SO-3 EELL – best quality model, custom specifications, choice of engraving motifs.

MSR $14,750	$13,500	$8,750	$7,500	$6,250	$5,250	$4,750	$3,950	

Add $2,000-$10,000 for master engraving.

SO-4 – 12 ga., sidelock, available in field, skeet, or trap configurations, custom specs., fluorescent sights, wide rib, cased. Disc. 1987, reintroduced 2001.

MSR $6,500	$5,650	$4,750	$4,225	$3,650	$3,250	$2,800	$2,400	

SO-5 COMPETITION – best quality O/U, extensively engraved, top quality checkered walnut stock (semi-pistol grip) and forearm, available in either Trap, Skeet, or Sporting configurations, leather cased, limited importation.

MSR $28,000	$22,000	$14,250	$10,250	$8,250	$6,400	$5,300	$4,500	

Add $10,000 for extra set of barrels. Add $3,500 for Trap Combo set (disc.).

SO-5 EELL – next to top-of-the-line model, available in either Trap, Skeet, or Sporting Clays configuration, custom built to customer dimensions.

The current MSR on this model is $37,500.

SO-6 COMPETITION – 12 ga. only high quality O/U, extensively scroll engraved, top quality checkered walnut stock (semi-pistol grip) and forearm, choice of Field (reintroduced during 1998), Trap, Skeet, or Sporting Clays configuration, built to customer specifications, leather cased, limited importation. Disc. 2002.

	$16,650	$13,500	$10,750	$8,500	$7,450	$6,350	$5,100	*$23,900*

Add $6,250 for extra set of barrels.

GRADING - PPGS™	100%	98%	95%	90%	80%	70%	60%	LAST MSR

SO-6 EL FIELD GRADE – 12 ga. only, available with rose and scroll engraving, 28, 30, or 32 in. barrels. New 2003.

MSR $27,500	$24,250	$19,750	$15,000	$11,000	$9,750	$8,750	$7,500

SO-6 EELL – 12 ga., current next to top-of-the-line model, field dimensions, custom built to customer specifications, leather cased.

MSR $55,000	$48,000	$42,000	$35,000	$30,000	$23,250	$18,000	$13,500

Add $7,000 for extra set of barrels.

Special engraving options are available on this model for an additional charge - contact the Gallery directly for pricing.

SO-6 EESS – 12 ga., features green enamel sideplates with diamond inlays. New 1998.

The current MSR on this model is $110,000.

* ***SO-6 EESS w/o Diamonds*** – features red or blue enamel sideplates, w/o diamonds. New 1998.

MSR $51,000	$40,000	$35,000	$27,250	$21,250	$16,750	$12,750	$10,750

SO-9 – 12, 20, 28 ga., or .410 bore, top-of-the-line sidelock model until 2003, 1990 was the first time the SO series was offered in smaller gauges, 28 ga. or .410 bore models have smaller proportionate frames. New 1990.

MSR $46,725	$35,000	$27,500	$20,500	$16,000	$12,000	$9,200	$7,000

Add $10,000 for extra set of barrels.
Add 10%-25% for well-known engravers.
Subtract 10% for 12 ga. on used specimens.

* ***SO-9 EELL Special*** – top-of-the-line O/U model.

Retail prices range from $125,000-$320,000, depending on individual custom-order engraving options. Pairs are also available from $287,500 to $690,000.

SO-10 – top-of-the-line O/U sidelock model, barrels made of nickel, chromium, and molybdenum steel. Limited availability beginning late 2003.

MSR $98,000	$83,750	$75,000	$69,000	$57,000	$47,000	$36,000	$29,500

Pairs are available for $207,000. Any level of engraving was available on this model in 20 ga. through 2005. 28 ga. or .410 bore models became available in 2006. Please contact the Beretta Gallery directly for more information about this model.

* ***SO-10 EELL Special*** – top-of-the-line O/U model, extra engraving.

Prices for single guns, depending on the amount of engraving, range from $125,000 - $320,000. Pairs are available from $287,500 to $747,500, depending on the amount of engraving. Please contact the Beretta Gallery directly for more information regarding availability and options.

GIUBILEO SPORTING – 12 or 20 ga., 28, 30, or 32 in. OptimaBore barrels, OptimaChokes, premium walnut oil finished stock and checkered forearm, coin finished boxlock engraved action with sideplates, scroll engraved receiver with P. Beretta logo, single trigger, available in Sporting configuration and combo, 6.6 - 7.3 lbs. New 2007.

MSR $18,000	$15,500	$12,750	$10,750	$9,000	$8,000	$7,000	$6,000

This model is available by special order through Beretta Galleries only.

DT10EELL SPORTING – 12 ga. only, scroll or game scene engraved, SST, sporting stock with extra fine wood. New 2010.

MSR $15,750	$13,950	$11,500	$9,750	$8,500	$7,250	$6,000	$4,750

This model is available by special order through Beretta Galleries only.

SHOTGUNS: SxS, RECENT MFG.

Subtract 20% on the following factory multi-choke models if w/o newer Beretta Optima-chokes (12 ga. only, became standard 2003).

MODEL 409 PB – 12, 16, 20, or 28 ga., 27, 28, and 30 in. barrels, various chokes, double triggers, plain extractors, checkered pistol grip stock. Mfg. 1934-1964.

12 or 16 ga.	$825	$725	$625	$550	$495	$440	$385

GRADING - PPGS™	100%	98%	95%	90%	80%	70%	60%	LAST MSR
20 ga.	$1,250	$1,100	$975	$850	$775	$700	$625	
28 ga.	$1,675	$1,400	$1,175	$925	$825	$750	$650	

MODEL 410 E – higher quality, auto ejector version of 409 PB.

12 ga.	$1,275	$1,000	$895	$775	$675	$575	$475	
20 ga.	$1,750	$1,550	$1,275	$1,000	$895	$775	$675	
28 ga.	$3,775	$3,300	$2,800	$2,275	$1,800	$1,450	$1,100	

MODEL 410 – similar to 410 E, except 10 ga. Mag., 32 in. barrel, full choke, heavier construction. Mfg. 1934-81.

	$1,200	$995	$880	$795	$700	$625	$550	

MODEL 411 E – similar to 409 PB, with false sideplates and finer finishing. Mfg. 1934-64.

12 ga.	$2,000	$1,750	$1,350	$1,050	$895	$775	$675	
20 ga.	$2,750	$2,325	$1,750	$1,300	$1,000	$895	$775	
28 ga.	$4,250	$3,775	$3,300	$2,800	$2,275	$1,800	$1,450	

MODEL 424-426 – 12 and 20 ga. (Model 426 only), 26 and 28 in. barrels, various chokes, boxlock, extractors, double triggers, light engraving, checkered straight stock.

	$1,195	$1,095	$975	$875	$750	$650	$600	

Add $115 for Model 426.
Add 50% for 20 ga.

MODEL 426 E – similar to 424, with auto ejectors, SST, select wood and more intricate engraving, silver pigeon inlay. Disc. 1983.

	$1,495	$1,300	$1,200	$1,075	$850	$775	$675	

MODEL 625 – 12 or 20 ga., 26-30 in. barrels, various chokes, boxlock, extractors, DTs or SST, light engraving, checkered straight stock. Imported 1984-86.

	$1,000	$925	$850	$775	$650	$600	$550	*$835*

Add 50% for 20 ga.
Add 15% for SST.

MODEL GR-2 – 12 or 20 ga., 26 and 28 in. barrels, various chokes, boxlock, extractors, double triggers, checkered pistol grip stock. Mfg. 1968-76.

	$900	$800	$700	$600	$400	$330	$275	

Add 50% for 20 ga.

MODEL GR-3 – similar to GR-2, with select wood and more engraving. Mfg. 1968-1976.

	$1,095	$995	$800	$550	$475	$425	$375	

Add 50% for 20 ga.

MODEL GR-4 – similar to GR-3, with auto ejectors. Mfg. 1968-1976.

	$1,300	$1,200	$1,075	$900	$775	$675	$600	

Add 50% for 20 ga.

SILVER HAWK – 12 ga. Mag. (3 in. chambers) or 10 ga. Mag. (3 1/2 in. chambers) with double triggers and extractors. Disc. 1967.

	$795	$700	$600	$400	$300	$275	$250	

Subtract 50% for 10 ga.

SILVER HAWK FEATHERWEIGHT – 12, 16, 20, or 28 ga., 26-32 in. barrels, high solid rib, various chokes, single or double triggers, checkered pistol grip stock, beavertail forearm. Disc. 1967.

Double trigger	$1,000	$925	$850	$775	$650	$600	$550	
Single trigger	$1,150	$975	$875	$800	$700	$625	$575	

Add 50% for 20 ga.
Add 100% for 28 ga.

GRADING - PPGS™	100%	98%	95%	90%	80%	70%	60%	LAST MSR

MODEL 470 SILVER HAWK (RECENT MFG.) – 12 or 20 ga., 3 in. chambers, 26 or 28 in. barrels with choice of fixed or multi-chokes (new 1999), satin chrome receiver finish, selector lever on forearm allows either automatic ejection or mechanical extraction, straight grip stock with matte finish, 5.9 or 6 1/2 lbs. Mfg. 1998-2002.

	100%	98%	95%	90%	80%	70%	60%	LAST MSR
	$1,950	$1,700	$1,475	$1,300	$1,175	$1,025	$875	*$2,596*

Add 15% for 20 ga.
Add $130 for MobilChokes (new 1999).

MODEL 470 EL – 12 or 20 ga., 3 in. chambers, 26 (20 ga. only) or 28 in. barrels with MC3 choke tubes, or OptimaBore barrels with OptimaChokes, case colored boxlock receiver with 4 gold inlays (doves and ducks) on sideplates, selector lever on forearm allows either automatic ejection or mechanical extraction, deluxe straight grip stock and splinter forearm with oil finish, 5.9 or 6 1/2 lbs. Mfg. 2002-2006.

	100%	98%	95%	90%	80%	70%	60%	LAST MSR
	$4,500	$4,350	$4,000	$3,750	$3,550	$3,200	$2,800	*$6,495*

This model was available only through select Beretta Showcase dealers.

MODEL 471 SILVER HAWK – 12 or 20 ga., 3 in. chambers, 26 (disc. 2011) or 28 in. barrels with MobilChokes or OptimaChokes, engraved satin chrome or color case hardened (disc. 2010) receiver finish, selector lever on forearm allows either automatic ejection or mechanical extraction, ST, choice of straight grip or pistol grip stock with matte finish, beavertail or splinter forearm (fixed chokes only), 5.9 or 6 1/2 lbs. New 2003.

	100%	98%	95%	90%	80%	70%	60%	LAST MSR
MSR $3,850	$3,660	$3,000	$2,700	$2,200	$1,800	$1,500	$1,200	

Add $625 for color case hardened frame with straight grip stock and splinter forearm (IC/IM fixed chokes only), disc. 2010. Last MSR for this option was $4,475.

MODEL 471 EL – 12 or 20 ga., 3 in. chambers, 26 or 28 in. VR barrels, color case hardened receiver with gold accents, satin finished straight grip English style stock. Mfg. 2005-2010.

	100%	98%	95%	90%	80%	70%	60%	LAST MSR
	$7,500	$6,500	$5,500	$4,500	$3,750	$3,150	$2,750	*$8,450*

MODEL 626 FIELD – 12 or 20 (disc. 1987) ga., 2 3/4 in. chambers, blue finish, 26 and 28 in. barrels, various chokes, boxlock, ejectors, single trigger, moderate engraving, pistol grip or straight checkered stock. Imported 1984-88.

	100%	98%	95%	90%	80%	70%	60%	LAST MSR
	$1,500	$1,300	$1,150	$995	$850	$775	$675	*$995*

Add 50% for 20 ga.

MODEL 626 ONYX – 12 or 20 ga., 3 in. chambers, 26 or 28 (new 1990) in. VR barrels with MobilChokes, matte finished metal, select checkered walnut stock and forearm. Imported 1988-1993.

	100%	98%	95%	90%	80%	70%	60%	LAST MSR
	$1,650	$1,350	$1,100	$925	$825	$750	$650	*$1,870*

* ***Model 626 Onyx Magnum*** – 12 ga. only, 3 1/2 in. chambers. Mfg. 1990-92.

	100%	98%	95%	90%	80%	70%	60%	LAST MSR
	$1,650	$1,250	$1,050	$925	$825	$750	$650	*$1,870*

MODEL 627 EL FIELD – 12 and 20 (disc. 1987) ga., 2 3/4 (disc. 1990) or 3 in. (became standard in 1991) chambers, 26 and 28 in. barrels, various chokes, boxlock, ejectors, single trigger, extensive engraving, pistol grip or straight checkered stock, cased. Imported 1985-93.

	100%	98%	95%	90%	80%	70%	60%	LAST MSR
	$2,250	$2,000	$1,800	$1,500	$1,275	$1,000	$900	*$3,270*

Subtract 10% for fixed chokes and 2 3/4 in. chambers.
Add 25% for 20 ga.

* ***Model 627 EL Sport*** – similar to Model 627 EL Field, except 12 ga. only, knurled rib, sporting clays dimensions. Importation disc. 1988.

	100%	98%	95%	90%	80%	70%	60%	LAST MSR
	$2,500	$2,200	$1,900	$1,625	$1,350	$1,100	$925	*$1,995*

Add 10% for 20 ga.

MODEL 627 EELL – 12 or 20 (disc. 1987) ga., 2 3/4 (disc.) or 3 (12 ga. only) in. chambers, 26 or 28 in. barrels, various chokes, boxlock, ejectors, single trigger, elaborate engraving, pistol grip or straight English checkered stock, cased. Imported 1985-1993.

	100%	98%	95%	90%	80%	70%	60%	LAST MSR
	$4,300	$3,675	$3,150	$2,700	$2,350	$1,975	$1,825	*$5,405*

Add 10% for 20 ga.
Add 25% for 28 in. barrels.

GRADING - PPGS™	100%	98%	95%	90%	80%	70%	60%	LAST MSR

Subtract 10% if fixed chokes only.

Multi-chokes became standard in 1991.

SHOTGUNS: SxS, CUSTOM GRADE

Current custom grade Beretta O/U and SxS shotguns are sold only by premium grade franchised Beretta dealers. For a listing of these dealers, contact a Beretta Gallery (see Trademark Index).

Where applicable, Beretta's new SST, with selector switch built into safety, is more desirable than older manufacture utilizing the discontinued single, non-selective trigger. Also, hand chased engraving on earlier mfg. (can be denoted by engraver's signature next to trigger guard) is more desirable, and may add a 10% premium, depending on condition.

MODEL 450 SERIES – 12 ga. only, built to individual customer order, various levels of engraving. Disc.

* ***Model 450 EL*** – incorporates H&H type sidelocks.

$8,000	$7,350	$5,900	$5,350	$4,750	$4,200	$3,600	

* ***Model 450 EELL*** – features third fastener with H&H type sidelocks.

$9,995	$8,000	$7,500	$6,000	$5,500	$4,850	$4,300	

SO-1 – 12 ga. only, entry level sidelock model with light engraving, ejectors, DT standard, cased with accessories. Mfg. 1934-disc.

$2,750	$2,300	$2,000	$1,800	$1,600	$1,400	$1,250	

SO-2 – 12 ga. only, similar to the SO-1 except has monobloc shoulders and fore-end, an engraved release lever, and English-style engraving. Mfg. 1930s-disc.

$3,750	$3,350	$3,000	$2,800	$2,575	$2,200	$1,995	

SO-3 – 12 ga. only, similar to the SO-2 except does not have swivels and plastic buttplate; instead has select walnut stock/forearm, floral motif engraving, and hand-finished diamond checkering. Mfg. 1930s-disc.

$5,500	$4,500	$3,950	$3,600	$3,000	$2,700	$2,400	

* ***SO-3 EL*** – similar to the SO-3 except has superior engraving, specially selected walnut, detachable sidelocks, simple screw takedown, and matted hand-knurled ventilated rib. Mfg. circa 1930s-disc.

$7,500	$6,500	$5,150	$4,500	$4,000	$3,600	$3,200	

» **SO-3 EELL** – similar to the SO-3 EL except has gold-plated interior parts, trigger, and locking pin, ivory bead front sight, and best quality engraving signed by artist. Mfg. 1930s-disc.

$12,500	$10,750	$9,500	$8,500	$7,500	$6,500	$5,500	

SO-4 – standard engraving motifs and custom stock dimensions, DT standard. Mfg. 1968-mid-1980s.

$5,500	$4,500	$3,950	$3,600	$3,000	$2,700	$2,400	

SO-6 – same general specifications and embellishments as the SO series O/U guns, but SxS, removable sidelocks, elaborate scroll engraving, cased with accessories. Mfg. 1988-disc.

$7,250	$6,500	$5,925	$5,300	$4,700	$4,250	$3,850	

* ***SO-6 EELL*** – similar to the SO-6 except has master engraved floral and traditional game scene, finest burl walnut. Mfg. 1988-disc.

$8,250	$7,250	$6,300	$5,500	$5,000	$4,500	$4,000	

SO-7 – top of the line SxS, finest quality wood, more elaborate engraving. Disc.

$8,950	$7,950	$6,875	$6,000	$5,250	$4,600	$4,000	

MODEL 451 SERIES – 12 ga., totally hand-made, sidelock action, ejectors, scroll engraving. Custom made to order with fitted luggage case, various grades have increasing embellishments in EL Models.

GRADING - PPGS™	100%	98%	95%	90%	80%	70%	60%	LAST MSR

* ***Model 451*** – disc. 1987.

	$6,250	$5,500	$4,875	$4,600	$4,300	$3,995	$3,600	*$12,375*

* ***Model 451 E*** – 12 ga. only, double triggers, specifications furnished by individual customer. Limited importation since 1989.

MSR $7,250	$6,750	$6,200	$5,500	$4,750	$4,000	$3,500	$2,750	

Add approx. 40% for extra set of barrels.
Add $750 for SST (disc.).

* ***Model 451 EL*** – limited importation, temporarily disc. 1984.

MSR $15,250	$14,500	$7,750	$6,750	$5,600	$5,000	$4,500	$4,100	

* ***Model 451 EELL*** – top-of-the-line for Model 451, choice of engraving motifs per customer specifications. Disc. 1987, reintroduced 1989.

MSR $18,500	$16,750	$8,500	$7,500	$6,500	$5,750	$5,150	$4,600	

MODEL 452 CUSTOM – 12 ga. only, next to top-of-the-line side-by side shotgun featuring H&H style detachable locks, built to customer's specifications, leather cased. New 1990.

MSR $35,000	$28,750	$15,750	$11,750	$8,750	$6,650	$5,500	$4,500	

Add $6,275 for extra set of barrels.

* ***Model 452 EELL Custom*** – 12 ga. only, top-of-the-line custom sidelock model featuring every refinement, built to customer's specifications, leather cased. Importation began 1992.

MSR $46,500	$38,950	$21,000	$15,750	$11,750	$9,000	$6,750	$5,600	

Add $6,275 for extra set of barrels.
Add approx. $8,500-$43,500 for special master engraving options.

MODEL 470 EL CUSTOM – 12 or 20 ga., mfg. by Beretta's custom shop per individual order, custom case hardened frame with 24Kt. bird inlays, upgraded wood with oil finish. New 1999.

MSR $9,350	$8,250	$7,000	$5,750	$3,600	$2,800	$2,300	$1,800	

MODEL JUBILEE II (MODEL 470 EELL) – 12 or 20 ga., scroll or game scene engraving signed by the engraver, select SO quality wood with Tru-oil finish, includes suede case, also available in pairs. New 1999.

MSR $18,000	$15,950	$13,750	$9,250	$7,750	$6,250	$5,250	$4,750	

Pairs are available in this model for $35,075.

This model was designated the Model 470 EELL through 1999.

GIUBILEO II – 12 or 20 ga., 3 in. chambers, 26 or 28 in. barrels with fixed chokes, oil finished premium English straight grip style walnut stock and checkered forearm, coin finished engraved boxlock action with sideplates, scroll and floral engraving, 6 1/2 lbs. New 2007.

MSR $18,000	$15,950	$13,750	$9,250	$7,750	$6,250	$5,250	$4,750	

IMPERIALE MONTE CARLO – 12 or 20 ga., best custom sidelock, top-of-the-line, built to customer's specifications with engraving options. New 2010.

Current MSR on this model is $131,000.
Add $20,000 - $25,000 for master engraving.

DIANA – 12 or 20 ga., external hammer, best quality custom model, completely handmade, available with engraving options. New 2010.

Current MSR on this model is $150,000.
Add $20,000 - $50,000 for master engraving.

SHOTGUNS: SINGLE BARREL, DISC.

MARK II TRAP – 12 ga., 32 or 34 in. wide vent. rib, full choke, boxlock with auto ejector, Monte Carlo stock, recoil pad. Mfg. 1972-76.

	$495	$435	$375	$335	$275	$225	$175	

GRADING - PPGS™	100%	98%	95%	90%	80%	70%	60%	LAST MSR

MODEL FS-1 SINGLE BARREL – 12, 16, 20, 28 ga., or .410 bore, 26 or 28 in. barrels, full choke, checkered semi-pistol grip, under lever break open, folds to length of barrel (also known as Companion).

	$175	$155	$130	$125	$95	$80	$60	

Subtract 20% for 12 ga.

TR-1 TRAP – 12 ga., 32 in. full choke barrel, under lever break open, Monte Carlo pistol grip stock with pad, engraved. Mfg. 1968-1971.

	$275	$250	$225	$195	$140	$110	$100	

TR-2 TRAP – similar to TR-1, with high rib. Mfg. 1969-1973.

	$295	$260	$230	$200	$150	$120	$110	

MODEL 412 – 12, 20, 28 ga., or .410 bore, monobloc construction, folding action, sling swivels, checkered walnut stock and forearm, 5 lbs. Importation disc. 1988.

	$195	$165	$140	$130	$100	$85	$65	*$215*

VANDALIA SPECIAL TRAP – 12 ga., sidelock action with crossbolt, fixed choke, coin finished receiver, light scroll hand engraving with borders, cased with accessories, never offically introduced or released commercially. 6 mfg. circa 1997.

	$9,975	$8,725	$7,475	$6,785	$5,475	$4,495	$3,400	

SHOTGUNS: SLIDE ACTION, MFG. 1960-1996

MODEL SL-2 – 12 ga., 26, 28, or 30 in. barrels, various chokes, vent. rib, checkered pistol grip stock. Mfg. 1968-71.

	$300	$275	$250	$220	$195	$165	$140	

SILVER PIGEON – 12 ga., various chokes, light engraving.

	$250	$200	$175	$160	$150	$140	$130	

GOLD PIGEON – 12 ga., various chokes, vent. rib, engraved.

	$475	$375	$310	$275	$240	$215	$195	

Add $200 for deluxe models.

RUBY PIGEON – 12 ga., various chokes, vent. rib, elaborately engraved, special deluxe walnut.

	$600	$475	$395	$350	$295	$260	$230	

SHOTGUNS: SEMI-AUTO

It is possible on some of the following models to have production variances occur including different engraving motifs, stock configurations and specifications, finishes, etc. These have occurred when Beretta changed from production of one model to another. Also, some European and English distributors have sold their excess inventory through Beretta U.S.A., creating additional variations/configurations that are not normally imported domestically. While sometimes rare, these specimens typically do not command premiums over Beretta's domestic models.

The following Beretta semi-auto models have been listed in numerical sequence, if possible, disregarding any alphabetical suffix or prefix.

Note: values are for unaltered guns.

Subtract 10% on the following factory multi-choke models if w/o newer Beretta Optima-chokes (12 ga. only, became standard 2003).

MODEL 60 – 12 ga., 2 3/4 in. chamber, gas operated with piston rod, 3 shot mag., 24, 26, or 28 in. plain barrel, approx. 7 lbs. Mfg. 1956-1960.

	$295	$260	$240	$220	$200	$185	$170	

Add 10% for Model 60 Deluxe with special embellishments.

MODEL 61 – 12 ga., improved version of the Model 60 with recoil spring located in stock, chromium plated action and fine engraving, 24, 26, or 28 in. VR barrel. Mfg. approx. 1961-1965.

	$335	$295	$260	$235	$210	$195	$175	

GRADING - PPGS™	100%	98%	95%	90%	80%	70%	60%	LAST MSR

SILVER LARK – 12 ga., various chokes.

	$295	$260	$240	$220	$200	$185	$170	

GOLD LARK – 12 ga., vent. rib, light scroll engraving, select walnut.

	$480	$400	$325	$260	$230	$210	$195	

RUBY LARK – 12 ga., vent. rib, heavy engraving, deluxe walnut.

	$675	$550	$475	$395	$350	$295	$260	

MODEL AL-1 – 12 and 20 ga., gas operated, 26, 28, and 30 in. plain barrel, various chokes, checkered pistol grip stock. Mfg. 1971-1973.

	$385	$360	$330	$300	$250	$195	$165	

MODEL AL-2 – 12 or 20 ga., 26, 28, or 30 in. barrels, vent. rib, various chokes, gas operated, checkered pistol grip stock. Mfg. 1973-75.

	$330	$305	$275	$250	$220	$195	$165	

MODEL AL-2 SKEET – similar to AL-2, with 26 in. wide rib skeet bored barrel. Mfg. 1973-75.

	$395	$360	$320	$275	$220	$200	$185	

MODEL AL-2 TRAP – similar to AL-2, with 30 in. full choke barrel, wide rib, Monte Carlo stock, with recoil pad. Mfg. 1973-75.

	$375	$345	$315	$285	$250	$195	$165	

MODEL AL-2 MAGNUM – 12 or 20 ga., 3 in. chamber, heavier action bar, 28 and 30 in. mod. or full choke. Mfg. 1973-75.

	$415	$385	$330	$275	$250	$230	$210	

MODEL AL-3 – continuation of the AL-2 series. Mfg. 1975-1976.

Field grade	$395	$360	$330	$260	$240	$220	$190	
Magnum grade	$395	$350	$300	$275	$250	$230	$210	
Skeet grade	$400	$360	$330	$260	$240	$220	$190	
Trap grade	$385	$350	$295	$250	$225	$210	$185	

MODEL AL-3 DELUXE TRAP – similar to AL-3, with fully engraved receiver, premium grade wood. Mfg. 1975-76.

	$600	$550	$500	$450	$425	$400	$375	

MODEL UGB25 XCEL TRAP – 12 ga., 2 3/4 in. chamber, unique two shot (second shell is located outside receiver on cartridge carrier), break open action featuring short recoil operating system, rising lock block system, light alloy black receiver with gold lettering, 30 or 32 (disc.) in. three alloy steel OptimaBore barrel, competition front sight, laser-checkered walnut stock with adj. comb, gold trigger, button safety, Gel-tek recoil pad, 7.7-9 lbs. Prototypes were introduced late 2004, but regular production started late 2007.

MSR $4,125	$3,625	$2,850	$2,280	$1,825	$1,450	$1,175	$950	

* ***Model UGB25 Xcel Gold Sporting*** – 12 ga., similar to UGB25 Xcel Trap, except does not have adj. comb, 28 or 30 in. barrel with OptimaChoke High Performance chokes, approx. 8 lbs. New 2010.

MSR $3,975	$3,575	$2,800	$2,280	$1,825	$1,450	$1,175	$950	

MODEL PINTAIL/ES100 PINTAIL (VITORIA) – 12 ga., 3 in. chamber, same action as the Benelli SL80 Series shotguns, 24, 26, or 28 (new 1999) in. VR barrel, matte black metal finish, choice of matte finished wood (disc. 1998) or black synthetic stock and forearm (new 1999), includes sling swivels, 7.3 lbs. Frame manufactured in Vitoria, Spain, and barrels were made in Italy. Mfg. 1993-2001, reintroduced 2003 only.

	$695	$625	$550	$500	$425	$325	$250	*$682*

Subtract 15-20% for wood stock and forearm.
Subtract 20% for Vitoria market guns.

In 1999, this model was renamed the ES 100 Pintail (with synthetic stock). This Beretta model is the same gun as the Benelli SL80 Series guns, with a few cosmetic changes.

GRADING - PPGS™	100%	98%	95%	90%	80%	70%	60%	LAST MSR

* ***Model ES100 Camouflage*** – 12 ga. only, features 100% Advantage Wetlands, Realtree Hardwoods HD (new 2003), or Mossy Oak Shadowgrass (new 2003) coverage, 28 in. VR barrel only, 7.3 lbs. Mfg. 2000-2003.

	$725	$685	$620	$540	$420	$300	$260	*$777*

* ***Model ES100 Rifled Slug (Pintail Rifled Slug)*** – 12 ga., 3 in. chamber, 24 in. rifled barrel with drilled and tapped upper receiver, barrel and upper receiver are permanently joined, anti-glare matte black metal finish, choice of matte finished wood (disc. 1998) or black synthetic (new 1999) stock and forearm, includes sling swivels, 7 lbs. Mfg. 1998-2001, reintroduced 2003 only.

	$725	$665	$620	$565	$445	$365	$280	*$749*

Add $148 for combo package (includes extra 28 in. smooth bore barrel with MC3 choke, mfg. 2001).

In 1999, the model nomenclature changed from Pintail Rifled Slug to ES100 Rifled Slug.

* ***Model ES100 Pintail Slug (Vitoria)*** – 12 ga. only, 24 in. slug barrel, includes rifle sights and rifle choke tubes, 7 lbs. Imported 1993-95.

	$575	$495	$415	$350	$280	$250	$230	*$700*

* ***Model ES100 NWTF Special Camouflage (Pintail)*** – 12 ga. only, 24 in. VR barrel with 3 dot TruGlo fiber optic sight system, includes Briley extended extra-full choke tube and 3 standard MobilChoke tubes, features Mossy Oak Break-Up treatment on synthetic stock and forearm, black matte anti-glare finish on metal components, includes nylon sling. Limited mfg. 1999, reintroduced 2002 only (limited mfg.).

	$640	$595	$525	$440	$365	$290	$265	*$966*

MODEL 300/301 – continuation of the AL-3 series, scroll engraved receiver. Mfg. approx. 1968-82.

Field grade	$395	$360	$330	$260	$240	$220	$190	
Magnum grade	$395	$385	$330	$275	$250	$230	$210	
Skeet grade	$395	$360	$330	$260	$240	$220	$190	
Trap grade	$385	$350	$295	$250	$225	$210	$185	

Beretta changed model nomenclature rapidly during the Model 300 Series. In approx. 10 months, the evolution of this model had progressed from the 300 to 303 Series. Beginning with the Model 303, all receivers were milled with a 3 in. ejection port window.

MODEL A300 OUTLANDER – 12 ga., 3 in. chamber, gas operation with compensating gas valve and self-cleaning piston, 28 in. VR barrel with F, M, and IC chokes, black synthetic, oiled wood, or Max-4 camo stock, fitted rubber recoil pad, crossbolt safety, front metal bead sight, 7.1 lbs. New 2012.

MSR $725	$625	$550	$475	$425	$375	$325	4295	

Add $100 for oiled wood or 100% Max-4 camo coverage.

MODEL 301 SLUG GUN – 22 in. barrel, with sights. Disc.

	$395	$360	$330	$305	$265	$230	$190	

MODEL 302 – 12 or 20 ga., self-compensating gas operation semi-auto, designed for both 2 3/4 and 3 in. shells, available with interchangeable chokes, slug barrel, trap and skeet models (disc.), VR, mag. cut-off. Mfg. 1982-87. This model was superceded by the Model 303.

	$395	$365	$340	$310	$280	$255	$225	*$480*

Add $30 for multi-choke set.

* ***Model 302 Super Lusso*** – same specifications as Model A302, but includes hand engraved receiver, many gold plated parts, and stock and forearm made from presentation grade walnut. Disc. 1986.

	$1,700	$1,500	$1,250	$1,025	$900	$800	$700	*$2,500*

MODEL A-303 FIELD – 12 (disc. 1993) or 20 ga., 2 3/4 or 3 in. chambers, same gas operation as the Model 302, 26 or 28 in. VR barrel, high-strength alloy receiver, select wood with choice of pistol grip or straight English stock, beavertail forearm, MobilChokes became standard 1987. Disc. 1996.

	$450	$400	$375	$335	$300	$270	$240	*$799*

Subtract 20% if without multi-chokes. Subtract $20 for straight grip English stock.

GRADING - PPGS™	100%	98%	95%	90%	80%	70%	60%	LAST MSR

* ***Model A-303 Upland*** – 12 (disc. 1993) or 20 ga., 2 3/4 or 3 in. chamber, 24 in. VR barrel with MobilChokes, English style straight stock, approx. 7 lbs. Imported 1989-1996.

$450	$400	$380	$335	$300	$270	$240	*$772*

* ***Model A-303 Waterfowl/Turkey*** – 12 ga. only, 3 in. chamber, choice of 24, 26, 28, or 30 in. VR barrel, matte finished wood and metal, MobilChokes are standard. Imported 1991 only.

$450	$400	$380	$335	$300	$270	$240	*$665*

* ***Model A-303 Sporting*** – 12 (disc. 1994) or 20 (new 1991) ga. only, 2 3/4 in. chambers, sporting clay dimensions, 28 or 30 (12 ga. only) in. VR barrel with MobilChokes. Mfg. 1988-1996.

$495	$450	$425	$375	$325	$300	$275	*$822*

Subtract 10% for 28 in. barrel.

* ***Model A-303 Skeet*** – 12 (disc. 1994) or 20 ga., 26 in. VR barrel with fixed skeet choking. Importation disc. 1995.

$400	$375	$350	$315	$275	$250	$225	*$736*

* ***Model A-303 Super Skeet*** – 12 ga. only, 28 in. VR fixed choke barrel, features factory porting, adj. LOP, and adj. separate cheekpiece on stock. Mfg. 1991-92.

$425	$375	$350	$315	$280	$240	$200	*$1,160*

* ***Model A-303 Trap*** – 12 ga. only, 30 or 32 in. VR barrel with fixed choking or MobilChokes. Importation disc. 1994.

$450	$400	$380	$350	$325	$300	$275	*$735*

Add $40 for MobilChokes (with Monte Carlo stock).

* ***Model A-303 Super Trap*** – 12 ga. only, 30 or 32 in. VR MobilChoke barrel with step tapered rib, features factory porting, adj. LOP, and adj. separate cheekpiece on stock. Mfg. 1991-1992.

$550	$525	$500	$450	$425	$365	$300	*$1,210*

* ***Model A-303 Slug*** – 12 or 20 ga., 3 in. chamber (12 ga. only), 22 in. cylinder bore barrel, iron sights. Importation disc. 1991.

$395	$350	$325	$300	$275	$265	$240	*$665*

* ***Model A-303 Youth*** – 20 ga. only, 2 3/4 or 3 (disc.) in. chamber, 24 in. VR barrel with MobilChokes, shortened stock, approx. 6 lbs. Mfg. 1988-1996.

$400	$375	$350	$325	$300	$270	$240	*$772*

MODEL A304 LARK – 12 ga., 2 3/4 in. chamber, 20 (Silver Slug), 22 (Silver Slug), 24, 26, 28, or 30 in. barrel, vent. rib (except Silver Slug model), MobilChoke or cylinder (Silver Slug) bore, ambidextrous safety, crossbolt, checkered walnut pistol grip stock and semi-beavertail forend, black recoil pad, black matte finished receiver with light scroll work, gold trigger, available in Silver Lark, Silver Slug, or Gold Lark. Mfg. 1994-disc.

$450	$400	$375	$335	$300	$270	$240	

Add 10% for Silver Lark with scroll engraved black receiver.

Add 20% for White or Black A304 Gold Lark Model with gold filled P. Beretta signature and game scene engraving.

MODEL AL390 FIELD SILVER MALLARD – 12 or 20 (new 1997) ga. only, 3 in. chamber, features gas system that accepts all 2 3/4 and 3 in. shotshells, single stainless steel piston with self regulating valve, mag. cut-off on left side of receiver, 22 slug (12 ga. only, new 1994), 24, 26, 28, or 30 (12 ga. only) in. VR barrel with MobilChoke system, choice of gloss or matte (includes sling swivels) wood finish on lightly engraved receiver, adj. checkered walnut stock, gold trigger, 6.4 (20 ga.) or 7.2 (12 ga.) lbs. Mfg. 1992-1999.

$495	$450	$415	$350	$300	$270	$240	*$860*

Add $25 for 20 ga.

Subtract $25 for 24 in. barrel.

Beginning 1997, Beretta introduced the "AL" Series of the 390, which is the lightweight variation of the 390. Prior to 1997, this model was designated the A390 Series.

GRADING - PPGS™	100%	98%	95%	90%	80%	70%	60%	LAST MSR

* ***Model AL390 Field Deluxe Gold Mallard*** – similar to Model 390 Field, except has gold accents on receiver frame, including a gold inlaid snipe, setter, and P. Beretta signature, deluxe walnut, 7.2 lbs. Mfg. 1993-99.

$595	**$550**	**$460**	**$400**	**$360**	**$320**	**$285**	***$1,025***

Add $30 for 20 ga.

* ***Model AL390 Lioness Limited Edition*** – 12 ga. only, 28 in. VR barrel with MC3 choke tubes, deluxe checkered walnut stock and forearm. Limited mfg. 2002.

$2,450	**$1,950**	**$1,600**	**$1,410**	**$1,160**	**$980**	**$800**	***$2,969***

* ***Model AL390 Silver Mallard Synthetic*** – 12 ga. only, 3 in. chamber, 24, 26, 28, or 30 in. barrel with MobilChoke, black synthetic stock and forearm with sling swivels, matte finish, approx. 7.2 lbs. Mfg. 1996-99.

$450	**$425**	**$400**	**$350**	**$300**	**$270**	**$240**	***$885***

* ***Model AL390 Silver Mallard Camouflage*** – 12 ga. only, 3 in. chamber, Advantage camo finish on entire gun, 24 or 28 in. VR barrel with choke tubes, synthetic stock and forearm, 7.2 lbs. Mfg. 1997-99.

$450	**$425**	**$400**	**$375**	**$300**	**$270**	**$240**	***$1,020***

* ***Model AL390 Silver Mallard Slug*** – 12 ga. only, 3 in. chamber, 22 in. non-rifled barrel with slug choke, gloss wood finish, adj. rear sight, approx. 6.8 or 7.4 (Model A390) lbs. Mfg. 1995-97.

$450	**$425**	**$400**	**$350**	**$300**	**$270**	**$240**	***$860***

* ***Model AL390 Silver Mallard Youth*** – 20 ga. only, 3 in. chamber, gloss wood finish, 24 in. VR barrel only with choke tubes, features youth stock dimensions, 6.4 lbs. Mfg. 1997-99.

$450	**$425**	**$400**	**$350**	**$300**	**$270**	**$240**	***$885***

* ***Model AL390 NWTF Special Camouflage*** – 12 ga. only, 3 in. chamber, 24 in. VR barrel with 3 dot TruGlo fiber optic sight system, includes Briley extended extra-full choke tube and 3 standard MobilChoke tubes, full Realtree X-tra Brown camo treatment (including synthetic stock and forearm), includes camo nylon sling. Special Edition released during 1999 only.

$525	**$500**	**$475**	**$450**	**$425**	**$400**	**$375**	***$1,105***

» **Model AL390 NWTF Special Synthetic** – similar to NWTF Special Camouflage, except has matte black anti-glare finish. Mfg. 1999 only.

$495	**$450**	**$400**	**$365**	**$315**	**$275**	**$240**	***$970***

* ***Model AL390 NWTF Special Youth*** – 20 ga. only, 3 in. chamber, 24 in. barrel, shorter stock dimensions with 13 1/2 in. LOP, matte finished wood stock and forearm, matte black metal anti-glare finish. Mfg. 1999 only.

$525	**$500**	**$425**	**$350**	**$300**	**$270**	**$240**	***$910***

MODEL AL390 SPORT SPORTING – 12 or 20 (new 1997) ga., 3 in. chamber, designed for sporting clays competition, similar to Model 390 Sport Skeet, 28 or 30 (12 ga. only) in. VR ported or unported barrel with choke tube, 6.8 (20 ga.) or 7.6 (12 ga.) lbs. Imported 1995-99.

$495	**$450**	**$425**	**$400**	**$325**	**$275**	**$240**	***$925***

* ***Model AL390 Sport Sporting Collection*** – 12 or 20 (Youth Model) ga., 3 in. chamber, 26 (20 ga. only), 28 in. VR barrel with MobilChoke, features multi-colored, gloss finished stock and forearm, 6.7 (20 ga.) or 7.6 (12 ga.) lbs. Mfg. 1998-99.

$525	**$475**	**$450**	**$400**	**$325**	**$275**	**$240**	***$965***

The 20 ga. in this model is a youth model with 13 1/2 in. LOP.

* ***Model AL390 Sport Sporting Gold*** – 12 ga. only, 28 or 30 in. VR barrel with MobilChokes, gloss finished wood, gold engraved receiver, 7.6 lbs. Mfg. 1997-99.

$725	**$650**	**$575**	**$525**	**$495**	**$460**	**$425**	***$1,145***

Subtract 10% for 28 in. barrel.

GRADING - PPGS™	100%	98%	95%	90%	80%	70%	60%	LAST MSR

* ***Model AL390 Sport Sporting Diamond*** – 12 ga. only, 3 in. chamber, silver sided receiver with multiple gold inlays, EELL quality stock and forearm with oil finish, matte 28 or 30 in. barrel with MobilChokes, oval nameplate on stock, 7.6 lbs. Mfg. 1998-99.

  $2,000 $1,650 $1,450 $1,275 $1,200 $995 $825 ***$3,075***

Subtract 10% for 26 in. barrel.

* ***Model AL390 Sport Sporting Youth*** – 20 ga. only, 3 in. chamber, matte finished checkered stock and forearm, 26 in. VR barrel only with choke tubes, features youth stock dimensions (13 1/2 in. LOP), 6.7 lbs. Imported 1997-1998 only.

  $500 $475 $450 $375 $300 $270 $240 ***$900***

MODEL AL390 SPORT SKEET – 12 ga. only, 3 in. chamber, 26 (disc.) or 28 in. SK bored VR barrel, matte finish on wood and metal, black rubber recoil pad, 7.6 lbs. Imported 1995-99.

$425 $400 $375 $350 $300 $270 $240 ***$890***

* ***Model AL390 Sport Super Skeet*** – 12 ga. only, 28 in. skeet choke VR ported barrels, includes adj. stock comb and LOP (using 3 different recoil pads) approx. 8.1 lbs. Mfg. 1993-99.

  $495 $450 $400 $375 $300 $270 $240 ***$1,160***

MODEL AL390 SPORT TRAP – 12 ga. only, 3 in. chamber, 30 or 32 in. VR barrel, matte finish on wood and metal, black rubber recoil pad, 7.8 or 8 1/4 (A390) lbs. Imported 1995-99.

$495 $450 $400 $375 $300 $270 $240 ***$890***

* ***Model AL390 Sport Trap Super*** – 12 ga. only, 30 or 32 in. VR MobilChoke ported barrels, adj. stock comb and LOP, approx. 8 lbs. Mfg. 1993-97.

  $600 $500 $450 $400 $375 $325 $295 ***$1,215***

MODEL AL391 URIKA – 12 or 20 ga., 3 in. chamber, features new self-compensating gas valve and receiver recoil absorber for internal shock reduction, satin finished checkered walnut stock and forearm, gas valve is located on the front bottom of the forearm, alloy receiver with thin design, cold hammer forged barrel, black anodized metal surfaces, gold trigger, beginning 2003, all 12 ga. AL391 Urika models include OptimaBore barrels with OptimaChoke Plus tubes, molded synthetic case included, 6.3-7.3 lbs. New 2000.

* ***Model AL391 Urika Standard*** – 12 or 20 ga., 24 (20 ga. only), 26, 28, or 30 (12 ga. only, disc. 2005) in. VR barrel, available in synthetic stock beginning 2004 at no charge, approx. 5.95 (20 ga.) or 7 1/4 lbs. Mfg. 2000-2006.

  $850 $725 $600 $525 $500 $400 $350 ***$1,050***

* ***Model AL391 Urika Synthetic Optima*** – 12 ga. only, 24 (disc. 2003), 26, 28, or 30 (disc. 2003) in. VR barrel with matte finish, features black synthetic stock with oversized grip area for a secure grip and recoil absorption and forearm, OptimaChokes became standard in 2004, approx. 7 1/4 lbs. Mfg. 2000-2006.

  $775 $650 $550 $475 $400 $350 $325 ***$998***

Subtract 20% for MobilChokes.

* ***Model AL391 Urika Camouflage*** – 12 ga. only, choice of 100% Hardwoods Green HD (mfg. 2003), RealTree Hardwoods HD (24 in. barrel only, turkey configuration), Max-4 HD (new 2004), or Advantage Wetlands camo (28 in. barrel only, waterfowl configuration, mfg. 2003) finish, with oversized stock grip, approx. 7 1/4 lbs. Mfg. 2000-2006.

  $895 $750 $650 $550 $525 $425 $350 ***$1,175***

* ***Model AL391 Urika Youth*** – 20 ga. only, 24 in. VR barrel only, shortened walnut stock and regular forearm, 5.95 lbs. Mfg. 2000-2006.

  $800 $675 $575 $495 $400 $350 $325 ***$1,050***

* ***Model AL391 Urika Gold*** – 12 or 20 ga., similar to Model AL391 Urika Standard, except has deluxe checkered walnut stock and forearm, choice of black (standard) or partial silver (lightweight configuration, 12 ga. only) receiver finish, multiple gold receiver inlays, 26 or 28 in. VR barrel, jewelled bolt, 5.9 (20 ga.), 6.6 (12 ga. lightweight), or approx. 7 1/4 lbs. Mfg. 2000-2002.

  $795 $725 $625 $495 $400 $350 $300 ***$1,213***

GRADING - PPGS™	100%	98%	95%	90%	80%	70%	60%	LAST MSR

* ***Model AL391 Urika Covey Quail Unlimited*** – 20 ga., matte black receiver with multiple gold quail inlays, deluxe checkered walnut stock and forearm, marked "1 of 1000." 1,000 mfg. 2003-2004.

$825	$775	$700	$650	$600	$500	$425	*$1,336*

* ***Model AL391 Urika Ringneck Pheasants Forever*** – 12 ga., matte black receiver with multiple gold pheasant inlays, deluxe checkered walnut stock and forearm, includes Gel-Tek recoil pad and OptimaBore barrel with OptimaChokes, marked "1 of 1000." 1,000 mfg. 2003-2004.

$995	$895	$825	$775	$675	$550	$450	*$1,377*

MODEL AL391 URIKA SPORTING – 12 or 20 ga., 3 in. chamber, gas operating system the same as Model Al391 Urika Standard, 28 or 30 in. wide VR barrel with 2 beads, features special competition checkered walnut sporting stock with rounded solid rubber recoil pad, satin black receiver with silver markings, gold trigger, MobilChoke tubes are standard on 20 ga., OptimaBore barrel with OptimaChoke Flush tubes became standard in 12 ga. during 2003 (AL391 Urika Sporting Optima), molded synthetic case included, 5.95 or 7.3 lbs. Mfg. 2000-2006.

$1,025	$825	$725	$650	$575	$475	$375	*$1,250*

* ***Model AL391 Urika Gold Sporting*** – similar to Model AL391 Urika Gold, except has deluxe walnut stock and forearm, with choice of black (disc.) or silver receiver and gold accents. Mfg. 2000-2006.

$1,150	$975	$825	$700	$650	$550	$450	*$1,500*

* ***Model AL391 Urika Diamond Sporting*** – 12 ga. only, 3 in. chamber, silver sided receiver with multiple gold inlays, EELL quality stock and forearm with oil finish, matte 28 in. barrel with MC4 chokes, oval nameplate on stock, 7.6 lbs. Mfg. 2002 only.

$2,000	$1,850	$1,700	$1,525	$1,200	$995	$775	*$3,139*

MODEL AL391 URIKA TRAP OPTIMA – 12 ga. only, 30 or 32 in. wide VR barrel with 2 beads, Monte Carlo stock with special trap recoil pad, satin black receiver with glossy side panels and silver markings, gold trigger, OptimaBore barrel with OptimaChoke flush tubes became standard in 12 ga. during 2003, molded synthetic case included, 7 1/4 lbs. Mfg. 2000-2006.

$950	$815	$695	$600	$500	$400	$350	*$1,250*

* ***Model AL391 Urika Trap Gold*** – similar to Model AL391 Urika Trap, except has black receiver with gold filled Beretta logo and P. Beretta signature, jewelled bolt and carrier, 7 1/4 lbs. Mfg. 2000-2002.

$995	$850	$725	$565	$450	$415	$395	*$1,254*

MODEL AL391 URIKA PARALLEL TARGET RL/SL – 12 ga. only, similar to Model AL391 Urika Trap, except features a Monte Carlo stock with parallel comb and reduced grip radius, RL suffix designates shorter LOP and slimmer grip, molded synthetic case included, 7 1/4 lbs. Mfg. 2000-2006.

$995	$825	$725	$675	$600	$500	$400	*$1,250*

MODEL AL391 TEKNYS – 12 or 20 ga., 3 in. chamber, multi-colored receiver with unique asymetrical patterns, X-tra Wood stock with Gel-Tek recoil pad, anti-glare receiver top, TruGlo Tru-bead front sight, choice of OptimaBore barrel with OptimaChokes or MobilChokes (20 ga.), includes molded case with 5 choke tubes, 5.9 (20 ga.) or 7.3 (12 ga.) lbs. Imported 2003-2005.

$1,050	$925	$795	$675	$525	$425	$375	*$1,425*

* ***Model AL391 Teknys Gold*** – 12 or 20 ga., 3 in. chamber, 26 or 28 in. VR barrel, receiver has engraved hunting scenes, jewelled breech bolt and carrier, checkered deluxe walnut stock and forearm with green colored enamel inserts in rear receiver and front of stock, includes Gel-Tek recoil pad, and stock recoil reducer. Mfg. 2003-2010.

$1,675	$1,425	$1,200	$1,000	$875	$750	$650	*$1,950*

GRADING - PPGS™	100%	98%	95%	90%	80%	70%	60%	LAST MSR

» ***Model AL391 Teknys Gold King Ranch*** – 12 or 20 ga., similar to AL391 Teknys Gold, except has 26 or 28 in. VR barrel, ranch stable engraving and rope bordered logo. Mfg. 2006-2011.

	$2,075	$2,050	$1,600	$1,225	$1,050	$850	$750	*$2,075*

* ***Model AL391 Teknys Gold Sporting*** – 12 or 20 ga., similar to Model AL391 Teknys Gold, except has 28 or 30 in. barrel, two-tone dark grey receiver with blue enamel inserts on stock and receiver, interchangeable rib, improved forearm checkering pattern, includes Gel-Tek recoil pad and stock recoil reducer, deluxe checkered walnut stock and forearm, includes hard case, 6.6 (20 ga.) or 7.9 (12 ga.) lbs. Importation began 2003.

MSR $2,325	$1,895	$1,525	$1,250	$1,050	$925	$775	$675	

* ***Model AL391 Teknys Gold Trap*** – 12 ga. only, 30 or 32 in. VR barrel, oil finished checkered walnut stock, gold trigger, Gel-Tek recoil pad, includes hardshell case. Imported 2004-2010.

	$1,975	$1,500	$1,225	$1,050	$875	$775	$675	*$2,300*

* ***Model AL391 Teknys Gold Target*** – 12 ga. only, 30 in. VR barrel with interchangable VRs and Optima-Plus choking, includes 8 1/2 oz. recoil reducer, deluxe checkered walnut stock w/adj. comb, satin nickel finished receiver with blue enamel accents on back of frame and stock. New 2007.

MSR $2,540	$2,075	$1,775	$1,425	$1,200	$1,050	$850	$750	

MODEL AL391 XTREMA2 3.5 (AL 391 XTREMA 3.5) – 12 ga. only, 3 1/2 in. chamber, features Gel-Tek recoil pad, spring mass and bolt travel recoil reducers lower felt recoil up to 20%, 24 (disc.), 26, or 28 in. VR OptimaBore barrel with OptimaChoke Plus tubes, gas operating system with rotating locking bolt, black synthetic stock and forearm with rubber inserts for firm control instead of traditional checkering, grooved receiver, removable trigger group, includes carrying case, 7.8 lbs. Mfg. 2002-2011.

	$1,150	$975	$850	$725	$625	$525	$475	*$1,350*

Add $250 for KO configuration (Kick-off recoil reduction).

This model's nomenclature changed to Xtrema2 during 2005.

* ***Model AL391 Xtrema2 Camouflage (AL391 Extreme Camouflage)*** – 12 ga. only, similar operating system to Model AL391 Xtrema 3.5, choice of 100% RealTree Hardwoods HD (24 in. barrel only, turkey configuration, disc. 2006), RealTree All-Purpose (new 2007), Max-4 HD (new 2004), Advantage Timber HD camo (26 in. barrel only, disc. 2004) or Advantage Wetlands (26 or 28 in. barrel, disc. 2004) finish, 7.8 lbs. Mfg. 2002-2012.

	$1,340	$1,075	$850	$675	$550	$500	$450	*$1,450*

Add $250 for KO configuration (Kick-off recoil reduction), disc. 2011.

* ***Model AL391 Xtrema2 Slug*** – 12 ga. only, 24 in. rifled OptimaBore barrel. Mfg. 2005-2007.

	$1,100	$950	$800	$675	$575	$475	$400	*$1,450*

Add $150 for KO configuration (Kick-off recoil reduction).

MODEL AL391 URIKA 2 – 12 or 20 ga., 3 in. chamber, features an improved gas system which is both faster and self-cleaning, various configurations. New 2007.

* ***Model AL391 Urika 2 Standard*** – 12 (disc.) or 20 ga., features Beretta's new proprietary X-Tra grain wood enhancement on stock and forearm, 26 or 28 in. VR barrel w/choice of OptimaChokes or MobilChokes, fine line scroll engraving on receiver.

MSR $1,565	$1,300	$1,050	$925	$800	$675	$550	$495	

* ***Model AL391 Urika 2 Youth*** – 20 ga., 24 in. VR barrel, similar to Standard, except has shorter dimensions.

MSR $1,565	$1,300	$1,050	$925	$800	$675	$550	$495	

GRADING - PPGS™	100%	98%	95%	90%	80%	70%	60%	LAST MSR

* ***Model AL391 Urika 2 Synthetic*** – 12 ga., similar to Standard model, except 28 in. barrel only, features black synthetic stock, available with or w/o Kick-Off recoil reducer (two shock absorbers).

MSR $1,105	$975	$815	$675	$575	$475	$400	$350	

Add $410 for Kick-Off recoil reduction.
Add $425 for Urika 2 Synthetic Sporting Model w/Kick-Off (mfg. 2008-2011).

* ***Model AL391 Urika 2 Camo*** – 12 ga., similar to Standard model, except features Advantage Max-4 or Realtree AP camo treatment, with or w/o Kick-Off recoil reducer.

MSR $1,215	$1,050	$875	$775	$650	$575	$475	$425	

Add $405 for Kick-Off recoil reduction.

* ***Model AL391 Urika 2 Gold*** – 12 or 20 ga., oil finished wood stock and forend, engraved receiver with gold game bird inlays. Disc. 2009.

	$1,375	$1,100	$875	$725	$625	$525	$475	*$1,550*

* ***Model AL391 Urika 2 Sporting*** – 12 or 20 ga., 28 or 30 in. barrel w/either OptimaChoke (12 ga.) or MobilChoke (20 ga.) choke tubes, features Beretta X-Tra Grain wood enhancement on stock and forearm. Disc. 2012.

	$1,300	$1,050	$925	$825	$700	$575	$500	*$1,565*

Add $375 for AL391 Urika 2 Gold Sporting (12 ga. only, includes gold inlays on receiver), disc. 2011.

* ***Model AL391 Urika 2 Parallel*** – 12 ga., 28, 30, or 32 in. VR OptimaBore barrel with OptimaChoke Plus tubes, X-Tra Grain wood enhancement on stock and forearm, available in RL (Youth) or SL configurations. Disc. late 2011.

	$1,300	$1,050	$925	$825	$700	$575	$500	*$1,565*

Add $325 for AL391 Urika 2 Gold Parallel (includes gold inlays on receiver), disc. 2011.

MODEL A400 XPLOR UNICO – 12 ga., Unico chambering with 2 3/4, 3, or 3 1/2 in. chamber, 26, 28, or 30 (KO only, new 2012) in. VR OptimaBore barrel with OptimaChoke, new Beretta Blink gas system, aluminum alloy receiver with light engraving and Beretta logo and green finish, chrome plated trigger, Xplor logo on trigger guard, metal bead front sight, X-Tra Grain pistol grip stock with oil finish, optional Kick-Off recoil reduction, 6.6 lbs. New late 2009.

MSR $1,755	$1,625	$1,300	$1,050	$875	$750	$600	$525	

Add $110 for Kick-Off recoil system.

MODEL A400 XPLOR LIGHT – 12 ga., similar to A400 Xplor Unico, except has 3 in. chamber, 26, 28, or 30 (available with Kick-off recoil only), approx. 6 1/4 lbs. Mfg. 2011-2012 only.

	$1,295	$1,150	$900	$800	$700	$600	$500	*$1,515*

Add $105 for Kick-Off recoil system.

MODEL A400 XCEL SPORTING – 12 ga., 3 in.chamber, Blink gas operating system, 28, 30, or 32 in. VR OptimaBore barrel with OptimaChoke tubes, features aqua blue aluminum receiver and forearm cap, choice of Micro-core recoil pad or optional Kick-Off recoil system, X-tra grain pistol grip stock and forearm with oil finish, optional Gun Pod system allows digital readout of ambient air temp, cartridge pressure of the last round fired and overall number of rounds fired through the shotgun, balance cap also has 3 interchangeable weights which allow changing the gun's balance, 7.7 lbs. New 2011.

MSR $1,755	$1,575	$1,350	$1,025	$950	$825	$700	$575	

Add $110 for either Kick-Off recoil system or Gun Pod electronics.

* ***Model A400 Xcel Parallel Target KO*** – 12 ga. only, 28, 30, or 32 in. VR barrel with external Optima chokes, includes Kick-Off stock. Mfg. 2012 only.

	$1,675	$1,425	$1,100	$1,000	$875	$725	$600	*$1,900*

MODEL A400 XPLOR ACTION W/GUNPOD – 12 ga., 3 in. chamber, featuring new Beretta Blink gas system, aluminum alloy brown receiver, 26, 28, or 30 in. VR barrel with OBF-HP chokes, chrome plated trigger, trigger guard with Xplor logo, pistol grip X-tra grain wood stock with oil finish and checkering with Beretta logo, features Gunpod electronics with digital readout in the pistol grip cap, with or without Kick-Off recoil system, metal bead front sight, 6.8 lbs. New 2012.

MSR $1,620	$1,495	$1,250	$1,050	$875	$750	$650	$575	

Add $205 for Kick-Off recoil system.

GRADING - PPGS™	100%	98%	95%	90%	80%	70%	60%	LAST MSR

MODEL A400 XTREME KICK-OFF – 12 ga., 2 3/4, 3, or 3 1/2 in. chamber, gas operated featuring new Beretta "Blink" system, aluminum alloy receiver, 26, 28 or 30 in. barrel with OBF-HP chokes, Kick-Off recoil system included, synthetic pistol grip stock with choice of Black synthetic, Max-4 Realtree camo, or Gore Optifade Marsh (new 2013) coverage, Micro-Core recoil pad, non-slip rubber grips, fiber optic front sight, 7.8 lbs. New 2012.

MSR $1,730	$1,575	$1,250	$1,025	$875	$750	$625	$550	

Add $110 for 100% Max-4 Realtree camo or Gore Optifade March (new 2013) coverage.

MODEL 1200 FIELD – 12 ga., inertia recoil system, 28 in. VR barrels with MobilChokes, checkered European walnut stock and forearm (pre-1989), matte black polymer stock and forearm (starting 1989), recoil pad, 4 shot mag., approx. 8 lbs. Imported 1984-1989.

	$375	$350	$300	$275	$250	$225	$200	*$580*

* ***Model 1200 Riot*** – 12 ga. only, 2 3/4 or 3 in. chamber, 20 in. cyl. bore barrel with iron sights, extended mag. Imported 1989-90 only.

	$400	$375	$350	$295	$250	$225	$200	*$660*

MODEL 1201 FIELD MAGNUM – 12 ga., 3 in. chamber, short recoil blowback action, 24, 26, or 28 in. VR barrel with two MobilChokes, matte black polymer stock and forearm. Imported 1989-94.

	$500	$395	$340	$285	$250	$225	$200	*$625*

The Model 1201 can be differentiated from the Model 1200 by stock spacers to adjust length.

* ***Model 1201 FP (Riot)*** – 12 ga., riot configuration featuring 18 (new 1997) or 20 (disc. 1996) in. cylinder bore barrel, 5 shot mag, choice of adj. rifle sights (disc.), Tritium sights (disc. 1998) or ghost ring (new 1999, Tritium front sight insert) sights, matte wood (disc.) or black synthetic stock and forearm, matte metal finish (disc.), 6.3 lbs. Mfg. 1991-2004.

	$725	$595	$500	$400	$300	$250	$200	*$890*

Add $80 for Tritium sights (mfg. 1997-98).
Add $45 for pistol grip configuration (Model 1201 FPG3 - mfg. 1994 only).

MODEL AL3901 – 12 or 20 (new 2003) ga., 3 in. chamber, 24 (new 2003), 26 (new 2003), or 28 in. VR barrel with three MobilChokes, choice of regular or shortened (Model AL3901RL) charcoal grey synthetic checkered wood, or Mossy Oak New Break-Up (new 2003), or Mossy Oak New Shadowgrass (new 2003) camo covered stock and forearm, gold trigger, matte metal finish, reversible crossbolt safety, 7 1/2 lbs. Mfg. 2002-2003.

	$450	$425	$375	$335	$280	$250	$230	*$730*

Add $50 for camo finish.

This model was available through Beretta Showcase Dealers only.

MODEL 3901 SERIES – 12 or 20 ga., 3 in. chamber, 26 or 28 in. VR barrel with three MobilChoke tubes, available in five configurations, including Citizen (synthetic stock), Statesman (wood stock, disc. 2010), Ambassador (X-Tra wood, disc. 2006), Target RL (12 ga. only, IC choke, shorter dimensions w/12-13 in. LOP and adj. comb, new 2006), or Rifled Slug (12 ga. only, 24 in. rifled slug barrel, new 2006), gas operating system, 26 or 28 in. steel alloy hammer forged barrel, Mobilchoke, removable trigger group, mfg. in America. Mfg. 2005-2011.

	$775	$650	$550	$450	$375	$325	$300	*$895*

Add $100 for Statesman configuration (disc. 2010).
Add $200 for Ambassador configuration (disc. 2006).
Add $105 for Target RL configuration (one IC choke only).
Subtract $25 for Rifled Slug Model (disc. 2010).

MODEL 3901 STANDARD SYNTHETIC – 12 ga., 3 in. chamber, 28 in. VR barrel with three MobilChoke tubes, black synthetic stock and forearm, gas operation, entry level model with full features, mfg. in America. Mfg. 2011 only.

	$575	$500	$450	$400	$365	$335	$295	*$645*

GRADING - PPGS™	100%	98%	95%	90%	80%	70%	60%	LAST MSR

TX4 STORM – 12 ga., 3 in. chamber, gas operated, dual lug action with rotating bolt, 18 in. OptimaBore barrel with OptimaChoke HP cylinder tube, optional TX4 Stand Off Device, 5 shot mag., matte black finish, alloy receiver with integral Picatinny rail, black synthetic stock, ghost ring rear sight, elevated post front sight, includes plastic case, approx. 6.4 lbs. Mfg. 2010-2011.

	100%	98%	95%	90%	80%	70%	60%	LAST MSR
	$1,200	$995	$850	$725	$625	$525	$450	*$1,450*

COMMEMORATIVES

MODEL A-303 DUCKS UNLIMITED – 12 or 20 ga., D.U. serialization, 5,500 mfg. in 12 ga. 1986-87, 3,500 mfg. in 20 ga. 1987-88.

	100%	98%	95%	90%	80%	70%	60%
12 ga.	$525	$450	$350	$285	$250	$215	$185
20 ga.	$575	$475	$375	$315	$270	$230	$200

These D.U. Models had no retail pricing from Beretta. Rather, they were auctioned off at D.U. dinners, and as a result, prices could vary substantially from region to region.

MODEL 687 O/U SHOTGUN TERCENTENNIAL – 12 ga., SST and ejectors. Limited production, only 300 manufactured.

	100%	98%	95%	90%	80%	70%	60%
	$2,500	$1,950	$1,400	$1,235	$1,000	$870	$700

MODEL 84 PISTOL TERCENTENNIAL – commemorative, only 300 manufactured. Fully engraved with gold inlays. Presentation case. Only 100 imported to U.S.

	100%	98%	95%	90%	80%	70%	60%
	$1,450	$1,100	$850	$740	$620	$515	$440

BERGARA

Current rifle and barrel manufacturer located in Bergara, Spain.

Bergara manufactures high quality rifle barrels, in addition to the single shot Apex rifles imported by Connecticut Valley Arms. Please refer to the Connecticut Valley Arms section for current rifle information and pricing (see Trademark Index).

BERGMANN

Previous manufacturer located in Gaggenau, Germany circa 1892-1944. Re-established in 1931 under Bergmann Erben.

PISTOLS: SEMI-AUTO

Prices established are for original guns with matching parts.

MODEL 1894 (ANTIQUE) – 8mm "Bergmann Schmeisser" cal. Extremely rare.

100%	98%	95%	90%	80%	70%	60%	50%	40%	30%	20%	10%
N/A	N/A	$18,500	$16,000	$12,000	$8,000	$7,500	$7,000	$6,500	$6,000	$5,500	$5,000

MODEL 1896-NO. 2 – 5mm cal., smaller type frame.

100%	98%	95%	90%	80%	70%	60%	50%	40%	30%	20%	10%
$6,500	$5,500	$4,500	$3,500	$3,000	$2,750	$2,500	$2,250	$2,000	$1,750	$1,200	$1,000

Add 50% for "folding trigger" version.

MODEL 1896-NO. 3 – 6.5mm cal., 80mm barrel.

100%	98%	95%	90%	80%	70%	60%	50%	40%	30%	20%	10%
$5,500	$4,500	$4,000	$3,500	$3,000	$2,750	$2,500	$2,250	$2,000	$1,750	$1,200	$1,000

Add 10% for early pistols without extractors and narrow grips.

Add 20% if hexagonal chamber.

*** *Model 1896-No. 3 Target***

100%	98%	95%	90%	80%	70%	60%	50%	40%	30%	20%	10%
$10,000	$8,000	$6,000	$5,000	$4,500	$4,000	$3,500	$3,000	$2,500	$2,000	$1,800	$1,600

MODEL 1896-NO. 4 – 8mm cal., military contract. Rarely seen.

100%	98%	95%	90%	80%	70%	60%	50%	40%	30%	20%	10%
$6,500	$5,500	$4,750	$4,000	$3,500	$3,000	$2,500	$2,000	$1,750	$1,500	$1,250	$1,000

MODEL 1897-NO. 5 – 7.8mm cal., commercial manufacture. May be fit with shoulder stock.

100%	98%	95%	90%	80%	70%	60%	50%	40%	30%	20%	10%
$9,500	$8,000	$7,000	$6,000	$5,000	$4,000	$3,000	$2,000	$1,500	$1,000	$800	$700

*** *Model 1897-No. 5 w/Shoulder Stock***

100%	98%	95%	90%	80%	70%	60%	50%	40%	30%	20%	10%
$17,000	$14,000	$11,000	$9,000	$7,000	$5,000	$4,000	$3,000	$2,000	$1,800	$1,600	$1,400

Add 20% if stock and pistol serial numbers match.

100%	98%	95%	90%	80%	70%	60%	50%	40%	30%	20%	10%

* ***Model 1897-No. 5 Long Barrel Carbine***

$25,000	$21,000	$16,500	$13,500	$10,500	$7,500	$6,000	$4,500	$3,000	$2,700	$2,400	$2,100

BERGMANN SIMPLEX – 8mm cal., 2.7 in. barrel, 10 shot mag., scaled down design, first and most common variation has mag. release button in front of mag. housing, later and much scarcer version has push button mag. release mounted on side of frame. Mfg. circa 1901-1914.

* ***Bergmann Simplex First Variation***

$4,000	$3,500	$3,000	$2,750	$2,500	$2,250	$2,000	$1,850	$1,650	$1,475	$1,350	$1,225

* ***Bergmann Simplex Second Variation***

$5,000	$4,500	$3,900	$3,650	$3,300	$3,050	$2,750	$2,350	$2,100	$1,800	$1,600	$1,475

BERGMANN MARS MODEL 1903 – .30 or 9mm Bergmann cal.

$7,500	$6,000	$5,500	$4,250	$3,000	$2,500	$2,000	$1,750	$1,500	$1,250	$1,000	$750

Add 25% if .30 caliber (first 100 pistols).

* ***Bergmann Mars Model 1903 w/Shoulder Stock***

$13,000	$11,000	$10,000	$8,000	$6,000	$5,000	$4,000	$3,500	$3,000	$2,500	$2,000	$1,500

MODEL 2 – .25 cal., small frame.

$400	$350	$300	$275	$250	$225	$200	$175	$150	$125	$100	$75

Add $100 for Model 2A.

MODEL 3 – .25 cal., small frame.

$400	$350	$300	$275	$250	$225	$200	$175	$150	$125	$100	$75

Add $100 for Model 3A.

ERBEN – .25 cal., Models I, II, and Special (.32 cal.).

$450	$400	$350	$300	$250	$215	$180	$160	$135	$115	$95	$80

PISTOLS: SEMI-AUTO - BERGMANN-BAYARD

Even though the Bergmann-Bayard models listed were manufactured only by Anciens Etablissements Pieper of Herstal, Belgium, these pistols are listed under this heading as they are most commonly referred to by this trademark designation.

MODEL 1908 STANDARD COMMERCIAL – 9mm Bergmann/Bayard cal., identified by a mounted knight on the left magazine housing and is without finger cuts at base of magazine housing.

$4,200	$3,800	$3,400	$2,750	$1,900	$1,600	$1,100	$900	$700	$600	$500	$400

Add 25% if backstrap is slotted for shoulder stock.

Add $3,500 for excellent original leather/wood shoulder stock.

MODEL 1908 SPANISH CONTRACT – 9mm Bergmann/Bayard cal., total contract was for 3,000 pistols, can be identified from standard commercial pistols by the Spanish military acceptance stamp struck on the receiver.

$3,700	$3,400	$3,000	$2,500	$1,600	$1,100	$900	$800	$700	$600	$500	$400

Add 10% for matched numbered magazine.

Prices are for guns with original finish and grips - many Spanish contract guns were arsenal refinished.

MODEL 1910 STANDARD COMMERCIAL – 9mm Bergmann/Bayard cal., mechanically similar to Model 1908 Standard Commercial except has finger cuts in bottom of magazine housing, circular grooves are present on each side of magazine base.

$3,500	$3,000	$2,750	$2,200	$1,700	$1,200	$900	$800	$700	$600	$500	$400

Add 10% for matching numbered magazine.

MODEL 1910 DANISH GOVERNMENT CONTRACT – 9mm Bergmann/Bayard cal., total contract was for 4,840 pistols with mfg. and delivery 1911-1914. This variation can be identified by the Danish proof mark on the left receiver side and Danish inventory number on right side of receiver. Most pistols were converted in Denmark, Trolite grips were part of the original conversion, followed later by wood replacements, Converted pistols are marked "1910/21". Few pistols escaped conversion and have just Trolite replacement

100%	98%	95%	90%	80%	70%	60%	50%	40%	30%	20%	10%

grips, those pistols lack the "1910/21" marking.

$2,650	$2,350	$2,000	$1,800	$1,300	$1,000	$900	$800	$700	$600	$500	$400

Add 15% for matching numbered magazine.

Add 25% for pistols that were not converted and lack the 1910/21 marking.

Subtract 25% for late wood replacement grips.

MODEL 1910/21 TOJHUS – 9mm Bergmann/Bayard cal., these pistols are marked "Haerens Tojhus" and are numbered from 1-900, original grips were black Trolit, replacement grips are either all smooth or with checkered circles above and below grip screw.

$2,950	$2,600	$2,200	$1,950	$1,450	$1,100	$900	$800	$700	$600	$500	$400

This contract was manufactured by the Danish Royal Arsenal located in Copenhagen.

MODEL 1910/21 RUSTKAMMER – 9mm Bergmann/Bayard cal., pistols are marked "Haerens Rustkammer", and numbered 901-2204, grip replacements are the same as noted for Haerens Tojhus.

$2,750	$2,350	$2,000	$1,800	$1,300	$1,000	$900	$800	$700	$600	$500	$400

This contract was manufactured by the Danish Royal Arsenal located in Copenhagen.

WAYNE BERGQUIST CUSTOM PISTOLS

Current custom pistolsmith and gun dealer established during 1980 and currently located in Naples, FL. The company should be contacted directly regarding its limited production custom pistol models and related gunsmithing services (see Trademark Index for current information).

BERNARDELLI, GIULIO

Current shotgun manufacturer located in Gardone, Italy.

Giulio Bernardelli Manifattura Armi manufactures both O/U and SxS (hammer or hammerless) boxlock shotguns in all gauges. Every gun is a special order manufactured per individual customer specifications. Please contact the company directly for a price quotation and length of delivery (see Trademark Index).

BERNARDELLI, VINCENZO

Current trademark of pistols and long arms mostly produced under private label by various manufacturers in Turkey, with headquarters located in Brescia, Italy beginning mid-2002. No current U.S. importation. Previously manufactured from 1721 to August, 1997 in Gardone, VT, Italy. Previously imported and distributed until 1997 by Armsport, Inc. located in Miami, FL. Previously imported and distributed by Magnum Research, Inc. located in Minneapolis, MN (1989-1992), Quality Arms, Inc. located in Houston, TX, Armes De Chasse located in Chadds Ford, PA, Stoeger located in New York, NY, and Action Arms, Ltd. located in Philadelphia, PA.

There is some confusion on the Bernardelli trademark as there have been three different companies (Pietro Bernardelli, Vincenzo Bernardelli, and Santini Bernardelli) that have produced firearms. During the late 1980s, there were quite a lot of Pietro Bernardellis that were "dumped" in the American marketplace - these guns do not have the quality of Vincenzo Bernardelli and are not covered within the scope of this text.

The Vincenzo Bernardelli trademark was purchased in early 2002, and many of the older discontinued models are once again back in production, in addition to some new models. Please contact the company directly for more information, including domestic model availability, pricing, and current importation (see Trademark Index).

GRADING - PPGS™	100%	98%	95%	90%	80%	70%	60%	LAST MSR

COMBINATION GUNS

MODEL 190 – 12, 16, or 20 ga. under .243 Win., .30-06, or .308 Win. cal., combination rifle/shotgun, boxlock action, DTs, extractors. Imported 1989 only.

$1,295	$1,025	$895	$800	$700	$600	$525	*$1,393*

Add $700 for extra set of 12 ga. O/U barrels.

GRADING - PPGS™	100%	98%	95%	90%	80%	70%	60%	LAST MSR

MODEL COMB 2000 – 12, 16, or 20 ga. under choice of rifle cals., ejectors, set trigger. Imported 1990-97.

$2,300	$1,550	$1,075	$875	$750	$675	$575	$2,920

Add $621 for extra set of O/U shotgun barrels (Model COMB 2000S - disc.).

MODEL 120 – 12 ga. over choice of 12 cals., deluxe checkered walnut stock and forearm, iron sights, double triggers, vent. recoil pad, coin washed receiver with light engraving.

$1,950	$1,585	$1,300	$1,050	$850	$760	$650	$2,411

Add $130 for extra set of shotgun barrels.

PISTOLS: SEMI-AUTO

VEST POCKET MODEL – .25 ACP cal., 2 1/8 in. barrel, fixed sights, blue, bakelite grips. Mfg. 1945-48.

$250	$195	$165	$140	$110	$90	$65

BABY SEMI-AUTO – .22 S or L cal., 2 1/8 in. barrel, fixed sights, blue, bakelite grips. Mfg. 1949-1968.

$250	$175	$150	$130	$100	$90	$80

SPORTER MODEL – .22 LR cal., 6, 8, or 10 in. barrels, target sights, blue, wood grips. Mfg. 1949-1968.

$305	$275	$220	$165	$140	$110	$85

MODEL 60 – .22 LR cal., .32 ACP, or .380 ACP cal., 3 1/2 in. barrel, fixed sights, blue, bakelite grips. Mfg. 1959-disc.

$220	$195	$180	$165	$155	$135	$120

This model was not imported domestically.

MODEL 68 – .22 Short or .22 LR cal., vest pocket model, 6 shot, bakelite grips, 8 1/2 oz. Disc.

$140	$120	$110	$100	$90	$80	$70

This model was not imported domestically.

MODEL 80 – .22 LR or .380 ACP cal., 3 1/2 in. barrel, adj. sights, blue, thumbrest plastic grips. Imported 1968-1988.

$185	$160	$150	$140	$130	$115	$100

Add $5 for .380 ACP.

Note: This model was produced to conform to import regulations of GCA 1968. Importation of this model was disc. 1988.

MODEL USA – .22 LR, .32 ACP (disc.), or .380 ACP. cal., semi-auto, single action, steel frame, loaded chamber indicator, adj. sights, target bakelite grips, 7 shot (.380 ACP) or 10 shot (.22 LR) mag. Disc. 1997.

$380	$295	$250	$215	$185	$165	$145	$425

Add $60 for chrome finish.

This model has the same technical specifications as the Model 60.

MODEL AMR – .22 LR, .32 ACP (disc.), or .380 ACP cal., similar action to USA Model except has 6 in. barrel and adj. rear sight. Disc. 1994.

$395	$325	$275	$225	$185	$165	$145	$445

MODEL 90 SPORT TARGET – .22 LR cal. or .32 ACP, similar to Model 80, with 6 in. barrel. Imported 1968-88.

$210	$185	$170	$155	$140	$120	$110	$245

MODEL 69 TARGET – .22 LR cal., target semi-auto, single action, 5.9 in. heavy barrel, 10 shot mag., wraparound checkered wood grips, 38 oz.

$575	$475	$400	$350	$275	$225	$185	$660

This model was previously designated Model 100.

GRADING - PPGS™	100%	98%	95%	90%	80%	70%	60%	LAST MSR

MODEL 100 TARGET – .22 LR cal., 5.9 in. barrel, adj. sight, blue, checkered wood, thumbrest grips, cased. Imported 1968-88.

$395	$325	$295	$260	$225	$190	$175	*$360*

P-ONE – 9mm Para. or .40 S&W cal., double action, 10 shot mag., choice of matte black or chrome finish. Imported 1993-97.

$580	$495	$400	$360	$330	$295	$265	*$684*

Add $36 for chrome finish.
Add $36 for wood grips.

* ***P-One Compact*** – compact variation of the P-One. Disc. 1997.

$595	$500	$400	$360	$330	$295	$265	*$702*

Add $48 for chrome finish.
Add $48 for wood grips.

MODEL P010 TARGET – .22 LR cal., single action, 5.9 in. barrel, adj. sights and trigger, matte black finish, large anatomic walnut stippled grips with thumbrest, 10 shot mag., 40 1/2 oz. Imported 1989-92, re-introduced 1995-97.

$675	$575	$495	$425	$375	$325	$275	*$768*

Add $132 for wood case and two sets of weights.

MODEL P018 – 7.65mm (disc. 1988), .380 ACP (mfg. 1993-94), or 9mm Para. cal., double action, semi-auto, steel construction, 4 7/8 in. barrel, 10 (C/B 1994) or 16* shot mag., black plastic (standard) or walnut checkered (disc. 1992) grips, blue (disc.), black (new 1994), or chrome finish, 36 oz. Imported 1985-96.

$485	$400	$350	$300	$275	$250	$230	*$560*

Add $40 for walnut grips (disc. 1992).
Add $60 for chrome finish.
Add $30 for carrying case w/combination lock (disc. 1989).

This model was extensively redesigned in 1989 and included a "cocked and locked" feature, thumb mag. release, loaded chamber indicator, as well as other improvements.

* ***Model P018 Compact*** – .380 ACP or 9mm Para. cal., similar to Model P018 except has 4 in. barrel and 10 (C/ B 1994) or 14* shot mag., approx. 2 lbs. Imported 1989-96.

$545	$430	$375	$310	$275	$250	$230	*$610*

Add $55 for chrome finish.

This model was also redesigned in 1989 to incorporate the same features as the Model P018.

PRACTICAL VB – 9x21mm cal., comp. gun built for IPSC competition, various configurations, black or matte chrome finish, 2, 4, or 6 port compensating system. Mfg. 1993-97.

$1,100	$925	$775	$675	$575	$475	$400	*$1,260*

Add $60 for 4 port compensator.
Add $60 for chrome finish.

* ***Practical VB Customized*** – state-of-the-art competition pistol featuring 4+2 port compensating system. Mfg. 1993-97.

$1,775	$1,325	$1,100	$975	$850	$725	$600	*$1,920*

Add $60 for chrome finish.

RIFLES: DOUBLE

EXPRESS VB – various cals., side-by-side sidelock action, ejectors, single or double triggers. Imported 1990-97.

$5,475	$4,100	$3,400	$2,725	$2,275	$1,900	$1,600	*$6,000*

Add $1,000 for Deluxe Model (double triggers).

EXPRESS 2000 – .30-06, 7x65R, 8x57JRS, or 9.3x74R cal., O/U boxlock design, single or double trigger, extractors, checkered walnut stock and forearm. Imported 1994-97.

$2,600	$1,995	$1,600	$1,275	$1,100	$975	$875	*$3,192*

Add $130 for single trigger.

GRADING - PPGS™	100%	98%	95%	90%	80%	70%	60%	LAST MSR

MINERVA EXPRESS – various cals., exposed hammers, extractors, double triggers, moderate engraving. Imported 1995-97.

	$4,975	$3,850	$3,250	$2,725	$2,275	$1,900	$1,600	*$5,850*

RIFLES: SEMI-AUTO

CARBINA .22 – .22 LR cal., blow back action. Imported 1990-97.

	$575	$375	$295	$210	$170	$150	$135	*$720*

SHOTGUNS: FOLDING MODELS

SINGLE BARREL – 12, 16, 20, 24, 28, 32 ga., or .410 bore, gun folds in half. Importation disc. 1990.

	$230	$185	$150	$135	$125	$115	$100	*$265*

DOUBLE BARREL – 12 and 16 ga., gun folds in half, double triggers. Previously available in Europe only.

	$570	$430	$370	$315	$285	$260	$230	

SHOTGUNS: O/U

MODEL 115 HUNTING – 12 ga. only, boxlock action, monobloc frame, inclined plane locking design, blue receiver, single trigger, ejectors. Importation disc. 1989.

	$1,770	$1,425	$1,225	$1,000	$895	$750	$650	*$1,915*

* ***Model 115S*** – similar to 115, except moderate engraving.

	$2,150	$1,925	$1,745	$1,500	$1,250	$1,025	$950	*$2,500*

* ***Model 115L*** – similar to 115S, except extensive scroll engraving on silver finish receiver.

	$2,600	$2,375	$2,050	$1,750	$1,450	$1,100	$850	*$3,170*

* ***Model 115E*** – sideplate, boxlock action, ejector, bulino game scene engraving.

	$4,650	$4,125	$3,600	$3,100	$2,650	$2,200	$1,800	*$5,200*

MODEL 115 TARGET – 12 ga. only, same specifications as Model 115, except trap dimensions. Importation disc. 1989.

	$1,800	$1,595	$1,375	$1,175	$1,000	$895	$750	*$2,160*

* ***Model 115S*** – same specifications as 115 Target, except light engraving. Importation disc. 1992.

	$3,275	$2,425	$1,825	$1,500	$1,250	$1,025	$895	*$3,920*

This model was available in either Pigeon, Skeet, Sporting Clays, or Trap configuration.

* ***Model 115L*** – similar to 115S, except extensive scroll engraving on silver finish receiver. Importation disc. 1990.

	$3,700	$2,995	$2,600	$2,375	$2,050	$1,750	$1,450	*$4,201*

* ***Model 115E*** – same specifications as 115S, except with extensively engraved sideplates. Importation disc. 1990.

	$5,950	$4,800	$4,125	$3,600	$3,100	$2,650	$2,200	*$6,827*

* ***Model 115S Trap/Skeet*** – 12 ga. only, available in Trap or Skeet configuration, ejectors, single trigger. Disc. 1997.

	$3,250	$2,450	$1,825	$1,425	$995	$875	$725	*$3,780*

* ***Model 115S Sporting Clays*** – 12 ga. only, SST, ejectors, choke tubes. Imported 1995-97.

	$3,875	$3,350	$2,775	$2,100	$1,750	$1,500	$1,350	*$4,200*

MODEL 190 TARGET – 12 ga, SST, ejectors, engraved silver receiver, select checkered walnut stock and forearm. Imported 1986-89.

	$1,425	$1,095	$925	$800	$700	$600	$525	*$1,572*

* ***Model 190 MC*** – similar to Model 190 Target except has Monte Carlo stock. Imported 1989 only.

	$1,000	$825	$700	$600	$525	$475	$450	*$1,155*

GRADING - PPGS™	100%	98%	95%	90%	80%	70%	60%	LAST MSR

* ***Model 190 Special*** – 12 ga. only, similar to Model 190 Target, except has better walnut and engraving. Imported 1988-89.

	$1,335	$1,000	$895	$800	$700	$600	$525	$1,456

Add $75 for single trigger (Model 190 Special MS).

These variations are hunting models.

MODEL 192 FIELD – 12 ga. only, single or double triggers, ejectors, choke tubes optional. Imported 1995-97.

	$1,175	$895	$750	$650	$550	$450	$375	$1,425

Add $65 for single trigger.
Add $200 for choke tubes.
Add $350 for 192 Special (includes double triggers, ejectors).

MODEL 192 MS COMPETITION – 12 ga. only, ejectors, selective or non-selective triggers, multi-chokes standard on Sporting Clays Model. Mfg. 1990-97.

	$1,725	$1,475	$1,150	$925	$775	$675	$575	$1,930

Add $120 for SST.
Add $200 for choke tubes.
Add $485 for Special Sport.

This model was available in either Pigeon, Skeet, Sporting Clays, Special Sport, or Trap configuration.

MODEL 192 MS-MC HUNTING – 12 ga. only, boxlock action with engraved coin finished receiver, 3 in. chambers, ejectors, SST, 26 3/4 or 28 in. VR barrels with choke tubes, steel shot compatible. Imported 1990-1992.

	$1,400	$995	$825	$700	$600	$525	$475	$1,833

* ***Model 192 MS-MC-WF*** – waterfowler variation which includes 3 1/2 in. chambers, 3 choke tubes, and SST. Imported 1990 only.

	$1,275	$950	$875	$775	$675	$575	$500	$1,444

MODEL 200 LIGHTWEIGHT MS – 12 ga. only, silver grey finished receiver with game scene engraving, ejectors, DTs. Imported 1988-89, resumed 1993-97.

	$1,325	$975	$850	$725	$650	$550	$450	$1,525

MODEL 220 MS HUNTING – 12 or 20 ga., silver grey finished receiver with engraving. Mfg. 1988-97.

	$1,350	$995	$850	$725	$650	$550	$450	$1,560

Add $75 for SST.
Add $180 for 12 ga. slug variation with DTs (new 1994).
Add $700 for extra set of 12 ga. barrels (disc. 1990).

This model was available with either a pistol grip or English grip (straight) stock.

MODEL LUCK – 12 ga., ejectors, boxlock action, choice of double or single trigger. Imported 1994-97.

	$1,450	$995	$725	$650	$550	$450	$375	$1,795

Add $275 for single trigger.

SATURNO MS-MC COMPETITION – 12 ga. only, sporter configuration, boxlock action with lightly engraved side plates, ejectors, DTs. Imported 1991-97.

	$2,325	$1,725	$1,150	$925	$775	$675	$575	$2,760

This model was available in either Pigeon, Skeet, Sporting Clays, or Trap configuration.

SATURNO MS-MC HUNTING – 12 ga. only, boxlock action with lightly engraved side plates, ejectors, SST, includes multi-chokes. Imported 1991-92.

	$2,275	$1,525	$1,050	$875	$750	$695	$600	$2,609

ORIONE S – 12 ga., double Purdey lock, VR, ejectors, engraved nickel finish receiver. Importation disc. 1989.

	$1,175	$1,025	$860	$760	$650	$560	$510	$1,425

GRADING - PPGS™	100%	98%	95%	90%	80%	70%	60%	LAST MSR

ORIONE L – similar to Orione S, single trigger, finer engraving, English or pistol-type select walnut stock. Importation disc. 1989.

	$1,285	$1,125	$950	$840	$750	$650	$550	*$1,550*

ORIONE E – top-of-the-line, deep relief engraving. Importation disc. 1989.

	$1,375	$1,200	$1,020	$900	$820	$710	$650	*$1,660*

SHOTGUNS: SxS

Bernardelli side-by-side shotguns were manufactured with straight grip, English style stocks with pistol grip available as a special order. Importation of Bernardelli shotguns was inconsistent over the years. A wide variety of special order options was available on these shotguns. Barrel choke markings for V. Bernardelli shotguns are as follows; Full: *, Impr. Mod: **, Mod: *, Impr. Cyl: ****, Cylinder: CL.**

MODEL 110 – 12 ga., trap or skeet model, separated barrels, high post rib.

	$2,000	$1,500	$1,300	$1,100	$1,000	$900	$800	

MODEL 110 EXTRAO – similar to Model 110, except engraved.

	$3,021	$2,265	$1,970	$1,665	$1,510	$1,360	$1,210	

S. UBERTO 1 GAMECOCK – 12, 16, 20, or 28 ga., 25 3/4 in. imp. cyl. and mod., 27 1/2 in. full and mod., hammerless, boxlock, extractors, two triggers, English style stock, checkered.

	$853	$635	$605	$550	$495	$440	$415	

Add 20% for ejectors.

BRESCIA HAMMER DOUBLE BARREL – 12, 16, or 20 ga., 25 3/4, 27 1/2, or 29 1/2 in. mod. and full, 12 ga., 25 1/2 in. imp. cyl. and mod., sidelock, extractors, two triggers, straight English stock, splinter forearm, checkered. Importation disc.

	$1,495	$1,150	$800	$600	$500	$400	$350	*$2,482*

ITALIA HAMMER DOUBLE BARREL – similar to Brescia, except higher grade engraving and wood. Importation disc.

	$1,750	$1,300	$925	$700	$600	$500	$450	*$2,844*

ITALIA EXTRA HAMMER – 12, 16, or 20 ga., hammer double. Top-of-the-line hammer model. Importation disc.

	$6,400	$3,150	$2,200	$1,650	$1,375	$1,050	$800	*$7,861*

MODEL 112 – 12 ga., entry-level model with extractors and DTs. Imported 1989 only.

	$850	$750	$675	$625	$550	$495	$450	*$998*

Add $65 for single trigger (Model 112 M - disc.).

MODEL 112 E – 12 ga., Anson & Deeley action, light engraving. Importation disc. 1989.

	$995	$850	$775	$695	$625	$550	$495	*$1,108*

MODEL 112 SI/S (EM) – similar to Model 112E, except has single or double triggers. Disc. 1997.

	$1,795	$1,000	$825	$725	$650	$550	$450	*$2,100*

Add $174 for ejectors.
Add $138 for ST.
Add $420 for choke tubes.

* ***Model 112 EM - MC*** – similar to Model 112 EM, except has 3 in. chambers and 5 choke tubes. Imported 1990-92.

	$1,600	$1,000	$850	$775	$675	$575	$495	*$1,971*

* ***Model 112 EM-MC-WF*** – includes 3 1/2 in. chambers, waterfowl model with matte finish, single trigger and 3 choke tubes. Importation disc. 1990.

	$1,275	$975	$850	$775	$675	$575	$495	*$1,444*

S. UBERTO 1 – 12, 16, 20, or 28 ga., Anson & Deeley action, Purdey locks, light engraving, case hardened receiver, double triggers, extractors.

	$1,050	$900	$800	$700	$625	$550	$495	*$1,164*

Add $65 for single trigger (Model S. Uberto 1M).

GRADING - PPGS™	100%	98%	95%	90%	80%	70%	60%	LAST MSR

* ***S. Uberto 1E*** – similar to S. Uberto 1, except with ejectors. Importation disc. 1990.

	$1,175	$950	$850	$740	$650	$565	$495	*$1,357*

Add $65 for single trigger (Model S. Uberto 1EM).

S. UBERTO 2 – 12, 16, 20, or 28 ga., Anson & Deeley action, Purdey locks, light scroll engraving, silver finished receiver, double triggers, extractors. Importation disc. 1989, resumed 1993-1997.

	$1,375	$1,150	$875	$725	$650	$550	$450	*$1,580*

Add $35 for single trigger (Model S. Uberto 2M - disc.).

* ***S. Uberto 2E*** – similar to S. Uberto 2, except with ejectors. Disc. 1997.

	$1,525	$1,300	$1,050	$875	$725	$650	$550	*$1,710*

Add $80 for single trigger (Model S. Uberto 2EM - disc.).

S. UBERTO FS – 12, 16, 20, or 28 ga., Purdey locks, relief engraved with hunting scenes on silver finished receiver, double triggers, extractors. Importation disc. 1989, resumed 1993-97.

	$1,695	$1,450	$1,125	$895	$750	$675	$575	*$1,915*

Add $65 for single trigger (Model S. Uberto FSM - disc. 1989).

* ***S. Uberto FSE*** – similar to S. Uberto FS, except with ejectors. Importation disc. 1989.

	$1,375	$1,100	$975	$850	$750	$625	$550	*$1,537*

Add $65 for single trigger (Model S. Uberto FSEM).

ROMA 3 – similar to S. Uberto, double triggers, extractors, false sideplates, case hardened receiver. Importation disc. 1989, resumed 1993-97.

	$1,425	$1,200	$895	$775	$675	$575	$475	*$1,625*

Add $65 for single trigger (Model Roma 3M - disc.).

* ***Roma 3E*** – similar to Roma 3, except with ejectors. Disc. 1997.

	$1,550	$1,325	$1,050	$875	$725	$650	$550	*$1,770*

Add $80 for single trigger (Model Roma 3EM - disc.).

ROMA 4 – more deluxe model than Roma 3, false sideplates, scroll engraved, silver finished receiver. Importation disc. 1989.

	$1,250	$1,025	$900	$800	$700	$625	$550	*$1,439*

Add $65 for single trigger (Model Roma 4M).

* ***Roma 4E*** – similar to Roma 4, except with ejectors. Disc. 1997.

	$1,775	$1,475	$1,150	$925	$775	$675	$575	*$2,000*

Add $80 for single trigger (Model Roma 4EM - disc.).

ROMA 6 – 12, 16, 20, or 28 ga., fully engraved sideplates with hunting scenes, Purdey locks, silver finish receiver, single trigger, finely figured English walnut. Importation disc. 1989.

	$1,395	$1,150	$975	$875	$775	$675	$600	*$1,619*

Add $175 for single trigger (Model Roma 6M).

* ***Roma 6E*** – similar to Roma 6, except with ejectors, 16 ga. was disc. 1989. Disc. 1997.

	$2,400	$1,825	$1,475	$1,150	$925	$775	$675	*$2,880*

Add $180 for single trigger (Model Roma 6EM).

ROMA 7 – 12 ga., ejectors, grade up from the Roma 6. Imported 1994-97.

	$3,200	$2,200	$1,675	$1,375	$995	$875	$750	*$3,840*

ROMA 8 – 12 ga., ejectors, grade up from the Roma 7. Imported 1994-97.

	$3,700	$2,700	$1,950	$1,675	$1,375	$995	$875	*$4,740*

ROMA 9 – 12 ga., ejectors, grade up from the Roma 8. Imported 1994-97.

	$4,550	$3,200	$2,500	$1,950	$1,675	$1,375	$995	*$5,520*

ELIO – 12 ga. only, lightweight, extractors, fine English style scroll engraving on silver finish receiver. Importation disc. 1989.

	$1,125	$925	$850	$740	$650	$565	$475	*$1,238*

Add $65 for single trigger (Model Elio M).

GRADING - PPGS™	100%	98%	95%	90%	80%	70%	60%	LAST MSR

* ***Elio E*** – similar to Elio, except with ejectors. Importation disc. 1989.

	$1,200	$1,000	$895	$795	$695	$595	$500	*$1,353*

Add $65 for single trigger (Model Elio EM).

SLUG GUN – 12 ga. only, 23 3/4 in. slug bored barrels, extractors, Anson & Deeley action, Purdey locks, lightly engraved, silver finish receiver. Importation disc. 1990.

	$1,325	$1,000	$895	$795	$695	$595	$500	*$1,575*

Add $65 for single trigger (Model Slug M).

SLUG LUSSO – 12 ga. only, 23 3/4 in. slug bored barrels, sideplates, with extensive engraving featuring hunting scenes, cheekpiece, ejectors, silver finished receiver. Importation disc. 1992.

	$2,325	$1,550	$1,200	$995	$875	$750	$650	*$2,793*

Add $80 for single trigger (Model Slug Lusso M).

This model was previously designated Slug Deluxe (1988 or earlier).

HEMINGWAY – 12, 20, or 28 (new 1992) ga., boxlock action, coin finished receiver with game scene engraving, 23 1/2 in. barrels, DTs, deluxe checkered walnut stock and forearm, 6 1/4 lbs. Disc. 1997.

	$2,050	$1,500	$1,050	$875	$750	$675	$575	*$2,520*

Add $70 for single trigger.
Add $120 for single selective trigger.

HEMINGWAY DE LUXE – similar to Hemingway, except is also available in 16 ga. and has sideplates, better wood, and more engraving. Disc. 1997.

	$2,350	$1,750	$1,150	$925	$775	$675	$575	*$2,874*

Add $126 for single trigger (Model Hemingway De Luxe M).

LAS PALOMAS PIGEON – 12 ga. live pigeon gun, single trigger, special dimensions for live pigeon shooting. Disc. 1997.

	$3,125	$2,550	$2,000	$1,700	$1,375	$995	$875	*$3,700*

Add $750 for Pigeon Model (includes single trigger).

HOLLAND V.B. LISCIO – 12 ga. only, Holland type sidelocks, light engraving, silver finish receiver, single trigger, ejectors, select walnut. Disc. 1997.

	$10,350	$5,300	$4,450	$3,900	$3,350	$2,850	$2,400	*$12,600*

HOLLAND V.B. INCISO – 12 ga. only, H&H sidelock action, Purdey locks, various barrel lengths, single trigger, ejectors, straight or pistol grip stock, 100% engraved on coin finished receiver. Importation disc. 1992.

	$10,700	$7,000	$5,500	$4,700	$4,200	$3,500	$3,000	*$12,929*

HOLLAND V.B. LUSSO – 12 ga. only, H&H sidelock action, Purdey locks, various barrel lengths, single trigger, ejectors, straight or pistol grip stock, same features as Holland V.B. Inciso, only extra select wood and game scene engraving. Importation disc. 1992.

	$8,900	$7,900	$6,500	$5,200	$4,750	$4,000	$3,450	*$14,377*

HOLLAND V.B. EXTRA – 12 ga. only, H&H style action, any barrel length and choke, double triggers, auto ejectors, straight or pistol grip stock, 100% engraved coin finished receiver. Prices are completely dependent upon individual customer specifications. Values are for engraving pattern No. 3. Importation disc. 1992.

	$13,250	$9,700	$7,450	$6,150	$5,200	$4,600	$3,950	*$16,549*

Add $1,034 for engraving pattern No. 4.
Add $4,551 for engraving pattern No. 12.
Add $8,895 for engraving pattern No. 20.
Add $621 for single trigger.

Older specimens ordered before 1992 could have values considerably lower than those listed.

HOLLAND V.B. GOLD – top-of-the-line model, made to individual order. Very limited production and ultra-rare. Importation disc. 1992.

	$47,500	$32,500	$24,000	$18,500	$13,000	$11,500	$9,950	*$57,922*

Older specimens ordered before 1992 could have values considerably lower than those listed.

GRADING - PPGS™	100%	98%	95%	90%	80%	70%	60%	LAST MSR

SHOTGUNS: SEMI-AUTO

MODEL 9MM FLOBERT – 9mm Flobert cal. (rimfire shot cartridge), 24.4 in. smooth bore barrel, 3 shot mag., steel receiver, walnut stock and forearm with sling and swivels, 5 lbs. 3 oz. Disc. 1997.

	$385	$265	$175	$150	$125	$100	$95	$474

BERSA

Current manufacturer established circa 1958 and located in Ramos Mejia, Argentina. Currently distributed exclusively by Eagle Imports, Inc. located in Wanamassa, NJ. Previously imported and distributed before 1988 by Rock Island Armory located in Geneseo, IL, Outdoor Sports Headquarters, Inc. located in Dayton, OH, and R.S.A. Enterprises, Inc. located in Ocean, NJ. Distributor sales only.

PISTOLS: SEMI-AUTO

THUNDER 9 – 9mm Para. cal., double action semi-auto, 3 1/2 in. barrel, 10 (C/B 1994) or 14* shot mag., ambidextrous manual safety and decocking lever, automatic firing pin safety, 3-dot sights, aluminum frame, wraparound matte black polymer grips, link-free locked breech design, non-glare matte blue, satin nickel (new 1995), or duo-tone (new 1995) finish. Imported 1993-95.

	$400	$350	$300	$270	$220	$180	$140	$475

Add $17 for duo-tone finish.
Add $50 for satin nickel finish.

THUNDER 22 (DISC. MODEL 23) – .22 LR cal., double action semi-auto, 9 shot mag., 3 1/2 in. barrel, black polymer (new 1997) or walnut (disc. 1996) grips, 24 1/2 oz. Imported 1988-98.

	$230	$200	$170	$155	$125	$100	$80	$265

Add $17 for satin nickel finish.

THUNDER 22 (CURRENT MFG.) – .22 LR cal., DA/SA, alloy frame/steel slide, 3 1/2 in. barrel with 3 dot sights, combat style trigger guard, integral locking system, choice of matte, satin nickel, or duo-tone (new 2012) finish, black checkered polymer grips, 10 shot mag. with finger extension, 18.9 oz.

MSR $335	$275	$230	$200	$180	$160	$140	$120	

Add $3 for duo-tone finish (new 2012).
Add $18 for nickel finish.

THUNDER 32 – .32 ACP cal., matte, duo-tone, or nickel finish, 10 shot mag. Mfg. 2012 only.

	$275	$225	$200	$185	$165	$145	$130	$323

Add $6 for duo-tone finish.
Add $19 for nickel finish.

THUNDER 380 – .380 ACP cal., double action, 3 1/2 in. barrel, fixed sights, 7 shot mag., deep blue, satin nickel, duo-tone (disc. 1995) finish, rubber grips, 25 3/4 oz. Imported 1995-98.

	$325	$295	$260	$230	$200	$185	$170	$275

Add $16 for satin nickel.
Add $16 for duo-tone finish (disc. 1995).

* ***Thunder 380 Deluxe*** – .380 ACP cal., 9 shot mag., black polymer grips, extended slide release and mag. bottom, polished blue, 3-dot sights, 23 oz. Mfg. 1997-2010.

	$295	$260	$230	$200	$185	$170	$150	$360

* ***Thunder 380 Plus*** – similar to Thunder 380, except has 15 shot mag. Mfg. 1995-1997.

	$265	$230	$200	$180	$145	$120	$95	$316

Add $32 for satin nickel finish.
Add $17 for duo-tone finish.

GRADING - PPGS™	100%	98%	95%	90%	80%	70%	60%	LAST MSR

THUNDER 380 (95) – .380 ACP cal., DA/SA, alloy frame/steel slide, 3 1/2 in. barrel, 3 dot sights fixed sights, 7 shot mag., combat trigger guard, matte blue, satin nickel, matte plus (new 2007-disc.) or duo-tone (3,000 mfg. 2001, reintroduced 2008) finish, black polymer grips, 20 oz. New 1995.

MSR $335	$275	$230	$200	$180	$160	$140	$120	

Add $2 for matte finish.
Add $18 for satin nickel finish.
Add $20 for matte black Combat Model (new 2012) with olive wrap-around grips.
Add $214 for Crimson Trace grips (7 shot, duo-tone finish only, new 2010).

* ***Thunder 380 Plus*** – similar to Thunder 380 Series, except has 15 shot mag., 20.5 oz.

MSR $406	$335	$295	$260	$230	$200	$180	$160	

Add $19 for nickel finish.

* ***Thunder 380 CC*** – .380 ACP cal., DA/SA, 3.2 in. barrel, 8 shot mag., low profile sights with notched rear and integral front sight, loaded chamber indicator, alloy frame/steel slide, ergonomic finger groove black polymer grips, matte black or duo-tone finish, 16.4 oz.

MSR $350	$285	$235	$210	$190	$170	$150	$140	

Add $10 for duo-tone finish.

THUNDER PRO 9MM ULTRA-COMPACT – 9mm Para. cal., DA/SA, 3 1/4 in. barrel, skeletonized hammer, loaded chamber indicator, ultra-compact dimensions, choice of matte black, nickel (disc. 2009), duo-tone (new 2008), or stainless steel (disc. 2008), 10 or 13 (new 2006) shot mag., Sig Sauer type interchangeable sights, current mfg. includes lower accessory rail, 23 oz. New 2004.

MSR $500	$425	$350	$315	$265	$235	$200	$175	

Add $58 for stainless steel (disc. 2008).

THUNDER PRO 40 ULTRA-COMPACT – .40 S&W cal., similar to Thunder Pro 9mm Ultra-Compact, except has 10 shot mag. New late 2004.

MSR $500	$425	$350	$315	$265	$235	$200	$175	

Add $10 for duo-tone.
Add $42 for stainless steel (disc.).
Add $20 for nickel finish (mfg. 2006-2009).

THUNDER PRO 45 ULTRA-COMPACT – .45 ACP cal., similar to Thunder Pro 9mm/40 Ultra-Compact, except has 3.6 in. barrel, 7 shot mag., choice of matte, duo-tone (mfg. 2003, reintroduced 2008), stainless steel (mfg. 2004-2007), or satin nickel (disc. 2009) finish, 27 oz. Importation began 2003.

MSR $500	$425	$350	$315	$265	$235	$200	$175	

Add $10 for duo-tone.
Add $36 for satin nickel finish (disc. 2009).
Add $58 for stainless steel (disc. 2007).

THUNDER PRO HC 9/40 – 9mm Para. or .40 S&W cal., DA/SA, 4 1/4 in. barrel with interchangeable Sig Sauer type 3 dot sights, alloy frame/steel slide, 17 (9mm Para. cal.), or 13 (.40 S&W cal.) shot mag., checkered black polymer grips, integral locking system, Picatinny lower rail, polygonal rifling, loaded chamber indicator, ambidextrous releases, matte black or duo-tone finish, 30.7 oz.

MSR $518	$440	$375	$325	$295	$250	$225	$195	

Add $7 for duo-tone finish.

FIRESTORM 380 – .380 ACP cal., PPK type design, DA/SA, 3 1/2 in. barrel, 7 shot mag., alloy frame with anatomic finger grooved rubber grips, steel slide with fixed sights, combat style trigger guard, integral locking system, matte black or duo-tone finish, 20 oz. New 2011.

While advertised during 2011, this model never went into production.

GRADING - PPGS™	100%	98%	95%	90%	80%	70%	60%	LAST MSR

* ***Firestorm 22*** – .22 LR cal., similar to Firestorm 380, except has 10 shot mag., 18.9 oz. New 2011.

While advertised during 2011, this model never went into production.

BP9/BP40CC – 9mm Para. or .40 S&W (disc. 2011) cal., 3.3 in. barrel, DAO, striker fired, 8 shot mag., interchangeable Sig Sauer type front and Glock type rear sights, loaded chamber indicator, black polymer frame with integral grips and front Picatinny rail, matte black or duo-tone finish, ambidextrous mag. release, steel slide, 21.5 oz. New 2010.

MSR $444	$380	$325	$295	$275	$250	$225	$195	

Add $11 for duo-tone finish.

MODEL 83 – .380 ACP cal., double action semi-auto, 3 1/2 in. barrel, blue or satin nickel finish, custom walnut grips, 6 shot mag., 24 1/2 oz. Imported 1988-94.

	$235	$205	$175	$160	$130	$105	$80	$288

Add $34 for satin nickel finish.

MODEL 85 – .380 ACP cal., similar specifications to Model 83 except has 12 or 13 shot mag., 30 1/2 oz. Imported 1988-94.

	$285	$250	$215	$195	$155	$130	$100	$340

Add $47 for satin nickel finish.

MODEL 86 – .380 ACP cal., blue matte or nickel finish, undercover model, wraparound rubber grips, 12 shot mag. Imported 1991-94.

	$315	$275	$235	$215	$175	$140	$110	$375

Add $29 for nickel finish.

MODEL 90 – 9mm Para. cal., single action, semi-auto, steel frame, checkered walnut grips, 13 shot mag., deep blue finish. Imported 1990-91 only.

	$325	$285	$245	$220	$180	$145	$115	$384

MODEL 223 – .22 LR cal., single action semi-auto, 10 shot mag., 3 1/2 in. barrel, blue finish, squared-off trigger guard, nylon grips. Importation disc. 1987.

	$200	$175	$150	$135	$110	$90	$70	$239

MODEL 224 – similar to Model 223, except has 4 in. barrel. Imported 1987 only.

	$200	$175	$150	$135	$110	$90	$70	$239

MODEL 225 – similar to Model 223, except has 5 in. barrel and 10 shot mag. Disc. 1987.

	$155	$135	$115	$105	$85	$70	$55	$170

MODEL 226 – similar to Model 225, except has 6 in. barrel. Importation disc. 1987.

	$200	$175	$150	$135	$110	$90	$70	$239

MODEL 323 – .32 ACP cal., single action semi-auto, 8 shot mag., thumbrest plastic grips, 25 oz. Disc. 1987.

	$105	$90	$80	$70	$60	$45	$35	$125

MODEL 383 – .380 ACP cal., single or double action semi-auto, 3 1/2 in. barrel, blue finish, nylon grips, 7 shot mag. Importation disc. 1988.

	$120	$105	$90	$80	$65	$55	$40	

Last MSR was $188 for single action.
Last MSR was $239 for double action.

Add $15 for double action.

REVOLVERS

FIRESTORM 38 – .38 Spl. + P cal., DAO, w/bobbed hammer, 2 in. barrel, 6 shot, fixed sights, black wood boot grips, choice of satin nickel, polished nickel, or parkerized finish, 24 oz. Mfg. by Armscor Precision. Limited importation 2011 only.

	$295	$250	$225	$200	$185	$170	$160	$364

BERTUZZI, F.LLI

Previous manufacturer located in Gardone, VT, Italy 1886-2009. Previously distributed during 2009 by Sporting Products, LLC, located in Palm Beach, FL, also by Dewing's Fly & Gun Shop, located in W. Palm Beach, FL, and by New England Arms Corp. located in Kittery Point, ME.

Bertuzzi made only best quality sidelock O/U and SxS shotguns, both with and w/o external hammers. Only 40-50 guns were mfg. annually, and all were custom ordered per individual specifications. Guns should be appraised indivdually for accurate evaluation.

SHOTGUNS: O/U

ZEUS – 12 ga., sidelock, auto ejector, deluxe engraving, deluxe wood checkering, SST. Importation disc. 1994.

This model was available on special order only. Retail prices generally ranged from $18,500-$27,500.

ZEUS EXTRA LUSSO – 12, 16, or 20 ga., sidelock, auto ejector, deluxe wood, deluxe checkering and engraving, SST. Disc. 2002.

This model was available on special order only. Prices generally ranged $35,000+.

ZEUS BOSS SYSTEM – 12 or 20 ga., features Boss locking system. Imported 1995-2009.

Prices began at $45,000.

ZEUS SEAGULL WINGS – elaborate O/U model with hinged swing open locks, all internal surfaces polished and engraved, exhibition wood, trigger plate action with lockplates exposed by a switch on the safety. Very limited mfg., approx. 1-2 guns per year.

Base model not including engraving was $135,000.
Add 10% for small frame.
Add 20% for matched pairs.

Engraving prices varied depending on style and engraver. Delivery time was approx. 4 years.

SHOTGUNS: SxS

MODEL ORIONE – 12 , 16, 20, or 28 ga., round boxlock action, DT or ST, ejectors, chopper lump barrels, base price includes English scroll engraving, deluxe Turkish walnut, and custom stock dimensions.

This model had a base model MSR of $27,950.
Add 10% for small frame.
Add 20% for matched pairs.

Additional engraving styles were available on this model.

VENERE BEST QUALITY SIDELOCK – various gauges, best quality sidelock model, ejectors, many options and engraving styles available, standard engraving is English rose and scroll.

This model had a base MSR of $31,950.
Add 10% for small frame.
Add 20% for matched pair.

Additional engraving options were available.

VENERE SEAGULL WINGS – elaborate model with hinged swing open locks, all internal surfaces polished and engraved, exhibition wood, trigger plate action with lockplates exposed from switch on safety, very limited mfg., approx. 1-2 guns per year.

This model not including engraving had a base MSR of $75,000.
Add 10% for small frame.
Add 20% for matched pair.

Engraving prices varied depending on style and engraver.

ARIETE HAMMER GUN – all gauges, upper tang safety, double triggers, fine quality engraving.

Prices started at $19,500. The self-cocking, auto-ejector mechanism is popular in this model and prices varied between $20,000-$40,000.

BESCHI, MARIO

Previous manufacturer until circa 1983 located in Italy.

GRADING - PPGS™	100%	98%	95%	90%	80%	70%	60%	LAST MSR

SHOTGUNS: O/U

BOXLOCK MODEL – 12 or 20 ga., standard model with light engraving.

	$3,000	$2,600	$2,300	$1,950	$1,600	$1,300	$995	

SHOTGUNS: SxS

EXTRA LUSSO SIDELOCK – 12 or 20 ga., elaborate game scene engraving.

12 ga.	$12,000	$10,750	$9,250	$8,000	$6,750	$5,500	$4,250	
20 ga.	$12,000	$10,750	$9,250	$8,000	$6,750	$5,500	$4,250	

BOXLOCK MODEL – prices assume moderate engraving.

	$1,650	$1,475	$1,300	$1,050	$850	$650	$500	

BETTINSOLI, TARCISIO, Srl

Current manufacturer located in Brescia, Italy. Currently imported on a private label basis by Franchi. Distributed in Europe by Bignami, located in Bolzano, Italy.

Bettinsoli manufactures fine quality O/U shotguns, express O/U rifles, and combination guns, with certain models private labeled under the Franchi trademark in the U.S., and distributed under the Bettinsoli name in Europe. Please contact the factory directly for more information (see Trademark Index).

BIG BEAR ARMS & SPORTING GOODS INC.

Previous firearms importer located in Carrollton, TX 1992-1999, specializing in the importation of both Russian military surplus and new firearms.

PISTOLS: SEMI-AUTO

IZH-70 MAKAROV – .380 ACP or 9mm Makarov cal., 8 shot mag., mfg. in Russia. Imported 1994-1999.

	$265	$185	$155	$135	$115	$100	$90	*$325*

RIFLES: SEMI-AUTO

SAIGA SPORTER RIFLE – 7.62x39mm cal., semi-auto with improved Kalashnikov design, checkered hardwood (disc.) or synthetic stock and forearm, 5 or 10 (disc.) shot mag. Imported 1996-99.

	$575	$400	$325	$250	$225	$200	$175	*$750*

Add $169 for 3.5X scope and mount.

SHOTGUNS

SAIGA SEMI-AUTO – .410 bore, 3 in. chamber, paramilitary configuration. Imported 1996-99.

	$425	$350	$295	$250	$200	$180	$165	*$499*

IJ-27 O/U – 12 ga., 2 3/4 in. chambers. Imported 1995-99.

	$425	$350	$295	$250	$200	$180	$165	*$499*

IJ-39E O/U – 12 ga., 2 3/4 in. chambers. Imported 1995-99.

	$760	$600	$495	$400	$360	$330	$295	*$895*

IJ-43 SxS – 12 ga., 2 3/4 in. chambers. Imported 1995-99.

	$325	$250	$200	$175	$155	$145	$135	*$399*

BIG HORN ARMORY INC.

Current rifle manufacturer located in Cody, WY.

RIFLES: LEVER ACTION

MODEL 89 – .500 S&W Mag., patterned after the Winchester Model 1886 lever action, 18 (carbine) or 22 (rifle) in. barrel, recessed crown, uncheckered American black walnut or hotwood maple stock, stainless steel action, sling swivels, aperture rear sight on receiver, blade front sight, satin stainless, Hunter Black, Blue, or case colored metal finish, approx. 7 1/2 lbs.

MSR $2,289	$2,075	$1,725	$1,450	$1,225	$995	$800	$725	

Add $50 for hotwood maple stock. Add $125 for Hunter Black, $300 for Blue, or $400 for case colored metal finish.

GRADING - PPGS™	100%	98%	95%	90%	80%	70%	60%	LAST MSR

SHOTGUNS: O/U

STERLING FIELD – 12 ga., 3 in. chambers, 26, 28, or 30 in. vent. rib alloy steel barrels, checkered Grade 3 Turkish walnut stock, includes ten choke tubes, SST, detachable trigger lock, engraved nitride receiver, ejectors, elongated forcing cones, 6 lbs. 14 oz - 7 lbs. 6 oz. Mfg. 2010-2012.

$2,750	$2,300	$1,950	$1,725	$1,500	$1,350	$1,100	*$2,999*

STERLING TARGET – 12 ga., 2 3/4 in. chambers, 28, 30 or 32 in. vent. rib barrels, engraved nitride receiver, checkered Turkish two-way adj. oil finished walnut stock, includes ten choke tubes, 7 lbs. 12 oz - 8 lbs. 4 oz. Mfg. 2010-2012.

$3,325	$2,950	$2,600	$2,300	$2,000	$1,700	$1,400	*$3,699*

STERLING REGAL – similar to Sterling Target and Field models, except has gold trigger and locks, exhibition grade walnut, special engraving, rust blued barrels, and bone charcoal case coloring.

While advertised, this model has not been manufactured.

BIG HORN ARMS CORP.

Previous manufacturer located in Watertown, SD.

PISTOLS: SINGLE SHOT

TARGET PISTOL – .22 Short cal. only, unique action permitting auto. ejection, ambidextrous stock made of molded Tufflex with carvings, 26 oz. Approx. 1,200 mfg. Disc. in the late 1960s.

$175	$150	$135	$125	$115	$105	$95

SHOTGUNS: SINGLE SHOT

LIL' MAGNUM SHOTGUN – .410 diameter reloadable shot cartridge, single shot open bolt operation, included reloading equipment, approx. 2,000 mfg. in the late 1960s.

$125	$100	$75	$65	$55	$50	$45

BIGHORN RIFLE CO.

Previous manufacturer located in Orem, UT.

PISTOLS: BOLT ACTION

BIGHORN PISTOL – .22 LR cal., bolt action design.

Lack of information on this pistol precludes accurate pricing.

RIFLES: BOLT ACTION

BIGHORN RIFLE – Mauser action, choice of calibers, custom made bolt action of high quality, interchangeable barrels (gun was supplied with 2 barrels), adj. trigger, deluxe walnut stock, many custom options. Mfg. 1984 only.

$2,100	$1,800	$1,600	$1,400	$1,200	$1,000	$850

BILL HANUS BIRDGUNS LLC

Current dealer and importer located in Newport, OR. Bill Hanus has imported select private label models from various manufacturers, including Fausti, Sabatti, Remington, Grulla, Merkel, Browning, and Fabarm. Previously, he had his own private label model manufactured by Armas Ugartechea (see separate listing) located in Eibar, Spain until 1997. Please contact the company directly for more information, including availability, delivery time, and pricing (see Trademark Index).

BINGHAM, LTD.

Previous manufacturer located in Norcross, GA circa 1976-1985.

Information regarding this manufacturer is available online free of charge in the Firearms section at www.bluebookofgunvalues.com.

BITTNER

Previously manufactured by Gustav Bittner located in Vieprty, Bohemia (Austria, Hungary), circa 1893.

GRADING - PPGS™	100%	98%	95%	90%	80%	70%	60%	LAST MSR

PISTOLS

BITTNER MODEL 1893 – 7.7mm Bittner cal., pistol with hand activated repeater mechanism, box magazine, checkered grips, limited manufacture circa 1893.

	$9,500	$8,500	$7,000	$6,000	$5,000	$4,000	$3,000	

BLACK FORGE

Current manufacturer of semi-auto rifles located in Florida.

RIFLES: SEMI-AUTO

Black Forge manufactures both AR-15 style and AK-47 design carbines and rifles, in addition to a modified Saiga 12 ga. shotgun. Current models include the Wolverine (MSR $1,350-$1,425), Badger (MSR $1,550), Tactical Black Poly ($1,350-$1,425), Tactical Plum Poly (MSR $1,475-$1,550), RPK ($1,650), WA-SPr 74 (MSR $2,375), Kalashnikov (MSR $1,975), Operator Gen2 (MSR $1,495-$1,725), Stinger (MSR $1,625), Vepr Tactical (MSR $1,650), A3 Flat top (MSR $899-$999), and M4 Tier (MSR $999-$1,199). Modified Izhmash, Saiga, and Vepr shotguns are also available in various configurations -prices range from $699-$1,899.

BLACKHEART INTERNATIONAL LLC

Current manufacturer located in Philippi, WV. The company also manufactures separate components for AR-15 style carbines/rifles, in addition to custom bolt actions and barreled actions.

PISTOLS

BHI manufactured a line of AR-15 style pistols in 5.56 NATO cal. including the BHI-15 with various options. MSRs started at $1,050.

RIFLES: BOLT ACTION

BHI also offered a line of tactical and sport bolt action models until 2012. They included the BBG Light Sniper - last MSR was $4,054, BBG Hunter - last MSR was $3,321, BBG F-Class - last MSR was $3,324, and BBG Tactical - last MSR was $4,579. Please contact the company directly for more information, including pricing and available options (see Trademark Index).

RIFLES: SEMI-AUTO

Blackheart International also makes a variety of NFA carbines for military and law enforcement.

IMPORTANT NOTE: On model(s) where *N/A has replaced the normal 100% value, it indicates current market conditions are too unstable to accurately ascertain 100%-60% values. Factory retail prices (MSRs) reflect most recent updates. For more up-to-date information on current pricing trends and additional useful information, please visit www.bluebookofgunvalues.com, select "Information & Services " from the menu, and click on "Additional Book Information".

BHI SOPMOD AK – 7.62x39mm cal., semi-auto AK-47 design, hammer forged chrome lined barrel, 30 shot polymer mag., Magpul CTR collapsible stock, SAW style pistol grip, black finish, widened mag. release lever, CCA aluminum quad rail forend, AK-103 muzzle brake, tritium front and rear sights, offset vertical grip, quick attach scope mount, enhanced selector lever.

MSR $1,850	*N/A	$1,425	$1,200	$995	$850	$700	$625	

BHI-15 (A) – 5.56 NATO cal., AR-15 style, 16 in. chrome lined barrel, semi-auto, mid-length gas system, 30 shot mag., manganese phosphate barrel finish, A2 flash hider, standard collapsible stock, polycarbonate hand guard, A3 flattop upper and aluminum lower, hard coat black anodized finish, standard charging handle, front post sight, rear aperture sight, Mil-Spec trigger group, Wolff springs, detachable carry handle.

MSR $1,245	*N/A	$975	$850	$725	$600	$500	$400	

BHI-15 (S) – 5.56 NATO cal., AR-15 style, 16 in. chrome lined barrel with Surefire flash hider/supressor adapator, flattop receiver with Picatinny rail, semi-auto, mid-length gas system, 30 shot mag., manganese phosphate barrel finish, Magpul CTR collapsible stock, aluminum free float tube, mid-length hand guard, hard coat black anodized finish, PRI Gasbuster charging handle, Geissele SSA 2-stage trigger, Stark SE-1 pistol grip.

MSR $1,888	*N/A	$1,425	$1,200	$995	$850	$700	$625	

This model is also available in a Short Barrel Rifle configuration with an 11 in. barrel for military/law enforcement.

GRADING - PPGS™	100%	98%	95%	90%	80%	70%	60%	LAST MSR

BHI-15 (SPR) SPECIAL PURPOSE RIFLE – 5.56 NATO cal., AR-15 style, 20 in. chrome lined barrel with Surefire flash hider/supressor adapator, flattop receiver with Picatinny rail, semi-auto, mid-length gas system, 20 shot mag., manganese phosphate barrel finish, Magpul PRS adj. stock, aluminum free float tube, rifle length hand guard, hard coat black anodized finish, PRI Gasbuster charging handle, Geissele SSA 2-stage trigger, Mil-Spec A3 flattop upper, aluminum lower, hard chromed titanium firing pin, adj. DPMS Panther Tactical grip, oversized magwell.

MSR $2,274	*N/A	$1,750	$1,525	$1,300	$1,100	$900	$750	

BHI-15 EXECUTIVE PACKAGE – AR-15 style, includes BHI-15 (S) rifle and pre-calibrated Aimpoint Micro-H1 sighting system mounted to a GG&G quick detach mount with integral flip-up lens covers, Harris 6-9 in. adj. bipod, Insight M3X Tactical Illuminator light, quick adj. padded sling, lightweight streamlined handguard, criterion barrel, Stark pistol grip, precision machined aluminum lower, Pelican Storm hard case with padded nylon case insert.

MSR $3,688	*N/A	$2,995	$2,500	$2,150	$1,800	$1,500	$1,250	

BLACKOPS TECHNOLOGIES

Current bolt action rifle manufacturer located in Columbia Falls, MT.

RIFLES: BOLT ACTION

BlackOps Technologies, in partnership with Mission Arms Group, currently manufactures both rimfire and centerfire bolt action rifles in various configurations. Current models include Ravage - MSR $4,725, Ranch Rifle - MSR $4,725, Kukri - MSR $4,725, Specter-BABR - MSR $6,625, and Recon - MSR $5,525.

BLACK RAIN ORDNANCE, INC.

Current rifle manufacturer established in 2008 and located in Neosho, MO. Dealer and distributor sales.

RIFLES: SEMI-AUTO

IMPORTANT NOTE: On model(s) where *N/A has replaced the normal 100% value, it indicates current market conditions are too unstable to accurately ascertain 100%-60% values. Factory retail prices (MSRs) reflect most recent updates. For more up-to-date information on current pricing trends and additional useful information, please visit www.bluebookofgunvalues.com, select "Information & Services" from the menu, and click on "Additional Book Information".

PG1 – .223 Rem. cal., gas or gas piston operation, 20 shot mag., 16 in. slim blast stainless steel barrel with flash suppressor, detachable folding sights, flat top Picatinny rail with 7 in. black barrel quad rail, black pistol grip and collapsible MOE stock, Pink Splash receiver finish.

MSR $1,959	*N/A	$1,555	$1,330	$1,205	$975	$800	$620	

Add $330 for PG1 with gas piston operation.

PG2 – .223 Rem. cal., gas or gas piston operation, 20 shot mag., 16 in. partially fluted black barrel with flash suppressor, flat top Picatinny rail with 7 in. FDE quad rail, FDE (flat dark earth) UBR stock, Digital Tan receiver finish, detachable folding sights.

MSR $2,339	*N/A	$1,840	$1,575	$1,430	$1,155	$945	$735	

Add $350 for PG2 with gas piston operation.

PG3 – .223 Rem. cal., gas or gas piston operation, 20 shot mag., 16 in. black/white finished partially spiral fluted barrel with flash suppressor, flat top Picatinny rail with 7 in. black quad rail, black UBR stock, Silver Skulls receiver finish, detachable folding sights.

MSR $2,339	*N/A	$1,840	$1,575	$1,430	$1,155	$945	$735	

Add $330 for PG3 with gas piston operation.

PG4 – .223 Rem. cal., gas operated, 20 shot mag., 24 in. partially fluted black bull barrel, flat top Picatinny rail with 12 in. black or FDE (disc. 2012) quad rail, black PRS stock, black or flat dark earth (disc. 2012) finish.

MSR $2,149	*N/A	$1,665	$1,425	$1,290	$1,045	$855	$665	

Add $30 for FDE finish (disc. 2012).

GRADING - PPGS™	100%	98%	95%	90%	80%	70%	60%	LAST MSR

PG5 – .223 Rem. cal., gas or gas piston operation, 20 shot mag., 16 in. partially fluted black barrel with flash suppressor, flat top Picatinny rail with 7 in. black quad rail, black MOE stock, black finish, detachable folding sights.

MSR $2,029	*N/A	$1,575	$1,350	$1,225	$990	$810	$630	

Add $310 for PG5 with gas piston operation.

PG6 – .223 Rem. cal., gas or gas piston operation, 20 shot mag., 16 in. partially fluted black barrel with flash suppressor, flat top Picatinny rail with 7 in. FDE quad rail, FDE MOE stock, black receiver finish, detachable folding sights.

MSR $2,029	*N/A	$1,575	$1,350	$1,225	$990	$810	$630	

Add $340 for PG6 with gas piston operation.

PG7 – Disc. 2011.

Last MSR was $1,989.

More research is underway for current values on this discontinued model.

PG8 – Disc. 2011.

Last MSR was $1,989.

More research is underway for current values on this discontinued model.

PG9 – .223 Rem. cal., gas or gas piston operation, 20 shot mag., 16 in. M4 partially fluted MACH barrel with flash suppressor, flat top Norguard finished receiver with 7 in. black quad rail, black pistol grip and MOE stock, detachable folding sights.

MSR $2,029	*N/A	$1,575	$1,350	$1,225	$990	$810	$630	

Add $330 for PG9 with gas piston operation.

PG10

More research is underway for current values on this discontinued model.

PG11 – .223 Rem. cal., gas operated, 20 shot mag., 18 or 20 in. partially fluted black barrel with compensator, no sights, flat top Picatinny rail with 12 in. black or flat dark earth modular rail, black or FDE UBR stock, Black, Digital Tan, Flat Dark Earth, Norguard, Pink Splash, or Silver Skulls receiver finish.

MSR $2,579	*N/A	$2,015	$1,725	$1,565	$1,265	$1,035	$800	

Add $40 for Digital Tan, Flat Dark Earth, Norguard, Pink Splash, or Silver Skulls finish.

PG12 – .308 Win. cal., 20 shot mag., 18 or 20 in. partially fluted black or stainless finished barrel with compensator, flat top Picatinny rail with 12 in. black or flat dark earth modular rail, black or FDE PRS stock, Black, Digital Tan, Flat Dark Earth, Norguard, Pink Splash, or Silver Skulls finish.

MSR $3,059	*N/A	$2,385	$2,045	$1,855	$1,500	$1,225	$955	

Add $40 for Digital Tan, Flat Dark Earth, Norguard, Pink Splash, or Silver Skulls finish.

PG13 – .308 Win. cal., 20 shot mag., 18 in. partially spiral fluted black/white finished barrel with flash suppressor, no sights, Silver Skull finished receiver with flat top Picatinny rail and 9 in. black modular rail, black pistol grip and UBR stock.

MSR $2,929	*N/A	$2,295	$1,970	$1,785	$1,445	$1,180	$920	

PG14 – .308 Win. cal., 20 shot mag., 18 in. partially fluted stainless barrel with flash suppressor, Norguard finished receiver with Picatinny rail and 9 in. black modular rail, black pistol grip and MOE stock, no sights.

MSR $2,589	*N/A	$2,015	$1,725	$1,565	$1,265	$1,035	$805	

PG15 – .308 Win. cal., 20 shot mag., 18 or 20 in. partially fluted black barrel with compensator, flat top Picatinny rail with 9 in. black modular rail, black MOE stock, black or FDE receiver finish. New 2013.

MSR $2,669	*N/A	$2,080	$1,780	$1,615	$1,305	$1,070	$830	

Add $30 for FDE (flat dark earth) finish.

PG16 – .308 Win. cal., 20 shot mag., 24 in. partially fluted black bull barrel, flat top Picatinny rail with 12 in. black or FDE modular rail, black or FDE pistol grip and PRS stock, black or FDE finish, no sights.

MSR $2,759	*N/A	$2,190	$1,875	$1,700	$1,375	$1,125	$875	

Add $30 for FDE (flat dark earth) finish.

GRADING - PPGS™	100%	98%	95%	90%	80%	70%	60%	LAST MSR

PG17 – .223 Rem. cal., 20 shot mag., 18 or 24 in. partially fluted black bull barrel, no sights, flat top Picatinny rail with 9 or 12 in. black or FDE modular rail, black or FDE pistol grip and UBR stock, black or FDE finish.

MSR $2,359	*N/A	$1,840	$1,575	$1,430	$1,155	$945	$735

Add $30 for FDE (flat dark earth) finish.

BLACK RIFLE COMPANY LLC

Current rifle and accessories manufacturer located in Clackamas, OR.

RIFLES: SEMI-AUTO

Black Rifle Company manufactures AR-15 style carbines. Current models include Billet Carbine - MSR $1,490, Mil-Spec Carbine - MSR $1,225, and 6.8 SPC Billet Carbine SASS - MSR $1,799.

BLAND, THOMAS & SONS GUNMAKERS LTD.

Current manufacturer located in England since 1840. This firm was purchased in 1990 by Woodcock Hill located in Benton, PA. Manufacturer direct sales only.

Woodcock Hill should be contacted directly (see Trademark Index) for more information (including current models and prices) regarding Thomas Bland & Sons firearms. Prices will vary depending on the exchange rate between the euro, pound, and dollar.

Record checks by serial number on all Thomas Bland & Sons rifles and shotguns are also available.

RIFLES: CUSTOM

Double rifles are available in most calibers and specifications. The standard model is "The Cape" with boxlock action and 40% engraving coverage - the current base price is £18,000 and includes leather case. Allow 6-8 months for delivery. The "Deluxe Cape II" has chopper lump barrels, is fully engraved, and fitted with sideplates if ordered - current MSR is £22,000. Bolt action rifles are available in any type of action, most popular calibers, and other special options. The bolt action models are not manufactured in England, and Woodcock Hill should be contacted directly for pricing. Prices vary, depending on configuration and special order features.

SHOTGUNS: CUSTOM

Boxlock, sidelock SxS and O/U best quality shotguns are available in all gauges, and pricing can vary depending upon configuration, finish, and accessories.

FAIRMOUNT MODEL – 12, 16, 20, or 28 ga., boxlock action, ejector, wood, accessories, finish, and engraving is per customer order.

Base price on this model is $14,500.

KENT MODEL – 12, 16, 20, or 28 ga., sidelock action, ejectors, wood, accessories, finish, and engraving is per customer order.

Each gun is priced individually per customer's specifications.

BLASER

Blaser

Currently manufactured by Blaser Jagdwaffen GmbH in Isny im Allgäu, Germany. Currently imported and distributed beginning late 2006 by Blaser USA, located in San Antonio, TX. Previously located in Stevensville, MD. Previously imported and distributed 2002-2006 by SIG Arms located in Exeter, NH, and circa 1988-2002 by Autumn Sales Inc. located in Fort Worth, TX. Dealer sales.

The Blaser Company was founded in 1963 by Horst Blaser. In 1986, the company was taken over by Gerhard Blenk. During 1997, the company was sold to SIG. In late 2000, SIG Arms AG, the firearms portion of SIG, was purchased by two Germans, Michael Lüke and Thomas Ortmeier, who have a background in textiles. Today the Lüke & Ortmeier group includes independently operational companies such as Blaser Jagdwaffen GmbH, Mauser Jagdwaffen GmbH, J.P. Sauer & Sohn GmbH, SIG-Sauer Inc., SIG-Sauer GmbH and SAN Swiss Arms AG.

GRADING - PPGS™	100%	98%	95%	90%	80%	70%	60%	LAST MSR

Blaser currently makes approximately 20,000 rifles and shotguns annually, with most being sold in Europe.

DRILLINGS

Blaser makes a D99 Drilling in a variety of combinations, including a rifle over two shotgun barrels, a single shotgun barrel with a rifle barrel on the top and on the side (Duo), and three rifle barrels (Trio). Many centerfire calibers are available, and the shotgun barrel is chambered for 3 in. 20 ga. This model is not currently imported into America, and is available by special order only. Please contact the importer directly for availability and pricing (see Trademark Index).

PISTOLS: BOLT ACTION

R-93 HHS (HUNTING HANDGUN SYSTEM) – various cals. between .222 Rem. - .375 H&H, features R93 right or left-hand straight pull bolt action, 14 in. hammer forged free floating barrel (interchangeable), matte black receiver with choice of wood, case colored, or game scene sideplates, Turkish walnut stock and pistol grip, 3-4 shot mag., 5 lbs. Limited importation 2004-2006.

	100%	98%	95%	90%	80%	70%	60%	LAST MSR
	$2,475	$2,050	$1,775	$1,500	$1,350	$1,200	$1,025	*$2,900*

Add $200 for left-hand bolt assembly.
Add $900 per interchangeable barrel.

RIFLES: BOLT ACTION

The R-93 rifle system's biggest advantage is its component interchangeability. Both barrels and bolt heads/assemblies can be quickly changed making the R-93 a very versatile rifle platform. Many special orders and features are available; please contact Blaser USA directly for additional information, including pricing and availability (see Trademark Index).

Add $395 for saddle scope mount on all current Blaser rifles.
Add $355 for left-hand stock available on currently manufactured R-8 and R-93 models.
Add $242 for Kickstop recoil pad on currently manufactured Blaser rifles.
Beginning late 2006, Blaser began offering graded wood between grades 3-11 on most models. Please refer to these listings under each current model.

R-8 PROFESSIONAL – available in many standard and metric cals. between .222 Rem.-10.3x60R cal., improved R-93 action featuring detachable mag. (includes double release buttons and locking device), Desmodromic mechanical trigger (available in both removeable or fixed trigger assemblies), optimized barrel bedding, and new stock design that decreases felt recoil, 20 1/2, 23, or 25 3/4 in. interchangeable barrel with white outline contrast sights on barrel, right or left hand action, Dark Green or Savannah (new 2013) synthetic one-piece stock is standard with black thermo elastic inlays, recoil pad, palm swell, and black forearm tip, approx. 6 3/8-8 3/4 lbs. New 2011.

	100%	98%	95%	90%	80%	70%	60%
MSR $3,625	$3,125	$2,725	$2,200	$1,900	$1,650	$1,375	$1,150

Add $1,161-$2,808 per interchangeable barrel, depending on caliber and configuration.
Add $445 for steel receiver (mfg. 2012 only).
Add $378 for rifle case.

This model is also available in additional higher grades, including the Jaeger (Grade 3 wood, MSR $4,195, new late 2010), Luxus (Grade 4 wood, MSR $5,245, new late 2010), Attache (Grade 7 wood, MSR $7,613), Custom (Grade 7 wood, disc. 2012 - last MSR was $12,425), Baronesse (Grade 8 wood, MSR $14,695), Super Luxus (Grade 7 wood, MSR $18,370), Exclusive (Grade 8 wood, currently POR, last published MSR was $22,232 in 2011), Super Exclusive (Grade 8 wood, currently POR, last published MSR was $29,615 in 2011), and Imperial (Grade 8 wood, currently POR, last published MSR was $43,511 in 2011).

Wood upgrade MSR's are as follows: Grade 3 - $1,507, Grade 4 - $1,722, Grade 5 - $2,247, Grade 6 - $3,092, Grade 7 - $3,938, Grade 8 - $4,499, Grade 9 - $5,481, Grade 10 - $7,586, Grade 11 - $9,692.

* ***R-8 Professional Success*** – similar to R-8 Professional, except has Dark Green or Dark Brown synthetic thumbhole stock, black thermo elastic inlays standard, or optional leather inlays (in Dark Brown only). New 2013.

	100%	98%	95%	90%	80%	70%	60%
MSR $4,148	$3,775	$3,225	$2,775	$2,125	$1,725	$1,475	$1,300

Add $1,050 for leather inlays.

GRADING - PPGS™	100%	98%	95%	90%	80%	70%	60%	LAST MSR

R-84 – .22-250 Rem. (disc. 1993), .243 Win., 6mm Rem., .25- 06 Rem., .270 Win., .280 Rem., or .30-06 standard cals., .257 Wby. Mag., .264 Win. Mag., 7mm Rem. Mag., .300 Win. Mag., .300 Wby. Mag., .338 Win. Mag., or .375 H&H cal., 23 or 24 (Mag. cals. only) in. interchangeable barrel, scroll engraving on receiver, short bolt action with 60 degree rotation, checkered Turkish walnut stock and forearm, approx. 7 lbs. Mfg. 1988-94.

$2,100 $1,575 $1,275 $1,050 $950 $850 $775 *$2,300*

Add $50 for left-hand action.

Add $600 per interchangeable barrel (w/scope mounts).

This model has the scope mounted directly to the barrel (and not the receiver). Since the scope mounts are on the barrel extension, this takedown rifle is unique in that it does not require re-zeroing when the rifle is reassembled.

* ***R-84 Deluxe*** – features a better grade of Turkish walnut with a North American game scene engraved on receiver, silver pistol grip cap with animal scene engraving.

$2,375 $2,025 $1,650 $1,200 $1,000 $925 $825 *$2,600*

Add $50 for left-hand action.

* ***R-84 Super Deluxe*** – best grade Turkish walnut with receiver featuring African game scene engraving (animals are in gold and silver), and silver pistol grip cap with gold animal engraving.

$2,675 $2,225 $1,775 $1,300 $1,100 $975 $895 *$2,950*

Add $50 for left-hand action.

R-93 CLASSIC – available in various domestic (.22-250 Rem. - .416 Rem. Mag.) and European (6.5x55mm and 7x57mm currently) calibers, 22, 24 (Mag. cals.), or 27 1/2 (disc.) in. barrel, unique patented rifle features straight pull bolt action (0 degree bolt lift), 360 degree radial locking system eliminates bolt rotation, unique safety offering cartridge in chamber capability, 3 shot mag., features interchangeable barrel system and newly designed bolt, searfree trigger mechanism, matte finished nickel receiver with engraving, non-glare "black velvet" barrel finish, integrated low scope mounts standard (1994-97 only), custom gun case with combination lock became standard 1998, 6 1/2 - 7 lbs. Importation began 1994, R-93 Classic introduced 1998, disc. May, 2002.

$2,600 $2,200 $1,850 $1,675 $1,500 $1,375 $1,250 *$2,950*

Add $595 per interchangeable barrel (w/o mounts).

During 1998, this model's nomenclature changed to the R-93 Classic. Scope mounts were no longer included. Between 1994-1997, this model retailed for approx. $2,800 and a Deluxe Grade was available for $3,100, while the Super Deluxe Grade retailed for $3,500.

* ***R-93 Classic Safari*** – .416 Rem. Mag. cal., features 24 in. heavy barrel, open sights, large forearm, 9 1/2 lbs., this model was renamed the R-93 Classic in 1998. Imported 1994-2002.

$3,575 $3,100 $2,650 $2,275 $1,825 $1,350 $1,150 *$4,140*

R-93 LUXUS – available in 20 calibers from .222 Rem. - .375 H&H., similar to the R-93 Classic, except has Grade 4 wood and ebony forend tip, choice of sideplates with game portraits or wood, available in right or left-hand action, case not included. Mfg. 2002-2010.

$4,150 $3,625 $2,850 $2,300 $1,850 $1,525 $1,350 *$4,594*

Add $700 for Luxus Plus Model with upgraded wood, black receiver and choice of color case hardened steel, wood, or animal sideplates (mfg. 2005-2007).

* ***R-93 Luxus Safari*** – .375 H&H or .416 Rem Mag. cal., similar to R-93 Classic Safari, except has higher quality walnut and ebony forend tip, available in right or left-hand action, case not included. Mfg. 2002-2008.

$4,875 $4,450 $3,700 $3,150 $2,400 $2,100 $1,800 *$5,470*

R-93 SUPER LUXUS – various cals., oil finished Grade 6 stock, engraved sideplates with animals and different styles of engraving were optional. Mfg. 2007-2010.

The last base price on this special order model was $10,643

GRADING - PPGS™	100%	98%	95%	90%	80%	70%	60%	LAST MSR

R-93 ATTACHE – various cals., features premium walnut stock and forearm with receiver wood panel inserts, wood bolt knob, ebony forearm tip, fluted barrel, current mfg. includes Grade 7 walnut, includes case, approx. 6 1/2 lbs. Mfg. 1998-2010.

	$5,895	$5,200	$4,550	$3,750	$3,250	$2,600	$2,025	*$6,360*

R-93 OCTAGON – various cals., Grade 6 wood, black receiver with wooden sideplates, full octagon barrel. Disc. 2008.

	$7,100	$6,000	$5,000	$4,000	$3,250	$2,650	$2,475	*$7,883*

R-93 GRAND LUXE – various cals., deluxe model with high grade checkered Grade 5 stock and forearm, fully hand engraved receiver with sideplates (various styles available), 3 shot mag., 6 1/2 - 7 lbs. Mfg. 1999-2003, reintroduced 2007-2010.

	$7,950	$6,800	$5,750	$4,600	$3,600	$2,750	$2,600	

Last MSR during 2003 was $5,160, and last MSR during 2010 was $8,409.

R-93 SELOUS – .375 H&H, .300 Win. Mag., or .416 Rem. cal., color case hardened steel receiver, compact design, Safari barrel, gold trigger, gold lined bolt handle, sling straps, named after big game hunter Frederick Courteney Selous, with Selous name in gold on receiver. Mfg. 2009-2010.

	$15,750	$12,750	$10,500	$9,000	$8,000	$7,000	$6,000	*$17,058*

Add $2,417 per interchangable barrel.

R-93 PROFESSIONAL – various cals., one-piece dark green synthetic stock with black thermo-elastic inlays, ergonomic pistol grip and rubber recoil pad, also available in Mossy Oak (disc. 2010) or Orange camo (disc.), approx. 6 3/4 lbs. Currently available exclusively through Mad Dog Guns. Importation began 2007.

MSR $3,145	$2,850	$2,450	$2,050	$1,625	$1,300	$1,100	$975	

Add $459 for left handed, EU style stock.
Add $1,746 for R-93 rimfire conversion kit (.17 HMR, .22 LR, or .22 WMR cal., includes barrel, magazine, bolt assembly, and bolt catch insert, mfg. 2008-2012).
Add $1,161 per extra R-93 barrel with standard taper (includes mag.).
Add $692 for semi-weight, $600 for match grade (disc. 2011), or $1,297 for Safari barrel configuration.
Add $1,134 for Professional Tracking Model with open sights and detachable sling swivels (disc. 2008).
Add $502 for camo coverage (disc. 2010).

The basic Professional Model was also available as a receiver, stock, and bolt assembly - last MSR (2011) was $2,001, or as a receiver and stock only - last MSR was $1,369 (2011).

Wood upgrade MSR's are as follows: Grade 3 - $1,365, Grade 4 - $2,149, Grade 5 - $2,103, Grade 6 - $2,936, Grade 7 - $4,329, Grade 8 - $4,321, Grade 9 - $5,289, Grade 10 - $7,643, Grade 11 - $9,741.

R-93 LRS 2 (LONG RANGE SPORTER 2) – various standard and metric cals., competition styled long range sporter with adj. trigger and stock, 5 or 10 (disc. 1999) shot removable box mag., free floating fluted barrel, many competition features, 10.4 lbs. New 1999.

MSR $4,405	$3,950	$3,325	$2,800	$2,150	$1,725	$1,400	$1,200	

Add $180 for left-hand action.
Add 10% for .338 Lapua cal. (disc. 2006).
Add $1,804 per interchangeable barrel (w/o mounts).
Add $358 for right hand bolt head, bolt assembly, and mag.
Add $1,600 for Package II or $2,600 for Package II in .338 Lapua cal. or $1,600 for Package III (includes Leupold scope, mounts, muzzle brake, bi-pod, and hard carry case). Disc. 2006.

R-93 SYNTHETIC – available in 21 cals. between .22-250 Rem. - .416 Rem. Mag., also available by special order in the same European cals. as the Model R-93 Repeater, features one-piece conventional black, wood grain (new 2004), or Mossy Oak camo (new 2004) synthetic stock, 22 or 26 in. barrel, without scope mounts and rings, 6 1/2 - 7 lbs. Mfg. 1998-2006.

	$1,800	$1,450	$1,150	$1,000	$875	$775	$675	*$2,100*

Add $400 for black synthetic Safari Model in .375 H&H or .416 Rem. Mag.
Add $600 for wood grain or camo stock.
Add $700 per interchangeable barrel (w/o mounts) in standard cals.

GRADING - PPGS™	100%	98%	95%	90%	80%	70%	60%	LAST MSR

R-93 TACTICAL 2 - please refer to listing in the Sig Sauer section under the Rifles: Bolt Action category.

This model is distributed by Sig Sauer Inc., located in Exeter, NH.

R-93 VARMINT - various cals., fluted match barrel, adj. comb, integrated rail, beavertail forend, removable sling swivels, Grade 3 wood. Imported 2007-2010.

	$4,675	$4,100	$3,650	$3,100	$2,650	$2,150	$1,725	*$5,145*

Add $306 for bipod.

* ***R-93 Varmint Success*** - similar to Varmint model, except has Grade 5 one-piece wood thumbhole stock. Mfg. 2008-2010.

	$6,375	$5,725	$5,150	$4,500	$3,650	$3,225	$2,500	*$6,802*

R-93 LX - similar cals. as Model R-93 Synthetic, features checkered walnut stock and forearm, coin finished stippled receiver sides, without scope mounts and rings, 6 1/2 - 7 lbs. Mfg. 1998-2002.

	$1,750	$1,425	$1,195	$1,000	$875	$795	$695	*$1,990*

Add $275 for Safari LX Model in .416 Rem. Mag. cal.
Add $595 per interchangeable barrel (w/o mounts).

R-93 PRESTIGE - similar to R-93 LX, except receiver has fine scroll engraving, and Grade 3 wood, case not included. Mfg. 2002-2010.

	$2,975	$2,600	$2,125	$1,750	$1,500	$1,300	$1,100	*$3,373*

Add $977 for Prestige Safari Model in .375 H&H or .416 Rem. Mag. cal. (disc. 2007).

R-93 EXCLUSIVE - various cals., high quality oil finished Grade 7 walnut stock, engraved sideplates, trigger guard, and bolt assembly, various levels of engraving available. Imported 2007-2010.

The last base price on this special order model was $15,448

R-93 SUPER EXCLUSIVE - various cals., similar to Exclusive, except has gold line engraving with deeper relief and Grade 8 stock and forearm.

The last base price on this special order model was $23,264

R-93 IMPERIAL - various cals., top-of-the-line R-93 model, Grade 9 wood, highest quality engraving with gold line and animal scenes, engraved bolt assembly and trigger guard, wood ball on bolt handle, titanium trigger and bolt head. Imported 2007-2010.

The last base price on this special order model was $32,615

R-93 STUTZEN - various cals., octagon barrel, full two-piece Grade 4 stock, sling swivels, various configurations available. Imported 2007-2010.

	$6,575	$5,925	$5,250	$4,500	$3,950	$3,500	$2,750	*$7,028*

This model was also available in the following special order configutations: Stutzen Attache ($10,432 Last MSR), Stutzen Grand Luxe ($10,208 Last MSR), Stutzen Super Luxus ($12,441 Last MSR), Stutzen Exclusive ($17,247 Last MSR), Stutzen Super Exclusive ($25,063 Last MSR), and the Stutzen Imperial ($34,413 Last MSR).

ULTIMATE BOLT ACTION - .22-250 Rem., .243 Win., .25-06 Rem., .270 Win., .308 Win., .30-06, 7x57mm, 7x64mm, .264 Win. Mag., 7mm Rem. Mag., .300 Win. Mag., .338 Win. Mag., or .375 H&H cal., unique bolt action design with 60 degree bolt throw, interchangeable barrel capability, 3 locking lugs, safety lever cocks and uncocks the firing pin spring, exposed hammer, 22 or 24 in. barrel, single set trigger, silver finished aluminum receiver has light engraving, select checkered walnut stock and forearm, 6 3/4 lbs. Extra interchangeable barrels were $545 each, extra bolt heads were $175 each. Mfg. 1985-89.

	$1,350	$1,100	$975	$925	$825	$750	$675	*$1,495*

All models were available in left-hand version at no extra charge.

ULTIMATE BOLT ACTION - SPECIAL ORDER - all of the following models may have been ordered with a buttstock cartridge trap - add $250-$500 depending on model. Mfg. was disc. 1989 on all models.

GRADING - PPGS™	100%	98%	95%	90%	80%	70%	60%	LAST MSR

* ***Ultimate Deluxe*** – similar to Ultimate, except better wood and game scene engraving.

	$1,425	$1,175	$1,000	$950	$850	$775	$700	*$1,595*

* ***Ultimate Deluxe Carbine*** – .243 Win. or .308 Win. cal. only, 19 1/2 in. barrel with full length forearm. Mfg. 1986-1989.

	$1,600	$1,375	$1,150	$1,000	$900	$825	$750	*$1,800*

* ***Ultimate Super Deluxe*** – similar to Ultimate Deluxe, except features better wood and game scene engraving. Mfg. 1986-1989.

	$3,750	$3,250	$2,900	$2,600	$2,300	$2,100	$1,850	*$4,030*

* ***Ultimate Exclusive*** – similar to Ultimate Super Deluxe, except features better wood and game scene engraving. Mfg. 1986-1989.

	$4,850	$4,300	$3,500	$2,975	$2,600	$2,275	$1,975	*$5,655*

Add $700 per interchangeable barrel.

* ***Ultimate Super Exclusive*** – similar to Ultimate Exclusive, except features better wood and game scene engraving. Mfg. 1986-1989.

	$7,700	$6,800	$5,750	$4,700	$3,950	$3,450	$2,950	*$8,905*

Add $950 per interchangeable barrel.

* ***Ultimate Royal*** – best quality Ultimate, featuring Bavarian cheekpiece and checkering/ carving on stock and forearm, elaborate game scene engraving, gold plated hammer. Mfg. 1986-1989.

	$9,000	$7,500	$6,750	$6,000	$5,375	$4,600	$4,000	*$11,500*

Add $1,200 per interchangeable barrel.

RIFLES: SxS

S2 – various cals. between .22 Hornet - .308 Win., including various metric cals., scalloped boxlock action false sideplates (higher grades only), 22.6 or 24 in. free floating barrels with quarter rib and iron sights, interchangeable easily regulated barrels, tilting lock block, manual cocking safety, checkered Turkish walnut stock and forearm (Grade 1 standard), approx. 7.7 lbs. for standard cals. Limited importation 2004-2005, reintroduced 2007.

MSR $7,954	$7,350	$6,650	$5,850	$5,100	$4,550	$3,995	$3,500	

Add $5,140 for extra set of standard cal. barrels.

This model is also available in higher grades by special order, including the S2 Luxus - $9,025 MSR, S2 Super Luxus -$15,087 w/sideplates, S2 Exclusive -POR, last published MSR was $17,765 in 2011, S2 Super Exclusive - POR, last published MSR was $23,305 in 2011, and the S2 Imperial - POR, last published MSR was $33,033 in 2011. Previously available in S2 Royal -last MSR was $29,000.

* ***S2 Safari*** – .375 H&H, .470 NE, .416 Rem. Mag. (disc.), .416 NE, or .500 NE cal., 24.4 in. barrel, Grade 1 wood standard, similar to S2 model, except has Monte Carlo stock with cheekpiece, Kickstop in buttstock, rubber recoil pad, and semi-beavertail forend.

MSR $11,060	$10,150	$8,900	$8,000	$7,150	$6,300	$5,550	$4,995	

Add $6,694 for extra set of standard cal. barrels (not interchangeable on the standard S2 model).

This model is also available in higher grades by special order, including the S2 Safari Luxus -$12,133 MSR, S2 Safari Super Luxus -$18,202 w/sideplates, S2 Safari Exclusive - POR, last published MSR was $20,583 in 2011, S2 Safari Super Exclusive - POR, last published MSR was $26,133 in 2011, and the S2 Safari Imperial - POR, last published MSR was $35,868.

RIFLES: SINGLE SHOT

MODEL BL 820 – various American and European cals., falling block action, adj. trigger, 26 1/2 in. barrel, available in Standard to Royal configurations. Mfg. 1982-89.

Standard Model	$1,550	$1,300	$1,075	$925	$800	$700	$600	*$2,900*

Add 30% for Royal configuration.

MODEL K77 A – .22-250 Rem., .243 Win., 6.5x55mm, .270 Win., 7x57R, 7x65R, or .30-06 standard cals., 7mm Rem. Mag., .300 Win. Mag. or .300 Wby. Mag. cal., break open

GRADING - PPGS™	100%	98%	95%	90%	80%	70%	60%	LAST MSR

action, 23 or 24 in. barrel, 3 piece take down, upper tang safety, checkered walnut stock and forearm, engraved silver finished receiver, sling swivels, 5 1/2 lbs. Imported 1988-90.

	$2,000	$1,675	$1,475	$1,300	$1,100	$925	$800	*$2,280*

Add $50 for Mag. calibers.

Add $730-$778 per interchangeable barrel.

K95 JAEGER (PRESTIGE) – .222 Rem., .22 Hornet (new 2006), .243 Win., .25-06 Rem. (new 2006), .270 Win., .308 Win., .30-06, 7mm Rem. Mag., .300 Win. Mag., or .300 Wby. Mag. cal., break open action, 22 (standard cals.) or 25 (Mag. cals.) in. barrel, upper tang safety/cocking lever, 3 piece takedown, checkered Grade 3 stock and forearm, scroll engraved sideplates, sling swivels. Importation began 2000.

MSR $5,251	$4,675	$4,100	$3,650	$2,950	$2,350	$1,800	$1,500

Add $1,418 for interchangable barrel.

Add $2,725 for octagonal barrel.

The following special order models are available in K95 configuration: K95 Luxus (Grade 4 wood, MSR $5,591), K95 Attache (Grade 7 wood, MSR $9,503), K95 Super Luxus (Grade 6 wood, MSR $12,595), K95 Baronesse (Grade 7 wood, MSR $16,931), K95 Exclusive (Grade 7 wood, POR, last published MSR was $16,156 in 2011), K95 Super Exclusive (Grade 8 wood, POR, last published MSR was $22,255 in 2011), and the K95 Imperial (Grade 9 wood, POR, last published MSR was $32,296 in 2011).

K95 LUXUS – similar to K95 Prestige, except has Grade 4 checkered stock and forearm, engraved sideplates and receiver. Importation began 2000.

MSR $5,325	$4,850	$4,325	$3,675	$3,100	$2,500	$2,000	$1,750

Add $1,350 for interchangable barrel.

Add $2,595 for octagonal barrel.

K95 STUTZEN LUXUS – various cals., features engraved aluminum frame, 20 in. octagon barrel and full length forearm, deluxe checkered Turkish Grade 4 wood, iron sights, 6 lbs. Importation began 2004.

MSR $8,453	$7,800	$6,950	$5,925	$5,000	$4,400	$3,850	$3,100

Add $2,798 for interchangable barrel.

The following special order models are available in K95 Stutzen configuration: K95 Attache (Grade 7 wood, MSR $12,331), K95 Super Luxus (Grade 6 wood, MSR $15,388), K95 Baronesse (Grade 7 wood, MSR $19,767), K95 Exclusive (Grade 7 wood, POR, last published MSR was $18,751in 2011), K95 Super Exclusive (Grade 8 wood, POR, last published MSR was $24,850 in 2011), and the K95 Imperial (Grade 9 wood, POR, last published MSR was $35,130 in 2011).

SHOTGUNS: O/U

Add $509 for adj. comb stock.

Add $142 for stock balancer or $294 for barrel balancer on all currently manufactured Blaser O/U shotguns (allows weight distribution, on both stock and forearm).

F3 GAME STANDARD – 12 or 20 (new 2008) ga., 3 in. chambers, boxlock action with satin oxide finish, SST, ejectors, 27, 28, or 29 in. VR barrels with 2 Briley choke tubes, similar to Competition model, except has Schnabel forearm, Grade 4 wood, 7.3 lbs. Mfg. 2007-2009.

	$5,750	$5,000	$4,250	$3,650	$2,975	$2,500	$2,150	*$6,197*

Add $3,274 per extra O/U barrel assembly.

This model was also available in the following special order configurations: Attache (Grade 7 wood, $8,875 MSR), Baroness (Grade 7 wood, $12,754 MSR), Luxus (Grade 5 wood, $7,804 MSR), Super Luxus (Grade 6 wood, $11,261 MSR), Exclusive (Grade 7 wood, MSR $14,609), Super Exclusive (Grade 8 wood, MSR $19,364), and the Imperial (Grade 9 wood, MSR $29,073).

F3 COMPETITION SPORTING STANDARD – 12, 20, 28 ga. or .410 bore, 3 in. chambers, boxlock action with monobloc barrels, 28 (12 ga. only), 30, 32, or 34 (12 ga. only) in. VR barrels with 5 Briley extended spectrum choke tubes, SST, ejectors, Grade 4 wood, greyed receiver finish, 8-8.4 lbs. New 2005.

MSR $7,613	$6,875	$6,000	$5,000	$4,000	$3,350	$2,650	$2,250

Add $3,012 per O/U barrel assembly.

GRADING - PPGS™	100%	98%	95%	90%	80%	70%	60%	LAST MSR

This model is also available in additional higher grades, including the Luxus (Grade 5 wood, MSR $9,340), Grand Lux (new 2012 -Grade 6 wood, $12,233), Super Luxus (Grade 6 wood, $13,913 MSR), Baroness (Grade 7 wood, $15,010 MSR), Exclusive (Grade 7 wood, POR, last published MSR was $15,575 in 2011), Super Exclusive (Grade 8 wood, POR, last published MSR was $23,750 in 2011), and the Imperial (Grade 9 wood, POR, last published MSR was $29,950 in 2011). Previously available in F3 Competition Royal ($25,895 last MSR) and the Attache ($9,085 last MSR).

Wood upgrade MSR's are as follows: Grade 4 - $2,153, Grade 5 - $2,704, Grade 6 - $3,754, Grade 7 - $4,673, Grade 8 - $5,350, Grade 9 - $6,295, Grade 10 - $8,395, Grade 11 - $10,505.

F3 SKEET – similar to F3 Competition Sporting Standard, original mfg. had choice of heavyweight (approx. 4 1/2 lbs.) or lightweight (LST, 3 1/2 lbs.) and 2 Briley choke tubes, current mfg. offers 28 (12 ga. only), 30, 32, or 34 (12 ga. only) in. VR barrels with 5 Briley extended spectrum choke tubes, Monte Carlo stock and semi-beavertail forearm, approx. 8.2 lbs. New 2007.

MSR $7,613	$6,875	$6,000	$5,000	$4,000	$3,350	$2,650	$2,250

Add $3,012 per O/U barrel assembly.

Please refer to the F3 Competition Sporting Standard model for current MSRs on the higher grades and wood upgrades.

F3 AMERICAN SUPER TRAP STANDARD – similar to F3 Competition Sporting Standard, except has 30 (disc. 2011), 32 in. barrels, also available as Unsingle with 34 in. barrel, approx. 8.1 lbs. New 2007.

MSR $8,689	$7,850	$6,700	$5,775	$4,825	$3,875	$2,900	$2,350

Add $3,355 for extra single barrel or O/U barrels.

Add $3,355 for combo package (includes either Unsingle or extra O/U barrel assembly) with adj. comb stock.

This model is also available in additional higher grades, including the Luxus (Grade 5 wood, MSR $10,453), Grand Lux (new 2012, Grade 6 wood, MSR $13,436), Super Luxus (Grade 6 wood, $14,963 MSR), Baroness (Grade 7 wood, $16,060), Exclusive (Grade 7 wood, POR, last published MSR was $16,561 in 2011), Super Exclusive (Grade 8 wood, POR, last published MSR was $24,736 in 2011), and the Imperial (Grade 9 wood, POR, last published MSR was $30,936 in 2011). Previously available in the Attache until 2009 (Grade 7 wood, $9,085 last MSR).

Wood upgrade MSR's are as follows: Grade 4 - $2,886, Grade 5 - $3,369, Grade 6 - $4,461, Grade 7 - $5,380, Grade 8 - $5,980, Grade 9 - $7,030, Grade 10 - $9,130, Grade 11 - $11,288.

F3 SUPERSPORT STANDARD – 12 ga. only, action similar to F3 Competion Sporting Standard, 3 in. chambers, 30 or 32 in. VR barrels with 5 Briley extended spectrum choke tubes and adj. rib, free floating barrels with adj. barrel hanger system, checkered walnut stock with adj. comb and Schnabel forearm, Grade 3 wood, 3 1/2 lb. trigger pull, approx. 9 lbs. New 2011.

MSR $8,689	$7,850	$6,700	$5,775	$4,825	$3,875	$2,900	$2,350

Add $3,355 per O/U barrel assembly (12 ga. only).

Please refer to the F3 American Super Trap Standard model for current MSRs on the higher grades and wood upgrades.

BLEIKER, HEINRICH

Current rifle and accessories manufacturer located in Bütschwil, Switzerland. No current U.S. importation.

RIFLES: BOLT ACTION

Please contact the factory directly for more information, including current U.S. availability on the following and other custom models (see Trademark Index).

CHALLENGER SERIES – .22 LR cal., Bleiker action featuring minimum firing pin resonance and precise head space, super match trigger, match barrel, choice of walnut, all aluminum or wood/aluminum laminated stock, many options available, including left-hand action. New 2002.

GRADING - PPGS™	100%	98%	95%	90%	80%	70%	60%	LAST MSR

MATCH/300 M FREE RIFLE – 6mm BR, .308 Win., or 7.5x55mm Swiss cal., alloy Bleiker action featuring titanium hardening/coating, integrated magazine, super match trigger, match barrel, many options available, including different colors. New 2002.

BLOW

Current trademark of airsoft and airguns manufactured by Ücyildiz Silah Sanayi Tic Ltd. Sti., located in Istanbul, Turkey. Currently distributed by Palco Sports, located in Maple Grove, MN. Previously distributed by KBI, located in Harrisburg, PA until early 2010.

BLUEGRASS ARMORY

Current rifle manufacturer located in Ocala, FL. Previously located in Richmond, KY. Consumer direct sales.

During 2010, Bluegrass Armory was purchased by Good Times Outdoors.

RIFLES: BOLT ACTION

VIPER MODEL – .50 BMG cal., single shot action with 3-lug bolt, 29 in. chrome moly steel barrel with muzzle brake, one-piece frame with aluminum stock (choice of gray, OD green, or black), incorporates Picatinny rail, includes detachable bipod, right or left hand, approx. 24 lbs. New 2003.

	100%	98%	95%	90%	80%	70%	60%	LAST MSR
MSR $4,200	*N/A	$3,550	$3,100	$2,750	$2,300	$1,775	$1,525	

Add $100 for OD Green or grey finish.

MOONSHINER – .308 Win., .300 Win. Mag., or .338 Lapua cal., Bullpup configuration with twin lugs, 21 in. barrel with muzzle brake, 8 in. Picatinny rail on top of receiver plus 3 on forearm, detachable mag., available in Desert Tan, OD Green, or Tactical Black finish, 11 lbs. New 2011.

	100%	98%	95%	90%	80%	70%	60%	LAST MSR
MSR $2,995	$2,750	$2,400	$2,100	$1,750	$1,475	$1,125	$975	

BOBCAT WEAPONS INC.

Previous manufacturer from April, 2003-circa 2006 and located in Mesa, AZ. During late 2006, the company name was changed to Red Rock Arms. Please refer to the R section for current information and pricing.

RIFLES: SEMI-AUTO

BW-5 MODEL – 9mm Para. cal., paramilitary design, stamped steel or polymer (Model BW-5 FS) lower receiver, roller locked delayed blowback operating system, 16 1/2 in. stainless steel barrel, choice of black, desert tan, OD green, or camo stock, pistol grip, and forearm, Model BW-5 FS has fake suppressor, paddle mag. release and 8 7/8 in. barrel, 10 shot mag., approx. 6.4 lbs. Mfg. 2003-2006.

	100%	98%	95%	90%	80%	70%	60%	LAST MSR
	*N/A	$995	$875	$800	$725	$650	$575	*$1,350*

Add $275 for Model BW-5 FS.

BOBERG ARMS CORPORATION

Current pistol manufacturer located in White Bear Lake, MN.

PISTOLS: SEMI-AUTO

XR9-S – 9mm Para. cal., DA only, 3.35 standard or 4.2 (optional) in. rotating barrel, lock breech, black polymer frame with stainless steel slide and barrel, choice of standard (two-tone), onyx (all black), or Platinum (all satin) finish, 7 shot mag., low profile 3-dot sights, unique compact design features no feed ramp into chamber, 17.4 oz. New 2013.

	100%	98%	95%	90%	80%	70%	60%	LAST MSR
MSR $995	$925	$825	$725	$625	$525	$425	$350	

Add $354 for onyx or platinum finish.
Add $100 for 4.2 in. barrel (XR9-L).

BOHICA

Previous manufacturer and customizer located in Sedalia, CO, circa 1993-1994.

RIFLES: SEMI-AUTO

M16-SA – .223 Rem., .50 AE, or various custom cals., AR-15 style, 16 or 20 in. barrel, A-2

GRADING - PPGS™	100%	98%	95%	90%	80%	70%	60%	LAST MSR

sights, standard handguard, approx. 950 were mfg. through September 1994.

	*N/A	$1,225	$1,000	$850	$725	$600	$525	

Add $100 for flat-top receiver with scope rail.

Add $65 for two-piece, free floating handguard.

In addition to the rifles listed, Bohica also manufactured a M16-SA Match variation (retail was $2,295, approx. 10 mfg.), a pistol version of the M16-SA in both 7 and 10 in. barrel (retail was $1,995, approx. 50 mfg.), and a limited run of M16-SA in .50 AE cal. (retail was $1,695, approx. 25 mfg.).

BOITO

Previous manufacturer located in Brazil. Previously imported by F.I.E. Corp. located in Hialeah, FL.

Boito shotguns were inexpensive, utilitarian shotguns that are shootable, but not collectible. Because of this, prices typically range between $75 - $175, depending on the gauge and condition.

BOLLINGER, JOHN

Please refer to Mountain Riflery, LLC.

BOND ARMS, INC.

Current manufacturer located in Granbury, Texas beginning 1998.

DERRINGERS: O/U

A key entry internal safety locking device was introduced for all Defender models beginning in 2000. This device locks the preexisting crossbolt safety in the on-safe position.

Add $15 for left-handed configuration (disc.)

Add $109 per extra set of 2 1/2 in. barrels, $139 for 3 in. barrels, $159 for 3 1/2 in. barrels or $189 for 4 1/4 in. barrels.

BOND MINI – .357/38 Special (Girl Mini) or .45 ACP cal., 2.5 in. barrel, Rosewood or Pink (Girl Mini) grips, blade front and fixed rear sights, 18-19 oz. New 2012.

MSR $394	$340	$300	$260	$230	$200	$165	$135	

TEXAS DEFENDER – .22 LR, .22 WMR, 9mm Para., 10mm, .32 H&R Mag., .327 Fed. (new 2012), .357 Mag./.38 Spl., .357 Max (disc.), .40 S&W, .44 Spl., .44 Mag. (disc.), .44-40 WCF, .45 GAP, .45 ACP, .45 LC, or .45 LC/.410 shot shell cals., O/U design, 3 in. barrels with spring loaded extractors, stainless steel, removable trigger guard, rebounding hammer, crossbolt safety, spring loaded cammed locking lever, 20 oz. New 1998.

MSR $415	$345	$300	$250	$225	$175	$140	$110	

CENTURY 2000 DEFENDER (C2K)/COWBOY CENTURY 200 – .357/.38 Spl. (new 2012), or .410 bore/.45 LC cal. with 2 1/2 in. chambers and 3 in. barrels, or .410 bore with 3 in. chambers and 3 1/2 in. barrels. New 1999.

MSR $435	$360	$310	$265	$230	$185	$150	$115	

COWBOY DEFENDER – similar cals. as Texas Defender, designed specifically for cowboy action shooting, w/o trigger guard, 19 oz. New 2000.

MSR $415	$345	$300	$250	$225	$175	$140	$110	

Add $25 for star grips.

SUPER DEFENDER – .450 AutoBond cal., 3 in. barrels, rosewood grips, stainless steel construction, 20 oz. Limited mfg. 2003-2004.

	$300	$260	$225	$205	$165	$135	$105	*$369*

SNAKE SLAYER – .357/.38 Spl. (new 2012) or .410 bore/.45 LC cal. with 3 in. chambers and 3 1/2 in. barrels, features larger grip frame with laser carved "Bond Arms" and logo on grips, 22 oz. New 2005.

MSR $489	$400	$350	$300	$265	$215	$175	$135	

SNAKE SLAYER IV – similar to the Snake Slayer, except has 4 1/4 in. barrels. and 23 1/2 oz. New mid-2006.

MSR $519	$450	$390	$335	$295	$235	$185	$145	

GRADING - PPGS™	100%	98%	95%	90%	80%	70%	60%	LAST MSR

RANGER – .410 bore/.45 LC cal., 4 1/4 in. barrel, black ash extended grips with star, hard shell carry case replaced black nylon bag in 2011, without triggerguard, includes black custom driving/concealed leather holster, 23.5 oz. New 2008.

MSR $634	$535	$470	$420	$365	$295	$250	$200

RANGER II – similar to Ranger, except has trigger guard. New 2011.

MSR $634	$525	$465	$415	$365	$295	$250	$200

TEXAS RANGER SPECIAL EDITION – various cals., Texas mesquite wood grips, features Texas Rangers and 200th Anniversary gold engraved on the barrel, includes custom glass top display case. Limited mfg. beginning 2012.

MSR $1,297	$1,125	$975	$850	N/A	N/A	N/A	N/A

USA DEFENDER – various rimfire and centerfire cals., 3 in. interchangeable barrels, design similar to Remington O/U Derringer, includes BAD Driving holster. 5,000 to be mfg. beginning 2012.

MSR $504	$450	$395	$335	$300	$225	$185	$155

PISTOLS: SEMI-AUTO

.450 AUTOBOND – .450 AutoBond/.45 ACP cal., based on Colt 1911 design, full size frame, 5 in. barrel.

While advertised during 2003, this model never went into production.

BORCHARDT

Previous pistol design originating in Germany circa 1894-1897.

PISTOLS: SEMI-AUTO

Prices below assume matching parts and original condition.

MODEL 1893 – 7.65mm Borchardt cal., original Luger design, 6 1/2 in. barrel, blue finish with fire-blue small parts, checkered walnut grips, 8 shot mag., distinguished by elongated spring mechanism housing located behind the toggle assembly, may include accessories (mags., holster, stock) and/or case.

* ***Model 1893 Ludwig Loewe Mfg.*** – serial numbered 1-1104.

$24,500	$20,900	$17,850	$14,550	$12,500	$10,500	$8,800

Original stocks (with attached leather holster) are priced starting at $5,000.

» **Model 1893 Ludwig Loewe Mfg. Cased With Accessories** – original cased gun was supplied with matching shoulder stock, detachable cheekpiece, leather holster, 3 regular mags. and a hold-open mag., plus tools.

$48,000	$37,750	$32,750	$26,750	$20,500	$17,500	$14,250

* ***Model 1893 DWM Mfg.*** – starting approx. 1895, serial numbered 1105-3000.

$23,000	$19,850	$17,000	$14,000	$11,500	$9,750	$8,000

Original stocks (with attached leather holster) are priced starting at $4,750.

» **Model 1893 DWM Mfg. Cased With Accessories** – original cased gun was supplied with shoulder stock, detachable cheekpiece, leather holster, 3 regular mags. and a hold-open mag., plus tools.

$46,000	$37,000	$32,000	$25,750	$20,500	$17,000	$14,000

* ***Model 1893 DWM Mfg.*** – starting approx. 1895, serial numbered 1105-3000.

$23,500	$20,250	$17,500	$14,250	$11,750	$9,950	$8,150

Original stocks (with attached leather holster) are priced starting at $4,750.

* ***Model 1893 DWM Mfg. Cased With Accessories*** – original cased gun was supplied with shoulder stock, detachable cheekpiece, leather holster, three regular and one hold-open mag., plus tools.

$46,950	$38,250	$32,650	$26,250	$20,950	$17,350	$14,350

At a recent nationally publicized auction a cased Borchardt with all major accessories in 90-95% condition sold for $36,350.

BORDEN RIFLES

Current bolt action rifle manufacturer located in Springville, PA. Consumer sales through FFL.

RIFLES: BOLT ACTION

Borden rifles feature a customer's choice of Alpine, Alpine Magnum, Timberline, Timberline Magnum or Rimrock custom left or right hand actions. Barrel sizes are available from No. 2 to No. 5 contour. Stocks are generally from McMillan. Variations include the Basic Rifle (MSR $2,975), Standard Hunting Rifle (MSR $3,730), Signature Rifle (MSR $5,325), Tactical/Long Range Rifle (MSR $3,995), Borden Prone and Tactical Rifle (MSR $4,300), "Walk Around" Varmint Rifle (MSR $3,325-$3,425), Bench Style Varmint Rifle (MSR $2,995-$3,295), Rimrock LV or HV Bench Rest Rifle (MSR $3,500), Rimrock/Alpine Hunter Bench Rest Rifle (MSR $3,295), and the 600/1000 Yard Bench Rest Light Rifle (MSR $3,295). Additionally, Borden Rifles offers a wide variety of custom and special order features. To obtain a firm quotation and delivery time based on a specific configuration, please contact the factory directly (see Trademark Index).

BOROVNIK, LUDWIG KG

Current long gun manufacturer located in Ferlach, Austria.

Ludwig Borovnik is a third generation gunmaker who manufactures long guns by custom order only. Please contact him directly for more information (see Trademark Index).

BOSIS, LUCIANO

Current manufacturer located in Travagliato, Italy. Currently imported beginning 2011 by Manchester Arms LLC, located in Manchester, VT. Larry's Trading Post located in Gaithersburg, Maryland, British Sporting Arms Ltd., located in Millsbrook, NY. Previously imported by JTH Agency, located in Pittsford, NY, Dewing's Fly & Gun Shop, located in W. Palm Beach, FL, Old Friends Hunting & Shooting Co., located in Livingston, MT, New England Arms, located in Kittery Point, ME, Sporting Products, LLC, located in Palm Beach, FL. and by William Larkin Moore & Co., located in Scottsdale, AZ.

All Luciano Bosis guns are truly Bespoke, and all are manufactured on a custom order only basis. Bosis works with only Italy's finest master engravers, and customers work directly with the engravers without a markup from Bosis. Annual production is approximately 25 best quality guns. Delivery time varies by the type of gun and engraving, as well as the engraver. Please contact the manufacturer or the importer directly for more information, including a custom order quotation, and delivery time (see Trademark Index). Used Bosis shotguns need to be appraised individually to accurately determine current value.

SHOTGUNS

Add 10% for matched pair on most models listed.
Add €500 for automatic safety. Add €800 for Briley thin wall choke tubes.
Add €800-2,000 for leather case, depending on configuration.

MICHAELANGELO SIDELOCK O/U – 12, 16, 20, 28 ga., or .410 bore, pinned Boss style sidelock action, 26-32 in. chopper lump barrels, scaled frame, supplied in the white, exhibition quality Turkish walnut, w/o engraving, optional case.

This model has a MSR of €50,000 without engraving.
Add 10% for 28 ga. or 20% for .410 bore.
Add €800 for single trigger.
Add €15,000 for extra set of barrels without forearm.

* ***Michaelangelo O/U Extra*** – 12, 16, 20, 28 ga., or .410 bore, pinless Boss style sidelock action, 28 in. chopper lump barrels, scaled frame, best quality Turkish walnut and engraving. Importation disc. 2010.

Last MSR on this model was €71,000 without engraving.

CHALLENGER TITANIUM SIDELOCK O/U – 12 ga. only, features 28-30 in. chopper lump barrels. New 2011.

The current MSR on this gun is €70,000 without engraving.

WILD COMPETITION O/U – 12 ga., boxlock action with optional sideplates, 26-34 in. monobloc barrels, 100% handmade stock and forearm with no CNC operations, normal or optional bluing, regular or round action, engraving per customer specifications, supplied in-the-white. New 2008.

This model has a current MSR of €23,500 without engraving.

Add €5,500 for extra set of barrels.

WILD ROUND BODY GAME GUN O/U – 12 or 20 ga., hand forged, 26-34 in. monobloc barrels. Importation began 2011.

The current MSR on this model is €18,000 without engraving.

Add €2,500 for sideplates.

Add €5,500 for extra set of barrels.

HAMMER GUN SxS – 12 ga., sidelock back action, regular or round action, stock and forearm are handmade, engraving depends on customer specifications, supplied in-the-white. Limited importation.

The current MSR on this gun is €30,000 without engraving.

QUEEN SIDELOCK SxS – 12, 16, 20, 28 ga., or .410 bore, H&H type sidelock action, hand forged 26-32 in. chopper lump barrels.

This model has a MSR of €30,000 without engraving.

Add 10% for 28 ga. or 20% for .410 bore.

Add €10,000 for extra set of barrels.

COUNTRY SxS – 12, 20, or 28 ga., Anson & Deeley type scalloped boxlock action, hand forged 26-32 in. chopper lump barrels, DT, checkered deluxe English straight grip stock and forearm.

This current MSR on this model is €28,000 without engraving.

Add €8,000 for extra set of barrels.

LAURA O/U – 12, 20, 28 ga. or .410 bore, 27-30 in. barrels, fixed or Briley screw-in chokes, solid or vent. rib, square back triggerplate action, checkered walnut stock, built on B. Rizzini frame, custom order engraving, with or w/o sideplates. New 2011.

This current MSR on this model is €9,000 without engraving.

BOSS & CO., LTD.

Current manufacturer located in London, England 1812 to date. Direct sales from the manufacturer only.

Boss manufactures some of the world's finest shotguns and rifles (best quality guns only). Their shotguns and rifles have always been custom built per individual order. Approximately 10,000 have been manufactured to date. The following currently manufactured models include best rose and scroll engraving and the customer's choice of exhibition grade wood. Base MSRs do not include special orders, optional engraving patterns, and other possible options. Values indicated below for manufacturer's suggested retail and 100% condition factors are listed in English pounds. All new prices do not include English VAT (currently at 20 %). Delivery time for new guns is approx. 3 years. Values for used guns in 98%-60% condition factors are priced in U.S. dollars.

BOSS COMPANY HISTORY

Boss & Co., Ltd. was founded in 1812 by Thomas Boss, who apprenticed under his gunmaker father, William, from 1804-1812, while working for Joseph Manton. Thomas left Manton in 1816 to set himself up as an independent gunmaker. Success soon followed, and after several relocations, Boss moved in 1839 to 73 St. James' Street. Thomas died in 1857, and the firm was managed by his widow Emma and managing partner Stephen Grant (who would later become an independent gunmaker in 1867). Boss & Co. continued to produce guns under nephews Edward and James Paddison.

After approximately 80 years of Boss family ownership, by 1891, Boss & Co had a new owner - Scottish-born inventor and craftsman John Robertson. Robertson was the factory manager for several years before buying the business. Many of the company's hallmarks that are still in use today are due to Robertson's inventive talents. Robertson was responsible for the Boss single trigger in 1894, the spiral spring driven ejectors in 1897, and the patent for the first O/U

GRADING - PPGS™	100%	98%	95%	90%	80%	70%	60%	LAST MSR

with a reliable single trigger in 1909. Robertson also cemented Boss' reputation for world class gunmaking with rounded action sidelocks, distinctive rose and scroll engraving, and the mechanical design of the sidelock O/U. Practically every best-quality gunmaker building O/Us today uses some aspect of Robertson's design.

The Robertson family retained control of the company for nearly 110 years, when it was sold to an investment group headed by Kenneth Finken in 1999 and moved to Mayfair's 16 Mount Street. In early 2001, Boss changed hands again and was sold to the Halsey family. Under managing director Graham Halsey, Boss & Co. expanded to include a 3,000 square foot factory and production was moved to near Kew Gardens in 2008, with retail offices remaining in Mayfair.

Boss & Co. continues to produce some of the world's finest SxS and O/U rifles and shotguns, with a maximum production of 20 guns annually.

Information appears courtesy of Vic Venters, David Grant, & Graham Halsey.

RIFLES: BOLT ACTION

BOSS BOLT ACTION – various cals., Mauser action with Walther premium sporter barrel, Win. Model 70 three-position side safety, box mag., includes mounts and Zeiss scope.

MSR £30,000	**£30,000**	**$25,000**	**$21,000**	**$17,500**	**$13,500**	**$10,000**	**$7,750**

RIFLES: O/U & SxS, CUSTOM

Boss Express O/U double rifles are quoted per individual request only. Current base price for the .375 H&H cal. starts at £147,000 (w/o VAT), larger calibers up to .700 NE are also available at additional cost. Approx. 12 1/2 lbs. The Boss SxS rifle starts at £104,750 (w/o VAT). These models have had very limited manufacture. Older Boss double rifles must be appraised individually.

SHOTGUNS: CUSTOM

Add 25% for self-opening action (extremely rare on small gauges).
Add 60% for 20 ga. on older mfg.
Add 75%-100% for 28 ga. or .410 bore (very rare) on older mfg., depending on condition.

BOSS O/U – 12, 16, 20, 28 ga., or .410 bore standard, barrel lengths and chokes to specifications, shell-framed sidelock, auto ejectors, double triggers or single non-selective, English straight stock standard to specifications, VR or pistol grip stock optional, best English bouquet & scroll fine engraving, limited production.

MSR £87,950	**£87,950**	**$93,000**	**$80,000**	**$70,000**	**$60,000**	**$50,000**	**$40,000**

Add £5,300 for 28 ga. or .410 bore on current mfg.

BOSS SxS – all gauges, barrel lengths and chokes to specifications, bar-action sidelock, easy open/close action (not self-opening), square or rounded action, checkered stock, pistol grip (optional) or straight grip stock, single (patented 3 pull system) or double triggers, splinter or beavertail (optional) forearm, best English bouquet & scroll engraving, limited production.

MSR £67,950	**£67,950**	**$70,000**	**$60,000**	**$50,000**	**$42,500**	**$37,500**	**$32,500**

Add £5,300 for 28 ga. or .410 bore on current mfg.

ROBERTSON O/U – 12 or 20 ga., boxlock action, fitted sideplates, single trigger, ejectors, 28 or 30 in. rota-hammer forged monobloc barrels, available with or w/o top rib, oil finished French walnut stock, six point multi-locking feature, hand engraved, color case hardened receiver. New 2005.

Current MSRs on this model range from £10,000 - £14,000.

ROBERTSON SxS – 12 or 20 ga., Anson & Deeley boxlock action, fitted sideplates, top tang safety, ejectors, single trigger, 28 or 30 in. barrels, Boss style concave rib, oil finished French walnut stock with splinter forearm, hand engraved, color case hardened receiver. New 2005.

Current MSRs on this model range from £6,000 - £10,000.

GRADING - PPGS™	100%	98%	95%	90%	80%	70%	60%	LAST MSR

BOSWELL, CHARLES

Current manufacturer established in 1869, and located in London, England. Currently imported by Chris Batha beginning 2004, and located in Okatie, SC. Previously imported by Saxon Arms, Ltd., located in Clearwater, FL. Consumer direct sales.

All new prices do not include English VAT. Delivery time for new guns 12 to 18 months.

CHARLES BOSWELL COMPANY HISTORY

Charles Boswell was not only a fine gunmaker but an expert shot in the sport of live pigeon shooting and accordingly specialized in the building of high quality competition shotguns and rifles. He founded his business in 1869 at Edmunton, but by 1884 had moved to 126 The Strand in central London. In 1914, Boswell's son, Osbourne George assumed management and in 1922 the firm moved to South Moulton Street. Charles Boswell died in 1924, and in 1932, the firm moved again to 15 Mill Street, where the company was bombed by the Luftwaffe in April of 1941. Osbourne George passed away a few months later, and his widow ran the business until 1944 - after which point the family connection apparently ends.

In 1988, Charles Boswell was purchased by U.S. interests and Cape Horn International (previously Cape Horn Outfitters) located in Charlotte, NC, was retained to sell and manufacture the Boswell Guns in the U.S. In addition to acquiring their entire inventory of English manufactured firearms, Charles Boswell fabricated new shotguns and double rifles in the U.S. using the best materials including English lock mechanisms and retained the Charles Boswell Co. trademark. Every gun was custom ordered to an individual client's requirements/specifications.

After several post WWII overseas ownerships, the brand was revived by British shooting instructor Chris Batha, with American owner Garfield R. Beckstead. Batha acquired the company name, records, and goodwill in January of 2004 and continues the heritage of building best guns of superior craftsmanship and outstanding quality of shotguns and rifles in all gauges and calibers.

Some information appears courtesy of David Grant and Vic Venters.

The most collectible Boswell guns are pre-WWII, including the hammer guns that were lightweight with great shooting dynamics.

RIFLES: BOLT ACTION

BOLT ACTION RIFLE – all standard calibers, built on Mauser or Mannlicher action, 3/4 rib with standard and two folding leaf rear sight, finest well figured hand checkered Turkish walnut, with pistol grip and cheekpiece. Delivered in leather motor case with accessories.

Current MSR for a base model is $22,500.

Pinless, scopes, Kurz or Magnum actions are available by individual quotation.

RIFLES: SxS

SIDELOCK DOUBLE RIFLE – all standard calibers, best quality reinforced sidelock ejector with pinless lock plates, folding leaf rear sight on 3/4 rib, finest well figured hand checkered Turkish walnut, with pistol grip and cheekpiece. Delivered in leather motor case with accessories.

The current MSR for base model is $71,950.

Deluxe and game scene engraving is POR.

BOXLOCK RIFLE – .300 Express, .375 H&H, .458 Win. Mag., or .500 NE cal., made to individual order, choice of game scene engraving, Anson & Deeley boxlock actions, select European hybrid walnut, double triggers, leather cased. Disc. 1996.

100%	98%	95%	90%	80%	70%	60%	LAST MSR
$17,500	$17,150	$16,625	$15,750	$14,000	$12,250	$10,500	*$35,000*

Add 40% for .458 Win. Mag. cal. or 50% for .500 NE cal.

*** *Boxlock Rifle .600 Nitro Express***

The 1991 MSR on this model was $123,000, and it was discontinued in 1996.

SIDELOCK RIFLE – .300 Express, .375 H&H, or .458 Win. Mag. cal., made to individual order, choice of game scene engraving, H&H sidelock action, select European hybrid walnut,

GRADING - PPGS™	100%	98%	95%	90%	80%	70%	60%	LAST MSR

double triggers, leather cased. Disc. 1996.

	$35,000	$29,500	$25,000	$20,000	$18,000	$17,000	$16,000	*$65,000*

Add 40% for .375 H&H cal. or 50% for .458 Win. Mag. cal.

* ***Sidelock Rifle .600 Nitro Express***

	$65,000	$55,000	$45,000	$37,500	$33,500	$29,500	$25,000	*$125,000*

SHOTGUNS: O/U, SIDELOCK

MERLIN – 12, 16, 20, 28 ga., or .410 bore, best quality sidelock ejector, pinless lock plates, single or double triggers, finest well figured hand checkered Turkish walnut. Delivered in leather motor case with accessories.

Current MSR for base model is $80,000.

PENDRAGON – 20 gauge only, best quality sideplate ejector pinless lock plates, trigger plate model with Boss style forend iron, finest well figured hand checkered Turkish walnut. Delivered in leather motor case with accessories.

Current MSR for base model is $40,000.

SHOTGUNS: SxS

MERLIN SIDELOCK MODEL – 12, 16, 20, 28 ga., or .410 bore, best quality sidelock ejector, pinless lock plates, single or double triggers, finest well figured hand checkered Turkish walnut. Delivered in leather motor case with accessories.

Current MSR for base model is $70,000.

BOXLOCK MODEL – previously made to individual order, choice of engraving - including game scenes with gold, Anson & Deeley boxlock actions, select European hybrid walnut, double triggers, leather cased. While each shotgun was priced per individual special order, the listed prices represented standard features and embellishments. Disc. 1996.

* ***Boxlock Model Best Quality***

	$5,950	$5,250	$4,500	$3,950	$3,425	$2,900	$2,250	*$9,500*

* ***Boxlock Model Deluxe Grade*** – game scene engraved.

	$7,450	$5,600	$4,800	$4,300	$3,850	$3,200	$2,650	*$10,500*

Add $900 for single trigger.
Add $2,800 for extra set of barrels.
Add $2,200 for 28 ga. or .410 bore.

FEATHERWEIGHT MONARCH GRADE – lavishly engraved with gold game scenes, lightweight model, specifications per individual customer special order. Mfg. 1989-96.

* ***Featherweight Monarch Grade Boxlock Model***

	$10,500	$8,150	$6,750	$5,500	$4,800	$4,150	$3,450	*$12,500*

* ***Featherweight Monarch Grade Sidelock Model***

	$18,000	$15,500	$13,250	$10,750	$9,100	$7,750	$6,750	*$25,000*

SIDELOCK MODEL – previously made to individual order, choice of game scene engraving, H&H sidelock action, select European hybrid walnut, double triggers, leather cased, while each shotgun was priced per individual special order, the listed values represented standard features and embellishments.

	$12,950	$10,500	$9,000	$7,600	$6,500	$5,500	$4,400	*$17,500*

Add $4,000 for smaller gauges except .410 bore - add $5,000.
Add $2,800 for extra set of barrels.
Add $2,800 for extra set of .410 bore barrels.
Subtract 50% for post-1988 mfg.

BOWEN, BRUCE & COMPANY

Current shotgun manufacturer established 1996 and located in Sturgis, SD. Consumer direct sales only. Bruce Bowen & Company is a division of NIP Manufacturing, Inc.

SHOTGUNS: SINGLE SHOT

BOWEN TRAP GUN – 12 ga. only, unique break open action similar to Seitz trap gun, 32, 33, 34, or 35 in. fixed full choke barrel with four different rib configurations, allowing for four different points of impact, both release and pull triggers included, deluxe checkered walnut with either regular or Monte Carlo stock, individually made per customer's specifications, 9 lbs.

The base price for the Bowen Trap Gun is $16,500 for fixed rib and $13,500 for adj. rib.

Please contact the factory directly for a firm price quotation with various options and a delivery date.

BOXALL & EDMISTON LTD.

Current shotgun manufacturer established during 2010 and located in Shropshire, U.K.

Boxall & Edmiston Ltd. was founded during 2010 by Peter Boxall, former manufacturing director of Holland & Holland, and James Edmiston, former managing director of the Sterling Armament Co.

SHOTGUNS: O/U

Current O/U models include a 12 ga. in either round (case colored action with choice of border or full scroll engraving) or square action (with sideplates and minimal engraving). MSRs are £10,900 for the border engraved round action, £12,900 for fully engraved round action, or £13,900 for square action.

SHOTGUNS: SxS

Boxall & Edmiston currently offers fine quality SxS Anson & Deeley boxlock shotguns in either 12 or 20 (new late 2012) ga. with and w/o sideplates. Prices start at £15,900 w/o sideplates, and £19,600 with sideplates. The company also offers a 12 or 20 (new late 2012) ga. sidelock SxS shotgun and prices start at £29,000. 30 in. barrels are standard. 16 or 28 ga. can be ordered on both shotguns for an additional £2,000. Engraving is available, and can be personalized. All guns are made to order and a variety of options are available, including small gauges, upgraded wood, and color case hardening. Prices include 20% VAT. Please contact the company for more information, including a custom quotation, delivery time, and availability (see Trademark Index).

BOY'S RIFLES

Rifle configuration generally denoting small caliber single shot rifles designed for youth circa 1890-early 1940s.

U.S. manufactured Boy's rifles are generally single shot, small caliber, rimfire rifles. The era of Boy's rifles is considered to be from the mid 1880s to the beginning of the US involvement in World War II in the early 1940s.

Many Boy's rifles are not marked with the maker's name, model, caliber, or serial number. Therefore, identification and evaluation should be left to an expert in the field for those unmarked guns. Many are clearly marked and are familiar to many gun enthusiasts. Many marked Boy's rifles are included in this book, e.g., Remington No. 4, Quackenbush Safety Rifles, Winchester Thumb Trigger, Stevens Favorite, et cetera. Unfortunately, due to various circumstances, many brands of Boy's rifles are not listed in this book, such as the various Hamilton guns, Davenport, Page Lewis, Meriden, Heal, Nicholson, Clive, et cetera.

In the beginning, Boy's rifles were all single shot and mostly falling block actions. Later when the bolt action became common, Boy's rifles started to appear with bolt actions. Then even later, repeaters started to emerge as Boy's rifles.

The most common caliber was .22 rimfire in all cartridge lengths. Some were available in .25 or .32 rimfire.

Most Boy's rifles were cheaply made and, therefore, barely safe. Those that have seen excessive wear or have a loose action are definitely not safe to be used with modern ammunition. They were designed to be inexpensive so children could afford them. Most were of diminutive size to suit young boys and girls. Most were made in the northeast and midwestern parts of the U.S.

It is not uncommon to find these in rough condition with poor bores. This is primarily due to the low quality steel used, lack of proper care by youngsters, and lack of proper cleaning (many Boy's rifles were used with black powder and/or corrosive ammunition) and are only worth a few dollars. However, one in excellent or close to like new condition

GRADING - PPGS™	100%	98%	95%	90%	80%	70%	60%	LAST MSR

with box and literature can command many thousands of dollars.

The publisher would like to thank Mr. John Groenewold for providing this information.

BRAVO COMPANY MFG. INC.

Current rifle manufacturer located in Hartland, WI.

CARBINES/RIFLES: SEMI-AUTO

Bravo Company Mfg., Inc. manufactures a line of AR-15 style rifles with many available options and accessories. The company is also a dealer/distributor for other companies that specialize in tactical gear.

IMPORTANT NOTE: On model(s) where *N/A has replaced the normal 100% value, it indicates current market conditions are too unstable to accurately ascertain 100%-60% values. Factory retail prices (MSRs) reflect most recent updates. For more up-to-date information on current pricing trends and additional useful information, please visit www.bluebookofgunvalues.com, select "Information & Services" from the menu, and click on "Additional Book Information".

CAR-16LW MOD 0 CARBINE - 5.56 NATO cal., 16 in. lightweight barrel, standard carbine length gas system, basic rifle with double heat shield handguards, no rear sight, black hardcoat anodized finish, adj. Magpul stock, mil spec F-marked forged front sight, M4 flat-top receiver, upper Picatinny rail, Mod 4 charging handle, chrome lined bore and chamber.

MSR $1,099	*N/A	$875	$750	$625	$550	$475	$395

CAR-16LW MOD 1 CARBINE - 5.56 NATO cal., similar to CAR-16LW, except has detachable carry handle with windage and elevation adj. 600m rear sight.

MSR $1,219	*N/A	$950	$825	$750	$600	$500	$425

M4 MOD 0 CARBINE - 5.56 NATO cal., 16 in. barrel, standard carbine length gas system, basic rifle with double heat shield handguards, no rear sight, black hardcoat anodized finish, adj. Magpul stock, mil spec F-marked forged front sight, M4 flat-top receiver, upper Picatinny rail, Mod 4 charging handle, chrome lined bore and chamber, MOE enhanced trigger guard, M4 feed ramp barrel extension.

MSR $1,099	*N/A	$875	$750	$625	$550	$475	$395

M4 MOD 1 CARBINE - 5.56 NATO cal., 16 in. barrel, standard carbine length gas system, double heat shield handguards, detachable carry handle with windage and elevation adj. 600m rear sight, black hardcoat anodized finish, adj. Magpul stock, mil spec F-marked forged front sight, M4 flat-top receiver, Mod 4 charging handle, chrome lined bore and chamber, MOE enhanced trigger guard, M4 feed ramp barrel extension.

MSR $1,219	*N/A	$950	$825	$750	$600	$500	$425

M4 MOD 2 CARBINE - 5.56 NATO cal., 16 in. barrel, standard carbine length gas system, drop in tactical handguard, folding rear battle sight, black hardcoat anodized finish, adj. Magpul stock, mil spec F-marked forged front sight, M4 flat-top receiver, quad rail, Mod 4 charging handle, chrome lined bore and chamber, MOE enhanced trigger guard, M4 feed ramp barrel extension.

MSR $1,379	*N/A	$1,050	$900	$775	$625	$525	$450

MID-16 MOD 0 CARBINE - 5.56 NATO cal., 16 in. barrel, mid-length gas system, basic rifle with Magpul MOE handguards, no rear sight, black hardcoat anodized finish, adj. Magpul stock, mil spec F-marked forged front sight, M4 flat-top receiver, upper Picatinny rail, Mod 4 charging handle, chrome lined bore and chamber, M4 feed ramp barrel extension.

MSR $1,119	*N/A	$875	$750	$625	$550	$475	$395

MID-16 MOD 2 CARBINE - 5.56 NATO cal., 16 in. barrel, mid-length gas system, drop in tactical handguard, folding rear battle sight, black hardcoat anodized finish, adj. Magpul stock, mil spec F-marked forged front sight, M4 flat-top receiver, quad rail, Mod 4 charging handle, chrome lined bore and chamber, MOE enhanced trigger guard, M4 feed ramp barrel extension.

MSR $1,395	*N/A	$1,075	$925	$775	$625	$525	$450

GRADING - PPGS™	100%	98%	95%	90%	80%	70%	60%	LAST MSR

MID-16LW MOD 0 CARBINE – 5.56 NATO cal., 16 in. lightweight barrel, mid-length gas system, M4 flat-top receiver, black hardcoat anodized finish, adj. Magpul stock, mil spec F-marked forged front sights, Mod 4 charging handle, chrome lined bore and chamber, Magpul MOE enhanced trigger guard. New 2011.

MSR $1,119	*N/A	$875	$750	$625	$550	$475	$395

RECCE-16 CARBINE – 5.56 NATO cal., 16 in. barrel, mid-length gas system, Magpul MOE handguards, black hardcoat anodized finish, adj. Magpul stock, M4 flat-top receiver, full length quad rail, Mod 4 charging handle, chrome lined bore and chamber, M4 feed ramp barrel extension, MOE enhanced trigger guard.

MSR $1,299	*N/A	$975	$850	$775	$625	$525	$450

Add $100 for Precision model configuration.

This model is also available with a 14 1/2 in. barrel for law enforcement/military.

A4 RIFLE – 5.56 NATO cal., standard rifle length gas system, polymer handguards, detachable carry handle with windage and elevation adj. 600m rear sight, black hardcoat anodized finish, fixed buttstock, mil spec F-marked forged front sights, M4 flat-top receiver, Mod 4 charging handle, chrome lined bore and chamber, MOE enhanced trigger guard, M4 feed ramp barrel extension.

MSR $1,219	*N/A	$950	$825	$750	$600	$500	$425

BRAZIER, JOSEPH, LTD.

Previous manufacturer established in circa 1700 and located in West Sussex, England. Previously represented in the U.S. by Joseph Brazier, Ltd - Karl Lippard, gunmaker, located in Colorado Springs, CO.

This firm was founded in approx. 1702 by William Brazier, Gunmaker, London (1721-1753), and was continued by his son, John Brazier, also of London, from 1741-1769. Benjamin Brazier was established in Wolverhampton from 1818-1835. Joseph Brazier was listed as a gun and lock maker at the same address (9 Brick Kiln Street) during 1827. From 1834 to 1887, the address was "The Ashes" on Great Brick Kiln Street, Wolverhampton. By 1838, the firm was also making implements, and had been appointed lock makers to the East India Company and the Board of Ordnance. In 1849, Joseph's elder son, also named Joseph, was made a partner, and the firm became known as Joseph Brazier & Son. By 1851, younger son Richard Brazier was made a partner, and the firm was renamed J & R Brazier. This company exhibited locks and accessories at the Great Exhibition of 1851.

During this same time, J & R Brazier was making gun furniture, sights, bullets, moulds, and breech loading actions. In 1855, Joseph Brazier patented a lever ramrod for Adams self-cocking pistols (No. 760) (single action later converted to double action), and the Adams revolvers, which he made under license. During 1858, Richard Brazier patented a loading device (No. 1593), and at least one revolver using this patent was made; the name engraved on the revolver was "Joseph Brazier & Son", which implied that Richard had died, and the firm's name had reverted.

By 1859, Joseph Brazier Jr. registered two designs, the first (No. 1056) was for a spring clamp, and the second (No. 1068) was for a lock vise. In 1864, Joseph Brazier Jr. reportedly patented a snap action breech loading mechanism (patent not traced). By 1872, the firm was classified as gun barrel makers, and in 1874 (as well as 1879-1880), the firm was recognized as gunmakers - breech loading. After 1874, the firm changed its name to Joseph Brazier & Sons, most likely indicating Joseph Sr. had retired after taking his sons into the business as partners. During 1876, the firm purchased a license to manufacture Anson & Deeley's famous patent boxlock. In 1887, William Mansfield Jr. became a senior partner, and the company moved from "The Ashes Works" to Lord Street. Mansfield was a lock maker on Lord Street from 1875-1896 and during 1887 under the name J. Brazier & Sons, patented the "Galwey Brazier Improved Game Scorer", which fitted into the forend or stock of a shotgun. By 1896, William Mansfield either retired or died, and G. Brazier together with W. Cashmore patented a safety for a hammerless gun.

It appears that after 1896, the Brazier family regained control of the business. Around 1920, the firm, which had approx. 26 employees, was bought by Edwin Chilton of

Wolverhampton, and Brazier named locks continued to be made until 1978, when Chilton closed down the company. After 1978, Joseph Brazier was registered as Magnum Arms Company Ltd. at 46 Newhampton Rd. West, Wolverhampton, West Midlands. In 1983, Joseph Brazier Ltd. was registered as a limited company, and by 1993 was acquired and incorporated.

Recently until 2010, Joseph Brazier manufactured complete guns, gunlocks for the HMS Victory, firearm locks, parts, accessories, and new technology Solid Solid one piece barrels for the trade. The firm also offered state of the art engineering services to the English gunmaking trade and was an engineering consultant to 14 major firearms manufacturers.

HANDGUNS

.357 Mag. cal. revolvers in stainless steel started at $2,050. Semi-auto 1911 A1 style pistols were available in a variety of configurations and began at $5,000.

RIFLES

A boxlock double rifle in .470 NE cal. was available starting at $14,750. The sidelock model started at $44,500.

SHOTGUNS

Brazier boxlock SxS shotguns were available in 20 or 28 ga., with DTs, ejector, and full hand engraving for $10,500.

A sidelock O/U Best gun was available in 12, 20, or 28 ga. and prices started at $29,500 and $32,500 if with SolidSolid barrels. Additionally, Watch and Signature sidelock models were available starting at $65,000, and the Exhibition Grade started at $85,000.

BREDA MECCANICA BRESCIANA

Current manufacturer located in Brescia, Italy. No current U.S. importation. Previous company name was Ernesto Breda. Previously imported 2007-2008 by Legacy Sports International located in Reno, NV, during 2002-2005 by Tristar, located in No. Kansas City, MO, during 2000-2001 by Gryphon International, located in Kansas City, MO, and by Diana Imports Co., located in San Francisco, CA. Dealer direct sales.

SHOTGUNS: O/U

Currently manufactured models include the Pegaso in 12 and 20 ga., and the Pegaso Anniversary in 12 ga. These models are not currently imported into the U.S.

VEGA SPECIAL – 12 or 20 ga., boxlock action, 26 or 28 in. barrels, single trigger, ejectors, blue only.

$575 $495 $460 $440 $400 $375 $350 ***$650***

VEGA SPECIAL TRAP – 12 ga. only, boxlock action, triggers and locks designed for competition shooting, 30 or 32 in. barrels, single trigger, ejectors, blue only.

$885 $820 $760 $720 $675 $635 $575 ***$1,114***

VEGA LUSSO – 12 ga. only, scalloped boxlock action, 3 in. chambers, SST, ejectors, 26 or 28 in. VR barrels, coin finished receiver with light perimeter engraving, deluxe checkered Circassian walnut stock and forearm. Imported 2001-2002.

$1,695 $1,375 $1,100 $975 $850 $725 $600 ***$1,858***

SIRIO STANDARD – 12 or 20 ga., boxlock action, 26 or 28 in. barrels, single trigger, ejectors, blue only, action extensively engraved. Also available in skeet model (28 in. barrels).

$2,000 $1,850 $1,630 $1,480 $1,320 $1,200 $1,050 ***$2,225***

PEGASO HUNTER – 12 or 20 ga., boxlock action, 3 in. chambers, 26, 28 (12 ga. only), or 30 (Sporting Clays only) in. VR barrels with 7mm (Hunter) or 11mm (Sporting Clays) rib, 5 interchangeable chokes, removable trigger group, engraved silver steel (Hunter Model) or blue finished (Sporting Clays), inertia SST, oil finished deluxe walnut stock and forearm, approx. 7-7 1/2 lbs. Imported 2004 only.

$2,400 $2,050 $1,850 $1,650 $1,425 $1,200 $950 ***$2,739***

GRADING - PPGS™	100%	98%	95%	90%	80%	70%	60%	LAST MSR

* ***Pegaso Sporting Clays*** – features upgraded wood, Breda logos in 24Kt. gold, removable trigger group, supplied with ABS fitted case. Imported 2004 only.

$3,300	$2,875	$2,400	$2,050	$1,700	$1,450	$1,200	*$3,644*

PEGASO HUNTING – 12 or 20 ga., 3 in. chambers, 28 in. blued VR barrels with three flush choke tubes, boxlock stainless steel receiver, SST, ejectors, checkered pistol grip stock and forearm, 6.2 - 6.8 lbs. Limited importation 2007.

$2,400	$2,000	$1,850	$1,650	$1,425	$1,200	$950	*$2,729*

PEGASO SPORTING – 12 or 20 ga., 3 in. chambers, 28 in. blued VR barrels with three flush choke tubes, blue boxlock receiver, SST, ejectors, checkered pistol grip stock and forearm, 7.9 lbs. Limited importation 2007.

$3,100	$2,600	$2,300	$2,000	$1,700	$1,400	$1,125	*$3,509*

PEGASO TRAP – 12 or 20 ga., 3 in. chambers, 28 in. blued VR barrels with three flush choke tubes, chrome plated boxlock receiver, checkered pistol grip stock and forearm, SST, ejectors, 7.8 lbs. Limited importation 2007.

$3,100	$2,600	$2,300	$2,000	$1,700	$1,400	$1,125	*$3,509*

SHOTGUNS: SxS

ANDROMEDA SPECIAL – 12 ga. only, single trigger, ejectors, select checkered walnut, satin finish receiver with elaborate engraving.

$640	$550	$480	$420	$365	$300	$250	*$685*

SHOTGUNS: SEMI-AUTO

Currently manufactured models include the Chiron, Xanthos, Echo, Grizzly, and the Altair. Models are available in a variety of gauges and configurations, and are not currently imported into the U.S.

Add approx. 5% for vent. rib on those discontinued models below where applicable.
Add approx. 10% for choke tubes on discontinued models.

GOLD SERIES – 12 or 20 (lightweight) ga., 2 3/4 in. chamber, 25 or 27 in. barrels, recoil operated, interchangeable choke tubes on recent mfg., vent. rib is standard.

* ***Antares Standard*** – all steel construction. Importation disc. 1988.

$440	$375	$340	$310	$285	$260	$240	*$495*

* ***Argus*** – lightweight standard, weighs only 6.6 lbs. Importation disc. 1988.

$450	$380	$340	$310	$285	$260	$240	*$510*

* ***Aries*** – Magnum, 3 in. chambers, 7.9 lbs. Importation disc. 1988.

$460	$395	$350	$320	$295	$270	$250	*$525*

STANDARD – 12 ga., 2 3/4 in. chamber, recoil operated, 25 or 27 in. barrel, lightly engraved, interchangeable choke tubes on recent mfg. Disc.

$300	$275	$255	$230	$215	$200	$180

GRADE 1 – 12 ga., similar to standard, except with fancier wood and engraving.

$575	$530	$485	$440	$410	$380	$350

GRADE 2 – 12 ga., exceeds Grade 1 embellishments.

$685	$620	$560	$500	$460	$420	$375

GRADE 3 – 12 ga., top-of-the-line semi-auto.

$850	$790	$700	$640	$590	$540	$480

MAGNUM MODEL – 12 ga. only, chambered for 3 in. shells.

$470	$415	$380	$350	$315	$290	$265

ALTAIR SPECIAL – 12 ga., 2 3/4 in. chamber, gas operated, 25 or 27 in. barrel, alloy construction, interchangeable choke tubes on recent mfg., vent. rib is standard, choice of blue or chromed receiver.

$440	$375	$340	$310	$285	$260	$240	*$495*

GRADING - PPGS™	100%	98%	95%	90%	80%	70%	60%	LAST MSR

ALTAIR – 12 or 20 ga., 3 in. chamber, gas operated, two-tone (disc.) or blue alloy receiver finish with 28 in. VR barrel and three choke tubes, checkered walnut stock and forearm, 5.7 - 6.1 lbs. Imported 2007-2008.

$1,150 $950 $850 $725 $625 $550 $475 *$1,320*

ASTRO – 12 (disc. 2002) or 20 ga., 3 in. chamber, inertia movement action, 22 (slug), 24, 26, 28, or 30 in. VR barrel with choke tube, choice of black synthetic, Advantage camo, or Circassian walnut stock (recoil pad on 20 ga. only) and forearm. Imported 2001-2004.

$1,050 $825 $675 $600 $525 $450 $425 *$1,215*

Add $100 for Advantage camo coverage (disc. 2002).

ASTROLUX – similar to Astro, except has two-tone receiver with engraving and deluxe checkered Circassian walnut stock and forearm. Imported 2001-2002.

$1,475 $1,200 $995 $875 $750 $625 $550 *$1,665*

ERMES SERIES (2000/2000 L) – 12 ga., 3 in. chamber, inertia recoil operating system, aluminum alloy receiver, nickel plated or blue (lower receiver only) finish, 24, 26, or 28 in. barrel with choke tube, deluxe checkered Circassian walnut stock and forearm. Imported 2001-2005.

$1,050 $925 $800 $700 $600 $500 $400 *$1,339*

Add $417 for Ermes 2000 L with nickel finished receiver.

* ***Ermes Silver*** – similar to Ermes 2000, except has engraved nickel plated finish on lower receiver. Imported 2002-2005.

$1,400 $1,200 $975 $825 $700 $575 $495 *$1,834*

* ***Ermes Gold*** – similar to Ermes 2000, except has nickel plated finish with engraving and 24Kt. animal gold inlays on lower receiver. Imported 2002-2005.

$1,550 $1,325 $1,075 $900 $775 $650 $550 *$2,060*

MIRA – 12 ga. only, 3 in. chamber, gas operated, Ergal aluminum alloy receiver, choice of anodized black metal or Advantage camo finish, 22 (slug), 24, 26, 28, or 30 in. VR barrel with choke tube, Circassian walnut or black synthetic (disc. 2002) stock and forearm. Imported 2001-2005.

$800 $700 $625 $550 $450 $375 $325 *$938*

Subtract 10% for black synthetic stock and forearm.
Add $12 for Sporting Clays configuration.

GRIZZLY – 12 ga., 3 1/2 in. chamber, inertia operation with rotary bolt, 28 in. VR barrel with choke tubes, choice of matte black receiver/barrel finish or 100% Advantage Timber HD camo, sling swivels, includes fitted case, 7 1/2 lbs. Imported 2004, resumed 2007-2008.

$1,495 $1,250 $1,050 $900 $800 $700 $600 *$1,826*

Add $295 for 100% camo coverage.

ARIES 2 – 12 ga. only, 2 3/4 in. chamber, gas operated, engraved two-tone receiver, 28 or 30 in. VR barrel, deluxe checkered Circassian walnut stock and forearm. Limited importation 2001 only.

$815 $725 $595 $550 $495 $445 $395 *$925*

ECHO – 12 or 20 ga., 3 in. chamber, inertia mechanism, blue, bronze, or nickel finished receiver with accents, 28 in. VR barrel and three choke tubes, grooved/checkered walnut stock and forearm, 6 - 6 1/2 lbs. Imported 2007-2008.

$1,550 $1,275 $1,050 $900 $800 $700 $600 *$1,897*

Add $317 for nickel finished receiver.
Add $72 for bronze finished receiver.

XANTHOS – 12 ga., 3 in. chamber, inertia operation, 28 in. VR blue barrel with three choke tubes, receiver colors include blue, grey, or chrome with accents, deluxe checkered walnut stock and forearm, 6 1/2 lbs. Imported 2007-2008.

$1,995 $1,750 $1,500 $1,250 $995 $850 $750 *$2,309*

Add $142 for grey receiver with colored accents.
Add $1,097 for chrome receiver with colored accents.

GRADING - PPGS™	100%	98%	95%	90%	80%	70%	60%	LAST MSR

BREEDING, RYAN

Current custom rifle manufacturer located in Nampa, ID. Previously located in Palmdale, CA.

RIFLES: BOLT ACTION

Ryan Breeding specializes in making high quality, custom built rifles in .22-.585 cal. On his safari rifles in larger cals., he features a 5 shot mag. and shorter barrel (19-24 in.) with optional muzzle brake. Base price for custom Kevlar stock models is $13,900, and go up to $15,900 depending on options. Custom safari rifles with wood stocks start at $17,500 for .30-06 cal. and go up to $21,500 for the .416 cal. Please contact Ryan Breeding directly for more information, including pricing and availability (see Trademark Index).

BRE-MAC SRL

Current manufacturer of Renato Gamba shotguns located in Gardone, Italy. Please refer to listings in the Renato Gamba section.

BREN 10 (PREVIOUS MFG.)

Previous trademark manufactured 1983-1986 by Dornaus & Dixon Ent., Inc., located in Huntington Beach, CA.

Bren 10 magazines played an important part in the failure of these pistols to be accepted by consumers. Originally, Bren magazines were not shipped in some cases until a year after the customer received his gun. The complications arising around manufacturing a reliable dual caliber magazine domestically led to the downfall of this company. For this reason, original Bren 10 magazines are currently selling for $150-$175 if new (watch for fakes).

PISTOLS: SEMI-AUTO

Note: the Bren 10 shoots a Norma factory loaded 10mm auto. cartridge. Ballistically, it is very close to a .41 Mag. Bren pistols also have unique power seal rifling, with five lands and grooves. While in production, Bren pistols underwent four engineering changes, the most important probably being re-designing the floorplate of the magazine to prevent the magazine from dislocating as the pistol recoiled.

100% values in this section assume NIB condition. Add 5% for extra original factory mag. Subtract 10% without box/manual.

BREN 10 STANDARD MODEL - 10mm cal. only, semi-auto selective double action design, blue slide/silver frame finish, 5 in. barrel, 11 shot, stainless steel frame, usually supplied with two mags. although early mfg. did not include a mag. because of design problems, "83SM" ser. no. prefix. Mfg. 1984-86.

	100%	98%	95%	90%	80%	70%	60%	LAST MSR
	$2,450	$2,100	$1,875	$1,300	$975	$700	$500	*$500*

Add $750 for .45 conversion unit.

BREN 10 MILITARY/POLICE MODEL - 10mm cal. only, identical to standard model, except has all black finish, "83MP" ser. no. prefix. Mfg. 1984-86.

	100%	98%	95%	90%	80%	70%	60%	LAST MSR
	$2,650	$2,300	$2,100	$1,850	$1,250	$900	$700	*$550*

BREN 10 SPECIAL FORCES MODEL - 10mm cal. only, commercial version of the military pistol submitted to the U.S. gov't. Model D has dark finish. Model L has light finish, "SFD" ser. no. prefix on Model D, "SFL" ser. no. prefix on Model L. Disc. 1986.

	100%	98%	95%	90%	80%	70%	60%	LAST MSR
Dark finish - Model D	$2,675	$2,250	$2,100	$1,850	$1,450	$975	$600	
Light finish - Model L	$3,675	$2,975	$2,750	$2,100	$1,650	$1,050	$675	*$600*

BREN 10 DUAL-MASTER PRESENTATION MODEL - 10mm and .45 ACP cal., supplied with extra slide and barrel (numbered to gun) to accommodate the .45 ACP, same mags. (two) for both cals., extra fine finish, light scroll engraving, with wood presentation case, "83DM" ser. no. prefix, less than 50 mfg. Disc. 1986.

	100%	98%	95%	90%	80%	70%	60%	LAST MSR
	$4,750	$3,985	$3,250	$1,800	$1,100	$900	$875	*$800*

Be wary of Standard Models with wooden cases and conversion kits - they are fakes!

GRADING - PPGS™	100%	98%	95%	90%	80%	70%	60%	LAST MSR

BREN 10 JEFF COOPER COMMEMORATIVE – 10mm cal. only, while 2,000 were annnounced for mfg., sources now believe that approx. 5 were actually made, 22Kt. gold plated detailing, laser engraved stocks, special presentation chest. Disc. 1986.

Last MSR was $2,000.

Extreme rarity factor precludes accurate pricing on this model. An individual appraisal is recommended. Current pricing guidelines, depending on condition, are approx. $5,000 - $7,500.

MARKSMAN MODEL – .45 ACP cal., approx. less than 250 mfg. (in its own ser. range) for "The Marksman" retail shop in Chicago, action similar to Bren 10 Standard Model, "MSM" ser. no. prefix.

	100%	98%	95%	90%	80%	70%	60%	LAST MSR
	$2,450	$2,100	$1,950	$1,750	$1,250	$950	$525	

Add $1,200 for 10mm conversion unit.

Add $400 for original nylon carrying case marked "Marksman."

Initial models were faulty and returned to D&D for repairs. Due to the closure of D&D, it is doubtful that all 250 guns were actually sent to Chicago.

BREN 10 (RECENT MFG.)

Previous trademark manufactured in limited quantities from 2010-2011 by Vltor Mfg., located in Tucson, AZ. Previously distributed exclusively until early 2011 by Sporting Products, LLC, located in W. Palm Beach, FL.

PISTOLS: SEMI-AUTO

SM SERIES – 10mm or .45 ACP cal., 5 in. barrel, stainless steel frame with blue slide, 10 (SM45) or 15 (SM10) shot mag., two-tone finish, synthetic grips, approx. 500 (SM10) or 300 (SM45) were scheduled to be mfg., but very few were produced mid-2010-2011.

	100%	98%	95%	90%	80%	70%	60%	LAST MSR
	$1,095	$995	$875	$750	$650	$550	$450	*$1,200*

SMV SERIES – 10mm or .45 ACP cal., 5 in. barrel, stainless steel frame, hard chrome slide, 10 (SMV10) or 15 (SMV15) shot mag., black synthetic grips, approx. 500 (SMV10) or 300 (SMV45) were scheduled to be produced, but very few were mfg. mid-2010-2011.

	100%	98%	95%	90%	80%	70%	60%	LAST MSR
	$1,175	$1,050	$925	$800	$700	$600	$495	*$1,299*

SFD45 – .45 ACP cal., 4 in. barrel, matte black finished frame and slide, synthetic grips, 10 shot mag., approx. 500 were scheduled to be produced, but very few were mfg. mid-2010-2011.

	100%	98%	95%	90%	80%	70%	60%	LAST MSR
	$995	$895	$800	$700	$600	$500	$425	*$1,100*

SFL45 – .45 ACP cal., 4 in. barrel, matte finished stainless steel frame, hard chrome slide, 10 shot mag., synthetic grips, two-tone finish, approx. 200 were scheduled to be produced, but very few were mfg. mid-2010-2011.

	100%	98%	95%	90%	80%	70%	60%	LAST MSR
	$1,095	$995	$875	$750	$650	$550	$450	*$1,200*

BRETTON-GAUCHER

Current manufacturer established in 2000, and located in Saint-Etienne, France. No current U.S. importation. Previously imported and distributed by Mandall Shooting Supplies, Inc. located in Scottsdale, AZ.

The Bretton trademark was established in 1934, and specialized in Baby lightweight shotguns. Gaucher dates back to 1834, and specialized in Express double rifles. The two companies merged in 2000.

RIFLES

Bretton-Gaucher manufactures a variety of single-shot and small caliber rifles, in addition to Express double rifles. To date, these guns have had little or no importation into the U.S. Please contact the factory directly for more information, including pricing and availability.

SHOTGUNS: O/U

All Bretton shotguns are extremely lightweight and well balanced because of their unique design (permitting total disassembly including barrels) and use of various composition alloys. Current MSR's reflect European pricing without shipping, export, and duty costs to the U.S.

GRADING - PPGS™	100%	98%	95%	90%	80%	70%	60%	LAST MSR

BABY STANDARD (SPRINT MODEL) – 12 or 20 ga. only, sliding breech action allows barrels to move straight forward, 27 1/2 in. separated barrels, double triggers, side opening lever, blue action and barrels, recoil pad, checkered walnut stock and forearm, 4.8 lbs. Limited importation.

MSR €1,090	$995	$885	$700	$625	$575	$475	$430	

Add €230 for Baby Luxe.

SPRINT DELUXE – 12, 16 (disc.), or 20 ga., action similar to Baby Standard, engraved coin finished receiver, 27 1/2 in. separated barrels, deluxe checkered walnut stock and forearm, extremely lightweight, 4.8 lbs. Limited importation.

	$895	$725	$625	$575	$475	$430	$395	*$975*

Prices reflect most recent importation information.

FAIR-PLAY – 12 or 20 ga., differs from Sprint Models in that action pivots like a normal O/U, 27 1/2 in. separated barrels, lightweight construction, 4.8 lbs. Limited importation.

MSR €1,335	$1,325	$1,125	$975	$850	$675	$625	$575	

Add €225 for Fair-Play Luxe model with engraved coin finished receiver.
Add €25 for Fair-Play MXT model with open sights (12 ga. only).
Add 10% for Fair-Play Limited Model.

TINY – 20 ga., double triggers, extremely lightweight, approx. 4.2 lbs.

Current French MSR on this model is €1,135.
Add €230 for Tiny Luxe model with coin finished receiver and engraving.

BRIGNOLI, SILVIO

Current firearms importer and distributor established in 1965 and located in Brescia, Italy.

Silvio Brignoli manufactures a Brescia Model boxlock SxS shotgun in most gauges and various configurations. Please contact the distributor/importer directly for current information on these models, including European pricing.

BRILEY

Current trademark of pistols and rimfire semi-auto rifles with choke tubes currently manufactured in Houston, TX. Current pistol and rifle manufacture is sub-contracted to other manufacturers using the Briley trademark. Briley has previously produced both pistols and rifles, including those listed, in addition to manufacturing a complete line of top quality shotgun barrel tubes and chokes since 1976. Additionally, beginning late March, 2006-2007 Briley Manufacturing imported and distributed Mauser Models 98 and 03 bolt action rifles from Germany.

PISTOLS: SEMI-AUTO

Briley still has some new old stock pistols remaining. Please check their website for availability and pricing (see Trademark Index).

FANTOM – 9mm Para., .38 Super, .40 S&W, or .45 ACP cal., features Caspian aluminum wide body frame, Briley match barrel, and many competition features, hot blue slide finish and armor coated frame, 8 or 10 shot mag, black synthetic grips, approx. 22-24 oz. Mfg. 1998-2003.

	$1,675	$1,300	$1,075	$875	$750	$625	$575	*$1,900*

Add $95 for hard chrome finish.
Add $75 for night sights.
Add $350 for 2 port barrel compensator.

ADVANTAGE – 9mm Para., .40 S&W, or .45 ACP cal., features 5 in. Briley match barrel, checkered walnut grips and front grip strap, hot blue finish. Mfg. 1998-2004.

	$1,495	$1,250	$1,050	$875	$750	$625	$575	*$1,650*

Add $175 for hard chrome finish.
Add $100 for stainless steel (new 2000).

GRADING - PPGS™	100%	98%	95%	90%	80%	70%	60%	LAST MSR

VERSATILITY PLUS – 9mm Para., .40 S&W, or .45 ACP cal., features steel or stainless steel (new 2000) 1911 Govt. length modular or Caspian frame, 5 in. barrel, checkered black synthetic grips and front grip strap, squared off trigger guard, hot blue finish. Mfg. 1998-2004.

	$1,625	$1,300	$1,050	$875	$725	$600	$550	*$1,850*

Add $175 for hard chrome finish.
Add $175 for stainles steel (new 2000).

SIGNATURE SERIES – .40 S&W cal. only, similar to Versatility Plus. Mfg. 1998-2004.

	$1,975	$1,650	$1,325	$1,125	$900	$775	$625	*$2,250*

Add $175 for hard chrome finish.

PLATE MASTER – 9mm Para. or .38 Super cal., features 1911 Govt. length frame, Briley TCII titanium barrel compensator, Briley scope mount, and other competition features, hot blue finish. Mfg. 1998-2004.

	$1,675	$1,325	$1,075	$895	$775	$625	$575	*$1,895*

Add $175 for hard chrome finish.

EL PRESIDENTE – 9mm Para. or .38 Super cal., top-of-the-line competition model with Briley quad compensator with side ports, checkered synthetic grips and front grip strap, squared off trigger guard. Mfg. 1998-2004.

	$2,250	$1,925	$1,625	$1,325	$1,075	$875	$750	*$2,550*

Add $175 for hard chrome finish.

LIMITED EDITION ADVANTAGE – .38 Super, 9mm Para., .40 S&W, or .45 ACP cal., patterned after the Colt M1911, features Briley frame, special Caspian slide, 5 in. match barrel on bushing, match trigger, checkered black grips, fit and finish by Pistol Dynamics. New 2012.

MSR $3,195	$2,800	$2,400	$1,995	$1,650	$1,375	$1,100	$995	

RIFLES: BOLT ACTION

Briley imported and distributed Mauser Models 98 and 03 bolt action rifles briefly circa 2006. Briley still has some stock rifles remaining. Please check their website for availability and pricing (see Trademark Index).

TRANS PECOS – .22-250 Rem., .243 Win., .260 Rem., .308 Win., or 7mm-08 Rem. cal., solid aluminum frame fits metal to metal with barreled action, bench rest grade Jewell trigger, match grade L. Walther barrel, 3 lug 45 degree one-piece bolt, choice of black synthetic (single shot) or checkered high gloss stock and forearm (repeater). Mfg. 1998-2002.

	$3,200	$2,750	$2,275	$1,950	$1,775	$1,525	$1,250	*$3,495*

Subtract $500 for single shot action.
This model was guaranteed to shoot 1/2 in. groups at 100 yards with factory ammo.

RIFLES: SEMI-AUTO

HUNTER – .22 LR cal., utilizes Ruger 10/22 action, 21 1/2 in. tapered match stainless steel barrel with crown, Hogue rubber or wood stock, 10 shot mag., includes Briley integral scope mount, approx. 6 1/4 - 6 5/8 lbs.

	$550	$475	$395	$360	$330	$300	$285	*$600*

Add $250 for wood stock. Add $100 for fluted barrel.

* ***Hunter Magnum*** – .22 WMR cal., similar to Hunter, except is 9 shot mag. and 21 1/2 in. bull barrel. Disc. 2003.

	$750	$575	$475	$425	$375	$325	$295	*$850*

Add $250 for walnut or laminate stock.
Add $100 for fluted barrel.

SPORTER – .17 HMR (new 2006) or .22 LR cal., similar to Hunter, except has 18 1/2 or 21 1/2 in. match stainless steel bull barrel with crown, Hogue rubber, brown laminate, or uncheckered walnut sporter stock, 10 shot mag., approx. 6 1/2 lbs.

	$550	$475	$395	$360	$330	$300	$285	*$600*

Add $250 for laminate or sporter style walnut stock.
Add $100 for fluted barrel.

GRADING - PPGS™	100%	98%	95%	90%	80%	70%	60%	LAST MSR

BMG – .22 LR cal., 17 in. match stainless steel bull barrel with target crown, includes 3 1/2 lbs. adj. match barrel weights, choice of Hogue rubber, brown laminate sporter, or walnut sporter stock, 10 shot mag., designed for match grade ammunition only.

	$675	$600	$525	$465	$425	$385	$350	*$750*

Add $250 for laminate or sporter style walnut stock.

SPECTRUM – .22 LR cal., uses Ruger 10-22 action, 16 1/2 in. threaded aluminum bull barrel (various colors), Picatinny rail on receiver top, features HawkTech Arms premium laminated wood stock, mfg. by Tactical Solutions located in Boise, ID. New 2012.

MSR $995	$895	$825	$750	$650	$550	$450	$350	

BRITARMS

Previous trademark manufactured by Berdan Gunmakers Ltd. located in England. Previously imported and distributed until 1994 by Mandall Shooting Supplies, Inc. located in Scottsdale, AZ, and by Action Arms Ltd. (1982-1983) located in Philadelphia, PA.

Britarms Target Pistols had very limited importation into the U.S. While Britarms manufactured other models, only the Model 2000 is listed since it was formally imported through U.S. firms.

PISTOLS: SEMI-AUTO

MODEL 2000 (MK II) – .22 LR cal., standard fire target semi-auto pistol, adj. trigger and rear sight, anatomical adj. grips, 5.82 in. barrel, 5 shot mag., 3 lbs., limited importation, including approx. 2000 through Action Arms Ltd.

	$995	$825	$700	$625	$550	$495	$450	*$1,295*

This model features a bolt hold-open mechanism which serves as a manual safety to allow importation.

BRNO ARMS (ZBROJOVKA BRNO)

Previously manufactured by Zbrojovka Brno located in Brno, Czech Republic (formerly Czechoslovakia) from 1918-2006. Brno 98 bolt action rifles and actions were imported by EAA Corp, located in Sharpes, FL until 2002. Also previously imported and distributed by Euro-Imports, located in El Cajon, CA until 2001 and by Bohemia Arms located in Fountain Valley, CA until 1997. Brno rifles, shotguns, and combination guns produced at the Brno factory were previously imported and distributed by Magnum Research Inc. located in Minneapolis, MN (c. 1994-1996). In the early '50s, Brno rifles were imported by Continental Arms Corp. located in New York City. Pragotrade located in Ontario, Canada also imported this trademark for Canada exclusively. Previously imported by T.D. Arms located in New Baltimore, MD.

As more history is becoming available on this important European trademark, the following biographical sketch will provide some information. Circa 1918, some military personnel took over the controlling interest of the Austro-Hungarian armament shop in Brno, Czechoslovakia, renaming it The State Armament and Engineering Works. Approximately a year later, the name was changed to Czechoslovak State Armament Works. The former provinces of Bohemia and Moravia had long been firearms manufacturing centers within their regions. Prior to 1924, this firm was involved mainly with Mauser Model 98 type rifles (both assembly and mfg.).

Pistol manufacture was tranferred from Brno to Ceská Zbrojovka, located in Strakonice, Czechoslovakia, circa 1923. During 1964-1966, the Czech government transferred the production of long guns from Zbrojovka Brno to Ceská Zbrojovka Uhersky Brod. During the 1970s & 1980s, the arms production of Zbrojovka Brno accounted for less than 3% of its total capacity. The activities of this company were deverted into the production of typewriters, diesel motors, and automatic machine tools. While many firearm designs originated in Brno, Zbrojovka Brno was not the manufacturer. Because of this, the long guns manufactured in the mid-1960s, including the ZKK 600 - 602 series and ZKM rimfires, were manufactured in CZ Uhersky Brod. Because of the Czech government's decision to

GRADING - PPGS™	100%	98%	95%	90%	80%	70%	60%	LAST MSR

merge manufacture within both companies, the Brno trademark was also used by Ceská Zbrojovka Uhersky Brod.

This relationship was terminated in 1983, when both companies became part of the Agrozet conglomerate. While confusing, the arms utlizing the Brno trademark were not produced in Brno during this time. All firearms exported from Czechoslovakia at the time carried the Brno logo, and most of them were manufactured by Ceská Zbrojovka Uhersky Brod.

Brno was declared bankrupt in March 2003. Shortly after, Brno emerged from bankruptcy, but fell back in during Oct. 2003. The company continued to trade under administration until Zbrojovka Brno finally closed in 2006. The facilities were bought by a Slovak firm, and the owners wanted to support various business activities in the future. The majority of the firm's employees transferred to Brno Rifles a subsidiary of Ceska Zbrojovka (CZ), which was established in Brno to continue production of Brno firearms. Please refer to Brno Rifles for current manufacture.

Brno's famous Z banner trademark was sold to an undisclosed buyer on November 6, 2007.

CZ PISTOLS & RIFLES

See separate listing under CZ in this text.

PISTOLS: SEMI-AUTO

MODEL ZBP-99 – 9mm Para. or .40 S&W cal., double action.

While advertised in 1998, this gun never went into production.

REVOLVERS

ZKR 551 – .32 S&W Long or .38 Spl. cal., double action, solid frame with Colt SAA style shrouded ejector rod, 6 shot cylinder, adj. sights, checkered wood grips with thumb rest, 6 in. barrel, approx. 2 lbs. Imported 1999-2002.

$1,375 $1,100 $978 $875 $775 $675 $600

RIFLES: BOLT ACTION

The Brno Lightweight Sporter was introduced in the late 1930s. A small quantity was manufactured during pre-war and WWII. Most production occured between 1946-1955. Total production of this model was approx. 40,000+ units. A design change was implemented at approximately serial number 23,000, at which time the receiver was changed to a double square bridge dovetailed to accept scope mounts.

Earlier mfg. had a rounded receiver and some had claw type scope mounts installed. These guns were referenced as Models 21 and 22 domestically, but no model designation appears on the gun. Available cals. were 6.5x57mm, 7x57mm, 7x64mm, 8x57mm, or 8x60mm. Configuration was small ring Mauser 98 receiver with double set trigger(s), butterknife bolt, checkered walnut pistol grip stock (half or full length), with cheekpiece and sling swivels, late production incorporated four variations and two barrel lengths (20.5 or 23.6 in.).

Brno rifles may be dated by the two digit date beside the proofmarks. Brno's rifle designations typically indicated the Brno Z brand and the designer. Hence, a ZG47 was manufactured by the factory in Zbrojovka Brno, G refers to Otakar Galas, the designer, and 47 is most likely the year of design.

HORNET SPORTER (MODEL ZKW 465) – various cals., miniature Mauser action, 22 3/4 in. barrel, 5 shot box mag., 3-leaf express sight, double set trigger(s), checkered pistol grip stock, also called Z-B Mauser, serial range noted is 00111-38262, approx. 40,000 mfg. between 1948-1974.

$1,200 $1,050 $900 $815 $660 $540 $420

There are few examples in .218 Bee and .222 Rem. cal. - premiums can be added.

This model was redesigned with a subsequent designation of ZKB 680 Fox in approx. 1971. Please refer to the CZ section for this model.

GRADING - PPGS™	100%	98%	95%	90%	80%	70%	60%	LAST MSR

MODEL ZG-47 – .270 Win., .30-06, 7x57mm, 7x64mm, 8x64S, 8x57mm, 9.3x62mm, or 10.75x68mm cal., large ring Mauser 98 action with 20mm dovetails on receiver ring and bridge, single trigger, hinged floorplate, rollover type safety and bolt handle designed for low scope mounting, 23 1/2 in. barrel, checkered pistol grip walnut stock with sling swivels and Schnabel forend, approx. serial range is 0-20,000, mfg. and exported world-wide between 1956-62 (approx.).

$1,125	$985	$845	$765	$620	$505	$395	

Early specimens of this model are marked "BRNO MADE IN CZECHOSLOVAKIA". This model is generally regarded as being one of the finest rifles that Brno has manufactured. Circa 1961-1966, Parker-Hale Limited, of Birmingham, England, built some Hussar and International model rifles on Brno Model ZG-47 actions. Calibers were .243, .270, .308, .30-06 and .308 Norma Mag. As no Brno/Czech markings appear on these guns, collectors should look for the integral scope mount dovetails on the receiver. Internationals were advertised in the 1963 *Gun Digest* for $149.95. The Magnum was an additional $10.

MODEL G 33-40 – 8mm cal., mfg. between 1940-42, prices below assume sporterized condition.

$350	$305	$260	$240	$190	$155	$120	

MODEL 21 – 6.5x57mm, 7x57mm, 7x64mm (scarce), 8x57mm, or 8x60mm cal., featherweight style design of the small ring Mauser type action, with (post-1949) or without 20mm dovetails on receiver ring and bridge, 20 1/2 or 23 in. barrel, butterknife style bolt handle, double set triggers, 2-leaf rear sight, checkered pistol grip walnut stock with cheekpiece and plastic buttplate/grip cap, small Schnabel forend, sling swivels included, noted serialization is 14,410-40,604, mfg. approx. 1946-1956.

$1,495	$1,325	$1,175	$1,050	$900	$825	$675	

The Brno Models 21 and 22 were available in 4 different variations: short barrel/short stock, short barrel/full length stock, long barrel/short stock, long barrel/full length stock. The left receiver rail on these models is marked "ZBROJOVKA BRNO, NARODNI PODNIK".

MODEL 22 – similar to 21, with full length stock. Disc.

$1,400	$1,225	$1,050	$950	$770	$630	$490	

The Brno Models 21 and 22 were available in 4 different variations: short barrel/short stock, short barrel/full length stock, long barrel/short stock, long barrel/full length stock. The left receiver rail on these models is marked "ZBROJOVKA BRNO, NARODNI PODNIK".

MODEL 1 – .22 LR cal., 22 3/4 in. barrel, 3-leaf sight, 5 shot box mag., 6 lbs. Mfg. 1945-1957.

$675	$595	$525	$450	$400	$325	$275	

Add a premium for the deluxe model with checkered pistol grip and walnut stock.

This model is also known as the Model ZKM 451.

ZKM 468 – .22 LR cal., single shot. Mfg. 1948.

$200	$175	$150	$135	$110	$90	$70	

MODEL 2 – similar to Model 1, except has 24.8 in. barrel and Mauser type tangent rear sight, walnut stock. Mfg. 1954-disc.

$635	$555	$475	$430	$350	$285	$220	

Add a premium for deluxe model with checkered walnut stock.

This model is also known as the Model ZKM 452.

MODEL 3 – .22 LR cal., target rifle model with 27 1/2 in. heavy barrel, adj. click target sights, 5 shot box mag., plain target style stock with large swivels, 9 1/2 lbs. Mfg. 1949-1956.

$635	$555	$475	$430	$350	$285	$220	

This model is also known as the Model ZKM 455.

MODEL 4 – similar to Model 3, except has improved trigger design and safety. Mfg. 1956-1962.

$700	$610	$525	$475	$385	$315	$245	

This model is also known as the Model ZKM 456.

GRADING - PPGS™	100%	98%	95%	90%	80%	70%	60%	LAST MSR

MODEL 5 (ZKM 573) – similar to Model 1, except has improved trigger design and safety. Noted mfg. 1957-1978.

	$750	$675	$595	$525	$450	$400	$325	

BRNO 98 STANDARD – .243 Win., .270 Win., .30-06, .308 Win., .300 Win. Mag., 6.5x55mm SE, 7mm Rem. Mag. (new 2000), 7x57mm, 7x64mm, 8x57 JS, or 9.3x62mm cal., Mauser 98 style action, 23.6 in. barrel with or without iron sights, checkered walnut stock with Bavarian cheekpiece, or synthetic stock (disc.) and forearms (new 2002) single or set trigger, 7 1/4 lbs. Disc.

	$525	$460	$395	$355	$290	$235	$185	

Subtract approx. $150 for synthetic stock (disc.).
Add $52 for Mag. cals.
Add $83 for single set trigger.
Add $22 for Battue ramp sights.

This model is historically significant as it was the last centerfire bolt action rifle assembled in the famous Brno factory. Guns were built on refurbished military M98 actions from various makers, primarily from the former Yugoslavia.

* ***Brno 98 Mannlicher*** – similar to Brno 98 Standard, except has full length stock and set trigger. Disc.

	$695	$610	$520	$470	$380	$315	$245	

Add $60 for Mag. cals.

MODEL ZOM-451 – .22 LR cal., straight pull bolt action, limited importation by Century International Arms during 1998.

	$215	$190	$160	$145	$120	$95	$75	

MODEL ZKM-451 – .22 LR cal. Imported 1995-2002.

	$595	$520	$445	$405	$325	$270	$210	

Add approx. 10% for Lux Model (deluxe checkered wood).

It is possible that these guns are refurbished Model 1s, and have been seen with older proof date stamps.

MODEL ZKM-456 LUX SPORTER – .22 LR cal., bolt action, 5 or 10 shot mag., 24.4 in. barrel, folding rear sight, blue finish, beechwood stock with pistol grip, 6.8 lbs., mfg. by Aeron. Imported 1992-1998.

	$315	$275	$235	$215	$175	$140	$110	*$370*

Add $18 for micrometer rear sight (ZKM-456 MI).

* ***Model 456 L/LK Target*** – .22 LR cal., Target variation of the ZKM-456 Lux featuring 25 or 28 in. barrel with adj. front and rear sights, 10.1 lbs., mfg. by Aeron. Imported 1992-1998.

	$305	$265	$230	$205	$170	$135	$105	*$358*

Add $7 for 25 in. barrel.

* ***Model 456 Match Single Shot*** – .22 LR cal., designed for UIT competition at 50 M, features 27 1/2 in. barrel, adj. cheekpiece and buttplate, aperture sights, 9.9 lbs., mfg. by Aeron. Imported 1992-1998.

	$375	$330	$280	$255	$205	$170	$130	*$459*

ZKK 600 – please refer to the CZ listing in this text for current information (recent mfg. is by CZ).

ZKK 601 – please refer to the CZ listing in this text for current information (recent mfg. was by CZ).

ZKK 602 – please refer to the CZ listing in this text for current information (recent mfg. is by CZ).

ZKB 680 (FOX/FOX II)

Please refer to the CZ section for this model.

GRADING - PPGS™	100%	98%	95%	90%	80%	70%	60%	LAST MSR

RIFLES: O/U

ZH-344, 348, & 349 – 7x57R (Model ZH-344), 7x65R (Model ZH-348), or 8x57JRS (Model ZH-349) cal., 23.6 in. VR barrels, double triggers, skip line checkering, sling swivels, approx. 7 1/2 lbs. Imported 1998-disc.

$1,100	$978	$875	$775	$675	$600	$550	

Add $324-$357 per additional set of shotgun barrels, $418 per additional rifle barrel, and $829 for additional Mag. cal. rifle barrels.

SUPER EXPRESS – 7x65R, 9.3x74R, .375 H&H, or .458 Win. Mag. (disc.) cal., sidelock action with Kersten breech crossbolt, hand engraved, skipline checkering, approx. 9 lbs. Importation disc. 1992.

$3,450	$2,875	$2,300	$1,875	$1,600	$1,375	$1,200	*$3,900*

This model previously could be ordered with 6 different types of engraving options. They were: Grade I - add $2,060, Grade II - add $1,030, Grade III - add $1,545, Grade IV - add $1,030, Grade V - add $620, Grade VI - add $660.

SUPER SAFARI – 7x64R, .375 H&H Mag., or 9.3x74R cal., action derived from the Super Express, sidelock, DT with set trigger built in, adj. point of impact, 23.6 in. barrels with open sights, deluxe skipline checkered walnut stock and forearm with vent. recoil pad, approx. 9 lbs. Imported 1992-disc.

$2,375	$1,975	$1,675	$1,450	$1,225	$1,000	$900	

MODEL 803 – various cals., includes set trigger.

$1,350	$1,175	$1,000	$875	$750	$650	$550	

RIFLES: SEMI-AUTO

ZKM-611 – .17 HMR (new 2006), .22 WMR cal., 20 1/2 in. barrel, 6, 10 (C/B 1994), or 12* shot mag., black metal finish, beechwood (new 1996) or checkered walnut stock and forend, grooved receiver, 6.2 lbs.

$800	$725	$650	$575	$500	$425	$350	

Add 20% for walnut stock (disc. 1999).

The prototype of this model was designed by Mr. Kautsky in 1962. Development was completed in early 1990, and production began in 1992.

MODEL 581 – .22 LR cal., select walnut stock, adj. sights, 5 shot mag. Mfg. 1959-disc.

$600	$540	$495	$440	$395	$350	$295	

RIFLES: SINGLE SHOT

ZK-05 – various cals., upgraded variation of the ZK-99, set trigger, many other design improvements.

$575	$500	$430	$390	$315	$260	$200	

ZK 99 – various cals., break open action with top lever, quarter rib on barrel, checkered walnut stock with cheekpiece and Schnabel forearm, includes swivels and slings, 5 3/4 lbs. Imported 2000-2003.

$875	$765	$655	$595	$480	$395	$305	

MODEL ZKB-110 – .22 Hornet, .222 Rem., 5.6x52R, 5.6x50R Mag., 6.5x57R (disc. 1999), 7x57R (disc. 1999), or 8x57JRS (disc. 1999) cal., single shot break open rifle/shotgun, top lever opening, 23.6 in. barrel, uncheckered (Standard Model) or checkered walnut stock with Bavarian cheekpiece and forearm (Lux Model), includes sling swivels, 6 lbs. Imported 1998-2003.

$225	$195	$170	$155	$125	$100	$80	

Add $77 for ZKB-110 Lux Model.
Add $205 for ZKB-110 Super Lux Model (new 2000).
Add $48 for 7x57R or 8x57JRS cal. (disc. 1999).
Add $132 (standard) or $142 (Lux) for an interchangeable 12 ga. shotgun barrel.

GRADING - PPGS™	100%	98%	95%	90%	80%	70%	60%	LAST MSR

EFFECT – .30-06 cal., 23.6 in. barrel, single set trigger, light engraved blue receiver, iron sights, sling swivels, checkered walnut stock, 6 lbs.

	$1,295	$1,135	$970	$880	$710	$585	$455	

Please refer to Brno Rifles section for current mfg.

SHOTGUNS/COMBINATION GUNS: O/U

Many of the following models were imported and distributed by Euro-Imports, located in El Cajon, CA.

ZH-300 SHOTGUN – 12 ga. only, double triggers with rear trigger doubling as single trigger, 27 1/2 in. barrels, 7 lbs. Imported 1986-92.

	$530	$465	$395	$360	$290	$240	$185	*$599*

This model was available in skeet, trap, or field configuration.

ZH-301 FIELD SHOTGUN – 12 or 16 ga. field, 27 1/2 in. barrels, optional Monte Carlo stock (disc.).

	$600	$525	$450	$410	$330	$270	$210	

Add $20 for Monte Carlo stock.

ZH-302 SKEET SHOTGUN – 12 ga., skeet model, 26 in. barrels, optional Monte Carlo stock (disc.).

	$650	$570	$485	$440	$355	$290	$225	

Add $20 for Monte Carlo stock.

ZH-303 TRAP SHOTGUN – 12 ga., trap model, 30 in. barrels, optional Monte Carlo stock (disc.).

	$650	$570	$485	$440	$355	$290	$225	

Add $20 for Monte Carlo stock.

ZH-300 SERIES COMBINATION GUNS – 7x57R x 12 ga. (ZH-304), 6x52R x 12 ga. (ZH-305), 6x50R Mag. x 12 ga. (ZH-306), .22 Hornet x 12 ga. (ZH-307), 7x65R x 12 ga. (ZH-308), 8x57JRS x 12 ga. (ZH-309), 7x57R x 16 ga. (ZH-324), 7x65R x 16 ga. (ZH-328), combination rifle/shotgun, optional adj. trigger and Monte Carlo stock. Importation disc. 1994 - reintroduced 1999-2003.

	$695	$610	$520	$470	$380	$315	$245	

Add $73 for cheekpiece and set trigger.
Add $35 for adj. trigger (disc.).
Add $20 for Monte Carlo stock (disc.).

ZH 300 Series over and unders are unique in that they permit 8 different interchangeable barrels including rifle and shotgun sets, interrupter on double trigger, blued action, engraving, diamond checkered walnut.

M6 SCOUT COMBINATION GUN – See separate listing under Springfield Armory.

MODEL ZH-300 COMBO SET – Model ZH-300 style engraving and features, equipped with 8 interchangeable O/U shotgun/shotgun and rifle/shotgun barrels in various gauges and calibers. Imported 1986-1991.

	$2,950	$2,580	$2,210	$2,005	$1,620	$1,325	$1,030	*$3,500*

MODEL 500/501 SHOTGUN – 12 ga. only, 28 in. VR barrels, double or single (disc. 1999) trigger.

	$845	$740	$635	$575	$465	$380	$295	

Add $50 for single trigger (disc. 1999).

* ***Model 500 Combo Set*** – shotgun/rifle set comprised of 4 barrels including 12 ga. over barrels with choice of 5.6x52R (disc.), 7x57R, 7x65R, or 12 ga. under barrels (in either field, skeet, or trap chokings), sling swivels, set trigger on rifle/shotgun combo, chemically engraved, about 7 1/2 lbs. Imported 1987-91.

	$1,925	$1,685	$1,445	$1,310	$1,060	$865	$675	*$2,169*

This model was available in limited quanitity.

GRADING - PPGS™	100%	98%	95%	90%	80%	70%	60%	LAST MSR

MODEL 502 SERIES COMBINATION GUN – 12 ga. only, ejectors, combination shotgun/rifle available in .222 Rem., .243 Win., .30-06, .308 Win., and 4 metric cals., fixed choke, acid etched engraving, skipline checkering and cheekpiece. Imported 1986-2003.

$1,050	$920	$785	$715	$575	$470	$365	

Add $699 for interchangeable 12 ga. shotgun barrels (new 1998).

BS-571/572 SHOTGUN/COMBINATION GUN – 12 ga. only, boxlock action with ejectors, 6x65R (disc.) or 7x65R rifle cal. only. Limited importation 1992-95.

$825	$720	$620	$560	$455	$370	$290	*$995*

Add approx. $115 for rifle/shotgun (12 ga. only) combination (Model 572).

MODEL 571 SUPER SERIES – 12 ga. field, skeet, and trap configuration as well as combination shotgun/rifle in 12 ga. x 7x57R or 7x65R cal. Importation disc. 1991.

$800	$700	$600	$545	$440	$360	$280	*$899*

Add $70 for single trigger or trap/skeet configuration (disc.).
Add $700 for extra set of 12 ga. field barrels.
Add $1,101 for hand engraving.

* ***Model 571 Super Combo*** – 3 barrel set including 12 ga., 7x57R, and 7x65R barrels. Imported 1987-90.

$1,925	$1,685	$1,445	$1,310	$1,060	$865	$675	*$2,169*

MODEL 801 SERIES SHOTGUN – 12 ga. only, 2 3/4 or 3 in. chambers, ejectors, SST, machine engraved receiver, checkered walnut stock and forearm, VR barrels with or without choke tubes, left-hand version in various configurations that include field, sporting, trap, and skeet available at no additional charge.

$875	$765	$655	$595	$480	$395	$305	

Add $276 for Sporting Model with 4 interchangeable choke tubes.

Please refer to Brno Rifles section for current manufacture (Models 801.1 and 801.2).

MODEL 802 COMBINATION GUN – 12 ga., 3 in. chamber, various American and metric cals., includes set trigger, extractors, machined engraved receiver, checkered walnut stock and forearm, interchangeable barrels.

$1,000	$875	$750	$680	$550	$450	$350	

COMBO RIFLE/SHOTGUN – .243 Win., .30-06, or .308 Win. cal. over 12 ga., 23 1/2 in. barrels, black receiver, checkered pistol grip walnut stock, extractors, sling mount on barrel, shotgun barrel fired by rear trigger, front trigger has set function for precision rifle shooting, 7 1/2 lbs.

$1,800	$1,575	$1,350	$1,225	$990	$810	$630	

SHOTGUNS: SxS

ZP-49 – 12 ga. only, ejectors, double triggers, true sidelock, Purdey-type top bolt, cocking indicators, walnut stock, swivels. Imported 1986-91.

$535	$460	$420	$385	$350	$320	$290	*$589*

Add $20 for engraving.

ZP-149 – 12 ga., similar to ZP-49, except has game scene engraving on sideplates, choice of English or pistol grip stock. Imported 1986-1998.

$575	$495	$425	$350	$300	$250	$225	*$676*

Add $23 for pistol grip stock.

ZP-349 – 12 ga. only, extractors, double triggers, true sidelock, Purdey-type top bolt, cocking indicators, walnut stock with cheek piece, beavertail forearm, swivels, 7.3 lbs. Imported 1986 only.

$450	$390	$360	$325	$300	$270	$250	*$520*

Add $20 for engraving.

SHOTGUNS: SINGLE SHOT

ZBK 100 – 12 or 20 ga., 3 in. chamber, walnut stock and forearm. Imported 1999-2003.

$180	$160	$140	$120	$105	$95	$85	

GRADING - PPGS™	100%	98%	95%	90%	80%	70%	60%	LAST MSR

BRNO RIFLES

Current manufacturer of fixed breech Brno O/U and single shot rifles, O/U shotguns, and O/U combination guns, established circa 2007, and located in Brno, Czech Republic. During 2010, the company changed its name to Zbrojovka Brno, and it remains as part of the CZUB Uhersky Brod group. Currently imported by CZ USA, located in Kansas City, KS.

COMBINATION GUNS

COMBO RIFLE/SHOTGUN - .243 Win., .30-06, or .308 Win. cal. over 12 ga., 23 1/2 in. barrels, black receiver, checkered pistol grip walnut stock, extractors, sling mount on barrel, shotgun barrel fired by rear trigger, front trigger has set function for precision rifle shooting, 7 1/2 lbs. Importation began 2009.

MSR $2,181	$1,875	$1,625	$1,400	$1,250	$900	$800	$700	

RIFLES: SINGLE SHOT

EFFECT - .30-06 or .308 Win. cal., 23.6 in. barrel, single set trigger, light engraved blue receiver, iron sights, sling swivels, checkered walnut stock, 6 lbs. Importation began 2009.

MSR $1,585	$1,295	$1,135	$970	$880	$710	$585	$455	

Add $114 for FS Model with Mannlicher full stock.

RIFLES: O/U

STOPPER - .375 H&H (new 2010), .416 Rigby (new 2010), or .458 Win. Mag. cal., black or hand engraved silver receiver with gold trigger, 23.7 in. separated barrels, checkered walnut stock with Schnabel forend, 9 lbs. Importation began 2009.

MSR $4,999	$4,500	$4,000	$3,650	$3,350	$3,000	$2,750	$2,500	

Add $3,000 for hand engraved silver receiver and gold trigger.

SHOTGUNS: O/U

MODEL 801.1 - 12 ga., 3 1/2 in. chambers, 30 in. barrels, engraved silver receiver, barrel selector, fixed chokes, checkered pistol grip walnut stock and forearm, SST, 7 lbs. Limited importation 2009-2010.

	$2,650	$2,320	$1,985	$1,800	$1,455	$1,190	$925	*$2,999*

MODEL 801.2 - 12 ga., 3 in. chambers, 30 in. barrels, engraved silver receiver, barrel selector, three screw in chokes, checkered pistol grip walnut stock and forearm, SST, 7 lbs. Limited importation 2009-2010.

	$2,650	$2,320	$1,985	$1,800	$1,455	$1,190	$925	*$2,999*

BROCKMAN'S RIFLES

Current custom rifle manufacturer and gunsmith established in 1986, and located in Gooding, Idaho. Consumer direct sales only.

Brockman's Custom Gunsmithing manufactures a wide variety of custom bolt action rifles typically based on Win. Model 70, Rem. Model 700, Dakota, or Nesika action. Please contact the company directly to find out more about their wide variety of custom rifles and gunsmithing services.

RIFLES: BOLT ACTION

Specific models and/or configurations include the Universal Hunter (complete gun base price $3,995), Dangerous Game (last MSR $2,450, disc. 2001), Premier Practical (base price $4,595), Model 70 Classic Practical (base price $3,995), Working Rifle (base price $4,199), Ladies rifles (base price was $2,100-$2,895 - disc. 2000), Scout rifles (last MSR $1,995 - disc. 2000), .50 Beowulf-Brockman (disc., base price was $995, includes case), and other handcrafted custom bolt action rifles.

RIFLES: LEVER ACTION

Brockman's lever action rifles are based on modified Marlin 1895G/SS actions. Models include the Presidential (new 2010, base price $2,850), Super Grade (new 2010, base price $3,900), Beast (base price $2,445), the SOB (is based on shorter and lighter Beast, disc. 2004,

GRADING - PPGS™	100%	98%	95%	90%	80%	70%	60%	LAST MSR

last MSR was $1,995), Master Guide Package (base price $1,329), and the Super Guide Package (base price $1,959).

BROLIN ARMS, INC.

Previous importer of handguns (FEG mfg.), rifles (older Mauser military, see Mauser listing), shotguns (Chinese mfg.), and airguns from 1995 to 1999. Previously located in Pomona, CA, until 1999, and in La Verne, CA until 1997.

PISTOLS: SEMI-AUTO, SINGLE ACTION

LEGEND SERIES MODEL L45 – .45 ACP cal., patterned after the Colt 1911 Government Model, features include throated match 5 in. barrel, polished feed ramp, flared ejection port, beveled mag well, flat-top slide, flat mainspring housing, front strap high relief cut, aluminum lightweight extended trigger, high visibility sights, 7 shot mag., commander style hammer and checkered walnut grips, 38 oz. Mfg. 1995-1998.

$425	$365	$325	$295	$275	$250	$225	*$500*

* ***Legend Series Model L45C (Compact)*** – similar to Model L45, except has 4 in. barrel, 35 oz. Mfg. 1995-98.

$440	$380	$330	$295	$275	$250	$225	*$520*

* ***Legend Series Model L45T*** – features standard frame with compact slide, 4 in. barrel, 36 oz. Mfg. 1997-98.

$440	$380	$330	$295	$275	$250	$225	*$520*

PATRIOT SERIES MODEL P45 COMP – .45 ACP cal., similar to Legend Series Model L45, except has one-piece match 4 in. barrel with integral dual port compensator, 7 shot mag., Millett or Novak combat sights (new 1997), test target provided, choice of blue or satin (frame only) finish, 38 oz. Mfg. 1996-97 only.

$585	$475	$415	$365	$325	$285	$250	*$649*

Add $70 for Novak combat sights (new 1997).
Add $20 for T-tone finish (frame only).

* ***Patriot Series Model P45C (Compact)*** – .45 ACP cal., similar to Model P45 Comp, except has 3 1/4 in. barrel with integral conical lock-up system, 34 1/2 oz. Mfg. 1996-97.

$610	$495	$425	$375	$325	$285	$250	*$689*

Add $70 for Novak combat sights.
Add $20 for T-tone finish (frame only).

* ***Patriot Series Model P45T*** – features standard frame with compact slide, 3 1/4 in. barrel, 35 1/2 oz. Mfg. 1997 only.

$620	$500	$425	$375	$325	$285	$250	*$699*

Add $60 for Novak combat sights (new 1997).
Add $10 for T-tone finish (frame only).

PRO STOCK MODEL COMPETITION PISTOL – .45 ACP cal., competition pistol featuring most state-of-the-art competitive improvements, 5 in. barrel, 8 shot mag., blue or satin (frame only) finish, signature wood grips, 40 oz. Mfg. 1996-97.

$685	$550	$475	$415	$360	$295	$260	*$779*

Add $20 for T-tone finish (frame only).

* ***Pro Comp Model Competition Pistol*** – similar to Pro Stock Model, except has 4 in. dual port compensated heavy match barrel, blue or satin (frame only) finish, 40 oz. Mfg. 1996-97.

$800	$650	$525	$435	$375	$325	$295	*$919*

Add $10 for T-tone finish (frame only).

TAC 11 – .45 ACP cal., 5 in. conical barrel w/o bushing, beavertail grip safety, 8 shot mag., T-tone or blue finish, Novak low profile combat or Tritium sights, black rubber contour grips, 37 oz. Mfg. 1997-98.

$595	$485	$425	$365	$325	$285	$250	*$670*

Add $90 for Tritium sights (disc. 1997).

GRADING - PPGS™	100%	98%	95%	90%	80%	70%	60%	LAST MSR

*** *Tac 11 Compact*** – similar to Tac 11, except has shorter barrel. Mfg. 1998 only.

	$610	$495	$435	$365	$325	$285	$250	*$690*

Add $60 for hard-chrome finish.

GOLD SERIES – .45 ACP cal., 5 in. barrel w/o barrel bushing and supported chamber, IPSC configuration with many features, adj. aluminum trigger, front and rear slide serrations, stainless steel construction with choice of natural stainless or blue stainless finish. Limited mfg. 1998 only.

	$715	$625	$525	$440	$385	$325	$280	*$800*

PISTOLS: SEMI-AUTO, DOUBLE ACTION

The following models had limited manufacture 1998 only.

TAC SERIES SERVICE MODEL – .45 ACP cal., full sized double action service pistol, single/double action, 8 shot single column mag., front and rear slide serrations, combat style trigger guard, royal or satin blue finish, low profile 3-dot sights. Mfg. 1998 only.

	$360	$315	$285	$260	$240	$220	$200	*$400*

Add $20 for royal blue finish.

TAC SERIES FULL SIZE MODEL – 9mm Para., .40 S&W, or .45 ACP cal., similar to Tac Series Service Model, except longer barrel, checkered walnut or plastic grips, 8 (.45 ACP only) or 10 shot mag. Mfg. 1998 only.

	$360	$315	$285	$260	$240	$220	$200	*$400*

Add $20 for royal blue finish.

TAC SERIES COMPACT MODEL – 9mm Para. or .40 S&W cal., shortened barrel/slide with full size frame, 10 shot mag. Mfg. 1998 only.

	$360	$315	$285	$260	$240	$220	$200	*$400*

Add $20 for royal blue finish.

TAC SERIES BANTAM MODEL – 9mm Para. or .40 S&W cal., super compact size, single/double action with concealed hammer, all steel construction, 3-dot sights. Mfg. 1998 only.

	$360	$315	$285	$260	$240	$220	$200	*$399*

BANTAM MODEL – 9mm Para. or .40 S&W cal., single or double action, super compact size, concealed hammer, all steel construction, 3-dot sights, royal blue or matte finish. Limited mfg. by FEG 1999 only.

	$360	$315	$285	$260	$240	$220	$200	*$399*

PISTOLS: CUSTOM

Brolin Arms manufactured a small quantity of high performance M1911 based custom combat and competition pistols during 1998 only. The Formula Z Model Custom Combat Model retail price range was $1,300-$1,600, the Formula One RS Limited Class Competition Model was priced at $2,000-$2,300, and the Formula One RZ Competition Race Gun Model topped the line at $2,450- $2,750.

SHOTGUNS: SEMI-AUTO

MODEL BL-12 – 12 ga. only, 3 in. chamber, 18 1/2 (security) or 28 (field) in. VR barrel with 3 choke tubes (Beretta compatible), satin blue finish, choice of wood or synthetic stock and forearm. Mfg. 1998 only.

	$375	$325	$300	$280	$260	$240	$220	*$430*

MODEL SAS-12 – 12 ga. only, 2 3/4 in. chamber, 24 in. barrel with IC choke tube, 3 (standard) or 5 shot (disc. late 1998) detachable box mag., synthetic stock and forearm, gas operated. Mfg. 1998-99.

	$445	$385	$335	$300	$280	$260	$240	*$499*

Add $39 for extra 3 or 5 (disc.) shot mag.

SHOTGUNS: SLIDE ACTION

Brolin shotguns were manufactured in China by Hawk Industries, and were unauthorized copies of the Remington Model 870. Most of these slide action models were distributed by

GRADING - PPGS™	100%	98%	95%	90%	80%	70%	60%	LAST MSR

Interstate Arms, and it is thought that Norinco or China North Industries were connected to the manufacturer during the importation of these shotguns.

FIELD SERIES – 12 ga. only, 3 in. chamber, 24, 26, 28, or 30 in. VR barrel with mod. choke tube, steel receiver and aluminum trigger guard, choice of black synthetic or wood stock, bead sights, 5 shot mag., matte finish, 7.3 lbs. Mfg. 1997-98.

$195	$170	$155	$140	$130	$120	$110	*$240*

* ***Field Combo*** – includes choice of extra 12 ga. 18 1/2 or 22 in. barrel, choice of regular or pistol grip stock. Mfg. 1997-98.

$230	$195	$175	$155	$140	$130	$120	*$270*

Add approx. $25 for rifled deer barrel.

LAWMAN MODEL – 12 ga. only, 3 in. chamber, action patterned after the Rem. Model 870 (disc. 1998) or the Ithaca Model 37 (new 1999) 18 1/2 in. barrel, choice of bead, rifle (disc. 1998), or ghost ring (disc. 1998) sights, matte (disc. 1998), nickel (disc. 1997), royal blue (new 1998), satin blue (new 1998) or hard chrome finish, black synthetic or hardwood stock and forearm, 7 lbs. Mfg. in China 1997-99.

$165	$155	$145	$135	$125	$115	$105	*$189*

Add $20 for nickel finish (disc. 1997).
Add $20 for hard chrome finish.
Add $20 for ghost ring sights.

SLUG SPECIAL – 12 ga. only, 3 in. chamber, choice of 18 1/2 or 22 in. barrel with either rifle sights, ghost ring, or cantilevered scope mount, wood or synthetic stock, choice of fixed IC choke, 4 in. extended rifled choke, or fully rifled barrel, 5 shot mag. Mfg. 1998 only.

$230	$180	$165	$150	$140	$130	$120	*$270*

Add $10 for rifled barrel.
Add $20 for cantilevered scope mount.

SLUGMASTER – 12 ga. only, 3 in. chamber, action patterned after the Model 37 Ithaca, bottom ejection, choice of royal blue metal finish with wood stock or satin blue metal with synthetic stock, rifle sights, mfg. in China. Limited importation 1999 only.

$165	$155	$145	$135	$125	$115	$105	*$189*

TURKEY SPECIAL – 12 ga. only, 3 in. chamber, 22 in. VR barrel with extra-full extended turkey choke, choice of wood or synthetic stock. Mfg. 1998 only.

$215	$165	$155	$145	$135	$125	$115	*$250*

BRONCO (PISTOLS)

Previous trademark manufactured by Echave Y Arizmendi, located in Eibar, Spain.

PISTOLS: SEMI-AUTO

MODEL 1918 POCKET AUTOMATIC – 7.65mm cal., 6 shot, 2 1/2 in. barrel, fixed sights, blue, hard rubber grips. Mfg. 1918-25.

$175	$150	$100	$80	$70	$60	$50

VEST POCKET AUTOMATIC – 6.35mm cal., small frame. Disc.

$160	$125	$110	$95	$80	$60	$40

BRONCO (LONG ARMS)

Previous trademark of rifles and shotguns imported by Firearms International Sporting Arms circa 1969-1970.

The Bronco was available in both a single shot rifle (.22 LR cal.) and .410 bore (3 in. chamber) shotgun. It featured a skeletonized aluminum stock and receiver with no forend. A forward trigger lever allowed a swing out action to pivot for loading, and the regular trigger operated a hammerless action. The Bronco also featured compact youth dimensions, crossbolt safety and adj. rear sight, and was approx. 3-3 1/2 lbs.

Average-above average condition specimens sell in the $150-$275 range - add approx. 10% more for .410 bore.

A.A. BROWN & SONS

Current long gun manufacturer established in 1938 and located in Birmingham, England.

A.A. BROWN COMPANY HISTORY

Albert Arthur Brown was an action maker who founded his business in 1929 in Birmingham's gun quarter. In 1938, he was joined by sons Albert Henry and Sidney Charles, and from that time on the firm was known as A.A. Brown & Sons. Much of the work done during the Depression era was for other British makers such as E.J. Churchill. During WWII, the company was involved in defense related contract work and the Sand Street premises were bombed.

By the late 1950s, A.A. Brown & Sons were building a wide variety of guns for Cogswell & Harrison, E.J. Churchill, and Holland & Holland. During 1960, the firm moved to Westley Richards' factory complex and built Westley's sidelocks. Robin Brown, grandson of the founder and son of Sidney Charles, joined as an apprentice in 1961. He left the Westley Richards location in 1974 to establish a factory in Alvechurch, south of Birmingham, and began building best quality sidelocks.

After the deaths of his father and uncle in 2001 and 2006, Robin Brown became the sole proprietor. Much of the work remains in-house, although Robin uses London trained barrel makers and stockers for his guns.

Information appears courtesy of David Grant and Vic Venters.

SHOTGUNS: SxS, CUSTOM

A.A. Brown & Sons manufactures high quality SxS English sidelock ejector shotguns in all gauges with many options available.

For more information, including VAT, customer options, availability and delivery time, please contact the company directly (see Trademark Index).

SUPREME DE LUXE – 12, 16, 20, 28 ga. or .410 bore, best gun with chopper lump barrels, sidelock ejector with standard or rounded action shape.

Prices for this model start at £38,000 for self or easy opening, un-assisted opening from £36,000. 28 ga. and .410 bore are built to special order, and start at £42,000. Pairing or matching sets start at £2500 per gun.

There are many engraving choices - both in terms of the engravers and engraving styles. Individual quotations are provided per order. As a guide, standard patterns range from £3500 to £12,000. Cases, cleaning kits, and other accessories are also available.

DAVID MCKAY BROWN (GUNMAKERS) LTD.

Current long gun manufacturer established in 1974 and located in Bothwell, Glasgow, Scotland. Available through the manufacturer directly or U.S. agents, Griffin & Howe, New York City and Bernardsville, NJ, and Wingshooting Adventures, located in Coopersville, MI.

Makers of Scottish Round Action SxS and O/U shotguns and rifles (approx. 30 guns mfg. annually), all guns made to customer order on round sidelock actions. Delivery is approximately 12 months, depending on the configuration.

Prices indicated below for manufacturer's suggested retail and 100% condition factors are listed in English pounds. Values for used guns in 98%-60% condition factors are priced in U.S. dollars.

All engraving is priced to order and subject to change due to the exchange rate of the euro.

DAVID MCKAY BROWN COMPANY HISTORY

David McKay Brown was born in 1941 in the mining town of Bellshil, and began his gunmaking career in 1958 as an apprentice with Alexander Martin, Ltd. in Glasgow. When Dickson purchased Martin in the early 1960s, McKay Brown trained in Edinburgh, and completed his apprenticeship making the firm's famous round action.

McKay Brown set himself up independently in March of 1967 in Hamilton, near Glasgow. He continued working for Dickson until establishing himself as an individual gunmaker building round

GRADING - PPGS™	100%	98%	95%	90%	80%	70%	60%	LAST MSR

actions under his own name in 1974. By 1980, the company had moved to Bothwell, near Glasgow. In 1992, David McKay Brown registered an O/U design and began making guns a year later.

Information appears courtesy of David Grant and Vic Venters.

RIFLES: CUSTOM, SxS

Please contact the agent/importer directly for a firm quotation on a SxS double rifle.

SHOTGUNS: CUSTOM

Add £250 for Pistol/Prince of Wales grip.
Add £1,000 for .410 bore.
Add £750 for single non-selective trigger.
Add £1,000 for best quality wood.
Add £450 for Nigel Teague precision chokes.
Engraving starts at £4,000 and final cost will be determined upon order confirmation.

SxS SHOTGUN – 12, 16, 20, 28 ga., or .410 bore, features rounded case colored action, double triggers, custom order only, base price does not include engraving.

MSR £34,000	£34,000	£40,000	£34,000	£26,000	£21,000	£17,000	£13,500	

O/U SHOTGUN – 12, 16, 20, 28 ga., or .410 bore, features rounded case colored action, double triggers, custom order only, base price does not include engraving.

MSR £38,000	£38,000	£47,500	£38,500	£31,500	£26,000	£22,000	£17,000	

ED BROWN CUSTOM, INC.

Please refer to Ed Brown Custom, Inc. located in the E section.

ED BROWN PRODUCTS, INC.

Please refer to Ed Brown Products, Inc. located in the E section.

BROWN PRECISION, INC.

Current manufacturer established in 1968, and located in Los Molinos, CA. Previously manufactured in San Jose, CA. Consumer direct sales.

Brown Precision Inc. manufactures rifles primarily using Remington or Winchester actions and restocks them using a combination of Kevlar, fiberglass and graphite (wrinkle finish) to save weight. Stock colors are green, brown, grey, black, camo brown, camo green, or camo grey. Chet Brown pioneered the concept of the fiberglass rifle stock in 1965. He started blueprinting actions and using stainless steel match grade barrels on hunting rifles in 1968, and became the first custom gunmaker to use high tech weather-proof metal finishes on hunting rifles.

PISTOLS: BOLT ACTION

CUSTOM XP-100 HIGH COUNTRY – various cals., includes highly tuned XP-100 single shot action with Shilen stainless match grade barrel, electroless nickel or Teflon finish, fiberglass stock. Limited mfg. 1993-96.

	$1,550	$1,375	$1,150	$950	$775	$650	$525	*$1,690*

RIFLES: BOLT ACTION

Brown Precision will also stock a rifle from a customer supplied action. This process includes a Brown Precision stock, custom glass bedding, recoil pad, stock finish, etc. Prices begin at $895.

CUSTOM HIGH COUNTRY – various cals. within the following factory barreled actions, choice of Rem. 700 ADL/BDL, Model 7, Ruger 77 (disc.), or Win. Model 70 push feed (disc.), or Winchester Model 70 Classic with controlled round feeding action and custom trigger guard, fiberglass/Kevlar stock (various colors), electroless nickel or Teflon metal finish, sling swivels and pad. New 1975.

MSR $5,195	$4,750	$4,100	$3,500	$3,100	$2,600	$2,100	$1,650	

Add $300 for left-hand action.
Add $135 for cryogenic barrel treatment.
Add $800 for take down action (new 2006).

GRADING - PPGS™	100%	98%	95%	90%	80%	70%	60%	LAST MSR

Subtract approx. $800 for Ruger M77 action and steel barrel (disc. 2012).
Subtract approx. $1,200 if action is supplied by customer.

Beginning 2006, this model's standard features include a choice of a fully blueprinted Winchester Model 70 (controlled round feeding), Rem. Model 700, or Rem. Model 7 action, and a match grade stainless steel barrel.

* ***Custom High Country ES II*** – similar to Custom High Country, except includes cryogenic barrel treatment and speed lock firing pin spring, includes 60 rounds of custom ammo. Disc. 2003.

	$3,400	$2,975	$2,550	$2,310	$1,870	$1,530	$1,190	*$3,995*

Add $100 for Rem. 700 BDL or Model 7 action.
Add $300 for stainless steel Rem. 700 BDL action.
Add $500 for Win. Model 70 Classic action with controlled round feeding.
Add $300 for left-hand action.
Subtract $700 if action is supplied by customer.

HIGH COUNTRY YOUTH RIFLE – various cals., choice of Rem. Model 7 or 700 factory barreled action, fiberglass stock. Mfg. 1993-2000.

	$1,250	$1,095	$935	$850	$685	$560	$435	*$1,435*

Add $145 for lengthening stock.

BROWN PRECISION WINCHESTER 70 – .270 Win. or .30-06 cal., 22 in. featherweight barrel, camo stock in four colors with black recoil pad, 6 1/4 lbs. Mfg. 1989-92.

	$650	$570	$485	$440	$355	$290	$225	*$750*

Add $20 for 7mm Rem. Mag. (24 in. sporter barrel).

BLASER BOLT ACTION RIFLE – standard Camex Blaser cals. and action, fiberglass stock and nickel plated barrel. Disc. 1989.

	$1,395	$1,220	$1,045	$950	$765	$630	$490	*$1,395*

MODEL 7 SUPER LIGHT – .223 Rem., .243 Win., 6mm Rem., 7mm-08 Rem., or .308 Win. cal., Model 7 action, 18 in. factory barrel, no sights, 5 lbs. 4 oz. Disc. 1992.

	$995	$870	$745	$675	$545	$450	$350	*$1,059*

This model could have been special ordered with similar options from the Custom High Country Model, with the exception of left-hand action.

LAW ENFORCEMENT SELECTIVE TARGET – .308 Win. cal., Model 700 Varmint action with 20, 22, or 24 in. factory barrel, O.D. green camouflage treatment. Disc. 1992.

	$995	$870	$745	$675	$545	$450	$350	*$1,086*

This model could have been special ordered with similar options from the Custom High Country Model, with the exception of left-hand action.

TACTICAL ELITE – various cals. and custom features, customized per individual order. New 1997.

MSR $5,295	$4,850	$4,100	$3,500	$3,100	$2,600	$2,000	$1,650	

Add $675 for 3 way adj. buttplate (disc.).
Subtract $1,100 if action is supplied by customer.

PRO/LIGHT VARMINTER – various cals., includes custom tuned Rem. Model 700 ADL action, Shilen match stainless steel barrel. New 1993, Light Varminter new 2006.

MSR $4,395	$3,975	$3,425	$2,875	$2,500	$2,050	$1,700	$1,400	

Add $300 for left-hand action.
Add $600 for optional Rem. Model 40-XB action with target trigger (disc. 2012).
Subtract $1,200 if action is supplied by customer.

PRO HUNTER – available in over 25 cals., Model 700 ADL action is standard, match grade stainless steel barrel, dull electroless nickel, blue, or teflon finish, express sights, synthetic stock (four different colors). New 1988.

MSR $5,695	$5,100	$4,350	$3,675	$3,175	$2,600	$2,100	$1,675	

Add $100 for left-hand action.

GRADING - PPGS™	100%	98%	95%	90%	80%	70%	60%	LAST MSR

Subtract $1,200 if action is supplied by customer.

In late 1991, improvements were made including decelerator recoil pad, barrel band swivel, and speed lock firing pin spring.

* ***Pro Hunter Elite*** – various cals., custom tuned Winchester Model 70 Super Grade action with controlled feed claw extractor, includes many custom order features. New 1993.

MSR $6,995	$6,450	$5,550	$4,700	$4,150	$3,350	$2,850	$2,225	

Add $794 for drop box trigger guard (allows additonal round in mag.).
Subtract $1,200 if action is supplied by customer.
Add $1,100 for take down action.

THE UNIT – .270 Win., .300 Win. Mag., .300 Wby. Mag., .338 Win. Mag., 7mm-08 Rem., 7mm Rem. Mag., or 7mm STW cal., Rem. 700 BDL or Win. Mod. 70 controlled feed action, various lengths match grade stainless steel barrel with cryogenic treatment, Teflon or electroless nickel finish, Brown Precision Kevlar or graphite reinforced fiberglass stock, includes 60 rounds of custom ammo. Limited mfg. 2001 only.

	$3,225	$2,820	$2,420	$2,195	$1,775	$1,450	$1,130	*$3,795*

Add $500 for Win. Model 70 Super Grade action with controlled round feeding.
Add $200 for left-hand action.
Subtract $600 if action was supplied by customer.

SUPER BOLT RIMFIRE – .22 LR or .22 WMR cal., modified Ruger 77/22 action, 20 in. heavy Shilen match grade steel or stainless steel barrel, extended mag. release, choice of lightweight fiberglass or Kevlar stock, blue or silver metal finish, 6 1/2 lbs. Disc. 2005.

	$1,600	$1,400	$1,200	$1,090	$880	$720	$560	*$1,895*

Add $100 for stainless steel barrel.
Add $200 for stainless steel action & barrel.

RIFLES: SEMI-AUTO

CUSTOM TEAM CHALLENGER – .22 LR cal., modified Ruger 10/22 action, 20 in. heavy Shilen match grade steel or stainless steel barrel, extended mag. release, choice of lightweight fiberglass or Kevlar stock, blue or silver metal finish, disc. 2005.

	$1,350	$1,075	$825	$675	$550	$450	$400	*$1,595*

Add $100 for stainless steel barrel.
Add $200 for stainless steel barrel & action.

BROWNING

Current manufacturer with U.S. headquarters located in Morgan, UT. Browning guns originally were manufactured in Ogden, UT, circa 1880. Browning firearms are manufactured by Fabrique Nationale in Herstal and Liège, Belgium. Beginning 1976, Browning also contracted with Miroku of Japan and A.T.I. in Salt Lake City, UT to manufacture both long arms and handguns. In 1992, Browning (including F.N.) was acquired by GIAT of France. During late 1997, the French government received $82 million for the sale of F.N. Herstal from the Walloon business region surrounding Fabrique Nationale in Belgium.

The category names within the Browning section have been arranged in an alphabetical format: - PISTOLS (& variations), RIFLES (& variations), SHOTGUNS (& variations), SPECIAL EDITIONS, COMMEMORATIVES & LIMITED MFG.

The author would like to express his sincere thanks to the Browning Collector's Association, including members Rodney Herrmann, Richard Spurzem, Jim King, Bert O'Neill, Jr., Anthony Vanderlinden, Richard Desira, Gary Chatham, Bruce Hart, and Glen Nilson for continuing to make their important contributions to the Browning section.

In addition to the models listed within this section, Browning also offered various models/variations that were available only at the annual SHOT SHOW beginning 2004. More research is underway to identify these models, in addition to their original MSRs (if listed).

BROWNING HISTORY

The Browning firm, first known as J.M. Browning & Bro., was established in Ogden, Utah about 1880. Later known as Browning Brothers and Browning Arms Company (BAC), the firm actually manufactured only one gun - the Model 1878 Single Shot which was John M.'s first patent. Winchester bought the production and distribution rights to this gun in 1883, bringing it out as the Winchester M1885. From that time until 1900, Mr. Browning sold Winchester the exclusive rights to 31 rifles and 13 shotguns, of which Winchester produced only 7 rifles (M1885SS: the lever actions M1886, 1892, 1894 and 1895: and the slide action .22s M1890 and 1906) and 3 shotguns (M1887, M1893 and M1897). The other models were bought from Browning simply to keep them out of the hands of other arms makers.

John M. Browning, perhaps the greatest firearms inventor the world has ever known, was directly responsible for an estimated 80 separate firearms that evolved from his 128 patents. During his most prolific period from 1894 to 1910, Browning sold the rights to his rifles, semi-auto pistols, shotguns and machine guns to Winchester, Remington, Colt and Stevens in this country and to Fabrique Nationale (Belgium) for sale outside the U.S. Every Colt and F.N. semi-auto pistol is based on a Browning patent. In 1902, Browning broke off relations with Winchester when the company refused to negotiate a royalty arrangement for his new semi-auto shotgun (A-5). Browning took the prototype to F.N. Since 1902, F.N. has produced numerous automatic pistols, 3 rifles and 2 shotguns designed by John M. Browning and is still a major producer of arms sold by Browning in the U.S. and by F.N. distributors worldwide.

Our American military was armed for many years with Browning designed weaponry, not the least of which is the venerable "Old Slabside" 1911 Govt. Model .45 ACP. Today, the firm that bears the Browning name still stands at the forefront with the other makers of fine sporting firearms.

BROWNING FACTS

Note: Between 1966-1971 Browning used a salt-curing process on some of its raw wood to speed the drying time needed to produce its walnut stock blanks. Unfortunately, the salt would be released from the wood and oxidize (rust) the metal surface(s) after a period of time. Although not all Browning guns were salty, those affected guns, especially bolt action rifles in all grades, some BARs, Superposed shotguns, and T-bolt models should be examined carefully around where the metal contacts with the wood for signs of freckling and rust. Discount values on guns which show tell-tale characteristics of salt corrosion range from 25%-40%, depending on how severe the rust damage is. Check all screws which have direct contact with wood and the wood under the buttplate as well. Original Superposed owners of salt wood guns who still have their original owner's warranty card are still eligible for Browning factory refurbishing of affected parts only without charge. Otherwise, Browning has a standardized repair charge for each model.

Since the inception and standardization of steel shot for hunting purposes, the desirability factor of shotguns has changed considerably. On newer manufacture, most shooters/buyers now expect choke tubes, and shotguns without choke tubes must be discounted somewhat. Browning does not recommend using steel shot in any Superposed (B-25) or older Belgian Auto-5 barrels.

Browning's Miroku plant in Japan, in addition to making models specifically for the Browning Arms Company (BAC) in the U.S., also makes a wide variety of makes and models specifically for European sale. These models are normally not imported into the U.S., and because of this, they are not included in this section. You may be able to find more information on the current European models by visiting Browning's international website: www.browningint.com.

BROWNING VALUES INFORMATION

Editor's Note: It is important to note the differences in values of Browning firearms manufactured in Belgium by F.N. and those made recently in Japan by Miroku. We feel that these values are somewhat higher because of collector interest in Belgian guns, and not as the result of any inferiority of the quality of Browning guns made anywhere else.

AS A FINAL NOTE: Most post-war Brownings are collectible only if in 95% or better condition as most models have relatively high mfg. and are not that old. Condition under 95% is normally very shootable, but not as collectible and values for 95% or less condition could be lower than shown in some areas.

GRADING - PPGS™	100%	98%	95%	90%	80%	70%	60%	LAST MSR

All add-ons or deductions on Browning's currently manufactured models reflect retail pricing without any discounting. On higher grade Browning firearms that are engraved, signed specimens by FN's master engravers Funken, J. Baerten, Vrancken, and Watrin will command premiums over the values listed.

BROWNING SERIALIZATION

In addition to the Belgian Browning serialization listed in the back of this text, the following codes will determine the year and origin of those guns made from 1975 to date. The 2 letters in the middle of the serial number are the code designations for year of manufacture. They represent the following: RV - 1975, RT - 1976, RR - 1977, RP - 1978, RN - 1979, PM - 1980, PZ - 1981, PY - 1982, PX - 1983, PW - 1984, PV - 1985, PT -1986, PR - 1987, PP - 1988, PN - 1989, NM - 1990, NZ - 1991, NY - 1992, NX - 1993, NW - 1994, NV - 1995, NT - 1996, NR - 1997, NP - 1998, NN - 1999, MM - 2000, MZ - 2001, MY - 2002, MX - 2003, MW - 2004, MV - 2005, MU - 2006, MT - 2007, MS - 2008, MN - 2009, ZM - 2010, ZZ - 2011, ZY-2012, ZX-2013, ZW-2014.

Since most recently manufactured Browning's use a 3-digit model identification code with the two-letter date code in the serial number (appearing before the year code on European and U.S. mfg. guns, and after the year code on Japanese mfg.) the configuration of a model can also be determined. For example, S/N 611RP2785 would be a Model B-2000 made in 1978 with 2785 being the shotgun's number. S/N 01001NY873 would be the first production example of a Citori Grade III 28 gauge Lightning Model shotgun manufactured in 1992. Refer to Browning Serialization in the back of this text of additional information on Browning model codes.

BROWNING CUSTOM SHOP

Browning's Custom Shop in Herstal, Belgium, continues to make a wide variety of firearms, a number of which have limited importation into the U.S. Current Custom Shop Superposed prices and model information have been provided in the Superposed section. For more information on the Browning Custom Shop's additional offerings, please look under the various category names for availability and current pricing. Please refer to Browning's web site at www.browning.com for more information on the wide variety of firearms available from the Browning Custom Shop in Belgium, or contact Browning directly.

PISTOLS: SEMI-AUTO, CENTERFIRE, F.N. PRODUCTION UNLESS OTHERWISE NOTED

MODEL 1899-FN – 7.65mm cal., first Belgian Browning, 4 in. barrel, similar to later M-1900 but w/o safety markings or lanyard ring, almost 15,000 mfg. 1899-1901.

100%	98%	95%	90%	80%	70%	60%	LAST MSR
$1,850	$1,500	$1,250	$1,000	$750	$600	$550	

Add 15% for guns manufactured in 1899 (ser. nos. 1-3900, without "A" prefix or suffix).
Add 50% for factory nickel finish (nickel finish with blue trigger and blue safety lever) - if 95% condition or better.
Add $800 for factory presentation case with accessories.

MODEL 1900-FN – 7.65mm cal., 4 in. barrel, standard safety markings are in French: Feu and Sur. 724,500 mfg. 1900-1914.

100%	98%	95%	90%	80%	70%	60%	LAST MSR
$1,200	$1,050	$900	$800	$600	$500	$350	

Add 50% for factory nickel finish (nickel finish with blue trigger and safety lever) - if 95% condition or better.
Add $800 for factory presentation case with accessories.
Add $750 for Imperial Russian contract (crossed rifles marking on blue or nickel guns).
Add $100 for Imperial German contracts with German safety markings (Feuer & Sicher).
Add $100 minimum for special contract or retailer markings.

MODEL 1903-FN – 9mm Browning Long cal., 5 in. barrel. 58,400 mfg. 1903-1927.

100%	98%	95%	90%	80%	70%	60%	LAST MSR
$2,000	$1,750	$1,500	$1,250	$1,000	$800	$600	

Add 100% if slotted to accept shoulder stock - beware of fakes.
Add $150 minimum for special contract or retailers markings.

This variation was also manufactured with a detachable shoulder stock. This accessory is rare and can add $1,500-$2,500 (shoulder stock w/o extended magazine) or $2,000-$3,000 (shoulder stock with extended magazine and cleaning rod) to the values listed.

GRADING - PPGS™	100%	98%	95%	90%	80%	70%	60%	LAST MSR

MODEL 1905-FN (VEST POCKET) – 6.35mm cal. (.25 ACP), 6 shot mag. dubbed "Vest Pocket" model, 2 in. barrel, manufactured by Fabrique Nationale, Herstal, Belgium. 1,086,133, mfg. 1906 to circa 1949.

* ***Model 1905-FN First Variation*** – no slide lock/safety lever.

	$600	$475	$375	$325	$275	$225	$175

Add 50% for factory nickel finish (nickel finish with blue trigger and blue safety lever) - if 95% condition or better.
Add $500 for factory presentation case.
Add $750 for Imperial Russian contract (crossed rifles marking on blue or nickel guns).
Add $150 minumum for special contract or retailers markings.

* ***Model 1905-FN Second Variation*** – post 1908, with slide lock/safety lever.

	$550	$425	$325	$275	$225	$175	$125

Add 50% for factory nickel finish (nickel finish with blue trigger and blue safety lever) - if 95% condition or better.
Add $500 for factory presentation case.
Add $750 for Imperial Russian contract (crossed rifles marking on blue or nickel guns).
Add $150 minimum for special contract or retailers markings.

MODEL 1907 HUSQVARNA MFG. – 9mm Browning Long cal., identical to FN Browning 1903, mfg. by Husqvarna in Sweden to supply the Swedish military. Mfg. started in 1917 because the FN Browning 1903 was not available from Belgium during WWI, produced 1917-1942. Most were arsenal refinished in Sweden featuring a dull blue finish over sandblasted metal. Many were imported into the U.S. and converted to .380 ACP cal. in the U.S.

	$1,000	$900	$800	$750	$650	$550	$450

Add 50% for original early factory high polish blue finish.
Add 20% for early "Browning's Patent" slide legend.
Add 10% for "System Browning" slide legend.
Subtract 20% for .380 ACP conversion.

MODEL 1910-FN (MODEL 1955) – 7.65mm (.32 ACP) or Browning 9mm short (.380 ACP) cal., 3 7/16 in. barrel. FN manufacture. 701,266 mfg. 1912-1983.

	$625	$475	$325	$275	$250	$195	$150

Add 20% if BAC marked and 7.65mm cal., or if FN marked and .380 ACP cal.
Add $100 minimum for special contract or retailer markings.

This model is also referred to as the Model 1910/55. BAC marked pistols were imported 1954-1968. Importation ceased after the 1968 GCA.

* ***Model 1955 Renaissance*** – Renaissance engraved model. Most often encountered with BAC slide legend, rarely encountered in the U.S. with "Fabrique Nationale" slide legend.

	$2,950	$2,375	$1,800	$1,400	$1,000	$850	$700

Add $100 for original Browning case.

MODEL 1922 OR 10/22 FN – 7.65mm (.32 ACP) or .380 ACP cal., 4 1/2 in. barrel, Model 10/22 and 1922 are the same. The Model 1910 was modified by FN technicians for sale to the Yugoslav military in 1922, includes a longer barrel, larger frame and magazine. Made primarily for police and military contracts, it was also sold in France, Holland, Greece, Germany, Turkey, and many other nations. Several hundred thousand were mfg. during the Nazi occupation of FN during 1940-44. Most common variations are wartime "WaA140" marked pistols.

	$525	$425	$375	$325	$275	$225	$200

Add 150% if .380 ACP and WaA613 marked on trigger guard.
Add 100% if .32 ACP and WaA613 marked.
Add 30% if WaA103 marked.
Add 30% if Wartime commercial Eagle N marked.
Add 25% for post liberation "A" prefix ser. no.
Add at least $100 for special prewar contract markings.
Subtract 10% for common WaA140 wartime marked pistols.

GRADING - PPGS™	100%	98%	95%	90%	80%	70%	60%	LAST MSR

FN "BABY" MODEL – 6.35mm (.25 ACP) cal., 6 shot mag., 2 in. barrel, w/o grip safety or slide lock lever, imported under BAC trademark from 1954-68+ in standard blue finish, lightweight nickel and alumnium frame, and engraved Renaissance models. Over 510,000 mfg. 1931-83. Reintroduced during the 1990s for the European market.

* ***FN "Baby" Model: FN Marked*** – slide marked "Fabrique Nationale", blue finish standard.

$775	$600	$475	$425	$350	$300	$225	

Add 20% for pre-war production (ser. no. 1-50140).
Add $100 for original cardboard or plastic box with extras.
Add $700 for pre-war factory presentation case.
Add $150 minimum for special contract or retailers markings.

* ***FN "Baby" Model: BAC Marked*** – slide marked "Browning Arms Co.", blue finish standard.

$550	$475	$400	$350	$250	$200	$150	

Add $50-$100 for original box and manual, or $25-$50 for original BAC pouch and manual.

* ***FN "Baby" Model: Lightweight Model*** – nickel or aluminum (introduced 1954) frame, with pearl grips.

$625	$525	$425	$375	$275	$225	$200	

* ***FN "Baby" Model: Renaissance Model*** – engraved, satin grey finish.

$2,400	$1,800	$1,500	$1,200	$900	$800	$600	

FN/BROWNING MODEL 10/71 – .380 ACP cal., 4 1/2 in. barrel, modified version of Model 1922 (10/22), grip safety, includes target sights and grips in addition to incorporating a magazine finger tip extension designed to comply with GCA of 1968. Sold in U.S. by BAC 1970-1974 as the "Standard .380," still mfg. by FN as Model 125.

$595	$500	$450	$400	$375	$350	$300	

* ***FN/Browning Model 10/71 Renaissance Model***

$2,250	$1,900	$1,500	$1,300	$1,150	$925	$700	

MODEL 1935 HI-POWER (HP) – 9mm Para. cal., 13 shot mag., 4 21/32 in. barrel, John M. Browning's last pistol design, mfg. 1935 to date in variations for commercial, military, and police use in over 68 countries, first imported under BAC trademark in 1954.

Please refer to the Fabrique Nationale section of this book for pre-1954 variations (including pre-WWII, WWII, and earlier commercial models), as well as contemporary production of those variations not imported by BAC.

HI-POWER: POST-1954 MFG. – 9mm Para. or .40 S&W (mfg. 1995-2010) cal., similar to FN model 1935, has BAC slide marking, 10 (C/B 1994) or 13* shot mag., 4 5/8 in. barrel, polished blue finish, checkered walnut grips, fixed sights, molded grips were introduced in 1986 (disc. in 2000), ambidextrous safety was added to all models in 1989, approx. 32 (9mm Para.) or 35 (.40 S&W) oz., mfg. by FN in Belgium, imported 1954-2000, reintroduced 2002.

* ***Hi-Power Standard - Polished Blue Finish (Imported 1954-2000)*** – 9mm Para. or .40 S&W (new 1995-) cal., includes fixed front and lateral adj. rear sight, 32 or 35 oz.

$875	$700	$550	$475	$425	$350	$325	

Add 50% for ring hammer and internal extractor.
Add 20% for ring hammer and external extractor (post 1962 mfg.).
Add 30% for thumb print feature.
Add 15% for T-prefix serial number.
Older specimens in original dark green, maroon, or red/black plastic boxes were mfg. 1954-1965 and are scarce - add $100+ in value. Black pouches (circa 1965-1968, especially with gold metal zipper) will also command a $25-$50 premium, depending on condition.

Major identifying factors of the Hi-Power are as follows: the "Thumb-Print" feature was mfg. from the beginning through 1958. Old style internal extractor was mfg. from the beginning through 1962, the "T" SN prefix (T-Series start visible extractor) was mfg. 1963-mid-1970s for all U.S. imports by BAC, 69C through 77C S/N prefixes were mfg. 1969-1977. Rounded type Ring Hammers with new external

GRADING - PPGS™	100%	98%	95%	90%	80%	70%	60%	LAST MSR

extractor were mfg. from 1962-1972 (for U.S. imports by BAC, much later on FN marked pistols). Spur Hammers have been mfg. 1972-present, and the "245" S/N prefix has been mfg. 1977-present. During 2010, all Hi-Powers featured a 75th Anniversary logo etched onto the top of the slide.

* ***Hi-Power Standard - Polished Blue Finish (Imported 2002-Current)*** – 9mm Para. or .40 S&W (mfg. 1995-2010) cal., includes fixed front and lateral adj. rear sight, 32 or 35 oz.

MSR $1,070	$850	$685	$535	$465	$415	$350	$325	

* ***Hi-Power Standard with Adj. Rear Sight*** – 9mm Para. or .40 S&W cal. (disc. 2010), similar to Hi-Power Standard blue, except has adj. rear sight.

MSR $1,150	$900	$715	$585	$485	$425	$385	$350	

* ***Hi-Power Standard - Polished Blue Finish 75th Anniversary Edition*** – 9mm Para. cal. only, similar to Hi-Power Standard Polished Blue Finish, except has "75 years 1935-2010" etched on the top of slide. Limited production 2011 only.

	$850	$685	$535	$450	$400	$350	$325	*$1,030*

Add $70 for adj. rear sight.

* ***Hi-Power Mark III*** – 9mm Para. or .40 S&W (mfg. 1994-2000, reintroduced 2003-2010) cal., non-glare matte blue (disc. 2005) or black epoxy (new 2006) finish, ambidextrous safety, tapered dovetail rear fixed sight, two-piece molded grips, Mark III designation became standard in 1994, approx. 35 oz. Imported 1985-2000, reintroduced 2002.

MSR $1,060	$845	$585	$485	$425	$365	$335	$300	

This model's finish may be confused with some other recent imports which have a "black" painted finish. These black finish guns are painted rather than blue, and some parties have been selling them as original military FNs.

» ***Hi-Power Mark III 75th Anniversary Edition*** – 9mm Para. cal. only, features "75th year" logo etched on top of slide. Limited production 2011 only.

	$825	$675	$525	$450	$400	$350	$325	*$1,030*

* ***Hi-Power Silver Chrome Finish*** – 9mm Para. or .40 S&W (new 1995) cal., entire gun finished in silver chrome, includes adj. sights and Pachmayr rubber grips, 36 (9mm Para.) or 39 (.40 S&W) oz. Assembled in Portugal, and imported 1991-2000.

	$795	$675	$550	$500	$425	$400	$375	*$718*

Add 50% for circa 1980 Belgian model marked "Made in Belgium."

* ***Hi-Power Practical Model*** – 9mm Para. or .40 S&W (new 1995) cal., features blue (disc. 2005) or black epoxy slide, silver-chromed frame finish, wraparound Pachmayr rubber grips, round style serrated hammer, and choice of adj. sights (mfg. 1993-2000) or removable front sight, 36 (9mm Para.) or 39 (.40 S&W) oz. Imported 1990-2000, reintroduced 2002-2006.

	$725	$600	$525	$450	$425	$400	$375	*$863*

Add $58 for adj. sights (disc. 2000).

* ***Hi-Power Nickel/Silver Chrome Finish*** – not to be confused with stainless steel (never offered in the Hi-Power), this nickel/silver chrome finish is different from the silver chrome finish released in 1991, gold trigger, checkered walnut grips. Approx. 11,609 mfg. 1980-85.

	$795	$675	$550	$500	$425	$400	$375	*$525*

Add 50% for circa 1980 Belgian model marked "Made in Belgium."

* ***Hi-Power .30 Luger cal.*** – .30 Luger cal., mfg. for European sales (most are marked BAC on slide), approx. 1,500 imported late 1986-89, similar specifications as 9mm Para. model.

	$925	$775	$625	$550	$450	$425	$375	

This model was never cataloged for sale by BAC in the U.S. A few earlier specimens have been noted with F.N. markings and ring hammer.

GRADING - PPGS™	100%	98%	95%	90%	80%	70%	60%	LAST MSR

* ***Hi-Power GP Competition*** – 9mm Para. cal., competition model with 6 in. barrel, detent adj. rear sight, rubber wraparound grips, front counterweight, improved barrel bushing, decreased trigger pull, approx. 36 1/2 oz.

$995	$895	$725	$600	$550	$500	$450	

The original GP Competition came in a black plastic case w/accessories and is more desirable than later imported specimens which were computer serial numbered and came in a styrofoam box. Above prices are for older models - subtract 10% if newer model (computer serial numbered). This model was never cataloged for sale by BAC in the U.S., and it is not serviced by Browning.

* ***Hi-Power Tangent Rear Sight*** – 9mm Para. cal., manufactured from 1965-1978. 50-500 meter tangent sight. A total of approx. 7,000 were imported by Browning Arms Co. Early pistols are designated by "T" prefix and were mfg. 1964-69, later pistols mfg. 1972-76, had spur hammers and followed the 69C-76C ser. no. prefixes.

$1,150	$975	$825	$600	$475	$400	$375	

Add $100 for "T" prefix.
Add $50 for original pouch and instruction manual.

* ***Hi-Power Tangent Capitan Polished Blue Finish*** – 9mm Para. cal., features 50-500 meter tangent rear sight, blue finish with walnut grips, slide is marked "Made in Belgium, Assembled in Portugal", 32 oz. Imported 1993-2000.

$925	$750	$600	$500	$400	$350	$300	*$764*

* ***Hi-Power Tangent Rear Sight & Slotted*** – 9mm Para. cal., variation with grip strap slotted to accommodate shoulder stock. Early pistols had "T" prefixes. Later pistols had spur hammers and are in the serial range 73CXXXX-74CXXXX.

$1,550	$1,300	$1,100	$900	$775	$650	$525	

Add $200 if with "T" prefix.
Add $50 for original pouch and instruction booklet.

This variation will command a premium; beware of fakes, however (carefully examine slot milling and look for ser. no. in 3 places).

Vektor Arms in N. Salt Lake, UT, imported this model again in limited quantities circa 2004 with both the "245" and seldom seen "511" (includes wide trigger, loaded chamber indicator and external extractor) ser. no. prefixes. These guns are not arsenal refinished or refurbished, and were sold in NIB condition, with two 13 shot mags. Original pricing was $895 for the "245" prefix, and $995 for the "511" prefix.

BCA EDITION HI-POWER – 9mm Para. cal., limited edition made specifically for the Browning Collectors Association in 1980, approx. 100 were delivered.

$950	$750	$575	N/A	N/A	N/A	N/A	

GOLD LINE HI-POWER – 9mm Para. cal., blue finish with gold line perimeter engraving.

$5,250	$4,500	$3,750	N/A	N/A	N/A	N/A	

Check this model carefully for factory originality - including the ring hammer, engraving and bluing, as most models encountered are reproductions.

RENAISSANCE HI-POWER – 9mm Para. cal., extensive scroll engraving on grey silver slide and frame, synthetic pearl grips, gold plated trigger. Disc. approx. 1978.

Round Hammer/ fixed sights	$3,795	$3,250	$2,950	N/A	N/A	N/A	N/A
Spur Hammer/ fixed sights	$3,250	$2,750	$2,250	N/A	N/A	N/A	N/A

Add $100 for internal extractor (pre-1962 mfg.)
Add $100 for "Thumb Print."
Add $50 for original pouch and booklet.
Add $600 for older individual blue leatherette European case.
Add $300-$500 for hi-polished silver finish, depending on condition.

Target sights do not affect the value of this model significantly.

Currently, the Browning Custom Shop in Belgium is making the following Renaissance models: Dore ($7,406 MSR), Nickele ($7,323 MSR), L1 ($4,377 MSR), I1 ($6,581 MSR), and the B2 ($4,571 MSR).

GRADING - PPGS™	100%	98%	95%	90%	80%	70%	60%	LAST MSR

HI-POWER: CUSTOM SHOP MODELS

Currently, the Browning Custom Shop in Belgium is making the following Hi-Power custom shop models: 75th Anniversary Model ($6,971 MSR), Renaissance "Dore" or Gold ($6,247 MSR), Renaissance Nickele ($6,185 MSR), L1 ($4,089 MSR), I1 ($5,225 MSR), and B2 ($4,089 MSR).

CASED RENAISSANCE SET – one pistol each in .25 ACP, .380 ACP (rarest cal. of the three), and 9mm Para. cal., Hi-Power Renaissance models in walnut or black vinyl case, ser. no. not related to other calibers. Offered 1954-1969.

	100%	98%	95%	90%	80%	70%	60%	LAST MSR
	$9,500	$8,250	$5,700	N/A	N/A	N/A	N/A	

Add 30% for coin finish/high polish in early walnut case.
Add $100 for "St. Louis" slide address.
Add $150 for old style Hi-Power extractor.

All original Renaissance cased sets had 9mm Para. Hi-Powers with Ring Hammers. The .380 ACP cal. is the rarest of this set, and will bring $2,500 if new.

CASED GRADE I (BLUE) SET – one pistol each in .25 ACP, .380 ACP, and 9mm Para. cal., Hi-Power Grade I Models in walnut or black vinyl case, ser. no. not related to other calibers.

	100%	98%	95%	90%	80%	70%	60%	LAST MSR
	$2,500	$2,100	$1,700	N/A	N/A	N/A	N/A	

Add $100 for walnut presentation case.
Add $100 for thumbprint.
Add $100 for "St. Louis" slide address.
Add $100 for old style Hi-Power extractor.

All original Grade I blue cased sets had 9mm Para. Hi-Powers with Ring Hammers.

CENTENNIAL MODEL HI-POWER – similar to fixed sight Hi-Power, chrome plated with inscription "Browning Centennial/1878-1978", engraved on side, checkered walnut grips with "B" in circle, cased, 3,500 mfg. in 1978. Original issue price was $495.

	100%	98%	95%	90%	80%	70%	60%	LAST MSR
	$1,100	$900	$750	N/A	N/A	N/A	N/A	

CENTENAIRRE MODEL HI-POWER 1 OF 100 – 9mm Para. cal., unique pattern chemically etched, signed by the engraver, checkered walnut grips with border. 100 mfg. during 1989 - approx. half were sold in U.S., the other half in Europe.

	100%	98%	95%	90%	80%	70%	60%	LAST MSR
	$5,000	$4,000	$3,250	N/A	N/A	N/A	N/A	

LOUIS XVI MODEL – 9mm Para., chemically etched throughout in leaf scroll patterns, satin finish, checkered grips, walnut case. Disc. 1984.

	100%	98%	95%	90%	80%	70%	60%	LAST MSR
	$1,900	$1,600	$1,100	N/A	N/A	N/A	N/A	

CLASSIC HI-POWER SERIES – 9mm Para. cal., less than 2,500 manufactured in Classic model and under 350 manufactured in Gold Classic. Both editions feature multiple engraved scenes, and a special silver grey finish, presentation grips, cased. Mfg. 1984-86.

	100%	98%	95%	90%	80%	70%	60%	LAST MSR
	$1,925	$1,700	$1,200	N/A	N/A	N/A	N/A	*$1,000*

* ***Gold Classic Hi-Power*** – 5 gold inlays, select walnut grips are both checkered and carved. Less than 350 mfg. 1984-1986.

	100%	98%	95%	90%	80%	70%	60%	LAST MSR
	$4,250	$3,700	$2,950	N/A	N/A	N/A	N/A	*$2,000*

125th ANNIVERSARY HI-POWER – 9mm Para. cal., silver nitride finish with scroll engraving, gold enhanced 125th Browning Anniversary logo with image of John M. Browning in gold on slide, 10 shot mag., fixed sights, smooth oil finished walnut grips. 125 mfg. 2003-2004 only.

	100%	98%	95%	90%	80%	70%	60%	LAST MSR
	$1,900	$1,600	$1,100	N/A	N/A	N/A	N/A	*$1,516*

BROWNING DOUBLE ACTION – this model was first listed in the Browning catalog in 1985 but was never imported commercially. The advertised 1985 retail price was $494.

BDM/BPM/BRM SINGLE/DOUBLE ACTION – 9mm Para. cal., double mode design featuring slide selector allowing choice between pistol (true double action operation) or revolver mode (full hammer decocking after each shot), available in double mode, single mode (BPM-D decocker, mfg. 1997), or double action only (BRM-DAO, mfg. 1997), dual purpose decocking lever/safety, 4.73 in. barrel, 10 (C/B 1994) or 15* shot mag., matte blue finish,

GRADING - PPGS™	100%	98%	95%	90%	80%	70%	60%	LAST MSR

black molded wraparound grips, unique breech block allows visible cartridge inspection, adj. rear sight, 31 oz. Mfg. in U.S. 1991-1997.

	$600	$450	$400	$350	$300	$280	$260	$551

This model features hammer block and firing pin block safeties.

* ***BDM Practical*** – similar to Standard BDM, except has matte blue slide and silver chrome frame. Mfg. 1997-98.

	$600	$450	$400	$350	$300	$280	$260	$571

* ***BDM Silver Chrome*** – similar to Standard BDM, except has silver chrome finish. Only 119 mfg. in 1997 only.

	$650	$500	$400	$350	$300	$280	$260	$571

FN DA 9 – 9mm Para. cal., choice of double action or double action only, 4 5/8 in. barrel, molded rubber grips, 10 shot mag., 31 oz. Mfg. by FN.

The retail price on this model was listed at $613.

While advertised in 1996, this model was never imported commercially.

PRO-9/PRO-40 – 9mm Para. or .40 S&W cal., single/double action, 4 in. barrel, 10, 14 (.40 S&W cal. only), or 16 (9mm Para. cal. only) shot mag., ambidextrous decocking and safety, black polymer frame with satin stainless steel slide, under barrel accessory rail, interchangeable backstrap inserts, fixed sights only, 30 (9mm Para.) or 33 oz. Mfg. in the U.S. by FNH USA 2003-2006.

	$525	$430	$370	$350	$315	$295	$260	$641

Please refer to FNH USA handgun listing for current manufacture.

BDA-380 – .380 ACP cal., double action, 10 (C/B 1994) or 14* shot, 3 13/16 in. barrel, fixed sights, smooth walnut grips, 23 oz., introduced 1978 - later production was by Beretta. Disc. 1997.

Blue finish	$595	$525	$450	$395	$325	$275	$225	$564
Nickel finish	$675	$595	$495	$450	$350	$295	$250	$607

BDA MODEL – 9mm Para. (9 shot, 2,740 mfg.), .38 Super (752 mfg.), or .45 ACP (7 shot) cal., mfg. from 1977-80 by Sig-Sauer of W. Germany (same as Sig-Sauer 220).

9mm Para.	$600	$550	$450	$375	$295	$250	$225
.38 Super	$795	$675	$600	$500	$450	$390	$350
.45 ACP	$650	$575	$500	$400	$325	$275	$250

PISTOLS: SEMI-AUTO, .22 CAL. RIMFIRE

NOMAD MODEL – .22 LR cal., 10 shot, 4 1/2 and 6 3/4 in. barrels, steel or alloy frame, adj. sights, blue finish, black plastic grips. Mfg. 1961-1974 by FN.

	$475	$400	$325	$300	$225	$200	$175

Add 10% for alloy frame.

CHALLENGER MODEL – .22 LR cal., 10 shot, 4 1/2 and 6 3/4 in. barrels, steel frame, adj. sights, checkered walnut or plastic (mfg. 1974 only) wraparound grips, gold plated trigger. Mfg. 1962-1975 by FN.

	$650	$575	$550	$500	$475	$400	$350

* ***Challenger Renaissance*** – engraved satin nickel finish, 437 mfg. total (121 with 4 1/2 in. barrel, and 316 with 6 3/4 in. barrel).

	$3,150	$2,350	$1,700	N/A	N/A	N/A	N/A

* ***Challenger Gold Line*** – blue finish, gold line border on perimeter of frame surfaces, 293 mfg. total (147 with 4 1/2 in. barrel, and 146 with 6 3/4 in. barrel).

	$3,250	$2,400	$1,750	N/A	N/A	N/A	N/A

CHALLENGER II – .22 LR cal., Salt Lake City mfg., 6 3/4 in. barrel, steel frame, plastic impregnated hardwood grips, 38 oz. Mfg. 1975-82.

	$350	$300	$275	$250	$200	$175	$150

GRADING - PPGS™	100%	98%	95%	90%	80%	70%	60%	LAST MSR

CHALLENGER III – .22 LR cal., Salt Lake City mfg., 5 1/2 in. bull barrel, 11 shot, alloy frame, adj. sights, 35 oz. Mfg. 1982-85.

	$295	$250	$200	$150	$135	$120	$110	$240

* ***Challenger III BCA Commemorative*** – .22 LR cal., mfg. to commemorate BCA's fourth anniversary.

	$500	$450	$400	N/A	N/A	N/A	N/A

CHALLENGER III SPORTER – .22 LR cal., similar to Challenger III, except has 6 3/4 in. round barrel, wide trigger, 29 oz. Mfg. 1983-1985.

	$295	$250	$200	$150	$135	$120	$110	$240

MEDALIST MODEL – .22 LR cal., 6 3/4 in. barrel, vent. rib, adj. target sights and barrel weights (3 supplied), blue finish, target walnut grips with thumbrest, dry-fire mechanism, 46 oz., black case with red cloth interior. 24,001 mfg. 1962-1976 by FN.

	$1,500	$1,300	$1,100	$950	$825	$725	$625

Subtract 20%-30% if without case and accessories, depending on condition.

The following is a breakdown on how many USA Medalists were manufactured per year: 1962 - 1,068, 1963 - 4,661, 1964 - 1,666, 1965 - 1,170, 1966 - 1,400, 1967 - 2,631, 1968 - 3,039, 1969 - 2,897, 1970 - 1,131, 1971 - 425, 1972 - 1507, 1973 - 708, 1974 - 906, 1975 - 792, 1976-10 (no case or accessories).

* ***Medalist Gold Line*** – 407 mfg. 1962-1975.

	$3,900	$3,150	$2,500	N/A	N/A	N/A	N/A

* ***Medalist Renaissance Model*** – 11 pistols were mfg. 1962-1967 with full coverage engraving, and 382 were mfg. 1970-1975 w/o full coverage engraving, early production guns were coin finished and later ones were satin chrome. Mfg. by FN 1964-1975.

	$4,200	$3,500	$2,750	N/A	N/A	N/A	N/A

* ***Medalist BCA Engraved Edition*** – this BAC edition was a special order (not regular production), featured full coverage engraving. 60 mfg. 1986 only.

	$5,250	$4,250	$3,150	N/A	N/A	N/A	N/A

The BCA Medalist features full coverage engraving (similar to 1962-67 Renaissance mfg.), and has a finish similar to 1970-75 Renaissance production.

INTERNATIONAL MEDALIST – target variation model manufactured 1971, 1974, and 1977-1980 (late model), 5 7/8 (early model) or flatsided 5 15/16 (late model, no production statistics) in. barrel, dull black finish, however 681 were mfg. with BCA markings and blue finish. Recently manufactured by FN in the parkerized international configuration.

Late Model	$850	$750	$600	$500	$400	$350	$325
Early Model	$1,250	$1,050	$825	$725	$600	$525	$400

BUCK MARK STANDARD URX – .22 LR cal., 10 shot mag., 5 1/2 in. bull barrel, aluminum frame, composite grips with skipline checkering (disc. 1990), molded rubber grips (mfg. 1991-2006), or URX grips (ambidextrous with finger grooves, new 2006, became standard during 2007), adj. sights, gold trigger, matte blue finish, 34-36 oz. New 1985.

MSR $460	$375	$295	$250	$200	$150	$125	$110

Add $58 for nickel finish (mfg. 1991-2005).

Subtract approx. 10% for composite or molded rubber grips.

Buck Mark models are manufactured in Salt Lake City, UT.

* ***Buck Mark Standard Stainless URX*** – similar to Buck Mark Standard, except stainless steel, 34 oz. New 2005.

MSR $500	$395	$325	$275	$225	$175	$150	$125

Subtract 10% for molded rubber grips (mfg. 2005-2006).

BUCK MARK MICRO STANDARD URX – similar to Buck Mark Standard, except has 4 in. barrel, choice of standard or nickel finish, URX grips became standard 2007, 32 oz. New 1992.

MSR $460	$375	$295	$250	$200	$150	$125	$110

Add $58 for nickel finish (disc. 2005). Subtract approx. 10% for composite or molded grips.

GRADING - PPGS™	100%	98%	95%	90%	80%	70%	60%	LAST MSR

* ***Buck Mark Micro Standard Stainless URX*** – similar to Buck Mark Micro Standard, except stainless steel, URX grips became standard 2007, 34 oz. Mfg. 2005-2010.

	$375	$295	$250	$200	$170	$145	$125	*$469*

* ***Buck Mark Micro Plus*** – similar to Micro Buck Mark, except has ambidextrous contoured laminated wood grips, nickel (new 1996) or blue finish. Disc. 2001.

	$325	$275	$225	$200	$170	$145	$125	*$350*

Add $33 for nickel finish.

BUCK MARK CHALLENGE – .22 LR cal., features smaller grip circumference for smaller hands, smooth (disc.) or checkered walnut grips with medallions, matte blue finish, 5 1/2 in. lightweight barrel, Pro-Target sights, 25 oz. Mfg. 1999-2010.

	$350	$295	$225	$175	$150	$125	$110	*$429*

* ***Buck Mark Micro Challenge*** – similar to Buck Mark Challenge, except has 4 in. barrel. 23 oz. Mfg. 1999-2000.

	$295	$240	$200	$175	$150	$125	$110	*$311*

BUCK MARK CAMPER – .22 LR cal., features 5 1/2 in. heavy barrel, ambidextrous molded black composite grips, matte blue or satin nickel finish, Pro-Target sights, 34 oz. Mfg. 1999-2012.

	$290	$225	$175	$125	$100	$95	$85	*$380*

Add $33 for satin nickel finish (disc. 2005).

* ***Buck Mark Camper Stainless*** – similar to Buck Mark Camper, except stainless steel, 34 oz. Mfg. 2005-2012.

	$315	$240	$190	$145	$110	$95	$75	*$420*

* ***Buck Mark Camper Stainless URX Field*** – .22 LR cal., alloy receiver, 5 1/2 in. stainless tapered bull barrel, ambidextrous Ultragrip RX grips, matte blued finish, Pro-Target adj. rear sight, Truglo/Marbles fiber optic front sight, 34 oz. Available from Full Line Browning dealers only. New 2008.

MSR $430	$325	$250	$195	$150	$115	$100	$80	

BUCK MARK CAMPER UFX – .22 LR cal., alloy frame, matte blue finish, tapered bull 5 1/2 in. barrel, 10 shot mag., Pro-Target adj. sights, ambidextrous overmolded black/grey UFX grips, 34 oz. New 2013.

MSR $380	$295	$235	$185	$135	$110	$100	$90	

* ***Buck Mark Camper Stainless UFX*** – similar to Buck Mark Camper UFX, except has satin finished stainless steel barrel and slide assembly, 34 oz. New 2013.

MSR $420	$325	$245	$190	$150	$115	$100	$85	

BUCK MARK HUNTER – .22 LR cal., features 7 1/4 in. round heavy barrel with integral scope base, Truglo front sight, smooth cocobolo target grips, matte blue finish, 38 oz. New 2005.

MSR $480	$370	$275	$210	$145	$110	$100	$90	

BUCK MARK PLUS UDX – similar to Buck Mark Standard, except has uncheckered laminated wood (disc. 2006) grips, or walnut ambidextrous DX Ultragrips (new 2007), Tru-Glo Marble front sight (new 2002), and choice of high polish blue or nickel (mfg. 1996-2006), 34 oz. Mfg. 1987-2007, reintroduced 2010.

MSR $520	$390	$290	$225	$170	$135	$120	$110	

Add approx. 10% for nickel finish (disc. 2006).

* ***Buck Mark Field Plus UDX (Classic Plus)*** – similar to Buck Mark Plus, except has rosewood grips (disc. 2006, reintroduced 2010) or DX Ultragrips (mfg. 2007), and Tru-Glo Marble front sight. Mfg. 2002-2007, reintroduced 2010.

MSR $520	$395	$295	$225	$165	$135	$120	$110	

This model is available from Full-Line dealers only.

GRADING - PPGS™	100%	98%	95%	90%	80%	70%	60%	LAST MSR

* ***Buck Mark Plus Stainless UDX*** – similar to Buck Mark Plus, except has stainless steel barrel/slide, choice of black or brown (disc. 2010) UDX laminate grips, 34 oz. Mfg. 2007, reintroduced 2010.

MSR $560	$450	$375	$295	$220	$190	$165	$150	

Subtract $35 for brown laminate grips.

BUCK MARK BULLSEYE TARGET – .22 LR cal., Bullseye model featuring 16 click per turn Pro-Target rear sight, 7 1/4 in. fluted barrel, matte blue finish, adj. trigger pull, contoured rosewood target or wraparound finger groove (disc.) grips, 10 shot mag., 36 oz. Mfg. 1996-2005.

	$495	$395	$295	$225	$190	$165	$150	*$604*

* ***Buck Mark Bullseye Target Stainless*** – similar to Buck Mark Bullseye Target, except is stainless steel and has laminated rosewood grips, 39 oz. Mfg. 2006-2011.

	$595	$475	$350	$285	$225	$175	$150	*$759*

* ***Buck Mark Bullseye Standard*** – similar to Buck Mark Bullseye Target, except has molded composite ambidextrous grips, 36 oz. Mfg. 1996-2006.

	$375	$295	$250	$200	$160	$145	$125	*$468*

BUCK MARK BULLSEYE URX – .22 LR cal., 7 1/4 in. fluted barrel, matte blue finish, URX ambidextrous grips with finger grooves, 39 oz. Mfg. 2006-2010.

	$460	$375	$300	$230	$190	$165	$150	*$579*

BUCK MARK 5.5 TARGET – .22 LR cal., same action as Buck Mark, 5 1/2 in. barrel with serrated top rib allowing adj. sight positioning, target sights, matte blue or nickel (mfg. 1994-2000) finish, choice of contoured walnut (disc. 2004), cocobolo (became standard 2005), or walnut wraparound finger groove grips (new 1992-disc.), 35 oz. Mfg. 1990-2009.

	$440	$350	$285	$225	$190	$170	$135	*$579*

Add $54 for nickel finish (mfg. 1994-2000).

* ***Buck Mark 5.5 Gold Target*** – similar to 5.5 Target, except has gold anodized frame and top rib. Mfg. 1991-99.

	$375	$295	$250	$200	$160	$145	$125	*$477*

BUCK MARK 5.5 FIELD – same action and barrel as the Target 5.5, except sights are designed for field use, anodized blue finish, choice of contoured walnut, cocobolo (became standard 2005), or walnut wraparound finger groove grips (new 1992-disc.), 35 1/2 oz. Mfg. 1991-2011.

	$450	$350	$295	$230	$190	$170	$135	*$619*

BUCK MARK LITE GREEN/GRAY – features alloy matte green or gray receiver, fluted alloy sleeved 5 1/2 or 7 1/4 (mfg. 2010 only) in. barrel, blowback action, Ultragrip RX ambidextrous grips, Pro-Target adj. rear sight and TruGlo/Marble's fiber optic front sight, 28-30 oz. New 2010.

MSR $560	$435	$350	$280	$220	$190	$165	$150	

Add $20 for 7 1/4 in. barrel (disc. 2010).

BUCK MARK LITE SPLASH URX – .22 LR cal., 5 1/2 or 7 1/4 in. round barrel, aluminum barrel and receiver feature gold splash annodizing, URX grips standard, adj. sights with TruGlo fiber optic front sight, 28 or 30 oz. Mfg. 2006-2009.

	$370	$290	$230	$180	$150	$135	$120	*$489*

Add $20 for 7 1/4 in. barrel.

BUCK MARK CONTOUR URX – .22 LR cal., 5 1/2 or 7 1/4 in. specially contoured steel or alloy (Lite) sleeved barrel with full length scope base, matte blue finish, URX grips, adj. rear sight, 28-36 oz. (Contour Lite variation is 8 oz. less than standard). New 2006.

MSR $540	$395	$300	$225	$170	$135	$120	$110	

Add $10 for 7 1/4 in. barrel.
Add $50 for Contour Lite variation (alloy sleeved barrel, 8 oz. less than steel, disc. 2010).

GRADING - PPGS™	100%	98%	95%	90%	80%	70%	60%	LAST MSR

BUCK MARK PRACTICAL URX – features alloy matte gray finished receiver, tapered 5 1/2 in. bull barrel, matte blue finish, Ultragrip RX ambidextrous grips, Pro-Target adj. rear sight, TruGlo/Marble's fiber optic front sight, 34 oz. New 2010.

MSR $430	$320	$235	$185	$140	$110	$95	$75	

BUCK MARK VARMINT – .22 LR cal., same action as Buck Mark, 9 7/8 in. barrel with serrated top rib allowing adj. sight positioning, laminated wood grips, choice of contoured walnut or walnut wraparound finger groove grips (new 1992), optional detachable forearm, matte blue, 48 oz. Mfg. 1987-99.

	$375	$300	$225	$175	$155	$135	$120	*$403*

BUCK MARK SILHOUETTE – .22 LR cal., silhouette variation of the Buck Mark, 9 7/8 in. bull barrel with serrated top rib allowing adj. sight positioning, hooded target sights, laminated wood stocks and forearm, choice of contoured walnut or walnut wraparound finger groove grips (new 1992), matte blue, 53 oz. Mfg. 1987-99.

	$395	$325	$250	$195	$170	$150	$135	*$448*

* ***Buck Mark Unlimited Silhouette (Match)*** – similar to Silhouette Model featuring 14 in. barrel with set back front sight, choice of contoured walnut or walnut wraparound finger groove grips (new 1992), 64 oz. Mfg. 1991-99.

	$495	$400	$350	$250	$195	$170	$150	*$536*

BUCK MARK COMMEMORATIVE – features 6 3/4 in. Challenger style tapered barrel, white bonded ivory grips with scrimshaw style patterning including "1 of 1,000 Commemorative Model" on sides, matte blue finish, gold trigger, 30 1/2 oz. 1,000 mfg. 2001 only.

	$395	$315	$250	N/A	N/A	N/A	N/A	*$437*

1911-22 – .22 LR cal., patterned after the Colt Model 1911-A1 .22 LR cal. Ace pistol, choice of 3 5/8 (Compact Model) or 4 1/4 (A1 Model) in. barrel, alloy frame and slide, matte black finish, fixed sights, checkered brown composite grips, 10 shot mag., approx. 15 oz. Mfg. in the USA beginning 2011.

MSR $600	$525	$450	$415	$385	$360	$340	$325	

Pistols made during 2011 include a limited edition canvas and leather zippered commemorative case, plus a collector's certificate.

1911-22 BCA EDITION – .22 LR cal., special 1911 Anniversary Edition, "BCA" is incorporated into the serial number, only 100 mfg. during 2011-2012.

	$925	$825	$725	N/A	N/A	N/A	N/A	*$850*

RIFLES: BOLT ACTION

MODEL 52 LIMITED EDITION – .22 LR cal., virtually identical to the original Winchester Model 52C Sporter, except for minor safety enhancements, bolt action, 24 in. drilled and tapped barrel, 5 shot detachable mag., pistol grip walnut stock with oil style finish, deep blue finish, adj. trigger, two-position safety, 7 lbs. 5,000 mfg. 1991-92.

	$950	$850	$700	N/A	N/A	N/A	N/A	*$500*

MODEL BBR – .25-06 Rem., .270 Win., .30-06, 7mm Mag., .300 Win. Mag. or .338 Win. Mag. cal., short action available in .22-250 Rem., 243 Win., 257 Roberts, 7mm-08 Rem., or 308 Win. cal., 24 in. standard or heavy barrel, 60 degree bolt throw, fluted bolt, adj. trigger, hidden detachable mag., no sights, checkered pistol grip, Monte Carlo stock. Mfg. 1978-84 by Miroku.

	$695	$600	$475	$400	$325	$250	$200	

Some rare production calibers will add premiums to the values listed (i.e., add 50% for .243 Win. cal.).

BBR RIFLE ELK ISSUE – 7mm Rem. Mag. cal., deeply blued receiver which has multiple animals gold inlaid, high grade walnut stock and forearm feature skipline checkering. 1,000 mfg. Disc. 1986.

	$1,800	$1,500	$1,100	N/A	N/A	N/A	N/A	*$1,395*

T-BOLT SPORTER/TARGET (NEW MFG.) – .17 HMR (new 2008), .22 LR, or .22 WMR (new 2008) cal., original straight pull action with enlarged bolt handle, 22 in. free floating

GRADING - PPGS™	100%	98%	95%	90%	80%	70%	60%	LAST MSR

medium sporter or heavy target barrel, 10 shot double helix rotary mag., blued steel receiver, satin finish sporter or target (w/cheekpiece) walnut stock with cut checkering, sling studs, gold trigger, no sights, top tang safety, right or left-hand (new 2009) action, 4 lbs., 14 oz. (sporter) or 5 1/2 (target) lbs. New 2006.

MSR $750	**$615**	**$515**	**$435**	**$380**	**$325**	**$250**	**$195**

Add $30 for Target/Varmint configuration (new 2007).

Add $40 for .17 HMR or .22 WMR cal. in sporter configuration, or $20 for same cals. in Target/ Varmint configuration.

Add $10 for left-hand.

* ***T-Bolt Composite Sporter/Target (New Mfg.)*** – similar to T-Bolt Sporter/Target, except has matte black composite stock, includes sling swivels, choice of 22 in. medium (Sporter) or heavy target (Target/Varmint) barrel, right or left-hand (new 2009) action, approx. 4 1/2 (Sporter) or 5 lbs. 2 oz. (Target/Varmint). New 2008.

MSR $750	**$615**	**$515**	**$435**	**$380**	**$325**	**$250**	**$195**

Add $30 for Target/Varmint configuration (new 2007).

Add $40 for .17 HMR or .22 WMR cal. in sporter configuration, or $20 for same cals. in Target/ Varmint configuration.

Add $10 for left hand.

T-BOLT T-1 – .22 LR cal., straight pull bolt action, 5 shot mag., 22 in. barrel, adj. rear sight, 5 1/2 lbs., plain pistol grip stock. Mfg. 1965-1974 by FN.

$600	**$525**	**$450**	**$410**	**$330**	**$270**	**$210**

Add 10%-15% for left-hand model (mfg. 1967-1974 only).

An aperture rear sight was standard for the first nine years of production.

Watch for salt wood.

T-BOLT T-2 – similar to T-1, only with select checkered walnut stock (lacquer finished), pinned front sight blade, 24 in. barrel, 6 lbs.

$875	**$765**	**$655**	**$595**	**$480**	**$395**	**$305**

Add 10%-15% for left-hand model (mfg. 1969-74 only).

Watch for salt wood.

* ***T-Bolt T-2 Late Production*** – features oil finished stock, press fit plastic front sight, and Browning computerized serialization.

$600	**$525**	**$435**	**$375**	**$305**	**$250**	**$195**

FN HIGH-POWER MODEL – .222 Rem. (Sako action), .222 Rem. Mag. (Sako action), .22-250 Rem. (Sako action), .243 Win., .257 Roberts, .264 Win. Mag., .270 Win., .284 Win. (Sako action), .30-06, .308 Win., 7mm Mag., .300 Win. Mag., .308 Norma Mag., .300 H&H, .338 Win. Mag., .375 H&H, or .458 Win. Mag. cal., standard Mauser type action with either short or long (more desirable) extractor, 22 or 24 in. (heavy available) barrel, folding leaf sight, checkered pistol grip stock. Mfg. 1960-1974 by FN.

The .243 Win. and .308 Win. cals. were built on the small ring Mauser action prior to using the Sako medium action.

Note: Grades differ in engraving, finish, checkering, and grade of wood. It should be noted that the salt wood problem is more common in these high powered models. Guns should be checked carefully for rust below wood surfaces.

* ***FN High-Power Safari Grade Basic Model*** – basic model with blue finish.

Standard cals.	**$1,675**	**$1,475**	**$1,275**	**$1,175**	**$995**	**$850**	**$550**
Mag. cals.	**$1,850**	**$1,650**	**$1,425**	**$1,275**	**$1,075**	**$900**	**$650**
.257 Roberts	**$2,825**	**$2,500**	**$2,150**	**$1,875**	**$1,500**	**$1,250**	**$1,150**
.308 Norma Mag.	**$2,250**	**$1,950**	**$1,550**	**$1,375**	**$1,250**	**$1,050**	**$975**
.338 Win. Mag.	**$1,995**	**$1,750**	**$1,400**	**$1,250**	**$1,050**	**$900**	**$800**
.375 H&H	**$2,195**	**$1,850**	**$1,500**	**$1,350**	**$1,150**	**$1,000**	**$900**

Add 15% for Magnum long extractor models.

Between 1963 and 1974, Browning also offered short and medium barrelled actions in the Safari,

GRADING - PPGS™	100%	98%	95%	90%	80%	70%	60%	LAST MSR

Medallion and Olympian Grades. These models have Sako barrelled actions and were stocked by FN. Medium weight barrels could also be ordered.

* ***FN High-Power Safari Grade Short Sako Action*** – .222 Rem. or .222 Rem. Mag. cal., short action.

$1,675	$1,475	$1,275	$1,175	$995	$850	$695	

* ***FN High-Power Safari Grade Medium Sako Action*** – .22-250 Rem., .243 Win., .284 Win. or .308 Win. cal., medium action.

$1,595	$1,375	$1,175	$1,050	$900	$750	$550	

Add 75% for .284 Win. cal. (mfg. 1965-76).

In .284 Win. cal., only 162 rifles were mfg. in Safari Grade, 29 in Medallion Grade, and 10 in Olympian Grade.

* ***FN High-Power Medallion Grade*** – features select figured walnut with skipline checkering, rosewood grip and forearm caps, blue/black lustre bluing, receiver and barrel portion scroll engraved, ram's head engraved on floor plate.

$3,250	$2,950	$2,500	$2,200	$1,850	$1,500	$1,200	

Add 20%-60% for rare calibers, depending on rarity.
Add 15% for Mag. cals. with long extractor.

Caliber rarity is as follows: .30-06 (least rare), .300 H&H, .375 H&H long extractor, .264 Win. Mag., .222 Rem./.222 Rem. Mag., .284 Win. (rarest).

This model was also available with a Sako short or medium action - cals. are the same as listed for the Sako Safari.

* ***FN High-Power Olympian Grade*** – top-of-the-line model featuring highly figured walnut stock that is both checkered and carved. Receiver, floor plate, and trigger guard are chrome plated in a satin finish that has deep relief animal scenes engraved, as well as deep scroll work on other metal parts.

$9,250	$8,000	$6,850	$6,200	$5,200	$4,400	$3,850	

Add 20%-60% for rare calibers, depending on the rarity.
Add 15% for Mag. cals. with long extractor.

Caliber rarity is as follows: .30-06 (least rare), .308 Norm. Mag., .300 H&H, .375 H&H long extractor, .264 Win. Mag., .222 Rem./.222 Rem. Mag., .284 Win. (rarest).

This model was also available with a Sako short or medium action - cals. are the same as listed for the Sako Safari.

ACERA MODEL – .30-06 or .300 Win. Mag. cal., features straight pull action, Teflon coated breech block face, 7 lug bolt, 22 or 24 (.300 Win. Mag.) in. barrel, available w/o sights, with sights (disc. 1999), or with BOSS, detachable box mag., checkered walnut stock, gloss metal finish, 7 lbs. 3 oz. - 7 lbs. 9 oz. Mfg. 1999-2000, reintroduced during 2002 only.

$895	$800	$650	$575	$475	$375	$285	*$896*

Add $34 for .300 Win. Mag. cal.
Add $24 for iron sights (disc. 1999).
Add $80 for barrel BOSS (.30-06 cal. mfg. 2002 only).

RIFLES: BOLT ACTION, CENTERFIRE A-BOLT I SERIES

A-BOLT HUNTER MODEL I – available in .25-06 Rem., .270 Win., .280 Rem. (new 1988), .30-06, 7mm Rem. Mag., .300 Win. Mag., or .338 Win. Mag. cal. in long action, short action available in .223 Rem. (new 1988), .22-250 Rem., .243 Win., .257 Roberts, .284 Win. (new 1989), 7mm-08 Rem., or .308 Win. cal., 3 or 4 shot mag., matte blue finish, 3 lug rotary bolt locking, 22 (short action only), 24 in. (disc. 1987), or 26 in. barrel (new 1988 - long action Mag. cals. only), 60 degree bolt throw, adj. trigger, hidden detachable mag., with or without sights, top tang thumb safety, checkered pistol grip stock, 6 lbs. 3 oz. - 7 lbs. 11oz. Mfg. 1985-93 by Miroku. Replaced by A-Bolt Model II in 1994.

$495	$425	$325	$295	$240	$195	$150	*$510*

Add $65 for open sights.

GRADING - PPGS™	100%	98%	95%	90%	80%	70%	60%	LAST MSR

* ***A-Bolt Hunter Medallion Model*** – same A-Bolt specifications, except also available in .375 H&H cal., features better grade walnut stock with rosewood pistol grip and forend cap, synthetic floor plate, high lustre bluing, no sights. Disc. 1993. Replaced by A-Bolt Medallion Model II in 1994.

$625 $525 $425 $355 $290 $235 $185 *$597*

Add $25 for left-hand action (avail. in long action cals. only).
Add $100 for .375 H&H cal. (open sights only).

Left-hand action available in .25-06 Rem., .270 Win., .280 Rem., .30-06, 7mm Rem. Mag., .300 Win. Mag., .338 Win. Mag., or .375 H&H cal.

* ***A-Bolt Hunter Micro Medallion Model*** – .223 Rem. (new 1988), .22-250 Rem., .243 Win., .257 Roberts, .284 Win., .308 Win., or 7mm-08 Rem. cal., scaled down variation of the A-Bolt Hunter Model, 20 in. barrel, short action only, 13 5/16 in. LOP, 3 shot mag., no sights, 6 lbs. 3 oz. for short action. Mfg. 1988-93. Replaced by A-Bolt Micro Medallion Model II in 1994.

$625 $525 $425 $355 $290 $235 $185 *$597*

* ***A-Bolt Hunter Gold Medallion Model*** – .270 Win., .30-06, .300 Win. Mag. (new 1993), or 7mm Rem. Mag. cal., similar to Medallion Model, except has extra select walnut stock with continental style cheekpiece, gold lettering and light engraving, no sights. Mfg. 1988-93. Replaced by A- Bolt Gold Medallion Model II in 1994.

$750 $650 $550 $500 $405 $330 $255 *$810*

* ***A-Bolt Hunter Euro-Bolt*** – .22-250 Rem., .243 Win., .270 Win., .30-06, .308 Win., or 7mm Rem. Mag. cal., features European styling including Schnabel style forearm, rounded rear receiver, Mannlicher style bolt, European cheekpiece on satin finished checkered stock, low-lustre bluing, hinged floor plate with removable mag., cocking indicator, upper tang thumb activated safety, 6 lbs. 14 oz. - 7 lbs. 6 oz. (Mag.). Mfg. 1993-96.

$675 $550 $475 $425 $345 $280 $220 *$700*

* ***A-Bolt Hunter Stainless Stalker*** – .22-250 Rem. (left-hand only, new 1993), .25-06 Rem., .270 Win., .280 Rem., .30- 06, 7mm Rem. Mag., .300 Win. Mag., .338 Win. Mag. or .375 H&H (new 1990) cal., action and barrel are stainless steel, matte black graphite fiberglass composite stock, dull stainless finish, no sights, 6 lbs. 11 oz. - 7 lbs. 3 oz. Mfg. 1987-93. Replaced by Stainless Stalker II in 1994.

$625 $525 $450 $410 $330 $270 $210 *$665*

Add $100 for .375 H&H cal.
Add $20 for left-hand action.

Originally, this model was offered in .270 Win., .30-06, or 7mm Rem. Mag. cal. only.

* ***A-Bolt Hunter Camo Stalker*** – .270 Win., .30-06, or 7mm Rem. Mag. cal., laminated black and green wood stock, matte finish on metal parts, no sights. Mfg. 1987-89.

$475 $425 $350 $300 $250 $190 $150 *$483*

* ***A-Bolt Hunter Composite Stalker*** – .25-06 Rem., .270 Win., .280 Rem., .30-06, 7mm Rem. Mag., .300 Win. Mag., or .338 Win. Mag. cal., black graphite fiberglass composite stock, matte non-glare metal finish, 6 lbs. 11 oz. - 7 lbs. 3 oz. Mfg. 1988-93. Replaced by Composite Stalker II in 1994.

$525 $425 $350 $300 $250 $190 $150 *$525*

A-BOLT BIGHORN SHEEP ISSUE – .270 Win. cal. only, 22 in. barrel, high grade walnut stock with gloss finish and skipline checkering, deep relief engraving on receiver barrel, floorplate, and trigger guard, two 24Kt. inlays depicting bighorn sheep. 600 mfg. 1986-87 only.

$1,450 $1,100 $950 $850 $725 $550 $500 *$1,365*

A-BOLT PRONGHORN ISSUE – .243 Win. cal., presentation grade walnut with skipline checkering and pearl borders, receiver and barrel engraving, multiple gold inlays on receiver top and floor plate. 500 mfg. 1987 only.

$1,450 $1,100 $950 N/A N/A N/A N/A *$1,302*

GRADING - PPGS™	100%	98%	95%	90%	80%	70%	60%	LAST MSR

RIFLES: BOLT ACTION, CENTERFIRE A-BOLT II SERIES

The A-Bolt II Series was introduced in 1994, and differs from the original A-Bolt variations (disc. 1993) in that a new anti-bind bolt featuring a non-rotating bolt sleeve has been incorporated in addition to an improved trigger system. Action feeding is similar to A-Bolt I Series, with a hinged floorplate featuring a detachable box magazine. Consumers also may have their name/inscription engraved on the flat bolt-face on any A-Bolt II Series variation for an additional $25. Browning introduced the BOSS (Ballistic Optimizing Shooting System) in 1994 as an option on A-Bolt rifles, except Micro-Medallion models. It is a user-adjustable barrel tuning attachment which greatly improves accuracy. The BOSS version has porting, which functions as a muzzle brake and reduces recoil by approx. 30%. The BOSS-CR (Conventional Recoil) is not ported, and does not have the substantially increased noise/muzzle blast of the BOSS.

During 2010, the A-Bolt celebrated its 25th Anniversary, and in commemoration, select A-Bolt rifles have a "25th Anniversary A-Bolt" etched on the floorplate.

A-BOLT HUNTER MODEL II – available in various cals. between .22-250 Rem. - .338 Win. Mag. (disc.), currently available in .270 WSM, 7mm WSM cals. (new 2002), .300 WSM (new 2001), or .325 WSM (new 2005) cal., 22 (disc.), 23 (.300 WSM cal. only), 24, or 26 in. barrel with (disc. 1998) or w/o open sights, walnut stock with gloss finish, top tang safety, low lustre bluing, 60 degree bolt throw, right hand action was disc. during 2007, except for Full Line dealer model, left hand action disc. 2010. 6 lbs. 7 oz. - 7 lbs. 3 oz. Disc. 2012.

$825	$630	$575	$475	$375	$335	$300	

Last MSR was $1,030 (right hand).

Subtract approx. $70 for left hand action (disc. 2010).
Subtract approx. $65 for Mag. cals. on left hand action.
Add approx. $60 for open sights (available in 8 cals., disc. 1998).

Beginning 2007, right hand action in this model was only available through Full Line Browning dealers.

* ***A-Bolt Hunter Model II WSSM*** – .223 WSSM, .25 WSSM (new 2004), or .243 WSSM cal., 3 shot mag., super short action, 21 or 22 (new 2004) in. barrel, walnut stock with satin finish and smaller dimensions, 6 1/4 lbs. Mfg. 2003-2007.

$650	$575	$450	$375	$325	$280	$240	*$770*

* ***A-Bolt Hunter Model II with BOSS*** – same cals. as Hunter Model II until 1999, available only in .22- 250 Rem., .243 Win., .270 Win., .280 Rem., .30-06, or .308 Win. cal. during 1999, features 22 or 26 (Mag. cals. only, disc. 1998) in. barrel with BOSS. Mfg. 1994-99.

$595	$500	$425	$350	$300	$275	$250	*$617*

A-BOLT HUNTER FIELD II (CLASSIC HUNTER) – .270 Win. (disc. 2001), .270 WSM (new 2002), .30-06 (disc. 2001), .300 Win. Mag. (disc. 2001), .300 WSM (new 2002), .325 WSM (new 2005) 7mm Rem. Mag. (disc. 2001), or 7mm WSM (new 2002) cal., 22 (disc. 2001), 23 (new 2002, WSM cals. only), or 26 (disc. 2001) in. barrel, 3-5 shot mag., features low-lustre bluing and select checkered satin finished Monte Carlo walnut stock and forend, approx. 6 1/2 - 7 1/4 lbs. Mfg. 1999-2006.

$695	$595	$475	$395	$325	$275	$250	*$808*

This model was available to Full-line and Medallion dealers only.

* ***A-Bolt Hunter Field II WSSM (Classic Hunter)*** – .223 WSSM, .25 WSSM (new 2004), or .243 WSSM cal., 3 shot mag., super short action, 22 in. barrel, satin finished Monte Carlo walnut stock with palm swell and double bordered checkering, low lustre bluing, 6 1/4 lbs. Mfg. 2003-2006.

$725	$600	$500	$400	$350	$300	$275	*$829*

This model was available to Full-line and Medallion dealers only.

A-BOLT RMEF SPECIAL HUNTER – .325 WSM cal., similar to Medallion Model II, except has satin finished Monte Carlo stock and special RMEF logo insert on floorplate. Mfg. 2007-2008.

$725	$625	$495	$395	$350	$300	$275	*$864*

GRADING - PPGS™	100%	98%	95%	90%	80%	70%	60%	LAST MSR

A-BOLT NRA WILDLIFE CONSERVATION COLLECTION – .243 Win. cal., 22 in. barrel, blue finish, features NRA Heritage logo laser engraved in satin finished walnut stock, approx. 6 1/2 lbs. Limited mfg. 2006-2007.

	$725	$625	$495	$395	$350	$300	$275	*$813*

A-BOLT MICRO HUNTER II – .22 Hornet (only available cal. in right hand action beginning 2009), .22-250 Rem. (disc. 2010), .223 Rem. (mfg. 2000-2005), .243 Win. (disc. 2010), .260 Rem. (disc. 2001), .270 WSM (mfg. 2003-2010), 7mm WSM (mfg. 2003-2010), .300 WSM (mfg. 2003-2010), .325 WSM (mfg. 2005-2010), .308 Win. (disc. 2010), or 7mm-08 Rem. (disc. 2010) cal., 3 shot mag., features shorter LOP and 20 or 22 in. barrel w/o sights, checkered walnut stock and forend, approx. 6 1/4 lbs. Mfg. 1999-2012.

	$675	$500	$385	$335	$285	$250	$225	*$870*

Add $60 for Mag. cals. (disc. 2009)
Add $30 for left-hand action (new 2003).

A-BOLT MEDALLION MODEL II – .375 H&H cal., previously available in various cals. between .22-250 Rem. (disc.) - .338 Win. Mag., similar to Medallion Model with A-Bolt II improvements, without sights, except for .375 H&H cal. (open sights standard), gloss finished walnut stock with rosewood grip and forend caps, right hand action w/o BOSS was disc. 2007, 6 lbs. 7 oz. - 7 lbs. 1 oz. Mfg. 1994-2011.

	$775	$625	$525	$400	$350	$295	$275	*$990*

Subtract approx. $30 for standard, non-Mag. cals., including WSM.
Subtract approx. $20 for right hand action w/o BOSS (only available in .375 H&H cal. beginning 2007).

* ***A-Bolt Medallion Model II WSSM*** – .223 WSSM, .25 WSSM (new 2004), or .243 WSSM cal., 3 shot mag., super short action, 22 in. barrel, engraved receiver, Monte Carlo gloss finished walnut stock with rosewood pistol grip and forend caps, palm swell and double bordered checkering, no sights, low lustre bluing, 6 1/4 lbs. Mfg. 2003-2007.

	$695	$575	$475	$425	$385	$365	$335	*$872*

* ***A-Bolt Medallion Model II with BOSS*** – various cals. between .223 WSSM - .375 H&H, similar to Medallion Model II, except has 22, 23 (new 2002, WSM cals. only), or 26 in. BOSS barrel. New 1994.

MSR $1,120	$885	$700	$565	$450	$400	$375	$335	

Add $30 for normal Mag. and WSM cals. or $51 for WSSM (disc. 2007) cals.
Add $32 for left-hand action (disc. 2005).

* ***A-Bolt Micro Medallion Model II*** – .22 Hornet, .22-250 Rem., .223 Rem., .243 Win., 7mm-08 Rem., .284 Win. (disc. 1997), or .308 Win. cal., similar to Micro Medallion Model with A-Bolt II improvements, 20 or 22 (.22 Hornet only) in. barrel without sights, 6 lbs. Mfg. 1994-98.

	$525	$465	$400	$350	$300	$275	$250	*$636*

A-BOLT CUSTOM TROPHY II – .270 Win., .30-06, .300 Win. Mag., or 7mm Rem. Mag. cal., features 24 or 26 (Mag. cals. only) in. octagon barrel with gold band at muzzle, no sights, gold outlines on barrel and receiver, checkered select American walnut stock with shadowline cheekpiece and skeleton pistol grip, approx. 7 1/2 lbs. Mfg. 1998-2000.

	$1,150	$925	$800	$660	$525	$450	$375	*$1,428*

A-BOLT GOLD MEDALLION MODEL II – .270 Win., .30-06, .300 Win. Mag., or 7mm Rem. Mag. cal., similar to Gold Medallion Model, except has A-Bolt II improvements, 22 or 26 in. barrel, approx. 7 1/2 lbs. Mfg. 1994-98.

	$695	$595	$450	$375	$335	$300	$265	*$855*

* ***A-Bolt Gold Medallion Model II with BOSS*** – mfg. 1994-97.

	$750	$625	$525	$450	$375	$325	$285	*$916*

A-BOLT WHITE GOLD MEDALLION MODEL II – .270 WSM (new 2004), .270 Win., .30-06, .300 Win. Mag., .300 WSM (new 2004), .325 WSM (new 2005), 7mm WSM (new 2004), or 7mm Rem. Mag. cal., stainless steel receiver and 22, 23 (new 2004), or 26 in. barrel, gold

GRADING - PPGS™	100%	98%	95%	90%	80%	70%	60%	LAST MSR

engraving, checkered high gloss Monte Carlo walnut stock with rosewood cap on forend and pistol grip, 6 lbs. 6 oz. - 7 lbs. 11 oz. Mfg. 1999-2009.

	$1,025	$775	$625	$525	$425	$360	$300	*$1,279*

Add $30 for Mag. cals.

* ***A-Bolt White Gold Medallion II RMEF*** – 7mm Rem. Mag. (disc. 2006) or .325 WSM (new 2007) cal., similar to White Gold Medallion, includes RMEF logo on pistol grip cap, gold engraved, stainless steel receiver and 26 in. barrel, select walnut stock, contrasting spacers and rosewood caps on forend and pistol grip, continental style cheekpiece and sling swivels, 7 lbs., 11 oz. Limited edition 2003-2008.

	$1,045	$785	$630	$515	$450	$375	$325	*$1,312*

* ***A-Bolt White Gold Medallion II with BOSS*** – similar to White Gold Medallion, except has barrel with BOSS, and not available in WSM cals. Disc. 2006.

	$985	$765	$610	$500	$435	$375	$320	*$1,235*

Add $28 for non-WSSM Mag. cals.

A-BOLT ECLIPSE HUNTER II WITH BOSS – .22-250 Rem. (disc. 1999), .243 Win. (disc. 1997), .270 Win., .30-06, .308 Win. (disc. 2000), or 7mm Rem. Mag. cal., features laminated thumbhole wood stock with cheekpiece, long action, 22 or 26 (7mm Rem. Mag. only) in. barrel with BOSS, approx. 7 1/2 lbs. New 1996.

MSR $1,430	$1,100	$850	$650	$550	$425	$350	$325	

Add $30 for 7mm Rem. Mag. cal.

* ***A-Bolt Eclipse Varmint II with BOSS*** – .22-250 Rem., .223 Rem., or .308 Win. cal., 24 in. heavy barrel with BOSS, 4 shot mag., otherwise similar to Eclipse Model, approx. 9 lbs. Mfg. 1996-99.

	$810	$655	$535	$455	$375	$325	$285	*$969*

A-BOLT ECLIPSE M-1000 II – .22-250 Rem. (new 2006), .270 WSM, 7mm WSM, .300 WSM, or .308 Win. (new 2006) cal., features 26 in. heavy blue barrel, 3 shot mag., 9 lbs. 14 oz. New 2004.

MSR $1,340	$1,050	$800	$665	$535	$400	$350	$300	

Add $20 for WSM cals.

* ***A-Bolt Eclipse M-1000 II with BOSS*** – .22-250 Rem. (new 2006), .300 Win. Mag., .308 Win. (new 2006), .270 WSM (new 2006), 7mm WSM (new 2006), or .300 WSM (new 2006) cal., features special 26 in. heavy target barrel, refined trigger system, 10 lbs.

MSR $1,440	$1,150	$925	$750	$635	$525	$425	$350	

Add $30 for Mag. cals.

* ***A-Bolt Eclipse M-1000 II Stainless*** – similar to Eclipse M-1000 II, except features 26 in. stainless bull barrel, 9 lbs., 14 oz. New 2004.

MSR $1,600	$1,325	$1,150	$975	$875	$700	$575	$475	

Add $100 for BOSS.
Add $40 for WSM cals.

A-BOLT VARMINT II WITH BOSS – .22-250 Rem., .223 Rem., or .308 Win. (new 1995) cal., features A-Bolt II improvements, 22 in. heavy barrel with BOSS, blue/gloss or satin/matte (new 1995, .223 Rem. disc. 1999) finish, black laminated wood stock with checkering, palm swell, and solid recoil pad, without sights, 9 lbs. Mfg. 1994-2000.

	$715	$600	$465	$380	$335	$300	$265	*$879*

A-BOLT EURO-BOLT II – .243 Win., .270 Win., .30-06, .308 Win., or 7mm Rem. Mag. cal., similar to Euro-Bolt with A-Bolt II improvements, 22 or 26 (7mm Rem. Mag. only) in. barrel w/o sights, 6 lbs. 7 oz. - 7 lbs. 3 oz. (Mag.). Mfg. 1994-96.

	$625	$510	$410	$355	$300	$265	$250	*$824*

* ***A-Bolt Euro-Bolt II with BOSS*** – .243 Win., .270 Win., or .308 Win. cal., 22 in. barrel with BOSS, 6 lbs. 7 oz.

	$725	$600	$500	$425	$350	$325	$295	*$922*

GRADING - PPGS™	100%	98%	95%	90%	80%	70%	60%	LAST MSR

A-BOLT STAINLESS STALKER II – similar to Stainless Stalker with A-Bolt improvements, available in various cals, between .22-250 Rem. - .375 H&H, .223 Rem. reintroduced during 2004 in super short action only, no sights, right hand action w/o Boss was disc. 2007, 6 lbs. 1 oz. - 7 lbs. 3 oz. Mfg. 1994-2010.

	$885	$625	$450	$375	$325	$275	$250	*$1,099*

Add $40 for normal Mag. or WSM cals.
Subtract approx. $20 for right hand action (available in .375 H&H cal. only beginning 2007).

* ***A-Bolt Stainless Stalker II WSSM*** – .223 WSSM, .25 WSSM (new 2004), or .243 WSSM cal., 3 shot mag., super short action, 21 (disc.) or 22 in. barrel, walnut stock with satin finish and smaller dimensions, 6 lbs., 1 oz. Mfg. 2003-2007.

	$790	$585	$425	$350	$300	$250	$215	*$966*

* ***A-Bolt Stainless Stalker II with BOSS*** – various cals. between .22-250 Rem. and .375 H&H, 22, 23 (new 2002, .300 WSM cal. only), 24 (.375 H&H cal. only) or 26 (Mag. cals. only) in. barrel with BOSS. Approx. 6 1/4 - 7 lbs.

MSR $1,240	$995	$750	$525	$400	$350	$300	$285	

Add $30 for normal Mag. or WSM cals., or $51 for WSSM cals. (mfg. 2004-2007).
Add $30 for left-hand action.

A-BOLT CARBON FIBER STAINLESS STALKER II – .22-250 Rem. or .300 Win. Mag. cal., features Christensen lightweight 22 or 26 in. carbon fiber barrel with steel liner, stainless steel action, black synthetic stock, 4 or 5 shot mag., approx. 6 1/4 or 7 1/4 lbs. Mfg. 2000-2001.

	$1,475	$1,225	$975	$860	$700	$600	$500	*$1,750*

A-BOLT COMPOSITE STALKER II – various cals. between .22-250 Rem. - .338 Win. Mag., similar to Composite Stalker with A-Bolt II improvements, 22, 23 (WSM cals. only), 24, or 26 (Mag. cals. only) in. barrel without sights, 6 lbs. 1 oz. - 7 lbs. 3 oz. Mfg. 1994-2007.

	$595	$525	$400	$350	$300	$250	$225	*$719*

Add $30 for all Mag. cals.

* ***A-Bolt Composite Stalker II WSSM*** – .223 WSSM, .25 WSSM (new 2004), or .243 WSSM cal., 3 shot mag., super short action, 21 (disc.) or 22 in. barrel, black composite stock with matte blued metal and smaller dimensions, 6.1 lbs. Mfg. 2003-2007.

	$650	$535	$435	$380	$335	$295	$260	*$770*

* ***A-Bolt Composite Stalker II with BOSS*** – various cals., 22, 23 (WSM cals. only), or 26 (Mag. cals. only) in. barrel with BOSS, 6 lbs., 6 oz. - 7 lbs., 3 oz.

MSR $1,000	$815	$625	$525	$425	$350	$300	$275	

Add $30 for standard Mag. and WSM cals., or $51 for WSSM cals. (mfg. 2004-2007).

A-BOLT VARMINT STALKER II – .22-250 Rem. or .223 Rem. (SSA only beginning 2004) cal., 24 or 26 (.22-250 Rem. cal. only) in. heavy barrel, features Dura-Touch armor coated composite stock with slight palm swell, matte blue metal, 4 or 6 shot mag., approx. 7 3/4 lbs. Mfg. 2002-2008.

	$715	$575	$450	$360	$300	$255	$230	*$895*

* ***A-Bolt Varmint Stalker II WSSM*** – .223 WSSM, .25 WSSM (new 2004), or .243 WSSM cal., 3 shot mag., super short action, 21 (mfg. 2003 only) or 24 (new 2004) in. barrel, features Dura-Touch armor coated composite stock with slight palm swell, matte blue metal, 7 lbs., 13 oz. Mfg. 2003-2007.

	$745	$580	$475	$395	$335	$295	$275	*$928*

A-BOLT II MOUNTAIN TI – .243 Win. (new 2006), .308 Win. (new 2006), 7mm-08 Rem. (new 2006), .270 WSM, .300 WSM, 7mm WSM, .223 WSSM (mfg. 2005-2010), .243 WSSM (mfg. 2005-2010), .25 WSSM (mfg. 2005-2010), or .325 WSM (new 2006) cal., features titanium short action receiver with composite bolt sleeve and stainless steel 23 in. barrel, fiberglass Bell & Carlson stock with Mossy Oak New Break-Up or Break-Up Infinity (new 2010) camo and Dura-Touch armor coating, Pachmayr Decelerator recoil pad, approx. 5 1/2 lbs. Mfg. 2004-2011.

	$1,565	$1,225	$985	$850	$725	$625	$525	*$1,960*

Add $30 for WSM cals.

GRADING - PPGS™	100%	98%	95%	90%	80%	70%	60%	LAST MSR

A-BOLT II GREYWOLF – .25-06 Rem., .270 Win., .280 Rem., .30-06, .300 Win. Mag., .338 Win. Mag., or 7mm Rem. Mag. cal., stainless steel, classic sporter with select walnut stock. Limited mfg. during 1994 only.

	$850	$675	$595	$525	$450	$400	$350	*$935*

A-BOLT TARGET II – .223 Rem., .308 Win., .300 WSM cal., 28 in. heavy contour bull barrel, 4 or 6 shot mag., matte blue finish, satin grey checkered laminated wood stock with adj. comb, right-hand palm swell, drilled and tapped, 13 lbs. New 2009.

MSR $1,480	$1,200	$925	$750	$650	$550	$450	$395	

Add $20 for .300 WSM cal.

* ***A-Bolt Target Stainless II*** – .223 Rem., .308 Win., .300 WSM cal., similar to A-Bolt Target, except has 28 in. stainless steel barrel. New 2009.

MSR $1,730	$1,425	$1,225	$1,050	$900	$775	$675	$575	

Add $50 for .300 WSM cal.

RIFLES: BOLT ACTION, CENTERFIRE X-BOLT SERIES

The X-Bolt Series was introduced during 2008, and features a new three-lever Feather trigger system, which is adjustable from 3-5 lbs. It also has a 3-4 shot detachable rotary mag., 60-degree bolt lift, top safety with bolt unlock button feature, free floating barrel, X-lock scope mounting system (four screws per base, instead of two), and a soft recoil pad using Inflex technology. The various models listed all have these features.

X-BOLT HUNTER – various cals. in both super short, short, and long action, right or left (new 2011) hand action, satin finished walnut stock with checkering, low luster blue finish, 22-26 in. barrel (depending on caliber) w/o sights, 3 or 5 shot mag., approx. 6 1/2 - 7 lbs. New 2008.

MSR $1,000	$775	$625	$500	$425	$375	$325	$295	

Subtract approx. $100 for 2008-2012 mfg. w/o raised cheekpiece on stock.
Add $40 for standard Mag. or WSM cals.
Add $20 for left-hand action (new 2011).

During 2013, this model became available throught Full Line Browning dealers only. The only difference is that models made from 2008-2012 have stocks without a cheekpiece, while the Full Line dealer model has a raised cheekpiece.

X-BOLT MICRO MIDAS – .22-.250 Rem., .243 Win., .308 Win., or 7mm-08 Rem. cal., short or super short action, low luster bluing with satin finished stock, 20 in. barrel w/o sights, 4 shot mag., 12 1/2 in. LOP stock, approx. 6 lbs. New 2011.

MSR $840	$675	$550	$475	$425	$360	$310	$275	

X-BOLT MICRO HUNTER – various cals., 20 or 22 in. blue barrel, right or left (new 2011) hand action, 3 or 4 shot mag., low luster blue finish, satin finished walnut stock, smaller dimensions, drilled and tapped, approx. 6 lbs. New 2009.

MSR $900	$715	$575	$465	$415	$360	$310	$275	

Add $40 for Standard Mag. or WSM cals.
Add $20 for left-hand action (new 2011).

X-BOLT RMEF SPECIAL HUNTER – .325 WSM cal., 23 in. steel barrel, 3 shot mag., low luster blue finish, checkered satin finished walnut stock with raised cheekpiece, rosewood grip cap with RMEF logo inset, drilled and tapped, 6 lbs., 14 oz. New 2009.

MSR $1,100	$875	$700	$525	$475	$425	$350	$325	

X-BOLT RMEF WHITE GOLD – .325 WSM cal., 23 in. stainless barrel, 3 shot mag., gold engraved matte finished receiver, drilled and tapped, checkered select gloss finish walnut stock with raised cheekpiece, rosewood grip cap, RMEF logo inset, 7 lbs., 3 oz. New 2009.

MSR $1,500	$1,075	$925	$785	$650	$575	$500	$450	

X-BOLT MEDALLION – similar to X-Bolt Hunter, except has a gloss finished walnut stock with rosewood pistol grip and forend caps, right or left (new 2011) hand action, 3-5 shot mag. New 2008.

MSR $1,030	$860	$675	$550	$450	$375	$325	$275	

GRADING - PPGS™	100%	98%	95%	90%	80%	70%	60%	LAST MSR

Add $40 for standard Mag., WSM, or .375 H&H (new 2012) cals.
Add $30 for left-hand action (new 2011).

X-BOLT WHITE GOLD – various cals., 22, 23, 24, or 26 in. barrel, 3-5 shot mag., stainless steel free floating receiver and barrel, scroll engraving, gloss finished walnut stock with rosewood forend grip and pistol grip cap, drilled and tapped, 6 lbs., 8 oz. - 7 lbs. New 2010.

MSR $1,400	$1,195	$1,050	$935	$850	$725	$600	$525	

Add $40 for Mag. cals.

X-BOLT COMPOSITE STALKER – similar cals. as X-Bolt Hunter, features matte black composite stock with palm swell and DuraTouch Armor coating, matte blued steel receiver and barrel, 22-26 in. barrel w/o sights, 3-5 shot mag., 6 lbs. 5 oz. - 6 lbs. 13 oz. New 2008.

MSR $840	$675	$550	$475	$415	$360	$310	$275	

Add $40 for standard Mag. or WSM cals.

X-BOLT STAINLESS STALKER – similar to X-Bolt Composite, except has matte finished stainless steel receiver and barrel. New 2008.

MSR $1,120	$925	$750	$625	$525	$425	$375	$350	

Add $40 for regular Mag. or WSM cals. or $40 for .375 H&H with open sights (new 2011).

X-BOLT VARMINT STALKER – .22-250 Rem., .223 Rem., .243 Win., or .308 Win. cal., 24 or 26 in. heavy blue barrel, low luster blue finish, 4 or 5 shot mag., matte black checkered composite stock with DuraTouch Armor coating and palm swell, approx. 8 lbs. New 2009.

MSR $1,120	$925	$750	$625	$525	$425	$375	$350	

RIFLES: BOLT ACTION, RIMFIRE A-BOLT SERIES

A-BOLT GRADE I RIMFIRE – .22 LR or .22 WMR (new 1989) cal., 60 degree bolt throw, 22 in. barrel, checkered walnut stock and forearm or laminated stock (scarce - approx. 1,500 mfg., 390 had no sights), 5 or 15 (optional) shot mag., adj. trigger, available with or without open sights, 5 lbs. 9 oz. Mfg. 1986-96.

* ***A-Bolt Grade I .22 LR cal.***

	$575	$495	$425	$350	$295	$250	$210	*$425*

Add $14 for open sights.

A 15 shot mag. was also available for this model at $45 retail.

* ***A-Bolt Grade I .22 WMR cal.***

	$650	$550	$450	$375	$325	$295	$250	*$493*

Add $21 for open sights.

A-BOLT GOLD MEDALLION RIMFIRE – .22 LR cal. only, similar to A-Bolt, except has high grade select walnut stock checkered 22 lines per inch, rosewood pistol and forend cap, high gloss finish, gold filled lettering and moderate engraving, solid recoil pad. Mfg. 1988-96.

	$625	$550	$450	$385	$325	$295	$250	*$567*

RIFLES: LEVER ACTION

BL-17 – .17 Mach 2 cal., otherwise similar to the BL-22, 5 lbs., 2 oz. New 2005.

* ***BL-17 Grade I*** – uncheckered stock with choice of blued or nickel (BL-17 Field) receiver, blued trigger. Mfg. 2005.

	$420	$370	$315	$285	$230	$190	$145	*$484*

Add $32 for nickel.

* ***BL-17 Grade II*** – features choice of engraved blued or nickel (Field) receiver, gold trigger, checkered stock and forearm. Mfg. 2005.

	$465	$405	$350	$315	$255	$210	$165	*$524*

Add $53 for nickel.

* ***BL-17 Grade II Field Octagon*** – similar to BL-22 Classic/Field octagon, 5 lbs., 6 oz., mfg. 2005 by Miroku.

	$750	$675	$600	$550	$400	$325	$250	*$744*

GRADING - PPGS™	100%	98%	95%	90%	80%	70%	60%	LAST MSR

BL-22 GRADE I – .22 S, L, and LR cal., 20 in. barrel, short throw (33 degree) lever, folding leaf sight, 15 shot (LR) mag., blue finish, exposed hammer, Western style gloss finished uncheckered stock and forearm, 5 lbs. Mfg. 1970-2003 by Miroku.

	$450	$395	$325	$280	$230	$185	$145	*$436*

* ***BL-22 Grade I (Classic/Field)*** – similar to BL-22 Grade I, except has choice of gloss or satin finished stock and forearm, 20 in. barrel, blue or nickel (new 2005) receiver. New 1999, mfg. by Miroku.

MSR $620	$485	$400	$350	$300	$240	$195	$150	

Add $40 for satin nickel finished frame and satin finished stock (Field, new 2005).

The satin nickel model is available through Full-Line and Medallion dealers only.

* ***BL-22 Grade I Micro Midas*** – .22 LR cal. only, features 19 3/8 in. barrel, 12 shot mag., and shortened 12 in. LOP uncheckered stock, 4 3/4 lbs. New 2011.

MSR $530	$435	$365	$315	$280	$230	$185	$150	

* ***BL-22 Grade I NRA*** – similar to BL-22 Grade I, except has NRA logo laser engraved in stock. Mfg. 2006-2007.

	$485	$400	$340	$305	$250	$205	$160	*$514*

BL-22 GRADE II – same general specifications as BL-22, except scroll engraved blue receiver and deluxe high gloss checkered walnut stock and forearm. Disc. 2003.

	$550	$475	$395	$325	$275	$225	$175	*$494*

* ***BL-22 Grade II (Classic/Field)*** – similar to BL-22 Grade II, except has choice of gloss or satin finished stock and forearm, engraved blue or nickel (new 2005) receiver. New 1999, mfg. by Miroku.

MSR $700	$565	$485	$400	$350	$275	$225	$175	

Add $50 for satin nickel receiver and satin finished stock and forearm (Field, new 2005).

This model is available through Full-Line and Medallion dealers only.

* ***BL-22 Grade II Classic/Field Octagon*** – features 24 in. octagon barrel and silver nitride finished receiver with scroll engraving, adj. buckhorn rear sight, checkered satin finished stock and forearm, 5 1/4 lbs. New 2004, mfg. by Miroku.

MSR $980	$815	$700	$575	$500	$400	$350	$295	

This model is available through Full-Line and Medallion dealers only.

MODEL 53 DELUXE LIMITED EDITION – .32-20 WCF cal. (round nose or hollow point bullets only), patterned after the original Winchester Model 53 (redesigned Model 1892), 7 shot tube mag., high polished blue metal, open sights, 22 in. tapered barrel, high grade checkered walnut stock featuring full pistol grip cap and shotgun style metal buttplate, 6 1/2 lbs. Only 5,000 mfg. in 1990.

	$925	$795	$675	N/A	N/A	N/A	N/A	*$675*

MODEL 65 GRADE I LIMITED EDITION – .218 Bee cal., patterned after the Winchester Model 65, round tapered 24 in. barrel, open sights (hooded front), blue metal finish, 7 shot tube mag., uncheckered pistol grip stock and semi-beavertail forearm, metal buttplate, 6 3/4 lbs. 3,500 total mfg. for Grade I in 1989 only, inventory depleted in 1990.

	$725	$625	$525	N/A	N/A	N/A	N/A	*$550*

* ***Model 65 High Grade*** – greyed receiver (and lever) with scroll engraving and gold plated animals, gold plated trigger, deluxe checkered walnut stock and semi-beavertail forearm. 1,500 total mfg. in 1989, inventory depleted in 1990.

	$1,050	$925	$800	N/A	N/A	N/A	N/A	*$850*

MODEL 71 LIMITED EDITION CARBINE – .348 Win. cal., reproduction of the Winchester Model 71 Carbine, 20 in. barrel, open sights, 4 shot mag., 8 lbs. New 1987 with inventory depleted in 1990.

* ***Model 71 Limited Edition Carbine Grade I*** – uncheckered satin finished walnut stock and forearm. 4,000 mfg. 1986-87 only.

	$875	$750	$650	N/A	N/A	N/A	N/A	*$600*

GRADING - PPGS™	100%	98%	95%	90%	80%	70%	60%	LAST MSR

* ***Model 71 Limited Edition Carbine High Grade*** – deluxe checkered walnut stock and forearm with high gloss finish, scroll engraved grey receiver with gold inlays and trigger. 3,000 mfg. 1986-1987 only.

$1,325	$1,075	$925	N/A	N/A	N/A	N/A	$980

MODEL 71 LIMITED EDITION RIFLE – .348 Win. cal., reproduction of the Winchester Model 71 Rifle, 24 in. barrel, open sights, 4 shot mag., 8 lbs. 2 oz. Mfg. 1986-87 only with inventory depleted in 1990.

* ***Model 71 Grade I Rifle*** – uncheckered satin finished walnut stock and forearm. 3,000 mfg. 1986-1987 only.

$895	$775	$675	N/A	N/A	N/A	N/A	$600

* ***Model 71 High Grade Rifle*** – deluxe checkered walnut stock and forearm with high gloss finish, scroll engraved grey receiver with gold inlays and trigger. 3,000 mfg. 1986-1987 only.

$1,425	$1,175	$900	N/A	N/A	N/A	N/A	$980

MODEL BLR SHORT ACTION – .22-250 Rem., .222 Rem. (disc. 1989), .223 Rem., .243 Win., .257 Roberts (disc. 1992), 7mm-08 Rem., .284 Win. (disc. 1994), .308 Win., or .358 Win. (disc. 1992) cal., steel receiver, rotary bolt locking lugs, 20 in. barrel with band, 3 (.284 Win. only) or 4 shot detachable mag., adj. rear sight, checkered straight grip stock, recoil pad, no sights optional 1988-89, approx. 7 lbs. Mfg. 1970-1981.

.243 Win. and .308 Win. cals. are the most popular in this model.

* ***Model BLR USA*** – .243 Win. or .308 Win. cal., this model was originally scheduled to be manufactured by TRW in Cleveland, OH for Browning. Originally assembled in 1966, these rifles are considered prototypes as they were never sold through regular channels and at one time were scheduled to be destroyed. Approx. 50-250 of these rifles exist, some still NIB.

$995	$870	$745	$675	$545	$450	$350

This variation has a 2-line legend on the right side marked "MADE IN USA" and "PATENT PENDING". This model is dangerous to operate and should not be fired.

* ***Model BLR Belgian*** – .243 Win. or .308 Win. cal., mfg. was moved to FN in Belgium with original assembly beginning 1969 and concluding in 1973. This FN model included a number of small dimensioning and engraving changes.

$925	$810	$695	$630	$510	$415	$325

* ***Model BLR Japan*** – .243 Win. or .308 Win. cal., mfg. was moved to Miroku in Japan 1974-1980. Early guns during 1974 had stocks with impressed checkering. By 1975, cut checkering and gloss wood finish was used on stocks and forearms. Last ser. no. for Belgian production was 27,XXX. Japanese mfg. started with ser. no. 30,000.

$775	$675	$575	$525	$425	$350	$275	$550

Add $40 without sights (scarce).

MODEL BLR '81 SHORT ACTION (MIROKU) – similar cals. and features as Model BLR short action, mfg. 1981-1995 by Miroku in Japan.

Standard cals.	$700	$625	$550	$450	$375	$300	$230	
.257 Roberts	$900	$790	$675	$610	$495	$405	$315	
.284 Win./.358 Win.	$900	$790	$675	$610	$495	$405	$315	
.222 Rem.	$1,550	$1,355	$1,165	$1,055	$855	$700	$545	$550

MODEL BLR '81 LONG ACTION – .270 Win., .30-06, or 7mm Rem Mag. cal., incorporates distinct design changes, 22 or 24 in. barrel, approx. 8 1/2 lbs. Mfg. 1991-95 by Miroku.

$750	$655	$565	$510	$415	$340	$265	$580

NEW MODEL LIGHTNING BLR (SHORT ACTION) – .22-250 Rem., .223 Rem. (disc. 1998), .243 Win., 7mm-08 Rem., or .308 Win. cal., rotary bolt locking lugs, 20 in. barrel w/o barrel band, similar action as the BLR 81, but features aluminum alloy receiver, checkered pistol grip stock and forearm, rack and pinion geared slide, fold down hammer, trigger

GRADING - PPGS™	100%	98%	95%	90%	80%	70%	60%	LAST MSR

travels with lever, 3-5 shot detachable mag., adj. rear sight, approx. 6 1/2 lbs. Mfg. by Miroku late 1995 - 2002.

	$625	$545	$470	$425	$345	$280	$220	*$681*

* ***BLR Lightweight Stainless Short Action*** – various cals., similar to BLR Lightweight Short Action, except has 20 or 22 in. stainless steel barrel, pistol grip stock, 6 1/2 - 7 lbs. New 2010.

MSR $1,100	$895	$775	$635	$565	$450	$365	$285	

Add $80 for WSM cals.
Add $130 for takedown.

NEW MODEL LIGHTNING BLR (LONG ACTION) – .270 Win., .30-06, .300 Win. Mag. (new 1997), or 7mm Rem. Mag. cal., 22 or 24 (Mag. cals.) in. barrel, approx. 7 1/4 - 7 3/4 lbs. Mfg. by Miroku 1995-2002.

	$650	$570	$490	$440	$360	$295	$230	*$721*

* ***BLR Lightweight Stainless Long Action*** – various cals., similar to BLR Lightweight Short Action, except has 20 (disc.), 22, or 24 in. stainless steel barrel, pistol grip stock, 7 1/4 or 7 3/4 lbs. New 2010.

MSR $1,150	$925	$785	$660	$600	$475	$390	$305	

Add $130 for takedown.

BLR LIGHTWEIGHT '81 (SHORT ACTION) – .22-.250 Rem., .223 Rem. (new 2010), .243 Win., .270 WSM (new 2004), 7mm-08 Rem., .325 WSM (pistol grip only, new 2005), .300 WSM (new 2004), 7mm WSM (new 2004), .308 Win., .358 Win., or .450 Marlin cal., 20 or 22 (WSM cals. only) in. barrel with barrel band, solid or takedown (new 2007) action, aluminum alloy receiver, choice of checkered Model 81 styled straight grip and forearm with gloss finish or checkered, gloss finished pistol grip with Schnabel forearm w/o barrel band (new 2005) stock, sling swivels (pistol grip only), rack and pinion geared slide with rotating breech head, fold down hammer, trigger travels with lever, 3-4 shot detachable mag., adj. rear sight, approx. 6 1/2 - 7 lbs. Mfg. by Miroku beginning 2003.

MSR $960	$775	$650	$540	$480	$380	$315	$245	

Add $80 for WSM cals. (new 2004).
Add $60 for checkered pistol grip stock and Schnabel forearm (new 2005).
Add $80 for takedown action (new 2007).
Add $70 for one-piece scope mount (new 2007).

BLR LIGHTWEIGHT '81 (LONG ACTION) – .270 Win., .30-06, .300 Win. Mag., or 7mm Rem. Mag. cal., 22 or 24 in. barrel, 7 1/4 or 7 3/4 lbs. Mfg. by Miroku beginning 2003.

MSR $1,020	$845	$725	$600	$540	$440	$350	$270	

Add $80 for takedown action (new 2007).
Add $60 for checkered pistol grip and Schnabel forend.

MODEL 1886 LIMITED EDITION GRADE I RIFLE – .45-70 Govt. cal. only, patterned after the Winchester Model 1886, blue receiver, 26 in. octagon barrel, 8 shot full mag., crescent buttplate, open sights. 7,000 mfg. 1986 only.

	$1,250	$1,075	$950	N/A	N/A	N/A	N/A	*$578*

* ***Model 1886 Limited Edition High Grade Rifle*** – same general specifications as Model 1886, except has checkered high grade walnut stock and forearm, greyed steel receiver, with game scene engraving including elk and American Bison, gold accenting with "1 of 3,000" engraved on top of barrel. 3,000 mfg. 1986 only.

	$2,050	$1,795	$1,540	N/A	N/A	N/A	N/A	*$935*

* ***Model 1886 Montana Centennial Rifle*** – similar to Model 1886 High Grade. 2,000 mfg. 1989 only to commemorate Montana Centennial.

	$1,975	$1,730	$1,480	N/A	N/A	N/A	N/A	*$935*

MODEL 1886 LIMITED EDITION GRADE I CARBINE – .45-70 Govt. cal. only, saddle ring carbine, patterned after the Winchester Model 1886 Carbine, blue receiver, 22 in. round barrel, 7 shot full mag., crescent buttplate, open sights. 7,000 total mfg. 1992-93.

	$1,095	$925	$800	N/A	N/A	N/A	N/A	*$750*

GRADING - PPGS™	100%	98%	95%	90%	80%	70%	60%	LAST MSR

* ***Model 1886 Limited Edition High Grade Carbine*** – same general specifications as Model 1886, except has checkered high grade walnut stock and forearm, greyed steel receiver, with game scene engraving including bear and elk, gold accenting, 3,000 total mfg. 1992-93.

	$1,695	$1,485	$1,270	N/A	N/A	N/A	N/A	*$1,175*

B-92 CARBINE – .357 Mag. or .44 Rem. Mag. cal., 20 in. barrel, patterned after the Winchester Model 92, 11 shot mag. (tubular), blue finish. Disc. 1986.

	$600	$525	$450	$410	$330	$270	$210	*$342*

Add 25% for .357 Mag. cal.

* ***B-92 Centennial*** – .44 Mag. cal., 6,000 mfg. in 1978.

	$685	$600	$515	N/A	N/A	N/A	N/A	*$220*

* ***B-92 BCA Commemorative*** – mfg. to commemorate BCA's third anniversary.

	$750	$650	$550	N/A	N/A	N/A	N/A	

MODEL 1895 LIMITED EDITION GRADE I – .30/40 Krag or .30-06 cal. only, patterned after the Winchester Model 1895, blue receiver, 24 in. barrel, 4 shot mag. (box type), select walnut, rear buckhorn sight, 8 lbs. Mfg. 1984 only.

.30/40 Krag	$925	$800	$700	N/A	N/A	N/A	N/A	
.30-06	$875	$750	$650	N/A	N/A	N/A	N/A	

Production totaled 6,000 in the .30-06 cal. and 2,000 in .30/40 Krag for this model.

* ***Model 1895 Limited Edition High Grade*** – same general specifications as Model 1895, except gold plated game scenes on satin finish receiver, gold trigger, and finely checkered select French walnut.

	$1,625	$1,420	$1,220	N/A	N/A	N/A	N/A	

Production totaled 1,000 in the .30-06 cal. and 1,000 in .30/40 Krag for this model.

RIFLES: O/U

Currently, the Browning Custom Shop in Belgium is producing the CCS25 double rifle in the following grades: B2E ($15,059 MSR), B5 ($15,059), D5G ($32,435 MSR), M1 ($43,343 MSR), Bavarian ($17,280 MSR), CCS Herstal ($11,150 MSR), and the 375 H&H African Classic ($27,256 MSR).

Previous custom shop models included: CCS Africa ($15,266 last MSR, disc. 2005), Bavarian ($25,149 last MSR), CCS25 D5G ($43,665 last MSR), and the M1 ($57,498 last MSR).

EXPRESS RIFLE – .270 Win., .30-06 cal., or 9.3x74R cal., Superposed Superlight style action. 24 in. barrels, checkered straight grip stock and forearm, auto ejectors, Fleur-de-lis engraving, single trigger, folding leaf rear sight, 6 lbs. 14 oz., cased. Disc. 1986.

	$6,000	$5,500	$4,775	$4,250	$3,500	$2,750	$2,250	*$3,125*

GRADE I CONTINENTAL SET – includes .30-06 O/U rifle barrels with extra set of 20 ga. O/U shotgun barrels (26 1/2 in.), rifle barrels are 24 in., 20 ga. frame, SST, ejectors, blue receiver with scroll engraving, straight grip checkered stock and forearm, supplied with 2 barrel takedown case. Mfg. 1978-86.

	$7,500	$6,500	$5,500	$4,850	$3,925	$3,225	$2,500	

RIFLES: SEMI-AUTO, .22 LR

Miroku manufactured .22s can be determined by year of manufacture in the following manner: RV suffix - 1975, RT - 1976, RR - 1977, RP - 1978, RN - 1979, PM - 1980, PZ - 1981, PY - 1982, PX - 1983, PW - 1984, PV - 1985, PT -1986, PR - 1987, PP - 1988, PN - 1989, NM - 1990, NZ - 1991, NY - 1992, NX - 1993, NW - 1994, NV - 1995, NT - 1996, NR - 1997, NP - 1998, NN - 1999, MM - 2000, MZ - 2001, MY - 2002, MX - 2003, MW - 2004, MV - 2005, MU - 2006, MT - 2007, MS - 2008, MN - 2009, ZM - 2010, ZZ - 2011, ZY - 2012, ZX - 2013, ZW - 2014.

Currently, the Browning Custom Shop in Belgium is making the following .22 LR cal. semi-auto models: Grade II ($2,386 MSR), and the Grade III ($3,407 MSR).

On the following FN (Belgian mfg.) models, add approx. 10% if in NIB condition.

GRADING - PPGS™	100%	98%	95%	90%	80%	70%	60%	LAST MSR

AUTO RIFLE GRADES I - VI – .22 LR or .22 Short (FN only, disc. - rare) cal., takedown design, 10 shot (16 for .22 Short) tube mag. in buttstock, 19 1/4 in. barrel for all .22 LR, .22 Shorts had various barrel lengths according to mfg. year: 19 1/4 in. for 1956, 22 3/8 in. for 1957, and 22 in. from 1958 until general production was disc. in 1983, checkered pistol grip stock, semi-beavertail forearm, stock has hole machined halfway to allow partial filling of tube mag., adj. folding rear or earlier wheel sight, grades differ in finish, amount of engraving, and quality of wood, 4 3/4-5 3/4 lbs. Early top loaders were mfg. from 1914 until approx. 1955. Modern tube loader mfg. 1956 to 1974 by FN Belgium. Mfg. beginning 1976 by Miroku in Japan.

* ***Auto Rifle Grade I - FN (Belgian Mfg.)***

	100%	98%	95%	90%	80%	70%	60%
	$875	$750	$650	$550	$450	$400	$350

Add 50% for guns in .22 Short cal., if in 98% or better condition.
Add 25% for wheel sight guns if in 98% or better condition.

FN Postwar Grade Is have a lightly engraved blue steel receiver, checkered walnut, blue trigger, and a variety of rear sights.

» **Auto Rifle Grade I - FN Custom Shop**

	100%	98%	95%	90%	80%	70%	60%
	$995	$900	$750	$650	$525	$450	$375

Add 10% for .22 Short cal.

* ***Auto Rifle Grade I - Miroku (Japan Mfg.)*** – .22 LR cal., 19 3/8 in. barrel, polished blue receiver finish with scroll engraving, gloss finished checkered walnut stock and forearm, 10 shot mag., approx. 5 1/4 lbs.

	100%	98%	95%	90%	80%	70%	60%
MSR $700	$535	$465	$385	$340	$275	$225	$175

* ***Auto Rifle Grade II - FN (Belgian Mfg.)***

	100%	98%	95%	90%	80%	70%	60%
	$1,650	$1,375	$1,100	$975	$825	$675	$525

Add $100 for guns initialed by the engraver.
Add $200 for guns fully signed by the engraver.
Add $150 for original box.
Add 35% for Grade II with wheel sight.
Add 50% for guns in .22 Short cal., if in 95% or better condition.

FN Grade IIs have grey receiver, deluxe wood with finer checkering, gold plated trigger, and engraving depicting two squirrels and two prairie dogs. Unsigned, signed, or initialed by engraver.

» **Auto Rifle Grade II - FN Custom Shop**

	100%	98%	95%	90%	80%	70%	60%
	$1,895	$1,500	$1,250	$1,050	$825	$675	$525

Add 10% for .22 Short cal.

* ***Auto Rifle Grade II - Miroku (Japan Mfg.)*** – disc. 1984.

	100%	98%	95%	90%	80%	70%	60%
	$795	$675	$575	$525	$425	$350	$275

Add $50 for original box.

* ***Auto Rifle Grade III - FN (Belgian Mfg.)***

	100%	98%	95%	90%	80%	70%	60%
	$3,300	$2,925	$2,500	$2,275	$1,950	$1,575	$1,225

Add 15% for guns signed by the engraver.
Add $200 for original box.
Add 50% for guns in .22 Short cal., if in 98% or better condition.

FN Grade IIIs have coin finish or grey chromed receiver, extra deluxe walnut with skipline checkering, gold plated trigger, and more elaborate game scene engraving usually featuring a dog flushing ducks or upland game. Signed or unsigned by engraver (Funken, J. Baerten, Vrancken, and Watrin will command premiums over values listed). A few were also special ordered with blue finish and special engraving - these command an extra premium.

» **Auto Rifle Grade III - FN Custom Shop**

	100%	98%	95%	90%	80%	70%	60%
	$3,500	$3,100	$2,600	$2,350	$2,000	$1,600	$1,250

Add 15% for guns signed by the engraver.
Add 50% for "transition" guns signed by FN engravers with barrels and boxes marked "Made in Japan."

GRADING - PPGS™	100%	98%	95%	90%	80%	70%	60%	LAST MSR

* ***Auto Rifle Grade III - Miroku (Japan Mfg.)*** – disc. 1983.

	$1,550	$1,375	$1,275	$995	$800	$675	$525	

* ***Auto Rifle Grade VI - Miroku (Japan Mfg.)*** – game scene engraved with gold plated animals (typically fox and squirrel on receiver sides), choice of blue or greyed receiver, deluxe walnut. New 1987.

MSR $1,580	$1,250	$1,050	$895	$795	$650	$550	$450	

Add at least 50% for small run of .22 Short cal. Grade VI mfg. during 2003.

* ***Auto Rifle Grade VI 125th Anniversary Miroku*** – features silver nitride receiver with gold enhanced 125th Anniversary logo and delicate scroll engraving. 500 mfg. 2003-2004.

	$1,275	$975	$795	N/A	N/A	N/A	N/A	*$1,271*

BAR-22 – .22 LR cal., 20 1/4 in. barrel, 15 shot tube mag., folding leaf sight, high polish steel receiver, checkered pistol grip stock, 5 lbs. 13 oz. Mfg. 1977-85 by Miroku.

	$695	$625	$550	$450	$350	$300	$250	*$245*

BAR-22 GRADE II – engraved model of BAR-22 featuring game scenes on silver greyed steel receiver, select French walnut. Disc. 1985.

	$1,050	$925	$775	$725	$575	$450	$350	*$350*

BUCK MARK RIFLE – .22 LR cal., Buck Mark pistol blowback action, 18 in. tapered barrel with Hi-Viz fiber optic sights (Sporter Rifle), heavy barrel w/o sights (Target or Field Target Rifle), or carbon composite barrel (disc. 2006), includes integral scope rail, uncheckered walnut or grey laminate (new 2002, no sights) Monte Carlo stock that attaches to non-detachable, one-piece skeletonized and enclosed rear grip assembly, separate forearm, 10 shot mag., 3 lbs. 10 oz. (Classic Carbon -disc. 2006), 4 lbs. 6 oz. (Sporter) or approx. 5 1/2 lbs. (Target & Classic Target). New 2001.

MSR $670	$525	$465	$385	$340	$275	$225	$175	

Add $20 for grey laminate stock (Classic/Field Target Rifle, new 2002).
Add $95 for carbon composite barrel (disc. 2006).

The Buck Mark Classic/Field Target with grey laminate stock & Classic/Field Carbon Rifles are available through Full-Line and Medallion dealers only.

RIFLES: SEMI-AUTO, BAR SERIES

Currently, the Browning Custom Shop in Belgium is making the following BAR custom shop rifles: Grade 4 VB ($9,086 MSR), Grade 4 PH ($9,086 MSR). Until 2006, the Custom Shop produced the Grade D ($6,543 last MSR).

BROWNING PATENT 1900 – please refer to model listing under F.N.

BAR SEMI-AUTO – .243 Win., .270 Win., .280 Rem. (new 1990), .308 Win., or .30-06 cal. available in standard model, Mag. cals. include 7mm Rem., .300 Win., and .338 Win. Mag. (reintroduced 1990), gas operated, blued steel receiver, 22 or 24 (Mag. only) in. barrel, rotary bolt with seven lugs, folding leaf sight, walnut stock, grades differ in engraving, finish, and quality of wood, in 1993, to celebrate the 25th Anniversary of the BAR, Browning introduced the BAR MK II Safari (see model listing), approx. 7 lbs. 6 oz. New 1967 (includes BAR MK II).

Add 20% for FN mfg. and assembled BARs (marked "Made in Belgium").
Add 10% for .338 Win. Mag. cal. (FN mfg. only).

Note: Original .338s were limited production, mostly seen in the deluxe Grade II only. During the last year of FN .338 production, several were delivered in a Grade I by FN. Although being rarer than the Grade II, it is not as desirable. The following prices are for Portuguese assembled guns, manufactured by FN, and so stamped on the barrel.

* ***BAR Grade I*** – standard grade without engraving, blue finish. Ordering this model without sights became an option in 1988. Disc. 1992.

	$725	$635	$545	$495	$400	$325	$250	*$633*

Add 15% for .280 Rem. cal. if in 98%+ condition.
Subtract $16 if without sights

FN mfg. and assembled Grade Is can be denoted by light scroll engraving on the receiver.

GRADING - PPGS™	100%	98%	95%	90%	80%	70%	60%	LAST MSR

* ***BAR Grade I Magnum*** – standard grade without engraving, with recoil pad, 8 lbs. 6 oz. Disc. 1992.

	$765	$675	$575	$525	$425	$350	$275	*$680*

Subtract $16 without sights.

Ordering this gun without sights became an option in 1988.

* ***BAR Grade II*** – blue receiver, engraved with big game heads. Mfg. 1967-74.

	$1,175	$1,025	$875	$800	$650	$525	$415	

This model was previously designated Deluxe.

* ***BAR Grade II Magnum*** – magnum version of Grade II. Mfg. 1967-74.

	$1,295	$1,100	$925	$875	$700	$550	$435	

* ***BAR Grade III*** – features antelope and deer game scenes etched on greyed steel receiver, select checkered stock and forearm. Disc. 1984.

	$1,750	$1,500	$1,275	$1,100	$950	$825	$725	

* ***BAR Grade III Magnum*** – magnum version of Grade III, features elk and moose game scenes. Disc. 1984.

	$1,850	$1,600	$1,375	$1,200	$1,050	$925	$825	

* ***BAR Grade IV*** – engraved satin finish greyed receiver depicts big game animal scenes and trigger guard, carved borders on checkering. Disc. 1989.

	$2,800	$2,500	$2,200	$1,825	$1,525	$1,275	$1,050	*$1,670*

* ***BAR Grade IV Magnum*** – magnum version of Grade IV. Disc. 1984.

	$2,950	$2,650	$2,350	$2,000	$1,650	$1,375	$1,150	*$1,720*

* ***BAR Grade V*** – more elaborate engraving than Grade IV, with gold inlays. Mfg. 1971-74.

	$6,500	$5,700	$4,900	$4,500	$3,515	$2,875	$2,250	

* ***BAR Grade V Magnum*** – magnum version of Grade V.

	$6,850	$5,995	$5,150	$4,650	$3,775	$3,075	$2,400	

BAR NORTH AMERICAN DEER RIFLE ISSUE – .30-06 cal. only, BAR style action with silver grey finish and engraved action, 600 total production, walnut cased with accessories. Disc. 1983 but were sold through 1989.

	$4,500	$3,950	$3,400	$3,100	N/A	N/A	N/A	*$3,550*

BAR MK II SAFARI – .22-250 Rem. (mfg. as prototype only during 1997), .25-06 Rem. (new 1997), .243 Win., .270 Win., .30-06, .308 Win., .270 Wby. Mag. (mfg. 1996-2000), 7mm Rem. Mag., .300 Win. Mag., or .338 Win. Mag. cal., improved BAR action featuring redesigned bolt release, new gas operating system, and reduced recoil, removable trigger assembly, 22, 23 (WSM cals. only, disc.), or 24 (Mag. cals. only) in. barrel with (adj. for windage and elevation) or without sights, BOSS became optional 1994, and is available with ported BOSS, (approx. 30% less recoil), or unported BOSS-CR (Conventional Recoil) muzzle brake, blue finish with scroll engraved receiver, checkered walnut stock and forearm, gold trigger, detachable 3 (.300 WSM cal. only), 4 (Mag. cals. only) or 5 shot box mag., approx. 7 lbs. 6 oz. except for Mag. cals. (8 lbs. 6 oz.). Mfg. by FN in Belgium. New 1993.

MSR $1,230	$995	$850	$725	$625	$525	$450	$375	

Add $120 for Mag. cals.

Add $19 for open sights (not available in .270 Wby. Mag., disc.).

The new BAR MK II Safari does not have interchangeable magazine capability with the older pre-1993 BARs.

* ***BAR Classic Mark II Safari*** – .270 Win. (disc. 2001), .270 WSM (new 2003), .30-06 (disc. 2001), 7mm Rem. Mag., (disc. 2001), 7mm WSM (new 2003), .300 Win. Mag. (disc. 2001), or .300 WSM (new 2002) cal., similar to BAR Mark II Safari, except has satin finished checkered stock and forearm, 7 lbs. 6 oz. or 8 lbs. 6 oz. Mfg. 1999-2003.

	$785	$685	$595	$525	$425	$350	$275	*$908*

Subtract approx. 10% for non-Mag. cals.

GRADING - PPGS™	100%	98%	95%	90%	80%	70%	60%	LAST MSR

Add $17 for open sights (disc. 2000).

This model was available through Full-line and Medallion dealers only.

* ***BAR Mark II Safari with BOSS*** – .243 Win. (disc. 1999), .308 Win. (disc. 1999), .270 Win., .270 WSM (new 2003), .30-06, 7mm Rem. Mag., 7mm WSM (new 2003), .300 Win. Mag., .300 WSM (new 2003), .338 Win. Mag. cal., similar to BAR MK II Safari, with BOSS (ballistic optimizing shooting system), no sights, approx. 7 1/2 or 8 1/2 lbs. New 1994.

MSR $1,390	$1,150	$995	$825	$725	$625	$525	$425	

Add $110 for Mag. and WSM cals.

* ***BAR Mark II Lightweight*** – .243 Win., .270 Win., .30-06, .308 Win., 7mm Rem. Mag. (new 1999), .300 Win. Mag. (new 1999), or .338 Win. Mag. (new 1999) cal., features alloy receiver and 20 or 24 (Mag. cals. only) in. barrel, matte wood and barrel finish, open sights, 7 lbs. 2 oz. or 7 lbs. 12 oz. Mfg. 1997-2003.

	$715	$625	$525	$475	$395	$325	$250	$850

Add $77 for Mag. cals. (new 1999).

* ***BAR MK II Lightweight with BOSS*** – 7mm Rem. Mag., .300 Win. Mag., or .338 Win. Mag. (disc. 1999) cal., similar to BAR Mark II Lightweight, except has 24 in. barrel with BOSS, 8 lbs., 6 oz. Mfg. 1999-2000.

	$800	$700	$600	$550	$450	$365	$275	$939

* ***BAR MK II Lightweight Stalker*** – .243 Win., .270 Win., .270 WSM (new 2003), .30-06, .308 Win., 7mm Rem. Mag. (disc. 2004), 7mm WSM (new 2003), .300 Win. Mag., .300 WSM (new 2002), or .338 Win. Mag. cal., similar to BAR Mark II Safari, except has aluminum alloy receiver and checkered black synthetic stock and forearm, matte metal finish, 20, 22, 23 (new 2002, WSM cals. only), or 24 (Mag. cals. only) in. barrel with open sights, 7 lbs. 2 oz. - 7 lbs. 12 oz. New 2001.

MSR $1,230	$995	$850	$725	$625	$525	$450	$375	

Add $110 for Mag. or WSM cals.

» ***BAR MK II Lightweight Stalker with BOSS*** – .270 WSM (new 2003), 7mm Rem. Mag., 7mm WSM (new 2003), .300 Win. Mag., .300 WSM (new 2002), or .338 Win. Mag. cal., similar to BAR Mark II Stalker, except has 23 (new 2002, WSM cals. only) or 24 in. barrel with BOSS, approx. 7 3/4 lbs. Mfg. 2001-2003.

	$835	$725	$625	$575	$450	$375	$295	$981

* ***BAR MK II High Grade*** – .270 Win., .30-06, .300 Win. Mag., or 7mm Rem. Mag. cal., satin finished receiver with either whitetail/mule deer or moose/elk etched game scenes and gold border, checkered high grade gloss finished walnut stock and forearm, no sights, 7 lbs. 6 oz. or 8 lbs. 6 oz. Mfg. 2001-2003.

	$1,475	$1,295	$1,100	$1,000	$815	$675	$515	$1,856

Add $58 for Mag. cals.

* ***BAR MK II Grade III*** – features Grade III engraving pattern. Mfg. by the FN custom shop 1996-99.

	$3,400	$2,975	$2,550	$2,300	$1,875	$1,525	$1,195	$3,754

* ***BAR MK II Grade IV*** – features Grade IV engraving pattern. Mfg. by the FN custom shop beginning 1996.

	$3,500	$3,075	$2,625	$2,375	$1,925	$1,575	$1,225	$3,859

BAR SHORTTRAC – .243 Win., .270 WSM, .300 WSM, .308 Win., 7mm-08 Rem. (new 2010), 7mm WSM, or .325 WSM (new 2009) cal., features new styling with black (disc. 2008) or satin nickel finished (new 2009) aluminum alloy gas operated short action receiver with light etching and gold Browning logo at rear, composite trigger guard and mag. floorplate, 22 or 23 in. hammer forged barrel w/o sights, mfg. in Belgium, drilled and tapped, checkered satin (disc. 2008) or oil (new 2009) finished walnut stock supplied with 6 adj. shims and squared off forearm, 3 or 4 shot detachable mag., 6 lbs. 10 oz (regular cals.) or 7 1/4 lbs. (WSM cals.). New 2004.

MSR $1,230	$995	$850	$725	$625	$525	$450	$375	

Add $110 for WSM cals. Add $40 for left-hand model with left-side ejection port.

GRADING - PPGS™	100%	98%	95%	90%	80%	70%	60%	LAST MSR

* ***BAR Shorttrac Stalker*** – similar to BAR Shorttrac, except has matte black metal finish and black composite stock and forearm. New 2006.

MSR $1,260	$1,050	$875	$750	$650	$525	$425	$325	

Add $90 for WSM cals.

* ***BAR Shorttrac Camo*** – similar to BAR Shorttrac, except has 100% Mossy Oak New Break Up (disc. 2009) or Break Up Infinity (new 2010) camo coverage. New 2007.

MSR $1,360	$1,175	$995	$850	$750	$650	$495	$375	

Add $120 for WSM cals.

BAR LONGTRAC – .270 Win., .30-06, .300 Win. Mag., or 7mm Rem. Mag. cal., similar to BAR Shorttrac, except has long action, 3 or 4 shot mag., 7 or 7 1/2 lbs. New 2004.

MSR $1,230	$995	$850	$725	$625	$525	$450	$375	

Add $90 for Mag. cals.
Add $40 for left-hand model with left-side ejection port.

* ***BAR Longtrac Stalker*** – similar to BAR Longtrac, except has matte black metal finish and black composite stock and forearm. New 2006.

MSR $1,260	$1,050	$875	$750	$650	$525	$425	$325	

Add $90 for Mag. cals.

* ***BAR Longtrac Camo*** – similar to BAR Longtrac, except has 100% Mossy Oak New Break Up (disc. 2009) or Break Up Infinity (new 2010) camo coverage. New 2007.

MSR $1,360	$1,175	$995	$850	$750	$650	$495	$375	

Add $100 for Mag. cals.

BAR ZENITH – various cals., features a manual cocking system on the upper tang and wood inserts in the receiver, 20 in. barrel with Battue/fixed rear sight and fiber optic front sight. European distribution only. New 2012.

This model is not available for U.S. importation, and is sold in Europe exclusively.

RIFLES: SEMI-AUTO, FAL & CAL SERIES

FN manufactured FALs and CALs imported by BAC can be found under the Fabrique Nationale heading.

	Above Average	Average	Below Average

RIFLES: SINGLE SHOT

MODEL 1878 STANDARD – various cals., J.M. Browning's first patent, falling block action, fewer than 600 made (highest known ser. no. is 542) by Browning Brothers in Ogden, Utah between 1878-1883, octagon barrel marked "Browning Bros. Ogden, Utah USA", plain wood stock and forearm with and without pistol grips, crescent steel buttplate, with or without ramrod, several receiver configurations, a very few were made in the deluxe model, seldom found in better than average used condition, with or w/o serial number. Approx. only 100 have survived - Browning Arms Co. and the Winchester Museum have no factory records on this model.

	Above Average	Average	Below Average
	$50,000 - $40,000	$35,000 - $30,000	$25,000 - $20,000

Add 50% for Deluxe Rifle (checkered stock and forearm), 10% for Early Rifle with Sharps Borchardt type lever, 40% for Early Rifle stamped "Ogden, U.T.", 20% for any caliber other than .40-70 SS or .45-70 Govt., 25% for Late Model with ramrod under barrel held by two thimbles (known as "Montana Model").
Subtract 20% if the original sights have been removed or replaced incorrectly.

Please refer to the grading explanation for Winchester lever actions regarding descriptions for the above condition factors.

Calibers in this model are listed from rarest to most commonly encountered: .50-70 Govt., .45 Sharps, .44 Rem., .40-90 Sharps, .44-77 Sharps, .45-70 Govt., and .40-70 Sharps Straight.

This model is rare since approx. only 550 were mfg. (approx. ser. range 1-550). This patent was sold to Winchester, which became their Model 1885 single shot. To date, less than 100 original Model 1878s have been encountered indicating a high mortality rate (most remaining specimens are in poor

GRADING - PPGS™ 100% 98% 95% 90% 80% 70% 60% *LAST MSR*

original condition). An inherent weakness of the original design was the way the stock attached to the action - Winchester later corrected this design flaw. A few remaining examples are not serial numbered. Barter guns are rifles which have Browning stamped actions but with another gunsmith's barrel.

MODEL B-78 – .22-250 Rem., 6mm Rem., .243 Win. (only 671 mfg.), .25-06 Rem., 7mm Mag., .30-06, or .45-70 Govt. (octagon barrel only) cal., 24 or 26 in. round or octagon barrel, lever activated falling block, no sights except .45- 70 Govt., checkered walnut stock, approx. 24,000 mfg. 1973-1982.

$1,495 $1,275 $1,125 $1,000 $825 $675 $525

Add 30% for .243 Win. cal.

Production statistics on the various calibers are as follows: .22-250 - 2,431 mfg. in round barrel, 3,482 mfg. in octagon, .243 Win. - 280 mfg. in round barrel, 391 mfg. in octagon, 6mm Rem - 1,280 mfg. in round barrel, 1,911 mfg. in octagon, .25-06 - 1,475 mfg. in round barrel, 3,293 mfg. in octagon, .30-06 - 1,588 mfg. in round barrel, 2,330 mfg. in octagon, .45-70 - 0 mfg. in round barrel, 3,839 mfg. in octagon, 7mm Rem. Mag. - 635 mfg. in round barrel, 961 mfg. in octagon.

The Model B-78 was superceded by the Model 1885 in 1985.

* ***Model B-78 Sporter*** – various cals., utilizes a Model 1885 barrelled action with B-78 wood (pistol grip and cheekpiece).

$1,495 $1,275 $1,125 $1,000 $825 $675 $525

MODEL 1885 HIGH WALL – .22-250 Rem., .223 Rem. (disc. 1994), .270 Win., .30-06, 7mm Rem. Mag., .45-70 Govt., or .454 Casull (new 1998) cal., falling block action, sear safety, 28 in. octagonal barrel, adj. gold trigger, no sights, checkered straight grip English walnut stock without cheekpiece and Schnabel forearm, exposed hammer, approx. 8 3/4 lbs. Mfg. 1985-2001.

$1,450 $1,270 $1,090 $985 $800 $655 $510 ***$1,027***

This model was equipped with open sights in .45-70 Govt. and .454 Casull cals.

MODEL 1885 LOW WALL – .22 Hornet, .223 Rem. (disc. 2000), .243 Win. (disc. 2000), or .260 Rem. (new 1999) cal., action patterned after the Winchester Low Wall receiver, features thinner 24 in. barrel, adj. trigger, 6 1/4 lbs. Mfg. 1995-2001.

$1,225 $1,070 $920 $835 $675 $550 $430 ***$997***

Add $100 for .260 Rem. cal.

MODEL 1885 HIGH WALL TRADITIONAL HUNTER – .30-30 Win., .38-55 WCF or .45-70 Govt. cal., High-Wall action, 30 in. octagon barrel with ejector, blue receiver, rear tang aperture sight, crescent buttplate, checkered stock and forearm, approx. 9 lbs. Mfg. 1997-2000.

$1,325 $1,160 $995 $900 $730 $595 $465 ***$1,220***

* ***Model 1885 High Wall Traditional Hunter 125th Anniversary*** – .45-70 Govt. cal., features delicate scroll receiver engraving and gold enhanced 125th anniversary logo with gold border. 500 mfg. 2003-2004 only.

$1,675 $1,465 $1,255 N/A N/A N/A N/A ***$1,516***

MODEL 1885 LOW WALL TRADITIONAL HUNTER – .357 Mag., .44 Mag., or .45 LC cal., 24 in. half-round, half-octagon barrel, case colored receiver and buttplate, gold bead front, semi-buckhorn rear, and rear tang aperture sights, 6 1/2 lbs. Mfg. 1998-2001.

$1,375 $1,205 $1,030 $935 $755 $620 $480 ***$1,289***

MODEL 1885 BPCR (BLACK POWDER CARTRIDGE RIFLE) – .40-65 Win. (black powder only) or .45-70 Govt. (black powder or smokeless) cal., case colored high wall action, 30 in. half-round, half-octagon barrel, checkered pistol grip stock with shotgun butt, w/o ejector system and shell deflector, vernier tang rear sight and globe front sight with spirit level, approx. 11 lbs. Mfg. 1996-2001.

$1,900 $1,665 $1,425 $1,290 $1,045 $855 $665 ***$1,766***

* ***Model 1885 BPCR Creedmoor*** – .45-90 cal., blue receiver, 34 in. half-round, half-octagon barrel with globe front and aperture rear tang sights, 11 3/4 lbs. Mfg. 1998-1999.

$1,900 $1,665 $1,425 $1,290 $1,045 $855 $665 ***$1,764***

GRADING - PPGS™	100%	98%	95%	90%	80%	70%	60%	LAST MSR

RIFLES: SLIDE ACTION

BPR – .243 Win., .270 Win., .30-06, .308 Win., .300 Win. Mag., or 7mm Rem. Mag. cal., 7 lug rotary bolt, blue alloy receiver, 22 or 24 (Mag. cals. only) in. barrel with open sights, features downward camming slide action assembly, checkered walnut stock and forend, cross-bolt safety, 3 or 4 shot mag., approx. 7 lbs. 3 oz. Mfg. 1997-2001.

	100%	98%	95%	90%	80%	70%	60%	LAST MSR
	$750	$650	$525	$475	$375	$315	$250	$725

Add $55 for Mag. cals.

BPR-22 – .22 LR or .22 WMR cal., short-stroke action, 20 1/4 in. barrel, 11 shot tube mag., mfg. 1977-1982.

	100%	98%	95%	90%	80%	70%	60%
	$550	$495	$425	$375	$315	$275	$225

Add 30% for .22 WMR cal.

* ***BPR-22 Grade II*** – similar to BPR-22, only engraved action, select walnut.

	100%	98%	95%	90%	80%	70%	60%
	$850	$750	$650	$550	$450	$400	$315

Add 30% for .22 WMR cal.

TROMBONE MODEL – .22 LR cal. only, slide action with tube mag., fixed sights, takedown, 24 in. barrel, hammerless, with either FN or U.S. (rare) barrel address, approx. 150,000 Grade I's were mfg.

Add $150 for original box.

* ***Trombone Model w/FN Barrel Address*** – most common variation.

	100%	98%	95%	90%	80%	70%	60%
	$1,375	$1,200	$1,025	$925	$750	$625	$475

* ***Trombone Model w/BAC Barrel Markings*** – approx. 3,200 Grade Is were imported by BAC during the late 1960s.

	100%	98%	95%	90%	80%	70%	60%
	$1,895	$1,650	$1,425	$1,295	$1,050	$850	$675

Add $250 for original box.

* ***Trombone Model Grade I*** – limited mfg. for the BCA circa 1985, 30 mfg., with only 10 sold individually, engraved by Custom Shop at FN for wholesaler.

	100%	98%	95%	90%	80%	70%	60%
	$1,650	$1,425	$1,175	N/A	N/A	N/A	N/A

* ***Trombone Grades I & II 2 Gun Set*** – limited mfg. for the BCA circa 1985, 10 sets mfg., available in 2 gun set.

	100%	98%	95%	90%	80%	70%	60%
	$3,925	$3,425	$2,950	N/A	N/A	N/A	N/A

* ***Trombone Grades I, II, & III 3 Gun Set*** – 10 sets mfg. for BCA circa 1985.

	100%	98%	95%	90%	80%	70%	60%
	$7,500	$6,575	$5,625	N/A	N/A	N/A	N/A

* ***Trombone Custom Shop Models*** – limited mfg. from the FN Custom Shop.

Values for 100% rifles are as follows: Grade I - $1,350, Grade II - $2,350, Grade III - $3,750, Grade III C or Grade III w/gold inlays (sometimes referred to as Grade IV) - $4,500, Grade V (wood and water or Squirrel gun) - $3,000.

SHOTGUNS: BOLT ACTION, A-BOLT SERIES

A-BOLT SHOTGUN MODEL (DISC.) – 12 ga. only, 3 in. chamber, 2 shot mag., same bolt system as A-Bolt II Rifle, 22 or 23 in. barrel (rifled or Invector with rifled tube), available in Stalker Model with graphite fiberglass composite stock or Hunter Model with select satin finished walnut stock, dull matte finished barrel and receiver, top tang safety, choice of no sights (new 1996) or adj. rear sight, drilled and tapped receiver, approx. 7 lbs. Mfg. by Miroku 1995-98.

* ***A-Bolt Stalker Model Shotgun***

	100%	98%	95%	90%	80%	70%	60%	LAST MSR
	$895	$825	$700	$625	$595	$475	$375	$720

Add $45 for open sights.
Add $150 for rifled barrel.

* ***A-Bolt Hunter Model Shotgun***

	100%	98%	95%	90%	80%	70%	60%	LAST MSR
	$895	$825	$700	$625	$595	$475	$375	$805

Add $40 for open sights.
Add $150 for rifled barrel.

GRADING - PPGS™	100%	98%	95%	90%	80%	70%	60%	LAST MSR

A-BOLT SHOTGUN HUNTER SERIES (CURRENT) – 12 ga. only, 3 in. chamber, 22 in. rifled barrel with adj. rear and Truglo fiber optic front sights, matte blued finish, 60 degree bolt lift, 2 shot detachable mag., choice of satin finish, checkered walnut stock (Hunter Model), black composite stock with Dura-Touch armor coating (Stalker Model), or Camo Model with Mossy Oak Break-Up Infinity camo finish with armor coating, vent. recoil pad, sling swivels, approx. 7 lbs. New 2011.

MSR $1,150	$975	$875	$750	$675	$650	$525	$400	

Add $130 for Hunter Model with wood stock.

Add $150 for Camo Model with Mossy Oak Break-Up Infinity finish.

SHOTGUNS: O/U, CYNERGY SERIES

During 2010, Vector Pro chokes became standard on 12 and 20 ga. models.

CYNERGY SERIES – 12, 20 (new 2005), 28 (new 2005) ga., or .410 bore (new 2007), silver nitride finished receiver, features new MonoLock hinge system allowing low receiver profile, mechanical striker based SST, reverse striker ignition system (triple trigger system included on Sporting models), 26 or 28 in. backbored and ported vent. barrels with VR, Vector Pro lengthened forcing cones became standard on all 12 and 20 ga. models beginning 2010, Invector-Plus chokes, choice of wood or composite (12 ga. only) stock and forearm, solid, vent., or Inflex recoil pad, impact ejectors. New 2004.

* ***Cynergy Field (Current)*** – 12, 20, 28 ga. or .410 bore, similar to discontinued Cynergy Field, except has Vector Pro lengthened forcing cones on 12 and 20 ga., engraving features pheasants and ducks on 12 ga., or quail and grouse on small gauge, gloss oil finished Grade II/III walnut stock, approx. 6 - 7 3/4 lbs. New 2010.

MSR $2,800	$2,420	$2,000	$1,800	$1,450	$1,150	$925	$775	

Add $50 for 20, 28 ga. or .410 bore.

* ***Cynergy Field (Disc.)*** – 12 (disc. 2006), 20, or 28 ga., 2 3/4 (28 ga. only) or 3 in. chambers, 26 or 28 in. non-ported barrels with 5/16 in. slanted VR, flush choke tubes, silver nitride finished receiver with clay pigeon motif, checkered Grade I walnut or non-glare black composite (disc. 2006) stock and forearm, stock has adj. comb with built in Inflex recoil pad system allowing LOP adjustment, approx. 6 1/4 - 7 1/2 lbs. Mfg. 2004-2007.

	$1,575	$1,200	$950	$875	$775	$700	$625	*$2,062*

Subtract approx. 10% for composite stock and forearm.

* ***Cynergy Classic Field*** – 12, 20 (new 2007), 28 ga. (new 2007), or .410 bore (new 2007), 3 in. chambers, features traditional satin finished walnut stock with standard vent. recoil pad and Schnabel forearm, etched mallard and pheasant on receiver sides, approx. 6 1/4 - 7 3/4 lbs. New 2006.

MSR $2,530	$2,350	$1,900	$1,500	$1,200	$950	$750	$700	

Add $60 for 20, 28 ga. or .410 bore.

* ***Cynergy Classic Field Grade III*** – 12 or 20 ga., 3 in. chambers, similar to Classic Field, except has gloss finished upgraded wood (Grade III/Grade IV) and fully engraved receiver, approx. 6-8 lbs. New 2007.

MSR $4,000	$3,475	$2,925	$2,600	$2,200	$1,875	$1,575	$1,200	

Add $50 for 20 ga.

* ***Cynergy Classic Field Grade VI*** – 12 or 20 ga., similar to Classic Field Grade III, except has upgraded wood (Grade V/VI), fully engraved receiver with multiple gold inlays. New 2007.

MSR $6,100	$5,260	$4,475	$4,000	$3,400	$2,890	$2,300	$1,800	

Add $30 for 20 ga.

* ***Cynergy Euro Field*** – 12, 20, 28 ga. or .410 bore, 26 or 28 in. barrel, jewelled monobloc, full coverage high relief engraving (pheasants and ducks on 12 ga., quail and grouse on 20 ga.) on receiver, forearm iron and top lever, gloss oil finished Grade II/III walnut stock and forearm, choke tubes, 5 lbs., 15 oz. - 7 lbs., 11 oz. Mfg. 2009.

	$2,300	$1,850	$1,475	$1,195	$950	$750	$700	*$2,509*

Add $20 for 20, 28 ga. or .410 bore.

This model's nomenclature was changed to the Cynergy Field during 2010.

GRADING - PPGS™	100%	98%	95%	90%	80%	70%	60%	LAST MSR

* ***Cynergy Feather*** – 12, 20 (new 2008), 28 (new 2008) ga. or .410 bore (new 2008), 3 in. chambers, choice of checkered black composite stock with adj. comb or checkered satin-finished walnut stock and Schnabel forearm, Inflex recoil pad, 26 or 28 in. barrels with flush Invector-Plus choke tubes, jewelled mono-bloc (new 2009), approx. 5 1/2 - 6 3/4 lbs. New 2007.

MSR $2,900	$2,525	$2,025	$1,650	$1,325	$1,100	$950	$800	

Add $30 for 20, 28 ga. or .410 bore.
Subtract $100 for black adj. composite stock and forearm (12 ga. only).

* ***Cynergy Sporting*** – 12 (disc. 2006), 20, or 28 ga., 2 3/4 in. chambers, 28, 30, or 32 in. ported barrels with tapered VR (non-tapered 5/16 in. rib on 28 ga.), Hi-Viz fiber optic front sight, silver nitride receiver with clay pigeon motif, oil finished checkered walnut (with or w/o adj. comb) or black composite (12 ga. only, disc. 2006) stock and forearm, stock has adj. comb with built in Inflex recoil pad system allowing LOP adjustment (disc. 2006), extended choke tubes, approx. 6 1/2 - 8 lbs. Mfg. 2004-2007.

	$1,875	$1,640	$1,405	$1,275	$1,030	$845	$655	*$3,080*

Add 25% for adj. comb (mfg. 2006 only).
Subtract approx. 20% for composite stock and forearm.

* ***Cynergy Classic Sporting*** – 12, 20 (new 2007), 28 ga. (new 2007) or .410 bore (new 2007), 2 3/4 or 3 in. chambers, 28, 30, or 32 in. ported barrels with extended choke tubes, features traditional oil finished walnut stock with solid recoil pad and Schnabel forearm, etched Browning logo on receiver sides, approx. 6 1/4 - 8 lbs. New 2006.

MSR $3,600	$3,100	$2,625	$2,375	$1,900	$1,600	$1,400	$1,100	

Add $30 for 20, 28 ga. or .410 bore.
Add $400 for adj. comb (new 2007, not available in 28 ga. or .410 bore).

* ***Cynergy Sporting (Euro Sporting)*** – 12 or 20 (new 2008) ga., 2 3/4 in. chambers, 28, 30, or 32 in. VR barrels with porting and extended choke tubes, features traditional checkered oil finished walnut stock and Schnabel forearm, or black composite (adj. comb only) stock with Inflex recoil pad, jewelled mono-bloc (new 2009), high relief scroll engraving on receiver forearm and top lever (new 2009), approx. 6 1/4 - 8 lbs. New 2007.

MSR $4,000	$3,525	$2,900	$2,400	$1,925	$1,650	$1,350	$1,175	

Add $500 for adj. comb (12 ga. only) with oil finished walnut stock and Schnabel forearm.
Add $30 for 20 ga.
Subtract $120 for adj. comb black composite stock and forearm (not available in 20 ga.).
Subtract 10% if w/o scroll engraving.

This model's nomenclature changed from Euro Sporting to Sporting during 2010.

* ***Cynergy Classic Trap*** – 12 ga. only, 2 3/4 in. chambers, 30 or 32 in. VR barrels with porting, extended Invector-Plus chokes and Hi-Viz fiber optic front sight, checkered walnut stock with or w/o adj. comb and competition forearm, vent. recoil pad, approx. 8 3/4 lbs. New 2007.

MSR $3,880	$3,340	$2,840	$2,550	$2,100	$1,785	$1,500	$1,300	

Add $400 for adj. comb.

* ***Cynergy Classic Trap Unsingle Combo*** – 12 ga. only, includes choice of 32 or 34 in. ported single barrel and choice of 30 or 32 in. O/U ported barrels with adj. top rib, gloss finished Grade III/VI walnut stock with adj. comb and semi-beavertail forearm with finger grooves, includes aluminum (disc.) or green canvas case, approx. 8 3/4 lbs. New 2008.

MSR $6,000	$5,180	$4,335	$3,685	$3,130	$2,665	$2,265	$1,800	

SHOTGUNS: O/U, CITORI HUNTING SERIES

All Citori shotguns which incorporate the Invector choke tube system may be used with steel shot. Invector Plus choke tubes are designed for backbored barrels. DO NOT USE Standard Invector choke tubes in barrels marked for the Invector Plus choking system. During 2010, Vector Pro chokes became standard on 12 and 20 ga. models.

GRADING - PPGS™	100%	98%	95%	90%	80%	70%	60%	LAST MSR

Hand engraving was replaced by machine engraving in late 1982 on all higher grade models.

Subtract $100 for 26 in. barrels on used guns.

CITORI HUNTING MODELS – 12, 16 (mfg. 1986-89), 20, 28 ga. (disc. 1994) or .410 bore (disc. 1994), 26, 28, or 30 in. barrels, various chokes, boxlock, auto ejectors, SST, vent. rib, features checkered semi-pistol grip stock with grooved semi-beavertail forearm, grades differ in amount of engraving, finish, and wood. Invector chokes became standard in 1988, Invector Plus chokes became standard 1995 on 12 or 20 ga., 6 lbs. 9 oz. - 8 lbs. 5 oz. Mfg. 1973-2001 by Miroku.

* ***Citori Hunting Grade I 12 or 20 ga.*** – blue finish with light scroll engraving beginning 1978.

» **Citori Hunting Grade I Earlier Mfg. without Invector Choking**

$950 $800 $700 $600 $575 $500 $450

Add 15% for 16 ga. if in 90%+ original condition.

Add approx. 40% for extra 20 ga. barrels originally ordered with gun.

» **Citori Grade I Hunter Model w/Invector Choking** – recent mfg. with Invector Choking, 12 or 20 ga., 3 in. chambers, 20 ga. available with Standard Invector or Invector Plus (new 1994) choking system, Invector Plus choking standard on recently mfg. 12 and 20 ga., 6 lbs. 9 oz. - 8 lbs. 5 oz. Disc. 2001.

$1,150 $950 $825 $700 $650 $575 $525 *$1,486*

Add $100 for Invector Plus choke tubes.

* ***Citori Hunting Grade I Smaller Gauges***

» **Citori Hunting Grade I 28 ga. or .410 bore** – without Invector choking. Disc. 1994.

$1,000 $850 $700 $600 $550 $500 $450 *$1,097*

* ***Citori Hunting Grade II*** – 12, 20, 28 ga., or .410 bore. Mfg. 1978-1983.

$1,200 $1,000 $800 $650 $600 $550 $500

* ***Citori Hunting Grade III*** – 12, 16 (mfg. 1986-89), 20, 28 ga. (disc. 1994), or .410 bore (disc. 1994), greyed steel receiver with engraved game scenes featuring grouse (20 ga.) and ducks (12 ga.), Invector chokes standard, Invector Plus became standard in 12 ga. in 1994. Mfg. 1985-95.

$1,900 $1,600 $1,300 $1,000 $800 $700 $600 *$1,875*

Add 15% for 16 ga. if in 90%+ original condition.

Add 15%-25% for 28 ga. or .410 bore (both disc. 1989).

Subtract $200 for standard Invector chokes.

* ***Citori Hunting Grade V*** – 12, 20, 28 ga., or .410 bore, extensive deep relief engraving with game scenes on satin grey receiver. Disc. 1984.

$2,750 $2,200 $1,850 $1,525 $1,300 $1,150 $995

Add 20% for 28 ga.

* ***Citori Hunting Grade VI*** – 12, 16 (mfg. 1986-89), 20, 28 ga. (disc. 1992), or .410 bore (disc. 1989), hand engraved (1983-1984 only) or machine engraving on blue or greyed receiver with extensive engraving including multiple gold inlays, Standard Invector (12 ga. disc. 1993) or Invector Plus chokes. Mfg. 1983-1995.

$2,750 $2,200 $1,900 $1,600 $1,350 $1,225 $1,100 *$2,715*

Add 35% for factory hand engraving mfg. 1983-1984 only.

Add 15% for 16 ga. if in 90%+ original condition.

Add 15%-25% for 28 ga.

Subtract $200 for standard Invector chokes.

* ***Citori Hunting 3 1/2 in. Magnum Model*** – 12 ga., 3 1/2 in. chambers, 28 or 30 in. VR barrels with back-bored Invector plus choke tubes, with recoil pad, approx. 8 lbs. 9 oz. Mfg. 1989-2000.

$1,250 $950 $825 $695 $600 $550 $495 *$1,563*

GRADING - PPGS™	100%	98%	95%	90%	80%	70%	60%	LAST MSR

* ***Citori Sporting Hunter*** – 12 or 20 ga., 3 or 3 1/2 (12 ga. only) in. chambers, 26, 28, or 30 (12 ga. only) in. barrels with Invector Plus choking, configured for both hunting and sporting clays shooting, Superposed style forearm, contoured recoil pad, front and middle bead sights, gloss or satin (3 1/2 in. only) wood finish, 6 lbs. 9 oz. - 8 lbs. 9 oz. Mfg. 1998-2001.

	$1,250	$950	$825	$695	$600	$550	$495	$1,607

* ***Citori Satin Hunter*** – 12 ga. only, 3 or 3 1/2 (disc. 2000) in. chambers, 26, 28, or 30 (3 1/2 in. Mag. only, disc. 1998) in. VR backbored barrels with Invector Plus choking, features satin wood finish, approx. 8 1/4 lbs. Mfg. 1998-2001.

	$1,150	$895	$700	$600	$500	$450	$375	$1,535

* ***Citori Upland Special*** – 12, 16 (mfg. 1989 only), or 20 ga. (2 3/4 in. chambers), shortened checkered straight grip walnut stock (14 in. LOP) and Schnabel forearm, 24 in. barrels, blue finish, Invector (12 ga. disc. 1993) or Invector Plus choking, 6-6 3/4 lbs. Mfg. 1984-2000.

	$1,195	$975	$725	$625	$500	$450	$375	$1,514

Add 15% for 16 ga. if in 90%+ original condition.
Subtract $200 for Invector choking.

* ***Citori White Upland Special*** – 12 or 20 ga., 2 3/4 in. chambers, similar to Upland Special, except features silver nitride finished receiver, 6 1/8 or 6 1/2 lbs. Mfg. 2000-2001.

	$1,250	$1,000	$875	$750	$650	$600	$550	$1,583

CITORI SATIN HUNTER MICRO MIDAS – 12 or 20 ga., 3 in. chambers, 24 or 26 in. VR barrels with Vector Pro lengthened forcing cones, includes 3 Invector Plus choke tubes, blued receiver, SST, checkered satin finished walnut stock and forearm, 13 in. LOP, vent. recoil pad on 12 ga., approx. 6 - 6 3/4 lbs. New 2011.

MSR $1,600	$1,395	$1,175	$1,055	$900	$750	$650	$500	

CITORI SUPERLIGHT MODELS – 12, 16, 20, 28 ga., or .410 bore, 2 3/4 in. chambers except for .410 bore, English stock, oil finish, Invector chokes became standard in 1988, Invector Plus became standard 1995 for 12 or 20 ga., approx. 5 lbs., 11 oz. - 6 3/4 lbs. New 1983.

* ***Citori Superlight Grade I 12, 16, or 20 ga.***

» **Citori Superlight Grade I Earlier Mfg. without Invector Choking**

	$995	$850	$750	$650	$600	$550	$500	

» **Citori Superlight Grade I w/Invector Choking** – recent mfg. with Invector Choking 12 or 20 ga., 20 ga. available with Standard Invector or Invector Plus (new 1994, became standard 1995) choking system, Invector Plus choking standard on recently mfg. 12 ga. Disc. 2002.

	$1,250	$1,025	$850	$750	$675	$600	$525	$1,590

Subtract $200 for Standard Invector choking in 12 or 20 ga.

* ***Citori Superlight Grade I 28 ga. or .410 bore*** – without Invector choking until 1993, Invector choking became an option in 1994 and standard in 1995. Disc. 2002.

	$1,300	$1,100	$875	$775	$700	$625	$550	$1,666

Subtract $200 if without Invector choke tubes.

* ***Citori Superlight Feather*** – 12 or 20 (new 2002) ga., 2 3/4 in. chambers, greyed alloy receiver, 26 in. Invector choked VR barrels, gloss finished straight grip English stock and scaled down Schnabel forearm, 5 3/4 or 6 1/4 lbs. New 1999.

MSR $2,390	$2,050	$1,650	$1,400	$1,175	$1,000	$850	$725	

* ***Citori Superlight Grade III*** – same gauges as Grade I, Standard Invector on 12 or 20 (disc.) ga. or Invector Plus (standard in 12 ga. beginning 1994) chokes. Mfg. 1986-2002.

	$1,900	$1,600	$1,300	$1,000	$800	$700	$600	$2,300

Add $270 for 28 ga. or .410 bore (disc. 1997).
Subtract $300 if without Invector choke tubes or $200 for standard Invector choke tubes.

GRADING - PPGS™	100%	98%	95%	90%	80%	70%	60%	LAST MSR

* ***Citori Superlight Grade V*** – sideplate available. Disc. 1984.

	$2,950	$2,300	$1,900	$1,500	$1,250	$1,075	$900	

* ***Citori Superlight Grade VI*** – older mfg. has Invector chokes standard (option on 28 ga. or .410 bore beginning 1994) or Invector Plus (standard and available in 12 or 20 ga. only) chokes, choice of blue or grey (new 1996) receiver finish. Mfg. 1983-2002.

	$2,750	$2,350	$2,000	$1,700	$1,450	$1,325	$1,200	*$3,510*

Subtract 10% for 28 ga. or .410 bore without choke tubes.
Subtract $200 for standard Invector choke tubes.
Add $270 for 28 ga. or .410 bore with Standard Invector choking.

* ***Citori Superlight Grade VI Sideplate*** – 20 ga. only. Disc.

	$3,350	$2,750	$2,250	$1,950	$1,825	$1,650	$1,475	

CITORI SPORTER MODELS – similar to Citori Superlight, except with 3 in. chambers, 26 in. barrels, various chokes, straight grip stock, Schnabel forearm. Disc. 1983.

	$1,100	$900	$825	$700	$600	$550	$500	

Add 10% for 28 ga. or .410 bore.

* ***Citori Sporter Grade II*** – 12, 20, 28 ga., or .410 bore.

	$1,350	$1,100	$1,000	$965	$880	$770	$715	

Add 10% for 28 ga.

* ***Citori Sporter Grade V*** – 12, 20, 28 ga., or .410 bore.

	$2,750	$2,200	$1,800	$1,600	$1,450	$1,300	$1,150	

Add 10% for 28 ga.

CITORI LIGHTNING MODELS – 12, 16 (disc. 1989), 20, 28 ga., or .410 bore, 2 3/4 (28 ga. only), or 3 in. (standard on 12 ga., 20 ga., and .410 bore) chamber, 26, 28, or 30 (disc.) in. barrels, Invector chokes standard on newer mfg. smaller ga.'s, Invector Plus became standard 1995 for 12 or 20 ga., boxlock, auto ejectors, SST, vent. rib, features checkered round knob pistol grip stock and slimmer forearm, grades differ in amount of engraving, finish, and quality of wood, approx. 6.5-8 lbs. Introduced 1988.

* ***Citori Lightning Grade I 12, 16 or 20 ga.***

» **Citori Lightning Grade I Earlier Mfg. w/o Invector Choking** – without Invector Choking.

	$995	$850	$750	$650	$600	$550	$500	

Add 15% for 16 ga.

» **Citori Lightning Grade I w/Invector Choking** – 12 or 20 ga., current mfg. with Invector Choking, 12 or 20 ga., Invector (disc. 1994) or Invector Plus choking (became standard on 12 ga. in 1994, 20 ga. in 1995), gloss finished walnut stock and forearm, buttplate replaced vent recoil pad in 2010, 6 1/2 - 8 lbs.

MSR $1,990	$1,725	$1,450	$1,200	$1,020	$875	$750	$625	

Subtract 10% for Standard Invector choking.

This model was supplied with scroll engraving with rosette design until 2004. Beginning 2004, standard engraving is high relief, intricate, and sculpted.

* ***Citori Lightning Grade I Smaller Gauges*** – 28 ga. or .410 bore, without Invector choking until 1993, Invector choking became an option in 1994, standard in 1995.

MSR $2,070	$1,785	$1,520	$1,290	$1,095	$900	$750	$625	

Subtract $200 if without Standard Invector choking.

* ***Citori Lightning Grade III*** – 12, 16 (disc. 1989), or 20 ga., greyed steel receiver with engraved game scenes (mallards/pheasants on 12 ga., quail/grouse on 20 ga.), older mfg. may or may not have Invector choking, Invector Plus choking is now standard on 12 or 20 ga. Mfg. 1988-2004.

	$1,865	$1,450	$1,250	$1,000	$800	$700	$600	*$2,464*

Subtract 10% if without Invector choking.
Add 15% for 16 ga. (disc. 1989).

GRADING - PPGS™	100%	98%	95%	90%	80%	70%	60%	LAST MSR

» **Citori Lightning Grade III 28 ga. or .410 bore** – features quail and grouse scene engraving. Disc. 2004.

	$1,950	$1,675	$1,500	$1,375	$1,250	$1,175	$995	*$2,754*

* ***Citori Lightning Grade IV*** – 12 or 20 ga., high relief engraving on grey receiver (pheasants on left, mallards on right on 12 ga., quail and grouse on 20 ga.) trigger guard and tang screws, high gloss finished walnut stock and forearm. Mfg. 2005-2012.

	$3,030	$2,380	$1,950	$1,575	$1,250	$1,030	$800	*$3,500*

» **Citori Lightning Grade IV 28 ga. or .410 bore** – features quail and grouse inlays. Disc. 2012.

	$3,095	$2,475	$2,100	$1,900	$1,700	$1,500	$1,100	*$3,590*

* ***Citori Lightning Grade VI*** – 12, 16 (disc. 1989), or 20 ga., blue or greyed receiver with extensive deep relief engraving with 7 gold inlays, including mallards/pheasants on receiver sides. Disc. 2004.

	$2,825	$2,400	$2,000	$1,650	$1,450	$1,225	$1,050	*$3,797*

Add 15% for 16 ga. (disc. 1989).

» **Citori Lightning Grade VI 28 ga. or .410 bore** – disc. 2004.

	$3,075	$2,550	$2,100	$1,750	$1,550	$1,325	$1,100	*$4,090*

* ***Citori Lightning Grade VII*** – 12 or 20 ga., deep relief engraving on grey or blue receiver, trigger guard, top tang, takedown lever and bracket, 24Kt. gold bird inlays (two flushing ringnecks and pointer on right side with three mallards on left side on 12 ga., quail and grouse on 20 ga.), high gloss finished walnut stock and forearm. Mfg. 2005-2012.

	$4,800	$3,840	$3,275	$2,625	$2,225	$1,895	$1,600	*$5,560*

» **Citori Lightning Grade VII 28 ga. or .410 bore** – features quail and grouse inlays. Disc. 2012.

	$4,875	$3,900	$3,300	$2,800	$2,400	$1,925	$1,650	*$5,660*

CITORI LIGHTNING FEATHER – 12 or 20 (new 2000) ga., 3 in. chambers, greyed alloy receiver with dovetailed steel breechface and steel hinge pin, 26 or 28 in. Invector Plus choked VR barrels, select checkered round knob walnut stock and forearm with gloss finish, vent. recoil pad, approx. 6 1/4 - 7 lbs. Mfg. 1999-2007.

	$1,400	$1,200	$1,000	$850	$550	$475	$450	*$1,944*

* ***Citori Lightning Feather Combo*** – includes set of 27 in. 20 ga. (3 in. chambers) and 28 ga. barrels with Invector Plus (20 ga.) and standard Invector (28 ga.) chokes, includes luggage case, approx. 6 1/4 lbs. New 2000.

MSR $3,580	$3,150	$2,525	$2,100	$1,800	$1,500	$1,350	$1,125	

CITORI FEATHER LIGHTNING – 12 or 20 ga., 3 in. chambers, greyed alloy receiver with dovetailed steel breechface and steel hinge pin, 26 or 28 in. Invector Plus choked VR barrels, select checkered round knob walnut stock and forearm with gloss finish, solid recoil plate, approx. 6 - 6 1/2 lbs. New 2012.

MSR $2,180	$1,875	$1,500	$1,225	$1,000	$850	$725	$625	

CITORI GRAN LIGHTNING (GL) MODEL – 12, 20, 28 ga. (new 1994), or .410 bore (new 1994) only, 2 3/4 (28 ga. only) or 3 in. chambers, similar to Lightning Model, except has Grade III walnut stock and forearm with satin/oil finish, includes recoil pad, 26 or 28 in. barrels, Invector chokes standard on newer mfg. smaller ga.'s, Invector Plus became standard 1995 for 12 or 20 ga., 6 1/4 - 8 lbs. Mfg. 1990-2005.

	$1,850	$1,575	$1,350	$1,150	$975	$850	$725	*$2,429*

Add $128 for 28 ga. or .410 bore.
Subtract $200 for standard Invector chokes on 12 or 20 ga.

Beginning 2004, high relief intricate sculpted engraving replaced rosette, scroll type engraving.

CITORI WHITE LIGHTNING – 12, 20, 28 (new 2000) ga., or .410 bore (new 2000), 3 in. chambers, silver nitride receiver with engraving, satin wood finish with round pistol grip

GRADING - PPGS™	100%	98%	95%	90%	80%	70%	60%	LAST MSR

stock and vent. recoil pad, 26 or 28 in. VR barrels with Invector Plus choking, 6 lbs. 7 oz - 8 lbs. 2 oz. New 1998.

MSR $2,070	**$1,785**	**$1,475**	**$1,250**	**$1,075**	**$925**	**$795**	**$695**	

Add $70 for .28 ga. or .410 bore (new 2000).

Beginning 2004, high relief intricate sculpted engraving replaced rosette, scroll type engraving.

CITORI MICRO LIGHTNING – 20 ga. only, 2 3/4 in. chambers, 24 in. VR barrels, Invector (disc. 1993) or Invector Plus (new 1994) choking, 13 3/4 in. LOP (1/2 in. shorter), 6 lbs. 3 oz. Mfg. 1991-2001.

* ***Citori Micro Lightning Grade I***

	$1,250	**$1,000**	**$850**	**$750**	**$650**	**$575**	**$525**	***$1,591***

Subtract 10% for standard Invector choking.

* ***Citori Micro Lightning Grade III*** – Invector (disc. 1993) or Invector Plus choking. Mfg. 1993-94.

	$1,600	**$1,300**	**$1,175**	**$950**	**$825**	**$700**	**$550**	***$1,850***

Subtract $200 for Standard Invector choking.

* ***Citori Micro Lightning Grade VI*** – Mfg. 1993-94.

	$2,025	**$1,725**	**$1,500**	**$1,250**	**$1,025**	**$900**	**$825**	***$2,680***

Subtract $200 for standard Invector choking.

CITORI CLASSIC LIGHTNING GRADE I – 12 or 20 ga., 3 in. chambers, 26 or 28 in. vent. rib barrels, Invector Plus chokes, silver nitride receiver with Grade I Superposed engraving, Grade II/III oil finished slender lightning style walnut stock and forearm with vent. recoil pad, 6 lbs. 10 oz. - 8 lbs., 2 oz. Mfg. 2005-2007.

	$1,600	**$1,300**	**$1,100**	**$850**	**$725**	**$650**	**$500**	***$1,968***

CITORI CLASSIC LIGHTNING FEATHER GRADE I – 12 or 20 ga., 3 in. chambers, 26 or 28 in. vent. rib barrels, Invector Plus chokes, lightweight alloy receiver with high relief sculpted engraving, Grade II/III satin finished lightning style stock and Schnabel forearm, vent. recoil pad, 6 lbs. 3 oz. - 7 lbs. Mfg. 2005-2006.

	$1,650	**$1,350**	**$1,100**	**$850**	**$725**	**$650**	**$550**	***$1,991***

CITORI SUPER LIGHTNING GRADE I – 12 or 20 ga., 3 in. chambers, 26 or 28 in. vent. rib barrels, Invector Plus chokes, deep blue receiver with gold border accents, Grade II/III gloss finished lightning style stock with buttplate and Schnabel forearm, 6 lbs. 7 oz. - 8 lbs. 2 oz. Mfg. 2005-2007.

	$1,500	**$1,200**	**$1,000**	**$825**	**$700**	**$600**	**$500**	***$1,941***

CITORI 525 FIELD – 12 (disc. 2007), 20, 28 (new 2003) ga. or .410 bore (new 2003), 3 in. chambers (except 28 ga.), engraved silver nitride receiver, 26 or 28 in. unported barrels featuring VR with forward angled posts, oil finished checkered walnut stock with pronounced pistol grip and European comb, flush fit Invector Plus choke tubes, vent. recoil pad, Schnabel forearm, 6 lbs. 6 oz. - 8 lbs. Mfg. 2002-2008.

	$1,650	**$1,395**	**$1,175**	**$1,000**	**$750**	**$650**	**$550**	***$2,144***

Add $31 for 28 ga. or .410 bore.
Subtract $50 for 12 ga.

CITORI 525 FIELD GRADE III – 12 ga. only, 3 in. chambers, similar to 525 Field, except has Grade III/VI wood and more engraving, includes case, approx. 8 lbs. Mfg. 2007.

	$1,950	**$1,650**	**$1,400**	**$1,200**	**$800**	**$700**	**$600**	***$2,532***

CITORI 525 FEATHER – 12, 20 (new 2008), 28 (new 2008) ga. or .410 bore (new 2008), 3 in. chambers, silver nitride alloy receiver featuring high relief engraving, traditional oil finished checkered stock and Schnabel forearm, approx. 6 1/4 lbs. Limited mfg. 2007-2008.

	$1,750	**$1,400**	**$1,200**	**$1,000**	**$800**	**$675**	**$550**	***$2,278***

Add $17 for 28 ga. or .410 bore.

GRADING - PPGS™	100%	98%	95%	90%	80%	70%	60%	LAST MSR

CITORI ESPRIT – 12 ga. only, 3 in. chambers, 28 in. barrels with VR and 3 choke tubes, features removable and interchangeable sideplates, satin finished receiver, choice of scroll or pointer engraving scenes, gold enhancements were optional, 8 1/4 lbs. Mfg. 2002-2003.

	$1,950	$1,350	$1,025	$875	$725	$625	$550	*$2,502*

CITORI PRIVILEGE – 12 or 20 (new 2001) ga., 3 in. chambers, boxlock with extensively hand engraved sideplates, silver finished receiver, 26 or 28 in. barrels with 5/16 in. VR and Invector Plus choking, approx. 8 lbs. Mfg. 2000-2003.

	$4,235	$3,600	$3,050	$2,600	$2,475	$2,025	$1,750	*$5,537*

CITORI 625 FIELD – 12 (disc. 2011), 20 (new 2009), 28 (new 2009) ga. or .410 (new 2009) bore, 3 in. chambers, 26 or 28 in. VR barrels with Vector Pro choking system with extended forcing cones, gloss finished Grade II/III special cut checkered walnut stock and Schnabel forearm, vent recoil pad, silver nitride finished receiver with etched engraving, approx. 6 1/2 - 7 3/4 lbs. New 2008.

MSR $2,630	$2,275	$1,825	$1,525	$1,300	$1,100	$950	$795

Add $30 for 28 ga. or .410 bore.

CITORI 625 FEATHER – 12 (disc. 2011), 20, 28 ga., or .410 bore, 2 3/4 (20 or 28 ga.) or 3 in. chambers, 26 or 28 in. lightweight VR barrels with three Invector Plus choke tubes (12 or 20 ga.) or Standard Invector (28 ga. or .410 bore), lightweight alloy receiver with steel breech face and hinge pin, high relief etched engraving, SST, ejectors, gloss finished Grade II/III pistol grip walnut stock with Schnabel forearm, approx. 5 lbs. 9 oz - 7 lbs. New 2009.

MSR $2,800	$2,425	$1,975	$1,575	$1,350	$1,100	$1,000	$800

Add $60 for 28 ga. or .410 bore.

CITORI 725 FIELD – 12 ga. only, 3 in. chambers, features lower profile silver nitride boxlock action receiver with engraving, 26 or 28 in. VR barrels with three Invector-DS choke tubes, Fire Lite mechanical gold single trigger, checkered gloss finished walnut stock and forearm with solid pad, approx. 7 1/4 lbs. New 2012.

MSR $2,470	$2,175	$1,750	$1,475	$1,250	$1,050	$925	$825

CITORI 725 FEATHER – 12 ga. only, 3 in. chambers, similar to 725 Field, except has lightweight alloy frame, approx. 6 1/2 lbs. New 2013.

MSR $2,470	$2,175	$1,750	$1,475	$1,250	$1,050	$925	$825

CITORI 725 GRADE III – 12 ga. only, 26 or 28 in. VR barrels with three invector-DS choke tubes, features engraved pheasants on left side of frame, mallards on the right side, and a dog on the bottom, Grade III/IV checkered walnut with high gloss finish, Inflex II recoil pad, Fire Lite mechanical SST trigger, includes ABS case, approx. 7 3/8 lbs. Only 300 to be mfg. during 2013.

MSR $3,730	$3,250	$2,725	$1,425	$1,950	$1,650	$1,450	$1,125

CITORI 725 GRADE V – 12 ga. only, 26 or 28 in. VR barrels with three invector-DS choke tubes, features gold enhanced pheasants on left and mallards on the right side, Grade V/VI checkered walnut with high gloss finish, Inflex II recoil pad, Fire Lite mechanical SST trigger, includes canvas/Crazy Horse leather case, approx. 7 3/8 lbs. Only 200 to be mfg. during 2013.

MSR $5,600	$4,950	$4,450	$3,700	$3,200	$2,700	$2,300	$1,950

SHOTGUNS: O/U, CITORI SKEET

During 2010, Vector Pro chokes became standard on 12 and 20 ga. models.

Hand engraving was replaced by machine engraving in late 1982 on all higher grade models.

Subtract 10%-15% for all Skeet models with 26 in. barrels.

CITORI SKEET/SPECIAL SKEET MODELS – 12, 20, 28 ga., or .410 bore, same action as Citori Field, only with high post target rib (standard 1985), 26 and 28 in. skeet barrels, recoil pad, Invector chokes became standard in 1990 in 12 and 20 ga., Invector Plus chokes with ported barrels were an option during 1992 and became standard on the 12 ga. in 1994, new Special Skeet models were introduced during 1995 with decreased weight (1/4 lb. lighter) and better swing/balance characteristics.

GRADING - PPGS™	100%	98%	95%	90%	80%	70%	60%	LAST MSR

* ***Citori Skeet Grade I***

» **Citori Skeet Grade I 12 or 20 Ga.** – Invector Plus choking, high-post target rib, and ported barrels became standard in 1994, 7 1/4 - 8 lbs. Disc. 2000.

$1,295	$1,095	$995	$800	$625	$575	$500	*$1,742*

Add $100 for factory adj. comb (mfg. 1995-98).
Subtract 10% if without Invector Plus chokes.
Subtract 30% for fixed chokes.
Add approx. 40% for extra 20 ga. skeet barrels originally ordered with gun.
Add $50 for 20 ga.

Earlier mfg. skeet guns had a low profile, wide VR.

» **Citori Skeet Grade I Smaller Gauges** – 28 ga. or .410 bore, 6 lbs. 15 oz. Disc. 1999.

$1,400	$1,000	$850	$650	$550	$500	$450	*$1,627*

Subtract 20% if without Invector chokes.

* ***Citori Skeet Grade II*** – 12, 20, 28 ga., or .410 bore, high rib. Disc. 1983.

$1,600	$1,235	$925	$740	$690	$650	$600	

* ***Citori Skeet Grade III*** – 12 or 20 ga., Invector chokes originally in 12 and 20 ga. and invector plus choking, high-post target rib, and ported barrels became standard in 1994. Mfg. 1986-1999.

$1,700	$1,300	$1,000	$800	$700	$650	$600	*$2,310*

Add $100 for factory adj. comb (mfg. 1995-98).
Subtract 10% if w/o Invector Plus choke system.

» **Citori Skeet Grade III Smaller Gauges** – 28 ga. or .410 bore, invector chokes became an option in 1994. Mfg. 1986-1999.

$1,800	$1,500	$1,300	$1,000	$700	$650	$600	*$2,316*

Subtract 20% if without standard Invector choking (new 1994).

* ***Citori Skeet Grade V*** – 12, 20, 28 ga., or .410 bore, high rib. Disc. 1984.

$2,500	$2,100	$1,800	$1,500	$1,250	$1,050	$850	

Add 20% for 20 ga. or 30% for 28 ga.or .410 bore.

* ***Citori Skeet Grade VI*** – 12 or 16 ga., choice of blue or grey finished receiver with multiple gold inlays, deluxe walnut, invector plus choking high post target rib and ported barrels became standard in 1994. Disc. 1995.

$2,400	$2,100	$1,800	$1,300	$1,100	$900	$800	*$2,555*

Add approx. 35% for hand engraving (mfg. 1983-1984 only).
Subtract 10% if w/o Invector Plus choke system.

» **Citori Skeet Grade VI Smaller Gauges** – 28 ga. or .410 bore, barrels are choked SK/SK.

$2,750	$2,250	$1,900	$1,400	$1,200	$1,000	$850	*$2,518*

Add approx. 35% for hand engraving (mfg. 1983-1984 only).

* ***Citori Skeet Golden Clays (GC)*** – 12 or 20 ga., 26 or 28 in. ported VR barrels with Invector (disc. 1995) or Invector Plus choking, high post target rib and ported barrels (12 ga. only), Skeet features, satin grey receiver with Grade VI level of engraving and gold inlays depicting a transitional hunting to clay pigeon scene. Mfg. 1993-1999.

$2,725	$2,400	$2,250	$2,000	$1,650	$1,300	$1,000	*$3,434*

Add $100 for factory adj. comb (mfg. 1995-98).
Subtract approx. 20% if without Invector Plus choking.

» **Citori Skeet Golden Clays Smaller Gauges** – 28 ga. or .410 bore, standard Invector or fixed SK/SK choking.

$3,000	$2,650	$2,400	$2,250	$1,800	$1,500	$1,250	*$3,356*

Subtract approx. 20% with fixed choking.

GRADING - PPGS™	100%	98%	95%	90%	80%	70%	60%	LAST MSR

CITORI XS SKEET – 12 or 20 (new 2001) ga., 2 3/4 in. chambers, ported 28 or 30 in. vent. barrels with raised 5/16 in. VR and Invector Plus choking, silver nitride receiver with gold accents, checkered walnut stock available with or without adj. comb, features similar to the Ultra XS Sporting Model, Hi-Viz fiber optic front sight, includes Triple Trigger System, approx. 7 - 8 1/4 lbs. New 2000.

MSR $3,180	$2,750	$2,350	$2,000	$1,700	$1,450	$1,200	$1,000	

Add $420 for adj. comb.

This model's nomenclature was changed from Ultra XS Skeet to Citori XS Skeet in 2002.

CITORI 3-GAUGE SKEET SETS – supplied with one 20 ga. frame and one forearm, and 3 barrels consisting of 20, 28 ga. and .410 bore, cased. Mfg. 1987-1996.

* ***Citori 3-Gauge Skeet Set Grade I*** – with high post target rib, standard Invector choking became standard 1994.

	$2,650	$2,200	$1,900	$1,450	$1,275	$1,050	$975	*$3,100*

* ***Citori 3-Gauge Skeet Set Grade III*** – with high post target rib, available with standard Invector choking (new 1994) or fixed SK/SK chokes.

	$3,400	$2,600	$2,100	$1,550	$1,395	$1,250	$1,125	*$3,900*

Subtract 20% for fixed SK/SK chokes.

* ***Citori 3-Gauge Skeet Set Grade VI*** – with high post target rib, fixed SK/SK chokes only. Disc. 1994.

	$3,600	$2,800	$2,300	$1,775	$1,600	$1,400	$1,275	*$3,990*

* ***Citori 3-Gauge Skeet Set Golden Clays*** – features Golden Clays accents and engraving, standard Invector choking. Mfg. 1994-95 only.

	$4,250	$3,075	$2,600	$2,100	$1,900	$1,750	$1,600	*$5,100*

CITORI 4-GAUGE SKEET SETS – supplied with one 12 ga. frame and forearm, and 4 barrels consisting of 12, 20, 28 ga., and .410 bore, cased. Imported 1985 only.

* ***Citori 4-Gauge Skeet Set Grade I*** – with high post target rib, choice of standard Invector (new 1994) or fixed SK/SK choking.

	$3,500	$2,850	$2,400	$1,975	$1,800	$1,775	$1,600	*$4,450*

Subtract 10% for fixed SK/SK choking.

* ***Citori 4-Gauge Skeet Set Grade III*** – with high post target rib, choice of standard Invector (new 1994) or fixed SK/SK choking.

	$4,250	$3,250	$2,700	$2,250	$1,950	$1,800	$1,700	*$5,450*

Subtract 20% for fixed SK/SK choking.

* ***Citori 4-Gauge Skeet Set Grade VI*** – with high post target rib, fixed SK/SK choking only. Disc. 1994.

	$4,600	$3,350	$2,775	$2,300	$2,100	$2,000	$1,900	*$5,225*

* ***Citori 4-Gauge Skeet Set Golden Clays*** – features Golden Clays accents and engraving, standard Invector choking. Mfg. 1994 only.

	$5,650	$4,100	$3,300	$2,600	$2,350	$2,100	$1,975	*$6,750*

SHOTGUNS: O/U, CITORI SPORTING CLAYS

All sporting clays models mfg. after 1994 have the Triple Trigger System which includes 3 interchangeable trigger shoes. During 2010, Vector Pro chokes became standard on 12 and 20 ga. models.

Subtract 10% for 28 in. barrels on used guns.

CITORI 325 GRADE II – 12 or 20 ga., 28, 30, or 32 (12 ga. only) in. 10mm VR barrels with Invector Plus choking, ported barrels, European styling featuring checkered walnut stock and Schnabel forearm, greyed nitrous finished receiver, top tang safety, SST, ejectors, 6 lbs. 12 oz. - 7 lbs. 15 oz. Mfg. 1993-94.

	$1,195	$995	$850	$715	$575	$495	$450	*$1,625*

GRADING - PPGS™	100%	98%	95%	90%	80%	70%	60%	LAST MSR

CITORI 325 GOLDEN CLAYS – 12 or 20 ga., 28, 30, or 32 in. ported (12 ga. only) or unported (20 ga. only) VR barrels, Invector Plus choking, Model 325 Grade II features, satin grey receiver with engraving and gold inlays depicting a transitional hunting to clay pigeon scene. Mfg. 1994 only.

	$2,450	$2,050	$1,450	$1,150	$975	$875	$825	$3,030

CITORI 425 SPORTING CLAYS GRADE I – 12 or 20 ga., 28, 30, or 32 (disc. 2000 - 12 ga. only, adj. comb) in. 10mm VR barrels with Invector Plus choking, 12 ga. has ported barrels, with or without adj. comb (disc. 2000), European styling featuring checkered walnut stock and Schnabel forearm, mono-bloc action with greyed nitrous finished receiver, top tang safety, SST, ejectors, solid pad, approx. 6 3/4 - 8 lbs. Mfg. 1995-2001.

	$1,625	$1,200	$1,000	$825	$725	$625	$525	$2,006

Add $231 for adj. comb.

CITORI 425 GOLDEN CLAYS – 12 or 20 ga., 28, 30, or 32 (disc. 1999) in. ported (12 ga. only) or unported (20 ga. only) VR barrels, with (disc. 1998) or without adj. comb, Invector Plus choking, Model 425 Grade I features, satin grey receiver with engraving and gold inlays depicting a transitional hunting to clay pigeon scene, 6 lbs., 13 oz. - 7 lbs., 14 oz. Mfg. 1995-2001.

	$2,725	$2,400	$2,250	$2,000	$1,650	$1,300	$1,000	$3,977

Add $100 for factory adj. comb (disc. 1998).

CITORI 425 WSSF – 12 ga. only, special dimensions for Women's Shooting Sports Foundation, features painted turquoise finish with WSSF logo on stock or natural walnut finish (new 1997), 7 1/4 lbs. Mfg. 1995-99.

	$1,750	$1,300	$1,100	$925	$800	$675	$550	$1,855

CITORI 525 SPORTING – 12, 20, 28 (new 2003) ga., or .410 bore (new 2003), 2 3/4 or 3 (.410 bore) in. chambers, 28, 30, or 32 (new 2003) in. vent. barrels with 8-11 mm (12 ga. only) or 10 mm (20 ga. only) width canted VR and porting (12 or 20 ga. only), silver nitride receiver finish with high relief engraving, Hi-Viz Pro-Comp sights, redesigned stock, includes full set of Midas Grade Invector Plus choke tubes (non-flush), oil finished European style checkered Grade III/IV walnut stock with palm swell and forearm, approx. 7-8 1/2 lbs. Mfg. 2002-2008.

	$2,425	$2,050	$1,750	$1,400	$1,000	$800	$695	$3,035

Add $11 for 28 ga. or .410 bore.
Add $298 for adj. comb stock (mfg. 2004-2007, 12 or 20 ga.).

* ***Citori 525 Sporting Grade I*** – 12 ga. only, 3 in. chambers, 28, 30, or 32 in. ported barrels, silver nitride receiver with light 525 style field engraving, oil finished Grade I American walnut stock and Schnabel forearm, right hand palm swell, tapered floating rib, triple trigger system, three flush Invector-Plus choke tubes, Hi-Viz Pro-Comp sight, approx. 8 lbs. Mfg. 2005-2007.

	$1,950	$1,675	$1,425	$1,200	$800	$675	$575	$2,461

CITORI 525 GOLDEN CLAYS – 12, 20, 28 (new 2003) ga. or .410 bore (new 2003), similar features to the Model 525 Sporting, except has oil finished Grade V/VI walnut stock with solid pad and Schnabel forearm, engraving pattern that depicts the transition of a game bird into a clay bird in 24Kt. gold, includes 5 Midas Grade Invector Plus choke tubes (non-flush), 7-8 1/2 lbs. Mfg. 2002-2007.

	$3,775	$3,000	$2,300	$1,850	$1,500	$1,250	$995	$4,722

Add $215 for 28 ga. or .410 bore.

CITORI 625 SPORTING – 12 (disc.), 20 (new 2009), 28 (new 2009) ga., or .410 bore (new 2009), 2 3/4 or 3 (.410 bore only) in. chambers, 28, 30, or 32 in. ported VR barrels with Vector Pro choking system with extended forcing cones, checkered gloss finished Grade III/IV walnut stock with or w/o adj. comb and Schnabel forearm, Triple Trigger System, Hi-Viz fiber optic front sight, silver nitride finished receiver with gold accents, approx. 7-8 lbs. New 2008.

MSR $3,550	$3,275	$2,425	$2,100	$1,750	$1,450	$1,200	$1,000	

Add $50 for adj. comb. (12 ga. only), disc. Add $30 for 28 ga. or .410 bore.

GRADING - PPGS™	100%	98%	95%	90%	80%	70%	60%	LAST MSR

CITORI 725 SPORTING – 12 ga. only, 3 in. chambers, features lower profile silver nitride boxlock action receiver, 28, 30, 32 in. vent ported barrels with VR and five Invector-DS choke tubes, adj. comb became an option during 2013, gold triple trigger system, oil finished Grade III/IV checkered forearm and walnut stock with Inflex II recoil pad, approx. 7 1/2 lbs. New 2012.

MSR $3,140	$2,775	$2,300	$1,950	$1,650	$1,375	$1,175	$1,000	

Add $390 for adj. comb. (new 2013).

CITORI 802 EXTENDED SWING (ES) SPORTING – 12 ga. only, 2 3/4 in. chambers, features 28 in. ventilated ported VR barrels (low post, 6.2mm wide) which accept either Invector Plus stainless steel 2 or 4 in. extension tubes (extends barrels to 30 or 32 in.), adj. pull trigger, slimmer checkered and Schnabel forearm, 7 lbs. 5 oz. Mfg. 1996-2001.

	$1,395	$1,100	$975	$800	$700	$600	$550	*$2,063*

CITORI GTI GRADE I – 12 ga. only, 28 or 30 in. barrel with 13mm vent. rib and barrels, red lettering on receiver during 1989 only - changed to gold lettering and borders with Browning logo in 1990, checkered stock and semi-beavertail forearm, ported barrels were introduced 1990 and became standard 1992, Invector chokes standard, back-bored Invector Plus chokes became standard in 1990, approx. 8 lbs. Mfg. 1989-1994.

	$1,100	$950	$850	$700	$625	$550	$475	*$1,450*

Subtract $100 for standard chokes.
Add $35 for Signature Painted Model.

The Signature Painted Model includes special paint treatment on stock and forearm featuring Browning logos and trademark - new 1993.

CITORI GTI GOLDEN CLAYS – 12 ga. only, 28, 30, or 32 in. ported VR barrels, Invector Plus choking, GTI features, satin grey receiver with Grade VI level of engraving and gold inlays depicting a transitional hunting to clay pigeon scene. Mfg. 1993-94.

	$2,350	$1,950	$1,600	$1,300	$1,050	$925	$825	*$2,930*

CITORI GRADE I SPECIAL SPORTING – 12 ga. only, 2 3/4 in. chambers, target dimensions, high-post tapered rib, 28, 30, or 32 in. barrels, full pistol grip with palm swell, adj. comb became optional in 1994, approx. 8 lbs. 3 oz. Mfg. 1989-99.

	$1,195	$925	$775	$635	$525	$495	$450	*$1,636*

Add $100 for factory adj. comb.
Add $35 for Signature Painted Model (disc. 1994).
Add $800 for 2 barrel set (28 and 30 in. barrels), disc. 1990.

The Signature Painted Model includes special paint treatment on stock and forearm featuring Browning logos and trademark - mfg. 1993-94.

Ported barrels were new in 1990 and became standard in 1992.

In 1990, the Grade I designation was added to this model. Changes include back-bored barrels with Invector plus choke tubes.

CITORI SPECIAL SPORTING GOLDEN CLAYS (GC) – 12 ga. only, 28, 30, or 32 in. ported barrels with high-post VR, Invector Plus choking, Special Sporting features, satin grey receiver with Grade VI level of engraving and gold inlays depicting a transitional hunting to clay pigeon scene. Mfg. 1993-98.

	$2,250	$1,900	$1,600	$1,250	$995	$875	$825	*$3,203*

Add $100 for factory adj. comb.

CITORI GRADE I SPECIAL SPORTING PIGEON GRADE – 12 ga. only, Invector Plus choking and ported barrels, higher grade of Special Sporting model featuring higher grade walnut and gold line receiver accents. Mfg. 1993-94.

	$1,395	$1,150	$950	$800	$700	$625	$550	*$1,630*

CITORI ULTRA SPORTER – 12 ga. only, 28, 30, or 32 in. barrels with vent rib separating barrels, low tapered 13-10mm VR, blue or grey (new 1996) receiver with gold accents, satin finished checkered pistol grip stock and forearm, Invector Plus choking, 7 lbs. 10 oz. - 8 lbs. 4 oz. Mfg. 1995-99.

	$1,400	$1,050	$875	$750	$575	$495	$450	*$1,800*

Add $210 for adj. comb (disc. 1998).

GRADING - PPGS™	100%	98%	95%	90%	80%	70%	60%	LAST MSR

This model was designated GTI until 1995.

* ***Citori Ultra Sporter Golden Clays (GC)*** – 12 ga. only, features better wood and satin finished engraved receiver with gold inlays clay target scene. Mfg. 1995-99.

$2,250	$1,900	$1,700	$1,500	$1,275	$1,075	$925	*$3,396*

Add $210 for adj. comb (disc. 1997).

CITORI FEATHER XS SPORTING – 12, 20, 28 ga., or .410 bore, 2 3/4 in. chambers (3 in. standard on .410 bore), 28 or 30 in. vent. barrels with tapered VR (12 ga. only) and Invector Plus choking on 12 and 20 ga. (standard Invector on 28 ga. and .410 bore, 28 in. barrels), alloy receiver with dovetailed steel breechface and hinge pin, satin finished checkered walnut pistol grip stock with Schnabel forearm, Hi-Viz comp. sighting system (includes 8 interchangeable colored light pipes), Nitex receiver finish, includes Triple Trigger System (3 interchangeable trigger shoes), 6 lbs. (28 ga. or .410 bore) - approx. 7 lbs. (12 ga., 30 in. barrels). Mfg. 2000-2002.

$1,700	$1,375	$1,150	$995	$875	$775	$675	*$2,311*

CITORI XS GOLDEN CLAYS – 12 or 20 ga. only, similar to 525 Golden Clays, except has traditional checkering pattern and 1/2 - 3/8 in. width VR, includes 3 choke tubes. Mfg. 2002-2003.

$3,150	$2,600	$2,050	$1,650	$1,400	$1,150	$925	*$3,914*

CITORI XS SPORTING (ULTRA) – 12, 20, 28 ga. (disc. 2003) or .410 bore (disc. 2003), greyed steel receiver with silver nitride finish, 24Kt. gold accents and light engraving, 28, 30, or 32 (new 2003) in. barrels, with or w/o (30 in. barrels only) barrel porting, 12 ga. features flush Invector Plus choking and right-hand palm swell, Hi-Viz Pro-Comp sight, Triple Trigger System, select checkered walnut stock with satin finish and Schnabel forearm, 6 lbs. 5 oz. - 8 lbs. Mfg. 1999-2007.

$1,900	$1,600	$1,300	$995	$875	$750	$650	*$2,597*

Add 10% for 28 ga. or .410 bore.

CITORI GRAND PRIX SPORTER – 12 ga. only, 2 3/4 in. chambers, steel receiver with silver nitride finish and gold enhanced engraving, 28, 30, or 32 in. VR ported barrels with extended Invector-Plus Midas Grade choke tubes and Hi-Viz fiber optic front sight, oil finished checkered pistol grip walnut stock and Schnabel forearm, select ejector system allows for either ejection or manual extraction, cased, approx. 8 1/4 lbs. Mfg. 2007-2009.

$2,800	$2,350	$1,800	$1,525	$1,250	$1,050	$925	*$3,439*

CITORI LIGHTNING SPORTING (GRADE I) – 12 ga. only, features 3 in. chambers, rounded pistol grip, Lightning style forearm, choice of high or low post VR, standard or adj. (new 1995) comb stock, "Lightning Sporting Clays Edition" inscribed and gold-filled on receiver, triple trigger system, 28 in. ported or 30 in. ported or unported (disc.) barrels, approx. 8 1/2 lbs. Mfg. 1989-2004.

$1,300	$1,045	$885	$765	$650	$550	$495	*$1,794*

Add $100 for adj. comb (disc. 1998).
Subtract $100 for low rib.

The Signature Painted Model includes special paint treatment on stock and forearm featuring Browning logos and trademark - mfg. 1993-94. Ported barrels were new in 1990 and became standard in 1992. Between 1990-2000, the Grade I designation was added to this model. Changes include back-bored barrels with Invector plus choke tubes.

* ***Citori Lightning Sporting Golden Clays (GC)*** – 12 ga. only, 28, 30, or 32 (disc.) in. ported barrels with choice of low or high-post VR, standard or adj. (new 1995) comb stock, Invector Plus choking, Lightning Sporting features, satin grey receiver with Grade VI level of engraving and gold inlays depicting a transitional hunting to clay birds scene, approx. 8 1/2 lbs. Mfg. 1993-98.

$2,600	$2,200	$1,750	$1,400	$1,175	$1,000	$875	*$3,092*

Add $100 for factory adj. comb.
Subtract $100 for low post rib.

GRADING - PPGS™	100%	98%	95%	90%	80%	70%	60%	LAST MSR

CITORI GRADE I LIGHTNING SPORTING PIGEON GRADE – 12 ga. only, higher grade model featuring higher grade walnut and gold line receiver accents. Mfg. 1993-94.

	$1,500	$1,200	$950	$700	$575	$495	$450	$1,566

Subtract $100 for low post rib.

CITORI SPORTING HUNTER – please refer to description and pricing under Shotguns: O/U Citori Hunting Series category.

SHOTGUNS: O/U, CITORI TARGET

During 2010, Vector Pro chokes became standard on 12 and 20 ga. models.

CITORI XS SPECIAL – 12 ga. only, 2 3/4 in. chambers, 30 or 32 in. vent. barrels, silver nitride receiver with XS Special engraving, satin finished stock with adj. comb and semi-beavertail forearm, low/regular or high-post (new 2007) floating 8-11mm tapered rib, includes Triple Trigger System and 5 Midas Grade Invector Plus chokes (non-flush), approx. 8 3/4 lbs. New 2004.

MSR $3,600	$3,100	$2,475	$2,100	$1,825	$1,525	$1,325	$1,150	

CITORI GTS GRADE I – 12 ga. only, 3 in. chambers, 28 or 30 in. 10mm VR barrels with flush Invector-Plus choke tubes, steel silver nitride finished receiver with game bird transforming into clay target engraving, oil finished checkered Grade II/III walnut pistol grip stock and Schnabel forearm, Hi-Viz front sight, includes case, approx. 8 1/4 lbs. Mfg. 2007-2009.

	$2,150	$1,750	$1,400	$1,150	$950	$800	$700	$2,349

CITORI GTS HIGH GRADE – 12 ga. only, similar to Grade I, except has gold game bird/clay target engraving. Mfg. 2007-2009.

	$3,475	$2,800	$2,350	$1,925	$1,600	$1,300	$1,175	$4,309

CITORI ULTRA XS PRESTIGE – 12 ga., similar to Citori GTS High Grade, except has gloss oil finished adj. stock and gold accented Ultra XS special engraving, ported barrels, Hi-Viz fiber optic sight, includes case, approx. 8 lbs. Mfg. 2008-2009.

	$4,000	$2,850	$2,000	$1,600	$1,350	$1,125	$1,000	$4,759

SHOTGUNS: O/U, CITORI TRAP

During 2010, Vector Pro chokes became standard on 12 and 20 ga. models.

Hand engraving was replaced by machine engraving in late 1982 on all higher grade models.

CITORI TRAP MODELS – 12 ga., similar to Standard Citori, 30 or 32 in. barrels, trap chokes, Monte Carlo stock, recoil pad. Invector chokes became standard in 1988, Invector Plus chokes with ported barrels became an option in 1992, and were made standard in 1993, new Special Trap models were introduced during 1995 with decreased weight (1/4 lb. lighter) and better swing/balance characteristics. Mfg. 1974-current.

* ***Citori Trap Grade I*** – w/o choke tube, mfg. 1974-1978, with choke tube 1979-1994.

w/o choke tube	$900	$800	$750	$650	$525	$495	$450	
w/ choke tube	$1,150	$1,025	$900	$800	$750	$650	$525	

* ***Citori Grade I Special Trap*** – approx. 8 1/2 lbs. Mfg. 1995-99.

	$1,395	$975	$795	$650	$525	$495	$450	$1,658

Add $100 for factory adj. comb.
Subtract 20% without Invector chokes or high rib.

* ***Citori Trap Combination Set*** – Grade I only, 32 in. O/U and 34 in. single barrel, or extra set of barrels in same ga., cased. Disc.

	$1,295	$1,100	$975	$900	$825	$775	$725	

Add approx. 40% for extra 20 ga. barrels originally ordered with gun.

* ***Citori Grade I Plus Trap*** – features adj. rib and stock, back-bored barrels, Invector Plus choke system. Mfg. 1990-94.

	$1,900	$1,525	$1,225	$995	$700	$600	$500	$2,005

Add 5% for ported barrels.

In 1991 this model included a travel vault gun case at no extra charge. Subtract $50 for older mfg. without travel case.

GRADING - PPGS™	100%	98%	95%	90%	80%	70%	60%	LAST MSR

* ***Citori Grade I Plus Trap Combo*** – includes ported barrels with Invector Plus choking and extra standard single ported barrel, luggage case. Mfg. 1992-94.

	$2,775	$2,475	$2,100	$1,900	$1,700	$1,500	$1,250	*$3,435*

* ***Citori Plus Trap Golden Clays*** – 12 ga. only, 30 or 32 in. ported VR barrels, Invector Plus choking, Trap features, satin grey receiver with Grade VI level of engraving and gold inlays depicting a transitional hunting to clay birds scene. Mfg. 1993-94.

	$3,000	$2,600	$2,000	$1,600	$1,400	$1,200	$995	*$3,435*

* ***Citori Plus Trap Golden Clays Combo*** – includes O/U ported barrels with Invector Plus choking and extra standard single ported barrel, luggage case. Mfg. 1993-94.

	$4,425	$3,300	$2,775	$2,250	$1,925	$1,800	$1,700	*$5,200*

* ***Citori XT Trap*** – 12 ga. only, features greyed receiver with 24Kt. gold accents and light engraving, Triple Trigger System (includes 3 interchangeable triggers for 1/8 in. adj. on LOP), 30 or 32 in. vent. backbored barrels with high-post VR, checkered high gloss Monte Carlo walnut stock and forearm, right hand palm swell, Hi-Viz front sight, waffle-style recoil pad, approx. 8 1/2 lbs. New 1999.

MSR $2,950	$2,550	$2,100	$1,575	$1,275	$1,000	$800	$650	

Add $440 for adj. comb.

* ***Citori XT Trap Gold*** – 12 ga. only, 2 3/4 in. chambers, features intricate "Golden Clays" engraving with game bird/clay bird, Grade V/VI American walnut stock and semi-beavertail forearm, vented 30 or 32 in. ported barrels with high post VR and Invector Plus choke system with five flush Midas Grade chokes, adj. comb, adj. GraCoil recoil reduction system, Triple Trigger System, Hi-Viz Pro-Comp, and mid-bead sights, approx. 9 lbs. New 2005.

MSR $5,700	$4,950	$3,850	$3,050	$2,375	$1,875	$1,475	$1,175	

* ***Citori Trap Pigeon Grade*** – 12 ga. only, features extra deluxe walnut, Invector Plus ported barrels, and receiver gold accents. Mfg. 1993-94.

	$1,715	$1,250	$950	$800	$700	$600	$500	*$2,225*

* ***Citori Trap Signature Painted*** – 12 ga. only, features painted red/black stock with Browning logos on stock and forearm, Invector Plus ported barrels. Mfg. 1993-94.

	$1,595	$1,200	$940	$800	$700	$600	$500	*$2,065*

* ***Citori Trap Grade II*** – high post rib. Mfg. 1978-1983.

	$1,200	$900	$800	$700	$650	$600	$500	

* ***Citori Trap Grade III*** – 12 ga. only, high post rib, Invector Plus choking and ported barrels became standard in 1994. Mfg. 1986-99.

	$1,500	$1,200	$900	$800	$725	$650	$550	*$2,310*

Add $100 for factory adj. comb.
Subtract 10% if without Invector Plus chokes or ported barrels.

* ***Citori Trap Grade V*** – high post rib. Mfg. 1978-1984.

	$1,750	$1,400	$1,100	$880	$795	$710	$620	

* ***Citori Trap Grade VI*** – 12 ga. only, Invector chokes became standard in 1985, Invector Plus chokes became standard in 1994. Disc. 1994.

	$1,995	$1,600	$1,300	$1,100	$960	$875	$825	*$2,555*

Add approx. 20% for hand engraving (mfg. 1983-1984 only).
Subtract $150 if without Invector Plus chokes or ported barrels.
Subtract $250 for fixed chokes.

* ***Citori Trap Golden Clays (GC)*** – 12 ga. only, 30 or 32 in. ported VR barrels, Invector Plus choking, Trap features, Monte Carlo or regular stock, satin grey receiver with Grade VI level of engraving and gold inlays depicting a transitional hunting to clay pigeon scene. Mfg. 1993-99.

	$2,750	$2,400	$2,100	$1,750	$1,500	$1,250	$1,025	*$3,434*

Add $220 for adj. comb (new 1995).

GRADING - PPGS™	100%	98%	95%	90%	80%	70%	60%	*LAST MSR*

CITORI XS PRO-COMP - 12 ga. only, 2 3/4 in. chambers, 28 or 30 in. vent. and ported VR barrels with spreader chokes, adj. comb, beavertail forearm, GraCoil recoil reduction system, right-hand palm swell, Triple Trigger System, features removable tungsten alloy forearm weight which approximates the same weight as barrel tubes, also has removable front barrel weight to adj. the swing through, approx. 9 lbs. Mfg. 2002-2004.

	100%	98%	95%	90%	80%	70%	60%	LAST MSR
	$2,750	$2,300	$1,900	$1,425	$1,100	$975	$850	*$4,027*

SHOTGUNS: O/U, SUPERPOSED GENERAL INFO & CHOKE CODES

SUPERPOSED MODEL - 12, 20 (introduced circa 1948-49), 28 ga. (introduced 1959) or .410 bore (introduced 1958), 26 1/2, 28, 30, or 32 in. barrels, various chokes, boxlock, auto ejectors, various trigger combinations (single & double), checkered pistol grip stock, mfg. 1931-40 and 1948-76 by FN, grades differ in amount of engraving, inlays, general quality of workmanship and wood.

NOTE: The use of steel shot is NOT recommended in any Superposed Series manufactured in Belgium (B-25 variations).

BROWNING CHOKES AND THEIR CODES (MARKED NEXT TO EJECTORS)

*** designates full choke (F).**

***- designates improved modified choke (IM).**

**** designates modified choke (M).**

****- designates improved cylinder choke (IC).**

****$ designates skeet (SK).**

***** designates cylinder bore (CYL).**

SKEET MODELS were available in every ga. and grade.

TRAP MODELS were available in every grade in 12 ga. only.

BROADWAY TRAP MODELS (mfg. 1961-75) featured a 5/8 in. wide vent. rib and were also available in every grade.

Please refer to the Browning Superposed serialization section in the Serialization section for determining year of manufacture.

SUPERPOSED: 1931-1940 MFG. (PRE-WWII)

Early pre-war guns had long slender forearms with a metal plate at the front called a horseshoe plate. Approx. circa 1936, the forearm was changed to the one used post war - smaller with a transverse bolt to hold the forearm on. The earlier forearm had a long bolt that ran from front to back through the metal plate. The earlier transverse bolts were recessed into the sides of the forearms. Later the head and fastener on the other side of the forearm were flush with the wood.

Pre-war cases were manufactured in black or brown, with a textured surface called elephant hide, in leather or tex leather. Insides were lined with grey or blue cloth, and the Browning brass label was on the inside top of the case, not the outside. Depending on original condition, these cases sell in the $200-$400 range - single barrel cases are more common than multi-barrel ones. Extra barrels (same ga. only) could be ordered with the original gun, and were supplied in a Browning hard case.

Very few pre-war Pigeon, Diana, and Midas Grades were signed by the engraver.

Add approx. 35%-50% per extra set of barrels (same ga. only), depending on condition.

Subtract 10%-25% for recoil pad (depending on originality, deterioration, and condition).

SUPERPOSED STANDARD GRADE/GRADE I/LIGHTNING - 12 ga. only, boxlock action, blue w/border receiver engraving until 1938, when a simple small center rosette engraving pattern was introduced, 4 trigger options until 1938, when the barrel selector was moved to the top tang, trigger options included: double normal, selective single with the selector on the bottom next to the trigger, twin single, and non-selective single, Standard model nomenclature was changed to Grade I during 1938, in addition to changing the trigger to SST with the barrel selector on the top tang, raised hollow or ventilated rib, Lightning Model introduced during 1936 in Standard grade with striped barrels - ribs were extra cost. Original buttplates featured intertwined twin circles and were made of horn.

	100%	98%	95%	90%	80%	70%	60%	LAST MSR
12 ga.	N/A	$2,900	$2,200	$1,800	$1,400	$1,200	$1,000	

GRADING - PPGS™	100%	98%	95%	90%	80%	70%	60%	LAST MSR

Original buttplates with unaltered (uncut) stock are very important to collectors for this period of Superposed manufacture.

First year production Superposed will command a premium (approx. ser. no. range 1-2,000). The twin single trigger is also very desirable for collectors.

Recoil pads were an extra option during this time, and even though they might be factory installed, they are not desirable to collectors, and as a result, prices could be reduced substantially based on pad deterioration. Pad makers included: Jostam, Hawkins, Noshoc, D&W, and Black Diamond - these pads were $5 options pre-WWII.

SUPERPOSED PIGEON GRADE - grey receiver with 2 pigeons on either side, these earlier guns had larger engraved pigeons than later production (1960 and later). Mfg. 1931-1940.

12 ga.	N/A	$5,950	$4,850	$3,950	$2,950	$2,200	$1,900	

The Pigeon Grade style of engraving is the only pre-war style that was continued after WWII.

SUPERPOSED DIANA GRADE - grey receiver with lighter style, delicate European style engraving, boars and stags were pictured in the 1931 catalog, but dogs and birds could also be special ordered at no additional cost until 1936, after which it became extra cost, dogs and birds engraving are more common than boars and stag. Mfg. 1931-1940.

12 ga.	N/A	$8,500	$6,750	$5,250	$4,150	$3,500	$2,750	

The Diana Grade was changed dramatically in post-WWII production.

SUPERPOSED MIDAS GRADE - featured gold inlaid pigeons with outstretched wings on blue frame sides and bottom plus trigger guard. This Germanic syle engraving also exhibited multiple gold escutcheons and gold lining, ejector trip rods, ejector hammers and firing pins are also 18Kt. gold plated, finest checkered walnut.

12 ga.	N/A	$10,500	$8,500	$6,750	$5,000	$4,000	$3,000	

The Midas Grade was changed dramatically in post-WWII production.

SUPERPOSED: 1948-1960 MFG. (POST-WWII)

Model nomenclature was changed from pre-war designations to Grades I-VI. During this period, extra barrels could only be ordered in the same gauge as the original gun. Hardshell cases from this era are referred to as Tolex cases - they have blue velvet lining, and a brass Browning label on the outside top.

Engraved guns signed by Browning's top engravers (Funken, Vrancken, Watrin, Doyen, Müller, and Magis) will command a premium over unsigned guns. Felix Funken retired in 1960, and died in 1966.

On most Superposed with added recoil pads, the stock has usually been cut to keep the LOP the same. The correct LOP on a Superposed is 14 1/4 inches, with or w/o a recoil pad.

The twin circle buttplate was always horn, and was used on very early post war guns until 1949-1950.

Barrel addresses appeared as follows: circa 1947-1958 "St. Louis, M.O." (earliest BAC markings) or "St. Louis, Missouri", 1959-1968 "St. Louis, Missouri and Montreal P.Q.", and 1969-1975 "Morgan, Utah and Montreal, P.Q.". Make sure barrel address date matches year of mfg. (see listings in the back of this text).

The original factory configuration of almost all Superposed shotguns can be verified by grade, gauge/ bore, and barrel length. To obtain information on a specific Belgian Superposed serial number, please contact the Browning historian directly (refer to Trademark Index for more information).

Add approx. 35%-50% per extra set of barrels (same ga. only), depending on condition.
Add $300-$500 for correct Tolex hardshell case with paperwork.
Subtract 25% for non-original recoil pads on Grade I models, depending on condition.
Subtract 25% for non-original recoil pads on the higher grades, depending on condition.
Special order Superposed with non-standard factory engraving, checkered buttstocks, 3 piece forearms, and other special orders will command premiums over standard configurations.

SUPERPOSED GRADE I STANDARD WEIGHT - 12 or 20 ga. (3 in. chambers were introduced in the 12 ga. during 1955, and in 20 ga. during 1957), otherwise similar to pre-war mfg., blue finish and triggers until 1955, gold trigger(s) became standard in 1955, raised (standard until 1959) or vent. rib only beginning in 1959, round knob long tang (RKLT) stock configuration, this earlier period of mfg. also featured smaller, narrower forearms and thinner pistol grip stock with horn buttplate (can be determined by the rounded "g" in

GRADING - PPGS™	100%	98%	95%	90%	80%	70%	60%	LAST MSR

Browning, not square), early post-war production had similar pre-WWII minimal engraving until circa 1952-53, more standard engraving continued through 1955, when Grade I models featured considerably more engraving, post-war 12 ga. serialization began at approx. 17,100, and with 200 on 20 ga. Mfg. 1948-1960.

12 ga.	N/A	$1,700	$1,475	$1,300	$1,000	$895	$675
20 ga.	N/A	$2,800	$2,500	$2,000	$1,500	$1,200	$1,000

Grade I models had 3 levels of standard engraving coverage.

* ***Superposed Grade I Lightning Hunting Model*** – 12 or 20 ga., 6 oz. lighter than Standard Weight. Introduced in all Grades beginning 1956.

12 ga.	N/A	$1,700	$1,475	$1,300	$1,000	$895	$675
20 ga.	N/A	$2,800	$2,500	$2,000	$1,500	$1,250	$1,100

* ***Superposed Grade I Magnum*** – 12 ga. only, 3 in. chambers, 28, 30, or 32 (rare) in. barrels with raised or vent. rib, recoil pad standard, introduced in all Grades in 1955.

	N/A	$1,850	$1,625	$1,450	$1,150	$950	$750

This model with 30 or 32 (rare) in. barrels is now popular again, as Sporting Clays shooters like this desirable configuration.

* ***Superposed Grade I Trap Standard Weight Model*** – 12 ga. only, various configurations. Introduced 1952.

	N/A	$1,825	$1,595	$1,450	$1,150	$950	$725

Pre-war trap guns and those manufactured post-war until approx. 1955 were virtually indistinguishable from field guns as they had field style forearms, round knob (semi-pistol grip) and long tangs. The only way to tell the difference is they had a longer LOP (14 1/2 in.) and a shorter drop at the heel - 1 3/4 in. vs. 2 1/2 in. for field stocks. These early trap guns did not come with recoil pads. Between 1956-1960, trap guns had the forearm changed to semi-beavertail. These late guns with semi-beavertail forearms are very desirable today due to their rarity and overall desirability.

SUPERPOSED GRADE II – 12 or 20 ga., featured pre-war Pigeon Grade engraving with large pigeons, some early post- war mfg. were signed by Funken.

12 ga.	N/A	$4,200	$3,675	$3,325	$2,650	$2,175	$1,675
20 ga.	N/A	$7,300	$6,395	$5,750	$4,600	$3,795	$2,925

SUPERPOSED GRADE III – 12 or 20 ga., European style engraving, commonly referred to as "fighting cocks," pheasants on right side, fighting cocks on left, most were signed by the engraver.

12 ga.	N/A	$4,800	$4,200	$3,795	$3,025	$2,500	$1,925
20 ga.	N/A	$9,000	$7,875	$7,100	$5,675	$4,675	$3,600

SUPERPOSED GRADE IV – 12 or 20 ga., features deeper European style engraving with dogs and foxes, most were signed by the engraver.

12 ga.	N/A	$8,000	$7,000	$6,325	$5,050	$4,150	$3,200
20 ga.	N/A	$12,500	$10,950	$9,875	$7,875	$6,500	$5,000

SUPERPOSED GRADE V – 12 or 20 ga., features deeper engraving than pre-war Diana Grade, pheasants and ducks on receiver, most were signed by the engraver - Doyen was prevalent on this model.

12 ga.	N/A	$7,000	$6,125	$5,525	$4,400	$3,650	$2,800
20 ga.	N/A	$12,000	$10,500	$9,475	$7,500	$6,250	$4,800

SUPERPOSED GRADE VI – 12 or 20 ga., engraving pattern similar to later production Midas Grade, almost all of these were signed by Müeller. Introduced in July, 1957, changed in 1960, limited production, and rarest of the 6 grades.

12 ga.	N/A	$10,000	$8,750	$7,900	$6,300	$5,200	$4,000
20 ga.	N/A	$20,000	$17,500	$15,800	$12,600	$10,400	$8,000

SUPERPOSED: 1960-1976 MFG.

In early 1960, a major change was made in the manner in which the various grades of Superposed

were designated. The Roman numerals used in the 1950s were dropped, and Browning once again returned to names. The Pigeon, Diana, and Midas names used for pre-war designations were brought back and replaced the Grade II, Grade V, and Grade VI respectively. Grades III & IV were dropped and replaced by the Pointer. The Grade I remained unchanged.

The Broadway Trap Model was introduced in 1961. Browning's lifetime Superposed warranty began in 1963. During 1965, the Hydro Coil stock (1 year only) and barrel Super Tubes were introduced. During 1966, a major change was implemented to save money when Browning switched from a long tang to short tang. During 1970-71, the stock configuration was once again changed to a full pistol grip (referred to as flat knob), and the long tang was brought back. Also at this time, mechanical triggers were implemented vs. the older inertial design, and silver solder vent. ribs vs. tin solder. As a result, this period of Superposed manufacture was mechanically better and more reliable. The Superlight Model was introduced in 12 ga. during 1967, 20 ga. during 1969, and became available in all Grades beginning in 1971. All gauge Skeet sets became available in all Grades during 1972.

During late 1966, Browning's salt wood problems began to emerge, and continued until 1970. The majority of salt wood Superposed models from this era are in the round knob short tang configuration (RKST), but some flat knob short tang (FKST) guns with salt problems have also been observed. Depending on the damage (it can vary a lot), values for salt damaged guns can be reduced by as much as 50% (heavy pitting and original salt wood). Those salt guns that have been restocked by Browning are accepted by the shooting fraternity, and can command as much as 90% of the value of non-salt original guns. To determine if a Superposed has salt damage, examine carefully any gun where the serial number is within the 1966-1971 production range (please refer to the Browning Superposed serialization section), and carefully inspect the wood around the buttplate, forearm, and where the wood joins the receiver metal for any telltale rusting or pitting.

Engraved guns signed by Browning's top engravers (Funken, Vrancken, Watrin, Magis, Müeller, and J. Baerten) will command a premium over unsigned guns. Also, more and more Superposed models are appearing with Angelo Bee's signature (while non-factory, Mr. Bee's work is universally recognized. He engraved in Belgium at FN from 1951-1974.) Louis Vrancken and Andre Watrin took over as heads of the engraving department in 1960.

The following values are for 1960-1976 Superposed production non-salt damaged guns. Most desirable period of mfg. is 1960-1966 (round knob, long tang, limited salt, rarely encountered with salt damage). Guns made during 1972-1976 (FKLT) are worth more than RKST. Lowest values are for 1966-1971 mfg. (round/flat knob, short tang - should be inspected carefully for potential salt wood problems). Many Browning collectors/dealers feel that round/flat knob, short tang Superposed are getting harder to sell every year.

Barrel addresses appeared as follows: circa 1947-1958 "St. Louis, M.O." (earliest BAC markings) or "St. Louis, Missouri", 1959-1968 "St. Louis, Missouri and Montreal P.Q.", 1969-1975 "Morgan, Utah and Montreal, P.Q." Make sure barrel address date matches year of mfg. (see listings in the back of this text).

The original factory configuration of almost all Superposed shotguns can be verified by grade, gauge/bore, and barrel length. To obtain information on a specific Belgian Superposed serial number, please contact the Browning historian directly (refer to Trademark Index for more information).

SUPERPOSED WITH EXTRA BARREL(S) OR SUPER-TUBES – The Superposed could be special ordered from the factory in the following combinations: 12 or 20 ga. with one extra set of barrels in same ga., 12 ga. with one extra set in 20 ga., 12 or 20 ga. with two extra barrel sets of same ga., 20 ga. with one extra set in either 28 ga. or .410 bore, 20 ga. with both 28 ga. and .410 bore barrel sets, and 28 ga. with extra set of .410 bore barrels. Super-Tubes were adaptable on 12 ga. guns only; came from the factory cased with accessories, 16 1/2 in. long, factory installation.

Add 40%-50% of the gun's value for each Grade I extra barrel set(s). For higher grades, add approx. $1,000-$2,500 per barrel set, depending on grade.

Add $250 for Super-Tubes - available for 12 ga. only, introduced in 1965.

GRADING - PPGS™	100%	98%	95%	90%	80%	70%	60%	LAST MSR

Add $400 for Super-Tube Set - 3 ga. set (20, 28 ga., and .410 bore).
Subtract $150-$500 for non-original recoil pads on Grade I models, depending on condition.
Subtract $250-$750 for non-original recoil pads on the higher grades, depending on condition.

SUPERPOSED VARIATIONS – On most Superposed with added recoil pads, the stock has usually been cut to keep the LOP the same. The correct LOP on a Superposed is 14 1/4 inches (14 1/2 in. on Trap & New Style Skeet), with or w/o a factory recoil pad, unless special ordered from the factory. Except for the Superlight Model, individual configurations have not been broken out on the Pigeon, Pointer, Diana, and Midas grades, but values will be similar to each other in most cases.

Subtract approx. 25%-40% for salt wood (depending on extent of damage).
Subtract 10% for new style Skeet configuration on models.
Subtract 15%-20% for Broadway Trap Model.
Special order Superposed with non-standard factory engraving, checkered buttstocks, 3 piece forearms, and other special orders will command premiums over standard configurations.

SUPERPOSED GRADE I STANDARD WEIGHT & LIGHTNING – 12, 20, 28 ga., or .410 bore (the 28 ga. & .410 bore were not cataloged until 1960), 28 ga. and .410 bore were built on a 20 ga. frame, the buttplate was changed from horn to plastic during 1961, 12 and 20 ga. Lightning Models were approx. 6 oz. lighter than Standard Weight.

12 ga.	$2,000	$1,600	$1,300	$975	$825	$750	$695
20 ga.	$3,500	$3,000	$2,800	$2,200	$1,550	$1,275	$1,100
28 ga.	$7,000	$6,500	$5,500	$4,250	$3,250	$2,650	$2,300
.410 bore	$5,500	$4,500	$3,500	$3,000	$2,200	$1,475	$1,225

Subtract 10%-15% for Grade I Standardweight (12 ga. only).
Add 20%-25% for round knob, long tang stock variations (pre-1966), unless Skeet choked.

* ***Superposed Grade I Magnum*** – 12 ga. only, 3 in. chambers, 28, 30, or 32 (rare) in. barrels with vent. rib, recoil pad standard.

12 ga.	$1,950	$1,600	$1,200	$1,000	$825	$775	$725

This model with 30 or 32 (very rare) in. barrels is now popular again, as Sporting Clays shooters like this desirable configuration.

* ***Superposed Grade I Superlight*** – 12 (mfg. 1967-1976), 20 (1969-1976), 28 (very rare, approx. 12-14 mfg.) ga. or .410 bore (mfg. 1970-76) features lightweight construction and straight grip stock. During 1971, the Superlight was offered in all Grades.

12 ga.	$3,375	$2,675	$2,175	$1,550	$1,075	$975	$875
20 ga.	$5,150	$4,425	$3,650	$2,850	$2,000	$1,650	$1,425
28 ga.	$17,500	$16,250	$13,750	$10,500	$8,125	$6,625	$5,750
.410 bore	$8,250	$6,750	$5,250	$4,500	$3,300	$2,200	$1,850

A Quail Unlimited limited edition was also available in the Superlight Series, add 10%-15% if in 98%+ original condition.
20 ga. with solid rib barrels are very rare and will command a premium over vent. rib variations.

* ***Superposed Grade I Skeet/New Model Skeet*** – 12, 20, 28 ga. or .410 bore, 26 1/2 or 28 in. VR barrels with fixed SK/SK chokes, New Model Skeet was introduced during 1968, and was available in both Standard and Lightning weights in 12 and 20 ga., this New Model featured a flat bottom pistol grip stock with factory vent. recoil pad and beavertail forearm, pre-'68 mfg. was basically a hunting model with skeet chokes. Mfg. circa 1950s-1976.

12 ga.	$1,675	$1,400	$1,100	$950	$825	$750	$700
20 ga.	$2,450	$2,100	$1,700	$1,250	$975	$850	$775
28 ga.	$4,950	$4,500	$3,500	$2,750	$2,250	$1,550	$1,275
.410 bore	$2,800	$2,400	$1,950	$1,450	$1,100	$925	$850

Add approx. 10%-15% for pre 1968 mfg. (w/o beavertail forearm and recoil pad.)
Subtract 20% for 26 in. (New Skeet style) barrels.

GRADING - PPGS™	100%	98%	95%	90%	80%	70%	60%	LAST MSR

* ***Superposed Grade I Four Gauge Skeet Set*** – includes 12, 20, 28 ga. and .410 bore barrels, 26 1/2 or 28 in. VR barrels, 12 ga. frame, beavertail forearm, includes fitted luggage case. Mfg. 1972-1976.

	100%	98%	95%	90%	80%	70%	60%	LAST MSR
	$5,250	$4,950	$4,500	$4,150	$3,850	$3,350	$2,650	

Subtract 20% for 26 in. (New Skeet style) barrels.

* ***Superposed Grade I Trap Model (Lightning and Broadway)*** – 12 ga. only, FKLT, Trap dimension stock with recoil pad, 14 3/8 in. LOP, semi-beavertail forearm, 30 or 32 (rare in Lightning model) in. barrels with either standard 5/16 in. VR (Lightning) or 5/8 in. Broadway VR, first cataloged in 1961, this new Lightning Model Trap was approx. 6 oz. lighter than previous mfg., front and middle ivory bead sights standard, Broadway is approx. 1 lbs. heavier than Lightning with same length barrels.

	100%	98%	95%	90%	80%	70%	60%	LAST MSR
	$1,950	$1,600	$1,200	$1,000	$825	$750	$700	

SUPERPOSED PIGEON GRADE – 12, 20, 28 ga. or .410 bore, features a silver grey receiver with 2 smaller flying pigeons surrounded by fine scroll engraving on each side of the frame, receiver bottom and tangs also exhibit fine scroll work. Disc. 1974.

	100%	98%	95%	90%	80%	70%	60%	LAST MSR
12 ga.	$5,500	$3,850	$2,900	$2,000	$1,700	$1,570	$1,485	
20 ga.	$9,000	$7,500	$6,000	$4,000	$2,750	$2,100	$1,850	
28 ga.	$12,500	$9,000	$7,800	$6,000	$4,500	$3,500	$2,500	
.410 bore	$9,000	$7,500	$6,000	$4,500	$3,300	$2,800	$2,200	

Add 20%-25% for round knob, long tang stock variations (pre-1966), unless Skeet choked.
Subtract 20% for newer Skeet style model with beavertail forearm and recoil pad.

Between 1948-1960, this model was designated the Grade II.

* ***Superposed Pigeon Grade Superlight*** – 12 (mfg. 1967-1976), 20 (1969-1976), 28 (very rare, approx. 6 mfg.) ga. or .410 bore (mfg. 1970-76) features lightweight construction and straight grip stock. During 1971, the Superlight was offered in all Grades.

	100%	98%	95%	90%	80%	70%	60%	LAST MSR
12 ga.	$8,500	$6,850	$5,500	$4,150	$3,100	$2,200	$1,800	
20 ga.	$11,500	$10,000	$8,750	$7,500	$6,250	$5,000	$4,000	
28 ga.	$15,000	$12,500	$9,250	$7,750	$6,150	$5,00	$3,750	
.410 bore	$12,000	$10,500	$9,250	$8,000	$6,750	$5,500	$4,500	

SUPERPOSED POINTER GRADE – features engraved silver grey receiver with a pointer on one side, and a setter on the other, select checkered walnut, early production was engraved by Funken, while the final design was executed by Vrancken. Mfg. 1959-disc. 1966, except for special orders.

	100%	98%	95%	90%	80%	70%	60%	LAST MSR
12 ga.	$8,750	$6,850	$5,500	$4,150	$3,100	$2,200	$1,800	
20 ga.	$15,000	$12,500	$9,250	$7,600	$6,000	$5,000	$3,750	
28 ga. (rare)	$21,500	$18,000	$15,500	$12,500	$8,000	$5,000	$3,800	
.410 bore (rare)	$17,500	$14,000	$12,250	$9,250	$6,000	$4,600	$3,500	

Add 40% for round knob, long tang stock variations (pre-1966), unless Skeet choked (add 40% if 28 ga.).
Subtract 20% for newer Skeet style model with beavertail forearm and recoil pad.

* ***Superposed Pointer Grade Superlight*** – this model was available by special order only, and was never cataloged by BAC (approx. 10 mfg. in 28 ga.).

	100%	98%	95%	90%	80%	70%	60%	LAST MSR
12 ga.	$12,250	$9,600	$7,700	$5,800	$4,350	$3,075	$2,525	
20 ga.	$21,000	$17,500	$12,950	$10,500	$8,400	$7,000	$5,250	
28 ga. (very rare)	$30,000	$25,750	$19,750	$15,000	$11,000	$8,500	$7,000	
.410 bore (very rare)	$25,000	$21,000	$15,500	$12,000	$9,000	$7,750	$6,000	

SUPERPOSED DIANA GRADE – deeper engraving with duck and pheasant game scenes - similar to 1948-60 mfg. Grade V. Disc. 1976.

	100%	98%	95%	90%	80%	70%	60%	LAST MSR
12 ga.	$7,750	$6,500	$4,300	$2,750	$2,450	$2,200	$1,975	
20 ga.	$13,000	$10,000	$8,500	$5,950	$4,850	$3,650	$3,150	
28 ga.	$22,500	$18,000	$15,000	$10,000	$7,350	$5,750	$4,750	
.410 bore	$14,500	$12,000	$9,000	$6,550	$5,000	$4,200	$3,650	

Add 20% for round knob, long tang stock variations (pre-1966, add 40% if 28 ga.).
Subtract 20% for newer Skeet style model with beavertail forearm and recoil pad.

Between 1948-1960, this model was designated the Grade V.

GRADING - PPGS™	100%	98%	95%	90%	80%	70%	60%	LAST MSR

* ***Superposed Diana Grade Superlight*** – 12 (mfg. 1967-76), 20 (1969-76), 28 (very rare, approx. 7-9 mfg.) ga. or .410 bore (mfg. 1970-76) features lightweight construction and straight grip stock. During 1971, the Superlight was offered in all Grades.

12 ga.	$11,650	$9,750	$6,450	$3,850	$3,425	$3,075	$2,775	
20 ga.	$18,000	$15,000	$11,500	$8,000	$6,500	$4,950	$4,000	
28 ga. (very rare)	$35,000	$30,000	$25,000	$21,000	$17,500	$14,000	$10,000	
.410 bore (very rare)	$27,500	$23,000	$17,000	$13,500	$10,000	$8,500	$7,250	

SUPERPOSED MIDAS GRADE – features new design by Vrancken with deep relief scroll engraving with gold inlaid ducks and pheasants on frame sides and a quail on the bottom, ejector trip rods, ejector hammers, and firing pins are also 18Kt. gold plated, best quality walnut with fine checkering. Disc. 1976.

12 ga.	$12,500	$10,500	$8,750	$6,250	$5,000	$4,000	$3,500	
20 ga.	$19,500	$16,500	$14,000	$11,750	$8,750	$7,250	$5,000	
28 ga.	$27,500	$23,000	$20,000	$16,500	$12,500	$9,000	$7,350	
.410 bore	$19,500	$16,500	$14,000	$11,750	$8,750	$7,250	$5,000	

Add 20% for round knob, long tang stock variations (pre-1966), unless Skeet choked (add 40% if 28 ga.).

Subtract 20% for newer Skeet style model with beavertail forearm and recoil pad.

Between 1948-1960, this model was designated the Grade VI.

* ***Superposed Midas Grade Superlight*** – 12 (mfg. 1967-76), 20 (1969-76), 28 (very rare, approx. 9 mfg.) ga. or .410 bore (mfg. 1970-76) features lightweight construction and straight grip stock. During 1971, the Superlight was offered in all Grades.

12 ga.	$15,625	$13,125	$11,000	$7,800	$6,250	$5,000	$4,375	
20 ga.	$24,375	$20,500	$17,500	$14,500	$11,000	$9,000	$6,250	
28 ga. (very rare)	$39,500	$33,500	$26,000	$21,000	$17,500	$14,750	$11,500	
.410 bore (very rare)	$27,250	$23,000	$19,500	$16,450	$12,250	$10,150	$7,000	

SUPERPOSED BICENTENNIAL SUPERLIGHT – specially engraved limited edition Model, 51 mfg. - one for each state and Washington, D.C. Left side has U.S. Flag, bald eagle and state emblem inlaid in gold. Right side has gold inlaid hunter and turkey. Blue receiver, fancy checkered English stock, Schnabel forend, velvet lined wood case. Made 1976 by FN.

	$12,000	$10,000	$8,000	N/A	N/A	N/A	N/A	

SUPERPOSED EXPOSITION/EXHIBITION MODEL – this specially manufactured Superposed saw limited production from pre-WWII through 1976. There are true exhibition models and a "C" series. Most "C" series did not have carved stocks, and were a special BAC sale of FN guns which did not sell well in Europe. True exhibition guns had gold lettering on the barrels in most cases, and many also had carved stocks. These guns were made for a very special reason, purpose, or person. Prices usually start in the 5 digit level - the C Series is typically priced between $20,000-$50,000, with the Exhibition guns comparably priced as long as they are not Trap or Skeet guns. Field choked RKLT and Superlite small bore guns bring the most, with small bore, all option side plated Exhibitions at the top of the heap, whether C Series or not.

SUPERPOSED PRESENTATION MODELS (P1-P4) – custom made versions of the Lightning Field, Super Light, Trap, and Skeet guns, specifications the same as Standard models, with differences in finish, engraving and inlay(s), and grade of wood and checkering. These guns were introduced by FN in 1977 and were disc. after 1984. Gauge premiums below refer to Models P1-P3.

Add 50% for 20 ga.

Add 75% for 28 ga.

Add 40% for .410 bore.

Add $1,500 for each P1 extra barrel set(s). For higher grades, add approx. $1,500-$2,500 per barrel set, depending on grade.

Subtract 25% for P Series Trap Models.

Subtract 25% for P Series Broadway Trap Models.

Subtract 20% for P Series Skeet 12 and 20 ga. guns.

GRADING - PPGS™	100%	98%	95%	90%	80%	70%	60%	LAST MSR

Since P Series Superposed were disc. in 1985, collector interest has increased substantially. Interestingly, the P series models are rarer than most of the pre-1976 high grade Superposed models.

* ***Superposed Presentation 1*** – silver grey or blue receiver, oak leaf and fine scroll engraved, choice of 6 different animal scenes.

	$3,300	$2,500	$2,100	$1,850	$1,500	$1,250	$1,000

* ***Superposed Presentation 1 w/gold inlays*** – similar to Presentation 1, only with gold inlays.

	$4,750	$3,500	$3,000	$2,100	$1,825	$1,700	$1,500

* ***Superposed Presentation 2*** – silver grey or blue receiver, high relief engraving, choice of 3 different sets of game scenes.

	$4,800	$4,000	$2,750	$2,050	$1,825	$1,700	$1,500

* ***Superposed Presentation 2 w/gold inlays*** – similar to Presentation 2, only with gold inlays.

	$7,000	$6,000	$4,200	$2,150	$1,925	$1,750	$1,550

* ***Superposed Presentation 3*** – silver grey or blue receiver, more elaborate high relief engraving with choice of partridges, mallards, or geese depicted on frame sides in 18Kt. gold.

	$9,000	$7,500	$5,500	$3,750	$3,200	$2,875	$2,300

* ***Superposed Presentation 4*** – features engraved side plates in either silver grey or blue finish, hand engraved game scenes include waterfowl on right frame side, 5 pheasants on left frame side, 2 quail on receiver bottom, and a retriever's head on trigger guard. Extra figure walnut stock and forearm.

	$8,000	$6,900	$5,250	$4,000	$3,350	$2,950	$2,375

Add 30% for 20 ga., 70% for 28 ga., or 50% for .410 bore.

* ***Superposed Presentation 4 w/gold inlays*** – similar to Presentation 4, only with game scenes inlaid in 18Kt. gold.

	$12,000	$10,500	$8,700	$6,000	$4,250	$3,650	$2,950

Add 50% for 20 ga., 75% for 28 ga., or 50% for .410 bore.

SUPERPOSED PRESENTATION SERIES SUPERLITE (PI - PIV) – available in various configurations including multi-barrel sets.

* ***Superposed Presentation I Superlite w/Gold*** – G, H, I, J, K, or L style engraving.

12 ga. (25 mfg.)	$6,750	$6,000	$5,200	$3,600	$3,000	$2,250	$1,800
20 ga. (80 mfg.)	$9,500	$8,000	$7,000	$5,500	$4,000	$3,200	$2,500
28 ga. (38 mfg.)	$13,000	$11,000	$9,800	$7,700	$6,200	$4,000	$3,400
.410 bore (47 mfg.)	$9,500	$8,500	$6,800	$5,500	$4,000	$3,200	$2,600

Add $1,500 per extra barrel.
Add 40% for an all option gun (checkered buttstock, oil finish, three piece forend, rare).
Add 15% for J. Baerten signed gun (rare).
Subtract 35% for Trap or Skeet Models.
Subtract 30% for A, B, C, D, E, or F models w/o gold.

* ***Superposed Presentation II Superlite*** – P, Q, or R style engraving.

12 ga. (23 mfg.)	$9,500	$9,000	$8,000	$7,000	$6,000	$4,500	$2,200
20 ga. (93 mfg.)	$14,000	$12,500	$9,500	$7,500	$6,000	$5,000	$3,000
28 ga. (57 mfg.)	$16,000	$14,500	$11,000	$9,000	$7,500	$6,000	$4,000
.410 bore (44 mfg.)	$14,000	$12,500	$9,500	$7,500	$6,000	$5,000	$3,000

Add $2,000 per extra barrel.
Add 40% for an all option gun (checkered buttstock, oil finish, three piece forend, rare, 50% if 28 ga.).
Add 15% for J. Baerten signed gun (rare).
Subtract 40% for Trap or Skeet Models.
Subtract 30% for M, N, or O models w/o gold.

GRADING - PPGS™	100%	98%	95%	90%	80%	70%	60%	LAST MSR

* ***Superposed Presentation III Superlite*** – S, T, or U style engraving.

12 ga. (16 mfg.)	$13,000	$12,000	$10,000	$8,500	$7,000	$5,000	$3,500	
20 ga. (85 mfg.)	$18,500	$17,000	$14,000	$10,000	$7,500	$5,500	$4,500	
28 ga. (36 mfg.)	$22,500	$20,500	$17,000	$14,000	$10,000	$8,000	$6,500	
.410 bore (37 mfg.)	$18,000	$16,500	$13,500	$9,500	$7,000	$5,000	$4,000	

Add $2,000 per extra barrel.
Add 30% for an all option gun (checkered buttstock, oil finish, three piece forend, 40% if 28 ga.).
Add 25% for an all option FKLT gun (very rare).
Add 15% for J. Baerten signed gun (rare).
Subtract 40% for Trap or Skeet Models.

* ***Superposed Presentation IV Superlite w/Gold*** – W style engraving.

12 ga. (14 mfg.)	$21,000	$20,000	$17,500	$14,000	$11,000	$8,500	$6,000	
20 ga. (44 mfg.)	$25,000	$23,000	$19,500	$15,000	$10,000	$8,000	$6,500	
28 ga. (20 mfg.)	$32,000	$30,000	$24,000	$18,000	$15,000	$12,000	$10,000	
.410 bore (35 mfg.)	$25,000	$23,000	$19,500	$15,000	$10,000	$8,000	$6,500	

Add $3,000 per extra barrel.
Add 40% for an all option gun (checkered buttstock, oil finish, three piece forend, 50% if 28 ga.).
Add 40% for an all option FKLT gun (very rare).
Add 15% for J. Baerten signed gun (rare).
Subtract 35% for Trap or Skeet Models.
Subtract 35% for plain models w/o gold.

LIEGE (FN B-26) – 12 ga., 26 1/2, 28 or 30 in. barrels, various chokes, boxlock, auto ejectors, non-selective single trigger, vent. rib, checkered pistol grip stock. Approx. 10,000 mfg. 1973-1975 by FN.

$1,325	$1,050	$850	$685	$610	$570	$540	

This model is also known as the B-26.

GRAND LIEGE – similar to Liege, except has deluxe checkered walnut stock and forearm, and engraved receiver. Disc.

$1,650	$1,225	$1,000	$850	$750	$700	$650	

B-26 – with BAC markings. Mfg. 1973-75.

$1,250	$1,000	$825	$685	$610	$570	$540	

B-27 – F.N. manufactured modified B-26, imported into the U.S. in 1984, same action as Liege (B 26), blue or satin finished receiver with light engraving, no BAC markings and never cataloged.

* ***B-27 Standard Game*** – 28 in. barrels, 9/32 in. vent. rib, pistol grip stock, Schnabel forearm, SST, blue receiver, choking M/F only.

$1,325	$1,050	$850	$685	$610	$570	$540	

Also available in Skeet model with gold "Browning" logo on blue receiver. Prices are the same.

* ***B-27 Deluxe Game (Grade II)*** – similar to Standard Grade, except has 30 in. barrels, better wood and English scroll engraved satin finished receiver, choking M/F only.

$1,425	$1,100	$1,000	$850	$750	$650	$550	

* ***B-27 Grand Deluxe Game*** – 28 in. IC/IM & M/F choked barrels, game scene engraved, signed by the engraver, 90% receiver coverage.

$1,575	$1,200	$1,075	$900	$775	$660	$595	

This model was also available in a Trap configuration - values are about the same as above.

* ***B-27 Deluxe Skeet*** – similar to Deluxe Game (Grade II), except is designed for skeet shooting.

$1,325	$1,050	$850	$685	$610	$570	$540	

International Skeet was also available at same price; hand fit pistol grip with stippling and International Type recoil pad.

GRADING - PPGS™	100%	98%	95%	90%	80%	70%	60%	LAST MSR

* ***B-27 Deluxe Trap*** – similar to Deluxe Game (Grade II), except is configured for trap shooting.

	$1,325	$1,050	$850	$685	$610	$570	$540	

* ***B-27 City of Liege Commemorative*** – limited edition of 250 units manufactured to commemorate the 1,000th anniversary of the city of Liege, cased. Only 29 imported into the U.S.

	$1,750	$1,500	$1,225	N/A	N/A	N/A	N/A	

ST-100 – 12 ga., Belgian mfg., O/U trap configuration with separated barrels and adj. point of impact, manufactured 1979-81 for European sale mostly, floating VR, ST, deluxe checkered walnut stock and forearm, non-BAC model.

	$3,500	$2,750	$2,000	$1,850	$1,200	$975	$825	

SUPERPOSED WATERFOWL SERIES – 12 ga., 500 made of each issue, 7 gold inlays with extensive engraving on French Grey receiver, lightning action, 28 in. barrels, checkered buttstock, full-length walnut case, factory inventories were depleted on Mallard, Pintail, and Black Duck Issues in 1989.

Add 20% for 3 gun set with same serial number.

* ***Superposed Waterfowl 1981 Mallard Issue***

	$9,500	$7,500	$6,000	N/A	N/A	N/A	N/A	$7,000

This issue was sold out in 1988.

* ***Superposed Waterfowl 1982 Pintail Issue***

	$9,500	$7,500	$6,000	N/A	N/A	N/A	N/A	$7,000

* ***Superposed Waterfowl 1983 Black Duck Issue***

	$9,500	$7,500	$6,000	N/A	N/A	N/A	N/A	$8,800

SUPERPOSED SHOTGUN: 1983-86 MFG. – 12 or 20 ga. In 1983, Browning announced renewed production of the famous Belgian "Superposed" O/U in Grade I only. Available in Lightning or Superlight models, 3 in. chambers in Lightning 20 ga., 26 1/2 or 28 in. barrels. Belgian manufactured from 1983-86.

* ***Superposed Shotgun Grade I (1983-86 mfg.)*** – limited mfg., not compatible with steel shot, featured select walnut stock/forearm and extra engraving.

Lightning	$2,800	$2,150	$1,550	$950	$800	$675	$550	
Superlight	$3,750	$3,300	$2,750	$1,850	$1,400	$1,000	$850	$1,995

Add 25% for 20 ga.

SUPERPOSED CLASSIC SERIES – 20 ga. only, 26 in. barrels, less than 2,500 manufactured in Classic model and under 350 manufactured in Gold Classic. Both editions feature multiple engraved scenes and a special silver grey finish. Select American walnut featuring oil finish. Available 1986 only.

	$4,000	$3,350	$2,750	N/A	N/A	N/A	N/A	$2,000

* ***Superposed Gold Classic*** – 8 gold inlays, select walnut forearm and stock are both checkered and carved, many were shipped back to Belgium due to poor sales domestically. Available 1986 only.

	$7,250	$6,000	$4,150	N/A	N/A	N/A	N/A	$6,000

SHOTGUNS: O/U, SUPERPOSED HIGH GRADES: 1985-PRESENT

Browning, in 1985, resumed production of the Superposed in Pigeon, Pointer, Diana, and Midas grades. They were available in 12 and 20 ga. only, in either a Lightning or Superlight configuration. These higher grades were custom ordered from the factory with delivery ranging from 8 to more than 12 months. Custom options could be special ordered on each grade with corresponding prices being higher than shown below. B-25 engraving patterns on these various grades will nearly duplicate those styles manufactured before 1976. Skeet models were not available.

Be wary of non-factory upgraded Superposed higher grade models. These upgraded guns have very nice workmanship, but are valued at approx. 50% less than a factory guns in similar grade/

GRADING - PPGS™	100%	98%	95%	90%	80%	70%	60%	LAST MSR

gauge, and barrel length. Non-factory engraving has been done by: R. Capece, Dubois, Diet, and Bee. It is strongly advised to get a factory letter from Glen Jensen in the Browning Historical Dept. to guarantee the original configuration of a Superposed.

Superposed: Custom Shop Current Pricing & Models

In 2000, Browning changed the nomenclature of their B-25 shotgun Series. Prices reflect current custom shop MSRs. These new boxlock grades include: Special Woodcock $16,558, Special Duck $16,968, Special Pigeon $18,091, Trap Evolution 2 $19,215, Traditionnel $16,968, Sporting 207 Gold 25 $17,273, Diana UK $21,913, and Grades B11 - $17,887 (disc. 2003, reintroduced 2006), B12 - $18,091 (disc. 2003, reintroduced 2006), B2G - $18,296 (disc. 2003, reintroduced 2004), C11 - $21,668, C12 - $22,896, C1G - $19,421, C2G - $22,896, C3 - $25,553, D11 - $30,970, D12 - $29,845, D2L $37,309, D4G $35,773, D5G - $35,773, Special Automn - $36,797, Cheverny - $41,907.

Additionally, the Browning Custom Shop also offers the following shotguns in various grades with engraved sideplates: Grade II - $23,234 (disc. 2003), C2S - $31,992, Grade E1 - $40,931 Grade F1 - $40,931, Grade I1 - $40,931, Grade M1 - $43,343, Grade M2 - $43,343, Special Perdrix - $54,058, Windsor Or - $54,058, Chenonceau - $56,376, Cheverny - $56,376, D5G Sideplate - $56,376, and the Special Automn $56,376. These new grades are special order only through the Browning Custom Shop.

Grade I Traditional, Pigeon Grade, Pointer Grade, Diana Grade, and Midas Grade Superposed are listed separately under the B-25 model listing.

Add 20% for 20 ga. on previously owned models.

Add approx. $1,250 for a previously owned extra set of barrels.

Add $6,479 - $11,954 per extra set of barrels on currently manufactured Superposed models, depending on the grade.

B-25 – 12 or 20 ga. only, original Superposed Model manufactured entirely from parts fabricated in Herstal, Belgium. Also available in Superlight configuration. This older nomenclature series was discontinued domestically in 1999, but the Custom Shop is still producing these grades.

* ***B-25 Grade I Traditional***

	100%	98%	95%	90%	80%	70%	60%	LAST MSR
	$10,500	$8,750	$6,500	N/A	N/A	N/A	N/A	*$19,433*

* ***B-25 Pigeon Grade***

	100%	98%	95%	90%	80%	70%	60%	LAST MSR
MSR $17,280	$12,500	$9,500	$7,250	N/A	N/A	N/A	N/A	

* ***B-25 Pointer C Grade***

	100%	98%	95%	90%	80%	70%	60%	LAST MSR
MSR $18,920	$14,500	$10,750	$8,500	N/A	N/A	N/A	N/A	

* ***B-25 Diana C Grade***

	100%	98%	95%	90%	80%	70%	60%	LAST MSR
MSR $19,886	$15,750	$11,750	$9,500	N/A	N/A	N/A	N/A	

* ***B-25 Midas D Grade***

	100%	98%	95%	90%	80%	70%	60%	LAST MSR
MSR $25,678	$17,750	$12,500	$10,000	N/A	N/A	N/A	N/A	

B-25 125th ANNIVERSARY – 12 ga. only, 2 3/4 in. chamber, 28 in. VR barrels with fixed M/F chokes and 8mm rib, Lightning style stock and forearm with oil finish and black buttplate, case colored receiver with gold border and gold enhanced 125th Anniversary logo. 10 mfg. 2003 only.

	100%	98%	95%	90%	80%	70%	60%	LAST MSR
	$13,750	$5,250	$3,750	N/A	N/A	N/A	N/A	*$15,219*

B-125 – 12 or 20 ga. only, retains all the features of the original Superposed, except parts were subcontracted worldwide to decrease production costs and were assembled "in the white" at Herstal's Custom Gun Shop in Belgium, choice of three different engraving styles and two receiver finishes. Mfg. 1988-2003.

* ***B-125 Hunting Model*** – available in either Hunting Lightning or Superlight configuration.

» **B-125 Hunting Model w/"A" Style Engraving** – blue frame with border engraving featuring Browning logo engraved on each side.

	100%	98%	95%	90%	80%	70%	60%	LAST MSR
	$3,400	$2,750	$2,150	$1,700	$1,450	$1,275	$1,050	*$3,925*

GRADING - PPGS™	100%	98%	95%	90%	80%	70%	60%	LAST MSR

» **B-125 Hunting Model w/"B" Style Engraving** – coin finished frame with smaller game scene engravings.

	$3,700	$3,100	$2,250	$1,800	$1,500	$1,300	$1,100	*$4,360*

» **B-125 Hunting Model w/"C" Style Engraving** – coin finished frame with elaborate scroll work and game scene engraving.

	$4,100	$3,475	$2,450	$1,900	$1,600	$1,400	$1,200	*$4,903*

* ***B-125 Sporting Clays Model*** – 12 ga. only, designed for sporting clays competition and included Invector-Plus choke tube system.

» **B-125 Sporting Clays Model w/"A" Style Engraving** – blue frame with border engraving featuring Browning logo engraved on each side.

	$3,400	$2,750	$2,150	$1,700	$1,450	$1,275	$1,050	*$3,925*

» **B-125 Sporting Clays Model w/"B" Style Engraving** – coin finished frame with smaller game scene engravings.

	$3,700	$3,100	$2,250	$1,800	$1,500	$1,300	$1,100	*$4,360*

» **B-125 Sporting Clays Model w/"C" Style Engraving** – coin finished frame with elaborate scroll work and game scene engraving.

	$4,100	$3,475	$2,450	$1,900	$1,600	$1,400	$1,200	*$4,903*

* ***B-125 Trap Model*** – standard F-1 style engraving.

	$4,950	$3,550	$2,325	$1,750	$1,450	$1,275	$1,050	*$5,452*

SHOTGUNS: SxS

The Browning Custom Shop in Herstal, Belgium offered several SxS sidelock models manufactured by Lebeau-Courally until circa 2006. Models include the LC1 (blued receiver, $17,516 last MSR), and LC2 (coin finished receiver, $22,799 last MSR).

B-SS – 12 or 20 ga., 26, 28, or 30 in. barrels, various chokes, engraved boxlock action, auto ejectors, checkered pistol grip walnut stock, beavertail forearm, SST. Mfg. 1971-1988 by Miroku.

12 ga.	$1,175	$1,000	$850	$725	$650	$550	$450	
20 ga.	$2,250	$2,000	$1,775	$1,525	$1,300	$1,100	$950	*$775*

Early guns had a single non-selective trigger (silver plated) - subtract 10%.

* ***B-SS Grade II*** – satin greyed steel receiver featuring an engraved pheasant, duck, quail, and dogs. Disc. 1983.

	$3,250	$2,850	$2,250	$1,775	$1,350	$1,100	$925	

B-SS SPORTER – 12 or 20 ga., straight grip stock, longer lower tang, slimmed down beavertail forearm, oil finish, 26 or 28 in. barrels. Disc. 1988.

	$2,000	$1,750	$1,500	$1,225	$950	$800	$650	*$775*

Add 50% for 20 ga., if in 95%+ condition.

* ***B-SS Sporter Grade II*** – satin greyed steel receiver featuring an engraved pheasant, duck, quail and dogs. Disc. 1983.

	$3,150	$2,700	$2,225	$1,800	$1,350	$1,100	$925	

Add 50% for 20 ga., if in 95%+ condition.

* ***B-SS "Bottle" Sporter Set*** – 12 and 20 ga., wild turkey and wood duck inlays on 12 ga., wood ducks only on 20 ga., straight grip sporter stock, shoulders are sculpted and engraved, Exhibition grade walnut, engraving was done in Belgium by custom shop, cased in Browning Airways case. Less than 100 mfg. circa 1976.

Set	$9,500	$8,750	$7,500	$6,250	$5,000	$4,500	$4,000	
12 ga.	$2,995	$2,750	$2,400	$2,100	$1,850	$1,600	$1,400	
20 ga.	$3,750	$3,300	$2,950	$2,650	$2,300	$2,000	$1,800	

This model got its nickname from a Mr. Bottles Sporting Goods store in Wichita, KS, who special ordered 100 sets of these guns circa 1976.

GRADING - PPGS™	100%	98%	95%	90%	80%	70%	60%	LAST MSR

B-SS SIDELOCK – 12 or 20 ga., engraved sidelock action in satin grey finish, ST, 26 or 28 in. barrels, English select walnut stock, splinter forend. Mfg. 1983-88 by Miroku in Japan.

12 ga.	$3,750	$3,300	$2,725	$2,275	$1,875	$1,500	$1,250	
20 ga.	$4,995	$4,300	$3,650	$2,900	$2,300	$1,875	$1,500	*$2,000*

SHOTGUNS: SEMI-AUTO, A-5 1903-1998, 2012-CURRENT MFG.

BROWNING CHOKES AND THEIR CODES (ON REAR LEFT-SIDE OF BARREL)

* designates full choke (F).
*- designates improved modified choke (IM).
** designates modified choke (M).
**- designates improved cylinder choke (IC).
**$ designates skeet (SK).
*** designates cylinder bore (CYL).
INV. designates barrel is threaded for Browning Invector choke tube system.
INV. PLUS designates back-bored barrels.

Miroku manufactured A-5s can be determined by year of manufacture in the following manner: RV suffix - 1975, RT - 1976, RR - 1977, RP - 1978, RN - 1979, PM - 1980, PZ - 1981, PY - 1982, PX - 1983, PW - 1984, PV - 1985, PT - 1986, PR - 1987, PP - 1988, PN - 1989, NM - 1990, NZ - 1991, NY - 1992, NX - 1993, NW - 1994, NV - 1995, NT - 1996, NR - 1997, NP - 1998, ZY - 2012, ZX - 2013, ZW - 2014.

Browning resumed importation from F.N. in 1946. On November 26, 1997, Browning announced that the venerable Auto-5 would finally be discontinued. Final shipments were made in February, 1998. Over 3 million A-5s were manufactured by Fabrique Nationale in all configurations between 1903-1976. 1976-1998 manufacture was by Miroku in Japan. The A-5 was reintroduced in 2012 with a Kinematic Drive System, aluminum receiver, and a fixed barrel.

NOTE: Barrels are interchangeable between older Belgian A-5 models and recent Japanese A-5s manufactured by Miroku, if the gauge and chamber length are the same. A different barrel ring design and thicker barrel wall design might necessitate some minor sanding of the inner forearm on the older model, but otherwise, these barrels are fully interchangeable.

NOTE: The use of steel shot is recommended ONLY in those recent models manufactured in Japan - NOT in the older Belgian variations.

The "humpback" design on the Auto-5 (both Belgian and Japanese mfg.) features recoil operation with a scroll engraved steel receiver. During 1909, Browning introduced the magazine cutoff, and moved the safety from inside to the front of the triggerguard. 1946-1951 mfg. has a safety in front of triggerguard. 1951-1976 mfg. has crossbolt safety behind the trigger. Post-war 16 ga. imports by Browning are chambered for 2 3/4 in., and have either a horn (disc. 1964) or plastic (1962-1976) buttplate, high luster wood finish (disc. 1962) or glossy lacquer (1962-1976) finish. Walnut buttstock has either round knob pistol grip (disc. 1967) or flat knob (new 1967). In today's Auto-5 marketplace, all gauges of the A-5 have become extremely collectible. Obviously, the Belgian A-5s are the most desirable. However, the pre-1998 Miroku guns are gaining in collectible popularity. It also has become very apparent that the demand for the FN lightweight 20 ga. has superceded the Sweet 16 due to availablilty. Both the lightweight 20 ga. and the Sweet 16 are the most desirable and have seen a dramatic increase in collectibility. Rarity of configurations such as choke designations, and barrel lengths are very important factors in determinging value. Older rare barrels such as the solid rib and the 16 and 20 ga. guns with shorter barrels and open chokes are more desirable than a 30 in. 12 ga. gun with full choke barrel.

The publisher would like to thank Mr. Richard "Doc" Desira for his recent contributions to the Auto-5/A-5 section.

Add 15% for NIB condition on Belgian mfg. Auto-5 models only, depending on desirability. Beware of reproduced boxes and labels, especially on the more desirable configurations.

Add 15% for the round knob (rounded pistol grip knob on stock, pre-1967 mfg.) variation on FN

GRADING - PPGS™	100%	98%	95%	90%	80%	70%	60%	LAST MSR

models only, depending on desirability.
Add $250-$500 per additional barrel, depending on the gauge, barrel length, choke, condition, and rarity (smaller gauge open chokes are the most desirable).
Add 15% on FN models with blonde stock and forearm - mfg. mid-1960s.

AUTO-5 STANDARD - 1903-1940 MFG. – 12 ga. (introduced in Sept., 1903, Browning discontinued imports Dec., 1903), 16 ga. (introduced in 1909, but not in the U.S.), in 1923, Browning resumed importing both 12 and 16 ga. in four grades that differ in engraving, inlays, and grade of wood, both gauges were available with 26-32 in. barrel, recoil operated, 4 shot mag. with cutoff, various chokes, checkered pistol grip stock, horn buttplate, also available in a 3 shot version with shorter magazine tube to limit capacity to 3 rounds from 1932-1940. Importation temporarily ceased in 1940 with the German occupation of Belgium, ser. no. range 1-224,596 (12 ga.) and 1-126,175 (16 ga.). Mfg. in Herstal, Belgium 1903-1940.

Grade 1	$925	$825	$700	$575	$525	$475	$450	
Solid matte rib	$1,175	$1,075	$975	$875	$775	$675	$625	
With vent. rib	$1,075	$975	$875	$775	$665	$575	$525	
Grade 2 (disc.1937)	$1,625	$1,375	$1,150	$1,025	$925	$850	$775	
Solid matte rib	$2,150	$1,925	$1,625	$1,350	$1,125	$1,075	$725	
With vent. rib	$2,050	$1,825	$1,525	$1,250	$1,025	$975	$875	
Grade 3 (disc. 1940)	$3,050	$2,725	$2,425	$2,175	$1,825	$1,600	$1,325	
Solid matte rib	$3,700	$3,250	$2,900	$2,625	$2,325	$2,025	$1,675	
With vent. rib	$3,600	$3,150	$2,800	$2,525	$2,225	$1,925	$1,575	
Grade 4 (disc. 1940)	$4,500	$4,050	$3,650	$3,300	$2,800	$2,300	$1,900	
Solid matte rib	$5,250	$4,650	$4,450	$3,550	$3,150	$2,650	$2,450	
Grade 4 w/vent. rib	$5,150	$4,550	$4,350	$3,450	$3,050	$2,550	$2,350	

Add 100% for first year production (No. 1-10,000) with "Browning Automatic Arms Co." marking on barrel.
Subtract 25% for pre-WWII 16 ga. A-5s chambered for 2 9/16 in. shells.

Early models with safety mounted in front of trigger guard are not as desirable as there are potential safety problems inherent in the design.

Pre-WWII 16 ga. A-5s could be chambered for 2 9/16 in. shells. These shotguns are considerably less desirable than 16 ga. A-5s chambered for 2 3/4 in. modern shotshells. Since some guns have been modified to 2 3/4 in., careful inspection is advised before purchasing or shooting. The 2 9/16 chambered guns can be modified by the Browning Service Dept. to accept 2 3/4 in. shells if so desired.

"AMERICAN BROWNING" AUTO-5 – 12, 16, or 20 ga., Remington-produced variation of the Browning Auto-5, very similar to the Remington Model 11, except with Browning logo, mag. cut-off, and different engraving, over 38,000 mfg. in 12 ga. (ser. no. range B5000-B43129), over 14,000 in 16 ga. (ser. no. range A5000-A19450), and 11,000 in 20 ga. (ser. no. range C5000- C16152), stocks have Remington style round knob pistol grip. Mfg. 1940-1947.

	$695	$575	$500	$450	$400	$375	$350	

Add 15% for 20 ga.

An easy way to identify this configuration is to look for the "A", "B", or "C" serial number prefix on the left side of receiver.

AUTO-5 STANDARDWEIGHT – 12 (disc. 1970) or 16 (disc. 1964) ga., 26-32 in. barrel, various chokes, checkered walnut stock and forearm, between 7 1/3-8 lbs. Browning resumed importation from F.N. in 1946.

Plain barrel	$1,150	$975	$800	$675	$600	$550	$500	
Matted rib (solid)	$1,450	$1,275	$1,100	$1,000	$900	$800	$700	
Vent rib	$1,350	$1,175	$1,000	$900	$800	$700	$600	

Add 20% for 16 ga.
Subtract 20% for front safety.

Note: Watch for cracked forearms on all A-5 models (due to barrel recoil.)

GRADING - PPGS™	100%	98%	95%	90%	80%	70%	60%	LAST MSR

Barrel addresses appeared as follows: circa 1930-1958 "St. Louis, M.O.", 1959-1968 "St. Louis, Missouri and Montreal P.Q.", 1969-1976 "Morgan, Utah and Montreal, P.Q.". Barrels are serial numbered to the gun until 1953. Make sure barrel address date matches year of mfg. (Refer to the information in the Serialization section.).

AUTO-5 LIGHTWEIGHT (LIGHT 12 & LIGHT 20) – 12 (new 1947) or 20 (new 1958) ga., recoil operated, 26, 28, or 30 in. barrel, various chokes, gold plated trigger, checkered pistol grip round knob (disc. 1967) or flat knob (mfg. 1967-1976) stock, approx. 10 oz. lighter than Standard weight.

FN model	$1,300	$1,125	$925	$850	$750	$650	$550	
FN-vent. rib	$1,525	$1,350	$1,125	$1,050	$950	$850	$750	

Add 60% for 20 ga.
Add 15% for round knob NIB condition.
Add 15% for blonde stock and forearm (mfg. mid-1960s).
Subtract 30% for Cutts or Polychoke.

* ***Auto-5 Light 12 Miroku*** – 12 ga. only, 22, 26, 28, or 30 in. VR (became standard 1986) barrel with Invector choke system, approx. 8-8 1/2 lbs. Mfg. 1976-Feb. 1998.

	$1,050	$925	$775	$700	$625	$550	$500	*$840*

Subtract 10% without Invector chokes.

* ***Auto-5 Light 20 Miroku*** – 20 ga. only, 2 3/4 in. chamber, similar to original Belgian Light 20, VR, 22 (new 1995), 26, or 28 in. barrel, Invector chokes standard until 1993, Invector Plus choking became standard 1994, 6 lbs. 12 oz - 7 lbs. 2 oz. Mfg. 1987-1997.

	$1,350	$1,225	$975	$900	$825	$750	$650	*$840*

AUTO-5 MAGNUM – 12 (new 1958) or 20 (new 1967) ga., 3 in. chamber, 26, 28, 30, or 32 in. barrels, various chokes, VR or etched, 8 1/2 - 9 lbs. Mfg. 1958-1976 by FN, 1976-Feb. 1998 by Miroku.

FN model	$1,150	$975	$800	$675	$600	$550	$500	
FN-vent. rib.	$1,350	$1,175	$1,000	$900	$800	$700	$600	

Add 50% for 20 ga.
Add 15% for round knob, NIB condition.
Add 15% for blonde stock and forearm (mfg. mid-1960s).

Between 1976-1985 approx. 2,000 Belgian 12 ga. A-5 Mags. were imported into the U.S. These late models can be differentiated by serialization - also, slight premiums may be asked.

* ***Auto-5 Mag. Miroku*** – 12 or 20 ga., VR barrel with Invector choke system until 1993, Invector Plus choking became standard 1994, 8 1/2 - 9 lbs. Disc. 1997.

	$1,025	$900	$750	$675	$595	$525	$475	*$866*

Add 30% for 20 ga.
Subtract 10% without Invector chokes.

AUTO-5 STALKER – 12 ga. only, 2 3/4 (Light-12) or 3 (Mag. Stalker) in. chamber, 22 (Light-12 only), 26, 28, 30, or 32 (Mag. only) in. VR barrel with Invector chokes, black matte finish graphite-fiberglass stock and forearm, matte finished metal, recoil pad, 8 lbs. 1 oz. - 8 lbs. 13 oz. Mfg. by Miroku 1992-1997.

	$975	$825	$675	$625	$550	$525	$450	*$840*

Add approx. $100 for Mag. Stalker.

AUTO-5 BUCK SPECIAL – 12, 16, or 20 ga., included Lightweight, Standardweight, and Magnum Models, 24 in. barrel, slug bore, adj. sight, optional sling studs and sling, between 1985-88, Buck Special barrels were available at additional cost. Introduced in 1962, mfg. by F.N. until 1976, and by Miroku from 1976-1984, and again in 1989.

* ***Auto-5 Buck Special FN Mfg. 12 Ga.***

	$1,375	$1,200	$1,000	$925	$825	$725	$625	

Add 75% for Sweet 16 model.
Add 60% for 20 ga.
Add 50% for Standard Weight 16 ga.

GRADING - PPGS™	100%	98%	95%	90%	80%	70%	60%	LAST MSR

This model was made in Light 12, Standard 12, 3 in. Mag. 12, Sweet 16, Standard 16, Lightweight 20 and Lightweight 20 Mag. (new 1967) configurations.

* ***Auto-5 Buck Special Miroku Model*** – mfg. 1989-97.

	$1,050	$925	$775	$700	$625	$575	$525	$829

AUTO-5 SKEET – 12, 16, or 20 ga., Lightweight models with 26 or 28 in. skeet bored, vent. rib barrel. Pre 1976 mfg. by F.N., 1976-1983 mfg. by Miroku.

* ***Auto-5 Skeet FN Mfg.***

	$1,325	$1,150	$950	$875	$775	$675	$575	

Add 20% for vent. rib.
Add 60% for 20 ga.

* ***Auto-5 Skeet Miroku Model***

	$1,000	$895	$750	$675	$600	$550	$500	

Add 30% for 20 ga.

AUTO-5 TRAP MODEL – 12 ga. only, similar to Standard, 30 in. full vent. rib barrel, 8 1/2 lbs., mfg. by FN until 1970.

	$1,300	$1,125	$925	$850	$750	$650	$550	

AUTO-5 SWEET 16 – 16 ga., 2 9/16 in. chamber from 1937-1940, and 2 3/4 in. chamber from 1947-1975, similar configuration to Lightweight, 12 and 20 ga., gold plated trigger, 10 oz. lighter than Standardweight Model 16 ga., 1937-1940 mfg. Sweet Sixteens were available in pre-war Grades I, III, and IV. Mfg. 1937-1975 by F.N.

Plain Barrel	$1,700	$1,400	$1,200	$1,100	$1,000	$875	$800	
Solid Matte Rib	$2,500	$2,100	$1,625	$1,425	$1,275	$1,175	$1,075	
Vent. Rib	$2,400	$2,000	$1,525	$1,325	$1,175	$1,075	$975	

Add 15% for round knob, NIB condition.
Add 15% for blonde stock and forearm (mfg. mid-1960s).
Subtract 20% for front safety.
Subtract 20% for 2 9/16 in. chamber.

* ***Auto-5 Sweet 16 Miroku*** – 16 ga. only, similar to original Belgian Sweet 16, VR, Invector choke standard. Mfg. 1987-92.

	$1,625	$1,325	$1,175	$1,075	$975	$825	$750	$720

AUTO-5 TWO MILLIONTH COMMEMORATIVE – 12 ga., 2,500 mfg., 1971-74 mfg., special walnut, engraving, high-lustre bluing, cased with Browning book. Issue price was $550-$700, serial range 2,000,000-1 to 2,000,000-2,500.

	$2,950	$2,250	$1,750	N/A	N/A	N/A	N/A	

Subtract 25%-40% for guns damaged from salt wood problems, depending on salt wood damage.

AUTO-5 POLICE CONTRACT – 12 ga. only, 5 or 8 (factory extended) shot mag., black enamel finish on receiver and barrel, can be recognized by the European "POL" police markings below serial number, 24 in. barrel. Imported in limited quantities during 1999.

5 shot mag.	N/A	$700	$650	$625	$575	$525	$500	
8 shot mag.	N/A	$1,300	$1,095	$995	$895	$850	$750	

A-5 CLASSIC SERIES – 12 ga., 5,000 mfg. in Classic model, 500 mfg. in Gold Classic. Both editions feature game scenes, John M. Browning's profile, and other inscriptions, special silver grey finished receiver. Introduced 1984.

* ***A-5 Gold Classic Model*** – features 4 gold inlays depicting duck hunting scenes, plus head silhouette of John Browning. 500 mfg. beginning 1986 with inventory depleted during 1989.

	$9,950	$7,450	$5,200	N/A	N/A	N/A	N/A	$6,500

* ***A-5 Classic Model*** – no inlays. Factory inventories were depleted in 1987.

	$2,850	$2,000	$1,750	N/A	N/A	N/A	N/A	$1,260

GRADING - PPGS™	100%	98%	95%	90%	80%	70%	60%	*LAST MSR*

FN CENTENARY EDITION – 12 or 16 ga., limited production mfg. 1989 to commemorate the 100th anniversary of FN, available for worldwide FN sales and not limited to Browning.

* ***FN Centenary Edition 12 ga.*** – 2 3/4 in. chamber, 28 in. VR barrel, Mod. choke, more engraving than a standard A-5, gold relief FN logo on left side of receiver, high grade French walnut flat knob pistol grip stock, 20 LPI checkering, ser. no. CENT 211 001 - 100, 100 mfg.

	100%	98%	95%	90%	80%	70%	60%	Last MSR
	$2,900	$2,200	$1,500	N/A	N/A	N/A	N/A	*$2,100*

* ***FN Centenary Edition 16 ga.*** – 2 3/4 in. chamber, 26 in. VR barrel, Mod. choke, ornate engraving with gold relief inlay (24 Kt.), commemorative FN medallion on left side of receiver, high grade French walnut flat knob pistol grip stock, 25 LPI checkering, ser. no. CENT 221 001 - 010, 10 mfg.

	100%	98%	95%	90%	80%	70%	60%	Last MSR
	$8,000	$6,250	$4,750	N/A	N/A	N/A	N/A	*$6,855*

A-5 BCA COMMEMORATIVE – 12 ga., 3 in. Mag., round knob, Belgian mfg., 1984 issue price was $595.

	100%	98%	95%	90%	80%	70%	60%
	$1,550	$1,275	$1,000	N/A	N/A	N/A	N/A

A-5 DU 50TH ANNIVERSARY

* ***A-5 DU Light 12*** – 12 ga. only, 5,500 mfg. in 1987 only for Ducks Unlimited chapters throughout North America.

	100%	98%	95%	90%	80%	70%	60%
	$2,100	$1,700	$1,200	N/A	N/A	N/A	N/A

* ***A-5 DU Sweet 16*** – 16 ga. only, companion 1988-89 DU auction gun, 4,500 mfg. 1988 only.

	100%	98%	95%	90%	80%	70%	60%
	$2,450	$2,050	$1,350	N/A	N/A	N/A	N/A

* ***A-5 DU Light 20*** – 20 ga. only, companion 1990 DU auction gun, 4,500 mfg. 1990 only.

	100%	98%	95%	90%	80%	70%	60%
	$2,200	$1,800	$1,350	N/A	N/A	N/A	N/A

A-5 FINAL TRIBUTE – 12 ga. only, limited edition of 1,000 guns, features elaborate engraving on white receiver, the last of the A-5 semi-autos. Mfg. 1999 only, sellout occurred during 2000.

	100%	98%	95%	90%	80%	70%	60%	Last MSR
	$3,200	$2,700	$2,300	N/A	N/A	N/A	N/A	*$1,330*

A5 HUNTER – 12 ga. only, 3 in. chamber, recoil operated humpback design with fixed barrel featuring Kinematic Drive System, aluminum receiver, bi-tone black anodized finish, 26, 28, or 30 in. VR barrel with 3 Invector-DS choke tubes, checkered gloss finish walnut stock with Inflex II recoil pad and forearm, speed loading/unloading, ergonomic bolt latch, includes extra stock spacers and ABS case, approx. 6 3/4 lbs. New 2012.

	100%	98%	95%	90%	80%	70%	60%
MSR $1,560	$1,375	$1,150	$925	$800	$675	$550	$495

A5 STALKER – 12 ga., similar to A5 Hunter, except has Dura-Touch armor coated black composite stock and forearm with textured gripping surfaces, matte black metal finish, approx. 7 1/4 lbs. New 2012.

	100%	98%	95%	90%	80%	70%	60%
MSR $1,400	$1,225	$1,025	$875	$750	$650	$550	$450

A5 CAMO – 12 ga., similar to A5 Stalker, except has 100% Mossy Oak Duck Blind (disc. 2012), Mossy Oak Break-Up Infinity, or Mossy Oak Shadow Grass Blades (new 2013) camo coverage, approx. 7 1/4 lbs. New 2012.

	100%	98%	95%	90%	80%	70%	60%
MSR $1,560	$1,375	$1,150	$925	$800	$675	$550	$495

SHOTGUNS: SEMI-AUTO, DOUBLE AUTO MODELS

Add 10% for NIB condition on the following models.

STANDARD DOUBLE AUTO – 12 ga. only, 2 shot, 26, 28, or 30 in. barrel, various chokes, checkered pistol grip stock and forearm, blued steel receiver, approx. 7 1/2 lbs. Mfg. 1952-1960.

	100%	98%	95%	90%	80%	70%	60%
	$825	$725	$550	$475	$375	$325	$300
Vent. or Raised Rib	$975	$850	$675	$600	$475	$375	$325

GRADING - PPGS™	100%	98%	95%	90%	80%	70%	60%	LAST MSR

LIGHTWEIGHT DOUBLE AUTO – similar to Standard Model, except has hiduminum (aircraft alloy) frame, anodized in velvet grey, dragon black, autumn brown, or forest green, approx. 6 3/4 lbs. Approx. 67,000 (all variations) mfg. 1952-1956.

	100%	98%	95%	90%	80%	70%	60%	LAST MSR
	$875	$750	$550	$475	$375	$325	$275	
Vent. or Raised Rib	$1,000	$875	$675	$600	$475	$375	$325	

Add 25% for autumn brown or forest green receiver.
Add 100%+ for all other colors (rare, only a few mfg.).

TWELVETTE DOUBLE AUTO – similar to Lightweight model, except has "Twelvette" stamped above loading port. Mfg. 1957-1971.

	100%	98%	95%	90%	80%	70%	60%	LAST MSR
	$875	$750	$550	$475	$375	$325	$275	
Vent. or Raised Rib	$1,000	$875	$675	$600	$425	$375	$325	

Add 25% for autumn brown or forest green receiver.
Add 100%+ for all other colors (rare, only a few mfg.).

TWENTYWEIGHT DOUBLE AUTO – similar to Twelvette, but 3/4 pound lighter, jet black finish with engraving accented with gold foil, "Twentyweight" stamped above loading port, 26 1/2 in. barrel only. Mfg. 1957-1971.

	100%	98%	95%	90%	80%	70%	60%	LAST MSR
	$950	$825	$625	$550	$450	$400	$300	
w/vent. rib	$1,050	$925	$725	$650	$525	$475	$400	

SHOTGUNS: SEMI-AUTO, MISC. - RECENT MFG.

BROWNING CHOKES AND THEIR CODES (ON REAR LEFT-SIDE OF BARREL)
*** designates full choke (F).**
***- designates improved modified choke (IM).**
**** designates modified choke (M).**
****- designates improved cylinder choke (IC).**
****$ designates skeet (SK).**
***** designates cylinder bore (CYL).**

Add $195-$375 per additional barrel, depending on the condition and configuration.

B/2000 STANDARD – 12 or 20 ga. (new 1975), 2 3/4 in. chamber, 26, 28, or 30 in. VR barrel, various chokes, gas operated, checkered pistol grip stock, Belgian manufactured but assembled in Portugal, approx. 115,000 imported (approx. 95,000 in 12 ga., and 20,000 in 20 ga.) into the U.S. between 1974-1983.

	100%	98%	95%	90%	80%	70%	60%	LAST MSR
	$495	$425	$375	$350	$325	$300	$275	*$475*

Add 20% for 20 ga.

This model could be converted to accept 3 in. Mag. shotshells by simply installing a barrel chambered for 3 in. shells. Even though production on this model ceased in 1979, assembly and sales were not discontinued until 1983.

B/2000 MAGNUM – similar to B/2000 Auto Shotgun, except with 3 in. chambered barrel (all receivers were the same), recoil pad, vent. rib.

	100%	98%	95%	90%	80%	70%	60%	LAST MSR
	$495	$425	$375	$350	$325	$300	$275	

B/2000 SKEET – similar to Standard, with 26 in. skeet bored barrel, floating vent. rib, skeet stock, pad.

	100%	98%	95%	90%	80%	70%	60%	LAST MSR
	$450	$395	$350	$325	$300	$275	$250	

B/2000 TRAP – similar to Standard, with 30 or 32 in. barrel bored F or IM, floating rib, Monte Carlo trap stock.

	100%	98%	95%	90%	80%	70%	60%	LAST MSR
	$450	$395	$350	$325	$300	$275	$250	

B/2000 BUCK SPECIAL – 12 or 20 ga., rifle sights on 24 in. barrel.

	100%	98%	95%	90%	80%	70%	60%	LAST MSR
	$450	$395	$350	$325	$300	$275	$250	

1976 CANADIAN OLYMPICS B2000 – 12 ga., 100 manufactured in 1976 for Canadian sales only, high polish blue with multiple gold inlays including Olympic crest, 30 in. barrel, cased. Issue price was $1,295.

	100%	98%	95%	90%	80%	70%	60%	LAST MSR
	$1,495	$1,095	$850	N/A	N/A	N/A	N/A	

GRADING - PPGS™	100%	98%	95%	90%	80%	70%	60%	LAST MSR

MODEL B-80 – 12 or 20 ga., offers 2 3/4 or 3 in. capability by changing barrel, gas operation, 4 shot, hunting models use choice of steel or aluminum receiver, anodized aluminum was used in the Superlight (12 ga. mfg. 1984 only), 6 to 8 lbs. 1 oz. Buck special disc. 1984. Components manufactured by Beretta of Italy and finished and assembled at FN's plant in Portugal. Mfg. 1981-late 1988, final inventory was sold in 1991. Invector chokes became standard in 1985.

	$450	$375	$325	$295	$275	$250	$230	*$562*

Add 10% for Invector chokes.

Steel frames were reintroduced into production again in 1988.

* ***Model B-80 Upland Special*** – 12 or 20 ga., 2 3/4 in. chamber, 22 in. vent. rib barrel, straight grip stock, Invector chokes. Mfg. 1986-88.

	$525	$450	$395	$350	$325	$300	$275	*$562*

MODEL B 80 DU COMMEMORATIVE – mfg. for American DU Chapters (The Plains and others), price fluctuates greatly as collector support is sometimes limited. Unless new, this model's values approximate those of the regular Model B-80. If NIB, values recently have been in the $795-$995 range.

A-500 (R) HUNTING – 12 ga. only, 3 in. chamber, new design utilizing short recoil system with a four-lug rotary bolt design, capable of shooting all 12 gauge loads interchangeably, magazine cut-off, 26, 28, or 30 in. VR barrel with Invector chokes standard, 24 in. barrel on Buck Special (fixed choke), high polished blue finish with red accents on receiver sides, gold trigger, checkered semi-pistol grip walnut stock with vent. recoil pad, 7 lbs. 11 oz. - 8 lbs. 1 oz. Mfg. 1987-1993.

	$525	$450	$395	$350	$325	$300	$275	*$560*

Add $33 for Buck Special variation (Invector chokes).

This model features fewer moving parts than many other semi-auto shotguns due to the short recoil operating system. From 1987-90, this model was the Model A-500 - R suffix was added in 1991.

A-500G HUNTING – similar to A-500, except is gas operated, distinguishable by "A-500G" in gold accents on receiver, capable of shooting all 2 3/4 or 3 in. shells interchangeably, approx. 8 lbs. Mfg. 1990-93.

	$575	$495	$425	$375	$340	$325	$295	*$653*

A Buck Special variation was mfg. until 1992. No premiums currently exist.

* ***A-500G Sporting Clays*** – 12 ga. only, Sporting Clays variation with 30 in. VR barrel, 8 lbs. 2 oz. Mfg. 1992-93.

	$575	$495	$425	$375	$340	$325	$295	*$653*

GOLD 3 IN. HUNTER – 12 or 20 ga., 3 in. chamber, self-cleaning piston rod gas action with self-regulation, alloy receiver with non-glare black finish and "Gold Hunter" on receiver side, 26, 28, or 30 (12 ga. only, disc. 2001) in. VR Invector Plus (12 ga. only) or Invector (20 ga. only) choked barrel with high polish bluing, cross-bolt safety, gloss finish checkered walnut stock and forearm with recoil pad (vent on 12 ga.), includes 3 choke tubes, 6 lbs. 12 oz. - 7 lbs. 10 oz. Parts mfg. in Belgium and final assembly in Portugal. Mfg. 1994-2005.

	$825	$575	$450	$375	$300	$275	$250	*$1,025*

Do not use 12 ga. 3 1/2 in. chambered barrels on either a 2 3/4 or 3 in. receiver, or vice versa.

* ***Gold Superlite Hunter*** – 12 or 20 ga., similar to Gold 3 in. Hunter, except has new alloy magazine, "Gold SL" on receiver sides, 6 lbs. 7 oz. - 7 lbs., 15 oz. Mfg. 2006-2008.

	$975	$750	$535	$425	$325	$275	$250	*$1,161*

GOLD 3 1/2 IN. HUNTER – 12 ga., 3 1/2 in. chamber, 24 (mfg. 2002-2003), 26, 28, or 30 (disc. 2003) in. VR barrel with Invector Plus choking, otherwise similar to Gold Hunter, 3-4 shot mag., approx. 7 3/4 lbs. Mfg. 1998-2005.

	$985	$725	$600	$550	$450	$375	$335	*$1,190*

* ***Gold 3 1/2 In. Superlite Hunter*** – 12 ga., similar to Gold 3 1/2 in. Hunter, except has new alloy magazine, "Gold SL" engraved on receiver sides, approx. 7 1/4 lbs. Mfg. 2006-2007.

	$1,075	$900	$700	$525	$425	$350	$300	*$1,279*

GRADING - PPGS™	100%	98%	95%	90%	80%	70%	60%	LAST MSR

* ***Gold 3 1/2 In. Turkey/Waterfowl Hunter*** – similar to Gold 3 1/2 in. Hunter, full coverage (including barrel) Mossy Oak Break-Up camo finish, 24 in. VR barrel with extra full choke tube, 7 1/4 lbs. Mfg. 1999-2000.

$875	**$695**	**$600**	**$500**	**$425**	**$375**	**$335**	***$1,038***

* ***Gold 3 1/2 In. NWTF Mossy Oak Break-Up*** – 12 ga. only, 3 1/2 in. chamber, 24 in. VR barrel with 4 choke tubes and Hi-Viz sight, full coverage Mossy Oak Break-Up camo pattern, Dura-Touch armor coating became standard 2003, 7 1/4 lbs. Mfg. 2001-2002.

$875	**$695**	**$600**	**$525**	**$450**	**$385**	**$335**	***$1,221***

* ***Gold 3 1/2 In. Mossy Oak New Break-Up/New Shadow Grass*** – similar to Gold 3 1/2 in. Hunter, choice of full coverage (including barrel) Mossy Oak Break-Up, New Break-Up (standard beginning 2004) or Shadow Grass camo finish, 24 (Mossy Oak Break-Up only, disc. 2001), 26 (Mossy Oak Shadow Grass only), or 28 (Mossy Oak Shadow Grass only) in. VR back-bored barrel with Invector Plus choke tubes, Dura-Touch armor coating became standard 2003, approx. 7 1/2 lbs. Mfg. 1999-2007.

$900	**$750**	**$650**	**$600**	**$500**	**$400**	**$350**	***$1,359***

* ***Gold 3 1/2 In. Mossy Oak Duck Blind*** – 12 ga. only, similar to Gold Mossy Oak New Break-Up, except has Mossy Oak Duck Blind camo coverage. Mfg. 2007.

$900	**$750**	**$650**	**$600**	**$500**	**$400**	**$350**	***$1,359***

* ***Gold 3 1/2 In. NWTF Ultimate Turkey Gun*** – 12 ga. only, similar to Gold NWTF Mossy Oak New Break-Up, except has extended full strut turkey choke tube and neoprene sling, 7 1/4 lbs. Mfg. 2003-2007.

$1,100	**$900**	**$725**	**$675**	**$600**	**$500**	**$450**	***$1,469***

GOLD FIELD HUNTER (CLASSIC) – similar to Gold Hunter, except has semi-hump back receiver design, magazine cutoff, adj. comb, and satin finished wood, 26 or 28 in. VR barrel. Mfg. 1999-2005.

$800	**$575**	**$450**	**$375**	**$300**	**$275**	**$250**	***$1,025***

This model was available through Full-line and Medallion dealers only.

* ***Gold Superlite Field Hunter*** – 12 or 20 ga., similar to Gold 3 in. Superlite Hunter, except is semi-humpback design, approx. 6 1/2 - 7 lbs. Mfg. 2006-2007.

$1,025	**$725**	**$525**	**$400**	**$300**	**$275**	**$250**	***$1,105***

* ***Gold Turkey/Waterfowl Hunter Camo*** – similar to Gold Hunter, full coverage (including barrel) Mossy Oak Break-Up camo finish, 24 in. VR barrel with Hi-Viz sights and extra full choke tube, 7 lbs. Mfg. 1999-2000.

$750	**$500**	**$400**	**$350**	**$295**	**$275**	**$250**	***$867***

* ***Gold Mossy Oak New Break-Up/Shadow Grass*** – 12 ga., similar to Gold 3 in. Hunter, choice of full coverage (including barrel) Mossy Oak New Break-Up or New Shadow Grass camo finish (New became standard in 2004), 24 (Mossy Oak Break-Up only, disc. 2004), 26, or 28 in. VR back-bored barrel with Invector Plus choke tubes, Dura-Touch armor coating became standard 2003, approx. 7 1/2 - 7 3/4 lbs. Mfg. 1999-2007.

$850	**$700**	**$525**	**$450**	**$325**	**$285**	**$250**	***$1,150***

* ***Gold Mossy Oak Duck Blind*** – 12 ga. only, similar to Gold Mossy Oak New Break-Up, except has Mossy Oak Duck Blind camo coverage. Mfg. 2007.

$850	**$700**	**$525**	**$450**	**$325**	**$285**	**$250**	***$1,150***

* ***Gold NWTF Mossy Oak New Break-Up*** – 12 ga. only, 3 in. chamber, drilled and tapped receiver, 24 in. VR barrel with 4 choke tubes and Hi-Viz sight, full coverage Mossy Oak New Break-up camo pattern, Dura-Touch armor coating became standard 2003, 7 lbs. Mfg. 2001-2007.

$850	**$700**	**$575**	**$450**	**$375**	**$300**	**$250**	***$1,226***

* ***Gold Classic High Grade Hunter*** – 12 (disc. 2001) or 20 ga. (new 2002), similar to Gold Classic Hunter, except has satin nickel finished receiver featuring multiple gold inlays with ducks, pheasants, and dogs (12 ga.) or doves and quail (20 ga.) and light scroll

GRADING - PPGS™	100%	98%	95%	90%	80%	70%	60%	LAST MSR

engraving, deluxe checkered gloss finished walnut stock and forearm, 28 in. barrel only, 6 lbs. 14 oz. Mfg. 1999-2004.

$1,575	$1,250	$1,050	$875	$725	$625	$550	*$1,838*

This model was available through Full-line and Medallion dealers only.

GOLD MICRO – 20 ga. only, 3 in. chamber, 24 (new 2002) or 26 in. VR barrel, features shorter stock (13 7/8 LOP) and lighter weight, 6 lbs., 10 oz. Mfg. 2001-2005.

$775	$575	$450	$375	$300	$275	$250	*$1,025*

* ***Gold Superlite Micro*** – 20 ga. only, 3 in. chamber, 26 in. VR barrel, features shorter stock (13 7/8 LOP) and lighter weight, 6 lbs., 3 oz. Mfg. 2006-2007.

$850	$650	$525	$400	$300	$275	$250	*$1,105*

GOLD UPLAND SPECIAL – 12 or 20 ga., 3 in. chamber, 24 or 26 (20 ga. only) in. VR barrel, checkered satin finished straight grip stock, 6 3/4 (20 ga.) or 7 lbs. Mfg. 2001-2005.

$775	$575	$450	$375	$300	$275	$250	*$1,025*

GOLD FUSION – 12 or 20 (new 2002) ga., 3 in. chamber, 26, 28, or 30 (12 ga. only, new 2002) in. wide profile lightweight VR barrel with 5 Invector Plus chokes and Hi-Viz Pro-Comp sight system, checkered oil finished Turkish walnut stock and forearm, shim adj. stock system, alloy mag. tube, includes hardshell case, 6.25 - 7 lbs. Mfg. 2001-2007.

$900	$650	$550	$400	$350	$295	$260	*$1,152*

* ***Gold Fusion High Grade*** – 12 or 20 ga., 3 in. chamber, silver nitride receiver with engraving and gold inlays (mallards and lab on 12 ga., quail and pointer on 20 ga.), 26, 28, or 30 in. barrel with five interchangeable Invector Plus chokes, high grade Turkish walnut stock and forearm, shim adj. stock system with 1/4 in. adj. range, Hi-Viz TriComp sight system, includes hard case, 6 lbs., 6 oz. - 7 lbs. Mfg. 2005-2007.

$1,825	$1,300	$1,125	$950	$850	$725	$625	*$2,137*

GOLD EVOLVE – 12 ga. only, 3 in. chamber, features updated engraved receiver, magazine cap, and canted VR design, 26, 28, or 30 in. barrel, includes shim adj. stock system, newly designed checkered satin finished walnut stock and forearm, alloy mag. tube, Hi-Viz Pro-Comp sight system, approx. 7 lbs. Mfg. 2004-2007.

$900	$650	$525	$425	$335	$285	$250	*$1,220*

* ***Gold Evolve Sporting*** – 12 ga. only, similar to Gold Evolve, except has 2 3/4 in. chamber, 28 or 30 in. ported barrel, gold receiver accents, includes case, approx. 7 lbs. Mfg. 2006-2007.

$950	$700	$550	$450	$350	$300	$250	*$1,287*

Subtract 10% for 28 in. barrel on used guns.

GOLD DEER HUNTER – 12 or 20 (new 2001) ga., 3 in. chamber, 22 in. barrel with choice of 5 in. rifled Invector choke (disc. 1998) or rifled plain barrel, checkered satin finished stock and forearm, cantilevered scope mount, sling swivels, 6 3/4 (20 ga.) or 7 3/4 lbs. Mfg. 1997-2007.

$900	$650	$525	$400	$325	$285	$250	*$1,154*

Subtract approx. 10% for rifled choke tube (disc. 1998).

* ***Gold Deer Hunter with Mossy Oak Break-Up Camo*** – 12 ga., similar to Gold Deer Hunter, except has full Mossy Oak Break-Up or New Break-Up (standard 2004) camo coverage, rifled barrel standard. Mfg. 1999-2007.

$950	$750	$625	$550	$450	$365	$335	*$1,242*

GOLD 3 IN. STALKER – 12 ga., similar to Gold Hunter (3 in. chamber), except has checkered black composite stock and forearm with sling swivels, approx. 7 3/8 lbs. Mfg. 1998-2007.

$800	$625	$475	$375	$300	$275	$250	*$1,001*

* ***Gold 3 In. Stalker Field (Classic)*** – similar to Gold Stalker, except has semi-hump back receiver design, magazine cutoff and adj. comb, 26 or 28 in. VR barrel. Mfg. 1999-2007.

$800	$625	$475	$375	$300	$275	$250	*$1,001*

This model was available through Full-line and Medallion dealers only.

GRADING - PPGS™	100%	98%	95%	90%	80%	70%	60%	LAST MSR

* ***Gold 3 In. Turkey/Waterfowl Stalker*** – similar to Gold Stalker, except has 24 in. VR barrel with extra full choke tube, Hi-Viz sights, matte non-glare wood and finish, 7 lbs. Mfg. 1999-2000.

$650	$500	$400	$350	$300	$275	$250	$850

* ***Gold 3 In. NWTF Stalker*** – 12 ga. only, 3 in. chamber, 24 in. VR barrel with 3 choke tubes and Hi-Viz sight, 7 lbs. Mfg. 2001-2002.

$635	$475	$415	$350	$300	$275	$250	$744

* ***Gold 3 In. Rifled Deer Stalker*** – 12 ga. only, 22 in. rifled barrel, cantilevered scope mount, sling swivels, 7 3/4 lbs. Mfg. 1997-2007.

$850	$625	$475	$400	$340	$300	$265	$1,108

GOLD 3 1/2 IN. STALKER – 12 ga., 3 1/2 in. chamber, 26, 28, or 30 (disc. 2002) in. VR barrel with Invector Plus choking, otherwise similar to Gold Stalker, 3-4 shot mag., approx. 7 lbs. 10 oz. Mfg. 1998-2007.

$985	$725	$625	$525	$425	$375	$335	$1,171

* ***Gold 3 1/2 In. Turkey/Waterfowl Stalker*** – similar to Gold 3 1/2 Stalker, except has 24 in. VR barrel with extra full choke tube, matte non-glare wood and finish, 7 1/4 lbs. Mfg. 1999-2000.

$800	$650	$595	$500	$420	$375	$335	$1,022

GOLD SPORTING CLAYS – 12 ga. only, similar specs as the Gold Hunter, except has 2 3/4 in. chamber, 28 or 30 in. ported barrel with Invector Plus choking, gloss finished walnut stock and forearm, adj. stock shims, Hi-Viz front sight, approx. 7 3/4 lbs. Mfg. 1996-2008.

$1,000	$850	$700	$600	$500	$400	$350	$1,184

This model was supplied standard with 2 interchangeable gas pistons for light or heavy loads.

* ***Gold Golden Clays*** – 12 ga. only, 2 3/4 in. chamber, engraved coin finished alloy receiver with gold accents and game birds, new scroll motif was introduced during 2005, deluxe satin finished checkered walnut stock and forearm, 28 or 30 in. VR ported barrel with Hi-Viz Tri-Comp front sight and mid-bead, approx. 7 3/4 lbs. Mfg. 1999-2008.

$1,650	$1,225	$950	$850	$750	$650	$550	$1,941

Subtract approx. 10% if with older engraving motif (non-scroll, disc. 2004).

* ***Gold Sporting Ladies/Youth*** – similar to Gold Sporting Clays, except has shorter 13 1/2 in. LOP stock, 28 in. barrel only, approx. 7 1/2 lbs. Mfg. 1999-2008.

$1,000	$850	$700	$600	$500	$400	$350	$1,184

» **Gold Golden Clays Ladies/Youth** – similar to Gold Sporting Ladies/Youth, except features coin finished receiver with "golden clays" rose motif and gold enhancements, satin finished select walnut stock and forearm. Mfg. 2005-2007.

$1,575	$1,175	$925	$850	$750	$650	$550	$1,848

GOLD NRA SPORTING – 12 ga. only, 2 3/4 in. chamber, similar to Gold Sporting Clays, except has NRA logo/banner on left side of receiver, approx. 7 3/4 lbs. Mfg. 2006-2007.

$950	$800	$650	$550	$450	$400	$350	$1,160

This model was supplied standard with 2 interchangeable gas pistons for light or heavy loads.

BSA 10 – while advertised, this gun had its model nomenclature changed to the Gold 10 Ga. before mfg. started.

GOLD LIGHT 10 GA. 3 1/2 IN. HUNTER/STALKER – 10 ga. Mag., 3 1/2 in. chamber, short stroke self-cleaning gas action, 4 shot mag., steel (disc. 2000) or aluminum (new 2001) receiver, choice of high polish (Hunter Model, disc. 2000), dull finish (Stalker Model, disc. 1999, reintroduced 2000) bluing, 24 (NWTF Model only with Break-Up, new 2001), 26, 28, or 30 (disc. 2001) in. VR standard Invector choke barrel, available with either high-gloss checkered walnut (Hunter, disc. 2002) stock/forearm, matte black fiberglass (Stalker, disc. 1998, reintroduced 2000-2003) stock/forearm, or choice of 100% camo treatment in Shadow Grass (disc. 2003), Break-Up (mfg. 2001-2003), New Shadow Grass (mfg. 2005-2008), Mossy Oak Duck Blind (new 2007), New Break-Up (mfg. 2004-2009),

GRADING - PPGS™	100%	98%	95%	90%	80%	70%	60%	LAST MSR

Break-Up Infinity (new 2010), or Mossy Oak Shadow Grass Blades (new 2013), vent. recoil pad, Dura-Touch armor coating became standard for camo finishes during 2003, approx. 9 1/2 lbs. (aluminum receiver) or 10 lbs. 10 oz. (steel receiver, disc. 2000), mfg. by Miroku, Japan. New 1994.

MSR $1,740	$1,425	$1,050	$875	$775	$675	$575	$500	

Add $130 for the NWTF Model with Mossy Oak New Break-Up.
Add 10% for extra 24 in. turkey barrel.
Subtract approx. 10% for matte black fiberglass stock and forearm.
Subtract 15% for steel receiver.

During 1999-2001, this model was packaged to include an extra 24 in. turkey barrel.

SILVER HUNTER – 12 or 20 ga., 3 in. chamber, semi-humpback design, silver finished aluminum alloy receiver, gas operating system similar to Gold Hunter, 26, 28, or 30 in. VR barrel with three Invector-Plus choke tubes, checkered satin finished stock and forearm with vent. recoil pad, includes three choke tubes, approx. 6 1/4 - 7 1/2 lbs. New 2006.

MSR $1,180	$1,025	$825	$650	$575	$495	$425	$375	

SILVER HUNTER MICRO MIDAS – 12 or 20 ga., similar to Silver Hunter, except has 24 or 26 in. VR barrel and 13 in. LOP, approx. 6 - 7 3/8 lbs. New 2011.

MSR $1,180	$1,025	$825	$650	$575	$495	$425	$375	

SILVER MICRO – 20 ga., 3 in. chamber, 26 in. VR barrel, lightweight aluminum alloy receiver, semi-humpback design, satin finished walnut stock and forearm, compact dimensions for smaller shooters, three Invector Plus choke tubes, 6 lbs., 3 oz. New 2008.

MSR $1,180	$1,025	$825	$650	$575	$495	$425	$375	

SILVER SPORTING – 12 ga. only, 2 3/4 in. chamber, 28 or 30 in. ported barrel with flush choke tubes, adj. satin finished walnut stock with Pachmayr Decelerator recoil pad, 7 1/2 lbs. New 2009.

MSR $1,300	$1,100	$925	$775	$675	$575	$475	$425	

SILVER SPORTING MICRO – 12 ga., 2 3/4 in. chamber, 28 in. VR ported barrel, lightweight aluminum alloy receiver, semi-humpback design, satin finished walnut stock and forearm, features 13 3/4 in. LOP adj. in 1/4 in. increments using three included adj. spacers, premium Pachmayr Decelerator pad, three Invector Plus chokes, 7 lbs. New 2008.

MSR $1,300	$1,100	$925	$775	$675	$575	$475	$425	

SILVER LIGHTNING – 12 ga., 3 in. chamber, 26 or 28 in. VR barrel, silver finished aluminum alloy receiver, semi-humpback design, gloss finished Lightning style walnut stock, three Invector Plus choke tubes, approx. 7 1/2 lbs. New 2008.

MSR $1,180	$1,025	$825	$650	$575	$495	$425	$375	

This model is available only through Browning Full Line and Medallion dealers.

SILVER NWTF MOSSY OAK CAMO – 12 ga., 3 in. chamber, 24 in. VR barrel, aluminum alloy receiver, composite stock and forearm with Dura-Touch Armor coating and 100% Mossy Oak New Break-Up (disc. 2009) or Break Up Infinity (new 2010) camo treatment, NWTF logo, Hi-Viz 4 in 1 fiber optic sight, three Invector Plus choke tubes, 7 lbs. Mfg. 2008-2012.

	$1,175	$1,000	$850	$675	$550	$500	$450	*$1,360*

SILVER RIFLED DEER MOSSY OAK CAMO – 12 or 20 (new 2009) ga., 3 in. chamber, 22 in. rifled deer barrel, aluminum alloy receiver, composite stock and forearm with Dura-Touch Armor coating and 100% Mossy Oak New Break-Up (disc. 2009) or Break-Up Infinity (new 2009) camo treatment, cantilever scope mount, 7 lbs., 12 oz. New 2008.

MSR $1,420	$1,220	$1,040	$885	$750	$600	$500	$400	

SILVER RIFLED DEER STALKER/SATIN – 12 or 20 ga., 3 in. chamber, 22 in. rifled deer barrel, choice of non-glare matte black finish composite stock and forearm (Stalker) or satin finished walnut stock with Dura-Touch Armor coating, cantilever scope mount, 7 lbs. 12 oz. New 2008.

MSR $1,280	$1,100	$875	$750	$650	$525	$475	$425	

Add $60 for satin finished walnut stock and forearm with matte grey finished receiver (20 ga.).

GRADING - PPGS™	100%	98%	95%	90%	80%	70%	60%	LAST MSR

SILVER 3 1/2 IN. HUNTER/STALKER – 12 ga. only, 26 or 28 in. VR barrel, semi-humpback design, choice of silver metal (Silver Hunter) or matte black (Silver Stalker) metal finish, choice of wood (Silver Hunter) or black composite (Silver Stalker) stock and forearm, includes three choke tubes, approx. 7 1/2 lbs. New 2006.

MSR $1,200	$1,050	$850	$725	$625	$525	$475	$425	

Add $140 for satin finished walnut stock and forearm (Silver Hunter).

* ***Silver 3 1/2 In. Camo*** – 12 ga. only, similar to Silver 3 1/2 In. Hunter/Stalker, except has choice of 100% Mossy Oak New Break-Up (disc. 2009), Break-Up Infinity (new 2010), Mossy Oak Duck Blind (mfg. 2007-disc.), New Shadowgrass (mfg. 2006 only), Mossy Oak Shadow Grass Blades (new 2013) camo finish, 26 or 28 in. VR barrel with 3 Invector Plus chokes, 7 1/2 lbs. New 2006.

MSR $1,340	$1,150	$950	$825	$725	$625	$495	$425	

SILVER 3 1/2 IN. LIGHTNING – 12 ga., similar to Silver Lightning 3 In., except has 3 1/2 in. chamber., 26 or 28 in. VR barrel with 3 Invector Plus choke tubes. New 2008.

MSR $1,360	$1,125	$850	$750	$625	$550	$500	$450	

This model is available only through Browning Full Line and Medallion dealers.

SILVER 3 1/2 IN. NWTF MOSSY OAK CAMO – 12 ga., 3 1/2 in. chamber, 24 in. barrel, aluminum alloy receiver, composite stock and forearm with Dura-Touch Armor coating and 100% Mossy Oak New Break-Up or Break-Up Infinity (new 2009) camo treatment, NWTF logo, Hi-Viz 4 in 1 fiber optic sight, three Invector Plus choke tubes, 7 1/4 lbs. New 2008.

MSR $1,540	$1,325	$1,125	$950	$800	$675	$500	$425	

MAXUS HUNTER 3 IN. – 12 ga., 3 in. chamber, 26, 28, or 30 in. VR barrel with Vector Pro lengthened forcing cone, similar to Maxus Stalker, except has satin nickel finished receiver with laser engraved duck and pheasant, checkered walnut stock with Inflex Technology recoil pad and forearm, removeable Lightning trigger and turnkey magazine plug and speed lock forearm, includes shims and spacers, approx. 7 lbs. New mid-2010.

MSR $1,500	$1,295	$1,100	$925	$800	$675	$500	$425	

* ***Maxus Hunter 3 1/2 In.*** – 12 ga., 3 1/2 in. chamber, otherwise similar to Maxus Hunter 3 in. except is also available with Mossy Oak Break-Up Infinity camo finish, approx. 7 lbs. New mid-2010.

MSR $1,640	$1,395	$1,025	$875	$750	$625	$525	$450	

Add $40 for Mossy Oak Break-Up Infinity camo finish.

MAXUS MOSSY OAK DUCK BLIND – 12 ga., similar to Maxus Stalker, except has Mossy Oak Duck Blind camo finish. Mfg. 2009-2012.

	$1,200	$1,025	$875	$750	$625	$525	$450	*$1,400*

* ***Maxus 3 1/2 In. Mossy Oak Duck Blind*** – similar to Maxus Mossy Oak Duck Blind, except has 3 1/2 in. chamber. Mfg. 2009-2012.

	$1,350	$975	$850	$725	$600	$525	$475	*$1,600*

MAXUS MOSSY OAK SHADOW GRASS BLADES – 12 ga., 3 in. chamber, similar to Maxus Stalker, except has 100% Mossy Oak Shadow Grass Blades camo coverage, approx. 7 lbs. New 2013.

MSR $1,470	$1,225	$900	$800	$700	$600	$500	$450	

* ***Maxus 3 1/2 In. Mossy Oak Shadow Grass Blades*** – 12 ga., similar to Maxus Mossy Oak Shadow Grass Blades, except has 3 1/2 in. chamber. New 2013.

MSR $1,600	$1,350	$1,025	$875	$750	$650	$550	$475	

MAXUS STALKER – 12 ga., 3 or 3 1/2 in. chamber, 26 or 28 in. VR barrel with three Invector Plus choke tubes, Vector Pro forcing cone became standard 2010, aluminum alloy receiver, gas operated with new Power Drive gas system (reduces recoil), matte black composite pistol grip stock with speedlock forearm and Dura-Touch Armor coating, turnkey magazine plug, Inflex recoil pad, approx. 6 lbs. 15 oz. New 2009.

MSR $1,340	$1,150	$950	$800	$700	$600	$500	$425	

GRADING - PPGS™	100%	98%	95%	90%	80%	70%	60%	LAST MSR

* ***Maxus 3 1/2 In. Stalker*** – similar to Maxus Stalker, except has 3 1/2 in. chamber. New 2009.

MSR $1,500	$1,250	$925	$825	$725	$625	$525	$450	

MAXUS ULTIMATE – 12 ga., 3 in. chamber, gas operated, engine turned bolt, 26, 28, or 30 in. flat VR barrel with three Invector Plus choke tubes, laser engraved featuring pheasant on right side, and mallard on left, checkered gloss oil finish Grade III walnut stock and forearm, Inflex Technology recoil pad, magazine cutoff includes spacers and hardshell ABS case, brass front bead sight, approx. 7 1/4 lbs. New 2013.

MSR $1,870	$1,550	$1,325	$1,100	$925	$800	$675	$575	

MAXUS RIFLED DEER CAMO – 12 ga., 3 in. chamber, 22 in. fully rifled barrel with cantilever sight base and w/o sights, 100% Mossy Oak Break-Up Infinity camo coverage, includes extra shims and spacer, approx. 7 1/4 lbs. New 2011.

MSR $1,590	$1,370	$1,150	$975	$825	$700	$600	$500	

MAXUS RIFLED DEER STALKER – 12 ga., 3 in. chamber, 22 in. fully rifled barrel with cantilever sight base and no sights, black composite stock and speed lock forearm, black metal finish, approx. 7 1/4 lbs. New 2011.

MSR $1,470	$1,275	$1,085	$925	$785	$675	$525	$425	

MAXUS SPORTING – 12 ga., 3 in. chamber, 28 or 30 in. VR barrel with Vector Pro lengthened forcing cone, includes 5 Invector Plus choke tubes, satin finished aluminum receiver with laser etched game birds transformed into clay birds, high grade gloss finish, walnut stock and speed lock forearm, HiViz front sight, Inflex Technology recoil pad, approx. 7 lbs. New 2011.

MSR $1,700	$1,475	$1,250	$1,050	$895	$750	$600	$500	

MAXUS SPORTING GOLDEN CLAYS – 12 ga., 3 in. chamber, 26, 28, or 30 in. VR barrel with three Invector Plus choke tubes, features satin nickel finished receiver with gold enhanced game birds transforming into a clay target on receiver sides, checkered gloss finished Grade III walnut stock and forearm with Inflex Technology recoil pad, engine turned bolt, includes ABS case, 7 1/4 lbs. New 2013.

MSR $2,000	$1,675	$1,450	$1,200	$1,000	$850	$750	$575	

MAXUS SPORTING CARBON FIBER – 12 ga., 3 in. chamber, 28 or 30 in. barrel, similar to Maxus Stalker, except has two-tone carbon fiber receiver finish and barrel, Dura-Touch armor coating, five Invector Plus choke tubes, approx. 7 lbs. New mid-2010.

MSR $1,500	$1,290	$1,095	$950	$800	$675	$550	$425	

SHOTGUNS: SINGLE BARREL, BT-99 & BT-100

During 2010, the Vector Pro lengthened 2 1/2 inch forcing cone became standard on the following current models.

BT-99 STANDARD TRAP GUN – 12 ga., 32 or 34 in. vent. rib barrel, mod., imp. mod., or full choke, boxlock, auto ejector, checkered pistol grip with Monte Carlo or conventional style stock, beavertail forearm. Invector chokes became standard in 1986 and ported barrel with Invector Plus chokes and back boring became standard in 1992. Values below assume Invector Plus choking with ported barrel. Mfg. 1968-94 by Miroku.

	$900	$800	$700	$600	$550	$500	$450	*$1,288*

Subtract $125 without Invector chokes or ported barrels.

* ***BT-99 2 Barrel Set*** – 12 ga., without Invector choking or barrel porting. Disc. 1983.

	$1,150	$995	$850	$750	$700	$650	$600	

* ***BT-99 Stainless*** – 12 ga., features all stainless construction with Invector Plus ported 32 or 34 in. black VR barrel. Mfg. 1993-1994.

	$1,500	$1,200	$1,000	$700	$575	$495	$450	*$1,738*

* ***BT-99 Current Mfg.*** – 12 ga., choice of 32 or 34 in. back bored unported barrel with 11/32 in. high post rib and one full Invector Plus choke tube, satin finished conventional or adj. comb stock, beavertail forearm, ejector only, 8 lbs. 5 oz. New 2001.

MSR $1,430	$1,230	$1,050	$900	$750	$600	$525	$450	

Add $250 for factory adj. comb stock.

GRADING - PPGS™	100%	98%	95%	90%	80%	70%	60%	LAST MSR

* ***BT-99 Micro*** – 12 ga., 30 or 32 in. high post VR barrel, similar to BT-99, except has shortened 13 3/4 LOP, approx. 7 3/4 lbs. New 2004.

MSR $1,430	$1,075	$900	$775	$675	$600	$525	$450	

* ***BT-99 Micro Midas*** – 12 ga., 2 3/4 in. chambers, 28 or 30 in. VR barrel with one Invector-Plus choke tube, compact variation with 13 in. LOP, blued finish, extractor, satin finished walnut stock, beavertail forearm, recoil pad, approx. 7 3/4 lbs. New 2013.

MSR $1,430	$1,075	$900	$775	$675	$600	$525	$450	

* ***BT-99 Pigeon Grade*** – 12 ga., features higher grade walnut and gold receiver accents, Invector chokes and ported barrels. Mfg. 1993-1994.

1978-1985 mfg.	$1,700	$1,500	$1,200	$1,100	$650	$575	$525	
1986-1994 mfg.	$1,395	$1,150	$875	$600	$525	$495	$450	*$1,505*

Older Pigeon Grade guns featured a satin grey receiver with deep relief, engraved pigeons in a fleur-de-lis background.

* ***BT-99 Signature Painted*** – 12 ga., features painted red/black stock with Browning logos on stock and forearm, Invector Plus ported barrels. Mfg. 1993-1994.

	$1,250	$1,050	$900	$700	$600	$500	$330	*$1,323*

BT-99 GRADE III – 12 ga., similar to BT-99, except has silver nitride receiver finished with gold accents, gloss finished Grade III/IV Monte Carlo stock with beavertail forearm, 32 or 34 in. ported barrel, approx. 8 1/2 lbs. New 2008.

MSR $2,540	$2,440	$2,075	$1,750	$1,485	$1,175	$950	$750	

Add $290 for adj. comb.

* ***BT-99 Golden Clays*** – 12 ga., features gloss finished Grade V/Grade VI wood and gold outline receiver and inlays depicting a transitional hunting to clay pigeon scene, current mfg. includes 32 or 34 in. ported barrel, adj. comb and LOP, and GraCoil recoil reduction, approx. 9 lbs. Mfg. 1994, reintroduced 2003.

MSR $4,340	$3,740	$3,180	$2,700	$2,300	$1,850	$1,475	$1,185	

Subtract 15% for older mfg. w/o current features.

BT-99 PLUS GRADE I – similar to BT-99, except has adj. rib to control point of impact and new recoil reduction system that reduces felt recoil by 50%, stock has adj. comb and buttplate (recoil pad), back-bored barrel, Invector chokes, 8 3/4 lbs. Mfg. 1989-94.

	$1,775	$1,525	$1,275	$1,100	$1,000	$800	$700	*$1,835*

Add 5% for ported barrel.

In 1990, the Grade I designation was added to this model. In 1991, this model was supplied with a travel vault gun case as standard equipment. Older mfg. will not have these cases as an original accessory.

Beginning 1991, a Micro Plus Model was introduced that incorporates smaller dimensions (shorter stock and choice of shorter barrel). Values are the same as listed.

* ***BT-99 Plus Stainless Grade I*** – features all stainless construction with Invector Plus ported 32 or 34 in. black VR barrel. Mfg. 1993-94.

	$1,950	$1,725	$1,425	$1,255	$1,020	$885	$715	*$2,240*

Beginning 1991, a Micro Plus Model was introduced that incorporates smaller dimensions (shorter stock and choice of shorter barrel). Values are the same as listed.

* ***BT-99 Plus Pigeon Grade Grade I*** – 12 ga., features higher grade walnut and gold receiver accents, Invector chokes and ported barrels. Mfg. 1993-disc.

	$1,875	$1,600	$1,250	$1,100	$895	$785	$630	*$2,065*

Beginning 1991, a Micro Plus Model was introduced that incorporates smaller dimensions (shorter stock and choice of shorter barrel). Values are the same.

* ***BT-99 Plus Signature Painted Grade I*** – features painted red/black stock with Browning logos on stock and forearm, Invector Plus ported barrels. Mfg. 1993-94.

	$1,750	$1,525	$1,250	$1,100	$895	$785	$630	*$1,890*

Beginning 1991, a Micro Plus Model was introduced that incorporates smaller dimensions (shorter stock and choice of shorter barrel). Values are the same.

GRADING - PPGS™	100%	98%	95%	90%	80%	70%	60%	LAST MSR

* ***BT-99 Plus Golden Clays Grade I*** – features high-grade wood and gold outline receiver and inlays depicting a transitional hunting to clay pigeon scene. Mfg. 1994 only.

	$2,700	$2,350	$2,050	$1,850	$1,700	$1,550	$1,395	*$3,205*

Beginning 1991, a Micro Plus Model was introduced that incorporates smaller dimensions (shorter stock and choice of shorter barrel). Values are the same.

BT-99 MAX – 12 ga. only, choice of blue steel with engraving or stainless steel barrel, receiver, and trigger guard, 32 or 34 in. high post VR ported barrel, thin forearm with finger grooves, select walnut pistol grip stock (regular or Monte Carlo) with high gloss finish, ejector/extractor selector, no safety, approx. 8 lbs. 10 oz. Mfg. 1995-96.

	$1,300	$1,000	$800	$600	$525	$495	$450	*$1,496*

Add $400 for stainless steel.

BT-100 STANDARD TRAP GUN – 12 ga. only, 32 or 34 in. steel high-post ported Invector Plus or fixed choked (F) barrel, without safety, choice of blue or stainless steel receiver, removable trigger assembly, ejector selector (either ejects or extracts) adj. comb and thumbhole stock (disc. 1999) are optional, approx. 8 lbs. 10 oz. Mfg. 1995-2002.

	$1,900	$1,600	$1,300	$795	$575	$495	$450	*$2,266*

Subtract approx. 10% for fixed choke.
Add $100 for adj. comb.
Add $558 for replacement trigger assembly (blue or stainless).

* ***BT-100 Stainless*** – features stainless steel barrel, receiver, trigger guard and top lever. Disc. 2002.

	$2,210	$1,800	$1,600	$1,000	$815	$695	$580	*$2,742*

Subtract approx. 10% for fixed choke.
Add $100 for adj. comb.
Add $558 for replacement trigger assembly (blue or stainless).

BT-100 SATIN (LOW LUSTER) – features 32 or 34 in. Invector Plus barrel, satin/low luster metal/wood finish, conventional type stock without Monte Carlo, quick removable trigger with adj. trigger pull, 8 lbs. 10 oz. Mfg. 1998-2000.

	$1,400	$1,200	$1,000	$775	$650	$575	$495	*$1,684*

SHOTGUNS: SINGLE BARREL, RECOILLESS TRAP

RECOILLESS SINGLE BARREL TRAP – 12 ga., special bolt action design that eliminates 72% of felt recoil, 27 (also available in Micro Model) or 30 in. high-post vent. rib Invector Plus choked back-bored barrel, rib adjusts for 3 points of impact (3, 6, or 9 in.), stock has adj. pull (2 sizes) and comb height, anodized receiver, no safety, approx. 8 1/2 lbs. Mfg. 1994-96.

	$995	$850	$750	$650	$525	$500	$450	*$1,995*

The Micro Model featured a 27 in. barrel and shorter length of pull.

* ***Recoilless Single Barrel Trap Signature Painted*** – features painted red/black stock with Browning logos on stock and forearm, Invector Plus ported barrels. Mfg. 1994 only.

	$995	$850	$750	$650	$525	$500	$450	*$1,900*

SHOTGUNS: SLIDE ACTION

Do not use BPS barrels chambered for 3 1/2 in. shotshells on a BPS 3 in. receiver or vice versa.

BPS HUNTER/FIELD MODEL – 12, 16 (new 2008), 20, 28 (new 1994) ga., or .410 bore (new 2000), 2 3/4 (28 ga. only) or 3 in. chamber, bottom ejection, double action bars, top tang safety, 5 shot capacity, vent. rib, all steel receiver with variety of finishes, receiver engraving became standard 1991 and was disc. during 1998, 20 and 28 ga. are approx. 1/2 lb. lighter than 12 ga. Field Models, Invector or Invector Plus (new 1994 in 20 ga.) choking, various barrel lengths, Invector Plus choking became standard 1995 (except 28 ga.), back bored barrels on 12 and 20 ga. BPS Models (except Game guns) became standard during 2003, 7 - 7 3/4 lbs. Mfg. by Miroku. New 1977.

MSR $650	$565	$450	$350	$275	$230	$195	$175

Add $40 for 16, 28 ga., or .410 bore.
Subtract 10% if without Invector Plus choke tubes.

GRADING - PPGS™	100%	98%	95%	90%	80%	70%	60%	LAST MSR

* ***BPS Stalker Model*** – 12 ga. only, 3 in. chamber, all metal parts have a dull matte finish, non-glare black synthetic composite stock and forearm, 24 (mfg. 1999-2000), 26, 28, or 30 in. VR barrel, approx. 8 lbs. New 1987.

MSR $650	$565	$450	$350	$275	$230	$195	$175	

* ***BPS Camouflage*** – 12 or 20 (disc. 2006) ga., 3 in. chamber, features Mossy Oak Shadow Grass (disc. 2006), Mossy Oak Duck Blind (new 2007), Mossy Oak Break-Up (mfg. 2000-2003), Break-Up Infinity (new 2010), New Break-Up (mfg. 2004-2009), Mossy Oak Shadow Grass Blades (new 2013) full camo treatment, 24 (standard model disc., or NWTF Model with Mossy Oak Break-Up camo - new 2001), 26, or 28 in. barrel, Dura-Touch armor coating became standard during 2003, approx. 8 lbs. New 1999.

MSR $780	$650	$550	$425	$350	$300	$275	$250	

Add $120 for NWTF Model with 24 in. barrel.

* ***BPS Pigeon Grade*** – 12 ga. only, 3 in. chamber, features high grade walnut and gold trimmed receiver, 26 or 28 in. VR barrel with Invector chokes, 7 lbs. 10 oz. Mfg. 1992-98.

	$550	$465	$395	$350	$310	$290	$275	*$603*

* ***BPS Upland Special*** – 12, 16 (new 2008), or 20 ga., 2 3/4 (16 ga.) or 3 in. chamber, 22 (12 and 20 ga.), 24, or 26 in. VR barrel, straight grip satin finished stock and forearm, Invector (pre-1994) or Invector Plus (new 1994, standard 1995) choking, 6 3/4 or 7 1/2 lbs. New 1985.

MSR $650	$595	$500	$400	$325	$230	$195	$175	

Add $50 for 16 ga. Subtract 10% if without Invector Plus choke tubes.

* ***BPS Turkey Special*** – 12 ga. only, 3 in. chamber, 20 1/2 in. lightened barrel, non-glare walnut stock, matte finished barrel and receiver, receiver is drilled and tapped for scope base, rifle-style stock dimensions, sling swivels, new extra-full Invector choke tube, 7 lbs. 8 oz. Mfg. 1992-2001.

	$400	$340	$275	$240	$215	$190	$175	*$500*

* ***BPS Micro*** – 20 ga. only, 22 in. vent. rib barrel, pistol grip stock (13 1/4 in. LOP), Invector Plus choking (includes 3 chokes), 6 3/4 lbs. New 2001.

MSR $650	$565	$480	$385	$300	$230	$195	$175	

* ***BPS Micro Midas*** – 12, 20, 28 ga., or .410 bore, 24 or 26 in. VR barrel with three standard Invector choke tubes, checkered satin finished walnut stock and forearm includes two stock spacers, 13 in. LOP, 7-7 1/2 lbs. New 2013.

MSR $650	$565	$480	$385	$300	$230	$195	$175	

Add $40 for 28 ga. or .410 bore.

* ***BPS Micro - Youth and Ladies Model*** – 20 ga. only, 22 in. vent. rib barrel, straight grip shortened stock (13 1/4 in. LOP), Invector (pre-1994) or Invector Plus (new 1994, standard 1995) choking, 6 3/4 lbs. Mfg. 1986-2002.

	$385	$300	$260	$225	$200	$185	$170	*$473*

Subtract 10% if without Invector Plus choke tubes.

* ***BPS Deer Hunter/Special (DG, DS or DH)*** – 12 or 20 (new 2007) ga., 3 in. chamber, 20 1/2 (disc. 2000) or 22 in. barrel with 5 in. rifled choke tube or rifled barrel (DH, cantilever scope mount with satin finish only, new 1997), iron sights, scope mount base, choice of gloss (DG, disc. 1997) or satin (DS, disc. 2000) finish checkered stock with recoil pad and forearm, sling swivels, polished or matte finished metal, approx. 7 1/2 lbs. New 1992.

MSR $780	$680	$580	$465	$375	$295	$200	$175	

Subtract approx. 10% for rifled choke tube.
Add $20 for 20 ga. (new 2007).

* ***BPS Deer Camo*** – 12 or 20 ga., 3 in. chamber, 22 in. rifled barrel with cantilever scope mount, 100% Mossy Oak New Break-Up (disc. 2009) or Mossy Oak Break-Up Infinity (new 2010) camo coverage, approx. 7 1/2 lbs. New 2007.

MSR $830	$715	$600	$485	$390	$300	$200	$175	

Add $100 for 20 ga.

GRADING - PPGS™	100%	98%	95%	90%	80%	70%	60%	LAST MSR

* ***BPS Buck Special*** – 12 or 20 (disc. 1984) ga., 3 in. chamber, 24 in. cyl. bore barrel, iron sights, 7 lbs. 10 oz. Reintroduced 1988-disc. 1998.

	$335	$275	$230	$200	$185	$175	$160	$409

BPS MAGNUM HUNTER/STALKER 12 GA. 3 1/2 IN. – 12 ga., 3 1/2 in. chamber, 24 (disc. 1997, reintroduced 1999-2000 - Stalker only), 26, 28, or 30 (disc. 1997) in. barrel with Invector chokes and vent. rib, 4 shot mag., 7 3/4 lbs. Hunter 3 1/2 in. Model disc. 2002.

MSR $750	$645	$500	$425	$365	$310	$275	$250	

In 1990, the back-bored Invector Plus choke tube system became standard in 12 ga. 3 1/2 in. chamber only.

* ***BPS Camo Magnum Hunter*** – 12 ga., similar to Magnum Hunter or Stalker 12 ga., features Mossy Oak Shadow Grass (disc. 2006), Mossy Oak Duck Blind (mfg. 2007-2012), Mossy Oak Break-Up Infinity (new 2010), Mossy Oak Break-Up (mfg. 2000-2009), or Mossy Oak Shadow Grass Blades (new 2013) full camo treatment, 24 (standard model disc., or NWTF Model with Mossy Oak Break-Up camo - new 2001), 26, or 28 in. VR barrel, Dura-Touch armor coating became standard during 2003, approx. 7 3/4 - 9 1/4 lbs. New 1999.

MSR $900	$775	$625	$550	$450	$375	$315	$275	

Add $80 for NWTF Model with 24 in. barrel (12 ga., available in Mossy Oak Break-Up from 2000-2009, Break Up Infinity beginning 2010).

* ***BPS Magnum Hunting Waterfowl*** – 10 ga., 3 1/2 in. Mag. with choice of 28 or 30 in. matte finished VR barrel with standard Invector choking, features higher grade walnut and gold trimmed receiver with Waterfowl outlined, approx. 9 lbs. 6 oz. Mfg. 1993-98.

	$615	$500	$400	$375	$350	$315	$285	$750

* ***BPS Magnum 3 1/2 In. Buck Special*** – 10 or 12 (disc. 1994) ga., 3 1/2 in. chambers, 24 in. cyl. bore barrel, 7 lbs. 10 oz. Mfg. 1990-1997.

	$500	$450	$400	$370	$335	$310	$290	$677

BPS MAGNUM HUNTER/STALKER 10 GA. – 10 ga., 3 1/2 in. chamber, 26 or 28 in. barrel with three standard Invector choke tubes, currently available in either Stalker (black synthetic stock and forearm), or camo - choice of Mossy Oak New Break-Up (disc. 2009), Mossy Oak Break-Up Infinity (new 2010), Mossy Oak Duck Blind (mfg. 2007-2012), New Shadowgrass (disc. 2006), or Mossy Oak Shadow Grass Blades (new 2013) - with Dura-Touch coating configuration, no longer available in Hunter Model, 10 1/2 lbs. Disc. 2001, reintroduced 2004.

MSR $750	$645	$500	$425	$365	$310	$275	$250	

Add $150 for 100% camo coverage.

* ***BPS 10 ga. NWTF*** – features 24 in. VR barrel with HiViz TriViz fiber optic sights and extra full XF extended turkey choke tube, 100% Mossy Oak New Break-Up (disc. 2009) or Break-Up Infinity (new 2010) camo coverage, NWTF logo on synthetic stock, 10 lbs. 3 oz.

MSR $980	$815	$600	$500	$400	$350	$300	$275	

BPS TRAP MODEL – 12 ga., 30 in. barrel. Disc. 1984 but trap barrels were available separately for several years.

	$360	$300	$270	$230	$210	$190	$170	

BPS TRAP (CURRENT MFG.) – 12 ga. only, 2 3/4 in. chamber, features dark grey receiver with full coverage engraving, 30 in. VR barrel with HiViz front sight, checkered satin finished Monte Carlo walnut stock and forearm, magazine cutoff, approx. 8 1/2 lbs. New 2007.

MSR $800	$695	$595	$475	$375	$300	$275	$225	

* ***BPS Micro Trap*** – 12 ga. only, similar to BPS Trap, except has 28 in. VR barrel and 13 3/4 in. LOP, approx. 8 lbs. New 2007.

MSR $800	$695	$595	$475	$375	$300	$275	$225	

BPS WILD TURKEY FEDERATION COMMEMORATIVE – only 500 manufactured. Disc. 1991.

	$495	$395	$325	N/A	N/A	N/A	N/A	

GRADING - PPGS™	100%	98%	95%	90%	80%	70%	60%	LAST MSR

BPS PACIFIC EDITION DU – limited mfg., DU serialization, cased.

	$595	$475	$350	$285	$250	$215	$185	

BPS COASTAL DU – limited mfg., DU serialization, cased.

	$595	$475	$350	$285	$250	$215	$185	

BPS WATERFOWL DELUXE – 12 ga. Mag., gold trigger and etching, Invector chokes, limited mfg.

	$625	$525	$450	$385	$335	$280	$235	

MODEL 12 LIMITED EDITION SERIES

* ***Model 12 Limited Edition Grade I 20 Ga.*** – 20 ga. only, 2 3/4 in. chamber only, reproduction of the famous Winchester Model 12 with slight design improvements, 26 in. VR barrel bored modified, 5 shot mag., high post floating rib, walnut stock and forearm with semi-gloss finish, take down, serialization format similar to 28 ga., 7 lbs. 1 oz. 8,000 mfg. in 1988 with inventory depleted 1990.

	$775	$650	$525	N/A	N/A	N/A	N/A	*$735*

* ***Model 12 Limited Edition Grade V 20 Ga.*** – similar specifications to Grade I, except has select walnut checkered 22 lines per inch with high gloss finish, extensive game scene engraving including multiple gold inlays serialization format similar to 28 ga. 4,000 mfg. 1988 only.

	$1,350	$1,125	$900	N/A	N/A	N/A	N/A	*$1,187*

* ***Model 12 Limited Edition Grade I 28 Ga.*** – 28 ga. only, similar to Grade I 20 Ga., except in 28 ga., 26 in. VR modified choke barrel, 5 digit ser. no. with NM872 suffix. 7,000 mfg. 1991-92.

	$1,050	$875	$700	N/A	N/A	N/A	N/A	*$772*

* ***Model 12 Limited Edition Grade V 28 ga.*** – 28 ga. only, similar to Grade V 20 ga., except in 28 ga., 26 in. VR modified choke barrel, 5 digit ser. no. with NM972 suffix. 5,000 mfg. 1991-92.

	$1,675	$1,350	$1,000	N/A	N/A	N/A	N/A	*$1,246*

MODEL 42 LIMITED EDITION

* ***Model 42 Limited Edition Grade I*** – .410 bore, 3 in. chamber, reproduction of the Winchester Model 42 with slight design improvements, 26 in. VR full choke barrel, select walnut stock, 5 digit ser. no. with NZ882 suffix, 6 lbs. 12 oz. 6,000 mfg. late 1991-1993.

	$895	$775	$550	N/A	N/A	N/A	N/A	*$800*

* ***Model 42 Limited Edition Grade V*** – .410 bore, engraving and embellishments similar to the Model 12 Grade V, 5 digit ser. no. with NZ982 suffix, 6,000 mfg. late 1991-1993.

	$1,495	$1,225	$925	N/A	N/A	N/A	N/A	*$1,360*

SPECIAL EDITIONS, COMMEMORATIVES, & LIMITED MFG.

Please refer to the *Blue Book of Modern Black Powder Arms* by John Allen (now online also) for more information and prices on Browning black powder rifles.

BICENTENNIAL 1876-1976 SET – .45-70 Govt. cal., Model 78 rifle with specially engraved receiver, silver finish, fancy wood, cased, with engraved knife and medallion, 1,000 sets mfg. in 1976. Issue price - $1,500.

	$1,975	$1,550	$1,200	N/A	N/A	N/A	N/A	

CENTENNIAL O/U RIFLE/SHOTGUN – 20 ga. O/U shotgun w/extra set of .30-06 O/U rifle barrels. Shotgun barrels are 26 1/2 in., rifle barrels are 24 in., SST, ejectors, elaborate scroll engraved receiver with 2 gold inlays, straight grip special oil finished walnut stock and forearm, deluxe walnut full-length case. 500 mfg. 1978 only.

	$6,750	$6,250	$5,250	N/A	N/A	N/A	N/A	*$7,000*

GRADING - PPGS™	100%	98%	95%	90%	80%	70%	60%	LAST MSR

CENTENNIAL SET – complete Browning set mfg. in 1978, includes the Centennial O/U rifle/shotgun, 9mm Hi-Power, B92 .44 Mag., Mountain Rifle, and a set of three knives.

	$8,750	$7,750	$6,250	N/A	N/A	N/A	N/A	

1 OF 50 BICENTENNIAL RIFLE – .30-06 cal., Model 78 single shot with 26 in. octagon barrel, includes special engraving by Neil Hartliep (non-factory), extra fine walnut, 4X wide angle scope, special luggage case. 50 mfg. (one for each state) during 1976 only and sold by silent mail order bidding (minimum bid was $3,100 in 1976).

As very few specimens are bought or sold each year, pricing is rather unpredictable. A few specimens have been sold in the $6,000 range recently. Remember, this is not a "factory edition" as the work on this gun was subcontracted by Centennial Guns (division of Frigon Guns located in Clay Center, KS).

BUCK MARK COMMEMORATIVE PISTOL – features 6 3/4 in. Challenger style tapered barrel, white bonded ivory grips with scrimshaw style patterning including "1 of 1,000 Commemorative Model" on sides, matte blue finish, gold trigger, 30 1/2 oz. 1,000 mfg. 2001-2002.

	$335	$275	$225	N/A	N/A	N/A	N/A	$437

BRUCHET

Previous trademark manufactured by Darne until circa 2011 and previous manufacturer located in Saint Etienne, France. Distributed exclusively from 1982-1989 by Wes Gilpin located in Dallas, TX. In 1989, Bruchet was able to get permission to use the older Darne trademark and all new manufacture can be found under the Darne listing.

Paul Bruchet manufactured his shotguns patterned after the Darne action circa 1981-2011, following his tenure at Darne as line foreman until 1979 (at which time the Darne plant closed). These new Bruchet Models were designated "A" or "B". All shotguns were totally hand made with approx. 50 guns being mfg. each year.

Since Paul Bruchet was able to retain the Darne trademark in 1989, please refer to the Darne section in this text for current manufacture.

SHOTGUNS: SxS

MODEL A – 12, 16, 20, 28 ga., or .410 bore, small key opening, ejectors, double triggers only, basically 4 variations (1, 1A, 2, and 2A), wide assortment of customer specified special orders.

Retail values were as follows: Model 1A started at under $2,000, the Model 2 started at $3,000, and the Model 2A started at $3,500.

Each additional grade represented more embellishments and better grade of walnut. Magnum chambers could be ordered at a small surcharge. Importation began 1982, values represent the last published retail prices from 1989.

MODEL B – 12, 16, 20, 28 ga., or .410 bore, large key opening, self-opening (assisted) action, ejectors, double triggers only, basically special ordered to individual customer specifications.

Retail values were as follows: Model B started at $5,800 and included deluxe carrying case.

Each additional upgrade represented more embellishments and a better grade of walnut. Magnum chambers could be ordered at a small surcharge. Importation began 1982, values represent the last published retail prices from 1989.

BRÜGGER & THOMET

Current manufacturer located in Thun, Switzerland. Currently imported by D.S.A., located in Barrington, IL. Brügger and Thomet also manufactures a wide variety of high quality paramilitary style and select-fire rifles and pistols. During 2004, the company purchased all rights to the TMP pistol, and SMG from Steyr Arms in Austria. After many design improvements the TP-9 pistol platform was released.

PISTOLS: SEMI-AUTO

TP-9 – 9mm Para. or .45 ACP (new late 2011) cal., 5.1 in. barrel, blow-back action, features

GRADING - PPGS™	100%	98%	95%	90%	80%	70%	60%	LAST MSR

ambidextrous and trigger safeties, polymer frame construction in choice of black, OD Green, or Desert Tan finish, full length upper integrated Picatinny rail with partial lower rail in front of trigger guard, 10 or 30 shot mag., adj. rear sight with post front sight, includes hard case, 44 oz. Disc. 2011.

MSR $1,795	$1,650	$1,475	$1,300	$1,125	$900	$800	$700	

This model is also available in a select-fire variation available to law enforcement and government agencies.

BRYCO ARMS

Previous manufacturer located in Irvine, CA until 2003. Previously distributed by Jennings Firearms, Inc. located in Carson City, NV.

PISTOLS: SEMI-AUTO, SINGLE ACTION

MODEL T-22 – while advertised during 1997 at a retail price of $179, this model was never produced.

MODEL J-25 – .25 ACP cal., aluminum alloy frame, 2 1/2 in. barrel, single action, synthetic ivory, walnut, or black combat grips, positive safety, 11 oz. Mfg. 1988-95, reintroduced 1999.

	$65	$55	$45	$40	$35	$30	$30	*$79*

This model was available in either satin nickel, bright chrome, or black teflon finish.

MODEL M-32/M-38 – .22 LR (disc.), .32 ACP, or .380 ACP cal., semi-auto single action, 2.8 in. barrel, pressure cast fabrication using non-ferrous alloy, chrome or blue finish, black combat grips, 16 oz. Mfg. 1991-disc.

	$65	$50	$40	$35	$30	$30	$30	*$79*

Add $20 for .380 ACP cal.

MODEL M-48 – .22 LR, .32 ACP, or .380 ACP cal., semi-auto single action, 4 in. barrel, larger frame variation of the M-38, chrome or blue finish, black combat grips, 24 oz. Mfg. 1991-95.

	$85	$75	$65	$55	$50	$45	$40	*$96*

MODEL M-5 – .380 ACP or 9mm Para. cal., 3 1/4 in. barrel, 10 or 12 shot mag., blue or nickel finish, black synthetic grips, 36 oz. Disc. 1995.

	$85	$75	$65	$55	$50	$45	$40	

Last MSR was $100 for the .380 ACP, $119 for 9mm Para.

Add $15 for 9mm Para. cal.

MODEL M-59 – .380 ACP or 9mm Para. cal., 4 in. barrel, 10 shot mag., blue or nickel finish, black synthetic grips, 36 oz. Disc. 1995.

	$95	$85	$75	$70	$65	$60	$55	*$119*

Add $15 for 9mm Para. cal.

JENNINGS NINE – 9mm Para. cal., single action, redesigned model 59, frame mounted ejector, contour grips, loaded chamber indicator, 30 oz. Mfg. 1997-2003.

	$120	$100	$85	$75	$65	$55	$50	*$145*

BUDISCHOWSKY

Previous manufacturer located in Mt. Clemens, MI.

PISTOLS: SEMI-AUTO

TP-70 .22 LR – .22 LR cal., double action, 2 1/2 in. barrel, stainless steel, fixed sights, plastic grips. Mfg. 1973-77.

	$440	$385	$330	$265	$230	$195	$175	

TP-70 .25 ACP – similar to TP-70, except .25 ACP cal. Mfg. 1973-77.

	$330	$275	$220	$175	$140	$125	$105	

Note: In 1977, Norton Arms marketed this pistol. Quality of workmanship is not on par with the early Budischowsky and values are approx. 35% less.

GRADING - PPGS™	100%	98%	95%	90%	80%	70%	60%	LAST MSR

SEMI-AUTO PISTOL – .223 Rem. cal., 11 5/8 in. barrel, 20 or 30 shot mag., fixed sights, a novel paramilitary designed type pistol.

$470	$415	$385	$360	$305	$250	$220	

RIFLES: SEMI-AUTO

IMPORTANT NOTE: On model(s) where *N/A has replaced the normal 100% value, it indicates current market conditions are too unstable to accurately ascertain 100%-60% values. Factory retail prices (MSRs) reflect most recent updates. For more up-to-date information on current pricing trends and additional useful information, please visit www.bluebookofgunvalues.com, select "Information & Services" from the menu, and click on "Additional Book Information".

PARAMILITARY DESIGN RIFLE – .223 Rem. cal., semi-auto, 18 in. barrel, wood paramilitary stock.

*N/A	$440	$415	$385	$330	$275	$250	

PARAMILITARY DESIGN RIFLE W/FOLDING STOCK

*N/A	$500	$450	$425	$395	$360	$330	

BUEHLER CUSTOM SPORTING ARMS

Current custom gun manufacturer established during 2005 and currently located in Medford, OR.

Reto Buehler manufactures custom order long guns. He also specializes in the repair and restocking of double rifles, shotguns, and combination guns. Since all guns are built or repaired per customer's specifications, please contact him directly for available options, pricing and delivery time (see Trademark Index).

BULLARD REPEATING ARMS COMPANY

Previous manufacturer located in Springfield, MA, circa 1882-1891.

Designed by prolific inventor James Bullard, the design, quality, and workmanship of Bullard rifles rivaled those of any competitor during the 1880s. Bullard made two basic rifles: a lever action repeater and a single shot. The repeater was made in two frame styles: large and small. The single shot was also made in two basic styles; solid frame and detachable-interchangeable barrel model. Total production is estimated at 2,800 rifles.

The author would like to thank Mr. Gene Weicht for providing information and values for this section.

100%	98%	95%	90%	80%	70%	60%	50%	40%	30%	20%	10%

RIFLES: LEVER ACTION

LEVER ACTION REPEATER – rack and pinion style lever activated mechanism, mag. mounted under barrel, loaded through underside of action while lever was opened, blue finish with various parts (including receiver) sometimes case hardened, approx. 1,700 mfg.

* ***Lever Action Large Frame*** – .45-70 Govt., .45-75, .50-95, .40-70 Bullard, .40-75 Bullard, .40-90 Bullard, .45-85 Bullard or .50-115 Bullard cal., 26 or 28 in. round, octagon, or part round barrel, crescent steel or hard rubber buttplates with elk motif, ser. no. range 1-1,500 and 2,000-3,000.

N/A	N/A	$3,850	$3,350	$2,675	$2,300	$2,150	$1,925	$1,525	$1,375	$1,175	$1,000

Add 25% for .40-90 Bullard, .50-95, or .50-115 Bullard cal.

Add 25% for deluxe checkered wood with pistol grip.

Various military and experimental models are found in this frame size and will command significant premiums.

Large frame repeating rifles up to ser. no. 113 will be marked "Bullard Repeating Arms Association". Ser. no. 114-4067 will be marked Bullard Repeating Arms Company.

* ***Lever Action Small Frame*** – .32-40 Bullard or .38-45 Bullard cal., (other calibers cataloged, but essentially unknown), 24, 26, or 28 in. round, octagon or part round barrel, crescent steel or hard rubber buttplates with turkey motif, ser. no. range 1,500-2,000. Approx. 500 mfg.

N/A	N/A	$3,300	$2,750	$2,400	$2,050	$1,800	$1,550	$1,225	$1,100	$975	$875

100%	98%	95%	90%	80%	70%	60%	50%	40%	30%	20%	10%

Add 25% for deluxe checkered wood with pistol grip.

Add 40% for any caliber other than .32-40 and .38-45.

Although the small frame saw less production and is scarcer than the large frame repeater, it is not as desirable among collectors, and is typically priced less than a large frame model.

RIFLES: SINGLE SHOT

SINGLE SHOT MODEL – thin receiver with full lever, similar in appearance to small frame repeater action, except shorter (several parts will interchange), 26, 28, or 30 in. round, octagon, or part round barrel, blue finish with various parts sometimes case hardened (including receiver), crescent steel or hard rubber (turkey motifs) buttplates, ser. no. range 3,500-4,100. Approx. 600 mfg.

* ***Single Shot Solid Frame*** – wide variety of cals. from .22 rimfire to .50 cal., (.22 and .32-40 are most common), made in both frame sizes, narrow width or wide width action.

100%	98%	95%	90%	80%	70%	60%	50%	40%	30%	20%	10%
N/A	N/A	$3,475	$2,975	$2,525	$2,175	$1,975	$1,825	$1,495	$1,340	$1,185	$1,050

* ***Single Shot Detachable-interchangeable Barrel Model*** – same cals. as small frame model with two frame sizes - small (.38 cal. and smaller) and large (usually .40 cal. and larger, but some small calibers were mfg.), interchangeable barrels could not be switched between the two frame sizes, barrel and breech detach from action, narrow or wide width action.

100%	98%	95%	90%	80%	70%	60%	50%	40%	30%	20%	10%
N/A	N/A	$3,350	$2,675	$2,425	$2,100	$1,900	$1,750	$1,450	$1,325	$1,160	$1,025

Add 15% for large frame models in less than .40 cal.

Add 30% for .50 cals.

Add 30% for extra barrel with forend (numbers matching).

Add 30% for Schuetzen model.

Add 25% for deluxe checkered wood with pistol grip.

Values are for models with original sights and no stock alterations - subtract 15% if not original.

BULLSEYE GUN WORKS

Previous manufacturer located in Miami, FL circa 1954-1959.

CARBINES

Bullseye Gun Works initially started as a gun shop circa 1954, and several years later, they started manufacturing M1 carbines using their own receivers and barrels. Approx. 2,000 2,500 were manufactured with their name on the receiver side until the company was reorganized as Universal Firearms Corporation circa late 1950s. Values are typically in the $200 - $350 range, depending on originality and condition.

BUL LTD. (TRANSMARK)

Current manufacturer located in Tel Aviv, Israel. Bul M1911 parts are currently being imported by All America Sales, Inc. located in Piggot, AR. Previously imported 2003-early 2010 by K.B.I., located in Harrisburg, PA. Previously imported and distributed in North America during 2009 by Legacy Sports International, located in Reno, NV, and during 2002 by EAA Corp., located in Sharpes, FL. Previously imported and distributed 1997-2001 by International Security Academy (ISA) located in Los Angeles, CA, and from 1996-1997 by All America Sales, Inc. located in Memphis, TN. Dealer sales only.

Bul Ltd

PISTOLS: SEMI-AUTO

Please refer to the Charles Daly section in this text for most recent information and prices on Charles Daly imported Bul Transmark pistols (domestic imports were marked Charles Daly 2004-early 2010). Non-domestic Bul Pistols are typically marked Bul M-5 on left side of slide except for the Cherokee and Storm models. M-5

frame kits were previously available at $399 retail.

BUL IMPACT – while advertised during 1999, this model was never produced.

BUL STORM & COMPACT – while advertised during 1999, this model was never produced.

GRADING - PPGS™	100%	98%	95%	90%	80%	70%	60%	LAST MSR

BUL 1911 GOVERNMENT (M-5 STANDARD) – .38 Super (disc.), 9mm Para. (disc.), .40 S&W (disc.), or .45 ACP cal., single action, 5 in. barrel, polymer double column frame, steel slide, aluminum speed trigger, checkered front and rear grip straps, blue or chrome (new 2000) finished slide, 10 shot staggered mag., 31-33 oz. Imported 1995-2000, reintroduced 2002-2003.

	$525	$460	$395	$355	$290	$235	$185	$559

Add 10% for .38 Super or .40 S&W cal.

* ***Bul Commander (M5 Standard)*** – similar to M-5 Government, except has 3.8, 4 1/3 or 4 1/4 in. barrel, 29-30 oz. Imported 1998-2000, reintroduced 2002-2003.

	$525	$460	$395	$355	$290	$235	$185	$559

Add 10% for .38 Super or .40 S&W cal.
Add 25% for early mfg. in 9mm Para. cal. with 18 shot mag. and bul frame.
Add $40 for matte chrome finished slide.

* ***Bul M-5 Stinger*** – similar to Bul 1911 Government, except has 10 shot mag., 3 in. barrel, 24 oz. Imported 2002-2003.

	$525	$460	$395	$355	$290	$235	$185	$559

* ***Bul M-5 Standard Street Comp.*** – similar to M-5 Standard Commander, except has single port compensated 4 1/4 in. barrel, 32 oz. Imported 1998-99.

	$960	$840	$720	$650	$530	$430	$335	$1,060

Add $28 for .38 Super or .40 S&W cal.

* ***Bul M-5 Multi Caliber*** – similar cals. as the M-5 Standard Government, includes 3 upper-ends including Commander length, another with adj. sights, and a third with a single port compensator, cased. Imported 1999-2000.

	$1,575	$1,380	$1,180	$1,070	$865	$710	$550	$1,768

BUL M-5 STANDARD IPSC – .38 Super, 9mm Para., .40 S&W, or .45 ACP cal., configured for IPSC competition, with custom slide to frame fit and match grade barrel bushing. Imported 1998-2001, reintroduced 2003.

	$925	$810	$695	$630	$510	$415	$325	$990

Add $111 for .38 Super or .40 S&W cal. (disc. 2001).
Add $70 for chrome finish (mfg. 2000-2001).

BUL M-5 STANDARD MATCH – IPSC custom race gun, includes multi-port compensator system. Imported 1998-99.

	$1,200	$1,050	$900	$815	$660	$540	$420	$1,655

Add $24 for .38 Super or .40 S&W cal.

BUL M-5 JET – same cals. as the M-5 Standard IPSC, features Commander length with 4 1/4 in. barrel and 4 port compensator on top of barrel, 31 oz. Imported 1999-2000.

	$875	$765	$655	$595	$480	$395	$305	$1,158

Add $51 for .38 Super or .40 S&W cal.

BUL M-5 MODIFIED – 9mm Para., .38 Super, .40 S&W, or .45 ACP cal., designed for Modified class competition, features new Optima 2000 optical sight fitted to slide, 5 port compensation on top of barrel, includes carrying case, 38 oz. Imported 1998-2001.

	$1,075	$940	$805	$730	$590	$485	$375	$1,430

BUL M-5 TARGET – same cals. as the M-5 Modified, features 6 in. slide and barrel, choice of sights, and match grade oversize barrel bushing, includes 3 mags and carrying case, 38 oz. Imported 1999-2001.

	$895	$785	$670	$610	$490	$405	$315	$1,196

Add $315 for Aristocrat Tri-state sights.

BUL M-5 ULTIMATE RACER – top-level IPSC competition gun, includes 3 mags. and carrying case, 38 oz. Imported 1998-2001.

	$1,050	$920	$785	$715	$575	$470	$365	$1,573

Add $306 for fitted C-more optical sight.

BUL CHEROKEE – 9mm Para. cal., full size polymer frame, integral Picatinny rail, DA, exposed

GRADING - PPGS™	100%	98%	95%	90%	80%	70%	60%	LAST MSR

hammer, double stack 17 shot mag., black polymer finger groove grips, squared off trigger guard, includes hard case, cleaning kit and two mags. Imported 2009.

$495	$435	$370	$335	$270	$225	$175	$575

*** *Bul Cherokee Compact*** – 9mm Para. cal., similar to the Cherokee, except is compact polymer frame. Imported 2009.

$495	$435	$370	$335	$270	$225	$175	$575

BUMAR

Current military supplier and exporter of armament, as well as manufacturing some makes/models available to the civilian marketplace. Distributed exclusively by Beryl ASG. The Bumar Group consists of 27 manufacturing and trading defense sector companies specializing in small arms, munitions, and large scale military weapons and accessories. Please contact the company directly for current civilian offerings, U.S. availability, and pricing (see Trademark Index).

THE BURGESS GUN CO.

Previous manufacturer located in Buffalo, NY circa 1892-1899.

Andrew Burgess was a prolific firearms designer that held many firearms patents and designed guns for Colt, Marlin and Whitney before forming The Burgess Gun Co. Burgess manufactured slide action rifles and shotguns of a unique design that incorporated an iron sleeve fitted over the wrist portion of the stock which operated the action.

RIFLES: SLIDE ACTION

Burgess rifles are very rare and need to be appraised individually. Also refer to the Colt section for the Colt-Burgess lever action model.

SHOTGUNS: SLIDE ACTION

Burgess shotguns have either a takedown or folding frame that was hinged on the bottom and manufactured in both plain/standard and fancy/deluxe grades. It is believed production may have reached a few thousand, with the vast majority being 12 gauge shotguns and only very few rifles. These long guns should be treated as a collectible and not fired. Solid frame shotguns are valued $300-$1,500 range, depending on condition. Folding frame shotguns are currently in the $600-$3,500 range, depending on original condition. Deluxe examples will bring premiums.

BUSHMASTER FIREARMS INTERNATIONAL

Current trademark of carbines, rifles, and pistols established in 1978, and currently manufactured in Ilion, NY beginning late 2011 and company headquarters located in Madison, NC. Previously located in Windham, ME until 2011. On March 31, 2011, Freedom Group Inc. announced that Bushmaster's manufacturing facility in Windham, ME would be closing, and new Bushmaster products would be produced in other Freedom Group facilities. The previous company name was Bushmaster Firearms, and the name changed after the company was sold on April 13, 2006 to Cerberus, and became part of the Freedom Group Inc. Older mfg. was by Gwinn Arms Co. located in Winston-Salem, NC 1972-1974. The Quality Parts Co. gained control in 1986. Distributor, dealer, or consumer direct sales.

During 2003, Bushmaster purchased Professional Ordnance, previous maker of the Carbon 15 Series of semi-auto pistols and rifles/carbines. Carbon 15s are still made in Lake Havasu City, AZ, but are now marked with Bushmaster logo. For pre-2003 Carbon 15 mfg., please refer to the Professional Ordnance section in this text.

Bushmaster formed a custom shop during 2009, and many configurations are now available by special order only. Please contact Bushmaster directly for more information and availability on these special order guns.

PISTOLS: SEMI-AUTO

IMPORTANT NOTE: On model(s) where *N/A has replaced the normal 100% value, it indicates current market conditions are too unstable to accurately ascertain 100%-60% values.

GRADING - PPGS™	100%	98%	95%	90%	80%	70%	60%	LAST MSR

Factory retail prices (MSRs) reflect most recent updates. For more up-to-date information on current pricing trends and additional useful information, please visit www.bluebookofgunvalues.com, select "Information & Services" from the menu, and click on "Additional Book Information".

BUSHMASTER PISTOL – .223 Rem. cal., AK-47 design, top bolt (older models with aluminum receivers) or side bolt (most recent mfg.) operation, steel frame on later mfg., 11 1/2 in. barrel, parkerized finish, adj. sights, 5 1/4 lbs.

	*N/A	$550	$450	$400	$375	$350	$300	*$375*

Add $40 for electroless nickel finish (disc. 1988).
Add $200 for matte nickel finish (mfg. circa 1986-1988).

This model uses a 30 shot M-16 mag. and the AK-47 gas system.

During 1985-1986, a procurement officer for the U.S. Air Force ordered 2,100 of this model for pilot use with a matte nickel finish. Eventually, this officer was retired or transferred, and the replacement officer turned down the first batch, saying they were "too reflective". Bushmaster then sold these models commercially circa 1986-1988.

CARBON-15 TYPE P21S/TYPE 21 – 5.56 NATO cal., ultra lightweight carbon fiber upper and lower receivers, 7 1/4 in. "Profile" stainless steel barrel, quick detachable muzzle compensator, ghost ring sights, 10 or 30 (new late 2004) shot mag., A2 pistol grip, also accepts AR-15 type mags., Stoner type operating sytem, tool steel bolt, extractor and carrier, 40 oz. Mfg. 2003-2012 (Bushmaster mfg.).

	*N/A	$710	$625	$550	$475	$400	$325	*$871*

Subtract approx. $200 if without full-length barrel shroud and Picatinny rail (Type 21, disc. 2005).

CARBON-15 TYPE 97/TYPE P97S – similar to Professional Ordnance Carbon 15 Type 20, except has fluted barrel, Hogue overmolded pistol grip and chrome plated bolt carrier, Type 97S has full length barrel shroud, upper and lower Picatinny rail, 46 oz. Mfg. 2003-2012 (Bushmaster mfg.).

	*N/A	$675	$625	$550	$475	$400	$325	*$825*

Add $78 for Model P97S with full length barrel shroud and lower Picatinny rail.
Subtract approx. $100 if w/o full length barrel shroud and lower Picatinny rail (disc.)

CARBON-15 9MM – 9mm Para. cal., blow-back operation, carbon fiber composite receiver, 7 1/2 in. steel barrel with A1 birdcage flash hider, A2 front sight, full-length Picatinny optics rail, Neoprene foam sleeve over buffer tube, 10 or 30 shot mag, 4.6 lbs. Mfg. 2006-2012.

	*N/A	$710	$625	$550	$475	$400	$325	*$871*

PIT VIPER AP-21 – 5.56 NATO cal., features 7 1/4 in. barrel with birdcage flash suppressor, visible upper gas transfer tube, receiver Picatinny rail, approx. 3 1/2 lbs. Limited mfg. 2011 only.

	*N/A	$715	$635	$550	$475	$400	$325	*$873*

XM-15 PATROLMAN'S AR PISTOL – 5.56 NATO cal., 7 or 10 1/2 in. stainless steel barrel with A2 flash hider, knurled free float tubular handguard, flat top receiver with Picatinny rail, Phase 5 ambi single point sling attachment, A2 pistol grip and standard trigger guard, aluminum pistol buffer tube with foam featuring laser engraved Bushmaster logo, 30 shot mag. New 2013.

MSR $949	*N/A	$750	$675	$600	$525	$450	$400	

XM-15 ENHANCED PATROLMAN'S AR PISTOL – 5.56 NATO cal., 7 or 10 1/2 in. stainless steel barrel with AAC 3 prong flash hider, free float lightweight quad rail handguard, Phase 5 ambi single point sling attachment, Magpul MOE pistol grip and trigger guard, aluminum pistol buffer tube with foam featuring laser engraved Bushmaster logo, 30 shot mag. New 2013.

MSR $1,099	*N/A	$925	$825	$725	$625	$550	$495	

RIFLES: BOLT ACTION

BA50 CARBINE/RIFLE – .50 BMG cal., 22 (carbine, disc. 2011) or 30 (rifle) in. Lothar Walther free floating barrel with vent. forend, 10 shot mag., left side bolt, full length receiver Picatinny rail, Magpul PRS adj. buttstock with LimbSavr recoil pad, high efficiency recoil reducing muzzle brake, steel bipod with folding legs, ErgoGrip deluxe tactical pistol grip,

GRADING - PPGS™	100%	98%	95%	90%	80%	70%	60%	LAST MSR

aluminum lower receiver, manganese phosphate finish on steel parts, hard anodized black finish on aluminum parts, includes Storm hardcase and two mags., 20 or 27 lbs. New 2009.

MSR $5,519	$4,995	$4,500	$4,000	$3,500	$3,000	$2,650	$2,300	

Last MSR on the carbine was $5,261.

RIFLES: SEMI-AUTO

All current AR-15 style Bushmaster rifles are shipped with a hard plastic lockable case. Most Bushmaster barrels are marked "5.56 NATO", and can be used safely with either 5.56 NATO (higher velocity/pressure) or .223 Rem. cal. ammo.

Information and values for state compliant variations are not listed.

IMPORTANT NOTE: On model(s) where *N/A has replaced the normal 100% value, it indicates current market conditions are too unstable to accurately ascertain 100%-60% values. Factory retail prices (MSRs) reflect most recent updates. For more up-to-date information on current pricing trends and additional useful information, please visit www.bluebookofgunvalues.com, select "Information & Services " from the menu, and click on "Additional Book Information".

During 2006, Bushmaster began offering a complete gas piston upper receiver/barrel assembly. Current MSRs range from $580-$990, depending on caliber and configuration.

300 AAC BLACKOUT – .300 AAC cal., 16 in. M4 contour barrel with AAC Blackout muzzle brake, Magpul ACS stock and MOE grip, free floating quad rail, 30 shot mag. (AR compatible), flat top receiver with Picatinny rail, 6 1/2 lbs. New 2012.

MSR $1,471	*N/A	$1,125	$900	$800	$700	$600	$500	

BUSHMASTER RIFLE – 5.56 NATO cal., semi-auto, top bolt (older models with aluminum receivers) or side bolt (current mfg.) operation, steel frame (current mfg.), 18 1/2 in. barrel, parkerized finish, adj. sights, wood stock, 6 1/4 lbs., base values are for folding stock model.

	*N/A	$625	$550	$500	$475	$425	$400	*$350*

Add $40 for electroless nickel finish (disc. 1988).
Add $65 for fixed rock maple wood stock.

This model uses a 30 shot M-16 mag. and the AK-47 gas system.

* ***Bushmaster Rifle Combination System*** – includes rifle with both metal folding stock and wood stock with pistol grip.

	*N/A	$675	$625	$575	$525	$475	$350	*$450*

TARGET/COMPETITION A-2/A-3 RIFLE (XM15-E2S) – 5.56 NATO cal., semi-auto patterned after the Colt AR-15, 20, 24 (disc. 2012), or 26 (disc. 2002) in. Govt. spec. match grade chrome lined or stainless steel (new 2002) barrel, 10 or 30 shot mag., manganese phosphate or Realtree Camo (20 in. barrel only, mfg. 2004 - late 2006) barrel finish, rear sight adj. for windage and elevation, cage flash suppressor (disc. 1994), approx. 8.3 lbs. Mfg. began 1989 in U.S.

MSR $1,150	*N/A	$850	$775	$700	$600	$500	$400	

Add $24 for A-3 removable carry handle.
Add $86 for stainless steel barrel with A-3 removable carry handle.
Add $194 for heavy 1 in. diameter competition barrel (disc. 2011).
Add $50 for fluted barrel or $40 for stainless steel barrel (mfg. 2002-2009).
Add $10 for 24 in. (disc. 2012) or $25 for 26 in. (disc. 2002) barrel.
Add $60 for Realtree Camo finish (disc.).

HEAVY BARREL CARBINE A-2/A-3 (XM15-E2S, SHORTY CARBINE) – 5.56 NATO cal., fixed (disc.) or telescoping buttstock, 11 1/2 (LE only, disc. 1995), 14 (LE only, disc. 1994), or 16 in. heavy barrel with birdcage flash suppressor, 30 shot mag., choice of A2 or A3 configuration, approx. 7.4 lbs. Mfg. began 1989.

MSR $1,182	*N/A	$925	$825	$725	$625	$475	$425	

Add $15 for A-3 removable carry handle.

This model does not have the target rear sight system of the XM15-E2S rifle.

* ***M4 Post-Ban Carbine (XM15-E2S)*** – 16 in. barrel, features fixed or telestock (new late 2004) tubular stock, pistol grip, phosphate or desert camo (stock, pistol grip, and

GRADING - PPGS™	100%	98%	95%	90%	80%	70%	60%	LAST MSR

forearm only, disc. 2005) finish, M4 carbine configuration with permanently attached Izzy muzzle brake, 30 shot mag. became standard in late 2004. New 2003.

MSR $1,300	*N/A	$1,025	$900	$825	$725	$625	$525	

Add $35 for desert camo finish (disc. 2005).
Add $85 for A3 removable carrying handle.
Subtract $55 for M4 Patrolman Carbine with A2 birdcage flash suppressor, collapsible stock, and 30 round magazine.

* ***XM-15 Limited Edition 20th Anniversary Rifle*** – 20 in. barrel, features 20th Anniversary engraving on upper and lower receiver, special medallion in buttstock, includes hardwood presentation case. Limited mfg. 1998-99.

	*N/A	$1,300	$1,125	$975	$875	$800	$725	

* ***XM-15 Limited Edition 25th Anniversary Carbine*** – features skeletonized tubular stock, pistol grip, A-3 type flatop with flip-up sights, laser engraved 25th anniversary crest on lower magwell, nickel plated ejection port. Limited mfg. of 1,500 during 2003.

	*N/A	$1,300	$1,125	$975	$875	$800	$725	*$1,695*

* ***E2 Carbine*** – 5.56 NATO cal., features 16 in. match chrome barrel with new M16A2 handguard and short suppressor, choice of A1 or E2 sights. Mfg. 1994-95.

	*N/A	$825	$725	$650	$600	$550	$500	

Add approx. $50 for E2 sighting system.

AK CARBINE – 5.56 NATO cal., 17 in. barrel featuring AK-47 style muzzle brake, tele-stock standard, choice of A2 or A3 configuration, ribbed oval forearm, approx. 7 1/2 lbs. Mfg. 2008-2010.

	*N/A	$950	$850	$750	$650	$550	$500	*$1,215*

Add $85 for A3 removable carry handle.

6.8mm SPC/7.62x39mm CARBINE – 6.8mm SPC or 7.62x39mm (new 2010) cal., gas operated, 16 in. M4 profile barrel with Izzy muzzle brake, six-position telescoping stock, available in A2 or A3 configuration, 26 shot mag., includes black web sling, extra mag. and lockable carrying case, approx. 7 lbs. New late 2006.

MSR $1,368	*N/A	$995	$875	$775	$675	$600	$550	

Add $100 for A3 configuration (disc. 2010).

.450 CARBINE/RIFLE – .450 Bushmaster cal., 16 (carbine) or 20 in. chrome-moly steel barrel, 5 shot mag., AR type gas operating system, forged aluminum receiver, A2 pistol grip, solid A2 buttstock with trapdoor, A3 flat-top upper receiver with Picatinny rail, 8 1/2 lbs. New 2008.

MSR $1,485	*N/A	$1,100	$925	$825	$725	$650	$575	

Add $15 for rifle.

DISSIPATOR CARBINE – 5.56 NATO cal., 16 in. heavy barrel with full length forearm and special gas block placement (gas block system is located behind the front sight base and under the rifle length handguard), A2 or A3 style with choice of solid buttstock or six-position telestock, 30 shot mag., lockable carrying case. Mfg. 2004-2010.

	*N/A	$950	$850	$750	$650	$550	$475	*$1,246*

Add $25 for tele-stock.
Add $50 for fluted barrel (disc. 2005).
Add $115 for A3 removable carrying handle.

MOE DISSIPATOR CARBINE – 5.56 NATO cal., mid-length gas system, 16 in. heavy barrel with muzzle brake, flat-top with Picatinny rail, pistol grip stock, features Magpul Original Equipment (MOE) accessories such as ACS adj. stock, MBUS rear flip sight, mid-length handguard, black, OD Green, or Flat Dark Earth finish, 6.42 lbs. New 2011.

MSR $1,298	*N/A	$950	$850	$750	$650	$550	$475	

MOE .223 MID-LENGTH – 5.56 NATO cal., similar to MOE Dissipator, except has standard barrel and half-length handguard, available in FDE finish only. New 2011.

MSR $1,298	*N/A	$950	$850	$750	$650	$550	$475	

GRADING - PPGS™	100%	98%	95%	90%	80%	70%	60%	LAST MSR

MOE 308 MID-LENGTH – .308 Win. cal., otherwise similar to MOE Mid-length, except has 10 shot mag., OD Green or FDE finsh, 6.1 lbs. New 2011.

MSR $1,508	*N/A	$1,150	$950	$850	$750	$650	$525	

SUPERLIGHT CARBINE – 5.56 NATO cal., 16 in. lightweight barrel, choice of fixed (disc.), 6-position telestock, or stub (disc.) stock with finger groove pistol grip, A2 or A3 type configuration, 30 shot mag., black finish, 5.8 - 6 1/4 lbs. New 2004.

MSR $1,259	*N/A	$875	$750	$650	$550	$475	$395	

Subtract 5% if without telestock.

Subtract approx. $75 if without A-3 removable carry handle.

MODULAR CARBINE – 5.56 NATO cal., 16 in. barrel with flash suppressor, includes many Bushmaster modular accessories, such as skeleton telestock and four-rail free floating tubular forearm, rear flip up and detachable sight, 10 or 30 (new late 2004) shot mag., 6.3 lbs. New 2004.

MSR $1,749	*N/A	$1,250	$1,025	$925	$825	$700	$575	

M4 A.R.M.S. CARBINE – 5.56 NATO cal., gas operated, 14 1/2 (law enforcement only) or 16 in. chrome-moly vanadium steel barrel with chrome lined bore and chamber, 30 shot mag., features A3 removable handle, black, foliage green (new 2010), or flat dark earth (new 2010) anodized finish, Magpul adj. buttstock with optional MOE (new 2010), Hogue pistol grip, optional Troy four rail handguard and front sights or A.R.M.S. 41-B front and rear flip-up sights (new 2010, became standard 2011), 6.2 lbs. Mfg. 2009-2011.

	*N/A	$950	$850	$750	$650	$550	$495	*$1,247*

Subtract approx. 10% if without A.R.M.S. front and rear flip up sights.

PATROLMAN'S CARBINE – 5.56 NATO, 6.8 SPC or 7.62x39mm NATO cal., gas operated, 16 in. standard barrel, choice of A2 (bullet button) or A3 configuration, two piece tubular handguard, six position adj. stock, black finish only, approx. 6 1/2 lbs.

MSR $1,275	*N/A	$900	$800	$700	$600	$550	$500	

Add $116 for 6.8 Rem. SPC or 7.62x39 NATO cal. (A3 configuration only).

M4 PATROLMAN'S CARBINE – 5.56 NATO cal., gas operated, 16 in. chrome-moly vanadium steel barrel with chrome lined bore and chamber, 30 shot mag., A2 birdcage suppressor, six position telestock, A3 configuration only, with or w/o quad rail, black anodized finish, approx. 6 1/2 lbs. New 2009.

MSR $1,211	*N/A	$900	$800	$650	$525	$450	$400	

Add $180 for quad rail (new 2011).

M4 A3 PATROLMAN'S CARBINE CERAKOTE – 5.56 NATO cal., 16 in. M4 barrel with A2 flash hider, A3 upper with removable carry handle, A2 carbine two-piece handguard, six position stock, 30 shot mag., choice of OD Green or FDE Cerakote finished receiver, 6.7 lbs. New 2013.

MSR $1,289	*N/A	$995	$895	$795	$695	$595	$495	

M4 MOE/A-TACS CARBINE – 5.56 NATO cal., includes Magpul adj. A-frame buttstock, 16 in. barrel with muzzle brake, available in black, OD Green, FDE or A-TACS camo (disc. 2012) finish (does not have Magpul features and 6-position telestock), 6.42 lbs. New 2011.

MSR $1,298	*N/A	$950	$850	$750	$650	$550	$475	

Add $104 for A-TACS camo w/o MOE features (disc. 2012).

ACR PATROL CARBINE – 5.56 NATO or 6.8mm SPC cal., 16 1/2 in. chrome-moly steel barrel with coated bore and chamber, AAC Blackout flash hider, ratchet-style supressor mounting, adj. two-position gas piston system, 30 shot mag., fixed stock, adj. cheekpiece, Picatinny rail, includes sling and three mags, 8.2 lbs. New 2010.

Current MSR on this model is POR.

ACR SPECIAL PURPOSE CARBINE – 5.56 NATO cal., similar to ACR Patrolman's Carbine, except has 6-position telescoping polymer stock, quad Picatinny rails, and includes three 30 shot PMAG magazines and soft nylon case, black finish only, 8.3 lbs. New 2011.

The current MSR on this model is POR.

GRADING - PPGS™	100%	98%	95%	90%	80%	70%	60%	*LAST MSR*

ACR BASIC A-TACS CARBINE – 5.56 NATO cal., similar to ACR Enhanced, except has fixed A-frame stock with rubber butt pod and sling mounts, black, Coyote Brown (disc. 2010), or camo finish, 8.2 lbs.

MSR $2,540	*N/A	$1,900	$1,725	$1,500	$1,275	$1,075	$850	

ACR ENHANCED – 5.56 NATO or 6.8mm SPC (while advertised in 2010, this caliber hasn't been mfg. to date) cal., Bushmaster proprietary gas operating system, modular design allows caliber interchangeability by changing the barrel, magazine, and bolt head, 16 1/2 in. chrome-moly steel barrel with coated bore and chamber, AAC Blackout NSM flash hider, ambidextrous controls, adj. two-position gas piston system, 30 shot mag., folding or six position telestock, black or coyote brown finish, three sided aluminum handguard, Magpul MBUS front/rear flip-up sights, upper and lower accessory rails, includes sling, hardcase and extra mag., 8.2 lbs. New 2010.

MSR $2,699	*N/A	$2,050	$1,800	$1,575	$1,325	$1,100	$875	

ACR BASIC FOLDER – .223 Rem. or 6.8 SPC (new 2013) cal., similar to ACR Basic, except has side folding, six-position telescoping stock, rubber buttpad, sling mounts, Magpul MBUS front, 16 1/2 in. barrel, rear flip up sights, adj. two-position gas piston system, 8.2 lbs. New mid-2011.

MSR $2,490	*N/A	$1,900	$1,700	$1,475	$1,225	$1,050	$800	

ACR BASIC ORC CARBINE – 5.56 NATO cal., 16 1/2 in. barrel with muzzle brake, features full-length top Picatinny rail w/o sights and fixed stock, 30 shot mag., black or Coyote Brown finish, 8.2 lbs. New 2011.

MSR $2,343	*N/A	$1,800	$1,625	$1,400	$1,175	$1,000	$775	

ACR STATE COMPLIANT CARBINE – 5.56 NATO cal., features 16 1/2 in. barrel with permanently attached "Izzy" muzzle brake, 10 shot mag., and fixed stock, includes sights. New 2011.

MSR $2,453	*N/A	$1,875	$1,650	$1,425	$1,175	$1,000	$775	

ORC (OPTICS READY CARBINE) ACR – 5.56 NATO or .308 Win. (mfg. 2010-2012) cal., 16 in. barrel with A2 birdcage suppressor, receiver length Picatinny rail with risers ready for optical sights, six position telestock, 30 shot mag., oval M4 type forearm, 6 lbs. New 2008.

MSR $1,112	*N/A	$865	$725	$625	$525	$425	$350	

Add $239 for .308 Win. cal. (mfg. 2010-2012).

ORC BASIC FOLDER CARBINE – 5.56 NATO cal., 16 1/2 in. barrel with muzzle brake, similar to ACR Enhanced Carbine, except does not have 3-sided aluminum hand guard with Picatinny rails, Black or Coyote Brown finish, 8.2 lbs. Mfg. 2011 only.

	*N/A	$1,900	$1,725	$1,500	$1,275	$1,075	$850	*$2,490*

ORC – 5.56 NATO or 7.62 NATO cal., mid-length gas system, 16 or 18 (disc.) in. heavy profile barrel with flash suppressor, full-length receiver Picatinny rail, heavy oval hand guard, 6-position telescoping stock, 10 or 30 shot mag., black finish, 7 3/4 lbs. New 2011.

MSR $1,056	*N/A	$875	$800	$725	$650	$550	$495	

Add $347 for 7.62 NATO cal.

MOE/ORC GAS PISTON CARBINE – 5.56 NATO cal., 16 in. barrel, MOE carbine features many Magpul accessories, is available in Black, OD Green, or Flat Dark Earth finish, ORC model does not have MOE features, but 6-position tactical stock and twin upper Picatinny rails for optics, approx. 6.3 lbs. New 2011.

MSR $1,247	*N/A	$975	$850	$725	$600	$500	$400	

Add $89 for ORC model.

Add $100-$149 for extra Magpul features on MOE model.

GAS PISTON CARBINE – 5.56 NATO cal., features gas piston operating system similar to AK-47s and FALs, 16 in. M4 profile barrel with flash suppressor, telestock, ribbed oval forearm with flip-up sight. Mfg. 2008-2010.

	*N/A	$1,400	$1,175	$975	$850	$750	$650	*$1,850*

GRADING - PPGS™	100%	98%	95%	90%	80%	70%	60%	LAST MSR

V-MATCH COMPETITION RIFLE – 5.56 NATO cal., top-of-the line match/competition rifle, flat-top receiver with extended aluminum barrel shroud, choice of 20, 24, or 26 (disc. 2002) in. barrel, 8.3 lbs. Mfg. 1994-2010.

	*N/A	$900	$750	$650	$575	$515	$465	$1,115

Add $50 for fluted barrel.
Add $10 for 24 in. or $25 for 26 (disc. 2002) in. barrel.
Add $117 for A-3 removable carry handle.

* ***V-Match Commando Carbine*** – similar to V-Match Competition Rifle, except has 16 in. barrel. Mfg. 1997-2010.

	*N/A	$900	$750	$650	$575	$515	$465	$1,105

Add $50 for fluted barrel.
Add $117 for A-3 removable carry handle.

VARMINTER – 5.56 NATO cal., includes DCM 24 in. extra heavy fluted or stainless steel varmint barrel, competition trigger, rubberized pistol grip, flat-top receiver with mini-risers (adds 1/2 in. height for scope mounting), free floating vented tube forearm, 5 shot mag., controlled ejection path, choice of black or A-TACS Digital camo (new 2011, compliant configuration only) finish. New 2002.

MSR $1,430	*N/A	$1,075	$875	$750	$625	$550	$500	

Add $71 for stainless steel barrel (compliant variation only).
Add $105 for A-TACS Digital camo coverage (compliant configuration only).

The stainless variation includes an adj., ergonomic pistol grip.

PREDATOR – 5.56 NATO cal., includes DCM (disc.) 20 in. extra fluted, or stainless steel (disc. 2006) varmint barrel, two-stage competition trigger, rubberized pistol grip, flat-top receiver with mini-risers (adds 1/2 in. height for scope mounting), free floating vented tube forearm, 10 shot mag., controlled ejection path, choice of black or A-TACS Digital Camo (new 2011, compliant configuration only) finish, 8 lbs. New 2006.

MSR $1,415	*N/A	$1,075	$900	$750	$625	$550	$500	

Add $104 for A-TACS Digital Camo finish (compliant configuration only).

The stainless variation included an adj. ergonomic pistol grip.

HUNTER – .308 Win. cal., 20 in. fluted barrel, features mid-length gas system and vented free floating aluminum forearm tube, 10 shot mag., Hogue rubberized pistol grip (Hunter) or A2 grip (Vista, disc. late 2011), Grey/Green or camo finish, 8.2 lbs. New 2011.

MSR $1,685	*N/A	$1,325	$1,125	$875	$750	$600	$525	

Add $100 for Vista Hunter model (disc. late 2011).

DCM COMPETITION RIFLE – 5.56 NATO cal., includes DCM competition features such as modified A2 rear sight, 20 in. extra heavy 1 in. diameter competition barrel, custom trigger job, and free-floating hand guard. Mfg. 1998-2005.

	*N/A	$1,125	$975	$875	$800	$725	$650	$1,495

DCM-XR COMPETITION RIFLE – 5.56 NATO cal., features dual aperature rear sight and competition ground for clarity front sight, 20 in. extra heavy competition barrel, free-floating ribbed forearm, competition trigger, choice of A2 solid or A3 removable carry handle, 13 1/2 lbs. Mfg. 2008-2010.

	*N/A	$875	$775	$700	$625	$550	$500	$1,150

Add $100 for A3 removable carry handle.

M17S BULLPUP – 5.56 NATO cal., semi-auto bullpup configuration featuring gas operated rotating bolt, 10 (C/B 1994) or 30* shot mag., 21 1/2 plain or 22 (disc.) in. barrel with flash-hider (disc.), glass composites and aluminum materials, phosphate coating, 8 1/4 lbs. Mfg. 1992-2005.

	*N/A	$650	$525	$475	$425	$400	$385	$765

GRADING - PPGS™	100%	98%	95%	90%	80%	70%	60%	LAST MSR

CARBON-15 R21 – 5.56 NATO cal., ultra lightweight carbon fiber upper and lower receivers, 16 in. "Profile" stainless steel barrel, quick detachable muzzle compensator, Stoner type operating system, tool steel bolt, extractor and carrier, optics mounting base, fixed tube stock, 10 or 30 (new late 2004) shot mag., also accepts AR-15 type mags., 3.9 lbs. Mfg. 2003-2009 (Bushmaster mfg.).

	*N/A	$800	$700	$600	$500	$450	$400	$990

* ***Carbon-15 Lady*** – 5.56 NATO cal., 16 in. barrel, includes overall tan finish (except for barrel) and webbed tube stock with recoil pad, chrome/nickel plating on small parts, supplied with soft case, 4 lbs. Mfg. 2004-2006.

	*N/A	$775	$675	$575	$500	$450	$400	$989

CARBON-15 (R97/97S) – 5.56 NATO cal., ultra lightweight carbon fiber upper and lower receivers, AR-15 style operating system, hard chromed tool steel bolt, extractor and carrier, 16 in. fluted stainless steel barrel, quick detachable muzzle compensator, optics mounting base, 10 or 30 (new late 2004) shot mag., quick detachable stock, also accepts AR-15 type mags., 3.9 or 4.3 (Model 97S) lbs. Mfg. 2003-2010.

	*N/A	$1,025	$900	$825	$725	$625	$525	$1,300

Subtract approx. $175 without Picatinny rail and "Scout" extension, double walled heat shield foregrip, ambidextrous safety, and multi-carry silent sling (Model Type 97, disc. 2005).

CARBON-15 .22 LR – .22 LR cal., similar to Carbon-15 R21, 16 in. barrel, Picatinny rail, 10 shot mag., fixed stock, approx. 4.4 lbs. Disc. 2009.

	$685	$575	$485	$415	$350	$300	$265	$790

Bushmaster also made a Carbon-15 .22 rimfire upper receiver/barrel assembly, which is exclusively designed for Bushmaster lower receivers - last MSR was $387 (new 2005).

CARBON-15 9MM – 9mm Para. cal., blow-back operation, carbon fiber composite receiver, 16 in. steel barrel with A1 birdcage flash suppressor, A2 front sight and dual aperture rear sight, Picatinny optics rail, collapsible stock, 10 or 30 shot mag., 5.7 lbs. Mfg. 2006-2012.

	*N/A	$765	$650	$550	$450	$375	$295	$933

CARBON-15 TOP LOADING RIFLE – 5.56 NATO cal., blow-back operation, carbon fiber composite receiver, 16 in. M4 profile barrel with Izzy suppressor, A2 front sight and dual aperture rear sight, Picatinny optics rail, collapsible stock, 10 shot top-loading internal mag., 5.8 lbs. Mfg. 2006-2010.

	*N/A	$875	$775	$700	$650	$600	$550	$1,100

CARBON-15 MODEL 4 CARBINE – 5.56 NATO cal., features carbon composite receiver, collapsible tube stock, 14 1/2 (LE only), or 16 (disc. 2012) in. barrel with compensator, 30 shot mag., semi-auto design styled after the military M4, 5 1/2 lbs. New 2005.

MSR $933	*N/A	$765	$650	$550	$450	$375	$295

CARBON-15 FLAT-TOP CARBINE – 5.56 NATO cal., similar to Carbon-15 Model 4 Carbine except has non-extended full-length Picatinny rail with dual aperture flip-up rear sight, 5 1/2 lbs. New 2006.

MSR $933	*N/A	$765	$650	$550	$450	$375	$295

CARBINE-15 COMPETITION – 5.56 NATO cal., various configurations, choice of extra heavy or heavy barrel in 20 or 24 in. with or w/o muzzle brake, A2 or A3 configuration, various type of sights, 8.5-13.85 lbs. Mfg. 2011 only.

	*N/A	$850	$775	$700	$600	$500	$400	$1,112

Add approx. $75 for A3 removeable carry handle.
Add $194 for heavy 1 in. diameter competition barrel.

CARBON-15 ORC – 5.56 NATO cal., 16 in. barrel with Izzy flash suppressor, 30 shot mag., features red dot optics. New 2012.

MSR $845	*N/A	$675	$600	$550	$495	$475	$450

CARBON-15 M4 QUAD RAIL – 5.56 NATO cal., similar to Carbon-15 Flat-top, except has quad rail handguard. New 2013.

MSR $845	*N/A	$675	$600	$550	$495	$475	$450

GRADING - PPGS™	100%	98%	95%	90%	80%	70%	60%	LAST MSR

CARBON-15 C22 COMBO - .22 LR and 5.56 NATO cals., includes two barrels chambered for .22 LR and 5.56 NATO cals., flat top receiver with Picatinny rail, 16 in. M4 style barrels with A2 flash hider, Mission First Tactical polymer quad rail with rail covers, 4-position stock, supplied with 25 shot (.22 LR cal.) and 30 shot (5.56 NATO) magazines. New 2013.

MSR $1,192	*N/A	$950	$875	$800	$725	$650	$595	

BUSHMASTER .308 SERIES - .308 Win. cal., 16 or 20 in. phosphate coated heavy alloy steel barrel with Izzy compensator, 20 shot mag., solid buttstock or skeletonized stock, available in A2 or A3 style with a variety of configurations, including muzzle brakes, flash suppressors, and sighting options. Mfg. late 2004-2005.

	*N/A	$1,250	$1,050	$825	$725	$625	$550	*$1,750*

Add $25 for A3 removable carry handle.
Add $10 for 20 in. barrel.
Add $50 (16 in. barrel) or $60 (20 in. barrel) for skeletonized stock.
Add approx. $100 for free-floating foream.

BUTLER ARMS USA

Current shotgun manufacturer located in Whitefish, MT.

SHOTGUNS: SEMI AUTO

BUTLER XX12 - 12 ga. only, 2 3/4 in. chamber, utilizes a proprietary HE (high efficiency) gas system and bottom barrel technology to reduce recoil, bottom ejection, side loading, quick detachable trigger, 30 in. barrel features adj. carbon fiber vent rib, includes Briley chokes and luggage travel case, checkered claro walnut stock with adj. comb. New 2012.

MSR $7,500	$7,250	$6,500	$5,500	$4,750	$4,000	$3,250	$2,500

BUTLER ASSOC., INC.

Previous manufacturer located in New Haven, CT.

DERRINGERS

SINGLE SHOT - .22 Short cal. only, side pivoting Thuer action, various metal finishes and grips, including wood and mother-of-pearl, spur trigger, uses same parts as Colt's Lord & Lady derringers, cased and uncased, B prefix serialization.

Derringer only	$150	$130	$95	$85	$75	$65	$60
Cased set	$375	$325	$275	$240	$200	$175	$150

BÜYÜK HUGLU

Current shotgun manufacturer located in Konya, Turkey. No current U.S. importation.

Büyük Huglu manufactures good quality O/U, slide action, and semi-auto shotguns under the trademarks Venus, Conquest, and Linberta. Please contact the company directly for more information, including pricing and U.S. availability (see Trademark Index).

C SECTION

C3 DEFENSE, INC.

Current manufacturer of AR-15 style rifles, upper/lower receivers, and related components located in Hiram, GA.

GRADING - PPGS™	100%	98%	95%	90%	80%	70%	60%	LAST MSR

RIFLES: SEMI-AUTO

C3 Defense also offers the short barrel C315 Clandestine Series for military/law enforcement.

IMPORTANT NOTE: On model(s) where *N/A has replaced the normal 100% value, it indicates current market conditions are too unstable to accurately ascertain 100%-60% values. Factory retail prices (MSRs) reflect most recent updates. For more up-to-date information on current pricing trends and additional useful information, please visit www.bluebookofgunvalues.com, select "Information & Services" from the menu, and click on "Additional Book Information".

C315 RANGER – .223 Rem. cal., 16 in. barrel, matte black finish, forged upper and lower, flared magwell, M4 feed ramps, mil-spec trigger group, A2 front post sight, 30 shot mag., six-position retractable stock, A2 grip, M16 bolt carrier group, Magpul rear MBUS.

MSR $995	*N/A	$775	$650	$525	$450	$400	$350

This model is also available with 10 1/2, 11 1/2 or 14 1/2 in. barrels for military/law enforcement.

C315 RECON – .223 Rem. cal., 16 in. barrel, matte black finish, forged upper and lower, flared magwell, M4 feed ramps, mil-spec trigger group, A2 front sight, 30 shot mag., Magpul MOE stock and grip, M16 bolt carrier group, Magpul MBUS and polymer extended trigger guard.

MSR $1,112	*N/A	$850	$700	$575	$500	$450	$400

This model is also available with 10 1/2, 11 1/2 or 14 1/2 in. barrels for military/law enforcement.

C315 SFR (STANDARD FULL RIFLE) – .223 Rem. cal., 16 in. barrel, matte black finish, billet upper and lower, flared magwell, tension screw, front textured grip, M4 feed ramps, mil-spec trigger group, A2 front sight, 30 shot mag., Magpul MOE stock, A2 grip, Magpul extended trigger guard, carbine length rail.

MSR $1,349	*N/A	$1,000	$875	$775	$675	$575	$475

This model is also available with 10 1/2, 11 1/2 or 14 1/2 in. barrels for military/law enforcement.

C315 EFR (ENHANCED FULL RIFLE) – .223 Rem. or .300 BLK cal., 16 in. barrel, matte black finish, enhanced billet upper and lower, flared magwell, tension screw, front textured grip, M4 feed ramps, mil-spec trigger group, 13 in. free float rail, 30 shot mag., Magpul MOE stock and grip, Magpul front and rear MBUS, Triad flash supressor, M16 bolt carrier group.

MSR $1,579	*N/A	$1,175	$1,000	$875	$750	$625	$525

This model is also available with 10 1/2, 11 1/2 or 14 1/2 in. barrels for military/law enforcement.

C315 EFR OW (OVERWATCH) – .223 Rem. or 6.8 SPC cal., 18 in. stainless steel barrel with fitted bolt, matte black finish, enhanced billet upper and lower, flared magwell, tension screw, front textured grip, M4 feed ramps, two-stage match trigger, 13 in. free float rail, chromed NM bolt carrier, 20 shot mag., Magpul UBR stock and MIAD grip, Magpul front and rear MBUS, Triad flash supressor.

MSR $2,539	*N/A	$2,000	$1,775	$1,525	$1,300	$1,150	$875

CETME

Previous manufacturer located in Madrid, Spain. CETME is an abbreviation for Centro Estudios Technicos de Materiales Especiales.

RIFLES: SEMI-AUTO

AUTOLOADING RIFLE – 7.62x51mm NATO cal., 17 3/4 in. barrel, delayed blowback action, utilizing rollers to lock breech, similar to HK-91 in appearance, wood military style stock, aperture rear sight.

$2,950	$2,650	$2,350	$2,000	$1,725	$1,500	$1,350

The H&K G3 is the next generation of this rifle, and many parts are interchangeable between the CETME and the G3.

GRADING - PPGS™	100%	98%	95%	90%	80%	70%	60%	LAST MSR

CFS GUNS

Previous firearms and airgun manufacturer circa 1997-2006, and located in Istanbul, Turkey.

CFS Guns manufactured a wide variety of O/U, SxS, slide action, and semi-auto shotguns. Some models were imported under the BSA trademark.

CMMG, INC.

Current manufacturer of AR-15 style carbines/rifles and related components and accessories established in 2002, and located in Fayette, MO.

RIFLES: SEMI-AUTO

All CMMG rifles feature hard chrome lined barrels and bores, recessed target crowns, anodized M-4 feed ramps, two 30 shot magazines, cleaning kit, sling, and USMC technical manual. All rifles can be upgraded and customized to specific customer needs, including stocks, grips, triggers, sights, optics, handguards, flash hiders, etc. Current MSRs are listed for the seven different series and include models within each series. 300 AAC Blackout series include: 16 in. w/4 rail $950, 16 in. $900, .22 LR Series include: M4LE22 - $700, Lightweight $700, Government Profile $730, M4LEP22 - $600, Quebec - last MSR was $500, M4LE22-A - $700, M4LEP22-A - $650, and the Quebec-A - last MSR was $550. 5.56 M4 Series include: F-M455-1474H - $1,126, F-M455-1454H - $1,126, F-M455-1604 - $1,076. 5.56 Govt. Series include: F-GP55-1455H - $1,126, F-GP55-1605 - $1,076, and the F-GP55-2006 - $1,076. 5.56 MedCon Series include: F-MC55-1608 - last MSR was $1,126, F-MC55-1609 - last MSR was $1,126, F-MC55-1809 - last MSR was $1,126, F-MC55-1604 - last MSR was $1,076, F-MC55-1605 - last MSR was $1,076, F-MC55-1606 - last MSR was $1,076, F-MC55-1805 - last MSR was $1,076, and the F-MC55-1806 - last MSR was $1,076. 5.56 LE Bull Series include: LE-BL55-1604 - $850, LE-BL55-1604PR - $1,100, LE-BL55-1604R - $1,000, LE-BL55-1805SST - $850, and the LE-BL55-2206SST - $850. LE Series include: LE-M455-1604-P - $1,000, and the LE-M455-1604 - $900. 9mm Series include: LE-M490-1604 - $1,000, 5.56 chrome lined include: M4 $1,000, mid-length MOE $1,250, M10 MOE $1,250, mid-length M10 $1,100, M10 rifle $1,100, mid-length Govt. Profile $1,100-$1,125, and MK308 series MK3 16 in. SS $1,500-$1,800, and MK3 18 in. SS $1,650-$1,800. Please contact the company directly for current options, availability, and a dealer listing (see Trademark Index).

C.O. ARMS

Previous manufacturer located in Millington, TN until 2011.

PISTOLS: SEMI-AUTO

SCORPION – .45 ACP cal., 4 1/4 in. stainless steel barrel, stainless steel slide with rear cocking serrations, diamond checkered wood grips, Novak sights, lightweight adj. trigger, beavertail grip safety, lowered and flared ejection port, full length guide rod, extended to rear slide stop.

$1,050	$925	$800	$700	$600	$500	$400	*$1,199*

AWP (ALL WEATHER PISTOL) – .45 ACP cal., 3 1/2 in. stainless steel bull barrel, carbon steel slide, aluminum frame, checkered front strap, XS Express big dot sights, Commander style hammer, solid adj. trigger, beavertail grip safety, lowered and flared ejection port, stippled synthetic grips, full length guide rod.

$1,425	$1,200	$1,025	$925	$825	$750	$675	*$1,599*

CVA

Please refer to the Connecticut Valley Arms listing in this section.

C Z (CESKÁ ZBROJOVKA)

Current manufacturer located in Uhersky Brod, Czech Republic since 1936. Previous manufacture was in Strakonice, Czechoslovakia circa 1923-late 1950s. Newly manufactured CZ firearms are currently imported exclusively by CZ USA located in Kansas City, KS. Previously imported by Magnum Research, Inc. located in Minneapolis, MN until mid-1994.

Previously imported before 1994 by Action Arms Ltd. located in Philadelphia, PA. Dealer and distributor sales.

For CZ manufactured airguns, please refer to the *Blue Book of Airguns* by Dr. Robert Beeman and John Allen (now online also).

CZ USA currently has four product lines, which include CZ (pistols, rifles, and shotguns), Safari Classics (best quality bolt action rifles), Dan Wesson (semi-auto pistols) and Brno (combination guns and rifles). Please refer to the individual listings for more information and current values.

CZ HISTORY

Ceská Zbrojovka simply means Czech weapons factory. CZ's full name is Ceská Zbrojovka a.s. Uhersky Brod, often abbreviated to CZUB a.s., meaning joint stock company. Uhersky Brod is the town the factory is located in. Zbrojovka Brno means weapons or arms factory located in Brno.

Zbrojovka Brno was built in 1916-1918, as a subsidiary of the Vienna Arsenal. After WWI, this factory was given the responsibility of providing the newly formed Czechoslovakian military with infantry weapons, specifically rifles and light machine guns. Circa 1923, pistol manufacture was transferred from Brno to Ceská Zbrojovka, located in the town of Strakonice, southwest of Bohemia. Since the location change, Zbrojovka Brno has never produced pistols on any great scale (please refer to the Brno section in this text for more information).

Ceská Zbrojovka Strakonice began developing many innovative and revolutionary pistol designs. These models, including the CZ-24, CZ-27, and CZ-52 are certainly well-known throughout the world. During the mid-1950s, CZ's facilities were converted to making motorcycles and precision engineering products.

Ceská Zbrojovka, located in the town of Uhersky Brod, was founded in 1936, as a subsidiary of Ceská Zbrojovka Strakonice, in a government decision designed to move firearms production further away from the German border, and out of the reach of German bombers. Uhersky Brod is located approx. 60 miles east of Brno. Before WWII, the factory produced aircraft machine guns (LK-30), the military pistol (CZ-38 in 9mm Para.), and rifle Models Z242-Z247. During WWII, the factory was taken over by the Germans, and the facilities were used for the production of aircraft machine guns (German designed MG 17s) and related components for other models of military weapons.

Shortly after WWII, Ceská Zbrojovka Uhersky Brod resumed production of firearms for the civilian marketplace, including the CZ 241 semi-auto shotgun, and some O/U shotguns. The production of pistols commenced during the mid-1950s, with the introduction of the Model CZ-50 and other small pistol models named DUO in 6.35mm cal. Up to this point, the main pistol producer in Czechoslovakia was CZ Strakonice as stated above. The CZ-52 pistol was the last model they produced. Since the end of the 1950s, Ceská Zbrojovka Uhersky Brod has become the sole producer of pistols.

After WWII, the Ceská Zbrojovka Uhersky Brod became massively involved in other types of production besides sporting and hunting firearms. Production reached a high during the 1980s, when hunting/sporting firearms manufacture resulted in approx. 30% of total production. The balance of manufacture was devoted to the production of power hydraulics for tractors, while gears and accessory drive boxes for speed reduction in turbo prop airplane engines made up the rest.

During 1964-1966, the Czech government transferred the production of long guns from Zbrojovka Brno to Ceská Zbrojovka Uhersky Brod. During the 1970s & 1980s, the arms production of Zbrojovka Brno accounted for less than 3% of its total capacity. The activities of this company were diverted into the production of typewriters, diesel motors, and automatic machine tools. While many firearm designs originated in Brno, Zbrojovka Brno was not the manufacturer. Because of this, the long guns manufactured in the mid-1960s, including the ZKK 600-602 series and ZKM rimfires, were manufactured in CZ Uhersky Brod. Because of the Czech government's decision to merge manufacture within both companies, the Brno trademark was also used by Ceská Zbrojovka Uhersky Brod.

This relationship was terminated in 1983, when both companies became part of the Agrozet conglomerate. While confusing, the arms utlizing the Brno trademark were not produced in Brno

GRADING - PPGS™	100%	98%	95%	90%	80%	70%	60%	LAST MSR

during this time. All firearms exported from Czechoslovakia at the time carried the Brno logo, and most of them were manufactured by Ceská Zbrojovka Uhersky Brod.

During 1975, Ceská Zbrojovka Uhersky Brod designed and began manufacture of the famous CZ-75 pistol. Production in quantity began in 1977. To date, over one million CZ-75s have been produced. This semi-auto has been made in many variations and/or modifications to suit many military and commercial contracts. During the mid-1980s, the CZ factory released the CZ-85, basically a CZ-75 with ambidextrous safety and slide stop. In the mid-1990s, production of the CZ-100 began - this new model featured a polymer frame. The CZ 550 line of rifles was also introduced at this same time.

During 2009, after the Brno factory closure, many of Brno's employees transferred to Brno Rifles, Ltd., a subsidiary of CZ, which was established in Brno to continue production of Brno firearms using the original Brno trademark. Please refer to the Brno section for current listings.

COMBINATION GUNS

CZ 584 SOLO – 12 ga. over choice of 7x57mm Mauser (importation disc. 1999), 7x57Rmm, 7x65Rmm, .222 Rem. (importation disc. 1999), .223 Rem. (imported 1994-99), .243 Win. (imported 1994-99), .30-06 (new 1994), 7mm Mauser (imported 1994-99), and .308 Win. (importation disc. 1999) cals., 24 1/2 in. barrels, similar action to CZ 581 O/U shotgun, extractors or ejectors, rifle sights, approx. 7.4 lbs. Importation disc. 1986, resumed 1994. Disc. 1995, importation resumed 1999. Disc. 2003.

$775	$655	$595	$515	$450	$385	$350	*$917*

Add 20% for ejectors.

PISTOLS: SEMI-AUTO, DISC.

The models listed below were made in Ceská Zbrojovka Strakonice, with the exception of some models manufactured in Ceská Zbrojovka Prague during the Nazi occupation of Czechoslovakia. The VZ38 was also produced in Uhersky Brod.

"DUO" POCKET AUTOMATIC – .25 ACP cal., 6 shot, 2 1/8 in. barrel, fixed sights, blue or nickel, plastic grips. Mfg. beginning 1926 (current Z pistol by Brno).

$250	$225	$200	$175	$150	$125	$100

Add 40% for WWII years.

This model was manufactured by Dushek and is similar to the Z pistol equivalent by Brno.

CZ 22 – .380 ACP cal., derived from Mauser variation and manufactured under license from Mauser. Mfg. 1923 only.

$750	$600	$500	$450	$400	$350	$300

CZ 24 – .380 ACP cal.

* ***CZ 24 Standard Frame*** – 8 shot mag. Over 175,000 mfg. 1924-1938. Over half issued to Czech Army. Same general design as CZ 22 except no gap between trigger and frame. Production continued to 1941.

Standard mfg.	$500	$400	$350	$325	$300	$275	$250
Kriegsmarine proofed	$1,275	$1,125	$975	$875	$800	$700	$600

Add $50 for Nazi proof.

Beware of counterfeit markings on Kriegsmarine proofed models.

* ***CZ 24 Long Frame*** – 9 shot mag.

$1,750	$1,500	$1,250	$1,000	$900	$800	$700

Add $750 if fit with stock slot (either standard frame or long frame).

CZ 27 – .32 ACP cal.

* ***CZ 27 "CESKA" Slide Legend Variation*** – slanted slide grooves, high polish, available as Prewar Commercial, DR proofed, or Nazi proofed. Ser. no. range 1 - 21,500.

$550	$450	$350	$300	$250	$200	$150

GRADING - PPGS™	100%	98%	95%	90%	80%	70%	60%	LAST MSR

* ***CZ 27 "BÖHMISCHE" Slide Legend Variation*** – vertical slide grooves, high or medium polish, standard or Nazi Police pistols dated 1941, 1942, or 1943 marked with Eagle/K on left trigger guard web, ser. no. range 21,500-261,000.

Standard mfg.	**$350**	**$300**	**$250**	**$200**	**$150**	**$135**	**$100**
1941 dated	**$775**	**$675**	**$550**	**$450**	**$325**	**$275**	**$225**
1942-1943 dated	**$700**	**$600**	**$500**	**$400**	**$300**	**$275**	**$200**
Kriegsmarine proofed	**$1,050**	**$900**	**$750**	**$600**	**$475**	**$400**	**$350**

Beware of counterfeit markings on Kriegsmarine proofed models.

* ***CZ 27 "fnh" Slide Legend Variation*** – medium polish or phosphate finish. Ser. no. range 261,000-476,000.

$325 $275 $225 $175 $150 $125 $100

Add 30% for late phosphate war finish.

* ***CZ 27 Sound Suppressor Barrel Variation*** – a small number of phosphate pistols were fitted with an extended barrel for suppressor attachment. Usually in 450,000-460,000 ser. no. range.

$3,500 $3,000 $2,500 $2,250 $2,000 $1,750 $1,500

* ***CZ 27 Post-WWII mfg.*** – dated 1945, 1946, 1947, 1948, 1949, 1950, 1951. These models will have the "NARODNI PODNIK" inscription on slide.

Currently, these variations average $250 in 95%+ condition while reworks (very common) average under $200.

CZ 28 – .32 ACP cal., blue finish, smooth hardwood grips, four slanted slide serrations on rear of slide, marked "C.S. STRAZ KARLOVY VARY" on right side, "CESKA ZBROJOVKA AS v PRAZE" on top of frame, and "CZ 28" on left side below serrations.

$300 $250 $200 $175 $150 $125 $100

VZ 36 – .25 ACP cal., 8 shot, 2 1/2 in. barrel, fixed sights, blue finish, plastic grips, DA, similar to VZ 45, but scarce, some examples mfg. with safety lever on the left frame, some made w/o the lever. Mfg. 1936-1942.

$600 $550 $500 $450 $400 $350 $300

VZ 38 DOUBLE ACTION AUTOMATIC – .380 ACP cal., 9 shot, double action only, 4 5/8 in. barrel, fixed sights, blue, plastic grips. Mfg. 1938-1939.

$650 $550 $450 $350 $300 $250 $200

Add 300% for Waffenamt proofed (E/WaA76 on barrel and left frame), usually phosphate finished and either unnumbered or in B291,000-B293,000 ser. no. range.

Changed to Model 39T after 1939.

VZ 38 "BULGARIAN CONTRACT" – .380 ACP cal., 9 shot, single or double action, prominent safety on left frame. Usually in 420,000-423,000 ser. no. range.

$3,250 $2,750 $2,250 $1,500 $1,000 $750 $500

VZ 45 – .25 ACP cal., 8 shot, 2 1/2 in. barrel, fixed sights, blue finish, plastic grips, DA, similar to VZ 36, but slightly modified and with no safety lever. Mfg. 1945-1952.

$300 $275 $250 $225 $200 $175 $150

PISTOLS: SEMI-AUTO, RECENT MFG.

CZ P-01 – 9mm Para. cal., based on CZ-75 design, but with metallurgical improvements, aluminum alloy frame, hammer forged 3.8 in. barrel, 10 or 14 (new 2005) shot mag., decocker, includes M3 rail on bottom of frame, checkered rubber grips, matte black polycoat finish, 27.2 oz. Importation began 2003.

MSR $608 $530 $475 $420 $365 $315 $275 $250

Add $99 for tactical block with bayonet (mfg. 2006-2012).
Add $67 for Crimson Trace laser grips (mfg. 2007-2010).

GRADING - PPGS™	100%	98%	95%	90%	80%	70%	60%	LAST MSR

CZ P-06 – .40 S&W cal., 10 shot mag., otherwise similar to CZ P-01. Mfg. 2008-2009, reintroduced 2011.

MSR $660	$555	$475	$400	$350	$300	$275	$250	

Add $99 for tactical block with bayonet (disc. 2012).

CZ P-07 DUTY – 9mm Para. or .40 S&W cal., SA/DA, 3.8 in. standard or threaded (new 2012) barrel, black polycoat or OD Green (new 2012) polymer frame with black slide, squared off trigger guard, 10 (9mm only),12 (.40 S&W only) or 16 shot mag., fixed sights, decocking lever, Omega trigger system, 27 oz. New 2009.

MSR $483	$435	$370	$325	$280	$260	$240	$220	

Add $13 for .40 S&W cal.
Add $6 for OD Green frame in 9mm Para. cal. with 16 shot mag. (new 2012).
Add $45 for threaded barrel (9mm Para. cal. only) with black finish (new 2012).

CZ P-09 DUTY – 9mm Para. or .40 S&W cal., full size variation of the P-07 Duty, 4 1/2 in. barrel, 15 (.40 S&W) or 19 (9mm Para.) shot staggered mag., includes lower Picatinny rail and low profile sights, Omega SA/DA trigger, black polymer frame and black steel slide, approx. 30 oz. New 2013.

MSR $514	$465	$395	$350	$315	$285	$250	$225	

Add $14 for .40 S&W cal.

CZ-40B/CZ-40P – .40 S&W cal. only, CZ-75B operating mechanism in alloy (CZ-40B) or polymer (CZ-40P) M1911 style frame, single/double action, black polycoat finish, 10 shot double column mag., fixed sights, firing pin block safety. Limited importation 2002 only, reintroduced 2007 only.

	$425	$365	$325	$290	$275	$250	$225	*$499*

* ***CZ-40 P Compact*** – .40 S&W cal., 1,500 imported 2004, reimported 2006.

	$325	$285	$265	$245	$225	$200	$175	*$370*

CZ-50/70 – .32 ACP cal., double action, blowback action, 3 3/4 in. barrel, loaded chamber indicator, 8 shot mag.

	$150	$125	$110	$100	$90	$80	$70	

CZ-52 – 7.62 Tokarev or 9mm Para. cal., single action semi-auto, roller locking breech system, 4.9 in. barrel, 8 shot mag. Mfg. in Strakonice.

	$250	$225	$195	$175	$150	$125	$100	

Add $40 for extra 9mm Para. barrel.
Currently imported used CZ-52 pistols are priced in the $125-$150 range, depending on condition, and will have the current importer's mark visible on the gun.

CZ-70 – 7.65mm/.32 ACP cal., double action, similar to Walther PP, 8 shot mag., 1 lb. 9 oz. Disc.

	$400	$350	$300	$275	$250	$225	$200	

A very limited quantity of this model was imported.

CZ-75, CZ-75 B, CZ-75 BD – 9mm Para. or .40 S&W (disc. 1997, reintroduced 1999) cal., Poldi steel, selective double action, double action only, or single action only, frame safety, 4 3/4 in. barrel, 10 (C/B 1994, standard for .40 S&W cal.), 15* (disc.), or 16 (9mm Para. cal. only) shot mag., currently available in black polycoat/polymer (standard, DA and SA only), matte blue (disc. 1994), high polish (disc. 1994), glossy blue (mfg. 1999-2010), dual tone (mfg. 1998-2012), satin nickel (mfg. 1994-2012), high polished stainless steel, or matte stainless steel (new 2006) finish, black plastic grips, non-suffix early guns did not have a firing pin block safety, reversible mag. release, or ambidextrous safety, and were usually shipped with two mags., B suffix model nomenclature was added 1998, and designated some internal mechanism changes, BD suffix indicates decocker mechanism, 34.3 oz.

MSR $499	$425	$385	$350	$300	$275	$250	$225	

Add $70 for .40 S&W cal.
Add $29 for Model CZ-75 BD (decocker).
Add $212 for high polished or matte stainless steel.
Add $70 for glossy blue (disc. 2011), dual tone (disc. 2012), or satin nickel (disc. 2012) finish.

GRADING - PPGS™	100%	98%	95%	90%	80%	70%	60%	LAST MSR

Add $391 for CZ-75 Kadet .22 LR Adapter I (mfg. 1998-2010), or Adapter II (includes .22 LR upper slide assembly and mag., fits Omega System (new 2012).
Add $56 for single action only (Model CZ-75 B SA, black polymer frame).
Add $81 for Crimson Trace laser grips (black poly coat finish only, mfg. 2007 only).
Add 10% with lanyard loop.
These early pistols sell for $1,200 if NIB condition, chrome engraved $1,650 (NIB), factory competition $1,500 (NIB).

"First Model" variations, mostly imported by Pragotrade of Canada, are identifiable by short slide rails, no half-cock feature, and were mostly available in high polish blue only. Current values range from $275-$595, depending on original condition.

* ***CZ-75 Shadow*** – 9mm Para. cal., DA or SAO (new 2013), black or dual-tone finish, competition hammer/trigger with beavertail frame, stainless steel guide rod, ambidextrous extended manual safety, new style 85 combat trigger, includes two 16 (SAO, new 2013), or 18 shot mags. and test target, fiber optic front sight and shadow rear sight, checkered black plastic grips, 39 oz. Mfg. in Czech Republic, assembled in USA. New 2011.

MSR $1,053 $915 $800 $725 $650 $575 $500 $425

Subtract $74 for SAO (new 2013, includes two 16 shot mags.).

* ***CZ-75 Shadow T*** – 9mm Para. cal., similar to CZ-75 Shadow, except is SA or DA, and has black rubber grips and full adj. rear sight. New 2011.

MSR $1,180 $1,075 $940 $815 $725 $650 $575 $500

CZ-75 SHADOW CTS LS-P – 9mm Para. cal., SA/DA, black polycoat frame/grips, satin nickel long slide, adj. sights. Mfg. by Custom Shop. New 2012.

MSR $1,521 $1,300 $1,150 $1,025 $875 $775 $675 $550

* ***CZ-75 B Military*** – 9mm Para. cal. Importation 2000-2002.

$365 $315 $270 $250 $225 $210 $195 ***$429***

* ***CZ-75 B Tactical*** – similar to CZ-75 B, except has OD green frame and matte black polymer slide, includes CZ knife. Limited importation during 2003.

$425 $355 $305 $270 $225 $210 $195 ***$499***

* ***CZ-75 B Target*** – similar to CZ-75, except is single action with custom shop target features. Limited importation 2010 only.

$1,182 $1,050 $900 $750 $625 $525 $525 $350

* ***CZ-75 B Limited Edition*** – similar to CZ-75 B, except is stainless steel, tritium night sights. Limited mfg. 2010 only.

$695 $625 $550 $475 $400 $350 $300 ***$806***

* ***CZ-75 Semi-Compact*** – 9mm Para. cal. only, 13 shot mag., choice of black polymer, matte, or high polish blue finish. Imported 1994 only.

$350 $300 $275 $250 $230 $250 $200 ***$519***

Add $20 for matte blue finish.
Add $40 for high polish blue finish.

* ***CZ-75 Compact*** – 9mm Para. or .40 S&W (mfg. 2005-2010) cal. only, otherwise similiar to CZ-75, full-size frame, except has 3.9 in. barrel, 10 (C/B 1994) or 13* (disc.), or 14 shot mag., checkered walnut grips, 33 oz. New 1993.

MSR $528 $445 $400 $360 $330 $295 $265 $235

Add $41 for glossy blue (disc. 2006), dual tone, or satin nickel finish.
Add $41 for .40 S&W cal. (disc. 2010).
Add $99 for tactical block with bayonet (.40 S&W cal. only) mfg. 2006-2012.
Add $391 for CZ Kadet .22 LR adapter I or II (includes .22 LR upper slide assembly and mag., new 1998).

* ***CZ-75 D PCR Compact*** – 9mm Para. cal., similar to CZ-75 Compact, except has black polymer alloy frame, decocker, PCR stands for Police of Czech Republic, 1.7 lbs. Importation began 2000.

MSR $582 $515 $465 $400 $350 $300 $265 $235

GRADING - PPGS™	100%	98%	95%	90%	80%	70%	60%	LAST MSR

* ***CZ-75 Compact SDP*** – 9mm Para. cal., SA/DA, 3.7 in. barrel, black alloy frame with black aluminum grips, lower Picatinny rail, low profile Tritium two-dot night sights, 14 shot mag., front and rear slide serrations, bobbed hammer, 28 1/2 oz. New 2013.

MSR $1,379	$1,195	$1,050	$925	$800	$700	$600	$500	

* ***CZ-75 Kadet*** – .22 LR cal., black polymer finish, 10 shot mag, 4.7 in. barrel, 37.9 oz. Mfg. 1999-2004, reintroduced 2006-2012.

	$560	$500	$450	$400	$350	$300	$275	*$690*

* ***CZ-75 25th Anniversary*** – 9mm Para. cal., features include 25th Anniversary markings. Limited mfg. of 500 during 2000 only.

	$625	$450	$375	$315	$270	$230	$200	*$699*

* ***CZ-75 Champion*** – 9mm Para. (mfg. 2000-2008) or .40 S&W cal., dual tone finish, IPSC competition features including 3 port compensator, finger grooved synthetic grips, target trigger and sights, 4 1/2 in. barrel, approx. 2.2 lbs. Imported 1999-2004, reintroduced 2006-2009.

	$1,425	$1,200	$1,050	$875	$725	$600	$500	*$1,739*

* ***CZ-75 Standard IPSC*** – .40 S&W cal., IPSC features, 5.4 in. barrel, dual tone finish, checkered wood grips, 10 or 16 (new 2005) shot mag., 45 oz. Mfg. 1999-2005.

	$1,000	$900	$750	$625	$550	$450	$350	*$1,152*

* ***CZ-75 Tactical Sport*** – 9mm Para. or .40 S&W cal., dual tone finish, steel frame, 10, 16 (.40 S&W cal.), or 20 (9mm Para. cal.) shot mag., 5.3 in. barrel, ambidextrous safety, checkered wood grips, fixed sights, 45 oz. New 2006.

MSR $1,272	$1,075	$950	$825	$700	$600	$500	$450	

* ***CZ-75 Modified*** – similar to Standard, except has dual port compensator and red dot reflex sight, approx. 2.8 lbs. Imported 2001-2002.

	$1,250	$1,075	$975	$875	$735	$600	$500	*$1,567*

* ***CZ-75 Special Editions*** – 9mm Para. cal., similar to CZ-75, except has optional special edition finishes including all matte nickel, bright nickel frame, matte chrome, all brushed chrome, bright chrome, or gold frame, choice of matching finish slide, master blue slide, gold small parts, or master blue slide with gold small parts, price line refers to all matte nickel finish. Imported 1993-94 by Action Arms only.

	$525	$465	$415	$375	$335	$310	$285	*$699*

Add approx. $120 for matte nickel frame with master blue small parts.
Add approx. $180 for matte nickel with gold small parts, matte nickel frame with master blue slide and gold small parts, master blue with gold small parts, or gold frame with master blue slide.

* ***CZ-75 30th Anniversary*** – 9mm Para. cal., features special 30th anniversary engraving with 24Kt. gold plated controls and accents, 10 or 15 shot mag., high gloss blue finish, birch grips with carved "30." 1,000 mfg. (ser. no. 1-1,000) 2005-2006.

	$875	$750	$625	$500	$450	$395	$350	*$999*

CZ-75 TS CZECHMATE – 9mm Para. cal., includes 2 barrels and all accessories necessary to shoot in IPSC open or limited division, aluminum grips, competition hammer, undercut trigger guard, package includes three 20 shot mags. and one 26 shot mag., black polycoat finish. Custom Shop mfg. New 2011.

MSR $3,220	$2,775	$2,425	$2,125	$1,800	$1,500	$1,250	$1,000	

CZ-75 SP-01 – 9mm Para. cal., 4 3/4 in. barrel, includes light rail, ambidextrous thumb safety, adj. tritium sights, matte black polycoat finish, decocker, checkered black rubber grips, includes two 10 or 18 shot mags, 38 oz. New 2006.

MSR $660	$560	$475	$400	$350	$300	$275	$250	

* ***CZ-75 SP-01 Phantom*** – 9mm Para. cal., SA/DA, polymer frame with accessory rail, steel slide, fixed sights, includes two interchangable grip inserts, decocking lever, 19 shot mag. (also fits standard CZ-75 models), black polycoat finish, squared off trigger guard, 28.2 oz. New 2009.

MSR $595	$520	$440	$375	$325	$275	$250	$225	

GRADING - PPGS™	100%	98%	95%	90%	80%	70%	60%	LAST MSR

CZ-75 SP-01 SHADOW – 9mm Para. cal., Custom Shop mfg. Limited mfg.

	$625	$550	$475	$425	$365	$335	$295	*$724*

* ***CZ-75 SP-01 Accu-Shadow*** – 9mm Para. cal., 4.6 in. barrel, features Accu-Bushing system enabling precise barrel placement and better accuracy, competition hammer, lighter springs, short reset disconnector, fiber optic front and Hajo serrated target rear sight, lower Picatinny rail, black finish, 38 1/2 oz. New 2013.

MSR $1,665	$1,450	$1,275	$1,075	$925	$800	$700	$600	

* ***CZ-75 SP-01 Shadow Custom*** – 9mm Para. cal., features adj. competition rear and fiber optic front sight, 19 shot mag., custom tuned action and trigger, competition hammer, reduced power springs, stainless guide rod, and thin black aluminum grips, dual tone finish, Custom Shop mfg. Mfg. 2011 only.

	$1,050	$900	$750	$600	$500	$400	$325	*$1,199*

* ***CZ-75 SP-01 Shadow Target*** – 9mm Para. cal., similar to SP-01 Series, except has custom shop target features, including Champion style hammer, fiber optic front sight and competition rear sight, extended mag. release, fully beveled magwell, 19 shot, rubber grips, 2.6 lbs., Custom Shop mfg. New 2010.

MSR $1,321	$1,150	$975	$800	$625	$525	$425	$350	

CZ-75 SP-01 TACTICAL – 9mm Para. or .40 S&W cal., light rail, decocker, 10 or 19 shot mag., tritium sights, black polycoat finish.

MSR $660	$560	$480	$400	$350	$300	$275	$250	

Add $77 for .40 S&W cal.

Add $99 for tactical block with bayonet (disc. 2012).

CZ-82 – 9x18mm Makarov cal., current Czech military sidearm, most recent exportation was to W. Germany in Makarov chambering.

This model is similar to the CZ-83 except for cal. Prices are similar to the model CZ-83.

CZ-83 – .32 ACP (disc. 1994, reintroduced 1999-2002 and 2006) or .380 ACP (new 1986), or 9mm Makarov (mfg. 1999-2001) cal., modern design, 3-dot sights, 3.8 in. barrel, choice of carry models, blue (disc. 1994), glossy blue (new 1998), satin nickel (new 1999, not available in .32 ACP), or black polymer (disc. 1997) finish, black synthetic grips, 10 (C/B 1994), 12* (.380 ACP) or 15* (.32 ACP) shot mag., 26.2 oz. Mfg. began 1985, but U.S. importation started in 1992. Importation disc. 2012.

	$375	$315	$265	$235	$200	$175	$160	*$452*

Add $36 for satin nickel.

* ***CZ-83 Special Editions*** – .380 ACP cal. only, similar to CZ-83, has optional special edition finishes including all matte nickel, master high polish blue, bright nickel, matte chrome, all brushed chrome, bright chrome, or gold frame, choice of matching finish or master blue slide with gold small parts, price line refers to all matte nickel or high polish blue finish. Importation disc. 1994.

	$425	$375	$335	$295	$250	$225	$200	*$569*

Add approx. $90 for matte nickel frame with master blue small parts.

Add approx. $175 for matte nickel with gold small parts, matte nickel frame with master blue slide and gold small parts, master blue with gold small parts, or gold frame with master blue slide.

CZ-85, CZ-85 B – 9mm Para. or 9x21mm (imported 1993-94 only) cal., variation of the CZ-75 with ambidextrous controls, new plastic grip design, sight rib, available in black polymer, matte blue (disc. 1994), glossy blue (mfg. 2001 only), or high-gloss blue (9mm Para. only, disc. 1994) finish, includes firing pin block and finger rest trigger, plastic grips, 10, 15 (disc.), or 16 shot mag. new 2005, B suffix model nomenclature was added during 1998, approx. 2.2 lbs.

MSR $582	$500	$450	$400	$365	$330	$295	$275	

Add $391 for CZ Kadet .22 LR adapter (includes .22 LR upper slide assembly and mag., mfg. 1998 only).

* ***CZ-85 Combat*** – similar to CZ-85B, except has fully adj. rear sight, available in black polymer, matte blue (disc. 1994), glossy blue (mfg. 2001-2010), dual-tone (disc.

GRADING - PPGS™	100%	98%	95%	90%	80%	70%	60%	LAST MSR

2012), satin nickel (disc. 2012), or high-gloss blue (disc. 2010) finish, walnut (disc. 1994) or black plastic (new 1994) grips, extended mag. release, drop free 15 (mfg. 1995-2011), or 16 shot mag. Importation began 1992.

MSR $615	$530	$450	$415	$375	$350	$325	$295	

Add $26 for glossy blue (disc. 2010) satin nickel (disc. 2012), or dual-tone (disc. 2012) finish.
Add $291 for CZ Kadet .22 LR adapter (includes .22 LR upper slide assembly and mag., mfg. 1998 only).

* ***CZ-85 Champion*** – .40 S&W or 9x21mm cal., similar to CZ-75 Champion. Imported 1999 only.

	$1,325	$1,100	$975	$850	$725	$600	$500	*$1,484*

* ***CZ-85 Special Editions*** – 9mm Para. cal., similar to CZ-85, has optional special edition finishes including all matte nickel, bright nickel, matte chrome, all brushed chrome, bright chrome, or gold frame, choice of matching finish slide, master blue slide, gold small parts, or master blue slide with gold small parts, price line refers to all matte nickel finish. Imported 1993-94 only.

	$575	$495	$450	$395	$350	$325	$285	*$749*

Subtract $60 for matte nickel frame with master blue slide.
Add $130 for matte nickel frame with master blue small parts, matte nickel with gold small parts, matte nickel frame with master blue slide and gold small parts, master blue with gold small parts or gold frame with master blue slide.

* ***CZ-85 Combat Special Editions*** – 9mm Para. cal., similar finishes to Model CZ-85 Special Editions, price line refers to all matte nickel finish. Limited importation 1994-95.

	$775	$725	$650	$595	$525	$450	$375	*$1,049*

Subtract $125 for matte nickel frame with master blue small parts.
Add $245 for matte nickel with gold small parts, matte nickel frame with master blue slide and gold small parts, master blue with gold small parts, or gold frame with master blue slide.

CZ-97 B – .45 ACP cal., SA or DA, manual safety with firing pin block safeties, 4.84 in. barrel with short recoil system, black polymer or glossy blue finish, checkered wood (disc. 2012) or aluminum (new 2013) grips, fixed (disc. 2012) or fiber optic (new 2013) front sight, double column 10 shot mag., last shot hold open slide, 40 oz. New 1998.

MSR $686	$580	$500	$450	$395	$350	$295	$265	

Add $27 for glossy blue finish.

* ***CZ-97 BD*** – .45 ACP cal., similar to CZ-97 B, except has black polymer frame, decocker, tritium night sights, black polycoat finish, 41 oz. New 2009.

MSR $792	$685	$575	$500	$450	$400	$350	$300	

CZ-100 – 9mm Para. or .40 S&W (disc.) cal., double action only, firing pin blocking safety, w/o external manual safety, black polymer finish, adj. 3-dot sights, high impact plastic frame, 10 or 12 (new 2005, 9mm Para. cal. only) shot mag., 3.9 in. barrel, approx. 24 oz. Mfg. 1996-2007, reintroduced 2009 only.

	$450	$395	$340	$285	$240	$220	$195	*$517*

CZ-122 B SPORT – .22 LR cal., semi-auto, single action only, 6 in. solid ribbed barrel with adj. rear sight, manual and firing pin block safety, last shot hold open slide, steel frame and slide with two-tone finish, ribbed black polymer grips, 10 shot mag., 30 oz. Limited mfg. 1998 only.

	$225	$190	$175	$160	$150	$140	$135	*$259*

CZ-2075 RAMI – 9mm Para. or .40 S&W cal., SA/DA operation, 3 in. barrel, double stack 7, (.40 S&W cal. new 2012), 8 (.40 S&W cal.), 10 (9mm Para. cal., flush fit) or 14 (9mm Para. cal.) shot mag. with finger extension, snag free sights, black polycoat finish with black checkered grips, alloy or polymer (mfg. 2006-2011) frame, 25 oz. New 2005.

MSR $595	$495	$435	$375	$325	$300	$250	$225	

Add $20 for .40 S&W with 7 shot mag. (new 2012).
Subtract approx. $100 for polymer frame with black polycoat finish (disc. 2011).

GRADING - PPGS™	100%	98%	95%	90%	80%	70%	60%	LAST MSR

* ***CZ-2075 RAMI BD*** – 9mm Para. cal., SA/DA operation, 3 in. barrel, 10 or 14 shot mag., similar to CZ-2075 RAMI, except has decocking lever, weight reduction scallop on slide, tritium 3-dot night sights, 23 1/2 oz. New 2009.

MSR $660 $575 $475 $425 $385 $350 $325 $295

CZ VZ 61 SKORPION – imported by CZ 2009-2010. Please refer to this model listing in the Skorpion section.

RIFLES: BOLT ACTION, RIMFIRE, COMMERCIAL MFG.

Ceská Zbrojovka began manufacturing rifles circa 1936. Long gun production was discontinued between 1948-1964, with the exception of the massive military contracts during that time period.

CZ 452 STYLE (ZKM-452) – .22 LR or .22 WMR (disc. 1998) cal., bolt action, 5, 6 (.22 WMR only), or 10 shot mag., 24.8 in. barrel, choice of black synthetic stock and matte nickel metal finish (new 1999) or uncheckered hardwood stock with Schnabel forend and blue metal finish (disc. 1998), adj. rear sight, 6.6 lbs. Importation began 1995 from CZ, earlier mfg. was by Brno. Reintroduced 2007-2011.

$360 $300 $260 $230 $200 $175 $150 *$443*

Add $50 for .22 WMR cal. (disc. 1998).

Satin nickel finish became the only finish on this model beginning 2011.

* ***CZ 452 Lux/Deluxe (ZKM-452D)*** – similar to CZ 452 Style (ZKM-452) only with checkered walnut stock, .22 WMR cal. in right hand action (disc. 2010). Importation began 1995.

MSR $451 $365 $310 $265 $230 $200 $175 $150

Add $34 for .22 WMR cal. (disc. 2010).

Left-hand action became standard on this model beginning 2011.

* ***CZ 452 Ultra Lux*** – .22 LR cal., beechwood stock, 10 shot mag., 28 in. barrel, features gold accents. New 2006.

MSR $409 $325 $270 $235 $200 $175 $150 $125

* ***CZ 452 American Classic (ZKM-452)*** – .17 HMR (new 2003), .17 Mach 2 (mfg. 2005-2009), .22 LR, or .22 WMR (disc. 2010) cal., 5 shot mag., 16 (new 2007) or 22 1/2 in. barrel w/ no sights, American style walnut stock, approx. 6 lbs. Importation began 1999.

MSR $451 $365 $310 $260 $230 $200 $175 $150

Add $26 for .17 HMR cal.

Add $34 for .22 WMR cal. (disc. 2010).

This model became standard with left-hand action only beginning 2011, except for 16 in. barrel.

* ***CZ 452 FS Mannlicher*** – .17 HMR (new 2005), .22 LR, or .22 WMR cal., 5 shot detachable mag., 21 in. barrel, features full length walnut Mannlicher stock, tangent rear adj. sight, 6.4 lbs. Mfg. 2004-2011.

$425 $365 $325 $275 $250 $225 $200 *$504*

Add $10 for .22 WMR or .17 HMR cal.

* ***CZ 452 Silouhette*** – .22 LR cal., similar to CZ-452 American Classic, except has black synthetic stock and blue metal, 5.3 lbs. Mfg. 2003-2011.

$335 $275 $230 $210 $180 $160 $145 *$414*

* ***CZ 452 Scout (ZKM-452)*** – .22 LR cal. only, youth configuration with shorter 16.2 in. barrel and uncheckered hardwood or pink synthetic (new 2009) stock, 5 shot mag., includes single shot adapter, 5 lbs. Importation began 2000.

MSR $303 $250 $215 $185 $165 $140 $120 $100

Add $15 for pink finish (disc. 2010).

* ***CZ 452 Special Military Training Rifle*** – .17 HMR (Special only) or .22 LR (disc. 2010, re-introduced 2013) cal., similar to CZ-452 Lux, except has beechwood stock and 5 shot mag., 6.4 lbs. New 2002.

MSR $395 $335 $285 $240 $210 $180 $150 $125

Subtract $21 for .22 LR cal.

GRADING - PPGS™	100%	98%	95%	90%	80%	70%	60%	LAST MSR

* ***CZ 452 Varmint (ZKM-452)*** – .17 HMR (new 2005), .17 Mach 2 (mfg. 2005-2009), .22 LR, or .22 WMR (new 2004) cal. only, similar to Model 452 Lux/Deluxe, except has 21 in. heavy barrel and no sights, 6.8 lbs. Imported 1998-2011.

	$385	$330	$290	$260	$225	$185	$165	*$448*

Add $16 for .22 WMR cal.
Add $26 for .17 HMR cal.
Add $65 for brown laminated thumbhole stock (new 2010).

CZ 453 AMERICAN/VARMINT – .17 Mach 2 (disc. 2006), .17 HMR (new 2007), or .22 LR cal., 5 shot detachable shot mag., 20.9 (Varmint) or 22 1/2 (American) in. fluted or non-fluted barrel, two-position safety, regular (disc. 2009) or single set trigger (became standard 2010), no sights, 6.1 (American) or 7 (Varmint) lbs. Mfg. 2006-2012.

	$455	$400	$350	$300	$265	$225	$200	*$534*

Add $27 for .17 HMR cal.
Add $13 for Varmint Model.
Add $74 for fluted barrel (.17 HMR cal. only).

CZ 455 AMERICAN – .17 HMR, .22 LR, or .22 WMR cal., 5 shot detachable mag., 20 1/2 in. barrel, w/o sights, black polymer (new 2013) or checkered walnut stock with sling swivels, adj. trigger, approx. 6.2 lbs. New 2010.

MSR $409	$335	$270	$240	$225	$200	$175	$150

Add $15 for .17 HMR or .22 WMR cal.
Add $27 for left hand action (mfg. 2012 only).
Subtract $35 for black polymer stock (new 2013).
Add $132 for American Combo (includes both .22 LR and .17 HMR cal. barrels), new 2011.

* ***CZ 455 FS Mannlicher*** – .17 HMR, .22 LR, or .22 WMR cal., features full length forearm, walnut stock, hooded front sight, 5 shot mag. Mfg. 2012.

MSR $500	$425	$385	$350	$325	$295	$265	$225

Add $24 for .17 HMR or .22 WMR cal.

* ***CZ 455 Varmint*** – .17 HMR, .22 LR, or .22 WMR cal., 21 in. heavy barrel without sights, 5 shot mag. New 2012.

MSR $456	$385	$350	$320	$295	$270	$250	$225

Add $27 for .17 HMR or .22 WMR cal.

* ***CZ 455 Varmint Evolution*** – .17 HMR (new 2013) or .22 LR cal., 20 1/2 in. heavy barrel, features blue laminated Boyds skeletonized stock and free floating heavy barrel w/o sights, adj. trigger, 5 shot mag., 7.2 lbs. New 2012.

MSR $522	$450	$415	$375	$335	$300	$275	$250

Add $27 for .17 HMR cal. (new 2013).

* ***CZ 455 Varmint Precision Trainer*** – .22 LR cal., 20 1/2 in. heavy barrel w/o sights, features tan Manners composite target stock, 5 shot mag., adj. trigger, 7.8 lbs. New 2012.

MSR $912	$785	$675	$600	$525	$450	$400	$350

* ***CZ 455 Varmint SST*** – .17 HMR or .22 LR cal., 20 1/2 in. heavy barrel w/o sights, features single set trigger, checkered walnut stock, 5 shot mag., 7 lbs. New 2013.

MSR $509	$440	$415	$375	$335	$300	$275	$250

Add $27 for .17 HMR cal.

* ***CZ 455 Varmint Thumbhole*** – .17 HMR or .22 LR cal., 20 1/2 in. heavy fluted barrel w/o sights, single set trigger, 5 shot mag., forest camo laminate thumbhole stock, 7 lbs. New 2013.

MSR $588	$495	$425	$375	$335	$300	$275	$250

Add $27 for .17 HMR cal.

* ***CZ 455 Lux*** – .22 LR or .22 WMR cal., features deluxe checkered Turkish walnut stock, adj. rear sight and hooded front sight, 6.1 lbs. New 2011.

MSR $427	$345	$290	$245	$220	$190	$175	$160

Add $29 for .22 WMR cal.

GRADING - PPGS™	100%	98%	95%	90%	80%	70%	60%	LAST MSR

* ***CZ 455 Super Match*** – .22 LR cal., 10 shot detachable box mag., 20 in. barrel, uncheckered beech wood pistol grip stock, adj. rear sight, approx. 6.2 lbs. New 2010.

While advertised in 2010, this model never went into production.

* ***CZ 455 Tacticool*** – .22 LR cal., 20 1/2 in. heavy barrel w/o sights, 5 shot mag., adj. trigger, black painted laminated composite stock featuring Monte Carlo cheekpiece and ambidextrous palm swells, beavertail forend, 7.4 lbs. New 2013.

MSR $522	**$450**	**$415**	**$375**	**$335**	**$300**	**$275**	**$250**	

CZ 513 HUNTER – .22 LR cal., entry level bolt action, 5 shot detachable mag., beechwood stock. Imported 1994 only.

	$195	**$175**	**$150**	**$125**	**$95**	**$80**	**$65**	***$225***

Add $30 for Farmer Model.

This model was imported exclusively by Action Arms.

CZ 513 BASIC – .22 LR cal., 5 shot detachable mag., 20.9 in. barrel, non-adj. trigger, uncheckered beechwood stock, iron sights, includes single shot adaptor, 5 3/4 lbs. Mfg. 2004-2005, reintroduced 2007-2012.

	$245	**$210**	**$180**	**$160**	**$140**	**$120**	**$100**	***$307***

RIFLES: BOLT ACTION, CENTERFIRE, COMMERCIAL MFG.

Ceská Zbrojovka began manufacturing rifles circa 1936. Long gun production was discontinued between 1948-1964, with the exception of the massive military contracts during that time period.

CZ USA MODEL 3 – .270 WSM, 7mm WSM, or .300 WSM cal., Mauser style claw extractor, adj. M-70 type trigger, bottom floorplate with 3 shot fixed mag., three position safety, blue or stainless matte finished action and 24 in. barrel, right or left-hand action, drilled and tapped, American black walnut stock with fleur-de-lis, no sights, mfg. in the U.S., 7.9 lbs. Limited mfg. 2005 only.

	$725	**$600**	**$550**	**$495**	**$450**	**$400**	**$350**	***$872***

Add $10 for left-hand action.

Add $21 for stainless steel action and barrel.

CZ 527 LUX – .22 Hornet, .222 Rem., or .223 Rem. cal., Mauser style bolt action with silent safety, 21.9 (disc.) or 23.6 in. barrel with open sights, 5 shot detachable mag., hardwood (disc.) or checkered walnut stock and forend, 6.2 lbs. Importation began 1995.

MSR $711	**$600**	**$475**	**$425**	**$360**	**$320**	**$275**	**$250**	

Add $44 for left-hand action (.223 Rem. cal. only).

* ***CZ 527 FS Mannlicher*** – similar to Model 527 Lux, except has checkered full length Mannlicher walnut stock with steel muzzle cap, vent. recoil pad, 6 1/4 lbs. Importation began 1995.

MSR $762	**$660**	**$585**	**$525**	**$450**	**$400**	**$325**	**$275**	

* ***CZ 527 American (Classic)*** – .17 Hornet (new 2013), .22 Hornet, .204 Ruger, .221 Fireball (new 2004), .222 Rem., or .223 Rem. cal., 21.9 in. barrel w/o sights, maple (disc.), brown laminate (disc.), spring camo laminate (disc.), sunset camo laminate (disc.), English walnut (disc.) or fancy American walnut stock, scope rings included, approx. 6 1/2 lbs. New 1999.

MSR $711	**$600**	**$475**	**$425**	**$360**	**$320**	**$275**	**$250**	

Add $53 for left-hand action (available in .204 Ruger or .223 Rem cal. only).

Add $122 for English walnut (disc.) stock or $178 for fancy American walnut stock.

Subtract $13 for laminated stock (disc.).

* ***CZ 527 M1 American*** – .223 Rem. cal., styling similar to U.S. military M1 carbine featuring 3 shot flush detachable mag., no sights, walnut or black polymer stock, approx. 6 lbs. New 2008.

MSR $645	**$540**	**$465**	**$420**	**$365**	**$335**	**$295**	**$250**	

Add $66 for walnut stock.

GRADING - PPGS™	100%	98%	95%	90%	80%	70%	60%	LAST MSR

* ***CZ 527 M1 Ultralight Predator*** – .223 Rem. cal., synthetic stock with 100% Badland West camo coverage, 22 in. sporter weight barrel, single set trigger, 3 shot detachable mag., no sights, 5 3/4 lbs. Mfg. 2009-2011.

	$695	$595	$500	$450	$400	$350	$295	$830

* ***CZ 527 Prestige*** – .22 Hornet (disc. 2008) or .223 Rem. (disc. 2006, reintroduced 2009) cal., similar to CZ 527 Lux, except has deluxe checkered walnut stock and forend, no sights, jewelled bolt, SST, scope rings included, 6.3 lbs. Limited mfg. 2001-2009.

	$895	$750	$625	$500	$400	$350	$300	$1,022

* ***CZ 527 Varmint*** – .17 Hornet (new 2013), .17 Rem. (mfg. 2005-2006, reintroduced 2007), .204 Ruger (new 2005), .222 Rem., or .223 Rem. cal., varmint configuration with heavy barrel and no sights, choice of walnut (.204 Ruger cal. only), maple (.223 Rem. cal., disc. 2006), laminated (new 2002), or H-S Precision Kevlar (new 2002) black stock, approx. 8 lbs. Importation began 2001.

MSR $704	$600	$475	$425	$360	$320	$275	$250	

Add $48 for grey laminate stock (.223 Rem. cal. only) or $178 for H-S Precision Kevlar stock (not available in .17 Rem.), disc. 2011.

* ***CZ 527 Varmint Target*** – .204 Ruger or .223 Rem. cal., 24 in. barrel, 5 shot detachable mag., vertical grip Kevlar stock with wide forearm and aluminum bedding. New 2012.

MSR $885	$775	$725	$625	$550	$500	$450	$400	

* ***CZ 527 Carbine*** – .223 Rem. (new 2001) or 7.62x39mm cal., carbine configuration with 18 1/2 in. barrel with sights, 5 shot detachable mag., 6 lbs. New 1999.

MSR $711	$600	$475	$425	$360	$320	$275	$250	

CZ 531 – .243 Win., .270 Win., .308 Win., .30-06, 7x64mm, 8x57mm, 8x60mm, 8x64mm, and 8x68mm, 4 shot detachable (.243 and .308 only) or internal 5 shot (4 shot, 8x58) mag., receiver drilled and tapped for scope bases, short extractor and plunger type ejector, double set trigger, tang safety with locking button, 23.6 in. (25.6 in., 8x68) barrel, adj. open sights, checkred walnut stock with Bavarian style cheekpiece, recoil crossbolts and vent. recoil pad, approx. 7-7 3/4 lbs. 766 rifles mfg. 1985-1988.

	$1,750	$1,500	$1,300	$1,150	$950	$800	$725	

CZ 531 was the firm's initial departure from the Brno-type (improved Mauser) centerfire rifle designs. Only .30-06 cal. rifles have been observed. Not until the introduction of CZ 555 in 2006 did CZ return to the push-feed style (short extractor, plunger ejector) action.

CZ 537 – .243 Win., .270 Win., .30-06, .308 Win., or 7x57mm cal., detachable 4 shot (.243 Win. and .308 Win. cals. only) or 5 shot fixed mag., choice of regular or Mannlicher (.30-06 or .308 Win. cal. only) stock, hooded ramp front sight, 7 1/4 lbs. Importation 1995 only.

	$495	$425	$370	$330	$300	$275	$250	$649

Add $100 for Mannlicher style stock.

* ***CZ 537 Mountain Carbine*** – .243 Win. cal. only, 19 in. barrel, 5 shot detachable mag., includes ring mounts, 7.1 lbs. Imported 1994 only.

	$525	$450	$375	$330	$300	$275	$250	$669

CZ 550 STANDARD – various cals. have been imported to date, 4 shot detachable (.243 Win. or .308 Win. only) or internal 5 shot mag., 23.6 in. barrel, receiver drilled and tapped for Remington 700 style scope base, no sights, checkered walnut stock and forearm, 7 1/4 lbs. Imported 1995-2000.

	$475	$395	$340	$310	$285	$260	$240	$561

Add $21 for .243 Win. or .308 Win. cal. with detachable mag.

* ***CZ 550 Lux*** – various cals., similar to CZ 550 Standard, except has deluxe checkered walnut stock with Bavarian style cheekpiece and vent. recoil pad. Mfg. 1998-2004.

	$495	$415	$350	$315	$285	$260	$240	$588

Add $20 for detachable mag. (.22-250 Rem., .243 Win., or .308 Win. cal., disc.).

GRADING - PPGS™	100%	98%	95%	90%	80%	70%	60%	LAST MSR

» **CZ 550 Battue Lux** – similar to CZ 550 Lux, except has 20 1/2 in. barrel with integral barrel fixed rear sight. Limited mfg. 1998 only.

	$450	$375	$330	$300	$280	$260	$240	*$519*

Add $30 for .243 Win. or .308 Win. cal. with removable mag.

* ***CZ 550 Prestige*** – .270 Win. or .30-06 cal., similar to CZ 550 Lux, except has deluxe checkered walnut stock and forend, no sights, scope rings included. Imported 2001, reintroduced 2003-2005.

	$740	$510	$405	$380	$325	$285	$260	*$854*

* ***CZ 550 American (Classic)*** – .22-250 Rem., .243 Win., .270 Win., .30-06, .308 Win., 6.5x55mm (new 2001), 7x57mm (disc. 2004), or 9.3x62mm cal., features American style walnut or Kevlar (.270 Win., .30-06, 6.5x55mm , or 9.3x62mm cals.) stock, fixed or detachable mag., scope rings included, no sights, approx. 8 lbs. New mid-1999.

MSR $815	$695	$575	$475	$425	$375	$325	$275	

Add $38 for 9.3x62mm cal.
Add $145 for Kevlar stock (new 2009).

* ***CZ 550 Varmint*** – .22-250 Rem. (new 2002) or .308 Win. cal., 25.6 in. barrel w/o sights, 4 shot detachable mag., checkered walnut (.308 Win. cal. only), H-S Precision Kevlar (new 2005), or laminated (new 2002) stock with vent. recoil pad, approx. 9 - 10 3/4 lbs. Importation began 2000.

MSR $840	$735	$600	$500	$450	$400	$350	$295	

Add $66 for laminated stock (new 2002).
Add $139 for H-S Precision Kevlar stock (new 2005).

* ***CZ 550 Carbine*** – .30-06 cal. or 9.3x62mm cal., features black Kevlar stock, 20.6 in. barrel with adj. rear iron sight and hooded front sight, fixed 4 shot mag., 7 lbs. New 2011.

MSR $1,049	$925	$800	$700	$600	$500	$400	$350	

Add $47 for 9.3x62mm cal.

* ***CZ 550 FS Mannlicher*** – .243 Win., .270 Win., .30-06, .308 Win., 6.5x55mm, or 9.3x62mm cal., similar to CZ 550 American Classic, except has Mannlicher stock and 20 1/2 in. barrel, fixed 5 shot or 4 shot detachable mag. (.243 Win. or .308 Win. cal. only), adj. sights, 7.4 lbs. Imported 1996-98, reintroduced 2001.

MSR $864	$765	$650	$550	$450	$400	$350	$295	

Add $47 for 9.3x62mm cal.

* ***CZ 550 Battue FS Mannlicher*** – similar to CZ 550 FS Mannlicher, except has integral barrel fixed rear sight. Limited mfg. 1998 only.

	$525	$465	$425	$395	$360	$330	$300	*$609*

Add $30 for .243 Win. or .308 Win. cal. with removable mag.

* ***CZ 550 Minnesota*** – similar to CZ 550 Lux, except has select walnut stock w/o cheekpiece, and barrel has no sights. Limited mfg. 1998 only.

	$445	$375	$330	$300	$280	$260	$240	*$505*

Add $30 for .243 Win. or .308 Win. cal. with removable mag.

* ***CZ 550 Medium Magnum*** – .300 Win. Mag. (disc. 2012) or 7mm Rem. Mag. cal., checkered walnut stock and forearm, open sights, (.300 Win. Mag. has Battue quarter rib, detachable mag. and fiber optic front sight), 23.6 in. barrel, 7 3/4 lbs. New 2007.

MSR $919	$795	$725	$625	$550	$495	$450	$395	

Add $177 for Kevlar stock (7mm Rem. Mag. only, new 2011).

CZ 550 MAGNUM STANDARD – .300 Win. Mag., .375 H&H, .416 Rem. Mag. (disc. 1998), .416 Rigby, .458 Win. Mag., or 7mm Rem. Mag. (importation disc. 1997) cal., 3-5 shot fixed mag., 25 in. barrel with express rear sight, checkered hardwood stock, 9 1/4 lbs. Limited mfg. 1998 only.

	$525	$475	$440	$400	$375	$350	$335	*$595*

Add $40 for .416 Rem. Mag., .416 Rigby, or .458 Win. Mag. cal.

GRADING - PPGS™	100%	98%	95%	90%	80%	70%	60%	LAST MSR

» **CZ 550 Magnum Standard Lux** – similar to CZ 550 Magnum, except has select checkered walnut, last cals. were .300 Win. Mag. and 7mm Rem. Mag., 7.7-9.4 lbs. Mfg. 1998-2005.

	$600	$500	$445	$395	$350	$335	$300	*$690*

Add $185 for .375 H&H., .416 Rigby, or .458 Win. Mag. (disc.) cal.

* ***CZ 550 Safari Magnum*** – .300 Win. Mag. (mfg. 2008-2009), .375 H&H, .416 Rigby, or .458 Win. Mag. cal., 25 in. barrel, express sights, single set trigger, checkered walnut stock with curved cheekpiece, fixed mag., 9.4 lbs. New 2004.

MSR $1,180	$975	$825	$700	$600	$500	$450	$395	

Add $100 for .416 or .458 Win. Mag. (new 2012).

* ***CZ 550 American Safari Field Magnum*** – .375 H&H, .416 Rigby, .458 Win. Mag., .458 Lott, or .505 Gibbs cal., 25 in. barrel, choice of field grade wood, brown, spring camo, or sunset camo laminate, or Kevlar (new 2009) stock, 9.9 lbs. New 2004.

MSR $1,180	$975	$825	$700	$600	$500	$450	$395	

Add $100 for .416 Rigby or .458 Win. Mag. cal. Add $128 for .458 Lott in Field grade.
Add $1,946 for .505 Gibbs cal.(Field grade only).
Add $207 for brown laminate, spring camo laminate, or sunset camo laminate stock.
Add $476 for Kevlar stock. Add $727 for fancy stock.
Add $764 for left hand action (.375 H&H cal. only) with premium walnut stock (disc. 2012).

* ***CZ 550 American Safari Deluxe Magnum*** – .375 H&H, .416 Rigby, .458 Win. Mag., or .458 Lott cal., similar to Field Grade, except has deluxe walnut stock. Mfg. 2004-2011.

	$1,700	$1,475	$1,225	$1,025	$925	$825	$725	*$1,911*

Add $57 for .458 Lott cal.

* ***CZ 550 Safari Classic (Custom Grade Safari Magnum)*** – .300 H&H (new 2007), .338 Lapua (new 2008), .338 Win. Mag. (new 2008), .375 H&H, .404 Jeffery, .416 Rem. (new 2008), .450 Rigby, .500 Jeffery (new 2007), or .505 Gibbs cal., custom Magnum action with two-position safety, single set trigger adjustable per individual requirements, glossy or matte blue metal finish, checkered fancy grade American walnut stock and forend, express sights, built per individual custom order. New 2005.

MSR $3,172	$2,725	$2,275	$1,900	$1,600	$1,300	$1,100	$995	

Add $397 for .338 Lapua, .500 Jeffery cal., or .505 Gibbs cal. (includes built-in recoil reducer and glass bedded action).
Subtract $530 for .375 H&H cal. with 20 in. barrel.

* ***CZ 550 Magnum H.E.T. (High Energy Tactical)*** – .300 Win. Mag., .300 Rem. Ultra Mag., or .338 Lapua cal., 28 in. barrel, flat black finish, Kevlar tactical stock, 4 to 6 shot fixed mag., SST, muzzle brake, oversized bolt handle, 13 lbs. New 2009.

MSR $3,929	$3,500	$3,125	$2,625	$2,250	$1,950	$1,575	$1,325	

* ***CZ 550 Urban Counter Sniper*** – .308 Win. cal., 16 in. barrel with SureFire muzzle brake, OD Green Kevlar stock, 10 shot mag. New 2010.

MSR $2,530	$2,275	$2,000	$1,750	$1,500	$1,250	$1,000	$825	

CZ 555 SPORTER – .30-06 or .308 Win. cal., push-feed style action, short extractor, side release 3 shot detachable mag., 24 in. hammer forged barrel with sights, single set trigger, two position safety, deluxe walnut stock with sling swivels, 7 1/4 lbs. Mfg. 2006-disc.

	$795	$725	$650	$575	$500	$450	$400	

CZ 557 SPORTER – .30-06 cal., forged steel receiver with integral scope dovetails, 20.6 hammer forged barrel w/o sights, short extractor and plunger style ejector, receiver mounted two-position safety, adj. trigger, checkered beechwood stock, matte blue metal finish, 7.8 lbs. New 2011.

While advertised in 2011, this model never went into production.

ZKK 600 – .270 Win., .30-06, or 7x57mm cal., improved Mauser type action, 23 1/2 in. barrel, checkered walnut stock, 5 shot internal mag., thumb safety, 7.2 lbs. Importation disc. 1995.

	$500	$425	$370	$330	$300	$275	$250	*$589*

GRADING - PPGS™	100%	98%	95%	90%	80%	70%	60%	LAST MSR

ZKK 601 – .222 Rem., .223 Rem., .243 Win. or .308 Win. cal., otherwise similar to ZKK 600. Importation disc. 1995.

	$500	$425	$370	$330	$300	$275	$250	*$589*

ZKK 602 – .300 Win. Mag. (disc.), .375 H&H, .416 Rigby (new 1996), .416 Rem. (new 1996), 8x68mm (disc.), or .458 Win. Mag. cal., similar to ZKK 600, except has 25.2 in. barrel and 3 leaf express rear sight, 9.3 lbs. Disc. 1997.

	$675	$575	$495	$450	$395	$350	$310	*$799*

ZKB 680 (FOX/FOX II) – .22 Hornet or .222 Rem. cal., 23 1/2 in. barrel, 5 shot mag., set triggers, 5 lbs. 12 oz. Importation disc. 1991.

	$445	$380	$340	$295	$255	$230	$200	*$499*

The Fox model in .222 Rem. cal. began production circa 1971. During the mid to late 1970s, this model was revamped into the Fox II, and was available in .222 Rem. and .22 Hornet.

CZ 700 SNIPER – .308 Win. cal., sniper design features forged billet receiver with permanently attached Weaver rail, 25.6 in. heavy barrel w/o sights, 10 shot detachable mag., black synthetic thumbhole stock with adj. cheekpiece and buttplate, large bolt handle, fully adj. trigger, 11.9 lbs. Limited importation 2001 only.

	$1,875	$1,575	$1,250	$1,025	$895	$775	$650	*$2,097*

CZ 700M1 SNIPER – .308 Win. cal., similar to CZ 700 Sniper, except has laminated stock, limited importation 2001 only.

	$1,875	$1,575	$1,250	$1,025	$895	$775	$650	

CZ 750 SNIPER – .308 Win. cal., sniper design, black synthetic thumbhole stock w/adj. comb, scope mounting via detachable Weaver rail or integral CZ 19mm dovetail, 26 in. barrel w/muzzle brake, includes two 10 shot mags., thread protector, and mirage shield, 11.9 lbs. Limited mfg. beginning 2006.

MSR $1,999	$1,775	$1,550	$1,250	$1,050	$925	$775	$675	

CZ ULTIMATE HUNTING RIFLE (UHR) – .300 Win. Mag. cal. only, extra craftsmanship guarantees one MOA accuracy to 600 yards, Kevlar (new 2011), or deluxe checkered stock and forend, 23.6 in. barrel, includes scope rings, 4 shot mag., 8 lbs. New 2007.

MSR $1,321	$1,175	$995	$850	$750	$625	$500	$425	

Add $2,097 for Nightforce 5.5-22x50 mm scope (disc).
Add $132 for Kevlar stock (new 2011).

RIFLES: O/U

CZ-589 STOPPER – .458 Win. Mag. cal. only, Kersten style boxlock action with Blitz type trigger, checkered Turkish walnut stock and forearm, fixed iron sights, includes sling swivels, 9.3 lbs. Approx. 5 mfg. and imported 2001 only.

	$2,695	$2,300	$2,000	$1,750	$1,500	$1,250	$1,050	*$2,999*

Add $1,000 for sideplates and special engraving/checkering.

RIFLES: SEMI-AUTO

CZ-M52 (1952) – 7.62x45mm Czech cal., semi-auto, 20 2/3 in. barrel, 10 shot detachable mag., tangent rear sight, this model was also imported briefly by Samco Global Arms, Inc. located in Miami, FL.

	$550	$450	$350	$300	$250	$200	$150	

CZ-M52/57 (1957) – 7.62x39mm cal., later variation of the CZ-M52.

	$425	$375	$325	$300	$250	$200	$150	

CZ-511 – .22 LR cal., blowback action, 22.2 in. barrel, uncheckered beechwood (disc. 2001) or checkered walnut (new 2006) stock, flip-up rear sight, receiver top slotted for scope mounts, 8 shot mag., approx. 5 1/2 lbs. Previously disc. 1986, importation resumed 1998-2001. Imported 2005-2006.

	$320	$275	$235	$200	$180	$160	$150	*$389*

CZ 512 – .22 LR or .22 WMR cal., dual guide rods, modular design with aluminum alloy upper receiver and fiberglass reinforced polymer lower receiver, 5 shot mag., hammer forged

GRADING - PPGS™	100%	98%	95%	90%	80%	70%	60%	LAST MSR

20.6 in. barrel with adj. rear and hooded front sight, uncheckered beechwood stock and forearm with sling swivels, integral 11mm dovetail on receiver, 5.9 lbs. New 2011.

MSR $465	$385	$340	$300	$275	$250	$225	$195	

Add $31 for .22 WMR cal.

VZ 58 MILITARY/TACTICAL SPORTER – 7.62x39mm cal., gas operated, AK-47 design, milled receiver, 16.14 in. barrel, tilting breech block, choice of Zytel skeletonized (Tactical) or plastic impregnated wood (Military) stock, alloy 30 shot mag., 7.32 lbs. Mfg. 2008-2011.

	$925	$850	$750	$650	$550	$450	$350	*$999*

Add $30 for Tactical Sporter model (available with synthetic or folding (new 2010) stock).

SHOTGUNS: O/U

CZ 581 SOLO – 12 ga., 2 3/4 in. chambers, boxlock action with Kersten upper locking mechanism, ejectors, checkered walnut stock and forearm, approx. 7.4 lbs. Importation disc. 1995, resumed 1999-2005.

	$740	$625	$570	$490	$425	$385	$350	*$872*

Add 10% for single trigger (disc.).

MALLARD (104A) – 12 or 20 ga., DT, extractors, 28 in. VR barrels with multichokes, coin finished alloy receiver, checkered Turkish walnut stock and forearm, 6 1/2 (20 ga.) or 7 1/2 (12 ga.) lbs. New 2005.

MSR $566	$475	$400	$350	$300	$275	$250	$225	

CANVASBACK (103D) – 12 or 20 ga., 3 in. chambers, 26 or 28 in. VR barrels with 5 choke tubes, black chrome finished receiver and barrels, extractors, blued frame with light perimeter engraving, SST, stock/forearm similar to Redhead, 6.3 - 7 1/2 lbs. New 2005.

MSR $786	$675	$550	$450	$400	$350	$300	$275	

REDHEAD DELUXE (103DE) – 12 or 20 ga., boxlock action, SST, ejectors, checkered round knob Turkish walnut pistol grip stock and Schnabel forearm, coin finished frame and trigger guard, 26 or 28 in. VR barrels with 5 screw-in chokes, 6.7 - 7.9 lbs. New 2005.

MSR $926	$795	$700	$625	$550	$500	$450	$395	

Subtract $78 for shortened LOP (20 ga. only, 24 in. barrels, and 13 in. LOP - new 2008).
Add $35 for retractable sling system (12 ga. only, disc.).

* ***Redhead 103 D (Mini)*** – 28 ga. or .410 bore, scaled down frame, otherwise similar to Redhead Deluxe, but w/o ejectors, 5.7 (.410 bore) or 6.2 lbs. New 2005.

MSR $960	$795	$725	$625	$550	$500	$450	$395	

* ***Redhead Custom Shop Enhanced*** – 12 ga., 28 in. barrels, similar to Redhead, except has hand rubbed oil finished stock, tuned action and trigger job from custom shop. Mfg. 2010 only.

	$1,675	$1,450	$1,250	$1,050	$900	$800	$700	*$1,899*

* ***Redhead Target*** – 12 ga. only, 30 in. barrels with stepped VR and standard choke tubes (disc. 2012), or 6 Kicks extended stainless steel choke tubes (new 2013), Monte Carlo checkered walnut stock and grooved forearm, silver finished receiver. New 2012.

MSR $1,348	$1,100	$950	$825	$725	$625	$525	$450	

Subtract 5% for standard choke tubes (disc. 2012).

WOODCOCK DELUXE 103FE – 12 or 20 ga., ejectors, SST, 26 or 28 in. barrels with screw-in chokes, color case hardened boxlock frame with sideplates and trigger guard, hand engraving, checkered round knob Turkish walnut stock and Schnabel forearm, 6.8 (20 ga.) or 7.8 (12 ga.) lbs. Mfg. 2005-2010.

	$1,075	$875	$725	$600	$500	$450	$395	*$1,246*

* ***Woodcock 103F Mini*** – 28 ga. or .410 bore, scaled down frame, otherwise similar to Woodcock Deluxe, but w/o ejectors, 6-6 1/4 lbs. Mfg. 2005-2010.

	$1,100	$900	$800	$700	$600	$500	$450	*$1,332*

WOODCOCK DELUXE CUSTOM GRADE – 20 ga. only, 28 in. barrels, features color case hardened frame, No. 4 deluxe checkered Circassian walnut stock and forearm. Mfg. 2006-2010.

	$1,895	$1,550	$1,325	$1,100	$950	$800	$700	*$2,309*

GRADING - PPGS™	100%	98%	95%	90%	80%	70%	60%	LAST MSR

UPLAND STERLING – 12 ga. only, 28 in. barrels with 5 screw-in choke tubes, two-toned CNC milled receiver and trigger guard, checkered walnut stock and forearm, 7 1/2 lbs. New 2013.

MSR $979	$875	$775	$700	$600	$500	$400	$325	

UPLAND ULTRALIGHT – 12 ga., 3 in. chambers, 26 or 28 in. VR matte black barrels with 5 choke tubes, matte black alloy receiver, checkered Turkish walnut pistol grip stock and forearm, 6 lbs. New 2010.

MSR $739	$640	$550	$495	$450	$415	$375	$335	

CZ SPORTER – 12 ga., boxlock action, ejectors, SST, 30 or 32 in. VR backbored barrels with standard choke tubes (disc. 2012), or 6 Kicks extended stainless steel choke tubes (new 2013), No. 3 Circassian walnut stock and forearm with adj. comb and palm swell, approx. 8 1/2 lbs. New 2008.

MSR $2,499	$2,100	$1,825	$1,625	$1,325	$1,100	$900	$775	

Subtract 5% if with standard choke tubes (disc. 2012).

CZ SPORTER STANDARD GRADE – 12 ga. only, 30 or 32 in. vent barrels with VR with 6 Kicks extended stainless steel choke tubes, checkered adj. Monte Carlo stock and Schnabel forearm, ejectors and SST, 8 1/2 lbs. New 2013.

MSR $1,799	$1,595	$1,375	$1,175	$1,000	$875	$750	$625	

LIMITED EDITION (DISC.) – 12 ga., 28 in. barrels, Circassian walnut stock and forearm, engraved boxlock action, gold trigger, 50 mfg. 2008-2009.

	$1,975	$1,725	$1,500	$1,300	$1,100	$900	$775	*$2,466*

CZ SUPER SCROLL LIMITED EDITION – 12 ga., 3 in. chambers, 28 in. barrels, boxlock, mechanical selective triggers, checkered Turkish walnut stock with Schnabel forend, ejectors, interchangeable choke tubes. Limited mfg. of 50 beginning 2011.

	$2,250	$1,975	$1,750	$1,525	$1,325	$1,125	$850	*$2,499*

WINGSHOOTER – 12, 20, 28 (limited mfg. 2011 only) ga. or .410 bore (limited mfg. 2011 only), 3 in. chambers, silver engraved boxlock action featuring black sideplates with gold inlayed birds, 28 in. VR barrels with 5 multi-chokes, SST, ejectors (12 and 20 ga.), or extractors (28 ga. and .410 bore), checkered Turkish walnut stock and forearm, 6 - 7.9 lbs. New 2011.

MSR $999	$875	$750	$625	$550	$495	$450	$395	

Add $41 for 28 ga. or .410 bore. (disc. 2011).

CZ SUPER SCROLL COMBO SET – includes 20 and 28 ga. 30 in. barrels with VR, coin finished receiver with hand engraved sideplates, ejectors, SST, includes 5 choke tubes, deluxe checkered walnut stock and forearm, supplied with aluminum Americase, 6.7 lbs. New 2013.

MSR $3,899	$3,475	$3,100	$2,750	$2,400	$2,100	$1,825	$1,600	

SHOTGUNS: SxS

DURANGO – 12 or 20 ga., hammerless contoured boxlock action with color case hardened frame, 20 in. barrels, single trigger, multichokes, checkered Turkish walnut round knob stock and splinter forearm, 6 (20 ga.) or 6.7 (12 ga.) lbs. Imported 2005-2006.

	$725	$625	$525	$425	$350	$300	$250	*$795*

AMARILLO – similar to Durango, except has double triggers, 5.9 (20 ga.) or 6 1/2 lbs. Imported 2005-2006.

	$625	$550	$475	$375	$300	$250	$200	*$695*

GROUSE – 12, 20, 28 ga., or .410 bore, 26 (28 ga. or .410 bore) or 28 (12 or 20 ga.) in. barrels, silver receiver, ST, choke tubes. Limited importation 2008.

	$875	$750	$650	$575	$500	$425	$350	*$995*

Add $211 for 28 ga. or .410 bore.

PARTRIDGE – 12, 20, 28 ga., or .410 bore, 26 (28 ga. or .410 bore) or 28 (12 or 20 ga.) in. barrels, silver receiver, DT, straight grip English stock, choke tubes. Limited importation 2008.

	$675	$600	$525	$450	$375	$300	$250	*$765*

Add $193 for 28 ga. or .410 bore.

GRADING - PPGS™	100%	98%	95%	90%	80%	70%	60%	LAST MSR

BOBWHITE (202B) – 12, 16 (new 2006), or 20 ga., 3 in. chambers, 26 or 28 in. barrels with multichokes (N/A in .410 bore), color case hardened boxlock action, DT, extractors, checkered Turkish walnut straight grip English style stock and semi-beavertail forearm, 6-7 lbs. New 2005.

MSR $756	$650	$575	$500	$425	$350	$300	$250	

Add $190 for 16 ga.

* ***Bobwhite Mini (202B)*** – 28 ga. or .410 bore, 26 in. barrels only, scaled down frame, otherwise similar to Bobwhite, 5.2 (.410 bore) or 5.6 (28 ga.) lbs. New 2005.

MSR $946	$850	$725	$625	$550	$475	$375	$325	

RINGNECK (201A) – 12, 16, or 20 ga., 3 in. chambers, features engraved boxlock action with sideplates, 26 or 28 in. barrels with multi chokes, ST, extractors, checkered straight (new 2012, 20 ga. only) or pistol grip walnut stock and splinter forearm, 6.3-7.1 lbs. New 2005.

MSR $993	$875	$775	$675	$575	$500	$425	$350	

Add $200 for 16 ga.

* ***Ringneck Mini (201A)*** – 28 ga. or .410 bore, proportional frame to gauge, otherwise similar to Ringneck 201A, 28 ga. is supplied with 5 choke tubes, 5 1/4 (.410 bore) or 6 (28 ga.) lbs. New 2005.

MSR $1,193	$1,025	$875	$775	$675	$575	$475	$400	

RINGNECK TARGET – 12 ga., 30 in. barrels with 5 choke tubes (disc. 2012) or 6 Kicks extended stainless steel choke tubes (new 2013), checkered walnut pistol grip stock and splinter forearm, case colored receiver with blued barrels. New 2012.

MSR $1,260	$1,075	$900	$800	$700	$600	$495	$425	

Subtract 5% if with standard choke tubes (disc. 2012).

RINGNECK DELUXE CUSTOM GRADE – 20 ga., 3 in. chambers, 28 in. barrels, features color case hardened engraved frame with sideplates, deluxe checkered pistol grip walnut stock and forearm, 6.3 lbs. Mfg. 2006-2012.

	$1,695	$1,450	$1,250	$975	$850	$725	$625	*$1,983*

RINGNECK COMPETITION – 12 ga., 28 in. ported barrels, adj. comb, lengthened forcing cones, hand honed action from custom shop. Mfg. 2010-2011.

	$2,725	$2,200	$1,825	$1,525	$1,375	$1,150	$995	*$3,189*

RINGNECK STRAIGHT GRIP – 20 ga. only, 3 in. chamber, 26 in. barrel with 5 choke tubes, straight grip English stock and semi-beavertail forearm, SST, color case receiver with sideplates, 6.3 lbs. New 2013.

MSR $993	$875	$775	$675	$575	$500	$425	$350	

HAMMER COACH MODEL – 12 ga., 3 in. chambers, color cased action, 20 in. barrels with fixed chokes bored C/C, DT, exposed hammers, 6.7 lbs. New 2006.

MSR $895	$775	$675	$575	$500	$400	$350	$295	

HAMMER CLASSIC MODEL – 12 ga., 3 in. chambers, similar to Hammer Coach Model, except has 30 in. barrels with multi chokes. New 2010.

MSR $934	$795	$675	$575	$500	$400	$350	$295	

SHOTGUNS: SEMI-AUTO

CZ-712/720 – 12 (Model 712) or 20 (Model 720) ga., 3 in. chamber, gas operated, checkered Turkish walnut stock, 20 (Utility model, new 2009), 26 or 28 in. VR barrel, matte black chrome, aluminum receiver, Mossy Oak Shadow Grass or Mossy Oak Obsession camo treatment (disc. 2005), multichokes, jeweled bolt, single trigger, 6.3 - 7.3 lbs. Limited mfg. 2005, reintroduced 2008.

MSR $488	$400	$350	$295	$260	$230	$200	$175	

Add $13 for 20 ga. (Model 720).

Add approx. 10% for 100% camo coverage (disc. 2005).

Add $11 for shortened 13 in. LOP (20 ga., 24 in. barrel, new 2008).

GRADING - PPGS™	100%	98%	95%	90%	80%	70%	60%	LAST MSR

* ***CZ-712 ALS*** – 12 ga., 26 or 28 in. barrel with 3 choke tubes, features fully adj. LOP, black adj. ATI polymer stock, fiber optic front sight. New 2012.

MSR $562	$475	$425	$365	$335	$300	$275	$250	

* ***CA-712 Target*** – 12 ga. only, 30 in. barrel with stepped VR and screw in chokes, fiber optic front sight. New 2012.

MSR $660	$575	$500	$425	$385	$350	$325	$295	

CZ-712 MAGNUM – 12 ga. only, 3 1/2 in. chamber, 24 or 28 in. barrel, matte black chrome, checkered walnut, Mossy Oak Shadowgrass (28 in. barrel) or Mossy Oak Obsession (24 in. barrel) camo treatment, single trigger, vent. rib., 7 1/2 lbs. Limited mfg. 2005.

	$425	$375	$325	$295	$265	$235	$200	*$499*

Add $100 for 100% camo coverage.

CZ-912/920 – 12 or 20 (new 2013) ga., 3 in. chamber, gas operated, black alloy receiver, 28 in. VR barrel with 5 choke tubes, high gloss Turkish checkered walnut stock and forearm, advanced design recoil pad, 6.4 or 7.3 lbs. New 2011.

MSR $528	$465	$400	$350	$315	$275	$250	$225	

Add $13 for 20 ga. (new 2013).

SHOTGUNS: SINGLE SHOT

COTTONTAIL – 20 ga. or .410 bore, 24 (Youth) or 28 in. barrel with Mod. choke, designed for beginning shooters, silver receiver with black hard chrome barrel finish, checkered pistol grip walnut stock, exposed hammer, transfer bar safety. Limited mfg. 2009.

	$195	$160	$130	$120	$115	$100	$90	*$255*

SHOTGUNS: SLIDE ACTION

CZ 612 HC-P – 12 ga., 20 in. barrel with cyl. choke tube, tactical configuration features black polymer pistol grip stock and grooved forearm, ghost ring sights with fiber dots, matte black metal finish, 6 1/2 lbs. New 2013.

MSR $349	$295	$275	$250	$225	$200	$185	$170	

CZ 612 HOME DEFENSE – 12 ga., 18 1/2 in. barrel with fixed cyl. choke and front bead sight, black synthetic stock and forearm, matte black metal finish, 6 lbs. New 2013.

MSR $290	$260	$230	$210	$190	$170	$150	$135	

CZ 612 WILDFOWL MAGNUM – 12 ga., 3 1/2 in. chamber, 26 in. VR barrel with M and XF choke tubes, 100% camo coverage, 6.8 lbs. New 2013.

MSR $409	$360	$325	$295	$260	$230	$210	$185	

CZ (STRAKONICE)

Current manufacturer established in 1919 and located in Strakonice, Czech Republic. No current U.S. importation. Previously imported by Adco Sales, Inc., located in Woburn, MA.

HISTORY OF THE CZ TRADEMARK

An aspect of the post-communist Czech economy is that there are now two rival manufacturing firms bearing the name of CZ (Ceska Zbrojovka). This company was started in Plzen in 1919, and moved to Strakonice in 1921, near the western border of Bohemia. The factory at Strakonice remained the primary center for Czech handgun manufacture until the 1960s. Additionally, pistols (and a great many rifles) were made at another CZ - Ceskaslovenska Zbrojovka of Brno. However, the manufacture of pistols was transferred at an early date to the CZ factory at Strakonice.

During the rise of Hitler and the Nazis, the Czechs were justifiably alarmed at having so much of their arms industry within easy reach of the Nazis. Consequently, the two CZs collaborated in opening a joint manufacturing facility in 1936, far from the German border at Uhersky Brod. While Czechoslovakia was united, Uhersky Brod was in the very middle of the country; now it is located only a few kilometers west of the Czech Republic's border with Slovakia.

The CZ facility at Uhersky Brod eventually took over most of Czechoslovakia's firearms manufacturing during the postwar years although handgun manufacture continued on a reduced

GRADING - PPGS™	100%	98%	95%	90%	80%	70%	60%	LAST MSR

scale at the plant at Strakonice.

The dismemberment of the state-owned communist economy in the early 1990s has resulted in the existence of the two competitive CZ firms - one based in Uhersky Brod, the other at the older plant at Strakonice. The Brno operation also retains the name "CZ". The CZ based in Uhersky Brod is represented in the U.S. by CZ-USA, based in Kansas City, KS. In recent years, the CZ based in Strakonice has had little or no importation, and the last company to do so was Adco Sales, Inc.

Some information appears courtesy of Jan Libourel and *Gun World* magazine.

PISTOLS: SEMI-AUTO

Older Strakonice manufacture can be found in the CZ (Ceska Zbrojovka) section.

CZ-75 – 9mm Para. cal., SA/DA, 4 3/4 in. barrel, steel frame, 10 shot mag., blue finish only. Limited importation 2004 only.

$475	$425	$375	$325	$295	$275	$225	*$569*

CZ-TT – 9mm Para., .40 S&W, or .45 ACP cal., SA/DA, polymer frame, 3.77 in. ported or unported barrel, matte finish, 10 shot mag., 26.1 oz. Imported 2004-2006.

$450	$415	$375	$325	$295	$275	$250	*$479*

Add $30 for ported barrel (disc.).
Add $40 for ported barrel and slide serrations (disc.).
Add $399 for conversion kit with one mag.

CZ-T POLYMER COMPACT – similar to CZ-TT, except has shorter barrel. Limited importation 2004 only.

$475	$425	$375	$325	$295	$275	$225	*$559*

ADCO/CZ 1911-A1 – .38 Super or .45 ACP cal., standard size government model with 5 in. barrel, black matte finish. Limited importation 2004.

$475	$425	$375	$325	$295	$275	$225	*$559*

Add $10 for .38 Super cal.

CZ ST9 – 9mm Para. cal., 5 in. barrel, 16 shot mag., DA, manual safety lever, matte blue finish, checkered wood grips.

This model has not been imported into the U.S.

RIFLES: SEMI-AUTO

CZ Strakonice also manufactures a .22 LR cal. AR-15 style training rifle, as well as .22 LR and .17 Mach 2 adapters for the AR-15. These guns are not imported into the U.S.

CABANAS

Previous trademark manufactured by Industrias Cabanas, S.A. in Aguilas, Mexico 1949-1999. Previously imported and retailed by Mandall Shooting Supplies, Inc. located in Scottsdale, AZ.

Cabanas manufactured a unique single shot bolt action rifle which shot oversized .177 pellets/BBs powered by .22 blanks at 1,150 feet per second. There were at least 8 variations, and secondary market prices today for 95%+ original condition ranges from approx. $65-$120. Transfer requires FFL. This trademark had limited U.S. importation.

CABELA'S INC.

Current sporting goods dealer and catalog company headquartered in Sidney, NE. Consumer direct (store or mail order catalog) sales only.

In addition to the models listed below, Cabela's has also offered many limited/special editions over the years. A trend has been for Cabela's to import special/limited editions that have the Cabela's private label. For more information on current special/limited editions, please visit www.cabelas.com.

To celebrate its 50th Annivesary during 2011, Cabela's commissioned special/limited editions from various manufacturers. These makes/models include: Winchester Model 94 with 24 in. octagon barrel and button mag. in .38-55 WCF cal., 750 total mfg. - MSR $1,600.

GRADING - PPGS™	100%	98%	95%	90%	80%	70%	60%	LAST MSR

Winchester Model 70 Super Grade Featherweight in .270 Win. cal. with recess crown and jewelled bolt and Cabela's special 50th Anniversary logo engraved on floorplate, 500 mfg. total - MSR $1,800. Winchester Model 70 Super Grade Safari rifle in .458 Win. Mag. cal., features original type express rear sight, checkered Grade III walnut and Cabela's special 50th Anniversary logo engraved on floorplate, 400 mfg. total - MSR $2,200. Cooper .22 Custom Classic with Neider style buttplate with Cabela's special 50th Anniversary logo engraved on it, 100 mfg. total - MSR $3,000. Ruger No. 1 rifle in .300 H&H cal. featuring open sights and gold Cabela's 50th Anniversary logo on bottom of frame, 500 mfg. total - MSR $500. Ruger 10-22 Rifle featuring checkered circassion walnut stock and Cabela's 50th Anniversary logo laser cut into the pistol grip cap, 750 mfg. total - MSR $400. The Ruger Single Six revolver with 5 1/2 in. barrel, old style medallion grips, special serial number and gold Cabela's 50th Anniversary logo engraved on backstrap, limited mfg. - MSR $550. S&W Model 29 Revolver, 4 screw design, pinned barrel, Cabela's 50th Anniversary logo engraved on right side of frame and includes wood box, limited mfg. - MSR $1,150.

Cabela's also imports black powder cartridge Sharps replicas, revolvers, and other reproductions, mostly manufactured in Italy by A. Uberti, Pedersoli, and Pietta (please see individual sections for more info).

Cabela's imports a wide variety of black powder muzzleloading rifles and pistols, in addition to replicas of popular older Colt and Winchester firearms.

Please refer to the *Blue Book of Modern Black Powder Arms* (also online) by John Allen for more information and prices on Cabela's lineup of modern black powder models. *Black Powder Revolvers - Reproductions & Replicas* and *Black Powder Long Arms & Pistols - Reproductions & Replicas* by Dennis Adler are also invaluable sources for most black powder reproductions and replicas, and they include hundreds of color images on most popular makes/models, provide manufacturer/trademark histories, and up-to-date information on related items/accessories for black powder shooting - www.bluebookofgunvalues.com

Cabela's should be contacted directly (see Trademark Index) to receive the most recent information on their complete firearms and black powder lineups, including both special and limited editions.

SHOTGUNS: O/U

VOLO – 12 or 20 ga., 3 in. chambers, 28 in. barrel, five interchangeable chokes, with or w/o gold inlay engraved sideplates (Volo Deluxe). Mfg. in Italy by Fausti. Importation began 2008.

MSR	100%	98%	95%	90%	80%	70%	60%
MSR $1,100	$1,050	$950	$775	$675	$575	$500	$450

Add $200 for gold inlay engraved sideplates.

SHOTGUNS: SxS

HEMINGWAY MODEL – mfg. for Cabela's by V. Bernardelli located in Italy, ST, ejectors. Disc. 1994.

100%	98%	95%	90%	80%	70%	60%	LAST MSR
$925	$775	$700	$640	$575	$525	$465	$975

AYA GRADE II CUSTOM – mfg. for Cabela's by AYA located in Eibar, Spain, ST, ejectors, similar to AYA Model II with Model 53 engraving and trim. Disc. and sold out.

100%	98%	95%	90%	80%	70%	60%
$3,650	$3,100	$2,500	$2,000	$1,650	$1,275	$1,000

CABOT GUN COMPANY LLC

Current pistol manufacturer located in Cabot, PA. Consumer and dealer sales. Cabot Guns is a division of Pen United Technologies, Inc.

PISTOLS: SEMI-AUTO

Add $180 for jeweled barrel and magazine on all models below (except for Jones Deluxe).

JONES 1911 – .45 ACP cal., full size CNC machined frame, 5 in. National Match grade barrel, polished feed ramp, lowered and flared ejection port, aluminum trigger, rear and front slide checkering, top slide serrations, right hand thumb safety, extended slide stop, 20 LPI front strap checkering, titanium firing pin, Novak adj. 3-dot sights, 8 shot Chip McCormack Power mag., bright blue hand polished finish, desert ironwood grips, includes customized aluminum Technoframes case and custom H.R. Gerstner & Sons oak display case, 40 oz. New 2012.

MSR	100%	98%	95%	90%	80%	70%	60%
MSR $5,950	$5,500	$4,850	$4,150	$3,600	$3,000	$2,500	$1,950

GRADING - PPGS™	100%	98%	95%	90%	80%	70%	60%	LAST MSR

JONES DELUXE – .45 ACP cal., similar to Jones 1911 with added refinements, including hand polishing and finishing, TriStar trigger, ironwood grips, beveled and chamfered magwell, CNC engraved star on guide rod. New 2012.

MSR $9,950	$9,400	$8,500	$7,500	$6,500	$5,500	$4,500	$3,500	

RANGEMASTER – .45 ACP cal., full size CNC machined frame, 5 in. National Match grade barrel, polished feed ramp, lowered and flared ejection port, aluminum trigger, rear and front slide checkering, top slide serrations, right hand thumb safety, extended slide stop, Novak adj. 3-dot sights, 8 shot Chip McCormack Power mag., semi-bright blue hand polished finish, Pachmayr American Legend grips, includes customized aluminum Technoframes case, 40 oz. New 2012.

MSR $5,250	$4,850	$4,150	$3,600	$3,050	$2,500	$2,000	$1,500	

CGI CLASSIC (CONTEMPORARY GOVERNMENT ISSUE CLASSIC) – .45 ACP cal., vintage M1911A1 style, full size CNC machined frame, 5 in. National Match grade barrel, polished feed ramp, aluminum skeletonized trigger, rear and front slide checkering, rear slide serrations, right hand thumb safety, extended slide stop, retro fixed style sights, 8 shot Chip McCormack Power mag., bright blue hand polished finish, box elder grips, includes customized aluminum Technoframes case, 40 oz. New 2012.

MSR $4,950	$4,600	$4,000	$3,500	$3,000	$2,500	$2,000	$1,500	

GI CLASSIC (GOVERNMENT ISSUE CLASSIC) – .45 ACP cal., vintage M1911A1 style, full size CNC machined frame, 5 in. National Match grade barrel, polished feed ramp, blued solid trigger with front stippling, rear slide serrations, right hand thumb safety, extended slide stop, arched main spring housing, retro fixed style sights, 8 shot original ordnance style mag., isonited glare resistant finish, ordinance style GI grips, includes customized aluminum Technoframes case, 40 oz. New 2012.

MSR $4,750	$4,400	$3,800	$3,300	$2,850	$2,300	$1,850	$1,475	

SOUTH PAW – .45 ACP cal., modern full size M1911 style, designed for left-handed shooters, National Match grade barrel, polished feed ramp, lowered and flared ejection port, recoil spring, aluminum trigger, rear slide serrations, top slide serrations, left hand thumb safety, extended slide stop, arched main spring housing, 20 LPI front strap checkering, Harrison design fixed rear sight, Rozic blind sight, 8 shot mag., hand polished grey nitride finish, box elder or CA olive wood grips, 40 oz. New 2012.

MSR $5,750	$5,375	$4,600	$4,000	$3,450	$2,850	$2,300	$1,700	

NATIONAL STANDARD – .45 ACP cal., modern full size M1911 style, stainless steel frame and slide, National Match grade barrel, polished feed ramp, lowered and flared ejection port, recoil spring, tristar trigger, rear slide serrations, top slide serrations, right hand thumb safety, extended slide stop, 20 LPI front strap checkering, Novak adj. 3-dot sights, 8 shot mag., mammoth ivory grips. New 2012.

MSR $6,250	$5,700	$5,000	$4,300	$3,700	$3,000	$2,400	$2,050	

NATIONAL STANDARD DELUXE – .45 ACP cal., similar to National Standard, except has closer tolerances, hand polished to a two micron finish, mammoth ivory grips. New 2012.

MSR $7,450	$6,995	$6,200	$5,500	$4,800	$4,000	$3,250	$2,450	

AMERICAN JOE – .45 ACP cal., modern full size 1911 style, enhanced frame to slide fit, similar to National Standard Deluxe, engraving design by Joe Faris, included exclusive custom design aluminum American flag grips. New 2013.

MSR $7,450	$6,995	$6,200	$5,500	$4,800	$4,000	$3,250	$2,450	

CAEM, RENATO

Previous manufacturer of small gauge SxS shotguns located in Marcheno Val Trompia, Italy until 2008.

Renato Caem manufactured approx. 5 best quality scalloped boxlock SxS shotguns annually, only in 20 ga., 28 ga., or .410 bore. This trademark has had very little importation into the U.S, and guns should be appraised individually.

GRADING - PPGS™	100%	98%	95%	90%	80%	70%	60%	LAST MSR

CAESAR GUERINI, s.r.l.

Current manufacturer located in Marcheno, Italy. Currently imported beginning 2003 by Caesar Guerini USA LLC.

CÆSAR GUERINI

SHOTGUNS: O/U, FIELD

Add $285 for double triggers on 12 ga.
Add $200 for left-hand with sideplates (disc. 2012).

APEX – 12, 20, 28 ga. or .410 bore, 26 (disc.), 28, or 30 (disc.) in. barrels with 5 choke tubes, full length trigger guard with skeletal grip cap, coin finished full coverage scroll engraved receiver, hand rubbed oil finish stock with Prince of Wales grip, brass bead front sight, approx. 8 lbs.

MSR $7,750	$6,575	$5,750	$4,925	$4,475	$3,600	$2,950	$2,300	

Combination sets are also available on this gun - prices range from $9,840-$12,100. .410 bore is only available in a combination set.

CHALLENGER SPORTING – 12 ga., 30 or 32 in. barrels, hand polished coin finished receiver, gold trigger, bold leaf and scroll engraving, DTS trigger system. New 2012.

MSR $4,995	$4,250	$3,725	$3,195	$2,875	$2,350	$1,925	$1,495	

Add $220 for left-hand.

ELLIPSE EVO – 12 (new 2012), 20 or 28 ga., 28 in. barrels, rounded action, checkered pistol grip walnut stock and forearm, alloy receiver with scroll and floral engraving. New mid-2010.

MSR $5,950	$5,050	$4,425	$3,795	$3,425	$2,775	$2,275	$1,775	

Add $1,925 for 20 and 28 ga. combo.
Add $220 for left-hand stock.
Add $220 for English style stock.

* ***Ellipse Evo Light*** – 20 or 28 ga., 28 in. barrels, similar to Ellipse Evo, except is lightweight, 5 1/2 lbs. New mid-2012.

MSR $5,950	$5,050	$4,425	$3,795	$3,425	$2,775	$2,275	$1,775	

Add $220 for left-hand or English straight grip stock.

* ***Ellipse Evo Sporting*** – 12 ga., 28 in. barrels, similar to Ellipse Evo, except has 30 or 32 in. barrels, bold leaf and scroll engraving. Limited mfg. mid-2012.

	$5,400	$4,000	$3,375	$3,125	$2,350	$2,000	$1,600	*$6,295*

Add $215 for left-hand stock.

ELLIPSE LIMITED – 20 or 28 ga., 28 in. barrels, 2 3/4 (28 ga.) or 3 (20 ga.) in. chambers, color case hardened receiver with light border line engraving, semi-deluxe checkered Turkish walnut stock with hand rubbed oil finish, gold trigger, approx. 6 1/2 lbs. Limited mfg. 2012.

	$3,350	$2,500	$2,100	$1,900	$1,500	$1,300	$1,100	*$3,995*

Add $215 for left-hand or English stock.
A combination set is available in this model for $5,825.

ESSEX FIELD – 12, 20, 28 ga. or .410 bore, 26 (disc.), 28, or 30 (20 ga. only) in. barrels, coin finished sideplates with English rose and scroll engraving, tapered solid rib, round knob pistol grip stock. Less than 100 mfg. for importation during 2006.

	$4,350	$3,500	$3,150	$2,675	$2,275	$1,950	$1,650	*$4,895*

Add $155 for .410 bore.
Combination packages were available on this model, and had MSRs in the $6,620-$8,500 range.

* ***Essex Limited*** – 20 or 28 ga., similar to Essex, except has case colored finish, full coverage English scroll engraving, 28 in. barrels. Mfg. 2009-2011.

	$4,550	$3,850	$3,450	$2,950	$2,500	$2,000	$1,500	*$5,095*

FLYWAY – 12 ga., 3 in. chambers, 28 or 30 in. barrels, beavertail forend, multichokes, blued boxlock receiver with satin finish and gold mallard on bottom, parallel 10mm top rib, shipped with hard case, 7 lbs. 14 oz. - 8 lbs.

	$1,795	$1,495	$1,295	$1,095	$895	$800	$725	*$2,295*

GRADING - PPGS™	100%	98%	95%	90%	80%	70%	60%	LAST MSR

FORUM - 12, 20, 28 ga., or .410 bore (new 2006), 2 3/4 or 3 in. chambers, 26 or 28 in. barrels, coin finished boxlock receiver, blind sideplates with no visible screws, Bulino style engraving with game scenes and floral scroll, Prince of Wales grip, Schnabel forend, checkered stock with oil finish, multichokes, factory hard case, 6 lbs. 5 oz.-7 lbs.

MSR $9,950	$8,450	$7,395	$6,350	$5,750	$4,650	$3,800	$2,950	

Combination packages were available on this model, and had MSRs in the $11,700-$13,915 range.

Left hand is available in this model by special order only.

MAGNUS LIGHT - 12, 20, 28 ga., or .410 bore (new 2006), 2 3/4 or 3 in. chambers, 26 or 28 in. barrels, case hardened sideplate boxlock alloy receiver with gold grouse, pheasant, and quail game scenes, Prince of Wales grip, Schnabel forend, oil finished wood, multichokes, factory hard case, 5 lbs. 4 oz.-6 lbs.

MSR $4,395	$3,725	$3,250	$2,795	$2,525	$2,050	$1,675	$1,300	

Add $165 for .410 bore.

Add $220 for left-hand or English stock.

Combination packages are available on this model, and have current MSRs in the $6,050-$7,870 range.

* ***Magnus*** - similar to Magnus Light, except has steel receiver, 28 or 30 in. barrels, 6 lbs. 4 oz.-7 lbs.

MSR $4,395	$3,725	$3,250	$2,795	$2,525	$2,050	$1,675	$1,300	

Add $165 for .410 bore.

Add $220 for left-hand or English stock.

Combination packages are available on this model, and have current MSRs in the $6,050-$7,870 range.

MAXUM FIELD - 12, 20, 28 ga. or .410 bore, 26 or 28 in. barrels, coin finished sideplates with deep relief floral scroll engraving, deluxe checkered oil finished Turkish walnut stock and forearm. Importation began 2006.

MSR $5,995	$5,095	$4,450	$3,825	$3,475	$2,800	$2,295	$1,785	

Add $220 for left-hand or English stock.

Combination packages are available on this model, and have current MSRs in the $7,875-$9,925 range.

* ***Maxum Light*** - similar to Maxum, except is lighter weight and available only with 28 in. barrels. Mfg. mid-2010-2012.

	$4,950	$3,950	$3,300	$2,800	$2,400	$2,000	$1,625	*$5,775*

Add $215 for left-hand or English stock.

Combination packages were available on this model, and had MSRs in the $7,595-$9,650 range

TEMPIO - 12, 20, 28 ga., or .410 bore (new 2006), 2 3/4 or 3 in. chambers, 26, 28, or 30 in. barrels, grey "Tinaloy" boxlock receiver featuring gold grouse, quail, and pheasant game scenes surrounded by scroll, Prince of Wales grip and Schnabel forend, oil finished wood, multichokes, factory hard case, 6 lbs. 4 oz.-7 lbs.

MSR $3,595	$3,050	$2,675	$2,295	$2,075	$1,675	$1,375	$1,075	

Add $170 for .410 bore.

Add $220 for left-hand or English stock.

Combination packages are available on this model, and have current MSRs in the $5,250-$7,070 range.

* ***Tempio Light*** - 12, 20, or 28 ga., similar to Tempio, except has lighter barrels and stock, 26 (disc.) or 28 in. barrels, case colored receiver with bulino style engraving and gold inlays. New mid-2008.

MSR $3,595	$3,050	$2,675	$2,295	$2,075	$1,675	$1,375	$1,075	

Add $220 for left-hand or English stock (new 2012).

A 20/28 ga. combination package is available in this model for $5,250.

WOODLANDER - 12, 20, 28 ga., or .410 bore (new 2006), 2 3/4 or 3 in. chambers, 26 (disc.), 28 (12 ga. only), or 30 in. barrels, case hardened boxlock receiver with Bulino style engraved (ruffed grouse in gold on bottom of receiver), Prince of Wales grip and Schnabel

GRADING - PPGS™	100%	98%	95%	90%	80%	70%	60%	LAST MSR

forend, 6mm top rib, multichokes, shipped with hard case, 6 lbs. 2 oz.-6 lbs. 14 oz.

MSR $3,250	$2,750	$2,400	$2,050	$1,875	$1,525	$1,250	$975	

Add $220 for left-hand or English stock.
Combination packages are available on this model, and have current MSRs in the $4,905-$6,725 range.

SHOTGUNS: O/U, SPORTING CLAYS

Add $285 for double triggers on 12 ga.
Add $200 for left-hand with sideplates (disc. 2012).

APEX SPORTING – 12 ga. only, 30 or 32 in. barrels, similar to Apex Field, except has high grade English walnut stock, approx. 8 lbs. New 2009.

MSR $8,250	$7,000	$6,125	$5,250	$4,750	$3,850	$3,150	$2,450	

Combination sets and left handed stocks are available on this model by special order only.

FORUM SPORTING – 12, 20, 28 ga., or .410 bore (new 2006), 30, 32, or 34 (12 ga. only, disc.) in. barrels, coin finished sideplate boxlock receiver, Bulino style game scene engraving, blind sideplates with no visible screws, approx. 8 lbs.

MSR $10,295	$8,750	$7,650	$6,575	$5,950	$4,800	$3,950	$3,075	

MAGNUS SPORTING – 12, 20, 28 ga., or .410 bore (mfg. 2006-2012), 30, 32, or 34 (12 ga. only) in. barrels, sideplate grey "Tinaloy" boxlock receiver featuring gold grouse, quail, and pheasant game scenes, 10mm parallel vent. top rib, vent. barrels, pistol grip stock and Schnabel forend, adj. trigger, extended choke tubes, factory hard case, 7 lbs. 4 oz.-8 lbs. 2 oz.

MSR $4,995	$4,250	$3,725	$3,195	$2,895	$2,350	$1,925	$1,495	

Add $165 for .410 bore (disc. 2012).
Add $220 for left-hand.
Add $325 for adj. comb.
Add $265 for case hardened receiver.
Combination packages are available on this model, and have current MSRs in the $6,795-$8,770 range.

* ***Magnus Sporting Limited Edition*** – 12 ga., 30, 32, or 34 in. barrels, case hardened receiver with engraved sideplates and gold inlays, deluxe grade oil finished Turkish walnut stock and forearm. Mfg. mid-2008-2012.

	$4,250	$3,300	$2,775	$2,350	$1,950	$1,650	$1,375	*$5,055*

Add $215 for left-hand.
Add $315 for adj. comb.

MAXUM SPORTING – 12, 20, 28 ga. or .410 bore, 28, 30, 32, or 34 in. barrels, coin finished sideplates with deep relief floral scroll engraving, deluxe checkered oil finished Turkish walnut stock and forearm, extended sporting chokes, approx. 7 1/2 - 8 lbs. Importation began 2006.

MSR $6,495	$5,525	$4,825	$4,150	$3,750	$3,050	$2,475	$1,925	

Combination packages are available on this model, and have current MSRs in the $8,495-$10,675 range.
Add $220 for left-hand.
Add $325 for adj. comb.

* ***Maxum Impact*** – 12 or 20 ga., 30, 32, or 34 in. barrels, also available in Unsingle Combo in 12 ga., 7 lbs. 11 oz. - 8 lbs., 7 oz. New mid-2010.

MSR $8,195	$6,975	$6,100	$5,225	$4,725	$3,825	$3,125	$2,425	

Add $2,300 for Unsingle Combo in 12 ga.
Add $220 for left-hand (not available in 20 ga.).

SUMMIT SPORTING – 12, 20, 28 ga., or .410 bore (new 2006), 30, 32, or 34 (12 ga. only) in. barrels, grey "Tinaloy" boxlock receiver with neo-modern engraving, 10mm parallel top vent. top rib with vent. barrels, adj. trigger, pistol grip stock, Schnabel forend, right hand palm swell, extended choke tubes, factory case, 7 lbs. 4 oz.-8 lbs. 2 oz.

MSR $3,595	$3,050	$2,675	$2,295	$2,075	$1,675	$1,375	$1,075	

Combination packages are available on this model, and have current MSRs in the $5,395-$7,370 range.

GRADING - PPGS™	100%	98%	95%	90%	80%	70%	60%	LAST MSR

Add $170 for .410 bore.
Add $220 for left-hand.
Add $325 for adj. comb.

* ***Summit Limited Sporting*** – similar to Summit Sporting, except has case hardened receiver.

MSR $4,295	$3,650	$3,195	$2,725	$2,475	$2,000	$1,650	$1,275	

Combination packages are available on this model, and have current MSRs in the $6,095-$8,070 range.
Add $170 for .410 bore.
Add $220 for left-hand.
Add $325 for adj. comb.

* ***Summit Impact*** – 12 or 20 ga., 30, 32, or 34 in. VR barrels, oil finished checkered walnut stock with adj. comb, satin blue receiver with light floral scroll engraving, DTS trigger system, Impact rib is 40% lower than usual, six choke tubes, approx. 8 lbs. New 2009.

MSR $5,295	$4,500	$3,925	$3,375	$3,050	$2,475	$2,025	$1,575	

An Unsingle combo is available for $7,595. A four gauge Skeet set is available for $7,880.
Add $220 for left-hand (not available in 20 ga.).

SUMMIT ASCENT – 12 ga., 30 or 32 in. barrels, 10mm high tapered top rib, checkered walnut stock with adj. comb, case colored hardened receiver with light engraving, gold trigger. New 2012.

MSR $4,495	$3,825	$3,325	$2,875	$2,600	$2,100	$1,725	$1,325	

Add $220 for left-hand.

ELLIPSE EVOLUTION – 12 ga., 32 in. barrels, bold leaf and scroll engraving, deluxe checkered Turkish walnut stock. New mid-2012.

MSR $8,195	$6,975	$6,100	$5,225	$4,725	$3,825	$3,125	$2,425	

Left hand stock is only available with a custom stock purchase.

CHALLENGER IMPACT – 12 ga., 2 3/4 in. chambers, 32 or 34 in. barrels, gold trigger, hand polished coin finished receiver with Acanthus leaf and scroll engraving, deluxe checkered wood stock, available in Skeet or Trap configurations, approx. 8 1/2 lbs. New 2012.

MSR $6,995	$5,950	$5,200	$4,475	$4,050	$3,275	$2,675	$2,075	

An Unsingle combination set is also available in this model for $9,315.
A four gauge Skeet set is available in this model for $9,580.
Add $220 for left-hand.

CHALLENGER SPORTING – 12 ga., 30, 32, or 34 in. barrels, coin finished receiver with Invisalloy finish, DTS trigger system, hand rubbed oil finished checkered walnut stock and forearm, vent. rib, six competition chokes, 7 lbs., 14 oz. - 8 lbs. 2 oz. New 2013.

MSR $4,995	$4,250	$3,725	$3,195	$2,895	$2,350	$1,925	$1,495	

Add $220 for left hand.

SHOTGUNS: O/U, TRAP

Add $215 for left-hand.

APEX TRAP – 12 ga., 32 or 34 in. barrels, available in Unsingle, Top Single Barrel, and combo set configuration, special production run, approx. 9 lbs. New 2010.

MSR $9,950	$8,450	$7,395	$6,325	$5,725	$4,650	$3,800	$2,950	

Combination sets are available starting at $12,295.

FORUM TRAP – 12 ga., 32 or 34 in. barrels, available in Unsingle, Top Single Barrel, and combo set configuration, special production run, approx. 9 lbs. Mfg. 2010-2012.

	$10,375	$9,250	$8,125	$7,100	$6,000	$5,000	$4,000	*$11,595*

Combination sets are available in this model starting at $13,845.

MAGNUS TRAP – 12 ga., 30, 32, or 34 (unsingle only) barrels, case colored action and sideplates, scroll engraved with gold game scenes, deluxe Turkish walnut, 8 - 9 lbs. Mfg. 2007-2012.

	$5,700	$4,650	$4,250	$3,825	$3,225	$2,750	$2,150	*$6,795*

A combination set of this model was available for $9,045.

GRADING - PPGS™	100%	98%	95%	90%	80%	70%	60%	LAST MSR

MAXUM TRAP – 12 ga., 30, 32, or 34 (unsingle only) in. barrels, coin finished hand polished action, deep engraved receiver, extra deluxe Turkish walnut stock, approx. 9 lbs. New 2007.

MSR $8,195	$6,975	$6,100	$5,225	$4,750	$3,825	$3,125	$2,450	

A combination set of this model is available for $10,495.
Add $220 for left hand stock.

SUMMIT TRAP – 12 ga., 30, 32, or 34 (unsingle only) in. barrels, grey alloy receiver with light scroll engraving, adj. comb, approx. 8-8 1/2 lbs. New 2007.

MSR $5,295	$4,500	$3,925	$3,375	$3,050	$2,475	$2,025	$1,575	

A combination set of this model is available for $7,595.
Add $220 for left hand stock.

CHALLENGER TRAP – 12 ga., 2 3/4 in. chambers, 32 or 34 in. barrels, gold trigger, hand polished coin finished receiver with Acanthus leaf and scroll engraving, deluxe checkered wood stock, approx. 9 lbs. New 2012.

MSR $6,995	$5,950	$5,200	$4,450	$4,050	$3,275	$2,675	$2,075	

An Unsingle combination set is also available in this model for $9,315.
Add $220 for left hand stock.

CALICO LIGHT WEAPONS SYSTEMS

Current manufacturer established during 1986, and located in Cornelius, OR, previously located in Hillsboro, OR from 2002-2010, located in Sparks, NV 1998-2001, and in Bakersfield, CA.

CARBINES

Extra magazines are currently priced as follows: $157 for 100 shot 9mm Para. cal., $131 for 50 shot 9mm Para. cal., or $141 for 100 shot .22 LR cal.

LIBERTY I/II & LIBERTY 50-100 – 9mm Para. cal., 16.1 in. barrel, downward ejection, retarded blowback CETME type action, aluminum alloy receiver, synthetic stock with pistol grip (some early post-ban specimens had full wood stocks with thumbhole cutouts), 50 or 100 shot helical feed mag., ambidextrous safety, 7 lbs. Mfg. 1995-2001, reintroduced late 2007.

MSR $807	$725	$650	$575	$500	$450	$400	$350	

Add $75 for Liberty 50 Tactical with quad rails (new 2010).
Add $215 for Liberty I Tactical with quad rails (new 2010), or $231 for Liberty II Tactical with quad rails (new 2010).
Add $135 for Liberty I with skeletal adj. stock, or $156 for Liberty II with fixed stock.
Add $52 for Liberty 100 (100 shot mag.), or $127 for Liberty 100 Tactical with quad rails (new 2010).
Current MSR is for the Liberty 50 Model.

M-100 – .22 LR cal., semi-auto carbine, blowback action, paramilitary design with folding buttstock, 100 shot helical feed mag., alloy frame, aluminum receiver, ambidextrous safety, 16.1 in. shrouded barrel with flash suppressor/muzzle brake, adj. sights, 4.2 lbs. empty. Mfg. 1986-1994, reintroduced late 2007.

MSR $651	$585	$500	$450	$400	$350	$300	$275	

* ***M-100 Tactical*** – similar to M-100, except has quad Picatinny rails. New 2010.

MSR $726	$625	$550	$475	$425	$375	$325	$300	

* ***M-100 FS*** – similar to M-100, except has solid stock and barrel does not have flash suppressor. Mfg. 1996-2001, reintroduced late 2007.

MSR $651	$585	$500	$450	$400	$350	$300	$275	

* ***M-100 FS Tactical*** – similar to M-100 FS, except has quad Picatinny rail. New 2010.

MSR $726	$625	$550	$475	$425	$375	$325	$300	

M-101 – while advertised, this model never went into production.

M-105 SPORTER – similar to M-100, except has walnut distinctively styled buttstock and forend, 4 3/4 lbs. empty. Mfg. 1989-1994.

	$650	$550	$495	$450	$350	$295	$250	*$335*

GRADING - PPGS™	100%	98%	95%	90%	80%	70%	60%	LAST MSR

M-106 – while advertised, this model never went into production.

M-900 – 9mm Para. cal., retarded blowback action, paramilitary design with wood (disc.) or collapsible buttstock (current mfg.), cast aluminum receiver with stainless steel bolt, static cocking handle, 16 in. barrel, fixed rear sight with adj. post front, 50 (standard) or 100 shot helical feed mag., ambidextrous safety, black polymer pistol grip and forend, approx. 3.7 lbs. Mfg. 1989-1990, reintroduced 1992-1993, again during 2007-2010.

	$775	$700	$650	$600	$500	$450	$400	*$875*

Add $157 for 100 shot mag.

* ***M-900S*** – similar to M-900, except has non-collapsible shoulder stock. Disc. 1993.

	$650	$550	$475	$400	$350	$300	$275	*$632*

* ***M-901 Canada Carbine*** – 9mm Para. cal., similar to M-900, except has 18 1/2 in. barrel and sliding stock. Disc. 1992.

	$675	$595	$550	$475	$350	$300	$285	*$643*

This model was also available with solid fixed stock (Model 901S).

M-951 TACTICAL CARBINE – 9mm Para. cal., 16.1 in. barrel, similar appearance to M-900 Carbine, except has muzzle brake and extra pistol grip on front of forearm, 4 3/4 lbs. Mfg. 1990-94.

	$750	$700	$675	$650	$600	$475	$450	*$556*

* ***M-951S*** – similar to M-951, except has synthetic buttstock. Mfg. 1991-94.

	$650	$595	$525	$450	$400	$350	$300	*$567*

PISTOLS: SEMI-AUTO

LIBERTY III – 9mm Para. cal., 6 in. ported barrel, choice of 50 or 100 shot mag., ribbed forend, 2 1/4 lbs. w/o mag. New 2010.

MSR $890	$795	$725	$650	$575	$500	$450	$395

Add $75 for Liberty III Tactical with quad rails (new 2011).

M-110 – .22 LR cal., blowback action, 6 in. barrel with muzzle brake, 100 round helical feed mag., includes notched rear sight and adj. windage front sight, 10 1/2 in. sight radius, ambidextrous safety, pistol grip storage compartment, 2.21 lbs. empty. Mfg. 1989-2001, reintroduced 2007.

MSR $703	$615	$540	$460	$375	$325	$275	$225

M-950 – 9mm Para. cal., same operating mechanism as the M-900 Carbine, 6 in. barrel, 50 (standard) or 100 shot helical feed mag., 2 1/4 lbs. empty. Mfg. 1989-1994, mfg. late 2007-2010.

	$775	$700	$650	$600	$500	$450	$400	*$872*

CAMEX-BLASER USA, INC.

Previous importer/distributor of Blaser Jagdwaffen Gmbh rifles.

Previously imported Camex-Blaser rifles can be located in the Blaser section.

CANIK55

Current trademark of pistols manufactured by Samsun Domestic Defence and Industry Corporation (a subsidiary of Aral Industry Corporation), established in 1997 and located in Samsun, Turkey. Currently imported being 2013 by Tristar, located in N. Kansas City, MO. Previously imported circa mid-2010-2011 by Canik-USA, located in Pueblo West, CO.

PISTOLS: SEMI-AUTO

Canik55 is a line of good quality semi-auto 1911-style pistols, including the Shark Series, Stingray Series, TP-9 Series (new 2012), Piranha Series, LSC Series, S-FC 100 Series, MKEK Series, and Dolphin Series. Currently, only some of these models are being imported into the U.S. Please contact the importer directly for more information, including pricing and U.S. availability (see Trademark Index).

GRADING - PPGS™	100%	98%	95%	90%	80%	70%	60%	LAST MSR

CAPRINUS

Previous shotgun manufacturer located in Varberg, Sweden.

SHOTGUNS: O/U

CAPRINUS SWEDEN – 12 ga., boxlock action, ejectors, ST, stainless steel receiver, unique design breaks down without forearm disassembly, 29 1/2 in. barrels with choke tubes, limited mfg. during early 1980s.

	100%	98%	95%	90%	80%	70%	60%	LAST MSR
	$3,750	$3,250	$2,850	$2,400	$2,000	$1,600	$1,200	*$5,955*

CARACAL

Current manufacturer of semi-auto pistols established in 2006, and located in the Abu Dhabi, United Arab Emirates. Currently imported beginning 2011 by Caracal USA, located in Trussville, AL. Previously located in Knoxville, TN. Currently distributed in Italy exclusively by Fratelli Tanfoglio Snc, located in Brescia, Italy.

PISTOLS: SEMI-AUTO

MODEL C – 9mm Para., 9x21mm, .357 SIG, or .40 S&W cal., modified Browning-type blowback design, double action, 3.66 in. barrel, 14 shot mag., ribbed black polymer frame with colored inserts and Picatinny rail in front of trigger guard, matte black slide with rear slide serrations and integral sights (fiber optic front sight), Glock style trigger safety, cocking indicator, approx. 25 oz.

	100%	98%	95%	90%	80%	70%	60%	LAST MSR
MSR $625	$550	$450	$415	$375	$335	$300	$275	

MODEL F – similar to Model C, except has 4.1 in. barrel and 18 shot mag., 26 1/2 oz.

	100%	98%	95%	90%	80%	70%	60%	LAST MSR
MSR $625	$550	$450	$415	$375	$335	$300	$275	

MODEL SC – 9mm Para. or 9x21mm cal., similar to Model C, except is compact variation with 3.38 in. barrel and 13 shot mag., approx. 23 oz. Limited mfg. 2009-2011.

	100%	98%	95%	90%	80%	70%	60%	LAST MSR
	$550	$450	$415	$375	$335	$300	$275	*$625*

RIFLES: BOLT ACTION

MODEL CSR – .308 Win. cal., 20 or 32 in. hammer forged threaded barrel, folding adj. skeletonized stock, pistol grip, quad rail, 10 shot mag., adj. match grade trigger, black finish, approx. 11 lbs. New 2012.

As this edition went to press, pricing information was not available.

RIFLES: SEMI-AUTO

MODEL CC10 – 9mm Para. cal., modern bull pup design with skeletonized stock with grip safety, full length Picatinny rail, sights integrated into the frame, 18 shot detachable mag., right hand ejection with bolt lever on left side, black finish, choice of 9.3 (CC10-SB, LE only) or 16.1 (CC10 LB) in. barrel. New 2012.

As this edition went to press, pricing information was not available.

CARBON 15

Please refer to the Professional Ordnance (discontinued mfg.) and Bushmaster (current mfg.) listings for more information on this trademark.

CARL GUSTAF

Previous manufacturer located in Eskilstuna, Sweden. Previously imported by Hansen & Co. located in Southport, CT during 1994-1995, and by Precision Sales International located in Westfield, MA during 1991-1993.

RIFLES: BOLT ACTION

MODEL CG 2000 STANDARD GRADE – 6.5x55mm, 7x64mm, 9.3x62mm, .243 Win., .270 Win., .30-06, .308 Win., 7mm Rem. Mag., or .300 Win. Mag. cal., bolt action, Monte Carlo walnut stock with checkering and Wundhammer grip, 24 in. barrel, detachable 3 or 4 shot mag., with or without sights, cold-swaged barrel and receiver, 60 degree bolt, 3-way slide safety, 7 1/2 lbs. Imported 1991-95.

	100%	98%	95%	90%	80%	70%	60%	LAST MSR
	$1,325	$1,050	$875	$725	$575	$475	$375	*$1,535*

Add $540 for Mag. cals.

GRADING - PPGS™	100%	98%	95%	90%	80%	70%	60%	LAST MSR

This model was supplied with individual 80 meter signed test targets. This model was also imported as the Fairfax 2000 series.

* ***Model 2000 Luxe Grade*** – .270 Win., .30-06, .308 Win., or 6.5x55mm cal., features choice of regular or Mannlicher deluxe walnut stock. Imported 1995 only.

$1,695	$1,400	$1,200	$975	$825	$650	$475	*$1,935*

A Model 2000 Super-Luxe was also available in 6.5x55mm or .30-06 cal. - retail was $4,250.

MODEL 3000 – various cals., features Sauer action with non-rotating bolt. Previously imported by Aimpoint.

$675	$575	$475	$400	$375	$350	$325

STANDARD BOLT ACTION RIFLE – 6.5x55mm, 7x64mm, .270 Win., 7mm Rem. Mag., .308 Win., .30-06, or 9.3x62mm cal., 24 in. barrel, folding rear sight, checkered classic style stock. Mfg. 1970-77.

$475	$425	$350	$315	$285	$250	$225

* ***Standard Bolt Action Rifle w/Monte Carlo stock***

$525	$450	$395	$350	$300	$275	$250

GRADE II – similar to Monte Carlo Standard, in .22-250 Rem., .25-06 Rem., 6.5x55mm, .270 Win., 7mm Rem. Mag., .308 Win., .30-06, or .300 Win. Mag. cal., select stock and rosewood pistol grip cap, and forearm tip.

$500	$425	$375	$325	$295	$275	$250

GRADE III – similar to Grade II, except fancy wood, deluxe high gloss finish.

$575	$475	$425	$350	$325	$300	$275

DELUXE – similar to Grade III, except engraved floorplate and trigger guard, Deluxe French walnut, and jeweled bolt.

$675	$575	$475	$400	$375	$350	$325

VARMINT TARGET MODEL – .222 Rem., .22-250 Rem., .243 Win., or 6.5x55mm cal., bolt action, fast lock time, 27 in. barrel, no sights, large bakelite bolt knob, target type stock. Mfg. 1970. Disc.

$550	$495	$440	$385	$360	$320	$290

GRAND PRIX SINGLE SHOT TARGET – .22 LR cal., fastest lock time bolt action, 27 in. heavy barrel with adj. weight, no sights, target stock, adj. buttplate. Mfg. 1970. Disc.

$550	$495	$440	$385	$360	$320	$290

CASARTELLI, CARLO

Previous manufacturer located in Brescia, Italy until 2000. Previously imported and distributed until 1999 by New England Arms Corp. located in Kittery Point, ME.

Casartelli rifles and shotguns were available through special order only. Virtually any custom gun configuration could be manufactured to the customer's exact specifications and requirements.

RIFLES

AFRICA MODEL - BOLT ACTION – various heavy and Mag. cals., square bridge Mauser action, full coverage game scene engraving appropriate to caliber, takedown, limited production.

$10,200	$7,500	$5,900	$5,300	$4,700	$4,100	$3,600	*$12,000*

SAFARI MODEL - BOLT ACTION – standard cals., regular Mauser action, full coverage game scene engraving, limited production.

$6,250	$5,900	$5,250	$4,950	$4,150	$3,650	$3,150	*$8,250*

KENYA - DOUBLE RIFLE – most standard and Mag. cals., sidelock action, elaborate game scene and/or scroll engraving, limited production.

$24,250	$21,500	$17,750	$14,750	$12,000	$9,950	$8,250	*$35,000*

GRADING - PPGS™	100%	98%	95%	90%	80%	70%	60%	LAST MSR

SHOTGUNS: SxS

SIDELOCK MODEL – various gauges, elaborate game scene and/or scroll engraving, limited production.

$13,000 $9,750 $7,900 $6,500 $5,200 $4,250 $3,750 *$17,000*

CASPIAN ARMS, LTD

Current parts manufacturer established during 1976, and located in Wolcott, VT. Dealer direct sales only. Caspian Arms, LTD. is a subsidiary of Foster Industries, Inc.

Caspian Arms currently fabricates high quality aluminum (new 2012), steel, stainless steel, titanium (new 2002), and alloy (disc. 2006) frames for the Colt Government Model 1911/A1, both in standard and high capacity frames. Frame sizes include the Government, Commander, and Officer's. Caspian Arms Ltd. also manufactures slides, including a damascus variation, and related small parts, in addition to having many special order machine operations available. Please contact them directly for current information on their extensive line of pistol-related components (see Trademark Index).

PISTOLS: SEMI-AUTO

VIETNAM COMMEMORATIVE – .45 ACP, total production was 1,000, hand engraved by J.J. Adams, nickel plated, service branch medallion installed in grips. Limited mfg. 1986-93.

$1,450 $995 $795 N/A N/A N/A N/A *$1,500*

Add $350 for gold plating.
Add $200 for serial numbers below RVN100.

This Vietnam Commemorative was also available in 24Kt. gold hand inlay edition for $14,000 - very limited production.

CASULL ARMS CORPORATION

Previous manufacturer and distributor located in Afton, WY 1996-2005.

PISTOLS: SEMI-AUTO

CA-3800 – .38 Casull or .45 ACP cal., single action, 6 in. match barrel, 8 shot mag., blue or stainless finish, checkered exotic wood grips, 2 piece guide rod, fully adj. rear sight and Casull mfg. adj. front sight, hand fitted slide to frame, slide features Dick Casull signature on left side, includes locking aluminum carrying case and 2 mags., 40 oz. Mfg. 2001-2005.

$2,395 $2,150 $1,975 $1,825 $1,675 $1,550 $1,425 *$2,495*

Add $300 for 6 in. .45 ACP barrel.
Add $400 for all stainless model.
Add $100 for either stainless steel frame and blue slide or vice versa.
Add $900 for both cals. with custom fitted extra slides.
Add $400 for compensator.

REVOLVERS

CA2000 MINI-FRAME REVOLVER – .22 LR or .32 ACP cal., double action, fold up trigger, hammerless, manual safety, hardwood grips. Mfg. 1997-2005.

$350 $295 $250 $225 $200 $185 $170 *$395*

CA3000 SMALL FRAME REVOLVER – while advertised during 1997 (MSR - $1,495), this model never went into production.

CA4000 LARGE FRAME REVOLVER – while advertised during 1997 (MSR - $1,995), this model never went into production.

RIFLES: BOLT ACTION

CAC5000 CONVENTIONAL – standard cals. include .270 Win., .300 Win. Mag., .375 H&H, .458 Win. Mag., or 7mm Rem. Mag. cal., featured improved bolt action with conventional extraction, box mag. Limited mfg. 1997-99.

$2,275 $1,950 $1,600 $1,410 $1,160 $980 $800 *$2,495*

GRADING - PPGS™	100%	98%	95%	90%	80%	70%	60%	LAST MSR

CRS7000 CASULL RIFLE SYSTEM – .30 Casull or 6.5 Casull cal., patented bolt and extraction system, featured all-metal bedding system allowing take-down and reassembly without affecting accuracy, box mag., stainless barrel without sights, uncheckered walnut stock, sporter or benchrest configuration. Limited mfg. 1997-99.

	100%	98%	95%	90%	80%	70%	60%	LAST MSR
	$2,700	$2,350	$2,000	$1,740	$1,495	$1,215	$1,000	$2,995

CAVALRY ARMS CORPORATION

Previous manufacturer located in Gilbert, AZ until 2010 and previously located in Mesa, AZ.

CARBINES/RIFLES: SEMI-AUTO

Cavalry Arms Corporation manufactured the CAV-15 Series, pattern after the AR-15 style carbine/rifle. Cavalry Arms also made paramilitary conversions for select slide action shotguns.

CAV-15 SCOUT CARBINE – .223 Rem. cal., 16 in. chrome lined barrel, A2 flash hider, A3 flat-top upper receiver, longer sight radius, longer gas system, stand alone rear sight, Black, Green, or Coyote Brown finish, C6 hand guards. Disc. 2010.

	100%	98%	95%	90%	80%	70%	60%	LAST MSR
	$765	$675	$575	$525	$425	$350	$275	$850

Add $199 for drop in rail system.
Add $259 for free float system.
Add $92 for YHM flip up front or rear sight.

CAV-15 RIFLEMAN – .223 Rem. cal., 20 in. chrome lined Govt. profile barrel, A2 flash hider, A3 flat-top upper receiver, stand alone rear sight, Black, Green, or Coyote Brown finish, A2 hand guard. Disc. 2010.

	100%	98%	95%	90%	80%	70%	60%	LAST MSR
	$765	$675	$575	$525	$425	$350	$275	$850

Add $279 mid-length free float system.
Add $310 for rifle length free float system.
Add $92 for YHM flip up front or rear sight.

CENTURION ORDNANCE, INC.

Previous importer located in Helotes, TX. Centurion Ordnance also imported Aguila ammunition.

SHOTGUNS: SLIDE ACTION

POSEIDON – 12 ga., 1 3/4 in. chamber (shoots "mini-shells" and slugs), 18 1/4 in. smoothbore barrel, 13 in. LOP, black synthetic stock and forearm, 6 shot mag., adj. rear sight, 5 lbs., 5 oz. Limited importation 2001.

	100%	98%	95%	90%	80%	70%	60%	LAST MSR
	$285	$250	$225	$200	$185	$170	$155	

While prototypes of this model were imported briefly during 2001, this gun never made it into the consumer marketplace.

Mini-shells retailed for $12.60 for a box of 20 (shot sizes include 7, #4 & #1 buckshot).

CENTURY ARMS

Previous manufacturer circa 1996-1998 located in Balwyn, Victoria, Australia.

RIFLES: SINGLE SHOT

REWA RIFLE – 4 bore ball, break open action, massive single shot with case colored and engraved action, deluxe checkered stock and forearm with ebony tip, iron sights, production limited to a few prototypes only (a convertible shotgun barrel was also planned).

Extreme rarity precludes accurate pricing on this model.

CENTURY INTERNATIONAL ARMS, INC.

Current importer and distributor founded in 1961 with current corporate offices located in Delray Beach, FL. Century International Arms, Inc. was previously headquartered in St. Albans, VT until 1997, and Boca Raton, FL from 1997-2004.

Century International Arms, Inc. imports a large variety of used military rifles, shotguns, and pistols. Because inventory changes daily, especially on paramilitary style rifles,

GRADING - PPGS™	100%	98%	95%	90%	80%	70%	60%	LAST MSR

carbines and pistols, please contact the company directly for the most recent offerings and pricing (see Trademark Index).

Additionally, Century International Arms imports a wide range of accessories, including bayonets, holsters, stocks, magazines, grips, mounts, scopes, misc. parts, new and surplus ammunition, etc., and should be contacted directly (see Trademark Index) for a copy of their most recent catalog, or check their web site for current offerings.

PISTOLS: SEMI-AUTO

Century International Arms Inc. also imports Arcus pistols from Bulgaria and Daewoo pistols from South Korea. Please refer to the individual sections for more information.

M-1911 STYLE PISTOLS – .45 ACP cal., patterned after the Colt Govt. Model 1911, choice of 4 1/4 (Blue Thunder Commodore, Commodore 1911, or GI-Officer's Model) or 5 (SAM Elite/SAM Standard or SAM Chief/Falcon) ported (disc. 2002) or unported barrel, 7 or 8 shot mag., various configurations and finishes, target features are available on select models, approx. 41 oz. Imported from the Phillippines beginning 2001, current mfg. is from Shooter's Arms.

No MSR	$400	$350	$300	$275	$225	$180	$140	

Add $35 for Commodore Blue Thunder Model with squared off trigger guard.

C93 PISTOL – 5.56 NATO or 7.62x39mm (new 2013) cal., patterned after the H&K MP-5 using the roller lock bolt system and fluted chamber, 8 1/2 in. barrel with flash suppressor, adj. rear sight, includes two 40 shot mags., 6.4 lbs. Importation began 2012.

No MSR	$750	$650	$550	$475	$400	$350	$300	

DRACO – 7.62x39mm cal., blonde wood forend, 12 1/4 in. barrel, 30 shot mag., approx. 5 1/2 lbs. Imported 2010-2012.

	$395	$350	$300	$265	$235	$200	$185	*$450*

CENTURION 39 AK PISTOL – 7.62x39mm cal., AK-47 design, features 11 3/8 in. barrel with M16 style birdcage muzzle brake, machined receiver, quad Picatinny rails, Tapco G2 trigger, ergonomic pistol grip, black polymer furniture, 5.4 lbs. Mfg. in the U.S. beginning 2011.

No MSR	$725	$625	$550	$495	$395	$325	$250	

CZ 999/CZ 999 COMPACT – 9mm Para. cal., 3 1/2 (Compact) or 4 1/4 in. barrel, 15 shot double column mag., ambidextrous controls, white dot sights, inertial firing pin, loaded chamber indicator, decocking lever, mfg. by Zastava. Importation began 2013.

As this edition went to press, pricing was not available on this model.

CZ 40/CZ 40 COMPACT – .40 S&W cal., 3 1/2 (Compact) or 4 1/4 in. barrel, 10 shot double column mag., ambidextrous controls, white dot sights, inertial firing pin, loaded chamber indicator, decocking lever, mfg. by Zastava. Importation began 2013.

As this edition went to press, pricing was not available on this model.

M57 – 7.62x25mm Tokarev cal., 4 1/2 in. barrel, Browning blowback action, based on Soviet TT design, 9 shot mag., solid steel, blue finish, factory installed safety, includes extra mag., 23 oz., mfg. by Zastava. Importation began 2013.

No MSR	$250	$225	$195	$175	$140	$115	$90	

M70A – 9mm Para. cal., 4 1/2 in. barrel, Browning blowback action, based on Soviet TT design, 9 shot mag., solid steel, blue finish, factory installed safety, includes extra mag., 23 oz., mfg. by Zastava. Importation began 2013.

No MSR	$250	$225	$195	$175	$140	$115	$90	

PAP M92 PV – 7.62x39mm cal., AK design, 10 in. cold hammer forged barrel, 30 shot mag., dual aperture Krinkov style rear sight, bolt hold-open notch on selector, chrome plated gas piston, steel alloy bolt and barrel, stamped receiver, hinged top cover, 6.6 lbs., mfg. by Zastava. Importation began 2013.

This model is POR.

PAP M85 PV – .223 Rem. cal., AK design, 10 in. cold hammer forged barrel, 30 shot mag., dual aperture Krinkov style rear sight, bolt hold-open notch on selector, chrome plated gas

GRADING - PPGS™	100%	98%	95%	90%	80%	70%	60%	LAST MSR

piston, steel alloy bolt and barrel, stamped receiver, hinged top cover, 6.4 lbs., mfg. by Zastava. Importation began 2013.

This model is POR.

COLEFIRE MAGNUM – 7.62 Tokarev cal., styled after the Sterling Mk7 pistol, manganese phosphate finish coated with black wrinkle paint, enlarged and knurled charging handle, 4 1/2 in. barrel, optional accessory rail. Importation began 2013.

No MSR	$250	$225	$195	$175	$140	$115	$90	

This model does not include a magazine (sold separately).

RIFLES: BOLT ACTION

Century International also imports a complete line of .22 LR and .22 WMR cal. rimfires. MSRs range from $140-$250. Please contact the company directly for current availability and pricing.

M70 – .243 Win., .270 Win., 30-06, .308 Win., 7mm Rem. Mag., or .300 Win. Mag. cal., right or left hand action, 20 or 23.6 in. barrel, 3, 4, or 5 shot integral mag., walnut Monte Carlo or Mannlicher style stock, 7.72 lbs., mfg. by Zastava. Importation began 2013.

No MSR	$400	$350	$300	$275	$225	$180	$140	

Add $40 for Mannlicher stock.
Add $30 for Mag. cals.

M85 "MINI MAUSER" – .223 Rem., 7.62x39mm, or .22 Hornet cal., right or left hand action, 18, 20, or 22 in. barrel, 5 shot integral or detachable (.22 Hornet cal. only) mag., walnut Monte Carlo or Mannlicher style stock, approx. 6.2 lbs., mfg. by Zastava. Importation began 2013.

No MSR	$400	$350	$300	$275	$225	$180	$140	

Add $20 for Mannlicher stock.

RIFLES/CARBINES: SEMI-AUTO

G-3 SPORTER – .308 Win. cal., mfg. from genuine G3 parts, and American made receiver with integrated scope rail, includes 20 shot mag., 19 in. barrel, pistol grip stock, matte black finish, refinished condition only, 9.3 lbs. Imported 1999-2006.

	$785	$685	$590	$535	$430	$355	$275	

FAL SPORTER – .308 Win. cal., U.S. mfg., new barrel receiver, synthetic furniture, 20 shot mag. Imported 2004-2006.

	$850	$745	$635	$580	$465	$380	$295	

CETME SPORTER – .308 Win. cal., new mfg. Cetme action, 19 1/2 in. barrel, 20 shot mag., choice of blue or Mossy Oak Break-Up camo (disc.) metal finish, wood (disc.) or synthetic stock, pistol grip, and vent. forearm, refinished condition only, 9.7 lbs. Imported 2002-2011.

	$550	$475	$400	$350	$300	$275	$250	*$635*

S.A.R. 1 – 7.62x39mm cal., AK-47 styling, 16 1/2 in. barrel, wood stock and forearm, scope rail mounted on receiver, includes one 10 and two 30 shot double stack mags., 7.08 lbs. Mfg. by Romarm of Romania. Importation disc. 2003.

	$750	$655	$560	$510	$410	$335	$260	

S.A.R. 2 – 5.45x39mm cal., AK-47 styling, 16 in. barrel, wood stock and forearm, includes one 10 and one 30 shot double stack mags., 8 lbs. Mfg. by Romarm of Romania. Importation disc. 2003.

	$750	$655	$560	$510	$410	$335	$260	

S.A.R. 3 – .223 Rem. cal., AK-47 styling, 16 in. barrel, wood stock and forearm, includes one 10 and one 30 shot double stack mags., 8 lbs. Mfg. by Romarm of Romania. Importation disc. 2003.

	$750	$655	$560	$510	$410	$335	$260	

GP WASR-10 LO-CAP – 7.62x39mm cal., AK-47 design, 16 1/4 in. barrel, wood stock and forearm, includes one 5 and one 10 shot single stack mags., 7 1/2 lbs. Mfg. by Romarm of Romania. Importation disc. 2011.

	$400	$350	$315	$275	$250	$225	$200	*$450*

GRADING - PPGS™	100%	98%	95%	90%	80%	70%	60%	LAST MSR

GP WASR-10 HIGH-CAP SERIES – 7.62x39mm cal., AK-47 styling, 16 1/4 in. barrel, various configurations, includes two 30 shot double stack mags., 7 1/2 lbs. Mfg. by Romarm of Romania.

No MSR	$440	$385	$325	$300	$240	$200	$150	

Add $10 for bayonet.
Add $133 for 100 shot drum mag.
Add $67 for recoilless buttstock with gun (new 2012).
Add $60 for 50th Anniversary model with Century Arms logo on back right of receiver (only 50 mfg. during 2012).

AK-74 BULLPUP – 5.45x39mm cal., AK-47 design, 16 1/4 in. barrel with muzzle brake, vent. handguard, top Picatinny rail, two 30 shot mags., 7.35 lbs. Limited importation 2010-2011.

	$575	$500	$425	$365	$335	$295	$275	*$650*

AKMS – 7.62x39mm cal., AK-47 design, 16 1/4 in. barrel with muzzle brake, features laminate wood handguards, pistol grip, and steel folding buttstock with skeleton buttplate, includes two 30 shot mags., 7.8 lbs. Importation began 2011.

MSR $700	$625	$550	$500	$425	$350	$275	$225	

L1A1/R1A1 SPORTER – .308 Win. cal., current mfg. receiver patterned after the British L1A1, includes carrying handle, synthetic furniture, 20 shot mag., 22 1/2 in. barrel, fold over aperture rear sight, 9 1/2 lbs. Mfg. in U.S., disc. 2010.

	$975	$850	$750	$650	$575	$500	$450	

Subtract approx. $200 for L1A1 Sporter.

DRAGUNOV – 7.62x54R cal., new CNC milled receiver, Dragunov configuration, thumbhole stock, 26 1/2 in. barrel, supplied with scope and cleaning kit. Mfg. in Romania. Disc. 2010.

	$975	$855	$730	$665	$535	$440	$340	

GOLANI SPORTER – .223 Rem. cal., 21 in. barrel, 35 shot mag., folding stock, optional bayonet lug, approx. 8 lbs., mfg. in Israel.

	$625	$550	$500	$425	$350	$275	$225	*$700*

Add $30 for bayonet lug (disc.).

TANTAL SPORTER – 5.45x39mm cal., 18 in. barrel, parkerized finish, side folding wire stock, flash hider, includes extra mag., 8 lbs.

	$475	$400	$350	$300	$275	$250	$225	*$550*

GORIUNOV SG43 – 7.62x54R cal., copy of Soviet model, gas operated, 28.3 in. barrel, 250 shot belt-fed, charging handle, spade grips, includes wooden crate, folding carriage, 3 ammo belts, 96 lbs. Importation disc. 2011.

	$4,750	$4,200	$3,750	$3,250	$2,650	$2,100	$1,850	*$5,325*

VZ2008 SPORTER – 7.62x39mm cal., copy of the Czech VZ58, 16 1/4 in. barrel, steel receiver, dull matte finish, bead blasted metal parts, wood or plastic buttstock, CA compliant, 7 lbs. Importation disc. 2011.

	$625	$550	$475	$400	$350	$300	$275	*$695*

M-76 SNIPER/SPORTER MODEL – 8mm Mauser cal., semi-auto version of the Yugoslav M76, new U.S. receiver and 21 1/2 in. barrel, includes original scope, mount, and 10 shot mag., 11.3 lbs. Importation disc. 2011.

	$1,495	$1,200	$1,000	$875	$750	$650	$550	*$1,725*

GP 1975 – 7.62x39mm cal., AK-47 design, 16 1/4 in. barrel, black synthetic furniture, new U.S. receiver and barrel, includes two 30 shot mags., approx. 7.4 lbs. Importation disc. 2011.

	$595	$425	$375	$325	$275	$250	$225	*$675*

Add approx. $140 for collapsible stock and Picatinny rail forearm.

DEGTYAREV MODEL – top mounted magazine, semi-auto version of the Soviet model, available in three variations.

GRADING - PPGS™ 100%	98%	95%	90%	80%	70%	60%	LAST MSR

* ***DP 28*** – 7.62x54R cal., 23.8 in. barrel, gas operated, 47 shot drum mag., full shoulder stock.

$3,500	$3,060	$2,625	$2,380	$1,925	$1,575	$1,225	

* ***DPM 28*** – 7.62x54R cal., 23.8 in. barrel, gas operated, 47 shot drum mag., pistol grip stock.

$3,500	$3,060	$2,625	$2,380	$1,925	$1,575	$1,225	

* ***DTX Tank Model*** – 7.62x54R cal., 23.8 in. barrel, 50 shot drum mag., collapsible stock, approx. 10 lbs.

$3,500	$3,060	$2,625	$2,380	$1,925	$1,575	$1,225	

STERLING SA – 9mm Para. cal., semi-auto version of the Sterling submachine gun, 16 1/4 in. barrel, American made receiver and barrel, original style crinkle painted finish, folding stock, includes two 34 shot mags., available in Type I or Type II.

$475	$400	$360	$330	$295	$275	$250	*$550*

C15A1 SPORTER – 5.56 NATO cal., AR-15 style, based on M16A1, triangular "Vietnam era" style handguard, 16 in. barrel with muzzle brake, fixed stock, includes two original Colt 30 shot mags. (disc. 2011) or fixed 10 shot mag. (current mfg.), choice of green polymer or walnut wood furniture, A3 carry handle and sights. Importation began mid-2010.

This model is POR.

Add 15% for High Cap Mag. model

CENTURION 39 SPORTER – 7.62x39mm cal., 16 1/2 in. barrel, V-shape Chevron compensator, black finish, fixed buttstock with pistol grip, four Picatinny rails, includes two 30 shot mags., 8.2 lbs. All parts mfg. in U.S. beginning mid-2010.

This model is POR.

AES10-B RPK STYLE – 7.62x39mm cal., 23 1/8 in. heavy barrel with folding bipod, laminated stock and forend, includes two AK style 40 shot mags., 10.9 lbs. Imported 2012.

$575	$500	$450	$400	$375	$350	$325	*$675*

DPM – 7.62x54R cal., semi-auto closed bolt copy of the WWII Soviet machine gun, 47 shot pan magazine mounted on top of receiver, 23.8 in. barrel, includes upper bipod, adj. sights, wood furniture, blued metal, 18 1/2 lbs. w/out mag. Imported 2011-2012.

$1,775	$1,575	$1,350	$1,150	$950	$750	$675	*$2,000*

CENTURION UC-9 CARBINE – 9mm Para. cal., patterned after the Israeli sub-machine gun, straight blowback action, 16 in. barrel, blue finish, closed bolt, folding steel stock, includes two 32 shot all steel double column mag., approx. 9 lbs. Importation began mid-2012.

This model is POR.

M70 AB2 – 7.62x39mm cal., based on Yugoslavian Paratrooper model, 16 1/4 in. barrel, includes two 30 shot double stack mags., classic wood furniture or black polymer upper and lower handguards, under folding stock, slant brake, bayonet lug, approx. 7 1/2 lbs. Limited importation beginning 2013.

This model is POR.

PAP SERIES – 7.62x39 or 7.62x51mm cal., 16 1/4 in. cold hammer forged barrel, choice of classic wood stock with pistol grip, black thumbhole stock with polymer handguard, or T6 collapsible stock with plastic handguard, 10 or 30 shot mag., accessory rail, 7.7-8 lbs. Mfg. by Zastava. Importation began 2013.

This series is POR.

PAP M77 PS – 308 Win. cal., 16 1/4 in. cold hammer forged barrel, 30 shot mag., black polymer thumbhole stock with upper and lower handguard, Picatinny rail, dust cover, mfg. by Zastava. Importation began 2013.

This model is POR.

RIFLES: SLIDE ACTION

PAR 1 OR 3 – 7.62x39mm (PAR 1) or .223 Rem. (PAR 3) cal., AK receiver styling, 10 shot mag., accepts double stack AK magazines, wood stock, pistol grip, and forearm, 20.9 in.

GRADING - PPGS™	100%	98%	95%	90%	80%	70%	60%	LAST MSR

barrel, 7.6 lbs. Mfg. by PAR, and imported 2002-2009.

	$360	$300	$275	$250	$225	$200	$175	

SHOTGUNS

ARTHEMIS (SUPER ARTHEMIS) O/U – 12, 20, 28 (new 2004) ga. or .410 bore, 3 in. chambers, 28 in. VR barrels, SST, extractors, checkered walnut stock and forearm, 5.3-7.4 lbs. Mfg. by Khan in Turkey, importation disc.

	$450	$395	$335	$305	$245	$200	$155	

Add $25 for 20 ga. or 28 ga.
Add $50 for .410 bore.

PHANTOM SEMI-AUTO – 12 ga. only, 3 in. chamber, 24, 26, or 28 in. VR barrels with 3 choke tubes, black synthetic stock and forearm. Mfg. in Turkey, importation disc.

	$265	$230	$200	$180	$145	$120	$95	

SAS-12 SEMI-AUTO – 12 ga. only, 2 3/4 in. chamber, detachable 3 (Type II) or 5 shot mag., black synthetic stock and forearm, 22 or 23 1/2 in. barrel. Mfg. by PRC in China.

	$225	$195	$170	$155	$125	$100	$80	

Add approx. $25 for ghost ring rear with blade front or bead sight.

JW-2000 COACH SxS – 12, 20 ga., or .410 bore (disc. 2012), exposed hammers, 20 in. barrels, DTs, steel contruction, checkered walnut stock and forearm, includes sling swivels. Mfg. in China.

No MSR	$240	$210	$180	$165	$125	$110	$85	

MODEL IJ2 SLIDE ACTION – 12 ga. only, 2 3/4 or 3 in. chamber, 19 in. barrel with ghost ring sights or fiber optic front sights, fixed choke only, 7.2 lbs. Mfg. in China.

	$200	$175	$150	$135	$110	$90	$70	

ULTRA 87 SLIDE ACTION – 12 ga., 3 in. chamber, 19 in. barrel with iron sights, optional pistol grip, metal heatshield (disc.), fixed black synthetic (current mfg.) or side folding (disc.) stock, 8.2 lbs.

	$185	$160	$145	$130	$115	$100	$90	*$200*

Add $65 for extra 28 in. barrel.

MKA 1919 – 12 ga., AR-15 style, gas operation, aluminum alloy upper, one piece polymer lower receiver, pistol grip fixed stock, matte black or 100% camo finish, right side magwell mag. release, bolt stop, 5 shot detachable mag., removable carry handle, three internal chokes, integral Picatinny rail, approx. 6 1/2 lbs. Imported from Turkey beginning mid-2012.

No MSR	$750	$650	$575	$500	$425	$325	$275	

CENTURY MFG., INC.

Previous manufacturer located in Knightstown, IN, Feb. 2002-late 2004. Previously manufactured in Evansville and Greenfield, IN 1973-circa 1999. Consumer direct and dealer sales.

This revolver design was originally manufactured in 1972 by Russell Wilson, who sandcasted the bronze frame (cloned from the Colt SAA configuration) in Evansville, IN. Gene Phelps purchased the manufacturing rights for this gun and formed a partnership with Earl Keller to produce a redesigned frame, also using sandcast bronze.

The original Century revolver was made in Evansville, IN beginning in 1973 (1973 was the 100th anniversary of the .45-70 Govt. cartridge - hence the term Century) and production was halted in 1976 at ser. no. 524. In late 1976, Phelps and Keller (the two original partners on the venture) dissolved their partnership and each began manufacturing their own version of the .45-70 revolver. Gene Phelps completely redesigned the gun's interior and began manufacturing the Heritage I, with an investment-cast steel frame, and without the Century's novel cross-bolt safety. Keller's Century Manufacturing, Inc. continued to produce the original Century, with some design refinements, and in 1985 the company was purchased by Dr. Paul Majors, who died in Dec. of 2001.

The most recent Century revolver featured a manganese bronze frame and other components in addition to having a cross-bolt safety. They were produced in .45-70 and

GRADING - PPGS™	100%	98%	95%	90%	80%	70%	60%	LAST MSR

various other cals., in Greenfield, IN. Earl Keller died in 1986. The second series was made in Greenfield, IN with limited production resuming in 1986. Earlier handmade "Evansville" Model 100s (disc.) are currently selling for between $2,500-$3,500, depending on the region.

In Feb. 2002, Century Mfg. was purchased by Dave Lukens and Jeff Yelton and moved to Knightstown, IN. New production guns also included a revolving rifle built on the Model 100 frame. These new production guns carried a limited lifetime guarantee.

REVOLVERS

Less than 3,000 Model 100s were manufactured 1976-2001. The values below are for .45-70 Govt. cal. Other calibers were priced from $2,000 on up.

MODEL 100 – .30-30 Win. (new 1987), .375 Win. (new 1986), .444 Marlin (new 1986), .45-70 Govt., .50-70 Govt. (new 1987), or .50-110 cal., single action 6 shot, manganese bronze frame, steel cylinder, 6 1/2, 8, 10, or 12 (disc.) in. round or octagon barrel, unique crossbolt safety that locks the hammer, adj. sights, walnut grips, 5 lbs. 14 oz. Disc. 2000, reintroduced 2002-2004.

* ***Model 100 .45-70 Govt. and other cals.*** – includes all cals. except .50-110.

	100%	98%	95%	90%	80%	70%	60%	LAST MSR
	$1,295	$1,100	$995	$900	$850	$800	$750	

Last MSR (2002-2004) was $1,295.
Previous mfg. last MSR was $2,000.

Add $200 for calibers other than .45-70 Govt.
Add $110 for normal octagon barrel.
Add $200 for stainless steel fabrication.

* ***Model 100 .50-110 cal.***

	100%	98%	95%	90%	80%	70%	60%	LAST MSR
	$2,895	$2,350	$1,950	$1,700	$1,500	$1,250	$1,025	*$2,895*

CHAMPLIN FIREARMS, INC.

Current custom manufacturer, gunsmith, and importer located in Enid, OK. Champlin Firearms was established in 1966. Direct sales only.

Champlin Firearms, Inc. manufactures handcrafted rifles built around a patented bolt action of their own design and manufacture. Most guns are built per individual customer order and specifications. Values will vary greatly depending on the configuration, desirability, and special order specifications. All Champlin rifles are built along classic lines with best quality wood and exemplary workmanship. They have been used successfully on safaris and have shot dangerous game throughout the world.

Champlin Firearms, Inc. also inventories a wide selection of high grade, top-quality shotguns and rifles (especially top trademark doubles and bolt actions). Contact George Caswell (owner) directly for a current listing (please refer to Trademark Index). Additional services include a complete gunsmithing service for all grades of English double rifles and shotguns. Custom stocks are also built to individual customer specifications. All double rifles are test fired and checked thoroughly upon completion of manufacture or repair. Again, Champlin Firearms should be contacted for consultation and quotation regarding this additional work.

RIFLES: BOLT ACTION

BOLT ACTION RIFLE – various cals., round or octagon barrel, adj. trigger, each rifle is built to customer specifications. Values below represent base gun with standard wood, no options, and no engraving.

	100%	98%	95%	90%	80%	70%	60%	LAST MSR
	$8,500	$8,000	$7,000	$6,750	$6,000	$5,250	$4,500	*$8,500*

CHAPARRAL ARMS

Current trademark of firearms manufactured in Brescia, Italy. Previously imported circa 2010-2011 by Chapparal Firearms Inc., located in Melbourne, FL. Previously imported by Tristar, located in Kansas City, MO, by Charter 2000, located in Shelton, CT, and K.B.I., located in Harrisburg, PA

Chaparral Arms manufactures quality reproductions of the Winchester Model 1866, 1873, 1876, Colt 1878, and Sharps 1874 rifles, and Colt 1873 SAA revolvers.

GRADING - PPGS™	100%	98%	95%	90%	80%	70%	60%	LAST MSR

RIFLES: LEVER ACTION, REPRODUCTIONS

MODEL 1866 – .357 Mag./.38 Spl. or .45 LC cal., 19 (round barrel carbine), 20 or 24 (octagon rifle) in. barrel. Imported late 2007-2008.

	$695	$625	$550	$475	$425	$375	$325	*$800*

MODEL 1873 – .357 Mag., .38-40 WCF, .44-40 WCF, or .45 LC cal., patterned after the Model 1873 Winchester, uncheckered straight grip stock, case colored frame, choice of 19 in. round (carbine), 20 or 24 in. octagon barrel. Imported late 2006-2008.

	$895	$775	$675	$600	$525	$450	$375	*$1,050*

MODEL 1876 – .40-60, .45-60, .45-75, or .50-95 (new 2008) cal., patterned after the Model 1876 Winchester, uncheckered straight grip stock and forearm, case colored frame, 22, 26, or 28 in. octagon barrel. Imported late 2006-2008.

	$1,095	$950	$850	$750	$650	$550	$450	*$1,250*

Add $100 for NWMP (Northwest Mounted Police) carbine with 22 in. barrel, and full length forearms, .45-75 cal. only.

CHAPUIS ARMES

Current manufacturer located in St. Bonnet Le Chateau, France. Currently imported by William Larkin Moore, located in Scottsdale AZ, Evolution USA, located in White Bird, ID, and Heirloom Armes, located in Howard Lake, MN. Previously imported by Chadick's, Ltd. (limited importation) located in Terrell, TX, by GSI, Inc. located in Trussville, AL until 1995 and by Armes De Chasse located in Chadds Ford, PA until 1993.

Chapuis rifles and shotguns are manufactured on a limited basis. Most of their emphasis is on high-quality double rifles and shotguns.

Importers have also had guns built to their own individual specifications and may have used different model names.

For further information regarding this respected French trademark, please contact the importers (see Trademark Index).

RIFLES: BOLT ACTION

Chapuis manufactures a high quality bolt action rifle in three configurations - Classic, Luxus, and Ambassaduer. Please contact the importers directly for pricing, availability, delivery time and available options (see Trademark Index).

RIFLES: O/U

SUPER ORION C15 MODEL – .300 Win. Mag. or .375 H&H cal., notched boxlock action with ejectors, coin finish only, 23.6 in. barrels with quarter rib, engraved action, approx. 8 lbs. Imported 1995-96.

	$8,250	$7,150	$6,250	$5,400	$4,200	$3,500	$3,150	*$9,195*

Add $2,900 for .375 H&H cal.

SUPER ORION C5 – 9.3x74R, 8x57 JRS, 7x65 R, .30-06, or 30R Blaser cal., 21 1/2 in. barrels, scalloped action, extractors, interchangeable recoil/headspace plate, AA fancy checkered walnut stock with pistol grip, drilled and tapped, alloy receiver with floral border and game scene engraving, DT or SST, fiber optic battue rear sight, walnut checkered buttplate, 6.8 lbs.

Please contact the importer directly for pricing on this model.

SUPER ORION C10 – 9.3x74R, 8x57 JRS, 7x65 R, .30-06, 30R Blaser, .300 Win. Mag., or .375 H&H cal., similar to Super Orion C5, except has ejectors and AAA grade fancy walnut stock, 6.8 lbs.

Please contact the importer directly for pricing on this model.

SUPER ORION C15 (CURRENT MFG.) – 9.3x74R, 8x57 JRS, 7x65 R, .30-06, 30R Blaser, .300 Win. Mag., or .375 H&H cal., similar to Super Orion C10, except has delicate rose and scroll engraving, AAAA fancy fine checkered walnut pistol grip stock with German style cheeckpiece, engraved steel grip cap, lengthened trigger guard, approx. 7 lbs.

Please contact the importer directly for pricing on this model.

GRADING - PPGS™	100%	98%	95%	90%	80%	70%	60%	LAST MSR

SUPER ORION C25 – 9.3x74R, 8x57 JRS, 7x65 R, .30-06, 30R Blaser, .300 Win. Mag., or .375 H&H cal., similar to Super Orion C15, except has sideplates with floral border motifs and game scenes, AAAA fine checkered walnut pistol grip stock with cheekpiece, approx. 7 lbs.

Please contact the importer directly for pricing on this model.

SUPER ORION EXPRESS – 9.3x74R, 8x57 JRS, 7x65 R, .30-06, 30R Blaser, or .300 Win. cal., 22 in. barrels, scalloped action, ejectors, interchangeable recoil/headspace plate, AAAAAA fancy checkered Circassian walnut stock with pistol grip and German style cheekpiece, drilled and tapped, alloy receiver with deep relief hand bulino style engraving, available in Excellence or Prestige configuration, approx. 7 lbs.

Please contact the importer directly for pricing on this model.

RIFLES: SxS

William Larkin Moore also has The Artisan Express Series III ($14,600 MSR), the Imperial Express (last MSR was $21,500 importation disc. 2010). Please contact them directly for more information.

RGEX EXPRESS MODEL – .30-30 Win., .30-06, .30R Blaser, .300 Win. Mag. (disc.), 7x65R, 8x57JRS, or 9.3x74R cal., double rifle, ejectors, boxlock action, 23.6 in. barrels, deluxe checkered walnut stock with cheekpiece, full line of options are available, 7 lbs. 6 oz. Limited importation beginning 1998.

MSR $7,625	$7,100	$6,450	$5,850	$5,350	$4,900	$4,450	$3,850

Add $390 for .30-06 or .30R Blaser cal.
Add $375 for round body (available in .30-30 Win. cal. only).
Add approx. $700 for .300 Win. Mag. cal. (disc.).
Add approx. 60% for HGEX Express Supreme Model (engraved, not avail. in .300 Win. Mag. cal.), disc.
Add 110% for HGEX Express Imperial Model (scroll engraved, not avail. in .300 Win. Mag. cal.), disc.

RGEX SERIES 3 – 9.3x74R, 8x57 JRS, 7x57R, 6.5x57R, or .30-30 Win. cal., similar to RGEX, except has hand engraved sideplates with deep relief engraving in "Royal" style game scenes, AAAA fancy walnut pistol grip stock and forearm with English style cheekpiece, hand rubbed oil finish, DT, approx. 6 lbs. New 2010.

MSR $8,140	$7,700	$6,875	$6,100	$5,250	$4,500	$3,750	$2,950

UGEX UTILITY GRADE EXPRESS – similar to RGEX, except has select walnut. New 1998.

MSR $6,515	$6,000	$5,475	$4,700	$4,000	$3,500	$2,950	$2,550

Add $500 for .300 Win. Mag. cal.

AFRICAN P.H. (PROFESSIONAL HUNTER) GRADE I – .30-06, .300 Win. Mag., .375 H&H, .416 Rigby, 9.3x74R, or .470 NE cal., notched boxlock action with English scroll border engraving, case colored receiver, selective ejectors, deluxe walnut stock with English cheekpiece.

MSR N/A	$10,500	$9,350	$8,475	$7,500	$6,500	$5,650	$4,600

Add $3,570 for .470 NE cal.
Add $3,099 for .416 Rigby cal.
Values are for .375 H&H or .300 Win. Mag cal. This model was previously designated Express Agex Brousse.

* ***African PH Grade II*** – similar to Grade I, except has master signed scroll engraving with game scene on bottom of coin finished receiver.

MSR N/A	$18,500	$15,250	$12,000	$10,000	$8,000	$7,000	$6,000

Values above assume .470 NE cal. Subtract for smaller cals.

BROUSSE SAFARI EXPRESS – .300 Win. Mag., .375 H&H, .416 Rigby, .450-400 NE, or .470 NE cal., similar to Grade I Professional Hunter, except has full rose and scroll engraving coverage on coin finished receiver. New 1998.

The current MSR on this model is $10,950.
Add $1,520 for .450-400 NE cal.
Add $2,900 for .470 NE cal.

GRADING - PPGS™	100%	98%	95%	90%	80%	70%	60%	LAST MSR

SAVANE MODEL – .30-06, .300 Win. Mag., .375 H&H, .416 R Chapuis (disc.), .416 Rigby, .470 NE, or 9.3x74R cal., deluxe version of the Agex Jungle, except has hand-engraved game scenes on action sides and Cape Buffalo head on floorplate of action, case colored (disc.) or coin finish.

The current MSR on this model is $23,000.
Add $2,000 for .470 NE cal.
Add $3,000 for .416 Rigby cal.
MSR is for .375 H&H cal.

JUNGLE SAFARI DELUXE EXPRESS – .30-06, .300 Win. Mag., .375 H&H, .416 R Chapuis (mfg. 1993- 96), .470 NE (new 1992), or 9.3x74R cal., boxlock action, case colored (disc.) or coin finish, special reinforced receiver with double underbites, 25 5/8 in. barrels, fine English scroll engraving with 3 African animals, ejectors, select French walnut with compartment in pistol grip cap.

The current MSR on this model in .470 NE cal. is $20,950.

* ***Jungle Second Grade*** – features elaborate engraving and best quality wood. Disc. 1996.

$26,000	**$22,500**	**$19,000**	**$16,000**	**$13,000**	**$10,000**	**$8,750**	***$29,395***

Add $3,900 for .470 NE cal.

EXPRESS AGEX AFRICA – same cals. as Jungle, notched boxlock action, master signed scroll engraving and African game scenes, selective ejectors, cased. Importation disc. 1994.

$19,250	**$17,750**	**$15,250**	**$13,500**	**$11,250**	**$10,000**	**$9,000**	***$20,954***

Add $2,896 for .470 NE cal.
Add $5,626 for .416 R Chapuis cal.

EXPRESS AGEX SAFARI – similar to AGEX Africa, except has top-of-the-line engraving and wood. Importation disc. 1994.

$29,000	**$26,550**	**$22,350**	**$19,150**	**$16,950**	**$14,000**	**$12,000**	***$30,375***

Add $2,040 for .470 NE cal.
Add $5,134 for .416 R Chapuis cal.

RIFLES: SINGLE SHOT

OURAL SERIES – .270 Win., .300 Win. Mag., 7mm Rem. Mag. cal., notched boxlock action, English scroll engraving, extractors, 23 5/8 in. barrel, fitted and engraved scope mounts. Importation disc. 1994, reintroduced 1999.

Add approx. 20% for Oural Luxe Model (features better engraving and wood).
Add approx. 58% for Oural Elite Model (features game scene engraving and presentation walnut).
Current pricing on this model is POR.

SHOTGUNS: RECENT IMPORTATION

SPORTING CLAYS MODEL O/U – 12 or 20 (3 in. Mag.) ga., scalloped boxlock action, 27 1/2 or 30 in. VR barrels, ST, case colored receiver with English scroll engraving. Limited importation 1997-98.

$3,675	**$3,300**	**$2,900**	**$2,500**	**$2,100**	**$1,675**	**$1,300**	***$3,995***

SUPER ORION SERIES O/U – 12, 16, 20, or 28 ga., various barrel lengths, round action, ejectors, available in C135 Artisan Upland, C140 Artisan Upland, C145 Artisan Woodcock, or C165 Woodcock configuration, hand carved and sculpted receiver with hand engraved bulino style game scenes, AAAAA grade English style straight grip checkered Circassian walnut stock, DT, C140 and C145 has sideplates, 5.7 - 6.6 lbs.

This model is not being imported currently.

SUPER ORION MODEL C30/C35/C60/C65 O/U – 12, 16, or 20 ga., available in Upland, Field, or Woodcock configuration, 23, 26, or 27 1/2 in. barrels, extractors (C30 or C60) or ejectors (C35 or C65), straight grip hand rubbed oil finish AA (C30 or C60) or AAA (C35 or C65) fancy checkered walnut stock, DT, scalloped and sculpted all steel action, alloy receiver with English style floral border and game scene engraving, fixed or interchangeable chokes.

These models are not being imported currently.

GRADING - PPGS™	100%	98%	95%	90%	80%	70%	60%	LAST MSR

SUPER ORION MODEL C40/C45 O/U – 12, 16, or 20 ga., similar to C35 and C65, except has engraved sideplates, ejectors, hand rubbed oil finish straight grip English style checkered AAAA fancy walnut stock.

These models are not being imported currently.

SUPER ORION UPLAND/WOODCOCK O/U – 12, 16, 20, or 28 ga., various barrel lengths, ejectors, available in C235, C240, or C245 Upland or Woodcock configuration, hand sculpted scalloped action, full coverage bulino style hand engraving, AAAAAA fancy grade English style Circassian walnut stock with hand checkering, 5.7 - 6.6. lbs.

These models are not being imported currently.

LUXUS/ROYAL SxS – 12, 16, or 20 ga., ejectors, various barrel lengths, available in Upland or Woodcock configuration, hand sculpted scalloped action, full coverage bulino style hand engraving, AAAAAA fancy grade English style Circassian walnut stock with hand checkering, approx. 6 lbs.

The current MSR on this model is $9,500.

Add $3,500 for Royal Model with sideplates.

These models are currently being imported by Heirloom Armes.

ST. BONNET MODEL SxS – 12, 16, or 20 (3 in. Mag.) ga., boxlock with case colored (disc.) or coin finished sideplates featuring fine English scroll (disc.) or game scene engraving, 27 1/2 in. monobloc barrels, DTs, ejectors, checkered straight grip walnut stock and forearm, hardshell case. Limited importation began 1997.

This model has not been imported recently, and needs to be individually appraised.

RGP/BLE MODEL SxS – 16 or 20 ga., boxlock action, semi-beavertail foream, concave rib, coin finished receiver with fine rose and scroll engraving. Importation began 2005.

MSR $3,600	$3,300	$2,775	$2,350	$2,050	$1,800	$1,600	$1,400

Add $625 for 20 ga.

RGP ARTISAN – 12, 16, or 20 ga., similar to UGP Model, except has ejectors and AAA fancy walnut stock. New 2010.

The current MSR on this model is $5,525.

This model is being imported by both William Larkin Moore and Heirloom Armes.

RP ARTISAN – similar to RGP Artisan, except is boxlock with sideplates and floral borders and bulino game scene.

The current MSR on this model is $7,000.

This model is currently being imported by Heirloom Armes.

RP ROUND DESIGN – 12, 16, or 20 ga., similar to RGP Model, except has engraved sideplates with English style game scene engraving, AAAA fancy walnut hand rubbed oil finish English style stock with cheekpiece. New 2010.

The current MSR on this model is $3,600.

This model is imported by Heirloom Armes.

UGP ROUND DESIGN SxS – 12, 16, or 20 ga., available in Upland, Field, or Woodcock configuration, 23, 26, or 27 1/2 in. barrels, extractors, straight grip hand rubbed oil finish AA fancy checkered walnut stock, splinter forend, recessed locking lever, DT, alloy receiver with English style game scene engraving, fixed or interchangeable chokes. New 2010.

This model is not being imported currently.

C50 COMBINATION GUN – 12, 16, or 20 ga. over 9.3x74R, 8x57 JRS, 7x65R, or 6.5x57R cal., scalloped and sculpted all steel action, engraved English style floral borders and game scenes.

This model is not being imported currently.

CHAPUIS, P. ETS

Previous manufacturer located in Saint-Bonnet le Chateau, France.

P. Chapuis specialized in custom order rifles and shotguns. This company developed a process to color the receiver sideplates while using traditional engraving techniques - resulting in a unique 3-D scene. This is a different company than Chapuis Armes.

GRADING - PPGS™	100%	98%	95%	90%	80%	70%	60%	LAST MSR

CHARLES DALY

See Daly, Charles listing in the D section.

CHARLIN ARMS

Previous manufacturer located in St. Etienne, France.

Charlin Arms previously made shotguns which were patterned after Darne firearms. Typically, they are very high quality and values seem to approximate the Darne guns. Once you have determined the comparable model in Darne, please refer to Darne.

CHARTER ARMS

Previously manufactured by Charco, Inc. located in Ansonia, CT 1992-1996. Previously manufactured by Charter Arms located in Stratford, CT 1964-1991.

The company's first model was the Undercover.

PISTOLS: SEMI-AUTO

MODEL 40 – .22 LR cal. only, double action semi-auto, 3.3 in. barrel, 8 shot mag., 21 1/2 oz., fixed sights, stainless steel. Mfg. 1984-86.

$265 $240 $220 $170 $135 $125 $105 ***$319***

MODEL 79K – .32 or .380 ACP cal., double action semi-auto, 3.6 in. barrel, 7 shot mag., 24 1/2 oz., fixed sights, stainless steel. Mfg. 1984-86.

$325 $300 $280 $230 $200 $170 $145 ***$390***

EXPLORER II & S II PISTOL – .22 LR cal., semi-auto survival pistol, barrel unscrews, 8 shot mag., black, gold (disc.), silvertone, or camouflage finish, 6, 8, or 10 in. barrels, simulated walnut grips. Disc. 1986.

$90 $80 $70 $60 $55 $50 $45 ***$109***

This model uses a modified AR-7 action.

Manufacture of this model was by Survival Arms located in Cocoa, FL.

MODEL 42T (COMPETITION II TARGET) – .22 LR cal. only, single action, 5.9 in. barrel, target model with checkered walnut grips, adj. sights, blue finish only. Mfg. 1984-85 only.

$490 $450 $395 $350 $300 $260 $220 ***$599***

REVOLVERS: DOUBLE ACTION

All Charter Arms revolvers had a hammer block safety system, 8 groove rifling, unbreakable beryllium copper firing pin, triple safety features, no sideplate, steel frames, and lifetime warranty to the original owner.

BONNIE & CLYDE SET – .32 H&R Mag. (Bonnie) and .38 Spl. (Clyde) cal., matched pair, 6 shot, 2 1/2 in. fully shrouded barrel, wood laminate grips (color coordinated), blue finish, pistols individually marked "Bonnie" or "Clyde" on barrels, supplied with gun rugs. Mfg. 1989-91.

$425 $365 $335 $295 $260 $240 $220

LADY ON DUTY – .32 S&W or .38 Spl. cal., 5 (.38 Spl.) or 6 shot, 2 in. shrouded barrel, fixed sights, rose neoprene grips, cased. Mfg. 1995-96.

$195 $165 $145 $130 $115 $100 $85 ***$219***

PATHFINDER – .22 LR or .22 WMR (disc. 1989) cal., 6 shot, 2, 3, or 6 (disc. 1985) in. barrels, round butt, adj. sights, walnut grips, wide trigger and spur hammer. Disc. 1990.

$185 $150 $125 $110 $90 $70 $50

* ***Pathfinder - Square Butt*** – .22 LR or .22 WMR (disc. 1989) cal., 6 in. barrel, square butt, otherwise similar to Pathfinder. Disc. 1990.

  $190 $155 $125 $110 $90 $70 $50

* ***Pathfinder Stainless*** – .22 LR or .22 WMR (disc. 1989) cal., stainless variation, 3 1/2 in. shrouded barrel. Disc. 1990.

  $185 $150 $130 $105 $90 $75 $70

GRADING - PPGS™	100%	98%	95%	90%	80%	70%	60%	LAST MSR

UNDERCOVER – .32 S&W (disc. 1989) or .38 Spl. cal., 5 shot in .38 Spl., 6 shot in .32 S&W, 2 (.38 Spl.) or 3 in. barrel, wide trigger and spur hammer, fixed sights, .38 Spl. was also available with pocket hammer. Disc. 1991.

$175 $145 $115 $100 $90 $85 $80

* ***Undercover Stainless*** – 2 in. shrouded barrel only. Disc. 1994.

$260 $195 $140 $110 $95 $80 $70 ***$304***

UNDERCOVERETTE – .32 S&W Long cal., similar to Undercover, 6 shot, 2 in. barrel, blue. Disc.

$155 $140 $110 $100 $90 $70 $55

BULLDOG – .44 Spl. cal., 5 shot, 2 1/2 or 3 (disc. 1988) in. barrels, wide trigger and spur or pocket hammer, checkered bulldog grips (walnut or neoprene), blue or electroless nickel finish. Disc. 1991, reinstated 1994. Disc. 1996.

$225 $195 $155 $125 $110 $90 $70 ***$268***

Add $22 for electroless nickel finish.

* ***Bulldog Stainless*** – 2 1/2 in. bull or 3 (disc. 1989) in. regular barrel. Disc. 1991.

$195 $155 $125 $100 $85 $70 $65

* ***Bulldog Target*** – .357 Mag. or .44 Spl. cal., 5 shot, 4 in. shrouded barrel, adj. sights, square butt only, blue finish. Mfg. 1976-1988.

$225 $150 $125 $100 $85 $70 $65 ***$255***

Subtract $10 for .357 Mag. cal.

* ***Bulldog Stainless Target*** – 9mm Federal, .357 Mag., or .44 Spl. cal., 5 shot, 5 1/2 in. shrouded VR barrel, adj. sights, square butt target grips only, matte finished, 28 oz. Mfg. 1989-91.

$250 $175 $125 $100 $85 $70 $65

BULLDOG PUG – .44 Spl. cal., 5 shot, 2 1/2 in. shrouded barrel, fixed sights, walnut or neoprene grips. Mfg. 1986-93.

$240 $195 $160 $130 $110 $100 $90 ***$279***

* ***Bulldog Pug Stainless*** – 2 1/2 in. shrouded barrel. Mfg. 1987-93.

$300 $235 $175 $135 $115 $100 $85 ***$334***

BULLDOG TRACKER – .357 Mag. (.38 Spl.) cal., 5 shot, 2 1/2, 4 (disc. 1989), and 6 (disc. 1989) in. bull barrels, adj. sights, blue only, checkered bulldog grips, square butt on 4 or 6 in. barrel only. Disc. 1986, reintroduced 1989-91.

$185 $150 $125 $110 $100 $90 $80

MAGNUM PUG – .357 Mag. cal., 5 shot, fixed sights, 2.2 in. shrouded barrel, blue finish. Mfg. 1995-96.

$225 $195 $155 $125 $110 $90 $70 ***$268***

POLICE BULLDOG – .32 H&R Mag., .38 Spl., or .44 Spl. cal., 5 (.44 Spl. only) or 6 shot, fixed sights, blue only, 3 1/2 or 4 in. barrel, Neoprene grips or square butt (.44 Spl. only). Disc. 1991.

$175 $140 $120 $105 $95 $85 $75

Add $20 for either .44 Spl. cal or 3 1/2 in. shrouded barrel.

* ***Bulldog Stainless Police*** – .32 Mag., .357 Mag. (new 1989), .38 Spl. (disc. 1988 - reintroduced 1990), or .44 Spl. (new 1989) cal., 5 (.357 Mag. or .44 Spl.) or 6 (.32 Mag. or .38 Spl.) shot, square butt, 3 1/2 or 4 in. shrouded barrel. Mfg. 1987-91.

$195 $160 $150 $140 $115 $95 $80

Add $20 for .357 Mag. or .44 Special cal.

Neoprene grips are standard on these models except for the .357 Mag. (square butt).

POLICE UNDERCOVER – .32 H&R Mag. or .38 Spl. cal., 6 shot, spur or pocket hammer, 2.2 in. shrouded barrel, checkered walnut grips, fixed sights, blue or electroless nickel (new 1994) finish. Disc. 1996.

$205 $175 $145 $120 $100 $85 $75 ***$238***

Add $14 for electroless nickel finish.

GRADING - PPGS™	100%	98%	95%	90%	80%	70%	60%	LAST MSR

* ***Police Undercover Stainless*** – similar to Police Undercover. Disc. 1993.

	$240	$185	$150	$120	$105	$90	$80	$276

OFF DUTY – .22 LR (new 1993), .22 WMR (new 1994), or .38 Spl. cal., 5 (.38 Spl.) or 6 (.22 LR) shot, 2 in. barrel, fixed sights, conventional or DA only, blue, matte black (disc.), or electroless nickel (new 1994) finish. Disc. 1996.

	$170	$145	$120	$105	$90	$85	$80	$200

Add $39 for electroless nickel finish.
Add $7 for double action only.

* ***Off Duty Stainless*** – similar to Off Duty. Disc. 1993.

	$235	$180	$145	$115	$100	$85	$75	$268

PIT BULL – 9mm Federal (rare), .357 Mag. (disc. 1989), or .38 Spl. (disc. 1989) cal., 5 shot, 2 1/2, 3 1/2, or 4 (disc. 1989) in. full shrouded barrel, Neoprene grips, approx. 26 oz. Mfg. 1989-91.

	$230	$180	$150	$125	$115	$100	$90	

* ***Pit Bull Stainless*** – 2 1/2 or 3 1/2 in. shrouded barrel. Disc. 1991.

	$240	$190	$155	$125	$115	$100	$90	

RIFLES: SEMI-AUTO

AR-7 EXPLORER RIFLE – .22 LR cal., takedown, barreled action stores in Cycolac synthetic stock, 8 shot mag., adj. sights, 16 in. barrel, black finish on AR-7, silvertone on AR-7S. Camouflage finish new 1986 (AR-7C). Mfg. until 1990.

	$125	$100	$85	$75	$65	$55	$50	$146

In 1990, the manufacturing of this model was taken over by Survival Arms located in Cocoa, FL. Current mfg. AR-7 rifles will be found under the Henry Repeating Arms Company and AR- 7 Industries.

CHARTER ARMS (CURRENT MFG.)

Current manufacturer located in Shelton, CT established during 1998. Previously marketed and distributed mid-2005-late 2010 by MKS Supply, Inc., located in Dayton, OH. Previous company name was Charter 2000, Inc. Dealer sales only.

Charter 2000, Inc. acquired the rights to reproduce the original Charter Arms Undercover Model. Otherwise, it is not affiliated with Charter Arms in any way, nor is it responsible for repair or service on older Charter Arms handguns.

DERRINGERS

DIXIE DERRINGER – .22 LR or .22 WMR cal., 5 shot, 1 1/8 in. barrel, choice of black frame with stainless cylinder (new 2011), or all stainless construction, spur trigger, hardwood grips, 6 oz. New 2002.

MSR $211	$180	$155	$130	$110	$90	$75	$65	

Add $10 for .22 WMR or black frame with stainless cylinder.
Add $53 for combo cylinder (new 2009).

REVOLVERS

Charter Arms also offers a multitude of various colored finishes the company refers to as "Guns of Color". These finish alternatives are available on the Undercover Lite frame. All are 5 shot .38 Spl. with a 2 in. barrel, fixed sights, and a traditional spur hammer. Please contact the company directly for more information on these variations and MSRs.

BULLDOG – .44 Spl. cal., 5 shot, 2 1/2 or 4 (Target Bulldog, adj. rear sights, new 2009) in. barrel, steel or stainless steel construction, hammer block safety, choice of standard or pocket hammer, round butt with finger groove or Crimson trace laser grips, Black and Tiger finish (new 2011), 21 oz. New late 1999.

MSR $414	$360	$310	$265	$235	$185	$150	$115	

Add $12 for stainless steel or $16 for DAO (new 2008).

GRADING - PPGS™	100%	98%	95%	90%	80%	70%	60%	LAST MSR

Add $65 for Target Bulldog model with adj. sights (4 in. barrel only, stainless steel, new 2009).
Add $172 for Crimson Trace laser grips (stainless steel only, new 2009).
Add $52 for Tiger finish (new 2011).

POLICE BULLDOG – .38 Spl. cal., 5 shot, large frame, 4 in. tapered or bull barrel, exposed ejector rod, full rubber grips, approx. 23 oz. Mfg. 2002-2007.

	$255	$225	$190	$175	$140	$115	$90	*$299*

* ***Heller Commemorative Bulldog*** – .44 Spl. cal., stainless steel, fully engraved, commemoratives Heller vs. DC court case, smooth finger groove wood grips, includes engraved knife, wood presentation case with glass etched top, and certificate of authenticity. 250 mfg. 2011 only.

	$1,475	$1,350	$995	N/A	N/A	N/A	N/A	*$1,595*

The proceeds from this gun were donated to the U.S. Bill of Rights Foundation.

UNDERCOVER – .38 Spl. cal., regular double action or DAO, 5 shot, 2 in. barrel, steel or stainless steel construction, checkered compact round butt (standard hammer) or super compact (concealed hammer) synthetic grips (full rubber or boot compact) with finger grooves, 16 oz. New late 1998.

MSR $319	$270	$235	$205	$185	$150	$120	$95

Add $7 for compact frame with DAO. Add $12 for stainless steel with standard frame, or $18 for stainless steel with compact frame.
Add $257 for Crimson Trace laser grips (new 2009).
Add $50 for Tiger stripe (mfg. 2011 only) or $35 for OD green finish (mfg. 2011 only), disc.

* ***Undercover Lite*** – .32 H&R Mag. or .38 Spl. cal., similar to Undercover, except has ultralight compact aluminum frame, fixed sights, standard or compact (new 2012) grips, available in blue, stainless, and a variety of colors. 12 oz. New 2009.

MSR $404	$350	$295	$250	$225	$180	$145	$110

Add $18 for red/stainless steel or red/black finish.
Add $41 for compact grips (new 2012).
Add $166 for Crimson Trace laser grips (Pink/stainless steel finish, .32 H&R Mag. cal. only), new 2012.

This model is available in a variety of colors including tiger/black, pink/stainless, lavender/stainless, red/stainless, red/black, gold/black, light bronze/black, green/black, Santa Fe blue, turquoise/stainless, turquoise/black, brown camo/black, black/grey, Shamrock green, or Liberty red/blue (disc. 2011) finish. Please contact the manufacturer directly for current prices.

* ***Undercover Southpaw*** – .38 Spl. cal., true left-hand design with cylinder release and opening from the right side, all aluminum one-piece frame with finger groove rubber grips, available in aluminum or two-tone Pink Lady (new 2009) finish. Mfg. 2008.

MSR $427	$355	$300	$260	$230	$195	$180	$140

Add $34 for Pink Lady finish.

UNDERCOVERETTE – .32 H&R Mag. cal., 5 shot, stainless steel frame, 2 in. barrel, rubber grips, available in stainless, pink and stainless, or gold and black finish, 12-16 oz. New late 2006.

MSR $378	$325	$275	$230	$210	$165	$135	$105

Add $50 for black and gold two-tone finish. Add $160 for Crimson Trace laser grips (new 2009) or $210 for Crimson Trace laser grips with pink/stainless finish. Add $45 for Lavender Lady model with lavender finish (disc. 2011).

POLICE UNDERCOVER – .38 Spl. cal., 6 shot, stainless, fixed sights, 2 or 4 (disc. 2007) in. barrel, rubber grips, 20 oz. New late 2006.

MSR $401	$345	$295	$250	$225	$175	$145	$110

CHIC LADY – .38 Spl. cal., aluminum frame, hammerless DAO or spur hammer, 5 shot, 2 in. barrel, pink and high polish stainless finish, includes pink faux alligator case, 12 oz. New 2012.

MSR $481	$395	$315	$275	$245	$200	$185	$150

Add $11 for DAO.

GRADING - PPGS™	100%	98%	95%	90%	80%	70%	60%	LAST MSR

OFF DUTY – .38 Spl. cal., DAO, 5 shot, 2 in. barrel, aluminum frame, enclosed hammer, combat synthetic or Crimson Trace laser (new 2009) grips, black or pink/stainless finish, 12 oz. New 2002.

MSR $410	$350	$295	$250	$225	$185	$145	$115	

Add $18 for black finish. Add $23 for Pink Lady model with pink/stainless finish. Add $160 for Crimson Trace laser grips (new 2009).

ON DUTY – .38 Spl. cal., SA or DA, 5 shot, 2 in. barrel, aluminum or stainless steel frame, semi-concealed hammer, 12 oz. New 2009.

MSR $410	$350	$295	$250	$225	$185	$145	$115	

Add $253 for Crimson Trace laser grips.

MAG. PUG – .357 Mag./.38 Spl., 5 shot, 2.2 or 4 (Target Model with adj. rear sight) in. ported barrel, blue or stainless steel, full rubber or Crimson Trace laser (new 2009) grips, 23 oz. New 2001.

MSR $395	$340	$290	$245	$220	$180	$140	$110	

Add $165 for Crimson Trace laser grips (new 2009). Add $5 for stainless steel or $8 for DAO.
Add $84 for 4 in. barrel (Target model with adj. sight).

PATHFINDER – .22 LR or .22 WMR cal., 6 shot, 2 or 4 (Target, new 2007) in. barrel, stainless construction, checkered walnut (disc.) or rubber grips with finger grooves, 19-20 oz. New 2002.

MSR $369	$310	$265	#225	$200	$160	$130	$100	

Add $41 for .22 WMR. Add $42 for 4 in. barrel (Target). Add $179 for combo with .22 LR/.22 WMR cylinder and adj. sights (disc. 2009, reintroduced 2011).

PATRIOT – .327 Federal cal., 2.2 or 4 in. barrel, 6 shot, stainless steel Bulldog frame, fixed or adj. sights, rubber finger groove grips, 23 oz. Mfg. 2009-2012.

	$345	$300	$260	$235	$190	$155	$120	*$390*

Add $180 for Crimson Trace laser grips and Kershaw knife. Add $50 for Target model.

RIFLES: BOLT ACTION

FIELD KING – .243 Win. (disc. 2000), .25-06 Rem., .270 Win., or .30-06 cal., blue or stainless Mauser long action, 4 shot mag., blue or stainless 22 in. E.R. Shaw barrel, checkered black fiberglass reinforced stock with recoil pad, 6 3/4 lbs. Mfg. 2000-2002.

	$300	$260	$225	$205	$165	$135	$105	*$345*

Subtract $46 for non-stainless standard blue rifle.

* ***Field King Carbine*** – .308 Win. only, similar to Field King, except is available in 18 in. barrel with compensator only, blue finish or stainless steel. Mfg. 2000-2002.

	$300	$260	$225	$205	$165	$135	$105	*$345*

CHEYTAC

Current manufacturer located in Arco, ID. Previously distributed by SPA Defense, located in Ft. Lauderdale, FL, and by Knesek Guns, Inc., located in Van Buren, AR. Dealer sales.

RIFLES: BOLT ACTION

Cheytac currently manufactures an advanced 5 shot bolt action design in .375 or .408 Cheyenne Tactical cal. The Intervention Model 200 Military weighs 27 lbs., and includes an advanced ballistic computer to help with accuracy. The M-325 model is also offered. Cheytac also builds an Intervention Model M310 Target Model. Please contact the company directly for more information, including pricing and commercial availability (see Trademark Index).

CHIAPPA FIREARMS LTD.

Current manufacturer established during 2008 and located in Dayton, OH. Marketed by MKS Supply, located in Dayton, OH with sales through various domestic distributors. Chiappa Firearms Ltd. is one division of the Chiappa Group, which includes Armi Sport (replica firearms manufacturer established in 1958), Chiappa Firearms Ltd. (firearms manufacturer), Kimar Srl (firearms manufacturer), Costa Srl (metal surface finish treatment), ACP (laser training system), and AIM (video/target simulations).

GRADING - PPGS™	100%	98%	95%	90%	80%	70%	60%	LAST MSR

Chiappa Firearms Ltd. manufacturers a wide variety of firearms including reproductions and replicas. The models listed in this section are marketed exclusively by MKS Supply, Inc., and are marked Chiappa Firearms on the guns. Chiappa also manufactures private label guns for Cimarron Firearms, Legacy Sports, and Taylor's and Company. Please refer to these sections for more information on those Chiappa mfg. models.

PISTOLS: SEMI AUTO

1911-22 – .22 LR cal., 5 in. barrel, blue steel or two tone finish, 10 shot mag., checkered wood grips, available in Standard, Target, OD (olive drab, new 2011), Tan (new 2011), and Tactical configuration, includes two mags., approx. 33 oz. New mid-2010.

MSR $300	$260	$225	$195	$175	$150	$125	$100

Add $30 for OD Green or Tan Model.

Add $89 for Target with adj. sights or $119 for Tactical Model with threaded barrel extension and fiber optic front sight.

M FOUR-22 – .22 LR cal., replica of the M4 carbine, 6 in. steel barrel, blue finish, fire control group, finger groove pistol grip, dust cover, adj. sights, 10 or 28 shot mag., faux flash hider, machined quad rail forearm, includes two mags. New 2011.

MSR $419	$375	$335	$300	$265	$250	$230	$210

Add $30 for red dot scope.

TACTICAL M9-22 – .22 LR cal., replica of the Beretta M9, available in Standard (fixed front sights, blue finish, choice of wood or checkered black plastic grips), or Tactical (blue finish, black plastic grips, faux suppressor, optional fiber optic sights) configuration, includes two 10 shot mags., 37 oz. New 2011.

MSR $369	$325	$295	$265	$235	$200	$175	$160

Add $50 for Tactical.

REVOLVERS

RHINO REVOLVER SERIES – .357 Mag. cal., barrel is in line with the lower cylinder chamber, matte black or brushed nickel (White Rhino) finish, hexagonal cylinder, checkered wood or neoprene grips, fixed or adj. sights, available in 2 (Model 200DS or Model 200D), 4 (Model 40DS), 5 (Model 50DS), or 6 (Model 60DS) in. barrel, with or w/o lower tactical rail, approx. 24 - 33 oz. New mid-2010.

* ***Rhino 200D*** – 2 in. barrel, DAO, matte black finish, 6 shot, aluminum frame, rubber grips, includes brown leather holster, 24 oz.

MSR $819	$725	$625	$525	$450	$375	$300	$250

* ***Rhino 200DS*** – 2 in. barrel, brushed nickel or matte black finish, 6 shot, aluminum frame, rubber grips, includes brown leather holster, 24 oz.

MSR $819	$725	$625	$525	$450	$375	$300	$250

Add $60 for White Rhino with brushed nickel finish.

* ***Rhino 40DS*** – 4 in. barrel, brushed nickel or matte black finish, 6 shot, aluminum frame, wood grips, 29.6 oz.

MSR $879	$775	$675	$575	$475	$400	$325	$275

Add $70 for White Rhino with brushed nickel finish.

* ***Rhino 50DS*** – 5 in. barrel, brushed nickel or matte black finish, 6 shot, aluminum frame, wood grips, 31.4 oz.

MSR $909	$795	$700	$595	$495	$450	$350	$300

Add $70 for White Rhino with brushed nickel finish.

* ***Rhino 60DS*** – 6 in. barrel, brushed nickel or matte black finish, 6 shot, aluminum frame, wood grips, 33.2 oz.

MSR $919	$800	$700	$600	$500	$450	$350	$300

Add $70 for White Rhino with brushed nickel finish.

SAA 1873 SCOUT REVOLVER – .22 LR cal., 4-3/4, 5-1/2, or 7-1/2 in. barrel, 6 shot, choice of black or antique finish, rotary safety on left recoil shield, black plastic checkered grips,

GRADING - PPGS™	100%	98%	95%	90%	80%	70%	60%	LAST MSR

Target variation has adj. rear sight, approx. 35 oz. New late 2011.

MSR $189	$165	$145	$130	$120	$110	$100	$90	

Add $10 for 7-1/2 in. barrel.

Add $40 for either dual cylinder (.22 LR/.22 WMR) or Target Model with adj. rear sight.

SAA 1873 – .22 LR cal., 6 shot, 4 3/4, 5 1/2, or 7 1/2 in. barrel, black plastic grips with "CF" medallions, approx. 2.2 lbs. New late 2011.

MSR $189	$170	$155	$140	$130	$120	$110	$100	

Add $40 for dual cylinder (includes .22 LR and .22 WMR cal. cylinders) or Target model with adj. rear sight.

RIFLES: LEVER ACTION

1886 KODIAK – .45-70 Govt. cal., 18 1/2 in. half octagon barrel, Express sights, drilled and tapped, straight grip black synthetic overmolded stock matte grey finish, 4 or 6 (Trapper Model with full-length mag.) shot mag., sling swivels. New 2011.

MSR $1,395	$1,250	$1,125	$1,000	$875	$725	$575	$450	

1886 KODIAK TRADITIONAL TRAPPER – .45-70 Govt. cal., 18 1/2 full octagon barrel, straight grip walnut stock, traditional sights, 6 shot, color case hardened finish. New 2011.

MSR $1,249	$1,100	$975	$850	$725	$600	$500	$400	

RIFLES: SEMI-AUTO

M-22 SERIES – While a Carbine, National Match, and Precision Match were advertised during 2011, this series never went into production and was not imported.

M FOUR-22 – .22 LR cal.,5, 10 or 28 shot, 16 in. barrel with flash hider, forward assist and bolt release, black or tan finish, fixed tube stock, ribbed tube-type forearm, A-4 adj. sights, Picatinny flat-top, detachable carry handle, accepts Mil Spec handguards, 5 1/2 lbs.

MSR $419	$360	$325	$300	$265	$230	$200	$180	

Add $30 for red dot scope.

Chiappa also offers an M Four-22 conversion unit (upper only) - current MSR is $319 (new 2012).

M1 CARBINE – please refer to listing under Citadel.

SHOTGUNS: LEVER ACTION

MODEL 1887 – Please refer to individual listings under Cimarron, Puma, and Taylors & Co. for more information and values.

CHIPMUNK RIFLES

Current trademark established in 1982 and currently manufactured by Keystone Sporting Arms, located in Milton, PA. Previously manufactured by Rogue Rifle Co., Inc., located in Lewiston, ID, 2001-2007. Previously located in Prospect, OR from 1997-2001. Previously manufactured by Oregon Arms, Inc. located in Prospect, OR 1988-1996, and by Chipmunk Manufacturing located in Medford, OR until 1988.

Rogue Rifle Co. Inc. was purchased by Keystone Sporting Arms, LLC in Jan. 2007. Keystone is also the manufacturer of Crickett rifles (see separate listing).

PISTOLS: SINGLE SHOT

SILHOUETTE PISTOL – .22 LR cal., bolt action design with 14 7/8 in. barrel, iron sights, rear grip walnut stock. Mfg. 1984-88.

	$135	$115	$95	$80	$70	$60	$50	*$150*

HUNTER/SILHOUETTE – .17 HMR (disc.), .17 Mach 2 (disc.), .22 LR, or .22 WMR (disc.) cal., 10 in. steel or stainless steel barrel with open or Truglo (disc.) sights, drilled and tapped, left-handed bolt, walnut or various color choices of laminate target style stock with ergonomic grip, current mfg. has Barracuda style forend. New 2005.

MSR $210	$185	$160	$145	$130	$115	$100	$85	

Add $25 for .17 HMR, .17 Mach 2 cal., or .22 WMR (disc.).

Add $28 for stainless steel (new 2006).

GRADING - PPGS™	100%	98%	95%	90%	80%	70%	60%	LAST MSR

RIFLES: BOLT ACTION, SINGLE SHOT

BARRACUDA CHIPMUNK – various cals., .22 LR cal. is current mfg., skeletonized thumbhole stock with ergonomic pistol grip, free floating (standard, disc.) or bull barrel, laminate stock is current mfg., blued steel or stainless steel barrel, w/o sights, receiver Picatinny rail.

MSR $240	$215	$180	$160	$145	$130	$120	$110	

Add $25 for .17 HMR, .17 Mach 2, or .22 WMR cal. (disc.).

CHIPMUNK STANDARD RIFLE – .17 HMR (new 2002), .17 Mach 2 (new 2005-disc.), .22 LR, .22 Short (disc. 2008), or .22 WMR (disc. 1987, reintroduced 1999-disc.) cal., manually cocked single shot, youth model with 16 1/8 in. blued steel or stainless steel barrel and 11 1/2 in. LOP, choice of walnut, black or brown laminate (new 1999), camo (new 2002, various colored woods), synthetic (new 2004), birch (new 2006), or uncheckered Monte Carlo walnut stock, iron sights (adj. aperture rear) or Truglo sights (mfg. 2005-disc.), 30 in. overall length, 2 1/2 (standard barrel) or 4 (bull barrel, disc.) lbs. New circa 1982.

MSR $180	$160	$140	$125	$110	$95	$85	$75	

Add $20 for .17 HMR, .17 Mach 2, or .22 LR cal. (disc.).
Add approx. 15% for bull barrel.
Add 100% for Chipmunk Special Edition with hand engraving (custom order only, limited mfg.).
Add 25% for deluxe rifle with hand checkered deluxe Monte Carlo walnut stock.
Add 75% for target rifle with 18 in. heavy barrel.
Subtract approx. 10% for black coated wood stock.

* ***Chipmunk Special Edition*** – similar to Deluxe Model, except has hand engraving.

This model was available by custom order only.

SHOTGUNS: SINGLE SHOT

CHIPMUNK .410 SHOTGUN – .410 bore, 18 1/4 in. smoothbore barrel, single shot, manual cocking, blue only, 11 1/2 in. LOP, walnut stock, approx. 3 1/4 lbs. Mfg. mid-2002-2005.

	$175	$150	$130	$100	$90	$80	$70	*$190*

CHRISTENSEN ARMS

Current rifle manufacturer established in 1995, and currently located in Gunnison, UT. Previously located in Fayette, UT during 2000-2010, and in St. George, UT during 1995-99. Direct sales only.

PISTOLS

CARBON ONE PISTOL SINGLE SHOT – various cals., graphite barrel lengths up to 14 in., uses Thompson Center Encore or Contender pistol frame, less than 1 in. grouping for 3 shots at 100 yards, satin nickel receiver, approx. 2.5-3 lbs. Limited mfg. beginning 1999.

This model is basically a special order, please contact the company directly.

CLASSIC GOVERNMENT LITE – 9mm Para., .40 S&W, or .45 ACP cal., patterned after Colt M1911, SA, 5.05 in. match barrel, titanium frame with a hand fit slide, front and rear slide serrations, extended ambidextrous thumb safety, SPRINCO recoil reducing system, carbon fiber grips, Trijicon/Novak Trinium sights, 8 (.45 ACP), 9 (.40 S&W), or 10 (9mm, disc. 2011) shot mag., 3 1/4-3 3/4 lb. trigger pull. New 2011.

MSR $3,195	$2,825	$2,400	$2,050	$1,775	$1,500	$1,250	$995	

COMMANDER LITE – similar to the Classic Government Lite, except has 4.29 in. match barrel, and flared magazine well. New 2011.

MSR $3,195	$2,825	$2,400	$2,050	$1,775	$1,500	$1,250	$995	

OFFICER LITE – similar to the Classic Government Lite, except has 3.65 in. barrel, low profile ambidextrous thumb safety, 7 (.40 S&W or .45 ACP cal.), or 8 (9mm) shot mag., 2 piece reverse plug recoil system, titanium pin and hammer strut, aluminum mainspring housing. New 2011.

MSR $3,195	$2,825	$2,400	$2,050	$1,775	$1,500	$1,250	$995	

GRADING - PPGS™	100%	98%	95%	90%	80%	70%	60%	LAST MSR

TACTICAL LITE – similar to Classic Government Lite, except has tactical accessory rail, and flared magazine well. New 2011.

MSR $3,350	$2,900	$2,400	$2,100	$1,775	$1,500	$1,250	$1,050	

1911 OFFICER – .45 ACP cal., titanium frame with natural finish, 3.65 in. barrel without bushing, stainless slide with black cerakote finish, Novak 3-dot Trijicon sights, skeletonized trigger, bobbed hammer, bi-directional textured black G10 grips, 6 shot mag., full length guide rod, 30 oz. New 2013.

MSR $3,295	$2,895	$2,500	$2,250	$2,000	$1,750	$1,500	$1,250	

1911 GOVERNMENT DAMASCUS – .45 ACP cal., 5 in. barrel without busing, titanium frame with natural finish, patterned damascus slide with front and rear serrations, stippled grip straps, skeletonized trigger and hammer, Novak 3-dot Trijicon sights, smooth carbon fiber grips, 7 shot mag., full length guide rod, 36 oz. New 2013.

MSR $4,595	$4,100	$3#,650	$3,175	$2,750	$2,375	$2,000	$1,700	

DAMASCUS – top-of-the-line 1911 with damascus patterned slide. New 2012.

Please contact the company directly for pricing and availability on this model (see Trademark Index).

RIFLES: BOLT ACTION

In addition to the models listed below, Christensen Arms also offers the Carbon One Custom barrel installed on a customer action (any caliber) for $1,100 ($875 if short chambered by competent gunsmith), as well as providing a Carbon Wrap conversion to an existing steel barrel ($675). Additionally, a Custom Long Range Package is available for $6,695, as well as an Extreme Long Range Package for $4,650.

Add $1,200 for titanium action, $195 for titanium muzzle brake, $225 for Jewell trigger, $150 for Teflon coated action, $150 for Realtree, Mossy Oak, King's Desert (new 2011), King's Snow (new 2011) or Natural Gear (disc. 2010) camo stock, and $250 for lightened action on the models listed below.

CARBON ONE CUSTOM – most popular cals., features Remington 700 BDL short action or Winchester Model 70 action, barrel (up to 32 in. long) features a match grade Shilen/Christensen precision 416R stainless steel barrel liner inside a larger diameter graphite/epoxy barrel casing with crown, black synthetic stock, Shilen trigger, 5 1/2 - 7 lbs. New 1996.

MSR $4,495	$3,995	$3,300	$2,700	$2,175	$1,750	$1,500	$1,325	

Add $1,955 for long range rifle package including Swarovski Z5 3-18x44mm BRH scope, Talley rings, 100 rounds of ammo, accessories, and custom rifle case (new 2011).

Variations have included the Carbon Lite (5 lbs.), Carbon King (6-7 lbs., .25-.308 cal.), Carbon Cannon (includes muzzle brake, 6 1/2-7 1/2 lbs., Magnum series), or Carbon Tactical (includes muzzle brake, 6 1/2 lbs., new 1997), or Carbon Conquest (new 1998).

CARBON ONE EXTREME – various cals., 18-26 in. carbon wrap free floating barrel, choice of carbon classic or thumbhole Christensen Arms stock, Teflon coated and lightened action, 3 lb. trigger pull, 5 1/2-7 lbs. New 2007.

MSR $3,295	$2,875	$2,400	$1,900	$1,500	$1,200	$975	$800	

CARBON ONE HUNTER – various popular cals., features Remington M700 (regular or stainless) or Winchester Model 70 stainless action, available with HS Precision (disc.), or synthetic (disc.), or Bell & Carlson stock with Dura touch (new 2011) finish, 18-26 in. large diameter graphite barrel with stainless steel barrel liner, 5 1/2 - 7 lbs. New 1999.

MSR $2,150	$1,825	$1,525	$1,250	$1,050	$900	$775	$650	

Subtract approx. 15% if without 2011 updates (drilled bolt handle, Bell & Carlson stock).

CARBON ONE R93 – various cals., features Blaser R93 action, 24 or 26 in. carbon fiber barrel with carbon classic stock, 5.5-7 lbs. New 2011.

MSR $4,195	$3,775	$3,150	$2,125	$2,150	$1,750	$1,500	$1,325	

CARBON ONE RANGER (CONQUEST) – .50 BMG cal., single shot (disc. 2010) or repeater (5 shot), McMillan stainless steel bolt action, max barrel length is 32 in. with muzzle brake, Christensen composite stock with bipod, approx. 16 (single shot) - 24 lbs. New 2001.

MSR $8,995	$8,200	$6,700	$5,450	$4,500	$3,750	$2,850	$2,500	

Subtract 20% for a single shot action (disc. 2010).

GRADING - PPGS™	100%	98%	95%	90%	80%	70%	60%	LAST MSR

CARBON RANGER – .50 BMG cal., large diameter graphite barrel casing (up to 36 in. long), no stock or forearm, twin rails extending from frame sides are attached to recoil pad, Omni Wind Runner action, bipod and choice of scope are included, 25-32 lbs. Limited mfg. 1998-2000 only.

	$9,950	$8,900	$8,000	$7,100	$6,200	$5,300	$4,400	*$10,625*

CARBONE ONE TACTICAL – various cals., grey synthetic stock, various barrel lengths, stainless steel free floating Shilen barrel with muzzle brake, glass bedded barrel assembly, precision trigger, many options available per customer request, 5.5-7 lbs. New 2010.

MSR $4,595	$4,150	$3,650	$3,250	$1,825	$2,300	$1,950	$1,700	

CARBON ONE 10TH ANNIVERSARY MODEL – .270 WSM, .300 WSM, or .325 WSM cal., Rem. titanium action, graphite stock, titanium muzzle brake, stainless floor plate, SST, laser engraving, individually numbered 1-50. Limited edition beginning mid-2005.

Please contact the company directly for more information on this model, including pricing and availability.

RIFLES: SEMI-AUTO

Christensen Arms also offered a Carbon One Challenge drop-in barrel (16 oz.) for the Ruger Model 10/22. Last MSR was $499 (disc. 2010).

IMPORTANT NOTE: On model(s) where *N/A has replaced the normal 100% value, it indicates current market conditions are too unstable to accurately ascertain 100%-60% values. Factory retail prices (MSRs) reflect most recent updates. For more up-to-date information on current pricing trends and additional useful information, please visit www.bluebookofgunvalues.com, select "Information & Services" from the menu, and click on "Additional Book Information".

CARBON ONE CHALLENGE (CUSTOM) – .17 HMR, .22 LR, or .22 WMR cal., features Ruger 10/22 Model 1103 action with modified bolt release, synthetic bull barrel with precision stainless steel liner, 2 lb. Volquartsen trigger, Fajen brown laminated wood (disc.) or black synthetic stock with thumbhole, approx. 3.5-4 lbs. Mfg. 1996-2010.

	$1,500	$1,250	$1,050	$875	$750	$600	$500	*$1,750*

Add $350 for .17 HMR or .22 WMR cal.

The 100% price represents the base model, with no options.

* ***Carbon One Challenge*** – .22 LR cal., non-custom shop variation, 4 lbs. New 1999.

	$550	$495	$440	$400	$365	$330	$295	*$599*

CARBON CHALLENGE II – similar to Carbon Challenge I, except has AMT stainless receiver and trigger, black synthetic stock, approx. 4 1/2 lbs. Limited mfg. 1997-1998 only.

	$1,150	$975	$875	$800	$725	$650	$525	*$1,299*

CA-10 RECON – .243 Win., 6.8 Creedmoor, .308 Win., or .338 Federal cal., features 16-24 in. carbon fiber match grade barrel, various stock configurations, flat-top receiver with Picatinny rail, adj. Timney trigger, carbon handguard, 20 shot mag., black carbon fiber or camo forearm finish, 6-8 lbs. New 2011.

MSR $3,495	*N/A	$2,650	$2,225	$1,900	$1,675	$1,450	$1,175	

Subtract $200 for steel barrel.

CARBON ONE CA-15 SERIES (AR-15) – .223 Rem. cal., forged aluminum upper and lower receiver, choice of round shroud with quad rails or integrated forearm with full Picatinny rail on top, adj. stock, carbon fiber wrapped stainless steel barrel, gas operated, ambidextrous charging handle, Timney adj. drop-in trigger, 30 shot detachable AR-15 style mag., 5.5 - 7 lbs. Mfg. 2009-2010.

	*N/A	$2,300	$2,000	$1,750	$1,500	$1,275	$995	*$2,950*

* ***CA-15 Predator*** – .223 Rem., .204 Ruger, 6.8 Spc., or 6.5 Grendel, 20 or 24 in. carbon fiber match grade barrel, collapsible stock, flat-top receiver with Picatinny rail, ambidextrous controls, adj. Timney trigger, 20 shot mag., Hogue pistol grip, black, King's Desert Shadow, or King's Snow Shadow finish, 5.5-7 lbs. New 2011.

MSR $2,995	*N/A	$2,350	$2,050	$1,775	$1,525	$1,300	$1,050	

GRADING - PPGS™	100%	98%	95%	90%	80%	70%	60%	LAST MSR

* ***CA-15 Recon*** – 5.56 NATO, .223 Wylde, or 6.8 SPC cal., 16 or 20 in. match grade carbon fiber barrel, carbon fiber handguard with built-in Picatinny rails, choice of adj. stock, adj. Timney trigger, piston drive, titanium birdcage flash suppressor, 30 shot mag., Hogue pistol grip, factory black synthetic, Digital Desert Brown, King's Desert Shadow, or King's Snow Shadow finish, 5.5-7 lbs. New 2011.

MSR $2,995	*N/A	$2,350	$2,050	$1,775	$1,525	$1,300	$1,050	

Subtract $200 for steel barrel.

CHURCHILL

Previous trademark imported and distributed by Ellett Brothers located in Chapin, SC until 1993. Previously imported (until 1988) by Kassnar Imports, Inc. located in Harrisburg, PA. Not affiliated with E.J. Churchill Gunmakers, Ltd.

In late 1988, the Churchill trademark was sold to Ellett Brothers located in Chapin, SC.

RIFLES: BOLT ACTION

HIGHLANDER – .25-06 Rem., .243 Win., .270 Win., .308 Win., .30-06, 7mm Rem. Mag., or .300 Win. Mag. cal., bolt action, 22 in. barrel, thumb safety, no sights, 3 or 4 shot mag., checkered walnut stock, 7 1/2 lbs. Importation disc. 1991.

$395	$350	$330	$300	$270	$240	$215	*$460*

Add $30 for iron sights (disc).

REGENT – same cals. as Highlander, deluxe checkered walnut with Monte Carlo comb and cheekpiece. Last imported by Kassnar in 1988.

$555	$455	$385	$340	$300	$280	$260	*$610*

Add $30 for iron sights.

RIFLES: SEMI-AUTO

ROTARY 22 – .22 LR cal., beginners rifle, bolt hold-open device, adj. rear sight, 10 shot rotary mag. Imported 1989 only.

$120	$105	$95	$85	$75	$65	$55	*$130*

SHOTGUNS: O/U

MONARCH – 12, 20, 28 (disc.) ga., or .410 (disc.) bore, 25 (disc.), 26, or 28 in. vent. rib barrels, SST, extractors, boxlock action, DT, silver finish receiver with fine scroll engraving, checkered European walnut stock and forearm, 6 1/2-7 1/2 lbs.

$460	$370	$340	$300	$250	$230	$210	*$520*

Add $67 for .410 bore with 26 in. barrels (disc.). Subtract $40 without SST.

* ***Monarch Turkey Gun*** – 12 ga. only, 24 in. barrels with matte finish. Imported 1990-91 only.

$460	$370	$340	$300	$250	$230	$210	*$529*

SPORTING CLAYS MODEL – 12 ga. only, designed for sporting clays competition with 28 in. VR ported barrels with choke tubes, ejectors, raised target style VR, checkered high gloss finish stock and forearm, 7 lbs. 6 oz. Imported 1992 only.

$800	$725	$650	$575	$500	$450	$395	*$900*

WINDSOR III – 12, 20 ga., or .410 bore (disc.), 27 or 30 in. barrels, double bottom lock, antique silver finish receiver with fine scroll engraving, extractors, SST, vent. rib, checkered pistol grip and forend. Importation disc. 1991.

$550	$495	$450	$380	$340	$300	$280	*$625*

Add $140 for Flyweight Model or choke tubes (disc.). Add $75 for .410 bore.

NEW WINDSOR IV – 12 or 20 ga., 3 in. chambers, boxlock action, silver receiver with full scroll engraving, 26 or 28 (12 ga. only) VR barrels with choke tubes, ejectors, SST, checkered walnut pistol grip stock with black rubber vent. recoil pad, finger grooved forearm, gloss finish, gold trigger, 5 year warranty. Mfg. 1992 only.

$625	$525	$450	$375	$325	$295	$275	*$690*

GRADING - PPGS™	100%	98%	95%	90%	80%	70%	60%	LAST MSR

WINDSOR IV - DISC. – 12, 20, 28 ga., or .410 bore, 26-30 in. barrels, double bottom lock, antique silver finish receiver with fine scroll engraving, ejectors, SST, vent. rib, checkered pistol grip and forend. Interchangeable chokes became standard in 1989. Importation disc. 1991.

$725	$640	$530	$470	$430	$395	$360	*$852*

Subtract $52 for 28 ga. or .410 bore.
Subtract $100 if without choke tubes.

REGENT V – 12 or 20 ga., 27 in. barrels, double bottom lock, antique silver finish receiver with extra fine scroll engraving, ejectors, single trigger, vent. rib, checkered pistol grip and forend. Interchangeable choke tubes standard. Disc. 1986, reintroduced 1990, disc. 1993.

$895	$795	$700	$620	$560	$510	$470	*$1,100*

This model was previously designated Regent VII until 1989 when it changed to the Regent V.

REGENT TRAP AND SKEET – 12 or 20 ga., 26 or 30 in. barrels, double bottom lock, antique silver finish receiver with sideplates engraved in fine scroll, ejectors, SST, vent. rib, checkered pistol grip and forend. Importation disc. 1991.

$795	$650	$575	$540	$485	$440	$390	*$963*

Add $40 for trap variation.

REGENT GRADE SHOTGUN/RIFLE COMBINATION – 12 ga. over either .222 Rem., .223 Rem., .243 Win. (disc.), .270 Win., .30-06, or .308 Win. cal., 25 in. barrels, double bottom lock, antique silver finish receiver with extra fine scroll engraving, ejectors, single trigger, vent. rib, checkered pistol grip and forend. Importation disc. 1991.

$800	$700	$635	$560	$510	$475	$440	*$927*

SHOTGUNS: SxS

WINDSOR I – 10 (disc. 1988), 12, 16, 20, 28 ga., or .410 bore, double barrel, 23-32 in. barrels, Anson and Deeley boxlock, antique silver finish receiver with fine scroll engraving, extractors, double triggers, checkered pistol grip and forend. Importation disc. 1991.

$550	$465	$450	$385	$300	$250	$230	*$653*

Add $150 for 10 ga.
Add $55 for 28 ga. or .410 bore.
Add $30 for Flyweight Models (25 in. barrels - disc. 1988).

WINDSOR II – 12 or 20 ga., 26-30 in. barrels, Anson and Deeley boxlock, antique silver finish receiver with fine scroll engraving, ejectors, double triggers, checkered pistol grip and forend. Add $100 for 10 ga. (disc.). Importation disc. 1987.

$595	$485	$415	$350	$315	$270	$240	*$638*

WINDSOR VI – 12 or 20 (disc.) ga., 25 or 28 in. barrels, sidelock, antique silver finish receiver with fine scroll engraving, ejectors, double triggers, checkered pistol grip and forend. Disc. 1987.

$840	$700	$600	$550	$510	$460	$420	*$900*

ROYAL – 10, 12, 20, 28 ga., or .410 bore, DTs, extractors, checkered walnut stock and forearm, case hardened receiver. Imported late 1988-91.

$485	$405	$370	$310	$275	$250	$230	*$540*

Add $20 for 28 ga.
Add $74 for .410 bore.

SHOTGUNS: SEMI-AUTO

STANDARD MODEL – 12 ga. only, gas operated and shoots different loads interchangeably without alterations, 24, 26, 28 in. VR barrel, magazine cut-off, hand checkered walnut with satin finish, matte metal finish, includes ICT choke tubes. Mfg. 1990-disc.

$495	$415	$375	$310	$275	$250	$230	*$550*

* ***Standard Turkey Model*** – similar to Standard Model, except has 24 in. barrel only. Mfg. 1990-disc.

$510	$425	$380	$315	$275	$250	$230	*$570*

GRADING - PPGS™	100%	98%	95%	90%	80%	70%	60%	LAST MSR

WINDSOR GRADE – 12 ga. only, 26, 28, or 30 in. barrels, gas operation, anodized alloy receiver, vent. rib, checkered pistol grip and forend, 7 1/2 lbs. Deluxe model included polished receiver with etching. Disc.

	$380	$320	$300	$275	$250	$225	$200	*$420*

Add $35 for choke tubes.
Add $55 for Deluxe model.

REGENT GRADE – 12 ga. only, 26, 28, or 30 in. barrels, gas operation, anodized alloy receiver, vent. rib, checkered pistol grip and forend, 7 1/2 lbs. Deluxe model included polished receiver with etching. Disc. 1986.

	$440	$365	$340	$320	$300	$285	$270	*$495*

Add $35 for choke tubes.
Add $55 for Deluxe model.

SHOTGUNS: SLIDE ACTION

WINDSOR GRADE – 12 ga. only, 26, 27, 28, or 30 in. barrels, dual action bars, anodized alloy receiver, vent. rib, checkered pistol grip and forend, 7 1/2 lbs. Disc. 1986.

	$385	$330	$310	$275	$250	$225	$200	*$430*

E.J. CHURCHILL GUNMAKERS

Current manufacturer established in 1891, and located in High Wycombe, England since 1996. Previously imported until 2001 by Aspen Outfitters, located in Aspen, CO. Previously manufactured in London, England. This company underwent various trading forms until Churchill, Atkin, Grant & Lang Ltd. closed in 1981. Currently, Churchill Gunmakers' rifles and shotguns are manufactured in High Wycombe, England.

Churchill Guns are very fine quality, and can be ordered with many custom features. We will list both discontinued and current models and approximate values, but strongly urge competent appraisal if purchase or sale is contemplated.

All new prices do not include English VAT. Please contact the company directly for current retail pricing (see Trademark Index).

Values for used guns in 98%-60% condition factors are priced in U.S. dollars.

E.J. CHURCHILL COMPANY HISTORY

Edwin John Churchill was apprenticed at William Jeffery of Dorchester before moving to London to work for F.T. Baker. He established his own business on Agar Street in 1891, making his reputation building pigeon guns. A crack shot, he was a superb gunfitter and his guns were popular among the professional shooting fraternity. Churchill's fortunes began declining as pigeon shooting fell out of popularity in the early 20th century. He fel into depression after the death of his son in 1902, and died in 1910. His nephew Robert raised capital and rescued the firm after Edwin's death and guided Churchill through WWII before incorporating the firm as E.J. Churchill (Gunmakers) Ltd. in 1917. Prior to WWI, Robert Churchill and general manager Jim Chewter began experimenting with short barreled guns, culminating in the early 1920s with the 'XXV' concept. Churchill declared longer barrels obsolete and began making fast-handling guns with 25 in. barrels - resulting in improved shooting. Churchill's claims resulted in tremendous publicity and by 1925, demand for the XXV outpaced the firms ability to build them. Many gunmakers tried to copy Churchill's style, and he wrote several books on shooting before his death in 1958.

During 1959, the firm was purchased and the name changed to Churchill (Gunmakers) ltd. and in 1964, the company acquired Atkin, Grant, & Lang. In 1971, the two firms were combined into Churchill, Atkin, Grant & Lang, Ltd. The firm suffered during the crippling inflation and spiralling costs, and by 1980, Churchill ceased operations. The remaining inventory was auctioned off in 1981.

Don Master, Churchill's former production manager, registered the name E.J. Churchill (Gunmakers) Ltd. in 1984. In 1996, West Wycombe Shooting Grounds Ltd. obtained rights to

GRADING - PPGS™	100%	98%	95%	90%	80%	70%	60%	LAST MSR

the Churchill Gunmakers name and began efforts to revive it. In addition to quality longarms, the company now offers a fine gun room, sporting agency, shooting school and a complete lineup of quality trademark clothing and accessories.

Information courtesy of David Grant and Vic Venters.

RIFLES: BOLT ACTION

"ONE OF ONE THOUSAND RIFLE" – .270 Win., 7mm Rem. Mag., .308 Win., .30-06, .300 Win. Mag., .375 H&H, or .458 Win. Mag. cal., Mauser type bolt action, 5 shot standard, 3 shot mag. Magnum, 24 in. barrel, classic French walnut stock, swivel recoil pad with trap, trap pistol grip cap. Mfg. 1973 for Interarms 20th Anniversary, only 100 mfg.

	100%	98%	95%	90%	80%	70%	60%	LAST MSR
	$3,995	$3,500	$2,950	$2,500	$2,000	$1,650	$1,350	

Add 50% for .375 H&H or .458 Win. Mag. cal.

BARONET RIFLE – various cals. from .30-06 to .375 H&H cal., standard Mauser 98 action with swept bolt handle, fully adj. trigger and 3 position side safety, border engraving, deluxe checkered European walnut stock and forearm, custom order only, allow 8-10 months for delivery, approx. 8.5-9 lbs. New 2001.

	100%	98%	95%	90%	80%	70%	60%	LAST MSR
MSR N/A	N/A	$15,000	$12,500	$10,000	$7,500	$5,000	$3,250	

Add £3,500 for Magnum Mauser action.
Add £2,535 for detachable scope mounts.

RIFLES: SxS

PREMIERE MODEL – various cals. up to .600 NE, pinless sidelock ejector mechanism with cocking indicators, 24 or 26 in. chopper lump barrels, double triggers, extended top tang, square or rounded body, full traditional fine scroll engraving, color case hardened action, allow 20-24 months for delivery, 9 1/2 - 12 1/2 lbs. Mfg. resumed 1998.

	100%	98%	95%	90%	80%	70%	60%	LAST MSR
MSR N/A	N/A	$65,000	$55,000	$45,000	$35,000	$27,500	$20,000	

Add £650 for hand detachable sidelocks.
Add £3,000 for .300-.500 NE cals. (cals. over .500 NE are P.O.R.)

SHOTGUNS: O/U

Please contact the company directly for a list of available options and pricing (see Trademark Index).

PREMIERE MODEL – 12, 16 (limited mfg.), 20, 28 ga., or .410 bore, 2 3/4 in. chambers, similar barrels and bores as Premiere SxS Model engraved, pinless sidelock ejector with cocking indicators, choice of monobloc (disc.) or chopper lump barrels, mechanical ST, auto ejectors, checkered pistol grip or straight stock, allow 18-24 months for delivery, 6.5 (20 ga.) or 7 (12 ga.) lbs.

	100%	98%	95%	90%	80%	70%	60%	LAST MSR
MSR POR	N/A	$52,500	$45,000	$37,500	$30,000	$22,500	$16,500	

Add £2,000 for 28 ga. or .410 bore.
Add £650 for hand detachable sidelocks.
Add £12,675 for extra set of barrels.
Add approx. 10% for ordering pair of matched guns.
Subtract approx. £1,500 for DT. (disc.).

IMPERIAL MODEL – 12 or 20 ga., 3 in. chambers, 30 in. barrels with customer specified chokes, tapering flat game rib, brass foresight bead, round body action with sideplates, ST, ejectors, brushed bright finish with English rose and scroll engraving, hand checkered best quality walnut stock with Prince of Wales grip and wooden butt plate.

This model is POR.

SHOTGUNS: SxS

Current models have a large array of available options and the company should be contacted directly for pricing and availability.

Discontinued models below were built or finished to customer specifications pertaining to choking, chambers, barrel lengths, stock measurements, weight, engraving patterns. Standardized patterns did exist, however, for each model. The "XXV" designation referred to the 25 in. barrel length, which was a Churchill specialty and was also a registered trademark.

GRADING - PPGS™	100%	98%	95%	90%	80%	70%	60%	LAST MSR

PREMIERE MODEL – most gauges, 2 3/4 in. chambers, best quality, easy opening or standard opening, 25 (XXV), 28, 30, or 32 (disc.) in. chopper lump barrels, any choke, sidelock, pinless sidelock ejector with cocking indicators, double triggers standard, engraved, color case hardened action, checkered, straight or pistol grip stock, allow 18-24 months for delivery, 5 lbs. 14 oz. (20 ga.) or 6 lbs. 6 oz. (12 ga.).

MSR POR	N/A	$44,500	$37,500	$31,250	$24,750	$20,750	$16,500	

Add £2,000 for 28 ga.
Add £8,950 for extra set of barrels.
Add £3,445 for ST.
Add approx. 10% for matched guns ordered as a pair.

IMPERIAL MODEL – most gauges, most barrel lengths, second quality sidelock model, ejectors, mostly standard opening, a few made as easy opening. Also mfg. in some double rifles. Disc.

	$13,500	$11,500	$9,500	$7,500	$6,500	$5,250	$4,000	

Add 20% for 20 ga., 40% for 28 ga., and $1,000 for SST, or 35% for double rifle.
Subtract 10% for 16 ga.

FIELD MODEL – 12 ga. only, most barrel lengths, third quality sidelock model. Disc.

	$9,000	$8,000	$7,000	$6,000	$5,000	$4,500	$3,500	

HERCULES MODEL – most gauges, 25-30 in. barrels, best quality boxlock model, ejectors, easy opening or standard opening. Also made in some double rifles in .22 Hornet and similar cals.

	$9,000	$8,000	$7,000	$6,000	$5,000	$4,500	$3,500	

Add 20% for 20 ga., 40% for 28 ga., $1,000 for SST, and 35% double rifle.
Subtract 10% for 16 ga.

UTILITY MODEL – all gauges (mostly encountered in 12 ga.), 25-30 in. barrels, second quality boxlock model, ejectors, checkered straight or pistol grip stock. Disc.

	$6,250	$4,500	$3,500	$3,000	$2,500	$2,000	$1,800	

Add 20% for 20 ga., 40% for 28 ga., 60% for .410 bore, and $500 for SST.
Subtract 10% for 16 ga.

CROWN MODEL – 12, 16, 20 ga., or .410 (rare) bore, third quality boxlock model, various barrel lengths. Disc.

	$4,500	$3,500	$3,000	$2,500	$2,000	$1,600	$1,200	

Add 20% for 20 ga., 40% for 28 ga., 60% for .410 bore, and $500 for SST.
Subtract 10% for 16 ga.

REGAL MODEL – 12, 16, 20, 28 ga., or .410 bore, second quality boxlock model introduced after WWII, released after Utility Model was disc. Premium for 28 ga. or .410 bore.

	$6,000	$4,300	$3,750	$3,100	$2,500	$2,000	$1,800	

Add 20% for 20 ga., 40% for 28 ga., 60% for .410 bore, and $500 for SST.
Subtract 10% for 16 ga.

* ***Regal Grade*** – 12, 20, 28 ga., or .410 bore, best quality boxlock model, ejectors, standard opening, limited production.

	$4,800	$4,000	$3,500	$3,000	$2,500	$2,000	$1,800	*$5,625*

CONTINENTAL SERIES – 12, 20, or 28 ga., 28 or 30 in. barrels, straight grip stock, DT, available in three grades. Mfg. in Spain.

* ***Crown Grade*** – square body entry level shotgun with rose and scroll engraving.

Prices start at £3,895.

* ***Regal Grade*** – 12 ga., 2 3/4 in. chambers, H&H assisted opening, ejectors, English splinter forend, fine scroll engraving, includes case.

Prices are POR.

* ***Hercules Grade*** – 12 or 20 ga., 2 3/4 in. chambers, H&H assisted opening, ejectors, best quality walnut stock with English splinter forend, Churchill silver scroll engraving, includes case.

Prices are POR.

GRADING - PPGS™	100%	98%	95%	90%	80%	70%	60%	LAST MSR

CIMARRON F.A. CO.

Current importer, distributor, and retailer located in Fredricksburg, TX. Cimarron is currently importing A. Uberti, D. Pedersoli, Chiappa Firearms, Pietta, and Armi-Sport firearms and black powder reproductions and replicas. Previous company name was Old-West Co. of Texas. Dealer sales only.

Please refer to the *Blue Book of Modern Black Powder Arms* by John Allen (also online) for more information and prices on Cimarron's lineup of modern black powder models.

Black Powder Revolvers - Reproductions & Replicas and *Black Powder Long Arms & Pistols - Reproductions & Replicas* by Dennis Adler are also invaluable sources for most black powder reproductions and replicas, and they include hundreds of color images on most popular makes/models, provide manufacturer/trademark histories, and up-to-date information on related items/accessories for black powder shooting - www.bluebookofgunvalues.com

DERRINGERS: O/U

DIABLO – .22 LR/.22 WMR, or .32 H&R Mag./.38 Spl. cal. 2 barrel set, 2.4 (.22 LR/.22 WMR cal.) or 2 3/4 (centerfire) in. VR barrels, chrome or black finish, tip-up action, spur trigger, walnut Cimarron grips with horse and rider logo, mfg. by Cobra Enterprises of Utah. New 2010.

MSR $220 $185 $160 $150 $130 $115 $100 $90

Add $13 for .32 H&R Mag. or .38 Spl.

TITAN – 9mm Para. or .45 LC/.410 shotshell cal., 3 1/2 in. VR rifled barrels with fixed front sight, 2 shot, SA, satin, brushed, or black stainless steel frame, rebounding hammer, rosewood grips with Cimarron logo, removable trigger guard, 16.4 oz. New 2011.

MSR $428 $375 $335 $295 $250 $200 $160 $145

Add $42 for snug case (9mm only, disc. 2011).

PISTOLS: SEMI-AUTO

MODEL 1911A1 – .45 ACP cal., 5 in. barrel, blue, polished, or nickel finish, mfg. by Armi Chiappa in Italy. Importation began 2011.

MSR $541 $460 $415 $365 $335 $300 $285 $250

Add $62 for polished finish. Add $92 for nickel finish.

MODEL 1911 22 TACTICAL – .22 LR cal., 5 in. barrel, 10 shot mag., fixed sights, diamond checkered walnut grips with CF logo, mfg. by Armi Chiappa in Italy. Imported 2011-2012.

$290 $260 $230 $200 $185 $170 $160 ***$335***

M4-22 – .22 LR cal., AR-15 style, 6 in. barrel with muzzle brake, quad rail, includes A2 carry handle, black finish, 5, 10, or 28 shot Atchison style conversion mag., cased with cleaning kit, 3.9 lbs. Mfg. by Armi Chiappa in Italy. Imported 2011-2012.

$485 $430 $385 $350 $325 $300 $275 ***$587***

REVOLVERS: REPRODUCTIONS, COLT

The Cimarron reproductions of the 1873 Colt Peacemaker, mostly mfg. by Uberti, with the exception of previous limited production by Armi San Marco, are available in two configurations listed below. Beginning in 1984, Cimarron arms reproductions began incorporating many of the features of the 1st Generation Colt SAAs. These SAA revolvers are extremely accurate reproductions of the original Colt pre-war Peacemaker and are marked (and machined) the same as the originals, including serial numbers on frames, backstrap, trigger guard, and cylinder. Barrels are radiused and cylinders are beveled. Frames are color case hardened, stocks are walnut - choice of 4 3/4, 5 1/2, or 7 1/2 in. barrel. All Cimarron SAAs are currently barrel marked "- CIMARRON F.A. MFG. Co. FREDERICKSBURG, TX. U.S.A. -". The "Old Model" configuration has the older style black powder frame, screw-in cylinder pin retainer, and circular "bullseye" ejector head. The Standard Model includes the post-1890 style frame with spring loaded cross-pin cylinder retainer and "half-moon" ejector head. Only the Old Model is available in the authentic old style "charcoal blue" finish (sometimes referred to as fire-bluing).

GRADING - PPGS™	100%	98%	95%	90%	80%	70%	60%	LAST MSR

During 1998, Cimarron introduced an Original Finish (antiqued) that resembles the older, worn finish seen on many of the well-used, original Colt revolvers. This distressed finish is a greyish-brown patina color, and certain areas of these guns (end of barrel, grip straps, frame/ cylinder edges, and grips) have been artifically aged to give them an authentic "been carried and used for 100 years" appearance.

Add $70 for Antique Original Finish (aged and antique looking) on SAAs listed below. Add approx. $70 for charcoal blue finish. Add $200 for antique custom nickel or custom nickel finish. Add $358 for silver plating. Add $250 for U.S. Armory finish utilizing bonemeal case coloring. Add $295 for old style color case hardening and Carbona blue finish (disc. 2003). Add $45 for hand checkered walnut grips (disc. 2003). Add $61 for various styles of grips. Add $140 for oversize grips (new 2011). Add $305 ($455 fitted) for Sumbar custom stag grips. Add $225 Izit ivory grips (disc. 2006). Add $325 for Izit ivory steer head grips (mfg. 2004-2006). Add $325 for Micarta grips. Add $845 for geniune ivory grips. Add $326 for mother-of-pearl grips (disc. 2006). Add $195 for Tru Ivory (stark white, slightly aged, antique or ultra antique ivory) grips (new 2007). Add $850 for "A" style engraving (30% coverage) on SAAs listed below (disc 2004). Add $904 for "B" style engraving (50% coverage) on SAAs listed below. Add $1,800 for "C" style engraving (70% coverage), on SAAs listed below (disc. 2004). Add $2,400 for "Texas Cattle Brands" or full (100% coverage) engraving pattern (disc. 2004). Add $1,091 for Patton engraving. Add $1,204 for Teddy Roosevelt laser engraving or $1,707 for Teddy Roosevelt hand engraving. Add $1,434 for Open Top Standard laser engraving. Add $2,600 for Judge Roy Bean engraving (disc.). Add $2,470 for Wild Bill conversion engraving (disc.).

1871-72 OPEN TOP – .38 Long Colt, .38 S&W Spl., .44-40 WCF, .44 Special (new 2011), .44 Russian, .45 Colt (new 2006), or .45 Schofield cal., 4 3/4 (new 2004, Navy size grips), 5 1/2 (Navy size grips), or 7 1/2 (Army size grips) in. barrel, patterned after the Colt 1871-1872 Open Top, Navy grip frame is available in brass or silver plated. Mfg. by A. Uberti beginning 1999.

MSR $493	$430	$395	$340	$300	$260	$210	$175	

Add $26 for Army grips (7 1/2 in. barrel only).
Add $40 for silver plated backstrap and trigger guard on Navy model only (disc. 2010).
Add $1,407 for standard engraving.
Add $2,334 for standard engraving and nickel finish (disc. 2010).

BADLANDS SAA MODEL – .357 Mag. or .45 LC cal., 4 3/4 in. barrel, brass backstrap and trigger guard, flat black frame and barrel finish, steel frame, smooth wood grips, case colored hammer. Mfg. 2005-2007.

	$275	$240	$205	$185	$150	$125	$95	*$325*

BUCKHORN – .44 Spl. or .44 Mag. cal., reinforced variation of the Cimarron SAA designed for more powerful cartridges, 4 3/4, 6, or 7 1/2 in. barrel, brass or steel backstrap, mfg. by Uberti. Disc. 1993.

	$355	$310	$265	$240	$195	$160	$125	*$400*

* ***Buckhorn Buntline*** – .44-40 WCF, .44 Spl., or .44 Mag. cal., 18 in. barrel, fixed or target sights. Disc. 1989.

	$370	$325	$275	$250	$205	$165	$130	*$419*

Add $30 for target sights.

* ***Buckhorn Carbine*** – .44-40 WCF, .44 Spl., or .44 Mag. cal., 18 in. barrel, includes non-detachable shoulder stock with brass hardware and lanyard ring. Disc. 1990.

	$375	$330	$280	$255	$205	$170	$130	*$429*

Add $30 for target sights.

* ***Buckhorn Convertible Model*** – .44 Mag. and .44-40 WCF cylinders, 4 3/4, 6, or 7 1/2 in. barrel. Disc. 1989.

	$375	$330	$280	$255	$205	$170	$130	*$427*

Add $12 for target sights.

* ***Buckhorn Target Model*** – .44 Spl. or .44 Mag. cal., 4 3/4, 6, or 7 1/2 in. barrel, adj. rear sight. Importation disc. 1991.

	$370	$325	$275	$250	$205	$165	$130	*$420*

GRADING - PPGS™	100%	98%	95%	90%	80%	70%	60%	LAST MSR

BUNTLINE MODEL – .357 Mag., .44-40 WCF, or .45 LC cal., 18 in. barrel, brass or steel gripstraps cut for shoulder stock. Disc. 1989.

	$355	$310	$265	$240	$195	$160	$125	*$400*

Add $10 for target sights.

BLACK EL DIABLO – .45 LC cal., 4 3/4 in. barrel. New 2012.

MSR $805	$695	$575	$495	$450	$395	$350	$295	

BISLEY SAA – .357 Mag., .44 Spl., .44-40 WCF, or .45 LC cal., 4 3/4, 5 1/2, or 7 1/2 in. barrel, Bisley configured grips, case colored receiver, standard blue finish, smooth walnut grips, flat-top target model available with 7 1/2 in. barrel in .44-40 WCF or .45 LC cal. only (disc. 2010), mfg. by Uberti. Importation began 2002.

MSR $597	$485	$435	$395	$350	$300	$250	$200	

Subtract $13 for .357 Mag./.38 Spl. with 7 1/2 in. barrel.

EVIL ROY SAA – .357 Mag./.38 Spl., .44-40 WCF, or .45 LC cal., 4 3/4 or 5 1/2 in. barrel, features wide square notch rear sight and constant width front sight, smooth or checkered slim grips, lightened trigger and hammer springs, color case hardened finish on frame, blue or stainless steel, Evil Roy signature on bottom of grip strap, mfg. by Uberti. New 2005.

MSR $740	$625	$525	$465	$410	$350	$300	$250	

Add $143 for stainless steel (new 2010).

HOLY SMOKER – .45 LC cal., 4 3/4 in. barrel, case hardened pre-war frame, standard blue finish, one-piece walnut grip with gold cross inlay on both sides, 2 1/4 lbs. Mfg. by Uberti.

MSR $761	$650	$575	$495	$425	$375	$325	$295	

Item code: MP310

JUDGE ROY BEAN COMMEMORATIVE – mfg. to commemorate Judge Roy Bean's Texas cattlebrand. Disc. 1996.

	$1,500	$1,310	$1,125	$1,020	$825	$675	$525	*$1,695*

LIGHTNING – .22 LR (new 2007), .38 Colt (disc.), .38 S&W Spl., or .41 LC (new 2007) cal., patterned after the original Colt Lightning, 3 1/2, 4 3/4, 5 1/2, or 6 1/2 (new 2012) in. barrel, one piece smooth walnut, birdshead, or checkered grips, standard blue finish. Mfg. by A. Uberti 1999-2001, reintroduced in 2003.

MSR $488	$415	$365	$315	$275	$230	$200	$175	

Add $122 for dual cylinder (.32-20 WCF/.32 H&R Mag. cal., new 2004).
Add $28 for .38 Spl. cal.
Add $44 for .41 LC cal.

MAN WITH NO NAME SAA – .45 LC cal., 4 3/4 or 5 1/2 in. barrel, case hardened pre-war frame, one-piece walnut grip with silver rattlesnake inlay on both sides, standard blue finish, approx. 2 3/4 lbs. Mfg. by Uberti.

MSR $774	$675	$575	$495	$425	$375	$325	$300	

Item code: MP410 and MP411

MODEL P SAA – .32-20 WCF, .38-40 WCF, .357 Mag., .44-40 WCF, .44 Spl., or .45 LC cal., features pinched frame (.45 LC cal. with 7 1/2 in. barrel only, disc. 2006), Old Model (OM) or Pre-War (PW) configuration, blue (standard), charcoal blue, or original finish, 4 3/4, 5 1/2, or 7 1/2 in. barrel. Importation began 1996.

MSR $520	$450	$400	$350	$315	$285	$225	$190	

Add $70 for charcoal blue finish.
Add $100 for original finish.
Add approx. $111 for convertible .45 ACP cylinder.
Add $1,029 for standard laser engraving (standard blue finish, 4 3/4 or 7 1/2 in. barrel only).
Add $60 for hard rubber grips (disc. 2010). Add $50 for target model with adj. sights and flattop frame (7 1/2 in. barrel and .45 LC or .44-40 WCF cal. only, disc. 2006).

* ***Model P Jr. SAA*** – .22 LR (new 2007), .38 Colt/S&W Spl., or .41 LC (mfg. 2007-2010) cal., features 20% smaller frame size than full size SAA, but with standard single

GRADING - PPGS™	100%	98%	95%	90%	80%	70%	60%	LAST MSR

action grip frame, 3 1/2, 4 3/4, or 5 1/2 in. barrel, blue finish, smooth walnut or checkered (disc. 2012) grips, brass (.22 LR cal. only) or steel backstrap. Mfg. by A. Uberti 2000-2001, reintroduced 2004.

MSR $501	$425	$385	$335	$295	$260	$210	$175	

Add $83 for dual cylinder (.32-20 WCF/.32 H&R Mag. cal., new 2004).
Subtract $63 for .22 LR cal. (w/brass backstrap).
Subtract $41 for .41 LC cal. (disc. 2010).
Add $45 for checkered walnut grips (disc. 2012).

* ***Model P Jr. Black Stallion*** – .22 LR/.22 WMR cal., dual cylinder, 4 3/4 in. barrel, black steel finish, brass backstrap and trigger guard, wood grips with gold medallions. New 2010.

MSR $506	$425	$365	$325	$300	$260	$230	$210	

* ***Model P Stainless*** – .357 Mag. or .45 LC cal., 4 3/4, 5 1/2, or 7 1/2 in. barrel, pre-war frame, smooth walnut grips. New 2004.

MSR $727	$595	$525	$450	$400	$350	$300	$250	

NEW SHERIFF – .357 Mag., .44-40 WCF, or .45 LC cal., 3 1/2 in. barrel, case hardened frame, blue finish only, smooth walnut grips. Mfg. by Uberti. New 2011.

MSR $520	$425	$385	$335	$295	$265	$230	$210	

Item code CA329, CA330, CA332.

PISTOLERO – .357 Mag. or .45 LC cal., similar to the Model P, except has brass gripstraps and trigger guard, 4 3/4, 5 1/2 (disc. 2010), or 7 1/2 (disc.) in. barrel, case hardened frame with blue barrel and cylinder (disc.) or Millenium (matte black) finish, one piece smooth walnut grips. Mfg. by Uberti 1997 only, reintroduced 2007.

MSR $454	$385	$325	$295	$275	$225	$200	$175	

PLINKERTON – .22 LR cal., 4 3/4 in. barrel, matte black metal finish, checkered black plastic or wood (mfg. 2011-2012) grips, 34 oz., mfg. by Chiappa. New 2007.

MSR $181	$150	$125	$115	$100	$80	$65	$50	

Add $37 for dual cylinders (.22 LR and .22 WMR).
Add $22 for wood grips (mfg. 2011-2012).

ROOSTER SHOOTER – .357 Mag., .44-40 WCF, or .45 LC cal., 4 3/4 in. barrel, replica of John Wayne's gun from many of his westerns, including *True Grit*, antique original finish, one-piece orange finger grooved grips. Mfg. by Uberti. Importation began 2010.

MSR $883	$725	$625	$525	$450	$375	$325	$275	

Item codes: RS400, RS410, RS420

THUNDERER – .357 Mag., .44 Spl., .44-40 WCF or .45 LC cal., patterned after Colt's Thunderer Model, 3 1/2, 4 3/4, or 5 1/2 (new 2000) in. barrel with full ejector rod housing, smooth or checkered walnut grips, choice of case colored or nickel finish, mfg. by Uberti. Importation began 1994.

MSR $545	$450	$395	$350	$295	$260	$230	$210	

Add $10 for .44 Spl. or .44 WCF cal.
Add $60 for hard rubber grips (disc. 2010).
Add $104 (3 1/2 in.) or $154 (4 3/4 in.) for convertible .45 ACP cylinder.
Add $156 for stainless steel (available in .357 Mag. or .45 LC in 3 1/2 or 4 3/4 in. barrel only).

* ***Thunderer Long Tom*** – .357 Mag., .44-40 WCF or .45 LC cal., 7 1/2 in. barrel, mfg. by Uberti. Mfg. 1997-2009.

	$445	$390	$335	$300	$245	$200	$155	*$534*

Add $45 for checkered walnut grips.

* ***Thunderer Doc Holliday*** – .357 Mag./.38 Spl., or .45 LC cal., 3 1/2 in. barrel, custom nickel finish, Tru Ivory grips, includes Huckleberry shoulder rig and numbered dagger, mfg. by Uberti. New late 2008.

MSR $1,689	$1,395	$1,125	$995	$850	$650	$550	$450	

GRADING - PPGS™	100%	98%	95%	90%	80%	70%	60%	LAST MSR

THUNDERSTORM – .357 Mag. or .45 LC cal., 3 1/2 or 4 3/4 in. barrel, pre-war configuration, standard blue finish or stainless steel.

MSR $714	$625	$550	$475	$400	$350	$300	$250	

Add $182 for stainless steel.

THUNDERSTORM COMPETITION – .45 LC cal., 3 1/2 or 4 3/4 in. barrel, checkered Model P or Thunderer grips, stainless steel or blue finish, wide front sights, deep rear notch sights, designed for competition shooting. New 2011.

MSR $818	$675	$575	$475	$400	$350	$300	$250	

Add $156 for stainless steel.
Add $26 for Thunderer grips.

U.S. ARTILLERY MODEL – Rinaldo A. Carr 1895 U.S. Artillery Model Commemorative, 5 1/2 in. barrel. Limited mfg.

	$430	$375	$320	$290	$235	$195	$150	*$499*

U.S.V. ARTILLERY (ROUGH RIDER) – .45 LC cal. only, 5 1/2 in. barrel, case colored Old Model frame, smooth walnut grips, standard blue or antique original finish. Mfg. by Uberti or Pietta. New 1996.

MSR $584	$495	$450	$400	$350	$300	$250	$215	

Add $100 for original finish.
Subtract $18 for Pietta mfg.

U.S. CAVALRY MODEL P (A.P. CASEY) – .45 LC cal. only, 7 1/2 in. barrel, Old Model frame. Mfg. 1996-97.

	$430	$375	$320	$290	$235	$195	$150	*$499*

7TH CAVALRY CASED SET – U.S. Cavalry Model in case with accessories. Disc. 1990.

	$695	$610	$520	$470	$380	$315	$245	*$780*

U.S. 7TH CAVALRY CUSTER MODEL – .45 LC cal., authentic reproduction of original Colt military cavalry contract SAA, 7 1/2 in. barrel, marked "U.S." on lower left frame, one-piece walnut grips with military cartouche, standard blue, charcoal blue, or original finish. Mfg. by Uberti or Pietta.

MSR $584	$495	$450	$400	$350	$300	$250	$215	

Add $70 for charcoal blue finish.
Add $100 for original finish.
Subtract $18 for Pietta mfg.

* ***U.S. 7TH CAVALRY CUSTER SCOUT MODEL*** – similar to U.S. 7th Cavalry Custer Model, except has nickel finish. Mfg. by Uberti.

MSR $771	$650	$575	$495	$450	$395	$350	$295	

WILD BILL ELLIOT TEXAS CATTLEBRAND – .45 LC cal. Mfg. 1994-96.

	$1,225	$1,070	$920	$835	$675	$550	$430	*$1,395*

WYATT EARP LIMITED EDITION BUNTLINE – .45 LC cal. only, Old Model case hardened frame, 10 in. barrel, one-piece walnut grip with inlaid sterling silver medallion, case colored receiver, standard blue finish, 2.69 lbs. Mfg. by Uberti. Importation began 2002.

MSR $881	$740	$640	$525	$450	$375	$325	$275	

Item Code: CA558

REVOLVERS: REPRODUCTIONS, COLT, FRONTIER MODELS

The following current models are all manufactured by F. LLI Pietta.

FRONTIER SIX SHOOTER (DISC.) – .22 LR (disc. 1995), .22 WMR (disc.), .357 Mag., .38 Spl. (disc.), .38-40 WCF, .44 Spl. (new 1998), .44-40 WCF, or .45 LC cal., 4 3/4, 5 1/2, or 7 1/2 in. barrel lengths, steel backstraps and trigger guard.

* ***Frontier Six-Shooter (USA Finish)*** – .32 WCF, .357 Mag., .38 WCF, .44 Spl., .44 WCF, or .45 LC cal., this variation is disassembled and then refinished in the U.S. in the same type of finish as the original Colt SAA from the late 19th century. Mfg. 2008-2010.

	$725	$650	$575	$485	$440	$355	$290	*$860*

GRADING - PPGS™	100%	98%	95%	90%	80%	70%	60%	LAST MSR

* ***Frontier Six-Shooter Standard or Old Model***

	$395	$345	$295	$270	$215	$180	$140	*$469*

Add $30 for convertible .45 ACP cylinder.

* ***Frontier Six-Shooter Sheriff's Model*** – .44-40 WCF or .45 LC cal., w/o ejector, 3 or 4 (disc. 1992) in. barrel, steel backstraps and trigger guard. Disc. 1998, reintroduced 2000-2001.

	$395	$345	$295	$270	$215	$180	$140	*$469*

* ***Frontier Six-Shooter New Sheriff Model*** – .357 Mag., .44-40 WCF, .44 Spl., or .45 LC cal., 3 1/2 in. barrel with ejector, Old Model frame only. Imported 1995-2010.

	$450	$385	$335	$295	$245	$210	$175	*$548*

Add $40 for charcoal blue finish (disc.).
Add $45 for checkered walnut grips.

* ***Frontier Six-Shooter Target Model*** – similar to Standard Model, except has fully adj. target rear sight, brass or steel backstrap. Importation disc. 1991.

	$355	$310	$265	$240	$195	$160	$125	*$400*

Add $40 for .357 Mag. cal.

This variation was available in the Standard Model configuration only and with standard finish.

FRONTIER (CURRENT MFG.) – .357 Mag., .44-40 WCF (new 2012) or .45 LC cal., features pinched frame, Old Model, or pre-war configuration, standard finish or charcoal blue (disc. 2012), 3 1/2 (PW only), 4 3/4, 5 1/2, or 7 1/2 in. barrel. Mfg. by Pietta. New 2011.

MSR $506	$450	$400	$360	$330	$280	$240	$195	

* ***Frontier Bird's Head*** – .45 LC cal., features pre-war configuration, standard blue finish, 3 1/2 or 4 3/4 in. barrel. Mfg. by Pietta. Limited importation 2011 only.

	$465	$425	$375	$325	$295	$235	$190	*$535*

* ***Frontier Stainless*** – .357 Mag./.38 Spl., or .45 LC cal., features pre-war configuration, stainless steel, 3 1/2, 4 3/4, 5 1/2, or 7 1/2 (new 2011) in. barrel, standard walnut grips. Mfg. by Pietta. New 2011.

MSR $688	$595	$525	$450	$400	$365	$335	$295	

* ***Frontier Sheriff*** – .45 LC cal., pre-war configuration, standard blue finish, 3 1/2 in. barrel. Mfg. by Pietta. Limited importation 2011 only.

	$475	$425	$375	$325	$295	$235	$190	*$546*

BIG IRON – .357 Mag. or .45 LC cal., brass gripstraps and trigger guard, 4 3/4 in. barrel, case hardened frame with blue barrel and cylinder or Millenium (matte black) finish, one piece smooth walnut grips, approx. 2 1/2 lbs. Mfg. by Pietta. New 2011.

MSR $441	$365	$315	$260	$230	$195	$175	$150	

HOLY SMOKER – .45 LC cal., 4 3/4 in. barrel, case hardened pre-war frame, standard blue finish, gold-plated sterling silver Jesus on the cross inlay on one or both sides of the one-piece walnut grips, accurate replica of Russell Crowe's gun from *3:10 to Yuma*, 2 1/4 lbs. Mfg. by Pietta. New 2010.

MSR $774	$675	$575	$495	$450	$395	$350	$295	

Add $168 for sterling silver cross inlay on both sides of the grips (disc. 2012).

Item code: PP310

MAN WITH NO NAME SAA – .45 LC cal., 4 3/4 or 5 1/2 in. barrel, case hardened pre-war frame, standard blue finish, walnut grips with sterling silver rattlesnake inlay on one or both sides, accurate replica of Clint Eastwood's spaghetti western gun. Mfg. by Pietta. New 2010.

MSR $748	$650	$575	$495	$450	$395	$350	$295	

Add $26 for 4 3/4 in. barrel.
Add $168 for sterling silver rattlesnake inlay on both sides (disc. 2012).

Item code: PP410 and PP411

GRADING - PPGS™	100%	98%	95%	90%	80%	70%	60%	LAST MSR

NEW SHERIFF – .45 LC cal., pre-war configuration, 3 1/2 in. barrel, standard blue finish. Mfg. by Pietta. Disc. 2012.

	$460	$410	$350	$300	$260	$210	$175	*$546*

ROOSTER SHOOTER – .45 LC cal., SA, 4 3/4 in. barrel, pre-war configuration, one-piece orange finger grooved grip, antique original finish, 2 1/2 lbs. Mfg. by Pietta.

MSR $883	$725	$625	$525	$450	$375	$325	$275

Item code: PPRS410

THUNDERBALL – .357 Mag. or .45 LC cal., patterned after Colt's Thunderer Model, 3 1/2 or 4 3/4 in. barrel with full ejector rod housing, birdshead grips, blue or stainless steel finish. Mfg. by Pietta. New 2011.

MSR $506	$435	$385	$335	$300	$285	$260	$240

Add $182 for stainless steel.

WYATT EARP LIMITED EDITION BUNTLINE – .45 LC cal. only, Old Model case hardened frame, 10 in. barrel, one-piece walnut grip with inlaid sterling silver medallion, case colored receiver, standard blue finish, 2.69 lbs. Mfg. by Pietta. Importation began 2002.

MSR $857	$700	$625	$525	$450	$375	$325	$275

Item code: PP558

REVOLVERS: REPRODUCTIONS, COLT CONVERSIONS

All guns are manufactured (current and previous) by Uberti.

Add approx. $60 for charcoal blue (disc. 2011) or $74 for Original finish (2011).

1851 NAVY RICHARDS-MASON – .38 Spl. cal., patterned after the original Richards-Mason 1851 Navy Conversion, 4 3/4, 5 1/2, or 7 1/2 in. barrel, available in standard blue, charcoal blue (disc. 2011), or original (disc. 2011) finish. Mfg. by Uberti. Importation began 2003.

MSR $519	$425	$375	$325	$285	$240	$215	$185

Add $25 for silver plated gripstraps and trigger guard (disc. 2006).

1851 MAN WITH NO NAME CONVERSION – .38 Colt/S&W Spl. cal., 7 1/2 in. barrel, blue finish, patterned after the original 1851 model used in the 1960s spaghetti westerns, one piece walnut grip. New 2007.

MSR $549	$450	$395	$350	$300	$250	$215	$185

Add $269 for right side sterling silver rattlesnake grip inlay or $448 for both sides (disc. 2012).

1860 ARMY RICHARDS-MASON – .38 Spl. (new 2007), .44 WCF and Russian, .45 LC (new 2007), or .45 Schofield cal., patterned after the original Richards-Mason 1860 Conversion, 4 3/4 (disc. 2010), 5 1/2 or 8 in. barrel, available in standard blue, charcoal blue (disc. 2011), or original (disc. 2011) finish. Mfg. by Uberti. Importation began 2003.

MSR $558	$450	$395	$350	$325	$295	$260	$230

1868 THUER CONVERSION OF 1860 ARMY – .44-40 WCF cal., Thuer conversion ring and cylinder, cartridge loading tool, all other specifications same as 1860 Army, prototype only.

This model required a special hand-loaded round in .44 cal for the Thuer Conversion. While it was advertised with a MSR $418, this model was only available as a prototype before being shelved by Uberti in 2002.

TYPE II RICHARDS TRANSITION MODEL – .38 Spl., .44 Colt, .44 Spl., or .45 LC cal., 5 1/2 or 8 in. barrel, blue finish, case hardened frame, one-piece walnut grips. New 2007.

MSR $592	$475	$425	$375	$335	$300	$260	$230

REVOLVERS: REPRODUCTIONS, REMINGTON

These guns are reproductions of the Models 1875 and 1890, and are manufactured by Uberti.

Add $90 for nickel plating, $10 for charcoal blue finish on models listed below.

MODEL 1875 OUTLAW – .357 Mag., .44-40 WCF, or .45 LC cal., 5 1/2 (new 2010) or 7 1/2 in. barrel, case colored frame, standard blue, charcoal blue (disc. 2012), or original (disc. 2012) finish, plain wood grips. Disc. 1993, reintroduced 2010.

MSR $545	$450	$385	$310	$265	$235	$200	$175

Last MSR in 1993 was $390.

Add $101 for dual cylinder (.45 LC/.45 ACP cal., 7 1/2 in. only).

GRADING - PPGS™	100%	98%	95%	90%	80%	70%	60%	LAST MSR

MODEL 1890 – .357 Mag., .44-40 WCF, or .45 LC cal., 5 1/2 or 7 1/2 (disc.) in. barrel, case colored frame, standard blue finish, plain wood grips, lanyard loop. Disc. 1993, reintroduced 2010.

MSR $571	$465	$395	$320	$290	$235	$200	$175	

Last MSR in 1993 was $390

Add $91 for dual cylinder (.45 LC/.45 ACP cal.).

1871 ROLLING BLOCK TARGET PISTOL – .22 LR, .22 Hornet (new 1990), .22 WMR, or .357 Mag. cal., 9 1/2 in. barrel. Importation disc. 1990.

	$250	$220	$185	$170	$135	$110	$85	*$280*

1858 ARMY NEW MODEL CONVERSION – .38 Spl., .44-40 WCF, or .45 LC cal., 5 1/2, 7 3/8, or 8 in. barrel, forged steel frame, blue finish, walnut grips. New 2007.

MSR $553	$465	$415	$365	$325	$260	$220	$190	

Add $72 for dual cylinder (.45 LC/.44 cal. Percussion, disc. 2010).

REVOLVERS: REPRODUCTIONS, SMITH & WESSON

These guns are S&W reproductions, and are manufactured by Uberti.

SCHOFIELD MODEL NO. 3 – .38 Spl. (disc. 1997), .38-40 WCF (disc. 1997), .44 Russian/Spl., .44-40 WCF, .45 Schofield, .45 ACP (disc.), or .45 LC cal., available in 7 (Civilian or Military) or 5 (Wells Fargo only) in. barrel. Mfg. by Armi San Marco 1996-99.

	$730	$640	$545	$495	$400	$330	$255	*$849*

Add $100 for nickel finish.
Add $150 for custom nickel finish.

This model was also available as a "Little Big Horn" variation with sub-inspector markings and "SBL" cartouche.

SCHOFIELD MODEL NO. 3 (CURRENT MFG.) – .38 Spl.,.44-40 WCF, or .45 LC cal., 3 1/2, 5, or 7 in. barrel, blue finish, mfg. by Uberti. New 2007.

MSR $1,039	$895	$800	$700	$600	$500	$400	$300	

MODEL NO. 3 RUSSIAN – .44 Russian or .45 LC cal., 6 1/2 in. barrel, blue finish, two-piece walnut grips, blue frame, mfg. by Uberti. New 2007.

MSR $1,127	$925	$825	$700	$600	$500	$400	$300	

RIFLES: CUSTOM SHOP OPTIONS

The following wood upgrades and special options apply to all rifles imported by Cimarron.

Add $200 for AA select wood (disc.), $520 for AAA premium select wood, or $1,040 for super premium (fine European walnut). Add $150 for fine hand oil finish (disc.) or $201 for super fine stock finish. Add $80 for antique finish.

RIFLES: REPRODUCTIONS, BURGESS

1883 BURGESS CARBINE/RIFLE – .44-40 WCF (new 2011) or .45 LC cal., 20 or 25 1/2 in. barrel, 10 (20 in. barrel) or 15 (25 1/2 in. barrel) shot mag., sliding dust cover over the loading port, side plate, lever action design, mfg. by Uberti. Importation began 2010.

MSR $1,403	$1,195	$1,025	$900	$800	$700	$625	$550	

Add $26 for rifle configuration.

RIFLES: REPRODUCTIONS, COLT

LIGHTNING MAGAZINE RIFLE – .357 Mag., .44-40 WCF, or .45 LC cal., 20, 24, or 26 in. round (not available with 24 or 26 in. barrel) or octagon barrel, walnut stock, blue or case colored frame, patterned after Colt Lightning rifle. Mfg. by Pedersoli. Imported 2006-2012.

	$1,375	$1,175	$975	$875	$700	$600	$500	*$1,581*

Add $98 for octagon barrel.
Add $243 for case colored frame.

RIFLES/CARBINES: REPRODUCTIONS, REMINGTON ROLLING BLOCK

MODEL 1871 ROLLING BLOCK BABY CARBINE – same cals. as Target Pistol, has 22 in. barrel and walnut stock and forearm, brass trigger guard and buttplate. Importation disc. 1990.

	$310	$270	$230	$210	$170	$140	$110	*$340*

GRADING - PPGS™	100%	98%	95%	90%	80%	70%	60%	LAST MSR

MODEL 1875 CARBINE – same cals. as Model 1875, 18 in. barrel, includes non-detachable shoulder stock with brass hardware and lanyard ring. Importation disc. 1990.

	$410	$360	$305	$280	$225	$185	$145	*$460*

ROLLING BLOCK SPORTING RIFLE – .45-70 cal., 30 in. barrel, walnut stock and forearm. Imported 1989-90 only.

	$625	$545	$470	$425	$345	$280	$220	*$620*

* ***Deluxe Rolling Block Sporting Rifle*** – similar to standard model, except has select wood. Importation disc. 1990.

	$725	$635	$545	$495	$400	$325	$255	*$720*

REMINGTON ROLLING BLOCK LONG RANGE CREEDMOOR – .45-70 Govt. cal., 30 in. tapered octagon barrel, deluxe checkered walnut stock. Importation began 1997.

	$1,125	$985	$845	$765	$620	$505	$395	*$1,295*

"ADOBE WALLS" ROLLING BLOCK – .45-70 Govt. cal., 30 in. octagon barrel, hand checkered walnut stock, case hardened receiver, German silver nose cap, optional Creedmoor sight, blue finish, 10.35 lbs. Mfg. by Pedersoli. Importation began 2004.

MSR $1,805	$1,500	$1,300	$1,100	$975	$825	$675	$575	

RIFLES/CARBINES: REVOLVING

BUNTLINE CARBINE – .22 LR/.22 WMR (convertible cylinders, disc.), .357 Mag., .44-40 WCF, or .45 LC cal., 18 in. barrel, includes non-detachable shoulder stock with brass hardware and finger extension trigger guard, mfg. by Uberti. Importation disc. 1991, reintroduced 2006.

MSR $811	$695	$575	$495	$450	$395	$350	$285	

Add 5% for target sights or .22 LR/.22 WMR combo (disc.).

THUNDERSTORM CARBINE – .45 LC cal., 6 shot, 18 in. barrel. Mfg. by Uberti. New 2012.

MSR $984	$825	$675	$575	$495	$425	$375	$325	

RIFLES: REPRODUCTIONS, SHARPS

SPORTING #1 RIFLE – .40-65 Win. or .45-70 Govt. cal., 32 in. octagon barrel, pistol grip stock. Mfg. by Pedersoli. Imported 2000-2002.

	$975	$855	$730	$665	$535	$440	$340	*$1,095*

SPORTING #1 SILHOUETTE RIFLE – .45-70 Govt. (disc. 2012) or .50-70 cal., 32 in. octagon barrel with silhouette sights, pistol grip stock. Mfg. by Pedersoli. Importation began 2003.

MSR $1,772	$1,475	$1,250	$1,050	$950	$750	$625	$550	

ARMI-SPORT BILLY DIXON MODEL 1874 SPORTING RIFLE – .38-55 WCF, .45-70 Govt., .45-90 Win., .45-110 (new 2003), or .50-90 (new 2003) cal., 32 in. barrel, nickel silver front blade and forearm cap, checkered deluxe walnut stock, double set triggers. Mfg. by Armi-Sport. Importation began 1997.

MSR $1,580	$1,375	$1,175	$995	$850	$750	$650	$550	

Add $42 for cals. other than .45-70 Govt.

PEDERSOLI BILLY DIXON MODEL 1874 SPORTING RIFLE – .45-70 Govt., .45-90 Win., or .50-70 (mfg. 2004-2006, reintroduced 2010 only) cal., 32 in. barrel, nickel silver front sight blade and forearm cap, checkered deluxe walnut stock, double set triggers. Mfg. by Pedersoli. Importation began 1997.

MSR $2,079	$1,750	$1,495	$1,300	$1,175	$950	$775	$650	

Add $208 for .45-90 cal.

ARMI-SPORT QUIGLEY II MODEL 1874 SPORTING RIFLE – .38-55 WCF (mfg. 2011-2012), .45-70 Govt., .45-90 Win. (disc. 2012), .45-110 (mfg. 2004-2012), .45-120 Sharps (disc. 2012), or .50-90 (mfg. 2002-2012) cal., 34 in. octagon barrel with storage compartment in stock. Mfg. by Armi-Sport. Importation began 2000.

MSR $1,754	$1,525	$1,300	$1,100	$925	$825	$725	$625	

Add $28 for cals. other than .45-70 Govt. (disc. 2012).

GRADING - PPGS™	100%	98%	95%	90%	80%	70%	60%	LAST MSR

PEDERSOLI QUIGLEY MODEL 1874 SPORTING RIFLE - .45-70 Govt., .45-90 Win., .45-110 (disc. 2012), .45-120 Sharps, .50-70 (mfg. 2004-2006), or .50-90 (new 2002) cal., 34 in. octagon barrel with storage compartment in stock. Mfg. by Pedersoli. Importation began 2000.

MSR $2,275	$1,925	$1,675	$1,425	$1,275	$1,050	$875	$725	

Add $33 for .45-90 Win. cal., $194 for .45-120 cal., or $314 for .50-70 (disc.) or .50-90 cal.

SHARPS BIG 50 LONG RANGE MODEL 1874 SPORTING RIFLE - .50-90 cal., 34 in. barrel, double set triggers, aperture rear sight, checkered stock and forearm. Mfg. by Pedersoli. Importation began 2004.

MSR $2,088	$1,750	$1,525	$1,300	$1,125	$950	$850	$750	

PEDERSOLI SHARPS "PRIDE OF THE PLAINS" MODEL 1874 - .45-70 Govt. cal., 32 in. matte black octagon barrel, hand checkered walnut stock, nickel receiver, Creedmoor rear sight. Mfg. by Pedersoli. Importation began 2004.

MSR $2,323	$1,875	$1,650	$1,350	$1,200	$975	$825	$725	

ARMI-SPORT SHARPS "PRIDE OF THE PLAINS" II MODEL 1874 - .45-70 Govt. cal., similar to original "Pride of the Plains", except comes with or w/o telescopic sight, silver forearm cap. Mfg. by Armi-Sport. Mfg. mid-2008-2009.

	$1,215	$1,065	$910	$825	$670	$545	$425	*$1,429*

Add $450 for extended tube telescopic sight.

SHARPS MCNELLY CARBINE MODEL 1874 (TEXAS RANGER) - .45-70 Govt. or .50-70 (disc. 2012) cal., 22 in. round blue barrel, American black walnut stock, case colored receiver, marked with TS initials with Lone Star in between on barrel. Mfg. by Armi Sport. Importation began 2004.

MSR $1,377	$1,175	$975	$825	$725	$625	$525	$450	

Add $42 for .50-70 cal. (disc. 2012).

SHARPS ROCKY MOUNTAIN II MODEL 74 - .45-70 Govt. cal., 30 in. octagon barrel, silver receiver, checkered walnut stock, available with optional 6X Malcolm rifle scope, mfg. by Armi Sport. Importation began 2010.

MSR $1,689	$1,495	$1,275	$1,000	$875	$775	$675	$575	

Add $619 for Malcolm scope.

SHARPS PROFESSIONAL HUNTER MODEL 1874 - .45-70 Govt. cal., 32 in. barrel, mfg. by Pedersoli. Importation began 2005.

MSR $1,525	$1,350	$1,150	$975	$875	$725	$575	$445	

SLOTTER & CO. SHARPS RIFLE - .45-70 Govt. cal., 34 in. barrel, choice of maple or walnut (disc.) stock, mfg. by Pedersoli. Importation began 2011.

MSR $2,379	$1,950	$1,675	$1,325	$1,175	$950	$825	$695	

LITTLE RASCAL MINI-SHARPS - .22 LR, .22 Hornet (new 2012), .30-30 Win. (new 2012), .38-55 WCF, or .45 LC cal., 3/4 scale Sharps rifle with original patent markings, 26 in. octagon barrel with blade front and aperture rear sight on upper tang, polished steel or standard blue color case hardened frame, mfg. by ArmiSport. Importation began 2011.

MSR $1,329	$1,175	$1,025	$850	$700	$600	$525	$450	

U.S.A. SHOOTING TEAM CREEDMOOR SHARPS - .45-70 Govt. cal., color case hardened frame, blue finish, 34 in. round barrel, walnut stock, mfg. by Armi-Sport.

MSR $1,559	$1,375	$1,175	$1,000	$900	$800	$675	$475	

Add $182 for carrying case.

Cimarron is donating a portion of the sales from this rifle to the U.S.A. shooting team.

RIFLES: REPRODUCTIONS, SPENCER

1860 SPENCER RIFLE - .56-50 cal., 30 in. barrel, uncheckered walnut stock and forearm, three barrel bands, case colored receiver, trigger guard, and hammer. Mfg. by Armi-Sport. Mfg. mid-2008-2012.

	$1,550	$1,325	$1,100	$975	$775	$625	$550	*$1,791*

GRADING - PPGS™	100%	98%	95%	90%	80%	70%	60%	LAST MSR

1865 SPENCER REPEATING RIFLE – .44-40 WCF (disc. 2012) .45 Schofield (disc. 2012), .45 LC, or .56-50 (disc. 2012) cal., case colored receiver, 20 or 30 (.56-50 cal. only, disc. 2009) in. barrel, blue finish, color case hardened frame, straight grip walnut stock, includes slings, mfg. by Armi-Sport. Importation began 2005.

MSR $1,788	$1,575	$1,325	$1,100	$950	$800	$725	$625	

Add $182 for 30 in. barrel (disc. 2009).

RIFLES: REPRODUCTIONS, WINCHESTER

The rifles listed below are manufactured by A. Uberti, unless otherwise indicated.

CIVILIAN HENRY RIFLE/CARBINE – .44-40 WCF, .44 Spl. (mfg. 1993-95), or .45 LC (new 1993) cal., brass or case colored steel (.44-40 WCF and .45 LC cal. only, new 2002) frame, 24 in. barrel on rifle, 22 (disc. 1995, .44-40 WCF cal. only) in. barrel on carbine, standard blue, charcoal, or original finish, mfg. by Uberti.

MSR $1,351	$1,150	$975	$850	$750	$650	$550	$475	

Add $100 for charcoal blue or $150 for original finish.
Add $65 for steel frame model.
Add $1,005 for standard engraving.
Add $1,273 for steel engraving.
Add $2,209 for Lincoln Presentation hand engraving (disc. 2009, reintroduced 2011).
Add $50 for in-the-white finish (disc.).
Previous to 1997, this model could also be special ordered with Grade A engraving ($450 extra), Grade B engraving ($550 extra), and Grade C engraving ($725 extra).

CIVIL WAR HENRY RIFLE – .44-40 WCF or .45 LC (new 1998) cal., 24 in. barrel, patterned after the U.S. issue original inspected by Chas. G. Chapman (C.G.C.) with military inspector's marks and cartouche, military sling swivels became standard in 1996, choice of standard blue, charcoal blue or original finish. Importation began 1993.

MSR $1,533	$1,325	$1,125	$950	$825	$700	$575	$495	

Add $100 for charcoal blue or $150 for original finish.
Add $65 for in-the-white finish (disc.).
Add $2,509 for standard hand engraving (disc. 2009).
Add $3,055 for standard hand engraving and deluxe wood (disc. 2009).
Add $4,225 for Lincoln hand engraving (disc. 2009).
Add $4,810 for Lincoln hand engraving and deluxe wood (disc. 2009).

1866 YELLOWBOY SPORTING RIFLE – .22 LR (disc. 1993, reintroduced 2012), .22 WMR (disc. 1993), .32-20 WCF (new 2002), .38 Spl. (new 1995), .38-40 WCF (new 2002), .44 Spl. (new 2006), .44-40 WCF, or .45 LC (new 1993) cal., brass receiver, 20 (new 2000, Short Rifle) or 24 in. octagon barrel, standard blue, charcoal, or original finish.

MSR $1,143	$995	$875	$775	$675	$575	$475	$375	

Add $39 for .32-20 WCF or .38-40 WCF cal. Add $136 for .22 LR cal.
Add $100 for charcoal blue (.44-40 WCF or .45 LC cal. only) or $150 for original finish (.44-40 WCF or .45 LC cal. only).
Add $1,000 for standard engraving (new 1997).
Add $2,946 for Mexican Eagle engraving (new 1997) or $2,535 for Red Cloud engraving (mfg. 2005-2008).
Add $500 (retail) for A engraving, $650 for B engraving, $1,175 for C engraving. Disc. 1996.

1866 YELLOWBOY CARBINE – .22 LR (new 2013), .32-20 WCF, .38 Spl., .38-40 WCF, .38-55 WCF (disc. 2011), .44 Spl., .44-40 WCF, or .45 LC cal., similar to Model 1866 Yellowboy Sporting Rifle, except has 19 in. round barrel with 2 bands, saddle ring, uncheckered walnut stock and forearm, mfg. by Uberti.

MSR $1,156	$1,025	$895	$750	$675	$575	$475	$375	

Add $26 for .32-20 WCF of .38-40 WCF cal.
Add $100 for charcoal blue (.44-40 WCF or .45 LC cal. only) or $150 for original finish (.44-40 WCF or .45 LC cal. only).
Subtract $52 for .22 LR cal. (new 2013).
Add $2,067 for standard engraving (disc. 2009).
Add $2,567 for standard engraving and deluxe wood (disc. 2009).

GRADING - PPGS™	100%	98%	95%	90%	80%	70%	60%	LAST MSR

Add $2,957 for deluxe engraving and deluxe wood (disc. 2009).
Add $4,875 for Mexican Eagle engraving with deluxe wood and silver accents (disc. 2009).
Add $4,095 for Red Cloud engraving, studded wood and blue finish (disc. 2009).

* ***1866 Trapper Carbine*** – .38 Spl. (new 2002), .44-40 WCF, or .45 LC (new 2005) cal., 16 in. round barrel, standard blue finish. Importation disc. 1990, reintroduced 2002.

MSR $1,104	$950	$825	$725	$650	$550	$425	$395	

Add $35 for saddle ring (disc.).

* ***1866 Yellowboy Indian Carbine*** – .22 LR (disc.), .22 WMR (disc.), .38 Spl. (disc.), .44-40 WCF (disc.) or .45 LC (new 2012) cal., 19 in. round barrel, photo engraved (disc. 1989) or plain brass frame includes tacks in forearm and rear of stock. Disc. 1989, reintroduced 2012.

MSR $1,299	$1,100	$900	$750	$675	$575	$475	$375	

Last MSR in 1989 was $649.

* ***1886 Red Cloud Commemorative Carbine*** – same cals. as Yellowboy Indian Carbine, includes special engraving representing Oglalla Indian tribe symbols, brass tacks in forearm and stock. Disc. 1989.

	$895	$785	$670	$610	$490	$405	$315	*$649*

1873 SPORTING RIFLE – .22 LR (disc. 1993), .22 WMR (disc. 1993), .32-20 WCF (new 2002), .357 Mag./.38 Spl., .38-40 WCF (new 2002), .44 Spl. (new 2002), .44-40 WCF, or .45 LC cal., 24 1/4 in. octagon barrel, case hardened receiver, full mag., iron sights, standard blue, charcoal, or original finish. Mfg. by Uberti.

MSR $1,234	$1,050	$900	$800	$700	$600	$500	$450	

Add $39 for .32-20 WCF, .38-40 WCF, or .44 Spl. cal.
Add $100 for charcoal blue (.44-40 WCF or .45 LC cal.) or $150 for original finish (.44-40 WCF or .45 LC cal. only).
Add $425 for old style color case hardening.
Add $104 for Deluxe Model with pistol grip and checkered walnut.
Add $1,034 for standard engraving or $2,005 for 1 of 1,000 engraving.
Add $500 (retail) for A engraving, $650 for B engraving, $1,075 for C engraving (disc. 2002).

* ***1873 Evil Roy Saddle Ring Rifle*** – .357 Mag., .44-40 WCF (new 2012), or .45 LC cal., 20 in. barrel, features Evil Roy shooting improvements, standard finish. Imported 2005-2007, reintroduced 2012 only.

	$1,750	$1,500	$1,300	$1,125	$1,020	$825	$675	*$2,027*

* ***1873 Larry Crow Signature Series Rifle*** – .357 Mag. or .45 LC cal., 20 in. barrel, features Larry Crow shooting improvements and signature. Imported 2005-2007.

	$1,850	$1,620	$1,385	$1,260	$1,015	$830	$645	*$2,275*

* ***1873 Short Rifle*** – .32-20 WCF (new 2002), .357 Mag./.38 Spl. (new 2000), .38-40 WCF (new 2002), .44 Spl. (new 2002), .44-40 WCF, or .45 LC cal., features 20 in. octagon barrel, case hardened receiver, iron sights, standard blue finish. Importation began 1990.

MSR $1,234	$1,050	$900	$800	$700	$600	$500	$450	

Add $39 for .32-20 WCF or .38-40 WCF cal.
Add $104 for Deluxe Border Model with pistol grip.

* ***1873 Long Range Rifle*** – .44-40 WCF or .45 LC cal., includes 30 in. octagon barrel with full mag., case hardened receiver, iron sights, standard blue finish. New 1990.

MSR $1,286	$1,150	$1,025	$925	$800	$700	$600	$500	

Add $351 for Deluxe Model with pistol grip.
Add $1,034 for standard engraving or $2,005 for 1 of 1,000 engraving.

* ***1873 Texas Brush Popper*** – .357 Mag./.38 Spl., .44-40 WCF, or .45 LC cal., features 18 in. half-round, half-octagon barrel w/o barrel bands, case colored receiver, choice of straight or checkered pistol grip stock.

MSR $1,273	$1,050	$900	$800	$700	$600	$500	$450	

Add $78 for Deluxe Model with pistol grip (new 2009).

GRADING - PPGS™	100%	98%	95%	90%	80%	70%	60%	LAST MSR

* ***1873 "Evil Roy" Texas Brush Popper*** – .357 Mag./.38 Spl., .44-40 WCF, or .45 LC cal., features 18 in. half-round, half-octagon barrel w/o barrel bands, choice of straight or checkered pistol grip stock, custom Marble sights, leather butt tamer, short stroke kit, tuned action, designed for competition cowboy action shooting. New 2010.

MSR $1,875	$1,700	$1,450	$1,225	41,000	$850	$750	$650	

Add $84 for Deluxe Model with pistol grip.

1873 SADDLE RING CARBINE – .22 LR (disc. 1993), .22 WMR (disc. 1993), .32-20 WCF (new 2002), .357 Mag./.38 Spl., .38-40 WCF (new 2002), .44 Mag. (new 2012), .44 Spl. (new 2002), .44-40 WCF, or .45 LC cal., blue steel receiver, saddle ring, 19 in. round barrel, standard blue, charcoal blue or original finish.

MSR $1,315	$1,125	$950	$800	$700	$600	$500	$450	

Add $70 for charcoal blue or $120 for original finish (.44-40 WCF or .45 LC cal. only).
Add $119 for .44 Mag. cal. (new 2012).
Add $90 for nickel plating (disc.).

* ***1873 Saddle Ring Shorty*** – .357 Mag./.38 Spl., .44-40 WCF, or .45 LC cal., 18 in. barrel with iron sights, standard action or with short stroke kit.

MSR $1,299	$1,100	$950	$825	$725	$625	$525	$450	

Add $78 for short stroke kit.

1873 TRAPPER CARBINE – .357 Mag. (new 1990, reintroduced 2004), .44-40 WCF (disc. 1990, reintroduced 2005), or .45 LC (mfg. 1990, reintroduced 2005) cal., 16 in. barrel, blue finish only, mfg. by Uberti. Importation disc. 1990, reintroduced 2004.

MSR $1,169	$975	$825	$725	$650	$550	$450	$395	

Add $65 for color case hardened frame (.44-40 WCF or .45 LC cal. only).

1876 CENTENNIAL SPORTING RIFLE – .40-60 WCF, .45-60 WCF, .45-75 WCF, or .50-95 WCF cal., 22 (Short rifle) or 28 in. octagon barrel, blue finish and case hardened frame, full mag., iron sights, walnut stock and forearm, mfg. by Uberti. Importation began 2006.

MSR $1,559	$1,350	$1,100	$995	$850	$750	$625	$525	

Add $104 for Short rifle.
Add $26 for .50-95 WCF cal.
Add $3,315 for standard engraving (disc. 2009).
Add $3,900 for standard engraving and deluxe wood (disc. 2009).

1876 CARBINE – .45-60 WCF or .45-75 cal., 22 in. round barrel with full length forend and barrel band, Crossfire model has color case hardened frame and is exact replica of carbine used in *Crossfire Trail*, Canadian Northwest Mounted Police variation has blued frame and saddle ring, mfg. by Uberti. Importation began 2010.

MSR $1,707	$1,495	$1,300	$1,100	$950	$800	$700	$595	

Add $42 for blue frame (N.W.M.P. Model).

1885 HI-WALL RIFLE – .30-40 Krag (new 2004), .348 Win. (new 2004), .38-55 WCF (new 2000), .405 Win. (new 2006), .40-65 WCF, .45-70 Govt., .45-90 WCF (new 2000), or .45-120 WCF (mfg. 2002-2004) cal., 28 (disc.) or 30 in. octagon barrel, case hardened finish on frame, iron sights (standard) or optional aperture rear and globe front sight (new 2002), mfg. by Uberti. New 1998.

MSR $1,034	$900	$800	$700	$600	$525	$450	$350	

Add $44 for cals. other than .45-70 Govt.
Add $148 for double set triggers.
Add $134 for Deluxe Model with adj. sights, and pistol grip (new 2002).
Add $1,034 for standard engraving, $1,676 for deluxe engraving, or $3,682 for deluxe gold line engraving.

1885 HI-WALL RIFLE (PEDERSOLI) – .38-55 WCF, .45-70 Govt., or .45-90 WCF cal., 32 in. heavy barrel, single set trigger, straight grip walnut stock, case colored receiver. Mfg. by Pedersoli. Limited importation 2010-2011 only.

	$1,975	$1,725	$1,525	$1,300	$1,100	$900	$725	*$2,278*

GRADING - PPGS™	100%	98%	95%	90%	80%	70%	60%	LAST MSR

1885 LOW WALL RIFLE – .22 LR, .22 Hornet, .22 WMR, .30-30 Win. (disc. 2007), .32-20 WCF, .357 Mag. (disc. 2007), .38-40 WCF, .44 Mag. (disc. 2007), .38-55 (disc. 2007), .44-40 WCF, .45-70 Govt. (custom shop only), or .45 LC cal., 30 in. barrel, hand checkered walnut stock, single or double set trigger, case colored frame. Mfg. by Uberti. Importation began 2005.

MSR $974	$850	$725	$625	$525	$475	$400	$350

Add $117 for Deluxe Model with adj. sights, and pistol grip.
Add $130 for double set triggers on Deluxe model.
Add $1,004 for standard engraving (.45-70 Govt. cal., custom shop only, mfg. 2010).
Add $1,285 for standard engraving with pistol grip (45-70 Govt. cal., custom shop only, mfg. 2010).

1886 CARBINE/RIFLE – .45-70 Govt. cal., 22 (carbine, disc. 2012) or 26 (rifle) in. octagon barrel, walnut stock and forearm, case colored frame, standard blue finish. Mfg. by ArmiSport. Importation began 2011.

MSR $1,559	$1,375	$1,175	$975	$850	$725	$600	$495

1892 RIFLE – .357 Mag., .44 Mag., .44-40 WCF, or .45 LC, 20 or 24 in. barrel, available in either solid or takedown (disc. 2010) frame, uncheckered walnut stock and forearm, case colored receiver, mfg. by ArmiSport. Importation began 2005.

MSR $1,189	$1,025	$875	$750	$650	$550	$450	$395

Add $28 for .44-40 WCF or .44 Mag. cals. Add $155 for takedown frame (disc. 2010).

1892 CARBINE – .357 Mag., .44 Mag. (new 2010), .44-40 WCF, or .45 LC cal., 16 (Trapper, disc. 2010), or saddle ring with 20 in. barrel only, solid frame, choice of big loop lever (El Dorado) or standard with 20 in. barrel, mfg. by ArmiSport. Importation began 2006.

MSR $1,189	$1,025	$875	$775	$650	$550	$450	$395

Add $28 for .44-40 WCF or .44 Mag. cal.
Add $54 for El Dorado model with Big Loop lever and 20 in. barrel (not available in .44 Mag. cal.).
Subtract $187 for Trapper model with 16 in. barrel (disc. 2010).

RIFLES: SEMI-AUTO

M4 22 TACTICAL – .22 LR cal., 19 in. solid steel barrel, fire control group, 28 shot, dust cover, adj. sights, pseudo flash hider, bayonet lug, forward assist, and bolt release, quad rail capable forearm, includes two mags, black polymer grips, matte black finish, 5 1/2 lbs., mfg. by Chiappa. Mfg. 2011-2012.

	$475	$400	$350	$315	$285	$260	$240	*$579*

PPS/50 CARBINE – .22 LR cal., patterned after the Russian WWII PPS military rifle, full length barrel shroud, 50 shot drum mag., walnut stock. Imported by Pietta. Imported 2012 only.

	$675	$525	$450	$395	$350	$300	$250	*$805*

SHOTGUNS: REPRODUCTIONS

1878 SxS COACH GUN – 12 ga., 3 in. chambers, 20 or 26 (new 2010) in. barrels, standard blue, original (disc. 2012), or USA (mfg. 2010-2012) finish, hammers, DT, uncheckered American walnut stock with pistol grip, mfg. in China by Polytech. Importation began 2007.

MSR $575	$475	$400	$350	$300	$250	$200	$150

Add $19 for 26 in. barrels.
Add $120 for Original finish (disc. 2012), or $170 for USA finish (mfg. 2010-2012).

1881 SxS COACH GUN – 12 ga., 2 3/4 in. chambers, 20 (mfg. 2010), 22, 26, 28, or 30 in. barrels with choke tubes, hammerless, straight grip walnut stock, DT, standard blue finish. Mfg. in China by Polytech. Importation began 2010.

MSR $722	$600	$525	$450	$400	$350	$300	$250

Add $39 for Deluxe model with deluxe wood.

1887 LEVER ACTION – 12 ga., 2 3/4 in. chamber, standard blue or Original (disc.) finish, 20 (disc.), 22 (disc.), 24 (mfg. 2010-disc.), or 28 in. barrel, uncheckered pistol grip stock, mfg. by ArmiSport Chiappa. Importation began 2010.

MSR $1,392	$1,175	$975	$825	$725	$600	$500	$400

Subtract $28 for Terminator model with 20 (mfg. 2010-disc.) or 22 in. barrel with blue or Original finish (mfg. 2010-disc.).

GRADING - PPGS™	100%	98%	95%	90%	80%	70%	60%	LAST MSR

1897 SLIDE ACTION – 12 ga., 2 3/4 in. chamber, 20 in. barrel with choke tubes, patterned after the Model 1897 Winchester, blue or original (disc. 2010) finish, uncheckered American walnut stock with pistol grip. Mfg. in China by Polytech. Imported 2007-2012.

	$475	$400	$350	$300	$250	$200	$150	*$561*

Add $86 for Original finish (disc. 2010).

1897 SLIDE ACTION – 12 ga., 2 3/4 in. chambers, 20 in. barrel with choke tubes, standard blue finish, approx. 7 1/4 lbs. New 2013.

MSR $561	$475	$395	$335	$295	$265	$235	$200

WYATT EARP SHOTGUN – 12 ga., SxS, 20 in. barrel, standard blue finish. New 2013.

MSR $1,554	$1,325	$1,125	$925	$825	$725	$625	$525

CITADEL

Current trademark imported beginning 2009 by Legacy Sports International, located in Reno, NV.

CARBINES: SEMI-AUTO

M1 CARBINE – 9mm Para. (new late 2013), or .22 LR cal., M1 design, 18 in. threaded (new 2013) barrel with fixed front sight and adj. rear sight, black synthetic, Harvest Moon camo (new 2013), Muddy Girl camo (new 2013), Outshine camo (new 2013), or wood (new 2012) stock, 10 shot mag., blued finish, 4.8 lbs. Mfg. by Chiappa in Italy, importation began 2011.

MSR $319	$265	$235	$200	$185	$170	$160	$150

Add $30 for threaded barrel (new 2013).
Add $40 for Harvest Moon, Muddy Girl, or Outshine camo (new 2013) stock.
Add $80 for wood stock (new 2012).

PISTOLS: SEMI-AUTO

M-1911 – .45 ACP cal., full size 1911 style frame, 5 in. barrel, matte black, brushed nickel (new 2010), or polished nickel (new 2010), steel slide, 8 shot, skeletonized hammer and trigger, Novak sights, lowered and flared ejection port, extended ambidextrous safety, checkered wood or Hogue wraparound (available in Black, Green, or Sand, new 2010) grips, includes two magazines and lockable plastic case, 2.3 lbs. New 2009.

MSR $589	$495	$425	$395	$365	$325	$275	$250

Add $100 for brushed nickel or $110 for polished nickel.
Add $250 for Wounded Warrior Project configuration with matte black finish.

* ***M-1911 Compact*** – .45 ACP cal., 3 1/2 in. barrel, 6 shot, similar to Citadel M-1911 FS, except has compact frame, not available in polished nickel, 2.1 lbs. New 2009.

MSR $589	$495	$425	$395	$365	$325	$275	$250

Add $50 for Hogue grips. Add $100 for brushed nickel.

M-1911 .38 SUPER – .38 Super cal., full size frame, 5 in. barrel, matte black, brushed nickel, or polished nickel, 8 shot, 2.35 lbs. New 2010.

MSR $589	$495	$425	$395	$365	$325	$275	$250

Add $100 for brushed nickel or $110 for polished nickel.

M-1911 9mm – 9mm Para. cal., full size frame, 5 in. barrel, matte black finish, 8 shot, 2.35 lbs. New 2013.

MSR $589	$495	$425	$395	$365	$325	$275	$250

» **M-1911 9mm Compact** – 9mm Para. cal., compact frame, 3 1/2 in. barrel, matte black finish, 7 shot, 2.1 lbs. New 2013.

MSR $589	$495	$425	$395	$365	$325	$275	$250

M-1911-22 TARGET MODEL – .22 LR cal., patterned after the M1911, 5 in. barrel, matte black finish, features wood (new 2012) or Hogue grips, standard (new 2012) or fiber optic sights and key operated safety, supplied with two 10 shot mags., lanyard loop, 2.1 lbs. Mfg. by Chiappa Firearms. New 2011.

MSR $310	$265	$235	$210	$195	$180	$170	$160

Add $39 for Hogue grips and fiber optic sights.

GRADING - PPGS™	100%	98%	95%	90%	80%	70%	60%	LAST MSR

SHOTGUNS: SLIDE ACTION

CITADEL LE TACTICAL – 12 ga., 20 (disc. 2011) or 22 (new 2012) in. barrel, 7 shot mag., matte black finish, available in Standard, Spec-Ops (features Blackhawk Spec-Ops stock with recoil reduction), Talon (features thumbhole stock with Blackhawk recoil reduction), or Pistol grip w/heat shield (features interchangeable stock and removeable pistol grip) configuration, approx. 5.8-7 lbs. Mfg. in the U.S. 2010-2012.

	$385	$335	$285	$240	$210	$180	$150	*$466*

Add $41 for Pistol grip w/heat shield or $166 for either Spec-Ops or Talon configuration.

CLARIDGE HI-TEC INC.

Previous manufacturer located in Northridge, CA 1990-1993. In 1990, Claridge Hi-Tec, Inc. was created and took over Goncz Armament, Inc.

All Claridge Hi-Tec firearms utilized match barrels mfg. in-house, which were button-rifled. The Claridge action is an original design and does not copy other actions. Claridge Hi-Tec models can be altered (Law Enforcement Companion Series) to accept Beretta 92F or Sig Model 226 magazines.

PISTOLS

Add $40 for polished stainless steel frame construction.

L-9 PISTOL – 9mm Para., .40 S&W, or .45 ACP cal., semi-auto paramilitary design, 7 1/2 (new 1992) or 9 1/2 (disc. 1991) in. shrouded barrel, aluminum receiver, choice of black matte, matte silver, or polished silver finish, one-piece grip, safety locks firing pin in place, 10 (disc.), 17 or 30 shot double row mag., adj. sights, 3 3/4 lbs. Mfg. 1991-1993.

	$595	$525	$375	$300	$265	$225	$200	*$598*

Add $395 for a trigger activated laser sight available in Models M, L, C, and T new mfg.

S-9 PISTOL – similar to L-9, except has 5 in. non-shrouded threaded barrel, 3 lbs. 9 oz. Disc. 1993.

	$695	$625	$550	$475	$350	$280	$250	*$535*

T-9 PISTOL – similar to L-9, except has 9 1/2 in. barrel. Mfg. 1992-93.

	$550	$495	$375	$300	$265	$225	$200	*$598*

M PISTOL – similar to L Model, except has 7 1/2 in. barrel, 3 lbs. Disc. 1991.

	$575	$515	$375	$300	$265	$225	$200	*$720*

RIFLES: CARBINES

C-9 CARBINE – same cals. as L and S Model pistols, 16.1 in. shrouded barrel, choice of black graphite composite or uncheckered walnut stock and forearm, 5 lbs. 12 oz. Mfg. 1991-1993.

	$650	$595	$525	$450	$395	$350	$300	*$675*

Add $74 for black graphite composite stock.
Add $474 for integral laser model (with graphite stock).

This model was available with either gloss walnut, dull walnut, or black graphite composite stock.

LAW ENFORCEMENT COMPANION (LEC) – 9mm Para., .40 S&W, or .45 ACP cal., 16 1/4 in. button rifled barrel, black graphite composition buttstock and foregrip, buttstock also provides space for an extra mag., available in either aluminum or stainless steel frame, matte black finish, available with full integral laser sighting system. Limited mfg. 1992-93.

	$750	$650	$575	$495	$425	$375	$325	*$749*

Add $400 for integral laser sighting system.

CLARK CUSTOM GUNS, INC.

Current custom gun maker and gunsmith located in Princeton, LA. Clark Custom Guns, Inc. has been customizing various configurations of handguns, rifles, and shotguns since 1950. It would be impossible to list within the confines of this text the many conversions this company has performed. Please contact the company directly (see Trademark Index) for an up-to-date price sheet and catalog on their extensive line-up of high quality competition pistols and related components. Custom revolvers,

GRADING - PPGS™	100%	98%	95%	90%	80%	70%	60%	LAST MSR

rifles, and shotguns are also available in addition to various handgun competition parts, related gunsmithing services, and a firearms training facility called The Shootout.

The legendary James E. Clark, Sr. passed away during 2000. In 1958, he became the first and only full-time civilian to win the National Pistol Championships.

PISTOLS: SEMI-AUTO

Clark Custom Guns manufactures a wide variety of M1911 style handguns, including the Bullseye Pistols (MSR $1,695-$3,100), the Custom Combat (MSR $1,925-$2,900), the Meltdown (MSR $1,995-$2,295), Millennium Meltdown (damascus slide, only 50 mfg. during 2000 - MSR was $3,795), .460 Rowland Hunter LS (last MSR $2,640), and the Unlimited (last MSR $3,395-$3,790). Clark will also build the above configurations on a customer supplied gun - prices are less. Please contact the company directly regarding more information on its wide variety of pistols, including availability and pricing (see Trademark Index).

CLASSIC DOUBLES

Previous trademark manufactured in Tochigi City, Japan until 1987. Previously imported and distributed by Classic Doubles International, Inc. located in St. Louis, MO.

The factory closed in 1987, and all Classic Doubles remaining in inventory were sold to GU Wholesalers located in Omaha, NE in 1990. To date, there has been little collectibility in the Classic Doubles trademark. As a result, values are determined by the shooting value each model has to offer against other competing models in the same configuration. Also, in some regions of the country, 98% condition or less specimens may be priced lower than values shown in this section.

In late 1987, Winchester/Olin discontinued importation of their Japanese shotgun models (Models 101 and 23). At that point, Classic Doubles International, Inc. became the sole importer of these shotguns. There were very few changes made during this changeover of importation. The late manufacture Classic Double shotguns (Models 101 and 201) do not have the Winchester trademark or definitive Winchester proofmark stamped on the barrels. The Model 201 was a new model designation.

SHOTGUNS: O/U, MODEL 101 - FIELD MODELS

The late manufacture Classic Doubles have an interchangeable choke tube system compatible with the older Winchester manufactured models. Prices listed include a luggage style carrying case.

100% values listed below for the Classic Doubles Shotguns assume NIB condition - subtract 10%-15% if without box, warranty card, and original shipping container (with packing materials).

CLASSIC FIELD GRADE I – 12 or 20 ga., 3 in. chambers, vent. rib, 25 1/2 or 28 in. vent. barrels with choke tubes, blue receiver with moderate scroll engraving, ejectors, checkered pistol grip or English stock and forearm, 6 1/4-7 lbs.

$1,400	$1,250	$1,100	$1,000	$900	$825	$750	*$1,905*

WATERFOWL MODEL – 12 ga. only, 3 in. chambers, 30 in. barrels with vent. rib and choke tubes, matte blue receiver with moderate engraving, low gloss walnut stock with vent. recoil pad, 7 3/4 lbs.

$1,300	$1,125	$950	$825	$700	$650	$600	*$1,520*

CLASSIC SPORTER – 12 ga. only, made for Sporting Clays competition, 28 or 30 in. vent. barrels and rib with choke tubes, quick detachable stock system, border engraved coin finished receiver with non-reflective matte surface on top frame and lever, checkered walnut stock and forearm, 7 3/4 lbs.

$1,995	$1,500	$1,295	$1,150	$1,000	$900	$775	*$1,980*

Add $965 for extra barrel.

CLASSIC FIELD GRADE II – 12, 20, 28 ga., or .410 bore, 28 in. VR barrels with choke tubes, deluxe walnut with round knob pistol grip stock and forearm with fine fleur-de-lis checkering, coin finished receiver (different sizes) with game scene engraving featuring hunting motifs on receiver sides and bottom, .410 bore bored M/F only, 6 1/4-7 lbs.

$1,795	$1,475	$1,275	$1,100	$1,000	$900	$795	*$2,190*

Add 15% for .410 bore (baby frame).

GRADING - PPGS™	100%	98%	95%	90%	80%	70%	60%	LAST MSR

Add 50% for 28 ga. (baby frame).

The lack of supply of the Winchester/Olin Model 101 28 ga. small frame has caused a significant increase in demand for the .410 bore or 28 ga. The Grade II .410 bore is the only round knob pistol grip produced in both Winchester and Classic Doubles manufacture.

CLASSIC FIELD GRADE II TWO BARREL SET – 12 and 20 ga. barrels, both with Winchokes, 26 in. barrels - 20 ga., 28 in. barrels - 12 ga., coin finished receiver with game scene engraving and borders, 6 1/2 (20 ga.) or 7 (12 ga.) lbs.

$2,695 $2,175 $1,825 $1,550 $1,375 $1,200 $1,075 ***$3,420***

SHOTGUNS: O/U, MODEL 101 - TARGET MODELS

CLASSIC TRAP SINGLE – 12 ga. only, over single 32 or 34 in. VR barrel with choke tubes, blue receiver with light engraving, choice of Monte Carlo or regular stock, recoil pad, 8 1/2 lbs.

$1,200 $1,100 $1,000 $900 $825 $750 $600 ***$2,070***

CLASSIC TRAP – 12 ga. only, 30 or 32 in. vent. barrels and rib with choke tubes, finish and engraving similar to Classic Trap Single, choice of Monte Carlo or standard stock with recoil pad, 8 3/4 or 9 lbs.

$1,300 $1,125 $1,000 $900 $825 $750 $675 ***$1,905***

CLASSIC TRAP COMBO – includes one set of O/U barrels (30 or 32 in.) and one over single barrel (32 or 34 in.), choke tubes, choice of Monte Carlo or standard stock, 8 3/4 or 9 lbs.

$2,400 $2,100 $1,875 $1,600 $1,475 $1,300 $1,175 ***$2,825***

CLASSIC SKEET – 12 or 20 ga., 27 1/2 in. vent. barrels and rib, choke tubes on 12 ga. only, smaller gauges are bored SK/SK, similar metal finish to Classic Trap models, 7 1/4 or 7 3/4 lbs.

$1,695 $1,375 $1,175 $1,025 $900 $825 $750 ***$1,905***

* ***Classic Skeet 4 ga. Set*** – similar to Classic Skeet except has 4 barrels (12, 20, 28 ga., and .410 bore), 12 ga. has choke tubes, smaller gauges are bored SK/SK.

$4,300 $3,875 $3,500 $3,100 $2,875 $2,600 $2,300 ***$4,765***

SHOTGUNS: SxS

MODEL 201 CLASSIC – 12 or 20 ga., 3 in. chambers, forged steel monobloc with improved lug design, 26 in. choke tube barrels with vent. rib, high lustre bluing, no engraving, SST, ejectors, premium walnut stock and beavertail forearm with fancy checkering pattern, solid red rubber recoil pad, 6 3/4-7 lbs.

$2,500 $2,150 $1,875 $1,650 $1,400 $1,200 $995 ***$2,190***

Add $120 for 20 ga.

The 12 ga. could be ordered with choke tubes at no extra charge. Only 63 were mfg. with choke tubes and slight premiums are being asked.

* ***Model 201 Classic Small Bore Set*** – 28 ga. and .410 bore two barrel set, similar to Model 201 Classic except has smaller frame and overall dimensions, 28 in. VR barrels only bored IC/M on 28 ga. and M/F on .410 bore, very limited importation, 6 or 6 1/2 lbs.

$4,250 $3,650 $3,250 $2,800 $2,400 $1,950 $1,475 ***$3,675***

CLERKE ARMS, LTD.

Previous manufacturer located in Raton, New Mexico 1997-2001.

PISTOLS: SINGLE SHOT

COMPETITOR PISTOL – available in 16 centerfire and 2 rimfire cals., 10, 12, 14, 16, or 20 (.410 bore only) in. barrel, features new uplifting C Breech gun system, Xtender slide can be fitted to all Colt .45 ACPs and replicas with no frame modification, matte finish, checkered wood grips. Mfg. 1998-2001.

$300 $285 $265 $240 $220 $200 $185 ***$325***

Add $135-$155 per interchangeable barrel, depending on length.

GRADING - PPGS™	100%	98%	95%	90%	80%	70%	60%	LAST MSR

CLERKE PRODUCTS

Previous manufacturer located in Santa Monica, CA.

REVOLVERS: DOUBLE ACTION

DOUBLE ACTION REVOLVER – .22 S, L, LR, or .32 S&W Long cal., inexpensive double action revolvers, which sold to dealers for $15 in 1971.

RIFLES: SINGLE SHOT

HI-WALL – available in most modern calibers, single shot, falling block replica of Winchester 1885 High Wall rifle, lever operated, case hardened receiver, 26 in. barrel, no sights, checkered walnut pistol grip stock, Schnabel forearm. Mfg. 1972-74.

	100%	98%	95%	90%	80%	70%	60%	LAST MSR
HI-WALL	$250	$225	$185	$175	$150	$140	$125	

DELUXE HI-WALL – similar to Hi-Wall, except half octagon barrel, select wood and recoil pad.

	100%	98%	95%	90%	80%	70%	60%	LAST MSR
DELUXE HI-WALL	$300	$275	$235	$210	$180	$160	$145	

CLIFTON ARMS

Previous manufacturer of custom rifles from 1992-1997 located in Medina, TX. Clifton Arms specialized in composite stocks (with or without integral, retractable bipod).

Clifton Arms manufactured composite, hand laminated stocks, which were patterned after the Dakota 76 stock configuration.

RIFLES: BOLT ACTION

CLIFTON SCOUT RIFLE – .243 Win. (disc. 1993), .30-06, .308 Win., .350 Rem. Mag., .35 Whelen, 7mm-08 Rem. (disc. 1993), or .416 Rem. Mag. cal., choice of Dakota 76, pre-64 Winchester Model 70, or Ruger 77 MK II (standard) stainless action with bolt face altered to controlled round feeding, Shilen stainless premium match grade barrel, Clifton synthetic stock with bipod, many other special orders were available. Mfg. 1992-97.

	100%	98%	95%	90%	80%	70%	60%	LAST MSR
CLIFTON SCOUT RIFLE	$3,000	$2,350	$1,650	$$1,455	$1,195	$1,010	$835	

This model was available as a Standard Scout (.308 Win. cal. with 19 in. barrel), Pseudo Scout (.30-06 cal. with 19 1/2 in. barrel), Super Scout (.35 Whelen or .350 Rem. Mag. with 20 in. barrel), or African Scout (.416 Rem. Mag. with 22 in. barrel).

COACH GUNS

A coach gun is a SxS shotgun with short barrels, which was used extensively in the American West for the protection of horse-drawn coach passengers, hence the name. They were also called guard guns, as they were used for guard duty and other security purposes.

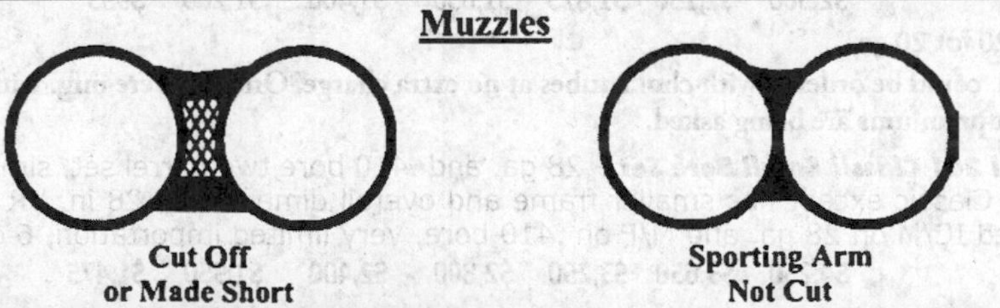

SHOTGUNS: SxS, COACH/GUARD GUNS

The author wishes to express his thanks to Jon Vander Bloomen for compiling much of the following information.

Extensive research indicates that three American gun companies made coach guns in the late 1800s and early 1900s - Colt, Parker, and Ithaca. Remington and Whitney may also have produced some, but there are no factory records to prove it. W.W. Greener of Birmingham, England may have made some short double barrel shotguns for guard use, but no one has seen any factory documentation to support this.

An "original" coach gun, properly called a guard gun, is a double barrel (SxS) shotgun originally manufactured with short barrels, not a long barreled sporting gun, which was cut off (see muzzle

diagram). However, the muzzles of an original coach gun and a gun whose barrels have been cut off look the same. On both, there is a gap between the muzzles, which is filled in with lead. The reason for this is because shotgun barrels are tapered. In order for the muzzles to touch on a 26 inch or shorter gun, the barrel walls would need to be thicker at the muzzle to eliminate the gap.

Some original coach guns may also have original factory markings, identification letters/numerals on the stock and other distinguishing features, which indicate that the gun was originally made and marked to identify it as company property. However, don't think that there's "safety in numbers." There are a lot more Wells Fargo marked guns today than there were 85 years ago.

The real question is, how can you tell an original coach gun from a sporting arm whose barrels have been cut down to potentially "enhance" its desirability factor? Hopefully, by obtaining factory documentation. To find out if a coach gun is an original or a "cut" gun, it is recommended that you contact the factory for documentation (if possible), giving the serial number of the gun and asking for the actual barrel length at the time the gun left the factory. Unfortunately, no Remington records exist. Parker records can be found in Vols. I & II of *The Parker Story*. W.W. Greener is still in business, and will look up a serial number, but it will take some time.

Colt records show that several double barrel shotguns left the factory with short barrels. Most of them were the Model 1878 hammer guns with 18 inch barrels. There where only three Model 1883 hammerless, boxlock guns made with short barrels; the lengths are as follows, 18, 22, and 24 inches. All of the Colt Damascus barrels were made in Belgium and shipped to the Colt factory in an unfinished state, so they were just Damascus tubes. Therefore when Colt got an order for a coach/guard gun, the barrels were custom made to length just as the longer barreled guns. These short barreled Colts are "original coach/guard guns". The extreme rarity of a Colt factory coach gun precludes accurate pricing evaluation.

Parker records show that several guns were made with short barrels. Not all short Parkers were made for guard use however, since some hunters preferred short barrels in the field (for fast upland birds). Parker purchased different grades of steel tubes and made their own barrels. When Parker received an order for a guard gun, the barrels were custom made to length. It would have been more costly for Parker to cut a long barreled choked gun, except in the case of used sporting arms that were cut for guard use. It is likely that the lower grade 10 and 12 ga. guns, which left the Parker factory with short barrels are "original" coach/guard guns. The extreme rarity factor of a Parker factory coach gun precludes accurate pricing evaluation.

Ithaca records show that 750 hammer doubles were made for Wells Fargo between 1909 and 1917. The first 200 guns had 26 in. barrels, and the remaining 550 had 24 in. barrels. Wells Fargo, as well as other express companies, used various makes of shotguns, mostly used lower grade models that were cut to a shorter length. There is no proof that any company other than Ithaca made guard guns for Wells Fargo. Buyers are cautioned to obtain original documentation when considering a purchase of a Wells Fargo coach gun or any other gun, which is claimed to have been used by a famous person. Average condition Wells Fargo coach guns are typically priced in the $4,000-$4,500 range, regardless if they are manufactured by Ithaca or are another trademark with cut barrels. What's important to the buyer is that the gun is a documented Wells Fargo gun, and should have some paperwork specifying that.

What's important to remember is that if there is no original documentation, there's no proof. And if there's no proof, the shotgun may or may not be an original coach gun. When buying, selling, or trading coach guns, the price tag should be proportional to the gun's originality and provenance. Anything less could result in an unwarranted premium for a tired out, "reconfigured" SxS plain Jane shotgun, with some added non-original markings/carvings.

Older sawed-off double barrel shotguns with no documentation that they were an express company gun, or a gun used by a famous person are valued in the $200 to $2,000 range, depending on trademark and condition, condition being most important. A good guide for pricing sawed-off doubles is to check the value of the same gun that has not been cut and then deduct 5% to 50%. If no price guide is available for that particular make, then consider availability. For example, tens of thousands of Belgian doubles were made in the 1800s. Because of the increase in collectibility of American western artifacts, original coach guns and all express company guns are highly prized and sought after, but the buyer must always be wary.

GRADING - PPGS™	100%	98%	95%	90%	80%	70%	60%	LAST MSR

COBB MANUFACTURING, INC.

Previous rifle manufacturer located in Dallas, GA until 2007.

On Aug. 20, 2007, Cobb Manufacturing was purchased by Bushmaster, and manufacture was moved to Bushmaster's Maine facility. Please refer to the Bushmaster section for current information.

RIFLES: BOLT ACTION

MODEL FA50 (T) – .50 BMG cal., straight pull bolt action, lightweight tactical rifle, standard A2 style stock, ergonomic pistol grip, parkerized finish, Lothar Walther 22 or 30 in. barrel, recoil reducing Armalite muzzle brake, padded Mil-spec sling, includes two 10 shot mags., detachable M60 bipod, watertight case, 29 lbs. Disc. 2007.

	100%	98%	95%	90%	80%	70%	60%	Last MSR
	$6,275	$5,300	$4,500	$3,900	$2,700	$2,300	$2,100	*$6,995*

Add $300 for 22 in. barrel.
Add $1,000 for Ultra Light model with lightweight 22 or 30 in. barrel.
Add $89 for additional 10 shot mag.

RIFLES: SEMI-AUTO

MCR (MULTI-CALIBER RIFLE) SERIES – available in a variety of calibers from 9mm Para. to .338 Lapua, offered in MCR 100, MCR 200, MCR 300, and MCR 400 configurations, variety of stock, barrel and finish options. Mfg. 2005-2007.

Prices on this series started at $3,000, and went up according to options chosen by customer.

COBRA

Current trademark imported by Tristar, located in Kansas City, MO. Please refer to the Tristar section.

COBRA ENTERPRISES OF UTAH, INC.

Current pistol manufacturer established in 2001, with headquarters in Salt Lake City, UT. During 2004, the name was changed from Cobra Enterprises to Cobra Enterprises of Utah, Inc.

DERRINGERS

Beginning 2008, all models come equipped with a lockable plastic case and cable gun lock.

COBRA DERRINGER – .22 LR, .22 WMR, .25 ACP, .32 ACP, .32 H&R Mag., .38 Spl., .380 ACP, or 9mm Para. cal., 2.4 (Standard Series), 2 3/4 (Big Bore Series), or 3.5 (Long Bore Series) in. barrel, tip-up action, spur trigger, internal hammer block safety, pearl, black, or laminated wood grips, chrome, black powder coat, or satin chrome finish, 9 1/2 oz.

MSR	100%	98%	95%	90%	80%	70%	60%
MSR $169	$140	$110	$95	$80	$75	$60	$50

Add $18 for big bore (.22 WMR, .32 H&R Mag., .38 Spl., .380 ACP, or 9mm Para cal. with 2 3/4 in. barrel).
Add $18 for long bore (.22 WMR, .38 Spl., or 9mm Para cal. with 3 1/2 in. barrel).
Add $69 for custom colored finishes, including black chrome, royal blue, ruby red, majestic pink, imperial purple, or King Cobra copper (special order).

TITAN DERRINGER – .45 LC/.410 shotshell or 9mm Para. cal., 2 shot, 3 in. barrel, stainless steel frame, SA, removable trigger guard, rosewood grips, polished stainless, brushed stainless, or black stainless. New 2010.

MSR	100%	98%	95%	90%	80%	70%	60%
MSR $399	$340	$285	$250	$225	$200	$185	$170

Add $40 for custom molded case (disc. 2011).

PISTOLS: SEMI-AUTO

Beginning 2008, all models come equipped with a lockable plastic case and cable gun lock.

CA (COBRA) SERIES – .32 ACP (CA32 Model) or .380 ACP (CA380 Model) cal., blowback single action, 2.8 in. barrel, 5 or 6 shot mag., fixed sights, chrome, black powder coat, or satin chrome finish, 22 oz.

MSR	100%	98%	95%	90%	80%	70%	60%
MSR $129	$110	$100	$90	$80	$70	$60	$55

Add $121 for custom colored finishes, including black chrome, royal blue, ruby red, majestic pink, imperial purple, or King Cobra copper (special order).

GRADING - PPGS™	100%	98%	95%	90%	80%	70%	60%	LAST MSR

FS (FREEDOM) SERIES – .32 ACP (FS32 Model) or .380 ACP (FS380 Model) cal., blowback single action, 3 1/2 in. barrel, 7 (.380 ACP) or 8 (.32 ACP) shot mag., fixed sights, bright chrome, black powder coat, satin nickel, two-tone (new 2012), or tri-colored (new 2012) finish, 2.1 lbs. New 2004.

MSR $129	$110	$100	$90	$80	$70	$60	$55	

Add $121 for custom colored finishes, including black chrome, royal blue, ruby red, majestic pink, imperial purple, or King Cobra copper (special order).

PATRIOT SERIES – .380 ACP or 9mm Para. cal., DAO, 3.3 in. barrel, polymer frame, 10 shot mag., loaded indicator, stainless steel, brushed or polished finish or optional black Melonite coating, 20 1/2 oz.

MSR $349	$295	$245	$210	$190	$175	$160	$145	

* ***Patriot 45*** – .45 ACP cal., DAO, black polymer frame with stainless steel slide, brushed, polished, or black Melonite coating, 3.3 in. barrel, 6 or 7 shot mag., 20 oz.

MSR $395	$340	$285	$250	$225	$200	$185	$170	

REVOLVERS

SHADOW – .38 Spl.+P cal., 5 shot, DAO, aluminum J-frame, stainless steel cylinder, fixed sights, available in brushed satin, black titanium, or pink finish, black rubber, rosewood, ebony (disc. 2010), or Crimson Trace Laser (new 2010) grips, concealed hammer, 15 oz. New 2009.

MSR $369	$315	$265	$235	$215	$200	$185	$165	

Add $26 for custom molded case.
Add $40 for Rosewood grips.
Add $256 for Crimson Trace laser grips (new 2010).

COBRAY INDUSTRIES

See listing under S.W.D. in the S section of this text.

COGSWELL & HARRISON (GUNMAKERS), LTD.

Current manufacturer established during 1770, and located in London, England. Previously imported by British Game Guns, located in Kent, WA. No current U.S. importation.

In 1993, Cogswell & Harrison came under new management and have concentrated on building best quality Beesley or Purdey type sidelocks, Woodward styled O/Us, and a round action boxlock. The company also provides a serialization service (free of charge), that provides the exact date of manufacture. A Certificate of Origin is also available for a fee, and indicates the original specifications and configuration - weights, dimensions, materials, points of choke, and original owner (including price paid). Cogswell & Harrison also offers a full repair and restoration service.

RIFLES: SxS

Please contact the company directly for an up-to-date quotation on the current models listed below. All new prices do not include VAT. Values for used guns in 98%-60% condition factors are priced in U.S. dollars. Allow 12-14 months for delivery on boxlocks, 18-24 months on sidelocks.

BOXLOCK MODEL – various cals. from .300 H&H - .600 NE, boxlock action, custom order only. New 1999.

Please contact the company directly for an up-to-date quotation on this model.

* ***Boxlock Model, Early Ejector Models*** – .400 or larger cals., mfg. circa 1900.

Original guns under .450 cal. are generally priced in the $20,000-$40,000 range depending on condition. On calibers .450-.600 NE, values are typically in the $40,000-$60,000 range depending on condition. A Certificate of Origin or individual appraisal is highly recommended.

SIDELOCK MODEL – standard cals. include .300 H&H, .375 H&H, .465, .470 NE, .577, and .600 NE, Beesley or Purdey type action standard, also available with H&H type system, individually made per customer specifications, 8 lbs. 10 oz.-14 lbs. 6 oz., depending on caliber. New 1999.

MSR POR	N/A	$60,000	$50,000	$43,000	$36,000	$29,000	$21,500	

GRADING - PPGS™	100%	98%	95%	90%	80%	70%	60%	LAST MSR

.375 H&H, .450 No. 2 NE, .450 NE, .465, and .470 NE cals. will command premiums over values listed above for both used and new guns.

* ***Sidelock Model Cals. .577 & .600 NE***

MSR POR	N/A	$72,000	$60,000	$50,000	$43,000	$36,000	$28,000	

SHOTGUNS: O/U, SIDELOCK

WOODWARD TYPE – Woodward style action, finest materials, each gun custom-built for individual specifications, delivery time approx. 18-23 months.

MSR POR	N/A	$47,250	$41,000	$36,000	$29,500	$22,350	$16,750	

Please contact the company directly for an up-to-date quotation on this model.

SHOTGUNS: SxS, OLDER MFG.

REGENCY – 12, 16, or 20 ga., 26, 28, or 30 in. barrels, any choke combination, hammerless Anson & Deeley system, boxlock, double triggers, auto ejectors, straight English stock.

$4,275	$3,750	$3,450	$3,125	$2,750	$2,500	$2,250	*$3,200*

AMBASSADOR MODEL – 12, 16, or 20 ga., 26, 28, or 30 in. barrel, boxlock with ornamental strengthening sideplates, auto ejectors, double triggers, engraved game scene or scroll rose motif, English stock.

$5,500	$4,950	$4,450	$3,950	$3,500	$3,100	$2,850	*$4,000*

MARKOR – 12, 16, or 20 ga., 27 1/2 or 30 in. barrel and choke, boxlock, double trigger, English stock. Disc.

$1,675	$1,475	$1,300	$1,050	$975	$825	$700

Add 20% for auto ejectors.

HUNTIC MODEL – 12, 16, or 20 ga., 25, 27, or 30 in. barrels, any choke, sidelock, auto ejectors, English style stock. Disc.

$3,900	$3,500	$3,200	$3,000	$2,800	$2,500	$2,175

Add $400 for SST.

AVANT TOUT SERIES – 12, 16, or 20 ga., 25, 27 1/2, or 30 in. barrels, boxlock, ornamental strengthening sideplates, straight English stock, auto ejectors, series disc.

$2,550	$2,250	$1,925	$1,700	$1,495	$1,350	$1,200

REX OR AVANT TOUT III – no sideplates.

$2,150	$1,800	$1,650	$1,500	$1,350	$1,200	$1,075

SANDHURST OR AVANT TOUT II

$2,800	$2,500	$2,300	$2,150	$2,000	$1,750	$1,500

KONOR OR AVANT TOUT I

$3,275	$2,850	$2,500	$2,250	$2,000	$1,750	$1,500

Add $400 for SST.
Add 20% for 20 ga.
Subtract 10% for 16 ga.

BEST QUALITY – 12, 16, or 20 ga., 25, 26, 28, or 30 in. barrels, any choke, hand detachable sidelock, auto ejectors, double triggers standard, English stock.

* ***Best Quality Primic Model*** – disc.

$6,200	$5,750	$4,650	$4,150	$3,650	$3,050	$2,500

* ***Best Quality Victor Model***

$9,250	$8,500	$7,250	$6,250	$5,000	$4,350	$3,740

Add $400 for SST.
Add 20% for 20 ga.

Note: Degree of engraving and grade of wood are the basic differences among models.

SHOTGUNS: SxS, BOXLOCK & SIDELOCK - CURRENT MFG.

Please contact the company directly for an up-to-date quotation on current models. All new prices do not include VAT. Values for used guns in 98%-60% condition factors are priced in U.S.

GRADING - PPGS™	100%	98%	95%	90%	80%	70%	60%	LAST MSR

dollars. Allow 9-12 months for delivery on boxlocks, 18-23 months on sidelocks.

All models below are available in 12, 20, or 28 ga.

REGENCY – scalloped boxlock action, DTs, 100% large scroll engraving coverage on receiver and tangs, light barrel engraving, checkered straight grip stock with teardrop. Introduced 1970 to commemmorate C&H's bicentennial.

MSR POR N/A $14,750 $12,250 $10,000 $8,000 $6,500 $4,950

VICTORIA – features scalloped round body boxlock action with 100% medium scroll engraving coverage on receiver and tangs, moderate barrel engraving, select checkered stock and forearm.

MSR POR N/A $16,950 $14,500 $12,250 $10,000 $7,800 $6,100

EXTRA QUALITY VICTORIA – similar to Victoria Model, except has better quality wood and more engraving.

MSR POR N/A $18,750 $16,250 $14,000 $11,750 $8,900 $7,350

Add £440 for 20 ga.
Add £890 for 28 ga.

EXTRA QUALITY (SPECIAL) VICTORIA – top-of-the-line round boxlock action with best quality walnut and chopperlump barrels, removable crosspin, and other refinements.

MSR POR N/A $22,350 $19,450 $16,350 $13,150 $10,250 $8,400

SELF-OPENING SLE SxS – sidelock action, best quality Beesley action and engraving, each gun custom-built per individual specifications, delivery time approx. 18-23 months.

MSR POR N/A $41,000 $36,000 $29,500 $22,350 $16,750 $12,500

COLE ARMS INC.

Previous manufacturer of custom trap shotguns from 1991 to 2012 and located in McMinnville, OR.

Cole Arms manufactured custom trap shotguns built per individual customer's specifications. Base guns started at $8,500 and went up depending on wood, engraving, and other customer choices.

COLT'S MANUFACTURING COMPANY, LLC

Current manufacturer with headquarters located in West Hartford, CT.

Manufactured from 1836-1842 in Paterson, NJ; 1847-1848 in Whitneyville, CT; 1854-1864 in London, England; and from 1848-date in Hartford, CT. Colt Firearms became a division of Colt Industries in 1964. In March 1990, the Colt Firearms Division was sold to C.F. Holding Corp. located in Hartford, CT, and the new company was called Colt's Manufacturing Company, Inc. The original Hartford plant was closed during 1994, the same year the company was sold again to a new investor group headed by Zilkha Co., located in New York, NY. During 1999, Colt Archive Properties LLC, the historical research division, became its own entity. In November 2002, Colt was divided into two separate companies, Colt Defense LLC (military/law enforcement) and Colt's Manufacturing Company LLC (handguns and match target rifles).

In late 1999, Colt discontinued many of their consumer revolvers, but reintroduced both the Anaconda and Python Elite through the Custom Shop. Production on both models is now suspended. The semi-auto pistols remaining in production are now referred to as Model "O" Series.

For more information and current pricing on both new and used Colt airguns, please refer to the *Blue Book of Airguns* by Dr. Robert Beeman & John Allen (also available online). For more information and current pricing on both new and used Colt black powder reproductions and replicas, please refer to the *Blue Book of Modern Black Powder Arms* by John Allen (also available online).

Black Powder Revolvers - Reproductions & Replicas and *Black Powder Long Arms & Pistols - Reproductions & Replicas* by Dennis Adler are also invaluable sources for most 2nd and 3rd Generation black powder reproductions and replicas, and include hundreds of color images on most popular makes/models, provide manufacturer/trademark histories, and

100%	98%	95%	90%	80%	70%	60%	50%	40%	30%	20%	10%

up-to-date information on related items/accessories for black powder shooting - www.bluebookofgunvalues.com

REVOLVERS: PERCUSSION

Prices shown for percussion Colts are for guns only. Original cased guns with accessories will bring a healthy premium over non-cased models (200-350% over a gun only is common). Be very careful when buying an "original" cased gun, as many fake cases have shown up in recent years.

If possible, it is advisable to procure a factory letter (available only within the following ser. no. ranges) before buying, selling, or trading Models 1851 Navy (ser. range 98,000-132,000), 1860 Army (ser. range 1,000-140,000), or 1861 Navy (ser. range 1-12,000). These watermarked letters are available by writing Colt Archive Properties LLC in Hartford, CT, with a charge of $300 or more per serial number (if they can research it). Some 1849 Pockets can also be researched for $200. Include your name and address, Colt model name, serial number, and check or credit card information to: COLT ARCHIVE PROPERTIES LLC, P.O. Box 1868, Hartford, CT 06144-1868. Please allow 90-120 days for a response.

Prices shown for extremely rare Colt's firearms might not include values in the 90%, 95%, 98%, and 100% condition columns. Prices are very hard to establish since these excellent to mint specimens are seldom seen or sold.

The author wishes to express his thanks to Greg Martin from Greg Martin Auctions for his pricing updates on Colt percussion revolvers, Conversions, Open Tops, Pocket models, and the New Line Series.

Revolvers: Percussion, Paterson Variations

PATERSON NO. 1 POCKET MODEL – also known as "Baby Paterson," .28 cal., single action with folding trigger, 5 shot, 2 1/2 in. to 4 3/4 in. octagon barrels, blue metal, varnished walnut grips. Serial range 1 to approx. 500. Standard bbl. marking "Patent Arms M'g Co. Paterson N.J.-Colt's Pt." Centaur scene with four horse head trademark and "COLT" on 1 1/16 in. cylinder of round or square type. Mfg. 1837-1838.

This and all other Paterson models have 5 shot cylinders and serial numbers are not commonly in evidence externally. Disassembly of the arm is usually necessary to determine the serial number.

The Pocket Model Paterson No. 1 (Baby Paterson) is the first production-made handgun in Colt's Paterson, N.J. facility. It is very small in size, almost appearing as a toy or miniature.

* ***Paterson No. 1 Pocket Model Standard Production Model*** – without attached loading lever.

100%	98%	95%	90%	80%	70%	60%	50%	40%	30%	20%	10%
N/A	N/A	$90,000	$80,000	$72,500	$65,000	$57,500	$55,000	$50,000	$45,000	$40,000	$35,000

* ***Paterson No. 1 Pocket Model Late Production Ehlers Model*** – with attached loading lever, 31/32 round back cylinder and recoil shield milled for ease of capping. Barrel marked "Patent Arms Paterson N.J.-Colt's Pt." Approx. 500 mfg. including the Ehlers Model under Belt Model No. 2 Mfg. 1840-1843.

100%	98%	95%	90%	80%	70%	60%	50%	40%	30%	20%	10%
N/A	N/A	$90,000	$75,000	$67,500	$60,000	$55,000	$50,000	$47,500	$45,000	$40,000	$35,000

PATERSON NO. 2 BELT MODEL – .31 or .34 cal., single action with folding trigger, 5 shot, 2 1/2 in. to 5 1/2 in. octagon barrels, blue metal, varnished walnut grips. Serial range 1-approx. 850 which includes the Belt Model No. 3. All standard production Belt Models No. 2 have straight bottom style grips. Standard bbl. markings "Patent Arms M'g Co. Paterson N-J. Colt's Pt." Centaur scene with four horse head trademark and "COLT" on cylinder of round or square backed type. Mfg. 1837-40. Somewhat heavier than the Pocket No. 1 revolver.

* ***Paterson No. 2 Belt Model Standard Production Model*** – without attached loading lever.

100%	98%	95%	90%	80%	70%	60%	50%	40%	30%	20%	10%
N/A	N/A	$80,000	$70,000	$65,000	$60,000	$55,000	$50,000	$47,500	$45,000	$40,000	$35,000

* ***Paterson No. 2 Belt Model Ehlers*** – with attached loading lever, 1 1/16 in. round back cylinder, recoil shield milled for ease of capping. Barrel marked "Patent Arms Paterson N-J. Colt's Pt." Approx. 500 mfg. including the Ehlers Model under Pocket Model No. 1. Mfg. 1840-43.

100%	98%	95%	90%	80%	70%	60%	50%	40%	30%	20%	10%
N/A	N/A	$90,000	$80,000	$77,500	$75,000	$70,000	$65,000	$57,500	$50,000	$45,000	$40,000

100%	98%	95%	90%	80%	70%	60%	50%	40%	30%	20%	10%

PATERSON NO. 3 BELT MODEL - .31 or .34 cal., single action with folding trigger, 5 shot, 3 1/2 in. to 5 1/2 in. octagon barrels, blue metal, a few having case hardened hammers. Varnished walnut grips. Serial range 1-approx. 850 which includes the Belt Model No. 2. All standard production Belt Models No. 3 have the flared bottom style grips. Standard barrel markings "Patent Arms M'g Co. Paterson N-J. Colt's Pt." The square backed cylinder is seen less often than the more common round back, both bearing the Centaur scene with four horse head trademark and "COLT," with both Belt Models, revolvers exhibiting attached loading levers are less common than those without a lever. Mfg. 1837-40.

* ***Paterson No. 3 Belt Model Standard w/o Lever*** - without attached loading lever.

N/A	N/A	$95,000	$85,000	$80,000	$75,000	$67,500	$60,000	$57,500	$55,000	$50,000	$45,000

* ***Paterson No. 3 Belt Model Standard With Lever*** - with attached loading lever and recoil shield milled for ease of capping (scarce).

N/A	N/A	$95,000	$85,000	$80,000	$75,000	$67,500	$60,000	$57,500	$55,000	$50,000	$45,000

PATERSON NO. 5 HOLSTER MODEL - also known as "Texas Paterson" - .36 cal., single action with folding trigger, 5 shot, 4 in. to 12 in. octagon barrels, blue metal with case hardened frame and hammer. All cylinders bear the stage coach hold-up scene. Varnished walnut grips of flared bottom style. Serial range 1 to approx. 1,000. As with all models of Patersons, the serial number usually cannot be seen without disassembly of the revolver. Very large and heavy compared to the other Paterson models. Enjoys more popularity with collectors because of its military and frontier use. Mfg. 1838-40.

Many specimens encountered in this variation show extreme use. Consequently, fine to mint specimens are quite rare and highly prized by collectors. Values are given for non-military marked specimens. Any specimen bearing an authenticated martial marking is truly a rarity and should be appraised individually. NOTE: Watch for fakes here. There are now many times more faked martial markings, often times on non-original Patersons, than there are originals.

* ***Paterson No. 5 Holster Model Standard Production Model w/o Lever*** - without attached loading lever, round or square backed cylinder.

N/A	N/A	$150,000	$125,000	$115,000	$100,000	$87,500	$75,000	$72,500	$70,000	$65,000	$60,000

* ***Paterson No. 5 Holster Model Standard Production Model With Lever*** - with attached loading lever, round backed cylinder and recoil shield milled for ease of capping.

N/A	N/A	$175,000	$125,000	$110,000	$90,000	$85,000	$80,000	$77,500	$75,000	$70,000	$65,000

Revolvers: Percussion, Walker Model

WALKER MODEL - .44 cal., 6 shot, 9 in. part round, part octagon barrel, blue metal with case hardened frame, lever and hammer. Cylinder left in the white without finish, brass trigger guard. One piece walnut grips. Mfg. 1847; total production approx. 1,100. Ser. numbers beginning with no. 1 were applied for each of five different military companies (A,B,C,D, & E). The total for the military issue Walkers was approx. 1,000 revolvers; the remaining approx. 100 revolvers were produced for civilian distribution. Barrels marked "Address SamL Colt New-York City," found on right side of barrel lug is "US" over "1847," cylinder bears Texas Ranger/Indian fight scene. Various metal parts and walnut grips stamped with Govt. Inspectors' marks.

Because of these arms being subjected to great extremes of use, they will exhibit high degrees of wear, often to the extent that most or all markings will be worn off. Replaced parts are common and many badly worn and damaged specimens have been extensively rebuilt and restored. NOTE: Use great caution when contemplating the purchase of a Walker. A multitude of out-and-out fakes and "antiqued" reproduction Walkers have been fed into the market over the past few decades. Some of these are old enough (and have aged enough naturally) to almost resemble an authentic specimen. Enlist the services of a qualified expert before your dollars are spent. Only 10-12% of the original production of approx. 1,100 specimens have been accounted for. The acquisition of an authenticated Walker revolver is the ultimate goal of serious Colt handgun collectors.

* ***Walker Standard Military Issue Model***

N/A	N/A	$850,000	$675,000	$500,000	$400,000	$300,000	$250,000	$200,000	$175,000	$150,000	$125,000

100%	98%	95%	90%	80%	70%	60%	50%	40%	30%	20%	10%

* ***Walker Limited Civilian Issue Model*** – serial range 1001 to approx. 1100. Similar to military model except Govt. inspectors' marks were not applied. Pricing is difficult on the civilian issue arms. They tend to be in considerably better condition than the much more common military specimens. The factors of scarcity and condition will often bring higher prices from the advanced collector of means, especially in the finer grades of condition. On the other hand, the collector appreciating military usage will pay more for military marked examples. This publication tries to reflect the latest trends on purchase of civilian models.

N/A	N/A	$850,000	$675,000	$500,000	$400,000	$300,000	$250,000	$200,000	$175,000	$150,000	$125,000

Revolvers: Percussion, Dragoon Series

WHITNEYVILLE HARTFORD DRAGOON – .44 cal., 6 shot, 7 1/2 in. part octagon, part round barrel, some of the left-over Walker parts were used in Dragoons, blue metal with case hardened frame, lever, hammer, brass trigger guard and steel cylinder bears Texas Ranger and Indian battle scene. Mfg. 1847. Total production approx. 240. Serial range approx. 1,100 to 1,340 in sequence following civilian Walkers.

* ***Whitneyville Hartford Dragoon w/Rear frame cut out for grips***

N/A	N/A	$350,000	$175,000	$140,000	$100,000	$87,500	$75,000	$70,000	$65,000	$57,500	$50,000

* ***Whitneyville Hartford Dragoon w/Straight rear frame***

N/A	N/A	$250,000	$150,000	$125,000	$90,000	$77,500	$65,000	$55,000	$45,000	$40,000	$35,000

FIRST MODEL DRAGOON – .44 cal., 6 shot, 7 1/2 in. round and octagon barrel, blue metal with case hardened frame, lever, hammer, brass grip straps, silvered straps for civilian market, serial range numbered after Hartford Dragoon, 1341 to around 8000. Mfg. 1848-50. Total production approx. 7,000. Oval cyl. slots, square back trigger guard, Texas Ranger and Indian fight scene on cylinder.

* ***First Model Dragoon Military Model***

N/A	N/A	$125,000	$80,000	$55,000	$30,000	$27,500	$25,000	$20,000	$15,000	$12,500	$10,000

* ***First Model Dragoon Civilian Model***

N/A	N/A	$80,000	$60,000	$40,000	$25,000	$22,500	$20,000	$17,500	$15,000	$12,500	$10,000

FLUCK MODEL DRAGOON – basically a First Model Dragoon, with 7 1/2 in. altered Walker barrels and fully martially marked, should be extensively checked over, used to replace defective Walkers. Mfg. 1848. Total production 300. Serial range approx. 2,216 to 2,515.

N/A	N/A	$85,000	$60,000	$55,000	$30,000	$25,000	$20,000	$17,500	$15,000	$13,500	$12,000

SECOND MODEL DRAGOON – .44 cal., 6 shot, 7 1/2 in. round and octagon barrel, serial range following the First Model Dragoon 8,000-10,700. Mfg. 1850-51. Texas Ranger and Indian fight scene on cylinder.

* ***Second Model Dragoon Military Model***

N/A	N/A	$85,000	$70,000	$50,000	$30,000	$25,000	$20,000	$16,000	$12,000	$10,000	$7,500

* ***Second Model Dragoon Civilian Model***

N/A	N/A	$75,000	$60,000	$40,000	$35,000	$22,500	$20,000	$17,500	$15,000	$11,000	$6,000

* ***Second Model Dragoon New Hampshire or Massachusetts*** – notice state markings on front portion of trigger guard.

N/A	N/A	$80,000	$65,000	$52,500	$40,000	$37,500	$25,000	$20,000	$15,000	$12,500	$10,000

THIRD MODEL DRAGOON – .44 cal., 6 shot, 7 1/2 in. round and octagon barrel, same basic features as earlier models, but with round trigger guard and rectangular cylinder slots, serial range approx. 10,200-19,600, some overlapping of numbers, with approx. 10,500 mfg. from 1851-61. Texas Ranger and Indian fight scene on cylinder.

* ***Third Model Dragoon***

N/A	N/A	$50,000	$35,000	$32,500	$30,000	$25,000	$17,500	$15,000	$12,000	$10,000	$7,500

* ***Third Model Dragoon Martially Marked U.S.***

N/A	N/A	$60,000	$40,000	$37,5000	$25,000	$22,500	$20,000	$17,500	$15,000	$12,000	$8,500

* ***Third Model Dragoon Third Model*** – 8 in. barrel.

N/A	N/A	$65,000	$45,000	$35,000	$27,500	$25,000	$22,000	$21,000	$19,500	$14,000	$9,500

100%	98%	95%	90%	80%	70%	60%	50%	40%	30%	20%	10%

* ***Third Model Dragoon First and Second Variation*** – shoulder stock model.

N/A N/A $60,000 $45,000 $35,000 $25,000 $22,500 $20,000 $17,500 $15,000 $12,500 $9,500

* ***Third Model Dragoon Third Variation***

N/A N/A $60,000 $45,000 $35,000 $25,000 $21,000 $17,500 $15,000 $12,000 $10,000 $7,500

* ***Third Model Dragoon C.L. Dragoon***

N/A N/A $65,000 $50,000 $40,000 $30,000 $26,000 $22,500 $19,000 $15,000 $12,500 $10,000

ENGLISH HARTFORD DRAGOON – basically a Third Model Dragoon, assembled at Colt's London factory, with unique serial range 1-700, some were assembled from earlier parts inventories, easy to spot with British proofs of crown over V and crown over GP, the blue was of the English type, many were engraved.

N/A N/A $55,000 $40,000 $32,000 $22,500 $19,000 $15,000 $12,500 $10,000 $8,750 $7,500

1848 BABY DRAGOONS – .31 cal., 5 shot, 3, 4, 5, or 6 in. octagon barrels, most without loading lever, serial range 1-15,500, a scaled down version of the .44 caliber Dragoons, early ones with Texas Ranger scene and later ones with the holdup scene.

* ***1848 Baby Dragoon Type I*** – left-hand barrel stamping, Texas Ranger and Indian scene, approx. serial range 1-150.

N/A N/A $25,000 $15,000 $11,000 $7,500 $7,000 $6,5000 $6,000 $5,500 $5,000 $4,500

* ***1848 Baby Dragoon Type II*** – with Texas Ranger and Indian scene, 11,600 serial range, without loading lever.

N/A N/A $17,500 $12,000 $9,500 $6,500 $6,250 $6,000 $5,200 $4,500 $4,000 $3,500

* ***1848 Baby Dragoon Type III*** – with Stagecoach scene and oval cylinder slots, serial range 10,400-12,000.

N/A N/A $17,500 $12,000 $9,500 $6,500 $6,250 $6,000 $5,200 $4,500 $4,000 $3,500

* ***1848 Baby Dragoon Type IV*** – with Stagecoach holdup scene, rectangle cylinder slots, serial range 11,000-12,500.

N/A N/A $17,500 $12,000 $9,500 $6,500 $6,250 $6,000 $5,200 $4,500 $4,000 $3,500

* ***1848 Baby Dragoon Type V*** – with Stagecoach holdup scene, rectangle cylinder slots and loading lever, serial range 11,600-15,500.

N/A N/A $17,500 $12,000 $9,500 $6,500 $6,250 $6,000 $5,200 $4,500 $4,000 $3,500

Revolvers: Percussion, Models 1849, 1851, 1855, 1860, 1861, 1862, & 1865

1849 POCKET MODEL – .31 cal., 5 or 6 shot, 3, 4, 5, and 6 in. octagon barrels, most with loading levers, blue metal with case hardened frame, lever and hammer, grip straps of brass (silver plated), or steel (silver plated or blue), stagecoach hold-up scene on cylinder, serial range 12,000 to 340,000. Mfg. 1850-73.

* ***1849 Pocket Model First Type*** – 4, 5, or 6 in. barrel, loading lever and small or large brass trigger guard.

N/A N/A $4,500 $3,000 $2,250 $1,500 $1,225 $950 $850 $750 $625 $500

* ***1849 Pocket Model Second Type*** – 4, 5, or 6 in. barrel, loading lever and steel grip straps.

N/A N/A $4,500 $3,000 $2,250 $1,500 $1,225 $950 $850 $750 $625 $500

* ***1849 Pocket Model Wells Fargo Model*** – 3 in. barrel, without loading lever and with small round trigger guard.

N/A N/A $15,000 $10,000 $8,500 $7,000 $5,500 $4,000 $3,250 $2,500 $2,250 $2,000

1849 LONDON POCKET MODEL – London pistols were of the same general configuration, but of better finish, serial range 1-11,000. Mfg. 1853-57.

* ***1849 London Pocket Model Early Type*** – serial numbered under 1500, with small trigger guard and brass grip straps.

N/A N/A $7,500 $4,500 $4,000 $3,500 $2,900 $2,250 $1,750 $1,200 $1,075 $950

* ***1849 London Pocket Model Late Type*** – oval trigger guard and steel grip straps.

N/A N/A $4,500 $3,000 $2,400 $1,750 $1,500 $1,200 $1,075 $950 $850 $750

100%	98%	95%	90%	80%	70%	60%	50%	40%	30%	20%	10%

1851 NAVY – .36 cal., 6 shot, 7 1/2 in. octagon barrel and loading lever, blue metal with case hardened frame, lever and hammer, one piece walnut finished grips, cylinder scene of Texas Navy battle with Mexico, serial range 1-highest recorded number was 215,348, three barrel addresses 1-74,000 (ADDRESS SAML COLT, NEW YORK CITY), 74,000-101,000 (ADDRESS SAML COLT, HARTFORD, CT.) 101,000-215,348 (ADDRESS COL. SAML COLT, NEW YORK, U.S. AMERICA). Mfg. 1850-73.

* ***1851 Navy First Model*** – square back trigger guard, bottom wedge screw, serial range 1-1,250.

N/A N/A $25,000 $20,000 $17,500 $15,000 $12,500 $10,000 $8,250 $6,500 $5,500 $4,500

* ***1851 Navy Second Model*** – square back trigger guard, top wedge screw, serial range 1,250-4,000.

N/A N/A $22,500 $18,000 $15,000 $12,000 $10,000 $7,500 $6,250 $5,000 $4,250 $3,500

* ***1851 Navy Third Model*** – small round brass trigger guard, serial range 4,200-85,000.

N/A N/A $7,500 $6,500 $5,250 $4,000 $3,000 $2,000 $1,600 $1,200 $1,100 $1,000

* ***1851 Navy Fourth Model*** – large round brass trigger guard, serial range 85,000-215,348.

N/A N/A $7,500 $6,500 $5,250 $4,000 $3,000 $2,000 $1,600 $1,200 $1,100 $1,000

* ***1851 Navy Iron Gripstrap Model*** – most often seen in fourth model.

N/A N/A $8,000 $7,000 $5,500 $4,000 $3,150 $2,200 $1,850 $1,500 $1,350 $1,200

* ***1851 Navy Martially Marked U.S. Navys*** – brass or iron gripstrap.

N/A N/A $22,500 $12,000 $9,750 $7,500 $6,000 $4,500 $4,000 $3,500 $3,000 $2,500

* ***1851 Navy Cut for shoulder stock*** – first and second type (like third model Dragoon).

N/A N/A $15,000 $10,000 $9,250 $8,500 $6,750 $5,000 $3,500 $2,000 $1,750 $1,500

* ***1851 Navy Third Type*** – four screw frame.

N/A N/A $9,000 $4,500 $3,750 $3,000 $2,750 $2,500 $2,150 $1,800 $1,650 $1,500

51 NAVY LONDON MODEL – basically the same gun as the Hartford piece with London barrel address, with British proof marks in serial range 1-42,000. Mfg. 1853-57.

* ***51 Navy London Early First Model*** – serial range below 2000, brass grip straps and small trigger guard.

N/A N/A $8,500 $4,500 $4,000 $3,500 $3,000 $2,500 $2,250 $2,000 $1,750 $1,500

* ***51 Navy London Late Second Model*** – balance of production, large round trigger guard, steel grip straps, all London parts.

N/A N/A $8,000 $4,500 $4,000 $3,5000 $3,000 $2,500 $2,000 $1,500 $1,350 $1,200

1855 SIDEHAMMER POCKET MODEL (ROOT MODEL) – .28 cal., had 3 1/2 in. octagon barrel, .31 cal. usually had 3 1/2 in. or 4 1/2 in. round barrel. Blue with case hardened lever and hammer, one piece wraparound style walnut grips.

Commonly called the "Root" Model by collectors, manufactured 1855 through 1870. The .28 cal. model serial numbered 1 through approx. 30,000. The .31 cal. round barrel model serial numbered 1 through approx. 14,000. Total production approx. 44,000.

Easily recognizable by its side mounted hammer and cylinder rotation ratchet at rear of frame.

* ***1855 Sidehammer Pocket Model 1 and 1A*** – .28 cal., 3 7/16 in. octagonal bbl., oct. load lever, Indian/cabin cyl. scene, Hartford barrel address. Serial range 1 to 384.

N/A N/A $12,500 $8,000 $6,500 $5,000 $4,250 $3,500 $3,000 $2,500 $2.250 $2,000

* ***1855 Sidehammer Pocket Model 2*** – .28 cal., 3 1/2 in. oct. bbl., Indian/cabin cyl. scene, Hartford barrel address with pointed hand. Serial range 476 to 25,000.

N/A N/A $3,500 $2,000 $1,600 $1,200 $1,075 $950 $850 $750 $625 $500

* ***1855 Sidehammer Pocket Model 3*** – .28 cal., 3 1/2 in. oct. bbl., full fluted cylinder, Hartford barrel address with pointed hand. Serial range 25,001 to 30,000.

N/A N/A $3,500 $2,500 $1,850 $1,200 $1,075 $950 $850 $750 $625 $500

* ***1855 Sidehammer Pocket Model 3A*** – .31 cal., 3 1/2 in. oct. bbl., full fluted cylinder, Hartford barrel address. Serial range 1 to 1,350.

N/A N/A $3,500 $2,500 $1,850 $1,200 $1,075 $950 $850 $750 $625 $500

100%	98%	95%	90%	80%	70%	60%	50%	40%	30%	20%	10%

* ***1855 Sidehammer Pocket Model 4*** – .31 cal., 3 1/2 in. oct. bbl., full fluted cylinder, Hartford barrel address. Serial range 1,351 to 2,400.

N/A	N/A	$4,000	$3,000	$2,400	$1,750	$1,500	$1,200	$1,075	$950	$850	$750

* ***1855 Sidehammer Pocket Model 5*** – .31 cal., 3 1/2 in. round bbl., full fluted cylinder, "COL. COLT NEW-YORK" barrel address. Serial range 2,401 to 8,000.

N/A	N/A	$4,500	$3,000	$2,400	$1,750	$1,500	$1,200	$1,075	$950	$850	$750

* ***1855 Sidehammer Pocket Model 5A*** – .31 cal., 4 1/2 in. round bbl., included in same serial range as Model 5.

N/A	N/A	$4,500	$3,500	$3,000	$2,250	$1,875	$1,500	$1,350	$1,200	$1,075	$950

* ***1855 Sidehammer Pocket Model 6*** – .31 cal., 3 1/2 in. round bbl., stage coach hold-up cylinder scene, "COL. COLT NEW-YORK" barrel address. Serial range 8,001 through 11,074.

N/A	N/A	$4,500	$3,500	$3,000	$2,250	$1,875	$1,500	$1,350	$1,200	$1,075	$950

* ***1855 Sidehammer Pocket Model 6A*** – .31 cal., 4 1/2 in. round bbl., included in same serial range as Model 6.

N/A	N/A	$4,500	$3,500	$3,000	$2,250	$1,875	$1,500	$1,350	$1,200	$1,075	$950

* ***1855 Sidehammer Pocket Model 7*** – .31 cal., 3 1/2 in. round bbl., stage coach hold-up cylinder scene, "COL. COLT NEW-YORK" barrel address. Cylinder pin retained by screw-in cylinder. Serial range 11,075 through 14,000.

N/A	N/A	$5,500	$4,000	$3,500	$3,000	$2,750	$2,500	$2,000	$1,500	$1,350	$1,200

* ***1855 Sidehammer Pocket Model 7A*** – .31 cal., 4 1/2 in. round bbl., including same cylinder scene, barrel address and serial range as Model 7.

N/A	N/A	$5,000	$4,000	$3,500	$3,000	$2,625	$2,250	$1,750	$1,200	$1,100	$1,000

1860 MODEL ARMY – .44 cal., 6 shot, 7 1/2 and 8 in. round barrels with loading lever, blue metal with case hardened frame, lever and hammer, one piece walnut grips, normally blue steel back strap and brass trigger guard, barrel markings were "ADDRESS SAM COLT, HARTFORD, CT." on early productions and "ADDRESS COL. SAM COLT, NEW YORK, U.S. AMERICA" on balance, serial range 1-about 200,500, Texas Navy scene on round cylinder model. Mfg. 1860-73.

* ***1860 Model Army Fluted Cylinder Model*** – Fluted Cylinder Model, full length cylinder flutes and no cylinder scene, 7 1/2 or 8 in. barrel, grips of Navy (very rare) or Army size, usually 4 screw frames.

N/A	N/A	$22,500	$15,000	$11,000	$7,500	$6,250	$5,000	$4,250	$3,500	$3,000	$2,500

* ***1860 Model Army Round Cylinder Model*** – roll engraved Texas Navy scene, some with early Hartford address, Army grips, four screw frame to about 50,000 range, most were sold to the U.S. Government and will be martially marked.

N/A	N/A	$15,000	$8,000	$6,500	$5,000	$4,250	$3,500	$3,000	$2,500	$2,000	$1,500

* ***1860 Model Army Civilian Model*** – same general configurations as Round Cylinder Model, but with 3 screw frame, no shoulder stock cuts and better blue finish than military pieces, late New York barrel address.

N/A	N/A	$10,000	$7,500	$4,250	$4,000	$3,250	$2,500	$2,000	$1,500	$1,350	$1,200

1861 MODEL NAVY – .36 cal., 6 shot, 7 1/2 in. round barrel with loading lever, blue metal with case hardened frame, lever and hammer, silver plated brass grip straps, the barrel address was "ADDRESS COL. SAM COLT, NEW YORK, U.S. AMERICA", serial range 1-38,843, cylinder scene of Texas Navy and Mexico Battle, mfg. 1861-73.

* ***1861 Model Fluted Cylinder Navy*** – in serial range 1-100, with fluted cylinder and without rolled cylinder scene.

N/A	N/A	$40,000	$35,000	$30,000	$25,000	$21,500	$17,500	$15,000	$12,000	$10,000	$7,500

* ***1861 Model Navy Regular Production model***

N/A	N/A	$20,000	$12,000	$10,000	$7,500	$6,250	$5,000	$4,250	$3,500	$2,750	$2,000

* ***1861 Model Martially Marked Navys*** – will bear the U.S. stamp and inspector's marks, those marked U.S.N. on butt were of a 650 piece order for the Navy.

N/A	N/A	$35,000	$20,000	$12,500	$8,500	$7,250	$6,000	$5,000	$4,000	$3,250	$2,500

100%	98%	95%	90%	80%	70%	60%	50%	40%	30%	20%	10%

* ***1861 Model London Marked Navy*** – with "ADDRESS COL. COLT, LONDON", for barrel address.

N/A	N/A	$22,500	$12,000	$10,000	$7,500	$6,250	$5,000	$4,750	$4,500	$3,250	$2,000

* ***1861 Model Shoulder Stock Cut Navy*** – 4 screw frames in serial range 11,000-14,000, made for third style stock (see Dragoon stocks).

N/A	N/A	$25,000	$15,000	$12,000	$9,000	$7,750	$6,500	$5,500	$4,500	$4,000	$3,500

1862 POLICE MODEL – .36 cal., 5 shot half fluted and rebated cylinder, 4 1/2, 5 1/2, and 6 1/2 in. round barrels (also 3 1/2 in. bbl. but quite rare) and loading lever. Mfg. 1861-73. Serial numbered with Model 1862 Pocket Navy, approx. 28,000 1862 Police Models were produced. Blue with case hardened frame, lever and hammer, grip straps silver plated, one piece walnut grips. Serial range 1 through approx. 47,000. Standard barrel marking "ADDRESS COL. SAML COLT NEW-YORK U.S. AMERICA" "COLTS/PATENT" on left side of frame, "PAT SEPT. 10TH 1850" stamped in cyl. flute.

Many Model 1862 Police and 1862 Pocket Navy revolvers were converted to cartridge with the advent of the metallic cartridge. Consequently these models in their original cap and ball chambering are quite desirable to collectors.

* ***1862 Police Early Model*** – "ADDRESS SAM COLT/HARTFORD CT" barrel address, silvered iron grip straps.

N/A	N/A	$6,000	$4,500	$3,750	$3,000	$2,650	$2,250	$2,000	$1,750	$1,500	$1,200

* ***1862 Police Early Model*** – same but silvered brass grip straps.

N/A	N/A	$6,000	$4,500	$3,750	$3,000	$2,650	$2,250	$2,000	$1,750	$1,500	$1,200

* ***1862 Police Standard Production Model*** – with New York barrel address.

N/A	N/A	$4,500	$3,000	$2,750	$2,500	$2,150	$1,750	$1,500	$1,250	$1,100	$950

* ***1862 Police Export Production Model*** – with "L" below serial numbers (for export to England), steel grip straps. Most often but not always bearing British proofs.

N/A	N/A	$4,500	$3,000	$2,750	$2,500	$2,150	$1,750	$1,500	$1,250	$1,100	$950

* ***1862 Police London Marked Model*** – similar to above, except with "ADDRESS, COL. COLT/LONDON" address on barrel.

N/A	N/A	$17,500	$12,000	$9,000	$6,000	$5,500	$5,000	$4,000	$3,000	$2,500	$2,000

POCKET MODEL OF NAVY CALIBER (MODEL 1865) – .36 or .38 cal., 5 shot rebated cylinder, 4 1/2 in., 5 1/2 in., and 6 1/2 in. octagonal barrels with loading lever. Mfg. 1865-1882. Blue with case hardened frame, lever and hammer, grip straps silver plated brass, one piece walnut grips. Standard barrel markings "ADDRESS COL. SAML COLT NEW-YORK U.S. AMERICA" "COLTS/PATENT" on left side of frame, stage coach hold-up scene on cylinder. Serial numbered with Model 1862 Police Model, approx. 19,000 produced. Serial range 1 through approx. 47,000. Mfg. began 1865.

This model has been identified for decades to collectors as the Model 1853 or the Model 1862 Pocket Model Navy. Recent research indicates that a more correct model name for this revolver is the Pocket Model of Navy Caliber.

Because of being produced during the advent of the metallic cartridge, the number remaining in the original cap and ball configuration is rather few; scarce with any serial number, but particularly so in numbers over approx. 19,800.

* ***Pocket Model of Navy Caliber Standard Model*** – 4 1/2, 5 1/2 or 6 1/2 in. barrel lengths.

N/A	N/A	$10,000	$7,500	$6,000	$4,500	$3,750	$3,000	$2,750	$2,500	$2,000	$1,500

* ***Pocket Model of Navy Caliber Export Production Model*** – with "L" below serial numbers (for export to England), steel grip straps. Often found with British proofs.

N/A	N/A	$10,000	$7,500	$6,000	$4,500	$3,750	$3,000	$2,750	$2,500	$2,000	$1,500

* ***Pocket Model of Navy Caliber London Marked Model*** – similar to above but "ADDRESS COL. COLT/LONDON" address on barrel.

N/A	N/A	$17,500	$12,500	$10,000	$7,500	$6,250	$5,000	$4,250	$3,500	$3,250	$3,000

100%	98%	95%	90%	80%	70%	60%	50%	40%	30%	20%	10%

REVOLVERS: PERCUSSION CONVERSIONS

Colt Thuer Conversions

Subtract approx. 50% for factory nickel plating on models listed below.

COLT THUER CONVERSIONS (c. 1868-1872) – .31, .36, and .44 CF cal., less than 5,000 produced in all models. This was Colt's first commercial attempt at converting percussion revolvers to fire fixed ammo. Standard features: usually threaded inside rammer for a Thuer loading tool, a hardened flat face on hammer, deepened loading cutout on right side of lug, Thuer ring and back of cylinder have matching assembly numbers. Beware of fakes! Only non-experimental Colt models are listed. Rarity by barrel length will not be considered here. Serial numbers are often missing on cylinder.

Prices for Colt Conversions reflect values for blue and case hardened examples. Nickel plated specimens are rarely seen, but typically sell for 20%-40% less than blue finish.

Any defects, excessive wear, or dulled blue will affect value. Nickeled conversions that have lost their translucence (become cloudy) should be discounted more than usual 20%-40% from blue and case hardened examples, especially on near-mint to mint specimens.

* ***Colt Thuer Conversion 1849 Pocket***

N/A	N/A	$70,000	$40,000	$32,500	$25,000	$21,500	$18,000	$15,000	$12,000	$10,000	$7,500

* ***Colt Thuer Conversion 1851 Navy***

N/A	N/A	$30,000	$27,500	$25,000	$22,000	$18,500	$15,000	$11,500	$8,500	$7,250	$6,000

* ***Colt Thuer Conversion 1860 Army*** – the most common Thuer, but popular because it's a large frame model.

N/A	N/A	$35,000	$27,500	$23,750	$20,000	$18,750	$17,500	$15,500	$12,500	$10,750	$9,000

* ***Colt Thuer Conversion 1861 Navy***

N/A	N/A	$35,000	$25,000	$21,000	$17,500	$16,250	$15,000	$12,500	$10,000	$8,750	$7,500

* ***Colt Thuer Conversion 1862 Police***

N/A	N/A	$22,500	$18,500	$16,750	$15,000	$13,500	$12,000	$10,250	$8,500	$7,500	$6,500

* ***Colt Thuer Conversion 1862 Pocket Navy***

N/A	N/A	$30,000	$27,000	$22,500	$17,500	$16,250	$15,000	$12,500	$10,000	$8,750	$7,500

Richards Conversions: All Variations

Subtract approx. 50% for factory nickel plating on models listed below.

RICHARDS CONVERSION, COLT 1860 ARMY REVOLVER – .44 CF cal., produced circa 1870s, special machining to barrel and breech of cylinder for conversion to a cartridge weapon. Produced in three serial ranges: one numbered under 10,000, a separate group generally in the 190,000 to 200,000 range, and approx. 9,000 produced 1873-1878 in the 24,000-144,000 serial range.

* ***1860 Army First Model Richards*** – quick ID: integral rear sight on breech plate. Floating firing pin in breechplate. Front edge of barrel lug is same as 1860 percussion Army. Breechplate extends over rear edge of cylinder.

N/A	N/A	$25,000	$15,000	$11,750	$8,500	$7,000	$5,500	$5,000	$4,500	$4,000	$3,500

* ***1860 Army Second Model Richards*** – quick ID: standard Richards type barrel. A space between face of conversion ring and rear of cylinder when viewed from the side. No integral sight on breechplate, cut away at top allowing hammer to directly strike the cartridge.

N/A	N/A	$25,000	$20,000	$14,500	$8,500	$7,750	$7,000	$5,750	$4,500	$4,250	$4,000

* ***1860 Army Twelve Stop Cylinder Variation Richards*** – quick ID: generally the same as the Second Model Richards except cylinder has extra "safety" notches between the locking notches. This variation was usually produced in the 100-300, 1,000-1,700 and 200,000 serial ranges. Cylinder locking notches over chambers often broken through. Watch for alterations.

N/A	N/A	$35,000	$25,000	$18,500	$12,000	$10,500	$9,000	$8,250	$7,500	$7,000	$6,500

100%	98%	95%	90%	80%	70%	60%	50%	40%	30%	20%	10%

* ***1860 Army U.S. Marked Richards*** – quick ID: generally the same as 1st Model Richards (many minor differences). Has "U.S." stamped on left barrel lug and "A" (Ainsworth) inspector marks in several places. They are converted 1860 percussion Armys, so original numbers are typically in 23,000-144,000 range plus a second set of assembly numbers. Oiled grips, military soft blue finish.

N/A	N/A	$35,000	$25,000	$18,500	$12,000	$10,500	$9,000	$8,250	$7,500	$7,000	$6,500

Richards-Mason Conversions: All Variations

Subtract approx. 50% for factory nickel plating on models listed below.

1860 ARMY RICHARDS-MASON – .44 CF cal., overall, much rarer than Richards Army Conversions, circa 1870s, approximately 2100 produced. A rare variation has an 1860 Army rebated cylinder and a barrel with a lug shaped similar to 1861 Navy Conversion.

* ***1860 Army Richards-Mason*** – quick ID: breechplate without integral rear sight, cutout at top so hammer can strike primer directly. A space can be seen between breechplate and rear of cylinder. Rear of lug is a vertical line instead of the bullet shape cutout seen on Richards models.

N/A	N/A	$30,000	$20,000	$17,500	$15,500	$12,500	$9,500	$8,000	$6,500	$5,750	$5,000

1851 NAVY RICHARDS-MASON – .38 CF and RF cal., circa 1870s. Produced in two different serial ranges. Has improved Richards-Mason breechplate that is flush with diameter of recoil shield. Difficult to locate in prime condition.

* ***1851 Navy Civilian Model Richards-Mason*** – quick ID: Richards-Mason breechplate which is same diameter as recoil shield, octagon barrel, mirrored civilian blue. Nickel finish commonly seen.

N/A	N/A	$17,500	$12,000	$9,500	$6,500	$5,500	$4,500	$4,000	$3,500	$2,500	$2,000

* ***1851 U.S. Navy Richards-Mason*** – quick ID: Richards-Mason breechplate, oiled grips, soft blue military finish, produced in US. percussion range of 40,000-90,000 ranges. Inconsistent "U.S.N." and other inspector markings. Iron straps, "U.S." on frame.

N/A	N/A	$20,000	$15,000	$12,000	$8,500	$7,500	$6,500	$5,500	$4,500	$4,000	$3,500

1861 NAVY RICHARDS-MASON – produced in civilian and military versions, circa 1870s, made in RF and CF cal. in two serial ranges. Round 7 1/2 in. barrel.

* ***1861 Navy Civilian Model Richards-Mason*** – quick ID: Richards-Mason breechplate, round 7 1/2 in. barrel with attached ejector housing, unrebated cylinder. When blue, has a commercial high gloss finish.

N/A	N/A	$25,000	$17,000	$13,750	$10,000	$8,750	$7,000	$6,250	$5,000	$4,000	$3,000

* ***1861 Navy U.S. Navy Richards-Mason*** – soft military blue finish, oiled grips, converted from percussion U.S. Navy revolvers, inconsistent military markings, centerfire, set of extra serial numbers often seen on cylinder.

N/A	N/A	$25,000	$20,000	$16,000	$12,000	$10,500	$8,000	$7,250	$6,000	$4,750	$3,500

COLT 1862 POLICE & POCKET NAVY RICHARDS-MASON CONVERSIONS (circa 1870s) – .38 RF and CF cal., parts for 1862 Police, Pocket Navy, as well as 1849 Pockets are often intermixed. As parts bins were depleted, Colt used whatever components that would fit, resulting in a tremendous amount of minor variations. Some barrels were converted from percussion models while others were newly made as cartridge barrels without rammer plugs and loading slots in the lug. There are five different serial ranges (1849, 1862 Police, Pocket Navy, Conversion). 3 1/2 to 6 1/2 in. barrels, again not all features available on all models.

Nickel plated conversions will bring 20%-40% less than blue and case hardened specimens.

* ***1862 Police & Pocket Navy Richards-Mason Conversion 4 1/2 in. Octagon Barrel Model*** – quick ID: 4 1/2 in. octagon barrel without ejector. Rebated Pocket Navy Cylinder.

N/A	N/A	$9,500	$6,500	$5,000	$3,500	$2,600	$1,750	$1,350	$950	$850	$750

* ***1862 Richards-Mason Conversion Round (Percussion) Barrel Pocket Navy with Ejector*** – quick ID: plug in rammer slot; ejector housing, loading cutout in right side of lug, barrel remachined from Pocket Navy percussion barrel, Pocket Navy rebated cylinder. Similar appearance to cartridge barrel variation.

N/A	N/A	$10,000	$8,000	$6,750	$5,000	$4,000	$3,000	$2,250	$1,500	$1,200	$850

100%	98%	95%	90%	80%	70%	60%	50%	40%	30%	20%	10%

1862 POLICE AND POCKET (1865 POCKET MODEL) NAVY CONVERSION – 4 1/2, 5 1/2, or 6 1/2 in. barrels with 1862 Police percussion profile and added ejector housing. Has rebated Pocket Navy cylinder or rarer half fluted 1862 Police cylinder. 6 1/2 in. barrel will bring a premium.

* ***1862 Police/Pocket Navy with Rebated Pocket Navy Cylinder*** – quick ID: 1862 Police profile barrel with ejector housing and rebated 1862 Pocket Navy cylinder.

N/A	N/A	$9,500	$6,000	$5,250	$4,000	$3,100	$2,250	$1,550	$850	$750	$650

* ***1862 Police/Pocket Navy with Half Fluted Cylinder*** – quick ID: 1862 Police profile barrel with ejector housing and 1/2 fluted Police cylinder.

N/A	N/A	$12,000	$8,500	$6,750	$5,000	$4,000	$3,000	$2,250	$1,500	$1,175	$850

Conversions with Round Cartridge Barrel

Subtract approx. 50% for factory nickel plating on models listed below.

ROUND CARTRIDGE BARREL WITH EJECTOR – .38 RF and CF cal., 4 1/2, 5 1/2, or 6 1/2 in. barrels produced as a cartridge component without rammer slots and lug cutouts inherent to a percussion barrel.

See Baby Open Top listing under Revolvers:"Open Top" models.

3 1/2 IN. ROUND CARTRIDGE BARREL CONVERSION – .38 RF or CF cal., sometimes seen with serial numbers that are from 1849 Pocket Model (300,000 range). Barrel newly made for cartridges, not converted from a percussion barrel.

* ***3 1/2 in. Round Cartridge Barrel*** – quick ID: only type conversion with 3 1/2 in. barrel. No ejector, no loading lever slot or loading cutout in lug area. Pocket Navy rebated cylinder.

N/A	N/A	$6,000	$4,000	$3,250	$2,500	$2,000	$1,500	$1,250	$1,000	$875	$750

REVOLVERS: "OPEN TOP" MODELS

If possible, it is advisable to procure a factory letter before buying/selling this Open Top Revolver. These watermarked letters are available by writing Colt Archive Properties LLC in Hartford, CT, with a charge of $200 or more per serial number (if they can research it). Send your name and address, Colt model name, serial number, and check or credit card information to: COLT ARCHIVE PROPERTIES LLC, P.O. Box 1868, Hartford, CT 06144-1868. Please allow 90-120 days for a response.

1871-72 OPEN TOP MODEL RIMFIRE – .44 RF cal., 6 shot, 7 1/2 in. barrel, without frame topstrap, blue metal with casehardened hammer, serial range 1-approx. 7,000, barrel address "ADDRESS COL. SAM COLT, NEW YORK, U.S. AMERICA", forerunner of the single action Army, quite desirable. Mfg. 1871-72.

Add 20% for blue finish on models listed below.

* ***Baby Open Top Prototype*** – much shorter lug area than similar model converted from percussion barrel, no slots or loading cutouts on barrel, with ejector housing and Pocket Navy rebated cylinder, only unnumbered and single digit serial numbers have been observed, very scarce.

N/A	N/A	$10,000	$6,000	$4,750	$3,500	$3,000	$2,500	$2,000	$1,500	$1,350	$1,200

* ***1871-72 Open Top Model Rimfire Regular Production Model*** – 7 1/2 in. barrel, New York address, Navy grips.

N/A	N/A	$45,000	$27,000	$24,000	$20,000	$16,500	$12,000	$10,000	$7,500	$6,250	$5,000

* ***1871-72 Open Top Model Rimfire Regular Production*** – with Army grips.

N/A	N/A	$45,000	$27,000	$24,000	$20,000	$16,500	$12,000	$10,000	$7,500	$6,250	$5,000

* ***1871-72 Open Top Model Rimfire Late Production*** – with address "COLT PT. F. A. MANUFACTURING CO., HARTFORD, CT., U.S.A."

N/A	N/A	$45,000	$25,000	$21,500	$17,500	$13,750	$10,000	$8,250	$6,500	$5,500	$4,000

Add 40% for models with 8 in. barrel or COLTS/PATENT frame markings.

REVOLVERS: PERCUSSION, 2ND & 3RD GENERATION BLACK POWDER SERIES

To learn more about the 2nd & 3rd Generation Percussion Black Powder Series, it is

100%	98%	95%	90%	80%	70%	60%	50%	40%	30%	20%	10%

recommended to purchase *Black Powder Revolvers - Reproductions & Replicas* and *Black Powder Long Arms & Pistols - Reproductions & Replicas* by Dennis Adler and the *Blue Book of Modern Black Powder Arms* by John Allen. The latest Edition contains more information on the Colt 2nd Generation Black Powder Series than anything else previously published. These definitive books are available from Blue Book Publications, Inc. To order, please call, fax, email, or visit www.bluebookofgunvalues.com.

DERRINGERS

FIRST MODEL DERRINGER – .41 RF cal., single shot, 2 1/2 in. barrel, scroll engraving standard, blue, nickel, or silver plated barrel, downward pivoting barrel, no grips, serial numbered 1-6,500. Mfg. approx. 1870-1890.

100%	98%	95%	90%	80%	70%	60%	50%	40%	30%	20%	10%
$3,325	$2,500	$2,150	$1,925	$1,700	$1,450	$1,275	$1,075	$875	$750	$675	$650

SECOND MODEL DERRINGER – .41 RF or CF cal., single shot, 2 1/2 in. barrel, scroll engraving standard, blue, nickel, or silver plated barrel, downward pivoting barrel, checkered and varnished walnut grips, "No 2" marked on top of barrel, serial numbered 1-9,000. Mfg. approx. 1870-1890.

100%	98%	95%	90%	80%	70%	60%	50%	40%	30%	20%	10%
$1,775	$1,475	$1,275	$1,100	$950	$850	$750	$650	$585	$535	$500	$475

* ***Second Model Derringer .41 Centerfire cal.***

100%	98%	95%	90%	80%	70%	60%	50%	40%	30%	20%	10%
$3,550	$2,950	$2,550	$2,200	$1,900	$1,700	$1,500	$1,300	$1,175	$1,050	$1,000	$950

THIRD MODEL DERRINGER (THUER MODEL) – .41 RF or CF (rare) cal., single shot, side pivoting 2 1/2 in. barrel, varnished walnut grips, blue barrels, bronze frames were either nickel or silver plated, engraving optional, Colt barrel address, spur trigger, serial numbered approx. 1-45,000. Mfg. approx. 1875-1912.

100%	98%	95%	90%	80%	70%	60%	50%	40%	30%	20%	10%
$1,500	$1,275	$950	$825	$725	$625	$550	$495	$450	$415	$385	$360

Add 30%-50% for .41 centerfire cal. Early models are worth considerably more.

GRADING - PPGS™	100%	98%	95%	90%	80%	70%	60%	*LAST MSR*

FOURTH MODEL DERRINGER (FIRING) – .22 Short cal., single shot similar in appearance to the 3rd Model, 2 1/2 in. barrel, approx. 112,000 mfg. 1959-1963 with either D or N suffix. A few were put in books (sometimes as pairs), picture frames, penholders, bookends, etc. (these will command premiums).

	100%	98%	95%	90%	80%	70%	60%	LAST MSR
Gun only	$100	$90	$75	$70	$55	$45	$35	
Gun w/accessories	$375	$330	$280	$255	$205	$170	$130	

* ***Fourth Model Derringer (non-firing)*** – this variation was normally used for decoration and is normally encountered in books, picture frames, penholders, bookends, etc. Values below assume all factory materials intact - if not, prices are reduced to $50-$75 for gun only.

100%	98%	95%	90%	80%	70%	60%	LAST MSR
$375	$330	$280	$255	$205	$170	$130	

Non-firing guns usually do not have the barrel notch, thus preventing the hammer from striking the cartridge.

LORD DERRINGER – .22 Short cal. only, side pivoting Thuer action, gold plated with black chrome barrel and walnut grips. Approx. 12,000 mfg. 1970-73 by Colt, cased.

100%	98%	95%	90%	80%	70%	60%	LAST MSR
$175	$155	$130	$120	$95	$80	$60	

LADY DERRINGER – .22 Short cal. only, side pivoting Thuer action, full gold plated finish with pearlite grips. Mfg. 3,000 approx. 1970-73 by Colt, cased.

100%	98%	95%	90%	80%	70%	60%	LAST MSR
$175	$155	$130	$120	$95	$80	$60	

LORD & LADY CASED SET – one each of the Lord & Lady Derringers or combinations, consecutive serial numbers, numbered 1,001-up, with DER suffix.

100%	98%	95%	90%	80%	70%	60%	LAST MSR
$495	$435	$370	$335	$270	$225	$175	

LADY CASED SET – cased pair of Lady Derringers. Approx. 12,000 pairs shipped first year.

100%	98%	95%	90%	80%	70%	60%	LAST MSR
$495	$435	$370	$335	$270	$225	$175	

LORD CASED SET – cased pair of Lord Derringers. Approx. 3,000 pairs shipped first year.

100%	98%	95%	90%	80%	70%	60%	LAST MSR
$495	$435	$370	$335	$270	$225	$175	

GRADING - PPGS™	100%	98%	95%	90%	80%	70%	60%	LAST MSR

BOOKCASE DERRINGER PAIR – .22 Short cal., consecutively numbered Derringers with synthetic ivory grips and nickel finish, cased inside unique hardcover "Colt Derringers" labeled book with red velvet lining, limited mfg. in early 1960s.

	100%	98%	95%	90%	80%	70%	60%	LAST MSR
	$350	$300	$265	$240	$195	$160	$125	

100%	98%	95%	90%	80%	70%	60%	50%	40%	30%	20%	10%

REVOLVERS: POCKET MODELS

If possible, it is advisable to procure a factory letter before buying/selling this variation (open top only). These watermarked letters are available by writing Colt Archive Properties LLC in Hartford, CT, with a charge of $200 or more per serial number (if they can research it). Send your name and address, Colt model name, serial number, and check or credit card information to: COLT ARCHIVE PROPERTIES LLC, P.O. Box 1868, Hartford, CT 06144-1868. Please allow 90-120 days for a response.

CLOVERLEAF HOUSE PISTOL – .41 Short or long RF cal., cloverleaf configured 4 shot cylinder, spur trigger, 1 1/2 or 3 in. barrel, blue or nickel plated, approx. 7,500 mfg. in ser. no. range 1-8,300 during 1871-76.

100%	98%	95%	90%	80%	70%	60%	50%	40%	30%	20%	10%
$2,550	$2,300	$1,850	$1,600	$1,400	$1,200	$1,100	$925	$825	$725	$650	$600

Add 30% for blue finish.

Add 80% for 1 1/2 in. barrel.

This model is sometimes referred to as the Jim Fisk model, as he was murdered by Edward Stokes with a Cloverleaf.

* ***5-shot Cloverleaf*** – similar to 4 shot model, except has round 5 shot cylinder and 2 5/8 in. barrel only, approx. 2,500 mfg. in ser. no. range 6,160-9,950 during 1871-76.

100%	98%	95%	90%	80%	70%	60%	50%	40%	30%	20%	10%
$2,175	$1,900	$1,600	$1,325	$1,150	$975	$850	$750	$650	$600	$550	$500

OPEN TOP REVOLVER (OLD LINE) – .22 Short or long RF cal., 2 3/8 or 2 7/8 in. barrel, 5 variations with a variety of finishes, engraving, and grips, first model has cone shaped firing pin that drops through frame (up to approx. ser. no. 125), without topstrap on frame, with or without integral ejector, varnished walnut grips were standard. Approx. 114,200 mfg. 1871-1877.

100%	98%	95%	90%	80%	70%	60%	50%	40%	30%	20%	10%
$1,450	$1,250	$1,150	$950	$850	$750	$700	$600	$550	$450	$375	$325

Add 30% for blue finish.

This model is also known as the Open Top .22 seven shot revolver, the Old Line .22, and the Open Top .22 Pocket. After 1873, Colt referred to this model as the O.M., or Old Model.

* ***Open Top Revolver (Old Line, Early Model)*** – has ejector and high hammer spur.

100%	98%	95%	90%	80%	70%	60%	50%	40%	30%	20%	10%
$3,195	$2,750	$2,525	$2,100	$1,875	$1,650	$1,550	$1,325	$1,200	$995	$825	$725

REVOLVERS: NEW LINE SERIES & VARIATIONS

If possible, it is advisable to procure a factory letter before buying/selling New Line Revolvers. These watermarked letters are available by writing Colt Archive Properties LLC in Hartford, CT, with a charge of $100 or more per serial number (if they can research it). Send your name and address, Colt model name, serial number, and check or credit card information to: COLT ARCHIVE PROPERTIES LLC, P.O. Box 1868, Hartford, CT 06144-1868. Please allow 90-120 days for a response.

Add 30% for blue finish on models listed below.

1ST MODEL – .22, .30, .32, .38, or .41 RF and CF cal., mfg. 1873-1876, 7 (.22 cal. only) or 5 shot, short cylinder flutes, cylinder stop slots cut on exterior of cylinder, 1 3/4, 2 1/4, or 4 in. barrel, full nickel or blue/case hardened finish, spur trigger. Many thousands mfg. 1873-1884.

100%	98%	95%	90%	80%	70%	60%	50%	40%	30%	20%	10%
$1,250	$1,050	$925	$825	$750	$675	$600	$550	$450	$350	$300	$250

2ND MODEL – similar to 1st Model, except has longer cylinder flutes and cylinder stop slots are on the back of cylinder, may or may not have loading gate. Mfg. 1876-1884.

100%	98%	95%	90%	80%	70%	60%	50%	40%	30%	20%	10%
$1,125	$995	$875	$800	$725	$650	$575	$500	$400	$325	$275	$235

Caliber rarity on both models from highest mfg. to lowest is: .22, .32, .30, .41, and .38.

100%	98%	95%	90%	80%	70%	60%	50%	40%	30%	20%	10%

NEW HOUSE MODEL - .38 or .41 CF cal., 5 shot, 2 1/4 in. barrel, spur trigger, checkered hard rubber grips. Approx. 4,000 mfg. 1880-1886 starting at ser. no. 10,300.

$1,475	$1,150	$1,000	$875	$775	$675	$600	$485	$425	$360	$325	$310

NEW POLICE MODEL - .32, .38, or .41 CF cal., 5 shot, 2 1/4, 4 1/2, 5, or 6 in. barrel, spur trigger, with or without ejector, stamped or etched "NEW POLICE" on barrel. Approx. 4,000 mfg. 1882-1886.

$1,800	$1,525	$1,275	$1,100	$925	$800	$725	$650	$600	$550	$525	$495

REVOLVERS: SAA, 1873-1940 MFG. (SER. NOS. 1-357,000)

The author wishes to express thanks to Charles Layson for making the following information available and reformatting the Colt 1st Generation SAA section.

The Colt SAA was produced in 36 calibers with many special order features or combinations available directly from the Colt factory. These factory special order features can greatly enhance the value of the revolver. The Single Action Colt, or "Peacemaker," as it is often called, is undoubtedly the most collectible handgun in the world, and as such, can command very high prices.

Standard barrel markings include the "short" two-line address on 4 3/4 in. or shorter barrels, or "long" one-line address on all other barrel lengths.

It is prudent to secure several professional opinions as to originality when contemplating an expensive purchase, since many SAAs have been altered or "improved" over the decades. Before he died, Keith Cochran, author of the *Colt Peacemaker Encyclopedia,* Vol. II, guesstimated that over 1/2 of all pre-WWII revolvers were no longer factory original. Because of this, it is advisable to procure a factory letter when buying or selling older or recently manufactured Colt Single Actions (hence guaranteeing original configuration and value credibility). These watermarked letters are based on the original factory handwritten shipping ledgers and are available by contacting Colt Archive Properties LLC in Hartford, CT. While not totally infallible, these letters are normally very accurate. The cost to document a 1st Generation SAA is $100. This research can be expedited by phone service for either $100 (2nd and 3rd Generation SAA), or $150 (First Generation SAA through ser. number 343,000). The expedite service provides a verbal report over the phone within 24 hours and a documentation letter follows in 2-3 weeks. Single actions shipped during the time period of 1933-1945 cannot be documented due to lost records. The serial number range typically affected is 354,000-357,859. Documentation letters for .44 rimfire SAA require a $200 research fee.

Additionally, historical research premium charges apply for factory engraving ($100-150, depending on if standard, expert, or master engraving with no gold inlays), and unique shipping destinations such as company executives, famous Western personalities or Colt family members ($50-$200). To contact the Archive Department for assistance call 1-800-962-2658, Ext. 1343. Once contacted, they can advise you what the exact historical research charge will be for the service you are requesting. The address to write to is COLT ARCHIVE PROPERTIES LLC, P.O. Box 1868, Hartford, CT 06144-1868. For a complete Archive Services price list, please refer to the Colt website at www.coltsmfg.com.

Values shown are for guns without special order features. Factory engraving, ivory grips, very rare special order barrel lengths, and special finishes would add considerably to the values shown below. One final word on single action Colts: Black Powder Colts (pre 165,000 serial range) should be scrutinized carefully for potential problems, including refinishing (including aging), replacement parts, restamped serial numbers, and added, non-factory special order features. This makes a major difference in pricing the SAA, since a genuine, original SAA's price tag will vary immensely from a non-original, made-up "parts gun."

SAA 1st Generation Civilian/Commercial (Mfg. 1873-1940)

One of the most well known handguns, and certainly the most collected revolver in the world, the Colt Single Action Army has been produced almost continuously since 1873, with only a minor interruption between 1940 and 1955. It is without a doubt, the most copied revolver with over fifteen clones currently in production.

Better known as the "Peacemaker", this firearm has appreciated in value at an accelerated rate over

100%	98%	95%	90%	80%	70%	60%	50%	40%	30%	20%	10%

the last fifty years. Spurred by the popularity of television westerns in the 1950s and 60s, a standard pre-war, 1st generation single action in excellent condition has gone from $250 in 1960 to approximately $10,000 today, and in some cases much higher.

Not every Colt Peacemaker, however, is worth thousands of dollars. While many factors determine the actual value, the single most important has to be the overall condition of the gun now, compared to the day it left the factory. Because of the demand for Peacemakers in excellent condition many have been reworked and/or reblued, both by private gunsmiths and by the Colt factory itself. Unfortunately only the factory marked its refinished guns, while private individuals normally did not.

The Colt company has used at least three different methods of marking handguns that are to be reworked and/or refinished, and while there is some disagreement among collectors as to exactly what these marks indicate, e.g., refinishing, major parts replacement, or both, it is the opinion of this writer that the first to be used was a six pointed star stamped on the rear right bow of the trigger guard, from approximately 1890 to 1920. The second was a small ampersand placed in the same location, from approximately 1920 to 1945. The third was completely different, and is occasionally found in addition to the ampersand. It was a series of three numbers stamped on most major parts. Called "bin" numbers, they correspond to the numbers on small boxes or "bins" in the custom shop, into which are placed all the parts of a disassembled handgun destined to be reworked and /or refinished. On the Single Action Army, these numbers were placed on the rear flat of the loading gate, visible when it is open (not to be confused with the assembly number stamped on the rear curve of the loading gate), on the front of the cylinder, on the left side of the grip straps, and on the bottom of the barrel, near the frame.

Any reworking or refinishing has a negative effect on the value of a gun to the collector, and the amount varies depending upon the age of the gun, what was actually done and the quality of the workmanship. For example, an early black powder single action that has been expertly refinished by the factory or a qualified restorer is worth only 10 to 20% of what the same gun would be worth in original, mint condition. A late smokeless powder Single Action similarly redone, however, is still worth 30%-40% of one in near new condition. In many cases, the factory had an irritating habit of adding then current markings to an earlier gun, e.g., a caliber designation added to the barrel of a pre-1890 Single Action, or a rampant Colt to the frame.

SINGLE ACTION ARMY (SAA) - STANDARD MFG. - over 30 cals., six shot single action revolver, three standard barrel lengths. The 4 3/4 in. barrel had a two line address, while the 5 1/2 in. and 7 1/2 in. had a one line address. Blue with color casehardened frame or full nickel finish were both available. Of the many (36) calibers offered, .45 Colt was by far the most popular, accounting for 42% of total production, followed by .44/.40 (18%), .38-40 (11%), .32-20 (8%) and .41 (4.5%). One piece, varnished walnut grips were standard for the first ten years, then gradually replaced with two piece hard rubber. When grips are "not listed" on Colt historical letters, you should assume that they were the standard for their time period, either wood or rubber; not the pearl or ivory that someone added at a later date.

* ***Pinch Frame SAA (ser. no. range 1-160)*** – very rare and seldom found with any original finish, .44 S&W American and .45 Colt calibers, 7 1/2 in. barrel, blue and casehardened finish, one piece varnished wood grips, distinctive rear sight situated one-half inch in front of hammer notch, which gives the impression that the top strap has been "pinched." Mfg. 1873.

100%	98%	95%	90%	80%	70%	60%	50%	40%	30%	20%	10%
N/A	N/A	N/A	$250,000	$225,000	$200,000	$180,000	$160,000	$150,000	$140,000	$130,000	$120,000

Add 50% for original .44 S&W American caliber (it is estimated that only 20-25 were produced in this caliber, and most were later converted).

Be aware! There are many counterfeits in this variation.

* ***Early Black Powder SAA (Mfg. 1873-1876, ser. no. range 160-22,000)*** - .45 LC cal., 7 1/2 in. barrel standard, blue or nickel finish, rear sight changed to standard "V" notch, first few hundred have German silver front sight, distinctive italic script style lettering used in barrel address, two line, two date patent marking on frame, one piece varnished wood grips has more distinctive flair at bottom rear on early guns, serial numbers

shared with early martial production, 5 1/2 in. barrels introduced in 1875 in guns for export. Mfg. 1873-76.

» **Ser. Nos. 160-999 (Mfg. 1873)**

100%	98%	95%	90%	80%	70%	60%	50%	40%	30%	20%	10%
N/A	N/A	$90,000	$82,000	$70,000	$65,000	$55,000	$48,000	$37,000	$30,000	$23,000	$16,000

» **Ser. Nos. 1,000 - 9,999 (Mfg. 1873-1874)**

100%	98%	95%	90%	80%	70%	60%	50%	40%	30%	20%	10%
N/A	N/A	$75,000	$68,000	$62,000	$55,000	$47,000	$40,000	$30,000	$25,000	$17,000	$14,000

» **Ser. Nos. 10,000 - 22,000 (Mfg. 1874 - 1876)**

100%	98%	95%	90%	80%	70%	60%	50%	40%	30%	20%	10%
N/A	$70,000	$65,000	$55,000	$44,000	$38,000	$31,000	$26,000	$20,000	$16,000	$13,000	$10,000

Subtract 50% for nickel finish.

* ***Intermediate Black Powder SAA (Mfg. 1876-1890, ser. no. range 22,000-130,000)*** – the italic style of lettering in the barrel address is changed to a block letter style in the 22,000 range, the first two piece gutta percha grips with eagle motif appear in 1882 and became the standard by 1888, the .44-40 (.44WCF) caliber is introduced in 1878, the round head ejector is changed to oval shape in the 52,000 serial range, 4 3/4 in. to 5 1/2 in. barrels are becoming more popular, and Colt gradually abandons the practice of placing serial numbers on the cylinders and barrels of civilian revolvers. Nickel plated single actions seldom have numbered barrels and cylinders after the 60,000 serial range. Blue guns normally have numbers on both up to the 110,000 range, and occasionally thereafter up to 125,000. Two line, two date patent markings change to three line, three dates by 1878.

Subtract 50% for nickel finish.
Add 30% for original box.
Add 10% for 4 3/4 in. barrel.
One-piece wood grips are more desirable than two-piece rubber grips.

» **Ser. Nos. 22,000 - 54,000 (Mfg. 1876 - 1880)**

100%	98%	95%	90%	80%	70%	60%	50%	40%	30%	20%	10%
N/A	$52,000	$45,000	$37,000	$30,000	$26,000	$20,000	$15,000	$12,000	$10,000	$8,000	$6,000

» **Ser. Nos. 54,000 - 130,000 (Mfg. 1880 - 1890)**

100%	98%	95%	90%	80%	70%	60%	50%	40%	30%	20%	10%
N/A	$42,000	$37,000	$31,000	$25,000	$20,000	$16,000	$12,000	$10,000	$8,500	$7,000	$5,500

* ***Late Black Powder SAA (Mfg. 1890 - 1896, ser. no. range 130,000-165,000)*** – three line patent date format changes to two lines with three dates, circled rampant Colt trademark is added to left side of frame, grips transition from wood and rubber w/ eagle to plain two piece rubber by 1892, and caliber designation is added to the barrel and eliminated from trigger guard.

100%	98%	95%	90%	80%	70%	60%	50%	40%	30%	20%	10%
N/A	$35,000	$32,000	$25,000	$18,000	$15,000	$12,000	$10,000	$8,500	$7,000	$6,000	$5,000

Subtract 35% for nickel finish.
Add 25% for original box.
Add 10% for 4 3/4 in. barrel.
Add 20% for wood or rubber w/eagle grips.

* ***Early Smokeless Powder SAA (Mfg. 1896 - 1908)*** – several important physical characteristics were changed during this transition period. Most notably, in 1896 the vertical screw retaining the cylinder pin was eliminated in favor of the horizontal latch. This was identical to what had already been used on the double action models since 1877. This change coincided with the introduction of ammunition loaded with white or smokeless powder, which was more powerful and less corrosive than black powder. It was necessary for firearms manufacturers, therefore, to modify and strengthen their products to safely use the new ammunition. By adopting the more modern and tool-free horizontal latch for the Single Action at this time, Colt gave its customers an easy way to tell the new from the old, the stronger from the weaker, and a good excuse to purchase a new Peacemaker! As a result, sales boomed and more Single Actions were sold in the next ten years, than any other ten year period in Colt's history. The knurling pattern on the hammer spur began a two step revision in 1906. Up until this time, the knurling was enclosed in a border with a line underneath. Beginning in 1906, for approximately two years, the border remained, but the line underneath was eliminated. By late 1908, the border was also eliminated, and thereafter, the

100%	98%	95%	90%	80%	70%	60%	50%	40%	30%	20%	10%

knurling ran to the very edges of the hammer spur. Although Colt advertised their improved smokeless powder Single Actions as early as 1897, they did not add the "VP" proof mark (verified proof, Colt's guarantee for smokeless powder use) to the trigger guard until 1904. While the highest production and sales figures were reached during this period, quality did not suffer. Many collectors feel that the fitting, polishing and finishing work performed during this period was superior to any other.

» **Ser. Nos. 165,000 - 182,000 (Mfg. 1896 - 1899)** – the first three years of this period, 1896 to 1899, have recently become known as the "blackpowder transition" period, to distinguish Single Actions made with the modern, stronger frame and yet still considered "antique" by federal law that uses January 1st, 1899 as the beginning of the modern gun era.

N/A	$28,000	$20,000	$15,000	$12,000	$9,500	$8,000	$6,500	$5,000	$3,800	$3,000	$2,500

» **Ser. Nos. 182,000 - 300,000 (Mfg. 1899 - 1908)**

N/A	$25,000	$18,000	$13,500	$9,000	$7,500	$6,000	$5,000	$4,000	$3,200	$2,500	$2,000

Add 25% for original box.
Subtract 25% for nickel finish.

* ***Intermediate Smokeless Powder SAA (Mfg. 1908 - 1920, ser. no. range 300,000-339,000)*** – physical changes continued to occur during this period. Rampant Colt medallions were inserted into pearl, ivory, and checkered walnut grips in 1909, the .44 Special caliber was introduced circa 1912, the blueing process was gradually changed, and the circled rampant Colt on the frame began to lose its circle as the die stamps wore. The company, however, did not quickly give up the use of black powder rifling (wide grooves and narrow lands) completely until 1914, although an experimentation and transition period with narrower grooves and wider lands had begun about 1910. Similarly, the small and low black powder front sight did not change to the larger and higher smokeless profile until 1914. WWI came and went, and SAA sales began to decline. The year 1920 is very significant to Single Action collectors since this was the year that the serial number relocation was completed. Those numbers on the trigger guard and backstrap were moved under the grips beginning in the late 338,000 serial range (1919), leaving only the number on the frame visible. This brought to a close a practice which had begun in the 1840s with the percussion revolvers. Many collectors regard this as the end of the "cowboy" period.

» **Ser. Nos. 300,000 - 328,000 (Mfg. 1908 - 1914)**

N/A	$20,000	$16,000	$10,000	$8,000	$6,000	$5,300	$4,000	$3,500	$3,000	$2,300	$1,900

Add 20% for original box.
Add 10% for smooth, two-piece walnut grips.
Add 25% for checkered, varnished walnut grips with deep set medallions.
Subtract 15% for nickel finish.

» **Ser. Nos. 328,000 - 339,000 (Mfg. 1914 - 1920)**

N/A	$16,000	$13,000	$9,000	$7,000	$5,500	$4,500	$3,500	$3,000	$2,500	$2,000	$1,700

Add 20% for original box.
Add 10% for smooth, two-piece walnut grips.
Add 25% for checkered, varnished walnut grips with deep set medallions.
Subtract 15% for nickel finish.

* ***Late Smokeless Powder SAA (ser. no. range 339,000-357,000)*** – single action sales continued to diminish after 1920, as sales of semi-automatics increased. Only 19,000 SAAs were sold in the twenty year period, with only 100 being produced in 1936. The complete serial number is visible only on the frame, but many cylinders are stamped on the rear with the last two or three digits. In 1928, the caliber marking on the left side of the barrel was changed to read "Colt Single Action Army," followed by the caliber. In 1930, the "V" notch rear sight was replaced with a square groove to match the wider front sight, and in 1935, the finish on the hammer was changed from color casehardened to blue with polished sides. Colt special order grip medallions also made a two step, transitional change in 1923. Since 1909, medallions on pearl, ivory or checkered walnut grips had been recessed into the grips and both horses faced

100%	98%	95%	90%	80%	70%	60%	50%	40%	30%	20%	10%

forward. They were first changed to a less expensive, flush mount design, still facing forward and then within the same year to a flush mount, with one facing forward and one backward, a cost cutting measure which required only one die. The finish on the checkered wood grips was also changed from a varnish to an oil finish in 1924.

It is important to remember that while special order grips such as pearl, ivory, or checkered wood may add as much as 25% to an SAA's value, they must be factory original to that particular gun, and be recorded as such in the factory records. Later add-ons enhance a gun's value by much less.

» **Ser. Nos. 339,000 - 350,000 (Mfg. 1920 - 1928)**

$12,000	$9,500	$8,800	$7,500	$6,200	$5,200	$4,500	$4,000	$3,500	$2,800	$2,300	$2,000

Add 20% for original box in good condition.
Add 25% for original checkered wood, pearl, or ivory grips.
Add 35% for original stag horn grips (very rare!).

» **Ser. Nos. 350,000 - 355,000 (Mfg. 1928 - 1935)**

$10,000	$8,500	$7,800	$6,500	$6,000	$5,000	$4,000	$3,500	$3,000	$2,500	$2,000	$1,800

Add 20% for original box in good condition.
Add 25% for original checkered wood, pearl, or ivory grips.
Add 35% for original stag horn grips (very rare!).

» **Ser. Nos. 355,000 - 357,000 (Mfg. 1935 - 1940)**

$9,000	$7,500	$6,800	$6,000	$5,400	$4,800	$3,500	$3,000	$2,500	$2,000	$1,800	$1,500

Add 20% for original box in good condition.
Add 25% for original checkered wood, pearl, or ivory grips.
Add 35% for original stag horn grips (very rare!).

SAA 1st Generation Commercial, Non-Standard Mfg.

SINGLE ACTION ARMY (SAA) - NON-STANDARD MFG. – between 1873-1940 Colt mfg. approx. 327,000 Pre-WWII SAA revolvers. There were several distinct types or configurations of SAAs that varied from the standard and therefore, have special significance to the collector.

* ***.44 Rimfire SAA*** – .44 Henry rimfire cal., 7 1/2 in. barrel, blue and nickel finishes, most were shipped to the southwest and saw hard use, rare with any original finish remaining, many barrels shortened during their period of use, serial numbered in their own range, 1 - 1,863, mfg. from 1875 to 1880.

N/A	N/A	N/A	N/A	$75,000	$60,000	$47,000	$35,000	$27,000	$22,000	$18,000	$15,000

Beware! Many have been found with cut and/or stretched barrels.
A factory letter on this model is available for $200.

* ***.22 Rimfire SAA*** – blue or nickel finish, 5 1/2 in. and 7 1/2 in. barrels, manufactured in two distinct runs, slightly less than 100 converted from unsold .44 RF still in inventory in the late 1880s, and approximately 20 mfg. new in 1891.

N/A	$40,000	$35,000	$32,000	$28,000	$25,000	$22,000	$20,000	$18,000	$15,000	$12,000	$9,000

Add 10% for rare 5 1/2 in. barrel.
Subtract 50% for factory refinished models.
Subtract 10% for those converted from .44 rimfire.

* ***Buntline Special Model SAA*** – .45 LC cal., long barrel model named after Ned Buntline, author of dime novels in the late 19th century. Only 28 believed mfg. with adjustable rear sights and extended hammer screw for attachment of metal skeleton shoulder stock, all in the 28,800 serial range, most with 12 in. or 16 in. barrels. Very rare.

Due to extreme rarity of this model, and the fact that so few ever come on the market, accurate pricing is difficult to determine.

While a model in excellent condition might sell for $300,000, another model with much less condition might bring just as much. Even a professionally restored or factory refinished model could bring $150,000. These guns are so rare that almost any price within reason could be obtained, depending on the market and competitive buyers. An individual appraisal is highly recommended.

* ***Etched Panel .44-40 SAA*** – refers to Single Actions in .44 WCF cal. with the words "Colt Frontier Six Shooter" acid etched in a panel on the left side of the barrel. This phrase was probably originated by one of Colt's New York distributors or possibly by

100%	98%	95%	90%	80%	70%	60%	50%	40%	30%	20%	10%

B. Kittredge & Co. of Cincinnati, OH, who had already advertised the .45 SA as the "Peacemaker" in March 1875, and later had double action Model 1878s etched with the word "OMNIPOTENT" on the barrel. The lowest known etched panel .44-40 is in the 41,000 serial range (1878) and the highest in the 129,000 range circa 1890.

N/A	$45,000	$38,000	$30,000	$22,000	$17,000	$14,000	$12,000	$10,000	$9,000	$8,000	$7,000

Subtract 30% for nickel finish.
Add 10% for 4 3/4 in. barrel.
Add 20% for 5 1/2 in. barrel.

* ***Sheriff's Model SAA*** – this term denotes Single Actions without ejectors and ejector housings. Most were produced in .45 and .44-40 cal., with 3 1/2 in. or 4 in. barrels, but 2 1/2 in., 3 in., 4 3/4 in., and 7 1/2 in. were made. According to collector and researcher Wynn Paul, the first ejectorless Sheriff's or Storekeeper's models were shipped from the factory on February 22, 1882 to Hibbard ,Spencer, Bartlett & Co., Chicago, IL, in two shipments of ten each, one group with 3 1/2 in. barrels, one group with 4 in. barrels. Approximately 1,000 were produced, most in the latter part of the 19th century.

Add 20% for .44-40 cal. w/etched panel.
Add 30% for original special order grips.
Add 50% for 2 1/2 in. or 7 1/2 in. barrel.
Subtract 15% for nickel finish.

» **Sheriff's Model SAA Smokeless Powder Frame**

N/A	$75,000	$65,000	$50,000	$38,000	$32,000	$26,000	$22,000	$18,000	$14,000	$10,000	$8,000

» **Sheriff's Model SAA Black Powder Frame** – pre-1896 mfg. with old style black powder frame.

N/A	$95,000	$82,000	$67,000	$50,000	$35,000	$28,500	$25,000	$20,000	$16,000	$12,000	$10,000

Beware of fakes! The *Blue Book of Gun Values* strongly recommends getting a historical letter from Colt, then checking the authenticity of the serial numbers. Many guns have had numbers altered to match records.

* ***Flat-top Target Model SAA*** – a target version of the SAA with flat-top frame and adj. sights, approximately 925 were manufactured from 1888-1896, both in 5 1/2 in. and 7 1/2 in. barrel and full blue finish, two-piece smooth walnut, two-piece rubber, or two-piece checkered walnut grips are known. Many calibers, from .22 RF to .476 Eley were available.

N/A	$25,000	$20,000	$16,000	$13,000	$11,000	$9,000	$8,000	$7,000	$6,000	$5,000	$4,500

Add 30% for 5 1/2 in. barrel.

Beware! Many target models were returned to the factory for refinishing.

* ***Long Flute Series SAA*** – in 1913, Colt decided to make use of approximately 1500 cylinders left over from the model 1878 double action production. Since it was necessary to add a bolt lock notch and a lead-in groove on these long flute cylinders, a block of serial numbers, 330,000 to 331,480, was set aside to be used for this special production. Manufactured in 1913 and 1914, specimens are known in .32 WCF, .38 WCF, .41 LC, .44 S&W Spl., and .45 Colt cals.

According to researchers Hull and Rowcliffe, whose survey includes 114 long flute Single Actions, no .44 WCF have been noted. The actual total mfg. may possibly exceed 1,500, and while quite rare, these long flute variations sell for only 5% to 10% more than other Single Actions of this period.

* ***Pre-war/Post-war Mfg. SAAs*** – made from pre WWII parts remaining in inventory after production of the Single Action Army had ended in 1940, many of these post-war guns were given as gifts to dignitaries and retiring Colt employees, known calibers include .30 Carbine, .357 Mag., .38 Spl., .44 Spl., .44-40 WCF and .45 Colt. Most are found with 5 1/2 in. barrels and blue and case hardened finish; nickel is rare. Shipping cartons vary from pre-war dark maroon and brown, hinged top, circa 1950, to black 2nd generation style. Approximately 338 were assembled and shipped between 1947-1961.

Add 10% for nickel finish.
Add 20% plus for important or well known recipient.

Most of these guns are found in 95% or better condition, and are valued like the last of the pre-war 1st generation Single Actions.

100%	98%	95%	90%	80%	70%	60%	50%	40%	30%	20%	10%

* ***Factory Engraved SAAs*** – slightly less than 1% (approximately 3,400) Single Actions are thought to have been engraved at the factory or elsewhere by authority from Colt between 1873 and 1940. Between 1873-circa 1929 Colt offered three basic grades of engraving with alphabetical designations - A (least coverage), B, and C (most coverage). Circa 1929-1936 Colt changed these alphabetical engraving designations to numerical, and became No. 1 (least coverage), 2, and 3 (most coverage). Many of these early SAA's also carried special inscriptions, initials, grips, etc., and because of this, the value ranges are very wide. Condition also plays a huge role here. Factory engraved black powder SAAs typically sell in the $10,000 to $100,000 range, while factory engraved smokeless powder SAAs usually peak in the $50,000 range. Very special or one of a kind pieces, such as the five known "panel" engraved guns, or one carried by a famous outlaw or lawman may bring upward of $300,000, depending on condition and particulars. Most factory work is documented in the records.

* ***Non-Factory Engraved SAAs*** – value depends on when and where the engraving was done. Early "New York" or "dealer" engraved Single Actions done outside the factory were usually shipped from Colt in the "soft" and w/o finish. The majority of these were done in the 1870s or 1880s, and condition being equal, are generally priced at 25% to 50% of factory original specimens. Later guns, well done by a known contemporary artist, are usually priced by adding the value of the gun to the cost of the engraving. Poor execution may actually lower the value of a plain, but original gun, much as refinishing would. The notation of "soft" in the factory records is desirable, since the large wholesalers in the northeast used many of the same engravers as Colt. There are and have been some 20th century engravers who stand out, however, and their work commands higher prices, e.g. Lynton McKenzie, Ben Lane, Cole Agee and Weldon Bledsoe - the two latter being famous for their "cattle brand" style, and Ben Lane for his meticulous duplication of the patterns of Cuno Helfricht, the most famous of all Colt factory engravers.

* ***Bisley Model SAA*** – numbered in the same serial range as the standard Single Action Army, the Bisley model featured a more curved forward and longer grip strap and a smaller, raked back hammer. It was designed with the target shooter in mind and named after Bisley, England, the location of the international shooting matches during the late 19th and early 20th century. It was offered in the same barrel lengths, the same finishes and most all of the more popular Single Action calibers, .32 WCF (.32-20) being the most popular. It was advertised from 1896 (approx. ser. no. 165,900) to 1912 (approx. ser. no. 323,000). The highest number known (331,916) was assembled in 1915, but not shipped until November, 1919. Slightly over 45,000 were produced.

N/A	$10,000	$8,500	$7,500	$6,200	$5,000	$4,200	$3,500	$2,800	$2,200	$1,800	$1,500

Add 25% for nickel finish.
Add 20% for original box.
Add 15% for pre-1899 serial number.

* ***Flat-top Target Bisley SAA*** – a target version similar to the flat-top target Single Action with adj. sights. Available in all standard calibers with a 7 1/2 in. barrel, blue finish and either walnut or rubber grips. Offered from 1894 to 1912, the most popular caliber was .455 Eley followed closely by .32 WCF. Only 976 were manufactured.

N/A	$20,000	$18,000	$15,000	$13,000	$11,000	$9,000	$8,000	$7,000	$6,000	$5,000	$4,000

Add 30% for any barrel length other than 7 1/2 in.

* ***Battle of Britain SAA*** – late 1st generation Single Action Armys purchased by the British government in anticipation of invasion from Germany in 1940. A total of 163, mostly .38 and .45 cal. in both blue and nickel finish were sent to England by Colt. These guns were fully inspected and proofed by the British, in many cases showing the exact specifications of the cartridge on the bottom of the barrel. Most, if not all, were unissued, and remain today in 90% plus condition.

$12,000	$10,000	$8,500	$7,500	$6,500	$5,500	$4,700	$4,200	$3,500	$3,000	$2,500	$2,000

Add 10% for blue and color casehardened finish.
Add 20% for original shipping carton.

* ***London Agency SAA*** – as with percussion revolvers and derringers, Colt shipped Single

Action Army revolvers to England for sale through its London Agency. John Kopec, author of *A Study of the Colt Single Action Army Revolver*, estimates that 18% of production during the first 2 1/2 years went to England. These early guns were marked with the standard Hartford address, and most were chambered in either .450 Eley or Boxer caliber, with a 7 1/2 or 5 1/2 in. barrel. A small number were shipped with 4 3/4 in. barrels in May of 1877. According to Kenneth Moore, author of *Single Action Army Revolvers and the London Agency*, and co-author of *A Study of the Colt SAA Revolver*, Baron Von Oppen, head of Colt's London Agency, requested in Oct. 1875 that Colt change the barrel address to "14 PALL MALL, LONDON" only, in an effort to increase sales and to prevent English customers from ordering direct from Hartford. Colt complied and sent 150 revolvers with the new barrel address in early 1876. This created a problem with English customs officials, since the guns were not made in England, they could not be marked "LONDON" only, and would not pass inspection. The London address could not be used. It is believed by Moore that these 150 Colt SAAs were the only ones marked with the London barrel address. By Jan. 1877, a compromise was reached and English customs authorized the use of the dual Hartford/London address to read "COLT'S PT. F.A. MNFG. CO. HARTFORD, CT USA DEPOT 14 PALL MALL LONDON". The London proofed SAAs were usually stamped at the bottom of the barrel, and in each flute of the cylinder, and had a high quality nickel or blue finish with case hardened frame, although some blue examples are known. Through 1890, several thousand SAAs were sold through the London Agency.

Values for the more common English proofed SAAs with the combined Hartford/London address are approx. 50% less than those SAAs sold during the same period in the United States. A gun with the Hartford only address would be more desirable, and one of the 150 with the London only address command substantially more than a model with the dual Hartford/London address, and perhaps more than an American counterpart. An original model with 4 3/4 in. barrel would also bring a premium.

SAA U.S. Military, Mfg. 1873-1903

Since many of the military models listed below are frequently encountered with no original finish remaining, prices for original no condition specimens will be approx. three quarters of the 10% prices listed below. With original specimens getting harder and harder to find, many guns are now observed with major parts replacements, including barrels, cylinders, grips, etc.

Beware of restorations that are purported to be original! One expert believes that as many as 90% of Colt SAA Cavalry & Artillery models currently offered for sale, especially at gun shows, have been intentionally faked, or "enhanced" in some way. Likewise, many "questionable" guns have been consigned to the auction houses for disposal. Many have been altered in the last 40 years in all inspector serial ranges. Some have now been skillfully "aged" to look more original. When making a substantial purchase, a letter of authentication from a reliable source is suggested in addition to a factory historical letter. Also ask for a guarantee of originality in writing from the seller. No factory information is available on U.S. Cavalry revolvers below ser. no. 30,600.

Blue Book Publications, Inc. would be happy to refer you to a credible source for authenticating the military revolvers listed below (very important). While a factory letter (if possible) verifies the configuration when shipped, it does not verify originality and/or authenticity. All inquiries are treated confidentially.

SINGLE ACTION ARMY (CAVALRY) - U.S. MILITARY CONTRACT – the Colt SAA was the primary sidearm of the U.S. military forces between 1873 and 1892. While sometimes called the "cavalry" model, this revolver was carried by commissioned officers in the regular army and the state militias, and issued to each man in the mounted units. A total of 37,063 were purchased by the U.S. government at an average cost of $12.50 each. Contract specifications called for 7 1/2 in. barrel, .45 Colt caliber, government blue and color casehardened finish (a softer blue color compared to the darker and more brilliant civilian finish, which required a higher polish and was therefore more expensive), and one piece, oil finished walnut grips. Each gun was stamped with the initial(s) of a U.S. ordnance principal sub-inspector and finally, with the letters "U.S." on the frame after being approved for delivery to the National Armory at Springfield, MA.

* ***Early U.S. Model SAA (Mfg. 1873 - 1875)*** – principal sub-inspectors of this early period used only the first letter of their last name to mark the revolvers which they inspected.

100%	98%	95%	90%	80%	70%	60%	50%	40%	30%	20%	10%

Chronologically, they were O.W. Ainsworth (A), S.B. Lewis (L), A.P. Casey(C) and W.W. Johnson (J).

While the lower serial numbers are generally the most desirable, the small number of guns inspected by Lewis, Johnson and Casey make them harder to find and perhaps more valuable than a higher numbered Ainsworth. These guns are in the same number sequence as guns made for the civilian market up to #20,000. There are no known "U.S." marked Single Actions between serial numbers 20,000 and 30,000. According to John Kopec, arguably the most knowledgeable and authoritative U.S. Single Action researcher and co-author of the widely respected work, *A Study of the Single Action Army Revolver*, the earliest known Ainsworth inspected Single Action is serial number "179".

» **Ainsworth Serial Range 179 - 999 (1873)**

N/A	N/A	$175,000	$140,000	$100,000	$80,000	$65,000	$55,000	$45,000	$35,000	$25,000	$20,000

» **Ainsworth Serial Range 1,000 - 9,999 (1873-1874)**

N/A	N/A	$140,000	$115,000	$90,000	$75,000	$60,000	$45,000	$35,000	$28,000	$24,000	$16,000

Ainsworth inspected guns between ser. nos. 4,500 and 6,500 were possibly issued to George Custer's 7th Cavalry, and therefore command a premium. Add 25% to 50% to this range.

» **Ainsworth Serial Range 10,000 - 15,000 (1874-1875)**

N/A	N/A	$120,000	$100,000	$80,000	$60,000	$50,000	$40,000	$24,000	$20,000	$16,000	$15,000

» **Lewis Serial Range 15,000-16,500 (1875)**

N/A	N/A	$140,000	$115,000	$90,000	$75,000	$60,000	$45,000	$35,000	$25,000	$18,000	$17,000

» **Johnson Serial Range 16,800-18,450 (1875)**

N/A	N/A	$135,000	$110,000	$85,000	$70,000	$58,000	$47,000	$36,000	$25,000	$18,000	$17,000

» **Casey Serial Range 16,400 - 19,530 (1875)**

N/A	N/A	$120,000	$100,000	$80,000	$60,000	$50,000	$40,000	$35,000	$25,000	$18,000	$17,000

More than a few Casey range guns are dual inspected, most with a "C" and a "J", but while interesting, this does not necessarily add a premium.

* ***Mid-Range U.S. Model SAA (1876 - 1887)*** – when military production resumed in the 30,000 serial range, the principal sub-inspectors during this eleven year period were John T. Cleveland (J.T.C.), Henry Nettleton (H.N.), and David F. Clark (D.F.C.). Starting in 1876, the marking procedure changed from one last name initial to two or all three of the inspector's initials. Also in 1876, the third patent date was added to the left side of the frame in a third line.

» **Cleveland Serial Range 30,690 to 35,570 (1876 - 1877)** – these are the very first of the U.S. Cavalry models to be recorded in the Colt records and the first ones that can be lettered by the factory. Slightly more than 2,000 were delivered under government contract, and were inspected by John T. Cleveland. For some reason, a small group of these guns show the initials of Lewis Draper "L.D." stamped on the frames, instead of the normal "J.T.C.", including the cartouche on the right grip. There is also an unusually high ratio of Civilian SAAs in this serial range with the condemned "C" mark on the frame, and there is existing correspondence from Colt and to the U.S. Ordnance Dept. complaining that Inspector Lt. David A. Lyle was being unduly hard to please. Perhaps Lewis Draper was a temporary replacement during this period. Regardless, this small group of "L.D." marked Single Action Cavalrys are an interesting variation and will command a slight premium.

N/A	N/A	$80,000	$65,000	$50,000	$38,000	$29,000	$20,000	$16,000	$15,000	$13,000	$11,000

Add 10% for "L.D." marked frames.

» **Early Henry Nettleton Serial Range 36,800 - 39,880 (1877)** – according to John Kopec's "Cavalry and Artillery Revolvers" there are a small group of known cavalry revolvers which were part of a large surplus of civilian SAAs which were inspected and accepted by the government. While some are Henry Nettleton inspected, most are marked with the "W" of E.C. Wheeler. It is thought that perhaps Wheeler substituted for Nettleton during an illness. Regardless, this is a very small and desirable group of Cavalry SAAs.

N/A	N/A	$87,000	$70,000	$55,000	$42,000	$36,000	$30,000	$25,000	$18,000	$16,000	$14,000

100%	98%	95%	90%	80%	70%	60%	50%	40%	30%	20%	10%

» **Early David F. Clark Serial Range 41,000-42,300 (1878) & Standard Henry Nettleton Serial Range 47,000-51,100 (1878 - 1879)**

100%	98%	95%	90%	80%	70%	60%	50%	40%	30%	20%	10%
N/A	N/A	$75,000	$50,000	$35,000	$28,000	$22,000	$18,000	$16,000	$15,000	$13,000	$10,000

» **Later David F. Clark Serial Range 53,000-121,000 (Mfg. 1880 - 1887)**

100%	98%	95%	90%	80%	70%	60%	50%	40%	30%	20%	10%
N/A	N/A	$55,000	$46,000	$32,000	$25,000	$18,000	$16,000	$14,000	$12,000	$10,000	$9,000

* ***Late U.S. Model SAA, Serial Range 131,187-140,361 (Mfg. 1890 - 1891)*** – this was the last of U.S. Single Action production. Four thousand were inspected by Rinaldo A. Carr during this sixteen month period. As hostilities in the west subsided, demand decreased and many revolvers of this group went to state militias or were left in storage. Consequently, a higher percentage of R.A.C. inspected SAAs are found in excellent condition than those of other inspectors, and this is reflected in their value. The last of this group was shipped from the factory on April 29, 1891.

100%	98%	95%	90%	80%	70%	60%	50%	40%	30%	20%	10%
N/A	$45,000	$41,000	$35,000	$27,000	$21,000	$18,000	$17,000	$16,000	$13,000	$10,000	$8,000

* ***Artillery Model SAAs*** – refers to U.S. government model SAA revolvers with 5 1/2 in. barrels, which were reworked and refinished between 1895 and 1903. In response to growing dissatisfaction with the stopping power of the newly adopted M1892 .38 LC cal. double action revolvers, the U.S. Ordnance Dept. directed Springfield Armory to collect all remaining quantities of .45 Colt Cavalry revolvers from storage, refurbish if necessary, and shorten the barrels from 7 1/2 in. to 5 1/2 in. The Colt Company did approximately 1,200 of these, while about 15,000 were done at Springfield Armory. Not all of these were refinished, since many were still new, in unissued condition, and simply had their barrels shortened. During this first re-work period from 1895 to 1898, care was taken to match serial numbered parts, and in some instances, parts were even renumbered to match. After seeing hard use in the Spanish American War and the Philippine Insurrection, approximately 6,000 of these same guns were returned to Colt between 1900 and 1903 for refurbishing, and others were apparently redone at Springfield Armory. Unfortunately, no attempt was made during this time period to match serial numbers. This shortcut minimized labor and saved the government $1.50 per gun.

* ***Standard Mixed Numbers Variation***

100%	98%	95%	90%	80%	70%	60%	50%	40%	30%	20%	10%
N/A	$16,000	$13,500	$9,500	$8,500	$7,500	$6,500	$5,500	$4,800	$4,200	$3,800	$3,400

Add 50% documented "Rough Rider" association.
Add 20% for 7-1/2 inch barrel matching frame.
Add 10% for Custer period frames (under #6000).

Only rarely will one be found with all the matching serial numbers, indicating that it had been refurbished at Colt's during 1896. (Factory letter advised). These guns will bring a premium price, and must be authenticated, as they may have been recently altered.

A few artillery models are believed to have been redone at various government arsenals, and this could explain the existence of several known artillery revolvers with blue frames. In fact, new information recently discovered by noted Single Action specialist Dave Lanara seems to confirm that some U.S. Artillery and Cavalry models were indeed refinished at the Manila Arsenal in the Philippines with blue frames, this was due to the lack of color case hardening capabilities at that location. Regardless, the artillery model is very popular with collectors and has become one of the most studied and interesting variants of the Colt Single Action revolver.

* ***Matching Numbers in Late Inspector Ranges (DFC & RAC)***

100%	98%	95%	90%	80%	70%	60%	50%	40%	30%	20%	10%
N/A	$20,000	$17,500	$15,000	$11,500	$9,750	$8,500	$7,000	$6,500	$5,500	$4,800	$4,500

* ***Matching Numbers in Early Inspector Ranges (A, C, J, LD, JTC, HN)***

100%	98%	95%	90%	80%	70%	60%	50%	40%	30%	20%	10%
N/A	$28,000	$26,500	$23,000	$20,000	$16,500	$15,000	$13,200	$12,000	$9,000	$6,500	$5,000

* ***Blued Frame Variation With Mixed Number***

100%	98%	95%	90%	80%	70%	60%	50%	40%	30%	20%	10%
N/A	$11,000	$9,500	$7,800	$6,500	$5,500	$4,750	$4,000	$3,800	$3,500	$3,200	$3,000

* ***New York State Militia SAA*** – in 1895 before work began on the artillery models, Colt refurbished 800 SAA revolvers supplied by Springfield Armory, especially for the New York State Militia. These guns retained their 7 1/2 inch barrels and all original parts wherever possible. Replacement parts were serial numbered to match, and strangely,

100%	98%	95%	90%	80%	70%	60%	50%	40%	30%	20%	10%

barrels and cylinders were given the missing first and second digits of the whole serial number which they had never before been applied. In addition to receiving a high polish blue and casehardened civilian finish, their hammers were blued instead of being color casehardened. Since most other Cavalry models in the government's possession were cut to 5 1/2 inches shortly thereafter, these 800 are quite possibly the only remaining 7 1/2 inch SAAs that could actually have seen service on the American frontier against hostiles. Most other 7 1/2 inch Cavalry revolvers that are seen today were likely issued to state militias rather than the U.S. Army. Some are found with unit markings on their buttstraps and/or grips or with lanyard swivels. These 800 Colt revolvers therefore may have played a very significant role in the history of the Indian wars.

N/A	$30,000	$26,000	$22,000	$16,000	$13,000	$10,000	$8,000	$6,750	$5,500	$4,800	$4,000

Since New York Militia revolvers are frequently encountered with a mismatched part, the question is often asked if the mismatched part affects value. If the serial number of the mismatched part can be attributed to another known New York Militia revolver, then the answer is no. Since the serial numbers of all 800 refurbished 1895 New York Militia models are recorded in the Colt ledgers, the serial number of the mismatched part should always belong to another documented New York example. In most cases, cylinders had been inadvertently switched by a New York Trooper, or back straps were refitted onto an incorrect revolver when the New York Militia armorer fitted the lanyard swivel.

CAUTION: Unscrupulous fakers have been known to restamp the mismatched part with the "host" revolver's primary serial number.

* ***Condemned U.S. Cavalry*** – throughout military contract production, a small percentage of SAAs did not pass inspection and were condemned, receiving a large "C" stamped on the frame, just over the serial number. These guns were set aside, and later completed as civilian revolvers. They are often found with the Ordnance sub-inspector's initials, such as J.T.C., on the bottom of the frame, but will not have a "U.S." on the left side. This does not have a negative effect on the value of these guns to the collector, and they should be regarded as normal civilian revolvers with an interesting history.

REVOLVERS: SAA, 2ND GENERATION: 1956-1975 MFG.

The author wishes to express his thanks to Charles Layson, and Carol and the late Don Wilkerson for their generous contributions to the 2nd & 3rd Generation Colt SAA information.

Popular demand brought back the Single Action Army in 1956 with minor modifications, most not detectable except to experts. Serial numbers began at 0001SA, and continued to 73,000SA before the "New Model" was introduced in 1976 (ser. no. 80,000SA). Premiums are paid for rare production variances in NIB condition. It should be noted "premium niches" exist in this model as collectors are establishing premiums paid for rarer production variances (the interrelation of barrel length, caliber, frame type, finish quality, year of manufacture, and other special features). The order of desirability on standard 2nd Generation SAAs is as follows: 4 3/4 in. barrels are the most desirable, followed by 7 1/2 in., and then 5 1/2 in. Caliber desirability is as follows: .45 LC has the most demand, followed by .44 Spl., .38 Spl., and then .357 Mag. It follows that desirable calibers found with desirable barrel lengths will command healthy premiums if production was unusually low for a particular configuration. Reference books specifically on the post-war SAA are a must when determining the rarity factors on these multiple production combinations. Buntlines, Sheriff's Models, and special orders through the Custom Gun Shop are in a class by themselves, and have to be evaluated one at a time.

It is advisable to procure a factory letter when buying or selling older or recently manufactured Colt single actions (hence, guaranteeing authenticity and value credibility). These watermarked letters are based on the original factory shipping records and are available by contacting Colt Archive Properties LLC in Hartford, CT. While not totally infallible, these letters are normally very accurate. The cost to document 2nd generation SAA's is $100. This research can be expedited for an additional $100. This expedite service provides a verbal report within 24-48 hours and a documentation letter follows in 2-3 weeks. Additionally, premium charges apply for factory engraved guns ($50-$150), or unique shipping destinations ($50-$200). To contact the Archive

GRADING - PPGS™	100%	98%	95%	90%	80%	70%	60%	LAST MSR

Department for assistance call 1-800-962-2658, Ext. 1343. Once contacted, they will tell you what the exact historical research charge will be for the service you are requesting. The address to write to is COLT ARCHIVE PROPERTIES LLC, P.O. Box 1868, Hartford, CT 06144-1868. For a complete Archive Services price list, please refer to the Colt website at www.coltsmfg.com.

SINGLE ACTION ARMY (SAA, 2ND GENERATION) – .357 Mag., .38 Spl., .44 Spl., or .45 LC cal., denoted by SA suffix, 3 (Sheriff's Model), 4 3/4, 5 1/2, 7 1/2, or 12 (Buntline) in. barrel length - 5 1/2, 7 1/2, and 12 in. barrels have the one-line barrel address, and are all blue, blue/case hardened, or nickel finished. 2nd Generation SAAs have been grouped into the following 3 categories.

* ***SAA Early 2nd Generation*** – ser. no. range 0001SA to approx. 39,000SA, shipped in one-piece black box similar to pre-war box. Mfg. from 1956-65.

.45 LC cal.	$2,800	$2,450	$2,100	$1,905	$1,540	$1,260	$980
.44 Spl. cal.	$2,600	$2,275	$1,950	$1,770	$1,430	$1,170	$910
.38 Spl. cal.	$2,400	$2,100	$1,800	$1,630	$1,320	$1,080	$840
.357 Mag. cal.	$2,000	$1,750	$1,500	$1,360	$1,100	$900	$700

Add 30% for original black box in good condition.
Add 20% for original nickel finish.
Add 15% for original 4 3/4 in. barrel.
Subtract 10% for rounded "fanning, quick draw" hammer configuration, where sharp corners above the firing pin were removed so as not to scratch the shooter's palm or thumb when trying to cock and fire quickly. Guns with this type of hammer fall between serial #26,500SA (1959) and #61,900SA (1972) approximately.

The very earliest models of this group, with serial numbers under 10,000 SA, have become more desirable when found in 100% new condition, with perfect black box, brush and papers - this configuration may bring an additional 20%.

* ***SAA Mid-Range 2nd Generation*** – approx. ser. no. range 39,000SA to 70,055SA, most were shipped in a red and white, two-piece, stagecoach box, but at approx. serial range 65,XXXSA a light wood grain box was used followed by a dark wood grain box. Mfg. 1965-1973.

.45 LC cal.	$2,000	$1,750	$1,500	$1,360	$1,100	$900	$700
.44 Spl. cal.	$1,900	$1,665	$1,425	$1,290	$1,045	$855	$665
.357 Mag. cal.	$1,800	$1,575	$1,350	$1,225	$990	$810	$630

Add 30% for original stagecoach box.
Add 10% for original light or dark grain wood box with styrofoam inserts.
Add 10% for original nickel finish.
Add 15% for original 4 3/4 in. barrel.

* ***SAA Late 2nd Generation*** – approx. ser. no. range 70,055SA to 73,205SA, shipped in a brown, wood grain cardboard shell with 2 styrofoam inserts. Mfg. 1973-1976.

.45 LC cal.	$1,800	$1,575	$1,350	$1,225	$990	$810	$630
.357 Mag. cal.	$1,700	$1,490	$1,275	$1,155	$935	$765	$595

Add 15% for original brown/styrofoam box.
Add 10% for original nickel finish.
Add 10% for original 4 3/4 in. barrel.

2nd Generation SAAs in stagecoach box w/o eagle black grips (ser. numbered under approx. 52,000SA) are more desirable than those with eagle. Also, flat-top hammers are more desirable than round top hammers found between ser. no. range 27,012SA-61,575SA (mfg. mid-1959-1972).

Colt manufactured approximately 100 screwless frames during the 1970s, and assembled approximately 50 guns at the time. The other 50 sat in the warehouse until Colt started assembling the screwless frames again during the 1990s. Most of these recent guns are engraved and in .38-40 WCF or .45 LC cal., and have either a 4 3/4 or 5 in. barrel. Typically, the engraver's name is part of the serial number. Bangor's distributed most of these guns, and in today's marketplace they are priced in the $7,500-$25,000 range.

GRADING - PPGS™	100%	98%	95%	90%	80%	70%	60%	LAST MSR

SHERIFF'S MODEL SAA (1961 MODEL) - .45 LC cal., distinictive configuration with 3 in. barrel and no ejector rod housing, ser. no. followed by SM suffix, 503 were mfg. for Centennial Arms Corp. - 478 had a blue/case hardened finish and 25 were done in nickel.

	$2,000	$1,750	$1,500	$1,360	$1,100	$900	$700	
Nickel finish	$7,750	$4,800	$4,200	$3,600	$3,000	$2,400	$2,100	

Add 25% for original two-piece box.

Original nickel finish is very rare on this model, watch for refinishing.

BUNTLINE SPECIAL SAA (2ND GENERATION) - .45 LC cal. only, 12 in. barrel, blue/case hardened finish, rubber (early mfg.) or walnut grips. Over 3,900 mfg. 1957-1975.

	$2,000	$1,800	$1,600	$1,500	$1,400	$1,200	$1,000	
Nickel finish	$3,400	$2,550	$2,000	$1,800	$1,700	$1,600	$1,500	

Add 30% for original black box.

Add 10% for black hard rubber grips.

Add 150% for nickel finish with black box, 50% for nickel with later tan box.

Original nickel finish is very rare on this model, watch for refinishing.

NEW FRONTIER SAA (2ND GENERATION) – .357 Mag., .38 Spl. (rare), .44 Spl., or .45 LC cal., denoted by flat-top frame, adj. rear sight, and "NF" after the serial number, 4 3/4 (scarce), 5 1/2 (scarce), or 7 1/2 (most common) in. barrel, case hardened frame/blue finish and smooth walnut grips were standard. Approx. 4,200 mfg. 1961-1975.

	$1,400	$1,200	$1,100	$950	$850	$750	$650	
.38 Spl., 5 1/2 in. bbl.	$3,750	$2,850	$2,600	$2,400	$2,200	$2,000	$1,800	

Add 15% for later brown/styrofoam box.

Add 20% for stagecoach or black box (must be in correct ser. no. range).

Add 35% for early black and gold box.

Add 50% for 4 3/4 in. barrel.

Add 25% for 5 1/2 in. barrel.

This model in .38 Spl. cal. with 7 1/2 in. barrel is very rare. NIB specimens can sell for as much as $8,750.

NEW FRONTIER BUNTLINE SAA (2ND GENERATION) - .45 LC cal. only, 12 in. barrel, flat-top frame and adj. rear sight. Approx. 72 mfg. 1962-67.

	$2,500	$2,190	$1,875	$1,700	$1,375	$1,125	$875	

Add 50% for original black or tan box (must be serial numbered to the gun).

FACTORY ENGRAVED 2ND GENERATION SAAs – approx. 350 revolvers were factory engraved with 90% being in .45 LC cal. Values range from 75%-100% higher than non-engraved specimens, with additional premiums paid for rare styles and configurations and/or for the notoriety of the engraver. Those SAAs done by Albert Herbert, A.A. White, Robert Burt, Leonard Francolini, and Dennis Kies are probably the highest-priced examples. Always check authenticity when buying, selling, or trading engraved 2nd Generation SAAs with the Colt Archive Dept. The charge for a factory letter per engraved gun is $150. $50 will be refunded if Colt cannot provide historical documentation.

Factory engraved 2nd Generation SAAs are at least 10 times rarer than engraved 3rd Generation pistols.

REVOLVERS: SAA, 3RD GENERATION: 1976-CURRENT MFG.

After a short break in production, Colt Firearms announced the resumption of full-scale production of the Single Action on Feb. 4th, 1976, at the N.S.G.A. (National Sporting Goods Association) Bi-Centennial show in Chicago.

The "New Model Colt Single Action Army" or the "Colt Post-War Single Action Army - New Model", as it was commonly referred to at the time, is known today to collectors as the "3rd Generation Colt Single Action Army". Minor changes include a modified, thin front sight contour, and a return of the cylinder pin bushing in late 2002, plus a few other "minor, modern manufacturing techniques that have not changed the appearance, feel, action, or performance of this historic handgun...," according to Colt's press release at the time.

Production began with ser. no. 80,000SA, and reached 99,999SA in 1978. At this point, the SA suffix changed to a prefix beginning with SA01,001. Serialization reached SA99,999 during 1993,

GRADING - PPGS™	100%	98%	95%	90%	80%	70%	60%	LAST MSR

and began over, this time separating the letters SA, and starting with S02,001A.

Starting at approximately ser. no. S34,000A, Colt reintroduced the full length cylinder bushing which had been eliminated in 1976, making these current 3rd Generation Single Actions essentially the same as the 1st and 2nd Generation guns. The factory still refers to these as 3rd Generation however, and not 4th Generation, as some collectors are now calling them.

For a listing of Colt's "P-Codes" (referring to the factory's model number designations specifying frame type, caliber, finish, and barrel length), please refer to the Colt Single Action Model Numbers section in the back of this book (located in Colt Serialization). As with 1st and 2nd Generation Single Actions, a factory letter authenticating configuration and shipping destination can be obtained by writing to: COLT ARCHIVE PROPERTIES LLC, P.O. Box 1868, Hartford, CT 06144-1868.

Please contact the Colt Custom Shop for a written quotation ($25) regarding a custom built SAA with special options/features. Their address is: Colt Manufacturing Company, Inc. P.O. Box 1868, Hartford, CT 06101, ATTN: Custom Shop.

POPULAR SAA CUSTOM SHOP SPECIAL ORDER OPTIONS

Add $329 for special barrel length, for "45 Colt" or two line address on barrel add $95, add $450 for caliber change, for custom-tuned action most recent MSR was $197, add $275 (available in .45 LC only beginning 2000) for extra regular fluted or unfluted cylinder, for extra long fluted cylinder most recent MSR was $308, add $152 for beveled front of cylinder, add $180 for fire blue package (screws, base pin, and ejector rod head), add $200 for mirror brite finish (disc.), add $1,618 for nickel finish, add $1,390 for blue/color case finish, add $1,390 for full blue finish, add $425, for gold or silver plating, last published MSR was $425, currently it's POR), add $105 for black eagle grips, add $305 for smooth walnut grips with medallions, add $275 for North American elkhorn grips (disc.), add $400 for red stag grips (disc.), add $450 for sambar stag grips (disc.), add $625 for stag grips, add $425 for buffalo horn grips, add $375 for mother-of-pearl grips (disc.), add $840 for one or two piece plain ivory grips, $425 for imitation ivory, approx. 10% for grip checkering, add $350 for scrimshaw engraving (3 initials only), add $65 for consecutive serial numbers, add $350 for individual unique serial number, add $105 to modify and shorten ejector housing, add $55 for bullseye ejector rod head, add $359 for birdshead grips, add $400 for extra long backstrap, for extended butt frame last MSR was $400, for special length barrel add $329, to regulate barrel for accuracy add $225, for qualify screws add $84, for wide spur hammer with blue finish add $225, for wide spur hammer with nickel or hard chrome finish add $255

While a few screwless frame SAAs have been mfg. to date (approx. 100), the Custom Shop now lists this option as a standard custom order feature. Price is POR

STANDARD/CUSTOM SINGLE ACTION ARMY SAA (3RD GENERATION) – .32-20 WCF (mfg. 2005-2011), .357 Mag. (disc. approx. 1983, reintroduced 2005), .38 Spl. (reintroduced 2005-2011), .38-40 WCF (reintroduced 2005-2011), .44 Spl. (disc. approx. 1983), .44-40 WCF (disc. 2011), or .45 LC cal., 4 (disc. 1988), 4 3/4, 5 (disc. 1987), 5 1/2, or 7 1/2 in. barrel, 5 1/2 and 7 1/2 in. barrels have the one-line barrel address, fixed sights, standard finishes include full blue (disc.), color case hardened/blue or nickel, plastic black eagle or walnut grips (used mostly during 1991-92) standard, current mfg. of black powder frames is available in .45 LC cal. only (see separate listing for current mfg.), most recent mfg. has blue shipping box with white slip cover. Mfg. 1976 to date. Original 1976 issue price was approx. $242.

MSR $1,349	$1,195	$995	$825	$725	$650	$600	$550

Add $202 for nickel finish (current mfg.).
Add 25% for original .38 Spl. cal. (disc.)
Add 10% for black powder frame mfg. pre-1996.
Add $700 for original two-piece ivory grips with screw.
Add $700 for original one-piece ivory grips w/o screw.
Add 5% for original brown box with styrofoam inserts (mfg. 1976-93).
Typically, the engraver's name is part of the serial number. Bangor's originally distributed most of these guns. In today's marketplace price range from $8,500-$25,000, depending on configuration and engraving.

GRADING - PPGS™	100%	98%	95%	90%	80%	70%	60%	LAST MSR

Through 2001, Colt offered the SAA as both Standard and Custom Models. The difference is that single actions, which are further customized with engraving, special barrel lengths, stocks, etc., are packaged more elaborately because of the added value of the customizing.

Beginning 2001, all orders for SAA models are processed through the Colt Custom Shop. The 2001 Custom Shop MSR for the Custom SAA was $2,100.

Various custom order barrel lengths have been available on this model for some time.

The .357 Mag. and .44 Spl. cals. were mostly discontinued by 1983.

Colt manufactured approximately 100 screwless frames during the 1970s, and assembled approximately 50 guns at the time. The other 50 sat in the warehouse until Colt started assembling the screwless frames again during the 1990s. Most of these recent guns are engraved and in .38-40 WCF or .45 LC cal., and have either a 4 3/4 or 5 in. barrel.

To reference factory coding for the various Standard Model P (SAA) configurations, please refer to the Colt Single Action Model Numbers within the Colt Serialization section in the back of this text.

BLACK POWDER FRAME SAA (3RD GENERATION) – .45 LC cal., 4 3/4, 5 1/2, or 7 1/2 in. barrel, features old style blackpowder frame. Mfg. 1984-1995, reintroduced 2008.

MSR $1,349	$1,195	$995	$825	$725	$650	$600	$550

COLT COWBOY SAA – .45 LC cal., 4 3/4 (disc. 1999, reintroduced 2002), 5 1/2, or 7 1/2 (disc. 1999) in. barrel marked "COLT COWBOY .45 COLT" on left side, transfer bar safety, all steel construction, frame assembly done in the U.S., charcoal case colors on frame with blue metal parts, rampant Colt black competition grips similar in design to those used on 1st generation SAAs, 40 oz. Not mfg. in U.S. While advertised beginning 1998, this model was not manufactured until 1999-2003.

$795	$650	$500	$450	$400	$375	$350	*$670*

* ***Cowboy SAA Collection Set*** – includes SAA in .45 LC cal., with 5 1/2 in. barrel, stag (very limited) or imitation ivory (more common) grips, blue/color case hardened finish, accessories include collector's Bowie knife, silver medallion and collector's case, marked "1 of 1,000". Limited mfg. 2000 only.

$1,250	$750	$625	$500	$425	$400	$400	*$1,600*

SHERIFF'S MODEL SAA (3RD GENERATION, MFG 1980-1985) – .44-40 WCF, .44 Spl., or .45 LC cal., 3 in. barrel w/o ejector rod, blue/case colored, nickel, or royal blue finish. Approx. 4,560 guns mfg. 1980-85.

.45 LC cal. (blue/CH)	$1,195	$1,050	$850	$750	$650	$600	$550
.44 Spl./.44-40 WCF	$1,075	$975	$850	$750	$675	$600	$525

Add 10% for extra convertible cylinder.
Add 10% for original nickel finish.
Add $550 for original ivory grips.
Subtract 20% for all blue finish.

* ***Sheriff's Model SAA (3rd Generation - Current Mfg.)*** – .44-40 WCF or .45 LC (most popular) cal., 3 or 4 in. barrel w/o ejector rod, blue/case colored (disc. 2009) or nickel finish, black plastic grips. Mfg. 2008-2010.

blue/cc finish (disc. 2009)	$1,150	$995	$825	$725	$650	$600	$550
nickel finish (disc. 2010)	$1,375	$1,075	$875	$775	$675	$625	$575

Last MSR was $1,490 (nickel finish) in 2010.

BUNTLINE SPECIAL MODEL SAA (3RD GENERATION) – .44-40 WCF or .45 LC cal. only, 12 in. barrel, blue/case hardened finish, walnut grips.

$1,195	$1,050	$850	$750	$650	$600	$550

Add 10% for original nickel finish.
Add $550 for original ivory grips.

NEW FRONTIER SAA (3RD GENERATION - 1978-1981 MFG.) – .357 Mag., .44-40 WCF (rare), .44 Spl., or .45 LC cal., denoted by "NF" serial suffix, 4 3/4, 5 1/2, or 7 1/2 in.

GRADING - PPGS™	100%	98%	95%	90%	80%	70%	60%	LAST MSR

barrel, blue/case hardened finish, flat-top frame, adj. rear sight, plain two-piece walnut grips. Mfg. 1978-1983.

	$1,095	$950	$825	$750	$700	$650	$600	

Subtract 10% for 5 1/2 in. barrel.
Subtract 15% for 7 1/2 in. barrel.
Add 5% for original brown box with styrofoam inserts.

Serial numbers on the New Frontier started at 01001NF, but during 1980 a few New Frontiers with 5 1/2 in. barrels were produced in the 7000NF serial range, where 2nd Generation New Frontiers left off. Therefore, a 3rd Generation New Frontier will either have a ser. no. starting with "O" or will have a higher number than 7288NF with no "O" prefix.

FRONTIER SIX SHOOTER SAA (3RD GENERATION) – .44-40 WCF cal., black powder frame, 4 3/4, 5 1/2, or 7 1/2 in. barrel with "Colt Frontier Six Shooter" acid etched in a panel on the left side of barrel, similar to 1st Generation SAAs, blue (disc. 2009) or nickel finish. Mfg. 2008-2010.

Blue finish (disc. 2009)	$1,350	$1,050	$850	$750	$650	$600	$550	
Nickel finish (disc. 2010)	$1,475	$1,125	$900	$800	$700	$625	$575	

The last MSR on nickel finish was $1,547 (2010).

NEW FRONTIER SAA (3RD GENERATION - NEW MFG.) – .357 Mag. (disc. 2011), .44 Spl., or .45 LC cal., 4 3/4, 5 1/2, or 7 1/2 in. barrel, royal blue/case hardened finish, flat-top frame, adj. rear sight, plain two-piece smooth walnut grips with medallions. New 2011.

MSR $1,455	$1,350	$1,150	$925	$825	$725	$625	$575	

NEW FRONTIER BUNTLINE SPECIAL SAA (3RD GENERATION) – .45 LC cal. only, 12 in. barrel, flat-top frame, adj. rear sight, limited mfg. as the New Buntline Commemorative during 1979. Please refer to the Colt Commemorative section for value information.

STOREKEEPER'S MODEL SAA (3RD GENERATION - 1984-85 MFG.) – .45 LC cal. only, black powder frame, 4 in. barrel w/o ejector rod, full nickel or royal blue/case hardened finish, ivory grips. Approx. 280 mfg. 1984-85.

	$1,700	$1,450	$1,300	$1,100	$900	$800	$750	

Add 10% for original nickel finish.

* ***Storekeeper's Model SAA (3rd Generation - Current Mfg.)*** – .44-40 WCF or .45 LC cal., 4 in. barrel w/o ejector rod, blue/case hardened (disc. 2009) or nickel (new 2010) finish. Mfg. 2008-2010.

Blue/cc finish (disc. 2009)	$1,290	$995	$825	$725	$650	$600	$550	
Nickel finish (2010)	$1,375	$1,075	$875	$775	$675	$625	$575	

Last MSR was $1,490 (nickel finish) in 2010.

COLT CLASSIC SAA – .45 LC cal., 5 1/2 in. barrel only, all blue finish, uncheckered wood grips with Colt medallions, twin gold barrel bands on back of cylinder and front of barrel. Limited mfg. 2010 only.

	$1,495	$1,275	$1,075	$925	$800	$700	$600	*$1,620*

HUGH O'BRIAN-WYATT EARP LIMITED EDITION – .45 LC cal., set includes one 4 3/4 in. and one 12 in. barreled Buntline SAA models, smooth walnut grips, case colored frame and hammer with polished blue barrel and cylinder, barrels are etched "Hugh O'Brian - Wyatt Earp Tribute" and backstrap features Hugh O'Brian's signature, set includes French fitted walnut case with hinged glass top and removeable drawer, includes replica marshall badge, certificates signed by Hugh O'Brian and double holster Buntline special gun belt, mfg. by Frontier Gunleather, total mfg. determined by orders taken by Dec. 31, 2010.

	$4,500	$4,100	$3,600	$3,100	$2,750	$2,350	$1,900	*$4,712*

Add $150 for holster set.

GRADING - PPGS™	100%	98%	95%	90%	80%	70%	60%	LAST MSR

COLT 175th ANNIVERSARY LIMITED EDITION SAA – .45 LC cal., Colt royal blue finish only, 175th Anniversary (1836-2011) Limited Edition with selective 24 Kt. gold plated scroll on frame, backstrap, barrel and cylinder, black powder frame, left side of barrel is marked "1836 - 175th Anniversary - 2011", 4 3/4, 5 1/2, or 7 1/2 in. barrel, black eagle plastic grips, 175 manufactured in each barrel length 2011 only.

	$1,795	$1,575	$1,325	$1,100	$950	$825	$700	*$1,580*

CUSTOM & SPECIAL ENGRAVED SAA EDITIONS (3RD GENERATION) – beginning in 1976, with the introduction of the "New Model" SAA (3rd Generation), the Colt Custom Shop produced many custom and special edition engraved Single Army Action revolvers. According to Mr. Don Wilkerson, author of *The Post-War Single Action Revolver 1976-1986*, "the term custom edition is defined as a group of identical revolvers assembled under the direction of the Custom Gun Shop at Colt's and sold through the normal distribution system. A custom edition differs from a special edition in that special editions are a group of revolvers made up to a customer's unique specifications, and sold as a group to one purchaser...." While the exact number is not known, it is thought that approx. 3,500 SAAs have been engraved since 1976. Since each edition is unique, values vary widely, depending upon the notability of the engraver, the amount and type of coverage, and the number produced. Models listed below are recent Colt Custom Editions.

* ***SAA Engraved European Model*** – 9mm Para. cal., nickel finish only, 4 3/4 (110 mfg.), 5 1/2 (110 mfg.), or 7 1/2 (50 mfg.) in. barrel, rosewood grips with silver medallions, 40-43 oz. Mfg. 1991-92 only.

	$1,950	$1,650	$1,395	$1,195	$1,065	$855	$750	*$1,990*

* ***SAA Engraved U.S. Model*** – .45 ACP cal., royal blue finish only, 4 3/4, 5 1/2, or 7 1/2 in. barrel, walnut grips, 40-43 oz. Mfg. 1991-92 only.

	$1,850	$1,325	$1,100	$985	$795	$675	$565	*$1,960*

* ***SAA Old World Engravers Sampler*** – .45 LC cal., 5 1/2 in. barrel, nickel finish, buffalo horn grips, includes four unique styles of engraving. Mfg. 1997-98, reintroduced 2001-2002.

	$2,975	$2,450	$2,000	$1,740	$1,495	$1,215	$1,000	*$3,445*

* ***Legend Rodeo/Legend Rodeo II SAA*** – disc. 1998.

	$1,950	$1,500	$1,250	$1,100	$895	$785	$630	*$2,450*

* ***125th Anniversary Edition SAA*** – beveled cylinder, fire blue finish, "45 COLT" on left side of barrel and address on top of barrel. 1,000 mfg. 1997-2002.

	$1,600	$1,150	$825	N/A	N/A	N/A	N/A	*$2,070*

* ***Model P w/Unsigned B Coverage Engraving*** – choice of cals. and barrel lengths, blue or nickel finish, features unsigned standard American scroll B engraving coverage. Disc. 2010.

	$2,250	$2,000	$1,750	$1,500	$1,250	$1,000	$875	*$2,319*

Add $231 for nickel finish.

* ***Modern Masters Model P w/Signed B Coverage Engraving*** – choice of cals. and barrel lengths, blue or nickel finish, features signed standard American scroll B engraving coverage. New 2009.

Current MSR on this model is $6,528.

SAA CUSTOM SHOP ENGRAVING PRICES - PRE-1997 – values below represent 1995 published SAA Custom Shop A-D engraving options before the company started separate Standard, Expert, and Master level pricing during 1997. For current Colt Custom Shop engraving prices, please refer to the "Colt Custom Shop Engraving - Current Mfg." section below.

Add $1,163 for Class "A" engraving (25% metal coverage).
Add $2,324 for Class "B" engraving (50% metal coverage).
Add $3,487 for Class "C" engraving (75% metal coverage).
Add $4,647 for Class "D" engraving (100% metal coverage).
Add an additional 13% (approx.) for Buntline engraving.

Standard Engraving was performed mostly by standard level factory engravers and engraving options generally included A-D style coverage. Typically, gold work was not performed by these engravers

and specimens are mostly unsigned. Expert Engravers executed classic American style scroll, w/o gold work, and may have signed their work.

FACTORY ENGRAVED SAAs (3RD GENERATION) - the rarity of the SAA configuration in addition to the notability of the engraver will make the difference on the premiums commanded. 3rd Generation factory engraved SAAs were produced in much greater numbers than were 2nd Generation SAAs. Over 80% of engraved 3rd Generation SAAs are .45 LC caliber, the majority have 7 1/2 in. barrels, and some variation of blue finish. Grade "C" (41% of engraved mfg.) and Grade "D" (24% of engraved mfg.) dominate production.

Current MSR on a Colt SAA with signed Master Level Engraving "B" coverage is $7,061.
Use the following add-ons as general guidelines for values on factory engraved recently manufactured 3rd Generation SAAs.
Add approx. 10% for original nickel finish.
Add 25% for 4 3/4 in. barrel.
Add 15% for 5 1/2 in. barrel.
Add 10% for calibers other than .45 LC.
Add 30% for factory ivory grips.
Add 10% for original blue cardboard or plastic box.
Unfortunately, the quality of the engraving on some early Third Generation SAAs has been substandard, and as a result, these guns usually cap at approx. $2,000.

During 1978-79, Colt engraved as many as 300-500 guns on a single factory order. If the level of quality is similar to today's SAAs, the price will also be similar.

COLT CUSTOM SHOP ENGRAVING, SAA & SEMI-AUTO, 1976-PRESENT

Prior to 1976, Colt had three factory engraving patterns - A, B, and C coverage. During 1976, they expanded the Custom Shop and a new class D pattern was added. To inaugurate the Custom Gun shop in 1976, Colt created a "Custom Edition" of deluxe engraved Model P revolvers. This custom edition was the first of many custom editions to be produced by the Custom Gun Shop over the years. The term "Custom Edition" is defined by Don Wilkerson as a group of identical revolvers assembled under the direction of the Custom Gun Shop and sold through Colt's normal distribution system. A "Custom Edition" differs from a "Special Edition" in that a special edition is a group of revolvers made per customer specifications, sold to one purchaser, and not through Colt's normal distribution system . An example of a custom edition: Twenty-five P-1970 revolvers were assembled on Custom Shop order #2622. All twenty-five .44-40 cal. Royal Blue and casehardened revolvers were assembled with unfluted cylinders and ivory stocks. This custom edition was shipped to the various Colt distributors in early 1984.

An example of a special edition: Two hundred P-1970 revolvers were ordered by the Powder Horn Gun Shop in Bozeman, Montana to commemorate the founding of the Bozeman trail. Each revolver in the edition was assembled with an unfluted cylinder and acid etched with gold leaf. All two hundred revolvers were contracted by and sold to the Powder Horn Gun Shop.

A large number of custom editions have been assembled by the Custom Gun Shop since 1976. The great majority of revolvers coming from the Custom Gun Shop are associated with either a "factory order" number or a "Custom shop" number. The end label of the shipping carton is the place where these two terms are most likely to be encountered. Custom Shop orders have varied from as few as a single revolver to as many as 100 revolvers.

The listings below represent both current and discontinued Custom Shop engraving prices for the various frame sizes, amount of engraving coverage (A = 25% coverage, B = 50% coverage, C = 75% coverage, and D = 100% coverage), and the three levels of engraving execution (i.e., Standard, Expert, and Master levels). SAAs are considered large frame, revolvers and full-size Government Models are considered medium frame, and Government Model 380s are considered small frame. Most buyers of engraved Colt SAAs today are very knowledgeable, and many of them are no longer satisfied with Standard types of patterns and styles. As a result, those engraved guns with the rarest production variances coupled with unique engraving done at an Expert or better level are currently more desireable than their counterparts with Standard engraving patterns. Colt currently employs three full-time engravers at the factory, in addition to several outside sources (at all engraving levels).

GRADING - PPGS™	100%	98%	95%	90%	80%	70%	60%	LAST MSR

The name of the engraver is available only when ordering either the Expert or the Master level of engraving.

Large Frame Size: Current SAAs and M1911s

The following is a listing of current Custom Shop engraving for both SAAs and M1911s. Other Custom Shop options are priced on request, including a wide variety of gold/silver inlays, panel scenes, color enamel inlays, gold/silver frame outlines, etc.

Add $1,130 for A Standard engraving.
Add $1,300 for B Standard, $2,075 for B Expert (signed), or $3,725 for B Master (signed) level engraving.
Add $1,700 for C Standard, $2,878 for C Expert (signed), or $5,415 for C Master (signed) level engraving.
Add $2,000 for D Standard, $4,280 for D Expert (signed), or $6,900 for D Master (signed) level engraving.
Add 20% to large frame pricing for Buntline Models (disc.).

Medium Frame Size

Medium frame engraving was discontinued.

Values listed reflect last published MSRs.
Add $900 for Standard A level engraving.
Add $1,200 for B Standard, $1,700 for B Expert, or $3,150 for B Master level engraving.
Add $1,400 for C Standard, $2,500 for C Expert, or $4,538 for C Master level engraving.
Add $1,600 for D Standard, $3,600 for D Expert, or $6,300 for D Master level engraving.

Small Frame Size

Factory small frame engraving was disc. 1998.

Values listed reflect last published MSRs. Subtract 20% from small frame pricing for Mustang Models.
Add $400 for A Standard, $600 for A Expert, or $800 for A Master level engraving.
Add $600 for B Standard, $800 for B Expert, or $1,000 for B Master level engraving.
Add $800 for C Standard, $1,100 for C Expert, or $1,500 for C Master level engraving.
Add $1,100 for D Standard, $1,300 for D Expert, or $1,900 for D Master level engraving.

REVOLVERS: SAA, SCOUT MODEL

100% values below assume NIB condition. Subtract 10% without box.

FRONTIER SCOUT (Q or F SUFFIX) – .22 LR or .22 WMR (introduced after 1960) cal., "Q" or "F" suffix, blue or bright alloy frame, all blue, or duotone (bright alloy frame disc. 1961), 4 3/4 or 9 1/2 (Buntline, blue only) in. barrel, available with interchangeable cylinders after 1964, black composition or walnut grips, approx. 246,000 mfg. 1957-1970.

	$500	$400	$325	$250	$200	$175	$150

Add 10% for extra cylinder.
Add 20% for Buntline model (marked "BUNTLINE SCOUT .22 CAL.")
Add 25% for "Q" suffix with duo-tone finish (mfg. 1957-58 only).
Add 10% for original box.
Add 50% for walnut grips (must have factory box or letter).

FRONTIER SCOUT (K SUFFIX) – Zamac alloy frame version of "Q" Model with "K" suffix, nickel finish with walnut stocks, approx. 44,000 mfg. 1960-1970.

	$600	$425	$325	$250	$200	$175	$150
Scout cased pair	$1,200	$900	$750	$550	$450	$350	$320
Buntline cased pair	$1,500	$1,125	$950	$675	$575	$425	$400

Add 20% for Buntline model (marked "BUNTLINE SCOUT .22 CAL.")
Add 10% for original box.

This model used the alloy Zamac for manufacture (as opposed to aluminum in the "Q" and "F" suffix models), and specimens are 6 oz. heavier as a result.

GRADING - PPGS™	100%	98%	95%	90%	80%	70%	60%	LAST MSR

FRONTIER SCOUT '62 (P SUFFIX) – blue finish version of "K" Model, except has "P" suffix, Staglite grips, approx. 68,000 mfg. 1962-1970.

	$600	$450	$375	$275	$225	$175	$160	
Scout cased pair	$1,200	$900	$750	$550	$450	$350	$320	
Buntline cased pair	$1,500	$1,125	$950	$675	$575	$425	$400	

Add 10% for original box.
Add 20% for Buntline model (marked "BUNTLINE SCOUT .22 CAL.")

PEACEMAKER 22 SCOUT – .22 LR/.22 WMR cal., color case hardened steel frame, 4.4, 4 3/4, 6, or 7 1/2 (nicknamed Buntline Model but may be marked Peacemaker or Buntline) in. barrel, black composition grips, furnished with interchangeable .22 LR/.22 WMR cylinders, approx. 190,000 mfg. 1970-1977.

$750	$600	$450	$350	$300	$200	$150	

Add 20% for 4.4 in. barrel.
Add 50% for 4 3/4 in. barrel (first year of production).
Add 10% for original box.
Add 25% for single cylinder model (must have original box with model number).
Subtract 10% if without extra cylinder.

This model can be identified by its "G" or "L" ser. no. prefix.

NEW FRONTIER 22 SCOUT – similar features as Peacemaker Model, except with flat-top frame, ramp front and adj. rear sight, mfg. 1970-1977, reintroduced in 1982 without convertible .22 WMR cylinder and added cross bolt safety, all blue finish became standard in 1985, models with safety are .22 LR only, G or L (1974 only) ser. no. prefix. Mfg. disc. 1986.

$600	$475	$350	$250	$200	$175	$150	*$181*

Add 50% for 4 3/4 in. barrel (first year of production).
Add 25% for single cylinder model w/o safety (must have original box with model number).
Add 20% for 4.4 in. barrel.
Add 10% for original box.
Subtract 10% if w/o extra cylinder (model w/o safety only).

PISTOLS: SEMI-AUTO, DISC.

Most of the semi-auto pistol models listed in the various pistol categories can have their original configuration confirmed with a Colt factory letter. To receive a letter, write: COLT ARCHIVE PROPERTIES, LLC, P.O. Box 1868, Hartford, CT, 06144. The research fee for these pistols is typically either $75 or $100, depending on the model. If they cannot obtain additional information on the variation you request, they will refund $50.

Until several years ago, the Single Action Army revolver commanded the most attention among Colt handgun collectors. Since 1987, Colt Semi-Autos have been in tremendous demand and have out-accelerated many other areas of Colt collecting. Because condition and originality play such a key role in determining Colt Semi-Auto prices, many variations have had their values pushed upward to the point where it is difficult to accurately determine a realistic price, especially on those models in 98% original condition or better. As a result, some of the rarer models rarely encountered in true 100% original condition have had their values deleted since extreme rarity precludes accurate price evaluation. As always, the hardest prices to ascertain when firearms market conditions are bullish are the 98-100% values.

MODEL 1900 – .38 ACP cal., 6 in. barrel, blue, plain walnut grips - checkered hard rubber grips after S/N 2,450, high spur hammer, sight safety. Mfg. 1900-03.

N/A	$15,000	$11,000	$7,600	$5,500	$4,000	$3,000	

Add 100% for U.S. marked 1st Army contracts (100 guns serial numbered 11-207).
Add 75% for U.S. marked Navy contracts (250 guns serial numbered 1,001-1,250).
Add 60% for U.S. marked 2nd Army contracts (200 guns serial numbered 1,501-1,700).
Subtract 30%-50% for altered sight safety (factory refinished).

This model is serial numbered approx. between 1-4,274.

Somewhere between serial number 2,200 and 2,450, Colt began altering the sights to fixed sights in

GRADING - PPGS™	100%	98%	95%	90%	80%	70%	60%	LAST MSR

the production process, shipping both types. By approx. serial number 3,300, most guns shipped were altered during production. Guns altered during production are not refinished. Altered guns below serial number 2,200 were refinished, or at least had the slides refinished.

MODEL 1902 SPORTING – .38 ACP, 6 in. barrel, blue, fixed sights, checkered hard rubber grips, no safety, high spur hammer or round hammer. Mfg. 1902-08.

N/A	$5,750	$4,250	$3,250	$2,500	$1,750	$900	

This model is serial numbered approx. 4,275-11,000 and 30,000-30,190.

MODEL 1902 MILITARY – .38 ACP cal., 6 in. barrel, blue, similar to 1902 Sporting, round hammer changed to spur type in 1908, checkered black hard rubber grips, lanyard swivel on bottom rear of left grip. Mfg. 1902-29.

N/A	$5,750	$4,500	$3,500	$2,500	$1,500	$900	

Add 30% for front slide serrations.

Add 20% with original box and instructions.

This model is serial numbered approx. 11,000-16,000 and 30,200-43,266.

MODEL 1902 MILITARY-U.S. ARMY MARKED – similar specifications to 1902 Military, only serial number range 15,001-15,200.

N/A	$18,000	$15,000	$12,500	$10,000	$8,750	$6,000	

MODEL 1903 POCKET HAMMER (.38 ACP) – .38 ACP cal., 4 1/2 in. barrel, blue finish standard, round or spur hammer, checkered black hard rubber grips, similar to 1902 Sporting, but 4 1/2 in. barrel, 7 1/2 in. overall. Mfg. 1903-29.

$5,000	$4,000	$2,750	$2,000	$1,250	$900	$750	

Add 30% for early round hammer.

Add 20% with original box and instructions.

This model is serial numbered approx. 16,000-47,226.

MODEL 1903 POCKET (MODEL M .32 ACP) – .32 ACP cal., 3 3/4 (Types II-IV) or 4 (Type I) in. barrel, charcoal blue, checkered hard rubber grips, hammerless, slide lock and grip safeties, barrel bushing. Mfg. 1903-1946.

$1,250	$1,050	$700	$550	$450	$375	$325	

Add 20% for nickel finish (mostly w/pearl grips).

Add 60% for first model (Type I) mfg. 1903-1911 if in 100%-98% condition. If lower than 98%, add 20%.

Add 30% for Type II if in 100%-98% condition.

Add 30% with original box and instructions.

Type I - 32 ACPs have a 4 in. barrel, barrel bushing, no magazine safety, and are serial numbered 1-71,999.

Type II - 32 ACPs still retain their barrel bushing but have a 3 3/4 in. barrel and were mfg. from 1908-1910. They are serial numbered 72,000-105,050.

Type III - 32 ACPs do not have a barrel bushing and were mfg. from 1910-1926. They are serial numbered 105,051-468,096.

Type IV - 32 ACPs have the added magazine safety (of which there are both the commercial and "U.S. Property" variations). They are serial numbered 468,097-554,446.

* ***Model 1903 Parkerized*** – U.S. Property, 3 1/4 in. barrel, no barrel bushing, magazine safety, serial numbered 554,447-572,214.

$2,400	$1,950	$1,200	$1,000	$850	$650	$600	

Add 50% for blue U.S. Property S/N 554,447 - approx. 562,000.

Add 20% with original box and instructions.

The 100% value on this model assumes NIB condition.

* ***Model 1903 General Officer's Pistol*** – .32 ACP cal., blue (mfg. until 1942) or parkerized (mfg. started 1942) finish.

Values assume issue to a General, and there must be paperwork to link the gun to the recipient. Otherwise, these values do not apply - see U.S. Property above for applicable values.

GRADING - PPGS™	100%	98%	95%	90%	80%	70%	60%	LAST MSR
*** Model 1903 Pocket Parkerized**								
	N/A	$3,000	$2,000	$1,700	$1,300	$1,050	$900	
*** Model 1903 Pocket Blue Finish**								
	N/A	$3,400	$2,700	$2,300	$1,850	$1,550	$1,250	

MODEL 1905 – .45 ACP cal., 5 in. barrel, blue, fixed sights, checkered walnut grips, similar to the Model 1902 Sporting. Mfg. 1905-1911.

	100%	98%	95%	90%	80%	70%	60%	LAST MSR
	N/A	$7,200	$5,000	$3,800	$3,000	$2,000	$1,500	

Add 50% for factory slotted specimens (500 manufactured).
Add 250% for 1907 U.S. Military Contract variation (205 manufactured).
The shoulder stock option for this pistol is exceedingly rare. Depending on the condition, this accessory can add $7,500-$10,000 to the price of the gun.

MODEL 1908 POCKET (MODEL M .380 ACP) – .380 ACP cal., first issue, 3 3/4 in. barrel only, similar to Model M .32 ACP, except chambered for .380 ACP. Mfg. 1908-1940.

	100%	98%	95%	90%	80%	70%	60%	LAST MSR
	$1,650	$1,475	$1,200	$900	$800	$700	$450	

Add 50% for Type I (see explanation below).
Add $100 for nickel finish.
Add 50% for factory pearl grips.
100% values assume NIB condition. Subtract 15% if without cardboard box. Pearl grips are normally encountered with nickel finish on this model.

Type I - 380 ACPs with barrel bushing and were mfg. 1908-1910 (6,251 mfg.). They are serial numbered 1-6,251.

Type II - 380 ACPs do not have a barrel bushing and were mfg. 1910-1926. They are serial numbered 6,252-92,893.

Type III - 380 ACPs have the added magazine safety (of which there are both the commercial and "U.S. Property" variations). They are serial numbered 92,894-134,499.

*** Model 1908 "U.S. Property"** – blue finish only, U.S. Property marking. Serial numbered 134,500-138,000.

	100%	98%	95%	90%	80%	70%	60%	LAST MSR
	N/A	$3,000	$2,250	$1,750	$1,300	$950	$750	

*** Model 1908 General Officer's Pistol** – .380 ACP cal., blue finish only.

	100%	98%	95%	90%	80%	70%	60%	LAST MSR
	N/A	$4,000	$3,250	$2,700	$2,300	$1,950	$1,550	

Values assume issue to a General, and there must be paperwork to link the gun to the recipient. Otherwise, these values do not apply - see U.S. Property above for appllcable values.

VEST POCKET MODEL 1908-HAMMERLESS – .25 ACP cal., 2 in. barrel, fixed sights, checkered hard rubber grips on early models, walnut on later, 6 shot mag., magazine disconnect added on guns made after 1916. Mfg. 1908-1946.

	100%	98%	95%	90%	80%	70%	60%	LAST MSR
*** Vest Pocket Model 1908 Blue finish**								
	$850	$750	$600	$500	$425	$350	$275	

Add 50% for factory pearl grips.
Add 50% for NIB condition if in 95% or better condition only.

	100%	98%	95%	90%	80%	70%	60%	LAST MSR
*** Vest Pocket Model 1908 Nickel finish**								
	$1,200	$1,000	$850	$650	$550	$450	$375	
U.S. Property marked	$4,800	$4,000	$3,400	$2,600	$2,200	$1,800	$1,500	

Add 50% for factory pearl grips.
Add 50% for NIB condition if in 95% or better condition only.
This model was also supplied with a suede purse. Add $150-$200, depending on condition.

MODEL 1909 – .45 ACP cal., straight handle design, 5 in. barrel, checkered walnut grips, approx. 22 mfg., ultra rare.

Extreme rarity factor precludes accurate price evaluation by individual condition factors. Specimens that are original and over 90% have sold for over $35,000 recently.

GRADING - PPGS™	100%	98%	95%	90%	80%	70%	60%	LAST MSR

MODEL 1910 – .45 ACP cal., while not a production model, this gun is probably the most desirable semi-auto Colt pistol.

A nice specimen at an auction was gavelled down at $195,000.

PISTOLS: SEMI-AUTO, GOVT. MODEL 1911 COMMERCIAL VARIATIONS

MODEL 1911 COMMERCIAL – .45 ACP cal., 5 in. barrel, fixed sights, 7 shot mag., flat main spring housing, polished blue finish only, checkered walnut grips. Denoted by "C" preceding serial number, approx. ser. no. range C1-C138,532. Watch for fakes. Colt licensed other companies to manufacture the military variation under government contracts, 39 oz. Mfg. 1912-1925.

Most M1911 variations listed below are not as collectible if under 60% original condition. However, they are still very desirable as shooters, and values (if in original condition) will approximate the 60% prices if in good mechanical condition.

Colt Model 1911s continue to enjoy high demand as of this writing and prices continue to be strong in the 95%-100% condition factors. Be careful on the 98%+ condition specimens, especially the rarer variations. Some collectors are now requiring a potential high-dollar Model 1911 to pass a metallurgical X-ray examination before purchasing.

* ***Model 1911 High Polish Blue*** – mfg. 1912 through ser. no. 4,500.

N/A	$15,000	$12,000	$9,000	$6,500	$4,000	$2,000

* ***Model 1911 Regular Finish*** – pistols mfg. after ser. no. 4,500.

N/A	$3,750	$2,750	$1,850	$1,200	$1,000	$750

Approx. 138,532 were mfg. between 1912-1925.

PISTOLS: SEMI-AUTO, GOVT. MODEL 1911 MILITARY VARIATIONS

All pistols in this section are .45 ACP (11.25mm) cal., unless otherwise noted. Values for original 98%+ M1911 Military Models have risen considerably in recent years, and as a result, values for original mint guns can double and even sometimes triple the values of 98% condition.

Over 2,550,000 M1911 pistols were ordered for WWI and WWII by the U.S. Government, but approx. 650,000 were mfg. between 1911-1925. Those pistols with a parkerized finish will indicate post-WWI reworking, usually marked with an arsenal code (ie. AA-AUGUSTA ARSENAL, SA-SPRINGFIELD ARSENAL, RIA-ROCK ISLAND ARSENAL, etc.). Please check individual listings for values of arseanl refinished pistols.

COLT MFG. MODEL 1911 MILITARY – right side of slide marked "MODEL OF 1911 U.S. ARMY", blue finish only (NOT parkerized unless reworked).

Recent sales for original mint examples of the Model 1911 Military are as follows: $14,000 for 1912 mfg., depending on the variation (there are three), $7,000 for 1913-1915 mfg., $7,500 for 1916 mfg., $6,000 for 1917-1918 mfg. and $6,000 for 1918 later mfg. (black Army finish).

* ***Model 1911 (1912 mfg.)*** – includes three variations.

N/A	$10,000	$7,750	$6,000	$5,000	$4,000	$3,000

* ***Model 1911 (1913-1915 mfg.)***

N/A	$5,000	$4,500	$4,000	$3,500	$2,000	$1,500

Add 300% for the first 114 pistols with oversize "United States Property" marking.
Add 150% for pistols in the ser. no. range 115-2,400.

* ***Model 1911 (1916 mfg.)*** – only 4,200 produced.

N/A	$5,500	$4,750	$4,000	$3,500	$2,000	$1,500

* ***Model 1911 (1917-1918 early mfg.)*** – early blue finish.

N/A	$4,250	$3,200	$2,050	$1,500	$1,200	$1,000

* ***Model 1911 (1917-1918 mfg.)*** – can be determined by black Army finish.

N/A	$4,250	$3,200	$2,050	$1,500	$1,200	$1,000

* ***Model 1911 (1919-1925 mfg.)***

N/A	$4,250	$3,500	$3,000	$2,000	$1,500	$1,200

GRADING - PPGS™	100%	98%	95%	90%	80%	70%	60%	LAST MSR

NORTH AMERICAN ARMS COMPANY – less than 100 mfg. in Quebec, Canada during 1918 only, blue finish. Be very aware of fakes, as this variation is perhaps the most desirable Colt WWI Govt. semi-auto.

N/A N/A $35,000 $30,000 $25,000 $20,000 $16,000

Note: a characteristic of the North American is the poor finish. The very best condition specimens will be in the 80%-90% range. All mint 100% specimens encountered in this model appear to have been refinished.

REMINGTON - UMC – over 21,500 mfg. (ser. numbered 1-21,676) in 1918-1919 only, blue finish.

N/A $6,950 $5,500 $3,850 $3,000 $2,500 $2,000

Most mint 100% specimens encountered in this model have been refinished - be careful. Mint original pistols are currently selling as high as $8,500.

SPRINGFIELD ARMORY – approx. 30,000 mfg. 1914-1915, blue finish.

N/A $6,750 $5,750 $3,750 $3,000 $2,500 $2,000

Mint original pistols are currently selling in the $7,500 range.

Serialization is 72,751-83,855, 102,597-107,596, 113,497-120,566, and 125,567-133,186.

Most mint 100% specimens encountered in this model have been refinished - be careful.

U.S. NAVY – over 31,000 mfg. for U.S. Navy contract between 1911-1914 in defined serial ranges, blue finish. Marked "MODEL OF 1911 U.S. NAVY" on right slide side.

N/A $8,500 $6,000 $4,500 $3,200 $2,200 $1,500

Add 100% for specimens under ser. no. 3,500.

U.S. Navy specimens are seldom found in over 80% original condition because of the corrosive conditions encountered while at sea.

U.S. MARINE CORPS. – approx. 13,500 mfg. between 1911-13 and 1916-18 in defined serial ranges, blue finish, right side of slide marked "MODEL OF 1911 U.S. ARMY".

N/A $7,500 $5,500 $4,500 $3,500 $3,000 $2,250

Mint original specimens are currently selling in the $13,000-$15,000 range.

WWI BRITISH SERIES – .455 cal., serialized W19,000-W110,695, marked "CALIBRE 455", blue finish, proofed with broad arrow British Ordnance stamp. Mfg. 1915-19.

N/A $5,750 $4,750 $2,950 $2,000 $1,200 $1,000

Subtract 30% if converted to .45 ACP cal.

Mint original specimens in this model have been selling in the $7,500 - $8,500 range.

Many WWI British-series M1911s were exported back to the U.S. following WWI and were converted to .45 ACP. Usually, a "5" has been crossed out of the original cal. designation.

A.J. SAVAGE MUNITIONS CO. – mfg. slides only, blue finish, marked in middle on left side of slide with flaming ordnance bomb with "S" in center.

N/A $3,000 $2,250 $1,750 $1,250 $1,000 $800

Mint original specimens have been selling in the $3,250 - $3,500 range.

NORWEGIAN TRIAL MODEL 1911 COLT – 11.25mm cal., approx. 300 mfg. with "C" prefix in 1913-14 and 1917, usually encountered in 90% or less condition.

N/A $4,500 $3,750 $2,750 $2,000 $1,200 $800

These guns were ordered for Norwegian service evaluation and were mfg. by Colt in Hartford, CT.

NORWEGIAN MODEL 1912 11.25MM – 11.25mm cal., mfg. under license from Colt's during 1917, "M1912" slide designation. Approx. 95 mfg.

N/A $8,500 $7,500 $6,000 $5,000 $4,000 $3,200

NORWEGIAN 1914 11.25MM – this model has a distinctive extended slide release, all parts should be serial numbered and have numerous matching numbers, approx. 32,750 mfg. 1918-1947, mostly military contract, commercial production was very limited. Most have been refinished.

N/A $2,250 $1,650 $1,450 $1,250 $850 $700

Add 250% for Waffenamt Nazi mfg. (mfg. 1945 only).

Serial ranges with corresponding year of manufacture on this model are as follows: 96-600 - 1918,

GRADING - PPGS™	100%	98%	95%	90%	80%	70%	60%	LAST MSR

601-1,150 - 1919, 1,151-1,650 (Naval Artillery) - 1920, 1,651-2,200 - 1921, 2,201- 2,950 - 1922, 2,951-4,610 - 1923, 4,611-6,700 - 1924, 6,701-8,940 - 1925, 8,941-11,820 - 1926, 11,821-15,900 - 1927, 15,901-20,100 - 1928, 20,101-21,440 - 1929, 21,441-21,940 - 1932, 21,941-22,040 - 1933, 22,041-22,141 - 1934, 22,142-22,211 - 1936, 22,212-22,311 - 1939, 22,312-22,361 - 1940, 22,362-26,460 - 1941, 26,461-29,614 - 1942, 29,615-32,335 (Waffenamt Nazi proofed) - 1945, 32,336-32,854 - (last original production) 1947.

Nazi production of the M1914 began in 1941. Between 1941-42, approx. 7,000 pistols were mfg. without Waffenamt stampings. Nazi proofed guns (all 1945 dated) began in the mid- 29,000 serial range, and 920 were mfg. with the Nazi Eagle.

ARGENTINE CONTRACT MODEL 1916 – identified by the Argentine seal on top of slide, with C prefix 5 digit ser. no., from 1914-1919, Colt delivered approx. 10,000 pistols to Argentina.

	100%	98%	95%	90%	80%	70%	60%
	N/A	$1,600	$1,450	$1,200	$800	$700	$600

Most specimens of this model have been refinished.

RUSSIAN CONTRACT – approx. 51,000 mfg. in U.S. as commerical guns with random serial numbers approx. C23000-C89000, blue finish, identified by cyrillic inscription on left side of frame (translates to English Order). Mfg. 1916-17.

	100%	98%	95%	90%	80%	70%	60%
	N/A	$8,750	$4,500	$4,000	$3,250	$2,500	$2,000

Mint original specimens have been selling in the $12,500 - $15,000 range.

This contract is seldolm encountered - beware of fakes.

1911 MILITARY REWORKS – .45 ACP cal., these are pistols that the government sent back to various military arsenals for reworking, arsenals include Augusta Arsenal (AA), Springfield Armory (SA), and Rock Island Arsenal (RIA), pistols may have original parts (matching) or parts from other manufacturers (mismatched), parkerized (most common), or arsenal blue finish.

	100%	98%	95%	90%	80%	70%	60%
Colt Mfg.	$1,400	$1,225	$1,050	$950	$770	$625	$495
Remington UMC Mfg.	$1,800	$1,575	$1,350	$1,225	$995	$815	$625
Springfield Mfg.	$1,800	$1,575	$1,350	$1,225	$995	$815	$625

Add 15% for box and DCM papers.
Add 15% for arsenal blue finish.
Subtract 40% if mismatched.

BRITISH RAF REWORK – this variation is the WWI British series re-issued to RAF officers in the early 1920s, blue finish, differentiated by hand-stamped "RAF" or "R.A.F." on left side of frame.

	100%	98%	95%	90%	80%	70%	60%
	N/A	$4,250	$3,250	$2,600	$2,000	$1,200	$1,000

Mint original specimens have been selling in the $5,500 - $6,000 range.

PISTOLS: SEMI-AUTO, GOVT. MODEL 1911A1 COMMERCIAL VARIATIONS

All pistols in this section are .45 ACP cal., unless otherwise noted.

GOVERNMENT MODEL 1911A1 – commercial blue finish or parkerized, checkered walnut grips, checkered arched mainspring housing relief cuts in frame for improved trigger reach, and longer grip safety spur. As in the Model 1911, Colt licensed other companies to produce under govt. contract during WWII. Mfg. 1925-1970.

Most M1911A1 variations listed below are not as collectible if under 60% original condition. However, they are still very desirable as shooters, and values (if in original condition) will approximate the 60% prices if in good mechanical condition.

MODEL 1911A1 PRE-WWII COLT COMMERCIAL – "C" preceding serial number, mfg. 1925-1942. Approx. ser. no. range C138,533-C215,000.

	100%	98%	95%	90%	80%	70%	60%
	N/A	$4,500	$3,500	$3,000	$2,500	$1,800	$1,000

Add 50% for nickel finish.
Add 20% with original box and instructions.
Add 20% for Swartz safety.

GRADING - PPGS™	100%	98%	95%	90%	80%	70%	60%	LAST MSR

MODEL 1911A1 1946-1970 COLT COMMERCIAL – 5 in. barrel, fixed sights, "C" prefix until 1950 when changed to "C" suffix. Approx. 196,000 mfg. 1946-1970.

* ***Model 1911A1 1946-1950 Mfg.*** – "C" Prefix with serial numbers C221,000-C240,227.

N/A	$1,850	$1,650	$1,350	$1,000	$875	$675	

* ***Model 1911A1 1950-1970 Mfg.*** – "C" Suffix with serial numbers 240,228C-336,169C.

N/A	$1,700	$1,500	$1,350	$950	$875	$675	

Add 10% for nickel finish.

SUPER .38 AUTOMATIC PISTOL – identical to Govt. Model .45, except chambered for .38 Super cal., blue or nickel finish. Mfg. 1928-70.

* ***Super .38 Automatic Pistol Pre-War***

N/A	$6,000	$5,750	$3,500	$2,250	$1,700	$1,200	

* ***Super .38 Automatic Pistol 2nd Model***

N/A	$2,750	$2,400	$1,800	$1,400	$1,100	$900	

* ***Super .38 Automatic Pistol 3rd Model***

$2,500	$2,000	$1,800	$1,200	$900	$750	$600	

* ***Super .38 Automatic Pistol 4th Model***

$2,200	$1,800	$1,600	$1,000	$800	$700	$600	

* ***Super .38 Automatic Pistol CS Prefix***

$2,200	$1,800	$1,600	$1,000	$800	$700	$600	

Add approx. 50% for nickel finish.

Pre-war variations are serialized below approx. 37,000.

The 2nd Model may be differentiated by noticing the heavier barrel and Rampant Colt on right side. The 3rd Model has a fat barrel with Rampant Colt on left side. The 4th Model has a thin barrel and Rampant Colt on left side.

SUPER MATCH .38 – similar to Super .38, but hand honed action, match grade barrel, recent research indicates that 2,392 had adj. sights, 857 were supplied with fixed sights, and on 557 models the type of sights was not indicated. 4,001 mfg. 1934-1947. Examine carefully for fakes.

Buyer beware - fakes are known to exist!

The first Super Match noted is ser. no. 15550, a fixed sight model, and was shipped on Feb. 9, 1934.

The lowest serial number is 14310, and was shipped on July 10, 1934. However, two serial numbers were much lower than the expected serial number ranges. Ser. no. 2253 was shipped on June 18, 1940 and ser. no. 10312 was shipped on Sept. 25, 1935. It is unknown if these guns were roll marked Super Match, but they were noted in the Colt Records as Super Match models.

The first adj. sight Super Match is ser. no. 17091, and was shipped on Feb. 7, 1935.

The last adj. sight Super Match noted is ser. no. 35731, and was shipped on Jan. 17, 1947.

The highest ser. no. Super Match is ser. no. 35999, a fixed sight model, and was shipped on Oct. 20, 1939.

Approx. 40 were mfg. with match barrels and/or hand fitted actions, w/o mention of the Super Match markings.

Total .38 Super Match pistols recorded in the Colt shipping records is 3,961. 2,250 were noted as having adj. sight, and 831 were noted as having fixed sights.

* ***Super Match .38 Fixed sights***

N/A	$10,000	$7,500	$6,000	$4,500	$3,000	$2,000	

* ***Super Match .38 Adj. sights***

N/A	$11,500	$9,000	$7,000	$5,500	$4,000	$3,000	

For adj. sight values to apply, the sight must be an original factory installed Stevens sight. After market adj. sights are not applicable. Be cautious of fixed sight Super Matches converted to adj. sight. A Colt historical letter is available for this model for $100.

GRADING - PPGS™	100%	98%	95%	90%	80%	70%	60%	LAST MSR

There were 3,909 .38 Super Matches manufactured from Feb. 16, 1934 - Jan. 17, 1947. 998 had fixed sights and 2,911 had adj. sights.

MATCH .38 AMU – .38 AMU cal. (semi-rimless .38 Spl., mfg. by Win.), this variation was mfg. by Colt from a .38 Super frame (and has .38 Super serialization) with a .38 AMU conversion kit slide, the Army took .45 frames and assembled their guns using .38 AMU kits, blue finish.

* ***Match .38 AMU Colt mfg. (unmodified)***

N/A	$3,500	$2,700	$2,200	$1,900	$1,675	$1,400	

* ***Match .38 AMU Army modified***

N/A	$2,250	$1,850	$1,275	$1,000	$800	$700	

* ***Match .38 AMU kit only***

$1,850	$1,700	$1,450	$1,150	$900	$700	$500	

On this configuration, the barrel, slide, and mag. were marked ".38 AMU".

SUPER MATCH .38 MS – .38 Super cal., 1961 mfg., serial numbered 101MS - 855MS, 754 total mfg, same configuration as the .38 AMU.

$5,500	$4,500	$3,500	$2,700	$2,000	$1,500	$1,300	

1968-1969 BB TRANSITIONAL – denoted by BB prefix on serial number.

$1,650	$1,375	$1,100	$945	$875	$750	$600	

.45 ACP TO .22 LR CONVERSION UNIT – consists of slide assembly, barrel, bushing, floating chamber, ejector, recoil spring and guide, fitted with Stevens adj. rear sight from 1938 to 1947 and Colt Master adj. sight from 1947 to 1954.

$650	$600	$550	$425	$350	$275	$200	

* ***.45 ACP to .22 LR Conversion Unit U Prefix*** – has "U" prefix on top of slide.

$2,000	$1,800	$1,650	$1,275	$1,050	$825	$600	

* ***.45 ACP to .22 LR Conversion Unit Marine Corps*** – should have pre-war Marine Corps documentation.

$2,500	$2,275	$2,100	$1,925	$1,475	$1,225	$950	

.22 LR TO .45 ACP CONVERSION UNIT – converted service Ace .22 to .45 ACP cal. Mfg. 1938-1942. Very rare - 112 mfg.

$6,500	$5,000	$4,000	$3,000	$2,250	$1,500	$1,100	

Add 50% for original box and instructions.

These units have "U" prefixed serial numbers on top of slide. Watch for fakes!

PISTOLS: SEMI-AUTO, GOVT. MODEL 1911A1 MILITARY VARIATIONS

All pistols in this section are .45 ACP (11.25mm) cal., unless otherwise noted. Values for original 98%+ M1911A1s have risen considerably in recent years, and as a result, values for original mint guns can double and even sometimes triple the values of 98% condition. Inspect carefully for arsenal reworks (so marked by proofing, normally on left side of frame above or behind trigger), and reparkerizing.

COLT MFG. MODEL 1911A1 MILITARY – approx. 438,527 mfg. between 1924- 1945, ser. nos. 700,000 - on up, right side of frame marked "M1911A1 U.S. ARMY", bright blue finish up to approx. ser. no. 780,000, parkerized finish after that. - standard military finish (WWII mfg.).

N/A	$3,500	$3,000	$2,500	$2,000	$1,600	$1,000	

Add 200% for 1937 Navy (S/N 710,001 - 712,345) Blue.

1937 Navy variations with blue finish are currently selling in the $1,000 - $7,000 range, depending on original condition.

Add 250% for 1938 Army (S/N 712,350 - 713,645) Blue.

1938 Army variations with blue finish are currently selling in the $1,500 - $9,000 range, depending on original condition.

Add 200% for 1939 Navy (S/N 713,646 - 717,281) Blue.

GRADING - PPGS™	100%	98%	95%	90%	80%	70%	60%	LAST MSR

1939 Navy varitions with blue finish are currently selling in the $1,000 - $7,000 range, depending on original condition.

Early 1911A1 military models with bright blue finish are currently selling in the $1,000 - $7,000 price range, depending on condition.

Add 150% for Blue guns outside these serial ranges.

Add 150% for 1942 Navy (S/N 793,658 - 797,639) Parkerized.

Add 25-50% for Schwartz safety variation depending on condition.

A large grouping of over 7,000 Commercial 1911A1s was transferred to the U.S. government. These pistols had their commercial serial numbers crudely removed (in ser. range 860,000 - 866,000) and re-stamped with a new military serial number. Some of these guns are unusual as the frames and slides have been cut for the Schwartz safety.

**** Model 1911A1 General Officer's Pistol***

N/A $5,000 $4,000 $3,500 $3,000 $2,000 $1,500

Values above assume issue to a General, and there must be paperwork to link the gun to the recipient.

DRAKE NATIONAL MATCH – Drake made slides only for use by the U.S. Army Marksmanship Unit to allow assembly of match guns.

N/A $2,000 $1,700 $1,400 $1,000 $850 $700

GOVERNMENT NATIONAL MATCH REWORKS – assembled by government armorers, all parts marked "NM", parkerized finish. Most will be "S.A." marked.

N/A $2,000 $1,700 $1,400 $1,000 $850 $700

Add 25% for Air Force pistols marked "AFPG" on slide.

These pistols were made specifically for the U.S. shooting team at Camp Perry.

ITHACA – .45 ACP cal., 7 shot mag., 5 in. barrel, parkerized finish, approx. 369,129 mfg. 1943-1945 in Ithaca, NY, ser. no. ranges 856,405-916,404, 1,208,674-1,279,673, 1,441,431-1,471,430, 1,743,847-1,890,503, 2,075,104-2,134,403, and 2,619,014-2,693,613.

N/A $2,200 $1,800 $1,500 $1,200 $1,100 $800

Add 20% for original shipping carton.

UNION SWITCH AND SIGNAL – approx. 55,000 mfg. 1943 only in Swissvale, PA, ser. no. range 1,041,405-1,096,404. Sandblast and blue finish.

N/A $5,500 $4,500 $3,500 $3,000 $2,200 $1,500

REMINGTON RAND – approx. 1,086,624 mfg. 1943-1945 in Syracuse, NY, ser. no. ranges 916,405-1,041,404, 1,279,649-1,441,430, 1,471,431-1,609,528, 1,743,847-1,816,641, 1,890,504-2,075,103, 2,134,404-2,244,803, and 2,380,014-2,619,013. Parkerized finish.

$2,500 $2,100 $1,900 $1,500 $1,200 $1,000 $900

Add 20% for original shipping carton (watch for fakes).

SINGER MFG. CO. – 500 mfg. 1941 in Elizabeth, NJ, ser. no. range S800,001-S800,500. Blue finish with plastic grips.

N/A N/A $65,000 $50,000 $40,000 $32,500 $24,000

The Singer 1911A1 variation is one of the most sought-after Colt models. In recent years, values have increased significantly, and as a result, some fakes have emerged. Most specimens are now recognized by ser. no. and be very cautious when contemplating a purchase. Some collectors unsure of authenticity are now requiring X-ray testing to determine originality (slide restampings, ser. no. changes, etc.).

GENERAL OFFICER'S PISTOL (M15) – standard military finish, issued by Rock Island Arsenal to Generals.

$7,500 $6,500 $5,500 $4,000 $3,200 $2,800 $2,200

MEXICAN CONTRACT – mfg. approx. 1921-27 with "C" prefix ser. nos., frames marked "EJERCITO MEXICANO", most surviving examples show much use.

N/A $4,500 $3,500 $2,500 $1,750 $1,200 $1,000

BRAZILIAN CONTRACT

N/A $5,500 $4,000 $3,000 $2,250 $1,800 $1,200

GRADING - PPGS™	100%	98%	95%	90%	80%	70%	60%	LAST MSR

ARGENTINE CONTRACT MODEL 1927 – serial numbered 1-10,000 under the mainspring housing and on the top of slide (should be matching), must have Argentine crest and "Model 1927" on right side of slide, external serial number applied to top of slide by the Argentine Arsenal, most have been Arsenal refinished.

	$1,500	$1,300	$1,100	$900	$800	$600	$500

Add 75% if original finish.

ARGENTINE MFG. – in 1927, the Argentina Arsenal "DGFM-FMAP" began manufacturing the Model 1911A1. The slide marking is two lines and reads "EJERCITO ARGENTINO SIST. COLT.CAL. 11.25mm MOD.1927", these guns were made in Argentina under license from Colt, with Colt machinery, and with help from Colt engineers, and are known as Model 1927 Systema Colt.

	$1,400	$1,200	$1,000	$800	$700	$600	$500

Add 50% if original finish.
Add 20% for Argentine Navy "ARMADA NACIONAL" (small shipments between 1912-1948). Markings vary on different types.
Add 30% for Air Force markings ("AERONAUTICA ARGENTINA" and winged crest).

This variation is not to be confused with the Ballester Molina/Rigaud Models (sold by Hispano Argentino Fábrica de Automóviles S.A., in Buenos Aires, Argentina - also known as the HAFDASA). Please refer to the Hispano Argentino Fábrica de Automóviles S.A. section.

ARGENTINE SERVICE MODEL ACE – .22 LR cal., conversion of the 1927 Argentine Contract Model, bottom right side of slide is marked "TRANSE A CAL .22 POR EST. VENTURINI S.A." Originally imported during 1996, this model was arsenal refinished and most pistols were in the 70%-95% condition range.

	$750	$700	$625	$575	$525	$500	$475

1911A1 MILITARY REWORKS – .45 ACP cal., these are pistols that the government sent back to various military arsenals for reworking, arsenals include Augusta Arsenal (AA), Springfield Armory (SA), and Rock Island Arsenal (RIA), pistols may have original parts (matching) or parts from other manufacturers (mismatched), finish is generally parkerized, but some pistols will have original finish with arsenal markings.

Colt Mfg.	$1,400	$1,225	$1,050	$950	$775	$625	$495
Remington Mfg.	$1,200	$1,050	$900	$815	$675	$550	$425
Ithaca Mfg.	$1,200	$1,050	$900	$815	$675	$550	$425
US & S Mfg.	$1,800	$1,575	$1,350	$1,225	$995	$815	$625
Singer Mfg.	N/A	$10,000	$8,000	$6,500	$5,250	$4,000	$3,500

Add 15% for box and DCM papers.
Add 100% if arsenal marked but with original finish.
Subtract 20% for mismatched slide and frame.

PISTOLS: SEMI-AUTO, ACE MODELS, 1931-1947 MFG.

COMMERCIAL ACE – .22 LR cal., similar to Government .45 ACP, but in .22 LR cal., 4 3/4 in. barrel, blue, adj. sights, checkered walnut grips, almost 11,000 mfg. (ser. no. range 1-10,935) 1931-41 and 1947.

	N/A	$4,500	$3,500	$2,500	$2,000	$1,500	$1,200

Add 20% for original box and instructions.

SERVICE MODEL ACE – .22 LR cal., 5 in. barrel, blue or parkerized finish, similar to .45 ACP National Match except for caliber, has floating chamber to simulate .45 ACP recoil, limited mfg. 1935-1945.

	N/A	$7,500	$6,000	$4,500	$3,250	$2,500	$2,000

Add 20% for original box and instructions.
Subtract 30% for parkerized finish.

This variation is marked "SERVICE MODEL" on left frame, serial numbers have "SM" prefix and have ranges to approx. 13,800. Other markings such as "U.S. PROP'Y" or "R.S." (inspectors' marks) have also been observed on this model, and can add a premium if original condition is 95% or more.

GRADING - PPGS™	100%	98%	95%	90%	80%	70%	60%	LAST MSR

PISTOLS: SEMI-AUTO, NATIONAL MATCH MODELS - PRE-WWII

NATIONAL MATCH – .45 ACP cal., similar to Government Model, except has hand-honed action, match grade barrel, blue or nickel finish, stamped "National Match" on left side of slide. There were a total of 4,813 National Matches manufactured between Feb. 9, 1932 - Sept. 16, 1941, serial numbered C162997-C204640. 3,339 had fixed sights, and 1,474 had adj. sights.

Add 20% with original box and instructions.

The first National Match and lowest ser. no. C162997, a fixed sight model, was shipped on Jan. 7, 1932.

The last National Match, ser. no. C200288, a fixed sight model, was shipped on Feb. 22, 1942.

The highest ser. no. is C204671, an adj. sight model, and was shipped on Aug. 20, 1941.

Of the total 4,813 National Match pistols, 1,474 were noted as having adj. sights, and 3,339 were noted as having fixed sights.

There were 45 nickel National Match models, four were engraved and two were inscribed.

There were 47 engraved National Match models, four of them nickel and eight with gold inlays.

There were fifteen inscribed National Match models, two of them nickel.

* ***National Match Fixed sights***

N/A $8,500 $7,000 $5,000 $4,000 $2,750 $2,000

* ***National Match Adj. sights***

N/A $10,000 $8,000 $6,500 $4,250 $3,200 $1,800

For adj. sight values to apply, the sight must be an original factory installed Stevens sight. After market adj. sights are not applicable. Be cautious of fixed sight National Match models that have been converted to adj. sight.

A Colt historical letter is available for this model for $100.

PISTOLS: SEMI-AUTO, NATIONAL MATCH MODELS - WWII & POST-WWII

Add 10% for NIB condition on discontinued models listed below.

Unless noted otherwise, all National Match models listed in this section will have "National Match" stamped on the left side of the slide.

NATIONAL MATCH – .45 ACP cal., match grade barrel, royal blue finish, new design bushing, beveld barrel bushing and recoil spring plug, flat or arched (mfg. approx. 1959-64) mainspring housing, long trigger w/adj. overtravel stop, hand fitted slide with enlarged ejection port, adj. target sights, gold medallions in grips, "NM" suffix. Mfg. 1957-1970.

$2,400 $1,800 $1,500 $1,00 $800 $650 $600

Note: This model was the first Gold Cup National Match Model manufactured following WWII.

MKII/MKIII NATIONAL MATCH MID-RANGE – .38 Spl. Mid-Range Wadcutter cal., similar to National Match, except chambered for .38 Spl. Mid-Range Wadcutter, "MR" suffix. Mfg. 1961-1971.

$2,000 $1,600 $1,200 $1,000 $800 $700 $600

Colt had problems with the original barrels of the Gold Cup .38 Mid-Range. The MKII was the first revision (very scarce), and the MKIII was the final revision.

MKIV/SERIES 70 GOLD CUP NATIONAL MATCH – .45 ACP cal., flat mainspring housing, Colt blue finish accurizer barrel and bushing, adj. trigger, target hammer, solid rib, Colt-Elliason rear sight. Mfg. 1970-1983.

$1,650 $1,400 $1,200 $1,000 $750 $650 $550

Add 10% for satin nickel.

MKIV/SERIES 70 GOLD CUP 75TH ANNIVERSARY NATIONAL MATCH – similar to Gold Cup, except was mfg. as a Camp Perry commemorative, 200 mfg. 1978 only.

$1,650 $1,400 $1,200 $1,000 $750 $650 $550

MKIV SERIES 80 GOLD CUP NATIONAL MATCH – .45 ACP cal., 5 in. barrel, flat mainspring housing, 7 or 8 shot mag., accurizer barrel and bushing, wide grooved adj. target trigger,

GRADING - PPGS™	100%	98%	95%	90%	80%	70%	60%	LAST MSR

target hammer, solid rib, Colt-Elliason rear sight, 39 oz. Mfg. 1983-1996.

	$1,050	$850	$750	$600	$550	$500	$450	*$937*

In 1992, this model was updated to accept an 8 shot mag. During 1997, this updated model was designated the Gold Cup Trophy.

* ***MKIV Series 80 Stainless Gold Cup National Match*** – similar to Gold Cup, only manufactured from stainless steel, matte finish. Mfg. late 1986-1996.

	$1,000	$800	$700	$550	$500	$450	$400	*$1,003*

Add $70 for "Ultimate" bright stainless steel finish.
Add 10% for NIB condition.

* ***Gold Cup MKIV Series 80 Elite IX Gold Cup National Match*** – 9mm Para. cal., stainless steel and blue, marked "GCNM" on right side, and "ELITE IX - 9mm Luger" on left side, "IX" prefix in ser. no. Mfg. 1989.

	$1,400	$1,100	$900	$700	$675	$550	$400	

Add 10% for NIB condition.

* ***Gold Cup MKIV Series 80 .38 Super Elite National Match*** – two-tone gun (stainless slide and blue frame), special edition by AcuSport. Mfg. 1987.

	$1,400	$1,100	$900	$700	$675	$550	$400	

* ***Gold Cup MKIV Series 80 .45 ACP Super Elite National Match*** – Mfg. circa 1987.

	$1,400	$1,100	$900	$700	$675	$550	$400	

* ***Gold Cup MKIV Series 80 Bullseye National Match*** – .45 ACP cal., hand-built, tuned, and adjusted by Colt's custom gunsmiths for precise match accuracy, includes factory-installed Bo-Mar sights, equipped with carrying case and 2 extra mags. Mfg. 1991-92.

	$1,450	$1,200	$1,000	$850	$725	$650	$600	*$1,500*

* ***Gold Cup MKIV Series 80 National Match Presentation*** – .45 ACP cal., similar to regular Gold Cup Series 80 National Match, except has a deep blue mirror bright finish accented by custom jeweled hammer, trigger, and barrel hood. Supplied with oak and velvet custom case. Mfg. 1991-92.

	$1,300	$1,100	$1,000	$925	$850	$750	$550	*$1,195*

GOLD CUP TROPHY NATIONAL MATCH (MODEL O) – .45 ACP cal., flat mainspring housing, 7 (disc.) or 8 shot mag., accurizer barrel and bushing, flat-top slide, adj. aluminum trigger, target hammer, Bo-Mar rear sight, checkered black wrap-around rubber grips, shipped with test target, 39 oz. Mfg. 1997-2010.

	$915	$800	$665	$595	$540	$450	$375	*$1,053*

This model replaced the MKIV/Series 80 Gold Cup National Match in 1997, and is only available from the Colt Custom Shop.

GOLD CUP NATIONAL MATCH O SERIES – .45 ACP cal., 5 in. National Match barrel, features fully adj. Bomar style rear sight, spur hammer, drilled wide target trigger, lowered and flared ejection port, rounded slide top, blue finish, wrap-around rubber grips with Colt medallions, 37 oz. New 2012.

MSR $1,158	$1,050	$950	$825	$725	$650	$575	$495	

PISTOLS: SEMI-AUTO, CUSTOM SHOP ENGRAVING PRICING, PRE-1991

Values below represent pre-1991 factory semi-auto Custom Shop A-D engraving options, before they started separate Standard, Expert, and Master level pricing (1997). It should also be understood that, in most cases, the quality of the engraving and notoriety of the engraver can be as important as the amount of coverage. Small Frame Engraving Options: includes Mustang, .380 ACP Government, Detective Special, and Diamondback models. Medium Frame Engraving Options: includes .45 ACP Gold Cup, Government Model, Officer's ACP, Python, Combat Commander, King Cobra, Trooper MKV, Lawman MKV, and Delta Elite models. Special engraving/options include inlays, seals, custom grips, and lettering. Prices were quoted upon request. Smooth ivory grips were $215 extra (1990 retail). Beginning in 1991, Colt began shipping all models in a distinctive blue plastic carrying case/shipping container. Please refer to

GRADING - PPGS™	100%	98%	95%	90%	80%	70%	60%	LAST MSR

the "Colt Custom Shop Engraving - Current Mfg." listing earlier in this section for current semi-auto engraving options and pricing. Semi-auto custom-order quotations from Colt are available at $25 each (deductible from work order).

Add $776-$969 for Class "A" Engraving (1/4 Metal Coverage) depending on frame size.
Add $959-$1,199 for Class "B" Engraving (1/2 Metal Coverage) depending on frame size.
Add $1,426-$1,783 for Class "C" Engraving (3/4 Metal Coverage) depending on frame size.
Add $1,814-$2,289 for Class "D" Engraving (Full Metal Coverage) depending on frame size.
Add 7% for 6 in. barrel, 14% for 8 in. barrel, or 25% for stainless steel construction.

PISTOLS: SEMI-AUTO, CURRENT CUSTOM SHOP ENGRAVING PRICING

The following Colt Custom Shop engraving options apply to M1911 variations only.

Add $1,130 for A Standard engraving.
Add $1,300 for B Standard, $2,075 for B Expert (signed), or $3,725 for B Master (signed) level engraving.
Add $1,700 for C Standard, $2,878 for C Expert (signed), or $5,415 for C Master (signed) level engraving.
Add $2,000 for D Standard, $4,280 for D Expert (signed), or $6,900 for D Master (signed) level engraving.

PISTOLS: SEMI-AUTO, SINGLE ACTION, RECENT MFG.

Factory Colt abbreviations used on its price sheets are as follows: F-H - Front Heinie sight, CC/B - colored case/blue, L/W - lightweight, BSTS - bright polished stainless steel, CCBS - Colt Champion Bo-Mar style sight, BRS - Bo-Mar rear sights, NNS - Novak night sights, WDS - white dot sights, FXS - fixed sights, HBAR - heavy barrel, HC - hard chrome, CCES - Colt Champion Elliason style sights, BPF - black powder frame, B - blue, STS - stainless steel, TT - two-tone, WDC - white dot carry, M - matte, and WDCN - white dot carry Novak sights.

Some Series 80 pistols, including Gold Cups and Defenders with slanted slide serrations, polished ejection port, and beavertail safety are more desirable than standard models without these features. See individual models for pricing.

JUNIOR COLT POCKET MODEL – .22 S or .25 ACP cal., 2 1/4 in. barrel, blue, checkered walnut grips, made by Astra in Spain 1958-1968.

.22 Short	$375	$350	$275	$250	$200	$180	$150
.25 ACP	$350	$325	$250	$225	$175	$160	$140

Add 10% for nickel finish.
A very few conversion kits were offered for this model. They are rare and asking prices are $250-$325 if in mint condition.

COLT AUTOMATIC CALIBER .25 – .25 ACP cal., mfg. by Firearms International for Colt 1970-1973.

$350	$325	$250	$225	$175	$160	$140

COMMANDER (PRE-70 SERIES) – 9mm Para, .38 Super, or .45 ACP cal., 4 1/4 in. barrel, full size grips, Colt alloy frame and mainspring housing. Mfg. 1950-1969.

9mm Para.	$1,200	$1,000	$950	$800	$650	$550	$450
.38 Super/.45 ACP	$1,400	$1,200	$1,125	$1,000	$900	$700	$600

* ***Commander General Officer's Pistol M1969*** – there were two shipments of the M1969 pistol. One was on 3/18/1969 to the Arsenal and were serialized 327248C, 327337C, 327338C, and 327673C. The second shipment was sent to military exchange in care of Robert Tremont on 5/2/1969, and were serialized CS-001868, CS-002019, CS-002023, CS-002027, CS-02248, and CS-002770.

$8,000	$7,500	$7,000	$6,000	$5,000	$4,000	$3,250

.38 SPECIAL/.45 ACP KIT GUNS – .38 Spl. or .45 ACP cal., left side slide marking includes either "COLT .38 SPEC. KIT", or "COLT .45 ACP KIT", these kit guns were designed to be used for competitive target shooting, and many of the guns were shipped without sights, with the buyer providing the sights of his/her choice, kit guns can be found with a myriad of various target sights. Approx. serial no. range is 00100-01164. Production began in

GRADING - PPGS™	100%	98%	95%	90%	80%	70%	60%	LAST MSR

1964, and fewer than 400 of the .38 Spl. Kit Guns were mfg. by 1970. It is estimated that approx. 1,050 .45 ACP Kit Guns were mfg. by the end of 1970.

	$2,300	$2,000	$1,500	$1,100	$800	$650	$550	

This model is also known as the Gil Hebard Model and is basically a .38 AMU.

SERIES 70 LIGHTWEIGHT COMMANDER – 7.65mm (.30 Luger), 9mm Para, .38 Super, or .45 ACP cal., 4 1/4 in. barrel, full size grips, this model is denoted by a "CLW" prefix. Mfg. 1970-83.

9mm Para.	$1,100	$875	$775	$675	$575	$500	$450	
.38 Super/.45 ACP	$1,100	$875	$775	$675	$575	$500	$450	
7.65mm	$2,500	$2,000	$1,575	$1,250	$995	$875	$750	

Add 10% for NIB condition.

500 Lightweight Commanders were mfg. in 7.65mm cal. during 1971. While most of these were mfg. for export trade, 5 were sold in the U.S.

SERIES 70 COMBAT COMMANDER – 9mm Para., .38 Super, or .45 ACP cal., similar to Series 70 Lightweight (LW) Commander, except has steel frame. Mfg. 1971-1980.

	$1,100	$1,000	$850	$750	$650	$575	$500	

Add 10% for NIB condition.
Add 10% for satin nickel.

This model was also available in satin nickel finish (scarce).

GOVERNMENT MODEL MKIV/SERIES 70 – .45 ACP, .38 Super, 9mm Para., or 9mm Steyr cal., 5 in. barrel, checkered walnut grips/medallion. Series 70 models were serial numbered with "SM" prefixes (approx. 3,000 mfg.), "70G" prefixes 1970-76, "70L" and "70S" prefixes also (see Serialization section for more information), "G70" suffixes 1976-80, "B70" suffixes 1979-81, and "70B" prefixes 1981-83. Mfg. 1970-83.

Blue finish	$1,000	$775	$600	$500	$450	$400	$375	
Nickel finish	$1,250	$1,000	$800	$675	$450	$400	$375	

Add 10% if in NIB condition, 20% for NIB with early two-piece box.
Add 10% for .38 Super, 9mm Para., or 9mm Steyr cal. if in 100% condition.
Add 10% for satin nickel.
9mm Steyr was made for export to Europe only. However, a few specimens have found their way into the United States. Prices for NIB specimens are in the $1,000 range.

* ***Series 70 Combat Govt.*** – .45 ACP cal., bluish-black metal finish, features modifications for combat shooting, forerunner to the Combat Elite.

	$1,250	$1,050	$950	$850	$775	$700	$650	

Add 10% for NIB condition.

* ***Government Model MKIV/Series 70 Conversion Unit*** – converts .45 ACP to .22 LR, mfg. 1954-84 with either Accro adj. rear or fixed sight.

Adj. Sight	$600	$550	$400	$350	$300	$250	$200	
Fixed Sight	$700	$600	$450	$375	$300	$250	$200	

Add 50% for conversion units in bright nickel finish (very scarce). Must be accompanied by original box w/nickel label.

1991 SERIES GOVERNMENT MODEL SERIES 70 MODEL O – .45 ACP cal., patterned after the original Series 70 pistol, high polish blue finish or stainless steel (new 2005), fixed sights, new release from the Custom Shop beginning 2002.

MSR $1,043	$895	$795	$675	$575	$495	$425	$375	

Add $35 for stainless steel (new 2005).

POST-WAR ACE SERVICE MODEL – .22 LR cal., similar specifications to previous pre-WWII manufacture, blue (most common) or electroless nickel Custom Shop finish, "SM" prefix (most common) or "B 70" suffix, approx. 30,000 mfg. between 1978-1989.

	$1,200	$950	$800	$700	$625	$500	$450	

Add 10% for NIB condition.

This model is serial numbered approx. SM14,001-SM43,830.

GRADING - PPGS™	100%	98%	95%	90%	80%	70%	60%	LAST MSR

GOVERNMENT 1911A1 GOLD CUP ACE .22 LR CAL. – .22 LR cal., 5 in. barrel, SA, fully adj. rear sight, w/o rail, 12 shot mag. only, Commander-style hammer, black checkered rubber wrap-around grips with diamond patterns, black anodized zinc alloy finish, manual and beavertail grip safeties, checkered front grip strap, skeleton trigger, 36 oz. Mfg. by Umarex GmbH in Germany under license from Colt beginning 2012, and distributed by Umarex USA.

MSR $500	$425	$365	$325	$295	$260	$230	$200	

GOVERNMENT MODEL MKIV/SERIES 80 – .38 Super, 9mm Para. (disc. 1992), 9x23mm Win. (mfg. 1997 only), or .45 ACP (disc. 1996) cal., single action, 5 in. barrel, 7- or 8- (new 1992) shot mag. in .45 ACP, approx. 38 oz., firing pin safety, checkered walnut (pre-1991 mfg.) or rubber combat style grips with medallion (new 1991). Production started in 1983 with ser. no. FG01000.

* ***Government Model MKIV/Series 80 Blue Finish*** – this finish was disc. in 1997.

	$900	$775	$650	$600	$525	$500	$450	*$600*

Add 5% for 9mm Para. (disc. 1992) cal.
Add 10% for NIB condition.

* ***Government Model MKIV/Series 80 Nickel Finish*** – .45 ACP (disc. 1986) or .38 Super (disc. in 1987) cal.

	$1,000	$775	$725	$625	$550	$500	$450	*$735*

Add 10% for NIB condition.

* ***Government Model MKIV/Series 80 Satin Nickel & Blue Finish*** – with Colt-Pachmayr grips. Disc. 1986.

	$1,000	$850	$750	$650	$575	$500	$450	*$557*

Add 10% for NIB condition.

* ***Government Model MKIV/Series 80 Stainless Steel*** – 9mm Para. (mfg. 1991-92), .38 Super (new 1990), .40 S&W (new 1992), or .45 ACP cal. Disc. 1998.

	$950	$850	$725	$650	$575	$525	$475	*$813*

Add 5% for 9mm Para. (disc. 1992) cal.
Add 10% for NIB condition.

* ***Government Model MKIV/Series 80 "Ultimate" Bright Stainless Steel*** – .38 Super (new 1991) or .45 ACP cal., high polish stainless finish. Mfg. 1986-96.

	$1,000	$850	$750	$650	$575	$500	$450	*$863*

Add 10% for NIB condition.

* ***Government Model MKIV/Series 80 Limited Class Model .45 ACP*** – .45 ACP cal., designed for tactical competition, includes parkerized matte finish, lightweight composite trigger, ambidextrous safety, upswept beavertail grip safety, beveled mag. well, accurized, includes signed target. Mfg. 1994-97.

	$1,000	$850	$750	$650	$575	$500	$450	*$936*

* ***Government Model MKIV/Series 80 Custom Compensated Model .45 ACP*** – .45 ACP cal., designed for serious competitive shooting, blue slide with full profile BAT Compensator, Bo-Mar rear sight, flared funnel mag. well. Mfg. by Custom Shop 1994-98.

	$2,000	$1,600	$1,350	$1,100	$975	$850	$725	*$2,428*

MODEL M1911A1 CUSTOM TACTICAL GOV'T - LEVEL I – .45 ACP cal., designed for tactical competition, Commander style hammer, beveled/contoured mag. well, nylon flat mainspring housing, ambidextrous safety, long nylon trigger with overtravel stop, available in Officer's or Commmander's length. Mfg. 1998-2001.

	$850	$750	$700	$650	$600	$525	$475	*$730*

In late 1999, this model was redesignated the Model O Custom Tactical Gov't.

* ***Model M1911A1 Custom Tactical Gov't. Model - Level II*** – similar to Level I, except has Videcki long aluminum trigger with overtravel stop, Heinie fixed combat sights, Colt match grade barrel bushing, high-ride grip safety with palm swell, double diamond stocks. Mfg. 1998-2001.

	$950	$875	$775	$700	$625	$525	$450	*$935*

GRADING - PPGS™	100%	98%	95%	90%	80%	70%	60%	LAST MSR

* ***Model M1911A1 Custom Tactical Gov't. Model - Level III*** – similar to Level II, except has Bo-Mar adj. rear sight, super match hammer. Mfg. 1998-2001.

	$1,150	$1,025	$875	$750	$650	$575	$495	*$1,350*

COMBAT GOVERNMENT SERIES 80 – .45 ACP cal., dark matte metal finish, features modifications for combat shooting, successor to the Series 70 Combat Govt. Mfg. 1983-1998.

	$950	$800	$650	$550	$475	$450	$400	

Add 10% for NIB condition.

* ***Combat Elite Series 80*** – .38 Super or .45 ACP cal., similar to Gold Cup, only with wraparound rubber grips, beveled magazine well, stainless steel frame with carbon steel slide, and Accro adj. sighting system. Mfg. 1986-1996.

	$975	$825	$675	$625	$575	$525	$450	*$895*

Note: Colt has issued a factory recall on the safety for this model sold after March 2007 in the following ser. no. range: CG10000E-CG11293E. These pistols must be returned to Colt's factory for part(s) replacement.

COMBAT GOVERNMENT SERIES 80 CONVERSION UNIT – converts Series 80 Govt. Model only to .22 LR or 9mm Para., mfg. 1984-86, 1995, and 1998, with Accro adj. rear sight.

9mm Para.	$725	$650	$500	$400	$325	$250	$200	
.22 LR (mfg. 1984-86)	$750	$650	$500	$400	$325	$250	$200	
.22 LR (mfg. 1995, rare)	$775	$675	$525	$425	$325	$250	$200	

Last MSR was $305 for .22 LR (mfg. 1984-86).

* ***Colt Ace II Conversion Unit*** – similar to above, except features an aluminum slide and barrel w/o floating chamber, does not have hold open feature. Mfg. 1998.

	$350	$295	$275	$225	$190	$175	$150	

COMBAT TARGET MODEL SERIES 80 – .45 ACP cal. only, 5 in. barrel, adj. sights, matte finish. Mfg. 1997 only.

	$750	$625	$525	$475	$450	$425	$400	*$768*

* ***Combat Target Model Stainless Series 80*** – similar to Combat Target Model, except stainless steel finish. Mfg. 1997 only.

	$800	$675	$550	$500	$450	$425	$400	*$820*

SPECIAL COMBAT GOVERNMENT COMPETITION MODEL SERIES 80 – .38 Super (new 2005) or .45 ACP cal., competition model featuring skeletonized trigger, custom tuning, polished ramp, 5 in. throated barrel, flared ejection port, and cut-out hammer. Supplied with two 8 shot mags., two-tone (new 2004) or hard chrome slide and frame, Bo-Mar rear and Clark dovetail front sight, flared mag. well, shipped with certified target. Mfg. by the Custom Shop. New 1992.

MSR $2,095	$1,775	$1,450	$1,125	$950	$775	$675	$575

SPECIAL COMBAT GOVERNMENT (CARRY MODEL) SERIES 80 – .45 ACP cal., similar to Special Combat Government, except has blue or royal blue (disc.), hard chrome, or two-tone finish, bar-dot-bar (disc. 2000) or Novak (new 2009) night sights, and ambidextrous safety. Mfg. 1992-2000, reintroduced 2009.

MSR $2,095	$1,775	$1,450	$1,125	$950	$775	$675	$575

SPECIAL COMBAT MARINE PISTOL – .45 ACP cal., full size with 5 in. National Match barrel, front and rear slide serrations, features Desert Tan cerakote finish, stainless steel receiver and slide, Novak 3-dot sights, serrated grip straps with lanyard loop, aluminum trigger, unique patterned grips, lower Picatinny rail, includes Pelican case with two 7 shot mags, cleaning kit, and test target. New 2013.

MSR $1,995	$1,795	$1,525	$1,300	$1,075	$925	$800	$700

COMMANDER LIGHTWEIGHT SERIES 80 – 9mm Para, .38 Super, or .45 ACP cal., 4 1/4 in. barrel, similar to Government Model, except shorter and lighter alloy frame, fixed sights,

GRADING - PPGS™	100%	98%	95%	90%	80%	70%	60%	LAST MSR

round spur hammer, 27 1/2 oz. Mfg. 1983-97.

	$875	$750	$625	$575	$525	$475	$450	*$735*

Add 10% for .38 Super or 9mm Para. (disc.) cals.

Some pistols are marked "Super Lite Commander - .38 Super - " on left side, and "Lightweight Commander Model" on right side. There may be an "M" on magazine floorplate, with the Colt logo.

COMBAT COMMANDER SERIES 80 – .38 Super (disc.), 9mm Para. (disc. 1992), or .45 ACP cal., similar to Lightweight, except has steel frame.

* ***Combat Commander Series 80 Blue Finish*** – disc. 1996.

	$875	$700	$600	$500	$450	$425	$400	*$735*

Add $20 for 9mm Para. (disc.) or .38 Super (disc.) cal.

* ***Combat Commander Series 80 Blue Slide/Stainless Steel Receiver*** – .45 ACP cal., two-tone matte finish, upswept grip safety, lightweight perforated trigger, black Hogue grips, 8 shot mag., 35 oz. Mfg. 1998 only.

	$800	$650	$550	$525	$500	$475	$450	*$813*

* ***Combat Commander Series 80 Stainless Steel*** – .38 Super (mfg. 1992-97) or .45 ACP cal. Mfg. 1990-98.

	$850	$675	$550	$475	$450	$425	$400	*$813*

* ***Combat Commander Series 80 Satin Nickel*** – disc. 1986.

	$975	$800	$675	$625	$575	$550	$475	*$550*

* ***Combat Commander Series 80 Gold Cup Commander*** – .45 ACP cal., features custom shop alterations including heavy duty adj. target sights, beveled mag. well, serrated front strap, checkered mainspring housing, wide grip safety, and Palo Alto wood grips. Mfg. 1991-93.

	$1,200	$1,050	$925	$875	$825	$700	$600	*$936*

* ***Combat Commander Series 80 Gold Cup Commander Stainless*** – stainless variation of the Gold Cup Commander. Mfg. 1992-disc.

	$1,200	$1,050	$925	$875	$825	$700	$600	*$949*

COMMANDING OFFICER'S LIGHTWEIGHT – 9mm Para. cal., 3 1/2 in. barrel, Officer slide, lightweight commander frame, three-dot sights, Officer's Model extended grip safety, round combat commander hammer, matte black finish, black pebble rubber grips with gold medallions, 500 mfg. by the Custom Shop.

	$1,100	$875	$775	$675	$575	$500	$450	

OFFICER'S ACP MODEL SERIES 80 – .45 ACP cal. only, 3 1/2 in. barrel, 34 oz., 6 shot mag., short version of the Government Model. Mfg. 1985-disc.

* ***Officer's ACP Model Series 80 Blue Finish*** – disc. 1996.

	$850	$700	$600	$500	$400	$350	$300	*$735*

* ***Officer's ACP Model Series 80 Matte Blue Finish*** – disc. 1991.

	$850	$750	$650	$550	$450	$425	$400	*$625*

* ***Officer's ACP Model Series 80 Stainless Steel*** – matte stainless steel finish. Mfg. 1986-97.

	$850	$750	$650	$550	$450	$425	$400	*$813*

Add $74 for "Ultimate" bright stainless steel finish (mfg. 1987-96).

* ***Officer's ACP Model Series 80 Lightweight*** – similar to Officer's ACP, except has alloy frame and weighs 24 oz. Mfg. 1985-1997.

	$900	$800	$700	$600	$500	$475	$425	*$735*

* ***Officer's ACP Model Series 80 Concealed Carry*** – .45 ACP cal., features matte stainless steel slide with matte blue aluminum alloy receiver, 7 shot mag., black contoured Hogue grips, upswept beavertail grip safety, lightweight perforated trigger, 26 oz. Mfg. 1998 only.

	$900	$800	$700	$600	$500	$450	$400	*$813*

GRADING - PPGS™	100%	98%	95%	90%	80%	70%	60%	LAST MSR

* ***Officer's ACP Model Series 80 Satin Nickel*** – disc. 1985.

	$950	$850	$750	$650	$550	$500	$450	*$513*

* ***General Officer's ACP Model Series 80*** – bright stainless steel with rosewood grips, special edition. Disc. 1996.

	$900	$800	$700	$600	$500	$475	$450	*$750*

DEFENDER SERIES MODEL O – 9mm Para., .40 S&W (mfg. 1999 only) or .45 ACP cal., 3 in. barrel with 3-dot (disc.) or white dot carry Novak sights, 7 shot mag., rubber wrap-around grips with finger grooves, lightweight perforated trigger, stainless steel slide and frame - frame finished in matte stainless, firing pin safety, 22 1/2 oz. New 1998.

MSR $1,066	$925	$775	$675	$575	$475	$425	$375	

Note: Colt has issued a factory recall on the safety for this model sold after March 2007 in the following ser. no. range: DR33036 - DR35948 X. Colt will send you a new recoil spring assembly kit that includes the Guide Pad to replace in your pistol.

* ***Defender Plus*** – .45 ACP cal., similar to Defender Model O, except has aluminum frame and 8 shot mag. Mfg. 2002-2003.

	$875	$775	$700	$625	$575	$550	$475	*$876*

COLT CONCEALED CARRY – .45 ACP cal., 3 in. barrel, aluminum frame with steel slide, Series 80 firing pin safety system, checkered double diamond walnut grips, front strap serrations, 25 oz. Mfg. 2007.

	$800	$725	$650	$575	$500	$450	$400	*$885*

XSE (XS) SERIES MODEL O – .45 ACP cal., 4 1/4 or 5 in. barrel, stainless brushed finish, front and rear slide serrations, checkered double diamond rosewood grips, 3-dot (disc.) or white dot carry Novak sights, new roll marking and enhanced tolerances, extended ambidextrous thumb safeties. New 2000.

* ***XSE Series Model O Government*** – .45 ACP cal., 5 in. barrel, blue (new 2002) or stainless brushed (SS Model) finish, 8 shot mag., 36 oz.

MSR $1,072	$900	$775	$675	$575	$475	$400	$350	

* ***XSE Series Model O Lightweight Government*** – .45 ACP cal., 5 in. barrel, features lightweight aluminum alloy frame, blue finish, 27 oz. New 2012.

MSR $1,072	$900	$775	$675	$575	$475	$400	$350	

* ***XSE Series Model O Combat Elite*** – .45 ACP cal., 5 in. barrel, two-tone finish, 8 shot, combat hammer with elongated slot, skeletonized trigger, checkered rosewood grips with Colt logo. New 2009.

MSR $1,083	$910	$775	$675	$575	$475	$425	$375	

Note: Colt has issued a recall for ser. nos. CG10000E - CG11293E X due to a problem with the safety and/or guide pad. Improper hardness may cause the safety or guide pad to crack and might not prevent the gun from an accidental firing. Please contact Colt directly if you have one of the pistols - recall@colt.com.

* ***XSE Series Model O Rail Gun*** – .45 ACP cal., stainless, two-tone, or Cerakote (new 2011) finish, similar to Government Stainless model, except has Picatinny rail underneath frame in front of trigger guard. New 2009.

MSR $1,141	$995	$875	$725	$625	$525	$450	$395	

Add $82 for Cerakote finish (new 2011).

* ***XSE Series Model O Concealed Carry Officers SS*** – features lightweight aluminum alloy frame, 4 1/4 in. barrel and 7 shot mag. Limited mfg. 2000 only.

	$800	$700	$600	$550	$500	$450	$400	*$750*

* ***XSE Series Model O Commander SS*** – .45 ACP cal., features 4 1/4 in. barrel and 8 shot mag., 33 1/2 oz.

MSR $1,072	$900	$775	$675	$575	$475	$400	$350	

GRADING - PPGS™	100%	98%	95%	90%	80%	70%	60%	LAST MSR

* ***XSE (XS) Series Model O Lightweight Commander SS*** – .38 Super (disc. 2011) or .45 ACP cal., features lightweight aluminum alloy frame, 4 1/4 in. barrel, and 8 shot mag., 27 oz.

MSR $1,072	$900	$775	$675	$575	$475	$400	$350	

Early production first series XS Series Lightweight Commander pistols manufactured during 2000 became the XSE Series Lightweight Commander SS pistols during 2001.

GOLD CUP NATIONAL MATCH MKIV/SERIES 80/MODEL O – please refer to the listings for Gold Cup National Match models under Pistols: Semi-Auto, National Match Models - WWII and Post-WWII.

GOLD CUP TROPHY STAINLESS – similar to Gold Cup Trophy National Match, except has round top slide, stainless steel, matte finish, 39 oz. New 1997.

MSR $1,180	$1,025	$875	$750	$625	$525	$425	$350	

1991 SERIES GOVERNMENT MODEL O (MKIV SERIES 80) – 9mm Para. (disc. 2001) or .45 ACP cal., 5 in. barrel, similar to original WWII issue pistols with government issue parkerized matte (disc.) or blue finish, fixed sights, checkered rosewood double diamond wood (blue only) or checkered black composite grips, 7 shot mag., early guns were marked Colt M1991A1 on left hand of slide, 38 oz., includes brown molded case. New 1991.

MSR $928	$800	$675	$575	$425	$375	$325	$295	

Add $93 for Custom Government Model in .45 ACP cal. with blue steel and low profile combat sights. New 2013.

This model is serialized consecutively with the last batch of Govt. military models manufactured during 1945.

* ***1991 Series Government Model O Stainless Steel*** – features matte stainless steel frame and slide, black checkered grips, white dot sights. New 1996.

MSR $989	$850	$725	$575	$475	$375	$325	$275	

1991 SERIES COMMANDER MODEL O (MKIV SERIES 80) – 9mm Para. (disc.) or .45 ACP cal., 4 1/4 in. barrel, full size grip, 7 shot mag., parkerized finish, 36 oz. Mfg. 1993-2005, reintroduced 2007.

MSR $946	$800	$675	$550	$425	$375	$325	$295	

Add 10% for 9mm Para. cal. (disc.).

» **1991 Series Commander SS** – .45 ACP cal., similar to Model M1991 A1 Commander, except is stainless steel. Mfg. 1999-2005, reintroduced 2007.

MSR $1,008	$850	$725	$600	$500	$400	$325	$275	

1991 SERIES OFFICER'S COMPACT (MKIV SERIES 80) – similar to Model M1991 Commander, except has 3 1/2 in. barrel, 6 shot mag., 34 oz. Mfg. 1992-1999.

	$600	$500	$425	$400	$375	$350	$325	*$556*

» **1991 Series Officer's Stainless Compact** – similar to Model M1991A1 Officer's Compact, except is stainless steel. Mfg. 1999 only.

	$650	$600	$550	$500	$475	$450	$400	*$610*

NEW AGENT SA MODEL O – 9mm Para. (disc. 2012) or .45 ACP cal., 3 in. barrel, Series 80 firing pin safety system, hammerless, 7 shot mag., double diamond slim fit or Crimson Trace (new 2012) grips, black anodized aluminum frame, blue finish, beveled mag. well, skeletonized trigger, snag free trench style sights, front strap serrations, captive recoil spring system. New 2008.

MSR $1,046	$895	$775	$650	$550	$450	$400	$350	

Add $260 for Crimson Trace laser grips (new 2012).

Note: Colt has issued a factory recall on the safety for this model sold after March 2007 in the following ser. no. range: GT01001-GT04505 XX. These pistols must be returned to Colt's factory for part(s) replacement.

1991 SERIES GOVERNMENT MODEL O .38 SUPER – .38 Super cal., 5 in. barrel, M1911 (bright stainless only) or M1911A1 style frame, Govt. Model, blue, 3-dot sights, checkered

GRADING - PPGS™	100%	98%	95%	90%	80%	70%	60%	LAST MSR

rubber or double diamond walnut (bright stainless only) grips, 9 shot mag., beveled mag. well. Mfg. 2003-2009, reintroduced 2011.

MSR $951	$825	$700	$600	$475	$400	$350	$325	

* ***.38 Super Model O Stainless*** – similar to .38 Super Model O, except is available in stainless steel. Disc. 2009.

	$775	$650	$525	$450	$415	$385	$350	*$866*

* ***.38 Super Model O Bright Stainless*** – similar to .38 Super Model O, except is bright stainless steel only. New 2003.

MSR $1,311	$1,175	$975	$850	$725	$600	$500	$400	

GUNSITE MODEL O – .45 ACP cal., M1911 style frame, Series 70 firing pin safety system, 4 1/4 (Commander configuration) or 5 in. barrel, checkered thin rosewood grips, blue or stainless steel, many shooting features are included, such as serrated flat mainspring housing, Gold Cup front strap serrations, Heinie front and Novak rear sights, two 8 shot Wilson mags., McCormick hammer and sear, slide marked with Gunsite logo. Mfg. 2003-2005.

	$1,300	$1,100	$900	$775	$700	$625	$575	*$1,400*

M1911 MODEL O SERIES 70 – .45 ACP cal., 5 in. barrel, accurate reproduction of the Model 1911 U.S. military sidearm, original style checkered walnut grips, carbonia blue finish, 7 shot mag., original WWI roll marks, original style packaging (cardboard box with wax paper), 4,400 were scheduled for mfg. by the Custom Shop, 38 oz. Mfg. 2003-2009.

	$975	$875	$775	$675	$575	$475	$425	*$990*

Note: Colt has issued a recall for ser. nos. 4597WMK - 5414WMK X due to a problem with the safety and/or guide pad. Improper hardness may cause the safety or guide pad to crack and might not prevent the gun from an accidental firing. Please contact Colt directly if you have one of the pistols - recall@colt.com.

M1911A1 REPLICA MODEL O – .45 ACP cal., 5 in. barrel, incorporates pre-Series 70 firing pin safety system, accurate reproduction of the Model 1911A1 U.S. military sidearm, original style composite grips, parkerized finish or stainless steel construction, 7 shot mag., original WWII roll marks, lanyard loop on arched serrated mainspring housing, wide spur hammer, safety and slide stop with original serrations, 38 oz., original style packaging (cardboard box with wax paper), approx. 4,000 mfg. by the Custom Shop. Mfg. 2001-2004.

	$995	$875	$775	$675	$575	$475	$400	*$940*

Colt has issued a factory recall on the safety for this model sold after March 2007 in the following ser. no. range: 4597WMK-5414WMK. These pistols must be returned to Colt's factory for part(s) replacement.

M1911 SERIES 70 MODEL 1918 REPLICA – .45 ACP cal., 5 in. barrel, accurate reproduction of the Model 1911 U.S. military sidearm manufactured during 1918, featuring black finish, original WWI roll marks, limited mfg. by the Custom Shop. Mfg. 2008-2009.

	$875	$775	$675	$575	$475	$425	$375	*$990*

Colt also offered this model in a Presentation Grade with blue or nickel finish and unsigned A engraving coverage - MSRs ranged from $2,278 - $2,378.

Note: Colt has issued a factory recall on the safety for this model sold after March 2007 in the following ser. no. range: 1001WW1-3431WW1X. These pistols must be returned to Colt's factory for part(s) replacement.

GOVERNMENT MODEL 1911A1 .22 CAL. – .22 LR cal., patterned after the Colt Post War Ace Service Model, features 5 in. barrel, checkered diamond patterned rubber grips, half-cock mechanism, all steel construction, 10 or 12 shot mag., standard 1911A1 model with removeable front and drift adj. rear sight, single slide serrations, 36 oz. Mfg. by Umarex in Germany beginning 2011, and distributed by Umarex USA, located in Fort Smith, AR.

MSR $400	$350	$300	$265	$225	$200	$185	$175	

This model is also available in a Gold Cup variation - please refer to the listing in the Pistols: Semi-Auto, National Match Models - WWII & Post-WWII category.

GRADING - PPGS™	100%	98%	95%	90%	80%	70%	60%	LAST MSR

GOVERNMENT MODEL 1911A1 .22 CAL. RAIL GUN – .22 LR cal., similar to Government Model 1911 .22 cal., except has lower Picatinny rail on frame, double slide serrations, skeleton trigger, low mount 3-dot combat style sights, beavertail grip safety and Commander style hammer, black or FDE (new 2013) finish, 36 oz. Mfg. by Umarex in Germany beginning 2011, and distributed by Umarex USA, located in Fort Smith, AR.

MSR $450	$385	$325	$285	$240	$215	$195	$185	

Add $50 for FDE finish (new 2013).

This model is also available in a Gold Cup variation - please refer to the listing in the Pistols: Semi-Auto, National Match Models - WWII & Post-WWII category.

M1911ANVII 100th ANNIVERSARY – .45 ACP cal., features 100th Anniversary of the M1911 with gold accents including slide banners, "Colt" and prancing stallion on rear sides of slide, royal blue metal finish, smooth Cocobolo grips with 100th Anniversary gold plated medallions, includes walnut display case, serial numbers beginning with 19110001. 750 mfg. 2011 only.

	$2,150	$1,775	$1,525	N/A	N/A	N/A	N/A	$2,295

M1911ANVIII 100th ANNIVERSARY – .45 ACP cal., based on Colt 1911A1 mfg. in 1918, custom military roll marks on frame and slide, brushed blue finish, walnut double diamond grips, special edition 100th Anniversary packaging, serialization begins with 00011911. Mfg. limited to all orders placed by Nov. 30, 2011.

	$1,075	$925	$795	N/A	N/A	N/A	N/A	$1,150

M1911 100th ANNIVERSARY CUSTOM SHOP – .45 ACP cal., 4 variations featuring either A, B, C, or D coverage standard engraving, gold inlayed serial number and "1911-2011" on slide, blue finish. 100 mfg. total in all four engraving patterns, mfg. 2011 only.

* ***M1911 100th Anniversary Custom Shop w/A Engraving*** – .45 ACP cal., featuring Custom Shop A coverage standard engraving. Mfg. 2011 only.

	$2,450	$2,100	$1,750	N/A	N/A	N/A	N/A	$2,640

* ***M1911 100th Anniversary Custom Shop w/B Engraving*** – .45 ACP cal., featuring Custom Shop B coverage standard engraving. Mfg. 2011 only.

	$2,675	$2,275	$1,875	N/A	N/A	N/A	N/A	$2,900

* ***M1911 100th Anniversary Custom Shop w/C Engraving*** – .45 ACP cal., featuring Custom Shop C coverage standard engraving. Mfg. 2011 only.

	$2,995	$2,550	$2,100	N/A	N/A	N/A	N/A	$3,265

* ***M1911 100th Anniversary Custom Shop w/D Engraving*** – .45 ACP cal., featuring Custom Shop D coverage standard engraving. Mfg. 2011 only.

	$3,200	$2,875	$2,475	N/A	N/A	N/A	N/A	$3,535

DELTA ELITE (1987-1996 MFG.) – 10mm cal., 5 in. barrel, black neoprene grips, high profile 3-dot sights, blue finish, 8 shot mag., 38 oz. Mfg. 1987-96.

	$925	$750	$625	$600	$500	$475	$450	$807

* ***Delta Elite First Edition (1991 Mfg.)*** – features laser engraving with gold-fill, smooth wood grips, includes presentation case. 500 mfg. 1991 only.

	$1,050	$850	$675	$625	$525	$500	$450	

* ***Delta Elite Stainless Steel*** – matte stainless steel finish. Mfg. 1989-96.

	$925	$725	$625	$600	$575	$550	$525	$860

Add $78 for "Ultimate" brite stainless steel finish (disc. 1993).

* ***Delta Elite First Edition (1988 Mfg.)*** – features stamped lettering on slide, ebony grips, and do not have display case. 1,000 mfg. 1988 only.

	$1,150	$900	$725	$650	$550	$500	$450	

DELTA ELITE – 10mm cal., 5 in. barrel, 8 shot mag., stainless steel, features diamond laser cut cocobolo grips with trademark Colt logo on both grips, white dot sights. New 2008.

MSR $1,061	$925	$800	$700	$600	$500	$425	$375	

GRADING - PPGS™	100%	98%	95%	90%	80%	70%	60%	LAST MSR

DELTA GOLD CUP STAINLESS – 10mm cal., target variation, includes Accro adj. rear sight and trigger (serrated also), wraparound combat grips. Mfg. 1989-93, re-released 1995-96.

$1,000	$800	$700	$600	$550	$525	$500	*$1,027*

* ***Delta Gold Cup Blue*** – similar to Delta Gold Cup Stainless, except has blue finish. Mfg. 1991 only.

$950	$825	$750	$675	$600	$550	$500	*$870*

.380 GOVERNMENT MODEL SERIES 80 – .380 ACP cal. only, single action, 3 1/4 in. barrel, 7 shot mag., fixed sights, composition stocks, 21 3/4 oz. Mfg. 1983-1997.

* ***.380 Government Model Series 80 Blue Finish*** – finish disc. in 1997.

$825	$700	$600	$550	$500	$450	$400	*$474*

* ***.380 Government Model Series 80 Nickel Finish*** – bright polish nickel finish with white composite grips. Disc. 1994.

$895	$775	$675	$600	$500	$450	$400	*$504*

* ***.380 Government Model Series 80 Coltguard Finish*** – employs a high-strength electroless matte nickel finish. Mfg. 1986-89.

$850	$750	$650	$575	$500	$450	$400	*$406*

* ***.380 Government Model Series 80 Stainless Steel*** – mfg. 1989-97.

$825	$700	$600	$525	$475	$450	$400	*$508*

GOVT. POCKETLITE L.W. – similar to .380 Series 80 Govt. Model, except frame is mfg. with alloy, blue or nickel/stainless (mfg. 1992-93) finish only, black composition grips, 14 3/4 oz. Mfg. 1991-97.

$750	$650	$525	$450	$400	$350	$325	*$462*

Add 15% for nickel/stainless finish (disc. 1993).

* ***Govt. Pocketlite Teflon Nickel/Stainless*** – similar to Govt. Pocketlite L.W., except has combination of Teflon nickel, stainless steel finish. Mfg. 1997-98.

$725	$600	$500	$400	$350	$300	$275	*$508*

MUSTANG – similar to .380 Series Govt., except has 2 3/4 in. barrel, single action, 5 or 6 (new 1992) shot mag., blue finish only, 18 1/2 oz. Mfg. 1986-1998.

$950	$825	$700	$575	$475	$375	$300	*$462*

* ***Mustang Nickel finish*** – bright polish nickel finish with white composite grips. Mfg. 1987-94.

$1,050	$900	$750	$650	$525	$425	$350	*$504*

* ***Mustang Stainless Steel*** – stainless steel variation of the Mustang. Mfg. 1990-97.

$995	$850	$725	$600	$500	$400	$325	*$508*

* ***Mustang Coltguard finish*** – employs a high-strength electroless matte nickel finish. Mfg. 1987.

$1,175	$975	$825	$700	$600	$500	$400	*$406*

MUSTANG PLUS II – .380 ACP cal. only, 2 3/4 in. barrel, blue finish, black composition grips, 7 shot mag., 20 oz. Mfg. 1988-96.

$775	$650	$550	$475	$400	$350	$275	*$462*

This model has the full grip length of the .380 Government Model.

* ***Mustang Plus II Stainless Steel*** – stainless steel variation of the Mustang Plus II. Mfg. 1990-1998.

$775	$650	$550	$475	$400	$350	$275	*$508*

MUSTANG POCKETLITE L.W. – similar to Mustang, except has aluminum alloy receiver and stainless slide, blue (disc. 1997) or nickel/stainless finish, black composite grips, 12 1/2 oz. Introduced 1987.

$775	$650	$525	$450	$375	$325	$300	*$462*

GRADING - PPGS™	100%	98%	95%	90%	80%	70%	60%	LAST MSR

* ***Mustang Pocketlite L.W. Nickel/Stainless Steel Finish*** – similar to Mustang Pocketlite, except has nickel finish frame and stainless steel slide. Mfg. 1991-96.

	$800	$700	$550	$450	$375	$325	$300	*$493*

* ***Mustang Pocketlite Teflon Nickel/Stainless*** – similar to Mustang Pocketlite L.W., except has combination of Teflon nickel, stainless steel finish. Mfg. 1997-99.

	$775	$650	$525	$450	$375	$325	$300	*$508*

* ***Mustang Pocketlite L.W. Lady Elite*** – features hard chrome receiver, blue slide with silver painted rollmark, finger extension mag., soft carrying case, limited mfg. 1995-96.

	$775	$650	$525	$450	$375	$325	$300	*$612*

* ***Mustang Pocketlite L.W. Nite Lite .380*** – .380 ACP cal., features bar-dot night sight, Teflon coated alloy receiver with stainless slide, finger extension mag., includes carrying case. Mfg. 1994 only.

	$775	$650	$525	$450	$375	$325	$300	*$577*

MUSTANG POCKETLITE, CURRENT MFG. – .380 ACP cal., SA only, 2 3/4 in. barrel, 7 shot mag., firing pin safety block, brushed stainless steel slide with electroless nickel finished frame, black composite grips with Colt medallions, 12 1/2 oz. New 2012.

MSR $649	$550	$465	$415	$350	$295	$250	$200	

PISTOLS: SEMI-AUTO, DOUBLE ACTION - RECENT MFG.

DOUBLE EAGLE SERIES 90 I & II – 9mm Para. (mfg. 1991 only), .38 Super (mfg. 1991 only), .45 ACP, or 10mm (disc. 1993) cal., double action semi-auto that operates on the Browning/Colt short recoil, pivoting link locking system used by the Govt. Model, 5 in. barrel, matte stainless steel only, 3 dot sighting system or Accro adj. rear sight (disc. 1994), checkered synthetic Xenoy grips, 8 shot mag. (9 shot in 9mm Para. or .38 Super cal.), decocking lever, squared off combat trigger guard, 39 oz. Mfg. 1990-96.

	$850	$650	$500	$430	$375	$315	$270	*$727*

Add $100 for 9mm Para. or .38 Super cal.
Add $20 for 10mm cal.
Add 10% for NIB condition.

The first edition (1,000 mfg. in 1989) on this model did not have a decocking lever - MSR was $916.

* ***Double Eagle Combat Commander*** – .40 S&W (new 1992) or .45 ACP cal., 4 1/4 in. barrel, 8 shot mag., white dot sights, 36 oz. Mfg. 1991-96.

	$850	$650	$500	$430	$375	$315	$270	*$727*

Add 100-200% for X serial number guns.

* ***Double Eagle Officer's Model*** – .45 ACP cal., 3 1/2 in. barrel, 8 shot mag., 35 oz. Mfg. 1991-disc.

	$850	$650	$500	$430	$375	$315	$270	*$727*

* ***Double Eagle Officer's Lightweight Model*** – .45 ACP cal. only, 3 1/2 in. barrel, alloy frame with blue finish only, white dot sights, 25 oz. Mfg. 1991-93.

	$900	$700	$500	$400	$365	$330	$295	*$696*

ALL AMERICAN MODEL 2000 – 9mm Para. cal. only, double action semi-auto, roller-bearing mounted trigger allowing double action only trigger pull every shot, recoil operated rotary action featuring integral locking lugs similar to the military M-16 rifle, hammerless, 4 1/2 in. barrel, matte finished steel slide and polymer receiver, 15 shot mag., 3-dot sighting system, ambidextrous mag. release, black synthetic checkered grips, internal striker block safety, checkered trigger guard and front grip strap, 29 oz. Manufacturing difficulty forced discontinuance and design and tooling were returned to Reed Knight. Mfg. 1991-93.

* ***Model 2000 - Polymer Frame***

	$750	$650	$525	$450	$375	$325	$275	*$575*

Add 10% for NIB condition.

This model could also be converted to a shorter version using a 3 3/4 in. barrel/bushing kit (no tools or other components were needed - $75 retail during 1993 only).

GRADING - PPGS™	100%	98%	95%	90%	80%	70%	60%	LAST MSR

* ***Model 2000 - Aluminum Frame*** – similar to polymer Model 2000, except frame is aluminum, serial numbered RK00001-RK03000 to commemorate the designer (Reed Knight). Mfg. 1993.

	$850	$700	$550	$465	$375	$325	$275	*$575*

Add 10% for NIB condition.

PONY SERIES 90 – .380 ACP cal., double action only, 2 3/4 in. barrel, bobbed hammer, 6 shot mag., stainless construction, brushed finish, fixed sights, black composition grips, 19 oz. Mfg. 1997-1998.

	$725	$650	$550	$450	$350	$300	$275	*$529*

* ***Pony Series 90 Pocketlite Lightweight*** – .380 ACP cal., similar to Pony Series 90, except utilizes aluminum and stainless steel construction, brushed finish, 13 oz. Mfg. 1997-1999.

	$750	$675	$550	$450	$350	$300	$275	*$529*

POCKET NINE – 9mm Para. cal., double action only, 2 3/4 in. barrel, aluminum frame, ultra slim profile, 6 shot mag., matte/brushed stainless steel, wraparound rubber grips, 3-dot sights, 17 oz. Mfg. 1999 only.

	$1,100	$925	$800	$700	$600	$500	$400	*$615*

COLT Z40 – .40 S&W cal., DAO, alloy frame, double column mag., firing pin safety, 3-dot sights, blue finish with black checkered synthetic grips and silver trigger, straight backstrap, marked "Colt Z40" on top of slide, while approx. 750-800 pieces were mfg. 1998-99 by CZ for a Colt subcontract, they were never shipped, and as a result, very few have made it into the U.S. to date from the Czech Republic.

	$800	$750	$700	$600	$550	$525	$500	

NEW AGENT DAO MODEL O – .45 ACP cal., DAO, 3 in. barrel, Series 80 firing pin safety system, hammerless, 7 shot mag., double diamond slim fit grips, black anodized aluminum frame, blue finish, beveled mag. well, snag free trench style sights, front strap serrations, captive recoil spring system. New 2008.

MSR $1,041	$900	$775	$675	$550	$450	$400	$350	

Note: Colt has issued a recall for ser. nos. GT01001 - GT04505 X X due to a problem with the safety and/or guide pad. Improper hardness may cause the safety or guide pad to crack and might not prevent the gun from an accidental firing. Please contact Colt directly if you have one of the pistols - recall@ colt.com.

1991 SERIES GOVERNMENT MODEL O LIGHTWEIGHT – .45 ACP cal., 5 in. barrel, DAO, features black anodized aluminum receiver with blued carbon steel slide, checkered double diamond slim fit grips, 7 shot mag., blue finish, white dot sights. New 2011.

MSR $1,068	$925	$800	$700	$600	$500	$425	$375	

PISTOLS: SEMI-AUTO, .22 CAL. - WOODSMAN SERIES & VARIATIONS

The publisher wishes to once again express his thanks to Major (ret.) Robert J. Rayburn for his continued generous contributions of information regarding the Colt Woodsman Series.

The Colt Woodsman was made for 62 years, and included a multitude of variations/options in models, sights, barrels, grips, markings, etc. Many of the variations are quite scarce and desirable, but generally known only to specialized collectors. The following price guidelines are for standard production models, and only for those specimens in unmodified, factory original condition.

Over 690,000 Woodsmans with variations were mfg. 1915-1977.

Factory engraved and special order Woodsmans are relatively rare and very desirable. Prices can fluctuate greatly, and auctions can sometimes be the only source of supply for these rarely encountered pistols.

Note: 100% "as new" 1st Series Colt Woodsmans with box and accessories are almost always locked up in existing collections and are not sold except when an entire collection is liquidated. Since the demand exceeds the supply, the price of such pristine items has been rising rapidly. The older or more rare versions in such condition can sell for double or even triple the price of a 98% gun. In the listings in this section, 100% means exactly that - absolutely perfect in every way, without a single

GRADING - PPGS™	100%	98%	95%	90%	80%	70%	60%	LAST MSR

blemish, not the slightest trace of blue wear or thinning. Such perfect examples can still be found for some versions. For others, where such condition is rarely, if ever, encountered, market values are too volatile to be listed in the 100% column.

PRE-WOODSMAN – .22 LR cal., 6 5/8 in. barrel. 10 shot mag., blue only, bottom mag. release, checkered wood grips, adj. front and rear sights, this model was officially named "Colt Automatic Pistol, Caliber .22 Target Model", magazine base has 2-line legend "CAL .22" "COLT". Standard velocity ammo. only. Approx. 54,000 mfg. 1915-1927.

$2,200	$1,600	$950	$675	$450	$325	$300	

Add 10% for pencil barrels (1915-1922 mfg. only, ser. nos. below 31000).

BEWARE: Because the early guns were used with corrosive ammo, many of them developed bad bores and have since been refitted with later barrels.

This model was manufactured to use standard velocity ammunition only (not high speed). Colt did offer a conversion kit for high velocity ammunition after the transition to high velocity in 1931.

Woodsmans mfg. between 1915-1922 had a lightweight pencil barrel (approx. serial range 1- 31,000).

The medium barrel was introduced in 1922 and was retained until the 90,000 serial range (approx. mfg. 1922-1934).

WOODSMAN 1ST SERIES – .22 LR cal., 10 shot mag., blue only, bottom mag. release, checkered wood grips, marked "The Woodsman" on receiver, adj. sights, mfg. from 1927-1947, total production was approx. 112,000.

Note: Guns made prior to 1931 were designed for standard velocity .22 LR ammunition only. The new style main spring housing, designed for high velocity ammunition, began appearing at approx. ser. no. 80,000 and was completely phased in by approx. ser. no. 85,000. Later guns, INCLUDING ALL PISTOLS MADE AFTER WWII, were designed for high velocity ammunition.

Between 1934 and 1947 a tapered barrel was standard production (approx. ser. range 90,000- 187,423).

151 factory engraved First Series Woodsmans were manufactured pre-WWII. The breakdown is 126 Target models, 14 Sport models, and 11 Match Target models. Values depend on engraving type/ coverage and original condition.

* ***Woodsman Sport Model*** – 4 1/2 in. barrel, this model was introduced in 1933.

$2,000	$1,600	$1,000	$650	$450	$350	$300	

Add 10% for adj. front sight (available beginning 1937).

Add 50% for medium weight barrel (1933-34 mfg. only), and an additional 50% for semi-circular "half moon" front sight (1933 mfg. only).

The vast majority of this model came with a fixed front sight, rounded at the front and serrated ramp at the rear.

Approx. serial range of the First Series Sport is 86,105-187,423 from 1933 to 1947.

* ***Woodsman Target Model*** – 6 5/8 in. barrel.

$1,800	$1,300	$750	$450	$325	$300	$275	

Note: Colt discontinued the 1st series in 1947. These guns are quite different from the 2nd series started later in 1947. Both the front and rear sights are adjustable.

WOODSMAN 1ST SERIES MATCH TARGET – .22 LR cal. only, 6 5/8 in. heavy barrel, commonly called "Bullseye" Match Target, mfg. 1938-44, production totaled around 16,000. Difficult to find in mint condition. Values listed assume original one-piece extended walnut grips.

$3,500	$2,700	$1,800	$1,100	$950	$900	$850	

In the lower conditions, much of the value derives from the original walnut "Elephant Ear" stocks. The value of the stocks, in excellent original condition, can actually exceed the value of a lower condition gun. The extended plastic stocks, as used on the military version of the Match Target, will fit on any 1st Series Colt Woodsman and are not to be confused with the one piece "Elephant Ear" stocks.

The correct magazine on this model has a 3-line legend "COLT WOODSMAN", "CAL. 22 L.R.", and "MATCH TARGET MOD".

* ***Woodsman 1st Series Match Target "U.S. Property" Marked*** – approx. 4,000 Match Target Woodsmans were sold to the U.S. Army and U.S. Navy during WWII. Most have serial

GRADING - PPGS™	100%	98%	95%	90%	80%	70%	60%	LAST MSR

numbers above MT12500, although some were shipped out of sequence with lower numbers. The wartime guns had elongated plastic stocks and standard blue finish, although some of them are now parkerized as the result of arsenal refinishing or other non-factory modifications. They are marked with either "US PROPERTY" or the ordnance wheel with crossed cannon, as well as the initials of the govt. inspector. Some also have additional markings.

N/A	$2,800	$1,900	$1,200	$925	$750	$575	

Since the military models have two-piece plastic grips, rather than the "Elephant Ear" stocks, the values in the lower condition categories are lower than those for the standard civilian model.

Check parkerized finish carefully for originality on this variation, as some "recent parkerizing" has been observed.

WOODSMAN 2ND SERIES – .22 LR cal. only, slide stop and hold open, push button mag. release on this model is located on the left side of frame, Colt Master rear sight was introduced during 1953, Coltwood plastic grips (mfg. 1947-1950) or brown plastic grips (mfg. 1950-55), total production on all 2nd Series was (not including the Challenger) approx. 146,000, serialization has "S" suffix. Mfg. 1947-1955.

* ***Woodsman 2nd Series Sport Model*** – 4 1/2 in. barrel.

$975	$825	$595	$450	$395	$325	$275	

* ***Woodsman 2nd Series Target Model*** – 6 in. barrel.

$895	$750	$525	$395	$325	$275	$250	

* ***Woodsman 2nd Series Match Target Model*** – this model is not marked Woodsman on the gun. It is marked MATCH TARGET.

4 1/2 in. heavy bbl.	$1,795	$1,500	$950	$650	$475	$450	$425	
6 in. heavy bbl.	$1,395	$1,200	$795	$595	$425	$375	$350	

CHALLENGER MODEL – similar to Woodsman 2nd Series, only with fixed sights, without hold open, and bottom mag. release, plastic grips, 4 1/2 and 6 in. barrels, mfg. 1950-1955 with total production reaching approx. 77,000.

$795	$650	$475	$295	$250	$225	$200	

WOODSMAN 3RD SERIES – .22 LR cal. only, slide stop and hold open, black plastic grips (mfg. 1955-60) or walnut grips (1960-77), 3rd Models can be differentiated from 2nd Models by their bottom mag. release. Total production of all 3rd series Woodsman models (not including the Huntsman or Targetsman) exceeded 100,000, serialization has "S" suffix. Mfg. 1955-1977.

* ***Woodsman 3rd Series Sport Model*** – 4 1/2 in. barrel.

$895	$795	$550	$375	$325	$300	$275	

* ***Woodsman 3rd Series Target Model*** – 6 in. barrel.

$795	$695	$450	$275	$250	$235	$225	

* ***Woodsman 3rd Series Match Target Model*** – 4 1/2 or 6 in. heavy barrel. This model is not marked Woodsman on the gun.

$1,250	$1,150	$795	$495	$395	$375	$325	

Add $200 for a 4 1/2 in. barrel if condition is 95% or better.

HUNTSMAN MODEL – .22 LR cal. only, fixed sights and no hold open, 4 1/2 and 6 in. barrels, black plastic grips to serial number 141094-C; walnut grips after that cutoff. Mfg. 1955-1977 with total production reaching over 100,000.

$750	$595	$450	$275	$225	$200	$195	

The Huntsman is very similar to the Challenger Model, except is built on a 3rd series frame.

* ***Huntsman Model S Master Series*** – approx. 400 Model S Masters were sold in 1983. This was a parts clean-up by Colt, using Huntsman frames leftover from the last days of production. They were equipped with automatic slide stop and Elliason rear sight, gold etching on the slide, and a French fitted walnut case marked "1 of 400". Approx. 285 had straight, non-tapered Huntsman barrel, while the remainder had the tapered

GRADING - PPGS™	100%	98%	95%	90%	80%	70%	60%	LAST MSR

Woodsman Sport barrel with pinned front sight.

Huntsman barrel	$1,600	$995	$600	N/A	N/A	N/A	N/A	
Woodsman barrel	$1,800	$900	$700	N/A	N/A	N/A	N/A	

Above values assume original walnut case included. Values for this model in 98%-60% original condition are hard to compute, as most are mint or new.

TARGETSMAN MODEL – similar to the Huntsman, except has adj. rear sight and thumbrest on left grip, 6 in. barrel only, approx. 65,000 mfg. 1959-1977.

$850	$695	$495	$395	$275	$250	$225	

CADET – .22 LR cal., 4 1/2 in. barrel, stainless steel, 10 shot mag., predecessor to the Colt 22 Model, originally introduced in 1994, fixed sights, this model was disc. by 1995 because of litigation involving the trademarked model name, 33 1/2 oz.

$450	$350	$300	$240	$210	$180	$155	

COLT 22 – .22 LR cal., 4 1/2 in. VR barrel, stainless steel, fixed sights, 10 shot mag., one-piece black Pachmayr rubber grips, 33 1/2 oz. Mfg. 1994-1998.

$425	$300	$250	$195	$165	$140	$120	*$248*

COLT 22 TARGET – .22 LR cal., 6 in. VR barrel with full length grooved sight rib, adj. rear sight, 40 1/2 oz. Mfg. 1995-1999.

$425	$300	$250	$195	$165	$140	$120	*$377*

100%	98%	95%	90%	80%	70%	60%	50%	40%	30%	20%	10%

REVOLVERS: DOUBLE ACTION

Most of the double action revolvers listed can have their original configuration confirmed with a Colt factory letter. To receive a letter, write: COLT ARCHIVE PROPERTIES, LLC, P.O. Box 1868, Hartford, CT, 06144. The research fee for these revolvers is typically either $75 or $100, depending on the model. If they cannot obtain additional information on the variation you request, they will refund $50.

Prices on top condition Colt DAs have continued to rise steadily, particularly for correctly boxed/cased guns. Be aware of ill-matched, wrong, or fake vintage boxes or grips being mated to an unmatched gun. Original boxes and grips will enhance the values of all Colt DAs.

MODEL 1877 (RAINMAKER) – .32 Colt cal., otherwise similar to the Model 1877 Lightning. 300 mfg. from 1877-1909.

$4,800	$3,600	$2,400	$2,200	$1,800	$1,200	$1,075	$925	$850	$775	$675	$575

Subtract approx. 15% for nickel plating.

Ejectorless versions, fitted also with a long, knurled cylinder pin will bring a 10%-15% premium, depending on condition.

Also, an etched barrel will command a 10%-15% over a roll marked barrel, depending on condition.

This model has a fragile mechanism - values are for working guns.

The "Rainmaker" name was used by dealers in period promotions, not by Colt.

MODEL 1877 (LIGHTNING) – .38 Colt cal., 1 1/2, 2, 2 1/2, 3, 3 1/2, 4, 4 1/2, or 6 in. barrels without ejector, 4 1/2, 5, 6, 7, or 7 1/2 in. barrels with ejector, 6 shot double action, long cylinder fluting, blue finish with case hardened frame and hammer, full nickel plating also available. Over 166,000 mfg. from 1877-1909.

$4,000	$3,000	$2,000	$1,700	$1,500	$1,000	$900	$775	$700	$650	$575	$475

Subtract approx. 15% for nickel plating.

Ejectorless versions, fitted also with a long, knurled cylinder pin will bring a 10%-15% premium, depending on condition.

Also, an etched barrel will command a 10%-15% over a roll marked barrel, depending on condition.

This model has a fragile mechanism - values are for working guns.

The "Lightning" and Thunderer names were used by dealers in period promotions, not by Colt.

MODEL 1877 (THUNDERER) – .41 Colt cal. only, otherwise same general specifications as Model 1877 Lightning.

$4,200	$3,200	$2,250	$2,100	$1,675	$1,125	$975	$850	$750	$700	$600	$500

100%	98%	95%	90%	80%	70%	60%	50%	40%	30%	20%	10%

MODEL 1878 DA – .32-20 WCF (scarce), .38 Colt (approx. 40 mfg.), .38-40 WCF, .41 LC (scarce, 308 mfg.), .44 Russian, .44 S&W, .44-40 WCF (Colt Frontier Six Shooter), .45 LC, .450 Eley, .455 Eley, or .476 Eley cal., 2 1/2 (scarce), 3 1/2, or 4 in. barrels without ejector, 4 3/4, 5 1/2, 7 1/2, 8, 8 1/2, 9, 10, or 12 in. with ejector. Mfg. 1878-1905. Over 51,000 made.

$5,775	$5,250	$4,750	$3,750	$3,250	$2,600	$1,750	$1,500	$950	$850	$750	$625

Approximately 80% of production for this model was in .44-40 WCF and .45 LC cals.

This model in .44-40 WCF was called the Colt Frontier Six Shooter, and this inscription is either acid etched or roll marked on the barrel. On the acid etched variation, the first few (approx. 3-500 and some later) .45 cal. guns shipped, especially to B. Kittredge were also acid etched "Omnipotent" and this represents the only non-caliber etching other than CFSS ever done by the Colt factory. An authentic Omnipotent ("All Powerful") will bring about a 30-50% premium over the same gun without the marking, especially in blue.

This model has an action that is weaker than that of the SAA, and should be carefully inspected to make sure the cylinder turns and locks up properly. Since original parts are scarce, at least $500 must be deducted for a non-working action.

Many original 1878 barrels have "found their way" on the front end of a SAA frame since the barrels are interchangable. Because of this, many "original" Model 1878 DAs may have an incorrect and/or later SAA Colt barrel attached. Watch yourself here! Also, scarce calibers should be verified with factory letter.

MODEL 1902/1904 (PHILIPPINE CONSTABULARY) – .45 LC cal., a variation of the Model 1878, except has oversized trigger guard and long trigger, 6 shot standard 1878 type cylinder with long flutes, pinched frame, 6 in. barrel, blue finish, hard rubber grips, many have been arsenal refinished.

* ***1902 Constabulary*** – 5,000 mfg., with a smaller number actually issued by the U.S. Army to the Philippine Constabulary (Police) Force (not to be confused with the Philippine Scouts, which were part of the U.S. Army), markings: "R.A.C." on left side of frame, 1902 date on right side of frame near grips, large "U.S." on right side of frame below cylinder, hard rubber grips, but some examples also show period correct wooden grips, perhaps from confirmed arsenal or Colt reworks.

N/A	N/A	$4,650	$3,650	$2,900	$2,200	$1,900	$1,800	$1,700	$1,600	$1,400	$1,300

Subtract 50% for arsenal or Colt refinish.

* ***1904 Constabulary Purchase*** – rare variation, approx. 50 more revolvers were delivered to the Army in 1904 within the 51,000 ser. no. range, use unknown, but assumed as Constabulary replacements with same overall configuration as 1902 version, last four digits of ser. no. are on the loading gate and cylinder, military inspection marks, wood grips.

Extreme rarity precludes accurate pricing evaluation on this model - only a few have been located.

This is the only model Colt ever sold to the military that was not specially marked by military inspectors for acceptance prior to delivery, so technically is a "contract purchase", not a unique model.

REVOLVERS: DOUBLE ACTION, SWING OUT CYLINDER

Most of the double action revolvers listed can have their original configuration confirmed with a Colt factory letter. To receive a letter, write: COLT ARCHIVE PROPERTIES, LLC, P.O. Box 1868, Hartford, CT, 06144. The research fee for these revolvers is typically either $75 or $100, depending on the model. If they cannot obtain additional information on the variation you request, they will refund $50.

In Oct. of 1999, Colt announced that all double action revolvers would be discontinued, including any custom shop manufacture. After over 120 years of continuous production, the series of swing out double action revolvers finally ended. As a result, interest and prices for this discontinued revolver configuration have increased greatly in recent years, even on recently discontinued models/configurations. For a few years starting in 2002, the Colt Custom Shop produced both the Anaconda and the Python Elite, but both have also since been discontinued.

Prices on top condition Colt DAs have continued to remain strong, particularly for correctly

100%	98%	95%	90%	80%	70%	60%	50%	40%	30%	20%	10%

boxed/cased guns. Pythons, Diamondbacks, Detective Specials, and good condition pre-war DAs have risen dramatically in price. Be aware of ill-matched or wrong vintage boxes or grips being mated to an unmatched gun. Also, reproduction box end labels for Colt revolvers are now being made. But original boxes and grips will enhance the values of all Colt DAs.

MODEL 1889 "NAVY" (NEW NAVY DA, MODEL OF 1889) – .38 Short and Long Colt, and .41 Short and Long Colt cal., 3, 4 1/2, and 6 in. barrel, blue (military and civilian) or nickel (civilian only) finish, wood (U.S.Navy) or hard rubber (civilian) grips with the world "Colt" in oval at top; the first solid frame, swing out cylinder with no visible locking latches (rotates counter-clockwise), sideplate is also on the right-hand side of frame, Colt produced approx. 31,000 mfg. 1889-1894, 1st 5,000 were ordered by U.S. Navy, with some additional orders later in production - hence name. Serial number is on the butt. US Navy versions (6 in. bbl. ONLY, also include Navy markings).

$2,250	$1,850	$1,550	$1,350	$1,050	$850	$700	$600	$500	$425	$350	$300

Add 40% for 3 in. barrel (civilian models only). Subtract $100-$200 for broken hard rubber grips or broken action.

Add 65%-100% for U.S. Navy Contract (ser. no. 1-5,000), U.S.N. on butt (.38 LC cal. only), depending on condition. Beware of fakes.

Note: Nearly all US Navy Military 1889 Navy issues were later converted to 1895 type actions. Unconverted Navy-marked specimens w/o notched cylinders will bring a premium, but must be authenticated by an expert - Fakes and re-assembled guns are common.

US ARMY MODELS 1892, 1894, 1896, 1901, 1903 (DA 38 "NEW ARMY" - US ARMY ISSUED MODELS – The US Army then followed Navy in adopting a modern 38 DA revolver. Based on Navy use, Army model has 2nd set of locking notches added to cylinder. 1892 and later DAs all look similar to 1889 Navy, except with double cylinder notches, double locking bolts, and shorter flutes, more square cyl. release thumb catch. Plain uncheckered wood grips (military models only) All Military models are all cal. 38 only and blue only. US Army military issue models include Model of 1892, Model of 1894, Model of 1896, Model of 1901, and Model of 1903. 1903 and 1901 models were made and survived in greater quantity and so are worth less than earlier models. Most military models have been altered, refinished, reworked or otherwise altered, which reduces value. Technical alterations by the Army itself - such as cylinder-open lock bolt and lanyard rings added later were part of this evolution. Most alterations reduce value, but a few are sought after (similar to finding a correct SAA Artillery model) . Unaltered examples of Models of 1892, 1894 and 1896 bring a premium. US Models 1901 and 1903 are common. Values below are only for US issued specimens marked on butt "US ARMY MODEL OF xxxx"; with original wood military grips, original barrel and with US Army military markings on the butt completely intact.

$1,950	$1,650	$1,050	$650	$500	$400	$300	$275	$250	$225	$195	$175

Add 100% for unaltered Models of 1892 or 1894 (consult expert). Add 20% for Model of 1896.

Subtract 90% for guns with butt markings removed. (very common - It seems a lot of these were "borrowed" from the government, and the butt or entire gun then reblued-usually very poorly.)

Subtract 75% for late factory/armory rebuilt versions of early models. Consult expert sources for details.

Subtract 90% for any barrel length other than 6 in., or for altered/damaged sights, target sights added, etc. All US Army issue models had 6 inch barrels, standard fixed sights, and are .38 caliber only.

MODEL 1892 & 1895 "NEW ARMY & NEW NAVY" - CIVILIAN & US NAVY VERSIONS – similar to 1889 Navy, but double cylinder notches, double locking bolts, and shorter flutes, square cyl. release thumb catch, hard rubber grips, .32-20 WCF cal. (uncommon) added in 1905. Mfg. 1892-1907.

$1,850	$1,650	$1,150	$700	$500	$400	$300	$275	$250	$225	$195	$175

Add $100-$750 for U.S.N. markings, depending on condition.

Add 40% for 3 in. barrel.

Subtract $100-$200 for broken hard rubber grips or broken action.

Models made before 1898 will bring a premium. Late models after about 1903 begin to show transitional details moving towards the later Army Special model. Serial numbers for all New Army

100%	98%	95%	90%	80%	70%	60%	50%	40%	30%	20%	10%

DA & New Navy DA are on the butt, not in the yoke. Numbers on yoke, latch etc. are always assembly numbers. Civilian New Navy grips have "COLT" in oval. Civilian New Army grips have the Rampant Colt.

NEW ARMY & NEW NAVY DA38 models after about 1894:

Much confusion ensues after about 1894 since in commercial production, both "NEW NAVY" civilian & NEW ARMY" civilian arms also have the dual notch system. The only difference between commercial examples was the type of hard rubber grips. "NEW NAVY" grips have only the word COLT, but no image of the rampant colt.

To add confusion, while the US Army continued to contract for special production with wooden grips and serial number markings different from commercial guns, the US NAVY after about 1894 simply purchased batches of specially produced and inspected commercial style guns. These include normal commercial markings and the regular hard rubber "New Navy" grips. Colt then included the Navy inspection markings (tridents or stars at various times) and US Navy markings on the butt. So US Issue Navy guns from about 1894 until 1903 have a commercial serial number in the commercial location on the butt, but are clearly marked as US Navy Models as well. (Because of this similarity to commercial prod'n, US Navy fakes are known to exist. Consult references and note the orientation of US Navy markings).

* ***Models 1892, 1894, 1895, 1896, 1901, 1903*** – these were variations of the Model 1892, military model (.38 Long Colt only) values will approximate those shown above, while civilian models will be approx. 10%-25% less, depending on condition.

OFFICER'S MODEL (FIRST ISSUE) – .38 Spl. or .38 Long Colt cal., 6 in. barrel, cylinder rotates counter-clockwise and sideplate is on right-hand side of frame, adj. front - adj. rear sights, high luster blue, flat-top, last patent date 1901. Mfg. 1904-08.

$1,850	$1,500	$1,250	$950	$775	$625	$550	$495	$395	$325	$275	$225

OFFICER'S MODEL (SECOND ISSUE) – .32 Colt or .38 Spl. cal., 4, 4 1/2, 5, 6, or 7 1/2 in. barrel, cylinder rotates clockwise, high luster blue through 1916, adj. front - adj. rear sights, checkered walnut grips, deep set medallions in grips were standard from 1913-1923. Mfg. 1908-1926. Last patent date July 4, 1905.

$1,750	$1,500	$1,150	$875	$675	$475	$375	$335	$300	$250	$225	$200

Add 100% for .32 Colt cal. in 6 or 7 1/2 in. barrel in .32 Colt cal. (rare).

Add 75% for 4, 4 1/2, or 5 in. barrel.

OFFICER'S MODEL TARGET (THIRD ISSUE) – similar design to the Second Issue, .22 LR cal. was added beginning 1930, heavy barrel was introduced in 1935. Mfg. 1927-1949. Last patent date Oct. 5, 1926.

$1,450	$1,200	$950	$700	$550	$475	$400	$325	$300	$275	$250	$225

Add 10% for .22 LR cal. (mfg. started 1930).

Add 50% for .32 Colt cal. (mfg. 1939-1941, w/heavy barrel, and production estimates are 800-1,500 units).

Add 75% for 4 or 5 in. barrel.

MODEL 1905 MARINE CORPS – .38 Short or Long cal., similar to New Navy Second Issue, except has a round butt, checkered wood grips w/o medallion, and 6 in. barrel only. Mfg. 1905-1909 in approx. ser. no. range 10,001-10,926, about 926 mfg.

$3,250	$3,000	$2,550	$1,850	$1,725	$1,425	$1,250	$1,000	$895	$795	$695	$595

Add 30% for Military issue marked "USMC" on butt (ser. nos. 1-812). Beware of fake USMC markings.

ARMY SPECIAL MODEL – .32-20 WCF, .38 (various), or .41 Colt cal., 4, 4 1/2, 5, and 6 in. barrels, hard rubber grips standard through 1923 - checkered wood with medallions beginning about 1924, blue finish, fixed sights, rounded checkered cylinder release thumb catch, smooth trigger, has heavier frame than New Navy, approx. ser. no. range 291,000-540,000, last patent date on barrel was July 4, 1905. Mfg. 1908-27.

$1,000	$900	$750	$600	$375	$325	$295	$275	$250	$225	$200	$175

Add 35% for nickel finish.

Subtract $50-$100 if hard rubber grips are chipped.

100%	98%	95%	90%	80%	70%	60%	50%	40%	30%	20%	10%

NEW SERVICE MODEL – .38 Spl., .357 Mag., .38-40 WCF, .44-40 WCF, .44 Russian, .44 Spl., .45 ACP, .45 LC, .450 Eley, .455 Eley, or .476 Eley cal., 4, 5, or 6 in. barrels in .357 Mag. and .38 Spl., 4 1/2, 5 1/2, and 7 1/2 in. barrel in all others, blue or nickel finish, bright blue finish was used through circa 1916, originally hard rubber (until approx. late '20s), with later guns having walnut grips with medallions. Mfg. 1898-1942.

Rare cals. (.450 and .476 Eley cals.) and 4 in. barrels will command premiums over values listed below.

Subtract $150 for broken, damaged, or heavily worn grips.

New Service revolvers with smooth bore barrel prices can range $6,500-$10,000+, depending on original condition.

New Service Models marked "NEW SERVICE 45 COLT" in .45 ACP cal. with shorter cylinder for rimmed cartridge are rare. Early models (first type) have flat latches. Later models (second type) have rounded cylinder latches.

Approx. 356,000 Colt New Service revolvers were mfg., but only approx. 122,800 were Commercial variations. 95% were mfg. with blue finish, while 5% were nickel plated (approx. 6,140 revolvers). Colt also mfg. a very limited number (probably less than 10) of New Service revolvers with smooth bores. When encountered, it is important to get a Colt factory letter confirming the smooth bore barrel.

* ***New Service Model Commercial***

$2,800	$2,450	$2,100	$1,800	$1,500	$1,325	$1,050	$900	$775	$675	$500	$425

Add 35% for nickel finish.

Add 40% for factory pearl, ivory or FDL walnut grips, if in perfect condition.

* ***New Service Model 1909 Army Model***

$3,200	$2,800	$2,450	$1,975	$1,650	$1,400	$1,100	$900	$800	$700	$575	$500

* ***New Service Model RNWMP & RCMP Model*** – .45 LC or .455 Eley cal., contract for Royal Canadian Northwest Mounted Police.

$1,995	$1,350	$1,175	$1,000	$925	$850	$775	$680	$590	$510	$435	$375

* ***New Service Model 1909 Navy Model*** – shortest production run of the Model 1909 variations.

$3,500	$3,100	$2,600	$2,150	$1,750	$1,500	$1,100	$900	$800	$725	$650	$525

* ***New Service Model 1909 - USMC***

$4,000	$3,650	$3,200	$2,750	$2,250	$1,875	$1,525	$1,250	$975	$850	$775	$675

* ***New Service Model 1917 Army***

$1,900	$1,600	$1,400	$1,125	$925	$775	$625	$525	$455	$390	$335	$295

* ***New Service Model 1917 Civilian/Commercial (1917 C/CM)*** – .45 ACP cal., 5 1/2 in. barrel only, last patent date is Oct. 5, 1926, checkered walnut grips with medallions, left side of barrel marked "Colt Model 1917 Auto Ctge". Approx. 1,000 mfg. during 1932, serialized 335,000-336,000.

$1,500	$1,275	$1,050	$850	$650	$525	$450	$415	$385	$350	$325	$295

* ***New Service Model 1917 Civilian/Commercial (Parts Model)*** – .38-40 WCF, .44-40 WCF, or .45 LC cal., 4 1/2 or 5 1/2 in. barrel, hard rubber grips, or checkered walnut with medallions, last patent date is July 4, 1905, approx. 1,000 mfg. serialized 336,450-337,500.

$1,375	$1,050	$925	$800	$625	$495	$415	$380	$360	$330	$300	$275

* ***New Service Model Target*** – similar to New Service Model, flat-top frame, hand-honed action and adj. front - adj. rear sights, 6 (scarce) or 7 1/2 in. barrel, square butt, round butt available after 1930, checkered grip straps, checkered walnut grips with medallion after 1913, blue or nickel (scarce) finish. Approx. 3,400 mfg. 1900-1940.

$3,450	$3,300	$2,775	$2,300	$1,850	$1,500	$1,250	$900	$750	$635	$550	$460

Add 40% - 60% for 6 in. barrel, depending on original condition.

Add 25% for flat latch "Old Models" with original high polish finish.

Approx. 1,000 were mfg. in .45 LC, 960 in .455 Eley, 700 in .44 Russian, 500 in .44 Spl., and 80 in .45 ACP cal.

100%	98%	95%	90%	80%	70%	60%	50%	40%	30%	20%	10%

* ***New Service Model Shooting Master*** – various cals. from 38 Spl. through .45 LC, 6 in. barrel, checkered walnut grips with Colt Medallion, machined grip straps, trigger, hammer, and ejector rod head, round or square butt, approx. 3,500 mfg. in ser. no. range 333,000-350,000.

» **New Service Model Shooting Master .38 Spl.** – approx. 2,500 mfg.

$1,950	$1,850	$1,650	$1,250	$1,000	$850	$750	$650	$550	$475	$400	$375

» **New Service Model Shooting Master .357 Mag.** – approx. 500 mfg.

$2,700	$2,500	$2,300	$1,950	$1,700	$1,475	$1,300	$1,100	$995	$850	$750	$650

» **New Service Model Shooting Master .45 ACP or .45 LC cals.** – approx. 156 mfg. in .45 LC and 250 mfg. in .45 ACP cal.

N/A	N/A	$3,850	$3,425	$3,050	$2,500	$2,050	$1,675	$1,350	$1,000	$750	$600

» **New Service Model Shooting Master .44 Spl. cal.** – approx. 94 mfg.

N/A	N/A	$4,600	$4,050	$3,500	$3,000	$2,500	$2,000	$1,575	$1,250	$1,000	$850

The Shooting Master could be ordered with a square butt after 1933.

OFFICIAL POLICE PRE-WAR – .32-20 WCF (disc. 1942), .38-200 (British), .41 Long (disc. 1930), .38 Spl., or .22 LR (introduced 1930 - 4 or 6 in. barrel only, 4 in. scarce) cal., blue finish, 6 shot, round (very scarce) or square butt, 2, 4, 5, or 6 in. barrels, checkered walnut grips, fixed sights, last patent date on barrel was Oct. 5, 1926. Mfg. 1927-1946.

$950	$850	$550	$425	$365	$325	$285	$250	$225	$200	$185	$165

Add 100% for round butt with factory verified letter.
Add 15% for nickel finish.
Add 20% for .22 LR cal.

OFFICIAL POLICE POST-WAR – .22 LR or .38 Spl. cal., 2, 4, 5, or 6 in. barrel, Coltwood plastic grips 1947-1954 - checkered walnut thereafter, fixed sights, no patent dates on barrel. Mfg. 1947-69.

$850	$700	$525	$400	$335	$275	$215	$195	$175	$165	$145	$125

Add 15% for nickel finish. Add 35% for .22 LR cal.

The 2 in. barrel in .38 Spl. cal. is scarce. .22 LR cal. was available with 4 or 6 in. barrel only.

MARSHAL MODEL – .38 Spl. cal., 2 (less common) or 4 in. barrel, round butt, differentiated by "M" suffix and "COLT MARSHAL" on barrel, about 2,500 mfg. 1954-1956 in approx. ser. no. range 833350-M through 845320-M.

$1,950	$1,650	$1,250	$900	$650	$500	$375	$325	$285	$260	$225	$200

Add 60% for 2 in. barrel. Add 50% for nickel finish.

COMMANDO MODEL – .38 Spl. cal., 2 in. (less common), 4 in. (common), or 6 in. (rare) barrel, should have plastic grips, parkerized finish, about 50,000 mfg. 1942-1945, 32 oz., marked "COLT COMMANDO" on barrel, last patent date on barrel was Oct. 5, 1926.

$1,900	$1,650	$1,400	$1,175	$950	$800	$675	$525	$450	$350	$300	$275

Add 15% for 2 in. barrel.

OFFICIAL POLICE MKIII – .38 Spl. cal., 4, 5, or 6 in. barrels, no patent dates on barrel. Mfg. 1969-75.

* ***Official Police MKIII Blue finish***

$550	$500	$450	$375	$285	$250	$225	$200	$185	$170	$150	$125

* ***Official Police MKIII Nickel finish***

$600	$500	$450	$375	$285	$250	$225	$200	$185	$170	$150	$125

METROPOLITAN MK III – .38 Spl. cal., similar to Official Police, except heavier 4 in. barrel only, blue finish. Mfg. 1969-72.

$625	$525	$425	$350	$275	$250	$225	$210	$190	$175	$165	$155

OFFICER'S MODEL SPECIAL (FOURTH ISSUE) – .22 LR or .38 Spl. cal., 6 in. barrel, blue, similar to Third Issue, only heavier non-tapered barrel, new style hammer and "Coltmaster Sight", checkered plastic grips, no patent dates on barrel. Mfg. 1949-52.

$1,025	$925	$825	$650	$525	$425	$375	$325	$275	$250	$225	$195

Add $75 for .22 LR cal.

100%	98%	95%	90%	80%	70%	60%	50%	40%	30%	20%	10%

OFFICER'S MODEL MATCH (FIFTH ISSUE) – .22 LR, .22 WMR (approx. 850 mfg.), or .38 Spl. cal., 6 in. barrel, single (rare) or double action, tapered heavy barrel, nickel finish is scarce in this model, wide spur hammer, Accro sight, large target grips (walnut). Mfg. 1953-1969.

$950	$900	$800	$775	$650	$500	$400	$350	$300	$275	$250	$225

Add $75 for .22 LR cal.

* ***Officer's Model Match (Fifth Issue) .22 Mag.*** – .22 WMR cal., approx. 850 mfg.

$1,900	$1,800	$1,600	$1,550	$1,300	$1,000	$800	$700	$600	$550	$500	$450

* ***Officer's Model Match Single Action only*** – limited mfg., must have accompanying factory letter.

$1,325	$1,200	$995	$925	$850	$775	$700	$650	$600	$550	$475	$425

OFFICER'S MODEL MATCH MK III (SIXTH ISSUE) – .38 Spl. cal. only, 6 in. shrouded VR barrel, wide spur hammer, Accro sights, target grips. 496 mfg. 1969-1971 only.

$1,850	$1,475	$1,350	$1,100	$950	$775	$700	$650	$600	$550	$475	$425

NEW POCKET – .32 Short and LC, or .32 Colt New Police cal., 2 1/2, 3 1/2, 5, or 6 in. barrel, first modern swing out DA, rubber grips, blue or nickel finish, round butt, last patent date on barrel was Nov. 6, 1888. Mfg. 1895-1905.

$1,350	$1,100	$850	$725	$525	$400	$300	$250	$215	$190	$170	$150

Subtract $75-$100 for chipped hard rubber grips (commonly found on this model).

POCKET POSITIVE (FIRST ISSUE) – similar to New Pocket, except has round butt and positive lock feature, also chambered for .32 Colt, .32 S&W, or .32 Colt New Police cal., last patent date on barrel was July 4, 1905. Mfg. 1905-27.

$1,250	$950	$700	$550	$425	$325	$295	$265	$235	$210	$185	$165

Add 15%-20% for nickel finish.

Add 15% for 90%+ condition early transitional guns that are double marked with "NEW POCKET" on frame.

Subtract $75-$100 for chipped hard rubber grips (commonly found on this model).

POCKET POSITIVE (SECOND ISSUE) – similar to Pocket Positive First Issue, except available in 2 in. barrel, stippled and matted top strap, last patent date on barrel was Oct. 5, 1926. Mfg. 1927-1940.

$1,250	$950	$700	$550	$425	$325	$295	$265	$235	$210	$185	$165

Add 15%-20% for nickel finish.

Add 15%-20% for 2 in. barrel.

Subtract $75-$100 for chipped hard rubber grips (commonly found on this model).

NEW POLICE – .32 Colt and .32 Colt New Police cal., 2 1/2, 4, and 6 in. barrels, fixed sights, same frame as New Pocket, except larger square butt gripstraps, rubber grips, last patent date on barrel was Nov. 6, 1888. Mfg. 1896-1907.

$1,250	$950	$750	$525	$400	$300	$225	$200	$175	$160	$150	$145

Add 25% for nickel finish.

Subtract $25-$50 for chipped hard rubber grips (commonly found on this model).

NEW POLICE TARGET – .32 Colt cal., 6 in. barrel, blue, late models use New Police frame, but include transistional improvements from later Police Positive Target Model (First Issue), last patent date on barrel was Nov. 6, 1888. Approx. 5,000 mfg. 1897-1907.

$1,850	$1,650	$1,100	$975	$725	$525	$475	$400	$350	$300	$275	$250

POLICE POSITIVE (FIRST ISSUE) – .32 Colt, .32 New Police, .38 New Police, or .38 S&W cal., 2 1/2 in. (.32 cal., only), 4, 5, or 6 in. barrel, improved "positive lock" version of the New Police, hard rubber grips standard through 1923, square butt, checkered walnut grips became standard 1924, denoted by 1905 last patent date and smooth top strap. Mfg. 1907-27.

$800	$650	$550	$350	$275	$250	$225	$200	$185	$170	$160	$150

Add 15%-20% for nickel finish.

Add 10% for 90%+ condition early transitional guns that are double marked with "NEW POLICE" on frame.

Subtract $75-$100 for chipped grips.

100%	98%	95%	90%	80%	70%	60%	50%	40%	30%	20%	10%

POLICE POSITIVE (SECOND ISSUE) – similar to Police Positive First Issue, except has 1926 last patent date, serrated top strap, and slightly heavier frame, walnut grips standard. Mfg. 1928-1947.

$850	$750	$525	$425	$350	$300	$275	$250	$225	$195	$175	$160

Add 10% for .38 cal.

POLICE POSITIVE TARGET MODEL (FIRST ISSUE, MODEL "G") – .22 LR, .22 WRF, .32 Colt, or .32 New Police cal., 6 in. barrel, blue, adj. sight, hard rubber grips standard through 1923, checkered walnut grips thereafter, last patent date on barrel was July 4, 1905, 22 oz. Mfg. 1907-1925.

$1,300	$1,100	$850	$575	$475	$425	$395	$375	$350	$325	$295	$275

Add 40% for .32 cal.

POLICE POSITIVE TARGET MODEL (SECOND ISSUE, MODEL "C") – similar to First Issue, except has slightly heavier frame and a last patent date of Oct. 5, 1926, blue finish, but a few were also mfg. in nickel, 26 oz. Mfg. 1926-41.

$1,200	$1,000	$775	$575	$475	$425	$395	$375	$350	$300	$270	$250

Add 40% for .32 cal.

Add 100% for nickel - extremely rare - must be verified by factory letter.

POLICE POSITIVE SPECIAL (FIRST ISSUE) – .32-20 WCF, .32 New Police, .38 New Police, or .38 Spl. cal., 4, 5, or 6 in. barrels, has a square butt and longer frame and cylinder to handle .38 Special and .32-20 WCF, fixed sights, frame longer to permit longer cylinder, denoted by 1905 last patent date on top of barrel, longer frame and smooth top strap, rubber grips. Mfg. 1907-27.

$800	$650	$450	$325	$300	$275	$250	$225	$200	$185	$175	$165

POLICE POSITIVE SPECIAL (SECOND ISSUE) – similar to Police Postitive Special (First Issue), except has 1926 last patent date on top of barrel, wood grips only, smooth (early mfg.) or checkered (later mfg.) trigger, and serrated top strap. Mfg. 1928-46.

$800	$650	$450	$325	$300	$275	$250	$225	$200	$185	$175	$165

CAMP PERRY MODEL – .22 LR cal., 8 in. (less common) or 10 in., Officer's Model frame modified to accept a flat single shot chamber. The model name was stamped on the left side of the chamber, the only single shot Colt on a revolver frame, last patent date on barrel was Oct. 5, 1926. 2,488 mfg. 1926-1941.

$2,400	$1,950	$1,650	$1,100	$900	$775	$715	$645	$575	$495	$425	$365

Add 35% for 8 in. barrel.

BANKER'S SPECIAL – 2 in. barrel, blue, square butt standard through 1933, round butt standard 1934-40, last patent date on barrel was Oct. 5, 1926. Mfg. 1926-40.

* ***Banker's Special .38 cal.*** – available in .38 Colt Police Positive (New Police) or .38 S&W cal.

$1,750	$1,250	$900	$700	$550	$425	$375	$275	$235	$205	$185	$165

Add 45% for nickel finish.

* ***Banker's Special .22 LR cal.***

$3,200	$2,500	$1,850	$1,650	$1,100	$750	$650	$550	$475	$425	$385	$355

Add 30%-50% for nickel finish, depending on original condition.

COURIER – .22 S/L/LR or .32 New Police (S&W) cal., double action, 6 shot, 3 in. barrel. Approx. 3,053 mfg. 1953-56.

$1,300	$1,100	$950	$750	$550	$475	$425	$395	$350	$325	$295	$260

Add 10% for .22 cal.

Even though fewer .22 cal. Couriers were mfg. than Banker's Specials, the Banker's Specials are still more desirable, as they are of pre-war quality, and are less frequently encountered in 95-100% condition.

Some .32 New Police (S&W) cal. models can be found with alloy or steel cylinders.

AIRCREWMAN – .38 Spl. cal., double action, aluminum frame and cylinder, 2 in. barrel, 11 oz., fixed sights, checkered walnut grips overlapping at top of frame, inset with silver Air Force medallions, mfg. 1951 mostly.

$4,000	$3,500	$2,750	$2,100	$1,700	$1,350	$1,075	$950	$850	$750	$675	$595

100%	98%	95%	90%	80%	70%	60%	50%	40%	30%	20%	10%

Approx. 1,200 mfg. within ser. no. range 2,900LW-7,775LW. Most were ordered destroyed. Perhaps less than 25 have survived.

BORDER PATROL (FIRST ISSUE) – .38 Spl. cal., double action, 6 shot, 4 in. heavy barrel, should have plastic grips, 400 mfg. during 1952 only in 823,000 ser. no. range.

$3000	$2,500	$1,500	$1,400	$1,125	$995	$875	$775	$675	$595	$525	$475

This model is built on the Official Police Model frame.

DETECTIVE SPECIAL PRE-WAR (FIRST ISSUE) – .38 Spl. cal., 2 in. barrel, blue, wood grips, square butt standard through 1932, round butt standard beginning 1933, last patent date on barrel was Oct. 5, 1926. Mfg. 1927-1946.

$2,150	$1,850	$1,625	$1,400	$1,200	$900	$795	$575	$400	$300	$250	$225

Add 20% for nickel finish.

Add 20% for square butt (early production only). Must be verified by factory letter and by ejector rod, since Police Positive Special (Second Issue) looks like a Detective Special.

DETECTIVE SPECIAL POST-WAR (SECOND ISSUE) – .32 NP, .38 NP, or .38 Spl. cal., 2 or 3 (scarce) in. barrel, can be distinguished from First Issue by 1/8 in. deeper frame (measured from hammer to bottom of frame behind trigger guard), plastic grips 1947-1954, wood grips 1955-1965, wraparound wood grips 1966-1972. Mfg. 1947-1972.

$1,350	$1,150	$950	$800	$550	$300	$250	$200	$185	$170	$160	$150

Add 20% for nickel finish.

Add 15% for 3 in. barrel.

There are four variations of the model - a pre-war design with post-war ser. nos., a "Transition" variation (late 1947-1952, with blue pre-war frame, late 1948-1952 have Coltwood grips), polished long grip frame (mfg. 1953-1966, round grip frame), and short grip frame (mfg. 1966-1972, walnut grip panels).

COBRA (FIRST ISSUE) – .22 LR, .32 Colt N.P., .38 Colt N.P., or .38 Spl. cal., first issue, 2, 3, or 4 (square butt on early model, later models had round butt) in. barrel, blue or nickel finish, similar to Detective Special, only alloy frame and available in .22 LR, very early guns had plastic grips with silver medallions, changed to plastic w/o medallions, and finally changed to wood grips. Mfg. 1950-72.

$950	$800	$650	$600	$495	$265	$225	$190	$160	$150	$140	$120

Add 20% for .22 LR cal.

Add 20% for nickel finish.

Add 15% for .38 cal. with 3 in. barrel.

The .22 LR cal. is available in 3 in. barrel only.

AGENT (FIRST ISSUE) – .38 Spl. cal., similar to Cobra first issue, except shorter grip frame. Mfg. 1962-1972.

$800	$700	$500	$325	$275	$235	$200	$190	$180	$170	$160	$150

AGENT L.W. (SECOND ISSUE) – .38 Spl. cal., similar to First Issue, except shrouded ejector rod, matte finish since 1982. Mfg. 1973-1991.

$625	$525	$425	$325	$275	$230	$200	$190	$180	$170	$160	$150

Last MSR was $260.

COBRA (SECOND ISSUE) – .38 Spl. cal., similar to Cobra first issue, except shrouded ejector rod, some were shipped with factory installed hammer shroud. Mfg. 1973-81.

$675	$625	$500	$400	$295	$275	$250	$210	$195	$165	$155	$150

DETECTIVE SPECIAL (THIRD ISSUE) – .38 Spl. cal., similar to Second Issue, shrouded ejector rod, 2 or 3 (scarce) in. barrel, integral long serrated ramp front sight, wraparound wood grips. Mfg. 1973-1986.

$975	$850	$750	$550	$475	$385	$350	$295	$200	$195	$185	$175

Last MSR was $429.

Add $50 for nickel.

Add 15% for 3 in. barrel.

Also available with class A engraving - add $600 if in 98% condition or better.

100%	98%	95%	90%	80%	70%	60%	50%	40%	30%	20%	10%

COMMANDO SPECIAL – .38 Spl. cal., similar to Detective Special with steel frame, shrouded ejector rod, 2 in. barrel, matte parkerized finish, rubber grips. Mfg. 1984-86.

$450	$395	$350	$295	$265	$235	$200	$190	$180	$170	$160	$150

Last MSR was $260.

POLICE POSITIVE SPECIAL (THIRD ISSUE) – .38 Spl. cal., similar to Detective Special Second Issue, except 4, 5, or 6 in. barrel. Mfg. 1947-76.

$550	$450	$350	$295	$250	$225	$200	$190	$180	$170	$160	$150

POLICE POSITIVE SPECIAL (FOURTH ISSUE) – .38 Spl. cal., shrouded ejector rod housing, steel frame, blue or nickel finish. Mfg. 1977-78.

$450	$395	$350	$275	$235	$210	$200	$190	$180	$170	$160	$150

Last MSR was $400.

Add 15% for nickel finish.

GRADING - PPGS™	100%	98%	95%	90%	80%	70%	60%	LAST MSR

POLICE POSITIVE MK V (FIFTH ISSUE) – .38 Spl. cal., full shrouded 4 in. barrel, steel frame, blue finish, rubber grips. Mfg. 1994-95.

	$450	$375	$325	$250	$195	$180	$165	

100%	98%	95%	90%	80%	70%	60%	50%	40%	30%	20%	10%

VIPER MODEL – .38 Spl. cal., similar to Police Positive Special (Fourth Issue), alloy frame, 4 in. barrel, shrouded ejector rod housing. Mfg. 1977-1984.

$1,495	$1,375	$1,125	$1,000	$875	$750	$625	$495	$375	$300	$225	$175

Add 25% for nickel finish.

DIAMONDBACK .22 CAL. – .22 LR or .22 WMR (rare) cal., 2 1/2 (scarce in .22 LR), 4, or 6 in. VR barrel, blue or nickel (more desireable) finish, adj. sights, steel frame, checkered walnut grips. Mfg. 1966-1991.

Add 20% for nickel finish. Some guns were produced in electroless nickel.

Note: .22 WMR cal. is rare, and values are difficult to accurately ascertain. Buyer beware - fakes do exist! Diamondbacks have risen in value so much that higher value guns based upon finishes, barrel length, etc. should be accompanied by a factory letter verifying details.

* ***Diamondback .22 cal. Blue w/2 1/2 In. Barrel***

$2,700	$2,500	$2,300	$1,950	$1,700	$1,475	$1,300	$1,100	$995	$850	$750	$650

A factory letter is now advisable on this configuration.

* ***Diamondback .22 cal. Nickel w/2 1/2 In. Barrel***

N/A	N/A	$3,500	$3,100	$2,600	$2,150	$1,500	$1,150	$1,000	$895	$775	$725

A factory letter is now advisable on this configuration.

* ***Diamondback .22 cal. Blue w/4 in. Barrel***

$1,750	$1,450	$1,150	$925	$625	$500	$425	N/A	N/A	N/A	N/A	N/A

* ***Diamondback .22 cal. Nickel w/4 in. Barrel***

$2,500	$2,300	$1,950	$1,700	$1,475	$1,300	$1,100	$995	$850	$750	$650	$475

* ***Diamondback .22 cal. Blue w/6 in. Barrel***

$1,850	$1,650	$1,100	$975	$725	$525	$475	$400	$350	$300	$275	$250

* ***Diamondback .22 cal., Nickel w/6 in. Barrel*** – approx. 2,200 mfg. circa 1979.

$2,650	$2,350	$2,150	$1,850	$1,600	$1,300	$1,000	$850	$700	$575	$500	$450

DIAMONDBACK .38 SPL. – .38 Spl. cal., 2 1/2 (scarce), 4, or 6 in. VR barrel, blue or nickel finish, adj. sights, steel frame, checkered walnut grips. Mfg. 1966-1991.

$1,250	$950	$700	$550	$425	$325	$295	$265	$235	$210	$185	$165

Last MSR was $461.

Add 20% for nickel finish.

* ***Diamondback .38 Spl. 2 1/2 in. Barrel***

$1,500	$1,275	$1,050	$850	$650	$525	$450	$415	$385	$350	$325	$295

100%	98%	95%	90%	80%	70%	60%	50%	40%	30%	20%	10%

Add 20% for nickel finish.

COLT .357 MAG – 4 in. or 6 in. barrel, heavy frame, Accro rear sight, blue or nickel finish, checkered walnut grips. Mfg. 1953-61.

Add 35% for nickel.

*** Colt .357 Mag. Standard hammer**

$900	$800	$725	$625	$475	$450	$350	$285	$270	$255	$240	$220

*** Colt .357 Mag. Wide hammer w/target grips**

$925	$825	$750	$650	$500	$475	$350	$300	$250	$225	$215	$200

In 1962, this model was absorbed into the Trooper line.

TROOPER – .22 LR (4 in. only, scarce), .357 Mag., or .38 Spl. cal., 4 or 6 in. barrel, blue or nickel finish, quick draw ramp front sight, adj. rear sight, checkered walnut grips. Mfg. 1953-69.

Add $75-$125 for .22 LR cal. (4 in. barrel only), depending on condition.
Add 25% for nickel finish.
Subtract 10% for .38 Spl. cal.

*** Trooper Standard hammer**

$800	$700	$625	$600	$500	$400	$325	$275	$225	$200	$185	$170

*** Trooper Wide hammer and target grips**

$825	$725	$650	$625	$525	$400	$325	$275	$225	$200	$185	$170

GRADING - PPGS™	100%	98%	95%	90%	80%	70%	60%	LAST MSR

TROOPER MK III – .22 LR, .22 WMR, .357 Mag., or .38 Spl. cal., 4, 6, or 8 in. solid rib barrel, adj. rear sight, walnut target grips, redesigned lock work to reduce amount of hand fitting needed on earlier Trooper versions. Mfg. 1969-1983.

Blue finish	$550	$475	$325	$250	$225	$200	$175	
Nickel finish	$600	$500	$350	$265	$235	$215	$185	

Add 50% for .22 WMR cal.

TROOPER MK V – .357 Mag. cal. only, 4, 6, or 8 in. barrel, adj. rear sight, walnut target grips, improved version of Mark III action, vent. rib barrel, a few made with solid rib, redesigned 1982. Disc. 1986.

Blue finish	$550	$375	$300	$265	$235	$215	$200	*$396*
Nickel finish	$575	$425	$325	$300	$265	$240	$225	*$362*

LAWMAN SKY MARSHAL – .38 Spl. cal., 2 in. barrel, experimental revolver with a replaceable plastic cylinder preloaded with plastic bullets, blue finish, checkered walnut grips, this model was designed to be carried on airliners by Federal Marshals during the 1970s.

	$925	$850	$775	$700	$625	$550	$475	

LAWMAN MK III – .357 Mag. cal., 2 in. and 4 in. barrel, unshrouded or shrouded ejector rod for 2 in. barrel, fixed sights, checkered walnut grips. Mfg. 1969-83.

Blue finish	$450	$375	$300	$180	$170	$160	$150	
Nickel finish	$500	$400	$325	$250	$200	$180	$170	

LAWMAN MK V – .357 Mag. cal., 2 or 4 in. barrel, shrouded ejector rod for 2 in. barrel, fixed sights, checkered walnut grips, improved version of MK III action. Mfg. 1984 and 1991 only.

Blue finish	$500	$450	$375	$325	$180	$165	$150	*$309*
Nickel finish	$550	$475	$400	$350	$250	$200	$180	*$328*

BORDER PATROL (SECOND ISSUE) – .357 Mag. cal., 4 in. heavy barrel, similar to Trooper Mark III frame, less polishing of frame. Limited mfg. 1970-75.

*** Border Patrol Blue Finish** – 5,356 mfg.

	$850	$700	$500	$300	$235	$200	$180	

GRADING - PPGS™	100%	98%	95%	90%	80%	70%	60%	LAST MSR

* ***Border Patrol Nickel Finish*** – 1,152 mfg.

	$950	$800	$600	$500	$400	$325	$275	

PEACEKEEPER – .357 Mag. cal. only, similar to Trooper MK V, 4 or 6 in. barrel, matte blue finish, rubber combat grips, adj. rear sight, about 42 oz. Mfg. 1985-1989.

	$575	$450	$325	$225	$195	$180	$165	*$330*

BOA – .357 Mag. cal., deep blue polish, full length ejector shroud with Mark V action, 600 each mfg. in 4 and 6 in. barrel lengths. Entire production run was purchased by Lew Horton Distributing Co., Inc. located in Southboro, MA. 1985 retail was $525.

	$1,600	$1,350	$1,100	$925	$800	$700	$600	

* ***Boa Set*** – 100 sets mfg. including 4 and 6 in. barrels with fully shrouded ejector rod housing, consecutive serial numbers, cases were supplied by Lew Horton. 1985 retail was $1,200.

	$4,500	$3,850	$3,000	$2,000	$1,740	$1,495	$1,215	

DETECTIVE SPECIAL (FOURTH ISSUE) – .38 Spl. cal., 6 shot, 2 in. barrel, steel frame, blue finish, black composition grips with gold medallions, 21 oz. Mfg. 1993-1995.

	$600	$500	$400	$375	$300	$200	$180	*$400*

* ***Bobbed Detective Special*** – .38 Spl. cal., double action only with bobbed hammer, front night sight, honed action, choice of hard chrome or standard blue finish. Mfg. 1994-1995.

	$725	$600	$500	$375	$300	$250	$200	*$599*

Add $30 for hard chrome finish.

COLT .38 SF-VI – .38 Spl. cal., 6 shot, 2 or 4 in. barrel, transfer bar safety, choice of matte (2 in.), bright polished (4 in.), or black (4 in.) finish, stainless steel, regular or bobbed (4 in. barrel only) hammer, fixed sights, black composition combat grips, 21 oz. Mfg. 1995-96.

	$550	$450	$350	$250	$200	$175	$155	*$408*

* ***Colt .38 Special Lady*** – while advertised during 1996, this model had very limited mfg.

COLT .38 DSII – .357 Mag. (new 1998) or .38 Spl. cal., 6 shot, 2 in. barrel, stainless steel, service hammer, rubber combat style checkered grips, 21 oz. Mfg. 1997-98.

	$600	$500	$400	$250	$210	$180	$155	*$435*

This model featured a redesigned trigger fire control group and is capable of shooting .38+P ammo.

COLT MAGNUM CARRY – .357 Mag. cal., 6 shot, 2 in. barrel, transfer bar safety, satin stainless steel, wraparound rubber grips with finger grooves, ramp front sight, 21 oz. Mfg. 1999 only.

	$595	$475	$360	$295	$235	$205	$175	*$460*

COMBAT COBRA – .357 Mag. cal., 2 1/2 in. barrel, special edition for Lew Horton with "CC" prefix and stainless steel construction. Mfg. 1986-1987.

	$1,200	$1,050	$900	$800	$675	$525	$395	

KING COBRA – .357 Mag. cal., blue metal, black neoprene round butt grips, 2 1/2 (new 1990), 4, or 6 in. solid rib barrel only, white outline rear sight, approx. 42 oz. (4 in. barrel). Mfg. 1986-92.

	$725	$625	$575	$475	$300	$250	$210	*$410*

KING COBRA STAINLESS – .357 Mag. cal., stainless steel construction, black neoprene round butt grips, 2 (mfg. 1988-94), 4, 6, or 8 (mfg. 1990-94) in. solid rib barrel, white outline rear sight, approx. 36 oz. (2 1/2 in. barrel). Mfg. late 1986-92, production resumed 1994, disc. 1998.

	$825	$725	$650	$550	$475	$400	$325	*$485*

* ***King Cobra "Ultimate" Bright Stainless*** – similar to King Cobra, except for bright stainless steel, 2 1/2 (new 1990), 4, 6, or 8 (new 1991) in. barrel. Mfg. 1988-92.

	$995	$875	$745	$675	$550	$450	$350	*$470*

PYTHON – .357 Mag. cal., 2 1/2 (disc. 1994), 3 (a.k.a Combat Python, disc., very scarce), 4, 6, or 8 in. barrel with vent rib, Royal Blue finish, fully shrouded ejector rod, adj. rear sight, checkered walnut grips (prior to 1991), rubber Hogue monogrips (2 1/2 or 4 in. barrel), or

GRADING - PPGS™	100%	98%	95%	90%	80%	70%	60%	LAST MSR

rubber target (6 or 8 in. barrel) grips, 38-48 oz. Mfg. 1955-96.

As one of the few hand fitted revolvers ever produced, Python values have risen dramatically in recent years. Smaller details of condition now make greater differences in value. Don't pay for claims of "mint" and "unfired" condition, unless the gun has been inspected by a competent Colt dealer/collector. Over time, the value distinctions group the Python into 4 overall groups by period. These four groups are as follows: Early (circa 1950's) production with full checkered grips and high polish blue, other early pre-suffix serial numbers up to about 1969, other production up to about 1990, and finally, 1990's production. In general, the older the Python, the higher the value.

* ***Python Blue or Royal Blue Finish (Mfg. 1955-1969)*** – first letter prefix or suffix used in ser. no., began in mid-1969 with the letter "E".

	100%	98%	95%	90%	80%	70%	60%	LAST MSR
	$2,100	**$1,975**	**$1,525**	**$1,200**	**$975**	**$700**	**$600**	

Add 20% for NIB condition.
Add 50% for very early production (circa 1950s) with checkered, non-varnished grips.
Add 50% for 3 in. barrel - purchase only with factory letter.

* ***Python Blue or Royal Blue Finish (Mfg. circa 1970-1996)***

	100%	98%	95%	90%	80%	70%	60%	LAST MSR
	$1,800	**$1,500**	**$1,100**	**$675**	**$625**	**$575**	**$450**	***$815***

Add 20% for NIB condition.
Add 50% for 3 in. barrel with factory letter.
Beware of loose 3 in. barrel models sold by GPC and others during the 1990s.

The standard Python was manufactured 1955-1996, and 1997-recent production is through the Colt Custom Shop by special order only (see Python Elite listing).

During 2001-2002, Colt shipped some Pythons to dealers with prices in $1,100 - $1,200 retail range. These guns had a slightly different (rougher) line checkering pattern on the cylinder release and hammer parts.

There were also a few Pythons mfg. in .256 Win. Mag. (circa 1961), .41 Mag., and .44 Spl. cals. While the .22 LR and the .22 WMR (.22 Mag.) were advertised in earlier factory catalogs, they were never mass-produced - only a few prototypes exist. At least one known example of a .22 cal. Python was found at an auction, but it had only a special factory barrel sleeve for photographic purposes, and was not a shootable gun. The amount of premium on these cals. depends on how serious (and deep-pocketed) the Python collector is.

A California distributor special ordered a quantity of the first 3 in. barreled Pythons, which at the time were not available directly from the factory. This variation is called the California Combat Python, with the words "CALIFORNIA COMBAT" underneath the "PYTHON 357" marking on the left side of the barrel. Later Colt made a special limited edition of 500 Combat Pythons, so marked for Lew Horton. These Lew Horton 3 inch Pythons are referred to as "Combat Pythons". A small number of the California Combat Pythons were mfg. in nickel finish, and are very rare.

* ***Python Nickel finish*** – available in polished or satin nickel, disc. 1985.

	100%	98%	95%	90%	80%	70%	60%	LAST MSR
	$1,900	**$1,500**	**$1,175**	**$725**	**$625**	**$525**	**$425**	
3 in. barrel w/nickel	**$7,000**	**$6,000**	**$5,000**	**$4,000**	**$3,250**	**$2,500**	**$1,750**	***$693***

Add 20% for NIB condition (except for 3 in. nickel).
Add 35% for satin nickel finish instead of polished nickel.

Satin nickel finish is so designated on original boxes as "Royal Coltguard" or "E NICK" (electroless nickel).

A Colt factory letter for the 3 in. barrel is mandatory if purchasing.

* ***Python Stainless Steel*** – stainless steel construction, matte or high polish finish, neoprene target or combat stocks, 2 1/2 (disc. 1994), 4, 6, or 8 (new 1989) in. barrel. Mfg. 1983-96.

	100%	98%	95%	90%	80%	70%	60%	LAST MSR
	$1,900	**$1,800**	**$1,700**	**$1,100**	**$900**	**$825**	**$750**	***$904***

Add 20% for NIB condition.
Add 100% for 2.5 inch ported barrel, Lew Horton edition of 1995.
Add 25% for Python Silver Snake (Factory Model #13060ESS), from Colt Custom Shop, 1982, laser etched.

Later production of the 6 in. barrel includes neoprene target stocks.

GRADING - PPGS™	100%	98%	95%	90%	80%	70%	60%	LAST MSR

* ***Python "Ultimate" Bright Stainless Steel*** – deluxe, highly polished stainless model, 2 1/2 (disc.), 4, 6, or 8 in. VR barrel. Mfg. 1985-disc.

$2,000	$1,900	$1,600	$1,100	$900	$775	$700	*$935*

Add 20% for NIB condition.

PYTHON ELITE – .357 Mag. cal., 4 or 6 in. VR barrel, choice of Royal Blue or stainless steel, adj. rear sight, rubber service style (disc.) or smooth walnut finger groove grips, later production roll-marked "Python Elite" on barrel, 38 or 43 1/2 oz. New 1997, disc. 1998, reintroduced 1999, again during 2002-2006.

$2,100	$1,850	$1,725	$1,150	$900	$825	$750	*$1,150*

Add 10% for NIB condition.

This model was available by custom order only through the Colt Custom Shop.

Some early production models have Colt-Elliason rear sights, and recent production used Colt Accro sights. Some guns were shipped with both wood and hard rubber grips until 1999.

* ***Python Elite Stainless*** – similar to Python Elite, except is stainless steel. Mfg. 1997-99, reintroduced 2002-2006.

$2,000	$1,900	$1,600	$1,100	$900	$775	$700	*$1,150*

Add 10% for NIB condition.

This model was available by custom order only through the Colt Custom Shop.

ULTIMATE PYTHON – .357 Mag. cal., specially tuned by the custom shop, supplied with both Colt-Elliason target and Accro white outline sighting systems, walnut and rubber grips also included, choice of Colt Royal Blue or Ultimate Stainless finish, 6 in. barrel only. Mfg. 1991-93.

$2,300	$2,050	$1,925	$1,350	$1,100	$750	$675	*$1,140*

Add $120 for Ultimate Stainless Model.
Add 10% for NIB condition.

Guns were delivered with 2 sets of Colt Python factory grips. Prices assume guns include both sets and accessories at time of resale.

PYTHON HUNTER – .357 Mag. cal., 8 in. barrel, includes Leupold 2x scope, Halliburton aluminum case, and accessories. Mfg. 1981 only.

$3,200	$2,750	$2,000	$1,950	$1,850	$1,800	$1,500	*$995*

Values assume undamaged Halliburton case, scope and accessories including plastic cartridge box.

PYTHON SILHOUETTE – .357 Mag. cal., 8 in. barrel, includes Leupold 2x scope, similar to Python Hunter, except barrel is roll marked with Silhouette name and scope position has been moved rearward, black luggage type case. Mfg. circa 1983.

$3,300	$2,850	$2,000	$1,950	$1,850	$1,800	$1,500

Values assume undamaged black luggage case, scope and accessories.

PYTHON .38 SPECIAL – 8 in. barrel, blue (3,489 mfg.) or nickel (251 mfg.) finish. Disc.

$1,800	$1,600	$1,350	$1,100	$800	$675	$525

Add 20% for NIB condition.
Add 50% for nickel finish.

PYTHON TEN POINTER – .357 Mag. cal., 8 in. barrel, includes 3x Burris scope, wooden grips, extra set of neoprene composite grips, carrying case. Disc.

$2,600	$2,200	$2,000	$1,700	$1,500	$1,100	$1,000

Add 20% for NIB condition.
Deduct 15% if original case is missing.

GRIZZLY – .357 Mag. cal., 6 in. barrel, matte stainless finish, approx. 500 mfg.

$1,900	$1,800	$1,700	$1,100	$1,000	$800	$700

Add 20% for NIB condition.

This model was mfg. by the Colt Custom Shop.

GRADING - PPGS™	100%	98%	95%	90%	80%	70%	60%	LAST MSR

WHITETAILER – .357 Mag. cal., 8 in. barrel, 2x matte stainless finish, aluminum hard shell case.

	$2,200	$2,000	$1,950	$1,800	$1,500	$1,100	$1,000	

Add 10% for NIB condition.
Deduct 15% if original factory case is missing.

* ***Whitetailer II*** – similar to Whitetailer, except has high polish finish, includes Burris 1.5-4x scope and Colt soft case.

	$2,200	$2,000	$1,950	$1,800	$1,500	$1,100	$1,000	

Add 10% for NIB condition.

KODIAK – .44 Mag. cal., 4 or 6 in. Mag-na-ported barrel with non-fluted cylinder, stainless steel, Pachmayr grips, built on Anaconda frame, "Colt Kodiak .44 Magnum" with outline of bear's footprint on left side of barrel, ser. nos. start with CKA. Approx. 2,000 mfg. in 1993 by Custom Shop.

	$2,500	$2,200	$1,900	$1,600	$1,350	$1,050	$800	

ANACONDA – .44 Mag. or .45 LC (mfg. 1992-99) cal., 4 (new 1991), 5 (not factory cataloged, special edition only, mfg. 1998), 6, or 8 in. VR barrel, transfer bar safety system, 6 shot, choice of matte (disc. 2003), Realtree Grey camo (.44 Mag. with 8 in. barrel only, mfg. 1996 only) finish, or stainless steel, black neoprene combat grips with Colt medallion, red ramp front sight, full length ejector rod housing, white outline rear adj. sight, approx. 47-59 oz. Mfg. 1990-99, reintroduced 2002-2006.

* ***Anaconda 2002-2006 Mfg.*** – from 2002-2006, the Anaconda was only available through the Colt Custom Shop.

	$1,050	$850	$600	$475	$350	$250	$215	*$1,000*

Add $50 for 8 in. barrel.

* ***Anaconda 1990-99 Mfg.*** – standard production, not mfg. by the Colt Custom Shop.

	$1,200	$1,050	$900	$800	$650	$550	$425	

Add 10% for .45 LC cal.

* ***Anaconda with scope*** – .44 Mag. cal. only, 8 in. barrel, Realtree Grey camo finish on gun and scope. Mfg. 1996 only.

	$1,595	$1,375	$1,075	$850	$575	$480	$410	*$999*

* ***Anaconda Hunter*** – .44 Mag. cal., supplied with Leupold 2x scope, carrying case, cleaning accessories, and both walnut and rubber grips, 8 in. barrel only. Mfg. 1991-93.

	$1,595	$1,375	$1,075	$850	$575	$480	$410	*$1,200*

* ***Anaconda Custom Ported*** – .44 Mag. cal., features 6 (disc.) or 8 in. Mag-na-ported barrel and Colt-Elliason rear sight, contoured trigger, and Pachmayr rubber grips, brushed stainless steel. Mfg. 1992-93, re-released 1995-96, again in 2002-2003.

	$1,150	$900	$700	$500	$425	$375	$325	*$1,050*

* ***Anaconda 1st Edition*** – .44 Mag. cal., Ultimate Stainless finish, special rollmark on left side of barrel reads "Colt Anaconda First Edition", with aluminum carrying case, ser. no. range MM00001-MM01000, 1,000 mfg. 1990 only.

	$1,750	$1,450	$1,150	$925	$625	$500	$425	

RIFLES/CARBINES: PRE-1904

A Colt letter of provenance for the Colteer, Courier, and Stagecoach models listed below is $75.00 per gun. The charge for Lightning models listed below is $100 per gun (limited records). Colt-Burgess model factory letters are also available at $100 per gun.

The author wishes to express his thanks to Mr. Wilmer Kellogg and Mr. Michael Kelly for providing much of the information on Colt-Burgess and Lightning rifles in this section.

FIRST MODEL RING LEVER – .34, .36, .38, .40, or .44 cal., 8 or 10 shot revolving cylinder, 32 in. octagon barrel, walnut stock, no forend, 200 mfg., percussion. Mfg. 1837-1838.

100%	98%	95%	90%	80%	70%	60%	50%	40%	30%	20%	10%

* ***First Model Ring Lever Standard Model***

N/A	N/A	N/A	$38,000	$28,500	$22,000	$17,000	$14,000	$11,500	$9,500	$8,000	$7,000

* ***First Model Ring Lever Improved Model*** – attached loading lever.

N/A	N/A	N/A	$41,500	$30,150	$23,250	$18,000	$15,000	$12,500	$10,500	$9,000	$8,000

SECOND MODEL RING LEVER – similar to First Model, w/o top strap over cylinder, .44 caliber only, percussion, 500 mfg., 1838-1841.

* ***Second Model Ring Lever Standard Model***

N/A	N/A	N/A	$34,000	$25,000	$17,500	$13,500	$11,500	$9,280	$7,700	$6,800	$6,150

* ***Second Model Ring Lever Improved Model***

N/A	N/A	N/A	$35,250	$26,500	$18,250	$13,800	$11,700	$9,400	$7,825	$6,890	$6,225

MODEL 1839 CARBINE – .52 smooth bore cal., 6 shot cylinder, 24 in. barrel, exposed hammer for cocking, blue, walnut stock, percussion, approx. 950 mfg., 1838-1841.

* ***Model 1839 Carbine Early Model*** – no loading lever.

N/A	N/A	N/A	$41,000	$39,000	$29,500	$22,500	$18,000	$15,250	$12,000	$9,850	$8,250

* ***Model 1839 Carbine Standard Model***

N/A	N/A	N/A	$34,500	$31,500	$23,000	$17,500	$14,000	$11,750	$9,500	$8,000	$7,100

MODEL 1855 REVOLVING – .36, .44, or .56 cal., various barrel lengths and stock styles, 5 or 6 shot cylinder, blue with walnut buttstock, no forend, percussion. Mfg. 1856-1864.

* ***Model 1855 Revolving 1/2 Stock Sporter*** – 24, 27, or 30 in. barrel, approx. 1,500 mfg.

N/A	N/A	N/A	$12,000	$9,500	$8,350	$7,500	$7,000	$6,500	$6,000	$5,600	$5,250

* ***Model 1855 Revolving Full Stock Sporter*** – 21, 24, 27, 30, or 31 in. barrel, approx. 2,000 mfg.

N/A	N/A	N/A	$14,000	$11,775	$9,650	$8,750	$8,000	$7,450	$7,000	$6,600	$6,250

* ***Model 1855 Revolving Military Model, U.S.*** – martially marked, 21-37 in. barrel, 9,310 mfg.

N/A	N/A	N/A	$18,000	$15,150	$12,400	$11,000	$10,300	$9,550	$8,950	$8,400	$7,975

* ***Model 1855 Revolving .36 Caliber Carbine Model*** – 15, 18, or 21 in. barrel, 4,400 mfg.

N/A	N/A	N/A	$17,650	$14,950	$12,160	$11,025	$10,100	$9,375	$8,775	$8,250	$7,800

* ***Model 1855 Revolving .56 Caliber Artillery Carbine*** – 5 shot, 21 in. barrel with bayonet lug and forestock, approx. 64 mfg.

N/A	N/A	N/A	$19,500	$17,000	$14,000	$11,375	$10,350	$9,600	$8,900	$8,450	$8,000

* ***Model 1855 Revolving Shotgun Model*** – 16 gauge or .60 cal., 10 ga. or .75 cal., smooth bore, 27, 30, 33, or 36 in. barrels, 1,100 mfg.

N/A	N/A	N/A	$13,250	$11,500	$9,500	$8,500	$7,750	$7,250	$6,800	$6,500	$6,100

BERDAN – .42 bottle-necked CF cal., breechloading, approx. 30,000 mfg. 1866-circa 1870. Scarce since most were sent to Russia and have Russian barrel markings, approx. 50-100 are Hartford marked.

* ***Berdan Rifle*** – 32 1/2 in. barrel, approx. 10 lbs.

N/A	N/A	N/A	$6,300	$5,300	$4,300	$3,800	$3,550	$3,300	$2,300	$1,650	$1,300

* ***Berdan Carbine*** – half stock, 18 1/4 in. barrel, approx. 50 mfg., both Russian and Hartford marked.

N/A	N/A	N/A	$8,600	$7,900	$7,025	$6,400	$5,800	$5,050	$4,250	$3,575	$3,050

MODEL 1861 MUSKET – .58 cal., percussion, muzzle loader, 40 in. barrel, with 3 bands, white metal parts, white walnut stock. 75,000 mfg., 1861-65.

N/A	N/A	N/A	$7,300	$5,300	$4,300	$3,800	$3,550	$3,300	$2,300	$1,650	$1,300

COLT-BURGESS LEVER ACTION – .44-40 WCF cal., 25 1/2 in. barrel, 15 shot tube mag., blue with case hardened lever and hammer, walnut stock. 6,403 mfg., 1883-1885.

N/A	N/A	N/A	$12,300	$9,300	$6,300	$5,300	$4,300	$3,800	$3,300	$2,800	$1,800

COLT-BURGESS CARBINE – similar to Rifle, with 20 in. barrel.

N/A	N/A	N/A	$18,300	$15,300	$12,300	$10,300	$8,300	$6,800	$5,300	$3,800	$2,800

100%	98%	95%	90%	80%	70%	60%	50%	40%	30%	20%	10%

COLT-BURGESS LIGHT CARBINE – lightened version of Carbine.

100%	98%	95%	90%	80%	70%	60%	50%	40%	30%	20%	10%
N/A	N/A	N/A	$21,500	$18,500	$15,500	$13,500	$11,500	$9,500	$7,500	$4,500	$3,500

LIGHTNING SLIDE ACTION RIFLE (CLMR) - SMALL FRAME – .22 S or L cal., 24 in. barrel, open sights, walnut straight stock, round or octagon barrel, approx. 90,000 mfg. 1887-1904.

100%	98%	95%	90%	80%	70%	60%	50%	40%	30%	20%	10%
N/A	N/A	N/A	$6,000	$4,500	$4,000	$3,500	$3,000	$2,700	$2,250	$1,700	$1,000

Add 25% for deluxe model.

LIGHTNING SLIDE ACTION RIFLE (CLMR) - MEDIUM FRAME – .32 CLMR (.32-20 WCF), .38 CLMR (.38-40 WCF), or .44 CLMR (.44-40 WCF) cal., similar to Small Frame, except with 26 in. barrel and larger frame. Approx. 90,000 mfg. 1884-1902.

100%	98%	95%	90%	80%	70%	60%	50%	40%	30%	20%	10%
N/A	N/A	N/A	$6,500	$5,500	$4,750	$4,250	$3,500	$3,000	$2,500	$2,000	$1,700

Add 25% for deluxe model.

23 Medium Frame rifles were shipped to A.G. Spalding and Brothers during 1897, a major sporting goods supplier located in Chicago. Most of these guns are factory engraved, and were probably used for display during the Chicago Exposition. These deluxe rifles represent some of the finest Colt rifles ever manufactured.

LIGHTNING CARBINE MEDIUM FRAME – similar to Medium Frame Rifle, with 20 in. barrel.

100%	98%	95%	90%	80%	70%	60%	50%	40%	30%	20%	10%
N/A	N/A	N/A	$8,500	$7,500	$6,500	$5,500	$4,500	$4,000	$3,500	$3,000	$2,500

LIGHTNING BABY CARBINE MEDIUM FRAME – lightened version of Medium Frame Carbine, one pound lighter.

100%	98%	95%	90%	80%	70%	60%	50%	40%	30%	20%	10%
N/A	N/A	N/A	$9,500	$7,500	$6,500	$5,500	$4,500	$4,000	$3,500	$3,000	$2,500

Add 50% for .50-95 Express cal.

LIGHTNING SLIDE ACTION RIFLE (CLMR) - LARGE FRAME – .38-56 WCF, .40-60 Marlin (most common), .45-60 WCF (rarest), .45-85 Marlin, or .50-95 Express (rare) cal., large version of previously described Lightnings, approx. 4,600 mfg. 1887-1894.

100%	98%	95%	90%	80%	70%	60%	50%	40%	30%	20%	10%
N/A	N/A	N/A	$11,500	$9,500	$8,000	$7,000	$5,500	$4,500	$3,500	$2,500	$2,000

Add 25% for .50-95 Express cal.

Add 25% for deluxe model. Add 25% for .45-60 cal. (approx. 8% mfg. in this cal.).

There may be a gap in the serial range of this model from ser. no. 2435 to 4444.

LIGHTNING CARBINE LARGE FRAME – similar to Large Frame Rifle, 22 in. barrel.

100%	98%	95%	90%	80%	70%	60%	50%	40%	30%	20%	10%
N/A	N/A	N/A	$13,700	$10,700	$8,700	$6,700	$5,700	$4,700	$3,950	$3,700	$3,200

LIGHTNING BABY CARBINE LARGE FRAME – lightened version of Large Frame Carbine, one pound lighter.

100%	98%	95%	90%	80%	70%	60%	50%	40%	30%	20%	10%
N/A	N/A	N/A	$13,700	$10,700	$8,700	$6,700	$5,700	$4,700	$3,950	$3,700	$3,200

Add 50% for .50-95 Express cal.

LIGHTNING MILITARY STYLE MUSKET – similar to Medium Frame Rifle, with bayonet lug.

100%	98%	95%	90%	80%	70%	60%	50%	40%	30%	20%	10%
N/A	N/A	N/A	N/A	N/A	N/A	$5,500	$4,500	$3,500	$2,500	$2,000	$1,500

Approximately 250 of these rifles with 27 in. round barrels, swivels, and carbine buttstocks, in serial ranges 50,000 and 51,000 were shipped to Costa Rica.

LIGHTNING SAN FRANCISCO POLICE – round barrel Medium Frame Rifle, with S.F. Police numbers.

100%	98%	95%	90%	80%	70%	60%	50%	40%	30%	20%	10%
N/A	$10,500	$9,250	$7,750	$5,500	$4,500	$4,000	$3,750	$3,500	$2,500	$1,850	$1,500

DOUBLE RIFLE SxS – various cals. in the .45 range, hammers, very limited production between 1878-1880. Most guns were owned by friends of Caldwell Colt - Sam Colt's son, the original designer. Colt Double Rifles are extremely rare and desirable, and should be examined carefully.

Prices typically range between $80,000-$110,000, if all original.

GRADING - PPGS™	100%	98%	95%	90%	80%	70%	60%	LAST MSR

COLTEER 1-22 – .22 LR or .22 WMR cal., single shot bolt action, 20, 22, or 24 (.22 WMR only, w/o sights) in. round barrel, adj. rear sight (20 or 22 in. barrel), plain walnut stock. Approx. 50,000 mfg. 1957-66.

GRADING - PPGS™	100%	98%	95%	90%	80%	70%	60%	LAST MSR
	$400	$325	$265	$225	$200	$175	$150	

Add 10% for .22 WMR cal.

GRADING - PPGS™	100%	98%	95%	90%	80%	70%	60%	LAST MSR

STAGECOACH – .22 LR cal., semi-auto, 16 1/2 in. barrel, 13 shot mag., deluxe walnut stock, saddle ring w/leather thong, roll-engraved hold-up scene. Over 25,000 mfg. 1965-mid 1970s.

	$400	$325	$265	$225	$200	$175	$150	

Subtract 5% if wood and finish are scratched in front of the barrel/forearm band.
Subtract 5-10% if w/o the front sight hood.
Subtract 10% if gold color is missing in stagecoach scene.

This model has a soft aluminum alloy painted receiver which was very easily scratched. It is quite common to find these guns in 80 to 85% condition with very little market interest. It is becoming common place to find these guns with the receiver repainted. There is a limited market interest in guns that are 98% condition and better. On the models that have the band around the barrel and forearm, it is common to see the wood and finish scratched where the band has been slid forward.

COLTEER – .22 LR cal., similar to Stagecoach, except 19 3/8 in. barrel, 15 shot mag., no engraving and plain walnut stock. Over 25,000 mfg. 1965-mid 1970s.

	$350	$325	$265	$225	$200	$175	$150	

Subtract 5% if wood and finish are scratched in front of the barrel/forearm band.
Subtract 5-10% if w/o the front sight hood.

This model has a soft aluminum alloy painted receiver which was very easily scratched. It is quite common to find these guns in 80 to 85% condition with very little market interest. It is becoming common place to find these guns with the receiver repainted. There is a limited market interest in guns that are 98% condition and better. On the models that have the band around the barrel and forearm, it is common to see the wood and finish scratched where the band has been slid forward.

COURIER – similar to Colteer semi-auto, except pistol-grip stock and enlarged forearm. Mfg. 1970-mid-1970s.

	$400	$325	$265	$225	$200	$175	$150	

Subtract 5% if wood and finish are scratched in front of the barrel/forearm band.
Subtract 5-10% if w/o the front sight hood.

This model has a soft aluminum alloy painted receiver which was very easily scratched. It is quite common to find these guns in 80 to 85% condition with very little market interest. It is becoming common place to find these guns with the receiver repainted. There is a limited market interest in guns that are 98% condition and better. On the models that have the band around the barrel and forearm, it is common to see the wood and finish scratched where the band has been slid forward.

RIFLES: BOLT ACTION, CENTERFIRE

COLT "57" – .243 Win. or .30-06 cal., FN Mauser action, mfg. by Jefferson Mfg. Co. in N. Haven, CT during 1957, approx. 5,000 mfg. starting at ser. no. 1, checkered American Monte Carlo walnut stock, rear aperture and wraparound front sight, drilled and tapped for scope.

	$695	$650	$600	$550	$500	$450	$400	

This model was also available in a deluxe version with deluxe hand checkered walnut stock - add 15%.

COLTSMAN STANDARD RIFLE – .223 Rem., .243 Win., .264 Win. Mag., .30-06, .300 Win. Mag., or .308 Win. cal., mfg. by Kodiak, Mauser or Sako action, 22 or 24 (.300 Win. Mag.) in. barrel, 5 or 6 shot mag. Approx. 10,000 (both models) mfg. 1958-66.

	$495	$450	$425	$400	$350	$325	$300	

COLTSMAN CUSTOM RIFLE – deluxe variation including deluxe walnut stock with skipline checkering and rosewood forearm cap.

	$695	$650	$600	$550	$500	$450	$400	

COLT SAUER RIFLE (STANDARD ACTION) – .25-06 Rem., .270 Win., or .30-06 cal., non-rotating bolt action, manufactured in Germany by J. P. Sauer & Sohn, 24 in. barrel, 4 shot detachable mag., no sights, checkered walnut stock with rosewood forend tip and pistol grip cap, recoil pad. Mfg. 1974-1985.

	$2,050	$1,700	$1,400	$1,250	$995	$825	$675	*$1,257*

Add 25% for .25-06 Rem. cal.

GRADING - PPGS™	100%	98%	95%	90%	80%	70%	60%	LAST MSR

COLT SAUER SHORT ACTION – similar to the standard except in .22-250 Rem., .243 Win., or .308 Win. cal. Mfg. 1976-85.

	$2,300	$1,900	$1,575	$1,375	$1,100	$850	$725	*$1,257*

Add 25% for .308 Win. cal.

COLT SAUER MAGNUM – similar to the standard except in 7mm Rem. Mag., .300 Win. Mag., or .300 Weatherby Mag. cal. Mfg. 1974-1985.

	$2,500	$2,100	$1,825	$1,500	$1,150	$900	$800	*$1,300*

COLT SAUER GRADE III – similar to Grade IV, except scroll engraved nitride/nickel receiver w/o game scenes, "Colt" stamped on flat knob.

	$4,100	$3,650	$3,150	$2,650	$2,200	$1,700	$1,500	

Add 10% for Magnum cals.

COLT SAUER GRADE IV – similar to the Magnum except has silver receiver, each caliber featured a different engraved animal.

	$4,825	$4,300	$3,800	$3,250	$2,750	$2,225	$2,000	

Add 10% for Magnum cals.

COLT SAUER GRAND ALASKAN – heavier version in .375 H&H cal., adj. sights. Mfg. 1978-1985.

	$2,625	$2,375	$1,975	$1,625	$1,375	$1,250	$1,050	

COLT SAUER GRAND AFRICAN – .458 Win. Mag. cal., 4 round capacity, 9 lb. 12 oz. Mfg. 1974-1985.

	$2,625	$2,375	$1,975	$1,625	$1,375	$1,250	$1,050	*$1,400*

COLT LIGHT RIFLE – .243 Win., .260 Rem., .270 Win., .280 Rem., .25-06 Rem., .30-06, .308 Win., 7x57mm, .300 Win. Mag., 7mm-08, or 7mm Rem. Mag. cal., short or long action, matte black synthetic stock, matte metal finish, adj. trigger, 3 position side-swing safety, approx. 5.4 lbs. in short action, manufactured by Saco Defense in the U.S. New 2000-disc.

	$675	$550	$500	$450	$400	$350	$295	*$779*

COLT PRECISION RIFLE (M2012SA308) – .308 Win. cal., tactical configuration featuring 22 in. spiral fluted stainless steel barrel with muzzle brake, skeletonized adj. rear stock, pistol grip, vent. aluminum handguard with 2/3 length Picatinny rail, 5 shot mag., black finish. Mfg. by Cooper Firearms of Montana. New 2013.

MSR $3,795	$3,300	$2,950	$2,600	$2,300	$2,000	$1,850	$1,625	

RIFLES: SINGLE SHOT, CENTERFIRE

COLT-SHARPS STANDARD OR DELUXE RIFLE – .17 Rem., .222 Rem. (one known), .22-250 Rem., .243 Win., .25-06 Rem., .270 Win., 7mm Rem. Mag., .30-06, .375 H&H (two known), .50-70 Govt. (two known) cal., 26 or 28 in. heavy (rare) barrel, Sharps falling block action with Timken roller bearings, high-gloss bluing, Canjar set trigger, deluxe checkered Monte Carlo walnut stock and forearm with cheekpiece and choice of beavertail or standard forearm, engraved cartridge trap door in stock and triggerguard, wood case with accessories, all guns were shipped with a Leupold VARI-X II 3-9x40mm scope with a special scope mount, supplied with either a full length wood and leather case (most desirable) or a green fiberglass case. Approx. 502 were mfg. 1970-1977 serial numbered CS000-CS502.

	$4,500	$3,995	$3,495	$2,900	$2,400	$1,900	$1,500	

Add 10% for 28 in. heavy barrel.
Subtract 10% for missing case and accessories or Leupold scope and mount.
Subtract 10% for Standard model (approx. 50 mfg. without Monte Carlo stock, cartridge trap, engraving, or case) - serial range starts at CS2000.

Above values are for the standard calibers .22-250 Rem., .243 Win., .25-06 Rem., .30-06, or 7mm Rem. Mag. with case, accessories, and Leupold scope and mount.

GRADING - PPGS™	100%	98%	95%	90%	80%	70%	60%	LAST MSR

DRILLINGS

COLT SAUER DRILLING – 12 ga./.30-06, 16 ga./.30-06 (rare), or .243 Win. cal., 25 in. barrels, engraved receiver, 8 lbs. Disc. 1985.

	$4,300	$3,600	$3,100	$2,675	$2,200	$1,800	$1,400	*$4,228*

RIFLES: SEMI-AUTO, CENTERFIRE, AR-15 & VARIATIONS

The AR-15 rifle and variations are the civilian versions of the U.S. armed forces M-16 model, which was initially ordered by the U.S. Army in 1963. Colt's obtained the exclusive manufacturing and marketing rights to the AR-15 from the Armalite division of the Fairchild Engine and Airplane Corporation in 1961.

Factory Colt AR-15 receivers are stamped with the model names only (Sporter II, Government Model, Colt Carbine, Sporter Match H-Bar, Match Target), but are not stamped with the model numbers (R6500, R6550, R6521, MT6430, CR6724). Because of this, if an AR-15 rifle/carbine does not have its original box, the only way to determine whether the gun is pre-ban or not is to look at the serial number and see if the configuration matches the features listed below within the two pre-ban subcategories.

AR-15 production included transition models, which were made up of obsolete and old stock parts. These transition models include: blue label box models having large front takedown pins, no internal sear block, 20 in. barrel models having bayonet lugs, misstamped nomenclature on receivers, or green label bolt assemblies.

Rifling twists on the Colt AR-15 have changed throughout the years, and barrel twists are stamped at the end of the barrel on top. They started with a 1:12 in. twist, changed to a 1:7 in. twist (to match with the new, longer .223 Rem./5.56mm SS109-type bullet), and finally changed to a 1:9 in. twist in combination with 1:7 in. twist models as a compromise for bullets in the 50-68 grain range. Current mfg. AR-15s/Match Targets have rifling twists/turns incorporated into the model descriptions.

Colt's never sold pre-ban lower receivers individually. It only sold completely assembled rifles.

A Colt letter of provenance for the following AR-15 models is $100 per gun.

AR-15, Pre-Ban, 1963-1989 Mfg. w/Green Label Box

Common features of 1963-1989 mfg. AR-15s are bayonet lug, flash hider, large front takedown pin, no internal sear block, and w/o reinforcement around the magazine release button.

AR-15 boxes during this period of mfg. had a green label with serial number affixed on a white sticker. Box is taped in two places with brown masking tape. NIB consists of the rifle with barrel stick down the barrel, plastic muzzle cap on flash hider, factory tag hanging from front sight post, rifle in plastic bag with ser. no. on white sticker attached to bag, cardboard insert, accessory bag with two 20 round mags., manual, sling, and cleaning brushes. Cleaning rods are in separate bag.

Pre-ban parts rifles are rifles, which are not assembled in their proper factory configuration. Counterfeit pre-ban rifles are rifles using post-ban receivers and assembled into a pre-ban configuration (it is a felony to assemble or alter a post-ban rifle into a pre-ban configuration).

Add $100 for NIB condition.

Add $300 for early green label box models with reinforced lower receiver.

SP-1 (R6000) – .223 Rem. cal., original Colt paramilitary configuration without forward bolt assist, 20 in. barrel with 1:12 in. twist, identifiable by the triangular shaped handguards/forearm, no case deflector, A1 sights, finishes included parkerizing and electroless nickel, approx. 6 3/4 lbs. Ser. no. range SP00001-SP5301 (1976). Mfg. 1963-1984.

	$2,100	$1,975	$1,850	$1,725	$1,600	$1,500	$1,200	

Add 40%-60% for mint original models with early two and three digit serial numbers.

Pre-ban serialization is ser. no. SP360,200 and lower.

Early SP-1s were packaged differently than later standard green box label guns.

* ***SP-1 Carbine (R6001)*** – similar to SP-1, except has 16 in. barrel, ribbed handguards, collapsible buttstock, high gloss finish.

	$2,900	$2,700	$2,425	$2,225	$2,075	$1,900	$1,650	

GRADING - PPGS™	100%	98%	95%	90%	80%	70%	60%	LAST MSR

Mint original condition models with early two and three digit serial numbers are selling in the $3,250 - $3,500 range.

Pre-ban serialization is ser. no. SP360200 and lower.

Early SP-1s were packaged differently than later standard green box label guns.

SPORTER II (R6500) – .223 Rem. cal., various configurations, receiver stamped "Sporter II", 20 in. barrel, 1:7 twist, A1 sights and forward assist, disc.

$1,875	$1,650	$1,475	$1,300	$1,175	$1,075	$995	

Serial numbers SP360200 and below are pre-ban.

* ***Sporter II Carbine (R6420)*** – similar to Sporter II, except has 16 in. barrel, A1 sights and collapsible buttstock.

$2,225	$2,000	$1,850	$1,675	$1,525	$1,425	$1,275	

Serial numbers SP360200 and below are pre-ban.

GOVERNMENT MODEL (R6550) – .223 Rem. cal., receiver is stamped Government Model, 20 in. barrel with 1:7 in. twist and bayonet lug, A2 sights, forward assist and brass deflector, very desirable because this model has the closest configurations to what the U.S. military is currently using.

$2,250	$2,100	$1,950	$1,800	$1,650	$1,400	$1,200	

In 1987, Colt replaced the AR-15A2 Sporter II Rifle with the AR-15A2 Govt. Model. This new model has the 800 meter rear sighting system housed in the receiver's carrying handle (similar to the M-16 A2).

Serial numbers GS008000 and below are pre-ban.

* ***Government Model (6550K)*** – similar to R6550, except does not have bayonet lug, originally supplied with .22 L.R. cal. conversion kit.

$2,050	$1,900	$1,750	$1,600	$1,450	$1,250	$1,100	

Subtract $300 w/o conversion kit.

Serial numbers GS008000 and below are pre-ban.

* ***Government Model (R6550CC)*** – similar to R6550, except has Z-Cote tiger striped camo finish, very scarce (watch for cheap imitation paint jobs).

$3,500	$3,350	$3,100	$2,800	$2,600	$2,400	$2,000	

Serial numbers GS008000 and below are pre-ban.

H-BAR MODEL (R6600) – H-Bar model with 20 in heavy barrel, 1:7 twist, forward assist, A2 sights, brass deflector, 8 lbs. New 1986.

$2,050	$1,900	$1,750	$1,600	$1,400	$1,200	$1,000	

Serial numbers SP360200 and below are pre-ban.

* ***H-Bar (R6600K)*** – similar to R6600, except has no bayonet lug, supplied with .22 LR cal. conversion kit.

$1,975	$1,825	$1,675	$1,525	$1,375	$1,225	$1,100	

Subtract $300 if w/o conversion kit.

Serial numbers SP360200 and below are pre-ban.

* ***Delta H-Bar (R6600DH)*** – similar to R6600, except has 3-9x rubber armored scope, removable cheekpiece, adj. scope mount, and black leather sling, test range selected for its accuracy, aluminum transport case. Mfg. 1987-1991.

$2,300	$2,150	$1,925	$1,775	$1,575	$1,375	$1,125	*$1,460*

Serial numbers SP360200 and below are pre-ban.

AR-15, Pre-Ban, 1989-Sept. 11, 1994 Mfg. w/Blue Label Box

Common features of 1989-1994 AR-15 production include a small front takedown pin, internal sear block, reinforcement around the mag. release button, flash hider, no bayonet lug on 20 in. models, A2 sights, brass deflector, and forward bolt assist. Models R6430 and 6450 do not have A2 sights, brass deflector, or forward bolt assist.

Blue label boxed AR-15s were mfg. between 1989-Sept. 11, 1994. Please refer to box

GRADING - PPGS™	100%	98%	95%	90%	80%	70%	60%	LAST MSR

description under Pre-1989 AR-15 mfg.

Pre-ban parts rifles are rifles which are not assembled in their proper factory configuration. Counterfeit pre-ban rifles are rifles using post-ban receivers and assembled into a pre-ban configuration.

Add $100 for NIB condition.

AR-15A3 TACTICAL CARBINE (R-6721) - .223 Rem. cal., M4 flat-top with 16 in. heavy barrel, 1:9 twist, A2 sights, pre-ban configuration with flash hider, bayonet lug, and 4-position, collapsible stock, removable carry handle, 134 were sold commercially in the U.S., most collectible AR-15. Mfg. 1994 only.

	100%	98%	95%	90%	80%	70%	60%	LAST MSR
S/N 134 and lower	$2,975	$2,500	$2,275	$2,050	$1,900	$1,775	$1,600	
S/N 135 and higher	$1,250	$1,075	$950	$850	$750	$650	$550	

On the R-6721, serial numbers BD000134 and below are pre-ban.

Please note the serial number cutoff on this model, as Colt shipped out a lot of unstamped post-ban law enforcement only "LEO" rifles before finally stamping them as a restricted rifle.

GOVERNMENT CARBINE (R6520) - .223 Rem cal., receiver is stamped Government Carbine, two-position collapsible buttstock, 800 meter adj. rear sight, 16 in. barrel bayonet lug, 1:7 twist, shortened forearm, 5 lbs. 13 oz. Mfg. 1988-94.

100%	98%	95%	90%	80%	70%	60%	LAST MSR
$2,275	$2,125	$2,025	$1,875	$1,750	$1,625	$1,425	*$880*

Add $200 for green label box.

On the R6520, serial numbers GC018500 and below are pre-ban.

Please note the serial number cutoff on this model, as Colt shipped out a lot of unstamped post-ban law enforcement only "LEO" rifles before finally stamping them as a restricted rifle.

This model was manufactured in both green and blue label configurations.

COLT CARBINE (R6521) - receiver is stamped Colt Carbine, similar to R6520, except has no bayonet lug, 16 in. barrel, 1:7 twist. Disc. 1988.

100%	98%	95%	90%	80%	70%	60%	LAST MSR
$2,150	$2,000	$1,850	$1,700	$1,625	$1,475	$1,300	*$770*

Serial numbers CC001616 and below are pre-ban.

SPORTER LIGHTWEIGHT (R6530) - .223 Rem. cal., receiver is stamped Sporter Lightweight, 16 in. barrel, 1:7 twist, similar to R6520, except does not have bayonet lug or collapsible stock.

100%	98%	95%	90%	80%	70%	60%	LAST MSR
$1,650	$1,500	$1,350	$1,100	$1,000	$900	$800	*$740*

Serial numbers SI027246 and below are pre-ban.

9mm CARBINE (R6430) - 9mm Para. cal., similar to R6450 Carbine, except does not have bayonet lug or collapsible stock. Mfg. 1992-1994.

100%	98%	95%	90%	80%	70%	60%	LAST MSR
$1,950	$1,800	$1,650	$1,500	$1,375	$1,275	$1,175	

Serial numbers NL004800 are pre-ban.

9mm CARBINE (R6450) - 9mm Para. cal., carbine model with 16 in. barrel, 1:10 twist, bayonet lug, w/o forward bolt assist or brass deflector, two-position collapsible stock, 20 shot mag., 6 lbs. 5 oz.

100%	98%	95%	90%	80%	70%	60%	LAST MSR
$2,250	$2,100	$1,950	$1,800	$1,725	$1,575	$1,400	*$696*

On the R6450, serial numbers TA010100 are pre-ban.

Please note the serial number cutoff on this model, as Colt shipped out a lot of unstamped post-ban law enforcement only "LEO" rifles before finally stamping them as a restricted rifle.

This model was manufactured with either a green or blue label.

7.62x39mm CARBINE (R6830) - 7.62x39mm cal., 16 in. barrel w/o bayonet lug, 1:12 twist, fixed buttstock. Mfg. 1992-1994.

100%	98%	95%	90%	80%	70%	60%	LAST MSR
$1,850	$1,700	$1,550	$1,400	$1,275	$1,175	$1,075	

Serial numbers LH011326 are pre-ban.

TARGET COMPETITION H-BAR RIFLE (R6700) - .223 Rem. cal., flat-top upper receiver for scope mounting, 20 in. H-Bar barrel (1:9 in. twist), quick detachable carry handle with a

GRADING - PPGS™	100%	98%	95%	90%	80%	70%	60%	LAST MSR

600-meter rear sighting system, dovetailed upper receiver grooved to accept Weaver style scope rings, 8 1/2 lbs.

	$1,850	$1,700	$1,550	$1,400	$1,200	$1,025	$875

Serial numbers CH019500 and below are pre-ban.

COMPETITION H-BAR CUSTOM SHOP (R6701) – .223 Rem. cal., similar to the R6700, but with detachable scope mount, custom shop enhancements added to trigger and barrel, 2,000 mfg. from Colt Custom Shop.

	$1,950	$1,800	$1,650	$1,500	$1,350	$1,200	$1,050

MATCH H-BAR (R6601) – heavy 20 in. H-Bar barrel with 1:7 twist, fixed buttstock. 8 lbs.

	$1,750	$1,600	$1,450	$1,300	$1,150	$1,025	$950

* ***Delta H-Bar (R6601DH)*** – similar to R6601, except has 3-9x rubber armored variable scope, removable cheekpiece, adj. scope mount, black leather sling, test range selected for its accuracy, aluminum transport case. Mfg. 1987-91.

	$2,450	$2,300	$2,150	$2,000	$1,850	$1,700	$1,550	*$1,460*

Serial numbers MH086020 and below are pre-ban.

SPORTER TARGET (R6551) – similar to R6601, except had 20 in. barrel with reduced diameter underneath handguard, 7 1/2 lbs.

	$1,750	$1,600	$1,450	$1,300	$1,150	$1,050	$950

On the R6551, serial numbers ST038100 and below are pre-ban.

AR-15, Post-Ban, Mfg. Sept. 12, 1994-Present

Due to Colt's current military contracts, the commercial availability of AR-15s and variations listed below has been somewhat limited in recent years.

During 2007, Colt released the M-5 Military Carbine and the LE 10-20, with 11 1/2, 14 1/2, or 16 in. barrel. These guns were only available for military and law enforcement.

During 2012, Colt started posting a variety of models for its law enforcement/military offerings in its commercial catalog. Current models include: LE6920 carbine ($1,155 MSR), LE6940 carbine ($1,502 MSR), LE6940P carbine ($2,105 MSR), LE6920MP-B carbine ($1,229 MSR), LE6920CMP-OD ($1,229-$1,258 MSR), LE6920MPFG ($1,395 MSR), LE6920MPHD ($1,476 MSR), LE6900 ($899 MSR), LE6920MP-FDE carbine ($1,258- $1,361 MSR), LE6920CMP-B carbine ($1,258 MSR), LE901-16S carbine .308 Win. ($2,129 MSR), and LE6920SOCOM carbine ($1,602 MSR).

IMPORTANT NOTE: On model(s) where *N/A has replaced the normal 100% value, it indicates current market conditions are too unstable to accurately ascertain 100%-60% values. Factory retail prices (MSRs) reflect most recent updates. For more up-to-date information on current pricing trends and additional useful information, please visit www.bluebookofgunvalues.com, select "Information & Services" from the menu, and click on "Additional Book Information".

Add $368 for Colt Scout C-More Sight (disc.).
Add $444 for Colt Tactical C-More Sight (disc.).

COMPETITION RIFLES – .223 Rem., 6.5 Grendel, or .308 Win. cal., various configurations with models including CRP-18, CRX-16E, CRG-20, and CRL-20. Manufactured under license by Bold Ideas beginning 2013.

Please visit www.coltcompetitionrifle.com for more information and prices on these models.

MATCH TARGET COMPETITION H-BAR RIFLE (MT6700/MT6700C) – .223 Rem. cal., features flat-top upper receiver for scope mounting, 20 in. barrel (1:9 in. twist), quick detachable carry handle which incorporates a 600-meter rear sighting system, counterbored muzzle, dovetailed upper receiver is grooved to accept Weaver style scope rings, supplied with two 5 (disc.), 8 (disc.), or 9 (new 1999) shot mags., cleaning kit, and sling, matte black finish, 8 1/2 lbs. New 1992.

MSR $1,230	*N/A	$925	$850	$750	$650	$575	$525

Add $57 for compensator (MT6700C, mfg. 1999-disc).

GRADING - PPGS™	100%	98%	95%	90%	80%	70%	60%	LAST MSR

TACTICAL ELITE MODEL (TE6700) – .223 Rem. cal., 20 in. heavy barrel, 1:8 in. twist, Hogue finger groove pistol grip, Choate buttstock, fine tuned for accuracy, scope and mount included, approx. 1,000 rifles made by the Custom Shop circa 1996-97.

	$1,650	$1,450	$1,250	$1,025	$900	$800	$700	

COLT ACCURIZED RIFLE (CR6720/CR6724) – .223 Rem. cal., 20 (CR6720) or 24 (CR6724, disc. 2012) in. stainless match barrel, matte finish, accurized AR-15, 8 (disc. 1998) or 9 (new 1999) shot mag., 9.41 lbs. New 1997.

MSR $1,374	*N/A	$1,050	$875	$795	$725	$650	$575	

MATCH TARGET COMPETITION H-BAR II (MT6731) – .223 Rem. cal., flat-top, 16.1 in. barrel (1:9 in.), 9 shot mag., matte finish, 7.1 lbs. Mfg. 1995-2012.

	*N/A	$925	$850	$725	$625	$575	$525	*$1,173*

MATCH TARGET LIGHTWEIGHT (MT6430, MT6530, or MT6830) – .223 Rem. (MT6530, 1:7 in. twist), 7.62x39mm (MT6830, disc. 1996, 1:12 in. twist), or 9mm Para. (MT6430, disc. 1996, 1:10 in. twist) cal., features 16 in. barrel (non-threaded per C/B 1994), initially shorter stock and handguard, rear sight adjustable for windage and elevation, includes two detachable 5, 8, or 9 (new 1999) shot mags., approx. 7 lbs. Mfg. 1991-2002.

	*N/A	$795	$725	$665	$600	$550	$495	*$1,111*

Add $200 for .22 LR conversion kit (disc. 1994).

TARGET GOVT. MODEL RIFLE (MT6551) – .223 Rem. cal., semi-auto version of the M-16 rifle with forward bolt assist, 20 in. barrel (1:7 in.), straight line black nylon stock, aperture rear and post front sight, 5, 8, or 9 (new 1999) shot mags., 7 1/2 lbs. Disc. 2002.

	*N/A	$925	$850	$775	$700	$650	$595	*$1,144*

Add $200 for .22 LR conversion kit (mfg. 1990-94).

MATCH TARGET M4 CARBINE (MT6400/MT6400R) – .223 Rem. cal., similar to current U.S. armed forces M4 model, except semi-auto, 9 or 10 shot mag., 16.1 in. barrel, 1:7 in. twist, matte black finish, fixed tube buttstock, A3 detachable carrying handle, 7.3 lbs. New 2002.

MSR $1,211	*N/A	$950	$850	$750	$650	$550	$500	

Add $341 for quad accessory rail (MT6400R).

MATCH TARGET 6400001 – 5.56 NATO cal., gas operation, 16.1 in. M4 barrel with flash suppressor, flat top receiver, fixed tube stock, 10 shot mag., Magpul Gen. II rear back up sight, two-piece ribbed handguard with post front sight, black finish, 7 lbs. New 2013.

MSR $1,461	*N/A	$1,250	$1,100	$995	$875	$775	$675	

MATCH TARGET 6400R001 – 5.56 NATO cal., gas operated, 16.1 in. M4 barrel with flash suppressor, 10 shot mag., flat top receiver with Picatinny rail integrated with quad rail handguard, Magpul Gen. II rear sight and flip-up adj. post front sight, black finish, 7.2 lbs. New 2013.

MSR $1,825	*N/A	$1,650	$1,475	$1,250	$1,100	$975	$850	

AR6520TRI – 5.56 NATO cal., gas operated, 16.1 in. barrel, matte black finish, 30 shot mag., adj. sights. New 2013.

MSR $1,223	*N/A	$995	$925	$825	$750	$675	$600	

AR6720LECAR – 5.56 NATO cal., 16.1 in. barrel, Magpul Gen. II rear sight with adj. post front sight, 30 shot mag., matte black finish, 6 lbs. New 2013.

MSR $1,468	*N/A	$1,250	$1,100	$995	$875	$775	$675	

MATCH TARGET H-BAR RIFLE (MT6601/MT6601C) – .223 Rem. cal., heavy 20 in. H-Bar barrel, 1:7 in. twist, A2 sights, 8 lbs. Mfg. 1986-2010.

	*N/A	$975	$875	$775	$675	$600	$550	*$1,218*

Add $200 for .22 LR conversion kit (mfg. 1990-94).
Add $1 for compensator (MT6601C, new 1999).

SPORTER CARBINE (SP6920) – .223 Rem. cal., has M-4 features including flat-top receiver with A3 removeable carry handle, 16.1 in. barrel with flash hider, 4-position collapsible

GRADING - PPGS™	100%	98%	95%	90%	80%	70%	60%	LAST MSR

buttstock, ribbed oval handguard, matte black finish, 5.95 lbs. Mfg. 2011 only.

	*N/A	$900	$800	$700	$600	$500	$400	*$1,155*

Add 15% for the legal LE6920 variation that were sold to civilians.

The last 100 carbines of the Model LE6920 marked "Law Enforcement Carbine" and "Restricted" were sold as commercial guns to FFL dealers. Each of these has a factory letter stating as such.

COLT SPORTER (SP6940) – .223 Rem. cal., flat-top receiver with full-length quad Picatinny rails, 16.1 in. fully floated barrel, flip up adj. sights, 4-position collapsible stock, 1-piece monolithic upper receiver, 20 shot mag., matte black metal finish, 6.1 lbs. Mfg. 2011 only.

	*N/A	$1,125	$1,000	$875	$775	$675	$575	*$1,500*

Add 15% for the legal LE6940 variation that were sold to civilians.

The last 100 carbines of the Model LE6940 marked "Law Enforcement Carbine" and "Restricted" were sold as commercial guns to FFL dealers. Each of these has a factory letter stating as such.

SP901 RIFLE – .308 Win. cal., 16 in. full floated heavy chrome lined barrel, direct gas system, locking bolt, matte black finish, one piece monolithic upper receiver with rail, upper receiver can be swapped out for .223, ambidextrous operating controls, flip up adj. post sights, bayonet lug and flash hider. New mid-2011.

Retail pricing is not available on this model.

COLT CARBINE (AR6450) – 9mm Para. cal., 16.1 in. barrel with flash suppressor, A3 detachable carrying handle, 32 shot mag., grooved aluminum handguard, A2 post front sight, adj. Rogers Super Stoc, matte finish, 6.35 lbs. Mfg. 2012 only.

	*N/A	$925	$850	$725	$625	$575	$525	*$1,176*

* ***Colt Carbine (AR6951)*** – 9mm Para. cal., similar to AR6450, except has flat top receiver and folding rear sight. New 2012.

MSR $1,248	*N/A	$995	$900	$775	$675	$575	$525	

COLT CARBINE (AR6720/AR6721) – 5.56 NATO cal., choice of 16.1 in. heavy (AR6721) or light (AR6720) barrel with flash hider and A2 front sight, ribbed aluminum forearm, A3 detachable carrying handle, 20 shot mag., matte finish, adj. stock, 6.2 or 7.3 lbs. New 2012.

MSR $1,136	*N/A	$925	$850	$725	$625	$575	$525	

COLT CARBINE (CR6724001) – 5.56 NATO cal., 24 in. stainless barrel without sights, one-piece flat top upper receiver with integrated 2/3 length quad Picatinny rail, fixed non-adj. stock, 10 shot mag., black finish, 8.8 lbs. New 2013.

MSR $1,653	*N/A	$1,295	$1,125	$995	$875	$775	$675	

AR15 A4 – 5.56 NATO cal., gas operated, 20 in. barrel with flash suppressor, flat top receiver with removable carry handle, A2 style buttstock and front sight, ribbed handguard, black finish, 7.7 lbs. New 2013.

MSR $1,270	*N/A	$995	$875	$775	$675	$575	$525	

AR15 A4MP-FDE – 5.56 NATO cal., 20 in. barrel with flash suppressor, Flat Dark Earth (FDE) furniture, 30 shot mag., 2/3 quad rail with cover, A2 front sight with Magpul Gen. II rear sight, fixed stock, matte black barrel and receiver finish, 7.4 lbs. New 2013.

MSR $1,304	*N/A	$1,020	$875	$775	$675	$575	$525	

AR-15 SCOPE (3X/4X) AND MOUNT – initially offered with 3x magnification scope, then switched to 4x. Disc.

	$395	$300	$240	$185	$160	$130	$115	*$344*

RIFLES: SEMI-AUTO, RIMFIRE, AR-15 & VARIATIONS

The following models are manufactured and by Carl Walther, located in Ulm, Germany, under license from New Colt Holding Corp., and imported/distributed by Umarex USA, located in Fort Smith, AR.

GRADING - PPGS™	100%	98%	95%	90%	80%	70%	60%	LAST MSR

M4 CARBINE – .22 LR cal., 16.2 in. shrouded barrel, flat-top receiver, 10 or 30 shot mag., detachable carry handle, single left-side safety lever, four position retractable stock, ribbed aluminum handguard, black finish, approx. 6 lbs. Mfg. by Umarex under license from Colt. New 2009.

MSR $500	$425	$375	$325	$300	$275	$250	$200

* ***M4 Ops*** – .22 LR cal., 16.2 in. barrel, 10 or 30 shot mag., aluminum upper and lower receiver, black finish, quad tactical rail interface system with elongated Picatinny rail on top of barrel and frame, inline barrel/stock design, cartridge case deflector, muzzle compensator, detachable rear sight, four position collapsible stock, ejection port cover, approx. 6 1/2 lbs. Mfg. by Umarex under license from Colt. New 2009.

MSR $579	$495	$425	$360	$330	$300	$275	$225

M16 – .22 LR cal., 21.2 in. barrel, 10 or 30 shot mag., flat-top receiver with detachable carry handle, fixed stock, elongated ribbed aluminum handguard, removable rear sight, ejection port cover, single left-side safety lever, black finish, approx. 6 1/4 lbs. Mfg. 2009-2010.

$575	$525	$475	$425	$395	$375	$350	*$599*

* ***M16 SPR (Special Purpose Rifle)*** – .22 LR cal., 21.2 in. barrel, 30 shot mag., black finish, fixed stock, aluminum upper and lower receiver, quad tactical rail interface system with Picatinny rail, flip up front and rear sights, inline barrel/stock design, cartridge case deflector, muzzle compensator. Mfg. 2009-2010.

$625	$575	$525	$475	$450	$415	$395	*$670*

SHOTGUNS: O/U

ARMSMEAR – 12 ga. only, 2 3/4 in. chambers, a few prototypes were mfg. by Worshipful Co. Gunmakers of London, boxlock action with engraved sideplates, checkered high-grade European walnut stock and forearm, 28 (HE) or 30 (LE) in. VR barrels with screw-in chokes, choice of light (Armsmear 12 LE) or heavy (Armsmear 12 HE) engraving, 7 1/2 lbs. This model was originally advertised in 1995.

While advertised, only several prototypes of this model were manufactured.

100%	98%	95%	90%	80%	70%	60%	50%	40%	30%	20%	10%

SHOTGUNS: SxS, DISC.

Strong, original case colors and vivid damascus barrel patterning will make the difference when determining values on the Models 1878 and 1883. Remember, the models listed below were designed to shoot black powder loads only, not smokeless powder.

A Colt letter of provenance for the models listed below is $100 per gun.

MODEL 1878 HAMMER SHOTGUN – 10 or 12 ga., 28-32 in. blue or browned damascus barrels, double triggers, sideplates, case hardened breech, extractors, semi-pistol grip stock, 22,683 mfg. between 1878-89. Many of these guns were ordered with special features - these original guns command premiums above the prices listed below.

$4,800	$4,300	$3,850	$3,500	$3,000	$2,600	$2,300	$1,975	$1,600	$1,275	$975	$825

MODEL 1883 HAMMERLESS – 8, 10, or 12 ga., 28-32 in. damascus barrels, many deluxe custom orders mfg. in this model from 1883-1895. Approx. serial range is 1-3,050 and 4,055-8,365. Seldom encountered in mint condition.

$4,250	$3,750	$3,350	$2,995	$2,675	$2,200	$1,925	$1,650	$1,475	$1,100	$995	$875

This model was generally a custom order gun with no standard grades being designated. Quality was extremely high, and the high cost of manufacture is a large reason why the gun never sold in large numbers commercially. The Model 1883 was discontinued after only 12 years of manufacture (it was one of the most expensive shotguns during its day). Values above assume moderate engraving and above average walnut.

* ***Model 1883 Hammerless 8 Ga.*** – 8 ga.

$12,750	$11,250	$10,000	$9,000	$8,075	$6,600	$5,775	$4,950	$4,425	$3,300	$2,975	$2,625

SxS SHOTGUN MFG. 1961-62 – 12 or 16 ga., various barrel lengths, DTs, checkered stock and forearm, mfg. in France 1961-62 by Fabrication Mechanique, estimated total between

GRADING - PPGS™	100%	98%	95%	90%	80%	70%	60%	LAST MSR

25-50 guns in serial range 467,000-469,000.

	$675	$595	$525	$450	$400	$360	$320	

SHOTGUNS: SEMI-AUTO

STANDARD AUTO SHOTGUN – 12 or 20 ga. (also available in Magnum), aluminum frame, 26, 28, 30, or 32 in. plain or VR barrel. Almost 5,300 mfg. (both models) mfg. by Franchi of Italy 1962-66.

	$375	$350	$325	$295	$260	$230	$200	

Add $50 for VR barrel.

CUSTOM AUTO SHOTGUN – similar to Standard Model, except deluxe walnut, hand engraved receiver. Mfg. 1962-1966.

	$475	$425	$375	$350	$325	$295	$260	

SHOTGUNS: SLIDE ACTION

COLTSMAN PUMP SHOTGUN – 12, 16, or 20 ga., Manufrance frame assembled by both Kodiak and Montgomery Wards, 26 or 28 in. plain barrel, aluminum frame. Approx. 2,000 mfg. 1961-1965.

	$325	$295	$260	$230	$200	$180	$165	

Add 30% for Riot model with extended magazine and 20 in. barrel (not cataloged).

FACTORY COMMEMORATIVES & SPECIAL/LIMITED EDITIONS

During the course of a year, we receive many phone calls and letters on Colt non-factory special editions and limited editions that do not appear in this section. It should be noted that Colt factory commemoratives and special/limited editions are guns that has been manufactured, marketed, and sold through the auspices of the specific trademark (in this case Colt). There have literally been hundreds of non-factory special and limited editions which, although mostly made by Colt (some were subcontracted), were not marketed or retailed by Colt. These guns are NOT factory Colt commemoratives or special/limited editions and for the most part, do not have the desirability factor that the factory commemoratives and special/limited editions have. Your best alternative to find out more information about the multitude of these special/limited editions is to write: COLT ARCHIVE PROPERTIES, LLC, P.O. Box 1868, Hartford, CT, 06144. If anyone could have any information, it will be the factory. Their research fee is $100 per gun, with a premium charge for factory engraving. If they cannot obtain additional information on the variation you request, they will refund $50. Unfortunately, in some cases, a special/limited edition may not be researchable. In situations like this, do not confuse rarity with desirability.

Typically, non-factory special and limited editions are made for distributors. These subcontracts seem to be mostly made to signify/commemorate an organization, state, special event or occasion, personality, etc. These are typically marketed and sold through a distributor to dealers, or a company/individual to those people who want to purchase them. These non-factory special/limited editions may or may not have a retail price and often times, since demand is regional, values may decrease rapidly in other areas of the country. In some cases, if the distributor/wholesaler who ordered the initial non-factory special/limited edition is known (and still in business), you may be able to find more information by contacting them directly (i.e. Lew Horton, Davidson's, etc.). Overall desirability is the key to determining values on these non-factory special/limited editions.

The word commemorative as it applies to firearms is almost an obsolete term - kind of like calling a flight attendant a stewardess these days. The last factory gun Colt designated a "Colt Commemorative" was manufactured back in the mid-1980s. One of the biggest reasons Colt dropped its commemorative program was because during this time period, it became more advantageous for Colt to sell large domestic distributors special order guns with the features these distributors wanted. This way Colt did not have to inventory, market, and sell these guns through the company. In today's marketplace, Colt is now producing factory special/limited editions which are marketed and sold through the auspices of Colt, so a line in the sand has now been drawn between factory Colt commemoratives and special/limited editions versus non-factory

GRADING - PPGS™	100%	Issue Price	Qty. Made

special/limited editions. The word commemorative has never applied to non-factory guns. In this text, recent Colt factory special/limited editions will appear as listings in those sections where their standard models are listed. Older factory special/limited editions will appear in this section.

Because the commemorative consumer is now more in charge (consumers now own most of the guns since distributor/dealer inventories are depleted) than during the 1980s, commemorative firearms are possibly as strong as they have ever been. When the supply side of commemorative economics has to be purchased from knowledgable collectors or savvy dealers and demand stays the same or increases slightly, prices have no choice but to go up. If and when the manufacturers crank up the commemorative production runs again (and it won't be like the good old days), the old marketplace characteristics may reappear. Until then, however, the commemorative marketplace remains steady, with values having become more predictable.

As a reminder on commemoratives, I would like to repeat a few facts, especially for the beginning collector, but applicable to all manufacturers of commemoratives. Commemoratives are current production guns designed as a reproduction of an historically famous gun model, or as a tie-in with historically famous persons or events. They are generally of very excellent quality and often embellished with select woods and finishes such as silver, nickel, or gold plating. Obviously, they are manufactured to be instant collectibles and to be pleasing to the eye. As with firearms in general, not all commemorative models have achieved collector status, although most enjoy an active market. Consecutive-numbered pairs as well as collections based on the same serial number may bring a premium. Remember that handguns usually are in some type of wood presentation case, and that rifles may be cased or in packaging with graphics styled to the particular theme of the collectible. The original factory packaging and papers should always accompany the firearm, as they are necessary to realize full value at the time of sale, and get more important every year.

NIB commemorative firearms should be absolutely new, unfired, and as issued, since any obvious use or wear removes it from collector status and lowers its value significantly. Many owners have allowed their commemoratives to sit in their boxes while encased in plastic wrappers for years without inspecting them for corrosion or oxidation damage. This is risky, especially if stored inside a plastic wrapper for long periods of time, since any accumulated moisture cannot escape. Periodic inspection should be implemented to ensure no damage occurs - this is important, since even light "freckling" created from touching the metal surfaces can reduce values significantly. A mint or unfired gun without its original packaging can lose as much as 50% of its normal value - many used commemoratives get sold as "fancy shooters" with little, if any, premiums being asked.

A final note on commemoratives: One of the characteristics of commemoratives/special editions is that over the years of ownership, most of them stay in the same NIB condition. Thus, if supply always is constant and in one condition, demand has to increase before price appreciation can occur. After 47 years of commemorative/special edition production, many model's performance records can be accurately analyzed and the appreciation (or depreciation) can be compared against other purchases of equal vintage. You be the judge.

1961 GENESEO, ILLINOIS 125TH ANNIVERSARY DERRINGER – ser. no. range, 87150D-87253D.

	100%	Issue Price	Qty. Made
	$650	$28	104

1961 125TH ANNIVERSARY MODEL SAA – ser. no. range, 1AM-7390AM.

	100%	Issue Price	Qty. Made
	$1,595	$150	7,390

1961 CIVIL WAR CENTENNIAL PISTOL .22 SHORT – ser. no. range, 50W-24189W (numbers 1W-49W and 124W-149W were not mfg.).

	100%	Issue Price	Qty. Made
	$250	$33	24,114

1961 KANSAS STATEHOOD CENTENNIAL FRONTIER SCOUT – ser. no. range, 001G-6201G.

	100%	Issue Price	Qty. Made
	$595	$75	6,201

1961 PONY EXPRESS CENTENNIAL FRONTIER SCOUT – ser. no. range, 1W-550W, 1E-500E.

	100%	Issue Price	Qty. Made
	$595	$80	1,007

GRADING - PPGS™	100%	Issue Price	Qty. Made

1961 SHERIFF'S MODEL – blue and case hardened, 3 in. barrel, "SM" suffix.

	$2,750	$130	478

1961 SHERIFF'S MODEL NICKEL – nickel, 3 in. barrel, "SM" suffix.

	$6,500	$140	25

1962 COLUMBUS, OHIO SESQUICENTENNIAL SCOUT – ser. no. range, 001CS-200CS.

	$650	$100	200

1962 FORT FINDLAY CASE PAIR – .22 LR and .22 WMR cals., ser. no. range, FF0001-FF0150, one hundred revolvers shipped as singles, forty shipped as cased pairs.

	$2,750	$185	20

1962 FORT FINDLAY, OHIO SESQUICENTENNIAL SCOUT – ser. no. range, FF0001-FF0150, 110 revolvers shipped as singles, 40 shipped as cased pairs.

	$750	$90	110

1962 FORT MCPHERSON, NEBRASKA CENTENNIAL DERRINGER – ser. no. range, 001McP-300McP.

	$495	$29	300

1962 NEW MEXICO GOLDEN ANNIVERSARY SCOUT – ser. no. range, 001NMA-1000NMA.

	$595	$80	1,000

1962 ROCK ISLAND ARSENAL CENTENNIAL MODEL – ser. no. range, 1RIA-550RIA.

	$250	$39	550

1962 WEST VIRGINIA STATEHOOD CENTENNIAL SCOUT – ser. no. range, WV5, WV8, WV9, WV50, and WV100-WV3546, not all shipped.

	$595	$75	3,452

1963 WEST VIRGINIA STATEHOOD CENTENNIAL SAA .45 – ser. no. range, 25WVC-624WVC, not all shipped.

	$1,595	$150	600

1963 ARIZONA TERRITORIAL CENTENNIAL SCOUT – ser. no. range, AT001-AT5355.

	$595	$75	5,355

1963 ARIZONA TERRITORIAL CENTENNIAL SAA .45 – ser. no. range, 100AT-129AT, and 24AC-1273AC.

	$1,595	$150	1,280

1963 BATTLE OF GETTYSBURG CENTENNIAL SCOUT – ser. no. range, 0001GC-1019GC.

	$595	$90	1,019

1963 CAROLINA CHARTER TERCENTENARY SCOUT – ser. no. range, 001CT-300CT.

	$595	$75	300

1963 CAROLINA CHARTER TERCENTENARY 22/45 COMBO – ser. no. range, Scout: 301CT-550CT and SAA: 301CCT-550CCT.

	$2,195	$240	251

1963 FORT STEPHENSON, OHIO SESQUICENTENNIAL SCOUT – ser. no. range, 001FS-200FS, records indicate 150 cased singles and 25 cased doubles.

	$650	$75	200

1963 GEN. JOHN HUNT MORGAN INDIANA RAID SCOUT – ser. no. range, 1JHM-100JHM.

	$750	$75	100

1963 H. COOK "1 OF 100" 22/45 COMBO – ser. no. range, Scout: 001HCK-100HCK and SAA: 001HC-100HC.

	$2,500	$275	100

1963 IDAHO TERRITORIAL CENTENNIAL SCOUT – ser. no. range, 0001TC-0902TC.

	$595	$75	902

GRADING - PPGS™	100%	Issue Price	Qty. Made

1964 CALIFORNIA GOLD RUSH SCOUT – ser. no. range, 0001GR-0500GR.

	$595	$80	500

1964 CHAMIZAL TREATY SCOUT – ser. no. range, 0001CS-0500CS, 350 singles and 50 cased pairs.

	$595	$85	450

1964 CHAMIZAL TREATY SAA .45 – ser. no. range, 0001CP-0100CP, 50 singles and 1 cased pair.

	$1,795	$170	50

1964 CHAMIZAL TREATY 22/45 COMBO – ser. no. range, Scout: 0001CS-0500CS and SAA: 0001CP-0100CP.

	$2,395	$280	50

1964 CHERRY'S SPORTING GOODS 35TH ANNIVERSARY 22/45 COMBO – ser. no. range, Scout: REC1-REC100 and SAA: EPC1-EPC100.

	$2,500	$275	100

1964 COL. SAM COLT SESQUI. PRESENTATION SAA .45 – ser. no. range, 0001SC-5000SC.

	$1,595	$225	4,750

1964 COL. SAM COLT SESQUI. DELUXE PRES. SAA .45 – ser. no. range, 2000SC-2200SC.

	$3,500	$500	200

1964 COL. SAM COLT SESQUI. SPEC. DELUXE PRES. SAA .45 – ser. no. range, 0001SC-5000SC, only numbers ending with 00 or 000.

	$5,500	$1,000	50

1964 GENERAL HOOD CENTENNIAL SCOUT – ser. no. range, 0001GH-1503GH.

	$595	$75	1,503

1964 MONTANA TERRITORIAL CENTENNIAL SCOUT – ser. no. range, 0001MF-2300MF.

	$595	$75	2,300

1964 MONTANA TERRITORIAL CENTENNIAL SAA .45 – ser. no. range, 0001MA-0850MA.

	$1,650	$150	851

Approx. 100-200 sets (including the Scout) were sold with matching ser. numbers.

1964 NEVADA STATEHOOD CENTENNIAL SCOUT – ser. no. range, 0001NS-1752NS, 1846NS, 1964NS, and 2001NS-4996NS.

	$595	$75	3,984

1964 NEVADA STATEHOOD CENTENNIAL SAA .45 – ser. no. range, 0001NC-1752NC, 1864NC, 1964NC, and 2001NC-2700NC.

	$1,595	$150	1,688

1964 NEVADA STATEHOOD CENTENNIAL 22/45 COMBO – ser. no. range, Scout: 0001NS-1752NS, 1846NS, 1964NS, and 2001NS-4996NS, SAA: 0001NC-1752NC, 1864NC, 1964NC, and 2001NC-2700NC.

	$2,195	$240	189

1964 NEVADA ST. CENT. 22/45 COMBO W/EXTRA ENGR. CYLS. – ser. no. range, Scout 0001NS-1752NS, 1846NS, 1964NS, and 2001NS-4996NS, SAA 0001NC-1752NC, 1864NC, 1964NC, and 2001NC-2700NC, records do not indicate how revolvers were cased.

	$2,395	$350	577

1964 NEVADA "BATTLE BORN" SCOUT – ser. no. range, 001BB-1001BB.

	$595	$85	981

1964 NEVADA "BATTLE BORN" SAA .45 – ser. no. range, 001NB-100NB, .45 cal., cased singles and cased pairs shipped.

	$1,895	$175	80

GRADING - PPGS™	100%	Issue Price	Qty. Made

1964 NEVADA "BATTLE BORN" 22/45 COMBO – ser. no. range, Scout: 001BB-100BB and S.A.A.: 001NB-100NB.

	$2,595	$265	20

1964 NEW JERSEY TERCENTENARY SCOUT – ser. no. range, 0001NJ-1001NJ.

	$595	$75	1,001

1964 NEW JERSEY TERCENTENARY SAA .45 – ser. no. range, 0001JT-0250JT.

	$1,595	$150	250

1964 PONY EXPRESS PRESENTATION SAA .45 – ser. no. range, 1W-500W and 1E-500E also 0E, 00E, 0W, 00W, X1-W, X1-E, and CAL-1.

	$1,750	$250	1,004

100% value assumes all accessory items included.

1964 ST. LOUIS BICENTENNIAL SCOUT – ser. no. range, 0251SL-1051SL.

	$595	$75	802

1964 ST. LOUIS BICENTENNIAL SAA .45 – ser. no. range, 0251SB-0450SB.

	$1,595	$150	200

1964 ST. LOUIS BICENTENNIAL 22/45 COMBO – ser. no. range, Scout: 0001SL-0250SL and SAA: 0001SB-0250SB.

	$2,195	$240	250

1964 WYATT EARP BUNTLINE SAA .45 – ser. no. range, 0001WE-0150WE.

	$2,995	$250	150

1964 WYOMING DIAMOND JUBILEE SCOUT – ser. no. range, 001DJ-2357DJ.

	$595	$75	2,357

1965 APPOMATTOX CENTENNIAL SCOUT – ser. no. range, 1000AK-2000AK.

	$595	$75	1,001

1965 APPOMATTOX CENTENNIAL SAA .45 – ser. no. range, 1000AP-1249AP.

	$1,595	$150	250

1965 APPOMATTOX CENTENNIAL 22/45 COMBO – ser. no. range, Scout: 0001AK-0250AK and SAA: 0001AP-0250AP.

	$2,195	$240	250

1965 FORTY-NINER MINER SCOUT – ser. no. range, 0001FN-0500FN.

	$595	$85	500

1965 GENERAL MEADE CAMPAIGN SCOUT – ser. no. range, 1GM-1197GM.

	$595	$75	1,197

1965 JOAQUIN MURIETTA 22/45 COMBO – ser. no. range, Scout: 001JMK-100JMK and SAA: 001JMP-100JMP.

	$2,500	$350	100

1965 OREGON TRAIL SCOUT – ser. no. range, 0001OT-1995OT.

	$595	$75	1,995

1965 OLD FT. DES MOINES RECONSTRUCTION SCOUT – ser. no. range, 0101DM-0800DM.

	$595	$90	700

1965 OLD FT. DES MOINES RECONSTRUCTION SAA .45 – ser. no. range, 0101FD-0200FD.

	$1,595	$170	100

1965 OLD FT. DES MOINES RECONSTRUCTION 22/45 COMBO – ser. no. range, Scout: 0001DM-0100DM and SAA: 0001FD-0100FD.

	$2,195	$290	100

1965 ST. AUGUSTINE QUADRACENTENNIAL SCOUT – ser. no. range, 1AQ-500AQ.

	$650	$85	500

GRADING - PPGS™	100%	Issue Price	Qty. Made
1965 KANSAS COWTOWN SERIES – Wichita Scout, ser. no. range, 1KW-500KW.	$595	$85	500
1966 ABERCROMBIE & FITCH "TRAILBLAZER" CHICAGO – Chicago, ser. no. range, 201AF-300AF.	$1,395	$275	100
1966 ABERCROMBIE & FITCH "TRAILBLAZER" NEW YORK – New York, ser. no. range, 001AF-200AF.	$1,395	$275	200
1966 ABERCROMBIE & FITCH "TRAILBLAZER" SAN FRANCISCO – San Francisco, ser. no. range, 301AF-400AF.	$1,395	$275	100
1966 CALIFORNIA GOLD RUSH SAA .45 – ser. no. range, 0001GP-0500GP, not all shipped.	$1,595	$175	130
1966 COLORADO GOLD RUSH SCOUT – ser. no. range, 0CG-1350CG.	$650	$85	1,350
1966 DAKOTA TERRITORY SCOUT – ser. no. range, 1DT-1000DT.	$595	$85	1,000
1966 GENERAL MEADE SAA .45 – ser. no. range, 0001MC-0200MC.	$1,595	$165	200
1966 INDIANA SESQUICENTENNIAL SCOUT – ser. no. range, 1IS-1745IS.	$595	$85	1,500
1966 KANSAS COWTOWN SERIES ABILENE – Abilene Scout, ser. no. range, 1KA-500KA.	$595	$95	500
1966 KANSAS COWTOWN SERIES – Dodge City Scout, ser. no. range, 1KD-500KD.	$595	$85	500
1966 OKLAHOMA DIAMOND JUBILEE – ser. no. range, 1OK-1343OK.	$595	$85	1,343
1966 PONY EXPRESS .45 SAA 4-SQUARE SET (4 GUNS) – ser. no. range with backstrap marking, PE001E-PE250E "SACRAMENTO TO FRIDAY'S STATION", PE251E-PE500E "SALT LAKE CITY TO FORT LARAMIE", PE001W-PE250W "ST. JOSEPH TO MARYSVILLE"' PE251W-PE500W "FORT KEARNEY TO JULESBURG".	$7,000	$1,400	unknown
1967 ALAMO SCOUT – ser. no. range, cased single 1051A22-4500A22 and cased pairs 251A22-1050A22.	$595	$85	4,250
1967 ALAMO SAA .45 – ser. no. range, 251A45-1000A45, 450 singles and 300 cased pairs.	$1,595	$165	750
1967 ALAMO 22/45 COMBO – ser. no. range, 1A22-250A22 and 1A45-250A45.	$2,095	$265	250
1967 KANSAS COWTOWN SERIES – Coffeyville Scout, ser. no. range, 1KC-500KC.	$595	$95	500
1967 KANSAS TRAIL SERIES – Chisolm Trail Scout, ser. no. range, 1CH-500CH.	$595	$100	500
1967 LAWMAN SERIES SAA – Bat Masterson SAA .45, ser. no. range, 1LMP-500LMP.	$1,795	$180	500
1967 LAWMAN SERIES SCOUT – Bat Masterson Scout, ser. no. range, 1LM-3000LM.	$695	$90	3,000

GRADING - PPGS™	100%	Issue Price	Qty. Made

1967 WWI SERIES – .45 ACP cal., Chateau Thierry, ser. no. range, 101CT-7500CT.

	$995	$200	7,400

1967 WWI SERIES DELUXE – Chateau Thierry Deluxe, ser. no. range, 26CT-100CT.

	$1,995	$500	75

1967 WWI SERIES SPECIAL DELUXE – Chateau Thierry Spec. Deluxe, ser. no. range, 1CT-25CT.

	$3,000	$1,000	25

1968 GEN. NATHAN BEDFORD FORREST SCOUT – ser. no. range, 1NBF-3000NBF.

	$595	$110	3,000

1968 KANSAS TRAIL SERIES PAWNEE TRAIL – Pawnee Trail Scout, ser. no. range, 1PT-500PT.

	$595	$110	501

1968 KANSAS TRAIL SERIES SANTA FE TRAIL – Santa Fe Trail Scout, ser. no. range, 1SF-500SF.

	$595	$120	501

1968 LAWMAN SERIES SAA – Pat Garrett .45 SAA, ser. no. range, 1PGP-500PGP.

	$1,695	$220	500

1968 LAWMAN SERIES SCOUT – Pat Garrett Scout, ser. no. range, 1PG-3000PG.

	$695	$110	3,000

1968 NEBRASKA CENTENNIAL SCOUT – ser. no. range, 1NEB-7000NEB.

	$595	$100	7,001

1968 WWI SERIES – .45 ACP cal., Belleau Wood, ser. no. range, 1BW-100BW and 201BW-7500BW.

	$995	$200	7,400

1968 WWI SERIES DELUXE – Belleau Wood Deluxe, ser. no. range, 126BW-200BW.

	$1,995	$500	75

1968 WWI SERIES SPECIAL DELUXE – Belleau Wood Special Deluxe, ser. no. range, 101BW-125BW.

	$3,000	$1,000	25

1968 WWI SERIES BATTLE OF THE MARNE – .45 ACP cal., 2nd Battle of the Marne, 1M2-200M2 and 301M2-7500M2.

	$995	$220	7,400

1968 WWI SERIES BATTLE OF THE MARNE DELUXE – 2nd Battle of the Marne Deluxe, ser. no. range, 226M2-300M2.

	$1,995	$500	75

1969 ALABAMA SESQUICENTENNIAL SCOUT – ser. no. range, 1AS-3098AS, not all shipped.

	$595	$110	3,001

1969 ALABAMA SESQUICENTENNIAL .45 SAA – ser. no. ALA1P.

	$17,500	unknown	1

1969 ARKANSAS TERRITORIAL SESQUICENTENNIAL SCOUT – ser. no. range, 1ARK-3500ARK.

	$595	$110	3,500

1969 CALIFORNIA BICENTENNIAL SCOUT – ser. no. range, 1CBI-5000CBI.

	$595	$135	5,000

1969 GOLDEN SPIKE SCOUT – ser. no. range, 1GS-11000GS.

	$650	$135	11,000

GRADING - PPGS™	100%	Issue Price	Qty. Made

1969 KANSAS TRAIL SERIES – Shawnee Trail Scout, ser. no. range, 1ST-500ST.

	$595	$120	501

1969 LAWMAN SERIES SAA – .45 SAA Wild Bill Hickok, ser. no. range, 1WBH-500WBH.

	$1,695	$220	500

1969 LAWMAN SERIES SCOUT – Wild Bill Hickok Scout, ser. no. range, 1WB-3000WB.

	$695	$117	3,000

1969 WWI SERIES BATTLE OF THE MARNE DELUXE – 2nd Battle of the Marne Spec. Deluxe, ser. no. range, 201M2-225M2.

	$3,000	$1,000	25

1969 WWI SERIES MEUSE-ARGONNE – .45 ACP cal., Meuse-Argonne, ser. no. range, 1MA-300MA and 401MA-7500MA.

	$995	$220	7,400

1969 WWI SERIES MEUSE-ARGONNE DELUXE – Meuse-Argonne Deluxe, ser. no. range, 326MA-400MA.

	$1,995	$500	75

1969 WWI SERIES MEUSE-ARGONNE SPECIAL DELUXE – Meuse-Argonne Spec. Deluxe, ser. no. range, 301MA-325MA.

	$3,000	$1,000	25

1970 KANSAS FORT HAYS – Ft. Hays Scout, ser. no. range, 1FH-500FH.

	$595	$130	500

1970 KANSAS FORT LARNED – Ft. Larned Scout, ser. no. range, 1FL-500FL.

	$595	$120	500

1970 KANSAS FORT RILEY – Ft. Riley Scout, ser. no. range, 1FR-500FR.

	$595	$130	500

1970 LAWMAN SERIES SAA – Wyatt Earp .45 SAA, ser. no. range, 1WYE-500WYE.

	$2,995	$395	500

1970 LAWMAN SERIES SCOUT – Wyatt Earp Scout, ser. no. range, 1LWE-3000LWE.

	$795	$125	3,000

1970 MAINE SESQUICENTENNIAL SCOUT – ser. no. range, 1MES-3000MES.

	$595	$120	3,000

1970 MISSOURI SESQUICENTENNIAL SCOUT – ser. no. range, 1MOS-3000MOS.

	$595	$125	3,000

1970 MISSOURI SESQUICENTENNIAL .45 SAA – ser. no. range, P1MOS-P900MOS.

	$1,595	$220	900

1970 TEXAS RANGER SAA .45 – ser. no. range, N/A.

	$2,250	$650	1,000

1970 TEXAS RANGER GRADE I (95% ENGRAVING COVERAGE) – ser. no. range, N/A.

	$6,000	N/A	90

1970 TEXAS RANGER GRADE II (75% ENGRAVING COVERAGE) – ser. no. range, N/A.

	$5,500	$2,250	80

1970 TEXAS RANGER GRADE III (50% ENGRAVING COVERAGE) – ser. no. range, N/A.

	$5,000	$2,950	90

1970 WWII SERIES EUROPEAN THEATRE – European Theatre, ser. no. range, 0001ETO-9959ETO, not all shipped.

	$995	$250	11,500

GRADING - PPGS™	100%	Issue Price	Qty. Made

1970 WWII SERIES PACIFIC THEATRE – Pacific Theatre, ser. no. range, 0001PTO-9960PTO, not all shipped.

	$995	$250	11,500

Note: A complete set of the WWI and WWII Series standard grade models (6 guns) with matching serial numbers in NIB condition is currently selling in the $4,750-$5,500 range.

1971 KANSAS SERIES – Ft. Scott Scout, ser. no. range, 1FSC-500FSC.

	$595	$130	500

1971 NRA CENTENNIAL GOLD CUP .45 ACP – ser. no. range, 1NRA-2500NRA, not all shipped.

	$1,295	$250	2,500

1971 NRA CENTENNIAL .45 SAA – ser. no. range, NRA1-NRA7000, not all shipped.

	$1,595	$250	5,000

1971 NRA CENTENNIAL .357 SAA – ser. no. range, NRA1-NRA7000, not all shipped.

	$1,495	$250	5,000

1971 1851 NAVY LEE-GRANT – Lee-Grant Set, ser. no. range, 1LGP-250LGP.

	$1,595	$500	250

1971 1851 NAVY U.S. GRANT – U.S. Grant, ser. no. range, 251USG-4398USG, not all shipped.

	$795	$250	4,750

1971 1851 NAVY ROBERT E. LEE – Robert E. Lee, ser. no. range, 251REL-4900REL.

	$795	$250	4,750

1972 ARIZONA RANGER SCOUT – ser. no. range, 1AR-3000AR.

	$595	$135	3,001

1972 FLORIDA TERRITORY SESQUICENTENNIAL SCOUT – ser. no. range, 1FLA-2000FLA.

	$595	$125	2,001

1975 PEACEMAKER CENTENNIAL .45 – ser. no. range, PC501-PC2000.

	$1,795	$300	1,500

1975 PEACEMAKER CENTENNIAL 44.40 – ser. no. range, 501PC-2000PC.

	$1,795	$300	1,500

1975 PEACEMAKER CENT. CASED PAIR – ser. no. range, .44-40 cal.: 1MPC-500MPC and .45 cal.: MPC1-MPC500.

	$3,500	$625	500

USS TEXAS BATTLESHIP SPECIAL EDITION (1975) – .45 ACP cal., Model 1911A1 with special embellishments, nickel finish, this model is not a factory commemorative, ser. no. range N/A.

	$1,150	unknown	500

USS ARIZONA BATTLESHIP SPECIAL EDITION (1975) – .45 ACP cal., Model 1911A1 with special embellishments, nickel finish, this model is not a factory commemorative, ser. no. range N/A.

	$1,150	unknown	500

1976 U.S. BICENTENNIAL SET – ser. no. range, SAA .45: 0001PM-1776PM, Python .357 Mag.: 0001PY-1776PY, and black powder Dragoon: 0001DG-1776DG, in walnut display case with drawers.

	$2,995	$1,695	1,776

1976 BICENTENNIAL SAA FREEDOM COLTS – consisted of A, B, and C sets, set As were engraved, Bs had gold work and accessories, Cs were similar to Bs, but had shoulder stock. Set A prices averaged $1,500-$3,000 in 1976, set B prices varied between $3,500-$20,000, and set C prices started at $5,000. Total mfg. was 4 set As, 6 set Bs, and 1 set C.

GRADING - PPGS™	100%	Issue Price	Qty. Made

These sets in today's marketplace are too rare to accurately evaluate and pricing is literally "what the market will bear."

These guns were all engraved by Dwain Wright located in Applegate, OR.

1977 2ND AMENDMENT .22 – ser. no. range, G0001RB-G3020RB.

	$595	$195	3,020

1977 U.S. CAVALRY 200TH ANNIVERSARY SET – ser. no. range, US0001-US3020 and 0001US-3020US, not all shipped.

	$1,450	$995	3,000

1978 STATEHOOD 3RD MODEL DRAGOON – ser. no. range, N/A.

	$7,500	$12,500	52

1979 NED BUNTLINE .45 SAA – ser. no. range, NB0001-NB3000.

	$1,295	$895	3,000

OHIO PRESIDENT'S SPECIAL EDITION (1979) – .45 ACP cal., Model 1911A1 with special Ohio embellishments, this is not a factory commemorative, ser. no. range N/A.

	$1,150	unknown	250

1979 TOMBSTONE CENTENNIAL .45 SAA – .45 LC cal., 7 1/2 in. barrel, nickel finish, two-piece walnut stocks, P-1876 Model, etched with scroll engraving and Western scenes. 300 mfg. (200 singles and 50 pairs), ser. no. range N/A.

	$1,495	$995	300

This model was not sold retail through the auspices of Colt.

1980 DRUG ENFORCEMENT AGENCY (DEA) .45 AUTO – ser. no. range N/A.

	$1,150	$550	910

This model was not sold at retail through the auspices of Colt.

1980 OLYMPICS ACE MODEL SPECIAL EDITION – ser. no. range N/A.

	$1,250	$1,000	200

This model was not sold at retail through the auspices of Colt.

1980 HERITAGE-WALKER .44 PERCUSSION – ser. no. range, 0001 C CO-1850 C CO.

	$950	$1,475	1,847

1981 "JOHN M. BROWNING" .45 ACP SEMI-AUTO – ser. no. range, CJMBC0001-CJMBC3000.

	$995	$1,100	3,000

1980-81 .45 ACP GOVT. SIGNATURE SERIES – .45 ACP cal., blue finished Govt. with gold auroplated or nickel finish. 250 mfg. in both finishes, ser. no. range N/A.

	$1,150	$833	250

Add $50 for blue finish.

1980-81 ACE SIGNATURE SERIES – .22 LR cal., featured Cocobolo grips with medallions, blue finish with photo engraving, cased. 1,000 mfg., ser. no. range N/A.

	$1,250	$955	1,000

1981 BUFFALO BILL SPECIAL EDITION – .44-40 WCF cal., 7 1/2 in. barrel, gold and silver plating, Class C engraved, scrimshaw ivory grips featuring Buffalo Bill and his TE Wyoming Ranch brand, leather cased, 250 mfg. serialized 1BB-250BB.

	$4,975	$3,750	250

This model was a special edition (not commemorative), which was made specifically for the Buffalo Bill Historical Center.

1982 JOHN WAYNE SAA STANDARD – ser. no. range, CJWC0001-CJWC3100.

	$2,250	$2,995	3,100

While advertising literature indicated 3,100 were mfg., 3,041 were sold.

GRADING - PPGS™	100%	Issue Price	Qty. Made

1982 JOHN WAYNE SAA DELUXE – ser. no. range, JWD001-JWD500.

	$8,000	$10,000	500

While advertising literature indicated 500 were mfg., only 90 were sold.

1982 JOHN WAYNE SAA PRESENTATION – ser. no. range, JWP001-JWP100.

	$13,500	$20,000	100

While advertising literature indicated 100 were mfg., only 47 were sold.

1983 BUFFALO BILL WILD WEST SHOW CENTENNIAL SAA .45 – ser. no. range, CBC0001-CBBC1236, not all shipped.

	$1,695	$1,350	500

1983 CCA LIMITED EDITION SAA – .44-40 WCF cal., 4 3/4 in. barrel, nickel finish, fleur-de-lis checkered walnut grips, two line barrel address and Colt Frontier Six Shooter roll marking. 250 mfg. in 1983 to commemorate Colt Collector's Assn., ser. no. range N/A.

	$1,595	$825	250

This model was not sold at retail through the auspices of Colt.

1983 "ARMORY MODEL" SAA .45 ACP – this model had limited production, and should not be considered a commemorative. So-called because it was shipped with extra .45 LC cylinder and the "Colt Armory Edition" book by E. Grant. 250 mfg. with nickel finish, 250 mfg. with blue finish, presentation cased, smooth ivory grips, ser. no. range N/A.

	$1,995	$1,125	500

20 Armory Models were available with class A engraving - $2,595, B engraving - $2,995, C engraving - $3,500, D engraving - $3,995.

1983 PYTHON SILVER SNAKE SPECIAL EDITION – .357 Mag. cal., 6 in. barrel, stainless steel with black chrome finish, Pachmayr grips with custom shop pewter medallions, etched engraving, includes custom gun pouch, ser. no. range N/A.

	$1,995	$1,150	250

1984 1ST EDITION GOVT. MODEL .380 ACP – ser. no. range, RC00000-RC01000.

	$850	$425	1,000

1984 JOHN WAYNE "DUKE" FRONTIER .22 – ser. no. range N/A.

	$895	$475	5,000

1984 COLT/WINCHESTER SET – 1 ea. of the Model 1894 Winchester carbine and Colt Peacemaker, serial numbered 1WC-4440WC, .44-40 WCF cal., elaborate gold etching, cased. Pistol became available for sale individually in 1986 - see individual listing below for values.

	$3,000	$3,995	2,300

Approx. 2,300 sets were actually put together in this combination. Some sets were split up with individual prices being discounted.

1984 COLT SAA ONLY FROM SET – .44-40 WCF cal., 7 1/2 in. barrel, gold etching, this commemorative was originally made as part of the 1984 Winchester/Colt rifle-pistol set, but was later able to be purchased individually. Originally mfg. 1984, ser. no. range N/A.

	$1,295	N/A	4,000

1984 USA EDITION SAA – .44-40 WCF cal., 7 1/2 in. barrel, old style black powder frame, bullseye ejector rod head, 3 line patent date, high polished blue with gold line engraving. 100 guns total mfg. - 1 for each state and its capitol, ser. no. range N/A.

	$3,500	$4,995	100

1984 KIT CARSON .22 NEW FRONTIER – 6 in. barrel, color case hardened frame, gold artwork, serial numbered KCC0001-KCC1000, cased.

	$595	$550	1,000

1984 SECOND EDITION GOVT. MODEL .380 ACP – serial numbered 00000RC- 01000RC.

	$850	$525	1,000

GRADING - PPGS™	100%	Issue Price	Qty. Made

1984 OFFICER'S COMMENCEMENT ISSUE – Officer's ACP with Marine Corps emblem, rosewood grips, silver plated oak leaf scroll, cased, ser. no. range N/A.

	$995	$700	1,000

This model was not sold retail through the auspices of Colt.

1984 THEODORE ROOSEVELT COMMEMORATIVE SAA – .44-40 WCF cal., 7 1/2 in. barrel, black powder frame, case colored receiver, factory "B" hand engraving, ivory stocks, cased, ser. no. range, TRC001-TRC500.

	$2,250	$1,695	500

1984 NORTH AMERICAN OILMEN SAA BUNTLINE – .45 LC cal., 12 in. barrel, non-fluted cylinder, elaborate gold etching, ebony grips with ivory inlays, stand-up glass case, ser. nos. 1-100 mfg. for Canada, 101-200 for the U.S.

	$3,250	$3,900	200

This model was not sold retail through the auspices of Colt.

1985 TEXAS 150th SESQUICENTENNIAL SAA – .45 cal., Sheriff's model, 4 3/4 in. barrel, mirror bright blue, gold etching, 24Kt. gold plated backstrap and trigger guard, smooth ivory grips, French fit oak presentation case. Mfg. 1985 only.

* ***1985 Texas 150th Sesquicentennial SAA Standard Model*** – 1,000 mfg., ser. no. range TX0001-TX1000.

	$1,595	$1,836	1,000

* ***1985 Texas 150th Sesquicentennial SAA Premier Model*** – elaborate engraving, 75 mfg., ser. no. range TEXAS0001-TEXAS0096, not all shipped.

	$5,000	$7,995	75

1986 150th ANNIVERSARY SAA – .45 LC cal., 10 in. barrel, 50% coverage engraving, royal blue finish, Goncalo Alves smooth grips, 150th anniversary logo in stocks, cherrywood case. 490 mfg. 1986 only, ser. no. range AM0001-AM1000, not all shipped.

	$1,995	$1,595	490

1986 150th ANNIVERSARY ENGRAVING SAMPLER SAA – various cals. and barrel lengths, 4 different engraving styles featuring Nimschke, Helfricht, Henshaw, and Contemporary (these names are scrimshawed on the ivory grips), approx. 75% coverage signed by the engraver, available in either blue or nickel finish, no special serialization. Mfg. 1986.

	$3,500	$1,613	unknown

1986 150th ANNIVERSARY ENGRAVING SAMPLER .45 M1911A1 – .45 ACP cal., 4 different engraving styles on metal surfaces, 75% coverage, ivory grips, signed by the engraver, available with either blue or nickel finish. New 1986, ser. no. range N/A.

	$1,995	$1,155	unknown

Add $60 for nickel.

1986 MUSTANG FIRST EDITION – .380 ACP cal., 1,000 manufactured serialized MU00001-MU01000 (the first thousand of production), rosewood stocks, walnut presentation case. Mfg. 1986 only.

	$850	$475	1,000

OFFICER'S ACP HEIRLOOM EDITION – .45 ACP cal., personalized with individual's choice for serial number (ie. John Smith 1), mirror brite bluing, jeweled barrel, hammer, and trigger, ivory grips, with historical letter and mahogany case. New 1986, ser. no. range N/A.

	$1,550	$1,643	open

1986 DOUBLE DIAMOND SET – Python Ultimate .357 Mag. revolver and Officer's Model .45 ACP, both guns in stainless steel, smooth rosewood grips, presentation cased. 1,000 sets mfg. 1986 only, serial numbered 1-1,000 (matched).

	$3,000	$1,575	1,000

DELTA MATCH H-BAR RIFLE – AR-15 A2 H-Bar rifle selectively chosen and equipped with 3-9x variable power rubber armored scope, leather sling, shoulder stock cheekpiece, cased. Mfg. 1987, ser. no. range N/A.

	$1,500	$1,425	open

GRADING - PPGS™	100%	Issue Price	Qty. Made

12TH MAN-'SPIRIT OF AGGIELAND' – .45 ACP cal., mfg. to commemorate Texas A&M University, serial numbered TAM001-TAM999, 24Kt gold plating including wreaths on left frame and inscription on right, cherrywood glass top presentation case, includes personalized class graduation inscription. Available 1987 only.

	$1,150	$950	999

This model was not sold retail through the auspices of Colt.

COMBAT ELITE CUSTOM EDITION – .45 ACP cal., with ambidextrous thumb safety, wide grip safety, hand tuned action, and carrying case, ser. numbered CG00001-CG00500. Mfg. 1987.

	$1,150	$900	500

1987 SHERIFF'S EDITION – set of 5 SAA Sheriff's configuration revolvers in .45 LC cal., barrel lengths include 2, 2 1/2, 3, 4, and 5 1/2 in., royal blue finish, smooth rosewood grips with medallions, supplied with glass top case which displays the revolvers in a circle around a brass sheriff's badge. Serialization has 3 numeral prefix (which is the same in each set), followed by the letters "SE", followed by 1 or 2 numerals (indicating barrel length) - i.e. serial number 002SE25 indicates the second set built, Sheriff's Edition (SE), and a barrel length of 2 1/2 inches.

	$6,000	$7,500	200 sets

1989 SNAKE EYES LIMITED EDITION – includes two Python revolvers (2 1/2 in. barrels), one finished in brite stainless steel and the other in Royal Blue finish, grips are ivory-like with scrimshaw "snake eyes" dice on left side and royal flush poker hand on right, includes chips and playing cards, 500 sets only of consecutive serial numbers. New 1989, ser. no. range N/A.

	$7,000	$3,500	500

1990 SAA HEIRLOOM II EDITION – .45 LC cal., 7 1/2 in. barrel, color case hardened frame and hammer, balance of metal finished in Colt Royal Blue, one-piece American Walnut grips with cartouche on lower left side, personalized inscription on backstrap, walnut cased. Available 1990 only, ser. no. range N/A.

	$1,595	$1,600	open

1990 JOE FOSS LIMITED EDITION .45 ACP GOVT. MODEL – .45 ACP cal., first limited edition in Colt's All American Hero Series, commemorates Joe Foss, famous American WWII Marine Fighter Pilot, gold etched scenes on slide sides, smooth walnut grips. While 2,500 were advertised, only 300+ were mfg. Serial numbered beginning with JF 0001. French fitted walnut presentation case, 38 oz. Mfg. 1990 only.

	$1,850	$1,375	300+

1911A1 50th ANNIVERSARY BATTLE OF THE BULGE – .45 ACP cal., special edition commemorating the Battle of the Bulge, silver plated with gold inlays, 300 mfg. serialized BB001-BB300.

	$1,595	$1,250	300

Add $150 for deluxe presentation case.

This special edition was sold exclusively by Cherry's located in Greensboro, NC.

1993 CCA LIMITED EDITION SAA – .38-40 WCF cal., 4 3/4 in. barrel, nickel finish, walnut grips, CCA markings on grip strap. 150 mfg. in 1993, ser. no. range N/A.

	$1,500	$1,165	150

This model was not sold at retail through the auspices of Colt.

COMANCHE

Current trademark manufactured in Argentina beginning 2001. Currently distributed (master distributor) beginning 2002 by Eagle Imports, located in Wanamassa, NJ. Distributor sales.

PISTOLS: SINGLE SHOT

SUPER COMANCHE – .45 LC cal./.410 bore or .22 WMR (new 2011) cal., 10 in. rifled barrel, blue, duo-tone (mfg. 2004-2005, reintroduced 2011), camo (mfg. 2006-2007) or satin

GRADING - PPGS™	100%	98%	95%	90%	80%	70%	60%	LAST MSR

nickel finish, black rubber grips and forearm, barrel release lever on front of trigger guard, adj. rear sight, transfer bar and manual safeties, 47 oz. New 2002.

MSR $220	$180	$160	$140	$120	$110	$90	$70	

Add $5 for duo-tone finish, $20 for satin nickel finish, or $33 for camo (disc. 2007).
Add $10 for .22 WMR cal. (new 2011).

This model is not available for sale in some states.

REVOLVERS: SA

COMANCHE I – .22 LR cal., 6 in. full lug barrel, 9 shot, blue, stainless, or alloy, adj. sights, rubber grips, 39 oz. Mfg. 2002-2009.

	$225	$195	$170	$155	$125	$100	$80	*$274*

Add $25 for stainless steel construction.
Subtract $66 for alloy (disc.).

COMANCHE II – .38 Spl. +P cal., 2 (mfg. 2006), 3 (new 2004), or 4 in. full lug barrel, 6 shot, blue or stainless (disc. 2010) finish, steel (disc. 2010) or alloy frame, adj. rear sight, approx. 30 oz. New 2002.

MSR $205	$175	$155	$125	$100	$85	$75	$65	

Add $15 for stainless steel construction (disc. 2010).
Add $9 for 2 in. barrel (disc.).

COMANCHE III – .357 Mag. cal., 2 (mfg. 2006), 3, 4, or 6 in. full lug barrel, 6 shot, blue or stainless, adj. rear sight, 29-39 oz. Mfg. 2002-2009.

	$240	$210	$180	$165	$130	$110	$85	*$289*

Add $27 for stainless steel construction.
Add $8 for 2 in. barrel.

COMANCHE IV – .44 Mag. cal., 6 in. barrel only with adj. rear sight, blue or stainless steel. Mfg. 2004.

	$250	$220	$185	$170	$135	$110	$85	*$308*

Add $25 for stainless steel construction.

COMBINATION GUNS

A two barrel long gun configuration of either SxS or O/U design, consisting of a rifle and a shotgun barrel. Combination guns originated in Europe.

Many imported combination guns designed for the U.S. have been known as turkey guns in the past, typically with a .22 rimfire/medium cal. centerfire rifle barrel over a 12 ga., 20 ga., or .410 bore shotgun barrel. European guns typically have metric rifle cals., and the shotgun barrel is usually 12 or 16 ga. European combination guns (see configurations below) need to be evaluated individually, since values will depend on the desirability of the gun's configuration in the U.S. (i.e., metric vs. American cals., gauge, type of lock, engraving, quality of wood, etc.). Most non-custom European boxlock combination guns with metric cals. in average condition are currently priced in the $750-$2,250 range. However custom ordered, top quality major trademark European combination guns with profuse engraving and best quality wood can sell for as high as $20,000. Typical American combination guns (the Savage Model 24 and others) are priced in the $375-$625 range, depending on condition.

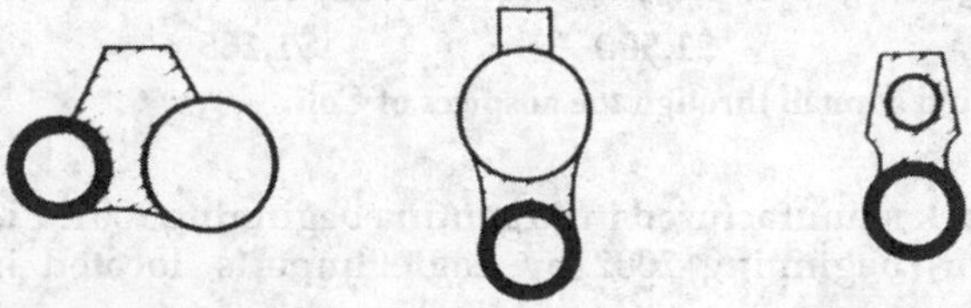

COMMANDO ARMS

Previous manufacturer located in Knoxville, TN.

Commando Arms became the new name for Volunteer Enterprises in the late 1970s.

GRADING - PPGS™	100%	98%	95%	90%	80%	70%	60%	LAST MSR

RIFLES: CARBINES

MARK 45 – .45 ACP cal., carbine styled after the Thompson sub-machine gun, 16 1/2 in. barrel.

	$495	$425	$350	$315	$280	$225	$195	

COMMANDO ARMS (NEW MFG.)

Current trademark of shotguns manufactured in Konya, Turkey. Currently imported under private label by Webley & Scott USA.

In addition to shotguns, parent company Komando Av Sa. Tic. Ltd. Sti. also manufactures air rifles.

SHOTGUNS

Current SxS models include the Estate, Prestige, and the Classic. Current O/U models include the Ultra, Hunter, Elite, Gold, Royal, Osso, and the Classic. Current semi-auto models include the Gold and Classic Series. Current single barrel models include the Star Series. Slide action defense guns include the Pump Series. None of these models are currently imported into the U.S. Please contact the company directly for more information, including U.S. availability and pricing on non-Webley & Scott labeled models (see Trademark Index).

COMPETITIVE EDGE GUNWORKS LLC

Current rifle manufacturer located in Bogard, OR.

RIFLES: BOLT ACTION

Competitive Edge Gunworks LLC builds custom order bolt action rifles based on its patented action. Tactical, Hunting, Varmint, and Competition configurations are available. Please contact the company directly for more information, including available options, delivery time and a price quotation (see Trademark Index).

COMPETITOR CORPORATION

Competitor

Current manufacturer established in 1988 and located in Jaffrey, NH. Previously located in New Ipswich, NH until 2001, and in West Groton, MA from 1988-1995. Dealer direct or distributor sales.

PISTOLS: SINGLE SHOT

COMPETITOR – available in over 400 cals. from .17 LR - .50 AE, ranging from small rimfire to large belted Magnums, 14 in. barrel standard, rotary cannon action, cocks on opening, dual sliding thumb and trigger safety, rotary style ejector, click adj. sights, matte blue or optional electroless nickel finish, choice of synthetic, laminated, or natural wood grips (ambidextrous), extractor or ejector. Approx. 59-73 oz. New 1988.

MSR $660	$575	$500	$425	$375	$300	$245	$190	

Add $30 for laminated wood stock.
Add approx. $50 for walnut grips (disc.).
Add $60 for electroless nickel finish (barreled action only, disc.).
Add $195 for extra 14 in. standard cal. barrel with sights.
Add $40 for less than 16 in. standard cal. barrel with sights.
Add $70 for 16-23 in. barrel.
Add $60-$80 for factory-installed muzzle brake.
Add $275 for rimfire or centerfire conversion kit.

CONCO ARMS

Previous importer of Hambrusch rifles located in Emmaus, PA.

RIFLES: SxS

PRO HUNTER BOXLOCK SxS – various cals. through .700 NE, Anson & Deeley action with double underlocking lugs and scalloped frame, ejectors, standard scroll engraving, H&H style frame reinforcement, checkered Circassian walnut stock and forearm, custom order only, mfg. by Hambrusch in Ferlach, Austria. Importation disc. 2004.

	$21,500	$18,750	$15,950	$12,500	$10,000	$8,700	$7,500	*$23,611*

Add $673 for .375 H&H, $1,061 for .470 NE, $1,987 for .500 NE, $12,816 for .577/.600 NE or $30,318 for .700 NE cal.

GRADING - PPGS™	100%	98%	95%	90%	80%	70%	60%	LAST MSR

PRO HUNTER SIDELOCK SxS – various cals. through .700 NE, full sidelock action with standard scroll engraving, ejectors, hinged DT, checkered Circassian walnut stock and forearm, custom order only, mfg. by Hambrusch in Ferlach, Austria.

	N/A	$26,000	$20,500	$16,750	$14,000	$11,000	$9,995	*POR*

Premiums exist for .375 H&H cal. and above.

CONNECTICUT SHOTGUN MANUFACTURING CO.

Current rifle and shotgun manufacturer established during 1995, and located in New Britain, CT. Consumer direct sales.

Connecticut Shotgun Manufacturing Co. has established itself as one of America's premier gunmakers, specializing in best quality O/U and SxS shotguns, in addition to a SxS double rifle. Please contact the company directly for more information, including pricing and availability (see Trademark Index).

RIFLES: SxS

MODEL 21 RIMFIRE – .22 LR or .22 WMR cal., based on a special order small frame, everything is scaled and proportioned to the caliber, open sights, base price is for Model 21-1 w/light scroll engraving and A fancy wood. New mid-2006.

MSR $25,000	$23,750	$20,000	$17,000	$13,500	$10,500	$8,750	$7,750

MSR for Grade 21-5 is $30,000, Grade 21-6 is $32,000, and Grand American is $34,000.

MODEL 21 CENTERFIRE – various centerfire calibers, based on the Model 21 action, Grand American styling and features, 4 game animals inlayed in 24Kt. gold, frame scaled proportionately to the caliber, iron sights, SST. Limited mfg. beginning 2002.

Each gun is custom-built to the customer's exact specifications and prices start at $35,000.

SHOTGUNS: O/U, SIDELOCK

A. GALAZAN MODEL – 12, 16, 20, 28 ga., or .410 bore, low profile sidelock action with Boss-style metal reinforced forearm, top-of-the-line model utilizing best quality materials and U.S. workmanship, wide choice of custom features and engraving options.

Each gun is custom-built to the customer's exact specifications, so price is POR.

A. GALAZAN ROUND BODY MODEL – 12, 16, 20, 28 ga., or .410 bore, round body, wide choice of custom features and engraving options.

Each gun is custom-built to the customer's exact specifications and base price is POR.

A-10 AMERICAN – 12, 20, or 28 ga., choice of 26, 28, 30, or 32 in. VR barrels, 12 ga. frame (20 ga. frame available by request), five TruLock choke tubes, XX grade American black walnut pistol or straight grip checkered stock and forearm, steel (standard A-10), platinum, or stainless steel receiver with light (not full coverage) rose and scroll engraving standard, SST, ejectors, hidden hand detachable sidelock with four exposed pins on each side, includes case. New 2010.

MSR $7,995	$7,500	$6,250	$5,250	$4,500	$3,750	$3,000	$2,500

Add $1,000 for the Deluxe Model with higher grade wood and more engraving coverage.
Add $2,000 for rose and scroll engraving, or add $7,000 for platinum engraving and wood upgrade.
Add $350 for 3X, $600 for 4x, $900 for exhibition, or POR quotation for Turkish wood walnut upgrades.

This model is available by contacting the company directly or can be ordered through Galazan Premium Galleries which include: Cook-Winston, Steve Barnett Fine Guns, Puglisi Gun Imporium, and John Foster Gunmakers, UK.

* ***A-10 American Sporting Clays*** – 12 ga. only, 3 in. chambers, sidelock action with choice of engraving and finish, 30 or 32 in. ported VR barrels with 5 extended choke tubes, adj. point of impact high top rib, weight distribution system under forend, XX walnut stock features adj. recoil pad and comb with stock weight balance system and target palm swell pistol grip, SST, ejectors, non-automatic safety, approx. 8 1/2 lbs. New 2012.

MSR $13,500	$12,000	$10,000	$8,500	$7,250	$6,000	$5,000	$4,000

INVERNESS – 20 ga., case colored rounded boxlock frame with fine scroll engraving, 28 or 30 in. file cut VR barrels with 5 choke tubes, SST, ejectors, checkered walnut straight or

GRADING - PPGS™	100%	98%	95%	90%	80%	70%	60%	LAST MSR

pistol grip stock with Galazan recoil pad, elongated top and bottom tangs, 6 lbs. 5 oz. New late 2011.

MSR $4,995	N/A	$2,700	$2,450	$2,100	$1,850	$1,600	$1,450

The normal MSR for this model is $8,995, but the first 500 customers get a special introductory price of $4,995. If the customer pays in full in advance, the MSR is $3,995. If the buyer is an existing Connecticut Shotgun customer and pays in full, the price is $2,995.

* ***Inverness Deluxe*** – 20 ga. only, 3 in. chambers, rounded action with trigger plate, 28 or 30 in. VR cryo-pattern barrels with 5 choke tubes, SST, AE, long tang straight or pistol grips, checkered forearm, Turkish walnut stock, engraved coin finished receiver. New late 2012.

MSR $6,995	$6,500	$5,750	$5,000	$4,200	$3,400	$2,600	$2,350

SHOTGUNS: SxS

Connecticut Shotgun Manufacturing Company will custom make a "Winchester" Model 21, with Winchester appearing on the barrel address. Please contact the factory directly for details and a price quotation (see Trademark Index).

Add $3,250 for extra set of 12, 16, or 20 ga. barrels on same gun, $4,500 for extra 28 ga. or .410 bore barrels on standard frame.

MODEL 21 – 12, 16, 20, 28 ga., or .410 bore, 4 frame sizes (12, 16, 20, and 28/.410 bore), various barrel lengths up to 32 in. with either matte solid or vent. rib and fixed chokes, best quality checkered wood, wide choice of custom features and engraving options, new mfg. not associated with Winchester production. Limited mfg. beginning 2002.

Each gun is custom-built to the customer's exact specifications.

* ***Model 21-1*** – features frame light scroll engraving patterned after Winchester's No. 1 style, A fancy wood. New 2002.

MSR $15,000	$15,000	$12,500	$9,995	$8,750	$7,250	$6,500	$5,750

Add $3,000 for 28 ga. or $3,500 for .410 bore.
Add $11,500 for 28 ga. or .410 bore on baby frame.

* ***Model 21-5*** – features both scroll and three hunting scenes engraving patterned after Winchester's No. 5 style on frame and barrels, AA fancy wood. New 2002.

MSR $18,000	$18,000	$14,500	$12,500	$9,950	$8,750	$7,250	$6,500

Add $2,000 for 28 ga. or $3,000 for .410 bore.
Add $11,500 for 28 ga. or .410 bore on baby frame.

* ***Model 21-6*** – features both tight scroll and dog/game bird engraving patterned after Winchester's No. 6 style on frame and barrels, AAA fancy wood. New 2002.

MSR $21,500	$21,500	$17,500	$13,750	$11,250	$9,250	$8,250	$7,000

Add $2,000 for 28 ga. or $3,500 for .410 bore.
Add $9,500 for 28 ga. or .410 bore on baby frame.

* ***Model 21 Grand American*** – top-of-the-line standard model with 2 sets of barrels, elaborate scroll engraving on barrels and frame, 5 gold inlays, including dogs and birds, B carved stock and forearm, AAA full fancy feather crotch American walnut. New 2002.

MSR $24,500	$24,500	$21,000	$17,000	$14,250	$11,650	$9,000	$7,500

Add $2,000 for 28 ga. or $5,500 for .410 bore.
Add $9,500 for 28 ga. or .410 bore on baby frame.

* ***Model 21 Royal Exhibition*** – top-of-the-line model with 2 sets of barrels, numerous engraving and gold inlay options, best quality wood. New 2002.

This model is built to customer's specifications and is POR only.

A. GALAZAN ROUND BODY MODEL – 12, 16, 20, 28 ga., or .410 bore, round body, top-of-the-line model utilizing best quality materials and U.S. workmanship, no visible pins or screws, wide choice of custom features and engraving options.

Each gun is custom built to the customer's exact specifications and price is POR depending on order.

GRADING - PPGS™	100%	98%	95%	90%	80%	70%	60%	LAST MSR

RBL EDITIONS – 12, 16, 20, 28 ga. or .410 (new late 2011) bore, rounded boxlock action, barrels with 5 choke tubes or fixed chokes, ejectors, DT or ST, XX walnut, choice of pistol or straight grip stock, case colored receiver, hammer, sears and triggers are treated in Hard Gold, recoil pad, canvas and leather cased with all accessories, choice of 14 1/4 or 14 3/4 LOP, approx. 5 1/2 (28 ga.) or 6 1/8 lbs. This series was introduced 2006.

Add $350 for XXX walnut, $600 for XXXX or $900 for Exhibition wood upgrade.
Add $400 for beavertail forearm.
Add $175 for SST (disc.)
Add $450 for assisted opening action (disc.)

* ***RBL 12 ga.*** – 12 ga., 26, 28, 30, or 32 in. barrels with 5 TruLock chokes, case colored receiver with light scroll and three ducks in flight on right and two pheasants on left, designed by Paul Lantuch. Mfg. 2009-2010, re-introduced 2012.

MSR $3,795	$3,350	$2,950	$2,650	$2,350	$2,000	$1,800	$1,600	

» **RBL 12 ga. Sporting Clays** – 12 ga., 30 or 32 in. raised VR barrels, exhibition grade checkered walnut stock with adj. comb, weight balancing system, and interchangeable recoil pads, case colored receiver with gold inlaid pigeons, non-automatic safety, beavertail forearm, 9 lbs. New 2011.

MSR $6,995	$6,650	$6,000	$5,250	$4,500	$3,750	$3,000	$2,250	

* ***RBL 16 ga.*** – 16 ga., scaled frame, 29 in. barrels, case colored receiver with light scroll engraving, features game scenes of a pointer and a setter, quick change recoil pad available in two lengths. Mfg. 2009-2010, re-introduced 2012.

MSR $3,795	$3,350	$2,950	$2,650	$2,350	$2,000	$1,800	$1,600	

* ***RBL 20 ga. Launch Edition*** – 20 ga., 28 in. barrels with 5 chokes, case colored receiver with scroll engraving by Richard Roy (launch edition) or French greyed receiver, metal grip cap, hard rubber buttplate, also available with fully rifled bore and open sights (Slug). Mfg. 2005-2010.

	$3,995	$3,500	$2,995	$2,500	$2,100	$1,750	$1,550	*$2,795*

Add approx. $650 for fully rifled barrels with open sights - mfg. approx. 2009-2010.

* ***RBL 28 ga.*** – 28 ga., 26, 28, or 30 in. barrels with choke tubes, case colored receiver features pointer and setter games scenes designed by James Demunk, splinter forend. Disc. 2010.

MSR $4,995	$4,500	$4,150	$3,650	$3,150	$2,750	$2,350	$2,050	

* ***RBL .410 Bore*** – .410 bore, 28 in. barrels with fixed chokes, case colored true baby frame, J. Purdey style rose and scroll engraving, 5 lbs. Only 500 to be mfg. New 2012.

MSR $6,995	$6,650	$6,000	$5,250	$4,500	$3,750	$3,000	$2,250	

* ***RBL Galleria*** – built to customer order, DT, stainless steel choke tubes, Exhibition black, English, or Turkish walnut, high gloss or rubbed oil finish, color case hardened or French greyed receiver, includes special leather case with canvas cover, RBL special label.

This model is POR.

* ***RBL NRA Special Wayne LaPierre Signature Edition*** – 20 ga., case colored receiver, straight or pistol grip stock, DT, splinter forend, 5 choke tubes, includes gold embossed NRA logo and gold Wayne LaPierre signature on trigger guard, many other options and upgrades available, includes leather case and accessories. New mid-2008.

Base price on this model starts at $4,350.

RBL GALLERY EDITION – 20 ga. only, many options and special orders are available per individual customer order. New 2011.

The price range on this model is $10,000-$40,000 depending on special order options and features.

* ***RBL Launch Edition Gallery Gun*** – 20 ga., 28 in. barrel with choke tubes, many options and special orders are available. New 2011.

Base price for this model starts at $12,000.

GRADING - PPGS™	100%	98%	95%	90%	80%	70%	60%	LAST MSR

RBL 20 GA. PROFESSIONAL SLUG GUN – 20 ga., 3 in. chambers, 24 in. fully rifled barrels with quarter rib and iron sights, walnut straight or pistol grip stock with splinter forearm, double triggers, ejectors, includes sling swivels. New 2011.

MSR $4,500	$4,150	$3,700	$3,200	$2,850	$2,400	$2,150	$1,800

RBL RESERVE EDITIONS – 12, 16, 20, or 28 ga., these editions were made at the end of the standard RBL production run. They can be distinguished by their special bluing, case colors, wood finish, and engraving. All are marked "Reserve" on the top rib, many options are available.

* ***RBL Reserve 12 ga.*** – 12 ga., case colored receiver with light scroll and three ducks in flight on right and two pheasants on left. Introduced 2010.

MSR $4,150	$3,950	$3,600	$3,250	$2,800	$2,400	$2,000	$1,650

* ***RBL Reserve 16 ga.*** – 16 ga., scaled frame, 29 in. barrels, case colored receiver with light scroll engraving, features game scenes of a pointer and a setter, quick change recoil pad available in two lengths. New 2010.

MSR $4,150	$3,950	$3,600	$3,250	$2,800	$2,400	$2,000	$1,650

* ***RBL Reserve 28 ga.*** – 28 ga., 26, 28, or 30 in. barrels with choke tubes, case colored receiver features dogs on point surrounded by full coverage scroll engraving. New 2010.

MSR $4,150	$4,150	$3,650	$3,150	$2,750	$2,350	$2,050	$1,750

* ***RBL Reserve Launch Edition*** – 20 ga., 28 in. barrels with choke tubes, similar to RBL 20 ga. Launch Edition, XXX American black walnut stock and forearm, many options and special orders are available. New 2011.

MSR $3,299	$3,000	$2,650	$2,300	$2,000	$1,700	$1,400	$1,100

RBL RESERVE SPECIAL EDITION – available in most gauges, this model typically has deeper engraving with gold inlays. Please contact the factory directly for availabilty, options, and a specific price quotation. New 2011.

Base price on this model starts at $12,999.

RBL RESERVE CAMBRIDGE SPECIAL – 20 ga. This model was released at the end of RBL 20 production, and features rose and scroll pattern engraving, model name is engraved on trigger guard, many options are available, including wood upgrades, engraving, etc. New 2011.

Base price on this model starts at $4,000.

CONNECTICUT VALLEY ARMS

Current importer of firearms, muzzle loaders, and muzzle loading accessories established during 1971 and located in Duluth, GA.

CVA is well known for their muzzleloading rifles and related black powder accessories. Please refer to the *Blue Book of Modern Black Powder Arms* by John Allen (now online also) for more information on these products - www.bluebookofgunvalues.com.

PISTOLS: SINGLE SHOT

SCOUT PISTOL – .357 Mag., .44 Mag., .45 LC/.410 shotshell cal., includes DuraSight scope mount. New 2010.

MSR $370	$295	$260	$225	$200	$180	$160	$140

RIFLES: SINGLE SHOT

APEX – .22 LR, .22-250 Rem., .222 Rem., .223 Rem., 243 Win., .270 Win., .30-06, .45-70 Govt., 7mm-08 Rem., .35 Whelen (new 2010), or.300 Win. Mag., .308 Win. cal., break open action, stainless steel standard contoured or full contoured fluted barrel, black or Realtree APG HD camo stock, DuraSight Z2 scope rail, mfg. by Bergara in Spain. New 2009.

MSR $692	$575	$475	$400	$350	$295	$250	$200

Add $85 for Realtree APG HD camo coverage.

GRADING - PPGS™	100%	98%	95%	90%	80%	70%	60%	LAST MSR

SCOUT – .243 Win., .270 Win., .30-06, .35 Whelen, .44 Mag. (new 2011), or 7mm-08 Rem. cal., similar to Apex model, 20 in. compact or 22 in. fluted stainless steel or blue barrel, black synthetic stock with Fibergrip, open sights (.243 Win. or 7mm-08 Rem. cal. only) or DuraSight scope mount, CrushZone recoil pad, reversible hammer spur, 5.8 lbs. New 2010.

MSR $341	$285	$240	$210	$185	$165	$150	$135	

Add $42 for stainless steel barrel.

Add $90 for mounted and bore sighted KonusPro scope with engraved reticle (various powers), DuraSights mounts, and soft case.

Subtract $10 for Scout Model with open sights.

ELITE STALKER – .35 Whelen, .444 Marlin, or .45-70 Govt. cal., blue or stainless steel barrel, black or camo finish, DuraSight Dead-On intergral mount. New 2012.

MSR $352	$290	$240	$210	$185	$165	$150	$135	

Add $43 for stainless steel.

Add $77 for camo.

SHOTGUNS: SINGLE SHOT

SCOUT – 12 ga., 22 in. rifled barrel with scope mount, choice of blued or stainless steel barrel. New 2011.

MSR $330	$275	$240	$210	$185	$165	$150	$135	

Add $40 for stainless steel barrel.

CONNECTICUT VALLEY CLASSICS, INC.

Previous trademark manufactured by Cooper Arms, located in Stevensville, MT 1996-1998. CVC, Inc. was a division of CVC Sports, Inc. Previous sales and marketing offices were located in Holyoke, MA until 1996 and in Westport, CT 1993-95.

SHOTGUNS: O/U

The models listed below have receiver dimensions built to the exact specifications of the original Classic Doubles Model 101. The only difference is that the tang spacer has been made an integral part of the frame.

Add $1,350 for each additional barrel set.

CLASSIC 101 SPORTER – 12 ga. only, boxlock action, monobloc, 28, 30, or 32 in. VR barrels with multi-chokes, SST, ejectors, nickel finished receiver with light engraving, checkered American black walnut stock and forearm with low luster finish, approx. 7 3/4 lbs.

	$1,875	$1,550	$1,225	$1,000	$825	$700	$600	*$2,195*

CLASSIC SPORTER SB – 12 ga. only, boxlock action, entry level sporter model. Mfg. 1997-98.

	$2,250	$1,875	$1,575	$1,175	$950	$775	$650	*$2,495*

GRADE I CLASSIC SPORTER – 12 ga. only, boxlock action, monobloc, 28, 30, or 32 in. vented barrels with VR, lengthened forcing cones, and 2 3/8 in. multi-chokes, SST, ejectors, stainless steel receiver with light engraving, checkered 20 LPI AA American black walnut stock and forearm with low luster finish, approx. 7 3/4 lbs. Disc. 1998.

	$2,695	$2,100	$1,675	$1,250	$1,000	$825	$700	*$2,995*

* ***Women's Classic Sporter*** – similar to Grade I Classic Sporter, except has smaller stock dimensions and 28 in. barrels only, 7 1/2 lbs. Mfg. 1996-98.

	$2,695	$2,100	$1,675	$1,250	$1,000	$825	$700	*$2,995*

This model was also available in Grade II or Grade III Women's Classic Sporter.

* ***Grade II Classic Sporter*** – similar to Grade I Classic Sporter, except has AAA American or Claro walnut with 22 LPI hand-checkering, 30 in. barrels only.

	$3,100	$2,350	$1,800	$1,325	$1,050	$850	$725	*$3,595*

* ***Grade III Classsic Sporter*** – similar to Grade II Classic Sporter, except has fleur-de-lis checkering patterns and gold accents. Disc. 1998.

	$3,600	$2,750	$1,975	$1,450	$1,175	$925	$750	*$4,195*

GRADING - PPGS™	100%	98%	95%	90%	80%	70%	60%	LAST MSR

GRADE I CLASSIC FIELD – 12 ga. only, similar to Grade I Classic Sporter, except has solid rib and standard flush-mounted choke-tubes, 27 1/2 in. barrels, 7 1/2 lbs. Mfg. 1996-98.

$2,695	$2,100	$1,675	$1,250	$1,000	$825	$700	*$2,995*

* ***Classic Waterfowler*** – 12 ga. only, 30 or 32 (disc. 1995) in. VR barrels, non-reflective surfaces, bird scene engraving, overbored barrels with lengthened forcing cones and four standard CVC chokes, 8 lbs. Mfg. 1993-98.

$2,495	$2,000	$1,575	$1,175	$950	$775	$650	*$2,795*

* ***Grade II Classic Field*** – similar to Grade I Classic Field, except has AAA American or Claro walnut with 22 LPI hand-checkering.

$3,025	$2,250	$1,750	$1,300	$1,050	$850	$725	*$3,495*

* ***Grade III Classic/English Field*** – similar to Grade II Classic Field, except has fleur-de-lis checkering patterns and gold accents, choice of straight English (25 1/2 in. VR barrels only) or pistol grip stock. Disc. 1998.

$3,575	$2,850	$2,025	$1,500	$1,200	$925	$750	*$4,195*

Add $100 for straight English stock.

* ***Classic Skeet*** – 12 ga. only, 29 in. vented barrels with 9mm VR, otherwise similar to Grade I Classic Sporter, 7 1/2 lbs. Mfg. 1996-98.

$2,695	$2,100	$1,675	$1,250	$1,000	$825	$700	*$2,995*

* ***Classic Flyer*** – 12 ga. only, live bird gun featuring AAA walnut and 22 LPI checkering, oil finish, 30 in. vented overbored barrels with 11mm tapered top rib and lengthened forcing cones, scroll engraving with pigeon scene on receiver bottom, 8 lbs. Mfg. 1996-98.

$3,100	$2,350	$1,800	$1,325	$1,050	$850	$725	*$3,595*

CONQUEST

Previous trademark of guns manufactured by various companies in Spain, Turkey, Germany, and Italy.

The Conquest trademark included shotguns in O/U, SxS, slide action, and semi-auto configuration. These models had little or no importation into the U.S.

CONSTITUTION ARMS

Current manufacturer located in Maplewood, NJ.

PISTOLS: SEMI-AUTO

PALM PISTOL – 9mm Para. cal., single shot, DAO, thumb operated trigger, polymer/metal frame, short barrel, may be fired by using either hand, three-position combination lock, grip safeties, optional Picatinny rail.

While this model has been advertised since 2009, it has yet to be manufactured.

CONTENTO/VENTURA

Previously imported by Ventura Imports in Seal Beach, CA. Ventura also imported Bertuzzi and Piotti.

SHOTGUNS: O/U

CONTENTO O/U – 12 ga., 32 in. barrels, boxlock, optional screw in choke tubes, high vent. rib, SST, auto ejectors, hand checkered Monte Carlo trap stock.

$1,045	$990	$935	$880	$770	$690	$635

MK 2 – with extra single barrel.

$1,375	$1,320	$1,265	$1,210	$1,100	$1,020	$965

MK 2 – leather cased, combination set.

$1,705	$1,650	$1,595	$1,540	$1,430	$1,350	$1,295

MK 3 – engraved, O/U.

$1,650	$1,570	$1,485	$1,375	$1,295	$1,185	$1,100

MK 3 – with extra single barrel.

$2,200	$2,035	$1,925	$1,815	$1,650	$1,595	$1,515

GRADING - PPGS™	100%	98%	95%	90%	80%	70%	60%	LAST MSR

MK 3 – leather cased, combination set.

	$2,750	$2,420	$2,200	$2,090	$1,955	$1,815	$1,760	

SHOTGUNS: SxS

MODEL 51 – 12, 16, 20, 28 ga., or .410 bore, 26-32 in. barrels, various chokes, extractors, boxlock, double triggers, checkered straight stock.

	$385	$360	$330	$305	$250	$220	$165	
Auto ejectors	$495	$440	$385	$360	$305	$275	$220	

MODEL 52 – 10 ga., double triggers only, otherwise similar to Model 51.

	$525	$495	$470	$415	$360	$305	$250	

MODEL 53 – deluxe version of Model 51, scalloped frame, auto ejectors.

	$470	$440	$415	$385	$330	$275	$220	
SST	$605	$550	$525	$495	$440	$385	$330	

MODEL 61 – 12 or 20 ga., 26, 27, 28, or 30 in. barrels, H&H sidelocks, various chokes, floral engraved, hand detachable locks, cocking indicators, select walnut pistol grip stock, auto ejectors.

	$880	$825	$770	$745	$690	$605	$550	
SST	$1,020	$965	$910	$855	$800	$715	$660	

MODEL 65 – similar to Model 61, with elaborate engraving and quality hand finishing.

	$1,100	$1,045	$990	$965	$880	$825	$770	

CONTINENTAL ARMS CORPORATION

Previous importer of high quality shotguns and rifles (usually Belgian), circa mid-1950s-mid-1970s.

RIFLES

BOLT ACTION – mostly large cals., typically custom Mauser action, makers include Defourney and Dumoulin.

Specimens should be evaluated individually due to the many configurations and embellishments encountered. This model is rarely seen in today's marketplace.

DOUBLE RIFLE – .270 Win., .303 British, .30-40 Krag, .348 Win., .30-06, .375 H&H, .400 Jeffery, .470, .475, .500, or .600 Nitro Express cal., 24 or 26 in. barrels, Anson & Deeley boxlock system, although some sidelocks were mfg., double triggers, checkered stock.

	$4,950	$4,350	$3,850	$3,300	$2,970	$2,750	$2,500	

Add 10% for boxlock with sideplates.
Add 15% for ejectors.
Add 30%-50% for .375 H&H and larger cals., depending on the size of the cal.

SHOTGUNS: O/U

Add 20% for .410 bore.
Add 30% for 28 ga.
Add 10% for Defourney mfg.

CENTAURE BOXLOCK – 12, 20, 28 ga., or .410 bore, ejectors, light engraving, chopper lump barrels with cross-bolt, double underlocks, SST, 3-piece forearm.

	$2,000	$1,675	$1,500	$1,250	$1,025	$875	$750	

CENTAURE LIEGE ROYAL CROWN GRADE – similar to Centaure Boxlock, except has game scene engraving, better figured wood and silver crown inlay.

	$3,150	$2,850	$2,600	$2,250	$1,900	$1,600	$1,400	

CENTAURE IMPERIAL CROWN GRADE – similar to Royal Crown Grade, except has higher grade wood, extensive game scene engraving, oak leaf engraving on barrels, and gold inlay on top lever.

	$4,500	$4,150	$3,750	$3,500	$3,200	$2,900	$2,700	

GRADING - PPGS™	100%	98%	95%	90%	80%	70%	60%	LAST MSR

SHOTGUNS: SxS

Add 20% for .410 bore.
Add 30% for 28 ga.
Add 10% for Defourney mfg.

CENTAURE – all gauges, basic boxlock action with double triggers and extractors.

$1,050 $950 $895 $850 $700 $500 $400

Add 35% for ejectors.

CENTAURE ROYAL CROWN GRADE – all gauges, single trigger, ejectors, checkered stock and forearm, game scene engraving, can be identified by silver crown inlaid on top lever.

$3,400 $3,150 $2,800 $2,600 $2,325 $2,100 $1,950

CENTAURE IMPERIAL CROWN GRADE – similar to Royal Crown, except gold inlay on top lever, extensive game scene engraving on receiver and barrels.

$4,275 $3,850 $3,500 $3,150 $2,850 $2,575 $2,300

COOEY, H.W., MACHINE & ARMS CO. LTD.

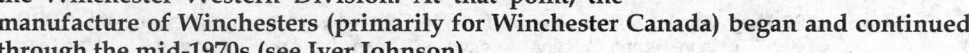

Previous manufacturer located in Cobourg, Ontario, Canada 1903-1961. During 1961, Cooey was sold to the Olin Corporation and placed under the supervision of the Winchester Western Division. At that point, the manufacture of Winchesters (primarily for Winchester Canada) began and continued through the mid-1970s (see Iver Johnson).

To date, there is limited collector demand for most models in this trademark and values should be based on the shooting utility rather than collector premiums due to rarity. Values for average condition guns will typically range between $75-$150.

RIFLES

Cooey manufactured a wide number of rifles, including bolt actions, single shots, and semi-autos. During the late 1920s-early 1930s, Cooey manufactured the Model X and 2X for Iver Johnson (please refer to Iver Johnson section).

Pre-1961 Cooey mfg. models include: 25, 35, 39, 55, 60, 62, 75, 78, 82, Ace, Ace 1, Ace 2, Ace 3, Ace Repeater, Ace Special, Bisley Sport, Canuck, Canuck 25, Canuck Junior, Canuck Western, Cooey Repeater, HWC, Mohawk, and several unnumbered single shot and repeating sporter rifles. Post-1961 Cooey firearms made for Winchester include: Model 10, Model 39, Model 60, Model 600, Model 64, Model 64 Deluxe, Model 64A, 64B, Model 71, 71 Carbine, Model 75, 750, and 750 Deluxe, Model 710, and Ranger.

SHOTGUNS

Cooey manufactured both double and single barrel shotguns for Iver Johnson (Hercules and Champion) during the late 1920s-early 1930s (see Iver Johnson section). Cooey also manufactured single shot shotguns. Pre-1961 Cooey mfg. models include: .22 rimfire smoothbore, 37A, 410, 84, Canuck 25, and Canuck 410. Post-1961 Cooey firearms made for Winchester include: Models 84 and 840.

COONAN ARMS

Previously manufactured by Dan Coonan, and distributed from November 1994-September 1998 by JS Worldwide Distribution Co. located in Maplewood, MN. Previously located in St. Paul, MN, approx. 1983-1996.

During 1985, Dan Coonan sold Coonan Arms to Bill Davis. In 1990, Dan Coonan left the company, and during July 1994, the company filed for Chapter 11. Coonan Arms was incorporated by JS Worldwide Distribution in November 1994. On Sept. 25, 1998, Coonan Arms and JS Worldwide Distribution was dissolved by the state of MN.

PISTOLS: SEMI-AUTO

COONAN .357 MAG. MODEL B – .357 Mag. cal. only, stainless steel and alloy construction, single action, semi-auto, design based on the Colt Model 1911, 7 shot mag., 5 or 6 (new

GRADING - PPGS™	100%	98%	95%	90%	80%	70%	60%	LAST MSR

1989) in. barrel, smooth or checkered (new 1996) walnut grips, Teflon finish options (new 1996), 42 oz. Mfg. 1983-1998.

	$795	$725	$650	$475	$400	$350	$295	$735

Add $40 for checkered walnut grips.
Add $33 for 6 in. barrel (new 1989).
Add $140 for Millett adj. rear sight.
Add $165 for Bo-Mar sight.
Add $45 for .38 Spl. conversion kit (new 1986).

This model could be differentiated from the Model A in that it had an extended grip safety lever, linkless barrel system, enclosed trigger bar slot, and recontoured rear grip strap. This model became standard in 1985.

* ***Coonan .357 Mag. Cadet Model*** – similar to .357 Mag. Model B, except is compact variation with 3.9 in. barrel and 6 shot mag., 39 oz. Mfg. 1993-98.

	$850	$775	$675	$500	$425	$375	$315	$855

Options were similar to those listed for the Model B.

* ***Coonan .357 Mag. Cadet II*** – features standard grip with 7/8 shot mag. Mfg. 1996-98.

	$850	$775	$675	$500	$425	$375	$315	$855

Options were similar to those listed for the Model B.

* ***Coonan .357 Mag. Model B Compensated*** – 6 in. barrel with compensator. Mfg. 1990-98.

	$1,000	$900	$800	$650	$540	$465	$385	$1,015

Options were similar to those listed for the Model B.

* ***Coonan .357 Mag. Model Classic Compensated*** – features 5 in. barrel with integral compensator, Millett white/orange outline sights, checkered black walnut grips, Teflon black and matte stainless two-tone finish, 42 oz. Mfg. 1996-98.

	$1,275	$1,025	$825	$675	$595	$525	$450	$1,400

COONAN .357 MAG. MODEL A – original model without above listed improvements, special order only, inventory depleted in 1991. Serialization is under 2,000 for this model (less than 1,200 were mfg.).

	$1,150	$775	$550	$460	$395	$335	$285	$625

Add approx. $350 for early variations with engraved slide.

This variation will also shoot .38+P loads. The first 25 Model As were engraved on both sides of slide.

COONAN .41 MAGNUM – .41 Mag. cal., 5 in. barrel, smooth or checkered walnut grips. Mfg. 1997-98.

	$875	$775	$675	$525	$450	$375	$315	$825

Options were similar to those listed for the .357 Mag.

COONAN, INC.

Current manufacturer established in 2009 and located in Blaine, MN.

PISTOLS: SEMI-AUTO

Coonan has partnered with Tactical Rifles for a rifle and pistol package consisting of a special limited edition 1 of 100 rifle and Coonan pistol. Please contact Tactical Rifles directly for more information on this limited edition set (see Trademark Index).

COONAN CLASSIC .357 MAGNUM AUTOMATIC – .357 Mag. cal., 5 in. barrel, compensated barrel became optional 2013, single action, 1911 style stainless steel frame, blue or digital camo (new 2013) finish, linkless barrel system, extended grip safety, 7 shot mag., dovetail front and rear fixed or adj. sights, smooth black walnut grips, includes case, 48 oz. New mid-2010.

MSR $1,249	$1,075	$925	$800	$700	$600	$500	$400

Add $90 for adj. sights.
Add $200 for night sights.

GRADING - PPGS™	100%	98%	95%	90%	80%	70%	60%	LAST MSR

COOPER FIREARMS OF MONTANA, INC.

Current manufacturer located in Stevensville, MT since 1991. Available through Cooper Firearms registered dealers only.

RIFLES: BOLT ACTION

Approx. 16,000 Cooper rifles have been manufactured in over 50 calibers to date.

Add $200 for left-hand action (custom order only) on the following models, except for Model 52, Model 54, and Model 56 - add $250.

MODEL 21 SINGLE SHOT – various medium size cals., 3 front locking lugs.

* ***Model 21 Classic*** – various cals., single shot, 24 in. chrome moly match grade barrel, stock is AA Claro walnut with 20 LPI hand checkering and hand rubbed oil finish, machined aluminum trigger guard, matte metal finish, approx. 7-7 1/4 lbs. New 1999.

MSR $1,795 $1,595 $1,375 $1,200 $995 $900 $725 $595

* ***Model 21 Custom Classic*** – includes Brownell No. 1 checkering pattern, ebony forend tip, and steel grip cap.

MSR $2,495 $2,175 $1,875 $1,600 $1,425 $1,150 $950 $750

* ***Model 21 Western Classic*** – various cals., features octagon barrel and case hardened action and metal work. New 1997.

MSR $3,395 $2,995 $2,600 $2,225 $1,995 $1,625 $1,325 $1,025

* ***Model 21 Varminter*** – various cals., 24 in. stainless steel match grade barrel, stock is AA Claro walnut with 20 LPI hand checkering and hand rubbed oil finish, machined aluminum trigger guard, approx. 7-7 1/4 lbs. New 1999.

MSR $1,695 $1,475 $1,225 $1,025 $900 $725 $600 $475

* ***Model 21 Varmint Extreme*** – various cals. between .17 Rem.-.223 Rem. (including metric cals.), features stainless barrel, checkered stock. New 1994.

MSR $2,255 $1,975 $1,700 $1,425 $1,250 $995 $825 $625

Add $465 for Benchrest Model with Jewell trigger (mfg. 1995-96).

* ***Model 21 Montana Varminter*** – various cals. New 2000.

MSR $1,795 $1,595 $1,375 $1,200 $995 $900 $725 $595

* ***Model 21 Varmint Laminate*** – similar to Varminter, except has laminated stock. New 2009.

MSR $1,695 $1,475 $1,225 $1,025 $900 $725 $600 $475

Add $200 for Jackson Varmint model.

* ***Model 21 Phoenix*** – 24 in. stainless match barrel, flat black or brown spider web synthetic stock, aluminum bedding block, matte metal finish. New 2005.

MSR $1,695 $1,475 $1,225 $1,025 $900 $725 $600 $475

MODEL 22 – various mid-length action cals., larger-sized version of the Model 21.

* ***Model 22 Classic*** – various mid-action cals., 24 in. chrome moly match grade barrel, stock is AA Claro walnut with 20 LPI hand checkering and hand rubbed oil finish, machined aluminum trigger guard, matte metal finish, approx. 7-7 1/4 lbs. New 1999.

MSR $1,795 $1,595 $1,375 $1,200 $995 $900 $725 $595

* ***Model 22 Custom Classic*** – includes Brownell No. 1 checkering pattern, ebony forend tip, and steel grip cap.

MSR $2,495 $2,175 $1,905 $1,630 $1,480 $1,195 $980 $760

* ***Model 22 Western Classic*** – various cals., features octagon barrel and case hardened action and bolt. New 1997.

MSR $3,395 $3,000 $2,625 $2,250 $2,040 $1,650 $1,350 $1,050

* ***Model 22 Varminter*** – various cals., otherwise similar to the Model 21 Varminter. New 2000.

MSR $1,695 $1,475 $1,225 $1,025 $900 $725 $600 $475

GRADING - PPGS™	100%	98%	95%	90%	80%	70%	60%	LAST MSR

* ***Model 22 Montana Varminter*** – various cals. New 2000.

MSR $1,825	$1,575	$1,350	$1,125	$1,000	$815	$665	$515	

* ***Model 22 Varmint Extreme*** – .220 Swift, .22 BR (new 1996), .22-250 Rem., .243 Win., .25-06 Rem., .308 Win., 6mm PPC, 6.5x55mm (new 1996), or 7.62x39mm (new 1996) cal., available in either Pro-Varmint, Benchrest, or Black Jack (black synthetic stock) configuration. New 1995.

MSR $2,255	$1,975	$1,700	$1,425	$1,250	$995	$825	$625	

Add $400 for Benchrest Model (disc. 2011).

* ***Model 22 Varmint Laminate*** – similar to Varminter, except has laminated stock. New 2009.

MSR $1,695	$1,475	$1,225	$1,025	$900	$725	$600	$475	

* ***Model 22 Phoenix*** – 24 in. stainless match barrel, flat black or brown spider web synthetic stock, aluminum bedding block, matte metal finish. New 2005.

MSR $1,695	$1,475	$1,225	$1,025	$900	$725	$600	$475	

MODEL 22 CLASSIC REPEATER – .22-250 Rem., .243 Win., .308 Win., or 7mm-08 Rem. cal., 3 shot mag. While advertised during 1996 only at $2,400 retail, this model was never mfg.

MODEL CUSTOM CLASSIC – .22 LR, .22 WMR, .22 Hornet, or .222 Rem. cal., features Anschutz Match 54 action with deluxe walnut stock with American features and smaller trigger guard. Mfg. 1996-99.

	$1,750	$1,530	$1,310	$1,190	$960	$785	$610	*$1,995*

MODEL CUSTOM MANNLICHER – .22 LR, .22 WMR, .22 Hornet, or .222 Rem. cal., features newest Anschutz Match 54 action with deluxe Mannlicher walnut stock and other special features. Mfg. 1996-99.

	$1,975	$1,730	$1,480	$1,345	$1,085	$890	$690	*$2,195*

MODEL 36 SPORTSMAN – .22 LR, .17 CCM, or .22 Hornet cal., without Shilen barrel, standard wood with rubber recoil pad. Mfg. 1994 only.

	$675	$590	$505	$460	$370	$305	$235	*$750*

MODEL 36 MARKSMAN – .22 LR, .17 CCM, or .22 Hornet cal., 4 shot mag., 23 in. chrome moly barrel, AA Claro walnut with 22 LPI checkering, 45 degree bolt lift, sling swivels, hand rubbed oil finish, 7 lbs. Mfg. 1992-94.

	$975	$855	$730	$665	$535	$440	$340	*$1,125*

* ***Model 36 Montana Trail Blazer*** – .22 LR cal. only, lightweight field gun with sporter barrel. Mfg. 1996 only.

	$1,300	$1,135	$975	$885	$715	$585	$455	*$1,475*

* ***Model 36 Classic*** – .22 LR cal. only, features choice of AAA Claro or AA French walnut with Monte Carlo cheekpiece. Disc. 1996.

	$1,500	$1,310	$1,125	$1,020	$825	$675	$525	*$1,695*

* ***Model 36 Varmint Extreme*** – various cals., stainless heavy bull barrel, checkered stock. Mfg. 1997 only.

	$1,525	$1,335	$1,145	$1,035	$840	$685	$535	*$1,695*

* ***Model 36 Western Classic*** – various cals., features octagon barrel and case hardened action and bolt. Mfg. 1997-99.

	$1,900	$1,660	$1,425	$1,290	$1,045	$855	$665	*$2,195*

* ***Model 36 Custom Classic*** – includes Brownell No. 1 checkering pattern, ebony forend tip, and steel grip cap. Disc. 1999.

	$1,625	$1,420	$1,220	$1,105	$895	$730	$570	*$1,850*

* ***Model 36 TRP-1*** – target variation of the Model 36 with ISU synthetic stock and adj. cheekpiece, 23 in. Wiseman/McMillan stainless steel or chrome moly barrel, single shot, fully adj. single stage trigger, vent. forearm. Mfg. 1992-93.

	$950	$830	$710	$645	$520	$425	$330	*$1,095*

GRADING - PPGS™	100%	98%	95%	90%	80%	70%	60%	LAST MSR

* ***Model MS-36 (TRP-1S)*** – silhouette variation of the Model 36 TRP-1, clear epoxy finish, silhouette style stock, Pachmayr buttpad. Mfg. 1992-93.

	$895	$785	$670	$610	$490	$405	$315	*$995*

* ***Model 36 BR-50*** – .22 LR cal., benchrest variation featuring black synthetic stock and heavy stainless barrel. Mfg. 1993-99.

	$1,675	$1,465	$1,255	$1,140	$920	$755	$585	*$1,950*

* ***Model 36 IR-50/50*** – .22 LR cal. only, lightweight sporter style competition rifle with heavy 20 in. barrel. Mfg. 1996-99.

	$1,675	$1,465	$1,255	$1,140	$920	$755	$585	*$1,950*

* ***Model 36 Featherweight*** – .17 CCM, .22 LR, or .22 Hornet cal., features matte black synthetic stock and metal, Jewell trigger. Mfg. 1994-99.

	$1,600	$1,400	$1,200	$1,090	$880	$720	$560	*$1,795*

MODEL 38 SPORTER – .17 CCM, or .22 CCM cal., 3 shot mag., 24 in. chrome moly barrel, AA Claro walnut with 22 LPI checkering, 45 degree bolt lift, sling swivels, hand rubbed oil finish, 8 lbs. Mfg. 1992-93.

	$965	$845	$725	$655	$530	$435	$340	*$1,095*

Add $100 for Standard Grade (AA Claro walnut).
Add $200 for Custom Grade.
Add $300 for Custom Classic Grade.

The custom grade includes choice of AAA Claro or AA French walnut with Monte Carlo cheekpiece.

The .17 CCM and .22 CCM cartridges are Cooper Centerfire Magnums. Basically, the .22 CCM is a centerfire derivative of the .22 WMR cal., and the .17 CCM is simply a necked down variation.

* ***Model 38 Repeater (Deluxe)*** – deluxe variation of the Model 38 Sporter. 650 mfg. 1992-1994.

	$1,750	$1,530	$1,310	$1,190	$960	$785	$610	

MODEL 38 SINGLE SHOT – small, mostly rimmed cals., 3 front locking lugs. New 1998.

* ***Model 38 Classic*** – various cals., single shot, 20 in. chrome moly match grade barrel, stock is AA Claro walnut with 20 LPI hand checkering and hand rubbed oil finish, machined aluminum trigger guard, matte metal finish, approx. 7-7 1/4 lbs. New 1999.

MSR $1,795	$1,595	$1,375	$1,200	$995	$900	$725	$595	

* ***Model 38 Custom Classic*** – includes Brownell No. 1 checkering pattern, ebony forend tip, and steel grip cap.

MSR $2,495	$2,175	$1,875	$1,600	$1,425	$1,150	$950	$750	

* ***Model 38 Western Classic*** – various cals., features octagon barrel and case hardened action and bolt. New 1997.

MSR $3,395	$2,995	$2,600	$2,225	$1,995	$1,625	$1,325	$1,025	

* ***Model 38 Varminter*** – various cals., single shot, 24 in. stainless steel match grade barrel, stock is AA Claro walnut with 20 LPI hand checkering and hand rubbed oil finish, machined aluminum trigger guard, approx. 7-7 1/4 lbs. New 1999.

MSR $1,695	$1,475	$1,225	$1,025	$900	$725	$600	$475	

* ***Model 38 Varmint Extreme*** – various cals. including the new .19-223, heavy stainless steel barrel w/o sights, checkered stock. New 1997.

MSR $2,255	$1,975	$1,700	$1,425	$1,250	$995	$825	$625	

* ***Model 38 Montana Varminter*** – various cals. New 2000.

MSR $1,795	$1,595	$1,375	$1,200	$995	$900	$725	$595	

* ***Model 38 Varmint Laminate*** – similar to Varminter, except has laminated stock. New 2009.

MSR $1,695	$1,475	$1,225	$1,025	$900	$725	$600	$475	

Add $200 for Jackson Varmint model.

GRADING - PPGS™	100%	98%	95%	90%	80%	70%	60%	LAST MSR

* ***Model 38 Phoenix*** – 24 in. stainless match barrel, flat black or brown spider web synthetic stock, aluminum bedding block, matte metal finish. New 2005.

MSR $1,695	$1,475	$1,225	$1,025	$900	$725	$600	$475	

MODEL 40 – .17 CCM (disc. 1995), .17 Ackley Hornet, .22 CCM (disc. 1995), .22 Hornet, or .22 K Hornet cal., 3 lug action, incorporates Anschütz mag., choice of Classic, Custom Classic, or Classic Varminter configuration. Mfg. 1995-96.

	$1,600	$1,400	$1,200	$1,090	$880	$720	$560	*$1,825*

Add $200 for Custom Classic or Classic Varminter (disc.) Model.

MODEL 52 – .25-06, .30-06, .270 Win. .280 Rem., .280 AI, .35 Whelen, or .338-06 cal., variety of stock options and barrel lengths, available in Classic, Jackson Game, Custom Classic, Western Classic, or Jackson Hunter configurations. New 2007.

* ***Model 52 Classic*** – AA Claro walnut, steel grip, four panel hand checkering, oil finished stock, matte metal finish, no options.

MSR $1,875	$1,650	$1,375	$1,125	$975	$800	$675	$525	

* ***Model 52 Custom Classic*** – includes Brownell No. 1 checkering pattern, ebony forend tip, and steel grip cap.

MSR $3,195	$2,850	$2,495	$2,135	$1,940	$1,565	$1,280	$995	

* ***Model 52 Western Classic*** – various cals., features octagon barrel and case hardened action and metal work.

MSR $3,895	$3,475	$3,040	$2,605	$2,365	$1,910	$1,565	$1,215	

* ***Model 52 Excalibur*** – 23 in. fluted steel barrel, synthetic version of the Classic with spiral fluted bolt and 3 shot mag.

MSR $1,995	$1,795	$1,575	$1,300	$1,175	$950	$775	$650	

* ***Model 52 Jackson Game*** – similar to Squirrel rifle, many available options.

MSR $2,095	$1,875	$1,625	$1,375	$1,225	$995	$850	$650	

* ***Model 52 Jackson Hunter*** – 22 in. blue match barrel, camo synthetic stock with aluminum bedding block, matte metal finish.

MSR $1,795	$1,595	$1,375	$1,200	$995	$900	$725	$595	

MODEL 54 – .22-250 Rem., .243 Win., .250 Savage, .260 Rem., .308 Win., or 7mm-08 Rem. cal., short action repeater, various configurations available for additional cost (similar to other models), values are for base model (Classic). New 2010.

MSR $1,875	$1,650	$1,375	$1,125	$975	$800	$675	$525	

This model is available in the following configurations as well: Phoenix ($1,875 MSR), Varminter ($1,875 MSR), Montana Varminter ($1,995 MSR), Varmint Laminate ($1,825 MSR), Varmint Extreme ($2,495 MSR), Excalibur ($1,995 MSR), Jackson Game ($2,095 MSR), Jackson Hunter ($1,795), Custom Classic ($3,195 MSR), and the Western Classic ($3,895 MSR).

MODEL 56 – various cals., 26 in. barrel, machined aluminum trigger guard with fully adj. trigger, matte metal finish, AA Claro walnut stock with Cooper multi-point checkering pattern, Pachmayr decelerator pad, 3 shot mag., Sako style extraction, values are for base model (Classic), 8 1/4 lbs. New 2012.

MSR $2,795	$2,500	$2,150	$1,825	$1,500	$1,250	$1,000	$925	

This model is also available in the following configurations: Custom Classic ($3,495), Excalibur ($2,895), Jackson Game ($2,995), Jackson Hunter ($2,795), and Western Classic ($4,395).

MODEL 57-M – . 17 Mach 2 (disc.), .17 HMR (new 2002), .22 LR, or .22 WMR (new 2001) cal., 3 rear locking lugs, 3 (.22 WMR or .17 HMR), or 4 (.17 Mach 2 and .22 LR cal.) shot mag., various configurations, barrel lengths, and features. New 2000.

* ***Model 57-M Classic*** – steel grip, 4-panel hand checkering, oil finished wood, matte metal finish, options not available. New 2000.

MSR $1,895	$1,650	$1,425	$1,150	$1,000	$825	$700	$575	

* ***Model 57 Custom Classic*** – new 2000.

MSR $2,595	$2,250	$1,950	$1,650	$1,450	$1,150	$950	$725	

GRADING - PPGS™	100%	98%	95%	90%	80%	70%	60%	LAST MSR

* ***Model 57 Western Classic*** – new 2000.

MSR $3,395	$2,995	$2,600	$2,225	$1,995	$1,625	$1,325	$1,025	

* ***Model 57 LVT*** – 24 in. stainless match barrel, oil finished AA select Claro hand checkered walnut, matte metal finish. New mid-2005.

MSR $1,895	$1,650	$1,425	$1,150	$1,000	$825	$700	$575	

* ***Model 57 Jackson Squirrel Rifle*** – 22 in. stainless match barrel, fluted forearm, oil finished hand checkered AA Claro walnut with roll over cheekpiece, steel grip cap, 6 1/2 lbs. New 2005.

MSR $1,995	$1,795	$1,575	$1,300	$1,175	$950	$775	$650	

* ***Model 57 Jackson Hunter*** – 22 in. blue match barrel, camo synthetic stock with aluminum bedding block, matte metal finish. New 2005.

MSR $1,795	$1,595	$1,375	$1,200	$995	$900	$725	$595	

* ***Model 57 TRP-3*** – .22 LR cal. only, 24 in. stainless match barrel, single shot, bench rest style, synthetic stock, matte metal finish, not available in left hand. New 2009.

MSR $1,755	$1,550	$1,375	$1,200	$995	$900	$700	$575	

RIFLES: SINGLE SHOT

MODEL 7 PEREGRINE FALLING BLOCK – various cals., falling block action with under lever, choice of varmint extreme or custom sporter configuration, 24 in. barrel, deluxe checkered walnut stock, tang mounted safety, approx. 6 lbs. Limited production 2001 only.

	$1,750	$1,400	$1,100	$925	$800	$675	$550	*$1,995*

Add $300 for custom sporter variation.

MODEL 16 – WSSM cals., 24 in. stainless match grade barrel, hand checkered, oil finished walnut stock, available in varmint styles only. Mfg. 2005-disc.

	$1,225	$975	$825	$725	$625	$550	$450	*$1,395*

Add $200 for Montana Varminter.
Add $400 for Varmint Extreme.

MODEL 72 MONTANA PLAINSMAN – various cals., single shot featuring case colored Win. Model 1885 action with heavy octagon barrel, double set triggers, deluxe checkered straight grip stock and forearm, no sights. While advertised during 1997 at a retail price of $2,195, this model never went into production.

COP

Previous derringer manufacturer located in Torrance, CA.

DERRINGERS

COP DERRINGER – .22 WMR or .357 Mag. cal., 4 shot, 3 in. barrel, stainless steel mfg., double action, wood grips, 28 oz. COP stands for Compact Off-Duty Police. Disc.

	$650	$575	$495	$425	$350	$275	$225	

Add 10% for box in 98%+ condition.

CORE 15

Current trademark of carbines and rifles manufactured by Good Time Outdoors, Inc. (GTO), located in Ocala, FL.

RIFLES: SEMI-AUTO

GTO Guns manufactures a complete line of AR-15 style carbines and rifles, in addition to uppers in various cals., lower receivers, and related accessories.

IMPORTANT NOTE: On model(s) where *N/A has replaced the normal 100% value, it indicates current market conditions are too unstable to accurately ascertain 100%-60% values. Factory retail prices (MSRs) reflect most recent updates. For more up-to-date information on current pricing trends and additional useful information, please visit www.bluebookofgunvalues.com, select "Information & Services" from the menu, and click on "Additional Book Information".

CORE15 M4 PISTON RIFLE – 5.56 NATO cal., AR-15 style, utilizes Core15/Adam Arms gas piston system, M1913 Picatinny optics rails, Tapco 6-position adj. stock, black furniture,

GRADING - PPGS™	100%	98%	95%	90%	80%	70%	60%	LAST MSR

16 in. barrel with muzzle brake, ribbed cylindrical handguard, flat-top receiver, matte black finish or custom colors also available, marked GTO near gas block, 5.9 lbs. New 2011.

MSR $1,200	*N/A	$925	$800	$700	$600	$500	$400

CORE15 M4 RIFLE – 5.56 NATO cal., utilizes standard gas impingement system, A-2 elevated front sight, with one Picatinny rail, otherwise similar to Core15 M4 Piston Rifle. New 2011.

MSR $900	*N/A	$725	$625	$550	$495	$400	$395

CORE15 MOE M4 RIFLE – 5.56 NATO cal., 16 in. M4 profile barrel with A2 flash hider, choice of gas impingement system or gas piston, 30 shot Magpul mag., includes many Magpul MOE accessories, approx. 6 lbs. New 2012.

MSR $1,080	*N/A	$875	$775	$650	$550	$475	$395

Add $420 for Core15 MOE M4 Piston rifle with gas piston assembly.

CORE15 TAC M4 RIFLE – 5.56 NATO cal., similar to Core15 MOE M4 rifle, except has TAC free floating quad rail, approx. 6 lbs. New 2012.

MSR $1,200	*N/A	$950	$825	$725	$625	$525	$425

Add $440 for Core15 TAC M4 Piston rifle with gas piston assembly.

CORE15 TAC M4 V.2 RIFLE – 5.56 NATO cal., 16 in. M4 profile barrel with A2 flash hider, choice of gas impingement system or gas piston, flat top model with full length Picatinny rail on top of receiver and quad rail, Magpul ACS six position stock and pistol grip, 30 shot Magpul mag., approx. 6 lbs. New 2012.

MSR $1,299	*N/A	$1,000	$850	$750	$650	$550	$450

CORE15 MOE MID-LENGTH RIFLE – 5.56 NATO cal., 18 in. heavy stainless steel barrel polygonal rifling and A2 flash hider, flat top receiver, choice of gas impingement system or gas piston, Magpul UBR buttstock and pistol grip, enclosed vent forearm, 8 lbs. New 2012.

MSR $1,329	*N/A	$1,025	$875	$775	$675	$575	$475

Add $375 for Core15 MOE Mid-Length Piston rifle with MOE Desert Tan hardware and gas piston operation (new 2012).

CORE15 TAC MID-LENGTH RIFLE – 5.56 NATO cal., 18 in. heavy barrel with polygonal rifling and A2 flash hider, choice of gas impingement system or gas piston, flat top receiver with mid-length quad rail, Magpul furniture, black finish, 30 shot mag., 8 lbs. New 2012.

MSR $1,599	*N/A	$1,225	$1,050	$925	$800	$675	$525

Add $220 for Core15 TAC Mid-Length Piston rifle with gas piston operation (new 2012).

CORONADO ARMS

Current bolt action rifle manufacturer located in Dixon, CA.

RIFLES: BOLT ACTION

Coronado Arms manufactures high quality bolt action rifles. Current models include Coloma - MSR $5,700, Palasade - MSR $5,400, Akando - MSR $5,100, and the Desperado - MSR $3,800. Please contact the manufacturer directly for availability and special order options on these models (see Trademark Index).

CORTONA

Previous trademark of shotguns manufactured exclusively by F.A.I.R. Techni-Mec, located in Marcheno, Italy for the Kalispel Case Line, an Indian tribe in Idaho. Previously imported until 2010 by Kalispel Case Line, located in Cusick, WA.

SHOTGUNS: O/U

Cortona shotguns utilized boxlock actions with a 3-lug system and Boss style frames in both aluminum and steel. Many variations are possible, and the lineup included the Legend Series with engraved sideplates (last MSR $3,085-$3,285), the Prestige Series with case colored and engraved sideplates and deluxe Turkish walnut stock and forearm (last MSR $3,610-$4,210) (also available in 16 ga.), the Grande Series (last MSR $2,095-$3,995), and the Alumino Series (last MSR $2,665-$2,800). A GR Series was also available in 12, 20, and 28 ga. MSRs ranged from $1,785 - $2,585 (disc. 2007).

GRADING - PPGS™	100%	98%	95%	90%	80%	70%	60%	LAST MSR

COSMI, AMERICO & FIGLIO

Current semi-auto shotgun manufacturer established during 1930, and located in Ancona, Italy. Consumer direct sales, no current U.S. importation. Previously distributed exclusively late 2005-2008 by Dewing's Fly & Gun Shop, located in West Palm Beach, FL. Previously imported 2005-2008 by Pacific Sporting Arms, located in Azuza, CA, from 2003-2004 by Old Friends Hunting & Shooting Co., from 1985-2003 by New England Arms Co., and from 2001-2002 by Autumn Sales, Inc., located in Fort Worth, TX. Please contact the factory directly for more information and model availability (see Trademark Index).

Approximately 8,200 Cosmi shotguns have been manufactured since 1930 (the design dates back to 1925). They are known for their unique mechanism and high-quality fabrication techniques. Since each gun's parts are made separately (and individually serial numbered), most components are not interchangeable from one gun to another.

SHOTGUNS: SEMI-AUTO

Add €2,250 for extra barrel, €2,500 for extra barrel with five multichokes.

STANDARD DELUXE MODEL – 12, 16, or 20 ga., 2 3/4 (16 ga. only) or 3 in. chamber, unique pivoting break open action loads cartridges into stock chamber from inside of receiver, 8 shot mag. with 3 shot reducer option, steel, alloy, or titanium frame, Boehler Antinit or stainless steel barrel (moves when shooting) available with or without choke tubes, all internal parts are mfg. from special chrome-nickel steel or titanium (new 1990), custom order gun only with dimensions specified by individual customer (approx. 6 month delivery time on 12 and 20 ga.). MSR and 100% values are listed in euros, but used pricing is in dollars.

* ***Standard DeLuxe Model*** – barrel and attached receiver assembly are blue, frame is chromed-nickel steel, w/o engraving, current importation is with best quality wood only and deluxe case.

MSR €11,000	€11,000	$12,000	$9,000	$7,500	$6,000	$4,500	$3,750	

Subtract approx. 25% for older mfg. w/o fancy wood and choke tubes.

* ***DeLuxe Engraved Models***

Please contact the company directly for a price quotation on the many Deluxe models it offers with a wide variety of engraving options.

* ***Standard Aluminum Model*** – 12 or 20 ga., receiver made out of machined aluminum, approx. 7 lbs. in 12 ga., approx. 5.9 lbs. in 20 ga., very limited mfg.

MSR N/A	N/A	$11,000	$9,250	$7,500	$5,000	$4,275	$3,750	

Subtract 15% if w/o choke tubes.

* ***Standard DeLuxe Titanium Model*** – 12 or 20 ga., receiver made out of machined titanium, approx. 6.8 lbs. in 12 ga., approx. 5.7 lbs. in 20 ga., MSR and 100% values are listed in euros, but used pricing is in dollars. New 1990.

MSR €17,000	€17,000	$15,500	$13,000	$11,250	$9,000	$7,000	$5,250	

Subtract 15% if w/o choke tubes.

» **DeLuxe Titanium Grade Engraved Models**

Please contact the company directly for a price quotation on the many Deluxe models it offers with a wide variety of engraving options.

COSTER, GEORGE & SON

Previous custom longarm maker circa 1920-1930, located in Glasgow, Scotland.

George Coster was the son of a German-born gunmaker, George Ernest Julius Coster, who left Germany to work for Alex Henry in 1869. Both Julius and George were talented gunmakers who worked for Alex Henry, and in 1886, Julius formed a partnership with a Mr. Hunter, trading as Coster & Hunter in Edinburgh until 1890. Julius continued to work independently until the late 1890s, when he moved to Glasgow and worked for Charles Ingram. Around 1920, father and son worked together as George Coster & Son. Julius died in 1927, and George carried on until 1930, when he went to work for Alex Martin. He stayed there until his retirement.

GRADING - PPGS™	100%	98%	95%	90%	80%	70%	60%	LAST MSR

In 1993, the Coster name was obtained by Glasgow Gunmakers Ltd. (now trading as Graham Mackinlay & Co Gunmakers). Since Mackinlay states that no company records have survived, it is highly recommended that an independent evaluation be done on any Coster firearm before purchase/selling.

Some information courtesy of David Grant and Vic Venters.

COUNTY, S.A.L.

Previous shotgun manufacturer located in Eibar, Spain.

SHOTGUNS: O/U

County manufactured a wide variety of both boxlock and sidelock O/Us, which had very limited U.S. importation.

CRESCENT FIRE ARMS CO. & CRESCENT-DAVIS ARMS CORP.

Previous manufacturers and trademarks manufactured circa 1888-1931 in Norwich, CT.

In 1888, George W. Cilley bought out the defunct Bacon Arms Co. of Norwich, CT. He then formed an alliance with Frank Foster, and borrowed enough money to form the Crescent Fire Arms Company. Cilley and Foster each held several firearms patents, and both were highly qualified in firearms design and manufacture. Production began with single shot tip-up shotguns, which had an external side hammer. Double barrel shotgun production was started in 1891. In 1893, they began making bicycle chains, and that same year, H&D Folsom took over the company's financial control. Early in the 1890s, Crescent built a rifle that resembled the Remington No. 4. A very rare Crescent was the .410 bore shotgun pistol, which was introduced in the 1920s. In 1929, N.R. Davis Firearms Co., then owned by Warner Arms Corp., merged with Cresent to become Crescent-Davis Arms Corp. Because of financial crisis, business continued to decline, and they were forced to sell out. Savage Arms Co. acquired Cresent-Davis in 1931, assembled guns from the remaining parts, and these guns were sold under the Crescent name only. In 1932, the city of Norwich, CT, took over the Crescent property for non-payment of back taxes. After the Norwich facility was closed, manufacture was moved to Chicopee Falls.

It is unknown whether or not Crescent did any high grade or custom work. However, a very well engraved SxS, with the Crescent logo, is known to exist in a private collection.

Crescent Fire Arms Company remains best known as a manufacturer of "house brand" shotguns (i.e., Crescent private labeled guns for retailers, distributors, mail-order houses, etc.). Over 100 different trademarks have been observed to date, manufactured by Crescent. Almost all the remaining specimens today are priced as shooters and have no collector value.

SHOTGUNS

Certain models may be considered Curios or Relics by the BATFE (subject to change). Other models fall under 1934 NFA legislation, and are subject to seizure w/o proper paperwork and registration. Please contact your local BATFE branch for clarification.

SINGLE SHOT MODEL – 12, 16, 20, 28 ga., or .410 bore, exposed hammer, various barrel lengths, walnut stock and forearm. Disc.

12 ga.	$140	$115	$100	$85	$75	$65	$50
16 or 20 ga.	$170	$140	$115	$100	$85	$75	$65
28 ga.	$225	$185	$160	$135	$115	$90	$75
.410 bore	$350	$300	$275	$250	$215	$185	$160

SxS MODEL – values below assume standard models with double triggers, extractors, original finish, and 100% working order. Most shotguns feature sidelock actions. Shotguns with exposed hammers can equal their hammerless counterparts if condition is 80% or better.

12 ga.	$375	$325	$295	$265	$230	$210	$185
16 ga.	$335	$295	$265	$210	$185	$165	$145
20 ga.	$375	$325	$295	$265	$230	$210	$185
28 ga./.410 bore	$1,000	$875	$750	$675	$550	$450	$350

KNICKERBOCKER – 20 ga., 14 in. nickel-plated barrels, case-hardened receiver, pistol grip, mfg. circa 1900s.

Extreme rarity factor precludes accurate pricing information.

GRADING - PPGS™	100%	98%	95%	90%	80%	70%	60%	LAST MSR

Guns not currently registered with the BATFE cannot be legally owned and are subject to seizure.

VICTOR EJECTOR – .410 bore, 12 in. single barrel, total production unknown, possibly prototype for Crescent Certified Shotgun.

Extreme rarity factor precludes accurate pricing information.

Guns not currently registered with the BATFE cannot be legally owned and are subject to seizure.

NEW EMPIRE – hammerless .410 bore or 20 ga., 12 1/4 in. barrels, extremely rare firearm whose total production and years of manufacture are unknown at this time (only known documentation is an "Auto Burglar Gun" in an advertisement by "Saul Ruben, The Gun Store, 68 E. Long St., Columbus, OH" of the October 1932 issue of *Hunter-Trader-Trapper,* which lists a $14.75 retail price). The receiver is marked "New Empire". At this time, 5 specimens are known in .410 bore, with ser. nos. scattered throughout the S-1 to S-19 range. The ser. no. appears on the metal under the forearm. The Crescent Auto & Burglar Gun may have been distributed by the H.& D. Folsom Arms Co. of New York City through its manufacturing division, the Crescent Firearms Co., Norwich, CT. Crescent's sellers included the Belknap Hardware Co., Louisville, KY and Hibbard-Spencer-Bartlett Co., Chicago, IL.

	$1,425	$1,200	$1,000	$900	$800	$700	$600

Guns not currently registered with the BATFE cannot be legally owned and are subject to seizure.

CRESCENT CERTIFIED SHOTGUN – .410 bore, 12 1/2 in. barrel, approx. 4,000 mfg. from approx. 1930-32 by the Crescent-Davis Arms Corp., and possibly thereafter until 1934 by the J. Stevens Arms Co., left receiver side is stamped "Crescent Certified Shotgun/ Crescent-Davis Arms Corp./Norwich, Conn. U.S.A." Also termed the "Ever-Ready" Model 200 and advertised with a blue frame, but specimens with "tiger stripe" and regular case coloring have been observed.

	$1,425	$1,200	$1,000	$900	$800	$700	$600

Add $100-$300 for original cardboard box.

Guns not currently registered with the BATFE cannot be legally owned and are subject to seizure.

CRICKETT RIFLE

Current trademark manufactured by Keystone Sporting Arms, located in Milton, PA.

RIFLES: BOLT ACTION

CRICKETT SPORTER – .22 Short (disc. 2008), .22 LR or .22 WMR (mfg. 2001-2004) cal., manually cocked single shot, 16 1/8 in. barrel with adj. rear aperture sight, steel or stainless steel (new 1999) construction, 11 1/2 in. LOP (youth dimension), choice of beech hardwood, walnut, colored laminate, camo, pink, desert tan, or black synthetic stock, stainless or blue barrel and receiver, 30 in. overall length, 2 1/2 lbs. New 1997.

MSR $180	$165	$140	$125	$110	$95	$85	$75

Add $10 for deluxe walnut stock.
Add $10-$30 for color laminated stock (various colors).
Add $50 for thumbhole stock (available with various stock colors).
Add $10 for stainless steel, and $30 for bull barrel.
Add $20 for adult model with 14 1/2 in. LOP (walnut only).
Add $25 for .22 WMR cal. (disc. 2004).

* ***Crickett Sporter Custom/Deluxe*** – features deluxe hand checkered stock. Mfg. 1998-2000.

$225	$195	$175	$150	$135	$120	$105	*$250*

Add $10 for deluxe configuration.

CROSS CANYON ARMS

Current bolt action rifle manufacturer located in West Haven, UT.

RIFLES: BOLT ACTION

Cross Canyon Arms manufactures custom bolt action hunting and tactical style rifles chambered for its proprietary Tejas cartridge. There are four base models: the Canyon, Grand Canyon, Grand Teton and Death Valley. A multitude of options and finishes are available. Please contact the company for more information, including options, delivery time, and pricing (see Trademark Index).

GRADING - PPGS™	100%	98%	95%	90%	80%	70%	60%	LAST MSR

CROSSFIRE LLC

Previous manufacturer located in La Grange, GA 1998-2001.

COMBINATION GUNS

CROSSFIRE MK-I – 12 ga. (3 in. chamber) over .223 Rem. cal., unique slide action O/U design allows stacked shotgun/rifle configuration, 18 3/4 in. shotgun barrel with invector chokes over 16 1/4 in. rifle barrel, detachable 4 (shotgun) and 5 (rifle) shot mags., open sights, Picatinny rail, synthetic stock and forearm, choice of black (MK-I) or RealTree 100% camo (MK-1RT) finish, single trigger with ambidextrous fire control lever, 8.6 lbs. Limited mfg. mid-1998-2001.

	100%	98%	95%	90%	80%	70%	60%	LAST MSR
	$1,295	$1,150	$995	$895	$795	$695	$595	$1,895

Add $100 for camo finish.

CROWN CITY ARMS

Previous pistol and pistol frame manufacturer located in Cortland, NY circa 1970s-1981.

PISTOLS: SEMI-AUTO

M1911 A1 – 9mm Para., .38 Super, or .45 ACP cal., patterned after the Colt MKIV Series 70 Govt. and Commander Models, 4 1/4 or 5 in. barrel, 7 shot mag., carbine steel, alloy, or stainless steel frame, smooth or checkered walnut grips, matte black oxide finish or brushed stainless steel, fixed or adj. sights, 27-39 oz. Disc. circa 1981.

	100%	98%	95%	90%	80%	70%	60%	LAST MSR
	$675	$600	$525	$450	$375	$325	$275	

Last MSR was approx. $200 (base model).

CUMBERLAND MOUNTAIN ARMS, INC.

Previous manufacturer located in Winchester, TN early 1993-99.

RIFLES: SINGLE SHOT

PLATEAU RIFLE – .40-65 or .45-70 Govt. cal., patterned after the Browning High Wall single shot, various barrel lengths up to 32 in., manual safety, blue receiver and barrel, Marble's style buckhorn rear sight, receiver drilled for scope mounts. Mfg. 1993-99.

	100%	98%	95%	90%	80%	70%	60%	LAST MSR
	$1,075	$825	$675	$575	$500	$450	$400	$1,295

Add approx. $200-$350 for deluxe wood.

CUSTOM GUN GUILD

Previous manufacturer located in Doraville, GA.

FIREARMS

WOOD'S MODEL IV SINGLE SHOT – various cals., custom manufactured, falling block type single shot, lightweight, only 5 1/2 lbs. Mfg. 1984 only.

	100%	98%	95%	90%	80%	70%	60%	LAST MSR
	$2,975	$2,500	$2,000	$1,850	$1,700	$1,500	$1,250	

CYLINDER & SLIDE, INC.

Current pistol manufacturer located in Fremont, NE. Direct consumer sales only through FFL.

William Laughridge has been making M1911 style custom pistols for decades. Currently he manufactures a historical Pocket Model based on the 1903/1908 Colt Pocket Model (MSR $3,995), the Trident Series (MSR $3,881-$3,988), in addition to building a new series of M1911s utilizing early 1913 patent markings - models include the U.S. Army, U.S. Navy, and U.S. Marine Corp. Please refer to the Turnbull Mfg. Co. in the T section for information and values on this new series.

CZECHPOINT INC.

Current distributor located in Knoxville, TN.

Czechpoint Inc. distributes paramilitary style semi-auto rifles, including a line of AK-47 design carbines/rifles with milled receivers in various configurations, Skorpion pistols (see model listing under Skorpion heading), and revolvers manufactured in the Czech Republic by D-Technik, Alfa Proj., and others. Please contact the company directly regarding current model availability and pricing (see Trademark Index).

D SECTION

D'ARCY ECHOLS & CO.

Current manufacturer beginning 1996, and located in Millville, UT.

RIFLES: BOLT ACTION

Models include the Legend Standard Sporter ($15,500 MSR), Legend Heavy Sporter, scoped or iron sight version ($15,500 MSR), Legend Long Range Sporter ($15,650 MSR), Classic Light Sporter ($32,000), Long Range (disc. 2010, last MSR was $13,700), Heavy Sporter (scoped or iron sight version, $32,000-$34,000 MSR). Additionally, many special orders and options are also available. Please contact the company for more information (see Trademark Index).

RIFLES: SINGLE SHOT

A new single shot rifle with Farquharson action in various calibers was released during 2012. Please contact the company directly for more information and a price quotation on this model.

DGS, INC.

Current custom rifle gunsmith and machinist located in Casper, WY.

Master gunsmith Dale A. Storey and custom machinist Robert J. Stone have a total of seventy-five years of experience in fine rifles and precision machining. DGS, Inc. offers a variety of rifles built per individual specification. Custom machining of octagon barrels in various configurations from assorted name brand blanks is also available. Please contact the company directly for more information and current prices on these quality custom rifles (see Trademark Index).

DPMS FIREARMS (LLC)

Current manufacturer established in 1986 and located in St. Cloud, MN. Previously located in Becker, MN. Previous company name was DPMS, Inc. (Defense Procurement Manufacturing Services, Inc.) assembles high quality AR-15 style rifles (including a conversion for .22 cal.), in addition to selling related parts and components. Distributor, dealer, and consumer direct sales.

In December 2007, Cerberus Capital Management acquired the assets of DPMS. The new company name became DPMS Firearms, LLC, and currently is DPMS Firearms.

GRADING - PPGS™	100%	98%	95%	90%	80%	70%	60%	LAST MSR

PISTOLS: SEMI-AUTO

DPMS .45 – .45 ACP cal., patterned after the Colt M1911A-1, 7 shot mag., 5 in. barrel, 38 oz. Limited mfg. 2001 only.

$475	$425	$360	$330	$300	$275	$250	*$519*

PANTHER .22 LR PISTOL – .22 LR cal., 8 1/2 in. heavy chrome-moly steel barrel, 10 shot mag., black aircraft aluminum flat-top upper receiver, black forged aircraft aluminum lower receiver, blowback action, phosphate and hard chrome finished bolt and carrier, aluminum trigger guard, ribbed aluminum tubular hand guard, no sights, 4 1/4 lbs. Limited mfg. 2006-2007.

$775	$700	$625	$550	$475	$425	$375	*$850*

PISTOLS: SLIDE ACTION

PANTHER PUMP PISTOL – .223 Rem. cal., slide action paramilitary design, 10 1/2 in. threaded heavy barrel, aluminum handguard incorporates slide action mechanism, pistol grip only (no stock), carrying handle with sights, 5 lbs. Disc. 2007.

$1,475	$1,200	$1,025	$925	$825	$700	$575	*$1,600*

RIFLES: BOLT ACTION

DPMS also distributed Evolution USA bolt action rifles until 2006. Please refer to the Evolution USA section for current models and pricing.

GRADING - PPGS™	100%	98%	95%	90%	80%	70%	60%	LAST MSR

RIFLES: SEMI-AUTO

Each new DPMS rifle/carbine comes equipped with two mags. (high cap where legal), a nylon web sling, and a cleaning kit. Post-crime bill manufactured DPMS rifles may have pre-ban features, including collapsible stocks, high capacity mags, and a flash hider/compensator. Models with these features are not available in certain states.

The Panther AR-15 Series was introduced in 1993 in various configurations, including semi-auto and slide action, and feature a paramilitary design in various barrel lengths and configurations, with a 10 or 30 shot mag.

IMPORTANT NOTE: On model(s) where *N/A has replaced the normal 100% value, it indicates current market conditions are too unstable to accurately ascertain 100%-60% values. Factory retail prices (MSRs) reflect most recent updates. For more up-to-date information on current pricing trends and additional useful information, please visit www.bluebookofgunvalues.com, select "Information & Services" from the menu, and click on "Additional Book Information".

300 AAC BLACKOUT – .300 AAC Blackout cal., 16 in. heavy chromelined barrel, equipped with Blackout suppressor adapter, or an inert slipover mock suppressor, AP4 stock, choice of carbine or mid-length handguard, 7-7 1/2 lbs. New 2012.

MSR $1,199	*N/A	$850	$725	$625	$525	$475	$425

COMPACT HUNTER – .308 Win. cal., 16 in. Teflon coated stainless steel barrel, B5 System Sopmod stock, two-stage match trigger, carbon fiber free float handguard, Hogue rubber pistol grip, 7 3/4 lbs. New 2012.

MSR $1,499	*N/A	$1,000	$850	$725	$600	$525	$450

LONG RANGE LITE – .308 Win. cal., 24 in. stainless steel barrel, A2 fixed stock, two-stage match trigger, carbon fiber free float handguard, Hogue rubber pistol grip, 10 1/4 lbs. New 2012.

MSR $1,499	*N/A	$1,000	$850	$725	$600	$525	$450

MOE WARRIOR – 5.56 NATO cal., 16 in. heavy barrel, Magpul MOE stock, handguard, and pistol grip, back-up sights, sling adapter, enhanced trigger guard, suppressor adapter, Black or Dark Earth Magpul MOE furniture, 7.3 lbs. New 2012.

MSR $1,159	*N/A	$850	$725	$625	$525	$475	$425

TPR – 5.56 NATO cal., 20 in. heavy stainless steel barrel with AAC flash hider, M111 modular handguard, Magpul MOE pistol grip and B5 Systems Sopmod stock, two stage trigger, 7 3/4 lbs. New 2012.

MSR $1,349	*N/A	$1,000	$875	$750	$650	$600	$550

TAC2 – 5.56 NATO cal., 16 in. barrel, Magpul ACS stock, MOE pistol grip, new M111 modular handguard system, utilizes a full rifle length gas system, Panther flash hider, 8 1/2 lbs. New 2012.

MSR $1,299	*N/A	$900	$775	$675	$575	$500	$450

TAC20 – .308 Win. cal., 20 in. heavy chromemoly barrel, A2 fixed stock, detachable carry handle, Panther flash hider, 11 1/2 lbs. New 2012.

MSR $1,299	*N/A	$900	$775	$675	$575	$500	$450

PANTHER A2/A3 CLASSIC – 5.56 NATO cal., 16 (disc.) or 20 in. heavy barrel, ribbed barrel shroud, A3 stock with detachable carrying handle with sights, or A2 fixed stock 9 lbs.

MSR $869	*N/A	$650	$575	$475	$425	$375	$335

Add $110 for A3 stock. Add $76 for left-hand variation (Southpaw Panther, disc.)

* ***Panther Classic Bulldog*** – 20 in. stainless fluted bull barrel, flat-top, adj. buttstock, vented free float handguard, 11 lbs. Disc. 1999.

	*N/A	$835	$725	$625	$550	$475	$425	*$1,219*

PANTHER 7.62x39mm CARBINE/RIFLE – 7.62x39mm Russian cal., 16 or 20 in. heavy barrel, black Zytel buttstock with trap door assembly, A2 flash hider, A2 pistol grip, 7-9 lbs. Mfg. 2000-2011.

	*N/A	$650	$575	$475	$425	$375	$335	*$850*

Add $10 for 20 in. barrel.

GRADING - PPGS™	100%	98%	95%	90%	80%	70%	60%	LAST MSR

PANTHER DCM – .223 Rem. cal., 20 in. stainless steel heavy barrel, National Match sights, two-stage trigger, black Zytel composition buttstock, 9 lbs. Mfg. 1998-2003, reintroduced 2006-2012.

	*N/A	$800	$675	$595	$525	$460	$415	*$1,129*

PANTHER LITE A1/A3 – 5.56 NATO cal., 16 (disc.) or 20 (new 2007) in. post-ban chromemoly barrel, 1:9 in. twist, non-collapsible fiberite CAR stock, choice of forged A1 upper with forward bolt assist or A3 (disc.) carry handle, black Teflon finish, 6-7.3 lbs. New 2002.

MSR $829	*N/A	$625	$525	$475	$395	$325	$250	

PANTHER LITE 308/338 – .308 Win. or .338 Federal cal., 18 in. free float barrel, no sights, carbon fiber free float hand guard, bipod stud, A3 style flat-top, Picatinny rail, various accessories and options available. New 2009.

MSR $1,499	*N/A	$1,100	$925	$800	$700	$600	$500	

PANTHER CLASSIC SIXTEEN – 5.56 NATO cal., 16 in. lightweight chromemoly (new 2012) or heavy (disc. 2011) barrel, adj. sights, black Zytel composition buttstock, 6 1/2 lbs. New 1998.

MSR $859	*N/A	$625	$550	$495	$400	$325	$250	

Add $55 for Panther Free Float Sixteen with free floating barrel and vent. handguard (disc. 2008).

PANTHER LO-PRO CLASSIC – 5.56 NATO cal., 16 in. bull barrel, A2 fixed stock, features flat-top lo-pro upper receiver with push pin, 7 3/4 lbs. Mfg. 2002-2012.

	*N/A	$625	$550	$450	$400	$360	$325	*$769*

PANTHER TUBER – 5.56 NATO cal., features 16 in. post-ban heavy free float barrel with full length 2 in. dia. aluminum free float handguard, adj. A2 rear sights. Mfg. 2002-2008.

	*N/A	$625	$565	$485	$435	$375	$335	*$754*

PANTHER A2 TACTICAL – 5.56 NATO cal., features 16 in. heavy manganese phosphated barrel, standard A2 handguard, 9 3/4 lbs. New 2004.

MSR $859	*N/A	$650	$550	$475	$425	$375	$335	

PANTHER AP4 CARBINE – 5.56 NATO cal., features 16 in. M4 contour barrel with A2 flash hider, with or w/o attached Miculek compensator, fixed fiberglass reinforced polymer M4 stock, 7 1/4 lbs. New 2004.

MSR $959	*N/A	$750	$625	$475	$425	$375	$335	

Add $54 for Miculek compensator.

* ***Panther AP4 Carbine (Disc.)*** – 6.8x43mm SPC or 5.56x45mm cal., 16 in. barrel, collapsible stock, includes carrying handle, 6 1/2 lbs. Disc.

	*N/A	$725	$600	$525	$450	$400	$360	*$904*

PANTHER AP4 A2 CARBINE – 5.56 NATO cal., 16 in. chromemoly steel heavy barrel with A2 flash hider, standard A2 front sight assembly, A2 fixed carry handle and adj. rear sight, forged aircraft aluminum upper and lower receiver, hard coat anodized teflon coated black AP4 six position telescoping fiber reinforced polymer stock, 7.1 lbs. New 2006.

MSR $959	*N/A	$725	$650	$550	$475	$425	$375	

PANTHER A2 CARBINE "THE AGENCY" – 5.56 NATO cal., 16 in. chrome-moly steel barrel with A2 flash hider, A3 flat-top forged receiver, two-stage trigger, tactical charging handle, package includes Surefire quad-rail and flashlight, EoTech and "Mangonel" rear sights, Ergo Suregrip forearm and collapsible stock, supplied with two 30 shot mags., 7 lbs. Mfg. 2007-2012.

	*N/A	$1,600	$1,425	$1,250	$1,025	$900	$775	*$2,069*

PANTHER 6.5 – 6.5 Creedmoor cal., 24 in. stainless steel free float bull barrel, single rail gas block, no sights, ribbed aluminum free float tube handguard, bipod stud, A3 style flat-top, black Teflon coated, standard A2 black Zytel mil spec stock, A2 pistol grip, 11.3 lbs. New 2009.

MSR $1,239	*N/A	$875	$750	$650	$575	$500	$450	

GRADING - PPGS™	100%	98%	95%	90%	80%	70%	60%	LAST MSR

PANTHER 6.8mm CARBINE/RIFLE – 6.8x43mm Rem. SPC cal., 16 (new 2007) or 20 in. chrome-moly manganese phosphated steel barrel with A2 flash hider, standard A2 front sight assembly, A3 flat-top upper receiver with detachable carry handle and adj. rear sight, aluminum aircraft alloy lower receiver, black standard A2 Zytel mil spec stock with trap door assembly, A2 handguard, includes two 25 shot mags., approx. 9 lbs. Mfg. 2006-2011.

	100%	98%	95%	90%	80%	70%	60%	LAST MSR
	*N/A	$800	$700	$600	$500	$425	$375	*$1,019*

Add $10 for 20 in. barrel.

PANTHER 6.8 SPCII HUNTER – 6.8x43mm Rem. SPC cal., 18 in. steel barrel with Miculek compensator, aluminum A3 flat-top with forward assist, black Zytel skeletonized A2 stock, mid-length carbine fiber free-floating forearm tube, 7.65 lbs. Mfg. 2011-2012.

	100%	98%	95%	90%	80%	70%	60%	LAST MSR
	*N/A	$950	$825	$725	$650	$600	$550	*$1,269*

PANTHER RECON MID-LENGTH CARBINE – 5.56 NATO cal., 16 in. stainless steel heavy barrel with AAC blackout flash hider, flat-top aluminum upper receiver with Magpul BUIS front and rear sights, mid-length quad rail free floating forearm tube, 7.7 lbs. New 2011.

	100%	98%	95%	90%	80%	70%	60%
MSR $1,129	*N/A	$795	$675	$595	$525	$460	$415

Add $430 for .308 Recon (new 2012).

PANTHER LBR CARBINE – 5.56 NATO cal., 16 in. lightweight stainless barrel with A2 flash hider, muzzle brake, flat-top receiver with integral Picatinny rail, Magpul MOE stock with A2 pistol grip, vent free floating handguard with front upper Picatinny rail, 7 1/4 lbs. New 2011.

	100%	98%	95%	90%	80%	70%	60%
MSR $979	*N/A	$750	$625	$475	$425	$375	$335

This model is also available in a DIVAS Edition with 16 in. chromemoly barrel and Leopard print especially for women (new 2012).

PRAIRIE PANTHER – 20 in. heavy fluted free float barrel, flat-top, vented handguard, 8 3/4 lbs. Disc. 1999.

	100%	98%	95%	90%	80%	70%	60%	LAST MSR
	*N/A	$750	$635	$550	$475	$425	$375	*$959*

PRAIRIE PANTHER (CURRENT MFG.) – .223 Rem. cal., 20 in. stainless steel fluted heavy barrel, target crown, carbon fiber free float tube, no sights, hard anodized finish, choice of black with carbon fiber handguard (new 2011), King's Desert Shadow (Desert), King's Snow Shadow (new 2011) or Mossy Oak Brush (Brush) camo coverage, A3 Picatinny rail flat-top, tactical charging handle assembly, Magpul winter trigger guard, skeletonized black Zytel mil spec stock with trap door assembly, A2 pistol grip, two-stage trigger, approx. 7.1 lbs. New 2010.

	100%	98%	95%	90%	80%	70%	60%
MSR $1,239	*N/A	$950	$825	$725	$625	$525	$425

Add $50 for camo finishes.

PANTHER BULL – .223 Rem. cal., features 16 (Sweet 16), 20, or 24 in. stainless free float bull barrel, flat-top, aluminum forearm, 10 lbs.

	100%	98%	95%	90%	80%	70%	60%
MSR $939	*N/A	$725	$600	$525	$450	$400	$360

Add $40 for 20 in. barrel. Add $60 for 24 in. barrel (Panther Bull 24).

* ***Panther Bull Classic*** – .223 Rem. cal., features 20 in. long, 1 in. bull barrel, adj. sights, 10 lbs. Mfg. 1998-2008.

	100%	98%	95%	90%	80%	70%	60%	LAST MSR
	*N/A	$725	$600	$525	$450	$400	$360	*$910*

Add $200 for SST lower.

* ***Panther Bull Twenty-Four Special*** – .223 Rem. cal., features 24 in. stainless fluted barrel, adj. A2 buttstock with sniper pistol grip. New 1998.

	100%	98%	95%	90%	80%	70%	60%
MSR $1,229	*N/A	$875	$725	$625	$525	$460	$415

* ***Panther Super Bull*** – .223 Rem. cal., 16, 20, or 24 in. extra heavy free float bull barrel, flat-top receiver, handguard; approx. 11 lbs. Mfg. 1997-98, 24 in. model reintroduced during late 2004, disc. 2006.

	100%	98%	95%	90%	80%	70%	60%	LAST MSR
	*N/A	$835	$725	$600	$525	$460	$415	*$1,199*

* ***Panther Super Bull 24*** – features 24 in. extra heavy stainless steel bull barrel (1 1/8 in. diameter barrel), flat-top, hi-rider upper receiver, skeletonized A2 buttstock, 11 3/4 lbs. Mfg. 1999-2004.

	100%	98%	95%	90%	80%	70%	60%	LAST MSR
	*N/A	$835	$715	$600	$525	$460	$415	*$1,199*

GRADING - PPGS™	100%	98%	95%	90%	80%	70%	60%	LAST MSR

ARCTIC PANTHER – .223 Rem. cal., 20 in. barrel, similar to Panther Bull, except has white powder coat finish on receiver and handguard, 10 lbs. New 1997.

MSR $1,129	*N/A	$800	$675	$595	$525	$460	$415	

PANTHER PARDUS – .223 Rem. cal., 16 in. stainless steel free float bull barrel, integrated compensator, titanium nitride plated steel bolt and carrier, three rail extruded upper receiver, aluminum alloy upper and lower receiver, Teflon coated tan or black six position telescoping fiber reinforced polymer stock, curved and serrated buttplate, four-rail aluminum handguard, no sights, includes two 30 shot mags., 8.1 lbs. Mfg. 2006-2008.

	*N/A	$1,150	$950	$800	$675	$575	$525	*$1,600*

PANTHER MK 12 5.56 NATO – 5.56 NATO cal., 18 in. stainless heavy free float barrel with flash hider, features one-piece four rail tube and six long rail covers, A3 flat-top receiver, 5-position collapsible stock with tactical pistol grip, two-stage trigger, two 30 round mags., 8 3/4 lbs. New 2007.

MSR $1,649	*N/A	$1,125	$950	$800	$700	$600	$500	

PANTHER MK 12 7.62 NATO – 7.62 NATO cal., 18 in. stainless steel heavy barrel, flash hider, Midwest Industries flip up rear sight, gas block with flip up front sight, A3 Picatinny rail flat-top, aluminum lower receiver, integral trigger guard, Magpul CTR adj. stock, Hogue rubber grip with finger grooves, two stage match trigger, hard anodized black finish, four rail free float tube, six rail covers, approx. 9.6 lbs. New 2010.

MSR $1,799	*N/A	$1,225	$975	$825	$725	$625	$550	

PANTHER SDM-R – .223 Rem. cal., 20 in. heavy stainless free float barrel with A2 flash hider, features four rail aluminum tube, pistol grip stock, National Match front sight, Harris bipod with rail adapter, two 30 shot mags., 8.85 lbs. Mfg. 2007-2008.

	*N/A	$1,075	$925	$825	$725	$650	$575	*$1,404*

PANTHER 20TH ANNIVERSARY – .223 Rem. cal., 20 in. stainless steel fluted bull barrel, phosphated steel bolt and carrier, hi-rider forged high polished chrome upper and lower receiver with commemorative engraving, chrome plated charging handle, semi-auto trigger group, aluminum trigger guard and mag. release button, A2 black Zytel mil spec stock with trap door assembly and engraved DPMS logo, no sights, vented aluminum handguard, includes two 30 shot mags., approx. 9 1/2 lbs. Limited mfg. of 100 rifles in 2006.

	*N/A	$1,750	$1,600	$1,475	$1,350	$1,225	$1,100	*$1,995*

PANTHER RACE GUN – .223 Rem. cal., 24 in. stainless steel barrel with Hot Rod hand guard, IronStone steel and aluminum stock with rubber buttplate and brass weights, 16 lbs. Mfg. 2001-2008.

	*N/A	$1,250	$1,050	$950	$850	$725	$600	*$1,724*

PANTHER SINGLE SHOT – 5.56 NATO cal., 20 in. barrel, A2 black Zytel stock and handguard, single shot only w/o magazine, 9 lbs. Disc. 2008.

	$725	$640	$560	$485	$435	$375	$335	*$819*

AP4 .22 CAL CARBINE – .22 LR cal., 16 in. barrel, GlacierGuard M4 handguard, A2 pistol grip and flash hider, AP4 stock with detachable carry handle.

MSR $935	$795	$695	$595	$550	$425	$350	$275	

.22 CAL. BULL CARBINE – .22 LR cal., 16 in. bull barrel, aluminum handguard, A2 pistol grip and flash hider, fixed A2 stock, no sights.

MSR $935	$795	$695	$595	$550	$425	$350	$275	

PANTHER .22 RIFLE – .22 LR cal., AR-15 style receiver, 16 in. bull barrel, black Teflon metal finish, Picatinny rail, black Zytel A2 buttstock, 7.8 lbs. Mfg. 2003-2008.

	$725	$625	$550	$475	$425	$375	$335	*$804*

PANTHER DCM .22 LR RIFLE – .22 LR cal., 20 in. fluted stainless steel H-Bar barrel with 1:16 in. twist, A2 upper receiver with National Match sights, black teflon finish, A2 stock and handguards, also available with optional DCM handguard system. Mfg. 2004-2008.

	$875	$775	$650	$550	$475	$425	$375	*$994*

GRADING - PPGS™	100%	98%	95%	90%	80%	70%	60%	LAST MSR

PANTHER AP4 .22 LR RIFLE – .22 LR cal., features 16 in. M4 contoured barrel with 1:16 in. twist, M4 handguards and pinned carstock, A3 flat-top upper receiver, detachable carry handle with A2 sights and black teflon finish, 6 1/2 lbs. Mfg. 2004-2008.

	$785	$675	$600	$500	$450	$400	$350	*$894*

This model was also available in a pre-ban configuration for law enforcement.

PANTHER LR-.308 – .308 Win. cal., 24 in. free float bull barrel with 1:10 in. twist, ribbed aluminum forearm tube, aircraft alloy upper/lower, A2 buttstock, black Teflon finish. New mid-2003.

MSR $1,199	*N/A	$875	$750	$650	$575	$500	$450	

* ***Panther LR-.308B*** – .308 Win. cal., similar features as the Long Range Rifle, except has 18 in. chrome-moly bull barrel and carbine length aluminum handguard. Mfg. late 2003-2012.

	*N/A	$875	$750	$650	$575	$500	$450	*$1,189*

* ***Panther LR-.308T*** – 7.62 NATO cal., similar features as the .308B, except has 16 in. H-Bar barrel. Mfg. 2004-2012.

	*N/A	$875	$750	$650	$575	$500	$450	*$1,189*

* ***Panther LR-.308 AP4*** – 7.62 NATO cal., similar to Panther .308 Long Range, except has AP4 six position telescoping fiber reinforced polymer stock. Disc. 2012.

	*N/A	$950	$825	$725	$650	$600	$550	*$1,299*

* ***Panther LR-.308 Classic*** – 7.62 NATO cal., similar to Panther LR-308, except has 20 in. barrel. New mid-2008.

MSR $1,199	*N/A	$800	$675	$595	$525	$460	$415	

PANTHER LRT-SASS – 7.62 NATO cal., 18 in. stainless steel contoured barrel with Panther flash hider, A3 style flat-top upper receiver solid alumnium lower receiver, AR-15 trigger group, ambi-selector, JP adj. trigger, black waterproof Vltor Clubfoot carbine 5 position (disc.) or Magpul stock, vented handguard and Panther tactical pistol grip, approx. 11 1/2 lbs. New 2006.

MSR $2,179	*N/A	$1,625	$1,350	$1,125	$950	$825	$700	

PANTHER MINI-SASS – 5.56 NATO cal., 18 in. stainless steel fluted barrel with Panther flash hider, forged A3 flat-top upper receiver, aircraft aluminum alloy lower receiver, aluminum trigger guard, tactical pistol grip, includes Harris bipod, 10 1/4 lbs. New 2008.

MSR $1,649	*N/A	$1,200	$950	$800	$675	$575	$525	

PANTHER LR-30S – .300 RSUM cal., 20 in. stainless steel free float fluted bull barrel, aluminum upper and lower receiver, hard coat anodized teflon coated black skeletonized synthetic stock, integral trigger guard, ribbed aluminum tube handguard, includes two 4 shot mags., nylon web sling and cleaning kit. Mfg. 2004-2008.

	*N/A	$925	$825	$725	$650	$600	$550	*$1,255*

PANTHER LR-204 – .204 Ruger cal., 24 in. fluted stainless steel bull barrel, no sights, A3 flat-top forged upper and lower receiver, semi-auto trigger group, standard A2 black Zytel mil spec stock with trap door assembly, includes two 30 shot mags., 10 1/4 lbs. New 2006.

MSR $1,059	*N/A	$825	$675	$575	$475	$425	$375	

PANTHER LR-243 – .243 Win. cal., 20 in. chrome-moly steel heavy (disc. 2012) or lightweight (Lite Hunter) free float barrel, no sights, raised Picatinny rail, aluminum upper and lower receiver, standard AR-15 trigger group, skeletonized black Zytel mil spec stock with trap door assembly, ribbed aluminum free float handguard, includes two 19 shot mags., 10 3/4 lbs. New 2006.

MSR $1,499	*N/A	$1,125	$950	$875	$700	$575	$450	

PANTHER LR-260 SERIES – .260 Rem. cal., 18 (mfg. 2007-2012, LR-260L), 20 (LR-260H, Lite Hunter) or 24 (LR-260) in. stainless steel fluted bull barrel, no sights, raised Picatinny rail, thick walled aluminum upper receiver, solid lower receiver, standard AR-15 trigger group, integral trigger guard, A2 black Zytel stock with trap door assembly, includes two 19 shot mags., 11.3 lbs. New 2006.

MSR $1,239	*N/A	$925	$795	$725	$575	$475	$375	

GRADING - PPGS™	100%	98%	95%	90%	80%	70%	60%	LAST MSR

Add $260 for 18 in. barrel (LR-260L) with skeletonized stock, Miculek compensator and JRD trigger (disc. 2012), or for 20 in. barrel (Lite Hunter).

PANTHER LR-308C – .308 Win. cal., 20 in. heavy steel free float barrel, features A3 flat-top receiver with detachable carrying handle, standard A2 front sight assembly, four rail standard length tube, two 19 shot mags., 11.1 lbs. Mfg. 2007-2008.

	100%	98%	95%	90%	80%	70%	60%	LAST MSR
	*N/A	$925	$825	$725	$650	$600	$550	*$1,254*

PANTHER ORACLE – 5.56 NATO (disc. 2012) or 7.62 NATO cal., 16 in. chrome-moly heavy barrel, A2 flash hider, gas block with single rail, no sights, GlacierGuards oval carbine length handguard, A3 Picatinny flat-top, hard anodized black finish, integral trigger guard, Pardus six position telescoping stock with cheekpiece, A2 pistol grip, curved and serrated buttplate, multiple sling slots, approx. 8.3 lbs. New 2010.

	100%	98%	95%	90%	80%	70%	60%
MSR $1,099	*N/A	$825	$700	$625	$525	$425	$325

Add $90 for ATACS Oracle Carbine (includes ATACS camo coverage), new 2011.

PANTHER SPORTICAL – 5.56 NATO (disc. 2012) or 7.62 NATO cal., 16 in. chrome-moly heavy or lite contour barrel, single rail gas block, A2 flash hider, various rails and accessories. New mid-2008.

	100%	98%	95%	90%	80%	70%	60%
MSR $1,029	*N/A	$775	$650	$595	$475	$395	$300

PANTHER REPR – 7.62 NATO cal., 18 in. chromemoly (disc.) or 20 in. fluted stainless steel free float barrel, Gem Tech flash hider/suppressor, micro gas block, A3 style flat-top upper receiver, milled aluminum lower receiver, hard coat anodized coyote brown finish, removable hinged trigger guard, Picatinny rail, four rail tube handguard, Magpul Precision Rifle Stock, Hogue rubber grip with finger grooves, 9 1/2 lbs. New 2009.

	100%	98%	95%	90%	80%	70%	60%
MSR $2,589	*N/A	$1,925	$1,650	$1,350	$1,125	$950	$825

PANTHER RAPTR CARBINE – 5.56 NATO cal., 16 in. chrome-moly steel contoured barrel, 30 shot mag., flash hider, A2 front sight, Mangonel flip up rear sight, Ergo Z-Rail two piece four rail handgard, Crimson Trace vertical grip with integrated light and laser combination, A3 Picatinny rail flat-top, hard coat anodized black finish, dust cover, aluminum trigger guard, AP4 six position telescoping polymer stock, Ergo Ambi-Sure grip, 8.2 lbs. Mfg. 2010-2011.

	100%	98%	95%	90%	80%	70%	60%	LAST MSR
	*N/A	$1,140	$950	$800	$700	$600	$500	*$1,649*

PANTHER CSAT TACTICAL – 5.56 NATO cal., 16 in. chrome-moly steel contoured barrel, 30 shot mag., A2 front sight assembly with A2 front sight post, detachable rear sight, four rail free float tube, A3 Picatinny rail flat-top, aluminum lower receiver, Magpul CTR adj. stock, Magpul MIAD pistol grip, 7.8 lbs. Mfg. 2010-2012.

	100%	98%	95%	90%	80%	70%	60%	LAST MSR
	*N/A	$1,250	$1,025	$850	$725	$625	$550	*$1,799*

PANTHER CSAT PERIMETER – 5.56 NATO cal., similar to Tactical, except has 16 in. heavy barrel, approx. 8 lbs. Mfg. 2010-2011.

	100%	98%	95%	90%	80%	70%	60%	LAST MSR
	*N/A	$1,250	$1,025	$850	$725	$625	$550	*$1,799*

PANTHER 3G1 – 5.56 NATO or 7.62 NATO (new 2012) cal., 18 in. stainless standard or heavy barrel, 30 shot mag., Miculek compensator, no sights, VTAC modular handguard, bipod stud, A3 Picatinny rail flat-top, black anodized finish, aluminum trigger guard, JP adj. trigger group, Magpul CTR adj. stock, Hogue rubber pistol grip, 7 3/4 lbs. New 2010.

	100%	98%	95%	90%	80%	70%	60%
MSR $1,299	*N/A	$900	$750	$650	$575	$500	$450

Add $400 for 7.62 NATO cal. (new 2012).

RIFLES: SLIDE ACTION

PANTHER PUMP RIFLE – .223 Rem. cal., paramilitary design, 20 in. threaded heavy barrel with flash hider, aluminum handguard incorporates slide action mechanism, carrying handle with sights, bayonet lug, designed by Les Branson, 8 1/2 lbs. Disc. 2009.

	100%	98%	95%	90%	80%	70%	60%	LAST MSR
	$1,525	$1,275	$1,050	$925	$775	$650	$575	*$1,700*

DSA INC.

Current manufacturer, importer, and distributor of semi-auto rifles and related components located in Barrington, IL. Previously located in Round Lake and Grayslake, IL.

GRADING - PPGS™	100%	98%	95%	90%	80%	70%	60%	LAST MSR

DSA Inc. is a manufacturer of FAL design and SA58 style rifles for both civilian and law enforcement purposes (L.E. certificates must be filled out for L.E. purchases). Until recently, DSA, Inc. also imported a sporterized Sig 550 rifle.

PISTOLS: SEMI-AUTO

SA58TAC – 7.62x51 cal., 8 in. barrel, based on SA58 FAL design, 20 shot mag., Type 1 or 2 receiver, Trident flash hider, black glass filled nylon furniture, Para extended scope mount, lightweight alloy lower receiver, SAW pistol grip, folding cocking handle, includes sling and hard case. New 2013.

MSR $1,695	*N/A	$1,275	$1,095	$975	$800	$650	$515	

RIFLES: BOLT ACTION

DS-MP1 – .308 Win. cal., 22 in. match grade barrel, Rem. 700 action with Badger Ordnance precision ground heavy recoil lug, trued bolt face and lugs, hand lapped stainless steel barrel with recessed target crown, black McMillan A5 pillar bedded stock, Picatinny rail, includes test target guaranteeing 1/2 MOA at 100 yards, black or camo Duracoat finish, 11 1/2 lbs. Mfg. 2004-2009.

	$2,500	$2,150	$1,800	$1,550	$1,250	$1,000	$850	*$2,800*

RIFLES: SEMI-AUTO

The SA-58 rifles listed are available in either a standard DuraCoat solid (OD Green or GrayWolf), or optional camo pattern finishes - add $250 for camo. Patterns include: Underbrush, Woodland Prestige, Desert MirageFlage, Urban MirageFlage, Wilderness MirageFlage, OD MirageFlage, Black Forest MirageFlage, Winter Twig, Tiger Stripe, Advanced Tiger Stripe, Vietnam Tiger Stripe, Marsh, AmStripe, Urban Camo, Belgian Camo, ACU, Afghan Camo, Multicolor or Mossy Oak Breakup (disc.). DSA Inc. makes three types of forged steel receivers, and they are distinguished by the machining cuts on Types I and II, and no cuts on Type III.

IMPORTANT NOTE: On model(s) where *N/A has replaced the normal 100% value, it indicates current market conditions are too unstable to accurately ascertain 100%-60% values. Factory retail prices (MSRs) reflect most recent updates. For more up-to-date information on current pricing trends and additional useful information, please visit www.bluebookofgunvalues.com, select "Information & Services" from the menu, and click on "Additional Book Information".

Add $300-$350 for camo, depending on pattern.

SA58 STANDARD RIFLE/CARBINE – .308 Win. cal., FAL design using high precision CNC machinery, 16 (carbine), 18 (carbine), 19 (disc. 2012), 21 (standard or bull), or 24 in. (bull only, disc. 2009) steel or stainless steel cyrogenically treated barrel, black synthetic stock, pistol grip (standard 2001) attached to frame, 10 or 20 shot mag., 8.7-11 lbs.

MSR $1,700	*N/A	$1,250	$1,050	$875	$775	$675	$575	

Add $250 for stainless steel barrel. Add $150 for bull barrel.

* ***SA58 Standard Rifle Predator*** – .243 Win., .260 Rem., or .308 Win. cal., Type 1 or Type 3 receiver, 16 or 19 in. barrel with target crown, green fiberglass furniture, Picatinny rail, 5 or 10 shot mag., approx. 9 lbs. Mfg. 2003-2012.

	*N/A	$1,250	$1,050	$875	$775	$675	$575	*$1,750*

* ***SA58 Standard Rifle Gray Wolf*** – .300 WSM (disc. 2005) or .308 Win. cal., Type 1 or Type 3 receiver, 21 in. bull barrel with target crown, gray aluminum handguard, synthetic stock and adj. pistol grip, Picatinny rail, 5 or 10 shot mag., approx. 13 lbs. Mfg. 2003-2010.

	*N/A	$1,750	$1,450	$1,250	$1,050	$875	$775	*$2,295*

* ***SA58 Tactical Carbine*** – similar to SA58 Standard Rifle, except has 16 1/4 in. barrel, 8 1/4 lbs. Mfg. 1999-2012.

	*N/A	$1,250	$1,050	$875	$775	$675	$575	*$1,700*

Add $275 for Para folding stock.
Add $200 for SA58 Lightweight Carbine with aluminum receiver components (disc. 2004).
Add $250 for SA58 Stainless Steel Carbine (included scope mount through 2000).
Subtract 5% if w/o fluted barrel (became standard 2009).

GRADING - PPGS™	100%	98%	95%	90%	80%	70%	60%	LAST MSR

* ***SA58 Carbine*** – .308 Win. cal., 16 1/4 or 18 in. threaded barrel, Type I or II receiver, standard synthetic or X-Series buttstock, pistol grip, threaded flash hider, lightweight alloy lower. New 2011.

MSR $1,700 *N/A $1,250 $1,050 $875 $775 $675 $575

* ***SA58 Standard Para. Rifle/Carbine*** – .308 Win. cal., 16 (carbine, fluted or non-fluted), 18 (carbine), or 21 in. threaded barrel, Type I or II receiver, standard synthetic, X-Series buttstock (disc. 2012), or Para. folding stock, pistol grip, threaded flash hider, lightweight alloy lower. New 2011.

MSR $1,975 *N/A $1,575 $1,350 $1,150 $950 $750 $625

* ***SA58 Medium Contour*** – .223 Rem. or .308 Win. cal., 21 in. medium contour barrel, Type I or II receiver, standard synthetic or X-Series buttstock, pistol grip, threaded flash hider, lightweight alloy lower. New 2011.

MSR $1,700 *N/A $1,250 $1,050 $875 $775 $675 $575

Add $150 for .223 Rem. cal.

* ***SA58 Standard Rifle Collectors Series*** – .308 Win. cal., configurations included the Congo ($1,970 - last MSR), Para Congo ($2,220 - last MSR), and the G1 ($2,000 - last MSR). Mfg. 2003-2010.

Add $230 for Dura-coat finish.

* ***SA58 Standard Rifle T48 Replica*** – .308 Win. cal., 10 or 20 shot fixed mag., stripper clip top cover, cryogenically treated barrel, wood furniture, replica Browning flash hider. Imported 2002-2008.

N/A $1,275 $1,050 $850 $725 $625 $525** ***$1,795

* ***SA58 SPR (Special Purpose Rifle)*** – .308 Win. cal., Type I forged receiver, 19 in. fully fluted premium barrel, match grade speed trigger, rail interfaced handguard, extended extreme duty scope mount, SPR side folding adj. stock, SAW pistol grip, Versa-Pod bipod and BUIS included, detachable 10 or 20 shot mag., includes adj. sling, hard case, 13.8 lbs. New 2009.

MSR $4,795 *N/A $3,950 $3,500 $3,100 $2,750 $2,450 $2,150

* ***SA58 Spartan*** – .308 Win. cal., Type 1 non-carry handle cut receiver with Spartan Series logo, aluminum lower receiver, 16 or 18 in. standard weight barrel with Steyr short flash hider or YHM Phantom flashider, DSA custom shop speed trigger, tactical para. rear sight, post front sight, standard synthetic buttstock, military grade handguard, black finish or black with OD Green furniture, three detachable 20 shot mags., adj. sling and case. New 2009.

MSR $2,595 *N/A $2,000 $1,750 $1,550 $1,325 $1,125 $950

Add $200 for Spartan TAC model with 16 in. medium contour fluted barrel, side folding stock, and A2 flash hider.

STG58 AUSTRIAN FAL – .308 Win. cal., features choice of DSA Type I or Type II upper receiver, carry handle, steel lower receiver, rifle has long flash hider, carbine has Steyr short flash hider, steel handguard with bipod cut, metric FAL buttstock and pistol grip, adj. front and rear sight, 10 or 20 shot detachable mag., 10 - 10.4 lbs. Imported 2006-2008, reimported 2011-2012.

N/A $900 $800 $700 $600 $500 $400** ***$1,150

Add $50 for carbine.
Add $290 for rifle with folding stock (disc. 2008).
Add $340 for carbine with folding stock (disc. 2008).

IMBEL 58 – .308 Win. cal., Imbel FAL standard rifle with 21 in. original Imbel barrel, DSA Type 1 carry handle cut receiver, original flash hider, U.S. humpback stock and handguard. Mfg. 2011-2012.

N/A $775 $650 $525 $450 $375 $325** ***$995

DS-S1 – .223 Win. cal., 16, 20, or 24 in. match chamber stainless steel free float bull barrel, A2 buttstock, aluminum handguard, Picatinny gas block sight base, forged lower receiver,

GRADING - PPGS™	100%	98%	95%	90%	80%	70%	60%	LAST MSR

NM two-stage trigger, forged flat-top upper receiver, optional fluted barrel, variety of Duracoat solid or camo finishes available, 8-10 lbs. Mfg. 2004-2005.

	*N/A	$775	$675	$600	$525	$450	$400	*$950*

DS-CV1 CARBINE – 5.56 NATO cal., 16 in. chrome-moly D4 barrel with press on mock flash hider, fixed Shorty buttstock, D4 handguard and heatshield, forged front sight base, forged lower receiver, forged flat-top upper receiver, variety of Duracoat solid or camo finishes available, 6 1/4 lbs. Mfg. 2004-2005.

	*N/A	$700	$625	$550	$500	$450	$400	*$850*

DS-LE4 CARBINE – 5.56 NATO cal., 14 1/2 or 16 in. chrome-moly D4 barrel with threaded A2 flash hider, collapsible CAR buttstock, D4 handguard with heatshield, forged lower receiver, forged front sight base with bayonet lug, forged flat-top upper receiver, Duracoat solid or camo finish, 6.15 or 6 1/4 lbs. Mfg. 2004-2012.

The 14 1/2 in. model was for military/law enforcement only.

DS-AR SERIES – .223 Rem cal., available in a variety of configurations including carbine and rifle, standard or bull barrels, various options, stock colors and features. Mfg. 2006-2008.

	*N/A	$800	$700	$600	$525	$450	$400	*$1,000*

Add $243 for SOPMOD Carbine. Add $30 for 1R Carbine. Add $150 for 1V Carbine. Add $130 for S1 Bull rifle. Add $500 for DCM rifle. Add $30 for XM Carbine.

Add $1,395 - $1,515 for monolithic rail platform. Add $675 for Z4 GTC Carbine with corrosion resistant operating system.

ZM-4 SERIES – .223 Rem. cal., 16 or 20 in. barrel, forged upper and lower receiver, various configurations, black finish, detachable magazine, hard case. New 2004.

* ***ZM-4 Standard*** – 20 in. chrome-moly heavy barrel with A2 flash hider, mil-spec forged lower receiver and flat-top upper, front sight base with lug, standard handguard with heat shield, fixed A2 buttstock, 9 lbs.

MSR $788	*N/A	$595	$500	$450	$375	$300	$235

Add $24 for A2 carry handle (mfg. 2011-2012)
Add $62 for chrome lined barrel.

* ***ZM-4 Mid-Length*** – similar to Standard, except has 16 in. barrel and M4 six position collapsible stock, 6.65 lbs.

MSR $834	*N/A	$625	$550	$475	$425	$395	$350

Add $13 for fluted barrel. Add $55 for A2 carry handle (disc.). Add $102 for Magpul MOE pistol grip and ACE FX fixed skeleton stock (new 2013).

* ***ZM-4 Standard Carbine*** – similar to ZM-4 Mid-Length, except has 16 in. non-fluted barrel, also available in OD Green, A2 carry handle.

MSR $831	*N/A	$650	$575	$500	$450	$400	$350

Add $219 for flat top receiver.

* ***ZM-4 Standard MRP*** – 16 or 18 in. chrome lined (16 in.) or stainless steel free float barrel, mil-spec forged lower receiver, LMT MRP forged upper receiver with 20 1/2 in. full length quad rail, LMT enhanced bolt, dual extractor springs, collapsible CAR stock, detachable 30 shot mag., A2 flash hider. Disc. 2010.

	*N/A	$2,050	$1,775	$1,550	$1,325	$1,125	$950	*$2,695*

Add $100 for stainless steel barrel.

* ***ZM-4 Gas Piston CQB*** – 16 in. chrome lined free floating barrel, Mil-spec forged lower receiver, LMT gas piston CQB forged upper receiver, one piece bolt carrier, quick change barrel system, collapsible CAR stock, detachable 30 shot mag., A2 flash hider. Disc. 2010.

	*N/A	$2,150	$1,625	$1,550	$1,325	$1,125	$950	*$2,870*

* ***ZM-4 Spartan*** – 16 in. fluted chrome-moly barrel, Yankee Hill Machine Phantom flash hider, mil-spec forged lower and flat-top upper receiver, mid-length gas system, forged front sight base with lug, M4 collapsible stock, Magpul trigger guard, Robar NP3 bolt, carrier, and charging handle, Hogue pistol grip, LEO model with Chip McCormick

GRADING - PPGS™	100%	98%	95%	90%	80%	70%	60%	LAST MSR

match trigger, SOPMOD collapsible stock, and two-piece rail system became standard 2013, 6.65 lbs.

MSR $1,455 *N/A $1,075 $925 $850 $675 $550 $430

* ***ZM-4 .300 Blackout*** – .300 Blackout cal., 16 in. blue or stainless steel barrel, matte black finish, A3 flat top alloy receiver, forged front sight base with bayonet lug, M4 handguard with heat shield, Trident flash hider, Hogue pistol grip, six position collapsible stock. New 2013.

MSR $853 *N/A $625 $550 $495 $400 $325 $250

Add $20 for stainless.

* ***ZM-4 Enhanced Carbine*** – 5.56 NATO cal., 16 in. Enhanced MK16 fluted M4 barrel, matte black finish, alloy flat top receiver, forged front sight base with bayonet lug, ambidextrous selector switch, YHM muzzle brake, Magpul MOE pistol grip, enhanced Delta ring, Magpul MOE handguard, six position MOE stock. New 2013.

MSR $929 *N/A $695 $595 $550 $425 $350 $275

RPD TRADITIONAL RIFLE – 7.62x39 cal., 20 1/2 in. barrel, billet machined receiver, belt-fed, wood stock, includes two 100 shot belt and drum sets, carry bag, sling, hard case, approx. 17 lbs. New 2013.

MSR $2,100 *N/A $1,575 $1,350 $1,225 $995 $815 $625

RPD CARBINE – 7.62x39 cal., 17 1/2 in. fluted barrel, billet machined receiver, belt-fed, quad rail handguard, SAW style pistol grip, fully adj. AR15 style stock, lightweight alloy lower trigger frame, includes two 100 shot belt and drum sets, carry bag, sling, hard case, approx. 14 lbs. New 2013.

MSR $2,850 *N/A $2,125 $1,825 $1,650 $1,325 $1,095 $850

DWM

Previous manufacturer located in Berlin, Germany circa 1900-1930. DWM (Deutsche Waffen und Munitionsfabriken) manufactured Lugers are listed in the Luger section.

PISTOLS: SEMI-AUTO

POCKET AUTOMATIC – 7.65mm cal., 3 1/2 in. barrel, blue, hard rubber grips. Mfg. 1921-1931.

$1,000 $850 $600 $500 $450 $400 $350

D.Z. ARMS

Current custom rifle manufacturer established in 1991 and located in Oklahoma City, OK.

D.Z. Arms manufactures replica Remington #3 Hepburn rifles, as well as bolt action benchrest and hunting rifles. The company also offers gunsmithing services. Please contact the company directly for more information, including pricing, options, and availability (see Trademark Index).

DAEWOO

Previous commercial firearms manufacturer located in Korea. Previous limited importation by Century International Arms, located in Delray Beach, FL. Previous importation included Kimber of America, Inc. until 1997, Daewoo Precision Industries, Ltd., until mid-1996, located in Southampton, PA, and previously distributed by Nationwide Sports Distributors 1993-96. Previously imported by KBI, Inc. and Firstshot, Inc., both located in Harrisburg, PA, and B-West located in Tucson, AZ.

Daewoo made a variety of firearms available for commercial use, and most of these were never imported into the U.S.

PISTOLS: SEMI-AUTO

DH380 – .380 ACP cal., double action design. Imported 1995-96.

$330 $285 $260 $235 $210 $185 $165 *$375*

GRADING - PPGS™	100%	98%	95%	90%	80%	70%	60%	LAST MSR

DH40 – .40 S&W cal., otherwise similar to DP51, 32 oz. Imported 1995-disc.

	$325	$270	$245	$225	$200	$185	$170	

DP51 STANDARD/COMPACT – 9mm Para. cal., "fast action" allows lowering hammer w/o depressing trigger, 3 1/2 (DP51 C or S, disc.) or 4.1 (DP51) in. barrel, 10 (C/B 1994), 12* (.40 S&W), or 13* (9mm Para.) shot mag., 3-dot sights, tri-action mechanism (SA, DA, or fast action), ambidextrous manual safety, alloy receiver, polished or sand-blasted black finish, 28 or 32 oz., includes lockable carrying case with accessories. Recently imported in various configurations circa 1991-2009.

No MSR	$315	$265	$240	$220	$200	$185	$170	

Add 10% for DP51 Compact (disc.).

DP52 – .22 LR cal., double action, 3.8 in. barrel, alloy receiver, 10 shot mag., blue finish, 23 oz. Imported 1994-96.

	$320	$275	$225	$200	$180	$165	$150	*$380*

RIFLES: SEMI-AUTO

MAX II (K2) – .223 Rem. cal., paramilitary design rifle, 18 in. barrel, gas operated rotating bolt, folding fiberglass stock, interchangeable mags. with the Colt M16, 7 lbs. Importation disc. 1986.

	$950	$875	$800	$725	$625	$550	$475	*$609*

MAX I (K1A1) – similar to Max II (K2), except has retractable stock. Importation disc. 1986.

	$1,050	$925	$850	$750	$650	$575	$500	*$592*

DR200 – .223 Rem. cal., paramilitary configuration with sporterized stock, 10 shot mag. Imported 1995-96.

	$650	$550	$475	$425	$395	$375	$350	*$535*

DR300 – 7.62x39mm cal., paramilitary configuration with or w/o thumbhole stock. Importation disc.

	$650	$550	$475	$425	$395	$375	$350	

DAISY

Current airgun manufacturer with headquarters located in Rogers, AR. Daisy manufactured firearms 1968-1991.

For more information and current pricing on both new and used Daisy airguns, please refer to the *Blue Book of Airguns* by Dr. Robert Beeman & John Allen (also online).

RIFLES: SINGLE SHOT, DISC.

As the V/L ammunition availability diminishes, the following values may fluctuate.

V/L STANDARD RIFLE – .22 V/L cal. (caseless air ignited cartridge), 1,100 FPS, 18 in. barrel, plastic stock, not particularly accurate. Approx. 19,000 mfg. 1968-69.

	$400	$350	$300	$275	$225	$180	$140	

V/L PRESENTATION – similar to Collector's Kit, except does not have owner's name inscribed on buttplate, walnut stock. 4,000 mfg. for dealers.

	$495	$425	$375	$325	$275	$225	$175	*$125*

V/L COLLECTOR'S KIT – comes with case, gun cradles, 300 rounds of ammo, and a gold plated brass buttplate with owner's name and serial number of gun. Approx. 4,000 mfg., available only by direct factory order.

	$700	$625	$525	$475	$375	$300	$250	*$125*

Note: The Daisy .22 V/L was discontinued because the BATFE ruled that the gun constituted a firearm, and since Daisy was federally licensed to manufacture air weapons only, the factory decided to discontinue manufacture.

RIFLES: BOLT ACTION, DISC.

All Legacy models have a removable trigger, slings and swivels, takedown barrel, dovetail receiver for scope mounting, rifled inner steel barrel with 12 lands and grooves, and an adj. rear sight. Weight is between 6 1/2-7 lbs.

GRADING - PPGS™	100%	98%	95%	90%	80%	70%	60%	LAST MSR

MODEL 8 – .22 S or LR cal., single shot, 16 in. barrel, black synthetic stock, 30,000 mfg. for Wal-Mart only 1987-88.

$275	$250	$200	$175	$150	$125	$95	

During 1987, Daisy assembled this model using left-over Iver Johnson parts.

LEGACY MODELS 2201/2211 – .22 LR cal., single shot, bolt action, plastic (2201) or walnut finished hardwood (2211) stock, models vary in features. Mfg. 1988-1991.

$275	$250	$200	$175	$150	$125	$95	

LEGACY MODELS 2202/2212 – .22 LR cal., bolt action repeater, 10 shot rotary mag., plastic (2202) or walnut finished hardwood (2212) stock, models vary in features. Mfg. 1988-1991.

$325	$275	$250	$225	$175	$150	$125	

Model 2202 has copolymer stock with adj. buttplate.

RIFLES: SEMI-AUTO

LEGACY MODELS 2203/2213 – .22 LR cal., 7 shot box mag., models vary in features. Mfg. 1988-1991.

$350	$300	$275	$250	$200	$150	$125	

Model 2203 has copolymer stock with adj. buttplate. Model 2213 has American hardwood stock.

DAIWA

Previous U.S. firearms importer and distributor.

Daiwa imported various firearms circa 1960s-early 1970s. Configurations included semi-auto shotguns mfg. by Nikko, Ltd. of Japan, and bolt action rifles. Values are based on the current utilitarian value, since there is little collectibility on these guns.

DAKIN GUN CO.

Previous importer located in San Francisco, CA, and Kansas City, MO, circa 1960s.

SHOTGUNS: O/U

MODEL 170 – 12, 16, 20 ga., or .410 bore, boxlock, light engraving, double triggers, vent rib.

$495	$400	$325	$275	$245	$220	$195	

SHOTGUNS: SxS

MODEL 100 – 12 or 20 ga., boxlock, engraved, double trigger.

$425	$350	$275	$240	$205	$190	$170	

MODEL 147 – 12 or 20 ga., boxlock, engraved, vent. rib, double trigger.

$495	$385	$300	$265	$235	$215	$195	

MODEL 160 – 12 or 20 ga., boxlock, single trigger, ejectors, vent. rib.

$825	$700	$595	$495	$450	$395	$360	

MODEL 215 – 12 or 20 ga., sidelock, heavy engraving, special walnut, single trigger, ejectors, vent. rib.

$2,250	$1,900	$1,675	$1,300	$1,100	$925	$775	

SHOTGUNS: SINGLE BARREL

Dakin imported a single barrel trap gun manufactured by Miroku while the company was located in Kansas City, MO.

DAKOTA ARMS, INC.

Current manufacturer and previous importer established in 1986, located in Sturgis, SD. Dealer and direct sales through manufacturer only. This company is not affiliated with Dakota Single Action Revolvers.

On June 5, 2009, Remington Arms Company purchased Dakota Arms, Inc.

Dakota Arms Inc. also owned the rights to Miller Arms and Nesika actions. Please refer to these individual sections for more information.

GRADING - PPGS™	100%	98%	95%	90%	80%	70%	60%	LAST MSR

Dakota Arms models listed below are also available with many custom options - please contact the factory directly for availability and pricing. Left-hand actions are available on all bolt action rifles at no extra charge. Actions (barreled or unbarreled) may also be purchased separately. Please contact the manufacturer directly for individual quotations.

RIFLES: BOLT ACTION

DAKOTA .22 RIFLE – .17 HMR (new 2004) .22 LR, .22 Win Mag. (new 2004), or .22 Hornet (disc.) cal., combines features of the Win. Model 52 Sporter and Dakota 76, full sized receiver, trigger and striker block safety similar to Dakota 76, 5 shot mag., 22 in. chrome-moly barrel, checkered XX walnut stock, no sights, 6 1/2 lbs. Mfg. 1992-98, reintroduced 2003-2004.

	100%	98%	95%	90%	80%	70%	60%	LAST MSR
	$2,650	$2,320	$1,985	$1,800	$1,455	$1,190	$925	*$3,000*

DAKOTA 76 TRAVELER – various cals. between .25-06 Rem. - .450 Dakota, in addition to Dakota proprietary calibers, 23 in. barrel, almost seamless take down rifle based on the Dakota 76 design, threadless disassembly ensuring scope stability and accuracy, in addition to no possibility of increasing the head space during repeated disassembly, wood stock, approx. 7 1/2 lbs. New 1999.

	100%	98%	95%	90%	80%	70%	60%
MSR $7,240	$6,500	$5,800	$5,000	$4,225	$3,750	$3,025	$2,475

Add $2,090 for Safari Traveler.
Add $3,300 for African Traveler.
Add $2,490 (standard cals.) or $2,720 (Safari cals.) per interchangeable barrel.
Add $2,950 for African barrel.

DAKOTA 76 CLASSIC GRADE – available in various cals. (short, standard, or long action), custom frame incorporating many Win. Model 70 features, 21 or 23 in. barrel, Mauser type extractor, checkered X English walnut stock, 7 1/2 lbs. New 1987.

	100%	98%	95%	90%	80%	70%	60%
MSR $ 6,030	$5,600	$4,900	$4,150	$3,550	$2,950	$2,675	$2,200

Add $1,980 for Classic Deluxe model with upgraded wood stock.

This Model is also available with a composite stock at no extra charge.

DAKOTA 76 .30-06 100TH ANNIVERSARY – .30-06 cal., 100 year banner on floor plate, Exhibition walnut with limited edition checkering pattern, stainless steel Model 76 Classic action and receiver, custom LOP, only 100 mfg. 2006-2007.

	100%	98%	95%	90%	80%	70%	60%	LAST MSR
	$8,350	$7,305	$6,260	$5,680	$4,590	$3,755	$2,920	*$8,945*

DAKOTA 76 VARMINT GRADE – available in 9 cals. between .17 Rem. and 6mm PPC, single shot bolt-action, heavy barrel. Mfg. 1994-97.

	100%	98%	95%	90%	80%	70%	60%	LAST MSR
	$2,275	$1,990	$1,705	$1,545	$1,250	$1,025	$795	*$2,500*

DAKOTA 76 SAFARI GRADE – available in various cals., 23 in. barrel, one-piece drop trigger guard assembly with hinged floor plate, checkered XXX English walnut stock with ebony forearm tip, 8 1/2 lbs. New 1987.

	100%	98%	95%	90%	80%	70%	60%
MSR $8,010	$7,500	$6,850	$5,650	$4,650	$4,100	$3,350	$2,725

Subtract $400 (retail) if ordered with composite stock (disc.).

DAKOTA 76 AFRICAN GRADE – .404 Jeffery, .416 Dakota, .416 Rigby, or .450 Dakota cal., 4 shot mag., select wood with cross bolts in the stock, other features similar to Safari Grade Model, 24 in. barrel, "R" prefix on serial number, 9 1/2 lbs. New 1989.

	100%	98%	95%	90%	80%	70%	60%
MSR $8,890	$7,995	$7,100	$6,100	$5,500	$4,750	$3,900	$2,850

DAKOTA 76 ALPINE GRADE – .22-250 Rem., .243 Win., 6mm Rem., .250-3000 Savage, 7mm-08 Rem., .308 Win., or .358 Win. cal., short action variation of the Classic Grade, 21 or 23 in. barrel, lighter weight model featuring a blind 4 shot mag., checkered X English walnut slimmer stock and barrel, serial numbered with a "K" prefix, 6 1/2 lbs. Mfg. 1989-1992, reintroduced 2008.

	100%	98%	95%	90%	80%	70%	60%
MSR $6,360	$5,500	$4,450	$3,700	$3,250	$2,600	$2,100	$1,800

Add $1,650 for Alpine Deluxe Model (new 2011).

Other calibers are available on a special order basis.

DAKOTA LONGBOW T-76 TACTICAL – .300 Dakota Mag., .300 Win. Mag. (new 2006), .330 Dakota Mag., .308 Win. (new 2006), .338 Lapua Mag., or .338 Dakota Mag. cal., 28 in.

GRADING - PPGS™	100%	98%	95%	90%	80%	70%	60%	LAST MSR

stainless barrel, long range tactical design, black synthetic stock with adj. comb, includes Picatinny optical rail, Model 70 style trigger, matte finish metal, controlled round feeding, and deployment kit, 13.7 lbs. Mfg. 1997-2009.

	$4,300	$3,760	$3,225	$2,925	$2,365	$1,935	$1,505	*$4,795*

DAKOTA SCIMITAR TACTICAL – .308 Win. or .338 Lapua cal., 24 or 27 in. match grade chrome-moly barrel, 2nd generation Longbow with solid top receiver, long and short action, one-piece bolt handle, oversized claw extraction system, true controlled round feed, three postition safety, non-glare matte black finish, synthetic stock, optical rail. Mfg. 2008-2009.

	$5,850	$5,120	$4,385	$3,980	$3,215	$2,630	$2,045	*$6,295*

DAKOTA MODEL 97 LIGHTWEIGHT HUNTER – available in most popular cals. between .22-250 Rem. and .308 Win., features fiberglass stock with black recoil pad, right hand only, 6 lbs. Mfg. 1998-2004.

	$1,925	$1,685	$1,445	$1,310	$1,060	$865	$675	*$2,195*

Add $300 for Wood Hunter 97 (includes semi-fancy wood and blind mag.).

* ***Dakota Model 97 Lightweight Hunter Deluxe*** – available in short or long action, matte blue finish, checkered AAA claro stock with cheekpiece, controlled round feed, three position safety, cloverleaf tang, 24 or 26 in. precision match chrome-moly blue or stainless barrel. Disc. 2010.

	$3,750	$3,280	$2,810	$2,550	$2,060	$1,685	$1,310	*$4,295*

Add $200 for stainless barrel.

* ***Dakota Model 97 Lightweight Hunter All Weather Outfitter*** – available in short or long action, matte blue finish, precision sand-colored composite stock, aluminum pillar bedding, controlled round feed, three position safety, cloverleaf tang, 24 or 26 in. precision match chrome-moly stainless barrel, right or left hand. Limited mfg. 2005.

	$2,650	$2,320	$1,985	$1,800	$1,455	$1,190	$925	*$2,995*

* ***Dakota Model 97 Outfitter Takedown*** – various cals., features takedown action, textured tan or grey synthetic stock, barrel assembly has ramped rear sight and hooded front sight, barrel band, drilled and tapped, tan or grey finish on barrel. New 2010.

MSR $5,150	$4,475	$3,825	$3,250	$2,750	$2,300	$1,850	$1,650	

DAKOTA MODEL 97 LONG RANGE HUNTER – available in 13 popular cals. between .25-06 Rem. and .375 Dakota Mag., composite black H-S Precision stock, 24 or 26 in. barrel, adj. match trigger, Model 76 ejector system, approx. 7.7 lbs. New 1997.

MSR $3,720	$3,350	$2,800	$2,400	$1,925	$1,750	$1,475	$1,250	

Add $300 for Wood Hunter 97 (includes semi-fancy wood and blind mag., disc. 2004).

Add $1,100 for Deluxe Model 97 (Hunter) - includes XX checkered walnut stock and matte blue finish.

DAKOTA MODEL 97 ALL WEATHER HUNTER (STAINLESS) – available in short or long action, matte blue finish, precision composite stock, aluminum pillar bedding, controlled round feed, three position safety, cloverleaf tang, 24 or 26 in. precision match chrome-moly stainless barrel, right or left hand. New mid-2008.

MSR $4,050	$3,650	$3,250	$2,800	$2,375	$2,125	$1,725	$1,425	

DAKOTA CLASSIC PREDATOR – various cals., special select checkered claro walnut sporter style stock with cheekpiece, 22 in. match grade stainless steel barrel, swivel studs. Mfg. 2005-2009.

	$3,650	$3,200	$2,800	$2,400	$2,000	$1,600	$1,375	*$4,295*

* ***Dakota Classic Predator Series*** – similar to Classic Predator, except has varmint type stock with semi-beavertail forend.

	$2,850	$2,495	$2,135	$1,940	$1,565	$1,280	$995	*$3,295*

* ***Dakota Classic Predator All-Weather*** – similar to Predator Serious, except has precision composite varmint type stock with semi-beavertail forend. Disc.

	$2,275	$1,990	$1,705	$1,545	$1,250	$1,025	$795	*$2,595*

GRADING - PPGS™	100%	98%	95%	90%	80%	70%	60%	LAST MSR

RIFLES: SxS

DOUBLE RIFLE – .470 NE, .500 NE, .570 NE, and most rimmed cals., round boxlock action similar to Dakota shotgun, 25 in. chopper lump barrels, selective ejectors, supplied with Americase, limited mfg. by Ferlib circa 2001-2005.

	$25,500	$21,250	$17,250	$14,00	$11,250	$9,500	$8,250	*$28,500*

RIFLES: SINGLE SHOT

DAKOTA MODEL 10 – available in most rimmed and rimless commercially loaded standard and Mag. cals., falling block standard or enlarged Magnum (new 1994) action designed by Don Allen, 23 in. round barrel, top tang safety, deluxe checkered XX English walnut stock and forearm, 6 lbs. New 1990.

MSR $5,260	$4,625	$4,200	$3,675	$3,150	$2,855	$2,310	$1,890	

Add $1,400 for Deluxe Model with case colored action and exhibition grade wood.

MODEL 10 .30-06 100TH ANNIVERSARY – .30-06 cal., 100 year banner on floor plate, Exhibition walnut with limited edition checkering pattern, custom LOP, color case hardened frame, jewelled bolt, only 100 mfg. 2006-2007.

	$7,600	$6,650	$5,700	$5,170	$4,180	$3,420	$2,660	*$8,195*

DAKOTA MODEL 97 VARMINT HUNTER – various varmint cals., rounded short action, 24 in. chrome-moly barrel, adj. trigger, black fiberglass stock standard, right-hand only, approx. 8 lbs. New 1998.

	$1,600	$1,400	$1,200	$1,090	$880	$720	$560	*$1,795*

Add $700 for Wood Varmint Hunter 97 (includes semi-fancy wood and blind mag.).

Add $1,200 for Deluxe Varmint Hunter 97 (includes semi-fancy wood and point panel checkering with floorplate).

DAKOTA VARMINTER (STANDARD PREDATOR) – various cals., XX walnut stock, matte stainless receiver, 24 in. barrel. New 2008.

MSR $2,840	$2,550	$2,250	$1,875	$1,575	$1,350	$1,150	$975	

Add $550 for Deluxe Model with panel hand-cut checkering (Predator Deluxe).

* ***Dakota Varminter Heavy Barrel (Predator Heavy Varmint)*** – various cals, choice of wood or green synthetic stock, 24 in. match grade stainless steel barrel w/o sights. New 2010.

MSR $2,840	$2,550	$2,250	$1,875	$1,575	$1,350	$1,150	$975	

Add $550 for All Weather with deluxe synthetic stock (Predator Heavy Varmint All Weather).

MILLER CLASSIC – various cals., falling block action, 24 in. round barrel, includes XXX hand checkered walnut stock and forearm, English style buttstock, choice of matte, matte blue, or stainles steel metal, actions include choice of Classic or Low Boy, custom built per individual order. New 2011.

MSR $5,590	$4,950	$4,500	$3,900	$3,400	$2,925	$2,475	$1,950	

DAKOTA SHARPS RIFLE – various cals. between .22 LR and .38-55 WCF, features scaled-down frame for smaller cals. (20% smaller than original Sharps), 26 in. octagon barrel, approx. 8 lbs. New 1998.

MSR $4,490	$3,950	$3,600	$3,250	$2,750	$2,350	$2,050	$1,650	

Add $265 for double set trigger.

SHOTGUNS: SxS

CLASSIC GRADE – 20 ga. only, case colored round boxlock action, 27 in. barrels with fixed chokes, DTs, straight grip checkered English walnut stock and splinter forearm, no engraving, 6 lbs. Mfg. 1996-98.

	$7,450	$6,520	$5,585	$5,065	$4,095	$3,350	$2,605	*$7,950*

PREMIER GRADE – 20, 28 ga. (new 2000), or .410 bore (new 2000), similar to Dakota Classic Field Grade, 27 in. barrels, exhibition grade English walnut, French grey metal finish, 50% engraving coverage, straight grip, splinter forend, DT, hand-rubbed oil finish stock, game rib with gold bead, ejectors, choice of chokes. Mfg. in conjunction with Ferlib.

	$13,950	$12,205	$10,460	$9,485	$7,670	$6,275	$4,880	*$14,950*

Add 10% for 28 ga. or .410 bore.

GRADING - PPGS™	100%	98%	95%	90%	80%	70%	60%	LAST MSR

DAKOTA AMERICAN LEGEND – 20, 28 ga., or .410 bore, fully scroll-engraved coin finish round boxlock action with gold inlays, French grey metal finish, special select English walnut mfg. to customer dimensions, 27 in. barrels with game rib and gold bead, straight grip, DT, round action, ejectors, choice of chokes, oak and leather trunk case, 6 lbs., mfg. by Ferlib 1996-2005.

	$16,000	$14,000	$12,000	$10,880	$8,800	$7,200	$5,600	*$19,000*

Add 10% for 28 ga. or .410 bore.

Only 100 guns were scheduled to be mfg. Also offered in a 12 ga. and .410 bore/28 ga. set.

DAKOTA CLASSIC FIELD GRADE SUPERLIGHT KNOCKABOUT – 12, 16, 20, 24 (new 2005), 28, 32 (new 2005) ga., or .410 bore, Anson & Deeley boxlock action, monobloc (12, 20, or 28 ga.) or chopper lump (16 ga. or .410 bore only) 28 or 30 in. barrels, ejectors, DT, custom dimensions, checkered Turkish walnut stock and splinter forearm with oil finish, includes scroll and border engraving. Mfg. 2004-2007.

	$4,200	$3,675	$3,150	$2,855	$2,310	$1,890	$1,470	*$4,600*

Add $600 for 16, 32 ga. or .410 bore.

Add $1,501 for Express Gun with rifled 24 1/2 in. barrels with quarter rib and folding leaf express sights (12 or 20 ga. only, disc. 2004).

DAKOTA CLASSIC GRADE II – similar to Field Grade, except has extra fancy Turkish walnut and game scene engraving. Mfg. 2004-2007.

	$5,100	$4,460	$3,825	$3,470	$2,805	$2,295	$1,785	*$5,600*

Add $700 for 16, 32 ga. or .410 bore.

Add $1,501 for Express Gun with rifled 24 1/2 in. barrels with quarter rib and folding leaf express sights (12 or 20 ga. only, disc. 2004).

DAKOTA CLASSIC GRADE III – similar to Grade II, except has XXX Turkish walnut and scroll and gold game scene engraving. Mfg. 2004-2007.

	$6,100	$5,335	$4,575	$4,150	$3,355	$2,745	$2,135	*$6,600*

Add $800 for 16, 32 ga. or .410 bore.

Add $1,501 for Express Gun with rifled 24 1/2 in. barrels with quarter rib and folding leaf express sights (12 or 20 ga. only, disc. 2004).

DAKOTA SINGLE ACTION REVOLVERS

Previous trademark of revolvers imported until mid-2008 by E.M.F. Company, Inc. located in Santa Ana, CA.

Dakota trademarked revolvers imported by E.M.F. company Inc. were initially manufactured by Armi Jager, located in Val Trompia, Italy circa mid 1970s-mid 1980s. Armi San Marco then began manufacturing Dakotas circa mid 1980s-early 1990s. Uberti was the last manufacturer to make this trademark, and it produced Dakota revolvers from the early 1990s until 2008.

Great Western II and Hartford revolvers (previously listed in this section) imported by E.M.F. can be found listed alphabetically under separate listings. Other firearms imported by E.M.F. Co., Inc. will be found in the E section.

REVOLVERS: REPRODUCTIONS

Add $125 for combo cylinder on the models listed (.45 ACP cal. only on Remingtons, .44-40 WCF, .44 Spl., or .45 ACP on Peacemaker SAAs).

OLD MODEL SAA – .22 LR, .32-20 WCF, .357 Mag., .38-40 WCF, .44 Spl., .44-40 WCF, or .45 LC cal., copy of the Colt SAA, 4 5/8, 5 1/2, or 7 1/2 in. barrels, blue finish, case hardened frame, 1-piece walnut grips, solid brass backstrap and trigger guard. Importation disc. 1991.

	$400	$350	$295	$265	$235	$200	$185	*$600*

Add $100 for nickel finish (disc.).

Add $110 for convertible cylinders.

* ***Old Model SAA Engraved Old Model*** – .32-20 WCF, .357 Mag., .38-40 WCF, .44-40 WCF, or .45 cal., 4 3/4, 5 1/2, or 7 1/2 in. barrel. Disc. 1993, reintroduced 1996, disc. 1998.

	$775	$695	$500	$425	$350	$325	$300	*$840*

Add $160 for nickel finish (disc).

GRADING - PPGS™	100%	98%	95%	90%	80%	70%	60%	LAST MSR

* ***Old Model SAA Cattlebrand Engraved*** – .44-40 WCF or .45 LC cal., 5 1/2, or 7 1/2 in. barrel, patterned after the famous Colt Cattlebrand variation (features various cattlebrands engraved on the barrel, frame and cylinder). Imported 1992-93, reintroduced 1996, disc. 1998.

	$775	$695	$500	$425	$350	$325	$300	*$840*

Add $140 for silver-plating.

NEW DAKOTA SAA – .357 Mag., .44-40 WCF, or .45 LC cal., features forged steel frame, black nickel backstrap and trigger guard, 4 (.45 LC cal. with standard grips), 4 3/4, 5 1/2, or 7 1/2 in. barrel, choice of case hardened or nickel frame, one piece walnut grips, original Colt type hammer (without transfer bar safety). Imported 1991-2004.

	$400	$350	$295	$265	$235	$200	$185	*$375*

Add $85 for combo. cylinder (disc. 2002).
Add $135 for satin nickel (disc.) or $175 for bright satin nickel finish.

* ***New Dakota SAA Sheriff Model*** – cals. similar to New Model, 3 1/2 in. barrel. Imported 1997-99.

	$395	$350	$295	$250	$220	$180	$160	*$435*

DAKOTA PREMIER SAA – .45 LC cal., black powder frame, initial mfg. was with 4 5/8 or 5 1/2 in. barrel, set screw cylinder pin release, steel backstrap and trigger guard, one-piece grips. This model was the predecessor to the New Hartford Model.

	$450	$375	$295	$250	$190	$170	$160	*$520*

FRONTIER MARSHAL SA – .357 Mag., .44-40 WCF (disc. 2004), or .45 LC cal., 4 3/4, 5 1/2, or 7 1/2 in. barrel, case colored frame, brass backstrap and trigger guard, blue barrel/cylinder. Imported 2003-2008.

	$395	$350	$295	$250	$220	$180	$160	*$450*

SHERIFF'S OLD/NEW MODEL SAA – .32-20 WCF (disc.), .357 Mag. (disc. 2000), .38-40 WCF (disc.), .44 Spl. (disc.), .44-40 WCF (disc. 2000), or .45 LC cal., 3 1/2 in. barrel only. Importation disc. 1991, resumed 1994-2000, again in 2003.

	$415	$335	$300	$265	$225	$175	$150	*$480*

U.S. ARMY SAA – variety of cals., premium quality construction. Disc. 1985.

	$400	$350	$295	$265	$235	$200	$185	*$395*

* ***U.S. Army SAA Commemorative*** – .45 LC cal., 7 1/2 in. barrel, serial numbered 1-500, blue finish, case hardened frame, steel backstrap and trigger guard, 1-piece walnut grips. Importation disc. 1987.

	$450	$375	$275	N/A	N/A	N/A	N/A	*$495*

CONVERTIBLE MODEL SAA – available with .22 LR/.22 WMR, .32-20 WCF/.32 H&R Mag., .357 Mag./9mm Para., .44-40 WCF/.44 Spl. cal., or .45 LC/.45 ACP double cylinders. Imported 1986-1990.

	$495	$450	$395	$350	$310	$275	$250	*$580*

FAST DRAW MODEL SAA – .22 LR, .22 WMR, .32-20 WCF, .32 H&R Mag., .357 Mag., .38-40 WCF, 9mm Para., .44 Spl., .44-40 WCF, .45 ACP, or .45 LC cal., case hardened frame, 4 5/8 in. barrel. Importation disc. 1990.

	$385	$340	$295	$225	$165	$150	$135	*$480*

BISLEY MODEL SAA – .22 LR (disc.), .22 WMR (disc.), .32-20 WCF (disc.), .32 H&R Mag. (disc.), .38-40 WCF (disc.), .357 Mag. (disc. 1999), 9mm Para. (disc.), .44 Spl. (disc.), .44-40 WCF (disc.), .45 ACP (disc.), or .45 LC (current mfg.) cal., 4 3/4 (disc. 1994, reintroduced 2001-2003 in .44-40 WCF cal. only), 5 1/2, or 7 1/2 in. barrel lengths. Imported 1986-91, reintroduced 1993-disc. 1995, reintroduced 1997-2008.

	$435	$385	$350	$315	$280	$250	$215	*$490*

Add $200 for bright or satin (disc.) nickel finish.
Add $112 for combo. cylinder (.45 ACP - disc.).

GRADING - PPGS™	100%	98%	95%	90%	80%	70%	60%	LAST MSR

* ***Bisley Model SAA Engraved*** – .32-20 WCF, .38-40 WCF, .357 Mag., .44-40 WCF, or .45 LC cal. (disc. 1990), 4 3/4, 5 1/2, or 7 1/2 in. barrel, action engraved throughout. Imported 1987-91.

	$600	$525	$450	$400	$350	$300	$275	*$570*

Add $100 for nickel finish.

1873 FRONTIER MODEL SAA – .22 LR cal., 4 3/4 in. barrel, case colored frame, black nickel backstrap and trigger guard. Mfg. by IAR, imported 1999-2002.

	$325	$275	$250	$225	$175	$150	$135	*$315*

Add $125 for bright nickel finish.

DALVAR OF USA

Previous importer of recently manufactured Radom pistols located in Henderson, NV. Please refer to the Radom listing in the R section.

DALY, CHARLES: PRUSSIAN MFG.

Previous trademark manufactured in Prussia, England, Belgium, and the U.S. circa 1875-pre-WWII.

Charles Daly was a gentleman (not a company) whose goal was to give the U.S. shotgun consumer a European-manufactured gun of similar quality to the premier American shotguns of the same era. Accordingly, he had various European firms fabricate shotguns with American shooting features and preferences. Many "Prussian" Dalys were built by various firms in Suhl, Germany. Importation ceased prior to WWII. These Prussian Charles Dalys utilized the finest materials and best workmanship of their time.

In 1865, Charles Daly was one of two partners who founded the sporting goods business named Schoverling & Daly. They were importers and dealers located in New York City. In 1873, the company reorganized to include a third partner, and the corporate name was changed to Schoverling, Daly & Gales.

Marking the Charles Daly name on firearms began some time around 1875. Daly's name was chosen because it had an appealing sound and would likely influence potential buyers to choose their firearms. Schoverling, Daly & Gales established their lofty reputation by dealing in top-quality merchandise. Because they were known for their high standard of excellence, the Charles Daly brand garnered much esteem.

Schoverling, Daly & Gales made every effort to select only the finest quality firearms for sale in the United States. Initially, manufacturers in Prussia, such as Schiller and Lindner, and later Heym and Sauer of Germany, were selected for their superbly constructed shotguns. Early manufacturers also included J&W Tolley of England, Newmann of Belgium, and even Lefever Arms of New York.

Schoverling, Daly & Gales changed ownership several times throughout the years. Eventually, the company's primary asset was the Charles Daly trademark. In 1910, Henry Modell bought the company, and controlled it for several years. In the 1920s, he sold out to the Walzer family, owners of Sloan's Sporting Goods of Ridgefield, CT. The Walzers established a branch of Sloan's in New York known as Charles Daly & Company. Sloan's imported quality shotguns from many companies, including Italian gun makers Beretta and Vincenzo Bernardelli, Miroku of Japan, and Garbi of Spain.

DRILLINGS

DRILLING MODEL – 12, 16, or 20 gauges and .25-20 WCF, .25-35 WCF, or .30-30 WCF cal., 3 barrel combination gun, extractors, double triggers, engraved action, select walnut, mfg. by both Linder and Sauer. Linder mfg. guns are extremely rare - very few specimens are to be found domestically. Sauer guns were not marked for grade, but rather had three levels of engraving which determined the grade. Most Sauer guns had a tang mounted aperture rear sight and a separate rifle cock and were sidelocks. Disc. 1933.

* ***Drilling Model Superior Quality*** – borderline engraving only.

Sauer mfg.	$4,500	$3,750	$3,000	$2,600	$2,300	$2,000	$1,700	

* ***Drilling Model Diamond Quality*** – full scroll engraving.

Sauer mfg.	$7,500	$6,500	$5,500	$4,800	$4,400	$4,000	$3,500	

GRADING - PPGS™	100%	98%	95%	90%	80%	70%	60%	LAST MSR

* ***Drilling Model Regent Diamond Quality*** – top-of-the-line model featuring full game scene coverage.

Linder mfg.	$20,000	$15,000	$12,000	$11,000	$10,000	$9,000	$7,000	
Sauer mfg.	$10,000	$8,000	$7,000	$6,700	$6,000	$5,000	$4,000	

Add approx. 25% for gold inlays.

RIFLES

BOLT ACTION GRADE I – .22 Hornet cal., mfg. by F. Jaeger & Co. of Suhl, Germany, 5 shot mag., 24 in. barrel, miniature Mauser bolt action, deluxe walnut. Very limited mfg.

	$2,000	$1,750	$1,500	$1,250	$1,025	$825	$650	

SHOTGUNS

In the higher grade Prussian Daly variations, there is quite a bit of difference in their manufacture, including engraving options, levels of wood embellishment, and other extra cost features at the time. H.A. Linder produced approx. 2,500 guns (ser. numbered accordingly), and many of the higher grades show a noticeable difference in the amount of engraving (from minimal to considerable game scene engraving). These guns can be either case colored only or have gold inlaid birds and animals (the number of which can also vary) and barrels can have various levels of engraving on both the breech and muzzle ends. All of these factors have considerable impact on the overall value of a particular specimen. It is estimated that it took three craftsmen one year to produce a single Diamond Regent gun.

Add 25% - 50% for 20 ga., depending on condition.
Add 200% for 28 ga. on higher grade models (very rare).
Add 100% for .410 bore on higher grade models.
Add approx. 20% for 10 ga. on the following models that apply.

COMMANDER O/U – 12, 16, 20, 28 ga., or .410 bore, Anson & Deeley boxlock action, single or double triggers, ejectors. Mfg. in Belgium circa 1947-1964.

Add 30% for 28 ga. or .410 bore.
Add 10% for single trigger.

* ***Commander O/U Model 100***

	$1,200	$975	$800	$700	$625	$550	$475	

Add $100 for single trigger.

* ***Commander O/U Model 200*** – similar to Model 100, except has deluxe walnut.

	$1,500	$1,275	$1,075	$900	$800	$700	$600	

EMPIRE O/U – 12, 16, or 20 ga., various barrel lengths, Anson & Deeley boxlock, ejectors and double triggers, fine engraving, deluxe walnut. Disc. 1933.

	$4,000	$3,400	$2,750	$2,375	$2,000	$1,825	$1,625	

DIAMOND O/U – similar to Empire model, only finer workmanship and materials.

	$6,000	$5,150	$4,300	$3,475	$3,000	$2,600	$2,300	

SUPERIOR SxS – 10, 12, 20, 28 ga., or .410 bore, Anson & Deeley boxlock, various barrel lengths, extractors. Disc. 1933.

10 ga.	$2,750	$2,300	$1,850	$1,600	$1,350	$1,125	$995	
12 ga.	$1,650	$1,425	$1,200	$975	$825	$675	$550	
20 ga.	$2,200	$1,875	$1,675	$1,400	$1,175	$995	$825	

28 ga. and .410 bore specimens are too rare to accurately evaluate, and should be appraised individually.

EMPIRE SxS – similar to Superior, only more engraving and better wood.

Linder mfg.	$5,500	$4,650	$4,150	$3,700	$2,950	$2,300	$1,500	
Sauer mfg.	$4,750	$3,850	$3,300	$3,000	$2,300	$1,800	$1,400	

DIAMOND SxS – similar to Empire model, only more elaborate engraving.

Linder mfg.	$11,000	$9,995	$9,000	$8,650	$7,450	$6,250	$4,500	
Sauer mfg.	$7,750	$6,500	$5,750	$5,100	$4,100	$3,000	$2,000	

GRADING - PPGS™	100%	98%	95%	90%	80%	70%	60%	LAST MSR

DIAMOND REGENT SxS – top-of-the-line Prussian side-by-side with or w/o engraving and gold inlays.

Linder mfg.	$18,500	$15,000	$12,000	$11,000	$8,500	$7,000	$5,000	
Sauer mfg.	$15,000	$12,000	$9,200	$8,000	$7,000	$6,000	$5,000	

Subtract 20% - 25% if w/o gold inlays.

EMPIRE SINGLE BARREL TRAP – 12 ga., 30-34 in. barrel, Anson & Deeley boxlock, ejector, vent. rib, finely engraved with select walnut, chopper lump extension, top quality. Disc. 1933.

Linder mfg.	$5,000	$4,500	$4,000	$3,500	$3,100	$2,800	$2,200	
Sauer mfg.	$4,000	$3,500	$3,100	$2,750	$2,350	$2,000	$1,700	

DIAMOND REGENT SINGLE BARREL TRAP – 12 ga., 30-34 in. barrel, six locking bolts, ejector, vent. rib, elaborately engraved and checkered.

Linder mfg.	$15,000	$12,750	$10,500	$8,500	$6,500	$5,000	$4,000	
Sauer mfg.	$10,500	$9,150	$8,000	$7,000	$6,000	$4,750	$3,750	

SEXTUPLE SINGLE BARREL TRAP EMPIRE QUALITY

Linder mfg.	$6,000	$5,400	$4,600	$4,150	$3,650	$3,100	$2,800	

SEXTUPLE SINGLE BARREL TRAP DIAMOND REGENT QUALITY

Linder mfg.	N/A	$18,000	$15,000	$12,000	$9,250	$7,500	$6,000	

DALY, CHARLES: JAPANESE MFG.

Private label of shotguns previously manufactured circa 1963-1972 by B.C. Miroku, located in Kochi, Japan.

In 1971, a typhoon almost destroyed the factory. Because of this, all factory records were lost, and these earlier models cannot be researched.

SHOTGUNS: O/U

In the early sixties, C. Daly guns were manufactured by the firm of B.C. Miroku in Kochi, Japan. This Japanese gun manufacturing company has produced guns for many companies, Browning being the biggest current customer. Miroku guns are high quality with excellent fit and finish. Many of them are highly engraved and are fine examples of the gunmaker's art. Charles Daly Miroku Guns are becoming quite collectible in some areas (smaller gauges with open chokes). Their production ceased in 1976.

O/U MODELS – 12, 20, 28 ga., or .410 bore, 26, 28, or 30 in. vent. rib barrels, various chokes, boxlock, auto ejectors, SST, select walnut checkered pistol grip stock, Superior and Diamond Grade Trap have Monte Carlo stocks, the grades differ in amount of engraving and wood. Mfg. 1963-1976 by Miroku.

Add 20% for 20 ga. on models listed below.
Add 50% for 28 ga. on models listed below.
Add 60% for .410 bore on models listed below.
Add 300% for original 28 ga. Lightweight models in 98%+ condition (rare).

Approx. 1,000 28 ga. Lightweight guns were manufactured. All 28 ga. Lightweights (approx. observed ser. range 230011-230998) have barrel spacing 3/4 in. center to center, while the normal 28 ga. has a measurement of 7/8 in. After the Charles Daly line of O/Us were mechanically redesigned, both the 28 ga. and .410 bore were only made on the new 20 ga. frame. To date, no one has observed a .410 bore Lightweight Charles Daly.

FIELD GRADE – 12 or 20 ga., light engraving.

	$1,000	$900	$825	$725	$625	$525	$375	

VENTURE GRADE – all gauges, moderate engraving.

	$1,150	$1,025	$900	$800	$700	$600	$495	

VENTURE SKEET – 26 in. barrels choked skeet and skeet.

	$1,050	$925	$825	$725	$625	$525	$400	

VENTURE TRAP – 30 in. imp. mod. and full.

	$895	$750	$625	$525	$425	$375	$350	

GRADING - PPGS™	100%	98%	95%	90%	80%	70%	60%	LAST MSR

SUPERIOR GRADE – all gauges, select checkered walnut stock with round knob, scroll engraving similar to Grade I Browning Superposed.

	$1,400	$1,200	$925	$825	$700	$650	$600	

SUPERIOR TRAP

	$1,200	$950	$675	$575	$500	$440	$390	

This model has an optional selective ejection system enabling the shooter to deactivate the ejectors.

DIAMOND GRADE – all gauges, extensive engraving with better quality wood.

	$2,600	$2,000	$1,425	$1,150	$995	$895	$775	

DIAMOND GRADE SKEET

	$2,400	$2,000	$1,450	$1,150	$1,000	$900	$775	

DIAMOND GRADE TRAP

	$1,900	$1,500	$1,050	$850	$775	$700	$625	

DIAMOND GRADE FLATTOP TRAP W/WIDE RIB

	$2,000	$1,600	$1,050	$850	$775	$700	$625	

DIAMOND REGENT GRADE – mostly 12 ga., extensive frame engraving with gold inlays, rare.

	$4,250	$3,650	$3,200	$2,550	$2,100	$1,800	$1,500	

SHOTGUNS: SxS

EMPIRE SHOTGUN – 12, 16, or 20 ga., 26, 28, or 30 in. barrels, various chokes, boxlock, extractors, single trigger, checkered pistol grip stock, early production guns were made by Beretta in Italy. Mfg. 1968-1971.

	$925	$825	$725	$625	$500	$425	$325	
Vent. rib	$1,050	$925	$775	$675	$575	$475	$375	

Add 25% for 20 ga.

MODEL 500 – 12 or 20 ga., 26 or 28 in. barrels with raised or vent. rib, DT, extractors.

	$750	$625	$495	$400	$325	$295	$260	

Add 20% for vent. rib.

1974 WILDLIFE COMMEMORATIVE – duck scene engraved, Diamond Grade, Trap, or Skeet, limited to 500 guns. Mfg. 1974 only.

	$2,000	$1,725	$1,500	N/A	N/A	N/A	N/A	

SHOTGUNS: SINGLE BARREL, TRAP

SUPERIOR GRADE SINGLE BARREL TRAP – 12 ga., 32 or 34 in. vent. rib, full choke barrel, auto ejector, Monte Carlo stock with recoil pad. Mfg. 1968-1976.

	$625	$575	$525	$495	$440	$385	$330	

DALY, CHARLES: 1976-2010

Previous manufactured trademark imported late 1996-early 2010 by KBI, Inc. located in Harrisburg, PA. Previously imported by Outdoor Sports Headquarters, Inc. located in Dayton, OH until 1995.

In 1976, Sloan's Sporting Goods sold the Daly division to Outdoor Sports Headquarters, Inc., a sporting goods wholesaler located in Dayton, OH. OSHI continued the importation of high-grade Daly shotguns, primarily from Italy and Spain. By the mid-1980s, the Charles Daly brand was transformed into a broad consumer line of excellent firearms and hunting accessories.

In 1996, OSHI was sold to Jerry's Sports Center, Inc. of Forest City, PA, a major wholesaler of firearms and hunting supplies. Within a few months of Jerry's acquisition of OSHI, K.B.I., Inc. of Harrisburg, PA, purchased the Charles Daly trademark from JSC. As it turned out, Michael Kassnar, president of K.B.I., Inc., had produced almost all of the Charles Daly products for OSHI from 1976-1985 in his capacity of president of Kassnar Imports, Inc. K.B.I., Inc. resurrected the complete line of O/U and SxS shotguns in early 1997.

In 1998, the line expanded to include rimfire rifles and the first pistol produced under the

GRADING - PPGS™	100%	98%	95%	90%	80%	70%	60%	LAST MSR

Daly name, a Model 1911-A1 in .45 ACP cal. In 1999, semi-auto and slide action shotguns were also reintroduced. In 2000, the additions included 3 1/2 in. slide actions and semi-autos, Country Squire .410 bore shotguns, bolt action centerfire rifles, and the DDA 10-45, the first double action pistol produced under the Charles Daly name.

During 2004, Charles Daly began importing Bul Transmark pistols from Israel. In 2007, the Little Sharps single shot rifles were introduced.

In 2008, a Charles Daly Defense line was established, which includes AR-15 style semi-auto rifles.

On Jan. 29, 2010, K.B.I. announced it was shutting its doors and discontinued importation of all models.

COMBINATION GUNS

SUPERIOR COMBINATION MODEL – 12 ga. (multi-chokes became standard in 2001) over choice of .22 Hornet, .22-250 Rem. (disc. 1998), .223 Rem., .243 Win. (disc. 1998), .270 Win. (disc. 1998), .30-06, or .308 Win. (disc. 1998) cal., boxlock action with dovetailed receiver (accepts scope mounts and iron sights), 23 1/2 in. barrels with iron sights, approx. 7 5/8 lbs. Mfg. by Sabatti in Italy. Imported 1997-2005.

$1,260	$1,105	$945	$855	$695	$565	$440	*$1,479*

EMPIRE COMBINATION MODEL – 12 ga. (multi-chokes became standard in 2001) over choice of .22 Hornet, .22-250 Rem. (disc. 1998), .223 Rem., .243 Win. (disc. 1998), .270 Win. (disc. 1998), .30-06, or .308 Win. (disc. 1998) cal., boxlock action, 23 1/2 in. barrels, engraved with choice checkered walnut stock and forearm. Mfg. by Sabatti in Italy. Imported 1997-2005.

$1,800	$1,575	$1,350	$1,225	$990	$810	$630	*$2,189*

HANDGUNS: LEVER ACTION

MODEL 1892 – .357 Mag. or .45 LC cal., similar to Model 1892 rifle, except has 12 in. blue barrel, color case hardened finish, walnut stock. Mfg. 2009.

$1,195	$1,050	$900	$775	$675	$575	$475	*$1,309*

PISTOLS: SEMI-AUTO

During 2001, the nomenclature on these 1911 models was changed to include a new "E" prefix. The "E" stands for enhanced, and features included extended high-rise beavertail grip safety, combat trigger, combat hammer, beveled magwell, flared and lowered ejection port, dovetailed front and low profile rear sights, and hand checkered double diamond grips. The Enhanced pistols were manufactured by Armscor of the Philipines. M-5 pistols are manufactured by Bul Transmark in Israel.

GOVERNMENT 1911-A1 FIELD EFS/FS – .38 Super (mfg. 2005-2007), .40 S&W (mfg. 2005-2007), .45 ACP cal., steel frame, single action, skeletonized combat hammer and trigger, ambidextrous safety, 8 or 10 shot mag., extended slide release and beavertail grip safety, oversized and lowered ejection port, 5 in. barrel with solid barrel bushing, matte blue (Field FS), stainless slide/blue frame (Superior FS, mfg. 1999-2002), or all stainless (Empire EFS, new 1999) finish, includes two 8 or 10 shot mags. and lockable carrying case, 39 1/2 oz. Mfg. 1998-2008.

$475	$415	$355	$325	$260	$215	$165	*$589*

Add $50 for Superior EFS Model (disc. 2002).
Add $199 for .22 LR conversion kit with adj. sight (disc. 1999).

* ***Government 1911A1 Field EFS Stainless Empire*** – .45 ACP cal. only, similar to Field FS, except is stainless steel. Disc. 2007.

$575	$505	$430	$390	$315	$260	$200	*$709*

GOVERNMENT 1911-A1 TARGET EFST/FST – similar to Government 1911-A1 Field FS, except has target sights. Imported 2000-2007.

$550	$480	$415	$375	$305	$250	$195	*$679*

Add $40 for Superior FST Model (disc. 2000).
Add $65 for Empire FST Model (disc. 2000).

GRADING - PPGS™	100%	98%	95%	90%	80%	70%	60%	LAST MSR

* ***Government 1911-A1 Target EFST Stainless Empire*** – .45 ACP cal. only, similar to Target EFST, except is stainless steel. Mfg. 2001-2007.

$650	$570	$490	$440	$360	$295	$230	$789

* ***Government 1911-A1 Target Field EFST*** – .45 ACP cal., 5 3/4 in. compensated barrel with 3 ports, blue or stainless steel, 44.5 oz. Limited importation 2001 only.

$550	$480	$415	$375	$305	$250	$195	$679

Add $100 for stainless steel (Empire EFSTC).

EMPIRE ECMT CUSTOM MATCH – .45 ACP cal., 5 in. barrel, match features, high polish stainless steel, 38 1/2 oz. Imported 2001-2007.

$750	$650	$575	$500	$425	$350	$275	$895

COMMANDER 1911-A1 FIELD EMS/MS – similar to Government 1911-A1, except has 4 in. Commander barrel and features, 37 oz. Imported 1999-2008.

$475	$415	$355	$325	$260	$215	$165	$589

Add $40 for Superior MS Model (includes stainless steel slide and blue frame, disc. 2000).

* ***Commander 1911-A1 Field EMS Stainless Empire*** – .45 ACP cal. only, similar to Field EMS/MS, except is stainless steel. Imported 1999-2007.

$575	$505	$430	$390	$315	$260	$200	$709

* ***Commander 1911-A1 Field EMSCC*** – carry comp., similar to Commander Field EMS, except has single port compensator, blue or stainless. Imported 2001 only.

$540	$475	$405	$365	$295	$245	$190	$619

OFFICER'S 1911-A1 FIELD ECS/CS – similar to Commander, except has 3 1/2 in. barrel and Officer's Model features, 34 1/2 oz. Imported 1999-2008.

$475	$415	$355	$325	$260	$215	$165	$589

Add $40 for Superior CS Model (includes stainless steel slide and blue frame, disc. 2000).

* ***Officer's 1911-A1 Field ECS Stainless Empire*** – .45 ACP cal. only, similar to Field ECS/CS, except is stainless steel. Imported 1999-2008.

$575	$505	$430	$390	$315	$260	$200	$709

* ***Officer's 1911-A1 Field ECSCC*** – carry comp., similar to Officer's Field ECS, except has single port compensator, blue or stainless. Importation began 2001.

$540	$475	$405	$365	$295	$245	$190	$619

Add $100 for Empire ECS Model (full stainless steel construction).

COMMANDER 1911-A1 POLYMER FRAME PC – .45 ACP only, features polymer frame, 4 in. barrel, available in matte blue (Field PC) or stainless slide/blue frame (Superior PC). Imported 1999-2000.

$460	$405	$345	$315	$255	$205	$160	$530

Add $25 for Superior PC Model (includes stainless steel slide and blue frame).

GOVERNMENT 1911-A2 FIELD EFS HC – .40 S&W or .45 ACP cal., 5 in. barrel, similar to Government 1911 A-1 Field EFS, 13 (.45 ACP cal.), or 15 (.40 S&W cal.) shot mag., blue finish only. Imported 2005-2007.

$595	$520	$445	$405	$325	$270	$210	$725

Add $124 for Target Model (.45 ACP cal. only, new 2005).

MODEL DDA 10-45 FS (DOUBLE ACTION) – .40 S&W (disc. 2001) or .45 ACP cal., single or double action, 4 3/8 in. barrel, polymer frame with checkering, double stack 10 shot mag. with interchangeable base plate (allowing for extra grip length), matte black or two-tone (new 2001) finish, 28 1/2 oz. Imported 2000-2002.

$450	$395	$340	$305	$250	$205	$160	$519

Add $40 for two-tone finish.

* ***Model DDA 10-45 CS*** – similar to Model DDA 10-45 FS, except has 3 5/8 in. barrel, 26 oz. Imported 2000-2002.

$450	$395	$340	$305	$250	$205	$160	$519

Add approx. $10 for colored frame (yellow, OD green, or fuschia, new 2001) and compensated barrel.

GRADING - PPGS™	100%	98%	95%	90%	80%	70%	60%	LAST MSR

FIELD HP HI-POWER – 9mm Para. cal., single action, 4 3/4 in. barrel, patterned after the Browning Hi-Power, blue or hard chrome (mfg. 2005) finish, 10 or 13 shot mag., XS Express sight system, mfg. in U.S. Mfg. late 2003 - 2006.

	$385	$335	$290	$260	$210	$175	$135	*$458*

Add $120 for hard chrome finish (mfg. 2005).

This model has been produced both by Dan Wesson (2003-2004) and Magnum Research (2005-2006).

CD9 – 9mm Para. cal., 4.46 in. barrel, black polymer frame and finish, striker fired, adj. sights, trigger safety, forward/lower accessory rail, 10 or 15 shot mag., three grip inserts. Imported 2009 only.

	$375	$330	$280	$255	$205	$170	$130	*$437*

G4 1911 SERIES – .45 ACP cal., 5 in. barrel, 7 shot, black finish or stainless steel, beveled mag well, flared and lowered ejection port, beavertail grip safety, internal extractor, Novak sights, three slot aluminum trigger, available in Standard, Target, and Tactical configurations, mfg. in Israel. Imported 2009 only.

	$750	$655	$565	$510	$415	$340	$265	*$867*

Add $96 for either Tactical or Target model.
Add $96 for stainless steel.
Add $354 for .22 LR conversion kit.

M-5 FS STANDARD (BUL 1911 GOVERNMENT) – 9mm Para. (new 2010), .40 S&W or .45 ACP cal., single action, 5 in. barrel, polymer double column frame, steel slide, aluminum speed trigger, checkered front and rear grip straps, blue or chrome finished slide, 10, 14, or 17 (9mm Para. cal.) shot staggered mag., 31-33 oz. Mfg. by Bul Transmark in Israel. Imported 2004-2009.

	$665	$580	$500	$450	$365	$300	$235	*$803*

* ***M-5 MS Standard Commander*** – .40 S&W or .45 ACP cal., similar to M-5 FS Standard, except has 4 1/3 in. barrel, 29-30 oz. Imported 2004-2009.

	$665	$580	$500	$450	$365	$300	$235	*$803*

* ***M-5 Ultra-X*** – 9mm Para. or .45 ACP cal., 10 or 12 (9mm Para. cal. only) shot mag., compact variation with 3.15 in. barrel. Imported 2005-2009.

	$665	$580	$500	$450	$365	$300	$235	*$803*

M-5 IPSC – .40 S&W, or .45 ACP cal., configured for IPSC competition, 5 in. barrel, with custom slide to frame fit and match grade barrel bushing. Mfg. by Bul Transmark in Israel. Imported 2004-2007.

	$1,250	$1,095	$940	$850	$690	$565	$440	*$1,439*

JERICHO SERIES – 9mm Para., .40 S&W, or .45 ACP cal., 3 1/2 (Compact), 3.82 (Mid-Size), or 4.41 (Full Size) in. barrel, DA/SA, 10, 12, 13, or 15 shot mag., polymer or steel frame with black or chrome (Mid-size .45 ACP cal. only) finish, combat style trigger guard, slide mounted thumb decocker, two slot accessory rail (except Compact), ergonomic grips, mfg. by IWI, Ltd. (formerly IMI) in Israel. Limited importation 2009.

	$595	$520	$445	$405	$325	$270	$210	*$699*

Add $198 for steel frame and chrome finish (Full or Mid-size only).

ZDA MODEL – 9mm Para. or .40 S&W cal., DA, 4 1/8 in. barrel, 12 (.40 S&W cal.) or 15 (9mm Para. cal.) shot mag., mfg. by Zastava. Limited importation 2005 only.

	$490	$430	$370	$335	$270	$220	$170	*$589*

REVOLVERS: DA

S222/S224/S226 SERIES – .22 LR cal., 2 (S222), 4 (S224) or 6 (S226) in. barrel, blue finish, 9 shot, rubber grips, fixed (S222) or adj. (S224 or S226) sights, steel construction. While advertised during 2006, this Series was never imported.

	$265	$230	$200	$180	$160	$140	$120	*$321*

GRADING - PPGS™	100%	98%	95%	90%	80%	70%	60%	LAST MSR

S352/S354/S356 SERIES – .357 Mag. cal., 2 (S352), 4 (S354), or 6 (S356) in. barrel, blue finish, 6 shot, fixed (S382) or adj. (S384 or S386) sights, rubber grips, steel construction. While advertised during 2006, this Series was never imported.

$300	$265	$240	$215	$185	$165	$145	$350

S382/S384/S386 SERIES – .38 Spl. cal., 2 (S382), 4 (S384), or 6 (S386) in. barrel, blue finish, 6 shot, fixed (S382) or adj. (S384 or S386) sights, rubber grips, steel construction. While advertised during 2006, this Series was never imported.

$265	$230	$200	$180	$160	$140	$120	$321

Z222/Z224/Z226 SERIES – .22 LR cal., 2 (Z222), 4 (Z224) or 6 (Z226) in. barrel, blue finish, 9 shot, rubber grips, fixed (Z222) or adj. (Z224 or Z226) sights. While advertised during 2006, this Series was never imported.

$200	$180	$160	$140	$120	$100	$80	$244

Z382 – .38 Spl. cal., 2 in. barrel, blue finish, 6 shot, fixed sights, rubber grips. While advertised during 2006, this Series was never imported.

$210	$185	$160	$140	$125	$110	$95	$249

REVOLVERS: SA

Models were manufactured by Flli. Pietta in Italy.

MODEL 1873 CLASSIC – .357 Mag. or .45 LC cal., 4 3/4, 5 1/2, or 7 1/2 in. barrel, case hardened frame, blue finish, choice of brass (.45 LC only) or steel backstrap and trigger guard. Imported 2004-2007.

$415	$365	$310	$280	$230	$185	$145	$485

Add $20 for steel backstrap and trigger guard.

* ***Model 1873 Classic Stainless*** – similar to Model 1873, except has matte finish, stainless construction with steel backstrap and trigger guard. Imported 2004-2006.

$515	$450	$385	$350	$285	$230	$180	$587

MODEL 1873 SONORA – similar to Model 1873 Classic, except has matte blue finish, and not available with steel backstrap and trigger guard. Imported 2006-2007.

$325	$285	$245	$220	$180	$145	$115	$399

MODEL 1873 BIRDSHEAD – .45 LC cal. only, 4 3/4 in. barrel, color case hardened finish, steel backstrap and trigger guard. Imported 2006-2007.

$445	$390	$335	$305	$245	$200	$155	$549

* ***Model 1873 Birdshead Sheriff*** – .45 LC cal. only, 3 in. barrel, color case hardened finish, steel backstrap and trigger guard. Imported 2006-2007.

$445	$390	$335	$305	$245	$200	$155	$549

MODEL 1873 LIGHTNING – .45 LC cal. only, 4 3/4 in. barrel, color case hardened finish, steel backstrap and trigger guard. Imported 2006-2007.

$445	$390	$335	$305	$245	$200	$155	$549

* ***Model 1873 Lightning Sheriff*** – .45 LC cal. only, 3 in. barrel, color case hardened finish, steel backstrap and trigger guard. Imported 2006-2007.

$445	$390	$335	$305	$245	$200	$155	$549

MODEL 1874 RUSSIAN – .44 Russian or .45 LC cal., 6 1/2 in. barrel, blue finish. Limited importation 2006.

$800	$700	$600	$545	$440	$360	$280	$931

RIFLES: BOLT ACTION

K.B.I. also imported a wide variety of Mauser and Mini-Mauser actions until 2006. MSRs ranged between $319-$659.

MAUSER 98 – various cals., Mauser 98 action, 22 (new 2001) or 23 (disc.) in. barrel, 3-5 shot, hinged floorplate, fiberglass/graphite composite (Field Grade) or checkered European walnut (Superior Grade) stock, open sights, drilled and tapped receiver, side safety. Mfg. by Zastava. Importation began 1998, and resumed 2001-2005.

GRADING - PPGS™	100%	98%	95%	90%	80%	70%	60%	LAST MSR

* ***Mauser 98 Field Grade*** – features fiberglass/graphite composite stock, matte blue finish or matte stainless steel.

$395	$345	$295	$270	$215	$180	$140	$459

Add $90 for stainless steel.
Add $30 for Mag. cals (.300 Win. Mag. or 7mm Rem. Mag.).
Add 50% for .375 H&H or .458 Win. Mag. cal. (disc.).

* ***Mauser 98 Superior Grade*** – features checkered European walnut stock and high polish blue finish.

$525	$460	$395	$355	$290	$235	$185	$599

Add $190 for .375 H&H or .458 Win. Mag. cal.
Add $30 for Mag. cals. (.300 Win. Mag. or 7mm Rem. Mag.).
Add $30 for left-hand action (.30-06 cal. only).

MINI-MAUSER 98 – .22 Hornet, .22-250 Rem. (disc.), .223 Rem., or 7.62x39mm cal., similar to Mauser 98, except has 18.1 (new 2001) or 19 1/4 (disc.) in. barrel, 5 shot.

* ***Mini-Mauser 98 Field Grade*** – features fiberglass/graphite composite stock.

$345	$300	$260	$235	$190	$155	$120	$399

* ***Mini-Mauser 98 Superior Grade*** – features checkered European walnut stock.

$525	$460	$395	$355	$290	$235	$185	$599

Add $30 for left-hand action (.223 Rem. cal. only).

FIELD HUNTER – .22 Hornet, .223 Rem., .243 Win., .270 Win., .30-06, .308 Win., .300 Rem. Ultra Mag., .300 Win. Mag., .338 Win. Mag., or 7mm Rem. Mag. cal., 22 or 24 (Mag. cals. only) in. barrel w/o sights, detachable mag. on short action cals. (.22 Hornet, .223 Rem., or .243 Win.), high polish bluing, checkered walnut stock and forend, right or left-hand action, gold trigger, approx. 7 1/3 lbs. Imported 2000 only.

$475	$415	$355	$325	$260	$215	$165	$565

Add approx. $31 for left-hand action (.223 Rem., .243 Win., .270 Win., .30-06, .300 Rem. Ultra Mag., or 7mm Rem. Mag.).

* ***Field Hunter Stainless/Polymer*** – similar to Field Hunter, except has stainless steel barrel and action, black polymer stock with checkering. Imported 2000 only.

$495	$435	$370	$335	$270	$225	$175	$580

FIELD GRADE .22 LR CAL. – .22 LR cal., 16 1/4 (True Youth Standard), 17 1/2 (Youth), or 22 5/8 (Standard) in. barrel, single shot (True Youth Standard) or 6 shot mag., all steel shrouded action, grooved receiver, walnut finished hardwood stock. Imported 1998-2002.

$110	$95	$85	$75	$60	$50	$40	$135

Add $14 for repeater Youth Model (6 shot, new 2000).
Add $20 for single shot True Youth Standard with shortened dimensions.

* ***Field Grade .22 LR Cal. Polymer/Hardwood*** – similar to Field Grade, except has stainless steel action and barrel with black polymer (disc.) or hardwood (new 2001) checkered stock, 6 1/3 lbs. Imported 2000-2002.

$120	$105	$90	$80	$65	$55	$40	$149

* ***Field Grade .22 LR Cal. Superior Grade*** – .22 LR (disc. 2001), .22 WMR, or .22 Hornet cal., 22 5/8 in. barrel, 5 or 6 shot mag., features checkered walnut finished stock with adj. rear sight. Imported 1998-2002.

$175	$155	$130	$120	$95	$80	$60	$209

Add $160 for .22 Hornet cal.
Subtract $20 for .22 LR cal. (disc. 2001).

* ***Field Grade .22 LR Cal. Empire Grade*** – similar to Superior Grade, except has checkered California walnut stock with rosewood grip and forend caps, high polish bluing and damascened bolt. Imported 1998-2001.

$290	$255	$220	$195	$160	$130	$100	$349

Add $20 for .22 WMR cal.
Add $130 for .22 Hornet cal.

GRADING - PPGS™	100%	98%	95%	90%	80%	70%	60%	LAST MSR

SUPERIOR II RIMFIRE – .17 HMR, .22 LR, or .22 WMR cal., 22 in. barrel, walnut stock. Limited importation 2005 only.

$215	$190	$160	$145	$120	$95	$75	*$259*

Add $40 for .22 WMR or $75 for .17 HMR cal.

RIFLES: LEVER ACTION, REPRODUCTIONS

MODEL 1866 – .38 Spl., .357 Mag., or .45 LC cal., brass or case colored blue (rifle, .357 Mag. cal. only) frame, choice of 19 (carbine), 20 (short rifle), or 24 1/4 (rifle) in. barrel, patterned after the Winchester Model 1866, mfg. by Chapparal. Limited importation 2008.

$725	$635	$545	$495	$400	$325	$255	*$849*

MODEL 1873 – .357 Mag. or .45 LC cal., case colored frame, choice of 18 (Trapper), 19 (carbine), 20 (short rifle), or 24 1/4 (rifle) in. barrel, patterned after the Winchester Model 1873, mfg. by Chapparal. Limited importation 2008.

$740	$660	$550	$475	$400	$350	$295	*$875*

Add $40 for half-round, half-octagon rifle or for Triwood stock.

MODEL 1876 – .45-60 WCF or .45-75 WCF cal., case colored or blue (NWMP short rifle) frame, choice of 22 (short rifle or musket), 26, or 28 in. barrel, patterned after the Winchester Model 1876, mfg. by Chapparal. Limited importation 2008.

$875	$765	$655	$595	$480	$395	$305	*$1,019*

Add $250 for NWMP short rifle or musket.
Add $90 for short rifle or $46 for Triwood stock.

1892 RIFLE/CARBINE – .357 Mag. or .45 LC cal., color case hardened frame, 20 (Carbine) or 24 1/4 (Rifle) in. barrel, patterned after the Winchester Model 1892, mfg. by Armi Sport. Disc. 2009.

$925	$810	$695	$630	$510	$415	$325	*$1,094*

* ***1892 Rifle/Carbine Takedown*** – .357 Mag. or .45 LC cal., color case hardened receiver, 20 (Carbine) or 24 1/4 (Rifle) in. barrel, takedown action. Disc. 2009.

$1,075	$940	$805	$730	$590	$485	$375	*$1,249*

RIFLES: O/U

SUPERIOR EXPRESS – .30-06 cal., 23 1/2 in. barrels with quarter rib and leaf sights, dovetailed receiver for scope mounting, silver finished boxlock receiver, gold SST, checkered walnut stock and forearm, 7 3/4 lbs. Imported 2000-2005.

$1,900	$1,665	$1,425	$1,290	$1,045	$855	$665	*$2,259*

EMPIRE EXPRESS – .30-06, .375 H&H (new 2005), or .416 Rigby (new 2005) cal., 23 1/2 in. barrels with quarter rib and leaf sights, dovetailed receiver for scope mounting, silver finished boxlock receiver with shoulders, gold SST, checkered European style walnut stock with Bavarian cheekpiece and forearm, 7 3/4 lbs. Imported 2000-2005.

$2,525	$2,210	$1,895	$1,715	$1,390	$1,135	$885	*$2,949*

Add $710 for .375 H&H or .416 Rigby cal.

RIFLES/CARBINES: SEMI-AUTO

All recently manufactured semi-auto rifles have forged aluminum alloy receivers that are hard coat milspec anodized and Teflon coated, manganese phosphate barrel (except stainless), radiused aluminum magazine release button, aluminum trigger guard, safety selector position on right side of receiver, dust cover, brass deflector, forward assist, and include one magazine and hard plastic carrying case. All recently manufactured rifles were covered by a lifetime repair policy.

SEMI-AUTO RIFLE – .22 LR cal., steel receiver, 20 3/4 in. barrel with adj. rear sight, 10 shot mag. Mfg. 1998-2002.

* ***Semi-Auto Rifle Field Grade*** – features uncheckered walnut finished hardwood stock.

$110	$95	$85	$75	$60	$50	$40	*$135*

GRADING - PPGS™	100%	98%	95%	90%	80%	70%	60%	LAST MSR

* ***Semi-Auto Rifle Field Grade Polymer/Hardwood*** – similar to Field Grade, except has stainless steel action and barrel with black polymer (disc.) or hardwood checkered stock, 6 1/8 lbs. Mfg. 2000-2002.

	$120	$105	$90	$80	$65	$55	$40	*$149*

* ***Semi-Auto Rifle Superior Grade*** – features checkered walnut finished stock. Disc. 2001.

	$175	$155	$130	$120	$95	$80	$60	*$209*

* ***Semi-Auto Rifle Empire Grade*** – features checkered California walnut stock. Disc. 2001.

	$275	$240	$205	$185	$150	$125	$95	*$334*

D-M4/D-M4P CARBINE – 5.56 NATO cal., 16 in. chrome-moly match barrel with M-203 mounting groove, 10, 20, or 30 shot mag., forged "F" front sight base with bayonet lug and rubber coated sling swivel, A3 detachable carry handle, T-Marked flat-top upper, six-position telestock, A2 birdcage flash hider, oval double heat shield M4 forend. Mfg. 2008-2009.

	$925	$810	$695	$630	$510	$415	$325	*$1,143*

Add $90 for M4 feed ramp (Model DM-4).

D-M4LE CARBINE – 5.56 NATO cal., similar to D-M4 carbine, except has mil spec diameter receiver extension with "H" buffer. Mfg. 2008-2009.

	$1,275	$1,115	$955	$865	$700	$575	$445	*$1,373*

D-M4S CARBINE – similar to D-M4 carbine, except has two Picatinny riser blocks, oval double heat shield M4 forend with QD sling swivel and swivel/bipod stud installed, Magpul enhanced trigger guard. Mfg. 2008-2009.

	$1,025	$895	$770	$695	$565	$460	$360	*$1,189*

D-M4LX CARBINE – 5.56 NATO cal., 16 in. chrome-moly H-bar fluted match barrel, M4 feed ramps, T-Marked flat-top upper, flip up rear sight, folding front gas block with bayonet lug, aluminum free floating quad rail forend with swiveling sling stud, nine 5-slot low profile ladder style quad rail covers, Ace M4 SOCOM standard length telestock with half buttpad, Phantom flash suppressor, Ergo Ambi AR grip. Mfg. 2008-2009.

	$1,650	$1,445	$1,240	$1,120	$910	$745	$580	*$1,783*

D-M4LT CARBINE – 5.56 NATO cal., Milspec diameter receiver extension with "H" buffer, chrome lined lightweight A1 barrel, permanently attached Phantom suppressor, slim carbine type forend, 30 shot Magpul PMAG black mag. Limited mfg. 2009.

	$1,275	$1,115	$955	$865	$700	$575	$445	*$1,373*

Add $890 for permanently attached Smith Vortex flash suppressor, Magpul CTR stock with buttpad, and Daniel Defense light rail (Model D-M4LTD, mfg. 2009 only).

Add $1,050 for Vltor Modstock, mid-length gas system, Smith Vortex suppressor, Daniel Defense light rail, and Magpul grip (Model D-M4MG, mfg. 2009 only).

Add $150 for A2 birdcage flash hider, full length hand guard, Troy flip up BUIS (Model D-M4MLL, mfg. 2009 only).

D-MCA4 RIFLE – .223 Rem. cal., 20 in. chrome lined govt. profile barrel, A3 detachable carry handle, A2 buttstock, A2 birdcage flash hider, A2 hand guard, forged front sight base, 30 shot mil spec mag. Limited mfg. 2009.

	$1,175	$1,030	$880	$800	$645	$530	$410	*$1,317*

Add $622 for KAC M5 quad rail with KAC panels (Model D-MCA4-M5).

D-M4LED CARBINE – 5.56 NATO cal., 16 in. chrome lined govt. profile barrel, flat Dark Earth finish, Magpul CTR mil spec buttstock, A2 birdcage flash hider, M4 feedramp, Daniel Defense light rail, Magpul MIAD grip, Troy rear BUIS. Limited mfg. 2009.

	$1,925	$1,675	$1,500	$1,250	$1,050	$875	$725	*$2,209*

D-MR20 RIFLE – 5.56 NATO cal., 20 in. Wilson Arms stainless steel fluted bull barrel, Magpul PRS II stock, three slot riser blocks, Daniel Defense light rail forearm with Picatinny rail gas block, two-stage match trigger, Phantom suppressor, 20 shot mag. Mfg. 2009.

	$1,825	$1,595	$1,370	$1,240	$1,005	$820	$640	*$1,979*

GRADING - PPGS™	100%	98%	95%	90%	80%	70%	60%	LAST MSR

DR-15 TARGET – 5.56 NATO cal., 20 in. chrome-moly match H-bar barrel, A2 upper with carry handle, fixed A2 buttstock, A2 birdcage flash hider, forged front sight tower with bayonet lug and rubber coated sling swivel. Limited mfg. 2008.

$895	$785	$670	$610	$490	$405	$315	$1,089

DV-24 MATCH TARGET/VARMINT – 5.56 NATO cal., 24 in. free float match stainless steel bull barrel, T-Marked flat-top upper, two Picatinny half riser blocks, ported aluminum tube forend with swivel/bipod stud installed, Ace skeletonized butt stock, Picatinny rail milled gas block, two-stage match trigger. Mfg. 2008-2009.

$1,250	$1,095	$940	$850	$690	$565	$440	$1,389

JR CARBINE – 9mm Para. (JR9), .40 S&W (JR40), or .45 ACP (JR45) cal., 16 1/4 in. triangular contoured barrel, 13 (.45 ACP), 15 (.40 S&W), or 17 (9mm) shot mag., features unique magwell interchangability, allowing the owner to use handgun magazine of choice, matte black synthetic six-position telescoping AR stock, anodized aluminum receiver, Picatinny rail, free float quad rail forearm, ergonomic AR grip, includes two mags., approx. 6 1/2 lbs. Disc. 2009.

$875	$775	$700	$625	$550	$475	$400	$987

RIFLES: SINGLE SHOT

FIELD GRADE – .22 Hornet, .223 Rem., .243 Win., or .270 Win. cal., single shot break open action, 22 in. barrel with mount base, drilled and tapped, adj. or no sights, checkered hardwood stock and forearm. Limited importation 2001 only.

$165	$145	$125	$110	$90	$75	$60	$189

Add $10 for adj. sights.

This model was also available in a Youth configuration at no extra charge.

MODEL 1874 LITTLE SHARPS – .17 HMR, .218 Bee, .22 LR (new 2008), .22 Hornet, .22 WMR (new 2009), .357 Mag., .30-30 Win., .38-55 WCF (new 2008), .44-40 WCF (new 2008), or .45 LC cal., 24 (rimfire only) or 26 in. tapered octagon barrel, case colored frame, straight grip uncheckered walnut stock and forearm, mfg. by Armi Sport. Mfg. 2007-2009.

$1,075	$940	$805	$730	$590	$485	$375	$1,249

SHOTGUNS: O/U

Recent O/U production was from Italy and Turkey.

PRESENTATION MODEL – 12 or 20 ga., with choke tubes, Purdey double underlug locking action with decorative engraved sideplates, French walnut, single trigger, ejectors. Disc. 1986.

$995	$870	$745	$675	$545	$450	$350	$1,165

COUNTRY SQUIRE MODEL – .410 bore only, 3 in. chambers, case colored boxlock action, gold DT, 25 1/2 in. vent. barrels with VR and F/F chokes, checkered straight grip stock and Schnabel forearm, approx. 6 lbs. Disc. 2002.

$640	$560	$480	$435	$350	$290	$225	$715

FIELD II HUNTER – 12, 16 (new 2001), 20, 28 ga., or .410 borc, similar to DeLuxe Model except has fixed chokes, extractors, machine-cut stock checkering, and blue receiver, 5 1/2 - 7 lbs., depending on ga./barrel lengths. Imported 1989-2005.

$850	$745	$640	$580	$470	$385	$300	$1,029

Add $100 for 28 ga. or .410 bore.

* ***Field II Hunter with Ejectors*** – similar to Field II Hunter, except has ejectors and multi-chokes (not available on 28 ga. or .410 bore), Monte Carlo stock. Imported 1997-2005.

$1,065	$900	$800	$675	$575	$475	$375	$1,279

* ***Field II Hunter Ultra-Light*** – 12 or 20 ga., alloy frame, 26 in. VR barrels only with fixed IC/M (disc. 2000) or multi-chokes (new 2001), thin forearm, approx. 5 1/2 lbs. Imported 1999-2005.

$965	$840	$725	$625	$525	$425	$325	$1,199

GRADING - PPGS™	100%	98%	95%	90%	80%	70%	60%	LAST MSR

DELUXE MODEL – 12, 20, 28 ga. (disc. 1995), or .410 bore (disc. 1995), boxlock with self adj. crossbolt, 26 or 28 in. chrome lined VR barrels with internal choke tubes, SST, ejectors, antique silver finish on receiver, deluxe hand checkered walnut stock and forearm. Imported 1989-96.

$650	$570	$490	$440	$360	$295	$230	*$770*

SPORTING CLAYS MODEL – 12 ga. only, SST, ejectors, silver engraved receiver, checkered walnut stock and forearm, screw-in chokes, 28 (disc.) or 30 (new 1996) in. VR ported barrels. Imported 1995-96.

$775	$680	$580	$525	$425	$350	$270	*$895*

SUPERIOR II – 12 or 20 ga., various chokes, boxlock action, single trigger, ejectors, engraved. Disc. 1988.

$675	$590	$505	$460	$370	$305	$235	*$875*

Add $35 for 12 ga. Mag. (disc. 1987).

FIELD III – 12 or 20 ga., various chokes, boxlock action, single trigger. Disc. 1989.

$395	$345	$295	$270	$215	$180	$140	*$450*

SUPERIOR II HUNTER – 12, 20, 28 ga. (new 1998), or .410 bore, 3 in. chambers (except 28 ga.), boxlock action, ejectors, 26, 28, or 30 in. VR barrels with multi-chokes (except 28 ga. and .410 bore), barrel porting became standard during 2000, select checkered walnut stock and forearm, 6 1/8-7 lbs. Imported 1997-2005.

$1,325	$1,160	$995	$900	$730	$595	$465	*$1,519*

Subtract $70 for 28 ga. or .410 bore.

* ***Superior II Hunter Sporting*** – 12 or 20 ga. (disc. 1998), 26 (disc. 1998), 28, or 30 (12 ga. only) in. 10mm VR barrels with multi-chokes and ported barrels. Imported 1997-2005.

$1,400	$1,225	$1,050	$950	$770	$630	$490	*$1,659*

* ***Superior II Hunter Trap*** – 12 ga. only, 30 or 32 (disc. 2001) in. VR barrels with choice of fixed chokes or multi-chokes, regular or Monte Carlo stock. Imported 1997-2005.

$1,450	$1,270	$1,090	$985	$800	$655	$510	*$1,699*

Subtract 10% if w/o multi-chokes with Monte Carlo stock.

* ***Superior II Hunter Skeet*** – 12 or 20 ga., 26 in. VR barrels with choice of Skeet fixed chokes or multi-chokes, regular or Monte Carlo stock. Imported 1997-98.

$935	$820	$700	$635	$515	$420	$325	*$1,039*

Add $120 for multi-chokes with Monte Carlo stock.

EMPIRE DL HUNTER – 12, 20, 28 ga., or .410 bore, boxlock action, silver receiver with game scene engraving, ejectors, SST, 26 or 28 (12 or 20 ga. only) in. VR barrels with multi-chokes (except 28 ga. and .410 bore). Imported 1997-98.

$1,025	$875	$750	$650	$550	$475	$395	*$1,159*

Add $65 for 28 ga. or $110 for .410 bore.

EMPIRE II EDL HUNTER – similar to Empire DL Hunter, except has engraved sideplates featuring game scenes. Imported 1998-2005.

$1,675	$1,465	$1,255	$1,140	$920	$755	$585	*$2,029*

Subtract $10 for 28 ga. or .410 bore.

* ***Empire II EDL Hunter Sporting*** – 12 or 20 ga. (disc. 1999), 26 (disc. 1999), 28, or 30 (12 ga. only) in. VR barrels with multi-chokes. Imported 1997-2005.

$1,675	$1,465	$1,255	$1,140	$920	$755	$585	*$2,049*

* ***Empire II EDL Hunter Trap*** – 12 ga. only, 30 or 32 (disc. 2000) in. VR barrels with choice of fixed chokes (32 in. barrel only) or multi-chokes, regular (disc. 1998) or Monte Carlo stock. Imported 1997-2005.

$1,700	$1,490	$1,275	$1,155	$935	$765	$595	*$2,099*

Subtract 10% if w/o multi-chokes.

GRADING - PPGS™	100%	98%	95%	90%	80%	70%	60%	LAST MSR

* ***Empire II EDL Hunter Mono Trap*** – features 30 or 32 in. single top barrel, standard or adj. Monte Carlo stock. Imported 1999-2005.

	$2,825	$2,400	$2,150	$1,800	$1,425	$1,150	$925	*$3,249*

Subtract approx. 20% if w/o adj. Monte Carlo stock.

* ***Empire II EDL Hunter Trap Combo*** – includes mono 32 in. barrel and extra set of 30 in. O/U barrels, standard or adj. Monte Carlo stock. Imported 1999-2005.

	$3,500	$3,150	$2,700	$2,250	$1,925	$1,625	$1,375	*$3,919*

Subtract approx. 20% if w/o adj. Monte Carlo stock.

* ***Empire II EDL Hunter Skeet*** – 12 or 20 ga., 26 in. VR barrels with choice of Skeet fixed chokes or multi-chokes, regular or Monte Carlo stock. Imported 1997-98.

	$1,050	$920	$790	$715	$580	$475	$370	*$1,189*

Add $125 for multi-chokes with Monte Carlo stock.

DIAMOND FIELD – 12 or 20 ga. (disc. 1986) Mag., with choke tubes. Same action as Presentation Model without sideplates, engraved, select walnut, single trigger, ejectors. Disc. 1986.

	$695	$610	$520	$475	$380	$315	$245	*$895*

* ***Diamond Field Trap or Skeet*** – 12 ga. only, 26 or 30 in. barrels only. Disc. 1986.

	$850	$745	$640	$580	$470	$385	$300	*$1,050*

Subtract $50 for Skeet Model.

DIAMOND GTX DL HUNTER – 12, 20, 28 ga., or .410 bore, sidelock action, ejectors, SST, elaborate engraving with select checkered walnut stock and forearm, 26, 28 (12 or 20 ga. only), or 30 (12 ga. only) in. VR barrels with multi-chokes (except 28 ga. and .410 bore). Imported 1997 only.

	$11,250	$9,845	$8,440	$7,650	$6,190	$5,065	$3,940	*$12,399*

* ***Diamond GTX EDL Hunter*** – more elaborate variation of the Diamond GTX DL Hunter. Imported 1997 only.

	$13,750	$12,030	$10,315	$9,350	$7,565	$6,190	$4,815	*$15,999*

DIAMOND GTX SPORTING – 12 or 20 (disc. 1998) ga., boxlock Boss action with light perimeter engraving, 28 or 30 (12 ga. only) in. VR barrels with multi-chokes and porting. Imported 1997-2001.

	$5,260	$4,605	$3,945	$3,575	$2,895	$2,365	$1,840	*$5,849*

DIAMOND GTX TRAP – 12 ga. only, boxlock Boss action with light perimeter engraving, 30 in. VR barrels with choice of fixed (disc. 1999) or multi-chokes with barrel porting, regular or adj. (new 1999) Monte Carlo stock. Imported 1997-2001.

	$5,865	$4,900	$4,400	$3,825	$3,175	$2,750	$2,175	*$6,699*

Subtract 10% w/o fixed chokes.

DIAMOND GTX MONO TRAP – features single top barrel, adj. Monte Carlo stock. Imported 1999-2001.

	$5,795	$4,850	$4,400	$3,825	$3,150	$2,750	$2,175	*$6,619*

* ***Diamond GTX Mono Trap Combo*** – includes 32 in. mono barrel and extra set of 30 in. O/U barrels, adj. Monte Carlo stock. Imported 1999-2001.

	$6,775	$5,930	$5,080	$4,605	$3,725	$3,050	$2,370	*$7,419*

DIAMOND GTX SKEET – 12 or 20 ga., 26 or 28 (20 ga. only with Monte Carlo stock) in. VR barrels with choice of Skeet fixed chokes or multi-chokes, regular or Monte Carlo stock. Imported 1997-98.

	$4,700	$4,115	$3,525	$3,195	$2,585	$2,115	$1,645	*$5,149*

Add $140 for multi-chokes with Monte Carlo stock.

DIAMOND REGENT GTX DL HUNTER – 12, 20, 28 ga., or .410 bore, sidelock action, ejectors, SST, best quality engraving with premium checkered walnut stock and forearm, 26, 28 (12 or 20 ga. only), or 30 (12 ga. only) in. VR barrels with multi-chokes (except 28 ga. and .410 bore). Imported 1997 only.

	$19,750	$17,280	$14,815	$13,430	$10,865	$8,890	$6,915	*$22,299*

GRADING - PPGS™	100%	98%	95%	90%	80%	70%	60%	LAST MSR

* ***Diamond Regent GTX EDL Hunter*** – top-of-the-line model incorporating best quality engraving and premium walnut. Imported 1997 only.

	$23,000	$20,125	$17,250	$15,640	$12,650	$10,350	$8,050	*$26,429*

MODEL 105 – 12 ga., 26 or 28 in. barrels, fixed chokes, extractors, DT, silver engraved receiver, Turkish walnut stock, mfg. in Turkey. Imported 2006-2007.

	$355	$310	$265	$240	$195	$160	$125	*$409*

MODEL 106 – 12, 20, 28 ga. or .410 bore, 26 or 28 in. barrels, SST, extractors, fixed (.410 bore) or multi-chokes, inlaid blue receiver, mfg. in Turkey. Imported 2006-2007.

	$525	$460	$395	$355	$290	$235	$185	*$599*

MODEL 206 – 12 ga., 3 in. chambers, extractors or ejectors, 26 or 28 in. VR barrels with three multichokes, SST, silver receiver, select Turkish Monte Carlo walnut stock, mfg. in Turkey. Imported 2007-2009.

	$685	$600	$515	$465	$375	$310	$240	*$793*

Add $126 for auto ejectors.

* ***Model 206 Sporting*** – 12 ga., 28 or 30 in. VR barrels with 5 multichokes, ejectors, SST. Imported 2007-2009.

	$925	$800	$700	$600	$500	$400	$350	*$1,059*

Add $240 for adj. comb.

* ***Model 206 Trap*** – 12 ga., 30 in. VR barrels with 5 multichokes, ejectors. Imported 2007-2009.

	$975	$850	$750	$650	$550	$450	$375	*$1,123*

Add $240 for adj. comb.

DALY UL – 12 ga., aluminum receiver, SST, ejectors, 26 in. barrels with five multi-chokes. Imported 2007 only.

	$525	$460	$395	$355	$290	$235	$185	*$599*

MAXI-MAG – 12 ga., 3 1/2 in. chambers, boxlock action, 26 or 28 in. VR barrels with three choke tubes, SST, extractors, checkered walnut stock and forearm. Imported 2007 only.

	$485	$425	$365	$330	$265	$220	$170	*$559*

Add $60 for Advantage Max-4 or Realtree HD camo finish.

SHOTGUNS: SxS

FIELD III – 12 or 20 ga., various chokes, boxlock action, single trigger. Disc.

	$350	$305	$265	$240	$195	$160	$125	

COUNTRY SQUIRE MODEL – .28 ga. or .410 bore, 3 in. chambers, case colored boxlock action, gold DT, 26 in. barrels with fixed chokes, checkered stock and splinter forearm, approx. 6 lbs. Disc. 2000.

	$600	$525	$450	$410	$330	$270	$210	*$680*

FIELD II HUNTER MODEL – 10 (disc. 2002), 12, 16 (new 2005), 20, 28 ga., or .410 bore, boxlock action, 26, 28, 30 (12 ga. only), or 32 (10 ga. only) in. barrels, fixed (disc. 2000) or multi-chokes (12 or 20 ga. only), 6-7 3/ 8 lbs., or 11 1/4 (10 ga.) lbs. Imported 1997-2005.

	$975	$875	$750	$650	$550	$450	$375	*$1,189*

Subtract $90 for 16 ga., 28 ga. or .410 bore (extractors only).

Subtract approx. 15% if w/o ejectors and multi-chokes (not available in 28 ga. or .410 bore).

SUPERIOR – 12 or 20 ga., boxlock action, various chokes, single trigger. Disc. 1985.

	$550	$480	$415	$375	$305	$250	$195	*$624*

SUPERIOR HUNTER – 12, 20, or 28 (new 1999) ga., or .410 bore (new 2000), 26 or 28 in. barrels with fixed (disc. 2000) or multi-chokes (new 2001, 12 or 20 ga. only), 5 7/8-6 3/4 lbs. Imported 1997-2005.

	$1,395	$1,220	$1,045	$950	$765	$630	$490	*$1,659*

Subtract $30 for 28 ga. or .410 bore.

GRADING - PPGS™	100%	98%	95%	90%	80%	70%	60%	LAST MSR

LUXE MODEL – 12 (disc. 1991) or 20 ga., boxlock action, SST, ejectors, 26 in. barrels with choke tubes, checkered pistol grip walnut stock with semi-beavertail forearm, recoil pad. Imported 1990-94.

$575	$505	$430	$390	$315	$260	$200	*$650*

This model was manufactured by Hermanos located in Spain.

EMPIRE HUNTER – 12, 20, or 28 (disc. 1998) ga., 26 or 28 in. barrels with fixed or multi-chokes (new 2001), 6-6 7/8 lbs. Imported 1997-2005.

$1,700	$1,490	$1,275	$1,155	$935	$765	$595	*$2,119*

DIAMOND DL – 12, 20, 28 ga., or .410 bore, case colored sidelock action with 3rd lever fastener, scroll engraving, select checkered walnut stock and splinter forearm, 26 or 28 in. barrels with fixed chokes. Importation began 1997.

$6,060	$5,305	$4,545	$4,120	$3,335	$2,725	$2,120	*$6,999*

DIAMOND REGENT DL – 12, 20, 28 ga., or .410 bore, sidelock action with best quality engraving and premium checkered walnut stock and forearm, 26 or 28 in. barrels with fixed chokes. Imported 1997 only.

$18,950	$16,580	$14,215	$12,885	$10,425	$8,530	$6,635	*$21,659*

MODEL 306 – 12 or 20 (new 2007) ga., 3 in. chambers, engraved boxlock action, 26 or 28 in. barrels with three multichokes, gold SST, extractors, checkered Turkish walnut stock and forearm, 6 1/2 - 7 lbs. Importation from Turkey 2006-2007.

$580	$510	$435	$395	$320	$260	$205	*$649*

CLASSIC COACH GUN – 12 ga., 3 in. chambers, engraved boxlock action, 20 in. barrels with three multichokes, gold SST, extractors, checkered Turkish walnut stock and forearm, 6.3 lbs. Imported 2007.

$550	$480	$415	$375	$305	$250	$195	*$635*

SHOTGUNS: LEVER ACTION

MODEL 1887 – 12 ga., patterned after the Winchester Model 1887, case-colored frame, 22 or 28 in. barrel. Imported 2007-2009.

$1,100	$950	$800	$700	$600	$500	$450	*$1,279*

Add $60 for 28 in. barrel.

SHOTGUNS: SEMI-AUTO

The Charles Daly "Novamatic" shotguns were produced in 1968 by Breda in Italy. The Novamatic series was not imported by Outdoor Sport Headquarters, Inc.

NOVAMATIC LIGHTWEIGHT MODEL – 12 ga., 26 or 28 in. barrel, various chokes, available with quick choke interchangeable tubes, checkered pistol grip stock, similar to the Breda shotgun. Mfg. 1968 only.

$305	$265	$230	$205	$170	$135	$105

Add $25 for vent. rib.
Add $15 for quick choke.

NOVAMATIC SUPER LIGHTWEIGHT – 12 or 20 ga., similar to Lightweight, except approx. 1/2 lb. lighter.

$330	$290	$250	$225	$180	$150	$115

Add $25 for vent. rib.
Add $15 for quick choke.

NOVAMATIC MAGNUM – 12 or 20 ga. with 3 in. chambers, similar to Lightweight, 28 or 30 in. vent rib barrel, full choke.

$330	$290	$250	$225	$180	$150	$115

NOVAMATIC TRAP – similar to Lightweight, with 30 in. full vent. rib barrel, Monte Carlo stock.

$360	$315	$270	$245	$200	$160	$125

MULTI-XII – 12 ga. only, 3 in. chamber, 27 in. VR multichoke barrel, self-adjusting gas operation, deluxe checkered walnut stock with recoil pad and forearm. Imported 1987-88 only.

$425	$370	$320	$290	$235	$190	$150	*$498*

GRADING - PPGS™	100%	98%	95%	90%	80%	70%	60%	LAST MSR

CHARLES DALY AUTOMATIC – 12 ga., 2 3/4 or 3 in. chambers, gas operation, alloy frame, pistol grip (high gloss) or English stock, vent. rib, 5 shot mag. Also available as slug gun with iron sights. Invector chokes became standard in 1986. Disc. 1988.

$320	$280	$240	$220	$175	$145	$110	$365

Add $15 for oil finished English stock.

FIELD GRADE ERCT – 12 or 20 ga., 22 in. barrel, adj. sight or cantilever scope mount, blue finish or RealTree Hardwoods camo coverage, extended rifle choke tube, deer variation, mfg. in Turkey. Imported 2006-2007.

$340	$300	$255	$230	$185	$155	$120	$399

Add $70 for Youth Model.
Add $10 for cantilever scope mount.
Add $60 for 100% camo coverage.

FIELD GRADE FRB – 12 ga., 22 in. fully rifled barrel with choice of fiber optic sights or cantilever scope mount, blue or camo finish, mfg. in Turkey. Imported 2007-2008.

$385	$335	$290	$260	$210	$175	$135	$449

Add $70 for 100% camo coverage.
Add $180 for combo variation with cantilever mount barrel and extra 28 in. multi-choke barrel.
Add $16 for cantilever scope mount.

FIELD IV (FIELD HUNTER) – 12, 20 (new 2002), or 28 (new 2002) ga., 3 in. chamber (12 or 20 ga.), gas operated, aluminum receiver, 22 (Youth or smoothbore slug), 24-30 in. VR barrel with multi-chokes, choice of standard wood/black metal or 100% Next (new 2009), Advantage (disc. 2001), Advantage Timber HD (mfg. 2002-2008), Realtree (disc. 2001), RealTree Hardwoods HD (disc. 2009), Advantage Max-4 HD (12 ga. only, mfg. 2004-2009), Realtree APG (mfg. 2008-2009), Advantage Wetlands (mfg. 2001-2003), or Advantage Classic (disc. 2001) camo coverage, synthetic stock and forearm, 6 7/8-7 1/8 lbs. Imported 1999-2009.

$440	$385	$330	$300	$240	$200	$155	$509

Add $74 for 100% camo coverage.
Add $20 for 28 ga.
Add $124 for Turkey Model with 24 in. barrel, pistol grip stock, and camo coverage (new 2009).
Add $28 for left-hand action (12 ga. only).
Add $20 for Advantage Timber HD camo (20 ga. only, disc. 2008).

* ***Field Hunter Slug*** – 12 ga. only, 22 in. cyl. bore barrel with adj. sights, black synthetic stock and forearm, nickel (disc. 2002) or black chrome finish, adj. open sights. Imported 1999-2003.

$355	$310	$265	$240	$195	$160	$125	$409

Add $20 for satin nickel finish (disc. 2002).
Add $40 for fully rifled barrel with adj. sights (new 2002).

FIELD HUNTER MAXI-MAG – 12 ga. only, 3 1/2 in. chamber, 24, 26 (new 2001), or 28 in. VR barrel with multi-choke, 7mm VR rib, choice of wood/metal or 100% camo coverage similar to Field Hunter, 6 7/8-7 1/8 lbs. Importation began 2000.

$440	$385	$330	$300	$240	$200	$155	$499

Add $75 for 100% camo coverage.

* ***Field Hunter Maxi-Mag Turkey*** – 12 ga. only, includes 24 in. barrel, Hi/TriViz fiber optic sights and XX full ported turkey choke tube, Advantage Timber or Realtree Hardwoods HD camo treatment, Uncle Mike's camo sling and sling swivels. Mfg. 2002-2009.

$550	$480	$415	$375	$305	$250	$195	$639

SUPERIOR II/IV HUNTER – similar to Field Hunter, except has 20 LPI checkered Turkish walnut stock and forearm, gold highlights and trigger. Imported 1999-2009.

$565	$495	$425	$385	$310	$255	$200	$675

Add $32 for 28 ga.
Add $100 for left-hand action (12 ga. only, disc. 2006).

Model nomenclature was changed from Superior II Hunter to Superior IV Hunter during 2009.

GRADING - PPGS™	100%	98%	95%	90%	80%	70%	60%	LAST MSR

* ***Superior II/IV Hunter Sporting*** – 12, 20, or 28 ga., similar to Superior Hunter, except has 28 or 30 in. ported 10mm VR barrels. Imported 1999-2009.

	$625	$525	$450	$410	$330	$270	$210	*$739*

Add $236 for adj. comb.
Add $30 for 28 ga.

* ***Superior II/IV Hunter Trap*** – 12 ga. only, 30 or 32 (disc. 2007) in. ported barrel with front and mid bead sights. Imported 1999-2009.

	$640	$540	$460	$420	$340	$275	$215	*$769*

Add $230 for adj. comb.

TACTICAL – 12 ga., 18 1/2 in. barrel, matte black synthetic pistol grip stock, Picatinny rail, ghost ring sights, extended tactical choke tube. Limited mfg. 2009.

	$495	$435	$370	$335	$270	$225	$175	*$587*

Add $80 for 100% A-Tacs camo finish (new 2010).

SHOTGUNS: SLIDE ACTION

FIELD ERCT – 12 or 20 ga., 22 in. barrel with rifled choke tubes, blue or RealTree Hardwoods HD camo finish, available with either adj. sights or cantilevered scope mount, also available in Youth Model (20 ga. only), deer variation. Imported 2006-2007.

	$220	$195	$165	$150	$120	$100	$75	*$259*

Add $10 for cantilevered scope mount.
Add $60 for 100% camo coverage.
Add $6 for Youth Model (20 ga. only).

FIELD HUNTER – 12 or 20 (new 2001) ga., 3 in. chamber, 22 (Youth, 20 ga. only), 24, 26, 28, or 30 in. VR barrel with multi-choke, black or pink (Youth only) synthetic stock and forearm, choice of standard wood/metal, chrome (Youth only) or 100% Next (new 2009), Advantage Timber HD (mfg. 2002-2008), Realtree APG (mfg. 2008-2009), Realtree AP HD (mfg. 2008-2009), Realtree Hardwoods HD 12 ga. only, (mfg. 2002-2008) or Advantage Classic (disc. 2001) camo coverage, 5 5/8-6 7/8 lbs. Imported 1999-2009.

	$240	$210	$180	$165	$130	$110	$85	*$299*

Add $14 for Youth model with pink synthetic stock (new 2009).
Add $80 for camo.
Add $124 for Turkey Model with pistol grip stock and camo (new 2009).

* ***Field Hunter Slug*** – 12 ga. only, 18 1/2 in. cyl. bore or 22 in. fully rifled (new 2002) barrel with adj. sights, black synthetic stock and forearm, black chrome or dull nickel finish. Imported 1999-2003.

	$210	$185	$160	$145	$115	$95	$75	*$229*

Subtract 15% for 18 1/2 in. barrel.

FIELD HUNTER MAXI-MAG – 12 ga. only, 3 1/2 in. chamber, 24, 26 (new 2001), or 28 in. VR barrel with multi-choke, 7mm VR rib, choice of wood/metal or 100% camo coverage similar to Field Hunter, approx. 6 3/4 lbs. Imported 2000-2009.

	$270	$235	$205	$185	$150	$120	$95	*$339*

Add $80 for camo.
Add $114 for Turkey Model with camo, Hi/TriViz fiber optic sights and XX full ported turkey choke tube - also includes sling and sling swivels (new 2002).

TACTICAL – 12 ga. or 20 (new 2009), 3 in. chamber, 18 1/2 in. cyl. bore barrel with front sight, black synthetic stock and forearm or 100% camo coverage (new 2009), matte blue metal or chrome finish, 6 lbs. Imported 2000-2009.

	$250	$220	$190	$170	$140	$115	$90	*$289*

Add $24 for Field Tactical AW with chrome finish and adj. sights.
Add $74 for pistol grip stock, ghost ring sights, and MC1 multichoke.
Add $134 for pistol grip stock, ghost ring sights, Picatinny rail, and extended choke tube.
Add $124 for camo with ghost ring and fiber optic sights (new 2009).

GRADING - PPGS™	100%	98%	95%	90%	80%	70%	60%	LAST MSR

DALY, CHARLES: 2011-PRESENT

Current trademark of shotguns imported by Samco Global Arms located in Miami, FL.

During Sept. 2012, Samco Global Arms, Inc. purchased the Charles Daly trademarks from the Kassnar family. On Akkar and Charles Daly shotguns imported by Samco during 2011-2012, service can be provided directly by Samco. Samco can also supply service parts and accessories for Charles Daly semi-auto, pump, and O/U shoguns imported by K.B.I., Inc. and made by the Akkar factory in Turkey, from 1999 through 2010. These models are identifiable by the serial number. Samco cannot provide direct service and/or parts for any other firearms imported by K.B.I. Inc. or others, that were sold under the Charles Daly name. Parts for other Charles Daly firearms imported by K.B.I., Inc., such as 1911 pistols made in the Phillipines - contact Armscor shotguns made in Italy, Sabatti, or Fausti. For Miroku shotguns made in Japan, contact Browning, etc.

SHOTGUNS

Current O/U models include the 206ASE Field - MSR $1,013, 206T Trap - MSR $1,199, 206SL - MSR $1,185, 206S Sporting - MSR $1,185. Current semi-auto models include the 600 Field Series - MSR $523-$611, 600S Sporting - MSR $739, 600T Trap - MSR $741, 600CY Compact - MSR $523-$611, 600SL mid-size - MSR $736, 635 Maxi Mag - MSR $556-$699. Current slide action models include the 300 Series - MSR $359-$493, 300SL mid range - MSR $467, 300CY Compact - MSR $359-449, 335 Maxi Mag - MSR $397-$447. Additionally, Samco also offers a line of both slide action and semi-auto configurations for home protection and tactical appplications. Slide action MSRs range from $333-$487, and semi-auto variations range from $499-$693. Please contact Samco directly for current availability and information.

DAN ARMS OF AMERICA

Previous trademark of shotguns manufactured in Italy by Silma. Previously imported by Dan Arms of America located in Allentown, PA and by Dan Arms of North America (previously called Sportsman's Emporium Ltd.) located in Fort Washington, PA.

All shotguns listed below were discontinued in early 1988.

SHOTGUNS: O/U

LUX GRADE I – 12 or 20 ga., 3 in. Mag. chambers, 26, 28, or 30 in. barrels, vent. rib, extractors, pistol grip, double trigger, European walnut.

100%	98%	95%	90%	80%	70%	60%	LAST MSR
$280	$220	$210	$200	$190	$180	$170	*$350*

LUX GRADE II – 12 ga. only, 3 in. Mag. chambers, 26, 28, or 30 in. barrels, vent. rib, extractors, pistol grip, single trigger, European walnut.

100%	98%	95%	90%	80%	70%	60%	LAST MSR
$320	$250	$240	$230	$215	$200	$190	*$395*

LUX GRADE III – 12 or 20 ga., 3 in. Mag. chambers, 26, 28, or 30 in. barrels, vent. rib, ejectors, pistol grip, single trigger, checkered European walnut.

100%	98%	95%	90%	80%	70%	60%	LAST MSR
$375	$300	$285	$270	$255	$240	$220	*$450*

LUX GRADE IV – 12 ga. only, 3 in. Mag. chambers, 28 in. barrels, vent. rib, ejectors, pistol grip, single trigger, checkered European walnut, multi-chokes with 5 tubes.

100%	98%	95%	90%	80%	70%	60%	LAST MSR
$460	$390	$350	$310	$285	$265	$245	*$550*

SKEET MODEL – 12 ga. only, 26 1/2 in. barrels, 10mm vent. rib, anatomical pistol grip.

100%	98%	95%	90%	80%	70%	60%	LAST MSR
$550	$450	$400	$355	$320	$300	$285	*$650*

TRAP MODEL – 12 ga. only, 30 in. barrels, 10mm vent. rib, anatomical pistol grip.

100%	98%	95%	90%	80%	70%	60%	LAST MSR
$550	$450	$400	$355	$320	$300	$285	*$650*

SILVERSNIPE – 12 or 20 ga., made to customer specifications, sideplates, select high grade walnut, name engraving upon request.

100%	98%	95%	90%	80%	70%	60%	LAST MSR
$1,300	$1,200	$1,050	$900	$800	$700	$600	*$1,475*

SHOTGUNS: SxS

FIELD MODEL – 12, 16, 20, 28 ga., or .410 bore, double triggers, extractors, 26 or 28 in. barrels.

100%	98%	95%	90%	80%	70%	60%	LAST MSR
$285	$220	$210	$200	$190	$180	$170	*$350*

GRADING - PPGS™	100%	98%	95%	90%	80%	70%	60%	LAST MSR

DELUXE FIELD MODEL – 12 or 20 ga., single triggers, ejectors, 26 or 28 in. barrels.

	$440	$375	$340	$310	$290	$260	$230	*$500*

DAN WESSON

Current trademark manufactured by Dan Wesson Firearms beginning 2005, and located in Norwich, NY. Distributed beginning 2005 by CZ-USA, located in Kansas City, KS. Previously manufactured by New York International Corp. (NYI) located in Norwich, NY 1997-2005. Distributor and dealer sales.

PISTOLS: SEMI-AUTO

Until 2005, Dan Wesson manufactured a complete line of .45 ACP 1911 style semi-auto pistols. Previously manufactured models include: Seven (last MSR was $999), Seven Stainless (last MSR was $1,099), Guardian (last MSR was $799), the Guardian Deuce (last MSR was $799), the Dave Pruit Signature Series (last MSR was $899), and the Hi-Cap (last MSR was $689).

CCO BOBTAIL – .45 ACP cal., SA, 4 1/4 in. barrel, similar to Commander Classic Bobtail, except has anodized black aluminum frame, stainless steel slide, black ceramic coat finish and tritium sights, wood stipled shadow grips, 26 oz. New 2009.

MSR $1,558	$1,350	$1,075	$950	$825	$650	$550	$475	

COMMANDER CLASSIC BOBTAIL – .45 ACP or 10mm cal., 4 1/4 in. barrel, stainless steel frame and slide, Colt Series 70 design, Ed Brown Bobtail mainspring housing, many target features, diamond checkered cocobolo grips, 34 oz. Mfg. 2005-2009.

	$1,050	$900	$775	$700	$600	$500	$450	*$1,191*

Add $33 for 10mm cal.
Add $339 for two-tone finish and black ceramic coated slide (10mm cal. only, new 2009).

ECO MODEL – 9mm Para. or .45 ACP cal., Officer sized model with 3 1/2 in. barrel and slide, SA, single stacked mag., G10 grips, black anodized finish on aluminum frame and steel slide, tritium night sights, 25 oz. New 2012.

MSR $1,623	$1,375	$1,175	$975	$850	$750	$650	$550	

Add $39 for .45 ACP cal.

ELITE SERIES HAVOC – .38 Super or 9mm Para. cal., 4 1/4 in. barrel with compensator, SA, all steel construction, designed for Open IPSC/USPSA Division, C-More sights, 21 shot mag., black finish, 38 oz. New 2011.

MSR $4,299	$3,700	$3,225	$2,800	$2,400	$2,000	$1,650	$1,400	

ELITE SERIES MAYHEM – .40 S&W cal., SA, Limited IPSC/USPSA, 6 in. bull barrel with tactical rail, 18 shot mag., adj. fiber optic sights, black finish, 38 3/4 oz. New 2011.

MSR $3,899	$3,400	$2,950	$2,550	$2,100	$1,800	$1,500	$1,325	

ELITE SERIES TITAN – 10mm cal., 4 3/4 in. bull barrel, 18 shot mag., all steel construction, lower frame tactical rail, black finish, tritium sights, 26 oz. New 2011.

MSR $3,829	$3,350	$2,925	$2,550	$2,100	$1,800	$1,500	$1,325	

GLOBAL – .45 ACP or 10mm cal., 5 or 6 in. barrel, full size frame, steel or stainless steel, choice of accessory light rail or full length dust cover. Disc. 2005.

	$1,000	$900	$800	$700	$600	$475	$350	*$1,149*

GUARDIAN – 9mm Para. or .45 ACP (new 2011) cal., 8 or 9 shot mag., 4 1/4 in. barrel, black light alloy commander frame, bobtail mainspring housing, tritium sight, checkered cocobolo grips, 28.8 oz. New 2010.

MSR $1,558	$1,350	$1,075	$950	$825	$650	$550	$475	

Add $61 for .45 ACP cal. (new 2011).

KO3 PANTHER SERIES – .45 ACP cal., full size, 5 in. barrel, Series 70 pistol with cast alloy frame, external extractor, Chip McCormick beavertail with Commander style hammer, forged conventional round top slide, fixed rear sight, matte bead blasted frame and slide top, slide sides are polished, blue or stainless, Hogue rubber grips. Disc.

	$595	$525	$450	$415	$385	$350	$325	

Add $20 for stainless steel.

GRADING - PPGS™	100%	98%	95%	90%	80%	70%	60%	LAST MSR

MARKSMAN – .45 ACP cal., stainless steel frame, 5 in. barrel, similar to Pointman, except slimmer design, 38 1/2 oz. Mfg. 2009.

	$1,225	$1,000	$900	$775	$650	$550	$475	*$1,391*

PATRIOT 1911 SERIES – .45 ACP or 10mm (Commander slide and frame only) cal., 4 1/4 (Commander) or 5 in. stainless steel match barrel, 1911 Series 70 action, external extractor, fitted parts, and many high-end components by McCormick, Ed Brown, Nowlin, etc., each gun shipped with test target, variations include Patriot Expert (blue or stainless, Bo-Mar style target sights), Patriot Marksman (blue or stainless, fixed sights), AAA cocobolo double diamond checkered grips with gold medallions, 2.3 lbs. Mfg. 2001-2005.

	$825	$750	$650	$550	$475	$425	$375	*$929*

Add $20 for 5 in. Patriot with blued action.
Add $70 for 5 in. barrel in stainless steel.
Add $30 for checkered front grip strap.
Add $70 for bobtail frame.

PM3-P MINOR SERIES – .45 ACP cal., full size, 5 in. barrel, Series 70 pistol with cast alloy frame, Chip McCormick beavertail with Commander style hammer, forged conventional round top slide, fixed rear sight, matte bead blasted frame and slide top, slide sides are polished, blue or stainless, checkered exotic hardwood grips. Disc.

	$515	$450	$415	$385	$350	$325	$295	

PM POINTMAN SERIES – .45 ACP or 10mm cal., full size, 5 in. target barrel, features Chip McCormick beavertail with Commander style hammer, forged conventional round top slide, high target rib or low profile Clark style sights with adj. white outline or Bo-Mar rear sight, blue or stainless, PM1-S is standard gun, checkered exotic hardwood grips. Disc. 2005.

	$725	$650	$575	$500	$425	$385	$350	*$809*

Add $50 for checkered front grip strap.
Add $50 for high or Ausi rib (Model PMA-S).
Add $100 for blue finish with Clark/Bo-Mar rib and sights (Model PMA-B, disc.).

POINTMAN SEVEN – .40 S&W (new 2009), .45 ACP or 10mm cal., 5 in. barrel, features stainless steel frame and slide, patterned after the Colt Series 70 semi-auto, 7 shot mag., double slide serrations, many target features, diamond checkered cocobolo grips, 38 oz. Mfg. 2005-2009.

	$1,050	$900	$775	$700	$600	$500	$400	*$1,158*

Add $33 for 10mm cal.
Add $31 for .40 S&W cal.
Add $111 for Desert Tan teflon finish with black grips and controls, (.45 ACP cal. only, new 2009).

POINTMAN NINE – 9mm Para. cal., similar to Pointman Seven, 5 in. barrel, stainless steel frame, front strap checkering, fiber optic front sight, cocobolo grips, 38 1/2 oz. New 2009.

MSR $1,558	$1,350	$1,150	$950	$825	$725	$625	$525	

RZ-10 RAZORBACK SPECIAL EDITION – 10mm cal., full size, 5 in. barrel, Colt Series 70 design with forged stainless frame and slide, Bo-Mar adj. rear sight, match barrel, bushing, and link, match grade trigger, sear, hammer, and beavertail, checkered synthetic or rubber (new 2006) grips, limited mfg. 2002-2004, and resumed 2006-2009.

	$1,050	$900	$775	$700	$600	$500	$450	*$1,191*

Add $257 for Sportsman Model with VZ G10 black operator grips, FO front sights and adj. sights (new 2009).

RZ-10 RAZORBACK – 10mm cal., SA, 5 in. barrel, stainless steel construction, checkered cocobolo grips, fixed sights, 9 shot mag., approx. 38-1/2 oz. New 2012.

MSR $1,350	$1,125	$975	$825	$725	$625	$525	$450	

RZ-45 HERITAGE – .45 ACP cal. only, 8 shot mag., 5 in. barrel, stainless steel frame, SA, fixed night sights, manual thumb safety, rubber grips, 38 1/2 oz. New 2009.

MSR $1,298	$1,075	$900	$800	$700	$600	$500	$400	

GRADING - PPGS™	100%	98%	95%	90%	80%	70%	60%	LAST MSR

SPECIALIST – .45 ACP cal., SA, 5 in. barrel, features serrated rib and tritium night sights, G10 VZ Operator II grips, two 8 shot mags., frame has lower Picatinny rail, matte stainless or black duty finish. New 2012.

MSR $1,558	$1,350	$1,150	$950	$825	$725	$625	$525	

Add $312 for black duty finish.

SS CUSTOM – .40 S&W cal., stainless steel construction, fiber optic front sight, ambidextrous safety, shark grips. Mfg. 2008-2009.

	$1,225	$1,000	$900	$775	$650	$550	$475	*$1,389*

VALOR – .45 ACP cal., 8 shot mag., 5 in. barrel, choice of black ceramic coated finish or matte stainless steel (new 2010), slimline VZ or G10 grips, adj. (disc.) or Heinie Ledge Straight 8 (new 2010) tritium night sights, 38 oz. New 2008.

MSR $1,701	$1,525	$1,225	$975	$850	$725	$625	$550	

Add $311 for black finish.

* ***Valor Bobtail Commander*** – similar to Valor, except has 4 1/4 in. barrel, and bobtail commander style features, 35.2 oz. New 2010.

MSR $1,766	$1,525	$1,225	$975	$850	$725	$625	$550	

Add $311 for black finish.

REVOLVERS: DOUBLE ACTION

Dan Wesson has also manufactured a variety of revolver packages that were available by special order only.

MODEL 44-AGS (ALASKAN GUIDE SPECIAL) – .445 SuperMag. cal., 6 shot, stainless steel, compensated 4 in. heavy barrel with VR and full ejector shroud, black Teflon metal finish, rubber wraparound finger groove grips, fully adj. sights. Mfg. 2002-2004, resumed 2006-2007.

	$1,075	$950	$850	$725	$650	$550	$475	*$1,295*

MODEL 715 SMALL FRAME SERIES – .357 Mag. cal., 6 shot, stainless steel, 2 1/2, 4, 6, 8, or 10 in. heavy barrel with VR and full ejector shroud, rubber wraparound finger groove grips, interchangeable barrels. Mfg. 2002-2004.

	$625	$550	$475	$425	$375	$325	$275	*$709*

Add $50 for 4 in., $90 for 6 in., $150 for 8 in., or $190 for 10 in. barrel.

This model was also available as a pistol pack with 4 barrels and case. MSR was $1,699.

MODEL 715 (CURRENT MFG.) – .357 Mag. cal., 6 shot, SA/DA, 6 in. heavy VR barrel with full shroud, stainless steel, adj. target rear sight with interchangeable front sight, Hogue finger grooved rubber grips, includes hard case, 38 oz. Mfg. 2011-2012.

	$1,025	$900	$775	$650	$525	$425	$325	*$1,168*

Barrel assemblies and grips for this model are interchangeable with those on the older Dan Wesson Model 15-2 and later variations.

MODEL 741 LARGE FRAME SERIES – .44 Mag. cal., 6 shot, stainless steel, 4, 6, 8, or 10 in. heavy barrel with VR and full ejector shroud, rubber wraparound finger groove grips, raked hammer, interchangeable barrels. Mfg. 2002-2004.

	$725	$650	$575	$500	$450	$400	$350	*$829*

Add $30 for 6 in., $110 for 8 in., or $170 for 10 in. barrel.

MODEL 7445 SUPERMAG FRAME SERIES – .445 SuperMag. cal., 6 shot, stainless steel, 4, 6, 8, or 10 in. heavy barrel with VR and full ejector shroud, rubber wraparound finger groove grips, interchangeable barrels. Mfg. 2002-2004, resumed 2006-2007.

	$965	$875	$775	$675	$600	$525	$450	*$1,070*

MODEL 7460 – .45 ACP, .45 Auto Rim., .445 Super Mag., .45 Win. Mag., or .450 Rowland cal., mfg. 1999-disc.

	$800	$725	$650	$575	$500	$450	$400	

RIFLES: BOLT ACTION

COYOTE CLASSIC – .22 LR or .22 WMR cal., 22 3/4 in. tapered barrel, 6 or 10 shot mag.,

GRADING - PPGS™	100%	98%	95%	90%	80%	70%	60%	LAST MSR

checkered hardwood stock and forend, adj. rear sight. Limited mfg. 2002 only.

	$200	$180	$160	$145	$130	$115	$100	*$239*

COYOTE TARGET – .22 LR or .22 WMR cal., 18 3/8 in. heavy bull barrel, 6 or 10 shot mag., uncheckered target hardwood stock with high cheekpiece, w/o sights. Limited mfg. 2002 only.

	$230	$200	$175	$155	$145	$135	$125	*$279*

DANIEL DEFENSE

Current AR-15 style rifle and related components manufacturer located in Savannah, GA.

CARBINES: SEMI-AUTO

In addition to the models listed below, Daniel Defense can build a custom rifle based on customer specifications. Please contact the company directly for this service (see Trademark Index).

IMPORTANT NOTE: On model(s) where *N/A has replaced the normal 100% value, it indicates current market conditions are too unstable to accurately ascertain 100%-60% values. Factory retail prices (MSRs) reflect most recent updates. For more up-to-date information on current pricing trends and additional useful information, please visit www.bluebookofgunvalues.com, select "Information & Services" from the menu, and click on "Additional Book Information".

DDM4 CARBINE SERIES – 5.56 NATO cal., 16 in. chrome lined barrel, A2 birdcage flash hider, 10, 20, or 30 shot mag., mil-spec enhanced mag. well, A4 feed ramp, A1.5 BUIS sight, pinned "F" marked front sight base, Omega X rails, Magpul 5 position extended buttstock, A2 vertical grip, includes plastic case.

* ***DDM4V1*** – 5.56 NATO cal., 16 in. chrome lined barrel, standard or lightweight (new 2012) barrel, original Daniel Defense rifle.

MSR $1,759	*N/A	$1,375	$1,125	$925	$800	$700	$600

* ***DDM4V2*** – 5.56 NATO cal., 16 in. chrome lined barrel, similar to DDM4V1, except lightweight configuration with Omega X 7.0 rail system, also available with lightweight carbine barrel (DDM4V2LW). New 2011.

MSR $1,759	*N/A	$1,375	$1,125	$925	$800	$700	$600

* ***DDM4V3*** – 5.56 NATO or 6.8 SPC (new 2012) cal., 16 in. chrome lined barrel, similar to DDM4V2, except has mid-length gas system, 9 in. free float Omega quad rail, also available with lightweight carbine barrel (DDM4V3LW).

MSR $1,759	*N/A	$1,375	$1,125	$925	$800	$700	$600

* ***DDM4V4*** – 5.56 NATO cal., 16 in. hammer forged carbine barrel, pinned low profile gas block, Omega X 9.0 rail system, available in lightweight profile (disc. 2011), no sights, fixed sights, or flip up sights.

MSR $1,639	*N/A	$1,275	$1,050	$875	$750	$625	$495

Add $120 for fixed sights.
Add $299 for flip up sights (disc. 2011).

* ***DDM4V5*** – 5.56 NATO or .300 Blackout (new mid-2012) cal., 16 in. hammer forged carbine barrel, 30 shot mag., pinned low profile gas block, Omega X 12.0 rail system, available in lightweight profile, no sights, fixed sights, or flip up sights, approx. 6 lbs.

MSR $1,709	*N/A	$1,350	$1,125	$925	$825	$725	$550

Add $120 for fixed sights.
Subtract $80 for 5.56 NATO cal.
Add $299 for flip up sights (disc. 2011).

* ***DDM4V7*** – 5.56 NATO or 6.8 SPC cal., 16 (5.56 NATO) or 18 (6.8 SPC) in. standard or lightweight barrel with flash hider, with or w/o sights, flat top receiver, full length top Picatinny rail, forearm features three modular Picatinny rails that are moveable, 30 shot mag. New 2012.

MSR $1,689	*N/A	$1,325	$1,075	$895	$775	$625	$550

Add $110 for fixed sights.

GRADING - PPGS™	100%	98%	95%	90%	80%	70%	60%	LAST MSR

DD CARBINE SERIES – 5.56 NATO or 6.8mm SPC cal., 16 in. chrome lined barrel, similar to DDM4 Series, except mil-spec buttstock. New 2010.

* ***DDXV/XV EZ*** – 16 in. cold hammer forged barrel, "F" marked fixed front sight base, flared mag well on lower receiver, Magpul enhanced trigger guard, M16 bolt carrier group, rear receiver QD sling swivel attachment, with (XV EZ) or w/o (XV, disc. 2011) EZ CAR 7.0 rail system and A1 fixed rear sight.

MSR $1,419 *N/A $1,100 $950 $825 $700 $575 $475

Add $68 for EZ CAR 7.0 rail system.
Add $129 for XVM model with mid-length barrel.

* ***DDV6.8*** – 6.8mm SPC cal., 16 in. cold hammer forged mid-length barrel, Omega X 9.0 VFG and A1.5 fixed rear sight. Disc. 2011.

N/A $1,275 $1,075 $900 $775 $650 $525 *$1,537

DARDICK

Previous manufacturer located in Hamden, CT.

CARBINES

DARDICK CARBINE CONVERSION – .22 or .38 Dardick Tround cal., 23 in. barrel (interchangeable), walnut stock. Limited mfg.

$1,795 $1,450 $1,150 $925 $825 $750 $700

PISTOLS: SEMI-AUTO

SERIES 1100 – .38 Dardick Tround cal., double action, 11 shot mag.

$2,500 $2,200 $1,900 $1,575 $1,250 $995 $875

Dardick ammunition in itself is collectible - currently, individual "Trounds" are selling in the $5- $10 range.

SERIES 1500 – .22, .30, or .38 Dardick Tround cal., double action, 15 shot mag.

$2,000 $1,795 $1,575 $1,125 $975 $850 $700

DARNE S.A.

Current manufacturer producing shotguns 1881-1979 and 1990 to date in Saint Etienne, France. Darne also began making double rifles circa 1996. Currently imported by Geoffroy Gournet, located in Easton, PA. Previously imported by The Drumming Stump, Inc. located in Circle Pines, MN circa 1996-2005, and by Wes Gilpin located in Dallas, TX until 1992.

For F. Darne Fils Ainé please refer to the F Section. Also, please refer to the Bruchet section for 1982-1990 mfg. utilizing the Darne action.

RIFLES: DOUBLE

DARNE DAMON PETRIK O/U – 8x57R, 9.3x74R, or .30R Blaser cal.

Base price for this model is €15,000.

MODEL R EXPRESS SxS – 8x57 JRS or 9.3x74R cal., double rifle version of the Darne Model R Series shotgun, many options available, including style of rib, sights, stock configuration, etc. Importation began 1996.

Base price for this model is €14,000.

EXPRESS SUPERPOSEÉ – .30-06, 8x57 JRS, or 9.3.74R cal., double rifle version of the Darne O/U shotgun, boxlock with false sideplates, straight grip stock, many options available. Importation began 1996.

Please contact the importer directly for a price quotation on this model.

MODEL V EXPRESS SxS – 8x57R, 9.3x74R, .30R Blaser, or .375 H&H cal., no obturators discs.

Base price for this model is €24,000. Base price for the .375 H&H cal. model is €26,000.

GRADING - PPGS™	100%	98%	95%	90%	80%	70%	60%	LAST MSR

SHOTGUNS: SxS, PRE-1980 MFG.

DARNE SLIDING BREECH SHOTGUN – 12, 16, 20, or 28 ga., SxS, unique action utilizes sliding breech lock-up, high quality mfg., 27 1/2 in. barrel standard with other lengths available, any choke combination, either straight grip or pistol grip stock, checkered, models differ in amount of engraving and grade of wood.

Model	100%	98%	95%	90%	80%	70%	60%	LAST MSR
*** *Darne Sliding Breech Shotgun Bird Hunter Model R11***	$1,500	$1,350	$1,100	$950	$825	$700	$600	
*** *Darne Sliding Breech Shotgun Pheasant Hunter Model R15***	$2,250	$2,000	$1,800	$1,625	$1,500	$1,425	$1,300	
*** *Darne Sliding Breech Shotgun Magnum Model R16***	$3,500	$3,150	$2,650	$2,300	$2,000	$1,750	$1,500	
*** *Darne Sliding Breech Shotgun Quail Hunter Model V19***	$4,500	$4,150	$3,700	$3,350	$2,850	$2,400	$1,950	
*** *Darne Sliding Breech Shotgun Model V22***	$5,750	$5,300	$4,600	$4,150	$3,650	$3,000	$2,500	
*** *Darne Sliding Breech Shotgun Hors Series No. 1 Model V***	$6,350	$5,750	$5,250	$4,500	$3,850	$3,150	$2,600	

SHOTGUNS: 1989-CURRENT MFG.

In 1990, Paul Bruchet (the old Darne plant superintendent) obtained permission to once again use the Darne trademark. Hence, all 1990 and later mfg. has been produced by Paul Bruchet.

All new mfg. Darnes can be choked to the customer's choice. All models listed have automatic ejectors, are oil finished by hand, and may be barreled to any length (except for Models R 11, 12, and 13). All prices are subject to change without notice.

O/U Models

SB1 – similar to SB3, traditional European O/U, DT, extractors, straight or semi-pistol grip stock. Importation began 1998.

MSR POR	N/A	N/A	$2,000	$1,650	$1,450	$1,100	$950	

SB2 – similar to SB3, except has scroll engraving, wood upgrade, and 28 in. barrels. Importation began 1996.

MSR POR	N/A	N/A	$2,400	$1,975	$1,625	$1,250	$1,000	

SB3 – 12 or 20 ga., scalloped boxlock action, extractors, 26 in. barrels, DTs, choice of English straight grip stock or semi-pistol grip. Importation began 1996.

MSR POR	N/A	N/A	$2,900	$2,300	$1,925	$1,800	$1,650	

DARNE DAMON PETRIK – 12, 16, 20 ga. or .410 bore (special order only), boxlock action, with or w/o ejectors.

This model is POR.

SxS Sliding Breech Models

Add $1,100 for single trigger on the following models.

R 11 – 12, 16, 20, 28 ga., or .410 bore, half pistol grip stock, light engraving.

The base price for this model is €7,600.

R 12 – similar to R 11, except with better engraving.

The base price for this model is $11,700.

R 13 – 12, 16, or 20 ga., straight or pistol grip stock, traditional action with bouquet engraving and obturator discs.

The base price for this model is €9,500.

R 14 – 12, 16, or 20 ga., slug gun, choice of forearms, light engraving, and optional cheek rest pistol grip stock was optional. Importation disc. circa 2002.

	N/A	$3,225	$2,675	$2,250	$1,950	$1,750	$1,200	*$6,600*

GRADING - PPGS™	100%	98%	95%	90%	80%	70%	60%	LAST MSR

R 15 – 12, 16, 20, 24, 28 ga., or .410 bore, select walnut stock and forearm with fine checkering, large scroll engraving, obturator discs.

The base price for this model is €11,000.

R 16 – same as R 15, except has 3 in. chambers. Importation disc. circa 2002.

	N/A	$3,450	$2,800	$2,350	$2,000	$1,750	$1,200	*$7,800*

R 17 – 12 (including Mag.), 16, 20, 24, 28 ga., or .410 bore, Magnum model (3 in. chambers), customer's choice engraving patterns, superior quality wood finish. Importation disc. circa 2002.

	N/A	$5,125	$4,600	$3,625	$2,900	$2,450	$1,975	*$8,900*

RHS – all gauges, top-of-the-line model incorporating customer's choice of engraving style, type of inlays, and checkering pattern, best quality wood. Due to the unique nature of this model, each specimen must be appraised individually. New guns are priced per individual customer order.

V 19 – all gauges, easy opening large key action, top quality walnut and checkering, full coverage rose and scroll engraving with chiseled fences.

The base price for this model is €17,000.

V 20 – similar to V 19, except has deep relief rosace engraving and chiseled fences. Importation disc. circa 2002.

	N/A	$6,600	$5,500	$4,400	$3,200	$2,550	$2,000	*$12,300*

V 21 – similar to V 19, except has 100% coverage English rose and scroll engraving and chiseled fences. Importation disc. circa 2002.

	N/A	$7,600	$6,500	$5,500	$4,400	$3,200	$2,550	*$14,400*

V 22 – similar to V 21, except has 100% engraving coverage featuring bouquet patterns and deeply chiseled fences, sculpted shoulders, best quality walnut.

The base price for this model is €22,500.

VHS – all gauges, top-of-the-line model incorporating customer's choice of engraving style, type of inlays, and checkering pattern, best quality wood. Due to the unique nature of this model, each specimen must be appraised individually. New guns are priced per individual customer order.

DAUDSONS ARMOURY

Current manufacturer located in Peshawar, Pakistan. No current U.S. importation.

Daudsons Armoury's orgins stretch back over two centuries dealing in the sporting arms and defense firearms trade. The company provides firearms for the armed forces of Pakistan as well as the Defense Ministry.

Daudsons Armoury manufactures the DSA line of 12 ga. shotguns. There are four basic models: DSA Shooter, DSA Commando, DSA Sure Shot, and the DSA Security. All are manufactured from high grade alloy steel, with black synthetic stocks and forearms, and all parts are completely interchangeable. Daudsons also manufactures double barrel rifles and a semi-auto .22 cal. rifle. For more information on these guns, including pricing and U.S. availability, please contact the company directly (see Trademark Index).

DAVID MILLER CO.

Current custom rifle manufacturer located in Tucson, AZ since 1973.

The David Miller Co., composed of David Miller and Curt Crum, is a custom rifle shop building best quality bolt-action rifles only. All guns are built per individual custom order and the company should be contacted directly for more information and price quotations.

All currently crafted rifles from the David Miller Co. are made using highly modified and finished Winchester Model 70 Classic actions or, on rare occasion, a Weatherby Mark V action. Three models of rifles are crafted in the Miller shop, the Classic, the Marksmen, and the GraGun. The Classic is the top-of-the-line in custom bolt action rifles available today and is priced starting at $55,000. The Marksmen is equally well constructed, but without many of the very labor-intensive features and is standard with a laminated wood stock rather than top quality walnut. The Marksmen is intended as a serious hunting rifle and has a starting price of $30,000. The latest model is the GraGun, with a base price starting at $32,000 and features a Bansner synthetic stock in two colors. The waiting period for

GRADING - PPGS™	100%	98%	95%	90%	80%	70%	60%	LAST MSR

any of the models is about 2-1/2 years. Please contact the David Miller Co. directly for a quotation on a new rifle (see Trademark Index).

Used rifles should be individually appraised to ascertain current values. Very few genuine Miller rifles ever appear on the used gun market. At the 2004 Safari Club International annual convention, an early David Miller Co. custom rifle, crafted around a much modified and refined Mauser G33/40 action and chambered for the .30-06 cartridge, equivalent to today's Classic rifle, sold used for $24,000. Another early used Miller rifle sold at the 2010 SCI convention for $20,000. These used rifles were authenticated by the David Miller Co. as being genuine examples coming from the Tucson shop.

DAVIDSON FIREARMS

Previously manufactured by Fábrica de Armas, located in Eibar, Spain.

SHOTGUNS: SxS

MODEL 63B – 12, 16, 20, 28 ga., or .410 bore, 25, 26, 28, or 30 in. barrels, Anson & Deeley boxlock, engraved and nickel plated frame, various chokes, walnut checkered stock. Mfg. 1963-disc.

	100%	98%	95%	90%	80%	70%	60%
	$350	$315	$275	$250	$225	$200	$175

Add 30% for 28 ga. or .410 bore.

* ***Model 63B Magnum*** – similar to 63B, except 10 ga. Mag., 12, or 20 ga. Mag., 32 in. barrel.

	100%	98%	95%	90%	80%	70%	60%
12 or 20 ga.	$395	$360	$325	$275	$230	$195	$165
10 ga.	$425	$375	$330	$300	$275	$250	$225

MODEL 69SL – 12 or 20 ga., true detachable sidelock action, engraved nickel plated action, 26 in. and 28 in. barrels, imp. cyl. and mod., mod. and full, checkered walnut stock. Mfg. 1963-76.

	100%	98%	95%	90%	80%	70%	60%
	$415	$395	$375	$340	$320	$290	$260

MODEL 73 STAGECOACH – 12 or 20 ga., detachable sidelock, exposed hammers, 3 in. chambers, 20 in. mod. and full barrels, checkered walnut stock. Mfg. 1976-disc.

	100%	98%	95%	90%	80%	70%	60%
	$275	$260	$220	$200	$175	$165	$155

DAVIDSON'S

Current distributor located in Prescott, AZ.

While Davidson's is not a manufacturer or an importer, this company has been responsible for many special and limited editions that are listed with quantities, but without used values, since they may vary greatly from region to region.

Make/Model	Qty. Made	Year Issued	Retail Price
SPECIAL/LIMITED EDITIONS/HANDGUNS			
BERETTA Stampede Ltd. Matched Pair	115	2006	$1,060
BROWNING BDA Special Limited Edition	N/A	2004	$630
BROWNING Buck Mark Camper Special Edition	N/A	N/A	$310
BROWNING Buck Mark Hunter Special Edition	N/A	2006	$340
BROWNING Buck Mark Grade I John Browning Endowment	2,500	2006	$500
BROWNING Buck Mark High Grade John Browning Endowment	1,001	2006	$655
BROWNING Buck Mark MS Camper w/Tru-Glo Sights	N/A	2011	$380
CHIAPPA 1911-22 Sport w/adj. sights	N/A	2011	$325
COLT Tiger Govt. Nickel .38 Super	N/A	1994	$1,000
COLT Panther Govt. .38 Super	250	1995	$1,070
COLT IPSC Standard Tactical Ltd. Ed.	1,500	1995	$1,398
COLT IPSC Superior Tactical Ltd. Ed.	500	1995	$1,802
COLT IPSC Deluxe Tactical Ltd. Ed.	250	1995	$2,660
FIRESTORM Government Special Edition	N/A	2004	$334

Make/Model	Qty. Made	Year Issued	Retail Price
LES BAER CUSTOM X-Treme Tactical .45 SS Pistol	N/A	2011	$2,310
PARA-ORDNANCE PXT 1911 SSP Single Stack Stainless	300	2007	$1,065
PARA-ORDNANCE PXT 1911 PDA .45 ACP SS	200	2008	$1,239
PARA-ORDNANCE PXT 1911 PDA 9mm SS	100	2008	$1,109
SMITH & WESSON Model 66 Combat Magnum Special .357 Mag.	N/A	2003	$641
SMITH & WESSON Model 629-5 Hunter .44 Mag.	N/A	2004	$1,059
SMITH & WESSON Model 657-5 Hunter .41 Mag.	N/A	2003	N/A
SMITH & WESSON Model 41 PC	N/A	2011	$1,305
SMITH & WESSON Model 637 SS DA Super Tuned	N/A	2011	$519
SMITH & WESSON Model 642 Centennial SS DA Super Tuned	N/A	2011	$519
SMITH & WESSON Model 686 Plus SS DA Super Tuned	N/A	2011	$1,008
SMITH & WESSON Model 18 Combat Masterpiece	N/A	2011	$1,090
SMITH & WESSON Model 442 Centennial DA Super Tuned	N/A	2011	$499
SMITH & WESSSON Model 41 Performance Center .22 LR	N/A	2011	$1,305
SPRINGFIELD ARMORY Leatham Legend Series TGO 1 Service Model	N/A	2003	$3,095
SPRINGFIELD ARMORY Leatham Legend Series TGO 3 Service Model	N/A	2003	$1,295
SPRINGFIELD ARMORY Leatham Legend Series TGO 2 Service Model	N/A	2003	$1,899
STEYR S-Series Special Edition	N/A	2004	$610
STEYR M-A1 Series Special Edition	N/A	2004	$610
STURM-RUGER WB Ruger NRA Limited Edition Mark II	N/A	2003	$334
STURM-RUGER Mark II Competition Target Special Edition	N/A	2003	$339
STURM-RUGER P90 Special Edition Series	N/A	2003	$448
STURM-RUGER P90 Guns & Ammo 45th Anniversary Special Edition	45	N/A	$560
STURM-RUGER Vaquero 45 Years of Guns & Ammo Special Ltd. Edition	N/A	2003	$599
STURM-RUGER Vaquero Dual Cylinder Special Limited Edition	N/A	2003	$600
STURM-RUGER New Vaquero Limited Edition .32-20 WCF	N/A	2004	$642
STURM-RUGER Bisley Single-Six Vaquero Special Edition	N/A	2004	$555
STURM-RUGER GP-100 Special Limited Edition .357 Mag.	N/A	2003	$555
STURM-RUGER GP-100 .357 Mag. Stainless	N/A	2008	$683
STURM-RUGER Super Blackhawk Hunter .41 Mag.	N/A	2004	N/A
STURM-RUGER Super Blackhawk Bisley Hunter .41 Mag.	N/A	2004	N/A
STURM-RUGER New Vaquero Montado	N/A	2007	$785
STURM-RUGER New Vaquero Montado Stainless	N/A	2008	$785
STURM-RUGER Vaquero Cowboy Fast Draw Spl. Ed.	1,000	2008	$663
STURM-RUGER Mark III 22/45	N/A	2007	$361
STURM-RUGER 22 Charger .22 LR w/Red/Purple Stock	N/A	2008	$387
STURM-RUGER Mark III 22/45 Hunter	N/A	2007	$345
STURM-RUGER SP101 DA Revolver	N/A	2009	$611
STURM-RUGER New Vaquero 4.62 in. Bbl.	N/A	2011	$807
STURM-RUGER New Vaquero 5 1/2 in. Bbl.	N/A	2011	$807
STURM-RUGER New Vaquero Stainless 4.62 in. Bbl.	N/A	2011	$807
STURM-RUGER New Vaquero Stainless 5 1/2 in. Bbl.	N/A	2011	$807
STURM-RUGER New Vaquero Montado SS .357 Mag. 3 3/4 in. bbl	N/A	2011	$823
STURM-RUGER GP100 .357 Mag. SS 5 in. hvy bbl.	N/A	2011	$754

Make/Model	Qty. Made	Year Issued	Retail Price
STURM-RUGER Super Blackhawk Hunter .41 Mag. SS 7 1/2 in. bbl.	N/A	2011	$857
STURM-RUGER New Vaquero Montado SS .45 LC 3 3/4 in. bbl.	N/A	2011	$823
STURM-RUGER Super Redhawk Alaskan .44 Mag. SS 2 1/2 in. bbl.	N/A	2011	$1,049
STURM-RUGER 22 Charger .22 LR w/Red Stock & Bi-pod	N/A	2011	$398
STURM-RUGER 22/45 Hunter .22 LR 5 1/2 in. fltd bbl	N/A	2011	$380
STURM-RUGER 22/45 Hunter .22 LR 5 1/2 in. fltd bbl Hi-Viz sgts	N/A	2011	$410
STURM-RUGER LCP-NRA Natural Gear Camo	N/A	2011	$411
TAURUS Model 17 Tracker Ltd. .17 Mag.	N/A	2005	N/A
TAURUS .45-410 Judge	N/A	2011	$1,305
TAURUS PT22 Satin Nickel ebony grips	N/A	2011	$273
TAURUS El Juez SS 3 in.	N/A	2011	$648
TAURUS 738TCP DA .380 raspberry grips	N/A	2011	$336
TAURUS 738TCP .380 SS raspberry grips	N/A	2011	$352
U.S. FIRE ARMS MFG. CO. 12/22 Plinker	N/A	2008	$1,220
U.S. FIRE ARMS MFG. CO. 12/22 Plinker Single Action	N/A	2008	$825
U.S. FIRE ARMS MFG. CO. New Woodsman Match .22	N/A	2010	$1,030
U.S. FIRE ARMS MFG. CO. Woodsman Match 4 1/2 in. Bbl.	501	2011	$1,030
U.S. FIRE ARMS MFG. CO. Sheriff's Spl. SA .45 LC	N/A	2008	$875
U.S. FIRE ARMS MFG. CO. 12/22 SA Plinker 4 3/4 in. bbl	N/A	2011	$1,095
U.S. FIRE ARMS MFG. CO. 12/22 Plinker Nickel 4 3/4 in. bbl	N/A	2011	$1,425
U.S. FIRE ARMS MFG. CO. 12/22 Plinker SA 5 1/2 in. bbl	N/A	2011	$1,095
U.S. FIRE ARMS MFG. CO. 12/22 Plinker Nickel 5 1/2 in. bbl	N/A	2011	$1,425
U.S. FIRE ARMS MFG. CO. 12/22 SA 7 1/2 in. bbl	N/A	2011	$1,095
U.S. FIRE ARMS MFG. CO. 12/22 Plinker Nickel 7 1/2 in. bbl	N/A	2011	$1,425
WALTHER P22 2 Barrel Set	N/A	2006	$450
WALTHER P22 Pink Camo	N/A	2008	$390
WALTHER P22 DA Desert Camo	N/A	2011	$410
WALTHER P22Q DA Desert Camo	N/A	2011	$410
SPECIAL/LIMITED EDITIONS/RIFLES			
AMERICAN TACTICAL IMPORTS GSG522-SD Carbine	N/A	2011	$469
BUSHMASTER E2SLE Optics Ready Carbine	N/A	2007	$1,115
BUSHMASTER E2S A3 M4 SOPMOD "DSC Exclusive"	N/A	2007	$1,235
BUSHMASTER E2S A3 M4 SOPMOD	N/A	2007	$1,500
BUSHMASTER E2S XM 15A4 Marine Corps	N/A	2007	$1,230
BUSHMASTER E2S XM 15A4 Marine Corps CH	N/A	2007	$1,295
BUSHMASTER LE A3 M4 Carbine w/tele-stock	N/A	2011	$1,224
BUSHMASTER LE M4 Optics Ready Carbine	N/A	2011	$1,067
BUSHMASTER E2S M4A1 Type Carbine	N/A	2011	$1,100
MARLIN Model 308SDT Stainless	251	2009	$845
MARLIN Model 336 Ltd. .35 Rem. cal.	1,001	2000	$515
MARLIN Model 336 Ltd. .30-30 SS Laminate	501	2008	$835
MARLIN Model 336 Ltd. .30-30 SS PG	501	2009	$845
MARLIN Model 1886 Ltd.	251	2005	$1,450
MARLIN Model 1894 Ltd. .41 Mag.	251	2005	$695
MARLIN Model 1894CC41-Ltd. .41 Mag. cal.	1,001	1999	$715
MARLIN Model 1894SC 44/45 Ltd	1,050	1997	$460

Make/Model	Qty. Made	Year Issued	Retail Price
MARLIN Model 1894 Cowboy Carbine .44-40 WCF	325	2000	$715
MARLIN Model 1894 Cowboy Carbine Limited .32-20 WCF	501	2005	$860
MARLIN Model 1894SS .357 Ltd.	351	2006	$660
MARLIN Model 1894SS .41 Ltd.	251	2006	$660
MARLIN Model 1894SS .44 Ltd.	351	2006	$660
MARLIN Model 1894SS .45 Ltd.	251	2006	$660
MARLIN Model 1895 Ltd I/II .45-70 Govt.	2,002	1997	$671
MARLIN Model 1895 Ltd. III .45-70 Govt.	1,001	1999	$715
MARLIN Model 1895 Ltd IV .45-70 Govt.	1,001	2000	$729
MARLIN Model 1895 Ltd. .45-70	501	2011	$845
MARLIN Model 1895 CD Ltd. .45-70	501	2011	$678
MARLIN Model 1895GS Ltd. Ed. Guide Gun .45-70	501	2006	N/A
MARLIN Model 1895 Trapper Ltd. .45-70 Govt. Stainless	501	2008	$835
MARLIN Model 917VSFT .17 Mag. Stainless	250	2007	$450
MOSSBERG Model 464 .30-30 Win.	N/A	2011	$535
PUMA Model 92 Ltd. Ed. .454 Casull & .480 Ruger	N/A	2004	$603
REMINGTON Model 700 VTR .223 w/Black Stock	250	2008	$805
REMINGTON Model 700 VTR .223 w/Tan Stock	250	2008	$805
REMINGTON Model 700 VTR .308 w/Tan Stock	500	2008	$805
STURM-RUGER 10/22 Compact .22 LR w/Black or Purple Laminate Stock	N/A	2008	$322
STURM-RUGER 10/22 Carbine .22 LR w/Black/Purple/Red Laminate Stock	N/A	2008	$322
STURM-RUGER 10/22 Sporter .22 LR Stainless	N/A	2008	$405
STURM-RUGER 10/22 Carbine w/Black/Green Stock	N/A	2011	$332
STURM-RUGER 10/22VLEB Hardwood w/bipod	N/A	2011	$500
STURM-RUGER 10/22RB-RBZ Carbine w/Black/Red Stock	N/A	2011	$359
STURM-RUGER 10/22RB-LGBZ w/Black/Green Stock	N/A	2011	$359
STURM-RUGER Mini-14 Ranch Rifle w/Laminate Stock	N/A	2008	$869
STURM-RUGER Mini-14 Ranch Rifle Stainless Black Laminate	N/A	2008	$995
STURM-RUGER Mini-14 Ranch Rifle Stainless Red/Black Lam.	N/A	2008	$967
WINCHESTER Model 1892 Limited Series	500	2004	$1,075
WINCHESTER Model 1892 Limited Series Trapper	N/A	2004	$1,075
WINCHESTER Model 1892 Deluxe Take Down Ltd.	501	2008	$1,875
WINCHESTER Model 9417 Limited .17 HMR	N/A	2004	$530
WINCHESTER Model 1885 Limited Series	N/A	2003	$1,360
WINCHESTER Model 1895 Take-Down Ltd. .405 Win.	1,001	2006	$1,475
WINCHESTER Model 1895 Saddle Ring Carbine Ltd.	501	2007	$1,640
WINCHESTER Model 1886 Solid Frame .45-70 Govt.	501	2006	$1,370
WINCHESTER Model 1886 Solid Frame .45-90 BPCR	501	2006	$1,370
WINCHESTER Model 1886 Take-Down .45-90 BPCR	501	2006	$1,450
WINCHESTER Model 1885 Ltd. Series .32-20 WCF	N/A	2006	N/A
WINCHESTER Model 1885 Ltd. Series .38-55 WCF	N/A	2006	N/A
WINCHESTER Model 1885 Ltd. Series .45-70	N/A	2006	N/A
WINCHESTER Model 1885 Ltd. Series .45-90	N/A	2006	N/A
WINCHESTER Model 1885 Ltd. Series .50-90	N/A	2006	N/A
WINCHESTER Model 1885 Ltd. Series Creedmoor .45-90	N/A	2006	N/A
WINCHESTER Model 1885 Ltd. Series High Wall Trapper	251	2008	$1,515
WINCHESTER Model 1885 Ltd. Series High Wall Trapper .45-70	376	2008	$1,515

Make/Model	Qty. Made	Year Issued	Retail Price
WINCHESTER Model 1885 Ltd. Series Short Hunter	N/A	2008	$1,515
WINCHESTER Model 1885 High Wall Sporter	N/A	2009	$1,405
WINCHESTER Model 1886 Deluxe Ltd. Series Takedown Octagon	501	2007	$2,080
WINCHESTER Model 1886 Deluxe Ltd. Series Takedown Round	N/A	2007	N/A
WINCHESTER Model 1886 Deluxe Take Down Ltd. .45-70	501	2007	$2,080
WINCHESTER Model 1885 Creedmoor Ltd. .50-90 cal.	126	2007	$2,227
WINCHESTER Model 1885 Creedmoor Ltd. .45-90 cal.	126	2007	$2,227
WINCHESTER Woodsman Match 6 in. Bbl.	501	2011	$1,030
SPECIAL/LIMITED EDITIONS/SHOTGUNS			
BROWNING Citori 525 Field Grade VI Combo	51	2007	$5,750
BROWNING Citori 525 Field Grade VI Combo 28/410	51	2007	$5,750
MOSSBERG Model 500 "3 in 1" Home Defense/Hunting/Cruiser	N/A	2007	$367
MOSSBERG Model 500 Tactical Cruiser	N/A	2007	$456
MOSSBERG Model 500 Tactical Cruiser w/Thumbhole Stock	N/A	2007	$447
MOSSBERG Model 500 12 ga. w/20 in. bbl	N/A	2011	$395
MOSSBERG Model 500 Cruiser w/18 1/2 in. bbl Desert Camo	N/A	2011	$502
MOSSBERG Model 500 3 in 1 Special	N/A	2011	$403

DAVIS INDUSTRIES

Previous manufacturer located in Chino, CA 1995-2001. Previously located in Mira Loma, CA until 1995.

Davis Industries provided a lifetime warranty on all products, which is now void.

GRADING - PPGS™	100%	98%	95%	90%	80%	70%	60%	LAST MSR

DERRINGERS

D-SERIES DERRINGER – .22 LR, .22 WMR, .25 ACP, .32 ACP, .32 H&R Mag. (new 1995), .38 Spl. (new 1992), or 9mm Para. cal., O/U steel construction, 2.4 or 2 3/4 (.38 Spl. only) in. vent. rib barrel, 9 1/2 or 11 1/2 oz., black Teflon or chrome finish. Disc. 2001.

	100%	98%	95%	90%	80%	70%	60%	LAST MSR
	$150	$125	$100	$80	$65	$55	$45	*$75*

Add $23 for Big-Bore series (larger frame) in .22 WMR, .32 H&R Mag., .38 Spl., or 9mm Para. cal.
Add $29 for Long-Bore cals. (.22 WMR, .32 H&R Mag. - disc., .38 Spl., or 9mm Para.).
In this series, the .25 ACP cal. is the Model D-25 and the .32 ACP cal. is the Model D-32.

LONG BORE DERRINGER – .22 WMR, .32 H&R Mag. (disc. 1998), .38 Spl., or 9mm Para. cal., similar to D Series, except has 3 3/4 in. barrel, 13 oz. Mfg. 1995-2001.

	100%	98%	95%	90%	80%	70%	60%	LAST MSR
	$185	$150	$125	$100	$85	$75	$65	*$104*

PISTOLS: SEMI-AUTO

P-32 – .32 ACP cal., single action, 6 shot mag., 2.8 in. barrel, black Teflon or chrome finish, laminated wood grips, 22 oz. Mfg. 1987-2001.

	100%	98%	95%	90%	80%	70%	60%	LAST MSR
	$125	$100	$75	$65	$55	$50	$45	*$88*

P-380 – .380 ACP cal., single action, similar to P-32, 5 shot mag., 2.8 in. barrel, bright chrome or black Teflon finish, internal recoil buffer, wood (disc.) or black synthetic grips, 22 oz. Mfg. 1989-2001.

	100%	98%	95%	90%	80%	70%	60%	LAST MSR
	$150	$125	$100	$85	$75	$65	$60	*$98*

DAVIS N.R.

Please refer to the Crescent Fire Arms Co. listing. in the C section.

DEFOURNEY

Previous long gun manufacturer located in Belgium.

Defourney specialized in both quality sidelock and boxlock (with or w/o sideplates) shotguns in both SxS and O/U configuration. Prices range from $750-$3,250 for boxlock

GRADING - PPGS™	100%	98%	95%	90%	80%	70%	60%	LAST MSR

shotguns and start in the $3,500 range for sidelock models, assuming 80% or better original condition.

DEHAAN SHOTGUNS LTD.

Current shotgun importer, repair center, and gunsmith for various Turkish shotgun manufacturers established in 1999, and located in Rigby, ID.

SHOTGUNS

DeHaan shotguns are good quality O/U and SxS models, with a wide variety of engraving and wood options available. Many guns are built per customer order. Please contact the company directly for more information (see Trademark Index).

DEL-TON INCORPORATED

Current rifle manufacturer located in Elizabethtown, NC. Dealer sales. Previously distributed until 2011 by American Tactical Imports, located in Rochester, NY.

CARBINES/RIFLES: SEMI-AUTO

Del-Ton manufactures a wide variety of AR-15 style carbines/rifles. Many options, accessories, and parts are also available. Please contact the company for more information, including current availability and options (see Trademark Index). All rifles includes a hard case, two mags., and buttstock cleaning kit.

IMPORTANT NOTE: On model(s) where *N/A has replaced the normal 100% value, it indicates current market conditions are too unstable to accurately ascertain 100%-60% values. Factory retail prices (MSRs) reflect most recent updates. For more up-to-date information on current pricing trends and additional useful information, please visit www.bluebookofgunvalues.com, select "Information & Services " from the menu, and click on "Additional Book Information".

SIERRA 316H MID-LENGTH CARBINE – .223 Rem. cal., 16 in. mid-length chrome-moly barrel, 30 shot mag., black furniture, six position M4 stock, CAR handguard with single heat shield, A2 flash hider, 7 lbs.

MSR $750	*N/A	$625	$550	$500	$450	$395	$350

SIERRA 216H A2 MID-LENGTH CARBINE – .223 Rem. cal., similar to Mid-Length Carbine, except has A2 fixed stock, 7.4 lbs.

MSR $750	*N/A	$625	$550	$500	$450	$395	$350

POST-BAN CARBINE – .223 Rem. cal., 16 in. heavy chrome-moly barrel with crowned end, 10 shot mag., fixed A2 or pinned M4 reinforced carbon fiber (Sierra 316P) buttstock, black furniture, CAR handguard with single heat shield, flat-top or A2 upper with carry handle, includes sling.

MSR $750	*N/A	$625	$550	$500	$450	$395	$350

Add $25 for Sierra 316P Model with M4 adj. stock.

M4 CARBINE – .223 Rem. cal., 16 in. chrome-moly barrel, 30 shot mag., black furniture, six position M4 stock, CAR handguard with single heat shield, A2 flash hider, includes sling.

MSR $750	*N/A	$625	$550	$500	$450	$395	$350

Add $9 for Tapco Model with Tapco buttstock, SAW grip, polymer mags., and short vertical grip (new 2012).

Add $25 for Echo 314/315 Model with pinned YHM Phantom flash hider (new 2012).

A2 DT-4 CARBINE – .223 Rem. cal., 16 in. chrome-moly barrel, six position M4 stock, 30 shot mag., CAR handguard with single heat shield, A2 flash hider, black furniture, includes sling.

MSR $750	*N/A	$625	$550	$500	$450	$395	$350

A2 CARBINE – .223 Rem. cal., 16 in. heavy chrome-moly barrel, fixed A2 stock, CAR handguard with single heat shield, A2 flash hider, black furniture, carry handle, includes sling.

MSR $750	*N/A	$625	$550	$500	$450	$395	$350

DTI-4 CARBINE – .223 Rem. cal., 16 in. chrome-moly M4 profile barrel, six position M4 stock, 30 shot mag., CAR handguard with single heat shield, A2 flash hider, black furniture,

GRADING - PPGS™	100%	98%	95%	90%	80%	70%	60%	LAST MSR

A3 flat-top or A2 upper with carry handle, includes sling.

MSR $750	*N/A	$625	$550	$500	$450	$395	$350

STANDARD GOVERNMENT PROFILE RIFLE – .223 Rem. cal., 20 in. chrome-moly standard or heavy profile barrel, standard gas system, fixed A2 buttstock, 30 shot mag., standard length handguard with heat shields, A2 flash hider, black furniture, A3 flat-top or A2 upper with carry handle, includes sling.

MSR $750	*N/A	$625	$550	$500	$450	$395	$350

DT SPORT CARBINE – .223 Rem. cal., M4 flat-top design, choice of collapsible or fixed stock, oval ribbed handguard with A3 front sight, 10 or 30 shot mag., 5.8 lbs. New 2011.

MSR $699	*N/A	$550	$475	$400	$365	$335	$295

DTI-15 CARBINE – .223 Rem. cal., 16.1 in. barrel, 30 shot mag., gas operated, hard anodized black oxide finish, adj. six position collapsible stock with M249-style pistol grip, fixed front sights, approx. 7 3/4 lbs. New mid-2011.

MSR $859	*N/A	$700	$625	$550	$500	$450	$400

DTI TRX MID-LENGTH RIFLE/CARBINE – 5.56 NATO cal., 16 in. barrel, black or tan finish, A2 flash hider, threaded muzzle, Troy TRX battlerail handguard, 30 shot mag., and BattleAx CQB adj. stock, 7.2 lbs. New 2012.

MSR $1,250	*N/A	$975	$850	$725	$625	$525	$425

ECHO/SIERRA 316 MOE – 5.56 NATO cal., 16 in. chrome moly barrel, mid-length gas system, threaded muzzle, A2 flash hider, OD Green, black or tan finish, A3 flat-top Magpul MOE grip and adj. buttstock, 30 shot PMag, forged T6 aluminum upper and lower receiver. New 2012.

MSR $830	*N/A	$675	$575	$525	$450	$395	$350

DTI EXTREME DUTY – 5.56 NATO cal., 16 in. hammer forged chrome lined barrel, carbine length gas system, black finish, T6 aluminum upper and lower receiver, M4 carbine handguard with double heat shield, M4 buttstock, 6.4 lbs. New 2012.

MSR $989	*N/A	$750	$625	$550	$475	$400	$350

DTI ECHO 216L A2 LIGHTWEIGHT CARBINE – 5.56 NATO cal., 16 in. chrome moly barrel, carbine length gas system with A2 flash hider and threaded muzzle, forged T6 aluminum upper and lower receiver, carbine length handguard with single heat shield, fixed A2 buttstock, 6.6 lbs. New 2012.

MSR $750	*N/A	$625	$550	$500	$450	$395	$350

DTI ECHO 316L LIGHTWEIGHT CARBINE – 5.56 NATO cal., 16 in. chrome moly barrel, carbine length gas system with A2 flash hider and threaded muzzle, forged T6 aluminum upper and lower receiver, carbine length handguard with single heat shield, M4 six position reinforced carbone fiber buttstock, 5.8 lbs. New 2012.

MSR $750	*N/A	$625	$550	$500	$450	$395	$350

DEMAS, ETS (L'ATELIER VERNEY-CARRON)

Current manufacturer of custom shotguns and rifles located in St. Etienne, France since 1967. Currently imported by Kebco LLC, located in Hanover, PA. Previously imported by Verney-Carron USA, Inc., located in Clay Center, KS until 2008, and by The Drumming Stump, located in Circle Pines, MN.

During 2004, Verney-Carron S.A., located in St. Etienne, France (please refer to separate listing) purchased Demas, which manufactures a full line of custom O/U and SxS rifles and shotguns. Prices vary according to configuration, engraving options, and quality of wood. Please contact the importer (or Verney-Carron directly) for more information, including current model availability and U.S. pricing regarding these fine firearms (see Trademark Index).

In December 2008, Verney-Carron legally absorbed its subsidiary and physically moved its facility to the Verney-Carron factory. The custom workshop is now known as "L'Atelier Verney-Carron".

Please refer to Verney-Carron in the V section listing for current models.

GRADING - PPGS™	100%	98%	95%	90%	80%	70%	60%	LAST MSR

DEMRO

Previous manufacturer located in Manchester, CT.

RIFLES: SEMI-AUTO

T.A.C. MODEL 1 RIFLE – .45 ACP or 9mm Luger cal., blow back operation, 16 7/8 in. barrel, open bolt firing system, lock-in receiver must be set to fire, also available in carbine model.

$650	$595	$525	$475	$425	$395	$360	

XF-7 WASP CARBINE – .45 ACP or 9mm Luger cal., blow back operation, 16 7/8 in. barrel.

$650	$595	$525	$475	$425	$395	$360	

Add $45 for case.

DEMYAN

Current manufacturer located in Moscow, Russia. No current U.S. importation.

Demyan manufactures good quality target pistols, including the SP-08 Khaydurov in .22 LR cal. Demyan also manufactured target rifles, including the T4 Bull Pup, and the T4 Karbine. Currently, Demyan manufactures target air rifles, and these models are not imported into the U.S. Please contact the factory directly for more information, including pricing and availability (see Trademark Index).

DEPAR

Previous manufacturer located in Istanbul, Turkey.

Depar manufactured both semi-auto and O/U shotguns.

SHOTGUNS

ATAK O/U – 12 ga. only, 2 3/4 in. chambers, ejectors, SST.

$425	$350	$295	$250	$225	$200	$185	*$350*

Add approx. 30% with scroll engraving and walnut stock and forearm.

ATILGAN SEMI-AUTO – 12 ga. only, 3 in. chamber, gas operated, includes multi-chokes.

$200	$175	$150	$135	$125	$115	$105	*$195*

* ***Atilgan Semi-Auto De Luxe*** – similar to Atilgan Semi-Auto, except has engraved receiver and deluxe walnut stock and forearm.

$350	$295	$250	$225	$200	$185	$170	*$350*

SAFARI SLIDE ACTION – 12 ga. only, 3 in. chamber, synthetic stock standard.

$170	$150	$135	$125	$115	$105	$95	*$170*

Add 10% for walnut stock and forearm.
Add approx. 50% for nickel chrome receiver finish and light scroll engraving.

DERYA HUNTING ARMS

Current shotgun manufacturer established in 2000, and located in Konya, Turkey.

SHOTGUNS

Derya Hunting Arms currently manufactures semi-auto, slide action, and single shot shotguns in various configurations. Please contact the factory directly for more information, values, and availability (see Trademark Index).

DESENZANI

Current manufacturer established approx. 1929 and located in Italy. Currently distributed by Kennedy Gunmakers, located in Cornwall, U.K.

Desenzani manufactures approx. 10 best quality shotguns per year, utilizing top quality wood, and customer's choice of engraver. Please contact the distributor directly for more information, including an individual price quotation and approx. delivery time (see Trademark Index).

DESERT EAGLE

Please refer to Magnum Research listing.

GRADING - PPGS™	100%	98%	95%	90%	80%	70%	60%	LAST MSR

DESERT INDUSTRIES, INC.

Previous manufacturer located in Las Vegas, NV 1991-1996. See listing under Steel City Arms, Inc. for older models.

In 1990, Desert Industries, Inc. was created - this new company was the same as Steel City Arms, Inc. More recently manufactured guns will have the Las Vegas slide address.

PISTOLS: SEMI-AUTO

THE DOUBLE DEUCE - .22 LR cal., double action, 2 1/2 in. barrel, matte stainless steel construction, 6 shot mag., rosewood grips, 15 oz. Limited mfg. 1991-96.

	$350	$295	$275	$225	$195	$165	$140	*$400*

TWO BIT SPECIAL - .25 ACP cal., double action, 2 1/2 in. barrel, similar to Double Deuce, except has 5 shot mag., 15 oz. Approx. 12 protoypes mfg. 1991-96.

	$375	$350	$295	$235	$205	$175	$150	*$400*

DESERT TACTICAL ARMS

Current rifle manufacturer located in Salt Lake City, UT.

RIFLES: SEMI-AUTO

STEALTH RECON SCOUT - .243 Win., .300 Win. Mag., .308 Win. or .338 Lapua cal., 22 or 26 in. match grade free floating barrel, 5 or 6 shot mag., bullpup designed to be eleven inches shorter than conventional M16A2 rifles, tactical stock with adj. LOP, pistol grip, black or olive drab hard coat anodizing, Black, Coyote Brown, or Olive Drab finish, full length rail, ambidextrous mag release, 9.4-15.1 lbs.

MSR $2,736	$2,500	$2,100	$1,850	$1,650	$1,350	$1,100	$925

Above values are for rifle or covert chassis and do not include a conversion kit. Add $1,390-$1,545, depending on caliber.

HTI SNIPER - .50 BMG or .375 Cheytac cal., 29 in. match grade, free floating, fluted barrel, designed to be lighter and more portable, compact bullpup design, 19.4 lbs. New 2012.

MSR $4,630	$4,300	$3,850	$3,300	$2,800	$2,300	$1,925	$1,775

DESERT TOYS

Current rifle manufacturer located in Mesa, AZ.

Desert Toys manufactures a single shot bolt action .50 BMG rifle called the Rebel. The standard Rebel is available with an 18 or 26 in. barrel in black finish. A variety of accessories and options are also available. Base price for this model is $2,950. Please contact the company directly for more information, including customer specifications and pricing on options (see Trademark Index).

DETONICS

Current semi-auto pistol manufacturer established in 2007 and located in Millstadt, IL.

PISTOLS: SEMI-AUTO

COMBAT MASTER HT - .40 S&W cal., 3 1/2 in. barrel, SA, 7 shot mag., two-tone cerakote finish, stainless steel frame, low profile sights, aluminum/dymondwood grips, 30 oz. New 2010.

MSR $1,849	$1,650	$1,450	$1,250	$950	$750	$550	$450

NEMESIS HT - .40 S&W cal., similar to Combat Master HT, except has 5 in. barrel, 9 shot, 38 oz. New 2011.

MSR $2,249	$1,950	$1,750	$1,550	$1,250	$995	$750	$550

DTX - 9mm Para. or .40 S&W cal., DAO, 4 1/4 in. barrel, two-tone cerakote finish, aluminum/polymer frame, 14 (.40 S&W) or 16 (9mm Para.) shot, low profile sights, aluminum/polymer grips, 25 1/2 oz. New mid-2011.

MSR $1,099	$995	$850	$725	$625	$500	$400	$300

DETONICS FIREARMS INDUSTRIES

Previous manufacturer located in Bellevue, WA 1976-1988. Detonics was sold in early 1988 to the New Detonics Manufacturing Corporation, a wholly owned subsidiary of "1045 Investors Group Limited."

GRADING - PPGS™	100%	98%	95%	90%	80%	70%	60%	LAST MSR

Please refer to the New Detonics Manufacturing Corporation in the "N" section of this text for complete model listings of both companies.

DETONICS USA

Previous manufacturer located in Pendergrass, GA circa 2004-mid-2007.

PISTOLS: SEMI-AUTO

COMBATMASTER – .45 ACP cal., 3 1/2 in. barrel, 6 shot, available in stainless steel (fixed sights), black bonded, two-tone, or mirror polish finish, 34 oz.

	$1,050	$875	$750	$650	$575	$500	$425	$1,200

Add $40 for two-tone finish, $100 for black bonded finish, $375 for mirror polish finish, or $550 for mirror polish finish w/stag grips.

9-11-01 – .45 ACP cal., 5 in. barrel, 7 shot, logo engraved checkered rosewood grips, low profile fixed combat sights, available in black bonded, two-tone, or mirror polish finish.

	$1,050	$875	$750	$650	$575	$500	$425	$1,200

Add $40 for two-tone finish, $100 for black bonded finish, or $375 for mirror polish finish.

STREETMASTER – .45 ACP cal., 5 in. barrel, 6 shot, low profile fixed combat sights, stainless steel construction, logo engraved checkered rosewood grips.

	$1,050	$875	$750	$650	$575	$500	$425	$1,200

SERVICEMASTER – .45 ACP cal., 4 1/4 in. barrel, 7 shot, stainless steel construction, low profile fixed combat sights, logo engraved checkered rosewood grips, choice of Standard or Compact frame, 39 oz.

	$1,050	$875	$750	$650	$575	$500	$425	$1,200

SCOREMASTER – .45 ACP cal., stainless steel construction, 5 in. barrel, 7 shot, MMC adj. rear sight, logo engraved checkered rosewood grips, available in Tactical (adj. sights and rail) or Target (Bo-Mar adj. sights, ext. slide stop, mag. release, and ambidextrous safety) configuration, 43 oz.

	$1,475	$1,250	$1,050	$925	$800	$775	$625	$1,650

MILITARY TACTICAL – .45 ACP cal., black bonded finish, adj. sights, includes rail, forward serrations, checkered front strap, and lanyard ring.

	$1,750	$1,525	$1,350	$1,125	$950	$800	$675	$1,975

DIAMOND SHOTGUNS

Please refer to the Adco Sales Inc. and Vega listings.

DIAMONDBACK FIREARMS

Current pistol and rifle manufacturer located in Cocoa, FL. Distributor and dealer sales.

PISTOLS: SEMI-AUTO

DB9 – 9mm Para. cal., micro compact design with 3 in. barrel, DAO, "ZERO Energy" striker fire system, 6 shot mag., mechanical firing pin block, matte black, orange, teal (disc. 2012), pink, flat dark earth (new 2013), or stainless steel (new 2013) finish, adj. sights, corrosion resistant coating, diamond checkered grips, 11 oz. New 2011.

MSR $490	$425	$365	$335	$300	$275	$250	$225	

Add $5 for Flat Dark Earth finish (new 2013).
Add $15 for DB9EXO coated slide.
Add $35 for DB9N model with two-tone nickel slide.
Add $35 for compensated (Model DB9C) model.
Add $50 for stainless steel or stainless steel black diamond (new 2013).
Add $85 for night sights (Model DB9NS).
Add $210 for Crimson Trace laser grip (Model DB9CTC).

DB380 – .380 ACP cal., 2.8 in. barrel, DAO, 6 shot mag., matte black, orange, pink, flat dark earth (new 2013), or stainless steel (new 2013) finish with FEA (finite element analysis) designed

GRADING - PPGS™	100%	98%	95%	90%	80%	70%	60%	LAST MSR

slide and barrel, corrosion resistant coating, "ZERO Energy" striker firing system, 8.8 oz.

MSR $445	$375	$325	$285	$250	$225	$200	$185	

Add $10 for Flat Dark Earth finish (DB380FDE, new 2013).
Add $20 for DB380EXO coated slide.
Add $35 for compensated (Model DB380C) model.
Add $55 for stainless steel (DB380SS, new 2013) or stainless steel black diamond (DBSSB, new 2013).
Add $210 for Crimson Trace laser grip (Model DB380CTC).
Add $90 for night sights (Model DB380NS).
Add approx. $30 for DB380MS model with machined sights (disc.).
Add $90 for DB380N model with two-tone nickel slide (disc. 2012).

RIFLES

DB15 5.56 NATO – 5.56 NATO cal., 16 in. standard handguard or M4 contour free floating barrel with A2 flash hider, A3 flattop upper receiver, 4-position M4 stock, Black or Flat Dark Earth finish, available with no sights, A2 front sights, or MagPul sights, 6.65 lbs. New 2013.

MSR $846	$775	$675	$600	$525	$450	$400	$350	

Add $133 for Flat Dark Earth finish.
Add $51 for MagPul sights.
Add $112 for M4 countour free-floating barrel with no sights.
Add $272 for Magpul CTR stock and Miad grip.

* ***DB15 Camo*** – 5.56 NATO cal., similar to DB15, except has Digital Green Camo or Digital Tan Camo finish. New 2013.

MSR $1,150	$1,000	$925	$825	$725	$625	$525	$450	

Add $104 for MagPul sights.

* ***DB15 Nickel*** – 5.56 NATO cal., 30 shot mag., 16 in. M4 contour free floating barrel with A2 flash hider, A3 flattop upper receiver, aluminum four rail handguard, nickel boron coating, 6-position MagPul CTR stock, Magpul MIAD grip, no sights, 6.65 lbs. New 2013.

MSR $1,118	$975	$900	$800	$700	$600	$500	$425	

Add $109 for MagPul sights.

DB15 .300 BLACKOUT – .300 AAC Blackout cal., similar to DB15 5.56 NATO.

MSR $962	$850	$775	$700	$650	$600	$550	$495	

Add $141 for Flat Dark Earth finish.
Add $48 for MagPul sights.
Add $112 for free floating quad rail.
Add $272 for Magpul CTR stock and Miad grip.
Add $302 for digital green camo or $406 for ATACS camo coverage.

DIARM S.A.

Previous manufacturing conglomerate (25 companies) located in Deba, Spain 1986-1989. Previously imported and distributed by American Arms, Inc. located in North Kansas City, MO. Older Diarm models can be found under the American Arms, Inc. heading in this publication.

DICKSON & MACNAUGHTON

Current trading company established in 1996, and located in Edinburgh, Scotland.

During 1999, the directors of James MacNaughton & Sons acquired the whole share capital of John Dickson & Son, from whom they purchased the MacNaughton manufacturing rights in 1996. The two companies now trade under the name of Dickson & MacNaughton, and trademarks currently owned are: John Dickson & Son, Dan'l Fraser, Alex Henry, James MacNaughton & Sons, Alex Martin, and Thomas Mortimer. See also listing for John Dickson & Son, Ltd.

Dickson & MacNaughton offers a gun research service for all the trademarks it owns. The charge is £20.00 per gun.

GRADING - PPGS™	100%	98%	95%	90%	80%	70%	60%	LAST MSR

JOHN DICKSON & SON, LTD.

Current trademark purchased during 1999 by James MacNaughton & Sons, located in Edinburgh, Scotland. During mid-2010, the company began making guns under the name John Dickson & Son, Ltd.

Currently, John Dickson & Son, Ltd. manufactures a round action O/U shotgun based on the original 1879 James MacNaughton design. Please contact the company directly for more information (see Trademark Index).

JOHN DICKSON & SON, LTD. COMPANY HISTORY

The original John Dickson was born in 1794 and was apprenticed to Edinburgh gunmaker James Wallace in the early nineteenth century. By 1840, he was trading as a gunmaker under his own name at 60 Princes Street in Edinburgh, moving nine years later to the old Wallace premises at 63 Princes, where the firm traded until 1929. By the late 1850s, Dickson's was manufacturing the new breechloaders, but in 1880, the company firmly established itself with the patent for the design of the Dickson Round Action. Three more patents followed between 1882-1887 before the gun design finally evolved. The company's heydays lasted from the 1880s through WWI. The last Dickson family member to manage the company died in 1923. The firm was run by successors and started purchasing its competitors, including Mortimer and Harkom in 1938, MacNaughton in 1947, and Martin and Henry during the 1960s. The company changed ownership several times until 1999, when the owners of James MacNaughton purchased Dickson, renaming the firm Dickson & MacNaughton, and taking over Dickson's Edinburgh premises at 21 Frederick Street, which Dickson had occupied since 1937. The firm continues to offer Dickson Round Actions, as well as new guns under the incorporated Scottish trademarks such as Alex Martin, Alex Henry, Thomas Mortimer, and Dan'l Fraser.

Information courtesy of David Grant and Vic Venters.

DIXIE GUN WORKS

Current importer, distributor, and catalog retailer established 1954, and located in Union City, TN.

In addition to importing a variety of firearms, Dixie Gun Works has also established itself as one of the leaders in black powder reproductions and replicas, related shooting accessories, and accoutrements. For more information regarding black powder reproductions and replicas and related shooting accessories, please contact the company directly and request a catalog. Please refer to the *Blue Book of Modern Black Powder Arms* by John Allen for more information on Dixie Gun Work's black powder reproductions and replicas.

Black Powder Revolvers Reproductions & Replicas and *Black Powder Long Arms & Pistols Reproductions & Replicas* by Dennis Adler are also invaluable sources for most black powder reproductions and replicas, and includes hundreds of color images on most popular makes/models, provides manufacturer/trademark histories, and up-to-date information on related items/accessories for black powder shooting - www.bluebookofgunvalues.com

RIFLES: REPRODUCTIONS

The following Pedersoli and Armi Sport models are a partial listing of rifles currently available from Dixie Gun Works. Please contact the company directly for more information, including current offerings and pricing.

1860 SPENCER REPEATING CARBINE – .56-50 cal., 20 in. barrel, uncheckered walnut stock and forearm, three barrel bands, case colored receiver, trigger guard, and hammer. 8 1/2 lbs. Mfg. by Armi-Sport.

MSR	100%	98%	95%	90%	80%	70%	60%
MSR $1,495	$1,495	$1,250	$1,125	$900	$775	$650	$525

1873 TRAPDOOR CARBINE/RIFLE – .45-70 Govt. cal., blued furniture, oil finished American walnut stock, 7 or 9 lbs. Mfg. by Pedersoli.

MSR	100%	98%	95%	90%	80%	70%	60%
MSR $1,150	$975	$800	$650	$550	$475	$400	$325

Add $350 for Officer's Model, with case colored lock and trigger guard, single set trigger.
Add $100 for Rifle.

GRADING - PPGS™	100%	98%	95%	90%	80%	70%	60%	LAST MSR

1874 SHARPS LIGHTWEIGHT HUNTER – .45-70 Govt. cal., reproduction of the Sharps No. 3 sporting rifle, 32 in. blued tapered octagon barrel, straight stock, case colored receiver and buttplate, vernier tang sight. Mfg. by Pedersoli. Disc. 2004.

	$865	$725	$600	$500	$400	$350	$300	*$975*

1874 SHARPS SILHOUETTE RIFLE – .40-65 or 45-70 Govt. cal., reproduction of the Sharps No. 1 sporting rifle, 30 in. blued tapered octagon barrel, pistol grip stock, case colored receiver and buttplate. Mfg. by Pedersoli.

MSR $1,150	$975	$800	$650	$550	$475	$400	$325

Add $900 for engraving with in-the-white receiver and buttplate.
Add $100 for .45-70 Govt. cal.

KODIAK MARK IV DOUBLE EXPRESS SxS RIFLE – .45-70 Govt. cal., back action, browned 24 in. barrels with triple leaf express sights, color case hardened frame, trigger guard, and hammers. Mfg. by Pedersoli.

MSR $4,500	$4,150	$3,600	$3,250	$2,850	$2,500	$2,000	$1,500

REMINGTON ROLLING BLOCK LONG RANGE RIFLE – .40-65 or .45-70 Govt. cal., 30 in. tapered octagon barrel, case colored receiver and buttplate, vernier tang sight. Mfg. by Pedersoli.

MSR $975	$825	$725	$595	$500	$400	$350	$325

Add $175 for .45-70 Govt. cal.

DLASK ARMS CORP.

Current manufacturer and distributor located in British Columbia, Canada. Direct sales.

PISTOLS: SEMI-AUTO

Dlask Arms Corp. manufactures custom M-1911 style custom guns for all levels of competition. Current models include the basic Dlask 1911 at $1,250 MSR, Dlask 1911 "Pro" at $1,560 MSR, and the Dlask 1911 "Pro Plus" at $2,500 MSR. Previous models included the TC Tactical Carry at $1,250 last MSR, Gold Team at $2,000 last MSR, Silver Team L/S at $1,700 last MSR, and the Master Class at $3,500 last MSR. Dlask also imported a DAC 394 during 1997-1998, it's a 9mm Para. copy of the Sig 225, limited importation. Current values range from $225-$400, depending on condition. In addition, Dlask also manufactures a wide variety of custom parts for the M-1911. For more information, please contact the company directly (see Trademark Index).

RIFLES

Current models include the DAR-701 semi-auto rifle in various configurations (AR-15 style) at $1,560 base MSR. Please contact the company directly for more information, including pricing and availability (see Trademark Index).

DOLPHIN GUN COMPANY

Current rifle manufacturer located in Lincolnshire, United Kingdom.

Dolphin Gun Company was founded circa 2006 by competitive shooters Mik Maksimovic and Pete Hobson. The company builds competition "F Class" and tactical style rifles, utilizing Accuracy International or tactical style stocks. Many calibers and options are available. Base price is £2355.00, including VAT. Please contact the company directly for more information, including pricing, delivery time, and availability (see Trademark Index).

DOMINGO, ACHA

Please refer to the Acha listing in the A section.

DOMINION ARMS

Previous trademark of slide action shotguns manufactured by Rauch Tactical, located in Blaine, WA.

Rauch manufactured 12 ga. tactical style slide action shotguns until circa 2010.

GRADING - PPGS™	100%	98%	95%	90%	80%	70%	60%	LAST MSR

DOMINO, IGI

Previous Italian company absorbed during 1990 by FAS (see separate listing in F section). Previously imported by Mandall Shooting Supplies located in Scottsdale, AZ.

PISTOLS: SEMI-AUTO

MODEL OP 601 MATCH PISTOL – .22 Short cal., 5 shot, 5.6 in. barrel, match sights, full target grips, vent. barrel and slide to reduce recoil, adj. and removable trigger.

	$1,300	$1,000	$715	$635	$550	$495	$440	*$1,495*

MODEL SP 602 MATCH PISTOL – .22 LR cal., 5 1/2 in. barrel, similar to 601, but .22 LR and slightly different trigger.

	$1,300	$1,100	$800	$700	$600	$550	$495	*$1,495*

DOUBLE STAR CORP.

Current manufacturer located in Winchester, KY. Distributed by JT Distributing. Dealer sales only.

PISTOLS: SEMI-AUTO

1911 COMBAT PISTOL – .45 ACP cal., forged steel frame, stainless steel slide, optional 1913 Picatinny rail, Novak white dot front and LoMount rear sights, memory groove beavertail grip safety, 8 shot mag., 25 LPI checkering, black nitride or nickel finish, 39 oz. New 2010.

MSR $1,500	$1,325	$1,175	$1,000	$875	$750	$575	$450

Add $100 for nickel finish.

DSC 7.5 AR PISTOL – 5.56 NATO cal., AR-15 style, direct gas impingement action, Picatinny rail gas block, 7 1/2 in. chrome moly steel barrel, free float aluminum tube handguard, flattop or standard A2 upper receiver, CAR length pistol receiver extension, standard A2 grip, 4.7 lbs.

MSR $1,010	$925	$825	$725	$650	$575	$500	$450

DSC 10.5 AR PISTOL – 5.56 NATO cal., AR-15 style, direct gas impingement action, Picatinny rail gas block, 10 1/2 in. chrome moly steel barrel, single heat shield CAR handguard, flattop or standard A2 upper receiver, CAR length pistol receiver extension, standard A2 pistol grip, 5 1/2 lbs.

MSR $970	$875	$775	$675	$575	$500	$425	$350

DSC 11.5 AR PISTOL – 5.56 NATO cal., AR-15 style, direct gas impingement action, Picatinny rail gas block, 11 1/2 in. chrome moly steel barrel, single heat shield CAR handguard, flattop or standard A2 upper receiver, CAR length pistol receiver extension, standard A2 pistol grip, 5.7 lbs.

MSR $970	$875	$775	$675	$575	$500	$425	$350

DSC STAR-15 PISTOL – .223 Rem. cal., AR-15 style, 7 1/2, 10 1/5, or 11 1/2 in. chrome-moly match barrel, A2 flash hider, front sight assembly or rail gas block. Disc. 2010.

	$875	$750	$675	$600	$525	$450	$395	*$950*

RIFLES/CARBINES: SEMI-AUTO

Double Star Corp. makes a complete line of AR-15 style carbines/rifles, as well as a line of SBRs (Short Barreled Rifles) for military/law enforcement.

IMPORTANT NOTE: On model(s) where *N/A has replaced the normal 100% value, it indicates current market conditions are too unstable to accurately ascertain 100%-60% values. Factory retail prices (MSRs) reflect most recent updates. For more up-to-date information on current pricing trends and additional useful information, please visit www.bluebookofgunvalues.com, select "Information & Services" from the menu, and click on "Additional Book Information".

DSC 3 GUN RIFLE – 5.56 NATO cal., AR-15 style, direct gas impingement system, 30 shot, 18 in. fluted stainless barrel with Carlson Comp muzzle brake, Samson 15 in. Evolution handguard, Ace ARFX buttstock, Timney trigger, Hogue or ERGO ambi sure grip, 7.51 lbs. New 2012.

MSR $1,600	*N/A	$1,275	$1,100	$975	$850	$750	$650

GRADING - PPGS™	100%	98%	95%	90%	80%	70%	60%	LAST MSR

DSC CRITTERSLAYER – .223 Rem. cal., AR-15 design, 24 in. fluted Shaw barrel, full length Picatinny rail on receiver and Badger handguard, two-stage match trigger, palmrest, ergonomic pistol grip with finger grooves, includes Harris LMS swivel bipod, flat-top or high rise upper receiver, 11 1/2 lbs. Disc. 2010.

	*N/A	$1,150	$925	$850	$750	$650	$550	*$1,430*

Add $40 for ported barrel.

* ***DSC CritterSlayer Jr.*** – similar to CritterSlayer, except has 16 in. barrel and fully adj. A2 style buttstock, DSC flat-top or high rise upper receiver. Disc. 2010.

	*N/A	$875	$775	$675	$575	$475	$400	*$1,150*

Add $65 for detachable carrying handle or $35 for removable front sight.

Add $200 for Enhanced CritterSlayer Jr. with 16 in. Expedition barrel, CAR hand guard, and adj. buttstock.

DSC DEER RIFLE – 6.8 SPC cal., AR-15 style, direct gas impingement action, 20 in. chrome moly heavy barrel with A2 phantom flash hider, 5 shot mag., Ace ARFX skeleton stock, Next Camo water transfer finish, winter trigger guard, 7 3/4 lbs. New 2012.

MSR $1,350	*N/A	$1,050	$825	$775	$700	$600	$500

DSC DS-4 – 5.56 NATO, 6.5 Grendel, 6.8 SPC, or 7.62x39mm cal., AR-15 style, patterned after the Military M-4, matte black, tactical pink, or OD Green finish, 16 in. chrome moly barrel, double heat shield handguard, A2 or flat top upper receiver, A2 pistol grip, 6-position buttstock, 6.3 lbs.

MSR $950	*N/A	$700	$600	$550	$450	$350	$275

DSC FDE DS-4 MOE – 5.56 NATO cal., AR-15 style, direct gas impingement action, 16 in. chrome moly barrel, Magpul MOE features include handguard, upper receiver, pistol grip, enhanced trigger guard, rear BUIS, 6 position commercial spec Magpul MOE stock, 30 shot mag., FDE (Flat Dark Earth) or OD Green finish, 6.3 lbs.

MSR $1,123	*N/A	$900	$800	$700	$600	$500	$400

DSC FDE DS-4 – 5.56 NATO cal., 16 in. chromemoly M4 barrel, Flat Dark Earth teflon conated finish, Picatinny rail gas block or "F" marked FSB, double heat shield two-piece polymer handguard, FDE flattop upper receiver, A2 pistol grip, six position buttstock, FDE lower, FDE Magpul Rear BUS. New mid-2012.

MSR $970	*N/A	$725	$625	$550	$450	$375	$295

DSC EXPEDITION CARBINE/RIFLE – 5.56 NATO cal., AR-15 style, direct gas impingement action, 16 or 20 (disc.) in. lightweight contour barrel with integrated muzzle brake, single heat shield CAR handguard, A2 or flat-top upper receiver, A2 pistol grip, A2 or 6-position commercial spec stock, 6.35lbs.

MSR $920	*N/A	$695	$595	$525	$425	$350	$275

Add $65 for detachable carry handle (disc.).

DSC MARKSMAN RIFLE – 5.56 NATO cal., AR-15 style, direct gas impingement action, 20 in. Wilson Arms stainless steel barrel, Daniel Defense free float handguard, Picatinny rail gas block, A2 Phantom flash hider, Magpul PRS buttstock, adj. LOP, Magpul MIAD pistol grip, two-stage trigger, front and rear flip sight, approx. 9 lbs.

MSR $1,700	*N/A	$1,275	$1,050	$875	$725	$600	$550

Add $185 for bipod.

DSC MIDNIGHT DRAGON – 5.56 NATO cal., AR-15 style, direct gas impingement action, 24 in. stainless steel bull barrel with spiral fluting and black nitride coating, aluminum free float handguard with bipod stud, A3 flat top upper receiver, ARFX buttstock, ERGO tactical pistol grip, DSC two-stage trigger, Badger TAC latch, DSC enhanced trigger guard, 9 1/4 lbs. New 2012.

MSR $1,250	*N/A	$975	$875	$775	$675	$575	$475

DSC PATROL CARBINE – 5.56 NATO cal., AR-15 style, direct gas impingement action, 16 in. chrome moly lightweight barrel with A2 phantom flash hider, Slimline quad rail handguard with three low profile rail covers, flip up rear sight, six position DS-4 buttstock, Hogue overmolded pistol grip, 6 1/2 lbs.

MSR $1,250	*N/A	$975	$875	$775	$675	$575	$475

GRADING - PPGS™	100%	98%	95%	90%	80%	70%	60%	LAST MSR

DSC STAR-CAR CARBINE – 5.56 NATO, 6.5 Grendel, or 6.8 SPC cal., AR-15 style, direct gas impingement action, 16 in. chrome moly steel heavy barrel, fixed post-ban CAR type stock, single heat shield CAR handguard, A2 or flat-top upper receiver, standard A2 pistol grip, 6.7 lbs.

MSR $880	*N/A	$750	$650	$550	$475	$425	$375	

Add $65 for detachable carrying handle.

DSC STAR M4 CARBINE – .223 Rem. cal., AR-15 M4 carbine design, fixed M4 style post-ban buttstock, 16 in. barrel, M4 handguard, 6.76 lbs. Disc. 2012.

	*N/A	$725	$650	$565	$500	$465	$430	*$910*

Add $85 for detachable carrying handle.

DSC STAR DISSIPATOR – 5.56 NATO cal., AR-15 style, direct gas impingement action, 16 in. dissipator chrome moly steel barrel with full length handguard, A2 or 6 position CAR buttstock, A2 or flat top upper receiver, 6.9 lbs.

MSR $930	*N/A	$765	$650	$550	$475	$425	$375	

Add $65 for detachable carrying handle.

DSC STAR-15 LIGHTWEIGHT TACTICAL – .223 Rem. cal., AR-15 design, 16 in. fluted H-Bar barrel with attached muzzle brake, shorty A2 buttstock, A2 or flat-top upper receiver, 6 1/4 lbs. Disc. 2004, reintroduced 2009-2010.

	*N/A	$750	$650	$550	$500	$465	$430	*$930*

Add $65 for detachable carrying handle.

DSC STAR-15 RIFLE/CARBINE – 5.56 NATO, 6.5 Grendel, 6.8 SPC, or 7.62x39mm cal., AR-15 style, 16 (disc.) or 20 in. match barrel, ribbed forearm, two-piece rifle handguard, standard A2 buttstock and pistol grip, A2 or flat top upper receiver, 8 lbs.

MSR $880	*N/A	$750	$650	$550	$475	$425	$375	

Add $65 for flattop with detachable carrying handle.
Add $75 for 6.5 Grendel, 6.8 SPC, or 7.62x39mm cal.

DSC STAR-15 9MM CARBINE – 9mm Para. cal., AR-15 design, 16 in. barrel, ribbed forearm, A2 or flat-top upper receiver, 7 1/2 lbs. Mfg. 2004, reintroduced 2009-2010.

	*N/A	$825	$725	$650	$575	$500	$450	*$1,080*

Add $65 for detachable carry handle.

DSC STAR-15 6.8 SPC RIFLE/CARBINE – 6.8 SPC cal., 16 or 20 in. chrome-moly barrel, A2 upper or flat-top, A2 (rifle) or 6-position DS-4 buttstock, 7-8 lbs. Disc. 2010

	$875	$750	$675	$600	$525	$450	$395	*$935*

Add $65 for detachable carry handle.

DSC STAR-15 6.8 SPC SUPER MATCH RIFLE – 6.8 SPC cal., 20, 22, or 24 in. free float super match stainless steel bull barrel, Picatinny rail gas block, two-piece NM free floating hand guard. Disc. 2010.

	$975	$850	$750	$650	$575	$500	$450	*$1,075*

DSC STAR-15 .204 RUGER RIFLE – .204 Ruger cal., 24 in. chrome-moly barrel, A2 buttstock, A2 flash hider. Disc. 2010.

	*N/A	$850	$750	$650	$575	$500	$450	*$1,050*

DSC STAR-15 6.5 GRENDEL CARBINE/RIFLE – 6.5 Grendel cal., 16 or 20 in. chrome-moly barrel, A2 or six position (Carbine) buttstock. Disc. 2010.

	$895	$775	$675	$600	$525	$450	$395	*$985*

Add $65 for detachable carry handle.

DSC STAR-15 6.5 GRENDEL SUPER MATCH RIFLE – 6.5 Grendel cal., 20, 22, or 24 in. free floating match bull barrel, A2 buttstock, Picatinny rail gas block, two-piece NM free floating hand guard. Disc. 2010.

	$1,050	$875	$775	$675	$575	$475	$400	*$1,125*

GRADING - PPGS™	100%	98%	95%	90%	80%	70%	60%	LAST MSR

DSC STAR-15 DCM SERVICE RIFLE – 5.56 NATO cal., AR-15 design, 20 in. free-float match barrel, National Match front and rear sights, two-stage match trigger, DCM handguard, 8 lbs. Disc.

	*N/A	$825	$725	$650	$550	$485	$440	*$1,000*

DSC SUPERMATCH RIFLE – 5.56 NATO, 6.5 Grendel, or 6.8 SPC cal., AR-15 style, direct gas impingement action, 16, 20, 22, or 24 in. free-float stainless steel Super Match barrel, flat-top or high rise upper receiver, includes Picatinny rail and one-piece National Match handguard, A2 stock, 9.2 lbs.

MSR $1,030	*N/A	$830	$725	$650	$575	$500	$450

DSC TARGET CARBINE – .223 Rem. cal., AR-15 design, features 16 in. dissipator barrel with full length round one-piece National Match handguard, flip-up sights, Picatinny rail, flat-top upper receiver. Disc.

	*N/A	$875	$775	$695	$625	$550	$485	*$1,175*

DSC ZOMBIE SLAYER – 5.56 NATO cal., AR-15 style, direct gas impingement action, 14 1/2 in. DS4 barrel with permanently attached A2 phantom flash hider, flat top upper receiver with detachable GI carry handle, two 30 shot magazines, 6 position D4 stock, double heat shield handguards, USMC multi-purpose bayonet, "Zombie Slayer" lasered lower, 6.1 lbs. New 2012.

MSR $1,250	*N/A	$975	$875	$775	$675	$575	$475

DSC .204 RUGER – .204 Ruger cal., 20 or 24 in. stainless steel fluted or non-fluted bull barrel, Picatinny rail gas block, mil-spec flattop, free float aluminum tube handguard, A2 pistol grip and buttstock. New 2013.

MSR $1,125	$975	$900	$800	$700	$600	$500	$400

DSC CONSTANT CARRY CARBINE – 5.56 NATO cal., 16 in. lightweight A-1 profile barrel, steel low profile gas block, Samson Evolution 9 inch handguard, mil-spec flattop with M4 feedramp, A2 pistol grip, Ace Ltd. AR-UL-E buttstock, Magpul MBUS front and rear sights, 5 1/2 lbs. New 2013.

MSR $1,225	*N/A	$925	$795	$715	$575	$475	$375

DSC .300 BLACKOUT – .300 Blackout cal., 16 in. HBAR barrel, black nitride coating, Picatinny rail gas block, CAR handguard, mil-spec flattop with M4 feed ramp, A2 pistol grip, six position commercial spec DS-4 stock. New 2013.

MSR $920	*N/A	$695	$595	$525	$425	$350	$275

DSC COMMANDO – 5.56 NATO cal., 16 in. chromemoly HBAR lightweight barrel, permanently attached flash hider, Picatinny rail gas block or "F" marked FSB, two-piece CAR length polymer handguard, mil-spec flattop or A2 upper receiver, A2 pistol grip, six position DS-4 buttstock, front sight base. New 2013.

MSR $930	*N/A	$765	$650	$550	$475	$425	$375

DSC LIGHTWEIGHT TACTICAL – 5.56 NATO cal., fluted 16 in. chromemoly HBAR barrel, Picatinny rail gas block or "F" marked FSB, single heat shield two-piece CAR length polymer handguard, mil-spec flattop or A2 upper receiver, D-4 six position buttstock. New mid-2012.

MSR $1,030	*N/A	$830	$725	$650	$575	$500	$450

DOUBLETAP DEFENSE, LLC

Current derringer manufacturer located in St. Louis, MO.

DERRINGERS: O/U

DOUBLETAP – 9mm Para. or .45 ACP cal., tip-up action with ambidextrous thumb latch for ejecting fired rounds, 3 in. ported or non-ported stainless steel barrels, DA trigger for two consecutive shots, design allows to carry two spare rounds in grip, choice of titanium or aluminum frame, checkered integral grips, only 5/8 in. wide, 12 (aluminum) or 14 (titanium) oz. New late 2012.

MSR $499	$450	$415	$385	$350	$325	$295	$275

Add $70 for ported barrels. Add $230 for titanium construction.
Add $199 per non-ported barrel assembly or $269 for ported barrel assembly.

GRADING - PPGS™	100%	98%	95%	90%	80%	70%	60%	LAST MSR

DOWNSIZER CORPORATION

Previous pistol manufacturer circa 1994-2007, and located in Santee, CA.

DERRINGERS

MODEL WSP (WORLD'S SMALLEST PISTOL) – 9mm Para. (disc. 1999), .357 Mag., .357 Sig. (disc. 1999), .40 S&W (disc. 1999), or .45 ACP cal., single shot pistol, tip-up 2.1 in. barrel with push-button release, internal firing pin block, double action only, synthetic grips, stainless steel, overall size is smaller than a playing card, 11 oz. Mfg. 1997-circa 2007.

	$415	$300	$235	$185	$150	$135	$110	*$499*

DREYSE

Previously manufactured by Rheinische Metallwaren und Machinenfabrik, located in Sommerda, Germany.

PISTOLS: SEMI-AUTO

MODEL 1907 AUTOMATIC – 7.65mm/.32 ACP cal., 8 shot, 3 1/2 in. barrel, blue, fixed sights, hard rubber grips. Mfg. 1907-14.

	$250	$185	$150	$120	$95	$75	$50	

MODEL 1910 – 9mm Para. cal., mfg. 1912-1915. Production estimated at 1,000 pistols, usually found in the 12xx-13xx ser. no. range. Seldom encountered.

	$6,500	$5,500	$4,500	$3,500	$2,500	$2,000	$1,500	

VEST POCKET AUTOMATIC – .25 ACP cal., 6 shot, 2 in. barrel, blue, fixed sights, hard rubber grips. Mfg. 1912-15.

	$325	$235	$150	$130	$100	$75	$65	

Add 100% for early version with double extractors.

RIFLES: SEMI-AUTO

1907 LIGHT RIFLE – 7.65mm (.32 ACP) cal., 18 3/4 in. barrel, staggered box 6-9 shot mag., used mostly for small game hunting, earlier rifles can be found with full "Rheinmetall" and "Dreyse" markings, and later rifles do not have markings, most have sporter stocks, some have military type stocks with cheekpieces and full forends to near the muzzle, other markings may include European sporting goods dealers and various police agencies, including the South American police. Mfg. 1907-circa 1913.

	$2,500	$2,200	$2,000	$1,800	$1,400	$1,000	$600	

Values shown are for the sporter type stock.

DRILLINGS

A Drilling is a three-barrel combination gun (two shotgun barrels and a rifle barrel, vice versa, or three shotgun barrels). Most Drillings have two triggers (very few have three triggers). The front trigger usually fires the right shotgun barrel, and the rear fires the left shotgun barrel. The rifle barrel is most often fired with the front trigger when it is selected. Most selectors are on top of the grip, but quite a few other designs can be found.

It is very important that owners familiarize themselves with a Drilling before shooting it.

The author would like to express his thanks to the German Gun Collectors Association, including members Dietrich Apel, Dick Hummel, and Steve Meyer for helping to compile the following information on Drillings.

Most well-made Drillings in above average condition are surprisingly accurate when using the rifle barrel(s), because of the stiffness gained with three barrels fixed together.

DRILLING CONFIGURATIONS & EXPLANATIONS

Please refer to illustrations below depicting the most commonly encountered Drilling barrel configurations. These various types are designed to accomodate the firing mechanism, which makes the Drilling slimmer, lighter, and more practical.

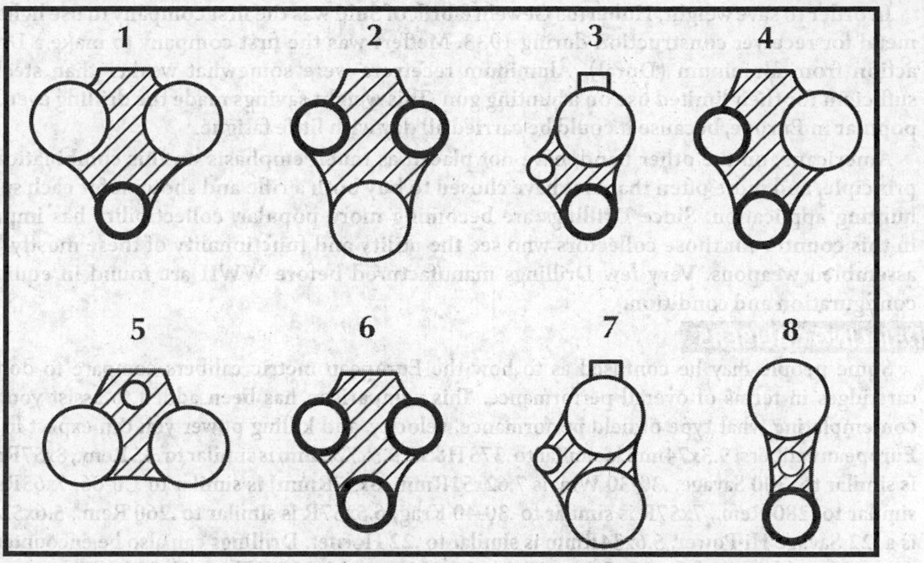

Illustration No. 1 – Normal Drilling configuration with 2 shotgun barrels over a rimmed, centerfire rifle (most are 16 ga. x 16 ga. by either 9.3x72R or 8x57JR cal.).

Illustration No. 2 – Two rifle barrels over a shotgun. This configuration will normally command twice the price as No. 1. German designation is "Doppelbüchsdrilling".

Illustration No. 3 – Three barrels with no two being the same gauge or caliber. This configuration is very collectible, especially if the smallest caliber is .22 LR. Again, price will be double of No. 1.

Illustration No. 4 – Sometimes called a Bock Drilling with one shotgun and two rifle barrels. This variation brings a good premium over No. 1.

Illustration No. 5 – Rib Drilling with rifle caliber generally small (.22 LR or .22 Hornet). German designation is "Schienendrilling".

Illustration No. 6 – Three shotgun barrels with the same gauge or three rifle barrels with different calibers. This configuration is quite rare and healthy premiums are charged over No. 1.

Illustration No. 7 – A variation of No. 3, this configuration features shotgun O/U barrels with a rifle barrel on the side. German designation is "Bock-Doppelflinte mit seitlichem Kleinkaliberlauf".

Illustration No. 8 – Very unusual - a 3-barrel drilling in vertical design - 2 rifle barrels under a shotgun barrel. This configuration is seldom encountered.

The following German nomenclatures apply as follows: single barrel rifle = Büchse; SxS double rifle = Doppelbüchse; O/U double rifle = Bock-Doppelbüchse; SxS double shotgun = Doppelflinte; O/U double shotgun = Bock-Doppelflinte; SxS double shotgun, rifle bbl. under = Drilling; SxS double shotgun, rifle bbl. on top = Schienendrilling; single shotgun, rifle bbl. under = Bock-Büchsflinte; single shotgun, rifle bbl. at side = Büchsflinte; single shotgun, rifle bbl. under and at side = Bock-Drilling; double rifle, shot bbl. under = Doppelbüchsdrilling; O/U double shotgun, rifle bbl. at side = Bock-Doppelflinte mit seitlichem Kleinkaliberlauf; SxS double shotgun, plus two rifle bbls. = Vierling.

DRILLING HISTORY

For over 150 years, Drillings have been the classic hunting gun of many European countries, especially Germany and Austria. Because a single hunting trip might require shooting both wildfowl and animals (often times within several hours), Europeans have long favored a single long-arm that could afford both rifle and shotgun shooting, be reliable, and not wear the hunter out while transporting it in the field. Another big reason the Europeans like the Drilling is that in recent years, ownership of firearms has become severely regulated and limited, thus making a versatile single firearm like the Drilling more desirable.

In order to save weight, Hubertus Gewehrfabrik of Suhl was the first company to use light alloy metal for receiver construction during 1933. Meffert was the first company to make a Drilling action from aluminum (Dural). Aluminum receivers were somewhat weaker than steel, but sufficient for their limited use on a hunting gun. This weight savings made the drilling even more popular in Europe, because it could be carried all day with little fatigue.

Americans, on the other hand, have not placed as much emphasis on this combination gun principle, and more often than not have chosen to buy both a rifle and shotgun for each specific hunting application. Since Drillings are becoming more popular, collectibility has improved in this country for those collectors who see the utility and functionality of these mostly hand-assembled weapons. Very few Drillings manufactured before WWII are found in equivalent configuration and condition.

DRILLING CALIBERS

Some people may be confused as to how the European metric calibers compare to domestic cartridges in terms of overall performance. This comparison has been added to assist you when contemplating what type of field performance, velocity, and killing power you can expect in these European calibers: 9.3x74mm is similar to .375 H&H, 9.3x72Rmm is similar to .35 Rem., 8x57RmmJS is similar to .300 Savage, .30-30 Win. is 7.62x51Rmm, 8x57RmmJ is similar to .30-06, 7x65Rmm is similar to .280 Rem., 7x57R is similar to .30-40 Krag, 6.5x57R is similar to .260 Rem., 5.6x52Rmm is a .22 Savage Hi-Power, 5.6x34Rmm is similar to .22 Hornet. Drillings can also be encountered in American calibers such as .270 Win., .30-06, .30-30 Win., .38-55 WCF, or .32-20 WCF.

DRILLING VALUES AND CONDITION FACTORS

Rather than list the various manufacturers of Drillings (there are hundreds), it should be noted that guns with major trademarks and established provenances (i.e. Charles Daly, Colt Sauer, Ferlach addressed, Heym, Krieghoff, J.P. Sauer, Berlin [rare] and Suhl addressed, etc.) will usually be more collectible than other, lesser-known brands, even if the quality of workmanship is similar. The overall quality, condition, engraving, wood type/fanciness, and carving all have to be taken into consideration when evaluating a Drilling. Some Drillings were assembled from manufactured parts by skilled and crafted gunsmiths and are sometimes better quality than factory specimens. Pre-war specimens are generally more desirable to collectors and to date, have outperformed post-war specimens in price appreciation. Pre-war guns required much more hand work, which made them more attractive. Many older pre-war specimens were designed for rimmed cartridges with lower breech pressures and should not be re-bored or reloaded for the "hotter" cartridges/loads available today.

Many pre-war guns have safeties that block only the triggers. Set triggers, also called hair triggers, can be dangerous when set.

Post-war guns have more functional designs which can be manufactured more efficiently with today's CNC equipment. Most modern Drillings now have hand cocking mechanisms for the rifle barrel, and set triggers, which unset themselves when the gun is opened.

It should be noted that since Drillings are more complex than a typical shotgun, most of the manufacture has been done by hand - some guns have taken individual craftsmen over a year to fabricate!

Ordering a new Drilling today would be a very expensive proposition, and buying a good used specimen will save you thousands of dollars (and maybe a year wait). For these reasons, many collectors feel Drillings today are under-priced since they can be purchased at a fraction of the cost of a new one (and may be better quality also).

Condition is another major consideration. A gun that shows much use and is not operationally intact/correct may bring several thousand dollars less than another similar specimen showing little wear and excellent original finish (including the case colors or coin finish).

Most above average condition boxlock Drillings in the above mentioned trademarks start in the $2,250 range and can go to $10,000 and higher if the configuration, features, and condition are all desirable. Average condition boxlock Drillings not made by a famous trademark usually sell in the $1,850-$3,250 range assuming moderate engraving, metric calibers, and some popular options. Sidelock Drillings typically start in the $3,500-$4,000 range, and can go well past $25,000, depending on the trademark, engraving, and desirable features. Also, while not many Drillings are available in

GRADING - PPGS™	100%	98%	95%	90%	80%	70%	60%	LAST MSR

the secondary marketplace, they have become increasingly popular due to shooting sports magazines and other gun publications. For these reasons, Drillings have to be evaluated one at a time and a COMPETENT appraisal/evaluation should be procured before buying or selling a specimen.

FEATURES THAT ADD VALUE TO DRILLINGS

Drillings with American calibers and smaller gauges will sometimes be more desirable (depending on engraving, case colors, or coin finish) than the European metric calibers (i.e. a gun configured 20 ga. x 20 ga. by .243 Win. will sell for more than a similar gun in 16 ga. x 16 ga. by 9.3 x 72Rmm cal.). The most commonly encountered gauges and calibers are 16 ga. (most pre-war guns are chambered for 2 9/16 in. shotshells). In addition, a sidelock action will be more desirable than a boxlock, and a lot more expensive if the locks are also detachable.

Drilling aficionados will mention there are four main things to look for when contemplating a drilling purchase - beauty, condition, quality, and features. Features and embellishments become very critical in ascertaining Drilling values also. A gun with deep relief engraving, carved stock, claw mounts w/scope, buffalo horn trigger guard and buttplate, cocking indicators, two position front sight (i.e. night sight), middle set of express sights, adj. trigger, concealed upper tang peep sight, a non-Greener safety system, lightweight (under 6 1/2 lbs.), separate rifle cocking, shotgun barrel inserts in .22 LR or .22 WMR cal. (approx. 8 or 11 in. long), cartridge trap, etc. is going to be A LOT more collectible than a plain-Jane hammer model with a loose action.

Drillings with original, detachable claw-mounted scopes (rail-mount or swing-off) are worth a 20%-50% premium, depending on overall desirability of the gun. Original Drilling scopes for pre-war Drillings are rare, as most were removed when the guns were turned in after WWII.

FEATURES THAT DETRACT VALUE FROM DRILLINGS

If a drilling is worn out and/or needs some service work or parts replaced, its eye appeal is compromised; values decrease significantly, and can end up in the three digits. Make sure that any drilling is mechanically inspected thoroughly, especially if it shows a lot of use, before contemplating a purchase.

DRULOV

Current trademark of pistols and rifles manufactured by PPK s.r.o., and located in Holice, Czech Republic. No current U.S. importation.

PISTOLS: SINGLE SHOT

PAV – .22 LR cal., single shot, 9 3/4 in. barrel, all steel construction. Imported 1986 only.

$95	$85	$75	$65	$60	$55	$50	*$105*

DRULOV 70 – .22 LR cal., single shot, wood grip with thumb rest.

As this edition went to press pricing information was not available on this model.

DRULOV 75 – .22 LR cal., single shot, set trigger, micrometer sights, short or long (with wood forearm) barrel. Also available in left-hand.

As this edition went to press pricing information was not available on this model.

DRULOV 78 – .22 LR cal., similar to Drulov 75. Imported 1986 only.

$275	$240	$200	$175	$150	$130	$110	*$180*

DRULOV 90 – .22 LR or .22 Hornet cal., single shot, target model with ergonomic thumb rest grip and wood forearm, target sights.

As this edition went to press, no information was available for pricing on this model.

DRULOV 97 MSP – .22 LR, .22 WMR, or .22 Hornet cal., short or long barrel, target model with weaver rail attached, micrometer sights, ergonomic grip with thumb rest and wood forearm.

As this edition went to press pricing information was not available on this model.

RIFLES: SINGLE SHOT

DRULOV RIFLE – .22 LR, .22 WMR, or .22 Hornet cal., single shot action, wood Monte Carlo stock with ergonomic pistol grip and grooved forearm, 16 in. barrel, micrometer target sights.

As this edition went to press pricing information was not available on this model.

GRADING - PPGS™	100%	98%	95%	90%	80%	70%	60%	LAST MSR

DUBIEL ARMS COMPANY

Previous manufacturer located in Sherman, TX. Dubiel Arms made custom bolt action rifles from 1975-approx. 1990.

RIFLES: BOLT ACTION

BOLT ACTION RIFLE – .22-250 Rem.-.458 Win. Mag. cals., custom made bolt action, barrel length and weight to order, no sights, Canjar trigger, all steel parts, custom made rifle stocks available in five styles. Disc.

$2,000	$1,750	$1,500	$1,275	$1,125	$975	$825	*$2,500*

DUCKS UNLIMITED, INC.

National wildlife organization established in 1937, with headquarters located in Memphis, TN.

SHOTGUNS: DINNER GUNS (GUN-OF-THE-YEAR)

The makes and models listed within this category reflect "dinner guns" only. Dinner guns (Gun-of-the-Year) refer to those shotguns sold at the various annual banquets held by Ducks Unlimited chapters. Dinner guns do not have a retail price. Rather, banquet auction prices can vary substantially from chapter to chapter, as can secondary market values. The price ranges listed below are general guidelines for DU dinner guns that are in unfired, NIB condition with all factory materials and boxes. Dinner guns that have been fired only a few times, have any type of storage freckling/problems, and/or are missing boxes and paperwork are not that collectible, and in many cases, a 98% DU dinner gun may be worth only slightly more than the make/model from which it was derived. This is why older, unfired NIB dinner guns are now in scarce supply - many owners used them for hunting. Also, do not expect to walk into your favorite pawn or gun shop and expect to get anywhere close to these values. The best way to liquidate an unfired, NIB DU dinner gun is to put it up on the various online auction sites with a reserve.

Manufacturer/Model	Quantity	Year	Issue Price
REMINGTON Model 1100 12 ga.	500	1973	N/A
Current values for this model in NIB condition range from $5,000-$6,000.			
REMINGTON Model 870 12 ga.	600	1974	N/A
Current values for this model in NIB condition range from $4,500-$5,500.			
WINCHESTER Model 12 12 ga.	800	1975	N/A
Current values for this model in NIB condition range from $4,000-$5,000.			
WINCHESTER Model Super X-1 12 ga.	900	1976	N/A
Current values for this model in NIB condition range from $3,500-$5,500.			
ITHACA Model 37 12 ga. (40th Ann'y)	1,125	1977	N/A
Current values for this model in NIB condition range from $3,500-$4,500.			
ITHACA Model 51 12 ga.	1,250	1978	N/A
Current values for this model in NIB condition range from $2,500-$3,000.			
WEATHERBY Model Patrician 12 ga.	1,600	1979	N/A
Current values for this model in NIB condition range from $1,500-$1,800.			
WEATHERBY Model Centurion 12 ga.	2,000	1980	N/A
Current values for this model in NIB condition range from $1,500-$1,800.			
REMINGTON Model 1100 12 ga. Mag.	2,400	1981	N/A
Current values for this model in NIB condition range from $1,000-$1,300.			
REMINGTON Model 870 12 ga. Mag.	3,000	1982	N/A
Current values for this model in NIB condition range from $1,000-$1,300.			
BROWNING Model B-80 12 ga.	3,400	1983	N/A
Current values for this model in NIB condition range from $800-$1,000.			
BROWNING Model BPS 12 ga.	3,800	1984	N/A
Current values for this model in NIB condition range from $800-$1,000.			

Manufacturer/Model	Quantity	Year	Issue Price
REMINGTON Model 1100 12 ga.	4,500	1985	N/A
Current values for this model in NIB condition range from $800-$1,000.			
BERETTA Model A303 12 ga.	5,500	1986	N/A
Current values for this model in NIB condition range from $1,000-$1,200.			
BERETTA Model A303 20 ga.	3,500	1987	N/A
Current values for this model in NIB condition range from $1,200-$1,400.			
BROWNING Model A5 12 ga. (50th Ann'y)	5,000	1987	N/A
Current values for this model in NIB condition range from $2,500-$3,000.			
BROWNING Model A5 16 ga.	4,500	1988	N/A
Current values for this model in NIB condition range from $2,500-$3,000.			
BROWNING Model A500 12 ga.	4,500	1989	N/A
Current values for this model in NIB condition range from $1,800-$2,000.			
BROWNING Model A5 20 ga.	4,500	1990	N/A
Current values for this model in NIB condition range from $2,000-$2,500.			
BERETTA Model A390 12 ga.	3,800	1991	N/A
Current values for this model in NIB condition range from $1,000-$1,200.			
FRANCHI Model Semi-Auto 12 ga.	4,200	1992	N/A
Current values for this model in NIB condition range from $700-$900.			
WINCHESTER Model 12 20 ga.	4,500	1993	N/A
Current values for this model in NIB condition range from $1,800-$2,000.			
BROWNING Model A500R 12 ga.	3,300	1994	N/A
Current values for this model in NIB condition range from $1,300-$1,500.			
BROWNING Model 12 Repro. 28 ga.	1,000	1995	N/A
Current values for this model in NIB condition range from $3,000-$3,500.			
BROWNING Model BPS 12 ga.	3,500	1996	N/A
Current values for this model in NIB condition range from $800-$1,000.			
BROWNING Model Gold Hunter	3,000	1997	N/A
Current values for this model in NIB condition range from $3,000-$3,500.			
This model commemorated DU's 60th anniversary.			
REMINGTON Model 11-87 12 ga.	3,500	1998	N/A
Current values for this model in NIB condition range from $1,700-$1,900.			
BROWNING Model BPS 20 ga.	3,500	1999	N/A
Current values for this model in NIB condition range from $1,000-$1,200.			
BERETTA Model AL390 12 ga.	3,500	2000	N/A
Current values for this model in NIB condition range from $1,400-$1,600.			
This dinner gun is the Gold Mallard variation of the Model AL390.			
FABARM Model Red Lion 12 ga.	3,600	2001	N/A
Current values for this model in NIB condition range from $600-$800.			
BROWNING Model BPS 28 ga.	3,500	2002	N/A
Current values for this model in NIB condition range from $1,200-$1,400.			
BERETTA Model AL391	3,500	2003	N/A
Current values for this model in NIB condition range from $1,200-$1,400.			
WINCHESTER SX2	2,800	2004	N/A
Current values for this model in NIB condition range from $1,000-$1,200.			
BERETTA Model White Onyx	3,200	2005	N/A
Current values for this model in NIB condition range from $2,500-$2,700.			
REMINGTON Model 11-87 Premier Grade	3,000	2006	N/A
Current values for this model in NIB condition range from $1,300-$1,400.			
BROWNING Silver Hunter 70th Anniversary	3,300	2007	N/A
Current values for this model in NIB condition range from $2,000-$2,500.			

Manufacturer/Model	Quantity	Year	Issue Price
BERETTA Model White Onyx 20 ga.	3,300	2008	N/A
Current values for this model in NIB condition range from $2,500-$2,700.			
BERETTA Model White Onyx 28 ga.	2,400	2009	N/A
Current values for this model in NIB condition range from $2,500-$2,700.			
WINCHESTER Model Super X3	1,450	2010	N/A
Current values for this model in NIB condition range from $2,000-$2,500.			
BERETTA Model 3901	2,400	2011	N/A
Current values for this model in NIB condition range from $2,000-$2,200.			
BROWNING Maxus 12 ga. (75th Ann'y)	2,700	2012	N/A
Current values for this model in NIB condition range from $2,000-$2,200.			
FAUSTI Silvery 12 ga. O/U	2,000	2013	N/A
As this edition went to press, current values could not be established.			

SHOTGUNS: SPECIAL/LIMITED EDITIONS

In addition to dinner guns, DU has also subcontracted for special/limited editions from various manufacturers. These guns should not be confused with banquet dinner guns. Manufacturers/importers of these limited/special editions include Remington, Beretta, Browning, etc. Collectibility on these DU limited/special editions to date has been minimal, with 100% values slightly above the standard make/model from which they were derived.

DUMOULIN, ERNEST S.P.R.L.

Current manufacturer located in Herstal, Belgium. Previously imported until 2011 by Empire Rifle Company, LLC, located in Meriden, NH. Previously imported from 1998-2000 by Armes De Chasse LLC, located in Hertford, NC, and on a very limited basis by Midwest Gun Sport located in Zebulon, NC until 1990 (formerly from Ellisville, MO). Older importation was by Abercrombie & Fitch located in New York, NY.

Most Ernest Dumoulin (son of Henri) drillings, rifles, and shotguns are essentially custom ordered firearms with a long list of available options which, in some cases, can easily double the values of models shown below. Because of this, these options are not listed individually. The company also produces their own A2000 LM (Long Magnum) action, based on the 1930s Mauser Oberndorf design, which is available separately.

Dumoulin manufactures 100-150 guns annually, and all firearms are marked Ernest Dumoulin. Please contact the importer directly regarding current information, including model availability and prices (see Trademark Index).

GRADING - PPGS™	100%	98%	95%	90%	80%	70%	60%	*LAST MSR*

COMBINATION GUNS

EAGLE MODEL – O/U configuration (shotgun barrel on bottom), 12 or 20 ga., .22 Hornet, .222 Rem., .222 Rem. Mag., 6mm Rem., .243 Win., .25-06 Rem., .30-06, 6.5x57Rmm, 7x57Rmm, 8x57RmmJS, or 9.3x74Rmm cal., boxlock action. 1989-disc.

	100%	98%	95%	90%	80%	70%	60%	LAST MSR
	$2,700	$2,400	$2,175	$1,850	$1,595	$1,400	$1,195	*$2,700*

RIFLES: BOLT ACTION

E. Dumoulin has had very limited importation since 1989. Beginning in 1998, some bolt action models have been imported into the U.S.

The current models employ the A2000 Dumoulin action featuring forged flattop receiver, 3 locking lugs with claw extractors, and one-piece bolt, handle, and knob.

BAVARIA DELUXE – .243 Win. through .458 Win. cals., 21 1/2, 24, or 25 1/2 in. octagonal barrel, French walnut stock with rosewood forend tip and pistol grip cap, no sights, essentially custom made with Sako (disc.) or Mauser action.

Add 15% for .375 H&H or .458 Win. Mag. cal.

Prices for this model begin at €12,000.

RIFLE MOUSQUETON – .243 Win. through .338 Win. cals., 20 in. barrel, Mannlicher style, French walnut stock and pistol grip cap, no sights, essentially custom made with Sako or

GRADING - PPGS™	100%	98%	95%	90%	80%	70%	60%	LAST MSR

Mauser action. Many engraving options available from $510-$1,900. Disc.

	$720	$620	$560	$510	$470	$420	$360	

CENTURION MODEL – .270 Win. through .458 Win. cals., 21 1/2, 24, or 25 1/2 in. barrels, French walnut stock with rosewood forearm tip and pistol grip cap, no sights, essentially custom made with Sako (disc.) or Mauser action, can be ordered with custom wood.

Prices for this model start at €13,000.

CENTURION CLASSIC – standard cals. only, similar to Centurion, Mauser 98 action only and has better wood.

	$1,525	$1,375	$1,175	$975	$800	$700	$600	*$1,525*

These models were also available in Mag. cals. that are divided into 4 groups - 1, 2, 3, and 4 Mag. Series. These options retailed in the $50-$300 price range.

* ***Centurion Classic Diane*** – grade up from Centurion Classic, 22 in. barrel, Mauser 98 action, M-70 safety, adj. steel trigger.

	$1,450	$1,250	$1,000	$825	$700	$600	$500	*$1,450*

* ***Centurion Classic Amazone*** – grade up from Diane, 20 in. barrel, full stock.

	$1,750	$1,525	$1,325	$1,075	$865	$750	$600	*$1,750*

* ***Centurion Classic Bavaria Deluxe*** – .243 Win. through .458 Win. cals., 21 1/2, 24, or 25 1/2 in. octagonal barrel, French walnut stock with rosewood forend tip and pistol grip cap, no sights, essentially custom made with Sako (disc.) or Mauser action.

	$1,900	$1,675	$1,450	$1,200	$995	$775	$650	*$1,900*

Many engraving options were available from $510 to $1,900.

* ***Centurion Classic Safari*** – Mag. cals. only.

	$2,350	$1,775	$1,475	$1,200	$995	$775	$650	*$2,350*

MANNLICHER MODEL – various cals., Mauser type bolt action, full stocked. Disc. 1985.

	$730	$660	$580	$520	$470	$430	$395	*$825*

* ***Mannlicher Model Classic*** – similar to basic Mannlicher, except has better walnut. Disc. 1985.

	$995	$890	$775	$650	$575	$530	$460	*$1,065*

MATCH MODEL – match target rifle, adj. sights and stock. Disc. 1985.

	$1,640	$1,490	$1,300	$1,050	$900	$800	$700	*$1,860*

* ***Match Model NATO*** – 7.62 NATO cal. match rifle. Disc. 1985.

	$2,640	$2,400	$2,175	$1,850	$1,595	$1,400	$1,195	*$3,000*

ST. HUBERT MODEL – Sako action, various cals. and barrel lengths. Disc. 1985.

	$1,900	$1,700	$1,495	$1,300	$1,150	$995	$850	*$2,125*

SAFARI SPORTSMAN – .416 Rigby, .375 H&H, .505 Gibbs, or .404 Jeffery cal., Mauser 98 action, 4 shot mag., limited availability in 1986.

	$5,250	$4,500	$3,550	$3,250	$2,800	$2,400	$2,000	*$4,000*

Add 10% for .505 Gibbs cal.

Add approx. $1,200-$1,500 for claw mounts and scope, depending on condition and trademark.

SAFARI PROFESSIONAL – various Mag. cals., K98 Mauser action.

Add €1,500 for .416 Rigby, .458 Win., .458 Lott, .378 Wby. Mag., 460 Wby. Mag., or .505 Gibbs cal.

Prices for this model start at €17,000.

AFRICAN PRO – similar to Safari Sportsman, except has ebony or buffalo horn forend tip, tilting hood for the front sight, multiple folding rear sight.

	$6,000	$5,350	$4,650	$3,750	$3,250	$2,800	$2,400	*$4,800*

GRAND CLASSIC – various cals., prices below reflect rifle w/o engraving. Limited importation.

	$9,000	$7,300	$6,500	$5,500	$4,500	$3,750	$3,000	*€9,500*

ADVENTURER SERIES – various cals. from .25-06 Rem. - .458 Win. Mag., configurations include Euro 2000 and Euroforest. Limited importation began 1999.

Please contact the importer directly for a price quotation on this model.

GRADING - PPGS™	100%	98%	95%	90%	80%	70%	60%	LAST MSR

GENTLEMAN HUNTER SERIES (LIEGE MODEL) – various cals. from .25-06 Rem. - .458 Win. Mag., including some additional Safari cals., configurations include Liege, Liege Safari, Liege Full Stock (Mannlicher), or Liege Thumbhole. Limited importation began 1999.

Please contact the importer directly for a price quotation on this model.

TRADITIONAL LIEGE CRAFTSMAN SERIES (HERSTAL MODEL) – various cals. from .25-06 Rem. - .458 Win. Mag., including many Safari cals., configurations include Herstal, Herstal Full Stock (Mannlicher), or Herstal Safari (5 shot mag.). Limited importation began 1999.

Depending on caliber and variation, prices on this model range from $7,950 - $10,950.

MODEL WHITE HUNTER SAFARI SPECIAL – .375 H&H, .416 Rigby, .416 Wby. Mag., .500 Jeffery, or .505 Gibbs cal., other cals. available upon request, this model features the proprietary Dumoulin Herstal A2000/LM (Long Magnum) action, hinged floorplate, express sights, deluxe checkered walnut stock with ebony forend. Limited importation began 1999.

Prices for this model start at $14,900.

TONY SANCHEZ-ARINO MAGNUM MAUSER – scroll engraved, animal inlays, extended tang and trigger guard, Tony's signature in gold. Importation began 2007.

Prices for this model start at $18,700.

RIFLES: SxS

EUROPA I – .22 Hornet, .222 Rem., .222 Rem. Mag., 6mm Rem., .243 Win., .25-06 Rem., .30-06, 6.5x57Rmm, 7x57Rmm, 8x57RmmJS, or 9.3x74Rmm cal., Anson & Deeley boxlock action, moderate engraving. 1989-disc.

$4,800	$4,200	$3,800	$3,500	$3,250	$2,995	$2,700	*$4,800*

CONTINENTAL I – same calibers as Europa I, sidelock action, 12 engraving options to choose from, many options available on special order. 1989-disc.

$8,600	$7,700	$6,995	$6,400	$5,600	$4,750	$4,150	*$8,600*

"PIONNIER" EXPRESS MODEL – assorted cals. from .22 Hornet through .600 Nitro Express, SxS configuration, heavily engraved, select walnut. Limited production, Anson & Deeley triple lock action, sideplates available at extra charge.

* ***"Pionnier" Express Model P-I and P-II*** – English style scroll or bouquet (P-II) engraving.

$7,850	$6,500	$5,825	$5,200	$4,650	$4,160	$3,700	*$7,850*

Add $400 for P-II engraving.

* ***"Pionnier" Express Model P III*** – English style lace engraving (tapestry style).

$8,640	$7,750	$7,000	$6,400	$5,600	$4,750	$4,150	*$8,640*

* ***"Pionnier" Express Model P-IV through P-VIII*** – various styles of royal engraving with or without hunting scenes.

$9,100	$7,995	$7,450	$6,800	$6,000	$5,000	$4,350	*$9,100*

Add $400 for gold inlays.

* ***"Pionnier" Express Model P-IX through P-XII*** – Louis XVI style engraving.

$9,540	$8,600	$7,800	$7,250	$6,400	$5,250	$4,500	*$9,540*

* ***"Pionnier" Express Model Magnum*** – .338 Win. Mag., .375 H&H, .416 Rigby, .416 Hoffman, .458 Win. Mag., .577 Nitro Express, or .600 Nitro Express cal. Boxlock action with Greener crossbolt.

$10,900	$9,400	$8,650	$7,800	$7,000	$6,450	$5,825	*$10,900*

PIONNIER RECENT IMPORTATION – .300 H&H, .300 Win. Mag., .338 Win. Mag., .375 H&H, .416 Rigby, .458 Win. Mag., or .470 NE cal., similar action as described above with or w/o sideplates, prices below reflect rifle w/o engraving.

Add $1,800 for sideplates. Add $2,800 for .375 H&H, .470 NE, or .500 NE cal.
Prices for this model start at €30,000.

ARISTOCRATE MODEL – available in all cals. up to .375 H&H (also in 20 ga.), single shot action with low profile, exhibition oil finished walnut stock and forearm. Values below assume standard model (12 engraving options available). Imported 1987-88 only.

$9,100	$8,450	$7,775	$7,000	$6,450	$5,825	$5,275	*$10,400*

GRADING - PPGS™	100%	98%	95%	90%	80%	70%	60%	LAST MSR

PRESTIGE SIDELOCK – similar cals. as the Pionnier Model, best quality sidelock, triple locking, 10 different presentation options available, values below reflect standard model without options. Custom order only, 1 year waiting period. Mfg. began 1986.

Prices for this model start at €60,000.

FLEURON SIDELOCK – 6.5x57Rmm, 7x57Rmm, 7x65Rmm, .30 Blaser, 8x57RmmJS, 8x57RmmS, or 9.3x74Rmm cal., made per individual customer specifications.

Prices for this model start at €50,000.

PIONNIER BOXLOCK – various dangerous game cals., with or w/o sideplates, ejectors, solid chrome molybdenum forged action, Greener or Purdey treble grip closure, options includes a variety of engraving patterns, sideplates, French grey or case color hardened finish.

Current MSR for the base model is $34,000, or $36,500 if w/sideplates.

PRESTIGE SIDELOCK – various dangerous game cals., sideplates, H&H ejectors with back action mechanism, DT, engraved sidelock action, options include a variety of engraving patterns, sideplates, French grey or case color hardened finish.

Current MSR for the base model is $62,400.

TONY SANCHEZ-ARINO BOXLOCK – scroll engraved, boxlock action, animal inlays, extended tang and trigger guard, Tony's signature in gold. Importation began 2007.

Prices for this model start at $39,500.

TONY SANCHEZ-ARINO SIDELOCK – scroll engraved, sidelock action, animal inlays, extended tang and trigger guard, Tony's signature in gold. Importation began 2007.

Prices for this model start at $67,400.

SHOTGUNS: O/U

BOSS ROYAL SUPERPOSED – 12, 20 or 28 ga., full sidelock, exhibition grade walnut, double triggers, top-of-the-line quality, built to special order. Values listed assume standard gun (12 engraving options available). 1987-disc.

	$18,500	**$16,000**	**$13,750**	**$11,000**	**$9,775**	**$8,000**	**$6,950**	***$18,500***

Add 6% for 28 ga.

SUPERPOSED EXPRESS "INTERNATIONAL" – O/U shotgun, includes extra set of rifle barrels, 20 ga., 7 choices of rifle cals., deluxe walnut. Elaborate engraving patterns available at extra charge, limited production. Disc. 1985.

	$2,400	**$2,000**	**$1,800**	**$1,575**	**$1,400**	**$1,200**	**$1,050**	***$2,490***

SHOTGUNS: SxS

EUROPA MODEL – 12, 20, 28 ga., or .410 bore, Anson & Deeley boxlock action, single or double trigger, moderately engraved, oil finished stock and forearm, choice of 6 engraving options. 1989-disc.

	$3,300	**$2,750**	**$2,350**	**$2,000**	**$1,800**	**$1,575**	**$1,400**	***$3,300***

LIEGE MODEL – 12, 16 (disc. 1986), 20, or 28 ga., Anson & Deeley locking action, elaborate engraving, deluxe walnut. 1986-disc.

* ***Liege Model Luxe***

	$5,300	**$4,600**	**$3,900**	**$3,300**	**$2,900**	**$2,600**	**$2,300**	

Last MSR was $5,900 (disc. 1988).

* ***Liege Model Grand Luxe***

	$6,900	**$6,000**	**$5,000**	**$4,300**	**$3,600**	**$3,200**	**$2,875**	***$6,900***

Add 15% for 28 ga.
Add 15% for sideplates.

Many engraving options and other special order features were available for the above models.

CONTINENTAL MODEL – 12, 20, 28 ga., or .410 bore, sidelock action, double or single trigger, deluxe oil finished walnut stock, choice of 6 engraving options. 1989-disc.

	$7,400	**$6,250**	**$5,200**	**$4,400**	**$3,700**	**$3,200**	**$2,875**	***$7,400***

GRADING - PPGS™	100%	98%	95%	90%	80%	70%	60%	LAST MSR

ETENDARD MODEL – 12, 20, 28 ga., or .410 bore, full sidelock, exhibition grade walnut, double triggers, top-of-the-line quality, built to special order. Values listed assume standard gun (many engraving options available). Mfg. began 1987, limited importation.

MSR POR	**N/A**	**$25,750**	**$21,750**	**$19,250**	**$16,750**	**$14,000**	**$11,750**	

Add $890 for 20, 28 ga. or .410 bore.

DUMOULIN, FRANCOIS

Previous shotgun manufacturer located in Liege, Belgium circa 1950s-1960s.

While Francois Dumoulin was well known for his shotguns, his company had no connection with any other Dumoulin family or trademark.

DUMOULIN, HENRI & FILS

Current manufacturer established circa 1950s and located in Herstal, Belgium. No current importation. Previously imported and distributed by New England Arms Corp. located in Kittery Point, ME.

Henri Dumoulin was the grandfather of the current owner of the Ernest Dumoulin and Dumoulin Herstal company. He began Henri Dumoulin & Fils during the late 1950s and worked with his 2 sons, Ernest and Noël. They were famous for their bolt action rifles based on k98 actions.

During the 1980s, Henri sold the company to Mr. Aukes from the Netherlands and worked with him until the early 1990s when his uncle died. Mr. Aukes continues the production of rifles under the name Henri Dumoulin & Fils. The company specializes in big-bore, high quality rifles, generally built on Mauser 98 or commercial Mauser actions. The improved double square bridge Imperial Magnum action was developed and introduced in 1987.

RIFLES: BOLT ACTION

GRAND LUXE BOLT ACTION – .300 Wby. Mag., .338 Win. Mag., .375 H&H, .378 Wby. Mag., .404 Jeffery, .416 Rigby, .460 Wby. Mag., or .505 Gibbs cal., 24, 25.6, or 26 in. barrel, European walnut stock with ebony forend tip and pistol grip cap, folding leaf rear sight, hooded front sight, custom made on the Dumoulin Imperial Magnum double square bridge action. Many engraving options are available.

MSR N/A	**N/A**	**$7,995**	**$7,525**	**$6,700**	**$5,750**	**$5,100**	**$4,400**	

Add $750 for left-hand action.
Add $1,150 for extended top and bottom tang.
Add $1,000 for claw mounts.
Add $1,000 for .505 Gibbs cal.

SOVEREIGN – available in same cals. as Grand Luxe Bolt Action, except with a higher quality finish, knurled bolt handles, gold inlayed lettering. Many engraving options are available.

Values on this model depend on engraving, wood and other options.

Imperial Magnum was also available in various stages of completion, barreled actions, actions in the white, etc.

RIFLES: SxS CUSTOM

Henri Dumoulin manufactures best quality boxlock and sidelock double rifles custom ordered to customer's specifications. Many options are available, including high quality wood and engraving. Prices start between $15,000 - $20,000. All guns should be individually appraised before buying or selling to determine accurate value.

SHOTGUNS: SxS, CUSTOM

Henri Dumoulin manufactured best quality boxlock and sidelock shotguns individually built to customer's specifications. Many options were available, including high quality wood and engraving. All guns should be individually appraised before buying or selling to determine accurate value.

DUMOULIN HERSTAL S.A.

Current company established in 1997 and located in Herstal, Belgium. This manufacturer's sister company is Ernest Dumoulin.

Dumoulin Herstal SA and Ernerst Dumoulin are two branches of the same company. Dumoulin-Hersal SA specializes in mechanical works and the production of parts for Ernest Dumoulin manufactured firearms.

E SECTION

84 GUN CO.

Previous manufacturer located in Eighty Four, PA. Circa early 1970s.

GRADING - PPGS™	100%	98%	95%	90%	80%	70%	60%	LAST MSR

RIFLES: BOLT ACTION

CLASSIC RIFLE – various calibers. Grades 1-4.

Grade 1	$420	$315	$275	$235	$210	$190	$170
Grade 2	$780	$585	$512	$430	$390	$355	$315
Grade 3	$860	$645	$560	$475	$430	$390	$345
Grade 4	$1,580	$1,185	$1,030	$870	$790	$715	$640

LOBO RIFLE – various calibers. Grades standard, 1-4.

Standard	$415	$315	$270	$230	$210	$190	$170
Grade 1	$540	$405	$355	$300	$270	$245	$220
Grade 2	$795	$600	$520	$440	$400	$360	$320
Grade 3	$1,600	$1,200	$1,040	$880	$800	$720	$640
Grade 4	$2,350	$1,765	$1,530	$1,295	$1,175	$1,060	$940

PENNSYLVANIA RIFLE – various calibers. Grades standard, 1-4.

Standard	$420	$315	$275	$235	$210	$190	$170
Grade 1	$540	$405	$355	$300	$270	$245	$220
Grade 2	$795	$600	$520	$440	$400	$360	$320
Grade 3	$1,600	$1,200	$1,040	$880	$800	$720	$640
Grade 4	$2,350	$1,765	$1,530	$1,295	$1,175	$1,060	$940

E. ARTHUR BROWN COMPANY INC.

Current manufacturer of single shot rifles and pistols located in Garfield, MN. E. Arthur Brown also sells a wide variety of shooting accessories including barrels, sights, scopes, scope mounts, and brass/bullets.

PISTOLS: SINGLE SHOT

BF PISTOL – .22 LR, 6.5mm BRM, or .44 Mag. cal., falling block action built on small frame, 10, 12, or 15 in. barrel w/o sights, Harrett grooved target grips with smooth forearm, includes scope mounts.

MSR $699	$625	$550	$495	$450	$395	$350	$295

RIFLES: SINGLE SHOT

MODEL 97D – available in most rimfire and centerfire calibers, falling block action, 24 in. heavy contour blue or stainless steel barrel w/o sights, French gray receiver, uncheckered walnut stock and forearm, includes Weaver rail, 6 1/2 lbs.

MSR $999	$925	$825	$725	$625	$550	$475	$395

Add $200 for stainless steel barrel.

E.D.M. ARMS

Current manufacturer established in 1997 and located in Hurricane, UT since 2008. Previously located in Redlands, CA 1997-2008. Dealer and consumer direct sales.

RIFLES: BOLT ACTION

WINDRUNNER MODEL 96 (XM107) – .338 Lapua (mfg. 2002-2010) or .50 BMG cal., takedown repeater action, EDM machined receiver, fully adj. stock, match grade 28 in. detachable barrel that removes within seconds, allowing exact head space every time the barrel is reinstalled, includes two 5 (.50 BMG cal.) or 8 (.338 Lapua) shot mags., Picatinny rail, and bipod, 24 (Lightweight Tactical Takedown) or 36 lbs.

MSR $6,750	$6,750	$6,200	$5,500	$5,000	$4,500	$4,000	$3,500

Add $1,000 for left hand action.

GRADING - PPGS™	100%	98%	95%	90%	80%	70%	60%	LAST MSR

* ***Windrunner Model 96 SS99*** – similar to Windrunner, except is single shot, w/o mag., includes bipod and sling, 32 lbs. New 2002.

MSR $5,250	$5,250	$4,600	$4,150	$3,450	$2,850	$2,250	$1,850	

MODEL 06 MINI-WINDRUNNER – .308 Win. cal., 20 in. barrel, 10 shot mag., Picatinny rail, lightweight, tactical, takedown version of the Windrunner Model 96, 11.2 lbs. Mfg. 2007-2010.

	$4,250	$3,750	$3,300	$2,900	$2,550	$2,175	$1,800	*$4,250*

MODEL XM04 CHEYENNE TACTICAL – .408 CheyTac cal., takedown repeater, tactical bolt action configuration, 5 shot mag., 30 in. fluted barrel with suppressor, desert camo finish, retractable stock, effective range is 2,500+ yards, 27 lbs. New 2002.

MSR $6,750	$6,750	$6,200	$5,500	$5,000	$4,500	$4,000	$3,500	

Subtract $1,400 for single shot action (disc.).

MODEL 12 – .223 Rem. or 7.62 NATO cal., fluted barrel with muzzle brake, 4 shot detachable mag., Savage AccuTrigger standard, includes twin rail adj. stock with heavy recoil pad, receiver with Picatinny rail, pistol grip, guaranteed one MOA at 100 yards. New 2012.

MSR $2,975	$2,975	$2,600	$2,250	$1,875	$1,600	$1,400	$1,200	

MODEL 50 – .50 BMG cal., bolt action, single shot, twin rail adj. skeletonized stock, Picatinny rail and bipod. Mfg. 2003.

	$4,250	$3,750	$3,250	$2,850	$2,450	$2,050	$1,650	*$4,250*

MODEL 98 – .338 Lapua cal., takedown repeating bolt action, single rail adj. stock, pistol grip, 22 lbs. New 2003.

MSR $6,750	$6,750	$6,200	$5,500	$5,000	$4,500	$4,000	$3,500	

510 DTC EUROP – .50 DTC Europ cal. (1 in. shorter than .50 BMG), designed for CA shooters and legal in CA. Mfg. 2007-2008.

	$7,500	$6,850	$6,200	$5,500	$5,000	$4,500	$4,000	*$7,500*

RIFLES: SEMI-AUTO

WINDRUNNER .50 CAL. – .50 BMG cal., 28 in. Lilja match grade chrome-moly barrel, integrated Picatinny rail, removable black stock with cheekrest and adj. buttpad. New 2006.

MSR $9,250	$8,750	$7,500	$6,750	$6,000	$5,250	$4,500	$3,750	

E.M.F. CO., INC.

Current importer and distributor established 1956 and located in Santa Ana, CA. Distributor and dealer sales. E.M.F. stands for Early & Modern Firearms Inc.

For information on Great Western, Dakota Single Action and Hartford revolvers, rifles and carbines imported by E.M.F., please refer to the Great Western, Dakota Single Action Revolvers and Hartford sections. Please refer to the *Blue Book of Modern Black Powder Arms* by John Allen (also online) for more information and prices on E.M.F.'s lineup of modern black powder models.

Black Powder Revolvers - Reproductions & Replicas and *Black Powder Long Arms & Pistols - Reproductions & Replicas* by Dennis Adler are also invaluable sources for most black powder revolver reproductions and replicas, and include hundreds of color images on most popular makes/models, provide manufacturer/trademark histories, and up-to-date information on related items/accessories for black powder shooting - www.bluebookofgunvalues.com

DERRINGERS: REPRODUCTIONS

STANDARD MODEL – .22 Short cal., copy of Colt Model Lord or Lady Derringer, blue, nickel, gold (disc.), or silver (disc.) gold finish. Importation disc. 1992.

	$95	$80	$70	$60	$55	$50	$45	*$125*

1872 STANDARD MODEL – .22 Short cal., copy of Colt Model Lord or Lady Derringer, nickel or silver/gold frame finish, hardwood grips, 7 oz. Disc. 2005.

	$75	$65	$60	$55	$50	$45	$40	*$90*

Add $30 for case, $95 for cased set with two Derringers.

GRADING - PPGS™	100%	98%	95%	90%	80%	70%	60%	LAST MSR

PISTOLS: REPRODUCTIONS

REMINGTON ROLLING BLOCK PISTOL – .357 Mag. cal., rolling block design. Disc. 1992.

	$300	$225	$185	$165	$155	$145	$135	*$395*

PISTOLS: SEMI-AUTO

All current semi-auto pistols are manufactured in the U.S.

HARTFORD 1911-A1 – .45 ACP cal., 5 in. barrel, 7 shot mag., patterned after original 1911, parkerized finish, fixed sights, flat or arched mainspring housing, black ergo, brown plastic military, ultra stag, or checkered hardwood grips, includes two mags. New 2009.

MSR $585	$515	$465	$400	$360	$330	$300	$275	

HARTFORD 1911 COMBAT MODEL – .45 ACP cal., 7 shot mag., similar to 1911-A1 model, except has choice of fixed Tritium low profile, or adj. sights with Tritium inserts, parkerized, blue, Duracoat, or nickel finish, black ergo or checkered hardwood grips, includes two mags, lock, and hard case. New 2009.

MSR $685	$595	$525	$450	$395	$360	$330	$300	

HARTFORD 1911 CCC MODEL – .45 ACP cal., 4 1/4 in. barrel, 8 shot mag., choice of fixed low profile, Novak style fixed night, or Bo-Mar adj. sights, parkerized, blue, stainless, Duracoat, or nickel finishes, includes two mags., lock, and hard case. New 2009.

MSR $1,075	$950	$825	$700	$575	$475	$425	$375	

Add $710 for night sights and skip checkered grips.

HARTFORD 1911-A1 COMMEMORATIVE MODEL – .45 ACP cal., 5 in. barrel, black finish with scrolled embellishments, ultra ivory grips with Army, Navy, Air Force, or Marines insignia, includes medallion and deluxe presentation case.

MSR $999	$895	$775	$650	N/A	N/A	N/A	N/A	

FMK MODEL 9C1 – 9mm Para. cal., 4 in. barrel, lightweight polymer frame, 10 shot mag., blue steel slide with engraved Bill of Rights, five interchangable front sights, eighteen interchangable rear sights, "Mag Out" safety, striker indicator, and loaded chamber indicator, includes two mags., lock, and case, 23 1/2 oz., mfg. by FMK Firearms. New 2009.

MSR $450	$395	$360	$325	$295	$275	$250	$225	

REVOLVERS: REPRODUCTIONS

Please refer to the Dakota Single Action Revolvers section in this text for previously imported revolvers under the Dakota trademark. Please also refer to the Great Western Arms and Hartford listings for trademarked guns imported by E.M.F.

RUSSIAN TOP-BREAK MODEL 1875 – .44 Russian (3rd Model only), or .45 LC cal., configurations include 2nd Model Hideout (3 1/2 in. barrel), Wells Fargo (5 in. barrel), 3rd Model Russian (6 1/2 in. barrel), or Cavalry (7 in. barrel), blue finish with walnut grips. Imported 2006-2008.

	$795	$675	$600	$525	$450	$400	$350	*$900*

REMINGTON 1875 SA ARMY/FRONTIER – .357 Mag., .44-40 WCF (disc. 2003, reintroduced 2006) or .45 LC (disc. 2003, reintroduced 2006) cal., available in either 5 1/2 (Frontier) or 7 1/2 (Army, disc. 2003, reintroduced 2006) in. barrel, blue and case colored metal finishes, walnut grips. Mfg. by A. Uberti.

MSR $520	$450	$385	$335	$275	$240	$200	$175	

Add $280 for laser engraving with custom patina finish.
Add $220 for nickel finish or case coloring (disc. 2010).
Add $15 for steel trigger guard (disc.).
Add $200 for bright or satin (disc. 2000) nickel plating.
Add $250 for engraving (disc.).
Add $85 for convertible cylinder (.45 LC/.45 ACP, disc.).

REMINGTON MODEL 1890 SA POLICE – .45 LC cal., standard blue or engraved frame with custom patina finish, 5 1/2 in. barrel, lanyard ring in buttstock, blue frame, walnut grips, mfg. by A. Uberti. Imported 1986-2009.

	$425	$365	$315	$260	$230	$200	$175	*$480*

GRADING - PPGS™	100%	98%	95%	90%	80%	70%	60%	LAST MSR

Add $210 for laser engraving with custom patina finish (disc.).
Add $10 for steel trigger guard (disc.).
Add $200 for bright or satin (disc. 2000) nickel plating.
Add $85 for convertible cylinder (.45 LC/.45 ACP, disc.).
Add $260 for engraving (disc.).

SCHOFIELD MODEL – .45 LC cal., replica of the original S&W Schofield, choice of 3 1/2 (Hideout), 5 (Wells Fargo), or 7 in. (Civilian/Cavalry) barrel, blue finish. Mfg. by Uberti. Imported 1999-2003.

	$575	$500	$450	$415	$385	$360	$340	*$625*

1851 CONVERSION – .38 Spl. cal., color case hardened frame, walnut grips, 5 1/2 or 7 1/2 in. barrel. Imported 2007-2008.

	$395	$340	$280	$235	$200	$180	$160	*$450*

1860 CONVERSION – .38 Spl. cal., 5 1/2 or 8 in. barrel, color case hardened frame, walnut grips. Imported 2007-2008.

	$415	$370	$340	$300	$270	$240	$210	*$475*

1871 OPEN TOP – .38 Spl. or .45 LC cal., 5 1/2 or 7 1/2 in. barrel, color case hardened frame, walnut grips. Imported 2007-2008.

	$375	$330	$280	$235	$200	$180	$160	*$440*

1873 STALLION STANDARD – includes .22 LR and .22 WMR 10 shot cylinders, 5 1/2 in. barrel, patterned after the Colt SAA, case colored frame, brass backstrap and trigger guard, mfg. by Uberti. Importation began 2009.

MSR $480	$350	$315	$285	$260	$240	$220	$200

1873 STALLION TARGET – .22 LR cal., 10 shot cylinder, 5 1/2 in. barrel with ramp front sight and adj. rear sight, otherwise similar to 1873 Stallion Standard, mfg. by Uberti. Importation began 2009.

MSR $530	$350	$315	$275	$240	$215	$195	$175

RIFLES: SxS

KODIAK MARK IV DOUBLE EXPRESS – .45-70 Govt. cal., back action, browned 24 in. barrels with triple leaf express sights, color case hardened frame, trigger guard and hammers.

MSR N/A	$3,725	$3,350	$2,800	$2,400	$1,950	$1,700	$1,500

RIFLES: SEMI-AUTO

J R CARBINE – 9mm Para., .40 S&W, or .45 ACP cal., blowback operation, utilizes standard M4/AR-15 furniture and trigger components, right or left hand action, Glock magazine, can be converted to other popular pistol mags., flattop receiver, quad rail forend, black adj. stock, extended pistol grip, tri-flatted barrel design, patented ejection and extration features, compatible with AR15 accessories, mfg. in U.S.A. by J R Carbines, LLC. New mid-2010.

MSR $750	$675	$600	$525	$475	$425	$400	$350

RIFLES: SEMI-AUTO, REPRODUCTIONS

These models are authentic shooting reproductions previously mfg. in Italy.

AP 74 – .22 LR or .32 ACP cal., copy of the Colt AR-15, 15 shot mag., 20 in. barrel, 6 3/4 lbs. Importation disc. 1989.

	$350	$295	$250	$200	$175	$155	$145	*$295*

Add $25 for .32 cal.

* ***AP74 Sporter Carbine*** – .22 LR cal. only, wood sporter stock. Importation disc. 1989.

	$375	$325	$275	$225	$195	$175	$160	*$320*

* ***AP74 Paramilitary Paratrooper Carbine*** – .22 LR cal. only, folding wire or black nylon stock on paramilitary design model. Importation disc. 1987.

	$395	$350	$300	$260	$215	$175	$165	*$325*

Add $10 for wood folding stock.

GRADING - PPGS™	100%	98%	95%	90%	80%	70%	60%	LAST MSR

* ***AP74 "Dressed" Military Model*** – with Cyclops scope, Colt bayonet, sling, and bipod. Disc. 1986.

	$395	$350	$300	$265	$240	$220	$200	*$450*

GALIL – .22 LR cal. only, reproduction of the Israeli Galil. Importation disc. 1989.

	$350	$295	$250	$200	$175	$155	$145	*$295*

KALASHNIKOV AK-47 – .22 LR cal. only, reproduction of the Russian AK-47, semi-auto. Importation disc. 1989.

	$350	$295	$250	$200	$175	$155	$145	*$295*

FRENCH M.A.S. – .22 LR cal. only, reproduction of the French bullpup combat rifle, with carrying handle, 29 shot mag. Importation disc. 1989.

	$375	$325	$265	$240	$220	$200	$185	*$320*

M1 CARBINE – .30 cal. only, copy of the U.S. Military M1 Carbine. Disc. 1985.

	$295	$250	$225	$200	$175	$150	$125	*$205*

Add 50% for Paratrooper variation.

RIFLES/CARBINES: COLT REPRODUCTIONS

LIGHTNING STANDARD – .357 Mag. (new 2009), .44-40 WCF or .45 LC cal., patterned after the Colt Lightning rifle, blue finish, 20 in. round or octagon, 24 in. octagon, or 26 in. octagon (disc. 2009) barrel, straight grip uncheckered walnut stock, drilled and tapped, semi-buckhorn rear sight. Mfg. by Pedersoli. New 2008.

MSR $1,450	$1,300	$1,175	$1,050	$925	$800	$675	$550	

Add $100 for rifle configuration with 20 in barrel, or $150 for 24 or 26 (disc.) in. barrel.

* ***Lightning Deluxe*** – .357 Mag., .44-40 WCF or .45 LC cal., patterned after the Colt Lightning rifle, 20, 24, or 26 in. barrel, color case hardened finish, checkered semi-fancy walnut stock, drilled and tapped, semi-buckhorn rear sight. Mfg. by Pedersoli. New 2008.

MSR $1,670	$1,450	$1,250	$1,050	$925	$800	$650	$525	

Add $20 for 24 in. or $40 for 26 in. barrel.

Add $280 for Super Deluxe Model with engraved coin finished frame and fine checkered fancy walnut stock.

RIFLES: REMINGTON REPRODUCTIONS

ROLLING BLOCK CARBINE/RIFLE – .45-70 Govt. cal., authentic reproduction of the Remington Rolling Block Rifle, standard (disc. 2003) or target model, 26 (carbine) or 30 (disc.) in. octagon barrel. Mfg. by Pedersoli. Imported 1991-2006, reintroduced 2009.

MSR $930	$825	$725	$625	$550	$475	$400	$325	

Subtract approx. $100 for standard model.

* ***Rolling Block Rifle Target Deluxe*** – .45-70 Govt. cal., similar to Rolling Block Rifle, except has 30 or 32 in. barrel, checkered pistol grip stock, and German silver forearm cap. Imported 2000-2002, reintroduced 2009.

MSR $1,125	$995	$875	$750	$625	$550	$475	$400	

BABY ROLLING BLOCK CARBINE/RIFLE – .357 Mag. cal., 22 or 26 in. barrel, color case hardened frame. Importation began 1992, reintroduced 2006, and 2009.

	$595	$525	$450	$375	$325	$275	$225	*$665*

Add $25 for 26 in. rifle configuration.

REVOLVING CARBINE – .357 Mag., .44-40 WCF (disc.), or .45 LC cal., 18 in. barrel, case colored frame, walnut grips, Model 1875 Army Single Action design, 5 lbs. Importation disc. 1995, reintroduced 2003.

	$450	$375	$315	$265	$230	$200	$185	*$560*

TEXAS CARBINE (1858 REMINGTON) – .22 LR cal., action patterned after Remington revolving carbine, 21 in. octagon barrel, wood stock and forearm, brass frame. Also available with extra .22 WMR cal. cylinder. Importation disc. 1998.

	$295	$225	$175	$150	$135	$125	$110	*$400*

GRADING - PPGS™	100%	98%	95%	90%	80%	70%	60%	LAST MSR

RIFLES: SHARPS REPRODUCTIONS

1874 SHARPS SPORTING OR MILITARY RIFLE – .45-70 Govt., .45 LC (mfg. 2004-2006), or .45-120 cal., copy of the Sharps Single Shot, 28 or 30 in. octagonal barrel, case hardened frame, single or double set triggers. Importation disc. 1999, reintroduced 2003-2008.

	$900	$800	$700	$625	$550	$475	$395	*$1,025*

Add $120 for checkered stock.
Add $180 for in-the-white (no metal finish, disc.).
Add $120 for brown finish (disc.)
Add $45 for target variation with 1/2 round, 1/2 octagon barrel (disc.)

* ***1874 Sharps Deluxe Rifle*** – .45-70 Govt. or .45-120 (disc.) cal., blue or brown finish, 32 in. tapered octagon barrel, double set triggers, checkered pistol grip and forearm, case hardened frame, silver forend tip. Disc. 2008.

	$1,325	$1,200	$1,025	$875	$775	$695	$625	*$1,500*

An engraved version of this model is still available for $2,500, and Super Deluxe with gold inlays is $3,150.

* ***1874 Sharps Silhouette*** – .45-70 Govt. cal., 32 in. tapered octagon barrel, double set triggers, checkered pistol grip stock and forearm, case colored frame. New 2009.

MSR $1,700	$1,525	$1,375	$1,225	$1,050	$900	$775	$625	

Add $200 for Billy Dixon variation with straight grip stock.
Subtract $400 for 1874 Business Rifle configuration in .45-70 Govt. cal. only.

* ***1874 Sharps Military Carbine*** – saddle ring carbine with 22 in. round barrel, single trigger. Disc. 2005.

	$695	$625	$550	$495	$450	$425	$400	*$760*

QUIGLEY SHARPS MODEL 1874 SPORTING RIFLE – .45-70 Govt., .45-90 (disc.), .45-110 (new 2007), or .45-120 (disc. 2003, reintroduced 2006) cal., 34 in. heavy octagon barrel with storage compartment in stock. Importation began 2000.

MSR $2,150	$1,825	$1,600	$1,400	$1,175	$975	$825	$750	

Add $100 for .45-110 or .45-120 cal.(disc.).

RIFLES: SPENCER REPRODUCTIONS

1865 SPENCER CARBINE – .44-40 WCF or .56-50 cal., 20 in. barrel with barrel band, case colored receiver and hammer, includes sling swivels, 8 lbs. Mfg. by Armi Sport 2006-2008.

	$1,095	$950	$825	$700	$600	$500	$400	*$1,280*

RIFLES: SPRINGFIELD REPRODUCTIONS

SPRINGFIELD 1873 TRAPDOOR CARBINE/RIFLE – .45-70 Govt. cal., trapdoor single shot action, 22 (carbine), 26 (Officer's Model), or 32 (Rifle) in. barrel, blue action, walnut stock. Mfg. by Pedersoli.

MSR $1,400	$1,200	$1,050	$900	$800	$700	$625	$550	

Add $190 for Rifle (disc. 2009) or $200 for Officer's Model.

RIFLES: WINCHESTER REPRODUCTIONS

DELUXE 1860 HENRY RIFLE – .44-40 WCF or .45 LC cal. only, brass or case colored steel frame, deluxe walnut, reproduction of New Haven Arms Co.'s Henry Rifle, 24 in. blue or white barrel. Mfg. 1987-2008.

	$925	$750	$525	$400	$350	$300	$275	*$1,050*

Add $135 for in-the-white barrel or for case colored steel (.45 LC cal. only) frame.

* ***Deluxe 1860 Henry Rifle Engraved*** – similar to deluxe Henry Rifle except has hand engraved receiver. Imported 1987-90.

	$1,350	$975	$700	$525	$400	$340	$295	*$1,598*

1866 YELLOWBOY CARBINE – .22 LR (disc. 2002), .22 WMR (mfg. 2000-2002), .32-20 WCF (mfg. 2000-2002), .38 Spl., .38-40 WCF (mfg. 2000-2002, reintroduced 2005), .44-

GRADING - PPGS™	100%	98%	95%	90%	80%	70%	60%	LAST MSR

40 WCF, or .45 LC (new 1993) cal., 19 in. barrel, brass frame, saddle ring carbine. Disc. 2003, reintroduced 2005-2008.

$725 $600 $475 $350 $275 $235 $200 *$870*

Add $330 for laser engraved Indian model (.45 LC cal. only).

* ***1866 Yellowboy Rifle*** – same cals. as 1866 Yellowboy Carbine, 20 (Border model short rifle, new 1999) or 24 1/4 (Sporting) in. barrel. Disc. 2008.

$775 $625 $495 $350 $275 $235 $200 *$920*

Add $50 for in-the-white barrel.

* ***1866 Yellowboy Border Rifle*** – .38 Spl. or .45 LC cal., 20 in. octagon barrel, brass frame, mfg. by Uberti. Importation began 2010.

MSR $1,075 $875 $725 $575 $425 $350 $285 $235

* ***1866 Yellowboy Carbine Engraved*** – .38 Spl. or .44-40 WCF cal. Importation disc. 1990.

$875 $575 $440 $330 $295 $260 $230 *$1,080*

1873 CARBINE – .22 WMR (disc.), .32-20 WCF (mfg. 1999-2000, reintroduced 2005-2006), .357 Mag. (disc. 2000, reintroduced 2003, and again in 2005), .38-40 WCF (mfg. 2000, reintroduced 2005-2006), .44 Spl. (mfg. 2000, reintroduced 2005-2006), .44-40 WCF (disc. 2000, reintroduced 2005), or .45 LC cal., 16 (Trapper model) or 19 in. round barrel, copy of the Winchester Model 1873 Carbine, blue (disc. 2000) or case hardened steel receiver. Disc. 2003, reintroduced 2005-2008.

$875 $700 $525 $425 $325 $275 $235 *$1,040*

* ***1873 Carbine/Rifle*** – .32-20 WCF, .357 Mag., .38-40 WCF, .44-40 WCF, or .45 LC cal., 20 (Border model short rifle, new 1999), 24 1/4, or 30 (limited importation 2000, reintroduced 2007) in. barrel, case hardened receiver. Disc. 2008.

$880 $700 $525 $425 $325 $275 $235 *$1,050*

Add $30 for 30 in. barrel.
Add $50 for Deluxe Border model.
Add $120 for Deluxe model with checkered pistol grip stock (.357 Mag. or .45 LC cal. only, disc. 2003).

* ***1873 Border Rifle*** – .357 Mag. or .45 LC cal., 20 in. octagon barrel, brass frame, mfg. by Uberti. Importation began 2010.

MSR $1,180 $950 $775 $625 $475 $395 $335 $295

* ***1873 Carbine/Rifle Youngboy*** – .22 LR cal., blue steel, 19 or 24 1/4 in. barrel. Imported 1995-96.

$800 $600 $450 $330 $295 $260 $230 *$1,050*

Add $50 for rifle barrel.

* ***1873 Carbine Rifle Engraved*** – .357 Mag. or .44-40 WCF cal. only. Importation disc. 1987.

$895 $635 $500 $450 $400 $360 $325 *$850*

PREMIER 1873 CARBINE & RIFLE – .45 LC cal., case hardened frame, uncheckered walnut stock and forearm, full mag., rifle has 24 1/4 in. barrel, carbine has 19 in. barrel. Imported 1988-1989 only.

$850 $595 $450 $330 $295 $260 $230 *$1,160*

1876 RIFLE – .40-60 or .45-75 cal., patterned after the Model 1876 Winchester, case hardened frame with 28 in. octagon barrel with open sights. Imported 2006-2008.

$1,050 $875 $750 $625 $500 $450 $400 *$1,265*

1885 HIGH WALL RIFLE (UBERTI MFG.) – .38-55 WCF (new 2000), .40-65 (mfg. 2005-2006), .45-70 Govt., or .45-90 (mfg. 2005-2006) cal., action patterned after the Winchester Model 1885 High Wall, 30 or 32 (mfg. 2003 only) in. barrel, checkered walnut stock. Mfg. by Uberti. Imported 1998-2003, reintroduced 2005-2008.

$925 $800 $675 $550 $500 $465 $435 *$900*

Add approx. 15% for deluxe model with checkered pistol grip stock.

GRADING - PPGS™	100%	98%	95%	90%	80%	70%	60%	LAST MSR

1885 HIGH WALL RIFLE (PEDERSOLI MFG.) – .38-55 WCF or .45-70 Govt. cal., case hardened frame, 30 or 32 in. blued octagon barrel, deluxe wood with cheekpiece. Importation began 2009.

MSR $1,890	$1,650	$1,425	$1,200	$995	$875	$750	$625	

SHOTGUNS

STAGECOACH SxS MODEL – 12 ga. only, features exposed hammers and 20 in. brown barrels, mfg. by S.I.A.C.E. Imported 2000-2002.

	$1,175	$900	$700	$500	$450	$400	$365	*$1,375*

MODEL 1878 SxS – 12 ga. only, exposed hammers, 20 in. barrels, patterned after the Colt Model 1878 shotgun. Importation began 2006.

MSR $475	$425	$385	$340	$300	$260	$230	$195	

MARK V CONQUEST SEMI-AUTO – 12 ga. only, 28 in. barrel with choke tubes. Limited importation 2003.

	$385	$325	$275	$240	$220	$200	$185	*$460*

MODEL 1897 SLIDE ACTION – 12 ga. only, 20 in. barrel, patterned after the Winchester Model 1897, exposed hammer. Imported 2006-2008.

	$440	$395	$350	$300	$260	$230	$195	*$515*

E.R. SHAW INC.

Current rifle and barrel manufacturer established circa 1913 and located in Bridgeville, PA. Consumer direct sales through FFL dealers.

RIFLES: BOLT ACTION

MK XII CUSTOM RIFLE – various cals., choice of stainless or chromemoly barrel, various stock options as well as many special features may be ordered. Please contact the company directly for a quotation on this model based on individual specifications and special orders. New 2012.

The base price on this model is $725.

EAGLE ARMS, INC.

Previous manufacturer located in Geneseo, IL. Previous division of ArmaLite, Inc. 1995-2002, located in Geneseo, IL. Manufacture of pre-1995 Eagle Arms rifles was in Coal Valley, IL.

During 1995, Eagle Arms, Inc. reintroduced the ArmaLite trademark. The new company was organized under the ArmaLite name. In 2003, Eagle Arms became a separate company, and no longer a division of ArmaLite.

Eagle Arms also made lower receivers only.

RIFLES: SEMI-AUTO, RECENT MFG.

On the following M-15 models manufactured 1995 and earlier, A2 accessories included a collapsible carbine type buttstock (disc. per 1994 C/B) and forward bolt assist mechanism. Accessories are similar, with the addition of National Match sights. The A2 suffix indicates the rifle is supplied with carrying handle, A4 designates a flat-top receiver, some are equipped with a detachable carrying handle.

AR-10 MATCH RIFLE – .308 Win. cal., very similar to the Armalite AR-10 A4 rifle, 20 or 24 (Match rifle) in. chrome-moly barrel, A2 (Service rifle) or A4 style flat-top upper receiver (no sights), black stock with pistol grip and forearm, 10 shot mag., 9.6 lbs. Mfg. 2001-2005.

	$1,125	$985	$845	$765	$620	$505	$395	*$1,000*

Add $65 for Service rifle with A2 front/rear sights.

Add $480 for 24 in. barrel and aluminum free-floating handguard.

MODEL M15 A2/A4 RIFLE (EA-15 E-1) – .223 Rem. or .308 Win. cal., patterned after the Colt AR-15A2, 20 in. barrel, A2 sights or A4 flattop, with (pre 1993) or w/o forward bolt assist, 7 lbs. Mfg. 1990-1993, reintroduced 2002-2005.

	$925	$810	$695	$630	$510	$415	$325	*$795*

Add $40 for .223 cal. flattop (Model E15A4B). Add $205 for .308 Win. cal. flattop.

GRADING - PPGS™	100%	98%	95%	90%	80%	70%	60%	LAST MSR

* ***Model M15 A2/A4 Rifle Carbine (EA9025C/EA9027C)*** – features collapsible (disc. per C/B 1994) or fixed (new 1994) buttstock and 16 in. barrel, 5 lbs. 14 oz. Mfg. 1990-95, reintroduced 2002-2005.

	$925	**$810**	**$695**	**$630**	**$510**	**$415**	**$325**	***$795***

Add $40 for flattop (Model E15A4CB).

1997 retail for the pre-ban models was $1,100 (EA9396).

Beginning 1993, the A2 accessory kit became standard on this model.

* ***Model M15 A2 H-BAR Rifle (EA9040C)*** – features heavy Target barrel, 8 lbs. 14 oz., includes E-2 accessories. Mfg. 1990-95.

	$1,025	**$895**	**$770**	**$695**	**$565**	**$460**	**$360**	***$895***

1997 retail for this pre-ban model was $1,100 (EA9200).

* ***Model M15 A4 Rifle Eagle Spirit (EA9055S)*** – includes 16 in. premium air gauged National Match barrel, fixed stock, full length tubular aluminum hand guard, designed for IPSC shooting, includes match grade accessories, 8 lbs. 6 oz. Mfg. 1993-95, reintroduced 2002 only.

	$1,025	**$895**	**$770**	**$695**	**$565**	**$460**	**$360**	***$850***

The 1995 pre-ban variation of this model retailed at $1,475 (EA9603).

* ***Model M15 A2 Rifle Golden Eagle (EA9049S)*** – similar to M15 A2 H-BAR, except has National Match accessories and two-stage trigger, 20 in. extra heavy barrel, 12 lbs. 12 oz. Mfg. 1991-1995, reintroduced 2002 only.

	$1,200	**$1,050**	**$900**	**$815**	**$660**	**$540**	**$420**	***$1,125***

The 1997 pre-ban variation of this model retailed at $1,300 (EA9500).

* ***Model M15 A4 Rifle Eagle Eye (EA9901)*** – includes 24 in. free floating 1 in. dia. barrel with tubular aluminum hand guard, weighted buttstock, designed for silhouette matches, 14 lbs. Mfg. 1993-95.

	$1,525	**$1,335**	**$1,145**	**$1,035**	**$840**	**$685**	**$535**	***$1,495***

* ***Model M15 Rifle Action Master (EA9052S)*** – match rifle, flattop, solid aluminum handguard tube, for free floating 20 in. barrel with compensator, N.M. accessories, fixed stock, 8 lbs. 5 oz. Mfg. 1992-95, reintroduced 2002 only.

	$925	**$810**	**$695**	**$630**	**$510**	**$415**	**$325**	***$850***

The 1995 pre-ban variation of this model retailed at $1,475 (EA5600).

* ***Model M15 A4 Rifle Special Purpose (EA9042C)*** – 20 in. barrel, flattop (A4) or detachable handle receiver. Disc. 1995.

	$1,050	**$920**	**$785**	**$715**	**$575**	**$470**	**$365**	***$955***

The 1995 pre-ban variation of this model retailed at $1,165 (EA9204).

* ***Model M15 A4 Rifle Predator (EA9902)*** – post-ban only, 18 in. barrel, National Match trigger, flattop (A4) or detachable handle receiver. Mfg. 1995 only.

	$1,325	**$1,160**	**$995**	**$900**	**$730**	**$595**	**$465**	***$1,350***

EAST RIDGE GUN COMPANY, INC.

Current rifle manufacturer located in Bancroft, WI.

RIFLES: BOLT ACTION, SINGLE SHOT

BIG BERTHA – .50 BMG cal., 36 in. Lothar Walther premium target bull barrel, muzzle brake, all steel bipod, special tactical or custom laminated wood stock, scope rail, approx. 40 lbs.

MSR $2,750	**$2,475**	**$2,165**	**$1,850**	**$1,685**	**$1,365**	**$1,115**	**$865**	

COMPETITOR 2000 – .50 BMG cal., 30 or 36 in. Lothar Walther fluted bull barrel, extra large muzzle brake, all steel bipod, adj. aluminum stock with military hard coat finish, scope mount, Jewell trigger, pistol grip with palm swell, accuracy guaranteed to be less than 1 minute of angle with custom ammo.

MSR $3,400	**$3,075**	**$2,695**	**$2,300**	**$2,095**	**$1,695**	**$1,385**	**$1,075**	

GRADING - PPGS™	100%	98%	95%	90%	80%	70%	60%	LAST MSR

LIGHT WEIGHT COMPETITOR – .50 BMG cal., 30 in. Lothar Walther fluted bull stainless or chrome-moly barrel, reduced weight muzzle brake, adj. skeletonized aluminum stock with black hard coat finish, scope mounting rail, Jewell trigger, sniper type pistol grip with palm swell, optional carrying handle, 28 lbs. Disc. 2010.

	$3,075	$2,695	$2,300	$2,095	$1,695	$1,385	$1,075	$3,400

Add $200 for stainless steel barrel.

REBEL – .50 BMG cal., 36 in. Lothar Walther bull barrel, muzzle brake, all steel bipod, adj. aluminum tactical stock with removable carrying handle, or custom laminated wood stock, scope rail, AR-15 grip, approx. 38 lbs.

MSR $2,450	$2,195	$2,000	$1,725	$1,550	$1,250	$1,025	$800	

Add $200 for custom laminated wood stock.

SHORTY – .50 BMG cal., 30 in. Lothar Walther tapered barrel, muzzle brake, all steel bipod, adj. aluminum tactical stock with removable carry handle, or custom laminated wood stock, scope rail, approx. 31 lbs.

MSR $2,250	$2,050	$1,795	$1,525	$1,395	$1,125	$925	$715	

Add $200 for custom laminated wood stock.

TITAN BENCH – .50 BMG cal., 30 in. Lothar Walther stainless steel fluted barrel, muzzle brake, adj. trigger, bench rest style laminated stock in choice of colors, precision ground tapered or flat steel scope base, 26 lbs. 6 oz.

MSR $2,550	$2,295	$2,015	$1,725	$1,560	$1,260	$1,035	$800	

ED BROWN CUSTOM, INC.

Current rifle manufacturer established during 2000 and located in Perry, MO. During 2009, the rifle division was transferred to Ed Brown Products, Inc.

Please refer to Ed Brown Products, Inc. for currently manufactured rifles.

RIFLES: BOLT ACTION

702 DENALI – various short and long action cals., designed as lightweight mountain hunting rifle, 22, 23 (disc.), or 24 in. lightweight barrel, glass bedded McMillian sporter stock with checkering and recoil pad, 3 position safety, 7 3/4 lbs. Mfg. 2002-2004.

	$2,895	$2,535	$2,170	$1,970	$1,590	$1,305	$1,015	$2,895

702 OZARK – various cals., lightweight hunting rifle utilizing Ed Brown custom short action, steel trigger guard and floorplate, 3 position safety, checkered lightweight fiberglass stock, match grade, hand lapped 21 in. barrel, approx. 6 1/2 lbs. Disc. 2003.

	$2,800	$2,450	$2,100	$1,905	$1,540	$1,260	$980	$2,800

702 LIGHT TARGET (TACTICAL) – .223 Rem. or .308 Win. cal., features Ed Brown short repeater action, aluminum trigger guard and floorplate, 21 in. match grade barrel, includes Talley scope mounts, approx. 8 3/4 lbs. Disc. 2005.

	$2,495	$2,185	$1,870	$1,695	$1,370	$1,125	$875	$2,495

A3 TACTICAL – various cals., top-of-the-line sniper weapon, 26 in. heavyweight match grade hand lapped barrel, Shilen trigger, McMillan fiberglass A-3 tactical stock, 11 1/4 lbs. Disc. 2008.

	$2,995	$2,620	$2,245	$2,035	$1,645	$1,350	$1,050	$2,995

ED BROWN PRODUCTS, INC.

Current manufacturer established during 1988 located in Perry, MO. Consumer direct sales.

PISTOLS: SEMI-AUTO

All the models in this category except the Classic Custom are available with Gen. III black coating at no extra charge.

The following MSRs represent each model's base price, with many options available at an additional charge.

Add $75 for ambidextrous safety on certain models.

GRADING - PPGS™	100%	98%	95%	90%	80%	70%	60%	LAST MSR

CLASSIC CUSTOM – .45 ACP cal., M1911 style, top-of-the-line model with highest level of cosmetic finishing, 5 in. barrel, incorporates all custom Ed Brown features, including slide and frame, choice of blue/blue, stainless/blue, or stainless/stainless frame and slide, exotic checkered cocobolo wood grips, adj. Ed Brown rear sight, 39 oz.

MSR $3,495	$3,325	$2,875	$2,450	$2,175	$1,775	$1,425	$1,100	

CLASSIC CUSTOM CENTENNIAL EDITION – .45 ACP cal., 5 in. barrel, hand relief engraved package, "Centennial Edition 1911-2011" special laser engraving on left hand side of slide, custom rib on top of slide, adj. sights, Tru-Ivory grips, special serial number starting with JMB prefix (signifies John Moses Browning). Limited mfg. 2010-2011.

	$6,995	$6,250	$5,500	$4,500	$3,500	$2,750	$2,250	*$6,995*

CLASSIC CUSTOM SIGNATURE EDITION – .45 ACP cal., marked "Signature Edition" on left side of slide and "Custom by Ed Brown" on right side of slide, hand engraved on frame and slide, custom rib. New 2012.

MSR $7,195	$6,900	$6,250	$5,550	$4,500	$3,500	$2,750	$2,250	

CLASS A LIMITED – available in 8 cals., M1911 style, basic custom pistol and features all custom Ed Brown accessories, including slide and frame, 7 shot mag., 4.25 (Commander) or 5 in. barrel length, Hogue exotic grips, 34 or 39 oz. Disc. 2003.

	$2,250	$1,970	$1,685	$1,530	$1,235	$1,010	$785	*$2,250*

Add $100 for stainless steel frame and all lower parts.
Add $100 for Novak night sights.

COMMANDER BOBTAIL – various cals., M1911 style, carry configuration, features round butt variation of the Class A Limited frame, incorporating frame and grip modifications, including a special housing w/o checkering, 4 1/4 in. barrel, Hogue exotic wood grips, 34 oz. Disc. 2003.

	$2,350	$2,055	$1,760	$1,600	$1,290	$1,055	$820	*$2,350*

EXECUTIVE TARGET – .45 ACP cal., similar to Executive Elite, except modified for target and range shooting, adj. Ed Brown rear sight, 5 in. barrel, single stack mag., matte stainless or matte black Gen. III stainless finish, cocobolo diamond checkered grips, approx. 38 oz. New 2006.

MSR $2,695	$2,495	$2,275	$1,950	$1,775	$1,425	$1,175	$925	

Add $75 for California Executive Target Model with matte blue frame/slide finish and black Gen II coating.

EXECUTIVE ELITE – .45 ACP cal., M1911 style, 5 in. barrel, choice of all blue (disc.) stainless blue (disc.), or full stainless slide/barrel, features Hardcore components, flared and lowered ejection port, Commander style hammer, 25 LPI checkering on front and rear grip strap, beveled magwell, fixed 3-dot night sights, checkered cocobolo wood grips, matte stainless or matte black Gen. III stainless finish, 34 oz. New 2004.

MSR $2,695	$2,525	$2,200	$1,875	$1,650	$1,325	$1,075	$850	

EXECUTIVE ELITE CENTENNIAL EDITION – .45 ACP cal., 5 in. barrel, traditional blue matte finish, "Centennial Edition 1911-2011" special laser engraving on left hand side of slide, Tru-Ivory grips, fixed sights, special serial number starting with JMB prefix (signifies John Moses Browning). Limited mfg. 2010-2011.

	$2,495	$2,175	$1,750	$1,675	$1,350	$1,100	$850	*$2,495*

EXECUTIVE CARRY – .45 ACP cal., similar to Executive Elite, except has 4 1/4 in. barrel and Bobtail grip, 34 oz. New 2004.

MSR $2,745	$2,625	$2,300	$1,975	$1,775	$1,450	$1,200	$925	

KOBRA – .45 ACP cal., M1911 style, 7 shot, 5 in. barrel, features "snakeskin" metal treatment on frame, mainspring housing and slide, 3-dot night sights, exotic wood grips, matte stainless or matte black Gen. III stainless finish, 39 oz. New 2002.

MSR $2,495	$2,325	$2,000	$1,725	$1,500	$1,225	$995	$775	

GRADING - PPGS™	100%	98%	95%	90%	80%	70%	60%	LAST MSR

KOBRA CARRY - .45 ACP cal., M1911 style, 4 1/4 in. barrel, features Bobtail and "snakeskin" metal treatment on frame, mainspring housing and slide, 3-dot night sights, matte stainless or matte black Gen. III stainless finish, 34 oz. New 2002.

MSR $2,745	$2,575	$2,250	$1,925	$1,700	$1,400	$1,100	$875	

* ***Kobra Carry Lightweight*** - .45 ACP, 7075 aluminum single stack commander frame and Bobtail housing, 4.25" barrel, 10-8 black sight, front night sight, slim cocobolo wood grips, black Gen. III coating, 27 oz. New 2010.

MSR $3,120	$2,925	$2,600	$2,200	$1,850	$1,525	$1,200	$975	

SPECIAL FORCES - .45 ACP cal., M1911 style, 7 shot mag, 5 in. barrel, Commander style hammer, special Chainlink treatment on front and rear grip straps, checkered diamond pattern cocobolo grips, 3-dot night sights, Generation III black coating applied to all metal surfaces, 38 oz. New 2006.

MSR $2,495	$2,325	$2,000	$1,725	$1,500	$1,225	$995	$775	

Add $100 for stealth gray Gen. III finish and carbon fiber grips (new 2011).

Add $75 for California Special Forces Model with matte blue frame/slide finish and black G3 coating.

SPECIAL FORCES LIGHT RAIL - .45 ACP cal., 5 in. barrel, forged Government style frame with integral light rail, Chainlink treatment on forestrap and mainspring housing, fixed 3-dot night sights, traditional square cut cocking serrations, diamond cut wood grips, approx. 40 oz. Mfg. 2009-2012.

	$2,275	$1,975	$1,725	$1,550	$1,275	$1,050	$825	*$2,395*

SPECIAL FORCES CARRY - .45 ACP cal., 4 1/2 in. Commander style barrel, single stack bobtail frame, chainlink treatment on forestrap and mainspring housing, fixed dovetail 3-dot night sights, diamond cut wood grips, approx. 35 oz. New 2009.

MSR $2,745	$2,445	$2,140	$1,835	$1,660	$1,345	$1,100	$855	

JIM WILSON SPECIAL LIMITED EDITION - .45 ACP cal., features black frame with Jim Wilson signature on slide, smooth Tru-Ivory grips, 7 shot mag., 38 oz. Limited mfg. 2007.

	$2,295	$2,010	$1,720	$1,560	$1,260	$1,035	$805	*$2,295*

JEFF COOPER COMMEMORATIVE LIMITED EDITION - .45 ACP cal., 5 in. barrel, Govt. style, forged frame and slide, matte finish, square cut serrations on rear of slide, Jeff Cooper signature on slide, fixed Novak Lo-mount dovertail rear sight, dovetail front sight, 7 shot mag., exhibition grade cocobolo grips with Jeff Cooper pen and sword logo, includes ltd. ed. leather bound copy of *Principles of Self Defense*, 38 oz. Ltd. mfg. 2008.

	$2,295	$2,010	$1,720	$1,560	$1,260	$1,035	$805	*$2,295*

MASSAD AYOOB SIGNATURE EDITION - .45 ACP cal., 4 1/4 in. commander bobtail stainless steel frame, 25 LPI checkering on frame and mainspring housing, Massad Ayoob signature on right side of slide, ambidextrous safety, fixed 3-dot sights, black G10 checkered grips, 4 1/2 lb. trigger pull, includes a copy of *Gun Digest Book of Concealed Carry* by Massad Ayoob. Limited mfg. 2009-2010.

	$2,700	$2,365	$2,025	$1,835	$1,485	$1,215	$945	*$2,700*

CHAMPION MOLON LABE 1911 - .45 ACP cal., 5 in. barrel, designed by certified law enforcement instructor Dave Champion, hand fitted and assembled, "Molon Labe" in Greek letters is laser engraved on the left side of the frame, "Champion" is laser engraved on the right side of the slide, custom G10 grips with engraved Spartan battle helmet, custom Snakeskin metal treatment on front and back grip straps, wide notch rear sight with Tritium front night sight, solid aluminum trigger, black Gen. III coating. Limited mfg. 2011 only.

	$2,595	$2,150	$1,850	$1,625	$1,450	$1,275	$1,050	*$2,595*

RIFLES: BOLT ACTION

In August of 2010, Ed Brown Products announced that all bolt action rifle production had been put on hold indefinitely. The following last MSRs represent each model's base price, and

GRADING - PPGS™	100%	98%	95%	90%	80%	70%	60%	LAST MSR

many options were available at additional cost. Beginning 2006, all M-702 actions were disc. in favor of Ed Brown's new Model 704 controlled feed action with spring-loaded extractor integral with the bolt. All recently manufactured rifles have stainless steel barrels and the entire rifle is coated with Generation III black coating (new 2007).

BUSHVELD – various short and long action cals., dangerous game rifle utilizing Ed Brown custom action, match grade 24 in. medium or heavyweight barrel, McMillan fiberglass stock with cheekpiece and recoil pad, approx. 8 1/2-9 lbs. Disc. 2008.

$2,995 $2,620 $2,245 $2,035 $1,645 $1,350 $1,050 ***$2,995***

Add $300 for .416 Rem. Mag or .458 Lott cals. (disc. 2005).

EXPRESS – .375 H&H, .416 Rem. Mag., or .458 Lott cal., dangerous game rifle utilizing Ed Brown custom M-704 fully controlled feed action, 4 shot internal mag, 24 in. barrel with iron sights and barrel band, Shilen trigger, hand-bedded McMillan fiberglass stock with Monte Carlo cheekpiece and Pachmayer Decelerator recoil pad, approx. 9-10 lbs. Mfg. 2006-2010.

$4,995 $4,370 $3,745 $3,395 $2,745 $2,250 $1,750 ***$4,995***

SAVANNA – various long and short action cals., hunting rifle utilizing Ed Brown custom action, McMillan checkered fiberglass stock with steel trigger guard and floor plate, Talley rings and bases, 24 or 26 in. match grade barrel, approx. 7.5-8 lbs. Disc. 2010.

$3,895 $3,410 $2,920 $2,650 $2,140 $1,755 $1,365 ***$3,895***

Add $100 for muzzle brake.

DAMARA – various cals., lightweight hunting rifle with Ed Brown repeater action, 23 in. barrel and ultra-lightweight McMillan graphite stock with Pachmayr Decelerator pad, 6.1 lbs. Mfg. 2004-2010.

$3,995 $3,475 $3,000 $2,600 $2,200 $1,850 $1,350 ***$3,995***

Add $100 for Mag. cals. with muzzle brake.

VARMINT/COMPACT VARMINT – various varmint cals., features Ed Brown action with steel trigger guard and adj. Jewell trigger., match grade 22 (mfg. 2006-2008, compact variation), 24 (Varmint), or 26 (optional, disc.) in. barrel, hand-bedded McMillan fiberglass stock and recoil pad, approx. 9 lbs. Disc. 2010.

$3,895 $3,410 $2,920 $2,650 $2,140 $1,755 $1,365 ***$3,895***

A5 TACTICAL – .300 Win. Mag. or .308 Win. cal., features adj. McMillan A-5 tactical stock, 5 shot detachable mag., black finish, Shilen trigger, 12 1/2 lbs. Mfg. 2008-2010.

$4,495 $3,935 $3,370 $3,055 $2,470 $2,025 $1,575 ***$4,495***

M40A2 MARINE SNIPER – .30-06 or .308 Win. cal., 24 in. match grade barrel, special McMillan GP fiberglass tactical stock with recoil pad, Woodlands camo is molded into stock, this model is a duplicate of the original McMillan Marine Sniper rifle used in Vietnam, except for the Ed Brown action, 9 1/4 lbs. Mfg. 2002-2010.

$3,695 $3,235 $2,770 $2,515 $2,030 $1,665 $1,295 ***$3,695***

EFFEBI SRL

Current manufacturer established in 1994 and located in Concesio, Italy. Previously imported and distributed 2004-2006 by American Outdoor Adventures, located in Leesburg, GA. Previously named Dr. Franco Beretta until 1994. Also refer to the Dr. Franco Beretta listing.

Effebi manufactures a variety of good quality shotguns in O/U, SxS, and single barrel configurations. Effebi also manufactures both SxS and O/U barrel assemblies. These models have limited importation into the U.S.

EGE SPORTING ARMS

Previous shotgun manufacturer located in Izmir, Turkey.

EGE Sporting Arms manufactured good quality O/U, slide action, and semi-auto shotguns that had limited importation into the U.S.

GRADING - PPGS™	100%	98%	95%	90%	80%	70%	60%	LAST MSR

EGEMEN

Current trademark of shotguns manufactured by Vatan Hunting Firearms Co., located in Konya, Turkey. Please refer to Vatan Hunting Firearms Company listing.

EGO ARMAS, S.A.

Previous manufacturer circa 1953-2006 and located in Eibar, Spain.

Ego Armas manufactured high quality sidelock double rifles ranging in price from approx. €5,000-€8,850 in cals. up to .375 H&H, and €13,100 for the .416 Rigby or .470 NE., in addition to a boxlock express model for €3,000. Mounted scopes were also available. Boxlock and sidelock shotguns were also available ranging in price from €770-€1,050 for a boxlock (hammer model also available), and €1,475-€2,200 for sidelock action with ejectors and English wood finish.

EKSEN ARMS INDUSTRY AND TRADE CO.

Current tactical semi-auto shotgun manufacturer located in Istanbul, Turkey. No current U.S. importation.

SHOTGUNS: SEMI-AUTO

MKE 1919 – 12 ga. only, 2 3/4 in. chamber, gas operated, AR-15 style design in either black finish or 100% camo coverage, 19 in. barrel with muzzle brake, 5 shot detachable mag., ribbed handguard with A2 front post sight and detachable carrying handle, 6 1/2 lbs. New 2012.

Please contact the manufacturer directly for possible U.S. importation and pricing.

EMPIRE RIFLE COMPANY LLC

Previous trademark of rifles manufactured by various independent gunmakers and located in Meriden, NH until 2011.

RIFLES: BOLT ACTION

Empire Rifle Company had a complete line of high quality custom Mauser bolt action rifles manufactured by various independent gunmakers. Calibers, barrel lengths, and other features were specified by the customer per individual order.

Values below did not include federal excise tax.

LEGACY MODEL – various cals. from .257 Roberts to .500 Jeffery, utilizes controlled feed Mauser 98 long double square bridge action, stainless match grade barrel, checkered walnut or Kevlar stock and forearm with cheekpiece, right hand only, integral bolt handle, available in chrome-moly or stainless steel receiver, approx. 7 1/2 lbs. Disc. 2008.

$4,350	$3,800	$3,250	$2,850	$2,500	$2,150	$1,850	*$4,785*

Add $200 for Guide Model with X walnut stock.
Add $1,360 for Professional Grade with AAA walnut stock.
Add $2,400 for Express Grade with all options included.

LIBERTY MODEL – over 40 various cals., lightweight model, similar action as Legacy Model, scaled down design for smaller shooters, walnut or Kevlar stock, stainless steel match grade barrel, approx. 6 lbs. Mfg. 2005-2011.

$5,450	$4,600	$4,150	$3,675	$3,300	$2,950	$2,500	*$5,785*

Add $200 for Guide model (disc. 2006).
Add $900 for Professional Grade with AAA walnut stock (disc. 2006).
Add $1,800 for Express Grade with all options included (disc. 2006).

STANDARD MODEL – various Magnum cals., features Empire 98S Mauser double square bridge action, stainless match grade barrel, checkered walnut or Kevlar stock and forearm, recoil pad, available in right or left hand, approx. 7 1/2 lbs. Mfg. 2005-2011.

$5,150	$4,675	$4,225	$3,800	$3,400	$3,000	$2,650	*$5,585*

Add $200 for Guide Model with X walnut stock.
Add $2,900 for Professional Grade with AAA walnut stock.
Add $4,300 for Express Grade with all options included.

GRADING - PPGS™	100%	98%	95%	90%	80%	70%	60%	LAST MSR

EAST AFRICA MODEL – various cals. up to .505 Gibbs, Mauser Magnum double square bridge action, right or left hand, checkered walnut or Kevlar pistol grip stock with recoil pad, straight bolt handle, integral box mag.

$8,850	$7,475	$6,850	$6,250	$5,400	$4,600	$3,950	*$9,445*

Add $1,250 for Professional Grade with AAA walnut stock.

Add $2,540 for Express Grade with all options included.

TITANIUM MODEL – features all titanium receiver, short action only, Kevlar pistol grip stock, 6 lbs., less than 30 mfg. 2005-2006.

$7,995	$7,200	$6,500	$5,700	$4,950	$4,000	$3,950	*$8,495*

EMPIRE 99 MODEL – various cals., restored Savage 99 action, hand bedded Kevlar stock, available in Professional or Express grade only. Mfg. 2011 only.

$6,450	$5,750	$5,150	$4,800	$3,950	$3,500	$2,900	*$6,885*

ENFIELD AMERICA, INC.

Previous manufacturer located in Atlanta, GA.

PISTOLS: SEMI-AUTO

MP-9 – 9mm Para. cal., paramilitary design, similar to MP-45. Mfg. 1985.

$550	$475	$425	$350	$295	$260	$240

Add $150 for carbine kit.

MP-45 – .45 ACP cal., paramilitary design, 4 1/2, 6, 8, 10, or 18 1/2 in. shrouded barrel, parkerized finish, 10, 30, 40, or 50 shot mag., 6 lbs. Mfg. 1985 only.

$550	$475	$425	$350	$295	$260	$240	*$350*

ENFIELDS

Originally manufactured by the Royal Small Arms Factory at Enfield situated on the northern outskirts of London, in Middlesex, England. Various Enfield rifles, carbines and revolvers were produced and/or converted by other British factories (B.S.A., L.S.A., S.S.A., N.R.F., P. Webley & Son, Webley & Scott Ltd., Albion Motors, W.W. Greener, Westley Richards, Vickers (VSM), ROF Fazakerley, ROF Maltby, BSA Shirley (M47C), as well as Australia at Lithgow (from 1913), in Canada at Long Branch (from 1941), the United States by Stevens-Savage (also from 1941), RFI Ishapore, India (from 1905), Nakhu, Pyuthan and Sundrijal in Nepal (from 1911), and at Wah Cantt in Pakistan (from the late 1950s).

The publisher would like to thank Mr. Ian Skennerton for making the following information available.

REVOLVERS

.450 ENFIELD REVOLVER Mk I & II – often called the ".476", which was a commercial ammunition designation. A 6 shot, hinged barrel with exposed knuckle-joint axis at front, a top break action with forward-sliding chamber for extraction. Mk I model (checkered grips) introduced in 1880 with a Mk II variant (plain wooden grips) in 1882. Designed by American Owen Jones and made at Enfield R.S.A.F., it was not liked due to its sliding chamber extraction and cumbersome proportions.

$1,950	$1,700	$1,450	$1,250	$1,050	$900	$800

.455 WEBLEY REVOLVER – purchased privately by officers as well on War Office contracts. Mk I model approved in 1887, Mk II in 1894, Mk III in 1897, Mk IV in 1899, Mk V in 1913, and the Mk VI in 1915, the Mark number is stamped on the revolver frame, composition grips. Enfield also made the Mk VI Webley during 1921-1926. Mfg. by Webley & Scott.

$1,500	$1,350	$1,250	$1,100	$950	$850	$700

Earlier Marks can sell at a 30-50% plus premium over the Marks V and VI as well as more scarce Enfield production (1921-1926).

Subtract 20% for cut cylinder for .45 ACP with rim clips.

GRADING - PPGS™	100%	98%	95%	90%	80%	70%	60%	LAST MSR

.380 WEBLEY REVOLVER – some purchased privately by officers as well as by police forces and security, early Marks and RIC (Royal Irish Constabulary) models by P. Webley & Son, the Mark or designation usually stamped on left side of revolver frame, wood or composition grips. Mfg. by Webley & Scott.

$900 $800 $750 $700 $600 $550 $495

Earlier Marks can sell at a 30-50% plus premium over the Mark IV Webley & Scott.

NO. 2 MK. I REVOLVER – .380 Enfield (based on .38 S&W with 200 gr. bullet), double action, 6 shot, fixed sights, blued or black finish, wood or composition grips, top break action, introduced in 1932. Essentially an Enfield copy of .380 Webley Mk IV.

$1,100 $1,000 $850 $750 $675 $600 $495

NO. 2 MK. I*/MK I REVOLVER** – .380 Enfield with hammer spur removed and other manufacturing concessions applied. Wartime production by Albion in England with very few by Howard Auto Cultivators (H.A.C.) in Australia which bring a huge premium due to a short run of only 355 revolvers. Enfield & Albion production only.

$900 $800 $750 $700 $650 $550 $450

Add $300+ for H.A.C. production.

RIFLES & CARBINES

.577 ENFIELD PATTERN 1853 RIFLE/CARBINE/MUSKET – adopted from 1853 as the general service issue rifle, percussion lock marked Tower, Enfield, B.S.A., L.S.A., or Windsor on the lockplate, available in 3-band long rifle, 2-band short rifle, engineer (Lancaster), artillery, and cavalry carbine configurations, many were supplied to the Confederacy during America's Civil War.

$2,200 $2,000 $1,850 $1,650 $1,250 $1,000 $900

Add 15% for Civil War production.
Subtract 20% for Indian issue.

.577 SNIDER-ENFIELD RIFLE/CARBINE – adopted in 1866 as a breech-loading conversion of the .577 Enfield, single shot, swing-over breech block, modified percussion lock, the Mk III improved locking breech in 1869 was new manufacture, safer to shoot.

$1,750 $1,650 $1,550 $1,350 $1,100 $900 $800

Subtract 10% for Indian issue. Subtract 15% for the more common carbine model.

.450 MARTINI-HENRY – Britain's first purpose built breech-loader in 1871, hinged falling block action with internal lock mechanism, early Mk I rifle had a safety catch, Mk II rifle introduced in 1876, Cavalry Carbine in 1877, Artillery Carbine in 1879, Mk III rifle in 1879, and the long lever "humpback" Mk IV in 1887 which was sent to India & Nepal.

$1,700 $1,550 $1,300 $1,150 $975 $825 $700

Subtract 10% for Indian issue.

.303 MARTINI-METFORD – conversion of .450 M.-H. with Metford rifling, converted markings are stamped on left side of receiver. Artillery & Cavalry carbines are more prolific than the rifles; Artillery models are marked "A.C." with Mark number on left side of the receiver, Cavalry models are marked "C.C." followed by the Mark number. Metfords are much rarer than ensuing Martini-Enfield models, only made between 1889 and 1895, with more carbines converted than rifles. A small number of rifles were converted only for the colonies of Natal, South Australia, Western Australia, and Canada. Most Martini-Metfords are marked "M.M. .303" on the left side of the action body whereas Martini-Enfields are marked "M.E. .303".

$2,100 $1,900 $1,550 $1,350 $1,100 $1,000 $850

Add 50% for Royal Cypher marked M.M. Rifles. Subtract 10% for commercial pattern. Subtract 20% for more common carbine model.

.303 MARTINI-ENFIELD – conversion of .450 M.-H., the conversion markings are stamped on the left side of the receiver. Artillery and Cavalry carbines are more prolific than the rifles, Artillery models are marked "A.C." with the Mark number on the left side of the receiver, and Cavalry models are marked "C.C.", followed by the Mark designation.

$1,500 $1,350 $1,150 $1,050 $1,000 $800 $650

GRADING - PPGS™	100%	98%	95%	90%	80%	70%	60%	LAST MSR

Add 50% for Royal Cypher marked M.E. Rifles. Subtract 10% for commercial pattern. Subtract 20% for more common carbine model.

.303 MAGAZINE LEE-METFORD – introduced in 1888 with 7-groove Metford segmental rifling and 8-round detachable magazine, rifles proceeded through Marks I, I*, II, and II* which is marked on the right side of the action body below the factory and year, underneath the closed bolt handle, rifles have 30.2 in. barrels, carbines have 20 3/4 in. barrels. Mk I and I* rifle have single-row 8 round magazine, carbines are 6 round, Mk II and II* rifles are 10 round staggered box. Mfg. by Enfield, BSA, LSA, and Nepal.

$3,300	$2,850	$2,650	$2,450	$2,300	$2,100	$1,850	

Add 50%+ for Mk I with Lewes sights.
Add 50% for Nepal mfg. (very limited).

.303 MAGAZINE LEE-ENFIELD – introduced in 1895 with 5-groove Enfield rifling for cordite loads, fitted with safety catch on the cocking piece, rifles and carbines went through Marks I and I*, Mk I* has no cleaning rod provision in forend or nosecap. Mfg. by Enfield, BSA, and LSA, repaired at Ishapore.

$2,500	$2,350	$2,100	$1,900	$1,700	$1,500	$1,250	

.303 CHARGER LOADING LEE-ENFIELD – M.L.M. and M.L.E. rifles with 30.2 in. barrels, modified for clip charger loading, after 1907 fitted with improved sights and foresight protector, conversions marked on left of receiver butt socket with factory and year (i.e., Enfield, BSA, LSA, VSM).

$2,250	$2,150	$2,000	$1,850	$1,700	$1,350	$1,100	

.22 LEE-ENFIELD LONG RIFLE – 22 LR cal., 30.2 in. barrel, tubed for rimfire cartridge, Mk I, Mk I*, and MK II variations, only a few were converted at Enfield and by the Royal Navy, some commercial models may be encountered. In the colonies, the .230 CF round was used in Long Rifle conversions, these were locally converted.

$2,500	$2,350	$2,200	$2,000	$1,850	$1,650	$1,350	

.303 S.M.L.E. Mk I (SHORT MAGAZINE, LEE-ENFIELD) – features a sliding charger guide on the bolthead, bone inserts on the rear sight slide and incurving nosecap foresight protector wings, 10 round staggered row detachable mag. with magazine cut-off provision in the receiver, also Mk I*, I**, I***, II Cd., II* Cd. upgrades and conversions. Introduced 1903, made at Enfield, BSA, and LSA until 1907.

$2,000	$1,900	$1,750	$1,600	$1,400	$1,250	$1,100	

Add 20% for an original unaltered Mk I S.M.L.E.

.303 S.M.L.E. Mk III (RIFLE No. 1 Mk III) – improved rear sight and rear handguard over the S.M.L.E. Mk I, still retains the magazine cut-off and volley sights of the Mk I S.M.L.E. model., approved in 1907, also made by Lithgow, Ishapore, and Nepal.

$1,600	$1,450	$1,250	$1,150	$1,000	$850	$750	

Add 50% for Nepal mfg. (limited production). Subtract 20% if later production w/o long range sights.

.303 RIFLE No. 1 Mk III* – later model that incorporates production shortcuts, no magazine cut-off, long range volley sights, or backsight windage adjustment. Made by Enfield, BSA, LSA, SSA, Lithgow, Ishapore, and Nepal, introduced in 1915.

$775	$625	$525	$425	$325	$250	$200	

Add 50% for Nepal mfg. (limited production).

.303 RIFLE No. 1 Mk III* H.T. SNIPER – factory fitted telescopic sight and heavy barrel, converted at Lithgow, Australia at the end of WWII, special bedding of furniture, some were also fitted with a cheekpiece, British and Lithgow actions.

$7,000	$6,000	$5,500	$5,000	$4,250	$3,750	$3,250	

Buyer beware - check for authentic serial nos., as there have been some fakes on this model.

.303 S.M.L.E. Mk V – features a folding aperture backsight on upper rear part of action body, reinforcing outer band at the base of the nosecap, full length top handguards, magazine

GRADING - PPGS™	100%	98%	95%	90%	80%	70%	60%	LAST MSR

cut-off, "V" marked safety catch with angled thumb grooves, limited production at Enfield in 1922-1924 of 20,000 rifles.

	$2,000	$1,750	$1,500	$1,250	$1,100	$1,000	$900	

Many found with damaged rearsight or wanting the upper reinforcing band - check for replacement parts. This reduces the value up to 30%.

.22 SHORT RIFLE Mk I, I*, & II – conversions from 1907 of M.L.M. and M.L.E. long rifles to short rifle configuration, 25.2 in. barrel, service conversions by R.S.A.F. Enfield for the War Office.

	$1,900	$1,750	$1,550	$1,350	$1,200	$1,000	$900	

.22 SHORT RIFLE Mk III – converted from .303 Cd. Mk II & II* SMLE for miniature range practice, external resemblance to SMLE Mk I, service conversions done at Enfield as well as by BSA and LSA.

	$1,700	$1,550	$1,400	$1,250	$1,000	$850	$750	

.22 PATT 1914 Nos. 1 & 2 – single shot WW1 conversions by the British gun trade. No. 1 model is from S.M.L.E. Mk I, No. 2 is from S.M.L.E. Mk III. Converted by A.G. Parker and Westley Richards.

	$1,350	$1,200	$1,000	$900	$800	$700	$600	

The .22 Patt. 1914 No. 1 can bring a 30%+ premium due to its earlier S.M.L.E. Mk I configuration.

.22 No. 2 Mk IV* – converted No. 1 rifle (S.M.L.E.) to single-loading trainer, modified in Britain, Lithgow (Australia), and Ishapore (India).

	$1,200	$1,100	$950	$850	$750	$600	$500	

.303 No. 3 Mk I* (PATTERN 1914 RIFLE) – U.S. manufactured British modified Mauser action during WWI, made by Winchester, Remington, and Eddystone, very similar to the U.S. .30 Model 1917, and shares many interchageable component parts.

	$1,350	$1,150	$1,000	$900	$800	$700	$600	

Add 40% for Winchester Mk I*(F) with fine adj. backsight.

.303 No. 3 Mk I* (T) (PATTERN 1914 SNIPER) – converted in England by Periscope Prism Co. (1918) & B.S.A. (1938) from Winchester rifles, the Pattern 1918 telescope on crawfoot mounts was fitted.

	$8,500	$7,500	$6,000	$5,250	$4,750	$4,000	$3,750	

.303 No. 3 Mk I* (T) A SNIPER – converted in England by Alex Martin in WWII from Winchester MK I* (F) rifles, Great War Aldis and P.P. Co. telescopes (ex-SMLE snipers) were fitted, original SMLE rifle engraved number is usually visible, usually scope is offset (left) of the bore line.

	$7,500	$6,750	$6,000	$5,250	$4,750	$4,000	$3,500	

Add 30% for overhead mount.

.410 MUSKET (INDIA) – conversion of the SMLE rifle after 1927 to single loader, smoothbore barrel, uses straight sided .303 cartridge equating to .410 medium length case. The .410 shot shell will not chamber.

	$750	$675	$600	$550	$475	$400	$325	

.303 SINGLE LOADER (S.L.) – similar configuration to .410 Musket, converted at Ishapore from 1923, but has rifled barrel and chambers the service .303 round, less common than the .410 Musket.

	$850	$775	$650	$600	$550	$475	$400	

.303 No. 4 Mk I & I* – WWII production Lee-Enfield, British R.O.F. Fazakerley, Maltby, BSA Shirley (M47C), and Wah Cantt (POF) from 1941, Britain only made the Mk I model, wartime U.S. Lend-Lease production marked "US PROPERTY", serial number contains letter "S", while Canadian Long Branch rifles contain an "L" (for Long Branch), U.S. and Canada made both Mk I and Mk I* models.

	$1,250	$1,150	$975	$875	$750	$625	$500	

Rare 1933 trials No. 4 rifles made at Enfield will bring a 50%+ premium.
Add 25% for Pakistan Wah Cantt (POF) made in Shirley plant in the late 1950s.

GRADING - PPGS™	100%	98%	95%	90%	80%	70%	60%	LAST MSR

.303 No. 4 Mk 2, Mk 1/2 & 1/3 – postwar Fazakerley [ROF(F)] production with the "hung" trigger and better quality fittings than wartime production, Mk 1/2 and 1/3 converted from Mk I and Mk I* rifles respectively, the No. 4 Mk 2 was of new manufacture, also made in the early 1970s at Wah Cantt, Pakistan on ex-Fazakerley machinery.

	$1,350	$1,100	$1,000	$925	$800	$675	$550

Add 30% for Mk 2.

.303 No. 4 Mk I (T) – converted by Holland & Holland (S51) during WWII in England, also by Long Branch in Canada from indigenous production, the No. 32 telescopic sight was generally fitted, made in England or by R.E.L. in Canada.

	$7,500	$6,500	$5,500	$4,750	$4,250	$3,900	$3,500
w/ scope mounts only	$2,500	$1,900	$1,500	$1,250	$1,100	$975	$800

Add 25%-30% for issue green painted rifle chest with telescope carrier and case.
Add 30% for matching nos.

.303 No. 5 MK. I JUNGLE CARBINE – 20 1/2 in. barrel with flash hider, lightened action body and shortened furniture. From 1944, for service in the Far East.

	$1,000	$900	$850	$750	$675	$625	$550

Subtract 20% for Indian service issues that have a transverse wood screw in the forend which is less desirable.

.22 No. 7 – postwar rimfire trainer on No. 4 action, British model has magazine feed, the Long Branch is designated "C No. 7" but is single shot only, originally issued in chest. Mfg. in England by BSA and in Canada by Long Branch.

	$1,750	$1,550	$1,350	$1,150	$1,000	$900	$800

Add $250-$350 for original marked Canadian chest.
Subtract 40% if w/o bolthead.

.22 No. 8 Mk I – postwar rimfire trainer, half-stock target rifle style made by BSA (M47C) and Fazakerley on a modified No. 4 action body.

	$1,500	$1,350	$1,200	$1,050	$950	$850	$750

.22 No. 9 Mk I – single shot only, full length rifle resembling the No. 4, British conversion of the No. 4 Mk I rifle by Parker Hale for the Royal Navy.

	$1,250	$1,100	$975	$850	$775	$700	$600

SKELETON ARMOURER & TRAINING ACTIONS – with shortened barrel, sometimes serial no. with SKN prefix. Models from MLM thru' to No.4. Some made at Enfield, others at Ordnance Depots. Beware of fakes.

	$1,000	$850	$750	$650	$575	$500	$450

* ***Skeleton Armourer & Training Actions Full Length Models*** – full-length models of SMLE made at Lithgow in short production run. Beware of fakes.

	$3,500	$2,500	$2,000	$1,800	$1,600	$1,300	$1,000

LONG BRANCH TRAINING RIFLE & SWIFT TRAINER – Non-guns with needle pointed striker at front of barrel, Canadian & British variants used with panoramic target in a frame.

	$1,850	$1,600	$1,350	$1,200	$950	$850	$725

.303 SHORTENED LIGHTENED NO. 1 RIFLE – Lithgow troop trials full-stock carbines, 20.2 in. barrel, serial numbered XP followed by 1-100 number, came with 10-inch bayonet. Rare. Late WWII production.

	$8,500	$7,500	$7,000	$6,500	$5,750	$4,950	$4,000

.303 No. 6 Mk I & I/I – Lithgow trials jungle carbines, Mk I has bed backsight, Mk I/I has aperture sight at rear of body, carbine length, marked XP followed by serial number. Rare.

	$8,500	$7,500	$7,000	$6,500	$5,750	$4,950	$4,000

.303 LONG BRANCH LIGHT RIFLE – Wartime short-run test rifle, One-piece stop, grooved forend with recess in butt and rubber recoil pad, carbine length, marked J5550 followed by serial number. Very rare.

	$10,000	$9,000	$8,250	$7,750	$7,000	$6,250	$5,000

GRADING - PPGS™	100%	98%	95%	90%	80%	70%	60%	LAST MSR

.303 EAL (EX-CAL LONG BRANCH) – sporter style survival, Ranger and surplus sale model, variations in sights, depending upon variant and applications, originally with orange color recoil pad. Mfg. late 1950s.

	$2,000	$1,750	$1,500	$1,300	$1,000	$850	$700	

.22 HORNET SLAZENGER SPORTER – Made at Lithgow under contract for Slazengers, Sporter model with modified 400yd. leaf rearsight, ramp front sight, pistol grip buttstock, 5 shot mag.

	$800	$700	$600	$525	$450	$400	$350	

.410 SLAZENGER SPORTER – sporter with short 'bobbed' fore-end, single loader, no rearsight, grooved top of action body for sighting, bead foresight, made at Lithgow under contract for Slazengers.

	$650	$575	$525	$475	$425	$375	$300	

7.62mm RIFLE 2A & 2A1 (INDIA) – new manufacture SMLE rifle in NATO cal., higher quality steel, 2A1 upgrade has metric rear sight graduated to 800m, and angled ramp on sight bed. Production from the mid-1960s.

	$750	$700	$650	$575	$525	$475	$375	

7.62mm L42A1 SNIPER – Enfield conversion and extensive rebuild of the No. 4 Mk I(T) sniper rifle, fitted with an upgraded No. 32 telescopic sight to L1A1, half-stocked furniture, 7.62mm magazine with integral ejector, with heavy target barrel.

	$8,500	$7,750	$7,250	$6,750	$5,750	$5,250	$4,500	

Add 20%+ for original green finished chest.

Add 30% for Iraq war issue with 6x Schmidt & Bender scope.

7.62mm L1A1 – Enfield, CAL, and Lithgow manufacture along with ensuing imports from South America and some domestic market action bodies (receivers) and parts, values can vary considerably, depending on the source of component parts, country of origin and markings, ATF and import restrictions apply to safety sear action bodies, as on original British, Canadian and Australian service models.

	$3,000	$2,500	$2,000	$1,500	$1,100	$950	$700	

Add 30% for original Lithgow SAF Model made for U.S. market (limited production).

Add a premium for heavy barrel, bipod, PNG flash hider, recoil reducer, optical sight, and wooden furniture.

.230 FRANCOTTE CADET MARTINI – turn of the century British empire trainer with Belgian Francotte patent, small size modular Martini action.

	$950	$850	$750	$675	$575	$525	$450	

Add 30% for take-down model.

Add 10% for colonial markings.

.310 CADET MARTINI – later production small Francotte action on Australian contract by W.W. Greener and BSA, circa 1910.

	$900	$800	$725	$650	$525	$475	$400	

RIFLES: U.S. MILITARY

Add 10% for Winchester mfg.

Add 10% for Type I guns.

Add 10% for British service models with red painted band around stock.

U.S. MODEL 1917 ENFIELD – .30-06 cal., bolt action, 5 shot, 26 in. barrel, original finish was high polish blue, although wartime and post war refurbished rifles may be parkerized or black matte, adj. sights, military stock, derived from English P14 Enfield, production run continued at Winchester, Remington, and Eddystone after British .303 cal. pattern contracts concluded, over two million mfg. 1917-18, but original guns in 90%+ condition are rare, some used in British service have red-painted band around stock to differentiate them from .303 Patt. '14.

* ***U.S. Model 1917 Enfield Rifle Original high polish blue***

	$2,700	$2,300	$1,900	$1,400	$1,100	$850	$650	

This model was manufactured primarily by Remington at the Eddystone plant in Eddystone, PA (Eddystone marked), the Ilion Remington plant, and by Winchester in New Haven, CT.

GRADING - PPGS™	100%	98%	95%	90%	80%	70%	60%	LAST MSR
* ***U.S. Model 1917 Enfield Rifle matte blue or parkerized reworks*** – most frequently encountered variation, many differences in the reworked matte blue and parkerized finishes, some also FTR'd (factory thorough repair) in British system and by subsequent users.	**$1,200**	**$1,000**	**$850**	**$700**	**$625**	**$575**	**$475**	

ENGLISH SHOTGUNS

Shotguns manufactured by various British makers.

Unlike American shotguns such as Parker, L.C. Smith, and A.H. Fox, the critical aspect of finish originality is not of premier importance with English shotguns. There are many English gunsmiths in both Britain and the U.S. who are capable of refinishing English guns on a level with the Old World masters. Of course, original guns with 100% original finish have the greatest desirability, but, when done properly, restored guns closely approach the same value of original guns. Do not confuse this with restored American guns, which are only worth a fraction of their "original" finish value.

Percentage of case colors on receivers and blue on barrels is not as critical in determining values, which diminish less drastically than with American guns. Tremendous fluctuations in value do occur in the smaller gauges (20, 28 ga. and .410 bore). The rarity and value of gauges, as they descend, are prodigious in English shotguns. However, the opposite is true in regard to double rifles, where bigger is better. A vintage English double with the original inside labeled trunk style case increases the gun's value $1,000 - $5,000+ depending on style, inclusive tools and accessories, and case materials. Cases with exotic leathers such as crocodile, elephant and ostrich are also very valuable.

A fine old English double, tastefully engraved and stocked with exhibition Turkish walnut by a master craftsman, is a work of art that is highly treasured by collectors, and should be appropriately valued. The same application can apply to American guns, but again, is subject to narrower limitations.

Also unlike most other shotguns, English guns are more delicate and sleek in design, eliminating any excess metal and wood, resulting in minimum weight and better balance. Because of this, there is far less margin for error in retaining necessary strength after modification such as chamber lengthening and back boring of barrels. Therefore, the importance of proof or reproofing after modification is a serious consideration. In Britain, it is serious enough to be a matter of law.

After years of hard use and sometimes neglect, rust pits appear in the bores which require back boring to restore them. Barrels can be cut and back bored to simulate chokes which are actually cylinder bore. This back boring must not result in more than a .015 in. increase in bore diameter from that of the original. Barrels more than .015 in. over original are considered "out of proof" and potentially dangerous. In any case, the barrel thickness should always exceed a minimum. Most authorities consider the minimum to be no less than .022 to .025 inch in wall thickness w/o a British reproof. The foregoing only applies to fluid steel barrels. Many consider "nitro proofed" damascus barrels safe to shoot - however, this is a dangerous crapshoot.

The above limitations are critical to overall value and their presence or absence must be established to buyer satisfaction prior to purchase. Bore micrometers and barrel thickness gauges are relatively inexpensive compared to the purchase of a $25,000 Purdey that has a true market value of only $10,000 because its aesthetically beautiful barrels are dangerously out of proof. New best English made chopper lump barrels currently cost at least $10,000, and original Purdey made barrels are about three times as much. Remember, the most important criteria for purchasing an English shotgun is the barrels.

Somewhat of a paradox is the later serial numbered guns. Albeit generally of lesser quality than early guns, they are generally more valuable on a sliding scale due to the ever increasing cost of currently manufactured guns.

The publisher would like to thank Mr. Larry Baer for providing the above information.

ENTRÉPRISE ARMS INC.

Current manufacturer located in Irwindale, CA, since 1996. Dealer and consumer sales.

GRADING - PPGS™	100%	98%	95%	90%	80%	70%	60%	LAST MSR

PISTOLS: SEMI-AUTO

The models listed are patterned after the Colt M1911, but have "Widebody" frames.

ELITE SERIES – .45 ACP cal., 3 1/4 in. barrel, features steel 1911 Widebody frame, flat mainspring housing, flared ejection port, 10 shot mag., bead blasted black oxide finish, tactical sights, 36 oz. New 1997.

* ***Elite Series P325***

MSR $700	$625	$565	$500	$450	$400	$360	$330	

* ***Elite Series P425*** – similar to Elite P325, except has 4 1/4 in. barrel, 38 oz. New 1997.

MSR $700	$625	$565	$500	$450	$400	$360	$330	

* ***Elite Series P500*** – similar to Elite P325, except has 5 in. barrel, 40 oz. New 1997.

MSR $700	$625	$565	$500	$450	$400	$360	$330	

TACTICAL SERIES – .45 ACP cal., 3 1/4 in. barrel, features Tactical Widebody with "De-horned" slide and frame allowing snag-free carry, narrow ambidextrous thumb safety, 10 shot mag., low profile Novak or ghost ring sights, squared trigger guard, flat main spring housing, matte black oxide finish, 36 oz. New 1997.

* ***Tactical Series P325***

MSR $979	$875	$750	$650	$575	$500	$450	$395	

* ***Tactical Series P325 Plus*** – similar to P325, except has short officer's length slide/barrel fitted onto a full government frame, designed as concealed carry pistol. New 1998.

MSR $979	$875	$750	$650	$575	$500	$450	$395	

* ***Tactical Series P425*** – similar to Tactical P325, except has 4 1/4 in. barrel, 38 oz. New 1997.

MSR $979	$875	$750	$650	$575	$500	$450	$395	

* ***Tactical Series P500*** – similar to Tactical P325, except has 5 in. barrel, 40 oz. New 1997.

MSR $979	$875	$750	$650	$575	$500	$450	$395	

MEDALIST SERIES (TITLEIST, P500 NATIONAL MATCH) – .40 S&W or .45 ACP cal., 5 in. barrel, features tighter tolerances and numerous custom features, 10 shot mag., front and rear slide serrations, blue slide, includes Bo-Mar low mount rear adj. sight, 40 oz. New 1997.

MSR $979	$875	$750	$675	$575	$525	$475	$425	

Add $120 for .40 S&W cal.

During 1999, this model's nomenclature changed from the Titleist Series to the Medalist Series.

BOXER SERIES – similar to Titleist Series, except has fully machined "high mass" frame and flattop slide. New 1998.

MSR $1,399	$1,200	$995	$850	$750	$625	$550	$500	

Add $100 for .40 S&W cal.

TOURNAMENT SHOOTER MODEL (TSM I-III) – .40 S&W or .45 ACP cal., 5, 5 1/2 (TSM III only), or 6 (.45 ACP only) in. barrel, blue finish, designed for IPSC competition, 10 shot mag., TSM II is standard, 40-44 oz. New 1997.

MSR $2,000	$1,800	$1,550	$1,325	$1,100	$950	$875	$750	

Add $300 for TSM I.
Add $700 for TSM III.

CARBINES, SEMI-AUTO

STG58C CARBINE/SCOUT – .308 Win. cal., paramilitary design, 16 1/2 in. barrel with muzzle brake, synthetic pistol grip stock, last shot bolt hold open, adj. gas system, mil-spec black oxide finish, 20 shot mag., 200-600 meter aperture sights, supplied with black nylon sling, various configurations, approx. 9 lbs. Mfg. 2000-2009.

* ***STG58C Carbine Scout*** – Entreprise Type 03 receiver, integral bipod, includes carry handle.

	$1,075	$875	$750	$625	$575	$500	$450	*$1,199*

GRADING - PPGS™	100%	98%	95%	90%	80%	70%	60%	LAST MSR

* ***STG58C Carbine*** – Entreprise Type 01 receiver, machined aluminum free-floating handguards, carry handle.

	$1,200	$995	$850	$750	$625	$550	$500	$1,399

FAL CARBINE MODEL – .308 Win. cal., 18 in. barrel, detachable 10 or 20 shot mag., parkerized finish, Entreprise Type 03 steel receiver, injection molded handguard and standard buttstock with pistol grip, zero climb muzzle brake, adj. gas system, carry handle, adj. front sight, adj. rear aperture sight, 9.3 lbs. New 2009.

MSR $979	$875	$775	$650	$550	$500	$450	$400	

FAL PARA CARBINE MODEL – .308 Win. cal., 18 in. barrel, detachable 10 or 20 shot mag., parkerized finish, Entreprise Type 03 steel receiver, paratrooper folding stock with pistol grip, zero climb muzzle brake, adj. gas system, carry handle, adj. front sight, adj. rear aperture sight, 9.8 lbs. New 2009.

MSR $1,249	$1,125	$900	$775	$650	$600	$500	$450	

RIFLES: SEMI-AUTO

STG58C RIFLE – .308 Win. cal., paramilitary design, choice of 16 1/2, 21, or 24 in. barrel with muzzle brake, synthetic pistol grip stock, last shot bolt hold open, adj. gas system, mil-spec black oxide finish, 20 shot mag., 200-600 meter aperture sights, supplied with black nylon sling, various configurations, 8 1/2-13 lbs. Mfg. 2000-2009.

* ***STG58C Rifle Lightweight Model*** – 16 1/2 in. barrel, Entreprise Type 03 receiver, 8 1/2 lbs.

	$1,050	$900	$800	$725	$650	$600	$550	$1,199

* ***STG58C Rifle Standard Model*** – 21 in. barrel, Entreprise Type 03 receiver, integral bipod, 9.8 lbs.

	$795	$700	$625	$525	$475	$425	$375	$899

Add $100 for CA configuration.

* ***STG58C Rifle Government Model*** – 21 in. barrel, Entreprise Type 01 receiver, integral bipod, 9 1/2 lbs.

	$1,050	$900	$800	$725	$650	$600	$550	$1,199

* ***STG58C Rifle Target Model*** – 21 in. free float barrel, Entreprise Type 01 receiver, with aluminum handguard, 11 1/2 lbs.

	$1,200	$995	$850	$750	$625	$550	$500	$1,399

* ***STG58C Rifle Match Target Model*** – 24 in. free-float match heavy barrel, Entreprise Type 01 receiver, with aluminum handguard, 13 lbs.

	$1,825	$1,650	$1,475	$1,200	$1,000	$850	$750	$1,999

FAL TARGET MODEL – .308 Win. cal., 21 in. barrel, detachable 10 or 20 shot mag., Entreprise Type 03 receiver, parkerized finish, injection molded free floating aluminum handguard, match grade trigger, lapped fitted bolt and carrier, iron sights, zero climb muzzle brake, injection molded standard buttstock with pistol grip, adj. front sight, adj. rear aperture sight, 9.9 lbs. New 2009.

MSR $1,199	$1,050	$900	$800	$725	$650	$600	$550	

FAL GOVERNMENT MODEL – .308 Win. cal., 21 in. barrel, detachable 10 or 20 shot mag., adj. gas system, carry handle, Entreprise Arm steel receiver, parkerized finish, steel handguard, zero climb muzzle brake, injection molded standard buttstock with pistol grip, adj. front sight, adj. rear aperture sight, 9.9 lbs. New 2009.

MSR $1,149	$1,000	$875	$775	$700	$600	$500	$450	

FAL STANDARD MODEL – .308 Win. cal., 21 in. barrel, detachable 10 or 20 shot mag., adj. gas system, carry handle, Entreprise Type 03 receiver, parkerized finish, injection molded handguard, zero climb muzzle brake, injection molded standard buttstock with pistol grip, adj. front sight, adj. rear aperture sight, 9 1/2 lbs. New 2009.

MSR $959	$850	$750	$650	$550	$500	$450	$400	

GRADING - PPGS™	100%	98%	95%	90%	80%	70%	60%	LAST MSR

ERA

Previous manufacturer located in Brazil.

SHOTGUNS

ERA O/U – 12 or 20 ga., 28 in. vent. rib barrel, full and mod., double triggers, extractors, checkered hardwood stock.

	$275	$250	$225	$200	$170	$150	$125	
Trap version	$300	$275	$250	$225	$200	$175	$150	
Skeet version	$300	$275	$250	$225	$200	$175	$150	

ERA SxS – 12, 20 ga., or .410 bore, 26, 28, or 30 in. barrels, various chokes, double triggers, extractors, checkered pistol grip stock.

	$165	$150	$135	$125	$110	$100	$85	

ERA RIOT SxS – 12 or 20 ga., 18 in. barrels.

	$185	$175	$150	$140	$125	$110	$95	

ERA QUAIL SxS – 12 or 20 ga., 20 in. barrels.

	$185	$175	$150	$140	$125	$110	$95	

ERHARDT, DENNIS

Current custom manufacturer and gunsmith located in Helena, MT.

Dennis Erhardt is a custom maker specializing in modern classic and European style custom rifles and shotguns. Many options and configurations are available. Please contact the company directly for more information and pricing (see Trademark Index).

ERMA SUHL, GmbH

Previous manufacturer located in Suhl, Germany January 1998 - circa 2004. Erma Suhl purchased the remaining assets of Erma-Werke.

RIFLES: BOLT ACTION

SR100 SNIPER RIFLE – .300 Win. Mag., .308 Win., or .338 Lapua Mag. cal., bolt action, tactical rifle featuring brown laminated wood stock with thumbhole, adj. buttplate/cheekpiece, and vent. forend, forged aluminum receiver, 25 1/2 or 29 1/2 in. barrel, muzzle brake, adj. match trigger, approx. 15 lbs. Limited importation 1997-98 only.

	$6,500	$5,750	$5,000	$4,350	$3,750	$3,000	$2,350	*$8,600*

This model was imported exclusively by Amtec 2000, Inc., located in Gardner, MA.

Most recent importation was in .300 Win. Mag., and included a Steyr scope mount.

ERMA-WERKE

Previous manufacturer located in Dachau, Germany (Erma-Werke production) until bankruptcy occurred in October of 1997. Pistols were previously imported and distributed by Precision Sales International, Inc. located in Westfield, MA, Nygord Precision Products located in Prescott, AZ, and Mandall's Shooting Supplies, Inc. located in Scottsdale, AZ. Previously distributed by Excam located in Hialeah, FL.

Erma-Werke also manufactured private label handguns for American Arms Inc. (refer to their section for listings).

PISTOLS: SEMI-AUTO

MODEL LA 22 – .22 LR cal., similar action and styling as the Luger. Mfg. 1964-1967.

	$395	$335	$275	$240	$200	$175	$140	

ERMA KGP68A/BEEMAN MP-08 – .32 ACP or .380 ACP cal., Luger type toggle action, 3 1/2 (Beeman) or 4 in. barrel, 6 shot mag., blue, 1.4 lbs. Mfg. 1968-disc.

	$450	$400	$335	$275	$240	$185	$145	*$500*

This model was imported exclusively by Mandall's Shooting Supplies, Inc. located in Scottsdale, AZ. From 1988-90, Beeman took over importation of this model in .380 ACP cal. only with new Luger

GRADING - PPGS™	100%	98%	95%	90%	80%	70%	60%	LAST MSR

style checkered walnut grips and 3 1/2 in. barrel. Previous models had plastic grips.

ERMA KGP69/BEEMAN P-08 – .22 LR cal., Luger type toggle action, 8 shot mag., 3 3/4 in. barrel, blue, plastic (disc.) or checkered walnut grips. Mfg. 1969-disc.

$335 $275 $240 $185 $145 $115 $95 *$390*

Beeman was the sole importer of this model between 1988-90.

MODEL ESP 85A SPORT/MATCH PISTOL – .22 LR or .32 S&W Long Wadcutter cal., blow back semi-auto, 6 in. barrel, 5 or 8 (.32 S&W only) shot mag., choice of sporting or adj. stippled match grips with thumbrest, fully adj. and interchangeable sights, gun is supplied with 1 extra weight, extra mag., sights, disassembly tools, and attaché style case ($134 option) with foam rubber cut-outs, 2 1/2 lbs. Imported 1989-97.

$1,225 $925 $800 $650 $550 $495 $450 *$1,785*

Subtract $315 for Junior Model.
Add $215 for .32 S&W cal.
Add $110 for Match Model (with anatomical grips).
Add $980-$1,390 for conversion unit.
Add approx. $215 for chrome finish.
Add $24 for left-hand action (Match Model only - disc. 1994).

ESP 85 refers to Junior Model (new 1995). The ESP 85 series was distributed by Precision Sales International, Inc. and Mandall Shooting Supplies, Inc.

* ***Model ESP 85A Sport/Match Pistol Complete Set*** – includes both .22 LR and .32 S&W Long Wadcutter barrels and mags., cased with accessories, complete set was disc. 1991.

$1,525 $1,350 $1,125 $950 $825 $750 $625 *$1,995*

EP-22 – similar to Model LA 22.

$395 $335 $275 $240 $200 $175 $140

ET-22 LUGER CARBINE – .22 LR cal., 11 3/4 in. barrel, blue rear ramp sight, checkered walnut grips and uncheckered forearm, adj. artillery type rear sight, rarely seen.

$500 $400 $350 $300 $250 $200 $175

Add 20% for leatherette case.

EP-25 – .25 ACP cal., 7 shot, 2 3/4 in. barrel, blue finish, fixed sights with grips.

$395 $335 $275 $240 $200 $175 $140

REVOLVERS: DOUBLE ACTION

These models were distributed by Precision Sales International, Inc. only.

ER-772 STANDARD/MATCH – .22 LR cal., standard or match gun with special adj. contoured grips with stippling, 6 in. barrel, action similar to ER-777, fully adj. and extended rear sight, interchangeable front sight, 3 lbs. Imported 1990-94.

$1,100 $875 $725 $625 $550 $495 $450 *$1,371*

ER-773 STANDARD/MATCH – .32 S&W Long Wadcutter cal., otherwise similar to ER-772 Match, 2.9 lbs. Imported 1990-95.

$925 $825 $695 $525 $475 $425 $385 *$1,068*

ER-777 STANDARD – .357 Mag. cal., 6 shot, 4 or 5 1/2 in. barrel, solid rib and full barrel shroud, adj. target rear sight, blue steel, checkered sport grips, 2 3/4 lbs. Imported 1990-95.

$875 $775 $650 $475 $425 $385 $350 *$1,019*

RIFLES

Models listed were available from Mandall Shooting Supplies, unless otherwise noted.

EM-1 .22 CARBINE – .22 LR cal., M1 copy, 10 or 15 shot mag., 18 in. barrel, rear adj. aperture sight, 5.6 lbs. Mfg. 1966-97.

$365 $295 $250 $215 $190 $175 $160 *$400*

EGM-1 – similar to EM-1 except for unslotted buttstock, 5 shot mag.

$260 $230 $195 $175 $150 $125 $100 *$295*

GRADING - PPGS™	100%	98%	95%	90%	80%	70%	60%	LAST MSR

EG-72 PUMP – .22 LR cal., outside hammer, 15 shot mag., 18 1/2 in. barrel. Mfg. 1970-76.

	$125	$95	$90	$75	$70	$65	$60	

EG-712 LEVER-ACTION – .22 LR cal., Win. Model 94 copy, tube mag., 18 1/2 in. barrel. Mfg. 1976-97.

	$260	$230	$195	$175	$150	$125	$100	*$295*

EG-73 – .22 WMR cal., similar to EG-712 12 shot mag. Mfg. 1973-97.

	$265	$230	$195	$175	$150	$125	$100	*$300*

ERN, MAX

Current custom rifle and shotgun manufacturer located in Leverkusen-Schlebusch, Germany. Direct sales through importer/FFL. Previously imported on a limited basis by New England Custom Gun Service, located in Claremont, NH until 2012.

Max Ern builds high quality double (SxS and O/U) rifles, bolt action rifles, and boxlock shotguns. Current models include bolt action Model 98, takedown bolt action Model 98, sidelock single barrel rifle, sidelock SxS double rifle, O/U sidelock double rifle, O/U shotgun, and SxS boxlock shotgun (20 ga.).

A variety of options and special orders are available. Please contact Max Ern directly for more information, including an individualized price quotation, availability, and delivery time (see Trademark Index).

ESCALADE

Previous trademark of slide action shotguns imported until circa 2008 by Mitchell's Mausers, located in Fountain Valley, CA.

SHOTGUNS: SLIDE ACTION

ESCALADE MODEL – 12 ga. only, 18 1/2, 22, or 28 in. chrome lined barrel with choke tubes (except Home Defense model), dual action bars, Turkish walnut checkered stock and grooved forearm, available in Home Defense (18 1/2 in.) or Hunting (22 or 28 in.) configurations. Importation from Turkey 2004-2007.

	$360	$295	$260	$220	$175	$150	$125	*$395*

ESCORT

Current trademark of shotguns manufactured by Hatsan Arms Co., located in Izmir, Turkey, and imported beginning 2002 by Legacy Sports International, located in Reno, NV. Previously located in Alexandria, VA.

SHOTGUNS: O/U

ESCORT – 12 ga. only, 3 in. chambers, 28 in. VR barrels with five choke tubes, boxlock action with choice of blue (disc. 2010) or silver finished receiver, Turkish walnut (disc., reintroduced 2011) or black synthetic stock and forearm with Cobblestone grip inserts, adj. comb, and Trio recoil pad (vent recoil pad became standard during 2009) with three adj. spacers, ST, extractors, fiber optic front sight, 7-8.2 lbs. Importation began 2007.

MSR $639	$550	$475	$425	$350	$315	$275	$250	

Add $50 for hardshell case.

Add $186 for AAA select walnut stock and silver finished receiver (disc.) or $17 for standard checkered walnut stock and forearm.

* ***Escort Shorty Home Defense*** – 12 ga. only, 3 in. chambers, 18 in. VR barrels with choke tubes, fiber optic front sight, accessory rail on lower barrel, nickel plated receiver, black synthetic stock with adj. comb and vent recoil pad, 7 lbs. New 2011.

MSR $659	$575	$500	$450	$365	$325	$285	$265	

SHOTGUNS: SEMI-AUTO

Beginning 2004, all models have a round back receiver with 3/8 in. dovetail milled along top for mounting sights. Beginning in 2009, all Escort semi-auto shotguns use a bottom feed system similar to a Remington 11-87.

GRADING - PPGS™	100%	98%	95%	90%	80%	70%	60%	LAST MSR

ESCORT SERIES - 3 IN. – 12 or 20 (new 2005) ga., 3 in. chamber, gas operated action with 2 position adj. screw (disc. 2003), 20 (disc. 2008), 22 (AS Youth and PS Slug, new 2005), 24 (disc. 2008), 26 (new 2005), or 28 in. VR barrel with 3 multi-chokes, blue finish, vent recoil pad, gold trigger, checkered walnut (Model AS) or polymer (Model PS) black or 100% camo coverage Mossy Oak Break Up (disc. 2004), Mossy Oak Obsession (mfg. 2005-2008), Shadowgrass (disc. 2008), King's Woodland (mfg. 2009-2010), King's Desert (mfg. 2009-2010), or King's Snow (mfg. 2009-2010) camo stock and forearm, 6.4-7 lbs. Importation began 2002.

MSR $489 $395 $350 $325 $285 $250 $225 $195

Add $169 for AS Supreme model with gloss finished walnut stock and forearm. Add $99 for Model PS Slug with rifled slug barrel and cantilever mount (disc. 2011).

Add $182 for AS Select Model with select walnut (mfg. 2007-2008). Add $100 for 100% camo coverage (disc. 2010). Add $74 for HiViz Spark front sight and King's Field metal finish (mfg. 2009). Add $175 for Model PS Slug Combo (mfg. 2006-2008). Add $81 for 24 in. barrel with Model PS TriViz sights and Mossy Oak Break Up camo coverage (disc. 2004).

* ***Escort Series 3 in. Youth AS*** – 20 ga. only, 3 in. chamber, choice of Black synthetic (new 2012) or wood (disc. 2011) or select wood (disc. 2011) stock and forearm, blued metal, 26 in. barrel. New 2009.

MSR $640 $525 $450 $395 $350 $315 $275 $240

Add $58 for select wood (disc. 2011).

* ***Escort Series - 3 in. - Aimguard*** – similar to Escort model, except has black chrome finish, black polymer stock, 18 (new 2006) or 20 (disc. 2005) in. barrel, cylinder bore. Imported 2004-2007.

$340 $295 $275 $250 $230 $215 $195 *$392*

* ***Escort Series - 3 in. - Waterfowl/Tukey Combo*** – includes camo stock and forearm, 24 in. barrel with HiViz and TriViz sights and 28 in. barrel with HiViz Spark sight, hard case. Imported 2003-2008, reintroduced 2010-2011.

$575 $495 $435 $375 $335 $300 $280 *$659*

* ***Escort Series 3 In. Home Defense*** – 12 ga., 18 in. barrel with cyl. bore choke, muzzle brake, receiver features upper Picatinny rail, adj. ghost ring rear sight and adj. fiber optic front sight, black MP-SA TacStock2 with cushioned pistol grip, forearm has Picatinny rail on bottom, 6.9 lbs. New 2011.

MSR $529 $450 $395 $350 $300 $265 $235 $195

ESCORT SERIES - 3 1/2 IN. – 12 ga., 3 1/2 in. chamber, polymer stock and forearm, blued steel or Mossy Oak Obsession (disc. 2008), Shadowgrass (mfg. 2007-2008), or King's (new 2009) camo coverage, 24 or 28 in. barrel with choke tubes, standard or choice of Spark front sight or TriViz sights, 7.6 lbs. Imported 2005-2010.

$400 $350 $315 $280 $250 $230 $215 *$489*

Add $100 for King's Field model with Spark front sight. Add $64 for 24 in. barrel with Model PS TriViz sights and camo coverage (disc. 2008).

EXTREME 3 IN. – 12 or 20 (new 2013, black synthetic only) ga., 3 in. chamber, 26 (new 2013, 20 ga. only) or 28 in. VR barrel with choke tubes, choice of black synthetic, Realtree Max4-HD or Realtree APHD 100% camo finish stock and forearm, 5 Hevi-Shot choke tubes, HiVis sights, right or left hand action, non-slip grip pads on forend and pistol grip, approx. 7.4 lbs. New 2012.

MSR $549 $475 $425 $365 $335 $295 $275 $250

Add $180 for 100% camo finish.

* ***Extreme 3 In. Turkey*** – 12 ga. only, 24 in. barrel with extended turkey choke tube, pistol grip stock, receiver Picatinny rail, 100% Realtree AP camo coverage, raised Hi-Vis sights, 7.4 lbs. New 2012.

MSR $659 $550 $475 $425 $365 $325 $285 $250

GRADING - PPGS™	100%	98%	95%	90%	80%	70%	60%	LAST MSR

EXTREME 3 1/2 IN. MAGNUM – 12 ga., 3 1/2 in. chamber, 28 in. VR barrel with choke tubes, choice of black synthetic, Realtree Max4-HD, or Realtree APHD 100% camo finish stock and forearm, 5 Hevi-Shot choke tubes, right or left hand action, HiVis sights, non-slip grip pads on forend and pistol grip, approx. 7.4 lbs. New 2012.

MSR $649	$550	$475	$400	$365	$335	$300	$275	

Add $150 for 100% Realtree Max4-HD or Realtree APHD camo finish.

EXTREME WATERFOWL 3 IN. – 12 ga., 28 in. nickel chromemoly lined barrel, multichokes, Hi Viz Magni fiber optic front sight, sling swivel studs, raised vent rib, black synthetic (mfg. 2011 only), 100% Avery Buckbrush, Killer Weed, Realtree Max4 (new mid-2011), or Realtree AP (new mid-2011) camo coverage, also available in left hand, 7.4 lbs. New 2011.

MSR $790	$695	$625	$550	$500	$450	$400	$350	

* ***Extreme Waterfowl Youth*** – 20 ga., 3 in. chamber, 22 in. VR barrel with M-3 Trio choke tubes, includes Trio recoil pad, choice of wood, black synthetic, Realtree Max-4 or Realtree AP 100% camo coverage, sling swivel studs, 6.35 lbs. New 2012.

MSR $499	$450	$395	$350	$300	$275	$250	$225	

Add $26 for wood stock.
Add $50 for Realtree Max-4 or Realtree AP camo coverage.

EXTREME WATERFOWL 3 1/2 IN. – 12 ga., 28 in. nickel chromemoly lined barrel, multichokes, Hi Viz Magni fiber optic front sight, sling swivel studs, raised vent rib, black synthetic (mfg. 2011 only), 100% Avery Buckbrush, Killer Weed, Realtree Max4 (new mid-2011), or Realtree AP (new mid-2011) camo coverage, also available in left hand, 7.4 lbs. New 2011.

MSR $873	$775	$675	$575	$500	$450	$400	$350	

SUPREME – 12 or 20 ga., SMART Valve self-regulating gas piston, aluminum alloy receiver, 26 or 28 in. nickel chrome moly barrel with raised vent. rib and 5 choke tubes, right or left-hand action, FAST loading system, premium Turkish walnut stock with two adjustment shims, sling swivels, fiber optic front sight, 7.4 lbs. New 2013.

MSR $603	$515	$450	$375	$350	$275	$225	$180	

TURKEY/COYOTE TACTICAL – FAST loading system, 24 in. chrome moly barrel, extended full choke Turkey tube, fiber optic ghost ring sights, 100% Realtree AP camo stock with cushioned pistol grip, built-in shell storage in the stock, upper and lower Picatinny rails, mag. cut off, sling swivel studs included. New 2013.

As this edition went to press, pricing had yet to be established on this model.

SHOTGUNS: SLIDE ACTION

ESCORT SERIES – 12 or 20 (new 2005) ga., 3 in. chamber, matte blue finish or 100% camo coverage with polymer stock and forearm, 18 (Aimguard or MarineGuard Model), 22 (Field Slug, new 2005), 24 (Turkey, includes extra turkey choke tube and FH TriViz sight combo with Mossy Oak Break Up [disc. 2004] or Obsession camo coverage), 26 (new 2005, Field Hunter), or 28 (Field Hunter) in. barrel, alloy receiver with 3/8 in. milled dovetail for sight mounting, trigger guard safety, 4 or 5 shot mag. with cut off button, two stock adj. shims, 6.4-7 lbs. Importation began 2003.

* ***Escort Series Field Hunter*** – 12 or 20 ga., 24 (disc. 2008), 26 (new 2009), or 28 in. barrel, black synthetic stock, 100% Mossy Oak Obsession (disc. 2008), Shadowgrass (disc. 2008), or King's Woodland (mfg. 2009-2010) camo coverage or matte blue finish, includes 3 choke tubes, 6-7.4 lbs.

MSR $379	$330	$275	$250	$225	$200	$180	$160	

Add $40 for Slug with rifled barrel and cantilever mount (disc. 2011).
Add $80 for 100% camo coverage. and Spark front sight (disc. 2010). Add $23 for combo in 12 ga. (disc. 2006). Add $100 for FH TriViz sights in Obsession camo finish with extra Turkey choke tube (disc. 2008). Add $144 for Slug Combo (disc. 2006).

* ***Escort Series Field Youth*** – 20 ga. only, 3 in. chamber, 22 in. barrel, black synthetic stock and forearm with Trio recoil pad, choice of blued metal or 100% King's Woodland (disc. 2010) camo coverage, 5.8 lbs. New 2009.

MSR $389	$350	$295	$260	$230	$200	$180	$160	

GRADING - PPGS™	100%	98%	95%	90%	80%	70%	60%	LAST MSR

Add $23 for Youth Slug model with 22 in. rifled barrel (mfg. 2011 only).
Add $80 for camo (disc. 2010).

* ***Escort Series Aimguard*** – 12 ga., 18 in. barrel with black synthetic stock, fixed cyl. bore choke, 6.4 lbs.

MSR $299	**$250**	**$225**	**$195**	**$175**	**$150**	**$135**	**$120**	

* ***Escort Series Marine Guard*** – 12 ga., 18 in. barrel with black synthetic stock, nickel receiver, 5 shot mag., fixed cyl. bore choke, 6.4 lbs.

MSR $369	**$325**	**$285**	**$250**	**$225**	**$200**	**$185**	**$150**	

* ***Escort Series Home Defense (Tactical Entry/Special Ops)*** – 12 ga. only, 3 in. chamber, 18 in. barrel, synthetic stock, cushioned vertical pistol grip, available in a variety of configurations, forearm features upper and lower Picatinny rail, current mfg. features the MP-P/A TacStock2 with pistol grip and built in holder for two extra shells, fiber optic front sight, fully adj. ghost ring rear, 6.85 lbs. New 2009.

MSR $399	**$350**	**$295**	**$260**	**$225**	**$200**	**$180**	**$160**	

Subtract approx. 15% if w/o TacStock2 (new 2010).

EUROARMS ITALIA Srl

Previous black powder replica manufacturer and current importer/exporter located in Concesio, Italy.

Euroarms Italia was the new name for Armi San Paolo, and was established during 2002. Euroarms Italia exported its black powder reproductions and accessories through Euroarms of America, Dixie Gun Works, Cabela's, and Navy Arms. It ceased operation during late 2011.

EUROARMS OF AMERICA

Previous black powder replica importer and distributor located in Winchester, VA circa 1970-2011. Manufactured by Euroarms Italia Srl, established 1970, and located in Concesio, Italy. The factory was previously named Armi San Paolo until 2002.

Euroarms imported a variety of firearms, including revolvers and rifles, mfg. by Armi San Paolo between 1970-1996. Values were determined by other similar competitive makes and models, and the condition factor.

Please refer to the *Blue Book of Modern Black Powder Arms* by John Allen (also online) for more information and prices on Euroarms of America's quality lineup of modern black powder reproductions and replicas.

Black Powder Revolvers - Reproductions & Replicas and *Black Powder Long Arms & Pistols - Reproductions & Replicas* by Dennis Adler are also invaluable sources for most black powder revolver reproductions and replicas, and include hundreds of color images on most popular makes/models, provide manufacturer/trademark histories, and up-to-date information on related items/accessories for black powder shooting - www.bluebookofgunvalues.com

EUROPEAN AMERICAN ARMORY CORP.

Current importer and distributor established in late 1990 and located in Rockledge, FL. Previously located in Sharpes, FL 1990-2006. Distributor and dealer sales.

EAA currently imports the Tanfoglio Witness series of semi-auto pistols, located in Italy, H. Weihrach revolvers, located in Germany, and select Zastava firearms, located in Serbia. All guns are covered by EAA's lifetime limited warranty. EAA has also imported various trademarks of long guns, including Saiga, and Izhmash. Please refer to those individual sections.

Baikal shotguns, Zastava Z98 and Z5 bolt actions, Sarpa slide action shotguns manufactured by Sarzilmaz, and Sabatti double rifles are currently imported by U.S. Sporting Goods Inc. Please refer to individual listings for more information and current pricing.

PISTOLS: SEMI-AUTO

EAA has issued a safety upgrade notice regarding any Witness style semi-auto pistol bearing a serial number between AE00000 - AE700000. Owners are requested to field strip the pistol and

GRADING - PPGS™	100%	98%	95%	90%	80%	70%	60%	LAST MSR

send the slide assembly directly to EAA. EAA will replace the firing pin and return it to you. See Trademark Index for contact information.

The following Witness pistols also have a .22 LR conversion kit available for $234.

WITNESS EA 9 SERIES – 9mm Para. cal., action patterned after the CZ-75, selective double action, 4 1/2 in. unported or ported (polymer, New Frame only, new 2002) barrel, steel or polymer frame/steel slide (new 1997), 10 (C/B 1994), 16*, or 18 (new late 2004) shot mag., choice of Wonder (new 1997), stainless steel (disc. 1996), blue, blue/chrome (disc. 1993), or brushed chrome (disc. 1996) finish, combat sights, black neoprene grips, 33 oz. Importation began late 1990.

MSR $557	$460	$410	$365	$315	$280	$230	$185	

Add $134 for 9mm Para/.22 LR combo. Subtract $32 for polymer New Frame.

* ***Model EA 9 Stainless*** – similar to EA 9, except is stainless steel. Imported 1992-96.

	$420	$365	$315	$285	$230	$190	$145	*$480*

* ***Model EA 9 (L) Compact*** – similar to EA 9, except has 3 5/8 in. unported or ported (polymer frame only, mfg. 2002-2006) barrel and 10 (C/ B 1994), 12 (new late 2004), or 13* shot mag., 27 oz.

MSR $557	$460	$410	$365	$315	$280	$230	$185	

Subtract $32 for polymer frame.

Add $10-$20 for ported barrel (polymer frame only, disc. 2006).

WITNESS EA 10 SUPER SERIES – 10mm cal., action patterned after the CZ-75, selective double action, 4 1/2 in. barrel, polymer or steel frame, 10, 12*, or 15 (new late 2004) shot mag., choice of stainless steel (disc.), blue, chrome (disc.), or Wonder (new 1999) finish, combat sights, black neoprene grips, 33 oz. Imported 1994 only, and 1999-current.

MSR $557	$460	$410	$365	$315	$280	$230	$185	

Add $30 for chrome finish (disc.).

Add $65 for stainless steel (disc.).

Subtract $32 for polymer frame.

* ***Model EA 10 Stainless*** – similar to EA 10, except is stainless steel.

	$495	$435	$370	$335	$270	$225	$175	*$566*

* ***Model EA 10 Carry Comp*** – similar to EA 10, except has 4 1/2 in. compensated barrel, blue or Wonder (new 2005) finish. Mfg. 1999-2005.

	$415	$365	$310	$280	$230	$185	$145	*$489*

Subtract $20 for blue finish.

* ***Model EA 10 Compact*** – similar to EA 10, except has 3 5/8 in. barrel, 8 or 12 (new late 2004) shot mag., 27 oz.

MSR $557	$460	$410	$365	$315	$280	$230	$185	

Subtract $32 for polymer frame.

WITNESS EA 38 SUPER SERIES – .38 Super cal., action patterned after the CZ-75, selective double action, 4 1/2 in. barrel, steel or polymer frame/steel slide (mfg. 1997-2004), 10 (C/B 1994), 18 (new late 2004) or 19* shot mag., choice of Wonder (heat treated grey satin finish, new 1997), stainless steel (disc. 1996), blue (disc.), blue/chrome (disc. 1994), or brushed chrome (disc. 1996) finish, combat sights, black neoprene grips, 33 oz. Importation began 1994.

MSR $557	$460	$410	$365	$315	$280	$230	$185	

Subtract $31 for polymer frame (disc. 2004).

* ***Model EA 38 Stainless*** – similar to EA 38, except is stainless steel. Imported 1994-96.

	$525	$460	$395	$355	$290	$235	$185	*$595*

* ***Model EA 38 Compact*** – similar to EA 38 Super Series, except has 3 5/8 in. unported or ported barrel, choice of matte blue or Wonder finish, 30 oz. Mfg. 1999-2004.

	$370	$325	$275	$250	$205	$165	$130	*$449*

Subtract $20 for polymer frame.

Add $20 for Wonder finish or ported barrel (polymer frame only).

GRADING - PPGS™	100%	98%	95%	90%	80%	70%	60%	LAST MSR

WITNESS EA 40 SERIES – .40 S&W cal., action patterned after the CZ-75, selective double action, 4 1/2 in. barrel, steel or polymer frame/steel slide (new 1997), 10 (C/B 1994), 12*, or 15 (new late 2004) shot mag., choice of Wonder (new 1997), stainless steel (disc. 1996), blue, blue/chrome (disc.), or brushed chrome (disc. 1996) finish, combat sights, black neoprene grips, 33 oz. Importation began late 1990.

MSR $557	$460	$410	$365	$315	$280	$230	$185	

Subtract $32 for polymer New Frame.

* ***Model EA 40 Stainless*** – similar to EA 40, except is stainless steel. Imported 1992-96.

	$455	$400	$340	$310	$250	$205	$160	*$509*

* ***Model EA 40 (L) Compact*** – similar to EA 40, except has 3 5/8 in. unported or ported barrel, 9 or 12 (new late 2004) shot mag.

MSR $557	$460	$410	$365	$315	$280	$230	$185	

Subtract $32 for polymer frame.
Add $10-$20 for ported barrel (polymer frame only, disc. 2005).

WITNESS EA 41 SERIES – .41 Action Express cal., action patterned after the CZ-75, selective double action, 4 1/2 in. barrel, steel frame, 11 shot mag., blue, blue/chrome, or brushed chrome finish, combat sights, black neoprene grips, 33 oz. Importation disc. 1993.

	$450	$395	$335	$305	$245	$200	$155	*$595*

Add $40 for blue/chrome or brushed chrome finish.

* ***Model EA 41 Compact*** – similar to EA 41, except has 3 1/2 in. barrel and 8 shot mag.

	$495	$435	$370	$335	$270	$225	$175	*$625*

Add $40 for blue/chrome or brushed chrome finish.

WITNESS EA 45 SERIES – .45 ACP cal., action patterned after the CZ-75, selective double action, 4 1/2 in. standard or compensated (mfg. 1998-2005) barrel, steel frame, polymer full size frame (new 2004), or polymer frame/steel slide (new 1997), 10 (C/ B 1994) or 11* shot mag., choice of Wonder (new 1997), stainless steel (disc. 1996), blue, blue/ chrome (disc. 1993), or brushed chrome (disc. 1996) finish, combat sights, walnut grips, 35 oz. Importation began late 1990.

MSR $557	$460	$410	$365	$315	$280	$230	$185	

Add $134 for .45 ACP/.22 LR combo.
Add $40 for ported barrel (steel only, with Wonder finish, disc. 2004).
Subtract $32 for polymer frame or blue finish.

* ***Model EA 45 Stainless*** – similar to EA 45, except is stainless steel. Imported 1992-96.

	$510	$445	$380	$345	$280	$230	$180	*$595*

* ***Model EA 45 (L) Compact*** – similar to EA 45, except has 3 5/8 in. unported or ported barrel and 8 shot mag., 26 oz.

MSR $557	$460	$410	$365	$315	$280	$230	$185	

Add $30 for ported barrel (polymer frame only, disc. 2004).
Add $50 for single port barrel compensator or carry configuration with compensator (disc.).
Subtract $32 for polymer frame.

WITNESS P CARRY – 9mm Para., 10mm, .40 S&W, or .45 ACP cal., SA/DA, 3.6 in. barrel, 10 (.45 ACP), 15 (10mm or .40 S&W), or 17 (9mm Para.) shot mag., full size polymer frame, compact slide, Commander style, Wonder finish, integral M-1913 rail, 27 oz. New 2006.

MSR $635	$525	$450	$395	$350	$300	$265	$220	

WITNESS CARRY COMP GUN – .38 Super (disc. 1997), 9mm Para. (disc. 1997), .40 S&W cal. (disc. 1997), 10mm (disc. 1994, reintroduced 1999), or .45 ACP cal., full size frame with compact slide and 1 in. compensator, 10 (C/B 1994), 12* (.40 S&W), or 16* (9mm Para.) shot mag., Wonder (new 1997), blue, Duo-Tone (disc. 1994) finish. Imported 1992-2004.

	$425	$370	$320	$290	$235	$190	$150	*$479*

Add $10 for Wonder finish.

GRADING - PPGS™	100%	98%	95%	90%	80%	70%	60%	LAST MSR

WITNESS SPORT – .38 Super, 9mm Para., .40 S&W, 10mm (disc. 1994), or .45 ACP cal., 4 1/2 in. barrel, full size frame, standard slide length, Duo-Tone finish, extended safety and high capacity mag., target sights. Imported 1994-95.

	$535	$470	$400	$365	$295	$240	$185	*$616*

Add $86 for .38 Super, 10mm, or .45 ACP cal.

WITNESS SPORT LONG SLIDE – .38 Super, 9mm Para., .40 S&W, 10mm (disc. 1994), or .45 ACP cal., long slide variation of the EA Series, except has 4 3/4 in. ported or unported barrel and slide, Duo-Tone finish, extended safety and high capacity mag., competition sights, 34 1/2 oz. Importation disc. 1995.

	$595	$520	$445	$405	$325	$270	$210	*$681*

Add $79 for .38 Super, 10mm, or .45 ACP cal.

WITNESS LIMITED CLASS – .38 Super, 9mm Para., .40 S&W, or .45 ACP cal., match frame, competition grips, high capacity mag., single action trigger, long slide with match barrel and super sight, extended safety, blue finish only. Imported 1994-98.

	$855	$750	$640	$580	$470	$385	$300	*$967*

* ***Witness Limited*** – 9mm Para., 10mm, .38 Super, .40 S&W, or .45 ACP cal., 4 3/4 in. barrel, competition hard chrome frame, 10 (.45 ACP), 15 (.40 S&W or 10mm), or 18 (9mm Para. or .38 Super) shot mag., square trigger guard, full length dust shroud, cone slide lock up, checkered frame and back strap, skeletonized hammer, low profile checkered walnut grips, 39 oz. Importation began 2005.

MSR $1,344	$1,175	$975	$825	$725	$595	$475	$375	

* ***Witness Limited Pro*** – similar to Witness Limited, except that small parts, including trigger, mag. release, hammer, rear sight, and frame controls are finished in black. New 2012.

MSR $1,028	$900	$800	$700	$625	$550	$450	$395	

WITNESS COMBO PACKAGE – includes one built up frame and 9mm Para./.40 S&W complete conversion kits, blue, chrome, or Duo-Tone (disc. 1994) finish, full size variation with 4 1/2 in. barrel. Imported 1992-97.

	$515	$450	$385	$350	$285	$230	$180	*$588*

Add $29 for chrome or Duo-Tone finish.

* ***Witness Combo Package (L) Compact*** – similar to Witness Combo Package, except has 3 5/8 in. barrels, blue only. Imported 1994-97.

	$515	$450	$385	$350	$285	$230	$180	*$588*

WITNESS MULTI-CLASS PISTOL PACKAGE – .38 Super, 9mm Para., 9x21mm, .40 S&W, or .45 ACP cal., consists of one Witness Limited Class Pistol and complete Unlimited Class top half (slide and barrel), dual chamber steel compensator, blue finish only. Imported 1994 only.

	$1,450	$1,270	$1,085	$985	$795	$650	$505	*$1,638*

WITNESS TRI-CALIBER PACKAGE – includes one built up frame and caliber conversions (9mm Para., .40 S&W, and .41 AE), which include slide, barrel, recoil guide, and spring, matte blue or chrome finish, compact or full size variations, includes carry case. Imported 1992-1993 only.

	$975	$855	$730	$665	$535	$440	$340	*$1,195*

Add $40 for chrome finish.

WITNESS SILVER TEAM – .38 Super, 9mm Para., 9x21mm, 10mm (disc. 1994), .40 S&W, or .45 ACP cal., dual chamber compensator, SA trigger, super sight, drilled and tapped for scope mount, competition features include hammer, extended safety, paddle mag. release, black rubber grips, double-dip blue finish, high capacity mag. Imported 1992-98.

	$855	$750	$640	$580	$470	$385	$300	*$967*

WITNESS GOLD TEAM – .38 Super, 9mm Para., 9x21mm, 10mm (disc. 1994), .40 S&W, or .45 ACP cal., triple chamber compensator, SA trigger, super sight, drilled and tapped for scope mount, top-of-the-line competition model featuring hand-fitted major components and 25 LPI checkering, hard chrome finish. Imported 1992-98.

	$1,875	$1,640	$1,405	$1,275	$1,030	$845	$655	*$2,150*

GRADING - PPGS™	100%	98%	95%	90%	80%	70%	60%	LAST MSR

This model was also available as a frame only - retail was $389.

* ***Witness Gold Team*** – 9mm Para., .38 Super, .40 S&W, or .45 ACP cal., 5 1/4 in. barrel, triple chamber compensator, 15 (.40 S&W or .45 ACP) or 18 (9mm Para. or .38 Super) shot mag., competition hard chrome frame, tapered cone slide/barrel lock up, checkered frame and back strap, competition hammer and safety, super sight, aluminum grips, 44 oz. Importation began 2005.

MSR $2,145	$1,875	$1,600	$1,350	$1,175	$940	$765	$595	

WITNESS FCP – .380 ACP, .38 Super, .38 Spl., 9mm Para., .40 S&W, or .45 ACP cal., polymer frame, DAO, blue finish, 6 shot non-detachable mag., 4 in. barrel, fast cycle tube chamber, utitlizes simple reusable tubes that encase each round, no detachable mag., 26 oz. Disc. 2007.

	$185	$160	$140	$125	$100	$85	$65	*$219*

WITNESS HUNTER – 10mm or .45 ACP cal., 6 in. barrel, competition hard chrome frame, 10 (.45 ACP) or 15 (10mm) shot mag., checkered frame, blue or camo finish, tapered cone slide/barrel lock up, drilled and tapped, single action, extended manual safety, low profile heavy duty adj. front sight, 41 oz. Importation began 2005.

MSR $1,187	$1,025	$895	$775	$675	$550	$450	$350	

WITNESS MATCH – 9mm Para., 10mm, .38 Super, .40 S&W, or .45 ACP cal., 4 3/4 in. polygonal rifled barrel, competition frame, SA, trigger over-travel, adj. rear sights, extended mag. release, rubber grips, two-tone finish, 33 oz. Importation began 2006.

MSR $715	$585	$495	$425	$375	$315	$265	$225	

WITNESS STOCK – 9mm Para., 10mm, .40 S&W, or .45 ACP cal., 4 1/2 in. barrel, competition hard chrome frame, 10 (.45 ACP), 15 (.40 S&W or 10mm) or 18 (9mm Para.) shot mag., tapered cone slide/barrel lock up, checkered frame and back strap, extended safety, adj. sights, diamond checkered walnut grips, heart shaped hammer, 33 oz. Importation began 2005.

MSR $1,013	$875	$775	$650	$550	$450	$375	$325	

Add $115 for SA/DA with full shroud.

F.A.B. 92 – 9mm Para. or .40 S&W cal., double action featuring hammer drop safety and decocker (Witness style), 4 1/2 in. barrel, 16* (9mm Para.), 12* (.40 S&W), or 10 (C/B 1994) shot mag., all steel construction, blue, chrome (disc. 1993), or Duo-Tone (disc. 1993) finish, smooth wood grips, 33 oz. Imported 1992-95.

	$335	$295	$250	$225	$185	$150	$115	*$386*

Add $40 for chrome or Duo-Tone finish.
Add $29 for .40 S&W cal.

F.A.B. designates Foreign American Brands.

* ***F.A.B. 92 Compact*** – similar to F.A.B. 92, except has 3 5/8 in. barrel, 13* (9mm Para.), 10 (9mm only, C/B 1994), or 9 (.40 S&W) shot mag., 30 oz. Imported 1992-95.

	$335	$295	$250	$225	$185	$150	$115	*$386*

Add $40 for chrome or Duo-Tone finish.
Add $29 for .40 S&W cal.

SAR K2 – 9mm Para., .40 S&W, 10mm or .45 ACP cal., 4 1/2 in. barrel, blue finish, DA/SA, 14 (.45 ACP), 17 (.40 S&W and 10mm), or 18 (9mm Para.) shot mag., steel frame and slide, ergonomic grip, accessory rail, extended beavertail, elongated trigger guard with serrations, removable dovetail front sight, mfg. by Sarsilmaz for Turkish military, 40 oz. Importation began mid-2011.

MSR $660	$550	$475	$425	$365	$315	$265	$235	

ZASTAVA EZ – 9mm Para., .40 S&W, or .45 ACP (disc. 2010) cal., DA/SA, ambidextrous controls, 10 (.45 ACP), 11 (.40 S&W), or 15 (9mm Para.) shot mag., 4 in. barrel, aluminum frame, accessory rail, spur hammer, blue or chrome finish, 33 oz. Imported 2007-2011.

	$495	$435	$375	$335	$285	$250	$215	*$573*

Add $47 for chrome finish (disc. 2010).

GRADING - PPGS™	100%	98%	95%	90%	80%	70%	60%	LAST MSR

* ***Zastava EZ Compact*** – similar to Zastava EZ Model, except has compact frame, 7 (.45 ACP), 8 (.40 S&W), or 12 shot mag., 3 1/2 in. barrel. Imported 2007-2010.

$495 $435 $375 $335 $285 $250 $215 *$573*

Add $47 for chrome finish (disc. 2010).
Subtract 10% if without ported barrel (disc. 2010).

ZASTAVA M88 – 9mm Para. or .40 S&W (disc. 2010) cal., SA, 6 or 8 shot mag., 3.6 in. barrel, blue finish, compact frame, 28 oz. Imported 2008-2011.

$265 $225 $190 $170 $135 $110 $85 *$309*

Add $16 for .40 S&W cal. (disc. 2010).

ZASTAVA EZ CARRY – 9mm Para. or .40 S&W cal., full size frame, 3 1/2 in. ported barrel, 10 or 14 shot mag. Imported 2010-2011.

$550 $495 $450 $395 $350 $300 $250 *$619*

PISTOLS: SEMI-AUTO, EUROPEAN SERIES

MODEL EA220 – .22 LR cal., 3.88 in. barrel, 10 shot mag., single action, steel frame, 26 oz., blue, chrome or blue/chrome, wood grips. Importation disc. 1992.

$185 $160 $140 $125 $100 $85 $65 *$225*

Add approx. $20 for chrome or blue/chrome finish.

MODEL EA22-T – .22 LR cal., 6 in. barrel, cocking indicator and grip safety, 5 or 12 shot mag., adj. trigger and grip, single action, steel frame, target model, 40 oz. Imported 1991-93.

$375 $330 $280 $255 $205 $170 $130 *$450*

EUROPEAN 32 (320) – .32 ACP cal., 3.88 in. barrel, 7 shot mag., single action, steel frame, 26 oz., blue, chrome or blue/chrome, wood grips. Importation 1991-95.

$130 $115 $95 $90 $70 $60 $45 *$161*

Add $14 for chrome finish.

EUROPEAN 380 – .380 ACP cal., single (new 1994) or double (disc. 1994) action, 3 7/8 in. barrel, blue, brushed chrome (disc. 1996), Wonder (new 1997), matte blue/chrome (disc. 1993), or blue/gold plated Duo-Tone (European Lady, disc. 1995) finish, 7 shot bottom release mag., steel construction, firing pin safety, external hammer, smooth wood or ivory rose polymer (European Lady) grips, 26 oz. Imported 1992-2001.

$145 $125 $110 $100 $80 $65 $50 *$179*

Add $9 for Wonder finish (new 1997).
Add $67 for European Lady model (disc. 1995).
Add $32 for double action design (disc. 1994).
Add $14 for brushed chrome or matte blue/chrome (disc. 1993) finish.
This model employed a unique patented magazine gun lock system.

PISTOLS: SINGLE SHOT

THOR RAPTOR – .223 Rem., .270 Win., .30-06, .300 Win. Mag., .308 Win., .375 Win., .44 Mag., .45-70 Govt., .500 S&W, 7mm-08 Rem., or 7mm Rem. cal., blue steel frame, 14 in. barrel with polygonal rifling, single action, rubber grips, auto ejector, integral sight base, 5 lbs. Imported 2005 only.

$895 $785 $670 $610 $490 $405 $315 *$1,099*

REVOLVERS: DOUBLE ACTION, WINDICATOR SERIES

WINDICATOR STANDARD GRADE – .22 LR (disc.), .22LR/.22 WMR combo. (disc.), .22 WMR (disc.), .32 H&R (disc. 1993), .357 Mag. (new 1994), or .38 Spl. (alloy frame only) cal., 2 (.32 H&R, .357 Mag., or .38 Spl. only), 4 (new 1997), or 6 (disc.) in. squared off barrel, blue, chrome (.38 Spl. only, new 1994-disc.) or nickel finish, steel or alloy frame, 6 (.38 Spl.), 7 (.32 H&R), or 8 (.22 LR/.22 WMR) shot, finger grooved rubber grips. Importation from Germany began 1992.

MSR $303 $260 $225 $185 $155 $125 $100 $80

Add $14 for 4 in. barrel.
Add $73 for nickel finish.

GRADING - PPGS™	100%	98%	95%	90%	80%	70%	60%	LAST MSR

Add $16 for steel frame in .357 Mag. cal.
Add $78 for .22 LR/.22 WMR combo. (disc.).

WINDICATOR TACTICAL GRADE – .38 Spl. cal. only, fixed sights, 6 shot, 2 in. (bobbed hammer) or 4 in. compensated barrel, blue finish only. Imported 1992-93.

	$220	$190	$165	$150	$120	$100	$75	*$295*

Add $80 for 4 in. compensated barrel.

WINDICATOR TARGET GRADE – .22 LR, .357 Mag., or .38 Spl. cal., 6 or 8 (.22 LR) shot, 6 in. squared off barrel, finger grooved hardwood stocks, adj. trigger pull and rear sight, blue finish only, 3.1 lbs. Imported 1992-1993.

	$425	$370	$320	$290	$235	$190	$150	*$550*

REVOLVERS: SAA, BOUNTY HUNTER SERIES

MODEL EASAB – .22 LR cal., single action revolver, 6 shot, 4 3/4 in. barrel, blue or chrome (disc. 1991) finish, wood grips. Importation disc. 1995.

	$70	$60	$50	$45	$40	$30	$25	*$85*

Add $20 for chrome finish.

MODEL EASAMB COMBO – includes .22 LR and .22 WMR cal. cylinders, 4 3/4 (standard), 6, or 9 in. barrel, blue finish, wood grips. Importation disc. 1995.

	$85	$75	$65	$55	$45	$40	$30	*$100*

Add $14 for 9 in. barrel.
Add $40 for gold plated gripstrap and trigger guard (disc.).

BIG BORE BOUNTY HUNTER – .357 Mag., .44-40 WCF (mfg. 2005-2008, 7 1/2 in. barrel only), .44 Mag., or .45 LC cal., 4 1/2 (new 1994), 5 1/2 (disc. 1993), or 7 1/2 in. barrel, 6 shot, choice of blue, chrome (mfg. 1994-95), nickel (new 1998), or case colored finish, gold plated trigger guard/gripstraps (disc. 1994), or gold (disc.) finish, 32-41 oz. New 1992.

MSR $446	$365	$315	$275	$240	$195	$165	$140	

Add $32 for nickel finish.
Add $20 for chrome finish (disc.).
Add $15 for gold-plated grip strap and trigger guard (disc.).
Add approx. $100 for gold plated finish (disc.)

* ***Small Bore Bounty Hunter Combo*** – includes .22 LR/.22 WMR cal. cylinders, 4 3/4 or 6 3/4 in. barrel, half cock mechanism and transfer bar safety, choice of 6, 8, or 10 shot, blue or nickel (new 1998) finish. New 1997.

MSR $320	$270	$230	$190	$170	$135	$110	$85	

Add $34 for nickel finish.
Add $132 for steel frame with 10 shot cylinder.

RIFLES

Some EAA rifles were manufactured by Sabatti in Italy (est. 1674), Lu-Mar in Italy, and H. Weihrauch in Germany (see separate listing in the H. Weihrauch section). Imported 1992-96.

SP1822 SEMI-AUTO SPORTER – .22 LR cal., semi-auto, 18 1/2 in. barrel, wood stock and forearm, adj. sights, 10 shot box mag., 5 1/4-6 1/2 lbs. Imported 1994-96.

	$180	$145	$120	$100	$90	$80	$70	*$206*

* ***SP1822 Semi-Auto Sporter Thumbhole*** – similar to Sporter, except has one-piece Bell & Carlson green synthetic thumbhole stock, without sights. Importation disc. 1995.

	$310	$260	$230	$200	$175	$150	$135	*$358*

ZASTAVA PAP 762 SEMI-AUTO – 7.62x39mm cal., patterned after the AK-47, blond hardwood thumbhole stock and furniture, 10 shot mag., 16 3/4 in. barrel, removable accessory rail, 10 lbs. Importation began 2008.

MSR $488	$435	$375	$335	$295	$265	$240	$220	

TANFOGLIO APPEAL SEMI-AUTO – .22 LR or .22 WMR cal., bull pup design, 16 in. barrel with muzzle brake, features elevated Picatinny rail, adj. front and rear sights, ambidextrous

GRADING - PPGS™	100%	98%	95%	90%	80%	70%	60%	LAST MSR

controls, black synthetic thumbhole stock with pistol grip has adj. LOP, 10 shot mag., black finish, 4.8 lbs. Importation began 2012.

MSR $414	$365	$315	$285	$260	$240	$220	$195	

Add $14 for .22 WMR cal.

ROVER 870 BOLT ACTION – .22-250 Rem., .243 Win., .25-06 Rem., .270 Win., .30-06, .308 Win., 7mm Rem. Mag., .300 Win. Mag., or .338 Win. Mag. cal., bolt action rifle featuring all-steel construction with 22 in. hammer-forged rifled barrel, staggered 5 shot internal mag., open sights. Imported 1993 only.

	$795	$695	$600	$550	$495	$450	$395	*$995*

M-93 BLACK ARROW BOLT ACTION – .50 BMG cal., Mauser action, 36 in. fluted heavy barrel with muzzle brake, adj. folding bipod, iron sights, detachable 5 shot mag., carry handle, detachable scope mount, wood case, 35 lbs. Mfg. by Zastava, imported 2007-2011.

	$6,400	$5,800	$5,000	$4,250	$3,500	$2,900	$2,300	*$6,986*

Z5 BOLT ACTION – .17 HMR (disc. 2010), .22 LR, or .22 WMR cal., 16 (Youth) or 20 in. blue barrel, 5 shot mag., checkered pistol grip walnut stock and forearm, mfg. by Zastava. Imported 2009-2011.

	$240	$210	$185	$170	$155	$140	$125	*$276*

Add $12 for .17 HMR (disc. 2010) or .22 WMR cal.

Z98 BOLT ACTION – .243 Win., .25-06 Rem. (Mfg. 2009), .270 Win., .30-06, .308 Win., 7mm Rem. Mag., .300 Win. Mag., .375 H&H, or .458 Win. Mag. cal., 22 or 24 in. blue or stainless (mfg. 2009) steel barrel, black synthetic pistol grip stock, controlled round feeding, steel floor plate, large claw extractor, drilled and tapped, non-glare finish, mfg. by Zastava. Imported 2009-2011.

	$450	$400	$375	$350	$325	$295	$275	*$522*

Add $21 for 7mm Rem. Mag. or .308 Win. Mag. cal.
Add $192 for .375 H&H or .458 Win. Mag. cal.
Add $22 for 7mm Rem. Mag. or .300 Win. Mag.

* ***Z98 Bolt Action Target*** – .270 Win., .30-06, .308 Win., 7mm Rem. Mag., or .300 Win. Mag. cal., 22 or 24 in. blue barrel, walnut thumbhole stock with raised cheekpiece, machined steel receiver, scope rail, short extractors, 3 or 4 shot detachable box mag., mfg. by Zastava. Imported 2009-2011.

	$925	$825	$725	$625	$525	$450	$375	*$1,070*

SHOTGUNS: O/U

SCIROCCO BASIC – 12 ga. only, single trigger, extractors, 26 or 28 in. fixed choke VR barrels, boxlock action, nickel engraved frame. Imported 1994-95.

	$425	$370	$320	$290	$235	$190	$150	*$478*

This model was mfg. by Lu-Mar located in Italy.

SCIROCCO SPORTING CLAYS – 12 ga. only, 28 or 30 in. barrels with 5 choke tubes and wide VR, SST, ejectors, Raybar front sight, nickel engraved frame. Imported 1994-95.

	$650	$570	$485	$440	$355	$290	$225	*$734*

This model was mfg. by Lu-Mar located in Italy.

FALCON – 12, 20 ga., or .410 bore, 3 in. chambers, 26, 28, or 30 in. fixed choke VR barrels, boxlock action, single or double trigger, extractors or ejectors, checkered pistol grip and forend. Imported 1993 only.

	$650	$570	$485	$440	$355	$290	$225	*$795*

Add $80 for .410 bore.
Add $100 for SST and ejectors.

SPORTING CLAYS PRO GOLD – 12 ga. only, 2 3/4 in. chambers, 28 or 30 in. screw-in choke barrels with wide VR, boxlock action, SST, ejectors, blue frame with engraving, recoil pad with custom carry case. Imported 1993-94.

	$850	$745	$635	$580	$465	$380	$295	*$978*

GRADING - PPGS™	100%	98%	95%	90%	80%	70%	60%	LAST MSR

SHOTGUNS: SxS

SABA – 12, 20, 28 ga., or .410 bore, 3 in. chambers, boxlock action with scrolled nickel finish, DT or SST, 26 or 28 in. fixed choke barrels with raised matted rib, ejectors, checkered stock and forearm with sling swivels. Imported 1993 only.

	$950	$830	$710	$645	$520	$425	$330	*$1,195*

Add $100 for SST.

SHOTGUNS: SEMI-AUTO

BUNDA SERIES – 12 ga. only, 2 3/4 or 3 in. chamber (depending on barrel) gas operated, 19, 26, 28 or 30 in. barrel with 4 choke tubes, choice of black synthetic or Turkish walnut stock and forearm, aluminum receiver. Limited importation 1998 only.

	$360	$315	$270	$245	$200	$160	$125	*$406*

Add $9 for Turkish walnut stock and forearm.

SHOTGUNS: SLIDE ACTION

MODEL PM2 – 12 ga. only, slide action, unique 7 shot detachable mag., 20 in. barrel, black wood stock and composite forearm, dual action bars, cross-bolt safety on trigger guard, available in matte blue or chrome finish, 6.81 lbs. Imported 1992 only.

	$550	$480	$410	$375	$300	$245	$190	*$695*

Add $200 for night sights.
Add $75 for matte chrome finish.

EVANS, WILLIAM, GUN & RIFLE MAKERS

Please refer to the W section in this text.

EVOLUTION USA

Current rifle manufacturer located in White Bird, ID since 1984. Distributor and dealer sales.

RIFLES: BOLT ACTION

Evolution USA uses four different types of actions for its rifles. They include the MSR-10 that is a faceted and highly customized Remington M700 receiver, the MSX-10 that uses a Post-64 Win. Model 70 with claw extractor, the Pre-64 Win. Model 70 action, and the Mauser Express 98 action manufactured by CZ USA. Most models can be ordered by selecting one of the previous receivers.

ARGALI – most short action cals., trued Rem. Model 700 action, Krieger ultra light barrel, synthetic stock, 5 1/2 lbs. Mfg. 2000-2004.

	$2,000	$1,700	$1,450	$1,225	$950	$775	$675	*$2,450*

COYOTE – available in various cals., blue printed Rem. Model 700 action, Grand Master (disc. 1999) or Kreiger match barrel with cryogenic treatment, Kevlar/graphite stock. Mfg. 1996-2004.

	$1,900	$1,600	$1,325	$1,100	$900	$825	$725	*$2,296*

COYOTE II – various cals., trued Remington M 700 action and customized trigger, matte black metal parts, HS Precision Kevlar graphite tactical stock with aluminum and fiberglass reinforced bedding. Mfg. 2001-2006.

	$1,900	$1,600	$1,325	$1,100	$900	$825	$725	*$2,295*

PHANTOM II – various cals. from .22 - .408, trued and blue printed custom Evolution (disc.) or choice of repeater action, Krieger match stainless steel barrel, Timney match trigger, McMillan A2 or A3 tactical stock, matte black metal, 1,000 yard competition rifle, 11 1/2 lbs. New 1999.

MSR $3,400	$3,150	$2,925	$2,650	$2,250	$1,900	$1,700	$1,400	

PHANTOM III – .50 BMG cal., Magnum single shot bolt action. New 2012.

MSR $5,800	$5,500	$4,995	$4,500	$3,950	$3,500	$3,000	$2,750	

GRADING - PPGS™	100%	98%	95%	90%	80%	70%	60%	LAST MSR

YELLOW WOLF SPORTER – available in various cals., designed for big game, blue printed Rem. Model 700 or Evolution M-1000 action, Kreiger match barrel, Kevlar graphite stock, available in Standardweight (7.2 lbs.), Lightweight (6.8 lbs.), Superlight (6.2 lbs.), and Ultralight (5 1/2 lbs.). New 1996.

MSR $3,286	$3,100	$2,650	$2,225	$1,875	$1,650	$1,300	$1,000	

Add $55 for Lightweight, $401 for Superlight, or $944 for Ultralight configuration.

IMPALA – most popular cals., Rem. Model 700 trued action w/o floor plate, lightweight sporter, Kevlar graphite stock. Mfg. 1998-99.

	$1,275	$1,050	$950	$750	$650	$575	$500	*$1,456*

KUDU – most standard length cals., Winchester Pre-64 Model 70 action, stainless steel match barrel, sporter style Kevlar graphite stock. Mfg. 1998-2006.

	$2,150	$1,850	$1,650	$1,350	$1,050	$875	$725	*$2,579*

Add $2,500 for presentation walnut stock.

SHI-AWELA – various cals., medium weight sporter, Evolution M1000 stainless action, stainless match barrel, Kevlar graphite stock. Mfg. 1999-2002.

	$2,600	$2,000	$1,750	N/A	N/A	N/A	N/A	*$3,052*

MBOGO – .375 H&H, .416 Rem., .458 Win. Mag., or .505 Gibbs cal., choice of Sako (disc.), Dakota (disc.), Rem. Model 700, CZ (new 2007), Win. Pre-64 Model 70 (disc. 2006), or stainless steel Evolution M1000 action, Krieger stainless steel match barrel, express style Kevlar graphite stock. New 1998.

This rifle with Evolution action requires 11% federal excise tax.

* ***Mbogo Recent Mfg.*** – disc.

	$1,550	$1,325	$1,100	$925	$750	$650	$575	*$1,828*

* ***Mbogo Current Mfg.*** – Evolution M-1000 action.

MSR $3,890	$3,500	$2,925	$2,450	$2,050	$1,750	$1,575	$1,300	

Add $1,768 for exhibition grade walnut stock.

* ***Mbogo Dakota Action***

	$2,775	$2,400	$2,000	$1,750	$1,500	$1,250	$1,000	*$3,142*

BOLT ACTION SNIPER/VARMINT SERIES – various cals., 3 different configurations included Sniper, Informal Target Varmint, and Field Grade Varmint, featured match barrel, action, and tuned trigger. Disc. 2000.

Prices for the Sniper rifle started at approx. $3,000 while the Varmint guns started at approx. $2,000.

RIFLES: SxS

DOUBLE RIFLE (NYATI) – various cals. from .30-06 to .500 NE, reinforced Chapuis Anson & Deeley action, choice of color case hardened or coin finished engraved receiver, blue chrome-moly barrels, various wood grades available, express sights. New 1999. Custom order only.

MSRs on this model are as follows: .30-06 - $6,000, .375 H&H - $9,500, .450/400 NE - $11,500, .470 NE - $11,800, .500 NE - $13,500.

NYALA – various standard cals., including .300 Win. Mag., 3 grades available, 7 lbs., 9 oz. Mfg. 2001-2006.

	$4,500	$4,000	$3,600	$3,150	$2,750	$2,350	$2,000	*$4,895*

RIFLES: SEMI-AUTO

WOLVERINE – .22 LR cal., Grand Master barrel, Kevlar graphite stock. Mfg. 1996-2000.

	$730	$650	$565	$515	$455	$400	$360	*$850*

GRENADA – .223 Rem. cal., paramilitary design based on the AR-15 with flat upper receiver, 17 in. stainless steel match barrel with integral muzzle brake, NM trigger. Disc. 2000.

	$985	$825	$675	$600	$525	$465	$400	*$1,195*

GRADING - PPGS™	100%	98%	95%	90%	80%	70%	60%	LAST MSR

DESERT STORM – similar to Grenada, except has 21 in. match barrel. Disc. 2003.

	$975	$825	$665	$560	$500	$450	$400	*$1,189*

IWO JIMA – features carrying handle incorporating iron sights, 20 in. stainless steel match barrel, A2 HBAR action, tubular handguard. Limited mfg.

	$1,000	$875	$775	$700	$600	$475	$425	

RIFLES : SINGLE SHOT

IMPALA – various standard cals., including .300 Win. Mag., 5 grades available, similar appearance and handling to the Nyala model. Mfg. 2001-disc.

This model was POR.

PHANTOM III SINGLE SHOT – .50 BMG or .700 NE cal., Evolution M-2000 stainless single shot action, 28 in. Lilja match barrel with flutes and muzzle brake, approx. 30 lbs. Mfg. 2000-2011.

	$4,700	$4,300	$3,850	$3,500	$2,950	$2,400	$2,250	*$4,700*

Add $1,700 for Delta Model (50-80 lbs.) or .700 NE cal. (24-30 lbs.), disc.

EXCAM

Previous importer and distributor located in Hialeah, FL, which went out of business late 1990. Excam distributed Dart, Erma, Tanarmi, Targa, and Warrior exclusively in the U.S. These trademarks will appear under Excam. All importation of Excam firearms ceased in 1990.

All Targa and Tanarmi pistols were manufactured in Gardone V.T., Italy. All Erma and Warrior pistols and rifles were manufactured in W. Germany. Senator O/U shotguns were manufactured by A. Zoli located in Brescia, Italy.

Due to space considerations, this section is now available online free of charge at www.bluebookofgunvalues.com.

EXCEL ARMS

Current trademark of pistols and rifles manufactured by Excel Industries, Inc., located in Chino, CA.

PISTOLS: SEMI-AUTO

ACCELERATOR MP – .17 HMR (MP-17), .17 Mach 2 (new 2007, SP-17), .22 LR (new 2007, SP-22), or .22 WMR (MP-22) cal., 6 1/2 (new 2007) or 8 1/2 in. barrel, polymer frame with stainless steel slide, adj. sights, 9 shot mag., 45 or 54 oz. Mfg. 2005-2009.

	$385	$325	$285	$260	$240	$220	$195	*$433*

Add $63 for red/green dot optic sight or $87 for 4x32mm scope with illuminated crosshairs.

Add $87 for choice of Realtree Hardwoods HD Green or Digital Desert camo coverage (new 2008).

MP-17 – .17 HMR cal., 8 1/2 in. barrel, 9 shot, stainless steel, polymer grip, adj. sights, available with red dot optic or scope and rings, matte black, Digital Desert or Realtree Hardwoods HD camo. Mfg. late 2008-2010.

	$375	$325	$285	$260	$240	$220	$195	*$433*

Add $63 for red dot optic front sight. Add $87 for scope and rings. Add $87 for camo.

MP-22 – .22 WMR cal., 6 1/2 or 8 1/2 in. barrel, 9 shot, stainless steel, polymer grip, adj. sights, available with red dot optic or scope and rings, matte black, Digital Desert (disc. 2010) or Realtree Hardwoods HD camo (disc. 2010), 3 3/8 lbs. New late 2008.

MSR $455	$385	$335	$295	$260	$240	$220	$195	

Add $66 for red dot optic front sight. Add $91 for scope and rings. Add $87 for camo (disc. 2010).

MP-5.7 – 5.7x28mm cal., stainless steel construction, 8 1/2 in. bull barrel with integral top Picatinny rail, fully adj. target sights, available with red dot optic or scope and rings, polymer grip, 9 shot mag., blow-back action, last round hole open, black Cerakote finish, 3 3/8 lbs. New 2011.

MSR $585	$525	$460	$420	$375	$325	$285	$250	

Add $66 for red dot optic sights. Add $91 for scope and rings.

GRADING - PPGS™	100%	98%	95%	90%	80%	70%	60%	LAST MSR

X-5.7P – 5.7x28mm cal., otherwise similar to X-30P, 10 or 25 shot mag., no sights or adj. iron sights (25 shot mag. only). New 2011.

MSR $715	$650	$575	$500	$450	$400	$350	$295	

Add $121 for adj. iron sights (25 shot mag. only).

X-22P – .22 LR cal., 4 1/2 in. barrel, black synthetic stock, 10 or 25 shot mag., adj. sights, Picatinny rail. New 2009.

MSR $415	$365	$310	$275	$240	$220	$200	$185	

X-30P – .30 Carbine cal., features aluminum frame with integral Picatinny rail, 8 1/2 in. partially shrouded barrel, delayed blow-back action, tilted black synthetic pistol grip with finger grooves, 10 or 20 shot mag., no sights or adj. iron sights (20 shot mag. only), 4 1/2 lbs. New 2011.

MSR $715	$650	$575	$500	$450	$400	$350	$295	

Add $121 for adj. iron sights (20 shot mag. only).

SP-17 – .17 Mach 2 cal., 6 1/2 or 8 1/2 in. barrel, 10 shot, stainless steel, polymer grip, adj. sights, available with red dot optic or scope and rings, matte black, Digital Desert or Realtree Hardwoods HD camo. Mfg. late 2008-2010.

	$375	$325	$285	$260	$240	$220	$195	*$433*

Add $63 for red dot optic front sight. Add $87 for scope and rings. Add $87 for camo.

SP-22 – .22 LR cal., 6 1/2 or 8 1/2 in. barrel, 10 shot, stainless steel, polymer grip, adj. sights, available with red dot optic or scope and rings, matte black, Digital Desert or Realtree Hardwoods HD camo. Mfg. late 2008-2010.

	$375	$325	$285	$260	$240	$220	$195	*$433*

Add $63 for red dot optic front sight. Add $87 for scope and rings. Add $87 for camo.

RIFLES: SEMI-AUTO

MR/SR SERIES – .17 HMR (MR17), .17 Mach 2 (SR17, new 2007), .22 LR (SR22, new 2007), or .22 WMR (MR22) cal., black composite stock with large thumbhole, fluted 18 in. stainless steel barrel and receiver with shroud, black, silver, or camo finish, fully adj. sights, 9 shot mag., standard package is supplied with red dot optic and hard sided case, 8 lbs. Mfg. 2004-2009.

	$435	$380	$325	$295	$240	$195	$150	*$488*

Add $195 for choice of Realtree Hardwoods HD Green or Digital Desert camo coverage (new 2008).
Add $35 for red dot optical sight.
Add $147 for iron sights or 3-9x40mm scope.
Add $231 for iron sights and 6x9 in. bipod.

CR-9 – 9mm Para. cal., stainless steel construction, 18 in. stainless bull barrel, full length Weaver rail and two side rails, adj. and detachable sights, 10 shot mag., nylon sling and detachable swivels. Mfg. 2008.

	$550	$480	$415	$375	$305	$250	$195	*$635*

X-22R – .22 LR cal., 18 in. barrel, fixed (new 2011) or collapsible black synthetic stock, blow back action, no sights, 10 or 25 shot mag., drilled and tapped, accepts Ruger 10/22 mags., 4 3/4 lbs. New 2009.

MSR $461	$415	$350	$300	$270	$215	$180	$140	

Add $15 for fixed stock (new 2011).
Add $87 for 3-9x40 scope.

X-30R – .30 Carbine cal., 18 in. partially shrouded barrel, features aluminum receiver with integral Picatinny top rail, blow-back action, fixed or collapsible stock, no sights or adj. iron sights (20 shot mag. only), 10 or 20 shot mag., approx. 6 1/4 lbs. New 2011.

MSR $795	$725	$650	$575	$500	$450	$400	$350	

Add $15 for fixed stock (10 shot mag. only).
Add $121 for adj. iron sights (20 shot mag. only).

GRADING - PPGS™	100%	98%	95%	90%	80%	70%	60%	LAST MSR

X-5.7R - 5.7x28mm cal., otherwise similar to the X-30R, 10 or 25 shot mag. New 2011.

MSR $795	$725	$650	$575	$500	$450	$400	$350	

Add $15 for fixed stock (10 shot mag. only).
Add $121 for adj. Iron Sights (25 shot mag. only).

MR-17 - .17 HMR cal., 18 in. bull barrel, 9 shot mag., silver or black shroud, available options include no sights, red dot optic, iron sights, scope and rings, sling, bipod, side rails, and flashlight, black, Digital Desert or Realtree Hardwoods HD Green camo. Mfg. late 2008-2010.

	$425	$370	$320	$290	$235	$190	$150	*$488*

Add $35 for red dot optic sights. Add $147 for iron sights or 3-9x40mm scope. Add $84 for bipod (iron sights or scope only). Add $257 for side rails and flashlight. Add $195 for camo.

The no sight model is only available with one magazine - all other variations include two.

MR-22 - .22 WMR cal., 18 in. bull barrel, 9 shot mag., silver or black shroud, full length top Picatinny rail, available options include no sights, red dot optic, iron sights, scope and rings, sling, bipod, side rails, and flashlight, blow back action, black, Digital Desert (disc. 2010) or Realtree Hardwoods HD Green camo (disc. 2010) finish, 8 lbs. New late 2008.

MSR $512	$440	$385	$335	$300	$250	$195	$150	

Add $37 for red dot optic sights. Add $155 for iron sights or 3-9x40mm scope. Add $243 for bipod (iron sights or scope only). Add $425 for side rails and flashlight. Add $195 for camo (disc. 2010).

The no sight model is only available with one magazine - all other variations include two.

MR-5.7 - 5.7x28mm cal., 18 in. fluted bull barrel, 9 shot mag., black or silver shroud, full length upper Picatinny rail, no sights, black synthetic pistol grip stock with thumbhole, last round hole open, 8 lbs. New 2011.

MSR $640	$575	$500	$450	$400	$350	$300	$275	

Add $155 for 3.9x40mm scope.

SR-17 - .17 Mach 2 cal., 18 in. bull barrel, 10 shot mag., silver or black shroud, available options include no sights, red dot optic, iron sights, scope and rings, sling, bipod, side rails, and flashlight, black, Digital Desert or Realtree Hardwoods HD Green camo. Mfg. 2008-2010.

	$425	$370	$320	$290	$235	$190	$150	*$488*

Add $35 for red dot optic sights. Add $147 for iron sights or 3-9x40mm scope. Add $84 for bipod (iron sights or scope only). Add $257 for side rails and flashlight. Add $195 for camo.

The no sight model is only available with one magazine - all other variations include two.

SR-22 - .22 LR cal., 18 in. bull barrel, 10 shot mag., silver or black shroud, available options include no sights, red dot optic, iron sights, scope and rings, sling, bipod, side rails, and flashlight, black, Digital Desert or Realtree Hardwoods HD Green camo. Mfg. late 2008-2010.

	$425	$370	$320	$290	$235	$190	$150	*$488*

Add $35 for red dot optic sights. Add $147 for iron sights or 3-9x40mm scope. Add $84 for bipod (iron sights or scope only). Add $257 for side rails and flashlight. Add $195 for camo.

The no sight model is only available with one magazine - all other variations include two.

EXEL ARMS OF AMERICA, INC.

Previous importer located in Gardener, MA. Exel Arms previously imported Lanber (Series 100), Ugartechea (Series 200), and Laurona (Series 300) shotguns. Please refer to the appropriate sections for more information on this series.

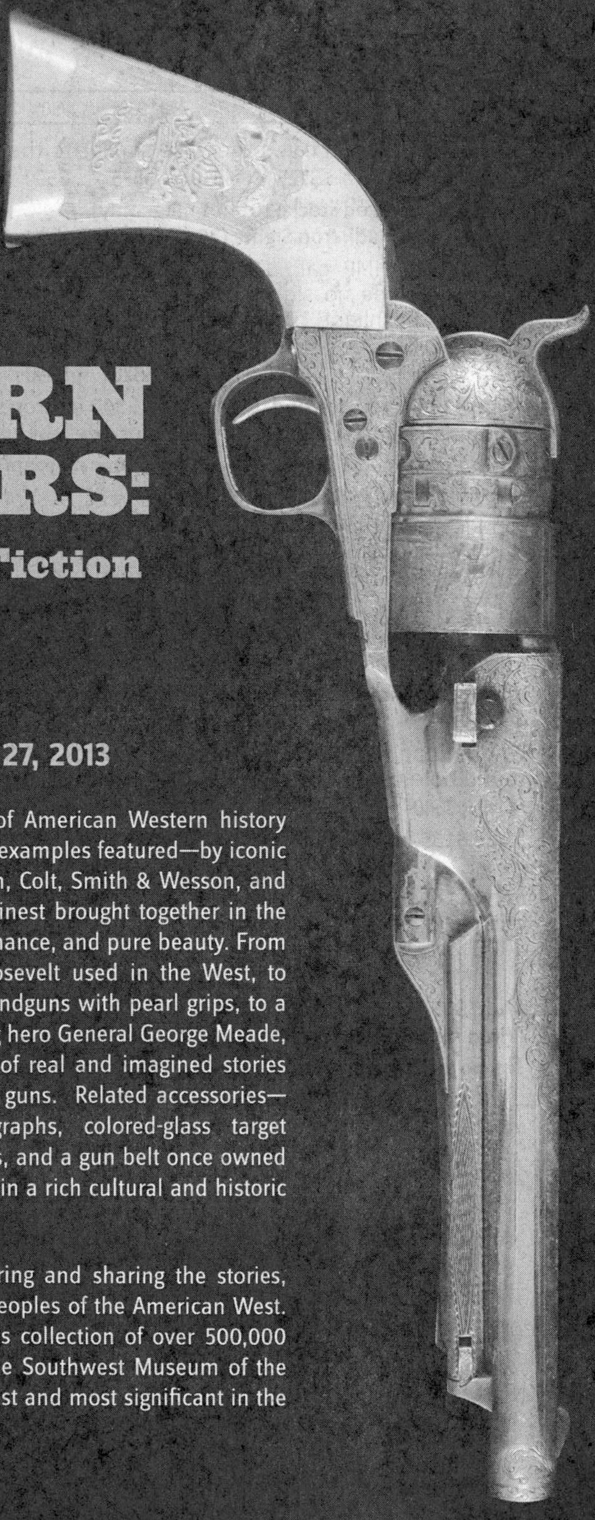

F SECTION

F. DARNE FILS AINÉ

Previous manufacturer located in St. Etienne, France.

Francisque Darne was the eldest son of Regis Darne, who developed the sliding breech gun. In 1910, Francisque left his father's company to form his own, "F. Darne Fils Ainé," producing high quality versions of the original 1894 patent R model Darne. Regis Darne updated most of his designs in 1909 and allowed the older patents to become public domain.

Francisque Darne died in 1917, but his company remained in production until 1955 under at least four different owners. SIFARM, a combination of the manufacturers Berthon Freres, Francisque Darne, Didier-Drevet, Gerest, and Ronchard-Cizeron, was absorbed in 1963 by Verney-Carron, along with the famous Canonnerie (barrel makers) Jean Breuil.

As is usually the case, the earlier production guns are by far the highest quality. Wide variations in quality exist in this marque, depending on the financial health of the owners at the time of production.

GRADING - PPGS™	100%	98%	95%	90%	80%	70%	60%	LAST MSR

SHOTGUNS: SxS, PRE-WAR MODELS

CLASSIC MODEL – 12 or 16 ga., an exact copy of the first Darne patent of 1894. Available in four grades.

* ***Classic Model Type A*** – standard French proof barrels, very light engraving, color case hardened, no quality stamps on barrel flats.

	100%	98%	95%	90%	80%	70%	60%
Type A	$1,200	$1,000	$800	$700	$600	$500	$450

* ***Classic Model Type B*** – French gray hardened or color case hardened, somewhat more engraving, 1 quality stamp on barrel flats.

	100%	98%	95%	90%	80%	70%	60%
Type B	$1,700	$1,400	$1,200	$900	$700	$600	$500

* ***Classic Model Type C*** – French gray hardening over modern or old English engraving, double proofed barrels with two quality stamps on barrel flats.

	100%	98%	95%	90%	80%	70%	60%
Type C	$2,000	$1,650	$1,350	$1,000	$800	$650	$550

* ***Classic Model Type E*** – French gray hardening over elaborate engraving. Better quality wood in either English or semi-pistol grip. Double proof barrels with four quality stamps on barrel flats.

	100%	98%	95%	90%	80%	70%	60%
Type E	$2,400	$2,000	$1,600	$1,300	$1,000	$900	$800

MODEL T – 12 or 16 ga., stylistic improvements to the 1894 patent R model. Two-piece stock, barrels removed by holding a button on forend, 4 grades, all were originally color case hardened, never blue.

Both the T 32 and T 34 were available in 10 ga. with 70mm or 75mm chambers and 72cm or 76cm barrels on special order. The barrels would carry triple proof in 10 ga.

* ***Model T 32 Type*** – lightly engraved, 3 quality stamps on barrel flats.

	100%	98%	95%	90%	80%	70%	60%
T 32	$1,950	$1,700	$1,250	$950	$700	$600	$500

Add 30% for 10 ga.

* ***Model T 34*** – better engraving and wood, 5 quality stamps on barrel flats.

	100%	98%	95%	90%	80%	70%	60%
T 34	$2,100	$1,800	$1,500	$1,100	$850	$675	$575

Add 30% for 10 ga.

* ***Model T 35*** – mono bloc barrels of superior French proof steel, better engraving and wood, 6 quality stamps on barrel flats.

	100%	98%	95%	90%	80%	70%	60%
T 35	$2,500	$2,200	$1,800	$1,400	$1,200	$1,000	$800

* ***Model T 36*** – mono bloc barrels of superior French proof steel, top-of-the-line T model, 7 quality stamps on barrel flats.

	100%	98%	95%	90%	80%	70%	60%
T 36	$2,800	$2,500	$2,100	$1,700	$1,400	$1,200	$850

GRADING - PPGS™	100%	98%	95%	90%	80%	70%	60%	LAST MSR

MODEL FIXED – 12 or 16 ga., further tinkering with the 1894 R model, these located the barrels in a rectangular block cut near the flats. Two grades.

* ***Model Fixed Type No. 3*** – color case hardened or French gray hardened. Good quality engraving and wood.

For pricing, see Type T 34.

* ***Model Fixed Type No. 4*** – better wood and engraving.

For pricing, see Type T 35.

MODEL PLATINUM – 12 or 16 ga., based on the model Fixed, these were top-of-the-line sliding breech guns. Four grades.

* ***Model Platinum Type No. 5*** – mono bloc barrels, English or art nouveau style engraving, chisled fences.

	$3,100	$2,800	$2,500	$2,200	$1,700	$1,400	$1,100

* ***Model Platinum Type No. 6*** – mono bloc barrels, English rose and scroll engraving or game scene or art nouveau style, high grade wood.

	$3,400	$2,900	$2,600	$2,350	$1,900	$1,600	$1,200

* ***Model Platinum Type No. 7*** – mono bloc barrels of top quality French proof steel, engraved in English rose and scroll or deep chiseled art nouveau style, superior wood. Pigeon model.

	$3,800	$3,500	$3,000	$2,800	$2,200	$1,900	$1,500

* ***Model Platinum Type No. 8*** – mono bloc barrels of top quality French proof steel. Top-of-the-line model with all details to customer's wishes. Very rare in any condition.

Rarity precludes accurate pricing.

SHOTGUNS: SxS, POST-WAR MODELS

Note: the model name of the following post-war guns is usually engraved on the side of the gun in front of the safety lever.

CLASSIC MODEL – 12 or 16 ga. with modified and full choke on 70 cm barrels, simple case colored gun with no engraving and plain wood in semi-pistol grip or straight stock, 2 quality stamps.

	$1,250	$1,000	$850	$700	$600	$525	$400

BARONNET-BROUSSARD – 12, 16, or 20 ga. with 70 cm barrels (two-piece stock on 12 and 16 ga.), lightly engraved with satin chrome receiver finish, Broussard model featured 80 cm barrels but was essentially the same, 3 quality stamps.

	$1,400	$1,200	$1,000	$800	$675	$550	$475

Add 20% for Broussard model.

GOUVERNEUR MODEL – 12, 16, or 20 ga., better engraving and one-piece stock of select walnut, French gray receiver, choice of barrel lengths in 12 ga. (70 cm, 72 cm, or 74 cm.) classic or modern style engraving, 5 quality stamps.

	$1,800	$1,650	$1,200	$1,000	$750	$600	$550

GOUVERNEUR PLUME AND PLUME MAGNUM – same as above, but with plume (swamped rib) on Plume Model, plume rib and 76mm chambers included on Plume Magnum Model.

Prices about 10% higher than previous models due to these having six quality stamps on flats of barrels in spite of being the same basic gun.

RAMBOUILLET MODEL – 12 or 16 ga., double sears in a large key action somewhat similar to the Darne V models stylistically, one-piece stock of select walnut, in semi-pistol grip or straight style, light engraving on color case hardening, choice of rib, 8 quality stamps.

	$1,500	$1,300	$1,100	$900	$700	$650	$575

AMBASSADEUR MODEL – 12 or 16 ga., large key model with double sears. French gray finish on breech with excellent engraving, one-piece stock of good quality walnut, top-of-the-line production model, 10 quality stamps.

	$2,700	$2,400	$2,200	$1,800	$1,500	$1,100	$850

GRADING - PPGS™	100%	98%	95%	90%	80%	70%	60%	LAST MSR

PRESTIGE MODEL – top-of-the-line custom gun, mono bloc barrels of Jacob Holtzer steel with plume swamped rib. Large key action with silent operation and double sears, one-piece stock of best quality walnut, in straight style only, 72 cm barrels, excellent full coverage engraving, eight month minimum wait, 12 quality stamps.

	$3,500	$3,100	$2,900	$2,600	$2,200	$1,700	$1,200	

F&D DEFENSE

Current manufacturer located in New Braunfels, TX.

RIFLES: SEMI-AUTO

FD308 – .308 Win. cal., FAL type action with gas piston operation, 17 or 21 in. stainless barrel with two chamber muzzle brake, full length Picatinny rail with folding battle tritium sights, side charging system with integrated forward asssist, removeable guide rails, GEISSELE trigger group, tan Magpul stock and pistol grip, storage compartment in the buttstock, 8.7 lbs. New 2012.

MSR $3,250	$3,100	$2,700	$2,450	$2,100	$1,800	$1,550	$1,250

F.A.I.R. srl

Current manufacturer established during 1971 (F.A.I.R. stands for Fabbrica Armi Isidoro Rizzini, owned by Isidoro Rizzini) and located in Marcheno, Italy. Currently imported, including private lables, on a limited basis by IFG (Italian Firearms Group), located in Rockledge, FL, beginning 2011. In 2003, the name changed from F.A.I.R. Tecni-Mec I. Rizzini to F.A.I.R. S.r.l. Previously imported and distributed exclusively by New England Arms Corp. located in Kittery Point, ME.

F.A.I.R. manufactures a wide variety of shotguns, rifles, double rifles, and combination guns, including O/Us and single shots in assorted configurations, with many options available. Please contact the IFG directly for more information, including current model availability and pricing (see Trademark Index).

COMBINATION GUNS

COMBI SERIES – 12 or 20 ga. over various cals., 24 in. smooth bore barrels, three chokes, extractors, DT, choice of De Luxe, Prestige, or De Luxe XLight configuration. Importation began 2012.

MSR $2,087	$1,795	$1,525	$1,300	$1,100	$900	$800	$700

Add $283 for De Luxe model, $507 for De Luxe XLight model, or $567 for Prestige model.

RIFLES

KIPPLAUF MODEL 500/500 DELUXE – various cals., single barrel stalking rifle, extractors, SST, checkered walnut stock and forearm. New 2002.

MSR $2,311	$2,050	$1,675	$1,400	$1,175	$950	$825	$725

Add $278 for De Luxe model.

SAFARI SERIES – various cals., 21 in. barrels, extractors, DT, silver engraved receiver, red fiber optic front sight, available in FXW, 500, De Luxe, and Prestige configurations. Importation began 2012.

MSR $3,354	$3,000	$2,650	$2,325	$2,050	$1,850	$1,600	$1,425

Add $431 for Safari 500, $904 for De Luxe model, or $1,193 for Prestige model.

SHOTGUNS

Due to space considerations, information regarding discontinued and currently imported (Models SLX800 and Pathos models) O/U shotguns is available online free of charge in the Firearms section at www.bluebookofgunvalues.com.

F.A.V.S. di FRANCESCO GUGLIELMINOTTI

Current manufacturer established in 1957, and located in Villar Focchiardo, Italy. No current U.S. importation. F.A.V.S. is an abbreviation for Fabbrica Armi Valle Susa.

GRADING - PPGS™	100%	98%	95%	90%	80%	70%	60%	LAST MSR

RIFLES: SINGLE SHOT

STRADIVARI – various cals., unique "shorty" bullpup configuration utilizing a break open single shot action and pivoting wood buttstock that opens/closes breech, 19 3/4, 24, or 29 in. barrel with muzzleweight, finger grooved pistol grip wood stock with short forend, standard walnut stock, 100% camo coverage, laminated birch/red stock, or deluxe finished wood stock, four variations are currently being mfg. - K, M, L, and MK, scope is mounted on front portion of barrel, approx. 6.8 lbs.

Current European MSRs on this model range from €2,470-€2,992, please contact the manufacturer directly for U.S. availability.

FAS

Current pistol and air pistol manufacturer located in Lainate, Italy. Previously located in Milan, Italy. Air pistols currently imported by Airguns of Airzona, located in Gilbert, AZ. No current U.S. importation of firearms. Previously imported and distributed by Nygord Precision Products located in Prescott, AZ, Mandall Shooting Supplies, located in Scottsdale, AZ, Beeman Precision Arms, Inc. located in Santa Rosa, CA, and Osborne's located in Cheboygan, MI.

PISTOLS: SEMI-AUTO

MODEL OP601 – .22 Short cal. only, competition pistol, 5.9 in. barrel, 5 shot mag., wraparound match wood grips, 41 1/2 oz.

$1,025	$875	$695	$640	$565	$500	$450	

MODEL 602 – .22 LR cal. only, competition pistol, 5.6 in. barrel, 5 shot mag., ergonomically designed match wood grips, 40 oz. Importation disc. 1994.

$895	$800	$625	$600	$525	$475	$425	*$1,100*

MODEL CF603 – .32 S&W Wadcutter cal. only, competition pistol, 5.3 in. barrel, 5 shot mag., ergonomically designed adj. or non-adj. match wood grips, 40 oz.

$975	$875	$695	$640	$565	$500	$450	

MODEL SP607 (LADY) – .22 LR cal. only, semi-auto competition pistol, similar to Model 602, except has removable barrel weights, 5.6 in. barrel.

$975	$875	$695	$640	$565	$500	$450	

FEG

Current manufacturer located in Hungary (FEG stands for Fegyver es Gepgyar) since 1891. Previously imported 2007-2010 by SSME Deutsche Waffen, Inc., located in Plant City, FL. A few models were imported by Century International Arms located in Delray Beach, FL (see additional information under the Century International Arms in this text). Previously imported and distributed by K.B.I., Inc. located in Harrisburg, PA, and distributed until 1998 by Interarms located in Alexandria, VA.

PISTOLS: SEMI-AUTO, INTERARMS IMPORTED

All FEG pistols were supplied with two mags.

MARK II AP22 – .22 LR cal., double action, 3.4 in. barrel, 8 shot mag., blue finish, black plastic grips, 23 oz. Imported 1997-98.

$235	$200	$175	$160	$145	$130	$115	*$269*

MARK II AP – .380 ACP cal., double action, patterned after the Walther PP, 3.9 in. barrel, 7 shot mag., blue finish, black plastic grips, 27 oz. Imported 1997-98.

$235	$200	$175	$160	$145	$130	$115	*$269*

MARK II APK – .380 ACP cal., similar to Mark II AP, except is patterned after the Walther PPK/S, 3.4 in. barrel, 7 shot mag., blue finish, black plastic grips, 25 oz. Imported 1997-98.

$235	$200	$175	$160	$145	$130	$115	*$269*

PISTOLS: SEMI-AUTO, RECENT IMPORTATION

In addition to the following imported models, FEG also makes additional models available

GRADING - PPGS™	100%	98%	95%	90%	80%	70%	60%	LAST MSR

mostly in Europe. Currently, these pistols include the RL61 (.22 LR cal.), the AP9/APK9 (.380 ACP cal.), P9RZ Compact (9mm Para cal.), and the AC/ACK (.45 ACP cal.).

MODEL PMK-380 – .380 ACP cal., patterned after Walther PP, alloy frame, double action, 4 in. barrel, plastic grips with thumbrest, blue finish, 21 oz. Importation by K.B.I. 1992-2003.

$205	$180	$160	$135	$120	$110	$100	*$239*

MODEL SMC-380 – .380 ACP cal., double action semi-auto, patterned after Walther PPK, alloy frame, 3 1/2 in. barrel, 6 shot mag., plastic grips with thumbrest, blue finish, 18 1/2 oz. Importation by K.B.I. 1993-2003.

$205	$180	$160	$135	$120	$110	$100	*$239*

* ***Model SMC-22*** – .22 LR cal., 8 shot mag., otherwise similar to Model SMC-380. Importation disc. 1997.

$210	$195	$180	$165	$150	$135	$115	*$235*

MODEL SMC-918 – 9x18mm Makarov cal., double action, semi-auto, 7 shot mag. Importation disc. 1997.

$175	$150	$130	$110	$95	$85	$75	*$235*

MODEL PA-63 – 9x18mm Makarov cal., single or double action, 3.93 in. barrel, blue or bright aluminum anodized frame with blued steel slide, fixed sights, plastic grips, decocking safety. Previously imported by Century International Arms.

$175	$150	$130	$110	$95	$85	$75	

MODEL PPH – .380 ACP cal., patterned after Walther PP, alloy frame, double action, plastic grips with thumbrest, blue finish. Imported 1986-87 only.

$200	$170	$140	$125	$115	$105	$95	*$225*

MODEL B9R – .380 ACP cal., little importation into the U.S., many are encountered with "Turkce Polis" (Turkish Police) on the slide, blue finish. Disc.

$250	$225	$200	$175	$150	$125	$100	

MODEL P9R (MBK-9HP OR R-9) – 9mm Para. cal., patterned after Browning Hi-Power, double action, 4 2/3 in. barrel, 14 shot mag., blue finish, steel construction, checkered wood grips, 36 oz. Imported 1992 only, reimported 2007-2011.

$450	$395	$350	$315	$275	$250	$225	*$499*

This model is the current Hungarian military/police pistol.

* ***Model MBK-9HPC*** – compact variation of the Model MBK-9HP with 4 in. barrel, 31 oz. Imported 1992 only.

$325	$275	$250	$225	$200	$185	$170	*$359*

MODEL P9M (PJK-9HP) – 9mm Para. cal., patterned after Browning Hi-Power, single action, all steel construction, 4 3/4 in. barrel, thumb safety, 10 (C/B 1994) or 13* shot mag., cleaning rod, 32 oz. Importation by K.B.I. 1992-2003, reimported 2007-2011.

$425	$375	$335	$300	$275	$250	$225	*$475*

Add approx. $60 for industrial hard chrome finish (Model PJK-9HPC - includes Uncle Mike's rubber grips, disc. 1999).
Add $175 for .40 cal. conversion kit.

* ***Model P9L*** – similar to P9M, except has 6 in. barrel and resembles the Browning HP. Imported 2007-2011.

$695	$600	$525	$450	$400	$365	$335	*$799*

MODEL P9RK (GKK-92C) – 9mm Para. cal., double action semi-auto, 4 in. barrel, 14 shot mag., improved variation of MBK models, includes same accessories as PJK-9H, 34 oz. Importation disc. 1993, reimported 2007-2011.

$450	$395	$350	$315	$275	$250	$225	*$499*

MODEL GKK-40C – .40 S&W cal., 9 shot mag., otherwise similar to GKK-45. Imported 1995-96.

$300	$265	$230	$200	$180	$160	$145	*$349*

GRADING - PPGS™	100%	98%	95%	90%	80%	70%	60%	LAST MSR

MODEL GKK-45 – .45 ACP cal., double action semi-auto, all steel, 4 1/4 in. barrel, blue (disc. 1994) or chrome (Model GKK-45C) finish checkered walnut grips, 8 shot mag., approx. 37 oz. Imported 1993-96.

	$300	$265	$230	$200	$180	$160	$145	*$349*

RIFLES: SEMI-AUTO

MODEL SA-85M – 7.62x39mm cal., sporter rifle utilizing AKM action, 16.3 in. barrel, 6 shot detachable mag., thumbhole stock, 7 lbs. 10 oz. Imported 1991, banned 1998.

	$550	$480	$410	$375	$300	$245	$190	*$429*

SA-85 S (SA-2000M) – .223 Rem. (disc. 2000) or 7.62x39mm cal., sporter rifle with skeletonized Choate synthetic stock, 16.3 (new 2007) or 17 3/4 (disc. 2000) in. barrel with muzzle brake, 6, 10, or 30 shot detachable mag. Imported 1999-2000, reimported 2007-2011.

	$950	$830	$710	$645	$520	$425	$330	*$1,075*

FIAS

Previous long gun and related components manufacturer located in Brescia, Italy. FIAS is an abbreviation for Fabbrica Italiana Armi Sabatti.

FIAS became part of the Sabatti Armi group circa 2002, and is based in Gardone VT, Brescia. Please refer to Sabatti for current information, including any domestic importation.

F.I.E.

Previous importer (F.I.E. is the acronym for Firearms Import & Export) located in Hialeah, FL until 1990.

F.I.E. filed bankruptcy in November of 1990 and all models were discontinued. Some parts or service for these older firearms may be obtained through Numrich Gun Parts Corp. (see Trademark Index), even though all warranties on F.I.E. guns are void.

Due to space considerations, this section is now available through our website: www.bluebookofgunvalues.com.

FMJ

Previous manufacturer located in Copperhill, TN, until circa 1998.

Little information is available regarding FMJ firearms (including short barrel derringers and pistols), except they were inexpensive shooters and have little collectibility, other than some oddball configurations. Their production records were turned in to the BATF during 1998.

FMK FIREARMS

Current pistol manufacturer located in Placentia, CA. Currently distributed by American Tactical Imports, located in Rochester, NY.

PISTOLS: SEMI-AUTO

FMK GENERATION II – 9mm Para. cal., 4 in. barrel, blue steel, DAO, features FAT trigger mechanism for quick and short trigger pull, polymer frame with steel slide, 10 or 14 shot mag., loaded chamber indicator, with or w/o Bill of Rights engraving, matte black, Dark Earth, or Pink finish, Picatinny rail, trigger safety, includes two mags. New 2010.

MSR $400	$350	$300	$265	$240	$220	$200	$180

FMK 9C2 LE COMPACT – 9mm Para. cal., 4 in. barrel, black tactical matte finish, polymer frame with carbon steel slide, fast action trigger, magazine free release, ergonomically grooved grips, 23.4 oz. New mid-2012.

MSR $400	$350	$300	$265	$240	$220	$200	$180

FMR

Current rifle manufacturer located in Pantin, France. No current U.S. importation.

RIFLES: BOLT ACTION

FMR owns the rights to the French trademark Unique, and manufactures a line of bolt action

GRADING - PPGS™	100%	98%	95%	90%	80%	70%	60%	LAST MSR

rifles based on the original Unique design. All rifles have an aluminum ERGAL or stainless steel action, interchangeable barrels and fully adjustable stocks. The RS1 Sniper is available as a single shot or a repeater, and has an MSR of €1,930. The RS1 Commando has a heavy barrel and muzzle brake and has an MSR of €1,570. Various options are also available, including an unmodified adjustable stock for the CZ22. Please contact the company directly for more information, including options, pricing, and U.S. availability (see Trademark Index).

FNH USA

Current manufacturer and importer established in 1998, and located in McLean, VA. Dealer and distributor sales.

In the U.S., FN (Fabrique Nationale) is represented by two entities - FNH USA, which is responsible for sales, marketing, and business development, and FNM, which stands for FN Manufacturing, which handles manufacturing. FNH USA has two separate divisions - commercial/law enforcement, and military operations. FN Manufacturing is located in Columbia, SC. Design, research and development are conducted under the authority of FN Herstal S.A. Some of the firearms that FNM currently produces for the U.S. government are M16 rifles, M249 light machine guns, and M240 medium machine guns. FNM also produces the FNP line of handguns for the commercial, military, and law enforcement marketplaces. FNM is one of only three small arms manufacturers designated by the U.S. government as an industry base for small arms production. In November 2004, the FN model was chosen by the U.S. Special Operations Command (USSOCOM) for the new SCAR paramilitary rifle.

CARBINES/RIFLES: SEMI-AUTO

PS90 - 5.7x28mm cal., blowback operation, bullpup configuration, 16 in. barrel, 10 or 30 shot box mag. runs horizontally along the top, empty cases are ejected downward, integrated muzzle brake, olive drab or black finish, configurations include PS90 RD with reflex sight module (mfg. 2009), PS90 USG with non-magnifying black reticle optical sight, and the PS90 TR with three M-1913 rails for optional optics, 6.3 lbs. Disc. 2011.

	$1,925	$1,675	$1,450	$1,295	$1,075	$925	$800	*$2,199*

* ***PS90 Standard*** - 5.7x28mm cal., similar to PS90, except no optical sights, 10 (new 2012) or 30 shot mag, black, OD Green, or olive drab (disc.) finish. New 2010.

MSR $1,695	$1,550	$1,325	$1,100	$975	$850	$725	$650

FS2000 STANDARD/TACTICAL - .223 Rem. cal., bullpup configuration, 17.4 in. barrel, gas operated with rotating bolt, 10 or 30 shot AR-15 style mag., empty cases are ejected through a forward port, includes 1.6x optical sighting package on Standard Model (disc. 2010), Tactical Model features emergency back up folding sights, CQB model features lower accessory rail, ambidextrous polymer stock, top mounted M-1913 rail, olive drab green or black finish, 7.6 lbs.

MSR $2,779	$2,425	$2,100	$1,825	$1,675	$1,450	$1,250	$995

SCAR 16S - .223 Rem. cal., semi-auto only version of U.S. SOCOM's newest service rifle, gas operated short stroke piston system, free floating 16 1/4 in. barrel with hard chrome bore, 10 or 30 shot detachable box mag., folding open sights, fully ambidextrous operating controls, three optical rails, side folding polymer stock, fully adj. comb and LOP, black or Flat Dark Earth finish on receiver and stock, 7 1/4 lbs. New 2009.

MSR $2,995	$2,695	$2,375	$2,050	$1,850	$1,575	$1,275	$1,050

SCAR 17S - .308 Win. cal., 10 or 20 shot mag., otherwise similar to SCAR 16S, 8 lbs. New 2009.

MSR $3,349	$2,925	$2,550	$2,175	$1,900	$1,575	$1,275	$1,050

FNAR STANDARD - .308 Win. cal., 16 (new 2010) or 20 in. light or heavy fluted contoured barrel, 10 or 20 shot detachable box mag., one-piece M-1913 optical rail, three accessory rails attached to forearm, matte black synthetic pistol grip stock with soft cheekpiece, adj. comb, ambidextrous mag. release, 8.8 - 9 lbs. New 2009.

MSR $1,699	$1,550	$1,325	$1,100	$975	$850	$725	$650

GRADING - PPGS™	100%	98%	95%	90%	80%	70%	60%	LAST MSR

PISTOLS: SEMI-AUTO

In addition to the models listed, FNH USA also imported the HP-SA ($800 last MSR), and the HP-SFS until 2006.

All FNP guns come standard with three magazines and a lockable hard case.

FNP-9 – 9mm Para. cal., 4 in. barrel, 10 or 16 (disc. 2010) shot mag., polymer frame, matte black or matte stainless steel slide, DA/SA, matte black or flat Dark Earth (mfg. 2010 only) finish, ambidextrous frame mounted decocker, underframe rail, interchangeable backstrap inserts, 25.2 oz. Disc. 2011.

	$575	$495	$435	$380	$340	$300	$275	*$649*

Add $125 for night sights (disc. 2009).

Add $50 for USG operation (DA/SA, ambidextrous frame mounted decocker/manual safety), disc. 2010.

FNP-9M – 9mm Para. cal., 3.8 in. barrel, 10 or 15 shot mag., polymer frame, similar to the FNP-9, except is smaller frame, 24.8 oz. Disc. 2008.

	$525	$450	$400	$365	$335	$300	$275	*$593*

Add $118 for night sights.

FNP-357 – .357 SIG cal., similar to FNP-9, black finish only, 14 shot mag., 27.2 oz. Mfg. 2009.

	$565	$475	$425	$375	$335	$300	$275	*$629*

Add $65 for USG operation (features ambidextrous frame mounted decocker/manual safety levers).

FNP-40 – .40 S&W cal., 4 in. barrel, 10 or 14 (disc. 2010) shot mag., DA/SA, black or flat Dark Earth (mfg. 2010 only) polymer frame, optional stainless steel slide, underframe rail, interchangeable backstrap, external hammer, 25.2 or 26.7 oz. Disc. 2011.

	$575	$495	$435	$380	$340	$300	$275	*$649*

Add $125 for night sights (disc. 2009).

Add $50 for USG operation (features ambidextrous frame mounted decocker/manual safety levers), disc. 2010.

FNP-45 – .45 ACP cal., 4 1/2 in. barrel, DA/SA, 10 (disc. 2011), 14, or 15 (new 2011) shot mag., polymer frame, matte black finish with optional stainless steel slide, or flat Dark Earth (new 2010) finish, external extractor, underframe rail, interchangeable backstraps, 33.2 oz.

MSR $795	$725	$625	$575	$525	$450	$400	$350

Add $125 for night sights (disc.).

Subtract approx. 5% if without USG operation (features ambidextrous frame mounted decocker/manual safety levers).

Add approx. $186 for pistol package, which include three mags., molded polymer holster, double mag. pouch, and training barrel (mfg. 2009 only).

* ***FNP-45 Competition*** – .45 ACP cal., DA/SA, matte black finish, 15 shot mag., lower accessory rail, interchangeable arched and flat backstrap inserts with lanyard holes, 33.2 oz. New 2011.

MSR $1,239	$1,075	$925	$825	$725	$625	$550	$475

* ***FNP-45 Tactical*** – .45 ACP cal., 5.3 in. threaded barrel, 15 shot mag., DA/SA, polymer frame with MIL-STD 1913 mounting rail and interchangeable backstraps with lanyard eyelets, serrated trigger guard, ambidextrous mag. release, manual safety, and slide stop, fixed combat sights, Black or Flat Dark Earth finish, stainless steel slide, includes fitted soft case. New 2010.

MSR $1,395	$1,200	$1,025	$875	$775	$675	$575	$495

FNS-9/FNS-40 – 9mm Para. or .40 S&W cal., DA, matte black or stainless steel slide, black polymer frame, 14 or 17 shot mag., fixed 3-dot night sights, loaded chamber indicator, front and rear cocking serrations, lower accessory rail, interchangeable backstrap inserts, serrated triggerguard, ambidextrous safety, 25.2 - 27 1/2 oz. New 2012.

MSR $699	$625	$525	$450	$395	$350	$300	$275

GRADING - PPGS™	100%	98%	95%	90%	80%	70%	60%	LAST MSR

FNX-9/FNX-40 – 9mm Para. or .40 S&W cal., 4 in. barrel, 10 (new 2012), 14 (.40 S&W) or 17 (9mm Para.) shot mag., DA/SA, matte black or matte black with stainless steel slide, front and rear cocking serrations, MIL-STD mounting rail, deep V fixed combat sights, serrated trigger guard, ambidextrous mag. release and manual safety, four interchangeable backstrap inserts, 21.9-24.4 oz. New 2010.

MSR $699	$625	$525	$450	$395	$350	$300	$275	

FNX-45/FNX-45 COMPACT – .45 ACP cal., DA/SA, Black or Flat Dark Earth finish, 10, 12, or 15 shot mag., matte black or stainless steel slide, low profile fixed 3-dot sights, matte black polymer frame, front and rear cocking serrations, four interchangeable backstrap inserts, lower accessory rail, ambidextrous decocking levers, ring style external hammers, approx. 32 oz. New 2012.

MSR $809	$725	$650	$575	$500	$425	$350	$295	

* ***FNX-45 Tactical*** – .45 ACP cal., similar to FNX-45, except has threaded barrel, 15 shot mag., high profile night sights, includes fitted Cordura nylon soft case, 33.6 oz. New 2012.

MSR $1,399	$1,200	$1,025	$875	$775	$675	$575	$495	

FIVE-SEVEN/USG – 5.7x28mm cal., 4 3/4 in. barrel, USG or standard action, 10 or 20 shot mag., reversible mag. release, textured grip, black, OD Green (disc. 2011) or Flat Dark Earth finish, polymer frame, MIL-STD mounting, choice of fixed 3-dot (standard mfg.), adj. (USG model), C-More fixed (disc.), or C-More fixed night sights (disc.), underframe rail, includes three mags., hard case and cleaning kit, 20.8 oz.

MSR $1,299	$1,125	$975	$850	$750	$650	$575	$495	

Add 10% for early mfg. that incorporated a larger trigger guard than current mfg.

RIFLES: BOLT ACTION

FNH USA imports a wide range of tactical rifle systems for military and law enforcement only. FNH USA also imported a line of modular system rifles, including the Ultima Ratio Intervention, the Ultima Ratio Commando II, and the .338 Lapua Model. Please contact the company directly for more information, including availability and pricing (see Trademark Index).

PBR (PATROL BOLT RIFLE) – .300 WSM (XP Model) or .308 Win. cal., 22 in. heavy free floating barrel standard, stippled black Hogue overmolded stock, Picatinny rail, four shot fixed or removable box mag., some models may be marked "FN Herstal", later production marked "FNH", approx. 9 1/2 lbs.

	$1,075	$925	$825	$750	$625	$500	$425	*$1,075*

Add $170 for XP Model in .300 WSM cal.

SPR A3 G (SPECIAL POLICE RIFLE) – .308 Win. cal., 24 in. fluted barrel with hard chromed bore, hinged floorplate, one-piece steel MIL-STD 1913 optical rail, A3 fiberglass tactical stock with adj. comb and LOP, steel sling studs, designed to achieve 1/2 MOA accuracy standard, 14.3 lbs.

MSR $3,395	$3,100	$2,710	$2,325	$2,110	$1,705	$1,395	$1,085	

SPR A1/A1a – .308 Win. cal., 20 in. fluted (A1a) or 24 in. non-fluted barrel, 4 shot detachable box mag., pre-'64 Model 70 action, external claw extractor, matte black McMillan fiberglass stock with adj. comb and LOP, textured gripping surfaces, 12.4 lbs.

MSR $2,095	$1,875	$1,625	$1,400	$1,250	$1,025	$825	$725	

Add $379 for SPR A1a with 20 in. fluted barrel.

SPR A2 – .308 Win. cal., similar to A1, 20 in. fluted or 24 in. non-fluted barrel, 11.6 or 12.2 lbs. Disc. 2009.

	$2,500	$2,185	$1,875	$1,700	$1,375	$1,125	$875	*$2,745*

SPR A5 M – .308 Win. or .300 WSM cal., 20 in. fluted (.308 Win. cal. only) or 24 in. non-fluted barrel, 3 or 4 shot mag., black synthetic tactical stock, 11.6 or 12.2 lbs.

MSR $2,895	$2,650	$2,325	$1,975	$1,750	$1,475	$1,250	$950	

Add $100 for traditional hinged floorplate in .300 WSM cal. or $200 for hinged floorplate .308 Win. cal.
Add $200 for TBM (tactical box mag.) with 20 or 24 in. fluted barrel (new 2011).

GRADING - PPGS™	100%	98%	95%	90%	80%	70%	60%	LAST MSR

PSR I – .308 Win. cal., 20 in. fluted or 24 in. non-fluted barrel, 3, 4, or 5 shot internal mag., FN tactical sport trigger system, hinged floorplate, matte black McMillan sporter style fiberglass stock, raised comb, recoil pad, steel sling studs, 7.7 or 8.7 lbs. Disc. 2009.

	$2,000	$1,750	$1,500	$1,360	$1,100	$900	$700	*$2,253*

PSR II/III – .308 Win. or .300 WSM (PSR II) cal., 22 in. fluted or 24 in. non-fluted barrel, 3, 4 (PSR III), or 5 shot internal or detachable box mag., FN tactical sport trigger system, matte olive drab McMillan sporter style fiberglass stock, raised comb, recoil pad, steel sling studs, 8.7 - 9.8 lbs. Disc. 2009.

	$2,000	$1,750	$1,500	$1,360	$1,100	$900	$700	*$2,253*

TSR XP/XP USA (TACTICAL SPORT RIFLES) – .223 Rem. (XP USA), 7.62x39mm (XP USA, disc. 2009), .300 WSM, or .308 Win. cal., Model 70 short (XP) or ultra short (XP USA) action, 20 in. fluted (disc. 2010), 20 or 24 in. non-fluted barrel, 3, 4 (detachable box mag., XP Model only), 5, or 6 shot mag., one-piece steel MIL-STD 1913 optical rail, full aluminum bedding block molded into FN/Hogue synthetic stock, olive drab overmolded surface, recoil pad, steel sling studs, 8.7 - 10.1 lbs.

MSR $1,199	$1,050	$925	$800	$700	$600	$500	$400

Add $100 for .300 WSM cal. with floorplate.

SHOTGUNS

FNH USA manufactured tactical style shotguns, including the FN Police Shotgun ($500 last MSR) and the FN Tactical Police Shotgun (with or w/o fixed stock, $923 last MSR).

MODEL SLP (SELF LOADING POLICE) – 12 ga., 18 (SLP Standard), or 22 in. standard cantilever Invector choked (Mark I/Tactical) or rifled (Mark I Rifled) barrel, 6 or 8 shot mag., adj. rear sight, black synthetic stock with half or full pistol grip, rail mounted adj. ghost ring rear sight, two gas pistons for heavy and light loads, 7.7 - 8.2 lbs.

MSR $1,299	$1,025	$975	$850	$725	$625	$525	$425

Add $50 for 18 in. barrel (SLP Standard) with adj. rear sight.
Add $50 SLP MK1 Competition Model with 22 in. cantilever barrel.
Add $100 for 22 in. Cantilever barrel (SLP MK1 Tactical) with pistol grip stock, rifle sight.
Add $150 for Tactical Model with pistol grip, 18 in. barrel and adj. rifle sights (6 shot mag.).

MODEL SC1 O/U – 12 ga., 2 3/4 in. chambers, 28 in. VR barrel with invector plus choking, silver receiver, blue/gray adj. comb laminate stock with recoil pad. New 2011.

MSR $2,199	$1,950	$1,725	$1,575	$1,375	$1,150	$1,000	$875

FTL

Previously manufactured by Wilkinson Arms located in Covina, CA for the FTL Marketing Corp. located in N. Hollywood, CA.

PISTOLS: SEMI-AUTO

FTL AUTO NINE – .22 LR cal., single action, hammerless, blowback action, 8 shot mag., checkered plastic grips, fixed sights. Disc.

	$200	$160	$125	$105	$95	$85	$75

FABARM, S.p.A.

Current manufacturer established in 1900 and located in Brescia, Italy. Currently imported by Fabarm USA beginning 2012, and located in Cambridge, MD. Previously imported by Tristar, located in Kansas City, MO circa 2007-2009. Select models retailed by Bill Hanus Birdguns, LLC, located in Newport, OR. Previously imported by SIG Arms during 2005, located in Exeter, NH, and by Heckler & Koch, Inc. 1998-2004. Certain models had limited importation by Ithaca Acquisition Corp. located in King Ferry, NY during 1993-1995. Previously imported and distributed (1988-1990) by St. Lawrence Sales, Inc. located in Lake Orion, MI. Previously imported until 1986 by Beeman Precision Arms, Inc. located in Santa Rosa, CA.

Fabarm currently manufactures approx. 35,000 long guns annually.

Fabarm manufactures a wide variety of shotguns, rifles, and double rifles in assorted configurations, with many options available. Most models, however, are not currently being imported into the U.S. at this time. Please contact the factory directly for more information, including current model availability and pricing (see Trademark Index).

Due to space considerations, this manufacturer is available online free of charge at www.bluebookofgunvalues.com.

FABBRI s.n.c.

Current manufacturer established during 1965, and currently located in Nave (Brescia), Italy (previously located in Concescio). Consumer direct sales.

Ivo Fabbri and Daniele Perazzi were partners in a shotgun manufacturing business beginning in 1960 - these guns are ser. no. 5001-5339. Circa 1965, Fabbri and Perazzi split up and formed their own individual companies. "Armi Fabbri" relocated from Brescia to Concesio during 1969 and underwent a name change from Armi Fabbri to Fabbri s.n.c. during 1989. The first CNC machine was installed during 1974. Currently, Fabbri s.n.c. engravers include Creative Art, Pedersoli, Torcoli, and Fracassi. Fabbri manufactures perhaps the highest quality shotguns available in today's marketplace - approx. 20-30 guns are mfg. annually. Delivery times range from 2-4 years.

SHOTGUNS: CUSTOM

SxS SHOTGUN – 12 or 20 ga., one of the world's best sidelock SxS shotguns, ejectors, full engraving, "E" prefix ser. no., two types of back action. Disc.

Older Fabbri SxS shotguns manufactured with type II actions and in mint condition are priced in the $65,000 range. Subtract $10,000 for scroll engraving, and/or approx. 50% for type I action.

O/U SHOTGUN – 12, 20, 28 ga. or .410 bore, top-of-the-line quality with advanced CNC metal fabrication, steel, stainless steel (new 2002), or titanium construction, any combination of engraving, wood, and other options. Unique full laser welded stainless steel barrels. Both the type/style of engraving and the engraver will make a big difference on the current value of a custom ordered Fabbri O/U shotgun. Because engraving alone can add $50,000+ to the cost of a new shotgun, a qualified appraisal from a reputable dealer/collector is advised when buying or selling recently manufactured Fabbri O/U shotguns.

Current retail on the Classic model starts at approx. €100,000, Full Stainless Steel model is €110,000, and Titanium/Stainless Steel model is €125,000. All prices are FOB Italy, w/o engraving. Please contact Fabbri directly for a firm price quotation and delivery times (see Trademark Index).Add 25% for matched pair.

O/U guns mfg. 1967-1983 (typically marked Ivo Fabbri) are currently priced in the $40,000-$80,000 range, depending on condition and engraving. O/U guns mfg. 1983-1989 (typically marked Ivo Fabbri) are priced in the $75,000-$110,000 range, depending on condition, notoriety of engraver, and amount of engraving coverage. Guns mfg. within the last 10 years are currently priced in the $100,000-$150,000 range, depending on condition, notoriety of engraver, and amount of engraving coverage.

During an auction at the 2012 SCI Show, a new Fabbri with American motif engraving sold for $105,000.

FABRIQUE NATIONALE

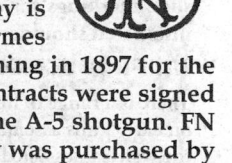

Current manufacturer located in Herstal, near Liege, Belgium. The current company name is "Group Herstal", however, the company is better known by "Fabrique Nationale" or "Fabrique Nationale d'Armes de Guerre". FN entered into their first contract with John M. Browning in 1897 for the manufacture of their first pistol, the FN 1899 Model. Additional contracts were signed and the relationship further blossomed with the manufacture of the A-5 shotgun. FN was acquired by GIAT of France in 1992. In late 1997, the company was purchased by the Walloon government of Belgium. Additional production facilities are located in Portugal, Japan, and the U.S.

Also see: Browning Arms under Rifles, Shotguns, and Pistols, and FNH USA for current offerings in the U.S.

The author would like to express his sincere thanks to Anthony Vanderlinden from the Browning Collector's Association for making FN contributions to this edition.

PISTOLS: SEMI-AUTO

For FN Models 1899, 1900, 1903, 1905, 1910, 1922 (10/22), Baby Model, Model 10/71, and BAC marked Hi-Powers (post 1954 mfg.), please refer to the Browning Pistol section in this text.

GRADING - PPGS™	100%	98%	95%	90%	80%	70%	60%	LAST MSR

PISTOLS: SEMI-AUTO, HI-POWER VARIATIONS

The F.N. Hi-Power (also known as P-35) was John Browning's last pistol design. A 9mm Para., single action, semi-auto pistol, it was the first to incorporate a staggered high capacity magazine. It has a 4 2/3 in. barrel, 13 shot mag., hammer and mag. safeties, a wide variety of finishes and sight options. It's probably the most widely used military pistol in the world.

For information on post-WWII BAC marked Hi-Powers, including model codes and identification, please refer to the Browning section under Serialization.

PRE-WAR COMMERCIAL AND MILITARY HP - 9mm Para. cal., single action, blue, wood grips, slotted for stock with tangent rear sight (fixed rear sight with unslotted rear grip strap not encountered in this model), 13 shot mag., commercial pistols display Liege proofs only, Belgian military pistols display Liege proofs and Belgian military acceptance markings. Mfg. 1935-1940.

	100%	98%	95%	90%	80%	70%	60%
Tangent sight & slotted	$2,750	$2,200	$1,700	$1,250	$950	$750	$650

Add $1,200 for original pre-war flat board stock with attached holster, commercial stocks are most often not numbered. Beware of post-war reproductions!

Add $1,400 for original prewar Belgian military flat board stock w/o attached holster. Check stock for small Belgian military acceptance marking.

Add $1,000 for correct Belgian military combination shoulder-stock - pistol holster.

PRE-WAR FOREIGN MILITARY CONTRACTS - mfg. under military contract for various countries.

	100%	98%	95%	90%	80%	70%	60%
Lithuanian Crest	N/A	$3,600	$2,950	$1,900	$1,350	$1,000	$900
Estonian Contract ("E.V." or "K.L.")	N/A	$3,700	$3,100	$2,500	$1,800	$1,350	$1,000
Finnish Contract ("SA" marked)	N/A	$2,800	$2,300	$1,900	$1,600	$1,100	$800
Paraguayan crest	N/A	$3,750	$3,000	$2,500	$2,250	$1,900	$1,750
Chinese, original finish	N/A	$2,400	$1,850	$1,500	$1,000	$850	$750

Add $1,200 for original (Finnish contract) pre-war flat board stock with attached holster.

Add $1,000 for original Finnish contract stock (ser. no. 11,000-15,000) with removed holster.

Add $200 for period Chinese inventory marking on Chinese contract pistols.

Subtract 50% for refinished Chinese contract pistols or reworks with Inglis parts.

Note: Finnish contract guns can be identified by the "SA" marking on frame, and/or slide, and/or mag. 2,400 pistols were shipped to Finland in 1940, all are in ser. no. range: 11,000 - 15,000.

Most Chinese contract pistols were refinished or reworked to include Inglis parts. Chinese contract pistols fall in the 6,000 - 11,000 and 20,000 - 21,000 ser. no. range.

Paraguayan contract guns are rare in the U.S. Numerous counterfeits have surfaced - check crest and slide markings for originality. Check bluing carefully, as most were refinished. Beware of matching numbered shoulder stocks as most are counterfeits or recently renumbered.

WWII PRODUCTION: WAFFENAMT PROOFED

There is a range of finishes during Nazi production that varies from the excellent pre-war commercial finish on early guns assembled from captured parts to the roughly milled, poorly finished specimens mfg. late in the war. Values listed assume all major parts (slide, barrel, and frame) are matching with original magazine.

In recent years, some Nazi production Hi-Powers have had the rear grip strap milled out and slotted to accept a shoulder stock. Careful observation is advised before purchasing a "rare" (and expensive) slotted and tangent sight specimen. Many HPs have been restored, since the restoration is easily accomplished by professionals.

* ***WWII Production: Waffenampt Proofed Type I*** - tangent slights, slotted, taken from existing pre-war Belgian production, quality is excellent, correct ser. range is quite limited, approx. 42,000-46,000+. Ser. range for production under German occupation is 50,001-52,500. All are proofed WaA 613.

	100%	98%	95%	90%	80%	70%	60%
	N/A	$5,200	$4,400	$3,700	$2,900	$2,450	$2,250

Beware of fakes and restorations. A large percentage of WaA613 pistols in the U.S. are counterfeits.

GRADING - PPGS™	100%	98%	95%	90%	80%	70%	60%	LAST MSR

* ***WWII Production: Waffenampt Proofed Type II*** – tangent sights, not slotted, approx. 90,000 mfg. with last ser. no. approx. 145,000, generally good quality finish, pistols are proofed WaA613, WaA103, some are WaA140.

N/A **$2,250 $1,650 $1,250 $1,000 $900 $800**

Add 25% if pistol is marked WaA613.
Add 15% if pistol is marked WaA103.

* ***WWII Production: Waffenampt Proofed Type III Standard Fixed Sights*** – not slotted, most common HP pistol produced during the war.

$1,200 $950 $700 $600 $500 $450 $400

Add 15% for late war Bakelite/synthetic grips.
Add 20% for eagle N proof instead of WaA140 proof, or for no WaA140 proof.

POST-OCCUPATION PRODUCTION – commercial assembly began September 1944 from wartime parts. Complete manufacturing from raw materials started in 1946. First imported with BAC markings in 1954 (see Browning HP section). Early (1944-1945) models are identifiable by an "A" serial number prefix and are not fitted with a magazine safety. Starting in 1947, the rear slide bushing was hardened by a new heat treatment process. Other design modifications were added in 1950. Many thousands manufactured for various government contracts.

Add $200-$2,000 for military pistols with crests, depending on condition and variation.

* ***Post-Occupation Production Tangent sight only***

$1,300 $1,100 $900 $700 $650 $550 $500

Add $100 for "T" prefix.

* ***Post-Occupation Production Tangent sight*** – slotted for stock, military or commercial mfg.

$1,500 $1,350 $1,100 $900 $750 $600 $500

Add $150 for "T" prefix.
Add $50 for internal extractor.

* ***Post-Occupation Production Fixed sight*** – most common variation.

$650 $525 $450 $400 $350 $325 $300

Add $100 for ring hammer.
Add 40% for "A" prefix, but only in 98%+ condition.

SULTAN OF MUSCAT AND OMAN CONTRACT

* ***Sultan Of Muscat And Oman Contract First Model*** – matte finish, reverse crest, scarce.

$4,500 $3,500 $2,500 $2,200 $2,000 $1,600 $1,300

* ***Sultan Of Muscat And Oman Contract Second Model*** – high polish finish, standard crest.

$4,000 $2,950 $1,750 $1,540 $1,265 $1,055 $875

INGLIS MANUFACTURED HI-POWERS – SEE INGLIS SECTION.

REVOLVERS

BARRACUDA – .357 Mag./9mm Para. cal., 4 in. barrel, blue finish, includes two cylinders chambered for .357 Mag. and 9mm Para. cal. Very limited importation.

$875 $775 $675 $600 $525 $450 $375

Add $175 for original styrofoam box, moon clips and documents.
Subtract $250 if sold with only one cylinder.

RIFLES: BOLT ACTION

FN MAUSER SPORTER DE LUXE – available in popular American and European calibers, 24 in. barrel, checkered pistol grip stock. Sold in the U.S. 1947-1963. Sold in the U.S. without rear sight installed or with a choice of Armstrong sights. No engraving. Note that barreled actions were also sold in the U.S.

$900 $750 $500 $450 $400 $350 $300

Add $100 for original FN box.
Prices assume original FN rifles with FN stock and FN buttplate, prices do not apply to FN barreled actions assembled by independent gunsmiths.

GRADING - PPGS™	100%	98%	95%	90%	80%	70%	60%	LAST MSR

FN MAUSER SPORTER DE LUXE SCROLL ENGRAVED – available in popular American and European calibers, 24 in. barrel, checkered pistol grip stock. Introduced shortly after the standard De Luxe model. Sold in the U.S. without rear sight installed or with a choice of Armstrong sights. FN scroll engraving in floral motif on receiver, buttplate and triggerguard. Note that scroll engraved barreled actions were also sold in the U.S.

	$2,000	$1,500	$1,000	$750	$500	$450	$350	

Prices assume original FN rifles with FN stock and FN buttplate, prices do not apply to scroll engraved FN barreled actions assembled by independent gunsmiths.
Add $100 for original FN box
Subtract $350 (95% or better) if the top of the engraved receiver is drilled and tapped for a scope.

FN MAUSER SPORTER (DE LUXE) PRESENTATION RIFLE – 30.06 or .270 Win. cal., other calibers only available on special order, 24 in. barrel, checkered pistol grip stock, rear sight installed on barrel, elaborate FN presentation grade engraving with dragon motifs on receiver, buttplate, triggerguard and barrel, engraved receiver and triggerguard are polished white and not blued, engraving design created and first executed by FN's Master Engraver Felix Funken. Note that presentation grade barreled actions were also sold in the U.S. Introduced 1954.

	$3,800	$3,200	$2,300	$1,250	$900	$800	$700	

Prices assume original FN rifles with FN stock and FN buttplate, prices do not apply to presentation grade FN barreled actions assembled by independent gunsmiths.
Add $100 for original FN box
Subtract $1,000 (95% or better) if the top of the engraved receiver is drilled and tapped for a scope.

FN SUPREME – .243 Win., .270 Win., 7mm Rem. Mag., .308 Win. or .30-06 cal., 24 in. barrel, peep sight, checkered pistol grip stock. Sold in the U.S. 1957-1975.

	$850	$725	$500	$450	$400	$350	$300	

FN SUPREME MAGNUM – .264 Win. Mag., 7mm Rem. Mag., .300 Win. Mag., or .375 H&H cal. Mfg. beginning circa 1957.

	$975	$850	$700	$550	$475	$425	$375	
.375 H&H cal.	$1,950	$1,700	$1,400	$1,100	$950	$850	$750	

FN SNIPER RIFLE (MODEL 30) – .308 Win. cal., this model was a Mauser actioned Sniper Rifle equipped with 20 in. extra heavy barrel, flash hider, separate removable diopter sights, Hensoldt 4x scope, hardcase, bipod, and sling. 51 complete factory sets were imported into the U.S., with additional surplus rifles that were privately imported.

	$4,750	$4,250	$4,000	$3,500	$3,000	$2,750	$2,500	

Subtract 15% if removable diopter sights or bipod is missing.
Subtract 10% if scope is not marked with F.N. logo.
Values assume complete factory outfit with all accessories.

RIFLES: SEMI-AUTO

BROWNING PATENT 1900 – .35 Rem. cal. only, usually features matted rib barrel and checkered stock and forearm, similar to Remington Model 8 auto-loading rifle. 4,913 mfg. 1910-1929 by FN, and not officially exported to the U.S.

	N/A	$3,500	$3,250	$3,000	$2,500	$2,000	$1,500	

Add 15% if rifle has plain barrel with tangent leaf rear sight.
Factory engraved rifles are very rare and will command substantial premiums.

MODEL 1949 – 7x57mm Mauser, 7.65mm Mauser, 7.92mm Mauser, or .30-06 cal., (.308 Win. cal. for Argentine conversion rifles), gas operated, 10 shot box mag. (20 round detachable mag. for Argentine conversions), 23 in. barrel, military rifle, tangent rear sight.

Columbia	$1,700	$1,400	$1,150	$1,000	$900	$750	$700	
Luxembourg	$1,500	$1,250	$1,000	$900	$800	$650	$600	
Venezuela	$1,350	$1,100	$900	$850	$700	$600	$550	
Argentina	N/A	$1,250	$1,100	$950	$850	$750	$650	
Egyptian	$1,600	$1,350	$1,100	$995	$895	$725	$675	

Add $100 for detachable grenade launcher.

GRADING - PPGS™	100%	98%	95%	90%	80%	70%	60%	LAST MSR

Subtract 30% for U.S. rebuilt, non-matching rifles with reproduction stocks.
Original FN-49 sniper rifles are extremely rare and may add $2,500+.

Beware of U.S. assembled "sniper" configurations, and Belgian military "ABL" scopes mounted on other contract rifles and sold as original sniper configurations.

FN-49 contract rifles not listed above are very rare in the U.S. and will demand a premium.

Carefully inspect black paint finish for factory originality, as all FN-49s were factory painted.

RIFLES: SEMI-AUTO, FAL/LAR/CAL/FNC SERIES

After tremendous price increases between 1985-88, Fabrique Nationale decided in 1988 to discontinue this series completely. Not only are these rifles not exported to the U.S. any longer, but all production has ceased in Belgium as well. The only way FN will produce these models again is if they are given a large military contract - in which case a "side order" of commercial guns may be built. 1989 Federal legislation regarding this type of paramilitary design also helped push up prices to their current level. FAL rifles were also mfg. in Israel by I.M.I.

F.N. FAL – semi-auto, French designation for the F.N. L.A.R. (light automatic rifle), otherwise similar to the L.A.R.

	100%	98%	95%	90%	80%	70%	60%
	$4,175	$3,950	$3,750	$3,475	$3,150	$3,100	$2,750

* ***F.N. FAL G***

	100%	98%	95%	90%	80%	70%	60%
Standard	$4,800	$4,000	$3,500	$2,950	$2,450	$2,150	$2,000
Paratrooper	$5,200	$4,400	$3,900	$3,350	$2,850	$2,550	$2,400
Heavy Barrel	$6,800	$6,250	$4,950	$4,400	$3,750	$3,250	$2,750
Lightweight	$5,200	$4,250	$3,750	$3,100	$2,600	$2,350	$2,100

Values listed assume inclusion of factory bipod.

The Standard G Series was supplied with a wooden stock and wood or nylon forearm. The Heavy Barrel variant had all wood furniture and was supplied with a bipod. The Lightweight Model had an aluminum lower receiver, piston tube and magazine.

G Series FALs were imported between 1959-1962 by Browning Arms Co. This rifle was declared illegal by the GCA of 1968, and was exempted 5 years later. Total numbers exempted are: Standard - 1,822, Heavy Barrel - 21, and Paratrooper - 5.

F.N. L.A.R. COMPETITION (50.00, LIGHT AUTOMATIC RIFLE) – .308 Win. (7.62x51mm) cal., semi-auto, competition rifle with match flash hider, 21 in. barrel, adj. 4 position fire selector on automatic models, wood stock, aperture rear sight adj. from 100-600 meters, 9.4 lbs. Mfg. 1981-83.

	100%	98%	95%	90%	80%	70%	60%
	$4,250	$4,025	$3,850	$3,625	$3,450	$3,175	$2,950

This model was designated by the factory as the 50.00 Model.

Mid-1987 retail on this model was $1,258. The last MSR was $3,179 (this price reflected the last exchange rate and special order status of this model).

* ***FN L.A.R. Competition Heavy barrel rifle (50.41 & 50.42)*** – barrel is twice as heavy as standard L.A.R., includes wood or synthetic stock, short wood forearm, and bipod, 12.2 lbs. Importation disc. 1988.

	100%	98%	95%	90%	80%	70%	60%
	$4,495	$4,275	$4,150	$4,000	$3,675	$3,500	$3,250

Add $500 for walnut stock.
Add $350 for match sights.

There were 2 variations of this model. The Model 50.41 had a synthetic buttstock while the Model 50.42 had a wood buttstock with steel buttplate incorporating a top extension used for either shoulder resting or inverted grenade launching.

Mid-1987 retail on this model was $1,497 (Model 50.41) or $1,654 (Model 50.42). The last MSR was $3,776 (this price reflected the last exchange rate and special order status of this model).

* ***FN L.A.R. Competition Paratrooper rifle (50.63 & 50.64)*** – similar to L.A.R. model, except has folding stock, 8.3 lbs. Mfg. 1950-88.

	100%	98%	95%	90%	80%	70%	60%
	$4,275	$3,700	$3,300	$3,000	$2,550	$2,300	$2,150

There were 2 variations of the Paratrooper L.A.R. Model. The Model 50.63 had a stationary aperture

GRADING - PPGS™	100%	98%	95%	90%	80%	70%	60%	LAST MSR

rear sight and 18 in. barrel. The Model 50.64 was supplied with a 21 in. barrel and had a rear sight calibrated for either 150 or 200 meters. Both models retailed for the same price.

Mid-1987 retail on this model was $1,310 (both the Model 50.63 and 50.64). The last MSR was $3,239 (this price reflected the last exchange rate and special order status of this model).

CAL – originally imported in 1980, FN's .223 CAL military rifle succeeded the .308 FAL and preceeded the .223 FNC, at first declared illegal but later given amnesty, only 20 imported by Browning.

$7,800	$7,000	$6,250	$5,500	$4,750	$4,100	$3,600

FNC MODEL – .223 Rem. (5.56mm) cal., lightweight combat carbine, 16 or 18 1/2 in. barrel, NATO approved, 30 shot mag., 8.4 lbs. Disc. 1987.

$2,950	$2,700	$2,550	$2,100	$1,900	$1,650	$1,500

Add $350 for Paratrooper model (16 or 18 1/2 in. barrel).

While rarer, the 16 in. barrel model incorporated a flash hider that did not perform as well as the flash hider used on the standard 18 1/2 in. barrel.

Mid-1987 retail on this model was $749 (Standard Model) and $782 (Paratrooper Model). The last MSR was $2,204 (Standard Model) and $2,322 (Paratrooper Model) - these prices reflected the last exchange rate and special order status of these models.

SHOTGUNS: SxS

FN ANSON STANDARD GRADE – 12 or 16 ga., 26, 28, or 30 (most common) in. barrels, boxlock action, with or w/o ejectors, DT, checkered walnut stock, Greener style crossbolt, FN legend roll engraved on bottom of boxlock, minor engraving on and around screws. Mfg. circa 1910-1940.

$1,500	$1,300	$950	$625	$550	$375	$325

Add $150 for factory checkered stock options or semi-pistol grip option.
Add $200+ for more elaborate engraving. FN offered six luxury engraving styles.
Subtract $50-$100 if w/o ejectors.
Subtract approx. $250 for replacement buttplate (not original), if in 95%+ original condition.

FN NEW ANSON STANDARD GRADE – 12 or 16 ga., 26, 28, or 30 (most common) in. barrels, boxlock action, with or w/o ejectors, DT, checkered walnut stock, FN legend hand engraved on top of the barrels, minor engraving on and around screws. Mfg. circa 1930-1968.

$1,400	$1,150	$850	$550	$475	$350	$300

Add $150 for factory checkered stock options or semi-pistol grip option.
Add $200+ for more elaborate engraving. FN offered six luxury engraving styles.
Subtract approx. $250 for replacement buttplate (not original), if in 95%+ original condition.

FN SIDELOCK STANDARD GRADE – 12 or 16 ga., 26, 28, or 30 (most common) in. barrels, sidelock action, ejectors, DT, checkered walnut stock, minor engraving on sideplates Mfg. 1921-1950. Improved in 1930, and often referred to as the Model 1930.

$1,500	$1,300	$950	$625	$550	$375	$325

Add $200+ for more elaborate engraving. FN offered six luxury engraving styles.
Subtract approx. $250 for replacement buttplate (not original), if in 95%+ original condition.

FABRYKA BRONI LUCZNIK - RADOM SP.ZO.O

Current manufacturer of commercial and military firearms located in Radom, Poland. No current U.S. importation.

Please contact the factory directly for possible U.S. importation and availability (see Trademark Index).

FALCO, srl

Current manufacturer established circa 1960, and located in Marcheno, Italy. Currently imported by Accardi Importer, located in Vacaville, CA. Previously represented in Europe by Effebi, snc. Some models were imported by K.B.I. until 2002.

Falco manufactures a variety of good quality shotgun and rifles in various configurations, including O/U, SxS, combinations, and single shots. Falco is well-known for its folding action design. Falco also manufactures a single shot, SxS pistol in either 9mm Flobert or

GRADING - PPGS™	100%	98%	95%	90%	80%	70%	60%	LAST MSR

.410 bore with approx. 19 3/4 in. barrels. Please contact the U.S. importer directly for information on current availability and pricing (see Trademark Index).

FALCON FIREARMS

Previous manufacturer located in Northridge, CA from 1986-1990.

PISTOLS: SEMI-AUTO

PORTSIDER – .45 ACP cal., patterned after Colt M 1911 A-1, stainless steel, fixed sights, 5 in. barrel, 7 shot mag., available in left-hand only. Mfg. 1986-90.

$500	$425	$375	$315	$270	$230	$200	*$580*

* ***Portsider Set*** – features right and left-hand models with matching serial numbers. Only 100 sets mfg. 1986-1987.

$1,300	$1,100	$895	$785	$655	$550	$465	*$1,400*

GOLD FALCON – .45 ACP cal., machined receiver made from solid 17Kt. gold alloy, stainless steel slide, diamond sighting system, choice of grips, standard or personalized engraving options. Only 50 mfg.

$25,000	$17,500	$11,500	N/A	N/A	N/A	N/A	*$30,500*

FAMARS di ABBIATICO & SALVINELLI SRL

Previous manufacturer established 1967-2012 by Mario Abbiatico and Remo Salvinelli, and located in Gardone, Italy. Famars USA is currently selling the remaining Famars inventory (see Trademark Index). Previously distributed and imported by Chris Batha, located in Okatie, SC, and by Robin Hollow Outfitters, located in Addieville, RI. Previously distributed by William Larkin Moore, located in Scottsdale, AZ, the First National Gun Banque, located in Colorado Springs, CO and by Fieldsport, located in Traverse City, MI. Previously imported by Dewing's Fly and Gun, located in West Palm Beach, FL, and by A&S of America, located in Jefferson Boro, PA.

A&S Famars manufactured some of the world's finest rifles and shotguns - approx. 100 were fabricated annually. Most Famars guns included a lifetime warranty. Because every A&S Famars longarm was an individual custom order, each Famars firearm must have its value ascertained on an individual appraisal basis, with the major considerations being original condition, bore/gauge or caliber, overall configuration, and both the amount of engraving and the notoriety of the engraver.

All A&S Famars shotguns incorporated a patented A&S Famars mechanism, and many were available in Hunting, Trap, Skeet, Sporting Clays, and Pigeon configurations.

Previously manufactured guns had base prices listed only, and values and options are in euros. On discontinued models, used gun prices in dollars. Further information and price quotations were available by contacting the distributors directly.

A&S Famars models currently manufactured and listed were broken down into three basic grades. The Extra grade was English scroll, Purdey style engraving, with quality 4 wood, and included leather case. The Prestige grade was game scene or full English scroll engraving, with quality 4 wood and included leather case. The De Luxe grade included very detailed, deep ornamental or ornamental and game scene engraving, exhibition quality wood, and leather case.

RIFLES: SxS, CUSTOM MFG.

Boxlock and sidelock rifles are all best quality and range in calibers between .22 LR and .600 Nitro Express.

AFRICA EXPRESS STANDARD, EXTRA, PRESTIGE, & DE LUXE – .243 Win., .30-06, 8x57RmmJS, 9.3x74Rmm, or .375 H&H cal., Anson & Deely boxlock action, chopper lump chrome steel barrels, fixed gold "V" notch front sight, DT, customer selected walnut.

Base price for this model in 2012 was €26,500.
Add €4,500 for Africa Extra.
Add €7,500 for Africa Express Prestige.
Add €11,500 for Africa Express De Luxe.
Add approx. 15% for .500 NE - .600 NE cals.

GRADING - PPGS™	100%	98%	95%	90%	80%	70%	60%	LAST MSR

EXCALIBUR EXPRESS – various cals. up to .470 NE cal., engraved round boxlock action with or w/o sideplates.

Base price for this model in 2012 was €15,000.
Add €2,500 for Extra.
Add €3,900 for Prestige.
Add €6,500 for De Luxe.

POSEIDON ROUND EXPRESS – available in calibers up to .375 H&H.

Base price for this model in 2012 was €26,000.
Add €4,000 for Extra.
Add €7,000 for Prestige.
Add €12,000 for De Luxe.

VENUS EXPRESS EXTRA, PRESTIGE, DE LUXE – dangerous game cals., removable sidelock action, ejectors, DT, chopper lump barrels, customer selected walnut.

Base price for this model in 2012 was €48,000.
Add €6,000 for Venus Express Prestige.
Add €14,000 for Venus Express De Luxe.
Add approx. 10% for .500 NE - .600 NE cals.

VENUS EXPRESS EXTRALUSSO – top-of-the-line model. Very limited mfg.

SHOTGUNS: O/U, CUSTOM MFG.

Each gun was manufactured per individual customer special order. Previously manufactured guns have the last MSRs listed when possible, and discontinued models were in euros.

JOREMA MODEL – 12 or 20 ga., sidelock. Disc. 1999.

	100%	98%	95%	90%	80%	70%	60%	LAST MSR
	$25,000	$19,750	$13,500	$10,250	$8,750	$7,500	$6,250	*$25,650*

Add 10% for 20 ga.

SOVEREIGN EXTRA, PRESTIGE, DE LUXE (JOREMA ROYAL, ARIES) – 12, 16, 20, 28 ga., or .410 bore, sidelock action, ejectors, DT or ST, chopper lump barrels, available with optional detachable sidelocks, customer selected walnut.

Base price for this model in 2012 was €40,000.
Add €5,000 for Prestige.
Add €9,000 De Luxe.
Add 10% for 28 ga. or .410 bore, depending on the grade.

This model was originally called the Jorema Royal, then renamed the Aries in 2000, and renamed the Sovereign in 2002.

ROYALE SH MODEL – 12, 20, 28 ga., or .410 bore, sidelock, bar action. Disc. 2002.

	100%	98%	95%	90%	80%	70%	60%	LAST MSR
	$34,000	$23,750	$17,750	$13,000	$10,000	$8,500	$7,250	*$38,875*

Add 20% for 28 ga. or .410 bore.

CASTORE EXTRA, PRESTIGE, DE LUXE – various gauges, sidelock action, customer selected walnut. Disc.

	100%	98%	95%	90%	80%	70%	60%	LAST MSR
	$33,500	$30,250	$26,900	$22,000	$17,000	$13,000	$10,500	*$37,000*

Add $4,000 for Prestige.
Add $11,000 for De Luxe.
Add approx. $4,000 for 28 ga. or .410 bore.

PEGASUS EXTRA, PRESTIGE, DE LUXE – features Famars patented sidelocks.

	100%	98%	95%	90%	80%	70%	60%	LAST MSR
	$26,750	$21,750	$16,500	$12,500	$10,000	$8,500	$7,250	

Add $2,820 for Prestige.
Add $10,800 for De Luxe.
Add 10% for 28 ga. or .410 bore.

EXCALIBUR COMPETITION MODELS – 12, 20, 28 ga., or .410 bore, current models include the BL, BLE (Extra), BLP (Prestige), BLX (sideplate), BLXE, BLXP, SL (sidelock), SLE, and SLP.

Add approx. 15% for 28 ga. or .410 bore. on the following models.

GRADING - PPGS™	100%	98%	95%	90%	80%	70%	60%	LAST MSR

* ***Excalibur BL*** – 12, 16, 20, 28 ga., or .410 bore, detachable locks, monobloc barrels, ST, ejectors, customer selected walnut.

Base price for this model in 2012 was €11,300.
Add €2,550 for Extra.
Add €3,600 for Prestige.
Add €6,500 for De Luxe.

* ***Excaliber BL Round*** – similar to BL, except round action.

Base price for this model in 2012 was $30,450.
Add approx. $3,000 for 28 ga. or .410 bore.

* ***Excalibur BL Round Titanium*** – titanium round action.

	100%	98%	95%	90%	80%	70%	60%	LAST MSR
	$21,750	$19,000	$17,000	$14,500	$11,250	$9,750	$8,500	*$24,816*

Add $2,376 for Extra.
Add $10,692 for De Luxe.

* ***Excalibur BLX*** – 12, 16, 20, 28 ga., or .410 bore, detachable trigger mechanism with sideplates and monobloc barrels, ejectors, ST, customer selected walnut.

Base price for this model in 2012 was $32,150.
Add approx. $3,300 for 28 ga. or .410 bore.

* ***Excalibur SL*** – sidelock action, monobloc barrels. Disc. 2002.

	100%	98%	95%	90%	80%	70%	60%	LAST MSR
	$21,000	$17,500	$13,250	$9,750	$8,200	$7,500	$6,750	*$23,750*

* ***Excalibur Sporting*** – 12 or 20 ga., removable trigger mechanism, SST, monobloc barrels with Briley chokes, ejectors, customer selected walnut, color case hardened receiver.

Base price for this model in 2012 was €13,500.
Add €2,800 for Extra.
Add €4,300 for Prestige.
Add €7,500 for De Luxe.

ROMBO VIERLING EXTRA, PRESTIGE, DE LUXE QUATTROCANNE – 28 ga. or .410 bore, Anson & Deeley locking system with sideplates, side opening lever, ST, four chopper lump barrels are arranged in a quad pattern, customer selected walnut, approx. 7 1/2 lbs. Limited mfg.

Base price for this model in 2012 was $130,000.

POSEIDON ROUND (BL) – 12, 20, 28 ga., or .410 bore., round action with monobloc or demibloc barrels.

Base price for this model in 2012 was $39,000.
Add $3,300 for 28 ga. or .410 bore.
Add approx. $5,000 for demibloc barrels (disc.).

* ***Poseidon Round w/Sideplates***

Base price for this model in 2012 was $44,780.
Add $4,470 for 28 ga. or .410 bore.

* ***Poseidon BL Round Titanium*** – titanium round action with demibloc barrels.

	100%	98%	95%	90%	80%	70%	60%	LAST MSR
	$27,250	$25,750	$21,000	$17,250	$14,750	$13,000	$11,750	

Add $2,160 for BL Extra.
Add $9,720 for De Luxe.

* ***Poseidon BLX*** – monobloc or demibloc barrels.

	100%	98%	95%	90%	80%	70%	60%	LAST MSR
	$17,250	$16,000	$13,750	$11,500	$9,650	$8,500	$7,250	

Add $1,200 for BLX Extra.
Add $3,480 for Prestige.
Add $13,172 for De Luxe.
Add $4,380 for demibloc barrels.

DOVE GUN – 20 or 28 ga., 27-32 in. barrel, round body frame, fixed or mobilchokes, ST or DT, customer selected Turkish walnut, four engraving choices, includes case. Limited mfg. of 100 beginning 2010.

Base price for this model in 2012 was $18,400.

GRADING - PPGS™	100%	98%	95%	90%	80%	70%	60%	LAST MSR

QUAIL GUN – 28 ga. or .410 bore, 26-32 in. barrels, customer selected Turkish walnut, boxlock sideplates, vent. rib, fixed or mobilchokes, ST or DT, two engraving choices, includes case, limited edition of 50 mfg. beginning 2010.

Base price for this model in 2012 was $21,900.

LEONARDO – various gauges, patented Famars pinless sidelock action, SST, ejectors, detachable sidelocks and titanium frame are an option.

The base price for this model in 2012 was $95,000.
Add $9,400 for 28 ga. or .410 bore.

SHOTGUNS: SxS

Each gun was manufactured per individual customer special order. Previously manufactured guns have last MSRs listed when available, and values are in dollars.

Add 10% for 28 ga. or .410 bore. on the following models.

CASTORE PRESTIGE/DE LUXE HAMMER GUN – various gauges, double barrel, exposed hammers, double triggers. Limited importation.

	100%	98%	95%	90%	80%	70%	60%	LAST MSR
	$30,000	$26,250	$23,000	$19,750	$16,750	$14,650	$12,000	

Add $3,168 for Prestige.
Add $11,880 for De Luxe.

BOXLOCK MODELS – various gauges, available with Anson & Deeley boxlock action, scalloped or rounded frame, various engraving patterns available.

* ***Zeus*** – 12 or 20 ga., features round action, side lever release, DT, limited mfg.

Base price for this model in 2012 was $49,000.
Add $10,000 for 28 ga. or .410 bore.

* ***Tribute Extra, Prestige, De Luxe Boxlock*** – 12 (disc.), 20 (disc.), 28 ga., or .410 bore (disc.), scalloped back drop lock action, 7 1/4 lbs., limited mfg.

	100%	98%	95%	90%	80%	70%	60%	LAST MSR
	$27,750	$24,250	$20,750	$15,250	$12,350	$10,750	$9,250	

Add $3,600 for Prestige.
Add $11,640 for De Luxe.
Add approx. 20% for 28 ga. or 10% for .410 bore.

SIDELOCK MODELS

* ***Highline (Veneri) Sidelock Model*** – various gauges, round body, back action, very limited mfg. Disc. 1999.

	100%	98%	95%	90%	80%	70%	60%	LAST MSR
	$25,500	$20,000	$16,000	$12,250	$10,000	$8,500	$7,250	*$30,000*

VENUS – features patented Famars sidelocks, back action.

Base price for this model in 2012 was $74,650.
Add $7,025 for 28 ga. or .410 bore.

VENUS EXPRESS – various gauges, chopper lump barrels, Famars patented sidelocks, sideplates featuring pins milled from solid steel, auto ejectors, manual safety.

Base price for this model in 2012 was $88,000.

AVANTIS – 12, 16, 20, 28 ga., or .410 bore, hand detachable sidelock mechanism is attached to removable trigger group, chopper lump barrels, uncheckered straight grip stock and forearm, customer selected walnut, round frame, 6 - 6 1/2 lbs.

Base price for this model in 2012 was $66,500.
Add $6,650 for 28 ga. or .410 bore.

FANZOJ, JOHANN

Current long gun manufacturer established in 1790 and located in Ferlach, Austria. Consumer direct sales.

Johann Fanzoj is the 9th generation in his family to manufacture top quality long arms. Today's configurations include double rifles in all possible calibers, double shotguns, bolt action rifles, stalking rifles, combination guns, and the new Tri-Bore three barrel shotgun. Drillings and Vierlings are also available by special order, but typically not imported into the U.S. Fanzoj was also a member of the Ferlach Guild, which was dissolved in 2004.

GRADING - PPGS™	100%	98%	95%	90%	80%	70%	60%	LAST MSR

RIFLES

Current MSR for a double rifle sidelock in-the-white is €54,000. Current MSR on an underlever stalking rifle in-the-white is €25,000. The Fanzoj bolt action rifle in-the-white starts at €12,500. A boxlock double rifle (new 2010) is currently POR.

SHOTGUNS

Tri-Bore shotguns are available in 12, 16, 20, 28 ga. or .410 bore. Current MSR for a Tri-Bore in-the-white is €47,000 for most gauges, and €51,700 for 28 ga. or .410 bore.

FARQUHARSON

Single shot rifle configuration designed by John Farquharson in 1871. The Farquharson was influential during the height of the British Empire, and was popular with sportsmen and soldiers alike.

Currently, Ballard Arms of Cody, Wyoming is building a rifle based on this configuration. Please contact the company directly for more information, including pricing, availability and delivery time (see Trademark Index).

FAUSTI STEFANO SRL

Current manufacturer established in 1948 and located in Marcheno, Italy. Shotguns currently imported beginning 2009 by Fausti USA, located in Frederickburg, VA.

FAUSTI STEFANO s.r.l.

Fausti manufactures a variety of excellent quality shotguns in O/U and SxS configuration, smoothbore and rifled. Fausti is a well established brand name in the European marketplace. New importation can be determined by the Fausti Stefano SRL markings.

RIFLES: DOUBLE

CLASS EXPRESS – 8x57JRS, 9.3x74R, .30R Blaser, .30-06, .444 Marlin, or .45-70 Govt., boxlock, 24 in. barrels, inertial single or double triggers, no selector, ejectors, fine deep chiseled engraving executed by laser, Bavarian or Classic A pistol grip walnut oil finished stock. New 2012.

MSR $4,990	$4,500	$4,000	$3,500	$3,000	$2,500	$2,000	$1,750

CLASS SL EXPRESS – 8x57JRS, 9.3x74R, .30R Blaser, .30-06, .444 Marlin, or .45-70 Govt., boxlock, 24 in. barrels,single trigger, ejectors, French grayed or color case hardened frame, hand engraving signed by the engraver, Bavarian or Classic AA pistol grip walnut oil finished stock with rubber recoil pad. New 2012.

MSR $7,600	$6,950	$6,200	$5,500	$4,750	$4,000	$3,250	$2,550

SHOTGUNS: O/U

Please refer to the Weatherby section for more information for previous O/U Fausti importation.

CALEDON – 12, 16, 20, 28 ga., or .410 bore, 2 3/4 or 3 in. chambers, boxlock, 26, 28, or 30 in. barrels, round pistol grip A+ walnut stock and foream, SST, ejectors, coin finished deep laser engraved receiver with gold inlays.

MSR $1,999	$1,795	$1,550	$1,325	$1,100	$900	$750	$650

Add $570 for 16, 28 ga. or .410 bore.

CALEDON YOUTH – 20 ga., 3 in. chambers, boxlock, 28 in. barrels, pistol grip A+ walnut stock and forearm, 12 1/2 LOP, SST, ejectors, coin finished deep laser engraved receiver with gold inlays.

MSR $1,999	$1,795	$1,550	$1,325	$1,100	$900	$750	$650

CALEDON SL – 12, 20, 28 ga., or .410 bore, 2 3/4 or 3 in. chambers, boxlock, 26, 28, or 30 in. barrels, round pistol grip AA+ walnut stock and forearm, SST, ejectors, coin finished deep laser engraved receiver with gold inlays, sideplates, scaled frame.

MSR $2,749	$2,450	$2,100	$1,800	$1,500	$1,225	$1,000	$875

Add $581 for 16, 28 ga. or .410 bore.

GRADING - PPGS™	100%	98%	95%	90%	80%	70%	60%	LAST MSR

CLASS – 12, 16, 20, 28 ga., or .410 bore, 2 3/4 or 3 in. chambers, boxlock, 26, 28, or 30 in. barrels, round pistol grip AA walnut stock and foream, SST, ejectors, coin finished deep laser engraved receiver with gold inlays, scaled frame.

MSR $2,449	$2,100	$1,900	$1,600	$1,350	$1,000	$900	$800

Add $550 for 16, 28 ga. or .410 bore.

CLASS SL – 12, 16, 20, 28 ga., or .410 bore, 2 3/4 or 3 in. chambers, boxlock, 26, 28, or 30 in. barrels, round pistol AA walnut stock and forearm, SST, ejectors, coin finished deep laser engraved receiver with gold inlays, side plates, scaled frame.

MSR $3,206	$2,800	$2,400	$2,000	$1,650	$1,275	$1,050	$995

Add $588 for 16, 28 ga. or .410 bore.

CLASS ROUND BODY – 16, 20, 28 ga., or .410 bore, 2 3/4 or 3 in. chambers, boxlock, 28 or 30 in. barrels, SST, ejectors, hand engraved case colored or coin finished receiver with gold inlays, AAA oil finished round pistol grip walnut stock and forearm, scaled frame.

MSR $4,950	$4,200	$3,675	$3,150	$2,850	$2,300	$1,875	$1,450

Add $590 for 16, 28 ga. or .410 bore.

SHOTGUNS: SxS

DEA – 12, 16, 20, 28 ga. or .410 bore, 2 3/4 in. (16 or 28 ga.) or 3 in. (12, 20 ga. or .410), chambers, boxlock, 26, 28, or 30 in. barrels, lightly engraved color case receiver with gold inlay, AAA checkered oil finished English walnut stock and forearm, single non-selective trigger, ejectors, scaled frames. New 2011.

MSR $3,350	$3,000	$2,650	$2,275	$1,850	$1,525	$1,300	$1,100

Add $640 for 16, 28 ga. or .410 bore.

DEA DUETTO – 28 ga. or .410 bore, 2 3/4 or 3 in. chambers, 26 (disc. 2013), 28, or 30 (disc. 2013) in. barrels, boxlock, lightly engraved case colored receiver with gold inlay, AAA checkered oil finished English walnut stock and forearm, single non-selective trigger, ejectors, scaled frame, approx. 5 lbs. Importation began 2010.

MSR $5,300	$4,750	$4,250	$3,650	$3,150	$2,600	$2,200	$1,775

DEA ROUND BODY – 12, 16, 20, 28 ga., or .410 bore, 2 3/4 (16 or 28 ga.) or 3 (12, 20 ga. or .410 bore) in. chambers, boxlock, 28 or 30 in. barrels, case colored or coin finished engraved receiver with gold inlay, AAA straight grip checkered walnut stock and forearm, recoil pad, DT, ejectors, scaled frame, 6 lbs. Importation began 2010.

MSR $5,899	$5,450	$4,775	$4,095	$3,700	$3,000	$2,450	$1,900

Add $590 for 16, 28 ga. or .410 bore.

CLASS – 12, 16, 20, 28 ga., or .410 bore, 2 3/4 or 3 in. chambers, 26, 28, or 30 in. barrels, straight grip AA walnut stock and foream, SST, ejectors, coin finished lightly engraved receiver with gold inlays, 5.8 - 7.3 lbs. Importation began 2010.

MSR $2,449	$2,175	$1,900	$1,625	$1,475	$1,195	$975	$750

Add $100 for 16 ga. or $500 for 28 ga. or .410 bore.

CLASS ROUND BODY – 16, 20, or 28 ga., 2 3/4 or 3 in. chambers, 28 or 30 in. barrels, SST, ejectors, lightly engraved case colored or coin finished receiver with gold inlay, AAA oil finished straight grip walnut stock and forearm, 5.8 - 6.3 lbs.

MSR $4,199	$3,825	$3,345	$2,875	$2,600	$2,100	$1,725	$1,350

Add $100 for 16 ga., or $400 for 28 ga.

CALEDON – 12, 16, 20, 28 ga., or .410 bore, 2 3/4 or 3 in. chambers, 26, 28, or 30 in. barrels, SST, ejectors, coin finished scroll engraved receiver with gold inlays, A+ oil finished walnut stock and forearm, 5.8-7 1/4 lbs. Importation began 2010.

MSR $1,999	$1,795	$1,570	$1,350	$1,225	$985	$810	$625

Add $100 for 16, 28 ga., or .410 bore.

SHOTGUNS: O/U, FAUSTI BOUTIQUE SERIES

Fausti manufactures a variety of custom guns models, they can be ordered through Fausti USA to the customers specifications. The following models belong to the Fausti Boutique line of guns that are entirely hand finished and feature stocks in select walnut, engravings signed by the artist,

GRADING - PPGS™	100%	98%	95%	90%	80%	70%	60%	LAST MSR

brands with outstanding ballistic performance and truly scaled frames. Extremely armonious lines, balance of shapes and attention to every detail converge into the creation of the Fausti Boutique line.

CLASS ROUND BODY THEME 1 – 16, 20, 28 ga. or .410 bore, boxlock, 2 3/4 or 3 in. chambers, 26 (new 2013), 28 or 29 in. barrels, SST, ejectors, hand scroll engraving signed by the author, French grayed receiver with gold inlay, AAAA oil finished Prince of Wales walnut stock and forearm, scaled frame.

MSR $14,600	$12,750	$10,000	$8,750	$7,500	$6,250	$5,500	$4,750

Add $640 for 16, 28 ga. or .410 bore.

* ***Class Round Body Theme 2*** – 16, 20, 28 ga. or .410 bore, boxlock, 2 3/4 or 3 in. chambers, 26, 28, or 29 in. barrels, similar to Class Round Body Theme 1, except has hand engraved rich scroll with gold inlay banners signed by the engraver, Frech grayed receiver, AAAA oil finished Prince of Wales walnut stock, scaled frame.

MSR $18,300	$16,500	$14,000	$11,750	$8,750	$7,250	$6,000	$5,000

Add $640 for 16, 28 ga. or .410 bore.

CLASS SL WOODCOCK DEDICATED – 12, 16, 20, 28 ga. or .410 bore, boxlock, 2 3/4 or 3 in. chambers, 26 (new 2013), 28 or 29 in. barrels, SST, ejectors, hand engraving signed by engraver, color case hardened or French grayed receiver, AAA oil finished straight grip with Prince of Wales walnut stock and forearm, sideplates, scaled frame.

MSR $7,990	$7,325	$6,500	$5,750	$5,000	$4,250	$3,500	$2,500

Add $640 for 16, 28 ga. or .410 bore.

CLASS SL DE LUXE – 12, 16, 20, 28 ga. or .410 bore, boxlock, 2 3/4 or 3 in. chambers, 26 (new 2013), 28 or 29 in. barrels, SST, ejectors, hand engraving signed by engraver, French grayed or color case hardened receiver, AAAA oil finished straight English walnut stock and forearm, sideplates, scaled frame.

MSR $9,950	$9,025	$7,750	$6,500	$5,250	$4,650	$3,800	$2,750

Add $640 for 16, 28 ga. or .410 bore.

MAGNIFICENT – 12, 16, 20, 28 ga. or .410 bore, boxlock, 2 3/4 or 3 in. chambers, 26 (new 2013), 28 or 29 in. barrels, SST, ejectors, ultimate 3-D laser chisel engraving with hand finishing, French grayed frame, AAA oil finished pistol grip walnut stock and forearm, scaled frame.

MSR $4,999	$4,500	$4,000	$3,500	$3,000	$2,500	$2,000	$1,675

Add $640 for 16, 28 ga. or .410 bore.

* ***Magnificent Sport Edition*** – 12, 16, 20, 28 ga. or .410 bore, boxlock, 2 3/4 or 3 in. chambers, 26 (disc.), 28, 30, or 32 (new 2013) in. barrels, SST, ejectors, ultimate 3-D laser chisel engraving hand finishing, French grayed frame, AAA+ oil finished pistol grip walnut stock and forearm, scaled frame. New 2012.

MSR $5,999	$5,300	$4,600	$4,100	$3,350	$2,750	$2,150	$1,775

Add $640 for 16, 28 ga. or .410 bore.

BRIXIAN XL (FUTURO ANTICO) – 12, 16, 20, 28 ga. or .410 bore, boxlock, 2 3/4 or 3 in. chambers, 26, 28, or 29 in. barrels, SST, ejectors, hand engraving signed by engraver, case color hardened or French grayed receiver, AAAAA oil finished W style pistol grip walnut stock and forearm, steel grip cap, scaled frame.

MSR $17,450	$15,750	$13,250	$10,750	$9,250	$8,250	$7,250	$6,000

Add $640 for 16, 28 ga. or .410 bore.

* ***Brixian LX (Futuro Antico) Theme 1*** – 12, 16, 20, 28 ga. or .410 bore, boxlock, 2 3/4 or 3 in. chambers, 26, 28, or 29 in. barrels, SST, ejectors, hand engraving signed by the engraver, French grayed frame, AAAAA oil finished W style pistol grip walnut stock and forearm, steel grip cap, side plates, scaled frame.

MSR $21,450	$18,750	$15,250	$13,000	$10,500	$8,750	$7,500	$6,250

Add $640 for 16, 28 ga. or .410 bore.

* ***Brixian LX (Futuro Antico) Theme 2*** – 12, 16, 20, 28 ga. or .410 bore, boxlock, 2 3/4 or 3 in. chambers, 26, 28, or 29 in. barrels, SST, ejectors, hand engraving signed by the

GRADING - PPGS™	100%	98%	95%	90%	80%	70%	60%	LAST MSR

engraver, bone charcoal frame, AAAAA oil finished W style pistol grip walnut stock and forearm, steel grip cap, side plates, scaled frame. New 2013.

MSR $21,450 $18,750 $15,250 $13,000 $10,500 $8,750 $7,500 $6,250

Add $640 for 16, 28 ga. or .410 bore.

* ***Brixian LX (Futuro Antico) Theme 3*** – 12, 16, 20, 28 ga. or .410 bore, boxlock, 2 3/4 or 3 in. chambers, 26, 28, or 29 in. barrels, SST, ejectors, hand engraving signed by the engraver, French grayed frame, AAAAA oil finished W style pistol grip walnut stock and forearm, steel grip cap, side plates, scaled frame. New 2013.

MSR $25,450 $21,625 $18,925 $16,225 $14,700 $11,895 $9,725 $7,550

Add $640 for 16, 28 ga. or .410 bore.

VENETIAN – 12, 16, 20, 28 ga. or .410 bore, boxlock, 2 3/4 or 3 in. chambers, 26, 28, or 29 in. barrels, SST, ejectors, hand engraving signed by the engraver, French grayed frame, AAAAA oil finished W style pistol grip walnut stock and forearm, steel grip cap, side plates, scaled frame. New 2013.

MSR $18,450 $15,675 $13,700 $11,750 $10,650 $8,625 $7,050 $5,475

Add $640 for 16, 28 ga. or .410 bore.

BRIXIAN VITTORIA ALATA – 12, 16, 20, 28 ga. or .410 bore, boxlock, 2 3/4 or 3 in. chambers, 26, 28, or 29 in. barrels, SST, ejectors, hand engraving signed by engraver, AAAAA oil finished straight English walnut stock and forearm, sideplates, scaled frame.

MSR $35,000 $31,000 $27,000 $23,000 $18,750 $15,500 $13,500 $11,750

Add $640 for 16, 28 ga. or .410 bore.

BRIXIAN BATTAGLIE BRESCIANE – 12, 16, 20, 28 ga. or .410 bore, boxlock, 2 3/4 or 3 in. chambers, 26, 28, or 29 in. barrels, SST, ejectors, hand engraving signed by engraver, AAAAA oil finished straight English walnut stock and forearm, sideplates, scaled frame.

MSR $35,000 $31,000 $27,000 $23,000 $18,750 $15,500 $13,500 $11,750

Add $640 for 16, 28 ga. or .410 bore.

SHOTGUNS: SxS, FAUSTI BOUTIQUE SERIES

DEA SL – 12, 16, 20, 28 ga. or .410 bore, boxlock, 2 3/4 (16 or 28 ga.) or 3 (12, 20 ga. or .410 bore) in. chambers, 26, 28, or 29 in. barrels, hand engraving signed by engraver, French grayed or color case frame, AAA checkered oil finished walnut stock and forearm, single non-selective trigger, ejectors, sideplates, scaled frames.

MSR $6,300 $5,000 $4,500 $4,000 $3,500 $3,000 $2,500 $2,000

Add $640 for 16 ga. or $1,500 for 28 ga. or .410 bore.

DEA SL WOODCOCK DEDICATED – 12, 16, 20, 28 ga. or .410 bore, boxlock, 2 3/4 (16 or 28 ga.) or 3 (12, 20 ga. or .410 bore) in. chambers, 26, 28, or 29 in. barrels, hand engraving signed by engraver, French grayed or color case frame, AAA checkered oil finished straight English walnut stock and forearm, single non-selective trigger, ejectors, sideplates, scaled frame.

MSR $7,990 $7,275 $6,500 $5,750 $5,000 $4,250 $3,500 $2,750

Add $640 for 16 ga. or $1,500 for 28 ga. or .410 bore.

DEA BRITISH – 16, 20, 28 ga. or .410 bore, boxlock, 2 3/4 (16 or 28 ga.) or 3 (12, 20 ga. or .410 bore) in. chambers, 26, 28, or 29 in. barrels, hand engraving signed by the engraver, French grayed or color case round frame with gold inlays, AAAA checkered oil finished straight English walnut stock and forearm, single trigger, ejectors, sideplates, scaled frame.

MSR $15,385 $14,000 $12,000 $10,000 $8,250 $7,000 $6,000 $5,000

Add $640 for 16 ga. or $1,500 for 28 ga. or .410 bore.

DEA BRITISH SL – 12, 16, 20, 28 ga. or .410 bore, boxlock, 2 3/4 (16 or 28 ga.) or 3 (12, 20 ga. or .410 bore) in. chambers, 26, 28, or 29 in. barrels, hand engraving signed by engraver, French grayed or color case frame, AAAA checkered oil finished straight English walnut stock and forearm, single non-selective trigger, ejectors, sideplates, scaled frame.

MSR $17,250 $15,750 $13,250 $11,000 $9,000 $7,750 $6,750 $5,750

Add $640 for 16 ga. or $1,500 for 28 ga. or .410 bore.

GRADING - PPGS™	100%	98%	95%	90%	80%	70%	60%	LAST MSR

* ***DEA British SL Theme 1*** – 12, 16, 20, 28 ga. or .410 bore, boxlock, 2 3/4 (16 or 28 ga.) or 3 (12, 20 ga. or .410 bore) in. chambers, 26, 28, or 29 in. barrels, hand engraving signed by the engraver, French grayed or color case frame, AAAA checkered oil finished straight English walnut stock and forearm, single non-selective trigger, ejectors, sideplates, scaled frame.

MSR $20,950 $18,500 $16,000 $12,500 $10,000 $8,750 $7,500 $6,500

Add $640 for 16 ga. or $1,500 for 28 ga. or .410 bore.

* ***DEA British SL Theme 2*** – 12, 16, 20, 28 ga. or .410 bore, boxlock, 2 3/4 (16 or 28 ga.) or 3 (12, 20 ga. or .410 bore) in. chambers, 26, 28, or 29 in. barrels, hand engraving signed by the engraver, French grayed or color case frame, AAAA checkered oil finished straight English walnut stock and forearm, single non-selective trigger, ejectors, sideplates, scaled frame.

MSR $22,800 $20,000 $17,000 $13,000 $10,500 $9,000 $7,750 $6,750

Add $640 for 16 ga. or $1,500 for 28 ga. or .410 bore.

* ***DEA British SL Theme 3*** – 12, 16, 20, 28 ga. or .410 bore, boxlock, 2 3/4 (16 or 28 ga.) or 3 (12, 20 ga. or .410 bore) in. chambers, 26, 28, or 29 in. barrels, hand engraving signed by the engraver, French grayed or color case frame, AAAA checkered oil finished straight English walnut stock and forearm, single non-selective trigger, ejectors, sideplates, scaled frame.

MSR $20,260 $18,000 $15,500 $12,000 $9,000 $8,250 $7,250 $6,250

Add $640 for 16 ga. or $1,500 for 28 ga. or .410 bore.

* ***DEA British SL Theme 4*** – 12, 16, 20, 28 ga. or .410 bore, boxlock, 2 3/4 (16 or 28 ga.) or 3 (12, 20 ga. or .410 bore) in. chambers, 26, 28, or 29 in. barrels, hand engraving signed by the engraver, French grayed or color case frame, AAAA checkered oil finished straight english walnut stock and forearm, single non-selective trigger, ejectors, sideplates, scaled frame.

MSR $21,950 $19,500 $16,500 $12,500 $10,250 $8,750 $7,500 $6,500

Add $640 for 16 ga. or $1,500 for 28 ga. or .410 bore.

* ***DEA British SL Theme 5*** – 12, 16, 20, 28 ga. or .410 bore, boxlock, 2 3/4 (16 or 28 ga.) or 3 (12, 20 ga. or .410 bore) in. chambers, 26, 28, or 29 in. barrels, hand engraving signed by the engraver, French grayed or color case frame, AAAA checkered oil finished straight English walnut stock and forearm, single non-selective trigger, ejectors, sideplates, scaled frame.

MSR $18,650 $16,750 $14,000 $11,750 $9,500 $8,00 $7,000 $6,000

Add $640 for 16 ga. or $1,500 for 28 ga. or .410 bore.

* ***DEA British SL Theme 6*** – 12, 16, 20, 28 ga. or .410 bore, boxlock, 2 3/4 (16 or 28 ga.) or 3 (12, 20 ga. or .410 bore) in. chambers, 26, 28, or 30 in. barrels, hand engraving signed by the engraver, French grayed or color case frame, AAAA checkered oil finished straight English walnut stock and forearm, single trigger, ejectors, sideplates, scaled frame.

MSR $21,950 $19,500 $16,500 $12,500 $10,250 $8,750 $7,500 $6,500

Add $640 for 16 ga. or $1,500 for 28 ga. or .410 bore.

* ***DEA British SL Theme 7*** – 12, 16, 20, 28 ga. or .410 bore, boxlock, 2 3/4 (16 or 28 ga.) or 3 (12, 20 ga. or .410 bore) in. chambers, 26, 28, or 29 in. barrels, hand engraving signed by the engraver, black and gold frame, AAAA checkered oil finished straight English walnut stock and forearm, single trigger, ejectors, sideplates, scaled frame. New 2012.

MSR $21,950 $19,500 $16,500 $12,500 $10,250 $8,750 $7,500 $6,500

Add $640 for 16 ga. or $1,500 for 28 ga. or .410 bore.

* ***DEA British SL Theme 8*** – 12, 16, 20, 28 ga. or .410 bore, boxlock, 2 3/4 (16 or 28 ga.) or 3 (12, 20 ga. or .410 bore) in. chambers, 26, 28, or 29 in. barrels, hand engraving signed by the engraver, French grayed or color case frame, AAAA checkered oil finished straight English walnut stock and forearm, single non-selective trigger, ejectors, sideplates, scaled frame. New 2012.

MSR $21,950 $19,500 $16,500 $12,500 $10,250 $8,750 $7,500 $6,500

Add $640 for 16 ga. or $1,500 for 28 ga. or .410 bore.

GRADING - PPGS™	100%	98%	95%	90%	80%	70%	60%	LAST MSR

NOBLESS THEME 1 – 12, 16, 20, or 28 ga., sidelock, 2 3/4 (16 or 28 ga.) or 3 (12 or 20 ga.) in. chambers, 26, 28, or 29 in. barrels, hand engraving signed by the engraver, color case hardened frame, AAAA checkered oil finished straight English walnut stock and forearm, double triggers, ejectors, sideplates. New 2012.

MSR $15,000	$13,500	$11,250	$9,000	$8,000	$7,000	$6,000	$5,000	

Add $640 for 16 ga. or $1,500 for 28 ga. or .410 bore.

* ***Nobless Theme 2*** – 12, 16, 20, or 28 ga., sidelock, 2 3/4 (16 or 28 ga.) or 3 (12 or 20 ga.) in. chambers, 26, 28, or 29 in. barrels, hand engraving signed by the engraver, color case hardened frame, AAAA checkered oil finished straight English walnut stock and forearm, double triggers, ejectors, sideplates. New 2012.

MSR $22,000	$18,500	$16,000	$13,750	$11,250	$9,000	$8,000	$7,250	

Add $640 for 16 ga. or $1,500 for 28 ga. or .410 bore.

SENATOR – 12, 16, 20, 28 ga. or .410 bore, detachable sidelock, 2 3/4 (16 or 28 ga.) or 3 (12, 20 or .410 ga) in. chambers, 26, 28, or 29 in. barrels, hand engraving signed by the engraver, French grayed frame, AAAA checkered oil finished straight English walnut stock and forearm, single non-selective trigger, ejectors, sideplates, many custom order options.

This model is POR.

FEATHER INDUSTRIES, INC.

Previous manufacturer located in Boulder, CO until 1995.

DERRINGERS

GUARDIAN ANGEL CENTERFIRE – 9mm Para. or .38 Spl. cal., O/U design, stainless steel, double action backup derringer. Mfg. 1988-89 only.

	$225	$190	$160	$130	$100	$80	$60	*$140*

This model has interchangeable loading blocks that allow shooting 9mm Para. or .38 Spl. There is no exposed hammer and trigger is totally enclosed.

GUARDIAN ANGEL RIMFIRE – .22 LR or .22 WMR cal., design is similar to 9mm Para./.38 Spl. model, loading block breech, 2 in. barrel, fixed sights, 12 oz. Mfg. 1990-95.

	$150	$125	$100	$75	$60	$55	$50	*$120*

Add $30 for individual extra loading blocks.

This model has interchangeable loading blocks that allow shooting .22 LR or .22 WMR. There is no exposed hammer and the trigger is totally enclosed.

PISTOLS: SEMI-AUTO

MINI-AT – .22 LR cal., pistol variation of the AT-22, 5 1/2 in. shrouded barrel, 20 shot mag., approx. 2 lbs. Mfg. 1986-89.

	$300	$265	$235	$195	$165	$145	$135	*$220*

RIFLES: SEMI-AUTO

AT-22 – .22 LR cal., semi-auto blowback action, 17 in. detachable shrouded barrel, collapsible metal stock, adj. rear sight, with sling and swivels, 20 shot mag., 3 1/4 lbs. Mfg. 1986-95.

	$325	$275	$250	$240	$230	$220	$215	*$250*

F2 – similar to AT-22, except is equipped with a fixed polymer buttstock. Mfg. 1992-95.

	$295	$240	$215	$200	$185	$175	$160	*$280*

AT-9 – 9mm Para. cal., semi-auto blowback action, 16 in. barrel, paramilitary design, available with 10 (C/B 1994), 25*, 32 (disc.), or 100 (disc. 1989) shot mag., 5 lbs. Mfg. 1988-95.

	$850	$775	$700	$650	$600	$550	$500	*$500*

Add $250 for 100 shot drum mag.

F9 – similar to AT-9, except is equipped with a fixed polymer buttstock. Mfg. 1992-95.

	$725	$675	$600	$550	$485	$450	$375	*$535*

GRADING - PPGS™	100%	98%	95%	90%	80%	70%	60%	LAST MSR

SATURN 30 – 7.62x39mm Kalashnikov cal., semi-auto, gas operated, 19 1/2 in. barrel, composite stock with large thumbhole pistol grip, 5 shot detachable mag., drilled and tapped for scope mounts, adj. rear sight, 8 1/2 lbs. Mfg. in 1990 only.

$800	$700	$625	$575	$525	$450	$425	*$695*

KG-9 – 9mm Para. cal., semi-auto blowback action, 25 or 50 shot mag., paramilitary configuration. Mfg. 1989 only.

$850	$775	$700	$650	$600	$550	$500	*$560*

Add $100 for 50 shot mag.

SAR-180 – .22 LR cal., semi-auto blowback action, 17 1/2 in. barrel, 165 shot drum mag., fully adj. rear sight, walnut stock with combat style pistol grip and forend, 6 1/4 lbs. Mfg. 1989 only.

$695	$625	$575	$525	$475	$440	$400	*$500*

Add $250 for 165 shot drum mag.
Add $200 for retractable stock.
Add $395 for laser sight.

This variation was also manufactured for a limited time by ILARCO (Illinois Arms Company), previously located in Itasca, IL.

KG-22 – .22 LR cal., similar to KG-9, 20 shot mag. Mfg. 1989 only.

$395	$350	$300	$275	$255	$245	$235	*$300*

FEATHER USA/AWI LLC

Current rifle manufacturer established 1996 and located in Eaton, CO.

RIFLES: SEMI-AUTO

Feather USA currently manufactures the following RAV models: .22 LR, 9mm, .45 ACP, 10mm, .40 S&W, .357 SIG, and .460 Rowland. All models except the .22 LR will accept Glock magazines, and many accessories and options are available. Prices range from $399-$950, not including options. Please contact the company directly for more information, including availability (see Trademark Index).

FEDERAL ENGINEERING CORPORATION

Previous manufacturer located in Chicago, IL.

RIFLES: SEMI-AUTO

XC-220 – .22 LR cal., semi-auto paramilitary design rifle, 16 5/16 in. barrel, 28 shot mag., machined steel action, 7 1/2 lbs. Mfg. 1984-89.

$495	$450	$400	$350	$320	$295	$275

XC-450 – .45 ACP cal. only, semi-auto paramilitary design carbine, 16 1/2 in. barrel length, 30 shot mag., fires from closed bolt, machined steel receiver, 8 1/2 lbs. Mfg. 1984-89.

$950	$825	$750	$675	$600	$550	$500

XC-900 – 9mm Para. cal., semi-auto paramilitary design carbine, 16 1/2 in. barrel length, 32 shot mag., fires from closed bolt, machined receiver action, 8 lbs. Mfg. 1984-89.

$950	$825	$750	$675	$600	$550	$500

FEDERAL ORDNANCE, INC.

Previous manufacturer, importer, and distributor located in South El Monte, CA from 1966-1992. Briklee Trading Co. bought the remaining assets of Federal Ordnance, Inc. in late 1992, and continued to import various firearms until circa 1998.

Federal Ordnance imported and distributed both foreign and domestic military handguns and rifles until 1992. In addition, they also fabricated firearms using mostly newer parts.

PISTOLS: SEMI-AUTO

In addition to the following Broomhandle models, Federal Ordnance also manufactured other special editions. These models include the British Model, Cut-Away, Cartridge Counter, Para La Guerra, and others. Prices are in the $800-$950 range (retail).

GRADING - PPGS™	100%	98%	95%	90%	80%	70%	60%	LAST MSR

MODEL 714 BROOMHANDLE – 7.63 Mauser or 9mm Para. cal., 5 1/2 in. barrel, new frame, exterior completely refinished, 10 shot detachable mag., "fair" bore, adj. rear sight. Mfg. 1986-91.

	$700	$600	$500	$450	$400	$350	$325	$820

Add $100 for new barrel.

* ***Model 714 Broomhandle Para La Guerra*** – 7.63 Mauser or 9mm Para. cal., remanufactured to duplicate Spanish Civil War configuration Broomhandle, includes 10 in. barrel with "Para La Guerra" engraved on side. Mfg. 1990-91 only.

	$750	$650	$550	$450	$400	$350	$325	$890

* ***Model 714 Broomhandle Bolo*** – similar to Model 714 Broomhandle, except has smaller grips, 3.9 in. barrel, 10 shot mag. standard. Mfg. 1988 only.

	$700	$600	$500	$450	$400	$350	$325	$890

STANDARD BROOMHANDLE – 7.63 Mauser or 9mm Para. cal., refurbished (new barrels, completely refinished, etc.) C-96 pistols, new springs, includes original Chinese shoulder/ holster stock. Disc. 1991.

	$650	$550	$485	$450	$420	$390	$380	$735

Subtract $150 without shoulder/holster stock.

* ***Standard Broomhandle Bolo*** – similar to Standard Broomhandle, except Bolo configuration (3.9 in. barrel and smaller grips). Includes original Chinese shoulder/ holster stock. Mfg. 1990-91 only.

	$600	$500	$450	$420	$390	$380	$370	$530

RANGER 1911A1 GI – .45 ACP cal., 5 in. barrel, 7 shot mag., steel construction throughout, checkered walnut grips, 40 oz. Mfg. 1988-92.

	$450	$395	$350	$310	$280	$260	$240	$440

Add $20 for Ranger Extended Model (40 oz. - new 1990).
Add $40 for Ranger Ambo (ambidextrous safety, 40 oz. - new 1990).
Add $15 for lightweight Ranger Lite Model (32 oz. - new 1990).

These pistols are patterned after the Colt 1911A1 Govt. Model.

* ***Ranger 1911A1 GI Ten*** – 10mm cal., otherwise similar to regular Ranger 1911A1. Mfg. 1990-91 only.

	$675	$525	$475	$450	$420	$395	$370	$780

RANGER SUPERCOMP – .45 ACP or 10mm cal., variation of the Ranger 1911A1 with 6 in. compensated barrel, slide, tuned trigger, and other competition features, 42 oz. Mfg. 1990-91 only.

	$1,250	$875	$775	$675	$600	$550	$495	$1,390

Add $10 for 10mm cal.

THE RANGER ALPHA – .38 Super, 10mm, or .45 ACP cal., 5 or 6 in. barrel, patterned after the Colt Govt. Model. Mfg. 1990-91 only.

	$895	$775	$675	$575	$475	$425	$380	$1,000

Add $16 for 10mm cal.
Add $16 for 6 in. barrel.
Add $9-$25 for ported 5 or 6 in. barrel depending on cal.

RIFLES/CARBINES

ALL AMERICAN SPORTER BOLT ACTION – .30-06 cal., Springfield M1903 receiver, new sporter stock, drilled and tapped for scope base (included), blue finish. Mfg. late 1991-92.

	$365	$345	$320	$300	$290	$280	$275	

MODEL 713 DELUXE MAUSER SEMI-AUTO CARBINE – 7.63 Mauser or 9mm Para. cal., 16 in. barrel, detachable stock, one 10 shot and one 20 shot detachable mag., deluxe walnut, leather case with accessories, adj. sights to 1,000 meters, 5 lbs. 1,500 mfg. 1986-1992.

	$1,750	$1,495	$1,250	$1,050	$935	$755	$640	$1,986

GRADING - PPGS™	100%	98%	95%	90%	80%	70%	60%	LAST MSR

* ***Model 713 Deluxe Mauser Semi-Auto Carbine Field Grade*** – 7.63 Mauser or 9mm Para. (new 1989) cal., 16 in. barrel, 10 shot fixed mag., nondetachable walnut stock. Mfg. 1987-92.

	$950	$775	$675	$600	$525	$475	$425	*$1,200*

M-14 SEMI-AUTO – .308 Win. cal., legal for private ownership (no selector), 20 shot mag., refinished original M-14 parts, available in either filled fiberglass, G.I. fiberglass, refinished wood, or new walnut stock. Mfg. 1986-91.

	$1,275	$1,075	$995	$940	$865	$800	$750	*$700*

Add $50 for filled fiberglass stock.
Add $110 for refinished wood stock.
Add $190 for new walnut stock with handguard.

During the end of production, Chinese parts were used on this model. Values are the same.

TANKER GARAND SEMI-AUTO – .30-06 or .308 Win. cal., original U.S. GI parts, 18 in. barrel, new hardwood stock, parkerized finish. Mfg. began late 1991.

	$975	$900	$850	$800	$750	$700	$625

CHINESE RPK 86S-7 SEMI-AUTO – 7.62x39mm cal., semi-auto version of the Peoples Republic of China RPK light machine gun, 75 shot drum mag., 23 3/4 in. barrel, with bipod. Imported 1989 only.

	$1,450	$1,275	$1,075	$1,000	$825	$775	$650	*$500*

Add $100 for 75 shot drum mag.

FEINWERKBAU

Current manufacturer established circa 1951, and located in Oberndorf, Germany. Currently imported beginning 2005 by Brenzovich Firearms Training Center (B.F.T.C.), located in Fort Hancock, Texas. Previously imported until 2004 by Nygord Precision, located in Prescott, AZ.

Feinwerkbau manufactures some of the world's finest quality target rifles and pistols (.22 LR rimfire and airgun). Target rifles and pistols have had limited importation into the U.S.

Feinwerkbau also manufactures world championship winning airguns and a black powder pistol. For more information and current pricing on both new and used Feinwerkbau airguns, please refer to the *Blue Book of Airguns* by Dr. Robert Beeman & John Allen (also online). For more information on the black powder pistol, please refer to the *Blue Book of Modern Black Powder Arms* by John Allen (also online).

PISTOLS: SEMI-AUTO, RIMFIRE

MODEL AW-93 – .22 LR cal., 6 in. barrel, 5 shot mag., ergonomically designed stippled walnut grips with adj. heel, unique damper prevents muzzle jump and recoil, satin nickel receiver finish, bolt burnished, top-of-the-line Target pistol, adj. two-stage trigger, adj. rear sight, right or left hand grip, current mfg. includes plastic case, approx. 2 1/2 lbs. New 1993.

MSR $2,443	$2,275	$1,925	$1,600	$1,400	$1,150	$950	$850

* ***Model AW-93 Lightweight*** – similar to standard Model AW-93, except has lightened frame, blue aluminum damper/weight underneath slide, 2 1/3 lbs. Limited importation began 2004.

MSR $2,527	$2,350	$1,975	$1,650	$1,425	$1,175	$975	$850

RIFLES: BOLT ACTION, RIMFIRE

MODEL 2000 – .22 LR cal. only, single shot, match target bolt action rifle, fully adj. trigger, walnut stocks, four variations featuring different specifications. Importation disc. 1988.

* ***Model 2000 Universal Model*** – 26 3/8 in. barrel, aperture sights, stippled pistol grip and forearm, 9 3/4 lbs.

	$1,150	$925	$850	$735	$650	$595	$550	*$1,395*

Add $350 for electronic trigger.
Add $160 for left-hand variation.

GRADING - PPGS™	100%	98%	95%	90%	80%	70%	60%	LAST MSR

* ***Model 2000 Mini (Junior)*** – 22 in. barrel, aperture sights, stippled pistol grip, 9 1/8 lbs.

	$1,025	$875	$825	$700	$625	$575	$525	*$1,225*

Add $350 for electronic trigger.
Add $150 for left-hand variation.

* ***Model 2000 Match Model*** – 26 1/4 in. barrel, adj. cheekpiece on stock, stippled pistol grip and forearm, aperture sights.

	$1,075	$895	$825	$700	$625	$575	$525	*$1,285*

Add $390 for electronic trigger.
Add $113 for left-hand variation.

* ***Model 2000 Running Target*** – adj. cheekpiece on stock, thumbhole stippled pistol grip, no sights, for running boar competition.

	$1,150	$925	$850	$735	$650	$595	$550	*$1,398*

Add $142 for left-hand variation.

MODEL 2600 UNIVERSAL – .22 LR cal. only, similar design to Model 600 air rifle, single shot, 26.3 in. barrel, aperture sights, 10.6 lbs. Imported 1986-94.

	$1,425	$1,125	$925	$850	$735	$650	$595	*$1,695*

Add $160 for left-hand variation.

MODEL 2600 ULTRA MATCH FREE RIFLE – .22 LR cal., single shot match gun based on Model 2600 action, 26.1 in. barrel, laminated stock with thumbhole, fully adj. aperture sights, 14 lbs. 1 oz. Mfg. 1986-94.

	$2,175	$1,750	$1,400	$1,150	$925	$850	$735	*$2,498*

Add $250 for electronic trigger (disc. 1988).
Add $152 for left-hand variation.

MODEL 2602 UNIVERSAL (UIT) RIFLE – .22 LR cal., designed for Match competition, state-of-the-art Target rifle with different color wood laminations possible, adj. cheekpiece, short or long barrel, two-stage trigger. Mfg. 1997-2003.

	$1,450	$1,275	$1,125	$975	$850	$725	$600	*$1,615*

Add $125 for left-hand action.

MODEL 2602 FREE RIFLE – .22 LR cal., standard Match rifle with red and blue anodized aluminum stock with adj. cheekpiece and buttplate, and adj. hand rest, 16 3/4 or 26 1/2 in. barrel with unique 13 3/4 in. squared-off barrel sleeve with sight, diopter sights, top-of-the-line competition rifle, approx. 13.86 lbs. Mfg. 1997-2003.

	$2,035	$1,800	$1,575	$1,350	$1,175	$1,000	$850	*$2,365*

Add $155 for left-hand action.

MODEL 2602 SUPER MATCH – .22 LR cal., Super Match variation featuring state- of-the-art design, adj. stock, comb, LOP, and trigger pull. Disc. 2003.

	$2,550	$2,175	$1,800	$1,575	$1,350	$1,175	$1,000	*$2,995*

Add $130 for left-hand action.
Subtract $130 for Model 2602 Sport RT.

MODEL 2602 SPORT – .22 LR cal., sporter variation of the Model 2602, short or long barrel, right or left-hand action, two-stage trigger, laminated wood stock with red stripes and thumbhole, adj. cheekpiece and buttplate, approx. 12 3/4 lbs. Mfg. 2000-2003.

	$1,950	$1,750	$1,525	$1,325	$1,175	$1,000	$850	*$2,240*

MODEL 2700 UNIVERSAL – .22 LR cal., competition rifle, single shot, features laminate stock and adj. cheekpiece, right or left hand action, adj. two-stage trigger, adj. aluminum buttplate, muzzle brake, approx. 12 lbs. New 2004.

MSR $2,484	$2,300	$1,900	$1,575	$1,275	$1,075	$875	$750	

MODEL 2700 FREE RIFLE SUPER MATCH – .22 LR cal., current top-of-the-line rifle, 27 in. barrel, single shot, right or left hand action, adj. two-stage trigger, features blue or silver aluminum stock, pivoting anatomical grip and interior sliding weight, adj. cheekpiece, adj. buttplate, sling holder with anatomical handstop, 12 1/4 - 13 1/2 lbs. New 2004.

MSR $3,601	$3,275	$2,850	$2,500	$2,225	$1,875	$1,575	$1,375	

GRADING - PPGS™	100%	98%	95%	90%	80%	70%	60%	LAST MSR

FELK TRAILERS PTY LTD.

Previous pistol manufacturer located in Australia circa 1998-2000.

PISTOLS: SEMI-AUTO

MTF919 – 9mm Para. cal., designed similar to a compact Glock with trigger safety, striker fire, black polymer frame, metal slide, 3 in barrel, 10 shot clear plastic mag., limited importation during the late 1990s.

$325	$275	$225	$200	$175	$150	$135	

FEMARU

Previously manufactured by Femaru-Fegyver es Gepgyar R.T. located in Budapest, Hungary.

PISTOLS: SEMI-AUTO

MODEL 1929 (29M) – .380 ACP cal., 3.93 in. barrel, 8 shot mag., identifiable by squared-off rear slide with vertical serrations, 2 piece walnut grips, approx. 50,000 mfg.

$795	$600	$400	$300	$200	$165	$145	

MODEL 1937 (37M) – .32 ACP or .380 ACP cal., 3.93 in. barrel, 8 shot mag., commercial blue finish, left slide marking "FEMARU FEGYVER ES GEPGYAR RT. 37M", vertically grooved 2-piece walnut grips, approx. 200,000 mfg. (.380 ACP cal.) for Hungarian service before Nazi variations began (dubbed "Pistole Modell 37 (ung)," circa 1941), Nazi marked "jhv 41" or "jhv 44", 27 oz.

$500	$400	$300	$250	$225	$200	$175	

Add 50% for Waffenamt proofing (.32 ACP only).
Add another 100% if with holster and 2 matching mags.

FROMMER STOP POCKET AUTO – .32 ACP or .380 ACP cal., 6 or 7 shot, 3 7/8 in. barrel, fixed sights, blue, rubber grips, locked breech, external hammer. Mfg. 1912-1920.

$395	$325	$250	$225	$200	$175	$150	

Add 50% for .380 ACP cal.

FROMMER BABY POCKET AUTO – similar to Stop Pocket Auto, except 2 in. barrel, 5 or 6 shot.

$300	$235	$180	$150	$115	$90	$70	

FROMMER LILIPUT AUTO – .25 ACP cal., blowback action, 6 shot, 2.14 in. barrel, blue, hard rubber grips. Mfg. in early 1920s.

$400	$300	$200	$145	$115	$90	$75	

FROMMER MODEL 1910 – 7.65mm Roth/Steyr cal., rare and only infrequently encountered. Estimated serial range 1-10,000.

$3,500	$3,000	$2,500	$2,000	$1,500	$1,100	$850	

FERLACH GUNS

Includes those firearms manufactured in Ferlach, Austria from 1558 to present. The Ferlach Guild (Genossenschaft) represented most of Ferlach's gunmakers until it was dissolved in 2004.

Many people mistakenly believe that Ferlach is a trademark - it is not. Rather, it is a small village in Austria where a gun guild was started as early as 1558. At that time, it was absolutely necessary that all the people involved in fabricating a firearm were located together in close proximity. This enabled the barrel maker, the stock maker, and the lock mechanism maker to work together closely to ensure that everyone was performing their task(s) correctly, effectively and efficiently. As the individual skills became better and more refined, more and more firearms were manufactured. Eventually, individual gunsmiths began to put their name on the barrel or frame of those guns which they had either manufactured solely or with the help of their fellow Ferlach craftsmen. Since all Ferlach firearms are essentially hand made per individual special order, very few are exactly alike. In the past, the gunsmiths of Ferlach have produced almost every type of shoulder arm imaginable, including such modern firearms as superposed and juxtaposed

GRADING - PPGS™	100%	98%	95%	90%	80%	70%	60%	LAST MSR

rifles and shotguns, hammerless drillings, repeating rifles, 3 barrel rifles, combination guns, 4 barrel rifles/shotguns/combination guns (called Vierlings), hammer guns of every type, etc. Some of these specimens represent the highest refinement in the gunmakers trade. Because of the almost unlimited variety of Ferlach variations, it is recommended that a COMPETENT appraisal is procured before buying or selling a specimen.

As is the case with many other European firearms, those models with desirable American features will generally outperform those with European specifications (i.e. a Ferlach sidelock combination gun that is 20 ga. x .243 Win. will be more valuable than a similar specimen chambered for 16 ga. x 5.6 by 50Rmm with sling swivels). Original condition and overall beauty are the primary factors to consider when contemplating buying or selling a Ferlach longarm. Other considerations include: type of action, difficulty of fabrication (Vierlings are very complicated to construct), caliber/gauge desirability, notoriety of gunsmith on barrel legend, elaborateness of embellishments, condition, rarity, accessories, and any provenance a specimen might have.

Today's master gunsmiths of Ferlach carry on the Old World tradition of quality in every respect. Most guns manufactured today are by individual special order with a wide range of calibers/gauges and other special features and options. As of this writing, these gunsmiths in alphabetical order are: Ludwig Borovnik, Johann Fanzoj, Wilfried Glanznig, Josef Hambrusch, Karl Hauptmann, Gottfried Juch, Josef Just, Jakob Koschat, Peter Michelitsch, Johann & Walter Outschar, Herbert Scheiring, Benedikt Winkler, and Josef Winkler. Anyone wishing to contact these master gunmakers should contact the indivudal gunmaker.

FERLACHER WAFFEN PRÄZISIONSTECHNIK PRODUCTIONS GmbH & CO. KG.

Current organization located in Ferlach, Austria.

When the Ferlach Guild was dissolved in 2004, gunmakers Fanzoj and Schiering bought the remaining assets and reopened the facility. The original function, namely to represent the gunmakers of Ferlach, has not changed.

Please refer to the Ferlach Guns listing for a complete explanation and list of gunmakers.

FERLIB

Previous manufacturer and trademark established circa late 1940s-2005, and located in Gardone V.T., Italy. During 2005-2009, Ferlib entered into a partnership with B. Rizzini, and the new company was called Rizzini & Tanfoglio srl (see separate listing). SxS rifles were imported and distributed by Dakota Arms, Inc. 1999-2005. Previously distributed until 1999 by Hi-Grade Imports located in Gilroy, CA.

RIFLES: SxS

Please refer to the Rizzini & Tanfoglio listing for recent information on this model.

SHOTGUNS: O/U

BOSS MODEL – features Boss style action, custom order gun, many engraving options.

This model was POR.

SHOTGUNS: SxS

The following models were available in 10, 12, 16, 20, 24, 28, 32 ga., or .410 bore. Also available for an additional charge were extra quality wood and upgraded engraving.

Add 10% for 24, 28, 32 ga., or .410 bore.
Add $1,050 for single trigger.
Add $1,600 for leather case.

MIGNON HAMMER MODEL – back action, exposed hammers, extensive scroll engraving, deluxe checkered walnut stock and forearm.

Please contact the company directly for a price quotation on this model.

MODEL F.VI – 12, 16, 20, 28 ga., or .410 bore, Anson & Deeley scalloped boxlock action, ejectors, double triggers, case hardened frame, select checkered stock and forearm. Disc. 1992.

	100%	98%	95%	90%	80%	70%	60%	LAST MSR
	$3,500	$2,950	$2,275	$1,975	$1,600	$1,250	$1,000	*$3,250*

GRADING - PPGS™	100%	98%	95%	90%	80%	70%	60%	LAST MSR

MODEL 7 (F.VII) – 12, 16, 20, 28 ga., or .410 bore, Anson & Deeley scalloped boxlock action, ejectors, double triggers, coin finish, full coverage English scroll or game scene engraving, select checkered stock and forearm.

$9,950 $8,750 $7,600 $6,500 $5,400 $4,500 $3,400

* ***Model 7 Rex*** – similar to Model 7, except has sideplates with extensive engraving.

$13,300 $10,650 $9,150 $8,100 $7,000 $6,000 $5,000

* ***Model 7 Premier*** – top-of-the-line boxlock model, similar to Model 7 Rex, except more extensive engraving with gold inlays, best quality walnut.

$15,000 $12,750 $10,950 $9,250 $8,100 $7,100 $6,100

MODEL F.VII/SC – 12, 16, 20, 28 ga., or .410 bore, Anson & Deeley scalloped boxlock action, ejectors, double triggers, coin finish, game scene with scroll accent engraving with gold inlays, select checkered stock and forearm. Importation disc. 1999.

$6,200 $5,500 $5,000 $4,500 $3,800 $3,300 $2,750 *$7,800*

SIDE PLATE MODEL (F.VII SIDEPLATE) – 12, 16, 20, 28 ga., or .410 bore, Anson & Deeley boxlock action with sideplates, ejectors, single trigger, coin finish, extensive English scroll or game scene and scroll accent engraving, select checkered stock and forearm.

$12,950 $10,500 $9,000 $8,000 $7,000 $6,000 $5,000

Subtract $400 if English scroll engraved.

* ***Sideplate Model F.VII/SC Gold*** – similar to F.VII Sideplate, except with gold inlays.

$13,450 $10,950 $9,250 $8,100 $7,100 $6,100 $5,100

PRINCE MODEL – various gauges, contoured Anson & Deeley action with rounded frame, choice of top or side lever opening, DT, deluxe checkered walnut stock and forearm.

$10,600 $9,250 $8,100 $6,800 $5,550 $4,600 $3,500

Add $2,550 for side lever opening.

FERRELL, ROGER

Current custom rifle manufacturer located in Fayetteville, GA.

Roger Ferrell manufactures custom made to order rifles. Many options and configurations are available. Please contact the company directly for more information (see Trademark Index).

FIALA ARMS AND EQUIPMENT CO.

Previous manufacturer located in New Haven, CT. Fiala Arms and Equipment Co. was founded circa 1920, and went bankrupt shortly thereafter. Fiala Outfits, Inc. of New York City, NY reportedly bought the remaining guns, parts, and inventory and sold them between circa 1922 until approximately 1930. Also see Schall & Co.

The author would like to thank Mr. John Stimson for making the following information available.

PISTOLS: SLIDE ACTION

FIALA REPEATING PISTOL – .22 LR cal., similar to Colt Woodsman, manual operation, blue finish, interchangeable 3, 7 1/2 (fixed or smoothbore), or 20 (smoothbore optional) in. barrel, optional detachable buttstock, smooth or ribbed walnut grips, rear sight is square notched blade that tips up into an elevated adj. aperture sight, marked "Fiala Arms and Equipment Co. Inc./New Haven Conn./Patents Pending" on right side of frame behind the grip, and "MODEL 1920/Made in U.S.A." on the right side of the frame above the trigger guard, left side of frame marked "FIALA ARMS" above the image of a polar bear with "TRADE MARK" below polar bear in area above the trigger guard. Most Fialas have serial numbers between 1 and 5566 with a few outliers in the 8000 range. The Columbia marked guns are scattered in the lower Fiala serial number range between 1059 and 2837. To date no surviving Botwinik marked guns have been reported to the Fiala, Columbia, and Schall registry.

* ***Fiala Repeating Pistol cased with all 3 barrels and screw attached stock***

$3,000 $2,750 $2,500 $2,250 $2,000 $1,825 $1,675

Add 15% for dovetail frame attachment. Add $100 for smooth bore 20 in. barrel.

This model was available with three different case variations - canvas, black, or tan leatherette (velvet lined

GRADING - PPGS™	100%	98%	95%	90%	80%	70%	60%	LAST MSR

and fitted with a lock). Some pistols are also marked "Columbia Arms Company" or "Botwinik Brothers". This model has been classified by the ATF as a Curio or Relic, and is collectible when complete with all accoutrements.

* ***Fiala Repeating Pistol (gun only)***

	$650	$575	$495	$425	$350	$315	$265	

Add $150 for uncased pistol with screw attached stock. Add $250 for uncased pistol with dovetail attached stock. Add $150 for extra 3 in. barrel, $90 for extra 7 1/2 in. barrel, $125 for extra 20 in. rifled barrel, or $175 for extra 20 in. smoothbore barrel.

57 CENTER LLC

Please refer to listing in front of the A section.

FINNCLASSIC

Current trademark owned and manufactured by Marocchi CD Europe, located in Brescia, Italy. Currently imported by Network Retailing LLC, located in Canby, OR.

RIFLES: O/U

FINNCLASSIC 512 SC RIFLE/COMBO – .30-06, .308 Win. cal., 12 ga. (3 1/2 in. w/choke tube) over .222 Rem. for combo, 23 1/2 in. barrels, SST, rifle has cocking indicators, boxlock action, checkered Monte Carlo walnut stock and forearm, 7.7 (combo) or 8 1/4 lbs.

MSR $1,575	$1,250	$1,050	$925	$825	$725	$625	$525	

Add $420-$1,675 for double rifle, depending on configuration.
Add $120 for SD Prestige model.
Add $200 for Bavarian Ti model.
Add $1,175 for Bavarian Gold Ti model.

SHOTGUNS: O/U

FINNCLASSIC 512 – 12 or 20 ga., 3 in. chambers, boxlock action, blue (Field), chrome, or matte nickel finished receiver, choice of Sporting (12 ga. only, 28, 30, or 32 in. VR barrels with 11mm VR), Youth/Ladies (shorter LOP), or Field, 7.4 lbs.

MSR $1,295	$1,050	$900	$775	$675	$600	$525	$450	

Add $100 for game scene engraving.
Add $280 for Prestige Gold model.
Add $1,355 for Bavarian Ti model.
Add $1,555 for Bavarian Gold Ti model.
Add $22 for Sporting Clays configuration with 5 choke tubes (disc.).
Add $314 for Youth/Ladies model (disc.).

FINNISH LION

Previous trademark manufactured by Valmet (now Tikka) located in Sweden. Limited importation into the U.S. by Mandall's Shooting Supplies, Inc. in Scottsdale, AZ.

RIFLES: BOLT ACTION

MATCH MODEL – .22 LR cal., bolt action, single shot, 29 in. barrel, extended aperture sight, globe front sight, thumbhole stock, adj. hook butt. Mfg. 1937-72.

	$495	$415	$360	$305	$250	$210	$195	

CHAMPION FREE MODEL – .22 LR cal., bolt action, single shot, 29 in. barrel, double set trigger, full target stock and accessories. Mfg. 1965-72.

	$580	$495	$440	$385	$330	$290	$265	

STANDARD ISU TARGET MODEL – .22 LR cal., bolt action, single shot, 27 in. barrel, full target stock and accessories. Mfg. 1966-1977.

	$330	$275	$250	$205	$180	$165	$150	

TARGET MODEL – .22 LR cal., target rifle with adj. stock and trigger, bolt action, single shot, aperture sights.

	$725	$595	$495	$440	$385	$340	$295	*$795*

GRADING - PPGS™	100%	98%	95%	90%	80%	70%	60%	LAST MSR

FIOCCHI OF AMERICA, INC.

Previous firearms importer and distributor located in Ozark, MO.

Fiocchi of America imported Pardini target pistols until 1990, and continues to manufacture a wide variety of ammunition domestically. Fiocchi also imported Antonio Zoli shotguns until 1988. These trademarks can be found in their respective sections of this text.

FIREARMS INTERNATIONAL CORP. (F.I.C.)

Previous importer and assembler located in Washington, D.C.

F.I.C. manufactured and imported various pistols, rifles, and shotguns, including AYA, Astra (mostly Star D models), Bronco (.22 LR cal. single shot rifles and .410 bore single shot shotguns - see listings under Bronco), FN Supreme Mauser bolt action rifles, Iver Johnson Pony handguns, Rossi .22 cal. rifles, Sako rifles, Star pistols, and Unique pistols and rifles.

F.I.C. sold less than 100 Pony .380 ACPs, which were marked Colt before the Mustang was introduced - these are rare. While some models are relatively rare, collectability to date has been minimal and most models sell in the $150-$295 range, depending on overall desirability and condition.

Please look under individual manufacturer listings for values on similar models.

FIREARMS INTERNATIONAL, INC.

Current manufacturer established in 1998, and located in Houston, TX. Dealer sales.

In September, 2004, a new company called Crusader Group Gun Company, Inc. was formed, and is the corporate parent of Firearms International, Inc., High Standard Manufacturing Co., AMT-Auto Mag, and Arsenal Line Products.

While IAI (Israel Arms International) was originally established to market firearms manufactured by Israel Arms, Ltd. through Firearms International, Inc., IAI defaulted on this agreement without any sales being made.

PISTOLS: SEMI-AUTO

During 1999, Firearms International, Inc. obtained permission to use older High Standard model nomenclature (Crusader & Supermatic Trophy) for use with their M-1911 pistols. Currently manufactured pistols are marked Firearms International Inc. on the frame, and High Standard on the slide.

Sharpshooter .45 ACP to .22 LR cal. conversion units are also available - fixed sight model retails for $280, adj. rear sight model retails for $340.

MODEL 1911 CRUSADER (CUSTOM SERIES) – 38 Super (mfg. 2002-2005, Two-tone finish only, reintroduced 2011) or .45 ACP cal., 5 in. barrel, 7 (disc.) or 9 (.38 Super cal. only) shot mag., many shooting enhancements are standard, stainless steel (disc.), blue, or Tu-tone (mfg. 2001-2005) finish, adj. sights, 40 oz. Mfg. 2000-2005, reintroduced 2007.

MSR $995 — $895 — $795 — $675 — $550 — $475 — $425 — $375

Add $50 for stainless steel (disc.)
Add $30 for Two-tone finish (disc.)

This model is sold exclusively through Lipsey's.

* ***Model 1911 Crusader Combat*** – similar to M-1911 Crusader, except has 4 1/4 (disc.) or 4 1/2 (new 2007) in. barrel and choice of fixed or adj. (disc. 2000) sights, 38 oz. Mfg. 2000-2005, reintroduced 2007.

$795 — $675 — $550 — $475 — $425 — $375 — $350 — *$895*

Add $50 for stainless steel (disc.)
Add $30 for Two-tone finish (disc.)

This model is sold exclusively through Lipsey's.

* ***Model 1911 Crusader Compact*** – 4 in. barrel, similar to Crusader Combat, except has shorter grip frame, 6 shot mag., 36 oz. Limited mfg. 2000 only.

$715 — $600 — $500 — $475 — $425 — $375 — $325 — *$775*

GRADING - PPGS™	100%	98%	95%	90%	80%	70%	60%	LAST MSR

*** *Model 1911 Crusader Compact Elite*** – .45 ACP cal., 3 5/8 in. barrel with Novak style sights.

MSR $1,045	$900	$725	$575	$500	$450	$400	$350	

SENTINEL – .45 ACP cal., 3 5/8 in. barrel, no sights. Mfg. 2010.

	$695	$625	$550	$475	$425	$375	$325	*$785*

STR-5S SUPERMATIC TROPHY MATCH (MATCH MODEL) – similar to M-1911 Crusader, except has National Match 5 or 6 in. barrel with bushing, polished feed ramp and throated barrel, lowered/flared ejection port, 40 oz. Mfg. 2000-2008.

	$950	$800	$700	$600	$525	$450	$375	*$1,095*

Subtract approx. 10% for blue finish (disc. 2001).
Subtract approx. 15% if w/o sights and no finish (disc.).
Add $300 for 6 in. barrel.

SUPERMATIC CUSTOM – .45 ACP cal., 6 in. match barrel, adj. sights, double diamond checkered wood grips, black teflon finish.

MSR $1,450	$1,250	$1,075	$900	$800	$700	$600	$500	

CAMP PERRY MODEL (TX5870FS/AS) – .45 ACP cal., 5 in. barrel, mil-spec slide, barrel, and barrel bushing, blue or Tu-Tone (mfg. 2001 only) finish, competition tuned, beveled mag. well, 40 oz. New 2000.

MSR $1,150	$1,025	$900	$795	$700	$600	$500	$400	

Subtract $70 if without adj. sights (disc. 2011).

G-MAN – .45 ACP cal., 5 in. barrel, special tolerances, including frame to slide fit, match grade stainless barrel and National Match bushing, polished feed ramp, throated barrel, slotted hammer, lightweight trigger, lowered and flared ejection port, beveled mag. well, checkered American walnut grips, black Teflon finish, includes two 8 shot mag., 39 oz. Mfg. 2001-2005, reintroduced 2007.

MSR $1,450	$1,250	$1,075	$900	$800	$700	$600	$500	

GI MODEL – .45 ACP cal., 5 in. barrel, parkerized finish, fixed sights, classic WWII design (1911A1 frame), 7 shot mag. Mfg. 2002-2005.

	$475	$425	$375	$335	$300	$285	$270	*$549*

ARMY SPECIAL – .45 ACP cal., 5 in. barrel, blue or parkerized finish, 7 shot mag., fixed sights, 39 oz. Limited mfg. 2000.

	$485	$435	$395	$365	$330	$300	$285	*$549*

NAVY MODEL – similar to Army Special, except is stainless steel, 39 oz. Limited mfg. 2000.

	$535	$465	$425	$395	$350	$325	$300	*$599*

AIR CREW MODEL – similar to Army Special, except is titanium, 26 oz. Introduced 2000.

While advertised, this model never went into production.

UNITED STATES M1911A1 – .45 ACP cal., 5 in. barrel, fixed sights. New 2007.

MSR $675	$575	$495	$435	$375	$335	$300	$260	

UNITED STATES M1926A1 – .38 Super cal., 5 in. barrel, fixed sights. New 2007.

MSR $725	$625	$550	$450	$375	$350	$300	$260	

RIFLES: SEMI-AUTO

M1 CARBINE – .30 Carbine cal., 18 in. barrel, parkerized finish, wood stock, adj. rear sight, 10 shot mag., mfg. in the U.S., and patterned after the WWII design, 5 1/2 lbs. Limited mfg. 2001-2003.

	$500	$425	$375	$335	$300	$275	$250	*$575*

P50 RIFLE/CARBINE – .50 BMG cal., designed by Robert Pauza, gas operation, 24 or 29 in. barrel, MOA accuracy at 1,000 yards, includes two 5 shot mags. and hard case, 25 (carbine) or 30 lbs. Limited mfg. 2001-2003.

	$7,500	$6,750	$5,750	$5,000	$4,500	$4,000	$3,500	*$7,950*

GRADING - PPGS™	100%	98%	95%	90%	80%	70%	60%	LAST MSR

FIRESTORM

Previous trademark of pistols and revolvers manufactured by Industria Argentina, Fabrinor, S.A.L., and Armscor. Distributed (master distributor) and imported from late 2000-2011 by SGS Imports, International Inc., located in Wanamassa, NJ.

PISTOLS: SEMI-AUTO

Beginning 2004, all Firestorm pistols were available with an integral locking system (ILS).

FIRESTORM SERIES – .22 LR, .32 ACP (disc. 2007), or .380 ACP cal., double action, 3 1/2 or 6 (.22 LR cal. only, Sport Model) in. barrel, matte or duo-tone finish, 7 (.380 ACP) or 10 (.22 LR or .32 ACP) shot mag., 3 dot combat sights, anatomic rubber grips with finger grooves, 23 oz. Imported 2001-2011.

$280	$235	$185	$155	$145	$135	$125	*$329*

Add $6 for duo-tone finish.

MINI-FIRESTORM – 9mm Para., .40 S&W, or .45 ACP (new 2002) cal., double action, 3 1/2 in. barrel, nickel, matte or duo-tone finish, 7 (.45 ACP cal.), 10, or 13 (9mm Para. only) shot mag., 3 dot sights, polymer grips, safeties include manual, firing pin, and decocking, 24 1/2 - 27 oz. Imported 2001-2009.

$365	$315	$275	$230	$195	$180	$165	*$425*

Add $10 for duo-tone finish.
Add $20 for nickel finish.

FIRESTORM 45 GOVERNMENT – .45 ACP cal., single action, 5 1/8 in. barrel, matte or duo-tone finish, 7 shot mag., anatomic rubber grips with finger grooves, 36 oz. Imported 2001-2005.

$260	$230	$200	$180	$165	$150	$135	*$309*

Add $8 for duo-tone finish.

* ***Firestorm 45 Government Compact*** – .45 ACP cal., 4 1/4 in. barrel, otherwise similar to Firestorm 45 Government, 34 oz. Imported 2001-2005.

$260	$230	$200	$180	$165	$150	$135	*$309*

Add $8 for duo-tone finish.

* ***Firestorm 45 Government Mini Compact*** – .45 ACP cal., 3 1/8 in. barrel, chrome or matte or duo-tone finish, 10 shot staggered mag., polymer grips, 31 oz. Imported 2001 only.

$280	$245	$215	$195	$180	$170	$155	*$324*

Add $17 for chrome finish.

FIRESTORM 45 GOVT. 1911 – .45 ACP cal., patterned after the M1911, choice of matte or deluxe blue finish, 7 shot mag., current mfg. has skeletonized hammer, forward slide serrations, Novak style sights, diamond checkered walnut grips, and flared ejection port, 36 oz. Imported 2006-2007, reintroduced 2009.

$395	$360	$330	$295	$275	$250	$200	*$460*

Add $39 for deluxe blue finish.

REVOLVERS

FIRESTORM .38 SPL. – .38 Spl. cal., 6 shot, 2 in. barrel, choice of satin nickel, polished nickel, or parkerized metal finish. Mfg. by Armscor. Imported 2011.

$285	$235	$185	$155	$145	$135	$125	*$349*

Add $10 for satin nickel finish or $20 for polished nickel finish.

FIRESTORM .380 – .380 ACP cal., 7 shot, double action, blue finish with nickel accents. Imported by Ellet Brothers 2011. Mfg. by Armscor.

$265	$235	$195	$175	$150	$125	$100	*$335*

FLAVIO FARÈ

Current custom bolt action rifle manufacturer located in Vinzaglio, Italy.

Flavio Farè manufactures high quality custom bolt action rifles. All guns are built per customer specifications. Please contact him directly for pricing, available options, and delivery time (see Trademark Index).

GRADING - PPGS™	100%	98%	95%	90%	80%	70%	60%	LAST MSR

FLODMAN GUNS

Current manufacturer established in 1978 and located in Järsta, Sweden. In 1992, Skullman Enterprise AB took over Flodman Guns. No current U.S. importation.

O/U: LONG GUNS

Flodman manufactures a variety of high quality shotguns, combination guns, and double rifles. They offer three designs - hunting, sporting, and luxury. All Flodman O/Us utilize a low profile, boxlock, stainless steel self-opening action, patented ejector (allows dry firing w/o ejector movement), and have no hammer, but a primed firing pin which moves perpendicularly, allowing a .002 second lock time. Barrels are available in either titanium, Sandvik steel, or stainless steel; shotguns are equipped with choke tubes. Please contact the factory directly for more information regarding an individual price quotation and delivery time (see Trademark Index).

FORBES RIFLE, LLC

Current bolt action rifle manufacturer established in 2011, and located in Westbrook, ME.

RIFLES: BOLT ACTION

M24B – .25-06 Rem., .270 Win., .30-06, .300 Win. Mag., or 7mm Rem. Mag. cal., CNC action, #2 profile 24 in. barrel with black oxide finish, black composite straight comb stock, no sights, two position safety, 3 or 4 shot internal mag., 5 1/4 lbs. New 2011.

	100%	98%	95%	90%	80%	70%	60%	LAST MSR
MSR N/A	$1,399	$1,275	$1,100	$1,075	$950	$825	$700	

Add $68 for stainless steel barrel or $100 for stainless steel barrel and action.
Add $85 for left-hand action.

FORT SOE SIA

Current trademark manufactured by the Science Industrial Association Fort of the Ministry of Internal Affairs of Ukraine, located in Vinnitsa, Ukraine. No current U.S. importation.

The Ministry manufactures a line of good quality semi-auto pistols and semi-auto rifles in various paramilitary configurations with a wide variety of options. Currently, these guns are not imported into the U.S. Please contact the company directly for more information, including pricing and availability (see Trademark Index).

FORT WORTH FIREARMS

Previous manufacturer located in Fort Worth, TX 1995-2000.

PISTOLS: SEMI-AUTO, RIMFIRE

MATCH MASTER STANDARD – .22 LR cal., 3 7/8, 4 1/2, 5 1/2, 7 1/2, or 10 in. bull barrel, double extractors, includes upper push button and standard mag. release, beveled mag. well, angled grip, flared slide, low profile frame. Mfg. 1995-2000.

	100%	98%	95%	90%	80%	70%	60%	LAST MSR
	$350	$310	$265	$230	$200	$185	$170	*$389*

Add $84 for 10 in. bull barrel.

* ***Match Master Standard Dovetail*** – similar to Match Master Standard, except has 3 7/8, 4 1/2, or 5 1/2 barrel with dovetail rib. Mfg. 1995-2000.

	100%	98%	95%	90%	80%	70%	60%	LAST MSR
	$425	$385	$325	$285	$240	$215	$190	*$473*

* ***Match Master Standard Deluxe*** – similar to Match Master Standard, except has Weaver rib on barrel. Mfg. 1995-2000.

	100%	98%	95%	90%	80%	70%	60%	LAST MSR
	$500	$450	$365	$315	$280	$240	$215	*$538*

Add $92 for 10 in. barrel.

SPORT KING – .22 LR cal., 4 1/2 or 5 1/2 in. barrel, blue finish, military grips, drift adjustable sight, 10 shot mag. Mfg. 1995-2000.

	100%	98%	95%	90%	80%	70%	60%	LAST MSR
	$325	$275	$245	$225	$200	$185	$170	*$313*

CITATION – .22 LR cal., 5 1/2 in. bull or 7 1/4 in. fluted barrel, military grips, 10 shot mag. Mfg. 1995-2000.

	100%	98%	95%	90%	80%	70%	60%	LAST MSR
	$350	$310	$265	$230	$200	$185	$170	*$389*

GRADING - PPGS™	100%	98%	95%	90%	80%	70%	60%	LAST MSR

TROPHY – .22 LR cal., 5 1/2 or 7 1/4 in. bull barrel, blue finish, military grips, 10 shot mag. Mfg. 1995-2000.

	$375	$330	$285	$240	$200	$185	$170	*$411*

Add $41 for left-hand action (5 1/2 in. barrel only).

VICTOR – .22 LR cal., 3 7/8, 4 1/2 (VR or Weaver rib), or 5 1/2 (VR or Weaver rib), 8 (Weaver rib), or 10 (Weaver rib) in. barrel, blue finish, military grips, 10 shot mag. Mfg. 1995-2000.

	$450	$395	$350	$295	$250	$215	$190	*$473*

Add $65 for 4 1/2 or 5 1/2 in. Weaver rib barrel.
Add approx. $148 for 8 or 10 in. Weaver rib barrel.

OLYMPIC – .22 LR or Short cal., 6 3/4 in. fluted barrel, blue finish, military grips, 10 shot mag. Mfg. 1995-2000.

	$525	$465	$415	$360	$330	$295	$265	*$600*

SHARP SHOOTER – .22 LR cal., 5 1/2 in. bull barrel, blue finish, military grips, 10 shot mag. Mfg. 1995-2000.

	$350	$300	$260	$230	$200	$185	$170	*$380*

RIFLES: BOLT ACTION

YOUTH RIFLE – .22 LR cal., bolt action, single shot, shortened stock dimensions. Mfg. 1995-96.

	$120	$105	$90	$80	$70	$60	$50	*$138*

SHOTGUNS: SLIDE ACTION

GL 18 – 12 ga. only, security configuration with 18 in. barrel with perforated shroud, thumb operated laser/xenon light built into end of 7 shot mag. tube, ammo storage. Mfg. 1995-96.

	$295	$265	$240	$210	$190	$170	$160	*$347*

FOX, A.H.

Current manufacturer located in New Britain, CT. The A.H. Fox trademark was brought to life once again during 1993 when the Connecticut Shotgun Manufacturing Company began producing an A.H. Fox 20 gauge in 5 different grades. Previously manufactured in Philadelphia, PA 1903-1930, and in Utica, NY from 1930-approx. 1946. Manufactured by Savage 1930-1988.

Depending on the remaining A.H. Fox factory data, a factory letter authenticating the configuration of a particular Fox shotgun (not to be confused with the more recent Savage/Stevens designed Fox doubles) may be obtained by contacting John T. Callahan (see Trademark Index for listings and address). If a model number is not known, please include a photo, the ser. no., gauge, barrel length and style, stock and forearm style, markings, patent dates, inspector stamps, etc. The charge for this service is $30.00 for the Sterlingworth Model, and $40.00 for graded models A-F and single barrel trap guns. Please allow 8 weeks for an adequate response.

Mr. Ansley H. Fox first started manufacturing shotguns in circa 1896. This first company was called the Fox Gun Co. and was located in Baltimore, MD. Relatively few guns were made and surviving specimens today are very rare. After this venture, Mr. Fox was employed by the Baltimore Gun Co. for several years (circa 1900-1903). Following this period, he formed the Philadelphia Gun Co. where the predecessors to the A.H. Fox Gun Co. models were manufactured. These Philadelphia Gun Co. models (circa 1904) were the same as the newer Fox shotguns except that the hinge pin was removed. Sources indicate that the lowest grade was an A with the highest being an E (fully engraved and ultra rare). Mr. Fox went on to form the A.H. Fox Gun Co. in 1906. In addition to being an entrepreneur and trend setter, Mr. Fox also had the reputation of being an expert shot in his own right, winning more than a few events on the East Coast around the turn of the century.

The A.H. Fox Gun Company of Philadelphia, Pennsylvania, began production in 1905 and produced high quality double barrel shotguns until 1930. The Savage Arms Company, then of Utica, New York, acquired the Fox Company and produced these guns until 1942, when all but the utilitarian model B series guns were discontinued.

A.H. Fox guns are considered an American classic comparable to L.C. Smith, Parker, and others. Collector interest is high and will undoubtedly grow. The guns do not command quite as high a price as the Smith and Parker guns, but represent a fine investment collectible value.

Savage-made guns from 1930-1942 are usually valued similarly to the early A.H. Fox guns. The recent production B series are just not in the same class and are obviously not intended to be. They are lower priced by today's standards and are designed as a utility grade hunting gun.

FOX COMPANY CHRONOLOGY

1906 - Company formed January 1906, A, B & C Grades introduced in 12 ga. only. D and F Grades introduced in 12 ga. in 1907. Ejector guns introduced in 1908. 1910 saw the introduction of the 12 ga. Sterlingworth - William H. Gough takes over as Chief of Engraving. Ansley Fox resigns in 1911 - first catalog showing Sterlingworth Model (called Model 1911). A-F Grades released in 16 and 20 ga. during 1912, as well as the addition of a 20 ga. Sterlingworth. 16 ga. Sterlingworth introduced in 1913. Fox/Kautsky single trigger introduced in 1914 - engineering transition complete. During 1915, the XE Grade was introduced. The B Grade was dropped in 1918. Single barrel trap guns (J, K, and L Grades) were introduced in 1919. 1920 saw the introduction of the M Grade single barrel trap. In 1922, both the G and HE Grades were released. Beavertail forend and vent. rib were introduced in 1927. 1929 was the Savage buy-out (November), GE Grade dropped. Company moved from Philadelphia, PA to Utica, NY in 1930. Skeeter Grade introduced in 1931 while the 20 ga. HE Grade was disc. 1932 saw the introduction of both the Trap Grade Double and SP Grade. Wildfowl Grade was introduced in 1934. 1935 was the last year of the K and L single barrel trap guns. 1937 was the last year for the J Grade single barrel trap gun. The last 16 and 12 ga. Sterlingworths were built in 1939. The outbreak of the war in 1941 saw the last FE Grade shipped, the Wildfowler Grade dropped, and the introduction of the Model B. 1942 was the last retail catalog. Factory records indicate that the last 12 ga. was shipped in 1945 and the last 20 ga. was shipped during 1946 (SP Grade shipped in December, 1946). However, guns continued to be assembled from left-over parts as late as the 1960s.

FOX SERIAL NUMBER ASSIGNMENTS

The publisher wishes to express his thanks to Mr. John Callahan and Mr. Gurney Brown for providing the model serialization and years of mfg. in this section.

Ser. # range 1-35,285 - 12 ga. Grades A-F
Ser. # range 200,000-203,975 - 20 ga. Grades A-F
Ser. # range 300,000-303,875 - 16 ga. Grades A-F
Ser. # range 50,000-161,556 - 12 ga. Sterlingworth
Ser. # range 250,000-271,304 - 20 ga. Sterlingworth
Ser. # range 300,000-378,481 - 16 ga. Sterlingworth
Ser. # range 400,000-450,568 - 12 ga. Single Barrel Traps, Grades J,K,L,M

FOX MODELS BY YEARS IN MFG.

Sterlingworth - 1910-1942 mfg.
Wildfowler - 1934-1940 mfg.
Trap Double - 1932-1936 mfg.
Skeeter - 1931 mfg.
SP - 1932-1946 mfg.
A - 1906-1942 mfg.
B - 1905-1918 mfg.
C - 1905-1942 mfg.
D - 1907-1942 mfg.
F - 1907-1940 mfg.
G - 1922-1929 mfg.
H - 1923-1942 mfg.
J - 1919-1939 mfg.
K - 1919-1934 mfg.
L - 1919-1934 mfg.
M - 1919-1936 mfg.
X - 1915-1942 mfg.

SHOTGUNS: SxS, CURRENT MFG.

Delivery time for custom orders is currently 10-14 months, depending on gauge and grade. The following models are manufactured by the Connecticut Manufacturing Co. located in New Britain, CT. These finely made shotguns have the following standard features: automatic safety, auto ejectors, DTs, Chromox 26, 28, or 30 in. barrels, individual barrel chokings, 2 3/4 in. chambers, scalloped receiver, Turkish Circassian walnut with hand-rubbed oil finish, choice of straight, semi-pistol, or full-pistol grip stock with custom dimensions, splinter forearm, ivory bead sights. Special order options are as follows: Krupp steel barrels ($350), Fox SST ($2,400),

GRADING - PPGS™	100%	98%	95%	90%	80%	70%	60%	LAST MSR

walnut upgrades ($800-$3,500), custom initials ($450-$1,000), personalized gold inlays on barrel ($1,000), skeleton steel buttplate ($900), beavertail forearm ($750), vent. rib ($1,000), and traditional leather trunk case with accessories ($650-$850). Multi-barrel sets (same or multi-gauge) are also available with prices ranging from $5,250-$9,000, depending on the grade.

28 ga. and .410 bore guns on the following models (except Exhibition Grade) are by quotation only.

CE GRADE – 16 (new 1995), 20, 28 ga. (new 1995), or .410 bore (new 1995), engraved with fine scroll and game scenes, Grade I Turkish Circassian walnut. New 1993.

MSR	100%	98%	95%	90%	80%	70%	60%
MSR $19,500	$19,500	$15,500	$13,560	$11,625	$10,540	$8,525	$6,975

XE GRADE – gauges similar to CE Grade, scroll work and engraved game scenes, Grade II Turkish Circassian walnut. New 1993.

MSR	100%	98%	95%	90%	80%	70%	60%
MSR $22,000	$22,000	$17,000	$14,875	$12,750	$11,560	$9,350	$7,650

DE GRADE – gauges similar to CE Grade, intricate and extensive engraving, Grade III highly figured Turkish Circassian walnut. New 1993.

MSR	100%	98%	95%	90%	80%	70%	60%
MSR $25,000	$25,000	$20,500	$17,935	$15,375	$13,940	$11,275	$9,225

FE GRADE – gauges similar to CE Grade, gold inlays surrounded by different types of scroll work, Grade IV highly figured Turkish Circassian walnut with finest checkering. New 1993.

MSR	100%	98%	95%	90%	80%	70%	60%
MSR $30,000	$30,000	$25,500	$22,310	$19,125	$17,340	$14,025	$11,475

EXHIBITION GRADE – gauges similar to CE Grade, individually built per customer specifications on a "cost-no-object" basis, includes best-quality leather trunk case with full accessories, Exhibition Grade Turkish Circassian walnut. New 1993.

This model is a special order only, and is POR. Please contact the company directly for an individual price quotation and available options.

100%	98%	95%	90%	80%	70%	60%	50%	40%	30%	20%	10%

SHOTGUNS: SxS & SINGLE SHOT, DISC.

STERLINGWORTH – 12, 16, or 20 ga., 26, 28, or 30 in. barrels, various chokes, boxlock, extractors, double trigger, checkered pistol grip stock. Mfg. 1910-1942.

100%	98%	95%	90%	80%	70%	60%	50%	40%	30%	20%	10%
N/A	$1,600	$1,400	$1,100	$875	$750	$575	$500	$450	$395	$350	$300

Add 33% for auto ejectors.
Add 75% for 20 ga. or 50% for 16 ga.
Add 25% for single trigger.

Ser. no. range on 12 ga. Sterlingworths is 50,000-161,556, 16 ga. is 300,000-378,481, and 20 ga. is 250,000-271,304.

STERLINGWORTH DELUXE – similar to Sterlingworth, with recoil pad and ivory bead front sight, 32 in. barrel available.

100%	98%	95%	90%	80%	70%	60%	50%	40%	30%	20%	10%
N/A	$2,100	$1,875	$1,475	$1,100	$950	$850	$750	$650	$550	$475	$425

Add 33% for auto ejectors.
Add 75% for 20 ga. or 50% for 16 ga.

A single trigger was not an option on this model.

STERLINGWORTH SKEET – similar to Sterlingworth, with 26 or 28 in. skeet boring, straight grip stock, beavertail forearm. Mfg. 1935-1945.

This model is very scarce (only several are known) and the extreme rarity factor precludes accurate price evaluation.

SUPER HE GRADE – 12 ga., 2 3/4 (very rare) or 3 in. chambered long range gun, 30 and 32 in. full choke, auto ejectors, otherwise similar to Sterlingworth.

100%	98%	95%	90%	80%	70%	60%	50%	40%	30%	20%	10%
N/A	$5,600	$5,200	$4,800	$4,400	$3,950	$3,400	$2,850	$2,300	$1,900	$1,625	$1,475

Add 10% for SST.

Original 3 in. chambered HE grades are marked "not warranteed, see instruction tag" on barrel flats. The HE grade was also manufactured in 20 ga. but is extremely rare. 2 3/4 in. chambers are rarer than 3 in. guns in this model.

100%	98%	95%	90%	80%	70%	60%	50%	40%	30%	20%	10%

HIGHER GRADE MODELS (A-F) – 12, 16, or 20 ga., the following higher grade Fox shotguns are similar to the Sterlingworth in configuration. The grades differ in engraving and inlays, grade of wood and general workmanship. The E designation means auto ejectors.

Add 50% for 16 ga. (made on same frame as 20 ga.).
Add 75% for 20 ga.
Add $200-$1,000 for SST, depending on grade.
Add $200-$1,000 for beavertail forearm, depending on grade.

Early A and B grades have very little engraving and are much less desirable than later models. The following values are for later guns.

Note: These guns were disc. in 1942 by Savage Arms after they mfg. them for 12 years. Pre-1930 guns were made by A.H. Fox Company.

* ***Higher Grade Model: A Grade***

N/A	$2,400	$2,175	$1,875	$1,625	$1,375	$1,075	$900	$825	$725	$650	$600

* ***Higher Grade Model: AE Grade (ejectors)***

N/A	$3,000	$2,700	$2,400	$2,075	$1,675	$1,400	$1,150	$1,000	$900	$850	$825

* ***Higher Grade Model: BE Grade (ejectors)***

N/A	N/A	$4,800	$4,450	$3,950	$3,475	$2,950	$2,500	$2,250	$1,975	$1,800	$1,675

This model is rarely encountered.

* ***Higher Grade Model: CE Grade (ejectors)***

N/A	N/A	$5,750	$5,200	$4,650	$4,150	$3,750	$3,300	$3,000	$2,700	$2,425	$2,150

* ***Higher Grade Model: XE Grade (ejectors)***

N/A	N/A	$8,000	$7,350	$6,750	$5,950	$5,225	$4,625	$4,100	$3,650	$3,200	$2,750

* ***Higher Grade Model: DE Grade (ejectors)***

N/A	N/A	$13,750	$11,650	$9,675	$8,750	$7,500	$6,750	$6,000	$5,300	$4,750	$4,300

* ***Higher Grade Model: FE Grade (ejectors)*** – top-of-the-line model, only infrequently encountered.

N/A	N/A	$22,000	$19,500	$16,450	$14,150	$12,000	$10,500	$9,750	$9,150	$9,000	$8,750

SINGLE BARREL TRAP – 12 ga., 30 or 32 in. vent. rib barrel, full choke, boxlock, auto ejector, checkered trap style stock with recoil pad. The grades differ in wood, engraving, and overall quality. ME grade is custom built and extremely high quality with gold inlays. These models were disc. 1942. 568 single barrel trap guns were mfg. between 1932-42 and have a ser. range of 400,000-400,568, with Monte Carlo stock.

Even though trap guns may be rarer than their SxS counterparts, to date their desirability is less since there are simply fewer collectors.

* ***Single Barrel Trap JE Grade***

N/A	$3,860	$3,550	$3,200	$2,800	$2,500	$2,100	$1,800	$1,600	$1,500	$1,425	$1,325

* ***Single Barrel Trap KE Grade***

N/A	$5,200	$4,650	$4,000	$3,500	$3,200	$2,800	$2,600	$2,400	$2,250	$2,100	$1,975

* ***Single Barrel Trap LE Grade***

N/A	N/A	$6,500	$5,750	$5,000	$4,500	$4,100	$3,750	$3,300	$3,000	$2,650	$2,300

* ***Single Barrel Trap ME Grade***

Extreme rarity factor precludes accurate percentage pricing on this model.

GRADING - PPGS™	100%	98%	95%	90%	80%	70%	60%	LAST MSR

MODEL B DOUBLE BARREL – 12, 16, 20 ga., or .410 bore, 24-30 in. barrels, various chokes, vent rib on newer models, boxlock, extractors, double triggers, handcut or pressed checkered pistol grip stock and forearm. Mfg. 1940-86.

12 or 16 ga.	$450	$395	$350	$295	$265	$235	$200	
20 ga.	$650	$575	$500	$450	$400	$365	$335	
.410 bore	$1,100	$975	$850	$750	$675	$600	$550	*$250*

GRADING - PPGS™	100%	98%	95%	90%	80%	70%	60%	LAST MSR

MODEL B-ST – similar to model B, with single trigger. Mfg. 1955-66.

12 or 16 ga.	$575	$475	$425	$350	$315	$275	$250	
20 ga.	$725	$650	$600	$550	$500	$425	$350	
.410 bore	$1,300	$1,075	$925	$800	$700	$600	$500	

MODEL B-DL – similar to model B-ST, with satin chrome frame, select wood. Mfg. 1962-65.

12 or 16 ga.	$600	$475	$425	$350	$315	$275	$250	
20 ga.	$750	$675	$600	$550	$500	$425	$350	
.410 bore	$1,350	$1,100	$925	$800	$700	$600	$500	

MODEL B-DE – similar to B-DL, with less checkering. Mfg. 1965-66.

12 or 16 ga.	$575	$475	$425	$350	$315	$275	$250	
20 ga.	$725	$650	$600	$550	$500	$425	$350	
.410 bore	$1,300	$1,075	$925	$800	$700	$600	$500	

MODEL B-SE – 12, 20 ga., or .410 bore, single trigger, selective ejectors, vent. rib, beavertail forearm, select walnut with pressed checkering. Mfg. 1966-88.

12 ga.	$850	$750	$675	$600	$550	$475	$400	
20 ga.	$1,000	$900	$800	$700	$625	$550	$475	
.410 bore	$1,550	$1,375	$1,125	$950	$850	$750	$650	*$525*

Even though there were multiple series designations assigned to this model, there seems to be little difference in desirability. For that reason, other designations will be priced similarly to values shown above.

FOX CARBINE

Previous rifle trademark manufactured by FoxCo Products Inc., located in Manchester, CT, and by Tri-C Corporation, located in Meridan, CT circa 1974-1976.

CARBINES: SEMI-AUTO

FOX CARBINE – 9mm Para. (mfg. by FoxCo Products) or .45 ACP (mfg. by Tri-C Corp.) cal., patterned after the Tommy Gun, 16 in. barrel with muzzle brake, grip safety, open bolt with fixed firing pin, removable wood rear stock and grooved forearm, uses M-3 30 shot mags., three safeties including a three-digit combination lock on left side of frame, loaded chamber indicator, adj. rear sight, matte metal finish, approx. 8 lbs.

	$995	$875	$750	$625	$550	$500	$450	

In 1977, the rights to manufacture the FoxCo carbine were sold to Demro Products Inc., which continued to manufacture this configuration until the mid-1980s.

FRANCHI, LUIGI

Current manufacturer established during 1868, and located in Brescia, Italy. This trademark has been imported for approximately the past 50 years. Currently imported exclusively by Benelli USA, located in Accokeek, MD, since 1998. Previously imported and distributed by American Arms, Inc. located in North Kansas City, MO. Some models were previously imported by FIE firearms located in Hialeah, FL.

Also see Sauer/Franchi heading in the S section.

RIFLES: SEMI-AUTO

CENTENNIAL MODEL – .22 LR cal., 21 in. barrel, open sight, commemorates Franchi's 100th anniversary. Mfg. 1968 only.

	$330	$250	$220	$195	$165	$150	$140	

* ***Centennial Model Engraved Deluxe***

	$415	$330	$305	$275	$240	$200	$165	

* ***Centennial Model Gallery***

	$220	$195	$160	$120	$100	$80	$60	

GRADING - PPGS™	100%	98%	95%	90%	80%	70%	60%	LAST MSR

SHOTGUNS: O/U

Currently manufactured Franchi O/U shotguns are supplied with a custom-fitted hard case, and use choke tubes that are compatible with both Beretta and Benelli shotguns.

ALCIONE MODEL – 12 ga., 28 in. barrels, less engraving than Alcione SL, separated barrels. Importation disc. 1989.

	$675	$550	$495	$460	$430	$380	$335	*$800*

Previously designated Diamond Model.

This model was imported exclusively by FIE Firearms located in Hialeah, FL.

ALCIONE SL – 12 ga., 27 or 28 in. barrels, 6 lbs. 13 oz., separated barrels, ejectors, single trigger, silver finished frame engraved with luggage case. Importation disc. 1986.

	$1,150	$995	$875	$800	$725	$640	$550	*$1,595*

ALCIONE 2000 SX (FIELD MODEL) – 12 ga., 3 in. chambers, 28 in. barrels, SST, separated barrels, ejectors, single trigger, engraved silver finished frame with gold accents, with case, 7 lbs. 4 oz. Imported 1997 only.

	$1,675	$1,495	$1,275	$1,025	$875	$750	$650	*$1,895*

ALCIONE FIELD – 12 ga. only, 3 in. chambers, blue (Classic Field, new 2004), polished steel (silver) alloy frame with game bird etching, SST, ejectors, 26 or 28 in. interchangeable barrels with choke tubes, checkered satin finished walnut stock and forearm, also available in left-hand, 7.4 lbs. Mfg. 1998-2005.

	$1,125	$960	$825	$725	$600	$500	$425	*$1,310*

Add $90 for Classic Field Model with blue receiver, gold trigger, and Schnabel forearm.

This model was previously designated 97-12 IBS.

* ***Alcione Field LF*** – 12 or 20 ga., 3 in. chambers (20 ga. only), lightweight alloy receiver with etching and gold fill, approx. 6.8 lbs. Mfg. 2000-2002.

	$1,150	$975	$875	$775	$650	$550	$425	*$1,305*

ALCIONE CLASSIC – 12 ga. only, 3 in. chambers, blue non-engraved receiver, SST, ejectors, 26 or 28 in. VR barrels with choke tubes, checkered satin finished walnut stock and forearm. 7 1/2 lbs. Mfg. 2004-2005.

	$1,125	$960	$825	$725	$600	$500	$425	*$1,320*

Add $475 for extra set of 12 or 20 ga. barrels.

ALCIONE SL SPORT – 12 ga. only, 2 3/4 in. chambers (can also be fitted for barrels with 3 in. chambers), polished stainless steel receiver, blue barrels, SST, manual safety, ejectors, 30 in. target rib ported barrels with choke tubes, detachable sideplates, available in left-hand, 7.7 lbs. Disc. 2005.

	$1,435	$1,200	$950	$850	$725	$625	$475	*$1,700*

This model was previously designated SL IBS.

ALCIONE SP – 12 ga. only, 3 in. chambers, satin silver finished boxlock action with engraved sideplates including mallard and pheasant gold inlays, gloss finished AA Grade checkered walnut pistol grip stock and Schnabel forearm, 28 in. VR barrels with choke tubes, 20 ga. barrels can be ordered w/o additional gunsmithing, 7 1/2 lbs. Imported 2003-2005.

	$2,325	$2,000	$1,750	$1,500	$1,275	$1,100	$975	*$2,780*

Add $490 for extra set of 20 ga. barrels.

ALCIONE SX – 12 ga. only, 3 in. chambers, 26 or 28 in. interchangeable vent. barrels with VR and 3 choke tubes, deluxe walnut, removable sideplates with etched game scenes, gold plated trigger, approx. 7.4 lbs. Imported 2001-2005.

	$1,535	$1,350	$1,050	$925	$800	$700	$575	*$1,855*

Add $490 for extra set of barrels.
Add $125 for Alcione Classic SX with blued receiver (new 2004).

ALCIONE TITANIUM (T) – 12 or 20 ga., 3 in. chambers, features receiver manufactured from aluminum alloy coupled with titanium inserts, 26 or 28 in. interchangeable vent.

GRADING - PPGS™	100%	98%	95%	90%	80%	70%	60%	LAST MSR

barrels with VR and 3 choke tubes, deluxe walnut, removable sideplates with etched game scenes, gold plated trigger with selector switch, approx. 6.8 lbs. Imported 2002-2005.

	$1,260	$1,050	$950	$875	$800	$750	$695	*$1,470*

Add $460 for 2 barrel set (includes extra 20 ga. barrels).

DE LUXE MODEL PRITI – 12 or 20 ga., boxlock action, ST, ejectors, 26 or 28 in. VR barrels with fixed chokes. Imported 1988-89 only.

	$395	$350	$315	$285	$240	$215	$185	*$460*

This model was imported exclusively by FIE Firearms located in Hialeah, FL.

VELOCE – 20 or 28 ga., 3 in. chambers on 20 ga., 26 or 28 (20 ga. only) in. vent. barrels with 3 choke tubes, aluminum frame with steel reinforcement, etched game scene receiver with gold filled inlays, skeletonized opening lever, deluxe oil finished checkered pistol grip or English (new 2002) stock and forearm, mechanical gold plated SST, 5.5 (28 ga.) or 5.8 (20 ga.) lbs. Imported 2001-2005.

	$1,260	$1,050	$950	$875	$800	$750	$695	*$1,470*

Add $75 for 28 ga.

* ***Veloce Grade II*** – similar to Veloce Model, except has semi-pistol grip deluxe walnut stock. Limited importation 2004 only.

	$1,750	$1,500	$1,250	$1,050	$925	$825	$725	*$2,000*

Add $75 for 28 ga.

* ***Veloce Squire Limited Edition*** – includes one set of 26 in. 20 ga. and one set of 26 in. 28 ga. barrels, cased, 5.7 lbs. Imported 2003-2005.

	$2,050	$1,750	$1,450	$1,125	$975	$875	$775	*$2,470*

VELOCE SP – 20 ga., 26 in. barrel, checkered oil finished AA walnut stock and forearm, deep relief engraving with gold game bird inlays, gold plated trigger, 5 1/2 lbs., available from World Class dealers only. Importation began 2007.

MSR $2,889	$2,525	$2,250	$1,975	$1,750	$1,525	$1,300	$1,100	

INSTINCT L – 12 or 20 ga., 26 or 28 in. barrels, 3 in. chambers, SST, checkered A Grade satin walnut stock and forearm, color case hardened receiver, 5 choke tubes, auto ejectors, red fiber optic front bead sights, comes with custom fitted hard case, 6.1-6.4 lbs. New 2012.

MSR $1,149	$995	$875	$775	$675	$600	$525	$425	

INSTINCT SL – 12 or 20 ga., 26 or 28 in. barrels, 3 in. chambers, checkered AA Grade satin walnut stock and forearm, coin finished aluminum alloy receiver, auto ejectors, 5 extended choke tubes, red fiber optic front bead sights, comes with custom fitted hard case, 5.3-5.7 lbs. New 2012.

MSR $1,349	$1,200	$1,050	$925	$800	$675	$550	$475	

RENAISSANCE FIELD – 12, 20, or 28 ga., 3 in. chambers (2 3/4 in. on 28 ga.), boxlock action with polished blue finish, 26 or 28 in. VR barrels with choke tubes, ejectors, SST, oil finished walnut stock and forearm, Twin Shock absorber recoil pad with gel insert, 5.5 - 6.2 lbs. Imported 2006-2010.

	$1,425	$1,200	$1,000	$875	$750	$650	$575	*$1,659*

Add $40 for 28 ga.

RENAISSANCE CLASSIC – similar to Renaissance Field, except has gold plated trigger, A Grade walnut and gold bird inlays. Imported 2006-2010.

	$1,575	$1,350	$1,125	$975	$875	$775	$650	*$1,820*

Add $70 for 28 ga.

* ***Renaissance Classic Combo*** – includes 26 in. 20 and 28 ga. barrels. Mfg. 2008-2010.

	$2,325	$1,925	$1,700	$1,500	$1,325	$1,150	$1,000	*$2,729*

RENAISSANCE ELITE – similar to Renaissance Classic, except has AA Grade walnut, deep relief engraving, gold game scene inlays. Imported 2006-2010.

	$2,000	$1,750	$1,475	$1,225	$995	$825	$700	*$2,329*

Add $110 for 28 ga.

GRADING - PPGS™	100%	98%	95%	90%	80%	70%	60%	LAST MSR

RENAISSANCE SPORTING – 12 ga., 3 in. chambers, 30 in. VR ported barrels with extended choke tubes, A Grade walnut stock with adj. comb, engraving, approx. 8 lbs. Imported 2007-2010.

$1,925	$1,675	$1,450	$1,250	$995	$825	$700	*$2,219*

BLACK MAGIC SPORTING HUNTER – 12 ga. only, 3 in. chambers, 28 in. separated barrels with VR and Franchokes, black frame with gold accents and gold plated trigger, SST, ejectors, checkered walnut stock and forearm, 7 lbs. Imported 1989-91.

$995	$875	$800	$725	$650	$575	$495	*$1,249*

The Black Magic Model Series was imported exclusively by American Arms, Inc. located in North Kansas City, MO.

* ***Black Magic Sporting Hunter Lightweight*** – similar to Black Magic Sporting Hunter except 2 3/4 in. chambers only, 26 in. separated barrels with VR and Franchokes, alloy frame, 6 lbs. Imported 1989-91.

$975	$850	$775	$700	$625	$550	$475	*$1,209*

SPORTING 2000 – 12 ga. only, design for sporting clays or hunting, 28 in. vent. ported (disc. 1993) or unported (new 1997) barrels with target VR and choke tubes, SST, ejectors, select walnut with checkering, solid pad, hard case, 7 3/4 lbs. Imported 1992-1993, resumed 1997, disc. 1998.

$1,275	$1,025	$875	$750	$650	$575	$500	*$1,495*

ARISTOCRAT FIELD – 12 ga., 26, 28, or 30 in. barrels, various chokes, vent. rib, auto ejectors, boxlock, selective single trigger, checkered pistol grip stock. Mfg. 1960-69.

$660	$470	$440	$395	$375	$340	$310

ARISTOCRAT MAGNUM – similar to Field, except 32 in. barrels, 3 in. chambers, full choke, pad. Mfg. 1962-65.

$660	$470	$440	$395	$375	$340	$310

ARISTOCRAT SKEET – similar to Field, but 26 in. vent. rib, bored skeet no. 1 and no. 2. Mfg. 1960-69.

$715	$525	$495	$450	$430	$395	$365

ARISTOCRAT SILVER KING – select wood, engraved coin finished frame. Mfg. 1962-69.

$750	$560	$535	$485	$470	$430	$400

ARISTOCRAT TRAP – 30 in. vent. rib barrels, bored mod. and full, trap stock Mfg. 1960-69.

$745	$550	$525	$480	$455	$415	$380

ARISTOCRAT DELUXE – finer wood, more engraving. Mfg. 1960-66.

$990	$870	$835	$810	$770	$715	$660

ARISTOCRAT SUPREME – gold inlaid game birds. Mfg. 1960-66.

$1,430	$1,265	$1,155	$1,075	$990	$935	$880

ARISTOCRAT IMPERIAL – high grade wood, more engraving. Mfg. 1967-69.

$2,640	$2,200	$2,090	$1,925	$1,815	$1,650	$1,430

ARISTOCRAT MONTE CARLO – highest grade wood, elaborate engraving and inlay, mfg. 1967-69.

$3,520	$3,080	$2,915	$2,640	$2,420	$2,090	$1,870

FALCONET S – 12 ga., lightweight model of the Alcione SL, 27 or 28 in. barrels, 6 lbs. 1 oz., separated barrels, moderate engraving on silver finish frame. Disc. 1985.

$895	$765	$660	$560	$510	$460	$410	*$1,015*

FALCONET FIELD – 12, 16, 20, 28 ga., or .410 bore, 24-30 in. barrels, various chokes, auto ejectors, SST, engraved alloy frame, checkered walnut stock. Mfg. 1968-75.

Buckskin (light)	$550	$495	$470	$440	$415	$385	$360
Ebony (black)	$550	$495	$470	$440	$415	$385	$360
Silver	$605	$550	$525	$495	$470	$415	$385

Add 25% for 28 ga. or .410 bore.

GRADING - PPGS™	100%	98%	95%	90%	80%	70%	60%	LAST MSR

FALCONET SKEET – 26 in. barrels, bored skeet no. 1 and no. 2, wide vent. rib, case hardened steel frame. Mfg. 1970-74.

	$935	$855	$825	$770	$715	$690	$650	

FALCONET INTERNATIONAL SKEET – higher grade wood, more engraving. Mfg. 1970-74.

	$1,045	$935	$865	$825	$770	$745	$700	

FALCONET STANDARD TRAP – 12 ga., 30 in. mod. and full, wide vent. rib, trap stock, pad. Mfg. 1970-74.

	$935	$855	$825	$770	$715	$690	$650	

FALCONET INTERNATIONAL TRAP – higher grade wood, more engraving. Mfg. 1970-74.

	$1,045	$935	$865	$825	$770	$745	$700	

FALCONET 2000 – 12 ga. only, boxlock with alloy frame featuring silver finish with gold plated game scenes, 26 in. separated barrels with VR and choke tubes, SST, ejectors, select checkered walnut stock and forearm, hard case, 6 lbs. Imported 1992-97.

	$1,245	$975	$850	$725	$650	$575	$500	*$1,375*

FALCONET 97-12 IBS – 12 ga. only, 2 3/4 in. chambers, ultra light alloy frame with gold inlays, scroll engraving, and nickel finish, SST, ejectors, 26 in. barrels with Franchokes, checkered walnut stock and forearm, includes hard case. Imported 1998-2000.

	$875	$750	$625	$550	$500	$450	$400	*$965*

PEREGRINE MODEL 451 – 12 ga., 26-28 in. barrels, various chokes, vent. rib, auto ejectors, alloy frame, SST, checkered pistol grip stock. Mfg. 1975.

	$605	$550	$525	$495	$440	$415	$360	

PEREGRINE MODEL 400 – similar to 451, except steel frame. Mfg. 1975.

	$660	$605	$570	$540	$495	$460	$385	

MODEL 2003 TRAP – 12 ga., 30 or 32 in. barrels, imp. mod. and full, or full and full, boxlock, auto ejectors, SST, high vent. rib, trap style stock, buttpad, cased. Mfg. 1976. Disc.

	$1,205	$1,090	$1,045	$910	$855	$770	$660	

MODEL 2004 TRAP – similar to 2003, except single barrel, cased. Mfg. 1976. Disc.

	$1,205	$1,090	$1,045	$910	$855	$770	$660	

MODEL 2005 COMBINATION TRAP – two sets of barrels, one single, one O/U, cased. Mfg. 1976. Disc.

	$1,815	$1,595	$1,515	$1,320	$1,210	$1,075	$935	

MODEL 2005/3 COMBINATION TRAP – three sets of barrels, cased. Mfg. 1976. Disc.

	$2,420	$2,090	$1,980	$1,705	$1,515	$1,485	$1,320	

UNDERGUN MODEL 3000 – radical competition trap, very high rib separated barrels, under single and O/U, drop in set screw chokes (hex drive), set aluminum cased. Disc.

	$2,750	$2,530	$2,310	$2,090	$1,980	$1,870	$1,760	

SHOTGUNS: SxS

AIRONE – 12 ga., choice of barrel length and chokes, Anson & Deeley box lock action, auto ejectors, double triggers, checkered English style stock, engraved. Mfg. 1940-50.

	$1,320	$1,100	$935	$825	$745	$715	$660	

ASTORE – similar to Airone, except less engraving, extractors. Mfg. 1937-60.

	$990	$910	$770	$715	$635	$580	$550	

ASTORE 5 – similar to Astore, except higher grade wood, more engraving, auto ejectors. Disc.

	$2,200	$1,925	$1,650	$1,540	$1,460	$1,375	$1,320	

ASTORE II – similar to Astore 5, except less elaborate, mfg. in Spain for Franchi.

	$1,210	$1,045	$935	$880	$800	$715	$660	

GRADING - PPGS™	100%	98%	95%	90%	80%	70%	60%	LAST MSR

HIGHLANDER – 12, 20, or 28 ga., 3 in. chambers except for 28 ga., English style straight grip walnut stock and splinter forearm, scalloped coin finished boxlock receiver, SST, extractors, 26 in. barrels with fixed chokes, includes fitted hardcase, 5.7-6.4 lbs. Limited importation 2003.

	$1,575	$1,275	$1,075	$950	$825	$700	$600	*$1,800*

HIGHLANDER (RECENT MFG.) – 12 or 20 ga., 3 in. chambers, scalloped boxlock action, SST, blued or case colored (20 ga. only) frame, 26 in. VR barrels with choke tubes, straight grip A Grade oil finished walnut stock and splinter forearm. Imported 2007-2009.

	$2,400	$2,100	$1,800	$1,500	$1,250	$1,000	$850	*$2,799*

SIDELOCK DOUBLE BARREL – 12, 16, or 20 ga., barrels and choke custom order, stock to order, hand detachable side lock, self-opening action, auto ejectors, six grades offered, they differ only in overall quality and ornamentation, and grade of wood used.

Condor	$7,700	$6,600	$6,050	$5,720	$5,500	$4,620	$3,960
Imperial	$10,450	$9,350	$8,800	$8,250	$7,480	$6,600	$5,720
Imperiales	$10,670	$9,570	$9,020	$8,470	$7,700	$6,820	$5,940

SIDE-LOCK DOUBLE BARREL – the following models are available through the Beretta Galleries and selected premium dealers only (see Trademark Index).

* ***Side-Lock Double Barrel No. 5 Imperial Monte Carlo***

	$30,000	$20,000	$16,000	$12,000	$10,000	$8,000	$6,500	*$35,000*

* ***Side-Lock Double Barrel No. 17 Imperial Monte Carlo***

	$37,500	$30,000	$25,000	$20,000	$15,000	$10,000	$7,500	*$42,500*

* ***Side-Lock Double Barrel Imperial Monte Carlo Extra*** – 12 or 20 ga.

Imperial Monte Carlo Extra is currently being mfg. by Beretta. Prices are $145,000 for single guns, and $325,000 - $345,000 for pairs.

DESTINO – 20 ga., 3 in. chambers, boxlock action with satin nickel finish and game scene engraving with gold inlays, SST, extractors, checkered straight grip AAA English walnut stock, fitted rubber buttpad, limited production of 250 during 2007-mid-2008.

	$3,100	$2,700	$2,300	$1,950	$1,575	$1,375	$1,150	*$3,495*

SHOTGUNS: SEMI-AUTO & SLIDE ACTION

BLACK MAGIC GAME – 12 ga. only, 3 in. chamber with gas metering system, interchangeable shell handling without gas system adjustments, two-tone black alloy receiver with gold plated accents and trigger, 24, 26, or 28 in. VR barrel with Franchokes, checkered walnut stock and forearm, 7 lbs. Imported 1989-91.

	$550	$450	$395	$330	$300	$270	$240	*$659*

* ***Black Magic Game Skeet*** – skeet variation of the Black Magic Game, 2 3/4 in. chamber, 26 in. ported VR barrel with fixed Tula skeet choke, skeet dimensioned stock, 7 1/4 lbs. Imported 1989-91.

	$580	$475	$425	$350	$325	$295	$265	*$699*

* ***Black Magic Game Trap*** – trap variation of the Black Magic Game, 2 3/4 in. chamber, 30 in. VR barrel with Franchoke system, trap dimensioned stock, 7 1/2 lbs. Imported 1989-91.

	$615	$495	$430	$350	$325	$295	$265	*$739*

48 AL FIELD MODEL – 12 (disc. 2001), 20, or 28 (new 1996) ga., 2 3/4 in. chamber, 24, 26, 28, or 30 (disc. in 1990) in. VR barrel with (beginning 1989) or w/o choke tubes, long recoil operation, alloy receiver, semi-humpback design, checkered pistol grip satin walnut stock and forearm, VR standard, standard choke tubes became available in 1989, 12 ga., 6 lbs. 9 oz. and 20 ga., 5 lbs. 6 oz. New 1950.

MSR $839	$695	$600	$500	$425	$375	$325	$285

Add $100 for 28 ga.
Add $20 for Youth Model.
Add $30 for 12 ga. 24 in. slug barrel (disc. 1994).
Subtract 10% if without choke tubes.

GRADING - PPGS™	100%	98%	95%	90%	80%	70%	60%	LAST MSR

This model is also available as a Youth Model (12 1/2 LOP, 20 ga. only). Starting in 1990, black receiver, gold accents, and choke tubes became standard.

* ***48 AL Field Model Deluxe*** – 20 or 28 ga., 26 in. barrel, similar to AL 48 Field, except has a high polish blue finish and upgraded walnut pistol grip, English (new 2002) or Prince of Wales (new 2012) stock and forearm, gold trigger and receiver accents, approx. 5 1/2 lbs. New 2000.

MSR $989	$850	$700	$600	$500	$400	$350	$325	

Add $120 for 28 ga.
Add $51 for Prince-of-Wales stock (new 2012).

STANDARD MAGNUM (48/AL) – similar to 48 AL Field, except has 3 in. chamber with 28 in. (disc. 1988) or 32 in. VR barrel, recoil pad. Mfg. 1954-1990.

	$415	$360	$300	$270	$250	$230	$210	*$482*

This model was slated to be replaced with the Combo S/T - however, while advertised, the Combo S/T was never mfg.

HUNTER MODEL (48/AL) – similar to 48 AL Field, except etched receiver, better wood, VR standard, Franchokes became available in 1989. Mfg. 1950-1990.

	$415	$360	$300	$270	$250	$230	$210	*$482*

Add $35 for internal Franchokes (3).

This model was imported exclusively by FIE Firearms located in Hialeah, FL.

FENICE – 20 or 28 ga., 26 or 28 in. barrel, checkered oil finished AA walnut stock and forearm, 5 shot mag., silver receiver with light scroll and gold game bird inlays, gold plated trigger, 5.4-5.7 lbs., available from World Class dealers only. Importation began 2007.

MSR $1,359	$1,225	$1,050	$900	$775	$650	$575	$475	

HUNTER MAGNUM – mfg. 1954-1973.

	$430	$380	$370	$340	$315	$290	$275	

AFFINITY – 12 or 20 ga., 26 or 28 in. barrel, 3 in. chamber, 4 shot mag., fiber optic red bar front sight, includes 3 choke tubes and shim kit, Black synthetic, Realtree Max-4, or Realtree APG 100% camo finish, 5.6 - 6 1/2 lbs. New 2012.

MSR $849	$725	$650	$575	$525	$475	$425	$375	

Add $100 for Realtree Max-4 or Realtree APG 100% camo finish.

PRESTIGE MODEL – 12 ga. only, gas operated, vent. rib, various barrel lengths, alloy receiver, Franchokes became available in 1989. Imported 1985-89.

	$575	$475	$395	$325	$310	$295	$275	*$720*

Add $40 for internal Franchokes (3).

This model was imported exclusively by FIE Firearms located in Hialeah, FL.

* ***Prestige Model Turkey*** – similar to Prestige Model except has dull matte black finish, Franchokes standard. Imported 1989 only.

	$615	$515	$425	$350	$320	$300	$280	*$760*

This model was imported exclusively by FIE Firearms located in Hialeah, FL.

ELITE MODEL – same general specifications as the Prestige Model, only etched receiver, Franchokes became available in 1989. Imported 1985-89.

	$595	$500	$425	$350	$320	$300	$280	*$740*

Add $45 for internal Franchokes (3).

This model was imported exclusively by FIE Firearms located in Hialeah, FL.

MODEL 610 VS – 12 ga., incorporates gas-operated Variopress System, adjusts for both 2 3/4 and 3 in. shells, 4 lug rotating breech bolt, alloy receiver, non-glare finish, 26 or 28 in. VR barrels with Franchokes, checkered walnut stock and forearm. Imported 1997 only.

	$650	$550	$425	$325	$275	$250	$225	*$750*

Add $45 for engraved receiver and bolt (Model 610 VSL).

GRADING - PPGS™	100%	98%	95%	90%	80%	70%	60%	LAST MSR

MODEL 612/620 (VS) – 12 (Model 612) or 20 (Model 620) ga., 3 in. chamber, features VarioSystem/Variomax gas operation utilizing reversible gas adjustment collar on mag. tube, advanced safety system, black receiver with (disc. 2001) or w/o gold borders (new 2002), 24, 26, or 28 in. barrel with choke tubes, last shot hold open, choice of checkered satin walnut, black synthetic (not available in 20 ga.) stock and forearm, 100% Realtree X-tra brown (disc. 1999), Realtree HD Timber (new 2002), Max-4 HD (new 2004, not available in 20 ga.), or Advantage (mfg. 2000-2002) camo coverage, 5.9-7 lbs. Mfg. 1998-2004.

$550	$475	$415	$350	$325	$300	$275	*$660*

Add $15 for satin finished walnut stock and forearm.
Add $105 for 100% camo coverage (Models 612/620 VS Camo).
Add $15 for 20 ga. or for Youth Model (20 ga. only, 12 1/2 LOP stock).

This model was previously designated the Variopress 612/620.

* ***Model 612 Sporting*** – 12 ga. only, features blue receiver with gold logo (new 2002), or silver receiver with black border and gold small parts (disc. 1998), matte black receiver with green logo (mfg. 2000-2002), or matte black top/polished sides receiver with gold lettering (new 2003), 28 (disc. 1998) or 30 (new 2000) in. ported target rib barrel with extended 4 in. forcing cone and elongated Franchokes, select checkered walnut stock and forearm, 7.1 lbs. Limited mfg. 1998, reintroduced 2000-2004.

$825	$750	$625	$525	$450	$375	$325	*$975*

This model was previously designated the Variopress 612 Sporting.

MODEL 612 DEFENSE – 12 ga. only, 18 1/2 in. barrel with cyl. bore, matte finish metal with black synthetic stock and forearm, 6 1/2 lbs. Imported 2000-2002.

$525	$450	$375	$325	$285	$265	$245	*$635*

This model was previously designated the Variopress 612 Defense.

MODEL 712 – 12 ga. only, 3 in. chamber, Benelli inertia recoil system with rotating bolt head, aluminum receiver, 24, 26, or 28 in. VR barrel, 5 shot mag., choice of synthetic, Weathercoat walnut, or 100% Advantage Timber HD or Max-4 HD camo coverage, recoil pad, approx. 7 lbs. Limited importation 2004 only.

$650	$575	$500	$450	$375	$325	$275	*$750*

Add $65 for walnut stock and forearm with Weathercoating.
Add $105 for camo finish.

* ***Model 712 Raptor*** – features 30 in. ported VR barrel with extended choke tubes, satin nickel receiver with green Franchi logo insert on right side, checkered Weathercoat pistol grip stock with recoil pad, blue finish, 5 shot mag., Benelli rotary bolt design, approx. 7 lbs. Mfg. 2005-2007.

$845	$700	$575	$500	$440	$395	$350	*$999*

MODEL 720 – 20 ga. only, 3 in. chamber, 26 or 28 in. barrel, similar to Model 712, except is not available with synthetic stock, also available with short LOP, blue or 100% Advantage Timber HD (disc. 2007) or Max 4-HD camo coverage, approx. 6 lbs. Mfg. 2004-2011.

$875	$725	$600	$500	$425	$375	$325	*$999*

Subtract $60 for short LOP.

* ***Model 720 Raptor*** – features 28 in. barrel with Weathercoat stock, blue finish, 5 shot mag. Mfg. 2005-2007.

$845	$700	$575	$500	$440	$395	$350	*$999*

* ***Model 720 Competition*** – 20 ga. only, 3 in. chamber, nickel finished receiver, 28 in. VR barrel with extended choke tube, Weathercoat stock and forearm, 6.2 lbs. Mfg. 2008-2011.

$950	$800	$700	$600	$525	$450	$400	*$1,109*

MODEL 912 – 12 ga. only, 3 1/2 in. chamber, VarioSystem/Variomax gas operation utilizing reversible gas adjustment collar on mag. tube, lightweight alloy receiver, 24, 26, 28, or 30 in. VR barrel with 3 choke tubes, choice of satin walnut stock (new 2002), black synthetic or 100% Advantage Timber HD or Max-4 HD (new 2004) camo coverage, magazine cutoff, includes hard case, 7.5-7.8 lbs. Imported 2001-2005.

$665	$575	$500	$450	$375	$325	$275	*$790*

GRADING - PPGS™	100%	98%	95%	90%	80%	70%	60%	LAST MSR

Add $110 for camo coverage.
Add $60 for satin finished walnut stock and forearm.
Add $60 for Model 912 steady-grip with 24 in. barrel and 100% Timber HD camo coverage.

This model was previously designated the Variopress 912.

I-12 INERTIA – 12 ga. only, 3 in. chamber, 24, 26, or 28 in. VR barrel, inertia operating system with free floating bolt which compresses an inertia spring upon recoil, choice of synthetic or satin walnut stock and forearm, blued, matte blue, Max-4 HD, APG HD (new 2007), or Timber HD (disc. 2007) camo coverage, Twin Shock Absorber recoil pad with gel insert, approx. 7 1/2 lbs. Mfg. 2005-2011.

$695 $575 $475 $400 $350 $325 $285 ***$839***

Add $100 for 100% camo coverage.
Add $100 for walnut stock and forearm.

I-12 LIMITED WHITE GOLD – 12 ga. only, similar to I-12 Inertia, except has AA Grade checkered walnut stock and forearm, 28 in. barrel only, engraved matte nickel receiver, includes hard case. Imported 2006-2011.

$1,425 $1,150 $975 $825 $725 $625 $525 ***$1,699***

I-12 UPLAND HUNTER – 12 ga. only, 3 in. chamber, 26 in. VR barrel with choke tubes, Weathercoat straight grip stock and forearm. Mfg. 2008-2009.

$1,075 $925 $800 $700 $600 $500 $400 ***$1,169***

I-12 SPORTING – 12 ga., 30 in. VR barrel with extended choke tubes, satin finished walnut stock and forearm, 7.8 lbs. Mfg. 2008-2011.

$1,175 $1,000 $875 $750 $650 $550 $475 ***$1,329***

SPAS-12 – 12 ga., 2 3/4 in. chamber, tactical shotgun, pump or semi-auto operation, 5 (new 1991) or 8 (disc.) shot tube mag., alloy receiver, synthetic stock with built-in pistol grip (limited quantities were also mfg. with a folding stock or metal fixed stock), one-button switch to change operating mode, 21 1/2 in. barrel, 8 3/4 lbs. Importation disc. 1994.

$1,000 $850 $700 $600 $500 $400 $300 ***$769***

This model was imported exclusively by FIE Firearms located in Hialeah, FL until 1990.

SPAS-15 – 12 ga. only, 2 3/4 in. chamber, tactical shotgun, pump or semi-auto operation, 6 shot detachable box mag., 21 1/2 in. barrel, lateral folding skeleton stock, carrying handle, one button switch to change operating mode, 10 lbs. Limited importation 1989 only.

Even though the retail was in the $700 range, demand and rarity have pushed prices up dramatically, with NIB examples in the $5,000 - $7,500 range.

This model had very limited importation (less than 200) as the BATFE disallowed further importation almost immediately.

SAS-12 – 12 ga. only, 3 in. chamber, slide action only, synthetic stock with built-in pistol grip, 8 shot tube mag., 21 1/2 in. barrel, 6.8 lbs. Imported 1988-90 only.

$415 $360 $300 $270 $250 $230 $210 ***$473***

This model was imported exclusively by FIE Firearms located in Hialeah, FL.

LAW-12 – 12 ga. only, 2 3/4 in. chamber, gas operated semi-auto, synthetic stock with built-in pistol grip, 5 (new 1991) or 8 (disc.) shot tube mag., 21 1/2 in. barrel, 6 3/4 lbs. Imported 1988-94.

$570 $485 $400 $360 $320 $300 $280 ***$719***

TURKEY GUN – 12 ga., similar to Standard Mag., 3 in. chamber only, turkey scene engraved. Mfg. 1963-65.

$415 $385 $370 $340 $315 $290 $275

SLUG GUN – 22 in. plain barrel, rifle sights.

$360 $330 $315 $295 $275 $255 $240

SKEET GUN – 26 in. skeet choke vent. rib barrel, select wood. Mfg. 1972-1974.

$385 $370 $350 $330 $310 $285 $265

GRADING - PPGS™	100%	98%	95%	90%	80%	70%	60%	LAST MSR

ELDORADO – fancy wood and gold filled engraved receiver. Mfg. 1954-75.

$450 $420 $395 $380 $360 $340 $320

CROWN GRADE – engraved hunting scene. Mfg. 1954-75.

$1,540 $1,320 $1,210 $1,045 $965 $910 $855

DIAMOND GRADE SILVER INLAID SCROLL – mfg. 1954-75.

$1,980 $1,735 $1,540 $1,430 $1,210 $1,045 $965

IMPERIAL GRADE – gold inlaid hunting scene.

$2,420 $2,090 $1,925 $1,760 $1,595 $1,485 $1,320

Note: Standard, Skeet and Slug with steel frame mfg. 1965-1972, designated "Dynamic" 12 ga., values are the same.

MODEL 500 STANDARD – 12 ga., 26 or 28 in. barrel, various chokes, vent. rib, gas operated, checkered pistol grip stock. Mfg. 1976-disc.

$330 $310 $305 $265 $230 $195 $165

MODEL 520 DELUXE – engraved receiver.

$385 $365 $330 $290 $260 $220 $195

MODEL 520 ELDORADO GOLD – fine wood, engraved gold, inlaid receiver. Mfg. 1977-disc.

$990 $770 $715 $660 $580 $525 $470

MODEL 530 AUTO TRAP – 12 ga., similar to 500, except 30 or 32 in. full choke barrel, very high rib, special trap stock, recoil pad.

$660 $550 $525 $440 $415 $385 $330

FRANCOTTE, AUGUSTE & CIE. S.A.

Current trademark owned by Connecticut Shotgun Manufacturing Company beginning 2011. Previous manufacturer located in Leige, Belgium 1805-2002. Previously imported until 1999 by Armes De Chasse located in Hertford, NC, Von Lengerke & Detmold between 1900-1930s, and Abercrombie & Fitch until approx. 1962.

It is important to note that original A. Francotte SxS rifles and shotguns should exhibit the "crown over AF" maker's mark amongst the proofmarks.

PISTOLS: SEMI-AUTO

SEMI-AUTO PISTOL – 6.35mm cal., 6 shot mag., frame marked "Francotte Liege." Mfg. 1912-1914.

$495 $450 $395 $335 $295 $260 $230

REVOLVERS

Francotte manufactured Pryse-type revolvers at the end of the 19th century, and these revolvers bore the name of the well-known British retailer. Encountered only infrequently domestically, these specimens found overseas are usually priced in the $250-$800 range.

RIFLES

All recently mfg. rifles in this section were custom made to the purchaser's individual specifications. Francotte took advantage of 5 different frame sizes for its double rifles.

Add 20%-50% for P. Grifnee engraving, depending on coverage and amount of detail.

BOLT ACTION MODEL – many calibers between .18 Bee and .505 Gibbs Mag., select checkered walnut stock, engraved mag. floor plate, gold inlays optional, the following values assume engraving.

* ***Bolt Action Model Short*** – cals. with shorter cartridges.

$9,400 $8,225 $7,050 $6,390 $5,170 $4,230 $3,290

Subtract $3,250 if without engraving.

GRADING - PPGS™	100%	98%	95%	90%	80%	70%	60%	LAST MSR

* ***Bolt Action Model Standard*** – cals. with medium cartridge lengths.

	$7,825	$6,845	$5,870	$5,320	$4,305	$3,520	$2,740	

Subtract $2,675 if without engraving.

* ***Bolt Action Model Magnum Action*** – cals. with longer cartridge lengths.

	$13,750	$12,030	$10,315	$9,350	$7,565	$6,190	$4,815	

Subtract $7,850 if without engraving.

SINGLE SHOT MOUNTAIN RIFLE – variety of cals., boxlock or sidelock action, custom order only.

* ***Single Shot Mountain Rifle Boxlock*** – 6.5x50Rmm, 7x57Rmm, or 7x65Rmm cal.

	$13,900	$12,165	$10,425	$9,450	$7,645	$6,255	$4,865	

Subtract $4,800 if without engraving.
Add 10% for optional sideplates.

* ***Single Shot Mountain Rifle Sidelock*** – 7x65Rmm or 7mm Rem. Mag. cal.

	$24,800	$21,700	$18,600	$16,865	$13,640	$11,160	$8,680	

Subtract $5,725 if without engraving.

BOXLOCK SxS RIFLE – .30-06, .375 H&H, .470 NE, .500-3 in., or 9.3x62mm cal., ejectors, case colored frame with border engraving (including screws), quarter rib on barrel, deluxe checkered pistol grip walnut stock and forearm. Mfg. 1997-disc.

	$13,750	$12,030	$10,315	$9,350	$7,565	$6,190	$4,815	

Add 50% for .375 H&H cal.
Add 100% for .470 NE or .500-3 in. cal.

SIDELOCK SxS RIFLE – .30-06, .375 H&H, .470 NE, .500-3 in., or 9.3x62mm cal., ejectors, case colored frame with border engraving (including screws), quarter rib on barrel, deluxe checkered pistol grip walnut stock and forearm. Mfg. 1997-disc.

	$26,000	$22,750	$19,500	$17,680	$14,300	$11,700	$9,100	
.470 NE or .500-3 in. cal.	$52,000	$45,500	$39,000	$35,360	$28,600	$23,400	$18,200	

Add 50% for .375 H&H, .470 NE, or .500 cal.

SHOTGUNS: SxS

Please contact CT Shotgun Manufacturing Company directly for availability and pricing on any new releases (see Trademark Index).

All recently manufactured shotguns in this section were custom made to purchaser's individual specifications. Basic types listed were also available in 24 or 32 ga. upon special order. Francotte took advantage of 5 different action sizes, one for each gauge. Auguste Francotte did not manufacture guns by model - all guns were custom order. Original A. Francotte SxS shotguns must have the "Francotte Choke Bore" marking on the water table. Be wary of fake barrel and frame markings, as some guns have recenty surfaced that are not Francotte, but have the Francotte name.

Add 50% for 20 ga.
Add 100% for 28 ga. or .410 bore, on the following models (except Jubilee), depending on condition.
Add 20%-50% for P. Grifnee engraving, (post-1970 mfg.) depending on coverage and amount of detail.

BOXLOCK MODEL – 12, 16, 20, 28 ga., or .410 bore, premium grade Belgium side-by-side, double triggers standard, auto ejectors, English scroll engraving, Anson & Deeley boxlock action.

	$15,450	$11,250	$8,000	$6,250	$5,000	$4,000	$3,250	

Subtract approx. 30% if without engraving.
Add approx. 15% for sideplates with engraving.

* ***Boxlock Model Deluxe Anson & Deeley*** – gold inlaid game scenes, and engraving was by customer's personal preference.

	$17,500	$14,250	$11,000	$8,750	$7,250	$6,000	$4,750	

GRADING - PPGS™	100%	98%	95%	90%	80%	70%	60%	LAST MSR

SIDELOCK MODEL – 12, 16, 20, 28 ga., or .410 bore, true sidelock action, Arabesque scroll engraving, various chokes and barrel lengths, custom order only.

	$27,300	$22,000	$18,750	$15,150	$12,000	$9,000	$7,750	

Subtract approx. 15% if without engraving.

* ***Sidelock Model Deluxe*** – gold inlaid game scenes and engraving were by customer's personal preference.

	$32,500	$27,500	$22,000	$18,750	$15,000	$12,000	$9,500	

JUBILEE MODEL – case colored frame with hand engraving, Von Lengerke & Detmold or Abercrombie & Fitch import. Mfg. circa 1920-1970.

Knockabout	$3,300	$2,950	$2,600	$2,100	$1,650	$1,450	$1,200	
No. 14	$4,100	$3,600	$3,000	$2,550	$2,200	$2,050	$1,750	
No. 18	$4,625	$4,000	$3,400	$2,950	$2,525	$2,075	$1,875	
No. 20	$5,500	$4,800	$4,100	$3,400	$2,925	$2,550	$2,100	
No. 25	$6,000	$5,500	$4,700	$4,100	$3,500	$2,850	$2,375	
No. 30	$7,800	$6,950	$6,100	$5,600	$5,050	$4,400	$3,850	
No. 45 Eagle Grade	$11,000	$9,900	$8,800	$7,700	$6,600	$5,500	$4,750	

Add 100%-150% for 20 ga., depending on condition.

Add approx. 300%-350% for 28 ga. or .410 bore, depending on condition.

Jubilee Models No. 20, 25, 30, and 45 Eagle Grade are boxlocks with sideplates.

FRANKLIN ARMORY

Current manufacturer of semi-auto pistols and rifles/carbines located in Morgan Hill, CA.

Franklin Armory specializes in producing legal firearms for restrictive jurisdictions such as California (07/FFL and Class II SOT manufacturer), as well as for the non-restrictive states.

PISTOLS: SEMI-AUTO

Current models include the 7.5 in. SE-SSP (MSR range $1,040-$1,195), 11.5 in. SE-SSP (MSR range $1,020-$1,200), XO-26 (MSR range $1,560-$1,770), XO26b (MSR range $1,130-$1,355), Salus Pistol (MSR $1,390-$1,445), and the XO-S Salus Pistol (MSR call). For more information and availability on these models, please contact the company directly (see Trademark Index).

RIFLES: SEMI-AUTO

M4-SBR-L (MSR $1,890), M4-L (MSR range $1,650-$1,700), 3GR-L (MSR $2,240), TMR-L (MSR range $1,950-1,975), V1-L (MSR $1,935), V2-L (MSR range $1,845-$1,985), M4 (MSR range $1,155-$1,180), M4-MOE (MSR range $1,200-$1,280), M4-HTF (MSR $1,735), 10-8 (MSR range $1,395-$1,550), HBAR 16 in. (MSR range $1,080-$1,240), HBAR 20 in. (MSR range $1,095-$1,260), LTW (MSR range $1,100-$1,125), 3GR (MSR $1,650), V1 (MSR $1,640), V2 (MSR range $1,560-$1,650), V3 (MSR range $1,110-$1,190), V4 (MSR range $1,095-$1,145), Featurless Rifle (MSR $1,200), CSW-V1 (MSR $2,300), CSW-V4 (MSR $1,690). For more information including pricing and availability on these models, please contact the company directly (see Trademark Index).

FRASER, DANL. & CO.

Current trademark owned by Dickson & MacNaughton located in Edinburgh, Scotland. Previously imported and distributed by Flying G Ranch, located in Carrizo Springs, TX.

Danl. Fraser & Co. has manufactured rifles since 1873 (originally located in Edinburgh, Scotland).

RIFLES: SINGLE SHOT

HIGHLANDER SINGLE SHOT – .22 LR or .22 Hornet cal., underlever falling block action (color case hardened), 24 in. (1/2 round, 1/2 octagon) barrel, folding express-style sights, pistol grip walnut stock with fine checkering. Disc.

	$415	$335	$300	$280	$260	$240	$220	*$475*

GRADING - PPGS™	100%	98%	95%	90%	80%	70%	60%	LAST MSR

* ***Highlander Single Shot Royal*** – .22 LR or .22 Hornet cal., mfg. in Scotland, rose and scroll engraving with 18Kt. inlays. Special order only.

FRASER FIREARMS CORP.

Previously manufactured by R.B. Industries, Ltd. until 1990. Previously distributed by Fraser Firearms Corp. located in Fraser, MI.

PISTOLS: SEMI-AUTO

FRASER 25 CAL. – .25 ACP cal. only, copy of the Bauer semi-auto pocket model, 6 shot mag., 2 1/4 in. barrel, stainless steel construction.

$120 $100 $90 $85 $80 $75 $70 *$133*

Add $17 for Model 2 (black nylon grips).
Add $115 for Model 3 (24 Kt. gold plated).

FREEDOM ARMS

Current manufacturer established during 1983, and located in Freedom, WY. Distributor and dealer sales.

REVOLVERS: MINI, STAINLESS STEEL

Because Freedom Arms' manufacturing capacity has been maximized due to the success of the .454 Casull revolver, the mini-revolver series was discontinued beginning 1989.

FA-S-22LR (PATRIOT) – .22 LR cal., 5 shot, 1, 1 3/4 (disc. 1988), or 3 (disc. 1988) in. barrel, Hi-Gloss finish. Disc. 1989.

$175 $135 $100 $90 $80 $75 $70 *$153*

Add $15 for 3 in. barrel model (FA-BG-22LR, Minute-Man, disc. 1988).

FA-S-22M (IRONSIDES) – .22 WMR cal., 4 shot, 1, 1 3/4 (disc. 1988), or 3 in. barrel, Hi-Gloss finish. Disc. 1989.

$200 $150 $110 $95 $85 $80 $75 *$177*

Add $43 for 3 in. barrel model (Bostonian).

FA-S-22-LR BUCKLE/REVOLVER COMBINATION – .22 LR cal., 1 in. barrel, pistol is housed in belt buckle. Disc. 1989.

$350 $295 $225 $185 $145 $120 $105 *$193*

* ***FA-S-22-LR Buckle/Revolver Combination .22 Mag. cal.***

$395 $350 $250 $200 $150 $125 $110 *$216*

REVOLVERS: SA, STAINLESS STEEL

Freedom Arms also offers a complete line of accessories and factory installed options. The factory should be contacted directly for an up-to-date listing and prices. Beginning in 1999, all revolvers are equipped with a locking safety device which slides into the muzzle and locks into the chamber under the firing pin, making it impossible to either load the top chamber or turn the cylinder.

Add $312 per interchangeable cylinder in different cals. on most of the following centerfire models.
Add $475 for octagon barrel.
Add $90 for non-standard barrel length.

MODEL 83 FIELD GRADE – .22 LR (w/match chamber), .357 Mag., .41 Mag., .44 Mag., .45 LC (disc. 1990), .454 Casull, .475 Linebaugh, .50 AE (disc. 2004) or .500 Wyoming Express (new 2006) cal., 5 shot, 4 3/4, 6, 7 1/2, 9 (.357 Mag. only), or 10 (not available in .500 Wyoming Express) in. barrel, fixed (disc.) or aluminum base adj. rear sight, replaceable blade front sight, matte stainless steel construction, manual sliding-bar safety system, Pachmayr presentation grips, 56 oz. (.454 Casull cal. with 7 1/2 in. barrel). New 1988.

MSR $1,985 $1,750 $1,500 $1,275 $1,025 $850 $775 $675

Add $105 for .454 Casull, .475 Linebaugh, .50 AE (disc. 2004), or .500 Wyoming Express cal.
Add $285 for .22 LR cal. with match chamber and 10 in. barrel.

GRADING - PPGS™	100%	98%	95%	90%	80%	70%	60%	LAST MSR

MODEL 83 HUNTER PAK FIELD GRADE – .357 Mag., .44 Rem. Mag., or .454 Casull cal., 7 1/2 in. barrel, plastic grips, field grade low profile adj. rear sight or no front sight base, sling and studs, locking aluminum carrying case with cleaning kit and tool. Mfg. 1990-93.

	$1,150	$975	$875	$775	$700	$625	$550	*$1,333*

Add $76 for low profile adj. sight and Pachmayr grips.

* ***Model 83 Hunter Pak Field Grade Premier*** – .357 Mag., .44 Rem. Mag., or .454 Casull cal., 7 1/2 in. barrel, ebony micarta grips, no sights or premier grade adj. sights, sling and studs, locking aluminum carrying case with cleaning kit and tool. Mfg. 1990-93.

	$1,395	$1,125	$925	$825	$750	$675	$500	*$1,611*

Add $100 for adj. sights.

MODEL 83 PREMIER GRADE – .357 Mag., .41 Mag., .44 Mag., .454 Casull, .475 Linebaugh, .50 AE (disc.), .500 Wyoming Express (new 2006) cal., 5 shot, 4 3/4, 6, 7 1/2, 9 (.357 Mag. only) or 10 (not available in .500 Wyoming Express) in. barrel, fixed or steel base adj. rear sight and replaceable blade front sight, stainless steel construction, bright brushed finish, manual sliding-bar safety system, and impregnated hardwood grips, 52.8 oz. New 1983.

MSR $2,365	$2,150	$1,850	$1,525	$1,250	$995	$875	$775	

Add $5 for adj. sights.
Add $95 for .454 Casull, .475 Linebaugh, .500 Wyoming Express, or .50 AE (disc.) cal. with adj. sight.

MODEL 83 VARMINT GRADE – .22 LR cal., 5 shot, dual firing pins, choice of 5 1/8 or 7 1/2 in. barrel, steel base adj. V notch rear sight and replaceable brass bead front sight, stainless steel construction, matte finish, manual sliding-bar safety system, pre-set trigger overtravel stop, impregnated hardwood grips, 58 oz. Disc. 2005.

	$1,525	$1,275	$950	$850	$775	$700	$650	*$1,828*

Add $264 for extra .22 WMR cylinder.

MODEL 83 CENTERFIRE SILHOUETTE – .357 Mag., .41 Mag., or .44 Mag. cal., 5 shot, 9 (.357 Mag. only) or 10 in. barrel, Pachmayr presentation grips, Iron Sight Gun Works silhouette rear sight and replaceable adj. front sight blade with hood, stainless steel construction, matte finish, manual sliding-bar safety system.

MSR $2,091	$1,850	$1,550	$1,275	$1,050	$900	$800	$700	

* ***Model 83 Centerfire Silhouette (.454 Casull Silhouette Model)*** – .454 Casull cal., includes 10 in. barrel, Pachmayr grips, field grade finish, silhouette competition sights, and trigger overtravel stop.

	$1,600	$1,275	$1,075	$925	$825	$750	$675	*$1,958*

* ***Model 83 Centerfire Silhouette Pak*** – .44 Mag. cal., includes 10 in. barrel, silhouette competition sight, honed action with 3 lb. trigger pull, plastic grips, locking aluminum carrying case with cleaning kit and tool. Mfg. 1990 only.

	$1,100	$950	$850	$775	$700	$650	$600	*$1,242*

* ***Model 83 Centerfire Silhouette .454 Casull Pak*** – .454 Casull cal., includes 10 in. barrel, silhouette competition sight, honed action with 3 lb. trigger pull, hardwood grips, locking aluminum carrying case with cleaning kit and tool. Mfg. 1990 only.

	$1,375	$1,175	$995	$850	$775	$700	$650	*$1,522*

MODEL 83 .22 CAL. SILHOUETTE CLASS – .22 LR cal., 5 shot, 10 in. barrel, wood (standard), black micarta (standard), or Pachmayr grips, Iron Sight Gun Works silhouette rear sight and replaceable adj. front sight blade with hood, stainless steel construction, matte finish, manual sliding-bar safety system, dual firing pins, lightened hammer for fast lock time, pre-set trigger overtravel stop, 63 oz. New 1991.

MSR $2,376	$2,075	$1,800	$1,550	$1,300	$1,050	$875	$725	

MODEL 97 PREMIER GRADE – .17 HMR (new 2004), .22 LR (new 2002), .224-32 F.A. (new 2009), .327 Federal (new 2010), .357 Mag., .32 H&R Mag. (mfg. 2004-2009), .41 Rem. Mag. (new 2000), .44 Spl. (new 2003), .45 LC (new 1999) cal., 5 (.41 Mag., .44. Spl., or .45 LC cal.) or 6 (.17 HMR, .22 LR or .357 Mag. cal.) shot, 3 1/2 (mfg. 2004-2005), 4 1/2

GRADING - PPGS™	100%	98%	95%	90%	80%	70%	60%	LAST MSR

(new 2000), 5 1/2, 7 1/2, or 10 in. barrel, fixed or steel base adj. rear sight and replaceable blade front sight, stainless steel construction, bright brushed finish, automatic transfer bar safety system, optional round butt grip, impregnated hardwood grips. New 1997.

MSR $1,995	$1,725	$1,400	$1,150	$975	$850	$750	$650	

Add $25 for .17 HMR or .22 LR cal. with sporting chambers.
Add $207 for optional round butt grip.
Add $215 for 3 1/2 in. barrel (disc.).
Subtract $140 for fixed sights (.32 H&R Mag., .357 Mag., .44 Spl. (new 2007), or .45 LC cal. only).

U.S. DEPUTY MARSHAL – 3 in. barrel only with no ejector, fixed or adj. sights, U.S. Marshal medallion in left hardwood grip. Mfg. 1990-93.

	$1,325	$900	$750	$640	$535	$450	$390	

Last MSR was $1475 (fixed sights).
Last MSR was $1,558 (adj. sights)
Add approx. $80 for adj. sights.

SIGNATURE EDITION – .454 Casull cal., high polish stainless steel, 7 1/2 in. barrel only, rosewood grips, cased with accessories, only 93 of 100 were actually mfg.

	$2,300	$1,750	$1,300	$1,150	$935	$815	$650	$2,684

PRIMUS INTER PARES – 1 of every 1,000 guns were made in this variation, includes octagonal barrel, ivory grips, 7 1/2 in. barrel, and cased. Disc. 1993.

Rarity factor precludes accurate pricing.

FRENCH MILITARY

Various configurations manufactured in several locations in France.

PISTOLS: SEMI-AUTO

P.38 configurations were manufactured in the French occupied Mauser factory in Oberndorf, Germany, after the end of WWII.

P.38 svw-45 STANDARD CONFIGURATION – 9mm Para. cal., blue or grey finish, French five pointed star proof located on right side of the slide, some parts may contain E/WaA135 German acceptance stamps, ser. no. range approx. 1g-4,500k. Mfg. by Mauser.

	$750	$675	$650	$500	$450	$400	$350	

Add 20% for French assembly with FN manufactured slide (marked ac-43 or ac-44 with E/WaA135 stamps).

P.38 svw-46 STANDARD CONFIGURATION – 9mm Para. cal., grey finish, French five pointed star proof located on right side of the slide, some parts may contain E/WaA135 German acceptance stamps, pressed steel grips are common, ser. no. range approx. 4501k-9999k. Mfg. by Mauser.

	$800	$750	$700	$650	$550	$500	$475	

P.38 svw-46 STANDARD CONFIGURATION (w/L Ser. Suffix) – 9mm Para. cal., black/blue finish, French five pointed star proof located on right side of the slide, ser. no. located on left side of slide (early) or under the rear tang of the frame, pressed steel grips common, ser. no. range 1L-500L. Mfg. by Mauser.

	$1,000	$900	$800	$700	$600	$550	$525	

MODEL 1935A AUTO PISTOL – 7.65mm French Long cal., 8 shot, 4.3 in. barrel, fixed sights, blue, checkered wood grips, French service sidearm. Mfg. 1935-1945.

	$450	$350	$275	$250	$225	$200	$175	

Add 50% if Nazi proofed.

* ***Model 1935S Auto Pistol*** – .32 ACP or .380 ACP cal., 4 1/3 in. barrel, enamel finish, Colt Govt. Model locking system, 26 oz.

	$325	$295	$260	$225	$195	$170	$150	

M.A.B. MODEL C – .32 ACP cal., design based on FN Browning Model 1910, 6.1 in. barrel. Introduced 1933.

	$250	$220	$190	$170	$150	$125	$110	

GRADING - PPGS™	100%	98%	95%	90%	80%	70%	60%	LAST MSR

M.A.B. MODEL D – .32 ACP cal., 3.96 in. barrel, single action, similar to Model C, mfg. commercially 1933-1940, many thousands mfg. for the German military during WWII (marked "Pistole MAB Kaliber 7.65mm").

$275	$225	$200	$175	$150	$125	$110	

MODEL M.A.B. PA - 15 – 9mm Para. cal., single action, 15 shot, formerly used by French military.

$650	$550	$450	$400	$365	$335	$300	

Subtract 10% for phosphate.

MODEL M.A.B. PA - 15 TARGET – rare target variation of PA-15, adj. rear sight, 6 in. barrel, cased.

$1,750	$1,250	$1,000	$750	$600	$550	$500	

MODEL 1950 – 9mm Para. cal., SA, 9 shot, most models saw heavy use, 221,900 mfg. by de Armes Chatellerault (MAC) from circa 1953-1963.

$1,295	$1,100	$900	$750	$600	$475	$325	

RIFLES

MODEL 1886 LEBEL BOLT ACTION – 8mm Lebel cal., 32 in. barrel, adj. sight, military stock. Mfg. 1886-WWII.

$450	$350	$300	$275	$250	$225	$200	

1936 MAS BOLT ACTION – 7.5x54mm MAS cal., 21 3/4 in. barrel, adj. sights, military stock, bayonet in forearm, distinguishable by forward bolt handle, housing machined from one piece forging, integral box. mag., loaded with stripper clips, no safety, 8 1/2 lbs. Mfg. 1936-1949.

$300	$225	$175	$145	$125	$100	$80	

MODEL 45 BOLT ACTION – .22 LR cal., trainer configuration, may have Mauser parts, aperture rear sight, post-war mfg.

$400	$360	$330	$275	$235	$200	$175	

MAS 49/56 SEMI-AUTO – 7.5x54mm MAS cal., gas operated (direct impingment) semi-auto rifle, 20 1/2 in. barrel w/NATO standard grenade launcher and adj. grenade sight, provision for bayonet, detachable 10 shot mag., gray finish, military stock, approx. 8 1/2 lbs.

$450	$395	$350	$300	$250	$200	$175	

FRIGON GUNS, INC.

Previously manufactured by Marocchi in Italy. Previously imported by Frigon Guns, Inc. located in Clay Center, KS.

SHOTGUNS

FT-I – 12 ga. only, single barrel trap gun, blue finish, 32 or 34 in. VR barrel, quick-change stock. Mfg. 1986-94.

$925	$675	$525	$435	$375	$350	$295	*$1,100*

FT-C – 12 ga. only, quick-change stock, trap combination gun includes 1 single barrel and 1 set of O/U barrels, cased. Mfg. 1986-94.

$1,700	$1,325	$1,050	$875	$775	$685	$620	*$1,975*

FS-4 – 4-barrel skeet set including 12, 20, 28 ga., or .410 bore, individual forearms, quick-change stock, vent. barrels (except for .410 bore), cased. Mfg. 1986-94.

$2,575	$1,975	$1,675	$1,475	$1,350	$1,250	$1,150	*$2,890*

FROMMER PISTOLS

Previously manufactured by Femaru-Fegyver es Gepgyar R.T., Budapest, Hungary.
Please refer to the Femaru listing in this section.

FULTON ARMORY

Current rifle manufacturer and parts supplier located in Savage, MD. Dealer sales.

RIFLES: SEMI-AUTO

Fulton Armory makes a comprehensive array of the four US Gas Operated Service Rifles: M1

Garand, M1 Carbine, M14 and AR-15-style, including corresponding commercial versions and upper receiver assemblies and related parts and components.

Current Fulton Armory M14-style rifles using Fulton Armory's semi-auto M14 receiver include: the M14 Service Rifle, M14 Competition Rifle (NRA/CMP Service Rifle Match-Legal), M14 JSSW with Sage Stock/Accuracy System, and the M14 Peerless Rifle (NRA/CMP Service Rifle Match-Legal).

Additionally, Fulton Armory manufactures U.S. military and enhanced civilian configurations of the M1 Garand and M1 Carbine, using genuine U.S.G.I. receivers. Models include: the M1 Garand Service Rifle, M1 Garand Carbine. M1 Garand Competition Rifle (John C. Garand Match-Legal) - $1,600 last MSR, M1 Garand Peerless Rifle (NRA/CMP Service Rifle Match-Legal) - $2,000 last MSR.

Fulton Armory FAR-15 models include: Legacy, a '60s semi-auto M16 replica, Classics, mirroring current military M16A2/A4 and M4 models, Guardian Carbines - disc., $1,000-$1,100 last MSR, Liberator and Phantom Tactical Carbines and Enhanced Battle Rifles, Mirage NRA/DCM National Match Rifles - $l,400-$1,800 last MSR, Accutron NRA Match Rifles - $1,300-$2,200 last MSR, Hornet Lightweight Rifle - $750 MSR, disc. 2003, and the Millennial Lightweight Rifle and Carbine - $750-$850 MSR, disc. 2002.

Previously manufactured rifles included: the UPR (Universal Precision Rifle) - $1,798 last MSR, the UBR (Universal Battle Rifle) - $1,100 last MSR, Predator Varmint Rifle - $1,100 last MSR, National Match - $1,375 last MSR, M14 - $2,500 last MSR, SOPMOD M14 - $3,370 last MSR, Titan UPR - $3,370 last MSR, and the Titan UPR - $1,100 last MSR.

Please contact the factory directly for more information, including current availability and pricing (see Trademark Index).

FURR ARMS

Current manufacturer located in Orem, UT.

Please refer to the Gatling Gun listing in the G section.

NOTES

G SECTION

GA PRECISION

Current manufacturer established in 1999, and located in N. Kansas City, MO.

RIFLES

GA Precision manufactures a wide variety of bolt action tactical and custom rifles in numerous configurations. Current models include Crusader - MSR $3,850, Hospitaller - MSR $4,325, GAP-10 (new 2012) - MSR $2,640, Non-typical - MSR $2,985, Base custom - MSR $2,900, Thunder Ranch (new 2012) - MSR $3,625, Rock - MSR $3,300, Gladius - MSR $3,950, and FBI HRT - MSR $4,425. Please contact the company directly for more information, including available options and pricing (see Trademark Index).

GALAZAN

Current trademark established in 1995, and manufactured by Connecticut Shotgun Manufacturing Co., located in New Britain, CT. Consumer direct sales.

The Galazan trademark has established itself as one of the premier names in best quality O/U shotguns and double rifles. All guns are custom order. For more information regarding current firearms, please refer to the Connecticut Shotgun Manufacturing Co. listing in this text.

GALEF SHOTGUNS

Previous importer of Zabala Hermanos (Spanish) and Antonio Zoli (Italian) shotguns.

GRADING - PPGS™	100%	98%	95%	90%	80%	70%	60%	LAST MSR

SHOTGUNS

COMPANION FOLDING SINGLE BARREL – 12, 16, 20, 28 ga., or .410 bore, 28 in. barrel, full choke, 30 in. full, 12 ga. only, hammerless, underlever, checkered pistol grip stock.

	100%	98%	95%	90%	80%	70%	60%	LAST MSR
	$155	$125	$100	$85	$75	$65	$55	

MONTE CARLO TRAP SINGLE BARREL – 12 ga., 32 in. full vent. rib, hammerless, underlever, recoil pad, checkered pistol grip Monte Carlo stock. Disc.

	100%	98%	95%	90%	80%	70%	60%	LAST MSR
	$225	$185	$175	$150	$135	$125	$100	

SILVER SNIPE O/U – 12 or 20 ga., 3 in. chambers, 26, 28, or 30 in. barrels, imp. cyl. and mod. or full and mod. vent. rib, checkered pistol grip stock, boxlock, extractors, single trigger. Mfg. by Angelo Zoli, disc.

	100%	98%	95%	90%	80%	70%	60%	LAST MSR
	$525	$500	$475	$400	$375	$325	$275	

GOLDEN SNIPE O/U – similar to Silver Snipe, except has auto ejectors.

	100%	98%	95%	90%	80%	70%	60%	LAST MSR
	$595	$525	$500	$475	$375	$350	$300	

SILVER HAWK SxS – 12 or 20 ga., 3 in. chambers, 26, 28, or 30 in. barrels, imp. cyl. and mod. or mod. and full, boxlock, extractors, checkered pistol grip and beavertail forearm. Mfg. by Angelo Zoli, 1968-72.

	100%	98%	95%	90%	80%	70%	60%	LAST MSR
	$450	$400	$375	$350	$300	$275	$250	

GALEF ZABALA SxS – 10, 12, 16, or 20 ga., 22, 26, 28, or 30 in. barrels, boxlock, extractors.

	100%	98%	95%	90%	80%	70%	60%	LAST MSR
10 gauge	$250	$230	$200	$175	$150	$140	$125	
Other gauges	$200	$175	$150	$130	$120	$110	$100	

GALENA INDUSTRIES INC.

Please refer to the AMT and Automag listings in the A section.

GALIL

Current trademark manufactured by Israel Weapon Industries Ltd. (IWI), formerly Israel Military Industries (IMI). No current consumer importation. Recent Galil semi-auto sporterized rifles and variations with thumbhole stocks were banned in April, 1998. Beginning late 1996, Galil rifles and pistols were available in selective fire mode only (law enforcement, military only) and are currently imported by UZI America, Inc., a subsidiary of O.F. Mossberg & Sons, Inc. Previously imported by Action Arms, Ltd.

GRADING - PPGS™	100%	98%	95%	90%	80%	70%	60%	LAST MSR

located in Philadelphia, PA until 1994. Previously imported by Springfield Armory located in Geneseo, IL and Magnum Research, Inc., located in Minneapolis, MN.

Magnum Research importation can be denoted by a serial number prefix "MR", while Action Arms imported rifles have either "AA" or "AAL" prefixes.

RIFLES: SEMI-AUTO

Models 329, 330 (Hadar II), 331, 332, 339 (sniper system with 6x40 mounted Nimrod scope), 361, 372, 386, and 392 all refer to various configurations of the Galil rifle.

MODEL AR – .223 Rem. cal. or .308 Win. cal., semi-auto paramilitary design rifle, gas operated - rotating bolt, 16.1 in. (.223 Rem. cal. only) or 19 in. (.308 Win. cal. only) barrel, parkerized, folding stock. Flip-up Tritium night sights. 8.6 lbs.

	100%	98%	95%	90%	80%	70%	60%	LAST MSR
	$3,150	**$2,650**	**$2,475**	**$2,150**	**$1,925**	**$1,750**	**$1,625**	***$950***

Add $500 for .308 Win. cal.

MODEL ARM – similar to Model AR, except includes folding bipod, vented hardwood handguard, and carrying handle.

	100%	98%	95%	90%	80%	70%	60%	LAST MSR
	$3,450	**$3,100**	**$2,850**	**$2,600**	**$2,300**	**$2,100**	**$1,900**	***$1,050***

Add $500 for .308 Win. cal.

GALIL SPORTER – similar to above, except has one-piece thumbhole stock, 4 (.308 Win.) or 5 (.223 Rem.) shot mag., choice of wood (disc.) or polymer hand guard, 8 1/2 lbs. Imported 1991-93.

	100%	98%	95%	90%	80%	70%	60%	LAST MSR
	$1,650	**$1,525**	**$1,375**	**$1,200**	**$1,100**	**$1,000**	**$950**	***$950***

Add $400 for .308 Win. cal.

HADAR II – .308 cal., gas operated, paramilitary type configuration, 1 piece walnut thumbhole stock with pistol grip and forearm, 18 1/2 in. barrel, adj. rear sight, recoil pad, 4 shot (standard) or 25 shot mag., 10.3 lbs. Imported 1989 only.

	100%	98%	95%	90%	80%	70%	60%	LAST MSR
	$1,575	**$1,375**	**$1,275**	**$1,050**	**$950**	**$825**	**$750**	***$998***

SNIPER OUTFIT – .308 Win. cal., semi-auto, limited production, sniper model built to exact I.D.F. specifications for improved accuracy, 20 in. heavy barrel, hardwood folding stock (adj. recoil pad and adj. cheekpiece) and forearm, includes Tritium night sights, bipod, detachable 6x40mm Nimrod scope, two 25 shot mags., carrying/storage case, 14.1 lbs. Imported 1989 only.

	100%	98%	95%	90%	80%	70%	60%	LAST MSR
	$6,500	**$5,750**	**$5,000**	**$4,350**	**$3,750**	**$3,250**	**$2,850**	***$3,995***

GAMBA, RENATO

RENATO GAMBA

Current trademark established in 1748, and located in Gardone V.T., Italy. Gamba firearms are currently manufactured by Bre-Mec srl beginning 2007, and are not currently being imported into the U.S. Previously imported in limited quantities circa 2005-2010 by Renato Gamba U.S.A., located in Walnut, CA. The U.S. service center is located in Bernardsville, NJ. Gamba of America, a subsidiary of Firing Line, located in Aurora, CO, was the exclusive importer and distributor for Renato Gamba long guns from 1996-2000. Pistols were previously imported and distributed (until 1990) by Armscorp of America, Inc. located in Baltimore, MD. Shotguns were previously (until 1992) imported by Heckler & Koch, Inc. located in Sterling, VA.

Filli Gamba (Gamba Brothers) was founded in 1946. G. Gamba sold his tooling to his brother, Renato, in 1967 when Renato Gamba left his brothers and S.A.B. was formed. Filli Gamba closed in 1989 and the Zanotti firm was also purchased the same year.

Renato Gamba firearms have had limited importation since 1986. In 1989, several smaller European firearms companies were purchased by R. Gamba and are now part of the Renato Gamba Group - they include Gambarmi and Stefano Zanotti. The importation of R. Gamba guns changed in 1990 to reflect their long term interest in exporting firearms to America. Earlier imported models may be rare but have not enjoyed much collectibility to date.

Due to space considerations, this section is now available through our website: www.bluebookofgunvalues.com.

GRADING - PPGS™	100%	98%	95%	90%	80%	70%	60%	LAST MSR

GARBI, ARMAS

Current manufacturer located in Eibar, Spain. Imported and distributed exclusively by William Larkin Moore & Co. located in Scottsdale, AZ.

Garbi typically manufactures approx. 60-70 shotguns and rifles annually.

RIFLES: SxS

Garbi also manufactures a deluxe SxS double rifle in 7x65R, 8x57JRS, 9.3x74R, .300 H&H, or .375 H&H cal. This model is POR. Please contact the importer or factory directly for more information (including special orders and prices) on this model.

SHOTGUNS: SxS, DISC.

Add $2,890 for Express No. 2 engraving.
Add approx. $3,850 for Purdey style, Prince Albert, or H&H Royal engraving pattern.
Add $4,950 for Prestige engraving.

MODEL 120 – 12, 16, 20, or 28 ga., Holland-pattern sidelock ejector double with chopper lump barrels of nickel-chrome steel, H&H type easy opening mechanism, game scene engraving - 3 patterns available. Well figured walnut stock. Importation disc. 1994.

	100%	98%	95%	90%	80%	70%	60%	LAST MSR
	$10,500	$9,750	$8,400	$7,300	$6,200	$5,100	$3,995	*$9,400*

SPECIAL WLM – 12, 16, 20, or 28 ga., top-of-the-line Holland-pattern sidelock ejector double with chopper lump barrels, full coverage large scroll engraving, fancy-figured walnut stock. Importation disc. 1994.

	100%	98%	95%	90%	80%	70%	60%	LAST MSR
	$10,500	$9,750	$8,400	$7,300	$6,200	$5,100	$3,995	*$9,400*

SPECIAL AG – 12, 16, 20, or 28 ga., top-of-the-line Holland-pattern sidelock ejector double with chopper lump barrels, large scroll engraving patterned after Lebeau-Courally, fancy figured walnut stock. Disc.

	100%	98%	95%	90%	80%	70%	60%	LAST MSR
	$10,500	$9,750	$8,400	$7,300	$6,200	$5,100	$3,995	*$9,200*

SHOTGUNS: SxS, RECENT MFG.

On the following models, add $455 for 28 ga., $2,885 for single trigger, $1,000-$3,000 for English or Turkish walnut wood upgrade, $960 for beavertail forearm. Subtract 20% for 12 ga. on values for used guns.

MODEL 100 – 12, 16, or 20 ga., Holland-pattern detachable sidelock ejector double, Purdey style scroll engraving, chopper lump barrels, oil finish, select walnut, articulated trigger.

	100%	98%	95%	90%	80%	70%	60%
MSR N/A	$5,500	$5,000	$4,350	$3,650	$2,950	$2,400	$1,900

This model is not currently being imported.

MODEL 101 – 12, 16, or 20 ga., round body action and smooth wood now standard, Holland-pattern sidelock ejector double with chopper lump barrels, scroll engraving, selected walnut stock.

	100%	98%	95%	90%	80%	70%	60%
MSR N/A	$6,500	$6,000	$5,500	$5,000	$4,350	$3,650	$2,950

This model is not currently being imported.

MODEL 103A – 12, 16, 20, or 28 ga., Holland-pattern sidelock ejector double with chopper lump barrels, fine scroll and rosette engraving, selected walnut stock.

	100%	98%	95%	90%	80%	70%	60%
MSR $15,450	$13,750	$12,250	$10,000	$8,500	$7,300	$6,200	$5,100

Add $3,700 for Express No. 2 engraving.
Add $5,050 for Purdey style, Prince Albert, or H&H Royal engraving pattern.
Add $5,975 for Prestige engraving.

MODEL 103B – 12, 16, 20, or 28 ga., Holland-pattern sidelock ejector double with chopper lump barrels of nickel-chrome steel, H&H type easy opening mechanism, fine scroll and rosette engraving, well figured walnut stock.

	100%	98%	95%	90%	80%	70%	60%
MSR $23,700	$21,500	$19,250	$16,500	$13,250	$8,950	$7,250	$6,300

Extra cost special order features for this model are the same as for the Model 103A.

MODEL 200 – 12, 16, 20, or 28 ga., Holland-pattern sidelock ejector double with chopper lump barrels of nickel-chrome steel, heavy-duty locks, magnum proofed, very fine

GRADING - PPGS™	100%	98%	95%	90%	80%	70%	60%	LAST MSR

Continental style floral scroll engraving, well figured walnut stock.

MSR $18,500	$17,000	$15,350	$12,750	$9,600	$7,250	$6,000	$4,750	

GARRAY RIFLES LTD.

Previous rifle manufacturer with headquarters located in Kelowna, British Columbia, Canada until 2008.

RIFLES: BOLT ACTION

GARRAY RIFLE – calibers range from .243 to .458, including all standard length cartridges, all other factory and big game calibers available, features exhibition grade walnut stock, Schnabel forend, barrel band, rounded pistol grip, and continental cheekpiece with client's initials in medallion on buttstock, various hand checkering designs available, modern Mauser 98 action, swivel (90 degree) release mounts, all rings and bases included, three position safety and Timney trigger standard.

All GarRay rifles were hand-built with an MSR of $6,995.

All rifles were supplied with a custom designed takedown case, including maker's name and customer's name embroidered on the inside.

GASTINNE RENETTE

Previous manufacturer and retailer 1812-2003, and located in Paris, France.

On Jan. 1, 2003, Gastinne Renette closed its doors at its famous location on Franklin D. Roosevelt Avenue in Paris. Gastinne Renette had limited U.S. importation and distribution, and most guns were subcontracted to other European manufacturers.

RIFLES: BOLT ACTION

Values listed are base prices for each model - since all guns were made to individual order. Wood, level of engraving, and other special features were available at an additional cost.

STANDARD MODEL MAUSER ACTION

	100%	98%	95%	90%	80%	70%	60%	LAST MSR
	$5,150	$4,450	$3,850	$3,150	$2,550	$1,900	$1,500	$6,000

DELUXE MAUSER ACTION

	100%	98%	95%	90%	80%	70%	60%	LAST MSR
	$9,950	$7,850	$6,850	$5,750	$4,750	$3,900	$2,750	$12,000

RIFLES: SxS, DOUBLE

BOXLOCK MODEL – variety of cals., features Anson & Deeley boxlock mechanism, color case hardened frame. Imported 1993-2002.

	100%	98%	95%	90%	80%	70%	60%	LAST MSR
	$8,950	$7,750	$6,950	$5,850	$4,950	$4,100	$3,200	$10,000

EUROPEAN SIDELOCK

	100%	98%	95%	90%	80%	70%	60%	LAST MSR
	$31,000	$27,000	$22,500	$18,750	$15,000	$12,500	$10,000	$36,000

AFRICAN SIDELOCK – various Mag. cals. Imported 1993-2002.

	100%	98%	95%	90%	80%	70%	60%	LAST MSR
	$33,000	$28,750	$23,500	$19,250	$15,500	$12,750	$10,000	$40,000

STANDARD TYPE G – 9.3x74Rmm, 7.65Rmm, .30-06, or .375 H&H cal., double bolt action, ejectors, reinforced stock, 23 3/4 in. barrels, bouquet style engraving with deluxe walnut stock and forearm, 7 lbs. 6 oz.

	100%	98%	95%	90%	80%	70%	60%	LAST MSR
	$2,995	$2,500	$2,150	$1,700	$1,560	$1,480	$1,340	

DELUXE TYPE R – 9.3x74Rmm, 7.65Rmm, .30-06, or .375 H&H cal., double bolt action, true sideplates, ejectors, reinforced stock, 23 3/4 in. barrels, animal engraving with deluxe walnut stock and forearm, 7 lbs. 6 oz.

	100%	98%	95%	90%	80%	70%	60%	LAST MSR
	$3,875	$3,325	$2,700	$2,175	$1,850	$1,700	$1,525	

PRESIDENT TYPE PT – 9.3x74Rmm, 7.65Rmm, .30-06, or .375 H&H cal., double bolt action, true sideplates, ejectors, reinforced stock, 23 3/4 in. barrels, light engraving with gold line inlays, best quality walnut, 7 lbs. 6 oz.

	100%	98%	95%	90%	80%	70%	60%	LAST MSR
	$4,250	$3,725	$3,200	$2,650	$2,250	$1,825	$1,600	

GRADING - PPGS™	100%	98%	95%	90%	80%	70%	60%	LAST MSR

RIFLES: SINGLE SHOT

FALLING BLOCK MODEL

	$9,750	$8,250	$6,750	$5,900	$5,000	$4,000	$3,000	$14,000

SIDELOCK MODEL – features breakdown action. Imported 1993-2002.

	$25,750	$21,250	$18,000	$14,750	$11,350	$9,250	$7,000	$34,000

SHOTGUNS: SxS

MODEL 105 – 12 or 20 ga., Anson and Deeley type triple bolt action, ejectors, double triggers, case hardened frame, 6 lbs. 8 oz.

	$2,250	$1,800	$1,400	$1,250	$1,125	$1,000	$900	

MODEL 98 – 12 and 20 ga., Purdey type triple bolt action, ejectors, double triggers, case hardened frame, 6 lbs. 8 oz.

	$2,995	$2,500	$2,000	$1,850	$1,580	$1,430	$1,260	

MODEL 202 – 12 or 20 ga., Purdey type triple bolt action, sidelocks, fine English engraving, first grade French walnut, ejectors, double triggers, coin finished frame, 6 lbs. 10 oz.

	$4,500	$3,950	$3,250	$2,500	$2,175	$1,875	$1,650	$5,250

MODEL 353 – 12 or 20 ga., Purdey type triple bolt action, hand detachable sidelocks, chopper lump barrels, fine English engraving, first grade French walnut, ejectors, double triggers, case hardened frame, best quality, 6 lbs. 10 oz.

	$17,500	$13,650	$11,000	$8,900	$6,700	$6,250	$5,750	$19,950

GATEWAY PRECISION ARMS

Previous manufacturer located in Affton, MO.

Current model information can be found under the RPM listing.

PISTOLS: SINGLE SHOT

XL HUNTER – over 40 cals., tip-up action, stainless steel frame, 5 1/16 in. under-lug, 12 or 14 in. Douglas chrome-moly (new 2004) or stainless steel barrel, ISGW rear and Patridge or hooded front sight, with (became standard 2000) or w/o external positive extractor. Mfg. 1995-2008.

	$1,375	$1,250	$995	$800	$700	$600	$500	$1,500

Add $250 for stainless steel barrel.
Add $250 for integral muzzle brake.
Add $50 for left-hand action.
Add approx. $400-$550 per extra barrel, depending on length.

GATLING GUNS

Gatling Gun refers to a rifle configuration utilizing multiple barrels and box magazine, which is operated by a rotating hand crank. Original full size Gatling guns were manufactured by Colt and some British manufacturers.

Full size Gatling reproductions are currently manufactured by Battery Gun Company.

Model Gatling guns include various models and scales of original Gatlings made from 1874 to 1893. Model cannons include the British Naval Cannon and the James Six Pounder. Prices vary according to the complexity of each model and are available by contacting Battery Gun Company.

For space considerations, no individual manufacturer/model listings or values are listed, but please check the internet and the Trademark Index for more information on currently produced full size and scale replica reproductions.

GAUCHER

Current manufacturer established in 1834, and located in St. Etienne, France. No current U.S. importation. Previously imported and distributed by Mandall Shooting Supplies located in Scottsdale, AZ. Gaucher merged with Bretton in 2000, and the new company name is Bretton-Gaucher (see Trademark Index).

GRADING - PPGS™	100%	98%	95%	90%	80%	70%	60%	LAST MSR

During 1997, Gaucher released four shooting rifles with unique sound suppression (approx. 71 dB) in 9mm Para., 12mm cal., or .410 bore. Additionally, Gaucher manufactures rifles (O/U and SxS double, bolt action rimfire, and semi-auto rimfire), shotguns (SxS, single shot), and 22 LR cal. target pistols. To date, there has been little importation of Gaucher firearms. Please contact the Bretton-Gaucher factory directly (see Trademark Index) for more information and up-to-date pricing regarding their current lineup of firearms.

PISTOLS: SINGLE SHOT, TARGET

MODEL GN1 – .22 LR cal., single shot silhouette pistol featuring 10 in. barrel, adj. sights, anatomically shaped grips, monobloc lever cocking, 2.42 lbs. Limited importation.

	100%	98%	95%	90%	80%	70%	60%	LAST MSR
	$360	$325	$290	$260	$230	$200	$185	*$380*

MODEL GP – similar to Model GN1, except has forearm integrated into grip. Limited importation.

	100%	98%	95%	90%	80%	70%	60%	LAST MSR
	$300	$275	$250	$225	$200	$185	$160	*$323*

GAZELLE ARMS

Previous trademark circa 1970-2008, and manufactured by Hisar Avcilik & Doga Sporlasi San Ve Tic. Ltd. Sti., located in Konak-Izmir, Turkey. Previously imported by EMA Distributors, LLC, located in Pineville, NC.

Gazelle Arms manufactured a line of good quality, inexpensive shotguns, including semi-autos, SxSs, single shots, and O/Us. Last MSRs on the semi-auto shotguns ranged from $345-$390, while the O/U was priced at $500.

GAVAGE

Previous manufacturer located in Liege, Belgium circa 1936-1943.

PISTOLS: SEMI-AUTO

GAVAGE PISTOL – .32 ACP/7.65mm cal., patterned after the Clement, fixed barrel, limited mfg.

	100%	98%	95%	90%	80%	70%	60%	LAST MSR
	$650	$550	$450	$400	$350	$300	$250	
Waffenamt proofmarks	$1,750	$1,350	$1,100	$800	$700	$600	$500	

This pistol is very rare with Waffenamt proofmarks.

GENTRY CUSTOM LLC

Current custom rifle maker located in Belgrade, MT. Previous company name was David Gentry - Custom Gunmaker.

David Gentry was a current custom rifle builder who usually fabricated rifles to individual custom order requests. His son Dennis took over the business after David's death in 2007. The company continues to build custom rifles as well as three position safeties for the Mauser 98 in right or left hand, as well as a variety of rifle accessories. Mr. Gentry should be contacted directly (see Trademark Index) for more information on options/prices.

GERMAN P.38 MILITARY & COMMERCIAL PISTOLS

Please refer to the P.38 entries in the P section.

GERMAN SPORT GUNS GmbH

Current firearms and air soft manufacturer and distributor located in Ense-Höingen, Germany. Currently imported by American Tactical Imports, located in Rochester, NY.

CARBINES: SEMI-AUTO

GSG-522 – .22 LR cal., semi-auto design patterned after the H&K MP-5 with forward bolt assist, 16.3 in. barrel with choice of flash hider or faux elongated suppressor, open sights, 10 or 22 shot detachable mag., rail system, black, camo, or nickel finish, synthetic, lightweight synthetic, or wood fixed stock with pistol grip, optional textured pistol grip, Weaver rail, and gold accents, 6.2-6.6 lbs. New 2002, importation began 2008.

	100%	98%	95%	90%	80%	70%	60%	LAST MSR
MSR $435	$375	$330	$295	$275	$250	$225	$200	

GRADING - PPGS™	100%	98%	95%	90%	80%	70%	60%	LAST MSR

Add $28 for nickel or $51 for camo finish (special order only, disc. 2011).
Add $47 for wood (disc. 2011).
Add $115 for gold accents.
Subtract $85 for lightweight synthetic stock.

GSG-522 SD – similar to GSG-522, except has textured pistol grip and integrated Weaver rail as standard, ribbed hand guard and barrel shroud, black finish only.

MSR $455	$415	$365	$310	$275	$250	$225	$200

Subtract $95 for lightweight stock.

KALASHNIKOV – .22 LR cal., patterned after the AK-47 design action, recoil operated, 10, 15 (disc.), 22 (disc.), or 24 (new 2011) shot mag., 16 1/2 in. barrel with protected front sight, available with black synthetic or hardwood pistol grip stock. New 2009.

MSR $385	$350	$315	$275	$250	$225	$200	$185

Add $174 for hardwood stock and gold receiver (new 2012).

GSG STG-44 – .22 LR cal., 17.2 in. barrel, 10 or 25 shot detachable mag., patterned after the Nazi Sturmgewehr 44, wood furniture, blue finish, includes WWII period style box. New 2012.

MSR $600	$550	$475	$425	$350	$325	$295	$275

PISTOLS: SEMI-AUTO

GSG-522 P – .22 LR cal., 10 or 22 shot mag., 9 in. barrel with flash suppressor, black finish, patterned after the MP-5 pistol, adj. diopter rear sight with optional Picatinny rail, top lever charging, integrated Weaver rail (new 2011), textured pistol grip, integrated sling bracket, 5.89 lbs. New 2009.

MSR $440	$385	$350	$315	$285	$265	$245	$225

GSG-522 PK – .22 LR cal., 10 or 22 shot mag., 4 5/8 in. barrel flush with top of frame, forward mounted charging lever, operating mechanism similar to GSG-522 P, integrated Weaver rail and textured pistol grip (new 2011), 5.2 lbs. New 2009.

MSR $435	$385	$350	$315	$285	$265	$245	$225

GSG-922 – .22 LR cal., 3.2 in. threaded barrel, with or w/o faux suppressor, beavertail and grip safety, black finish, Picatinny rail, checkered black plastic grips, compatible with 1911 parts. New mid-2012.

MSR $360	$325	$295	$275	$250	$225	$200	$185

Add $20 for faux suppressor.

GSG 1911 SERIES – .22 LR cal., patterned after the M1911, 5 in. barrel, front and rear slide serrations, checkered diamond walnut (GSG 1911) or black plastic (GSG Black) grips, skeletonized trigger and hammer, beavertail grip safety, 10 shot mag., available with Picatinny rail and false supressor (GSG Ad Ops). New 2009.

MSR $360	$325	$295	$275	$250	$225	$200	$185

Add $40 for Ad Ops Model.
Subtract $10 for GSB Black Model.

GEVARM

Previous manufacturer located in Saint Etienne, France.

RIFLES: SEMI-AUTO

E-1 AUTOLOADING RIFLE – .22 LR cal., 19 in. barrel, open sights, walnut pistol grip stock.

	$300	$250	$225	$195	$180	$165	$150

GIANI, VITTORIO

Please refer to MAG Rifles listing in the M section.

GIB

Previous trademark manufactured in Spain.

GRADING - PPGS™	100%	98%	95%	90%	80%	70%	60%	LAST MSR

SHOTGUNS: SxS

10 GAUGE MAGNUM – 10 ga., 3 1/2 in. chambers, 32 in. full choke barrel, case hardened frame, matted rib, rubber pad, checkered pistol grip walnut stock. Disc.

	100%	98%	95%	90%	80%	70%	60%	LAST MSR
	$275	$250	$235	$220	$200	$175	$150	

GIBBS, GEORGE

Current trademark established 2007, and located in Wiltshire, U.K. Previous gunmaker circa 1830-1929, located in Bristol, U.K.

George Gibbs began manufacturing guns in Bristol circa 1830. He built a new factory in 1873, and became famous for big game rifles popular during the Victorian and Edwardian eras. The .505 Gibbs cartridge became widely known. In 1874, the maker patented the Gibbs & Pitt gun - sometimes dubbed the first commercially successful hammerless shotgun - a triggerplate design that cocked via its underlever (later a toplever-cocking variant was also produced). In 1906, Gibbs moved to 35 Savile Row. The firm's founder, George C. Gibbs, died in 1918, and company ownership passed out of family hands and into a partnership. By 1929, the firm went bankrupt, but survived for a time in smaller quarters off Baldwin Street in Bristol. During 1964, Gibbs was purchased by Bath gunmaker I.M. Crudgington and Norman Harper. In 2007, Crudgington's son, stockmaker Mark Crudgington, purchased the name and continues to make guns under the Gibbs name.

Information courtesy of David Grant and Vic Venters.

GIBBS GUNS, INC.

Previously manufactured by Volunteer Enterprises in Knoxville, TN and previously distributed by Gibbs Guns, Inc. located in Greenback,TN.

CARBINES

MARK 45 CARBINE – .45 ACP cal. only, based on M6 Thompson machine gun, 16 1/2 in. barrel, 5, 15, 30, or 90 shot mag. U.S. mfg. Disc. 1988.

	100%	98%	95%	90%	80%	70%	60%	LAST MSR
	$750	$625	$525	$450	$375	$330	$300	*$279*

Add $200 for 90 shot mag.
Add 10% for nickel plating.

GIBBS RIFLE COMPANY, INC.

Current manufacturer, importer, and distributor located in Martinsburg, WV. Gibbs manufactured rifles with the Gibbs trademark in Martinsburg, WV 1991-1994, in addition to importing Mauser-Werke firearms until 1995. Dealer and distributor sales.

In the past, Gibbs Rifle Company, Inc. imported a variety of older firearms, including British military rifles and handguns (both original and refurbished condition), a good selection of used military contract pistols and rifles, in addition to other shooting products and accessories, including a bipod patterned after the Parker-Hale M-85.

Gibbs Rifle Company, Inc. imported and manufactured military collectibles, historical remakes, and special sporting rifles. All rifles were carefully inspected, commercially cleaned and boxed to ensure their quality, and all had a limited lifetime warranty. Gibbs Rifle Company, Inc. also offered membership in the Gibbs Military Collectors Club, an organization dedicated to military firearms collectors.

RIFLES: BOLT ACTION

M-71/84 MAUSER – 11mm Mauser cal., 31 1/2 in. barrel, available in good original or refurbished condition, 10 lbs. Imported 1999-2004.

	100%	98%	95%	90%	80%	70%	60%	LAST MSR
	$165	$135	$120	$110	$100	$90	$85	*$190*

Add $110 for refurbished condition (all parts are historically correct and have been cleaned and hand inspected).

This rifle cannot be safely shot with modern ammunition.

GRADING - PPGS™	100%	98%	95%	90%	80%	70%	60%	LAST MSR

M1871/84 "SAMURAI" MAUSER – built on original Mauser action, replica wood stock, gold trigger guard, designed by Robert "Rock" Galotti for the movie *"The Last Samurai"*. New 2010.

MSR $550	$495	$450	$400	$365	$335	$295	$275	

M-1888 MAUSER – 8mm Mauser (7.92x57mm) cal., good original condition, 30 in. barrel, 10 lbs. Imported 1999-2004.

	$85	$75	$65	$55	$45	$40	$35	*$100*

This rifle cannot be safely shot with modern ammunition.

M-98K ISRAELI MAUSER – .308 Win. cal., rebarreled by the Israeli Arsenal Ha'as, various makers, 23.6 in. barrel, original condition (offered in 3 grades), 9 lbs. Imported 1999-2003.

	$275	$225	$175	$150	$125	$115	$105	*$170*

Add 10% for Grade 2, or 20% for Grade 1.

M-98 MAUSER SPORTER – .270 Win. or .30-06 cal., Mauser M-98 type action, blue finish, sporterized checkered hardwood stock and forend, 24 in. Wilson barrel. Mfg. in Martinsburg, WV 1998-99.

	$350	$295	$265	$245	$225	$210	$195	*$330*

2A HUNTER RIFLE/CARBINE – .308 Win. cal., sporterized action features black enamel refinish, synthetic stock, 12 shot mag, and choice of 18 (carbine) or 22 1/2 (rifle) in. barrel with Parker-Hale muzzle brake, approx. 10 lbs. Mfg. 1999 only.

	$325	$285	$260	$23.	$195	$175	$150	*$275*

ENFIELD NO. 5 JUNGLE CARBINE – .303 British cal., older No. 4 Enfield barreled action with newly manufactured stock, bayonet lug and flash hider have been added, 20 in. barrel, 7 3/4 lbs. Imported 1999-2004, reintroduced 2010 with camo synthetic stock.

	$700	$650	$575	$525	$450	$375	$295	

A bayonet and scabbard were also available for this model.

ENFIELD NO. 7 JUNGLE CARBINE – .308 Win. cal., older 2A action with reconfigured original wood, flash hider and bayonet lug have been added, 20 in. barrel, 8 lbs. Imported 1999-2004.

	$275	$225	$175	$155	$125	$115	$105	*$200*

QUEST EXTREME CARBINE – .303 British cal., updated No. 5 Enfield action with 20 in. barrel with compensator and flash hider, electroless nickel metal finish, new buttstock with survival kit packaged in butt trap, 7 3/4 lbs. Imported 2000-2004.

	$295	$265	$225	$185	$170	$160	$150	*$250*

QUEST II – .308 Win. cal., modern 2A Enfield barreled action, mfg. from chrome vanadium steel, 20 in. barrel with compensator/flash-hider and adj. rear sight, front sight protector, pre-fitted see-through scope mount accepts all Weaver based optics and accessories, electroless nickel finish, hardwood stock with survial kit included, 12 shot mag., 8 lbs. Imported 2001-2004.

	$375	$325	$265	$235	$200	$185	$170	*$280*

QUEST III – .308 Win. cal., similar to Quest II, except has black synthetic stock, w/o survival kit. Imported 2002-2004.

	$395	$345	$280	$240	$200	$185	$170	*$300*

SUMMIT FRONTIER .45-70 CARBINE – .45-70 Govt. cal., remanufactured No. 4 Enfield action, new 21 in. button rifled barrel with front sight, blue action and barrel, checkered hardwood sporting stock, 3 shot mag., 8 1/2 lbs. Imported 2000-2005.

	$450	$375	$325	$275	$255	$230	$210	*$385*

GIBBS ECONOMY SPORTER – 8mm Mauser cal., sporterized military action with good barrel and sporting sights, walnut finished checkered hardwood stock. Mfg. 1993-94.

	$275	$225	$185	$150	$135	$120	$100	*$205*

GIBBS MAUSER SPORTER – .243 Win., .270 Win., .30-06, or .308 Win. cal., features M-98 action, walnut finished checkered hardwood stock, action is drilled and tapped, flip-up rear sight and ramp front. Mfg. 1993-94.

	$375	$325	$275	$225	$195	$175	$150	*$295*

GRADING - PPGS™	100%	98%	95%	90%	80%	70%	60%	LAST MSR

MODEL 81 CLASSIC – available in 11 cals. between .22-250 Rem. and 7mm Rem. Mag., 24 in. barrel, open sights, 4 shot mag., select checkered walnut with sling swivels, 7 3/4 lbs.

	$795	$595	$475	$395	$340	$300	$280	*$900*

* ***Model 81 Classic African*** – .375 H&H or 9.3x62mm cal., similar specifications as Model 81 Classic with quarter rib and express sights, engraved action, Pachmayr recoil pad, 9 lbs.

	$925	$725	$600	$500	$425	$360	$330	*$1,050*

MODEL 85 SNIPER RIFLE – .308 Win. cal., bolt action, 24 in. heavy barrel, 10 shot mag., camo green synthetic McMillan stock with stippling, built in adj. bipod and recoil pad, enlarged contoured bolt, adj. sights, 12 lbs. 6 oz.

	$1,825	$1,450	$1,275	$1,050	$875	$750	$625	*$2,050*

MODEL 87 TARGET – .243 Win., 6.5x55mm, .308 Win., .30-06, or .300 Win. Mag. cal., target stock, aperture sights. Mfg. disc. 1992.

	$1,375	$1,100	$900	$775	$650	$550	$495	*$1,500*

MODEL 1000 STANDARD – .22-250 Rem., .243 Win., 6mm Rem., 6.5x55mm, 7x57mm, 7x64mm, .270 Win., .30-06, or .308 Win. cal., 22 in. barrel, 4 shot built in mag., checkered walnut stock with cheekpiece, open sights, 7 1/4 lbs.

	$425	$375	$325	$290	$260	$240	$220	*$495*

* ***Model 1000 Standard Clip*** – similar to Model 1000 Standard, except has detachable 4 shot mag.

	$460	$395	$350	$300	$270	$240	$220	*$535*

MODEL 1100 LIGHTWEIGHT – available in 9 cals. between .22-250 Rem. and .308 Win., 22 in. barrel, open sights, 4 shot mag., 6 1/2 lbs.

	$435	$380	$325	$290	$260	$240	$220	*$510*

* ***Model 1100M Lightweight African*** – .375 H&H, or .458 Win. Mag. cal., 24 in. barrel, 4 shot mag., 9 1/2 lbs.

	$825	$650	$575	$500	$450	$425	$400	*$930*

MODEL 1200 SUPER – .22-250 Rem., .243 Win., 6mm, 6.5x55mm, 7x64mm, .270 Win., .30-06, or .308 Win. cal., bolt action, Mauser type action, 24 in. barrel, folding sight, skip checkered walnut stock, pad swivels, rosewood pistol grip cap and forend tip.

	$495	$400	$350	$325	$285	$270	$255	*$595*

* ***Model 1200 Super Clip*** – similar to Model 1200 Super, except has detachable 4 shot box mag.

	$525	$425	$375	$350	$300	$280	$265	*$640*

MODEL 1300S SCOUT – .243 Win. or .308 Win. cal., 20 in. barrel with muzzle brake, internal 5 shot or detachable 5/10 shot mag., laminated checkered birchwood stock, sling swivels, 8 1/2 lbs.

	$425	$375	$325	$290	$260	$240	$220	*$495*

Add $30 for detachable mag. (Model 1300C).

MODEL 1500S SURVIVOR – .308 Win. cal., bolt action, matte stainless construction, black composite (Kevlar/fiberglass) stock, 22 in. barrel, 4 shot mag., 7 lbs. Mfg. began 1993. Disc.

	$395	$350	$300	$270	$240	$210	$185	*$450*

Add $30 for detachable mag. (Model 1500C).

This model was made for the Gibbs Rifle Co. by Bell & Carlson, Inc.

M1903-A4 SPRINGFIELD SNIPER MODEL – .30-06 cal., replica of original M1903-A3 Springfield, drilled and tapped, Redfield replica rings and mounts, new C stock, barrel marked with modern dates of mfg., includes U.S. issue leather sling and OD Green canvas carrying case. M73G2 scope became standard during 2012. New 2009.

MSR $1,099	$975	$875	$775	$675	$575	$475	$375	

GRADING - PPGS™	100%	98%	95%	90%	80%	70%	60%	LAST MSR

M1903-A4-82 SPRINGFIELD SNIPER MODEL – .30-06 cal., similar to M1903, except has improved M82 rifle scope and 7/8 in. rings. New 2010.

MSR $1,200	$1,075	$950	$825	$700	$600	$500	$400	

M1903-A4-84 SPRINGFIELD SNIPER MODEL – .30-06 cal., similar to M1903A4-82, except has improved M84 rifle scope and 7/8 in. rings. New 2010.

MSR $1,250	$1,100	$950	$825	$700	$600	$500	$400	

RIFLES: BOLT ACTION, MIDLAND SERIES

MODEL 2100 MIDLAND DELUXE – similar to Model 2600 Midland, except has checkered walnut stock and pistol grip cap.

	$375	$325	$275	$235	$210	$190	$180	*$390*

MODEL 2600 MIDLAND – .22-250 Rem., .243 Win., 6mm Rem. (disc. 1994), 6.5x55mm (disc. 1994), 7x57mm (disc. 1994), 7x64mm (disc. 1994), .270 Win., .30-06, or .308 Win. cal., 22 in. barrel, 4 shot mag., checkered hardwood stock with Monte Carlo cheekpiece, open sights, drilled and tapped action, 7 lbs. Disc. 1997.

	$400	$360	$310	$260	$220	$185	$165	*$400*

This model was re-introduced during late 1996, utilizing a 1903 Springfield action with choice of 5 shot fixed mag. with hinged floorplate or 3 shot detachable mag.

MIDLAND 2700 LIGHTWEIGHT – lightweight variation of the Model 2100 Midland Deluxe featuring tapered barrel, anodized aluminum trigger housing and lightened stock with full pistol grip and recoil pad, Schnabel forend, 6 1/2 lbs.

	$400	$360	$310	$260	$220	$185	$165	*$415*

MIDLAND 2800 – similar to Model 2600 Midland, except has laminated birchwood stock, re-introduced during late 1996, utilizing a 1903 Springfield action, 7 lbs. Disc. 1997.

	$385	$325	$265	$215	$195	$185	$175	*$430*

SHOTGUNS: SINGLE SHOT

MIDLAND STALKER – 12 ga., trigger bar safety, unique squeeze break open action and cocking system, 28 1/2 in. barrel bored F, hardwood stock and forearm, 6 lbs.

	$90	$65	$55	$45	$35	$30	$25	*$110*

GIL, ANTONIO & CO.

Current manufacturer located in Eibar, Spain. Limited U.S. importation. Previously imported and distributed exclusively late 2000-2004 by New England Arms Corp., located in Kittery Point, ME.

All Antonio Gil shotguns are handmade, and can be built to each customer's exact measurements at no extra cost. All models are equipped with chopper lump barrels as a standard feature. Please contact the company directly for more information, including current U.S. pricing and availability (see Trademark Index).

SHOTGUNS: SxS

All models are sidelock only.
Add 10% for 20, 28 ga. or .410 bore.
Add $500-$1,500 for wood upgrade.
Add $1,000-$1,250 per extra set of barrels.
Add $500 for non-selective trigger.

LAGA – 12, 16, 20, 28 ga., or .410 bore, sidelock action with color case hardened receiver and scroll engraving, demi-bloc barrels, DT, deluxe checkered walnut stock and forearm. Importation began 2001.

MSR N/A	$2,250	$1,750	$1,500	$1,350	$1,200	$1,100	$995	

OLIMPIA – 12, 16, 20, 28 ga., or .410 bore, sidelock action, features traditional rose and scroll engraving on coin finished receiver. Importation began 2001.

MSR N/A	$2,575	$2,250	$1,750	$1,500	$1,350	$1,200	$1,050	

GRADING - PPGS™	100%	98%	95%	90%	80%	70%	60%	LAST MSR

ALHAMBRA – 12, 16, 20, 28 ga., or .410 bore, sidelock action, features elaborate full coverage floral scroll engraving on coin finished receiver and wood upgrade. Importation began 2001.

MSR N/A	$3,625	$3,150	$2,575	$2,250	$1,750	$1,500	$1,350	

DIAMOND – 12, 16, 20, 28 ga., or .410 bore, sidelock action, top-of-the-line model with best engraving and best quality wood. Importation began 2001.

MSR N/A	$5,475	$4,650	$4,125	$3,625	$3,050	$2,500	$2,000	

GILA RIVER GUN WORKS

Current custom rifle manufacturer located in Pocatello, ID, and previously located in Yuma, AZ.

RIFLES: CUSTOM

Michael Scherz specializes in high-quality, bolt action rifles in .550 Magnum caliber. During late 2011 Gila River Tactical was formed and is a division of Gila River Gunworks. This tactical division offers a wide variety of long range precision tactical rifles. Please contact the company directly for more information, including pricing and availability (see Trademark Index).

GIRSAN MACHINE & LIGHT WEAPON INDUSTRY COMPANY

Current handgun and shotgun manufacturer established in 1994, and located in Giresun, Turkey. No current U.S. importation.

Girsan manufactures a complete line of good quality semi-auto pistols under the trademark Yavuz 16 in a variety of configurations, calibers, frame sizes, and finishes. Many options are available. During 2012, the company also expanded its line into the 312 series of semi-auto hunting shotguns. Please contact the company directly for more information, including U.S. availability and pricing (see Trademark Index).

GLANZIG PRÄZISIONS-UND SPORTWAFFEN JAGDZUBEHÖR

Current custom long gun manufacturer located in Ferlach, Austria.

Glanzig manufactures custom long guns, built per individual customer specifications. Please contact the company directly for a price quotation, available options, and delivery time (see Trademark Index).

GLENFIELD

Previous trademark of promotional rifles sold by the Marlin Firearms Company circa 1960-1966.

Please refer to the Marlin Firearms Company listing in the M section.

GLISENTI

Please refer to the Italian Military Arms listing in the I section.

GLOCK

Currently manufactured by Glock GmbH in Austria beginning 1983. Sales in the U.S. began in 1986. Glock also opened a production facility for manufacturing its polymer frames and assembling complete pistols in Smyrna, GA during late 2005. Exclusively imported and distributed by Glock, Inc. USA, located in Smyrna, GA. Distributor and dealer sales.

All Glock pistols have a "safe action" constant operating system (double action mode) which includes trigger safety, firing pin safety, and drop safety. Glock pistols have only 35 parts for reliability and simplicity of operation. With approximately 170 or more variations, over 8 million Glock semi-auto pistols had been manufactured since 1983.

In 1995 the Glock Collector's Association was formed. To date Glock has manufactured commemoratives (see Pistols: Semi-Auto, Commemoratives in this section), specially marked, and engraved models, plus the agency and police marked variations. By joining the Glock Collector's Association, members can find out the history of the most desirable G17-G39 civilian models. Please refer to Firearms/Shooting Organizations for more information on the Glock Collector's Association, including how to join.

GRADING - PPGS™	100%	98%	95%	90%	80%	70%	60%	LAST MSR

PISTOLS: SEMI-AUTO

To date, there have been four generations of Glock pistols. Generation 1, circa 1986-1988 features a pebbled finish frame without horizontal grooves on the front or back strap. Generation 2, circa 1988-1997 can be identified by a checkered grenade finish with horizontal grooves on both the front and rear grip straps. Generation 3, circa 1995-2013 started out with transition finger grooves and no front rail with thumbrests, then transitioned into finger grooves and a rail with thumb rests, checkered finished frame. This was followed by Variant 2 which is identified by an (extreme polymid traction) Rough Texture Frame (RTF-2), finger grooves, rail, with recessed thumb rests. During 2010, Glock introduced Generation 4 (RTF-4) Rough Textured Frame, this enables standard frame Glock pistols to adopt the new short frame technology, which can be almost instantly fitted to any hand size, and features the (less polymid traction) Rough Textured Frame with recessed thumb rests, finger grooves, rail, and interchangeable frame back straps. It also includes a reversible enlarged magazine catch, dual recoil spring assembly, and a new trigger system. Glock has been transitioning all its pistols to Gen.4 since 2010.

Add $18 for adj. rear sight, $22 for Glock steel sights (new 2004), or $47 for Glock night sights (new 2004).

Add $80 for fixed Meprolight sight or $105 for fixed Trijicon sight (disc. 2003-2004, depending on model.)

Add $25 for internal locking system (ILS) on most currently manufactured models listed below (new 2004).

Add $95 for tactical light or $284 for tactical light with laser for most currently manufactured pistols listed below.

MODEL 17/17C SPORT/SERVICE (GEN1-3) – 9mm Para. cal., striker fired constant double action mode, polymer frame, mag., trigger and other pistol parts, 4.48 in. hexagonal rifled barrel, Gen1 (new 1986), Gen2 (new 1989), Gen3 (new 1998) or Gen4 (new 2010), with (Model 17C, new 1997) or w/o ports, steel slide and springs, 5 1/2 lb. trigger pull, 10 (C/B 1994), 17* (reintroduced late 2004), or 19* (reintroduced late 2004) shot mag., adj. (Sport Model) or fixed (Service Model) rear sight, includes a lockable pistol box, cable lock, cleaning rod, and other accessories, extra mag. and a spare rear sight, 24 3/4 oz. Importation began late 1985.

MSR $599	$475	$425	$395	$365	$335	$295	$250

Add $22 for Model 17C with fixed rear sight (new 1997).

Add $119 for competition model w/adj. sights (Model 17CC, mfg. 2000-2003).

This model is still available with the RTF-2 finish (Model 17 RFT-2 mfg. 2009).

During 2011 Glock released its 25th Silver Anniversary Limited Edition of the Model 17 Gen4. It featured a 25 year marking on the top of the slide in addition to special 25th year silver medallion inletted in polymer frame - only 2,500 were produced.

All Gen3-4 models have recessed thumb rests and finger grooved mounting accessories rail, except Gen3 Trasistion models (mfg. 1995-1998) have finger grooves, but no mounting accessories rail.

* ***Model 17 Gen4*** – 9mm Para. cal., similar to Model 17, except features (less polymid traction) Rough Textured Frame (RTF-4) with recessed thumb rests, finger grooves rail, and interchangeable frame back straps, includes a reversible enlarged magazine catch, dual recoil spring assembly, and a new trigger system, fixed rear, adj. rear Glock steel, or Glock night sights. All Gen4 models shipped with 3 magazines. New 2010.

MSR $649	$500	$440	$400	$375	$335	$295	$250

* ***Model 17 Gen4 25th Silver Anniversary Limited Edition*** – 9mm Para. cal., Glock steel sights only, features 25th year silver medallion inletted in polymer frame and special inscription in back of slide on top, includes silver case. 2,500 to be mfg. during 2011.

MSR $850	$700	$600	$500	$450	$375	$350	$295

* ***Model 17L Sport/Service Competition Model*** – 9mm Para. cal., 6.02 in. barrel, slotted relieved slide, recalibrated trigger pull (4 1/2 lb. pull), adj. rear sight, 26.3 oz. mfg. Gen1 pebbled grip (new 1988), Gen2 checkered grip, has no mounting accessories rail (new

GRADING - PPGS™	100%	98%	95%	90%	80%	70%	60%	LAST MSR

1990), Gen3 has thumb rests, finger grooves, mounting accessories rail (new 1998).

MSR $750	$625	$550	$475	$425	$350	$325	$275	

Add $28 for adj. sight.

Early Gen1 production with barrel ports, will command a high premium (new 1988).

This model is a long barreled competition version of the Model 17 "pebbled frame". Gen1 production non ported model (new 1988).

MODEL 19/19C COMPACT SPORT/SERVICE – 9mm Para. cal., 4.01 in. barrel with hexagonal rifling ported (Model 19C, new 1997), or unported barrel and checkered grip Gen2 has no accessories rail, (new 1988). 10 (C/B 1994), 15* (reintroduced late 2004), or 17* (reintroduced late 2004) shot mag., fixed (Service Model) or adj. (Sport Model) rear sight, 23 1/2 oz., Gen1 pebbled grip, has no mounting accessories rail. Gen3 early transition model has finger grooves, thumb rests, no mounting accessories rail, (new 1997). Later Gen3 models ported/non-ported barrel have thumb rests, finger grooves, mounting accessories rail, (new 1997-1998). New 1988.

MSR $599	$475	$425	$395	$365	$335	$295	$250	

Add $22 for Model 19C with fixed sight (new 1997).

Add $119 for competition model w/adj. sights (Model 19CC, mfg. 2000-2003).

This model is still available with RTF-2 finish (extreme polymid traction, Rough Textured Frame, Model 19 RTF-2, mfg. 2009).

This model is similar to Model 17, except has scaled down dimensions.

During 1996, AcuSport Corp. commissioned Glock to make a special production run of matching 9mm Para. cal. sets. Each set consists of a Model 19 and 26 with serialization as follows: Model 19 (ser. range AAA0000-AAA0499) and Model 26 (ser. range AAB0000-AAB0499).

* ***Model 19 Gen4*** – 9mm Para. cal., similar to Model 19, except features (less polymid traction) Rough Textured Frame (RTF-4) with recessed thumb rests, finger grooves, rail, and interchangeable frame back straps, includes a reversible enlarged magazine catch, dual recoil spring assembly, and a new trigger system, fixed rear, adj. rear Glock steel, or Glock night sights. New 2010.

MSR $649	$500	$440	$400	$375	$335	$295	$250	

MODEL 20/20C SPORT/SERVICE – 10mm Norma cal., similar to Model 17 features except has 4.61 in. barrel ported Model 20C, Gen3 with hexagonal rifling, early transition model has recessed thumb rests, finger grooves, no mounting accessories rail (new 1997), 10 (C/B 1994) or 15* (reintroduced late 2004) shot mag., larger slide and receiver, fixed (Service Model) or adj. (Sport Model) rear sight, 30 oz. Gen2 non-ported barrel, checkered grip, has no mounting accessories rail, Gen3 ported/non-ported barrel have recessed thumb rests, finger grooves, mounting accessories rail, (new 1997-1998). New 1990.

MSR $637	$500	$440	$410	$375	$350	$325	$295	

Add $39 for compensated barrel (Model 20C, fixed sight only, new 1997).

Add $145 for competition model w/adj. sights (Model 20CC, mfg. 2000-2003).

* ***Model 20SF*** – 10mm Norma cal., similar to Model 20, except has Gen3 (short frame), have recessed thumb rests, finger grooves, mounting accessories rail, 4.61 in. barrel with hexagonal rifling, 15 shot mag., all Glock sight options available, new trigger position, 30.7 oz. New 2009.

MSR $637	$500	$440	$410	$375	$350	$325	$295	

* ***Model 20 Gen4*** – 10mm Norma cal. similar to Model 20 except features (less polymid traction) Rough Textured Frame (RTF-4) with recessed thumb rests, finger grooves, rail and interchangeable frame back straps, includes a reversible enlarged magazine catch, dual recoil assembly and new trigger system, fixed rear, adj. rear Glock steel or Glock night sights. New 2012.

MSR $687	$535	$460	$385	$330	$300	$265	$230	

MODEL 21/21C SPORT/SERVICE – .45 ACP cal., similar to Model 17, features except has 4.61 in. barrel with octagonal rifling ported Model 21C, Gen3 early transition model has recessed thumb rests, finger grooves, no mounting accessories rail (new 1997), 10 (C/B 1994) or

GRADING - PPGS™	100%	98%	95%	90%	80%	70%	60%	LAST MSR

13* (reintroduced late 2004) shot mag., 29 oz. Gen2 non-ported barrel, checkered grip, has no mounting accessories rail, Gen3 ported/non-ported barrel, have recessed thumb rests, finger grooves, mounting accessories rail (new 1997-1998). New 1990.

MSR $637	$500	$440	$410	$375	$350	$325	$295

Add $39 for compensated barrel (Model 21C, fixed rear sight only, new 1997).

Add $145 for competition model w/adj. sights (Model 21CC, mfg. 2000-2003).

* ***Model 21 Gen4*** – .45 ACP cal., similar to Model 21, except features (less polymid traction) Rough Textured Frame (RTF-4) with recessed thumb rests, finger grooves rail and interchangeable frame back straps, includes a reversible enlarged magazine catch, dual recoil spring assembly, and a new trigger system, fixed rear, adj. rear Glock steel, or Glock night sights. New 2011.

MSR $687	$535	$460	$385	$330	$300	$265	$230

* ***Model 21SF/21SF (RTF-2)*** – .45 ACP cal., similar to Model 21, except has Gen3 (short frame), recessed thumb rests, finger grooves, mounting accessories rail, 4.61 in. barrel with octagonal rifling, 13 shot mag., 29 oz. (new 2007). Gen3 RTF-2 (extreme polymid traction) Rough Textured Frame (new 2009).

MSR $637	$500	$440	$410	$375	$350	$325	$295

MODEL 22/22C SPORT/SERVICE – .40 S&W cal., similar to Model 17, except has 4.48 in. barrel with hexagonal barrel ported Model 22C, 10 (C/B 1994), 15* (reintroduced late 2004), or 17 shot mag., all Glock sight variations available, 25.5 oz., Gen2 has non-ported barrel, checkered grip has no mounting accessories rail, Gen3 has ported/non-ported barrel, have recessed thumb rests, finger grooves mounting accessories rail (new 1997-1998). New 1990.

MSR $599	$475	$425	$395	$365	$335	$295	$250

Add $22 for Model 22C with compensated barrel (fixed rear sight only, new 1997).

Add $119 for competition model with adj. sights (Model 22CC, mfg. 2000-2004).

This model is still available with RTF-2 finish (less polymid traction, Rough Textured Frame, Model 22 RTF-2, mfg. 2009).

200 Model 22s were originally shipped with serial numbers beginning with "NY-1." Somehow, they probably were erroneously numbered at the factory (probably thinking that they somehow were part of the New York State Troopers shipment of Model 17s) during 1990. Premiums will occur on this variation.

* ***Model 22 Gen4*** – .40 S&W cal., similar to Model 22, except features (less polymid traction) Rough Textured Frame (RTF-4) with recessed thumb rests, finger grooves rail and interchangeable frame back straps, includes a reversible enlarged magazine catch, dual recoil spring assembly, and a new trigger system, fixed rear, adj. rear Glock steel, or Glock night sights. New 2010.

MSR $649	$500	$440	$400	$375	$335	$295	$250

MODEL 23/23C COMPACT SPORT/SERVICE – .40 S&W cal., compact variation of the Model 22, 4.01 in. barrel with hexagonal rifling ported (Model 23C), 10 (C/B 1994), 13* (reintroduced 2004), or 15 shot mag., available in all Glock sight variations, 23 1/2 oz., Gen2 as non-ported barrel, checkered grip has no mounting accessories rail, Gen3 ported/non-ported barrel have recessed thumb rests, finger grooves, mounting accessories rail (new 1997-1998.) New 1990.

MSR $599	$475	$425	$395	$365	$335	$295	$250

Add $22 for compensated barrel (Model 23C, fixed rear sight only).

Add $145 for competition model w/adj. sights (Model 23CC, mfg. 2000-2003).

This model is still available with RTF-2 finish (extreme polymid traction) Rough Textured Frame (Model 22 RTF-2 mfg. 2009).

During 1996, AcuSport Corp. commissioned Glock to make a special production run of matching .40 S&W cal. sets. Each set consists of a Model 23 and 27 with serialization as follows: Model 23 (ser. range AAC0000-AAC1499) and Model 27 (ser. range AAD0000-AAD1499).

GRADING - PPGS™	100%	98%	95%	90%	80%	70%	60%	LAST MSR

* ***Model 23 Gen4*** – .40 S&W cal., similar to Model 23 Compact, except features (less polymid traction) Rough Textured Frame (RTF-4) with recessed thumb rests, finger grooves, rail, and interchangeable frame back straps, includes a reversible enlarged magazine catch, dual recoil spring assembly, and a new trigger system, fixed rear, adj. rear Glock steel, or Glock night sights. New 2010.

MSR $649	$500	$440	$400	$375	$335	$295	$250	

MODEL 24/24C SPORT/SERVICE COMPETITION – .40 S&W cal., Gen3, 6.02 in. barrel with hexagonal rifling, internally compensated, recessed thumb rest, finger grooves, accessory rail (Model 24C, new 1999), adj. rear sight, 10, 15, or 17 shot mag., recalibrated trigger pull (4 1/2 lb. pull), Gen2 had checkered grip with no rail, "P" ported/non-ported series, 29 1/2 oz. New 1994.

MSR $750	$625	$550	$475	$425	$350	$325	$275	

Add $40 for compensated barrel (Model 24C).

MODEL 25 COMPACT SPORT/SERVICE – .380 ACP cal., similar to Model 19 Compact, except has 4.02 in. barrel, 15 or 17 shot mag., recessed thumb rest, finger grooves, accessory rail, 22.5 oz. New 2008.

This model is available for law enforcement only.

MODEL 26 SUB-COMPACT – 9mm Para. cal., sub-compact variation of the Model 19 Compact, except has shortened grip, 3.42 in. barrel with hexagonal rifling, 10 or 12 shot mag., available with all Glock sight variations, thumb rest, finger grooves, no rail, 21 3/4 oz. New 1995.

MSR $599	$475	$425	$395	$365	$335	$295	$250	

* ***Model 26 Sub-Compact Gen4*** – 9mm Para. cal., similar to Model 26 Sub-Compact, except features (less polymid traction) Rough Textured Frame (RTF-4) with recessed thumb rests, finger grooves, and interchangeable frame back straps, includes a reversible enlarged magazine catch, dual recoil spring assembly, and a new trigger system, fixed rear, adj. rear Glock steel, or Glock night sights. New 2010.

MSR $649	$500	$440	$400	$375	$335	$295	$250	

MODEL 27 SUB-COMPACT – .40 S&W cal., sub-compact variation of the Model 23 Compact, except has shortened grip, 3.42 in. barrel with hexagonal rifling, 9 or 10 shot mag., all Glock sight variations available, thumb rest, finger grooves, no rail, 21 3/4 oz. New 1995.

MSR $599	$475	$425	$395	$365	$335	$295	$250	

* ***Model 27 Sub-Compact Gen4*** – .40 S&W cal., similar to Model 27 Sub-Compact, except features (less polymid traction) Rough Textured Frame (RTF-4) with recessed thumb rests, finger grooves, and interchangeable frame back straps, includes a reversible enlarged magazine catch, dual recoil spring assembly, and a new trigger system, fixed rear, adj. rear Glock steel, or Glock night sights. New 2010.

MSR $649	$500	$440	$400	$375	$335	$295	$250	

MODEL 28 SUB-COMPACT – .380 ACP cal., similar to Model 26/27/33/39 Sub-Compact, except has scaled down dimensions with 3.42 in. barrel, thumb rest, finger grooves, accessory rail, approx. 20 oz. New 1996.

This model is available for law enforcement only.

MODEL 29 SUB-COMPACT – 10mm Norma cal., sub-compact variation of the Model 20, featuring 3.77 in. barrel with hexagonal rifling, 10 shot mag., all Glock sight variations are available, thumb rest, finger grooves, with or w/o (early mfg.) rail, 27 oz. New 1996.

MSR $637	$500	$440	$410	$375	$350	$325	$295	

* ***Model 29SF*** – 10mm Norma cal., 3.77 in. barrel, Gen3, short frame, all Glock sight options available, new trigger position, thumb rest, finger grooves, rail, otherwise similar to Model 29. New 2009.

MSR $637	$500	$440	$410	$375	$350	$325	$295	

* ***Model 29 Gen4*** – 10mm Norma cal, similar to Model 29 Sub-compact except features (less polymid traction) Rough Textured Frame (RTF-4) with recessed thumb rest, finger

GRADING - PPGS™	100%	98%	95%	90%	80%	70%	60%	LAST MSR

grooves, rail and interchangeable frame back straps, reversible enlarged magazine catch, dual recoil spring assembly, and new trigger system, fixed rear, adj. rear Glock steel, or Glock night sights. New 2012.

MSR $637 $500 $440 $410 $375 $350 $325 $295

MODEL 30 SUB-COMPACT – .45 ACP cal., sub-compact variation of the Model 21 featuring 3.77 in barrel, with octagonal rifling, mag. extension, 10 shot mag., all Glock sight options available, thumb rest, finger grooves, with or w/o (early mfg.) rail, 26 1/2 oz. New 1996.

MSR $637 $500 $440 $410 $375 $350 $325 $295

* ***Model 30SF*** – .45 ACP cal., 3.77 in. barrel, Gen3 short frame, all Glock sight options available, new trigger position, thumb rest, finger grooves, accessory rail, otherwise similar to Model 30. New 2008.

MSR $637 $500 $440 $410 $375 $350 $325 $295

* ***Model 30S*** – .45 ACP cal., 3.78 in. barrel, Gen3 short frame, all Glock sight options available, new trigger position, recessed thumb rest, finger grooves, accessory rail, otherwise similar to Model 30SF. Model 36 slim style slide. New 2012.

MSR $637 $500 $440 $410 $375 $350 $325 $295

* ***Model 30 Gen4*** – .45 ACP cal, similar to Model 30 Sub-compact except features (less polymid traction) Rough Textured Frame (RTF-4) with recessed thumb rest, finger grooves, rail and interchangeable frame back straps, reversible enlarged magazine catch, dual recoil spring assembly, and new trigger system, fixed rear, adj. rear Glock steel, or Glock night sights. New 2012.

MSR $637 $500 $440 $410 $375 $350 $325 $295

MODEL 31/31C SPORT/SERVICE – .357 SIG cal., similar to Model 22, 4.48 in. barrel with hexagonal rifling, ported (Model 31C Gen3, new 1999) or unported (Gen2, checkered grips w/o rail), all Glock sight options available, 10, 15, or 16 shot mag., thumb rest, finger grooves, with or w/o accessory rail, 26 oz. New 1997.

MSR $599 $475 $425 $395 $365 $335 $295 $250

Add $22 for compensated barrel (Model 31C, fixed rear sight only, new 1998).

Add $119 for competition model w/adj. sights (Model 31CC, mfg. 2000-2004).

* ***Model 31 Gen4*** – .357 SIG cal., similar to Model 31, except features (less polymid traction) Rough Textured Frame (RTF-4) with recessed thumb rests, finger grooves, and interchangeable frame back straps, includes a reversible enlarged magazine catch, dual recoil spring assembly, and a new trigger system, accessory rail, fixed rear, adj. rear Glock steel, or Glock night sights. New 2010.

MSR $649 $500 $440 $400 $375 $335 $295 $250

MODEL 32/32C COMPCT SPORT/SERVICE – .357 SIG cal., similar to Model 19, except has 4.02 in. ported (Model 32C) or unported barrel, 10, 13, or 14 shot mag., all Glock sight options are available, 24 oz. New 1998.

MSR $599 $475 $425 $395 $365 $335 $295 $250

Add $22 for compensated barrel (Model 32C, fixed rear sight only, new 1998).

Add $119 for competition model w/adj. sights (Model 32CC, mfg. 2002-2004).

* ***Model 32 Gen4*** – .357 SIG cal., similar to Model 32 Compact, except features (less polymid traction) Rough Textured Frame (RTF-4) with recessed thumb rests, finger grooves, rail, and interchangeable frame back straps, includes a reversible enlarged magazine catch, dual recoil spring assembly, and a new trigger system, fixed rear, adj. rear Glock steel, or Glock night sights. New 2012.

MSR $649 $500 $440 $400 $375 $335 $295 $250

MODEL 33 SUB-COMPACT – .357 SIG cal., sub-compact variation of the Model 32 Compact, shortened grip, 3.42 in. barrel with hexagonal rifling, 9 or 10 shot mag., thumb rest, finger grooves, no rail, 22 oz. New 1997.

MSR $599 $475 $425 $395 $365 $335 $295 $250

GRADING - PPGS™	100%	98%	95%	90%	80%	70%	60%	LAST MSR

* ***Model 33 Gen4*** – .357 SIG cal., similar to Model 33 Sub-compact, except features (less polymid traction) Rough Textured Frame (RTF-4) with recessed thumb rests, finger grooves, rail, and interchangeable frame back straps, includes a reversible enlarged magazine catch, dual recoil spring assembly, and a new trigger system, fixed rear, adj. rear Glock steel, or Glock night sights. New 2012.

MSR $614 $535 $450 $375 $325 $295 $260 $225

MODEL 34 SPORT/SERVICE COMPETITION – 9mm Para. cal., similar features as the Model 17, except has 5.31 in. barrel with hexagonal rifling, extended slide stop lever and magazine catch, adj. rear sights, target grips with finger grooves, thumbrest, receiver has rails for mounting accessories, 10, 17, or 19 shot mag., 25.75 oz. New 1998.

MSR $679 $525 $450 $375 $325 $295 $260 $225

* ***Model 34 Gen4*** – 9mm Para. cal., similar to Model 34, except features (less polymid traction) Rough Textured Frame (RTF-4) with recessed thumb rests, finger grooves, rail, and interchangeable frame back straps, includes a reversible enlarged magazine catch, dual recoil spring assembly, and a new trigger system, adj. rear sight only. New 2011.

MSR $729 $575 $475 $400 $350 $325 $295 $265

MODEL 35 SPORT/SERVICE COMPETITION – .40 S&W cal., 10, 15, or 16 shot mag., recessed thumb rest, finger grooves, accessory rail, otherwise similar to Model 34, 27.5 oz. New 1998.

MSR $679 $525 $450 $375 $325 $295 $260 $225

* ***Model 35 Gen4*** – .40 S&W cal., similar to Model 35, except features (less polymid traction) Rough Textured Frame (RTF-4) with recessed thumb rests, finger grooves, rail, and interchangeable frame back straps, includes a reversible enlarged magazine catch, dual recoil spring assembly, and a new trigger system, adj. rear sight only. New 2010.

MSR $729 $575 $475 $400 $350 $325 $295 $265

MODEL 36 SUB-COMPACT – .45 ACP cal., similar to Model 30 Sub-compact, except has single column 6 shot mag., 3.77 in. barrel with hexagonal rifling, recessed thumb rest, finger grooves, no rail, all Glock sight options are available, slimmest Glock for concealment, 22 1/2 oz. New 1999.

MSR $637 $500 $440 $410 $375 $350 $325 $295

MODEL 37 SPORT/SERVICE – .45 G.A.P. (Glock Automatic Pistol) cal., 4.48 in. barrel with octagonal rifling, all Glock sight options are available, similar to Model 17, except has extended slide stop lever, wider and heavier slide, improved locking block and ejector, 10 shot double column mag., recessed thumb rest, finger grooves, accessory rail, 28 3/4 oz. New 2003.

MSR $614 $535 $450 $375 $325 $295 $260 $225

* ***Model 37 Gen4*** – .45 G.A.P. (Glock Automatic Pistol) cal. similar to Model 37, except features (less polymid traction) Rough Textured Frame (RTF-4) with recessed thumb rests, finger grooves, rail, and interchangeable frame back straps, includes a reversible enlarged magazine catch, dual recoil spring assembly, and a new trigger system, fixed rear, adj. rear Glock steel, or Glock night sights. New 2010.

MSR $664 $515 $450 $375 $325 $295 $260 $225

MODEL 38 COMPACT SPORT/SERVICE – .45 G.A.P. cal., similar to Model 37, except has 4.01 in. barrel with octagonal rifling, 8 shot double column mag., thumb rest, finger grooves, accessory rail, all Glock sight options are available, 26 oz. New 2005.

MSR $614 $535 $450 $375 $325 $295 $260 $225

MODEL 39 SUB-COMPACT – .45 G.A.P. cal., sub-compact variation of the Model 38 Commpact, except has shortened grip, 6 shot single column mag., 3.42 in. barrel with octagonal rifling, all Glock sight options are available, recessed thumb rest, finger grooves, no rail, 22 oz. New 2005.

MSR $614 $535 $450 $375 $325 $295 $260 $225

PISTOLS: SEMI-AUTO, COMMEMORATIVES, ENGRAVED, & SPECIAL/LIMITED EDITIONS

The author wishes to express his thanks to Mr. Stanley J. Ruselowski Jr. and the Glock Collector's Association for providing the following information.

During 1991, Glock inc. USA released its first commemorative, "Desert Storm Commemorative" Model G-17 2nd generation, "checkered grenade" frame pistols. The top of the slide was engraved with all 30 coalition countries and the side of the slide was engraved with "New World Order" and "Operation Desert Storm, Jan. 16-Feb. 27th, 1991". 1,000 were mfg. Serial prefix was UD000US-UD999US. Fifty wood display cases in mahogany were designed with a place for a field knife and a G-17 rd + 2 bottom magazine. The cases were desert camo inside.

During 1996, 2,000 "Centennial Georgia Olympic Games" Model G-17 2nd generation "checkered grenade" frame pistols were produced. Serial prefix was BZF000US-BZF999US and CAE000US-CAE999US. The side of slide was engraved "Atlanta, Georgia, Security Team USA 1996". These pistols included a walnut display case.

Also in 1996, Model G-23, commemorative 2nd generation "checkered grenade" frame pistols were produced and engraved with the "Bell Helicopter 50 year 'Ping' " logo on the right side of the slide and the 1996 Olympic logo on the top of the slide. The 73 pistols Serial Prefix BELL000US-BELL072US commemorate the 50th Anniversary of Bell Helicopter. They included cherry wood display cases.

During 1997, "1 only", "1 of 1" Model G-27 3rd generation "FG" finger grooves (only) no rail frame "Ducks Unlimited" "Great Outdoors" pistol was produced. The side of the slide was gold laser engraved with "Ducks Unlimited" "Great Outdoors" with a high polish blue finish on the slide; Serial Prefix CNS777US. Included hardwood presentation case.

During 1999, 100 "Alaska Statehood" Model G-27 3rd generation "FG" finger grooves (only) no rail frame pistols were produced. The side of the slide was engraved with "40 Years of Alaska Statehood 1959-1999" with an outline picture of the state. Serial Prefix DBW000US-DBW099US.

During 2000, 725 "NRA" Model G-22 3rd generation "FGR" finger grooves and rails frame pistols were produced. The side of the slide was engraved with "NRA". These pistols were produced for raffles at various NRA dinners across the United States. Serial Prefix DFY000US-DFY724US.

During 2001, a limited number of Model G-17 "GSSF" 3rd generation "FGR" finger grooves and rails frame pistols Serial Prefix GSSF000-GSSF999 were produced. The side of the slide was engraved with "GSSF" and "Ten Years of Safe Shooting 1991-2001". There are thousands of members of the Glock Shooting Sports Foundation. These pistols were produced for members only.

During 2002, 1,000 pistol runs of the Models G-17, G-21, and G-22, 3rd generation "FGR" finger grooves and rails frame pistols "America's Heroes", were produced in memory of the Sept. 11, 2001 attack on the World Trade Center. The Model G-17 Serial Prefix was USA0000-USA0999, Model G-21 Serial Prefix was USA1000-USA1999, and Model G-22 Serial Prefix was USA2000-USA2999. They used 0, 1, and 2 in front of each serial number to keep the USA prefix on all three models. On one side of the slide next to each other was gold laser engraved "PD" in a seven sided star, "America's Heroes" in scroll, and "FD" in a Maltese cross. 9-11-01 is underneath. Accusport Corp. distributed these pistols to dealers to honor the NYPD and NYFD for their extraordinary heroism during the attack on the World Trade Center buildings. The sale proceeds from the pistols are going to the victims' funds established after the attack and disaster.

Glock Inc. Anniversary USA "1986-2006" 20 years of Perfection and Integrity. Model G-17 3rd Generation "FGR" finger grooves and rails frame pistol slide bears the lasered autograph of its inventor, Mr. Gaston Glock. The pistols were produced in October 2006. There were 2006 pistols produced in honor of 20 years of business in the USA. Serial Prefix, KLX000-KLX999, KNC000-KNC999, and KFU987-KFU992.

Glock Inc. Silver Anniversary USA "1986-2011" 25 years of Perfection and Integrity. Model G-17 Gen 4 (RTF) Rough Textured Frame "FGR" finger grooves and rails frame pistols = Interchangeable frame backstraps, (SF) Short frame, to standard, to large size grip, reversible enlarged magazine catch, dual recoil spring assembly and new trigger system with a solid silver medallion inledded in the

GRADING - PPGS™	100%	98%	95%	90%	80%	70%	60%	LAST MSR

polymer frame. this will be a run of 2,500 Model G-17 Gen 4 (RTF) pistols with a silver carrying case produced in January 2011. Serial Prefix 25Y001-25Y2500.

Unusual Specially Marked and Engraved Glocks USA

During 1996, there were 500 matching 9mm Para. cal. pistol sets produced consisting of the G-19 and G-26 and 1,500 matching .40 AUTO pistol sets produced consisting of the G-23 and G-27. These sets were called "Defense Set". Mathematically, only 500 sets of 4-pistol sets exist. Realistically, it is believed less than 80 4-pistol sets were sold to specific dealers. It is possible these 80 dealers further broke up the sets. Accusport Corp. was unable to effectively sell the 2-pistol sets; thus, most were broken up with single pistols being sold individually to dealers across the country. The side of the slide is engraved with "Defense Set" 1 of 2 and 2 of 2 with no US suffix.

Model 19 "Defense Set" "1 of 2" Serial Prefix AAA0000-AAA0499, 2nd Generation "Checkered Grenade" frame - Model 26 "Defense Set" "2 of 2", Serial Prefix AAB0000-AAB0499, 3rd Generation "FG" finger grooves (only) no rail frame - Model 23 "Defense Set" "1 of 2", Serial Prefix AAC0000-AAC1499, 2nd Generation "Checkered Grenade" frame - Model 27 "Defense Set" "2 of 2", Serial Prefix AAD0000-AAD1499, 3rd Generation "FG" finger grooves (only) no rail frame.

Therefore, to have a set of 4 pistols with the same serial number is less likely than 80 out of 500 or less likely than 80 if they were broken up further. A low serial number will command a higher premium.

Also during 1999, the "2 Millionth Glock" 17 pistol was produced, Serial Prefix DAP000US. It was auctioned off at a Sheriff's Police gun show. It has been appropriately engraved "My Two Millionth Pistol" and it bears the engraved autograph of its inventor, Mr. Gaston Glock. The slide has been uniquely engraved with a rather unusual geometric pattern. The proceeds were donated to a law enforcement foundation. A sister pistol, ser. no. 2,000,001 was also auctioned off in Nuremberg, Germany. These two pistols were 3rd generation "FGR" finger grooves and rails frame.

During 2006, there were 1,000 model G-19 3rd Generation "FGR" finger grooves and rails frame pistols produced Serial Prefix KNF000-KNF999 and 1,400 model G-23 3rd generation "FGR" finger grooves and rails frame pistols Serial Prefix KWG100-KWG999, KWR500-KWR999. The side of the slide is gold laser engraved "Homeland Defender" with a small circle and the United States of America flag in the middle. Ellett Bros. was the distributor of these pistols to dealers.

To date, there are hundreds of unusual specially marked and engraved Glocks for law enforcement and other agencies.

MODEL 17 SPORT/SERVICE DESERT STORM COMMEMORATIVE – 9mm Para. cal. 1,000 mfg. in 1991 only.

$1,195	$925	$725	N/A	N/A	N/A	N/A	$995

This model features coalition forces listing on top of barrel, inscription on the side of slide is "NEW WORLD ORDER". This is the first Limited Edition Commemorative model.

ENGRAVED, UNUSUALLY MARKED, AND MISCELLANEOUS GLOCK COMMEMORATIVES – These pistols feature laser engraving inscriptions on top and side of slides.

$1,195	$925	$725	N/A	N/A	N/A	N/A	$995

Low serial number will command a higher premium.

GOLAN

See KSN Industries Ltd. listing in the K section.

GOLDEN EAGLE

Previous trademark of rifles/shotguns produced by Nikko Limited located in Tochigi, Japan, circa 1975-1981.

Please refer to the Nikko Firearms Limited listing in this text for a complete chronological history of Nikko - Japan's previous long gun manufacturer.

RIFLES: BOLT ACTION

MODEL 7000 GRADE I – bolt action, all popular American calibers, including .270 Win., and .300 Wby. Mag., 24 or 26 in. barrels, select skipline checkered walnut stock, rosewood

GRADING - PPGS™	100%	98%	95%	90%	80%	70%	60%	LAST MSR

forend tip, golden eagle head engraved in pistol grip cap, recoil pad. Mfg. 1976-81.

	$600	$550	$525	$450	$375	$340	$290

MODEL 7000 GRADE I AFRICAN – .375 H&H and .458 Win. Mag. cal., similar to 7000, open sights.

	$650	$590	$555	$480	$400	$365	$315

MODEL 7000 GRADE II – scroll engraving, better grade wood.

	$690	$625	$590	$510	$430	$395	$340

SHOTGUNS: O/U

MODEL 5000 GRADE I (FIELD) – 12 or 20 ga., 26, 28, or 30 in. barrels, various chokes, vent. rib, engraved frame, gold eagle head inlay, auto ejectors, SST, checkered pistol grip beavertail stock. Mfg. 1975-81.

	$850	$775	$700	$625	$560	$510	$440

MODEL 5000 GRADE I SKEET – similar to 5000 Field, except 26 or 28 in. skeet bored, wide rib.

	$875	$800	$725	$650	$580	$510	$440

MODEL 5000 GRADE I TRAP – similar to 5000 Field, except 30 or 32 in. barrel, mod. and full, imp. mod. and full, or full and full choke, wide rib, trap stock with pad.

	$875	$800	$725	$650	$580	$510	$440

MODEL 5000 GRADE II – available in Field, Trap, and Skeet, more engraving, better grade wood, with screaming eagle on frame in gold.

	$950	$875	$790	$710	$630	$540	$460
Skeet	$975	$895	$810	$725	$640	$540	$460
Trap	$975	$895	$810	$725	$640	$540	$460

GRANDEE GRADE III – similar to 5000 Grade II, except elaborate engraving, inlays, and better grade wood.

	$2,500	$2,200	$1,900	$1,575	$1,250	$1,000	$850

GOLDEN STATE ARMS

Previous importer located in Pasadena, CA. Golden State Arms imported and subcontracted various firearms constructed by European and Japanese manufacturers - achieving private label status on some guns.

Most firearms previously imported by Golden State Arms (including private labels) are not that collectible. In many cases, the shooting value will determine the price of a specimen. In some models or configurations which are currently desirable, however, premiums may exist.

GONCZ ARMAMENT, INC.

Previous manufacturer located in North Hollywood, CA circa 1984-1990.

While advertised, BATF records indicate very few Goncz pistols or carbines were actually produced. All of these guns were prototypes or individually hand-built and none were ever mass produced through normal fabrication techniques.

In 1990, Claridge Hi-Tec, Inc. purchased Goncz Armament, Inc.

GRAND POWER s.r.o.

Current manufacturer established in 2002 and located in the Slovakia. Currently imported beginning 2007 by STI International, located in Georgetown, TX.

Grand Power s.r.o. manufactures a 9mm Para. cal. lightweight semi-auto polymer pistol in various configurations. Please contact the importer directly for more information, including availability and pricing (see Trademark Index).

GRANGER, G.

Current manufacturer established during 1902, and located in Saint Etienne, France. Current U.S. agent is Jean-Jacques Perodeau, located in Enid, OK.

All guns are made on a custom order basis. Please contact the U.S. agent directly for more information (please refer to Trademark Index).

SHOTGUNS: SxS, SIDELOCK

GRANGER SxS – 12, 16, 20, or 28 ga., case hardened receiver, Granger sidelock mechanism and plates, DT or SNT, choice of pistol or straight grip, deluxe French walnut stock and forearm, prices will vary per older customer specifications and appointments, delivery time is 12-36 months. Limited mfg.

Engraving is available by request.

Please contact the importer directly for pricing and availability.

GRANITE MOUNTAIN ARMS, INC.

Current rifle and action manufacturer located in Phoenix, AZ. Previously located in Prescott, AZ. Consumer and dealer sales.

Granite Mountain Arms, Inc. currently manufactures precision rifle actions and related components. In the past, various custom gun makers manufactured rifles per individual special order. Additionally, custom rifle manufacturers also use Granite Mountain Arms, Inc. actions to build their own bolt action rifles. Please contact the company directly for more information, including availability and pricing (see Trademark Index).

GRANT, STEPHEN

Current trademark manufactured by Atkin, Grant & Lang, established in 1867, and located in Hertfordshire, England.

The Stephen Grant trademark is primarily used on custom order SxS rifles and shotguns. Shotguns can be top or side lever and are equipped with sidelocks and a self-opening mechanism. Please contact the company directly for current information, availability, delivery time, and custom order pricing.

Atkin, Grant & Lang provide a useful historical research service on older Stephen Grant shotguns and rifles. The charge for this service is £25 per gun, and the company will give you all pertinent factory information regarding the history.

STEPHEN GRANT COMPANY HISTORY

Stephen Grant was born in 1821 in Tipperary, Ireland. Young Grant served his apprenticeship with Dublin's William Kavanaugh before moving to London in 1843 to work with Charles Lancaster. In 1850, Grant moved to Thomas Boss and when Boss died in 1857, his widow made Grant a managing partner. In 1867, Grant decided to work for himself, taking pains in 1871 to publicly disassociate himself with Boss. That same year he was appointed gunmaker to the Prince of Wales, and over the next quarter century, he would establish the Grant name as one of the finest gunmakers in London. Grant and his two sons were clever inventors and were also quick to adopt promising patents by other talents. By the time of his death in 1898, Stephen Grant was one of London's most respected gunmakers.

Grant's widow and family continued the business, but by the early 1920s, deaths in the family and associated tragedies meant the business had to be sold. In 1923, the firm was purchased by Scotsman William Robson, who amalgamated it with Joseph Lang & Sons in 1925. Under Robson's tutelage, Grant & Lang went on to absorb many of its competitors during the Depression, including Harrison & Hussey, Charles Lancaster, Watson Bros, and Frederick Beesley. The company merged with Henry Atkin Ltd. in 1960 and then became Churchill, Atkin, Grant & Lang in 1971. The name lanquished for a time until Cyril Adams of Texas purchased Atkin, Grant & Lang in the mid-1980s and best quality gunmaking resumed. In 1999, Ken Duglan purchased the firm and moved it to Broomhill Shooting Grounds north of London. In 2011, Duglan sold the company to Diggory Hadoke.

Today, Grant remains best known for its elegant sidelever sidelocks. The firm also restores vintage Grant guns.

Information courtesy of David Grant & Vic Venters.

RIFLES: SxS

Prices on current custom order rifles and shotguns do not include VAT or importation costs.

GRADING - PPGS™	100%	98%	95%	90%	80%	70%	60%	LAST MSR

SIDELOCK MODEL – various cals. between .300 H&H - .577 NE, best quality sidelock, individually made per customer specifications.

MSR N/A	N/A	$39,250	$35,000	$31,000	$27,000	$24,000	$20,500	

SHOTGUNS: O/U

Prices on current custom order rifles and shotguns do not include VAT or importation costs.

SIDELOCK MODEL – 12, 16, 20, 28 ga., or 410 bore, best quality sidelock ejector, individually made per customer specifications.

MSR N/A	N/A	$18,500	$15,000	$12,000	$10,000	$8,850	$7,500	

Add 20% for 20 ga.
Add 30% for 28 ga. and .410 bore.

SHOTGUNS: SxS

Prices on current custom order rifles and shotguns do not include VAT or importation costs.

SIDELOCK MODEL – 12, 16, 20, 28 ga., or .410 bore, best quality sidelock ejector, top or side lever opening, individually made per customer specifications.

MSR N/A	N/A	$12,000	$9,900	$8,700	$7,500	$6,250	$5,000	

Add 20% for 20 ga.
Add 30% for 28 ga. and .410 bore.

GREAT WESTERN

Current trademark of revolvers manufactured by Pietta of Italy and imported by E.M.F. Company, Inc., located in Santa Ana, CA.

REVOLVERS: REPRODUCTIONS

GREAT WESTERN II CUSTOM 1873 SA – .357 Mag., .44-40 WCF, or .45 LC cal., 4 3/4, 5 1/2, or 7 1/2 in. barrel, four metal finishes include all blue, blue w/case colored frame, bright nickel, or satin nickel, ultra ivory grips, mfg. by Pietta. Imported 2003-2009.

	$725	$625	$550	$475	$400	$325	$275	*$810*

Add $125 for ultra stag grips or $960-$1,300 for engraving options.
Add $25 for Express birdshead grips (4 3/4 in. barrel only).

* ***Great Western II Custom/Deluxe 1873 SA Californian*** similar to Great Western II, except has standard charcoal case colored frame and blue finish, also available in Buntline configuration with 12 in. barrel. Importation began 2003.

MSR $520	$450	$400	$350	$300	$250	$215	$185	

Add $85 for Alchimista model with checkered walnut grips.
Add $55 for Buntline Model with walnut grips.
Add $250 for custom bone case coloring or for bright nickel finish.
Add $40 for Deluxe Model with ultra ivory or checkered walnut grips (.357 Mag. or .45 LC cal. only, 4 3/4 in. barrel).
Add $225 for ultra stag fitted grips.
Add $20 for Express birdshead grips (4 3/4 in. barrel only).

* ***Great Western II Custom 1873 Stainless*** – .357 Mag. or .45 LC cal., 3 1/2 (Pony Express Model) or 4 3/4 in. barrel, similar to Great Western II, except is stainless steel construction, choice of walnut or ultra-ivory grips. Importation began 2006.

MSR $720	$625	$550	$475	$400	$350	$300	$275	

Add $40 for ultra-ivory or checkered walnut grips.
Add $10 for birdshead Express grips (4 3/4 in. barrel only).
Add $105 for Pony Express model with 3 1/2 in. barrel and walnut grips.

GREAT WESTERN II DELUXE PHOTO ENGRAVED MODEL – .357 Mag. or .45 LC cal., 4 3/4 in. barrel, all blue finish with photo engraving, ultra ivory grips. New 2008.

MSR $825	$700	$575	$450	$400	$350	$300	$275	

GRADING - PPGS™	100%	98%	95%	90%	80%	70%	60%	LAST MSR

GREAT WESTERN ARMS COMPANY

Previous manufacturer located in Los Angeles, CA circa 1954-1964.

Most firearms enthusiasts are more or less familiar with Great Western Arms Co., an enterprise initially organized in Los Angeles through the efforts of Hy Hunter and established by three partners; Dr. Hassam, a prominent surgeon, Dan Reeves, owner of the L.A. Rams, and Dan Fortmann. Bill Wilson, a former production engineer at North American Aviation, served as president.

Wilson established his shop in a tin covered building on Minor Street in Southgate, CA and staffed it with a small group of employees, some taken from Weatherby. As time went by, as many as fifty workers were busy producing guns.

Hy Hunter's American Weapons Corp. in Burbank was chosen by the partners to be the exclusive distributor. Hunter so aggressively marketed the Frontier Six Shooter that his name became synonymous with Great Western and many believed that he was the owner of the company.

With Bob Green as financial officer and Bill Hensley as plant superintendent, machining of parts to manufacture exact copies of the original Colt Model P began in early 1954. Fitting, de-burring, polishing, finishing and assembly began slowly in the spring, with initial production and sales generated by notoriety of the proprietary .357 Atomic cartridge.

Great Western Arms Co. operated for approximately ten years, during which time they were reorganized by at least five different owners. Even though the company was well funded with $250,000 initially, it was never stable, lacking in manufacturing expertise and management skills. But the employees made up for it with enthusiasm and a genuine desire to accommodate their customers.

Appearing in early Great Western brochures and catalogues were spokesmen John Wayne and Audie Murphy. Exhibition shooters Dee Woolem and Sam Toole represented the company with their fast draw talents.

The Great Western revolver line-up offered a well-rounded variety of models with sub-variants. A good selection of barrel lengths, finishes, decoration and calibers were available. They offered interchangeable auxiliary cylinders and a variety of other special and innovative accessories.

The author would like to thank Mr. John Dougan for providing information and values for this section.

Due to space considerations, some portions of this manufacturer's listing are available online free of charge at www.bluebookofgunvalues.com.

DERRINGERS

GREAT WESTERN DERRINGER – .38 S&W or .38 S&W Spl. cal. (not interchangeable). Basically an improved version of the Remington Double Derringer frame.

	100%	98%	95%	90%	80%	70%	60%	LAST MSR
	$800	$750	$700	$600	$550	$500	$450	

Add a premium for engraving, plating and presentation case.

One verified .22 WRM prototype is known.

Some derringers were shipped with plated finishes and several are known to have been engraved. One cased salesman sample, serial number 1838 was engraved by Carl Courts, it is gold & silver plated and fitted with pearl grip panels.

Derringer serial number 25 was given to Elvis.

There were two distinct frame configurations specific to the hinge, at first the hinge was in identical proportion to the original Remington, and like the originals many failed. A more robust hinge was introduced and is visually discernable. The original configuration was referred to in Great Western catalogs and parts lists as the Old Model and the guns with the larger hinge lug were of course referred to as the New Model. The change occurred at approximately serial number 1800.

REVOLVERS: SINGLE ACTION

FRONTIER SIX SHOOTER – chambered for .22 LR/WMR and a variety of centerfire calibers, 4 3/4, 5 1/2, 7 1/2, or 12 in. barrel, plastic faux stag (standard), walnut, stag, pearl, or

GRADING - PPGS™	100%	98%	95%	90%	80%	70%	60%	LAST MSR

ivory grips, cyanide case colored, blue, chrome, or nickel plated finish, Christy Gun Works firing pin mounted in recoil shield.

$650	$600	$550	$450	$400	$350	$300	

Add a premium for plating or presentation case.
Add $100 for 12 in. Buntline model.

A .22 LR/.22 WMR convertible model was listed in the catalog.

SHERIFF'S MODEL – .45 LC cal., nickel, blue, cyanide case colored finish, plastic faux stag grips standard.

$750	$700	$650	$550	$500	$450	$400	

Add a premium for plating or presentation case.

Aside from the definitive short barrel, Sheriffs Models were made with three features which distinguished them from the rest of the guns. Oral history is that Great Western purchased Colt's existing inventory of single-action parts, cylinder frames, and some tools when they began operations.

When viewed from the bottom, the Sheriffs Model offers strong evidence of this; all Sheriffs Models examined feature a full radius to the front of the cylinder frame, whereas the Great Western frames exhibit a pinched and elliptical appearance. Further, all of the Sheriffs Models examined feature a Colt hammer with the firing pin and a hole through the recoil shield. It is believed that these cylinder frames were actually made by Colt.

To make a Sheriffs Model, the ejector rod housing lug was simply removed. It has been noted that Sheriffs Models are serial numbered below 400.

The words "GREAT WESTERN" were roll marked on the side of the barrel, there was not enough space on top of the barrels.

FAST DRAW MODEL – solid brass backstrap and trigger guard, 4 3/4 in. barrel, blue finish, plastic faux stag grips.

$675	$625	$575	$475	$425	$375	$325	

Dee Woolem initiated the Fast Draw project and personally fitted and set-up each gun. Based on the Frontier Six Shooter, these revolvers came from the factory fitted with a solid brass back-strap and trigger-guard. The hammer spur was slightly longer and turned upward. The action was smoothed-up.

TARGET MODEL – most .22 LR cal., blue or case colored finish.

$700	$650	$600	$500	$450	$400	$350	

Again, based on the Frontier Six Shooter, this model was fitted with a MICRO front blade and adjustable rear sights. The top strap was planed or milled flat and the rear sight mounted with two screws. Various calibers and barrel lengths were shipped, most were .22 LR cal. Blue or case colored examples are known.

DEPUTY MODEL – .22 LR, .38 Spl., or .357 Mag. cal., 4 in. barrel, deluxe blue finish, walnut grips.

$800	$750	$700	$600	$550	$500	$450	

Announced in 1956, the first of these special revolvers were intended only for Great Western Arms Co. distributors and dealers. The accepted quantity is sixty guns. They all feature a 4" barrel with a full length sight rib with adjustable rear sight. These are the rarest of the cataloged Great Western revolvers, according to Great Western's service manager John McCormick, they number less than 100 and until recent years, many believed that only prototype Deputy Models were made. They appear in the 17XXX - 19XXX serial number range.

ENGRAVED MODEL

Values will vary depending on the configuration, engraver, case, provenance, and verification of authenticity.

Offered from the beginning, this model could be ordered with any amount of coverage in any style of engraving and inlay. Cattle brand engraving was popular. Finishes were gold, silver, nickel, and blue.

Carl Courts was Great Western's primary artist and engraved most of the verifiable revolvers, including the following cased presentation pairs - serial numbers GW1 & GW2 for Bill Wilson, serial numbers GW3 & GW4 for Dan Fortmann and serial numbers GW9828 & GW9737 for Mel Torme, and a brace with 4 3/4 in. barrels for John Wayne which were later used in *The Shootist*, his last movie in 1976.

Special engraved single examples were: serial number, GW73 factory sales sample, GW5000 for President Eisenhower, and A.A. White engraved serial number 17694. Carl Courts engraved another for the Duke. George Montgomery received GW5571 & GW5572 and 17856 & 17857, the officers and crew of the USS Taluga presented Capt. R.H. Caldwell with serial numbers 12250 & 12251. Nickel plated serial number 12838 was received by film actor Arvo Ojala. Exhibition shooters Sam Toole and Dee Woolem were presented with cased pairs. Dozens of other notable personalities were presented revolvers and Derringers. Ruger engraver Charles H. Jerred completed at least one gun, serial number 11390 in November 1955 and the correspondence between Wilson and Jerred suggest that he may have engraved others.

Cole Agee was a well known and popular engraver at the time and according to John McCormick, engraved the pair of 5 1/2 in. Frontier Models, which John Wayne is pictured holding in the photograph on the back of Great Western catalogs. Agee is also credited with engraving a Derringer for the Duke.

KIT GUNS

Unassembled in box - $650.
Unassembled with no box - $400.
Assembled - depending on quality of fit and finish - $200 - $300.

Unthinkable in today's climate of litigation, Great Western sold guns, which could be assembled and completed at the kitchen table with a few basic tools and average skills. The kit guns came with all machining complete, all holes were drilled and tapped and the final contours roughed out. To finish the gun, the customer would de-burr and final polish all surfaces. Of course the lock-work had to be cleaned-up and honed and the preferred finish applied.

According to service manager John McCormick there could have been as many as 1000 Kit Guns shipped.

Typically, the first digit of the serial number on Kit Guns is zero, followed by five numbers, i.e. 020173. The Kit Guns first made their debut in the 1956 catalog and were priced at $59.95. Unassembled Kit Guns in the original box with assembly instructions are extremely rare.

GREEN, ROGER

Current custom gun maker located in Evansville, WY.

Roger Green builds high quality custom made rifles and shotguns to order per customer's specifications. A variety of gunsmithing services are also available. Please contact him directy for more information, including pricing, availability, and custom order options (see Trademark Index).

GREENER, W.W., LIMITED

Current manufacturer established in 1829 in Newcastle Upon Tyne, and currently located in Hagley, England, with sales and administration offices located in Wiltshire, England. Current U.S. agent is Kirk Merrington, located in Kerryville, TX. Until 1994, Gibbs Rifle Co. located in Martinsburg, WV was the U.S. agent.

Currently, all guns are built to the customer's specifications.

RIFLES: SxS

A few "Limited Edition" Presentation grade double rifles are being made in .375 caliber to meet the requirements of big game hunters.

Barrels - made of the highest quality steel, bored and rifled to individual requirements, will be of the correct caliber to suit the quarry.

Actions - rifles have side-lock or Facile Princeps actions.

Engraving - fine scroll work, exquisite game scenes and the best chiselled relief engraving designed to cater for all discerning customer requirements.

Calibers - new double rifles in .375 caliber are presently being built but other calibers can be built on request.

GRADING - PPGS™	100%	98%	95%	90%	80%	70%	60%	LAST MSR

Presently the company cannot accept any orders for rifles of any caliber due to the number of guns presently being built.

SHOTGUNS: SINGLE SHOT

GENERAL PURPOSE (GP Mk I) – 12 ga., improved Martini action, 26, 28, 30, 32, or 34 in. barrel, full or mod., auto ejector, straight hand stock, was also produced as a Multi-choke shotgun with a set of five interchangeable chokes and as a Trap model with raised ventilated rib and better quality stock. Disc. 1967.

$330	$305	$275	$220	$195	$165	$160	

Add 50%-100% for Trap model.

GP MK II – 12 ga. only, famed general purpose (GP) English shotgun configuration featuring Greener Martini action, 28 or 30 in. barrel, walnut stock and forearm. Disc. 1999.

$525	$450	$400	$350	$300	$250	$195	

Older, used military contract variations of this model may be offered for sale - typically seen in the $165-$200 range.

Many of these have shaped chambers and three pronged firing pins which can only be used with special ammunition which is no longer made or available. These guns may not be suitable for conversion for use with modern ammunition.

SHOTGUNS: SxS

Presently the company makes new 'Exhibition' shotguns using traditional W.W. Greener designs in 12, 16, 20 and 28 bores. Recently a 12 bore hammer gun was completed and all of the current production are of the very best Presentation or Exhibition quality.

Barrels - are made of the highest quality steel and bored to maintain the famous choke boring improvements, made by W.W. Greener in the 1870s, to optimize shooting performance. These ensure patterns of shot guaranteed to meet customers' exact requirements whether for game, wildfowl, or clay pigeon shooting. A few pairs of Limited Edition shotguns were made with interchangeable steel and damascus barrels.

Actions - Sidelock actions can incorporate the 3 teardrop, 5 pin bridle invented by Harry Greener in 1914. The Facile Princeps, reintroduced in 1998 is, weight for weight, the strongest action ever produced and features the traditional Greener cross-bolt adding extra strength and safety to these weapons. Recently two 'Unique' ejector shot guns were finished. This 'Unique' type of ejecting shotgun was also invented by Harry Greener as an improvement to the 'self-acting' ejector of 1881.

Stocks - are made from the very best walnut and customers can make their own choice from a wide selection when ordering their guns. Dimensions, including stock length, cast, comb and drop, with straight, half pistol or full pistol hand, are all carefully tailored to meet each individuals' shooting characteristics.

Engraving - Only the very best engravers are employed to design and execute the finest scroll work, game scenes, or other exquisite artistic designs. Chiselled relief engraving is a speciality and this may be embellished with gold and precious metal inlays to further enhance the beauty of the very best guns made in England today.

Degree of engraving and grade of wood are the basic differences between the models.

NO. 5 NEEDHAM EJECTOR – 12 ga. only, one mfg. in 1987.

Extreme rarity precludes accurate pricing on this model.

G 60 ROYAL – 12, 16, 20 ga., or .410 bore, best Self-acting or Unique ejector model with fine scroll, game scenes or deep carved engraving and gold crown. Disc. 1967.

$22,000	$15,000	$10,000	$9,000	$8,000	$6,500	$6,000	

G 70 IMPERIAL – 12, 16, 20 ga., or .410 bore, 2 1/2 or 3 in. chambers, very best presentation exhibition quality Unique or Self-acting ejector model with steel or damascus barrels with deep carved scroll and game scene engraving, gold crown and scepter. Disc. 1967.

$35,000	$30,000	$25,000	$20,000	$15,000	$11,000	$8,500	

GRADING - PPGS™	100%	98%	95%	90%	80%	70%	60%	LAST MSR

L 40/L 50/L 120 – 12, 16, 20 ga., or .410 bore, best sidelock ejector model with dovetail lump barrels, fine scroll engraving with choice of bright or color case hardened frame finish. Disc. 1967.

$35,000 $30,000 $25,000 $20,000 $15,000 $10,000 $6,000

L 60/L 80/L 150 – 12, 16, 20 ga., or .410 bore, 2 1/2 or 3 in. chambers, very best sidelock ejector model with chopper lump barrels and easy-opening device, bright or color case hardened frame finish. Disc. 1967.

$35,000 $30,000 $25,000 $20,000 $15,000 $10,000 $6,000

L 70/L 90/L 500 – 12, 16, 20 ga., or .410 bore, 2 1/2 or 3 in. chambers, very best side-lock ejector model with chopper lump barrels and easy-opening device, bright or color case hardened frame finish. Disc. 1967.

$125,000 $110,000$90,000 $75,000 $60,000 $45,000 $32,500

FARKILLER GRADE F35 – 12 ga., 28, 30, or 32 in. barrels, hammerless boxlock, checkered straight or semi-pistol grip stock. Disc. 1967.

$2,420 $2,200 $2,090 $1,870 $1,760 $1,650 $1,540

FARKILLER GRADE F35 LARGE BORE – 8 or 10 ga., similar to F35. Disc. 1967.

$2,750 $2,585 $2,310 $2,090 $1,980 $1,815 $1,650

HAMMERLESS EJECTOR (DH/FH) AND NON-EJECTOR (D/F) MODEL – 12, 16, 20, 28 ga., or .410 bore, 26, 28, or 30 in. barrels supplied with any choke combination, auto ejectors, single or double triggers, straight or semi-pistol grip stock, DH models have Anson & Deeley type actions, FH have Facile Princeps type actions. Disc. 1967, except for DH Presentation Model.

Subtract 50% for non-ejectors.

* ***Hammerless Ejector Model Grade DH35/FH35/FH25/F20*** – medium grade model with forend ejectors and some scroll engraving. Disc. 1967.

$4,000 $3,500 $3,000 $2,000 $1,650 $1,540 $1,375

Subtract 50% for F20 model.

* ***Hammerless Ejector Model DH 40/F40*** – medium grade model with ejectors, except has better engraving than DH35 and deluxe walnut stock and forearm. Disc. 1967.

$6,700 $5,900 $5,000 $4,250 $3,500 $2,850 $2,100

Subtract 50% for F40 Model.

* ***Hammerless Ejector Model Crown Grade DH55/FH45/F40*** – medium grade model with ejectors, has better engraving than DH35 and deluxe walnut stock and forearm. Disc. 1967.

$5,000 $4,500 $4,000 $3,500 $3,000 $2,000 $1,750

Subtract 50% for F40 Model.

* ***Hammerless Ejector Model DH 75/FH70*** – 12 ga. only, 2 3/4 in. chambers, best quality of the medium grade guns, scalloped action, 27, 28, or 30 in. barrels, case hardened receiver, choice of engraving (game scene or fine scroll work). Disc. 1967.

$15,000 $12,000 $10,000 $7,250 $6,000 $4,950 $3,875

Add $500 for SST.

* ***Hammerless Ejector Model DOH 90*** – 12 ga., 3 in. chambers, best Anson & Deeley scalloped action with Greener easy opening device, French walnut stock, DT. Mfg. 1988-1989.

$22,000 $19,250 $16,500 $14,950 $12,100 $9,900 $7,700

EMPIRE – 12 ga. only, 2 3/4 or 3 in., any choke, 28, 30, or 32 in. barrel, hammerless, boxlock, straight stock or semi pistol grip. Disc. 1967.

	100%	98%	95%	90%	80%	70%	60%
	$1,760	$1,540	$1,320	$1,100	$935	$825	$770
Auto ejectors	$1,980	$1,760	$1,540	$1,320	$1,155	$1,045	$990

GRADING - PPGS™	100%	98%	95%	90%	80%	70%	60%	LAST MSR

EMPIRE DELUXE – similar to Empire, only better grade wood. Disc. 1967.

Non-ejector model	$1,980	$1,760	$1,540	$1,320	$1,155	$1,045	$990	
Auto ejectors	$2,200	$1,980	$1,760	$1,540	$1,375	$1,265	$1,100	

Add $1,500 for Blue Rock versions.

GREIFELT AND COMPANY

Previous manufacturer located in Suhl, Germany (formerly East Germany).

GRENDEL, INC.

Previous manufacturer located in Rockledge, FL, circa 1990-1995.

PISTOLS: SEMI-AUTO

MODEL P-10 SERIES – .380 ACP cal., blowback double action, 10 shot mag., small dimensions, hammerless, matte blue finish, 15 oz. Disc. 1991.

$200	$175	$165	$155	$145	$140	$135	*$155*

Add $15 for electroless nickel finish.

Add $15 for nickel green finish.

Green finish was available at no extra charge.

MODEL P-12 – .380 ACP cal., double action only, 3 in. barrel, steel construction with polymer grip area, no external safety, 11 shot Zytel mag., blue or electroless nickel finish, 11 lb. trigger pull, 13 oz. Mfg. 1992-95.

$200	$175	$165	$155	$145	$140	$135	*$175*

Add $20 for nickel finish.

Add $50 for threaded barrel with muzzle brake parts option.

MODEL P-30 – .22 WMR cal., blowback similar action to P-12, 5 in. barrel, hammerless, matte black finish, 10 (C/B 1994) or 30* shot mag., 21 oz. Mfg. 1990-95.

$300	$250	$225	$200	$185	$175	$165	*$225*

Add $25 for electroless nickel finish (disc. 1991).

Add $35 for scope mount (Weaver base).

* ***Model P-30M*** – similar to Model P-30, except has 5.6 in. barrel with removable muzzle brake. Mfg. 1990-95.

$300	$250	$225	$200	$185	$175	$165	*$235*

Add $25 for electroless nickel finish (disc. 1991).

MODEL P-30L – similar to Model P-30, except has 8 in. barrel with removable muzzle brake, 22 oz. Mfg. 1991-92.

$350	$325	$285	$250	$230	$220	$190	*$280*

Add $15 for Model P-30LM that allows for fitting various accessories.

MODEL P-31 – .22 WMR cal., same action as P-30, except has 11 in. barrel, enclosed synthetic barrel shroud and flash hider, 48 oz. Mfg. 1990-95.

$450	$400	$365	$325	$290	$265	$235	*$345*

RIFLES & CARBINES

MODEL R-31 – similar design to Model P-31, except has 16 in. barrel and telescoping stock, 64 oz. Mfg. 1991-95.

$465	$425	$375	$335	$310	$285	$265	*$385*

SRT-20F COMPACT – .243 Win. or .308 Win. cal., bolt action based on the Sako A-2 action, 20 in. match grade finned barrel with muzzle brake, folding synthetic stock, integrated bipod rest, no sights, 9 shot mag., 6.7 lbs. Disc. 1989.

$775	$725	$675	$595	$565	$540	$520	*$525*

Grendel previously manufactured the SRT-16F, SRT-20L, and SRT-24 - all were disc. 1988. Values are approx. the same as the SRT-20F.

GRADING - PPGS™	100%	98%	95%	90%	80%	70%	60%	LAST MSR

GREYBULL PRECISION

Current rifle manufacturer located in Loveland, CO.

Greybull Precision manufactures the P105 bolt action rifle, available in a variety of configurations, including calibers, optics, and stocks. Base price is $6,000. Please contact the company directly for more information, including pricing, options, and availability (see Trademark Index).

GRIFFIN & HOWE

Griffin & Howe

Current custom gunsmith, rifle manufacturer, and importer established in 1923, with store locations in Bernardsville, NJ (gunsmithing also), and Greenwich, CT. Griffin & Howe also had a NY City store location until April, 2003.

Founded in 1923 by Seymour Griffin and James Howe, Griffin & Howe continues to build its custom rifles as well as providing the full spectrum of gunsmithing services and importation of fine English guns.

Griffin & Howe has been building custom rifles since 1923. They also perform a variety of custom gunsmithing services. Prices may vary greatly depending on configuration, desirability, condition, and special features. Most used Griffin & Howe Custom Rifles in average condition and without special engraving start at $4,500+ and rise according to condition and nature of the individual gun. Since 1923, fewer than 2,800 have been made. In 1930, Griffin & Howe became a subsidiary of Abercrombie & Fitch and remained with them until 1976, when it became a privately held company. Because all Griffin & Howe rifles are essentially special ordered, accurate pricing can be ascertained only by examining each individual gun. Elaborate specimens by this maker/trademark will command over $10,000. Engraving by Joseph Fugger, Winston Churchill, Robert Swartley, or Rudolph Kornbrath will add considerably to the value.

During 2011, Griffin & Howe acquired the sales records of Von Lengerke & Detmold and Abercrombie & Fitch. These records cover the recording sales and inventory between 1901-1976. Within the records, most of the "new sales" are grouped by make and model. Please visit www.griffinhowe.com for more information on how to access these older records.

Pricing on new custom rifles, with a wide selection of options, is available directly from Griffin & Howe.

RIFLES: BOLT ACTION

Values represent a standard gun with no upgrades or options.

G&H CLASSIC FRENCH WALNUT STOCK – most popular cals., custom honed action with lapped lugs, Douglas premium barrel, hand engraving, French walnut sporter stock with ebony forend tip, G&H pistol grip cap, "Griffin & Howe, New York" barrel address, custom order.

Current MSR on this model is $15,000.

WIN M70 STANDARD ACTION – for .243 Win., .270 Win., .30-06, or .308 Win. cal.

$5,750 $5,000 $4,500 $4,250 $3,750 $3,300 $2,750

WIN M70 MEDIUM – .300 Win. Mag., 7mm Rem. Mag., or .338 Win. Mag. cal.

$6,750 $6,250 $5,500 $4,750 $4,000 $3,450 $2,950

WIN M70 MAGNUM – .375 H&H or .416 Rigby cal.

$7,000 $6,500 $5,650 $4,850 $4,100 $3,550 $3,000

WIN M52 – .22 LR cal.

$5,000 $4,500 $4,000 $3,400 $3,100 $2,700 $2,400

WIN HIGHWALL

$4,500 $4,150 $3,800 $3,500 $3,150 $2,850 $2,500

SPRINGFIELD 1903

$4,950 $4,400 $3,750 $3,450 $3,150 $2,800 $2,550

GRADING - PPGS™	100%	98%	95%	90%	80%	70%	60%	LAST MSR
SPRINGFIELD 1922								
	$4,500	$4,100	$3,650	$3,350	$3,000	$2,750	$2,500	
MAUSER STANDARD								
	$5,750	$5,000	$4,500	$4,250	$3,750	$3,300	$2,750	
MAUSER MAGNUM								
	$9,850	$9,000	$8,500	$7,850	$6,850	$5,950	$4,950	
SAVAGE 99								
	$3,500	$3,175	$2,850	$2,550	$2,250	$2,000	$1,850	

G&H PRE-'64 MODEL 70 CLASSIC SYNTHETIC STOCK – most popular cals., features glass bedded synthetic classic sporter stock in black or woodgrain finish, Douglas premium barrel, "Griffin & Howe, New York" barrel address, custom order. Disc. 2002.

	$4,750	$4,450	$4,000	$3,700	$3,500	$3,300	$3,100	*$2,250*

SHOTGUNS: O/U

MADISON – 12, 20, 28 ga., or .410 bore, case hardened frame, 26 1/2, 28, or 30 in. VR barrels, scroll engraved with gold accents. Mfg. by the Belgian Browning custom shop using a B25 action, 1999-2006.

	$9,000	$8,250	$7,750	$7,150	$6,450	$5,500	$4,500	*$9,750*

CLAREMONT – 12 ga. only, case hardened frame, shallow frame BOSS style lock-up, 30 in. VR barrels standard, scroll engraving with gold accents. Mfg. by Gamba beginning 1999.

MSR $8,750	$8,000	$7,500	$7,100	$6,250	$5,750	$5,000	$4,300

EXTRA FINISH CLAREMONT – similiar to Claremont, except has coin finished frame with full coverage acanthus scroll engraving and drop out trigger group. Importation began 1999.

MSR $11,500	$10,800	$9,950	$8,500	$7,300	$6,500	$5,700	$5,200

CLAREMONT LUSSO – similar to Extra Finish Claremont, except has fully engraved sideplates. Importation began 2000.

MSR $18,000	$17,250	$16,750	$14,800	$12,000	$10,250	$9,000	$8,000

BROADWAY – 12 or 20 ga., case hardened frame, 26, 28, or 30 in. VR barrels, scroll engraving with gold accents. Mfg. by the Belgian Browning custom shop using a B125 action, 1999-2003.

	$5,750	$5,250	$4,600	$4,150	$3,650	$2,950	$2,550	*$5,750*

SUPERBRITTE – 12 or 16 ga., unique side opening design, built by Britte company in Liege, Belgium before WWII, purchased by G&H in 2001.

	$32,000	$29,000	$25,750	$23,500	$21,250	$18,500	$16,750	*$25,000*

BLACK RAM – 12 or 20 ga., boxlock action, inertial cocking system, single bolt locking system, SST, 30 or 32 in. barrels with Briley chokes, traditional checkered Turkish walnut stock with pistol grip and recoil pad, 8 1/4 lbs. Mfg. by Zoli, importation began 2007.

MSR $5,450	$4,950	$4,500	$4,000	$3,500	$3,000	$2,500	$2,000

SILVER RAM – 12 or 20 ga., boxlock action, inertial cocking system, single bolt locking system, SST, 30 or 32 in. barrels with Briley chokes, traditional checkered Turkish walnut stock with pistol grip and recoil pad, game scene engraving, 8 1/4 lbs. Mfg. by Zoli, importation began 2007.

MSR $8,450	$7,750	$6,700	$5,900	$5,100	$4,300	$3,600	$2,950

SHOTGUNS: SxS

ROUND BODY GAME GUN – 12, 16, 20, 28 ga., or .410 bore, case colored round frame with sidelock action, "SAFE" in gold, H&H style selective ejectors, 25-30 in. barrels, double triggers, checkered straight grip stock and splinter forearm, G&H name inlaid in gold, cased (optional 2004). Mfg. by Arrieta, importation began 1989.

MSR $5,950	$5,500	$5,100	$4,750	$4,150	$3,600	$3,100	$2,500

Add $500 for 20 ga., $900 for 28 ga. or .410 bore.

Add $1,150 for single trigger.

GRADING - PPGS™	100%	98%	95%	90%	80%	70%	60%	LAST MSR

* ***Round Body Game Guns Pair*** – 12, 16, 20, 28 ga. or .410 bore, scroll engraved with case colored hardened finish, "SAFE" in gold, round sidelock action, H&H style selective ejectors, 25-30 in. barrels, double triggers, checkered straight grip and splinter forearm, G&H name inlaid in gold, built as a pair, and gold numbered 1 & 2 on barrels, forend, and top lever. Mfg. by Arrieta.

MSR $12,950 $11,950 $10,500 $9,500 $8,500 $7,650 $6,850 $6,000

Add $1,000 for pair of 20 ga.

Add $3,000 for assisted opening.

EXTRA FINISH ROUND BODY GAME GUN – same action as Round Body Game Gun, except has coin finished frame and game scene engraving with gold accents, upgraded wood. Importation began 1999.

MSR $8,950 $8,300 $7,850 $7,200 $6,400 $5,600 $4,900 $4,000

Add $800 for 20 ga. or $1,000 for 28 ga. or .410 bore.

Add $1,150 for single trigger.

* ***Extra Finish Round Body Game Guns Pair*** – built as a pair, gold numbered 1 & 2 on barrels, forend, and top lever.

MSR $19,750 $18,500 $16,500 $14,750 $13,500 $11,500 $9,750 $8,500

Add $1,250 for pair of 20 ga.

Add $3,000 for assisted opening.

BRITTE – 12 ga. only, best quality sidelock ejector, built by Britte company in Liege, Belgium before WWII, purchased by G&H in 2001.

$13,750 $12,900 $11,700 $10,500 $9,250 $8,400 $7,500 ***$15,000***

CONTINENTAL SIDELOCK – 12 ga. only, best quality Britte action, finished by current Belgian gunmakers such as Lebeau-Courally, various scroll patterns, case colored or bright finish, finest European walnut stock. Disc. 2006.

$17,000 $15,000 $13,100 $11,000 $9,250 $8,300 $6,900 ***$18,500***

* ***Continental Sidelocks Pair*** – 12 ga. only, built as a pair, gold numbered 1 & 2 on barrels, forend, and top lever. Disc. 2006.

$35,500 $31,400 $28,750 $26,750 $23,500 $19,500 $17,750 ***$38,500***

TRADITIONAL GAME GUN – 12, 16, 20, 24, 28 ga., or .410 bore, square body action, color case hardened with bright brush finish, DT, seven pin lock assemblies, 29 in. barrels with IC/Mod chokes, English style straight checkered Turkish walnut stock, available with optional game scene engraving, 6 3/4 lbs. Importation began 2007.

MSR $7,500 $6,750 $5,900 $5,100 $4,300 $3,600 $3,100 $2,650

Add $750 for 20 ga.

Add $825 for 28 ga. or .410 bore.

Add $3,000 for game scene engraving.

* ***Traditional Game Gun Pair*** – 12 and 16 ga.

MSR $16,000 $14,500 $13,250 $12,000 $10,000 $8,950 $7,750 $7,000

Add $3,000 for assisted opening.

Add $1,500 for 20 ga.

Add $6,000 for game scene engraving.

GRIFFON

Previously manufactured until 2003 by Continental Weapons (Pty) Ltd. established in 1996, and located in Midrand, Johannesburg, South Africa. Previously imported and distributed by Griffon USA, Inc., a subsidiary of 21st Century Technologies, Inc., located in Ft. Worth, TX, and by First Defense International located in San Clemente, CA.

PISTOLS: SEMI-AUTO

GRIFFON 1911 A1 COMBAT – .45 ACP cal., patterned after the Colt M1911, single action,

GRADING - PPGS™	100%	98%	95%	90%	80%	70%	60%	LAST MSR

4.13 in. barrel, 7 shot mag., ported barrel/slide, black Teflon finish, Commander hammer, tritium sights, 36.5 oz. Mfg. 1997-2003.

	$445	$375	$335	$300	$275	$250	$225	

GRIFFON CW 11 – 9mm Para. cal., 8 shot mag., 4 in. barrel without porting, combo blue/chrome finish, perforated trigger, 3 dot sighting system. Mfg. 1997-2003.

	$445	$375	$335	$300	$275	$250	$225	

GRISEL, H.L.

Previous custom rifle manufacturer located in Bend, OR.

H.L. "Pete" Grisel co-founded Dakota Arms in 1986, and was a founding member of the American Custom Gunmakers Guild. He built many custom rifles using actions of various types, including six using his own proprietary action. Grisel designed the Dakota 76 action and built some of Dakota's early guns, including the Leupold 40th anniversary rifle. Grisel also designed the Kimber Model K770 bolt action prototype, which Kimber never put into production. Grisel retired from gunmaking circa 2006-2007. Since Grisel guns were essentially custom made, each gun should be evaluated individually in order to determine value and shootability.

GRULLA ARMAS

Current manufacturer located in Eibar, Spain since 1932. Currently imported by Harry Marx Hi-Grade Imports, located in Los Banos, CA. Previously imported and distributed until 2009 by Merkel USA, located in Trussville, AL, Fieldsport, located in Traverse City, MI, Lion Country Supply, located in Port Matilda, PA, and by Dale's Decoy Den, located in Nelsonville, OH.

Grulla Armas manufactures a complete line of quality SxS shotguns in addition to both SxS and bolt action rifles.

RIFLES

C-95 BOLT ACTION – .270 Win. Mag., 7mm Rem. Mag., .300 Win. mag., .338 Win. Mag., .375 H&H, or .416 Rigby cal., deluxe bolt action featuring extensively scroll engraved square bridge receiver with elongated upper tang, K98 action, octagon barrel with quarter rib and express sights, 4 shot mag., drilled and tapped, hand finished deluxe checkered wood with ebony forend tip, custom made per individual order. New 1996.

Current retail is $16,995.

E-95 SxS DOUBLE RIFLE – various cals., top-of-the-line double rifle utilizing H&H type sidelocks with customer choice of engraving, forged steel action with matte finish, skeleton steel buttplate, chopper lump barrels, ejectors, DT, beavertail forend, exhibition grade select walnut with hand rubbed oil finish, gold oval with initials, custom-made per individual order, includes case. New 1996.

Current retail is $24,395. The H&H engraved model retails for $30,995.

SHOTGUNS: SxS, SIDELOCK

The following models are currently available in 12, 16, 20, 28 ga., or .410 bore. All guns have double triggers with hinged front, selective auto-ejectors, and straight grip stock with splinter forearm. Values represent standard models with no options.

MODEL 209 - HOLLAND – choice of case colored, antique silver, or coin finished receiver, scroll engraving, hand rubbed oil finish stock, 27 or 28 in. chopper lump barrels, gas escape valves. Importation disc. 2008.

Current retail is $8,995.

MODEL 215 – similar to Model 209, except has rose and scroll engraving and nicer wood.

Current retail is $9,295.

MODEL 216 – 12, 16, 20, 28 ga. or .410 bore, color case hardened or old silver coin finished reciever, round or traditional action, Bellota steel chopper lump barrels, ejectors, Purdey style rose and scroll engraving, DT, hand rubbed oil finished figured checkered walnut stock and forearm, five pin sidelock mechanism with double safety sears.

Current retail is $9,650.

GRADING - PPGS™	100%	98%	95%	90%	80%	70%	60%	LAST MSR

MODEL 216RB – round body version of the Model 216, similar Purdey style rose and scroll engraving, upgraded wood stock.

Current retail is $9,995.

MODEL 216RL – 12, 20, or 28 ga., round body, H&H style sidelocks, deluxe checkered straight grip walnut stock and forearm, 28 in. chopper lump barrels, 6-7.1 lbs. Imported 2004-2009.

	$9,250	$8,400	$7,600	$6,850	$6,400	$5,500	$4,750	

Add $1,000 for Elite Model.

This model was imported exclusively by Merkel USA.

MODEL 216 RL SUPREME – 12, 16, 20, 28 ga., or .410 bore, features drop forged round body steel frame, disc strikers, H&H style assisted self-opening action, ejectors, case colored receiver, chopper lump barrels, articulated DT, seven-pin sidelock mechanisms with intercepting sears and cocking indicators, best quality Exhibition oil finished walnut stock and forearm, includes leather covered trunk style fitted case. Imported 2008-2009.

	$16,500	$13,500	$10,750	$8,750	$7,500	$6,500	$5,750	

MODEL 216SL – 12, 16, 20 ga., or .410 bore, 28 in. barrels, H&H style sidelock, DT, ejectors, straight grip English stock, luxury grade wood, coin finished receiver with hand engraved Purdey style rose and scroll.

	$9,250	$8,400	$7,600	$6,850	$6,400	$5,500	$4,750	

Add $400 for 28 ga. or .410 bore.

MODEL 217RB – various gauges., game gun, 3 in. chambers, flat file rib, 10 in. semi-beavertail forearm, select wood.

	$7,200	$6,200	$5,200	$4,350	$3,650	$3,150	$2,600	*$7,995*

Add $300 for 28 ga. or .410 bore.

MODEL 219 – features more elaborate engraving and better wood.

	$5,325	$4,950	$4,000	$3,550	$2,950	$2,475	$1,995	*$6,050*

MODEL 219-P

	$7,050	$6,225	$5,600	$4,850	$4,100	$3,200	$2,600	*$7,750*

CONSORT – 12, 16, 20, 28 ga. or .410 bore, case colored or old silver coin finished receiver, chopper lump barrels, H&H style assisted opening action, DT, five pin sidelocks with double safety sears, silver oval with customer initials, light scroll engraving coverage, straight grip exhibition grade checkered walnut stock.

Current retail is $12,195.

WINDSOR – similar to Consort Model, except has more engraving.

Current retail is $12,795.

Add $3,100 for Windsor Woodcock model.

SUPER MH – best quality sidelock with Purdey style engraving, seven pin H&H lock, H&H style assisted opening, chrome nickel steel barrels, fitted leather case, select XXX walnut stock, deluxe hand rubbed oil finish.

	$11,400	$9,500	$8,475	$7,425	$6,200	$5,000	$4,150	*$12,395*

NUMBER 1 – next to the top-of-the-line gun with best quality features.

	$13,175	$10,625	$8,800	$7,575	$6,350	$5,150	$4,200	*$15,550*

ROYAL – 12, 16, 20 , 28 ga. or .410 bore, top-of-the-line model with H&H, Purdey, or Churchill style scroll engraving, seven pin H&H lock, H&H style assisted opening, traditional or round body action, choice of color case hardened or old silver finish, ejectors, chrome nickel steel barrels, fitted leather case, select exhibition grade hand rubbed oil finished walnut stock, gold oval with customer's initials.

Current retail for H&H Model is $24,695, Purdey is $25,795, and Royal is $26,995.

SUPREME – 12, 16, 20, 28 ga. or .410 bore, special style round body forged steel action, ejectors, H&H style assisted opening, chopper lump nickel chromium steel barrels, DT, seven pin sidelocks with intercepting sears and cocking indicators, case colored finish,

GRADING - PPGS™	100%	98%	95%	90%	80%	70%	60%	LAST MSR

exhibition grade hand rubbed oil finished straight grip checkered walnut stock, includes truck style fitted case.

Current retail is $24,395.

GRUND, KARL

Current rifle manufacturer located in Ferlach, Austria. No current U.S. importation.

Karl Grund manufactures high quality custom double rifles in a variety of configurations, including drillings and express rifles. Please contact him for more information, including pricing, U.S. availability, or a price quotation (see Trademark Index).

GRÜNIG & ELMIGER AG

Current rifle manufacturer located in Malters, Switzerland. Currently represented in the U.S. by Gunsmithing, Inc., located in Colorado Springs, CO, Champion's Choice, located in Lavergne, TN, and by Brenzovich Firearms Training Center, located in Ft. Hancock, TX.

Grünig & Elmiger AG is a third generation Swiss company that manufactures both rimfire and centerfire high quality competition and sporter rifles in various configurations. Numerous options and accessories are available. Please contact the U.S. representatives directly for current U.S. availability and pricing (see Trademark Index).

GUERINI, CAESAR

Please refer to Caesar Guerini in the C section.

GUN 1

Previous trademark owned by Savage Arms, Inc.

RIFLES

GUN 1 SERIES – .22 LR cal., 16 (Junior) or 19 (Youth) in. barrel, short LOP, Accutrigger. Mfg. 2008.

$180	$165	$150	$140	$130	$120	$110	*$213*

Add $9 for 19 in. barrel.

* ***Gun 1 Series Youth Centerfire*** – .243 Win. cal., 22 in. barrel, Accutrigger, similar to Gun 1 Series, short LOP. Mfg. 2008.

$550	$495	$450	$400	$350	$300	$250	*$605*

GUN ROOM CO., LLC

Please refer to the Only Long Range listing in the O section.

GUN WORKS, LTD.

Previous manufacturer and distributor located in Buffalo, NY. Early guns were made in Tonawanda, NY.

HANDGUNS

X-CALIBER – .44 Mag. cal., single shot, tip up pistol, 8 in. barrel, matte type blue finish, ergonomic hardwood grips, probably used older Sterling Arms parts and restamped the barrel address. Limited mfg.

$350	$300	$260	$230	$200	$175	$150	

MODEL 9 – .357 Mag., 9mm Para., .38 Super, or .38 Spl. cal., O/U derringer, electroless nickel finish, 2 1/2 in. barrel, wood grips, Millett sights, 15 oz. Disc. 1986.

$135	$120	$105	$95	$65	$55	$50	*$149*

GUNCRAFTER INDUSTRIES

Current pistol manufacturer located in Huntsville, AR.

PISTOLS: SEMI-AUTO

MODEL NO. 1 – .45 ACP or .50 GI cal., 1911 style, 7 shot mag., 5 in. heavy match grade barrel, parkerized or hard chrome finish, front strap checkering, Heinie Slant Pro tritium

GRADING - PPGS™	100%	98%	95%	90%	80%	70%	60%	LAST MSR

sights, Aluma checkered grips, includes two mags. and cordura case, 41.3 oz.

MSR $2,985	$2,750	$2,325	$2,000	$1,775	$1,575	$1,350	$1,075	

Subtract $300 for .45 ACP cal. "American" model.

MODEL NO. 2 – .45 ACP or .50 GI cal., 1911 style, 7 shot mag., 5 in. heavy match grade barrel, full profile slide with dust cover frame, integral light rail, parkerized or hard chrome finish, front strap checkering, Heinie Slant Pro tritium sights, Aluma checkered grips, includes two mags. and cordura case, 45.9 oz.

MSR $2,985	$2,750	$2,325	$2,000	$1,775	$1,575	$1,350	$1,075	

MODEL NO. 3 – .50 GI cal., similar to Model No. 1, except has Commander style frame. New 2010.

MSR $2,985	$2,750	$2,325	$2,000	$1,775	$1,575	$1,350	$1,075	

PISTOL WITH NO NAME – .45 ACP cal., similar to Model No. 3, available with 5 in. or 4 1/2 in. barrel. New 2010.

MSR $2,495	$2,250	$1,970	$1,690	$1,530	$1,240	$1,015	$790	

GUNSMOKE

Current manufacturer and gunshop with gunsmithing services located in Wheat Ridge, CO. Consumer direct sales.

Gunsmoke manufactures custom order firearms built per individual customer specifications. Additionally, Gunsmoke offers a complete line of gunsmithing services. Please contact the company directly for more information, availability, and pricing (see Trademark Index).

GUNSMOKE ENTERPRISES

Current manufacturer located in Okeechobee, FL.

Gunsmoke Enterprises manufactures AR-15 style pistols, rifles and carbines, as well as match grade rifles. Please contact the company directly for more information (see Trademark Index).

GUNWERKS

Current rifle manufacturer located in Cody, WY.

RIFLES: BOLT ACTION

Many options are available, including caliber, muzzle brakes, left hand action, etc. Please contact the company directly for a quotation on these custom made rifles.

LR LIGHTWEIGHT (LR-800) – various cals., custom action, one piece bolt and side bolt release, target trigger, match grade contoured lightweight stainless steel barrel, synthetic stock with recoil pad, includes case.

Base price on this model is $5,250.

LR-1000 – various cals., precision action, positive extractor, side bolt release, Jewell trigger, long range style stock in black or grey synthetic, includes all weather case.

Base price on this model is $4,500.

GUSTAF, CARL

Please refer to Carl Gustaf listing in the C section.

GYROJET

See MBA Gyrojet listing in the M Section of this text.

H SECTION

HHF

Please refer to the Huglu section.

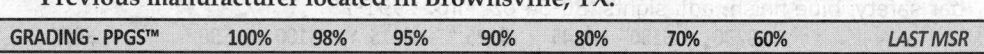

H.J.S. INDUSTRIES, INC.

Previous manufacturer located in Brownsville, TX.

GRADING - PPGS™	100%	98%	95%	90%	80%	70%	60%	LAST MSR

DERRINGERS

FRONTIER FOUR – .22 LR cal., 4 shot derringer, stainless steel construction, 5 1/2 oz.

$115	$90	$80	$75	$70	$60	$50	

LONE STAR – .38 S&W cal., single shot derringer, stainless steel construction, 6 oz.

$137	$105	$95	$80	$75	$65	$50	

HMS PRÄZISIONSTECHNIK GmbH

Current bolt action rifle manufacturer located in Eugendorf, Austria.

RIFLES: BOLT ACTION

STRASSER RS 05 – .243 Win., 6.5x55mm, .270 Win., .30-06, 7x64Rmm, .308 Win., 8x57Rmm, 8.5x63mm, 9.3x62mm, 7mm Rem. Mag. or .300 Win. Mag. cal., 22 or 24 in. barrel, 2 or 3 shot mag., Dr. Horst J.E. Blaser's latest straight pull design featuring ultra short bolt action, with or w/o deep relief engraved sideplates, front sling swivel, interchangable barrels, silent firing pin block safety, breech bolt locks directly into the barrel, ergonomic mag. release, right or left hand ejection, removable trigger group, all metal open sights, integral scope mount, dust cover, available in Standard, Premium, Deluxe (all with sideplates), Consul I, II, or III (non-sideplates) configurations, 7 - 7 1/4 lbs.

Please contact the company directly for more information on this model, including pricing, delivery time, and U.S. availability (see Trademark Index).

H & R 1871, LLC. (HARRINGTON & RICHARDSON)

Current trademark with headquarters located in Madison, NC, beginning 2008. Currently manufactured by Remington in Ilion, NY beginning early 2011. Previous manufacturer with production facilities and corporate headquarters located in Gardner, MA 1991-2008. During 2000, Marlin Firearms Co. purchased the assets of H&R 1871, Inc., and the name was changed to H&R 1871, LLC.

H & R 1871, LLC utilizes the original H & R trademark and does not accept warranty work for older (pre-1986 mfg.) Harrington & Richardson, Inc. firearms. Distributor sales only.

The use of the original Harrington & Richardson trademark was permitted during 1991. All new manufacture will use this trademark, but older H & Rs manufactured by Harrington & Richardson, Inc. are not the responsibility of H & R 1871, LLC.

REVOLVERS

Additional revolvers using the New England Firearms trademark may be located in the N section. During 1997-1999, all H & R 1871, Inc. revolvers were supplied with a lockable plastic case.

929 SIDEKICK – .22 LR cal., 9 shot, blue metal, swing-out cylinder, 4 in. heavy barrel, square butt with brown laminate grips, fixed sights, 30 oz. Mfg. 1996-99.

$150	$120	$100	$85	$75	$65	$55	*$173*

* ***929 Sidekick Trapper Edition*** – similar to 929 Sidekick, except has grey laminate grips and special barrel markings, limited mfg. 1996 only, distributed through 1996.

$150	$115	$95	$85	$75	$65	$55	*$175*

939 PREMIER WESTERN TARGET – .22 LR cal., 9 shot, blue metal, swing-out cylinder, target model with ribbed 6 in. heavy barrel and adj. rear sight, hardwood grips, 36 oz. Mfg. 1995-99.

$150	$125	$105	$90	$75	$65	$55	*$190*

GRADING - PPGS™	100%	98%	95%	90%	80%	70%	60%	LAST MSR

FOURTY-NINER (WESTERN 949) – .22 LR cal., 9 shot fixed cylinder, case colored frame, 5 1/2 or 7 1/2 in. barrel, hardwood grips, fixed sights, approx. 37 oz. Mfg. 1995-99.

	$150	$125	$105	$90	$75	$65	$55	*$190*

SPORTSMAN 999 – .22 LR cal., single or double action, top break action with auto shell ejection, 9 shot, 4 or 6 in. barrel with fluted solid rib, smooth hardwood stocks, transfer bar safety, blue finish, adj. sights, 30-34 oz. Mfg. 1991-99.

	$230	$180	$145	$125	$115	$100	$90	*$285*

RIFLES: SINGLE SHOT

H&R 1871 began providing the Trigger Guardian trigger locking system beginning Dec. 1, 1999 at no extra charge. During 2008, H&R 1871 reintroduced its Ultragon rifling on its rifled slug barrels, which feature six oval lands and grooves w/o sharp corners. All H&R models are built in the U.S.A.

ULTRA HUNTER MODEL – .22 WMR (mfg. 2002-2007), .22-250 Rem. (disc. 1994), .223 Rem. (disc. 1997, reintroduced 2002-2008), .25-06 Rem. (mfg. 1995-2008), .243 Win. (disc. 2008), .270 Win. (mfg. 2005-2006), .30-06 (mfg. 2005-2007), .308 Win. (mfg. 1995-2008), .357 Rem. Max. (mfg. 1996-98), .450 Marlin (mfg. 2001-2004), .45-70 Govt. (new 2008), 7x57mm (mfg. 1997 only), or 7x64mm (mfg. 1997 only) cal., single shot break-open action with ejector, side-lever release, 22 in. heavy (.22-250 Rem. or .223 Rem.), 22 in. normal (.22 WMR, .308 Win. or .450 Marlin), 24 in. bull (.223 Rem. or .243 Win. cal., new 2006) or 26 in. (.25-06 Rem.) steel or stainless (new 2008) barrel with scope mount rail, checkered curly maple (disc. 1994), laminated cinammon hardwood Monte Carlo stock with black line recoil pad (disc. 2008), or thumbhole stock (new 2008), sling swivel studs, 7-8 lbs. New 1993.

MSR $517	$445	$375	$325	$265	$230	$195	$160
Cals. other than .45-70	$325	$275	$235	$200	$175	$150	$125

Subtract approx. 10% for metric cals. (disc.).

This model featured a scope rail on .25-06 Rem. and .308 Win. cals.

* ***Ultra Model .22 Mag.*** – .22 WMR cal. only, 22 standard or 24 in. heavy (disc.) in. barrel. Disc. 2008.

	$150	$125	$105	$90	$85	$80	$75	*$183*

* ***Ultra Model Varmint*** – .204 Ruger (mfg. 2005-2009), .22-250 Rem. (new 2005), .223 Rem., .243 Win. (disc. 2004, reintroduced 2006), .25-06 Rem., or .308 Win. cal., features heavy 24 in. fluted (mfg. 2005-2009) or unfluted barrel, blue finish, natural finish cinnamon laminate Monte Carlo stock with (new 2008) or w/o thumbhole, or skeletonized black synthetic stock (new 2005, fluted barrel only, disc. 2010), includes scope mount rail, 7 lbs. New 1998.

MSR $381	$330	$275	$240	$210	$185	$160	$140

Add $73 for thumbhole stock (.22-250 Rem., .223 Rem., or .243 Win. cal. only).

Add $44 for fluted barrel and skeletonized stock (disc. 2010).

Subtract approx. 15% if w/o fluted barrel.

* ***Ultra Model Comp.*** – .270 Win. or .30-06 cal., features 23 in. barrel with integral compensator, blue finish, multi-color checkered laminate wood stock and forearm. Approx. 7-8 lbs. Mfg. 1997-2003.

	$310	$240	$195	$150	$125	$105	$95	*$376*

* ***Ultra Model Rocky Mountain Elk Foundation Commemorative 1st Ed.*** – .280 Rem. cal., 26 in. blue barrel, features RMEF medallion in stock, high gloss bluing, 7-8 lbs. Mfg. 1995-96.

	$220	$175	$135	N/A	N/A	N/A	N/A	*$270*

* ***Ultra Model Rocky Mountain Elk Foundation Commemorative 2nd Ed.*** – .35 Whelen cal., 26 in. blue barrel, features RMEF medallion in multi-color laminate stock and forearm, high gloss bluing, 7-8 lbs. Mfg. 1996-97.

	$260	$215	$160	N/A	N/A	N/A	N/A	*$300*

GRADING - PPGS™	100%	98%	95%	90%	80%	70%	60%	LAST MSR

HANDI-MAG – 7mm Rem. Mag. or .300 Win. Mag. cal., blued receiver, 26 in. stainless barrel w/o sights, black polymer synthetic Monte Carlo stock, includes scope mount rail, approx. 7 1/2 lbs. Mfg. 2008.

	$265	$225	$165	$135	$120	$110	$100	*$319*

WHITETAILS UNLIMITED COMMEMORATIVE RIFLE – .30-30 (new 1998) or .45-70 Govt. cal., Topper style break-open action, 22 in. barrel, blue frame with special etching, checkered American walnut stock (with medallion) and forearm. 7 lbs. Mfg. 1997-98.

	$250	$210	$170	N/A	N/A	N/A	N/A	*$290*

BUFFALO CLASSIC – .45 LC (new 2007) or .45-70 Govt. cal., top lever break open action, 20 (.45 LC cal.) in. barrel with carbine front sights or 32 in. barrel with Williams rear receiver and Lyman front target sights with aperture inserts, case hardened frame, checkered walnut stock and forearm, 8 lbs. New 1995.

MSR $479	$420	$365	$315	$265	$230	$200	$180	

This model was also produced under the Wesson & Harrington trademark.

TARGET RIFLE – .38-55 WCF cal., 28 in. heavy barrel, target sights, blue finish 7 1/2 lbs. Mfg. 1998-2007.

	$345	$280	$230	$180	$145	$125	$105	*$395*

This model was also produced under the Wesson & Harrington trademark.

HANDI-RIFLE – .204 Ruger, .22-250 Rem., .223 Rem., .243 Win. (new 2009), .25-06 Rem., .270 Win. (disc.), .280 Rem. (disc. 2011), .30-30 Win., .30-06, .35 Whelen (new 2010), .308 Win., .444 Marlin, .45-70 Govt., 7mm-08 Rem., or .500 S&W cal., break open single shot action, 22 or 26 in. regular or bull barrel, blue receiver, regular or Monte Carlo walnut stained hardwood stock, scope mount rail or ramp front and adj. rear sights, sling swivels, 7 lbs. New 2008.

MSR $314	$270	$235	$200	$165	$140	$120	$100	

Add $46 for 3-9x32mm scope (.223 Rem. or .243 Win. cal. only).

* ***Handi-Rifle Compact*** – .243 Win. or 7mm-08 Rem. cal., break open single shot action, 22 in. blue barrel, blue receiver, walnut stained hardwood stock, no sights, hammer extension, scope mount rail, sling swivels, 7 lbs. New 2008.

MSR $314	$270	$235	$200	$165	$140	$120	$100	

Add $46 for 3-9x32mm scope (.243 Win. cal. only).

* ***Handi-Rifle Synthetic*** – .22 Hornet, .223 Rem., .243 Win., .270 Win., .30-06, .35 Whelen (new 2010), .357 Mag., .44 Rem. Mag., .444 Marlin, or .45-70 Govt. cal., 22 in. barrel, blue finish, features black synthetic stock and forearm, adj. sights on some cals., drilled and tapped, scope base mount only on others, 7 lbs. New 2008.

MSR $323	$280	$240	$200	$165	$140	$120	$100	

* ***Handi-Rifle Synthetic Handi-Grip*** – .204 Ruger, .22-250 Rem., .223 Rem., .25-06 Rem., .243 Win., .45-70 Govt., or .308 Win. cal., 22, 24 (heavy), or 26 in. barrel, ambidextrous synthetic thumbhole stock, black finish. New 2010.

MSR $341	$290	$245	$205	$170	$150	$135	$120	

* ***Handi-Rifle Synthetic Stainless*** – .270 Win., .30-06, 7mm Rem. Mag. or .300 Win. Mag. cal., similar to Handi-Rifle Synthetic, features 22 or 26 in. matte stainless steel barrel with matte blue or nickel finished receiver, 7 lbs. Mfg. 2008.

	$255	$200	$160	$120	$80	$70	$60	*$319*

HANDI-RIFLE/SLUG COMBO SERIES – includes 12 (disc.) or 20 ga. Slug barrel with 3 in. chamber and choice of 22 in. .243 Win., .270 Win., or .30-06 barrel, 22 (available with compact stock and .243 Win. only), 24 (disc.) or 26 (new 2010) in. rifled slug barrel, black synthetic stock, blue finish, hammer extension. Mfg. 2009-2011.

	$315	$260	$225	$200	$170	$150	$135	*$350*

SUPERLIGHT HANDI-RIFLE – .223 Rem. or .243 Win. cal., break open single shot, 20 or 22 in. barrel, black synthetic stock and forearm, drilled and tapped, blue finish, Compact model with 11 3/4 in. LOP became standard during 2010. New 2008.

MSR $323	$280	$240	$200	$165	$140	$120	$100	

Add $37 for 3-9x32mm mounted and bore sighted scope (.243 Win. cal., Youth only).

GRADING - PPGS™	100%	98%	95%	90%	80%	70%	60%	LAST MSR

SPORTSTER – .17 HMR (new 2002), .17 Mach 2 (mfg. 2005-2007), .22 LR, or .22 WMR (new 2001) cal., 20 (mid-weight) or 22 (.17 HMR cal. only, heavy) in. barrel with Weaver style scope rail, no iron sights, available in either adult or youth (.22 LR cal. only) dimensions, black polymer stock and forearm. New 1999.

MSR $217	$175	$145	$120	$100	$85	$75	$65	

SURVIVOR – .223 Rem. or .308 Win. cal., similar in design to the Survivor Series shotgun, removable forearm for ammo storage, thumbhole design with storage compartment, no iron sights, 22 or 24 in. bull barrel, blue finish, scope mount rail, 6 lbs. New 2008.

MSR $327	$275	$235	$190	$160	$135	$110	$100	

SHOTGUNS: O/U

PINNACLE – 12 or 20 ga., 3 in. chambers, boxlock action, 26 (12 ga.) or 28 (20 ga.) in. vent. rib barrels with choke tubes, SST, ejectors, checkered walnut pistol grip stock with fluted comb, vent. recoil pad, bead front sight, 6 3/4 lbs. Limited importation 2005 only.

	$675	$525	$450	$400	$365	$335	$295	*$886*

SHOTGUNS: SEMI-AUTO

In 2008, H&R 1871 decided to import all semi-auto shotguns under its New England Firearms trademark. Please refer to this section for currently imported semi-auto shotguns.

EXCELL AUTO 5 – 12 ga., 3 in. chamber, 28 in. VR barrel with choke tubes, 5 shot mag., black synthetic, walnut, or Realtree Advantage Wetlands 100% camo covered pistol grip stock with fluted comb, vent. recoil pad, bead front sight, approx. 7 lbs. Mfg. 2005-2007.

	$300	$250	$210	$180	$160	$140	$120	*$374*

Add $29 for walnut stock or $82 for 100% camo coverage (Waterfowl model).

* ***Excell Auto 5 Turkey*** – 12 ga., 3 in. chamber, 5 shot mag., 22 in. vent. rib barrel with choke tubes and fiber optic sights, Realtree Advantage Hardwoods camo covered pistol grip stock and barrel, 7 lbs. Mfg. 2005-2007.

	$395	$345	$300	$265	$230	$195	$170	*$456*

* ***Excell Auto 5 Combo*** – includes 24 in. rifled slug barrel and 28 in. regular barrel, synthetic stock only. Mfg. 2005-2007.

	$425	$380	$330	$290	$260	$230	$200	*$512*

SHOTGUNS: SINGLE SHOT

H&R 1871 began providing the Trigger Guardian trigger locking system beginning Dec. 1, 1999 at no extra charge.

TOPPER (098) – 12, 16 (mfg. 1992-2007), 20, 28 (mfg. 1992-95, reintroduced 1998-2005) ga., or .410 bore, 2 3/4 (16 and 28 ga.) or 3 in. chamber, 26 or 28 in. fixed choke barrel, break open side lever release action, transfer bar safety, ejector, satin nickel frame with blue barrel, black finish hardwood stock with full pistol grip and forearm, 5-6 lbs. Mfg. 1991-2011.

	$140	$110	$95	$80	$70	$60	$50	*$161*

Add $24 for screw-in choke on 12 ga. only (Topper Deluxe).

* ***Topper 3 1/2 in.*** – 12 ga. only, 3 1/2 in. chamber, satin nickel frame with blue barrel, 28 in. barrel with 1 choke tube, black finish hardwood stock (with recoil pad) and forearm, 5-6 lbs. Mfg. 1991-2008.

	$125	$110	$90	$75	$60	$50	$40	*$164*

* ***Topper Deluxe Classic*** – 12 or 20 (new 2005) ga., 3 in. chamber, 26 (20 ga. only, mfg. 2005-2010) or 28 (12 ga. only) in. VR barrel with Mod. choke tube, matte nickel plated receiver, checkered American walnut pistol grip stock and forearm with recoil pad, 6-7 lbs. Mfg. 2004-2011.

	$200	$175	$145	$120	$95	$80	$70	*$238*

* ***Topper Deluxe Rifled Slug Gun*** – 12 ga. only, 3 in. chamber, 24 in. compensated barrel, rifle sights, dark American hardwood stock and forearm, satin nickel frame, approx. 5 1/2 lbs. Mfg. 1996-99.

	$150	$115	$95	$85	$75	$65	$55	*$170*

GRADING - PPGS™	100%	98%	95%	90%	80%	70%	60%	LAST MSR

* ***Topper Jr.*** – 20 ga. or .410 bore, smaller variation of the Topper 098 with youth dimensions including 22 in. fixed choke barrel and shortened hardwood stock with recoil pad, satin nickel frame with blue barrel, 12 1/2 in. LOP, 5-6 lbs. Mfg. 1991-2011.

	$145	$120	$100	$80	$70	$60	$50	*$169*

* ***Topper Jr. Classic*** – 20, 28 (disc. 2004) ga., or .410 bore, 22 in. fixed choke barrel, checkered American black walnut stock and forearm, recoil pad, 12 1/2 in. LOP, 5-6 lbs. Mfg. 1991-2011.

	$175	$150	$125	$100	$90	$80	$70	*$208*

* ***Topper Trap*** – 12 ga., 3 in. chamber, 30 in. VR barrel with IM extended choke tube, checkered walnut stock and forearm with decelerator recoil pad, nickel finished receiver with blue barrel, 7 lbs. Mfg. 2008-2011.

	$365	$315	$265	$225	$200	$180	$160	*$416*

* ***Topper NWTF Turkey Mag.*** – 10 (mfg. 1996 only) or 12 (mfg. 1991-95) ga., 3 1/2 in. chamber, 24 in. drilled and tapped barrel with 1 choke tube, entire gun is covered in Mossy Oak camo, includes sling and swivels, 6 lbs. Mfg. 1991-96.

	$145	$120	$100	$85	$75	$65	$55	*$180*

This model was part of the National Wild Turkey Federation (NWTF) sponsorship program.

* ***Topper 1994 NWTF Youth Turkey Gun*** – 20 ga., 3 in. chamber, 22 in. full choke barrel, features Realtree camo finish and sling, limited mfg. 1994-95.

	$140	$110	$95	$85	$75	$65	$55	*$160*

* ***Topper 2000 NWTF/Youth Edition*** – 12 or 20 ga., 3 in. chamber, 20 ga. is NWTF Youth Edition with 22 in. barrel, camo finished laminate stock and forend with NWTF laser engraved frame, includes sling and swivels. Mfg. 2000-2004.

	$175	$130	$115	$95	$80	$70	$60	*$207*

Add $9 for NWTF Edition - 12 ga. with 24 in. barrel.

THE TAMER – 20 ga. (new 2007) or .410 bore, 3 in. chamber, synthetic thumbhole stock is designed to hold 3 or 4 shells, transfer bar system, 19 or 20 (20 ga. only) in. full choke barrel, electroless nickel finish, 6 lbs. New 1994.

MSR $223	$185	$150	$125	$100	$85	$75	$65	

SB1-920 ULTRA SLUG HUNTER – 20 ga. only, utilizes 12 ga. action and barrel that has been under-bored to 20 ga. and fully rifled, hardwood Monte Carlo stock and forearm, matte black frame. Mfg. 1996-disc.

	$190	$155	$125	$100	$85	$75	$65	*$225*

ULTRA SLUG HUNTER – 12 or 20 ga., 3 in. chamber, 22 (20 ga., Youth Model) or 24 in. fully rifled heavy barrel, side-release lever, black Monte Carlo hardwood stock with recoil pad, matte finished frame, 8-9 lbs. New 1995.

MSR $291	$250	$215	$175	$140	$110	$90	$80	

Add $46 for 3-9x32mm scope (new 2007).
Add $3 for 20 ga. (standard stock or Youth model).

* ***Ultra Slug Hunter Deluxe*** – similar to Ultra Slug Hunter, except has checkered camo laminate wood and scope mount rail (scope optional), adj. rear sight. New 1997.

MSR $359	$320	$280	$230	$200	$175	$150	$125	

Add $4 for 20 ga.

* ***Ultra Light Slug Hunter*** – 12 or 20 ga., 3 in. chamber, 24 in. rifled barrel w/o sights, blue finish, walnut stained hardwood stock and forearm, 5 1/4 lbs. New 2008.

MSR $290	$240	$195	$170	$150	$125	$100	$85	

Add $3 for 20 ga.

* ***Ultra Slug Hunter Thumbhole*** – 12 or 20 ga., 3 in. chamber, features colored laminate thumbhole stock and forearm, 24 in. rifled barrel w/Weaver rail type scope base, blue finish, 8 1/2 lbs. New 2008.

MSR $401	$355	$295	$265	$230	$200	$180	$160	

GRADING - PPGS™	100%	98%	95%	90%	80%	70%	60%	*LAST MSR*

WHITETAILS UNLIMITED RIFLED SLUG GUN – 12 ga., 3 in. chamber, 24 in. fully rifled heavy barrel, hand checkered Monte Carlo black laminate stock and forend, Whitetails medallion, hammer extension, swivels and sling. Mfg. 1998-99.

	$220	$185	$145	$120	$100	$85	$75	*$255*

PARDNER – 12, 20, 28 ga., or .410 bore, 2 3/4 (28 ga.) or 3 in. chamber, single shot, break open action, safety transfer bar mechanism on hammer, side lever release, color case hardened receiver, 14 in. LOP, 26, 28, or 32 (12 ga. only, new 2009) in. barrel, fixed or mod. choke tube (12 or 20 ga. only, with black synthetic stock and forearm), extractor, walnut stained hardwood or black synthetic (disc., 12 or 20 ga. only) stock and forearm, 5-6 lbs. New 2008.

MSR $156	$125	$100	$85	$75	$65	$55	$45	

Add $19 for 32 in. barrel (12 ga. only).
Add $23 for modified choke tube with black synthetic stock and forearm (12 or 20 ga. only, disc. 2009).

* ***Pardner Compact (Youth)*** – 20, 28 (disc. 2011) ga., or .410 bore, similar to Pardner, except has 22 in. barrel and straight grip stock with recoil pad, 12 1/2 in. LOP, 5-5 1/2 lbs. New 2008.

MSR $175	$140	$120	$95	$75	$65	$55	$45	

Add $12 for modified choke tube (20 ga. only with black synthetic stock and forearm, disc. 2009).

* ***Pardner Turkey Gun*** – 10, 12, or 20 (Youth only) ga., 3 (20 ga.) or 3 1/2 in. chamber, 22 (20 ga.) or 24 in. barrel with fixed or full choke tube, camo or matte black wood finish, 5 1/2 - 9 lbs. New 2008.

MSR $227	$185	$150	$125	$110	$95	$85	$75	

Add $95 for 10 ga. with camo wood finish.
Add $10 for Mossy Oak Break-Up camo in 12 ga. with full choke bore (disc. 2009).

* ***Pardner Waterfowl*** – 10 ga., 3 1/2 in. chamber, 30 or 32 in. barrel, blue barrel and receiver, walnut or Mossy Oak Break Up camo (disc.) finish on stock and forearm, recoil pad, 9 1/2 lbs. Mfg. 2008-2009.

	$185	$150	$125	$100	$85	$65	$55	*$228*

SURVIVOR – .410 ga./.45 LC cal., 3 in. chamber, 20 in. barrel with screw-in modified choke, blue or nickel finish, black synthetic stock with open pistol grip, 6 lbs.

MSR $327	$250	$210	$180	$160	$135	$115	$100	

Add $20 for nickel finish.

TRACKER II SLUG MODEL – 12 or 20 ga., 3 in. chamber, 24 in. rifled slug barrel, 14 in. LOP, walnut finished hardwood stock, adj. iron sights, 5 1/4 lbs. New 2008.

MSR $291	$240	$195	$165	$130	$110	$90	$80	

Add $44 for Tracker II 12 ga. Slug Gun/Huntsman .50 cal. black powder muzzleloader (disc. 2002).

SHOTGUNS: SLIDE ACTION

PARDNER PUMP – 12 or 20 ga., 3 in. chamber, 18 1/2 (no rib), or 26 or 28 in. VR barrel with choke tube, choice of walnut or black synthetic stock and forearm. New 2008.

MSR $227	$185	$165	$145	$130	$120	$110	$100	

Add $27 for walnut stock and forearm.

* ***Pardner Pump Compact*** – 20 ga. only, 3 in. chamber, 21 in. VR barrel with choke tube features compact stock dimensions. New 2008.

MSR $227	$185	$165	$145	$130	$120	$110	$100	

H-S PRECISION, INC.

Current custom pistol and rifle manufacturer established 1990 and located in Rapid City, SD. H-S Precision, Inc. also manufactures synthetic stocks and custom machine barrels as well. Dealer and consumer direct sales.

H-S Precision introduced the aluminum bedding block for rifle stocks in 1981, and has been making advanced composite synthetic stocks and custom ballistic test barrels for more than two decades.

In addition to the following models, H-S Precision, Inc. also built rifles using a customer's

GRADING - PPGS™	100%	98%	95%	90%	80%	70%	60%	LAST MSR

action (mostly Remington 700 or Winchester Post-'64 Model 70). 2004 MSRs ranged from $1,520-$1,830.

PISTOLS: SINGLE SHOT

PRO-SERIES 2000 VP/SP – various cals., stainless steel receiver, 15 in. fluted stainless steel barrel, 3 position safety, laminated composite Pro-Series stock, Teflon coated receiver and barrel, choice of varmint (VP, no sights) or silhouette (SP, drilled and tapped for sights) configuration, choice of stock colors. New late 1997.

MSR $2,760	$2,325	$2,035	$1,750	$1,575	$1,275	$1,050	$815

RIFLES: BOLT ACTION, PRO-SERIES 2000

All H-S Precision rifles feature Kevlar/graphite laminate stocks, cut rifle barrels, and other high tech innovations including a molded aluminum bedding block system. Beginning in 1999, H-S Precision began utilizing their H-S 2000 action, and model nomenclature was changed to begin with Pro-Series 2000.

Add approx. $170-$275 for left-hand action, depending on the model.

PRO-SERIES 2000 BENCH REST (BCR) – .22 PPC or 6 PPC cal., 20-26 in. fluted barrel, right hand short action only, Yellow/Black stock. New 2012.

MSR $3,580	$3,050	$2,675	$2,295	$2,075	$1,675	$1,375	$1,075

PRO-SERIES 2000 CLASSIC HUNTING RIFLE (CHR) – various long action cals., 20-26 in. fluted, w/o sights, right hand action only, internal blind box magazine, Tan/Black stock, approx. 7.1 lbs. New 2012.

MSR $3,710	$3,150	$2,750	$2,365	$2,140	$1,735	$1,425	$1,100

PRO-SERIES 2000 F CLASS RIFLE (FCR) – 6.5x284 cal., 20-26 in. fluted barrel, short or long action, Black/Red stock, approx. 9.3 lbs. New 2012.

MSR $3,580	$3,050	$2,675	$2,295	$2,075	$1,675	$1,375	$1,075

PRO-SERIES 2000 VARMINT TAKEDOWN (VTD) – various cals., accurized Remington Model 700 receiver (disc. 1999) or H-S 2000 action (new 2000), H-S stainless steel cut rifled and fluted barrel, 5 or 10 shot detachable mag, Teflon coated metal Urban camo finish, approx. 8.9 lbs. New 1997.

MSR $4,950	$4,600	$4,200	$3,600	$3,200	$2,750	$2,250	$1,750

Add $100 for extended barrel port (Model VTD EP, disc.).
Add $2,750 - $3,300 for extra take-down barrel, depending on cartridge case head size.

PRO-SERIES 2000 SPORTER/VARMINT (VAR/SPR/SPL) – various short and long action cals., Remington ADL action only, each rifle is built per individual specifications, fluted barrel became standard 2006. New 1990.

MSR $3,250	$2,750	$2,400	$2,065	$1,875	$1,515	$1,240	$965

Add $145 for 2000 Varmint VAR model.
Add $245 for 2000 SPL model (lightweight, 7 lbs.).
Add $100 for extended barrel port (Model VAR/SPR EP, disc.).
Add $880 for extra stainless barrel (disc.).

PRO-SERIES 2000 PRO-HUNTER RIFLE (PHR) – available in 10 Safari cals., 24 or 26 in. fluted stainless steel barrel with cut rifling, Teflon finish, Pro-Series sporter stock, long action only.

MSR $3,555	$3,000	$2,625	$2,250	$2,040	$1,650	$1,350	$1,050

Add $2,500 - $3,000 for extra take-down barrel, depending on head size.

PRO-SERIES 2000 PRO-HUNTER LIGHTWEIGHT (PHL) – short action only, various cals. including WSM, 20 or 22 in. fluted barrel, Teflon coated action and barrel, green/tan camo stock, 5 1/2 lbs. New 2004.

MSR $3,705	$3,150	$2,750	$2,365	$2,140	$1,735	$1,420	$1,100

PRO-SERIES 2000 PRO-HUNTER TAKEDOWN (PTD) – various cals., features takedown action and 20 or 22 in. fluted barrel with muzzle brake, Sand finish, approx. 9.4 lbs. New 2012.

MSR $5,000	$4,625	$4,200	$3,600	$3,200	$2,750	$2,250	$1,750

GRADING - PPGS™	100%	98%	95%	90%	80%	70%	60%	LAST MSR

PRO-SERIES 2000 LONG RANGE (HEAVY TACTICAL MARKSMAN, HTR) – various cals., stainless fluted barrel standard, Remington BDL (disc. 1999) or Pro-Series 2000 (new 2000) action. New 1990.

MSR $3,580	$3,050	$2,675	$2,295	$2,075	$1,675	$1,375	$1,075	

Add $20 for Heavy Tactical Model.
Add $100 for extended barrel port (Model HTR EP, disc.).

PRO-SERIES 2000 SHORT TACTICAL (STR) – .308 Win. cal., 20 in. fluted barrel, matte Teflon finished action and barrel, 20 in. fluted barrel with standard porting, Pro Series Tactical stock. New 2004.

MSR $3,600	$3,050	$2,675	$2,295	$2,075	$1,675	$1,375	$1,075	

PRO-SERIES 2000 TAKEDOWN TACTICAL LONG RANGE (TTD) – various short and long action cals., stainless steel barrel, Remington BDL takedown action, matte blue finish. Mfg. 1990-2005, reintroduced 2008.

MSR $5,500	$4,995	$4,500	$4,100	$3,700	$3,200	$2,750	$2,250	

Add $100 for extended barrel port (Model TTD EP, disc.).
Add $2,500 - $3,000 for extra take-down barrel, depending on cartridge case head size.

PRO SERIES 2000 RAPID DEPLOYMENT RIFLE (RDR) – .308 Win. cal., Pro-Series 2000 stainless steel short action only, 20 in. fluted barrel, black synthetic stock with or w/o thumbhole, black teflon metal finish, approx. 7 1/2 lbs. New 2000.

MSR $3,395	$2,875	$2,525	$2,150	$1,950	$1,575	$1,295	$1,000	

Add $205 for RDT model (new 2006).
Add $125 for PST60A Long Range stock (disc.).

TAKEDOWN LONG RANGE (TACTICAL MARKSMAN) – .223 Rem., .243 Win., .30-06, .308 Win., 7mm Rem. Mag., .300 Win. Mag., or .338 Win. Mag. cal., includes "kwik klip" and stainless fluted barrel. Mfg. 1990-97.

	$2,895	$2,225	$1,675	$1,350	$995	$850	$750	*$2,895*

A complete rifle package consisting of 2 calibers (.308 Win. and .300 Win. Mag.), scope and fitted case was available for $5,200 retail.

HWP INDUSTRIES

Previous manufacturer located in Milwaukee, WI circa 1989.

REVOLVERS

THE SLEDGEHAMMER – .500 HWP Mag. cal., 5 shot revolver, double action, stainless steel, full shrouded 4 in. barrel (quick change), Pachmayr grips. Limited mfg. 1989 only.

	$1,150	$895	$750	$640	$535	$450	$390	*$1,295*

HAENEL, C.G. (OLD MFG.)

Previous firearms and airguns manufacturer located in Suhl, Germany 1840-1946.

The firm was originally established by Carl Gustav Haenel. Herbert Haenel, grandson of the firm's founder, ran the organization from his father's death in 1917 until the firm was taken over by government decree on July 24, 1946. After the second World War, Haenel was disowned without compensation by the so-called "Thueringer Gesetz". At the same time the name of the company was stricken from the register and became a part of VEB Ernst-Thaelmann. The firm's old plant then operated under the name Ernst-Thaelmann-Werke VEB until Germany was re-united.

During 1840-WWII, C.G. Haenel manufactured a variety of sporting longarms, mostly concentrating on bolt action rifles, drillings, and SxS shotguns. Some of these guns are extremely well executed, and must be appraised individually. If quality, condition, and overall desirability are at a level similar to pre-war Sauers, Krieghoffs, etc., Haenel values could be similar to the trademarks just mentioned. However, a standard grade Haenel rifle/shotgun/drilling, in an obscure metric caliber with no engraving in 70% or less original condition, gets priced for its utilitarian shooting value as opposed to adding a collector premium.

For more information and current values on Haenel, C.G., airguns, please refer to the *Blue*

GRADING - PPGS™	100%	98%	95%	90%	80%	70%	60%	LAST MSR

Book of Airguns by Dr. Robert Beeman & John Allen (also online).

The author would like to thank Mr. Dietrich Apel and the German Gun Collectors Association for providing the company history.

PISTOLS: SEMI-AUTO

SCHMEISSER MODEL 1 & 2 – .25 ACP cal., similar to Baby Browning.

$500 $400 $300 $275 $230 $200 $180

MODELS 200-205 – see Hämmerli-Walther.

RIFLES: BOLT ACTION

MAUSER-MANNLICHER SPORTING RIFLE – 7x57mm, 8x57Rmm, or 9x57Rmm cal., Model 88 Mauser type action, 22 or 24 in. octagon barrel, Mannlicher box mag., double set triggers, raised rib on barrel, leaf sight, sporter stock.

$775 $700 $625 $575 $525 $475 $425

MODEL 1900 – metric cals., features round receiver, mag. guide reinforcement, separate ejector housing, latch release on floorplate.

$900 $800 $700 $625 $575 $525 $475

MODEL 1909 – metric cals., round receiver bridge, bolt does not have a guide rib, two-piece ejector/bolt stop housing, push button mag. release on left side of trigger guard, no dovetail guiding on cocking piece.

$1,100 $925 $800 $700 $625 $575 $525

HAENEL, C.G., GmbH (NEW MFG.)

Current trademark established during 2006 and manufactured by various gunmakers/craftsmen from the Suhl Arms Alliance, located in Suhl, Germany.

During 2006, the Suhl Arms Alliance was founded by a group of industrial manufacturers and gunsmithing craftspeople located in Suhl, Germany. All guns manufactured by this alliance are proofed in the Suhl firearms proof house.

Currently manufactured Haenel trademarked guns include a Jaeger.10 bolt action rifle, Model SLB2000+ semi-auto rifle, Jaeger.9 single shot rifle, Jaeger.810 O/U combination gun, Jaeger.811 O/U shotgun, Jaeger 11 O/U shotgun, an RS8 and RS9 tactical rifle utilizing a modular design. Please contact the company directly for more information including U.S. availabilty and pricing (see Trademark Index).

HAKIM

Previous trademark of rifle adopted by the Egyptian army during the early 1950s.

RIFLES: SEMI-AUTO

HAKIM – 7.92x57mm or 8x57mm cal., gas operated, 25.1 in. barrel with muzzle brake, cocking the bolt is done by sliding the top cover forword, then pulling it back, manual safety is located in rear of receiver, 10 shot detachable box mag., can also be reloaded using stripper clips, adj. rear sight, hardwood stock, 9.7 lbs. Approx. 70,000 mfg. circa 1950s-1960s, with Swedish machinery.

$495 $450 $400 $360 $320 $285 $245

A scaled down variation of the Hakim rifle was manufactured later, and called the Rasheed - it was produced in small numbers.

HALO ARMS, LLC

Current rifle manufacturer established in 2003, and located in Phoenixville, PA. Dealer and consumer direct sales.

Halo Arms also manufactures custom alloy stocks.

RIFLES

Halo Arms, LLC manufactures good quality AR-15 style rifles in commercial, military, and law enforcement configurations.

GRADING - PPGS™	100%	98%	95%	90%	80%	70%	60%	LAST MSR

HA 50 FTR SINGLE SHOT – .50 BMG cal., 22 in. chrome-moly barrel, special order only, matte black finish or optional colors, muzzle brake, vertical aluminum front grip, bipod, Picatinny rail, flip up front sights, rear iron sights, standard AR trigger, unique bottom load/eject operation.

MSR $4,350	$4,100	$3,850	$3,500	$3,150	$2,700	$2,400	$2,000	

Add $300 for deployment package, which includes Storm hard case, cleaning rods, and ammo pouch.

HA 50 LRR SINGLE SHOT – .50 BMG cal., long range rifle. Disc. 2008.

	$4,200	$3,900	$3,500	$3,150	$2,700	$2,400	$2,000	*$4,500*

HA 308 FTR BOLT ACTION – .308 Win. cal., field tactical rifle, 24 in. heavy contour chrome-moly barrel, 5 shot internal mag. with screw removable floorplate, three position safety, matte black finish or optional colors, Picatinny rail, right hand bolt and ejection port, full length vented free float tube with rail attachment points, hand tuned trigger, 11 1/2 lbs. Disc. 2009.

	$1,295	$1,100	$925	$800	$675	$575	$475	*$1,375*

F-BAR BOLT ACTION – .204 Ruger, .22-250 Rem., .223 Rem., .243 Win., or .308 Win. cal., matte black finish standard, custom colors available, 24 in. heavy contour chrome-moly barrel, 5 shot, full length vented free float tube, Picatinny rail, hand tuned trigger, 11 1/2 lbs.

MSR $1,455	$1,375	$1,200	$1,025	$900	$775	$650	$525	

Add $18 for tube Picatinny rail.
Add $25 for vertical grip or bipod mount.
Add $45 for monopod.

MAXIMUS BOLT ACTION – .416 Barrett or .50 BMG cal., 22 or 30 in. sporter contour chrome-moly target barrel, matte black finish standard, custom colors available, benchrest single shot, integral flat bottom, full length forearm, Picatinny rail, dual stock struts, muzzle brake, Jewell trigger, two-position safety, 25 lbs.

MSR $5,185	$4,750	$4,250	$3,600	$3,000	$2,500	$2,000	$1,625	

Add $18 for Picatinny rail forearm.
Add $25 for vertical grip.
Add $30 for bipod mount.
Add $55 for monopod.

M-BAR MONOLITH BOLT ACTION – .204 Ruger, .22-250 Rem., .223 Rem., .243 Win., or .308 Win. cal., matte black finish standard, custom colors available, 24 in. heavy contour chrome-moly barrel, 5 shot, Picatinny rail, hand tuned trigger, three position safety, 11 1/2 lbs.

MSR $1,395	$1,325	$1,175	$1,000	$875	$750	$650	$525	

Add $18 for tube Picatinny rail.
Add $25 for vertical grip or bipod mount.
Add $45 for monopod.

HAMBRUSCH JAGDWAFFEN GmbH

Current manufacturer established in 1752, and located in Ferlach, Austria. Previously imported and distributed exclusively by CONCO Arms, located in Emmaus, PA.

Hambrusch Jagdwaffen was a member of the Ferlach Gun Guild until it was dissolved in 2004. This company manufactures many types of high-grade long arms, including SxS shotguns, combination guns, drillings, double rifles, and single shot rifles. The combinations of these configurations are almost endless. During 2002, Hambrusch introduced a new proprietary big game cartridge, the .600/538 MM (Mega Magnum with 722 grain bullet). All guns are built per customer specifications. Please contact the company directly for more information, availability, and current pricing (see Trademark Index).

HÄMMERLI AG

Current trademark purchased during 2006 by Walther, and firearms are currently manufactured in Ulm/Donau, Germany beginning 2008. Previous manufacture was located in Lenzburg, Switzerland until late 2005. Currently imported by Umarex USA, located in Ft. Smith, AR. Currently distributed by Larry's Guns, located in Gray, ME, Brenzovich

GRADING - PPGS™	100%	98%	95%	90%	80%	70%	60%	LAST MSR

Firearms, located in Fort Hancock, TX, Champion's Choice, located in LaVergne, TN. Previously imported by SIG Arms Inc. located in Exeter, NH, Gunsmithing Inc., located in Colorado Springs, CO, Hämmerli Pistols USA, located in Groveland, CA, and by Beeman Precision Arms located in Santa Rosa, CA.

For more information and current pricing on both new and used Hämmerli airguns, please refer to the *Blue Book of Airguns* by Dr. Robert Beeman & John Allen (also online).

PISTOLS: SINGLE SHOT, RIMFIRE

Values listed below for recently manufactured pistols reflect older mfg. by Hämmerli in Lenzburg, Switzerland.

FP-10 FREE PISTOL – .22 LR cal., top-of-the-line Hämmerli pistol. Imported 2000-2004.

	$1,525	$1,200	$950	$850	$750	$650	$575	*$1,749*

MODEL 33MP – .22 LR cal., similar to the Model 100, except not available in a deluxe model. Mfg. 1933-49.

	$925	$725	$650	$550	$470	$440	$385

MODEL FP 60 – .22 LR cal., refined ergonomic design from the FP-10, 12 3/4 in. barrel, increased stability, adj. rear sight with integral front sight, many accessories available, approx. 2 1/2 lbs. Importation began 2005.

MSR N/A	$2,068	$1,675	$1,450	$1,275	$1,050	$875	$750

MODEL 100 FREE PISTOL – .22 LR cal., 11 1/2 in. octagon barrel, blue, martini action single shot, set trigger, micro rear sight, walnut stock and forearm. Mfg. 1950-56.

	$880	$660	$605	$550	$470	$440	$385

Add 15%-20% for Olympic rings, "London", and "1948" markings (indicative of Swiss shooting team).

* ***Model 100 Free Pistol Deluxe Model*** – carved stock.

	$990	$770	$715	$660	$580	$550	$495

MODEL 101 – similar to Model 100, but heavy round barrel, improved action and sights, matte finish. Mfg. 1956-60.

	$880	$660	$605	$550	$470	$440	$385

MODEL 102 – similar to Model 101, except high polished finish. Mfg. 1956-60.

	$880	$660	$605	$550	$470	$440	$385

* ***Model 102 Deluxe Model***

	$990	$770	$715	$660	$580	$550	$495

MODEL 103 FREE PISTOL – similar to Model 101, except lighter octagon polished barrel. Mfg. 1956-60.

	$935	$715	$660	$605	$580	$550	$495

MODEL 104 MATCH PISTOL – similar to Model 103, except lighter round barrel, redesigned stock, mfg. 1961-65.

	$760	$660	$550	$495	$470	$440	$385

MODEL 105 MATCH PISTOL – similar to Model 103, except redesigned action and stock, octagon barrel. Mfg. 1962-65.

	$935	$715	$660	$605	$580	$550	$495

MODEL 106 MATCH PISTOL – similar to Model 105, except improved trigger.

	$910	$690	$580	$525	$495	$470	$415

MODEL 107 MATCH PISTOL – similar to Model 105, except improved trigger.

	$990	$770	$660	$550	$525	$495	$440

* ***Model 107 Match Pistol Deluxe model*** – engraved and carved wood.

	$1,320	$990	$880	$660	$635	$605	$550

GRADING - PPGS™	100%	98%	95%	90%	80%	70%	60%	LAST MSR

MODEL 120-1 SINGLE SHOT FREE PISTOL – .22 LR cal., bolt action, 9.9 in. barrel, blue barrel and receiver, side lever operated, anodized aluminum lever and frame, walnut checkered grips.

	$625	$550	$475	$425	$375	$325	$295	

MODEL 120-2 – similar to 120-1, except stocks hand contoured.

	$700	$600	$550	$475	$425	$375	$325	

MODEL 120 HEAVY BARREL – similar to 120-1, with 5.7 in. bull barrel, 1,000 mfg.

	$800	$700	$600	$550	$475	$425	$375	

This model was cased with test target and tools.

MODEL 150 FREE PISTOL – .22 LR cal., 11.3 in. barrel, improved Martini-type action, set trigger, innovative design incorporating many unusual features. Disc. 1989.

	$1,850	$1,495	$1,275	$1,120	$980	$900	$850	*$1,980*

Add $113 for left-hand variation.

The Model 150 was replaced by the Model 151.

MODEL 151 FREE PISTOL – replacement for the Model 150 Free Pistol. Imported 1990-93.

	$1,850	$1,495	$1,275	$1,120	$995	$900	$800	*$1,980*

MODEL 152 FREE PISTOL – .22 LR cal., 11.3 in. barrel. improved Martini-type action, electronic trigger release, innovative design incorporating many unusual features. State-of-the-art target pistol. Disc. 1992.

	$1,995	$1,600	$1,350	$1,195	$1,090	$990	$895	*$2,105*

Add $57 for left-hand variation.

MODEL 160 FREE PISTOL – .22 LR cal., similar to Model 150, except has poly-carbon fiber forend, includes carrying case. Mfg. 1993-2002.

	$1,725	$1,475	$1,175	$900	$800	$700	$595	*$1,850*

Add $290 for smaller adj. grips.

MODEL 162 FREE PISTOL – .22 LR cal., replacement for the Model 152 Free Pistol, includes poly-carbon fiber forend, includes carrying case. Imported 1993-2000.

	$2,150	$1,700	$1,375	$1,125	$900	$800	$700	*$2,410*

Add $290 for smaller adj. grips.

PISTOLS: SEMI-AUTO

Values listed below are for both pistols manufactured by Hämmerli in Lenzburg, Switzerland, and by Walther in Ulm/Donau, Germany (beginning 2008).

MODELS 200-205 – see Hämmerli-Walther.

INTERNATIONAL MODEL 206 – .22 Short or .22 LR cal., semi-auto, 7 1/16 in. barrel with muzzle brake, adj. sights, walnut grips, blue. Mfg. 1962-69.

	$675	$625	$525	$450	$395	$365	$330	

INTERNATIONAL MODEL 207 – similar to 206, except adj. grip heel.

	$725	$650	$550	$475	$425	$375	$350	

INTERNATIONAL MODEL 208 – .22 LR cal., 9 shot, 6 in. barrel, blue, adj. sights, checkered walnut grips with adj. heel. Mfg. 1966-88.

	$2,000	$1,700	$1,450	$1,150	$925	$825	$725	*$1,755*

This model was replaced by the Model 208S.

* ***International Model 208S*** – similar to Model 208, except has redesigned trigger guard and safety with interchangeable rear sight element. Imported 1988-2000.

	$2,450	$2,150	$1,750	$1,450	$1,150	$925	$825	*$2,021*

Add $125 for factory scope mount.

Add $180 for smaller adj. grips.

* ***International Model 208 Deluxe*** – similar to Model 208, except has carved grips and elaborate engraving. Importation disc. 1988.

	$2,995	$2,500	$1,995	$1,735	$1,495	$1,215	$1,000	*$3,250*

GRADING - PPGS™	100%	98%	95%	90%	80%	70%	60%	LAST MSR

* ***International Model 208C (Commemorative)*** – limited edition commemorative. Disc. 1987.

	$2,100	$1,750	$1,400	N/A	N/A	N/A	N/A	*$2,225*

INTERNATIONAL MODEL 209 – .22 Short cal., semi-auto, 5 shot, 4 3/4 in. barrel, muzzle brake, adj. sights, blue, walnut stock. Mfg. 1966-70.

	$800	$690	$635	$550	$525	$485	$440	

INTERNATIONAL MODEL 210 – similar to 209, but grips have adj. heel. Mfg. 1966-70.

	$800	$715	$660	$590	$540	$525	$495	

MODEL 211 – .22 LR cal., semi-auto, 9 shot, 6 in. barrel, adj. sights, blue, similar to Model 208 except non-adj. walnut stocks. Importation disc. 1990.

	$1,550	$1,275	$1,050	$950	$880	$835	$770	*$1,669*

MODEL 212 HUNTER – .22 LR cal., semi-auto, hunter's pistol, 9 shot, 5 in. barrel, adj. sights, blue, walnut stocks. Importation disc. 1993.

	$2,000	$1,800	$1,650	$1,400	$1,200	$850	$675	*$1,395*

MODEL 215 – .22 LR cal., semi-auto, commercial target version with Model 208 specifications, 9 shot, 5 in. barrel, adj. sights, blue, walnut stocks. Importation disc. 1990.

	$2,300	$1,950	$1,775	$1,550	$1,300	$1,150	$995	*$1,505*

Add $300 for Model 215S.

MODEL 230 RAPID FIRE PISTOL – .22 S cal., semi-auto, 5 shot, 6.3 in. barrel, blue, adj. sights, smooth walnut grips. Mfg. 1970-83.

	$705	$635	$580	$530	$485	$450	$415	

MODEL 230-2 – similar to 230, except checkered grips with adj. heel. Mfg. 1970-83.

	$735	$655	$605	$570	$515	$485	$470	

MODEL 232-1 RAPID FIRE PISTOL – .22 S cal., semi-auto, 6 shot, 5.1 in. barrel, blue, adj. sights, contoured walnut grips. Importation disc. 1993.

	$1,395	$1,125	$950	$850	$750	$700	$650	*$1,505*

Add $25 for wraparound grips sizes S-M-LG (Model 232-2).

MODEL 280 – .22 LR or .32 S&W Wadcutter cal., new modular pistol design utilizing carbon fiber synthetic material to replace frame and other critical parts, adj. grips, trigger, and rear sight, 4.6 in. barrel, 5 or 6 shot mag., approx. 2.2 lbs. Imported 1988-2000.

	$1,450	$1,125	$900	$800	$675	$575	$475	*$1,643*

Add $200 for .32 S&W Wadcutter cal.
Add $765 (.22 LR) or $965 (.32 S&W Wadcutter) for conversion kit.
Add $200 for smaller adj. grips.
A package was also available with both calibers, magazines, and hard case for $2,595.

MODEL SP 20 – .22 LR or .32 S&W Wadcutter cal., replacement for Model 280, features low-level sight line, colored alloy receiver (blue, red, gold, violet, or black), adj. "JPS" buffer system that varies recoil characteristics per individual preference, black Hi-Grip anatomical grips. New 1998.

MSR N/A	$1,749	$1,500	$1,325	$1,075	$925	$800	$700	

Add $246 for .32 S&W Wadcutter cal.
Add $499 for .22 LR conversion (disc.), $599 for .32 S&W Wadcutter conversion (disc.).

MODEL SP 20 RRS – .22 LR or .32 S&W Wadcutter cal., state-of-the-art target pistol featuring composite frame with redesigned ergonomic grips, RRS designates recoil reducing system, fully hand adj. rear sight, various slide colors available. Mfg. 2002-2005.

	$1,430	$1,250	$1,125	$1,025	$925	$825	$725	

Add $113 for .32 S&W Wadcutter cal.
Add $795 for .22 LR conversion, or $850 for .32 Wadcutter conversion.

MODEL P-240 – see SIG-Hämmerli for this model.

TRAILSIDE PL 22 – .22 LR cal., single action, 4 1/2 or 6 in. barrel, two-tone finish, choice of ultralight polymer composite grips or target variation which includes wood grips and adj.

GRADING - PPGS™	100%	98%	95%	90%	80%	70%	60%	LAST MSR

rear sight, 10 shot mag., cased with trigger lock, lower cost variation of the X-Esse, 28 or 30 oz. Imported exclusively by SigArms. Mfg. 1999-2006.

	$395	$350	$300	$275	$250	$225	$200	*$455*

Add $79 for 4 1/2 in. barrel with target sights, or $95 for 6 in. barrel with target sights.

This model was also available as one of SIG Arms' limited editions in Jan. 2004 - it included a BSA 30mm red dot optical sight with integrated mount and 6 in. barrel. Last MSR was $709.

* ***Trailside Competition*** – includes 6 in. barrel with blue anatomical stippled grips and adj. bottom rest, cased with trigger lock, 37.2 oz. Limited importation 2000-2005.

	$580	$500	$400	$350	$300	$265	$225	*$710*

X-ESSE – .22 LR cal., available in Sport, Long, and Short configurations, 4 1/2 or 6 in. barrel, polymer or anatomic stippled polymer target (Competition model) grips, adj. hand rest, 10 shot mag. Mfg. in the Walther factory located in Ulm beginning 2008. Importation began 2009.

MSR N/A	$699	$650	$575	$500	$450	$400	$365	

Add $50 for 6 in. target barrel.

Add $266 for Competition (Sport) Model with anatomic grips, adj. front and rear sights, and barrel weight.

Add $380 for IPSC variation with 6 in. barrel (standard grips).

RIFLES: BOLT ACTION, TARGET

OLYMPIC 300 METER – .30-06 cal., bolt action, single shot free rifle, U.S.A. import, 7x57mm overseas, 20 1/2 in. heavy barrel, double set trigger, aperture rear and globe front sight, free rifle stock with thumbhole pistol grip, beavertail forearm, Swiss style target butt. Mfg. 1945-59.

	$880	$745	$605	$550	$470	$440	$415	

HÄMMERLI-TANNER 300 METER FREE RIFLE – similar to Olympic 300, except 7.5x55mm standard, also was available in other calibers. Mfg. 1962-disc.

	$895	$825	$770	$715	$660	$580	$520	*$935*

MODEL 45 SMALLBORE MATCH RIFLE – .22 LR cal., bolt action, single shot, 27 1/2 in. heavy barrel, same sights and stock type as Hämmerli-Tanner. Mfg. 1945-57.

	$660	$550	$470	$440	$385	$360	$330	

MODEL 54 SMALLBORE MATCH RIFLE – similar to 45 Smallbore, except adj. butt. Mfg. 1954-57.

	$670	$560	$480	$450	$395	$370	$340	

MODEL S 205 – 6mm BR, 7.5x55mm, or .308 Win. cal., designed for 300 meter competition, adj. blue aluminum or wood stock, 5 shot mag., Hammerli aperture rear sight, Sauer produced 205 action with 26 in. heavy free floating barrel, 12 lbs. Mfg. 2004-2005.

	$3,995	$3,650	$3,300	$3,000	$2,650	$2,300	$1,850	

Add $723 for adj. aluminum stock.

MODEL 503 SMALLBORE FREE RIFLE – similar to 54 Smallbore, except free style stock.

	$660	$550	$470	$440	$385	$360	$330	

MODEL 505 MATCH RIFLE – match stock with aperture sights.

	$690	$580	$495	$470	$415	$385	$360	

MODEL 506 SMALLBORE MATCH RIFLE – similar to 503 Smallbore. Mfg. 1963-66.

	$690	$580	$495	$470	$415	$385	$360	

SPORTING RIFLE – various calibers, set triggers, Mauser repeating action.

	$725	$650	$490	$425	$360	$325	$300	

RIFLES: SEMI-AUTO

MODEL 22SA SPORT – .22 LR cal., 21 1/4 in. barrel, 17 shot tube mag., pistol grip uncheckered wood or synthetic stock, ambidextrous manual safety, adj. rear fiber optic sight, rubber recoil pad, 3.3 lbs.

While advertised, this model has yet to go into production.

GRADING - PPGS™	100%	98%	95%	90%	80%	70%	60%	LAST MSR

HÄMMERLI-WALTHER

Previously manufactured semi-auto target pistols made under joint effort from Hämmerli and Walther.

PISTOLS: SEMI-AUTO, RIMFIRE

MODEL 200 OLYMPIA – .22 Short or LR cal., 7 1/2 in. barrel, 1952 type, adj. sights, barrel weight, blue, checkered walnut grips. Mfg. 1952-58.

	100%	98%	95%	90%	80%	70%	60%
	$660	$605	$550	$440	$415	$385	$360

MODEL 200 OLYMPIA – 1958 type, similar to 1952 type, except has muzzle brake. Mfg. 1958-63.

	100%	98%	95%	90%	80%	70%	60%
	$715	$605	$550	$495	$470	$415	$385

MODEL 201 – similar to 200, 1952 type, except 9 1/2 in. barrel. Mfg. 1955-57.

	100%	98%	95%	90%	80%	70%	60%
	$660	$605	$550	$440	$415	$385	$360

MODEL 202 – similar to 201, except adj. heel grips. Mfg. 1955-57.

	100%	98%	95%	90%	80%	70%	60%
	$715	$605	$550	$495	$470	$415	$385

MODEL 203 – similar to 200, except has adj. heel grip.

* ***Model 203 1955 Type*** – no muzzle brake.

	100%	98%	95%	90%	80%	70%	60%
	$715	$605	$550	$495	$470	$415	$385

* ***Model 203 1958 Type*** – muzzle brake.

	100%	98%	95%	90%	80%	70%	60%
	$770	$660	$605	$550	$525	$470	$440

MODEL 204 – similar to 200, except .22 LR cal. only.

* ***Model 204 1956 Type*** – no muzzle brake.

	100%	98%	95%	90%	80%	70%	60%
	$745	$635	$580	$525	$495	$470	$440

* ***Model 204 1958 Type*** – muzzle brake.

	100%	98%	95%	90%	80%	70%	60%
	$800	$690	$635	$550	$525	$495	$470

MODEL 205 – .22 LR cal., similar to 204, except adj. heel grips.

* ***Model 205 1956 Type*** – no muzzle brake.

	100%	98%	95%	90%	80%	70%	60%
	$800	$690	$635	$550	$525	$495	$470

* ***Model 205 1958 Type*** – muzzle brake.

	100%	98%	95%	90%	80%	70%	60%
	$855	$745	$715	$635	$580	$525	$495

HARRINGTON & RICHARDSON, INC.

Previous manufacturer located in Gardner, MA - formerly from Worcester, MA. Successors to Wesson & Harrington, manufactured from 1871 until January 24, 1986. H & R 1871, LLC was formed during 1991 (an entirely different company, see listing in the front of this section). H & R 1871, LLC is not responsible for the warranties or safety of older pre-1986 H & R firearms.

A manufacturer of utilitarian firearms for over 115 years, H & R ceased operation on January 24, 1986. Even though new manufacture (under H & R 1871, LLC) is utilizing the H & R trademark, the discontinuance of older models in either NIB or mint condition may command slight asking premiums, but probably will not affect values on those handguns only recently discontinued. Most H & R firearms are still purchased for their shooting value rather than collecting potential. In recent years, Pre-1950s examples have become increasingly more collectible.

Further recent research indicates that many H&R frames were manufactured and stamped with serial numbers in the mid-1930s, but not assembled as complete guns until the WWII era. Therefore, H&R serial numbers alone will not always indicate the variation number.

Please refer to H & R listing in the Serialization section for alphabetical suffix information on how to determine year of manufacture for most H & R firearms between 1940-1982.

The author would like to thank Mr. Jim Hauff and the late Mr. W.E. "Bill" Goforth for providing pricing and information on many of the H&R models.

GRADING - PPGS™	100%	98%	95%	90%	80%	70%	60%	LAST MSR

HANDGUNS: 1871-1986

Single Action Spur Trigger Revolvers: 1871-1883

WESSON & HARRINGTON MARKED SINGLE ACTION SPUR TRIGGER (BLACK POWDER) – .22 Short, .32 rimfire, .38 rimfire, or .41 rimfire cal., 5 or 7 shot, 2 1/2 (Third type), 3 3/16 (First type, No. 3), or 3 1/2 in. octagon barrel, First type has brass frame silver-plated, patented cartridge ejector, birds-head grip frame, rosewood grips, Second type has iron frame nickel-plated patented cartridge ejector, birds-head grip frame, rosewood grips, Third type has iron frame nickel-plated birds-head grip frame, no cartridge ejector pull pin cylinder release. No. 2 is 7 shot, .22 Short, small frame, 3 3/16 in. octagon barrel, No. 3 is 5 shot, .32 rimfire cal., medium frame, 3 3/16 octagon barrel, No. 4 is 5 shot, .38 rimfire cal., large frame, 3 1/2 in. octagon barrel. Both First and Second type will be marked with Feb.7 and June 13, 1871 patent dates. Mfg. 1871-1876.

First Type (rare)	$1,200	$1,000	$865	$765	$660	$575	$495
Second Type No. 2, 3, & 4	$600	$520	$440	$390	$340	$285	$245
Third Type	$400	$350	$300	$265	$225	$190	$165

Add 50% for late production with Harrington & Richardson barrel markings.

H&R MODEL 1 SPUR TRIGGER SINGLE ACTION (BLACK POWDER) – .32 or .38 rimfire cal., 5 or 7 shot, pull pin cylinder release, 3 inch octagon barrel, birds-head grip frame, hard rubber grip panels, only slightly changed version of the Wesson & Harrington Third Type marked with patent date May 23, 1876. Mfg. 1876-1883.

$500	$440	$375	$325	$275	$235	$200

H&R SPUR TRIGGER SINGLE ACTION (BLACK POWDER) – pull pin cylinder release, nickel finish only, most will be marked with patent date May 23, 1876 and company name and address on left side of barrel, sometimes called 'New Design of 1878", saw handle grip. Mfg. 1878-1883.

Subtract 50%-70% for models not marked H&R.

The above model as well as modified Wesson & Harrington Models can be found marked with the following Brand Names: AETNA, VICTOR, BANGUP, CROWN, EAGLE, ELY & WRAY, GREAT WESTERN, PANTHER, SMOKY CITY and maybe more names.

* ***Model 1 1/2*** – .32 rimfire cal. 5 shot, 2 1/2 in. octagon barrel (actual barrel length may vary slightly), medium frame.

$400	$350	$300	$265	$225	$190	$165

* ***Model 2 1/2*** – .32 rimfire cal., 7 shot, 3 1/4 in. octagon barrel (actual barrel length may vary slightly), large frame.

$400	$350	$300	$265	$225	$190	$165

* ***Model 3 1/2*** – .38 rimfire cal., 5 shot, 3 1/2 in. octagon barrel (actual barrel length may vary slightly), large frame.

$400	$350	$300	$265	$225	$190	$165

* ***Model 4 1/2*** – .41 rimfire cal., 5 shot, 3 1/2 in. octagon barrel (actual barrel length may vary slightly), large frame, rare.

$700	$600	$525	$450	$385	$340	$285

Solid Frame Revolvers: 1880-1952

MODEL 1880 MEDIUM DOUBLE ACTION, (BLACK POWDER) – .32 or .38 centerfire cal., 5 or 6 shot, 2 1/2 in. round barrel, nickel finish, pull pin cylinder release, side plate on left side of frame, hard rubber grip panels with floral design, marked with patent date January 20, 1880 and company name and address on left side of barrel. Mfg. 1880-1883.

$550	$475	$415	$360	$315	$265	$230

AMERICAN DOUBLE ACTION FIRST MODEL, (BLACK POWDER) – .32, .38, or .44 cal., 5 (.38 or .44) or 6 (.32 cal.) shot, 2 1/2, 4 1/2, or 6 in. barrel, nickel (standard) or blue (rare) finish, pull pin cylinder release, marked on top strap "THE AMERICAN DOUBLE ACTION", first variation has round barrel and nickel trigger guard with rear retaining pin offset to rear slightly (1884 only), second variation has round barrel and nickel trigger

GRADING - PPGS™	100%	98%	95%	90%	80%	70%	60%	LAST MSR

guard (1884-1887), third variation has octagon barrel and nickel trigger guard (1888-1897), fourth variation has octagon barrel, blue trigger guard and company name and address on left side of barrel (1898-1904). Mfg. 1884-1904.

$225	$195	$170	$140	$125	$110	$95	

Add 50% for first variation (rare).
Add 15% for blue finish.
Add 10% for 4 1/2 or 6 in. barrel.
Add 5%-10% for nickel trigger guard (pre-1898 mfg.).

BULLDOG FIRST MODEL LARGE FRAME (BLACK POWDER) – .32 or .38 rimfire cal., 5 (.38 cal.) or 6 (.32 cal.) shot, 2 1/2, 4 1/2, or 6 in. barrel, variation of the American Double Action First Model marked on the top strap "H&R BULL DOG". Mfg. 1888-1904.

$235	$200	$180	$150	$125	$110	$95	

SAFETY HAMMER DOUBLE ACTION FIRST MODEL (BLACK POWDER) – .32, .38, or .44 cal., 5 (.38 or .44) or 6 (.32 cal.) shot, 2 1/2, 4 1/2, or 6 in. barrel, nickel (standard) or blue (rare) finish, patented spurless hammer, marked on top strap "SAFETY HAMMER DOUBLE ACTION". Mfg. 1888-1904.

$235	$200	$180	$150	$125	$110	$95	

AMERICAN DOUBLE ACTION SECOND MODEL (SMOKELESS POWDER) – .32, .38, or .44 Webley (disc. 1921) cal., 5 (.38 or .44 cal.) or 6 (.32 cal.) shot, 2 1/2, 4 1/2, or 6 in. barrel, nickel or blue finish, pull pin cylinder release, the difference between First Model and Second Model is the caliber markings on the left side of the barrel, .44 Webley has a larger frame, after 1930 this model was listed in catalogs as: AMERICAN DOUBLE ACTION No. 60 .32 Caliber 6 shot, and AMERICAN DOUBLE ACTION No. 65 .38 Caliber 5 shot. Mfg. 1905-1941.

$225	$195	$170	$140	$125	$110	$95	

Add 15% for blue finish or 10% for 4 1/2 or 6 in. barrel.

BULLDOG SECOND MODEL LARGE FRAME (SMOKELESS POWDER) – .32 or .38 rimfire cal., 5 (.38 cal.) or 6 (.32 cal.) shot, 2 1/2, 4 1/2, or 6 in. barrel, nickel or blue finish, variation of the American Double Action Second Model, except the top strap is marked "H&R BULL DOG". Mfg. 1905-1923.

$235	$200	$180	$150	$125	$110	$95	

SAFETY HAMMER DOUBLE ACTION SECOND MODEL (SMOKELESS POWDER) – .32, .38, or .44 Webley (disc. 1921) cal., 5 (.38 or .44 cal.) or 6 (.32 cal.) shot, 2 1/2, 4 1/2, or 6 in. barrel, nickel or blue finish, patented spurless hammer, patent date may be marked on hammer, and the top strap is marked "SAFETY HAMMER DOUBLE ACTION". Mfg. 1904-1940.

$235	$200	$180	$150	$125	$110	$95	

VEST POCKET FIRST MODEL MEDIUM FRAME (BLACK POWDER) – .32 S&W cal., 5 shot, 1 1/4 in. round or 2 in. octagon barrel (rare), double action, pull pin cylinder release, spurless hammer, blue (rare) or nickel finish, markings on top strap are "VEST POCKET SELF COCKER" "VEST POCKET SAFETY HAMMER" or "VEST POCKET". The First Variation has 1 1/4 in. round or 2 in. octagon barrel, nickel finish and nickel trigger guard (mfg. 1891-1897), the Second Variation has 1 1/4 in. round or 2 in. octagon barrel, nickel finish, and a blue trigger guard (mfg. 1897-1904). Mfg. 1891-1904.

$215	$195	$165	$135	$120	$100	$90	

Add 50% for 2 in. octagon barrel or 15% for blue finish.

VEST POCKET SECOND MODEL SMALL FRAME (SMOKELESS POWDER) – .22 rimfire cal., 7 shot, 1 1/4 in. round barrel, spurless hammer, nickel or blue finish, pull pin cylinder release, top strap markings are "VEST POCKET SAFETY HAMMER" or "VEST POCKET". The company name and address is marked on bottom of butt. After 1930 the catalog listing is: VEST POCKET No. 77 .22 rimfire caliber 7 shots. Mfg. 1905-1941.

$220	$190	$165	$140	$125	$110	$95	

Add 5% for blue finish.

See American Double Actions for the differences between the First and Second models.

GRADING - PPGS™	100%	98%	95%	90%	80%	70%	60%	LAST MSR

VEST POCKET SECOND MODEL MEDIUM FRAME (SMOKELESS POWDER) - .32 S&W cal., 5 shot, 1 1/4 in. round barrel, spurless hammer, medium frame, nickel or blue finish. Mfg. 1905-1941.

	$195	$175	$155	$125	$110	$95	$85	

Add 15% for blue finish.

This model is similar to the Small Frame model.

YOUNG AMERICA DOUBLE ACTION FIRST MODEL (BLACK POWDER) - .22 rimfire or .32 S&W cal., 2, 4 1/2, or 6 in. round or octagon barrel, small (.22 cal.) or medium (.32 cal.) frame, pull pin cylinder release, nickel or blue (rare) finish, marking on top strap only "YOUNG AMERICA DOUBLE ACTION" or "YOUNG AMERICAN DOUBLE ACTION". The First Variation has a round barrel and nickel trigger guard (mfg. 1884-1887), the Second Variation has an octagon barrel and nickel trigger guard (mfg. 1888-1897), Third Variation has octagon barrel, blue trigger guard and company name and address on left side of barrel (mfg. 1897-1904). Mfg. 1884-1904.

First Variation	$300	$275	$245	$210	$170	$145	$120	
Second & Third Variations	$250	$225	$195	$170	$140	$125	$110	

Add 15% for blue finish or 10% for 4 1/2 or 6 in. barrel.

YOUNG AMERICA SAFETY HAMMER FIRST MODEL (BLACK POWDER) - .22 rimfire or .32 S&W cal., 2, 4 1/2, or 6 in. round or octagon barrel, small (.22 cal.) or medium (.32 cal.) frame, nickel or blue (rare) finish, spurless hammer, pull pin cylinder release, top strap only is marked "YOUNG AMERICA DOUBLE ACTION" or "YOUNG AMERICAN DOUBLE ACTION". Mfg. 1884-1904.

	$235	$200	$180	$150	$125	$110	$95	

YOUNG AMERICA BULLDOG FIRST MODEL MEDIUM FRAME (BLACK POWDER) - .32 Short rimfire cal., 5 shot. Mfg. 1888-1904.

	$235	$200	$180	$150	$125	$110	$95	

YOUNG AMERICA DOUBLE ACTION SECOND MODEL SMALL FRAME (SMOKELESS POWDER) - .22 Short cal., 7 shot, 2, 4 1/2, or 6 in. barrel, pull pin cylinder release, nickel or blue finish, caliber and company name and address marked on side of barrel, top strap will be marked "YOUNG AMERICA DOUBLE ACTION" or "YOUNG AMERICAN DOUBLE ACTION". After 1930 listed in catalogs as: YOUNG AMERICA No. 70 DOUBLE ACTION. Mfg. 1905-1941.

	$250	$235	$200	$180	$150	$125	$110	

Add 15% for blue finish or 10% for 4 1/2 or 6 in. barrel.

See American Double Actions for the differences between the First and Second models.

YOUNG AMERICA DOUBLE ACTION SECOND MODEL MEDIUM FRAME (SMOKELESS POWDER) - .32 S&W cal., 5 shot, 2, 4 1/2 or 6 in. barrel, pull pin cylinder release, nickel or blue finish, caliber and company name and address marked on side of barrel, top strap will be marked "YOUNG AMERICA DOUBLE ACTION" or "YOUNG AMERICAN DOUBLE ACTION". After 1930 listed in catalogs as: YOUNG AMERICA No. 73 DOUBLE ACTION .32 Rimfire short 5 shot and YOUNG AMERICA No. 74 DOUBLE ACTION .32 S&W 5 shot. Mfg. 1905-1941.

	$250	$225	$195	$170	$140	$125	$110	

Add 15% for blue finish or 10% for 4 1/2 or 6 in. barrel.

See American Double Actions for the differences between the First and Second models.

YOUNG AMERICA BULLDOG MEDIUM FRAME SECOND MODEL (SMOKELESS POWDER) - .32 Rimfire cal., 5 shot. Mfg. 1905-1923.

	$225	$195	$170	$140	$125	$110	$95	

This model was only advertised as a separate model until 1923.

YOUNG AMERICA SAFETY HAMMER MEDIUM FRAME SECOND MODEL (SMOKELESS POWDER) - .32 S&W cal., 5 shot. Mfg. 1905-1939.

	$205	$185	$165	$130	$120	$100	$90	

This model was only advertised as a separate model until 1939.

GRADING - PPGS™	100%	98%	95%	90%	80%	70%	60%	LAST MSR

VICTOR (BRAND NAME VERSION OF AMERICAN DOUBLE ACTION AND YOUNG AMERICA DOUBLE ACTION SERIES, SMOKELESS POWDER) – .32 S&W Long or .38 S&W cal., 5 (.38 cal.) or 6 (.32 cal.) shot, 2 1/2 or 4 1/2 in. round barrel (Large Solid Frame), .32 S&W cal., 5 shot, 2 or 4 in. barrel (Medium Solid Frame Double Action), or .22 rimfire cal., 7 shot, 2 or 4 in. barrel (Small Solid Frame Double Action), marked "VICTOR DOUBLE ACTION" and have a round barrel and unfluted cylinder, pull pin cylinder release, and may have company name and address marked on frame or bottom of the butt (not listed in any H&R catalogs). Mfg. 1913-1936.

$195 $175 $155 $125 $110 $95 $85

MODEL 1904 LARGE SOLID FRAME DOUBLE ACTION (SMOKELESS POWDER) – .38 S&W cal., 5 shot, 2 1/2, 4 1/2 or 6 in. barrel, hard rubber target logo grips, pull pin cylinder release, blue or nickel finish, marked with company name and address on left side of the barrel and on top strap in two lines "H&R DOUBLE ACTION MODEL 1904 .38 CAL.", after 1930 listed in catalogs as: H&R MODEL 4 DOUBLE ACTION No. 83 .38 S&W CALIBER 5 shot. Mfg. 1905-1941.

$230 $195 $175 $150 $125 $110 $95

MODEL 04 LARGE SOLID FRAME DOUBLE ACTION – .32 S&W cal., 6 shot, 2 1/2, 4 1/2 or 6 in. barrel, pull pin cylinder release, blue or nickel finish, hard rubber target logo grips, marked with company name and address on left side of barrel and on top strap in two lines "H&R DOUBLE ACTION MODEL 04 .32 6 SHOT". After 1930 listed in catalogs as: H&R MODEL 4 DOUBLE ACTION No. 80 .32 S&W Long Caliber 6 shot. Mfg. 1905-1941.

$220 $190 $165 $140 $125 $110 $95

MODEL 1905 MEDIUM SOLID FRAME DOUBLE ACTION – .32 S&W cal., 5 shot, 2 1/2, 4 1/2, or 6 in. barrel, pull pin cylinder release, hard rubber target logo grips, blue or nickel finish, marked with company name and address on left side of barrel and on top strap in two lines "H&R DOUBLE ACTION MODEL 1905 .32 CAL." After 1930 listed in catalogs as: H&R MODEL 5 DOUBLE ACTION No. 90 .32 S&W CALIBER 5 shot. Mfg. 1905-1941.

$225 $195 $170 $140 $125 $110 $95

MODEL 1906 SMALL SOLID FRAME DOUBLE ACTION – .22 rimfire cal., 7 shot, 2 1/2, 4 1/2, or 6 in. barrel, hard rubber target logo grips, blue or nickel finish, marked with the company name and address on left side of barrel and on top strap in two lines "H&R MODEL 1906 22 CAL. R.F." After 1930 listed in catalogs as: H&R MODEL 6 DOUBLE ACTION No. 96 .22 RF CALIBER 7 shot. Mfg. 1905-1941.

$185 $165 $140 $120 $100 $90 $80

TRAPPER SMALL SOLID FRAME DOUBLE ACTION – .22 rimfire cal., 7 shot, 6 in. octagon barrel, two-piece oversize walnut grips, pull pin cylinder release, blue finish only, marked "H&R TRAPPER" on the top strap. After 1930 listed in catalogs as: TRAPPER MODEL 722 SMALL SOLID FRAME DOUBLE ACTION .22 RIMFIRE 7 shot. Mfg. 1924-1941.

$365 $315 $275 $225 $200 $165 $140

HUNTER SMALL SOLID FRAME DOUBLE ACTION – .22 rimfire cal., 7 shot, 2 1/2 (rare), or 10 in. octagon barrel, also mfg. with round frame (rare), two piece oversize walnut or small two-piece target logo hard rubber (2 1/2 in. barrel only) grips, pull pin cylinder release, blue finish only, marked "H&R HUNTER" on the top strap, some with the "HUNTER" marking were assembled late in production with short 2 1/2 inch barrel and the small two piece Target Logo hard rubber grips. Mfg. 1926-1929.

$475 $425 $355 $300 $260 $220 $195

HUNTER LARGE SOLID FRAME DOUBLE ACTION – .22 rimfire cal., 9 shot, (built on the M922 frame), 10 in. octagon barrel only, pull pin cylinder release, blue finish only, two-piece oversize walnut grips, marked on top strap "H&R HUNTER" or just "HUNTER". After 1930 catalogs listed as: MODEL 933 DOUBLE ACTION. Mfg. 1929-1939.

$565 $$485 $415 $360 $310 $260 $225

MODEL 922 DOUBLE ACTION FIRST MODEL LARGE SOLID FRAME – .22 rimfire cal., 9 shot, 6 in. octagon barrel, pull pin cylinder release, blue finish, two piece oversize walnut saw handle grips, marked with company name and address on top of barrel, right side of

GRADING - PPGS™	100%	98%	95%	90%	80%	70%	60%	LAST MSR

barrel marked H&R 922 and caliber marked on left side of barrel. Mfg. 1927-1952.

	$195	$175	$150	$125	$110	$95	$85	

Add 40% for First Variation, or 20% for Second, Third, Fourth, or Fifth Variations.

First Variation 1927-1930, serial number range 125,270*-143,000*(estimate).

Second Variation 1931, Difference: new grip shape (saw handle shape eliminated) serial number range 144000*-160000*(estimate).

Third Variation 1932-1937, Difference: new safety cylinder, serial number range 160000*-171000*(estimate).

Fourth Variation 1938-1939, Difference: new grip frame and round barrel, serial number range 171000*-192000*(estimate).

Fifth Variation 1940- 1947, Difference: same as 4th variation except letter code prefix to serial number A thru H.

Sixth Variation 1948-1949, Difference: a new barrel length, serial number letter codes I and J.

Seventh Variation 1949-1952, Difference: all-in-one cartridge extraction system, serial number letter codes J thru M.

Eighth Variation 1952, models for M922 Camper and M922 Bantam weight (see Revolvers: Recent Mfg.).

MODEL 923 DOUBLE ACTION FIRST MODEL LARGE SOLID FRAME – .22 rimfire cal., 6 in. barrel, similar to Model 922 Sixth and Seventh Variations, except has chrome finish. Mfg. 1949-1952.

	$205	$185	$165	$135	$120	$100	$90	

The Model 923 Sixth Variation has serial number letter codes I and J (mfg. 1948-1949), and the Seventh Variation features an all-in-one cartridge extraction system, and has serial number letter codes J thru M (mfg. 1949-1952).

Top Break Revolvers: 1885-1952

MANUAL EJECTING MODEL (MANUAL SHELL EXTRACTOR, BLACK POWDER) – .32 S&W or .38 S&W cal., 5 (.38 cal.) or 6 (.32 cal.) shot, 3 1/4 in. barrel, manual ejector rod under barrel, hard rubber grip panels with floral design, nickel finish, modified American Double Action mechanism and frame, first variation marked on top of barrel with company name and address only, and two guide rods for ejector (1885-1887), second variation has patent date 10-4-87 marked on top of barrel along with company name and address, extractor does not have guide rods (1887-1889). Mfg. 1885-1889.

	$525	$465	$395	$340	$295	$250	$220	

MANUAL EJECTING SECOND MODEL BLACK POWDER – .32 S&W or .38 S&W cal., 5 or 6 shot, new frame (same as Second Model Auto Ejecting), 3 1/4 in. barrel, hard rubber grips with target logo, nickel or blue finish, one patent date marking, very rare. Mfg. 1890 - disc.

	$600	$520	$440	$390	$340	$285	$245	

AUTOMATIC EJECTING FIRST MODEL (BLACK POWDER) – .32 S&W or .38 S&W cal., 5 (.38 cal.) or 6 shot cylinder, hard rubber grip panels with floral design, 3 1/4 in. barrel, modified American Double Action mechanism and frame, nickel finish, First Variation marked on top of barrel with company name and address only and two guide rods for ejector (1885-1886), Second Variation patent date 10-4-87 marked on top of barrel along with company name and address, extractor does not have extra guide rods (1887-1889). Mfg. 1885-1889.

	$325	$285	$250	$200	$175	$150	$125	

Add 30% for First Variation.

Factory 2, 5, and 6 inch barrel examples were seen in 2011.

AUTOMATIC EJECTING MODEL 1 1/2 (BLACK POWDER) – .32 S&W or .38 S&W cal., different double action mechanism, trigger, trigger guard and hammer, 5 (.38 S&W cal.) or 6 (.32 S&W cal.) shot, new frame, nickel or blue finish, hard rubber grips with target logo, 3 1/4 in. barrel, marked with two patent date 10-04-87 and 12-25-88 (only revolver to use this date), rare. Mfg. 1889-1890.

	$600	$520	$440	$390	$340	$285	$245	

A second variation was found in 2011 with a new frame and Target Logo grips, rare. Mfg. 1890-unknown.

AUTOMATIC EJECTING SECOND MODEL (BLACK POWDER) – .32 S&W or .38 S&W cal., 5 (.38 S&W cal.) or 6 (.32 S&W cal.) shot, new frame shape and new hard rubber grip

GRADING - PPGS™	100%	98%	95%	90%	80%	70%	60%	LAST MSR

panels with target logo, nickel or blue finish, 2 1/2 (rare), 3 1/4 (standard), 4, 5, or 6 in. barrel, if there is no caliber marking on the left side of the barrel, then it was manufactured for black powder, top of barrel markings include company name and address and patent dates. Mfg. 1890-1904.

	$300	$195	$170	$140	$125	$110	$95

Add 75% for 2 1/2 in. barrel or 25% for 4, 5, or 6 in. barrels.
Add 15% for blue finish.
Add 10% for First, Second, Third, or Fourth Variations with nickel trigger guard and nickel finish.

First Variation; one patent date OCT-4-87 only (1890-1892).

Second Variation one patent date marked OCT-4-1887 (year marked in full) (1890-1892*).

Third Variation three patent dates, Oct-4-1887, May 14 & Aug-6-89 (1893-Only*).

Fourth Variation three patent dates Oct-4-87, May-14 & Aug-6-89 (note 87 date does not have full year markings) (1894-1896*).

Fifth Variation five patent dates Oct-4-87, May 14 & Aug-6-89, April-2-95, April-7-96 (1897-1904*).

***Serial numbers found on the bottom side of the top strap will have letter codes.**

AUTOMATIC EJECTING POLICE SECOND MODEL (BLACK POWDER) – similar to Auto-Ejecting Second model except has a patented spurless Hammer, the Police Model will be found in all variations and calibers of the Second Model. Mfg. 1890-1904.

	$235	$200	$180	$150	$125	$110	$95

AUTOMATIC EJECTING THIRD MODEL (SMOKELESS POWDER) – .32 S&W Long or .38 S&W cal., 5 (.38 cal.) or 6 (.32 cal.) shot, hard rubber grip panels with target logo, blue or nickel finish, 2 1/2 (rare), 3 1/4 (standard), 4, 5 or 6 in. barrel, top of barrel markings include company name and address and early production has patent dates, the one recognizable difference in the Second and Third Models is the caliber marking on the left side of the barrel on the Third Model, which indicates, it was manufactured for smokeless powder. Mfg. 1905-1940.

	$235	$200	$180	$150	$125	$110	$95

Add 75% for 2 1/2 in. barrel, or 25% for 4, 5, or 6 in. barrel.
Add 15% for blue finish.

First Variation 4 patent dates (5-14 & 8-6-89, 4-2-95, 4-7-97) model name and caliber on left side of barrel (1905-1908).

Second Variation 2 patent dates (8-6-89 and 10-8-95) model name and caliber on left side of barrel (1909-1912).

Third Variation no patent dates the name of the state is marked as MASS (1913-1915).

Fourth Variation no patent dates the state name of Massachusetts is spelled out (1916-1924).

Fifth Variation new grip frame, it is now the same size as the rest of the frame with no step down for the grip panel (1925-1941).

After 1931 listed in Catalogs as: AUTOMATIC EJECTING No. 10 .32 S&W LONG CALIBER 6 shots.

After 1931 listed in Catalogs as: AUTOMATIC EJECTING No. 25 .38 S&W CALIBER 5 shots.

After 1932 listed in Catalogs as: AUTOMATIC EJECTING No. 20. .38 S&W CALIBER 5 shots.

AUTOMATIC EJECTING POLICE THIRD MODEL (SMOKELESS POWDER) – similar to Auto-Ejecting Third Model except has a patented spurless hammer, Police Model will be found in all variations and calibers of the Third Model until 1939. Mfg. 1905-1939.

	$275	$215	$185	$150	$125	$110	$95

AUTOMATIC EJECTING KNIFE MODEL – similar to regular Auto-Ejector Model except 4 in. barrel with a 2 1/4 inch double edge knife attached under the barrel, 6 (.32 S&W) and 5 (.38 S&W) shot, only finish listed in catalogs was nickel but some blue finish examples have been observed, Second Model Black Powder mfg. 1901-1904, Third Model Smokeless Powder mfg. 1905-1917.

	$2,000	$1,700	$1,500	$1,150	$850	$700	$625

Add 10% for blue finish.
Subtract 60% if knife is missing.

GRADING - PPGS™	100%	98%	95%	90%	80%	70%	60%	LAST MSR

.22 SPECIAL LARGE FRAME TOP BREAK – .22 rimfire or .22 WRF cal., 6 in. barrel, 7 or 9 shot, blue finish, two-piece walnut grips (after 1932 one-piece grips). Mfg. 1925-1941.

$330	$290	$255	$200	$175	$150	$125	

Add 50% for .22 WRF cal., 15% for First Variation, or 10% for Fourth and Fifth Variation.

First Variation, 7 shot, .22 rimfire only, oversized 2 piece saw handle shaped walnut grips (serial number range above 490000*) (1926-1928).

Second Variation, 9 shot, .22 rimfire and 7 shot, 22WRF, (serial number range 497000-559100*) (1928-1930).

Third Variation, new rounded two-piece grip (saw handle grip eliminated) (serial number range unknown) (1931-1932).

Fourth Variation, safety cylinder and new grip frame (RICE FRAME) (serial number range 559100-590000*) (1933-1938).

Fifth Variation, automatic cylinder stop (serial number range above 590000*) (1939-1942).

After 1930 listed in catalogs as: MODEL 944 LARGE FRAME TOP BREAK .22 RIMFIRE CALIBER 9 shots.

After 1930 listed in catalogs as: MODEL 945 LARGE FRAME TOP BREAK .22 Winchester Rim Fire CALIBER 7 shots.

22 EXPERT LARGE FRAME TOP BREAK – similar to .22 Special Large Frame Top Break, except has 10 in. barrel. Mfg. 1927-1941.

$430	$370	$320	$275	$235	$195	$175	

Add 50% for .22 WRF cal.

After 1930 listed in catalogs as: MODEL 955 LARGE FRAME TOP BREAK .22 RIMFIRE CALIBER 9 shot, or MODEL 956 LARGE FRAME TOP BREAK .22WRF CALIBER 7 shot.

H&R BOBBY LARGE FRAME TOP BREAK – .32 or .38 centerfire cal., double action, 5 or 6 shot, round ribbed 4 inch barrel, fixed sights, blue finish, one piece oversize checkered walnut grips (some furnished with one piece plastic grips), free wheeling cylinder, only the .32 caliber seems to have been purchased by London's Metropolitan Police, these will be marked MK-II, on the top strap as well as having the company name and address on the top of the barrel rib, No. 15 model is .32 cal. 6 shot, No. 25 model is .38 cal. 5 shot, own serial number range, overall length 9 inches, 23 oz. Mfg. 1939-1942.

$300	$255	$220	$175	$150	$125	$115	

Add 100% for Metropolitan Police marked model (MK-II on top strap, M.P. P on front of grip frame.
Subtract $25 for plastic grips.

H&R HAMMERLESS FIRST MODEL LARGE FRAME TOP BREAK (BLACK POWDER) – .38 S&W cal., 5 shot, double action, double top post barrel latch, nickel or blue finish, hard rubber grips with a target logo at the top, 3 1/4 (standard), 4, 5 or 6 in. barrel, rebounding hammer; automatic cylinder stop, top of barrel is marked with the same 5 patent dates as the Auto-Ejector Second Model 5th Variation, no caliber markings on left side of barrel means designed for black powder cartridge pressures only. Mfg. 1899-1904.

$295	$260	$220	$180	$160	$140	$120	

Add 10% for blue finish or 20% for 4, 5, or 6 in. barrel.

Serial number range is approximately 01* to 45000* (No letter codes): Highest known 43308 (* Estimate).

H&R HAMMERLESS SECOND MODEL LARGE FRAME TOP BREAK (SMOKELESS POWDER) – .38 S&W cal., 5 shot, double top post barrel latch, nickel or blue finish, grips are hard rubber with a target logo at the top; 3 1/4 (standard), 4, 5, or 6 in. barrel, rebounding hammer, automatic cylinder stop, cylinder was lengthened to take the .32 S&W long cartridge and the catalogs now listed the calibers as: 6 shot .32 S&W, .32 S&W Long, .32 Colt New Police cartridges, also offered in 5 shot .38 S&W and .38 Colt New Police, caliber marked on left side of barrel, designed for smokeless powder cartridge. Mfg. 1905-1941.

$325	$285	$250	$200	$175	$150	$125	

Add 10% for blue finish. Add 20% for 4, 5, or 6 in. barrel.

First variation, 5 patent dates same as First model with caliber marked on left side of barrel, serial number range 45000*-55000* (estimate) - 1905.

Second Variation, patent dates, 5-14 & 8-6-89, 4-2-95, 4-7-96, serial number range: 55000*-100000*(estimate) - 1906-1908.

GRADING - PPGS™	100%	98%	95%	90%	80%	70%	60%	LAST MSR

Third Variation, patent dates 8-6-1889, 10-8-1895, serial number range: 100000*-120000*(estimate) - 1909-1912.

Fourth Variation, no patent dates, state in address not spelled out (MASS.), serial number range: 120000*-160000*(estimate) - 1913-1915.

Fifth Variation, no patent dates, state name in address is spelled out (MASSACHUETTS), serial number range: 160000*-190000*(estimate) - 1916-1924.

Sixth Variation, new grip frame same as Auto-Ejector, serial number range: unknown - 1925-1940.

There is some indication production of the hammerless model stopped somewhere in the early 1920's but it was carried in catalogs until 1941.

After 1930 listed in Catalogs as: H&R HAMMERLESS No. 50 TOP BREAK .32 S&W LONG 6 shot.

After 1930 listed in Catalogs as: H&R HAMMERLESS No. 55 TOP BREAK .38 S&W 5 shot.

H&R HAMMERLESS FIRST MODEL SMALL FRAME TOP BREAK (BLACK POWDER) – .32 S&W cal., 5 shot, double top post barrel latch, nickel or blue finish, hard rubber grips with a target logo at the top, 3 1/4 (standard), 4, 5, or 6 in. barrel, rebounding hammer, automatic cylinder stop, no caliber markings on left side of barrel, designed for black powder cartridge pressures. Mfg. 1899-1904.

$255	$225	$195	$155	$130	$115	$100	

Add 10% for blue finish. Add 20% for 4, 5, or 6 in. barrel.

First Variation, patent dates 10-4-87, 4-2-95, 4-7-96, serial number range: 01*-82000* (Estimate) - 1899-1903.

Second Variation, patent dates 5-14-89,4-2-95, 4-6-96, serial number range: 82000*-90000* (Estimate) - 1904.

H&R HAMMERLESS BICYCLE FIRST MODEL – .32 S&W cal., 5 shot, similar to H&R Hammerless First Model, except has 2 in. barrel only. Mfg. 1899-1904.

$275	$245	$210	$170	$145	$120	$110	

Add 10% for blue finish.

H&R HAMMERLESS SECOND MODEL SMALL FRAME TOP BREAK (SMOKELESS POWDER) – .22 rimfire or .32 S&W cal., 5 (.32 cal.) or 7 (.22 cal.) shot, double top post barrel latch, nickel or blue finish, hard rubber grips with target logo at the top, 3 (standard), 4, 5, or 6 in. barrel, rebounding hammer, automatic cylinder stop, caliber marking on left side of barrel, designed for smokeless powder cartridge pressures only. Mfg. 1905-1941.

$265	$235	$200	$160	$135	$110	$100	

Add 10% for blue finish. Add 20% for 4, 5, or 6 in. barrel, or 20% for .22 rimfire cal.

First Variation, patent dates 5-14-89, 4-2-95, 4-7-96, serial number range: 90000*-100000* (estimate) - 1905-1906.

Second Variation, patent dates 4-2-95, 4-7-96, serial number range: 100000*-120000* (estimate) - 1907-1909.

Third Variation, patent date 10-8-95, serial number range: 120000*-180000* (estimate) - 1910-1913.

Fourth Variation, no patent dates small font used for company name, serial number range: 180000*-190000* (estimate) - 1914.

Fifth variation, large font used in company name and state not spelled out (MASS), serial number range: 190000*-200000* (estimate) - 1915.

Sixth Variation, state name in address spelled out (MASSACHUSETTS), serial number range: 200000*-220000* (estimate) - 1916-1924.

Seventh Variation, new grip frame, it is now same width as rest of frame, no step down for grips, serial number range: unknown - 1925-1942.

After 1930 listed in catalogs as: HAMMERLESS No. 40 TOP BREAK .22 Rimfire 7 shot.

After 1930 listed in catalogs as: HAMMERLESS No. 45 TOP BREAK .32 S&W 5 shot.

H&R HAMMERLESS BICYCLE SECOND MODEL – .22 rimfire or .32 S&W cal., 5 or 7 shot, similar to H&R Hammerless Second Model, except has 2 in. barrel only, not listed as a separate model after 1920 but 2 inch barrel was still available. Mfg. 1905-1920.

$295	$260	$225	$185	$160	$140	$120	

Add 10% for blue finish or 20% for .22 rimfire cal.

GRADING - PPGS™	100%	98%	95%	90%	80%	70%	60%	LAST MSR

H&R PREMIER FIRST MODEL SMALL FRAME TOP BREAK (BLACK POWDER) – .22 rimfire or .32 centerfire cal., 5 or 7 shot, double top post barrel latch, free wheeling cylinder (no automatic cylinder stop), nickel with case harden hammer and barrel latch, 3 (standard), 4, 5, or 6 in. barrel, features a scaled down version of the new frame and double action mechanism introduced in 1890 on the Auto-Ejecting Second Model, does not have caliber marking on left, manufactured for black powder cartridge pressures. Mfg. 1895-1904.

$285	$255	$220	$175	$150	$125	$115	

Add 10% for blue finish, 20% for 4, 5, or 6 in. barrel, or 20% for .22 rimfire cal.

First Variation, patent dates 10-4-87, 5-14-89, 2-23-92, serial number range 01*-15,000 (estimate) - 1895-April 1896.

Second Variation, patent dates 10-4-87, 5-14-89, 4-2-95, 4-7-96, serial number range 15,000*-20,000* (estimate) - May 1896.

Third Variation, patent dates 10-4-87, 4-2-95, 4-7-96, serial number range 20,000* to 100,000* (estimate) - 1897-1898.

Fourth Variation, automatic cylinder stop, same patent dates as 3rd variation several different serial number series that may have letter codes - 1899-1903.

Fifth Variation, use different font in barrel markings and may have an A letter code in the serial number - 1904.

H&R PREMIER BICYCLE MODEL FIRST MODEL TOP BREAK (BLACK POWDER) – similar to Premier First Model, except has 2 in. barrel only. Mfg. 1895-1904.

$295	$260	$220	$180	$160	$140	$120	

Add 10% for blue finish or 20% for .22 rimfire caliber.

H&R PREMIER POLICE (SPURLESS HAMMER, BLACK POWDER) – similar to Premier First Model, except has patented spurless hammer. Mfg. 1895-1904.

$300	$265	$225	$185	$160	$140	$120	

Add 10% for blue finish, 20% for .22 rimfire caliber, or 20% for 4, 5, or 6 in. barrel.

H&R PREMIER POLICE BICYCLE FIRST MODEL (BLACK POWDER) – similar to Premier First Model, except has 2 in. barrel and patented spurless hammer. Mfg. 1895-1904.

$315	$280	$235	$190	$165	$145	$125	

Add 10% for blue finish or 20% for .22 rimfire caliber.

H&R PREMIER SECOND MODEL SMALL FRAME TOP BREAK R.F. & C.F. – .22 rimfire or .32 S&W cal., double top post barrel latch, 5 or 7 shot, automatic cylinder stop, nickel finish with case hardened hammer and barrel latch, 2, 3 (standard), 4, 5, and 6 in. barrel, caliber markings on left side of barrel, manufactured for smokeless powder cartridge pressures. Mfg. 1905-1941.

$265	$235	$200	$160	$135	$110	$100	

Add 10% for blue finish, 20% for 4, 5, or 6 in. barrel, 20% for .22 rimfire cal., or 10% for Seventh Variation.

There has not been enough data gathered on serial number ranges for the different variations.

First Variation, model name & caliber marked on left side of barrel, patent dates 5-14-89, 4-2-95, 4-7-96; 1905.

Second Variation, model name & caliber marked on left side of barrel, patent dates 4-2-95, 4-7-96; 1906-1908.

Third Variation, caliber only marked on left side of barrel, patent date 10-8-95; 1909-1913.

Fourth Variation, caliber only marked on left side of barrel, no patent date, state not spelled out in address (MASS); 1914-1915.

Fifth Variation, caliber only marked on left side of barrel, same as 4th except different font used in barrel markings; 1914-1915.

Sixth Variation, caliber only marked on left side of barrel. State name in barrel marking spelled out (MASSACHUSETTS); 1916-1924.

Seventh Variation, new grip frame, there is no step down for the grip panels to fit into - 1925-1942.

After 1930 listed in catalogs as: PREMIER No. 30 .22 Rimfire 7 shot or PREMIER No. 35 .32 S&W 5 shot.

GRADING - PPGS™	100%	98%	95%	90%	80%	70%	60%	LAST MSR

H&R PREMIER BICYCLE SECOND MODEL (SMOKELESS POWDER) – similar to Premier Second Model, except has 2 in. barrel, not listed as a separate model after 1919. Mfg. 1905-1920.

	$285	$255	$220	$175	$150	$125	$115

Add 10% for blue finish or 20% for .22 rimfire caliber.

H&R PREMIER POLICE SECOND MODEL (SMOKELESS POWDER) – similar to Premier Second Model, except has spurless hammer, not listed as a separate model after 1938. Mfg. 1905-1939.

	$275	$245	$210	$170	$145	$120	$110

Add 10% for blue finish, 20% for .22 rimfire caliber, or 20% for 4, 5, or 6 in. barrel.

H&R PREMIER POLICE BICYCLE SECOND MODEL (SMOKELESS POWDER) – similar to Premier Second Model, except has 2 in. barrel and patented spurless hammer, not listed as a separate model after 1919. Mfg. 1905-1920.

	$285	$255	$220	$175	$150	$125	$115

Add 10% for blue finish or 20% for .22 rimfire caliber.

H&R TARGET SMALL FRAME TOP BREAK (AKA MODEL 766) – .22 rimfire cal., 7 shot, blue finish, 6 in. barrel, double action, oversized two-piece walnut grips, marked on left side of barrel "H&R TARGET", 22 rimfire on the right side of the barrel,company name and address on the top of the barrel rib. Mfg. 1925-1934.

	$325	$285	$250	$200	$175	$150	$125

After 1930 listed in the catalogs as: MODEL 766 TARGET SMALL FRAME TOP BREAK REVOLVER 7 SHOT.

MODEL 299 NEW DEFENDER LARGE FRAME TOP BREAK – .22 rimfire cal., 9 shot, 2 in. barrel, large frame top break revolver, adj. sights, one piece walnut grips, pocket size, marked on right side of barrel with model name and caliber, modified "Rice Frame", automatic cylinder stop, finger rest trigger guard, overall length only 6 1/4 inches, serial number range unknown, but believed to be in the same series as the Model 999 Sportsman. Mfg. 1935-1939.

	$525	$465	$395	$340	$295	$250	$220

H&R DEFENDER SPECIAL MODEL 299 LARGE FRAME TOP BREAK – .38 S&W cal., 5 shot, 2 and 4 in. flat sided barrel, large frame double action top break revolver, adj. front and rear sight, blue finish, finger rest trigger guard, birds-head grip frame shortened for special one-piece pocket size checkered walnut grips, automatic cylinder stop, overall length 6 1/4 in., serial number range unknown. Mfg. 1935-1939, limited production from 1939-1949.

	$600	$520	$440	$390	$340	$285	$245

DEFENDER NO MODEL NUMBER LARGE FRAME TOP BREAK – .38 S&W cal., 5 shot, large frame double action, 4, 5 or 6 inch flat sided barrel, fixed sights, blue finish, no finger rest on trigger guard, birds-head grip frame, one-piece oversized checkered walnut grips, automatic cylinder stop, hammer mounted firing pin, top of barrel marked with company name and address, left side of barrel is marked "DEFENDER 38" and right side is marked "38 S&W CTGE". Mfg. 1939-1942.

	$400	$285	$250	$200	$175	$150	$125

Add 20% for 5 or 6 (scarce) in. barrel.

Most likely this is the beginning of the Defender 38 Model 25, but the literature for the Model 25 shows a slightly different revolver. The literature for this revolver refers to it as the Defender 38. Believed to be in a separate serial number range and possibly have letter code prefixes. Early examples will not be marked "Defender".

DEFENDER NO. 25 LARGE FRAME TOP BREAK – .38 S&W cal., 5 shot, 4 in. flat sided barrel, double action, adj. front and rear sights, blue finish, no finger rest on trigger guard, birds-head grip frame, one-piece oversized checkered black plastic grips, automatic cylinder stop, cylinder release via push button on left side of barrel lug, right side of barrel is marked with company name and address and caliber, left side of barrel marked "DEFENDER 38", serial numbers is believed to be a separate range. Mfg. 1943-1945.

	$350	$300	$265	$210	$180	$150	$125

GRADING - PPGS™	100%	98%	95%	90%	80%	70%	60%	LAST MSR

DEFENDER MODEL 925 LARGE FRAME TOP BREAK – .38 S&W cal., 5 shot, 4 in. flat sided barrel, adj. front and rear sights, blue finish, no finger rest on trigger guard, birds-head grip frame, one-piece oversized checkered black plastic grips, automatic cylinder stop, cylinder release via push button on left side of barrel lug, overall length 9 inches, 25 oz. Mfg. 1946-1947.

	$325	$285	$250	$200	$175	$150	$125

Add 50% for manual ejecting model.

There has been one model 925 that is a factory manual ejection revolver with a serial number low enough that it actually may be a Model 25. It has company name and address on top of the barrel, "DEFENDER" on right side of barrel and the caliber on the left side of the barrel.

ULTRA SPORTSMAN MODEL 777 LARGE FRAME TOP BREAK – .22 rimfire cal., 9 shot, large frame single action top break, 6 in. flat top oval shaped barrel (same as the Model 199), adj. front and rear sight, elevation screw on front of barrel just above muzzle, oversized one-piece checkered walnut grips (eleven different styles available), straight trigger, arched hammer spur, cylinder release is a vertical lever on the right side of barrel lug, rear of cylinder has the patented H&R safety rim, finger rest trigger guard, trigger pull factory set 2 1/2 to 3 pounds, hammer mounted firing pin, serial numbered in its own series U01 to at least U900, top of barrel markings in two lines: "HARRINGTON & RICHARDSON ARMS CO. WORCESTER, MASS. U.S.A.", left side of barrel in three lines: "H&R NO. 777 ULTRA SPORTSMAN", right side of barrel, one line: ".22 LONG RIFLE CTCG." Mfg. 1938-1939.

	$800	$685	$600	$535	$475	$325	$275

EUREKA SPORTSMAN MODEL 196 – .22 rimfire cal., 6 shot, large frame single action top break, cylinder chambers individually recessed, 6 in. flat top oval heavy barrel, adj. front and rear sight (has a different configuration than found on any other H&R adj. rear sight), oversized one-piece checkered walnut grips (eleven different styles available), trigger guard is heaver and wider than Model 777, trigger pull factory set 2 1/2 to 3 pounds, with over travel adjustment, curved trigger and heavy straight hammer spur, hammer mounted firing pin, birds-head shaped grip frame, top of barrel markings in two lines: "HARRINGTON & RICHARDSON ARMS CO., WORCESTER, MASS U.S.A.", left side of barrel in three lines: "H&R NO. 196 EUREKA SPORTSMAN", right side of barrel, one line: "22 LONG RIFLE CTGE", overall length approx. 10 3/4 inches, 30-32 oz. Mfg. 1940 only.

	$1,000	$860	$770	$680	$525	$450	$395

Add $250 for fitted case (rare).

At a recent auction, a Eureka Sportsman Model 196 in 90% condition sold auction for $1,500.

SPORTSMAN SINGLE ACTION MODEL 199 LARGE FRAME TOP BREAK – .22 LR cal., 9 shot, safety rim cylinder, blue finish, 6 in. round heavy rib barrel, automatic cylinder stop, adj. front and rear sights, finger rest trigger guard, one-piece oversized checkered walnut grips, birds-head grip frame, top of barrel marked with company name and address, left side of barrel marked in two lines: "H & R SPORTSMAN SINGLE ACTION", right side of barrel marked: "22 LONG RIFLE CTGE", serial numbered in series from 01 up and early production will have S letter code denoting single action. Mfg. 1932-1951.

	$575	$495	$415	$340	$285	$250	$210

Add 15% for First Variation or 10% for Fifth Variation.

First Variation; heavy ribbed barrel with non-adjustable front sight - Oct. 1932-April 1933.

Second Variation; oval shaped barrel with flat top, fully adjustable sights - May 1933-disc.

Third Variation; very small lettering on cylinder patent date - unknown-1936.

Fourth Variation; firing pin moved to the hammer - 1937-1941.

Fifth Variation; limited production (1949=J101-J148, 1950=K101-K265, 1951=L111-L112) - 1949-1951.

SPORTSMAN DOUBLE ACTION MODEL 999 LARGE FRAME TOP BREAK – .22 LR or .22 WRF cal., 7 (.22 WRF cal.) or 9 shot, blue finish, 6 in. ribbed barrel, safety rim cylinder, automatic cylinder stop, adj. rear sight, three different front sights - fixed full blade, Partridge type, and Partridge type pinned to barrel top rib, finger rest trigger guard, one-piece oversized checkered walnut grips, birds-head grip frame (Rice frame), frame

GRADING - PPGS™	100%	98%	95%	90%	80%	70%	60%	LAST MSR

mounted firing pin, hammer face is flat, cylinder release is long pivoting lever on right side of frame (there are two different version of this), serial numbered in its own series from 01 up to at least 89761 by the end of 1939, starting in 1940 letter codes were used. Mfg. 1932-1952.

	$525	$450	$375	$300	$265	$225	$195	

Add 15% for First Variation, 50% for 7 shot, .22 WRF cal. variation, or 30% for 3 in. barrel (scarce).

Early production until about 1933 the letter code "D" was used to denote double action.

First Variation; round heavy weight ribbed barrel with non-adjustable front sight blade - 1932- to before April 18,1933.

Second Variation; adjustable front sight - 1933 (after 4-18-1933).

Third Variation; firing pin moved to hammer - 1934.

Fourth Variation; three inch barrel was offered - 1935.

Fifth Variation; two patent dates marked on cylinder (before there was only one) - 1936 (after 3-17)-1937.

Sixth Variation; top of barrel markings moved to right side of barrel - 1937-1939.

Seventh Variation; .22 WFR caliber dropped, 3 inch barrel dropped - 1940-1941.

Eighth Variation; one piece over size plastic grips are standard, limited production during WWII years - 1942-1952.

PISTOLS: SEMI-AUTO

H&R SELF LOADING .25 ACP – .25 ACP cal., 6 shot mag. (magazines may be either blue, nickel, or in-the-white), 2 in. barrel, blue finish, markings on right side of slide "HARRINGTON & RICHARDSON ARMS CO. WORCESTER, MASS. U.S.A. PAT. AUG.20.'07. APRIL 13, 1909" in three lines on left side of slide, "H&R SELF-LOADING CALIBER 25" in two lines on left side of frame at rear ser. no., the ser. no. is in its own series numbered from 01 to about 16,500. One source lists manufacture date between 1912 and 1916, however, it was featured in the catalogs until 1920. Mfg. 1912-1920.

First Variation	$565	$485	$415	$355	$300	$250	$225	
Second Variation	$525	$465	$395	$340	$295	$250	$220	

The First Variation is serial numbered from 01 to approx. 10,000, with 12 slide serrations, magazine follower is flat and straight, right side of slide markings middle line is stretched out.

The Second Variation is serial numbered from approx. 10,000 to 16,500+, 16 slide serrations, magazine follower is curved and stepped at rear, right side of slide markings middle line compacted and in line with other markings.

H&R SELF LOADING .32 ACP – .32 ACP cal., 8 shot mag. (magazines with either be blue, nickel, or in-the-white), 3 1/2 in. barrel, blue finish, marking on right side of slide: "HARRINGTON & RICHARDSON ARMS CO. WORCESTER, MASS. U.S.A. PAT. AUG.20.'07. APRIL 13, 1909" in three lines, left side of slide "H&R SELF-LOADING CALIBER 32" in two lines at rear ser. no., the ser. no. is in its own series numbered 01 to approx. 34,500. Mfg. 1914-1924.

First Variation	$525	$465	$395	$340	$295	$250	$220	
Second Variation	$495	$435	$370	$320	$275	$235	$200	

The First Variation is serial numbered 01 to approx. 2,000, 12 slide serrations, magazine follower is flat and straight, on right side of slide markings, the middle line is stretched out.

The Second Variation is serial numbered approx. 2,000 to 34,500+, 16 slide serrations, magazine follower is curved and stepped at rear, on the right side of slide markings the middle line is compacted and in line with other markings.

In order to take advantage of the wartime shortage of handguns, H&R offered the remaining inventory of the .32 Self-Loader in the 1939 and 1940 catalogs. Since this model was not sold in ser. no. sequence, it is impossible to tell when any one pistol was shipped between 1914-1924 or 1939-1940.

HK-4 – please refer to listings under Heckler & Koch section.

PISTOLS: SINGLE SHOT

HANDY GUN SMOOTH BORE – 28 ga. or .410 bore, smooth bore pistol with shotgun type break open action, blue finish, color case hardened frame, built on H&R's small frame Model 1915 Single Barrel Shotgun action, 28 ga. standard factory loads (early production

GRADING - PPGS™	100%	98%	95%	90%	80%	70%	60%	LAST MSR

2 1/2 inch and late production 2 3/4 inch chamber), black and smokeless powder, .410 bore chambered for 2 1/2 inch shells, 8 and 12 1/4 inch barrel lengths, oversized uncheckered one-piece walnut saw handle grips, detachable wire stock offered after 1932. Serial number in a separate series from 01 up to about 54,000 with both gauges in the same series classified by the government as NFA Curio & Relic, if registered with the ATF. Guns not already registered are illegal to own and subject to seizure. Mfg. 1924-1934.

Legal smooth bore Handy Guns are typically prices between $1,200-$2,500, depending on original condition.

After 1930 listed in catalogs as HANDY GUN No. 141 SINGLE SHOT SMOOTH BORE .410 BORE.
After 1930 listed in catalogs as HANDY GUN No. 128 SINGLE SHOT SMOOTH BORE .28 GAUGE.

HANDY GUN RIFLED BARREL – .22 LR or .32-20 WCF cal., blue finish with color case hardened frame, shotgun type break open action, built on H&R's small frame Model 1915 Single Barrel Shotgun action, 12 1/4 in. barrel, oversized one-piece checkered rounded walnut grips, short uncheckered walnut forend, .22 LR is serial numbered in a separate series 1 (or 101) to approx 300, and .32-20 in same series as smooth bores. Mfg. 1931-1934.

This model is rarely seen, and legal original specimens are typically valued in the $1,250-$2,250 range.

Listed in catalog as HANDY GUN No. 122 SINGLE SHOT RIFLED BARREL .22 RF CALIBER, and as HANDY GUN No. 132 SINGLE SHOT RIFLED BARREL .32-20 WCF CALIBER.

MODEL 195 H&R SINGLE SHOT PISTOL TOP BREAK (aka U.S.R.A. MODEL) – .22 LR cal., large frame, blue finish, oversized checkered walnut grips, adj. sights, automatic ejector, serial number location is on the front of the grip strap or on the left side of the grip frame under the grips and on the bottom of the breech block, original production has a 10 inch barrel only, later production could be ordered with a 7 or 8 inch barrel, birds-head grip frame (called by collectors "Rice Frame"), serial numbered in its own series from 01 up to about 40,000, after 1930 this model is known as the U.S.R.A. Model. Mfg. 1928-1942.

N/A	N/A	$1,800	$1,475	$1,000	$775	$625	

Add 25% for rare square plate type ejector.
Add $300 for fitted case and accessories.

There are many sub-variations of this model due to special orders and factory reworks.

First Variation; two piece walnut grips, round ribbed barrel with non-adj. front sight, 10 inch barrel only - 1928.

Second variation; features a plunger type (round head) ejector, one-piece walnut grips - 1928-1929.

Third Variation; grooved trigger, name and model markings changed to U.S.R.A. Model 195 -1930.

Fourth Variation; 7 inch barrel length added, new front & rear sight and different shaped rib - 1931-1932.

Fifth Variation; grooved trigger, new barrel shape - 1933-1934.

Sixth variation; lever type automatic ejector - 1935-1942.

REVOLVERS: RECENT MFG.

MODEL 504 SQUARE BUTT – .32 H&R Mag. cal., 5 shot, blue finish, 3, 4, or 6 in. barrel, transfer bar ignition, solid frame, DA, swing out cylinder, square butt. Mfg. 1984-1986.

$235	$200	$175	$140	$125	$110	$95	*$185*

Add 10% for 3 in. barrel, or 15% for 6 in. barrel.

* ***Model 504 Round Butt*** – compact design available with 3 or 4 in. barrel only. Disc. 1985.

$165	$145	$135	$120	$110	$100	$90	*$185*

MODEL 532 – .32 H&R Mag. cal., blue finish, 2 1/2 or 4 in. barrel, case colored hardened frame, 5 shot, DA, solid frame, transfer bar ignition, pull pin cylinder release. Mfg. 1983-1986.

$165	$145	$125	$110	$90	$80	$70	*$115*

MODEL 586 – .32 H&R Mag. cal., 5 shot, similar to Model 686, Western-style revolver, double action, 4 1/2, 5 1/2, 7 1/2, or 10 in. barrels, adj. rear sight, antique finish frame with blue cylinder and barrel, black plastic or walnut grips. Mfg. 1983-1985.

$275	$245	$210	$170	$145	$120	$110	*$195*

Add 30% for 10 in. barrel.

GRADING - PPGS™	100%	98%	95%	90%	80%	70%	60%	LAST MSR

MODEL 600 FORTY-NINER – .22 LR cal., 9 shot, 5 1/2 in. barrel, DA, solid frame, rod ejection, blue finish, Western style grips. Mfg. 1960 only.

$275	$225	$185	$150	$125	$100	$90	

MODEL 603 – .22 WMR cal., similar to Model 903 but is 6 shot, 6 in. full round bull barrel, DA, transfer bar ignition, swing out cylinder. Mfg. 1980-83.

$300	$245	$195	$160	$125	$100	$90	

MODEL 604 – .22 WMR cal., 6 shot, blue finish, 6 in. flat sided bull barrel, DA, solid frame, swing out cylinder, square butt. Mfg. 1980-1983.

$300	$245	$195	$160	$125	$100	$90	

MODEL 622 – .22 S-L-LR cal., solid frame, DA, 6 shot, 2 1/2, 4, 6, or 10 in. barrels, blue finish, round or square butt, plastic grips, pull pin cylinder release. Mfg. 1957-1973.

$200	$165	$130	$110	$90	$75	$65	*$104*

* ***Model 622 Second Model*** – similar to Model 622, except round butt only, 2 1/2 or 4 in. barrel, transfer bar ignition system. Mfg. 1974-1986.

$250	$185	$145	$120	$95	$85	$70	

MODEL 623 – similar to Model 622, chrome/nickel finish only. Mfg. 1957-1964.

$260	$195	$155	$130	$110	$95	$80	

* ***Model 623 Second Model*** – similar to Model 622 Second Model, except electroless nickel finish, transfer bar ignition system. Mfg. 1977-1979.

$250	$155	$130	$115	$95	$85	$75	

MODEL 632 – .32 S&W cal., 6 shot, blue finish, large solid frame, DA, round or square butt, 2 1/2 or 4 in. barrel, pull pin cylinder release. Mfg. 1952-1959.

$165	$145	$125	$110	$90	$80	$70	

* ***Model 632 Second Model*** – .32 S&W Long cal., 2 1/2 or 4 in. barrel, blue finish, 6 shot, transfer bar ignition system, DA, solid frame, pull pin cylinder, round or square butt. Mfg. 1973-1986.

$175	$155	$130	$115	$95	$85	$75	

MODEL 633 – similar to the Model 632, except chrome/nickel finish, 2 1/2 in. barrel only, round butt. Mfg. 1953-1959.

$185	$165	$140	$120	$100	$90	$80	

* ***Model 633 Second Model*** – similar to Model 632 Second Model, except nickel finish, 2 1/2 in. barrel only, transfer bar ignition system. Mfg. 1977-1979.

$195	$175	$150	$125	$110	$95	$85	

MODEL 642 – .22 WMR cal., 2 1/2 or 4 in. barrel, 6 shot, blue finish, DA, solid frame, pull pin cylinder release, round butt, transfer bar ignition. Mfg. 1980-1983.

$195	$175	$150	$125	$110	$95	$85	

MODEL 649 CONVERTIBLE – .22 LR or .22 cal., furnished with extra cylinder, similar to Model 949, Western style, double action, side loading, 5 1/2 or 7 1/2 in. barrel, 6 shot, walnut grips, blue finish, transfer bar ignition system. Mfg. 1976-1985.

$290	$235	$185	$150	$125	$100	$90	*$160*

MODEL 650 CONVERTIBLE – similar to Model 649, except with nickel finish and only available with 5 1/2 in. barrel. Mfg. 1975-1986.

$295	$240	$190	$155	$130	$110	$100	*$175*

MODEL 660 GUNFIGHTER – .22 LR cal., 6 shot, blue finish, 6 in. barrel, DA, solid frame, Western style grip. Mfg. 1960-1961.

$325	$285	$250	$200	$175	$150	$125	

MODEL 666 CONVERTIBLE – .22 LR or .22 WMR cal., 6 shot, 6 in. barrel, blue finish, plastic grips, square butt, extra cylinder, transfer bar ignition system. Mfg. 1975-1979.

$145	$125	$110	$90	$80	$75	$70	

GRADING - PPGS™	100%	98%	95%	90%	80%	70%	60%	LAST MSR

MODEL 676 CONVERTIBLE – .22 LR/.22 WMR cal., similar to the Model 649, except has finger spur on trigger guard, blue/case colored finish, 6 shot, 4 1/2, 5 1/2, 7 1/2, or 12 in. barrel, side load and eject, one piece walnut stock, fixed sights. Mfg. 1975-1980.

$300 $260 $215 $170 $145 $120 $110

Add 20% for 12 in. barrel.
Subtract $35 if with only one cylinder.

MODEL 686 CONVERTIBLE – .22 LR or .22 WMR cal., similar to Model 676 except with adj. target sights, larger frame, 4 1/2, 5 1/2, 7 1/2, or 12 in. barrel, transfer bar ignition. Mfg. 1980-1986.

$315 $270 $225 $175 $150 $125 $110

Add 20% for 12 in. barrel.
Subtract $35 if with only one cylinder.

MODEL 732 GUARDSMAN – .32 S&W cal., similar to Model 929, 6 shot, 2 1/2 and 4 in. barrels, DA, fixed sights, swing out cylinder, blue finish, round or square butt, black plastic grips. Mfg. 1957-1973.

$185 $165 $140 $120 $100 $90 $80

* ***Model 732 Guardsman Second Model*** – similar to Model 732 Guardsman, except with transfer bar ignition. Mfg. 1974-1986.

$195 $175 $150 $125 $110 $95 $85

MODEL 733 GUARDSMAN – similiar to the Model 732, except chrome/nickel finish, 2 1/2 in. barrel, round butt. Mfg. 1957-1986.

$195 $175 $150 $125 $110 $95 $85

* ***Model 733 Guardsman Second Model*** – .32 S&W Long cal., 6 shot, nickel finish, 2 1/2 or 4 (rare) in. barrel, transfer bar ignition, solid frame, DA, swing out cylinder, round butt. Mfg. 1973-1986.

$195 $175 $150 $125 $110 $95 $85

Add 10% for 4 in. barrel.

MODEL 826 – .22 WMR cal., 6 shot, 3 in. barrel, adj. rear sight, solid frame, DA, swing out cylinder, transfer bar ignition. Mfg. 1981-1983.

$190 $175 $150 $125 $110 $95 $85

MODEL 829 – .22 LR cal., 9 shot, blue finish, 3 in. barrel, adj. rear sight, solid frame, DA, swing out cylinder, transfer bar ignition. Mfg. 1981-1983.

$190 $175 $150 $125 $110 $95 $85

MODEL 830 – similar to Model 829, but with nickel finish. Mfg. 1982-1983.

$195 $175 $150 $125 $110 $95 $85

MODEL 832 – .32 S&W Long cal., similar to Model 830. Mfg. 1981-1983.

$190 $175 $150 $125 $110 $95 $85

MODEL 833 – similar to Model 832, but with nickel finish. Mfg. 1982-1983.

$195 $175 $150 $125 $110 $95 $85

MODEL 900 – .22 S, L, or LR cal., 9 shot, 2 1/2, 4, or 6 in. barrels, snap out cylinder, DA, blue finish, black plastic grips, solid frame. Mfg. 1962-1973.

$180 $150 $125 $90 $85 $70 $65

MODEL 901 – similar to Model 900, but chrome finish with white tenite grips. Mfg. 1962-1964.

$185 $155 $125 $110 $90 $80 $70

MODEL 903 – .22 LR cal., successor to the Model 939, 6 in. heavy barrel with raised rib, 9 shot, blue finish, adj. sights, DA, solid frame, swing out cylinder, transfer bar ignition. Mfg. 1980-1983.

$300 $195 $170 $140 $125 $110 $95

GRADING - PPGS™	100%	98%	95%	90%	80%	70%	60%	LAST MSR

MODEL 904 – .22 S, L, or LR cal., SA, similar to Model 903 except has 4 or 6 in. round bull barrel, target grade, 9 shot, adj. sights. Mfg. 1980-1985.

$300	$260	$215	$170	$145	$120	$110	*$168*

MODEL 905 – similar to Model 904, except with nickel finish and 4 in. round bull barrel only. Mfg. 1980-1986.

$300	$260	$215	$170	$145	$120	$110	*$185*

MODEL 922 BANTAM WEIGHT – .22 LR cal., blue finish, 2 1/2 in. barrel, 9 shot, DA, solid frame, pull pin cylinder release, round butt. Mfg. 1952-1961.

$215	$195	$165	$135	$120	$100	$90

MODEL 922 CAMPER – .22 LR cal., similar to Model 922 Bantam Weight, except has 4 in. barrel. Mfg. 1952-1955.

$215	$195	$165	$135	$120	$100	$90

MODEL 922 THIRD MODEL – .22 LR cal., features new frame, 2 1/2, 4, or 6 in. barrel, 9 shot, blue finish, solid frame, DA, pull pin cylinder release, round or square butt. Mfg. 1953-1961.

$195	$175	$150	$125	$110	$95	$85

MODEL 922 FOURTH MODEL – .22 LR cal., similar to Model 922 Second Model, except has transfer bar ignition. Mfg. 1973-1979.

$200	$180	$160	$130	$120	$100	$90

MODEL 923 FIRST MODEL BANTAM WEIGHT – .22 LR cal., 9 shot, chrome finish, 2 1/2 in. barrel, DA, solid frame, pull pin cylinder release, round butt. Mfg. 1953-1961.

$215	$195	$170	$135	$120	$100	$90

MODEL 923 FIRST MODEL CAMPER – .22 LR cal., similar to Model 923 Bantam Weight, except has 4 in. barrel. Mfg. 1952-1955.

$215	$195	$165	$135	$120	$100	$90

MODEL 923 SECOND MODEL – .22 LR cal., similar to Model 922 Second Model, features new frame. Mfg. 1953-1961.

$205	$185	$165	$135	$125	$100	$90

MODEL 923 THIRD MODEL – .22 LR cal., similar to 922 Third Model. Mfg. 1977-1979.

$210	$190	$165	$135	$120	$100	$90

MODEL 925 DEFENDER SECOND MODEL TOP BREAK – .22 LR or .38 S&W cal., new frame version of pre-1953 Model 925, blue or matte black finish, 2 1/2 or 4 (disc. 1969) in. barrel, top break, DA, 5 (.38 cal.) or 9 (.22 cal.) shot, birds-head grip, square butt (4 in. barrel 1968-69). Mfg. 1964-1972.

$265	$215	$180	$140	$125	$110	$95

Add 10% for 4 in. barrel.
Add 75% for 4 in. barrel (.22 cal.).
Add 15% for matte black finish.

MODEL 925 DEFENDER THIRD MODEL TOP BREAK – .38 S&W cal., similar to Second Model, except 2 1/2 in. barrel only, 5 shot, transfer bar ignition. Mfg. 1973-1978.

$265	$215	$180	$140	$125	$110	$95

MODEL 926 MANUAL EJECTOR TOP BREAK – .22 LR or .38 S&W cal., 5 (.38 S&W) or 9 (.22 LR) shot, 4 in. barrel, blue finish, DA, square butt, manual ejection, adj. rear sight, top break, walnut grips. Mfg. 1968-1972.

$265	$215	$180	$140	$125	$110	$95

Add 10% for .22 LR cal.

MODEL 926 MANUAL EJECTOR SECOND MODEL TOP BREAK – .22 LR or .38 S&W cal., 5 (.38 S&W) or 9 (.22 LR) shot, 4 in. barrel, blue finish, DA, square butt, manual ejection, adj. rear sight, top break, walnut grips, transfer bar ignition. Mfg. 1973-1978.

$265	$215	$185	$150	$125	$110	$95

GRADING - PPGS™	100%	98%	95%	90%	80%	70%	60%	LAST MSR

MODEL 929 SIDEKICK – .22 LR cal., 9 shot, 2 1/2, 4, or 6 in. barrels, swing out cylinder, plastic grips, blue finish, DA, round or square solid frame, DA, round or square butt. Mfg. 1956-1973.

	$200	$165	$135	$115	$95	$85	$75	$127

MODEL 929 SIDEKICK SECOND MODEL – .22 LR cal., 9 shot, 2 1/2, 4, or 6 in. barrels, swing out cylinder, plastic grips, blue finish, DA, round or square butt, transfer bar ignition. Mfg. 1974-1986.

	$210	$175	$150	$125	$110	$95	$85	$127

MODEL 930 SIDEKICK – similar to 929 Sidekick Second Model, except chrome/nickel finish and not available with 6 in. barrel. Mfg. 1957-1986.

	$215	$195	$170	$135	$120	$100	$90	$140

MODEL 930 SIDEKICK SECOND MODEL – similar to Model 930 Sidekick, except has transfer bar ignition, nickel finish. Mfg. 1974-1986.

	$220	$190	$165	$135	$120	$95	$80

MODEL 935 DEFENDER TOP BREAK – similar to Model 925 Third Model, top break, DA, nickel finish, transfer bar ignition. Mfg. 1977-1978.

	$275	$245	$210	$170	$145	$120	$110

MODEL 939 ULTRA SIDEKICK – .22 S, L, or LR cal., 9 shot, 6 in. flat sided bull barrel, swing out cylinder, vent rib, adj. sights, blue finish, solid frame, DA, square butt. Mfg. 1957-1972.

	$310	$265	$220	$180	$155	$135	$115

In 1962, the hammer mounted cylinder release button was discontinued. A key lock for safety was added in 1962, and discontinued in 1972. This model was H&R's second most expensive revolver.

MODEL 939 ULTRA SIDEKICK SECOND MODEL – similar to Model 939 Ultra Sidekick, except has transfer bar ignition. Mfg. 1973-1980.

	$300	$265	$225	$185	$160	$140	$120

MODEL 940 ULTRA SIDEKICK – similar to Model 939, except has 6 in. full round bull barrel. Mfg. 1970-1972.

	$300	$265	$225	$185	$160	$140	$120

MODEL 940 ULTRA SIDEKICK SECOND MODEL – similar to Model 940 Ultra Sidekick, except has transfer bar ignition. Mfg. 1973-1980.

	$275	$225	$175	$150	$125	$100	$90

MODEL 949 "FORTY NINER" – .22 S, L, or LR cal., 5 1/2 in. barrel, DA, solid frame, 9 shot, side load and Western style ejection, adj. rear sight, walnut grips. Mfg. 1961-1972.

	$275	$225	$175	$150	$125	$100	$90	$127

MODEL 949 "FORTY NINER" SECOND MODEL – .22 S, L, or LR cal., similar to Model 949 Forty Niner, except has transfer bar safety. Mfg. 1973-1986.

	$285	$235	$200	$160	$140	$115	$100

MODEL 950 – similar to Model 949, except with nickel finish. Mfg. 1974-1986.

	$290	$245	$210	$170	$145	$120	$110	$145

MODEL 976 – .22 LR cal., 9 shot, 7 1/2 in. barrel, rod ejection, solid frame, DA, Western style grips, blue finish, case colored hardened frame, fixed sights, transfer bar ignition, catalog number 97603, in 1978 catalog advertised as a 6 in. barrel. Mfg. 1978-1981.

	$310	$265	$220	$180	$155	$135	$115

Subtract $35 if with only one cylinder.

MODEL 976 DELUXE – .22 LR cal., 9 shot, 7 1/2 in. barrel, rod ejection, solid frame, DA, Western style grips, blue finish, case colored hardened frame, adj. sights, transfer bar ignition, catalog number 97602. Mfg. 1978-1981.

	$325	$280	$225	$185	$160	$140	$120

Subtract $35 if with only one cylinder.

GRADING - PPGS™	100%	98%	95%	90%	80%	70%	60%	LAST MSR

MODEL 999 ENGRAVED – similar to 999, only engraved throughout, 6 in. barrel only. Disc. 1985.

	$600	$500	$425	$365	$325	$285	$225	*$525*

MODEL 999 SPORTSMAN SECOND MODEL (NEW FRAME, TOP BREAK) – .22 LR cal., 9 shot, 6 in. barrel, adj. sights, top break, DA, blue finish. Mfg. 1953-1972.

	$575	$475	$410	$350	$210	$170	$150

MODEL 999 SILVER SPORTSMAN TOP BREAK – .22 LR cal., 9 shot, 6 in. barrel, top break, DA, chrome finish, serial number letter codes Z, AA, AB, AC only. Mfg. 1963-1966.

	$600	$500	$425	$365	$325	$285	$225

MODEL 999 SPORTSMAN THIRD MODEL TOP BREAK – .22 LR cal., 9 shot, 4 (new 1979) or 6 in. barrel, top break, DA, blue finish, adj. sights. Mfg. 1973-1986.

	$575	$475	$410	$350	$210	$170	$150

In 1979, this model was advertised as the Model 999 Automatic Ejecting and was offered as a 6 shot in .32 S&W Long cal.

MODEL 999 SPORTSMAN 1 of 999 TOP BREAK – .22 LR cal., top break, DA, 9 shot, 6 in. barrel, adj. sights, engraved, fitted wood case. Mfg. 1979-1986.

	$750	$625	$525	$450	$385	$340	$285

Values are only for unfired models with all original tags, manuals, commemorative medallion, wooden presentation case and cardboard box. Use Model 999 Third Model values if not intact.

RIFLES

MODEL 12 TARGET BOLT ACTION – .22 LR cal., single shot, 28 in. heavy barrel, high polish blue finish, no sights, drilled and tapped, walnut stained birch target stock, bolt cocks on closing, adj. trigger, accessory rail, palm rest, same military specs as the Winchester Model 52, internal company model name is M12 JROTC, 11 lbs. Mfg. 1981-1986.

	$850	$700	$600	$500	$425	$365	$310

Subtract 25% if w/o sights.

MODEL 58 (058) COMBO SINGLE SHOT – .22 Hornet or .30-30 Win. cal., or 20 ga., single shot side lever action, 22 in. rifle barrel and 24 in. smooth bore barrel, drilled and tapped, modified choke, blade front sight, adj. folding rear sight (rifle barrel only), color case frame with blue barrels, walnut stained pistol grip buttstock, 6 1/2 lbs. Mfg. 1975-1986.

	$225	$195	$170	$140	$125	$110	$95

While marked Model 58, the catalogs listed this gun as the Model 058.

MODEL 58C SEMI-AUTO (H&R MODEL 65) – .22 LR cal., blow back action, 23 in. heavy barrel, military designation for the H&R Model 65, has Model 58C and U.S. PROPERTY markings, 10 shot detachable box mag., protected front blade sight, manual bolt hold open, buttstock dimensions same as M-1 Garand, sling swivels, 9 lbs. Mfg. 1944-1945.

	$1,200	$995	$850	$765	$660	$575	$495

MODEL 60 REISING SEMI-AUTO – .45 ACP cal., delayed blow back action, 18 1/4 in. barrel, parkerized finish, 10 or 20 shot detachable box mag., front post and adj. rear sight, pistol grip walnut stock, sling swivels, semi-auto verson of the Model 50. Mfg. 1944-1946.

	$2,800	$2,400	$1,925	$1,575	$1,275	$1,050	$900

MODEL 65 H&R GENERAL SEMI-AUTO – .22 LR cal., blow back action, civilian version of the Model 58C, 23 in. heavy barrel, manual bolt hold open, 10 shot detachable box mag., front blade sight, rear adj. aperture sight, buttstock dimensions same as M-1 Garand, sling swivels, 9 lbs. Mfg. 1944-1945.

	$450	$395	$335	$285	$245	$210	$180

MODEL 150 LEATHERNECK SEMI-AUTO – .22 LR cal., blow back action, 22 in. heavy barrel, blue finish, 5 or 10 shot detachable box mag., adj. rear open sight, ramped front blade sight, plain walnut stock, 7 1/4 lbs. Mfg. 1948-1952.

	$300	$265	$225	$185	$160	$140	$120

GRADING - PPGS™	100%	98%	95%	90%	80%	70%	60%	LAST MSR

MODEL 151 LEATHERNECK SEMI-AUTO – .22 LR cal., blow back action, 22 in. heavy barrel, blue finish, 5 or 10 shot detachable box mag., Redfield M70 rear aperture sight, ramped front blade sight, plain walnut buttstock, 7 1/4 lbs. Mfg. 1948-1952.

$375 $325 $285 $235 $210 $175 $150

MODEL 155 SHIKARI SINGLE SHOT – .45-70 Govt. or .44 Mag. cal., single shot side lever break action, 24 or 28 in. blue barrel, drilled and tapped, blade front sight, adj. folding rear sight, case colored frame, walnut stained hardwood straight grip buttstock, brass cleaning rod, 7 - 7 1/4 lbs. Mfg. 1973-1981.

$275 $225 $190 $155 $130 $115 $100

Add 10% for .45-70 Govt. cal.

MODEL 157 SINGLE SHOT – .22 Hornet (mfg. 1976-1977), .22 WMR (1976-1977), or .30-30 Win. cal., single shot side lever break action, 22 in. blue barrel, drilled and tapped, blade front sight, adj. folding rear sight, case colored hardened frame, walnut stained hardwood pistol grip stock with Mannlicher-style forearm with nose cap, sling swivels, 6 1/2 lbs. Mfg. 1975-1983.

$295 $260 $225 $185 $160 $140 $120

MODEL 158

* ***Model 158 Topper 30/Topper Jet*** – .22 S&W Jet or .30-30 Win. cal., side lever break action, 22 in. blue barrel, case colored hardened frame, drilled and tapped, walnut stained hardwood pistol grip stock, blade front sight, folding rear sight, 6 1/2 lbs. Mfg. 1963 only.

$225 $195 $170 $140 $125 $110 $95

Add 25% for extra .22 Jet barrel.

* ***Model 158 Topper 4 in 1*** – standard with four barrels in .30-30 Win., .22 Jet, 20 ga. (mod. choke), and .410 bore (full choke). Mfg. 1964-1967.

$450 $395 $335 $285 $245 $210 $180

* ***Model 158 Topper Combo*** – standard with one rifled and one smoothbore barrel in .22 Jet (1968-1975), .22 Hornet (new 1975), or .30-30 Win., and 20 ga., straight grip stock. Mfg. 1968-1975.

$350 $320 $275 $225 $200 $165 $140

* ***Model 158 Rifle*** – 20 ga. shotgun barrel was disc. and model became rifle only in .22 Hornet or .30-30 Win. cal. Mfg. 1976-1984.

$225 $195 $170 $140 $125 $110 $95

MODEL 163 MUSTANG SINGLE SHOT – .30-30 Win. cal., 22 in. blue barrel, side lever break action, drilled and tapped, blade front sight, adj. folding rear sight, blue finished frame, gold plated trigger, straight grip walnut stock with contoured forearm, 6 1/2 lbs. Mfg. 1965-1966.

$225 $195 $170 $140 $125 $110 $95

MODEL 164 SINGLE SHOT – similar to Model 163 Mustang, except nickel finished frame. Mfg. 1966.

$225 $195 $170 $140 $125 $110 $95

MODEL 165 LEATHERNECK SEMI-AUTO – .22 LR cal., blow back action, 23 in. round tapered blue barrel, 10 shot detachable box mag., Redfield M79 rear aperture sight, ramped blade front sight, plain walnut stock, sling swivels. Mfg. 1946-1947 and 1959-1961.

$250 $225 $195 $170 $140 $125 $110

MODEL 171 SPRINGFIELD CAVALRY CARBINE – .45-70 Govt. cal., replica of Model 1873 Springfield Trapdoor Cavalry carbine, heavy 22 in. blue barrel, plain walnut stock with metal buttplate, adj. rear sight, blade front sight, color case hardened receiver, lock plate and buttplate, 7 lbs. Mfg. 1972-1986.

$650 $600 $525 $450 $395 $325 $275

GRADING - PPGS™	100%	98%	95%	90%	80%	70%	60%	LAST MSR

MODEL 171 SPRINGFIELD CAVALRY RIFLE – similar to Carbine, except has 26 in. barrel. Mfg. 1972-1973.

	$675	$585	$500	$435	$375	$325	$275

MODEL 171 DELUXE SPRINGFIELD CAVALRY CARBINE – similar to Model 171 Carbine, except has engraved receiver and lock plate, extra fancy walnut stock, original style rear sight. Mfg. 1974-1986.

	$750	$645	$560	$485	$420	$365	$310

MODEL 172 SILVER PLATE CARBINE – .45-70 Govt. cal., 22 in. heavy barrel, similar to Model 171 Carbine, except hand checkered select walnut stock with metal buttplate and grip adaptor, adj. tang mounted aperture rear sight, blade front sight, silver plated engraved receiver and lock plate, 7 1/4 lbs. Mfg. 1975 and 1977-1980.

	$1,650	$1,495	$1,250	$1,050	$875	$750	$625

MODEL 173 OFFICER MODEL RIFLE – .45-70 Govt. cal., 26 in. heavy blue barrel, plain walnut stock, metal buttplate and grip adaptor, adj. tang mounted aperture rear sight, blade front sight, color case hardened receiver, lock plate, and buttplate, cleaning rod mounted under barrel, 7 lbs. Mfg. 1975-1981.

	$800	$675	$550	$495	$425	$375	$325

MODEL 178 SPRINGFIELD RIFLE – .45-70 Govt. cal., 32 in. heavy blue barrel, full length American walnut stock, metal buttplate, ladder type rear sight, blade front sight, color case hardened receiver, lock plate, and buttplate, cleaning rod mounted under barrel, available in three variations - a Commemorative (ser. no. SPR-1 to SPR-1000, mfg. 1973-1975), Rifle (unknown ser. nos. and quantity, mfg. 1976), and the Infantry Rifle (unknown ser. nos. and quantity, mfg. 1977). Mfg. 1973-1977.

	$700	$600	$525	$450	$385	$340	$285

Add 50% for Commemorative model.

MODEL 250 SPORTSTER BOLT ACTION REPEATER – .22 LR cal., 23 in. round blue barrel, 5 shot detachable mag., plain walnut grip stock, ramped blade front sight, step adj. rear sight, 6 1/2 lbs. Mfg. 1948-1950.

	$195	$175	$150	$125	$110	$95	$85

MODEL 251 SPORTSTER BOLT ACTION REPEATER similar to Model 250 Sportster, except has Lyman No. 55H adj. aperture rear sight. Mfg. 1948-1950.

	$225	$195	$170	$140	$125	$110	$95

MODEL 258 HANDY GUN II SINGLE SHOT COMBO – .22 Hornet, .30-30 Win., .357 Mag., .357 Max., or .44 Mag. and 20 ga. smooth bore, side lever break action, 22 in. rifled barrel, drilled and tapped, electroless nickel finish, walnut stained hardwood pistol grip buttstock, includes fitted canvas carrying case, 6 1/2 lbs. Mfg. 1982-1986.

	$250	$220	$190	$155	$130	$115	$100

MODEL 264 TARGETEER BOLT ACTION REPEATER – .22 LR cal., 22 in. round blue barrel, 10 shot detachable box mag., plain walnut pistol grip stock, ramped blade front sight, step adj. rear sight, 6 3/4 lbs. Mfg. 1947-1948.

	$185	$165	$140	$120	$100	$90	$80

MODEL 265 TARGETEER BOLT ACTION REPEATER – similar to Model 264, except has adj. Lyman rear aperture sight. Mfg. 1946-1950.

	$285	$250	$215	$170	$145	$120	$110

* ***Model 265 Targeteer Jr.*** – .22 LR cal., similar to Model 265, except has shortened LOP stock. Mfg. 1948-1950.

	$250	$220	$190	$155	$130	$115	$100

MODEL 300 ULTRA BOLT ACTION – .22-250 Rem., .243 Win., .270 Win., .30-06, .308 Win., 7mm Rem. Mag., or .300 Win. Mag. cal., Mauser (mfg. by FN 1965-1972), Sako (mfg. 1973-1977), or Mauser Mark X (Mfg. by Zastava 1978-1983) repeater action, 3 or 5 shot internal mag., 22 in. blue barrel, drilled and tapped, ramped front blade sight, adj. rear sight, hinged floorplate, adj. trigger, checkered American walnut Monte Carlo stock with

GRADING - PPGS™	100%	98%	95%	90%	80%	70%	60%	LAST MSR

rollover cheekpiece and pistol grip stock, contrasting wood on pistol grip cap and forend, recoil pad, sling swivels, 7 3/4 lbs. Mfg. 1965-1981.

	$700	$525	$425	$350	$295	$250	$220	

MODEL 301 ULTRA BOLT ACTION CARBINE – .22-250 Rem., .243 Win., .270 Win., .30-06, or .308 Win. cal., repeater action similar to Model 300, 3 or 5 shot internal mag., 18 in. blue barrel, drilled and tapped, ramped front blade sight, adj. rear sight, hinged floorplate, adj. trigger, checkered Mannlicher American walnut Monte Carlo stock with rollover cheekpiece and pistol grip, contrasting wood on pistol grip cap and forend, recoil pad and sling swivels, 7 1/4 lbs. Mfg. 1967-1981.

	$650	$495	$400	$325	$275	$225	$200	

MODEL 317 ULTRA WILDCAT BOLT ACTION – .17/223 H&R Wildcat, .17 Rem., .222 Rem., or .223 Rem. cal., 6 shot internal mag., 20 in. blue barrel, hinged floor plate, no sights, drilled and tapped, hand checkered American walnut stock with cheekpiece and pistol grip, recoil pad, early mfg. used leftover inventory of the O'Brien Rifle Co. of Las Vegas, NV, which H&R purchased in the late 1960s, early production barrels were mfg. by Ackley and Shilen, later mfg. used Sako actions, 5 1/4 lbs. Mfg. 1968-1976.

	$600	$520	$440	$390	$340	$285	$245	

* ***Model 317P Presentation Grade Ultra Wildcat*** – similar to Model 317, except has basket weave pattern hand checkered American walnut stock with contrasting wood pistol grip cap and forend tip. Mfg. 1968-1976.

	$675	$585	$500	$435	$375	$325	$275	

MODEL 322 BOLT ACTION REPEATER – .222 Rem. cal., 5 shot mag., Sako short action, 24 in. medium weight barrel, adj. trigger, hand checkered European walnut Monte Carlo stock with cheekpiece, sling swivels, no sights. Mfg. 1973.

	$415	$350	$315	$275	$235	$195	$175	

MODEL 330 BOLT ACTION REPEATER – .243 Win., .270 Win., .30-06, or .308 Win. cal., 22 in. blue barrel, drilled and tapped, Mauser action, ramped front blade sight, adj. rear sight, hinged floorplate, adj. trigger, plain American walnut Monte Carlo stock with pistol grip, recoil pad, sling swivels, 7 1/8 lbs. Mfg. 1968-1972.

	$400	$350	$300	$265	$225	$190	$165	

MODEL 340 BOLT ACTION REPEATER – .22-250 Rem., .243 Win., .270 Win., .30-06, .308 Win., or 7x57mm cal., 3 shot internal mag., 22 in. blue barrel, blue finish, no sights, drilled and tapped, hinged floorplate, adj. trigger, American walnut Classic style stock, vent. recoil pad, sling swivels, 7 1/4 lbs. Mfg. 1981-1983.

	$400	$350	$300	$265	$225	$190	$165	

MODEL 360 ULTRA SEMI-AUTO – .243 Win. or .308 Win. cal., gas operated, side ejection, manual bolt stop, 3 shot detachable box mag., 22 in. blue barrel, drilled and tapped, ramped front sight, adj. open rear sight, checkered American walnut Monte Carlo stock with cheekpiece and pistol grip, contrasting wood on forearm tip and pistol grip cap, 7 1/2 lbs. Mfg. 1965-1977.

	$500	$440	$375	$325	$275	$235	$200	

MODEL 361 ULTRA DELUXE SEMI-AUTO – similar to Model 360, except has extra fancy American walnut stock with full rollover cheekpiece for right or left hand. Mfg. 1970-1973.

	$525	$465	$395	$340	$295	$250	$220	

MODEL 365 REG'LAR (A.K.A. ACE) – .22 LR cal., bolt action single shot, 22 in. round blue barrel, bolt cocks on closing, plain full size walnut pistol grip stock, ramped blade front sight, Lyman No. 55 rear sight, 6 1/2 lbs. Mfg. 1946-1947.

	$145	$125	$110	$100	$85	$75	$65	

MODEL 370 ULTRA MEDALIST BOLT ACTION – .22-250 Rem., .243 Win., 6mm Rem. Mag., repeater Mauser action, blue finish, 5 shot internal mag., 24 in. bull barrel with recessed muzzle crown, no sights, hinged floorplate, drilled and tapped, adj. trigger, target style American walnut oil finished stock with rollover cheekpiece, semi-beavertail forend, recoil

GRADING - PPGS™	100%	98%	95%	90%	80%	70%	60%	LAST MSR

pad, adj. sling swivels, 9 1/2 lbs. Mfg. 1968-1973.

	$515	$450	$395	$340	$295	$250	$220

MODEL 422 SLIDE ACTION – .22 LR cal., repeater action, 21 shot tube mag., 24 in. barrel, ramped front sight, step adj. rear sight, blue finish, plain walnut stock, grooved slide handle, 6 lbs. Mfg. by Noble Firearms Co. 1956-1958.

	$325	$285	$250	$200	$175	$150	$125

MODEL 424 BOLT ACTION – .22 LR cal., single shot, 22 in. round barrel, manual cocking, shortened plain walnut pistol grip stock, ramped blade front sight, step adj. rear sight, beginner's or boy's model, mfg. by Nobel Firearms Co. 1960-1961.

	$135	$120	$100	$85	$75	$65	$50

MODEL 450 MEDALIST BOLT ACTION – .22 LR cal., 26 in. round barrel, 5 shot detachable mag., repeater action, plain walnut pistol grip stock, no sights, blue finish, 9 1/2 lbs. Mfg. 1948.

	$375	$325	$285	$235	$210	$175	$150

MODEL 451 MEDALIST BOLT ACTION – similar to Model 450, except has Lyman No. 524 extension rear aperture sight. Mfg. 1948-1950 and 1959-1961.

	$400	$350	$300	$265	$225	$190	$165

MODEL 550 PAL BOLT ACTION – .22 LR cal., single shot, 22 in. round tapered barrel, bolt cocks on closing, plain full size walnut pistol grip stock, blade front sight, step adj. rear sight, blue finish, 5 lbs. Mfg. 1947-1948.

	$145	$125	$110	$100	$85	$75	$65

MODEL 565 PAL BOLT ACTION – .22 LR cal., single shot, 22 in. round tapered barrel, bolt cocks on closing, plain full size walnut pistol grip stock, blade front sight, Lyman adj. rear sight, blue finish, 5 lbs. Mfg. 1947.

	$175	$155	$130	$115	$95	$85	$75

MODEL 700 SEMI-AUTO – .22 WMR cal., blow back action, 22 in. round blue barrel, 5 or 10 shot detachable box mag., open adj. folding rear sight, ramped blade front sight, full size Monte Carlo style pistol grip walnut stock, high polish blue finish, composite buttplate, 6 1/2 lbs. Mfg. 1975-1986.

	$425	$365	$315	$275	$235	$195	$175

* ***Model 700 DL Deluxe*** – similar to Model 700, except has extra fancy checkered Monte Carlo walnut stock. Mfg. 1978-1986.

	$475	$425	$355	$300	$260	$220	$195

MODEL 749 SLIDE ACTION – .22 LR cal., 15 shot tube mag., 19 in. barrel, bead front sight, step adj. rear sight, walnut stained straight grip stock, grooved slide handle, 4 1/2 lbs. Mfg. 1970-1971.

	$150	$130	$115	$100	$85	$75	$65

This model was manufactured by Rossi and imported from Brazil. It was not listed in any H&R catalog.

MODEL 750 BOLT ACTION – .22 LR cal., 22 (mfg. 1966-1969) or 24 in. round barrel, bolt cocks on closing, plain full size sporter walnut pistol grip, rounded (mfg. 1978-1986) or Monte Carlo comb (mfg. 1963-1964) stock, finger grooved forend (mfg. 1965), bead front sight, step adj. rear sight, blue finish. Mfg. 1953-1986.

	$125	$110	$100	$85	$75	$65	$50

MODEL 751 BOLT ACTION – similar to Model 750, except has Mannlicher stock, 5 1/4 lbs. Mfg. 1971-1972.

	$155	$130	$115	$100	$85	$75	$65

MODEL 755 SAHARA SINGLE SHOT – .22 S, L, or LR cal., blow back action, automatic ejection, 18 in. blue barrel, walnut stained hardwood Mannlicher pistol grip stock, blade front sight, step adj. rear sight, 4 lbs. Mfg. 1963-1970.

	$145	$125	$110	$100	$85	$75	$65

GRADING - PPGS™	100%	98%	95%	90%	80%	70%	60%	LAST MSR

MODEL 760 SINGLE SHOT – similar to Model 755, except has regular Monte Carlo style stock. Mfg. 1965-1970.

	$165	$145	$125	$110	$90	$80	$70	

MODEL 765 PIONEER BOLT ACTION – .22 S, L, or LR cal., single shot, 24 in. blue barrel, pistol grip walnut stock, "RED DEVIL" hooded front (designed by Walter Roper) or dovetailed bead sight (mfg. 1950-1952), step adj. rear sight, safety on right side of receiver, "redi-feed" loading platform, 5 lbs. Mfg. 1948-1952.

	$175	$155	$130	$115	$95	$85	$75	

MODEL 766 PIONEER BOLT ACTION – similar to Model 765, except has nickel finish. Mfg. 1949-1950.

	$200	$180	$160	$130	$120	$100	$90	

MODEL 800 LYNX SEMI-AUTO – .22 LR cal., blow back action, 22 in. round barrel, blue finish, 10 shot detachable box mag., full size plain pistol grip walnut stock, bead front sight, open step adj. rear sight, 6 lbs. Mfg. 1958-1961.

	$300	$265	$225	$185	$160	$140	$120	

MODEL 880 LYNX DELUXE – similar to Model 800, except has nickel finish. Mfg. 1958-1959.

	$375	$325	$285	$235	$210	$175	$150	

MODEL 852 FIELDSMAN BOLT ACTION – .22 LR cal., repeater action, 21 shot tube mag., 24 in. tapered barrel, full size pistol grip walnut stained hardwood stock, blue finish, bead front sight, step adj. rear sight, 5 1/2 lbs. Mfg. 1952-1954.

	$175	$155	$130	$115	$95	$85	$75	

MODEL 865 PLAINSMAN BOLT ACTION – .22 LR cal., repeater action, 22 (mfg. 1966-1969) or 24 in. round tapered barrel, 5 shot detachable box mag., full size oil finished or satin (mfg. 1959-1961) walnut, blonde Monte Carlo (mfg. 1962-1964), or walnut stained hardwood (mfg. 1970-1975) pistol grip stock, ramped white bead front sight, step adj. rear sight, blue finish, single claw extractor, stamped steel trigger guard, 5 lbs. Mfg. 1949-1986.

	$135	$120	$100	$85	$75	$65	$50	

Add 10%-50% for stock options, depending on grade.

MODEL 866 BOLT ACTION – similar to Model 865, except has Mannlicher stock. Mfg. 1971-1972.

	$175	$155	$130	$115	$95	$85	$75	

MODEL 5200 TARGET BOLT ACTION – .22 LR cal., single shot, bolt cocks on closing, 28 in. heavy barrel, no sights, drilled and tapped, full size walnut stained birch target stock, accessory rail, palm stop, adj. trigger, high polish blue finish, fluid feed loading platform, similar to mil spec version of the Winchester Model 52. Mfg. 1981-1986.

	$550	$475	$415	$360	$315	$265	$230	

MODEL 5200S SPORTER BOLT ACTION – .22 LR cal., repeater action, 24 in. bull barrel, 5 shot detachable box mag., hand checkered American walnut pistol grip stock, adj. trigger, hooded ramped blade front sight, adj. Lyman aperture sight, blue finish, 6 1/2 lbs. Limited mfg. 1982-1983.

	$650	$565	$485	$425	$360	$310	$265	

MODEL M-4 SURVIVAL – .22 Hornet cal., 5 shot mag., 14 or 16 in. barrel, wire folding stock, mfg. for U.S. military during the 1950s.

	$2,000	$1,650	$1,425	$1,125	$965	$855	$750	

Add $400 for barrels less than 16 in. (sales restricted).

This model was packaged in survival kits for U.S. pilots, and is usually encountered with a replacement barrel of 16 inches or more.

MODEL M-1 GARAND – .30-06 cal., semi-auto, 8 shot internal mag., some may be arsenal refinished, mfg. for the U.S. military during the 1950s.

	$1,550	$1,325	$1,150	$895	$750	$625	$495	

Subtract 60% if w/o correct parts.

GRADING - PPGS™	100%	98%	95%	90%	80%	70%	60%	LAST MSR

MODEL T-48 FAL/T223 (H&R MFG. FAL) – .308 Win. cal., 20 shot mag., selective fire, approx. 200 mfg. for U.S. military during the 1960s.

Recent values are approx. $10,000 for 98% condition.

Since sales of this rifle are restricted, it is not often encountered in the used marketplace.

M-14 RIFLE/GUERILLA GUN – .308 Win. cal., selective fire, 20 shot mag., Guerilla gun mfg. in prototype only, mfg. for the U.S. military during the 1960s.

Recent values are approx. $20,000 for 98% condition.

Since sales of this rifle are restricted, it is not often encountered in the used marketplace.

M-16 AUTOMATIC BATTLE RIFLE – 5.56 Nato cal., selective fire, 20 or 30 shot mag., mfg. for the U.S. military during the 1960s-1970s.

Recent values are approx. $15,000 for 98% condition.

Since sales of this rifle are restricted, it is not often encountered in the used marketplace.

T-223 (H&R MFG. H&K 93) – .223 Rem. or .308 Win. cal., selective fire, 20 shot mag., approx. 200 mfg. for the U.S. military during the 1960s.

Recent values are approx. $15,000 for 98% condition.

Since sales of this rifle are restricted, it is not often encountered in the used marketplace.

SLIDE ACTION CENTERFIRE RIFLE – .300 Sav. cal., prototype, only 2 known to exist, one complete firing model, and one non-firing model, based on Eugene Reising's patent. Mfg. during the 1940s-1950s.

Extreme rarity precludes accurate pricing on this model.

SHOTGUNS: BOLT ACTION

MODEL 120 – 16 ga., 2 3/4 in. chamber, 5 shot tube mag., blue finish, 26 in. barrel with choke tubes, safety on right side of receiver, oil finished walnut pistol grip stock, vent. rubber recoil pad, 7 1/2 lbs. Mfg. 1941-1942.

$145	$125	$110	$95	$85	$75	$65	

H&R sold the rights to this shotgun to Sears Roebuck & Co, and it was mfg. by High Standard.

MODEL 121 – 20 ga., 2 3/4 in. chamber, otherwise similar to Model 120. Mfg. 1941-1942.

$145	$125	$110	$95	$85	$75	$65	

H&R sold the rights to this shotgun to Sears Roebuck & Co, and it was mfg. by High Standard.

MODEL 348 GAMESTER – 12 or 16 ga., 28 in. barrel, 3 shot tube mag., blue finish, safety located on the right side of the receiver, oil finished pistol grip walnut stock with fluted comb, hard rubber recoil pad, 7 1/2 lbs. Mfg. 1949-1954.

$165	$145	$125	$110	$90	$80	$70	

MODEL 349 GAMESTER DELUXE – 12 or 16 ga., 26 in. barrel, 3 shot tube mag., H&R's "VARI-CHOKE" adj. choke, oil finished pistol grip walnut stock with fluted comb, 7 1/2 lbs. Mfg. 1952-1955.

$175	$155	$130	$115	$95	$85	$75	

MODEL 351 HUNTSMAN – similar to the Model 349 Deluxe, except has new model number and walnut stained hardwood stock. Mfg. 1956-1958.

$175	$155	$130	$115	$95	$85	$75	

SHOTGUNS: DOUBLE

ANSON & DEELEY DOUBLE BARREL SxS – 10 or 12 ga., 28, 30, or 32 in. damascus barrels, hammerless boxlock action, 4 grades of European walnut stock and forend, 4 levels of engraving, Anson & Deeley markings on lockplate, H&R markings on barrels, ser. no. 01-3000+. Mfg. 1883-1887.

N/A	$1,000	$865	$765	$660	$495	$450	

SMALL BORE DOUBLE BARREL HAMMER GUN – 20, 28 ga., or .410 bore, 26 or 28 in. barrels, SxS, sidelock action with exposed hammers, English checkered walnut pistol grip stock, DT, cross bolt barrel locking, forged steel case hardened frame, 5 1/4 - 6 1/4 lbs. Mfg. 1909-1919.

N/A	$1,500	$1,225	$1,050	$875	$675	$550	

GRADING - PPGS™	100%	98%	95%	90%	80%	70%	60%	LAST MSR

MODEL 404 DOUBLE BARREL SxS – 12, 20 ga., or .410 bore, hammerless boxlock action, DT, 26 or 28 in. barrels, walnut stained Brazilian hardwood stock with beavertail forend, with (Model 404) or w/o (Model 404C) machine checkering. Mfg. by Rossi 1970-1971.

	$250	$220	$190	$155	$130	$115	$100

Add 15% for Model 404C.

HARRICH #1 O/U – 12 ga., 2 3/4 in. chambers, hammerless boxlock action, single barrel mfg. on O/U frame from Ferlach, Austria, raised vent. rib, 30 or 32 in. barrel, blue finish, engraved receiver, European walnut buttstock and beavertail forearm, Anson & Deeley crossbolt with double locking lugs. Mfg. 1971-1975.

	$1,950	$1,635	$1,425	$1,125	$965	$855	$750

MODEL 1212 O/U – 12 ga., 2 3/4 in. chambers, boxlock hammerless action, European walnut stock and beavertail forearm, SST, extractors, 28 in. barrels with vent. rib, gold bead front sight, 7 lbs. Mfg. by Lanber 1975-1980.

	$400	$365	$325	$285	$250	$200	$175

* ***Model 1212WF*** – similar to Model 1212, except has 3 in. chambers, 30 in. barrels, 7 1/2 lbs. Mfg. by Lanber 1975-1980.

	$350	$320	$275	$225	$200	$165	$140

SHOTGUNS: SINGLE BARREL, 1900-1942 MFG.

MODEL 1900 – 12, 16, or 20 ga., 28, 30, or 32 in. barrel, top lever break action, two-piece takedown via removable hinge pin, full choke, case hardened frame, walnut pistol grip stock with short forearm, hard rubber buttplate, 5 3/4 - 6 3/8 lbs. Mfg. 1901-1916.

	$175	$155	$130	$115	$95	$85	$75

This model may have been available under a store brand name through mail order catalogs.

MODEL 1905 – many gauges, small frame version of the Model 1900. Mfg. 1906-1916.

	$175	$155	$130	$115	$95	$85	$75

Add 25% for auto-ejector model in .44 cal., 14mm, and .410 Eley chambering (mfg. 1911-1916).

This model may have been available under a store brand name through mail order catalogs.

MODEL 1908 – 12, 16, 20, 24 (disc. 1923), 28 ga. (disc. 1923), or .410 bore (new 1925), top lever break action, case hardened frame, 26, 28, 30, or 32 in. barrel, three piece takedown (non-removable hinge pin), non-adj. barrel lock, walnut pistol grip stock and forearm, hard rubber buttplate, 5 3/4 - 6 3/8 lbs. Mfg. 1909-1942.

	$195	$175	$150	$125	$110	$95	$85

Add 25% for 24 or 28 ga.
Subtract 25% for store brand model.

The first variation (mfg. 1909-1921) has a 2 1/2 in. chamber and short forearm, the second variation (mfg. 1922-1930) has a 2 3/4 in. chamber and slim, long forearm, third variation (mfg. 1925-1942) featured .410 bore, and the fourth variation (mfg. 1931-1942) had a wider forearm and was known as the No. 8 Standard, and "STANDARD" is marked on the left side of frame.

This model was available under a store brand name through mail order catalogs.

MODEL 1915 – 24, 28 ga., or .410 bore, top lever break action, 26, 28, or 30 in. barrel, small frame, non-adj. barrel lock, three piece take down (non-removable hinge pin), case hardened frame, walnut pistol grip stock and forearm, hard rubber buttplate, 4 - 4 3/4 lbs. Mfg. 1916-1942.

	$375	$325	$285	$235	$210	$175	$150

The .410 bore can be dated by its markings: 410-44 (mfg. 1916-1921), 410-12MM (Mfg. 1922-1936), and 410 (mfg. 1937-1941 - only pre-WWII model chambered for the 3 in. shell).

This model was available under a store brand name through mail order catalogs.

The first variation (mfg. 1916-1921) has a short forearm, the second variation (mfg. 1922-1930) has a long forearm and squared off pistol grip, the third variation (mfg. 1931-1936) was known as the No. 5 Standard (may be marked on the frame), and the fourth variation (mfg. 1937-1942) is a .410 bore chambered for 3 in. shells.

GRADING - PPGS™	100%	98%	95%	90%	80%	70%	60%	LAST MSR

BAY STATE & COLUMBIA BRAND NAME – 12, 16 ga., or .410 bore, top lever break action, blue finish, 26, 28, 30, or 32 in. barrel, three piece takedown (non-removable hinge pin), walnut pistol stock and forearm, hard rubber buttplate, 5 3/4 - 6 3/8 lbs. Mfg. 1916-1942.

$200 $180 $160 $130 $120 $100 $90

This model was a brand name shotgun and can be found under the following trade names: No. 7 Bay State, No. 7 Bay State Lightweight Gun, No. 9 Columbia, No. 9 Bay State, No. 9 Bay State Lightweight and others.

H&R FOLDING MODEL – 12, 16, 20 ga., or .410 bore, 26 in. barrel, top lever break action, case hardened frame, blue finish, walnut pistol grip stock and forearm, 5 3/4 - 6 1/2 lbs. Mfg. 1928-1942.

$375 $325 $285 $235 $210 $175 $150

The .410 bore model was available with a 3 in. chamber after 1937. This model was known after 1931 as the No. 4 Folding Model.

H&R LIGHTWEIGHT FOLDING MODEL – 28 ga. or .410 bore, 26 in. barrel, top lever break action, case hardened small frame, blue finish, walnut pistol grip stock and forearm, 5 3/4 - 6 1/2 lbs. Mfg. 1925-1930.

$400 $350 $300 $265 $225 $190 $165

The .410 bore model was available with a 3 in. chamber after 1937. This model was known after 1931 as the No. 4 Folding Lightweight Model.

H&R HAMMERLESS – 12, 16, 20 ga., or .410 bore, top lever break action, 26, 28, 30, 32, 34, or 36 in. barrel, three piece take down (non-removable hinge pin), snap-on forearm, walnut pistol grip stock, 6 1/4 - 7 1/4 lbs. Mfg. 1925-1941.

$400 $350 $300 $265 $225 $190 $165

The .410 bore model was available with a 3 in. chamber after 1937. After 1931, this model was listed in catalogs as the No. 3 Hammerless Model.

H&R RE-ENFORCED BREECH (A.K.A. HEAVY BREECH) – 10 (new 1931), 12, 16, or 20 (new 1933) ga., large heavy frame, top lever break action, 30, 32, 34, or 36 in. barrel, case hardened frame, walnut pistol grip stock and forearm, hard rubber buttplate, 7 - 7 3/8 lbs. Mfg. 1913-1941.

$385 $330 $285 $235 $210 $175 $150

Add 15% for 10 ga.

After 1931 this model is known as the No. 6 Heavy Breech Model, and is marked "RE-ENFORCED" on the frame.

H&R TOP RIB MODEL – 12, 16, or 20 ga., top lever break action, 28 or 30 in. barrel with chokes, case hardened frame, three piece take down (non-removable hinge pin), non-adj. barrel lock, walnut pistol grip stock, hard rubber buttplate, 5 1/4 - 6 1/4 lbs. Mfg. 1926-1932.

$325 $285 $250 $200 $175 $150 $125

After 1931, this model was listed in catalogs as the No. 2 Top Rib Model.

SHOTGUNS: SINGLE BARREL, 1943-1986 MFG.

TOPPER MODEL HISTORY – The Topper name was applied to a large series of single barrel shotguns therefore there were several different models that used the Topper name starting with the Model 48 in 1943 and continuing through the early Model 058/098. All other single barrel shotguns are variations of these basic models except for the Hammerless Model manufactured between 1925 and 1942. The Topper name was last used in the 1974 catalog. The Model 088 was actually introduced in 1979 but did not become the main line model until 1982. The Topper name has also been used by New England Firearms and H&R 1871 after the purchase by Marlin, but these models are not considered true H&R Topper single barrel shotguns.

MODEL 47 TOPPER DELUXE – similar to Model 48 Topper, except has all chrome finish. Mfg. 1947.

$165 $145 $125 $110 $90 $80 $70

GRADING - PPGS™	100%	98%	95%	90%	80%	70%	60%	LAST MSR

MODEL 48 TOPPER – 12, 16, 20 ga., or .410 bore, 26 to 32 in. barrel with chokes, case hardened frame, top lever break open action, rebounding hammer, self-adj. barrel latch, auto-ejector, three-piece takedown (snap on forearm), oil finished walnut pistol grip stock, semi-beavertail forearm, hard rubber buttplate, this model was the first to use the Topper name. Mfg. 1943-1956.

	100%	98%	95%	90%	80%	70%	60%	LAST MSR
	$150	$130	$115	$100	$85	$75	$60	

MODEL 058 TOPPER – 12, 16, 20 ga., or .410 bore, 26 to 36 in. barrel with chokes, case hardened frame, side lever break open action, self-adj. barrel latch, walnut stained pistol grip hardwood stock, semi-beavertail forearm, hard rubber buttplate, 13 3/4 in. LOP, rebounding hammer (mfg. 1974-1976) or transfer bar ignition system (mfg. 1977-1981). Mfg. 1974-1981.

	100%	98%	95%	90%	80%	70%	60%	LAST MSR
	$165	$145	$125	$110	$90	$80	$70	

Guns are marked Model 58.

MODEL 088 AMERICAN CLASSIC – 12, 16, 20, 28 ga., or .410 bore, 25 to 36 in. barrel with chokes, side lever break open action, transfer bar ignition system, case colored frame, walnut stained semi-pistol grip hardwood stock and semi-beavertail forearm, hard rubber buttplate, 13 3/4 in. LOP, 5 - 6 1/2 lbs. Mfg. 1979-1986.

	100%	98%	95%	90%	80%	70%	60%	LAST MSR
	$165	$145	$125	$110	$90	$80	$70	

The name "American Classic" was not added until the 1982 catalog.

Guns are marked Model 88.

* ***Model 088 American Classic Junior*** – similar to Model 088 American Classic, except only 20 ga. or .410 bore, 12 3/4 in. LOP, 5 lbs. Mfg. 1979-1986.

	100%	98%	95%	90%	80%	70%	60%	LAST MSR
	$165	$145	$125	$110	$90	$80	$70	

MODEL 098 TOPPER DELUXE – 12 (new 1977), 20 ga., or .410 bore, deluxe version of the Model 058, 26 in. barrel with chokes, nickel frame, black hardwood pistol grip stock, 5 1/2 lbs. Mfg. 1974-1981.

	100%	98%	95%	90%	80%	70%	60%	LAST MSR
	$185	$165	$140	$120	$100	$90	$80	

Guns are marked Model 98.

MODEL 099 AMERICAN CLASSIC DELUXE – 12, 16, 20 ga., or .410 bore, deluxe version of the Model 088, 25 to 28 in. barrel with choke, electroless nickel frame, walnut stained pistol grip hardwood stock, semi-beavertail forearm, transfer bar ignition system, hard rubber buttplate, 5 1/4 - 6 1/2 lbs. Mfg. 1982-1986.

	100%	98%	95%	90%	80%	70%	60%	LAST MSR
	$185	$165	$140	$120	$100	$90	$80	

Guns are marked Model 99.

MODEL 148 TOPPER – 12, 16, 20 ga., or .410 bore, similar to Model 48 Topper, except has vent. rubber recoil pad. Mfg. 1957-1958.

	100%	98%	95%	90%	80%	70%	60%	LAST MSR
	$150	$130	$115	$100	$85	$75	$65	

* ***Model 148A Topper*** – similar to the Model 148 Topper, except has a side lever break open action. Mfg. 1958-1961.

	100%	98%	95%	90%	80%	70%	60%	LAST MSR
	$155	$135	$120	$100	$85	$75	$65	

MODEL 158 TOPPER – 12, 16, 20 ga., or .410 bore, 28 to 36 in. barrel with chokes, side lever break open action, rebounding hammer, self-adj. barrel latch, three piece takedown with snap on forearm, case hardened frame, blue finish, glossy-satin finished pistol grip walnut stock, semi-beavertail forearm, vent. rubber recoil pad. Mfg. 1962-1973.

	100%	98%	95%	90%	80%	70%	60%	LAST MSR
	$155	$135	$120	$100	$85	$75	$65	

MODEL 158 COMBO RIFLE/SHOTGUN – please refer to the Rifle section.

MODEL 159 GOLDEN SQUIRE – 12 or 20 ga., side lever break open action, 28 (20 ga.) or 30 (12 ga.) in. barrel with chokes, rebounding hammer, self-adj. barrel latch, three piece takedown, snap on forearm, case hardened frame, high polish blue finish, glossy satin finished straight grip walnut stock, Schnabel forearm, custom recoil pad, gold hammer, trigger, gold filled lettering. Mfg. 1964-1966.

	100%	98%	95%	90%	80%	70%	60%	LAST MSR
	$225	$195	$170	$140	$125	$110	$95	

GRADING - PPGS™	100%	98%	95%	90%	80%	70%	60%	LAST MSR

MODEL 162 TOPPER BUCK – 12 or 20 (mfg. 1973-1978) ga., side lever break open action, 22 or 24 in. barrel, rebounding hammer, self-adj. barrel latch, case hardened frame, blue finish, three piece takedown, screw retained forearm, pistol grip walnut stained hardwood stock, semi-beavertail forearm, vent. rubber recoil pad, adj. rear aperture sight. Mfg. 1968-1986.

$185	$165	$140	$120	$100	$90	$80	

MODEL 176 MAGNUM – 10, 12, 16, or 20 ga., heavy frame, 32 or 36 in. barrel, chokes, side lever break open action, self-adj. barrel latch, three piece takedown, case hardened frame, blue finish, walnut stained pistol grip hardwood stock, semi-beavertail forearm, vent. rubber recoil pad, approx. 9 1/2 lbs. Mfg. 1975-1986.

$350	$320	$275	$225	$200	$165	$140	

Add 15% for 10 ga. with 36 in. barrel.

MODEL 176 SLUG GUN – 10 ga., 3 1/2 in. chamber, 28 in. barrel, heavy frame, side lever break open action, cylinder bore choke, three piece takedown, bored special for rifled slugs, case hardened frame, walnut stained pistol grip hardwood stock, semi-beavertail forearm, vent., rubber recoil pad, 9 1/4 lbs. Mfg. 1982-1986.

$375	$325	$285	$235	$210	$175	$150	

MODEL 188 TOPPER DELUXE – .410 bore, 3 in. chamber, 28 in. barrel with chokes, chrome frame, top lever break open action, rebounding hammer, deluxe variation of the Model 148, black lacquer pistol grip stock, semi-beavertail forearm, vent., rubber recoil pad. Mfg. 1957-1958.

$175	$155	$130	$115	$95	$85	$75	

* ***Model 188A Topper Deluxe*** – similar to Model 188 Topper Deluxe, except has multi-colored lacquered stock. Mfg. 1958-1961.

$185	$165	$140	$120	$100	$90	$80	

MODEL 198 TOPPER DELUXE – 20 ga. (mfg. 1970-1973) or .410 bore, 3 in. chamber, 26 or 28 in. barrel, side lever break open action, deluxe variation of the Model 158, rebounding hammer, chrome finish, three piece takedown, snap-on forearm, glossy satin finished ebony painted pistol grip stock, semi-beavertail forearm, approx. 5 1/2 lbs. Mfg. 1962-1973.

$185	$165	$140	$120	$100	$90	$80	

MODEL 459 GOLDEN SQUIRE JR. – 20 ga. or .410 bore, side lever brake open action, gold hammer, trigger, and gold filled lettering, rebounding hammer, 26 in. barrel with chokes, three piece takedown, snap on forearm, case hardened frame, high polish blue finish, straight grip walnut stock with Schnabel forearm, custom recoil pad, short LOP. Mfg. 1964.

$235	$200	$175	$145	$125	$110	$95	

MODEL 480 TOPPER JR. – 20 ga. or .410 bore, Junior version of the Model 148, 12 1/2 in. LOP, 26 in. barrel with chokes, satin lacquered stock and forearm, hard rubber buttplate, approx. 5 lbs. Mfg. 1958-1961.

$155	$135	$120	$100	$85	$75	$65	

MODEL 488 DELUXE SPORTER – 12, 16, 20 ga., or .410 bore, 28 or 30 in. barrel with chokes, deluxe edition of the Model 48, top lever break open action, rebounding hammer, chrome finished frame, hard rubber buttplate, pistol grip walnut stock and semi-beavertail forearm, approx. 6 lbs. Mfg. 1951-1957.

$195	$175	$150	$125	$110	$95	$85	

MODEL 490 TOPPER JR. – 20, 28 ga., or .410 bore, side lever break open action, junior verson of the Model 158, 26 in. barrel, rebounding hammer, three-piece takedown, case hardened frame, walnut stained pistol grip hardwood stock, semi-beavertail forearm, vent. rubber recoil pad, short LOP, 5 lbs. Mfg. 1961-1983.

$155	$135	$120	$100	$85	$75	$65	

MODEL 490 GREENWING – 20, 28 ga., or .410 bore, based on the Model 158, transfer bar ignition system, 26 in. barrel, high polished blue frame, walnut stained pistol grip hardwood stock, semi-beavertail forearm, hard rubber buttplate, gold trigger, gold markings, short LOP, 5 lbs. Mfg. 1978-1983.

$185	$165	$140	$120	$100	$90	$80	

GRADING - PPGS™	100%	98%	95%	90%	80%	70%	60%	LAST MSR

MODEL 580 TOPPER JR. DELUXE – 20 ga. (new 1959) or .410 bore, junior version of the Model 148, 26 in. barrel, chrome frame finish, ebony painted pistol grip stock, satin lacquered semi-beavertail forearm, short LOP, 5 lbs. Mfg. 1958-1960.

	$195	$175	$150	$125	$110	$95	$85	

MODEL 590 TOPPER JR. DELUXE – 20 ga. or .410 bore, junior version of the Model 158, similar to Model 580 Topper Jr. Deluxe, except has satin finished forearm. Mfg. 1961-1963.

	$165	$145	$125	$110	$90	$80	$70	

SHOTGUNS: SEMI-AUTO

MODEL 403 – .410 bore, gas operated, hammerless small size receiver, 3 in. chamber, 6 shot tube mag., 26 in. barrel, blue finish, walnut pistol grip stock, vent. rubber recoil pad, 5 3/4 lbs. Mfg. by Noble Firearms Corp. 1964.

	$200	$180	$160	$130	$120	$100	$90	

H&R MANUFRANCE – 12 ga., 3 in. chamber, 4 shot tube mag., recoil operated, takedown model with interchangeable barrels, checkered walnut buttstock. Mfg. by Manufrance 1969.

	$250	$220	$190	$155	$130	$115	$100	

SHOTGUNS: SLIDE ACTION

MODEL 400 – 12 or 16 ga., 2 3/4 chamber, 6 shot tube mag., hammerless standard size receiver, 28 in. barrel, blue finish, vent. rubber recoil pad, walnut pistol grip stock, 7 1/4 lbs. Mfg. by Noble Firearms Corp. 1958-1967.

	$165	$145	$125	$110	$90	$80	$70	

MODEL 401 – 12 or 16 ga., similar to Model 400, except has fancy checkered walnut, adj. "VARI-CHOKE", 7 1/4 lbs. Mfg. by Noble Firearms Corp. 1958-1963.

	$185	$165	$140	$120	$100	$90	$80	

MODEL 402 – similar to Model 400, except is .410 bore, small frame, 26 in. barrel, 5 1/2 lbs. Mfg. by Noble Firearms Corp. 1959-1967.

	$200	$180	$160	$130	$120	$100	$90	

MODEL 440 – 12, 16 (2 3/4 in. chamber), or 20 ga., 4 shot tube mag., 26 or 28 in. barrel, hammerless standard size receiver, push button safety at rear of trigger, bolt release at front of trigger, side ejecting, blue finish, walnut pistol grip stock and semi-beavertail forearm, vent. rubber recoil pad, 6 1/4 - 6 1/2 lbs. Mfg. by Manufrance 1968-1973.

	$165	$145	$125	$110	$90	$80	$70	

MODEL 442 – similar to Model 440, except has extra fancy checkered walnut stock and forearm. Mfg. 1969-1972.

	$195	$175	$150	$125	$110	$95	$85	

MODEL 500 – 12, 16, or 20 ga., 2 3/4 in. chamber, 3 or 4 shot detachable box mag., 28 or 30 in. barrel, oil finished walnut stock, 6 1/4 - 6 3/4 lbs. Mfg. 1946.

This model never appeared in any H&R catalog, and likely exists in prototype form only. Design appears to be based on a Eugene Reising patent.

COMMEMORATIVES

CHISHOLM TRAIL MODEL 999 – 300 mfg., not listed in catalogs. Mfg. 1967.

	$495	$435	$370	$320	$270	$230	$195	

NEBRASKA CENTENNIAL – letter coded "NE" serial numbers, presentation case, unknown number mfg. 1967.

	$1,000	$865	$765	$660	$575	$495	$450	

MODEL 926 ABILENE KANSAS CENTENNIAL – .22 LR cal., barrel is marked "Abilene Kansas" and "1869 Centennial 1969", not listed in catalogs, 300 mfg. 1969 only.

	$350	$320	$275	$225	$200	$165	$140	

MODEL 999 1 of 999 – similar to previous Model 999 1 of 999, except listed in 1981 catalog, values are for complete set. Mfg. 1981-1986.

	$700	$600	$525	$450	$385	$340	$285	

GRADING - PPGS™	100%	98%	95%	90%	80%	70%	60%	LAST MSR

MODEL 171 AND 171 DELUXE – please refer to listings under Rifles section.

MODEL 172 SILVER CARBINE – please refer to listing under Rifles.

CUSTER MEMORIAL ISSUE (MODEL 177) – .45-70 Govt. cal., limited production, deluxe walnut stock, highly engraved, gold inlaid, mahogany display case and two volumes on Custer history - *Reno Court of Inquiry* and *Men with Custer*. Each weapon bears the name of one who fell at Little Big Horn, originally 25 Officer models and 243 Enlisted Men models were scheduled to be mfg., but only 100 total were actually made. Total number made of each model is unknown.

* ***Custer Memorial Issue Officer's Model*** – 26 in. heavy barrel, tang mounted rear sight, must be NIB w/original box and accessories, 8 lbs.

	$3,995	$3,150	$2,400	$2,100	$1,900	$1,500	$1,200	*$3,000* *(1973)*

* ***Custer Memorial Issue Enlisted Men's Model*** – 22 in. heavy barrel, original ladder style rear sight, must be NIB w/original box and accessories, 7 lbs.

	$1,995	$1,400	$900	$785	$655	$550	$465	*$2,000* *(1973)*

MODEL 174 LITTLE BIG HORN CARBINE – .45-70 Govt. cal., replica of Model 1873 Springfield Trapdoor Cavalry carbine, heavy 22 in. blue barrel, plain walnut stock with metal buttplate and grip adaptor, adj. rear sight, blade front sight, color case hardened receiver, lock plate and buttplate, engraved lock and receiver, includes box with the book *In the Valley of the Little Big Horn*, 7 lbs., 4 oz. Mfg. 1972-1983.

	$850	$725	$640	$550	$490	$425	$375

MODEL 178 SPRINGFIELD COMMEMORATIVE RIFLE – please refer to Rifles section.

MODEL 1871-1971 H&R CENTENNIAL COMMEMORATIVE OFFICERS RIFLE – .45-70 Govt. cal., 26 in. heavy blue barrel, select hand checkered walnut stock, metal buttplate, forend cap, and grip adaptor, tang mounted adj. rear sight, blade front sight, cleaning rod mounted under barrel, color case hardened receiver, lock plate, and buttplate, original production was going to be 10,000, but number actually mfg. is unknown. Mfg. 1971.

	$1,250	$995	$825	$725	$675	$600	$500

Subtract $225 for ser. nos. 1501-3000 or $300 for ser. nos. 3001-10000.

HARRIS GUNWORKS

Previous firearms manufacturer located in Phoenix, AZ 1995-March 31, 2000. Previously named Harris-McMillan Gunworks and G. McMillan and Co., Inc. (please refer to the M section for more information on these two trademarks).

RIFLES: BOLT ACTION

BENCHREST COMPETITOR – .222 Rem. (disc.), .243 Win., 6mm Rem., 6mm PPC, 6mm BR, or .308 Win. cal., benchrest configuration. Mfg. 1993-2000.

	$2,675	$2,425	$1,950	$1,675	$1,425	$1,200	$1,025	*$3,050*

NATIONAL MATCH COMPETITOR – .308 Win., or 7mm-08 Rem. cal. Mfg. 1993-2000.

	$3,125	$2,675	$2,300	$1,875	$1,650	$1,325	$1,100	*$3,500*

LONG RANGE TARGET MODEL – .300 Win. Mag., .300 Phoenix, .30-378 Wby. Mag., .30-416 Rigby, .338 Lapua, or 7mm Rem. Mag. cal., black synthetic fully adj. stock, w/o sights, grey barrel finish. Mfg. 1996-2000.

	$3,225	$2,700	$2,325	$1,900	$1,650	$1,325	$1,100	*$3,620*

TALON SPORTER – available in various cals. between .22-250 Rem. and .416 Rem., receiver available in either 4340 chrome molybdenum or 17-4 stainless steel, drilled and tapped, match grade barrel. Mfg. 1992-2000.

	$2,600	$2,075	$1,725	$1,375	$1,050	$895	$800	*$2,900*

The Talon action was patterned after the Winchester pre-64 Model 70. It featured a coned breech, controlled feed, claw extractor, and 3 position safety.

GRADING - PPGS™	100%	98%	95%	90%	80%	70%	60%	LAST MSR

SIGNATURE CLASSIC SPORTER – various cals. available between .22-250 Rem. and .416 Rem., premium wood stock, matte metal finish, buttoning used on rifling for 22 or 24 in. stainless steel barrel, McMillan action made from 4340 chrome moly steel (either left- or right-handed), 3 or 4 shot mag. supplied with 5 shot test target. Mfg. 1988-2000.

$2,450	$2,000	$1,675	$1,325	$1,000	$895	$800	*$2,700*

SIGNATURE VARMINTER – similar to Signature Model, except is available in 12 cals. between .22-250 Rem. and .350 Rem. Mag., hand bedded fiberglass stock, adj. trigger, 26 in. heavily contoured barrel. Mfg. 1988-2000.

$2,450	$2,000	$1,675	$1,325	$1,000	$895	$800	*$2,700*

SIGNATURE TITANIUM MOUNTAIN RIFLE – .270 Win., .280 Rem., .30-06, .300 Win. Mag., .338 Win. Mag., or 7mm Rem. Mag. cal., lighter weight variation with shorter stainless steel or graphite/steel composite barrel, 5 3/4 (w/graphite barrel), or 6 1/2 lbs. Mfg. 1990-2000.

$2,950	$2,575	$2,300	$1,925	$1,650	$1,325	$1,100	*$3,300*

Add $400 with graphite barrel.

SIGNATURE ALASKAN – available in many cals. between .270 Win. and .458 Win. Mag. Mfg. 1990-2000.

$3,425	$2,725	$2,275	$1,650	$1,250	$1,125	$900	*$3,800*

TALON SAFARI – available in many cals. between .300 Win. Mag. and .460 Wby. Mag., hand bedded fiberglass stock, 4 shot mag., 24 in. stainless steel barrel, matte black finish, 9 1/2 lbs. Mfg. 1988-2000.

$3,650	$2,850	$2,500	$2,150	$2,000	$1,850	$1,700	*$3,900*

Add $300 for .300 Phoenix, .30-416 Rigby, .30-378 Wby. Mag., .338 Lapua, .335-378, .338-378, .378 Wby. Mag., .416 Wby. Mag. or Rigby, or .460 Wby. Mag. cal.

The Talon action was patterned after the Winchester pre-64 Model 70. It featured a coned breech, controlled feed, claw extractor, and 3 position safety. Older Signature action rifles do not have this new Talon action.

M-40 SNIPER RIFLE – .308 Win. cal., Remington action with McMillan match grade heavy contour barrel, fiberglass stock with recoil pad, 4 shot mag., 9 lbs. Mfg. 1990-2000.

$1,825	$1,450	$1,125	$925	$800	$700	$600	*$2,000*

M-86 SNIPER RIFLE – .300 Phoenix (disc. 1996), .30-06 (new 1989), .300 Win. Mag., or .308 Win. cal., fiberglass stock, variety of optical sights. Mfg. 1988-2000.

$2,450	$2,000	$1,675	$1,325	$1,000	$895	$800	*$2,700*

Add $300 for .300 Phoenix cal. with Harris action (disc. 1996).
Add $200 for takedown feature (mfg. 1993-96).

.300 PHOENIX – available in most popular .30 cals., special fiberglass stock with adj. cheekpiece and buttplate, right or left-hand action, 12 1/2 lbs. Mfg. 1997-2000.

$3,025	$2,650	$2,325	$1,925	$1,675	$1,325	$1,100	*$3,380*

M-87 LONG RANGE SNIPER RIFLE – .50 BMG cal., stainless steel bolt action, 29 in. barrel with muzzle brake, single shot, camo synthetic stock, accurate to 1500 meters, 21 lbs. Mfg. 1988-2000.

$3,450	$2,800	$2,375	$2,000	$1,850	$1,700	$1,575	*$3,885*

* ***M-87R Long Range Sniper Rifle*** – similiar specs. as Model 87, except has 5 shot fixed box mag. Mfg. 1990-2000.

$3,725	$2,950	$2,550	$2,200	$2,000	$1,850	$1,700	*$4,000*

M-88 U.S. NAVY – .50 BMG cal., reintroduced U.S. Navy Seal Team shell holder single shot action with thumbhole stock (one-piece or breakdown two-piece), 24 lbs. Mfg. 1997-2000.

$3,250	$2,600	$2,200	$1,625	$1,250	$1,125	$900	*$3,600*

Add $300 for two-piece breakdown stock.

M-89 SNIPER RIFLE – .308 Win. cal., 28 in. barrel with suppressor (also available without), fiberglass stock adj. for length, and recoil pad, 15 1/4 lbs. Mfg. 1990-2000.

$2,875	$2,525	$2,250	$1,875	$1,650	$1,325	$1,100	*$3,200*

Add $425 for muzzle suppressor (disc. 1996).

GRADING - PPGS™	100%	98%	95%	90%	80%	70%	60%	LAST MSR

M-92 BULL PUP – .50 BMG cal., bullpup configuration with shorter barrel. Mfg. 1993-2000.

	$4,300	$3,250	$2,750	$2,300	$2,050	$1,850	$1,700	*$4,770*

M-93 – .50 BMG cal., similar to M-87, except has folding stock and detachable 5 or 10 shot box mag. Mfg. 1993-2000.

	$3,800	$3,250	$2,750	$2,300	$2,000	$1,850	$1,700	*$4,150*

Add $300 for two-piece folding stock or dovetail combo. quick disassembly fixture.

M-95 TITANIUM/GRAPHITE – .50 BMG cal., features titanium alloy M-87 receiver with graphite barrel and steel liner, single shot or repeater, approx. 18 lbs. Mfg. 1997-2000.

	$4,650	$4,175	$3,475	$2,875	$2,300	$2,050	$1,850	*$5,085*

Add $165 for fixed mag. Add $315 for detachable mag.

M-96 SEMI-AUTO – .50 BMG cal., gas-operated with 5 shot detachable mag., carry handle scope mount, steel receiver, 30 lbs. Mfg. 1997-2000.

	$6,200	$5,625	$5,075	$4,650	$4,175	$3,475	$2,875	*$6,800*

RIFLES SxS

BOXLOCK MODEL – various cals. from .270 Win. - .500 NE, engraved boxlock action, 3 leaf express rear sights, AAA wood, high polish barrel blue, equipped with aluminum case and chain, custom order. Mfg. 1998-2000.

	$12,000	$10,000	$8,500	$7,000	$6,000	$5,000	$4,000	*$12,000*

Add $1,000 for quick detachable claw scope mounts.
Add $6,000 for additional set of rifle barrels.
Add $5,000 for additional set of shotgun barrels.

SIDELOCK MODEL – various cals. from .375 H&H - .577 NE, engraved sidelock action, 3 leaf express rear sights, AAA wood, high polish barrel blue, equipped with aluminum case and chain, custom order. Mfg. 1998-2000.

	$18,200	$15,750	$12,000	$10,000	$8,500	$7,000	$6,000	*$18,200*

Add $1,000 for quick detachable claw scope mounts.
Add $6,000 for additional set of rifle barrels.
Add $5,000 for additional set of shotgun barrels.

HARRISON & HUSSEY LTD.

Current trademark founded in 1919 and currently owned by Cogswell & Harrison, located in Slough, England.

Harrison & Hussey Ltd. was founded in 1919 and purchased by Stephen Grant & Joseph Lang Ltd. in 1930. Boss & Co. took over Harrison & Hussey's original 41 Albermarle Street location and remained there until 1961.

Harrison & Hussey guns are best quality English longarms. It is recommended that an appraisal be obtained before purchase. Harrison & Hussey records have remained intact, and Cogswell & Harrison can provide owners with a date of manufacture free of charge, providing there is a serial number. A full repair and restoration service is also offered. Please contact Cogswell & Harrison for more information about these services (see Trademark Index).

HARTFORD

Current trademark of reproductions manufactured in Italy and Brazil, and imported by E.M.F., located in Santa Ana, CA. Previously manufactured by Armi San Marco.

REVOLVERS: REPRODUCTIONS

HARTFORD 1873 SAA (NEW OR OLD STYLE FRAME) – .22 LR (disc. 1992), .32-20 WCF, .357 Mag., .38-40 WCF, .44-40 WCF, .44 Spl., or .45 LC cal., features forged steel New or Old style frame, backstrap, and trigger guard, exact reproduction of Colt's 1st or 2nd generation SAA, choice of black powder (with cylinder pin frame set screw) or 2nd generation (push button cylinder pin release) frame, case hardened frame, original Colt markings, 4 (.45 LC cal. with standard grips), 4 3/4, 5 1/2, or 7 1/2 in. barrel. Imported 1991-2008.

	$450	$395	$350	$310	$275	$240	$210	*$490*

Add $135 for satin nickel (disc.) or $220 for bright satin nickel finish or case colored hardening.
Add $10 for .32.-20 WCF cal.

GRADING - PPGS™	100%	98%	95%	90%	80%	70%	60%	LAST MSR

* ***Hartford 1873 SAA Old West (Antique) Finish*** – .45 LC cal. only, black powder frame, finish has been aged for older appearance. Mfg. 2001-2003, reintroduced 2005-2006.

$375	$325	$265	$230	$185	$155	$125	$430

* ***Hartford 1873 SAA Pinkerton Model*** – .357 Mag., .38-40 WCF (disc. 1999), or .45 LC cal., birdshead grips, 4 or 4 3/4 in. barrel. Mfg. 1994-2006.

$365	$335	$300	$270	$240	$210	$180	$415

* ***Hartford 1873 SAA Deputy Model*** – .45 LC cal., 3 1/2 (new 2003) or 4 (disc. 2000) in. barrel with full length ejector shroud, standard SAA grips. Imported 2000, reimported 2003.

$415	$335	$300	$265	$225	$175	$150	$480

* ***Hartford 1873 SAA Express Model*** – .45 LC cal., features "Lightning" grips, 4 or 4 3/4 in. barrel, New Model. Imported 1999-2000.

$340	$300	$265	$225	$175	$150	$125	$375

* ***Hartford 1873 SAA Cavalry Model*** – .45 LC cal., 7 1/2 in. barrel, faithful reproduction of the original Colt Cavalry Model, one-piece walnut grips with inspector cartouche, case hardened frame and hammer. Imported 1991-2008.

$450	$395	$350	$310	$275	$240	$210	$505

* ***Hartford 1873 SAA Artillery Model*** – .45 LC cal., similar to Cavalry Model, except has 5 1/2 in. barrel. Imported 1991-2008.

$450	$370	$340	$300	$270	$240	$210	$505

* ***Hartford 1873 SAA Stallion Model*** – .38 Spl. cal., 3 1/2 (bird's head grips only) or 4 3/4 in. (walnut grips only) barrel with ejector rod housing, case colored frame, steel backstrap and trigger guard. Imported 2005-2008.

$395	$320	$290	$255	$220	$195	$160	$450

Add $20 for 3 1/2 in. barrel with bird's head grips.

* ***Hartford 1873 SAA Texas Sesquicentennial*** – .45 LC cal., 4 3/4 in. barrel, 50 mfg. for Texas Sesquicentennial with special engraving, includes numbered belt buckle and presentation case. Disc. 1991.

$1,200	$925	$725	$610	$515	$425	$375	

Original list price was $4,550.

* ***Hartford 1873 SAA Target Model*** – .357 Mag., .44-40 WCF, or .45 LC cal., 5 1/2, or 7 1/2 in. barrel, case hardened frame, brass backstrap. Imported 1987-90.

$325	$240	$185	$150	$140	$130	$120	$500

* ***Hartford 1873 SAA Buntline Model*** – .357 Mag. (disc.), .44-40 WCF (disc.), or .45 LC cal., blue only, 10 (mfg. 1997-2002) or 12 in. barrel. Importation disc. 1990, reintroduced 1997-2008.

$465	$415	$365	$325	$285	$260	$230	$535

Add $200 for bright or satin (disc.) nickel finish, $110 for ultra ivory or stag grips (disc.).

* ***Hartford 1873 SAA Revolver/Carbine*** – .357 Mag. or .45 LC cal., features 18 in. barrel and fixed stock with crescent buttplate, finger extension on trigger guard. Disc. 2008.

$550	$475	$400	$350	$295	$250	$210	$670

* ***Hartford 1873 SAA Buckhorn Model*** – 16 1/4 in. barrel, otherwise similar to Buntline. Importation disc. 1987.

$295	$250	$180	$170	$160	$150	$140	$495

HARTFORD PREMIER 1873 SA – .357 Mag., .32-20 WCF, or .45 LC cal., 4 3/4, 5 1/2, or 7 1/2 in. barrel, charcoal bone case colored frame, high polish blue, choice of black Colt style checkered or ultra stag grips, tuned action with light hammer pull. Imported 1999-2004.

$550	$475	$425	$375	$325	$275	$240	$625

GRADING - PPGS™	100%	98%	95%	90%	80%	70%	60%	LAST MSR

RIFLES: REPRODUCTIONS

In December 2008, Rossi Firearms sold its 1892 Rifle manufacturing to Taurus International. As a result of Taurus having declined continuing to manufacture the Hartford 1892's for EMF, once the inventory is depleted these models will no longer be available. Please check with EMF for existing availability.

HARTFORD 1892 CARBINE – .357 Mag. (disc.), .44 Mag. (disc. 2003, reintroduced 2005), .44-40 WCF, .45 LC (disc.) cal., case colored, blued (disc.), brass (disc.), or stainless steel frame, 16 (stainless steel only), 20 in. round barrel with or w/o (disc.) saddle ring, buckhorn sights, standard stock with crescent buttplate and forearm, mfg. by Rossi. Importation began 2003.

MSR $550	$475	$425	$350	$315	$275	$235	$200

Add $50 for Deerhunter Model in .44 Mag. cal.
Add $30 for stainless steel - .357 Mag. (disc.) or .45 LC cal.

HARTFORD 1892 RIFLE – .357 Mag., .44-40 WCF, .44 Mag., or .45 LC cal., case colored, blued, brass (disc.), or stainless steel frame, 20 (short rifle) or 24 in. octagon barrel with buckhorn sights, standard stock with crescent buttplate and forearm, mfg. by Rossi. Importation began 1998.

MSR $600	$525	$450	$400	$350	$300	$260	$230

Add $10 for case colored frame, $70 for brass frame (disc. 2009), or $40 for stainless steel frame.
Add $20 for Target Model with case colored receiver, and 1/2 round, 1/2 octagon barrel (disc. 2003).
Add $50 for Deerhunter Model in .44 Mag. cal. with padded recoil pad. This model was also packaged with the Great Western II 1873 SA revolver - combination sets range from $950-$1,200 (disc.).

* ***Model 1892 Takedown Rifle*** – .45 LC cal., 20 or 24 in. barrel, takedown action, 6.9 lbs. Mfg. by Armi-Sport, importation disc. 2009.

$950	$825	$700	$600	$500	$425	$375	*$1,100*

SHOTGUNS

HARTFORD MODEL STAGECOACH SxS SHOTGUN – 12 ga., exposed hammers, 20 in. barrels, checkered walnut stock and forearm, color case hardened frame, mfg. in Spain by Aral. Limited importation 2001-2005.

$575	$500	$450	$420	$375	$340	$325	*$650*

HARTFORD ARMORY

Previous manufacturer located in Collinsville, CT circa 2003-2006.

REVOLVERS: REPRODUCTIONS

MODEL 1875 – .357 Mag., .44 Mag., .44-40 WCF, or .45 LC cal., reproduction of original Remington Model 1875 with reinforced barrel, 5 3/4 or 7 1/2 in. barrel, blue metal finish standard (optional frame case colors by Doug Turnbull), or stainless steel construction, includes wooden presentation box with six brass snap caps. Limited mfg. 2004-2005.

$1,325	$1,100	$875	$700	$600	$500	$450	*$1,495*

Add $325 for stainless steel.
Add $325 for case colored frame.

MODEL 1890 – .357 Mag., .44 Mag., .44-40 WCF, or .45 LC cal., reproduction of original Remington Model 1890, 5 3/4 or 7 1/2 in. barrel, blue metal or stainless steel, includes wooden presentation box with six brass snap caps. Limited mfg. 2004-2005.

$1,325	$1,100	$875	$700	$600	$500	$450	*$1,495*

Add $325 for stainless steel.
Add $325 for case colored frame.

HARTFORD ARMS & EQUIPMENT COMPANY

Previous manufacturer located in Harford, CT 1925-1932. Established in 1925, this firm was bankrupt when purchased by the High Standard Company in 1932.

The company made the two rimfire pistols listed and a .22 caliber bolt action rifle which is seldom seen.

GRADING - PPGS™	100%	98%	95%	90%	80%	70%	60%	LAST MSR

PISTOLS: SEMI-AUTO, RIMFIRE

HARTFORD AUTOMATIC TARGET MODEL 1925 – .22 LR cal., 6 3/4 in. round barrel, checkered black hard rubber or ribbed/vertical striation walnut grips, 10 shot, frame marked "Manfd. by/the Hartford Arms and Equip. Co./Hartford, Conn./Patented/.22 cal./ Long Rifle" on left side in front of breech. Approx. 5,000 mfg. 1926-1930. There are three major variations of this pistol. Highest known serial number 4962. Some models have a "S" prefix. The highest serial number known with the "S" prefix is approx. S437. It is not currently known if this was a separate series or if some guns were marked with the prefix within the regular serial number series. Known examples are between serial number 1 and 36. The .22 short pistols can have mottled/case colored frames, slides with adj. rear sights.

$775 $675 $600 $500 $425 $325 $300

Add $250 for guns in original Hartford Arms box (Type 1) numbered to gun (pistol illustrated with text on box).

Add $300 for guns in original Hartford Arms box (Type 2) numbered to the gun. (Written text only on box).

HARTFORD REPEATING PISTOL – The existence of this pistol is in doubt. If encountered, please have the gun checked for authenticity by an expert. The interrelationship of Fiala, Hartford, and Schall through the common gun designer suggests that if this gun exists, then it is probably a Hartford marked repeater like the Fiala and Schall models. Numerous examples of unmarked Schall pistols exist, and some have confused the Schall as a Hartford repeater. None of the factory advertisements or documents mention a repeating pistol.

PISTOLS: SINGLE SHOT

HARTFORD SINGLE SHOT TARGET – .22 LR cal., single shot, manual operation, 6 3/4 in. round barrel, fixed sights, ribbed/vertical striation walnut or composition grips, frame marked "Manfd. by/the Hartford Arms and Equip. Co./Hartford, Conn./Patented/.22 cal./ Long Rifle" on the left side in front of the breech, resembles a semi-auto, no mag.

$850 $725 $650 $575 $500 $425 $350

Add $350 for guns in original Hartford Arms box (Type 1) numbered to gun.

Add $300 for guns in original High Standard box (Type 2) numbered to gun. (Written text only on box)

High Standard assembled with slight modifications a number of these models in 1932 and 1933 with the majority sold by J.L. Galef. These guns were mfg. from Hartford parts and carried the Hartford markings. Boxes for High Standard manufactured guns carry the High Standard and Hartford names. Hartford production is unknown, but probably less than 800. Some models have a "S" prefix S/N. The highest serial number known with the "S" prefix is approx. S439. It is not currently known if this was a separate series, some guns were marked with the prefix within the regular serial number series. High Standard produced less than 900 pistols. There are a small number of the single shot that were made with 10 inch barrels. The 10 in. barreled pistols can have mottled/case colored frames and adj. rear sights that sit forward on the slide that has been reduced for an unobstructed sight picture. Known examples are between serial number 1 and 10.

HARTMANN & WEISS GmbH

Current manufacturer established during 1965 and located in Hamburg, Germany.

Hartmann and Weiss, previously employed by James Purdey & Sons, Ltd., manufactures only top quality longarms, including sidelock SxS shotguns and rifles, O/U shotguns and rifles, falling block single shot rifles (including the Heeren and Hagn action), and bolt action rifles with three lengths of action. Please contact the manufacturer directly for more information and/or a price quotation (see Trademark Index).

HASKELL MANUFACTURING

Previous manufacturer of .45 ACP cal. semi-auto pistols located in Lima, OH. Previously distributed by MKS Supply located in Mansfield, OH.

Refer to listing under Hi-Point Firearms in the H section.

GRADING - PPGS™	100%	98%	95%	90%	80%	70%	60%	LAST MSR

HATCHER GUN COMPANY

Current custom pistol, rifle, and shotgun manufacturer located in Elsie, NE and established in 1983.

Hatcher Gun Company manufactures custom pistols, rifles, and shotguns for both the civilian and law enforcement marketplaces. Rifles include a series of AR-15 models in various barrel lengths and configurations, pistols include a bolt action model based on the Remington XP-100, and shotguns include a modified Saiga semi-auto with a short barrel (LE only). Please contact the company directly for more information, availability, and pricing (see Trademark Index).

HATFIELD GUN CO., INC.

Previous manufacturer located in St. Joseph, MO. The following shotguns were previously manufactured until 1996 by the Hatfield Gun Co., Inc. (designated Hatfield Rifle Works until 1986).

Due to space considerations, information regarding this manufacturer is available online free of charge in the Firearms section at www.bluebookofgunvalues.com.

HATFIELD GUN COMPANY LLC

Current importer of sidelock O/U and SxS shotguns manufactured in Turkey, established 2005 and located in Des Plains, IL. Previously located in Sagle, ID.

Hatfield Gun Company LLC represents the Hatfield trademark on shotguns manufactured in Turkey. Current models include the Mayfair sidelock O/U and London sidelock SxS. These shotguns feature the Hatfield seven pin jeweled lock plate, and semi-chopper lump barrels with double locking underlugs. Many options are available, including wood upgrades. Please contact the company directly for more information, including availability and pricing (see Trademark Index).

Shotguns imported into North America by Kimber can be found in the Kimber section.

HATFIELD'S

Current manufacturer established during 2003, and located in St. Joseph, MO.

SHOTGUNS: O/U

HATFIELD 1 OF 100 – 28 ga., small frame O/U, 28 in. barrels with five choke tubes, vent. rib, chrome lined bores, SST, extractors, matte blue finish, checkered Circassian pistol grip stock and forend. New 2007.

MSR $1,695	$1,550	$1,375	$1,175	$975	$825	$700	$600

SHOTGUNS: SxS

UPLANDER 28 – 28 ga., small scalloped boxlock frame, extractors, SST or DT, 26 in. monobloc barrels with matte rib, checkered Circassian walnut straight grip stock and splinter forearm, case colored frame, 4 lbs. New 2004.

MSR $1,499	$1,350	$1,200	$1,000	$875	$700	$550	$475

Add $100 for single trigger.

HATSAN ARMS COMPANY

Current shotgun manufacturer established in 1976, and located in Izmir, Turkey. Currently imported by Legacy Sports International LLC, located in Reno, NV. Previously located in Alexandria, VA.

Hatsan Arms Company manufactures the Escort line of shotguns imported by Legacy. Please refer to the Escort section for current model availability and pricing.

KARL HAUPTMANN JAGDWAFFEN

Current long arm manufacturer established in 1939 and located in Ferlach, Austria. Consumer direct sales.

Karl Hauptmann II was a member of the Ferlach Guild until it was dissolved in 2004. His son Gerd Hauptmann is currently the managing director of the company. Hauptmann Jagdwaffen manufactures high quality shotguns, combination guns, and double rifles, and a very unique, three barrel SxSxS rifle. Since every gun is custom made according to each customer's specifications, please contact the factory directly for an individual price quotation and delivery time (see Trademark Index).

HAUSMANN & CO. GmbH

Current rifle manufacturer located in Ferlach, Austria.

Hausmann & Co. manufactures high quality rifles in various configurations. Since every gun is manufactured per individual customer specifications, please contact the company directly for a price quotation and availability (see Trademark Index).

HAWES FIREARMS

Previously manufactured by J.P. Sauer & Sohn in Eckernforde, Germany. Previously imported by Hawes Firearms in Van Nuys, CA.

Hawes Firearms was created after Hy Hunter discontinued their gun line in the early 1960s.

REVOLVERS

Rather than give an individual listing of the various single action and double action (including Medallion models) revolvers that have been imported, a generalized price range is as follows: centerfire single actions usually are in the $225-$450 range, centerfire double actions are $175-$325, while .22 rimfire models are typically valued between $100-$200.

HEAD DOWN PRODUCTS LLC

Current semi-auto rifle manufacturer located in Dallas, GA. Currently distributed by American Tactical Imports, located in Rochester, NY.

RIFLES: SEMI-AUTO

HD5V9 - .300 AAC Blackout or 5.56 NATO cal., flat top Picatinny receiver with integrated 9, 13, or 15 in. Provectus quad rail, billet upper/lower receiver, 16 in. barrel with flash suppressor, HDF 6-position buttstock, pistol grip, 30 shot mag. New 2013.

MSR $1,760 $1,595 $1,400 $1,225 $1,050 $925 $800 $700

Add $85 for 13 in., or $350 for 15 in. Provectus quad rail.
Add $100 for .300 AAC Blackout cal.

MK12 – 5.56 NATO cal., similar to PV9, except has 15 in. Provectus quad rail and 18 in. match grade barrel with muzzle brake. New 2013.

MSR $2,299 $2,000 $1,800 $1,600 $1,400 $1,200 $1,000 $850

HECKLER & KOCH

Current manufacturer established in 1949, and located in Oberndorf/Neckar, Germany. Currently imported and distributed beginning mid-2008 by H & K USA, located in Columbus, GA. Previously imported by Merkel USA, located in Trussville, AL, by Heckler & Koch, Inc. located in Sterling, VA (previously located in Chantilly, VA). During 2004, H & K built a new plant in Columbus, GA, primarily to manufacture guns for American military and law enforcement. In early 1991, H & K was absorbed by Royal Ordnance, a division of British Aerospace (BAE Systems) located in England. During December 2002, BAE Systems sold Heckler & Koch to a group of European investors. Heckler & Koch, Inc. and HKJS GmbH are wholly owned subsidiaries of Suhler Jag und Sportwaffen Holding GmbH and the sole licensees of Heckler & Koch commercial firearms technology.

PISTOLS: SEMI-AUTO, RECENT MFG.

USP and USP Compact (with bobbed hammer) Models are divided into 10 variants. They include: USP Variant 1 (DA/SA with control safety decocking lever on left), USP Variant 2 (DA/SA with control safety decocking lever on right), USP Variant 3 (DA/SA with control safety decocking lever on left), USP Variant 4 (DA/SA with control safety decocking lever on right), USP Variant 5 (DAO with control safety decocking lever on left), USP Variant 6 (DAO with control safety decocking lever on right), USP Variant 7 (DAO with no control lever), USP

GRADING - PPGS™	100%	98%	95%	90%	80%	70%	60%	LAST MSR

Variant 9 (DA/SA with safety control lever on left), and USP Variant 10 (DA/SA with safety control lever on right). Please contact your H&K dealer for pricing on these variants.

LEM refers to Law Enforcement Modification (enhanced DAO and conventional SA/DA with serrated decocking button on rear of frame).

All currently manufactured H&K pistols feature a patented lock-out safety device which blocks the hammer strut and slide.

Add $65 for variant change or night sights prior to shipping on currently manufactured USP and USP Compact models.

Add $387 for laser sighting device BA-6 (mfg. 2002-2005).

HK-4 – First and Second Variations. Mfg. 1968-1973.

* ***HK-4 First Variation*** – .22 LR, .25 ACP, .32 ACP, or .380 ACP, DA, blow back action; 8 (.380 ACP), 9 (.32 ACP), or 10 (.22 LR or .25 ACP) shot mag., high polished blue finish on slide, matte black finish, brown checkered plastic grips with HK logo, fixed front sight, adj. rear sight, firing pin block safety mounted on the left side of the slide, 18 oz. Mfg. 1967-1970.

	$485	$435	$360	$300	$265	$220	$195	

An early four barrel set with in all calibers with recoil springs, 4 mags., .22 cal. ejector, bolt tool and four plastic fitted cases is currently priced in the $2,000 range.

A late four barrel set with in all calibers with recoil springs, 4 mags., .22 cal. ejector, bolt tool and two cardboard fitted cases is currently priced in the $1,500 range.

* ***HK-4 Second Variation*** – .380 ACP cal., 8 shot mag., DA, blue finish, blowback action, adj. rear sight, 22 LR cal. conversion kit offered as optional 10 round magazine, fixed front sight, adj. rear sight, firing pin block safety mounted on the left side of the slide, 18 oz. Mfg. 1971-1973.

	$475	$425	$355	$300	$260	$220	$195	

Add approx. 10%-15% for .22 LR cal. conversion kit.

HK-4 COMMEMORATIVE COMBO – includes one .22 LR cal. and one .380 ACP cal. barrel, in wooden presentation with gold plating for H&R. Mfg. 1971.

	$950	$850	$750	$650	$550	$450	$400	

P9S – .45 ACP or 9mm Para. cal., double action combat model, 4 in. barrel, blue (early mfg.) or phosphate finish, sculptured plastic grips, fixed sights. Although production ceased in 1984, limited quantities were available until 1989.

	$950	$875	$775	$650	$525	$450	$375	*$1,299*

Add 20% for .45 ACP.

Add 50% for pistols marked "P9".

P9S TARGET – .45 ACP or 9mm Para. cal., 4 in. barrel, phosphate finish, adj. sights and trigger. Although production ceased in 1984, limited quantities were available until 1989.

	$1,500	$1,275	$1,050	$925	$800	$700	$600	*$1,382*

Add 20% for .45 ACP cal.

P9S COMPETITION KIT SPORT MODEL – 9mm Para. or .45 ACP (rare) cal., similar to P9S Target, except extra 5 1/2 in. barrel and weight, competition walnut grip, 2 slides, with factory case. Disc. 1984.

Sport 1	$3,000	$2,650	$2,300	$2,050	$1,800	$1,600	$1,400	
Sport 2	$4,000	$3,500	$3,000	$2,500	$2,000	$1,600	$1,400	
Sport 3	$5,000	$4,500	$4,000	$3,500	$3,000	$2,500	$2,000	*$2,250*

P7 PSP – 9mm Para. cal., older variation of the P7 M8, without extended trigger guard, ambidextrous mag. release (European style), or heat shield. Standard production ceased 1986. A reissue of this model was mfg. in 1990, with approx. 150 produced. Limited quantities remained through 1999.

	$1,200	$1,075	$900	$800	$700	$600	$500	
European Model	$2,000	$1,800	$1,500	$1,300	$1,000	$800	$700	*$1,111*

The PSP is serial numbered 001-239. The PSP/P7 is serial numbered 240-251, and the P7 serialization starts at 252.

GRADING - PPGS™	100%	98%	95%	90%	80%	70%	60%	LAST MSR

P7 M8 – 9mm Para. cal., unique squeeze cocking single action, extended square combat type trigger guard with heat shield, 4.13 in. fixed barrel with polygonal rifling, 8 shot mag., ambidextrous mag. release, fixed 3-dot sighting system, stippled black plastic grips, black phosphate or nickel (mfg. 1992-2000) finish, includes 2 mags., 28 oz. Disc. 2005.

	$1,500	$1,250	$975	$800	$700	$600	$500	*$1,515*

Add 30% for nickel/hard chrome finish.
Add $100 for Tritium sights (various colors, new 1993).
Add $1,200 for .22 LR conversion kit (barrel, slide, and two mags., disc. 1999).

P7 M13 – similar to P7 M8, only with staggered 13 shot mag., 30 oz. Disc. 1994.

	$2,500	$2,250	$1,875	$1,600	$1,350	$1,125	$950	*$1,330*

Add 20% for nickel/hard chrome finish.
Add $85 for Tritium sights (various colors, new 1993).
Add $150 for factory wood grips.

P7 M10 – .40 S&W cal., similar specifications as P7 M13, except has 10 shot mag., 39 oz. Mfg. 1991-1994.

	$2,800	$2,500	$2,200	$2,000	$1,800	$1,500	$1,200	*$1,315*

Add 20% for nickel/hard chrome finish.
Add $85 for Tritium sights (various colors, new 1993).

P7 K3 – .22 LR or .380 ACP cal., uses unique oil-filled buffer to decrease recoil, 3.8 in. barrel, matte black or nickel (less common) finish, 8 shot mag. (includes 2), 26 1/2 oz. Mfg. 1988-94.

	$2,200	$1,950	$1,750	$1,475	$1,250	$1,050	$875	*$1,100*

Add $1,500 for .22 LR conversion kit.
Add $1,000 for .32 ACP conversion kit.
Add $85 for Tritium sights (various colors, new 1993).

HK45 – .45 ACP cal., SA/DA and variants (10), 10 shot mag., 4.53 in. O-ring barrel with polygonal rifling, features black polymer frame with finger groove grips, integrated Picatinny rail, low profile 3-dot sights, interchangable grip panels, twin slide serrations, internal mechanical recoil reduction system reduces recoil 30%, 27.7 oz. New 2008.

MSR $1,193	$1,025	$900	$800	$675	$550	$500	$450

Add $67 for LEM trigger, DAO.

* ***HK45 Tactical*** – .45 ACP cal., choice of SA/DA with safety decocking lever on left or LEM trigger, DAO and no safety/decocking lever, with threaded barrel, choice of black, tan, or green frame, supplied with night sights and one additional grip. New 2013.

MSR $1,392	$1,225	$1,050	$925	$800	$675	$550	$475

Add $69 for LEM trigger, DAO.

* ***HK45 Compact*** – similar to HK45, except has 3.9 in. barrel, 8 or 10 shot mag., small grip frame, and bobbed hammer, 28.5 oz. New 2008.

MSR $1,193	$1,025	$900	$800	$675	$550	$500	$450

Add $67 for LEM trigger, DAO.

* ***HK45 Compact Tactical*** – .45 ACP cal., similar to HK45 Compact, except has 4.57 in. threaded barrel, and 10 shot mag. with extended floorplate, safety/decocking lever on left side, and spur hammer, 29 oz. New 2011.

MSR $1,392	$1,225	$1,050	$925	$800	$675	$550	$475

Add $69 for decocking lever on left side.

P30 – 9mm Para. or .40 S&W (new 2011) cal., 3.86 in. barrel with polygonal rifling, 10 (CA only), 13 (.40 S&W cal.) or 15 (9mm Para. cal. only) shot mag., 3-dot sights, lower Picatinny rail, self decocking DA spur hammer, multiple trigger variants including regular (disc. 2012) or lightened LEM DAO (new 2012) trigger, firing pin block safety, loaded chamber indicator, ergonomic grips with interchangeable side panels and backstraps, double slide serrations, internal recoil reduction system, approx. 23 oz. Importation began mid-2007.

MSR $1,054	$925	$775	$650	$550	$450	$400	$375

GRADING - PPGS™	100%	98%	95%	90%	80%	70%	60%	LAST MSR

* ***P30L*** – similar to P30, except has 4.5 in. barrel and 1/2 in. longer slide, 27.5 oz. New 2009.

MSR $1,108	$950	$800	$675	$575	$475	$425	$400	

P2000 – 9mm Para., .357 SIG (mfg. 2005-2012), or .40 S&W cal., SA/DA or LEM (Law Enforcement Modification) DAO (w/o control lever), compact design, patterned after USP Compact Model, features pre-cocked hammer system with very short trigger reset distance, lockout safety device, 3-dot sights, 3.66 in. barrel with polygonal rifling, 10 or 12 shot mag. with finger extension, or optional 13 shot mag. (new late 2004), with or w/o decocker, interchangeable rear grip panels, black finish, approx. 25 oz.

MSR $992	$850	$750	$650	$525	$450	$400	$375	

Subtract approx. $50 for .357 SIG cal. (mfg. 2005-2012).

* ***P2000 SK SubCompact*** – similar to P2000, choice of LEM (Law Enforcement Modification) or regular DA/SA trigger system, 3.26 in. barrel, 9 (.357 SIG (disc. 2012) or .40 S&W cal.) or 10 (9mm Para.) shot mag., approx. 24 oz. Importation began 2005.

MSR $1,037	$950	$800	$675	$550	$495	$450	$375	

Subtract approx. $50 for .357 SIG cal. (mfg. 2005-2012).

USP CUSTOM COMBAT – 9mm Para. or .40 S&W cal., DA/SA, Variant 1, Novak combat sight system, includes jet funnel kit and two 16 (.40 S&W cal.) or 18 (9mm Para. cal.) shot mags. Mfg. 2009.

	$1,150	$975	$875	$775	$675	$550	$450	*$1,295*

USP COMBAT COMPETITION – 9mm Para. or .40 S&W cal., 4 1/4 in. barrel, includes jet funnel kit with two 16 (.40 S&W) or 18 (9mm Para) mags., Novak combat sight system, LEM trigger became standard mid-2008, lower accessory rail on frame, 26 1/2 oz. Imported 2007-2010.

	$1,250	$1,025	$925	$825	$700	$600	$500	*$1,450*

Subtract approx. $100 if w/o LEM trigger.

USP COMPETITION – similar to USP Combat Competition, except features LEM match trigger system. Imported 2007-2008.

	$1,125	$975	$850	$750	$625	$500	$450	*$1,279*

USP 9 – 9mm Para. cal., available in regular DA/SA mode or DA only (10 variants), 4 1/4 in. barrel with polygonal rifling, Browning-type action with H & K recoil reduction system, polymer frame, all metal surfaces specially treated, can be carried cocked and locked, stippled synthetic grips, bobbed hammer, 3-dot sighting system, multiple safeties, 10 (C/B 1994), 15 (new late 2004), or 16* shot polymer mag., 26.5 oz. New 1993.

MSR $952	$825	$725	$600	$500	$450	$400	$350	

Add $67 for LEM trigger, DAO.
Add $107 for Tritium sights (various colors, mfg. 1993-2010).

* ***USP 9 SD*** – similar to USP 9, except has target sights and 4.7 in. threaded barrel, approx. 27 oz. Imported 2004-2006, reintroduced 2011.

MSR $1,313	$1,150	$975	$875	$725	$600	$500	$450	

* ***USP 9 Stainless*** – similar to USP 9, except has satin finished stainless steel slide. Mfg. 1996-2001.

	$700	$565	$475	$415	$360	$300	$255	*$817*

USP 9 COMPACT – 9mm Para. cal., compact variation of the USP 9 featuring 3.58 in. barrel, 10 or 13 (new late 2004) shot mag., LEM trigger became available 2003, 25.5 oz. New 1997.

MSR $992	$850	$750	$650	$525	$450	$400	$375	

Add $68 for LEM trigger, DAO.

* ***USP 9 Compact Stainless*** – similar to USP 9 Compact, except has satin finished stainless steel slide. Mfg. 1997-2004.

	$735	$595	$500	$430	$375	$315	$270	*$849*

GRADING - PPGS™	100%	98%	95%	90%	80%	70%	60%	LAST MSR

* ***USP 9 Compact LEM*** – 9mm Para. cal., DAO, blue finish only, LEM trigger mechanism decreases trigger pull to 7 1/2 - 8 1/2 lbs., 24 1/2 oz. Imported 2003-2004.

	$695	$575	$495	$450	$400	$350	$315	*$799*

USP 9x19 TACTICAL – 9mm Para. cal. enhanced variation of the USP 9, 4.92 in. threaded barrel with rubber o-ring, 10 or 15 shot mag., adj. target type sights and trigger, approx. 28 1/2 oz. Mfg. 2007-2010.

	$975	$850	$750	$625	$525	$450	$400	*$1,112*

USP 357 – .357 SIG cal., available in 4.25 (Standard, disc. 2004) or 3.58 (Compact) in. barrel, 10 or 12 (optional beginning 2004) shot mag., black finish, approx. 24.5 oz. Imported 2001-2005.

	$695	$560	$500	$450	$395	$350	$300	*$799*

Subtract $30 for Standard Model (disc. 2004).

USP 40 – .40 S&W cal., similar to USP 9, 9 variants of DA/SA/DAO, 10 (C/B1994), 13* (reintroduced late 2004), or 16 (optional, new 2005, needs jet funnel modification) shot mag., LEM trigger (new 2013), 27.75 oz. New 1993.

MSR $952	$825	$725	$600	$500	$450	$400	$350	

Add $67 for LEM trigger (new 2013).
Add $107 for Tritium sights (various colors, mfg. 1993-disc.).

A desert tan finish became available during 2005 at no extra charge (includes matching nylon carrying case). Limited mfg. 2005-2006.

* ***USP 40 Stainless*** – similar to USP 40, except has satin finished stainless steel slide. Mfg. 1996-2003.

	$700	$565	$470	$415	$360	$300	$255	*$817*

USP 40 COMPACT – .40 S&W cal., compact variation of the USP 40 featuring 3.58 in. barrel, 10 or 12 (new late 2004) shot mag., LEM trigger became available 2002, 27 oz. New 1997.

MSR $992	$850	$750	$650	$525	$450	$400	$375	

Add $68 for LEM trigger, DAO.

A desert tan finish became available during 2005-2006 at no extra charge (includes matching nylon carrying case). Grey was also available in limited quantites during 2005 only.

* ***USP 40 Compact Stainless*** – similar to USP 40 Compact, except has satin finished stainless steel slide. Mfg. 1997-2004.

	$735	$595	$500	$430	$375	$315	$270	*$849*

* ***USP 40 Compact LEM*** – .40 S&W cal., DAO, blue finish only, LEM trigger mechanism decreases trigger pull to 7 1/2 - 8 1/2 lbs., 24 1/2 oz. Imported 2002-2005.

	$695	$575	$495	$450	$400	$350	$315	

USP 40 TACTICAL – .40 S&W cal., enhanced variation of the USP 40, 4.92 in. threaded barrel with rubber o-ring, 10 (standard) or 13 shot mag., adj. target type sights and match trigger, 30 1/2 oz. New 2005.

MSR $1,333	$1,150	$995	$850	$750	$625	$550	$495	

USP 45 – .45 ACP cal., similar to USP 9, 9 variants of DA/SA/DAO, 10 (C/B 1994), 12 (new late 2004) or 13* shot mag., 27 3/4 oz. New 1995.

MSR $988	$850	$750	$650	$525	$450	$400	$375	

Add $68 for LEM trigger, DAO (new 2011).
Add $107 for Tritium sights (various colors, mfg. 1993-2010).

A desert tan or green finish became available during 2005-2006 at no extra charge (includes matching nylon carrying case). Grey was also available in limited quantities during 2005 only.

* ***USP 45 Stainless*** – similar to USP 45, except has satin finished stainless steel slide. Mfg. 1996-2003.

	$760	$600	$500	$430	$375	$315	$270	*$888*

GRADING - PPGS™	100%	98%	95%	90%	80%	70%	60%	LAST MSR

* ***USP 45 Match Pistol*** – .45 ACP cal., features 6.02 in. barrel with polygonal rifling, micrometer adj. high relief and raised rear sight, raised target front sight, 10 shot mag., barrel weight, fluted, and ambidextrous safety, choice of matte black or stainless steel slide, supplied with additional o-rings and setup tools, 38 oz. Mfg. 1997-98.

	$2,150	$1,850	$1,575	$1,300	$1,050	$900	$800	*$1,369*

Add $72 for stainless steel slide model.

USP 45 COMPACT – .45 ACP cal., compact variation of the USP 45, featuring 3.8 in. barrel, 8 shot mag., 28 oz. New 1998.

MSR $1,040	$895	$775	$650	$550	$475	$425	$375

Add $68 for LEM trigger, DAO (new 2011).

* ***USP 45 Compact Stainless*** – similar to USP 45 Compact, except has satin finished stainless steel slide. Mfg. 1998-2004.

	$775	$615	$510	$440	$385	$325	$275	*$894*

* ***USP 45 Compact 50th Anniversary*** – commemorates the 50th year of H & K (1950-2000), 1 of 1,000 special edition featuring high polish blue slide with 50th Anniversary logo engraved in gold and silver, supplied with presentation wood case and commemorative coin. Limited mfg. 2000 only.

	$1,150	$895	$795	N/A	N/A	N/A	N/A	*$999*

USP 45 TACTICAL PISTOL – .45 ACP cal., enhanced variation of the USP 45, 5.09 in. threaded barrel with rubber o-ring, 10 or 12 (new late 2004) shot mag., adj. 3-dot target type sights and match trigger, limited availability, 36 oz. New 1998.

MSR $1,352	$1,175	$1,000	$875	$775	$650	$550	$495

A desert tan finish became available during 2005-2006 at no extra charge (includes matching nylon carrying case).

* ***USP 45 Tactical Pistol Compact*** – .45 ACP cal., compact variation of the USP 45 Tactical, 3.78 in. barrel, 8 shot mag., 28 oz. Imported 2006-2012.

	$1,100	$950	$850	$750	$650	$550	$450	*$1,242*

USP EXPERT – 9mm Para. (mfg. 2003-2005, reintroduced 2013), .40 S&W (mfg. 2002-2009) or .45 ACP (disc. 2009)cal., features new slide design with 5.2 in. barrel, 10 (standard), 12 (.45 ACP, disc. 2009), 13 (.40 S&W, disc. 2009), 15 (9mm Para.) or 18 (new 2013) shot mag., match grade SA or DA trigger pull, recoil reduction system, reinforced polymer frame, adj. rear sight, approx. 30 oz. Imported 1999-2009, reintroduced 2013.

MSR $1,372	$1,225	$1,075	$925	$825	$725	$625	$525

Add $123 for jet funnel frame and two 18 shot mags. (new 2013).

USP ELITE – 9mm Para. (disc. 2005) or .45 ACP cal., long slide variation of the USP Expert, 6.2 in. barrel, match trigger parts, target sights, ambidextrous control levers, blue finish, includes two 10 shot mags. or 12 (.45 ACP) or 15 (9mm Para.) shot mag. Imported 2003-2009.

	$1,375	$1,150	$1,000	$900	$800	$700	$600	*$1,406*

MARK 23 SPECIAL OPERATIONS PISTOL – .45 ACP cal., 5.87 in. threaded barrel with O-ring and polygonal rifling, polymer frame with ribbed integral grips, 3-dot sights, 10 or 12 (optional beginning late 2004) shot mag., squared off trigger guard, lower frame is grooved for mounting accessories, mechanical recoil reduction system, 39 oz. Limited availability. New 1996.

MSR $2,253	$2,000	$1,750	$1,500	$1,250	$1,000	$875	$775

The "MK23" is the official military design that is not available to civilians.

A desert tan finish became available during 2005-2006 at no extra charge (includes matching nylon carrying case).

SP 89 – 9mm Para. cal., recoil operated delayed roller-locked bolt system, 4 1/2 in. barrel, 15 shot mag., adj. aperture rear sight (accepts HK claw-lock scope mounts), 4.4 lbs. Mfg. 1990-1993.

	$4,950	$4,500	$4,150	$4,000	$3,750	$3,625	$3,500	*$1,325*

GRADING - PPGS™	100%	98%	95%	90%	80%	70%	60%	LAST MSR

VP 70Z - 9mm Para. cal., 18 shot, double action only, 4 1/2 in. barrel, parkerized finish, plastic receiver/grip assembly. Disc. 1984.

	$750	$675	$600	$550	$500	$450	$400	

Add 125% if frame cut for shoulder stock (Model VP 70M, NFA Class III).

The majority of pistols that were cut for shoulder stock are the Model VP 70M, and are subject to NFA Class III regulation. A complete M stock with sear is also considered NFA.

HK-416 – .22 LR cal., 10 or 20 shot mag., pistol variation of the Model 416 rifle, blowback action, 9 in. barrel, steel receiver, fixed front sight, external safety, quad Picatinny rail with open sights, including diopter adj. rear sight, black finish, approx. 5 lbs, mfg. by Carl Walther in Ulm, Germany, and imported by Umarex USA. New mid-2009.

MSR $450	$395	$360	$330	$300	$265	$235	$215	

RIFLES: BOLT ACTION

BASR – .22 LR, .22-250 Rem., 6mm PPC, .300 Win. Mag., .30-06, or .308 Win. cal., Kevlar stock, stainless steel barrel, limited production. Special order only. Mfg. 1986 only.

	$5,750	$5,000	$4,500	$4,000	$3,650	$3,300	$2,600	*$2,199*

Less than 135 of this variation were manufactured and they are extremely rare. Contractual disputes with the U.S. supplier stopped H & K from receiving any BASR models.

RIFLES: SEMI-AUTO

Most of the models listed, being of a paramilitary design, were disc. in 1989 due to Federal legislation. Sporterized variations mfg. after 1994 with thumbhole stocks were banned in April, 1998.

In 1991, the HK-91, HK-93, and HK-94 were discontinued. Last published retail prices (1991) were $999 for fixed stock models and $1,199 for retractable stock models.

In the early '70s, S.A.C.O. importers located in Virginia sold the Models 41 and 43 which were the predecessors to the Model 91 and 93, respectively. Values for these earlier variations will be higher than values listed.

G3 SEMI-AUTO – .308 Win. cal., patterned after the H&K G3 select-fire military rifle, two variations were imported by Golden State Arms circa 1962.

	$8,500	$7,500	$6,500	$5,500	$4,750	$4,000	$3,250	

SR-9 – .308 Win. cal., semi-auto sporting rifle, 19.7 in. barrel, Kevlar reinforced fiberglass thumbhole stock and forearm, 5 shot mag., diopter adj. rear sight, accepts H & K claw-lock scope mounts. Mfg. 1990-93.

	$2,075	$1,725	$1,400	$1,225	$1,075	$950	$850	*$1,199*

While advertised again during 1998, this model was finally banned in April, 1998.

SR-9T – .308 Win. cal., precision target rifle with adj. MSG 90 buttstock and PSG-1 trigger group, 5 shot mag. Mfg. 1992-93.

	$2,795	$2,375	$2,050	$1,775	$1,375	$1,295	$1,050	*$1,725*

While advertised again during 1998, this model was finally banned in April, 1998.

SR-9TC – .308 Win. cal., similar to SR-9T except has PSG-1 adj. buttstock. Mfg. 1993 only.

	$3,350	$2,925	$2,600	$2,275	$1,925	$1,475	$1,250	*$1,995*

While advertised again during 1998, this model was finally banned in April, 1998.

PSG-1 – .308 Win. cal. only, high precision marksman's rifle, 5 shot mag., adj. buttstock, includes accessories (Hensholdt illuminated 6x42mm scope) and case, 17.8 lbs. Importation disc. 1998.

	$13,950	$12,500	$10,950	$9,500	$8,500	$7,500	$7,000	*$10,811*

MODEL 41 A-2 – .308 Win. cal., predecessor to the Model 91 A-2, originally imported by Golden State Arms.

	$4,500	$4,000	$3,750	$3,500	$3,350	$3,200	$3,000	

MODEL 43 A-2 – predecesor to the Model 93 A-2. Disc.

	$4,500	$4,000	$3,750	$3,500	$3,350	$3,200	$3,000	

GRADING - PPGS™	100%	98%	95%	90%	80%	70%	60%	LAST MSR

MODEL 91 A-2 – .308 Win. cal., paramilitary design, roller locked delayed blowback action, attenuated recoil, black cycolac stock, 17.7 in. barrel, 20 shot mag., 9.7 lbs. Importation disc. 1989.

* ***Model 91 A-2 Fixed stock model***

$2,350	$2,000	$1,800	$1,600	$1,400	$1,250	$1,000	*$999*

Add $200 for desert camo finish.
Add $275 for NATO black finish.

* ***Model 91 A-2 SBF (Semi-Beltfed)*** – supplied with bipod and M60 link (200 shot with starter tab) and MG42 modified belt (49 shot with fixed starter tab), limited mfg. Disc.

$10,500	$9,500	$8,500	N/A	N/A	N/A	N/A	

* ***Model 91 A-3*** – with retractable metal stock.

$3,100	$2,900	$2,700	$2,500	$2,150	$2,000	$1,895	*$1,114*

Add $775 for .22 LR conversion kit.

* ***Model 91 A-2 Package*** – includes A.R.M.S. mount, B-Square rings, Leupold 3-9x compact scope with matte finish. Importation disc. 1988.

$3,150	$2,750	$2,400	$2,150	$1,900	$1,700	$1,475	*$1,285*

Add 30% for retractable stock.

MODEL 93 A-2 – .223 Rem. cal., smaller version of the H & K 91, 25 shot mag., 16.14 in. barrel, 8 lbs.

* ***Model 93 A-2 Fixed stock model***

$2,500	$2,250	$2,000	$1,750	$1,500	$1,250	$1,000	*$946*

Add 10% for desert camo finish.
Add 15% for NATO black finish.

* ***Model 93 A-3*** – with retractable metal stock.

$3,400	$3,250	$3,000	$2,800	$2,650	$2,500	$2,250	*$1,114*

* ***Model 93 A-2 Package*** – includes A.R.M.S. mount, B-Square rings, Leupold 3-9x compact scope with matte finish. Importation disc. 1988.

$3,500	$3,100	$2,850	$2,550	$2,400	$2,100	$1,895	*$1,285*

Add 10% for retractable stock.

MODEL 94 CARBINE A-2 – 9mm Para. cal., semi-auto carbine, 16.54 in. barrel, aperture rear sight, 15 shot mag. New 1983.

* ***Model 94 Carbine A-2 Fixed stock model***

$3,950	$3,750	$3,500	$3,400	$3,000	$2,600	$2,500	*$946*

* ***Model 94 Carbine A-3*** – retractable metal stock.

$4,150	$3,900	$3,700	$3,550	$3,200	$2,800	$2,700	*$1,114*

* ***Model 94 Carbine A-2 Package*** – includes A.R.M.S. mount, B-Square rings, Leupold 3-9x compact scope with matte finish. Importation disc. 1988.

$4,300	$3,875	$3,650	$3,300	$3,000	$2,800	$2,500	*$1,285*

Add 10% for retractable stock.

* ***Model 94 Carbine A-2 SGI*** – 9mm Para. cal., target rifle, aluminum alloy bipod, Leupold 6X scope, 15 or 30 shot mag. Imported 1986 only.

$3,950	$3,750	$3,500	$3,000	$2,750	$2,500	$2,150	*$1,340*

MODEL 270 – .22 LR cal., sporting rifle, 19.7 in. barrel with standard or polygonal rifling, 5 or 20 shot mag., high luster blue, plain walnut stock, approx. 5.7 lbs. Disc. 1985.

$975	$895	$725	$675	$525	$400	$350	*$200*

MODEL 300 – .22 WMR cal., 5 or 15 shot, polygonal rifling standard, otherwise similar to H & K 270 with checkered walnut stock. Importation disc. 1989.

$1,350	$1,050	$925	$775	$700	$600	$550	*$608*

Add $350-$400 for factory H & K scope mount system.

GRADING - PPGS™	100%	98%	95%	90%	80%	70%	60%	LAST MSR

* ***Model 300 Package*** – includes A.R.M.S. mount, B-Square rings, Leupold 3-9x compact scope with matte finish. Importation disc. 1988.

	$1,625	$1,275	$1,075	$900	$800	$700	$650	*$689*

MODEL HK 416 – .22 LR cal., 10 or 20 shot mag., blowback action with hold open bolt, 16.1 in. barrel with muzzle brake, H&K style diopter sight, black ergonomic pistol grip with storage compartment, manual safety, steel flat-top receiver with quad Picatinny rail, H&K style 5 position buttstock with storage compartment and recoil pad, black finish, 6.8 lbs, mfg. by Carl Walther in Ulm, Germany. Mfg. mid-2010-2011.

	$500	$450	$400	$375	$350	$325	$295	*$569*

MODEL 416 D145RS – .22 LR cal., blowback action, 16.1 in. barrel, fixed front sight, adj. rear sight, external safety, 10 or 20 shot mag., metal receiver, black finish, upper and lower rail interface system, pistol grip with compartment, adj. buttstock, functional dust cover, 6.8 lbs., mfg. by Carl Walther in Ulm, Germany, and imported by Umarex USA. New late 2009.

MSR $600	$550	$495	$450	$395	$350	$300	$275	

MODEL 630 – .223 Rem. cal., roller locked delayed blowback action, 17.7 in. barrel with or w/o muzzle brake (early mfg.), reduced recoil, checkered walnut, 4 or 10 shot mag., 7.04 lbs. Importation disc. 1986.

	$1,650	$1,400	$1,200	$1,100	$1,000	$850	$750	*$784*

Add $350-$400 for factory H & K scope mount system.

The .222 Rem. cal. was also available in this model. Most were French contracts.

MODEL 770 – .308 Win. cal., 3 or 10 shot mag., 19.7 in. barrel with or w/o muzzle brake (early mfg.), otherwise similar to Model 630, 7.92 lbs. Importation disc. 1986.

	$2,150	$1,900	$1,650	$1,375	$1,150	$1,000	$900	*$797*

Add $350-$400 for factory H & K scope mount system.

Significant price increases stopped the importation of this model.

Approx. 6 Model 770s were imported in .243 Win. cal. during 1984. Values for the .243 Win. cal. will be considerably higher than listed for the .308 Win. cal.

MODEL 911 – .308 Win. cal., earlier importation. Disc.

	$1,900	$1,700	$1,500	$1,275	$1,050	$900	$775	

MODEL 940 – .30-06 cal., 21.6 in. barrel with or w/o muzzle brake (early mfg.), otherwise same as Model 770, 8.62 lbs. Importation disc. 1986.

	$1,950	$1,750	$1,500	$1,250	$995	$875	$750	*$917*

Add $350-$400 for factory H & K scope mount system.

Cals. 7x64mm and 9.3x62mm were also available in this model.

Significant price increases stopped the importation of this model.

* ***Model 940K*** – similar to Model 940, except has 16 in. barrel and higher cheekpiece. Two imported 1984 only.

Rarity precludes accurate price evaluation.

SLB 2000 – .30-06 or .308 Win. (new 2003) cal. (bolt head dimension allows cartridge interchangeability), short stroke piston actuated gas operating system, alloy receiver with black weather resistant coating, gold accents on receiver, 19.69 in. barrel (interchangeable), checkered walnut stock and specially angled pistol grip, tang mounted safety blocks hammer and trigger, 2, 5, or 10 shot mag., iron sights, 7.28 lbs. Imported 2001-2003.

	$1,150	$995	$895	$825	$775	$700	$650	*$1,299*

MODELS SL6 & SL7 CARBINE – .223 Rem. or .308 Win. cal., 17.71 in. barrel, roller locked delayed blowback action, reduced recoil, vent. wood hand guard, 3 or 4 shot mag., 8.36 lbs., matte black metal finish, HK-SL6 is .223 Rem. cal., HK-SL7 is .308 Win. cal. Importation disc. in 1986.

	$1,650	$1,450	$1,250	$1,050	$925	$800	$650	

Add $250-$300 for factory H & K scope mount system.

Add $200 for .308 Win. cal.

GRADING - PPGS™	100%	98%	95%	90%	80%	70%	60%	LAST MSR

These models were the last sporter variations H & K imported into the U.S. - no U.S. importation since 1986.

MODEL SL8-1 – .223 Rem. cal., short stroke piston actuated gas operating system, advanced grey carbon fiber polymer construction based on the German Army G36 rifle, thumbhole stock with adj. cheekpiece and buttstock, 10 shot mag., modular and removable Picatinny rail, removable sights, 20.8 in. cold hammer forged heavy barrel, adj. sights, 8.6 lbs. Imported 2000-2003, reimported 2007-2010.

	100%	98%	95%	90%	80%	70%	60%	LAST MSR
	$1,950	$1,650	$1,500	$1,350	$1,200	$1,000	$900	*$2,449*

Add $338 for carrying handle with 1.5X-3x optical sights (disc. 2009).
Add $624 for carrying handle with 1.5X-3x optical sights and red dot reflex sight (disc. 2009).

MODEL SL8-6 – .223 Rem. cal., similar to SL8-1, except has elevated Picatinny rail that doubles as carrying handle. Mfg. 2010-2011.

	100%	98%	95%	90%	80%	70%	60%	LAST MSR
	$1,950	$1,650	$1,500	$1,350	$1,200	$1,000	$900	*$2,388*

MODEL USC .45 ACP CARBINE – .45 ACP cal., similar design/construction as the Model SL8-1, except is blowback action, and has 16 in. barrel and grey skeletonized buttstock, 10 shot mag., 6 lbs. Imported 2000-2003, reimported beginning 2007-2011.

	100%	98%	95%	90%	80%	70%	60%	LAST MSR
	$1,500	$1,275	$1,050	$925	$825	$725	$625	*$1,788*

MR556A1 CARBINE – 5.56 NATO cal., gas piston operation, 10 or 30 shot steel mag., 16 1/2 in. heavy barrel with muzzle brake, free floating rail system hand guard with four Mil Std 1913 Picatinny rails, Picatinny rail machined into top of upper receiver, two-stage trigger, diopter sights, black anodized finish, adj. buttstock with storage compartment, pistol grip with optional configurations. Mfg. in the U.S. using American and German made components. New 2009.

	100%	98%	95%	90%	80%	70%	60%
MSR $3,295	$2,995	$2,600	$2,300	$2,000	$1,700	$1,500	$1,250

MR762A1 CARBINE – 7.62x51mm cal., 16 1/2 in. barrel, gas piston operation, free floating rail system, flip up front and diopter rear sights, black anodized finish, 10 or 20 shot polymer mag., upper and lower accessory rails, adj. buttstock with storage compartment, pistol grip with optional configurations, 9.84 lbs. Limited mfg. in the U.S. New late 2009.

	100%	98%	95%	90%	80%	70%	60%
MSR $3,995	$3,600	$3,150	$2,700	$2,350	$1,950	$1,725	$1,400

MODEL MP5 A5 – .22 LR cal., blowback action, 10 or 25 shot mag., 16.1 in. barrel with compensator, black finish, metal receiver, Navy pistol grip, H&K adj. front and rear sights, 3 lug, standard forearm, retractable stock, external safety, 5.9 lbs., mfg. by Carl Walther in Ulm, Germany, imported by Umarex USA. New late 2009.

	100%	98%	95%	90%	80%	70%	60%
MSR $480	$450	$395	$360	$330	$300	$275	$250

MODEL MP5 SD – .22 LR cal., blowback action, 10 or 25 shot mag., 16.1 in. barrel with compensator, black finish, metal receiver, adj. rear sights, interchangeable front post sight, 3 lug imitation, SD type ribbed forearm, Navy pistol grip, retractable stock, external safety, 5.9 lbs. Mfg. by Carl Walther in Ulm, Germany, imported by Umarex USA. New late 2009.

	100%	98%	95%	90%	80%	70%	60%
MSR $550	$475	$425	$395	$360	$330	$300	$275

SHOTGUNS: SEMI-AUTO

Benelli shotguns previously imported by H&K can be found under Benelli.

MODEL 512 – 12 ga. only, mfg. by Franchi for German military contract, rifle sights, matte finished metal, walnut stock, fixed choke pattern diverter giving rectangular shot pattern. Importation disc. 1991.

	100%	98%	95%	90%	80%	70%	60%
	$1,500	$1,300	$1,100	$925	$800	$700	$600

Last Mfg.'s Wholesale was $1,895

SLS 2002 – 12 ga. only, 3 in. chamber, IQ-port gas operation (excess gas is vented forward through forearm cap), various barrel lengths, including slug barrel, double slide rails, deluxe checkered walnut stock and forearm, phosphate black finish, prototypes only in Europe, approx. 6 3/4 lbs.

While advertised during 2002, this gun was never manufactured past the prototype stage.

GRADING - PPGS™	100%	98%	95%	90%	80%	70%	60%	LAST MSR

N.L. HEINEKE, INC.

Current custom bolt action rifle manufacturer located in Laramie, WY.

RIFLES: BOLT ACTION, CUSTOM

Nathan Heinke manufactures high quality bolt action rifles on a custom order basis only. The base price is $15,000, and many options and accessories are available, including engraving. Please contact the company directly for more information, including delivery time (approx. 12 months), custom options, and availability (see Trademark Index).

HEINIE SPECIALTY PRODUCTS

Previous pistol manufacturer established in 1973, and located in Quincy, IL. Heinie currently manufactures sights only.

Heinie manufactured both scratch built personal defense and tactical/carry 1911 packages in a wide variety of chamberings.

HEIZER DEFENSE

Current pistol manufacturer established in 2011 and located in St. Louis, MO.

DERRINGERS

DOUBLETAP – 9mm Para. or .45 ACP cal., O/U, 3 in. ported or non-ported barrels utilizing tip-up design, aluminum or titanium construction, double action trigger system, thumb latch ejects spent rounds, grip housing contains two additional rounds, grey Mil/Std. finish, 14 oz. (titanium). New late 2011.

MSR $499	$450	$415	$385	$350	$325	$295	$275

Add $70 for ported barrels.
Add $230 for titanium construction.

HELLIS, CHARLES

Current trademark of shotguns established in 1884 and located in London, England.

SHOTGUNS: CUSTOM

Charles Hellis manufactures high quality traditional SxS and O/U shotguns with a unique spring assisted opening mechanism. All guns are entirely hand made to custom order. SxS prices begin at £32,500, and O/U prices begin at £39,950. Please contact the company directly for more information, including pricing, availability and delivery time (see Trademark Index).

HELWAN

Previous trademark imported by Navy Arms Co. and Interarms until 1995.

PISTOLS: SEMI-AUTO

BRIGADIER – 9mm Para. cal., single action, 4 1/2 in. barrel, all steel construction, 8 shot mag. with finger extension, black plastic grips, 32.6 oz. Imported 1988-94.

$295	$250	$225	$195	$150	$125	$115	*$260*

Add 20% for early mfg. with better finish.

This model is patterned after the Beretta Model 951 Brigadier. They were manufactured at the Helwan arsenal in Egypt.

MODEL 920 – 9mm Para. cal., patterned after the Beretta M92, blue finish, bottom mag. release, mfg. in Egypt, limited importation in 1997 by Intrac.

$425	$375	$325	$275	$250	$225	$195

HENDRY, RAMSAY & WILCOX

Previous manufacturer located in Perth, Scotland.

Hendry, Ramsay & Wilcox manufactured top quality shotguns and rifles which were priced per individual quotation. The company, now called Hendry, Ramsay & Waters, Ltd., is a hunting and sporting outfitter.

HENRY, ALEX

Current trademark owned and manufactured by Dickson & MacNaughton, located in Edinburgh, Scotland.

GRADING - PPGS™	100%	98%	95%	90%	80%	70%	60%	LAST MSR

Please contact Dickson & MacNaughton directly for more information regarding this trademark, including current availability and pricing (see Trademark Index).

HENRY REPEATING ARMS COMPANY

Current rifle manufacturer established during 1997, and located in Bayonne, NJ beginning 2008. Previously located in Brooklyn, NY. Distributor and dealer sales.

RIFLES

HENRY MINI-BOLT – .22 S & LR cal., single shot, 16 1/4 in. barrel, stainless steel receiver and barrel, Williams Fire Sights, manual safety, 11 1/2 in. LOP, black or orange (new 2009) synthetic stock, 3 1/4 lbs. New 2002.

MSR $260	$215	$175	$145	$120	$95	$90	$85	

HENRY ACU-BOLT – .17 HMR, .22 LR or .22 WMR cal., scaled down action, 20 in. stainless steel barrel and receiver, checkered black fiberglass stock, includes 4X scope with cantilever mount, 4 1/4 lbs. New 2004.

MSR $400	$335	$285	$225	$185	$160	$140	$120	

HENRY LEVER ACTION – .17 HMR (disc. 2010), .22 S-L-LR, or .22 WMR (new 2000) cal., side ejection, blue steel receiver, 16 1/8 (Youth Model), 18 1/4 (.22 LR only), 19 1/4 (.22 WMR only, disc. 2005) in. round or 20 in. octagon (mfg. 2006-2010) barrel, 11 (.22 WMR) or 15 (.22 LR) shot mag., deluxe American walnut stock and forearm, adj. rear sight and hooded front, 5 1/2 lbs. New 1997.

MSR $325	$275	$225	$185	$165	$150	$130	$120	

Add $150 for .22 WMR cal.
Add $100 for octagon barrel (disc. 2010).
Add $225 for .17 HMR cal. with octagon barrel (disc. 2010).

This model is also available as a Youth Model, with 13 in. LOP and shorter barrel.

* ***Henry Lever Action Carbine Large Loop*** – similar to Henry Lever Action, except has 16 1/8 in. barrel and large loop lever, 4 1/2 lbs. New 1998.

MSR $355	$290	$230	$185	$165	$150	$130	$120	

* ***Henry Lever Action Varmint Express*** – .17 HMR cal., similar to Henry Lever Action, except has 20 in. barrel, includes cantilever scope mount, Williams Fire Sights, 11 shot tube mag., Monte Carlo stock, 5 3/4 lbs. New 2003.

MSR $540	$475	$385	$325	$250	$200	$175	$150	

* ***Henry Lever Action Octagon Frontier*** – .17 HMR, .22 S, L, or LR, or .22 WMR cal., 20 in. blue octagon barrel, 11, 12, 16 or 21 shot, American walnut stock, Marbles adj. semi-buckhorn rear sight, brass beaded front sight.

MSR $430	$350	$295	$225	$185	$160	$140	$120	

Add $115 for .22 WMR or $110 for .17 HMR cal.

* ***Henry Lever Action BSA Venturing Edition*** – .22 S-L-LR cal., 18 1/4 in. round blue barrel, 15 (.22 LR), 16 (.22 Long), or 21 (.22 Short) shot mag., straight grip American walnut stock, "10th Anniversary Venturing" logo on receiver, adj. rear sight, hooded front sight, 5 1/4 lbs. Mfg. 2008.

	$385	$340	$300	$265	$235	$200	$175	*$430*

* ***Henry Lever Action Golden Boy*** – .17 HMR, .22 S-L-LR, or .22 WMR cal., features brasslite receiver, buttplate, and buckhorn sight, 16 1/4 (Youth Model), 20, or 20 1/2 (.22 WMR cal. only) in. blue octagon barrel, 16 shot mag., approx. 6 3/4 lbs. New mid-1999.

MSR $515	$430	$350	$275	$210	$175	$160	$140	

Add $80 for .22 WMR cal. (new 2002).
Add $100 for .17 HMR cal. (new 2005).
Add $150 for personalized 20-word inscription on right side of receiver.

This model is also available as a Youth Model, with 13 in. LOP and shorter barrel.

GRADING - PPGS™	100%	98%	95%	90%	80%	70%	60%	LAST MSR

* ***Henry Lever Action Golden Boy Deluxe II*** – .17 HMR (mfg. 2006-2012) or .22 S-L-LR cal., features hand engraved gold and silver brasslite receiver, deluxe uncheckered walnut stock and forearm. New 2004.

MSR $1,585	$1,400	$1,225	$1,035	$900	$750	$600	$525	

Add $29 for .17 HMR cal. (disc. 2012).

This model has been made in two editions - the original first edition of the one of 1,000 (disc.), and the second edition of one of 1,000 (current mfg.).

* ***Henry Lever Action Golden Boy Lincoln Bicentennial*** – .22 S-L-LR cal., 20 in. barrel, 16 or 21 shot mag., brasslite receiver, brass buttplate, blue barrel and lever, straight grip American walnut stock, replica of Lincoln's ser. no. 6 Henry rifle, brass replica of Lincoln memorial embedded in stock, Marbles adj. semi-buckhorn rear sight, brass bead front sight, 6 3/4 lbs. New 2009.

MSR $1,200	$1,075	$925	$800	$700	$600	$500	$400	

* ***Henry Lever Action Golden Boy BSA Venturing Edition*** – .22 S-L-LR cal., 20 in. octagon blue barrel, 16 or 21 shot mag., straight grip American walnut stock, "10th Anniversary Venturing" logo in buttstock, Marbles adj. semi-buckhorn rear sight with reversible diamond insert, brass bead front sight, brasslite receiver, buttplate, and barrel band. Mfg. 2008.

	$575	$500	$425	$350	$300	$265	$235	*$650*

* ***Henry Lever Action Golden Boy Eagle Scout Tribute*** – .22 S, L, or LR cal., 20 in. barrel, 16 or 21 (.22 S cal.) shot mag., American walnut stock with Eagle Scout embedded logo, Marbles adj. semi-buckhorn rear sight, brasslite receiver, brass buttplate, metal barrel band, 6 3/4 lbs. New 2011.

MSR $1,050	$975	$875	$750	$625	$525	$425	$350	

* ***Henry Lever Action BSA Centennial Edition Golden Boy*** – .22 S-L-LR cal., 20 in. round/ octagon barrel, 16 or 21 (.22 S cal.) shot mag., brasslite receiver with Scout Law engraved on right side, Scout Oath on left side, "100 Years of Scouting" medallion on stock, brass buttplate, blue barrel, lever, and barrel band, straight grip American walnut stock, adj. buckhorn rear sight, brass bead front sight, 6 3/4 lbs. New 2009.

MSR $900	$795	$700	$625	$550	$475	$400	$325	

* ***Henry Lever Action Golden Boy Military Service Tribute*** – .22 S, L, or LR cal., 20 in. barrel, 16 or 21 (.22 S cal.) shot mag., American walnut stock with American flag and "God Bless America" embedded logo, Marbles adj. semi-buckhorn rear sight, blue steel or brass receiver, brass buttplate, metal barrel band, drilled and tapped, 6 3/4 lbs. New 2011.

MSR $1,200	$1,075	$925	$800	$700	$600	$500	$400	

A portion of the proceeds from each gun will benefit the American Legion, VFW, Wounded Warrior Project and the Fisher House for military families.

HENRY MARE'S LEG .22 LR CAL. – .22 LR cal., features cut-down American walnut stock and forearm, 12 7/8 in. round barrel with open sights and barrel band, includes saddle ring carbine, large loop lever, blued metal finish, approx. 4 1/2 lbs. New 2011.

MSR $415	$365	$315	$280	$255	$235	$210	$190	

HENRY MARE'S LEG CENTERFIRE – .357 Mag. (new 2013), .44 Mag. (new 2013), or .45 LC cal., brass frame w/o saddle ring carbine, 12.9 in. barrel with Marbles adj. sights and brass barrel band, cut down American walnut stock with brass buttplate, large loop lever, Brasslite receiver and blued barrel and lever, 5.8 lbs. New 2011.

MSR $975	$865	$735	$600	$525	$450	$400	$350	

HENRY "BIG BOY" LEVER ACTION – .38 Spl./.357 Mag. (new 2008), .44 Mag./.44 Spl. or .45 LC (new 2004) cal., brass receiver, buttplate, and barrel band, 20 in. octagon barrel with 10 shot tube mag., buckhorn rear sight, straight grip walnut stock and forearm, 8.68 lbs. New 2003.

MSR $900	$785	$650	$550	$450	$400	$350	$300	

Add $420 for Wildlife Edition or Cowboy Edition (mfg. 2006-2007).

GRADING - PPGS™	100%	98%	95%	90%	80%	70%	60%	LAST MSR

* ***Henry Big Boy Deluxe II*** – .38 Spl./.357 mag. (new 2008), .44 Mag. or .45 LC cal., features hand engraved brass frame and barrel band, deluxe uncheckered walnut stock and forearm, 1,000 mfg. beginning 2007.

MSR $1,995	$1,725	$1,500	$1,225	$995	$850	$700	$575	

This model has been made in two editions - the original first edition of the one of 1,000 (disc.), and the second edition of one of 1,000 (current mfg.).

* ***Henry Big Boy BSA Venturing Edition*** – .44 Mag. cal., 20 in. octagon blue barrel, 10 shot mag., straight grip American walnut stock, Marbles adj. semi-buckhorn rear sight with reversible diamond insert, brass bead front sight, solid brass receiver, buttplate, and barrel band. Mfg. 2008.

	$875	$750	$675	$600	$525	$475	$400	*$1,000*

* ***Henry Big Boy "Cowboy" Edition II*** – .44 Mag. or .45 LC cal., 20 in. octagon barrel, 10 shot mag., straight grip American walnut stock, solid top brass receiver, brass buttplate and barrel band, Marbles adj. semi-buckhorn rear sight, brass beaded front sight, cowboy motif embedded in stock. New 2011.

MSR $1,400	$1,275	$1,125	$1,000	$900	$750	$600	$475	

This model has been made in two editions - the original first edition of the one of 1,000 (disc.), and the second edition of one of 1,000 (current mfg.).

* ***Henry Big Boy "Wildlife" II*** – similar to Henry Big Boy "Cowboy" II, except has wildlife scenes painted on stock and forearm.

MSR $1,400	$1,275	$1,125	$1,000	$900	$750	$600	$475	

This model has been made in two editions - the original first edition of the one of 1,000 (disc.), and the second edition of one of 1,000 (current mfg.).

HENRY PUMP ACTION – .22 S-L-LR or .22 WMR (new 2006) cal., blue grooved receiver, 18 1/4 in. round (disc. 2005) or 20 1/2 octagon (new 2006) barrel, walnut straight grip stock and forearm, 12 (.22 WMR) or 16 (.22 LR) shot mag., adj. buckhorn rear sight, approx. 5 1/2 lbs. New 1999.

MSR $510	$450	$350	$265	$215	$175	$160	$140	

Add $75 for .22 WMR cal.

HENRY U.S. SURVIVAL .22 SEMI-AUTO – .22 LR cal., patterned after the Armalite AR-7 with improvements, takedown design enables receiver, 2 mags., and barrel to stow in ABS plastic stock, 100% Mossy Oak Break-Up camo (mfg. 2000-2010) or weather resistant silver or black (new 1999) stock/metal finish, two 8 shot mags., adj. sights, 16 1/2 in. long when disassembled and stowed in stock, includes plastic carrying case, approx. 2 1/2 lbs. New 1997.

MSR $280	$225	$195	$170	$150	$130	$115	$100	

Add $70 for 100% camo finish (new 2000).

HENRY .30-30 LEVER ACTION – .30-30 Win. cal., lever action, 6 shot mag., 20 in. round or octagon barrel, straight grip American checkered walnut stock and forearm with buttplate, Marbles semi-buckhorn rear sight and brass bead front sight or XS Ghost ring sights (steel frame only), blue steel or brass receiver, with or w/o barrel band, drilled and tapped, 8.3 lbs. New 2008.

MSR $750	$675	$600	$525	$450	$395	$335	$275	

Add $200 for octagon barrel with brass receiver.

HENRY RIFLE

Please refer to the Winchester section in this text for this model.

HERA ARMS

Current firearms manufacturer located in Triefenstein, Germany. No current importation.

Hera Arms manufactures a complete line of AR-15 style semi-auto rifles in .223 Rem cal., as well as several styles of conversions for SIG, Glock, Walther, CZ, and H&K pistols. Hera Arms also manufactures a variety of tactical accessories geared towards military, law enforcement, and sport shooters. Please contact the company directly for more information, including options, US availability, and pricing (see Trademark Index).

GRADING - PPGS™	100%	98%	95%	90%	80%	70%	60%	LAST MSR

HERITAGE MANUFACTURING, INC.

Current manufacturer located in Opa Locka, FL since 1992.

In May 2012, Heritage Manufacturing Inc. was sold to Taurus International. Currently, Heritage remains a stand alone facility and manufacturing continues in Opa Locka, FL.

PISTOLS: SEMI-AUTO

H-25/25S – .25 ACP cal., 6 shot mag. with finger extension, single action, external hammer, choice of blue or blue/gold finish, 13 1/2 oz. Mfg. 1995-99.

	100%	98%	95%	90%	80%	70%	60%	LAST MSR
	$125	$110	$95	$85	$70	$55	$45	*$150*

Add $10 for nickel steel.
Add $10 for Model H-25G (blue/gold finish with checkered grips).

STEALTH SHADOW COMPACT – 9mm Para. or .40 S&W cal., striker firing mechanism, stainless steel slide and 3.9 in. barrel, black polymer frame, manual safety, 10 shot mag. with finger extension, fixed sights, choice of stainless slide, two-tone stainless slide, or all black (Shadow) finish, 20.5 oz. Mfg. 1996-2000.

	100%	98%	95%	90%	80%	70%	60%	LAST MSR
	$255	$225	$190	$175	$140	$115	$90	*$300*

Add $30 for .40 S&W cal.

REVOLVERS

Rough Rider SAA models are made in the U.S.A.

ROUGH RIDER SAA RIMFIRE SERIES – .17 HMR (new 2003), .22 LR, or .22 LR/.22 WMR cal. combo, SAA design with choice of alloy (33.4 oz.) or steel (35 oz., new 2000) frame, hammer block safety, blue, nickel (disc. 2001), black satin (new 2002), satin (new 2001), or silver satin (new 2005) finish, 3 1/2, 4 3/4, 6 1/2, or 9 (combo only) in. barrel, fixed or adj. (new 2001) rear sight, bird's head, white mother-of-pearl, pink mother-of-pearl, smooth or camo (new 2003) wood grips, approx. 33 1/2 oz. New 1993.

* ***Rough Rider SAA Series Steel Frame*** – .17 HMR (disc. 2009) or .22 LR cal., available in blue, black satin (mfg. 2003, reintroduced 2013), or case hardened (mfg. 2003) finish, includes extra .22 WMR cylinder, choice of regular or bird's head grips.

	100%	98%	95%	90%	80%	70%	60%	LAST MSR
MSR $330	$265	$230	$200	$175	$155	$125	$100	

Add $51 for nickel finish (combo package only, disc. 2001).
Add $50 for .17 HMR cal. with adj. sights (mfg. 2003-2008, not available in 4 3/4 in. barrel).
Add $10 for 9 in. barrel (available with combo package only).
Subtract $50 for alloy frame with combo package (disc. 2002).

* ***Rough Rider SAA Series Fixed Sight*** – .22 LR/.22 WMR cal. combo only, 4 3/4, 6 1/2, or 9 in. barrel.

	100%	98%	95%	90%	80%	70%	60%	LAST MSR
MSR $240	$200	$170	$150	$125	$110	$100	$80	

Add $50 for satin or $40 for black satin finish.
Add $30 for faux mother-of-pearl grips.
Add $20 for 9 in. barrel.
Add $50 for 9 shot model (new 2012).
Add $40 for case colored frame (new 2006).
Subtract $30 if with .22 LR cylinder only.

* ***Rough Rider SAA Series Adjustable Sight*** – .17 HMR (mfg. 2006-2008) or .22 LR/.22 WMR cal. combo, 4 3/4, 6 1/2, or 9 in. barrel.

	100%	98%	95%	90%	80%	70%	60%	LAST MSR
MSR $290	$250	$220	$195	$170	$155	$135	$120	

Add $60 for satin or $40 for black satin finish.
Add $30 for .17 HMR cal. (disc. 2008).
Add $80 for steel frame (disc. 2002, reintroduced 2012).
Add $50 for 9 in. barrel.

During 2004, a Williams red ramp front sight and Millett adj. microclick rear sight became available on the 6 1/2 in. barrel.

GRADING - PPGS™	100%	98%	95%	90%	80%	70%	60%	LAST MSR

* ***Rough Rider SAA Series Illuminator*** – .22 LR/.22 WMR cal. combo only, features Adco Hot Shot Red Dot frame mounted sight, 6 1/2 in. barrel only. Disc. 2007.

	$160	$140	$120	$110	$90	$70	$55	*$200*

* ***Rough Rider SAA Series with Birds Head Grip*** – .22 LR/.22 WMR cal. combo only, choice of 2 3/4 (disc. 1997), 3 (disc. 1994), 3 1/2, or 4 3/4 in. barrel, bird's head, white mother-of-pearl bird's head, or pink mother-of-pearl grips. New 1993.

MSR $250	$215	$185	$160	$140	$125	$100	$85	

Add $70 for black satin finish or $20 for mother-of-pearl grips.
Add $30 for nickel finish (disc. 2001).

ROUGH RIDER SAA CENTERFIRE SERIES – .32 H&R Mag. (blue finish only), .357 Mag., .44-40 WCF, or .45 LC cal., 3 1/2 (.32 H&R cal. only, with birdshead grips), 4 3/4, 5 1/2, 6 1/2 (.32 H&R cal. only), or 7 1/2 in. barrel, blue, nickel, stainless steel or case hardened frame, one piece cocobolo grips, 6 shot, fixed open sight, approx. 36 oz. Mfg. by Pietta.

MSR $480	$425	$375	$325	$300	$275	$250	$225	

Add $20 for case hardened frame.
Add $70 for nickel finish.
Add $50 for 3 1/2 or 4 3/4 in. barrel with birdshead grips and case colored finish.
Add $120 for distressed bluing and wood (.45 LC cal., 4 3/4 or 5 1/2 in. barrel, disc. 2009).
Add $110 for stainless steel (disc.).
Subtract $150 for .32 H&R cal. (black satin finish only).

ROUGH RIDER SAA SHOTSHELL SERIES – .45 LC/.410 shotshell cal., 4 3/4 in. barrel, black satin finish, 6 shot, steel frame, red fiber optic front sight, fixed rear sight, smooth rosewood grips, 44 oz. Mfg. 2012 only.

	$400	$350	$300	$275	$250	$225	$200	*$450*

SENTRY DA SERIES – .22 WMR (disc. 1996), .32 Mag. (disc. 1996), .38 Spl., or 9mm Para. (disc. 1996) cal., snubnose design, with 2 or 4 (.22 LR or .38 Spl.) in. barrel, 6 (centerfire) or 8 (rimfire) shot, transfer bar safety, blue or nickel finish, black polymer grips, ramp front sight. Mfg. 1993-97.

	$110	$95	$80	$75	$60	$50	$40	*$130*

Add $10 for nickel finish.

ROUGH RIDER COMMEMORATIVE PRESENTATION SET – .22 LR/.22 WMR cal. combo, 6 1/2 in. micro threaded barrel, hammer block safety, faux ivory grips with scrimshaw Confederate state battle flags, includes presentation cedar box with corresponding matching battle flag for each Confederate state. New 2013.

MSR $270	$225	$195	$175	N/A	N/A	N/A	N/A	

HEROLD RIFLE

Previously manufactured by Franz Jaeger, located in Suhl, Germany.

RIFLES: BOLT ACTION

SPORTING RIFLE – .22 Hornet cal., miniature Mauser action, 24 in. barrel, leaf sight, double set trigger, select checkered stock, imported by Daly & Stoeger, pre-WWII.

	$990	$880	$825	$770	$660	$550	$495	

HERTERS

Previous importer, distributor, and retailer headquartered in Waseca, MN from early 1960s - 1979. Herters also had additional retail stores scattered throughout the upper Midwest.

Herters subcontracted various manufacturers (mostly European) to fabricate Powermag revolvers, U-9/J-9 rifles, and shotguns which were mostly patterned after more famous original models. Most of these copies were designed to undersell the competition at the time and while quality in most cases was quite good, consumer sales were not strong enough to continue production. While many Herters models are relatively rare, collectibility to date has been minimal. Herters model values are usually under the original trademarks from which they were derived and to date have been based more on the shooting utility than the collector potential.

GRADING - PPGS™	100%	98%	95%	90%	80%	70%	60%	LAST MSR

HESSE ARMS

Previous manufacturer located in Inver Grove Heights, MN.

Hesse Arms manufactured very limited quantities of semi-auto pistols, bolt action rifles, and semi-auto rifles. Due to space considerations, this information is available free of charge on www.bluebookofgunvalues.com.

HEYM AG

Current manufacturer established in 1865 and located in Gleichamberg, Germany since 1995. Currently imported beginning 2006 by Double Gun Imports LLC, located in Dallas, TX. Limited importation 1999-2005 by New England Custom Gun Service, Ltd., located in Plainfield, NH. During 1998, Heym underwent a management change. The company name was changed from Heym Waffenfabrik AG to Heym AG during mid-2007. Previously manufactured in Muennerstadt, Germany circa 1952-1995 and Suhl, Germany between 1865-1945. Originally founded in 1865 by F.W. Heym. Previously imported by JagerSport, Ltd. located in Cranston, RI 1993-94 only, Heckler & Koch, Inc. (until 1993) located in Sterling, VA, Heym America, Inc. (subsidiary of F.W. Heym of W. Germany) located in Fort Wayne, IN, and originally by Paul Jaeger, Inc. 1970-1986.

Please contact the importer for more information, current pricing and domestic model availability (see Trademark Index).

Pre-war guns in 95%+ original condition will bring a premium over values listed.

COMBINATION GUNS

MODEL 22 S2 O/U – rifle/shotgun combination, 12, 16, or 20 ga. (3 in.), under rifle (17 cals. available), single set trigger, takedown feature (standard 1990), coin finish with engraving, 5 1/2 lbs.

$3,675	$3,000	$2,450	$1,875	$1,575	$1,325	$1,100	*$4,125*

Subtract $380 without engraving.

This model featured a dampened rifle barrel which prevents the "climbing" of groups, thereby enhancing accuracy.

MODEL 25 O/U – rifle/shotgun combination, 12, 16, or 20 ga. over various rifle cals., 23 3/4 in. barrels with iron sights, checkered walnut stock and forearm, 5.9 lbs.

$2,425	$1,725	$1,350	$1,125	$950	$800	$700	

Add $800 for deluxe game scene engraving.

MODEL 55 BF O/U – rifle/shotgun combination, popular U.S. and European cals., shotgun barrels interchangeable in 12 (disc.), 16, or 20 ga., 25 or 28 in. barrels, boxlock, auto ejectors, silver finish, fine German engraving, folding leaf sight, checkered pistol grip stock.

$6,500	$5,400	$4,950	$4,525	$3,950	$3,615	$3,210	*$7,485*

Add $3,250 for O/U rifle and $2,250 for O/U shotgun or shotgun/rifle combination extra barrels.

MODEL 88 BF SxS – 2 barrel set with 20 ga. barrels and an extra set of rifle barrels available in cals. .375 H&H Mag., .458 Win. Mag., .470 N.E., or .500 N.E.

$13,100	$10,750	$9,600	$8,150	$6,900	$5,850	$4,850	*$15,060*

This model is a larger frame variation of the Model 88 B.

* ***Model 88B/F SxS Safari*** – includes set of rifle and shotgun barrels, choice of .375 H&H, .458 Win. Mag., .470 NE, or .500 NE cal. and extra set of 20 ga. 3 in. chamber barrels.

$16,150	$14,100	$11,950	$10,250	$8,950	$6,750	$5,250	*$18,530*

MODEL 88 F SxS – available in various cals. and 20 ga. with 2 3/4 or 3 in. chambers.

$13,300	$11,250	$10,100	$9,400	$8,000	$6,950	$5,800	*$14,650*

DRILLINGS

MODEL 33 BOXLOCK STANDARD – 16 or 20 ga., boxlock, Arabesque engraving, shotgun barrels over popular European cals., and .222 Rem., .243 Win., .270 Win., .308 Win., and .30-

GRADING - PPGS™	100%	98%	95%	90%	80%	70%	60%	LAST MSR

06 cal. rifle barrel, 25 in. full and mod. barrels, set trigger on rifle, checkered pistol grip stock.

$6,075 $5,300 $4,525 $3,950 $3,350 $2,750 $2,150

* ***Model 33 Boxlock Standard Deluxe*** – similiar specifications as Standard Model, only hunting scene engraved.

$6,450 $5,425 $4,650 $4,025 $3,400 $2,750 $2,150

MODEL 35 STANDARD – 3 barrels, (two rifle and one shotgun), choice of cals. with top barrel either 16 or 20 ga., light border engraving, 8 1/4 lbs.

$13,650 $11,000 $9,250 $8,000 $6,850 $5,700 $4,600 *$15,100*

Add $2,430 for hunting scene engraving.

MODEL 37F SIDELOCK STANDARD – 12, 16, or 20 ga. 25 in. SxS barrels over rifle barrel in .22 Hornet, .30 Blaser, 5.6x50R, 5.6x52R, 5.6x57R, 6x70R, 6.5x57R, 6.5x65RWS, 7x57R, 7x65R, 8x57JRS, 8x75RS, or 9.3x74, (other chamberings available by request), sidelock action with Greener crossbolt, cocking indicators, non-automatic safety, set front trigger, hand engraved, case colored or coin finished, other barrel lengths available by request, select French walnut stock, approx. 8 lbs.

MSR $25,000 $21,750 $18,250 $15,000 $12,500 $10,500 $8,500 $6,950

* ***Model 37B Sidelock Standard Deluxe*** – 12, 20, 16, 28 ga. or .410 bore over same rifle cals. as the Model 37, available in right or left hand, more engraving.

MSR $28,000 $24,000 $20,500 $16,500 $13,250 $11,000 $9,000 $7,500

MODEL 37 B STANDARD – rifle barrels over shotgun (20 ga.), sidelock, border engraved, about 8.6 lbs.

$13,250 $10,875 $9,500 $8,400 $7,550 $6,500 $5,650 *$15,065*

* ***Model 37 B Standard Deluxe*** – similar to Model 37 B Standard, except has large hunting scene engraving.

$15,600 $12,750 $10,700 $9,450 $8,200 $7,050 $5,750 *$17,620*

RIFLES: BOLT ACTION

On most of the models listed, the "N" suffix in the model denotes standard calibers, whereas "G" refers to Mag. cals.

MODEL SR 10 SPORTER – various cals., originally mfg. by H & K. Limited mfg.

$1,325 $1,100 $950 $850 $750 $650 $550

MODEL SR 20N & CLASSIC – available in 18 cals., Mauser type bolt action, single trigger, French walnut, 24 in. Krupp steel barrel except Mag. (25 in.). Importation disc. 2001.

$1,825 $1,425 $1,100 $900 $800 $700 $600 *$2,100*

Subtract $70 without iron sights.
Add $430 for left-hand variation.
Add $300 for Mag. cals. (G suffix).
Add $1,140 for .375 H&H cal. (Model SR20 G Etoscha).
Add $260 for Classic Model.
Add $300 for carbine Classic Model.

* ***Model SR 20 Hunter*** – similar to Model SR 20N, except has classic style fiberglass stock with either matte blue or parkerized metal finish. Imported 1988-90.

$1,500 $1,225 $1,050 $900 $800 $700 $600 *$1,750*

* ***Model SR 20L*** – Mannlicher style stock, European configuration, 18 in. barrel, 7 lbs.

$1,475 $1,225 $985 $895 $785 $720 $650 *$1,700*

SR 20 TROPHY – available in all SR 20 cals., bolt action, 22 or 24 (Mag. cals. only) in. octagonal barrel, classic stock configuration with cheekpiece and recoil pad. Importation began 1989.

$2,550 $2,100 $1,800 $1,500 $1,250 $985 $895 *$2,815*

Add $120 for Mag. cals.

This model was also available in either right-hand or left-hand action.

GRADING - PPGS™	100%	98%	95%	90%	80%	70%	60%	LAST MSR

SR 20G CLASSIC SPORTER – available in various cals., bolt action, 22 or 24 in. round barrel, steel grip cap. Importation began 1989.

	$1,875	$1,600	$1,300	$1,050	$900	$785	$720	*$2,235*

Subtract $70 without iron sights.

This model was also available in either right-hand or left-hand action.

SR 20 ALPINE – available in standard cals. between .243 Win. and 9.3x62mm, mountain style rifle with Mannlicher forend and classic buttstock, supplied with mounted open sights. Importation began 1989.

	$1,900	$1,650	$1,325	$1,075	$925	$800	$750	*$2,165*

This model was also available in either right-hand or left-hand action.

SR 20 MATCH – .308 Win. cal., 24 in. heavy barrel, target stock with accessory rail, large bolt handle, supplied without sights, 9 lbs. Imported 1991-94.

	$1,860	$1,600	$1,300	$1,050	$900	$785	$720	*$2,200*

SR 20 CLASSIC SAFARI – .375 H&H, .404 Jeffery (disc.), .425 Express, or .458 Win. Mag. cal., 24 in. barrel only, express rear sight and large front post sights, tight grained walnut stock. Imported 1989-94.

	$2,150	$1,650	$1,250	$1,050	$875	$800	$700	*$2,530*

This model was also available in either right-hand or left-hand action.

SR 21 CLASSIC (N) – 24 standard and metric cals., 22 or 24 in. barrel, traditional bolt action that is bascially a Mauser M90 design with modern extractor recessed in the bolt face, set or standard trigger, unique interchangeable barrel/receiver, detachable mag., 3 position side safety, right or left-hand action, with or w/o open sights, approx. 7 lbs. New 2001.

Add $325 for carbine (disc.)
Add $1,325 for Model SR 21 N Concorde (disc.)
Add $110 for Model SR 21 N Keiler (disc.)
This model is POR.

SR 30 CLASSIC (N) – various cals., 22 or 24 in. barrel, straight pull bolt which locks in the receiver head, with or w/o open sights, deluxe checkered walnut stock with rosewood pistol grip cap and forend tip, sling swivels, set or standard trigger, detachable mag., 7-7 1/2 lbs.

Add $264 for carbine (disc.).
Add $1,505 for SR 30 N Concorde Model (disc.).
Add $155 for SR 30 N Wild Boar Model (disc.).
This model is POR.

EXPRESS SERIES RIFLE – .338 Lapua Mag. (disc.), .375 H&H, .378 Wby. Mag. (disc.), .404 Jeffery (disc. 1992, reintroduced), .416 Rigby, .450 Ackley (disc.), .450 Rigby, .458 Win. Mag., .458 Lott, .460 Wby. Mag., .500 NE (new 1994), .500 A-Square (disc.), or .505 Gibbs (disc.) cal., double square bridge Mauser action, express sights, Timney single trigger, available in right or left hand. New 1989.

MSR $11,000	$9,995	$8,750	$7,500	$6,250	$5,000	$4,000	$3,250	

Add $525 for .460 Wby. Mag. - .505 Gibbs cal.
Add $375 for muzzle brake (included installation, disc.).
Add $555 for left-hand action (disc. 1992).

* ***Express Series Rifle .577 NE & .600 NE Cals.*** – .577 NE (disc.) or .600 NE cal., 24 in. barrel, reinforced action, 2 shot mag. New 1991.

MSR $21,000	$18,950	$16,500	$14,500	$12,500	$10,500	$8,500	$6,500	

RIFLES: O/U

MODEL 26 B – .223 Rem., 7x65R, .30R Blaser, .30-30 Win., .30-06, 8x57RJS, or 9.3x74R cal., double lock system, manual cocking, ST, buttstock with slightly curved stock comb and Bavarian cheekpiece, game scene engraving with stag and boar, extractors, other calibers available by request. New 2006.

MSR $5,400	$4,875	$4,400	$3,900	$3,450	$3,000	$2,650	$2,300	

Add $550 for Luxus model (disc.).

This model was also available in Luxus variation, with higher grain wood, wild boar sights, and hunting scene engraving.

GRADING - PPGS™	100%	98%	95%	90%	80%	70%	60%	LAST MSR

MODEL 55 BOXLOCK – various cals. up to .500 NE, boxlock action, Greener crossbolt, double Purdey underbite, right or left hand, case colored or coin finish, 26 in. barrels standard, other lengths available by request, ejectors, steel grip cap, express sights, intercepting sears, cocking indicators, non-automatic safety, articulated front trigger, hand engraved.

MSR $22,000 $19,995 $17,500 $15,500 $13,500 $11,500 $9,500 $7,500

Add $1,500 for NE calibers.

* ***Model 55BF*** – similar to Model 55 Boxlock, except has shotgun barrel on bottom in 12, 16, 20, 28 ga. or .410 bore.

MSR $18,000 $16,000 $14,000 $12,000 $10,000 $8,000 $6,750 $5,500

MODEL 55 SIDELOCK – O/U rifle only with different caliber for each barrel, double set triggers, "Bergstutzen" design. Disc.

$9,350 $8,000 $6,850 $5,950 $5,125 $4,500 $3,975

Add $1,000 for Deluxe Model.

* ***Model 55 SS Sidelock*** – various cals. up to .500 NE, pinless sidelock action, Greener crossbolt, double Purdey underbite, right or left hand, case colored or coin finish, 26 in. barrels standard, other lengths available by request, ejectors, steel grip cap, express sights, intercepting sears, cocking indicators, non-automatic safety, articulated front trigger, hand engraved.

MSR $28,000 $25,000 $22,250 $19,250 $17,000 $15,000 $12,750 $9,250

RIFLES: SxS

MODEL 80 B – various cals., modified boxlock action with top sear bars, small frame, regular or manual cocking, 23 3/4 in. barrels with quarter rib and iron sights, DT or ST, deluxe checkered walnut stock and forearm, extractors, available with splinter or semi-beavertail forend with interchangable rifle or shotgun barrels, hand made, limited production, 6.6 lbs.

MSR $12,000 $10,750 $9,500 $8,250 $7,000 $5,750 $4,750 $3,950

Add $600 for ST with hand cocking (disc.), $700 for DT with hand cocking (disc.).

MODEL 88 B – available in most safari cals. between .300 Win. Mag. - .458 Win. Mag. boxlock action, 25 in. Krupp steel barrels, double underlocking lugs with Greener crossbolt, ejectors, checkered Circassian walnut stock and forearm, built to customer specifications, hand engraved with case colored or coin finish, splinter or semi-beavertail forend, interchangable rifle or shotgun barrels available by request, steel grip cap., express sights, 7 1/2 lbs.

MSR $17,000 $15,250 $13,500 $11,500 $9,500 $7,750 $6,500 $5,500

Add $550 for .416 Rigby - .500 NE cal. (disc.)

* ***Model 88 B SS*** – similar cals. as Model 88B, pinless sidelock model with interceptor sears.

MSR $22,000 $19,995 $17,500 $15,500 $13,500 $11,500 $9,500 $7,500

This model was also available in both .577 NE and .600 NE cal. Prices started at $28,575 for the .577 NE, and $32,500 for .600 NE.

* ***Model 88 B PH Boxlock*** – available in various safari cals., boxlock action, 26 in. barrels, Greener crossbolt, right or left hand, ejectors, cocking indicators, intercepting sears, non-automatic safety, atriculated front trigger, no engraving, case colored or coin finish, steel grip cap, short trigger guard, express sights, splinter or semi-beavertail forend with interchangable rifle or shotgun barrels to order, other barrel lengths available by request. New 2007.

MSR $17,000 $15,250 $13,500 $11,500 $9,500 $7,750 $6,500 $5,500

* ***Model 88 B Safari*** – similar to PH Model, except has more detailed hand shaping on action and action bolsters, long trigger guard extending to steel grip cap, higher grade of wood and hand engraved to order.

MSR $22,000 $19,995 $17,500 $15,500 $13,500 $11,500 $9,500 $7,500

* ***Model 88 B Safari Sidelock*** – similar to Safari Model, except has pinless sidelock action.

MSR $28,000 $25,000 $22,250 $19,250 $17,000 $15,000 $12,750 $9,250

GRADING - PPGS™	100%	98%	95%	90%	80%	70%	60%	LAST MSR

* ***Model 88 B Jumbo*** – .470 NE, .500 NE, .577 NE, or .600 NE cal., large frame, 26 in. barrels, best grade pinless sidelock action with hidden Purdey fastener, ejectors, cocking indicators, non-automatic safety, case colored or coin finished with hand engraving, express sights, intercepting sears, articulated front trigger, steel grip, other barrel lengths available by request, splinter or semi-beavertail forend with interchangable rifle or shotgun barrels available by request.

MSR $50,000 | $45,000 | $38,500 | $33,000 | $27,000 | $23,000 | $19,000 | $16,500

IVORY HUNTER – large dangerous game cals. only, sidelock model, Purdey locking system, custom engraving, steel pistol grip cap, steel trigger guard, Classic stock with German cheekpiece, rubber recoil pad, custom order only, 12.8 lbs.

This model was available POR.

RIFLES: SINGLE SHOT

MODEL HR 30N – available in many cals., Ruger No. 1 falling block action, 24 in. barrel, French walnut with Bavarian cheekpiece, round barrel, Sporter or full length carbine style French walnut stock, engraved coin finished receiver, 6.6 lbs.

$3,500 | $2,975 | $2,350 | $1,950 | $1,675 | $1,350 | $1,175 | *$4,040*

Add $440 for Mag. cals.
Add $1,710 for Mannlicher stocked Carbine Model.
Add $850 for hunting scene engraving (minimum extra charge).

MODEL HR 38 N – available in many cals., Ruger No. 1 falling block action, 24 in. barrel, octagon barrel, French walnut with Bavarian cheekpiece, Sporter, or full length carbine style French walnut stock, engraved coin finished receiver, 6.6 lbs.

$4,150 | $3,450 | $2,875 | $2,300 | $1,950 | $1,675 | $1,350 | *$4,835*

Add $235 for Mag. cals.
Add $2,400 for sideplates with engraved large game hunting scenes.

MODEL 44 B – various standard and metric cals., single lock action with thumbpiece and sideplates, open sights with barrel quarter rib, deluxe checkered stock and forearm, 6.6 lbs.

$4,900 | $4,350 | $3,550 | $3,025 | $2,350 | $2,000 | $1,750

Add $1,100 for Deluxe Model.

SHOTGUNS: O/U

MODEL 55 F – 12, 16, or 20 ga., boxlock action, Greener crossbolt, various barrel lengths up to 28 in., non-automatic safety, case colored or coin finished receiver, cocking indicators, extractors or ejectors, right or left hand, hand made, limited production. Importation disc. 1992, reintroduced 2009.

MSR $12,000 | $10,750 | $9,500 | $8,250 | $7,000 | $5,750 | $4,750 | $3,950

MODEL 55 SS – sidelock version of Model 55 F, large engraved hunting scenes.

MSR $18,000 | $16,000 | $14,000 | $12,000 | $10,000 | $8,000 | $6,750 | $5,500

MODEL 200 – 20 ga., 3 in. chambers, boxlock action, DTs, 28 in. VR barrels, light engraving, previous importation.

$895 | $795 | $700 | $650 | $600 | $550 | $500

VIERLINGS

MODEL 37 V – 4 barrel configuration, various cals. and gauges, special order only. Limited mfg.

MSR $42,000 | $37,500 | $32,000 | $28,000 | $24,000 | $21,000 | $18,000 | $15,000

HIENDLMAYER, KLAUS

Please refer to Waffen Hiendlmayer listing in the W section.

HI-POINT FIREARMS

Current trademark marketed by MKS Supply, Inc. located in Dayton, Ohio. Hi-Point firearms have been manufactured since 1988. Dealer and distributor sales.

GRADING - PPGS™	100%	98%	95%	90%	80%	70%	60%	LAST MSR

Prior to 1993, trademarks sold by MKS Supply, Inc. (including Beemiller, Haskell Manufacturing, Inc., Iberia Firearms, Inc., and Stallard Arms, Inc.) had their own separate manufacturers' markings. Beginning in 1993, Hi-Point Firearms eliminated these individualized markings and chose instead to have currently manufactured guns labeled "Hi-Point Firearms". All injection molding for Hi-Point Firearms is done in Mansfield, OH.

CARBINES

MODEL 995TS – 9mm Para. cal., 16 1/2 in. barrel, one-piece camo (disc.) or black polymer stock features pistol grip (target stock became standard 2013), 10 shot mag., aperture rear sight, parkerized or chrome (disc. 2007) finish. New 1996.

MSR $286	$230	$185	$140	$120	$100	$85	$75

Add $109 for laser sight.
Add $33 for 4x scope or $30 for red dot scope.
Add $23 for forward grip or $52 for forward grip and light.
Add $128 for 4x RGB scope.
Add $153 for forward grip, light, and laser sight (new 2011).
Add $49 for Pro Pack Kit with target stock (new 2011).
Add $15 for camo stock (mfg. 2002-disc.).
Add $85 for detachable compensator, laser, and mount (mfg. 1999-2010).
Add $10 for chrome finish (disc. 2007).

This model is manufactured by Beemiller, located in Mansfield, OH.

MODEL 4095TS – .40 S&W cal., 17 1/2 in. barrel, one-piece camo (disc.) or black polymer stock features pistol grip (target stock became standard 2013), 10 shot mag., aperture rear sight, parkerized or chrome (disc. 2007) finish. Mfg. 2003-2008, reintroduced 2011.

MSR $315	$250	$190	$150	$125	$110	$90	$80

Add $84 for laser sight.
Add $136 for forward grip, light, and laser sight (new 2011).
Add $32 for Pro Pack Kit with target stock (new 2011).
Add $13 for 4x scope or red dot scope.
Add $111 for 4x RGB scope (new 2013).
Add $6 for forward grip or $35 for forward grip and light.
Add $85 for detachable compensator, laser, and mount (mfg. 1999-2010).

This model is manufactured by Beemiller, located in Mansfield, OH.

MODEL 4595TS – .45 ACP cal., 17 1/2 in. barrel, black polymer stock (target stock became standard 2013), 9 shot mag., aperture rear sight, black finish. New 2011.

MSR $319	$250	$195	$160	$130	$115	$90	$80

Add $90 for laser sight.
Add $152 for forward grip, light, and laser sight (new 2011).
Add $49 for Pro Pack Kit with target stock (new 2011).
Add $32 for 4x scope or $30 for red dot scope.
Add $106 for 4x RGB scope (new 2013).
Add $22 for forward grip or $51 for forward grip and light.

This model is manufactured by Beemiller, located in Mansfield, OH.

PISTOLS: SEMI-AUTO

Beginning 2000, all compact models feature magazine disconnect safety and last shot hold open, and all pistols are shipped with a rear adj. aperture sight (which can replace the standard rear adj. sight).

MODEL CF-380 POLYMER – .380 ACP cal., single action, 3.5 or 4 (new 2002) in. barrel, polymer frame, 3-dot adj. sights, 8 shot mag. with thumb activated release, chrome slide (disc.) or two-tone black satin finish, 29 oz. New 1995.

MSR $149	$120	$100	$85	$65	$55	$50	$45

Add $6 for hard case.
Add $21 for compensator (new 2013).
Add $15 for 4 in. barrel with compensator and two mags. (Model 380 Comp, disc. 2007).

This model is manufactured by Beemiller, located in Mansfield, OH.

GRADING - PPGS™	100%	98%	95%	90%	80%	70%	60%	LAST MSR

JS-9 – 9mm Para. cal., single action, 4 1/2 in. barrel, thumb safety, fixed (disc. 1999) or adj. (new 2000) sights, 8 shot mag., non-glare military blue finish (early mfg.) or black satin finish (new 1991), copolymer synthetic grips, 39 oz. Mfg. 1990-2000.

	$140	$110	$95	$80	$70	$65	$60	*$159*

Add 10% for nickel finish (disc.).

This model was manufactured by Beemiller, Inc. located in Mansfield, OH.

* ***JS-9 Compact (Model C-9)*** – compact variation of the Model JS-9 with 3 1/2 in. barrel and 8 shot mag., choice of alloy or polymer (new 1994, various slide/frame finishes) frame, 3-dot adj. sights became standard in 2000, 32 (polymer) or 29 oz. New 1993.

MSR $189	$145	$110	$100	$80	$60	$50	$45	

This model is manufactured by Beemiller, Inc. located in Mansfield, OH.

* ***JS-9 Comp*** – features 4 in. barrel with compensator, with (new 1999) or w/o laser sight package, adj. sights, 10 shot mag. Mfg. 1998-2006.

	$135	$115	$100	$90	$80	$75	$70	*$159*

Add $61 for laser sights and mount.

JS-40 – .40 S&W cal., single action, steel frame, black or nickel (disc. 1994) finish, 4 1/2 in. barrel, 3-dot adj. sights, 8 shot mag., 39 oz. Mfg. 1992-2002.

	$135	$110	$100	$90	$80	$75	$70	*$159*

Add $7 for nickel finish (disc. 1994).

This model was manufactured by Iberia Firearms, Inc. located in Iberia, OH.

JC-40 – .40 S&W cal., single action, polymer frame, black finish or OD Green slide with camo grips (new 2009), 4 1/2 in. barrel, 3-dot adj. sights, accessory rail (new 2004), 10 shot mag., 32 oz. New 2002.

MSR $199	$165	$135	$110	$95	$85	$75	$70	

Add $51 for laser sight.

This model is manufactured by Iberia Firearms, Inc. located in Iberia, OH.

JS-45 – .45 ACP cal., single action, steel frame, similar to JS-9, except has 7 shot mag. and 4 1/2 in. barrel, adj. sights, 39 oz. Mfg. 1991-2002.

	$135	$110	$100	$90	$80	$75	$70	*$159*

Add $10 for nickel finish (disc. 1994).

This model was manufactured by Haskell Mfg., Inc. located in Lima, OH.

JH-45 – .45 ACP cal., single action, polymer frame, similar to JS-9, except has 9 shot mag. and 4 1/2 in. barrel, accessory rail (new 2004), adj. sights, black finish or OD Green slide with camo grips (new 2009), 32 oz. New 2003.

MSR $199	$165	$135	$110	$95	$85	$75	$70	

Add $51 for laser sight.

This model is manufactured by Haskell Mfg., Inc. located in Lima, OH.

HIGGINS, J.C.

Previous trademark used on Sears & Roebuck rifles and shotguns manufactured between 1946-1962.

The J.C. Higgins trademark has appeared literally on hundreds of various models (shotguns and rifles) sold through the Sears & Roebuck retail network. Most of these models were manufactured through subcontracts with both domestic and international firearms manufacturers. Typically, they were "spec." guns made to sell at a specific price to undersell the competition. Most of these models were derivatives of existing factory models (i.e., Browning, High Standard, Marlin, Mossberg, Savage, Stevens, Winchester, etc.) with less expensive wood and perhaps missing the features found on those models from which they were derived.

To date, there has been minimal interest in collecting J.C. Higgins guns, regardless of rarity. Rather than list J.C. Higgins models, a general guideline is that values generally are less than models of their "1st generation relatives" (listed above). The Ranger trademark was also used by Sears & Roebuck - it is not any more desirable than those guns marked

"J.C. Higgins". As a result, prices are ascertained by the shooting value of the gun, rather than its collector value.

To find the original manufacturer of a J.C. Higgins model, please refer to the Store Brand Crossover List.

HIGH STANDARD

Previous manufacturer located in New Haven, Hamden, and East Hartford, CT. High Standard Mfg. Co. was founded in 1926. They entered the firearms business when they purchased Hartford Arms and Equipment Co. in 1932. The original plant was located in New Haven, CT. During WWII High Standard operated plants in New Haven and Hamden. After the war, the operations were consolidated in Hamden. In the late 1940's and early 1950's the pistol plant was located in East Haven but the guns continued to be marked New Haven. In 1968, the company was sold to the Leisure Group, Inc. A final move was made to East Hartford, CT in 1977 where they remained until the doors were closed in late 1984. In early 1978, the Leisure Group sold the company to the management and the company became High Standard, Inc.

Many collectors have realized the rarity and quality factors this trademark has earned. 13 different variations (Models C, A, D, E, H-D, H-E, H-A, H-B First Model, G-380, , GD, GE, and Olympic, commonly called the GO) had a total production of less than 28,000 pistols. For these reasons, top condition High Standard pistols are getting more difficult to find each year.

As a final note on High Standard pistols, they are listed under the following category names: Letter Series, Letter Series w/Hammer, Lever Letter Series, Lever Name Series, 100 Series, 101 Series, 102 Series, 103 Series, 104 Series, 105 Series, 106 Series - Military Models, 107 Series, Conversion Kits, and SH Series.

Note: catalog numbers were not always consistent with design series, and in 1966-1967 changed with accessories offered, but not design series.

The approx. ser. number cut-off for New Haven, CT marked guns is 442,XXX.

The approx. ser. number range for Hamden, CT marked guns is 431,XXX-2,500,811, G 1,001-G 13,757 (Shipped) or G15,650 (Packed) or ML 1,001-ML 23,065. One exception is a 9211 Victor serial number 3,000,000 shipped 1 March, 1974.

The first gun shipped 16 June, 1977 from E. Hartford was a Victor 9217 serial number EH0001.

The approx. ser. number ranges for E. Hartford, CT manufacture is ML 25,000-ML 86,641 and SH 10,001-SH 34,034. One exception is a single gun numbered ML90,000.

All "V" marked guns were shipped during June 1984 or later independent of serial number.

Original factory boxes have become very desirable. Prices can range from $50-$100 for a good condition Model 106 or 107 factory box to over $150 for an older box of a desirable model.

DERRINGERS

DERRINGER MODELS - .22 or .22 WMR cal., double action only O/U, 2 shot, 3 1/2 in. barrels.

The first derringer was mfg. about 1962, at the approximate serial number 1,261,903 in Hamden, CT. The serial numbers continued in the handgun serial number series until serial number 2,500,464 in 1975, when the derringers were put into a separate serial number group with a D prefix, D 1,001 through D 96,098 V. Serial number D 12,047 was the last Hamden made gun, with E. Hartford production beginning with D 13,000. After 1976, the guns were made in East Hartford.

Three different styles of roll marking methods were used during production.

The First style is marked with the caliber and "D-100" or "DM-101" on left side of frame, "Hi-Standard Derringer" with eagle logo on left side of barrel.

The Second style is marked with the caliber and "D-100", "D-101", or "DM-101" on left side of frame, "Hi-Standard Derringer" with trigger logo on left side of barrel. Both the first and second types were marked "HIGH STANDARD MFG. CORP./-HAMDEN, CONN. U.S.A.-"

GRADING - PPGS™	100%	98%	95%	90%	80%	70%	60%	LAST MSR

The Third style is marked with the caliber and "D-101" or "DM-101" on left side of frame, "Derringer" on left side of barrel. The third style was marked with different addresses and company names on the right side of the barrel. Style 3A is marked on the right side of the barrel the same as types one and two. Type 3B is marked with "HIGH STANDARD MFG. CORP./-E. HARTFORD, CONN. US.A.-" and type 3C is marked "HIGH STANDARD INC./-E. HARTFORD, CONN. U.S.A.-" Later third style is not marked with the "D-101" or "DM-101". The early derringers had a grooved back grip strap, which changed to a smooth grip strap just before the move to E. Hartford.

Near the end of production, a "V" suffix was added to some visually impaired guns, which were sold at discount. These guns were guaranteed to function properly, but the company would not allow them to be returned for appearance reasons. Numerous guns' earlier serial numbers, held back because of visual flaws, were also marked with the "V" and were shipped in 1984. The earliest V suffix gun found to date is D 25,945V.

* ***Derringer Model Blue Finish*** – .22 LR or .22 WMR cal ., blue, white or black grips.

$295	$250	$200	$165	$135	$105	$95

Add $25 for hinged maroon case.

.22 LR D-100 First series, catalog #9193, mfg. 1962-67, ser. no. 1,261,903. .22 LR D-100 Second series, catalog #9193, mfg. 1967-1969, ser. no. 1,6XX,XXX. .22 LR D-101 Second series, catalog #9193, mfg. 1969-1970, ser. no. 2,1XX,XXX. .22 LR D-101 Third series, catalog #9193, mfg. 1970-75, ser. no. 2,497,125. .22 LR Third series, catalog #9193, mfg. 1975-77, ser. no. D 02,809-D 13,319. .22 LR Third series, catalog #9193, mfg. 1982-84, ser. no. D 73,100-D 96,098 V. .22 WMR DM-101 First series, catalog #9194, mfg. 1963-67, ser. no. 1,301,611. .22 WMR DM-101 Second series, catalog #9194, mfg. 1967-1970, ser. no. 1,6XX,XXX. .22 WMR DM-101 Third series, catalog #9193, mfg. 1970-1975, ser. no. 2,500,464. .22 WMR Third series, catalog #9193, mfg. 1975-1982, ser. no. D 01,001. .22 WMR Third series, catalog #9193, mfg. 1982-84, ser. no. D95,217 V.

* ***Derringer Model Nickel Finish*** – .22 LR or .22 WMR cal., nickel, black grips, ivory grips were used on some early models, introduced 1970.

$340	$295	$260	$200	$150	$120	$100

.22 LR D-101 Third series, catalog #9305, mfg. 1970-75, ser. no. 2,182,780-2,476,0XX. .22 LR Third series, catalog #9305, mfg. 1975-77, ser. no. D05,543-D 13,426. .22 WMR. DM-101 Third series, catalog #9306, mfg. 1970-75, ser. no. 2,182,380-2,500,464. .22 WMR Third series, catalog #9306, mfg. 1975-1984, ser. no. D 01,001-D 95,217 V.

* ***Derringer Model Gold Plated*** – .22 LR or .22 WMR cal., with black grips, includes presentation case, introduced 1964.

$595	$525	$450	$295	$250	$200	$175

Add $85 for derringers with 1-3 digit serial numbers.
Subtract $75 if w/o presentation case.

#9195 derringers found in the regular serial number series around 1,339,002-1,339,080 beginning the end of 1963. #9196 found in regular serial number series around 2,366,556-2,366,561, 2,398,810-2,397,819 in 1973, and D 81,122 in 1982. Others are in a separate serial number series running from 1 through 123 which contains about 25 #9195 and 30 #9196 derringers. .22 LR D-100 First Series, catalog #9195, mfg. 1963-1973. .22 WMR DM-101 First Series, catalog #9196, mfg. 1964-1973. .22 LR D-100 First Series, cased pair, catalog #9197. .22 WMR DM-101 First Series, cased pair, catalog #9198.

While matched sets did have factory catalog numbers, rarity and lack of known sales preclude accurate valuation.

* ***Derringer Model Electroless Nickel Finish*** – . 22 LR or .22 WMR cal., checkered walnut grips.

$350	$300	$250	$200	$150	$125	$100

.22 LR Third series, catalog #9421, mfg. 1981-83, ser. no. D 74,351 - D 87,705. .22 WMR Third series, catalog #9420, mfg. 1981-83, ser. no. D 63.390 - D 93,632.

PRESIDENTIAL DERRINGER – .22 WMR cal., gold plated, smooth walnut grips, includes walnut case marked "PRESIDENTIAL DERRINGER".

$595	$525	$450	$375	$300	$250	$215

Subtract $100 if w/o presentation case.

Third series, catalog #9196, mfg. 1974-78. Serial numbers DM1 through DM 416 (353 guns) and HDM153 through HDM160 (7 guns) and a few special prefixes on about 10 guns.

GRADING - PPGS™	100%	98%	95%	90%	80%	70%	60%	LAST MSR

PRESENTATION DERRINGER

* ***Presentation Derringer Gold Plated*** – .22 WMR cal., smooth walnut grips, includes presentation case marked "PRESENTATION DERRINGER", ser. no GP0 through GP1000, approx. 917 produced in 1980 in E. Hartford.

$525 $475 $395 $350 $275 $225 $195

Subtract $75 if w/o presentation case.

Third series, catalog #9196, mfg. 1980 only.

* ***Presentation Derringer Silver Plated*** – .22 WMR cal., faux mother-of-pearl grips, includes presentation case marked "PRESENTATION DERRINGER", ser. nos. SP0 through SP500, 501 were mfg. 1981.

$575 $525 $450 $375 $300 $225 $200

Subtract $100 if w/o presentation case.

Third series, catalog #9341.

PISTOLS: SEMI-AUTO, LETTER SERIES

These were the first models made and used letters to designate the various models. A few guns from this series were sold after WWII. Catalog numbers for this series were assigned after the war in order to utilize the record keeping system of that time. This design series utilized three different takedowns. Types I-A and I-B takedowns have the takedown lever on the left side of the frame. Type I-A takedown has a round retracting rod protruding through the rear of the slide off center to the left side. Type I-B takedown is an improved, more durable design with a rectangular retracting rod. Type II takedown has the takedown lever in the right side of the frame with a round pick-up button on the top of the slide. Type I-A takedown was utilized from 1932 to February 1938 and the type I-B takedown was utilized from that time until August 1939. Models B and C are the only models with the Type I-A takedown. The Model B and other Letter Models utilized type I-B and II takedowns. Guns with original boxes and original papers can add significant premiums but, like the guns, the condition is very important as is the requirement that the box be numbered to the gun. Those guns listed as a Curio or Relic by BATFE are noted in this text with a C-R abbreviation at the end of the model description. Serial number ranges are best estimates as of this printing and may change with further research. All serial numbers are located on the front gripstrap.

Add approx. 15% for original box with papers in the same condition as gun on the following models.

MODEL B – .22 LR cal., original High Standard pistol, basically the same gun as Hartford Arms 1925 Automatic, small frame, 4 1/2 or 6 3/4 in. lightweight barrel (approx .63" diameter at frame), fixed Patridge type front and rear sights, checkered hard rubber grips (later production versions have checkered grips impressed with the High Standard monogram), 10 shot mag. Beginning ser. no. 5,000. Approx. 65,000, early production utilized Hartford front sight, safety and takedown levers. Post War models have the frame contour of the B-US. C-R.

$625 $495 $395 $325 $250 $200 $125

Add $75 for I-B Type takedown.

Add $75 for early models with Hartford Arms parts.

Add $50 for post-war versions (ser. nos. greater than 146,000).

4 1/2 in. barrel #9000 1932 - 1942 & 1946. 6 3/4 in. barrel #9001 1932 - 1942 & 1946. Most guns found in serial number ranges from 5,000 to about 95,894 and from about 148,198 to about 151,021.

MODEL B-US – a version of the Model B with slight contour modification to the back of the frame. 4 1/2 in. barrel only. 14,000 made for the US government during 1942-1943. Most are marked "PROPERTY OF U.S." on the top of the barrel and on the right side of the frame above trigger guard. Crossed cannon ordnance stamp usually found on the right side of the frame. Monogrammed hard rubber grips. Type II takedown only. Note the early Model Bs shipped to the government and marked "PROPERTY OF U.S." had the original frame contour with transition to the B-US contour between ser. no. 99,261 and 100,972, .22 LR cal., 10 shot mag.

$850 $725 $595 $475 $370 $270 $195

Most guns found in serial number range from about 92,344 to about 111,631.

GRADING - PPGS™	100%	98%	95%	90%	80%	70%	60%	LAST MSR

MODEL S – .22 LR cal., chambered for .22 LR shot shell cartridge, essentially a Model B with a 6 3/4 in. smooth bore barrel only without choke, ivory bead front sight, left side of slide is stamped "HI-STANDARD MODEL S .22 LR SHOT ONLY", this variation was never a production model, ten are registered as Model S. Additional five with Model C slides are registered, Model C/S. Others may exist but only 15 are registered with BATFE (see serial numbers below). Manufactured in 1939 and 1940. Values for both variations are equal. 6 3/4 in. barrels. C-R.

	$4,750	$4,320	$3,900	$3,325	$2,850	$2,450	$2,100

Serial numbers: Model S - 48,142, 48,143, 48,144, 48,145, 48,146, 59,474 , 59,496, 59,458, 59,459, 59,493, Model C/S: 59,279, 59,460, 59,469, 59,473, 59,478. S/N 59,484 is listed as a Model S in the factory records but is not currently registered with the BATFE.

MODEL C – .22 Short cal. only, identical to Model B in appearance, small frame, 4 1/2 or 6 3/4 in. light weight barrel, fixed rear sight, checkered hard rubber grips with or without H.S. monogram, this action was adapted for the decreased power of the .22 Short cartridge. Early production in separate serial number series beginning with 500 and continuing through 3,116. Joined regular serial number series at 42,806. There are numerous Model Cs in the regular serial number series earlier than 42,806 around 25,600 which shipped a date later than the Model Bs in the same serial number range. C-R.

	$925	$750	$550	$425	$305	$215	$175

Add $75 for I-A takedown.
Add $175 for I-B takedown.

Most guns found in serial number ranges from 500 to 3,116 and from about 42,806 to about 86,249. This model was used primarily for plinking and gallery shooting. The Model C was made in all 3 variations of takedowns - I-A, I-B, and Type II. 4 1/2 in. barrel #9061 1936 -1942. 6 3/4 in. barrel #9062 1936 -1942.

MODEL A – .22 LR cal., similar to Model B, except grip part of frame is lengthened with a squared-off butt, 4 1/2 or 6 3/4 in. light weight barrel, adj. rear sight, checkered walnut grips, checkered thumb rest walnut grips optionally available separately, automatic slide lock, 10 shot mag. Approx. 7,300 mfg. C-R.

	$795	$695	$550	$440	$310	$230	$180

Add $175 for I-B takedown.

Most guns found in serial number range from about 33,209 to about 97,734. A very few guns found in serial number range between 500 and 555. 4 1/2 in. barrel #9005 1938 - 1942. 6 3/4 in. barrel #9006 1938 - 1942.

MODEL D – .22 LR cal., identical to Model A except 4 1/2 or 6 3/4 in. medium weight barrel (approx .79" diameter at frame), adj. sights, walnut grips, checkered thumb rest walnut grips optionally available separately, slide lock, trigger stop, 10 shot mag. Approx. 2,500 mfg. C-R.

	$995	$825	$600	$455	$330	$230	$190

Add $175 for I-B takedown.

4 1/2 in. barrel #9063 1938 - 1942. 6 3/4 in. barrel #9064 1938 - 1942. Most guns found in serial number range from about 33,216 to about 95,206. A very few guns found in serial number range between 500 and 555.

MODEL E – .22 LR cal., high quality, deluxe model of the hammerless series, adj. sight, 4 1/2 or 6 3/4 in. heavy bull barrel (approx .90" diameter at frame), checkered walnut target grips with thumb rest, automatic slide lock, trigger stop, 10 shot mag. Approx. 2,600 mfg. C-R.

	$1,225	$995	$825	$675	$500	$370	$245

Add $175 for I-B takedown.

4 1/2 in. barrel #9067 1938 - 1942. 6 3/4 in. barrel #9068 1938 - 1942. Most guns found in serial number range from about 34,419 to about 98,306.

PISTOLS: SEMI-AUTO, LETTER SERIES W/HAMMER

Second series of models made, like the letter models with external hammers. Letters were still used to designate the various models. Most were produced before the war, but a few models were produced after the war. Catalog numbers for this series were assigned after the war in order to utilize the record keeping system of that time. Type II takedown only. Guns with original boxes and original papers can add significant premiums but, like the guns, condition is very important,

GRADING - PPGS™	100%	98%	95%	90%	80%	70%	60%	LAST MSR

as is the requirement that the box be numbered to the gun. Those guns listed as a Curio or Relic by BATFE are noted - C-R. Serial number ranges are best estimates as of this printing and may change with further research. All ser. numbers are located on forestrap of frame.

Add approx. 15% for original box with papers in the same condition as the gun on the following models.

MODEL H-D – .22 LR cal., first exposed hammer model, similar to Model D, 4 1/2 or 6 3/4 in. medium weight barrel, adj. sight, trigger stop, slide lock, checkered walnut grips, (checkered thumb rest walnut grips optionally available separately), no external safety, 10 shot mag, pistols in the 135,990 to 145,439 range have a safety and are marked "Model HD" but do not have the adjustable sight or trigger overtravel screw. Fewer than 700 mfg. C-R.

$1,225 $1,050 $825 $600 $450 $325 $235

Most guns found in serial number ranges from about 45,463 to about 93,164 and from about 135,990 to about 145,439. 4 1/2 in. barrel #9065 1940 - 1941 & 1945. 6 3/4 in. barrel #9066 1940 - 1941.

USA-MODEL-HD – .22 LR cal., this model was developed because the government needed a training pistol similar to the Colt Model 1911 .45 ACP, the result was a Model HD with external safety and fixed sight, 4 1/2 in. medium weight barrel, the barrel is marked "Property of USA", black checkered hard rubber grips, first models mfg. had high gloss blue finish, changed to a parkerized finish around ser. no. 128,000 to 130,000. Approx. 34,000 mfg. 1943-1945. C-R.

$1,075 $925 $750 $650 $525 $400 $325

Add 20% for early blue finish.

Add $150 for box.

Most guns found in serial number range from about 103,863 to about 145,700.

MODEL USA-HD-MS – .22 LR cal., variation of the USA-Model-HD with integral silencer, mfg. for U.S. Government for the OSS during 1944 and 1945, ownership requires NFA transfer, approx. 2,000 mfg. Only a few registered with BATFE for civilian ownership.

$6,000 $5,600 $5,250 $4,875 $4,540 $4,250 $3,750

Most guns found in serial number range from about 110,074 to about 130,040.

MODEL H-D MILITARY – .22 LR cal., though called H-D Military, this model was not mfg. for the government, essentially a Model H-D with an external safety, 4 1/2 or 6 3/4 in. barrel, plastic (early mfg.) or checkered walnut grips (later mfg,) trigger stop (later manufacture), 10 shot mag. Approx. 143,000 mfg. C-R.

$650 $525 $450 $375 $275 $195 $135

4 1/2 in. barrel #9050 1945 - 1950. 6 3/4 in. barrel #9051 1945 - 1950. Most guns found in serial number range from about 145,196 to about 334,751.

MODEL H-E – .22 LR cal., deluxe model of exposed hammer series, 4 1/2 or 6 3/4 in. heavy barrel, adj. sight, trigger stop, slide lock, deluxe hand checkered walnut grips with thumb rests, no external safety, 10 shot mag. Rare - approx 1,000 mfg. 1941-42. C-R.

$2,200 $1,875 $1,550 $1,000 $725 $575 $450

4 1/2 in. barrel #9026 1940 - 1942. 6 3/4 in. barrel #9027 1940 - 1942. Most guns found in serial number range from about 51,802 to about 90,588.

MODEL H-A – .22 LR cal., similar to Model A, 4 1/2 or 6 3/4 in. lightweight barrel, adj. sight, slide lock, plain checkered walnut grips, no external safety, 10 shot mag. Rare - approx. 1,000 mfg. C-R.

$1,325 $1,125 $950 $725 $500 $350 $225

4 1/2 in. barrel #9007 1940 - 1942. 6 3/4 in. barrel #9008 1940 - 1942. Most guns found in serial number range from about 53,176 to about 92,816.

MODEL H-B – .22 LR cal., duplicate of Model B with external hammer, 4 1/2 or 6 3/4 in. lightweight barrel, fixed sight, checkered hard rubber grips with or w/o H.S. monogram, no external safety, 10 shot mag. Approx. 2,200 mfg. C-R.

$775 $650 $510 $385 $275 $225 $175

4 1/2 in. barrel 1940 - 1941. 6 3/4 in. barrel 1940 - 1941. Most guns found in serial number range from about 52,405 to about 86,155.

GRADING - PPGS™	100%	98%	95%	90%	80%	70%	60%	LAST MSR

* ***Model H-B Second Model*** – reintroduced as the H-B second model similar to first model, except with external safety. C-R.

	$675	$595	$450	$325	$225	$185	$150	

4 1/2 in. barrel #9003 1948 - 1949 274,197 - 311,535. 6 3/4 in. barrel #9004 1948 - 1949 274,996 - 311,520.

PISTOLS: SEMI-AUTO, LEVER LETTER SERIES

These were the third design models made, which incorporate interchangeable barrels with a lever takedown. The .22 caliber guns evolved from the Model G-380, High Standard's first production removable barrel gun which is included in this section. Like the letter models with external hammers, these .22 caliber models still use letters to designate the various models. New to this series was the adjustable Davis sight. Also introduced in this series was a breech face shrouded by the slide. Significant premiums can be asked for guns with the combination of both barrels, if verified by factory records that the gun shipped as a combination. (Buyer beware - many "combinations" have been created after leaving the factory). Non-factory combinations should have additional value equal to the value of an extra barrel. Guns with original boxes and papers can add significant premiums but, like the guns, the condition is very important, as is the requirement that the box be numbered to the gun. Those guns listed as a Curio or Relic by BATFE are noted - C-R. Serial number ranges are best estimates, and may change with further research. Ser. numbers are on the right side of slide and rear right side of frame. Mfg. 1949-1950.

Add approx. 15% for original box with papers in the same condition as gun on the following models.

MODEL G-380 CENTERFIRE – .380 ACP cal., only in-house production of a center-fire pistol, transition model to the G-series using a lever takedown, exposed hammer, fixed sights, checkered black plastic grips, external safety, 5 in. barrel only, 6 shot mag. Approx. 7,400 mfg. in a serial number series of its own but a few examples exist in the regular serial number range around 329,337. C-R.

	$650	$550	$450	$350	$250	$225	$185	

5.00" barrel #9060 1947 - 1950 123 - 7,551

MODEL G-B – .22 LR cal., similar to Model B with light barrel, small frame, external safety, fixed sight, monogrammed checkered brown plastic grips, interchangeable 4 1/2 or 6 3/4 in. barrel with lever takedown, 10 shot mag., last short frame model produced. Approx. 4,900 mfg. C-R.

	$650	$550	$400	$325	$245	$210	$180	

Add $225 for factory combination.

4 1/2 in. barrel #9010 1949 - 1950 310,449 - 335,278. 6 3/4 in. barrel #9011 1949 - 1950 309,578 - 335,095. Combination with both barrels #9012 1949 - 1950 311,001 - 335,066.

MODEL G-D – .22 LR cal., large frame, medium weight, interchangeable 4 1/2 or 6 3/4 in. barrel with lever takedown, adj. Davis sight (named for designer G.F. Davis), sight is adj. for both windage and elevation, trigger stop, slide lock, grips avail. in plain checkered walnut or deluxe with thumb rest, 10 shot mag. Approx. 3,300 mfg. C-R.

	$1,025	$900	$750	$535	$400	$300	$225	

Add $325 for factory combination.
Add $75 for factory target grips.

4 1/2 in. barrel standard walnut grips #9020 1949 - 1950 315,445 - 335,279. 6 3/4 in. barrel standard walnut grips #9021 1949 - 1950 311,804 - 335,300. Combination with both barrels and standard walnut grips #9022 1949 - 1950 312,001 - 335,247. 4 1/2 in. barrel thumb rest walnut grips #9023 1949 - 1950 316,623 - 326,850. 6 3/4 in. barrel thumb rest walnut grips #9024 1949 - 1950 311,804 - 335,222. Combination with both barrels and thumb rest walnut grips #9025 1949 - 1950 317,914 - 335,278.

MODEL G-E – .22 LR cal., deluxe top-of-the-line model, large frame, interchangeable 4 1/2 or 6 3/4 in. heavy bull barrel with lever takedown, Davis adj. sight, deluxe walnut hand checkered grips with thumb rest, trigger stop, slide lock, 10 shot mag. Approx. 2,900 mfg. C-R.

	$1,425	$1,225	$875	$740	$465	$350	$250	

Add $375 for factory combination.

4 1/2 in. barrel #9030 1949 - 1950 314,050 - 335,275. 6 3/4 in. barrel #9031 1949 - 1950 314,027 -

GRADING - PPGS™	100%	98%	95%	90%	80%	70%	60%	LAST MSR

335,198. Combination with both barrels #9032 1949 - 1950 312,002 - 335,200.

OLYMPIC (G-O) – .22 Short cal., adaptation of Model GE in .22 Short cal., also known as First Model Olympic, deluxe top-of-the-line quality, interchangeable 4 1/2 or 6 3/4 in. heavy bull barrel with lever takedown, Davis adj. sight, deluxe hand checkered walnut grips with thumb rests, trigger stop, slide lock, grooved fore and rear strap, first High Standard production gun with aluminum slide. special curved magazine, about 32 early guns exist which utilized a curved magazine with a straight back, the majority of these Olympics use the curved magazine with a humped back, grooved surface on top of barrel and slide. Rare - approx. 1,250 mfg. C-R.

$1,725	**$1,425**	**$1,150**	**$825**	**$550**	**$525**	**$425**	

Add $375 for factory combination.

Add $500 for the straight back magazine variation.

4 1/2 in. barrel #9040 1949 - 1950 325,929 - 334-735. 6 3/4 in. barrel #9041 1949 - 1950 307,734 - 334,979. Combination with both barrels #9012 1949 - 1950 329,590 - 334,399.

PISTOLS: SEMI-AUTO, LEVER NAME SERIES

These models were the fourth design evolving from the lever letter series with slight changes. This series followed the precedent set by the Olympic (G-O) of naming the models instead of utilizing letters. The upscale models, the Supermatic and Olympic, incorporated a rib dovetailed to the top of the barrel and a dovetail slot on the bottom of the barrel for mounting balance weights. This series continued the breech face shrouded by the slide design. Significant premiums can be asked for combination guns which have both barrels, if verified by factory records that the gun shipped as a combination. (Buyer beware - many "combinations" have been created after leaving the factory). Non-factory combinations should have additional value equal to the value of the extra barrel. Adjustable sight models continued to use the Davis sight. No guns in this series were offered with barrels incorporating the integral stabilizer but stabilizer barrels were offered in 1954 after the series ended. Most guns in this series utilized a single screw to retain the grips. However, the earliest Olympics used a screw for each side before changing to a single screw. Guns with original boxes and original papers can add significant premiums but, like the guns, the condition is very important, as is the requirement that the box be numbered to the gun. Serial number ranges are best estimates, and may change with further research. Those guns which have Curio or Relic status by virtue of being over 50 years old are noted C-R.

Add approx. 15% for original box with papers in the same condition as gun on the following models.

SPORT-KING (FIRST MODEL) – .22 LR cal., 10 shot mag., similar to Field-King except has fixed sight and lightweight interchangeable 4 1/2 or 6 3/4 in. barrel featuring lever takedown, early models did not have a slide hold back when the magazine became empty, early variation w/o hold back was produced in about twice the quantity as the later models incorporating this feature. C-R.

$450	**$375**	**$325**	**$250**	**$200**	**$150**	**$100**	

Add $25 for guns with hold back.

Add $200 for factory combination.

4 1/2 in. barrel #9080 1950 - 1954 335,001 - 442,605. 6 3/4 in. barrel #9081 1950 - 1954 335,012 - 442,572. Combination with both barrels #9082 1951 - 1953 337,699 - 442,574.

FIELD-KING (FIRST MODEL) – .22 LR cal., plain version of Supermatic, 10 shot mag., interchangeable 4 1/2 or 6 3/4 in. barrels with lever takedown, Davis adj. sight, trigger stop, slide lock, 10 shot mag., no rib on barrels or provisions for weights. C-R.

$650	**$575**	**$475**	**$350**	**$275**	**$225**	**$175**	

Add $225 for factory combination.

4 1/2 in. barrel #9090 1951 - 1953 342,703 - 439,658. 6 3/4 in. barrel #9091 1951 - 1953 341,751 - 439,665. Combination with both barrels #9092 1951 - 1953 348,762 - 439,660.

SUPERMATIC (FIRST MODEL) – .22 LR cal., 4 1/2 or 6 3/4 in. interchangeable barrel with lever takedown, Davis adj. sight, trigger stop, 10 shot mag., slide lock, grooved front and back straps, brown plastic thumb rest grips, serrated rib between front and rear sight, adj.

GRADING - PPGS™	100%	98%	95%	90%	80%	70%	60%	LAST MSR

2 oz. and 3 oz. weights which dovetail into and beneath barrel, a filler strip was provided for when the weights were not used. C-R.

	$825	$675	$550	$415	$320	$225	$175	

Add $250 for factory combination.
Add $30 for each weight and $25 for filler strip if present with gun.

Price is for pistol without both weights and filler strip. 4 1/2 in. barrel with provisions for weights #9070 1951 - 1953 340,103 - 438,698. 6 3/4 in. barrel with provisions for weights #9071 1951 - 1953 338,210 - 438,726. Combination with both barrels #9072 1951 - 1953 340,101 - 438,714.

OLYMPIC (SECOND MODEL) – .22 Short cal., identical in all respects to the Supermatic, except has aluminum slide for rapid recoil, 10 shot mag., interchangeable 4 1/2 or 6 3/4 in. barrel with lever takedown, also available as combination with both barrels, Davis adj. sight, ribbed barrels and provisions for weights, 2 oz. and a 3 oz. weight were provided with this model, as was a filler strip for when the weights were not used, grooved front and back straps on frame. Some, perhaps a few hundred, of the early guns exist which utilize the hump back curved magazine from the previous series, but the majority of these Olympics use a newly developed straight magazine. C-R.

	$1,250	$995	$795	$600	$500	$400	$300	

Add $250 for factory combination.
Add a slight premium for curved magazine version.
Add $30 for each weight and $25 for filler strip if present with gun.
Price is for pistol without both weights and filler strip.

Note: Conversion kits for converting from .22 LR to .22 Short became available in 1956 (see the information at the end of the 101 section).

4 1/2 in. barrel with provisions for weights #9043 1951 - 1953 341,795 - 428,989. 6 3/4 in. barrel with provisions for weights #9044 1951 - 1953 341,788 - 428,982. Combination with both barrels #9045 1951 - 1953 348,505 - 428,990.

PISTOLS: SEMI-AUTO, 100 SERIES

The 100 Series firearms were the fifth design models evolving from the Lever Name Series designs. This series introduced the small, push button barrel release takedown, and deleted the shrouded breech. This series featured slanted plastic grips as standard issue. The upscale models continued with the ribbed barrel and a dovetail slot on the bottom of the barrel for mounting balance weights. Adjustable sight models continued to use the Davis sight. New to this series was the introduction of an aluminum frame on the Flite King and the Sport King Lightweight. Significant premiums can be asked for guns with the combination of both barrels, if verified by factory records that the gun shipped as a combination. Buyer beware - many "combinations" (over 50% of those researched) have been created after leaving the factory. Non-factory combinations should have additional value equal to the value of the extra barrel. Guns with original boxes and original papers can add significant premiums but, like the guns, the condition is very important, as is the requirement that the box be numbered to the gun. There are some pistols that represent a transition between the 100 Series in the Field King, Supermatic, and Olympic models where the slides are marked with the 100 Series, but the barrels are from the 101 Series. These transistion pistols are generally listed as 101 Series pistols and only the factory records will tell the tale. Serial number ranges starting points are best estimates, and may change with further research. Those guns which have Curio or Relic status by virtue of being over 50 years old are noted C-R.

Add approx. 15% for original box with papers in the same condition as gun on the following models.

SPORT-KING (SECOND MODEL) – .22 LR cal., similar to Flite-King but with steel slide and frame, SK 100 stamped on right side of slide, front and rear grip straps on this model are smooth, slide lock, fixed rear sight. C-R.

	$425	$375	$295	$200	$175	$150	$100	

Add $200 for factory combination.
Add $350 for ARMAMEX version.

In late 1958, Col. Rex Applegate imported about three hundred into Mexico. These guns are marked with his company's name, ARMAMEX. Marked "ARMAMEX, MEXICO" on the right side of the barrel and

GRADING - PPGS™	100%	98%	95%	90%	80%	70%	60%	LAST MSR

"SPORT KING / CAL. 22 L.R." on the left side of the barrel. Customary "HI-STANDARD" marking on the left side of the slide. Serial numbers around 870,084-870,383. Note that the Applegate guns were made after the 102 series was in production. Armamex catalog number 1910.

4 1/2 in. barrel #9100 1954 - 1957 436,311 - 804,081. 6 3/4 in. barrel #9101 1954 - 1957 436,308 - 804,080. Combination with both barrels #9102 1954 - 1957 443,651 - 804,075.

SPORT-KING LIGHTWEIGHT – .22 LR cal., similar to standard Sport-King, except has forged aluminum alloy frame, "Lightweight" is inscribed in script on the left side of frame, also available in nickel.

	$550	$425	$350	$250	$175	$150	$100	

Add $150 for nickel finish.
Add $200 for factory combination.

4 1/2 in. barrel blue #9156 1955 - 1964 506,248 - 1,333,056. 6 3/4 in. barrel blue #9157 1955 - 1964 506,243 - 1,333,043. Combination with both barrels blue #9158 1956 - 1959 506,320 - 1,030,619. C-R. 4 1/2 in. barrel nickel #9166 1957 - 1960 726,752 - 1,136,533. C-R. 6 3/4 in. barrel nickel #9167 1957 - 1960 726,745 - 1,136,534. C-R. Combination with both barrels nickel #9168 1957 - 1959 726,909 - 1,025,505. C-R.

FLITE-KING (FIRST MODEL) – .22 Short cal., 10 shot mag., blued finish with black anodized aluminum frame and slide, 4 1/2, 6 3/4 in. barrel, or a combination with both barrel lengths, brown plastic checkered thumb rest grips, fixed sights. C-R.

	$625	$500	$425	$340	$260	$180	$135	

Add $200 for factory combination.

4 1/2 in. barrel #9103 1953 - 1957 431,297- 1,090,206. 6 3/4 in. barrel #9104 1953 - 1957 431,286 - 1,131,844. Combination with both barrels #9105 1954 - 1957 431,532 - 1,039,917.

FIELD-KING (SECOND MODEL) – .22 LR cal., 4 1/2 or 6 3/4 in. interchangeable barrel with push-button takedown, FK 100 stamped on right side of slide, 10 shot mag., front and rear grip straps on this model are smooth, slide lock, trigger stop, adj. rear sight. Mfg. briefly in 1954. C-R.

	$800	$675	$550	$425	$350	$250	$150	

Add $325 for factory combination.

4 1/2 in. barrel #9106 1954 - 1954 446,645. 6 3/4 in. barrel #9107 1954 - 1954 446,595. Combination with both barrels #9108 1954 - 1954 446,601.

SUPERMATIC (SECOND MODEL) – .22 LR cal., 4 1/2 or 6 3/4 in. interchangeable barrel with push-button takedown, "S-100" stamped on right side of slide, 10 shot mag., adj. 2 oz. or 3 oz. weights, slide lock, trigger stop, adj. rear sight, grooved front and back straps on frame, a 2 oz. and a 3 oz. weight were provided with this model as was a filler strip for when the weights were not used. Mfg. briefly in 1954. A few were sold to the U.S. government. C-R.

	$875	$750	$650	$500	$350	$250	$150	

Add $350 for factory combination.
Add $30 for each weight and $25 for filler strip if present with gun.
Price is for pistol without both weights and filler strip.

4 1/2 in. barrel with provisions for weights #9109 1954 - 1954 446,516. 6 3/4 in. barrel with provisions for weights #9110 1954 - 1954 446,445. Combination with both barrels #9111 1954 - 1954 446,705 -

OLYMPIC (THIRD MODEL) – .22 Short cal., 4 1/2 or 6 3/4 in. interchangeable barrel with push-button takedown, 10 shot mag., "O-100" stamped on right side of alloy slide, adj. 2 oz. or 3 oz. weights, adj. rear sight, slide lock, trigger stop, grooved front and back straps on frame, a 2 oz. and a 3 oz. weight were provided with this model as was a filler strip for when the weights were not used. Mfg. briefly in 1954. C-R.

	$1,175	$925	$750	$575	$425	$300	$200	

Add $350 for factory combination.
Add $30 for each weight and $25 for filler strip if present with gun.
Price is for pistol without both weights and filler strip.

Note: Conversion kits for converting from .22 LR to .22 Short became available in 1956 - see the information at the end of the 101 section.

GRADING - PPGS™	100%	98%	95%	90%	80%	70%	60%	LAST MSR

4 1/2 in. barrel with provisions for weights #9112 1954 - 1954 447,209. 6 3/4 in. barrel with provisions for weights #9113 1954 - 1954 447,210. Combination with both barrels #9114 1954 - 1954 447,205.

PISTOLS: SEMI-AUTO, 101 SERIES

The 101 Series were the sixth design models evolving from the 100 Series. This series continued the small push button barrel release takedown. The ribbed barrel was dropped from the upscale models, but the dovetail slot on the bottom of the barrel for mounting balance weights continued. Adjustable sight models continued to use the Davis sight (Note: the Flite-King, Sport King, and Sport King Lightweight did not upgrade to this series). Significant premiums can be asked for guns with the combination of both barrels, if verified by factory records that the gun shipped as a combination. Buyer beware - many "combinations" (over 50% of those researched) have been created after leaving the factory. Non-factory combinations should have additional value equal to the value of the extra barrel. Guns with original boxes and papers can add significant premiums, but like the guns, the condition is very important, as is the requirement that the box be numbered to the gun. Serial number ranges are best estimates and may change with further research.

Add approx. 13% for original box with papers in same condition as gun on the following models.

FIELD-KING (THIRD MODEL) – .22 LR cal., 4 1/2 or 6 3/4 in. interchangeable barrel with push-button takedown, FK 101 stamped on right side of slide, 10 shot mag., front and rear grip straps on this model are smooth, adj. rear sight, slide lock, trigger stop, brown plastic thumb rest grips, 6 3/4 in. barrel incorporates a muzzle brake with one slot either side of the front sight. A few shipped in 1959 around ser. no. 1,039,1XX. C-R.

	100%	98%	95%	90%	80%	70%	60%
	$650	$550	$475	$425	$350	$235	$175

Add $300 for factory combination.

4 1/2 in. barrel #9115 1954 - 1957 447,149. 6 3/4 in. barrel #9116 1954 - 1957 447,146 - 799,260. Combination with both barrels #9117 1954 - 1957 - 799,259.

SUPERMATIC (THIRD MODEL) – .22 LR cal., 4 1/2 or 6 3/4 in. interchangeable barrel with push-button takedown, "S 101" stamped on right side of slide, 10 shot mag., adj. 2 oz. or 3 oz. weights and a filler strip for when the weights were not used, 6 3/4 in. barrel incorporates a muzzle brake with one slot either side of the front sight, slide lock, trigger stop, adj. rear sight, brown plastic thumb rest grips, grooved front and back straps on frame, about 3,700 were produced with U.S. marking for the military and another approx. 1,600 made for the USMC which typically are not US marked. C-R.

	100%	98%	95%	90%	80%	70%	60%
	$750	$675	$550	$475	$350	$235	$175

Price is for pistol without both weights and filler strip.
Add $350 for factory combination.
Add $30 for each weight and $25 for filler strip if present with gun.

4 1/2 in. barrel with provisions for weights #9118 1954 - 1957 447,586 -. 6 3/4 in. barrel with provisions for weights and integral stabilizer #9119 1954 - 1957 446,511 -. Combination with both barrels #9120 1954 - 1957 447,595 -.

OLYMPIC (FOURTH MODEL) – .22 Short cal., 4 1/2 or 6 3/4 in. interchangeable barrel with push-button takedown, "O-101" stamped on right side of alloy slide, 10 shot mag., adj. 2 oz. or 3 oz. weights and a filler strip for when the weights were not used, 6 3/4 in. barrel incorporates a muzzle brake with one slot either side of the front sight, adj. rear sight, slide lock, trigger stop, brown plastic thumb rest grips, grooved front and back straps on frame. A very small number were sold to the U.S. government. C-R.

	100%	98%	95%	90%	80%	70%	60%
	$1,150	$950	$750	$595	$450	$325	$200

Price is for pistol without both weights and filler strip.
Add $350 for factory combination.
Add $30 for each weight and $25 for filler strip if present with gun.

4 1/2 in. barrel with provisions for weights #9121 1954 - 1957 447,230 -. 6 3/4 in. barrel with provisions for weights and integral stabilizer #9122 1954 - 1957 447,214 -.Combination with both barrels #9123 1954 - 1957 447,227 -.

GRADING - PPGS™	100%	98%	95%	90%	80%	70%	60%	LAST MSR

* ***Olympic (Fourth Model) Conversion kits*** – kits for converting .22 LR guns to .22 Short were announced in both the 1956 catalog and in a 1956 brochure. Kits include a barrel, an aluminum slide, and magazine (.22 short to .22 LR conversion had a steel slide).

	$525	$435	$375	$315	$270	$230	$200	

Values are for kits in original boxes - subtract 20% if w/o box.

Cat.# 9150 Supermatic/Field King to 22 Short, 4 1/2 Bbl. Cat.# 9151 Supermatic/Field King to 22 Short, 6 3/4 Bbl. Cat.# 9152 Olympic to Supermatic 22 LR, 4 1/2 Bbl. Cat.# 9153 Olympic to Supermatic 22 LR, 6 3/4 Bbl. Cat.# 9154 Olympic to Field King 22 LR, 4 1/2 Bbl. Cat.# 9155 Olympic to Field King 22 LR, 6 3/4 Bbl. Kits were also offered for the earlier lever name series and the 100 Series guns. Catalog numbers are unknown for conversion kits for lever name series or the 100 series guns.

PISTOLS: SEMI-AUTO, DURA-MATIC SERIES

The Dura-Matic pistols are a striker fired design that was designed and patented by O.O. Sunderland, a former designer for High Standard. The design was shopped around, and High Standard became the producer of this low cost plinker. The basics of this design can also be found in the Colt Cadet, Colt 22 and the Beretta U22 Neos.

Add approx. 10% for original box with papers in same condition as gun on the following models.

DURA-MATIC M-101 – .22 LR cal., 4 1/2 or 6 1/2 in. barrel, fixed sight, oversized plastic grips, "M-101" stamped on right side of slide (mfg. 1954 to 1970), later appeared renamed "Plinker" M-101 during 1971 to 1973.

	$325	$250	$200	$160	$125	$100	$80	

Add $150 for factory combination.

Add $80 for Plinker with case in original box.

The Plinker was not available with both barrel combination. During the first year, the Plinker came with a zippered carrying case. The Dura-matic was sold by Sears Roebuck & Co. as the J.C. Higgins Model 80. This Sears variation had some minor exterior differences but, mechanically it was the same - including a unique thumb screw takedown, push-button mag. release and oversized trigger guard. A slightly modified version was sold by Sears Roebuck & Co. as the J. C. Higgins M-80.

* ***Dura-Matic M-101***

4 1/2 in. barrel #9124 1955 - 1970 47X,XXX. 6.50" barrel #9125 1955 - 1970 47X,XXX. Combination with both barrels #9126 1955 - 1959 47X,XXX - 1,030,956.

* ***Dura-Matic Sears M-80***

4 1/2 in. barrel #9133 1955 1962 477,292. 6.50" barrel #9134 1955 1962 477,649. Combination with both barrels #9135 1955-1962 477,303.

* ***Dura-Matic M-101 Plinker***

4 1/2 in. barrel #9214 1971 - 1973. 6 3/4 in. barrel #9215 1971 - 1973.

DURA-MATIC M-100 – .22 LR cal., 4 1/2 or 6 1/2 in. barrels, fixed sight, striker fired, oversized plastic grips, M-100 stamped on right side of slide, unique thumb screw takedown, pushbutton release for the thumb screw, push-button mag. release and oversized trigger guard. Mfg. 1954.

	$350	$295	$235	$175	$150	$125	$100	

Add $150 for factory combination.

4 1/2 in. barrel #9124 1954 - 1954 458,801 - 47X,XXX. 6 1/2 in. barrel #9125 1954 - 1954 458,802 - 47X,XXX. Combination with both barrels #9126 1954 - 1954 459,675 - 47X,XXX.

PISTOLS: SEMI-AUTO, 102 SERIES

The 102 Series was a major design change, incorporating a new frame with a large push button takedown release, and a superb adjustable sight. There is little difference between the two series. Pistols in this series are marked Model 102 on right side of the slide. Three variations of ejectors were utilized during the 102 Series. No premiums exist for these variations. Significant premiums can be asked for guns with the combination of both barrels, if verified by factory records that the gun shipped as a combination. Buyer beware - many "combinations" have been created after leaving the factory. Non-factory combinations should have additional value equal to the value

GRADING - PPGS™	100%	98%	95%	90%	80%	70%	60%	LAST MSR

of the extra barrel. The 102 Series was produced from 1958 to 1960, ending at approx. ser. no. 1,12X,XXX. Guns with original boxes and papers can add significant premiums but, like the guns, the condition is very important as is the requirement that the box be numbered to the gun.

Original cased 102 Series Trophy, Olympic Citation models, and Special Presentation combinations in 98%+ condition are currently in great demand and are bringing asking prices in the $1,700-$2,600 range.

Add approx. 15% for original box with papers in same condition as gun on the following models.

SPORT-KING – .22 LR cal., 10 shot mag., 4 1/2 or 6 3/4 in. lightweight, round and tapered barrels, blued finish, fixed sights, checkered plastic grips, smooth grip straps, also available as a combination with both barrel lengths. C-R.

	$395	$325	$275	$215	$160	$120	$90	

Add $200 for factory combination.

4 1/2 in. tapered barrel blued #9200 1958 - 1960 778,028. 6 3/4 in. tapered barrel blued #9201 1958 - 1960 778,021. Combination with both barrels #9202 1958 - 1959 778,026.

FLITE-KING – .22 Short cal., otherwise similar to the Sport King Models 102 and 103, steel frames with an alloy slide. C-R.

	$525	$450	$365	$310	$240	$170	$120	

Add $200 for factory combination.

4 1/2 in. tapered barrel blued #9220 1958 - 1960 791,149. 6 3/4 in. tapered barrel blued #9221 1958 - 1960 791,150. Combination with both barrels #9222 1958 - 1959 791,169.

SUPERMATIC TOURNAMENT – .22 LR cal., 10 shot, 4 1/2 or 6 3/4 in. tapered barrel, brown diamond checkered plastic slant grips, adj. sight, push button takedown, smooth front and back grip straps. C-R.

	$695	$595	$495	$375	$300	$220	$150	

Add $200 for factory combination.
Add $50 for factory guns marked U.S.

4 1/2 in. tapered barrel #9270 1958 - 1960 796,555. 6 3/4 in. tapered barrel #9271 1958 - 1960 796,536. Combination with both barrels #9272 1958 - 1959. The U.S. Govt. ordered the Model 102 Tournaments to use for training. These models were marked "U.S." on left side of frame.

SUPERMATIC CITATION – .22 LR cal., 10 shot, 6 3/4, 8, and 10 in. tapered barrels, diamond checkered plastic slant grips, adj. sight, push-button takedown, one grade above Tournament, grooved front and back grip straps, trigger stop, trigger pull adjustment, adj. sight located on 8 and 10 in. barrel, detachable stabilizer and 2 or 3 oz. barrel weights available. C-R.

	$850	$700	$600	$450	$340	$250	$180	

Price is for pistol without both weights and muzzle brake.
Add $150 for 8 in. barrel.
Add $200 premium for 10 in. barrel.
Add $50 for each weight and $90 for muzzle brake if present with gun.
Add $50 for factory guns marked U.S.

6 3/4 in. tapered barrel with provisions for weights and stabilizer #9260 1958 - 1960 803,303. 8 in. tapered barrel with provisions for weights and stabilizer #9261 1958 - 1960 795,726. 10 in. tapered barrel with provisions for weights and stabilizer #9262 1958 - 1960 771,275. The U.S. Govt. ordered a quantity of Model 102 Citations to be used for training, marked "U.S." on left side of frame.

SUPERMATIC TROPHY – .22 LR cal., 10 shot, 6 3/4 in., 8 in. and 10 in. tapered barrels, high gloss "Trophy" finish, detachable barrel weights and stabilizer also available, walnut checkered thumb rest grips, grooved front and back grip straps, trigger stop, trigger pull adjustment, gold trigger, gold safety button and gold inlaid lettering, adj. sight and push-button takedown. The U.S. government ordered a small number of the Model 102 Trophys. C-R.

	$1,250	$995	$800	$615	$445	$325	$215	

Price is for pistol without both weights and muzzle brake.
Add $175 for 8 in. barrel.
Add $225 for 10 in. barrel.
Add $60 for each weight and $120 for muzzle brake if present with gun.

GRADING - PPGS™	100%	98%	95%	90%	80%	70%	60%	LAST MSR

6 3/4 in. tapered barrel with provisions for weights and stabilizer #9250 1958 - 1960 812,641. 8 in. tapered barrel with provisions for weights and stabilizer #9251 1958 - 1960 791,247. 10 in. tapered barrel with provisions for weights and stabilizer #9252 1958 - 1960 791,246.

OLYMPIC – .22 Short cal., similar to Citation, adj. sight located on 8 and 10 in. barrel and on the slide of the 6 3/4 in barrel, early models marked "Olympic Citation", then changed to "Olympic" only about 1960, grooved front and back straps on frame, checkered plastic grips, trigger stop, trigger pull adjustment. C-R.

$1,250	$995	$800	$615	$445	$325	$215	

Add $175 for 8 in. barrel.
Add $225 for 10 in. barrel.
Add $350 for "Olympic Citation" marked guns.
Add $50 for each weight and $90 for muzzle brake if present with gun.

6 3/4 in. tapered barrel with provisions for weights and stabilizer #9280 1958 - 1960 812,365. 8 in. tapered barrel with provisions for weights and stabilizer #9281 1958 - 1960 796,924. 10 in. tapered barrel with provisions for weights and stabilizer #9282 1958 - 1960 796,930.

PISTOLS: SEMI-AUTO, 103 SERIES

The 103 Series is much the same as the later 102 Series pistols. There is little difference between the two Series. This Series is marked Model 103 on right side of the slide. Significant premiums can be asked for guns with the combination of both barrels, if verified by factory records that the gun shipped as a combination. Buyer beware - many "combinations" have been created after leaving the factory. Non-factory combinations should have additional value equal to the value of the extra barrel. The 103 Series was produced 1960 to 1963, except for the Sport King, the Flite King, the Supermatic Tournament, and the Sharpshooter - see date ranges of the individual models below. After mid-1975, the Sport King and the Sharpshooter appeared in the "G" prefix serial numbered series - see serial number chart. Guns with original boxes and papers can add significant premiums but, like the guns, the condition is very important as is the requirement that the box be numbered to the gun.

Original cased 103 Series Trophy, Olympic Trophy, Olympic Citation models, and Special Presentation combinations in 98%+ condition are currently in great demand, with asking prices in the $1,700-$2,600 range.
Add approx. 15% for original box with papers in the same condition as gun on the following models.

SPORT-KING – .22 LR cal., 4 1/2 or 6 3/4 in. lightweight, round and tapered barrel, 10 shot mag., blue finish, fixed sights, checkered plastic grips, smooth grip straps, available as a combination with both barrel lengths.

$350	$300	$250	$200	$150	$120	$90	

Add $100 for nickel finish.

4 1/2 in. tapered barrel blued #9200 1960 - 1970 & 1973 - 1977. 6 3/4 in. tapered barrel blued #9201 1960 - 1970 & 1973 - 1978. 4 1/2 in. tapered barrel nickel #9208 1973 - 1977. 6 3/4 in. tapered barrel nickel #9209 1973 - 1977. Note that later production models were not marked 103. 254 Sport Kings (#9200 & #9201) shipped in May, 1977 with serial numbers between G160,000 - G162,590. 116 guns, #9201 Sport Kings, shipped April and May 1978 serial numbers G20,106 - G20,223.

FLITE-KING – .22 Short cal., similar to Sport King Model 103, steel frame with an alloy slide. There were 44 specials with 6 3/4 in. barrels made with adjustable sights for export in April 1962. There were two export only models made in 1966 and 1967, catalog numbers 9224 and 9225. The export models were made in relative small numbers and to date none have been reported in the US.

$525	$425	$360	$310	$240	$170	$120	

Add $200 for factory combination.

4 1/2 in. bull tapered barrel #9220 1960 - 1965. 6 3/4 in. fluted tapered barrel #9221 1960 - 1965.

SUPERMATIC TOURNAMENT – .22 LR cal., 4 1/2, 5 1/2 bull (avail. 1963), or 6 3/4 in. tapered barrel, 10 shot mag., brown diamond checkered plastic slant grips, adj. sight, push button takedown, this model featured smooth front and back grip straps.

$675	$575	$475	$375	$300	$220	$150	

GRADING - PPGS™	100%	98%	95%	90%	80%	70%	60%	LAST MSR

Add $50 for factory guns marked U.S.

4 1/2 in. tapered barrel #9270 1960 - 1962. 6 3/4 in. tapered barrel #9271 1960 - 1965. 5 1/2 in. bull barrel with provisions for weights and stabilizer #9275 1962 - 1965.

SHARPSHOOTER – .22 LR cal., 5 1/2 in. bull barrel, 10 shot mag., blue finish, adj. sights, checkered plastic grips, smooth grip straps, some mfg. with Model 103 marked slides.

	$550	$450	$350	$240	$200	$160	$125	

Add $25 for "SPORT KING" marked guns.

5 1/2 in. bull barrel #9205 1971 - 1977. Although the Model 103 marked guns have 1969 and later serial numbers, they were shipped after the introduction of the Sharpshooter in 1971, and were probably converted from unsold Sport Kings. Some early Sharpshooters have "Sport King" on the left side of the frame.

SUPERMATIC CITATION – .22 LR cal., 6 3/4, 8, or 10 in. tapered barrels, 10 shot, diamond checkered plastic slant grips, adj. sight, push-button takedown, one grade above Tournament, grooved front and back grip straps, trigger stop, trigger pull adjustment, adj. sight located on 8 and 10 in. barrel (a 5 1/2 in. target bull barrel became avail. in 1962), detachable stabilizer and 2 or 3 oz. barrel weights available.

	$825	$650	$525	$430	$340	$250	$180	

Add $150 for 8 in. barrel.
Add $200 for 10 in. barrel.
Add $50 for each weight and $90 for muzzle brake if present with gun.
Add $50 for factory guns marked U.S.
Add $125 for extra magazine (#9263 only).
Price is for pistol without weights and muzzle brake.

6 3/4 in. tapered barrel with provisions for weights and stabilizer #9260 1960 - 1964. 8 in. tapered barrel with provisions for weights and stabilizer #9261 1960 - 1964. 10 in. tapered barrel with provisions for weights and stabilizer #9262 1960 - 1963. 5 1/2 in. bull barrel #9263 1962 - 1963. The U.S. Govt. ordered a quantity of Model 103 Citations to be used for training, marked "U.S." on left side of frame.

SUPERMATIC TROPHY – .22 LR cal., 6 3/4 in., 8 or 10 in. tapered barrels, 5 1/2 bull and 7 1/4 in. fluted barrels became avail. in 1962, high gloss "Trophy" finish, 10 shot, detachable barrel weights and stabilizer were also available, walnut checkered thumbrest grips, grooved front and back grip straps, trigger stop, trigger pull adjustment, gold trigger, gold safety button and gold inlaid lettering, adj. sight and push-button takedown.

	$1,175	$975	$800	$650	$475	$350	$225	

Values are for pistol w/o weights and muzzle brake.
Add $175 for 8 in. barrel.
Add $225 for 10 in. barrel.
Add $60 for each tapered barrel weight, $30 for each fluted or bull barrel weight, and $120 for muzzle brake if present with gun.

6 3/4 in. tapered barrel with provisions for weights and stabilizer #9250 1960 - 1962. 8 in. tapered barrel with provisions for weights and stabilizer #9251 1960 - 1962. 10 in. tapered barrel with provisions for weights and stabilizer #9252 1960 - 1962.

ISU OLYMPIC – .22 Short cal., 6 3/4 in. barrel with integral stabilizer, 10 shot, grooved grip straps, checkered walnut thumbrest grips, trigger stop, trigger pull adjustment, alloy slide.

	$1,250	$995	$825	$525	$475	$350	$225	

Price is for pistol without weights and muzzle brake.
Add $1,000 for Model 9289 marked "Olympic Trophy" if in 98% or better condition.
Add $50 for each weight if present with gun.

6 3/4 in. tapered barrel with integral stabilizer - with accessories #9299 1961 - 1963. 6 3/4 in. tapered barrel with integral stabilizer - with accessories #9289 1961 - 1962. 5 1/2 in. bull barrel #9294 1963 - 1963. There was also an Olympic ISU with a Supermatic Trophy finish (catalog number 9289) - fewer than 500 were produced.

OLYMPIC – .22 Short cal., similar to Citation, adj. sight located on 8 in and 10 in. barrel and on the slide of the 6 3/4 in barrel, grooved front and back straps on frame, checkered plastic grips, trigger stop, trigger pull adjustment.

	$1,250	$995	$825	$525	$475	$350	$225	

GRADING - PPGS™	100%	98%	95%	90%	80%	70%	60%	LAST MSR

Values are for pistol w/o weights and muzzle brake.
Add $175 for 8 in. barrel.
Add $225 for 10 in. barrel.
Add $50 for each weight and $90 for muzzle brake if present with gun.

6 3/4 in. tapered barrel with provisions for weights and stabilizer #9280 1960 - 1963. 8 in. tapered barrel with provisions for weights and stabilizer #9281 1960 - 1963. 10 in. tapered barrel with provisions for weights and stabilizer #9282 1960 - 1963.

PISTOLS: SEMI-AUTO, 104 SERIES

The 104 Series is the last of the slant grip gun designs. Early production marked "Model 104". Later production is unmarked. The trigger stop screw moved from the right side of the frame to the trigger on the up scale models with that feature. During the production of this series, the accessories were deleted in lieu of a price increase. The serial numbers of later guns produced after mid-1975 utilized a new serial numbering system with the slant grip models utilizing a "G" prefix on the serial number. This series was produced from 1963 to 1978. Guns with original boxes and papers can add significant premiums but, like the guns, the condition is very important as is the requirement that the box be numbered to the gun.

Add approx. 12% for original box with papers in same condition as gun on the following models.

SUPERMATIC CITATION – .22 LR cal., similar to Model 102/103 Series, 10 shot mag., blue finish, adj. sights, brown plastic grips were standard on the 6 3/4, 8, and 10 in. guns, or thumbrest walnut checkered grips standard on the 5 1/2 in. model, grooved front and back straps.

$775	**$650**	**$525**	**$430**	**$340**	**$250**	**$180**	

Values are for pistol w/o weights and muzzle brake.
Add $150 for 8 in. barrel.
Add $250 for 10 in. barrel.
Add $50 for each tapered barrel weight, $30 for each bull barrel weight, and $90 for muzzle brake if present with gun.
Add $125 for extra magazine (#9263 only).

103 guns, #9244 Citations, shipped March-May, 1978 serial numbers G20,000-G-20,105. 6 3/4 in. tapered barrel with provisions for weights and stabilizer #9260 1963 - 1965. 8 in. tapered barrel with provisions for weights and stabilizer #9261 1963 - 1965. 10 in. tapered barrel with provisions for weights and stabilizer #9262 1963 - 1963. 5 1/2 in. bull barrel with extra magazine #9263 1963 - 1966. 5 1/2 in. bull barrel w/o extra magazine #9244 1967 - 1978.

SUPERMATIC TROPHY – .22 LR cal., similar to Model 102/103 Series, top-of-the-line target model, 5 1/2 in. bull, or 7 1/4 in. fluted barrel, extra mag., muzzle brake and weights were supplied with gun, grooved front and back straps, super polished blue finish, adjustable sights, 2 and 3 oz. adjustable weights, checkered walnut thumb rest grips, grooved front and back straps on frame. Mfg. 1964-65.

$1,100	**$1,000**	**$750**	**$375**	**$325**	**$240**	**$170**	

Price is for pistol without weights and muzzle brake.
Add $150 for high polish blue finish.
Add $40 for each weight and $120 for muzzle brake if present with gun.

5 1/2 in. bull barrel with accessories #9254 1963 - 1965. 7.25" fluted barrel with accessories #9255 1963 - 1965.

OLYMPIC – .22 LR cal., similar to Model 102, grooved front and back straps, checkered plastic grips.

$1,100	**$1,000**	**$750**	**$465**	**$325**	**$240**	**$170**	

Price is for pistol without weights and muzzle brake.
Add $50 for each weight and $90 for muzzle brake if present with gun.

8 in. barrel #9281 1963 - 1963.

ISU OLYMPIC – .22 Short cal., similar to Model 102, grooved front and back straps, 6 3/4 in. barrel with integral muzzle brake, the 5 1/2 in. bull barrel was supplied with muzzle

GRADING - PPGS™	100%	98%	95%	90%	80%	70%	60%	LAST MSR

brake and weights, wts. avail., walnut checkered thumbrest grips standard, 5 1/2 in. barrel introduced 1964.

	$1,150	$1,025	$775	$475	$325	$240	$170	

Values are for pistol w/o weights and muzzle brake.
Add $50 for each weight and $90 for muzzle brake on bull barrel if present with gun.
Add $125 for extra magazine (#9299 only).

5 1/2 in. barrel w/accessories #9295 1964 - 1965. 6 3/4 in. tapered barrel with integral stabilizer - with accessories #9299 1963 - 1966. 6 3/4 in. tapered barrel with integral stabilizer - w/o accessories #9237 1967 - 1977. Catalog and price lists refer to #9295 as both the Olympic and Olympic ISU. This model met ISU regulations and included a removable muzzle brake and weights.

THE VICTOR (SLANT GRIP) – .22 LR cal., 10 shot mag. 4 1/2 in. or 5 1/2 in. slab sided barrels with either ventilated or solid ribs, adj. sights are integral with the rib, blue finish, barrel tapped for weight, checkered walnut thumb rest grips, grooved front and back straps on frame, trigger is adj. for both pull force and over travel, probably 600 of these slant grip Victors were mfg. in all configurations, and probably fewer than 40 each of the 4 1/2 in. guns. Most guns are in the ser. no. range above 2,401,860 to 2,460,614, with a possible few in the ML serial number series. All but a few of the just over 200 guns produced in 1974 were exported, making finding one in the U.S. more difficult.

	$3,200	$2,650	$1,975	$850	$550	$250	$200	

Add $75 for steel rib.
Add $200 for solid rib.
Add $300 for 4 1/2 in. barrel.
Add $30 for original weight if present with gun.

4 1/2 in. slabbed barrel with ventilated steel rib #9218 1973 - 1973. 5 1/2 in. slabbed barrel with ventilated steel rib #9219 1973 - 1973. 4 1/2 in. slabbed barrel with solid aluminum rib #9226 1973 - 1974. 5 1/2 in. slabbed barrel with solid aluminum rib #9229 1973 - 1974. 4 1/2 in. slabbed barrel with ventilated aluminum rib #9218 1974 - 1974. 5 1/2 in. slabbed barrel with ventilated aluminum rib #9219 1974 - 1974. Note the early vent. rib. barrels were steel, and the later ones were aluminum - w/o a change in the catalog numbers. Buyer beware - fakes exist.

CONVERSION KITS MODEL 102/103/104

	$500	$450	$400	$325	$275	$200	$150	

Add $250 for Trophy Conversions.
Add $125 for 8 in. barrel.
Add $225 for 10 in. barrel.

Cat. # 9266 Olympic to Supermatic Citation, 6 3/4 Bbl., Cat. # 9264 Olympic to Supermatic Citation, 8 Bbl., Cat. # 9265 Olympic to Supermatic Citation, 10 Bbl., Cat. # 9283 Supermatic Citation to Olympic, 6 3/4 Bbl., Cat. # 9284 Supermatic Citation to Olympic, 8 Bbl., Cat. # 9285 Supermatic Citation to Olympic, 10 Bbl., Cat. # 9286 Supermatic Trophy to Olympic, 6 3/4 Bbl., Cat. # 9287 Supermatic Trophy to Olympic, 8 Bbl., Cat. # 9288 Supermatic Trophy to Olympic, 10 Bbl.

PISTOLS: SEMI-AUTO, 105 SERIES

Note: High Standard designed the Model 105 but did not produce it. The 105 Series was to have been a 104 Series gun with the bridge style sight that appeared on the 106 series.

PISTOLS: SEMI-AUTO, 106 SERIES, MILITARY MODELS

Referred to as military models, this series was designed to provide same grip angle and feel of the Colt Military Model 1911. This design was introduced in 1965, and continued through most of 1968. The design utilized the tooling of the 104 Series guns, which resulted in the occasional appearance of a bullet shaped brass design in the rear grip strap when the spring hole was not properly plugged. This design appears as both a full bullet shape or only the outline. There is no premium for this feature. The magazines in this series have a red plastic bottom. The right side of the frame is marked "MODEL 106"/"MILITARY". During the production of this series, the accessories were deleted in lieu of a price increase. This resulted in two catalog numbers for each model. Guns with original boxes and papers can add significant premiums but, like the guns, the condition is very important as is the requirement that the box be numbered to the gun.

Add approx. 12% for original box with papers in same condition as gun on the following models.

GRADING - PPGS™	100%	98%	95%	90%	80%	70%	60%	LAST MSR

SUPERMATIC TOURNAMENT MILITARY – .22 LR cal., entry level target pistol, early guns had smooth front and back straps and no trigger stop, later models had stippled grip straps and a trigger stop, slide mounted rear sight instead of bridge sight, 5 1/2 in. bull or 6 3/4 in. tapered barrel with military grips.

	$650	$495	$375	$250	$200	$150	$125	

Add $125 for guns with boxes and accessories if factory records verify model numbers.

5 1/2 in. bull barrel with accessories #9230 1965 - 1966 1,484,801 - 1,602,XXX. 6 3/4 in. barrel with accessories #9231 1965 - 1966 1,484,817 - 1,599,XXX. 5 1/2 in. bull barrel w/o accessories #9232 1967 - 1968 1,594,XXX - 1,93X,XXX. 6 3/4 in. barrel w/o accessories #9233 1967 - 1968 1,598,XXX - 1,94X,XXX.

SUPERMATIC CITATION MILITARY – .22 LR cal., 5 1/2 in. bull or 7 1/4 in. fluted barrel, mid-level target pistol, trigger stop, trigger pull adjustment, stippled front and back straps, new rear bridge type sight.

	$750	$625	$495	$375	$275	$200	$175	

Add $150 for guns with boxes and accessories if factory records verify model numbers.
Add $30 for each weight and $90 for muzzle brake if present with gun.

5 1/2 in. bull barrel with accessories #9240 1965 - 1966 1,465,195 - 1,595,XXX. 7.25" fluted barrel with accessories #9241 1965 - 1966 1,467,353 - 1,595,XXX. 5 1/2 in. bull barrel w/o accessories #9242 1967 - 1968 1,595,XXX - 1,98X,XXX. 7.25" fluted barrel w/o accessories #9243 1967 - 1968 1,592,XXX - 1,98X,XXX.

SUPERMATIC TROPHY MILITARY – .22 LR cal., 5 1/2 bull or 7 1/4 in. fluted barrel, high gloss "Trophy" finish on early guns, top-of-the-line target pistol, trigger stop, trigger pull adjustment, stippled front and back straps, gold plated trigger, safety and magazine release, gold filled lettering, new rear bridge type sight.

	$1,050	$875	$675	$500	$375	$225	$175	

Add $100 for high polish blue finish.
Add $200 premium for guns with boxes and accessories if factory records verify model numbers.
Add $30 for each weight and $90 for muzzle brake if present with gun.
Add $10 per weight or $20 for muzzle brake with high gloss Trophy finish.

5 1/2 in. bull barrel with accessories #9245 1965 - 1966 1,436,172 - 1,595,XXX. 7.25" fluted barrel with accessories #9246 1965 - 1966 1,436,170 - 1,595,XXX. 5 1/2 in. bull barrel w/o accessories #9247 1967 - 1968 1,595,XXX - 1,97X.XXX. 7.25" fluted barrel w/o accessories #9248 1967 - 1968 1,595,XXX - 1,97X,XXX.

OLYMPIC MILITARY – listed in catalog but not in shipping records.

Catalog number #9235 for 5 1/2 in. barrel.

OLYMPIC ISU MILITARY – .22 Short cal., target pistol, 6 3/4 in. tapered barrel with integral stabilizer, trigger stop, trigger pull adjustment, stippled front and back straps, rear bridge type sight, military grips, supplied with extra mag. and weights.

	$1,100	$875	$700	$500	$375	$225	$175	

Add $50 for each weight if present with gun.
Add $200 if w/box and accessories and factory records can verify model.

6 3/4 in. tapered barrel with integral stabilizer - with accessories #9238 1966 - 1966. 6 3/4 in. tapered barrel with integral stabilizer - w/o accessories #9236 1967 - 1968 1,511,284.

PISTOLS: SEMI-AUTO, 107 SERIES

The 107 Series was the evolutionary successor to the 106 Series. This Series had the frame redesigned to eliminate the plugging of the spring hole produced with the old tooling. During the time of this series' production, the "MODEL 107" and the "MILITARY" marking on the frame was removed at about serial number 2,330,000. Then later the "MILITARY" marking reappeared at about serial number 2,4XX,XXX and remained until the end of the traditional serial number series. The "MILITARY" marking is absent from the guns with the "ML" prefixed serial numbers. There is no premium associated with these variations. These marking changes were not a change in design series, but rather only a change in markings. The traditional serial number series ran until August of 1975. The serial numbers on guns produced beginning July 1975 utilized a new

GRADING - PPGS™	100%	98%	95%	90%	80%	70%	60%	LAST MSR

serial numbering system. The Military models utilized an "ML" prefix on the serial number. Early production utilized the red bottomed magazines. Later guns had magazines with blued steel bottoms. The 107 Series was produced from 1968 until Sept 1981. Production was at Hamden, CT from 1968 to 1976 (S/N ML23,065), and at East Hartford 1977 (S/N ML25,000) to 1981 (S/N ML 86,641). Note that early E. Hartford pistols used up old stock of Hamden marked barrels.

The desirability factor for Hamden guns is higher than for East Hartford guns. Guns with original boxes and papers can add significant premiums, but like the guns, the condition is very important as is the requirement that the box be numbered to the gun.

Add approx. 12% for original box with papers in same condition as gun on the following models.
Subtract about 10% for East Hartford mfg.
Use 106 Series pricing for weights and muzzle brakes if present with gun.

SPORT KING – .22 LR cal., similar to previous Sport-Kings, except has military grips, labeled "SPORT KING-M." Mfg. in East Hartford only.

$325	$250	$200	$175	$150	$125	$100	

4 1/2 in. barrel #9258 1978 - 1981 ML35,454 - ML86,493. 6 3/4 in. barrel #9259 1978 - 1981 ML35,453 - ML86,488. 6 3/4 in. barrel (123 guns) #9259 1980 - 1980 MLG20,224 - MLG20,408.

SHARPSHOOTER – .22 LR cal., early models were marked "SHARPSHOOTER", later models were labeled "SHARPSHOOTER-M." Mfg. in East Hartford only.

$425	$365	$300	$250	$200	$150	$125	

5 1/2 in. bull barrel #9210 1977 - 1981 ML29,215 - ML86,641

* ***Sharpshooter Survival Pack*** – introduced 1981, includes Sharpshooter-M pistol, electroless nickel, 5 1/2 in. bull barrel, push-button takedown, packaged in canvas carrying case with extra nickel magazine.

$625	$550	$450	$350	$250	$200	$150	

Subtract $100 for guns without the case.
Subtract $65 for guns without the extra magazine for guns in exc. condition.

5 1/2 in. bull barrel #9424 1981 - 1981 ML 85,635 - ML86,044

SUPERMATIC TOURNAMENT MILITARY – .22 LR cal., similar to Model 106 Series, last of the Tournament pistols, adj. sight mounted on slide, smooth front and back straps on frame. About 1,600 are U.S. marked on the right side and were sold to the U.S. government.

$550	$475	$375	$300	$250	$150	$125	

5 1/2 in. bull barrel #9232 1968 - 1971. 6 3/4 in. barrel #9233 1968 - 1971.

SUPERMATIC CITATION MILITARY – .22 LR cal., similar to Model 106 Series, 7 1/4 fluted and 5 1/2 in. bull barrel available, mid-level target pistol.

$675	$575	$460	$340	$280	$230	$175	

5 1/2 in. bull barrel #9242 1968 - 1981. 7.25" fluted barrel #9243 1968 - 1981.

SUPERMATIC TROPHY MILITARY – .22 LR cal., similar to Model 106 Series, top-of-the-line target pistol.

$900	$750	$575	$450	$325	$250	$175	

5 1/2 in. bull barrel #9247 1968 - 1981. 7.25" fluted barrel #9248 1968 - 1981.

1972 OLYMPIC COMMEMORATIVE – .22 LR cal., highly engraved version of a Supermatic Trophy Military Model 107, high polish blue finish, 5 1/2 in. bull barrel, has 5 Olympic gold rings on right side of receiver, ser. no. has a "T" prefix, came with a lined presentation case, early models were marked "MODEL 107", and were not high polished. C-R.

$6,500	$5,000	$4,000	N/A	N/A	N/A	N/A	*$605*

Values assume guns in original presentation cases.

5 1/2 in. bull barrel #9207 1972 - 1975 T0,000,000 - T0,000,999

This model was a limited edition with 1,000 guns planned, but only 108 guns were listed in the shipping records, plus one frame manufactured due to their high price. A couple of prototypes are believed to exist in the regular serial number series. The original Issue price was $550. One fully engraved gun is known. Buyer beware - fakes may exist.

GRADING - PPGS™	100%	98%	95%	90%	80%	70%	60%	LAST MSR

OLYMPIC ISU MILITARY – .22 Short cal., target pistol for Olympic Style Rapid Fire Events, 6 3/4 in. fluted barrel with integral stabilizer and two detachable weights.

	$1,050	$875	$675	$575	$475	$325	$250	

Add $50 for each weight if present with gun.

6 3/4 in. barrel #9238 1968 - 1977

1980 OLYMPIC COMMEMORATIVE – engraved, right side of slide has the five gold ring Olympic logo, "USA" prefix on serial numbers from 0001 to 1000, lined presentation case, a limited edition of the Model 107 Olympic ISU with 1000 being produced. C-R.

	$1,350	$1,000	$875	N/A	N/A	N/A	N/A	

Values assume complete guns with box, papers, and presentation case - subtract $250 for guns in exc. condition w/o box, papers and presentation case. Subtract $100 for guns with presentation case but w/o box and papers.

6 3/4 in. barrel #9239 1980 - 1980 USA 0001 - USA 1000

THE VICTOR – .22 LR cal., 4 1/2 or 5 1/2 in. slab sided barrels with either ventilated or solid ribs, 10 shot mag., adjustable sights are integral with the rib, blue finish, barrel tapped for weight, checkered walnut thumb rest grips, stippled front and back straps on frame, earliest ventilated steel ribs (1971) were smooth on top, later steel ventilated ribs were grooved, aluminum replaced the steel on later ventilated ribs, still later a clearance groove was added for spent shell ejection behind the barrel, solid aluminum ribs introduced 1973, early models marked "THE VICTOR" on the left side of the barrel, later guns marked simply "VICTOR" on the left side of the frame, a few transition guns are marked in both locations, early wts. are rectangular with round bottoms, later weights were flat bottomed with three grooves.

	$795	$650	$550	$425	$300	$200	$150	

Add $150 for smooth topped vent. steel rib from first year of production.
Add $125 for steel ribs.
Add $150 for solid rib guns.
Add $100 for 4 1/2 in. barrel.
Add $140 for Hamden guns (7digit serial numbers and ML prefix serial numbers below ML 23,066).
Add $35 if weight is present with gun.

4 1/2 in. slabbed barrel with ventilated steel rib #9216 1971 - 1973. 5 1/2 in. slabbed barrel with ventilated steel rib #9217 1971 - 1973. 4 1/2 in. slabbed barrel with solid aluminum rib #9206 1973 - 1977. 5 1/2 in. slabbed barrel with solid aluminum rib #9211 1973 - 1977. 4 1/2 in. slabbed barrel with ventilated aluminum rib #9216 1973 - 1979. 5 1/2 in. slabbed barrel with ventilated aluminum rib #9217 1973 - 1981.

10X – .22 LR cal., 5 1/2 in. bull barrel, push-button takedown. Specifically designed for top flight shooting, hand-picked parts and precisely assembled by one of only five High Standard Master Gunsmiths (with his initials under the left grip of each gun), black matte finish, black painted checkered walnut grips, stippled front and back straps. Mfg. in East Hartford.

	$2,800	$2,300	$1,950	$1,300	$950	$725	$575	

Values are for guns with box and papers including test target - subtract $150 if missing.

5 1/2 in. bull barrel #9372 1980 - 1981 ML71,116 - ML86,123

PISTOLS: SEMI-AUTO, CONVERSION KITS

These kits for the conversion of .22 LR cal. to .22 Short cal. contained an aluminum slide, the barrel and accessory listed below, and two Short mags., and comes in "gun size box" set in styrofoam. Manufactured in E. Hartford 1979-1982

VICTOR KIT – includes 5 1/2 in. barrel with aluminum vent rib and barrel weight, designated #9370 when mfg.

	$550	$450	$350	$285	$250	$215	$185	

TROPHY/CITATION KIT – includes a 5 1/2 in. bull barrel and a stabilizer, designated #9371 when mfg.

	$550	$450	$350	$285	$250	$215	$185	

GRADING - PPGS™	100%	98%	95%	90%	80%	70%	60%	LAST MSR

SILHOUETTE KIT – includes a .22 LR cal., 10 in. bull barrel with front sight and rear sight adapter for adj. rear sights, barrel will work with either large push button takedown or socket head screw takedown.

$550	$450	$350	$285	$250	$215	$185	

PISTOLS: SEMI-AUTO, SH SERIES

This was the final series of High Standard pistols and can be differentiated from the 107 Series by the new barrel release in place of the push button takedown. An allen head screw attached the frame to the barrel. This was a cost reduction design change. Shipped from late May 1981-October 1984. Serial No. range was SH10,001-SH34,034. Near the end of production, a "V" suffix was added to some visually impaired guns which were sold at discount. These guns were guaranteed to function properly, but the company would not allow them to be returned for appearance reasons. A few guns were made in this Series with an "SH" prefix serial number with the Model 107 pushbutton takedown. Serial number ranges are best estimates, and may change with further research.

Add approx. 10% for original box with papers in same condition as gun on the following models.
Add $25 for push button takedown.
Use 106 Series pricing for weights or muzzle brakes if present with gun.

SPORT KING - M – .22 LR cal., similar to ML series, except has allen screw takedown, 4 1/2 or 6 3/4 in. barrel, electroless nickel finish also available, also called the "SPORT KING-M."

$275	$235	$215	$185	$150	$125	$100	

Add 15% for the electroless nickel guns.
Values are for the blued guns.

4 1/2 in. barrel blued #9258 1981 - 1984 SH10,889 - SH33,964. 6 3/4 in. barrel blued #9259 1981 - 1983 SH10,001 - SH28,232. 4 1/2 in. barrel electroless nickel #9450 1983 - 1983 SH27,003 - SH31,436. 6 3/4 in. barrel electroless nickel #9451 1983 - 1983 SH27,004 - SH31,054.

SHARPSHOOTER - M – .22 LR cal., "SH" prefix serial no. with allen screw takedown, military grips, electroless nickel version utilized in some survival kits.

$350	$285	$240	$200	$175	$150	$125	

5 1/2 in. bull barrel #9210 1981 - 1982 SH10,8XX - SH25,074

SUPERMATIC CITATION MILITARY – .22 LR cal., similar to previous Citation model, except with allen screw takedown and military grips.

$500	$435	$350	$275	$225	$175	$150	

5 1/2 in. bull barrel #9242 1981 - 1982 SH10,550 - SH25,166. 7.25" fluted barrel #9243 1981 - 1982 SH10,513 - SH25,167.

CITATION II – .22 LR cal., 10 shot, new variation of the Supermatic Citation, 5 1/2 or 7 1/4 in. slab sided barrel, checkered military-type wood grips, allen screw takedown, SH prefix serial no., slab sided barrel, rear sight mounted on slide, electroless nickel model also available in the survival pack, this model replaced the Sharpshooter and the Supermatic Citation.

$475	$400	$325	$275	$225	$175	$150	

5 1/2 in. slab sided barrel #9348 1982 - 1984 SH25,326 - SH31,495. 7.25" slab sided barrel #9349 1982 - 1984 SH25,575 - SH31,496.

SUPERMATIC TROPHY MILITARY – .22 LR cal., similar to previous Trophy Model with "SH" prefix, except has allen screw takedown, military grips.

$650	$525	$375	$300	$250	$200	$150	

5 1/2 in. bull barrel #9247 1981 - 1984 SH10,865 - SH32,630. 7.25" fluted barrel #9248 1981 - 1984 SH10,492 - SH33,828.

VICTOR – .22 LR cal., similar to previous Victor, new allen screw takedown, "SH" prefix, military grips, 5 1/2 in. vent. barrel only mfg. in this Victor Series, some Victor ser. numbers had a "V" suffix.

$525	$465	$375	$275	$180	$140	$120	

Add $35 if weight is present with gun.

GRADING - PPGS™	100%	98%	95%	90%	80%	70%	60%	LAST MSR

5 1/2 in. slabbed barrel with vent. aluminum rib 9217 1984 - 1984 SH10,321 - SH34,034

10-X – .22 LR cal., top-of-the-line model similar to previous 10-X, but with allen screw takedown, also available with 7 1/4 in. fluted barrel and a 5 1/2 in. ribbed barrel like a Victor.

$2,125	$1,795	$1,450	$1,025	$795	$675	$575	

Add $1000-$900 for ribbed barrel model.
Add $500-$600 for fluted barrel.
Values are for guns with box and papers including test target - subtract $150 if missing.

5 1/2 in. bull barrel #9372 1981 - 1983 SH10,200 - SH29,640. 7.25" fluted barrel #9249 1983 - 1983 SH27,536 - SH29,641. 5 1/2 in. Slabbed barrel w/vent. rib #9434 1983 - 1983 SH26,657 - SH29,601.

Buyer beware - fakes are known to exist.

SURVIVAL PACK – .22 LR cal., Sharpshooter "M" or Citation II electroless nickel, allen screw takedown, packaged in canvas carrying case with extra nickel magazine (two different fabrics utilized during production).

$550	$500	$375	$300	$250	$200	$175	

Subtract $100 for guns without the case and $65 for guns without the extra magazine for guns in exc. condition.

Sharpshooter version #9424 1981 - 1982 SH10,048 - SH25,XXX. Citation II version #9424 1982 - 1984 SH25,XXX - SH31,312.

REVOLVERS: POLICE STYLE

The Sentinel revolvers begin with the R-100 design series, and continue through the R-109 design series. Later steel framed Sentinels carry no design series markings. A change of design series designation indicates design changes to the guns. The R-105 has the fewest known survivors. The design series designations and the associated catalog numbers which follow are best estimates, and may require further research. Earliest Sentinels in 1955 were in a separate serial number series from 1 through approximately 45,000. Then they were included in a serial number series common to all handguns. In 1974, they were again put in a separate serial number series with a prefix - S101 through S79946. Many of the later guns had a "V" suffix which indicates it was visually impaired, but guaranteed to work properly. High Standard private labeled the aluminum framed Sentinels for both Sears and Western Auto. A few were also provided to Col. Rex Applegate for his ARMAMEX company in Mexico.

R-100, R-101, and R-102 models are all C-R.

Add 20% for extra convertible cylinder (.22 LR/.22 Mag.) on those models listed that apply.
Add $30 for box and papers unless otherwise specified.

SENTINEL – .22 S, L, or LR cal., aluminum frame, nine shot, SA or DA, swing out cylinder, 2 3/8, 3, 4, 5, or 6 in. barrel, fixed sights, return spring on ejector beginning with R-102 Series, until 1960 the 2 3/8 in. barrel model had a bobbed hammer, beginning in 1961 this changed to a standard spur hammer with no change in Cat. No.

* ***Sentinel Blue finish***

$225	$200	$140	$100	$85	$70	$55	

* ***Sentinel Nickel finish***

$250	$225	$200	$115	$95	$85	$65	

Subtract $15 for early models without spring return ejector.
Add $25 for 5 in. barrel.

R-100, R-101, R-102 Series 3 in. bbl., brown sq. butt, plastic grips, blue, #9127, mfg. 1955-1960. R-100, R-101, R-102 Series 3 in. bbl., brown sq. butt, plastic grips, nickel #9136, mfg. 1956-1960. R-100 Series 5 in. bbl., brown sq. butt, plastic grips, blue, #9128, mfg. 1955 only.

* ***Sentinel R-100, R-101, R-102 Series 6 in. bbl.***

Brown sq. butt, plastic grips, blue, #9128 mfg. 1956-1964. White sq. butt, plastic grips, nickel #9137 mfg. 1956-1964.

GRADING - PPGS™	100%	98%	95%	90%	80%	70%	60%	LAST MSR

* ***Sentinel R-102, R-103 Series 4 in. bbl.***

Brown sq. butt, plastic grips, blue #9159 mfg. 1957-1964. White sq. butt, plastic grips, nickel #9160 mfg. 1957-1964.

* ***Sentinel R-102, R-103 Series 2 3/8 in. barrel*** – faux ivory round butt, plastic grips.

Blue #9144 mfg. 1957-1966. Nickel #9145 mfg. 1957-1966.

* ***Sentinel w/Dura-Tone colors*** – 2 3/8 in. barrel, offered in three different color anodized frames, featured nickel plated cylinders, triggers, and hammers, round butt ivory colored plastic grips, mahogany finished case.

Add $40 for R-102 models. Add $100 for R-103 models.
Subtract $50 if w/o wood presentation case.

	100%	98%	95%	90%	80%	70%	60%	LAST MSR
* ***Sentinel Turquoise finish***	$595	$525	$425	$250	$195	$150	$120	
* ***Sentinel Pink finish***	$595	$525	$425	$250	$195	$150	$120	
* ***Sentinel Gold finish***	$550	$450	$375	$250	$195	$140	$120	

Gold R-101, R-102 Series #9161 mfg. 1957-1962 710,397 - 1,221,102. Turquoise R-101, R-102 Series #9162 mfg. 1957-1962 710,463 - 1,221,101. Pink R-101, R-102 Series #9163 mfg. 1957-1962 710,393 - 1,160,442.

SENTINEL IMPERIAL – similar to Sentinel, except has adj. sights, two piece walnut grips, mfg. 1962-64.

	100%	98%	95%	90%	80%	70%	60%	LAST MSR
* ***Sentinel Imperial Blue finish***	$275	$250	$225	$135	$115	$100	$90	
* ***Sentinel Imperial Nickel finish***	$275	$250	$225	$150	$115	$100	$90	

R-104 Series 4 in. bbl., blue #9187 mfg. 1962-1964. R-104 Series 6 in. bbl., blue #9188 mfg. 1962-1964. R-104 Series 4 in. bbl., nickel #9191 mfg. 1962-1964. R-104 Series 6 in. bbl., nickel #9192 mfg. 1962-1964.

SENTINEL DELUXE – similar to Sentinel, except has two piece walnut square butt grips and fixed sights, wide trigger, 24 or 26 oz.

	100%	98%	95%	90%	80%	70%	60%	LAST MSR
* ***Sentinel Deluxe Blue finish***	$250	$225	$195	$125	$100	$90	$80	
* ***Sentinel Deluxe Nickel finish***	$275	$250	$225	$125	$100	$90	$80	

R-106, R-107 Series 4 in. bbl., blue #9146 mfg. 1965-69, 1972-73. R-106, R-107 Series 4 in. bbl., nickel #9148 mfg. 1965-1973. R-106, R-107 Series 6 in. bbl., blue #9147 mfg. 1965-69, 1972-73. R-106, R-107 Series 6 in. bbl., nickel #9149 mfg. 1965-1973.

SENTINEL SNUB – similar to Sentinel Deluxe, except has checkered bird's-head grip, blue or nickel finish, 2 3/8 in. barrel, 20 oz.

	100%	98%	95%	90%	80%	70%	60%	LAST MSR
* ***Sentinel Snub Blue finish***	$250	$225	$175	$125	$100	$90	$80	
* ***Sentinel Snub Nickel finish***	$275	$250	$225	$150	$115	$95	$85	

R-108 Series, brown round butt, plastic grip. Blue #9344 mfg. 1967-69, 1972-73. Nickel #9345 mfg. 1967-69, 1972-73.

KIT GUN – 22 LR cal., swing out cylinder, 9 shot, 4 in. barrel, adj. sights, blue finish, aluminum frame, round butt walnut grips.

	100%	98%	95%	90%	80%	70%	60%	LAST MSR
	$275	$225	$215	$150	$125	$110	$95	

R-109 Series #9304 mfg. 1971-1973.

GRADING - PPGS™	100%	98%	95%	90%	80%	70%	60%	LAST MSR

CAMP GUN – 22 LR or .22 WMR cal., 6 in. barrel, blue, adj. rear sight, checkered walnut grips, also available as a combination with both cylinders.

	$275	$250	$225	$175	$120	$110	$100	

Add $50 for combination with both cylinders.

R-109 Series, .22 S/L/LR #9342 mfg. 1976-77. R-109 Series, .22 WMR #9343 mfg. 1976-77. R-109 Series, Combination #9393 mfg. 1977-1984.

SENTINEL MARK I – .22 S, L, or LR cal., SA or DA, swing out cylinder, 2, 3, or 4 in barrel, steel frame, fixed sights, blue or nickel finish, adj. sights on 3 or 4 in. barrel, smooth wood, square butt grips.

* ***Sentinel Mark I Blue finish***

	$265	$225	$200	$175	$120	$100	$90	

* ***Sentinel Mark I Nickel finish***

	$295	$250	$225	$175	$150	$125	$100	

$25 premium for adj. sights.

2 in. bbl., fixed sights, blue #9350 mfg. 1974-77. 2 in. bbl., fixed sights ,nickel #9351 mfg. 1974-77. 3 in. bbl., fixed sights, blue #9352 mfg. 1974 only. 3 in. bbl., fixed sights, nickel #9354 mfg. 1974 only. 4 in. bbl., fixed sights, blue #9356 mfg. 1974-77. 4 in. bbl., fixed sights, nickel #9358 mfg. 1974-77. 4 in. bbl., adj. sights, blue #9357 mfg. 1974-77. 4 in. bbl., adj. sights, nickel #9359 mfg. 1974-77.

The following versions were in the catalogs and proive lists but only one sample cat. No. 9353 has been found in the shipping records.

3 in. bbl., fixed sights, blue #9352 mfg. 1974 only. 3 in. bbl., fixed sights, nickel #9354 mfg. 1974 only. 3 in. bbl., adj. sights, blue #9353 mfg. 1974 only. 3 in. bbl., adj. sights, nickel #9355 mfg. 1974 only.

SENTINEL MARK IV – similar to Sentinel Mark I, except .22 WMR cal.

* ***Sentinel Mark IV Blue finish***

	$275	$225	$200	$175	$130	$115	$100	

* ***Sentinel Mark IV Nickel finish***

	$300	$275	$225	$200	$150	$130	$110	

Add $25 for adj. sights.

2 in. bbl., fixed sights, blue #9360 mfg. 1974-77. 2 in. bbl., fixed sights, nickel #9361 mfg. 1974-77. 3 in. bbl., fixed sights, blue #9362 mfg. 1974-77. 3 in. bbl., fixed sights, nickel #9363 mfg. 1974-77. 3 in. bbl., adj. sights, blue #9364 mfg. 1974-77. 3 in. bbl., adj. sights, nickel #9365 mfg. 1974-77. 4 in. bbl., fixed sights, blue #9366 mfg. 1974-77. 4 in. bbl., fixed sights, nickel #9367 mfg. 1974-77. 4 in. bbl., adj. sights, blue #9368 mfg. 1974-77. 4 in. bbl., adj. sights, nickel #9369 mfg. 1974-77.

POWER PLUS – .38 Spl. cal., 5 shot, SA or DA, swing out cylinder, blue finish, steel frame, serial numbers between PG 1010 and PG1273, only 177 mfg. 1983-84.

	$550	$500	$425	$360	$250	$200	$150	

Catalog number 9438 .

SENTINEL COMBO – similar to Mark I Sentinel, except without the Mark I markings, steel frame, blue finish, offered as a combination with cylinders for .22 LR and .22 WMR cal.

	$295	$275	$250	$225	$200	$175	$150	

Values are for guns with both cylinders.
Add $25 for adj. sights.
Subtract $50 for guns with only one cylinder.

2 in. bbl., fixed sights #9390 mfg. 1978-1984. 4 in. bbl., adj. sights #9392 mfg. 1978-1984.

SENTINEL MARK II – .357 Mag. cal., SA or DA, 6 shot, swing out cylinder, blue finish, steel frame, fixed sights, produced by Dan Wesson for High Standard from 1974-75.

	$295	$275	$250	$225	$200	$175	$150	

Serial numbers had an "H" prefix H10001 to H35100. A few preproduction guns were sold to employees (H1 to about H28). 2 1/2 in. bbl., #9401, 4 in. bbl., #9402. 6 in. bbl., #9403.

GRADING - PPGS™	100%	98%	95%	90%	80%	70%	60%	LAST MSR

SENTINEL MARK III – similar to Mark II, except adj. sights, mfg. by Dan Wesson.

	$315	$275	$250	$200	$175	$150	$140	

2 1/2 in. and 6 in. bbl. #9407. 4 in. bbl. #9408. 6 in. bbl. #9409.

CRUSADER – planned production only in .357 Mag., .44 Mag. or .45 Colt cal., swing-out cylinder, unique geared action, adj. sights.

.357 Mag., 4 1/4 in. barrel, medium frame, catalog #9458 advertised 1979-1980. .357 Mag., 6 1/2 in. barrel, medium frame, catalog #9459 advertised 1979-1980. .357 Mag., 4 1/4 in. barrel, large frame, catalog #9471 advertised 1979-1980. .357 Mag., 6 1/2 in. barrel, large frame, catalog #9472 advertised 1979-1980. .44 Mag., 4 1/4 in. barrel, large frame, catalog #9452 advertised 1979-1980. .44 Mag., 6 1/2 in. barrel, large frame, catalog #9453 advertised 1979-1980. .44 Mag., 8 3/4 in. barrel, large frame, catalog #9454 advertised 1979-1980. .45 Colt, 4 1/4 in. barrel, large frame, catalog #9455 advertised 1979-1980. .45 Colt, 6 1/2 in. barrel, large frame, catalog #9456 advertised 1979-1980. .45 Colt, 8 3/4 in. barrel, large frame, catalog #9457 advertised 1979-1980.

Only a few prototypes with "EX" prefix serial numbers of this model exist, and pre-production Crusaders with serial numbers C1001 and C1002 exist.

CRUSADER 50TH ANNIVERSARY – .44 Mag. or .45 LC cal., 51 mfg. for each cal. in 8 3/8 in. barrel with 1/3 coverage engraving (ser. no. 0-50), double action employing gear assembly, blue with a gold crusader figure on the side plate, and an anniversary rollmark to commemorate High Standard's 50th anniversary, cased.

* ***Crusader 50th Anniversary Standard Model w/o engraving***								
	$825	$750	$675	$475	$415	$325	$275	
* ***Crusader 50th Anniversary 8 3/8 in. barrel***								
	$1,550	$1,350	$1,175	$925	$775	$675	$525	

Add 25% for single digit serial number.
Limited availability might affect asking prices considerably. Two gun sets with matching serial numbers were also available - current asking prices are over $3,250.

Advertising materials at the time listed 450 revolvers of each cal. in a 6 1/2 in. barrel (ser. no. 51-500). Serial numbers for the 8 3/4 in. barrels are 44M0 through 44M50 (shipped 1979 through 1981) and 45C0 through 45C50 (shipped in 1981). Serial numbers 44M51 through 44M500 (approx 425 guns shipped 1978 through 1983). Serial numbers 45C51 through 45C487 (approx 339 guns shipped 1981 through 1983).

.44 Mag., 8 3/4 in. bbl., first 51 of 501 commemoratives #9601 mfg. 1979-1981. .44 Mag., 6 1/2 in. bbl., balance of 501 commemoratives #9603 mfg. 1978-1983. .45 Colt, 8 3/4 in. bbl., first 51 of 501 commemoratives #9600 mfg. 1981 only. .45 Colt, 6 1/2 in. bbl., balance of 501 commemoratives #9602 mfg. 1981-1983.

REVOLVERS: WESTERN STYLE

The Western style revolvers begin with the W-100 design series and continue through the W-106 design series. The changes of design series designations indicate design changes to the guns. The design series designations and the associated catalog numbers which follow are best estimates. Early western revolvers were in the serial number series common to all handguns. In 1972, they were put in a separate serial number series with an "M" prefix - M 1001 through M90916. Many of the later guns had a "V" suffix which indicated the gun was visually impaired but guaranteed to work properly. All "V" marked guns were shipped during June 1984 or later independent of serial number. High Standard private labeled the aluminum frame Western style revolvers for both Sears and Western Auto.

DURANGO – .22 S, L, or LR cal., single/double action, 9 shot, blue or nickel finish, aluminum or steel frame, 4 1/2 or 5 1/2 in. barrel, fixed or adj. sights, square butt walnut grips, two models have their grip straps and trigger guard nickel plated.

Durango W-105 Series, aluminum frame - 4 1/2 in. bbl., blue with brass trim #9302 mfg. 1970-73. Durango W-105 Series, aluminum frame - 5 1/2 in. bbl., blue #9307, mfg. 1971-73. Durango W-105 Series, aluminum frame - 5 1/2 in. bbl., nickel #9308 mfg. 1971-73. Durango W-106 Series, steel frame - 5 1/2 in. bbl., blue with nickel trim, #9316 mfg. 1974 only. Durango W-106 Series, steel frame - 5 1/2

GRADING - PPGS™	100%	98%	95%	90%	80%	70%	60%	LAST MSR

in. bbl., nickel #9317 mfg. 1974 only. Durango W-106 Series, steel frame - 5 1/2 in. bbl., adj. sights, blue/nickel #9318 mfg. 1974 only.

* ***Durango Blue Finish***

	100%	98%	95%	90%	80%	70%	60%	LAST MSR
	$275	$225	$200	$150	$115	$90	$75	

* ***Durango Nickel Finish***

	100%	98%	95%	90%	80%	70%	60%	LAST MSR
	$300	$250	$225	$150	$125	$100	$85	

Add $25 for steel frame.
Add $25 for adj. sights.
Values assume aluminum frames.

HOMBRE – similar to Double Nine aluminum frame, but no ejector rod housing, 4 1/2 in. barrel, fixed sights and square butt walnut grips.

* ***Hombre Blue finish***

	100%	98%	95%	90%	80%	70%	60%	LAST MSR
	$275	$225	$200	$150	$110	$90	$75	

* ***Hombre Nickel finish***

	100%	98%	95%	90%	80%	70%	60%	LAST MSR
	$295	$250	$225	$150	$125	$100	$75	

W-105 Series, blue #9300 mfg. 1970-1972. W-105 Series, nickel #9301 mfg. 1970-1972.

LONGHORN – .22 LR or .22 WMR cal., DA, 4 1/2, 5 1/2, or 9 1/2 in. barrel, 9 shot, swing out cylinder, fixed sights except for one model.

* ***Longhorn 1958-1970 Mfg.*** – .22 S, L, or LR cal., SA or DA, aluminum frame guns, blue finish, fixed sights, square butt grips, one model has grip straps and trigger guard with gold plating contrasting with the blue frame.

	100%	98%	95%	90%	80%	70%	60%	LAST MSR
	$350	$325	$300	$225	$175	$125	$100	

Subtract $15 for early models w/o spring return ejector.

These guns are found in the W-100, W-101, W-102, W-103, and W-104 design series.

* ***Longhorn Aluminum Frame***

4 1/2 in. bbl., faux ivory plastic grips #9175 mfg. 1961 only. 5 1/2 in. bbl., faux ivory plastic grips #9176 mfg. 1961 only. 9 1/2 in. bbl., ivory colored plastic grips #9177 mfg. 1961 only. 4 1/2 in. bbl., pearl style plastic grips #9178 mfg. 1961-65. 5 1/2 in. bbl., stag style plastic grips #9179 mfg. 1961-65. 9 1/2 in. bbl., walnut grips #9180 mfg. 1961-65. Sears version #9184 9 1/2 in. bbl., walnut grips, gold colored trim #9199 mfg. 1966 only. 9 1/2 in. bbl., walnut grips #9399 mfg. 1967-1970.

* ***Longhorn Steel Frame 1971-1984 Mfg.*** – .22 S, L, LR, or .22 WMR cal., steel frame, or a combination with both cylinders.

	100%	98%	95%	90%	80%	70%	60%	LAST MSR
	$350	$325	$300	$225	$175	$125	$100	

Add $45 for combination models.
Add $25 for adj. sights

* ***Longhorn Steel Frame W-106 Series***

9 1/2 in. bbl., .22 S/L/LR #9397 mfg. 1984 only. 9 1/2 in. bbl., .22 WMR #9327 mfg. 1971-74. 9 1/2 in. bbl., combination #9326 mfg. 1971-76. 9 1/2 in. bbl., combination, adj. sights #9328, mfg. 1976-1984.

DOUBLE NINE SERIES

* ***Double Nine 1958-1970 Mfg*** – .22 S, L, or LR cal., SA or DA, aluminum frame, one model has grip straps and trigger guard with gold plating contrasting with the blue frame, return spring on ejector beginning with W-102 Series.

» **Double Nine 1958-1970 Mfg Blue finish**

	100%	98%	95%	90%	80%	70%	60%	LAST MSR
	$235	$200	$175	$125	$100	$80	$70	

Subtract $15 for early models without spring return ejector.

» **Double Nine 1958-1970 Mfg Nickel finish**

	100%	98%	95%	90%	80%	70%	60%	LAST MSR
	$250	$215	$190	$140	$95	$80	$70	

Subtract $15 for early models without spring return ejector.

These guns are found in the W-100, W-101, W-102, W-103, and W-104 design series.

GRADING - PPGS™	100%	98%	95%	90%	80%	70%	60%	LAST MSR

Catalog Nos.: Blue with faux ivory plastic grip #9169 mfg. 1958-1965. Nickel with black plastic grips #9170 mfg. 1958-1970. Sears version, Blue, "Ranger" #9171. Sears version, Nickel, "Ranger" #9174. Blue/gold colored trim, stag style grips #9129, mfg. 1966 only. Blue, stag style grips #9329 mfg. 1967-1970.

* ***Double Nine 1971-1984 Mfg.*** – steel frame, walnut grips.

» **Double Nine 1971-1984 Mfg. Blue finish**

$275	$250	$225	$175	$150	$115	$100	

» **Double Nine 1971-1984 Mfg. Nickel finish**

$315	$275	$250	$195	$150	$125	$100	

Add $45 for combination models.

W-106 Series, blue, combination #9320 mfg. 1971-79. W-106 Series, blue, .22 WMR #9321 mfg. 1971-73. W-106 Series, nickel, combination #9322 mfg. 1971-73. W-106 Series, nickel, .22 WMR #9323 mfg. 1971-76. W-106 Series, blue, combination, adj. sights #9324 mfg. 1971-1984. W-106 Series, blue, .22 WMR, adj. sights #9325 mfg. 1971-73.

THE GUN/HIGH SIERRA – .22 S, L, LR cal., single/double action, 9 shot, available as a combination model with a second cylinder in .22 WMR, blue finish with gold plated grip straps and trigger guard, steel frame, 7 in. octagon barrel, fixed or adj. sights and square butt walnut grips, gold plated grip frame.

$350	$300	$275	$215	$175	$125	$100	

Add $40 for presentation case.
Add $45 for combination models.
Add $25 for adj. sights.

This gun was introduced as "The Gun" in the February 1973 price list and the name changed to "High Sierra" by the November 1973 price list. Note that the early production had neither "High Sierra" markings nor any other name. The name High Sierra was the result of a "name the gun" contest after the gun was introduced.

.22 S, L, LR, in a case #9313 mfg. 1973-74. Combination, in a case #9314 mfg. 1973-74. Combination, in a case, adj. sights #9315 mfg. 1973-74. Combination, without a case #9374 mfg. 1975 only. Combination, without a case, adj. sights #9375 mfg. 1975-1984. .22 S, L, LR, without a case #9379 mfg. 1984 only.

POSSE – similar to Double Nine aluminum, except has 3 1/2 in. barrel, blue, brass grip frame, fixed sights, walnut grips.

$275	$250	$225	$150	$125	$100	$75	

W-104 and W-105 Series #9181 mfg. 1961-1965. Sears version #9183

NATCHEZ – .22 S, L, LR cal., SA or DA, 9 shot, blue finish, aluminum frame, 4 1/2 in. barrel, fixed sights, faux ivory bird's head grips.

$450	$375	$350	$250	$200	$150	$125	

Add $50 for box and papers.

W-104 and W-105 Series #9182 mfg. 1961-1965. Sears version #9186.

MARSHAL – .22 S, L, LR cal., SA or DA, 9 shot, blue finish, aluminum frame, fixed sights, 5 1/2 in. long barrel, square butt stag style plastic grips.

$250	$215	$195	$125	$115	$100	$90	

Values are for gun alone. Add $50 if box, papers and accessories are present and in excellent condition.

Catalog number 9330 , mfg. 1971-73.

Offered in a special promotion package with a holster, trigger lock, and spray can of G-96 gun scrubber.

RIFLES/CARBINES

SPORT-KING FIELD SEMI-AUTO RIFLE – .22 S, L, or LR cal., 22 1/4 in. barrel, walnut stock, open sights, 15, 17, or 21 shot tube mag.

$200	$175	$150	$115	$90	$80	$65	

A-100, A-103. Catalog number #8000 mfg. 1960-1965.

GRADING - PPGS™	100%	98%	95%	90%	80%	70%	60%	LAST MSR

SPORT-KING SPECIAL – similar to Field Model, except has beavertail forearm and Monte Carlo stock.

	$225	$195	$150	$125	$110	$95	$75	

A-100, A-103. Catalog number #8001 mfg. 1960-1965.

SPORT-KING SEMI-AUTO CARBINE – .22 S, L, or LR cal., 18 1/4 in. barrel, straight grip walnut stock with barrel band and sling, open sights, 12, 14, or 17 shot tube mag.

	$225	$200	$175	$150	$115	$100	$75	

A-101, A-102. Catalog number #8002 mfg. 1962-1971.

SPORT-KING DELUXE / SPORT KING SEMI-AUTO RIFLE – revised nomenclature for the Sport-King Special, catalog number 6005 is also the same gun but called Sport-King, a special promotional package (catalog number 8007) was offered which included the Sport-King rifle, a zippered gun case, a plastic trigger lock, and G-96 gun lubricant.

	$225	$195	$150	$125	$110	$95	$75	

Add 10% for complete 8007 package in original box.

A-1041 Sport King Deluxe Catalog number #8005 mfg. 1966-1971. Sport King Catalog number #8007 mfg. 1971 only. Sport King Catalog number #6005 mfg. 1973-1976.

HI-POWER FIELD CENTERFIRE BOLT ACTION – .270 Win. or .30-06 cal., Mauser type action, 4 shot mag., 22 in. barrel, folding rear sight, plain stock.

	$475	$425	$375	$350	$300	$250	$200	

H-100 .30-06 Catalog number #8507 mfg. 1962-1965. H-100 .270 Catalog number #8509 mfg. 1962-1965.

HI-POWER DELUXE – similar to Field, except has checkered Monte Carlo stock and sling swivels.

	$500	$450	$400	$350	$300	$250	$200	

H-100 .30-06 Catalog number #8506 mfg. 1962-1965. H-100 .270 Catalog number #8508 mfg. 1962-1965. H-100 .308 Catalog number #8511 mfg. 1965-1965. H-100 .243 Catalog number #8513 mfg. 1965-1965.

SPORT-KING/FLITE-KING SLIDE ACTION RIFLE – .22 S, L, or LR cal., 24 in. barrel, tube mag., hammerless, Patridge sight, Monte Carlo stock with pistol grip, semi beavertail forearm.

	$225	$195	$150	$125	$110	$95	$75	

P-100 Sport-King Catalog number #8004 mfg. 1963-1965. P-1011 Sport-King Catalog number #8006 mfg. 1966-1971. Flite-King Catalog number #6006 mfg. 1973-1976.

SHOTGUNS: BOLT ACTION

MODEL 514 – some of the Sears versions of this shotgun were recalled for safety considerations in the late 1990s.

	$135	$120	$90	$70	$60	$50	$40	

CATALOG NUMBERS

Series Barrel Full Choke Adj Choke Single Shot Full Choke Date Range - 12 Ga 514 Plain 8370 8373 8376 Unknown. 16 Ga 514 Plain 8371 8374 8377 Unknown. 20 Ga 514 Plain 8372 8375 8378 Unknown. The catalog numbers shown are from a parts book which does not provide production dates.

SHOTGUNS: SEMI-AUTO

High Standard began making shotguns for Sears Roebuck in the late 1940s. In 1960, High Standard began marketing shotguns under their own name and the approximately 200 models in the following listing is derived from the High Standard catalogs and price lists of that time. A redesign of the shotgun line occurred with new models introduced in 1966. In 1973, High Standard introduced their new "Trophy Line" of shotguns and this marked a change in catalog numbers from the number beginning with the numeral 8 to the number beginning with the numeral 6. At this time the previous catalog numbers were referred to as the "Regular Line". Some regular line guns were cataloged in 1973, but this was the last year for them except the

GRADING - PPGS™	100%	98%	95%	90%	80%	70%	60%	LAST MSR

Police models. The 12 gauge pumps in the Trophy line were the guns which had interchangeable barrels. Serial numbers began appearing on the High Standard shotguns during mid to late 1967. Beginning about 1958, many of the shotguns had a two letter date code.

Additionally, there are over 150 catalog numbers for both semi-auto and slide action shotguns not listed here which represent models with High Standard markings but with special roll marking or other features which High Standard produced for several large distributors. Many of these distributor specials had their own model names which included Point Right, Pointer, Birdwing, NATO Pintail Field Classic Mallard Model 200 (J.C. Penney 20 ga. semi-auto), Model 220, and Sport Deluxe. These distributor label guns are not listed in the following data.

The choke markings used by High Standard are: * Full, ** Modified, *** Improved Cylinder, and **** Skeet Bore. Cylinder Bore has no mark.

SUPERMATIC FIELD – 12 or 20 ga., 2 3/4 (12 ga.) or 3 (20 ga.) chambers, 28 or 30 in. barrel, full or modified choke, improved cylinder, gas operated, blue finish, plain pistol grip walnut stock and forearm, 4 shot mag. capacity.

	$225	$210	$185	$170	$150	$140	$120

Add 10% for 20 gauge.

Supermatic Field models were superceded by models in the Supermatic Deluxe group beginning in 1966.

SUPERMATIC FIELD CATALOG NUMBERS: Series Barrel 30 in. Full 28 in. Modified 26 in. Imp. Cyl. 27 in. Adj.Date Range. 12 ga. C-100 Plain 8203 8200 8201 8202 1960-1965. 20 ga. C-200 Plain 8270 8271 8273 1963-1965.

SUPERMATIC SPECIAL – 12 or 20 ga., similar to the Supermatic Field except has 27 in. barrel with 6 position click stop adjustable choke, 2 3/4 (12 ga.) or 3 in. (20 ga.) chambers.

	$230	$210	$195	$175	$150	$140	$120

Add 10% for 20 ga.

Supermatic Special models were superceded by models in the Supermatic Deluxe group beginning in 1966.

C-100 catalog #8250 mfg. 1961-65. C-200 catalog #8272 mfg. 1963-65.

SUPERMATIC DELUXE – 12 or 20 ga., 2 3/4 (12 ga.) or 3 (20 ga.) in. chambers, gas operated, blue finish, 26, 27, 28, or 30 in. barrel, checkered pistol grip, walnut stock and forearm, 4 shot mag., recoil pad (new 1966).

	$270	$245	$205	$175	$150	$140	$130

Add $20 for vent rib versions.

Add 10% for 20 ga.

SUPERMATIC DELUXE CATALOG NUMBERS - 12 Ga Series Barrel 30" Full 28" Full 28" Modified 26" Imp Cyl 27" adj. Date Range. C-100 Plain 8213 8210 8211 8212 1960-1965. C-100 Vent Rib 8214 8215 8216 1960-1965. C-1200 Plain 8207 8204 8205 8206 8251 1966-1972. C-1200 Vent Rib 8224 8225 8226 8227 1966-1973 Late Plain 6207 6205 1973-1975. Late Vent Rib 6224 6225 6226 6232 1973-1976. 20 Ga Series Barrel 28" Full 28" Modified 26" Imp Cyl 27" adj. Date Range. C-200 Plain 8274 8276 1963-1965. C-2011 Plain 8280 8283 8279 8275 1966-1973. C-2011 Vent Rib 8284 8285 8282 1966-1974. Late Plain 6280 6283 6279 1973-1975. Late Vent Rib 6284 6285 - 6282 1973-1976.

SUPERMATIC CITATION – similar to Supermatic Trophy model except w/o vent. rib, 2 3/4 in. chambers, 6 click stop adjustable choke.

	$245	$230	$210	$190	$160	$140	$115

Catalog #8220 has a compensator integral with the adjustable choke. 12 ga., 27 in. barrel, adjustable catalog #8220 mfg. 1960. C-100, 12 ga., 27 in. barrel, adjustable catalog #8221 mfg. 1961-62.

SUPERMATIC TROPHY – 12 or 20 ga., 2 3/4 (12 ga.) or 3 (20 ga.) in. chamber, gas operated, blue finish, checkered walnut stock and forend, 4 shot mag., 6 click stop adjustable choke.

	$255	$235	$210	$190	$165	$145	$120

Add 10% for 20 ga.

Catalog #8230 has a compensator integral with the adjustable choke. 12 ga., 27 in. barrel, Adjustable Vent Rib, catalog #8230 mfg. 1960. C-100, 12 ga., 27 in. barrel, Adjustable Vent Rib, catalog #8231 mfg. 1961-65. C-200, 20 ga., 27 in. barrel, Adjustable Vent Rib, catalog #8281 mfg. 1963-65.

GRADING - PPGS™	100%	98%	95%	90%	80%	70%	60%	LAST MSR

SUPERMATIC DUCK – 12 ga., 3 in. magnum chamber, (also fits 2 3/4 in. shells), blue finish, checkered pistol grip walnut stock and forearm, 5 (2 3/4 in. shells) or 4 (3 in. shells) shot mag.

$285	$255	$205	$175	$145	$125	$110	

Add $20 for vent rib.

C-101, 12 ga., 3 in., 30 in. barrel, Full Choke Vent Rib, catalog #8240 mfg. 1960 only. C-101, 12 ga., 3 in., 30 in. barrel, Full Choke, catalog #8241 mfg. 1961-62. 12 ga., 3 in., 30 in. barrel, Full Choke Vent Rib, catalog #8242 mfg. 1961-65. 12 ga., 3 in., 30 in. barrel, Full Choke, catalog #8243 mfg. 1963-65. C-1211, 12 ga., 3 in., 30 in. barrel, Full Choke, catalog #8244 mfg. 1966-1973. C-1211, 12 ga., 3 in., 30 in. barrel, Full Choke Vent Rib, catalog #8247 mfg. 1966-1973. 12 ga., 3 in., 30 in. barrel, Full Choke Vent Rib, catalog #6247 mfg. 1973-75.

SUPERMATIC DEER GUN – similar to Supermatic Deluxe, except has 22 in. cylinder bore barrel, rifle sights, checkered stock and forearm, recoil pad.

$250	$225	$195	$175	$150	$125	$115	

Receiver tapped for aperture sight on cat no. 8246. 12 ga., 22 in. barrel, Cylinder Bore, catalog #8245 mfg. 1965 only. C-1200, 12 ga. , 22 in. barrel, Cylinder Bore, catalog #8246 mfg. 1966-1972.

SUPERMATIC SKEET – similar to Supermatic Deluxe, except has select American walnut stock and forearm, 2 3/4 (12 ga.) or 3 (20 ga.) in. chamber.

$300	$275	$250	$225	$200	$175	$150	

Add 10% for 20 ga.

C-100, 12 ga., 26 in. barrel, Skeet Choke, Vent Rib, catalog #8260 mfg. 1962-63. 12 ga., 26 in. barrel, Skeet Choke, Vent Rib, catalog #8262 mfg. 1964-65. C-1200, 12 ga., 26 in. barrel, Skeet Choke, Vent Rib, catalog #8264 mfg. 1966-72. 12 ga., 26 in. barrel, Skeet Choke, Vent Rib, catalog #6264 mfg. 1973-75. 20 ga. , 26 in. barrel, Skeet Choke, Vent Rib, catalog #8277 mfg. 1964-65. C-2011, 20 ga., 26 in. barrel, Skeet Choke, Vent Rib, catalog #8287 mfg. 1964-1972. 20 ga., 26 in. barrel, Skeet Choke Vent Rib, catalog #6287 mfg. 1973-75.

SUPERMATIC TRAP – similar to Supermatic Deluxe, except has select American walnut stock and forearm and recoil pad.

$300	$275	$225	$200	$180	$160	$140	

Catalog number 8266 is the Executive Trap model with Fajen Monte Carlo stock and 2 3/4 in. chamber. C-100, 12 ga., 30 in. barrel, Full Choke, Vent Rib, catalog #8261 mfg. 1962-63. 12 ga., 30 in. barrel, Full Choke, Vent Rib, catalog #8263 mfg. 1964-65. C-1200, 12 ga., 30 in. barrel, Full Choke, Vent Rib, catalog #8265 mfg. 1966-1972. 12 ga., 30 in. barrel, Full Choke, Vent Rib, catalog #8266 mfg.1970-72. 12 ga., 30 in. barrel, Full Choke, Vent Rib, catalog #6265 mfg. 1973-75.

SHOTGUNS: SLIDE ACTION

FLITE-KING FIELD – 12, 16, 20 ga. or .410 bore, 2 3/4 (12 or 16 ga.) or 3 (20 ga. or .410 bore) in. chamber, blued finish, 4 or 5 shot mag., plain pistol grip walnut stock and forend.

$200	$175	$150	$130	$115	$105	$95	

Add 50% for .410 bore, add 5% for 16 ga., and 10% for 20 ga.

FLITE-KING FIELD CATALOG NUMBERS - Series Barrel 30" Full 28" Full 28" Modified 26" Imp Cyl Date Range. 12 Ga K-100 Plain 8103 8100 8101 8102 1960-1965. 16 Ga K-160 Plain - 8300 8301 8302 1960-1965. 20 Ga K-200 Plain - 8400 8401 8402 1960-1965. .410 bore Plain - - - 8450 1962-1965.

FLITE-KING SPECIAL – 12, 16, or 20 ga., 2 3/4 (12 or 16 ga.) or 3 (20 ga.) in. chamber, 5 shot mag., blued finish, 27 in. barrel, 6 click adj. choke, walnut stock and forend.

$200	$175	$150	$130	$115	$105	$95	

Add 5% for 16 ga., or 10% for 20 ga.

K-100, K-10, 12 ga., catalog #8110 mfg. 1961-65. K-160, 16 ga., catalog #8310 mfg. 1961-64. K-200, 20 ga., catalog #8410 mfg. 1961-65.

FLITE-KING DELUXE – 12, 16, 20, 28 ga., or .410 bore, 2 3/4 (12, 16, 28 ga.) or 3 (20 ga. or .410 bore) chamber, blued finish, checkered walnut pistol grip stock and forearm, 5 shot mag., 6 click adj. choke, available with and without a vent rib, recoil pad beginning 1966 except .410 models.

$205	$185	$160	$140	$120	$100	$90	

Add 5% for 16 ga. or 10% for 20 ga.

GRADING - PPGS™	100%	98%	95%	90%	80%	70%	60%	LAST MSR

Add $20 for vent rib.
Add 50% for plain barrel in 28 ga. or .410 bore.
Add 70% for ribbed barrel in 28 ga. or .410 bore.
Add $25 for catalog numbers 6135-6142 with interchangeable barrels capability.

Catalog nos. 8411 and 6411 were the Converta Pump sold with two stocks - one youth sized and one adult size. The 12 ga. models with catalog nos. 6115 through 6142 are models with provisions for interchangeable barrels.

12 Ga Series Barrel 30" Full 28" Full Modified 26" Imp Cyl 27" Adj Date Range. K-100 Plain 8123 8120 8121 8122 1961-1962. K-100 Vent Rib 8127 8124 8125 8126 1961-1965. K-121/1221 Plain 8135 8132 8133 8134 8115 1966-1972. K-121/1221 Vent Rib 8136 8137 8138 6142 1973-1975. Late Plain 6135 6132 6133 6134 6115 1973-1975. Late Vent Rib 6136 6137 6138 6142 1973-1975. 16 Ga Series Barrel 28" Full 28" Modified 26" Imp Cyl Date Range. K-160 Plain 8320 8321 8322 1961-1962. K-160 Vent Rib 8324 8325 8326 1961-1965. 20 Ga Series Barrel 28" Full 28" Modified 26" Imp Cyl 27" Adj Date Range. K-200 Plain 8400 8401 8402 1961-1962

K-200 Vent Rib 8425 8426 8427 1961-1965. K-2011 Plain 8403 8404 8405 1966-1972. K-2011 Vent Rib 8429 8430 8443 8442 1966-1972. Late Plain 6403 6404 1973-1975. Late Vent 6429 6430 6443 6442 1973-1975. 28 Ga Series Barrel 26" Full 26" Modified Date Range. K-2800 Plain 8332 8333 1966-1972. K-2800 Vent Rib 8334 8335 1966-1972. Late Plain 6332 6333 1973-1975. Late Vent Rib 6334 6335 1973-1975. .410 Bore Series Barrel 26" Full 26" Skeet Date Range. K-4111 Vent Rib 8451 8452 1963-1965. Plain Vent Rib K-4111 Plain 8453 8454 1966-1972. Late 26" Full 6453 6454 1973-1975.

MODEL 200 – 12 ga., also sold as part of a promotional package beginning in 1971, which included the Model 200, a zippered gun case, a plastic trigger lock, and G-96 gun lubricant.

	100%	98%	95%	90%	80%	70%	60%	LAST MSR
	$175	$160	$140	$120	$105	$95	$90	

Add $20 premium for entire promotional package in original box.

FLITE-KING CITATION – 12 or 16 ga., 2 3/4 in. chamber, similar to Flite-King Trophy, except does not have vent rib.

	100%	98%	95%	90%	80%	70%	60%	LAST MSR
	$210	$195	$175	$150	$120	$100	$90	

Add 5% for 16 ga.

Catalog #8130 has a compensator integral with the adjustable choke. K-100, 12 ga., 26 1/2 in. barrel, 6 click stop adjustable,catalog #8130 mfg. 1960. K-10, 12 ga., 27 in. barrel, 6 click stop adjustable, catalog #8131 mfg. 1961-62. K-160, 16 ga., 27 in. barrel, 6 click stop adjustable, catalog #8331 mfg. 1961-62.

FLITE-KING TROPHY – 12, 16, or 20 ga., 2 3/4 (12 or 16 ga.) or 3 (20 ga.) in. chamber, blued finish, walnut stock and forend, 5 shot mag, vent. rib.

	100%	98%	95%	90%	80%	70%	60%	LAST MSR
	$220	$210	$180	$160	$130	$110	$100	

Add 5% for 16 ga. or 10% for 20 ga.

Catalog #8140 has a compensator integral with the adjustable choke. K-100, 12 ga., 26 1/2 in. barrel, 6 click stop adjustable, vent rib, catalog #8140, mfg. 1960. K-10, 12 ga., 27 in. barrel, 6 click stop adjustable, vent rib, catalog #8141, mfg. 1961-65. K-160, 16 ga., 27 in. barrel, 6 click stop adjustable, vent rib, catalog #8341, mfg. 1961-64. K-200, 20 ga., 27 in. barrel, 6 click stop adjustable, vent rib., catalog #8441, mfg. 1962-65.

FLITE-KING BRUSH – 12, ga., 2 3/4 in. chamber, similar to the Flite-King Field, except has adjustable rifle sights, receiver is tapped for the Williams sight and provisions exist for sling swivels, deluxe models have Williams receiver sight, a leather sling and a recoil pad.

	100%	98%	95%	90%	80%	70%	60%	LAST MSR
	$325	$275	$250	$225	$135	$100	$90	

Add $10 for deluxe model.
Add $25 for catalog no. 6166 with interchangeable barrel capability.

K-102, K-101, 12 ga., 20 in. barrel, cylinder bore, catalog #8105 mfg. 1962-65. K-102, 12 ga., 20 in. barrel, Cylinder Bore Deluxe, catalog #8106 mfg. 1964-65. K-101, 12 ga., 26 in. barrel, Cylinder Bore, catalog #8107 mfg. 1962-63. K-102, 12 ga., 26 in. barrel, Cylinder Bore Deluxe, catalog #8108 mfg. 1964-65. K-102, 12 ga., 18 in. barrel, Cylinder Bore, catalog #8109 mfg. 1964-65. K-120, K-1200, 12 ga., 20 in. barrel, Cylinder Bore, catalog #8116 mfg. 1966 - 1972. K-120, K-1200, 12 ga., 20 in. barrel, Cylinder Bore Deluxe, catalog #8117 mfg. 1966 - 1972. 12 ga., 20 in. barrel, Improved Cylinder, catalog #6116 mfg. 1973-75.

GRADING - PPGS™	100%	98%	95%	90%	80%	70%	60%	LAST MSR

FLITE-KING SKEET – 12, 20, 28 ga. or .410 bore, 2 3/4 (12 or 28 ga.) or 3 (20 ga. or .410 bore) in. chamber, similar to Flite-King Deluxe except has select American walnut stock and forearm and no recoil pad.

	$290	$260	$230	$185	$150	$120	$100	

Add 50% for 28 ga. or .410 bore.

Add 10% for 20 ga.

Cat #6164 is a model with provisions for interchangeable barrels - add $25. K-10, 12 ga., 26 in. barrel, Skeet Bore, Vent Rib, catalog #8160, mfg. 1962-63. 12 ga., 26 in. barrel, Skeet Bore, Vent Rib, catalog #8162, mfg. 1964-65. K-121, K-1211, 12 ga., 26 in. barrel, Skeet Bore, Vent Rib, catalog # 8164, mfg. 1966 - 1972. 12 ga., 26 in. barrel, Skeet Bore, catalog #6164, mfg. 1973-75, K-200, 20 ga., 26 in. barrel, Skeet Bore, catalog #8428, mfg. 1964-65. K-2011, 20 ga., 26 in. barrel, Skeet Bore, catalog #8431, mfg. 1966 -1972. 20 ga., 26 in. barrel, Skeet Bore, catalog #6431, mfg. 1973-75. K-2800, 28 ga., 26 in. barrel, Skeet Bore, catalog #8336, mfg. 1968 - 1972.28 ga., 26 in. barrel, Skeet Bore, catalog #6336, mfg. 1973. .410 bore , 26 in. barrel, Skeet Bore, catalog #8452, mfg. 1964 -65. K-4111, .410 bore, 26 in. barrel, Skeet Bore, catalog #8455, mfg. 1968 - 1972. .410 bore, 26 in. barrel, Skeet Bore, catalog #6455, mfg. 1973.

FLITE-KING TRAP – 12 ga., 2 3/4 in. chamber, similar to Flite-King Deluxe, except has select American Walnut stock and forearm and recoil pad, 30 in. barrel.

	$275	$225	$195	$175	$150	$130	$110	

Add $25 for Fajen Monte Carlo stock.

Cat. #8166 is the Executive trap model with Fajen Monte Carlo stock. Add $25 for Cat. #6165 - a model with provisions for interchangeable barrels. K-10, 12 ga., 30 in. barrel, Full Choke, Vent Rib, catalog #8161, mfg. 1962-63. 12 ga., 30 in. barrel, Full Choke, Vent Rib, catalog #8163, mfg. 1964-65. K-121, K-1211, 12 ga. 30 in. barrel, Full Choke, Vent Rib, catalog #8165, mfg. 1966 - 1972. 12 ga. , 30 in. barrel, Full Choke, Vent Rib, catalog #8166, mfg. 1970-71. 12 ga., 30 in. barrel, Full Choke, Vent Rib, catalog #6165, mfg. 1973-75.

SHOTGUNS: IMPORTED

SUPERMATIC SHADOW INDY O/U – 12 ga., boxlock, selective auto ejectors, single trigger, fully engraved receiver, skipline checkered walnut stock with pistol grip, vent. forearm, recoil pad, special "Airflow" rib. Imported from Nikko in Japan.

	$860	$820	$770	$720	$625	$550	$500	

12 ga., 2 3/4 in., 271/2 in. barrel, Skeet / Skeet Choke, catalog #54230, imported 1974-75. 12 ga., 2 3/4 in., 29 3/4 in. barrel, Full / Full Choke, catalog #54231, imported 1974-75. 12 ga., 2 3/4 in., 29 3/4 in. barrel, Imp.Mod / Full Choke, catalog #54232, imported 1974-75.

SUPERMATIC SHADOW SEVEN – similar to Shadow Indy, except has a standard size vent. rib, conventional forearm, no recoil pad, standard checkering, and less engraving. Imported from Nikko in Japan.

	$695	$660	$620	$575	$480	$430	$390	

12 ga., 2 3/4 in., 27 1/2 in. barrel, Skeet / Skeet Choke, catalog #54220, imported 1974-75. 12 ga., 2 3/4 in., 27 1/2 in. barrel, Mod./ Imp. Choke, catalog #54221, imported 1974-75. 12 ga., 2 3/4 in., 27 1/2 in. barrel, Full / Mod. Choke, catalog #54222, imported 1974-75. 12 ga., 2 3/4 in., 29 3/4 in. barrel, Full / Full Choke, catalog #54223, imported 1974-75. 12 ga., 2 3/4 in., 29 3/4 in. barrel, Imp. Mod./ Full Choke, catalog #54224, imported 1974-75.

SUPERMATIC SHADOW AUTOMATIC – 12 or 20 ga., semi-auto, gas operated, interchangeable barrels, checkered walnut stock and forearm, special "Airflow" rib. Imported from Nikko in Japan.

	$400	$370	$345	$270	$200	$175	$150	

12 ga., 2 3/4 in., 28 in. barrel, Imp. Mod. Choke, catalog #54200, imported 1974-75. 12 ga., 2 3/4 in., 28 in. barrel, Mod. Choke, catalog #54201, imported 1974-75. 12 ga., 2 3/4 in., 26 in. barrel, Skeet Choke, catalog #54203, imported 1974-75. 12 ga., 2 3/4 in., 28 in. barrel, Full Choke, catalog #54204, imported 1974-75. 12 ga., 2 3/4 in., 30 in. barrel, Full Choke, catalog #54205, imported 1974-75. 12 ga., 2 3/4 in., 30 in. barrel, Trap Choke, catalog #54206, imported 1974-75. 12 ga., 2 3/4 in., 30 in. barrel, Imp. Mod. Choke, catalog #54207, imported 1974-75. 20 ga., 3 in., 28 in. barrel, Imp. Mod. Choke, catalog #54210 , imported 1974-75. 20 ga., 3 in., 28 in. barrel, Mod. Choke, catalog #54211, imported 1974-75. 20 ga., 3 in., 26 in. barrel, Imp. Choke, catalog #54212, imported 1974-75. 20 ga., 3 in., 26 in. barrel,

GRADING - PPGS™	100%	98%	95%	90%	80%	70%	60%	LAST MSR

Skeet Choke, catalog #54213, imported 1974-75. 20 ga., 3 in., 28 in., barrel, Full Choke, catalog #54214, imported 1974-75.

SHOTGUNS: DEFENSE & LAW ENFORCEMENT

SEMI AUTOMATIC MODEL – 12 ga., 20 in. cylinder bore barrel, 4 shot mag., recoil pad walnut stock and forearm.

$325 $300 $275 $250 $225 $200 $150

C-1200, 12 ga., 20 in. barrel, cylinder bore, Riot 20-5, catalog #8294, mfg. 1969. C-1200, 12 ga., 20 in. barrel, cylinder bore, rifle sights, Riot 20-5, catalog #8295, mfg. 1969.

MODELS 10A/10B SEMI-AUTO – 12 ga., combat model, 18 in. barrel, semi-auto, unique bullpup design incorporates raked pistol grip in front of receiver and metal shoulder pad attached directly to rear of receiver, black cycolac plastic shroud and pistol grip, very compact size (28 in. overall). Disc.

* ***Model 10-A Semi-Auto*** – 4 shot mag., fixed carrying handle and integral flashlight. Between 1,700 and 1,800 were produced beginning 1967.

$875 $795 $725 $650 $575 $500 $425

12 ga., 18 in. barrel, cylinder bore, catalog #8290, mfg. 1967-69.

* ***Model 10-B Semi-Auto*** – 12 ga., folding carrying handle, provisions made for attaching a Kel-lite flashlight to receiver top, extended blade front sight, 4 shot mag., carrying case.

$850 $775 $715 $650 $575 $515 $450

Add 15% for flashlight.

Cat. No. 50284 optional carrying case and attachable flashlight; Cat. No. 50285 sold optionally. 12 ga., 18.13 in. barrel, cylinder bore, catalog #8291, mfg. 1970-77.

SLIDE ACTION RIOT SHOTGUN – 12 ga. only on the Flite King Action, 18 or 20 in. barrel, police riot gun, available with or w/o rifle sights, plain pistol grip oiled walnut stock & forearm, changed to walnut stained and lacquered birch in the mid-1970s.

$325 $275 $250 $200 $175 $125 $115

Catalog #8111/#8113 magazine capacity 6. # 8104/#8129 magazine capacity 5. A 1963 flyer mentions the #8105 Flite King Brush 20 in. and the #8107 Flite King Deluxe 20 in. as riot guns. The data on the #8105 and #8107 is listed under the Flite King Brush. K-101, K-120, K-1200, 12 ga., 20 in. barrel, cylinder bore, Riot 20-6, catalog #8104, mfg. 1963-1977. K-120, K-1200, 12 ga., 18 1/8 in. barrel, cylinder bore, Riot 18-7, catalog #8111, mfg. 1964-1978. K-120, K-1200,12 ga., 18 in. barrel, cylinder bore, rifle sights, Riot 18-7, catalog #8113, mfg. 1965-1978. K-120, 12 ga., 18 1/8 in. barrel, cylinder bore, rifle sights, Riot 18-6, catalog #8118, mfg. 1968. 12 ga., 20 in. barrel, cylinder bore, rifle sights, catalog #8129, mfg. 1976-77. K-102, 12 ga., 20 in. barrel, cylinder bore, catalog #8112, 1964-65. 12 ga., 18 in. barrel, cylinder bore, rifle sights, catalog #8128, mfg. 1976-77.

HIGH STANDARD MANUFACTURING CO.

High Standard is a current trademark of firearms manufactured by Firearms International Inc., established in 1993 and located in Houston, TX.

This company was formed during 1993, utilizing many of the same employees and original material vendors which the original High Standard company used during their period of manufacture (1926-1984). During 2004, Crusader Group Gun Company, Inc. was formed, and this new company includes the assets of High Standard Manufacturing Co, Firearms International Inc., AMT-Auto Mag, Interarms, and Arsenal Line Products.

PISTOLS: SEMI-AUTO, RIMFIRE

SPORT KING – .22 LR cal., 4 1/2 or 6 3/4 in. barrel, blue finish, military grips, fixed sights, 10 shot mag. Limited edition produced in small quantities.

MSR $835 $750 $665 $575 $500 $450 $395 $325

GRADING - PPGS™	100%	98%	95%	90%	80%	70%	60%	LAST MSR

PLINKER – .17 High Standard (advertised, but never mfg.) or .22 LR cal., same design as former Ram-Line pistol, 4, 6, or 8 in. barrel with adj. rear sight, uses many plastic materials, interchangeable barrels, 10 shot mag., 14 1/4 oz. Limited mfg. 2011 only.

	$450	$400	$350	$300	$250	$200	$175	*$495*

DURAMATIC PLINKER – .22 LR cal., 4 1/2 in. barrel, fixed sights, parkerized metal finish, black plastic grips, 10 shot mag., 44 oz. New 2013.

MSR $525	$450	$400	$365	4335	$300	$275	$250	

SUPERMATIC CITATION – .22 LR cal., 5 1/2 or 7 1/4 (disc. 1995) in. barrel, matte blue (disc. 1996) or parkerized finish, military grips, open sights (disc. 2001) or universal scope base, 9 shot mag., 44 oz. Mfg. 1994-2003.

	$415	$325	$260	$225	$200	$185	$170	*$490*

Add $317 for .22 Short conversion kit (includes barrel, slide, and 2 mags.).

SUPERMATIC CITATION MS – .17 High Standard (new 2003-disc.) or .22 LR cal., features 10 in. barrel, mounting bracket with scope base, designed for the Metallic Silhouette shooter, 54 oz. New 1997.

MSR $940	$825	$725	$575	$475	$375	$300	$275	

Add approx. $119 for RPM sights (scope base only, disc).

SUPERMATIC CITATION 10X – .22 LR cal., 5 1/2 in. barrel, blue finish, military grips, High Standard's most accurate pistol, choice of either factory or Shea custom tuning, 10 shot mag., approx. 45 oz., custom shop only. New 1994.

* ***Supermatic Citation 10X Factory Tuned***

MSR $1,275	$1,075	$950	$825	$700	$600	$500	$400	

* ***Supermatic Citation 10X Custom Shea*** – limited mfg. (approx. 150 pistols annually), hand-built by Bob Shea. New 1995.

MSR $1,490	$1,325	$1,125	$1,000	$850	$750	$650	$550	

SUPERMATIC TOURNAMENT – .22 LR cal., choice of 4 1/2 (disc. 1995), 5 1/2, or 6 3/4 (disc. 1995) in. barrel, matte blue, non-adj. trigger, approx. 44 oz. Mfg. 1995-97, reintroduced 2004 through the custom shop.

MSR $965	$850	$735	$625	$550	$475	$375	$300	

SUPERMATIC TROPHY – .17 High Standard (mfg. 2003-2009) or .22 LR cal., 5 1/2 or 7 1/4 in. barrel, blue finish, scope base became standard on 5 1/2 in. barrel in 2000, 2002 for 7 1/4 in. barrel, fixed (disc.) or adj. iron sights, military grips, 10 shot mag., 44 or 46 oz. New 1994.

MSR $905	$800	$700	$625	$550	$475	$375	$300	

Add $85 for 7 1/4 in. barrel.
Subtract approx. 10% if with fixed sights.
Add $450 for .22 Short conversion kit (includes barrel, slide, and 2 mags.). Disc.

VICTOR – .17 High Standard (mfg. 2003-2009) or .22 LR cal., 4 1/2 or 5 1/2 in. barrel, blue or parkerized (new 1995, 5 1/2 in. barrel only) finish, military grips, fixed (disc.) or adj. sights, or universal scope base mount (HSUM, blue only, new 1996, standard mfg. currently), 10 shot mag., approx. 45 oz., custom shop only. New 1994.

MSR $905	$795	$675	$585	$535	$450	$350	$275	

Add $85 for adj. sights and VR barrel.
Add $50 for open sights (5 1/2 in. barrel only, disc.).
Add $440 for .22 Short conversion kit (includes VR barrel, slide, and 2 mags.). Disc.

* ***Victor 10X*** – factory tuned and individually tested, includes test target signed by the gunsmith, 46 oz. New 1997.

MSR $1,375	$1,225	$1,075	$900	$800	$725	$625	$525	

* ***Victor 10X Shea*** – parkerized finish, 5 1/2 in. barrel only, 150 built by Bob Shea annually, 46 oz. New 1996.

MSR $1,605	$1,425	$1,150	$975	$850	$750	$650	$550	

GRADING - PPGS™	100%	98%	95%	90%	80%	70%	60%	LAST MSR

LIMITED EDITIONS - during 1996, High Standard offered several limited editions. They included the Victor (fully engraved, 6 mfg., $1,862 MSR), the Tournament (non-engraved, 26 mfg., $608 MSR), and the engraved Tournament (50% engraved, 6 mfg. $1,062 MSR). Additionally, only 5 sets were mfg. with 4 guns included - the Olympic 8 in. Space Gun, Tournament, Flite King, and Victor. Retail was $3,200 (non-engraved) or $7,200 (engraved). A 3 gun set was also available (w/o Olympic) for $2,150 (non-engraved) or $5,150 (engraved).

Extreme rarity of these guns precludes accurate pricing.

OLYMPIC I.S.U. – .22 Short cal., 6 3/4 in. fluted barrel with integral muzzle brake, blue finish, military grips, 10 shot mag. Mfg. 1994-95 only.

	$550	$450	$385	$315	$250	$200	$185	*$625*

OLYMPIC MILITARY – .22 Short cal., 5 1/2 in. fluted bull barrel with removable stabilizer, aluminum alloy slide with steel frame, scope base or open sights. New 1995.

MSR $1,010	$865	$700	$575	$450	$400	$350	$325	

Subtract approx. $60 if w/o open sights.

OLYMPIC RAPID FIRE – .22 Short cal., 4 in. VR barrel with integral muzzle brake and forward mounted compensator, gold-plated small parts, matte finish, special grips with rear support, adj. trigger, 46 oz., custom shop only. New 1996-2003.

	$925	$725	$625	$525	$425	$375	$325	*$1,027*

OLYMPIC TROPHY "SPACE GUN" – .22 LR cal., blue/black finish, updated version of 1960 Olympic gold medal pistol, 6 3/4, (disc. 2010) 8, or 10 in. barrel, 10 shot mag., checkered walnut grips with thumbrest, muzzle brake, 39 - 43 oz. New 2010.

MSR $1,275	$1,100	$975	$850	$725	$600	$500	$400	

RIFLES/CARBINES: SEMI-AUTO

HSA-15 – 5.56 NATO or 6x45mm (new 2012) cal., AR-15 style, A2 configuration, 16 (carbine), or 20 (rifle) in. barrel with muzzle brake, fixed (rifle) or collapsible (carbine) stock, 30 shot mag., with or w/o adj. sights.

MSR $925	$850	$750	$650	$575	$525	$475	$425	

Add $40 for adj. sights.
Subtract $72 for 6x45mm cal. (new 2012).

HSA-15 NATIONAL MATCH – 5.56 NATO cal., AR-15 style, available with either 20 in. (National Match) or 24 in. (Long Range Rifle) fluted barrel, includes Knight's military two-stage trigger. Mfg. 2006-2012.

	$1,125	$950	$850	$750	$650	$550	$495	*$1,238*

Add $12 for Long Range Rifle.

M-4 CARBINE – 5.56 NATO or 9mm Para. cal., 16 in. barrel, fixed A2 (.223 Rem. cal. only, new 2010) or six position adj. stock, fixed or adj. sights. New 2009.

MSR $880	$825	$725	$625	$550	$475	$400	$350	

Add $30 for 9mm Para. cal. (adj. stock only).
Add $35 for adj. sight (disc.).
Add $65 for quad rail with Picatinny gas block.
Add $450 for chrome lined barrel, free floating quad rails, flip up sights, flash hider and two-stage match trigger (.223 Rem. cal. only, disc. 2009).

M-4 ENFORCER CARBINE – 5.56 NATO cal., 16 in. barrel with A2 flash hider, Socom style six position collapsible stock, flip up battle sights, full length flat top receiver, YHM quad rail with smooth sides, ergo grip, 30 shot mag. New 2012.

MSR $2,275	$1,950	$1,700	$1,475	$1,250	$1,050	$875	$725	

HIGH TECH CUSTOM RIFLES

Current custom manufacturer of bolt action rifles located in Colorado Springs, CO.

RIFLES: BOLT ACTION, CUSTOM

High Tech Custom Rifles manufactures a complete line of custom built, high quality bolt action rifles, including the Shadow (base price $2,200), Shadow II, Falcon Series (base price $2,450),

Varmint Hunter (base price $2,200), Alaskan Pro Hunter (base price $2,800) and Mountain Hunter (base price $2,200). They also manufacture and install their own proprietary muzzle brake (60%-80% recoil reduction). Please contact the company directly for more information, including pricing, availability and a custom quotation (see Trademark Index).

HILL COUNTRY RIFLE COMPANY

Current manufacturer of bolt action rifles established in 1996, and located in New Braunfels, TX. Consumer direct sales.

RIFLES: BOLT ACTION

Hill Country Rifles currently manufactures a complete line of custom built, high quality bolt action rifles, including the Custom Sheep, (MSR - $4,295), Field Stalker (MSR - $4,295), Compact Sporter (MSR - $4,295), Tactical Rifle (MSR - $4,595), Safari Synthetic with Dakota 76 action (MSR - $5,995), Dangerous Game (MSR - $5,995), Genesis (MSR - $5,995), Long Range Hunter (MSR - $4,495), Harvester (MSR $1,995), Harvester Plus (MSR $2,995), Harvester Tactical (MSR - $2,495), Long Range Tactical (MSR - $5,995), and the Harvester Safari (MSR $4,595).

Previously manufactured models include Harvester Semi-Custom (MSR - $1,995), American Classic (POR), American Classic Dangerous Game (POR), Custom Hunter (last MSR - $2,495, disc. 2010), Custom Varmint (last MSR - $2,950, disc. 2010), Hill Country Classic (last MSR - $2,895, disc. 2010), Dangerous Game (last MSR - $5,400, disc. 2006), Semi-Custom (last MSR - $1,595, disc. 2006). All synthetic custom rifles are built on either a customer, or Hill Country provided action, and feature a McMillan synthetic stock. Hill Country Rifles also accurizes rifles and performs complete gunsmithing services. For current model availability, features, special orders, and pricing information (including a custom quotation and delivery time), please contact the factory directly (see Trademark Index).

HISPANO ARGENTINO FABRICADE AUTOMOVILES SA (HAFDASA)

Previous car manufacturer located in Buenos Aires, Argentina.

This company accepted and sold both commercial and military pistols manufactured by Ballester-Rigaud initially, followed by Ballester-Molina. Please refer to the Ballester-Molina listing.

GEORGE HOENIG, INC.

Current custom rifle builder located in Emmett, ID. Previously located in Boise, ID.

LONG GUNS

George Hoenig builds a unique patented rotary round action O/U rifle, shotgun, or combination gun. Opening is achieved by rotating barrels quarter turn to the right, then sliding barrel assembly forward. Because of this, there is no top opening lever. Standard features include double triggers, extractors, rotary safety on stock, and coin finished scroll engraved frame. Prices for a 20, 28 ga. or .410 bore game gun start at $22,500 (approx. 6-6 1/4 lbs., 12 month delivery time), while the double rifle (add $2,000 for mag. cals. up to .450 NE), approx. 7 1/3 - 8 1/3 lbs., and combination guns have a base price of $27,500. During 2009, George Hoenig introduced a four-barrel Vierling (20 ga.x20 ga., .223 Rem., and .22 LR barrels), which has a base price of $50,000. For more information, delivery time, and current pricing, please contact George Hoenig directly (see Trademark Index).

HOFER-JAGDWAFFEN, PETER

Current custom gun manufacturer and master gunsmith located in Ferlach, Austria.

Peter Hofer manufactures custom order only, best quality rifles (most configurations), combination guns, drillings, and shotguns (O/U and SxS), all made per individual order. Prices usually start in the $20,000 range, and can go up to over $600,000! Information (including an individualized quotation) can be obtained by contacting Mr. Hofer directly (see Trademark Index).

GRADING - PPGS™	100%	98%	95%	90%	80%	70%	60%	LAST MSR

HOGAN MANUFACTURING LLC

Current AR-15 style carbine/rifle manufacturer located in Glendale, AZ.

RIFLES: SEMI-AUTO

Hogan Manufacturing currently manufactures a H-223 series chambered for 5.56 NATO cal. in a variety of configurations. MSRs range from $1,699-$2,774. A H-308 series is also available in 7.62 NATO cal. MSRs currently range from $2,899-$3,249. Please contact the company directly for more information and availability (see Trademark Index).

P.L. HOLEHAN, INC.

Current custom rifle manufacturer located in Tucson, AZ. Consumer direct sales.

P.L. Holehan, Inc. is a custom rifle maker fabricating best quality bolt action rifles only. The company is also known for its integral return to zero scope mounting system. All guns are essentially built per individual custom order and the company should be contacted directly for more information, including special order options/features (see Trademark Index).

RIFLES: BOLT ACTION

SAFARI HUNTER – various Safari cals., features Win. M-70 controlled feed claw extractor, double square bridge action, premium grade barrel, satin blue metal finish, fiberglass (disc. 2005) or oil finished premium walnut stock with ebony forend tip, Pachmayr decelerator pad, hinged floor plate, 9 1/2 lbs.

MSR $14,250	$14,250	$11,750	$9,500	$7,250	$6,000	$5,000	$4,500

AFRICAN HUNTER – various Safari cals., similar to Safari Hunter, except features Dakota Magnum action, 10 1/4 lbs. New 2002.

MSR $14,950	$14,950	$12,000	$9,650	$7,500	$6,500	$5,500	$5,000

CLASSIC HUNTER – available in most popular non-Safari cals., walnut stock, hinged floor plate, standard or blind box mag., 7 1/2 - 8 lbs.

MSR $12,400	$12,400	$9,995	$8,750	$7,850	$6,750	$5,500	$4,500

LONG RANGE HUNTER – various cals., choice of short or long action, 26 in. fluted barrel, satin blue or matte Teflon metal finish, laminated stock, 8 3/4 lbs.

MSR $11,700	$11,700	$9,650	$8,650	$7,750	$6,750	$5,500	$4,500

LIGHTWEIGHT CLASSIC HUNTER – various cals., features short action, Win. M-70 controlled feed claw extractor, checkered walnut stock, customer choice of barrel weight and length, standard or blind box mag., 6 1/2 - 7 lbs.

MSR $12,250	$12,250	$9,850	$8,750	$7,800	$6,750	$5,500	$4,500

Add $1,550 for left hand.

ALPINE HUNTER – various cals., Win. M-70 short or standard length action with controlled feeding, blind box mag., fiberglass (disc.), Kevlar, or McMillian (new 2005) stock, approx. 6-6 3/4 lbs. New 2000.

MSR $6,500	$6,500	$5,900	$5,250	$4,500	$3,900	$3,300	$2,800

HOLLAND & HOLLAND LTD.

HOLLAND & HOLLAND
Established 1835

Current manufacturer established in 1835 and located in London, England since 1835, with gun showrooms currently located in New York City, NY, and London, England. The Paris, France location closed during 2007.

Holland & Holland over the years has justly earned the reputation of producing some of the finest firearms ever manufactured, exhibiting outstanding quality and superior craftsmanship. Most of these fine arms were made to order for the famous, wealthy, or royalty of their day. Because of the individual nature of each firearm, these early guns, as with any high grade item, must be individually appraised.

All H&H long guns are built per individual special order. Orders may be placed directly with the office in England (see Trademark Index).

GRADING - PPGS™	100%	98%	95%	90%	80%	70%	60%	LAST MSR

The early double rifles were proofed and regulated with the black powder ammunition of their day. These exposed hammer rifles were almost exclusively sold cased with accessories by Holland & Holland, and are seldom encountered today. Purchase of these as well as any high grade firearm should include trusted appraisal.

RIFLES: MODERN

During 2003, H&H released two new large proprietary cartridges. They are: .400 H&H Mag. Belted Rimless (400 grain bullet with 400 H&H headstamp), and .465 H&H Belted Rimless (480 grain bullet with 465 H&H headstamp).

All currently manufactured H&H rifles are priced in English pounds, and 98%-60% values are not included. All older and recently manufactured used rifles are priced in dollars.

ROOK RIFLE – .250, .295/.300, .360, .380 black powder cals., single shot, break-open action, various levels of embellishment - Royal Models were made but most Rook rifles were base models with few extra features. Disc.

Values today range from $1,000 (average condition, small cal.) to $3,000 (larger cal., engraving, better wood, perhaps cased).

BEST QUALITY MAGAZINE RIFLE – Mauser 98 (current mfg.) or Enfield (disc.) action, various cals., built per individual customer specifications, checkered French walnut stock available in traditional configuration or with Monte Carlo pattern.

*** *Best Quality Magazine Rifle Current Mfg.***

The current MSR on this model is £19,250.
Add £1,750 for calibers .375 H&H and greater.
Add £2,700 for full length carbine stock.
Add £1,250+ for deluxe grade walnut.
Add £2,700 for takedown.
The values listed represent the standard model without additional options or engraving (of which there are a wide array).

*** *Best Quality Magazine Rifle Older & Recent Mfg.***

	100%	98%	95%	90%	80%	70%	60%
	N/A	$17,750	$15,530	$14,025	$11,185	$9,230	$7,100

Subtract 25% for Enfield action.

DE LUXE MAGAZINE RIFLE – similar to Best Quality, except with deluxe grade walnut and various engraving options, very limited mfg.

There is no standard base price on this model - rather, individual options are custom ordered and are individually priced.

CENTENARY MAGAZINE RIFLE – .375 H&H cal., limited mfg. beginning 2011 to commemorate the 100th year of the .375 H&H caliber.

Please contact the company directly for more information, availability, and pricing on this limited commemorative model.

DOMINION GRADE NO. 2 MODEL DOUBLE RIFLE SxS – various British and American cals., 24-28 in. barrels, sidelock, folding leaf sight, checkered French walnut stock, auto ejectors.

	100%	98%	95%	90%	80%	70%	60%
	$22,500	$19,690	$16,875	$15,300	$12,375	$10,125	$7,875
.400-.500 cal.	$33,750	$28,500	$24,000	$21,000	$18,000	$15,000	$13,125
larger than .500 cal.	$45,000	$38,000	$32,000	$28,000	$24,000	$20,000	$17,500

Subtract 25% for extractors.

ROYAL DOUBLE SxS RIFLE - OLDER & RECENT MFG. – similar to No. 2, except has deluxe finish and more engraving.

	100%	98%	95%	90%	80%	70%	60%
.300 H&H cal. or less	N/A	N/A	$52,250	$44,000	$39,600	$33,000	$27,500
Up to .375 H&H cal.	N/A	N/A	$65,000	$55,000	$48,000	$40,000	$36,000
Up to .577 NE cal.	N/A	N/A	$92,500	$82,500	$72,500	$60,000	$55,000
.577NE-.600 NE cal.	N/A	N/A	$135,000	$115,000	$100,000	$85,000	$72,500

Add 50% for self-opening action.
Subtract 25% if w/o ejectors.
Subtract 25% if w/o reinforced action.

GRADING - PPGS™	100%	98%	95%	90%	80%	70%	60%	LAST MSR

ROYAL DE LUXE SxS RIFLE - CURRENT MFG. – same cals. as the Royal Double SxS, except also available in .700 H&H cal., top-of-the-line model, every refinement, 22-26 in. chopper lump barrels, traditional royal scroll engraving, color case hardened frame or bright finish, built to individual order only with almost any option possible, includes aluminum travel case, 8 3/4 - 15 lbs.

* ***Royal De Luxe - .240 H&H, 7mm, or 8mm cal.***

Current MSR on this model is £78,500.

* ***Royal De Luxe - .275 H&H (disc.), .300 H&H, or 9.3mm cal.***

Current MSR on this model is £81,500.

* ***Royal De Luxe - .375 H&H or .500/.465 H&H cal.***

Current MSR on this model is £87,500.

* ***Royal De Luxe - .577 NE or .600 NE cal.***

Current MSR on this model is £96,000.

H&H .700 BORE SxS DOUBLE RIFLE – .700 H&H cal., 3 1/2 in. chambers, 1,000 grain jacketed bullet, approx. 19 lbs. with 26 in. barrels. This is the largest caliber rifle available in the world today.

* ***SxS Double Rifle Royal Model*** – this model is not currently mfg. 1997 retail was $115,920.

* ***SxS Double Rifle Royal De Luxe Model***

Current MSR on this model is £138,000.

ROUND ACTION SIDELOCK SxS DOUBLE RIFLE – available in standard flanged cals., rounded back action sidelock with DT, 24 in. chopper lump barrels, English rose and fine scroll and border engraving, color case hardened or bright finish frame, 8-10 3/4 lbs. New 2004.

Current MSR on this model is £50,000.

SHOTGUNS: O/U

All currently manufactured H&H shotguns are priced in English pounds, and 98%-60% values are not included. All older and recently manufactured used rifles are priced in dollars.

ROYAL OLD MODEL – 12 ga., customer specifications as to barrel length and choke, hand detachable sidelocks, auto ejectors, checkered straight grip stock. Mfg. until 1951. Very rare, very few mfg., but not nearly as desirable as newer model.

100%	98%	95%	90%	80%	70%	60%
$37,500	$32,000	$28,000	$23,500	$20,000	$18,000	$16,500

Add 5% for single trigger.

ROYAL NEW MODEL – similar to Old Model, with improved narrow action. Mfg. until 1960, fewer than 30 mfg.

100%	98%	95%	90%	80%	70%	60%
$36,000	$31,000	$27,000	$22,500	$19,000	$17,000	$15,500

ROYAL SIDELOCK GAME GUN – 12, 20, 28 (new 1997) ga., or .410 bore (new 1997), somewhat similar to New Model, with improved cocking, striking and ejection, slimmer action body, DT, 25 to 30 in. game or VR barrels, 2 3/4 in. chambers, finest checkered walnut straight hand or pistol grip stock, scroll engraved receiver with color case hardened or bright finish, prototype testing has finished and guns are available for demonstration, includes aluminum case, 5 lbs. 1 oz - 7 lbs. 8 oz. Written quotations on this re-released model are available by contacting H&H directly (see Trademark Index). Values listed are for base models only and reflect the most recent factory information.

* ***Royal Sidelock Game Gun 12 or 20 ga.***

Current MSR on this model is £63,500.
Add £3,200 for 28 ga. or .410 bore.
Add £1,500 for inertia type single trigger.
Add £12,700 per extra set of barrels.

ROYAL DE LUXE MODEL – similar to Royal Sidelock Game Gun, except choice of more elaborate engraving and exhibition wood.

This model is quoted per individual special order only.

GRADING - PPGS™	100%	98%	95%	90%	80%	70%	60%	LAST MSR

SPORTING MODEL – 12, 16, 20, or 28 ga., 2 3/4 or 3 in. chambers, designed with a trigger plate action, Game or Sporting Clays configuration featuring detachable SST mechanism, 25 to 32 in. game or VR barrels, medium scroll engraving, bright finish only. Options on specifications to include screw-in chokes, 12 ga. - 7 1/4-8 lbs., 28 ga. - 6 lbs. New 1993. Values listed reflect most recent factory information.

Current MSR on this model is £42,500
Add £1,250 for color case hardened action with gold name inlay.
Add £9,600 per extra set of barrels.

SPORTING DE LUXE MODEL – similar to Sporting O/U Model, except with choice of more elaborate engraving and exhibition wood. New 1993.

This model is quoted per individual special order only.

SHOTGUNS: SxS

Holland & Holland currently manufactures the Royal De Luxe Game Gun and Royal Game Gun (limited mfg.) models in sidelock configuration. In addition to the sidelock models, H&H also manufactured the boxlock models Cavalier, Cavalier De Luxe, Northwood, and Northwood De Luxe until recently. The following values assume standard model with double triggers, game rib, standard walnut, or casing. Additional special order features will add considerable value to the price of a new custom order.

In 1988, Holland & Holland absorbed W & C Scott and manufactured the Chatsworth, Bowood, and Kinmount boxlock models until they were discontinued in late 1990. H&H has phased this trademark out, and more information can be found in the W & C Scott section of this text.

All currently manufactured H&H shotguns are priced in English pounds, and 98%-60% values are not included. All older and recently manufactured used rifles are priced in dollars.

NORTHWOOD SxS BOXLOCK – 12, 16 (disc. 1992), 20, or 28 (disc. 1992) ga., 28 or 30 in. barrels, scalloped-case colored receiver, boxlock, auto ejectors, double triggers, border engraving, checkered pistol grip or straight stock. The values shown are for standard model. Disc. 1993.

$5,950	$5,200	$4,450	$3,850	$3,300	$2,800	$2,300	*$6,705*

Add approx. 10% for 20 ga.
Add approx. 20% for 28 ga.

* ***Northwood SxS Boxlock De Luxe*** – 12, 16, 20, or 28 ga., scalloped-case colored receiver with moderate engraving and select walnut, double triggers. Disc. 1993.

$6,950	$5,950	$5,000	$4,250	$3,500	$3,000	$2,500	*$7,450*

Add approx. 10% for 20 ga.
Add approx. 20% for 28 ga.

CAVALIER SxS BOXLOCK – 12, 20, or 28 (disc. 1992) ga., best quality model boxlock with scalloped frame, double triggers, ejectors, and case colored receiver. Disc.

$9,500	$7,750	$6,350	$5,500	$4,850	$4,100	$3,500	*$11,175*

Add approx. 10% for 20 ga.
Add approx. 20% for 28 ga.

* ***Cavalier SxS Boxlock De Luxe*** – similar to Cavalier Model, except has deluxe walnut and better engraving. Disc. 1993.

$9,950	$8,000	$6,500	$5,600	$4,950	$4,200	$3,600	*$11,920*

Add approx. 10% for 20 ga.
Add approx. 20% for 28 ga.

DOMINION GAME GUN – 12, 16, or 20 ga., 25-30 in. barrels, any choke, sidelock, auto ejectors, double triggers, checkered straight grip stock. Disc. 1990.

$6,750	$6,150	$5,650	$4,750	$4,150	$3,650	$3,250

Add 50% for 20 gauge.
Add 100% ejector sidelock model with 2 in. chamber.

GRADING - PPGS™	100%	98%	95%	90%	80%	70%	60%	LAST MSR

ROUND ACTION SIDELOCK – 12 or 20 ga., 2 3/4 in. chambers, rounded frame with back action sidelock, DT, 25-30 in. chopper lump barrels with game rib, scroll and border engraving, color case hardened or bright finish. New 2004.

Current MSR on this model is £42,500.

ROUND ACTION SIDELOCK PARADOX – 12 ga., 2 3/4 or 3 in. chambers, rounded back action sidelock design, DT, 28 in. chopper lump barrels with paradox rifled chokes, two-leaf folding rear sight regulated for 50 and 100 yards, bright or case colored finish, approx. 7 1/4 or 8 lbs. New 2005.

Current MSR on this model is £42,000.

ROYAL HAMMERLESS EJECTOR SIDELOCK (OLDER & RECENT MFG.) – 12, 16, 20, 28 ga., or .410 bore, non-self (disc.) or self-opening (recent mfg.), customer specifications as to barrel length and chokes, hand detachable sidelocks, stocked in pistol grip or straight style to specifications. Mfg. 1885-disc.

	100%	98%	95%	90%	80%	70%	60%	LAST MSR
12 ga.	N/A	$42,500	$37,500	$32,500	$27,750	$25,000	$23,000	
20 ga.	N/A	$50,000	$45,000	$40,000	$36,000	$33,000	$30,000	
28 ga.	N/A	$70,000	$65,000	$60,000	$55,000	$50,000	$45,000	
.410 bore	N/A	$85,000	$75,000	$65,000	$60,000	$57,500	$51,000	

Add 15% for self-opening action.
Add 10%-15% if cased with accessories.
Subtract approx. 10%-15% on 12 ga. with 2 1/2 in. chambers.

Values listed are for older, previously manufactured specimens.

ROYAL GAME GUN (CURRENT MFG.) – 12, 16, 20, 28 ga., or .410 bore, best quality sidelock self-opening game gun. Mfg. per individual customer specifications, includes aluminum travel case, 4 3/4 - 10 3/4 (12 ga.) lbs. The following values reflect most recent factory information. Mfg. 1922 to date.

* ***Royal Game Gun (Current Mfg.) 12, 16, or 20 ga.***

Current MSR on this model is £52,500.
Add £2,500 for 28 ga. or .410 bore.
Add £1,500 (inertia type) or £4,100 (mechanical type) for ST.
Add £10,800 per extra set of barrels.
Add $3,100 for VR (disc.).

ROYAL DE LUXE GAME GUN – 12, 16, 20, 28 ga., or .410 bore, top-of-the-line sidelock self-opening shotgun. Mfg. per individual customer specifications. Current production.

This model is quoted per individual special order only.
Older mfg. is sometimes referred to as the De Luxe Model.

BADMINTON SIDELOCK – 12, 16, or 20 ga., similar to Royal model, except has traditional rose and scroll engraving and does not have self-opening action. Disc.

	100%	98%	95%	90%	80%	70%	60%	LAST MSR
12 or 16 ga.	N/A	$25,000	$22,000	$20,000	$18,000	$16,000	$14,000	
20 ga.	N/A	$34,500	$31,000	$28,000	$24,000	$22,000	$20,000	

Add $1,000 for SST.

* ***Badminton Sidelock Game Gun*** – 12 or 20 ga., double or single trigger. Disc. 1988.

	100%	98%	95%	90%	80%	70%	60%	LAST MSR
	N/A	$31,000	$27,000	$24,000	$21,000	$18,000	$16,000	*$28,000*

RIVIERA SIDELOCK – similar to Badminton model, with two sets of barrels. Mfg. until 1967.

	100%	98%	95%	90%	80%	70%	60%	LAST MSR
12 or 16 ga.	N/A	$31,000	$28,000	$25,000	$22,000	$19,000	$17,000	
20 ga.	N/A	$33,000	$29,500	$26,000	$23,000	$20,000	$18,000	

CENTENARY SIDELOCK – 12 ga., 2 in. chambers, lightened version of Royal, Badminton, and Dominion grades, mfg. until 1962.

Add 35% over standard 12 ga. chambered guns.

SHOTGUNS: SINGLE SHOT

SINGLE BARREL TRAP GUN – 12 ga., 30 or 32 in. full choke barrel, vent. rib, boxlock, auto ejector, Monte Carlo pistol grip stock, pad. Disc.

	100%	98%	95%	90%	80%	70%	60%	LAST MSR
	N/A	$9,250	$8,000	$6,750	$5,800	$4,750	$3,950	*$28,420*

GRADING - PPGS™	100%	98%	95%	90%	80%	70%	60%	LAST MSR
*** Single Barrel Trap Guns - Older Mfg.**								
Standard Grade	N/A	$4,500	$4,000	$3,250	$2,500	$2,250	$2,000	
De Luxe Grade	N/A	$7,000	$6,250	$5,000	$4,500	$3,750	$3,000	
Exhibition Grade	N/A	$8,950	$7,500	$6,000	$5,500	$5,000	$4,250	

HOLLENBECK GUN COMPANY

Previous manufacturer located in Wheeling, WV circa 1901-1903, and Moundsville, WV circa 1903-1910.

The Hollenbeck Gun Company began circa 1901, moved to Moundsville, WV in 1903 and stayed until they went out of business in 1910. The company name changed in 1905 to The Three Barrel Gun Company (circa 1905-1909), and then to The Royal Gun Company (circa 1909-1910). The company made a total of approx. 1,500 three barrel guns, as well as a few SxS models. After going out of business, an unknown Florida man bought the name and all the assets. He assembled and sold some three barrel guns as late as 1930.

Pricing on these three-barrel shotguns with unique, sculpted recoil shields in average original condition typically ranges from $950 - $1,500 for both damascus (most common) and steel barrels. There were two basic grades - 0 and 1, but there are also shotguns with more elaborate engraving which will command a premium.

Information appears courtesy of AntiqueGuns.com and the Gurnmeister.

HOLLOWAY & NAUGHTON GUNMAKERS

Current trade name of long guns manufactured since 1909 in Leicestershire, England. Consumer direct sales.

Founded by Thomas Naughton and G. O'Connor Holloway, Holloway & Co. manufactured traditional sidelock and boxlock shotguns, double and bolt action rifles in Birmingham. Naughton managed the company for approx. 15 years, when it was sold to H. Ludlow England, owner of Midland Gun Co. Naughton stayed on as manager, eventually buying back the company in early 1909, and changing the name to Holloway & Naughton. In 1911, the firm bought the name J.W. Tolley. Naughton died in 1921, and his son T.J. continued the business until the early 1950s.

Holloway & Naughton currently produces very high quality long guns, with many options, and a delivery time between 6 - 24 months. Please contact the factory directly (see Trademark Index) for more information including individual quotations. Holloway & Naughton makes 7-10 best quality, custom order only guns annually. They also perform all services, including engraving, in-house.

SHOTGUNS: CUSTOM

During 2010, Holloway & Naughton was comissioned to create a commemorative shotgun for the 38th Ryder Cup, held in Newport, South Wales. The gun was displayed during the golf tournament and was engraved by Welsh engraver Phil Coggan.

BLENHEIM TRIGGER PLATE O/U FIELD & SPORTING CLAYS MODELS – 12 or 20 ga., trigger plate action, 27-34 in. barrels with flush or extended proprietary chokes, choice of triggers & engraving, standard English scroll or individual customer specifications (extra charge), includes fitted canvas case. Delivery approx. 1 year. 10 year warranty.

Current MSRs on this model start at £29,000.

BRITANNIA SIDELOCK O/U FIELD & SPORTING CLAYS MODELS – 12 or 20 ga., sidelock action, 27-34 in. barrels with flush or extended proprietary chokes, choice of triggers & engraving: standard English scroll or individual customer specifications (extra charge), includes fitted leather case. Delivery time approx. 1 year. 10 year warranty.

Current MSRs for this model start at £55,000.

PREMIER SIDELOCK O/U MODEL – 12, 16, 20, 28 ga., or .410 bore, various Field grade models, choice of Holloway & Naughton lightweight case colored or coin finished action with reinforced forearm, exhibition grade stock standard, choice of engraving: traditional bouquet rose and scroll, or individual specifications (extra charge), chopper lump barrels

GRADING - PPGS™	100%	98%	95%	90%	80%	70%	60%	LAST MSR

range from 27 to 32 in., choice of fixed or multi-chokes, solid, graduated or parallel rib, including hand made fitted English toe-under leather case with accessories and tools, 7-7 1/2 lbs. Delivery for special orders 12-18 months approx. 10 year warranty.

Current MSRs for this model start at £67,000.

PREMIER SIDELOCK SXS MODEL – 12, 16, 20, 28 ga. or .410 bore, Holloway & Naughton Beesley style action, available in Field/Game configurations, features lightweight case colored or coin finished action, exhibition grade stock standard, choice of Standard Engraving: traditional bouquet rose and scroll, or individual specifications (extra charge), barrels range from 27-31 in., choice of fixed or multi-chokes, solid, concave ribs, includes hand made fitted English toe-under leather case with accessories and tools, 6-7 lbs. Delivery for special orders approx. 12-18 months. 10 year warranty.

Current MSRs for this model start at £55,000.

HOLLOWAY ARMS CO.

Previous manufacturer located in Fort Worth, TX.

Holloway made very few rifles or carbines before operations ceased and existing specimens are scarce.

RIFLES: SEMI-AUTO

HAC MODEL 7 RIFLE – .308 Win. cal., gas operated semi-auto paramilitary design rifle, 20 in. barrel, adj. front and rear sights, 20 shot mag., side folding stock, right or left-hand action. Mfg. 1984-85 only.

$3,750	$3,350	$3,100	$2,800	$2,650	$2,350	$2,000	*$675*

* ***HAC Model 7C Rifle Carbine*** – 16 in. carbine, same general specifications as Model 7. Disc. 1985.

$3,750	$3,350	$3,100	$2,800	$2,650	$2,350	$2,000	*$675*

Also available from the manufacturer were the Models 7S and 7M (Sniper and Match models).

HOLMES FIREARMS

Previous manufacturer located in Wheeler, AR. Previously distributed by D.B. Distributing, Fayetteville, AR.

PISTOLS: SEMI-AUTO

These pistols were mfg. in very limited numbers, most were in prototype configuration and exhibit changes from gun to gun. These models were open bolt and subject to 1988 federal legislation regulations.

MP-83 – 9mm Para. or .45 ACP cal., paramilitary design pistol, 6 in. barrel, walnut stock and forearm, blue finish, 3 1/2 lbs.

$700	$600	$500	$450	$400	$375	$350	*$450*

Add 10% for deluxe package.
Add 40% for conversion kit (mfg. 1985 only).

MP-22 – .22 LR cal., 2 1/2 lbs., steel and aluminum construction, 6 in. barrel, similar appearance to MP-83. Mfg. 1985 only.

$395	$360	$320	$285	$250	$230	$210	*$400*

SHOTGUNS

COMBAT 12 – 12 ga., riot configuration, cylinder bore barrel. Disc. 1983.

$795	$720	$650	$595	$550	$500	$450	*$750*

HOPKINS & ALLEN ARMS COMPANY, 1902-1914

Previous manufacturer located in Norwich, CT. H&A started their firearms business in 1867, manufacturing percussion revolvers.

Before 1870, they were producing rimfire cartridge guns and eventually centerfire handguns and long guns. Prior to 1896, H&A guns were marked "HOPKINS & ALLEN MANUFG. CO. NORWICH CONN." or other private trade names, including Merwin, Hulbert & Company. Hopkins & Allen guns are about equally priced with Stevens, N.R. Davis,

GRADING - PPGS™	100%	98%	95%	90%	80%	70%	60%	LAST MSR

Crescent Firearms Co., etc. There are many exceptions due to the numerous limited production guns, examples of which are the AA GRADE double shotgun and the "PARROT BEAK" Derringer. Hopkins & Allen also manufactured firearms which were not described in their catalogs. Compiled from Hopkins & Allen catalogs by Charles E. Carder.

HANDGUNS

Most H&A handguns were nickel plated, with blue finish originally costing $.50 extra, grips were hard rubber, wood or pearl. Some had engraving from low to very good quality. Revolver barrel lengths varied from 1 3/4-6 in. Calibers were .22 rimfire (.22 S, L, or LR) up to .38-40 WCF. Specific calibers have not been listed in this section.

FOREHAND MODEL TOP BREAK – .32 cal., top break, double action, five shot.

$190 $160 $140 $120 $100 $85 $75

FOREHAND MODEL TOP BREAK HAMMERLESS – similar to above except hammerless. (This model was offered in large and small frame).

$190 $160 $140 $120 $100 $85 $75

FOREHAND MODEL LARGE FRAME W/FULL HAMMER – large frame as above in .32 and .38 centerfire cal. with full hammer or "bobbed" hammer.

$190 $160 $140 $120 $100 $85 $75

FOREHAND MODEL SOLID FRAME – solid frame and hard rubber grips, otherwise as above in small frame.

$170 $140 $120 $100 $85 $75 $65

FOREHAND MODEL FOLDING HAMMER – similar to above models, with "folding hammer." .22 rimfires were seven shot, while .32 and .38 centerfires were five shot. By 1909, the Forehand logo was dropped from these revolvers.

$295 $265 $235 $195 $170 $150 $130

H&A NEW MODEL AUTOMATIC HAMMER REVOLVER – similar to top break with hammer, produced in small and large frame, in .22 rimfire, .32 and .38 centerfire cal.

$170 $140 $120 $100 $85 $75 $65

H&A SOLID FRAME – .32 and .38 centerfire cal., five shot, double action, hammer or "bobbed" hammer.

$175 $140 $120 $100 $85 $70 $55

H&A XL MODEL – similar to above in .22, .32 and .38 cal.

$160 $140 $120 $100 $85 $70 $55

H&A RANGE MODEL – .22, .32 and .38 cal., solid frame, loading gate on right side, wood target style grips, single or double action (two models, large and small frames).

$200 $175 $140 $120 $100 $85 $70

H&A TRIPLE ACTION SAFETY POLICE REVOLVER – .22, .32 and .38 cal., top break with newly designed locking mechanism, hard rubber or pearl grips (considered to be one of the best designed breaktops in its time). Other options for this model included hammerless, engraved, and wood target or pearl grips.

$375 $340 $310 $275 $235 $200 $185

H&A NEW VEST POCKET DERRINGER – .22 Short rimfire cal., single shot, tip up, single action, 3 1/2 in. overall length, folding trigger, blue or nickel finish, wood or pearl grips with golden monograms. This model was first listed about 1910 and known as the "Parrot Beak." It is estimated that less than one thousand were produced, and they are very rare.

$2,375 $2,100 $1,800 $1,550 $1,250 $950 $650

H&A NEW MODEL TARGET PISTOL – .22 rimfire cal., single shot top break with the same new locking mechanism as the Safety Police Revolver, wood target grips with golden monograms, blue finish and 6, 8, or 10 in. barrels.

$565 $495 $440 $375 $325 $285 $250

GRADING - PPGS™	100%	98%	95%	90%	80%	70%	60%	LAST MSR

H&A NEW MODEL SKELETON STOCK TARGET PISTOL – similar to above, with rounded hard rubber grips with logo, detachable "skeleton metal stock", 18 in. barrel, and blue finish.

	$850	$775	$675	$600	$550	$500	$465

RIFLES

Hopkins & Allen started building "falling block" rifles circa 1887-1914 with the buy-out of the Baystate Arms Company. Most commonly seen is the "Junior" model, known after 1902 as 922, 925, and 932. These numbers were in reference to the catalog numbers, not model numbers. In the very late 1890s or early 1900s, the Number 722, 822, and 832 rifles were added. In 1906, a "bolt action" repeater was added to their line, followed in 1909 by a "bolt action" single shot "military". Specific calibers have not been listed in this section.

Add $60-$75 for Lyman tang sights on the following models.

NUMBER 922 – .22 cal. rimfire, round barrel, falling block, lever operated.

	$310	$245	$195	$195	$165	$125	$110

NUMBER 925 – similar to above in .25 cal. rimfire.

	$390	$310	$245	$195	$150	$110	$95

NUMBER 932 – similar to above in .32 cal. rimfire.

	$310	$245	$195	$150	$110	$95	$80

NUMBER 938 – similar to above in .38 S&W centerfire.

	$440	$350	$285	$225	$200	$175	$150

NUMBER 1922 – similar to above in .22 cal. rimfire with octagon bbl.

	$310	$250	$200	$180	$165	$150	$125

NUMBER 1932 – similar to above in .32 cal. rimfire.

	$310	$250	$200	$165	$125	$110	$90

NUMBER 2922 – similar to above in .22 cal. rimfire, with checkering.

	$420	$335	$265	$225	$195	$175	$150

NUMBER 2932 – similar to above in .32 cal. rimfire.

	$420	$335	$265	$225	$195	$175	$150

NUMBER 3922 – similar to above in .22 cal. rimfire, "SCHUETZEN RIFLE", nickeled Swiss buttplate, octagon barrel (Schuetzen rifles in good cond. are somewhat rare).

	$775	$620	$495	$450	$400	$365	$325

NUMBER 3925 – similar to above in .25-20 WCF (this caliber rifle is more rare than the .22 cal. rimfire).

	$1,010	$810	$650	$600	$550	$500	$450

NUMBER 44XL – chambered for the .44XL shotshell, similar to Number 922, except has smooth bore (referred to as "TAXIDERMIST'S" or "LADIES GUN").

	$530	$430	$350	$325	$275	$235	$200

NUMBER 722 – .22 cal. rimfire, rolling block, thumb operated.

	$300	$240	$195	$165	$125	$110	$90

SCOUT MILITARY RIFLE – similar to above with military style stock and with a "Bonneted Indian" stamped on the left side of frame (these are somewhat rare).

	$505	$405	$325	$285	$250	$200	$175

NUMBER 822 – .22 cal. rimfire, rolling block, lever operated.

	$300	$240	$195	$175	$150	$125	$100

NUMBER 832 – .32 cal. rimfire, otherwise similar to Model 822 (this model was offered first with "pig tail" type levers and later with "loop" type levers. The "loop" levers are somewhat rare).

	$350	$280	$225	$200	$175	$150	$125

GRADING - PPGS™	100%	98%	95%	90%	80%	70%	60%	LAST MSR

NUMBER 4922 – .22 rimfire cal., bolt action, repeater.

	$260	$205	$165	$135	$120	$100	$80

NUMBER 5022 – similar to above with deluxe checkering.

	$340	$270	$215	$175	$150	$135	$100

MILITARY RIFLE – similar to above, except single shot with military style stock and sling (in good condition, these are somewhat rare).

	$490	$395	$315	$250	$225	$200	$185

NOISELESS – .22 rimfire, similar to the Number 922, except for checkered wood and the addition of a noise suppressor attached to the muzzle, by means of mating threads inside of suppressor and outside of barrel. The machining/threading is so precise that it is difficult to recognize the suppressor. The front sight is attached to a dovetail slot in the suppressor. These rifles are listed under the National Firearms Act of 1934 and must have proper licensing. Very rare.

	$690	$625	$575	$500	$450	$395	$325

SHOTGUNS: SxS

Hopkins & Allen purchased Forehand Arms Co. and W.H. Davenport and continued to produce their line of firearms, and after a few years dropped the Forehand name. In 1902, they offered the Forehand double boxlocks with or without outside hammers. Most models were offered in 12, 16 & 20 gauge. Sidelocks were added 1906-09. In 1902, the AA GRADE, a very high quality boxlock, was offered for $100 to $125. It had fine damascus barrels, straight grip, plain or automatic ejectors, fine wood, and engraving, and was competitive with some Remingtons, L.C. Smiths, Bakers and other fine guns of that era. This gun was very short lived and today is rare. One feature found on all H&A double barrel guns is the "rib extension" or "doll's head."

BOXLOCK – Anson & Deeley type frame, damascus, twist, and steel barrels.

	$315	$275	$235	$195	$160	$130	$95

BOXLOCK – similar to above, except with outside hammers.

	$315	$275	$235	$195	$160	$130	$95

SIDELOCK – hammerless, damascus, twist, and steel barrels.

	$315	$275	$235	$195	$160	$130	$115

SIDELOCK – similar to above, except with outside hammers.

	$315	$275	$235	$195	$160	$130	$95

SHOTGUNS: SINGLE SHOT

H&A produced a "falling block" shotgun in most gauges circa 1887-early 1900s. Falling Blocks (FBs) in 12 ga. were built on heavy frames with the 20 and 16 gauges sharing a medium frame. Prior to 1902, some FBs were chambered for .45-70 shotshells and, today, these are rare if in good condition. From the 1890s through 1914, 38XL, 44XL shotshell guns were periodically offered in the Junior frame. After 1902, "tip-over" single shotguns were offered in Forehand designs and, later, the Davenport designs.

FALLING BLOCK – lever operated, outside hammer.

	$275	$235	$210	$180	$160	$145	$125

BOXLOCK – with outside hammer, damascus, twist, and steel barrels.

	$190	$170	$150	$130	$110	$95	$80

BOXLOCK – hammerless, top safety.

	$190	$170	$150	$130	$110	$95	$80

GOOSE GUNS – outside hammer, 8, 10, or 12 ga., were offered with barrels up to 40 inches long.

	$250	$225	$190	$170	$150	$135	$115

GRADING - PPGS™	100%	98%	95%	90%	80%	70%	60%	LAST MSR

"SAFETY SINGLE GUN" – engraved with outside hammer and top safety. Was offered in 1911 and recommended for trap shooting for $15.00.

	$250	$225	$195	$175	$155	$140	$125	

HORTON, LEW, DIST. CO.

See Lew Horton Dist. Co. listing in the L section.

HOULDING PRECISION FIREARMS

Current AR-15 style manufacturer located in Madera, CA.

RIFLES: SEMI-AUTO

Houlding Precision Firearms currently manufactures the HPF-15 Series in various configurations. Please contact the company directly for more information, pricing, and availability (see Trademark Index).

HOWA

Current manufacturer established in 1967, and located in Tokyo, Japan. Howa sporting rifles are currently imported beginning Oct., 1999 by Legacy Sports International, LLC, located in Reno, NV. Previously located in Alexandria, VA. Previously imported until 1999 by Interarms/Howa, located in Alexandria, VA, Weatherby (Vanguard Series only), Smith & Wesson (pre-1985), and Mossberg (1986-1987).

RIFLES: BOLT ACTION

Howa also manufactures barreled actions in various configurations. MSRs range from $476-$596. During mid-2011, detachable magazines became available for all Model 1500s.

MODEL 1500 HUNTER – various cals., 3 (Mag. or WSM cals. only) or 5 shot, 22 or 24 in. barrel, adj. rear sight and trigger, checkered walnut stock, blue metal finish or stainless steel (new 1999) construction, approx. 7.6 lbs. Imported by Interarms 1988 only, reintroduced by Legacy 1999-2006.

	$460	$400	$345	$310	$255	$205	$160	*$574*

Add $21 for Mag. cals.
Add $108 for stainless steel.

MODEL 1500+/1500 LIGHTNING – various cals., lightweight variation of the Model 1500 Hunter featuring heavy (new 2007) or lightweight regular or Carbolite (disc.) black synthetic stock with cheekpiece and pressed checkering or Realtree camo (new 2005), 22 or 24 in. barrel, no sights, 3 or 5 shot mag., blue or stainless steel, approx. 7-7.6 lbs. Imported 1988-1991, reimported 1993-2008.

	$435	$380	$325	$295	$240	$195	$150	*$506*

Add $21 for standard Mag. cals. or $27 for WSM cals.
Add $187 for camo stock and stainless steel barrel.
Add $77 for camo stock (scope not included).
Add $99 for heavy blue barrel w/camo stock.
Add $223 for heavy stainless barrel w/camo stock.
Add $156 for scope package with Leupold VX-I scope.

The Model 1500+ was introduced during 2005, and featured a three position safety.

During 2007, this model was supplied with a Nikko Sterling scope with rings and bases (black polymer stock only).

MODEL 1500+/1500 ULTRALIGHT – .22-250 Rem., .223 Rem., .243 Win., .308 Win. (new 2003), or 7mm-08 Rem. (new 2003) cal., 20 in. barrel, short bolt throw, non-glare blue, blue/black metal, or stainless steel finish, laminated hardwood stock with black textured coating, 5 shot mag., w/o sights, Youth model with 12 5/8 in. LOP introduced 2003, 6.4 lbs. Imported 2002-2008.

	$485	$425	$365	$330	$265	$220	$170	*$599*

Add $149 for stainless steel (.308 Win. or 7mm-08 cals. only).
Subtract $16 for Nikko scope package.

The Model 1500+ was introduced during 2005, and featured a three position safety.

GRADING - PPGS™	100%	98%	95%	90%	80%	70%	60%	LAST MSR

MODEL 1500 VARMINT – .204 Ruger (new 2006), .22-250 Rem., .223 Rem., .243 Win. (new 2005), or .308 Win. (mfg. 1990-92, reintroduced 2001) cal., 24 in. heavy barrel without sights, 5 shot mag., blue steel or stainless steel (new 1999) construction, black polymer (new 1999), 100% Realtree camo (new 2005), or walnut stock, approx. 9.3 lbs. Imported 1988-92, and from 2001-2006.

	100%	98%	95%	90%	80%	70%	60%	LAST MSR
	$450	$395	$335	$305	$245	$200	$155	*$546*

Add $64 for wood stock.
Add $36 for camo.
Add $118 for stainless steel.

MODEL 1500 AXIOM VARMINTER – various cals., 20, or 24 in. heavy blue barrel, 4 or 5 shot mag., choice of black aluminum (disc. 2008), black, green (mfg. 2010-2012), sand (mfg. 2010-2012), or desert camo (new 2010) synthetic, or camo synthetic adj. Blackhawk/Knoxx stock (with cheekpiece allowing LOP to be adjusted from 11 1/2 to 15 1/2 in.), pistol grip, patented recoil reduction, Picatinny top rail, approx. 10 lbs. New 2007.

	100%	98%	95%	90%	80%	70%	60%	LAST MSR
MSR $853	$725	$625	$550	$495	$400	$325	$250	

Add $140 for desert camo stock.
Add $360 for black aluminum stock (disc. 2008).
Add $143 for rifle package with Nikko Platinum scope, rings and bases.

MODEL 1500 AXIOM STANDARD – .204 Ruger, .22-250 Rem., .223 Rem., .243 Win., .25-06 Rem., .270 Win., .308 Win., .300 Win. Mag., .338 Win. Mag., or 7mm Rem. Mag. cal., 22 blue barrel, 4 or 5 shot mag., choice of black aluminum (disc. 2008) or camo synthetic adj. Blackhawk/Knoxx stock (with cheekpiece allowing LOP to be adjusted from 11 1/2 to 15 1/2 in.), pistol grip, patented recoil reduction. Mfg. 2007-2009.

	100%	98%	95%	90%	80%	70%	60%	LAST MSR
	$625	$545	$470	$425	$345	$280	$220	*$699*

Add $20 for Mag. cals.
Add $120 for rifle package with Nikko scope, rings and bases.
Add $360 for black aluminum stock (disc. 2008).

MODEL 1500+/1500 SUPREME – available in various standard and Mag. cals. between .22-250 Rem. - .338 Win. Mag., 22 or 24 in. barrel, 3 or 5 shot mag., choice of JRS Classic, black (Varminter only), Thumbhole Sporter, Varminter, or Thumbhole Varminter stock configuration available in either pepper or nutmeg finish, blue metal finish or stainless steel, 8-9.9 lbs. Importation began 2003.

The Model 1500+ was introduced during 2005, and features a three position safety.

* ***Model 1500+/1500 Supreme JRS Classic*** – standard stock configuration, w/o sights, 8 lbs. Imported 2003-2006.

	100%	98%	95%	90%	80%	70%	60%	LAST MSR
	$515	$450	$385	$350	$285	$230	$180	*$646*

Add $109 for stainless steel.
Add $29 for Mag. cals.

* ***Model 1500+/1500 Supreme Varminter*** – .204 Ruger (new 2006), .22-250 Rem., .223 Rem., .243 Win. (new 2005) or .308 Win. cal., 24 in. bull barrel, blue or stainless steel, nutmeg, pepper, or black synthetic (disc. 2008) stock with raised comb and rollover cheekpiece, vented beavertail forend, 9.3 lbs. Imported 2003-2009.

	100%	98%	95%	90%	80%	70%	60%	LAST MSR
	$615	$540	$460	$420	$340	$275	$215	*$679*

Add $100 for stainless steel.

* ***Model 1500+/1500 Supreme Varminter Thumbhole*** – similar to Supreme Varminter, except has thumbhole stock configuration, nutmeg (disc. 2011) or woodland laminate stock, grooved forend, Picatinny rail, approx. 10 lbs. Importation began 2003.

	100%	98%	95%	90%	80%	70%	60%	LAST MSR
MSR $813	$695	$600	$525	$475	$375	$315	$250	

Add $105 for stainless steel.

* ***Model 1500+/1500 (Supreme) Thumbhole Sporter*** – similar to Thumbhole Varminter, except has 22 in. barrel, nutmeg (blue only, disc. 2010), woodland, or pepper (stainless only, disc. 2009) colored laminated stock, no sights or Picatinny rail, sporterized

GRADING - PPGS™	100%	98%	95%	90%	80%	70%	60%	LAST MSR

forend, 7.6 lbs. Importation began 2003.

MSR $773	$650	$575	$495	$450	$350	$295	$225	

Add $126 for stainless steel.
Add $66 for standard Mag. cals. or $60 for WSM (disc. 2008) cals.

MODEL 1500 CUSTOM – .300 Win. Mag. or .300 WSM cal., 22 or 24 (.300 Win. Mag. cal. only) in. barrel, black polymer or laminate wood in either the Classic JRS or thumbhole configuration, 3 shot mag., blue (.300 Win. Mag. cal. only) or stainless steel barrel and action, 7.6-8.1 lbs. Imported 2002-2004.

	$775	$680	$580	$525	$425	$350	$270	*$858*

Add $30 for JRS nutmeg finish stock and blued finish.
Add $102 for JRS laminate stock.
Add $131 for thumbhole laminate stock in pepper finish.

MODEL 1500 TEXAS SAFARI – .270 Win. or .300 Win. Mag. cal., features Howa M-1500 barreled action with Bill Wiseman recontoured bolt sleeve and receiver, bolt release, and 3-position safety, 3 or 5 shot mag., non-glare blue Teflon metal finish, brown laminate glass bedded stock, individually test fired, approx. 7.8 lbs. Imported 2002-2003.

	$1,350	$1,180	$1,010	$920	$740	$605	$470	*$1,580*

Add $240 for .300 Win. Mag. cal.

This model was also available as a complete custom rifle with many options and special orders.

MODEL 1500 PCS – .308 Win. cal., police counter sniper rifle featuring 24 in. barrel, choice of blue metal or stainless steel, black synthetic or checkered walnut stock, no sights, approx. 9.3 lbs. Imported 1999-2000.

	$385	$335	$290	$260	$210	$175	$135	*$465*

Add $20 for wood stock.
Add $60 for stainless steel.

MODEL 1500 TROPHY – .22-250 Rem., .223 Rem., .243 Win., .270 Win., .308 Win., .30-06, .300 Win. Mag., .338 Win. Mag., or 7mm Rem. Mag. cal., 3 (Mag. cals. only) or 5 shot, 22 or 24 in. barrel, adj. rear sight and trigger, select Monte Carlo stock with skipline checkering. Imported 1988-92.

	$528	$460	$395	$360	$290	$235	$185	*$528*

Add $20 for Mag. cals.

MODEL 1500 HOWA/HOGUE – .204 Ruger, .223 Rem., .22-250 Rem., .243 Win., .25-06 Rem., .270 Win., .30-06, .308 Win., 6.5x55mm (new 2010), .300 Win. Mag., .338 Win. Mag., .375 Ruger (new 2009), 7mm Rem. Mag., .300 WSM (disc. 2008), .270 WSM (disc. 2008), or 7mm WSM (disc. 2008) cal., 22 or 24 in. blue or stainless regular or heavy varmint barrel, fluted barrels became optional 2011, 3, 4, or 5 shot mag., choice of black, sand, green. Harvest Moon (new 2013), Muddy Girl (new 2013), or Outshine (new 2013) camo Hogue overmolded stock, with or w/o HiViz (new 2009) sights, 7.6 - 9.3 (heavy barrel) lbs. New 2007.

MSR $570	$475	$415	$350	$325	$260	$215	$165	

Add $110 for .270 Win. or .30-06 cal.
Add $29 for standard Mag. cals. or approx. $60 for WSM cals. (disc.).
Add $140 for stainless steel.
Add $71-$165 for varmint configuration w/heavy barrel, depending on caliber (disc.).
Add $75 for Nikko Stirling Platinum Night Eater 3-10x42mm scope package.
Add $40 for Gameking Combo with 3.5-10x44 Nikko scope and one piece base (new 2012).
Add $217-$267 for Targetmaster Combo with 20 in. heavy fluted or non-fluted barrel (new 2012).
Add $55 for Harvest Moon, Muddy Girl, or Outshine camo finish (new 2013) or $98 if w/scope.

* ***Model 1500 Howa/Hogue Youth*** – similar to Model 1500 Howa/Hogue, except has short LOP, 20 in. standard barrel, 2-N-1 combo package with scope and extra adult sized OD green stock became standard during 2011. New 2009.

MSR $669	$550	$475	$415	$375	$300	$250	$195	

Add $30 for scope package.
Add $9 for Harvest Moon, Muddy Girl, or Outshine camo finish or $40 if w/scope.

GRADING - PPGS™	100%	98%	95%	90%	80%	70%	60%	LAST MSR

LIGHTNING WOODGRAIN – .243 Win., .270 Win., .30-06, .308 Win., or 7mm Rem. Mag. cal., features lightweight Carbolite synthetic stock with simulated wood grain and checkering, 22 in. barrel, 5 shot mag., no sights, 7 1/2 lbs. Imported 1994 only.

	$450	$395	$335	$305	$245	$200	$155	*$537*

Add $19 for 7mm Rem. Mag. cal.

REALTREE CAMO RIFLE – .270 Win. or .30-06 (disc. 1993) cal., 22 in. barrel, 5 shot mag., monobloc receiver, drilled and tapped, thumb safety, entire rifle is coated with a Realtree brown leaf camo pattern, no sights, 8 lbs. Imported 1993-94.

	$495	$435	$370	$335	$270	$225	$175	*$620*

HOWA/CHRISTENSEN CARBON FIBER RIFLE – .204 Ruger, .223 Rem., .22-250 Rem., .243 Win., or .308 Win. cal., 24 in. Christensen carbon fiber barrel, 4 or 5 shot mag., pepper colored TH Varminter stock, includes green Howa soft case, 8 lbs. Limited production 2007-2008.

	$1,675	$1,465	$1,255	$1,140	$920	$755	$585	*$1,923*

Add $153 for Nikko Stirling Night Eater scope package.

HOWA/HOGUE RANCHLAND COMPACT – various cals., 20 in. free floating lightweight barrel, forged steel flat bottomed receiver, large recoil lug, one-piece bolt, two locking lugs, M16 style extractor, three position safety, Hogue fiberglass reinforced stock in black, coyote sand, OD green, King's Desert Shadow camo (new 2009, package only), Harvest Moon (new 2013), Muddy Girl (new 2013), or Outshine (new 2013) camo, 7 lbs. New 2008.

MSR $585	$495	$425	$375	$325	$275	$225	$175

Add $125 for scope package with Nikko Stirling 3-10x42mm Night Eater scope, rings, and tactical rail.
Add $197 for scope package with Desert Camo finish (new 2009).
Add $72 for Harvest Moon, Muddy Girl, or Outshine camo finish.

HOWA HUNTER – various standard and Mag. cals., 24 in. blue or stainless steel barrel, one piece high grade checkered pistol grip walnut stock, rubber recoil pad, sling swivels, two-stage match trigger, approx. 7 1/2 lbs. New 2012.

MSR $709	$600	$525	$450	$410	$325	$275	$210

Add $48 for Mag. cals.
Add $144 for stainless steel.
Add $64 for Gameking Combo with 3.5-10x44 Nikko scope and one-piece base.

MODEL 1500 TALON THUMBHOLE VARMINTER – various cals., 20, 22, or 24 in. standard or heavy barrel, fluted barrel became optional during 2011, black Axiom thumbhole stock with two-stage Knoxx recoil compensator, vent. and grooved cutaway forend, 8.3 - 9.7 lbs. New 2010.

MSR $814	$695	$600	$525	$475	$375	$315	$250

Add $26 for fluted barrel.
Add $39 heavy barrel.
Add $86 for 4-16x44 scope with Picatinny mounting rail.

HOWA CLASSIC LAMINATE VARMINTER – .204 Ruger, .22-250 Rem., .223 Rem., .243 Win., or .308 Win. cal., short action, 24 in. blue or stainless steel barrel, two-stage match trigger, nutmeg or pepper laminate stock with full pistol grip and palm swell, dual sling swivel studs, three position safety, beavertail forend with large cooling vents, forged one piece bolt with two locking lugs, approx. 10 lbs. New 2012.

MSR $813	$695	$600	$525	$475	$375	$315	$250

Add $105 for stainless steel barrel.

HUG-SAN

Previous shotgun manufacturer located in Huglu, Turkey until 2000.

Hug-San manufactured slide action, semi-auto, and O/U shotguns, in various configurations and gauges.

HUGLU

Current shotgun manufacturer established in 1962, and located in Huglu, Turkey. Currently imported beginning 2005 by CZ-USA, located in Kansas City, KS, and beginning 2010 by TR Imports, located in Keller, TX. Previously imported 2002-2004 by Armsco Firearms Corp., located in Des Plaines, IL, and from 1999-2002 by Huglu USA, located in Rigby, ID.

Huglu makes a wide variety of quality O/U, semi-auto, and SxS shotguns available in all gauges, and are now imported by CZ-USA and TR Imports. Please refer to the CZ section for models and pricing for gun imported by CZ USA.

TR Imports imports the Silver Eagle line of shotguns, including O/U, SxS and semi-autos. Please refer to the TR Imports section for a listing of current models. Some Huglu models were imported 1999-2002 by Huglu USA, and are stamped "Huglu USA, Rigby, ID" on the barrel. Huglu USA Ltd. Co. was reorganized in January 2003 as H-Legacy Shotguns Ltd. Co., and is now a Huglu dealer. For more information, including current models, prices, and U.S. availability, please contact CZ-USA directly (see Trademark Index).

SHOTGUNS: O/U

Armsco previously imported the 103 Series. Models with last MSRs included: 103D - $679 MSR, 103D Mini (28 ga. or .410 bore) - $849 MSR, 103DE (ejectors) - $849 MSR, 103C (case colored receiver) - $799 MSR, 103C Mini - MSR $999, 103CE - $949 MSR, 103F - $949, 103F Mini - $1,199 MSR, 103FE - $1,099 MSR, 103FEC - $1,199 MSR, 103FC Mini - $1,299 MSR., 104A $499 - MSR, and 104A Mini - $699 MSR.

SHOTGUNS: SxS

Armsco's previous lineup of Huglu SxS shotguns through 2003 with last MSRs included: 201A - $899 MSR, 201AC (choke tubes) - $999 MSR, 201A Mini - $1,099, 201AC Mini - $1,199, 202B - $599 MSR, 202B Mini - $799 MSR, 202BCB - $599 MSR, and the 200ACB - $799 MSR.

Current SxS models include: the Bobwhite - $699 MSR, Bobwhite Silver - $899 MSR, Ringneck - $999 MSR, Ringneck Small Gauge - $1,199 MSR, Woodcock - disc. 2004, last MSR was $1,049, Woodcock Small Gauge - disc. 2004, last MSR was $1,299, Woodcock Deluxe - disc. 2004, last MSR was $1,199, Amarillo - $699 MSR, and the Durango - $849 MSR.

SHOTGUNS: SEMI-AUTO

Armsco previous lineup of Huglu's semi-auto shotguns through 2003 with last MSRs included: 501GA - $499 MSR, 501GB - $499 MSR, 601GA - $499 MSR, 601GB - $499 MSR, 601GM (3 1/2 in. chamber) - $599 MSR, 701GA - $499 MSR, and the 701GB - $499 MSR.

SHOTGUNS: SINGLE SHOT

Armsco imported the Model 301A. MSR was $199.

HULDRA ARMS

Current manufacturer of AR-15 style carbines/rifles and located in Brainerd, MN.

RIFLES: SEMI-AUTO

Huldra Arms manufactures various AR-15 style models chambered for 5.56 NATO and 5x45 Russian cal. Current models include: PRE-1 (MSR $2,000), Mark IV 5.56 (MSR $1,000), Mark IV Tactical Elite (MSR $1,500), Mark IV Tactical EVO (MSR $1,350), and Mark IV 5.45x39 (MSR $1,050).

HUNTER ARMS COMPANY

Previous manufacturer located in Fulton, NY circa 1891-1945.

The Hunter Arms Company was formed to manufacture L.C. Smith shotguns circa 1891. During 1915, Hunter Arms began producing its own line of shotguns. Please refer to the L.C. Smith section in this text for further information regarding this manufacturer (including Fulton, Fulton Special, and Hunter Special models).

HUSQVARNA

Previous manufacturer located in Husqvarna, Sweden.

Also see: Lahti Pistols.

GRADING - PPGS™	100%	98%	95%	90%	80%	70%	60%	LAST MSR

RIFLES: BOLT ACTION

HI-POWER – .220 Swift, .270 Win., or .30-06 cal., Mauser type action, open sights, checkered beech wood. Mfg. 1946-51, early models found in 6.5x55mm, 8x57Rmm, 9.3x57mm cals.

$625 $550 $500 $450 $400 $365 $335

MODEL 1951 – similar to Hi-Power, except high profile stock.

$500 $465 $425 $385 $340 $300 $270

SERIES 1100 DELUXE – similar to Model 1951, except has European walnut and jeweled bolt. Mfg. 1952-56.

$520 $480 $440 $360 $330 $310 $290

SERIES 1000 SUPER GRADE – similar to Model 1951, has walnut Monte Carlo stock. Mfg. 1952-56.

$520 $480 $440 $360 $330 $310 $290

SERIES 3100 CROWN GRADE – .243 Win., .270 Win., .30-06, 7x57mm, or .308 Win. cal., improved HVA Mauser action, 24 in. barrel, walnut stock, black forend tip and pistol grip cap. Mfg. 1954-72.

$575 $525 $475 $400 $360 $330 $315

SERIES 3000 CROWN GRADE – similar to 3100, except has Monte Carlo stock.

$660 $595 $525 $475 $400 $360 $330

SERIES 4100 LIGHTWEIGHT – HVA Mauser action, calibers same as 3100, 20 1/2 in. barrel, open sights, lightweight walnut stock, pistol grip, Schnabel forend. Mfg. 1954-72.

$575 $525 $475 $400 $360 $330 $315

SERIES 4000 LIGHTWEIGHT – similar to 4100, except has Monte Carlo stock, no sights.

$660 $595 $525 $475 $400 $360 $330

MODEL 456 LIGHTWEIGHT – similar to 4000/4100, except full length stock. Mfg. 1959-70.

$675 $600 $550 $495 $415 $385 $330

SERIES 6000 IMPERIAL GRADE – similar to 3100, except has select wood, 3 leaf folding rear sight. Mfg. 1968-70.

$795 $695 $625 $575 $495 $470 $440

SERIES 7000 IMPERIAL LIGHTWEIGHT – similar to 6000 Imperial, except 20 1/2 in. barrel, lightweight stock.

$850 $775 $695 $625 $575 $495 $470

SERIES P-3000 PRESENTATION – similar to Crown, except engraved action, special wood. Mfg. 1968-70.

$1,100 $1,000 $925 $850 $775 $675 $575

MODEL 9000 CROWN GRADE – cals. similar to Model 3100 Crown Grade, except also available in .300 Win. Mag. cal., Husqvarna action, 23 1/2 in. barrel, adj. trigger, adj. sight, walnut stock. Mfg. 1971-72.

$575 $525 $475 $400 $360 $330 $315

MODEL 8000 IMPERIAL – similar to 9000, but jeweled bolt, engraved floor plate, no sights and deluxe stock. Mfg. 1971-1972.

$750 $675 $595 $525 $495 $470 $415

SHOTGUNS

Husqvarna also manufactured limited quantities of SxS and underlever shotguns in various configurations, including a Model 20 SxS in 12 or 16 ga. with exposed hammers (popular with cowboy action shooting). Most of these shotguns are currently selling in the $375-$1,200 range, depending on the desirability of the configuration and original condition.

GRADING - PPGS™	100%	98%	95%	90%	80%	70%	60%	LAST MSR

HY-HUNTER INC. FIREARMS MANUFACTURING CO.

Previous trademark imported by Hy-Hunter Inc., located in Hollywood, CA.

Hy-Hunter Inc. imported single action revolvers in various calibers and O/U derringers manufactured in West Germany. Typically, prices are determined by their shooting value rather than their collector value. Prices generally range from $100-$175 depending on caliber and finish.

HYPER

Previous manufacturer located in Jenks, OK.

RIFLES: SINGLE SHOT

SINGLE SHOT RIFLE – all calibers, all standard lengths and contours, falling block trigger guard lever activated, adj. trigger, no sights, stocked to customer specifications, in AA grade walnut. Disc. 1984.

100%	98%	95%	90%	80%	70%	60%	LAST MSR
$2,200	$1,980	$1,925	$1,870	$1,650	$1,540	$1,375	

Add $75 for stainless barrel.
Add $85 for octagon barrel.

The results of the Blue Book Company Shootout .22 competition. David Kosowski was the winner, but Clint Schmidt took a respectable 2nd place - not bad for a first time shooter!
Photo courtesy S.P. Fjestad

I SECTION

I.A.B. srl

Previous manufacturer (Industria Armi Bresciane) of modern firearms, black powder replicas and historical Sharps rifles located in Gardone, Valtrompia, Brescia, Italy. Previously imported by E.M.F., located in Santa Ana, CA, Dixie Gun Works, located in Union City, TN, Kiesler's, located in Jeffersonville, IN, American Arms, located in Kansas City, MO, and by Tristar Sporting Arms, located in Kansas City, MO. Previously distributed by Sporting Arms International, Inc. located in Indianola, MS.

I.A.B. also manufactured shotguns (O/U and single barrel trap or skeet) in various styles and configurations including combo sets. These guns employed a boxlock action, had ejectors, and various amounts of engraving. Prices for 100% condition usually started in the $650-$1,000 price range. Values for older models will be determined by their shooting value, not collector value, as there are very few I.A.B. collectors.

IAC

Please refer to Interstate Arms corp. listing.

IAI

Please refer to Intrac Arms International LLC listing.

IAI INC. - AMERICAN LEGEND

Previous manufacturer, importer, and distributor located in Houston, TX. Firearms were manufactured by Israel Arms International, Inc., located in Houston, TX. IAI designates Israel Arms International, and should not be confused with Irwindale Arms, Inc. (also IAI).

The models listed were part of an American Legend Series that are patterned after famous American and Belgian military carbines/rifles and semi-auto pistols.

GRADING - PPGS™	100%	98%	95%	90%	80%	70%	60%	LAST MSR

CARBINES/RIFLES

MODEL 888 M1 CARBINE – .22 LR or .30 Carbine cal., 18 in. barrel, mfg. from new original M1 parts and stock by IAI (barrel bolt and receiver) and unused GI parts, 10 shot mag., choice of birch or walnut stock, parkerized finish, metal or wood handguard, 5 1/2 lbs. Mfg. by IAI in Houston, TX 1998-2004.

	100%	98%	95%	90%	80%	70%	60%	LAST MSR
	$675	$595	$565	$435	$395	$315	$295	*$556*

Add $11 for .22 LR cal.
Add $31 for walnut/metal forearm or $47 for walnut/wood forearm.

MODEL 333 M1 GARAND – .30-06 cal., patterned after the WWII M1 Garand, 24 in. barrel, internal magazine, 8 shot en-bloc clip, parkerized finish, 9 1/2 lbs. Mfg. 2003-2004.

	100%	98%	95%	90%	80%	70%	60%	LAST MSR
	$950	$875	$775	$625	$525	$400	$350	*$972*

PISTOLS: SEMI-AUTO

MODEL 2000 – .45 ACP cal., patterned after the Colt Govt. 1911, 5 or 4 1/4 (Commander configuration, Model 2000-C) in. barrel, parkerized finish, plastic or rubber finger groove grips, 36-38 oz. Mfg. in South Africa 2002-2004.

	100%	98%	95%	90%	80%	70%	60%	LAST MSR
	$415	$365	$325	$295	$275	$250	$225	*$465*

I A I

Please refer to the Irwindale Arms, Inc. heading in this section.

IAR, Inc.

Previous importer and distributor since 1995 located in San Juan Capistrano, CA. During late 2009, E.M.F. bought the remaining assets of IAR and discontinued any importation under the IAR name.

IAR, Inc. (International Antique Reproductions, Inc.) imported and distributed a wide variety of firearms, including SA revolvers, rolling block pistols, rolling block target rifles, Henry rifle reproductions, baby rolling block carbines, exposed hammer shotguns, and reproduction

GRADING - PPGS™	100%	98%	95%	90%	80%	70%	60%	*LAST MSR*

rifles and carbines. IAR, Inc. also imported black powder reproductions and replicas, plus a complete lineup of blank firing arms and ammunition, including pistols, revolvers, and rifles.

Black Powder Revolver Reproductions & Replicas and *Black Powder Long Arms & Pistols - Reproductions & Replicas* by Dennis Adler are also invaluable sources for most black powder reproductions and replicas, and include hundreds of color images on most popular makes/models, provide manufacturer/trademark histories, and up-to-date information on related items/accessories for black powder shooting - www.bluebookofgunvalues.com

I.F.G.

Current importer established during 2011 for the importation of select Italian makes/models. I.F.G. is an abbreviation for the Italian Firearms Group, formed to import and distribute select models into the U.S. civilian marketplace. The Italian Firearms Group represents the following Italian firearms manufacturers: F.A.I.R., Pedersoli, Sabatti, and Tanfoglio. Please refer to these individual listings for more information.

I G A

Current trademark with manufacturing facilities located in Veranopolis, Brazil (O/U and SxS shotguns only), and by Vursan Manufacturing (semi-auto shotguns only) beginning in 2000, located in Istanbul, Turkey. Currently imported by Stoeger Industries, Inc. located in Accokeek, MD. Previously located in Wayne, NJ.

During 2000, Stoeger Industries was purchased by Beretta USA Corp., located in Accokeek, MD. Guns manufactured before 2000 were made by E.R. Amantino, located in Brazil, and were marked I G A/E.R. Amantino. Currently manufactured shotguns have Stoeger markings. Amantino still makes O/U and SxS guns for Stoeger, but guns made since 2002 may be marked E.R. Amantino and/or Stoeger.

Please refer to the Stoeger Industries section for recently manufactured shotguns.

SHOTGUNS: O/U

CONDOR MODEL – 12 ga. only, single trigger, ejectors, presentation walnut, chrome lined bores. Disc. 1985.

$580	$500	$450	$410	$375	$350	$325	*$667*

CONDOR II DOUBLE TRIGGER – 12 or 20 (disc.) ga., boxlock action, VR, checkered walnut, separated barrels. Disc. 1997.

$350	$295	$260	$230	$195	$170	$150	*$459*

CONDOR SUPREME – 12 or 20 ga., boxlock action, single trigger, ejectors, 26 or 28 in. VR barrels with choke tubes, deluxe checkered walnut stock and forearm. Imported 1995-2000.

$500	$450	$395	$360	$320	$280	$240	*$629*

TURKEY SERIES – 12 ga. only, 3 in. chambers, 26 in. VR barrels with choke tubes, ST, ejectors, Advantage camo on wood and metal (except receiver). Mfg. 1997-2000.

$615	$525	$450	$380	$335	$300	$270	*$729*

HUNTER CLAYS MODEL – 12 ga. only, ST, ejectors, 28 in. barrels with choke tubes, deluxe checkered stock and forearm, gold trigger. Mfg. 1997-99.

$595	$515	$435	$375	$335	$300	$270	*$699*

WATERFOWL SERIES – 12 ga. only, 3 in. chambers, similar to Turkey Series, except has 30 in. barrels. Mfg. 1998-2000.

$615	$525	$450	$380	$335	$300	$270	*$729*

TRAP SERIES – 12 ga., features SST, ejectors, 30 in. VR barrels with choke tubes, deluxe checkered Monte Carlo stock and forearm. Mfg. 1998-99.

$595	$515	$435	$375	$335	$300	$270	*$699*

ERA 2000 MODELS – 12 ga. only, 26 or 28 in. VR barrels with choke tubes, single trigger. Imported 1992-94.

$585	$375	$315	$250	$215	$195	$180	*$710*

GRADING - PPGS™	100%	98%	95%	90%	80%	70%	60%	LAST MSR

SHOTGUNS: SxS

DELUXE MODEL – 12, 20, 28 ga., or .410 bore, features better quality checkered walnut stock and forearm, gold triggers, 12 and 20 ga. have choke tubes, 28 ga. and .410 bore have fixed chokes. Mfg. 1997-99.

$425	$365	$310	$270	$230	$195	$170	*$559*

Subtract $40 for 28 ga. or .410 bore (fixed chokes only).

TURKEY SERIES MODEL – 12 ga. only, 3 in. chambers, 24 in. barrels, DT, choke tubes. Mfg. 1997-2000.

$425	$365	$310	$270	$230	$195	$170	*$559*

SHOTGUNS: SINGLE BARREL

REUNA SINGLE BARREL – 12, 20 ga., or .410 bore, exposed hammer with half-cock, extractor. Disc. 1998.

$95	$70	$60	$50	$45	$40	$35	*$120*

Add $22 for choke tubes (12 ga. new 1992, 20 ga. new 1993).

* ***Reuna Single Barrel Youth*** – 20 ga. or .410 bore, 22 in. barrel, features rubber recoil pad. Imported 1993-98.

$100	$75	$60	$50	$45	$40	$35	*$132*

SINGLE BARREL CLASSIC – 12, 20 ga., or .410 bore, 3 in. chamber, break open action activated by moving trigger guard rearward, exposed hammer or hammerless (new 2003), 26 or 28 in. barrel with (new 2003) or w/o VR (disc. 2003), hardwood stock and forend, matte metal finish, Youth Model also available in 20 ga. or .410 bore (13 in. LOP), approx. 5 1/2 lbs. Mfg. 2002-2005.

$95	$80	$65	$55	$45	$40	$35	*$119*

Add $6 for Special Model with matte finished stainless steel receiver (new 2004).

IMI

Please refer to listing under Israel Military Industries.

I.O., INC.

Current manufacturer established in 2008, and located in Monroe, NC.

PISTOLS: SEMI-AUTO

I.O. Inc. makes several semi-auto pistols, including the Hellpup AK-47 design model - current MSR is $864, the Hellcat DA concealed pocket pistol in .380 ACP cal. - current MSR is $280-$310, and the Polish PPs43C - current MSR is $450.

RIFLES: SEMI-AUTO

I.O. Inc. currently makes the following AK-47 style semi-auto rifles in 7.62x39mm cal.: STG2000-C with fixed, folding, or collapsible stock (MSR $864), the AK47-C with fixed, folding, collapsible or polymer stock (Galil-type forearm), synthetic or wood stock (last MSR was $500-$670, disc. 2010), an AK-22 rifle (last MSR was $500, disc. 2010), STG-22 rifle (last MSR was $500, disc. 2010), a CASAR AK series of rifles (last MSR was $648, disc. 2011), the Hellhound Tactical (MSR $936, new 2011), the Sporter (MSR $720, new 2011), Laminate Sporter (POR), Sporter-Econ (MSR $677), and the Sporter-Wood (MSR $750). Please contact the company directly for availability and more information (see Trademark Index).

ISSC HANDELSGESELLSCHAFT

Current manufacturer of semi-auto firearms located in Ried, Austria. Currently imported by Legacy Sports International located in Reno, NV beginning late 2011. Previously imported by Austrian Sporting Arms, located in Ware, MA until 2011.

PISTOLS: SEMI-AUTO

M22 – .22 LR cal., patterned after the Glock semi-auto, 4, 4 3/4 (new 2012), or 5 1/2 (new 2012) in. threaded (new 2012), standard, or target (new 2012) barrel, SA, 10 shot mag., black polymer frame with contoured grip, adj. rear sight, tactical rail, black, two-tone desert tan, OD Green, pink, Harvest Moon camo (new 2013), Outshine camo (new 2013),

GRADING - PPGS™	100%	98%	95%	90%	80%	70%	60%	LAST MSR

or Muddy Girl camo (new 2013) finish, with or w/o brushed chrome (new 2012) slide, 21 oz. New 2009.

MSR $428	$365	$325	$285	$265	$245	$225	$200

Add $30 for brushed chrome slide.
Add $41 for Harvest Moon camo, Outshine camo, or Muddy Girl camo (new 2013) stock.
Add $111 for 4 3/4 in. threaded barrel.
Add $37 for 5 1/2 in. target barrel.

RIFLES: BOLT ACTION

SPA STRAIGHT PULL ACTION – .17 HMR, .22 LR, or .22 Mag. cal., 10 shot detachable box mag., straight pull Biathlon Style action, 20 in. match barrel w/o sights, black synthetic or Hunter wood stock with raised cheekpiece, 7.84 lbs. New 2013.

MSR $489	$440	$395	$350	$315	$275	$250	$225

Add $10 for .17 HMR or .22 Mag. cal.
Add $100 for wood stock.

* ***Spa Target Straight Pull Action*** – .17 HMR, .22 LR, or .22 Mag. cal., similar to Spa Straight Pull Action Rifle, except features a Target adj./folding thumbhole stock, adj. cheekpiece, and butt spike, 7.84 lbs. New 2013.

MSR $689	$595	$525	$450	$395	$350	$300	$275

Add $10 for .17 HMR or .22 Mag. cal.

RIFLES: SEMI-AUTO

MK22 – .22 LR cal., 10 or 22 shot mag., 16.6 in. L. Walther match barrel with muzzle brake, multiple charge bar locations on right and left side of receiver, ambidextrous safety and mag. release, Back or Desert Tan (new 2012) finish, variable and folding adj. open sight, Picatinny quad rail, fixed, folding or collapsible stock with adj. cheekpiece, features Ucas system (Universal cocking adaptation system), 6 1/2 lbs. New 2011.

MSR $664	$575	$500	$450	$400	$365	$335	$300

Add $35 for Desert Tan finish.

I.W.I

Please refer to lising under Israel Weapon Industries Ltd.

IBERIA FIREARMS

Current manufacturer of .40 S&W cal. pistols located in Iberia, OH. Distributed by MKS Supply located in Dayton, OH. Distributor sales only.

Please refer to the Hi-Point section in this text.

IMPALA PRECSION

Previous rifle manufacturer located in London, England.

IMPERIAL GUN CO. LTD

Previous manufacturer located in Surrey, Great Britain circa 1992-1995. The Imperial Gun Co. Ltd. had limited importation into the U.S.

Imperial Gun secondary marketplace values must be based realistically on their competitive shooting value, not collectibility.

INDIAN ARMS

Previous trademark manufactured by Indian Arms Corporation located in Detroit, MI.

PISTOLS: SEMI-AUTO

INDIAN ARMS .380 – .380 ACP cal., patterned after Walther PPK, stainless steel, 3 1/4 in. barrel, 6 shot mag., natural or blue finish, with (early specimens) or without key lock safety, with or without VR barrel, walnut grips, 20 oz. Mfg. 1975-77.

	$395	$350	$300	$275	$250	$225	$195

This model had limited manufacture with approx. 1,000 guns being made.

GRADING - PPGS™	100%	98%	95%	90%	80%	70%	60%	LAST MSR

INDUSTRIA ARMI GALESI

Previous manufacturer located in Brescia, Italy.

PISTOLS: SEMI-AUTO

GALESI MODEL 6 POCKET AUTO – .22 LR or .25 ACP cal., 6 shot, 2 1/4 in. barrel blue, fixed sights, plastic grips. Mfg. 1930-disc.

	100%	98%	95%	90%	80%	70%	60%
	$165	$145	$125	$110	$90	$75	$60
Chrome engraved	$330	$290	$250	$225	$180	$150	$115

GALESI MODEL 9 POCKET AUTO – .22 LR, .32 ACP, or .380 ACP cal., 8 shot, 3 1/4 in. barrel, blue, fixed sights, plastic grips. Mfg. 1930-disc.

	100%	98%	95%	90%	80%	70%	60%
	$195	$170	$145	$135	$105	$90	$70
Chrome engraved	$395	$345	$295	$270	$215	$180	$140

INFALLIBLE

Previous trademark manufactured by Warner Arms Corp. located in Norwich, CT, and Davis-Warner Arms Corp. located in Assonet, MA.

PISTOLS: SEMI-AUTO

INFALLIBLE PISTOL – .32 ACP cal., 3.2 in. barrel, 7 shot mag., 24.7 oz.

* ***Infallible Pistol Type I*** – mfg. and marked "Warner Arms Corp., Norwich, Conn.", serial range is 501-2,299.

100%	98%	95%	90%	80%	70%	60%
$450	$325	$295	$270	$250	$225	$200

* ***Infallible Pistol Type II*** – marked "Davis-Warner Arms Corporation, Assonet, Massachusetts", serial range is 2,300-5,299.

100%	98%	95%	90%	80%	70%	60%
$400	$300	$250	$225	$195	$170	$150

* ***Infallible Pistol Type III*** – marked "Warner Arms Corporation, Norwich, Connecticut", serial range is 5,300-7,400.

100%	98%	95%	90%	80%	70%	60%
$400	$300	$250	$225	$195	$170	$150

INFINITY FIREARMS

Current trademark manufactured by Strayer-Voight Inc. since 1994 and located in Grand Prairie, TX. Currently distributed by JP Enterprises, located in White Bear Lake, MN. Distributor and dealer sales.

PISTOLS: SEMI-AUTO

Strayer-Voight manufactures a complete line of custom high quality M1911-based semi-auto pistols in a wide variety of finishes, materials (including titanium), options, and special orders. Some models have included the Tiki, Titanium Model, Bushing, Comp. Gun, Hybricomp, IED 1911, Duotone 1911, PPC Masterpiece, and Competition Gun. Please contact JP Enterprises directly for more information on pricing and availability regarding Infinity firearms (see Trademark Index).

INGLIS HI-POWERS

Previously manufactured by John Inglis Co. Limited of Toronto, Canada. Over 151,000 Inglis Hi-Powers were manufactured between February 1944 and September 1945 under military contractual agreements.

PISTOLS: SEMI-AUTO

For more information on Inglis serialization and model coding, please refer to the Serialization section.

CHINESE CONTRACT PATTERN 35

* ***Chinese Contract Pattern 35 No. 1*** – 9mm Para. cal., large Chinese characters (2-6) on left slide, slotted for stock and tangent sights, can be denoted by no numerical prefix before the "CH" in serial number.

100%	98%	95%	90%	80%	70%	60%
$3,500	$3,250	$2,750	$2,250	$1,750	$1,250	$1,000

Add approx. $375 for original wood holster stock (beware of reproductions).
Add $350-$450 for early front sight (approx. first 100 pistols only).

GRADING - PPGS™	100%	98%	95%	90%	80%	70%	60%	LAST MSR

CH SERIES MILITARY

* ***CH Series Military MK 1-No. 1 Inglis*** – 9mm Para. cal., tangent sight, slotted, contracts included Canadian, Chinese, and other countries.

$1,325	$1,050	$875	$725	$650	$550	$450	

Add 10%-20% for decal on front strap.
Add approx. $350 for original wood holster stock. Beware of reproductions.
This model has been recently imported again. Most recent imports have been painted black or refinished, and are priced in the $350-$575 range.

T SERIES CANADIAN MILITARY

* ***T Series Canadian Military MK 1-No. 2 Inglis*** – 9mm Para. cal., fixed sight, without slot, numerical ser. no. prefix (0-10) references the sequence of guns in increments of 10,000. Scarcer variations include: 0, 9, and 10.

$1,000	$750	$600	$400	$350	$295	$275	

Add 10%-20% for original decal on front strap.
Add 15% for 0 variation prefix.
Add 10% for 9 variation prefix.
Add 30% for 10 variation (ser. no.) prefix.
Most recent imports are priced $350-$650.

Since the original decals are very fragile, most are observed with approx. 10%-90% of the decal remaining.

This model has been recently imported again.

* ***T Series Canadian Military Inglis "DIAMOND" logo*** – refers to Inglis trademark in diamond shaped logo on left side of slide, only a few prototypes were mfg. 1946-47.

$3,500	$3,250	$2,750	$2,250	$1,750	$1,250	$1,000	

Add 50% for polished steel (parkerized finish is more common).
Add 50% for 5 CH Series.

All Inglis diamond variations are in the 5CH or 9T ser. no. range.

Be careful of fakes!

* ***T Series Canadian Military MK 1-No. 2 Inglis*** – fixed sight, slotted. Inspect slot very carefully, and provenance verification is advised.

$1,950	$1,250	$1,100	$900	$800	$650	$500	

INGRAM

Previously manufactured until late 1982 by Military Armament Corp. (MAC) located in Atlanta, GA.

PISTOLS: SEMI-AUTO

MAC 10 – .45 ACP or 9mm Para. cal., open bolt, semi-auto version of the sub machine gun, 10 (.45 ACP cal.), 16 (9mm Para. cal.), 30 (.45 ACP cal.), or 32 (9mm Para. cal.) shot mag., compact all metal welded construction, rear aperture and front blade sight. Disc. 1982.

$950	$875	$800	$700	$650	$575	$525	

Add approx. $160 for accessories (barrel extension, case, and extra mag.).

MAC 10A1 – similar to MAC 10 except fires from a closed bolt.

$395	$375	$350	$280	$265	$225	$210	

MAC 11 – similar to MAC 10 except in .380 ACP cal.

$750	$695	$650	$575	$550	$535	$485	

INLAND

Previous WWII subcontractor of M1 carbines. Former division of General Motors, located in Dayton, OH.

Please refer to U.S. M1 Carbines/Rifles listings under U.S. Military.

GRADING - PPGS™	100%	98%	95%	90%	80%	70%	60%	LAST MSR

INNOGUN

Current long gun manufacturer located in Obersfeld, Germany. No current U.S. importation.

InnOGun makes two models currently. The InnOGun Hybrid is a unique O/U interchangeable two-barrel gun with a box magazine feeding the lower barrel which has a slide action operation. The top barrel is a single shot rifle, and the gun has a break-open style action with top opening lever. This allows it to be a combination gun in shotgun/rifle, rimfire/centerfire, or centerfire/centerfire configurations. The InnOGun Impuls model is a single shot repeater available in various cals. Please contact the manufacturer directly for more information on its unique designs, current U.S. availability, and pricing (see Trademark Index).

INTERARMS

Previous importer and distributor located in Alexandria, VA, from circa 1956-1999.

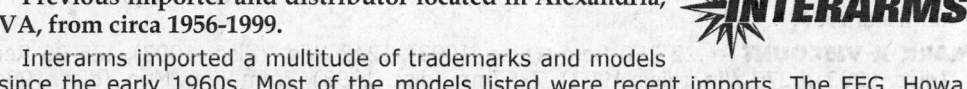

Interarms imported a multitude of trademarks and models since the early 1960s. Most of the models listed were recent imports. The FEG, Howa, Rossi, and Walther trademarks will be found in their own sections listed alphabetically in this text.

PISTOLS: SEMI-AUTO, FEG & HELWAN MFG.

Please refer to the FEG & HELWAN sections in this text.

REVOLVERS: SA, VIRGINIAN SERIES

Virginian Revolvers were previously manufactured in Europe by various manufacturers (including Hämmerli of Switzerland). They were also manufactured in Midland, VA from 1976-1984. Older models with exceptional quality (including Hämmerli guns) are worth a premium over values listed.

VIRGINIAN DRAGOON STANDARD – .41 Mag., .44 Mag., or .45 LC (mfg. 1982-84) cal., improved action patterned after Colt SAA design, 6 shot, 6, 7 1/2, 8 3/8, or 12 (Buntline) in. barrel, blue finish, smooth walnut grips, adj. rear sight, 51 oz. with 7 1/2 in. barrel.

$340	$295	$255	$225	$205	$190	$180	*$315*

Add 15% for Buntline Model.

* ***Virginian Dragoon Standard Stainless*** – .41 Mag., .44 Mag., or .45 LC cal., 6 (disc.), 7 1/2 (disc.), or 8 3/8 in. barrel, same general specifications as Standard Dragoon.

$375	$325	$275	$235	$215	$190	$180	*$315*

DRAGOON SILHOUETTE – .357 Mag. or .44 Mag. cal., stainless steel, 7 1/2, 8 3/8, or 10 1/2 in. (standard on .357 Mag.) barrel, special sights and grips.

$475	$325	$365	$320	$275	$225	$195	*$425*

DRAGOON ENGRAVED – .44 Mag. cal. only, choice of stainless steel or blue finish, 6 or 7 1/2 in. barrel., "Sic Semper Tyrannis" inscription on butt with a 5 point star.

$650	$575	$500	$450	$395	$360	$320	*$625*

Add $75 for presentation case.

DRAGOON "DEPUTY" – .357 Mag. or .44 Mag. cal., blue barrel, case hardened frame, 5 in. barrel only.

$340	$295	$255	$225	$205	$190	$180	*$295*

* ***Dragoon "Deputy" Stainless*** – similar to Dragoon "Deputy", except .44 Mag. available in 6 in. barrel only, stainless steel.

$375	$325	$275	$235	$215	$190	$180	*$295*

VIRGINIAN .22 CONVERTIBLE – .22 LR/.22 WMR cal. cylinders, 5 1/2 in. barrel only, adj. rear sight, 38 oz.

$215	$185	$155	$145	$135	$125	$115	*$219*

* ***Virginian .22 Convertible Stainless*** – stainless steel fabrication, otherwise similar to above.

$240	$200	$170	$155	$125	$110	$95	*$239*

GRADING - PPGS™	100%	98%	95%	90%	80%	70%	60%	LAST MSR

RIFLES: BOLT ACTION, DISC.

MODEL JW-15 – .22 LR cal., 5 shot detachable mag., 23.8 in. barrel, open sights, blue finish, Model 70 style safety, patterned after the Brno Model ZKM, 5 1/2 lbs. Mfg. by Norinco. Imported 1990-96.

$135	$115	$85	$70	$60	$50	$40	*$109*

ENFIELD NO. 4 – .303 British cal., genuine British Commonwealth issue, 25 1/4 in. barrel, 10 shot box mag., 9 lbs. Importation disc. 1996.

$495	$450	$400	$350	$300	$275	$250	*$86*

RIFLES: BOLT ACTION, HOWA MFG.

Please refer to the Howa section in this text.

RIFLES: BOLT ACTION, MAUSER ACTIONS

Whitworth rifles were mfg. in England. Mark X rifles were mfg. in Yugoslavia by Zastava Arms until late 1997.

MARK X VISCOUNT – .22-250 Rem. (disc. 1993), .243 Win. (disc. 1993), .25-06 Rem. (disc. 1993), .270 Win. (disc. 1993), 7x57mm (disc. 1993), 7mm Rem. Mag. (disc. 1994), .308 Win. (disc. 1994), .30-06, or .300 Win. Mag. (disc. 1994) cal., 5 shot, 3 shot mag., 24 in. barrel, adj. rear sight and trigger, classic style Monte Carlo stock. Disc. 1983, re-introduced 1985, disc. 1996.

$425	$375	$300	$265	$240	$225	$205	*$471*

Add $15 for 7mm Rem. Mag. or .300 Win. Mag. cal.

This model is often referred to as the Viscount. Early manufacture was done in Manchester, England. Recent manufacture was in Yugoslavia. Earlier Manchester guns (before approx. 1980) will bring a slight premium over the values listed.

* ***Mark X Viscount Mini*** – .223 Rem. or 7.62x39mm (new in 1990) cal., miniature M98 Mauser System action, 20 in. barrel with iron sights, checkered hardwood stock, 5 shot mag., adj. trigger, 6.35 lbs. Imported 1987-94.

$410	$360	$295	$265	$240	$225	$205	*$455*

* ***Mark X Viscount Lightweight*** – .22-250 Rem. (new 1994), .270 Win. (disc.), .30-06 (disc. 1994), or 7mm Rem. Mag. (disc.) cal., similar to Mark X Viscount, except has Carbolite (synthetic) stock and 20 in. barrel, 7 lbs. Imported 1988-90, reintroduced 1994-97.

$395	$350	$290	$265	$240	$225	$205	*$438*

CAVALIER – similar to Viscount, except modern style stock, roll-over cheekpiece, rosewood pistol grip cap and forend tip, recoil pad. Disc.

$425	$375	$335	$305	$290	$265	$230

MANNLICHER STYLE CARBINE – similar to Cavalier, except 20 in. barrel, full length stock, no Magnum or varmint calibers. Disc.

$550	$500	$450	$395	$350	$300	$275

CONTINENTAL CARBINE – similar to Mannlicher Style, except with double set trigger. Disc.

$600	$550	$495	$440	$400	$325	$295

THE MARQUIS – .243 Win., .270 Win., .308 Win., 7x57mm, or .30-06 cal., 20 in. barrel, adj. trigger. Mannlicher style carbine. Disc. 1984.

$550	$500	$450	$395	$350	$300	$275

ALASKAN – similar to Mark X, except .375 H&H or .458 Win. Mag. cal., recoil pad and extra stock crossbolt. Disc. 1984.

$650	$595	$550	$500	$450	$395	$350

MARK X REALTREE – .270 Win. or .30-06 cal., features Realtree Camo finish. Imported 1994-96.

$460	$390	$365	$320	$275	$250	$225	*$549*

GRADING - PPGS™	100%	98%	95%	90%	80%	70%	60%	LAST MSR

MARK X WHITWORTH – .270 Win., .30-06, and .300 Win. Mag. cals., Mauser action, 24 in. barrel, open sights, 5 shot mag. (.300 Win. Mag. is only 3), checkered deluxe walnut stock with ebony forearm tip, thumb safety, sling swivels, adj. trigger, rubber recoil buttplate, 7 lbs. Imported 1984-96.

	$475	$400	$365	$320	$275	$250	$225	*$565*

Add $19 for 7mm Rem. Mag. (disc.) or .300 Win. Mag. cal.

This model was the Whitworth American Field Series until 1987. Early manufacture was done in Manchester, England. Later manufacture was by Zastava located in Yugoslavia. Earlier Manchester guns (before approx. 1980) will bring a slight premium over the values listed.

WHITWORTH MANNLICHER STYLE CARBINE – .243 Win., .270 Win., .308 Win., 7x57mm, or .30-06 cal., bolt action with full length walnut Mannlicher style stock, open sights, sling swivels, thumb safety, 20 in. barrel, 5 shot mag., 7 lbs. Imported 1984-87.

	$675	$600	$525	$450	$415	$375	$340	*$675*

WHITWORTH EXPRESS RIFLE – .375 H&H (disc. 1993) or .458 Win. Mag. cal., 3 shot, 24 in. barrel, 3 leaf express sight, English style walnut stock, checkered pistol grip and forend, 8 1/2 lbs. Imported 1974-96.

	$995	$895	$825	$750	$650	$550	$450	*$703*

RIFLES: SEMI-AUTO

22-ATD – .22 LR cal. only, patterned after the Browning Semi-Auto, 19.4 in. barrel, 11 shot mag. in stock, blue finish, checkered hardwood stock, take-down design, adj. rear sight, 4.6 lbs. Mfg. by Norinco 1987-96.

	$250	$225	$195	$175	$150	$125	$100	*$121*

Add $16 for camo case (disc.).

INTERARMS ARSENAL

Current trademark of firearms imported and distributed by High Standard Manufacturing Company, located in Houston, TX.

RIFLES: SEMI-AUTO

POLISH MODEL WZ.88 TANTAL – 5.45x39mm cal., choice of side folding stock with wood forend furniture or fixed stock, chrome lined barrel, mfq. in U.S.

MSR $619	$525	$465	$415	$365	$335	$300	$275

Add $10 for side folding stock.

HUNGARIAN ADM 65 STYLE AKM – 7.62x39mm cal., side folding stock.

MSR $586	$495	$450	$400	$365	$335	$300	$275

AKM SERIES – 7.62x38mm cal., black polymer stock, Russian, Egyptian or Polish configurations.

MSR $619	$525	$465	$415	$365	$335	$300	$275

Add $40 for Polish import with under folding stock (AKMS Model).

AK-74 – 5.45x39mm cal., Bulgarian style mfg., choice of wood or polymer furniture.

MSR $679	$575	$500	$450	$400	$350	$300	$275

AK-47 – 7.62x39mm cal., AK-47 design with milled receiver, choice of Yugoslavian Zastava or other Easter Bloc mfg.

MSR $1,195	$1,050	$925	$800	$675	$550	$475	$400

AR-15 A2 RIFLE – 5.56 NATO cal., AR-15 style, choice of flat-top (no sights), or A2 configuration, 20 in. barrel with flash hider, choice of black synthetic fixed or collapsible stock, 30 shot mag.

MSR $935	$825	$750	$675	$600	$525	$450	$400

Add $40 for A2 adj. sights.

M4 CARBINE – 5.56 NATO cal., 16 in. barrel with muzzle brake, choice of flat-top or A2 configuration, M4 6-position collapsible stock.

MSR $925	$825	$750	$675	$600	$525	$450	$400

Add $35 for A2 configuration.

GRADING - PPGS™	100%	98%	95%	90%	80%	70%	60%	LAST MSR

INTERCONTINENTAL ARMS INC.

Previous importer located in Los Angeles, CA circa 1970s.

Intercontinental Arms Inc. imported a variety of SA revolvers, an AR-15 type semi-auto rifle, a derringer, a rolling block single shot rifle, and a line of black powder pistol reproductions and replicas. While these firearms were good, utilitarian shooters, they have limited desirability in today's marketplace. The single action revolvers manufactured by Hämmerli are typically priced in the $200-$395 range, the derringer is priced in the $115-$175 range, the AR-15 copy is priced in the $425-$675 range, and the single shot rolling block rifle is priced in the $150-$200 range, depending on original condition.

INTERDYNAMIC OF AMERICA, INC.

Previous distributor located in Miami, FL 1981-84.

PISTOLS: SEMI-AUTO

KG-9 – 9mm Para. cal., 3 in. barrel, open bolt, paramilitary design pistol. Disc. approx. 1982.

	100%	98%	95%	90%	80%	70%	60%	LAST MSR
	$850	$800	$700	$675	$650	$600	$575	

KG-99 – 9mm Para. cal., 3 in. barrel, semi-auto paramilitary design pistol, closed bolt, 36 shot mag., 5 in. vent. shroud barrel, blue only, a stainless steel version of the KG-9. Mfg. by Interdynamic 1984 only.

	100%	98%	95%	90%	80%	70%	60%	LAST MSR
	$425	$375	$325	$275	$250	$225	$195	

* ***KG-99M Mini Pistol***

	100%	98%	95%	90%	80%	70%	60%	LAST MSR
	$495	$450	$400	$325	$275	$250	$225	

INTERNATIONAL BUSINESS MACHINE CORP. (IBM)

Previous WWII subcontractor of M1 carbines located in Poughkeepsie, NY.

Please refer to U.S. M1 Carbines/Rifles listings under U.S. Military.

INTERNATIONAL HARVESTER CORP.

Previous WWII subcontractor of M1 Garand rifles.

Please refer to U.S. M1 Carbines/Rifles listings under U.S. Military.

INTERSTATE ARMS CORP.

Current importer located in Billerica, MA.

Interstate Arms Corp. imports a variety of Chinese made cowboy action shotguns and reproductions, as well as pistols from Turkey.

PISTOLS: SEMI-AUTO

REGENT R100 1911 – .45 ACP cal., 5 in. stainless steel barrel, matte black finish, 7 shot mag., checkered brown plastic grips, mfg. by Tisas in Turkey. Importation began 2010.

	100%	98%	95%	90%	80%	70%	60%	LAST MSR
MSR $560	$495	$450	$395	$365	$335	$300	$275	

SHOTGUNS: SxS

MODEL 99 COACH GUN – 12 or 20 ga., 3 in. chambers, exposed hammers, 20 in. barrels with cyl./cyl. fixed chokes, blue finish with checkered stock and forearm, 7.2 lbs. Importation began 1999, manufactured by SD2 Linyi. Disc. 2009.

	100%	98%	95%	90%	80%	70%	60%	LAST MSR
	$295	$255	$225	$190	$175	$155	$145	*$340*

SHOTGUNS: LEVER ACTION

MODEL 87W – 12 ga. only, 2 3/4 in. chamber, patterned after the Winchester Model 1887, 20 in. barrel, walnut stock and forearm, previous mfg. by SD1 Rizhou, current mfg. by Sun City Machinery Ltd. Importation began mid-2003.

	100%	98%	95%	90%	80%	70%	60%	LAST MSR
MSR $560	$465	$385	$345	$280	$235	$200	$180	

SHOTGUNS: SLIDE ACTION

MODEL 97W HAMMER – 12 ga. only, patterned after the Win. Model 97, hammer, 20 or 26 (new 2008) in. plain barrel with cylinder bore fixed choke, solid frame, oil finish American walnut (new 2005) or hardwood (disc. 2004) stock with grooved "corn

GRADING - PPGS™	100%	98%	95%	90%	80%	70%	60%	LAST MSR

cob" forearm, previous mfg. by SD1 Rizhou, current mfg. by Sun City Machinery Ltd. Importation began 2001.

MSR $425	$365	$315	$275	$225	$200	$175	$160	

MODEL 97T WWI TRENCH GUN – 12 ga. only, authentic reproduction of the original Winchester WWI Trench Gun, complete with shrouded barrel, proper markings, finish, and wood. Imported mid-2002-2006, reintroduced 2010. Mfg. by Sun City Machinery Ltd.

MSR $425	$345	$295	$265	$225	$195	$175	$160	

MODEL 372 – 12 ga., 3 in. chamber, 18 1/2 in. barrel with heat shield and ghost ring sights, bottom ejection port, cylinder choke, black synthetic stock and forearm. Limited importation 2007-2009.

While advertised, this model had limited mfg. with no established pricing.

MODEL 982T (981) – 12 ga. only, 3 in. chamber, defense configuration with 18 1/2 in. cylinder bore barrel with fixed choke, black synthetic stock and forearm, matte black metal finish, current mfg. uses ghost ring sights. Importation began 2001.

MSR $230	$195	$170	$150	$125	$115	$95	$85	

MODEL 1893/97 – similar to Model 97, except built on receiver patterned after Winchester Model 1893, mfg. by SD1 Rizhou. Limited importation mid-2006-2007.

	$325	$285	$250	$220	$190	$175	$160	*$399*

INTRAC ARMS INTERNATIONAL INC.

Previous importer located in Knoxville, TN. Intrac imported trademarks manufactured by Arsenal Bulgaria, and by IM Metal Production facility in Croatia late 2000-2004. Previously imported by HS America, located in Knoxville, TN.

PISTOLS: SEMI-AUTO

HS 2000 – 9mm Para, .357 SIG, or .40 S&W cal., short recoil locked breech mechanism, polymer frame, trigger and grip safety, 3 dot low profile sights, loaded chamber indicator, black finish, 23 oz. Importation from Croatia 2000-2004.

	$400	$340	$285	$235	$210	$185	$175	*$419*

MAKAROV – .380 ACP or 9x18mm cal., double action, black phosphate finish, black grips, supplied with two 8 shot mags. and holster. Imported 2002-2004.

	$175	$150	$125	$100	$85	$80	$75	*$159*

RIFLES: SEMI-AUTO

ROMAK 1 & 2 – 7.62x39mm (Romak 1) or 5.45x39mm (Romak 2) cal., AK-47 copy with 16 1/2 in. barrel and scope mount on left side of receiver, wood thumbhole stock, includes 5 and 10 shot mags., and accessories. Imported 2002-2004.

	$595	$550	$525	$475	$450	$400	$350	*$329*

SLR-101 – similar to Romak, except has 17 1/4 in. cold hammer forged barrel and black polymer stock and forearm, includes 2 mags. and accessories. Imported 2002-2004.

	$650	$575	$500	$450	$425	$350	$325	*$359*

ROMAK 3 – 7.62x54R cal., based on current issue PSL/FPK sniper configuration, 5 or 10 shot mag., last shot bolt hold open, 26 1/2 in. barrel with muzzle brake, mil-spec scope with range finder, bullet drop compensator and illuminated recticle. Imported 2002-2004.

	$900	$825	$750	$650	$575	$525	$475	*$899*

INTRATEC

Previous manufacturer circa 1985-2000 located in Miami, FL.

INTRATEC

PISTOLS: SEMI-AUTO

PROTEC-25 – .25 ACP. cal., double action only, 2 1/2 in. barrel, 8 shot mag., 13 oz. Disc. 2000.

	$110	$80	$65	$45	$35	$30	$25	*$137*

Add $5 for Tec-Kote finish or black slide/frame finish (disc.).

GRADING - PPGS™	100%	98%	95%	90%	80%	70%	60%	LAST MSR

TEC-DC9 – 9mm Para. cal., paramilitary design pistol, 5 in. shrouded barrel, matte black finish, 10 (C/B 1994) or 32* shot mag. Mfg. 1985-94.

$475	$425	$375	$300	$275	$225	$200	*$269*

* ***TEC-9DCK*** – similar to TEC-9, except has new durable Tec-Kote finish with better protection than hard chrome. Mfg. 1991-94.

$495	$465	$425	$375	$325	$295	$260	*$297*

* ***TEC-DC9S*** – matte stainless version of the TEC-9. Disc. 1994.

$550	$500	$450	$400	$350	$300	$250	*$362*

Add $203 for TEC-9 with accessory package (deluxe case, 3-32 shot mags., paramilitary design grip, and recoil compensator).

TEC-DC9M – mini version of the Model TEC-9, including 3 in. barrel and 20 shot mag. Disc. 1994.

$495	$465	$425	$375	$325	$295	$260	*$245*

* ***TEC-DC9MK*** – similar to TEC-9M, except has Tec-Kote rust resistant finish. Mfg. 1991-94.

$525	$450	$400	$350	$300	$250	$200	*$277*

* ***TEC-DC9MS*** – matte stainless version of the TEC-9M. Disc. 1994.

$575	$500	$450	$400	$350	$300	$275	*$339*

TEC-22 "SCORPION" – .22 LR cal., paramilitary design, 4 in. barrel, ambidextrous safety, military matte finish, or electroless nickel, 30 shot mag., adj. sights, 30 oz. Mfg. 1988-94.

$375	$325	$275	$225	$200	$175	$160	*$202*

Add $20 for TEC-Kote finish.

* ***TEC-22N*** – similar to TEC-22, except has nickel finish. Mfg. 1990 only.

$395	$345	$300	$275	$250	$230	$220	*$226*

Add $16 for threaded barrel (Model TEC-22TN).

TEC-22T – threaded barrel variation of the TEC-22 "Scorpion." Mfg. 1991-94.

$395	$350	$300	$250	$225	$195	$175	*$161*

Add $23 for Tec-Kote finish.

SPORT-22 – .22 LR cal., 4 in. non-threaded barrel, 10 shot Ruger styled rotary mag., matte finish, adj. rear sight, 29 1/2 oz. New 1995.

$195	$175	$150	$125	$100	$85	$75	*$170*

Add $15 for stainless steel barrel.

CAT-9, CAT-45, CAT-380 – .380 ACP (new 1995), 9mm Para., or .45 ACP (new 1995) cal., double action only, black finish, polymer frame, sight channel, in slide, only 27 parts, blowback action on 9mm Para., locked breech on .45 ACP, 6 (.45 ACP cal.) or 7 (.380 ACP or 9mm Para.) shot mag., 3 or 3 1/4 (.45 ACP only) in. barrel, 18-21 oz. Mfg. 1993-2000.

$235	$200	$175	$150	$125	$100	$90	*$260*

Subtract $25 for .380 ACP cal.
Add $20 for .45 ACP cal.
Add $15 for Fire Sights.

This series was designed by N. Sirkis of Israel.

AB-10 – 9mm Para. cal., design similar to Luger, 2 3/4 in. non-threaded barrel, choice of 32* (limited supply) or 10 shot mag., black synthetic frame, firing pin safety block, black or stainless steel finish, 45 oz. Mfg. 1997-2000.

$325	$275	$235	$200	$180	$160	$150	*$225*

Add $20 for stainless steel (new 2000).
Add $100 for 32 shot mag.

INTRATEC U.S.A., INC.

Previous manufacturer located in Miami, FL.

CARBINES

TEC-9C – 9mm Para. cal., carbine variation with 16 1/2 in. barrel, 36 shot mag.

Only 1 gun mfg. 1987 - extreme rarity precludes pricing.

GRADING - PPGS™	100%	98%	95%	90%	80%	70%	60%	LAST MSR

DERRINGERS

TEC-38 DERRINGER – .22 WMR, .32 H&R Mag., .357 Mag., or .38 Spl. cal., O/U, 3 in. blue barrel, synthetic black frame, double action, 13 oz. Mfg. 1986-1988.

$110	$95	$85	$75	$65	$60	$55	*$125*

PISTOLS: SEMI-AUTO

PROTEC-22 – while advertised for $112 MSR during 1993, this model never went into production.

TEC-9 – 9mm Para. cal., paramilitary design, 5 in. shrouded barrel, 32 shot mag. Disc.

$550	$495	$450	$395	$350	$295	$250	

INVESTARM, s.p.a.

Current manufacturer located in Marcheno, Italy. Previously distributed by Kimber until 2005, located in Yonkers, NY.

Investarm manufactures a wide variety of shotguns in various configurations, including folding single shots and folding O/Us, which are not currently imported into the U.S. The company also manufactures muzzle loading black powder rifles and pistols. Please contact the company directly for more information, including pricing and availability (see Trademark Index).

INVESTMENT ARMS INC.

Previous company specializing in limited/special editions located in Fort Collins, CO.

Investment Arms Inc. subcontracted various gun manufactures to produce their own limited editions/special editions. These guns were typically marketed within a limited geographic area (usually county or state), and featured various engraving motifs, configurations, and other embellishments. Secondary marketplace liquidity is difficult to determine, based on relative desirability and limited collectibility.

IRON BRIGADE ARMORY

Current rifle manufacturer located in Jacksonville, NC established 1979. Consumer direct sales through FFL.

Iron Brigade Armory makes four bolt action rifles currently, including the XM-3, Chandler Sniper Rifle, Super/Standard Grade, and the Tactical Precision. Please contact the company directly for more information, availability, and current prices (see Trademark Index).

IRWIN PEDERSON ARMS CO.

Previous WWII subcontractor of M1 carbines located in Grand Rapids, MI.

Please refer to U.S. M1 Carbines/Rifles listings under U.S. Military.

IRWINDALE ARMS, INC. (IAI)

Previous manufacturer located in Irwindale, CA 1988-1991.

PISTOLS: SEMI-AUTO

In June, 1991, AMT reacquired the manufacturing rights to all IAI models. Please refer to the AMT section for recent models.

AUTOMAG III – .30 Carbine or 9mm Win. Mag. (mfg. 1990-92) cal., stainless steel only, 6 3/8 in. barrel, patterned after Colt Govt. Model, Millett adj. sights with white outline, grooved Lexan grips, 8 shot mag., 43 oz. Mfg. 1989-91.

$550	$475	$395	$330	$285	$240	$210	*$606*

AUTOMAG IV – .45 Win. Mag., or 10mm cal., semi-auto, 6 1/2 or 8 5/8 (mfg. 1991) in. barrel, 7 shot mag., Millett adj. sights, stainless steel only, 46 oz. Mfg. 1990-91.

$565	$485	$500	$430	$375	$315	$270	*$630*

JAVELINA – 10mm cal., semi-auto, 5 (disc. 1991) or 7 in. barrel, 8 shot mag., Millett adj. sights, wraparound Neoprene grips, stainless steel, wide adj. trigger, long grip safety, 48 oz. Mfg. 1990-91.

$525	$450	$375	$315	$270	$230	$200	*$570*

GRADING - PPGS™	100%	98%	95%	90%	80%	70%	60%	LAST MSR

BACKUP PISTOL – .380 ACP cal., semi-auto action, 2 1/2 in. barrel, stainless steel, Lexan grips, 5 shot mag., 18 oz. Older disc. walnut grip models are worth a slight premium. Disc. 1989.

$200 $165 $135 $110 $95 $75 $65 *$243*

ISRAEL ARMS INTERNATIONAL, INC.

Previous importer (please refer to IAI listing) and manufacturer located in Houston, TX, 1997-2004.

ISRAEL ARMS LTD.

Previous manufacturer located in Kfar Saba, Israel. Imported and distributed exclusively by Israel Arms International, Inc. located in Houston, TX 1997-2001.

PISTOLS: SEMI-AUTO

MODEL 1500 HI POWER – 9mm Para. cal., single action, 3.85 (Compact) or 4.64 (Standard, disc. 1998) in. barrel, two-tone finish, rubberized grips, regular or Meprolite sights, 10 shot mag., 33.6 oz. Imported 1997-98 only.

$360 $305 $255 $225 $200 $185 $170 *$413*

Add approx. $160 for two-tone finish with Meprolite sights.

* ***Model 1500/1501 Hi-Power Compact*** – 9mm Para. or .40 S&W cal., compact variation with 3.85 in. barrel, choice of two-tone (Model 1500) or blue (Model 1501) finish, 32.2 oz. Imported late 1999-2000.

$360 $305 $255 $225 $200 $185 $170 *$412*

MODEL 2500 – 9mm Para. or .40 S&W cal., single or double action, ambidextrous safety with decocking feature, steel slide with alloy frame, 3 7/8 in. barrel, 10 shot mag., matte black finish, 34 oz.

While advertised during 1999, this model had very limited importation.

MODEL 3000 – 9mm Para. cal., double action. Limited importation 2000-2001.

$335 $295 $260 $230 $200 $175 $150 *$374*

MODEL 4000 – .40 S&W cal., double action. Limited importation 2000-2001.

$335 $295 $260 $230 $200 $175 $150 *$374*

MODEL 5000/5001 COMBAT – .45 ACP cal., single action, 4 1/4 in barrel, combat configuration with ambidextrous safety, competition trigger, hammer, and slide stop, front and rear slide serrations, blue (Model 5001) or two-tone (Model 5000) finish, wraparound rubber grips, 42 oz., mfg. in Philipines. Imported 1999-2001.

$395 $365 $330 $295 $265 $235 $210 *$448*

MODEL 6000/6001 STANDARD – .45 ACP cal., single action, 5 in. stainless steel barrel, features beveled feed ramp, extended slide stop, safety and magazine release, ambidextrous safety, beavertail grip safety, combat style hammer, blue (Model 6001) or two-tone (Model 6000, disc. 2000) finish, 38 oz., mfg. in Philipines. Imported 1999-2001.

$395 $365 $330 $295 $265 $235 $210 *$448*

MODEL 7000/7001 WIDE FRAME – .45 ACP cal., single action, similar to Model 6000/6001, except has double stack mag., blue (Model 7001) or two-tone (Model 7000) finish, 40 oz. Imported 1999-2000.

$445 $395 $350 $300 $255 $225 $200 *$490*

RIFLES

MODEL 333 M1 GARAND – .30-06 cal., 24 in. barrel, parts remanufactured to meet GI and mil specs, parkerized finish, 8 shot en-bloc clip, 9 1/2 lbs. Mfg. 2000-2001.

$895 $850 $800 $700 $600 $500 $400 *$852*

MODEL 444 FAL – .308 Win. cal., patterned after the FN FAL model. Mfg. by Imbel, located in Brazil, 2000-2001.

$925 $850 $795 $725 $675 $595 $550 *$897*

GRADING - PPGS™	100%	98%	95%	90%	80%	70%	60%	LAST MSR

ISRAEL MILITARY INDUSTRIES (IMI)

Previous manufacturer established 1933-circa 2009, and located in Israel.

IMI manufactured guns (both new and disc. models) include Galil, Jericho, Magnum Research, Timberwolf, Uzi, and others, and can be located in their respective sections.

ISRAEL WEAPON INDUSTRIES LTD. (I.W.I.)

Current manufacturer established circa 2009, and located in Israel. Currently imported beginning 2013 by I.W.I USA, Inc. located in Harrisburg, PA.

Israel Weapon Industries (I.W.I.) is part of a group of companies specializing in development, manufacturing and marketing a variety of products for the international and national military and law enforcement. In early 2011 Carl Walther from Ulm, Germany indicated that it had reached a licensing agreement with I.W.I. Ltd. to manufacture a series of Uzi pistols in .22 LR cal. In late 2012, I.W.I. US was created to import the Tavor semi-auto rifle and centerfire Uzi Pro pistol. Please refer to listings in the Uzi and Tavor sections.

ITALIAN MILITARY ARMS

Previous Italian popular military models mfg. since 1891.

PISTOLS: SEMI-AUTO

GLISENTI MODEL 1910 – 9mm Glisenti cal., 4 in. barrel, 7 shot mag., checkered wood grips, official Italian service pistol of both WWI and WWII, 32 oz.

$1,500 $1,250 $1,000 $800 $700 $600 $500

Warning: 9mm Para. ammunition (9x19mm) cannot be used in this pistol - only 9mm Glisenti, as it is approx. 25% less powerful than the 9mm Para.

BRIXIA – similar to Glisenti Model 1910, except utilizes simplified mfg. techniques, mostly sold to civilians.

$2,000 $1,500 $1,250 $1,000 $750 $600 $500

SOSSO – 9mm Para. cal., large experimental semi-auto, early pistols were double action and marked "Sosso", late guns were single action and built by FNA. All Sosso pistols feature a unique continuous "chain link" 19 or 21 shot mag. Approx. 5 guns mfg.

Extreme rarity factor precludes accurate price evaluation.

CARBINES/RIFLES: BOLT ACTION

MODEL 1891 MANNLICHER-CARCANO – 6.5x52mm Carcano cal., integrated 6 shot mag. that forms front part of trigger guard housing, 18 (carbine) or 31 (rifle) in. barrel, straight bolt handle, adj. sight, military stock, carbine has either folding or detachable bayonet, mfg. in Italian Govt. Arsenals, located in Terni, Brescia, Torre Annuziata, and Torino circa 1891-1918. Approx. 3.5-4 million mfg.

$225 $175 $150 $125 $100 $85 $70

MODEL 38 TERNI MILITARY RIFLE – 7.35x52mm Carcano cal., similar to 1891, except turned down bolt handle, 21 in. barrel and folding bayonet.

$225 $175 $150 $125 $100 $85 $70

ITHACA CLASSIC DOUBLES

Previous importer and SxS shotgun manufacturer 1998-2003, and located in Victor, NY from 1999-2003 and Mendon, NY until 1999.

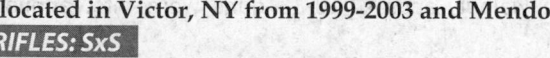

RIFLES: SxS

DOUBLE RIFLE – many popular cals., including .45-70 Govt., also available in 20 ga. with 26 in. fully rifled barrels, express sights, German claw type scope mounts, DT, ejectors, exhibition walnut standard, many options were available. Limited importation only.

Advertised MSR was $8,500, w/o engraving or other special orders/features.

SHOTGUNS: SxS

All Ithaca Classic Doubles shotguns were handmade to order in the U.S. Frames were made from the traditional forgings and internal parts from solid steel. Barrels were hammer forged from geniune Krupp steel. Metal finishing, checkering, oil finish, and engraving were done completely by hand. All guns were fitted to customer's specifications and wood selection. Guns were available in .410 bore through 12 ga., with full rifle barrels available in 12 or 20 ga. and .45-

GRADING - PPGS™	100%	98%	95%	90%	80%	70%	60%	LAST MSR

70 Govt. cal. Each gauge has its own frame size, and serial numbers were continued from the last gun Ithaca manufactured in 1948 (ser. no. 469,999).

The Ithaca custom shop manufactured custom orders, including special options and features.

For Special Combination Sets - add $3,000 (4E, 5E, 6E) and $3,750 (Grades 7E & Sousa) for extra set of 16 (20 ga. frame) or 28 (.410 bore frame) ga. barrels.

Add $600-$2,150 for canvas, canvas and leather, leather, or oak and leather cases.

Add $1,125 for SST and vent. rib.

Add $950 for VR.

SKEET GRADE (SPECIAL FIELD) – 16 (new 2001), 20, 28 ga., or .410 bore, designed for field and clay shooting, DT, ejectors, 26, 28, or 30 in. barrels with fixed chokes, light perimeter hand engraving with metal stippling on shoulders and in front of top opening lever, Turnbull bone and charcoal case colors, checkered pistol grip or English feather crotch walnut stock and forearm, 5lbs. 5 oz.-6 lbs. 6 oz. Mfg. late 1998-2002.

$5,500	$4,750	$3,750	$3,250	$2,650	$2,175	$1,775	*$5,999*

Add 20% for SST or vent. rib option.

CLASSIC COMPETITION GRADE – all gauges, competition features. Mfg. 2002-2003.

$5,500	$4,750	$3,750	$3,250	$2,650	$2,175	$1,775	*$5,995*

GRADE 4E CLASSIC – 16 (new 2001), 20, 28 ga., or .410 bore, features gold plated triggers, jewelled barrel flats, hand tuned locks, hand engraved three game scenes with floral scroll, deluxe walnut stock and forearm with fleur-de-lis pattern and 22 LPI checkering, other specifications similar to Special Field/Skeet Grade. Mfg. 1998-2003.

$6,750	$5,750	$4,900	$4,100	$3,300	$2,500	$1,850	*$7,500*

STAR MODEL COMPETITION – competition model. Limited mfg. 2003.

$6,750	$5,750	$4,900	$4,100	$3,300	$2,500	$1,850	*$7,500*

GRADE 5E CLASSIC – step up from Grade 4E, with more elaborate frame engraving and gold inlays on frame sides, upgraded walnut. Mfg. 2002-2003.

$7,500	$6,500	$5,750	$4,850	$4,100	$3,500	$2,500	*$8,500*

GRADE 6E CLASSIC – step up from Grade 5E, with fine scroll engraving and gold dog inlays on frame sides, upgraded walnut. Mfg. 2002-2003.

$8,500	$7,500	$6,500	$5,750	$4,950	$4,150	$3,250	*$9,999*

GRADE 7E CLASSIC – 16 (new 2001), 20, 28 ga., or .410 bore, features hand engraved oak leaf scroll on frame and barrels, and 24Kt. flat gold game scene inlays, including a bald eagle on floor plate, exhibition grade American walnut with 12 checkered panels in fleur-de-lis pattern, other specifications similar to Special Field/Skeet Grade. Mfg. 1998-2003.

$9,250	$8,250	$7,250	$6,150	$5,350	$4,450	$3,500	*$11,000*

SOUSA SPECIAL – 16 (new 2001), 20, 28 ga., or .410 bore, top-of-the-line model with every possible refinement, each gun individually hand fitted, jewelled, and polished, includes famous 24Kt. Sousa mermaid on trigger guard, other specifications similar to Special Field/Skeet Grade. Special order only, limited mfg. 1998-2003.

$16,750	$14,000	$12,000	$10,000	$8,250	$7,000	$5,750	*$18,000*

SUPERLATIVE CLASS – custom order, best quality model with a wide choice of engraving options and inlays, exhibition grade walnut, approx. 10-15 guns were mfg. annually. Limited mfg. 2002-2003.

Prices for this model started at $20,000.

SHOTGUNS: SINGLE SHOT

KNICKERBOCKER SINGLE BARREL TRAP – limited mfg. of 100 guns during 2003.

Prices for this model started at $9,000, w/o engraving.

ITHACA GUN COMPANY (NEW MFG.)

Current manufacturer established in 2006 and located in Upper Sandusky, OH.

During December of 2007, Ithaca Gun Company bought out the remaining assets and equipment of Ithaca Gun Company LLC and moved production to Upper Sandusky, OH. Please contact the company directly for more information, including price and options on available models (see Trademark Index).

GRADING - PPGS™	100%	98%	95%	90%	80%	70%	60%	LAST MSR

PISTOLS: SEMI-AUTO

MODEL 1911 – .45 ACP cal., hand lapped frame and slide, 5 in. barrel, rear slide serrations, blue finish, skeletonized trigger, extended beavertail, double diamond checkered walnut grips. New mid-2011.

MSR $1,799	$1,595	$1,350	$1,150	$1,000	$875	$725	$575	

Add $50 for adj. sights or $150 for adj. sights and ambidextrous safety.

SHOTGUNS

Ithaca currently offers shotguns in 12, 16, 20 and 28 ga. (2 3/4 or 3 in. chambers).

M37 SERIES – 12, 16, 20 (2 3/4 and 3 in. chamber), or 28 ga. (2 3/4 in. chamber), 26, 28, or 30 in. barrel, 5 or 8 shot, wood, synthetic, or laminated stock, vent. rib or field barrel, brass bead front sight, fixed scope mount (DeerSlayer only), or Marble Arms rear sight (Featherweight Upland), bottom ejection action, Pachmayr recoil pad, high luster, matte blue or Perma-Guard finish, 5.8-8.2 lbs. New 2007.

Current models with MSRs are as follows: Featherlight Series - $799-$999 MSR, Featherlight Combo - $1,059 MSR, 28 ga. Featherlight Deluxe - $999-$1,589 MSR, Featherlight Waterfowl - $759-$799 MSR, Featherlight Youth Model - $799-$824 MSR, Featherlight Trap - $899 MSR, Ultralight - disc. 2012, last $859-$959 MSR, Deerslayer - $899-$1,224 MSR, Turkeyslayer - $699-$999 MSR, Hogslayer - $759-$779 MSR, new 2012), Tactical - $699-$769 MSR, and the Home Defense Model - $685-$769 MSR.

ITHACA GUN COMPANY LLC (OLDER MFG.)

Previous manufacturer located in Ithaca, NY from 1883-1986, King Ferry, NY circa 1989-2005, and Auburn, NY right before it closed in June, 2005.

Ithaca Gun Company, LLC had resumed production on the Model 37 slide action shotgun and variations during 1989, and then relocated to King Ferry, NY shortly thereafter. In the past, Ithaca also absorbed companies including Syracuse Arms Co., Lefever Arms Co., Union Fire Arms Co., Wilkes-Barre Gun Co., as well as others.

COMBINATION GUNS

LSA-55 TURKEY GUN – O/U shotgun-rifle combo, 12 ga., .222 Rem., 24 1/2 in. ribbed barrel, exposed hammer, folding rear sight, checkered Monte Carlo stock. Mfg. by Tikka, Finland 1970-81.

	$650	$575	$475	$450	$425	$385	$330	

HANDGUNS

ITHACA WWII MILITARY MFG.

For more information on other WWI and WWII M1911/A1 military contracts, please refer to the Colt's Manufacturing section Pistols: Semi-Auto, Govt. M1911/1911A1 Military Variations in this text.

ITHACA 50TH SEMI-AUTO ANNIVERSARY MODEL – .45 ACP cal., 5 in. match barrel with bushing, blue polished or tactical matte finish, checkered diamond pattern walnut grips, extended beavertail grip safety, includes plastic case and certificate, only 125 mfg. with special serialization 1995-97. Disc.

	$695	$625	$550	$500	$450	$400	$360	*$795*

This model was offered exclusively by All American Sales, Inc. located in Memphis, TN.

X-CALIBER SINGLE SHOT – .22 LR or .44 Mag. (advertised only) cal., break open action with contoured wood grip and forearm, 8, 10 or 15 in. barrel, unique dual firing pin detonates both rimfire and centerfire cartridges. While advertised in 1988, the Models 20 & 30 were never retailed. Approx. 300 units were mfg. in 22 cal. only.

	$1,200	$950	$825	$695	$550	$425	$300	

RIFLES: BOLT ACTION

LSA-55 STANDARD – .222 Rem., .22-250 Rem., 6mm Rem., .243 Win., or .308 Win. cal., Mauser type action, 22 in. barrel, leaf sight, 3 shot mag., checkered Monte Carlo stock. Mfg. in Finland by Tikka from 1969-77.

	$400	$375	$350	$310	$275	$250	$230	

The LSA Model designation stands for Light, Strong, Accurate.

GRADING - PPGS™	100%	98%	95%	90%	80%	70%	60%	LAST MSR

LSA-55 DELUXE – similar to Standard, except rollover cheekpiece, rosewood pistol grip cap and forend tip, skipline checkering, no sights, scope mounts furnished.

$495 $450 $425 $400 $365 $345 $325

LSA-55 HEAVY BARREL – similar to LSA-55, except .222 Rem. or .22-250 Rem. cal. only, target heavy barrel, special beavertail stock, 8 1/2 lbs.

$450 $425 $400 $375 $350 $325 $300

LSA-65 – similar to LSA-55, except long action for calibers .25-06 Rem., .270 Win., or .30-06. Mfg. 1969-77.

$400 $375 $350 $310 $275 $250 $230

LSA-65 DELUXE – similar to LSA-55, except has deluxe checkered walnut stock, .25-06 Rem.,.270 Win., or .30-06.

$495 $450 $425 $400 $365 $345 $325

RIFLES: LEVER ACTION

MODEL 49 SADDLEGUN – .22 LR or .22 WMR cal., lever action, single shot. Mfg. 1961-78. Martini-style action.

$145 $130 $110 $80 $65 $50 $40

Add 15% for .22 WMR cal. Add 20% for Deluxe Model.

MODEL 49R – similar to Model 49 Saddlegun, except is slide action repeater. Mfg. 1965-1971.

$265 $250 $235 $200 $175 $150 $125

Add 15% for .22 WMR cal.

MODEL 49 PRESENTATION – similar to Model 49 Saddlegun, except gold-plated trigger, hammer, engraved receiver, fancy walnut. Mfg. 1962-1974.

$295 $275 $250 $235 $200 $165 $135

MODEL 49 ST. LOUIS BICENTENNIAL – like Deluxe Model 49, except inscription on receiver. 200 mfg. 1964.

$325 $255 $215 $165 $130 $115 $95 *$35*

MODEL 72 SADDLEGUN – .22 or .22 WMR cal., lever action, 18 1/2 in. barrel, hooded front sight. Mfg. 1973-78 by Erma Werke, W. Germany.

$375 $325 $275 $200 $175 $145 $125

MODEL 72 DELUXE – similar to Model 72, except has silver finished engraved receiver, deluxe walnut, octagon barrel. Mfg. 1974-76.

$450 $400 $300 $250 $225 $175 $145

RIFLES: SEMI-AUTO

MODEL X5 LIGHTNING – .22 LR cal., 7 shot mag., grooved forearm, Model X5-T Lightning has tube mag., Model X5-C has box mag. Mfg. 1958-1964.

$195 $165 $125 $100 $80 $70 $60

MODEL X-15 LIGHTNING – .22 LR cal., similar to X5-C, except forearm is not grooved. Mfg. 1964-1967.

$195 $165 $125 $100 $80 $70 $60

RIFLES: SINGLE SHOT

MODEL 89 – .243 Win., .30-06, .375 H&H, .416 Rigby, or 7x57mm cal., falling block action, 26 or 28 in. Shilen barrel, full-length uncheckered walnut stock.

While advertised at $658 MSR during 1994, this model never went into production.

SHOTGUNS: O/U, PREVIOUS IMPORTATION

Note: Ithaca was the sole importer for Perazzi in the '70s. All new and used models will be in the P section under Perazzi. Perazzi currently distributes their own firearms.

Note: Please refer to the Fabarm section in this text for those models previously imported by Ithaca (imported 1994-95).

Note: Previously imported SKB O/U shotguns can be found under the SKB heading.

GRADING - PPGS™	100%	98%	95%	90%	80%	70%	60%	LAST MSR

SHOTGUNS: SxS, PREVIOUS IMPORTATION

Note: Previously imported SKB SxS shotguns can be found under the SKB heading.

SHOTGUNS: SxS, 1880-1948 MFG.

AUTO & BURGLAR SxS – 20 ga., 10 in. barrels, case hardened finish, pistol grip, Model A (approx. 2,500 mfg.) has grip spur, Model B (approx. 2,000 mfg.) has squared grip; both were mfg. in lots of about 100 according to demand, and serial numbers are mixed with those of regular Ithaca shotguns. Guns not currently registered with BATFE cannot be legally owned and are subject to seizure. Mfg. 1922-34.

* ***Auto & Burglar SxS Model A*** – serial no. range is 343,336-398,365.

100%	98%	95%	90%	80%	70%	60%
$1,850	$1,450	$1,200	$975	$775	$675	$575

* ***Auto & Burglar SxS Model B*** – serial no. range is 425,000-464,699.

100%	98%	95%	90%	80%	70%	60%
$1,450	$1,200	$975	$775	$675	$575	$465

Add $300-$500 for original holster (very rare). Prototype or special order guns (in 16, 28 ga., or .410 bore) are extremely rare and command premiums of 100%+.

ITHACA HAMMERLESS – 12, 16, 20, 28 ga., or .410 bore, 26-32 in. fluid steel or damascus barrels, boxlock, extractors, double triggers, any standard choke, checkered pistol grip stock and forearm, grades shown differ in overall quality, ornamentation, grade of wood, and style of checkering. In 1925, the rotary bolt and stronger frame were adapted (ser. numbers after 400,000 - commonly referred to as NID or New Ithaca Double). Values are the same as for pre-400,000 serial range shotguns. Ithaca doubles incorporated a number of design changes made on the action - they are referred to as the Lewis, Crass, Flues, and Minier frame variations.

Add $200 for SST.
Add $150 for SNT.
Add $350 for VR on Grades 4, 5, 7, and $2,000 Grade.
Add $200 for VR - lower grades.
Add $175 for beavertail forearm.
Add 33% for auto ejectors on Grades No. 1, 2, and 3.
Subtract 33% if without ejectors on Grades 4E-7E.
Early hammer doubles in average condition are approx. valued between $175-$450. However, if 60%+ condition remains (including original case colors), values can approximate those listed.

100%	98%	95%	90%	80%	70%	60%	50%	40%	30%	20%	10%

FIELD GRADE

* ***Field Grade 10 ga. Mag.***

100%	98%	95%	90%	80%	70%	60%	50%	40%	30%	20%	10%
N/A	N/A	$1,500	$1,400	$1,300	$1,200	$1,100	$950	$825	$775	$675	$630

3 1/2 in. chambered 10 ga. Mags. are serial numbered over 500,000. Total mfg. was approx. 850 guns for all grades. 2 7/8 in. chambered 10 gauges are priced the same as a 12 ga. A 12 ga., 3 in. model was also made on the 10 ga. frame - only 87 were mfg. and specimens are noted in the 500,000 serial range.

* ***Field Grade 12 ga.***

100%	98%	95%	90%	80%	70%	60%	50%	40%	30%	20%	10%
$1,000	$800	$600	$550	$500	$450	$415	$380	$350	$325	$300	$280

* ***Field Grade 16 ga.***

100%	98%	95%	90%	80%	70%	60%	50%	40%	30%	20%	10%
$1,500	$1,200	$1,000	$800	$700	$650	$600	$550	$500	$425	$375	$340

* ***Field Grade 20 ga.***

100%	98%	95%	90%	80%	70%	60%	50%	40%	30%	20%	10%
$1,600	$1,300	$1,100	$1,000	$850	$800	$750	$700	$600	$550	$500	$440

* ***Field Grade 28 ga.***

100%	98%	95%	90%	80%	70%	60%	50%	40%	30%	20%	10%
N/A	N/A	$3,000	$2,700	$2,400	$2,300	$2,250	$2,200	$2,100	$2,050	$2,025	$2,000

* ***Field Grade .410 bore***

100%	98%	95%	90%	80%	70%	60%	50%	40%	30%	20%	10%
N/A	N/A	$3,500	$3,000	$2,500	$2,300	$2,250	$2,200	$2,100	$2,050	$2,025	$2,000

GRADE NO. 1 – manufactured in both Flues and NID models, similar to Field Grade.

* ***Grade No. 1 12 ga.***

100%	98%	95%	90%	80%	70%	60%	50%	40%	30%	20%	10%
$1,225	$1,000	$800	$600	$550	$500	$450	$415	$380	$350	$325	$315

	100%	98%	95%	90%	80%	70%	60%	50%	40%	30%	20%	10%
*** Grade No. 1 16 ga.**	$1,700	$1,550	$1,275	$1,150	$925	$825	$750	$700	$650	$600	$550	$500
*** Grade No. 1 20 ga.**	$1,950	$1,700	$1,400	$1,200	$1,000	$900	$850	$800	$750	$700	$600	$550
*** Grade No. 1 28 ga.**	N/A	N/A	$4,200	$3,900	$3,600	$3,000	$2,725	$2,400	$2,100	$1,900	$1,600	$1,300
*** Grade No. 1 .410 bore**	N/A	N/A	$4,500	$4,100	$3,750	$3,200	$2,900	$2,500	$2,200	$2,000	$1,725	$1,500
GRADE NO. 2												
*** Grade No. 2 10 ga. Mag.**	$2,400	$2,000	$1,800	$1,600	$1,400	$1,300	$1,200	$1,100	$950	$900	$800	$735
3 1/2 in. chambered 10 ga. Mags. are serial numbered over 500,000. Total mfg. was approx. 850 guns for all grades. 2 7/8 in. chambered 10 gauges are priced the same as a 12 ga.												
*** Grade No. 2 12 ga.**	$1,950	$1,700	$1,550	$1,275	$1,150	$925	$825	$750	$700	$650	$600	$550
*** Grade No. 2 16 ga.**	$1,500	$1,200	$1,000	$900	$800	$750	$700	$650	$600	$550	$500	$475
*** Grade No. 2 20 ga.**	$2,150	$1,950	$1,700	$1,400	$1,200	$1,000	$900	$850	$800	$750	$700	$600
*** Grade No. 2 28 ga.**	N/A	N/A	$5,500	$5,000	$4,400	$4,000	$3,600	$3,200	$2,800	$2,400	$2,000	$1,725
*** Grade No. 2 .410 bore**	N/A	N/A	$5,750	$5,150	$4,500	$4,000	$3,600	$3,200	$2,800	$2,400	$2,000	$1,725
GRADE NO. 3												
*** Grade No. 3 10 ga. Mag.**	$3,500	$2,900	$2,300	$1,850	$1,600	$1,400	$1,300	$1,200	$1,100	$950	$825	$735
3 1/2 in. chambered 10 ga. Mags. are serial numbered over 500,000. Total mfg. was approx. 850 guns for all grades. 2 7/8 in. chambered 10 gauges are priced the same as a 12 ga.												
*** Grade No. 3 12 ga.**	$2,300	$2,075	$1,850	$1,500	$1,200	$1,000	$800	$750	$700	$650	$600	$550
*** Grade No. 3 16 ga.**	N/A	N/A	$1,950	$1,700	$1,400	$1,200	$1,000	$900	$850	$800	$750	$700
*** Grade No. 3 20 ga.**	N/A	N/A	$2,150	$1,950	$1,700	$1,400	$1,200	$1,000	$900	$850	$800	$750
*** Grade No. 3 28 ga.** – only 5 mfg. Extreme rarity factor precludes accurate pricing evaluation.												
*** Grade No. 3 .410 bore** – only 7 mfg. Extreme rarity factor precludes accurate pricing evaluation.												
GRADE NO. 4E – auto ejectors.												
*** Grade No. 4E 10 ga. Mag.**	$5,800	$5,350	$4,650	$4,100	$3,350	$2,650	$2,100	$1,975	$1,875	$1,750	$1,650	$1,550
3 1/2 in. chambered 10 ga. Mags. are serial numbered over 500,000. Total mfg. was approx. 850 guns for all grades. 2 7/8 in. chambered 10 gauges are priced the same as a 12 ga.												
*** Grade No. 4E 12 ga.**	N/A	$3,750	$3,325	$3,000	$2,500	$2,100	$1,700	$1,550	$1,325	$1,200	$1,100	$995
*** Grade No. 4E 16 ga.**	N/A	N/A	$4,100	$3,750	$3,325	$3,000	$2,400	$2,000	$1,875	$1,650	$1,550	$1,450

100%	98%	95%	90%	80%	70%	60%	50%	40%	30%	20%	10%

* ***Grade No. 4E 20 ga.***

N/A	N/A	$5,000	$4,625	$4,250	$3,725	$3,525	$3,300	$3,100	$2,950	$2,700	$2,300

* ***Grade No. 4E 28 ga.***

Extreme rarity factor precludes accurate pricing evaluation.

* ***Grade No. 4E .410 bore***

Extreme rarity factor precludes accurate pricing evaluation.

GRADE NO. 5E – auto ejectors.

* ***Grade No. 5E 10 ga.*** – only 9 mfg.

Extreme rarity factor precludes accurate pricing evaluation.

* ***Grade No. 5E 12 ga.***

N/A	N/A	$4,750	$4,200	$3,750	$3,325	$3,000	$2,700	$2,200	$1,875	$1,650	$1,325

* ***Grade No. 5E 16 ga.***

N/A	N/A	$5,400	$4,750	$4,200	$3,750	$3,325	$3,000	$2,700	$2,200	$1,875	$1,650

* ***Grade No. 5E 20 ga.***

N/A	N/A	$6,000	$5,400	$4,750	$4,200	$3,750	$3,325	$3,000	$2,700	$2,200	$1,875

* ***Grade No. 5E 28 ga.***

Extreme rarity factor precludes accurate pricing evaluation.

* ***Grade No. 5E .410 bore***

Extreme rarity factor precludes accurate pricing evaluation.

GRADE NO. 6E – auto ejectors, total mfg. N/A.

Rarity factor precludes accurate price evaluation on this model.

GRADE NO. 7E – auto ejectors, only 22 mfg. in all gauges.

Extreme rarity factor precludes accurate pricing evaluation on this model.

$2,000 GRADE – 12 ga., top-of-the-line model, auto ejectors, single selective trigger.

N/A	N/A	$8,450	$7,400	$6,500	$5,650	$4,750	$4,000	$3,250	$2,600	$2,100	$1,700

PRE-WAR $1,000 GRADE – 12 ga., top-of-the-line models, auto ejectors, single selective trigger.

N/A	N/A	$9,500	$8,450	$7,400	$6,500	$5,650	$4,750	$4,000	$3,250	$2,600	$2,250

SOUSA GRADE – has mermaids on trigger guard in gold, only 11 manufactured (including one .410 bore). This model is very rare and prices are hard to establish. Recently, the price range has been approx. $15,000-$40,000, depending on gauge and original condition.

The famous band director and composer, John Phillip Sousa, assisted in the development of this model.

GRADING - PPGS™	100%	98%	95%	90%	80%	70%	60%	LAST MSR

SHOTGUNS: SEMI-AUTO

MODEL 51A FEATHERLIGHT STANDARD – 12 or 20 ga., 30 in. full, 28 in. full or mod., 26 in. imp. cyl., gas operated, autoloading, checkered pistol grip stock. Vent. rib became standard during late production. Mfg. 1970-1985.

Older models								
w/o VR	$250	$230	$200	$180	$165	$150	$130	
Vent. rib	$295	$265	$235	$210	$190	$175	$165	

Last MSR with VR was $477.

MODEL 51A MAGNUM – similar to 51 Standard, except 3 in. shells only, blue finish, recoil pad, VR became standard in 1984. Disc. 1985.

Older models								
w/o VR	$265	$235	$220	$205	$180	$165	$150	
Vent. rib	$325	$275	$250	$225	$200	$185	$170	

GRADING - PPGS™	100%	98%	95%	90%	80%	70%	60%	LAST MSR

MODEL 51A MAGNUM WATERFOWLER – similar to 51 Standard, except 3 in. shells only, matte finished metal, flat finished walnut, recoil pad. Vent. rib standard. Mfg. 1984-86.

$325	$295	$275	$250	$230	$200	$180	*$625*

Add $40 for camouflaged exterior finish (mfg. 1986 only).

MODEL 51A SUPREME TRAP – similar to 51 Standard, except 12 ga. only, 30 in. barrel, 7 post rib, full choke, select wood, pad, trap style stock. Add $36 for Monte Carlo. Mfg. 1970-86.

$450	$375	$325	$295	$270	$250	$230	*$869*

MODEL 51A SUPREME SKEET – similar to 51 Standard, except 26 in. VR barrel, skeet choke, select wood, 20 ga. was available 1983. Mfg. 1970-1986.

$465	$395	$340	$300	$280	$260	$240	*$858*

MODEL 51A DEERSLAYER – similar to 51 Standard, with 24 in. slug barrel, rifle sights, recoil pad, no rib. Mfg. 1972-83.

$350	$300	$260	$230	$195	$180	$165	*$477*

MODEL 51A TURKEY GUN – 12 ga. Mag. only, 26 in. barrel, matte finish, sling and swivels included. Mfg. 1984-86.

$360	$305	$275	$265	$250	$230	$210	*$625*

MODEL 51 DUCKS UNLIMITED – similar to 51 Deluxe, with D/U emblem on receiver.

$425	$375	$335	$300	$280	$260	$230	

MODEL 51 PRESENTATION – 12 ga., blue, engraved, gold engraved receiver with deluxe walnut. Mfg. 1984-86.

$1,325	$1,050	$875	$700	$575	$450	$325	*$1,658*

MODEL XL 300 – 12 or 20 ga., gas operated, various barrel lengths with or w/o VR.. Mfg. 1973-76.

$250	$230	$200	$180	$165	$150	$130	

Add 15% for VR barrel.

MODEL XL 900 – 12 or 20 ga., gas operated, various barrel lengths with VR. Mfg. 1973-78.

$295	$275	$245	$210	$185	$170	$150	

Add 10% for skeet, trap, or slug variations.

Shotguns: Semi-Auto, Mag-10 Series

All Ithaca Mag-10s were disc. 1986.

MAG-10 – 10 ga., 3 1/2 in. Mag., various barrel lengths, stainless steel breech block assembly, gas operated, various chokes, plain barrel, 11 lbs. Mfg. 1975-1986.

100% values assume NIB condition - if without, subtract 10%.

* ***Mag-10 Standard Grade*** – dull finished, plain uncheckered walnut stock, plain barrel, matte finished metal.

$675	$600	$550	$500	$460	$430	$395	*$726*

* ***Mag-10 Standard Grade with VR*** – available in 22, 26, 28, or 32 in. barrel lengths - otherwise similar to Standard Grade.

$750	$650	$550	$495	$450	$400	$360	*$781*

Add $60 for camouflaged exterior finish.
Add $60 for interchangeable choke tubes (3) - became available in 1986.

* ***Mag-10 Deluxe Vent*** – select checkered walnut stock and forearm with sling swivels, 22, 26, 28, or 32 in. barrels, high lustre wood finish.

$800	$700	$600	$550	$495	$450	$400	*$924*

* ***Mag-10 Supreme Grade*** – extra-select checkered walnut stock and forearm with sling swivels, otherwise similar to Deluxe Vent.

$995	$800	$725	$675	$595	$550	$495	*$1,124*

* ***Mag-10 Mag. 10 Roadblocker*** – 22 in. cylinder bored ribless barrel, parkerized finish.

$750	$625	$575	$500	$460	$430	$400	*$741*

GRADING - PPGS™	100%	98%	95%	90%	80%	70%	60%	LAST MSR

* ***Mag-10 National Wild Turkey Fed. Special Edition*** – mfg. in 1985 only.

	$950	$795	$625	N/A	N/A	N/A	N/A	

MAG-10 PRESENTATION OR CENTENNIAL – 10 ga. Mag., blue, engraved, gold inlaid receiver, extra fancy walnut. Limited production. Approx. 200 mfg. in Presentation Grade 1983-86.

	$1,875	$1,550	$1,300	$1,050	$915	$830	$745	*$1,727*

This configuration was also offered as a 3 gun set - a NIB set is currently selling in the $4,750 range.

SHOTGUNS: SINGLE SHOT, LEVER ACTION

MODEL 66 – 12, 20 ga., or .410 bore single shot lever action, field gun only. Mfg. 1963-78.

	$150	$125	$100	$75	$70	$65	$55	

Add 33% to .410 bore.
Add 25% for VRs that were also available on special order.

* ***Model 66 RS*** – 20 ga. slug gun with 22 in. barrel and rifle type sights, recoil pad.

	$195	$165	$135	$115	$90	$80	$70	

Add 25% for special order VR.

SHOTGUNS: SINGLE BARREL TRAP

CENTURY TRAP – please refer to the SKB section.

CENTURY II TRAP – please refer to the SKB section.

SINGLE BARREL TRAP – 12 ga., 30, 32, or 34 in. barrels, VR, boxlock, auto ejector, checkered pistol grip and forearm, grades differ in engraving, overall workmanship, and grade or wood and checkering. Values on these models sometimes vary greatly depending on originality of finish, customer alterations, and other variations trap shooters might use to alter dimensions for their particular shooting requirements. Values represent trap guns in original, unaltered condition.

Note: Flues model mfg. prior to 1921 with serial numbers under 400,000 generally have better engraving than NID (New Ithaca Double) models over serial number 400,000 (also referred to as Knick models).

Trap guns under 60% original condition will be within 25% of the value shown in the 60% column.

* ***Single Barrel Trap Victory Grade*** – disc. 1938.

	$1,250	$995	$850	$775	$675	$575	$495	

* ***Single Barrel Trap No. 4E*** – disc. 1976.

	$2,950	$2,675	$2,450	$2,200	$2,000	$1,825	$1,625	

* ***Single Barrel Trap No. 5E*** – 12 ga., 32 or 34 in. barrel, custom order only, elaborate engraving, quality worksmanship throughout. Originally mfg. 1925-86, mfg. resumed 1988-91.

	$4,000	$3,500	$3,000	$2,550	$2,175	$1,900	$1,725	*$7,500*

* ***Single Barrel Trap No. 6E*** – this model was available by special order only. Rarity factor precludes accurate pricing.

* ***Single Barrel Trap No. 7E*** – disc. 1964.

	$6,500	$5,500	$4,700	$4,000	$3,500	$3,000	$2,500	

* ***Single Barrel Trap Dollar Grade*** – 12 ga., 32 or 34 in. barrel. Top-of-the-line model custom built to customer specifications. Original mfg. was stopped 1986 and resumed 1988-91.

	$6,750	$5,950	$5,200	$4,600	$3,850	$3,250	$2,775	*$10,000*

* ***Single Barrel Trap $5,000 Grade*** – similar to Pre-War $1,000 grade.

	$9,500	$8,900	$8,175	$7,650	$6,725	$5,825	$4,950	

* ***Single Barrel Trap Sousa Grade*** – extremely rare.

Extreme rarity factor precludes accurate pricing evaluation. Prices will be higher than the $5,000 Grade.

GRADING - PPGS™	100%	98%	95%	90%	80%	70%	60%	LAST MSR

SHOTGUNS: SLIDE ACTION

In 1987, Ithaca Acquisition Corp. reintroduced the Model 37 as the Model 87. Recently manufactured Model 87s are listed in addition to both new and older Model 37s (produced pre-1986). During late 1996, Ithaca Gun Co., LLC resumed manufacture of the Model 37, while discontinuing the Model 87.

Over 2 million Model 37s have been produced.

Model 37s with ser. nos. above 855,000 will accept both 2 3/4 and 3 in. chambered barrels interchangeably. Earlier guns have incompatible threading for the magnum barrels.

MODEL 37 TRENCH AND RIOT GUNS – see separate listing under Trench Guns in the T Section.

MODEL 37 DS POLICE SPECIAL – 12 ga. only, 18 1/2 in. barrel with rifle sights, Parkerized finish on metal, oil finished stock, typically subcontracted by police departments or law enforcement agencies, with or without unit code markings.

$325	$275	$235	$200	$185	$170	$160	

MODEL 37 $1000 GRADE – all gauges, deluxe engraving and checkering, gold inlaid, select figured walnut, hand-finished parts. Mfg. 1937-40.

$5,750	$5,200	$4,750	$4,250	$3,750	$3,250	$2,650	

MODEL 37 $5000 GRADE – similar to $1000 Grade, post-war designation. Mfg. 1947-67.

$5,250	$4,850	$4,250	$3,850	$3,250	$2,850	$2,250	

MODEL 37V – similar to 37, except VR. Mfg. 1962-disc.

$315	$260	$240	$195	$180	$170	$165	

All recently manufactured Model 37s have the Featherlight designation. Prices are for older manufactured Model 37s.

MODEL 37D – similar to 37, except recoil pad, beavertail forearm, checkered wood. Mfg. 1954-1981.

$295	$275	$235	$200	$185	$175	$160	

MODEL 37DV – similar to 37D, except VR. Mfg. 1962-81.

$375	$325	$265	$225	$200	$185	$170	

MODEL 37 AMERICANA – 12 ga., 28 in. VR barrel with modified choke, uncheckered walnut stock, corncob forearm, roll engraved eagle on a banner with "Heritage. The Ithaca Gun Company, Pride." Approx. 2,200 mfg. circa 1972 with ser. nos. A0001-A2200.

$275	$250	$225	$185	$165	$145	$125	

MODEL 37 ULTRA FEATHERLIGHT – 20 ga. only, bottom ejection, 4 shot mag., 26 or 28 in. VR barrel, standard choke, approx. 4 3/4 lbs. Disc.

$395	$340	$275	$235	$210	$190	$175	

MODEL 37 ULTRA FEATHERLIGHT RUFFED GROUSE SOCIETY SPECIAL EDITION – 20 ga. only, bottom ejection, aluminum receiver, 22 or 24 in. barrel, English style American walnut stock. Limited mfg. 2003-2004.

$715	$565	$435	$375	$300	$260	$230	*$840*

MODEL 37 FIELD GRADE MAGNUM – 12 or 20 ga., 3 in. chambers, VR, walnut stock and corncob forearm, supplied with three choke tubes. Mfg. 1984-86.

$300	$240	$195	$180	$170	$165	$150	*$428*

MODEL 37 FIELD GRADE STANDARD – 12 or 20 ga., economy model, corncob style forearm, 26, 28, or 30 in. barrel. Mfg. 1983-1985 only.

$245	$225	$195	$175	$160	$140	$120	*$298*

MODEL 37 ULTRALIGHT – 12 (disc.) or 20 ga., new manufacture features checkered pistol grip (with Sid Bell red grip cap) and forearm, most recent mfg. was in deer configuration, 20 ga. only with 20 or 25 in. smooth bore barrel. Mfg. 1996-2002.

$475	$380	$340	$300	$275	$250	$225	*$600*

GRADING - PPGS™	100%	98%	95%	90%	80%	70%	60%	LAST MSR

MODEL 37 ENGLISH ULTRALIGHT DELUXE – 12 (disc.), 16 or 20 ga., 24, 25 (disc.), 26 or 28 in. barrels, choice of English straight grip stock with checkered forearm or pistol grip stock and grooved forearm, aluminum receiver, world's lightest pump, 20 ga. weighs 4 3/4 lb., 12 ga. weighs 5 1/2 lbs. Mfg. 1983-1986, reintroduced 1999-2005.

	$520	$410	$300	$250	$225	$200	$185	*$659*

* ***Model 37 English Ultralight Deluxe Classic*** – 16 or 20 ga., choice of pistol grip or English straight grip deluxe checkered walnut stock and forearm, 24, 26, or 28 in. VR barrel with three choke tubes, 5 1/4 lbs.

	$700	$555	$425	$375	$300	$260	$230	*$834*

MODEL 37/37R STANDARD – 12, 16, or 20 ga., solid rib, checkered walnut stock and forearm (mfg. 1937-1946), smooth pistol grip and grooved forearm (mfg. 1946-1952). Mfg. 1937-1952.

Plain stock	$295	$200	$175	$145	$130	$110	$90	
Checkered stock	$335	$245	$200	$175	$165	$145	$120	

Add 20% for 16 or 20 ga.

MODEL 37R DELUXE – similar to 37R, except fancy wood. Mfg. 1937-1955.

	$600	$550	$475	$400	$325	$250	$200	

MODEL 37R FEATHERLIGHT – 12, 16, or 20 ga., bottom ejection, 4 shot mag., 26, 28, or 30 in. barrel, hammerless, take down, any standard choke. Mfg. 1952-1985.

	$600	$550	$475	$400	$325	$250	$200	

Add 25% for 16 or 20 ga.

MODEL 37 PROTECTION SERIES – 12 ga. only, 18 1/2 or 20 in. smoothbore barrel w/o chokes, 5 or 8 shot tube mag., approx. 6 3/4 lbs. Limited mfg. 2005.

	$425	$375	$325	$275	$250	$225	$195	*$482*

Add $27 for 20 in. barrel.

TURKEYSLAYER – 12 (Storm) or 20 (new 2000, Storm Light)) ga., 3 in. chamber, choice of matte blue or 100% camo coverage in Realtree Hardwoods (disc. 2002), Realtree Hardwoods HD (new 2003), Realtree Timber (disc. 2002), or Advantage (disc. 2001) pattern, 22 (disc. 2002) or 24 in. barrel with extended choke tube, Truglo fiber optic sights standard beginning 2003, 7 lbs. Mfg. 1996-2004.

	$375	$335	$300	$275	$250	$225	$200	*$459*

Add $20 for ported choke tube (disc.).

* ***Turkeyslayer Youth*** – 20 ga. only, features 22 in. barrel and shortened youth dimension stock. Mfg. 1998-2003.

	$500	$375	$295	$225	$175	$160	$145	*$615*

TURKEYSLAYER II GUIDE SERIES – 12 ga. only, 3 in. chamber, 20 in. interchangeable barrel with turkey choke, choice of Realtree Hardwoods Green or 100% Mossy Oak Break Up camo coverage, pistol grip stock, includes 30mm red dot scope and sling, fiber optic sights. Limited production 2005 only.

	$500	$425	$365	$330	$300	$275	$250	*$599*

WATERFOWLER – 12 (Storm) or 20 (Storm Light) ga., features black finish or Wetlands (disc.), Realtree Hardwoods HD Green, or Realtree Max 4 camo treatment, 24, 26, 28 (standard) or 30 in. barrel designed for shooting steel shot. Mfg. 1998-2004.

	$425	$375	$335	$300	$275	$250	$225	*$499*

Add $50 for Realtree Max 4 camo.

MODEL 37 DELUXE W/VR – 12, 16 (Featherlight, new 1999), or 20 ga., similar to Model 87 Field Grade except has cut checkering, 26, 28, or 30 (disc. 2002) in. VR barrel, high gloss lacquer finish, and gold trigger, newer mfg. includes 3 choke tubes. Mfg. 1996-2005.

	$500	$380	$285	$230	$175	$160	$145	*$627*

Add $30 for 20 ga. Youth Model.

GRADING - PPGS™	100%	98%	95%	90%	80%	70%	60%	LAST MSR

*** *Model 37 Deluxe W/VR English*** – 12 (new 2000) or 20 ga., features 24, 26, or 28 in. English style vent. rib barrel, approx. 7 lbs. Mfg. 1998-2003.

	$485	$365	$275	$225	$175	$160	$145	*$600*

Add $30 for 20 ga.

MODEL 37 CLASSIC – 12, 16 (Featherlight, new 1999), or 20 ga., features knuckle cut receiver, corncob style forearm, hand checkering, and sunburst recoil pad, 26 or 28 in. VR barrel with choke tubes, choice of pistol grip or English straight grip deluxe checkered walnut stock and forearm, 6 1/2 - 7 lbs. Limited production 1998-2005.

	$680	$540	$425	$375	$300	$260	$230	*$812*

*** *Model 37 Classic NRA Women's*** – 16 or 20 ga., 24 in. VR barrel with three choke tubes, 5 1/4 or 6 1/2 lbs. Mfg. 2003-2004.

	$715	$565	$435	$375	$300	$260	$230	*$840*

MODEL 37 SUPREME – 12, 16, or 20 ga., deluxe checkered walnut stock and forearm, 28 or 30 in. VR barrel, engraved receiver, approx. 7 3/4 lbs. Originally mfg. 1967-1986, reintroduced late 1996, disc. 1997, reintroduced 2003-2004.

	$895	$650	$550	$450	$400	$350	$425	
1967-1997 Mfg.	$675	$575	$495	$425	$375	$325	$295	*$1,185*

MODEL 37S SKEET GRADE – similar to 37, except Knicker VR, large forearm, fancy wood. Mfg. 1937-55.

	$495	$445	$375	$335	$300	$275	$250	

Add 20% for 16 or 20 ga.

MODEL 37 SPORTING CLAYS – 12 ga. only, 24 (disc.), 26 (disc.), 28, or 30 (disc.) in. VR ported (standard 2001) or unported (disc. 2000) barrel with 3 Briley choke tubes, similar in appearances and features to Model 37 Trap. Mfg. 2000-2004.

	$1,275	$1,075	$925	$800	$650	$525	$450	*$1,495*

MODEL 37T TRAP GRADE – similar to 37S, except trap stock, select walnut, recoil pad. Mfg. 1937-55.

	$475	$425	$375	$325	$295	$275	$250	

Add 20% for early models with fleur-de-lis checkering.

MODEL 37 TRAP – 12 ga. only, 30 in. VR ported (standard 2001) or unported (disc. 2000) barrel with 3 Briley choke tubes, antique silver finished receiver with scroll style engraving and gold inlays on receiver sides, optional adj. cheekpiece stock. Mfg. 2000-2004.

	$1,275	$1,075	$925	$800	$650	$525	$450	*$1,495*

MODEL 37T TARGET GRADE – replaced 37S and 37T. Mfg. from 1955-61.

	$475	$425	$375	$325	$295	$275	$250	

MODEL 37 DEERSLAYER – 12, 16, or 20 ga., original Deerslayer, smooth bore with fixed choke only, rifle sights. Mfg. circa 1959-1986.

	$300	$240	$195	$180	$170	$165	$150	

MODEL 37 SUPER DELUXE DEERSLAYER – similar to Model 37 (87) Deerslayer, except Williams aperture rear sight and fancy wood. Mfg.1962-1985.

	$375	$335	$300	$270	$235	$210	$185	*$447*

MODEL 37 DEERSLAYER DELUXE – 12, 16 (new 1999 - smooth bore only, rifled beginning 2000) or 20 ga., 20, 24, or 25 (disc.) in. smooth bore (disc.) or rifled barrel, 100% Realtree Hardwoods 20/200 camo (mfg. 2000-2002, 12 ga. only) or walnut stock and forearm with cut checkering, light receiver engraving. Mfg. 1959-2005.

	$495	$410	$330	$285	$240	$210	$185	*$591*

Add $50 for Hardwoods camo (disc.).

DEERSLAYER II – 12, 16 (new 2001), or 20 ga., 20, 24 (new 2003) or 25 (disc.) in. barrel with 1:34 rifling (also available with fast twist 1:25 rifling, 12 ga. only, disc.), Monte Carlo stock and forearm with cut checkering, receiver is drilled and tapped for scope mounting, 6.25-7 lbs. Mfg. 1996-2005.

	$520	$390	$310	$230	$175	$160	$145	*$642*

GRADING - PPGS™	100%	98%	95%	90%	80%	70%	60%	LAST MSR

* ***Deerslayer II Model 37 Storm*** – 12 or 20 (Storm Light) ga., 24 in. smooth bore barrel with choke tube and open rifle sights, 100% DSS treatment on stock, approx. 6 1/2 lbs. Mfg. 2003-2004.

$350	$300	$275	$250	$225	$200	$185	*$399*

DEERSLAYER II GUIDE SERIES – 12 or 20 ga., 20 or 24 in. rifled barrel with fiber optic sights, 3 in. chamber, blued metal, grey camo laminate pistol grip stock and forearm. Limited production 2005.

$500	$415	$330	$285	$240	$210	$185	*$599*

DEERSLAYER III – 12 ga., 26 in. smooth bore barrel with DSR-1 choke tube, 11 lbs. Mfg. 2003-2004.

$750	$675	$600	$525	$450	$375	$300	*$900*

MODEL 37 BICENTENNIAL – 12 ga., engraved, fancy wood, cased with pewter buckle, 1,776 mfg. 1976, 100% value assumes NIB condition with case and belt buckle.

$595	$450	$325	$265	$230	$195	$170	

MODEL 37 2500 SERIES CENTENNIAL – 12 ga., customized version of the Model 37 commemorating Ithaca's 100th year anniversary, silver plated, etched antique finish receiver, deluxe walnut. Mfg. 1980-84.

$775	$625	$450	$385	$335	$280	$235	*$919*

MODEL 37 60TH ANNIVERSARY LIMITED EDITION – 20 ga., scroll engraving by A&A Engraving on both sides of nickel receiver with dog game scene/eagle motif, supreme grade wood, includes case. 200 mfg. 1997 only.

$1,450	$850	$475	$415	$360	$300	$255	*$2,000*

MODEL 37 PRESENTATION – 12 ga., blue, engraved, gold mounted receiver with extra-fancy walnut, cased, limited production. Mfg. 1981-86.

$1,500	$1,245	$1,080	$915	$830	$745	$665	*$1,658*

A 3 gun set was also available - an NIB set is currently priced in the $4,500 range.

MODEL 37 DUCKS UNLIMITED – 12 ga., VR. Please refer to the Ducks Unlimited section.

MODEL 37 60TH ANNIVERSARY – 20 ga., 3 in. chamber, 26 in. VR barrel, checkered Supreme wood, engraved, cased. 200 mfg. 1997 only.

$1,750	$1,250	$850	$740	$620	$515	$440	

MODEL 87 FIELD (BASIC) – 12 or 20 ga., 3 in. chamber, economy model, walnut stock and forearm with pressed checkering, 26, 28, or 30 (disc.) in. barrel with 3 choke tubes standard. Reintroduced 1987-96.

$360	$290	$240	$195	$170	$160	$145	*$477*

* ***Model 87 Field Basic Combo*** – 12 or 20 ga., includes 20/25 in. deer barrel with special bore and 28 in. VR multi-choke field barrel, uncheckered walnut stock and corncob forearm, 7 lbs. Mfg. 1989-92.

$400	$315	$275	$235	$210	$190	$170	*$459*

Add $32 for rifled bore barrel.
Add $104 for laminated wood (includes rifle bored barrel).

* ***Model 87 Field Camo*** – 12 ga. only, 3 in. chamber, 24, 26, or 28 in. VR barrel, camo-seal rust resistant finish on exterior parts. Available in either green or brown camo finish. Mfg. began 1986, resumed 1988, disc. 1996.

$425	$315	$260	$200	$175	$160	$145	*$542*

* ***Model 87 Field Turkey*** – 12 ga. only, 24 in. VR barrel with choice of fixed full choke or full choke tube, camo or matte blue finish. Mfg. 1989-96.

$365	$285	$235	$190	$170	$160	$145	*$466*

Add $85 for camo finish. Add $43 for full choke tube.

GRADING - PPGS™	100%	98%	95%	90%	80%	70%	60%	LAST MSR

MODEL 87 ULTRALITE FIELD – 12 or 20 ga., 3 in. chamber, aluminum receiver, 20 (disc. 1988), 24, 25 (disc. 1988), or 26 in. barrel. 20 ga. weighs 5 lbs., 12 ga. weighs 5 3/4 lbs, multi-chokes (3) became standard in 1989. Originally mfg. 1985-86, reintroduced 1988-90.

	$445	$375	$295	$240	$210	$190	$170	*$481*

Add $50 for slim grip model (12 1/2 in. stock - disc. 1985).
Subtract $42 if without multiple choke feature.

The 20 and 25 in. barrels were disc. when mfg. was resumed 1988.

* ***Model 87 Ultralite Field Deluxe*** – similar to Model 87 Ultralite Field except has cut checkering, high gloss lacquer finish, and gold trigger. Mfg. 1989-1991.

	$425	$360	$300	$250	$220	$190	$170	*$514*

MODEL 87 ENGLISH – 20 ga. only, 3 in. chamber, 24 or 26 in. VR barrel with 3 choke tubes, steel receiver, checkered walnut stock and forearm, recoil pad, 6 3/4 lbs. Mfg. 1991-96.

	$425	$315	$260	$200	$175	$160	$145	*$545*

MODEL 87 DELUXE – similar to Model 87 Field Grade except has cut checkering, 26, 28, or 30 in. VR barrel, high gloss lacquer finish, and gold trigger, newer mfg. includes 3 choke tubes. Mfg. 1989-96.

	$415	$310	$255	$200	$175	$160	$145	*$533*

Add $54 for combo package (includes 20 in. special bore deer barrel, disc. 1992).
Add $87 for combo package with 20 or 25 in. rifled bore deer barrel, disc. 1992.

* ***Model 87 Deluxe Magnum*** – 12 or 20 ga., 3 in. chambers, VR, deluxe wood with checkered forearm. Mfg. 1981-86, production resumed 1988 only.

	$320	$270	$230	$210	$200	$185	$165	*$395*

Add $77 for Combo package (extra 28 in. barrel).

Recent mfg. 20 ga. shotguns were available with a 25 in. barrel only (with choke tubes).

MODEL 87 SUPREME GRADE – 12 or 20 ga., presentation walnut, high luster blue, limited production, previously available in either trap, skeet, or field models, fixed chokes. Mfg. 1988-96.

	$640	$475	$395	$325	$295	$270	$250	*$809*

BASIC DEERSLAYER – 12 ga. only, 20 or 25 in. special bore or rifled barrel, oil finished stock and corncob style forearm with no checkering, iron sights, matte metal finish, 7 lbs. Mfg. 1989-1996.

	$345	$280	$240	$195	$175	$160	$145	*$425*

Add $40 for rifled barrel.

MODEL 87 FIELD DEERSLAYER – 12 or 20 ga., rifle slug barrel, 20 or 25 in. special smooth bore barrel with open sights. Mfg. 1959-86, reintroduced 1988-93.

	$300	$250	$210	$180	$160	$150	$140	*$364*

MODEL 87 DELUXE DEERSLAYER – similar to Field Deerslayer except stock has cut checkering and high gloss lacquer finish, gold trigger. Mfg. 1989-96.

	$365	$285	$235	$190	$170	$160	$145	*$465*

Add $34 for rifled bore.
Add $120 for combo package (28 in. multi-choke barrel).

* ***Model 87 Deluxe Deerslayer Ultra*** – similar to Deluxe Deerslayer except has aluminum frame. Mfg. 1989-90 only.

	$350	$285	$245	$200	$175	$160	$145	*$444*

MONTE CARLO DEERSLAYER II – 12 ga. only, 20 or 25 in. barrel with rifling, Monte Carlo stock and forearm with cut checkering, receiver is drilled and tapped for scope mounting, 7 lbs. Mfg. 1989-96.

	$445	$335	$270	$210	$175	$160	$145	*$567*

DEERSLAYER II FAST TWIST – 12 ga. only, 25 in. rifled permanently fixed barrel, Monte Carlo stock with checkering, receiver is drilled and tapped. Mfg. 1992-93.

	$440	$385	$325	$275	$235	$200	$180	*$550*

GRADING - PPGS™	100%	98%	95%	90%	80%	70%	60%	LAST MSR

MODEL 87 MILITARY & POLICE – 12 (3 in.) or 20 (new 1989) ga., short barrel Model 37 w/ normal stock or pistol grip only, 18 1/2, 20, or 24 3/4 (scarce) in. barrel, choice of front bead or rifle sights, front blade was usually a flourescent orange plastic, 5, 8, or 10 shot. Originally disc. 1983, reintroduced 1989-95.

	$265	$230	$200	$180	$170	$160	$150	$323

Add $104 for nickel finish (mfg. 1991-92 only).

IVER JOHNSON ARMS, INC. (NEW MFG.)

Current manufacturer established during 2004 and located in Rockledge, FL.

The new Iver Johnson Arms, Inc. company was formed during 2004, and currently manfactures a line of 1911A1 pistols in .45 ACP cal. Current models include: The 1911 Officer (MSR $581-$743), Thrasher (MSR $608-$817), Model 1911A1 (MSR $581-$743), the Eagle (MSR $675-$729), the Eagle LR (new 2011, MSR $824-$985), the Falcon (MSR $587), and the Hawk (MSR $641-$675). Additionally, Iver Johnson Arms, Inc. imports a line of PAS 12 slide-action shotguns manufactured by Armed in Turkey (MSRs range from $270-$432), and during 2013, introduced a 1911A1 Carbine/Rifle with Mech-Tech Systems upper and Iver Johnson lower.

Iver Johnson Arms, Inc. previously manufactured the Raven Series in both .22 LR and .45 ACP cals. until 2009, and the last MSR was $532. Also discontinued during 2009 was the Frontier Four Derringer and the Model PM 30G M1 Carbine. The Trojan was discontinued in 2012 (last MSR was $574).

Please contact the company directly for more information, including availability and pricing (see Trademark Index).

IVER JOHNSON ARMS & CYCLE WORKS

Previously located in Worchester, MA, 1883-1890, Fitchburg, MA, 1890-1975, Middlesex, NJ 1975-1983 (name changed to Iver Johnson Arms Inc.) and Jacksonville, AR 1984-1993. Formerly Johnson Bye & Co. 1871-1883. Renamed Iver Johnson's Arms & Cycle Works mid-year 1894-1975 (incorporated as Iver Johnson's Arms & Cycle Works Inc. in 1915). Renamed Iver Johnson's Arms & Cycle Works in 1891 with manufacturing moving to Fitchburg, MA. In 1975 the name changed to Iver Johnson's Arms, Inc., and two years later, company facilities were moved to Middlesex, NJ. In 1982, production was moved to Jacksonville, AR under the trade name Iver Johnson Arms, Inc. In 1983, Universal Firearms, Inc. was acquired by Iver Johnson Arms, Inc.

IVER JOHNSON HISTORY & DATES OF INTEREST

1841: Iver Johnson born in Nordjford, Norway. 1857: Became apprentice gunsmith in Bergen, Norway. 1862: Opened gunshop in Christiania, Norway. 1863: Immigrated to the United States (Boston) went to work for Allen & Wheelock Co. in Worcester Mass. Married Mary Elizabeth Speirs, children: Fredrick Iver, John Lovell, Walter Clof and Mary Louise. 1871: Formed partnership with Martin Bye as Johnson & Bye Gunsmith in Worcester, Mass. 1873: Company moved to new five-story building on Central St. in Worcester, Mass. First bicycles introduced. 1883: Partnership with Martin Bye ended: became Iver Johnson & Co. some firearms marked "Iver Johnson Maker" or "Iver Johnson's Arms Co." Company remained at the central street location in Worcester. 1888: Iver Johnson becomes a U.S. citizen. 1890: Company moved to Fitchburg, Mass. Owl's head first appeared on revolver's grips. 1894: Company became Iver Johnson's Arms & Cycle Works of Fitchburg, Mass. Purchased bicycle shop in Fitchburg, Mass. and opened first retail sporting goods store in Fitchburg. 1895: August 3rd, Iver Johnson dies (age 54) eldest son Fred became president of company. 1896: First catalog issued, opened retail stores in Worchester, Boston and Keene, New Hampshire. 1900: Purchased J.P. Lovell Co. (wholesale and retail store in Boston). 1903: Opened sales offices in New York City, Chicago, San Francisco, Hamburg (Germany), Paris (France), London (England), and Constantinople (Turkey). 1904: Slogan "Hammer the Hammer" first used. 1909: All firearms manufactured for smokeless powder pressure. John L., second eldest son, became president of company. 1910: First Patent for semi-automatic pistol issued to Fred I. Johnson (no prototype). 1911: Motorcycles introduced. L.H. Cobb received a patent for a semiautomatic pistol (no prototype built). 1915: Mary Elizabeth Johnson dies (Iver's wife). Company incorporated as Iver Johnson's Arm's & Cycle Works Inc. Family retains control of the majority of stock. 1916:

100%	98%	95%	90%	80%	70%	60%	50%	40%	30%	20%	10%

William Barnes received patent for .25 ACP pistol (one prototype known). 1935: Walter O., youngest of Iver's sons, becomes president. 1953: Luther M. Otto III becomes president of company (Iver's grandson and son of Mary Louise, Iver's daughter). 1971: Company celebrates its 100th birthday. 1973: Company sold to Louis Imperato (owner of John Jovine Company of New York City). 1975: Purchased Plainsfield Machine Co. (makers of M-1 carbine), moved to Middlesex, New Jersey. Name changed to Iver Johnson's Arms Co. 1978: First semi-automatic pistol manufactured. 1980: Company sold to Interstate Dist. Co. of Little Rock, Arkansas. 1983: Company moved to Jacksonville, Arkansas. 1985: Purchased Universal Firearms Co. (Universal Carbines appeared in 1986 catalog only). 1986: October 22 - company filed for Chapter 11 bankruptcy, production ceased and plant closed in December. 1987: Louis Imperato re-assumed control, renamed Iver Johnson Arms by AMAC. 1988: Resumed limited production of M-1 carbine and semiautomatic pistols. A few new prototype firearms were designed by AMAC but none of them ever reached full production. 1993: Doors shut for good, auction held and equipment sold.

HANDGUNS: SOLID FRAME, DOUBLE ACTION MODELS MFG. 1878-1978

AMERICAN EAGLE (EAGLE/LION/OLD HICKORY) – .22 rimfire (small frame) or .32 rimfire (medium frame) cal., saw handle grip frame with eagle design on hard rubber grip panels, 2 1/4 (small) or 2 7/16 (medium) in. round rifled barrel, 5 (medium) or 7 (small) shot, usually marked with the model name and patent dates "June 4, 1878" or "Feb. 25, 1879", 9 1/4 or 11 7/8 oz. Mfg. 1878-1881.

$425	$365	$315	$275	$235	$195	$175	$155	$130	$115	$95	$85

AMERICAN BULLDOG FIRST MODEL (LION/OLD HICKORY) – .22 rimfire (small frame), .32 rimfire and centerfire (medium frame), .38 rimfire and centerfire (extra large frame), .44 Webley or .44 Bulldog cal., nickel finish, 2 1/2 in. round, 2 7/16 in. octagon (extra large frame), 4 1/2, 6, or 6 in. half-octagon/half-round barrel (extra large frame, 5 or 7 (small frame) shot, saw handle shaped grip frame, eagle design on hard rubber grip panels, model name marked on top strap, 9 5/8 - 19 7/8 oz., sold under the brand names Lion, Old Hickory, Navy Favorite and Ajax Army. Mfg. 1882-1884.

$425	$365	$315	$275	$235	$195	$175	$155	$130	$115	$95	$85

Add 25% for .22 cal. small frame or .44 cal. extra large frame.

AMERICAN BULLDOG SECOND MODEL – .22 rimfire (small frame), .32 rimfire or centerfire (medium frame), .38 rimfire or centerfire (extra large frame), .44 Webley, or .44 Bulldog cal., nickel finish, 2 1/4 (small frame), 2 1/2 (medium frame), or 2 7/16 (extra large frame) in. octagon barrel, longer barrel lengths of 4 1/2 or 6 were available on medium, rounded grip frame with square butt, hard rugger grip panels with dog's head design on large and extra large frame, small and medium frame have eagle design, 5 (large and extra large frames) or 7 shot, model name marked on top of barrel, sold under the brand names Lion, Old Hickory, Navy Favorite, and Ajax Army, 9 5/8 - 19 5/8 oz. Mfg. 1885-1899.

$350	$320	$275	$225	$200	$165	$140	$120	$100	$85	$75	$65

Add 25% for small .22 cal. frame or extra large .44 cal. frame.

AMERICAN BRITISH BULLDOG – similar to the American Bulldog, except has birdshead grip frame shape and checkered hard rubber grip panels. Mfg. 1882-1887.

$450	$395	$335	$285	$245	$210	$180	$160	$140	$120	$100	$85

Variations of the American Bulldog First Model have also been marked "BRITISH BULL DOG".

BOSTON BULLDOG – .22 rimfire (small frame), .32 centerfire (medium frame), or .38 centerfire (large frame) cal., nickel finish, 2 1/4 (small frame) or 2 15/32 in. octagon barrel, nickel finish, 5 (medium or large) or 7 shot, hard rubber grips panels, small and medium frames have floral design, large frame has dog's head design, 8 3/8 - 16 oz. Mfg. 1887-1899.

$435	$370	$320	$275	$235	$195	$175	$155	$130	$115	$95	$85

LOVELL SAFETY DOUBLE ACTION REVOLVER (MODEL 1879) – .38 centerfire cal., 2 7/8 in. ribbed barrel, hard rubber grip panels with dog's head design, nickel finish, one-piece frame and barrel, not marked with model name, only marked "Iver Johnson Co. Maker", cylinder swings to the right, 17 oz. Mfg. 1883-1889.

$600	$520	$440	$390	$340	$285	$245	$220	$190	$155	$130	$115

GRADING - PPGS™	100%	98%	95%	90%	80%	70%	60%	LAST MSR

This model was the first double action revolver manufactured in the U.S. with a side swing cylinder for loading and unloading.

I.J. MODEL 1900 – .22 rimfire (small frame), .32 rimfire or centerfire (medium frame), or .38 centerfire (large frame) cal., 2 1/4 (small frame), 2 1/2 (medium/large frame) in. octagon barrel or various optional barrel lengths, nickel or blue finish, hard rubber grips panels with owl's head logo, 7 (.22 cal.), 5 (.32/.38 cal.), or 6 (.32 cal. large frame only after 1930) shot, does not have hammer the hammer action, pull pin cylinder release, 11 - 18 oz. Mfg. 1900-1941.

	$150	$135	$125	$100	$85	$75	$65

The large frame model was introduced in 1903.

* ***I.J. Model 1900 Target Small Frame*** – .22 rimfire cal., built on the small frame Model 1900, blue finish, 6 or 9 in. octagon barrel, oversize two-piece checkered wood grips, 7 shot, does not have hammer the hammer action, pull pin cylinder release, 12 7/8 - 14 3/8 oz. Mfg. 1925-1928.

6 in. barrel	$200	$180	$160	$130	$120	$100	$90
9 in. barrel (rare)	$250	$220	$190	$155	$130	$115	$100

* ***I.J. Model 1900 Target Large Frame*** – .22 rimfire cal., built on the large frame Model 1900, 6 or 10 in. octagon barrel, oversize saw-handle shape checkered grips, 7 or 9 shot, does not have hammer the hammer action, pull pin cylinder release, 24 -27 oz. Mfg. 1921-1941.

6 in. barrel	$200	$180	$160	$130	$120	$100	$90
10 in. barrel (rare)	$250	$220	$190	$155	$130	$115	$100

In the 1938 Iver Johnson Arms & Cycle Works catalog, this revolver was given a model number - Model 69 (6 in. barrel) or Model 79 (10 in. barrel).

I.J. PETITE – .22 rimfire cal., 6 shot, 1 1/4 in. barrel, folding trigger, pull pin cylinder release, hard rubber grip panels with large IJAC molded into them, 4 7/8 oz. Ltd. production run of less than 1,000, most likely 500 to 600. Mfg. 1909 only.

	$600	$520	$440	$390	$340	$285	$245

This model is one of the smallest double action revolvers ever built in the U.S.

U.S. REVOLVER CO. DOUBLE ACTION – .22 rimfire (small frame), .32 centerfire (medium or large frame), or .38 centerfire (large frame), 5 (.32 or .38 cal.), 6 (.32 cal.), or 7 (.22 cal.) shot, 2 1/2 in. round barrel with unfluted cylinder, hard rubber grip panels with U.S. on top or optional two-piece oversized hard rubber grips, approx. 17 oz. Mfg. 1911-1935.

	$135	$120	$100	$85	$75	$65	$50

This model was manufactured for sale through mail order catalogs, and it was never listed in any Iver Johnson catalog.

I.J. TARGET SEALED 8 FIRST MODEL (LARGE FRAME OCTAGON BARREL) – .22 rimfire cal., 8 shot, 6 or 10 in. octagon barrel, does not have hammer the hammer action, large solid frame, double action with pull in cylinder release, cylinder features recessed chambers that fully enclose the cartridge case head, one piece checkered wood grips, 24-27 oz. Mfg. 1932-1941.

	$250	$220	$190	$155	$130	$115	$100

This model is the first major improvement of the solid frame double action model since its introduction in 1900. The 1938 catalog refers to the 6 in. model as the Model 68, and the 10 in. barrel as the Model 78.

I.J. TARGET SEALED 8 SECOND MODEL (LARGE FRAME ROUND BARREL) – .22 rimfire cal., 8 shot, 4 1/2 or 6 in. round barrel, blue finish, does not have hammer the hammer action, but does have recessed chambers in the cylinder, pull pin cylinder release, oversized checkered wood or plastic grips, 24-27 oz. Mfg. 1947-1954.

	$240	$215	$190	$155	$130	$115	$100

This model was introduced after WWII with only minor modifications, and the model number continued to be the Model 68.

GRADING - PPGS™	100%	98%	95%	90%	80%	70%	60%	LAST MSR

I.J. SEALED 8 SNUB MODEL 68S (LARGE FRAME ROUND BARREL) - .22 rimfire cal., 8 shot, 2 1/2 in. round barrel, blue finish, does not have hammer the hammer action, but does have recessed chambers in the cylinder, pull pin cylinder release, two-piece wood pocket-size grips, 20 1/2 oz. Mfg. 1952-1954.

$265	$235	$210	$190	$155	$130	$115	

I.J. TARGET MODEL 55 - .22 rimfire cal., 8 shot, blue finish, 4 1/2 or 6 in. barrel, pull pin cylinder release, recessed chambers and flash control front rim (unfluted cylinder until 1958), oversized one-piece Tenite plastic grips, does not have hammer the hammer action, 26-27 oz. Mfg. 1955-1960.

$225	$195	$170	$140	$125	$110	$95	

Beginning in 1955, Iver Johnson Arms & Cycle Works introduced a newly designed solid frame double action revolver. Over the next few years, IJ introduced at least one new model a year, and during the first year, two new models were introduced.

* ***I.J. Target Model 55A (Iver Johnson Sportman)*** - .22 rimfire cal., similar to I.J. Target Model 55, except has a loading gate on right side of frame, approx. 29-30 oz. Mfg. 1961-1978.

$225	$195	$170	$140	$125	$110	$95	

This model was also called the Iver Johnson Sportman from 1974-1978.

I.J. CADET MODEL 55S - .22 rimfire cal., 8 shot, blue finish, 2 1/2 in. barrel, two-piece Tenite grips, does not have hammer the hammer action, recessed chambers with flash control front rim (unfluted cylinder until 1958), similar to the Model 55, 24 oz. Mfg. 1955-1960.

$225	$195	$170	$140	$125	$110	$95	

* ***I.J. Cadet Model 55SA*** - .22 rimfire cal., 8 shot, blue finish, similar to Cadet Model 55A, except has loading gate on right side of frame, approx. 27 oz. Mfg. 1961-1978.

$225	$195	$170	$140	$125	$110	$95	

I.J. MODEL 56 STARTER REVOLVER - .22 rimfire blank cal., built on the older Model Target Sealed 8 frame, half-length cylinder, 8 shot, pull pin cylinder release, 2 1/2 in. barrel, hard rubber or wood grips, does not have hammer the hammer action, 10 oz. Mfg. 1956-1960.

$120	$100	$85	$75	$65	$60	$50	

* ***I.J. Starter Model 56A*** - .22 rimfire or .32 centerfire blank cal., 5 (.32) or 8 (.22) shot, similar to the Model 56 Starter Revolver, except has loading gate on right side of frame, approx. 12 oz. Mfg. 1961-1978.

$120	$100	$85	$75	$65	$60	$50	

I.J. TARGET MODEL 57 - .22 rimfire cal., 8 shot, 2 1/2, 4 1/2, or 6 in. barrel, similar to the Model 55, except has adj. front and rear sights, oversize molded plastic grips with thumb rest, 27-30 1/2 oz. Mfg. 1957-1960.

$235	$200	$175	$140	$125	$110	$95	

* ***I.J. Target Model 57A (Sportsman Deluxe)*** - .22 rimfire blank cal., similar to the Model 57, except has loading gate on right side of frame. Mfg. 1961-1978.

$235	$200	$175	$140	$125	$110	$95	

This model was also called the Iver Johnson Sportsman Deluxe between 1974-1978.

I.J. SIDEWINDER MODEL 50/50A - .22 rimfire cal. (.22 WMR combo new 1974), blue or nickel (new 1974) finish, oversize western style wood or plastic imitation stag (new 1968) grips, 8 shot, recessed chambers, flash control, 4 3/4 (new 1974) or 6 in. barrel, fixed front sight, adj. rear sight (new 1974), does not have hammer the hammer action, 30-31 oz. Mfg. 1961-1978.

$250	$220	$190	$155	$130	$115	$100	

During 1963, this model's nomenclature changed to Model 50A. After 1974, this model had different model numbers for different finishes, barrel lengths, calibers, and rear sight combinations.

GRADING - PPGS™	100%	98%	95%	90%	80%	70%	60%	LAST MSR

NEW AMERICAN BULLDOG SERIES – .22 rimfire, .22 WMR, or .38 Spl. cal., blue or satin nickel finish, 2 1/2 or 4 in. barrel, 5 or 6 shot, large oversize plastic one-piece or small pocket two-piece grips, ramp front sight, adj. rear sight, pull pin cylinder release, does not have hammer the hammer action, heavy full length rib, 26-30 oz. Mfg. 1973-1978.

$275 $240 $215 $190 $155 $130 $115

I.J. ROOKIE – .38 Spl. cal., 5 shot, blue finish, 4 in. barrel, pull pin cylinder release, oversized one-piece plastic grips with molded thumb rest, fixed sight, does not have hammer the hammer action, 29 oz. Mfg. 1973-1978.

$235 $200 $175 $140 $125 $110 $95

I.J. SWINGOUT CYLINDER PROTOTYPE – .22 rimfire, .32 S&W Long, or .38 Spl. cal., blue finish, hammer the hammer action, large frame, (modified Model 55), ramp front sight, fixed or adj. rear sight, only five models known, each is different, .22 rimfire cal. has 6 in. barrel, full length vent. rib and under lug, 8 shot, two piece oversized wood grips, .32 S&W Long cal. has 2 1/2 in. barrel, full length solid rib and under lug, 5 shot, two piece combat wood grips, second .32 S&W Long model (tool room model) has plain round barrel, 5 shot, no sights, no grips, and no finish, .38 Spl. cal. has 4 in. barrel, half under lug, no top rib, fixed rear sight, (groove in top strap), two piece service style composite grips, third .32 S&W Long cal. model is 5 shot, similar to .38 Spl., except has homemade grips. Mfg. 1976.

Values range from $600 for 100% condition to $400 for 60% condition.

This model is rare and only three have shown up in the used marketplace.

PISTOLS: SEMI-AUTO

.25 ACP PROTOTYPE – .25 ACP cal., only one example known to exist, patent #1173161 issued on Feb. 29, 1916 to William O. Barnes, who assigned it to Mary E. Spears Johnson, Iver's widow. Mfg. 1916.

Extreme rarity factor precludes accurate pricing.

An individual appraisal would be recommended if this specimen is ever encountered. One other early semi-auto pistol patent was assigned to Iver Johnson - #992854, issued to L.H. Cobb. No known examples of this patent exist.

MODEL X300 PONY MEDIUM FRAME SINGLE ACTION – .380 ACP cal., blue, nickel, or matte blue finish, checkered wood grips, front blade sight, adj. rear sight, 3 in. barrel, 6 shot mag., no mag. safety, 20 oz. Mfg. in Middlesex, NJ 1978-1982, Jacksonville, AR 1983-1988, and Jacksonville, AR by AMAC 1989-1991.

$385 $335 $290 $260 $210 $175 $135

Add 10% for nickel finish.

I.J. SUPER ENFORCER (M1 CARBINE) – .30 Carbine cal., gas operated pistol version of the M1 Carbine, 5, 10, or 15 shot mag., walnut stock, fires from closed bolt, 9 1/2 in. barrel, 4 lbs. Mfg. 1978-1993.

$850 $745 $640 $580 $470 $385 $300

TP SERIES 25 – .25 ACP cal., double action, small frame, 2.85 in. barrel, black plastic wraparound grips, blue or nickel finish, fixed sights, hammer block safety mounted on slide, 7 shot mag., does not have slide hold open device, designed by Erma Werke in Germany, 14 1/2 oz. Mfg. 1981-1982.

$250 $220 $190 $170 $140 $115 $90

TP SERIES 22 – .22 LR cal., double action, black plastic wraparound grips, 2.85 in. barrel, 7 shot, blue or nickel finish, fixed sights, hammer block safety and patented firing pin block safety, does not have a slide hold open or mag. safety, designed by Erma Werke. Mfg. 1982-1989.

$275 $240 $205 $185 $150 $125 $95

NEW TRAILSMAN – .22 LR cal., large frame, single action, copy of Colt Woodsman, blue finish, plastic or wood grip panels, 4 1/2 or 6 in. barrel, 10 shot mag., sear block safety, internal hammer mechanism, fixed sights, slide hold open latch, push button mag. release, 64 oz. First 500 mfg. in Argentina and assembled in the USA (not all of these 500 were assembled). Mfg. 1985-1991.

$275 $240 $205 $185 $150 $125 $95

GRADING - PPGS™	100%	98%	95%	90%	80%	70%	60%	LAST MSR

9MM PROTOTYPE – redesigned .380 ACP Pony model chambered for 9mm Luger cal., never put into production, but one prototype is known to exist, double action, medium frame. Mfg. 1986.

Extreme rarity factor precludes accurate pricing.

UNIVERSAL ENFORCER (M1 CARBINE) – .30 Carbine cal., gas operated, blue finish, single action, pistol version of the M1 carbine, 5, 10, or 15 shot mag., 9 1/2 in. barrel, hard wood stock, fires from close bolt, trigger block safety, 4 lbs. Mfg. 1986.

	100%	98%	95%	90%	80%	70%	60%	LAST MSR
	$850	$745	$640	$580	$470	$385	$300	

COMPACT 25 – .25 ACP cal., 6 shot, single action, 2 in. barrel, checkered plastic grips, matte blue finish, bright blue slide, trigger block safety, packaged in jewelry presentation case, also available as a Compact Elite with 24Kt. gold finish and Ivorex grips, 9.3 oz. Mfg. 1991-1993.

	100%	98%	95%	90%	80%	70%	60%	LAST MSR
	$250	$220	$190	$170	$140	$115	$90	
Compact Elite	$500	$440	$375	$340	$275	$225	$175	

100%	98%	95%	90%	80%	70%	60%	50%	40%	30%	20%	10%

PISTOLS: SINGLE SHOT MFG. 1871-1899

UNCLE SAM PERCUSSION DERRINGER – .28, .30, or .36 cal., 2 1/4 in. barrel, smoothbore, muzzle loading, spur trigger, center mounted hammer, brown finish, one piece frame and barrel, 4 1/2 oz. Mfg. 1871-1873.

100%	98%	95%	90%	80%	70%	60%	50%	40%	30%	20%	10%
$400	$350	$320	$275	$225	$200	$150	$140	$120	$110	$100	$90

Add 25% for engraved "Prince" model.

A deluxe engraved version with detachable barrel and nickel finish was called the "Prince" model.

ECLIPSE CARTRIDGE DERRINGER – .22 (small frame), .32, or .38 (large frame) rimfire cal., smoothbore, 2 in. half-round, half-octagon barrel, swings to side for loading, nickel frame, brown barrel, spur trigger, center mounted hammer, wood, hard rubber, or mother-of-pearl grips. Mfg. 1871-1899.

100%	98%	95%	90%	80%	70%	60%	50%	40%	30%	20%	10%
$350	$325	$285	$250	$200	$175	$150	$125	$110	$100	$90	$80

Add 25% for the engraved "Star" model.

A deluxe engraved version was called the "Star" model, featuring a fully engraved frame and fancy grips.

GEM BLANK PISTOL – .22 rimfire blank cal., spur trigger, Flobert type action. Mfg. 1880-1890.

100%	98%	95%	90%	80%	70%	60%	50%	40%	30%	20%	10%
$250	$200	$180	$160	$130	$120	$100	$90	$80	$75	$70	$65

REVOLVERS: SA, MFG. 1873-1899

Model names for these guns included: Defender, Eagle, Encore, Enterprise (Enterprise Gun Works), Eureka, Favorite, Invincible, J.T. Johnson, J.S.T. Co., Lion, Navy Favorite, Old Hickory, Red Hot, Smoker, Tiger, and Tycoon.

SQUARE BUTT MODELS – .22 (small frame), .32 (medium frame), .38, or .41 (large frame) rimfire cal., 2 1/16 in. smoothbore (small frame), 2 15/16 in. (medium frame) with three straight grooves, or 2 3/8 in. octagon rifled bore (large frame) barrel, 5 (medium or large frame) or 7 shot, 7-14 oz. Mfg. 1873-1888.

100%	98%	95%	90%	80%	70%	60%	50%	40%	30%	20%	10%
$250	$220	$200	$190	$175	$155	$130	$115	$100	$90	$75	$60

Barrel lengths as long as 10 inches have been seen.

BIRD'S HEAD GRIP MODELS – .22 (small frame), .32 (medium frame), .38 or .41 (large frame) rimfire cal., 2 1/2 in. smoothbore (small or medium frame) or 2 7/16 in. rifled bore (large frame) barrel, 5 or 7 shot. Mfg. 1873-1888.

100%	98%	95%	90%	80%	70%	60%	50%	40%	30%	20%	10%
$250	$220	$200	$190	$175	$155	$130	$115	$100	$90	$75	$60

Barrel lengths as long as 10 inches have been seen.

Not all spur trigger single action revolvers marked with the Defender name were manufactured by Iver Johnson (Johnson & Bye Gunsmith). All of these brand names were actually owned by J.P. Lovell Co. Before Iver Johnson (Johnson & Bye) started manufacturing revolvers, J.P. Lovell Co. had Hopkins & Allen manufacture the Defender (and quite possibility some of the other names associated with

100%	98%	95%	90%	80%	70%	60%	50%	40%	30%	20%	10%

Iver Johnson). The main difference in these Hopkins & Allen Defenders is that the cylinder locking notches are at the front of the cylinder. The era of manufacture for the Hopkins & Allen manufactured Defenders was 1868 - 1872.

DEFENDER 89 SERIES – .22 (small frame), .32 (medium frame), .38 or .41 (large frame) rimfire cal., 2 1/16 (small frame), 2 7/16 (medium frame), or 2 3/8 (large frame) in. round or octagon barrel, improved version of the older Defender series, not sold under any other brand name, square butt and bird's head grip variations, wood or hard rubber grips, 5 or 7 shot, frame sizes are similar to earlier Defender series, may also be found with same names as the earlier series of single action spur trigger revolvers. Mfg. 1889-1899.

$265	$240	$220	$200	$175	$160	$140	$120	$100	$90	$75	$60

GRADING - PPGS™	100%	98%	95%	90%	80%	70%	60%	LAST MSR

REVOLVERS: SA

Between 1973-1978, Iver Johnson imported single action revolvers, as well as a line of black powder reproductions and replicas manufactured by Uberti in Italy.

CATTLEMAN SERIES – .357 Mag., .44 Mag., or .45 LC cal., 4 3/4, 5 1/2, or 7 1/4 in. barrel, blue finish, case hardened large frame, rod ejection, brass trigger guard and backstrap, one-piece European walnut grips, fixed (Magnum) or adj. (Buckhorn Magnum) sights, 6 shot, automatic hammer block safety, some very early Buckhorn models were imported with a 12 in. barrel and shoulder stock attachments, 41-44 oz. Mfg. by Uberti, imported 1973-1978.

$350	$320	$275	$225	$200	$154	$140

Add 25% for 12 in. barrel.
Subtract approx. 10% for Cattleman Magnum model.

* ***Cattleman Buckhorn Buntline*** – similar to Cattleman Buckhorn Magnum, except has 18 in. barrel with detachable stock, front blade sight, rear sight dovetailed into frame top strap.

$400	$350	$300	$265	$225	$190	$165

* ***Cattleman Trailblazer*** – .22 LR or .22 WMR cal., 5 1/2 or 6 1/2 in. barrel, medium frame, otherwise similar to Cattleman Magnum, 40 oz.

$350	$320	$275	$225	$200	$154	$140

100%	98%	95%	90%	80%	70%	60%	50%	40%	30%	20%	10%

REVOLVERS: TOP BREAK, MFG. 1887-1978

LOVELL SAFETY HAMMERLESS AUTOMATIC – .38 centerfire cal., 5 shot, nickel finish, 3 1/4 in. barrel, hard rubber grips panels with dog's head design, does not have hammer the hammer action, not marked with model name or number, "Iver Johnson & Co." on the barrel top rib, 18 1/8 oz. Mfg. 1887-1889.

$600	$520	$440	$390	$340	$285	$245	$220	$190	$155	$130	$115

LOVELL SWIFT REVOLVER HAMMER & HAMMERLESS MODELS – .38 centerfire cal., 5 shot, 3 1/4 in. barrel, nickel finish, hard rubber grip panles with owl's head at top, marked on barrel top rib with patent dates and "Iver Johnson Co. Worchester Mass." marked on barrel top strap, with model name "SWIFT", does not have hammer the hammer action, only sold through J.P. Lovell Co., 16 7/8 - 17 7/8 oz. Mfg. 1890-1894.

$450	$395	$335	$285	$245	$210	$180	$160	$140	$120	$100	$85

Add $50 for hammerless model.

FIRST MODEL SAFETY AUTOMATIC HAMMER (BLACK POWDER CARTRIDGE) – .22 rimfire, .32 centerfire, or .38 centerfire cal., nickel (standard) or blue finish, hard rubber grips with owl's head design, small or large frame, 5 or 7 shot, 3 (small) or 3 1/4 in. barrel, single top post barrel latch (release lever mounted on left side of top strap), flat leaf hammer spring, first revolver marked "Iver Johnson's Arms & Cycle Works", some early models were marked "Iver Johnson & Co.", uses hammer the hammer action, main ser. no. location on left side of grip frame, 12-17 1/4 oz. Mfg. 1894-1895.

$290	$260	$180	$160	$140	$120	$110	$100	$90	$80	$70	$60

100%	98%	95%	90%	80%	70%	60%	50%	40%	30%	20%	10%

Add 10% for models marked "Iver Johnson & Co."

SECOND MODEL SAFETY AUTOMATIC HAMMER (BLACK POWDER CARTRIDGE) – .22 rimfire, .32 centerfire, or .38 centerfire cal., 5 or 7 shot, 3 or 3 1/4 in. barrel, nickel (standard) or blue finish, hard rubber grips with owl's head at top, double top post latch, flat leaf hammer spring, two cross pins in lower frame, uses hammer the hammer action, main ser. no. located on left side of grip frame, 12-17 1/4 oz. Mfg. 1896-1908.

$275	$245	$220	$200	$175	$160	$140	$120	$100	$90	$75	$60

Add 100% for Bourne Knuckleduster.

FIRST MODEL SAFETY AUTOMATIC HAMMERLESS (BLACK POWDER CARTRIDGES) – .32 centerfire, or .38 centerfire cal., small or large frame, 5 shot, 3 (small) or 3 1/4 in. barrel, nickel (standard) or blue finish, hard rubber grips with owl's head logo at top, single top post barrel latch (release lever mounted on left side of top strap), flat leaf hammer spring, two cross pins in lower frame, uses hammer the hammer action, main ser. no. location on left side of grip frame, 12-17 1/4 oz. Mfg. 1895-1896.

$300	$265	$185	$160	$140	$120	$110	$100	$90	$80	$70	$60

SECOND MODEL SAFETY AUTOMATIC HAMMERLESS (BLACK POWDER CARTRIDGE) – .32 centerfire, or .38 centerfire cal., small or large frame, 5 shot, 3 (small) or 3 1/4 in. barrel, nickel (standard) or blue finish, hard rubber grips with owl's head at top, double top post latch, flat leaf hammer spring, two cross pins in lower frame, uses hammer the hammer action, main ser. no. located on left side of grip frame, 12 1/2-17 1/4 oz. Mfg. 1896-1908.

$285	$250	$225	$200	$175	$160	$140	$120	$100	$90	$75	$60

Add 100% for Bourne Knuckleduster.

GRADING - PPGS™	100%	98%	95%	90%	80%	70%	60%

THIRD MODEL SAFETY AUTOMATIC HAMMER (SMOKELESS POWDER CARTRIDGE) – .22 rimfire, .32 centerfire, or .38 centerfire cal., 5 or 7 shot, small or large frame, 3 or 3 1/4 in. barrel, hard rubber grips with owl's head on top, optional oversized wood or hard rubber grips, all coil springs, redesigned model for smokeless powder, double top post barrel latch, hammer the hammer action, coil hammer spring, four cross pins in lower frame, main ser. no. located on left side of grip frame, 13-19 oz. Mfg. 1909-1941.

$250	$220	$200	$190	$175	$155	$130

THIRD MODEL SAFETY AUTOMATIC HAMMERLESS (SMOKELESS POWDER CARTRIDGE) – .22 rimfire, .32 centerfire, or .38 centerfire cal., 5 or 7 shot, small or large frame, 3 or 3 1/4 in. barrel, hard rubber grips with owl's head on top, optional oversized wood or hard rubber grips, all coil springs, redesigned model for smokeless powder, double top post barrel latch, hammer the hammer action, coil hammer spring, four cross pins in lower frame, main ser. no. located on left side of grip frame, 13 1/2 - 19 1/4 oz. Mfg. 1909-1941.

$260	$225	$200	$190	$175	$155	$130

U.S. REVOLVER CO. AUTOMATIC HAMMER – .22 rimfire, .32 or .38 centerfire cal., large or small frame, blue or nickel finish, 5 or 7 shot, 3 or 3 1/4 in. barrel (5 in. barrels have been seen), does not have hammer the hammer action, safety notch on hammer, hard rubber grips with U.S. at top, oversized two piece hard rubber grips optional, brand name revolver mfg. by Iver Johnson's Arms & Cycle Works sold through the wholesale trade, never listed in any IJ catalog, although it was listed in some European catalogs as an original Iver Johnson product, main ser. no. located on left side of grip frame, 12-17 3/4 oz. Mfg. 1910-1935.

$225	$195	$170	$140	$125	$110	$95

U.S. REVOLVER AUTOMATIC HAMMERLESS – .32 or .38 centerfire cal., similar to Hammer model, except has rebounding hammer, 12 1/2-18 oz. Mfg. 1910-1935.

$225	$195	$170	$140	$125	$110	$95

SECRET SERVICE SPECIAL HAMMER – same model as the U.S. Revolver Co., except for markings on the barrel, large and small frame, does not have hammer the hammer action, top of barrel marked for .38 SMITH & WESSON cartridge" (or .32 for small frame), and "SECRET SERVICE SPECIAL" on left side of barrel, main ser. no. location on left side of grip

GRADING - PPGS™	100%	98%	95%	90%	80%	70%	60%	LAST MSR

frame, mfg. for Fred Biffar Co. of Chicago., four other companies also manufactured this gun - Meriden Firearms Co., Hopkins & Allen Firearms Co., H&R Arms Co., and an unknown Spanish company. Mfg. 1912-disc.

$225 $195 $170 $140 $125 $110 $95

Subtract 10% for H&R Arms Co., 15% for Hopkins & Allen Co., 20% for Meriden Firearms Co., or 25% for Spanish mfg.

SECRET SERVICE SPECIAL HAMMERLESS – same model as the U.S. Revolver Co. hammerless, except for markings on the barrel and grips, mfg. for Fred Biffar Co. of Chicago., four other companies also manufactured this gun - Meriden Firearms Co., Hopkins & Allen Firearms Co., H&R Arms Co., and an unknown Spanish company. Mfg. 1912-disc.

$225 $195 $170 $140 $125 $110 $95

Subtract 10% for H&R Arms Co., 15% for Hopkins & Allen Co., 20% for Meriden Firearms Co., or 25% for Spanish mfg.

SECRET SERVICE MODEL W/HAMMER BLOCK SAFETY – similar to U.S. Revolver Automatic Hammer, except has patented hammer block safety, patented by Prospero Donaldo and assigned to Fred Biffar Co. of Chicago. Mfg. 1917-disc.

$250 $220 $200 $190 $175 $155 $130

.22 SUPERSHOT AUTOMATIC (LARGE FRAME) – .22 rimfire cal., blue finish, 6 in. barrel, one piece checkered wood grips, features hammer the hammer action, Model 70 (7 shot) or Model 90 (9 shot), built on the Safety Automatic Hammer Third Model large frame with similar specs, left side of barrel marked "22 SUPERSHOT", 24 oz. Mfg. 1928-1941.

$250 $220 $200 $190 $175 $155 $130

.22 SUPERSHOT SEALED EIGHT FIRST MODEL (LARGE FRAME) – .22 rimfire cal., blue finish, 8 shot, 6 in. barrel, oversized checkered wood grips, hammer the hammer action, cylinder with recessed chambers that full enclose the cartridge case head, large frame top break, left side of barrel marked "22 SUPERSHOT SEALED EIGHT", main ser. no. located on left side of grip frame, ser. nos. below L26601, 24 oz. Mfg. 1932-1941.

$275 $245 $220 $200 $175 $160 $140

Add 20% for adj. sight model.

The 1938 catalog identifies this model as the Model 88 (fixed sights), the Model 833 (adj. rear sight), and the Model 834 (adj. rear sight and adj. finger rest).

.22 SUPERSHOT SEALED EIGHT SECOND MODEL (LARGE FRAME) – .22 rimfire cal., blue finish, similar to First Model, except has altered grip frame, and was also available in 4 1/2 in. barrel, ser. nos. above L26600, 26 3/4-28 3/4 oz. Mfg. 1947-1954.

$275 $245 $220 $200 $175 $160 $140

.22 SUPERSHOT THIRD MODEL (MODEL 844) – .22 rimfire cal., blue finish, similar to Second Model, except has unfluted cylinder, known and marked as the Model 844, 24-27 oz. Mfg. 1955-1957

$300 $275 $245 $220 $200 $175 $160

PROTECTOR SEALED EIGHT LARGE FRAME – .22 rimfire cal., blue finish, 2 1/2 in. barrel, hammer the hammer action, cylinder has 8 recessed chambers, pocket size one piece checkered wood grips, marked on left side "PROTECTOR SEALED EIGHT", listed as the Model 84 in the 1938 catalog, 20 oz. Mfg. 1932-1941.

$415 $350 $315 $275 $235 $195 $175

Add 10% for serial numbers above L26600.

MODEL 36T TRIGGER COCKING, LARGE FRAME SINGLE ACTION – .22 rimfire cal., 8 shot, blue finish, 6 in. barrel, oversize checkered wood grips with finger rest, adj. rear sight, patented trigger cocking action, first pull of trigger cocks the hammer and next pull releases it, main ser. no. located on left side of grip frame, scarce, 24 oz. Mfg. 1938-1941.

$495 $425 $375 $325 $275 $225 $200

This model Iver Johnson's was first attempt at a true adj. sight target revolver. The patent rights to the action were obtained early in the 1900s and experimented with for many years.

GRADING - PPGS™	100%	98%	95%	90%	80%	70%	60%	LAST MSR

I.J. CHAMPION MODEL 822 SINGLE ACTION TARGET – .22 rimfire cal., blue finish, 6 in. barrel, 8 shot, based on .22 Supershot Sealed Eight frame, oversize fancy checkered wood grips with finger rest, does not have hammer the hammer action, large frame, design for target shooting, recessed chambers in the cylinders, 24 oz. Mfg. 1939-1947.

	$450	$400	$350	$300	$275	$210	$195

ARMSWORTH MODEL 855 – .22 rimfire cal., 6 in. barrel, flat side with round bottom, full length top rib, adj. sights, does not have hammer the hammer action, combination of earlier Champion single action and .22 Supershot Third Model, has Champion single action mechanism and barrel, grips, and cylinder of the .22 Supershot, unfluted cylinder with recessed chambers and flash control front rim, 30 oz. Mfg. 1955-1957.

	$425	$365	$315	$275	$235	$195	$175

I.J. TRAILSMAN MODEL 66 LARGE FRAME – .22 rimfire cal., 4 1/2 or 6 in. barrel, blue finish, double action, oversized plastic Tentite grips with molded thumbrest, adj. rear and front sight, manual ejection, hammer mounted firing pin, 8 shot, cylinder has recessed chambers and flash control front rim, main ser. no. located on front of the grip strap until 1961, then on right side of frame below cylinder, 31-34 oz. Mfg. 1958-1978.

	$225	$195	$170	$140	$125	$110	$95

* ***I.J. Trailsman Model 66S Snub Large Frame*** – .22 rimfire, .32 centerfire (new 1962), or .38 centerfire (new 1962) cal., similar to the Trailsman Model 66, except has two piece plastic grips, 2 3/4 in. barrel, manual extractor, 5 or 8 shot, main ser. no. located on front of grip strap until 1961, then moved to right side of frame below cylinder, 25 oz. Mfg. 1959-1963.

	$235	$200	$175	$140	$125	$110	$95

HIJO QUIK BREAK LARGE FRAME – similar to Trailsman Model 66, nickel finish, 2 3/4 in. barrel, double action, does not have hammer the hammer action, small two piece pocket size grips, mfg. for sale through NYC mail order companies, 25 oz. Mfg. 1961.

	$235	$200	$175	$140	$125	$110	$95

MODEL 67 VIKING LARGE FRAME – .22 rimfire cal., 8 shot, blue finish, 4 1/2 or 6 in. chrome lined barrel, redesigned Model 66 double action incorporating the hammer the hammer feature, oversized plastic grips with molded thumb rest, adj. rear and front sight, cylinder has recessed chambers and flash control front rim, main ser. no. located on right side of frame below cylinder, 31-34 oz. Mfg. 1964-1978.

	$250	$220	$200	$190	$175	$155	$130

* ***Model 67S Viking Snub Large Frame*** – .22 rimfire, .32 or .38 centerfire cal., similar to Model 67 Viking, except has small two piece plastic grips, 2 3/4 in. barrel, 5 or 8 shot, 25 oz. Mfg. 1964-1978.

	$260	$225	$200	$190	$175	$155	$130

MODEL 69 STARTER DELUXE LARGE FRAME – .22 rimfire blank or .32 centerfire blank, double action, 2 3/4 in. solid barrel, does not have hammer the hammer action, fixed sights, action similar to Trailsman Model 66, small two piece plastic pocket size grips, 5 or 8 shot, blue finish, manual ejection, main ser. no. located on right side of frame below cylinder, 22 oz. Mfg. 1964-1978.

	$125	$100	$85	$75	$65	$60	$50

RIFLES

Iver Johnson's first rifle was manufactured in 1928 and remained the only rifle manufactured entirely within the Iver Johnson factory in Fitchburg. The later .22 cal. rifles were all imported from either Canada or Germany, except the Lil Champ Model, which was manufactured in Jacksonville, AR. The M1 Carbine models were manufactured in either Middlesex, NJ or Jacksonville, AR.

I.J. X BOLT ACTION EARLY MODEL – .22 rimfire cal., bolt action, single shot, fixed open rear sight, blade front sight, 22 in. round tapered barrel, thumb screw take down, solid block walnut stock with large knob at front of forend, patented automatic safety, steel buttplate, 4 lbs. Mfg. 1928-1941.

	$250	$220	$190	$155	$130	$115	$100

GRADING - PPGS™	100%	98%	95%	90%	80%	70%	60%	LAST MSR

I.J. X BOLT ACTION LATE MODEL – .22 rimfire cal., bolt action, similar to Early model, except larger, heavier stock, 4 1/2 lbs.

	$250	$220	$190	$155	$130	$115	$100

I.J. 2X BOLT ACTION – .22 rimfire cal., single shot, adj. rear sight, post front sight, round tapered 24 in. barrel, blue finish, thumb screw take down, checkered full pistol grip stock with finger grooves in forend, steel buttplate, chromium plated bolt and trigger, patented automatic safety, 4 1/2 lbs. Mfg. 1930-1955.

	$285	$250	$215	$175	$145	$120	$110

* ***I.J. 2XA Bolt Action*** – .22 rimfire cal., single shot, similar to Model 2X, except has Lyman #55 adj. rear sight, Lyman #3 bead front sight, sling swivels, leather sling strap, tapered 24 in. proofed and targeted barrel, 4 5/8 lbs. Mfg. 1930-1941.

	$325	$300	$275	$250	$200	$175	$150

I.J. LIL CHAMP BOLT ACTION – .22 rimfire cal., single shot, 16 1/4 in. blue barrel, blue receiver, nickel bolt and trigger, step adj. rear sight, ramp front sight, black plastic molded shortened stock, designed for smaller shooters, 3 1/8 lbs. Mfg. 1985-1990.

	$175	$155	$130	$115	$95	$85	$75

I.J. TRAILBLAZER SEMI-AUTO – .22 LR cal., recoil operated, blue finish, 10 shot detachable mag., Monte Carlo style hardwood stock, post front sight, step adj. rear sight, plastic buttplate, 18 1/2 in. barrel, imported from Canada. Mfg. 1984-1986.

	$150	$130	$115	$100	$85	$75	$65

I.J. WAGONMASTER LEVER ACTION – .22 Rimfire or .22 WMR cal., 12 (.22 WMR), 15, 17, or 21 shot mag., tubular mag. under the barrel, 18 1/2 in. barrel, hooded ramp front sight, step adj. rear sight, walnut finished hardwood stock and forend, plastic buttplate, imported from Germany, 5 3/4 lbs. Mfg. 1985-1990.

	$325	$300	$275	$250	$200	$175	$150

* ***I.J. Wagonmaster Junior*** – .22 rimfire cal., similar to I.J. Wagonmaster, except has 16 1/4 in. barrel, 14, 15, or 18 shot mag., imported from Germany, 5 1/4 lbs. Mfg. 1985-1990.

	$325	$300	$275	$250	$200	$175	$150

I.J. TARGETMASTER SLIDE ACTION – .22 rimfire cal., 12, 15, or 19 shot mag., tubular magazine under the barrel, 18 1/2 in. barrel, hooded ramp front sight, step adj. rear sight, blue finish, walnut finished hardwood stock, plastic buttplate, imported from Germany, 5 3/4 lbs. Erma Mfg. 1985-1990.

	$325	$300	$275	$250	$200	$175	$150

I.J. SEMI-AUTO CARBINE – .22 LR cal., 15 shot mag., recoil operated, blue finish, copy of the M-1 carbine, 18 1/2 in. barrel, military type front sight protected by wings, rear aperture adj. sight, walnut finished hardwood stock and handguard, sling swivels, imported from Germany, 5 3/4 lbs. Mfg. 1985-1990.

	$425	$365	$315	$275	$235	$195	$175

I.J. MAGNUM SEMI-AUTO CARBINE – .22 WMR cal., gas operated, otherwise similar to Semi-Auto Carbine, imported from Germany. Mfg. 1985-1990.

	$525	$465	$395	$340	$295	$250	$220

I.J. PLAINSFIELD SEMI-AUTO CARBINE – .30 Carbine, 9mm Para. (new 1986), or 5.7mm (disc. 1986) cal., gas operated, copy of WWII U.S. Military Carbine, 5, 10, 15, or 30 shot detachable mag., stainless steel or blue finish, 18 in. barrel, American walnut or hardwood stock, model names and numbers changed several times, M2 full auto model available during the 1980s, 6 1/2 lbs. Mfg. 1978-1993.

	$450	$395	$335	$285	$245	$210	$180

Add 10% for walnut stock.
Add 20% for stainless steel.
Add 35% for 5.7mm cal. (Spitfire Model) or 9mm Para. cal.

GRADING - PPGS™	100%	98%	95%	90%	80%	70%	60%	LAST MSR

I.J. PARATROOPER SEMI-AUTO CARBINE – .30 Carbine cal., gas operated, copy of WWII U.S. Military Carbine, 5, 10, 15, or 30 shot detachable mag., stainless steel or blue finish, 18 in. barrel, American walnut or hardwood stock, with collapsible stock extension model names and numbered changed several times, M2 full auto model available with 12 in. barrel, 4 1/2 lbs. Mfg. 1978-1989.

	100%	98%	95%	90%	80%	70%	60%	LAST MSR
	$595	$550	$500	$460	$430	$395	$360	

Add 10% for walnut stock.
Add 20% for stainless steel.

I.J. SURVIVAL CARBINE SEMI-AUTO – .30 Carbine or 5.7mm cal., gas operated, copy of WWII military carbine, 5, 10, 15, or 30 shot detachable mag., stainless steel or blue finish, Zytel black plastic pistol grip stock, 6 1/2 lbs.

	100%	98%	95%	90%	80%	70%	60%	LAST MSR
	$450	$395	$335	$285	$245	$210	$180	

Add 20% for stainless steel.
Add 35% for 5.7mm cal. (Spitfire Model).

* ***I.J. Survival Carbine Semi-Auto w/Folding Stock*** – .30 Carbine or 5.7mm cal., similar to Survival Carbine, except has folding stock. Mfg. 1983-1989.

	100%	98%	95%	90%	80%	70%	60%	LAST MSR
	$585	$500	$425	$375	$325	$275	$235	

Add 20% for stainless steel.
Add 35% for 5.7mm cal. (Spitfire Model).

I.J. UNIVERSAL CARBINE SEMI-AUTO – .30 Carbine or .256 Win. Mag. cal., gas operated, GI military type carbine, 5 or 10 shot detachable mag., 18 in. barrel, stainless steel or blue finish, walnut stained hardwood, sling swivel, drilled and tapped, known as Model 1003 (.30 Carbine) or Model 1256 (.256 Win. Mag., 5 shot only). Mfg. 1986.

	100%	98%	95%	90%	80%	70%	60%	LAST MSR
	$450	$395	$335	$285	$245	$210	$180	

Iver Johnson marked models are rare.

I.J. UNIVERSAL PARATROOPER SEMI-AUTO CARBINE – 30 Carbine cal., similar to Universal Carbine model, except has Schmeisser-type hardwood folding stock, 5 or 10 shot detachable mag., drilled and tapped. Mfg. 1986.

	100%	98%	95%	90%	80%	70%	60%	LAST MSR
	$550	$475	$415	$360	$315	$265	$230	

Iver Johnson marked models are rare.

MODEL 5100 BOLT ACTION SNIPER – .338 Win., .416 Win., or .50 BMG cal., single shot, free floating 29 in. barrel, no sights, drilled and tapped, marketed with Leupold Ultra M1 20X scope, adj. composite stock, adj. trigger, two different model numbers, ltd. mfg., 36 lbs. Mfg. 1985-1993.

	100%	98%	95%	90%	80%	70%	60%	LAST MSR
	$4,550	$3,775	$3,375	$3,000	$2,600	$2,300	$2,000	

SHOTGUNS: O/U

IVER JOHNSON SILVER SHADOW O/U – 12 ga., 3 in. chambers, boxlock action, 26, 28, or 30 in. barrels with chokes, full length vent. rib, extractors, DT or non-SST, checkered European pistol grip walnut stock and forend, plastic buttplate, pistol grip cap, imported from Italy, 7 1/2 lbs. Mfg. 1973-1977.

	100%	98%	95%	90%	80%	70%	60%	LAST MSR
	$500	$440	$375	$325	$275	$235	$200	

SHOTGUNS: SxS

There are two basic double barrel designs - the early monobloc breech models (mfg. 1913-1923) and one piece barrel/breech models originally called the Hercules Grade (mfg. 1924-1935), and later called Hammer Forged (mfg. 1936-1941). These are mass produced high quality field grade guns. The later Skeeter (mfg. 1933-1943) doubles were specially built high quality with excellent fit and finish. However, there is no difference in the internal mechanism of any of these guns.

HAMMERLESS MONOBLOC – 12 ga., boxlock, 28, 30, or 32 in. browned barrels with chokes, case hardened receiver, breech sleeve area is solid one piece (monobloc), dropped forged, hammers can be lowered w/o snapping them on empty chambers, automatic safety, extractors, DT, checkered pistol grip American black walnut stock and forend, hard rubber buttplate, 7 1/2 lbs. Mfg. 1914-1923.

	100%	98%	95%	90%	80%	70%	60%	LAST MSR
	$600	$525	$440	$390	$340	$285	$245	

GRADING - PPGS™	100%	98%	95%	90%	80%	70%	60%	LAST MSR

HAMMERLESS HERCULES GRADE – 12, 16, 20, or 28 ga., boxlock action, case hardened receiver with hunting dog etched on left side, 30 in. blued barrels and lug forged as one piece and joined together, hand checkered American black walnut stock and forend with pistol grip cap, plain extractor model has slim forend, D&E fastener, hard rubber buttplate, automatic safety, DT, some seen with Canadian markings, most likely mfg. by Cooey, approx. 7 3/4 lbs. Mfg. 1924-circa 1935.

	100%	98%	95%	90%	80%	70%	60%
	$1,100	$900	$795	$695	$595	$495	$450
28 ga.	$2,200	$1,800	$1,575	$1,395	$1,175	$995	$900

Add 15% for ejectors or 25% for single trigger.

A special run of this model was manufactured in the 1930s for Montgomery Wards and marked "Western Field Model 53".

HAMMERLESS HERCULES GRADE .410 BORE – .410 bore, boxlock action, hammerless design, top lever break open (cocks on opening), small case colored frame, straight grip American black walnut stock and forend, extractors or ejectors (ejector model has D&E fastener), 26 in. fully choked blue barrels, barrels and lug forged as one piece, hunting dog etched on left side of frame, approx. 5 3/4 - 6 lbs. Mfg. 1924-circa 1935.

	100%	98%	95%	90%	80%	70%	60%
	$2,600	$2,250	$1,850	$1,350	$995	$895	$800

HAMMERLESS SUPERTRAP HERCULES GRADE – 12 ga., boxlock action, 32 in. fully choked barrels and lug forged as one piece then joined together after proof test, full length raised vent. rib, selective ejectors, DT, two Lyman ivory sights, hunting dog etched on left side of frame, automatic safety, hand checkered American black walnut stock and beavertail forend, D&E fastener, hard rubber pistol grip cap and anti-flinch recoil pad, approx. 7 3/4 lbs. Mfg. 1924-circa 1935.

	100%	98%	95%	90%	80%	70%	60%
	$1,600	$1,375	$1,050	$925	$825	$725	$625

HAMMERLESS HAMMER FORGED MODEL – similar to Hercules Grade, except left side of frame is marked "IVER JOHNSON HAMMER FORGED" in two lines and right side of frame marked with company name and address. Mfg. circa 1936-1943.

	100%	98%	95%	90%	80%	70%	60%
	$1,100	$900	$795	$695	$595	$495	$450

HAMMERLESS SUPERTRAP (HAMMER FORGED BARREL) – similar to Hammerles Hercules Grade, except left side of frame is marked "IVER JOHNSON HAMMER FORGED" in two lines and right side of frame is marked with company name and address. Mfg. circa 1936-1941.

	100%	98%	95%	90%	80%	70%	60%
	$1,600	$1,375	$1,050	$925	$825	$725	$625

HAMMERLESS HAMMER FORGED MODEL .410 BORE/28 GA. – 28 ga. or .410 bore, boxlock action, similar to Hercules Grade, except left side of frame marked "IVER JOHNSON HAMMER FORGED" in two lines and right side of frame marked with company name and address. Mfg. circa 1936-1941.

	100%	98%	95%	90%	80%	70%	60%
	$2,600	$2,250	$1,850	$1,350	$995	$895	$800

Add 50% for 28 ga.

SKEET-ER – 12, 16, 20, or 28 ga., 26 or 28 in. special skeet bored barrels, boxlock action, barrel and lug forged as one piece, proofed, then joined together, select fancy figured hand checkered lacquer finished high grade American black walnut pistol grip or straight grip stock and large beavertail forend, D&E fastener, extractors or ejectors, automatic or manual safety, Lyman #10 front sight, Jostam anti-flinch recoil pad, Miller single selective or non-selective trigger, 8 1/2 lbs. Mfg. 1930-1941.

	100%	98%	95%	90%	80%	70%	60%
	$2,195	$1,795	$1,500	$1,150	$1,050	$825	$725
16 or 28 ga.	$4,400	$3,600	$3,000	$2,300	$1,100	$1,650	$1,550

Add 30% for ejectors, 50% for SST, 20% for non-selective trigger, 100% for factory VR, 30% for 20 ga., 200% for rare factory engraving (be wary of upgrades) and 50% for scarce factory case colors (be wary of new colors).

SKEET-ER .410 BORE – .410 bore, boxlock action, 3 in. chambers, 26 or 28 in. special skeet choked barrels, high grade American black walnut straight grip or pistol grip stock with beavertail forend, extractors or ejectors (w/D&E fastener), hard rubber buttplate, Lyman #10 ivory front sight, SST, single non-selective trigger or DT, same small frame as .410 Hammerless Hercules Grade, 6 lbs. Mfg. 1931-1943.

	100%	98%	95%	90%	80%	70%	60%
	$4,000	$3,500	$3,000	$2,500	$2,000	$1,800	$1,500

GRADING - PPGS™	100%	98%	95%	90%	80%	70%	60%	LAST MSR

Add 25% for Miller NST or 40% for Miller SST.
Add 25% for scare 30 in. barrels.

.410 bore is the most commonly encountered gun and was made on a special small frame. This model was probably responsible for more Skeet records than any other American .410 bore SxS shotgun.

* ***Skeet-er Italian Mfg.*** – .410 bore, straight grip, DT, Arkansas address, extractors, figured wood, a few were imported during the late 1970s-early 1980s as a possible reintroduction of the Skeet-er Model, not cataloged, rare.

$2,500 $2,150 $1,825 $1,600 $1,300 $1,100 $875

100%	98%	95%	90%	80%	70%	60%	50%	40%	30%	20%	10%

SHOTGUNS: SINGLE BARREL

Some single barrel shotguns may have Canadian markings, as parts were probably shipped to Canada and assembled there.

On the following models where applicable, add 10% for 16 ga., 20% for 20 ga., 50% for 24, 28, or 32 ga., and 100% for .410 bore.

CHAMPION TOP SNAP – 12 ga., 30 in. plain twist steel barrel, top lever break open mechanism, rebounding hammer, double locking bolt, extractors, American black walnut stock and forend, nickel frame, browned barrel (imported from Belgium), marked "Champion" on top of barrel and possibly with patent date of July 27, 1880. Mfg. 1880-1900.

$300 $275 $250 $200 $175 $150 $125 $110 $100 $90 $80 $70

CHAMPION SIDE SNAP – 12 ga., 30 in. plain twist steel choked browned barrel (imported from Belgium), side lever opening mechanism, double locking bolts, rebounding hammer, extractors, American black walnut stock and forend, nickel frame, marked with Champion name on top of barrel and patent date of July 27, 1880, 6 1/2 lbs. Mfg. 1880-1900.

$300 $275 $250 $200 $175 $150 $125 $110 $100 $90 $80 $70

CHAMPION SIDE SNAP HAMMERLESS – 12 ga., concealed hammer, 30 or 32 in. plain twist steel choke barrel (imported from Belgium), side lever break open mechanism, cocks on opening, double locking bolt, extractors, American black walnut stock and forend, nickel frame, marked with Champion name on top of barrel and patent date of July 27, 1880, 6 1/2 lbs. Mfg. 1880-1900.

$325 $300 $275 $250 $200 $175 $150 $125 $110 $100 $90 $80

IVER JOHNSON EJECTOR SEMI-HAMMERLESS (RING TRIGGER) – 12 ga., semi-hammerless (does not have spur), ring trigger break open mechanism (ring in front of trigger opens action), 28, 30, or 32 in. plain twist steel choked brown barrel, rebounding hammer, ejector, American black walnut stock and forend, case hardened frame, 7 lbs. Mfg. 1897-1899.

$325 $300 $275 $250 $200 $175 $150 $125 $110 $100 $90 $80

GRADING - PPGS™	100%	98%	95%	90%	80%	70%	60%	LAST MSR

IVER JOHNSON EJECTOR SEMI-HAMMERLESS IMPROVED MODEL 1900 (RING TRIGGER) – 12 or 16 ga., 28, 30, 32, or 34 in. browned barrel, semi-hammerless break open, ring in front of trigger opens action, rebounding hammer, ejector, improved barrel take down, American black walnut stock and forend, case hardened frame, 6 1/4 lbs. Mfg. 1900-1908.

$300 $275 $250 $200 $175 $150 $125

IVER JOHNSON EJECTOR SEMI-HAMMERLESS JUNIOR MODEL (RING TRIGGER) – 12 or 16 ga., 26 or 28 in. browned barrel, semi-hammerless break open, ring in front of trigger opens action, rebounding hammer, single locking bolt, shortened American black walnut stock and forend, case hardened frame, hard rubber buttplate, 5 1/2 - 6 lbs. Mfg. 1901-1908.

$300 $275 $250 $200 $175 $150 $125

IVER JOHNSON TOP SNAP IMPROVED MODEL 1901 – 12 or 16 ga., 28, 30, 32, or 34 in. steel choke bored browned barrel, hammer top lever operated break open mechanism, ejectors, American black walnut pistol grip stock and forend, case hardened frame, hard rubber butt plate, pistol grip cap, approx. 6 lbs. Mfg. 1901-1904.

$300 $275 $250 $200 $175 $150 $125

GRADING - PPGS™	100%	98%	95%	90%	80%	70%	60%	LAST MSR

This model is also know as the New White Powder Wonder or White Powder Wonder, and was manufactured for Sears, Roebuck & Co.

(IVER JOHNSON) CHAMPION TOP SNAP – 12 or 16 ga., similar to Iver Johnson Top Snap Improved Model 1901, top lever opening, 28, 30, or 32 in. browned steel barrel, with chokes, case hardened receiver, ejectors, rebounding hammer, American black walnut stock and forend, hard rubber buttplate, marked "CHAMPION", approx. 6 lbs. Mfg. 1905-1908.

$300	$275	$250	$200	$175	$150	$125	

IVER JOHNSON TRIGGER ACTION SINGLE GUN – 12 ga., 28, 30, or 32 in. brown barrel with full choke, trigger action break open mechanism, when hammer is in rebound position, a pull on it will release the barrel locking bolt, fired by manually cocking the hammer, then pressing a small trigger insert into main trigger, American black walnut stock and forend, case hardened frame, ejector, hard rubber buttplate, pistol grip cap, approx. 6 lbs. Mfg. 1905-1908.

$325	$300	$275	$250	$200	$175	$150	

There are two different version of the trigger action and not enough information has turned up to give details as to when each version was manufactured.

IVER JOHNSON TRIGGER ACTION JUNIOR MODEL – 12 or 16 ga., 26 or 28 in. browned barrel with full choke, similar to Trigger Action Model, except has shortened American black walnut stock and forend, approx. 5 1/2 lbs. Mfg. 1905-1908.

$325	$300	$275	$250	$200	$175	$150	

CHAMPION MODEL 36 – 10, 12, 16, 20, 24 (new 1913), 28 (new 1913), 32 ga., or .410 bore, 28, 30, or 32 in. barrel (barrel and lug forged into one piece), rebounding center mounted hammer, top lever operated break open design, full choke, case hardened or nickel receiver, extractors or ejectors, American black walnut stock and forend, name changed to Champion Single Barrel in 1923, approx. 6 3/4 lbs. Mfg. 1909-1922.

$250	$220	$190	$155	$130	$115	$100	

Add 20-40% for 12, 20, 28, 32 ga. or .410 bore.

CHAMPION SINGLE BARREL – 10, 12, 16, 20, 24 (new 1913), 28 (new 1913), 32 ga., or .410 bore, 28, 30, or 32 in. barrel (barrel and lug forged into one piece), same model as Champion Model 36, except smaller gauges are built on same frame as large gauges, exact year production stopped not determined, some seen with Canadian markings, most likely because they were shipped to Canada, as there is no evidence that Iver Johnson ever had a production facility in Canada. Mfg. 1923-approx. 1978.

$250	$220	$190	$155	$130	$115	$100	

Add 20-40% for 24, 28, 32 or .410 ga.

CHAMPION MODEL 36 JUNIOR – 12, 16, or 20 ga., 26 or 28 in. barrel, similar to Champion Model 36, except has shortened buttstock and forend, 6 1/4 lbs. Mfg. 1909-1916.

$300	$250	$220	$190	$155	$130	$115	

CHAMPION MODEL 39 – 24, 28 ga., .410 bore (mfg. 1911-1915), or .44 cal. (mfg. 1911-1915), smaller frame than the Model 36, center mounted rebounding hammer, top lever break open mechanism, 28 or 30 in. plain full choke barrel, extractors or ejectors, case hardened or nickel frame, American black walnut stock and forend, pistol grip cap, hard rubber buttplate, 5 3/4 lbs. Mfg. 1909-1916.

$325	$300	$275	$250	$200	$175	$150	

CHAMPION MODEL 39 JUNIOR – 24, 28 ga., .410 bore (mfg. 1911-1915), or .44 cal. (mfg. 1911-1915), similar to Model 39, except has shortened stock, 26 or 28 in. barrel, extractors, 5 1/4 lbs. Mfg. 1909-1916.

$325	$300	$275	$250	$200	$175	$150	

CHAMPION JACKETED BREECH – similar to Champion Model 36, except has reinforced barrel breech to accept heavier loads that were available for waterfowl hunting. Mfg. 1912-1918.

$300	$275	$250	$200	$175	$150	$125	

GRADING - PPGS™	100%	98%	95%	90%	80%	70%	60%	LAST MSR

CHAMPION MATTED RIB MODEL – 12, 16, 20 ga., or .410 bore (new 1928), 28, 30, or 32 in. fully choked blue barrel, center mounted rebounding hammer, top lever break open, solid raised full length rib, finely matted, extractors or ejectors, case hardened frame, American black walnut full checkered pistol grip stock and forend, may also be marked with the Western Field brand name, 7 1/4 lbs. Mfg. 1912-1941.

$315	$285	$260	$200	$175	$150	$125	

Add 10% for .410 bore.

CHAMPION SEMI-OCTAGON – 12 or 16 ga., 28, 30, or 32 in. blue full choke barrel, center mounted rebounding hammer, top lever break open, top half of barrel is octagon, matted top surface, case hardened frame, American walnut stock and forend with or w/o (later production) pistol grip cap, hard rubber buttplate, extractors or ejectors, 6 1/2 - 6 3/4 lbs. Mfg. 1912-1920.

$300	$275	$250	$200	$175	$150	$125	

I.J. SPECIAL TRAP – 12 ga., 32 in. full choke brown barrel with full length raised vent. rib, finely matted, top lever break open, two Lyman ivory sights, blue frame, hand checkered American black walnut stock and forend with pistol grip cap and hard rubber buttplate, ejectors, anti-flinch recoil pad optional, approx. 7 lbs. Mfg. 1927-1941.

$400	$350	$300	$265	$225	$190	$165	

EXCEL – 12, 16, 20 ga., or .410 bore, 26, 28, 30, or 32 in. fully choked blue barrel (barrel and lug forged in one piece), blue or nickel receiver, rebounding center mounted hammer, top lever operated break open design, extractors, walnut stock and forend, approx. 6 3/4 lbs. Mfg. 1910-1935.

$175	$155	$130	$115	$95	$85	$75	

This was the economy model of the Champion single barrel that was offered to mail order houses and other wholesalers, and can also be found under the following brand names: T. Barker (H&D Folsum CO., NY), Blackfield (Hibbard-Spencer & Bartlett Co., Chicago), Blackimp K-S-CO (Keith Simmons Co, San Francisco), Challenger (George Worthington Co, Cleveland), Diamond Arms Co. (Shapleigh Hardware Co., St. Louis), Eastern Arms Co. (Sears, circa pre and post WWII), Famous (Hirch Mercantile Co., San Francisco), Falcon (National Lead Co., San Francisco), Hermitage K-S-CO (Keith Simmons Co., Nashville), Ideal (Charles Williams Stores, Brooklyn), King Nitro (Shapleigh Hardware Co., St. Louis), Marshfield (could also be Marshwood, Charles Williams Stores, Brooklyn), Moniter (Paxton & Gallager Co., Omaha), Newport (Hibbard-Spencer & Bartlett Co., Chicago), Olympic Arms Co. (Morley & Murphy Hardware, Green Bay or Morley Brothers, Saginaw), Ranger (Sears, circa pre and post WWII), Revonoc (Rev-o-noc, Richardson & Conover Hardware Co, Kansas City, or Hibbard-Spencer & Bartlett), Scout (Frankfurth Hardware Co., Milwaukee), Sioux (Larson Hardware Co., SD), Triumph (Montgomery Wards), True Blue (Shapleigh Hardware Co., St. Louis), Volunteer (Belknap Hardware Co., St. Louis), Western Field (Montgomery Wards), XLCR (W. Bingham Co., Cleveland). Some of these names will also be found on guns manufactured by other makers, as some names were the property of the wholesaler/retailer.

GRADING - PPGS™	100%	Issue Price	Qty. Made

COMMEMORATIVES

100TH YEAR COMMEMORATIVE FOUR GUN CASE SET – set contains one each of the following models: Model 50A Sidewinder (E code), Model 55A Target (H code), Model 57A Target (J code), Model 67 Viking (A code), all serial numbered the same except for the letter code, ser. nos. 1-450, all were bright blue finish, white plastic grips with gold owl's head on top, ser. no. marked on lower right side of frame and 1871-1971 on upper right frame. Mfg. 1971.

$1,000	$299	450

100TH YEAR COMMEMORATIVE SINGLE CASED GUN – an unknown number of cased single guns were mfg. using the same models and letter codes as the four gun case set, finish and grips were the same, included a metal box with vinyl covering, ser. nos. starting at 451. Mfg. 1971.

$300	N/A	N/A

GRADING - PPGS™	100%	Issue Price	Qty. Made

The issue price of each gun were as follows: Model 67 was $85, Model 50A was $73, Model 57A was $72.50, and the Model 55A was $69.50.

U.S. BORDER PATROL COMMEMORATIVE – .380 ACP Pony model with engraving, some sold as match pairs, wooden presentation case, 500 mfg.

	$650	N/A	500

D-DAY COMMEMORATIVE CARBINE – includes carbine model with two 15 shot mags., double magazine pouch, web sling, oiler, full color poster depicting invasions, one set of dog tags (could be returned to have original owner's name stamped on them), special edition of Bill Mauldin's book *Up Front*, brown cardboard box encased in a color sleeve depicting the invasion. Mfg. 1980.

	$1,500	N/A	N/A

Subtract $500 for non-NIB.
Subtract 50% if w/o accessories.

WWII COMMEMORATIVE CARBINE – engraved with gold filled markings, packaged in special wood and glass display case, includes papers, mfg. for American Historical Foundation circa mid-1980s.

	$1,500	N/A	2,500

Subtract $500 for non-NIB.
Subtract 50% if w/o display case and papers.

50th ANNIVERSARY CARBINE – did not include accessories, production number unknown. Mfg. 1991-1993.

	$700	N/A	N/A

Subtract 40% for non-NIB.

NATIONAL GUARD CARBINE – did not include accessories, production number unknown. Mfg. 1991-1993.

	$700	N/A	N/A

Subtract 40% for non-NIB.

IZHMASH

Current manufacturer located in Izhevsk, Russia. Currently imported exclusively beginning 2012 by RWC Group LLC, located in Tullytown, PA. Previously imported and distributed by Russian American Armory, located in Scottsburg, IN, and until 2004 by European American Armory (certain models only), located in Sharpes, FL. Other models were also imported by Kalashnikov USA, located in Port St. Lucie, FL. Previously distributed by Interstate Arms Corp., located in Billerica, MA, and by L.A. Austin International, Inc., located in Surprise, AZ.

Current Izhmash trademarks include Saiga (see separate listing in S section), Hesse-Saiga, Krebs-Saiga, Romak, Sobol, Korshun, LOS, Maral (not imported), and Dragunov (not imported).

GRADING - PPGS™	100%	98%	95%	90%	80%	70%	60%	*LAST MSR*

RIFLES: BOLT ACTION

URAL 5.1 MATCH RIFLE – .22 LR cal., single shot, competition model with eccentric bolt, adj. cheekpiece, trigger, and buttplate, 26 1/2 in. barrel with aperture sights, 11.3 lbs. Imported 2000.

	$1,075	$950	$825	$700	$600	$500	$425	

URAL 6-1 MATCH RIFLE – .22 LR cal., U.I.T. configuration with adj. buttplate and 26 3/4 in. barrel, aperture sights, various accessories included, 10 2/3 lbs. Imported 2000-2002.

	$550	$500	$450	$400	$360	$330	$300	*$625*

URAL 6-2 MATCH RIFLE – .22 LR cal., features laminated stock. Imported 2000-2002.

	$1,000	$875	$750	$650	$550	$450	$350	*$1,125*

GRADING - PPGS™	100%	98%	95%	90%	80%	70%	60%	LAST MSR

BIATHLON BASIC – .17 HMR (new 2003), 22 LR, or .22 WMR (new 2003) cal., entry level biathlon model, beech stock, heavy barrel with Weaver rail, 6.1 lbs. Imported 2002-2004.

	$315	$275	$240	$195	$175	$160	$145	

Add $10 for .22 WMR or $20 for .17 HMR cal.
Add $50 for adj. sights.

BIATHLON 7-4 – .22 LR cal., features pivoting crank right or left hand action, extra mags. that can be stored on the stock, 19.7 in. barrel with aperture sights, includes biathlon harness, spare mags., and counter weights, safety slings, cased, with or w/o chrome barrel exterior, 9.1 lbs. Imported 2000-2004, reimportation began 2012.

	$895	$725	$650	$550	$450	$350	$300	
MSR $1,543	$1,350	$1,150	$1,000	$875	$750	$625	$550	

Add $95 for left-hand action.
Add $392 for Version 8 Model or $524 foir Version 10 Model w/chrome barrel exterior.

CM-2 – .22 LR cal., light match rifle, similar overall to Ural 6-1, 19.8 in. (Youth) or 26.7 in. barrel. Imported 2000-2002, reintroduced 2003.

	$365	$325	$285	$250	$225	$200	$180	

LOS 7-1 SPORTER – .223 Rem. (disc.), .308 Win., or 7.62x39mm (disc.) cal., 21.8 in. hammer forged barrel with two lug bolt lockup, detachable 5 shot mag., adj. trigger, checkered hardwood stock with vent. recoil pad, includes scope, 7.3 lbs. Imported 2000-2002, reimported beginning 2012.

	$360	$330	$300	$270	$240	$210	$190	
MSR $1,200	$1,050	$950	$850	$750	$650	$550	$450	

Subtract 10% if w/o scope.

BARS 4-1 – .223 Rem., 5.6x39mm, or 7.62x39mm cal., birch stock, 21 in. barrel. Importation began 2012.

MSR $1,130	$1,000	$900	$800	$700	$600	$500	$450	

RECORD – 7.62x54R, .308 Win., or .338 Lapua cal., hardwood stock, monopod, bipod. Importation began 2012.

MSR $8,330	$7,500	$6,500	$5,500	$4,750	$4,000	$3,250	$2,650	

Add $1,410 for 7.62x54R or .338 Lapua cal.

KORSHUM – .22 LR cal., 19 in. heavy barrel, birch stock. Importation began 2012.

MSR $1,040	$950	$850	$750	$650	$550	$500	$400	

SM-2 – .22 LR cal., adj. birch target stock, optional Cadet configuration. Importation began 2012.

MSR $955	$850	$725	$600	$500	$400	$350	$300	

Add $103 for Cadet configuration.

BI-7-2-KO BASIC – .22 LR cal., birch stock. Importation began 2012.

MSR $1,035	$950	$850	$750	$650	$550	$500	$400	

SABLE (SOBOL) – .22 LR cal., birch stock. Importation began 2012.

MSR $925	$825	$700	$600	$500	$400	$350	$300	

SHOTGUNS

Please refer to the Saiga section for more information about these models.

J SECTION

J.B. CUSTOM INC.

Current manufacturer and restorer located in Huntertown, IN. Previously located in Fort Wayne, IN. Consumer direct sales.

J.B. Custom also offers service parts and restoration services for Winchester commemorative lever action rifles and carbines.

GRADING - PPGS™	100%	98%	95%	90%	80%	70%	60%	LAST MSR

PISTOLS: LEVER ACTION

MODEL 1892 MARE'S LEG – .357 Mag., .44-40 WCF, .44 Mag. or .45 LC cal., blue finish, 12 in. barrel, 6 shot, adj. rear sight, dovetail front sight, big loop lever, saddle ring, straight grip walnut stock, also available in takedown.

MSR $1,295	$1,175	$1,050	$925	$800	$700	$600	$500

Add $500 for takedown.
Custom engraved models are available beginning at $15,000.

MODEL MARE'S LEG – .30-30 Win., .32 Win. Spl., or .38-55 WCF cal., 10 1/2 to 12 in. octagon or round barrel, adj. rear sight, dovetail front sight, big loop lever, saddle ring, straight grip walnut stock, blue, nickel, or case colored finish. New 2012.

MSR $1,395	$1,250	$1,100	$950	$825	$700	$600	$500

Add $100 for nickel or $300 for case colored finish.

MODEL BEAR'S LEG – .45-70 Govt. cal., octagon barrel, blue or case colored finish, adj. rear sight, dovertail front sight, big loop lever, saddle ring, straight grip walnut stock.

MSR $1,795	$1,595	$1,325	$1,100	$925	$800	$675	$575

PISTOLS: SEMI-AUTO

J.B. Custom builds custom semi-auto pistols based on the 1911 design, including the Diamond Match (MSR $2,595), the Tactical Masterpiece (MSR $2,595), the Diamond Jim Gambler (MSR $2,895), the Elite Officer (MSR $1,995), and the Elite Command (MSR $1,995).

REVOLVERS: SINGLE ACTION

J.B. Custom builds single action revolvers in .45 Colt cal., based on the Model 1873, including the Shane (MSR $1,295), the Doc Holliday (MSR $995), and the Bat Masterson (MSR $995).

RIFLES: LEVER ACTION

J.B. Custom builds a replica of Chuck Connor's Model 1892 from *The Rifleman* TV Series. It is available in .357 Mag., .44-40 WCF, .44 Mag., or .45 Colt cal., has a 20 in. barrel, large D-loop, case colored receiver and walnut stock. MSR is $1,095.

RIFLES: SEMI-AUTO

J.B. Custom builds two types of AR-15 style rifles in .223 Rem. cal. - the Target Sniper (MSR$1,195) and the M-4 (MSR $995).

SHOTGUNS: LEVER ACTION

J.B. Custom builds lever action shotguns based on the Model 1887 - the T2 (MSR $795), the Wells Fargo (MSR $695), and the Deluxe (MSR $695). All are 12 ga. with walnut stocks.

J.C. HIGGINS

Please refer to listing in the H section.

J.L.D. ENTERPRISES, INC.

Previous rifle manufacturer located in Farmington, CT. In 2006, the company name was changed to PTR 91, Inc.

Please refer to PTR 91, Inc. listing for current information.

J.O. ARMS

Previous importer of KSN Industries, Ltd. pistols until 1997.

GRADING - PPGS™	100%	98%	95%	90%	80%	70%	60%	LAST MSR

J. ROBERTS & SON (GUNMAKERS) LTD.

Current manufacturer, import agent, and dealer established during 1950, and located in London, England.

Please contact J. Roberts & Son (Gunmakers) Ltd. directly for more information on their current inventory of custom rifles and shotguns, in addition to other services (see Trademark Index).

J. Roberts & Son also owns the trademark W.J. Jeffery & Co. Please refer to this section for more information.

JMC FABRICATION & MACHINE, INC.

Previous manufacturer located in Rockledge, FL 1997-99.

RIFLES: BOLT ACTION

MODEL 2000 M/P – .50 BMG cal., rapid takedown, 30 in. barrel, matte black finish, cast aluminum stock with Pachmayr pad, fully adj. bipod, 10 shot staggered mag., two-stage trigger, includes 24X U.S. Optics scope, prices assume all options included, 29 1/2 lbs. Limited mfg. 1998-99.

	100%	98%	95%	90%	80%	70%	60%	LAST MSR
	$7,950	$7,400	$6,800	$6,150	$5,500	$4,900	$4,200	*$8,500*

Subtract $2,800 if w/o options.

JO. LO. AR.

Previous semi-auto pistol manufacturer circa 1924-disc. and located in Eibar, Spain.

PISTOLS: SEMI-AUTO

SEMI-AUTO PISTOL – .25 ACP, .32 ACP, .380 ACP, 9mm Largo, or .45 ACP (rare) cal., designed for one handed cocking, presumably for the cavalry, features rotating lever on the right side of the slide, most sales were commercial but a few pistols in 9mm Largo were purchased by the Peruvian military, available in four frame sizes.

	100%	98%	95%	90%	80%	70%	60%	LAST MSR
.25 ACP cal.	$2,750	$2,350	$2,000	$1,600	$1,200	$975	$775	
.32 ACP cal.	$1,500	$1,250	$1,000	$800	$600	$500	$400	
.380 ACP cal.	$1,500	$1,250	$1,000	$800	$600	$500	$400	
9mm Largo cal.	$1,500	$1,250	$1,000	$800	$600	$500	$400	
.45 ACP cal. (rare)	$6,500	$5,750	$5,000	$4,250	$3,500	$2,750	$2,000	

JP ENTERPRISES, INC.

Current manufacturer and customizer established in 1978, and located in Hugo, MN beginning 2010, previously located in White Bear Lake, MN 2000-2009, Vadnais Heights, MN 1998-2000, and in Shoreview, MN 1995-98. Distributor, dealer, and consumer sales.

JP Enterprises is a distributor for Infinity pistols, and also customizes Remington shotgun Models 11-87, 1100, and 870, the Remington bolt action Model 700 series, Glock pistols, and the Armalite AR-10 series.

JP Enterprises also manufactures a complete line of high quality parts and accessories for AR-15 style rifles, including upper and lower assemblies, sights and optics, machined receivers, barrels/barrel kits, fire control kits, handguards, etc. and gunsmithing services. Please contact the company directly for more information and pricing regarding these parts, accesssories, and services (see Trademark Index).

PISTOLS: SEMI-AUTO

Level I & Level II custom pistols were manufactured 1995-97 using Springfield Armory slides and frames. Only a few were made, and retail prices were $599 (Level I) and $950 (Level II).

RIFLES: BOLT ACTION

MOR-07 – .260 Rem., 7mm WSM (new 2009), or .308 Win. cal., 24 in. stainless steel cryo-treated bull barrel, benchrest quality bolt action, Picatinny rail, JP Tactical Chassis system, Timney trigger, benchrest or tactical style forend, Precision grip system, matte black hard coat anodizing, 10 shot detachable, includes hard case. Disc. 2010.

	100%	98%	95%	90%	80%	70%	60%	LAST MSR
	$4,250	$3,850	$3,350	$2,925	$2,500	$2,000	$1,600	*$4,499*

GRADING - PPGS™	100%	98%	95%	90%	80%	70%	60%	LAST MSR

MR-10 – .260 Rem. (new 2012), 7mm WSM (new 2012), .308 Win., .300 WSM, or 6.5 Creedmoor cal., 3 lug short through bolt action with upper Picatinny rail, spiral cut bolt, 24 in. JP Supermatch fluted stainless steel barrel with large profile JP compensator, folding Magpul stock with tactical grip including palmrest, benchrest style forend or JP modular handguard system. New 2011.

MSR $3,999	$3,850	$3,500	$3,150	$2,700	$2,300	$1,900	$1,650	

RIFLES: SEMI-AUTO

The rifles in this section utilize a modified AR-15 style operating system.

IMPORTANT NOTE: On model(s) where *N/A has replaced the normal 100% value, it indicates current market conditions are too unstable to accurately ascertain 100%-60% values. Factory retail prices (MSRs) reflect most recent updates. For more up-to-date information on current pricing trends and additional useful information, please visit www.bluebookofgunvalues.com, select "Information & Services" from the menu, and click on "Additional Book Information".

BARRACUDA 10/22 – .22 LR cal., features customized Ruger 10/22 action with reworked fire control system, choice of stainless bull or carbon fiber superlight barrel, 3 lb. trigger pull, color laminated "Barracuda" skeletonized stock. Mfg. 1997-2003.

	$1,075	$950	$775	$650	$575	$475	$400	*$1,195*

A-2 MATCH – .223 Rem. cal., JP-15 lower receiver with JP fire control system, 20 in. JP Supermatch cryo-treated stainless barrel, standard A-2 stock and pistol grip, DCM type free float forend, MIL SPEC A-2 upper assembly with Smith National Match rear sight. Mfg. 1995-2003.

	*N/A	$1,300	$1,100	$925	$825	$700	$600	*$1,695*

JP-15 & VARIATIONS (GRADE I A-3 FLAT TOP) – .204 Ruger (new 2012), .223 Rem., or 6.5 Grendel (new 2012) cal., features Eagle Arms (disc. 1999), DPMS (disc. 1999) or JP15 lower assembly with JP fire control system, Mil Spec A-3 type upper receiver with 18 or 24 in. JP Supermatch cryo-treated stainless barrel, 10 shot mag., synthetic modified thumbhole (disc. 2011), synthetic A2 or ACE ARFX buttstock (new 2012), or laminated wood thumbhole (disc. 2002) stock, JP vent. two piece free float forend, JP adj. gas system and recoil eliminator, black teflon hard coat anodized finish, JP Compensator muzzle treatment, Hogue pistol grip. New 1995.

MSR $1,999	*N/A	$1,575	$1,250	$1,000	$900	$775	$650	

Add $400 for NRA Hi-Power version with 24 in. bull barrel and sight package (disc. 2002).
Add $200 for laminated wood thumbhole stock (disc. 2002).
Subtract $34 for Kyle Lamb signature rifle (JP-15/VTAC).
Subtract $300 for Duty Defense rifle (JP-15D).
Subtract $500 for LE/Military rifle (JP-15LE).

* ***JP-15 Grade I IPSC Limited Class*** – similar to Grade I, except has quick detachable match grade iron sights, Versa-pod bipod. Mfg. 1999-2004.

	*N/A	$1,400	$1,150	$995	$775	$625	$550	*$1,795*

* ***JP-15 Grade I Tactical/SOF*** – similar to Grade I, all matte black non-glare finish, 18, 20, or 24 in. Supermatch barrel. Mfg. 1999-2003.

	*N/A	$1,225	$1,050	$925	$800	$700	$600	*$1,595*

Add $798 for Trijicon ACOG sight with A-3 adapter.

GRADE II – .223 Rem. cal., features MIL SPEC JP lower receiver with upper assembly finished in a special two-tone color anodizing process, JP fire control and gas system, 18-24 in. cryo treated stainless barrel, composite skeletonized stock, Harris bipod, choice of multi-color or black receiver and forend, includes hard case. Mfg. 1998-2002.

	*N/A	$1,450	$1,200	$1,025	$825	$700	$600	*$1,895*

Add $200 for laminated wood thumbhole stock.

GRADE III (THE EDGE) – .223 Rem. cal., RND machined match upper/lower receiver system, 2-piece free floating forend, standard or laminated thumbhole wood stock, 18 to 24 in. barrel (cryo treated beginning 1998) with recoil eliminator, includes Harris bipod, top-of-the-line model, includes hard case. Mfg. 1996-2002.

	*N/A	$2,125	$1,750	$1,450	$1,150	$875	$750	*$2,795*

Add $250 for laminated thumbhole stock.

GRADING - PPGS™	100%	98%	95%	90%	80%	70%	60%	LAST MSR

AR-10T – .243 Win. or .308 Win. cal., features Armalite receiver system with JP fire control, flat-top receiver, vent. free floating tubular handguard, 24 in. cryo treated stainless barrel, black finish. Mfg. 1998-2004.

	*N/A	$1,825	$1,600	$1,450	$1,150	$875	$750	$2,399

Add $150 for anodized upper assembly in custom color.
Add $350 for laminated wood thumbhole stock.

* ***AR-10LW*** – lightweight variation of the Model AR-10T, includes 16-20 in. cryo treated stainless barrel, composite fiber tubular handguard, black finish only, 7-8 lbs. Mfg. 1998-2004.

	*N/A	$1,825	$1,600	$1,450	$1,150	$875	$750	$2,399

Add $200 for detachable sights.

CTR-02 COMPETITION TACTICAL RIFLE – .204 Ruger (new 2012), .223 Rem., or 6.5 Grendel (new 2012) cal., state-of-the-art advanced AR design with many improvements, integral ACOG interface, beveled mag well, black synthetic A2 or ACE ARFX buttstock, rifle or mid-length adj. gas system, 10 shot mag., JP recoil eliminator and fire control system, 1/4 MOA possible, JP Supermatch polished stainless steel barrel, rifle or mid-length JP modular hand guard system, Hogue pistol grip, JP low mass or full mass operating system, black teflon over hard coat anodized finish. New 2002.

MSR $2,599	*N/A	$1,925	$1,450	$1,150	$925	$825	$750

Add $599 for presentation grade finish (disc. 2011).

LRP-07 – .260 Rem., .308 Win., 6.5 Creedmoor (new 2012), or .338 Federal (new 2012) cal., 18 (LRP-07H, Hunter's package) or 22 in. stainless steel cryo-treated barrel, left side charging system (new 2009), tactical compensator, matte black hard coat anodizing, aluminum components, 10 or 19 shot mag., A2 or ACE ARFX black synthetic stock, JP modular hand guard, rifle or mid-length adj. gas system, JP low mass operating system, Hogue pistol grip, upper accessory rail.

MSR $3,299	*N/A	$2,725	$2,275	$1,900	$1,500	$1,250	$1,000

PSC-11 – .204 Ruger (new 2012), .223 Rem., or 6.5 Grendel (new 2012) cal., practical side charging rifle with left side charge system, upper has same features as SCR-11 model, but lower unit is cross compatible with any standard AR-15 platform, black teflon hardcoat anodized finish, A2 or ACE ARFX buttstock with Hogue pistol grip, small frame with upper accessory rail. New 2011.

MSR $2,599	*N/A	$1,925	$1,500	$1,200	$950	$825	$750

PSC-12 – .260 Win., .308 Win., 6.5 Creedmoor, or 6.5 Grendel cal., similar to PSC-11, except has larger frame, dual charging upper assembly compatible with DPMS lower receivers. New 2012.

MSR $3,499	*N/A	$2,850	$2,375	$1,950	$1,525	$1,275	$1,050

SCR-11 – .204 Ruger, .223 Rem., or 6.5 Grendel cal., competition side-charging rifle with left side charge system, features JP Supermatch polished stainless barrel with JP compensator, flat-top receiver with Picatinny rail, vent. modular handguard, choice of A2 or ACE ARFX buttstock, Hogue pistol grip, matte black anodizing on aluminum components. New 2011.

MSR $2,799	*N/A	$2,100	$1,575	$1,250	$1,000	$900	$800

J R CARBINES, LLC.

Current manufacturer of AR-15 style carbines distributed by EMF Company Inc.

Please refer to the EMF listing in the E section.

J R DISTRIBUTING

Current manufacturer located in Moorpark, CA. J R Distributing is a division of J R Sports Distribution Corporation. Dealer and consumer sales.

RIFLES: SEMI-AUTO

.22 MAG. CUSTOM RIFLE – .22 WMR cal., choice of Ruger 10/22 or AMT action, 20 in. bull barrel with laminate or synthetic stock, 9 shot rotary mag., supplied with hard case. New 1998.

MSR $795	$725	$650	$550	$500	$450	$400	$360

GRADING - PPGS™	100%	98%	95%	90%	80%	70%	60%	LAST MSR

JSL (HEREFORD)

Previous manufacturer located in Hereford, England. Imported until 1994 by Specialty Shooters Supply, Inc. located in Fort Lauderdale, FL.

PISTOLS: SEMI-AUTO

SPITFIRE (G1) – 9mm Para. or 9x21mm cal., patterned after the Czech CZ-75/85, 3.7 in. barrel, ambidextrous safety, commander style hammer, black non-slip rubberized grip panels, investment cast stainless steel fabrication, 10 (C/B 1994) or 15* shot mag., 2.2 lbs. Imported 1992-94.

* ***Spitfire Standard*** – includes fixed rear sight, 2 mags., presentation case, and allen key.

	100%	98%	95%	90%	80%	70%	60%	LAST MSR
	$1,332	$1,100	$925	$810	$670	$565	$475	*$1,332*

Add $81 for adj. rear sight (Sterling Model).

JACKSON HOLE FIREARMS

Previous manufacturer located in Jackson Hole, WY circa mid-70s.

RIFLES: BOLT ACTION

STANDARD RIFLE – various cals., Mauser 98 action utilizing patented system for interchangeable barrels, checkered walnut stock.

	100%	98%	95%	90%	80%	70%	60%
	$1,050	$875	$800	$725	$650	$575	$495

Jackson Hole Firearms manufactured a limited quantity of their unique interchangeable barrel bolt action rifles. Collectibility to date has been minimal, and values are affected by the J.P. Sauer Models 90 and 200 which also feature the interchangeable barrel design.

JACKSON RIFLES

Previous rifle manufacturer located in Castle Douglas, Scotland. Currently, the company manufactures and distributes parts for custom rifles.

Jackson Rifles manufactured high quality long-range competition rifles, including the J5-P (single shot) and the J5-T (bolt action repeater), available in both right and left-hand actions.

JAEGER, FRANZ

Previous manufacturer located in Suhl, Germany circa 1900-1945. Franz Jaeger firearms included pistols, rifles, and shotguns.

Franz Jaeger, the founder, obtained many firearms patents and many Jaeger firearms were manufactured in a wide variety of configurations. Perhaps the company's most famous gun was an auto-loading pistol manufactured between 1914-1918 that featured sheet metal stampings (approx. 13,000 were manufactured). Values for Jaeger firearms today depend on the overall desirability factor and original condition.

HISTORY OF FRANZ JAEGER

Franz Jaeger's inventions still play an important role in the guns of today. He was born in 1876 in Rampitz, Merseburg County. Jaeger apprenticed as an actioner in Zella Mehlis, opened his own gunshop in Halle, then moved to America. He found employment as a gunsmith in New York, met and married Fanny Strauss, also from Germany. After their first son Paul was born, Franz began to develop his own ideas and he took out his first patent for a single trigger mechanism. Franz opened his own business with a partner (Bittner & Jaeger) on Broadway in New York.

Around the turn of the century, the family returned to Germany and settled in Suhl. Franz installed single triggers for other manufacturers and gun owners. Between 1901-1914, Franz Jaeger obtained eight patents. The catalogs of that period showed a wide variety of guns, most of them with Jaeger patents.

Franz Jaeger designed the "Jaeger Pistol" in a period of 3 months. It used steel stampings and castings, something unheard of at the time. The army rejected it for official use with one word: "Blech" (sheet metal). Nevertheless, the Jaeger factory produced about 15,000 of the pistols.

The following year Franz Jaeger was drafted into the army. Finally the "Hindenburg Proclamation" discharged skilled craftsmen and brought him home for the rest of the war. The post-war German economy and subsequent worldwide Great Depression had a very negative effect on his firearms business.

An order from abroad for good but reasonably priced stalking rifles brought the Magnus brothers

together with Franz Jaeger to establish the Magnus-Jaeger Company. They set up manufacturing facilities in Maebendorf near Suhl, but soon barely escaped a bankruptcy.

The Hitler years brought an improvement of the economy and work for Suhl's gunmakers. However, the extermination of Jews in Europe became a reality, and Fanny Jaeger was Jewish. She was transported to the concentration camp in Theresienstadt but survived.

During this time, Franz Jaeger and 2 to 3 loyal employees continued to make hunting guns, and the family was reunited after the war. But then the Americans left and the Russian troops arrived. Under a communist government, private initiative was not tolerated. Younger members of the family slipped to West Germany illegally, but Franz Jaeger and his wife turned down the offer to emigrate to America.

Two of his important patents are still used by major gun companies today.

JAGD-UND SPORTWAFFEN SUHL GmbH

Previous company name of Merkel, located in Suhl, Germany since 1535.

Currently, the famous Merkel trademark (mfg. by Merkel Jagd-Und Sportwaffen Suhl GmbH) is imported by Merkel USA, located in Trussville, AL. Previously imported by Heckler & Koch, located in Sterling, VA. Please refer to the Merkel listing in this text for current information regarding this older European trademark. See the Trademark Index in this text for current factory information.

JAMES RIVER ARMORY

Current restoration company specializing in the restoration of military firearms from WWI and WWII and located in Baltimore, MD.

James River Armory currently restores selected U.S. Military WWI and WWII rifles, and puts on new Criterion barrels and in some cases, new stocks. When completed, all rifles are test fired for safety. Current offerings include: M1 Garand (MSR range $1,295-$1,495), M1D Sniper rifle (MSR $1,895), M1903 (MSR $1,099), M1903USMC Sniper Model 1942 (MSR $2,195), Model 1903A3 (MSR range $795-$1,195), Model 1903A4 (MSR $1,395), M1 Carbine (disc. 2012), M14SA (MSR $2,495), Model 25 (MSR $2,795), K98 Mauser (MSR $1,095), K98 Mauser Sniper (MSR $1,595), and JR AK-47 (MSR range 4895-$1,095). Please contact the company directly for more information, availability, and additional pricing (see Trademark Index).

JANZ GmbH

Current revolver manufacturer established in 2000, and located in Malente, Germany. No current importation. Previously imported 2007-2009 by Brenzovich, located in Fort Hancock, TX. Previously imported 2003-2004 by Rocky Mountain Armoury, located in Silverthorne, CO.

REVOLVERS

Please contact the factory directly for current pricing and availability.

JTL-E – .22 LR, .357 Mag./.38 Spl., .44 Mag., .45 Win. Mag., .454 Casull/.45 LC, or .500 S&W (new 2005) cal., DA, 5 (.500 S&W), 6, or 7 (.357 Mag.) shot, 4-10 in. barrel with full lug, ergonomic stippled wood grips, target sights, quick change cylinder. New 2000.

Prices on this model start at €3,295 for the .22 LR cal., and will increase according to caliber and barrel length.

JTL-S – .22 LR, .357 Mag./.38 Spl., .44 Mag., .45 Win. Mag., or .454 Casull/.45 LC cal., DA, 6 or 7 (.357 Mag.) shot, unique interchangeable barrels and cylinders allow cals. to be changed rapidly, 4-10 in. barrel with full lug, ergonomic stippled wood grips, target sights. New 2003.

Prices on this model start at €1,200 for the .22 LR cal., and go up according to caliber and barrel length.

This model is also available as a package with .357 Mag., .44 Mag., and .454 Casull barrels.

JAPANESE MILITARY

Previously manufactured prior to and during WWII in Japan by various manufacturers.

PISTOLS: SEMI-AUTO

Please refer to the Nambu section for further information on Nambus and variations.

GRADING - PPGS™	100%	98%	95%	90%	80%	70%	60%	LAST MSR

HAMADA VARIATIONS

* ***Hamada Variations Type I*** – .32 ACP cal., similar to FN Model 1910, except has 9 shot mag., early production pistols have chrysanthemum and Japanese characters on left slide, salt blue. Mfg. estimated at 5,000, but examples are scarce and usually in the 2,000-3,000 ser. range.

	100%	98%	95%	90%	80%	70%	60%	LAST MSR
	$7,500	$6,750	$5,750	$4,750	$3,500	$2,500	$1,750	

Add 10% for early variation.

* ***Hamada Variations Type II*** – 8mm cal., designed to replace the Type 94 Nambu, larger than Type I and with a more squared profile, essentially a pre-production gun, all known examples are roughly finished in the white and are serial numbered 1-50.

	100%	98%	95%	90%	80%	70%	60%	LAST MSR
	$9,500	$8,000	$7,000	$6,000	$5,000	$4,000	$3,000	

REVOLVERS

1893 REVOLVER (MODEL 26) – 9mm Japanese cal., double action only, 4.7 in. barrel, blue, wood grips. Approx. 59,000 mfg. 1893-1925.

	100%	98%	95%	90%	80%	70%	60%	LAST MSR
	$1,500	$1,250	$1,000	$750	$500	$400	$300	

Subtract 25% for arsenal rework.

Add 100% for early mfg. with internal numbers (approx. first 300 revolvers), or final Kokura assembled pistols in 58,971-59,183 serial range.

RIFLES: MILITARY

Subtract 20% if National Crest (chrysanthemum flower) has been ground off front receiver ring.

Subtract 20% if serial numbers are not matching (does not apply to sniper rifles, as they are only rarely found with matching scopes and mounts).

Subtract 10%-40% for training rifles of each type.

MODEL 38 ARISAKA RIFLE – 6.5x51R Arisaka cal., Jap. Mauser type bolt action, 31 in. barrel, adj. sight, adopted 1905.

	100%	98%	95%	90%	80%	70%	60%	LAST MSR
	$625	$525	$400	$300	$250	$200	$100	

MODEL 38 A & B CAVALRY CARBINE – 6.5x51R Arisaka cal., similar to Model 38 Arisaka Rifle, except has 19 in. barrel. Mfg. 1911.

	100%	98%	95%	90%	80%	70%	60%	LAST MSR
	$625	$550	$450	$325	$250	$200	$100	

Add 300% for paratrooper variation with hinged stock (often referenced as Type I, has crude construction and cast iron hinge).

MODEL 44 CAVALRY ARISAKA CARBINE – 6.5x51R Arisaka cal., similar to Model T38 Carbine, features 19 in. barrel and folding bayonet.

	100%	98%	95%	90%	80%	70%	60%	LAST MSR
	$1,150	$950	$800	$650	$500	$400	$325	

MODEL 97 SNIPER RIFLE – based on Model 38 Arisaka Rifle.

	100%	98%	95%	90%	80%	70%	60%	LAST MSR
	$3,500	$2,750	$2,200	$1,950	$1,650	$1,375	$1,100	

Add $1,000-$2,000 if complete with scope.

MODEL 99 SERVICE RIFLE – 7.7x58mm Arisaka cal., WWII version of Model 38 Arisaka Rifle, mostly encountered with shorter barrels (26 in. or less) than the Model 38 Arisaka Rifle.

	100%	98%	95%	90%	80%	70%	60%	LAST MSR
	$500	$400	$300	$250	$200	$150	$100	
Sniper rifle w/4X scope	$3,800	$3,450	$3,000	$2,600	$2,200	$1,800	$1,400	

Add 20% for monopod (non-Sniper).

Add 75% for 31.4 in. long barrel (non-Sniper).

Add 50% for externally adjustable scope.

MODEL 99 PARATROOPER TAKEDOWN VERSION – 7.7x58mm Arisaka cal., adopted 1940, crossbolt barrel lock.

	100%	98%	95%	90%	80%	70%	60%	LAST MSR
Type 2	$2,900	$2,500	$2,000	$1,500	$1,250	$1,000	$750	

JARRETT RIFLES, INC.

Current manufacturer established in 1979, and located in Jackson, SC. Direct custom order sales only.

GRADING - PPGS™	100%	98%	95%	90%	80%	70%	60%	LAST MSR

HANDGUNS

CUSTOM XP-100 HUNTER – various cals., re-machined Remington XP-100 action, Jarrett match grade stainless steel barrel, McMillan fiberglass stock, various options. Limited mfg.

$3,450 $2,650 $2,150 $1,750 $1,350 $1,050 $995

ULTIMATE REDHAWK – .44 Mag. cal., features Hogue grips and muzzle brake. Mfg. 1995-2000.

$1,150 $1,025 $850 $675 $575 $500 $450 *$1,150*

RIFLES: BOLT ACTION

Jarrett Rifles, Inc. is justifiably famous for its well-known Beanfield rifles (refers to shooting over a beanfield at long range targets). A Jarrett innovation is the Tri-Lock receiver, which has 3 locking lugs, and a semi-integral recoil lug. Jarrett blueprints every action for proper dimensioning and rigid tolerances, and this explains why their rifles have set rigid accuracy standards.

A wide variety of options are available for Jarrett custom rifles (holders of 16 world records in rifle accuracy). Jarrett also manufactures its own precision ammunition for discriminating shooters/hunters. The manufacturer should be contacted directly for pricing and availability regarding these special order options, and custom gunsmithing services (see Trademark Index).

Current pricing does not include 11% excise tax or scope.

STANDARD HUNTING RIFLE – various cals., Remington Model 700 right-hand or left-hand action, McMillan fiberglass stock, blue receiver, Jarrett satin finish match grade barrel, sling studs and leather sling, rings and base, weights vary. Disc. 2003.

$4,625 $4,150 $3,650 $3,150 $2,750 $2,150 $1,750 *$4,625*

WALK ABOUT – various cals. in short action only, features Remington Model 7 action (left-hand utilizes Rem. Model 700 short action), weights vary. Mfg. 1995-2003.

$4,625 $4,150 $3,650 $3,150 $2,750 $2,150 $1,750 *$4,625*

TRUCK GUN – various small bore cals., 19-20 in. barrel, black synthetic stock. Mfg. 1999-2003.

$4,625 $4,150 $3,650 $3,150 $2,750 $2,150 $1,750 *$4,625*

BENCHREST/YOUTH/TACTICAL – various cals., various configurations depending on application. New 1999.

$4,625 $4,150 $3,650 $3,150 $2,750 $2,150 $1,750 *$4,625*

SERIES RIFLE – various cals., various configurations, only 100 made of each series. Mfg. 1993-2003.

* ***Series Rifle Standard*** – various cals.

$5,025 $4,450 $3,850 $3,250 $2,850 $2,250 $1,850 *$5,025*

* ***Series Rifle Coup de Grace*** – various cals. Mfg. 1996-99.

$3,295 $2,750 $2,300 $1,800 $1,500 $1,250 $995 *$3,495*

* ***Series Rifle Nombre Unique*** – various cals., 100 mfg. 1999 only.

$3,495 $2,900 $2,400 $1,850 $1,550 $1,250 $995 *$3,695*

SIGNATURE SERIES – various cals., Jarrett tri-lock stainless steel receiver, fiberglass, wood laminate, or deluxe walnut stock, helical fluted bolt with three lugs, built to special order only. New 2004.

MSR $7,640 $6,495 $5,695 $4,875 $4,425 $3,575 $2,925 $2,275

WIND WALKER SERIES – various cals. up to .30 cal., Rem. M-700 ADL action only, lightweight design, 24 in. tapered barrel with muzzle brake, Brown Precision stock, 7 1/4 lbs. New 1999.

MSR $7,380 $6,275 $5,495 $4,700 $4,265 $3,450 $2,825 $2,195

RIDGE WALKER – various cals., various barrel lengths, Jarrett Tri-lock receiver, aluminum floorplate, with or w/o muzzle brake, Kevlar/fiberglass pistol grip stock available in a variety of colors, 8 lbs. New 2009.

MSR $7,640 $6,495 $5,695 $4,875 $4,425 $3,575 $2,925 $2,275

CUSTOM RIFLE – various cals., features Jarrett short action.

MSR $6,330 $5,375 $4,700 $4,025 $3,650 $2,950 $2,425 $1,875

GRADING - PPGS™	100%	98%	95%	90%	80%	70%	60%	LAST MSR

LONG RANGER – .300 Jarrett cal., 26 in. (hunting) standard or 27 in. (target) heavy barrel, Jewell trigger, highly polished metal (choice of colors), Kevlar/fiberglass pistol grip stock (choice of colors), 8 (hunting) or 12 (target) lbs. New 2009.

MSR $7,640	$6,495	$5,695	$4,875	$4,425	$3,575	$2,925	$2,275	

PRESTIGE SERIES – New 2013.

MSR $9,640	$8,195	$7,175	$6,150	$5,575	$4,500	$3,695	$2,875	

ORIGINAL BEANFIELD RIFLE – built on customer supplied action, choice of caliber, stock style, color, barrel length and finish, with or w/o muzzle brake, supplied with 20 rounds of ammo and test target. New 2005.

MSR $5,380	$5,380	$4,850	$4,250	$3,825	$3,400	$3,000	$2,600	

PROFESSIONAL HUNTER – Mag. cals. to customer's specifications, starting with .375 H&H, features Winchester controlled round feed Model 70 action with claw extractor and 3 position bolt shroud safety, Jarrett match grade stainless steel barrel, McMillan stock, quarter rib with iron sights, includes 2 sets of detachable rings and two 1.75-6x32mm Leupold scopes, takedown action, includes custom built Americase.

MSR $10,400	$8,850	$7,750	$6,650	$6,025	$4,875	$3,985	$3,100	

.50 CAL. – .50 BMG cal., McMillan custom receiver, choice of repeater or single shot, 30 or 34 in. barrel with muzzle brake, 28-45 lbs. Mfg. 1999-2003.

	$8,050	$6,500	$5,300	$4,350	$3,650	$3,000	$2,500	*$8,050*

Add $300 for repeater action.

CLASSIC SERIES – various cals., 100 mfg. 1989 only.

	$3,195	$2,650	$2,100	$1,650	$1,375	$1,150	$875	

INVESTOR SERIES – various cals., 100 mfg. 1989 only.

	$3,195	$2,650	$2,100	$1,650	$1,375	$1,150	$875	

ACCURACY LEGEND SERIES – various cals., similar to Jarrett Custom Rifle, except has many accuracy tune-ups incorporated as well as muzzle brake. 100 mfg. 1993 only.

	$3,495	$2,850	$2,300	$1,850	$1,500	$1,250	$995	*$3,495*

COUP de MAIM – various cals., similar to the Jarrett Custom Rifle, includes muzzle brake, matte black or olive drab finish, Model 70 style bolt release. 100 mfg. 1995 only.

	$2,750	$2,300	$1,800	$1,500	$1,250	$995	$775	*$3,495*

PRIVATE COLLECTION – various cals., similar quality as the Jarrett Custom Rifle, except many extra cost special order options are included, ser. numbered 1-100. Mfg. 1994 only.

	$3,495	$2,850	$2,300	$1,850	$1,500	$1,250	$995	*$3,495*

SILENT PARTNER SERIES – various cals., only 10 mfg. 1994 only.

	$3,495	$2,850	$2,300	$1,850	$1,500	$1,250	$995	

ULTIMATE HUNTER SERIES – various cals., 100 mfg. 1989 only.

	$3,495	$2,850	$2,300	$1,850	$1,500	$1,250	$995	

RIFLES: RIMFIRE, SEMI-AUTO

SQUIRREL KING – .22 LR cal., reworked Ruger 10/22 action, 18 in. barrel, McMillan or Brown Precision synthetic stock. Mfg. 1999-2003.

	$1,650	$1,300	$1,050	$900	$700	$575	$475	*$1,800*

Add $195 for Target King variation.

SHOTGUNS: SLIDE ACTION

JARRETT ULTIMATE SHOTGUN – 12 ga., Remington Model 870 action with 21 in. hand lapped barrel with interchangeable chokes, 8 shot mag. extension, matte black or olive drab green finish. Disc. 1999.

	$900	$825	$675	$550	$450	$350	$295	*$1,000*

JEAN-MARC STEVAUX, S.P.R.L.

Current custom gun manufacturer located in Malonne, Belgium.

Jean-Marc Stevaux builds high quality custom order long guns. Currently, he does not have a U.S. importer. For more information, including pricing, availability, delivery time and variety of options, please contact him directly (see Trademark Index).

JEFFERY, W.J. & CO. LTD

Current trademark established in 1888, and manufactured by J. Roberts & Son (Gunmakers) Ltd., located in London, England. Previous manufacture was also in London, England.

J. Roberts & Son (Gunmakers) Ltd. currently manufactures W.J. Jeffery shotguns, double rifles, and bolt action rifles. Many options are available, including calibers, special engraving, etc. Please contact the company directly for more information, including pricing, delivery time and availability (see Trademark Index).

In addition to making a complete line of their own shotguns and rifles, W.J. Jeffery also was subcontracted by many other exporters, distributors, and retailers, including London's famous Army & Navy department store (see separate listing). Many models were produced and, rather than list them individually, a generalized format has been adopted for determining values on both discontinued rifles and shotguns.

Current MSRs do not include English VAT.

RIFLES, CURRENT MFG.

BOLT ACTION RIFLE – various cals. between .243 Win. - .500 Jeffery, manufactured with both original Mauser actions and recent production (non-Mauser mfg.) actions, other commercial actions are available upon request.

Current MSR on this model starts at $38,000, and can go up depending on configuration, features, accessories, engraving, and grade of wood. Delivery time is approx. 6-15 months.

SxS MODEL – standard cals. are 9.3x74R, .375 H&H, .470 NE, or .500 Jeffery, choice of boxlock or sidelock action, ejectors, includes deep scroll engraving and case.

Current MSR for the boxlock ejector model starts at £20,000, depending on caliber, configuration, features, and grade of wood. The sidelock ejector rifle MSR starts at £40,000 (£30,000 for 9.3x74R cal.), depending on caliber, features, configuration, and grade of wood.

RIFLES, DISC.

SINGLE SHOT – various cals., falling block action, checkered walnut stock and forearm, usually multiple folding leaves rear sight (also tangent), excellent quality.

Prices start in the $750 range for poor condition specimens in obsolete or undesirable cals. and can go up to $6,500 for 100% condition in .600 Nitro Express.
Subtract substantially for the Martini action variation.

BOXLOCK DOUBLE RIFLE – many cals., various engraving patterns, top or under (usually large cals.) lever opening, multiple folding leaves rear sight, checkered walnut stock and forearm.

Prices usually start in the $1,750 range for poor condition in undesirable cals. and can exceed $10,000 if encountered with elaborate engraving in .475 Express or larger cals.
Subtract approx. 40% if with hammers, over 50% if with damascus barrels.

SIDELOCK DOUBLE RIFLE – various cals., available in No. 1 or No. 2 grade, top-lever opening, best quality engraving, deluxe checkered walnut stock and forearm, almost any custom order could be filled.

Prices start in the $7,500 range for 60% condition in smaller cals. and can easily go to $25,000+ when found in excellent condition in the larger cals.
Subtract approx. 40% if with hammers, over 50% if with damascus barrels.

SHOTGUNS, CURRENT MFG.

Please contact the company directly (see Trademark Index) for more information on currently manufactured W.J. Jeffery shotguns, including the sidelock ejector models, and the London finished SxS and O/U Italian and Spanish shotguns manufactured under J. Roberts & Son patterns.

GRADING - PPGS™	100%	98%	95%	90%	80%	70%	60%	LAST MSR

SXS SIDELOCK MODEL – 12 or 20 ga., choice of H&H self-opening style or Beesley/Purdey action, deep scroll engraving is standard.

Current MSR on this model starts at $52,000.

SHOTGUNS: SxS, DISC.

BOXLOCK SHOTGUN – most ga., many combinations of options available, top-lever opening, many ranges of engraving, high quality and worksmanship.

Values usually start in the $950 range if in poor condition and can go to $5,500+ if in a small ga. in near new condition.

Subtract approx. 40% if with hammers, over 50% if with damascus barrels.

SIDELOCK SHOTGUN – most ga., many combinations of options available, top-lever opening, many ranges of engraving, high quality and worksmanship.

Values usually start in the $2,250 range if in poor condition and can go to $20,000+ if in a small ga. in near new condition.

JEFFERY SHARPS

Current rifle configuration manufactured by Ballard Arms, located in Cody, WY.

The original Jeffery Sharps was crafted during the late 1880s by W.J. Jeffery of London, and was based on the Winchester Model 1885.

New guns built in Cody are based on the original design and will come in calibers from .400 Jeffery to .577 NE. Pricing is POR. (Last base price published was $5,250 in 2011). Please contact Ballard Arms directly for more information, including a price quotation and delivery time (see Trademark Index).

JENNINGS FIREARMS

Previous trademark and distributor established 1978 and located in City of Industry, CA until 1985. Jennings was a brand name for Bryco Arms, and was also the exclusive distributor for Bryco. Jennings also distributed Sundance and Accu-Tek.

PISTOLS: SEMI-AUTO

MODEL J-22 – .22 LR cal., 6 shot, single action, 2 1/2 in. barrel, positive safety locks sear, satin nickel, bright chrome or black teflon finish, 13 oz. Disc. 1985.

$65	$50	$40	$35	$30	$30	$30	*$79*

JERICHO

Previous trademark of Israel Military Industries (I.M.I.). Previously imported by K.B.I., Inc. located in Harrisburg, PA.

PISTOLS: SEMI-AUTO

JERICHO 941 – 9mm Para. cal. or .41 Action Express (by conversion only) cal., semi-auto double action or single action, 4.72 in. barrel with polygonal rifling, all steel fabrication, 3 dot Tritium sights, 11 or 16 (9mm Para.) shot mag., ambidextrous safety, polymer grips, decocking lever, 38 1/2 oz. Imported 1990-92.

$625	$550	$475	$425	$375	$325	$295	*$649*

Add $299 for .41 AE conversion kit.

Industrial hard chrome or nickel finishes were also available for all Jericho pistols.

* ***Jericho 941 Pistol Package*** – includes 9mm Para. and .41 AE conversion kit, cased with accessories. Mfg. 1990-91 only.

$850	$775	$700	$625	$575	$495	$450	*$775*

JIMENEZ ARMS

Current manufacturer located in Henderson, NV. Previously located in Costa Mesa, CA until 2005. Distributed by Shining Star Investments, LLC, located in Lewisville, TX.

Paul Jimenez, former plant manager of Bryco Arms, bought the remaining assets of Bryco in 2004.

GRADING - PPGS™	100%	98%	95%	90%	80%	70%	60%	LAST MSR

SEMI-AUTO PISTOLS

JA-NINE – 9mm Para. cal., SA, 3 3/4 in. barrel, adj. rear sight, high visibility front sight, 30 oz.

MSR $199	$175	$150	$125	$110	$100	$90	$85

JA-.22LR/JA-.25 AUTO – .22 LR or .25 Auto cal., SA, 2 1/2 in. barrel, easy recoil, cocking indicator, 13 oz.

MSR $149	$125	$110	$95	$85	$75	$65	$55

JA-.380 – .380 ACP cal., SA, 2 3/4 in. barrel, extended finger rest, 19 oz.

MSR $159	$130	$115	$100	$90	$80	$70	$60

JOHANNSEN RIFLES

Currently manufactured by Reimer Johannsen GmbH, located in Neumünster, Germany. Previously imported by New England Custom Gun Service, located in Plainfield, NH. Previously imported until 2003 by Johannsen, Inc.

RIFLES: BOLT ACTION

Johannsen rifles feature high quality short, medium, and Magnum Mauser actions in many calibers. Actions are manufactured by Orth, using sophisticated CAD and CNC technology, in addition to Old World gunsmithing techniques.

Johannsen take down express rifles are unique in that the bolt locks into the barrel with the same precision every time. This design ensures that point of impact remains identical after each assembly/disassembly. Please contact the company directly for more information, including domestic availability and current pricing.

Add approx. $6,400 for take down action on all models listed, except the Classic Safari. Johannsen 98 double square bridge actions range from $4,160-$5,990 depending on size and caliber. Johannsen 98 double square bridge barreled actions range from $4,690-$6,740 depending on size and caliber. Prices do not include duty and VAT (approx. 20% extra), FOB Hamburg.

PROFESSIONAL MODEL – .500 Jeffery or .505 Gibbs cal., double square bridge action, adj. trigger, flag safety, English stock, various options available.

MSR $13,140	$12,650	$10,850	$9,750	$8,400	$7,100	$6,000	$5,000

Add $1,560 for .505 Gibbs cal.

CLASSIC SAFARI – various cals., single square bridge action with thumbcut, express sight with two leaves, safari English style stock, open sights, 8 lbs. 3 oz.

MSR $11,360	$10,950	$9,000	$8,150	$7,100	$6,000	$5,000	$4,000

SAFARI RIFLE – various cals. between .25-06 to .500 Jeffery, features medium or Magnum double square bridge action, adj. trigger, three position safety, express sight with two leaves, safari English stock with satin oil finish.

MSR $11,200	$10,750	$8,900	$8,000	$7,000	$6,000	$5,000	$4,000

Add $1,196 for .375 H&H, .404 Jeffery, .416 Rigby, .450 Rigby, .458 Lott, or .500 Jeffery cal.
Add $2,700 per extra takedown barrel.

TRADITION RIFLE – various cals. between .17 Rem. to .458 Lott, available in mini, short, medium, or Magnum action, adj. trigger, three position safety, low bolt handle, pivot insert in front square bridge, express sight with one leaf, straight grip stock with satin oil finish.

MSR $11,800	$11,150	$9,100	$8,100	$7,150	$6,000	$5,000	$4,000

Add $2,520 for mini-action, $1,690 for short action, or $1,195 for Magnum action.
Add $2,700 per extra takedown barrel.

MOUNTAIN RIFLE – various cals. between .243 Win. to 9.3x62mm, short or medium action, double square bridge action, adj. trigger, three-position safety, low bolt handle, integral scope mount in rear square bridge, express sight with one leaf, satin oil finished high gloss stock, lightweight. New 2007.

MSR $11,800	$11,150	$9,100	$8,100	$7,150	$6,000	$5,000	$4,000

Add $1,695 for short action, $3,670 for mini action.

GRADING - PPGS™	100%	98%	95%	90%	80%	70%	60%	LAST MSR

JOHNSON AUTOMATICS, INC.

Previous manufacturer located in Providence, RI. Johnson Automatics, Inc. moved many times during its history, often with slight name changes. M.M. Johnson, Jr. died in 1965, and the company continued production at 104 Audubon Street in New Haven, CT as Johnson Arms, Inc. mostly specializing in sporter semi-auto rifles with Monte Carlo stocks in .270 Win. or 30-06 cal.

RIFLES: SEMI-AUTO

MODEL 1941 – .30-06 or 7x57mm cal., 22 in. removable air cooled barrel, recoil operated, perforated metal handguard, aperture sight, military stock. Most were made for Dutch military, some used by U.S. Marine Paratroopers, during WWII all .30-06 and 7x57mm were ordered by South American governments.

$7,350	$6,750	$6,000	$5,250	$4,500	$3,950	$3,250

MilTech offers a restored version of this model. Inspect this model carefully for originality before considering a possible purchase. Values are somewhat lower for restored guns.

J. JONGMANS ARMS COMPANY PTY. LTD.

Previous manufacturer established circa 1979-1980 through 1993, and located in Hikutaia, New Zealand from 1979-1986, and Ipswich, Queensland, Australia from 1987-1993.

J. Jongmans was founded by Dutch-born John Jongmans. He built custom rifles, and manufactured a line of high quality rifles, actions, and barrels. Early bolt action receivers, whether octagonal or round, were made from the same (octagonal) investment castings and had a high parts rejection rate. Later receivers and bolt bodies were fully machined on CNC equipment.

Jongmans also built Miller (formerly De Haas-Miller) single shot rifles and actions under license. The late Dean Miller had contracted with Jongmans to supply approx. 150 actions, but investment casting again proved to be a problem with quality. Miller only made approx. 10-15 rifles with Jongmans' actions. Approx. 200 actions were made under the Jongmans brand, and most ended up in New Zealand or Australia.

Jongmans also supplied Farquharson-type single shot actions to the Farquharson Rifle Company of Melbourne, Australia. One completed rifle was purchased by Holland and Holland of London.

During 2009-2010, John Jongmans assembled a few Miller-type rifles using leftover parts. Any Jongmans gun should be evaluated individually for its features and shootability.

JUCH-GRUND JAGDWAFFEN INH. KARL GRUND

Please see listing under Grund, Karl in the G section.

JUNG, WAFFEN, GMBH

Please refer to Waffen Jung GmbH in the W section.

JURRAS, LEE E.

Previous custom pistolsmith located in Hagerman, New Mexico. Howdah pistols were distributed by J & G Sales located in Prescott, AZ.

Ammunition for Jurras pistols was manufactured by Robert Davis, Jr. located in Athens, TN.

Lee Jurras was the founder and president of Super Vel Cartridge Corporation. Mr. Jurras also made custom AutoMags (see AutoMag section). He established the Outstanding American Handgunner Awards, and was a pioneer of the first metallic silhouette shooting matches.

PISTOLS

100 LEJ Howdah pistols were custom built in the late 1970s. The action was based on the Thompson/Center Contender receiver. Almost any caliber, barrel length, finish, and stock was available by special order. Original MSR was approx. $800.

HOWDAH – most common in .375, .416, .460, .475, .500, or .577 Jurras cals., action based on Thompson/Center Contender receiver, 12 in. bull barrel, satin nickel, nickel, or blue

GRADING - PPGS™	100%	98%	95%	90%	80%	70%	60%	LAST MSR

finish, adj. rear sight, ebony, mesquite, or walnut stocks, special order serial number range from 001-100, limited mfg. (100).

* ***Howdah Custom Grade***

	$1,150	$925	$800	$725	$650	$575	$500	

* ***Howdah Presentation Grade*** – .375 Jurras or .460 Jurras cals. standard, deluxe Claro walnut stock and forearm.

	$2,000	$1,750	$1,500	$1,250	$1,050	$950	$825	

Special order .416, .475, .500, or .577 Jurras calibers command a premium on this model.

JUST, JOSEF

Current custom long gun manufacturer and gunsmith established in 1790, and located in Ferlach, Austria.

Josef Just was a member of the Ferlach Guild until it was dissolved in 2004, and manufactures a variety of high quality long gun configurations (including SxSs, O/Us, drillings, vierlings, combination guns, and single shot), all to custom order. Delivery time is up to three years. Please contact Mr. Just directly for more information and an individual price quotation (see Trademark Index).

JUST RIGHT CARBINES

Current trademark of carbines established in 2011 and distributed by LDB Supply LLC located in Dayton, OH beginning 2013. Previously distributed by American Tactical Imports (ATI), located in Rochester, NY.

CARBINES: SEMI-AUTO

JUST RIGHT CARBINE – 9mm Para., .40 S&W, or .45 ACP (new mid-2011) cal., blowback action, 16 1/4 in. barrel, features ambidextrous bolt handle and ejection, flat-top receiver with Picatinny rail and half length barrel quad rail, uses Glock or M1911 (.45 ACP only) magazines, collapsible 6-position stock, matte black, Desert Camo (new 2013), or Muddy Girl (new 2013) finish, approx. 6 1/2 lbs. New 2011.

MSR $749	$650	$575	$500	$450	$400	$350	$300	

Add $25 for .40 S&W cal.
Add $50 for .45 ACP cal.
Add $50 for Desert Camo or Muddy Girl camo coverage.
Add $65 for Reaper Z Green and 33 shot mag. (new 2013).
Add $100 for tactical package (includes red dot scope, forward folding grip, Tuff1 grip cover and two magazines.

JUSTIN CUSTOM GUNS

Current custom rifle manufacturer located in Toquerville, UT.

RIFLES: CUSTOM

Justin Custom Guns builds both single shot and bolt action rifles, including a take-down bolt action in various cals. The standard bolt gun has a base price of $9,900, the Safari bolt gun has a base price of $11,800, the large bore Safari bolt gun has a base price of $13,500, a barrel take-down option is $1,800, and additional barrels are $2,400 each, quarter rib and express sights are $1,250. Upgrade options are POR. Please contact the company directly for more information, a quotation, and delivery time (see Trademark Index).

K SECTION

K.B.I., INC.

Previous importer and distributor located in Harrisburg, PA until Jan. 29, 2010. Distributor sales.

K.B.I., Inc. imported Charles Daly semi-auto pistols, Bul Transmark semi-auto pistols, SA revolvers, AR-15 style rifles, and shotguns in many configurations, including O/U, SxS, semi-auto, lever action, and slide action. K.B.I. also imported Armscor (Arms Corp. of the Philippines), FEG pistols, and Liberty revolvers and SxS coach shotguns. These models may be found within their respective alphabetical sections. K.B.I. previously imported the Jericho pistol manufactured by I.M.I. from Israel. Older imported Jericho pistols may be found under its own heading in this text, and more recently imported pistols are listed under the Charles Daly listing.

GRADING - PPGS™	100%	98%	95%	90%	80%	70%	60%	*LAST MSR*

RIFLES: BOLT ACTION

KASSNAR GRADE I – available in 9 cals., thumb safety that locks trigger, with or w/o deluxe sights, 22 in. barrel, 3 or 4 shot mag., includes swivel posts and oil finished standard grade European walnut with recoil pad, 7 1/2 lbs. Imported 1989-93.

	$445	$385	$325	$275	$225	$195	$175	*$499*

NYLON 66 – .22 LR cal., patterned after the Remington Nylon 66. Imported until 1990 from C.B.C. in Brazil, South America.

	$125	$110	$95	$85	$75	$70	$65	*$134*

MODEL 122 – .22 LR cal., bolt action design with mag. Imported from South America until 1990.

	$125	$110	$95	$85	$75	$70	$65	*$136*

MODEL 522 – .22 LR cal., bolt action design with tube mag. Imported from South America until 1990.

	$130	$115	$100	$85	$75	$70	$65	*$142*

BANTAM SINGLE SHOT – .22 LR cal., youth dimensions. Imported 1989-90 only.

	$110	$90	$85	$75	$70	$65	$60	*$120*

SHOTGUNS

GRADE I O/U – 12, 20, 28 ga., or .410 bore, gold plated SST, extractors, vent. rib, checkered walnut stock and forearm. Imported 1989-93.

	$525	$425	$350	$295	$265	$240	$220	*$599*

Add $70 for 28 ga. or .410 bore.
Add $50 for choke tubes (12 and 20 ga. only).
Add $150 for automatic ejectors (with choke tubes only).

GRADE II SxS – 10, 12, 16, 20, 28 ga., or .410 bore, boxlock action, case hardened receiver, English style checkered European walnut stock with splinter forearm, chrome barrels with concave rib, extractors, double hinged triggers. Imported 1989-90 only.

	$515	$435	$375	$325	$275	$250	$225	*$575*

Add $95 for 28 ga. or .410 bore.
Add $85 for 10 ga.

KDF, INC.

Previous rifle manufacturer until circa 2007 and current custom riflesmith specializing in restocking and installing muzzle brakes, in addition to supplying specialized rifle parts. Located in Seguin, TX. KDF utilized Mauser K-15 actions imported from Oberndorf, Germany for many rifle models. Previously, KDF rifles were manufactured by Voere (until 1987) in Vöhrenbach, W. Germany.

Older KDF rifles were private labeled by Voere and marked KDF. Since Voere was absorbed by Mauser-Werke in 1987, model designations changed. Mauser-Werke does not

GRADING - PPGS™	100%	98%	95%	90%	80%	70%	60%	LAST MSR

private label (i.e. newer guns are marked Mauser-Werke), and these rifles can be found under the Mauser-Werke heading in this text.

Due to space considerations, information regarding this manufacturer is available online free of charge at www.bluebookofgunvalues.com.

K.F.C.

Previously manufactured by Kawaguchiya Firearms Co., Ltd. Previously imported and distributed by La Paloma Marketing, Inc. located in Tucson, AZ.

SHOTGUNS

MODEL 250 SEMI-AUTO – 12 ga. only, semi-auto incorporating a patented, cushioned piston assembly, 26, 28, or 30 in. barrel, matte blue finish, vent. rib standard, checkered premium walnut, 7 lbs. Manufactured 1980-86.

$360 $290 $270 $250 $235 $220 $205 *$485*

Add $60 for multi-chokes.

* ***Model 250 Semi-Auto Deluxe*** – same specifications as Model 250, except has scrolled acid etching panels on both sides of normally black receiver. Disc. 1986.

$395 $310 $290 $270 $250 $225 $210 *$520*

FIELD GUN O/U – 12 ga. only, VR, premium grade walnut, semi pistol grip stock, F&IC chokes. Disc. 1986.

$645 $565 $530 $495 $470 $445 $410 *$748*

E-1 TRAP OR SKEET O/U – 12 ga. only, VR, oil finished premium grade walnut, semi pistol grip stock, engraved. Disc. 1986.

$935 $800 $750 $700 $625 $550 $495 *$1,070*

E-2 TRAP OR SKEET O/U – 12 ga. only, VR, oil finished premium grade walnut, semi pistol grip stock, detailed engraving. Disc. 1986.

$1,450 $1,250 $1,075 $950 $850 $750 $650 *$1,660*

KSN INDUSTRIES LTD.

Previous distributor (1952-1996) located in Houston, TX. Previously imported until 1996 exclusively by J.O. Arms, Inc. located in Houston, TX. Currently manufactured Israel Arms, Ltd. pistols may be found under their individual listing.

PISTOLS: SEMI-AUTO

The pistols listed were mfg. by Israel Arms, Ltd.

KAREEN MK I – 9mm Para. cal., patterned after the Browning HP, round or spur hammer, blue finish, wood grips, limited importation by Jo Lo Arms.

$725 $650 $575 $500 $425 $350 $275

KAREEN MK II – 9mm Para. or .40 S&W (new late 1994) cal., single action, 4.64 in. barrel, two-tone finish, rubberized grips, regular or Meprolite sights, 10 (C/B 1994), 13*, or 15* shot mag., 33 oz. Imported 1993-96.

$360 $305 $255 $225 $200 $185 $170 *$411*

Add approx. $160 for two-tone finish with Meprolite sights.

* ***Kareen Mk II Compact*** – compact variation with 3.85 in. barrel. Imported 1993-96.

$415 $360 $315 $255 $225 $200 $185 *$497*

GOLAN MODEL – 9mm Para. or .40 S&W cal., single or double action, ambidextrous safety with decocking feature, steel slide with alloy frame, 3 7/8 in. barrel, matte black finish, 29 oz. Imported 1994-96.

$565 $515 $460 $410 $360 $330 $295 *$650*

Add $35 for .40 S&W cal.

K-VAR CORP.

Current importer located in Las Vegas, NV. MSR Distribution is the distributor for K-Var Corp.

GRADING - PPGS™	100%	98%	95%	90%	80%	70%	60%	LAST MSR

K-VAR Corp. currently distributes Saiga rifles and shotguns, in addition to importing select Zastava bolt action rifles and pistols, Vepr rifles mfg. by Molot, Arsenal Inc. SLR series, AK-47 design rifles and an RPK milled rifle. Additionally, K-Var Crop. manufactures a Model SA M-7 SFK AK-47 design rifle in the U.S. See separate listings for Saiga rifles/shotguns, Zastava bolt action rifles, Vepr rifles, Arsenal, and the RPK model. Please contact the company directly for availability and pricing (see Trademark Index).

KAHR ARMS

Current manufacturer established in 1993, with headquarters located in Blauvelt, NY, and manufacturing in Worchester, MA. Distributor and dealer sales.

PISTOLS: SEMI-AUTO

All Kahr pistols are supplied with two mags (except CW Series), hard polymer case, trigger lock, and lifetime warranty. Except for the CW Series, all pistols feature Lothar Walther polygonal rifled match grade barrels.

CW380 – .380 ACP cal., 2 5/8 in. barrel, black polymer frame, matte stainless steel slide. New 2013.

MSR $419 $350 $300 $265 $240 $195 $160 $125

P380 – .380 ACP cal., 2 1/2 in. barrel, black polymer frame, matte stainless steel slide, 6 shot mag., approx. 10 oz. New 2010.

MSR $649 $535 $460 $425 $360 $320 $290 $260

Add $41 for matte blackened stainless slide.
Add $109 for night sights.
Add $84 for mag disconnector and load chamber indicator (new 2011).
Add $150 for Crimson Trace trigger guard laser (new 2011).
Add $300 for custom engraved slide (Custom Shop only), new 2012.

CM9 – 9mm Para. cal., compact design with 3 in. barrel, black polymer frame, matte stainless steel slide, 6 shot mag., DAO, textured polymer grips, adj. white bar-dot combat sights, 14 oz. New 2011.

MSR $517 $450 $400 $350 $315 $285 $250 $225

CM40 – .40 S&W cal., 3 in. barrel, black polymer frame with matte stainless slide, CW configuration, includes one mag. New 2012.

MSR $517 $450 $400 $350 $315 $285 $250 $225

CW9 – 9mm Para. cal., black polymer frame, matte stainless steel slide, 7 shot mag., DAO, 3.6 in. barrel, textured polymer grips, adj. rear sight, pinned in polymer front sight, white dot combat sights, 15.8 oz. New 2005.

MSR $485 $425 $375 $325 $295 $275 $250 $225

CW40 – .40 S&W cal., black polymer frame, matte stainless steel slide, 6 shot mag., DAO, 3.6 in. barrel, textured polymer grips, adj. rear sight, pinned in polymer front sight, white dot combat sights, 16.8 oz. New 2008.

MSR $485 $425 $375 $325 $295 $275 $250 $225

CM45 – .45 ACP cal., 3.14 in. barrel, black polymer frame, matte stainless steel slide. New 2013.

MSR $517 $450 $400 $350 $315 $285 $250 $225

CW45 – .45 ACP cal., otherwise similar to CW40, 19.7 oz. New 2008.

MSR $485 $425 $375 $325 $295 $275 $250 $225

E9 – 9mm Para. cal., economized version of the K9 Compact, matte black finish or duo-tone (new 2003), supplied with one mag. Mfg. 1997 only, reintroduced 2003 only.

$425 $365 $335 $300 $280 $265 $250 ***$490***

K9 COMPACT – 9mm Para. cal., trigger cocking, double action only with passive striker block, locked breech with Browning type recoil lug, steel construction, 3 1/2 in. barrel with polygonal rifling, 7 shot mag., wraparound black polymer grips, matte black, black

GRADING - PPGS™	100%	98%	95%	90%	80%	70%	60%	LAST MSR

titanium (Black-T, mfg. 1997-98), or electroless nickel (mfg. 1996-99) finish, 25 oz. Mfg. 1993-2003.

	$560	$485	$435	$385	$340	$315	$285	*$648*

Add $74 for electroless nickel finish (disc.).
Add $126 for black titanium finish (Black-T, disc.).
Add $103 for tritium night sights (new 1996).

* ***K9 Compact Economy*** – features black matte finish, shipped with one mag. only. Limited mfg. 1999 only.

	$350	$300	$275	$250	$230	$210	$190	*$399*

* ***K9 Compact Stainless*** – similar to K9 Compact, except is matte finished stainless steel, NYCPD specs became standard 2006 (trigger LOP is 1/2 in. compared to 3/8 in.). New 1998.

MSR $855	$750	$665	$550	$450	$385	$335	$280	

Add $130 for tritium night sights.
Add $36 for matte black finish (new 2004).

* ***K9 Compact Elite 98 Stainless*** – similar to K9 Compact, except has high polish slide and specially designed combat trigger utilizing shorter trigger stroke. New 1998.

MSR $932	$785	$700	$600	$500	$425	$375	$300	

Add $122 for tritium night sights.

* ***K9 Compact Wilson Custom Package*** – includes Wilson customizing with Metalloy hard chrome frame, black slide, checkered front strap and beveled mag. well. Limited quantities mfg. 1998.

	$1,175	$995	$875	$775	$700	$625	$550	*$1,310*

* ***K9 Compact Kahr Lady*** – similar to K9 Compact, except has lightened recoil spring, not available in black titanium finish, 25 oz. Mfg. 1997-99.

	$480	$435	$395	$365	$315	$285	$250	*$545*

Add $74 for electroless nickel finish.
Add $85 for tritium night sights (new 1996).

P9 POLYMER COMPACT – 9mm Para. cal., similar to K9 Compact, except has 3.6 in. barrel, lightweight polymer frame, 7 shot mag., matte stainless slide, 17.9 oz. New 1999.

MSR $739	$630	$525	$450	$375	$325	$285	$250	

Add $118 for tritium night sights (new 2000).
Add $47 for matte black stainless slide (new 2004).
Add $137 for external safety and loaded chamber indicator with new enhanced trigger (new 2012).

* ***P9 Polymer Compact Covert*** – similar to K9 Polymer Compact, except has 1/2 in. shorter frame, supplied with one 6 and one 7 (with grip extension) shot mag., 16.9 oz. Limited mfg. 1999, reintroduced 2002 - 2006.

	$595	$495	$430	$365	$325	$285	$250	*$697*

Add $111 for tritium night sights (new 2000).

MK9 MICRO SERIES – 9mm Para. cal., micro compact variation of the K9 Compact featuring 3 in. barrel, double action only with passive striker block, overall size is 4 in. H x 5 1/2 in. L, duo-tone finish with stainless frame and black titanium slide, includes two 6 shot flush floor plate mags. Mfg. 1998-99.

	$650	$575	$515	$465	$425	$395	$375	*$749*

Add $85 for tritium night sights.

* ***MK9 Micro Series Box*** – similar to MK9 Micro, except has matte stainless steel frame with steel matte black slide, duo-tone finish. Limited mfg. 2003, reintroduced 2004-2005.

	$400	$325	$285	$235	$200	$170	$145	*$475*

Add $100 for tritium night sights (disc.).

* ***MK9 Micro Series Stainless*** – similar to MK9 Micro, except is stainless steel, supplied with 6 and 7 shot mag., 24 oz. New 1998.

MSR $855	$695	$575	$475	$375	$325	$260	$225	

Add $103 for tritium night sights.

GRADING - PPGS™	100%	98%	95%	90%	80%	70%	60%	LAST MSR

* ***MK9 Micro Series Elite 98 Stainless*** – similar to MK9 Micro, except has high polish slide and specially designed combat trigger utilizing shorter trigger stroke, 24 oz. New 1998.

MSR $932	**$795**	**$675**	**$595**	**$475**	**$415**	**$360**	**$300**	

Add $122 for tritium night sights.

* ***MK9 Micro Series Elite 2000 Stainless*** – similar to MK9 Elite 98 Stainless, except features black stainless frame and slide, black Roguard finish. Mfg. 2001-2002.

	$575	**$485**	**$425**	**$360**	**$315**	**$260**	**$225**	***$694***

PM9 MICRO POLYMER COMPACT – 9mm Para. cal., 3 in. barrel with polygonal rifling, black polymer frame, trigger cocking DAO, blackened stainless steel slide, 6 or 7 (with mag. grip extension, disc.) shot mag., 16 oz. New 2003.

MSR $786	**$665**	**$550**	**$460**	**$400**	**$350**	**$300**	**$275**	

Add $122 for tritium night sights.
Add $51 for matte black stainless slide (new 2004).
Add $138 for external safety, loaded chamber indicator (new 2010), and enhanced trigger (new 2012).
Add $168 for stainless slide with Crimson Trace trigger guard laser (new 2010).
Add $263 for custom engraved slide (Custom Shop only), new 2012.

MP9 COMPACT POLYMER – 9mm Para. cal., features lightweight polymer frame and matte stainless steel slide, 3 in. barrel, DAO with passive striker block, supplied with 6 and 7 shot mag. with grip extension, includes hard case and trigger lock, 15.9 oz. Mfg. 2002-2003.

	$565	**$485**	**$415**	**$380**	**$340**	**$300**	**$275**	***$660***

Add $101 for tritium night sights.

T9 – 9mm Para. cal., 4 in. barrel with polygonal rifling, matte stainless steel construction, checkered Hogue Pau Ferro wood grips, 8 shot mag., Elite 98 trigger, MMC (disc.), white bar-dot (new 2006) or optional Novak low profile night sights, 28 oz. New 2002.

MSR $831	**$695**	**$565**	**$460**	**$395**	**$345**	**$285**	**$240**	

Add $137 for Novak night sights.

TP9 – 9mm Para. cal., similar to T9, except has black polymer frame and standard sights, 20 oz. New 2004.

MSR $697	**$600**	**$500**	**$425**	**$360**	**$315**	**$260**	**$225**	

Add $141 for Novak night sights.

K40 COMPACT – .40 S&W cal., similar to K9, except has 6 shot mag., matte black or electroless nickel finish (disc. 1999), 26 oz. Mfg. 1997-2003.

	$560	**$485**	**$435**	**$385**	**$340**	**$315**	**$285**	***$648***

Add $103 for tritium night sights (new 1997).
Add $74 for electroless nickel finish (disc. 1999).
Add $126 for black titanium finish (Black-T, disc. 1998).

* ***K40 Compact Stainless*** – similar to K40 Compact, except is stainless steel. New 1997.

MSR $855	**$695**	**$575**	**$475**	**$375**	**$325**	**$260**	**$225**	

Add $130 for tritium night sights.
Add $36 for matte black stainless steel (new 2004).

* ***K40 Compact Elite 98 Stainless*** – similar to K40 Compact, except has high polish slide and specially designed combat trigger utilizing shorter trigger stroke. New 1998.

MSR $932	**$785**	**$700**	**$600**	**$500**	**$425**	**$375**	**$300**	

Add $122 for tritium night sights.

* ***K40 Compact Wilson Custom Package*** – includes Wilson customizing with Metalloy hard chrome frame, black slide, checkered front strap, and beveled mag. well. Limited quantities mfg. 1998.

	$1,175	**$995**	**$875**	**$775**	**$700**	**$625**	**$550**	***$1,310***

* ***K40 Compact Covert Stainless (KS40 Small Frame)*** – .40 S&W cal., similar to Kahr Compact K40, except grip is 1/2 in. shorter, supplied with 5 and 6 shot mags., 25 oz. Mfg. 1998-2000.

	$500	**$440**	**$400**	**$335**	**$290**	**$245**	**$215**	***$580***

Add $88 for tritium night sights.

GRADING - PPGS™	100%	98%	95%	90%	80%	70%	60%	LAST MSR

P40 COMPACT POLYMER – .40 S&W cal., similar to P9 Compact Polymer, 6 shot mag., 18.9 oz. New 2001.

MSR $739	$630	$525	$450	$375	$325	$285	$250	

Add $118 for tritium night sights.
Add $47 for matte black stainless slide (new 2004).

* ***P40 Compact Polymer Covert*** – similar to P40 Compact Polymer, except has 1/2 in. shorter frame, matte stainless slide, supplied with one 6 and one 7 (with grip extension) shot mag., 16.9 oz. Mfg. 2002-2006.

	$600	$500	$425	$370	$325	$285	$250	$697

Add $111 for tritium night sights.

MK40 MICRO – .40 S&W cal., micro compact variation of the Compact K40, featuring 3 in. barrel, matte stainless frame and slide, supplied with one 5 shot and one 6 shot (with grip extension) mag., 25 oz. New 1999.

MSR $855	$750	$665	$550	$450	$385	$335	$280	

Add $103 for tritium night sights.

* ***MK40 Micro Elite Stainless*** – similar to MK40 Micro, except has high polish slide and specially designed combat trigger utilizing shorter trigger stroke. New 2000.

MSR $932	$785	$700	$600	$500	$425	$375	$300	

Add $122 for tritium night sights.

PM40 COMPACT POLYMER – .40 S&W cal., black polymer frame, 3 in. barrel, supplied with one 5 shot and one 6 shot (with grip extension) mag., matte finished stainless slide, 17 oz. New 2004.

MSR $786	$665	$550	$460	$400	$350	$300	$275	

Add $122 for tritium night sights.
Add $51 for matte black stainless slide (new 2005).
Add $168 for stainless slide and Crimson Trace trigger guard laser (new 2010).
Add $42 for external safety and loaded chamber indicator with enhanced trigger (new 2012).

T40 – .40 S&W cal., 4 in. barrel with polygonal rifling, matte stainless steel construction, checkered Hogue Pau Ferro wood grips, 7 shot mag., Elite 98 trigger, MMC (disc. 2005), white bar dot (standard, new 2006), or optional Novak low profile night sights, 29 oz. New 2004.

MSR $831	$695	$565	$460	$395	$345	$285	$240	

Add $137 for Novak night sights (T40 Tactical).

TP40 – .40 S&W cal., similar to T40, except has polymer frame. New 2006.

MSR $697	$600	$500	$425	$370	$325	$285	$250	

Add $141 for Novak night sights (TP40 Tactical).

P45 POLYMER – .45 ACP cal., DAO, black polymer frame with matte or black stainless steel slide, 3.54 in. barrel, 6 shot mag., ribbed grip straps, low profile white dot combat sights, 18 1/2 oz. New 2005.

MSR $805	$685	$560	$460	$410	$340	$290	$250	

Add $116 for Novak night sights.
Add $50 for black stainless slide (new 2006).

PM45 POLYMER – similar to TP45 Polymer, except has 3.14 in. barrel and 5 shot mag., approx. 19 oz. New 2007.

MSR $855	$750	$665	$550	$450	$385	$335	$280	

Add $119 for Novak night sights.
Add $48 for black stainless steel slide (new late 2008).
Add $89 for Crimson Trace trigger guard laser (new 2011).

TP45 POLYMER – .45 ACP cal., DAO, 4.04 in. barrel, 7 shot mag., matte stainless slide only, otherwise similar to P45, approx. 23 oz. New 2007.

MSR $697	$595	$495	$430	$365	$325	$285	$250	

Add $142 for Novak sights.

GRADING - PPGS™	100%	98%	95%	90%	80%	70%	60%	LAST MSR

KASSNAR IMPORTS, INC.

Previous importer and distributor located in Harrisburg, PA. Kassnar Imports operations ceased April, 1989.

Kassnar also imported Churchill and Omega shotguns which can be found in their individual section.

PISTOLS: SEMI-AUTO

PJK-9HP – 9mm Para. cal., single action, patterned after the Browning Hi-Power, 4 3/4 in. barrel, 13 shot mag., cone hammer, checkered walnut grips, 32 oz.

	100%	98%	95%	90%	80%	70%	60%	LAST MSR
	$325	$295	$270	$250	$225	$200	$175	

Add $25 for VR barrel.

This pistol was imported from Hungary. Approx. 18,000 (including the MBK-9HP) were imported until importation was disc. because of Federal ramifications.

MBK-9HP – 9mm Para. cal., double action, patterned after the Browning Hi-Power, 4 2/3 in. barrel, spur hammer, blue metal, checkered walnut grips, 14 shot mag., 36 oz. Limited importation was stopped in late 1985.

	100%	98%	95%	90%	80%	70%	60%	LAST MSR
	$425	$375	$325	$275	$225	$200	$185	

PMK-380 – .380 ACP cal., double action, patterned after the Walther PP, plastic grips with thumbrest, 4 in. barrel, 7 shot mag., 21 oz. Limited importation.

	100%	98%	95%	90%	80%	70%	60%	LAST MSR
	$275	$235	$200	$185	$175	$165	$155	

This model was imported in very limited quantities before Interarms began exclusive importation.

KEBERST INTERNATIONAL

Previously manufactured and distributed by Kendall International located in Paris, KY.

RIFLES: BOLT ACTION

KEBERST MODEL 1A – .338 Lapua Mag., .338-416 Rigby, or .338-06 cal., muzzle brake and unique recoil pad, camouflaged synthetic stock, package includes 3-9 power Leupold scope, stainless steel cleaning rod, custom designed case, built to special order only. Mfg. 1987-88 only.

	100%	98%	95%	90%	80%	70%	60%	LAST MSR
	$3,475	$2,850	$2,475	$2,100	$1,750	$1,400	$1,150	*$3,750*

Add $275 for 10X Ultra scope.

KEL-TEC CNC INDUSTRIES, INC.

Current manufacturer established in 1991, and located in Cocoa, FL. Dealer sales.

CARBINES/RIFLES: SEMI-AUTO

RFB CARBINE – .308 Win. cal., bullpup configuration with pistol grip and rear detachable mag., 18 (Carbine), 24 (RFB Hunter/Sporter), or 32 (Target, disc. 2012) in. barrel with muzzle brake, Picatinny rail, front ejection from tube located above barrel, 10 or 20 shot mag., accepts FAL type mags., tilting breech block design, ambidextrous controls, black synthetic lower, adj. trigger, choice of Black, Canadian Green, or Tan finish, 8.1-11.3 lbs. New 2009.

	100%	98%	95%	90%	80%	70%	60%	LAST MSR
MSR $1,927	$1,795	$1,550	$1,375	$1,150	$900	$800	$700	

Add $158 for Canadian Green or Tan finish.
Add $277 for 24 in. barrel (RFB Hunter/Sporter).

SUB-9/SUB-40 CARBINE – 9mm Para. or .40 S&W cal., unique pivoting 16.1 in. barrel rotates upwards and back, allowing overall size reduction and portability (16 in. x 7 in.), interchangable grip assembly will accept most popular double column high capacity handgun mags., including Glock, S&W, Beretta, SIG, or Kel-Tec, tube stock with polymer buttplate, matte black finish, 4.6 lbs. Mfg. 1997-2000.

	100%	98%	95%	90%	80%	70%	60%	LAST MSR
	$365	$335	$300	$265	$235	$200	$180	*$700*

Add $25 for .40 S&W cal.

GRADING - PPGS™	100%	98%	95%	90%	80%	70%	60%	LAST MSR

SUB-2000 CARBINE – 9mm Para. or .40 S&W (new 2004) cal., similar to Sub-9/Sub-40, choice of blue (disc.), parkerized or hard chrome (disc.) finish, 4 lbs. New 2001.

MSR $425	$375	$340	$300	$265	$235	$200	$180	

This model accepts magazines from the Glock 17, 19, 22, or 23, Beretta 92 or 96, S&W Model 59, or Sig 226.

SU-16 SERIES CARBINE/RIFLE – 5.56 NATO cal., unique downward folding stock, forearm folds down to become a bipod, 16 (new 2005) or 18 1/2 in. barrel, Picatinny receiver rail, M16 breech locking and feeding system, choice of Black, OD Green (new 2012), or Tan (new 2012) synthetic stock (stores extra mags.) and forearm, approx. 4.7 lbs. New 2003.

* ***SU-16A*** – 5.56 NATO cal., features 18 1/2 in. barrel, 10 shot AR-15 compatible mag., right hand reciprocating bolt handle and mag. catch, buttstock can store two 10 shot mags., 5 lbs.

MSR $682	$635	$550	$500	$450	$400	$365	$335	

Add $140 for OD Green or Tan finish.

* ***SU-16B*** – 5.56 NATO cal., similar to SU-16, except has lightened 16 in. barrel, 4 1/2 lbs.

MSR $736	$660	$580	$525	$465	$415	$365	$335	

Add $139 for OD Green or Tan finish.

* ***SU-16C*** – .300 AAC Blackout (new 2013) or 5.56 NATO cal., similar to SU-16A, except front sight is integrated into the gas block, and also has a true folding stock, parkerized finish with black polymer components, 4.7 lbs.

MSR $788	$725	$650	$600	$550	$500	$450	$400	

Add $141 for OD Green or Tan finish.

* ***SU-16E*** – .223 Rem. or .300 AAC Blackout cal., 16 in. barrel, flat top Picatinny receiver, collapsible buttstock, pistol grip, small quad rail, accepts AR-15 compatible magazines, 4.7 lbs. New 2012.

MSR $901	$825	$750	$675	$600	$550	$500	$450	

Add $138 for OD Green or Tan finish.

* ***SU-16F*** – 5.56 NATO cal., similar to SU-16A, except features Canadian Black or choice of OD Green or Tan finish. New 2012.

MSR $682	$635	$550	$500	$450	$400	$365	$335	

Add $140 for OD Green or Tan finish.

SU-22 RIFLE SERIES – similar to SU-16, except is .22 LR cal., parkerized finish, Picatinny rail on top of receiver and bottom of aluminum quad forearm, open sights, 27 shot mag., 4 lbs. New 2008.

MSR $460	$410	$360	$320	$285	$266	$245	$225	

Add $10 for under folding stock with 15 shot mag. (SU-22C).
Add $41 for pistol grip style AR stock (SU-22E).
Add $126 for OD Green or Tan finish.

RMR-30 CARBINE – .22 WMR cal., 16.1 in. threaded barrel, rifle version of the PMR-30 featuring a skeletonized collapsible stock, upper and lower Picatinny rails, flat-top design, ambidextrous operating handles, aluminum construction, 30 shot mag., 3.8 lbs. New 2011.

MSR $588	$525	$465	$425	$385	$350	$325	$295	

PISTOLS: SEMI-AUTO

P-3AT – .380 ACP cal., developed from the P-32, 2.76 in. barrel, 6 shot mag., black composite frame with parkerized steel slide, 8.3 oz. New 2003.

MSR $331	$275	$220	$180	$160	$150	$135	$125	

Add $43 for parkerized finish.
Add $61 for hard chrome finish.

P-11 – 9mm Para. cal., double action only, locked breech design, 3.1 in. barrel, composite frame with steel slide, transfer bar safety, matte blue, parkerized (new 1997), hard chrome (new 1999), or electroless nickel (disc. 1995) finish, black, grey, or green (disc. 1998)

GRADING - PPGS™	100%	98%	95%	90%	80%	70%	60%	LAST MSR

synthetic grips, 10 shot double column mag., 14.4 oz. New 1995.

MSR $340	$280	$225	$185	$165	$150	$135	$125	

Add $45 for parkerized finish (choice of grips).
Add $60 for hard chrome finish (new 1999).
Add $30 for electroless nickel finish (disc. 1995).
Add $85 for night sights (mfg. 1997-2003, reintroduced 2007).
Add $175 for 9mm Para. to .40 S&W cal. conversion kit (disc. 2002).

* ***P-11 Stainless*** – similar to P-11, except is stainless steel, available with black (P- 11SB), grey (P-11SGY), or green (P-11SGN) grips. Mfg. 1996-98.

	$350	$275	$230	$180	$140	$125	$105	*$408*

P-32 – .32 ACP cal., double action only with internal hammer block safety, 7 shot mag., composite frame with steel slide, 2.68 in. barrel, choice of parkerized, blue, or hard chrome finish, choice of light blue, dark blue, grey, green or full ivory grips, 6.6 oz. New 1999.

MSR $326	$270	$215	$180	$160	$150	$135	$125	

Add $43 for parkerized finish.
Add $59 for hard chrome finish.

P-40 – .40 S&W cal., double action only with internal hammer block safety, composite frame with steel slide, 3.3 in. barrel, choice of parkerized, blue, or hard chrome finish, 9 or 10 shot mag., 15.8 oz. Mfg. 1999-2001.

	$275	$225	$190	$175	$160	$140	$130	*$331*

Add $41 for parkerized finish.
Add $58 for hard chrome finish.

PLR-16 – 5.56 NATO cal., gas operation, 9.2 in. threaded barrel, upper frame has integrated Picatinny rail, 10 shot detachable mag., black composite frame, 3.2 lbs. New 2006.

MSR $682	$600	$550	$500	$460	$420	$380	$340	

Add $119 for OD Green or Tan finish.

PLR-22 – .22 LR cal., similar to PLR-16, except has 26 shot mag., 2.8 lbs. New 2008.

MSR $400	$340	$300	$275	$250	$225	$200	$185	

Add $193 for OD Green or Tan finish.

PF-9 – 9mm Para. cal., similar operating system as P-11, 3.1 in. barrel, single stack 7 shot mag., includes lower accessory rail, black finish, 12.7 oz. Limited mfg. 2006, reintroduced 2008.

MSR $340	$275	$220	$185	$165	$150	$135	$125	

Add $45 for parkerized finish.
Add $60 for hard chrome finish.

PMR-30 – .22 WMR cal., 4.3 in. barrel, 30 shot mag., blowback action, manual safety, fiber optic sights, steel slide and barrel, black finished aluminum frame, lower Picatinny rail, 19 1/2 oz. New 2010.

MSR $436	$375	$325	$295	$275	$250	$225	$200	

Add $27 for OD Green or Tan finish.

SHOTGUNS: SLIDE ACTION

KSG – 12 ga., 2 3/4 in. chamber, unique bullpup configuration, utilizing an 18 1/2 in. cyl. bore barrel, twin mag. tubes under the barrel allow 14 shot capacity, downward ejection, steel and polymer construction, upper and lower Picatinny rails w/o sights, pistol grip, 26.1 in. overall length, 6.9 lbs. New 2011.

MSR $924	$850	$775	$700	$650	$600	$550	$500	

Add $144 for OD Green or Tan finish.

KEMEN

Current competition shotgun manufacturer established in 1990, and located in Elgoibar, Spain. Currently imported exclusively by Fieldsport (all models), located in Traverse City, MI. Previously imported by Target Shotguns, located in Arden, NC, American Shooting Centers, located in Houston, TX, by Fly and Field, located in Bend, OR, and by New England Custom Gun Service (Model KM-4 only), located in Plainfield, NH.

Gun service is available through Briley.

Due to space considerations, information regarding this manufacturer is available online free of charge at www.bluebookofgunvalues.com.

KENDALL INTERNATIONAL

Previous importer and distributor located in Paris, KY. Kendall International also imported Australian Automatic Arms, and the Keberst Rifle. Air rifles can be found in the *Blue Book of Airguns* by Dr. Robert Beeman & John Allen (also online).

KENTUCKY RIFLES

U.S. flintlock/percussion long rifle configuration originating in Pennsylvania. Kentucky rifles are a field unto themselves, and should be evaluated by an experienced and known source for accurate identification and/or price evaluation.

KENTUCKY RIFLES IDENTIFICATION & PRICING

The author wishes to express his thanks once again to Mr. James Buelow for updating the following information.

The Kentucky rifle was the creation of early settlers from Europe. This new American configuration combined the architectural elements of the English Fowler with the ornamental features of the German Jaeger.

The earliest recorded use of the term "Kentucky rifle" was in a ballad written after the battle of New Orleans. The battle was won by the American Long Rifle, in the hands of 2,000 frontiersmen. During that period, the area west of the 13 colonies was known as Kentucky; hence the name Kentucky rifle.

Kentucky rifles began appearing around the middle of the 18th century and disappeared by the middle of the 19th century. Their origin is credited to eastern Pennsylvania, but soon spread to many other states, including Maryland, Virginia, Tennessee, North Carolina, and areas where the rifle maker found a market for his skills.

The styles vary, but they have two things in common: they are long, and most had curly maple stocks. The bores are found both rifled and smooth. The rifles most prized by the collector are the ones that have relief or incised carving. Original carved Kentucky rifles are now considered one of America's earliest art forms and have become a functional example of important early Americana. Present values may range from as low as $1,500 all the way up to almost $200,000! Non-carved or plain Kentuckys are most often encountered.

The present value of an uncarved, original flintlock Kentucky rifle in average condition is approx. $3,500. An uncarved percussion specimen in average original condition is approx. $2,500. These prices diminish when the Kentucky rifle lacks a maker's name, usually found on the top of the barrel, or if it does not have a patch box. Kentucky rifle values vary greatly, due to maker popularity, quality of carving, condition, rifle style, and a multitude of other factors.

During the past several decades, many fine contemporary Kentucky rifles have been built by craftsmen who understand the trade. Many of these guns are now available in the secondary marketplace. A large percentage have outstanding craftsmanship, and are highly sought after. These specimens sell in the $2,000-$10,000 range, depending on the notoriety of the builder and the sophistication of the work. Because of this, these guns have to be evaluated one at a time.

The best way to find out the value of a Kentucky rifle is to seek out a knowledgeable Kentucky rifle collector. To find such a person in your area, contact the Kentucky Rifle Association's Administrative Assistant: Ruth Collis, 2319 Sue Ann Dr., Lancaster, PA, 17602. For information regarding contemporary Kentucky rifles makers (with some contact information), visit the Contemporary Longrifle Association at www.longrifle.ws, or see their listing under Firearms Associations.

KEPPELER - TECHNISCHE ENTWICKLUNGEN GmbH

Current rifle manufacturer located in Fichtenberg, Germany. No current U.S. importation.

Keppeler manufactures a wide variety of top quality rifles, in many target configurations (including UIT-CISM, Prone, Free, and Sniper Bullpup). Both metric and domestic calibers are available as well as a variety of special order options. Keppeler also manufactures precision caliber conversion

GRADING - PPGS™	100%	98%	95%	90%	80%	70%	60%	LAST MSR

tubes for the shotgun barrel(s) on combination guns and drillings. Please contact the factory directly for more information and current pricing (see Trademark Index).

KEPPLINGER, ING. HANNES

Please refer to the Kufsteiner Waffenstube section.

KESSLER ARMS CORPORATION

Previous manufacturer located in Silver Creek, NY.

SHOTGUNS

LEVERMATIC MODEL – 12, 16, or 20 ga., lever action, 26 or 28 in. full choke barrel, takedown, plain pistol grip stock. Disc. 1953.

	100%	98%	95%	90%	80%	70%	60%	LAST MSR
	$175	$150	$125	$100	$85	$65	$55	

BOLT ACTION MODEL – 12, 16, or 20 ga., 26 or 28 in. full choke barrel, takedown, plain stock. Mfg. 1951-53.

	100%	98%	95%	90%	80%	70%	60%	LAST MSR
	$90	$65	$50	$45	$35	$35	$35	

KESSLER, WAFFEN

Please refer to Waffen Kessler listing.

KEYSTONE SPORTING ARMS

Current manufacturer established 1996, and located in Milton, PA. Distributor and dealer sales.

Keystone manufactures the Chipmunk and Crickett lines of youth bolt action rifles and pistols. In January 2007, Keystone purchased the remaining assets of Rogue Rifle Co., manufacturer of Chipmunk rifles. Please refer to the Crickett and Chipmunk sections for current models and pricing. In addition to Chipmunk and Crickett rifles and pistols, Keystone currently manufactures a Model 10 bolt action shotgun and a Hunter .22 caliber bolt action pistol. Additionally, the company makes a wide variety of conventional and thumbhole stocks and forearms in many different colors. Please contact the company directly for more information and pricing on these guns (see Trademark Index).

KHAN

Current trademark of shotguns established in 1985, and manufactured in Istanbul, Turkey. Currently imported on a private label basis by Mossberg. Previously imported late 2004-2005 by Legacy Sports International, LLC, located in Alexandria, VA.

In addition to the O/U and hammer SxS shotguns listed, Khan also manufactures a K303 hammerless SxS model, and a K107/K142 single barrel folding action shotgun.

SHOTGUNS: O/U

ARTHEMIS ELITE FIELD/DELUXE – 12, 20, 28 ga., or .410 bore, 3 in. chambers (except for 28 ga.), 26 or 28 in. VR barrels with multichokes (fixed chokes on .410 bore), extractors, SST, matte blue (Field) or bright blue (Deluxe) metal finish, light engraving, choice of satin finish (Field) or polished select finish (Deluxe) walnut stock, 5.7-7.9 lbs.

	100%	98%	95%	90%	80%	70%	60%	LAST MSR
	$500	$450	$400	$350	$300	$265	$235	*$617*

Add $15 for 20 ga.
Add $22 for 28 ga. or .410 bore.
Add $174 for Deluxe Model with bright blue metal and polished select wood stock (12 or 20 ga. only).

* ***Arthemis Elite Field/Deluxe Sporting Clays*** – 12 ga., 2 3/4 in. chambers, ejectors, 28 in. barrels, ST, otherwise similar to Arthemis Field, 8 lbs.

	100%	98%	95%	90%	80%	70%	60%	LAST MSR
	$925	$825	$725	$650	$575	$495	$425	*$1,104*

SHOTGUNS: SxS

COACH GUN – 12 ga., 2 3/4 in. chamber, bright blue metal, hammerless boxlock action, extractors, polished select wood stock and forearm, 20 in. barrels with fixed cyl. bore chokes, 6.9 lbs.

	100%	98%	95%	90%	80%	70%	60%	LAST MSR
	$675	$595	$525	$450	$375	$300	$225	*$784*

GRADING - PPGS™	100%	98%	95%	90%	80%	70%	60%	LAST MSR

KILIMANJARO RIFLES

Current custom rifle manufacturer established in 2010 with headquarters located in Honolulu, HI and manufacturing facilities located in Kalispell, MT.

Kilimanjaro Rifles purchased the Serengeti name, model lines, and patents so it could continue making the Serengeti and Jaguar models, in addition to its new flagship Kilimanjaro rifle.

RIFLES: CUSTOM

Kilimanjaro Rifles manufactures high quality custom rifles, including the bolt action Kilimanjaro ($17,500 MSR), The New Serengeti ($14,500 MSR), the Jaguar (last MSR in 2012 was $5,995), the Tigercat ($14,500 MSR), the Artemis ($14,500 MSR), and the Doctari ($19,500 MSR), as well as the Kilimanjaro lever action rifle ($9,995 MSR, special order only). Many options are available - please contact the company directly for a listing of these options and current pricing. Additionally, Kilimanjaro manufactures full custom versions of various historical rifles. These rifles are built to customer specifications and are POR. Please contact the company directly for more information, including pricing, available options, and delivery times (see Trademark Index).

KIMAR srl

Current division of Armi Sport Chiappa Silvia e. C. S.N.C., located in, Brescia, Italy. Currently imported by Traditions, located in Old Saybrook, CT. Previously imported by IAR, located in San Juan Capistrano, CA, and by Valor Corp., located in Sunrise, FL.

Kimar is well known for its starter/signal revolvers and pistols in many popular configurations. Additionally, the company also manufactures a single shot folding barrel shotgun in small hunting calibers. Please contact the importer directly for more information and U.S. availability (see Trademark Index).

J. KIMBALL ARMS CO.

Previous manufacturer located in Detroit, MI circa 1958.

PISTOLS: SEMI-AUTO

AUTOMATIC PISTOL - .30 Carbine or .22 Hornet (very rare) cal., 7 shot, 3 in. (Combat Model) or 5 in. (Target Model) barrel, approx. 32 oz. Less than 300 mfg. in 1958 only.

$1,950 $1,875 $1,500 $1,325 $1,050 $875 $750

Add 50% for .22 Hornet cal.

Functional weaknesses of this pistol caused discontinuance. Surviving specimens should be checked carefully for slide failures and other potential problems. Values assume no operational damage to the pistol.

KIMBER

Current trademark manufactured by Kimber Mfg., Inc., established during 1997, with company headquarters and manufacturing located in Elmsford, NY. Previously located in Yonkers, NY until 2011. Previous rifle manufacture was by Kimber of America, Inc., located in Clackamas, OR circa 1993-1997. Dealer sales.

PISTOLS: SEMI-AUTO

Kimber pistols, including the very early models marked "Clackamas, Oregon", have all been manufactured in the Yonkers, NY plant. Prior to the 1998 production year, the "Classic" model pistols were alternately roll-scrolled "Classic", "Classic Custom" or "Custom Classic". During 1997-98, the "Classic" moniker was dropped from Kimber pistol nomenclature as a specific model.

All Kimber 1911 pistols are shipped with lockable high impact synthetic case with cable lock and one magazine, beginning 1999.

Beginning in 2001, the "Series II" pistol, incorporating the Kimber Firing Pin Safety System, was again phased into some centerfire models. All pistols incorporating the firing pin block have the Roman Numeral "II" following the name of the pistol presented on the slide directly under the ejection port. This conversion was completed by February 2002, and about 50% of

GRADING - PPGS™	100%	98%	95%	90%	80%	70%	60%	LAST MSR

subsequent Kimber 1911 pistol production has been Series II. There was no "Series I" pistol per se, but pre-series II models are often referred to in that manner.

During 2003, external extractors were phased many .45 ACP models. Due to consumer demand, production was phased back to traditional (internal) extractors during 2006.

All three changes (disuse of the term "Classic" for pistols, Series II safety system, and external extractor) were "phased in" throughout normal production cycles. Therefore, no distinctive cut-off dates or serial numbering series were established to identify specific product runs or identify when these features were incorporated.

Almost all Kimber pistols (exceptions are Royal II, Classic Carry Pro, rimfires and some pistols sold in California) have stainless steel match grade barrels beginning 2013.

Add $339 for .22 LR cal. or $344-$379 for .17 Mach 2 cal. (mfg. 2005-2006) conversion kit for all mil-spec 1911 pistols (includes complete upper assembly, lightweight aluminum slide, premium bull barrel, and 10 shot mag.). Available in satin black and satin silver. Kimber began manufacture of these kits in early 2003. Prior to that, they were manufactured by a vendor.

CUSTOM II – .45 ACP cal., patterned after the Colt Government Model 1911, 5 in. barrel, various finishes, 7 shot mag., steel frame, match grade barrel, bushing and trigger group, dovetail mounted sights, frame machined from solid steel, high ride beavertail grip safety, choice of rubber, laminated wood (disc.), walnut or rosewood (disc.) grips, 38 oz. New 1995.

MSR $871	$725	$625	$525	$475	$375	$325	$265

Add $34 for walnut or rosewood (disc.) grips.
Add $117 for night sights.
Add $185 for Royal II finish (polished blue and checkered rosewood grips, disc. 2010, and replaced by new Custom Shop version with same name.)

This series' nomenclature added the Roman numeral "II" during 2001.

* ***Custom Target II*** – .45 ACP cal., similar to Custom II, except features Kimber adj. rear sight. New 1998.

MSR $974	$850	$750	$625	$550	$450	$360	$280

CUSTOM II STAINLESS II – .38 Super (advertised in 1999, mfg. late 2005-2008), 9mm Para. (advertised in 1999, new 2008), .40 S&W (mfg. 1999-2007), or .45 ACP cal., similar to Custom II, except has stainless steel slide and frame.

MSR $998	$850	$750	$650	$550	$440	$360	$280

Add $18 for 9mm Para. or $11 for .40 S&W (disc. 2007) cal.
Add $130 for night sights (.45 ACP cal. only).
Add $143 for high polish stainless in .38 Super cal. only (mfg. late 2005-2008).
Subtract $27 for Stainless Limited Edition marked "Stainless LE" (disc. 1998).

* ***Custom II Stainless Target II*** – similar to Stainless II, except is available in .38 Super (new 2002), 9mm Para., 10mm (new 2003), or .45 ACP cal., features Kimber adj. rear sight. New 1998.

MSR $1,108	$975	$850	$725	$625	$500	$425	$350

Add $30 for .40 S&W cal. (disc. 2002).
Add $84 for .38 Super, 10mm or 9mm Para. cal.
Add $130 for high polish stainless in .38 Super cal. only (mfg. late 2005-2008).

CUSTOM II ROYAL II – .45 ACP cal., 5 in. barrel, similar to Custom II, except features charcoal blue slide and frame, solid bone grips, 38 oz. New 2010.

MSR $2,020	$1,850	$1,575	$1,325	$1,100	$950	$825	$700

GOLD MATCH II – .45 ACP cal., features Kimber adj. sight, 5 in. stainless steel match barrel and bushing, premium aluminum match grade trigger, ambidextrous thumb safety became standard in 1998, 8 shot mag., fancy checkered rosewood grips in double diamond pattern, high polish blue, hand fitted barrel by Kimber Custom Shop, 38 oz.

MSR $1,393	$1,250	$1,125	$950	$850	$700	$575	$450

This series' nomenclature added the Roman numeral "II" during 2001.

GRADING - PPGS™	100%	98%	95%	90%	80%	70%	60%	LAST MSR

* ***Gold Match Stainless II*** – .38 Super (advertised in 1999, never mfg.), 9mm Para. (advertised in 1999, new 2008), .40 S&W (mfg. 1999-2007), or .45 ACP cal., similar to Gold Match, except is stainless steel, 38 oz.

MSR $1,574	$1,375	$1,175	$1,025	$900	$750	$625	$550	

Add $50 for 9mm Para. or .40 S&W (disc. 2007) cal.

* ***Gold Match II Team Match II*** – 9mm Para. or .45 ACP cal., 5 in. barrel, features two-tone finish and extended magazine well, 30 lpi front strap checkering, G10 grips, adj. rear sight, 8 or 9 shot mag., 39 oz. New 2013.

MSR $1,868	$1,695	$1,425	$1,200	$1,050	$900	$775	$675	

Add $14 for 9mm Para. cal.

TEAM MATCH II – 9mm Para. (new 2009), .45 ACP, or .38 Super (limited mfg. 2003-2004, reintroduced 2006-2010) cal., same pistol developed for USA Shooting Team (2004 Olympics Rapid Fire Pistol Team) competition, satin finish stainless steel frame and slide, 5 in. match grade barrel, 30 LPI front strap checkering, match grade trigger, Tactical Extractor system (disc.) or internal extractor, extended magazine well, 8 shot mag., laminated red/white/blue grips, 38 oz. Total production just over 10,000 units. Revised to new version with gold logo on slide, red/blue grips and black DLC coating on slide in 2013. Mfg. 2003-2012.

	$1,315	$1,150	$975	$775	$725	$575	$450	*$1,563*

Add $13 for 9mm Para. cal.
Add $48 for .38 Super cal. (disc. 2010).

A $100 donation is made to the U.S.A. Shooting Team for every Team Match II sold.

GOLD COMBAT II – .45 ACP cal. only, 5 in. barrel (bushingless bull became standard 2008), full size carry pistol based on the Gold Match, steel frame and slide, stainless steel match grade barrel and bushing, matte black KimPro finish, rear night sight, serrated flat-top and scalloped French shoulders also became standard 2008, tritium night sights, checkered walnut (disc. 2008) or 24 LPI herringbone pattern micarta grips, ambidextrous thumb safety, extended and beveled mag. well, full length guide rod, 38 oz, mfg. by Custom Shop. Mfg. 1994-2008, reintroduced 2011.

MSR $2,307	$2,075	$1,800	$1,575	$1,350	$1,100	$900	$750	

This series' nomenclature added the Roman numeral "II" during 2001.

* ***Gold Combat Stainless II*** – similar to Gold Combat, except is all stainless steel. Mfg. 1994-2008, reintroduced 2011.

MSR $2,251	$2,000	$1,775	$1,550	$1,375	$1,100	$900	$700	

* ***Gold Combat RL II*** – similar to Gold Combat, except has Picatinny rail machined into the lower forward frame to accept optics and other tactical accessories. Mfg. 1994-2008, reintroduced 2011.

MSR $2,405	$2,100	$1,800	$1,575	$1,375	$1,125	$925	$800	

SUPER MATCH II – .45 ACP cal. only, 5 in. barrel, top-of-the-line model, two-tone stainless steel construction, KimPro finish on slide, match grade trigger, Custom Shop markings, accuracy guarantee, 38 oz. New 1999.

MSR $2,313	$2,075	$1,800	$1,575	$1,350	$1,100	$900	$750	

This series' nomenclature added the Roman numeral "II" during 2001.

LTP II – .45 ACP cal., designed for Limited Ten competition, Tactical Extractor, steel frame and slide, KimPro finish, 20 LPI front strap checkering, 30 LPI checkering under trigger guard, tungsten guide rod, flat-top serrated slide, beveled mag. well, ambidextrous thumb safety, adj. rear sight. Mfg. by Custom Shop 2002-2006.

	$1,850	$1,620	$1,385	$1,260	$1,015	$830	$645	*$2,106*

RIMFIRE TARGET – .17 Mach 2 (mfg. 2004-2005) or .22 LR cal., 5 in. barrel, 10 shot mag., aluminum frame in silver or black anodized finish (disc. 2006), black oxide steel or satin stainless slide (.17 Mach 2 cal. only), black synthetic grips, Kimber adj. rear sight, 28 oz. New 2003.

MSR $871	$775	$675	$575	$500	$400	$325	$275	

Add $39 for .17 Mach 2 cal. (disc. 2005).

GRADING - PPGS™	100%	98%	95%	90%	80%	70%	60%	LAST MSR

RIMFIRE SUPER – .22 LR cal., similar to Rimfire Target, except has flat-top slide with aggressive fluting on upper sides, premium aluminum trigger, ambidextrous safety, rosewood grips with logo inserts, guaranteed to fire a sub-1.5 in. 5 shot group at 25 yards, test target included, 23 oz., mfg. by Kimber Custom Shop. New 2004.

MSR $1,220	$1,075	$925	$800	$700	$600	$500	$425	

POLYMER MODEL – .45 ACP cal., features widened black polymer frame offering larger mag. capacity, choice of fixed (Polymer Model) or adj. Kimber target (Polymer Target Model, disc. 1999) rear sight, matte black slide, 10 shot mag., 34 oz. Mfg. 1997-2001.

	$675	$595	$500	$450	$375	$300	$225	*$795*

Add $88 for Polymer Target Model.

All Polymer Models were disc. in 2002 in favor of the new "Ten" Series with improved Kimber made frame. Magazines are interchangeable.

* ***Polymer Model Stainless*** – .38 Super (advertised in 1999, never mfg.), 9mm Para. (advertised in 1999, never mfg.), .40 S&W (mfg. 1999 only), or .45 ACP cal., similar to Polymer Model, except has satin finish stainless steel slide. Mfg. 1998-2001.

	$745	$650	$550	$500	$410	$335	$250	*$856*

Add $88 for Polymer Stainless Target Model (disc. 1999).

* ***Polymer Model Gold Match*** – .45 ACP cal. only, similar to Gold Match, except has polymer frame, supplied with 10 shot double stack mag., 34 oz. Mfg. 1999-2001.

	$925	$810	$695	$630	$510	$415	$325	*$1,041*

» **Polymer Model Gold Match Stainless** – similar to Gold Match, except has polymer frame and stainless steel slide, 34 oz. Mfg. 1999-2001.

	$1,025	$895	$770	$695	$565	$460	$360	*$1,177*

* ***Polymer Model Pro Carry*** – .45 ACP cal. only, 4 in. bushingless bull barrel, steel slide, 32 oz. Mfg. 1999-2001.

	$725	$635	$545	$495	$400	$325	$255	*$814*

» **Polymer Model Pro Carry Stainless** – similar to Polymer Pro Carry, except has stainless steel slide. Mfg. 1999-2001.

	$755	$660	$565	$515	$415	$340	$265	*$874*

* ***Polymer Model Ultra Ten*** – .45 ACP cal., black polymer frame with aluminum frame insert, stainless slide, 3 in. barrel, 10 shot staggered mag., low profile sights, lighter version of the Polymer Series frame, Kimber Firing Pin Safety, 24 oz.

While advertised during 2001 with an MSR of $896, this model never went into production.

COMPACT II – .45 ACP cal., features 4 in. barrel, .4 in. shorter aluminum or steel frame, 7 shot mag., Commander style hammer, single recoil spring, low profile combat sights, checkered black synthetic grips, 28 (aluminum) or 34 (steel) oz. Mfg. 1998-2001.

	$635	$555	$475	$430	$350	$285	$220	*$764*

* ***Compact Stainless II*** – .40 S&W (mfg. 1999-2001) or .45 ACP cal., features stainless steel slide, 4 in. bull barrel, 4 in. shorter aluminum (disc., reintroduced 2009) or stainless (mfg. 2002-2008) frame, 7 shot mag., Commander style hammer, single recoil spring, low profile combat sights, black synthetic grips, 34 oz. New 1998.

MSR $1,052	$925	$825	$725	$625	$525	$450	$350	

Add $32 for .40 S&W cal. (disc. 2001).

This model's nomenclature added the Roman numeral "II" during 2001.

COMBAT CARRY – .40 S&W or .45 ACP cal., 4 in. barrel, carry model featuring aluminum frame and trigger, stainless steel slide, tritium night sights, and ambidextrous thumb safety, 28 oz. Limited mfg. 1999 only.

	$940	$825	$700	$650	$515	$425	$325	*$1,044*

Add $30 for .40 S&W cal.

GRADING - PPGS™	100%	98%	95%	90%	80%	70%	60%	LAST MSR

PRO CARRY II – 9mm Para. (new mid-2005), .40 S&W (disc. 2001) or .45 ACP cal., 4 in. barrel, features full length grip similar to Custom Model, aluminum frame, steel slide, 7 or 8 shot mag., 28 oz. New 1999.

MSR $919	$825	$725	$625	$525	$450	$350	$295

Add $50 for 9mm Para. cal.
Add $35 for .40 S&W cal. (disc.).
Add $120 for night sights (.45 ACP cal. only).

This series' nomenclature added the Roman numeral "II" during 2001.

* ***Stainless Pro Carry II*** – similar to Pro Carry, except has stainless steel slide, not available in 9mm Para. cal. New 1999.

MSR $1,016	$900	$800	$700	$600	$500	$400	$300

Add $50 for 9mm Para (new 2008) or $38 for .40 S&W (disc. 2007) cal.
Add $112 for night sights (.45 ACP cal. only).
Add $295 for Crimson Trace grips (.45 ACP cal. only, disc. 2009).

* ***Pro Carry HD II*** – .38 Super (new 2002) or .45 ACP cal., similar to Pro Carry Stainless, except has heavier stainless steel frame, 35 oz. New 2001.

MSR $1,046	$925	$825	$700	$600	$500	$425	$350

Add $48 for .38 Super cal.

ULTRA CARRY II – .40 S&W (disc. 2001) or .45 ACP cal., 3 in. barrel, aluminum frame, 7 shot mag., 25 oz. New 1999.

MSR $919	$795	$675	$575	$525	$450	$375	$325

Add $120 for night sights.
Add $39 for .40 S&W cal. (disc. 2001).
Add $375 for Crimson Trace grips (disc. 2009).

This series' nomenclature added the Roman numeral "II" during 2001.

* ***Stainless Ultra Carry II*** – 9mm Para. (new 2008), .40 S&W (disc. 2007), and .45 ACP cal., similar to Ultra Carry, except has stainless steel slide. New 1999.

MSR $1,016	$895	$775	$650	$575	$475	$400	$350

Add $50 for 9mm Para. (new 2008) or $45 for .40 S&W cal. (disc. 2007).
Add $109 for night sights (.45 ACP cal. only, disc. 2009).

CLASSIC CARRY PRO – .45 ACP cal., features 4 in. bushingless match grade bull barrel, charcoal blue metal finish, uncheckered bone grips, night sights, front strap checkering, 35 oz. New 2012.

MSR $2,056	$1,825	$1,575	$1,350	$1,150	$950	$825	$700

SUPER CARRY SERIES – .45 ACP cal., 3 (Ultra), 4 (Pro), or 5 (Custom) in. barrel, stainless steel slide, aluminum frame, KimPro II finish, night sights, rounded edges, checkered double diamond wood or Micarta (Ultra+, new 2011) grips, recessed slide stop pin with surrounding bevel, rear slide serrations. New 2010.

MSR $1,596	$1,350	$1,150	$975	$875	$775	$650	$525

* ***Super Carry Pro HD*** – .45 ACP cal., 3 (Ultra), 4 (Pro), or 5 (Custom) in. barrel, similar to Super Carry, except has matte black finish and checkered blue/black Micarta grips, 32 oz. New 2011.

MSR $1,699	$1,525	$1,300	$1,100	$950	$825	$700	$575

MASTER CARRY – .45 ACP cal., 3 (Ultra), 4 (Pro), or 5 (Custom) in. stainless steel barrel, aluminum frame on Carry Pro and Carry Ultra models, stainless steel frame on Carry Custom, black KimPro II finish on slide and satin finish frame, skeletonized trigger, includes Crimson Trace master series laser grips with red beam, round heel frame, tactical wedge night sights, 25-30 oz. New 2013.

MSR $1,568	$1,325	$1,175	$1,025	$900	$775	$650	$550

SOLO CARRY – 9mm Para. cal., micro-compact aluminum frame, single action, 2.7 in. barrel, 6 or 8 (extended mag.) shot, matte black (Solo Carry) or satin silver (Solo Carry Stainless)

GRADING - PPGS™	100%	98%	95%	90%	80%	70%	60%	LAST MSR

KimPro II finish, stainless steel slide and barrel, amidextrous thumb safety, removable grips, amidextrous mag. release, steel sights, 17 oz. New 2011.

MSR $815	$725	$625	$525	$450	$395	$340	$315

* ***Solo CDP (LG)*** – 9mm Para. cal., matte black aluminum frame with satin stainless steel slide, 6 or 8 shot mag., features fixed 3 dot Tritium night sights and rosewood Crimson Trace laser grips, 17 oz. New late 2011.

MSR $1,223	$1,050	$875	$750	$675	$550	$450	$350

* ***Solo Carry DC*** – 9mm Para. cal., SA striker fired trigger, features black DLC finished slide and barrel, night sights, Carry Melt treatment, 6 shot mag., 17 oz. New 2013.

MSR $904	$825	$750	$675	$600	$550	$500	$450

Add $300 for Crimson Trace laser grips.

MICRO CDP – .380 ACP cal., 2 3/4 in. barrel, SA, 6 shot mag., stainless steel slide and barrel, aluminum frame, 30 LPI front strap checkering, steel dovetail mounted 3-dot night sights, ambidextrous thumb safety, high cut under the trigger guard, double diamond checkered rosewood grips, matte black finish, checkered mainspring housing, 13.4 oz. New late 2012.

MSR $1,121	$1,000	$900	$800	$700	$600	$500	$400

Add $305 for Crimson Trace laser grips (LG Model).

MICRO CARRY – .380 ACP cal., SA, stainless steel slide, 2 3/4 in. stainless steel barrel, aluminum frame, all satin or black frame finish, 6 shot mag., steel sights, 15.4 oz. New 2013.

MSR $651	$575	$500	$450	$415	$385	$350	$295

Add $18 for all satin finish.

ECLIPSE II SERIES – 10mm (Eclipse Custom II, new 2004) or .45 ACP cal., stainless steel slide and frame, black matte finish with brush polished flat surfaces for elegant two-tone finish, Tritium night sights, target models have adj. bar/dot sights, silver/grey laminated double diamond grips, black small parts, 30 LPI front strap checkering, include Eclipse Ultra II (3 in. barrel, short grip), Eclipse Pro II and Eclipse Pro-Target II (4 in. barrel, standard grip, disc. 2012), Eclipse Custom II, and Eclipse Target II (full size). New 2002.

MSR $1,289	$1,150	$1,000	$875	$775	$625	$500	$395

Add $62 for Eclipse Custom II in 10mm cal.
Add $104 for Eclipse Target II or Eclipse Pro-Target II (disc. 2012).

The initial Custom Shop version of these pistols was mfg. during late 2001, featuring an ambidextrous thumb safety, and "Custom Shop" markings on left side of slide, 7,931 were mfg.

TLE II – 10mm (new 2012) or .45 ACP cal., 5 in. barrel, tactical law enforcement pistol (TLE) with exactly the same features as the Kimber pistols carried by LAPD SWAT, black oxide coated frame and slide, same features as Custom II, except has 30 LPI front strap checkering and night sights, approx. 38 oz. New 2003.

* ***Custom TLE II*** – .45 ACP cal., features 5 in. barrel, black finish, low-profile 3 dot sights, double diamond black synthetic grips, 38 oz.

MSR $1,080	$950	$825	$700	$625	$525	$425	$350

Add $61 for 10mm cal. (new 2013).
Add $274 for Crimson Trace laser grips (disc. 2010).

* ***Custom TLE/RL II*** – 10mm (new 2013) or .45 ACP cal., similar to Custom TLE II, except has Picatinny rail machined into the frame to accept optics and other tactical accessories. New 2003.

MSR $1,178	$1,050	$925	$825	$725	$600	$500	$425

Add $74 for 10mm cal. (new 2013).

* ***Stainless TLE II*** – .45 ACP cal., similar to TLE II, except has stainless steel slide and frame. New 2004.

MSR $1,211	$1,050	$925	$800	$725	$600	$500	$425

GRADING - PPGS™	100%	98%	95%	90%	80%	70%	60%	LAST MSR

* ***Stainless TLE/RL II*** – .45 ACP cal., similar to Custom TLE/RL II, except is stainless. New 2004.

MSR $1,322	$1,150	$975	$825	$750	$650	$550	$450	

* ***Pro TLE/RL II*** – .45 ACP cal., similar to Custom TLE/RL II, except has 4 in. bushingless bull barrel. New 2004.

MSR $1,248	$1,075	$950	$825	$725	$625	$525	$425	

* ***Pro TLE II (LG)*** – .45 ACP cal., similar to Custom TLE/RL II, except has 4 in. bushingless bull barrel and Crimson Trace laser grips (disc. 2008 only). Mfg. 2006-2008, reintroduced 2010.

MSR $1,150	$995	$850	$725	$650	$575	$500	$425	

Subtract $240 if w/o Crimson Trace laser grips (mfg. 2008 only).

* ***Stainless Pro TLE II*** – .45 ACP cal., similar to Pro TLE II, except is stainless steel, and Crimson Trace laser grips optional.

MSR $1,253	$1,075	$950	$825	$725	$625	$525	$425	

Add $265 for Crimson Trace laser grips.

* ***Stainless Pro TLE/RL II*** – .45 ACP cal., similar to Stainless TLE/RL II, except has 4 in. bushingless bull barrel. New 2004.

MSR $1,379	$1,225	$1,050	$900	$800	$700	$600	$475	

ULTRA TLE II – .45 ACP cal., 3 in. bull barrel, 7 shot mag., dovetail mounted night sights, matte black finish, aluminum frame. New 2010.

MSR $1,150	$950	$825	$700	$600	$500	$425	$350	

Add $243 for Crimson Trace laser grips.

* ***Stainless Ultra TLE II*** – .45 ACP cal., similar to Ultra TLE II, except is stainless steel. New 2010.

MSR $1,253	$1,075	$950	$825	$725	$625	$525	$425	

Add $265 for Crimson Trace laser grips.

TACTICAL II SERIES – 9mm Para. (Tactical Pro II, new 2004) or .45 ACP cal., lightweight tactical pistol, gray anodized (disc. 2008) or gray KimPro II finished frame with black steel slide, fixed tritium Meprolight 3-dot night sights, extended magazine well, 30 LPI front strap checkering, black/gray laminated logo grips, 7 shot mag. with bumper pad, available in Tactical Ultra II (3 in. barrel, short grip, 25 oz.), Tactical Pro II (4 in. barrel, standard grip, 28 oz.), Tactical Custom II (5 in. barrel, standard grip, 31 oz.). Tactical Custom HD II (.45 ACP only, new 2009), or Tactical Entry II (.45 ACP only, includes integral rail and night sights). New 2003.

MSR $1,317	$1,125	$975	$850	$725	$600	$525	$450	

Add $34 for Tactical Pro II in 9mm Para. cal.
Add $70 for Tactical Custom HD II.
Add $163 for Tactical Entry II.

A Custom Shop version of the Pro Tactical II was manufactured in 2002, but w/o checkering and night sights.

STAINLESS TEN II SERIES – .45 ACP cal., high capacity polymer frame, stainless steel slide with satin finish, impressed front grip strap checkering and serrations under trigger guard, textured finish, polymer grip safety and mainspring housing, 10 or 13 (new 2005) round double stack mag., includes Ultra Ten II (3 in. barrel, short grip, disc. 2003), Pro Carry Ten II (4 in. barrel, standard grip), Stainless Ten II (full size), and Gold Match Ten II (stainless steel barrel, polished stainless steel slide flats, hand fitted barrel/bushing to slide, adj. sight), 14 (pre-ban) round mags. also available, accepts magazines from older Kimber mfg. polymer pistols. Mfg. 2002-2007.

	$715	$625	$535	$485	$395	$320	$250	*$812*

Add $9 for Pro-Carry Ten II, $35 for Ultra Ten II (disc. 2003), or $294 for Gold Match Ten II.

* ***BP Ten II*** – similar to Stainless Ten II, except has black oxide carbon steel slide, and aluminum frame for lighter weight. Mfg. 2003-2007.

	$570	$500	$425	$385	$315	$255	$200	*$652*

GRADING - PPGS™	100%	98%	95%	90%	80%	70%	60%	LAST MSR

* ***Pro BP Ten II*** – similar to Pro Carry Ten II, except has black oxide carbon steel slide, and aluminum frame for lighter weight. Mfg. 2003-2007.

	$570	$500	$425	$385	$315	$255	$200	*$666*

CDP II (CUSTOM DEFENSE PACKAGE) SERIES – 9mm Para. (new 2008), .40 S&W (disc. 2007), or .45 ACP cal., Custom Shop pistol featuring tritium night sights, stainless steel slide with black anodized aluminum frame, 3 in. (Ultra CDP II, 25 oz.), Ultra+ (3-inch barrel with full length grip, new 2011), 4 in. (Pro CDP II and Compact CDP II, 28 oz.), or 5 in. (Custom CDP II, 31 oz.) barrel, carry bevel treatment, ambidextrous thumb safety, double diamond pattern checkered rosewood grips, 30 LPI checkered front strap and under trigger guard (new 2003), two-tone finish. New 2000.

MSR $1,331	$1,150	$1,000	$875	$775	$625	$525	$400

Add $28 for 9mm Para cal. (new 2008).
Add $300 for Crimson Trace laser grips (new 2010).
Add $40 for .40 S&W cal., available in either Ultra CDP II or Pro CDP II configuration (disc. 2007).

The Pro CDP II has a full length grip frame.

This series' nomenclature added the Roman numeral "II" during 2001.

ULTRA TEN II CDP – .45 ACP cal., tritium night sights, stainless steel slide with black polymer frame, 3 in. barrel, carry bevel treatment, standard manual safety, 10 shot mag., 24 oz. Mfg. 2003 only.

	$825	$720	$620	$560	$455	$370	$290	*$926*

RAPTOR II – .45 ACP cal., full size carbon steel or stainless steel (new 2008) frame with "scales" on front strap, continuing on slide in lieu of standard serrations, flats on frame and slide polished, black oxide finish, back cut flattop, 5 in. stainless barrel with engraved "Raptor II" and "Custom Shop", black anodized trigger, ambidextrous safety, scaled Zebra wood grip panels with Kimber logo, fixed slant night sights, 38 oz. New mid-2004.

MSR $1,434	$1,250	$1,075	$925	$800	$700	$600	$475

Add $134 for stainless steel frame (new 2008).

PRO RAPTOR II – .45 ACP cal., full size stainless steel frame with "scales" on front strap, continuing on carbon steel slide in lieu of standard serrations, flats on frame and slide polished, black oxide finish, back cut flattop, 4 in. stainless barrel with engraved "Pro Raptor II" and "Custom Shop", black anodized trigger, ambidextrous safety, scaled Zebra wood grip panels with Kimber logo, fixed slant night sights, 38 oz. New mid-2004.

MSR $1,295	$1,100	$975	$850	$725	$600	$500	$450

Add $120 for Stainless Pro Rapter II (new 2009).

ULTRA RAPTOR II – .45 ACP cal., all-matte black finish, 3 in. ramped bushingless barrel, lightweight aluminum frame, lizard scale serrations on flat-top slide and frontstrap, feathered logo wood grips, flats on frame and slide polished, night sights, mfg. by Custom Shop. New 2006.

MSR $1,295	$1,100	$975	$850	$725	$600	$525	$450

Add $120 for Stainless Ultra Raptor II.

GRAND RAPTOR II – .45 ACP cal., full-size stainless steel frame, blued slide, flats on frame and slide polished, two-tone finish, lizard scale rosewood grips with Kimber logo, extended ambidextrous thumb safety, bumped beavertail grip safety, night sights, mfg. by Custom Shop. New 2006.

MSR $1,657	$1,425	$1,250	$1,050	$925	$800	$675	$525

WARRIOR – .45 ACP cal., production began following adoption of this pistol by the Marine Expeditionary Unit (MEU) Special Operations Capable (SOC), Detachment 1 (Det. 1), civilian version with 5 in. barrel, Series I (no firing pin block), carbon steel slide and frame, integral Picatinny light rail, internal extractor, lanyard loop, bumped grip safety, G-10 material grip (coyote brown), wedge night sights, ambidextrous safety, GI length (standard) guide rod finished in black KimPro II, 38 oz. New mid-2004.

MSR $1,512	$1,325	$1,150	$975	$850	$725	$600	$550

GRADING - PPGS™	100%	98%	95%	90%	80%	70%	60%	LAST MSR

* ***Warrior SOC*** – .45 ACP cal., tan/green KimPro11 finish, features lower front rail with removable Desert tan Crimson Trace Rail Master laser sight, ambidextrous thumb safety, lanyard ring, textured G10 grips, 40 oz. New 2013.

MSR $1,665	$1,495	$1,300	$1,100	$1,025	$900	$775	$650	

DESERT WARRIOR – .45 ACP cal., similar to Warrior, except has Dark Earth KimPro II metal finish and light tan G-10 grips. New mid-2005.

MSR $1,512	$1,325	$1,125	$950	$825	$700	$600	$500	

COVERT II SERIES – .45 ACP cal., 3 (Ultra Covert II), 4 (Pro Covert II), or 5 (Custom Covert II) in. bushingless barrel in 3 and 4 in. models, Custom Covert II has Kimber logo and digital camo pattern, carry bevel treatment, 30 LPI front strap checkering, night sights, Desert Tan finish, matte black oxide slide, approx. 25-30 oz. New 2007.

MSR $1,657	$1,400	$1,225	$1,025	$925	$750	$625	$475	

KPD – while advertised during 2006-2007, this model never went into production.

SIS SERIES – .45 ACP cal., stainless steel slide, frame, and serrated mainspring housing, 7 or 8 shot mag., 3 (Ultra), 4 (Pro), or 5 (Custom or Custom RL) in. barrel, SIS Night Sight, cocking shoulder for one-hand cocking, lightweight hammer, solid trigger, slide serrations, gray KimPro II finish, beavertail grip safety, stippled black laminate logo grips, ambidextrous thumb safety, choice of rounded frame and mainspring housing (SIS Ultra), Picatinny rail (SIS Pro & Custom RL), standard length guide rod (Custom & Custom RL), 31-39 oz. Mfg. 2008-2009.

	$1,250	$1,095	$935	$850	$685	$560	$435	*$1,427*

Add $95 for SIS Custom RL model with standard length guide rod and Picatinny rail.

AEGIS II SERIES – 9mm Para. cal., 3 (Ultra), 4 (Pro), or 5 (Custom) in. barrel, 8 or 9 shot mag., aluminum frame w/satin silver premium KimPro II finish, matte black slide, thin rosewood grips, 30 LPI front strap checkering, high relief cut under trigger guard, Tactical Wedge night sights, bumped and grooved grip safety, hammer, thumb safety and mag. release button are bobbed, carry melt treatment on both frame and slide, 25 oz. New 2006.

MSR $1,331	$1,125	$975	$850	$725	$625	$525	$450	

ULTRA RCP II – .45 ACP cal., (Refined Carry Pistol), black anodized frame, carry melt treatment, matte black slide with premium KimPro II finish, no sights, bobbed mag. release, hammer, beavertail grip safety and thumb safety, round mainspring housing and rear of frame, thin black micarta grip panels, older mfg. had distinctive "hook" on hammer, new mfg. has straight hammer, 25 oz. Mfg. 2003-2005 by Custom Shop, reintroduced 2007.

MSR $1,351	$1,150	$975	$850	$725	$600	$525	$450	

CRIMSON CARRY II – .45 ACP cal., satin silver aluminum frame, 3 (Ultra), 4 (Pro), or 5 (Custom) in. barrel, matte black slide with black sights, shortened slide stop pin, beveled frame, rosewood Crimson Trace laser grips. New mid-2008.

MSR $1,206	$1,050	$900	$800	$700	$600	$500	$400	

Add $87 for Crimson Trace laser grips with green beam (new 2013).

Pistols: Kimber Non-Cataloged Models

Over the past several years, Kimber has manufactured a number of pistols that did not appear in their catalog. To help identify non-cataloged models, pistols are listed in two categories: Custom Shop/Special Edition Pistols and Limited Edition Pistols.

Pistols: Kimber Custom Shop/Special Editions

Beginning in 1998, the Kimber Custom Shop began producing special edition pistols. Special edition models have been issued in either fixed numbers, or time limited. Where available, time limited models show the actual number produced. All models are .45 ACP caliber unless otherwise specified.

ROYAL CARRY – compact aluminum frame, 4 in. bushingless barrel, highly polished blue, night sights, ambidextrous safety, hand checkered rosewood grips, 28 oz. 600 mfg. 1998.

Last MSR was $903.

GRADING - PPGS™	100%	98%	95%	90%	80%	70%	60%	LAST MSR

GOLD GUARDIAN – highly polished stainless steel slide and frame, hand fitted 5 in. match barrel and bushing, tritium night sights, ambidextrous safety, extended magazine well, skeletonized match trigger, hand checkered rosewood grips, 38 oz. 300 mfg. 1998.

Last MSR was $1,350.

ELITE CARRY – black anodized compact aluminum frame, stainless slide, 4 in. barrel, meltdown treatment on slide and frame, tritium night sights, 20 LPI checkered front strap, ambidextrous safety, aluminum match trigger, hand checkered rosewood grips, 28 oz. 1,200 mfg. 1998.

Last MSR was $1,019.

STAINLESS COVERT – meltdown stainless slide and frame finished in silver KimPro, 4 in. barrel, 30 LPI front strap checkering, 3-dot tritium night sights, hand checkered rosewood grips, 34 oz. 1,000 mfg. 1999.

Last MSR was $1,135.

PRO ELITE – aluminum frame with silver KimPro finish, stainless slide with black KimPro finish, full meltdown treatment on slide and frame, 4 in. barrel, 30 LPI front strap checkering, 3-dot tritium night sights, hand checkered rosewood grips, 28 oz. 2,500 mfg. 1999.

Last MSR was $1,140.

ULTRA ELITE – aluminum frame with black KimPro finish, satin stainless slide, full meltdown treatment on slide and frame, 3 in. barrel, 30 LPI front strap checkering, 3-dot tritium night sights, hand checkered rosewood grips, 25 oz. 2,750 mfg. 1999.

Last MSR was $1,085.

HERITAGE EDITION – black oxide steel frame and slide, 30 LPI front strap checkering,ambidextrous safety, premium aluminum trigger, NSSF Heritage medallion and special markings on slide, ser. no. begins with KHE, 38 oz. 1,041 mfg. 2000.

Last MSR was $1,065.

STAINLESS GOLD MATCH SE II – .38 Super or .45 ACP cal., stainless steel frame and slide, 5 in. barrel, serrated flat-top slide, 30 LPI front strap checkering, hand checkered rosewood grips, ambidextrous safety, polished flats, ser. no. begins with KSO, 38 oz. 260 (.38 Super) and 294 (.45 ACP) mfg. 2001.

Last MSR was $1,487.

Add $88 for .38 Super cal.

ULTRA SHADOW II – black steel slide and anodized aluminum frame, 3 in. barrel, fixed tritium night sights, 30 LPI front strap checkering, grey laminate grips, silver grip and thumb safeties and mainspring housing, ser. no. begins with KUSLE, 25 oz.

Last MSR was $949.

PRO SHADOW II – black steel slide and anodized aluminum frame, 4 in. barrel, fixed tritium night sights, 30 LPI front strap checkering, grey laminate grips, silver grip and thumb safeties and mainspring housing, ser. no. begins with KPSLE, 28 oz.

Last MSR was $949.

ULTRA CDP ELITE II – .45 ACP cal., first Kimber .45 pistols with ramped match grade barrels, black anodized aluminum frame, black oxide carbon steel slide, 3 in. barrel, carry melt treatment for rounded and blended edges, Meprolight 3-dot tritium night sights, 30 LPI checkering on front strap and under trigger guard, ambidextrous thumb safety and charcoal/ruby laminated logo grips, 25 oz. Mfg. 2002-Jan., 2003.

Last MSR was $1,216.

ULTRA CDP ELITE STS II – .45 ACP cal., first Kimber .45 pistols with ramped match grade barrels, silver anodized aluminum frame, satin stainless steel slide, 3 in. barrel, carry melt treatment for rounded and blended edges, Meprolight 3-dot tritium night sights, 30 LPI checkering on front strap and under trigger guard, ambidextrous thumb safety and charcoal/ruby laminated logo grips, 25 oz. Mfg. 2002-Jan. 2003.

Last MSR was $1,155.

ULTRA SP II – special anodized frame colors (black/blue, black/red, and black/silver) with black oxide slide, 7 shot mag., 3 in. bushingless barrel, 3-dot sights, carry melt, ball milled micarta grips, standard fixed sights, 25 oz. Mfg. 2003-2005.

	100%	98%	95%	90%	80%	70%	60%	LAST MSR
	$1,025	$900	$800	$725	$625	$575	$495	*$1,175*

GRADING - PPGS™	100%	98%	95%	90%	80%	70%	60%	LAST MSR

25th ANNIVERSARY CUSTOM LIMITED EDITION – .45 ACP cal., black oxide frame and slide, 5 in. barrel, premium aluminum trigger, fancy walnut anniversary logo grips, "1979-2004" engraving on slide, Series I safeties and traditional extractor, ser. no. range is KAPC0001-KAPC1911. Limited production of 1,911 during 2004-2005.

	100%	98%	95%	90%	80%	70%	60%	LAST MSR
	$825	$725	$650	$575	$500	$425	$350	*$923*

* ***25th Anniversary Custom Limited Edition Gold Match*** – blued frame and slide, deep polish on flats, 5 in. stainless barrel, premium aluminum trigger, ambidextrous safety, adj. sights, fancy walnut anniversary logo grips, "1979-2004" engraving in slide, Series I safeties and traditional extractor, ser. no. range KAPG0001-KAPG0500, 38 oz. Limited production of 500 during 2004-2005.

	100%	98%	95%	90%	80%	70%	60%	LAST MSR
	$1,175	$995	$875	$775	$700	$625	$550	*$1,357*

* ***25th Anniversary Custom Limited Edition Pistol Set*** – includes one Custom (ser. no. range KMSC0001-KMSC250) and one Gold Match (ser. no. range KMSG0001 - KMSG250), matched ser. nos., wood presentation case. Limited production of 250 during 2004-2005.

	100%	98%	95%	90%	80%	70%	60%	LAST MSR
	$2,250	$2,000	$1,775	$1,525	$1,300	$1,100	$900	*$2,620*

CENTENNIAL EDITION – .45 ACP cal., steel frame with finish by Turnbull Restoration, ivory grips, adj. target sights, light scroll engraving, aluminum trigger, includes presentation case, Limited mfg. of 250 during 2010.

	100%	98%	95%	90%	80%	70%	60%	LAST MSR
	$3,995	$3,650	$3,275	N/A	N/A	N/A	N/A	*$4,352*

SAPPHIRE ULTRA II – 9mm Para. cal., 3 in. barrel, G10 grips, polished stainless steel slide and small parts feature a bright blue PVD finish with fine engraved border accents, rounded heel, ambidextrous thumb safety, Tactical Wedge nightsights. New 2012.

	100%	98%	95%	90%	80%	70%	60%
MSR $1,652	$1,425	$1,200	$1,000	$875	$750	$650	$550

Pistols: Kimber Limited Editions

Kimber has produced limited runs of pistols for dealer groups, NRA Events, sporting goods stores, law enforcement agencies, special requests, etc. Limited run pistols can be as small as 25 mfg.

PRO CARRY SLE – all stainless steel slide and frame, 4 in. barrel, identicial to Stainless Pro Carry Model, except has stainless frame, mfg. for Kimber Master Dealers, cataloged in 2001, later production known as Pro Carry HD II, 1,329 mfg. during 2000.

Last MSR was $815.

PRO COMBAT – black oxide stainless steel frame and slide, 4 in. barrel, ambidextrous safety, tritium 3-dot night sights, match grade aluminum trigger, 30 LPI front strap checkering, hand checkered rosewood grips, 35 oz. Marketed by RGuns. 52 mfg. 2000.

Last MSR was $860.

TARGET ELITE II – two-tone stainless frame and slide, black oxide coating on frame, slide natural stainless, adj. rear sight, rosewood double diamond grips, sold through stores affiliated with Sports Inc. buying group, 38 oz. 220 mfg. 2001.

Last MSR was $950.

CUSTOM DEFENDER II – two-tone stainless frame and slide, black oxide coating on frame, slide natural stainless, fixed low profile rear sight, double diamond rosewood grips, sold only through stores affiliated with National Buying Service, 38 oz. 290 mfg. 2001.

Last MSR was $839.

CUSTOM ECLIPSE II – stainless slide and frame, 5 in. barrel, black oxide finish brush polished on the flats, 30 LPI front strap checkering, adj. night sights, laminated grey grips, ser. no. begins with KEL, 38 oz. 4,522 mfg. 2001.

Last MSR was $1,121.

PRO ECLIPSE II – stainless steel frame and slide, 4 in. barrel, black oxide finish brush polished on the flats, 30 LPI front strap checkering, fixed 3-dot night sights, laminated grey grips, ambidextrous safety, ser. no. begins with KRE, 35 oz. 2,207 mfg. 2001.

Last MSR was $1,065.

GRADING - PPGS™	100%	98%	95%	90%	80%	70%	60%	LAST MSR

ULTRA ECLIPSE II – stainless steel frame and slide, 3 in. barrel, black oxide finish brush polished on the flats, 30 LPI front strap checkering, fixed 3-dot night sights, laminated grey grips, ambidextrous safety, 34 oz. 1,202 mfg. 2001.

Last MSR was $1,054.

STRYKER TEN II – Ultra Ten II with black polymer frame and frame insert and small parts, natural stainless slide, 25 oz. 200 mfg. 2002.

Last MSR was $850.

LAPD SWAT – black oxide coated stainless frame and slide, 5 in. barrel, low profile Meprolight 3-dot night sights, 30 LPI front strap checkering, black rubber double diamond grips, 38 oz. 300 mfg. 2002.

Following extensive testing to select a duty pistol, LAPD SWAT chose a Kimber Stainless Custom II and had it enhanced to their specifications. This model was made strictly for law enforcement and not sold to the public. A civilian version called the Tactical law Enforcement (TLE) Series went into production in 2003.

NRA EPOCH II – stainless slide and frame, 5 in. barrel, black oxide finish brush polished on flats, 30 LPI front strap checkering, standard safety, fixed tritium night sights, laminated grey grips, ser. no. begins with KNRAE, Friends of NRA pistol available only at NRA banquets, 38 oz. 58 mfg. 2002.

This model had no established MSR.

THE BOSS II – limited edition to commemorate Blythe Sports 50th anniversary, stainless steel slide and frame, carry melt treatment, fixed white dot sights, premium aluminum 2 hole trigger, 5 in. barrel, engraved "The BOSS II" on ejection port side, and "SPECIAL EDITION", black and sliver laminate grips with Blythe 50th anniversary logo in center on white insert, ser. no. KBSS000-KBSS024, 25 mfg.

This model had no established MSR.

ECLIPSE CLE II – 5 in. barrel, Eclipse Custom II finish on slide with black over stainless frame (no front strap checkering), charcoal/ruby Kimber logo grips, sold only through stores affiliated with National Buying Service, 38 oz. 271 mfg. 2003.

Last MSR was $917.

* ***Eclipse PLE II*** – similar to Eclipse CLE II, except has 4 in. bushingless barrel, sold only through stores affiliated with Sports Inc. buying group, 35 oz. 232 mfg. 2003.

Last MSR was $877.

* ***Eclipse ULE II*** – Eclipse Ultra II finish on slide with black over stainless frame (no front strap checkering), 3 in. bushingless barrel, charcoal/ruby Kimber logo grips, sold only through stores affiliated with National Buying Service, 34 oz. 227 mfg. 2003.

Last MSR was $890.

TEAM MATCH II 38 SUPER – .38 Super cal., identical to original Team Match II, with .38 Super ramped barrel, match grade chamber, bushing and trigger group, special Team Match features, including 30 LPI checkered front strap, adj. sight, extended magazine well, premium aluminum trigger and red, white, and blue USA Shooting Team logo grips, 38 oz. Mfg. 2003-2004.

$1,150	$995	$875	$775	$675	$575	$475	*$1,352*

MCSOCOM ICQB (2004) – .45 ACP cal., at the request of the Marine Corps Special Operations Command (MCSOCOM) Detachment 1 (Det. 1), Kimber produced Interim Close Quarters Battle (ICQB) 1911 patterned pistols in accordance with very high specific requirements: steel frame and slide finished in matte black, internal extractor, GI length guide rod and plug, light rail, bumped grip safety and ambidextrous manual safety, lanyard loop, Simonich G-10 "Gunner" grips, and Novak Lo-Mount night sights.

There was no MSR on this model, as it was not available for sale to the general public.

The civilian version of this pistol is called the Warrior.

TARGET MATCH – .45 ACP cal., oversized 5 in. stainless steel barrel, matte black frame and slide with brush polished flats, high relief cut under trigger guard, wide cocking serrations,

GRADING - PPGS™	100%	98%	95%	90%	80%	70%	60%	LAST MSR

solid match trigger, engraved bullseye inlaid burl walnut logo grips, 30 LPI checkering on front strap and under trigger guard, special ser. no. starting with "KTM", 38 oz. 1,000 mfg. 2006-2009.

	$1,215	$1,025	$875	$775	$700	$600	$500	*$1,427*

CLASSIC TARGET II – .45 ACP cal., two-tone stainless steel frame, matte black oxide slide, no cocking serrations, adj. sights, premium match grade trigger, smooth/stippled logo grips, match grade chamber, barrel, and barrel bushing, 38 oz. Sold exclusively through Gander Mountain. Mfg. 2006-2008.

	$825	$675	$555	$460	$395	$350	$300	*$999*

FRANKLIN CUSTOM II – similar to Custom II, silver finished slide stop, bushing, mag. release, grip safety and mainspring housing, red, white and blue laminate grips with Franklin's Gun Shop logo, commemorates 44th anniversary of Franklin's Gun Shop, ser. no. KFGS01 - KFGS50, 50 mfg. 2006.

This model had no established MSR.

RIFLES: BOLT ACTION

Rimfire Models, Repeating and Single Shot

A three position Win. Model 70 type safety became a standard feature on all Kimber .22 LR and .17 Mach 2 cal. rifles in early 2004.

HUNTER – .17 Mach 2 (new 2007) or .22 LR cal., similar to Classic, except has grade A walnut, clear stock finish, straight barrel contour, 6.7 lbs. Mfg. 2002-2007.

	$715	$595	$515	$455	$400	$350	$300	*$863*

Add $40 for .17 Mach 2 cal.

YOUTH – .22 LR cal., similar to Hunter, except has 12 1/4 in. LOP.

While this model was cataloged during 2002-2003 with an MSR of $746, it never went into production.

CLASSIC – .22 LR cal., Mauser claw extractor with 2 position Model 70 type safety, unique eccentric bolt that allows a "centerfire-type" firing pin for faster lock time and greater strength, AA walnut sporter stock with 20 LPI 4-point panel checkering and hand rubbed oil finish, 22 in. match grade sporter barrel with match chamber and Custom Sporter contour, 5 shot mag., steel grip cap, pillar bedding, bead blasted blue finish, adj. trigger, approx. 6 1/2 lbs. Mfg. 1999-2007.

	$1,025	$875	$765	$655	$550	$450	$350	*$1,223*

Through 2002, all Kimber .22 cal. Classic rifles had an A grade claro walnut stock, 2-point checkering pattern, urethane finish, and straight barrel taper contour.

* ***Classic Varmint*** – .17 Mach 2 (new mid-2004) or .22 LR cal., similar to Classic, except has A Grade walnut and 20 in. stainless fluted barrel in a heavy sporter contour. Mfg. 2003-2007.

	$975	$825	$725	$600	$500	$425	$375	*$1,125*

* ***Classic Pro Varmint*** – .17 Mach 2 (new mid-2004) or .22 LR cal., similar to Classic Varmint, except has grey laminate uncheckered stock, brush polished stainless 20 in. barrel with black flutes. Mfg. 2004-2007.

	$995	$850	$760	$655	$550	$450	$350	*$1,182*

Add $46 for .17 Mach 2 cal.

* ***Custom Classic*** – .22 LR cal., similar to Classic, except has 24 LPI wrap checkering, ebony forend tip and AAA walnut stock, 6 1/2 lbs. Mfg. 2003-2007.

	$1,375	$1,150	$900	$775	$650	$550	$475	*$1,607*

SUPERAMERICA MODEL – .22 LR cal., top-of-the-line model with AAA claro walnut with 24 LPI full wrap checkering, highly polished blue finish, hand rubbed oil finish, Custom Sporter barrel contour, ebony forend tip, cheekpiece and black recoil pad, 5 shot mag., 6 1/2 lbs. Limited mfg. 2001-2007.

	$1,675	$1,375	$1,100	$925	$825	$700	$600	*$1,988*

Through 2001, all Superamerica rifles had urethane finish and straight taper barrel contour.

GRADING - PPGS™	100%	98%	95%	90%	80%	70%	60%	LAST MSR

* ***SuperAmerica Model Custom Match 25th Anniversary Ltd. Ed.*** – .22 LR cal., similar to SuperAmerica model, except has AAA French walnut stock, black oxide matte finish barrel and receiver, steel buttplate, engraved grip cap, specially marked barrel and jeweled bolt. Limited production of 300 sequentially numbered rifles during 2004-2005.

	$2,325	$2,000	$1,700	$1,400	$1,100	$900	$750	*$2,852*

SVT (SHORT VARMINT/TARGET) MODEL – .17 Mach 2 (new mid-2004) or .22 LR cal., 18 in. fluted stainless steel bull barrel, uncheckered grey laminate wood stock with high comb target design, matte blue action and satin stainless steel barrel, 5 shot mag., no sights, 7 1/2 lbs. Mfg. 1999-2007.

	$945	$800	$700	$575	$475	$375	$300	*$1,073*

Add $52 for .17 Mach 2 cal.

HS (HUNTER SILHOUETTE) MODEL – .22 LR cal., features 24 in. half-fluted medium sporter match grade barrel w/o sights, checkered walnut high comb Monte Carlo stock with clear stock finish, adj. trigger, matte blue finish, 7 lbs. Mfg. 1999-2007.

	$850	$700	$585	$515	$425	$350	$275	*$976*

Through 2001, all HS Models had urethane finish.

MODEL 82C CLASSIC – .22 LR cal., 22 in. barrel, drilled and tapped receiver, repeater with 4 shot mag., checkered A claro walnut stock, polished and blue metal, 6 1/2 lbs. Mfg. 1995-99.

	$775	$625	$550	$475	$400	$360	$330	*$917*

The C suffix on this model designates manufacture by Kimber of America.

* ***Model 82C Classic Stainless*** – .22 LR cal., features stainless steel barrel with matte blue action. Approx. 600 mfg. 1997-98.

	$800	$650	$565	$470	$400	$345	$295	*$968*

* ***Model 82C Classic Stainless Varmint*** – .22 LR cal., features 20 in. fluted stainless steel barrel, A claro walnut with 18 LPI side panel checkering. Approx. 1,000 mfg. 1995-98.

	$825	$675	$575	$500	$425	$350	$275	*$1,002*

MODEL 82C SVT – .22 LR cal., single shot, features 18 in. fluted heavy stainless barrel with uncheckered high comb target style walnut stock, matte blue action, 7 1/2 lbs. Mfg. 1997 only.

	$675	$550	$495	$425	$375	$315	$270	*$825*

SVT designates Short Varmint/Target.

MODEL 82C HS – while advertised during 1997, this model never went into production.

MODEL 82C SUPERAMERICA – .22 LR cal., 22 in. drilled and tapped barrel, 4 shot mag., AAA claro checkered walnut stock with steel pistol grip cap, polished and blue metal, 6 1/2 lbs. Mfg. 1993-99.

	$1,275	$995	$875	$750	$650	$575	$400	*$1,488*

MODEL 82C CUSTOM MATCH – .22 LR cal., features AA French walnut with 22 LPI wraparound checkering, steel Neidner-style buttplate, matte rust blue finish. Mfg. 1995-99.

	$1,900	$1,525	$1,225	$975	$775	$650	$525	*$2,158*

MODEL 82C SUPER CLASSIC – .22 LR cal., features AAA claro walnut with 18 LPI side panel checkering, polished and blue metal. Mfg. 1995-96.

	$975	$875	$775	$675	$600	$550	$450	*$1,090*

Centerfire Models

The models listed feature a Mauser style action with controlled round feeding and extraction.

MODEL 84C SINGLE SHOT CLASSIC – while advertised during 1996-97, this model never went into production.

MODEL 84C SINGLE SHOT SUPERAMERICA – while advertised during 1996-97, this model never went into production.

MODEL 84C SINGLE SHOT VARMINT STAINLESS – while advertised during 1997, this model never went into production.

GRADING - PPGS™	100%	98%	95%	90%	80%	70%	60%	LAST MSR

MODEL 84C SINGLE SHOT VARMINT – .17 Rem. or .223 Rem. cal., features 24 (first 200 rifles only), or 25 in. stainless match grade fluted barrel with recessed crown, matte blue receiver finish, checkered A claro walnut stock with beavertail forend, 7 1/2 lbs. Mfg. 1997-99.

	$895	$785	$675	$610	$495	$400	$315	*$1,032*

Add $150 for .17 Rem. cal. (less than 100 mfg.).

MODEL 84L CLASSIC – .270 Win., .25-06 Rem. (disc.) or .30-06 Springfield cal., similar to Model 84M Classic. New 2010.

MSR $1,223	$1,025	$875	$750	$650	$550	$450	$395	

* ***Model 84L Classic Select Grade*** – .25-06 Rem., .270 Win., .280 Ack Imp. (new 2011), .30-06 Springfield, or .35 Whelen (new 2012) cal.

MSR $1,427	$1,250	$1,050	$900	$800	$700	$600	$500	

* ***Model 84L Classic Stainless Select Grade*** – .25-06 Rem., .270 Win., .280 Ack. Imp., or .30-06 Springfield cal. New 2012.

MSR $1,495	$1,250	$1,050	$900	$800	$700	$600	$500	

* ***Model 84L Montana*** – .25-06 Rem., .270 Win., .280 Ack. Imp., or .30-06 Springfield cal., similar to Montana 84M. New 2011.

MSR $1,359	$1,175	$1,000	$875	$775	$675	$575	$450	

MODEL 84M – .22-250 Rem., .204 Ruger (new 2004), .223 Rem. (new 2004), .243 Win. (new 2004), .260 Rem., .308 Win., or 7mm-08 Rem. cal., true Mauser action, much improved version of the Model 84C, longer and stronger receiver, 2 position Model 70 type safety, match grade barrel and trigger, 3-5 shot mag., walnut or laminated stock with sculpted steel floorplate. New 2001.

A three position Win. Model 70 type safety became a standard feature on all Kimber 84M rifles in early 2004.

* ***Model 84M Classic*** – .22-250 Rem. (disc.), .223 Rem. (mfg. 2009-2011), .243 Win., .260 Rem. (disc. 2009), .308 Win., 7mm-08 Rem., or .338 Federal (mfg. 2007-2011) cal., 22 in. light sporter barrel, checkered walnut stock and forend, 5 lbs. 10 oz. New 2001.

MSR $1,223	$1,025	$875	$750	$650	$550	$450	$395	

* ***Model 84M Classic Stainless*** – .243 Win., .308 Win., or 7mm-08 Rem. cal., stainless steel action and barrel.

	$1,025	$875	$750	$650	$550	$450	$395	*$1,223*

* ***Model 84M Classic Select Grade*** – .223 Rem., .243 Win., .25-06 Rem. (disc.), .257 Roberts, 7mm-08 Rem., or .308 Win. cal., features checkered Claro or French (disc. 2007) walnut stock. New 2006.

MSR $1,427	$1,250	$1,050	$900	$800	$700	$600	$500	

Add $164 for Classic Select Grade with French walnut (mfg. 2006-2007).

* ***Model 84M Classic Stainless Select Grade*** – .243 Win., 7mm-08 Rem., or .308 Win. cal., stainless steel action and barrel. New 2012.

MSR $1,495	$1,295	$1,075	$925	$825	$725	$625	$500	

* ***Model 84M LongMaster Classic*** – .223 Rem., .243 Win. (disc. 2007), or .308 Win. cal., 24 in. heavy stainless steel fluted barrel, 7 lbs. 5 oz. New 2002.

MSR $1,291	$1,125	$995	$875	$750	$650	$550	$425	

* ***Model 84M LongMaster VT*** – .22-250 Rem. cal. only, 26 in. stainless bull match grade barrel, match grade trigger, 5 shot mag. with sculpted steel floorplate, grey/black laminate target stock with high comb and extended pistol grip, 10 lbs. New 2001.

MSR $1,427	$1,175	$995	$850	$725	$600	$500	$450	

* ***Model 84M SVT*** – .223 Rem cal., short barrel variation of the Model 84M Longmaster VT.

MSR $1,427	$1,175	$995	$850	$725	$600	$500	$450	

GRADING - PPGS™	100%	98%	95%	90%	80%	70%	60%	LAST MSR

* ***Model 84M Varmint*** – .204 Ruger or .22-250 Rem. cal., features 26 in. heavy stainless steel fluted barrel, 7 lbs. 5 oz. New 2001.

MSR $1,291	$1,125	$995	$875	$750	$650	$550	$425	

* ***Model 84M Pro Varmint*** – .204 Ruger, .22-250 Rem., or .223 Rem. cal., grey laminate uncheckered stock, brush polished 24 in. stainless steel barrel with black flutes. New 2004.

MSR $1,427	$1,175	$995	$850	$725	$600	$500	$450	

MODEL 84M SUPERAMERICA – .223 Rem. (disc. 2009), .243 Win. (disc. 2009), .260 Rem. (disc. 2009), 7mm-08 Rem., .308 Win., or .338 Federal (disc. 2009) cal., similar to Model 84M Repeater, except has 24 LPI wrap checkering, ebony forend tip, AAA walnut, highly polished blue action and barrel. New 2003.

MSR $2,240	$1,925	$1,700	$1,450	$1,275	$1,025	$875	$750	

MODEL 84M MONTANA – .204 Ruger (new 2009), .223 Rem. (new 2009), .243 Win., .257 Roberts (new 2008), .260 Rem. (disc. 2009), 7mm-08 Rem., .308 Win., or .338 Federal (mfg. 2007-2011) cal., synthetic stock and satin stainless steel barreled action, 5 lbs. 2 oz. New 2003.

MSR $1,359	$1,175	$1,000	$875	$775	$675	$575	$450	

Add $248 for Montana Black KimPro in .308 Win. cal. only (disc.).

MODEL 84M/L MOUNTAIN ASCENT – .270 Win., .280 Ack. Imp., .30-06, or .308 Win. cal., 84 M (.308 Win. cal. only) or 84L action, ultra lightweight model with 22 in. fluted barrel, satin stainless steel barreled action, Kevlar/carbon fiber stock with Gore Optifade Open Country Concealment finish, fluted bolt and bolt handle, hollow bolt knob, removable muzzle brake, Talley lightweight matte black one inch ring mounts, full length Mauser claw extractor, three position safety, 4 lbs. 13 oz. New 2012.

MSR $2,040	$1,800	$1,600	$1,400	$1,200	$1,000	$850	$700	

MODEL 84M LONGMASTER PRO – .22-250 Rem. or .308 Win. cal., similar to Longmaster VT, except has synthetic stock, 24 (.308 Win. cal.) or 26 (.22-250 Rem. cal.) in. brush polished stainless bull barrel with black flutes.

While this model was cataloged during 2003 with an MSR of $1,189, it never went into production.

MODEL 84M LPT (LIGHT POLICE TACTICAL) – .223 Rem. or .308 Win. cal., 24 in. matte blue heavy sporter contour fluted barrel, 5 shot mag., black laminate stock with panel stippling, Picatinny rail, oversize bolt handle, sling swivels, recoil pad, full length Mauser claw extractor, 3-position Model 70 style safety, adj. trigger, 8 lbs., 7 oz. New 2008.

MSR $1,495	$1,295	$1,075	$925	$825	$725	$625	$500	

MODEL 84M LIMITED EDITION – .257 Roberts or .308 Win. cal., Classic Select Grade French walnut stock and forearm, limited mfg. Mfg. 2010-2011.

	$1,575	$1,375	$1,175	N/A	N/A	N/A	N/A	*$1,767*

MODEL 8400 CLASSIC – .25-06 Rem. (mfg. 2006-2009), .270 WSM, .270 Win. (mfg. 2006-2009), 7mm Rem. Mag. (mfg. 2009-2011), 7mm WSM (disc. 2009), .300 WSM, .300 Win. Mag. (new 2006), .30-06 (mfg. 2006-2009), .325 WSM (mfg. 2005-2011), or .338 Win. Mag. (mfg. 2006-2011) cal., a walnut stock, 20 LPI panel checkering, 3-position Model 70 type safety, 24 in. sporter match grade blue barrel, match grade adj. trigger. New 2003.

MSR $1,223	$1,025	$875	$750	$650	$550	$450	$395	

While a left-hand version of this model was cataloged during 2003, they were never produced.

* ***Model 8400 Classic Stainless*** – .270 WSM, or .300 WSM cal., stainless steel action and slide. Disc. 2011.

	$1,025	$875	$750	$650	$550	$450	$395	*$1,223*

* ***Model 8400 Classic Select Grade*** – .270 WSM, .300 WSM, or .325 WSM (disc.), 7mm Rem. Mag., .300 Win. Mag., or .338 Win. Mag. cal., Claro or French (disc. 2007) walnut finish. New 2006.

MSR $1,427	$1,250	$1,050	$900	$800	$700	$600	$500	

GRADING - PPGS™	100%	98%	95%	90%	80%	70%	60%	LAST MSR

* ***Model 8400 Classic Stainless Select Grade*** – .270 WSM, .300 WSM, .300 Win. Mag., or .338 Win. Mag. cal., stainless steel action and slide. New 2012.

MSR $1,495	$1,295	$1,075	$925	$825	$725	$625	$500	

MODEL 8400 SUPERAMERICA – .270 Win. (mfg. 2009), .30-06 (mfg. 2009), .270 WSM, 7mm WSM (disc. 2009), .300 WSM, .300 Win. Mag. (new 2006), .325 WSM (mfg. 2005-2009), or .338 Win. Mag. (new 2006) cal., similar to Model 8400 Classic, except has AAA walnut stock, 24 LPI panel checkering, ebony forend tip, highly polished blue action, and 24 in. custom sporter barrel. New 2003.

MSR $2,240	$1,925	$1,700	$1,450	$1,275	$1,025	$875	$750	

MODEL 8400 MONTANA – .25-06 Rem. (mfg. 2006-2009), .270 Win. (mfg. 2006-2009), .270 WSM, .280 Ackley Improved (disc. 2009), 7mm WSM (disc. 2009), .300 WSM, .300 Win. Mag. (new 2006), .30-06 (mfg. 2006-2009), .325 WSM (mfg. 2005-2011) or .338 Win. Mag. (new 2006) cal., similar to Model 8400 Classic, except has synthetic stock and 24 or 26 in. satin stainless steel custom sporter barrel, 6 lbs., 2 oz. New 2003.

MSR $1,359	$1,175	$1,000	$875	$775	$675	$575	$450	

MODEL 8400 TACTICAL SERIES – .300 Win. Mag. or .308 Win. cal., matte blue (Tactical) or KimPro II Dark Earth (Advanced Tactical) finish, grey (Tactical) or Desert Camo (Advanced Tactical) McMillan synthetic stock, 24 in. fluted bull barrel, 5 shot mag., 9 lbs., 4 oz. New 2007.

MSR $1,971	$1,675	$1,450	$1,250	$1,125	$900	$750	$575	

Add $680 for Advanced Tactical with desert tan or black Pelican case.

MODEL 8400 PATROL/POLICE TACTICAL – .300 Win. Mag. or .308 Win. (new 2010) cal., features 20 (Patrol), 24, or 26 in. match grade barrel, chamber, and trigger, trued bolt face, custom McMillan glass bedded stock, fixed Picatinny rail, enlarged bolt handle and knob, 8 3/4 lbs. New 2009.

MSR $1,495	$1,325	$1,160	$995	$900	$725	$595	$475	

MODEL 8400 CAPRIVI – .375 H&H, .416 Rem. Mag. (new 2010), or .458 Lott cal., 24 in, contoured blue barrel, 4 shot mag., Mauser claw extractor, 3-position Model 70 style safety, adj. trigger, oil finished checkered pistol grip AA Grade French walnut stock, pancake cheekpiece, ebony forend tip, swivel studs, three leaf express sight, double cross bolts, recoil pad, 8 lbs., 7 oz. New 2008.

MSR $3,263	$2,850	$2,450	$2,125	$1,800	$1,500	$1,275	$1,075	

* ***Model 8400 Caprivi Special Edition*** – .375 H&H cal., similar to Caprivi, except has AAA grade French walnut stock and color case hardened receiver, approx. 9 lbs. Mfg. 2011-2012.

	$4,500	$4,150	$3,600	N/A	N/A	N/A	N/A	*$5,031*

MODEL 8400 TALKEETNA – .375 H&H cal., stainless barrel with single leaf express sight, Kevlar/carbon fiber pistol grip stock, 7 3/4 lbs. New 2008.

MSR $2,175	$1,825	$1,595	$1,350	$1,225	$995	$850	$725	

MODEL 8400 SONORA – .25-06 Rem., .30-06 (disc. 2009), .300 Win. Mag., 7mm Rem. Mag., or .308 Win. (disc. 2009) cal., brown laminate stock, fluted stainless steel match grade barrel w/o sights, approx. 9 1/2 lbs. Mfg. 2008-2011.

	$1,100	$960	$825	$750	$600	$495	$385	*$1,359*

MODEL K770 CLASSIC – while advertised during 1997, this model never went into production. Prototypes only.

MODEL K770 SUPER AMERICA – while advertised during 1997, this model never went into production. Prototypes only.

Mauser 96 Sporters

MODEL 96 SPORTER – .308 Win. cal., features M-96 action with stainless steel fluted heavy barrel. Mfg. 1995-97.

	$450	$415	$365	$300	$260	$225	$200	*$520*

Retail prices ranged from $340-$415 for the Standard Sporter, while the Varmint/Heavy barrel

GRADING - PPGS™	100%	98%	95%	90%	80%	70%	60%	*LAST MSR*

variation was priced at approx. $510. Sporter variations were also available as a combo package with scope and hardshell case - add approx. $30.

During 1995-96, Kimber began sporterizing the Swedish Mauser Model 96 military surplus rifles. They featured stainless steel fluted barrels and a black synthetic Ramline stock, receivers were drilled and tapped to accept Weaver scope mounts, bead blasted bluing, and original reprofiled military bolt. The Sporter configuration included .243 Win., 6.5x55mm, or .308 Win. cal., while the heavy fluted barrel models were available in .22-250 Rem. or .308 Win. (Varmint or Heavy Barrel).

Mauser 98 Sporters

MODEL 98 SPORTER – .220 Swift (100 mfg.), .257 Roberts (100 mfg.), .270 Win., .280 Rem. (100 mfg.), .30-06, .300 Win. Mag., .338 Win. Mag., or 7mm Rem. Mag. cal., features Mauser M-98 action with stainless match grade fluted barrel, choice of synthetic or claro walnut stock, and Warne bases, matte black finish receiver. Mfg. 1996-98.

$465	**$425**	**$375**	**$315**	**$270**	**$230**	**N/A**	***$535***

Add $25 for Mag. cals.
Add $100 for Claro walnut stock.

* ***Mauser 98 Sporter Matte*** – .300 Win. Mag., .338 Win. Mag., or 7mm Rem. Mag. cal., features 25 in. non-fluted sporter barrel, synthetic stock, and Weaver style bases. Disc. 1998.

$275	**$250**	**$225**	**$200**	**$185**	**$170**	**$155**	***$339***

SHOTGUNS: O/U

AUGUSTA SERIES – 12 ga., 2 3/4 (Trap & Skeet) or 3 (Sporting & Field) in. chambers, Boss type boxlock action with shallow frame, blue (Trap & Skeet) or polished metal (Field & Sporting) frame, ejectors, SST, tang safety with ejector, 26-34 in. vent. barrel lengths with VR backbored to .736 in., available in Field, Sporting, Skeet, and Trap variations, beavertail or Schnabel forend, Pachmayr Decelerator recoil pad, 7 lbs., 2 oz-7 lbs., 13 oz. Mfg. in Italy by Investarm 2002-2005, limited delivery 2003-2005.

$4,750	**$4,250**	**$3,750**	**$3,250**	**$2,750**	**$2,250**	**$1,850**	***$5,676***

MARIAS SERIES – 12 or 20 ga., 3 in. chambers, 26, 28, or 30 in. VR barrels with 5 choke tubes, ejectors, charcoal case colored detachable sidelock action with engraving, deluxe checkered walnut English or pistol grip stock and forearm, available in Grade I with Grade III Turkish walnut or Grade II with Grade IV Turkish walnut, imported from Turkey. Imported 2006-2008.

$4,995	**$4,375**	**$3,750**	**$3,250**	**$2,700**	**$2,200**	**$1,825**	***$5,799***

SHOTGUNS: SxS

VALIER SERIES – 16 (new 2006) or 20 ga., 26 or 28 in. barrels, hand engraved sidelock action with seven pins, hand checkered Turkish walnut straight grip English stock, DT, fixed chokes, hand engraved blue (20 ga. only), case colored, or optional bone charcoal case colored action, extractors, approx. 6 1/2 lbs., mfg. in Turkey 2005-2007.

$3,525	**$3,050**	**$2,675**	**$2,200**	**$1,850**	**$1,450**	**$1,100**	***$3,999***

* ***Valier Grade II*** – similar to Grade I, except has ejectors, with or w/o (disc. 2007) charcoal case colored frame, mfg. in Turkey. Imported 2005-2008.

$4,495	**$3,995**	**$3,050**	**$2,675**	**$2,200**	**$1,850**	**$1,450**	***$4,999***

Subtract approx. $600 if w/o bone charcoal case colors.

KIMBER OF OREGON, INC.

Previous manufacturer located in Clackamas, OR circa 1980-1991.

Kimber of Oregon went out of business with its final sale in 1991. In some models, magazines for these fine quality rifles are getting extremely hard to find with healthy premiums being asked. Once "B" suffix models were introduced, older manufacture started being referred to as "A" models.

Kimber of Oregon, Inc. was started by Jack Warne, who was originally from Australia and moved to Oregon in 1969 as an executive for Omark Industries. The Warne's purchased all rimfire tooling from Omark Industries after the manufacture of Australian Sportcos ceased. Jack Warne, together with his son Greg, started Kimber in the late 1970s. By 1980, the

GRADING - PPGS™	100%	98%	95%	90%	80%	70%	60%	LAST MSR

first Model 82s in .22 rimfire were being shipped. The name Kimber was originally derived from the small town in South Australia named Kimba. The spelling was changed due to commercial considerations.

PISTOLS: BOLT ACTION

PREDATOR MODEL – .221 Fireball, .223 Rem., 6mm TCU (disc. 1987), 7mm TCU, or 6x45mm (disc. 1987) cal., single shot Model 84 action with shortened 14 7/8 in. barrel, scope use only, one piece deluxe walnut stock with contoured pistol grip, 5 1/4 lbs., rare cals. will command a premium. Approx. 200 mfg. 1987-88 only.

* ***Predator Model Hunter Grade*** – AA Claro walnut without checkering. Disc. 1988.

  $1,995 $1,750 $1,500 $1,250 $950 $800 $700 *$995*

* ***Predator Model Super Grade*** – similar to Hunter Grade, except has select French walnut with ebony forend tip and 22 lines/in. checkering. Disc. 1988.

  $3,000 $2,650 $2,250 $2,000 $1,750 $1,400 $1,250 *$1,195*

RIFLES: BOLT ACTION

Note: No suffix in Kimber models denotes pre-1986 action design, "B" suffix models incorporate the new action with improved cocking system, faster lock time, swept-back bolt design, improved recoil lug, and are right-handed. Pre '83 rifles had no bolt release.

Add $175 for skeleton grip cap on models listed below.
Add $275 for skeleton buttplate on models listed below.
Add $100 for checkered bolt handle on models listed below.
Add $300 for raised quarter rib.
Add $100 for forend tip.
Extra fancy walnut on any Kimber will always command a premium.
10 shot mags. will typically bring $80-$100.

Model 82, .22 Cal. Series

Add $200-$500 for .22 Hornet or .22 WMR. cal. on the models listed, depending on the variation.

STANDARD MODEL 82 – .22 LR, .22 WMR, or .22 Hornet cal., Mauser type rear locking bolt action, 3 (.22 Hornet), 4 (.22 WMR), or 5 (.22 LR) shot mag., 22 in. (Sporter) or 24 in. (Varmint) barrel, deluxe claro walnut, steel buttplate, rocker style safety, right or left-hand action, 6 1/2 lbs.

* ***Standard Model 82 Classic*** – disc. 1988.

  $885 $775 $665 $600 $485 $400 $310 *$750*

* ***Standard Model 82 Cascade*** – Monte Carlo cheekpiece, disc. 1988.

  $885 $775 $665 $600 $485 $400 $310

Add 150% for Custom Cascade Model, with higher grade walnut, ebony forend tip, and Niedner style buttplate (34 mfg).

* ***Standard Model 82 Custom Classic*** – higher grade claro walnut, ebony forearm tip, Niedner style steel buttplate. Disc. 1988.

  $1,500 $1,400 $925 $800 $725 $625 $525

  .218 Mashburn cal. $2,350 $2,100 $1,850 $1,575 $1,450 $1,150 $950 *$995*

Add 25% for .218 Bee cal. (approx. 130 standard mfg.).
Add 10% for .22 WMR cal.

Also available in .25-20 (approx. 200 mfg. single shot only) cals. Mfg. 1985 only (retail price was $695).

* ***Standard Model 82 Deluxe Grade*** – .22 LR cal. only, similar to Custom Classic Model, AA walnut, 5 or 10 (optional) shot mag., 6 1/2 lbs. Mfg. 1989-90 only.

  $1,500 $1,400 $790 $715 $580 $475 $370 *$1,195*

A left-hand variation was also available at no extra charge, but had limited mfg. in 1990.

SPORTER MODEL – .17 Ackley Hornet (approx. 9 mfg.), .17 K. Hornet (approx. 88 mfg.), or .22 LR cal., includes Model 82A action, 22 in. sporter weight barrel, 4 shot mag., round top receiver with bases, checkered stock and forend, 6 1/2 lbs. Mfg. 1991 only.

$940 $825 $700 $640 $515 $425 $330 *$995*

GRADING - PPGS™	100%	98%	95%	90%	80%	70%	60%	LAST MSR

Add approx. 100% for .17 K Hornet or .17 Ackley Hornet cals.

There is some speculation that this model may not have been produced.

RIMFIRE VARMINTER – .22 LR cal. only, Model 82A action, free floating 25 in. medium heavy barrel, laminated stock, 5 or optional 10 shot mag., rubber buttpad, 8 1/4 lbs. Mfg. 1990-91 only.

$1,100	$995	$670	$610	$490	$400	$315	*$795*

The barrels were left over All-American Match rifle production, which had an accuracy guarantee of .3 @ 50 yards with match ammo.

HUNTER GRADE – .22 LR cal. only, similar to Rimfire Varminter with Super America configured barrel and action with low glare metal finish. Mfg. 1990 only.

$1,000	$925	$595	$535	$430	$350	$275	*$895*

MINI CLASSIC – .22 LR cal. only, Model 82 action, 18 in. barrel, steel buttplate, sling swivels. Mfg. 1988 only.

$900	$825	$525	$475	$385	$315	$245	*$795*

GOVERNMENT MODEL 82A TARGET – .22 LR cal. only, specifically designed for U.S. Army training, 25 in. heavy target barrel including scope blocks, oversized stock, some rifles are "star" marked indicating an accuracy guarantee, 10 3/4 lbs. Mfg. 1987-91.

$650	$600	$550	$500	$400	$325	$250	*$595*

20,000 rifles were mfg. 1987-1989 to fill the initial U.S. government contract. These rifles were all transferred to the CMP for resale to the public and are all marked "US" over the serial number. Commercial guns were manufactured for the private sector pending an accuracy test of .3 @ 50 yards with match ammo. These guns were marked with a "Star" stamp over the serial number. Add $300 for a "Star" marked rifle.

ALL AMERICAN MATCH – .22 LR cal. only, precision rifled 25 in. free floating target grade barrel, stock is adj. both vertically and for length of pull, fully adj. single stage trigger, approx. 9 lbs. Mfg. 1990-91 only.

$1,100	$995	$595	$535	$435	$355	$275	*$895*

CONTINENTAL – .22 LR, .22 WMR, or .22 Hornet cal., Sporter action only, full length Mannlicher stock, open sights, deluxe walnut. New 1987.

This model was only available as a special order with prices on request from the factory.

Add $200 for .22 WMR or .22 Hornet cal.

* ***Continental Super*** – similar to Continental, except has AAA claro walnut with 22 lines/in. checkering. Mfg. 1987-88.

$2,200	$2,000	$1,275	$1,150	$925	$765	$595	*$1,465*

Add 100% if model is one of three known laminated stock variations with cheekpieces that were mfg., all in .22 LR cal.

S SERIES – .22 LR (535 mfg.), .22 Hornet (354 mfg.), or .22 WMR (88 mfg.) cal., top-of-the-line limited production model, grooved for scope mounting, Neidner checkered steel buttplate, best quality walnut, continental cheekpiece, ebony forend tip, Sporter configuration only. Mfg. early 1980s.

$1,900	$1,850	$1,050	$950	$770	$630	$490	

SUPER AMERICA – top-of-the-line model, includes detachable scope mounts, Niedner checkered steel buttplate and best quality walnut, cheekpiece and ebony forend tip added after 1983, available in Sporter configuration only. This model was disc. 1988, and reintroduced 1990-91.

$2,100	$1,995	$1,175	$1,090	$880	$720	$560	*$1,295*

* ***Super America Super Grade*** – similar to Super America, AAA walnut, beaded cheekpiece, 5 or 10 (optional) shot mag., 6 1/2 lbs. Mfg. 1989 only.

$2,100	$1,995	$1,175	$1,090	$880	$720	$560	*$1,295*

GRADING - PPGS™	100%	98%	95%	90%	80%	70%	60%	*LAST MSR*

CUSTOM MATCH – .22 LR or .22 WMR cal., limited edition of 217 rifles, match dimension chamber, French walnut stock with 22 L.P.I. checkering, rust blue finish, other custom rifle features. Introduced 1984.

$3,000	$2,750	$1,875	$1,700	$1,375	$1,125	$875	

Add $500 for .22 WMR cal.

BROWNELL – .22 LR cal., only 500 mfg. to commemorate the late Leonard Brownell, Mannlicher style extra deluxe claro walnut stock. Mfg. 1986 only.

$2,750	$2,325	$1,500	$1,325	$1,085	$930	$750	*$1,500*

CENTENNIAL – .22 LR cal. only, limited edition (100 rifles) to commemorate centennial of .22 LR cal., includes hand-picked checkered walnut, moderate engraving, special Wilson Arms match barrel, skeleton buttplate and other refinements, serial numbered C1-C100, shipped in a quality pine shipping container. Mfg. 1987 only.

$4,000	$3,775	$2,150	$1,950	$1,580	$1,295	$1,000	*$2,950*

TENTH ANNIVERSARY ISSUE – .22 LR cal., limited edition, French walnut stock featuring slim forend design with shadowed cheekpiece, Neidner steel buttplate and other refinements. Mfg. 1989 only.

$2,200	$1,995	$1,400	$1,235	$1,000	$870	$700	

Add $100 for matte finish.

Model 84 Centerfire Series

Model 84 caliber rarity is as follows: .222 Rem. and .223 Rem. are common. 6x45mm or 47mm, .221 Fireball, .17 Rem., and .17 Mach IV are less common and more desirable. .222 Rem. Mag. is rare, while 5.6x50mm is extremely rare.

Add $200-$375 for rare calibers.

Add $75 for forend tip - option A. Add $300 for iron sights - option B. Add $100 for checkered bolt handle - option C. Add $200 for skeleton grip cap - option D. Add $300 for skeleton buttplate - option G. Add $250-$300 for 3-position safety in this series.

STANDARD MODEL 84 – .17 Rem., .17 Mach IV (disc. 1987), 6x45 or 47mm (disc. 1987), 5.6x50mm (disc. 1987), .221 Fireball, .222 Rem., .222 Rem. Mag. (disc. 1987), or .223 Rem. cal., "Mini-Mauser" type head locking bolt action, 5 shot mag., 22 (Sporter) or 24 (Varmint) in. barrel, deluxe Claro walnut, steel buttplate, rocker style safety, 6 1/2 lbs.

* ***Standard Model 84 Classic*** – disc. 1988.

$1,095	$1,000	$875	$750	$600	$500	$400	*$885*

Add $55 for disc. Cascade Model (Monte Carlo cheekpiece).
Add 20% for left-hand action.

Also available in left hand action in .22 Hornet, .222 Rem., .223 Rem., 6x45mm, 6x47mm, .17 Rem., and .17 Mach IV (very limited mfg.).

CUSTOM CLASSIC MODEL – higher grade Claro walnut, ebony forearm tip, Niedner style steel buttplate. Disc. 1988.

$1,400	$1,200	$1,000	$825	$675	$550	$450	*$1,130*

* ***Custom Classic Model Deluxe Grade Sporter*** – .17 Rem., .221 Rem., or .223 Rem. cal., Mauser action, AA walnut, similar to Custom Classic Model, 6 1/4 lbs. Mfg. 1989-90.

$1,400	$1,200	$1,000	$825	$675	$550	$450	*$1,295*

Also available in left-hand action (.223 Rem. cal. only), limited mfg.

CONTINENTAL – .221 Fireball (extremely rare, mfg. 1988 only) .222 Rem. or .223 Rem. cal., Sporter action only, full length Mannlicher stock, open sights, deluxe walnut. New 1987.

Extreme rarity precludes accurate price evaluation on this model.

* ***Continental Super*** – similar to Continental (same cals.), except has AAA Claro walnut with 22 lines/in. checkering. Mfg. 1987-88.

$2,100	$1,850	$1,500	$1,250	$1,000	$800	$700	*$1,600*

Add 100% if model is one of three known laminated stocks that were mfg. in .223 Rem. cal.

GRADING - PPGS™	100%	98%	95%	90%	80%	70%	60%	LAST MSR

HUNTER GRADE – .17 Rem., .222 Rem., or .223 Rem. cal., laminated stock, Super America configured action and barrel with low glare metal finish. Mfg. 1990 only.

$995	$875	$750	$650	$550	$475	$400	*$995*

SPORTER – .17 Rem., .22 Hornet, .222 Rem., .22-250 Rem., or .223 Rem. cal., 22 in. sporter weight barrel, A grade Claro walnut, round top receiver with bases, 4 shot mag., hand checkering. Mfg. 1991 only.

$1,020	$850	$725	$625	$550	$500	$495	*$1,095*

This model was available in either right or left-hand action.

* ***Sporter Big Bore*** – .250 Savage or .35 Rem. cal., similar action to Sporter Model, except has 3/4 in. red Pachmayr Decelerator recoil pad. Mfg. 1991 only.

Last MSR was $1,095

Extreme rarity precludes accurate price evaluation on this model.

Consult an expert when buying/selling this model. This model was available in either right or left-hand action.

SUPER AMERICA/SUPER GRADE – .17 Rem., .17 MK IV, .221 Fireball, .22 Hornet, .222 Rem., .222 Rem. Mag., .22-250 Rem., .223 Rem., 5.6x56mm, or 6x47mm cal., 22 in. sporter weight barrel, top-of-the-line, with detachable scope mounts, available in Sporter configuration only, cheekpiece and ebony forend tip added after 1983, 4 shot mag., right or left hand action. Disc. 1988, reintroduced 1990-91.

$1,825	$1,575	$1,250	$1,000	$850	$725	$675	*$1,495*

Be careful when buying rare cals. and/or options on this model.

* ***Super America/Super Grade Big Bore*** – .250 Savage or .35 Rem. cal., similar action to Super America Model, except has 3/4 in. red Pachmayr Decelerator recoil pad. Mfg. 1991 only.

$2,100	$1,775	$1,425	$1,125	$925	$800	$700	*$1,495*

CUSTOM MATCH – .222 Rem. or .223 Rem. cal., limited edition of 200 rifles, match dimension chamber, French walnut stock with 22 L.P.I. checkering, rust blue finish, other custom rifle features. Introduced 1986.

$2,500	$2,000	$1,800	$1,500	$1,100	$1,000	$750	

TENTH ANNIVERSARY ISSUE – .223 Rem. cal., limited edition, French walnut stock featuring slim forend design with shadowed cheekpiece, 22 in. barrel, roundtop receiver with mounts, Neidner steel buttplate and other refinements. Mfg. 1989 only.

$1,995	$1,650	$1,250	$1,100	$895	$785	$630	

Add $100 for matte finish.

ULTRA VARMINTER – .17 Rem., .22 Hornet (rare, new 1991), .221 Rem. (disc. 1990), .222 Rem., .22-250 Rem. (rare), or .223 Rem. cal., 24 in. medium weight stainless steel barrel, laminated birch stock, plain buttstock, right or left-hand action, 7 3/4 lbs. Mfg. 1989-91 only.

$1,600	$1,300	$1,175	$1,000	$850	$750	$675	*$1,295*

* ***Ultra Varminter Super*** – similar to Ultra Varminter except has steel barrel, AAA walnut stock with beaded cheekpiece, 7 1/4 lbs. Mfg. 1989-91 only.

$2,000	$1,850	$1,500	$1,200	$975	$775	$675	*$1,495*

Model 89 Centerfire, Big Game Series

Fewer than 5,000 Model 89 BGRs were mfg. Note: fancy wood is harder to find in Model 89s.

MODEL 89 BGR – .270 Win., .280 Rem., 7mm Rem. Mag., .30-06, .300 Win. Mag., .338 Win. Mag., or .375 H&H cal., new action incorporates features from both Mauser 98 and Win. pre-64 Model 70, three position safety, 22 or 24 in. barrel, matte blue finish will command a premium. Introduced late 1988.

* ***Model 89 BGR Classic Model*** – deluxe Claro walnut checkered 18 lines/in. with steel buttplate. Disc. 1988.

$875	$725	$600	$500	$415	$350	$300	*$985*

Add $200 for .375 H&H cal. Add $100 for matte finish.

GRADING - PPGS™	100%	98%	95%	90%	80%	70%	60%	LAST MSR

* ***Model 89 BGR Custom Classic Model*** – higher grade Claro walnut, ebony forearm tip, Niedner style steel buttplate. Disc. 1988.

	$1,125	$950	$775	$650	$525	$450	$375	*$1,230*

Add $200 for .375 H&H cal.

DELUXE GRADE – similar to Custom Classic Model, round top receiver with Model 70 scope mount hole configuration, AA walnut stock with ebony forend tip and rubber recoil pad (no cheekpiece), 22 or 24 in. barrel, 7 1/2-8 1/2 lbs. New 1989.

* ***Deluxe Grade Featherweight Barrel Model*** – .257 Roberts (rare), .25-06 Rem., 7x57mm (rare, disc. 1990), .270 Win., .280 Rem., or .30-06 cal., 5 shot mag., 22 in. Featherweight barrel, right-hand action only, 7 1/2 lbs. Disc. 1990.

	$1,600	$1,225	$1,000	$850	$700	$600	$525	*$1,795*

Add 25% for 7x57mm cal.
Add $470 for Super America Grade with square bridge, dovetail receiver.
Add $100 for matte finish.

The Super America Grade will accept Kimber double lever scope mounts and has one grade better wood than the Deluxe Grade with beaded cheekpiece.

* ***Deluxe Grade Medium-weight Barrel Model*** – .300 Win. Mag., .300 H&H (rare, disc. 1990), .300 Wby. Mag. (very rare, new 1991), .338 Win. Mag., .35 Whelen (rare, disc. 1990), or 7mm Rem. Mag. cal., 3 shot mag., 24 in. medium-weight barrel, right-hand action only, 7 3/4-8 1/2 lbs. Disc. 1990.

	$1,675	$1,250	$1,025	$875	$725	$625	$550	*$1,895*

Add a premium for rare cals.
Add $495 for Super America Grade with square bridge, dovetail receiver.
Add $100 for matte finish.

The Super America Grade will accept Kimber double lever scope mounts and has one grade better wood than the Deluxe Grade with beaded cheekpiece.

* ***Deluxe Grade Heavy-weight Barrel Model*** – .375 H&H Mag. cal., 3 shot mag., 24 in. heavy weight barrel, right-hand action only, 9 lbs. Disc. 1990.

	$2,000	$1,750	$1,500	$1,250	$1,000	$800	$700	*$1,995*

Add $495 for Super America Grade with square bridge, dovetail receiver.
Add $100 for matte finish.

The Super America Grade will accept Kimber double lever scope mounts and has one grade better wood than the Deluxe Grade with beaded cheekpiece.

SPORTER MODEL – same cals. as Deluxe/Super America Models, 22 in. featherweight or 24 in. medium or heavy barrel, double square bridge dovetail receiver, A grade Claro walnut stock with 3/4 in. red Pachmayr Decelerator recoil pad (Mag. cals. only with 24 in. barrel). Mfg. 1991 only.

	$1,395	$1,050	$900	$775	$650	$500	$450	*$1,595*

Add $100 for medium Magnum action.
Add $200 for heavy Magnum action (.375 H&H and .458 Win. Mag. cals.).

HUNTER GRADE – .270 Win., .30-06, .300 Win. Mag., .338 Win. Mag., or 7mm Rem. Mag. cal., laminated stock, Super America configured action and barrel with low glare metal finish. Mfg. 1990-91 only.

	$1,325	$1,025	$895	$750	$625	$525	$450	*$1,495*

Add $100 for Mag. cals.

SUPER GRADE – similar to Super America Model, square top frame, AAA walnut, 22 or 24 in. barrel, plain buttstock, 7 1/2-8 1/2 lbs. Mfg. 1989 only.

	$1,575	$1,325	$995	$825	$695	$550	$500	*$1,495*

Add $100 for .375 H&H cal.
Add $100 for matte blue metal finish.

The 24 in. barrel was available in Mag. cals. only.

GRADING - PPGS™	100%	98%	95%	90%	80%	70%	60%	LAST MSR

LIMITED WILDLIFE EDITION SERIES – series of 5 guns, includes .257 Roberts (Whitetail Deer Edition), .270 Win. (Mule Deer Edition), .338 Win. Mag. (Rocky Mt. Elk Edition), 7mm Rem. Mag. (Big Horn Sheep Edition), and .375 H&H (Grizzly Bear Edition) cals. included, hand select walnut, special Shilen Rifle barrel, gold plated trigger, receivers are stamped "Wildlife Edition", special prefix serialization, only 25 sets were to be manufactured in 1991 only, includes rings, swivels, and hard case.

Retail price was scheduled to be $3,595.

While advertised, only one .270 Win. Mule Deer model was mfg.

MODEL 89 AFRICAN – .375 H&H (rare), .416 Rigby (most common) cal., or .505 Gibbs (rare) cal., Magnum action, 24 in. heavy barrel, AA English walnut stock with beaded cheekpiece and rubber recoil pad, includes twin recoil cross bolts, express sights on quarter rib, drop box magazine, 10-10 1/2 lbs. Mfg. 1990-91 only.

$5,500	**$4,500**	**$4,000**	**$3,500**	**$2,750**	**$2,250**	**$1,650**	***$3,595***

.375 H&H or .505 Gibbs cal. will command a premium.

KIMEL INDUSTRIES, INC.

Previously manufactured until late 1994 by A.A. Arms located in Monroe, NC. Previously distributed by Kimel Industries, Inc. located in Matthews, NC.

CARBINES

AR-9 CARBINE – 9mm Para. cal., carbine variation of the AP-9 with 16 1/2 in. barrel, 20 shot mag., and steel rod folding stock. Mfg. 1991-94.

$625	**$550**	**$475**	**$425**	**$365**	**$315**	**$275**	***$384***

PISTOLS: SEMI-AUTO

AP-9 PISTOL – 9mm Para. cal., paramilitary design, blowback action with bolt knob on left side of receiver, 5 in. barrel with vent. shroud, front mounted 10 (C/B 1994) or 20* shot detachable mag., black matte finish, adj. front sight, 3 lbs. 7 oz. Mfg. 1989-94.

$475	**$425**	**$375**	**$325**	**$300**	**$275**	**$250**	***$279***

* ***AP-9 Pistol Mini*** – compact variation of the AP-9 Model with 3 in. barrel, blue or nickel finish. Mfg. 1991-94.

$550	**$500**	**$425**	**$375**	**$325**	**$300**	**$275**	***$273***

* ***AP-9 Pistol Target*** – target variation of the AP-9 with 12 in. match barrel with shroud, blue finish only. Mfg. 1991-94.

$600	**$550**	**$475**	**$425**	**$375**	**$350**	**$325**	***$294***

* ***P-95 Pistol*** – similar to AP-9, except without barrel shroud and is supplied with 5 shot mag., parts are interchangeable with AP-9. Mfg. 1990-91 only.

$395	**$350**	**$300**	**$250**	**$200**	**$175**	**$150**	***$250***

KING'S GUN WORKS, INC.

Previous custom handgun and accessories manufacturer 1949-circa 2011 located in Glendale, CA.

King's Gun Works manufactured a complete line of custom pistols patterned after Colt M-1911, in addition to many related accessories and/or after-market parts.

KINTREK, INC.

Previous rifle manufacturer located in Owensboro, KY.

RIFLES: SEMI-AUTO

BULLPUP MODEL – .22 LR cal., bullpup configuration, hinged dust cover, clear Ram-Line type coil spring mag., black synthetic thumbhole stock, A-2 type front/rear sight. Disc.

$350	**$300**	**$250**	**$225**	**$200**	**$175**	**$150**

KLEINGUENTHER FIREARMS CO.

KLEINGUENTHER®

Previous custom rifle manufacturer located in Seguin, TX until circa 2001. The original KDF Co. was started by Mr. Robert Kleinguenther and sold in the early 1980s. Mr. Kleinguenther then started a new company called

GRADING - PPGS™	100%	98%	95%	90%	80%	70%	60%	LAST MSR

Kleinguenther Firearms Co.

RIFLES: BOLT ACTION

Values listed are for base models only with no additional customer special order options. Mr. Kleinguenther also custom built rifles utilizing customer actions.

BOLT ACTION RIFLE – various cals., individual customer special order rifle with a variety of options, guns are guaranteed to shoot 1/2 M.O.A., choice of actions, various weights.

* ***Bolt Action Rifle Winchester Model 70 Custom***

	100%	98%	95%	90%	80%	70%	60%	LAST MSR
	$975	$800	$675	$575	$500	$450	$400	*$975*

* ***Bolt Action Rifle Sako Action*** – various cals., newer guns feature the ballistic recoil muzzle brake system (60-70% recoil reduction), most newer stocks are mfg. out of high tech laminated wood with 28-32 resin coated panels.

	100%	98%	95%	90%	80%	70%	60%	LAST MSR
	$1,550	$1,325	$1,100	$950	$825	$725	$625	*$1,750*

Add $155 for ballistic recoil muzzle brake system.

* ***Bolt Action Rifle K-15***

	100%	98%	95%	90%	80%	70%	60%	LAST MSR
	$1,375	$1,100	$950	$800	$675	$575	$500	*$1,375*

KNIGHT'S ARMAMENT COMPANY

Current manufacturer established in 1983, and located in Titusville, FL. Previously located in Vero Beach, FL. Dealer and consumer direct sales.

RIFLES: SEMI-AUTO

Some of the models listed were also available in pre-ban configurations. SR-25 Enhanced Match model has 10 or 20 shot mag. Some of the following models, while discontinued for civilian use, may still be available for military/law enforcement.

IMPORTANT NOTE: On model(s) where *N/A has replaced the normal 100% value, it indicates current market conditions are too unstable to accurately ascertain 100%-60% values. Factory retail prices (MSRs) reflect most recent updates. For more up-to-date information on current pricing trends and additional useful information, please visit www.bluebookofgunvalues.com, select "Information & Services" from the menu, and click on "Additional Book Information".

STONER SR-15 M-5 RIFLE – .223 Rem. cal., 20 in. standard weight barrel, flip-up low profile rear sight, two-stage target trigger, 7.6 lbs. Mfg. 1997-2008.

	100%	98%	95%	90%	80%	70%	60%	LAST MSR
	*N/A	$1,475	$1,225	$1,025	$900	$825	$725	*$1,837*

* ***Stoner SR-15 M-4 Carbine*** – similar to SR-15 rifle, except has 16 in. barrel, choice of fixed synthetic or non-collapsible buttstock. Mfg. 1997-2005.

	100%	98%	95%	90%	80%	70%	60%	LAST MSR
	*N/A	$1,175	$950	$850	$775	$700	$650	*$1,575*

Add $100 for non-collapsible buttstock (SR-15 M-4 K-Carbine, disc. 2001).

* ***Stoner SR-15 URX E3 Carbine*** – features 16 in. free floating barrel with URX forearm, E3 type rounded lug improved bolt. New 2004.

	100%	98%	95%	90%	80%	70%	60%	LAST MSR
MSR $2,207	*N/A	$1,700	$1,325	$1,075	$900	$775	$675	

STONER SR-15 MATCH RIFLE – .223 Rem. cal., features flattop upper receiver with 20 in. match grade stainless steel free floating barrel with RAS forend, two-stage match trigger, 7.9 lbs. Mfg. 1997-2008.

	100%	98%	95%	90%	80%	70%	60%	LAST MSR
	*N/A	$1,525	$1,200	$975	$850	$750	$700	*$1,972*

STONER SR-25 SPORTER – .308 Win. cal., 20 in. lightweight barrel, AR-15 configuration with carrying handle, 5, 10, or 20 (disc. per C/B 1994) shot detachable mag., less than 2 MOA guaranteed, non-glare finish, 8.8 lbs. Mfg. 1993-97.

	100%	98%	95%	90%	80%	70%	60%	LAST MSR
	*N/A	$2,250	$1,900	$1,600	$1,300	$1,000	$850	*$2,995*

* ***Stoner RAS Sporter Carbine (SR-25 Carbine)*** – 16 in. free floating barrel, grooved non-slip handguard, removable carrying handle, 7 3/4 lbs. Mfg. 1995-2005.

	100%	98%	95%	90%	80%	70%	60%	LAST MSR
	*N/A	$2,550	$2,125	$1,750	$1,500	$1,250	$1,000	*$3,495*

Subtract 15% if w/o RAS.

In 2003, the Rail Adapter System (RAS) became standard on this model.

GRADING - PPGS™	100%	98%	95%	90%	80%	70%	60%	LAST MSR

SR-25 STANDARD MATCH – .308 Win. cal., free-floating 24 in. match barrel, fiberglass stock, includes commercial gun case and 10 shot mag. Disc. 2008.

	*N/A	$3,300	$2,950	$2,600	$2,300	$2,000	$1,600	*$3,918*

SR-25 RAS MATCH – similar to SR-25 Standard, except has 24 in. free floating match barrel and flat-top receiver, less than 1 MOA guaranteed, RAS became standard 2004, 10 3/4 lbs. Mfg. 1993-2008.

	*N/A	$2,800	$2,300	$1,800	$1,500	$1,250	$1,000	*$3,789*

Subtract approx. 15% if w/o Rail Adapter System (RAS).

Over 3,000 SR-25s were mfg.

* ***SR-25 RAS Match Lightweight*** – features 20 in. medium contour free floating barrel, 9 1/2 lbs. Mfg. 1995-2004.

	*N/A	$2,450	$2,125	$1,750	$1,500	$1,250	$1,000	*$3,244*

Add approx. 15% for Rail Adapter System.

SR-25 ENHANCED MATCH RIFLE/CARBINE – .308 Win. cal., 16 or 20 in. barrel, 10 or 20 shot mag., URX rail system, two-stage trigger, ambidextrous mag. release, integrated adj. folding front sight, micro adj. folding rear sight, EM gas block, combat trigger guard, chrome plated multi-lug bolt and bolt carrier, fixed or nine position adj. stock, black anodized finish, flash hider (carbine only), approx. 8 1/2 lbs.

MSR $4,994	*N/A	$4,250	$3,750	$3,250	$2,750	$2,250	$1,875	

Add $625 for 16 in. carbine.

SR-25 MK11 MOD O CIVILIAN DELUXE SYSTEM PACKAGE – .308 Win. cal., consumer variation of the Navy Model Mark Eleven, Mod O, w/o sound suppressor, includes Leupold 3.5-10X scope, 20 in. military grade match barrel, backup sights, cell-foam case and other accessories. Mfg. 2003-2008.

	$7,950	$7,250	$6,350	$5,850	$5,100	$4,500	$4,000	*$8,534*

SR-25 MK11 MATCH RIFLE – .308 Win. cal., includes MK11 Mod O features and 20 in. heavy barrel. Mfg. 2004-2008.

	$5,675	$5,200	$4,775	$4,400	$3,750	$3,150	$2,700	*$6,325*

SR-25 MK11 CARBINE – .308 Win. cal., includes MK11 Mod O features and 16 in. match grade stainless steel barrel with muzzle brake, URX 4x4 rail forend, 4-position buttstock. New 2005.

MSR $6,636	$6,000	$5,500	$4,950	$4,550	$3,875	$3,250	$2,800	

SR-25 BR CARBINE – .308 Win. cal., similar to SR-25 MK11 Carbine, except has chrome lined steel barrel. Mfg. 2005-2008.

	$5,675	$5,200	$4,775	$4,400	$3,750	$3,150	$2,700	*$6,307*

SR-M110 SASS – 7.62x51mm cal., 20 in. military match grade barrel, full RAS treatment on barrel, civilian variation of the Army's semi-auto sniper rifle system, includes Leupold long-range tactical scope, 600 meter back up iron sights, system case and other accessories. Mfg. 2006-2009.

	$13,000	$11,000	$9,500	$8,000	$7,000	$6,000	$5,000	*$14,436*

"DAVID TUBB" COMPETITION MATCH RIFLE – .260 Rem. or .308 Win. cal., incorporates refinements by David Tubb, top-of-the-line competition match rifle, including adj. and rotating buttstock pad. Mfg. 1998 only.

	$5,200	$4,000	$3,600	$3,150	$2,700	$2,300	$1,995	*$5,995*

STONER SR-50 – .50 BMG cal., features high strength materials and lightweight design, fully locked breech and two lug rotary breech bolt, horizontal 5 shot box mag., tubular receiver supports a removable barrel, approx. 31 lbs. Limited mfg. 2000, non-commercial sales only.

Last MSR was $6,995.

KODIAK CO.

Previous manufacturer located in North Haven, CT circa 1963-66.

Kodiak Co. was in business for only a short time. They produced the first .22 WMR semi-auto rifle (Model 260), as well as a centerfire bolt action (Model 158 Deluxe), and a slide

GRADING - PPGS™	100%	98%	95%	90%	80%	70%	60%	LAST MSR

action shotgun (Model 458). While Kodiak long guns are rare and extremely well made, collectability to date has been minimal with most specimens selling at a slight premium over similar quality trade name counterparts of that era. Prior to 1963, Kodiak firearms were marketed under the trade name of Jefferson.

KOFS LTD.

Current shotgun manufacturer located in Isparta, Turkey. No current U.S. importation.

Kofs Ltd. manufactures a complete line of good quality boxlock O/U and SxS shotguns, many grades and options are available. Please contact the company directly for more information including U.S. availability and pricing (see Trademark Index).

KOLAR ARMS

Current manufacturer located in Racine, WI. Dealer direct sales.

SHOTGUNS

Kolar Arms manufactures fine quality O/U and single barrel boxlock shotguns in Skeet, Sporting Clays, and Trap configurations. Many options are available, including custom orders, wood upgrades, and engraving. Please contact the company directly for more information, including model availability, delivery time, and pricing (see Trademark Index).

KOLIBRI

Previous trademark manufactured 1914-1925 by Georg Grabner located in Rehberg, Austria.

PISTOLS: SEMI-AUTO

KOLIBRI PISTOL – 2.7 or 3mm centerfire cal., unrifled barrel, 5 shot box mag., world's smallest semi-auto centerfire pistol.

100%	98%	95%	90%	80%	70%	60%	LAST MSR
$2,500	$2,250	$1,950	$1,750	$1,500	$1,350	$1,175	

Add approx. $300 for original case.
Add approx. 20% for nickel finish (rare).

Individual rounds of 2.7 or 3mm (more rare) ammunition are currently trading in the $75 range as it has the distinction of being the world's smallest centerfire shell (shooting a 3 grain bullet at approx. 475 fps and generating 1.75 ft./lbs. of muzzle energy!).

KONGSBERG

Previous manufacturer circa 1814-1998 located in Kongsberg, Norway. Previously imported and distributed 1996-98, by Kongsberg America L.L.C. located in Fairfield, CT, and by Lew Horton Distributing Co., Inc. until 1996, located in Westboro, MA.

RIFLES: BOLT ACTION

Add $50 for iron sights on models listed below.

393 SERIES – .22-250 Rem., .243 Win., .270 Win., .30-06, .308 Win., 6.5x55 Swedish, 7mm Rem. Mag., .300 Win. Mag., or .338 Win. Mag. cal., available in either Classic, De Luxe, Thumbhole (.22-250 Rem. or 308 Win. only), or Select (Standard) configuration, checkered pistol grip, forend mounted recoil lug which connects to stock, 3-position rear safety, fixed rotary mag., fully adj. trigger. Imported 1994-98.

*** *393 Series Classic Model***

100%	98%	95%	90%	80%	70%	60%	LAST MSR
$875	$750	$675	$575	$495	$440	$385	*$995*

Add $114 for Mag. cals.
Add $138 for left-hand action.

*** *393 Series Select Model (Standard Model in Europe)***

100%	98%	95%	90%	80%	70%	60%	LAST MSR
$860	$735	$660	$560	$495	$440	$385	*$980*

Add $113 for Mag. cals.
Add $138 for left-hand action.

*** *393 Series De Luxe Model***

GRADING - PPGS™	100%	98%	95%	90%	80%	70%	60%	LAST MSR
	$940	$795	$700	$595	$515	$450	$395	$1,124

Add $112 for Mag. cals.
Add $137 for left-hand action.

* ***393 Series Thumbhole Model*** – .22-250 Rem. or .308 Win. cal., features thumbhole stock. Mfg. 1996-98.

GRADING - PPGS™	100%	98%	95%	90%	80%	70%	60%	LAST MSR
	$1,350	$1,175	$1,000	$875	$750	$625	$500	$1,580

Add $138 for left-hand action.

KORA BRNO

Current revolver trademark manufactured by Kroko a.s., located in Brno, Czech Republic. No current U.S. importation.

To date, the Kora Brno revolver/revolver carbine line has had little or no importation into the U.S. Models include many configurations of both .22 LR, .22 WMR, and .38 Spl. cals. Please contact the factory directly for more information (see Trademark Index).

KORRIPHILA

Previous trademark manufactured until 2004 by Intertex, located in Eislingen, Germany. Previously imported 1999-2004 by Korriphila, Inc., located in Pineville, NC., and by Osborne's located in Cheboygan, MI until 1988.

PISTOLS: SEMI-AUTO

Less than 30 Korriphila pistols were made annually.

HSP 701 – 7.65 Luger (disc.), .38 Spl. (disc.), 9mm Para., 9mm Police (disc.), 9mm Steyr (disc.), .45 ACP, or 10mm Norma (disc.) cal., double action, Budischowsky delayed roller block locking system assists in recoil reduction, 40% stainless steel parts, 4 or 5 in. barrel, blue or satin finish, walnut grips, 7 or 9 shot mag., approx. 2.6 lbs, very limited production.

GRADING - PPGS™	100%	98%	95%	90%	80%	70%	60%	LAST MSR
	$6,500	$5,500	$3,750	$2,950	$2,150	$1,850	$1,675	

* ***HSP 701 Odin's Eye (Damascus)*** – similar to HSP 701, except is completely made from one block of Damascus stainless steel, rosewood grips with Manta skin inlays, custom order only.

GRADING - PPGS™	100%	98%	95%	90%	80%	70%	60%	LAST MSR
	$12,250	$10,250	$8,500	N/A	N/A	N/A	N/A	

KORTH

Current manufacturer established 1954, and located in Lollar, Germany. Previously located in Ratzeburg, Germany. Currently imported since 1994 by Korth USA, a division of Earl's Repair Service, Inc., located in Tewksbury, MA. Previously imported 1997-99 by Keng's Firearms Specialty, Inc. located in Atlanta, GA. Previously imported by Mandall Shooting Supplies, Inc. located in Scottsdale, AZ, Beeman Precision Arms, located in Santa Rosa, CA and by Osborne's in Cheboygan, MI.

Korth handguns are very high quality and are literally manufactured one-at-a-time, resulting in limited mfg. (less than 100 annually) and importation. 7,140 revolvers in 10 different configurations were manufactured between 1964-1981.

Retail values listed below reflect the most recent U.S. pricing available from Korth USA.

PISTOLS: SEMI-AUTO

KORTH SEMI-AUTO – 9mm Para., .357 SIG (disc. 2002), .40 S&W (disc. 2004), .45 ACP (Tactical Model, mfg. 2003-2004) or 9x21mm IMI (disc.) cal., double action, 4, 4 1/2 threaded, or 5 (disc.) in. barrel, all steel construction, 8 (.45 ACP cal.), 9 (.40 S&W and .357 SIG) or 10 (9mm Para. or 9x21mm IMI) shot mag., adj. sights, checkered walnut grips, top quality manufacture throughout. Introduced 1986 with first guns shipped 1988, very limited mfg.

The most recent MSR on this model is $6,495.
Add $587 for .45 ACP Tactical Model.
Add $2,000 for Model Schalldampfer (9mm Para cal. only, threaded barrel, new 2003).
Add $285 for silver matte plasma finish.

Add $740 for silver polished plasma finish.
Add $845 for polished blue plasma finish.
Add $1,440 per interchangeable barrels.
Add $180 for extra mag.

Base values are for high polished blue finish.

JAEGER MODEL – 9mm Para. cal., 4 in. barrel, ivory grips with hunting scene, left side has hunter and dog, right side has deer in forest, gold inlaid, grey "pickled" finish, fully engraved in Arabesque style.

The most recent MSR on this model is $19,200.

WILLIE KORTH "JUBILEE" 50th ANNIVERSARY MODEL – 9mm Para. cal., 4 in. barrel, combat trigger guard, gold inlaid with head of Willie Korth and dates (1954-2004), 50 Jahre oak leaf, and acorn engraving in high polish blue, deluxe hand engraved wood grips. Only 5 to be mfg. beginning 2004.

The most recent MSR on this model is $18,000.

A special case which holds both the anniversary pistol and the revolver, as well as a matching commemorative knife is also available.

REVOLVERS

The crane of the main cylinder and of the extra cylinder (.22 LR/.22 WMR or .357 Mag./9mm Para.) are cut from the same billet of steel, and for reasons of smallest tolerance that Korth guarantees, once a gun is made with a single cylinder, the extra convertible cylinder cannot be ordered at a later date. Korth currently produces the world's most expensive revolver.

Add $255 for silver matte plasma finish. Add $520 for silver polished plasma finish. Add $620 for bright blue polished plasma finish.
Subtract approx. $550-$700 if w/o interchangeable different cal. cylinder on Combat, Sport, and Target Models.
Currently, most used Combat, Sport, and Target models encountered in the secondary marketplace are priced in the $2,250-$3,750 price range, depending on condition and configuration.

TROJA MODEL – .22 LR, .22 WMR, or .357 Mag. cal., 4 or 6 in. barrel, matte finish, smooth oversized walnut finger groove grips. New 2003.

The most recent MSR on this model is $4,500.

COMBAT MODEL – .22 LR, .22 WMR, .38 Spl., or .357 Mag. cal., 3 (solid only), 4 VR, 5 1/4 VR, 6 VR, or 8 in. barrel, steel or stainless steel (disc., limited mfg.) construction, 6 shot, fixed or fully adj. combat sights, full length shrouded or unshrouded ejector rod, adj. trigger, checkered and oil finished walnut grips, 2.6 lbs. Introduced circa early 1960s.

The most recent MSR on this model is $6,880.

Used specimens of this model are infrequently encountered, and secondary values are difficult to determine.

SPORT MODEL – .22 LR, .32 S&W Long, .38 Spl., or .357 Mag. cal., 2 1/2 (disc., scarce), 4, 5 1/4, 6 VR, or 8 in. barrel, 5 (early mfg.) or 6 shot, fixed or micro adj. sights, full length shrouded or unshrouded ejector rod, adj. trigger, checkered and oil finished walnut grips, 2.6 lbs. Introduced circa early 1960s.

The most recent MSR on this model is $7,000.
Subtract approx. 50% for 5 shot, depending on condition.

Used specimens of this model are infrequently encountered, and secondary values are difficult to determine.

TARGET MODEL – .22 LR, .32 S&W Long, .38 Spl., or .357 Mag. cal., 5 1/4 or 6 VR in. barrel, 6 shot, micro adj. sights, adj. trigger, stippled oversized target walnut grips, 2.6 lbs.

The most recent MSR on this model is $7,240.

Used specimens of this model are infrequently encountered, and secondary values are difficult to determine.

WECHSEL MODEL – centerfire and .22 LR/.22 WMR cals., both cylinder and barrel can be changed. Mfg. 2003-2004.

Last MSR was $10,000.

GRADING - PPGS™	100%	98%	95%	90%	80%	70%	60%	LAST MSR

Revolvers: Special/Limited Editions

MODEL EVEREST 40 YEARS KORTH SPECIAL EDITION – .357 Mag., 5 1/4 in. barrel only, deeply engraved frame and barrel with gold inlays, smooth select walnut grips, cased, only 25 mfg. 1994 only.

	$8,950	$6,350	$4,500	N/A	N/A	N/A	N/A	*$8,500*

WILLIE KORTH "JUBILEE" 50th ANNIVERSARY MODEL – .357 Mag., 4 in. barrel, gold inlaid with head of Willie Korth and dates (1954-2004), 50 Jahre oak leaf, and acorn engraving in high polish blue, deluxe hand engraved wood grips. Only 5 to be mfg. beginning 2004.

Last MSR was $18,000.

A special case which holds both the anniversary pistol and the revolver, as well as a matching commemorative knife was also available.

ANNO DOMINI 2000 – 357 Mag., 4 in. combat model, PVD gold plasma coating, deep relief engraving featuring thorns, includes black leather briefcase, only 10 mfg. during 2000.

Extreme rarity precludes accurate pricing on this model - manufacturer's suggested retail was $10,000.

PLATINUM MODEL – .357 Mag. cal., 6 shot, 4 in. barrel, platinum engraved model with deluxe grips, includes black leather briefcase. New 2002.

The last MSR on this model was $9,600.

ARABESQUE MODEL – .357 Mag. cal., 6 shot, 4 in. barrel, arabesque engraved model with deluxe grips, includes black leather briefcase. New 2003.

The last MSR on this model was $9,600.

EICHENLAUB MODEL – .357 Mag. cal., 6 shot, 4 in. barrel, oak leaf engraved model with deluxe grips, includes black leather briefcase. New 2003.

The last MSR on this model was $12,000.

JAEGER MODEL – .357 Mag. cal., 4 in. barrel, ivory grips with hunting scene, left side has hunter and dog, right side has deer in forest, gold inlaid, grey "pickled" finish, fully engraved in Arabesque style.

The last MSR on this model was $19,200.

MODEL BELLEZZA – .357 Mag. cal., 6 in. barrel, ruby and diamonds with palladium finish, special female figured grips, Arabesque engraving, includes case, very limited mfg.

The last MSR on this model was $150,000.

"Bellezza" comes from a Handel opera, and means "the triumph over sorrow and disappointment."

CUSTOM PRESENTATION MODEL – deluxe variation of Sport/Combat model.

This variation is available with engraving and other special options that are priced per individual quotation from the factory.

KOSCHAT, JAKOB

Current longarm manufacturer located in Ferlach, Austria. No current U.S. importation.

Jakob Koschat manufactures high quality shotguns and double rifles in a variety of sporting configurations. Many options are available. Please contact him directly for more information, including pricing, availability, and delivery time (see Trademark Index).

KRAG-JORGENSEN (30/40 KRAG)

Previous U.S. magazine fed military rifle. Official government designation is United States Magazine Rifle and Carbine, Caliber 30. First U.S. (.30-40 Krag) military repeating rifle to shoot smokeless powder ammunition. Approx. 475,000 mfg. by Springfield Armory 1894-1904.

There have been many alterations and conversions of Krag-Jorgensen rifles - some of which are hard to identify. As a rule, these alterations and conversions almost remove any collectibility, and pricing is determined mostly by its competitive shooter value. Since prices for upper condition (95%+), original Krag-Jorgensens have increased significantly in recent years, beware of non-original guns, conversions, and in some cases, fakes.

GRADING - PPGS™	100%	98%	95%	90%	80%	70%	60%	LAST MSR

RIFLES: BOLT ACTION

MODEL OF 1892 RIFLE (DATED 1894) – traditionally, these models have been categorized as either Type I (solid upper band) or Type II (double strap upper band), but this is too simple a definition - there were many variations. Ordnance documents list approx. 14 changes that were made during the production run, and examination of original rifles have found many more. 24,562 mfg.

	$12,000	$10,000	$7,500	$5,000	$3,000	$2,000	$1,200	

Early rifles in original condition will have numbered bolt parts (below S/N 500) and magazine parts (below S/N 1,500) - they will command a premium.

It is essential that anyone considering purchasing this model thoroughly research the sequence and scope of the changes.

Only one rifle that has all the appropriate bolt and magazine parts numbered to the receiver is known.

* ***Model of 1892 Rifle Carbine*** – rare, only 2 known - one in a government museum, and the other in a private collection.

Extreme rarity precludes accurate pricing on this model.

MODEL 1892/1896 RIFLE (ARSENAL ALTERED) – numerous variations of Model 1892 rifles arsenal altered to Model 1896. 21,264 altered.

	$1,000	$875	$775	$675	$600	$525	$375	

Add a small premium for models upgraded in 1897 by being restocked but retaining the Model 1892 extractor, and a receiver with no notch.

MODEL 1892 CADET RIFLE – rare, 2 variations - 400 in the 18-19,000 serial number range, with 1894 dated receiver, 4 in the 35,XXX serial number range with 1896 receiver, both have 1896 dated cartouches, three of the 400 were surveyed or condemned, and the remainder were converted to service rifle configuration. 3 of the group of 4 are known - 2 are in private collections and one is at West Point. 404 mfg.

Extreme rarity precludes accurate pricing on this model.

MODEL 1895/1896 TRANSISTION RIFLE – these rifles were produced prior to the official introduction of the Model 1896, receiver dates 1895 or 1896 with the MODEL prefix, cartouche dates will be 1896. 1,368 mfg.

	$4,000	$3,000	$1,750	$950	$650	$500	$400	

MODEL OF 1896 RIFLE – receivers marked Model 1896, cartouche dates are 1896, 1897, and 1898. 60,528 mfg. - receivers stamped "MODEL 1896", with 1896, 1897, 1898, or 1901 dated cartouches (rare), rear leaf sight, first type graduated for 700 to 2,000 yards, second type graduated for 200 to 2,000 yards. 14,942 mfg.

	$4,000	$3,000	$1,750	$950	$650	$500	$400	

Add a premium for rifles with 1897 dated cartouches impressed sideways.

Add a premium for rifles with 1901 dated cartouches.

* ***Model 1895/1896 Rifle Transition Carbine*** – a "crash" program was started in the spring of 1895 and completed in May, 1896 to arm the regular cavalry, receivers dated 1894 (rare) 1895, or 1896 with no MODEL prefix, 1896 cartouche date. 7,111 mfg.

	$5,000	$4,500	$2,750	$1,850	$1,150	$825	$600	

Add a premium for rare early version with two cleaning rod holes in the butt, stacked one above the other.

* ***Model of 1896 Rifle Carbine*** – rear sight leaf graduated for 700 to 2,000 yards and will be stamped at the top right with a "C" and the base will have a "C" on the right side.

	$5,000	$4,500	$2,750	$1,850	$1,150	$825	$600	

Buyer beware - some models may have fake sights.

MODEL OF 1898 RIFLE – some 25 variations exist in this model. 342,526 mfg.

	$3,000	$2,500	$1,000	$700	$600	$500	$400	

Subtract 20%-40% for "as modified" guns.

Collectors must be aware of the correct combination of serial number, sight variation, and cartouche date of a rifle in original "as made" condition.

GRADING - PPGS™	100%	98%	95%	90%	80%	70%	60%	LAST MSR

* ***Model of 1898 Rifle Carbine*** – scarce and rare in authentic original condition. 5,002 mfg.

	$5,000	$4,500	$3,500	$1,800	$1,500	$1,200	$1,000	

Beware of fakes.

* ***Model of 1898 Rifles with Parkhurst Device*** – scarce/rare, most were destroyed. 100 modified.

Extreme rarity precludes accurate pricing on this model.

MODEL OF 1899 CARBINE – numerous variations, sight and hand guard changes. 36,052 mfg.

	$5,000	$4,000	$2,350	$1,450	$1,100	$850	$600	

Subtract 20% - 40% for "as modified" or parts guns.

Collectors must be aware of the correct combination of serial number, sight variation, hand guard, and stock cartouche date.

* ***Model of 1899 Carbine with Parkhurst Device*** – scarce/rare, most were destroyed. 100 modified.

Extreme rarity precludes accurate pricing on this model.

BOARD OF ORDNANCE RIFLE – 26 in. barrel, rare. 100 mfg.

Extreme rarity precludes accurate pricing on this model.

PHILIPPINE CONSTABULARY RIFLE – records from the Bureau of Insular Affairs show that the civil government of the Philippines purchased Model of 1899 carbines, and had them modified by the U.S. military at the Manila Ordnance Facility. 4,980 converted.

The absence of an authenticated example of this model precludes accurate pricing.

SCHOOL GUN – officially known as the United States Magazine Carbine, Model of 1899, Modified for Use with Knife Bayonet and Gun Sling, these were carbines and stocks modified between 1906-1916 at both Springfield and Rock Island, examples of Springfield modification have been observed with a block J.F.C. cartouche. 3,371 carbines and 6,118 stocks converted.

	$4,500	$3,800	$1,800	$1,200	$1,000	$800	$600	

DCM/NRA CARBINE – original carbines and cut down rifles were sold by the DCM to NRA members and others during the 1930s-40s, widely imitated by commercial vendors.

	$1,500	$1,200	$1,000	$800	$600	$500	$400	

Buyer beware - this gun should have original documentation before considering a purchase.

KRAL AV

Current manufacturer established circa 1983, and located in Konya, Turkey. No current U.S. importation.

Kral AV manufactures a complete line of good quality O/U, SxS, single shot, semi-auto, and slide action shotguns. The company also manufactures air rifles and blank pistols. Currently, no products are being imported into the U.S. Please contact the company directly for more information, including pricing and availability (see Trademark Index).

KRASSNIK, VALENTIN

Current custom long gun manufacturer located in Ferlach, Austria.

Valentin Krassnik is a member of the Ferlacher Waffen Präzisionstechnik Produktions GmbH & Co KG, established after the Ferlach Guild was dissolved. Krassnik manufactures custom long guns, built per individual customer specifications. Please contact him directly for a price quotation, available options, and delivery time (see Trademark Index).

KRICO

Current trademark manufactured by Kriegeskorte Handels GmbH, located in Pyrbaum, Germany. No current U.S. importer. Previously imported exclusively mid-2005-2010 by Northeast Arms LLC, located in Fort Fairfield, ME. Previously distributed by Precision Sales, Int'l, located in Westfield, MA 1999-2002. Previously manufactured in Vohburg-Irsching, Germany 1996-1999, and in Fürth-Stadeln, Germany by Sportwaffenfabrik

GRADING - PPGS™	100%	98%	95%	90%	80%	70%	60%	LAST MSR

Kriegeskorte GmbH pre-1996.

During 2000, Krico was purchased by Marocchi. Krico has been imported/distributed by over ten U.S. companies/individuals. Krico manufactures high quality rifles, and to date, has mostly sold their guns in Europe. Many of the discontinued models listed may still be current within the European marketplace. Please contact the factory directly for more information, including availability and pricing (see Trademark Index). The Krico name is an abridgement of the family name Kriegeskorte.

Due to space considerations, information regarding this manufacturer is available online free at www.bluebookofgunvalues.com.

H. KRIEGHOFF GUN CO. (SHOTGUNS OF ULM)

Current manufacturer located in Ulm, Germany since circa 1954. Previous manufacture was in Suhl, Germany 1886-1947. Currently imported and distributed by Krieghoff International, Inc. located in Ottsville, PA. Dealer direct sales only.

KRIEGHOFF

Currently, Krieghoff manufactures 2,000 guns annually, in all configurations.

DRILLINGS

H. Krieghoff drillings can be ordered with a variety of cals. (.222 Rem., .243 Win., .270 Win., or .30-06) and special order features. The universal trigger system (UAS) and Combi-cocking device are standard on all Plus, Steingass, Optima, and Quadro drillings. Prices shown below are for standard guns with no options. Better models will have a finer grade walnut and exhibit more elaborate deep relief engraving.

Add $450 for free floating rifle barrels on Trumpf and Neptun Models listed below (both regular steel frame and Dural variations).
Add $1,390 for Pivot scope mount.
Add $1,290 for 3-claw scope mount system (disc.).

PLUS MODEL – 12, 16, or 20 ga. over rifle barrel (.222 Rem., .243 Win., .270 Win., or .30-06 cal.), boxlock action, includes universal trigger system (UAS) as standard, light engraving, choice of soldered or free floating rifle barrel with adj. point of impact (Thermo TS Stabil - Model Plus TS). Mfg. 1988-2004.

$5,125 $3,650 $2,800 $2,200 $1,825 $1,525 $1,200 ***$6,275***

Add $1,700 for full length stock (Model Steingass, 20 ga. only).

OPTIMUS TS MODEL – 12 or 20 ga. over 21 1/2 in. rifle barrel (various rifle cals.), features Thermo Stabil barrels, standard engraving is small arabesque, includes soft case. Mfg. 2003-2009.

$9,350 $8,200 $7,100 $6,500 $5,500 $4,500 $3,500 ***$10,950***

Add $2,800 for Quadro 20 Model with double rifle and 20 ga. shotgun barrel configuration.
Add $2,295 - $2,595 for KS full length rifled barrel insert, depending on caliber (up to 9.3x74R).
Add $1,975 for pivot mount for installed and sighted in pivot mount.
Add $975 for single trigger, or $1,295 for single/double trigger.

During 2009, this model was dropped in favor of the new Optima Series.

QUADRO AFRICAN DRILLING – .20 ga. under rifle barrels (.375 Flanged Mag. NE, .500/.416 NE, or .470 NE), 20 ga. drilling frame with reinforced sidewalls, hinged front trigger, similar sights as the Classic Big 5 double rifle. Mfg. 2003-2009.

This gun was available by custom order only.

TRUMPF MODEL – 12, 16, or 20 ga. O/U, or rifle shotgun combo., various cals., boxlock, 25 in. barrels, 7 1/2 lbs.

This model is POR.

* ***Trumpf Model Dural*** – Dural aluminum frame variation of the Trumpf, 6.8 lbs., cased. Disc. 2003.

$8,300 $6,300 $5,350 $4,250 $3,300 $2,750 $2,200 ***$9,950***

GRADING - PPGS™	100%	98%	95%	90%	80%	70%	60%	LAST MSR

NEPTUN MODEL – 12, 16, or 20 ga., variety of cals., elaborate engraving, sidelocks. Mfg. began pre-WWII. Disc. 2011.

	$13,250	$10,400	$9,000	$7,550	$6,200	$5,100	$4,150	*$16,500*

* ***Neptun Model Dural*** – Dural aluminum frame variation of the Neptun, cased. Disc. 2011.

	$13,250	$10,400	$9,000	$7,550	$6,200	$5,100	$4,150	*$16,500*

NEPTUN PRIMUS MODEL – similar to Neptun Model, only hand detachable sidelocks and elaborate deep relief engraving. Disc. 2011.

	$18,500	$13,650	$10,450	$8,400	$7,100	$5,850	$4,950	*$24,500*

* ***Neptun Primus Model Dural*** – Dural aluminum frame variation available at no extra charge. Disc. 2011.

	$18,500	$13,650	$10,450	$8,400	$7,100	$5,850	$4,950	*$24,500*

OPTIMA – 12 or 20 ga. over various cals., 21 1/2 in. barrels, universal trigger system, combi-cocking device, Arabesque engraving on 20 ga., includes soft case.

MSR $11,495	$9,750	$8,450	$7,225	$6,600	$5,500	$4,500	$3,500	

Add $1,995 for Pivot scope mount.

* ***Optima Double Rifle Drilling*** – 20 ga. over various cals., 3 in. chambers, 21 1/2 in. barrels, universal trigger system, combi-cocking device, Arabesque engraving, includes soft case.

MSR $14,495	$12,750	$10,750	$8,650	$7,225	$5,800	$4,750	$4,150	

* ***Optima Big Five (Africa)*** – 20 ga. over .375 Flanged Mag. NE, .500/.416 NE, or .470 NE cal., 21 1/5 in. barrel, universal trigger system, combi-cocking device, includes soft case.

MSR $23,500	$20,750	$16,500	$13,500	$10,500	$8,750	$7,250	$6,600	

PISTOLS: SEMI-AUTO

WWII Krieghoff Lugers will appear in the Luger section.

KRIEGHOFF LUGER – 9mm Para. cal., 8 shot mag., toggle lock action, based on the WWII production with Bakelite grips, 4 in. barrel, and special ser. no. range. Only 200 mfg. beginning 2006, serial numbered 18001-18200.

MSR $17,545	$15,995	$14,250	$12,000	$9,000	$7,000	$5,000	$4,000	

RIFLES: O/U & SxS

Various grades differ in style and amount of engraving, choice of walnut and various options that can be special ordered.

Add $1,950 for 4-claw scope mount (standard or European).

TECK O/U – .30-06, .300 Win. Mag. (disc. 1994), .308 Win., 7x56R (disc. 1994), 7x65R (new 1995), 8x57JRS, 8x75RS (new 1995), 9.3x74R, .375 H&H (disc. 1988), or .458 Win. Mag. cal., 25 in. barrels, boxlock action, cocking indicators, hard case included.

	$8,725	$6,475	$5,200	$4,300	$3,650	$3,300	$3,000	*$10,500*

Add $1,400 for .375 H&H or .458 Win. Mag. cal.
Add $990 for DTs with front set trigger.

* ***Teck-Handspanner O/U*** – 7x65R, .30-06, or .308 Win. cal. on 16 ga. receiver frame, manual cocking.

	$10,200	$7,950	$6,675	$5,175	$4,375	$3,950	$3,200	*$12,495*

ULTRA TS O/U – various cals. up to 9.3x74R, features unique manual cocking/self cocking device and interchangeable muzzle wedge for adjustable point of impact. New 1993.

MSR $9,395	$8,400	$7,200	$6,100	$5,000	$4,275	$3,500	$2,950	

Add $995 for single trigger.
Subtract $1,100 for combination gun with 20 ga., 3 in. chambers, and a variety of rifle cals.

ULM O/U – similar to Teck Double Rifle, except has any combination of cals., with sidelocks and more elaborate engraving.

	$14,300	$10,350	$8,550	$6,900	$6,100	$5,500	$4,950	*$17,900*

Add $695 for hand detachable sidelocks. Add $1,775 with single/double trigger.

GRADING - PPGS™	100%	98%	95%	90%	80%	70%	60%	LAST MSR

* ***Ulm O/U Dekor*** – sidelock with light scroll engraving. Importation disc. 1991.

	$10,450	$9,150	$8,000	$6,750	$5,600	$5,000	$4,400	*$12,500*

* ***Ulm O/U Primus*** – deluxe sidelock. Disc. 2004.

	$19,750	$13,000	$10,250	$8,100	$6,550	$5,700	$5,300	*$26,000*

TRUMPF SxS – boxlock action, similar to Teck model, except in .30-06, 8x57JRS, or 9.3x74R cal. Disc. 1994.

	$13,200	$9,700	$8,350	$6,900	$6,100	$5,500	$4,950	*$16,150*

CLASSIC SxS STANDARD – current cals. include .30-06, .308 Win., 7x57R, 7x65R, .30R Blaser, 8.5x63R, 8x57JRS, 8x75RS, and 9.3x74R, boxlock action, 21 1/2 (optional) or 23 1/2 in. regulated barrels, DTs, Combi cocking device, removable wedge and integrated front sight in cals. up to .375 H&H, extractors, choice of standard or Bavarian style stock, light engraving, with or w/o sideplates, various engraving options, 7 1/2 - 11 lbs. New 1995.

MSR $9,995	$9,200	$8,000	$6,750	$5,600	$4,650	$3,700	$3,300	

Add $4,400 for a set of 20 ga., 3 in. chambered barrels.
Add $6,150 per set of interchangeable rifle barrels.
Add $3,975 for sideplates with standard scroll engraving or $1,895 for boxlock standard engraving.

* ***Classic SxS Standard Big Five (Big Bore)*** – .375 H&H, .375 Flanged Mag. NE (new 1996), .416 Rigby, .458 Win. Mag., .450/400 NE, .470 NE, .500/.416 NE (new 1996), or .500 NE cal., hinged front trigger, non-removable muzzle wedge, 23 1/2 in. barrels with express style quarter rib, 9 1/2 - 10 1/2 lbs. New 1995.

MSR $12,995	$11,250	$8,950	$7,750	$6,750	$5,800	$5,300	$4,750	

Add $4,400 for a set of 20 ga./3 in. barrels.
Add $6,150 per set of interchangeable rifle barrels.
Add $3,975 for sideplates with standard scroll engraving or $1,895 for boxlock standard engraving.
Add $3,600 for Big Game Grade II with small game scene engraving and best quality select wood (new 2012).

NEPTUN SxS – sidelock double rifle, same features as the Ulm model. Importation disc. 1991.

	$12,750	$10,400	$8,700	$7,350	$6,000	$5,450	$4,995	*$15,500*

RIFLES: SINGLE SHOT

HUBERTUS RIFLE – available in .22-250 Rem., .222 Rem., .243 Win., .270 Win., .30-06, .308 Win., .270 Wby. Mag. (disc.), .300 Win. Mag., 7mm Rem. Mag., and in 12 metric cals. between 5.6x50R Mag. - 9.3x74R, single shot stalking rifle with Kickspanner (unique manual cocking device), engraved boxlock action, 23 1/2 in. barrel with quarter rib, fast lock time, double underlugs, approx. 6 1/2 lbs. Importation began circa 1997.

MSR $6,495	$5,850	$4,900	$4,150	$3,550	$3,000	$2,600	$1,900	

Add $1,000 for Mag. cals.
Add $3,975 for sideplates with standard scroll engraving.
Add $3,395 per extra interchangeable barrel on standard U.S. or European cals.

RIFLES: SLIDE ACTION

SEMPRIO – .223 Rem., .243 Win., .270 Win., 7x64, 6.5x55mm, .30-06, .308 Win., 8x57IS, 9.3x62mm, 7mm Rem. Mag., .300 Win. Mag., .338 Win. Mag. (disc. 2009), or .375 Ruger cal., unique in-line action is operated by using the forearm to slide the barrel assembly forward (not backward), fluted bolt, full take-down capability, 3 (mag. cals.) or 4 shot detachable mag., 21.7 or 25 (Mag. cals.) in. barrel, open sights, checkered pistol grip stock, universal trigger system, drilled and tapped, black or nickel anodized finish, Combi cocking device, sling swivels, rubber recoil pad, approx. 7 1/2 lbs. New 2007.

MSR $4,690	$4,250	$3,750	$3,250	$2,750	$2,250	$1,775	$1,575	

Add $300 for Mag. cals.
Add $1,390 (standard cals) or $1,690 (Mag. cals.) per extra barrel, depending on configuration.

SHOTGUNS: O/U

Subtract 15% for 26 in. barrels on used models.
Subtract 25% for 26 in. barrels on used higher grade models.
Add $2,395 - $2,600 for "KS" full length rifle insert barrel, depending on caliber - available in 12, 16, or 20 ga. (new 2006).

GRADING - PPGS™	100%	98%	95%	90%	80%	70%	60%	LAST MSR

MODEL 32 STANDARD – 12, 20, 28 ga., or .410 bore, O/U, 28-32 in. high rib barrels, ejectors, boxlock, single trigger, select wood. Disc. 1983.

Standard	$2,750	$2,500	$2,250	$2,000	$1,900	$1,700	$1,500	
San Remo	$5,750	$5,250	$4,500	$3,750	$3,000	$2,250	$1,950	
Monte Carlo	$7,500	$6,750	$5,625	$4,875	$4,125	$3,000	$2,250	
Crown	$8,750	$7,500	$6,000	$5,250	$4,500	$3,375	$2,625	
Super Crown	$10,500	$9,000	$7,500	$6,000	$5,250	$3,750	$3,000	

* ***Model 32 Standard Low Rib*** – 28 ga. or .410 bore.

	$3,950	$3,575	$2,875	$2,650	$2,200	$1,900	$1,600	

Add approx. 20% for two-barrel set.

MODEL 32 4-BARREL SKEET SET – 12, 20, 28 ga., or .410 bore, O/U, matched barrels in case, grades differ in engraving and wood quality. Disc. 1983.

Standard	$8,450	$7,450	$6,500	$5,600	$4,650	$3,725	$2,775	
München Grade	$9,950	$8,450	$7,450	$6,500	$5,600	$4,650	$3,725	
San Remo Grade (unmarked)	$12,750	$10,350	$8,250	$6,750	$5,850	$4,950	$4,750	
Monte Carlo (Silver Crown 50 mfg.)	$18,750	$16,000	$13,750	$11,000	$9,000	$7,800	$6,600	
Crown Grade (400 mfg.)	$24,995	$21,000	$17,750	$14,750	$12,100	$10,350	$9,650	
Super Crown Grade (48 mfg.)	$29,995	$25,750	$20,750	$16,750	$14,775	$12,650	$10,350	

K-20 SPORTING AND FIELD – 20, 28 ga., or .410 bore, compact 20 ga. frame, incorporates all of the technical refinements of the K-80, nickel plated receiver with satin grey finish and classic scroll engraving, 28 (disc.), 30 or 32 in. separated barrels (28 ga. and .410 bore barrels can be purchased separately but must be fitted) with tapered flat rib, SST, AE, checkered walnut stock and Schnabel forearm, includes 5 choke tubes, approx. 7 1/4 lbs., includes fitted aluminum case. Importation began 2000.

MSR $10,995	$9,700	$8,350	$7,650	$6,425	$5,750	$4,850	$4,000	

Add $100 for 28 ga. or .410 bore.
Add $300 for Pro Sporter variation including 5 titanium choke tubes.
Add $4,195 for extra set of 20 ga. barrels, or $4,295 for 28 ga. or .410 bore.
Add $950-$3,700 for wood upgrades, depending on quality.
Add $4,295 for 20/28 ga. set or $8,590 for 3 gauge set.

A 20/28 ga. set with 10 choke tubes and hard case is also available for $13,945. A 3 gauge set (20, 28 ga. and .410 bore) with 15 choke tubes and hard case is also available for $18,115.

Additional options for the K-20 include case colors ($4,295), and K-20 models with engraving options include Super Standard ($13,895 MSR), Super Scroll ($15,995 MSR), Suhl Scroll ($17,695 MSR), Parcours Special ($16,995 MSR), Gold Super Scroll (coin or blue finish, $19,395 MSR), Bavaria (disc. 2004), Bavaria Royale (new 2005, $19,195 MSR), Gold Uplander (coin or blue finish, $22,695 MSR), Gold Plantation Scroll (coin or blue finish, $22,695 MSR), Plantation Scroll/Uplander (nickel or blue finish, $18,395 MSR), Millennium (currently POR, last MSR was $28,695 in 2011, new 2005), Waterfowl Medallion Nitride ($27,395, new 2005), and Bavaria Suhl ($25,645 MSR).

K-80 TRAP – 12 ga. only, available in O/U, Unsingle, Top Single (single top barrel, disc. 2005 w/fixed rib), and Combo (O/U with extra trap barrel) configurations, standard model has silver finished receiver, adj. rib allowing variable points of impact (new 1993). In O/U configuration the barrels are separated, about 8 1/2 lbs. A wide variety of custom order options can be ordered on this model.

Add $475 for 3 screw-in chokes capability (single barrel guns only).
Add $3,495 (O/U) or $5,275 (Unsingle) per extra barrel(s), w/o choke tubes.
Add $595 for single release trigger or $995 for double release trigger.
Subtract 20% for old style receiver with "K-80" on side.

Additionally, Krieghoff offers many more custom engraving options. Please contact Krieghoff International Inc. for current engraving options and pricing on the K-80 Series.

GRADING - PPGS™	100%	98%	95%	90%	80%	70%	60%	LAST MSR

* ***K-80 Trap Standard Unsingle*** – 32 or 34 in. lower barrel with either fixed choke or choke tubes.

MSR $12,075	$10,950	$8,850	$7,850	$6,600	$5,600	$3,550	$3,200	

Add $420 for choke tubes.
Add $505 for Trap Special Unsingle (new 2007).
Add approx. 30% for Combo (includes unsingle and O/U barrels), or approx. 35%-75% for Trap Special Combo CTIII (new 2005), depending on grade.

* ***K-80 Trap Standard O/U*** – 30 or 32 in. barrels with either fixed chokes or choke tubes.

MSR $10,295	$9,825	$8,000	$7,000	$5,950	$5,100	$4,350	$3,600	

Add $700 for choke tubes.
Add $525 for Trap Special Model (new 2007).
Add approx. 50% for Combo Standard K-80 variations.
Subtract 20% for top single variation (very limited mfg.).

* ***K-80 Trap Centennial Model*** – 12 ga. only, available in combo configuration only, 100 only mfg. 1986 to commemorate Krieghoff's centennial year, ser. no. 14501-14600, H. Krieghoff's signature inlaid in gold on frame sides.

	$6,750	$5,500	$4,650	$3,900	$3,500	$3,000	$2,600	*$7,650*

K-80 SKEET/SKEET SPECIAL – 12 ga. only, available in Standardweight (8mm rib) or International (12mm rib) configuration, 28 (limited availability) or 30 in. barrels, approx. 8 3/4 lbs.

Beginning 2000, options for the K-80 Skeet include case colors ($4,295 MSR), and K-80 models with engraving options include: Super Standard (new 2005, $12,700 MSR), Super Scroll ($14,800 MSR), Suhl Scroll ($16,500 MSR), Parcours Special ($15,800 MSR), Gold Super Scroll (coin or blue finish, $18,200 MSR), Gold Uplander (coin or blue finish, $21,500 MSR), Gold Plantation Scroll (coin or blue finish, $19,800 MSR), Plantation Scroll/Uplander (nickel or blue finish, $17,200 MSR), and Bavaria Suhl ($24,500 MSR).

Additionally, Krieghoff offers many more custom engraving options. Please contact Krieghoff International Inc. for current engraving options and pricing on the K-80 Series.

* ***K-80 Skeet/Skeet Special Standard Model*** – available in Standardweight frame, hard case optional.

MSR $9,800	$8,800	$7,250	$6,125	$4,900	$3,650	$2,950	$2,450	

Add $700 for choke tubes.
Add $3,495 per extra set of barrels with fixed chokes, $4,195 with choke tubes (Skeet Special), or $3,550 for heavy Skeet barrels (disc.).
Subtract 20% for receivers with "K-80" on side.

* ***K-80 Skeet Special Model*** – similar to Standard Model, except includes 5 choke tubes and tapered flat rib.

MSR $10,500	$9,400	$7,750	$6,600	$5,000	$4,100	$3,350	$2,850	

Subtract 20% for receivers with "K-80" on side.

* ***K-80 Special Centennial Skeet*** – available in skeet configuration - special features as noted above on Centennial Model description listed under K-80 Trap. Mfg. 1986 only.

	$3,675	$3,150	$2,700	$2,425	$2,100	$1,800	$1,650	*$3,980*

K-80 2-BARREL LIGHTWEIGHT SKEET SET – 12 ga., includes one set of 28 in. barrels with Tula chokes and one set of carrier barrels allowing use of sub-gauge tubes (carrier barrels cannot be used for 12 ga.), 8mm rib, hard case standard. Mfg. 1988-99.

* ***K-80 2-Barrel Lightweight Skeet Set Standard Grade***

	$8,750	$7,000	$5,150	$4,300	$3,875	$3,300	$3,000	*$11,840*

Subtract $1,845 for heavy barrel variation, which does not include sub-gauge tubes.
Retail price for 2 barrel heavy set with choke tubes was $9,995.

* ***K-80 2-Barrel Lightweight Skeet Set Bavaria Model*** – game scene engraved silver receiver with light perimeter scroll work, select walnut. Imported 1988-99.

	$12,950	$10,000	$8,000	$7,200	$6,200	$5,250	$4,800	*$16,990*

Subtract $1,845 for heavy barrel variation, which does not include sub-gauge tubes.

GRADING - PPGS™	100%	98%	95%	90%	80%	70%	60%	LAST MSR

Retail price for 2 barrel heavy set with choke tubes was $15,145.

* ***K-80 2-Barrel Lightweight Skeet Set Danube Model*** – fine English scroll work on receiver sides and floor plate. Imported 1988-99.

	$22,945	$15,250	$17,750	$9,400	$7,750	$7,000	$6,650	*$28,090*

Subtract $1,845 for heavy barrel variation, which does not include sub-gauge tubes.

Retail price for 2 barrel heavy set with choke tubes was $26,245.

* ***K-80 2-Barrel Lightweight Skeet Set Gold Target Model*** – deep chiseled scroll engraving with gold line accents, 100% coverage finest quality walnut. Importation disc. 1999.

	$25,975	$20,500	$15,950	$12,375	$9,950	$8,700	$7,500	*$31,635*

Subtract $1,845 for heavy barrel variation.

Retail price for heavy 2 barrel set with choke tubes was $29,790.

K-80 4-BARREL SKEET SET – 1 barrel each of 12, 20, 28 ga., and .410 bore, 12 ga. is Tula choked (even patterning), 8mm tapered flat or standard VR, includes hard case. Since most shooters prefer different gauge insert tubes (Briley, etc.) rather than barrel sets, values have gone down considerably recently for these 4 gauge sets.

* ***K-80 4-Barrel Skeet Set Standard Grade*** – satin finished receiver with skeet scroll engraving. Importation disc. 1999.

	$10,000	$8,000	$6,500	$5,350	$4,500	$4,000	$3,650	*$16,950*

* ***K-80 4-Barrel Skeet Set Bavaria Model*** – game scene engraved silver receiver with light perimeter scrollwork, select walnut. Importation disc. 1999.

	$14,000	$12,000	$9,500	$8,250	$6,900	$5,400	$4,350	*$22,100*

* ***K-80 4-Barrel Skeet Set Danube Model*** – fine English scroll work on receiver sides and floor plate. Importation disc. 1999.

	$22,500	$17,000	$13,000	$10,500	$8,700	$7,500	$6,250	*$33,200*

* ***K-80 4-Barrel Skeet Set Gold Target Model*** – deep chiseled scroll engraving with gold line accents, 100% coverage finest quality walnut. Importation disc. 1999.

	$29,650	$17,350	$13,000	$10,500	$8,700	$7,500	$6,250	*$36,745*

K-80 PIGEON – 12 ga. only, available with 28 or 30 in. barrels, standard tapered step rib, IM/F choking, available in Standardweight configuration.

Beginning 1992, the K-80 Pigeon Model is available by special order only. Rather than list the various Pigeon models separately, their current values will be approximately the same as the corresponding K-80 Trap/Skeet Models listed.

ULM-P LIVE PIGEON – 12 ga. only, live pigeon gun with hand detachable sidelocks, 28 or 30 in. VR barrels, standard grade has light scrollwork engraving.

	$17,500	$12,000	$9,175	$7,700	$6,000	$5,450	$4,995	*$22,500*

* ***ULM-P Live Pigeon Bavaria Grade*** – similar to Ulm-P, only with elaborate game scene engraving.

	$22,000	$16,000	$12,000	$9,000	$7,250	$6,000	$5,500	*$29,500*

K-80 SPORTING CLAYS – 12 ga. only, 28 (disc.), 30 (new 1991), 32 (new 1993), or 34 (mfg. 2003-2009) in. barrels with 5 choke tubes, choice of 8mm VR skeet, tapered flat (broadway), or step rib (special order), sporting clay stock dimensions. New 1988.

For options on the Model K-80 Sporting, please refer to the options on the K-80 Skeet, as they are similar in price.

* ***K-80 Sporting Clays Standard Grade*** – satin finished receiver with sporting scroll engraving.

MSR $10,995	$9,750	$8,300	$7,600	$6,400	$5,800	$5,200	$4,400	

Add $4,195 for extra set of O/U barrels with 5 choke tubes or $3,595 w/o choke tubes (disc.).
Subtract 10% for 28 in. barrels.

GRADING - PPGS™	100%	98%	95%	90%	80%	70%	60%	LAST MSR

KS-2 SERIES – any ga., full H&H type sidelocks, priced by individual special order. Prices started at $24,000. Disc. 1988.

K-80 PROSPORTER/PROSKEET – 12 ga., 3 in. chamber, 30 or 32 in. barrels with extended choke tubes, bead sights, case hardened nickel plated receiver, optional SST, top tang push button safety, choice of checkered Turkish walnut stock with adj. comb and choice of Pro Sporter #3/#7 Schnabel or Pro Skeet #3/#6 forend, approx. 8 3/4 lbs. New 2008.

MSR $11,295	$9,950	$8,300	$7,850	$6,600	$5,800	$5,200	$4,400	

Engraving options and special orders are the same as the Sporting Clays model.

K-80 PARCOURS – 12 ga. only, 3 in. chambers, features 32 in. non-separated (soldered rib) barrels with flat 6mm tapered VR, choice of fixed or optional Briley thin wall chokes, choice of case colored or nickel plated steel receiver with satin gray finish, SST, top tang safety, redesigned checkered adj. Monte Carlo stock and slim profile forearm, includes fitted aluminum case, 8 lbs. New 2013

MSR $9,500	$8,850	$8,150	$7,500	$6,700	$5,800	$4,900	$4,000	

SHOTGUNS: O/U OR COMBINATION GUNS

Add $695 for hand detachable sidelocks (Ulm only).
Add $1,290 for 4-claw scope mount system (disc.).
Add $1,150 for pivot mount system.

TECK MODEL – 12 and 16 ga., O/U shotgun or rifle/shotgun combo., various cals. (7x57R, 7x64mm, 7x65R, .30-06, or .308 Win.), boxlock action, Kersten double crossbolt, auto ejectors, 7 1/2 lbs. Importation disc. 2004.

	$6,650	$5,100	$4,400	$3,550	$3,000	$2,600	$2,295	*$7,750*

* ***Teck Model Dural*** – dural aluminum frame variation of the Teck, 6.8 lbs. Importation disc. 2004.

	$6,625	$5,100	$4,400	$3,550	$3,000	$2,600	$2,295	*$7,750*

ULM – similar to Teck, except sidelock and fully engraved with leaf arabesques.

MSR $14,500	$12,325	$9,250	$7,950	$6,350	$5,250	$4,400	$3,500	

* ***Ulm Dural*** – dural aluminum frame variation of the Ulm. Importation disc. 2004.

	$12,325	$9,250	$7,950	$6,350	$5,250	$4,400	$3,500	*$14,500*

ULM PRIMUS – similar to Ulm, except game scene engraved with English arabesques. Disc. 2011.

	$19,000	$13,750	$10,000	$8,750	$7,500	$6,250	$5,500	*$22,850*

* ***Ulm Primus Dural*** – dural aluminum frame variation of the Ulm Primus. Disc. 2011.

	$19,000	$13,750	$10,000	$8,750	$7,500	$6,250	$5,500	*$22,850*

ULTRA TS COMBINATION GUN – 12 (disc. 2007) or 20 ga., combination O/U, various calibers (lower barrel), 25 in. barrels, "Kickspanner" mechanism allows manual cocking from thumb safety, satin finish receiver, VR, 6 lbs. New 1985.

MSR $8,295	$7,250	$6,000	$5,100	$4,350	$3,650	$2,950	$2,300	

* ***Ultra-B TS Combination Gun*** – similar to Ultra, except features a selector to switch the front set trigger to the top shotgun barrel. Disc. 1995.

	$6,750	$5,600	$4,500	$3,950	$3,400	$2,750	$2,100	*$4,990*

SHOTGUNS: SxS

ESSENCIA SIDELOCK – 12, 16, 20 , 28 ga., or .410 bore, 2 3/4 or 3 (20 ga.) in. chambers, back action sidelock, 26 1/2 (disc.), 28, or 30 in. barrels choked IC/Mod., three frame sizes, ejectors, DTs, color case hardened receiver with fine English scroll engraving, gold plated cocking indicators and Krieghoff engraved in gold on receiver sides, Turkish walnut straight grip or pistol grip stock with semi-beavertail forearm, Krieghoff leather case, 6 3/4 - 7 lbs. New 2003.

MSR $29,895	$26,000	$22,950	$18,750	$15,750	$13,250	$11,000	$9,500	

Add $1,000 for 28 ga.
Add $4,055 for 28 ga. on small frame (sidelock only).

GRADING - PPGS™	100%	98%	95%	90%	80%	70%	60%	LAST MSR

Add $5,055 for .410 bore on 28 ga. frame (sidelock only).
Add $1,500 for Briley thin wall choke tubes.
Add $1,450 for single non-selective trigger. Add $2,000 for wood upgrade. Add $1,500 for oak and leather case.
Add $10,450 - $12,750 for extra set of interchangable barrels, depending on ga./bore.

Krieghoff also manufactures special editions of this gun on a private label basis for LeArmes, featuring a North American Game Bird Series (including Woodland Grade, Upland Grade, and Sierra Nevada Grade).

ESSENCIA BOXLOCK – 12, 16, 20 , or 28 ga. 2 3/4 in. chambers, round body boxlock action, 28 or 30 in. barrels choked IC/Mod., two frame sizes, ejectors, DTs, color case hardened receiver with fine English scroll engraving, gold plated cocking indicators and Krieghoff engraved in gold on receiver sides, Turkish walnut straight grip stock with semi-beavertail forearm, includes leather case, 6 1/4 - 7 lbs. New 2003.

MSR $25,950	$22,575	$19,000	$16,000	$13,000	$9,995	$8,500	$7,500	

Add $1,000 for 28 ga.
Add $4,000 for 28 ga. with 30 in. barrels.
Add $1,450 for single non-selective trigger.
Add $2,000 for wood upgrade.

Krieghoff also manufactures special editions of this gun on a private label basis for LeArmes, featuring a North American Game Bird Series (including Woodland Grade, Upland Grade, and Sierra Nevada Grade).

SHOTGUNS: SINGLE BARREL TRAP

MODEL 32 – 12 ga., same action as Model 32 O/U, 32-34 in. barrel, VR, mod., imp. mod., or full choke.

	$2,000	$1,800	$1,675	$1,550	$1,425	$1,300	$1,200	

KS-5 – 12 ga. only, 32 or 34 in. barrel, adj. point of impact, innovative trigger configuration, optional choke tubes, redesigned streamlined receiver (new 1993). Mfg. 1985-99.

	$2,500	$2,250	$2,100	$2,000	$1,875	$1,625	$1,400	*$3,675*

Add $2,100 per additional barrel.
Add $200 for screw-in choke option.
Add $200 for factory adj. comb stock.
Subtract $250 if w/o factory aluminum case.
Subtract 20% for blued receiver.
Subtract 15% for receiver with "KS-5" engraved on sides.
Subtract 10% for 32 in. barrel.

Adj. point of impact on this model is achieved by means of different, optional front hangers.

* ***KS-5 Special*** – 12 ga. only, 32 or 34 in. barrel, features adj. rib and comb stock, cased. Mfg. 1990-99.

	$3,500	$3,000	$2,650	$2,200	$2,050	$1,750	$1,500	*$4,695*

Add $2,750 per additional barrel.
Add $200 for screw-in choke option.
Subtract 10% for 32 in. barrel.

KX-5 – 12 ga. only, 2 3/4 in. chamber, 32 (disc. 2005) or 34 in. barrel, adj. point of impact, innovative adj. trigger (pull or release type), adj. stock comb, light scroll engraving, includes choke tubes and aluminum case. Mfg. 2002-2011.

	$4,295	$3,650	$3,200	$2,700	$2,400	$2,100	$1,850	*$5,495*

Add $425 for factory release trigger.
Subtract 10% for 32 in. barrel.

KX-6 – 12 ga. only, 3 in. chamber, 34 in. barrel with ventilated and fully adj. tapered high rib with three screw-in chokes, right or left hand Krieghoff parallel off-set trap stock, matte black receiver finish, includes Krieghoff fitted case. New 2012.

MSR $5,490	$4,400	$3,775	$3,300	$2,750	$2,450	$2,100	$1,850	

Add $475 for adj. buttplate (new 2013).

GRADING - PPGS™	100%	98%	95%	90%	80%	70%	60%	LAST MSR

KRISS SYSTEMS SA

Current manufacturer of civilian and law enforcement firearms established in 2008 with factories located in Nyon, Switzerland and Virginia Beach, VA. Dealer sales.

Kriss Systems SA is a division of the Gamma Applied Visions Group SA, a Swiss-based global technology development firm. The company's previous name was Transformational Defense Industries, Inc. In late 2010, the company acquired Swiss pistol maker Sphinx Sytems Ltd.

Kriss Systems SA also manufactures a semi-auto pistol variation of its SBR (short barrel rifle) with a standard 5 1/2 in. barrel and other lengths available.

Please contact Kriss USA directly for more information, including configurations, availability, and pricing (see Trademark Index).

PISTOLS: SEMI-AUTO

KRISS VECTOR SDP – .45 ACP cal., pistol variation of the Kriss Vector carbine, 5 1/2 or 6 1/2 in. threaded or unthreaded (optional) barrel, full length Picatinny receiver rail, accepts Glock 21 mags., 5.4 lbs. New 2011.

	100%	98%	95%	90%	80%	70%	60%
MSR $1,895	**$1,750**	**$1,550**	**$1,375**	**$1,200**	**$1,100**	**$1,000**	**$900**

RIFLES: SEMI-AUTO

Kriss also manufactures a .45 ACP Vector submachine gun for military and law enforcement only.

KRISS VECTOR CRB - .45 ACP cal., delayed blowback utilizing patented Super V System redirects recoil downward and away from the shooter, 16 in. steel barrel w/o sights, Ultramid Nylon 6/6 polymer receiver with A2 steel plates, 13 shot Glock type mag., Picatinny rail, flip up front and rear sights, two-stage trigger, folding vertical forearm grip, rail type folding stock, 5.8 lbs. New 2011.

	100%	98%	95%	90%	80%	70%	60%
MSR $1,895	**$1,750**	**$1,550**	**$1,375**	**$1,200**	**$1,100**	**$1,000**	**$900**

Add $100 for Kriss Vector SBR model with 5 1/2 or 6 1/2 in. barrel (NFA weapon).
Add $884 for TacPac option (includes tactical sling, bipod grip pod system, Surefire tactical light, and L-3 Eotech holographic sight system), new 2012.

KUFSTEINER WAFFENSTUBE

Current rifle manufacturer located in Kufstein, Austria.

RIFLES

Kufsteiner rifles are essentially built per individual order, and should be appraised by a knowledgeable person for an accurate price evaluation based on condition, quality of materials/construction and special features.

In addition to his unique bolt action, he also manufactures other bolt action designs and O/U rifles as well.

KAISERBUCHSE 3-S SYSTEM BOLT ACTION RIFLE – various cals. including Magnum calibers, unique short action allows for straight on cartridge loading, high strength alloy main parts, grip safety on lower pistol grip, unique uncocking device allowing manual cocking/decocking of the firing pin spring, 23.6 in. standard barrel, 3 shot detachable mag., iron sights, receiver drilled for scope mounts, best quality wood, available in either Schnabel forearm or Mannlicher configuration, many styles of engraving are optional, 7.14 lbs.

JAGERBUCHSE REPEATING RIFLE – various cals., bolt action, 3 front locking lugs, firing pin safety, ST, removable 5 shot mag., European walnut stock with Bavarian cheekpiece and Schnabel forearm, 5.8-10 lbs.

KUPEC, PAVEL

Previous longarm manufacturer located in the Czech Republic.

Pavel Kupec manufactured high quality hunting and sporting longarms made to custom order. These guns had little importation into the U.S.

L SECTION

L.A.R. MANUFACTURING, INC.

Current rifle manufacturer located in West Jordan, UT. Dealer sales.

In addition to its .50 cal. bolt action rifles, L.A.R. also makes upper receiver assemblies, and associated parts/accessories for AR-15 style carbines/rifles. Please contact the factory directly for both up-to-date information and pricing on these items (see Trademark Index).

GRADING - PPGS™	100%	98%	95%	90%	80%	70%	60%	LAST MSR

PISTOLS: SEMI-AUTO

GRIZZLY WIN. MAG. MARK I – .357 Mag., .357/.45 Grizzly Win. Mag. (new 1990), .45 ACP, 10mm, or .45 Win. Mag. cal., single action, based on the Colt 1911 design, 5.4 in. (new 1986), 6 1/2 in., 8 in. (new 1987), or 10 in. (new 1987) barrel, parkerized finish, 7 shot mag., ambidextrous safeties, checkered rubber grips, adj. sights, 48 oz. empty. Also can be converted to .45 ACP, 10mm (new 1988), .357 Mag., or .30 Mauser (disc.). Mfg. 1984-1999.

* ***Grizzly Win. Mag. Mark I Short Barrel Lengths*** – 5.4 or 6 1/2 in. barrel.

	$875	$675	$625	$525	$495	$475	$450	*$1,000*

Add $14 for .357 Mag. cal.
Add $150 for hard chrome or nickel frame.
Add $260 for full hard chrome or nickel frame.
Add $233-$248 for cal. conversion units.

Conversion units include .357 Mag., 10mm, .40 S&W (1991-1993 only), and .45 ACP cals.

* ***Grizzly Win. Mag. Mark I Long Barrel Lengths*** – .357 Mag., .45 Win. Mag., or .357/.45 Grizzly Win. Mag. (new 1990) cal., 8 or 10 in. barrel, extended slides. Disc. 1995.

	$1,195	$975	$895	$800	$725	$650	$575	*$1,313*

Add $62 for 10 in. barrel.
Add $24 for .357 Mag.
Add $143 for scope mounts (disc.).
Add $110 for muzzle compensator.

* ***Grizzly Win. Mag. Mark I State Special Edition*** – .45 Grizzly Win. Mag., 50 mfg. beginning 1998 to commemorate each state (ser. numbers match the order each state was admitted to the union), features gold etchings on frame, gold small parts, faux mother-of-pearl grips, cased. Limited mfg. 1998-99.

Regional demand/interest preclude accurate pricing on this model.

GRIZZLY .44 MAG. MARK 4 – .44 Mag. cal., choice of lusterless blue, parkerized, chrome, or nickel finish, 5.4 or 6 1/2 in. barrel, adj. sights. Mfg. 1991-99.

	$875	$715	$635	$550	$495	$475	$450	*$1,014*

GRIZZLY .50 MARK 5 – .50 Action Express cal., single action semi-auto, 5.4 or 6 1/2 in. barrel, 6 shot mag., checkered walnut grips, 56 oz. Mfg. 1993-99.

	$1,475	$1,275	$1,050	$895	$775	$700	$625	*$1,152*

Add $178-$189 per coversion unit (new 1996).

GRIZZLY WIN. MAG. MARK II – similar to Mark I, except has fixed sights, standard safeties, and different metal finish. Mfg. 1986 only.

	$625	$550	$525	$495	$475	$450	$425	*$550*

Add $25 for .357 Mag.

RIFLES: BOLT ACTION

GRIZZLY BIG BOAR COMPETITOR RIFLE – .50 BMG cal., single shot, bolt action design in bullpup configuration, alloy steel receiver and bolt, 36 in. heavy barrel with compensator, thumb safety, match or field grade, includes bipod, scope mount, leather cheek pad and hard carry case, 30.4 lbs. Mfg. 1994-2011.

	$2,150	$1,725	$1,575	$1,375	$1,175	$1,050	$950	*$2,350*

GRADING - PPGS™	100%	98%	95%	90%	80%	70%	60%	LAST MSR

Add $100 for parkerizing.
Add $250 for nickel trigger housing finish.
Add $350 for full nickel frame (disc. 2010).
Add $250 for stainless steel Lothar Walther barrel (disc. 2010).
Add $522 for redesigned (2002) tripod and pintle mount.
Last MSR was $4,841 for the Big Bore Hunter Rifle Package in 2011. This included: Nightforce scope and rings, cleaning kit, tripod with pintle mount, drag bag, and hard carry case.

GRIZZLY T-50 – .50 BMG cal., single shot, 32-36 in. barrel with muzzle brake, extended barrel shroud with top and bottom Picatinny rails, black parkerized finish, cheek saddle on frame, carry handle in front of trigger guard, extended bolt handle, 30 1/2 - 32 lbs. Mfg. 2009-2012.

	100%	98%	95%	90%	80%	70%	60%	LAST MSR
	$3,000	$2,800	$2,600	$2,400	$2,200	$2,000	$1,800	*$3,200*

Current MSR on the A T-50 Tactical Package is $5,618. This package includes: Nightforce scope and rings, cleaning kit, heavy duty bipod, carry handle, Accu-Shot monopod, drag bag, and hard carry case.
While discontinued during 2012, limited quantities remain on this model as this edition went to press.

RIFLES: SEMI-AUTO

GRIZZLY 15 – .223 Rem. cal., patterned after the AR-15, available in either A2 or A3 configuration, limited mfg. 2004-2005.

	100%	98%	95%	90%	80%	70%	60%	LAST MSR
	$825	$725	$650	$575	$525	$475	$425	*$795*

Add $85 for detachable carry handle.

GRIZZLY A2 SPEC CARBINE – 5.56 NATO cal., AR-15 style, 16 in. M4 chrome moly threaded barrel with A2 Bird cage flash suppressor, 5 position collapsible carbine stock, Grizzly A2 aluminum upper receiver, mil spec forged aluminum LAR Grizzly lower receiver, mil spec or LAR split carbine quad rail handguard, A2 front sight, standard trigger group, A2 mil spec pistol grip. New 2011.

	100%	98%	95%	90%	80%	70%	60%
MSR $999	$895	$775	$675	$575	$525	$475	$425

GRIZZLY A3 SPEC CARBINE – 5.56 NATO cal., similar to Grizzly A2 Spec Carbine, except has Grizzly A3 aluminum flat top upper receiver. New 2011.

	100%	98%	95%	90%	80%	70%	60%
MSR $979	$880	$765	$675	$575	$525	$475	$425

OPS-4 GRIZZLY H-TACTICAL – 5.56 NATO cal., AR-15 style, 16 in. M4 chrome moly threaded barrel with A2 Bird cage flash suppressor, 5 position collapsible carbine stock, LAR side charged forged aluminum flat top upper receiver, mil spec forged aluminum LAR Grizzly lower receiver, mil spec or LAR split carbine quad rail handguard, adj. gas piston with rail, hard anodized aluminum charging handle. New 2011.

	100%	98%	95%	90%	80%	70%	60%
MSR $1,111	$975	$850	$725	$625	$550	$500	$450

OPS-4 GRIZZLY HUNTER – 5.56 NATO or .223 Wylde cal., AR-15 style, 18, 20, or 24 in. bull chrome moly (20 or 24 in.) or stainless steel (18 or 20 in.) barrel, standard A2 black stock, standard trigger or 2 stage match trigger group, OPS-4 side charged forged aluminum flat top upper receiver, mil spec forged aluminum LAR Grizzly lower receiver, LAR free float tube rifle length handguard, LAR aluminum gas block, hard anodized aluminum charging handle. New 2011.

	100%	98%	95%	90%	80%	70%	60%
MSR $989	$885	$765	$675	$575	$525	$475	$425

OPS-4 GRIZZLY OPERATOR – 5.56 NATO cal., AR-15 style, 16 in. chrome moly heavy threaded barrel with 5 port muzzle brake and compensator, Magpul CTR collapsible stock, Hogue rubber grip with finger grooves or Magpul MIAD pistol grip, standard trigger group, OPS-4 side charged forged aluminum flat top upper receiver, mil spec forged aluminum LAR Grizzly lower receiver, LAR mid length quad rail handguard, LAR aluminum gas block with rail, hard anodized aluminum charging handle. New 2011.

	100%	98%	95%	90%	80%	70%	60%
MSR $1,099	$975	$825	$725	$625	$550	$500	$450

OPS-4 GRIZZLY PRECISION OPERATOR – .223 Wylde cal., AR-15 style, 18 or 20 in. bull stainless steel barrel, Magpul PRS stock, Magpul pistol grip and trigger guard or Magpul MIAD, standard trigger or 2 stage match trigger group, LAR rifle length free float quad rail handguard, LAR aluminum low profile gas block, otherwise similar to OPS-4 Grizzly Operator. New 2011.

	100%	98%	95%	90%	80%	70%	60%
MSR $1,299	$1,125	$950	$825	$725	$625	$550	$475

GRADING - PPGS™	100%	98%	95%	90%	80%	70%	60%	LAST MSR

OPS-4 GRIZZLY SPEC CARBINE – 5.56 NATO cal., AR-15 style, 16 in. M4 chrome moly threaded barrel with A2 Bird cage flash suppressor, standard trigger group, 5 position collapsible carbine stock, OPS-4 side charged forged aluminum flat top upper receiver, mil spec forged aluminum LAR Grizzly lower receiver, A2 front sight, mil-spec or LAR split carbine quad rail handguard, hard anodized aluminum charging handle. New 2011.

MSR $959	$865	$750	$675	$575	$525	$475	$425

OPS-4 GRIZZLY SPEC RIFLE – 5.56 NATO cal., AR-15 style, 20 in. chrome moly heavy threaded barrel with A2 Bird cage flash suppressor, standard trigger or 2 stage match trigger group, standard A2 black stock, otherwise similar to OPS-4 Grizzly Spec Carbine. New 2011.

MSR $999	$895	$775	$675	$575	$525	$475	$425

OPS-4 GRIZZLY STANDARD CARBINE – 5.56 NATO cal., AR-15 style, 16 in. M4 chrome moly threaded barrel with A2 Bird cage flash suppressor, standard trigger group, 5 position collapsible carbine stock, LAR side charged forged aluminum flat top upper receiver, mil spec forged aluminum LAR Grizzly lower receiver, LAR aluminum gas block with rail, full chrome bolt carrier and gas key, hard anodized aluminum charging handle. New 2011.

MSR $999	$895	$775	$675	$575	$525	$475	$425

OPS-4 GRIZZLY STANDARD RIFLE – 5.56 NATO cal., AR-15 style, 20 in. chrome moly heavy threaded barrel with A2 Bird cage flash suppressor, standard trigger or 2 stage match trigger group, standard A2 black stock, otherwise similar to OPS-4 Grizzly Standard Carbine. New 2011.

MSR $1,099	$975	$850	$725	$625	$550	$500	$450

OPS-22 TERMINATOR – .22 LR cal. New 2011.

MSR $649	$575	$500	$425	$375	$325	$295	$275

L E S INCORPORATED

Previous manufacturer located in Morton Grove, IL.

PISTOLS: SEMI-AUTO

P-18 ROGAK – 7.65mm Para. (limited mfg.) or 9mm Para. cal., double action, 18 shot, 5 1/2 in. barrel, stainless steel, black plastic grips with partial thumb rest. Disc.

	$450	$395	$350	$325	$295	$275	$250
High Polish Finish	$525	$450	$395	$375	$325	$295	$275

Add 25% for 7.65mm Para. cal.

This pistol was patterned after the Steyr Model GB. Approx. 2,300 P-18s were mfg. before being disc.

LMT

Please refer to the Lewis Machine & Tool section.

LRB ARMS

Current manufacturer located in Floral Park, NY. Currently distributed by LRB of Long Island, NY.

RIFLES: SEMI-AUTO

Current AR-15 style carbines/rifles include: M14SA Base (MSR range $2,541-$2,674), M14SA Classic (MSR range $2,641-$2,724), M14SA Tanker (MSR range $2,663-2,882), M14SA Medium Match (MSR $3,005), M25 Medium Match (MSR $3,090), and 10th Anniversary Special (MSR $2,593). Additionally, LRB also manufactures AR-15, M-14, and M-25 receivers and barreled actions. Please contact the company directly for more information (see Trademark Index).

LWRC INTERNATIONAL, INC.

Current pistol and rifle manufacturer located in Cambridge, MD. Dealer and distributor sales.

PISTOLS: SEMI-AUTO

PSD (PERSONAL SECURITY DETAIL) PISTOL – 5.56 NATO cal., 8 in. ultra compact hammer forged steel barrel, A2 flash hider, 30 shot Magpul P-Mag, MIAD pistol grip, shortened

GRADING - PPGS™	100%	98%	95%	90%	80%	70%	60%	LAST MSR

recoil system, Troy front sight, folding BUIS rear sight, NiCorr surface treatment, 5 1/2 lbs.

MSR $2,216	$1,995	$1,775	$1,550	$1,325	$1,100	$950	$775	

RIFLES: SEMI-AUTO

LWRC manufactures a complete line of short-stroke, gas-piston operated AR-15 style, M-16, and M-4 semi-auto rifles. These models have a wide variety of sights, accessories, and related hardware available. Please contact the company directly for more information on the available options (see Trademark Index).

IMPORTANT NOTE: On model(s) where *N/A has replaced the normal 100% value, it indicates current market conditions are too unstable to accurately ascertain 100%-60% values. Factory retail prices (MSRs) reflect most recent updates. For more up-to-date information on current pricing trends and additional useful information, please visit www.bluebookofgunvalues.com, select "Information & Services" from the menu, and click on "Additional Book Information".

M6-SL – 5.56 NATO or 6.8mm SPC cal., 16.1 in. light contour cold hammer forged barrel, six position Magpul CTR stock, MOE mid length handguard and pistol grip, 30 shot mag., A2 flash hider, EXO (nickel boron) plated advanced combat bolt, one piece coated carrier, and enhanced fire control group, Daniel Defense fixed rear sight, fixed A2 front sight, 7.2 lbs.

MSR $1,675	*N/A	$1,300	$1,100	$900	$775	$650	$575	

This model is also available with a 10 1/2, 12.7, and 14.7 in. barrel for law enforcement/military. A M6A1-S Patrolman's Carbine is also available with 14.7 in. barrel and M4 collapsible stock.

M6A2 – 5.56 NATO or 6.8mm SPC cal., 16.1 in. cold hammer forged match grade barrel, six position Vltor EMod stock, Magpul MIAD pistol grip, 30 shot mag., A2 flash hider, folding BUIS front and rear sights, mid-length free float rail system, black, olive drab, or desert tan finish, 7.3 lbs.

MSR $2,217	*N/A	$1,725	$1,550	$1,375	$1,125	$975	$775	

This model is also available with a 10 1/2 or 14.7 in. barrel for law enforcement/military. A M6A2 DEA variation is also available with 14.7 in. barrel.

* ***M6A2-SPR (Special Purpose Rifle)*** – 5.56 NATO or 6.8mm SPC cal., 16.1 in. cold hammer forged fluted barrel, Magpul ACS stock, Magpul MIAD pistol grip, 30 shot mag., A2 flash hider, folding BUIS front and rear sights, black, olive drab, or desert tan finish, SPR-MOD rail, Brovo Company Mod4 Gunfighter charging handle, nickel coated bolt carrier and fire control group, mid-length piston system, Skirmish sights, 7.3 lbs.

MSR $2,479	*N/A	$1,850	$1,625	$1,425	$1,150	$995	$800	

This model is also available with a 14.7 in. barrel for law enforcement/military.

M6A3 – 5.56 NATO or 6.8mm SPC cal., 16.1 or 18 in. barrel, Vltor EMod adj. stock, Magpul MIAD pistol grip, adj. gas system, integrated flip down sight, ARM-R free float rail system, front sight is folding and incorporated in gas block, 30 shot mag., A2 flash hider, olive drab or black finish, 7.3 lbs.

	*N/A	$1,775	$1,575	$1,400	$1,125	$975	$800	*$2,317*

M6-G – 5.56 NATO or 6.8mm SPC cal., 16.1 in. hammer forged steel barrel, short stroke piston system, Magpul MOE pistol grip stock, folding BUIS front and rear sights, 30 shot mag., enhanced fire control group, black finish, approx. 7 lbs.

While advertised during 2011, this model has yet to be manufactured.

M6A4 – 5.56 NATO or 6.8mm SPC cal., 16 1/2 in. hammer forged steel barrel, short stroke piston system, Vltor EModel adj. stock, Magpul MIAD pistol grip, folding rear BUIS sight, folding front sight incorporated in gas block, 30 shot mag., black finish, four position adj. gas block, front handle, quad rail, 7.4 lbs.

While advertised during 2011, this model has yet to be manufactured.

IC-M6 – 5.56 NATO cal., 16 in. barrel, Monoforge upper receiver, integrated rail base, brown, black or black/tan Cerakote finish, FDE furniture, available in standard, A5 (law enforcement only), SPR, PSD, and MK configurations, wide variety of options available. New 2013.

MSR $2,499	*N/A	$1,850	$1,595	$1,450	$1,175	$950	$750	

Add $100 for fluted barrel.

GRADING - PPGS™	100%	98%	95%	90%	80%	70%	60%	LAST MSR

R.E.P.R. (RAPID ENGAGEMENT PRECISION RIFLE) – 7.62mm NATO cal., variations include 16 (medium light), 18 (DMR, medium), and 20 (Sniper, heavy) in. cold hammer forged barrel, six position Vltor Emod, Magpul UBR, or Magpul PRS stock, 5, 10, or 20 shot mag., Magpul MIAD pistol grip, folding BUIS sights, sculpted ARM-R top rail, adj. four position gas block, ambidextrous bolt release, left side mounted charging handle, A2 flash hider, 9 1/2 - 11 1/4 lbs.

MSR $3,600 *N/A $2,900 $2,550 $2,175 $1,650 $1,425 $1,200

SIX8 – 6.8mm SPCII cal., 16.1 in. barrel nickel boron coated bolt carrier group, enhanced fire control group, claw extractor, black, tan, or OD green finish, pistol grip, full length Picatinny quad rail. New 2013.

MSR $2,499 *N/A $1,850 $1,595 $1,450 $1,175 $950 $750

LA ARMERIA DE MADRID

Please refer to the Armeria De Madrid, LA listing in the A section.

LABANU INCORPORATED

Labanu, Inc. SKSs were manufactured by Norinco in China, and imported exclusively until 1998 by Labanu, Inc., located in Ronkonkoma, NY.

RIFLES: SEMI-AUTO

MAK 90 SKS SPORTER RIFLE – 7.62x39mm cal., sporterized variation of the SKS with thumbhole stock, 16 1/2 in. barrel, includes accessories, 5 lbs. Importation began 1995, banned 1998.

$625 $550 $475 $425 $375 $325 $295 *$189*

LAHTI PISTOL

Previous manufacturer located in Husqvarna, Sweden. Also mfg. by Vkt (state rifle factory) in Jyvaskyla, Finland.

PISTOLS: SEMI-AUTO

SWEDISH MODEL 40 – 9mm Para. cal., 4 3/4 in. barrel, blue finish, fixed sights, plastic grips, mfg. 1940-44.

$650 $550 $425 $300 $260 $250 $240

Add 10% for Holster-Rig.

It is important to note that there are diversely marked variations of this pistol, such as RPLT (Danish State Police); such police markings add value by about 10%.

FINNISH L-35 – 9mm Para., 4 basic variations - only the first 2 types have the more desirable shoulder stock lug. Military pistols are usually "SA" marked, approx. 9,100 mfg. 1938-1954.

* ***Finnish L-35 1st Variation*** – can be identified by "hump" for yoke locking piece and loaded indicator, ser. no. range 1001-3700.

  $4,200 $3,250 $2,750 $2,250 $1,750 $1,250 $1,000

* ***Finnish L-35 2nd Variation*** – does not have the "hump" for yoke locking piece, scarcer than 1st Variation, ser. no. 3701-4700.

  $3,700 $3,000 $2,500 $2,000 $1,750 $1,250 $1,000

* ***Finnish L-35 3rd Variation*** – can be identified by small changes in loaded indicator, most are marked "Valmet", ser. no. range 4701-6800.

  $1,750 $1,350 $850 $750 $700 $650 $600

* ***Finnish L-35 4th Variation*** – w/o loaded indicator, marked "Valmet," and sold commercially, ser. no. range 6801-9100.

  $1,500 $1,250 $850 $750 $700 $650 $600

* ***Finnish L-35 Shoulder Stocks*** – the shoulder stock for this model (w/o serial numbers) features a sheet metal compartment which contains a cleaning rod and extra magazine. Original stocks (only 50 mfg.) are currently selling in the $5,000 range, while more recently manufactured stocks utilizing original hardware are currently priced in the $2,500 range.

GRADING - PPGS™	100%	98%	95%	90%	80%	70%	60%	LAST MSR

LAKE FIELD ARMS LTD.

Previous manufacturer located in Ontario, Canada. Lake Field Arms Ltd. was acquired by Savage Arms, Inc. during late 1994. Distributor sales only through most major U.S. distributors.

Lake Field rifles manufactured after the Savage acquisition are marked Savage - please refer to the Savage listing in the S section for current mfg.

RIFLES: .22 RIMFIRE

MARK I – .22 LR cal., single shot bolt action, 20 3/4 in. rifled or smooth bore barrel, adj. rear sight, thumb rotary safety, walnut finish hardwood stock, 5 1/2 lbs. Disc.

$110	**$75**	**$65**	**$55**	**$50**	**$40**	**$30**	***$135***

Add $14 for left-hand variation.

This model was also available in youth dimensions (19 in. barrel) at no extra charge (Model Mark I-Y).

MARK II – .22 LR cal., bolt action, 10 shot mag., 20 3/4 in. barrel, adj. rear sight, thumb operated rotary safety, walnut finish hardwood stock, 5 1/2 lbs. Disc.

$120	**$80**	**$70**	**$60**	**$50**	**$40**	**$30**	***$140***

Add $15 for left-hand variation (mfg. 1993-95).

This model was also available in youth dimensions (19 in. barrel) at no extra charge (Model Mark II-Y).

MODEL 64B – .22 LR cal., semi-auto, side ejection, 10 shot mag., 20 1/4 in. barrel, adj. rear sight, thumb operated rotary safety, walnut finish hardwood stock, 5 1/2 lbs. Disc.

$120	**$85**	**$75**	**$65**	**$55**	**$45**	**$40**	***$143***

MODEL 90B (BIATHLON) – .22 LR cal., biathlon rifle, includes five 5 shot mags., 21 in. barrel, aperture sights, one-piece natural finish hardwood stock, 8 1/4 lbs. Mfg. 1991-95.

$430	**$300**	**$225**	**$195**	**$170**	**$150**	**$130**	***$570***

Add $55 for left-hand variation (new 1993).

MODEL 91T – .22 LR cal., target rifle, single shot, 25 in. barrel with aperture sights, dark hardwood finished stock, 8 lbs. Mfg. 1991-95.

$340	**$255**	**$215**	**$175**	**$150**	**$135**	**$115**	***$455***

Add $45 for left-hand variation (mfg. 1993-95).

* ***Model 91TR*** – repeater version of the Model 91T, 5 shot mag. Mfg. 1993-95.

$360	**$265**	**$215**	**$175**	**$150**	**$135**	**$115**	***$485***

Add $45 for left-hand variation (mfg. 1993-95).

MODEL 92S – .22 LR cal., 5 shot detachable mag., 21 in. barrel, hardwood stock with Monte Carlo cheekpiece, 8 lbs. Mfg. 1993-95.

$300	**$240**	**$200**	**$175**	**$160**	**$150**	**$135**	***$388***

Add $37 for left-hand variation.

MODEL 93M – .22 WMR cal., 5 shot mag., thumb operated rotary safety, 20 3/4 in. barrel, hardwood stock, 5 3/4 lbs. Mfg. 1995 only.

$140	**$120**	**$100**	**$85**	**$75**	**$65**	**$55**	***$168***

LAKELANDER

Previous trademark circa 1976-1999. Manufacture was by MIPRO AB (c. 1946-1999) in Sweden. Previously imported and distributed 1996-98 by Lakelander U.S.A., Inc. located in Gulfport, MS.

RIFLES: BOLT ACTION

LAKELANDER 389 – .270 Win., .30-06, or .308 Win. cal., unique design with many shooter enhancements, 4 shot integrated mag. with rotary swing plate, 3 configurations including Premium (22 in. barrel with skip-line checkering and Monte Carlo stock), Classic (22 in. barrel, standard stock with checkering), and Match-Maker (target model with 21.7 in. barrel and competition stock and adj. cheekpiece, .308 Win. only), 7.3-8.4 lbs. Mfg. 1996-98.

$1,425	**$1,225**	**$995**	**$850**	**$700**	**$600**	**$500**	***$1,599***

Add $500 for Match-Maker Model.

GRADING - PPGS™	100%	98%	95%	90%	80%	70%	60%	LAST MSR

LAKESIDE MACHINE LLC

Current manufacturer located in Horseshoe Bend, AR. Previously located in Pound, WI.

RIFLES: SEMI-AUTO

Lakeside manufactures half-scale, semi-auto, belt fed replicas of many of America's famous machine guns, including the 1919 A4 ($3,995 MSR), 1919 M37 ($3,895 last MSR, only 2 mfg.), 1917 A1 ($4,495 MSR), M2 HB ($4,995 MSR), M2 WC ($5,495 MSR), and a dual mount M2 HB (POR). Calibers include: .22 LR, .17 Mach 2 (optional), and .22 WMR. Additionally, Lakeside also manufactures a semi-auto, closed bolt, belt fed .22 LR cal. Model Vindicator BF1 with 16 1/4 in. shrouded barrel ($2,695 MSR).

LAMBOY, S.R. & CO. INC.

Previous importer located in Victor, NY until 2003. S.R. Lamboy manufactured Ithaca Classic Doubles and imported Renato Caem and other high quality, low production long guns from Italy. Please check indivdual listings for more information.

LAMES

Previous manufacturer located in Italy.

SHOTGUNS: O/U

FIELD MODEL – 12 ga., 26, 28, or 30 in. barrels, various chokes, VR, engraving, SST, auto ejectors, checkered pistol grip stock with pad.

$400 $380 $365 $350 $325 $300 $275

Add 25% for separated barrels.

STANDARD TRAP – similar to Field, 30 or 32 in. various trap bore barrels, with wide VR, trap style Monte Carlo stock.

$600 $575 $550 $525 $425 $400 $450

CALIFORNIA TRAP – similar to Standard Trap, with separated barrels.

$700 $675 $650 $625 $525 $500 $450

SKEET MODEL – similar to Field, with 26 in. skeet bore barrels, skeet stock and separated barrels.

$600 $575 $550 $525 $425 $400 $350

LANBER

Current shotgun (O/U and semi-auto only) trademark manufactured by ComLanber, S.A., located in Zaldibar, Spain, and established in 1973. No current U.S. importation. Previously imported beginning late 2006-late 2011 by Lanber USA, located in Westfield, MA. Previously located in Blakely, GA. Previously imported 1999-2006, O/U shotguns by Wingshooting Adventures, located in Coopersville, MI, 1996-99 by ITC International, Inc. located in Marietta, GA, until 1994, by Eagle Imports, Inc. located in Wanamassa, NJ, by Exel Arms of America, Inc., located in Gardener, MA, and by Lanber Arms of America located in Adrian, MI.

Due to space considerations, information regarding this manufacturer is available online free of charge at www.bluebookofgunvalues.com.

Lanber makes a wide range of quality O/U and semi-auto shotguns.

LANCER SYSTEMS

Current rifle and accessories manufacturer located in Allentown, PA.

RIFLES: SEMI-AUTO

L15 COMPETITION – 5.56 NATO cal., 18 in. stainless steel barrel, Wheaton Arms compensator, extra long free floating handguard, EFX-A2 fixed stock, Ergo grip, CMC trigger, 7.7 lbs. New 2013.

MSR $2,121 $1,900 $1,700 $1,450 $1,200 $1,000 $850 $750

GRADING - PPGS™	100%	98%	95%	90%	80%	70%	60%	LAST MSR

* ***L15 Super Competition*** – 5.56 NATO cal., upgraded version of the L15 Competition featuring 17 in. stainless steel Krieger barrel, Wheaton Arms SS compensator, Lancer extra long handguard, EFX-A2 fixed stock, Ergo grip, CMC trigger, 7.8 lbs. New 2013.

MSR $2,328	$2,150	$1,800	$1,525	$1,250	$1,050	$875	$775	

L15 SHARP SHOOTER – 5.56 NATO cal., 20 in. heavy profile Krieger barrel, Lancer extra long free-float handguard, tactical Magwell lower receiver, EFX-A2 fixed stock, Ergo grip, CMC trigger, 8.9 lbs. New 2013.

MSR $2,017	$1,800	$1,600	$1,350	$1,100	$950	$750	$675	

L15 SPORTER – 5.56 NATO cal., mid-length gas system, 16 in. lightweight CHF chrome lined barrel with A2 flash hider, Lancer handguard with 2 in. sight rail, tactical Magwell lower receiver, F93 Pro stock, Ergo grip, Milspec trigger, 7.2 lbs. New 2013.

MSR $1,655	$1,495	$1,325	$1,100	$900	$775	$675	$575	

LANG, JOSEPH

Current trademark established in 1821 and manufactured by Atkin, Grant & Lang, located in Hertfordshire, England. No current U.S. importation.

During 1925, the company of Joseph Lang & Son amalgamated with Steven Grant & Son, forming the new company of Grant & Lang, Ltd. The company achieved notoriety for its unique thumbnail and key lock hand detachable sidelocks.

Prices indicated are for manufacturer's suggested retail and 100% condition factors are listed in English pounds. All new prices do not include VAT. Values for used guns in 98%-60% condition factors are priced in U.S. dollars.

Please contact the factory directly for more information and model availability (see Trademark Index). Atkin, Grant & Lang provide a useful historical research service on older Joseph Lang shotguns and rifles. The charge for this service is £25 per gun, and the company will give you all pertinent factory information regarding the history.

RIFLES: SxS

JOSEPH LANG DOUBLE RIFLE – available in cals. between .300 H&H - .577 NE, best quality double rifle, individually made per customer specifications.

MSR N/A	N/A	$30,000	$26,000	$21,000	$19,000	$16,250	$14,750	

Add 25% for .450 NE - .577 NE cals.

SHOTGUNS: SxS

IMPERIAL SIDELOCK EJECTOR – 12, 16, 20, 28 ga., or .410 bore, best quality sidelock ejector model, individually made per customer specifications.

MSR N/A	N/A	$28,875	$24,750	$20,750	$17,250	$15,000	$13,250	

Add 50% for 20 ga., 75% for 28 ga. or 100% for .410 bore.

Add 15% for key hand detachable locks, or 25% for thumbnail hand detachable locks.

LAPORTE HOLDING

Previous shotgun manufacturer until circa 2005 and located in Biot, France.

Laporte Holding manufactured a unique reduced recoil 12 ga. O/U shotgun called the SwingTrap/Pro II, reducing recoil by 50% and noise by 75%. This was accomplished by the barrels being surrounded by a round shroud, which dissipated most of the recoil and noise. These guns had little or no importation into the U.S.

The company continues to manufacture trap throwers and related equipment.

LARUE TACTICAL

Current manufacturer located in Leander, TX.

RIFLES: SEMI-AUTO

IMPORTANT NOTE: On model(s) where *N/A has replaced the normal 100% value, it indicates current market conditions are too unstable to accurately ascertain 100%-60% values. Factory retail prices (MSRs) reflect most recent updates. For more up-to-date information on current pricing trends and additional useful information, please visit www.bluebookofgunvalues.com, select "Information & Services" from the menu, and click on "Additional Book Information".

GRADING - PPGS™	100%	98%	95%	90%	80%	70%	60%	LAST MSR

OBR (OPTIMIZED BATTLE RIFLE) – 5.56 NATO (new 2011) or .308 Win. cal., AR-15 style, 16.1, 18, or 20 in. stainless steel barrel, adj. gas block, 20 shot box mag., flared magwell, A2 fixed stock, black anodized finish, Mil-Std 1913 one piece upper rail, Troy front and optional BUIS rear sight, A2 flash hider, detachable side rails, approx. 10 lbs.

MSR $2,245 *N/A $1,850 $1,675 $1,425 $1,295 $1,050 $850

A variety of accessories are available on this model for additional cost.
Add $1,125 for .308 Win. cal.

TACTICAL PREDATAR – 5.56 NATO or .308 Win. (new 2013) cal., 16.1 or 18 in. contoured stainless steel barrel, skeletonized handguard, low profile gas block, A2 flash hider, quad rail forend, black phosphate finish, six position Magpul stock, 30 shot mag., charging lever, forward assist, Giselle two-stage trigger, approx. 6 1/2 lbs. New mid-2011.

MSR $1,682 *N/A $1,495 $1,250 $1,075 $975 $785 $640

Add $1,125 for .308 Win. cal.

COSTA SIGNATURE EDITION – 5.56 NATO cal., 16.1 in. barrel, SureFire muzzle brake, FDE KG GunKote finish, "COSTA LUDUS" logo engraved on left side of receiver, black parts and rail covers, first 500 units are match numbered on the upper and lower. New 2013.

MSR $2,895 *N/A $2,375 $2,150 $1,850 $1,675 $1,350 $1,100

LASERAIM ARMS, INC.

Previous distributor located in Little Rock, AR. Previously manufactured until 1999 in Thermopolis, WY. Laseraim Arms, Inc. was a division of Emerging Technologies, Inc.

PISTOLS: SEMI-AUTO

SERIES I – .40 S&W, .400 Cor-Bon (new 1998), .45 ACP, or 10mm cal., single action, 3 3/8 (Compact Model), 5, or 6 in. barrel with compensator, ambidextrous safety, all stainless steel metal parts are Teflon coated, beveled mag. well, integral accessory mounts, 7 (.45 ACP) or 8 (10mm or .40 S&W) shot mag., 46 or 52 oz. Mfg. 1993-99.

$325 $295 $265 $215 $185 $150 $125 *$349*

Add $120 for wireless laser combo (new 1997).

* ***Series I Compact*** – .40 S&W or .45 ACP cal., features 3 3/8 in. non-ported slide and fixed sights. Mfg. 1993-99.

$325 $295 $265 $215 $185 $150 $125 *$349*

Series I Illusion and Dream Team variations were made during 1993-94. Retail prices respectively were $650 and $695.

SERIES II – .40 S&W (disc. 1994), .45 ACP, or 10mm cal., similar technical specs. as the Series I, except has non-reflective stainless steel finish, fixed or adj. sights, and 3 3/8 (Compact Model, .45 ACP only), 5, or 7 (.45 ACP only) in. non-compensated barrel, 37 or 43 oz. Mfg. 1993-96.

$485 $385 $300 $240 $210 $180 $155 *$550*

Series II Illusion and Dream Team variations were made during 1993-94. Retail prices respectively were $500 and $545.

SERIES III – .45 ACP cal., 5 in. ported barrel, serrated slide, Hogue grips. Mfg. 1994-disc.

$595 $465 $415 $375 $345 $310 $275 *$675*

SERIES IV – .45 ACP cal., 3 3/8 (Compact Model) or 5 in. ported barrel, serrated slide, diamond checkered wood grips. Mfg. 1994-disc.

$550 $450 $400 $360 $330 $300 $265 *$625*

LASALLE

Previous manufacturer located in France.

SHOTGUNS

SLIDE ACTION SHOTGUN – 12 or 20 ga., 26, 28, or 30 in. barrels, various chokes, alloy frame, checkered pistol grip stock.

$250 $225 $200 $175 $150 $125 $100

GRADING - PPGS™	100%	98%	95%	90%	80%	70%	60%	LAST MSR

SEMI-AUTO SHOTGUN – 12 ga., 26, 28, or 30 in. barrels, various chokes, gas operated, checkered pistol grip stock.

	$300	$275	$250	$225	$200	$175	$150	

LAUER CUSTOM WEAPONRY

Current manufacturer of AR-15 style of carbines/rifles located in Chippewa Falls, WI.

RIFLES: SEMI-AUTO

Currently, Lauer Custom Weaponry makes the following AR-15 style carbines/rifles include: LCW15 Series (call for price), and the Vindicator Belt Fed .22 (MSR $2,595). Please contact the company directly for more information including pricing and availability (see Trademark Index).

LAURONA ZABALA

Current trademark established in 2011, and manufactured by Armas Eibar, S.A.L., located in Eibar, Spain. Previous trademark was Laurona from 1941-2011. During 2010, Laurona was absorbed by Norica, and the new company name was Norica Laurona. No current U.S. importation. Previously imported until 1993 by Galaxy Imports located in Victoria, TX.

Laurona was founded in Eibar during 1941 by four craftsmen (hence the name Laurona, which in Basque means "of the four"), each a specialist in a discipline of shotgun mfg. Laurona made SxS guns until 1978, at which time they discontinued SxS models in order to concentrate on the O/U marketplace.

Laurona manufactures good quality O/U shotguns and O/U express rifles/combination guns. Beginning 1992, Laurona switched from a one-piece, demi-block type of fabrication to a monobloc system which has improved strength characteristics while reducing weight in their X-Series line of shotguns and express rifles.

Laurona long guns come standard with a black chrome metal finish that is extremely resistant to oxidation. Left hand stocks are available for the 83 MG Super Game, 85 MS Super Game, Trap, and Super Skeet, Silhouette Trap models, and Silhouette Sporting Clays.

Suffix designations on Laurona shotguns refer to the following: G - twin non-selective triggers, S - selective single trigger, M - multi-chokes, T - Tulip, BV - beavertail, U - single non-selected triggers.

All Super Game Models were available with a deluxe package which includes a recoil pad, mid-bead sight, and select wood for an additional $250. Special order dull matte finished barrels (with multi-chokes) were available for an additional $200 - extra barrels were priced between $635 (20 ga.) or $800 (12 ga.) per set.

Due to space considerations, information regarding this manufacturer is available online free of charge at www.bluebookofgunvalues.com.

LAW ENFORCEMENT ORDNANCE CORPORATION

Previous manufacturer located in Ridgway, PA until 1990.

SHOTGUNS: SEMI-AUTO

STRIKER-12 – 12 ga., semi-auto, paramilitary design shotgun featuring 12 shot rotary mag., 18 1/4 in. alloy shrouded barrel with PG extension, folding or fixed paramilitary design stock, 9.2 lbs., limited mfg. 1986-90.

	$1,000	$875	$750	$675	$600	$550	$500	*$725*

Add $200 for folding stock.

Add $100 for Marine variation ("Metal Life" finish).

Earlier variations were imported and available to law enforcement agencies only. In 1987, manufacture was started in PA and these firearms could be sold to individuals (18 in. barrel only). This design was originally developed in South Rhodesia.

HARRY LAWSON LLC

Current custom gunsmith established during 1965 and currently located in Tucson, AZ. Consumer direct sales.

Harry Lawson is well-known for custom stock work. This company also customizes its own line of sporting rifles, most feature an innovative thumbhole stock design. Please contact the company directly for more information regarding customized models, pricing on stocking services, and related gunsmithing services (see Trademark Index).

RIFLES: BOLT ACTION

Harry Lawson manufactures the 650 Series in both Mountaineer and Ultralite configurations. These bolt action rifles are custom order, and can be built on a customer supplied Remington 700 barreled action or the action can be purchased separately from $650 - $850. With a customer supplied action, prices start at $3,115 for Grade II XX wood. Prices start at $2,665 for Grade II XX wood.

Current MSR is $4,730 for a Lawson 650 Series Weatherby Mark V factory barreled action in .300 Wby. Mag. cal. or smaller with Grade 5 EF French or claro walnut stock, or $4,080 for a similar gun with a Remington 700 action.

LAZZERONI ARMS COMPANY

Current manufacturer located in Tucson, AZ since 1995. Direct/dealer sales.

RIFLES: BOLT ACTION

Lazzeroni ammunition is precision loaded in Lazzeroni's Tucson facility under rigid tolerances. All ammunition is sealed for absolute weatherproofing. Lazzeroni proprietary calibers are already established as being extremely effective at long distances.

SAKO MODEL TRG-S – 7.21 Firebird (.284, new 2002) or 7.82 Warbird (.308) cal., features Sako TRG action with free floating 26 in. barrel, 3 shot detachable mag., fully adj. trigger, and scope rings, 7.9 lbs. Mfg. 1999-2004.

$825 $700 $600 $495 $430 $365 $315 ***$900***

Add $400 for metal finish upgrade or $1,200 for metal finish upgrade with Burris 4-16x50mm mil-dot scope.

SAVAGE 16LZ – 7.21 Tomahawk (.284, disc. 2001) or 7.82 Patriot (.308) cal., stainless steel action with 2 locking lugs, 24 in. stainless barrel, detachable box mag., injection molded composite stock, 6.8 lbs. Mfg. 2001-2004.

$475 $400 $350 $285 $250 $215 $185 ***$550***

Add $100 for left-hand action.
Add $400 for Cabela's 4.5-14x42mm scope.

MODEL 700ST – various Lazzeroni cals., Rem. M-700 action, features remachined bolt face, squared recoil lug and receiver, mag. and follower are replaced with Lazzeroni style units, steel (disc.) or stainless steel (new 1999) action, blue steel or stainless steel 24 in. barrel. Mfg. 1998-99.

$2,150 $1,750 $1,425 $1,255 $1,020 $885 $715 ***$2,395***

MODEL 2000 SERIES – available in either Lazzeroni short magnum (6.17 Spitfire - .243 cal., 6.71 Phantom - .264 cal., 7.21 Tomahawk - .284 cal., 7.82 Patriot - .308 cal., 8.59 Galaxy - .338 cal., or 10.57 Maverick - .416 cal.) or Lazzeroni long magnums (6.53 Scramjet - .257 cal., 7.21 Firebird - .284 cal., 7.82 Warbird - .308 cal., 8.59 Titan - .338 cal., or 10.57 Meteor - .416 cal.), features precision machined steel (disc.) or stainless steel (new 1999) receiver, helically fluted bolt with heavy duty extractor, stainless steel match barrel with integral muzzle brake, adj. benchrest trigger, matte finish metal, 3 position firing pin safety on most models (new 1999), 2 or 3 (new 1999) shot internal mag., various stock configurations. Mfg. 1996-2005.

* ***Model L2000ST*** – features 27 in. barrel with conventional fiberglass stock, 8.1 lbs.

$5,250 $4,100 $3,175 $2,650 $2,300 $1,950 $1,650 ***$5,899***

* ***Model L2000ST-28*** – .308 Warbird cal., shoots 130 grain BarnesX boattail at 4,000 fps, 28 in. stainless steel fluted barrel, includes Schmidt & Bender 4-16x50mm scope, stainless action, black synthetic stock, approx. 8.3 lbs. Mfg. 1999-2001.

$5,875 $5,250 $4,750 $4,250 $3,600 $3,100 $2,650 ***$6,310***

This model was advertised as the flattest shooting hunting rifle then manufactured, and was at zero at 100, 200, and 300 yards.

GRADING - PPGS™	100%	98%	95%	90%	80%	70%	60%	LAST MSR

* ***Model L2000ST-W*** – features 27 in. barrel with conventional black wood laminate stock. Mfg. 1996 only.

	$4,400	$4,050	$3,600	$2,550	$2,200	$1,925	$1,625	$4,795

* ***Model L2000ST-WF Package*** – features 27 in. barrel with one conventional fiberglass and one black wood laminate stock. Disc. 1997.

	$4,875	$4,450	$4,050	$2,650	$2,400	$2,100	$1,750	$5,295

* ***Model L2000DG*** – .375 Saturn or .416 Meteor cal. only, features Fibergrain stock finish, removable muzzle brake, 3 shot mag., 24 in. barrel, includes sling swivels, 10.1 lbs. Mfg. 1998-2005.

	$5,575	$4,850	$4,350	$3,275	$2,800	$2,500	$2,000	$6,199

* ***Model L2000LLT*** – .257 Scramjet, .284 Firebird, .308 Warbird, or .338 Titan cal., lightweight variation with 26 in. barrel and detachable muzzle brake, 4 shot mag., right or left-hand action, 7.4 lbs. Mfg. 2004-2005.

	$5,400	$4,750	$4,250	$3,175	$2,750	$2,450	$1,950	$5,899

* ***Model L2000SA*** – .243 Spitfire, .264 Phantom, .284 Tomahawk, .308 Patriot, .338 Galaxy, .358 Eagle, .375 Hellcat, or .416 Maverick cal., short action cals. only, lightweight mountain configuration with 24 in. fluted barrel, 6.8 lbs. Mfg. 1998-2004.

	$4,750	$4,350	$3,800	$2,600	$2,350	$2,050	$1,750	$5,499

* ***Model L2000SLR*** – features 28 in. extra heavy fluted barrel and conventional fiberglass stock, not chambered in .338 Titan. Disc. 1999.

	$3,775	$3,400	$2,975	$2,600	$2,300	$2,000	$1,800	$4,195

* ***Model L2000SP*** – 25 in. fluted barrel, thumbhole fiberglass stock, 7.8 lbs. Disc. 2004.

	$4,750	$4,350	$3,800	$2,600	$2,350	$2,050	$1,750	$5,499

* ***Model L2000SP-W*** – 23 in. barrel, thumbhole black wood laminate stock.

	$4,400	$4,050	$3,600	$2,550	$2,200	$1,925	$1,625	$4,795

* ***Model L2000SP-FW Package*** – features 23 in. barrel with one thumbhole fiberglass and one black wood laminate thumbhole stock. Disc. 1997.

	$4,875	$4,450	$4,050	$2,650	$2,400	$2,100	$1,750	$5,295

MODEL L2012/L2005 GLOBAL HUNTER SERIES – available in various Lazzeroni proprietary cals., various configurations including Short Magnum Lite, Long Magnum Lite, Long Magnum Thumbhole, Long Magnum Special Long Range (disc. 2010), Short Magnum Dangerous Game (disc. 2010) and Long Magnum Dangerous Game, features stainless steel receiver, match grade fluted or unfluted barrel with muzzle brake, Jewell competition trigger, diamond fluted or helical cut bolt shaft, titanium firing pin, Limbsavr recoil pad, slim line graphite composite stock, approx. 6.1-8.7 lbs. New 2005.

MSR $5,000	$4,650	$4,250	$3,600	$3,100	$2,650	$2,150	$1,675

Add $1,000 for Long Magnum Lite or Sporter (Model L2012-LLT, new 2011).
Add $1,700 for Thumbhole (Model L2012-LTH/LSP).
Add $2,000 for Long Range Sporter (Model L2012-LSP, new 2012).
Add $1,000 for heavy barrel Long Magnum (disc. 2010).
Add $3,000 for Dangerous Game (Model L2012-LDJ) or Long Magnum Tactical (Model L2012-TAC, new 2011).

LEADER ARMS TECHNOLOGY

Current long arms manufacturer located in Trabzon, Turkey, with offices located in Ankara, Turkey.

SHOTGUNS

Leader Arms Technology manufactures single shot, O/U, slide action, and semi-auto shotguns under the Alpha Arms trademark. Please contact the company directly for more information, including U.S. availibility and pricing (see Trademark Index).

GRADING - PPGS™	100%	98%	95%	90%	80%	70%	60%	LAST MSR

LEBEAU-COURALLY

Current manufacturer established during 1865 and located in Liege, Belgium. Currently imported by Griffin & Howe, located in Bernardsville, NJ, and William Larkin Moore, located in Scottsdale, AZ. Previously imported by Heirloom Armes, located in Howard Lake, MN.

Lebeau-Courally manufactures only best quality rifles and shotguns. Approximately 30 are manufactured annually. Base prices listed do not include engraving on some models, and also do not include VAT (approx. 20%). Please contact the importer directly for a firm quotation on a Lebeau-Courally rifle or shotgun (see Trademark Index).

RIFLES: BOLT ACTION

Currently, Lebeau-Courally is building a bolt action rifle using a Mauser action, available in most calibers, and built to customer's specifications. This model is called the Marquis and has a current MSR of €22,000. Please contact the importers directly for more information and pricing on this model, including engraving options.

RIFLES: O/U

VICOMTE – various plains game and dangerous game cals., top-of-the-line model.

Base price on this model is currently €95,000.

RIFLES: SxS

AFRIQUE BOXLOCK EJECTOR – various cals., Anson & Deeley boxlock, ejectors, select French walnut stock, built per customer's specifications (disc.).

Base price on this model is currently €43,000.

ARDENNES BOXLOCK EJECTOR – various cals., Anson & Deeley boxlock, ejectors, select French walnut stock, built per customer's specifications (disc.).

Base price on this model is currently €33,000.

BIG FIVE SIDELOCK EJECTOR EXPRESS RIFLE – various dangerous game cals., top-of-the-line model.

Base price on this model is currently €95,000.

DAUPHIN SIDELOCK EJECTOR EXPRESS RIFLE – various plains game cals., features light construction, chopper lump barrels, reinforced action, select French walnut stock, quarter rib with ramp front sight, engraving not included, approx. 8 lbs.

Base price on this model is currently €70,000.

RIFLES: SINGLE SHOT

ARCHIDUE – various cals., best quality, top lever break open sidelock action with ejector, built per customer's specifications.

Base price on this model is currently €45,000.

CHEVALIER – various cals., falling block takedown action.

Base price on this model is currently €23,000.

SHOTGUNS: O/U

BARON – 12, 16, or 20 ga., several options available per individual custom order.

Current MSR on this model is €60,000.

BOSS VERREES – 12, 16, or 20 ga., top-of-the line sidelock ejector model.

Current MSR on this model is $85,000.

BOXLOCK WITH SIDEPLATES – various gauges, black pewter or case colored frame and sideplates, gold inlays around perimeter of receiver. New 2000.

Current MSR on this model is $22,256.

SIDELOCK – 12, 20, or 28 ga., Greener locking system.

Currently, this model is POR.

VERSAILLES – 12, 16, or 20 ga., includes ornamental engraving, top-of-the line sidelock.

MSR $30,000	$25,000	$20,000	$18,500	$16,000	$14,000	$12,000	$10,000

Subtract 10% for engraving styles other than ornamental.

100%	98%	95%	90%	80%	70%	60%	50%	40%	30%	20%	10%

SHOTGUNS: SxS

Older mfg. Lebeau-Courally shotguns have a completely different action and locking system than the newer models.

SOLOGNE BOXLOCK EJECTOR – 12, 16, or 20 ga., choice of classic or rounded action, with or without sideplates, select French walnut stock, choice of numerous engraving patterns (optional), 26, 28, or 30 in. barrels, double trigger.

Base price on this model is currently €27,000.

PRINCE SIDELOCK EJECTOR – 12, 16, 20, 28 ga., or .410 bore, choice of classic or rounded action, 26, 28, or 30 in. chopper lump barrels, select French walnut stock, base price includes fine scroll full coverage engraving, choice of numerous engraving patterns (optional), double triggers.

Base price on this model is currently €52,000.
Add €8,000 for 20, 28 ga. or .410 bore.

LECHNER & JUNGL GES.m.b.H.

Current manufacturer established circa 1874 and located in Graz, Austria.

Lechner & Jungl's history actually dates back to 1821, but the company started building guns circa 1874. All rifles and shotguns are high quality and are available in a wide variety of configurations, including drillings, vierlings, and combination guns. Since each gun is built per custom order, please contact the company directly for more information, including price, availability, options, and delivery time (see Trademark Index).

Lechner & Jungl also has a store in Graz stocked with a complete line of hunting, shooting, and sporting accessories.

LEFEVER ARMS COMPANY

Previous shotgun manufacturer located in Syracuse, NY circa 1885-1948.

SHOTGUNS: SxS

The Lefever was the first commercially successful hammerless double barrel shotgun made in America. They were made in Syracuse, NY from 1885-1916, at which time the company was acquired by Ithaca Gun Company. Ithaca made the Lefever after 1916. In 1921, the Box Lock Nitro Special was introduced and in 1934, the Lefever Grade A was introduced. Production of Lefever guns ceased in 1948.

The practice of assigning new serial numbers to guns returned to the factory for alterations absorbed approximately 5,000 numbers. Also, the serial number series started with 5,000, so approx. 62,000 guns were built.

The following is a percentage breakdown of gauges made between 1885-1916 (totaling 100%): 8 ga.-1/2%, 10 ga.-25%, 12 ga.-60%, 14 ga.-1/2%, 16 ga.-8%, 20 ga.-6%. Total serial numbers used was approx. 72,000 during this period. Damascus specimens of this trademark are worth approximately the same if in 60% or better original condition as their fluid steel barrel counterparts because of the rarity and desirability factors. Hammer guns are valued the same as damascus hammerless guns (grade for grade). Subtract 10%-30% on values with respective condition factors 50%-10%. Prices shown for 90% and up condition are very difficult to evaluate and are meant as a guide only - any Lefever shotgun in over 95% is rare and hard to evaluate.

SIDEPLATE MODELS – 10, 12, 16, or 20 ga., 26-32 in. barrels, any choke, boxlock action (even though model nomenclature referred to sidelock model), cocking indicators on all but DS and DSE grades, double triggers standard, checkered straight or pistol grip stock, auto ejectors designated by letter E after grade, most lower grades marked at water table near serial number. Mfg. 1885-1919.

Add 50% for 16 ga.
Add 100% for 20 ga.
Add 10% for SST.
Add 10% for AE.

*** *Model I Grade***

100%	98%	95%	90%	80%	70%	60%	50%	40%	30%	20%	10%
N/A	$1,525	$1,375	$1,250	$1,025	$925	$850	$775	$700	$630	$565	$500

100%	98%	95%	90%	80%	70%	60%	50%	40%	30%	20%	10%
* ***Model DS Grade***											
N/A	$1,525	$1,375	$1,250	$1,025	$925	$850	$775	$700	$630	$565	$500
* ***Model DSE Grade***											
N/A	$2,000	$1,800	$1,575	$1,275	$1,100	$950	$850	$775	$715	$650	$600
* ***Model H Grade***											
N/A	$2,175	$1,975	$1,700	$1,375	$1,200	$1,100	$1,000	$950	$900	$800	$750
* ***Model HE Grade***											
N/A	$3,000	$2,750	$2,350	$1,800	$1,600	$1,400	$1,250	$1,100	$1,000	$900	$850
* ***Model G Grade***											
N/A	$2,175	$1,975	$1,700	$1,500	$1,400	$1,300	$1,200	$1,100	$1,000	$900	$800
* ***Model GE Grade***											
N/A	$3,125	$2,850	$2,200	$1,800	$1,700	$1,500	$1,400	$1,300	$1,200	$1,100	$1,000
* ***Model F Grade***											
N/A	N/A	$2,375	$2,150	$1,700	$1,600	$1,500	$1,400	$1,100	$1,000	$900	$800
* ***Model FE Grade***											
N/A	N/A	$3,250	$2,950	$2,400	$2,000	$1,800	$1,600	$1,400	$1,300	$1,100	$1,000
* ***Model E Grade***											
N/A	N/A	$3,600	$3,000	$2,500	$2,100	$1,900	$1,800	$1,600	$1,400	$1,200	$1,100
* ***Model EE Grade***											
N/A	N/A	$7,400	$6,750	$3,750	$3,150	$2,700	$2,500	$2,300	$2,100	$1,900	$1,800
* ***Model D Grade***											
N/A	N/A	$4,550	$4,150	$3,250	$2,750	$2,150	$1,800	$1,600	$1,500	$1,400	$1,200
* ***Model DE Grade***											
N/A	N/A	$6,600	$5,700	$4,800	$3,700	$3,200	$2,700	$2,200	$2,000	$1,800	$1,600
* ***Model C Grade***											
N/A	N/A	$10,350	$8,500	$6,850	$4,000	$3,200	$2,700	$2,400	$2,200	$2,000	$1,900
* ***Model CE Grade***											
N/A	N/A	$11,400	$9,500	$7,500	$5,500	$4,800	$4,400	$3,600	$3,200	$2,800	$2,400
* ***Model B Grade***											
N/A	N/A	$13,300	$11,100	$9,500	$6,000	$5,200	$4,800	$4,000	$3,400	$3,000	$2,500
* ***Model BE Grade***											
N/A	N/A	$19,900	$17,750	$10,900	$6,600	$5,700	$5,100	$4,400	$3,800	$3,400	$3,150
* ***Model A Grade*** – auto ejectors standard.											
N/A	N/A	$28,500	$25,500	$23,750	$19,250	$11,250	$8,150	$7,200	$6,300	$5,400	$4,700
* ***Model AA Grade*** – auto ejectors standard.											
N/A	N/A	$46,000	$43,000	$38,000	$33,000	$25,000	$20,250	$18,250	$17,150	$16,500	$16,000

* ***Model Optimus Grade*** – auto ejectors standard.

Prices typically range from $60,000-$85,000, depending on original condition.

* ***Model Thousand Dollar Grade*** – auto ejectors standard.

Only one known to exist - last paid price at approx. $250,000.

GRADING - PPGS™	100%	98%	95%	90%	80%	70%	60%	*LAST MSR*

NITRO SPECIAL – 12, 16, 20 ga., or .410 bore, 26-32 in. barrels, various chokes, boxlock, extractors, checkered pistol grip stock. Mfg. 1921-48.

	100%	98%	95%	90%	80%	70%	60%
12 ga.	$725	$650	$575	$450	$395	$350	$300
16 ga.	$895	$825	$725	$650	$575	$475	$400
20 ga.	$1,225	$1,100	$975	$875	$775	$675	$575
.410 bore	$3,500	$3,150	$2,800	$2,450	$2,150	$1,725	$1,400

Add 10% for ST.

GRADING - PPGS™	100%	98%	95%	90%	80%	70%	60%	LAST MSR

GRADE A FIELD MODEL – 12, 16, 20 ga., or .410 bore, 26-32 in. barrels, various chokes, boxlock, checkered pistol grip stock. Mfg. 1934-42.

12 ga.	$1,100	$975	$875	$800	$725	$650	$575
16 ga.	$1,275	$1,125	$950	$875	$775	$675	$600
20 ga.	$1,650	$1,450	$1,250	$995	$875	$775	$675
.410 bore	$3,995	$3,550	$3,100	$2,750	$2,450	$2,150	$1,725

Add 33% for auto ejectors.
Add 10% for ST.

GRADE A SKEET MODEL – similar to Grade A, with 26 in. skeet bore barrels, auto ejector, single trigger and beavertail forearm standard.

12 ga.	$1,650	$1,450	$1,275	$1,075	$925	$800	$675
16 ga.	$2,000	$1,750	$1,475	$1,250	$1,075	$950	$800
20 ga.	$2,575	$2,300	$1,975	$1,700	$1,500	$1,250	$995
.410 bore	$4,500	$4,000	$3,500	$2,750	$2,450	$2,150	$1,725

SHOTGUNS: SINGLE BARREL

TRAP GUN – 12 ga. only, 30 or 32 in. VR barrel, full choke, boxlock, auto ejector, checkered pistol grip stock. Disc. 1942.

$600	$550	$440	$385	$330	$275	$250

LONG RANGE FIELD – 12, 16, 20 ga., or .410 bore, 26-32 in. barrel, boxlock, extractor, checkered pistol grip stock. Disc. 1942.

$395	$350	$295	$265	$225	$170	$140

LEFEVER, D.M.

Previous manufacturer circa 1901-1906. Company names and locations have been D.M. Lefever & Sons, Syracuse, NY (1901), D.M. Lefever, Sons & Co., Syracuse, NY (1901-1902), D.M. Lefever Gun Mfg., Defiance OH (1903-1904), and D.M. Lefever Co., Bowling Green, OH (1905-1906).

"Uncle Dan Lefever" founded the Lefever Arms Co. in 1884. He left the company in 1901 to found the above listed companies. While all were short-lived, the last was dissolved in 1906 the year of his death. Lefever Arms Co. continued manufacturing shotguns until sold to Ithaca Gun Co. in 1916. Ithaca assembled the Lefever gun until circa 1921, when they started building the "Nitro Special".

SHOTGUNS

"Uncle Dan" Lefever, founder of Lefever Arms, designed and manufactured the first breech loading double hammerless shotgun made in the U.S. Production started in 1872 and continued in the Syracuse, NY plant until he sold his interest in the Lefever Arms Company during the early 1900s. He then moved to Ohio and started another factory under the name D.M. Lefever & Son. After his death a few years later the Ohio factory was closed, while his old company (Lefever Arms Co.) continued manufacturing Lefevers until being sold to Ithaca Gun Company in 1916. From that point, Lefever Arms Co. was a branch of Ithaca and continued to make shotguns until shortly after WWII.

Total production on D.M. Lefever shotguns between 1901-1904 totaled less than 1,200. Because of their inherent rarity, values listed show only 10%-80% condition specimens. D.M. Lefever specimens are so rare in 80%+ condition that prices cannot be accurately ascertained.

On all Lefevers, the overall condition is so important to its value. Have a competent Lefever gunsmith check out the gun prior to purchasing is important. Also note that many times the barrels have been cut back to open up the shot pattern. And this effects the value of the gun considerably. The barrels should be exactly even lengths from 24-32 in. Also many sellers think their gun is a 60% level gun and others might grade it at 10%.

Also a note to all Lefever buyers: there seems to be a supply of faked and upgraded Lefevers on the market from time to time. The Lefever club keeps serial number records with the original grade as produced from the factory. Research and caution is recommended when purchasing the higher grades.

100%	98%	95%	90%	80%	70%	60%	50%	40%	30%	20%	10%

SHOTGUNS: SxS

NEW LEFEVER MODEL – 12, 16, or 20 ga., boxlock action, any length barrel and choke on order, auto ejectors standard on all grades except O Excelsior, double triggers standard on all except Uncle Dan grade, optional single triggers available, checkered walnut pistol grip or straight stock, grades differ as to engraving, wood, checkering and overall quality. Mfg. 1901-1906.

Add 50% for 16 ga. or 20 ga.

100%	98%	95%	90%	80%	70%	60%	50%	40%	30%	20%	10%
* *New Lefever Model O Excelsior Grade*											
N/A	N/A	N/A	N/A	$2,800	$2,425	$1,925	$1,650	$1,475	$1,350	$1,175	$950
* *New Lefever Model Excelsior Grade w/ejectors*											
N/A	N/A	N/A	N/A	$3,150	$2,725	$2,300	$1,925	$1,595	$1,450	$1,300	$1,045
* *New Lefever Model F Grade, No. 9*											
N/A	N/A	N/A	N/A	$3,150	$2,725	$2,300	$1,925	$1,595	$1,450	$1,300	$1,045
* *New Lefever Model E Grade, No. 8*											
N/A	N/A	N/A	N/A	N/A	$4,000	$3,600	$3,100	$2,700	$2,300	$1,900	$1,600
* *New Lefever Model D Grade, No. 7*											
N/A	N/A	N/A	N/A	N/A	$4,950	$4,500	$4,125	$3,850	$3,375	$2,975	$2,750
* *New Lefever Model C Grade, No. 6*											
N/A	N/A	N/A	N/A	N/A	$7,500	$6,950	$6,250	$5,600	$4,800	$4,300	$3,900
* *New Lefever Model B Grade, No. 5*											
N/A	N/A	N/A	N/A	N/A	$7,925	$7,250	$6,600	$5,850	$5,000	$4,500	$4,000
* *New Lefever Model AA Grade, No. 4*											
N/A	N/A	N/A	N/A	N/A	$11,100	$10,000	$9,250	$8,500	$7,700	$6,600	$5,500

UNCLE DAN GRADE – extremely rare, original specimens are selling for $100,000+.

OPTIMUS – extremely rarity precludes accurate pricing on this model.

It is highly recommended that this model be professionally checked out by a competent Lefever gunsmith prior to selling or buying.

SHOTGUNS: SINGLE BARREL TRAP

TRAP GUN – 12 ga., 26-32 in. full choke, auto ejector, boxlock, checkered pistol grip stock. Mfg. 1904-06.

100%	98%	95%	90%	80%	70%	60%	50%	40%	30%	20%	10%
N/A	N/A	N/A	$6,500	$5,750	$4,900	$3,500	$2,750	$2,000	$1,500	$1,000	$750

LE FORGERON

Previous manufacturer located in Belgium. Previously imported and distributed by Midwest Gun Sport in Zebulon, NC.

GRADING - PPGS™	100%	98%	95%	90%	80%	70%	60%	LAST MSR

RIFLES: SxS

MODEL 6020 – 9.3x74R cal., boxlock action, beavertail forearm, pistol grip stock.

100%	98%	95%	90%	80%	70%	60%	LAST MSR
$4,450	$4,025	$3,750	$3,475	$3,100	$2,800	$2,550	*$4,900*

Add $700 for sideplates (Model 6040).

MODEL 6030 – sidelock action, engraved action with deluxe French walnut stock and forearm.

100%	98%	95%	90%	80%	70%	60%	LAST MSR
$8,475	$7,900	$7,100	$6,300	$5,500	$4,700	$4,000	*$8,950*

SHOTGUNS: SxS

Prices represent the importer's last available information (1989).

BOXLOCK EJECTOR – 20 or 28 ga. only, with or without sideplates, select French walnut stock, choice of engraving patterns (optional), single trigger.

100%	98%	95%	90%	80%	70%	60%	LAST MSR
$3,975	$3,650	$3,325	$2,995	$2,600	$2,250	$1,900	*$4,400*

Add $1,000 for sideplates.

GRADING - PPGS™	100%	98%	95%	90%	80%	70%	60%	LAST MSR

SIDELOCK EJECTOR – 20 or 28 ga. only, select French walnut stock, choice of engraving patterns (optional), rounded action, single trigger.

	100%	98%	95%	90%	80%	70%	60%	LAST MSR
	$10,200	$9,250	$8,500	$7,900	$7,100	$6,300	$5,500	$11,600

LE FRANCAIS PISTOLS

Previous trademark manufactured by Manufacture Francaise d'Armes et Cycles de Saint-Etienne, located in Saint Etienne, France. Trade name was MANUFRANCE.

PISTOLS: SEMI-AUTO

POCKET MODEL AUTOMATIC – .25 ACP cal., double action, 7 shot, 2 3/8 in. hinged barrel, blue, fixed sights, hard rubber grips. Mfg. 1914-1966.

	100%	98%	95%	90%	80%	70%	60%
	$300	$250	$210	$180	$150	$125	$100

Add 50%-100% for engraved models, depending on amount of coverage.

TYPE POLICEMAN MODEL AUTOMATIC – .25 ACP cal., similar to Pocket Model, except has 3 1/2 in. hinged barrel, some are marked "FRANCO". Mfg. 1922-1968.

	100%	98%	95%	90%	80%	70%	60%
	$400	$300	$250	$210	$180	$150	$125

Add 50%-100% for engraved models, depending on amount of coverage.

.32 AUTOMATIC MODEL – .32 ACP cal., double action, 8 shot, 3 1/4 in. hinged finned barrel, blue, fixed sights, rubber grips. 10,000 mfg. 1950-1969, very few imported into the U.S.

	100%	98%	95%	90%	80%	70%	60%
	$1,250	$1,000	$850	$750	$600	$500	$400

TYPE ARMY MODEL AUTOMATIC – 9mm Browning Long cal., double action, 8 shot, 5 in. hinged barrel, blue, fixed sights, checkered walnut grips, some are marked "FRANCO". 4,000 mfg. 1928-1938. Early model with plain tapered barrel (1928), later model with finned barrel (1931).

	100%	98%	95%	90%	80%	70%	60%
	$2,250	$1,750	$1,250	$1,000	$750	$625	$500

Add 10% for later model with finned barrel (1931).
Add 50%-100% for engraved models, depending on amount of coverage.

LEGACY SPORTS INTERNATIONAL

Current importer located in Reno, NV. Previously located in Alexandria, VA.

Legacy Sports International imports a wide variety of firearms trademarks in various configurations, including pistols, rifles, and shotguns. Trademarks include: Citadel, Escort, Howa, ISSC, Puma, and Verona (disc.). Please refer to these individual listings.

LEGEND

Previous rifle trademark manufactured circa 1996-2006 by D'Arcy Echols & Co. and located in Millville, UT.

RIFLES: BOLT ACTION

Previous Legend rifles utilized an extensively modified and refined Winchester Model 70 claw extractor action. Synthetic stocks were built by special order. Current rifles may be found under the D'Arcy Echols & Co. listing in the D section.

LEGION FIREARMS

Current firearms and accessories manufacturer located in Temple, TX.

Legion Firearms makes a variety of AR-15 style carbines/rifles, semi-auto pistols in various configurations, and accessories. Please contact the company directly for more information on their models including price and availability (see Trademark Index).

LEGION USA INC.

Previous importer until 2011 of Saiga firearms manufactured by Izhmash, located in Izhevask, Russia.

LEITNER-WISE DEFENSE, INC.

Current AR-15 style parts/accessories manufacturer located in Alexandria, VA. The company discontinued its semi-auto line of rifles circa 2010.

GRADING - PPGS™	100%	98%	95%	90%	80%	70%	60%	LAST MSR

RIFLES: SEMI-AUTO

M.U.L.E. MOD. 1 (MODULAR URBAN LIGHT ENGAGEMENT CARBINE) – 5.56 NATO cal., 16 in. steel barrel standard, other lengths optional, op-rod operating system, single stage trigger, Magpul ACS buttstock, MOE pistol grip, black finish, upper and lower rails, 30 shot mag., flared magwell, E sights, includes one mag., manual, and cleaning kit, 7.9 lbs. Disc. circa 2010.

$1,550 $1,375 $1,175 $1,000 $850 $700 $575 *$1,680*

Add $100 for precision trigger.

M.U.L.E. MOD. 2 (MODULAR URBAN LIGHT ENGAGEMENT CARBINE) – .308 Win. cal., 16 or 20 in. steel barrel, similar to Mod. 1, except has heavier barrel, 8 1/2 lbs. Disc. circa 2010.

$1,895 $1,700 $1,500 $1,300 $1,100 $900 $700 *$2,100*

Add $100 for 20 in. barrel.

LEITNER-WISE RIFLE CO. INC.

Previous manufacturer located in Springfield, VA circa 2006. Previously located in Alexandria, VA 1999-2005.

RIFLES: SEMI-AUTO

LW 15.22 – .22 LR or .22 WMR cal., paramilitary configuration patterned after the AR-15, forged upper and lower receivers, choice of carry handle or flat-top upper receiver, forward bolt assist, last shot hold open, 16 1/2 or 20 in. barrel, 10 or 25 shot mag. Mfg. 2000-2005.

$775 $675 $600 $550 $500 $450 $425 *$850*

Add $50 for A2 carrying handle.

LW 15.499 – .499 (12.5x40mm) cal., receiver and action patterned after the AR-15, mil spec standards, 16 1/2 in. steel or stainless steel barrel, flat-top receiver, 5 (disc.), 10, or 14 (new 2006) shot mag., approx. 6 1/2 lbs. Mfg. 2000-2005.

$1,350 $1,150 $995 $875 $750 $675 $600

Add $92 for stainless steel barrel.

LW 6.8/5.56 S.R.T. – 5.56x45mm NATO or 6.8x43mm SPC cal., 16.1 in. barrel, hard chrome lined bore, gas operated, locking bolt, Troy front and rear sights, forged T7075 aluminum flat-top upper receiver, six position collapsible stock, Picatinny rail, removable carry handle, A2 flash hider, LW forged lower receiver, 28 or 30 shot mag., 5.38 lbs. Ltd. mfg. 2006.

$2,050 $1,800 $1,600 $1,400 $1,200 $1,000 $850

Add $100 for 6.8x43mm SPC cal.

LES BAER CUSTOM, INC.

Current manufacturer and customizer established in 1993, and located in LeClaire, IA since 2008. Previously located in Hillsdale, IL until 2008. Dealer sales only.

PISTOLS: SEMI-AUTO, 1911 SERIES

The following current models are available with the following features unless otherwise noted: lowered and flared ejection port, tuned and polished extractor, Baer extended ejector, and beveled mag. well.

Add $70 for Tactical Package (rounds the edges of the pistol).

ULTIMATE MASTER COMBAT SERIES – .38 Super, .400 Cor-Bon, or .45 ACP cal., steel frame and slide with blued finish, compensated, 5 or 6 in. barrel, two 8 shot mags., checkered Cocobolo grips, low mount LBC adj. sight with hidden rear leaf, dovetailed front sight, double serrated slide, deluxe Commander hammer and sear, full length recoil rod, extended ambi safety, speed trigger.

* ***COMPENSATED MODEL*** – .38 Super or .45 ACP cal., compensated barrel.

MSR $2,880 $2,500 $2,250 $2,000 $1,750 $1,575 $1,350 $995

Add $260 for .38 Super cal.

* ***5 INCH MODEL*** – .38 Super, .400 Cor-Bon, or .45 ACP cal., 5 in. barrel.

MSR $2,790 $2,425 $2,150 $1,900 $1,650 $1,525 $1,275 $925

Add $50 for .400 Cor-Bon cal. Add $100 for .38 Super cal.

GRADING - PPGS™	100%	98%	95%	90%	80%	70%	60%	LAST MSR

* ***6 INCH MODEL*** – .38 Super, .400 Cor-Bon, or .45 ACP cal., 6 in. barrel.

MSR $2,790	$2,425	$2,150	$1,900	$1,650	$1,525	$1,275	$925	

Add $70 for .400 Cor-Bon cal. Add $180 for .38 Super cal.

NATIONAL MATCH HARDBALL PISTOL – .45 ACP cal., NM steel frame, slide, and 5 in. barrel with stainless bushing, 7 shot mag., blued finish, checkered front strap, checkered Cocobolo grips, low mount LBC adj. sight with hidden rear leaf, dovetailed front sight, rear serrated slide, match trigger.

MSR $1,960	$1,725	$1,550	$1,325	$1,100	$975	$825	$675	

BULLSEYE WADCUTTER PISTOL – .45 ACP cal., NM frame, slide, and barrel with stainless bushing, 7 shot mag., blued finish, checkered Cocobolo grips, double serrated slide, high checkered front strap, Baer deluxe hammer and sear, beavertail grip safety with pad, Baer speed trigger, optical scope mount.

MSR $2,140	$1,900	$1,675	$1,450	$1,225	$1,025	$850	$700	

Add $50 for 6 in. slide with Lo-Mount LBC adj. sights and Baer optical mount.

PPC DISTINGUISHED MATCH PISTOL – 9mm Para. or .45 ACP cal., NM steel frame, slide, and barrel with stainless bushing, 8 shot mag., 5 in. barrel, blued finish, checkered Cocobolo grips, PPC sight, Baer dovetail front sight, double serrated slide, Baer deluxe Commander hammer and sear, beavertail grip safety with pad, Baer speed trigger, extended ambi safety.

MSR $2,240	$2,000	$1,775	$1,525	$1,275	$1,050	$875	$725	

Add $390 for 9mm Para. cal. with supported chamber.

PPC OPEN CLASS – 9mm Para. or .45 ACP cal., similar to PPC Distinguished Match, except features 6 in. barrel.

MSR $2,350	$2,100	$1,850	$1,600	$1,325	$1,100	$900	$750	

Add $390 for 9mm Para. cal. with supported chamber.

PREMIER II 5 INCH MODEL – .38 Super, .400 Cor-Bon, or .45 ACP cal., NM steel frame, slide, and barrel with stainless bushing, 5 in. barrel, low mount LBC adj. sight with hidden rear leaf, dovetail front sight, two 8 shot mags., blued finish or stainless steel, checkered Cocobolo grips, beavertail grip safety with pad, speed trigger, extended ambi safety.

MSR $1,905	$1,675	$1,425	$1,225	$1,050	$925	$775	$650	

Add $45 for stainless steel.
Add $185 for .400 COR-BON cal. Add $365 for .38 Super cal. Add $505 for .45 ACP/.400 COR-BON dual cylinder combo.

PREMIER II 6 INCH MODEL – .38 Super or .45 ACP cal., similar to Premier II 5 Inch Model, except features 6 in. barrel, blued finish only.

MSR $2,090	$1,825	$1,600	$1,375	$1,175	$995	$825	$675	

Add $100 for .400 COR-BON cal. Add $420 for .38 Super cal.

PREMIER II SUPER-TAC – .38 Super, .400 Cor-Bon, .45 ACP, or .45 ACP/.400 Cor-Bon combo cal., NM steel frame, slide, and barrel with stainless bushing, double serrated slide, low mount LBC adj. rear sight and Baer dovetail front sight, both fitted with tritium night sights, two 8 shot mags., Dupont S coating, checkered Cocobolo grips, deburred for tactical carry, beavertail grip safety with pad, Baer speed trigger, extended ambi safety.

MSR $2,370	$2,125	$1,850	$1,600	$1,325	$1,100	$900	$750	

Add $25 for .400 Cor-Bon cal.
Add $200 for .38 Super cal.
Add $520 for .45 ACP/.400 Cor-Bon dual cylinder combo.

BOSS – .45 ACP cal., similar to the Premier II series, except features blued slide, extended combat safety, rear cocking serrations on the slide, fiber optic front sight, chromed complete lower, special tactical package.

MSR $2,260	$2,025	$1,775	$1,525	$1,275	$1,050	$875	$725	

GRADING - PPGS™	100%	98%	95%	90%	80%	70%	60%	LAST MSR

PROWLER III – .45 ACP cal., NM steel frame, slide, and 5 in. barrel with tapered cone stub weight, Bear reverse plug, slide fitted to frame, double serrated slide, low mount BoMar sight with hidden leaf rear, dovetail front sight, checkered slide stop, Baer speed trigger, deluxe Commander hammer, beavertail grip safety with pad, extended ambi safety, blued finish, two 8 shot mags., checkered Cocobolo grips.

MSR $2,710	$2,400	$2,125	$1,800	$1,575	$1,300	$1,100	$925

CUSTOM CARRY – .38 Super (4 1/4 in. only), or .45 ACP cal., NM steel frame, slide, and barrel with stainless bushing, 4 1/4 (Comanche length) or 5 in. throated barrel, blued or stainless steel finish, deluxe fixed combat sight, dovetail front sight, improved ramp style night sights, double serrated slide, checkered slide stop, Baer speed trigger, extended ambi safety, two 8 shot mags., checkered Cocobolo grips.

MSR $1,920	$1,700	$1,525	$1,300	$1,075	$950	$800	$650

Add $120 for stainless steel finish.

Add $300 for .38 Super cal. with 4 1/4 in. barrel and stainless steel finish.

SUPER COMANCHE – .38 Super cal., steel construction only, 4 1/4 in. throated barrel, NM slide with rear serrations only, stainless steel bushing, deluxe fixed combat rear sight with night sight, dovetail front sight ramp style with night sight, blue finish or optional chrome or DuPont S finish, checkered slide stop, speed trigger, extended ambi safety, checkered Cocobolo grips, high checkered front strap, two 9 shot mags. with base pads. New 2013.

MSR $2,220	$1,995	$1,775	$1,525	$1,275	$1,050	$875	$725

ULTIMATE RECON PISTOL – .45 ACP cal., full size Caspian frame with integral Picatinny rail system for frame mounted light, comes standard with a Streamlight TLR-1, NM slide and 5 in. barrel with stainless bushing, deluxe fixed combat rear sight with night sights, dovetail front sight, double serrated slide, bead blast blue finish or optional bead blast chrome finish, deluxe hammer and sear, checkered slide stop, speed trigger, tactical style extended combat safety, checkered Cocobolo grips, high checkered front strap, two 8 shot mags.

MSR $2,370	$2,125	$1,850	$1,600	$1,325	$1,100	$900	$750

Add $240 for bead blast chrome finish.

ULTIMATE TACTICAL CARRY – .45 ACP cal., steel NM frame and slide with front and rear serrations, slide fitted to frame, 5 in. barrel with stainless match bushing, LBC deluxe fixed combat rear sight with tritium inserts, dovetail front sight with tritium insert, blued finish, deluxe hammer and sear, checkered slide stop, combat extended safety, aluminum match trigger, deluxe special slim line grips, three stainless steel 8 shot mags.

MSR $1,930	$1,695	$1,450	$1,225	$1,050	$925	$775	$650

THUNDER RANCH SPECIAL – .45 ACP cal., similar to Ultimate Tactical Carry, except has beavertail grip safety with pad, high checkered front strap, deluxe special slim line grips with Thunder Ranch logo, three stainless steel 7 shot mags., special Thunder Ranch logo engraved on slide, special serial numbers with "TR" prefix.

MSR $1,980	$1,695	$1,495	$1,225	$1,050	$925	$775	$650

SHOOTING USA CUSTOM PISTOL – .45 ACP cal., similar to Premier II 5 in. model, except also features tactical extended safety, a special serial number prefix with "S USA" and the number, the famous Shooting USA logo engraved on the right side of the slide, blued finish, two 8 shot stainless steel mags., and a special DVD produced by Shooting USA.

MSR $1,905	$1,675	$1,425	$1,225	$1,050	$925	$775	$650

CUSTOM CENTENNIAL MODEL 1911 PISTOL – .45 ACP cal., made to commemorate the 100th anniversary year of "Old Ironsides", similar to Premier II 5 in. model, except features rear serrated slide with the model name engraved on the slide, ivory grips, deluxe charcoal blue finish, extended tactical safety, three 8 shot mags., special presentation box.

MSR $4,050	$3,600	$3,200	$2,750	$2,250	$1,875	$1,500	$1,350

1911 S.R.P. (SWIFT RESPONSE PISTOL) – .45 ACP cal., NM steel frame and slide with front and rear serrations, 4 1/4 (Comanche Model) or 5 in. barrel with stainless match bushing, deluxe fixed combat sight, dovetail front sight, checkered slide stop, speed trigger, deluxe Commander hammer, beavertail grip safety with pad, tactical style ambi safety, Tritium night sights installed front and rear, Deburred for tactical carry, Dupont S

GRADING - PPGS™	100%	98%	95%	90%	80%	70%	60%	LAST MSR

coating on complete pistol, three 8 shot mags., checkered Cocobolo grips, special wooden presentation box with glass lid.

MSR $2,490	$2,150	$1,800	$1,575	$1,300	$1,050	$875	$775

MONOLITH – .38 Super or .45 ACP cal., NM steel Monolith frame, Monolith flat bottom double serrated slide, 5 in. barrel with stainless match bushing, low mount LBC adj. sight with hidden rear leaf, Baer dovetail front sight, checkered slide stop, speed trigger, deluxe Commander hammer, beavertail grip safety with pad, extended ambi safety, two 8 shot mags., checkered Cocobolo grips, blued finish, extra long dust cover.

MSR $1,990	$1,695	$1,495	$1,225	$1,050	$925	$775	$650

Add $400 for supported chamber .38 Super.

* ***Monolith Heavyweight*** – .38 Super or .45 ACP cal., similar to Monolith, except has a heavier frame.

MSR $2,060	$1,750	$1,525	$1,250	$1,075	$950	$800	$675

Add $335 for supported chamber .38 Super.

MONOLITH COMANCHE – .45 ACP cal., NM steel Monolith frame, Monolith flat bottom double serrated slide, 4 1/4 in. barrel with stainless match bushing, Tritium night sights front and rear and deluxe fixed rear sight, checkered slide stop, speed trigger, deluxe Commander hammer, beavertail grip safety with pad, extended ambi safety, two 8 shot mags., checkered Cocobolo grips, blued finish, extra long dust cover.

MSR $1,995	$1,725	$1,450	$1,225	$1,050	$925	$775	$650

* ***Monolith Comanche Heavyweight*** – .45 ACP cal., similar to Monolith Comanche, except dust cover is slightly thicker to add weight and is flat on the bottom.

MSR $2,060	$1,750	$1,525	$1,250	$1,075	$950	$800	$675

.38 SUPER STINGER – .38 Super cal., NM Stinger frame, NM Commanche length slide with rear serrations only, 4 1/4 in. barrel with supported chamber and stainless steel bushing, deluxe fixed combat rear sight with night sight, dovetail ramp type with night sight, checkered slide stop, speed trigger, deluxe Commander hammer, beavertail grip safety with pad, tactical ambi safety, three 8 shot mags. with pads, checkered Cocobolo grips, blue finish or optional chrome or Dupont S finish. New 2013.

MSR $2,495	$2,250	$1,975	$1,700	$1,475	$1,225	$1,050	$850

STINGER MODEL – .45 ACP cal., NM Stinger frame, NM Commanche length slide with rear serrations, slide fitted to frame, 4 1/4 in. barrel with stainless bushing, low mount combat fixed rear sight, dovetail front sight, checkered slide stop, speed trigger, deluxe Commander hammer, beavertail grip safety with pad, extended ambi safety, two 7 shot mags., checkered Cocobolo grips, blued finish.

MSR $1,930	$1,695	$1,450	$1,225	$1,050	$925	$775	$650

* ***Stinger Model Stainless*** – .45 ACP cal., similar to Stinger Model, except features stainless steel frame and slide.

MSR $1,990	$1,695	$1,495	$1,225	$1,050	$825	$725	$650

CONCEPT I/CONCEPT II – .45 ACP cal., NM steel frame and slide, 5 in. barrel with stainless bushing, slide fitted to frame, double serrated slide, LBC adj. deluxe low mount rear sight with hidden leaf, dovetail front sight, or deluxe fixed combat sight (Concept II), checkered slide stop, fitted speed trigger with action job, deluxe Commander hammer, beavertail grip safety with pad, extended ambi safety, two 8 shot mags., checkered Cocobolo grips, blued finish.

MSR $1,770	$1,595	$1,350	$1,150	$975	$825	$700	$575

* ***Concept III/Concept IV*** – .45 ACP cal., similar to Concept I/Concept II, except has stainless steel frame and blued steel slide, and checkered front strap.

MSR $1,910	$1,675	$1,450	$1,225	$1,050	$925	$775	$650

* ***Concept V*** – .45 ACP cal., similar to Concept I, except both frame and slide are stainless steel, available with 5 or 6 in. barrel, LBC adj. rear sight, checkered front strap.

MSR $1,940	$1,700	$1,450	$1,225	$1,050	$925	$775	$650

Add $85 for 6 in. barrel.

GRADING - PPGS™	100%	98%	95%	90%	80%	70%	60%	LAST MSR

* ***Concept VI*** – .45 ACP cal., similar to Concept V, except has 5 in. barrel, Baer deluxe fixed combat rear sight.

MSR $1,910	$1,675	$1,450	$1,225	$1,050	$925	$775	$650	

* ***Concept VII*** – .45 ACP cal., similar to Concept I, except has Commanche size 4 1/4 in. barrel, all blued steel, Baer deluxe fixed combat rear sight, and checkered front strap.

MSR $1,920	$1,675	$1,450	$1,225	$1,050	$925	$775	$650	

* ***Concept VIII*** – .45 ACP cal., similar to Concept I, except has Commanche size 4 1/4 in. barrel, all stainless steel, Baer deluxe fixed combat rear sight, and checkered front strap.

MSR $1,955	$1,695	$1,450	$1,225	$1,050	$925	$725	$650	

HEMI 572 – .45 ACP cal., inspired by Chrysler's fast and fearsome 1970 Hemi Cuda, double serrated slide, fiber optic front sight with green insert, Hex head grip screws, special tactical package with ambi safety, VZ black recon grips, complete hard chrome finish on all major components, Dupont S coating on slide stop, mag. catch and mag. catch lock, two 8 shot mags. New 2013.

MSR $2,395	$2,050	$1,725	$1,500	$1,225	$1,000	$825	$725	

LIMITED EDITION LES BAER PRESENTATION GRADE 1911 – .45 ACP cal., similar to Premier II, except also features detailed hand chiseled engraving, special charcoal blueing on all polished surfaces, rich nitre blue is used on pins, thumb safety, slide stop, grip screws, mag catch lock and hammer, real ivory grips, "LBC" engraving on top of the slide is inlaid with gold, optional to add name of the recipient engraved on the slide with the legend "To (name) by Les Baer", includes special presentation box.

MSR $6,590	$5,950	$5,500	$4,750	$4,000	$3,250	$2,500	$2,100	

Add $100 for name engraving on slide.

CUSTOM 25TH ANNIVERSARY SPECIAL COLLECTORS MODEL – .45 ACP cal., similar to Premier II, except also includes hand engraving on both sides of the slide and frame, Les Baer's actual signature and the legend "25th Anniversary" have been engraved, then inlaid with white gold on the top of the slide, rich charcoal blue finish, real ivory grips, also includes a special presentation box.

MSR $6,995	$6,250	$5,750	$4,850	$4,100	$3,300	$2,550	$2,200	

RIFLES: BOLT ACTION

CUSTOM TACTICAL VARMINT CLASSIC – .243 Win., .260 Rem., .300 Win. Mag. (new 2011) or .308 Win. cal., 24 in. match grade barrel, Still Tac 30 action and thick lug, Timney match trigger, front and back of action are glass bedded and lug is bedded into Bell & Carlson precision varmint stock, fitted Wyatts precision floorplate with box mag., Picatinny one piece rail, Dupont S coated finish. Mfg. 2010-2011.

	$3,250	$2,850	$2,450	$2,000	$1,650	$1,375	$1,125	*$3,410*

Add $150 for .300 Win. Mag. cal. with Harris bipod and muzzle brake.

CUSTOM TACTICAL/TACTICAL RECON – .243 Win., .260 Rem., .308 Win., .338 Lapua, 6.5x284 Norma, or .300 Win. Mag. cal., 24, 26, or 27 in. match grade barrel with or w/o muzzle brake, Still Tac 30 action and thick lug, Timney match trigger, front and back of action are glass bedded and lug is bedded into Bell & Carlson adj. stock, fitted Wyatts precision floorplate with box mag., Picatinny one piece rail, Dupont S coated finish, Harris bipod. Limited mfg. 2011 only.

	$3,300	$2,950	$2,500	$2,075	$1,695	$1,375	$1,125	*$3,560*

Add $200 for .300 Win. Mag. with enforcer muzzle brake or $330 for .338 Lapua with enforcer muzzle brake.

RIFLES: SEMI-AUTO

CUSTOM ULTIMATE AR MODEL – .204 Ruger (new 2004), .223 Rem., or 6.5 Grendel (mfg. 2007-2009) cal., 18-24 in. stainless steel barrel, Picatinny flat top rail, individual rifles are custom built with no expense spared, everything made in-house ensuring top quality and tolerances, all models are guaranteed to shoot 1/2-3/4 MOA groups, various configurations include Varmint Model (disc.), Super Varmint Model, NRA Match Rifle, Super Match Model

GRADING - PPGS™	100%	98%	95%	90%	80%	70%	60%	LAST MSR

(new 2002), M4 Flattop Model, Custom Special Tactical (new 2011), and IPSC Action Model. New 2001.

MSR $2,240	$2,100	$1,900	$1,700	$1,500	$1,300	$1,100	$900	

Add $950-$1,305 for Super Varmint scope packages (includes Leupold Vari-X III 4.5-14x40mm scope). Add $140 for Super Match model. Add $90 for M4 flat-top model. Add $320 for IPSC action model. Add $349 for Thunder Ranch rifle (disc. 2010). Add $849 for CMP competition rifle. Add $240 for NRA match rifle w/o sights. Add $245 for Super Varmint model (.204 Ruger cal.) Add $210 for 6.5 Grendel cal. with M4 style barrel. Add $110 for Custom Special Tactical rifle (new 2011).

.264 LBC-AR – .264 LBC-AR cal., 18-24 in. stainless steel barrel, available in Ultimate Super Varmint, Ultimate Super Match, and Ultimate M4 Flat-top configurations, fixed stock, black finish, 14 shot mag., features similar to Ultimate Model in .223 cal. New 2010.

MSR $2,240	$2,100	$1,900	$1,700	$1,500	$1,300	$1,100	$900	

Add $50 for Super Varmint model.
Add $150 for Super Match model.

6x45 ULTIMATE AR – 6x45mm cal., 18-24 in. stainless steel barrel, available in Super Varmint, Super Match, and M4 Flattop configurations, black finish, fixed stock, similar to Ultimate AR in .223 configuration. New 2010.

MSR $2,240	$2,100	$1,900	$1,700	$1,500	$1,300	$1,100	$900	

Add $50 for Super Varmint model.
Add $150 for Super Match model.

POLICE SPECIAL – .223 Rem., .264 LBC-AR (disc.), or 6x45mm (disc.) cal., 16 in. precision button rifled steel barrel, 14 or 30 shot mag., removable carry handle with rear sight, Picatinny flat-top upper rail, National Match chromed carrier, flip up front sight, six position ATI collapsible stock with adj. cheekpiece and grip, Picatinny four-way handguard, A2 flash hider, Timney match trigger group, lockable sling swivel mounted on stud on four-way handguard, includes two mags. New 2010.

MSR $1,790	$1,625	$1,425	$1,150	$1,000	$875	$750	$625	

.308 LBC ULTIMATE MATCH/SNIPER – .308 Win. cal., 18 or 20 in. stainless steel barrel with precision cut rifling, matte black finish, 20 shot mag., machined upper and lower, no forward assist, Picatinny flat-top rail, steel gas block, free float handguard with lock ring, two-stage trigger group, Dupont S coating on barrel, Harris bipod, fixed or adj. Magpul stock, with or w/o enforcer muzzle brake, available in Match or Sniper configuration. New 2011.

MSR $3,190	$2,850	$2,725	$2,600	$2,275	$1,750	$1,500	$1,250	

Add $30 for Match model with PRS Magpul stock or $310 for Sniper model with adj. stock and enforcer muzzle brake.

.308 ULTIMATE MONOLITH SWAT MODEL – .308 Win. cal., 18 or 24 in. stainless steel barrel with precision cut rifling, matte black finish, 20 shot mag., similar to .308 Ultimate Match/Sniper, except has integrated Mil-Std 1913 Picatinny rail system, Magpul PRS adj. stock, Versa pod and adapter, integral trigger guard is bowed on bottom so shooter can wear gloves. New 2011.

MSR $3,940	$3,750	$3,475	$3,000	$2,725	$2,450	$2,250	$1,750	

Add $250 for Enforcer muzzlebrake.

LEW HORTON DIST. CO.

Current firearms distributor located in Westboro, MA. While Lew Horton is not a manufacturer or an importer, this company has been responsible for many special and limited editions which are listed with quanities, but without prices, since they may vary greatly from region to region. Special/Limited Editions began in 1983.

SPECIAL/LIMITED EDITIONS

In addition to the special/limited editions listed, Lew Horton also subcontracted special editions that were sold from company flyers and other promotional materials. They include the following Smith & Wesson Models - Classic Hunter M29 (500 mfg. 1989), Model 63 2 in. (500 mfg. 1989), Model 36 2nd Amendment (200 mfg. 1989), Model 60 25th Anniversary (100 mfg. 1989), Model

Make/Model	Qty. Made	Year Issued	Retail Price

629 Classic Hunter (mfg. 1986), Model 5967 (500 mfg. 1990), and the Model 3914 (200 mfg. 1990). There are two Remington models - the M1100 Special Field (200 mfg. 1987-88) and the M700 BDL .257 Roberts cal. (500 mfg. 1990). There are three Colt models - the Combat Python (750 mfg. 1987-88), the Pocketlite (350 mfg. 1989), and the Custom Cobra Stainless Sets (2 sets, mfg. 1989).

Current values are not listed on the following special/limited editions, as pricing can vary greatly depending on each gun's unique desirability factor, which depends on the configuration, caliber, finish, geographical area, options, and accessories.

SPECIAL/LIMITED EDITIONS HANDGUNS: COLT

Make/Model	Qty. Made	Year Issued	Retail Price
COLT SAA Horse Pistol	100	1983	$1,100
COLT Presidential - Gold SAA & Det. Spec. w/Gold Eye	600	1985	$525
COLT Boa (includes both 4 & 6 in. barrel)	1,200	1985	$525
COLT Ultimate Officer's .45 ACP	500	1989	$777
COLT Lt. Commander .45 ACP	800	1985	$590
COLT Combat Cobra 2 1/2 in.	1,000	1987	$500
COLT Lady Colt (MK IV .380 ACP)	1,000	1989	$547
COLT Night Commander .45 ACP	250	1989	$725
COLT El Presidente .38 Super Govt.	350	1990	$800
COLT El Comandante .38 Super Govt.	500	1991	$800
COLT El General .38 Super Govt.	500	1991	$850
COLT El Capitan .38 Super	500	1991	$875
COLT Detective Special	100	1992	$430
COLT Elite Ten/Forty	100	1992	$900
COLT El Patron	500	1992	$850
COLT El Jefe	500	1992	$849
COLT El Dorado	750	1992	$1,099
COLT El Teniente	400	1992	$1,037
COLT El Teniente	300	2001	N/A
COLT El Coronel	750	1993	$900
COLT Classic Gold Cup	300	1993	$1,285
COLT Classic Single Action	180	1993	$680
COLT Night Officer	350	1993	$680
COLT El Presidente Premier Edition	10	1993	$3,000
COLT Classic Government	300	1993	$965
COLT Night Government	300	1993	$705
COLT El Caballero	500	1994	$986
COLT El Potro	500	1994	$1,025
COLT Frontier Six Shooter	100	1994	$1,849
COLT McCormick Factory Racer	500	1994	$1,149
COLT Springfield Armory Bicentennial Edition	400	1994	$1,000
COLT Springfield Armory Premier Bicentennial	200	1994	$1,213
COLT Classic 45 Special Edition	500	1995	$960
COLT Comp Commander .45 ACP Ported	350	1998	$889
COLT Defender Custom .45 ACP 3 in. w/4 Ports	100	1998	$900
COLT Delta 98 10mm 5 in. Matte SS	100	1998	$800
COLT El Aquila Supreme .38 Sup. Engraved	20	1999	$3,000
COLT El Aquila .38 Sup. 5 in. RB	350	1999	$1,000
COLT El Cabo .38 Sup. 5 in. Bright SS	350	1999	$1,200
COLT El Campecon .38 Super Blue	550	1997	$870
COLT El Centauro .38 Sup. BTS	350	1997	$798
COLT El Embajador .38 Sup. BTS/Gold	350	1998	$1,000

Make/Model	Qty. Made	Year Issued	Retail Price
COLT El General 5 Star Deluxe 38 Sup. Engr.	10	1997	$2,000
COLT El Jefe Supremo Supreme 38 Sup. Engr.	20	1999	$3,000
COLT El Jefe Supremo 38 Sup BSTS/Fire Bl.	350	1999	$1,410
COLT El Official .38 Super/Blue w/gold	450	1998	$1,003
COLT El Sargento .38 Super 5 in. RB/SS	350	1999	$1,000
COLT El Soldado 38 Super 5 in. Ryl Blue/Pearlite grips	350	2000	$1,020
COLT El Soldado Supreme 38 Super A Engraved	20	2000	$2,996
COLT El Soldado Supreme	20	2001	N/A
COLT El Soldado Supreme Proposed	20	2001	N/A
COLT El Senador	350	2001	N/A
COLT El Senador Supreme	20	2001	N/A
COLT El Toro 38 Super Bl w/jeweled parts	350	2000	$1,020
COLT El Toro	350	2001	N/A
COLT El Toro Supreme	20	2001	N/A
COLT El Obra Maestra .38 Super Royal Blue/Gold	350	2001	$1,130
COLT El Matadore .38 Super 5 in. Bright Stainless w/Gold	350	2001	$1,425
COLT El Rey Hi Polish Stainless Steel Blue .38 Super	350	2001	$1,050
COLT McCormick Combat Cmdr 45 Engr.	50	1995	$1,213
COLT McCormick Combat Cmdr 45 Chrome	500	1995	$1,073
COLT McCormick Officer Cmdr 45 Chrome	300	1995	$1,073
COLT Night Officer II Chrm 45 Night Sight	100	1994	$829
COLT Night Officer III SS/Matte 45	200	1996	$810
COLT Officers Ultimate .45 ACP Bl/SS	500	1995	$900
COLT Officers Ultimate .45 ACP Engr.	10	1995	$1,995
COLT SAA CC/B Mop. Std. Eng.	15	1999	$5,345
COLT SAA .45 LC Nickel Bird's Head Mother-of-Pearl, Std. C	30	2001	$5,715
COLT U.S. Shooting Team .45 ACP	750	1995	$1,150
COLT Govt. Model XSE w/gold scroll	20	2006	$1,170
COLT M1991A1 w/scroll & gold detail	20	2006	$1,000
COLT El Caballo De Oro Deluxe	200	2008-2009	$5,000
COLT El Jefe de Jefes	200	2008-2009	$2,500
COLT El Caballo De Oro	200	2008-2009	$2,296
COLT El Jefe de Jefes Maximo	200	2008-2009	N/A
COLT Col. Colt. .45 Signature Blue	200	2008-2009	$3,795
COLT Col. Colt .45 Signature Stainless	100	2008-2009	$3,195
COLT Rampant Colt .45 Blue	100	2008-2009	$3,599
COLT Rampant Colt .45 Stainless	100	2008-2009	$3,599
COLT SAA Golden Eagle .45 LC 4 3/4 in.	100	2008-2009	$2,795
COLT SAA Silver Scroll Ltd. .45 LC 5 1/2 in.	100	2008-2009	$2,200
COLT SAA Gold Scroll Ltd. .45 LC 5 1/2 in.	100	2008-2009	$2,200

SPECIAL/LIMITED EDITIONS HANDGUNS: SMITH & WESSON

Lew Horton is a major distributor of S&W's Heritage Series and Performance Center models. Please contact Lew Horton directly to find out more information on this wide variety of handguns, including current availability and pricing.

SMITH & WESSON Model 25-3 Lew Horton Special	100	1977	$500
SMITH & WESSON Model 29-3 Lew Horton Special	5,000	1984	$425
SMITH & WESSON Model 629-3 Lew Horton Special	5,000	N/A	$400
SMITH & WESSON Model 24-3 Lew Horton Special	5,000	1983-84	$380
SMITH & WESSON Model 686 Lew Horton Special	N/A	1984	$450
SMITH & WESSON Model 657-3 Lew Horton Special	5,000	1986	$410

Make/Model	Qty. Made	Year Issued	Retail Price
SMITH & WESSON Model 624-2 Lew Horton Special	7,000	1986-87	$395
SMITH & WESSON Model 640 Carry Comp	250	1991	$750
SMITH & WESSON .40 Compensated	150	1992	$1,699
SMITH & WESSON .40 Tactical	200	1992	$1,499
SMITH & WESSON Shorty Forty	N/A	1992	$950
SMITH & WESSON Model 629 Hunter	200	1992	$1,234
SMITH & WESSON Model 629 Carry Comp	300	1992	$1,000
SMITH & WESSON Model 686 Carry Comp 4 in.	300	1992	$1,000
SMITH & WESSON Model 657 Classic Hunter	350	1993	$545
SMITH & WESSON Model 356 Shorty	N/A	1993	$999
SMITH & WESSON Model 356 Tactical	N/A	1993	$1,350
SMITH & WESSON Model 629 Hunter II	200	1993	$1,234
SMITH & WESSON Model 629 Carry Comp II	100	1993	$1,000
SMITH & WESSON Model 686 Carry Comp 3 in.	300	1993	$1,000
SMITH & WESSON Model 686 Competitor	400	1993	$1,100
SMITH & WESSON Model 686 Hunter	200	1993	$1,153
SMITH & WESSON Model 5906 Shorty Nine	200	1993	$999
SMITH & WESSON Model 60 Carry Comp	300	1993	$800
SMITH & WESSON Model 629 Unfluted	300	1993	$1,234
SMITH & WESSON Model 629 Hunter III	300	1994	$1,234
SMITH & WESSON Model 640 Paxton Quigley	250	1994	$800
SMITH & WESSON Model 625 Classic Snub	300	1994	$603
SMITH & WESSON Model 629 Classic Hunter	500	1994	$1,234
SMITH & WESSON Model 629 Quad-magnaported .44 Mag.	150	1994	$900
SMITH & WESSON Shorty Forty Mark II	150	1995	$999
SMITH & WESSON Shorty .40 Mark III	500	1997	$1,025
SMITH & WESSON Shorty .45	225	1997	$1,096
SMITH & WESSON Shorty .45 Mark II	N/A	1997	N/A
SMITH & WESSON Model 625 Hunter .45 LC Fluted	150	1997	$1,234
SMITH & WESSON Model 629 Hunter .44 Mag. Unfluted	500	1997	$1,234
SMITH & WESSON Model 686 Hunter 7 Shot Unfluted	300	1997	$1,234
SMITH & WESSON Model 640 Quadport .357 Mag. 2 in.	500	1997	$836
SMITH & WESSON Model 681 Quadport .357 Mag. 7 Shot	300	1997	$700
SMITH & WESSON PC M627 2 5/8 in. 8 shot RRWO Unfluted	450	2000	$1,025
SMITH & WESSON Model 686 7 Shot Night Sight	300	1997	$1,000
SMITH & WESSON F Comp. 3 in. Comp. Barrel	500	1997	$800
SMITH & WESSON Model 629 Classic Carry 3 in. Unfluted	300	1997	$590
SMITH & WESSON M625 .45 LC 3 in. RRWO	400	1998	$755
SMITH & WESSON M625 .45 Colt 3 in. Rosewood RRWO	150	2000	$755
SMITH & WESSON M657 Classic Hunter .41 Mg 6.5 in. wood flt.	150	1997	$614
SMITH & WESSON M657 Classic Hunter .41 Mg 6.5 in. wood unflt.	400	1997	$614
SMITH & WESSON PC M629 6 in. Hunter w/barrel cut out, unfluted	350	2000	$1,300
SMITH & WESSON PC M629 12 in. FL, Bomar sights	400	2000	$1,059
SMITH & WESSON PC M1006 Classic Ser 10mm 5 9 shot	28	1998	$550
SMITH & WESSON PC M27 .357 Mag. 5 in. fluted cyl. SB	16	1999	$670
SMITH & WESSON PC M29 Classic Ser .44 Mag. 7.5 in.	19	1998	$1,060
SMITH & WESSON PC M41 Classic Ser .22 LR 7 in.	14	1998	$801

Make/Model	Qty. Made	Year Issued	Retail Price
SMITH & WESSON PC M4516 Classic Ser .45 ACP	7	1998	$866
SMITH & WESSON PC M4563 CQB .45 ACP 4 Alloy Frame	100	1998	$1,235
SMITH & WESSON PC M4563 CQB .45 ACP 4 two-tone	200	1998	$1,235
SMITH & WESSON PC M4566 CQB .45 ACP 4 SS frame	100	1998	$1,235
SMITH & WESSON PC M4567 Classic Ser .45 4.5 two-tone	14	1998	$1,010
SMITH & WESSON PC M627 Htr .357 6 in. 8 shot unf. wood	200	1997	$1,060
SMITH & WESSON PC M627 .357 Mg. 5 in 8 shot ported	100	1997	$1,050
SMITH & WESSON PC M627 .357 2 5/8 8 shot RRWO unflt.	300	1999	$1,025
SMITH & WESSON PC M627 .357 5 in. 8 shot unf. wood cmbt	1,200	1997	$1,000
SMITH & WESSON PC M627 .357 5 in. 8 shot unf. rosewood	200	1998	$1,000
SMITH & WESSON PC M627 .357 6.5 in. 8 shot fluted rosewood	200	1998	$1,025
SMITH & WESSON PC M629 .44 Mg. 6 1/2 in. flt. 6 sht RMB	200	1998	$1,020
SMITH & WESSON PC M629 .44 Mg. 2 5/8 in. 6 sht rosewood	300	1999	$1,026
SMITH & WESSON PC M629 6 Htr w/bbl CO Unf port	100	1999	$1,060
SMITH & WESSON PC M657 Classic Ser .41 Mg. 3 in.	7	1994	$550
SMITH & WESSON PC M657 Classic Ser .41 Mg. 4 in.	25	1998	$550
SMITH & WESSON PC M657 41 Mg. 6 1/2 in. FL 6 sht	200	1998	$1,020
SMITH & WESSON PC M686 .357 3 in. 7 sht ss night sights	500	1996	$1,000
SMITH & WESSON PC M686 .357 6 in. 7 sht Hntr w/port	175	1996	$1,024
SMITH & WESSON PC M686 .357 Mg. 7 sht profile bbl	125	1998	$1,025
SMITH & WESSON PC M9 Shorty 9 MKII 9mm Compact	150	1995	$1,050
SMITH & WESSON PC M625 3 in.	N/A	2004	$1,110
SMITH & WESSON PC M329 .44 cal., Clear Scandium frame, 3 in. Stainless bbl	100	2004	$1,200
SMITH & WESSON PC M329 .44 cal., Black Scandium frame, 3 in. bl. bbl.	500	2004	$1,200
SMITH & WESSON PC M629 .44 Mag. cal., 7.5 in. bbl Comped Hunter TDA	500	2004	$1,171
SMITH & WESSON M15 .38 Spl. 4 in. color case blue	200	2001	$770
SMITH & WESSON M15 .38 Spl. 4 in. nickel	200	2001	$750
SMITH & WESSON M15 .38 Spl. 5 in. nickel McGivern	150	2001	$1,070
SMITH & WESSON M15 .38 Spl. 6 in. blue McGivern	150	2001	$1,040
SMITH & WESSON M15 .38 Spl. 6 in. color case blue	100	2001	$1,070
SMITH & WESSON M17 .22 LR 6 in. AS blue	200	2001	$1,040
SMITH & WESSON M17 .22 LR 6 1/2 in. color case blue	150	2001	$1,070
SMITH & WESSON M24 .44 Spl. 6 1/2 in. color case frame	300	2001	$1,110
SMITH & WESSON M24 .44 Spl. 6 1/2 in. fluted blue	150	2001	$1,050
SMITH & WESSON M25 (1917) .45 ACP 5 1/2 in. 6 shot	200	2001	$1,047
SMITH & WESSON M25 .45 Colt 6 1/2 in. color case blue frame	150	2001	$1,111
SMITH & WESSON M25 .45 Colt 6 1/2 in. fluted blue	150	2001	$1,050
SMITH & WESSON M25 (1917) .45 ACP 5 1/2 in. color case blue	100	2001	$1,110
SMITH & WESSON M25 (1917) .45 ACP 5 1/2 in. Military	150	2001	$1,050
SMITH & WESSON M27 5 1/2 in. Nickel	100	2007	$1,510
SMITH & WESSON M27 3 1/2 In. Nickel	100	2007	$1,500
SMITH & WESSON M29 .44 Mag. 6 1/2 in. blue	250	2001	$1,045
SMITH & WESSON M29 .44 Mag. 6 1/2 in. nickel	200	2001	$1,070
SMITH & WESSON Schofield M3 .45 S&W	100	2001	$1,520
SMITH & WESSON Schofield 7 in. bright nickel	100	2001	$1,520

Make/Model	Qty. Made	Year Issued	Retail Price
SMITH & WESSON Model SW1911 "United We Stand"	250	2005	$1,127
SMITH & WESSON PC Model 625 .45 LC Scandium SS 2 in.	100	2005	$1,291
SMITH & WESSON SW 1911 SS .45 ACP Engraved	50	2006	$1,005
SMITH & WESSON PC Model 500 SS .500 Mag.	1,000	2004	$1,350
SMITH & WESSON PC Model 625-10 Scandium SS .45 ACP	800	2003	$1,110
SMITH & WESSON Model 36 .38 Spl, nickel/blue	250	2006	$857
SMITH & WESSON SW1911 Land of the Free w/gold	150	2004	$1,137
SMITH & WESSON SW1911 Gold Eagle Ltd.	60	2005	$2,000
SMITH & WESSON PC M460 Spl. Ed. .460 S&W Mag. SS 3 1/2 in.	500	2005	$1,600
SMITH & WESSON PC M460 Spl. Ed. .460 S&W Mag. SS 6 1/2 in.	750	2005	$1,500
SMITH & WESSON SW1911 SS Long May It Wave w/gold	100	2004	$1,137
SMITH & WESSON SW1911 SS Rebel Flag Ltd. Ed.	100	2005	$1,137
SMITH & WESSON SW1911 SS Mexican Eagle Ltd. Ed.	100	2004	$1,147
SMITH & WESSON PC M460 .460 S&W Mag. Two-tone 3 1/2 in.	100	2006	$1,600
SPECIAL/LIMITED EDITIONS HANDGUNS: MISC MANUFACTURERS			
BERETTA Lady Beretta	100	1985	$285
EUROPEAN AMERICAN ARMORY Witness Competitor 45 Ported	100	1998	$460
EUROPEAN AMERICAN ARMORY Witness Competitor Polymer 45 Ported	100	1998	$460
EUROPEAN AMERICAN ARMORY Witness Defender II 45 Ported	100	1998	$460
EUROPEAN AMERICAN ARMORY Witness Defender Polymer 45 Ported	100	1998	$496
EUROPEAN AMERICAN ARMORY Witness Tactical .40 S&W 12rd	300	1997	$400
EUROPEAN AMERICAN ARMORY Witness Tactical .45 ACP 10rd	300	1997	$400
H&R 1871, INC. 999 Premier Edition	100 pr.	1993	$345
SIGARMS P220 Premium Edition .45 ACP	200	1994	$850
SPRINGFIELD Night Light Compact 1911-A1 Lightweight	500	1997	$749
SPRINGFIELD Night Light Standard 1911-A1 Lightweight	300	1997	$749
SPRINGFIELD M1911 Ltw Compact .45 ACP bi-tone 7rd	125	1998	$675
SPRINGFIELD M1911 Ltw Std. .45 ACP bi-tone 8rd	300	1998	$675
SPRINGFIELD Springfield Armory Bicentennial Edition	500	1994	$775
TAURUS Model PT-92AF	250	1990	$454
TAURUS Model 85 3 in. Ported Blue	500	1995	$229
TAURUS Model 85 3 in. Ported Stainless	500	1995	$349
TAURUS SAA Gold Laurel .32-20 WCF	100	2008-2009	$2,699
SPECIAL/LIMITED EDITIONS RIFLES			
REMINGTON Model 541J Curly Maple	500	1994	$500
REMINGTON Model 700 Police .308 Win., 26 in. fluted	500	2004	$1,000
REMINGTON Model 700 Police .308 Win. grn. stock	500	2004	$930
SAVAGE 10FP Tactical .223 Rem. Short Action	200	1999	$492
SAVAGE 10FP Tactical .308 Win. HB 20	550	1999	$500
SAVAGE 30 Joshua Stevens .22 LR	250	2001	$400
SPECIAL/LIMITED EDITIONS SHOTGUNS			
MOSSBERG Night Persuader Special Edition	300	1990	N/A

GRADING - PPGS™	100%	98%	95%	90%	80%	70%	60%	LAST MSR

LEWIS MACHINE & TOOL COMPANY (LMT)

Current paramilitary rifle and accessories manufacturer established in 1980, and located in Milan, IL.

RIFLES: SEMI-AUTO

LMT manufactures AR-15 style rifles and carbines.

IMPORTANT NOTE: On model(s) where *N/A has replaced the normal 100% value, it indicates current market conditions are too unstable to accurately ascertain 100%-60% values. Factory retail prices (MSRs) reflect most recent updates. For more up-to-date information on current pricing trends and additional useful information, please visit www.bluebookofgunvalues.com, select "Information & Services" from the menu, and click on "Additional Book Information".

CQB SERIES – 5.56 NATO cal., gas piston operating system, 16 in. chrome lined barrel, 30 shot mag., standard trigger, SOPMOD stock, monolithic rail platform, tactical charging handle assembly, includes sling, manual, tactical adj. front and rear sights, torque wrench/driver, and three rail panels, 6.8 lbs.

MSR $2,100	*N/A	$1,550	$1,350	$1,215	$975	$800	$625

* ***CQB16 6.8*** – 6.8 SPC cal., similar to CQB16 Standard, except has 25 shot mag. New 2010.

MSR $2,509	*N/A	$1,850	$1,595	$1,450	$1,175	$955	$750

* ***CQBPS16*** – 5.56 NATO cal., 16 in. barrel, gas piston operating system, tactical charging handle assembly, Defender lower with SOPMOD buttstock, 30 shot mag., standard trigger group, includes sling, tactical front and rear sights, torque wrench/driver, and three rail panels. New 2010.

MSR $2,351	*N/A	$1,750	$1,500	$1,360	$1,100	$900	$700

* ***CompCQB16*** – 5.56 NATO cal., similar to CQB16 Standard Model, except has 10 shot mag.

MSR $2,100	*N/A	$1,550	$1,350	$1,215	$975	$800	$625

COMP16 – 5.56 NATO cal., 16 in. chrome lined barrel, standard flat-top upper receiver, 10 shot mag., tactical charging handle assembly, Defender lower with fixed SOPMOD buttstock, standard trigger group, includes sling, tactical adj. rear sight.

MSR $1,685	*N/A	$1,250	$1,075	$975	$795	$650	$500

STD16 – 5.56 NATO cal., 16 in. chrome lined barrel, standard trigger and bolt, choice of SOPMOD or Gen. 2 collapsible stock, 5.9 - 6.2 lbs.

MSR $1,594	*N/A	$1,175	$1,025	$925	$750	$615	$475

SPM16 – 5.56 NATO cal., similar to STD16, except has Generation 2 buttstock. New 2010.

MSR $1,371	*N/A	$1,025	$875	$800	$650	$525	$410

LM8MWS – .308 Win. cal., 16 in. steel or stainless steel barrel, 20 shot mag., monolithic rail platform, gas piston operating system, Defender lower with SOPMOD stock, two stage trigger, includes sling, manual, tactical front and rear sights, torque wrench/driver, and three rail panels. New 2010.

MSR $3,149	*N/A	$2,350	$2,000	$1,825	$1,475	$1,200	$935

Add $536 for matte black stainless steel barrel.
Add $340 for Pigman Signature Model (new 2012).

LM8MRP – 5.56 NATO cal., otherwise similar to LM8MWS. New 2012.

MSR $2,254	*N/A	$1,695	$1,450	$1,300	$1,050	$875	$675

Add $133 for 16 in. stainless steel barrel.

LM308MWSE/MWSF – .308 Win. cal., 16 in. barrel, two stage trigger group, Sopmod buttstock, tactical sights, 20 shot mag., includes 3 rail panels. New 2012.

MSR $3,003	*N/A	$2,225	$1,925	$1,725	$1,400	$1,150	$895

Add $563 for matte black stainless steel barrel.

GRADING - PPGS™	100%	98%	95%	90%	80%	70%	60%	LAST MSR

LM308 COMP16 – .308 Win. cal., standard 16 in. crowned target barrel, 10 shot mag., includes 3 rail panels. New 2012.

MSR $3,003	*N/A	$2,225	$1,925	$1,725	$1,400	$1,150	$895	

LM308MWSK – .308 Win. cal., 20 in. stainless steel barrel with matte black finish, Sopmod buttstock, two stage trigger, 20 shot mag., includes three rail panels. Limited mfg. 2012.

	*N/A	$2,750	$2,400	$2,100	$1,800	$1,500	$1,200	*$3,396*

LM8308SS SHARPSHOOTER WEAPON SYSTEM – .308 Win. cal., 16 in. stainless steel matte black barrel, tactical charging handle, Sopmod buttstock, flip up sights, includes eight 20 shot magazines, cleaning kit, Harris bipod and pelican case, Flat Dark Earth furniture. New 2012.

MSR $5,198	*N/A	$3,875	$3,325	$3,000	$2,425	$1,995	$1,550	

LIBERATOR

Previously manufactured by the Guide Lamp Corporation (division of General Motors) circa 1942.

100%	98%	95%	90%	80%	70%	60%	50%	40%	30%	20%	10%

PISTOLS: SINGLE SHOT

LIBERATOR PISTOL – .45 ACP cal., simplistic design and action utilizing nonstrategic WWII materials, mfg. for European resistance movement during WWII, very limited number used in Europe, most used in Philipines and China, each gun was individually packaged in a paraffin-coated cardboard box with wood ejector rod, wood spacer, and a smaller box containing 10 rounds of .45 ACP ammo with a graphics only instruction sheet on top, 4 in. smooth bore barrel, sheet steel stamping mfg. with welds, no ser. no., 1 million mfg. 1942 only.

N/A	$3,000	$2,750	$2,500	$2,250	$2,000	$1,750	$1,500	$1,250	$1,000	$850	$725

Add $600-$800 for original box.
Add $400-$600 for original B&W instruction sheet.

An authentic instruction sheet will have a watermark reading "WHITING MUTUAL BOND RAG CONTENT", and all ammo will have a headstamp of "FA 42". This is the only pistol that could be mfg. (6.6 sec.) faster than it could be loaded (10 sec.). While the Liberator's appearance is crude, remember that the entire production run (1 million) was mfg. and ready for overseas shipment in 10-11 weeks.

Even though 1 million of these pistols were mfg., remaining specimens brought into the U.S. are rare. Complete pistols in original box are extremely rare.

LIBERTY

Previous trademark imported 1997-2003 by K.B.I., Inc. located in Harrisburg, PA.

GRADING - PPGS™	100%	98%	95%	90%	80%	70%	60%

REVOLVERS: SAA

FRONTIER MODEL – .38-40 Win. (disc. 1998), .357 Mag. (disc. 1998, reintroduced 2000 only), .44-40 WCF (disc. 2000), or .45 LC cal., 4 3/4, 5 1/2, or 7 1/2 in. barrel, case hardened, bright nickel, or antique silver (new 1999) frame, choice of brass or steel backstrap and trigger guard, mfg. by Uberti. Imported 1997-2001.

$295	$250	$235	$210	$195	$175	$160	*$339*

Add $45 for steel backstrap and trigger guard.
Add $80 for antique silver finish (new 1999).
Add $25 for bright nickel finish (.44-40 WCF or .45 LC only).

TARGET MODEL – similar to Frontier Model, except is not available in .357 Mag. cal., and has adj. rear sight. Imported 1997-98.

$300	$265	$240	$220	$200	$180	$165	*$319*

BISLEY MODEL – .44-40 WCF or .45 LC cal., features Bisley grip configuration, 4 3/4, 5 1/2, or 7 1/2 in. barrel, case hardened or bright nickel finish, steel backstrap and trigger guard. Limited importation 1999 only.

$415	$365	$325	$295	$260	$230	$200	*$459*

Add $60 for bright nickel finish.

GRADING - PPGS™	100%	98%	95%	90%	80%	70%	60%	LAST MSR

LIBERTY I/II – .357 Mag., .44-40 WCF, or .45 LC cal., 4 3/4, 5 1/2, or 7 1/2 in. barrel, case hardened frame, blue finish, choice of brass or steel backstrap and trigger guard.

$275 $250 $235 $210 $195 $175 $160 *$319*

Add $70 for steel backstrap and trigger guard.

This model changed nomenclature to Charles Daly Model 1873 during 2004 - please refer to the Charles Daly 1976-present section for current information on this model.

RIFLES: LEVER ACTION

MODEL 1892 CARBINE – .357 Mag. or .45 LC cal., choice of case hardened or brass plated receiver, 20 in. round barrel. Limited importation 2000 only.

$595 $525 $475 $425 $395 $360 $330 *$665*

Add $15 for brass plated receiver.

MODEL 1892 RIFLE – .357 Mag., .44-40 WCF, or .45 LC cal., choice of case hardened, brass plated, or antique silver finished receiver, 24 in. octagon barrel. Limited importation 2000 only.

$610 $535 $485 $430 $400 $360 $330 *$680*

RIFLES: REPRODUCTIONS

SHARPS TRAPDOOR CARBINE/RIFLE/BUSINESS – .45-70 Govt. cal., case hardened receiver finish, choice of 22 (Carbine), 28 (Rifle), or 32 (Business, limited importation 2000 only) in. round barrel, single or double set triggers. Imported from Pedersoli 2000-2001.

$675 $575 $500 $450 $400 $350 $300 *$769*

Add $20 for Hunter rifle.

Add $60 for Business Model (limited importation 2000 only).

ROLLING BLOCK CARBINE/RIFLE – .357 Mag., .45 LC, or .45-70 Govt. cal., case hardened receiver finish, 22 in. round (Carbine) or 28 in. octagon (Rifle) barrel. Imported from Pedersoli 2000-2001.

$615 $550 $475 $425 $375 $325 $275 *$689*

Add $10 for Rifle.

SPRINGFIELD TRAPDOOR CARBINE/RIFLE – .45-70 Govt. cal., case hardened receiver finish, 22 (Carbine) or 26 (Rifle) in. round barrel. Imported from Pedersoli 2000-2001.

$725 $650 $600 $550 $475 $425 $375 *$815*

Add $34 for rifle with 26 in. barrel.

RIFLES: SxS

LIGHTNING EXPRESS DOUBLE RIFLE – .44-40 WCF, .45 LC, or .45-70 Govt. cal., exposed hammers, 22 in. barrels, choice of case hardened, bright nickel (disc.), or antique silver (new 2000) finish. Limited importation 1999-2000.

$750 $650 $550 $475 $425 $375 $325 *$840*

Add $40 for antique silver finish.

SHOTGUNS: SxS

LIBERTY I/II COACH GUN – 12 ga. only, exposed hammers, 20 or 24 (disc. 2000, reintroduced 2002) in. barrels, choice of case hardened or antique silver finish, fixed chokes (cyl./cyl., 20 in. barrels only, or IC/M, 24 in. barrels only). Imported 1999-2003.

$475 $435 $375 $345 $315 $285 $250 *$559*

* ***Liberty I/II Coach Gun/Express Rifle Combination Set*** – includes 20 in. 12 ga. barrels, and choice of 22 in. rifle barrels in any Lightning Express cal., blue finish only. Limited importation 1999 only.

$1,025 $875 $750 $625 $550 $475 $425 *$1,159*

LIBERTY ARMS INTERNATIONAL LLC

Current importer and manufacturer currently located in Victoria, TX. Previously located in Albion, NY until 2010.

RIFLES: SEMI-AUTO

Liberty Arms assembles an AK-47 design carbine manufactured from U.S. milled or stamped receivers, U.S. chrome lined barrels, and Bulgarian manufactured part kits. MSRs are $900 for

GRADING - PPGS™	100%	98%	95%	90%	80%	70%	60%	LAST MSR

the milled receiver, and $750 for the stamped receiver. Additionally, the company imports a variety of European firearms and ammunition. Please contact the company directly for current surplus offerings, availability, and pricing (see Trademark Index).

LIBERTY ARMS WORKS, INC.

Previous manufacturer located in West Chester, PA circa 1991-1996.

PISTOLS: SEMI-AUTO

L.A.W. ENFORCER – .22 LR, 9mm Para., 10mm, .40 S&W (new 1994), or .45 ACP cal., patterned after the Ingram MAC 10, single action, 6 1/4 in. threaded barrel, closed bolt operation, manual safety, 10 (C/B 1994) or 30* shot mag., 5 lbs. 1 oz. Mfg. 1991-96.

	100%	98%	95%	90%	80%	70%	60%	LAST MSR
	$575	$500	$450	$415	$385	$335	$295	*$545*

LIEGEOISE D'ARMES

Previous manufacturer located in Belgium.

Small manufacturer that specialized in boxlock shotguns, normally engraved and with ejectors. Prices usually range from $600-$1,200, depending on condition and engraving.

LIGNOSE (BERGMAN)

Previous manufacturer located in Suhl, Germany.

PISTOLS: SEMI-AUTO

EINHAND MODEL 2A POCKET AUTOMATIC – 6.35mm/.25 ACP cal., 6 shot, 2 in. barrel, blue, rubber grips, can be cocked by rearward pressure on trigger guard.

	100%	98%	95%	90%	80%	70%	60%
	$395	$325	$225	$185	$150	$120	$90

MODEL 2 POCKET AUTOMATIC – similar to 2A, without one hand cocking trigger guard.

	100%	98%	95%	90%	80%	70%	60%
	$325	$265	$215	$165	$90	$75	$55

MODEL 3 POCKET AUTOMATIC – similar to 3A, except without one hand cocking trigger guard.

	100%	98%	95%	90%	80%	70%	60%
	$300	$250	$200	$165	$140	$110	$85

MODEL 3A POCKET AUTOMATIC – similar to 2A, except longer grip, 9 shot capacity.

	100%	98%	95%	90%	80%	70%	60%
	$450	$350	$250	$200	$140	$110	$85

LILIPUT

Previous trademark manufactured by August Menz, located in Suhl, Germany.

PISTOLS: SEMI-AUTO

4.25mm cal. – 4.25mm centerfire Liliput cal. (shoots 12 grain bullet), blue or nickel finish, limited 1920s mfg.

	100%	98%	95%	90%	80%	70%	60%
	$750	$700	$550	$425	$385	$340	$300

Ammunition for this caliber is very rare, and is selling for approx. $20 per round.

6.35mm cal. – .25 ACP cal., mfg. in large quantities pre-WWII.

	100%	98%	95%	90%	80%	70%	60%
	$250	$200	$140	$110	$90	$75	$55

LIND, AL

Current custom long gun maker located in Tacoma, WA, previously located in Lakewood, WA until 2010.

Al Lind is a member of the American Custom Gunmakers Guild and manufacturers custom made shotguns and rifles, all built to customer specifications, with base prices starting at $3,600 for bolt rifles and $4,000 for sidelock shotguns. Many options and accessories are available. Please contact him directly for more information, including pricing, delivery time, and availability (see Trademark Index).

LINDNER GUN COMPANY

Previous manufacturer located in Sandornville, NH circa 2007-2010.

While Lindner Gun Company advertised in many trade magazines, it appears that the company made no guns for consumers other than a few prototypes.

GRADING - PPGS™	100%	98%	95%	90%	80%	70%	60%	LAST MSR

LINEBAUGH, JOHN

Current pistolsmith located in Cody, WY.

Mr. John Linebaugh has been making specialized, custom sixguns since 1980. He is the inventor of the .475 Linebaugh cartridge (introduced 1988), and the .500 Linebaugh caliber (the first successful .50 caliber revolver and cartridge introduced in 1986). Current pricing on current models is $2,400-$2,700. Please contact him directly for more information, including a price quotation (see Trademark Index).

LIPPARD, KARL

Current manufacturer and importer located in Colorado Springs, CO.

Karl Lippard is a well-known firearms designer, importer, shooter, and author of books on Perazzi and Fabbri. He invented the first interchangeable part sidelock O/U shotgun.

PISTOLS: SEMI-AUTO

NCO 1911A2 COMBAT – .45 ACP cal., 5 in. barrel, includes two barrels, available in commercial production and close quarters battle pistol configurations.

	100%	98%	95%	90%	80%	70%	60%
MSR $3,250	$3,250	$2,900	$2,600	$2,300	$1,950	$1,600	$1,275

Add $250 for NCO production variation, $1,750 for NCO commercial variation.

RIFLES: CUSTOM

BOXLOCK DOUBLE RIFLE – .375 H&H or .470 NE cal., boxlock action, SolidSolid barrels made from one piece of steel, interchangeable parts, best quality wood.

Base price for this model starts at $14,750.

Add $4,500 for Solidsolid barrels.

SIDELOCK DOUBLE RIFLE – .375 H&H or .470 NE cal., similar to Boxlock Double rifle, except is sidelock action.

Base price for this model starts at $44,500.

BOLT ACTION RIFLE – SolidRifle action made from one solid piece of steel, best quality wood.

Base price for this model starts at $11,500.

Add $11,000 for signature solid rifle.

SHOTGUNS: CUSTOM

CLASSIC O/U – 12, 20, or 28 ga., sidelock action, interchangeable parts, one-piece MonoSolid barrel, all metal parts (except springs) are S7 vacuum arc remelt steel, classic English scroll engraving, best quality checkered wood.

Base price on this model is $38,500. SolidSolid barrel models are additional.

SPECIAL O/U – similar to Classic, except has more engraving, better quality wood, other custom options. Limited mfg.

Base price on this model was $32,950.

BOXLOCK MODEL – best quality sculpted action boxlock, hidden third fastener, removable/replaceable hidden hinge pin, Joseph Brazier locking bolt, MonoSolid barrels, best quality wood.

Base price on this model was $10,500.

SIGNATURE SERIES – 12, 20, or 28 ga., best quality wood, special engraving, wood treatment, acoutrements, interior engraving, personally designed by Karl Lippard, limited mfg. of 10 guns.

Base price on this model was $65,000.

WATCH MODEL – SolidSolid barrels, each gun is paired with a special wristwatch made exclusively to pair with the gun, watchmaker's design elements, each gun is individually unique, best quality wood.

Base price on this model was $65,000.

EXHIBITION MODEL – each gun engraved with unique historical subjects, SolidSolid barrels, best quality wood.

Base price on this model was $85,000.

GRADING - PPGS™	100%	98%	95%	90%	80%	70%	60%	LAST MSR

PREMIER MODEL – 12, 20, or 28 ga., sidelock action, many special orders/features are available per individual order.

Base price on this model is $75,000.

LITTLE SHARPS RIFLE MFG.

Current rifle manufacturer established in 1996, and located in Big Sandy, MT. Consumer direct sales through FFL licensed dealers.

RIFLES: SINGLE SHOT

DELUXE SHARPS RIFLE – various rimmed cals. between .22 LR and .375 LSR, features scaled down frame for smaller cals. (20% smaller than original Sharps), octagon barrel, current mfg. features XXX wood, gold inlays, and engraving, various barrel choices. Mfg. in America beginning 1998.

MSR $5,000	$4,750	$4,250	$3,600	$3,000	$2,500	$2,150	$1,650	

Subtract approx. 40% if without engraving, gold inlays, and deluxe XXX walnut stock and forearm.

LIL RELIABLE – .17 HMR, .218 Bee, .22 LR (new 2008), .22 Hornet, .22 WMR (new 2009), .357 Mag., .30-30 Win., .38-55 WCF (new 2008), .44-40 WCF (new 2008), or .45 LC cal., 24 (rimfire only) or 26 in. tapered octagon barrel, case colored frame, mfg. by Armi Sport. Limited importation from Italy 2010-2011.

	$1,125	$1,000	$900	$800	$725	$650	$575	*$1,229*

LJUNGMAN

Previously manufactured by Carl Gustaf, located in Eskilstuna, Sweden.

RIFLES: SEMI-AUTO

AG 42 – 6.5x55mm Swedish cal., 10 shot mag., wood stock, tangent rear and hooded front, bayonet lug, designed in 1941.

	$850	$700	$600	$495	$450	$400	$365	

This was the first mass produced, direct gas operated rifle. This weapon was also used by the Egyptian armed forces and was known as the Hakim, and chambered in 8x57mm Mauser.

LJUTIC LLC

Current shotgun manufacturer established circa 1955 and located in Yakima, WA. Dealer direct and retail sales.

Prior to 1960, Ljutic Industries, Inc. did business as Ljutic Gun Co. The name changed again in 2006 to Ljutic LLC.

SHOTGUNS: O/U

LM 6 – 12 ga. only, supplied with one set of O/U barrels, deluxe wood and checkering, separated barrels on O/U.

	$17,500	$15,750	$11,000	$9,250	$8,400	$7,500	$6,600	*$19,995*

Add $7,000 for extra set of O/U barrels.
Add $9,000 for top single barrel (includes 2 pull trigger groups, and 2 forearms).

DYNA BICENTENNIAL – 12 ga. only, includes one set of O/U barrels, steel or stainless steel frame, deluxe wood and checkered stock and forearm. Mfg. 2000-2007.

	$16,500	$14,750	$10,000	$9,000	$8,000	$7,000	$6,000	*$18,995*

Subtract $2,000 for steel frame.

SHOTGUNS: SEMI-AUTO

BI MATIC AUTO LOADER – 12 ga., 2 shot, 26-32 in. barrels, low recoil, trap or skeet models available, stock and choking to customer specifications. Limited mfg. until 1999.

	$5,995	$4,450	$2,500	$2,100	$1,750	$1,250	$900	*$5,995*

Add $2,000 for extra barrel.
Add $750 for extra release trigger.

SHOTGUNS: SINGLE BARREL TRAP

To date approx. 15,000 target shotguns have been manufactured total (all models).

GRADING - PPGS™	100%	98%	95%	90%	80%	70%	60%	LAST MSR

DYNATRAP MODEL – 12 ga., 33 in. barrel, full choke, push button opening, extractor, trap stock.

	100%	98%	95%	90%	80%	70%	60%	LAST MSR
	$2,500	$2,150	$1,600	$1,475	$1,300	$1,200	$1,100	

Add $300 for release trigger.
Add $400 for extra release trigger.
Add $250 for extra pull trigger.

MODEL X-73 MODEL – 12 ga., 33 in. barrel. full choke, push button opening, high rib fancy Monte Carlo stock.

	100%	98%	95%	90%	80%	70%	60%	LAST MSR
	$2,500	$2,250	$2,000	$1,850	$1,700	$1,600	$1,500	

Add $300 for extra pull trigger.
Add $500 for extra release trigger.

DYNOKIC MODEL – 12 ga., 32 (disc.) or 33 in. barrel with 2 choke tubes, patented recoil reduction system reduces felt recoil by 50%, checkered walnut stock, many options available. Mfg. 1997-2003.

	100%	98%	95%	90%	80%	70%	60%	LAST MSR
	$4,795	$4,000	$3,450	$2,900	$2,500	$2,000	$1,650	*$4,795*

Add $1,000 for stainless steel construction.

* ***Dynokic Model Supreme*** – similar to Dynokic Model, except has deluxe walnut stock with checkering. Mfg. 2000-2004.

	100%	98%	95%	90%	80%	70%	60%	LAST MSR
	$5,595	$4,250	$3,400	$3,000	$2,650	$2,300	$1,900	*$5,595*

* ***Dynokic Model Centennial Pro Stainless*** – 12 ga., high grade walnut stock and forearm, 33 in. stainless steel barrel with 2 chokes, recoil reduction system reduces recoil by 50%.

	100%	98%	95%	90%	80%	70%	60%	LAST MSR
	$7,995	$6,250	$4,875	N/A	N/A	N/A	N/A	*$7,995*

MONO GUN – 12 ga., 34 in. barrel, custom choked, custom stocked, pull or release trigger, a "built to customers specifications" trap gun. Also known as Standard Rib or Medium Rib.

* ***Mono Gun Standard, Medium, or Olympic Rib Model***

	100%	98%	95%	90%	80%	70%	60%	LAST MSR
MSR $7,495	$7,495	$6,850	$6,200	$4,750	$4,250	$3,500	$2,500	

Add $400 for stainless choke tubes.
Add $1,000 for stainless steel construction.
Add $1,500 for stainless steel SLE Pro Model.
Add $1,000 for SLE Pro Package (includes Laib adj. comb, adj. alum. base plate with 2 pads, and Pro barrel with special bore).

* ***Mono Gun LTX (Deluxe Mono Trap)*** – similar to Mono Gun except has 33 (disc.) or 34 in. medium rib barrel and exhibition wood and checkering. Disc. 2006.

	100%	98%	95%	90%	80%	70%	60%	LAST MSR
	$7,995	$6,800	$5,725	$4,750	$3,800	$2,900	$2,350	*$7,995*

Add $500 for extra pull trigger.
Add $650 if with release trigger.
Add $300 for choke tube barrel with 2 chokes.
Add $850 for extra release trigger.
Add $2,499 for extra barrel.
Add $1,200 for stainless steel package.

* ***Mono Gun Pro 3 (Deluxe Mono Trap)*** – similar to Mono Gun except is lighter weight, 34 in. medium rib ported barrel, exhibition wood and checkering, Briley Series 12 choke tubes, pull trigger. New 2000.

	100%	98%	95%	90%	80%	70%	60%	LAST MSR
MSR $8,995	$8,995	$7,400	$6,100	$5,000	$4,000	$3,000	$2,500	

Add $1,000 for adj. comb.
Add $499 for adj. rib.
Add $750 for extra pull trigger.
Add $650 if with release trigger.
Add $850 for extra release trigger assembly.
Add $2,599 for extra barrel with fixed chokes or $2,995 with SIC.
Add $1,000 for stainless steel Pro 3 Package.

PRO 3 – 12 ga. only, 34 in. barrel with three different rib variations and a choice of fixed or adj. chokes, features McCarthy trigger, checkered walnut stock and forearm. New 2011.

	100%	98%	95%	90%	80%	70%	60%	LAST MSR
MSR $899	$875	$795	$725	$650	$575	$500	$450	

GRADING - PPGS™	100%	98%	95%	90%	80%	70%	60%	LAST MSR

SPACE GUN – 12 ga. only, single barrel, unusual design permits in-line round stock with recoil pad, circular forearm wraps around barrel, high post rib on muzzle half of barrel, patented recoil reduction system reduces recoil by 50%. Disc. 1999.

	$5,995	$4,150	$3,375	$2,825	$2,300	$2,000	$1,750	*$5,995*

LLAMA - Fabrinor S.A.L.

Previous manufacturer established during 1904, and located in Alava, Spain from 1992-2005. Previously located in Vitoria, Spain until 1992. Previously distributed until 2005 by Import Sports, Inc. located in Wanamassa, NJ. Previously imported and distributed by Stoeger Industries, Inc. located in South Hackensack, NJ until 1993, and by R.S.A. Ent., Inc., located in Ocean, NJ. Previous company name was Llama - Gabilondo y Cia S.A.

During 1992, Llama Gabilondo/Vitoria went bankrupt. In January 2000, after arranging new financing, manufacture was taken over by approx. 60 employees of Gabilondo under the name Fabrinor S.A.L. - a cooperative which closed in 2006.

PISTOLS: SEMI-AUTO

Most of the pistols listed were imported by Stoeger, long time exclusive U.S. importer, and are so marked on the guns.

MODEL IIIA – .380 ACP cal., 7 shot, 3 in. barrel, adj. sights, blue, plastic grips., vent. rib slide. Mfg. 1951-disc.

	$325	$250	$200	$160	$140	$120	$110	

MODEL XA – similar to Model IIIA, except .32 ACP.

	$295	$225	$180	$160	$140	$120	$110	

MODEL XV – similar to Model XA, except .22 LR.

	$295	$225	$180	$160	$140	$120	$110	

Add 50% for airweight.

MODEL XVII – .22 S cal.

	$325	$250	$200	$160	$140	$120	$110	

Add 50% for Deluxe Executive Model if engraved and chromed. Add 100% if engraved and gold plated.

Add $2,500 if gold damascened in 95%+ condition.

MODEL XVIII – .25 ACP cal., blue finish standard, available with optional chrome or gold finish and stag grips.

	$300	$250	$200	$160	$140	$120	$110	

Add 50% for Deluxe Executive Model if engraved and chromed. Add 100% if engraved and gold plated.

Add $2,500 if gold damascened in 95%+ condition.

MODELS C-IIIA, C-XA, C-XV – similar to Model C, except engraved chrome.

	$500	$400	$300	$275	$250	$225	$200	

MODELS BE-IIIA, BE-XA, BE-XV – similar to Model CE, except engraved, blue.

	$450	$375	$275	$225	$180	$155	$140	

Deluxe Models or chrome engraved with simulated pearl grips, add $20.

MODEL G-IIIA – similar to IIIA, except gold damascened, simulated pearl grips.

	$3,500	$3,000	$2,500	$2,000	$1,500	$1,250	$1,000	

MODEL VIII – .38 Super or 9mm Para. cal., 9 shot, 5 in. barrel, fixed sights, wood grips. Mfg. 1952-disc.

	$350	$295	$235	$195	$180	$165	$140	

Add 100% for 9mm Para. cal.

MODEL IXA – 9mm Para. or .45 ACP, vent. rib slide.

	$350	$295	$235	$195	$180	$165	$140	

Add 100% for 9mm Para. cal.

GRADING - PPGS™	100%	98%	95%	90%	80%	70%	60%	LAST MSR

MODEL XI – similar to Model IXA, except 9mm Para.

	$350	$295	$235	$195	$180	$165	$140	

Add 100% for pistols mfg. 1946-1952.

MODELS C-VIII, C-IXA, C-XI – similar to Model VIII, except satin chrome.

	$375	$325	$285	$260	$220	$195	$165	

MODELS CE-VIII, CE-IXA, CE-XI

	$425	$350	$310	$285	$265	$220	$195	

MODELS BE-VIII, BE-IXA, BE-XI – similar to Model CE, except blue, engraving.

	$495	$395	$295	$275	$250	$210	$180	

Add $20 for Deluxe Models (simulated pearl grips).

OMNI – .45 ACP or 9mm Para. cal., double action, all steel construction, 2 sear bars, 3 safeties, 4 1/4 in. barrel, 7 shot mag. in .45 ACP, 13 shot mag. in 9mm Para., blue finish. Importation disc. 1986.

9mm Para.	$440	$380	$330	$295	$260	$225	$200	$546
.45 ACP	$395	$360	$320	$285	$250	$220	$195	$500

SMALL FRAME MODEL – .22 LR (disc. 1994), .32 ACP (disc. 1993), or .380 ACP cal., Colt 1911A1 design, single action, 3 11/16 in. barrel, 7 shot mag., 23 oz. Also available in satin chrome, optional engraving patterns. Disc. 1997.

	$325	$250	$200	$160	$140	$120	$110	$259

Add $60 for duo-tone finish (.380 ACP only, mfg. 1991-1993).
Add $33 for satin chrome finish (not avail. in .32 ACP cal.).

COMPACT FRAME MODEL (IX-B) – 9mm Para. (disc.) or .45 ACP cal., scaled down variation of the Large Frame Model, 4 1/4 in. barrel, 7 or 9 shot mag., 34 or 37 oz. Mfg. 1986-97.

	$325	$255	$200	$180	$160	$155	$150	$409

Add $16 for satin chrome finish.
Add $90 for duo-tone finish (mfg. 1990-1993).

GOVERNMENT MODEL (IX-C) – 9mm Para. (disc.), .38 Super (mfg. 1988-1996), or .45 ACP cal., similar to Small Frame Model, 5 1/8 in. barrel, 36 oz., 9 shot mag. in 9mm Para., 10 shot mag. in .45 ACP. Engraved and deluxe models available also. Disc. 1997.

	$325	$255	$200	$180	$160	$150	$140	$409

Add $16 for satin chrome finish (.45 ACP only).
Add $90 for duo-tone finish (.45 ACP only, mfg. 1991-1993).

MAX I MODEL – 9mm Para. or .45 ACP cal., patterned after the Colt Govt. Model, 4 1/4 (Compact Model) or 5 1/2 in. barrel, SA, 3-dot combat sights, 7 (.45 ACP) or 9 (9mm Para.) shot mag., matte blue, satin chrome, or duo-tone finish, rubber grips, 34 or 36 oz. Mfg. 1995-99.

	$295	$265	$225	$200	$180	$160	$150	$299

Add $10 for duo-tone finish (.45 ACP cal. only).
Add $16 for satin chrome finish (new 1996).

* ***Max-I Model Compensated*** – .45 ACP only, 7 or 10 shot mag., features compensated barrel. Disc. 1997.

	$445	$385	$330	$250	$200	$180	$160	$492

Add $25 for 10 shot model.

MINI-MAX – 9mm Para. (disc. 1999), .40 S&W (disc. 2004), or .45 ACP cal., mini-compact variation featuring 6 or 8 shot mag., choice of matte, satin chrome, duo-tone (.45 ACP only), or stainless steel finish/construction, 34 oz. Mfg. 1996-2005.

	$265	$230	$190	$170	$150	$140	$130	$309

Add $25 for satin chrome finish.
Add $7 for duo-tone finish (.45 ACP only).
Add $66 for stainless steel construction (disc.).
Add 100% if with Jordain Crest (only 200 mfg., blue finish with numbered mags.).

GRADING - PPGS™	100%	98%	95%	90%	80%	70%	60%	LAST MSR

* ***Mini-Max Sub Compact*** – 9mm Para. (disc. 2000), .40 S&W (disc. 2000), or .45 ACP cal., 3.14 in. barrel, all steel construction, 3-dot combat sights, 10 shot mag., polymer grips, choice of matte, satin chrome, or duo-tone finish, 31 oz. Mfg. 1999-2005.

$270	$235	$195	$175	$150	$140	$130	*$316*

Add $26 for satin chrome finish.
Add $9 for duo-tone finish (.45 ACP cal. only).

MICRO-MAX – .32 ACP (mfg. 1999-2004, matte finish only) or .380 ACP cal., features standard or lightweight steel design, polymer grips, 7 or 8 shot mag., 3 dot combat sights, slimline slide and frame, non-glare matte or satin chrome finish, 23 oz. Mfg. 1998-2005.

$250	$220	$200	$170	$160	$150	$140	*$282*

Subtract $15 for Ultra Lite Model (disc.).
Add $18 for satin chrome finish (.380 ACP cal. only, beginning 1999).

MAX II – 9mm Para. or .45 ACP cal., 4.25 (Compact) or 5 1/8 (Government) in. barrel, 3-dot combat sights, anatomically designed polymer grips, 13 (.45 ACP) or 17 (9mm Para.) shot mag., 39-41 oz. Limited mfg. 2005.

$275	$240	$200	$180	$155	$140	$130	*$325*

MODEL 82 – 9mm Para. cal., double action, 4 1/4 in. barrel, blue finish, 3-dot sighting system, 15 shot mag., ambidextrous safety, loaded chamber indicator, black polymer grips, 39 oz. Imported 1988-93.

$550	$500	$450	$400	$350	$300	$275	*$975*

MODEL 87 COMPETITION – 9mm Para. cal., competition variation of the Model 82, includes built in ported compensator, oversize magazine and safety release, fixed barrel bushing, beveled rapid load magazine well, 14 shot mag., extended and serrated trigger guard, and adj. trigger. Imported 1989-93.

$995	$850	$750	$700	$625	$575	$500	*$1,450*

REVOLVERS: DOUBLE ACTION

MARTIAL MODEL – .22 LR or .38 Spl. cal., 6 shot, 4 and 6 in. barrels, target sights, blue, checkered wood grips. Mfg. 1969-76.

$220	$200	$180	$165	$140	$120	$100

DELUXE MARTIAL – similar to Martial, except finish as follows:

Satin chrome	$275	$250	$220	$195	$165	$140	$120
Chrome, engraved	$600	$525	$450	$400	$350	$300	$250
Blue, engraved	$650	$575	$500	$450	$375	$300	$250
Gold, damascened	$3,500	$2,950	$2,350	$1,750	$1,200	$1,000	$800

COMANCHE I – .22 LR cal., similar to Martial DA, mfg. 1977-82.

$255	$220	$195	$165	$155	$140	$110

COMANCHE II – .38 Spl. cal., similar to Martial DA, mfg. 1977-82 and 1986 in .22 LR and .22 WMR cal. only.

$240	$220	$195	$165	$155	$140	$110	*$272*

COMANCHE III – .22 LR (disc.) or .357 Mag. cal., 6 shot, 4, 6, or 8 1/2 (disc. 1986) in. barrel, blue, adj. sights, checkered walnut grips. Mfg. 1975-95. Before 1977, it was called "Comanche."

$280	$245	$200	$165	$155	$140	$130	*$339*

* ***Comanche III Satin Chrome Finish (disc.)***

$330	$270	$230	$205	$185	$170	$160	*$395*

* ***Comanche III Gold Damascene Finish (disc.)***

$3,200	$2,750	$2,250	$1,700	$1,200	$1,000	$800

SUPER COMANCHE IV – .44 Mag. cal., 6 or 8 1/2 in. VR barrel, adj. sights, blue only. Disc. 1998.

$400	$325	$275	$250	$225	$200	$175	*$440*

GRADING - PPGS™	100%	98%	95%	90%	80%	70%	60%	LAST MSR

SUPER COMANCHE V – .357 Mag. cal., 6 shot, 4, 6, or 8 1/2 in. VR barrel, adj. sights, blue only. Importation disc. 1988.

	$375	$325	$275	$250	$225	$200	$175	*$414*

LOKI WEAPON SYSTEMS, INC.

Current manufacturer and distributor established in 2009 and located in Coalgate, OK.

Loki Weapon Systems manufactures AR-15 style tactical rifles and 1911 style pistols. Loki was also the U.S. distributor for A.M.S.D., located in Geneva, Switzerland until 2012.

CARBINES/RIFLES: SEMI-AUTO

Other calibers are available by request. Loki offers a limited lifetime warranty on all rifles and carbines.

FENRIR – 5.56 NATO, .300 Whisper, .458 SOCOM, 6.5 Grendel, 6.8 SPC, or 6.8 Grendel cal., 16 in. barrel, 40 shot mag., mid length gas operating system, M4 ramps and extension, machined upper and lower, Fail Zero coated bolt carrier group, 12 in. eight sided forend with full length Picatinny rail, YHM Phantom flash hider, Ergo F93 eight position stock, hard case, approx. 8 lbs. Mfg. 2009-2011.

	$1,450	$1,295	$1,125	$900	$800	$700	$600	*$1,575*

Subtract $125 for ambidextrous safety selector and 15 in. eight sided forend.

HUNTING RIFLE – .223 Wylde cal., 20 in. varmint barrel, eight sided forend with three Picatinny rails, single stage trigger, 10 shot mag., fixed stock with ERGO grip, includes hard case. Mfg. mid-2010-2011.

	$1,475	$1,295	$1,125	$900	$800	$700	$600	*$1,625*

PRECISION SNIPER TACTICAL RIFLE – .223 Wylde cal., M4 upper and lower, 18 in. fluted stainless steel barrel, three port compensator, eight sided forend with full length Picatinny rail, ambidextrous safety, two-stage trigger, 30 shot mag., F93 ERGO stock and grip, includes hard case. Disc. 2011.

	$1,625	$1,475	$1,295	$1,125	$900	$800	$700	*$1,795*

LWSF 3G COMPETITION – 5.56 NATO cal., 18 in. double fluted stainless steel barrel, 15 in. vented carbon fiber forend, Vltor A2 fixed stock, adj. gas block, lightened buffer system and carrier, standard mil-spec charging handle, hardcoat anodized teflon coated black finish, two-stage trigger, integrated CQB Magwell grip with XL magwell and ERGO pistol grip, Nordic Corvette compensator, approx. 6 1/2 lbs. New 2012.

MSR $1,850	$1,675	$1,450	$1,225	$1,050	$900	$750	$675

LWSF DMR (DESIGNATED MARKSMAN) – .223 Wylde cal., 20 in. fluted stainless steel SDMR contoured barrel with Rolling Thunder compensator, standard mil-spec charging handle, A2 stock with Magpul MOE grip, hardcoat anodized Teflon coated black finish, multiple picatinny rails, LOKI 14.5 handguard, pinned Lo Pro gas block, M4 feed ramps, 7.8 lbs. New 2012.

MSR $1,645	$1,495	$1,300	$1,100	$900	$700	$600	$550

LWSF MAGPUL MOE – .264 LBC, .300 BLK, or 5.56 NATO cal., 16.1 in. chrome-moly vanadium alloy barrel, A2 birdcage flash hider, Magpul MOE stock with pistol grip, mid-length forend and low profile gas block or YHM flip sight tower gas block, integrated picatinny rail, oversized trigger guard, hardcoat anodized teflon coated finish, forward assist and dust cover, polished M4 feed ramps, fail zero full-auto bolt carrier, nickel-boron coated charging handle and fire control group, approx. 6 1/2 lbs. New 2012.

MSR $1,349	$1,195	$1,000	$850	$725	$600	$500	$450

LWSF PATROL – .264 LBC, .300 BLK, or 5.56 NATO cal., 16 (.300 BLK cal.), 18 (.264 LBC) or 18 in. double fluted stainless steel barrel, mid-length gas block, phantom flash hider, Vltor EMOD retractable stock with Magpul MOE grip, full length picatinny rail, free floating forend, integrated winter trigger guard, creep-adj. polished trigger, M4 feed ramps, forward assist and dust cover, black hard coat anodized finish, also available with optional tactical comp or Battlecomp, 7 1/2 lbs. New 2012.

MSR $1,479	$1,275	$1,075	$975	$775	$625	$525	$475

GRADING - PPGS™	100%	98%	95%	90%	80%	70%	60%	LAST MSR

LWSF STD – .300 BLK, 6.5 Grendel, or 5.56 NATO cal., 16.1 in. chrome-moly vanadium alloy barrel, A2 birdcage flash hider, Magpul MOE stock, low profile gas block with rail, black hard coat anodized finish, mid-length free floating forend, standard M4 pistol grip, oversized trigger guard, integrated CQB Magwell grip with XL magwell, fail zero full-auto rated bolt carrier, polished M4 feed ramps, forward assist and dust cover, optional YHM flip sight tower gas block, Vltor EMOD or Ergo F93 stock, 6.7 lbs. New 2012.

MSR $1,349	$1,195	$1,000	$850	$725	$600	$500	$450

LWSF TACTICAL – .300 BLK or 5.56 NATO cal., 16 in. nitride treated M4 barrel, 14 1/2 in. modular forend, A2 birdcage flash hider, Vltor EMOD six-position retractable stock with Magpul MOE grip, black hard coat anodized teflon coated finish, Nib-X coated full-auto rated bolt carrier, integrated winter trigger guard, CQB Magwell grip with XL magwell, creep-adj. polished trigger, optional 9 in. top rail and three 3 in. rails or Troy TRX Extreme handguard, standard mil-spec charging handle, forward assist and M4 feed ramps. New 2012.

MSR $1,525	$1,300	$1,100	$1,000	$800	$650	$550	$500

LWS M4 MOE – 5.56 NATO cal., 16 in. nitride treated barrel, M4 extension, A2 birdcage flash hider, six-position Magpul MOE stock with pistol grip and trigger guard, standard A2 sight post low profile gas block with integrated rail or YHM gas block with integrated flip up front sight, mil-spec BCG nickel boron bolt carrier, midlength handguard, black hardcoat anodized teflon coated finish, forward assist and dust cover, creep-adj. hand stoned trigger, standard mil-spec charging handle. New 2012.

MSR $999	$895	$825	$750	$650	$550	$450	$350

LWS M4 PATROL – .300 BLK or 5.56 NATO cal., 16 in. nitride treated barrel, M4 extension, A2 birdcage flash hider, choice of six-position Magpul MOE stock with pistol grip and trigger guard, EMOD or F93 collapsible stock and ERGO pistol grip, mil-spec BCG nickel boron bolt carrier, Loki 12 rifle length handguard, black hardcoat anodized teflon coated finish, forward assist and dust cover, creep-adj. hand stoned trigger, standard mil-spec charging handle, optional 12 in. top picatinny rail and three 3 in. side and bottom rails. New 2012.

MSR $1,199	$1,050	$925	$825	$700	$600	$500	$400

LWS M4 STD – .300 BLK or 5.56 NATO cal., 16 in. nitride treated barrel, M4 extension, six-position Magpul MOE stock with M4 pistol grip and trigger guard, black, flat Dark Earth, or OD Green hardcoat anodized teflon coated finish, M4 flattop upper, 30 shot PMAG, creep-adj. hand stoned single stage trigger, standard mil-spec charging handle, low profile gas block with integrated rail, midlength handguard, includes case. New 2012.

MSR $1,049	$925	$850	$775	$675	$575	$475	$375

LWS M4 TACTICAL – .300 BLK or 5.56 NATO cal., 16 in. nitride treated M4 barrel, 14 1/2 in. free floating forend, A2 birdcage flash hider, choice of six-position Magpul MOE, EMOD, or F93 stock with ERGO pistol grip, black hard coat anodized teflon coated finish, standard mil-spec charging handle, forward assist and dust cover, midlength gas system, optional 9 in. picatinny rail, three 3 in. side and bottom rails, hand stoned trigger, XL modular handguard. New 2012.

MSR $1,225	$1,075	$925	$825	$700	$600	$500	$400

PISTOLS: SEMI-AUTO

Loki manufactures custom built 1911 style pistols in .45 ACP cal. Base price begins at $1,800 and goes up according to options and accessories.

LON PAUL CUSTOM GUNS

Current custom rifle manufacturer located in Mountain Center, CA.

Lon Paul builds high quality custom rifles with a variety of options. Please contact him directly for an individualized price quotation, including specifications and delivery time (see Trademark Index).

LONE STAR ARMAMENT, INC.

Previous pistol manufacturer circa 1970-2004, and located in Stephenville, TX. During 2003, Lone Star Armament was absorbed by STI, located in Georgetown, TX.

GRADING - PPGS™	100%	98%	95%	90%	80%	70%	60%	LAST MSR

PISTOLS: SEMI-AUTO

Lone Star Armament manufactured a lineup of M1911 style pistols. Models included: Ranger Match ($1,595 last MSR), Lawman Match ($1,595 last MSR), Lawman Series ($1,475 last MSR), Ranger Series ($1,475 last MSR), and the Guardian Series ($895 last MSR).

LONE STAR RIFLE CO., INC.

Previous rifle manufacturer circa 1992-2011 and located in Conroe, TX. The company specialized in Remington Rolling Block rifle reproductions.

RIFLES: REPRODUCTIONS

REMINGTON ROLLING BLOCK SERIES – various black powder cartridge cals., configurations, and options, case colored or nickel plated receiver, rust or nitre blue barrel, extra select checkered walnut, single or double set triggers.

* ***Remington Rolling Block Creedmoor*** – features competition long range 34 in. full octagon or half octagon/half round barrel with pistol grip and shotgun butt, single trigger set at 3 lbs., per Creedmoor rules, 10 lbs.

  $2,000 $1,650 $1,275 $995 $875 $725 $600 *$2,195*

* ***Remington Rolling Block Silhouette (Target)*** – designed for silhouette competition, with 30, 32, or 34 in. full octagon or half octagon/half round barrel with pistol grip and shotgun butt. Disc. 2011.

  $2,250 $2,000 $1,650 $1,275 $995 $875 $725 *$2,495*

* ***Remington Rolling Block Silhouette Standard Rifle*** – .40-65 or .45-70 Govt. cal., similar to #5 Sporting Standard Rifle, except has 32 or 34 in. barrel, steel shotgun butt plate, pistol grip stock, 11 lbs. Mfg. 1999-2006.

  $1,400 $1,150 $900 $750 $600 $550 $475 *$1,595*

* ***Remington Rolling Block Cowboy Action Rifle*** – .32-40 WCF, .38-55 WCF, .40-65 WCF, .44-77, .45 LC (disc. 2002), .45-70 Govt., or .50-70 cal., heavy 28 in. barrel, 8 1/2 lbs. Mfg. 1999-2006.

  $1,400 $1,150 $900 $750 $600 $550 $475 *$1,595*

* ***Remington Rolling Block #5 Sporting Standard Rifle*** – .25-35 WCF (new 2002), .30-30 Win. (new 2000) or .30-40 Krag cal., 26 in. round barrel, single trigger, case colored frame, standard American walnut stock and forearm, 6 lbs. Mfg. 1999-2006.

  $1,400 $1,150 $900 $750 $600 $550 $475 *$1,595*

* ***Remington Rolling Block Classic #5*** – .22 Hornet, .25-35 WCF, .30-30 Win., .30-40 Krag, or .33 WCF cal., rapid taper octagon barrel, approx. 6 lbs. Mfg. 2007-2009.

  $3,250 $2,750 $2,375 $2,000 $1,750 $1,550 $1,250 *$3,500*

* ***Remington Rolling Block #7 Sporting Rifle*** – .25-20 WCF, .32-20 WCF, or .22 Hornet cal. Mfg. 2002-2007.

  $3,000 $2,650 $2,350 $1,950 $1,725 $1,500 $1,200 *$3,500*

* ***Remington Rolling Block Sporting Rifle*** – various cals., standard sporting rifle designed for accuracy, 28, 30, or 32 in. barrel, straight grip stock. Disc. 2011.

  $2,250 $2,000 $1,650 $1,275 $995 $875 $725 *$2,495*

* ***Remington Rolling Block Deluxe Sporting Rifle*** – deluxe variation of the Sporting Rifle with 28, 30, or 32 in. full octagon or half octagon/half round barrel with pistol grip and shotgun butt, buckhorn rear sight and choice of front sight.

  $2,000 $1,650 $1,275 $995 $875 $725 $600 *$2,195*

* ***Remington Rolling Block Custer Rifle*** – .50-70 cal., an exact reproduction of Gen. G.A. Custer's original Remington Rolling Block, 28 in. octagon barrel with SST, straight grip, crescent buttplate, and Schnabel forearm tip. Disc. 2011.

  $3,000 $2,650 $2,350 $1,950 $1,725 $1,500 $1,200 *$3,500*

* ***Remington Rolling Block Buffalo Rifle*** – various cal., features relic finish enabling a new gun to appear somewhat worn, double set triggers, exact copy of the original, 16 lbs.

  MSR $3,200 $3,200 $2,850 $2,400 $1,900 $1,625 $1,400 $1,200 *$3,200*

GRADING - PPGS™	100%	98%	95%	90%	80%	70%	60%	LAST MSR

* ***Remington Rolling Block Take Down Model*** – features take down action. Mfg. 2001-2002.

	$3,600	$3,150	$2,750	$2,300	$1,995	$1,700	$1,375	*$4,000*

GOVE ROLLING BLOCK – various cals., new rolling block with underlever design by Carlos Gove. Mfg. 1998-2002.

	$2,650	$2,250	$1,875	$1,625	$1,400	$1,200	$1,000	*$2,995*

LONE STAR TACTICAL SUPPLY

Current firearms manufacturer and dealer located in Tomball, TX.

Lone Star Tactical Supply manufactures a line of 1911-style semi-auto pistols in 9mm Para. or .40 S&W cal. Base price is $750.The company also manufactures the AR-15 style Border Patrol semi-auto tactical rifle - MSR is $1,025, and tactical rail kits for the Remington Model 870. Lone Star is also a dealer for Saiga rifles, and offers many shooting accessories. Please contact the company for more information (see Trademark Index).

LONGTHORNE GUNMAKERS

Current long gun manufacturer established in mid-2010 and located in Lancashire, England. Consumer direct sales.

SHOTGUNS: O/U

Descriptions include base gun with standard options. A variety of options are available at the customer's request.

Prices do not include U.K. VAT.

"HESKETH" GAME GUN (L1-GM) – 12 ga., 28 to 32 in. solid barrels, sidelock, SST, low profile action, English scroll engraving, semi-pistol grip or straight grip Turkish walnut stock, right or left hand, includes green canvas case with hand sewn leather corners and Longhorne emblem, approx. 7 lbs.

Base price for this gun is £10,639.

"HESKETH" DELUXE – similar to Hesketh Game Gun, except has deep scroll engraving. New 2012.

Base price for this gun is £14,583.

RUTLAND – similar to Hesketh Game Gun, except has elaborate engraving with gold inlays and wood upgrades. New 2012.

Base price for this gun is £20,416.

SPORTER (L1-SP) – 12 ga., 28 to 32 in. solid barrels, sidelock, SST, low profile action, English scroll engraving, semi-pistol grip or straight grip Turkish walnut stock, right or left hand, includes green canvas case with hand sewn leather corners and Longhorne emblem, approx. 7 lbs., 8 oz.

Last base price in 2012 for this gun was £10,650.

LORCIN ENGINEERING CO., INC.

Previous handgun manufacturer located in Mira Loma, CA, 1989-1999.

DERRINGERS: O/U

STAINLESS MODEL – .357 Mag. or .45 LC cal., 3 1/2 in. barrel, synthetic grips, tip-up action, rebounding hammer, fixed sights. Mfg. 1996-98.

	$175	$155	$140	$125	$110	$100	$90	*$110*

PISTOLS: SEMI-AUTO

During the height of production in the mid-90s, Lorcin was making 40,000 semi-auto pistols a month. One year, its production totalled 400,000 units.

Before buying any Lorcin pistol, it is recommended that a competent gunsmith check it out.

L-22 MODEL – .22 LR cal., similar to L-25 Model, except 2.55 in. barrel and 9 shot mag., black or chrome finish, 16 oz. Mfg. 1992-99.

	$75	$60	$50	$45	$40	$35	$35	*$89*

GRADING - PPGS™	100%	98%	95%	90%	80%	70%	60%	LAST MSR

L-25 MODEL – .25 ACP cal., single action, 6 shot mag., 2.4 in. barrel, anatomically designed grips to fit hand better, choice of black and gold, chrome and pearl, satin chrome and pearl, Teflon camo finish (new 1992), or black and pearl finish, 13.5 oz. Mfg. 1989-99.

$65	$50	$45	$40	$35	$35	$35	$79

Add $20 for lightweight frame (Model LT 25, new in 1990).

* ***L-25 Model Lady Lorcin*** – same specifications as the L-25 Model, except is available in chrome, satin chrome, or black exterior finish with pink grips. Mfg. 1990-99.

$70	$60	$50	$45	$40	$35	$35	$79

L-32 – .32 ACP cal., single action, 7 shot mag., 3 1/2 in. barrel, available in black or chrome finish, 23 oz. Mfg. 1992-99.

$80	$70	$60	$50	$45	$40	$35	$89

L-380 – .380 ACP cal., single action, 7 shot mag., 3 1/2 in. barrel, available in black or chrome finish, 23 oz. Mfg. 1992-99.

$85	$75	$65	$55	$50	$45	$40	$100

LH-380 – .380 ACP cal., similar to L9MM, 36 oz. Mfg. 1995-99.

$125	$115	$100	$90	$85	$80	$75	$149

L9MM – 9mm Para. cal., single action, 10 (C/B 1994) or 13* shot mag., 4 1/2 in. barrel, grip safety, black finish, 3-dot sights, 36 oz. Mfg. 1994-99.

$125	$115	$100	$90	$85	$80	$75	$149

Add $20 for disc. 13 shot mag. variation.

LORENZO, CRESS

Current rifle manufacturer located in Minersville, UT.

Custom gunmaker Cress Lorenzo specializes in custom express rifles built to customer specifications. Many options are available, in addition to general gunsmithing services. Please contact Mr. Lorenzo directly for more information, including models, options, availability and pricing (see Trademark Index).

LOSOK CUSTOM ARMS

Current semi-auto rifle manufacturer located in Delaware, OH.

RIFLES: SEMI-AUTO

VALKYR – various cals. between .30-06-.458 Win. Mag., various barrel configurations 18 in. to 28 in. sporter through heavy, choice of M1 Garand or M14 operating system, milled receiver, modified M1918 Browning BAR magazine, McMillan stock, Picatinny top rail, 16 1/2 lbs. New 2012.

Please contact the company directly for more information on this model including availability, pricing, and options (see Trademark Index).

LUCCHINI, SANDRO

Current manufacturer located in Sarezzo (Brescia), Italy. Currently imported by Springbrook Manufacturing, Ltd., located in Alberta, Canada.

Sandro Lucchini manufactures high quality, made to order, double rifles and SxS shotguns (approx. 10-20 guns annually). Starting prices for shotguns are as follows (not including engraving) - Purdey style rose and scroll is approx. €1,750, while elaborate work by a master engraver can exceed €18,000. Shotguns: €7,000 for Anson action without sideplates (add €1,200 for sideplates), €15,700 for standard sidelock, manual cocking extractor hammer guns start at €7,800, self cocking ejectors are €17,200. Add 10% for 28 ga. or .410 bore, and €450 for single trigger. All shotgun barrels are demi-bloc construction. New O/U scaled frame 20 and 28 ga. shotguns begin at €7,100, including fine line gold inlay and case colors. Double rifles start at €26,500 for calibers under .375 H&H, and are available up to .600 NE. All double rifles feature Ferlach barrels.

Please contact the importer directly for more information, including an individual price quotation and delivery time (see Trademark Index).

LUGERS WITH VARIATIONS

Semi-auto pistol design originated by Georg Luger, circa 1899. Many previous manufacturers - see main text for more information. Previous post-WWII manufacture (through 1997) was by Mauser-Werke Oberndorf Waffensysteme, located in Oberndorf, Germany.

Note: The Luger section in this book is arranged chronologically by year of manufacture under individual manufacturer/city arsenal headings.

Often times, year of production can be hard to nail down, especially on commercial models. An easier way to initially identify your Luger is to categorize by toggle marking first - then by chamber marking within groups (chronologically for dated chambers). Once you know period of manufacture, simply refer to the appropriate subheading in this section. While some rare variations will be excluded in this generalized overview, it will be very helpful to establish correct, basic knowledge about your particular Luger.

While many recently imported Lugers would make workable shooters, they have in no way lowered prices on 90%+ condition specimens with all matching original parts due to normal collector activity in original condition only pistols. Recently imported Lugers should have the importer's name visibly stamped on an exterior surface. Most of these recent imports are in the 9mm Para. - 4 in. barrel configuration. Recently imported Lugers with the importer's markings visible are typically priced in the $450-$700 range.

Every year more and more reblued, restrawed, regripped, reframed, and rebarreled Lugers are sold to unknowing military handgun collectors as rare variations. On any expensive contract variation, careful inspection for originality on all parts must be made before potentially purchasing. If in doubt, secure 2 or 3 additional appraisals/observations from qualified individuals. Lugers are a field in themselves and a specialized Winchester dealer would not be qualified to guesstimate the originality of these German handguns.

A final note on Lugers: Original pistols in 90%-100% condition have not been affected by the influx of recent imports as these newly imported guns are usually in 80% and lower condition or have been reblued.

It seems that every year the prices of top quality (98%+ condition) original Lugers get more expensive and less predictable. For this reason, the 100% values on many Lugers have been omitted intentionally, since rarity precludes accurate price evaluation in this condition factor. In many cases, the value for a mint original military Luger can double the 98% price listed.

For Borchardt models, please refer to Borchardt listing.

Values for all variations of Lugers assume a proper magazine and matching parts. All Lugers that were originally manufactured with numbered magazines should increase in value if that Luger has one or both original matching magazines.

REFERENCE GUIDE BY TOGGLE MARKING

DWM TOGGLE IDENTIFICATION

DWM stands for Deutsche Waffen-und Munitionsfabriken.

DWM MODELS

* ***DWM MODELS*** – mfg. from 1900 to 1930 in Berlin, Germany.
* ***DWM Models 1900*** – grip safety and "Dished" Toggles, ser. nos. 1-24,999.
* ***DWM Models 1906*** – grip safety, many chamber markings, ser. nos. 25,000-74,000.
* ***DWM Models 1908 Commercial*** – no grip safety, 9mm Para., ser. nos. 39,000-74,000.
* ***DWM Models 1908 Military*** – no stock lug.
* ***DWM Models 1914 Military*** – stock lug, dated 1913-18.
* ***DWM Models 1920 Commercial*** – no grip safety, usually 3 7/8 in. barrel. Most common Luger, undated chamber, 7.65mm Para. or 9mm Para.

Note: Lugers with 4 inch barrels are most frequently encountered in military and commercial models. 6 in. barrels usually denote "Navy" models. 8 in. barrels usually denote "Artillery" models. Guns with barrels over 8 inches are rare and should be checked carefully for originality.

DWM COMMERCIAL LUGERS

DWM stands for Deutsche Waffen-und Munitionsfabriken. These are models manufactured from 1900-1923 found in the five digit serial range.

MODEL 1900 – ser. range 1-20,000. Configuration: 4 3/4 in. x .30 Commercial, American Eagle, Swiss.

MODEL 1900 – ser. range 20,001-21,000. Configuration: 4 3/4 in. x .30 Bulgarian.

MODEL 1902 – ser. range 21,001-25,000. Configuration: 9mm Para. x 4 in. "Fat Barrels" and 11 3/4 in. x 7.65mm Para. Carbine models, intermixed with 4 3/4 x 7.65mm Para. American Eagles and Commercials.

MODEL 1906 – ser. range 25,001-39,000. Configuration: Commercial American Eagle, Navy Commercial and Swiss, both 4 3/4 in. x 7.65mm Para. and 9mm Para. x 4 in. grip safety models.

MODEL 1908 – ser. range 39,001-71,000. Configuration: First 9mm Para. x 4 in. without grip safety, M1908 Commercials were interspersed with 7.65mm Para. and 9mm Para. Eagles, Commercials, Navy Commercials, and a few Carbines and Swiss.

MODEL 1914 – ser. range 71,001-74,000. Configuration: Last pre-WWI Commercial Lugers, made with stock lug, with a few 9mm Para. Commercials mixed in.

MODEL 1920 – ser. range 2,000i-9,999u. Configuration: Post-WWI Commercials, mostly 3 7/8 in. x 7.65mm Para. cal.

MODEL 1923 – ser. range 89,001-91,000. Configuration: The last thousand or so made have "safe" on lever and "loaded" on the extractor, 3 7/8 in. x 7.65mm Para. barrels.

ERFURT TOGGLE IDENTIFICATION

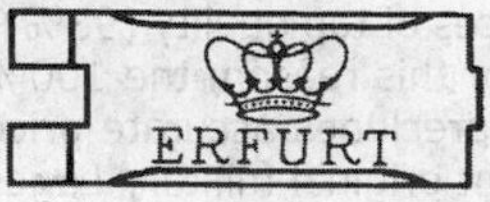

ERFURT MODELS – produced from 1910-1914 and 1916-1918 in Erfurt, Germany. Military Model - Chamber dated 1911-1914 and 1916-1918. Erfurt models exhibit the most proof marks or individual parts numbering. Walnut grips.

SIMSON & CO. TOGGLE IDENTIFICATION

SIMSON & CO. – manufactured 1925 to 1934 in Suhl, Germany. During this period, Simson manufactured approx. 12,000 Lugers. Simson Lugers are military models (9mm - 4 in. barrels). During this 12 year period, Simson supplied the German Army with Lugers exclusively. Can be dated 1925 or 1926 or not dated at all. Many reworks of WWI DWM Military Lugers were refurbished by Simson, and can be detected by the Simson "Eagle-over-6" proof on repaired parts. Toggles are marked "Simson" or "S".

SWISS TOGGLE IDENTIFICATION

SWISS BERN MODELS – Manufactured 1918 to 1947 by WAFFENFABRIK Bern, Switzerland. Relatively rare - these Swiss models have "improved" changes (flat and curved front grip strap), 4 3/4 in. barrels, walnut or plastic grips, grip safety. 1929 model (flat front grip strap) has Swiss Cross in shield on front link.

MAUSER TOGGLE IDENTIFICATION

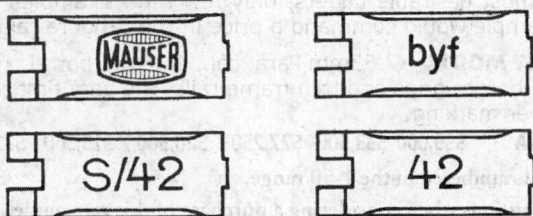

MAUSER VARIATIONS – Manufactured 1934-1942 in Oberndorf, Germany. Between 1930 and 1934 Mauser Werke was primarily engaged in reworking older Lugers, since transfer of machinery and personnel to the DWM plant in Berlin was completed in 1931. Mauser "Banner" models were made from 1934 to 1942, many are dated from 1939-1942 on the chamber. S/42 models are MOSTLY MILITARY contract guns manufactured between 1934 and 1940, usually chamber marked. "42" toggle marked guns (Mauser code) were mfg. 1939 and 1940 and are dated. "byf" marked toggles indicate guns made for German military use after 1940 and are more common than other military models. The Mauser Werke trademark also appears on those Lugers made in the 1970s.

KRIEGHOFF TOGGLE IDENTIFICATION

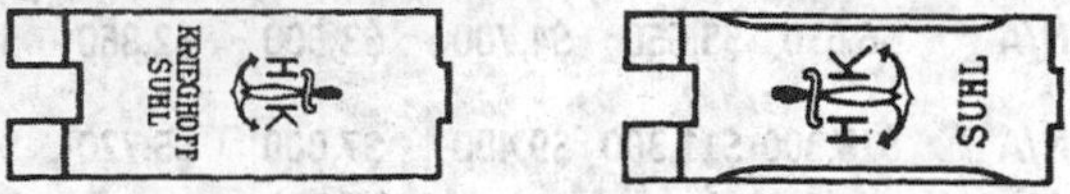

KRIEGHOFF MODELS – Manufactured between 1934-1946 in Suhl, Germany. Early Krieghoffs are side frame inscribed. The German Luftwaffe contracted with Krieghoff for military guns in 1935. Early military Krieghoffs have "S" marked chambers, most are chamber dated between 1936 and 1945. Krieghoff Lugers are prized for their quality fit and finish and command higher prices because of their rarity factor. The vast majority of commercial Krieghoff Lugers have the letter P before the serial number. Estimated total Krieghoff produced between 13,000 and 14,000.

VICKERS TOGGLE IDENTIFICATION

VICKERS – Manufactured by Vickers, Ltd., circa 1921 in England, probably from DWM parts for military contract sale to the Netherlands. Added barrel date is a date of arsenal refinish or refurbishing. Distinguishable by Vickers toggle and "Rust" marked safety. Serial range is 1-10,100. Grips can be finely checkered with shallow contour or very coarsely checkered. Configuration is 9mm Para., 4 in. barrel, and grip safety.

LUGERS: MATCHING MAGAZINE(S) & MILITARY HOLSTER ADD ONS

Values for all variations of Lugers listed assume a proper original magazine and matching parts.

Add approx. 50% for one original matching magazine on all Lugers listed below that were originally manufactured/issued with numbered magazines.

Add approx. 75%-100% for two original matching magazines on all Lugers listed in the following sections that were originally manufactured/issued with numbered magazines, depending on condition.

Add approx. $250-$400 for original military holster (4 in. barrel only), depending on condition.

PISTOLS: SEMI-AUTO, LUGERS & VARIATIONS

Lugers: Pre-1900 & 1900 DWM Mfg.

Values on most 100% Lugers have been omitted intentionally since rarity precludes accurate price evaluation in this condition factor.

GRADING - PPGS™	100%	98%	95%	90%	80%	70%	60%	LAST MSR

1898/99 BORCHARDT LUGER TRANSITIONAL – 7.65mm Para. cal., 5 in. barrel, this is perhaps one of the most desirable Lugers, only few mfg. Examples scarce, no reported sales, an original example would command a price in the 5-figure range.

1899/1900 SWISS TEST MODEL – 7.65mm Para. cal., 4 3/4 in. barrel, 100 or less mfg., pre-production with wide border grips and thin frame rails, the very first true Luger. Engraved "Swiss Cross" chamber marking.

	N/A	$39,000	$33,500	$27,250	$20,500	$15,500	$11,000	

Approx. 50 pistols serial numbered in the 1-50 range.

Buyers should be very cautious when considering a purchase of this rare model, as good fakes do exist.

1900 COMMERCIAL DWM – 7.65mm Para. cal., 4 3/4 in. barrel, approx. 5,500 mfg.

	N/A	$6,900	$5,600	$4,600	$3,275	$2,650	$2,100	

1900 SWISS COMMERCIAL DWM – 7.65mm Para. cal., 4 3/4 in. barrel, 2,000 commercially mfg.

	N/A	$6,650	$5,600	$4,700	$3,500	$2,850	$2,250	
Unrelieved grip frame	N/A	$13,300	$11,200	$9,400	$7,000	$5,700	$4,500	

Add 15% for wide trigger (found only in ser. no. range 4,000).

At a recent nationally publicized auction, a 1900 Swiss Commercial Luger with a three digit serial number and an unrelieved frame, an original case and accessories, and in 98-99% overall condition sold for $31,625.

1900 SWISS MILITARY DWM – 7.65mm Para. cal., 4 3/4 in. barrel, 3,000 military mfg.

	N/A	$6,650	$5,650	$4,700	$3,500	$2,860	$2,250	
Unrelieved grip frame	N/A	$13,300	$11,300	$9,400	$7,000	$5,720	$4,500	

Add 15% for wide trigger (found only in ser. no. range 4,000).

1900 AMERICAN EAGLE DWM – 7.65mm Para. cal., 4 3/4 in. barrel, approx. 12,000 mfg.

	N/A	$6,885	$5,500	$5,100	$3,350	$2,700	$2,100	

Add 40% for U.S. Test Model (approx. ser. no. range 6,009 - 7,500) - not marked Germany, has no proofmarks, has last two digits of ser. no. on right side of locking bolt.

1900 BULGARIAN DWM – 7.65mm Para. cal., 4 3/4 in. barrel, 1,000 mfg., very rare in U.S., most often seen in the 60% and lower condition.

	N/A	$10,750	$9,000	$7,000	$5,100	$4,200	$3,500	

Subtract 30% if rebarreled.

Lugers: 1902-DWM Mfg.

1902 COMMERCIAL – 9mm Para. cal., 4 in. barrel, serial number range 22,300-22,400 and 22,900-23,500 (500-600 mfg.). Commonly called "Fat Barrel" model.

	N/A	$13,500	$11,000	$9,000	$7,000	$5,000	$4,000	

1902 AMERICAN EAGLE – 9mm Para. cal., 4 in. barrel, 600-700 mfg., commonly called the "Fat Barrel." Same ser. range as 1902 Commercial Model.

	N/A	$16,500	$13,500	$11,000	$9,000	$7,500	$6,000	

1902 CARTRIDGE COUNTER AMERICAN EAGLE – 9mm Para. cal., only 50 mfg. with the Powell Indication Device; be extremely wary of fakes. Ser. no. range 22,401- 22,450.

	N/A	$45,150	$38,600	$30,100	$20,450	$14,800	$12,825	

1902 DANZIG TEST – 7.65mm Para. or 9mm Para. cal., blank toggle, 4 in. barrel, Crown D proofs.

	N/A	$7,850	$6,500	$5,500	$4,500	$3,700	$2,950	

1902 CARBINE – 7.65mm Para. cal., 11 3/4 in. barrel, approx. 2500 mfg.

Gun w/ matching stock	N/A	$18,900	$16,275	$13,520	$10,675	$7,800	$6,775	
Gun only	N/A	$12,000	$10,100	$8,100	$6,250	$5,700	$3,800	

Add approx. 40% for American Eagle variation.

Subtract 20% for non-matching stock.

GRADING - PPGS™	100%	98%	95%	90%	80%	70%	60%	LAST MSR

1902/06 TRANSITIONAL CARBINE – 11 3/4 in. barrel, 50-100 mfg., may have new model frame. Ser. nos. start at 50,000.

N/A	$11,500	$9,000	$6,850	$4,850	$4,500	$4,250	

Subtract 30% if without matching stock.

1903 COMMERCIAL – 7.65mm Para. cal., 4 in. barrel, 50 mfg., extractor marked "charge," ser. range 25,000-25,050, with 90 degree toggle checkering.

N/A	$8,250	$7,450	$6,000	$5,600	$4,850	$3,500	

Lugers: 1904-DWM Mfg.

1904 NAVY DWM – 9mm Para. cal., 6 in. barrel, limited mfg., a Transitional Navy, "Fat Barrel" with 90 degree toggle checkering and toggle lock, should have 2-digit ser. no.

Extreme rarity precludes pricing for individual condition factors. Good condition (70%-95%), no problem, original specimens are currently selling in the $30,000 - $50,000 range.

Most of these pistols available for sale are fakes - buyer beware!

Lugers: 1906-DWM Mfg.

1906 COMMERCIAL 7.65mm Para. W/"GESICHERT" MARKED SAFETY – 7.65mm Para. cal., 4 3/4 in. barrel, "GESICHERT" marked safety, long frame. Approx. 750 mfg.

N/A	$4,150	$3,550	$2,950	$2,100	$1,450	$1,150	

1906 COMMERCIAL 9mm Para. – 9mm Para. cal., 4 in. barrel, 3,500-4,000 mfg. Scarcer than 7.65mm Para.

N/A	$4,150	$3,550	$2,950	$2,100	$1,450	$1,150	

1906 COMMERCIAL 7.65mm Para. – 7.65mm Para. cal., 4 3/4 in. barrel, area under safety polished bright, 5,000 mfg.

N/A	$3,425	$3,000	$2,300	$1,725	$1,150	$950	

1906 AMERICAN EAGLE – 9mm Para. cal., 4 in. barrel, American Eagle stamped in front of breech, approx. 3,000 mfg.

N/A	$4,500	$4,000	$3,350	$2,350	$1,700	$1,350	

1906 AMERICAN EAGLE – 7.65mm Para. cal., 4 3/4 in. barrel, 7,500-8,000 mfg.

N/A	$4,000	$3,500	$3,000	$2,100	$1,550	$1,150	

Add 40% for long frame.

1906 NAVY COMMERCIAL – 9mm Para. cal., 6 in. barrel, approx. 2,500 mfg.

N/A	$5,550	$4,750	$3,850	$3,025	$2,325	$1,500	

Add 50% for 7.65mm Para. cal. with 6 in. barrel.

1906 NAVY MILITARY FIRST ISSUE – 9mm Para. cal., 6 in. barrel, first issue, 19,000 mfg., mostly altered safety marking - "GESICHERT" in upper position. Ser. no. range 1-9,000a.

N/A	$6,600	$5,500	$4,550	$3,550	$2,700	$1,800	

Add 10% for Navy unit markings. Add 25% for unaltered safety variation.

1906 NAVY MILITARY SECOND ISSUE – 9mm Para. cal., 6 in. barrel, second issue, 2,000 mfg. Ser. range 9,000a-1,000b.

N/A	$6,500	$5,400	$4,500	$3,500	$2,675	$1,700	

Add 10% for Navy unit markings.

Lugers: 1906-1918 DWM & Erfurt Mfg.

Most common variations in good supply within this section in 50% or less condition will approximate the 60% value. This reflects its value as a representative shooter rather than a higher priced collector's gun.

1906 SWISS COMMERCIAL – 7.65mm Para. or 9mm Para. cal., 4 3/4 in. barrel, less than 1,000 mfg., Swiss "Cross in Sunburst", short frame.

N/A	$3,850	$3,250	$2,750	$2,100	$1,500	$1,100	

Add 20% for "Cross in Shield".

1906 SWISS MILITARY – 7.65mm Para. cal., 4 3/4 in. barrel, long frame, Swiss Police has either "Cross in Shield" or "Cross in Sunburst."

N/A	$3,725	$3,150	$2,650	$1,950	$1,535	$1,180	

GRADING - PPGS™	100%	98%	95%	90%	80%	70%	60%	LAST MSR

1906/23 DUTCH – 9mm Para. cal., 4 in. barrel, approx. 4,000 mfg., often seen as arsenal rework.

N/A $3,550 $3,100 $2,800 $2,225 $1,850 $1,425

Original finish & bbl. N/A $14,200 $12,400 $11,200 $8,900 $7,400 $5,700

1906 BRAZILIAN – 7.65mm Para. cal., 4 3/4 in. barrel, 5,000 mfg., extremely rare in fine condition.

N/A $3,525 $3,000 $2,570 $2,050 $1,690 $1,300

1906 BULGARIAN – 7.65mm Para. cal., 4 3/4 in. barrel, 1,500 mfg., most rebarrelled to 9mm Para.

N/A $6,300 $5,515 $4,975 $3,970 $3,275 $2,520

Subtract 60% for versions rebarreled to 9mm Para. cal.

This is the rarest Bulgarian - most are fakes or have been restored.

1908 BULGARIAN – 9mm Para. cal., 4 in. barrel, "DWM" on chamber, 10,000 mfg., extremely rare in mint condition.

N/A $3,850 $3,400 $3,100 $2,500 $2,100 $1,600

1906 PORTUGUESE ARMY – 7.65mm Para. cal., 4 3/4 in. barrel, "Manuel II" crest on chamber. Approx. 5,000 mfg.

N/A $3,375 $2,950 $2,500 $2,000 $1,700 $1,300

1906 ROYAL PORTUGUESE NAVY – 9mm Para. cal., 4 in. barrel, "Anchor & Crown" on chamber, very rare. Most are fakes.

N/A $10,750 $9,400 $8,500 $6,800 $5,600 $4,300

1906 REPUBLIC OF PORTUGAL NAVY – 7.65mm Para. cal., "Anchor R.P." on chamber, very rare. Most are fakes.

N/A $10,750 $9,400 $8,500 $6,800 $5,600 $4,300

1906 RUSSIAN – 9mm Para. cal., 4 in. barrel, approx. 1,000 mfg., only 7 reported.

N/A $17,500 $15,500 $13,825 $11,025 $9,100 $7,000

1906 VICKERS DUTCH – 9mm Para. cal., 4 in. barrel, approx. 10,000 assembled by Vickers Ltd. from DWM supplied parts.

N/A $4,350 $3,700 $3,275 $2,000 $2,145 $1,650

1906 FRENCH COMMERCIAL – 7.65mm Para. cal., 4 3/4 in. barrel.

N/A $3,375 $2,950 $2,525 $2,000 $1,650 $1,275

w/case & accessories N/A $6,400 $5,600 $5,050 $4,000 $3,330 $2,550

1908 DWM COMMERCIAL AND MILITARY – 9mm Para. cal., 4 in. barrel, Test/Acceptance Model, approx. 500 mfg. Ser. no. range 69,000-71,200.

N/A $2,550 $2,250 $1,750 $1,385 $1,145 $880

1908 NAVY COMMERCIAL – 9mm Para. cal., 6 in. barrel.

N/A $6,500 $5,500 $5,000 $4,250 $3,500 $2,750

Add 50% for 7.65mm Para. with 6 in. barrel.

1908 DWM MILITARY – 9mm Para. cal., 4 in. barrel, undated 1st issue or dated 1910-1913, no stock lug, except for a few late 1913 mfg. guns.

N/A $2,500 $2,000 $1,750 $1,400 $1,150 $900

Add 20%+ for Imperial unit markings (depends on history of unit).

Add 20% for undated or for 1913 date w/stock lug.

Approx. 25,000 1st issue pistols were mfg., 20,000 dated 1910, 15,000 dated 1911, 10,000 dated 1912, 25,000 dated 1913.

1908 DWM COMMERCIAL – 9mm Para. cal., 4 in. barrel, no stock lug or hold open, blank chamber.

N/A $2,500 $2,000 $1,750 $1,400 $1,150 $900

1911-1914 DATED 1908 ERFURT MILITARY – 9mm Para. cal., 4 in. barrel (dated 1910-1914), 1910, 1911, 1912, and most 1913 chamber dates do not have stock lugs.

N/A $2,450 $2,150 $1,775 $1,425 $1,175 $925

GRADING - PPGS™	100%	98%	95%	90%	80%	70%	60%	LAST MSR

Add 20%+ for Imperial unit markings (depends on history of unit).
Add 50% for 1910 chamber date.
Add 20% for 1913 chamber date with stock lug.
Add 20% for 1914 date.
Add $250 for original holster in average+ condition.

WWI ERFURT MILITARY SERIAL RANGES

CHAMBER DATE	OBSERVED LOW SERIAL	OBSERVED HIGH SERIAL	APPROXIMATE QTY. MADE
1911	575	9548	10,000
1912	255	866b	22,000
1913	575	2563b	25,000
1914	2137	539A	25,000
1915	none observed		
1916	13	5764b	80,000
1917	844	2854n	150,000
1918	304	5816s	180,000

Production data appears courtesy of Jan C. Still.

1908 NAVY – 9mm Para. cal., 6 in. barrel, scarce. Ser. no. range 1,000B-10,000B, 9,000 mfg.
N/A $8,400 $7,575 $6,320 $5,040 $4,160 $3,200

1908 BOLIVIAN CONTRACT – 9mm Para. cal., 4 in. barrel.
N/A $4,000 $3,550 $3,160 $2,520 $2,080 $1,600

1913 COMMERCIAL DWM – 9mm Para. cal., 4 in. barrel, grip safety and stock lug, horizontal "N" proof mark, 71,000 ser. no. range, rare.
N/A $3,850 $3,250 $2,850 $2,250 $1,850 $1,500

1914 COMMERCIAL DWM – 9mm Para. cal., 4 in. barrel, undated, stock lug, horizontal crown-N proofed.
N/A $2,650 $2,225 $1,895 $1,510 $1,250 $1,000

1914 NAVY – 9mm Para. cal., 6 in. barrel, scarce. Dated 1916 and 1917.
N/A $5,975 $5,250 $4,295 $3,215 $2,700 $2,295

Add 20% for 16 date.

Watch for fakes made from 1920 Commercials with new barrels and rear toggles added. Crown M proofs and date will look "fresh" (1917 date usually encountered).

1914-1918 DATED ERFURT MILITARY – 9mm Para. cal., 4 in. barrel, dated 1916-18, there are no known 1915 chamber dated Erfurts.
N/A $2,150 $1,895 $1,550 $1,225 $1,050 $875

Add 20% for 1914 date. Add 20%+ for Imperial unit markings (depends on history of unit).
Add $250 for original holster in average+ condition.

Note: Date stamped on top frame is date of production; thus dates could be 1914, 1916, 1917, or 1918. All are military P.08s, however, 98%-100% Erfurts are rare.

1914 ERFURT ARTILLERY – 9mm Para. cal., 1914 date is only one seen, 8 in. barrel.
N/A $4,650 $3,950 $3,475 $2,770 $2,290 $1,800

Add 20%+ for Imperial unit markings (depends on history of unit).

1910-1918 DATED WWI DWM MILITARY – 9mm Para. cal., 4 in. barrel. 1910-1918 dated. Most frequently encountered WWI military Luger, w/stock lug mid-1913-1918.
N/A $2,150 $1895 $1,550 $1.225 $1,050 $875

Add approx. 20% for 1910-1913 chamber dated mfg.
Add 20%+ for Imperial unit markings (depends on history of unit).
Add $250 for original holster in average+ condition.

GRADING - PPGS™	100%	98%	95%	90%	80%	70%	60%	LAST MSR

Note: Date stamped on top frame is date of production; thus, dates could be 1910 through 1918, but all are military P.08s.

WWI DWM MILITARY SERIAL RANGES

CHAMBER DATE	OBSERVED LOW SERIAL	OBSERVED HIGH SERIAL	APPROXIMATE QTY. MADE
1908	(undated) 34	2636b	25,000
1910	5095b	5358d	20,000
1911	1524c	4825e	13,000
1912	599	9974	10,000
1913	2617	3850d	25,000
1914	282	6212c	40,000
1915	1398	2557d	100,000
1916	287	5438q	180,000
1917	587	3521m	60,000
1918	110	9018n	190,000

Production data appears courtesy of Jan C. Still.

1914-1918 DATED DWM ARTILLERY – 9mm Para. cal., 8 in. barrel. Dated 1914-18.

N/A $3,500 $3,000 $2,500 $2,000 $1,850 $1,500

Add $750-$1,000 for matching stock, depending on condition.
Add $350 for proper non-matching stock.
Add $550 for original leather holster with shoulder strap.
Add 200% for rare 1914 chamber date.
Add 20% for 1915 chamber date.
Add 20%+ for Imperial unit markings (depends on history of unit).

Lugers: 1920-1930 DWM

Most common variations in good supply within this section in 50% or less condition will approximate the 60% value. This reflects its value as a representative shooter rather than a higher priced collector's gun.

1920 DWM OR ERFURT – 9mm Para. cal., 4 in. barrel, military and police, reworked and issued to police units, many thousand reworked, double date also, 1920 and 1921 dated.

N/A $1,400 $1,155 $975 $800 $675 $550

1920 COMMERCIAL – 7.65mm Para. or 9mm Para. cal., 3 7/8-4 in. barrel, available in many configurations, since these guns were assembled using the parts of previously manufactured Lugers, including 1900-06 mfg. with the grip safety on the frame.

N/A $1,425 $1,175 $995 $815 $700 $550

Add 25% for 9mm Para. cal.

These prices reflect original condition, and are not to be confused with recent imports (with import markings).

1920 NAVY COMMERCIAL – 9mm Para. cal., 6 in. barrel, very rare rework, Navy rear sight.

N/A $3,600 $3,145 $2,425 $1,775 $1,185 $1,050

Add 20% for 7.65mm Para. with 6 in. barrel.

1920 COMMERCIAL ARTILLERY – 9mm Para. cal., 8 in. barrel, very rare rework.

N/A $4,725 $4,150 $3,375 $2,300 $1,600 $1,300

1920 "LONG BARREL" COMMERCIAL – 7.65mm Para. or 9mm Para. cal., 10-20 in. barrel, extremely rare.

N/A $4,325 $3,785 $3,125 $2,125 $1,500 $1,185

Watch for fakes - these guns have to be evaluated one at a time. Barrel should have matching nos. and Crown N proof.

GRADING - PPGS™	100%	98%	95%	90%	80%	70%	60%	LAST MSR

1920 NAVY CARBINE – 7.65mm Para. cal., 11 3/4 in. barrel, long frame (if short frame, be wary of fakes, very few produced). Navy rear sight, no forearm under barrel.

	N/A	$4,775	$4,100	$3,200	$2,400	$1,545	$1,185	

1920 CARBINE – 7.65mm Para. cal., 11 3/4 in. barrel, very rare.

Gun only	N/A	$7,425	$6,100	$4,800	$3,800	$2,975	$2,250	
Gun with stock	N/A	$10,500	$8,925	$6,775	$5,725	$4,850	$3,800	

1920 SWISS REWORK – 7.65mm Para. cal., 3 5/8-6 in. barrel, several hundred produced.

	N/A	$2,325	$1,950	$1,525	$1,050	$925	$850	

ABERCROMBIE & FITCH COMMERCIAL – 7.65mm Para. or 9mm Para. cal., long frame, 4 3/4 in. barrel, 100 mfg., total for both cals.

	N/A	$5,475	$4,625	$3,850	$3,025	$2,600	$2,250	

Add 30% for 6 in. barrels (rare).

Inspect barrel legend very carefully (as in beware of fakes) - must have reinforced frame (look for rib in rear frame well).

1920/21-DWM – 9mm Para. cal., 4 in. barrel.

	N/A	$1,275	$1,100	$975	$750	$575	$475	

Subtract 20% if arsenal reworked.

1920/23 STOEGER AMERICAN EAGLE – 7.65mm Para. or 9mm Para. cal., 3 5/8-24 in. barrels, less than 1,000 mfg., made by DWM for Stoeger, sold in USA, longer barrel models have higher value.

3 7/8 - 6 in. barrels	N/A	$5,650	$4,775	$4,000	$3,125	$2,675	$2,325	
8 in. barrel	N/A	$6,300	$5,250	$4,325	$3,075	$2,575	$2,300	

Add 50% for Mauser mfg., safe and loaded extractor, or V ser. no. suffix.

Be extremely careful when examining the frame markings on this variation as there are many fakes in the marketplace.

1923 DWM COMMERCIAL – 7.65mm Para. cal., 3 5/8 in. barrel, 14,000 mfg. ser. range 74,000-89,000.

	N/A	$1,550	$1,350	$1,125	$850	$650	$550	

1923 DWM "SAFE AND LOADED" COMMERCIAL – 7.65mm Para. cal., "safe and loaded" marked on frame and extractor, 7.65mm Para. cal., 3 7/8 in. barrel, safety and extractor marked in English, 2,000 mfg. ser. range 89,000-91,000.

	N/A	$2,450	$2,050	$1,575	$1,125	$975	$900	

1923 FINNISH LUGER – 7.65mm Para. cal., approx. 5,000-7,000 units made for Finnish military contract (Army and Navy), marked "SA" surrounded by a rectangle, most have been recently imported into the U.S.

	N/A	$1,275	$1,150	$975	$750	$600	$475	

Lugers: Krieghoff Mfg.

Please refer to the Krieghoff section for recently manufactured Krieghoff Lugers.

1923 DWM/KRIEGHOFF COMMERCIAL – 7.65mm Para. (3 7/8 in. barrel only) or 9mm Para. (4 in. barrel only), few mfg., reworked by Krieghoff, chamber dated 1921 or unmarked, most in "i" range, Krieghoff stamped on back of frame. Be wary of fakes.

	N/A	$2,325	$1,950	$1,525	$1,050	$975	$850	

DWM/KRIEGHOFF COMMERCIAL – 7.65mm Para. or 9mm Para. cal., 4 in. barrel, a few hundred made, side frame marked Krieghoff. Most are fake.

	N/A	$3,625	$3,050	$2,600	$1,875	$1,575	$1,250	

KRIEGHOFF COMMERCIAL SIDE FRAME – 7.65mm Para. or 9mm Para. cal., 4 or 6 in. barrel, approx. 1500 mfg., 1,000 with side frame marking, and 500 without side frame marking.

	N/A	$7,100	$6,125	$5,100	$3,825	$3,325	$2,550	

Add 30% for side frame marked 7.65mm Para.
Add approx. 30% if w/o side frame marking.

Almost all Krieghoff Commercial Lugers have the letter P before the serial number.

GRADING - PPGS™	100%	98%	95%	90%	80%	70%	60%	LAST MSR

KRIEGHOFF S CODE EARLY – 9mm Para. cal., 4 in. barrel, approx. 1,800 mfg., German Luftwaffe. Has fat walnut grips, "H-K Suhl" toggle.

	N/A	$4,650	$4,000	$3,250	$2,500	$1,525	$1,350

KRIEGHOFF S CODE MID SERIES – 9mm Para. cal., 4 in. barrel, approx. 500-700 mfg., Luftwaffe, ser. no. range 1600-2500, finely checkered plastic grips.

	N/A	$5,050	$4,250	$3,550	$3,150	$1,675	$1,450

KRIEGHOFF S CODE LATE – 9mm Para. cal., 4 in. barrel, approx. 1,800 mfg., Luftwaffe, ser. no. range 2300-4200.

	N/A	$4,450	$3,800	$3,125	$2,275	$1,400	$1,300

KRIEGHOFF 36 DATE – 9mm Para. cal., 4 in. barrel, approx. 500-700 made, Luftwaffe military, 2 digit date, coarsely checkered plastic grips.

	N/A	$4,550	$3,900	$3,225	$2,150	$1,525	$1,350

KRIEGHOFF 1936-1945 DATED – 9mm Para. cal., 4 in. barrel, approx. 9,000 mfg., 4 digit chamber date, 1936, 1937, and 1940 most common.

1936-37 & 1940	N/A	$5,500	$4,750	$4,000	$3,250	$2,600	$1,850
1938	N/A	$6,000	$5,000	$4,150	$3,350	$2,725	$1,900
1941	N/A	$7,000	$6,000	$5,000	$4,100	$3,250	$2,650
1942-43	N/A	$10,000	$8,000	$6,000	$4,150	$3,350	$2,750
1944	N/A	$16,500	$12,500	$10,000	$8,250	$6,750	$5,000
1945	N/A	$20,000	$15,000	$11,500	$9,000	$8,000	$7,000

The 1941 "large date" is very rare - watch for fakes (re-dated frames) on this model in general.

POST-WAR KRIEGHOFF TYPE I – 9mm Para. cal., 4 in. barrel, approx. 150 mfg. for occupation forces, H-K marked toggle link.

	N/A	$3,875	$3,325	$2,875	$2,150	$1,725	$1,425

POST-WAR KRIEGHOFF TYPE II – 9mm Para. cal., 4 in. barrel, approx. 150 mfg., unmarked toggle link, many parts proofed "Eagle-over-2".

	N/A	$3,875	$3,325	$2,875	$2,150	$1,725	$1,425

POST-WAR KRIEGHOFF COMMERCIAL – 7.65mm Para. cal., 4 in. barrel, approx. 100-200 mfg., unmarked toggle, many parts proofed "Eagle-over-2".

	N/A	$3,325	$2,950	$2,075	$1,625	$1,175	$975

Lugers: Mauser Mfg.

Most common variations in good supply within this section in 50% or less condition will approximate the 60% value. This reflects its value as a representative shooter rather than a higher priced collector's gun.

1935-06 PORTUGUESE GNR – 7.65mm Para. cal., 4 3/4 in. barrel, 564 mfg., "GNR" on chamber, Portuguese marked safety and extractor.

	N/A	$3,525	$3,000	$2,645	$2,110	$1,740	$1,340

1934/06 MAUSER SWISS COMMERCIAL – 7.65mm Para. cal., 4 3/4 in. barrel, a few hundred produced, "Cross in Sunburst" or blank chamber, grip safety.

	N/A	$4,150	$3,575	$3,120	$2,490	$2,055	$1,580

1934 MAUSER BANNER COMMERCIAL – 7.65mm Para. or 9mm Para. cal., 4 in. barrel, hundreds produced, unmarked chamber, "v" suffix ser. no.

	N/A	$4,350	$3,750	$3,120	$2,490	$2,055	$1,580

Add 15% for "Kal. 7.65" barrel marking.

S/42 K DATE – 9mm Para. cal., 4 in. barrel, approx. 10,000 mfg. during 1934 only for military.

	N/A	$7,650	$6,775	$5,500	$4,350	$3,430	$2,675

Add 100% for "large eagle over M Navy" proofmark.

S/42 G DATE – 9mm Para. cal., 4 in. barrel, many thousand produced 1935 only.

	N/A	$2,850	$2,350	$2,035	$1,620	$1,340	$1,030

Add 50% for Navy markings.

GRADING - PPGS™	100%	98%	95%	90%	80%	70%	60%	LAST MSR

S/42 DATED CHAMBER – 9mm Para. cal., 4 in. barrel, many thousands produced, "S/42" stamped rear toggle, chamber dated 1936-1940. One of the most frequently encountered WWII military Lugers.

	N/A	$2,250	$2,050	$1,620	$1,290	$1,050	$950
w/Navy/ Police markings	N/A	$4,500	$4,100	$3,240	$2,580	$2,100	$1,900

Add 20% for 1936 date.

Add 30% for "strawed" 1937 date.

Add $250 for original holster in average+ condition.

The last regular production S/42 Models were mfg. approx. April of 1939.

MAUSER PERSIAN (IRANIAN) CONTRACT – 9mm Para. cal., 4 and 8 in. barrels, approx. 1,000 mfg. with 8 in. barrel, and 2,000-3,000 mfg. in 4 in. barrel, Farsi numerals.

4 in. barrel	N/A	$4,000	$3,850	$3,250	$2,750	$2,250	$1,750
Artillery (8 in.)	N/A	$4,500	$4,000	$3,500	$2,850	$2,350	$1,850
Cutaway	N/A	$6,500	$5,750	$5,000	$4,000	$3,000	$2,500

Add 50% for Artillery with matching rig.

Mauser produced fifty 4 in. barrel cutaways with the Persian contract for training purposes.

1936-1942 DATED MAUSER BANNER – 9mm Para. cal., 4 in. barrel, over 1,000 mfg., commercial and contract sales, wood grips, no sear safety, often have strawed small parts.

N/A	$3,950	$3,250	$2,900	$2,075	$1,860	$1,430

MAUSER BANNER DUTCH CONTRACT – 9mm Para. cal., 4 in. barrel, 1,000 mfg., safety marked "Rust". Dated 1936-40.

N/A	$3,750	$3,130	$2,825	$2,250	$1,860	$1,430

Add 25% for 1936, 1937, 1938, or 1939 chamber date.

MAUSER BANNER SWEDISH CONTRACT – 275 mfg. in 9mm Para. cal., 4 3/4 in. barrels, dated 1938, 25 mfg. in 9mm Para. cal., dated 1939, 30 mfg. in 7.65mm Para. cal., dated 1939, very rare in 7.65mm Para. dated 1940.

N/A	$4,050	$3,425	$3,040	$2,425	$2,000	$1,540

Add 15% for 7.65mm Para. cal. (4 3/4 in. barrel).

CODE "S/42" COMMERCIAL CONTRACT – 9mm Para. cal., 4 in. barrel, a few hundred produced, dated 1938. Commercial proof marks only.

N/A	$2,950	$2,580	$2,330	$1,860	$1,535	$1,180

CODE "42" – 9mm Para. cal., 4 in. barrels, dated 1939-1940, rear toggle marked "42." One of the most frequently encountered WWII military Lugers.

	N/A	$2,150	$1,900	$1,550	$1,275	$1,200	$1,075
w/Navy markings	N/A	$4,300	$3,800	$3,100	$2,550	$2,400	$2,150

Add $250 for original holster in average condition.

At a recent nationally publicized auction, a 1940 dated code "42", condition a strong 99%, with two matching magazines and original holster sold for $8,337.50

MAUSER BANNER POLICE – 9mm Para. cal., approx. 30,000 mfg., dated 1939-1942, police contract, have sear safeties, blue small parts. A few observed dated 1938.

N/A	$3,200	$2,750	$2,290	$1,825	$1,510	$1,160

Add 30% with 1938 chamber date (rare).

CODE "41-42" – 9mm Para. cal., 4 in. barrel, 2-digit date, approx. 7,000 mfg. in January of 1941, "41" dated chamber, "42" code, most 42 dates are reworks.

N/A	$4,250	$3,720	$3,360	$2,680	$2,210	$1,700

Add $250 for original holster in average condition.

CODE "byf" – 9mm Para. cal., 4 in. barrel, thousands made, chamber dated "41" and "42". Rear toggle is stamped "byf", standard magazine was "fxo" marked and had an un-numbered plastic bottom. One of the most frequently encountered WWII military Lugers.

N/A	$2,150	$1,900	$1,540	$1,230	$1,050	$780

Add 30% for original black bakelite grips.

GRADING - PPGS™	100%	98%	95%	90%	80%	70%	60%	LAST MSR

Add $250 for original holster in average condition.

Code "byf" Lugers with black bakelite grips are referred to as the "Black Widow" variation.

AUSTRIAN BUNDES HEER – 9mm Para. cal., 4 in. barrel, several hundred produced, Austrian Federal Army, no serial letter suffix-same ser. placement as Mauser 42KU. Rarely encountered in mint condition.

	100%	98%	95%	90%	80%	70%	60%
	N/A	$2,900	$2,400	$2,095	$1,670	$1,380	$1,060

MAUSER 1934 CODE BYF, S/42 AND 42 KU – 9mm Para. cal., 3,500 mfg. Post-1942 Luftwaffe subcontract.

	100%	98%	95%	90%	80%	70%	60%
	N/A	$3,475	$3,000	$2,375	$2,000	$1,850	$1,300

Lugers: Reworks

DEATH'S HEAD REWORK – 9mm Para. cal., 4 in. barrel, very rare, possible early SS unit issue. Most are fakes.

	100%	98%	95%	90%	80%	70%	60%
	N/A	$2,500	$2,190	$1,975	$1,575	$1,300	$1,000

SIMSON REWORK – 9mm Para. cal., 4 in. barrel, DWM toggles, Simpson Eagle proofs on reworked parts.

	100%	98%	95%	90%	80%	70%	60%
	N/A	$1,325	$1,150	$990	$790	$650	$500

DOUBLE DATED DWM/ERFURT – 9mm Para. cal., 4, 6, or 8 in. barrel, very scarce. 1920 over 1910-1918 chamber dates. Often with sear safety and mag. safety remnant.

	100%	98%	95%	90%	80%	70%	60%
	N/A	$1,500	$1,325	$1,100	$875	$750	$700
w/intact mag. safety	N/A	$3,000	$2,650	$2,200	$1,750	$1,500	$1,400

Add 40% for 8 in. barrel.

KONZENTRATION LUGER REWORK – 9mm Para. cal., 4 in. barrel, 200-300 marked "KI 1933" and issued to guards working in the first concentration camps - most went to Dachau. Most are fakes.

	100%	98%	95%	90%	80%	70%	60%
	N/A	$1,925	$1,685	$1,520	$1,215	$1,000	$770

Lugers: Simson Mfg.

SIMSON & COMPANY – 7.65mm Para. or 9mm Para. cal., 3 7/8 or 4 in. barrel, military and possibly limited commercial sales, approx. 12,000 produced but rarely found.

	100%	98%	95%	90%	80%	70%	60%
	N/A	$4,250	$3,600	$2,950	$2,300	$2,000	$1,300

SIMSON MILITARY DATED – 9mm Para. cal., 4 in. barrel, possibly 2,000 mfg., dated 1925.

	100%	98%	95%	90%	80%	70%	60%
	N/A	$6,250	$5,200	$4,250	$3,350	$2,900	$1,850

This model is encountered with a 1925 or 1926 (rare) chamber date.

SIMSON S CODE/SIMSON MARKED TOGGLE – 9mm Para. cal., 4 in. barrel. Undated, scarce.

	100%	98%	95%	90%	80%	70%	60%
	N/A	$5,500	$4,075	$3,300	$2,575	$2,225	$1,500

Lugers: Swiss Bern

1906 BERN – 7.65mm Para. cal., 4 3/4 in. barrel, "Waffenfabrik Bern" on toggle, Swiss military, bordered checkered walnut grips, exactly 17,874 mfg.

	100%	98%	95%	90%	80%	70%	60%
	$3,750	$3,250	$2,750	$2,250	$2,000	$1,750	$1,500

1929 SWISS BERN – 7.65mm Para. or 9mm Para. (rare) cal., 4 3/4 in. barrel, 29,857 mfg., many machining changes to simplify production, straight front grip strap, P prefix designates commercial model, brown or black plastic grips.

	100%	98%	95%	90%	80%	70%	60%
	$2,750	$2,250	$2,000	$1,750	$1,500	$1,250	$1,000

Add 20% for red plastic grips and mag. bottom.

Add 150% for 9mm Para. cal. (rare).

Lugers: KDF, Interarms, Stoeger, & Recent Import

Note: Post-WWII Lugers have been manufactured by Mauser Werke in Oberndorf, W. Germany during the 1970s, and by both Stoeger Industries and Mitchell Arms (see separate listing under Mitchell Arms) in recent years. Earlier Mauser importation was by Precision Imports, Inc. located in San Antonio, TX and Interarms of Alexandria, VA (and so marked on these guns).

Prices for 100% condition Lugers assume NIB status. If without box and accessories, deduct 15%.

GRADING - PPGS™	100%	98%	95%	90%	80%	70%	60%	LAST MSR

INTERARMS MAUSER P.08 – 7.65mm Para. or 9mm Para. cal., 4 or 6 in. barrel, fully-contoured front grip strap.

	$1,500	$1,200	$900	$700	$600	$500	$400	

INTERARMS "SWISS-STYLE" MAUSER EAGLE – 7.65mm Para. or 9mm Para. cal., "straight" front grip strap, American eagle logo on top of frame.

	$1,200	$850	$700	$600	$500	$400	$350	

Add 10% for 6 in. barrel in 9mm Para. cal.

STOEGER .22 CAL. LUGER – .22 LR cal., toggle action, all steel or aluminum construction, 4 1/2 or 5 1/2 in. barrel, right or left-hand safety, 10 shot mag., previously mfg. in the U.S. until 1985.

	$295	$265	$225	$190	$145	$120	$100	*$200*

* ***Stoeger .22 Cal. Luger "1 of 1,000"*** – .22 LR cal., 1,000 mfg. in 1984-85, includes wooden box and extra mag.

	$375	$325	$250	N/A	N/A	N/A	N/A	

STOEGER LUGER – 9mm Para. cal., choice of 4 or 6 (Navy) in. barrel, stainless steel construction, choice of polished stainless or matte black (new 1996) upper frame finish, American eagle engraved on top of frame, curved front grip strap, 7 shot mag., plastic mag. bottom, approx. 30 oz. Mfg. 1994-disc.

	$750	$625	$475	$425	$375	$325	$295	*$720*

Add $79 for matte black finish.

NEW MODEL CARBINE WITH STOCK – 9mm Para. cal., authentic reproduction of the original Luger Carbine complete with matching stock, accessories, and case. Inventory was depleted during 1998.

	$8,000	$6,250	$5,000	N/A	N/A	N/A	N/A	*$7,431*

CARTRIDGE COUNTER – 9mm Para. cal., left grip is slotted and contains a numbered metal strip. Manufacture began 1983, and inventory was depleted during 1998.

	$4,000	$2,750	$2,000	N/A	N/A	N/A	N/A	*$3,865*

COMMEMORATIVE BULGARIAN – 7.65 Para. cal., 100 available on U.S. market.

	$2,500	$1,650	$1,250	N/A	N/A	N/A	N/A	

Add $200 for leather case.

COMMEMORATIVE RUSSIAN – 9mm Para. cal., 100 available on U.S. market.

	$2,900	$2,150	$1,500	N/A	N/A	N/A	N/A	

Add $200 for leather case.

* ***Commemorative Russian Matched pair of each***

	$5,000	$2,675	$1,950	N/A	N/A	N/A	N/A	

COMMEMORATIVE NAVY 75TH YEAR – 9mm Para. cal., complete with leather briefcase and accessories, 250 mfg., but Interarms only imported 10 pistols.

	$3,700	$3,000	$2,500	N/A	N/A	N/A	N/A	

MAUSER SPORT PARABELLUM – 7.65mm Para. or 9mm Para. cal., imported target barrel and adj. sights. 10 mfg. of each cal.

	$3,500	$2,500	$2,000	N/A	N/A	N/A	N/A	

* ***Mauser Sport Parabellum Consecutive Pair*** – 7.65mm Para. or 9mm Para. cal.

	$5,250	$4,500	$3,500	N/A	N/A	N/A	N/A	

Lugers: Special Interest

SPANDAU LUGER – be wary of originality on this model.

MO4/05 G.L. BABY LUGER – 7.65mm Para. or 9mm Para. cal., 3 1/4 in. barrel, G.L. proofed, hand made under Georg Luger's supervision, two known to exist. Made with shortened barrel, mag., and grip frame.

BABY LUGER 1925/26 – .380 ACP/.32 ACP cal., prototype, probably 4 mfg., only one known is .380. Only Luger documented by the manufacturer.

GRADING - PPGS™	100%	98%	95%	90%	80%	70%	60%	LAST MSR

VONO REWORK – 7.65mm Para. or 9mm Para. cal., 4 in. barrel, commercial, rework by W.P. Von Nordheim.

	$1,575	$1,350	$1,125	$950	$850	$725	$625	

1900 DWM CARBINE – 7.65mm Para. cal., 11 3/4 in. barrel, probably 100 mfg., only one known to exist. Characterized by "Ski slope" sight on rear toggle.

Extreme rarity precludes accurate pricing on this model.

1907 U.S. ARMY TEST TRIAL – .45 ACP cal., at least four originally mfg., serial numbered 1-4, plus an un-numbered prototype.

Extreme rarity precludes accurate pricing on this model. Undoubtedly, this is the most desirable semi-auto pistol ever manufactured, and would be priced accordingly.

CONVERSIONS: JOHN MARTZ – John Martz of Lincoln, CA has converted WWII P.38s (please refer to P.38 section) and WWI or WWII Lugers into various configurations since 1968. These conversions are known for their quality workmanship and functional accuracy. Below is a generalized listing of variations he has fabricated and their values to date with production totals.

* ***Conversions: John Martz .380 ACP Baby Luger*** – 6 fabricated, disc.

	$6,300	$3,375	$2,525	N/A	N/A	N/A	N/A	

* ***Conversions: John Martz 7.65mm Para. Baby Luger (Grip Safety)*** – 213 mfg. total, includes 9mm Baby Luger also.

	$3,150	$2,625	$2,000	N/A	N/A	N/A	N/A	

* ***Conversions: John Martz 9mm Para. Baby Luger*** – 2 1/4 (disc.), 2 1/2 (disc.), or 2 5/8 in. barrel.

	$3,150	$2,625	$2,100	N/A	N/A	N/A	N/A	

* ***Conversions: John Martz Big-Bore .45 ACP Luger*** – 89 fabricated (5 are babies), .45 ACP cal., fixed sights, 2 3/4, 4, 6, or 8 in. barrel. Disc.

	$5,775	$3,525	$2,525	N/A	N/A	N/A	N/A	

* ***Conversions: John Martz .45 ACP Luger Reproduction*** – made to original 1907 U.S. Army test trial specifications by Mike Krause (limited mfg.).

This variation typically sells in the $8,500-$12,500 range, depending on condition.

* ***Conversions: John Martz Navy Model*** – .45 ACP cal., 6 or 8 in. barrel, adj. rear Navy sight, estimated mfg. is 25 pistols, disc.

	$6,000	$4,675	$3,475	N/A	N/A	N/A	N/A	

Add 10% for Navy Model with 100-200 meter rear sight.

* ***Conversions: John Martz Navy Model Ltd. Edition*** – .38 Super cal., 6 in. barrel, adj. rear Navy sight, 10 fabricated, disc.

	$5,250	$4,150	$3,250	N/A	N/A	N/A	N/A	

Subtract 10% for fixed rear sight (standard model with 4 in. barrel).

* ***Conversions: John Martz Standard Model*** – .38 Super cal., 4 to 8 in. barrel, fixed sight, 3 fabricated.

	$4,500	$3,325	$2,525	N/A	N/A	N/A	N/A	

* ***Conversions: John Martz Target Luger*** – .22 WMR cal., 6 or 9 in. barrel, fixed sight, 11 fabricated, disc.

	$7,875	$5,675	$3,575	N/A	N/A	N/A	N/A	

* ***Conversions: John Martz Luger Carbines (with shoulder stock)*** – .22 WMR (disc.), 7.65mm Para., 9mm Para., or .38 Super cal., 11-18 in. barrel with adj. rear sights. Disc.

	$8,300	$5,950	$3,775	N/A	N/A	N/A	N/A	

Add 20% for .22 WMR cal. (2 fabricated).

83 Luger carbines with 16 in. barrels were fabricated with shoulder stocks.

42 Luger carbines with 12 in. barrels were fabricated w/o shoulder stocks.

* ***Conversions: John Martz Experimental Lugers*** – experimental pistols have been made in .40 S&W (disc.), .41 AE (disc.), .357 SIG (11 mfg., 7, 8, or 9 in. barrel) and .357 Mag. Most have 8 in. barrels (except for .40 S&W cal., disc.). Extreme rarity (and not for

GRADING - PPGS™	100%	98%	95%	90%	80%	70%	60%	LAST MSR

sale status) precludes accurate price evaluation.

The .357 SIG model had a retail price of $3,500.

LUGERS: ACCESSORIES

"SNAIL DRUM" CANVAS CARRIER/POUCH

	$2,000	$1,700	$1,450	$1,225	$1,050	$900	$750

"RADIUM" FILLED REMOVABLE FRONT SIGHT FOR ARTILLERY LUGER

	$2,000	$1,700	$1,450	$1,225	$1,050	$900	$750

Conversion Units - .22 cal.

ERMA – postwar-in green cardboard box.

	$950	$800	$725	$575	$475	$375	$325

ERMA-PREWAR IN WOODEN BOX

	$2,625	$2,325	$1,850	$1,500	$1,250	$1,050	$750

Add 50% for Nazi Navy property numbered. Subtract 20% for mismatched.

Detachable Stocks

ARTILLERY TYPE FLAT BOARD

	$650	$575	$525	$420	$325	$275	$250

ARTILLERY HOLSTER RIG, COMPLETE

	$3,200	$2,850	$2,250	$1,925	$1,625	$1,350	$1,125

Subtract 20% if shoulder strap is missing.

NAVAL-TYPE FLAT BOARD

	$2,850	$2,525	$2,000	$1,700	$1,450	$1,200	$975

NAVAL HOLSTER RIG, COMPLETE

	$5,625	$4,800	$4,250	$3,700	$2,850	$1,975	$1,575

Subtract 20% if shoulder strap is missing.

CARBINE CONTOURED (ORIGINAL)

	$4,650	$4,000	$3,400	$2,750	$1,875	$1,325	$1,100

IDEAL TELESCOPING WITH GRIPS mfg. in U.S. by Ideal Corp.

	$3,000	$2,800	$2,300	$1,600	$1,200	$850	$650

"Snail" Drum Magazines

1ST ISSUE – machined telescoping winder.

	$2,250	$2,000	$1,750	$1,500	$1,250	$1,000	$750

2ND ISSUE TYPE I – stamped hinged winder with no drum reinforcement rings.

	$2,000	$1,675	$1,425	$1,250	$1,000	$900	$725

2ND ISSUE TYPE II – stamped hinged winder with reinforcement rings.

	$1,700	$1,475	$1,275	$1,150	$900	$775	$650

LOADING TOOL

	$1,275	$1,100	$900	$800	$675	$575	$500

WWI – "Snail Drum" canvas carrier/pouch.

	$2,200	$1,700	$1,450	$1,225	$1,045	$900	$750

WWI "RADIUM" – "Radium" filled removable front sight for the artillery Luger.

	$2,000	$1,700	$1,450	$1,225	$1,045	$900	$750

SHOTGUNS: O/U

CLASSIC MODEL – see listing under Stoeger Industries, Inc. in the S section.

SHOTGUNS: SEMI-AUTO

ULTRA-LIGHT MODEL – see listing under Stoeger Industries, Inc. in the S section.

GRADING - PPGS™	100%	98%	95%	90%	80%	70%	60%	LAST MSR

LU-MAR s.r.l.

Previous shotgun manufacturer located in Gardone, Italy. Limited U.S. importation.

Lu-Mar made a wide variety of O/U shotguns. In addition to their fine O/U lineup, Lu-Mar also manufactured SxS shotguns. These guns had little or no importation into the U.S.

LUNA

Previous manufacturer located in Germany.

PISTOLS: SINGLE SHOT

MODEL 200 FREE PISTOL – .22 LR cal., 11 in. barrel, blue, target sights, checkered target grips, pre-WWII.

	100%	98%	95%	90%	80%	70%	60%	LAST MSR
	$1,100	$990	$855	$770	$660	$605	$525	

RIFLES: SINGLE SHOT

TARGET RIFLE – .22 LR or .22 Hornet cal., falling block action, 20 in. barrel, adj. sights, target type stocks, pre-WWII.

	100%	98%	95%	90%	80%	70%	60%	LAST MSR
	$990	$880	$800	$690	$605	$550	$495	

LUSA USA

Current manufacturer located in Hooksett, NH. Dealer and distributor sales.

CARBINES

Lusa USA manufactures a 9mm Para. cal. carbine with a 16 in. barrel in three configurations - the 94 LE (MSR $1,295), 94 SP89 Pistol (MSR $999), 94 SA (A2 Standard, MSR $999), the 94 PDW (side folding stock, MSR $1,099), and the 94 AWB (fixed stock, MSR $999-$1,099). Please contact the company directly for more information, including options and availability (see Trademark Index).

LUXUS

Current manufacturer and importer located in Mt. Orab, OH. Previously located in Milford, OH until 2010.

Luxus is well known for their premium Turkish walnut stocks. Luxus Products imports high quality double rifles, as well as SxS and O/U shotguns from Italy. Each gun is custom order, and delivery time is approximately one year. Luxus Arms manufactures a single shot Model 11 in calibers from .22 Hornet to .375 H&H. Base price is $2,995 and there are many options available. Please contact the company directly for an individual price quotation (see Trademark Index).

LYMAN

Current trademark of firearms, black powder reproductions, reloading supplies, and related accessories manufactured by Lyman-Pachmayr-Trius Products, and located in Middletown, CT.

REPRODUCTIONS: LITTLE SHARPS

LITTLE SHARPS – .17 HMR, .22 LR, .22 WMR, .22 Hornet, .218 Bee, .30-30 Win., .38-55 WCF, .44 Win., or .45 LC cal., 20% smaller version of the original Sharps rifle, 24, 26, or 32 in. octagon barrel, double set triggers, rear tang aperture sight, case colored frame, 5.9 lbs. Mfg. by Armi-Sport. Importation began 2011.

	100%	98%	95%	90%	80%	70%	60%	LAST MSR
MSR N/A	$1,150	$975	$850	$750	$575	$475	$400	

LYNX

Current trademark of bolt action rifles manufactured by Pirkan Ase Ltd., established in 1979, and located in Tampere, Finland. No current U.S. importation.

RIFLES: BOLT ACTION

Please contact the company directly for current availability and pricing on these models (see Trademark Index).

LYNX – available in standard or metric cals., features straight pull bolt system, variations include the Hunter with traditional checkered walnut stock, and the Target model with 10 shot mag. and thumbhole stock with adj. cheekpiece.

LYNX X.O./X.X.O. – various standard metric and Magnum (Model X.X.O.) cals., features 60 degree bolt, traditional styling, 3 shot mag.

M SECTION

M+M, INC.

Current importer and distributor located in Eastlake, CO.

GRADING - PPGS™	100%	98%	95%	90%	80%	70%	60%	LAST MSR

RIFLES: SEMI-AUTO

M10-762 RIFLE – 7.62x39mm cal., AK-47 design, 16 1/4 in. barrel, 30 shot mag., RPK graduated rear sight. Imported from Romania with six U.S. made parts and assembled in America.

No MSR	$625	$550	$495	$450	$400	$375	$350	

PISTOLS: SEMI-AUTO

SAN P553 – 5.56 NATO cal., upper receiver has Picatinny rail with integrated triangular hand guard, pistol grip, muzzle brake, 30 shot mag. Mfg. in Switzerland. Importation began 2013.

As this edition went to press, prices have yet to be established on this model.

MAB

Military MAB listings can be found under the French Military heading.

PISTOLS: SEMI-AUTO

MODEL R – 9mm Para. cal., blowback action, blue finish, rotating barrel, commercial mfg., approx. 1,000 mfg., some imported by Western Arms Co.

	$550	$495	$450	$400	$350	$300	$250	

MAC (METROARMS CORP.)

Current trademark of pistols imported and distributed by Eagle Imports, located in Wanamassa, NJ. Please see listings under the MetroArms Corporation section.

MAC (MILITARY ARMAMENT CORP.)

Please refer to FMJ and Ingram sections in this text. MAC was located in Ducktown, TN.

MAG CUSTOM RIFLES

Current custom rifle manufacturer located in Brescia, Italy.

Vittorio Giani, the owner of Manifattura Armi Giani (MAG) specializes in custom order bolt action rifles, as well as SxS rifles and shotguns. All guns are built per customer specifications. Please contact him directly for more information, including an individualized price quotation and delivery time (see Trademark Index).

MAS

Previously manufactured by D'Armes St. Etienne (MAS) located in France.

Please refer to the French Military heading in this text.

MBA ASSOCIATES

Previous manufacturer circa 1966-1969 located in San Ramon, CA.

PISTOLS: SEMI-AUTO

MARK I GYROJET PISTOL (ROCKETEER AUTOMATIC ROCKET) – 12mm or 13mm cal., caseless, uses spin-stabilized rocket projectiles that accelerate to 1,250 FPS in .12 seconds, 2 in. (rare) or 5 in. barrel, 6 shot semi-auto action drives rocket projectile (primer activated) into fixed firing pin, smooth walnut grips, black, antique nickel, or gold-plated finish, 13 or 16 oz., "A" prefix until ser. no. 49, "B" prefixes followed, there are also other variations and experimental models in addition to the production models listed. Without rifling, this gun wasn't particularly accurate.

The rocket ammunition for this model is rare and typically sells in the $30-$35/round range per shell.

* ***Mark I Gyrojet Pistol Model A Cased*** – 13mm, black finish, smooth walnut grips, walnut cased with 10 rounds and medal.

	$2,495	$2,150	$1,800	$1,400	$1,125	$950	$875	

Add 20% if gold plated and marked "experimental".

GRADING - PPGS™	100%	98%	95%	90%	80%	70%	60%	LAST MSR

* ***Mark I Gyrojet Pistol Model B Cased*** – 13mm, black, nickel, satin, or green finish, many variations with different grips, casings, and barrel lengths, wood cased, includes 10 dummy rounds and bronze medal honoring rocket pioneers Robert H. Goddard and Joseph J. Stubbs.

	$2,195	$1,825	$1,500	$1,250	$975	$850	$725	

Add approx. 25% for satin finish.

* ***Mark I Gyrojet Pistol Model B Uncased or Cardboard*** – either with cardboard case or no case, black finish.

	$1,500	$1,050	$850	$750	$625	$500	$400	

* ***Mark II Gyrojet Pistol Model C Uncased or Cardboard*** – 12mm, black finish, walnut grips.

	$1,500	$1,050	$850	$750	$625	$500	$400	

This variation was manufactured in 12mm to conform with the 1968 GCA, since any caliber over .50 was classified as a destructive device (i.e., 12mm = .49 cal. and 13mm =.51 cal.). In 1982, the 13mm guns were reclassified as curios and relics.

RIFLES: SEMI-AUTO, CARBINES

MARK I MODEL A or B CARBINE – 13mm cal., same action as Mark I pistol, black (Model A, AR-15 type "space gun") or satin (Model B) finish, full stock with pistol grip extension, 18 in. barrel, nickel finish, 4 1/2 lbs. Limited mfg.

Model A	$3,500	$3,000	$2,650	$2,250	$1,850	$1,700	$1,475	
Model B	$2,895	$2,000	$1,700	$1,425	$1,150	$950	$850	

MG ARMS INCORPORATED

Current manufacturer established in 1980, and located in Spring, TX. MG Arms Incorporated was previously named Match Grade Arms & Ammunition. Consumer direct sales.

REVOLVERS

CUSTOM BIG 5 – .45 LC+P, .454 Casull, .475 Linebaugh, .50 AE, or .500 Linebaugh cal., Ruger frame, stainless 5 shot cylinder, custom barrels, standard finish or optional camo coverage. Mfg. 2000-2007.

	$1,175	$975	$875	$775	$700	$625	$525	*$1,295*

MG Arms also offered a conversion package for $795 (customer supplies Ruger revolver).

DRAGON SLAYER – .44 Mag., .44 Colt, .454 Casull, .50 AE (disc. 2011), .475 Linebaugh, .500 Linebaugh, .445 Super Mag. (disc. 2011), .450 Marlin (disc. 2011), .460 S&W Mag. (disc.), or .500 S&W Mag. (disc. 2011) cal., single action, 5 shot, stainless steel construction, choice of grips, includes 20 rounds of custom loaded ammo, 2 1/2 lb. trigger. Mfg. 2008-2011, reintroduced 2013.

MSR $1,895	$1,675	$1,350	$1,100	$950	$825	$725	$625	

DRAGONFLY – .32 H&R Mag., .38 Spl., .44 Colt, or .44 Mag. cal., SA, finely tuned trigger, corrosion resistant PTFE metal finish (customer choice of color pattern), choice of cowboy (quick draw) or target (backpacking) configuration. Mfg. 2010-2011.

	$995	$875	$750	$625	$525	$450	$375	*$1,095*

RIFLES: BOLT ACTION

ULTRA-LIGHT MODEL – various cals., lightened and skeletonized Wby. Vanguard (disc. 2004) or Rem. 700 (new 2005) action, MGA button rifled barrel, Teflon metal finish, epoxy stock with Pachmayr decelerator pad, Super Eliminator muzzle brake, variety of camo finishes on stock, 5 1/2 lbs.

MSR $3,795	$3,475	$3,100	$2,875	$2,450	$2,075	$1,750	$1,425	

Add $200 for Win. M70 action (disc. 2006).

VARMINTER – various cals., squared and lapped Rem. M700 action, stainless steel National Match barrel with Super Eliminator muzzle brake, black Teflon metal finish, camo epoxy stock.

MSR $2,895	$2,625	$2,300	$2,000	$1,650	$1,325	$1,050	$925	

GRADING - PPGS™	100%	98%	95%	90%	80%	70%	60%	LAST MSR

SIGNATURE CLASSIC – various cals., Nesika Hunter action, Hart stainless steel barrel with Super Eliminator muzzle break, Jewell trigger, fiberglass or claro walnut stock. Limited mfg. (approx. 10 guns per year) beginning 2000.

MSR $6,195	$5,750	$5,300	$4,700	$4,150	$3,650	$3,000	$2,450	

MGA SILVER EDITION – various cals., Model 7015 action, match grade #3 taper barrel, tuned trigger, 20 oz. fiberglass stock, PTFE metal finish. Mfg. 2009-2010.

	$2,450	$2,200	$1,925	$1,700	$1,500	$1,300	$1,050	*$2,635*

BANSHEE – various cals., blueprinted Rem. action, cryogenically treated stainless steel National Match barrel, 5 or 10 shot detachable mag., 2 1/2 lb. custom trigger, Varmint weight fully adj. or lightweight non-adj. for Banshee Lite, includes Picatinny scope base. New 2012.

MSR $3,095	$2,850	$2,500	$2,150	$1,825	$1,650	$1,375	$1,075	

RIFLES: SEMI-AUTO

K-YOTE VARMINT SYSTEM – various cals. from .17 Rem. - .458 Lott, AR-15 style, target trigger, stainless match grade free floating barrel, standard or camo finish four rail aluminum hand guard, adj. stock, A3 flattop upper receiver, machined lower receiver, scope rail. New 2009.

MSR $3,695	$3,450	$3,100	$2,850	$2,550	$2,300	$2,250	$1,995	

CK-4 – .223 Rem. or .300 Fireball cal., AR-15 style, MGA 3-piece lower receiver, A3 flat-top receiver, 5 position collapsible stock, 16 in. barrel with flash hider, free floating quad rail handguard, choice of PTFE resin finish, basic, or camo coverage. New 2011.

MSR $1,795	$1,600	$1,475	$1,275	$1,075	$950	$800	$625	

TARANTS – 5.56 NATO cal., AR-15 style, 16 in. lightweight match grade tapered barrel with titanium flash hider, upper receiver with flat top Picatinny rail, carbon fiber handguard, CTR 6-position collapsible stock, 20 or 30 shot mag., PTFE resin, basic, or zebra camo finish. New 2013.

MSR $1,995	$1,800	$1,625	$1,375	$1,125	$975	$825	$650	

PISTOLS: SEMI-AUTO

WRAITHE – .45 ACP cal., M1911 design, 4 1/2 in. match grade barrel, choice of fixed or night sights, 3 1/2 lb. trigger, custom grip panels, choice of Olive Drab, Black, Desert Tan, or titanium finish. New 2013.

MSR $2,595	$2,300	$2,050	$1,775	$1,400	$1,150	$925	$850	

MGI

Current rifle manufacturer located in Old Town, ME. Previously located in Bangor, ME until late 2010.

RIFLES: SEMI-AUTO

The MARCK-15 (Hydra) is a completely modular paramilitary AR-15 rifle, consisting of a quick change barrel upper receiver and a modular lower with interchangeable magazine wells, and current cartridge offerings include .22 LR, .223 Rem., 5.56 NATO, 7.62x39mm, 6.8 SPC, 6.5 Grendel, .204 Ruger, .450 Thumper, .458 Socom, and .50 Beowulf cal. No tools are required, and it utilizes standard barrels. MSR on the MARCK base gun in 5.56 NATO cal. is $1,299. A wide variety of configurations are available. During 2012, MGI modified the Hydra to accept Glock 9mm Para., .40 S&W, and .45 ACP cal. magazines. Additionally, MGI also manufactures a belt fed MARCK-15 - current MSR is $4,499. Please contact the company directly for more information, including available options and pricing (see Trademark Index).

M-K SPECIALTIES INC.

Previous rifle manufacturer circa 2000-2002 located in Grafton, WV.

RIFLES: SEMI-AUTO

M-14 A1 – .308 Win. cal., forged M-14 steel receiver using CNC machinery to original government specifications, available as Rack Grade, Premier Match, or Tanker Model,

GRADING - PPGS™	100%	98%	95%	90%	80%	70%	60%	LAST MSR

variety of National Match upgrades were available at extra cost, base price is for Rack Grade. Mfg. 2000-2002.

	$1,475	$1,275	$995	$875	$750	$625	$500	*$1,595*

National Match upgrades ranged from $345-$955.

MK ARMS INC.

Previous manufacturer located in Irvine, CA circa 1992.

CARBINES

MK 760 – 9mm Para. cal., paramilitary design carbine configuration, steel frame, 16 in. shrouded barrel, fires from closed bolt, 14, 24, or 36 shot mag., parkerized finish, folding metal stock, fixed sights. Mfg. 1983-approx. 1992.

	$725	$650	$575	$525	$475	$415	$375	*$575*

MKE

Current manufacturer located in Ankara, Turkey. No current U.S. importation. Previously imported beginning 2011 by American Tactical Imports, located in Rochester, NY. Previously distributed by Mandall Shooting Supplies, Inc., located in Scottsdale, AZ.

MKE manufactures a wide variety of military and law enforcement models, in addition to a line of consumer semi-auto hunting rifles and a semi-auto pistol. Please contact the importer directly for more information, including pricing and availability (see Trademark Index).

PISTOLS: SEMI-AUTO

KIRIKKALE AUTOMATIC – 7.65mm Para. (disc.) or .380 ACP cal., double action, 7 shot, blue, fixed sights, checkered plastic grips. Disc. 1987.

	$365	$295	$240	$215	$185	$170	$155	*$395*

This model is a close copy of Walther's PP and the Turkish Army's standard service pistol.

AT-94P – 9mm Para. cal., MP5 style, 16.4 in. barrel, matte black finish, roller delayed blowback system, 30 shot mag. Imported 2011-2012.

	$1,395	$1,200	$1,000	$850	$700	$600	$525	*$1,596*

AT-94K – 9mm Para. cal., MP5 style, roller delayed blowback system, 4 1/2 in. barrel, matte black finish, 30 shot mag., open sights. Imported 2011-2012.

	$1,395	$1,200	$1,000	$850	$700	$600	$525	*$1,596*

RIFLES/CARBINES: SEMI-AUTO

AT-94R2 CARBINE – 9mm Para. cal., 16.4 in. barrel, patterned after H&K Model 94, roller delayed blowback action, A2 style MP5 stock, steel receiver, matte black finish, 10 shot detachable box mag. Imported 2011-2012.

	$1,350	$1,125	$900	$800	$700	$600	$500	*$1,550*

AT-43 RIFLE – .223 Rem. cal., 17 in. barrel, patterned after H&K Model 93, roller delayed blowback action, A2 style fixed stock, steel receiver, matte black finish, 30 shot detachable box mag. Imported 2011-2012.

MSR $1,495	$1,300	$1,075	$875	$775	$675	$575	$475	

MKS SUPPLY, INC.

Marketing company representing various companies including Chiappa Firearms Ltd. and Hi-Point Firearms. MKS firearms are manufactured by Chiappa Firearms Ltd. located in Dayton, OH.

RIFLES

MKS Supply, Inc. currently offers the following rifles: Aimpro Tactical 590 A1 with choice of 18 1/2 or 20 in. barrel with Hogue standard stock, and TacStar side saddle - MSRs are $897 and $945, Aimpro Tactical 590 A1 Breacher - MSR $868, and the Aimpro Tactical 590 A1 Elite with holographic sight and other accessories - MSR $1,495. Please contact the company directly for more information and availability (see Trademark Index).

GRADING - PPGS™	100%	98%	95%	90%	80%	70%	60%	LAST MSR

M.O.A. CORPORATION

Current manufacturer located in Sundance, WY since 2005. Previously located in Eaton, OH. Dealer direct sales only.

PISTOLS: SINGLE SHOT

Approx. 500-600 Maximum pistols are produced annually. Allow 4-6 months for delivery.

MAXIMUM – available in 30 standard chamberings between .22 Rimfire and .454 Casull cal., additional custom calibers are also available upon special order, single shot lever action pistol, falling block action, Chromoly receiver (disc. 1991), Armoloy coated Chromoly (disc. late 1992), or stainless steel (new 1991, standard 1992) receiver, 8 3/4 (new 1989), 10 1/2, or 14 in. interchangeable barrel, transfer bar safety, adj. open sights, walnut grips and forearm. New 1986.

MSR $865	$740	$650	$550	$450	$400	$375	$350	

Subtract 10% for older steel receiver.
Add $60 for scope mounts.
Add $101 for stainless steel barrel on either receiver.
Add $125 for muzzle brake.
Add $269 per extra steel barrel.
Add $336 per extra stainless steel barrel.

Barrels must be fitted to individual receivers at the factory initially. Afterwards, they can be changed by the customer with the spanner wrench (included with extra barrels).

* ***Maximum Carbine Model*** – cals. up to .250 Sav., stainless receiver, otherwise similar to Maximum, except has 18 in. blue barrel. Mfg. began 1986, and production has been disc. several times.

	$925	$850	$750	$650	$575	$525	$475	*$1,023*

M.R. NEW SYSTEM ARMS

Current designer and handgun manufacturer located in Cerrione, Italy. No current U.S. importation.

FIREARMS

Inventor and designer Marco Rigido manufactures a Mauser Model 92 carbine in both standard/Mag. cals. (€3,500), or a Safari Model in African calibers (€6,000). He also manufactures both SxS and O/U express rifles with either boxlock or sidelock action. Boxlocks start at €4,000, and the sidelock in Africa cals. is POR. Other products include both O/U and SxS shotguns with prices starting at €2,500 (O/U boxlock).

Perhaps his most famous guns are the 5 shot SA Model Cucciolo in .728 MR cal. (€30,000) and both a single shot pistol and rifle chambered for 1.000 caliber, the largest caliber ever offered for consumers. Please contact the company directly for more information, including U.S. availability and pricing (see Trademark Index).

MTs ARMS

Current trademark manufactured by Sporting and Hunting Guns Central Design and Research Bureau, a subsidiary of the State Unitary Enterprise, Instrument Design Bureau, (GUP "KBP" - "TsKIB SOO"), located in Tula, Russia. No current U.S. importation.

MTs Arms manufactures a variety of firearms, including SxS and O/U shotguns, combination guns, self-loading shotguns, slide action shotguns, bolt action rifles, drillings, competition guns, and semi-auto rifles. TsKIB SOO is the only manufacturer of quality hunting guns in Russia and the countries of the CIS (Commonwealth of Independent States). Please contact the company directly for more information regarding this trademark and current domestic availability (see Trademark Index).

JAMES MacNAUGHTON & SONS

Current trademark owned and manufactured by Dickson & MacNaughton, located in Edinburgh, Scotland.

GRADING - PPGS™	100%	98%	95%	90%	80%	70%	60%	LAST MSR

The firm of James MacNaughton was founded in Edinburgh, Scotland in 1864. During 1947, the company was acquired by John Dickson and during 1996, the ownership of the company changed again, having purchased the manufacturing rights from Dickson. In 1999, the directors of James MacNaughton & Sons acquired the whole share capital of John Dickson & Son, and the two companies now trade as one under the name of Dickson & MacNaughton. Please contact Dickson & MacNaughton directly for more information regarding this trademark, including current availability and pricing (see Trademark Index).

RIFLES: SxS

SIDELOCK RIFLE – .375 H&H or .470 NE cal., specifications per individual customer order.

Please contact the manufacturer directly regarding domestic availability and pricing.

SHOTGUNS

SxS SIDELOCK MODEL – 20 or 28 ga., lightweight construction.

Please contact the manufacturer directly regarding domestic availability and pricing.

MAADI-GRIFFIN CO.

Previous rifle manufacturer located in Mesa, AZ until 2003. Consumer direct sales.

RIFLES: SEMI-AUTO

MODEL MG-6 – .50 BMG cal., gas operated, bullpup configuration, one piece cast lower receiver, 5, 10, or 15 shot side mounted mag., 26-30 in. barrel, includes bipod, hard carrying case, and 3 mags. 23 lbs. Mfg. 2000-2003.

100%	98%	95%	90%	80%	70%	60%	LAST MSR
$5,500	$4,750	$3,850	$3,250	$2,600	$2,200	$1,800	*$5,950*

Add $450 for MK-IV tripod.

RIFLES: SINGLE SHOT

MODEL 89 – .50 BMG cal., one piece cast lower receiver, 36 in. barrel, felt recoil is less than 12 ga., tig-welded interlocking assembly, no screws, tripod optional, 22 lbs. Mfg. 1990-2003.

100%	98%	95%	90%	80%	70%	60%	LAST MSR
$3,100	$2,750	$2,400	$2,050	$1,775	$1,500	$1,250	*$3,150*

Add $600 for stainless steel.

MODEL 92 CARBINE – .50 BMG cal., 20 in. barrel, 5 lbs. trigger pull, 18 1/2 lbs. Mfg. 1990-2003.

100%	98%	95%	90%	80%	70%	60%	LAST MSR
$2,950	$2,550	$2,225	$1,875	$1,650	$1,400	$1,200	*$2,990*

Add $650 for stainless steel.

MODEL 99 – .50 BMG cal., similar to Model 89, except has 44 in. barrel, 28 lbs. Mfg. 1999-2003.

100%	98%	95%	90%	80%	70%	60%	LAST MSR
$3,150	$2,725	$2,450	$2,050	$1,775	$1,500	$1,250	*$3,350*

Add $650 for stainless steel.

MAGNUM RESEARCH, INC.

MAGNUM RESEARCH, INC.

Current trademark of pistols and rifles with company headquarters located in Blauvelt, NY beginning 2010, with manufacturing facilities located in Pillager, MN, and by I.W.I. (Baby and Desert Eagle Series), located in Israel. During June of 2010, Kahr Arms purchased the assets of Magnum Research, Inc. Desert Eagle Series was manufactured 1998-2008 by IMI, located in Israel. Previously manufactured by Saco Defense located in Saco, ME during 1995-1998, and by TAAS/IMI (Israeli Military Industries) 1986-1995. .22 Rimfire semi-auto pistols (Mountain Eagle) were previously manufactured by Ram-Line. Single shot pistols (Lone Eagle) were manufactured by Magnum Research sub-contractors. Distributed by Magnum Research, Inc., in Minneapolis, MN. Dealer and distributor sales.

MRI CUSTOM SHOP

In addition to the standard models listed, Magnum Research can also provide a variety of special order options through their custom shop, including many choices of Desert Eagle finishes, in addition to various sight systems and grips.

MRI's current custom shop Desert Eagle (not Baby Eagle) finish options with MSRs (vary slightly depending on caliber) with 6 in. barrels are as follows: Polished hard chrome (PC) - MSR is $1,838-$1,912, matte chrome (MC) - MSR - $1,838-$1,912, brushed hard chrome (BC) - MSR

GRADING - PPGS™	100%	98%	95%	90%	80%	70%	60%	LAST MSR

- $1,838-$1,912, black chrome - disc. 2007, MSR was $1,949, bright nickel (BN) - MSR is $1,838-$1,912, satin nickel (SN) - MSR is $1,838-$1,912, polished blue (PB) - disc. 2010, last MSR was $1,838, or gold accents - disc. 2010, last MSR was $274, 24Kt. gold (GO) finish, titanium gold finish (TG, new 2000), titanium gold with tiger stripes (new 2005, .50 AE cal. only), or titanium carbon nitride (TCN, mfg. 2002-2010) - MSR is $2,070-$2,153.

PISTOLS: SEMI-AUTO, RIMFIRE

THE MOUNTAIN EAGLE – .22 LR cal., single action, 6 (new 1995) or 6 1/2 (disc. 1994) in. polymer and steel barrel, features alloy receiver and polymer technology, matte black finish, adj. rear sight, 15 or 20 shot mag. 21 oz. Mfg. 1992-96.

$185	$155	$135	$115	$100	$85	$75	*$239*

* ***The Mountain Eagle Compact Edition*** – similar to Mountain Eagle, except has 4 1/2 in. barrel with shortened grips, adj. rear sight, 10 or 15 shot mag., plastic case, 19.3 oz. Mfg. 1996 only.

$165	$135	$120	$105	$95	$80	$70	*$199*

* ***The Mountain Eagle Target Edition*** – .22 LR cal., Target variation of the Mountain Eagle, featuring 8 in. accurized barrel, 2-stage target trigger, jeweled bolt, adj. sights with interchangeable blades, 23 oz. Mfg. 1994-96.

$235	$185	$150	$135	$120	$105	$95	*$279*

PICUDA MLP-1722 – .17 Mach 2 or .22 LR cal., 10 in. graphite barrel, no sights, features MLR-22 frame, choice of laminated nutmeg, forest camo, or pepper colored Barracuda stock, integral scope base, target trigger, 10 shot mag., approx. 3 lbs. Mfg. 2007-2009.

$595	$525	$450	$400	$350	$300	$250	*$699*

PISTOLS: SEMI-AUTO, CENTERFIRE

IMI SP-21 – 9mm Para., .40 S&W, or .45 ACP cal., DA or SA, traditional Browning operating system, polymer frame with ergonomic design, 3.9 in. barrel with polygonal rifling, 10 shot mag., finger groove grips, 3 dot adj. sights, reversible mag. release, multiple safeties, matte black finish, decocking feature, approx. 29 oz. Limited importation from IMI late 2002-2005.

$475	$395	$335	$300	$280	$260	$240	*$499*

The IMI SP-21 uses the same magazines as the Baby Eagle pistols. This model is referred to the Barak SP-21 in Israel.

PISTOLS: SEMI-AUTO, CENTERFIRE - EAGLE SERIES

Magnum Research also offers a Collector's Edition Presentation Series. Special models include a Gold Edition (serial numbered 1-100), a Silver Edition (serial numbered 101-500), and a Bronze Edition (serial numbered 501-1,000). Each pistol from this series is supplied with a walnut presentation case, 2 sided medallion, and certificate of authenticity. Prices are available upon request by contacting Magnum Research directly.

Alloy frames on the Desert Eagle Series of pistols were discontinued in 1992. However, if sufficient demand warrants, these models will once again be available to consumers at the same price as the steel frames.

Beginning late 1995, the Desert Eagle frame assembly for the .357 Mag., .44 Mag., and .50 AE cals. is based on the .50 caliber frame. Externally, all three pistols are now identical in size. This new platform, called the Desert Eagle Pistol Mark XIX Component System, enables .44 Mag. and .50 AE conversions to consist of simply a barrel and a magazine - conversions to or from the .357 Mag. also include a bolt.

The slide assembly on the Mark I and Mark VII is physically smaller than the one on a Mark XIX. Also, the barrel dovetail on top is 3/8 in. on a Mark I or Mark VII, while on a Mark XIX, it is 7/8 in., and includes cross slots for scopes.

Individual Desert Eagle Mark XIX 6 in. barrels are $389-$564, depending on finish, and 10 in. barrels are $459-$634, depending on finish. Add $129 for Trijicon night sights (new 2006). Add $49-$89 for Hogue Pau Ferro wooden grips (new 2007) or $49 for Hogue soft rubber grips with finger grooves (disc. 2008).

GRADING - PPGS™	100%	98%	95%	90%	80%	70%	60%	LAST MSR

MR9/MR40 EAGLE – 9mm Para. or .40 S&W cal., striker fire design, fully adj. rear sight, 4 (9mm Para. cal.) or 4.15 (.40 S&W cal.) in. barrel, interchangeable palm swells, 10, 11(.40 S&W cal.), or 15 (9mm Para. cal.) shot mag., lower Picatinny rail, internal safeties, square trigger guard, cooperative manufacturing effort with Carl Walther supplying the black polymer frame with integral steel rails, while the stainless steel slide and barrel are manufactured and assembled in Pillager, MN, approx. 25 oz. New 2011.

MSR $559	$475	$425	$375	$325	$295	$275	$250	

MICRO DESERT EAGLE – .380 ACP cal., 2.2 in. barrel, DAO, blue or nickel Teflon finish, 6 shot mag., fixed sights, aluminum alloy frame, steel slide, oversized trigger guard, checkered black grips, 14 oz. New 2009.

MSR $467	$425	$375	$325	$275	$250	$225	$195	

Add $12 for nickel finish or nickel frame with blue slide and barrel (new 2010).

THE BABY EAGLE – 9mm Para., .40 S&W, .41 AE (disc.), or .45 ACP (3.7 in. barrel only, new 2000) cal., double action, all steel or polymer (3.5 or 3.7 in. barrel, 9mm Para. or .40 S&W only) frame construction, 3.5 (new 2000), 3.62 (mfg. 1993-99), 3.7 (new 2000), or 4.52 in. barrel, short recoil operation, polygonal rifling, combat styled trigger guard, decocking slide safety or frame mounted safety (Model 9mmF), blued (disc. 1995), standard black (new 1996), or chrome (disc. 1999) finish, 10 (C/B 1994), 13 (.40 S&W only, new 2005), 16* (9mm Para., disc.), 11* (.41 AE), or 15 (9mm Para. only, new 2005) shot mag., shipped with two magazines beginning 2006, 38 1/2 oz. Imported 1991-96. Reintroduced mid-1999-2007.

* ***The Baby Eagle Full Size*** – 9mm Para. or .40 S&W cal., 4.52 in. barrel, steel frame only. Disc. 2007.

	$465	$385	$320	$275	$235	$210	$190	*$569*

Add $239 for conversion kit (9mm Para. to .41 AE or .41 AE to 9mm Para., includes barrel, spring, and mag.), disc. 1996.

This model was also available in various optional finishes, including brushed or polished chrome - MSR was $804, titanium gold - MSR was $1,069, or titanium carbon nitride - MSR was $1,069.

* ***The Baby Eagle Semi-Compact*** – 9mm Para, .40 S&W, or .45 ACP cal., same general specifications as Baby Eagle, except has 3.7 in. barrel, .45 ACP not available in polymer, 36 oz. (steel) or 29 oz. (polymer). Disc. 2007.

	$465	$385	$320	$275	$235	$210	$190	*$569*

This model was also available in brushed or polished chrome finish - MSR was $804, titanium gold or titanium nitride - MSR was $1,069.

* ***The Baby Eagle Compact*** – 9mm Para. or .40 S&W cal., same general specifications as Baby Eagle, except has 3 1/2 in. barrel, 10 or 12 (9mm Para. only) shot mag., 27 oz. (polymer) or 34 oz (steel). Disc. 2007.

	$465	$385	$320	$275	$235	$210	$190	*$569*

This model was also available in brushed chrome finish - MSR was $804.

THE BABY EAGLE II – 9mm Para., .40 S&W, or .45 ACP cal., 10, 12, or 15 shot mag., similar specs as the Baby Eagle, except has improved rear sight and Picatinny rail, choice of black polymer or steel frame, black, brushed chrome, or custom finishes. Mfg. by I.W.I. in Israel. New 2008.

* ***The Baby Eagle II Full Size*** – 9mm Para., or .40 S&W cal., 4 (mfg. 2010 only), 4.2 (mfg. 2010 only), or 4.52 in. barrel with ergonomic rear sight and lower Picatinny rail, 25 oz. New 2008.

MSR $630	$550	$475	$425	$375	$325	$275	$225	

Add $235 for brushed or polished chrome (disc. 2009).
Add $500 for titanium gold (disc. 2009).
Subtract $14 for polymer frame.

* ***The Baby Eagle II Semi-Compact*** – 9mm Para., .40 S&W, or .45 ACP cal., similar to Baby Eagle II Full Size, except has 3.7 (disc.), or 3.93 (new 2011) in. barrel with ergonomic rear sight and lower Picatinny rail. Importation began 2008 by I.W.I.

MSR $630	$550	$475	$425	$375	$325	$275	$225	

Add $235 for brushed or polished chrome (disc. 2009).
Subtract $14 for polymer frame.

GRADING - PPGS™	100%	98%	95%	90%	80%	70%	60%	LAST MSR

* ***The Baby Eagle II Compact*** – 9mm Para. cal. only, similar to Baby Eagle II Semi-Compact, except has 3.64 in. barrel w/o Picatinny rail. Importation began 2008 by I.W.I.

MSR $630	$550	$475	$425	$375	$325	$275	$225	

Add $235 for brushed chrome (disc. 2009).
Subtract $14 for polymer frame.

MARK I DESERT EAGLE .357 MAG – .357 Mag. cal., similar to Mark VII, except has standard trigger and safety lever is teardrop shaped, and slide catch release has single serration. Disc.

	$925	$825	$725	$625	$525	$450	$400	

MARK XIX .357 MAG. DESERT EAGLE – features .50 cal. frame and slide, standard black finish, 6 or 10 (disc. 2011) in. barrel, full Picatinny top rail with fixed sights became standard late 2009 (U.S. mfg.), 4 lbs., 6 oz. Mfg. by Saco 1995-98, by IMI 1998-2009, and domestically beginning 2010.

MSR $1,563	$1,350	$1,125	$875	$775	$650	$550	$475	

Add $87 for 10 in. barrel (disc. 2011).

As this edition went to press, Magnum Research announced that this model would not be available again until the first quarter of 2013.

MARK VII .357 MAG. DESERT EAGLE – .357 Mag. cal., gas operated, 6 (standard barrel length), 10, or 14 in. barrel length with 3/8 in. dovetail rib, steel (58.3 oz.) or alloy (47.8 oz.) frame, adj. trigger, safety lever is hook shaped, slide catch/release lever has three steps, adaptable to .44 Mag. with optional kit, 9 shot mag. (8 for .44 Mag.). Mfg. 1983-95, limited quantities were made available again during 1998 and 2001.

	$1,100	$1,000	$875	$750	$650	$550	$475	*$929*

Add approx. $150 for 10 or 14 in. barrel (disc. 1995).
Add $495 for .357 Mag. to .41 Mag./.44 Mag. conversion kit (6 in. barrel). Disc. 1995.
Add approx. $685 for .357 Mag. to .44 Mag. conversion kit (10 or 14 in. barrel). Disc. 1995.

* ***Mark VII .357 Mag. Desert Eagle Whitetail Special*** – 14 in. barrel, includes scope mount, target walnut grips, and Desert Eagle premiums. Mfg. 1990-92.

	$1,175	$1,050	$900	$775	$650	$550	4475	*$1,088*

Add $50 for stainless steel frame.

* ***Mark VII .357 Mag. Desert Eagle Stainless Steel*** – similar to .357 Mag. Desert Eagle, except has stainless steel frame, 58.3 oz. Mfg. 1987-95.

	$1,100	$1,000	$875	$750	$650	$550	$475	*$839*

Add approx. $150 for 10 or 14 in. barrel.

MARK VII .41 MAG. DESERT EAGLE – .41 Mag. cal., similar to .357 Desert Eagle, 6 in. barrel only, 8 shot mag., steel (62.8 oz.) or alloy (52.3 oz.) frame. Mfg. 1988-95, limited quantities available during 2001.

	$1,050	$975	$850	$725	$625	$525	$475	*$899*

Add $395 for .41 Mag. to .44 Mag. conversion kit (6 in. barrel only).

* ***Mark VII .41 Mag. Desert Eagle Stainless Steel*** – similar to .41 Mag. Desert Eagle, except has stainless steel frame, 58.3 oz. Mfg. 1988-95.

	$1,100	$1,000	$875	$750	$650	$550	$475	*$949*

MARK I DESERT EAGLE .44 MAG – .44 Mag. cal., similar to Mark VII, except has standard trigger and safety lever is teardrop shaped, and slide catch release has single serration. Disc.

	$1,200	$1,075	$925	$775	$675	$575	$495	

MARK XIX .44 MAG. DESERT EAGLE – features .50 cal. frame and slide, standard black finish, 6 or 10 in. barrel, full Picatinny top rail with fixed sights became standard late 2009 (U.S. mfg.), 4 lbs., 6 oz. Mfg. by Saco 1995-98, by IMI 1998-2009, domestically by CCI beginning 2009, and by I.W.I. beginning 2012.

MSR $1,534	$1,350	$1,125	$875	$775	$650	$550	$475	

Add $116 for 10 in. barrel.
Add $29 for U.S. mfg.
Add $199 for black muzzle brake (limited mfg. 2010 only).

GRADING - PPGS™	100%	98%	95%	90%	80%	70%	60%	LAST MSR

MARK VII .44 MAG. DESERT EAGLE – .44 Mag. cal., similar to .357 Desert Eagle, 8 shot mag., steel (62.8 oz.) or alloy (52.3 oz.) frame. Originally mfg. 1986-95, re-released 1998-2000.

	$1,100	$1,000	$875	$750	$650	$550	$475	*$1,049*

Add $100 for 10 (current) or 14 (disc. 1995) in. barrel.
Add $475 for .44 Mag. to .357 Mag. conversion kit (6 in. barrel). Disc. 1995.
Add $675 for .44 Mag. to .357 Mag. conversion kit (10 or 14 in. barrel). Disc. 1995.
Add $395 for .44 Mag. to .41 Mag. conversion kit (6 in. barrel). Disc. 1995.

* ***Mark VII .44 Mag. Desert Eagle Stainless Steel*** – similar to .44 Mag. Desert Eagle, except has stainless steel frame, 58.3 oz. Mfg. 1987-95.

	$1,175	$1,050	$900	$775	$675	$575	$475	*$949*

Add approx. $210 for 10 or 14 in. barrel.

HUNTER EDITION MARK VII – .357 or .44 Mag. cal., 6 in. barrel with extra 14 in. hunting barrel, includes Leupold 2X EER scope, scope mount. Mfg. late 1987-93.

	$1,200	$975	$825	$675	$550	$475	$425	*$1,350*

Add $110 for .44 Mag. cal.

MARK VII .50 MAG. DESERT EAGLE – .50 AE cal., 6 in. barrel with 7/8 in. rib with cross slots for Weaver style rings, steel only, black standard finish, frame slightly taller than the Mark VII .357 Mag./.44 Mag., 7 shot mag., 72.4 oz. Mfg. 1991-95 by IMI, limited quantities were made available again during 1998 only.

	$1,175	$950	$825	$700	$575	$500	$450	*$1,099*

This cartridge utilized the same rim dimensions as the .44 Mag. and was available with a 300 grain bullet. The .50 Action Express cal. has 20%-25% more stopping power than the .44 Mag., with a minimal increase in felt recoil.

MARK XIX CUSTOM 440 – .440 Cor-Bon cal., similar to Mark XIX .44 Mag. Desert Eagle, 6 or 10 in. barrel, standard black finish, rechambered by MRI Custom Shop, limited mfg. 1999-2001.

	$1,175	$995	$850	$725	$575	$500	$450	*$1,389*

Add $40 for 10 in. barrel.

MARK XIX .50 MAG. DESERT EAGLE – .50 AE cal., larger frame, standard black finish, 6 or 10 in. barrel, full Picatinny top rail with fixed sights became standard late 2009 (U.S. mfg.), 4 lbs., 6 oz. Mfg. by Saco 1995-98, by IMI (1998-2008 disc.), I.W.I. (new 2009), and CCI in the U.S. beginning 2010.

MSR $1,563	$1,350	$1,125	$875	$775	$650	$550	$475	

Add $120 for 10 in. barrel.
Add $31 for domestic mfg.
Add $240 for muzzle brake (black finish, 6 in. barrel only).
Add $199 for black muzzle brake (mfg. 2010 only), or $623 for muzzle brake with brushed chrome finish (new 2011).

MARK XIX 3 CAL. COMPONENT SYSTEM – includes Mark XIX .44 Mag. Desert Eagle and 5 barrels including .357 Mag. (6 and 10 in.), .44 Mag., and .50 AE (6 and 10 in.) cals., .357 bolt assembly and ICC aluminum carrying case. Also available in custom finishes at extra charge. Mfg. 1998-2011.

	$3,900	$3,450	$2,800	$2,400	$2,000	$1,750	$1,500	*$4,402*

* ***Mark XIX 3 Cal. Component System (6 or 10 in. Barrel)*** – includes component Mark XIX system in 6 or 10 in. barrel only. Mfg. 1998-2011.

	$2,550	$2,225	$1,775	$1,500	$1,250	$1,000	$850	*$2,910*

Add $262 for 10 in. barrel (disc. 2011).

MODEL 1911 DESERT EAGLE – .45 ACP cal., 4.3 or 5 in. barrel, SA, 8 shot mag., black oxide finish, double diamond checkered wood grips, fixed sights, grip safety, extended thumb safety, 36.2 oz. New 2010.

MSR $874	$750	$650	$595	$550	$495	$450	$395	

Add $350 for .22 LR conversion kit (disc 2011).

GRADING - PPGS™	100%	98%	95%	90%	80%	70%	60%	LAST MSR

PISTOLS: SINGLE SHOT

LONE EAGLE (SSP-91) – .22 LR (disc. 1992), .22 WMR (disc. 1992), .22 Hornet, .22-250 Rem., .223 Rem., .243 Win., .260 Rem. (new 1997), .30-30 Win., .30-06, .300 Win. Mag. (Ltd. ed., mfg. 1997-99), .308 Win., 6mmBR (disc. 1992), 7mm-08 Rem., 7mmBR, .35 Rem., .357 Max. (disc. 1997, reintroduced 2001), .358 Win., .44 Mag., .440 Cor-Bon (new 1999), .444 Marlin, or 7.62x39mm (new 1996) cal., circular rear breech action, quick change 14 in. barrels (drilled and tapped), black or chrome (new 1997) finish, black synthetic Valox ambidextrous pistol grip, 4 lbs. 3 oz.-4 lbs. 7 oz. Mfg. 1991-2001.

	100%	98%	95%	90%	80%	70%	60%	LAST MSR
	$380	$315	$275	$230	$200	$185	$170	*$438*

Add $40 for chrome finish.
Add $35 for adj. hunting sights.
Add $129 for adj. silhouette sights by RPM.
Add $319 for standard black finish barrel, $418 for standard barrel with muzzle brake, $359 for chrome barrel, and $469 for chrome barrel with muzzle brake.

The grip assembly ($119) and barreled actions were available individually on this model.

REVOLVERS

BFR LONG CYLINDER – .30-30 Win. (new 2004), .444 Marlin, .45 LC/.410 bore, .450 Marlin (mfg. 2002-2012, 10 in. barrel only), .45-70 Govt., .460 S&W Mag. (new 2006), or .500 S&W Mag. (new 2003) cal., single action, 5 shot, stainless steel, various barrel lengths, checkered rubber grips, 4 - 4.36 lbs. New 1999.

	100%	98%	95%	90%	80%	70%	60%	LAST MSR
MSR $1,050	$950	$825	$725	$650	$550	$450	$350	

This model was originally advertised as the BFR Maxine, then was changed to BFR (Biggest Finest Revolver).

BFR SHORT CYLINDER – .22 Hornet (disc. 2011), .44 Mag. (new 2010), .45 LC+P (disc. 2001), .454 Casull, .475 Linebaugh (disc. 2011), .480 Ruger (new 2002), or .50 AE (disc. 2001, reintroduced 2004, disc. 2011), .500 JRH (limited mfg. 2012 only) cal., similar to BFR Model, various barrel lengths, 3.2-4.36 lbs. New 1999.

	100%	98%	95%	90%	80%	70%	60%	LAST MSR
MSR $1,050	$950	$825	$725	$650	$550	$450	$350	

This model was originally advertised as the BFR Little Max, then was changed to BFR (Biggest Finest Revolver).

RIFLES: BOLT-ACTION

MOUNTAIN EAGLE RIFLE – .223 Rem. (new 2000), 270 Win., .280 Rem., .30-06, 7mm STW (mfg. 1998-99), .300 Win. Mag., .300 Wby. Mag., .338 Win. Mag., .340 Wby. Mag. (disc. 1997), 7mm Rem. Mag., .375 H&H, or .416 Rem. Mag. cal., Sako action, adj. trigger, 4 or 5 shot mag., match grade Krieger barrel with cut rifling, H-S Precision composite stock with aluminum bedding block, includes carrying case. Mfg. 1994-2000.

	100%	98%	95%	90%	80%	70%	60%	LAST MSR
	$1,325	$1,075	$900	$775	$625	$550	$495	*$1,499*

Add $200 for muzzle brake.
Add $50 for left-hand action.
Add $300 for .375 H&H or .416 Rem. Mag. cal.

* ***Mountain Eagle Rifle Varmint*** – .222 Rem. or .223 Rem. cal., 26 in. stainless steel heavy fluted barrel, w/o sights, approx. 9 3/4 lbs. Mfg. 1996-2000.

	100%	98%	95%	90%	80%	70%	60%	LAST MSR
	$1,425	$1,100	$925	N/A	N/A	N/A	N/A	*$1,629*

MOUNTAIN EAGLE MAGNUM LITE – .223 Rem. (varmint only), .22-250 Rem. (varmint only), .280 Rem., .30-06, .300 Win. Mag., .300 WSM (new 2003), 7mm WSM (new 2003), or 7mm Rem. Mag. cal., custom-built Rem. short action or Sako (disc.) action with one-piece forged bolt, adj. trigger, 24 in. sport tapered or 26 in. varmint bull graphite barrel with stainless steel liner, no sights, black swirl H-S Precision Kevlar graphite or Hogue overmolded (7mm WSM or .300 WSM only) stock, 4 or 5 shot mag, approx. 7 1/4 lbs. Mfg. 2001-2011.

	100%	98%	95%	90%	80%	70%	60%	LAST MSR
	$1,925	$1,700	$1,400	$1,100	$825	$700	$575	*$2,173*

Magnum Lite graphite barrels are available in 3 configurations for $599 (disc. 2011).

GRADING - PPGS™	100%	98%	95%	90%	80%	70%	60%	LAST MSR

MOUNTAIN EAGLE TACTICAL RIFLE – .223 Rem. (new 2002), .22-250 Rem. (new 2002), .308 Win., .300 Win. Mag., or .300 WSM (new 2002) cal., accurized Rem. M-700 action, 26 in. Magnum Lite barrel, H-S Precision tactical stock, adj. stock and trigger, 9 lbs., 4 oz. Mfg. 2001-2011.

	$2,150	$1,825	$1,475	$1,150	$850	$700	$575	*$2,475*

Add $96 for any cal. other than .300 WSM (disc. 2011).

MAGNUM LITE 77 – .17 HMR cal., features 22 in. graphite barrel. Mfg. 2006-2008.

	$875	$750	$625	$500	$400	$325	$250	*$999*

RIFLES: SEMI-AUTO

Magnum Lite .22 graphite barrels are also available individually starting at $269. For the .17 Mach 2 barrel a bolt kit is also included. MLR 17/22 barrels will also fit Ruger 10/22 rifles.

Add $140 for Clark custom upgrade (includes Clark deluxe trigger kit, tuned extractor, and bolt release) on the models listed (not available in .17 HMR cal., disc. 2006).

MAGNUM LITE RIFLE – .17 HMR (mfg. 2004-2009), .17 Mach 2 (mfg. 2005-2010), .22 LR or .22 WMR (new 2000) cal., features Ruger 10/22 WMR (.17 HMR or .22 WMR only beginning 2006) or one-piece Model 17/22 MLR receiver featuring large bolt handle machined from solid billet of aluminum (available in .22 LR or .17 Mach 2 cal.), with Acculite (disc.) or graphite (new 1999) barrel utilizing uni-directional graphite carbon fiber with stainless steel liner, barrel weighs 13 oz. New 1997.

* ***Magnum Lite Rifle Standard Stock*** – choice of walnut (mfg. 2006-2009), black Hogue Overmolded or Fajen high stock (disc. 1999) in either midnight or coffee color, 4.3 (.22 LR cal.) or 5.4 (.22 WMR cal.) lbs. with Hogue stock. New 1997.

MSR $665	$595	$525	$450	$400	$360	$330	$295	

Add $126 for .22 WMR or .17 HMR (disc. 2009) cal.
Add $159 for walnut stock (only available in .17 Mach 2 or .22 LR cal., Model 17/22, disc. 2009).

* ***Magnum Lite Rifle w/Fajen Thumbhole Stock*** – features choice of Fajen thumbhole sporter or thumbhole silhouette in midnight or coffee color. Mfg. 1997-99.

	$625	$525	$450	$395	$360	$330	$275	*$699*

Add $100 for thumbhole silhouette stock configuration.

* ***Magnum Lite Rifle w/Barracuda Stock*** – features skeletonized sporter stock with thumbhole, choice of green (disc.), nutmeg (new 2006), forest camo (new 2006), pepper (new 2006) or coffee (disc.) laminate, choice of blued, red (disc. 2009), or blue (disc. 2009) anodized receiver, 4.4 (.22 LR cal.) or 5.4 (.22 WMR) lbs. New 1997.

MSR $819	$725	$650	$550	$485	$440	$395	$325	

Add $116 for .17 HMR (disc. 2009) or .22 WMR cal. (Model 10/22 only).
Add $40 for red or blue anodized receiver (.17 Mach 2 or .22 LR cal. only, disc. 2009).

* ***Magnum Lite Rifle w/Graphite Ambidextrous Thumbhole Stock*** – .22 LR cal., black synthetic ambidextrous thumbhole stock only. New 2012.

MSR $599	$525	$450	$395	$360	$330	$300	$275	

MAGNUM HEAVY VARMINT – .17 HMR (disc. 2009) or .22 WMR cal., choice of blued steel (disc. 2010) or stainless steel barrel, choice of Hogue overmolded stock or Barracuda with skeletonized sporter stock. New 2008.

MSR $727	$640	$565	$480	$425	$375	$325	$275	

Add $179 for Barracuda forest camo (disc. 2010), nutmeg (disc. 2010), or pepper colored laminate skeletonized stock.

MAGTECH

Current importer and distributor of CBC (Companhia Brasileria de Cartuchos) ammunition located in Centerville, MN. Previously located in Madison, CT 1999-2001 and in Las Vegas, NV until 1999. Magtech previously imported firearms manufactured by CBC located in Brazil.

RIFLES

MODEL 7022 SEMI-AUTO – .22 LR cal., Ruger 10/22 style action, 10 shot, 18 in. barrel,

GRADING - PPGS™	100%	98%	95%	90%	80%	70%	60%	LAST MSR

choice of hardwood or synthetic stock. New 2001.

	$120	$100	$85	$75	$70	$65	$60	

MODEL 122 BOLT ACTION – .22 LR cal., 6 shot detachable mag., safety lever disconnects trigger from firing mechanism, uncheckered hardwood stock, 5.7 lbs. Imported 1992 only.

	$115	$95	$80	$70	$60	$50	$40	*$131*

SHOTGUNS

MODEL 151 SINGLE SHOT – 12, 16, 20 ga., or .410 bore, 26, 28, or 30 in. barrel, exposed hammer, ejector, front trigger guard opening mechanism, some plastic used for buttons, levers, and bushings, 5-6 1/2 lbs. Imported 1992 only.

	$95	$80	$70	$60	$50	$40	$35	*$109*

MODEL 199 – 12, 16, 20, 28 ga., or .410 bore, all steel construction, exposed hammer with underlever opening, unique hammer/firing pin safety, 24 or 28 in. barrel, uncheckered Brazilian stock and forearm, recoil pad supplied on Youth Models (20 ga. or .410 bore only), New 2001.

	$100	$85	$75	$70	$65	$60	$55	

MODEL MT-586-2 SLIDE ACTION – 12 ga. only, 3 in. chamber, standard Field model shotgun, 28 in. barrel with fixed chokes, hardwood stock and forearm, double slide bars. Imported 1993-95.

	$190	$175	$160	$140	$130	$120	$110	*$229*

The Model MT-586 preceded the MT-586-2. The MT-586 was disc. 1994.

* ***Model MT-586-2-VR Slide Action*** – similar to Model MT-586, except has choice of 26 or 28 in. VR barrel with interchangeable chokes. Imported 1993-95.

	$220	$185	$170	$155	$140	$130	$120	*$259*

MODEL MT-586 SLIDE ACTION SLUG – 12 ga. only, slug gun featuring 24 in. cylinder bore barrel with rifle sights, matte finished metal parts, and special Monte Carlo stock. Imported 1993-95.

	$195	$180	$165	$145	$130	$120	$110	*$239*

MODEL MT-586-2P – 12 ga. only, 3 in. chamber, slide action, 19 in. cylinder bore barrel, 7 shot mag., double slide bars, steel construction, hardwood stock, 7.3 lbs. Imported 1992-96.

	$185	$170	$155	$140	$130	$120	$110	*$219*

MAJESTIC ARMS, LTD.

Previous firearms manufacturer established during 2000, and located on Staten Island, NY. The company now produces firearms components, conversion kits, and accessories.

CARBINES: SEMI-AUTO

MA 2000 – .22 LR cal., Henry Repeating Arms Co. AR-7 takedown action, fiberoptic sights, American walnut forearm, pistol grip, and buttplate, fixed tubular stock with butt bag, 16 1/4 in. Lothar Walther barrel with crown, black teflon or silver bead blast finish, 4 lbs. Mfg. 2000-2008.

	$350	$295	$250	$225	$195	$175	$150	*$389*

MA 4 – .17 HMR, .17 Mach 2 (new 2005), .22 LR (new 2005), or .22 WMR cal., takedown action, traditional or wire frame stock, interchangeable barrel/bolt assembly.

While intially advertised during 2004 with a MSR of $399, this model did not go into production past the prototype stage.

SHOTGUNS: SLIDE ACTION

BASE-TAC – 12 or 20 ga., 3 in. chamber, based on M870 Remington action, approx. 18 in. barrel with ghost ring sights, black synthetic (12 ga.) or hardwood stock and forearm, extended 6 shot tube mag., 6-7 lbs. Mfg. 2004-2010.

	$675	$575	$500	$450	$400	$350	$300	*$759*

Add $30 for 20 ga.

GRADING - PPGS™	100%	98%	95%	90%	80%	70%	60%	LAST MSR

MAKAROV

Pistol design originating from the former Soviet Union. Russian manufactured Makarovs may be found under the "Russian Service Pistol and Rifle" heading in this text. Pistols listed have recently been imported by various companies, including Century International Arms, Inc. located in St. Albans, VT.

PISTOLS: SEMI-AUTO

MAKAROV COPIES – 9mm Makarov cal., patterned after the Soviet PM pistol, mfg. in eastern Germany, Czechoslovakia, Bulgaria, and China, double action, blowback design, all steel, slide mounted safety that doubles as a decocking lever, 3.6 in. barrel, 8 shot mag., 25 oz.

No MSR	$185	$145	$125	$105	$95	$85	$75	

Add approx. $35-$40 for polished blue or silver matte finish (Bulgarian mfg. only).

The importation of this type of pistol increased beginning 1992.

MALIN, F.E.

Previous manufacturer located in England. Previously imported by Saxon Arms, Inc. located in Clearwater, FL. Charles Boswell purchased Malin shortly before manufacture stopped.

SHOTGUNS: SxS, CUSTOM

BOXLOCK – made to individual order, choice of game scene engraving, Anson & Deeley boxlock actions, select European hybrid walnut, double triggers, leather cased.

Prices started at $3,750 and each shotgun was priced per individual special order.

SIDELOCK – made to individual order, choice of game scene engraving, H&H sidelock action, select European hybrid walnut, double triggers, leather cased.

Prices started at $5,000 and each shotgun was priced per individual special order.

MAMBA

Previously manufactured by Viper Mfg. Co. (a division of Sandock Austral Boksburg) located in South Africa.

PISTOLS: SEMI-AUTO

AUTO PISTOL – 9mm Para. cal., double action, 5 in. barrel, 14 shot mag., designed in Rhodesia, manufacture was not successful due to the non-hardened steel used in the investment cast construction process, poor exterior finish, less than 80 imported into the U.S., and 25 prototypes were built for Navy Arms.

Rarity factor precludes accurate pricing and values vary greatly in different regions.

MANCHESTER ARMS INC.

Previous manufacturer located in Lenoir, TN.

PISTOLS: SEMI-AUTO

COMMANDO MARK 45 – .45 ACP cal., paramilitary type design with detachable mag., wood pistol grip, 5 in. barrel with muzzle brake. Disc.

	$600	$525	$450	$395	$350	$300	$265	

MANDALL SHOOTING SUPPLIES, INC.

Previous importer, distributor, and retailer located in Scottsdale, AZ.

Mandall Shooting Supplies distributed and imported various firearms including pistols, revolvers, rifles, and shotguns, as well as other models.

MANIFATURRA ARMI ART

Current longarm manufacturer located in Gardone, Italy. Currently imported beginning 2004 by William Larkin Moore & Co., located in Scottsdale, AZ.

Denis Fontana from Manifattura Armi Art manufactures high quality custom long guns, including rifles and shotguns. Guns may be marked "Art Armi" or "Denis Fontana". Please contact the importer (see Trademark Index) directly for more information, including availability and pricing.

GRADING - PPGS™	100%	98%	95%	90%	80%	70%	60%	LAST MSR

Currently imported models include a SxS Anson & Deeley boxlock action with rose and scroll engraving, a H&H type sidelock SxS shotgun with choice of H&H or Purdey style engraving, bolt action rifle in small and large calibers, and a SxS sidelock rifle in .375 H&H, .470 NE, or .500 NE cal., with rose and scroll engraving. All models are POR. Please contact the importer directly for more information, including pricing and delivery time (see Trademark Index).

MÄNNEL SPORT SHOOTING GmbH

Current rifle and airgun manufacturer located in Kronstorf, Austria. No current U.S. importation.

Männel manufactures the ASB (advanced small bore) target rifle noted for its almost infinite amount of adjustments, including the forearm, stock, and trigger guard, in addition to a target air pistol. Please contact the manufacturer directly for pricing and U.S. availabilty (see Trademark Index).

MANNLICHER PISTOLS

Previously manufactured in Austria and Switzerland starting circa 1894.

PISTOLS: SEMI-AUTO

MODEL 1894 – 6.5mm or 7.6mm cal., unique blow forward design, fewer than 100 mfg. by Fabrique d' Armes in Neuhausen Switzerland, and OWGS, Austria.

$19,500 $17,500 $15,000 $12,500 $10,000 $7,500 $6,000

Add 20% for 7.6mm cal.

MODEL 1897 – 7.63mm Mannlicher cal., first Mannlicher pistol with detachable mag. (matching), unique cocking lever on right frame, approx. 1,000 mfg.

$9,500 $8,000 $6,500 $5,000 $4,000 $3,500 $3,000

Add 150% for Model 1896 prototype in similar configuration, but with fixed mag.
Add 100% for extended barrel version with adj. sight and detachable shoulder stock.
Subtract 15% for rifle (carbine).

MODEL 1899 – 7.63 Mannlicher cal., rear sight mounted on barrel, large safety lever on left frame, approx. 300 mfg.

$8,500 $7,000 $5,500 $4,500 $4,000 $3,500 $3,000

MODEL 1901 – 7.63 Mannlicher cal., rear sight mounted on barrel, safety on rear of right slide, approx. 1,000 mfg.

$6,000 $4,500 $3,500 $2,750 $2,250 $1,750 $1,250

MODEL 1905 – 7.63 Mannlicher cal., final and most common variation.

$3,500 $2,500 $1,500 $1,000 $750 $650 $550

ARGENTINE MODEL 1905 – 7.65mm cal., Argentine crest on right panel is usually machined off. Values assume matching numbers but removed crest.

$900 $800 $700 $600 $500 $400 $300

*** *Argentine Model 1905*** – with Original Military Crest.

$4,500 $3,500 $3,000 $2,500 $2,000 $1,500 $1,000

MANNLICHER SCHOENAUER SPORTING RIFLES

Originally manufactured by Oesterreich Waffenfabrik Gesellschaft Steyr in Steyr, Austria from 1900 until the occupation of Austria by Germany in 1938. The current manufacturer is Steyr-Mannlicher, also of Steyr, Austria. Products made from 1968 to date are listed under Steyr-Mannlicher current production. Please refer to the Steyr-Mannlicher section.

Only a few sporting rifles were produced during the war period and were marked "Made in Germany". Production started agin in 1950 with serial number 1 until 1973 with serial number 61154. The last rifle was manufactured in 7x64 cal.

RIFLES: BOLT ACTIONS, PRE-WWII

The M1924 is properly known as the "Sequoia Importing Co." model because of a San Francisco company that ordered 1,000 units in .30-06 cal. for sale in the U.S. Apparently, these rifles did not

GRADING - PPGS™	100%	98%	95%	90%	80%	70%	60%	LAST MSR

sell well, and several of them were returned to Steyr where they were re-stamped 7.62x63mm cal. on the receiver ring. By 1933, Sequoia listed the .30-06 as the M1925 indicating that the changeover must have taken place rapidly. Meanwhile, the Steyr Company began chambering the basic M1924 action in six assorted calibers (7x57, 7x64, .30-06, 8x60S, 9.3x62, and 10.75x68) and marketing the improved rifle as the M1925. This was in addition to their continued production of the M1903, M1905, M1908, and M1910, and other chamberings were available on special order.

Starting with the M1925, Steyr began to engrave the caliber on the receiver ring, as it is standard in all Post WWII models. A Mannlicher-Schoenauer with the caliber engraved upon the barrel has been rebarreled by a European gunsmith and reproved by the local proof authority.

A proper Mannlicher-Schoenauer will have either no caliber marking on the receiver, as caliber was assigned via model only, or that caliber will be engraved upon the receiver ring as the final line in the description. For example, KAL 7x64. If the caliber is engraved or stamped upon the barrel only, the rifle was rebarreled by a gunsmith.

Add approx. 25% for all takedown pre-war models.

MODEL 1900 – 6.5x54mm Mannlicher Schoenauer cal., bolt handle with round knob, carbine, rifle, and takedown rifle configurations.

N/A	$2,750	$2,300	$1,975	$1,750	$1,500	$1,225

MODEL 1903 CARBINE – 6.5x54mm Mannlicher Schoenauer cal., 5 shot, 17.7 in. barrel, rotary mag., two leaf rear sight, double set trigger, full length stock.

N/A	$2,750	$2,300	$1,975	$1,750	$1,500	$1,225

This caliber may also be referred to as 6.5x53mm. This model is normally encountered in poor condition.

The Greek government ordered over 100,000 M1903 rifles, and many of these have been modified to a sporting configuration. These converted guns can be difficult to differentiate from true commercial Model 1903s, and values above are for original sporting carbines.

MODEL 1903 RIFLE – 6.5x54mm Mannlicher Schoenauer cal., 5 shot, various barrel lengths up to 23 inches, otherwise similar to Carbine.

N/A	$2,500	$2,200	$1,950	$1,750	$1,500	$1,225

Full stocked rifles may be encountered.

The Greek government ordered over 100,000 M1903 rifles, and many of these have been modified to a sporting configuration. These converted rifles can be difficult to differentiate from true commercial Model 1903s, and values above are for original sporting rifles.

MODEL 1905 CARBINE – similar to Model 1903, except 9x56mm Mannlicher Schoenauer cal., 19.7 in. barrel, flat butterknife bolt handle.

N/A	$1,900	$1,625	$1,275	$975	$850	$725

This model is normally encountered in poor condition. It is perhaps the least desirable of pre-war models because of the wide variation in bore diameters.

MODEL 1905 RIFLE – similar to Model 1905 Carbine, except available in various barrel lengths up to 25 inches, flat butterknife bolt handle, also available in take down configuration.

N/A	$1,900	$1,625	$1,275	$975	$850	$725

MODEL 1908 CARBINE – 8x56mm Mannlicher Schoenauer cal., 5 shot rotary mag., 19.7 in. barrel, two leaf rear sight, double set or single trigger, full length stock, flat butterknife bolt handle.

N/A	$1,900	$1,625	$1,275	$975	$850	$725

This model is frequently noticed in better condition factors. Some exceptional takedown variations also exist within this model.

MODEL 1908 RIFLE – similar to Model 1908 Carbine, except available in various barrel lengths up to 24 inches, flat butterknife bolt handle, also available in take down configuration.

N/A	$1,575	$1,300	$1,025	$875	$725	$600

GRADING - PPGS™	100%	98%	95%	90%	80%	70%	60%	LAST MSR

MODEL 1910 CARBINE – 9.5x57mm Mannlicher-Schoenauer (.375 Rimless Nitro Express or 9.5x57mm Mauser cal.), 7x57mm, 8x57mm, and other custom calibers, 19.7 in. barrel, 5 shot rotary magazine, two leaf rear sight, double set trigger, full length stock.

	N/A	$1,800	$1,575	$1,225	$950	$850	$725	

MODEL 1910 RIFLE – 9.5x57mm Mannlicher-Schoenauer cal., similar to 1910 Carbine, except available in various barrel lengths up to 26 inches.

	N/A	$1,575	$1,300	$1,025	$875	$725	$600	

Fully stocked rifles may be encountered.

MODEL 1925 (HIGH VELOCITY SPORTING RIFLE) – .30-06, 7x64mm, 8x60mm, 9.3x62mm, or 10.75x68mm cal., 23.6 in. barrel, three leaf rear sight, half stock, double set or single trigger.

	N/A	$2,200	$1,850	$1,625	$1,350	$1,195	$975	
10.75x68mm cal.	N/A	$4,500	$4,000	$3,600	$3,200	$2,750	$2,000	

Fully stocked rifles may be encountered.

This model was referred to as the Model 1925 in Europe. The difference is that the Model 1925 has the caliber engraved on the receiver ring, and the Model 1924 does not.

RIFLES: BOLT ACTION, POST-WWII-1971 MFG.

Values represent standard models with no engraving. Original engraving will add at least $500-$1,500 to prices listed with some heavily engraved Premier & Alpine models selling for large premiums. A variation of the 1950-1952 Series is called the "GK" because of its traditionally styled European stock, which is a variant of the pre-war style and approaches the design of the Model 1951 MCA. Of the calibers listed for post-WWII models, the 6.5x54mm is considered one of the most desirable, as well as the 9.3x62mm.

In 1951, Steyr (at Stoeger's request) made the following changes to the Model 1950 (named Improved Model 1950). These include: an ebony tip and fuller forend, left-side dummy plate cuts for side mount, left side of receiver was flattened to facilitate side scope mount, and flatter bolt handle requiring slot inside of stock.

In 1952, changes included a carved cheekpiece, change from 3/4 in. sling swivels to 1 in., swept back bolt handle, wood on left-side of stock over the dummy sideplate cutout thickened to strengthen the stock with a side mount in place, and removal of loading ears and clip guides, thereby streamlining the receiver and enabling lower scope mounting.

At one time Stoeger listed 18 versions of the M1950-52 family, defined as #S-1 through #S-18, with three major differences existing within each block of Model 1950, Improved Model 1950, and Model 1952. The differences were: single and double set triggers (DST), rifle or carbine style, 6.5mm Carbine, single trigger, or DST. The "GK" stock design was available as a special order variant during the entire post WWII production run.

From the M1950 through the improved M1952, these rifles were in continuous change and parallel production, thus rifles can be found with 1950 characteristics and proofmarks as late as 1954. Some examples are found with "nonstandard" markings such as "Model 1952" and no reference to the "Improved" standard. After mid-1965, U.S. market rifles were drilled and tapped for the Redfield scope mount. Some rifles were chambered for 8x57mm and 7x64mm.

During 1952-55, a small amount of Deluxe and Super Deluxe Mannlicher-Schoenauer were manufactured. These are typically encountered with better grade wood and model nomenclature is the same as the standard guns.

A method of differentiating Mannlichers made for the European market versus the U.S. market is by looking at the bolt. A blued bolt usually indicates a European market piece, while a polished bolt indicates a U.S. market piece. This is a usual identification; however, it is not always correct. A Stoeger logo on the floorplate is definite U.S. market proof.

Post World War II catalogs often list 6.5mm and 7mm as available calibers, but the actual calibers offered from the factory were 6.5x54mm, 6.5x55mm, 6.5x57mm, 7x57mm, and 7x64mm.

Add approx. 35% for 6.5x54mm, 9.3x62mm, .257 Roberts, or .244 Remington cal.

GRADING - PPGS™	100%	98%	95%	90%	80%	70%	60%	LAST MSR

MANNLICHER-SCHOENAUER MAGNUM RIFLE – .257 Wby. Mag., 6.5x68mm, .264 Win. Mag., 8x68mm, 9.3x64mm, .338 Win. Mag., or .458 Win. Mag., similar to Model 1956 MC, except has straight bolt handle, 5 shot rotary mag., 22 in. barrel with half stock, double set or single trigger.

	N/A	$4,000	$3,500	$2,700	$2,250	$1,800	$1,600	

MODEL 1950 RIFLE – .270 Win., .30-06, 6.5x54mm, or 9.3x62mm Mauser, bolt action, 5 shot rotary mag., 24 in. barrel, straight style bolt handle, double or single set trigger, half stock.

	$2,150	$1,700	$1,300	$1,000	$850	$725	$600	

MODEL 1950 CARBINE – 6.5x54mm cal., similar to Model 1950, except has 18 1/4 in. barrel and full length stock.

	$2,250	$1,800	$1,350	$1,050	$900	$750	$600	

IMPROVED MODEL 1952 RIFLE – .257 Roberts, .270 Win., .30-06, or 9.3x62mm cal., 24 in. barrel, 5 shot rotary mag., rear angled bolt handle, double set or single trigger, half stock.

	$2,000	$1,725	$1,300	$1,050	$900	$750	$600	

IMPROVED MODEL 1952 CARBINE – .257 Roberts, 6.5x54mm, .270 Win., 7x57mm, .308 Win. (new 1953), or .30-06 cal., 18.25 (6.5x54mm cal. only) or 20 in. barrel, rear angled bolt handle, double or single trigger.

	$2,000	$1,725	$1,300	$1,050	$900	$750	$600	

MODEL 1956 MC RIFLE – .243 Win., 6.5x55mm, 6.5x57mm, 7x57mm, 7x64mm, 8x57mm, 8x60mm, 9.3x62mm, .244 Rem, .257 Rob, .270, .280, .308, .30-06, .358 WCF, or .30-06 cal., similar to Model 1952, high comb stock design, 5 shot rotary mag., 22 in. barrel, half length stock, double set or single trigger. Mfg. 1956-1961.

	$2,000	$1,725	$1,300	$1,050	$900	$750	$600	

Add 20%-30% for advertised special order calibers such as 8x57mm, 7x64mm, and 9.3x64mm, depending on original condition.

MODEL 1956 MC CARBINE – .243 Win., 6.5x54mm, .257 Roberts, 6.5x55mm, 6.5x57mm, 7x64mm, 8x57mm, 8x60mm, .244 Rem, .280 Rem., 7x57mm, .270 Win., .30-06, .308 Win., or .358 Win. cal., similar to Model 1956 MC Rifle, except has 20 in. barrel with full stock, double set or single trigger. Mfg. 1956-1961.

	$2,000	$1,725	$1,300	$1,050	$900	$750	$600	

Add 20%-30% for advertised special order calibers such as 8x57mm, 7x64mm, and 9.3x64mm, depending on original condition.

MODEL 1961 MCA RIFLE – .243 Win., .270 Win., or .30-06 cal., similar to Model 1956 Rifle, except has Monte Carlo stock, 5 shot rotary mag., 22 in. barrel with half stock, double set or single trigger. Mfg. 1961-1971.

	$1,800	$1,425	$1,100	$925	$750	$650	$550	

Subtract $250 for models with plastic tang safety.

MODEL 1961 MCA CARBINE – .243 Win., 6.5x54mm, .270 Win., .30-06, 7x57mm, .308 Win., or .358 Win. (rare) cal., 20 in. barrel with full stock, similar to Model 1956 Carbine, except has Monte Carlo stock. Mfg. 1961-1971.

	$2,000	$1,725	$1,300	$1,050	$900	$750	$600	

Subtract $250 for models with plastic tang safety.

During production, the European market included the Model NO (Model MC/MCA) with GK stock and a straight pre-war bolt handle, produced in metric calibers such as 6.5x55mm Swedish, 7x64mm, and 8x57mm.

PREMIER/CUSTOM MODELS – 8x57mm or 7x64mm cal., these models were available from 1956 to 1968 and featured custom engraving of the metalwork and stock woodcarving. Some versions were also made for the market and such adornments were provided per the craftsmen at Steyr. These usually included individual engraved animal insets on the floor plate, receiver ring, and trigger guard, woodcarving in the oak leaf style, and wild animal figures on the butt stock. Gold inlays were available as well as monograms. All of these rifles offered single or double set triggers, and Steyr factory scope mounts, which

GRADING - PPGS™	100%	98%	95%	90%	80%	70%	60%	LAST MSR

were also engraved. Over a dozen standard engraving designs were offered for these rifles in any chambering.

	$6,500	$6,250	$5,750	$5,250	$4,750	$4,300	$3,995

ALPINE MODEL – .243 Win. or .30-06 cal., an MCA-1961 variant, offered between 1965 and 1968 as a version between the standard Mannlicher-Schoenauer and the Premier. It featured an engraved bolt handle and tasteful oak leaf carving on the pistol grip and fore end. The Alpine was offered in carbine length only.

	$4,000	$3,650	$3,250	$2,875	$2,500	$2,250	$2,000

RIFLES: BOLT ACTION, CURRENT PRODUCTION 1972-PRESENT

Current production guns are now called Steyr-Mannlicher models and can be located under this trademark in the S section.

MANU-ARM

Current rifle and airgun manufacturer located in Veauche, France. No current U.S. importation.

Manu-Arm manufactures good quality utilitarian .22 cal. bolt action and semi-auto rifles, in addition to an O/U in 9mm Para., .410 bore, and 32 ga. Please contact the factory directly for more information, including U.S. availability and pricing.

MANUFRANCE

Current manufacturer established circa 1887 and located in St. Etienne, France. No current U.S. importation.

Manufrance currently manufactures both SxS rifle and shotgun variations (the Robust Models being the most popular) that are not being currently imported into the U.S. Please contact the factory directly for more information, including model availability, parts, and domestic prices (see Trademark Index).

SHOTGUNS: DISC.

SEMI-AUTO MODEL – 12 ga., 26, 28, or 30 in. imp. cyl., mod. and full, 2 3/4 or 3 in. chamber, gas operated, walnut stock, black matte receiver, VR.

	$330	$305	$290	$275	$255	$240	$220

FALCOR O/U – 12 ga., VR, 26 in. imp. cyl. and mod., 28 in. mod. and full, SST, auto ejector, chrome lined barrel, walnut checkered stock.

	$715	$665	$635	$605	$550	$495	$470

MANURHIN

Current trademark manufactured by Manufacture d. Armes de tir Chapuis beginning in 1998, and located in Saint Bonnet Le Chateau, France. No current U.S. importation. During 1998, Chapuis Armes purchased Manurhin, and new revolvers are currently being manufactured in the new Manufacture d. Armes de tir Chapuis facility located in Saint Bonnet Le Chateau, France, utilizing the original production machinery. Previously manufactured by Manurhin Equipment 1972-1998, located in Mulhouse, France. Currently available by contacting the factory directly. Previously owned by Matra Manurhin Defense. Previously imported and distributed by Sphinx U.S.A. located in Meriden, CT. Previously imported (1984-86) directly by Matra-Manurhin International, Inc., located in Fort Lauderdale, FL.

Manurhin in France has been manufacturing models PP, PPK, and PPK/S since 1952. Previously, these guns were imported from 1953 by Tholson Co. of San Francisco, CA, and from 1956 by Interarms out of Alexandria, VA. In 1984, Manurhin imported their new models directly and they were marked Manurhin on the left front slide assembly. This differs from the previous Walther stamped guns. Also, no Interarms logo appears on the right side.

PISTOLS: SEMI-AUTO, DISC.

P-1 – 9mm Para. cal., similar to W. German P-38, double action, 5 in. barrel.

	$350	$325	$300	$275	$230	$215	$200

GRADING - PPGS™	100%	98%	95%	90%	80%	70%	60%	LAST MSR

MODEL P4 – 9mm Para. cal., P.38 variation issued to the French Police when in Berlin during post-WWII.

	$375	$340	$300	$245	$230	$215	$200	

MODEL PP – .22 LR, .32 ACP, or .380 ACP cal., 3 7/8 in. barrel, 10 shot mag.-.22 LR, 8 shot mag.-.32 ACP, 7 shot mag.-.380 ACP, blue only, all steel construction, double action with positive steel hammer block safety, 24 oz. Add $10 for .22 LR cal., $46 for Durgarde finish. Imported 1984-86.

	$360	$320	$275	$230	$205	$185	$170	*$419*

* ***Model PP Collector Model*** – blue finish, special engraving. Imported 1986 only.

	$465	$415	$350	$285	$250	$215	$185	*$529*

* ***Model PP Presentation Model*** – blue finish, special ornamentation. Imported 1986 only.

	$720	$650	$500	$430	$375	$315	$270	*$819*

Also available with various engraving options in either blue, nickel, or gold finish - prices range from $222-$540.

MODEL PPK/S – .22 LR, .32 ACP, or .380 ACP cal., 3 1/4 in. barrel, 10 shot mag.-.22 LR, 8 shot mag.-.32 ACP, 7 shot mag.-.380 ACP, blue only, all steel construction, double action with positive steel hammer block safety, 23 oz. Imported 1984-86.

	$360	$320	$275	$230	$205	$185	$170	*$419*

Add $10 for .22 LR cal.

* ***Model PPK/S Durgarde*** – similar to PPK/S, only with bonded brushed chrome finish.

	$410	$365	$325	$290	$265	$250	$240	*$465*

Add $14 for .22 LR cal.

* ***Model PPK/S Collector Model*** – blue finish, special engraving. Imported 1986 only.

	$465	$415	$350	$285	$250	$215	$185	*$529*

* ***Model PPK/S Presentation Model*** – blue finish, special ornamentation. Imported 1986 only.

	$720	$650	$500	$430	$375	$315	$270	*$819*

Also available with various engraving options in either blue, nickel, or gold finish - prices range from $222-$540.

PP SPORT – .22 LR cal. only, double action, 6.1 or 8.1 in. barrel, blue finish only, precision adj. sights, contoured plastic grips with thumbrest, 25 oz. New Manurhin design for 1985. Imported 1984-86.

	$795	$650	$500	$450	$400	$350	$300	*$635*

Add 10% for 8.1 in. barrel.

* ***PP Sport-C*** – similar to PP Sport, except has single action with lightened trigger pull.

	$750	$650	$500	$450	$400	$350	$300	*$635*

REVOLVERS

MODEL 73 DEFENSE – .357 Mag./.38 Spl. cal., 6 shot, 2 1/2, 3, or 4 in. barrel, checkered wood stocks, mfg. to precise tolerances, 31-33 1/2 oz. Importation began 1988.

MSR N/A	$1,200	$1,000	$850	$725	$600	$500	$425	

MODEL 73 GENDARMERIE – .357 Mag./.38 Spl. cal., 6 shot, similar to Model 73 Defense except has adj. sighting components and also is offered in 5 1/4, 6, or 8 in. barrel lengths. Manufactured for police requirements. Importation began 1988.

MSR N/A	$1,675	$1,125	$900	$750	$625	$525	$450	

MODEL 73 SPORT – .357 Mag./.38 Spl. cal., 6 shot, sport shooting features include minimized hammer stroke, micrometer rear sight, and free release trigger with fitted adj. sights. Importation began 1988.

MSR N/A	$1,675	$1,125	$900	$750	$625	$525	$450	

MODEL 73 CONVERTIBLE – includes choice of .22 LR/.38 Spl. or .22 LR/.32 Long cal. cylinders and barrels (5 3/4 in. for .38 Spl. and 6 in. for .22 LR/.32 Long). Imported 1988-95.

	$1,925	$1,675	$1,325	$1,125	$950	$800	$700	*$2,200*

GRADING - PPGS™	100%	98%	95%	90%	80%	70%	60%	LAST MSR

* ***Model 73 Convertible 3 Cylinder*** – similar to Model 73 Convertible except includes 3 calibers (.22 LR, .32 Long, and .38 Spl.). Imported 1988-95.

	$2,375	$1,950	$1,700	$1,375	$1,150	$975	$850	*$2,690*

MODEL 73 SILHOUETTE – .22 LR or .357 Mag. cal., Silhouette variation with fully adj. rear sight and either 10 (.22 LR) or 10 3/4 (.357 Mag.) in. heavy barrel with full shroud, contoured wooden target grips, approx. 4 lbs. Importation began 1988.

MSR N/A	$1,750	$1,175	$925	$750	$625	$525	$450

Add $13 for .357 Mag. cal.

MODEL MR 88 – .357 Mag. cal., stainless steel, 4, 5, or 6 in. barrel, fixed sights, rubber grips. Importation began 1996.

MSR N/A	$775	$625	$450	$385	$335	$280	$235

MODEL MR 96 – .357 Mag. cal., black finish, 3, 4, 5, or 6 in. VR barrel, adj. rear sight, ergonomic rubber grips. Importation began 1996.

MSR N/A	$750	$615	$425	$375	$350	$325	$295

This model allows the user to unlock, swing the cylinder out, and eject the cases with one movement of the hand.

MARATHON PRODUCTS, INC.

Previously manufactured by Santa Barbara Armaments exclusively for Marathon Products, Inc. Most of the models listed were also available in kit form, but are not shown in this book.

PISTOLS: SINGLE SHOT

HOT SHOT MODEL – .22 LR cal., single shot, fixed sights, 14 3/4 in. barrel, hardwood stock with target grip configuration. Mfg. 1986-87.

$55	$45	$40	$35	$35	$30	$30	*$60*

RIFLES: BOLT ACTION

.22 FIRST SHOT – .22 LR cal., single shot, 16 1/2 in. barrel, hardwood stock, open sights, 31 in. total length, 3.8 lbs. Mfg. 1985-87.

$55	$45	$40	$35	$35	$30	$30	*$60*

* ***.22 First Shot Super*** – similar to First Shot, except with 24 in. barrel and regular dimension stock. Mfg. 1985-87.

$55	$45	$40	$35	$35	$30	$30	*$60*

CENTERFIRE MODEL – .243 Win., .270 Win., 7x57mm, 7mm Rem. Mag., .30-06, .300 Win. Mag., or .308 Win. cal., Mauser type action, 5 shot fixed box mag., 24 in. barrel, select walnut with recoil pad, adj. trigger, open sights, 7.9 lbs. Available 1985-86 only.

$295	$240	$215	$195	$180	$170	$160	*$320*

MARBLE ARMS & MFG. CO.

Current firearms manufacturer established circa 1907, and located in Gladstone, MI. Marble Arms (current company name) also manufactures sights, knives, and compasses.

In addition to axes and compasses, Marble Arms & Mfg. Co. also manufactured its Game Getter O/U combination gun from approx. 1907 to the early 1950s. During this period of production, the gun underwent quite a few changes including sights (an aperture sight mounted on the rear backstrap was optional in 1908), different configuration folding metal stock, and other changes.

During 2009, Marble Arms announced plans to release the third generation of its Game Getter. None have been made to date.

COMBINATION GUNS

Marble Arms manufactures replacement parts for first and second generation 1908 and 1921 models. Turnbull Manufacturing Co. will have replacement parts, as well as repair and/or replace barrels and other components.

GRADING - PPGS™	100%	98%	95%	90%	80%	70%	60%	LAST MSR

GAME GETTER MODELS

* ***Game Getter Model 1908*** – starting manufacture in 1908, 2 variations of the Model 1908 Game Getter were offered, the 1908A featured a flexible rear sight mounted behind the hammer and the 1908B had a filler blank in that space. The 1908s featured a .22 cal. rifled top barrel, and in standard configuration, a smooth bored bottom barrel chambered for the .44 round ball or .44 shot. Very late in production, chambering for the 2 in. .410 could be ordered. Standard barrel lengths were 12 in., 15 in., and 18 in., but Marbles was ready to please their customers, and on special order, 8 in., 10 in., 17 in., and 22 in. barrels were made, some were even shipped from the factory fitted with silencers, and very few guns were ordered without the milling for the round tubular folding stock. A pivoting striker on the hammer was used to select the barrel to be fired, and the tip-up barrels were opened by pressing the trigger guard to the rear. The top frame featured a folding leaf sight, and the front barrel band incorporated the front sight, the grips were checkered black hard rubber with fleur-de-lis design. On very early 1908 guns, the buttplate was a separate piece secured to the tubing with 2 screws and later stocks were all one piece. A few guns were built with bottom barrels chambered for .25-20 & .32-20, but these are very rare. The gun was shipped in a dovetailed wooden box with sliding lid, and included a shoulder holster, cleaning rod, and directions for use. The first 1908 was shipped from the factory June 21, 1909, and serial letters A-M were used. Then, starting with serial number 1, they continued through 9981, and the last gun was shipped from the factory May 22, 1918.

	$2,500	**$2,300**	**$1,900**	**$1,700**	**$1,600**	**$1,400**	**$1,200**

Add $500 for Model 1908A with original flexible tang sight.
Add $100-$200 for original holster, depending on condition of leather.
Add $1,000-$1,200 for correct original box, depending on condition.

* ***Game Getter Model 1921*** – the 1921 was an entirely new gun, with similar barrel lengths (12, 15, or 18 in.), not nearly as pleasing in appearance as the 1908. The same barrel lengths were standard, but the bottom barrel was chambered for the 2 in. .410. In 1924, the standard chamber was changed to 2 1/2 in. .410. It featured a bag style, oiled walnut grip, and a unique "Triple Combination Rear Sight," which was developed and made only for this model. A number of guns in the 14,000 to 16,000 serial number range can be found with brown plastic grips, conventional "v" notch rear sight adjustable for elevation. The 1921 featured a folding and hinged 3 piece stock with an improved lock which eliminated wobble, but had no adjustment for drop. It also had a shorter action than the 1908, which was a faster action, and the hammer rebounded to a safety notch after firing. As with the 1908 Model, Marbles would accomodate the wishes of the customer, and barrels as short as 8 in. can be found. Some guns were ordered choke bored, and some were chambered just for .44 Game Getter on the bottom barrel. A few had no provision for stock, at least 2 were shipped in .32-20, and as records are not complete, .38-40 cal. models are known to exist and calibers like the .25-20 are thought to exist. Supplied with a heavy cardboard box, shoulder holster, cleaning rod and instructions. First shipment was serial number 10,001 - shipped to William L. Marble, the west coast representative, on Oct. 4, 1921. Serial range 10,000-20,076.

	$2,000	**$1,800**	**$1,600**	**$1,400**	**$1,200**	**$1,100**	**$1,000**

Add $150-$200 for original holster if in good condition.
Add $1,000-$1,200 for correct original box, depending on wood condition (very early 1921 only).
Add $300-$500 for cardboard box, depending on condition (just cardboard lift-off lid).

The first 200-300 of this model were shipped in 1908 boxes with 1921 yellow end label on the box.

Values assume legal 18 in. barrels or correct registration. If not legal configuration, the gun is basically a black market item subject to BATFE confiscation. The U.S. government and foreign countries continued to purchase 15 in. guns after the 1934 law was passed, and the last gun was shipped during the mid 1950s. 200 M1921 models with 15 in. barrels were assembled from parts and sold by Marbles as collector's items in 1960.

Not all, but many 1921s in this serial range approx. 14,000 - 16,000 had parkerized finish, no flip rear sight, one piece cardboard box with end flaps and no holster.

GRADING - PPGS™	100%	98%	95%	90%	80%	70%	60%	LAST MSR

* ***Game Getter Model 3rd Generation*** – .22 LR cal. over .410 bore, 18 1/2 in. barrels, patterned after the Game Getter Model 1921, folding sporting rear sight, aperture tang sight, original barrel band beaded front sight, includes replica leather holster and slide top pine wood box, assembled and finished by Doug Turnbull Restoration. Only prototypes were mfg.

While advertised at $1,995 circa 2011, this gun was never put into standard production.

MARCEL THYS & SONS

Previous SxS rifle and shotgun manufacturer circa 1960-2004 and located in Crisnée, Belgium. The U.S. agent was Jean-Jacques Perodeau, located in Enid, OK.

Marcel Thys & Sons manufactured fine quality double rifles and shotguns, with many engraving options and special orders. Since these guns were custom-made per individual order, each gun must be individually appraised.

MARGOLIN

Original pistol design by M.V. Margolin developed after WWII as a training firearm for members of the Russian shooting team. The Margolin is currently manufactured at the Izhevsk mechanical plant located in Izhevsk, Russia, and known as the "MTsN" sporting pistol. Limited importation.

PISTOLS: SEMI-AUTO

TARGET MODEL – .22 LR cal., originally developed from the TT (Tula Tokarev), manufactured to precise tolerances, many specimens are made to individual shooters' specifications, seldom encountered in the U.S., while rare, desirability to date has been limited, current mfg. - limited importation.

100%	98%	95%	90%	80%	70%	60%	LAST MSR
$875	$825	$750	$675	$600	$525	$450	

While currently imported Chinese copies are considerably less expensive, they do not have the quality (or accuracy) of the Russian Margolins.

MARLIN FIREARMS COMPANY

Current trademark with headquarters located in Madison, NC beginning 2010. Currently manufactured by Remington in lion, NY beginning early 2011. Previous manufacturer located in North Haven, CT (1969-2010), and in New Haven, CT (1870-1969). The Marlin company manufactured firearms between 1870-2010. Distributor sales only.

On Nov. 10th, 2000, Marlin Firearms Company purchased H&R 1871, Inc. This includes the brand names Harrington & Richardson, New England Firearms, and Wesson & Harrington (please refer to individual sections in this text).

During 2005, Marlin Firearms Company once again started manufacturing a L.C. Smith line of both SxS and O/U shotguns.

Remington Arms Company, Inc. and The Freedom Group acquired Marlin Firearms Company, H&R 1871, LLC., New England Firearms (NEF), and L.C. Smith brand in January of 2008. The Freedom Group, Inc. announced the closure of its Marlin manufacturing facility, located in North Haven, Connecticut. During 2011, production was moved to Ilion, NY. Marlin Firearms Company had been a family-owned and operated business from 1921-2007.

PISTOLS: DERRINGERS AND REVOLVERS

Many of the more common variations in average condition sell in the $150-$250 range, while rarer specimens with 90%+ original condition will be priced in the $450-$1,750 range, depending on rarity and condition.

RIFLES: LEVER ACTION, ANTIQUE & OLDER MFG.

Factory information by individual serial number may be available from the Cody Firearms Museum in Cody, WY on the following models with serial numbers 4001-355,504: Models 1881, 1888, 1889, 1892, 1893, 1894, 1895, and 1897. Marlin had only one series of serial numbers for all lever action repeating rifles from 1883-1906: therefore serial numbers do not reflect the place in production or sequence number of a gun within a model. Sometimes, a record shows two or even three guns with the same serial

100%	98%	95%	90%	80%	70%	60%	50%	40%	30%	20%	10%

number from the same time period.

Values are for standard models only without special order features. 98% and 100% prices have been intentionally replaced with N/As (not applicable), since these condition factors are seldom encountered and hard to accurately price, as their values have dramatically increased during the past 3-5 years.

Add a premium for all mint condition guns with vibrant case coloring on receivers.

MODEL 1881 – .32-40 WCF, .38-55 WCF, .40-60 Marlin, .45-70 Govt., or .45-85 Marlin cal., tube mag., 28 in. octagonal barrel standard, top ejection, blued finish with case hardened hammer, lever, and buttplate. Approx. 20,000 mfg. 1881-1892.

N/A	N/A	$3,750	$3,100	$2,600	$2,000	$1,750	$1,450	$1,250	$1,100	$925	$725

Add approx. 15% for .45-70 or .45-85 cal.
Add 200-300% premium for rare First models (pre-ser. no. 600).
Add a premium for very early First models with hand engraved script barrel markings - approx. first 60 rifles mfg.

This model came in 3 frame styles for various calibers.

MODEL 1888 – .32-20 WCF, .38-40 WCF, or .44-40 WCF cal., 24 in. octagonal barrel most frequently encountered, top ejection, blued finish with case hardened hammer, lever, and buttplate, short throw lever action principle. Approx. 4,800 mfg. 1888-1889. Ser. range approx. 19,560-27,850.

N/A	N/A	$3,400	$2,750	$2,150	$1,850	$1,550	$1,300	$1,050	$875	$750	$625

Add 40% for half-round, half-octagon barrel (23 mfg.).
Add 20% for round barrel (266 mfg.).
Add 25% for half magazine (78 mfg.).

MODEL 1889 – .25-20 WCF (very rare), .32-20 WCF, .38-40 WCF, or .44-40 WCF cal., 24 (approx. 39,300 mfg.) or 28 (approx. 2,260 mfg.) in. octagonal barrel most frequently encountered, side ejection with solid top frame, blued finish with case hardened hammer, lever, and buttplate, short throw lever action principle. Approx. 55,000 mfg. 1889-1899. Ser. range approx. 25,000-100,000.

N/A	N/A	$1,850	$1,550	$1,150	$800	$625	$450	$375	$325	$275	$250

Add 300%-500% for Musket.
Add 25% for carbine.
Add 15% for .44-40 WCF cal.
Factory special orders/features will add premiums, depending on the desirability of each option and the gun's original condition factor.

Also available as Carbine with either a 15 in. (only 367 mfg.) or 20 in. (approx. 10,000 mfg.) barrel or Musket (30 in. barrel - very rare).

MODEL 1891 – .22 Rimfire and .32 Rimfire/Centerfire cal., 24 in. octagonal barrel most often encountered, choice of side loading (1st variation) or tube loading (2nd variation), blued finish with case hardened hammer, lever, and buttplate, sear safety system on lever action. Approx. 18,650 mfg. between 1891-1897. Ser. no. range is approx. 37,500-118,000.

N/A	N/A	$2,500	$2,150	$1,600	$1,300	$1,050	$950	$800	$700	$625	$550

Add 50% for deluxe, pistol grip checkered model.
Subtract 40% for tube loading model (.32 Centerfire).
Add $100 each for special sights (including correct Lyman, Marbles, Beeches combo, etc.).
Factory special orders/features will add premiums, depending on the desirability of each option and the gun's original condition factor.

MODEL 1892 – .22 S, L, or LR, .32 S or L cal., 16, 24, 26, or 28 in. barrel, tubular mag., open sight, plain straight stock. Mfg. 1892-1916.

N/A	N/A	$2,000	$1,550	$1,150	$975	$800	$675	$575	$500	$450	$400

Add 10% for .22 cal.
Subtract 10% for .32 cal.
Add $100 each for special sights (including correct Lyman, Marbles, Beeches combo, etc.).
Factory special orders/features will add premiums, depending on the desirability of each option and the gun's original condition factor.

100%	98%	95%	90%	80%	70%	60%	50%	40%	30%	20%	10%

MODEL 1893 RIFLE – .25-36 Marlin, .30-30 Win., .32 Spl., .32-40 WCF, or .38-55 WCF cal., 20-32 in. round or octagonal barrels, blue (Model B) or case colored receiver, 10 shot tube mag., straight grip stock. Mfg. 1893-1936.

N/A	N/A	$3,300	$2,750	$2,100	$1,550	$1,150	$825	$625	$525	$425	$350

Add 15%-20% for calibers other than .30-30 Win. or .32 Spl.
Add 15%-20% for takedown model, depending on condition.
Add approx. 20% for special Lightweight Model.
Subtract 10%-20% for the Model B with blue receiver.
Factory special orders/features will add premiums, depending on the desirability of each option and the gun's original condition factor.

Although incorrect, more than a few people refer to all 20 in. barrels as "Lightweight" models. Technically, the Lightweight variation has a 7 1/2 in. forearm rather than the standard 9 in.

Later production guns were marked "Model '93" and have less value. This model had two barrel variations - one was marked "special smokeless steel" while the other was marked "for Black Powder". The latter (also known as Model B) are 1st Models only and have blue receivers rather than case colored.

* ***Model 1893 Musket*** – similar to the Model 1893 Rifle, except has 30 in. barrel and military style forearm.

N/A	N/A	$6,000	$5,300	$4,750	$3,950	$3,400	$3,000	$2,650	$2,300	$1,850	$1,450

MODEL 1893 CARBINE – .30-30 Win., .32 Spl., .32-40 WCF cal., or .38-55 WCF cal., 15 (only 61 mfg.) or 20 in. round barrel, case colored receiver, 7 shot tube mag., straight or pistol grip stock. Mfg. 1893-1935.

Add 15%-20% for calibers other than .30-30 Win. or .32 Spl.
Factory special orders/features will add premiums, depending on the desirability of each option and the gun's original condition factor.

* ***Model 1893 Carbine 1st Model*** – with saddle ring. Mfg. 1893-1915.

N/A	N/A	$2,100	$1,575	$1,300	$1,050	$850	$650	$525	$425	$375	$350

Strong, original case colors over 95% condition can result in $2,500 asking prices.

* ***Model 1893 Carbine 2nd Model*** – .30-30 Win. or .32 HPS (High Power Special) cal., has "Bull's-eye" in stock, no saddle rings. Mfg. 1922-35.

N/A	N/A	$1,100	$875	$675	$525	$450	$400	$350	$325	$300	$285

* ***Model 1893 Carbine Sporting*** – .30-30 Win. or .32 Spl. cal., 20 in. round barrel, 2/3 mag., 5 shot, carbine style front sight, Rocky Mountain rear, straight stock, hard rubber buttplate, bull's-eye in stock. Mfg. 1923-35.

N/A	N/A	$1,800	$1,375	$1,125	$875	$775	$650	$550	$450	$375	$350

Subtract 40% for 2nd Model made in 1935 with "S" steel buttplate and ivory bead front sight.

MODEL 1894 – .25-20 WCF, .32-20 WCF, .38-40 WCF, or .44-40 WCF cal., case colored receiver, 10 shot tube mag., 24 in. round or octagon barrel, straight or pistol grip stock. Mfg. 1894-1934.

N/A	N/A	$3,250	$2,500	$2,000	$1,450	$1,000	$750	$600	$500	$400	$350

Add 25% for saddle ring carbine.
Add 10% for .44-40 WCF cal.
Add 40% for Baby Carbine with 18 in. barrel and 1/2 mag.
Add 15%-20% for takedown model, depending on condition.
Factory special orders/features will add premiums, depending on the desirability of each option and the gun's original condition factor.

Later production guns were marked "Model '94" and have less value. This model was also available in both a Carbine and Musket variation.

* ***Model 1894 Musket***

N/A	N/A	$5,500	$5,000	$4,500	$3,750	$3,250	$2,600	$2,000	$1,500	$1,000	$850

MODEL 1895 – .33 WCF, .38-56 WCF, .40-65 WCF, .40-70 WCF, .40-82 WCF, .45-70 Govt., or .45-90 cal., case colored receiver, 9 shot tube mag., 24 or 26 in. round or octagon barrel standard, other lengths were available, open sights, plain straight or pistol grip stock. Mfg. 1895-1915.

N/A	N/A	$4,250	$3,500	$3,000	$2,350	$1,750	$1,400	$1,150	$850	$675	$550

100%	98%	95%	90%	80%	70%	60%	50%	40%	30%	20%	10%

Premiums exist for .40-70 WCF (approx. 60 mfg.), .45-70 Govt., and .45-90 WCF cal.
Factory special orders/features will add premiums, depending on the desirability of each option and the gun's original condition factor.

In 1912, a lightweight variation was introduced with hard rubber buttplate and half-magazine, cals. were .33 WCF and .45-70 Govt. (commands a premium), and round barrels were either 22 or 24 in. A Carbine variation was also offered with approx. 200 mfg. - premiums may run as high as 150% over rifle values listed.

MODEL 1897 – .22 S, L, or LR cal., tube mag., 16, 24, 26, or 28 in. barrel, case colored receiver, takedown, open sights, plain straight or pistol grip stock. Mfg. 1897-1922.

N/A	N/A	$3,000	$2,250	$1,675	$1,425	$1,150	$975	$750	$575	$475	$375

Add 100% for 16 in. barrel "Bicycle Rifle."
Add 15%-20% for takedown model, depending on condition.
Add $100 each for special sights (including correct Lyman, Marbles, Beeches combo, etc.).
Factory special orders/features will add premiums, depending on the desirability of each option and the gun's original condition factor.

RIFLES: MODERN PRODUCTION INFORMATION

Year of manufacture can be determined from 1946-1968 by the following letter/numeral prefixes: 1946-C, 1947-D, 1948-E, 1949-F, 1950-G, 1951-H, 1952-J, 1953-K, 1954-L, 1955-M, 1956-N, 1957-P, 1958-R, 1959-S, 1960-T, 1961-U, 1962-V, 1963-W, 1964-Y,Z, 1965-AA, 1966-AB, 1967-AC, 1968-AD, 1969-69, 1970-70, 1971-71, 1972-72. Starting in 1973, the year can be determined by subtracting the first 2 numbers of the serial number from 100.

GRADING - PPGS™	100%	98%	95%	90%	80%	70%	60%	LAST MSR

RIFLES: CENTERFIRE

Rifles: Centerfire, Bolt Action

The models listed are in alphabetical sequence first, followed by numerical sequence for easy reference.

Machine cut checkering became standard on many Marlins beginning 1995. Safety locks have been shipped with every new rifle/shotgun beginning 1999.

MODEL MR-7 – .22-250 Rem. (advertised in 1998, but never mfg.), .243 Win. (advertised in 1998, but never mfg.), .25-06 Rem. (new 1997), .270 Win., .280 Rem. (new 1998), .30-06, or .308 Win. (advertised in 1998, but never mfg.) cal., 4 shot box mag. with removable hinged floorplate, 3 position safety, adj. 3-6 lb. trigger, 22 in. barrel, checkered American walnut stock, cocking indicator, forged receiver, damascened bolt, includes sling swivels, with or without sights, approx. 7 1/2 lbs. Mfg. 1996-99.

	$550	$450	$375	$315	$275	$240	$215	*$603*

Add $40 for open sights (.270 Win., .280 Rem., or .30-06).

* ***Model MR-7B*** – .270 Win. or .30-06 only, similar to Model MR-7, except has birch stock and forearm with cut checkering. Mfg. 1998-99.

	$475	$450	$350	$185	$165	$150	$130	*$483*

Add $40 for open sights (mfg. 1998 only).

MODEL X7 SERIES – various cals., barrel joined to receiver by barrel nut, no sights, 4 shot internal mag., Pro-Fire adj. trigger system, two-position safety, recoil pad, fluted bolt, fully enclosed bolt shroud with cocking indicator, recessed target style muzzle crown, steel sling swivel studs. New 2008.

* ***Model X7*** – .223 Rem. (new 2012), .243 Win., .25-06 Rem., .270 Win., .30-06, .308 Win. or 7mm-08 Rem. cal., short or long action, 22 in. barrel w/o sights, features black synthetic stock, blue metal finish, scope base included, approx. 6 1/2 lbs. New 2008.

MSR $391	$350	$295	$260	$230	$210	$190	$170

Add $52 for 3-9x40mm mounted scope and bore sighted (new 2012).

* ***Model X7S*** – similar to Model X7, except has stainless steel barrel. Mfg. 2009-2011.

	$415	$345	$310	$265	$240	$215	$190	*$505*

GRADING - PPGS™	100%	98%	95%	90%	80%	70%	60%	LAST MSR

* ***Model X7C*** – .243 Win., .25-06 Rem., .270 Win., .30-06, .308 Win., 7mm-08 Rem. cal., 22 in. barrel w/o sights, features Realtree APG HD camo stock. Mfg. 2008-2011.

	$365	$310	$275	$240	$220	$195	$175	$426

* ***Model X7W*** – .270 Win. or .30-06 cal., similar to Model X7, except has walnut stock. Mfg. 2009-2011.

	$465	$395	$360	$300	$260	$225	$200	$580

* ***Model X7L*** – similar to Model X7W, except has laminate stock. Mfg. 2009-2011.

	$465	$395	$360	$300	$260	$225	$200	$580

* ***Model X7 Varmint Heavy Barrel*** – .22-250 Rem., .223 Rem. (new 2012) or .308 Win. cal., similar to Model X7, except has black synthetic stock, 24 (disc.) or 26 in. heavy barrel. 7 3/4 lbs. New 2011.

MSR $397	$345	$295	$260	$230	$210	$190	$170	

* ***Model X7Y*** – .243 Win., .308 Win., or 7mm-08 Rem. cal., similar to Model X7, except has shortened black stock, 6 1/2 lbs. New 2008.

MSR $391	$350	$295	$260	$230	$210	$190	$170	

Add $52 for 3-9x40mm mounted scope and bore sighted (new 2012).

MODEL 322 VARMINT – .222 Rem. cal., Sako Mauser type action, 3 shot mag., 24 in. medium weight barrel, 2 position aperture sight, checkered stock. Approx. 5,850 mfg. 1954-57.

	$550	$500	$475	$400	$325	$300	$250	

MODEL 455 SPORTER – .30-06, or .308 Win. cal., FN Mauser action with Sako trigger, 24 in. stainless steel barrel, Lyman aperture sight, checkered Monte Carlo pistol grip stock. 1,079 were mfg. in .30-06 cal., 59 in .308 Win. cal. Mfg. 1957-1959.

	$650	$525	$375	$250	$220	$195	$165	

Add 20% for .308 Win. cal.

Rifles: Centerfire, Lever Action

MODEL 30/30A – .30-30 Win. cal., 20 in. barrel, promotional Glenfield model with birch stock and pressed checkering. Mfg. 1964-83.

	$250	$195	$160	$135	$120	$110	$100	

This model was replaced by the Model 30AS in 1983.

* ***Model 30TK*** – .30-30 Win. cal., 20 in. micro-grooved barrel, 6 shot, birch straight grip stock, sling swivels, sold through K-Mart.

	$250	$195	$160	$135	$120	$110	$100	

MODEL 30AS – please refer to Model 336A/336AS listing.

MODEL 36 - 1ST VARIATION – same as Model 1936 - called Model 36 in catalog only. Mfg. 1937-40.

	$725	$650	$500	$350	$250	$200	$150	

Add 10% for rifles and sporting carbines.

The Model 36 - 1st Variation has an upper tang inscription "Model 1936" and a case colored receiver. Also, the Model 36 - 1st variation did not have a letter prefix in the ser. no.

MODEL 36 - 2ND VARIATION – similar to Model 1936, still has case colored receiver with "Model 1936" on upper tang, coiled main spring, buttstock is heavier style and no longer has fluted comb, buttplate is a thicker, slightly curved style - hard rubber, forearm is a heavier beaver-tailed style, "B" prefix in ser. no. Mfg. 1941.

	$750	$500	$400	$300	$250	$200	$165	

Add 10% for rifles and sporting carbines.

MODEL 36 ADL DELUXE RIFLE – similar to Model 1936, case colored receiver, checkered pistol grip buttstock and forearm, pistol grip cap, Winchester quick detachable swivels with 1 in. sling, "B" prefix in ser. no., has "Model 1936" on upper tang. Less than 50 mfg. in 1945 only.

	$1,150	$1,000	$800	$600	$400	$275	$250	

Both the rear and front swivel bases are attached with two wood screws and are not inletted into the wood.

GRADING - PPGS™	100%	98%	95%	90%	80%	70%	60%	LAST MSR

MODEL 36 - 3RD VARIATION – .30-30 Win. or .32 SPEC cal., blued receiver, no upper tang markings, model no. and cal. marked on barrel, rifles have "A" suffix, Sporting Carbine has "SC" suffix, and regular carbine has "RC" suffix, small case "c" prefix in 1946, and large "D" prefix in 1947. Mfg. 1946-47.

	$500	$425	$350	$225	$165	$150	$125	

Add 10% for rifles and sporting carbines.

Some standard rifles may have the "ADL" barrel markings in 1946-47. 1946 mfg. has a lowercase "c" prefix and 1947 mfg. has a capital "D" prefix in ser. no.

* ***Model 36 3rd Variation ADL Deluxe*** – similar to Model 36 3rd Variation, has checkered pistol grip stock and forearm, forearm has checkering on sides and underneath, round swivel stud in buttstock and on forearm cap, deluxe quick detachable swivels and 1 in. leather sling, does not have model designation on upper tang or pistol grip cap, hooded front ramp screw on front sight, Rocky Mountain rear, letter prefix in ser. no. is "C" or "D."

	$850	$700	$550	$450	$400	$375	$350	

MODEL 62 LEVERMATIC – .256 Mag. or .30 Carbine cal., 4 shot mag., 23 in. barrel, open sight, pistol grip Monte Carlo stock. Mfg. 1963-69.

.256 Mag.	$500	$450	$400	$325	$300	$195	$175	
.30 Carbine	$400	$350	$300	$250	$225	$175	$150	

MODEL 308MX – .308 Marlin Express cal., 22 in. barrel, walnut pistol grip stock and forearm, blue finish, 5 shot tube mag, 7 1/4 lbs. New 2007.

MSR $686	$550	$450	$395	$340	$280	$235	$200	

This model was developed to take advantage of the Hornady LEVERevolution ammunition, which greatly improves range, energy, and accuracy.

* ***Model 308MXLR*** – similar to Model 308MX, except has 24 in. stainless steel barrel and laminated stock, fluted bolt, 7 1/2 lbs. New 2007.

MSR $905	$740	$600	$465	$375	$325	$275	$225	

This model was developed to take advantage of the Hornady LEVERevolution ammunition, which greatly improves range, energy, and accuracy.

MODEL 336A (DISC.) – improved 36A, .30-30 Win., .35 Rem., or .32 Spl. cal., round breech bolt, 24 in. barrel with 2/3 mag. Mfg. 1948-1962, re-introduced 1973-1980.

	$500	$450	$400	$350	$300	$195	$175	

Add 20% for 1st Model mfg. 1948-52. Add 10% for 1953-62 mfg.

The .35 Rem. cal. was added in 1950, .32 Spl. was disc. in 1962.

* ***Model 336ADL*** – similar to Model 336A Rifle, except has deluxe checkered walnut stock and forearm, quick detachable swivels and 1 in. sling. Mfg. 1948-62.

	$625	$550	$500	$450	$375	$325	$275	

Add 20% for 2nd Model (1957-1962).
Add 20% for .32 Spl. or .35 Rem. cal.

The 336ADL 1st Model (mfg. 1948-56) did not have a raised comb or cheekpiece. The 2nd Model (mfg. 1957-62) is identifiable by a Monte Carlo buttstock with raised comb and cheekpiece. Wood was supplied by Bishop.

MODEL 336A/336AS (30AS) – .30-30 Win. cal. only, 20 in. barrel, 6 shot tube mag, walnut finished birch stock (pressed checkering became standard 1995, cut checkering became standard 1998), open sights (adj. rear sight became standard 1995), no frills version of the 336CS, 7 lbs. Mfg. 1983-2007.

	$375	$275	$200	$150	$125	$120	$115	$423

Add $50 for 4X scope (disc. 2006) or $41 for 3-9x32mm bore sighted scope.

Prior to 2000, this was designated the Model 30AS. The Model 30AS was formerly part of the Glenfield line. During 2001, this model's nomenclature was changed from 336AS to 336A.

* ***Model 336W (30AW)*** – similar to Model 30AS, except has carbine barrel with band and gold trigger, laminate stock became standard 2012, 7 lbs.

MSR $500	$415	$335	$285	$245	$215	$195	$160	

GRADING - PPGS™	100%	98%	95%	90%	80%	70%	60%	LAST MSR

Add $53 for 4X scope (disc. 2006).
Add $48 for 3-9x32mm bore sighted scope (new 2007).

This model was previously sold by Wal-Mart only. Model nomenclature was changed during 1998.

* ***Model 336Y SpikeHorn*** – similar to Model 336W, 5 shot tube mag, 16 1/2 in. barrel, shorter stock (12 1/2 in. LOP) with vent. recoil pad, 6 1/2 lbs. Mfg. 2003-2005.

	$425	$325	$215	$165	$135	$125	$115	*$566*

* ***Model 336CC*** – similar to Model 336W, except has Mossy Oak Breakup camo stock and forearm, 7 lbs. Mfg. 2001-2004.

	$400	$325	$285	$190	$155	$135	$125	*$503*

MODEL 336RC CARBINE – .30-30 Win., .32 Spl., or .35 Rem. cal., standard model carbine. Mfg. 1948-68.

	$495	$425	$350	$315	$275	$200	$175

Add 10% for 1st Model mfg. 1948-52.

MODEL 336BL – .30-30 Win. cal., 20 in. blue barrel, 6 shot tube mag., brown laminated hardwood stock with pistol grip, large loop lever, 7 1/2 lbs. New 2010.

MSR $622	$515	$415	$350	$265	$210	$185	$150

MODEL 336C CARBINE (DISC.) – .30-30 Win., .32 Spl., or .35 Rem. cal., standard model carbine with 20 in. barrel. Mfg. 1969-83.

	$450	$375	$300	$250	$220	$200	$175

Add 10% for .35 Rem. cal.

MODEL 336SC SPORTING CARBINE – similar to Model 336C, with 20 in. barrel and 2/3 length mag. tube, raised comb buttstock (1957-63). Mfg. 1948-63.

	$625	$550	$475	$400	$350	$300	$250

Add 10% for 1st Model mfg. 1948-52.

MODEL 336SC .219 ZIPPER – similar to Model 336SC, in .219 Zipper cal., 5 shot mag. 3,230 mfg. 1955-60.

	$800	$700	$600	$550	$500	$450	$400

MODEL 336SD CARBINE (SPORTING DELUXE) – .30-30 Win., .32 Spl., or .35 Rem. cal., deluxe sporting carbine with 20 in. barrel, checkered stock and forearm, raised comb, no cheekpiece, quick detachable swivels and 1 in. sling. Mfg. 1954-62.

	$800	$700	$600	$425	$275	$200	$185

MODEL 336C (336CS) CARBINE – .30-30 Win. or .35 Rem. cal., 6 shot tube mag., 20 in. barrel, hammer block safety, American black walnut pistol grip stock (cut checkering became standard 1994), 7 lbs. Introduced 1984.

MSR $592	$475	$415	$350	$260	$200	$175	$150

During 2001, this model's nomenclature was changed from 336CS to 336C.

MODEL 336SS (336M) – .30-30 Win. cal. only, similar to Model 336W/30AW, except is stainless steel, 6 shot tube mag., 7 lbs. New 2000.

MSR $727	$585	$500	$415	$350	$295	$250	$200

During 2001, this model's nomenclature was changed from 336M to 336SS.

MODEL 336Y – .30-30 Win. cal., 16 1/4 in. barrel, features hardwood stock with 12 1/2 in. LOP and forearm, laminate stock became standard 2012. New 2011.

MSR $500	$385	$295	$250	$220	$200	$175	$150

MODEL 336XLR – .30-30 Win. or .35 Rem. (mfg. 2007-2011) cal., features stainless steel finish with 24 in. barrel, broached rifling, fluted bolt, 5 shot mag., black/grey laminate stock with deluxe recoil pad, adj. folding semi-buckhorn rear sight, hammer block safety, 7 1/2 lbs. New 2006.

MSR $905	$725	$595	$465	$385	$330	$295	$265

This model was developed to take advantage of the Hornady LEVERevolution ammunition, which greatly improves range, energy, and accuracy.

GRADING - PPGS™	100%	98%	95%	90%	80%	70%	60%	LAST MSR

MODEL 336LTS CARBINE – .30-30 Win. cal. only, 16 1/4 in. barrel, 5 shot tube mag., 6 1/2 lbs. 2,671 mfg. 1988-89 only.

$450	$400	$350	$200	$175	$165	$150	*$346*

MODEL 336 COWBOY – .30-30 Win. (disc. 2001) or .38-55 WCF cal., 8 shot tube mag., squared off finger lever, 24 in. tapered octagon barrel with deep cut Ballard-type rifling (6 grooves), cut checkered (disc. 2001) straight grip walnut stock and forearm, adj. Marbles semi-buckhorn rear and carbine front sight, ser. no. is on left side of receiver, instead of on tang, 7 1/2 lbs. Mfg. 1999-2004.

$550	$475	$385	$310	$275	$250	$225	*$735*

Add 10% for .30-30 Win. cal.

MODEL 336ER (EXTRA RANGE) – .356 Win. cal., 5 shot tube mag., 20 in. barrel, walnut pistol grip stock, open sights, 7 lbs. 2,441 mfg. 1983-86.

$550	$475	$325	$225	$200	$175	$150	*$350*

Although advertised, this model was never manufactured in .307 cal.

MODEL 336T CARBINE "TEXAN" – .30-30 Win., .35 Rem., or .44 Mag. (1965-1967 only) cal., similar to 336C, with straight stock, 18 1/2 (1983 only) or 20 in. barrel, saddle ring (1965-1971 only). Mfg. 1954-83.

$450	$400	$350	$300	$250	$200	$150

MODEL 336DT CARBINE (DELUXE TEXAN) – .30-30 Win. or .35 Rem. cal., select stock version of 336T, longhorn and map of Texas carved on buttstock. Mfg. 1962-63.

$750	$625	$450	$300	$200	$150	$135

Add 10% for .35 Rem. cal.

MODEL 336TS TEXAN – similar to 336 CS, except is .30-30 Win. cal., 18 1/2 in. barrel, straight grip stock and squared finger lever, crossbolt safety. Mfg. 1984-87.

$325	$275	$225	$175	$150	$130	$120	*$314*

MODEL 336 OCTAGON RIFLE – .30-30 Win. cal. only, with 22 in. octagon barrel, standard model. 2,414 mfg. 1973 only.

$500	$425	$300	$250	$200	$175	$150

MODEL 336 MARAUDER CARBINE – .30-30 Win. or .35 Rem. cal., 16 1/4 in. barrel. 5,856 mfg. 1963-64.

$550	$475	$425	$350	$275	$235	$210

Add 10% for .35 cal.

Approx. 65% were mfg. in .30-30 Win. cal., and 35% were mfg. in .35 Rem. cal.

Be careful of re-barreled examples of this model.

MODEL 336 MAGNUM CARBINE – .44 Mag. cal., 20 in. standard carbine configuration, w/o saddle ring. 2,823 mfg. 1963-64 only.

$450	$400	$350	$300	$250	$200	$175

MODEL 336T – .44 Mag. cal., with saddle ring, 13,895 mfg. 1965-67.

$375	$325	$295	$250	$200	$170	$160

MODEL 336 ZANE GREY CENTURY CARBINE – .30-30 Win. cal., similar to 336 Octagon, 22 in. octagon barrel, Zane Grey medallion inlaid in receiver, select walnut stock, pistol grip, brass buttplate and forearm cap. 7,871 mfg. in 1971.

$525	$450	$350	$300	$250	$225	$200

This model was mfg. to commemorate the 100th anniversary of the birth of Zane Grey.

MODEL 336 PRESENTATION RIFLE – .30-30 Win. cal., one of the pair in the "Brace of 1,000," 22 in. octagon barrel, engraved receiver, sold with Model 39 Presentation. Mfg. 1970 only.

$750	$650	$525	$425	$325	$250	$225

Add a premium for serial numbers under 100.

GRADING - PPGS™	100%	98%	95%	90%	80%	70%	60%	LAST MSR

CENTENNIAL MATCHED PAIR (MODELS 336 & 39) "BRACE OF 1,000" – Model 336 and Model 39 serial numbered the same, .30-30 Win. or .22 LR cal., engraved by Robert Kain and Winston Churchill, deluxe wood, inlaid medallions, cased. 1,000 mfg. sets in 1970.

$1,500 $1,350 $900 $785 $655 $550 $465 *$750*

MODEL 338MX – .338 Marlin Express cal., 22 in. barrel, walnut pistol grip stock and forearm, blue finish, 5 shot tube mag., 7 1/2 lbs. Mfg. 2009-2011.

$515 $425 $375 $325 $275 $235 $200 *$643*

* ***Model 338MXLR*** – similar to Model 338MX, except has 24 in. stainless steel barrel and laminated stock, fluted bolt. Mfg. 2009-2011.

$695 $575 $450 $375 $325 $275 $225 *$848*

MODEL 375 – similar to Model 336 CS, except is .375 Win. cal. 16,315 mfg. 1980-83.

$450 $400 $350 $300 $250 $200 $150

MODEL 444P OUTFITTER – .444 Marlin cal., 5 shot tube mag., 18 1/2 in. ported barrel with deep cut Ballard-type rifling (6 grooves), adj. semi-buckhorn folding rear sight with ramp front, checkered straight grip walnut stock and forearm, tapped for scope mount, approx. 7 lbs. Mfg. 1999-2002.

$495 $395 $315 $245 $195 $180 $170 *$631*

MODEL 444 – .444 Marlin cal., 4 shot tube mag., 24 in. barrel, open sights, straight grip, Monte Carlo stock, recoil pad, swivels, sling, 1st Model. Mfg. 1965-71.

$425 $375 $275 $225 $200 $185 $160

MODEL 444 (444SS) SPORTER – .444 Marlin cal., similar to Model 444, with 22 in. barrel and hammer block safety, pistol grip stock without Monte Carlo configuration (cut checkering became standard 1994), 7 1/2 lbs. Mfg. 1984-2011.

$525 $450 $365 $300 $250 $225 $195 *$649*

During 2001, this model's nomenclature was changed from 444SS to 444.

* ***Model 444S*** – similar to Model 444, except has pistol grip stock. Mfg. 1972-83.

$325 $265 $225 $200 $185 $165 $150

MODEL 444XLR – .444 Marlin cal., features stainless steel construction with 24 in. barrel, broached rifling, fluted bolt, 5 shot mag., black/grey laminate stock with deluxe recoil pad, adj. folding semi-buckhorn rear sight, hammer block safety, 7 1/2 lbs. Mfg. 2006-2010.

$695 $575 $450 $375 $325 $275 $225 *$861*

This model was developed to take advantage of the new Hornady LEVERevolution ammunition, which greatly improves range, energy, and accuracy.

MODEL 1894 (1969-1984 MFG.) – .44 Spl. or .44 Mag. cal., 20 in. bbl., 10 shot tube mag., adj. sights, straight grip walnut stock and forearm, 6 lbs. Mfg. 1969-84.

$375 $300 $250 $195 $165 $145 $130

MODEL 1894 (1894S) – .41 Mag. (disc. 1991), .44 Mag./.44 Spl., or .45 LC (mfg. 1988-91, reintroduced 2005 only) cal., Model 1894 with addition of cross bolt ("S" suffix) and hammer block safety, 20 in. barrel, 10 shot tube mag., adj. sights, straight grip walnut stock and forearm (cut checkering became standard 1994), 6 lbs. Disc. 2002, reintroduced 2005.

MSR $708 $575 $485 $375 $260 $185 $150 $140

During 2001, this model's nomenclature was changed from 1894S to 1894.

MODEL 1894C CARBINE – .357 Mag. cal., 18 1/2 in. barrel, w/o hammer block safety, 6 lbs. Mfg. 1979-84.

$400 $350 $275 $225 $185 $165 $130

MODEL 1894 SPORTER – .44 Mag. cal. only, 6 shot half mag. tube, crescent shaped hard rubber buttplate, 1,398 mfg. 1973 only.

$600 $500 $425 $350 $300 $250 $200

GRADING - PPGS™	100%	98%	95%	90%	80%	70%	60%	LAST MSR

MODEL 1894C SERIES CARBINE (1894CS) CURRENT MFG. – .357 Mag./.38 Spl. cal., copy of original Model 1894, 9 shot mag., 18 1/2 in. round barrel, open sights (hooded front became standard 1999), straight grip stock (cut checkering became standard 1994), squared finger lever, 6 lbs. New 1984.

MSR $708	$575	$485	$375	$260	$185	$150	$140	

During 2001, this model's nomenclature was changed from 1894CS to 1894C.

* ***Model 1894CP Carbine*** – similar to Model 1894C, except has 16 1/4 in. ported round barrel, 8 shot mag., approx. 5 3/4 lbs. Mfg. 2001-2002.

	$550	$450	$350	$250	$200	$175	$150	*$566*

* ***Model 1894CL Carbine*** – .32-20 Win. cal., 6 shot tube mag., 22 in. barrel with button rifling and barrel band, Marble sights, American walnut stock and forearm with cut checkering, 6 lbs. New 2005-2007.

	$595	$515	$425	$350	$300	$250	$225	*$755*

MODEL 1894P CARBINE – .44 Mag./.44 Spl. cal., 16 1/4 in. ported barrel with deep-cut Ballard type 6 groove rifling, 8 shot tube mag., checkered straight grip walnut stock with vent. recoil pad, 5 3/4 lbs. Mfg. 2000-2002.

	$550	$450	$350	$250	$200	$175	$150	*$566*

* ***Model 1894S Carbine Limited*** – .44 Mag./.44 Spl. cal., features 16 1/4 in. barrel with "The Marlin Limited" roll stamped on barrel, approx. 1,500 mfg. 1996 only.

	$550	$450	$350	$250	$200	$175	$150	

MODEL 1894FG – .41 Mag. cal., similar to Model 1894, except has pistol grip stock with cut checkering and 10 shot mag., 6 1/2 lbs. Mfg. 2003-2007.

	$525	$400	$300	$200	$175	$150	$130	*$588*

MODEL 1894PG – .44 Mag. cal., similar to Model 1894FG. Mfg. 2003-2004.

	$490	$340	$255	$190	$160	$145	$130	*$622*

MODEL 1894SBL – .357 Mag./.38 Spl. or .44 Mag./.44 Spl. cal., stainless steel, 16 1/4 in. barrel, gray/black laminate stock and forearm, big loop lever, XS Ghost ring sights, includes scope mount. Limited mfg. 2011 only.

	$875	$750	$625	$525	$425	$375	$325	*$1,062*

MODEL 1894SS/1894CSS – .357 Mag./.38 Spl. (new 2010), or .44 Mag./.44 Spl. cal., stainless steel, 20 in. barrel, 10 shot tube mag., straight grip, checkered black walnut stock and forearm, offset hammer spur, approx. 6 lbs. Mfg. 2002-2011.

	$725	$595	$475	$350	$275	$225	$185	*$829*

MODEL 1894 COWBOY (COWBOY II) – .32 H&R Mag. (mfg. mid-2004-2006), .357 Mag. (new 1997), .44-40 WCF (mfg. 1997-99), .44 Mag. (new 1997), or .45 LC cal., 10 shot tube mag., incorporates "cowboy action shooting" features, straight grip stock w/o or with checkering (disc. 2001), adj. Marbles-type rear sight, blued finish, 20 (new 2003, n/a in .45 LC cal.) or 24 (disc. 2009) in. tapered octagon barrel, 7 1/2 lbs. New 1996.

MSR $1,010	$895	$750	$625	$525	$375	$325	$275	

The Model 1894 Cowboy II refers to the three new cals. introduced in 1997. This model in .32 H&R Mag. cal. (new 2004) loads through a port in the front of the mag. tube, not a receiver port like the other cals.

* ***Model 1894 Cowboy Competition*** – .38 Spl. or .45 LC (new 2003) cal., 10 shot tube mag., 20 in. tapered octagon barrel with deep cut Ballard type rifling, hammer block safety, Marbles sights, case colored receiver, lever, and bolt, "factory tuned" to meet the demands of competitive shooters. 6 1/2 lbs. Mfg. 2002-2005.

	$795	$675	$525	$425	$375	$325	$295	*$986*

MODEL 1894CL – .218 Bee (new 1990), .25-20 WCF or .32-20 WCF cal., 6 shot (two-thirds length) tube mag., 22 in. barrel, 6 1/4 lbs. Mfg. 1988-94.

	$475	$400	$350	$250	$200	$175	$150	*$502*

Add 20% for .218 Bee cal.

GRADING - PPGS™	100%	98%	95%	90%	80%	70%	60%	LAST MSR

MODEL 1894 CENTURY LIMITED – .44-40 WCF cal., limited edition commemorative mfg. to celebrate the Model 1894's 100th Anniversary, 24 in. tapered octagon barrel with full 12 shot tube mag., features Giovanelli engraved receiver, bolt, and lever, receiver is case colored using traditional methods, checkered straight grip stock and forearm, crescent buttplate, 6 1/2 lbs. 2,500 mfg. 1994 only.

	100%	98%	95%	90%	80%	70%	60%	LAST MSR
	$1,200	$975	$675	N/A	N/A	N/A	N/A	*$1,088*

MODEL 1894 CENTURY LIMITED (EMPLOYEE SPECIAL EDITION) – employee special edition featuring gold inlaid Marlin horse and rider logo. 100 mfg. 1994-95 in ser. no. range 1-100.

	100%	98%	95%	90%	80%	70%	60%	LAST MSR
	$3,850	$2,850	$1,850	N/A	N/A	N/A	N/A	

MODEL 1894 OCTAGON – similar to 1894 Carbine, with octagon barrel. Mfg. 1973.

	100%	98%	95%	90%	80%	70%	60%	LAST MSR
	$550	$475	$425	$350	$275	$225	$200	

MODEL 1895 – .45-70 Govt. cal., 4 shot tube mag., 22 in. barrel, open sights, straight grip stock with curved buttplate, forearm cap, sling and swivels. Mfg. 1972-1984.

	100%	98%	95%	90%	80%	70%	60%	LAST MSR
	$450	$400	$350	$300	$250	$225	$200	

Add 10% for guns mfg. 1972-1978.
Add 10% for pre-micro-groove.

Early new Model 1895 Marlins had cut rifling suitable for cast bullets, while later mfg. was switched to Marlin's "Micro Groove" shallow rifling. Changes were also made from a straight stock to a pistol grip stock and from a traditional receiver to one with the newer hammer- block, push-button safety. Early guns with a straight grip stock, traditional receiver, and cut rifling command premiums over later mfg. Deep cut rifling (ser. no. to approx. 10,000) occured during the first year of production only. More recently mfg. models have pistol grip, Micro Groove rifling, and hammer-block safety - these newer guns are the least desirable from a collector's standpoint.

* ***Model 1895S*** – similar to Model 1895, except has pistol grip stock and straight buttpad.

	100%	98%	95%	90%	80%	70%	60%	LAST MSR
	$475	$300	$275	$200	$175	$150	$140	

MODEL 1895 (1895SS) – .45-70 Govt. cal., similar to Model 1895, checkered pistol grip stock, hammer block safety, cut checkering became standard 1994, 7 1/2 lbs. New 1983.

	100%	98%	95%	90%	80%	70%	60%	LAST MSR
MSR $675	$565	$465	$325	$250	$200	$175	$150	

During 2001, this model's nomenclature was changed from 1895SS to 1895.

* ***Model 1895SS Cody Stampede 75th Anniversary*** – .45-70 cal., includes semi-fancy checkered walnut stock with medallion, serial numbered CS-001-CS-200, 200 mfg. 1994 only.

	100%	98%	95%	90%	80%	70%	60%	LAST MSR
	$750	$500	$400	$335	$290	$245	$215	*$695*

* ***Model 1895 LTD V*** – .45-70 Gov't. cal., 24 in. half round/half octagon barrel, full length 8 shot mag. tube, checkered walnut stock and forearm. Mfg. 2001.

	100%	98%	95%	90%	80%	70%	60%	LAST MSR
	$695	$595	$495	$425	$350	$300	$275	

MODEL 1895XLR – .45-70 Govt. cal., features stainless steel construction with 24 in. barrel, broached rifling, fluted bolt, 4 shot mag., black/grey laminate stock with deluxe recoil pad, adj. folding semi-buckhorn rear sight, hammer block safety, 7 1/2 lbs. Mfg. 2006-2011.

	100%	98%	95%	90%	80%	70%	60%	LAST MSR
	$695	$575	$450	$375	$325	$275	$225	*$848*

This model was developed to take advantage of the Hornady LEVERevolution ammunition, which greatly improves range, energy, and accuracy.

MODEL 1895SBL – .45-70 Govt. cal., similar to Model 1895MXLR, except has 18 1/2 in. barrel, Picatinny rail. New 2009.

	100%	98%	95%	90%	80%	70%	60%	LAST MSR
MSR $1,039	$865	$775	$675	$600	$525	$450	$350	

MODEL 1895M – .450 Marlin Mag. cal. (belted), 4 shot tube mag., 18 1/2 in. ported barrel, checkered straight grip walnut stock and forearm, vent. recoil pad, adj. folding buckhorn rear sight, 7 lbs. Mfg. 2000-2010.

	100%	98%	95%	90%	80%	70%	60%	LAST MSR
	$585	$500	$400	$325	$275	$250	$225	*$715*

GRADING - PPGS™	100%	98%	95%	90%	80%	70%	60%	LAST MSR

MODEL 1895MR – similar to Model 1895M, except has 22 in. barrel, 7 1/2 lbs. Mfg. 2003-2004.

$610 $485 $395 $325 $285 $255 $225 *$761*

MODEL 1895MXLR – .450 Marlin cal., features stainless steel construction with 24 in. barrel, broached rifling, fluted bolt, 4 shot mag., black/grey laminate stock with deluxe recoil pad, adj. folding semi-buckhorn rear sight, hammer block safety, 7 1/2 lbs. Mfg. 2006-2009.

$675 $525 $435 $365 $315 $260 $225 *$806*

This model was developed to take advantage of the Hornady LEVERevolution ammunition, which greatly improves range, energy, and accuracy.

MODEL 1895CB COWBOY – .45-70 Govt. cal., features 26 in. tapered octagon barrel and 9 shot tube mag., uncheckered straight grip walnut stock and forearm, Marble front and rear (adj.) sights, 8 lbs. Mfg. 2001-2011.

$725 $575 $450 $375 $325 $260 $225 *$815*

MODEL 1895G GUIDE GUN – .45-70 Govt. cal., features 18 1/2 in. ported barrel with Ballard style cut rifling, cut checkered American stock and forearm, adj. folding buckhorn rear sight, 4 shot tube mag., vent. recoil pad, Porting was discontinued in 2002, approx. 7 lbs. 2,500 to be mfg. beginning 1998.

MSR $680 $575 $465 $330 $230 $185 $165 $150

* ***Model 1895GS Guide Gun*** – similar to Model 1895G, except is stainless steel. New 2001.

MSR $813 $700 $525 $375 $275 $225 $175 $150

* ***Model 1895GBL*** – .45-70 Govt. cal., similar to Model 1895G, except has large loop lever. New 2010.

MSR $713 $595 $475 $340 $225 $185 $165 $150

MODEL 1895RL – .480 Ruger/.475 Linebaugh cal., 6 (.480 Ruger) or 5 (.475 Linebaugh) shot tube mag., 18 1/2 in. barrel, walnut pistol grip stock, otherwise similar to Model 1895, 7 lbs. Limited mfg. 2004 only.

$565 $455 $380 $315 $275 $250 $225 *$695*

MODEL 1895 CENTURY LIMITED (CLTD) – .45-70 cal., commemorates Marlin's 125th Anniversary, engraving includes grizzly bear on left side, Marlin horse and rider logo on right, 24 in. half-round half-octagonal barrel, crescent buttplate, satin finished receiver, checkered walnut stock and forearm. Approx. 2,500 mfg. 1995 only.

$1,200 $975 $675 $525 $425 $350 $295 *$1,104*

A Marlin Collector's Association Edition was also mfg. and was the same as the Model 1895 Century Limited.

* ***Model 1895 Century Limited (CLTD) Employee Edition*** – features 3 elk on left side and gold inlaid Marlin horse and rider logo on right. 100 mfg. 1995-96 in ser. no. range 1-100.

$2,900 $2,175 $1,425 N/A N/A N/A N/A

MODEL 1936 – .30-30 Win. or .32 HPS (High Power Special) cal., similar to Model 36 1st variation, 6 shot, 20 or 24 in. barrel, tubular mag., open sights, pistol grip stock, barrel band, leaf mainspring, thinner "perch belly" forearm, case colored receiver, upper tang, buttstock has a fluted comb and flat hard rubber buttplate. Mfg. 1936-37.

$825 $675 $500 $350 $275 $200 $150

Add 10% for vivid case colors with strong greens, reds, and yellows.
Add 10% for rifles and sporting carbines.

Rifles have "A" suffix, sporting carbine has "SC" suffix, and regular and carbine has "RC" suffix.

The Model 1936 has an upper tang inscription "Model 1936" and a case colored receiver. Also, the Model 1936 did not have a letter prefix in the ser. no.

Rifles: Centerfire, Miscellaneous

MODEL 9 CAMP CARBINE SEMI-AUTO – 9mm Para. cal. only, 16 1/2 in. barrel, 12 or 20 shot mag. (disc. 1989), 4 shot mag. became standard in 1990, sand blasted steel receiver, open sights, last shot automatic hold-open, 6 3/4 lbs. Mfg. 1985-99.

$525 $375 $275 $250 $225 $200 $175 *$443*

Add 10% for nickel plating (mfg. 1991-94, Model 9N).

A new high visibility orange front sight post with cutaway hood was added in 1989.

GRADING - PPGS™	100%	98%	95%	90%	80%	70%	60%	LAST MSR

MODEL 27 SLIDE ACTION – .25-20 WCF, or .32-20 WCF cal., 2/3 tube mag., 7 shot, 24 in. octagon barrel, open sight, plain straight grip stock. Mfg. 1910-11.

$1,850	$1,650	$1,500	$1,250	$1,000	$800	$700	

Subtract 15% for .25RF cal.

MODEL 27S SLIDE ACTION – .25RF, .25-20 WCF, or .32-20 WCF cal., similar to Model 27, except has safety button on right side of receiver, round or octagonal barrel added in 1913.

$1,550	$1,350	$1,200	$1,000	$850	$700	$600	

MODEL 45 CARBINE SEMI-AUTO – .45 ACP cal. only, 7 shot mag., sandblasted steel receiver, 16 1/2 in. barrel, last shot hold open device, pressed checkering, adj. rear sight, 6 3/4 lbs. Mfg. 1986-99.

$525	$375	$275	$250	$225	$200	$175	*$443*

A new high visibility orange front sight post with cutaway hood was added in 1989.

RIFLES: RIMFIRE

From 1930 to date, Marlin has made a number of .22 cal. rimfire rifles, bolt action single shots, bolt action repeaters and auto loaders. These have normally been good quality, inexpensive weapons. In 1960, the name Glenfield was also used in connection with these guns. We will list these models for reference purposes with price ranges appearing at the end of each listing.

The models listed are in numerical sequence first, followed by alphabetical sequence, then end with promotional models for easy reference.

Machine cut checkering became standard on many Marlins beginning 1995. Safety locks have been shipped with every new rifle/shotgun beginning 1999. In 2004, the T-900 fire control system became standard on all Marlin 900 Series rifles, except the Papoose and the Model 717M2. This improved trigger has a pull of 3-5 lbs., features a new safety mechanism with positive click positions for fire and safe, and a crisp let-off.

In 2007, Marlin changed its bolt action rimfire synthetic stocks to a new classic design featuring a fluted comb, deep molded checkering, and sling swivel studs.

Rifles: Rimfire, Bolt Action

MODEL 15YN "LITTLE BUCKAROO" SINGLE SHOT – .22 S, L, or LR cal., single shot, 16 1/4 in. barrel, youth dimensions with 12 LOP, adj. rear sight, grooved receiver, pressed checkering, 4 1/4 lbs. Disc. 2003.

$175	$140	$105	$80	$75	$70	$65	*$209*

* ***Model 15YS "Little Buckaroo" Single Shot Stainless Steel*** – similar to Model 15YN, except is stainless steel and has Fire Sights. Mfg. 2002-2003.

$215	$175	$135	$85	$75	$70	$65	*$233*

MODEL 17V – .17 HMR cal., 7 shot detachable mag., 22 in. heavy barrel, walnut finished checkered hardwood Monte Carlo stock and forend, red cocking indicator, grooved receiver, includes scope mounts, 6 lbs. Mfg. 2002-2003.

$250	$200	$180	$170	$160	$145	$130	*$269*

* ***Model 17VS*** – similar to Model 17V, except has bead blasted stainless steel barrel and receiver, laminated black/grey hardwood Monte Carlo stock, 7 lbs. Mfg. 2002-2004.

$350	$275	$225	$175	$140	$125	$105	*$402*

MODEL 25MB – .22 WMR cal., bolt action, 16 1/4 in. micro-groove barrel, 7 shot mag., hardwood stock, takedown action, 6 lbs. Mfg. 1987-88 only.

$145	$115	$95	$85	$75	$70	$65	*$173*

This model included both a scope and gun case.

MODEL 25MG GARDEN GUN – please refer to the Marlin bolt action shotgun section for information on this model.

MODEL 25MN – .22 WMR cal., bolt action, 7 shot mag., 22 in. barrel, choice of walnut finished hardwood or Mossy Oak Breakup camo (new 2001) stock (pressed checkering became

GRADING - PPGS™	100%	98%	95%	90%	80%	70%	60%	LAST MSR

standard 1994), grooved receiver, adj. rear sight (new 1995), 6 lbs. Mfg. 1989-2003.

$185	$140	$105	$85	$75	$70	$65	*$241*

Add $6 for 4X scope (disc. 2000).
Add $37 for Mossy Oak Breakup camo stock.

MODEL 25N – .22 LR cal., 7 shot mag., 22 in. barrel, press checkered Monte Carlo stock, 5 1/2 lbs. Disc. 2003.

$155	$135	$110	$80	$75	$70	$65	*$212*

Add $8 for 4X scope.

* ***Model 25NC*** – similar to Model 25N, except has Mossy Oak Breakup camo stock. Disc. 2003.

$190	$145	$105	$85	$75	$70	$65	*$248*

MODEL 81TS – .22 S, L, or LR cal., 22 in. barrel with 17-25 shot tube mag., black synthetic stock with molded checkering, adj. rear sight, 6 lbs. Disc. 2003.

$165	$130	$100	$80	$75	$65	$60	*$213*

MODEL 83TS – .22 WMR cal., 22 in. barrel, 12 shot mag., otherwise similar to Model 81TS, 6 lbs. Disc. 2003.

$195	$150	$125	$95	$85	$75	$70	*$259*

MODELS 780, 781, 782, and 783 – .22 LR or .22 WMR (Models 782 and 783) cal., tube or mag., 22 in. barrel. Disc. 1988.

$110	$85	$75	$70	$65	$55	$50	*$162*

Add $17-$25 for Models 782 and 783.

MODELS 880/881 – .22 LR or .22 WMR cal., replacement for Models 780, 781, Model 880 is .22 LR with 7 shot detachable mag. and 22 in. barrel, (cut checkering became standard 1994), Model 881 is .22 LR with 17 shot tube mag. and 22 in. barrel, 6 lbs. Mfg. 1989-97.

$185	$145	$100	$85	$75	$70	$65	*$251*

Add $10 for Model 881.

This model was also available in a Biathlon configuration - approx. 100 were mfg.

* ***Model 880SS*** – similar to Model 880, except is stainless steel, black fiberglass synthetic stock, approx. 6 lbs. Mfg. 1994-2003.

$240	$175	$115	$90	$75	$60	$40	*$316*

* ***Model 880SQ (Squirrel Rifle)*** – similar to Model 880, except has black fiberglass filled synthetic stock with checkering and heavy 22 in. barrel, without sights and grooved receiver, matte finish, 7 lbs. Mfg. 1996-2003.

$245	$190	$135	$100	$80	$70	$65	*$330*

MODELS 882/883 – .22 WMR cal., 7 shot detachable (Model 882) or 12 shot tube mag. (Model 883), 22 in. barrel, checkered (cut checkering became standard 1994), black walnut Monte Carlo stock with Mar-Shield finish, adj. semi-buckhorn rear sight and hooded front, thumb safety, 6 lbs. Mfg. 1989-2003.

$240	$185	$130	$95	$85	$75	$70	*$324*

Add $13 for Model 883.
Add $35 for nickel finish on Model 883N (disc. 1993).

The Models 882 and 883 are the replacements for Models 782 and 783.

* ***Model 882SS*** – .22 WMR cal., similar to Model 882, except is stainless steel and stock is black synthetic with molded-in checkering, fire sights (red fiberoptic inserts with cutaway hood) became standard 1998, approx. 6 lbs. Mfg. 1995-2003.

$250	$190	$130	$100	$85	$70	$65	*$345*

* ***Model 882SSV*** – .22 WMR cal., features 22 in. bead blasted stainless barrel and receiver with black fiberglass reinforced synthetic stock, 7 shot mag., grooved receiver, w/o sights, ring mounts included, 7 lbs. Mfg. 1997-2003.

$245	$185	$125	$100	$85	$70	$65	*$338*

GRADING - PPGS™	100%	98%	95%	90%	80%	70%	60%	LAST MSR

* ***Model 882L*** – similar to Model 882, except has two-tone brown laminated hardwood stock, 6 1/4 lbs. Mfg. 1992-2003.

	$250	$200	$140	$100	$85	$75	$70	$342

* ***Model 883SS*** – .22 WMR cal., 12 shot tube mag., similar to Model 883, except barrel is stainless steel and stock is laminated two-tone brown birch with Monte Carlo cheekpiece. Mfg. 1993-2003.

	$265	$205	$145	$115	$100	$85	$75	$358

MODEL 915Y "LITTLE BUCKAROO" SINGLE SHOT – .22 S, L, or LR cal., 16 1/4 in. barrel, features T-900 fire control system, cocks on opening, youth dimensions, adj. rear sight, thumb safety, grooved receiver, walnut finished hardwood stock, 4 1/4 lbs. Mfg. 2004-2010.

	$175	$145	$115	$80	$75	$70	$65	$219

Add $26 for front fiber optic fire sight (Model 915YS, new 2004).

MODEL 917 – .17 HMR cal., black synthetic stock, 4 and 7 shot mags. supplied standard beginning 2007, T-900 fire control system, 22 in. barrel with sights, thumb safety, cocking indicator, adj. rear sight, 6 lbs. Mfg. 2006-2010.

	$200	$170	$150	$120	$110	$100	$90	$253

Add $49 for stainless steel finish (Model 917S, new 2007).

MODEL 917M2 – .17 Mach 2 cal., otherwise similar to Model 917V, 6 lbs. Mfg. 2005-2007.

	$185	$160	$145	$130	$100	$90	$80	$232

* ***Model 917M2S*** – similar to Model 917M2, except has laminated grey/black hardwood Monte Carlo stock and stainless steel barrel, 7 lbs. Mfg. 2005-2006.

	$300	$225	$175	$150	$125	$110	$100	$410

MODEL 917V SERIES – .17 HMR cal., 4 and 7 shot detachable mags. supplied standard beginning 2007, 22 in. heavy barrel, features T-900 fire control system, walnut finished checkered hardwood Monte Carlo stock, thumb safety, no sights, scope base included, 6 lbs. Mfg. 2004-2010.

	$225	$190	$160	$140	$120	$100	$90	$279

Add $41 for 3-9x32mm bore sighted scope (new 2007).

* ***Model 917VR*** – similar to Model 917, except has 22 in. heavy barrel, 7 lbs. Mfg. 2006-2010.

	$210	$175	$155	$135	$115	$100	$90	$266

* ***Model 917VS*** – similar to Model 917V, except has laminated grey/black hardwood Monte Carlo or synthetic carbon fiber pattern (mfg. 2007-2008) stock and stainless steel barrel. Mfg. 2004-2010.

	$315	$265	$210	$165	$135	$110	$100	$396

Add $24 for fluted barrel (Model 917VSF, new 2005).
Subtract $17 for synthetic stock (mfg. 2007-2008).

* ***Model 917VT*** – .17 HMR cal., features 22 in. heavy blue bull barrel, 4 or 7 shot mag., two-tone brown laminate stock with thumbhole pistol grip, swivel studs, rubber butt pad, no sights, drilled and tapped, 7 lbs. Mfg. 2008-2010.

	$325	$265	$200	$165	$135	$120	$110	$402

* ***Model 917VST*** – .17 HMR cal., similar to Model 917VT, except has stainless steel barrel, grey laminated thumbhole stock. Mfg. 2008-2010.

	$365	$275	$215	$175	$150	$125	$110	$451

MODEL 925 SERIES – .22 LR cal., 7 shot detachable mag., features T-900 fire control system, 22 in. barrel, thumb safety, adj. rear sight, grooved receiver, walnut finished hardwood stock with swivel studs, 5 1/2 lbs. Mfg. 2004-2010.

	$175	$140	$115	$80	$75	$70	$65	$221

Add $10 for 4x scope (disc. 2006).

GRADING - PPGS™	100%	98%	95%	90%	80%	70%	60%	LAST MSR

* ***Model 925C*** – similar to Model 925, except has Mossy Oak Break Up camo stock. Mfg. 2004-2010.

$200 $160 $130 $100 $80 $70 $65 ***$258***

* ***Model 925R*** – similar to Model 925, except has Monte Carlo black synthetic stock, 5 1/2 lbs. Mfg. 2006-2010.

$175 $145 $115 $80 $75 $70 $65 ***$213***

Add $41 for 3-9x32mm bore sighted scope (new 2007).

MODEL 925M – .22 WMR cal., 4 and 7 shot detachable mags. supplied standard beginning 2007, features T-900 fire control system, 22 in. barrel, thumb safety, adj. rear sight, grooved receiver, walnut finished hardwood stock with swivel studs, 6 lbs. Mfg. 2004-2010.

$200 $165 $135 $100 $90 $80 $75 ***$252***

Add $40 for Model 925MC with Monte Carlo stock and Mossy Oak Break-Up camo finish (disc. 2006).

* ***Model 925RM*** – .22 WMR cal., similar to Model 925M, except has checkered black fiberglass synthetic stock with full pistol grip, 6 lbs. Mfg. 2009-2010.

$190 $160 $130 $95 $85 $80 $75 ***$239***

MODEL 980S – .22 LR cal., 7 shot detachable mag., 22 in. stainless steel barrel, other metal parts stainless steel/nickel plated, T-900 fire control system, black fiberglass synthetic stock with molded checkering, thumb safety, adj. buckhorn rear sight, approx. 6 lbs. Mfg. 2004-2010.

$250 $200 $165 $130 $110 $95 $85 ***$315***

Add $30 for black synthetic stock with carbon fiber pattern (Model 980S/CF).

* ***Model 980V*** – similar to Model 980S, except has 22 in. heavy steel barrel with recessed muzzle, double bedding screws, swivel studs, no sights, grooved receiver with scope bases, drilled and tapped, 7 lbs. Mfg. 2004-2006.

$265 $210 $170 $145 $120 $100 $80 ***$349***

MODEL 981T – .22 S, L, or LR cal., 17-25 shot tube mag., 22 in. barrel, black fiberglass synthetic stock, features T-900 fire control system, thumb safety, adj. rear sight, approx. 6 lbs. Mfg. 2004-2010.

$180 $145 $110 $90 $80 $70 $60 ***$221***

Add $65 for stainless steel barrel (new 2010).

MODEL 982 – .22 WMR cal., 7 shot detachable mag., 22 in. regular barrel, T-900 fire control system, checkered American Monte Carlo stock, adj. buckhorn rear sight, thumb safety, rubber buttplate, 6 lbs. Mfg. 2004-2006.

$255 $210 $170 $145 $120 $100 $80 ***$341***

Add $20 for Model 982L with two-tone brown laminated stock (new 2004).
Add $23 for Model 982S with stainless steel barrel and nickel/stainless steel small parts (mfg. 2004-2005).

* ***Model 982VS*** – similar to Model 980, except has black synthetic stock and 22 in. heavy stainless barrel, 4 and 7 shot mags. supplied standard beginning 2007. Mfg. 2004-2010.

$265 $210 $175 $150 $125 $110 $90 ***$326***

Add $41 for synthetic stock with carbon fiber pattern (mfg. 2007-2009).

MODEL 983 SERIES – .22 WMR cal., 12 shot tube mag., 22 in. barrel, features T-900 fire control system, checkered walnut Monte Carlo stock, adj. folding buckhorn sight, 6 lbs. Mfg. 2004-2010.

$265 $210 $175 $150 $125 $105 $85 ***$325***

* ***Model 983T*** – .22 WMR cal., 12 shot tube mag., 22 in. barrel, features T-900 fire control system, black fiberglass synthetic stock with molded-in checkering, adj. rear sight, 6 lbs. Mfg. 2004-2010.

$210 $175 $150 $130 $110 $90 $75 ***$249***

* ***Model 983S*** – similar to Model 983T, except has stainless steel barrel and nickel plated/ stainless steel parts, two-tone brown hardwood laminate stock, 6 lbs. Mfg. 2004-2010.

$275 $225 $185 $145 $125 $105 $90 ***$355***

GRADING - PPGS™	100%	98%	95%	90%	80%	70%	60%	LAST MSR

MODEL 2000 TARGET – .22 LR cal., single shot (can be converted), 22 in. heavy barrel with match chamber and Lyman adj. sights, 2 stage target trigger, molded synthetic stock made from fiberglass and Kevlar with twice baked blue enamel, adj. buttplate, aluminum forearm rail, 8 lbs. Mfg. 1991-95.

	$525	$410	$350	$300	$275	$250	$225	*$602*

Add $34 for 5-shot conversion unit (for summer biathlon competition).

* ***Model 2000A Target*** – similar to Model 2000 Target, except has adj. comb, ambidextrous pistol grip, and molded-in logo. Mfg. 1994 only.

	$550	$425	$365	$315	$290	$260	$230	*$625*

* ***Model 2000L Target*** – .22 LR cal., updated version of the Model 2000, featuring grey/black laminated stock, adj. aperture rear and aperture insert front sight, double bedding screws, factory test target supplied with each gun, 8 lbs. Mfg. 1996-2002.

	$600	$475	$380	$320	$280	$250	$225	*$745*

MODEL XT SERIES – .17 HMR (XT-17 Series), .22 LR (XT-22 Series), or .22 WMR (XT-22M Series), 16 1/4 (Youth), or 22 in. barrel, features ProFire adj. trigger allowing 3-6 lb. trigger pull with zero creep, detachable or tubular mag., red cocking indicator, thumb and trigger safeties, black synthetic ergonomic stock with palm swell pistol grip, with or w/o (Varmint models) sights. New 2011.

* ***Model XT-17 Series*** – .17 HMR cal., 22 in. regular, varmint, or fluted varmint barrel, includes 4 and 7 shot mags., blue finish or stainless steel, 6-7 lbs. New 2011.

» **Model XT-17R** – features black synthetic stock, 22 in. regular barrel with sights, and blue finish.

MSR $260	$215	$185	$165	$145	$130	$120	$110

» **Model XT-17SR** – similar to Model XT-17R, except is stainless steel.

MSR $310	$250	$220	$190	$165	$150	$135	$115

» **Model XT-17VR** – features varmint barrel.

MSR $273	$220	$190	$165	$145	$130	$120	$110

» **Model XT-17V** – features hardwood stock, 22 in. varmint barrel and blued finish.

MSR $287	$230	$195	$170	$150	$130	$120	$110

Add $40 for 3x32mm mounted and bore sighted scope (Model XT-17VO).

» **Model XT-17VSL** – features black/gray laminate stock, stainless steel, and 22 in. varmint barrel.

MSR $407	$330	$285	$240	$210	$180	$150	$130

Add $24 for 22 in. fluted varmint barrel w/o scope base blocks (Model XT-17VSFL).

» **Model XT-17VLB** – features brown laminate thumbhole stock, 22 in. varmint barrel, blue finish.

MSR $414	$335	$285	$240	$210	$180	$150	$130

» **Model XT-17VSLB** – features black/gray laminate thumbhole stock, stainless steel, 22 in. varmint barrel.

MSR $464	$395	$325	$265	$230	$200	$175	$150

* ***Model XT-22 Series*** – .22 S, L, or LR cal., 16 1/4 or 22 in. barrel, 7 shot detachable or tube (25 shot with .22 S, 19 shot with .22 L, or 17 shot with .22 LR) mag., blue finish or stainless steel, 6-7 lbs. New 2011.

» **Model XT-22TR** – features black synthetic stock and blue finish. New 2011.

MSR $227	$175	$145	$120	$100	$85	$70	$60

Add $55 for stainless steel (Model XT-22TSR).

» **Model XT-22Y1** – features compact hardwood stock, 16 1/4 in. barrel, single shot, blue finish. New 2011.

MSR $219	$175	$145	$120	$100	$85	$70	$60

GRADING - PPGS™	100%	98%	95%	90%	80%	70%	60%	LAST MSR

» **Model XT-22YS1** – features compact hardwood stock, 16 1/4 in. barrel, stainless steel, and fiber optic sights. New 2011.

MSR $238	$185	$150	$120	$100	$85	$70	$60	

» **Model XT-22YR** – features compact black synthetic stock, 16 1/4 in. barrel, blue finish.

MSR $226	$180	$145	$120	$100	$85	$70	$60	

» **Model XT-22YSR** – features compact black synthetic stock, stainless steel, 16 1/4 in. barrel, fiber optic sights. New 2011.

MSR $247	$195	$155	$125	$100	$85	$70	$60	

» **Model XT-22** – features .22 LR cal. only, hardwood stock, 22 in. barrel, blue finish. New 2011.

MSR $221	$175	$145	$120	$100	$85	$70	$60	

» **Model XT-22R** – features .22 LR cal. only, black synthetic stock, 22 in. regular or threaded (Model XT-22RZ) barrel, blue finish. New 2011.

MSR $213	$175	$145	$120	$100	$85	$70	$60	

Add $41 for 3-9x32mm mounted and bore sighted scope (Model XT-22RO), disc. late 2011.

» **Model XT-22RC** – features .22 LR cal. only, synthetic camo stock, 22 in. barrel, blue finish. New 2011.

MSR $258	$200	$155	$125	$100	$85	$70	$60	

» **Model XT-22VR** – features .22 LR cal. only, black synthetic stock, 22 in. heavy varmint barrel, blue finish. New 2011.

MSR $225	$180	$145	$120	$100	$85	$70	$60	

» **Model XT-22SR** – features .22 LR cal. only, black synthetic stock, stainless steel, 22 in. barrel with semi-buckhorn folding rear sight and hooded ramp front sight. New 2011.

MSR $314	$260	$225	$190	$165	$150	$135	$115	

» **Model XT-22RO** – features adj. trigger, black synthetic stock, 22 in. barrel with blue finish. New 2012.

MSR $255	$200	$155	$125	$100	$85	$70	$60	

» **Model XT-22RZ** – similar to Model XT-22RO, except has threaded barrel. New 2012.

MSR $243	$190	$150	$120	$100	$85	$70	$60	

* ***Model XT-22M Series*** – .22 WMR cal., 4 and 7 shot clip mag., or 12 shot tube mag., 22 in. barrel with or w/o sights, blue or stainless finish, 6 lbs. New 2011.

» **Model XT-22M** – hardwood stock, blue finish and adj. ramp sights. New 2011.

MSR $252	$200	$155	$125	$100	$85	$70	$60	

» **Model XT-22MR** – features black synthetic stock, adj. ramp sight, blue finish. New 2011.

MSR $239	$185	$150	$120	$100	$85	$70	$60	

» **Model XT-22MTR** – features black synthetic stock, 12 shot tube mag., adj./ramp sights, blue finish. New 2011.

MSR $249	$200	$155	$125	$100	$85	$70	$60	

» **Model XT-22MTSL** – features brown laminate stock, stainless steel, 12 shot tube mag., and semi-buckhorn folding rear sight with hooded ramp front sight. New 2011.

MSR $355	$285	$250	$220	$190	$170	$150	$130	

» **Model XT-22MTW** – features walnut stock, 12 shot tube mag., semi-buckhorn folding rear sight with hooded ramp front sight, blue finish. New 2011.

MSR $325	$265	$230	$190	$165	$150	$135	$115	

» **Model XT-22MVSR** – features black synthetic stock, stainless steel. New 2011.

MSR $326	$265	$230	$190	$165	$150	$135	$115	

GRADING - PPGS™	100%	98%	95%	90%	80%	70%	60%	LAST MSR

MARLIN PROMOTIONAL MODELS – Models 15 (disc.), 15Y (disc.), 15N (mfg. 1998-99, last MSR $188), 15YN (refer to individual listing), 25 (disc.), 25M (disc.), 25N (refer to individual listing), 25NC (refer to individual listing), 70 (disc.), 70HC (mfg. 1989-95, last 1995 MSR was $167), 75C (disc.), 81TS (refer to individual listing), and 795 Semi-Auto (refer to individual listing), are inexpensive, utilitarian .22 LR or .22 WMR cal. (Model 25M only), rifles designed for inexpensive shooting.

Series 15 and 25 Models designate bolt action, Series 60 and 70 designate semi-auto design.

REPEATING PROMOTIONAL MODELS

Model 80 - 1934-1939. Price Range $50 - $95.
Model 80E - 1934-1940. Price Range $55 - $100.
Model 80C - 1940-1970. Price Range $55 - $100.
Model 80DL - 1940-1965. Price Range $70 - $105.
Model 80G - 1960-1965, Marlin Glenfield. Price Range $45 - $80.
Model 20 - 1966-disc., Marlin Glenfield. Price Range $45 - $80.
Model 780 - 1971-1988. Price Range $50 - $85.
Model 781 - 1971-1988. Price Range $50 - $85.
Model 782 - 1971-1988, .22 WRM. Price Range $75 - $135.
Model 783 - 1971-1988, .22 WRM. Price Range $75 - $135.
Model 980 - 1962-1970, .22 WRM. Price Range $75 - $135.
Model 81 - 1937-1940. Price Range $50 - $95.
Model 81E - 1937-1940. Price Range $65 - $110.
Model 81C - 1940-1970. Price Range $65 - $110.
Model 81DL - 1940-1965. Price Range $65 - $100.
Model 81G - 1960-1965 Marlin Glenfield. Price Range $55 - $85.

SINGLE SHOT PROMOTIONAL MODELS

Model 65 - 1932-1938. Price Range $40- $75.
Model 65E - 1932-1938. Price Range $50 - $85.
Model 100 - 1936-1941. Price Range $50 - $85.
Model 100S Tom Mix Special - disc. Price Range $140 - $275.
Model 100SB - 1936-1941. Price Range $55 - $95.
Model 101 - 1941-1977. Price Range $50 - $85.
Model 101 DL - disc. Price Range $65 - $100.
Model 101 Crown Prince - 1959. Price Range $85 - $165.
Model 101G - 1960-1965, Marlin Glenfield. Price Range $45 - $80.
Model 10 - 1966-disc., Marlin Glenfield. Price Range $45 - $75.
Model 122 - 1966-disc. Price Range $45 - $70.

Rifles: .22 Cal., Lever Action

MODEL 39 – .22 S, L, or LR cal., 24 in. octagon barrel with tube mag., open sights, takedown, case hardened receiver and lever, S-shaped pistol grip stock, bluing on barrel, forend tip, mag. tube, bolt, hammer, and screws, various qualities of walnut (X, 2X, or 3X), hard rubber buttplate. Approx. 40-50,000 mfg. 1922-38.

	N/A	N/A	$4,500	$3,250	$2,750	$2,200	$1,600	

Early models with fancy 2X-3X wood will bring a considerable premium.

Excellent original condition in this model is extremely hard to find since most specimens were well used due to the 16/25 shell mag. capacity, reliability, and the fact that the balance point of the gun (the receiver) normally wore first due to carrying wear. Earlier guns without a prefix or with an "S" prefix are noted for their superior workmanship and fine finish. Later "HS" prefix (High Speed) are not quite as valuable as these earlier guns, but offer practical shooting value.

MODEL 39A – similar to Model 39, with case hardened receiver (mfg. 1939-1945), includes 1st and 2nd Models with round barrel. 3rd Model 1st Variation was introduced in 1946 and has blue receiver, 3rd Model 2nd Variation has flutes in buttstock comb and was introduced in 1951, and 3rd Model 3rd Variation has Micro-Groove rifling, no pistol grip cap, and was introduced in 1954.

* ***Model 39A 1st Model*** – case colored frame, no prefix. Mfg. 1939 only.

	N/A	$2,200	$1,700	$1,350	$950	$775	$650	

The first variation of the Model 39A mfg. in 1939 is distinguishable by a buttstock and lever similar to those on earlier Model 39s.

GRADING - PPGS™	100%	98%	95%	90%	80%	70%	60%	LAST MSR

* ***Model 39A 2nd Model*** – case colored frame, "B" prefix. Mfg. 1941.

	N/A	$1,850	$1,375	$1,050	$900	$650	$550	

The second variation had a rounded lever like current production and no "S" shape to bottom of pistol grip.

* ***Model 39A 3rd Model 1st Variation*** – features blued receiver, new ramp front sight, hard rubber buttplate, and Ballard rifling. Mfg. 1946-1950.

	N/A	N/A	$750	$575	$475	$400	$350	

* ***Model 39A 3rd Model 2nd Variation*** – similar to 3rd Model 1st Variation, except has flutes in buttstock comb, white plastic spacer next to buttplate, and pistol grip cap with white spacer and brass insert. Mfg. 1951-53.

	N/A	$550	$450	$375	$300	$275	$250	

* ***Model 39A 3rd Model 3rd Variation*** – similar to 3rd Model 2nd Variation, except has Micro-Groove rifling, and no pistol grip cap. Mfg. 1954-57.

	N/A	$450	$375	$325	$300	$250	$200	

GOLDEN 39A – similar to Model 39A, with gold-plated trigger, sling swivels. Mfg. 1957-87.

	$475	$375	$300	$250	$200	$175	$150	

Add 30% to pre-1970 (oil finished stock) models.

GOLDEN 39M – similar to Golden 39A, except is carbine variation. Mfg. 1972-1987.

	$550	$425	$365	$300	$250	$150	$125	

MODEL 39A "MOUNTIE" – straight grip stock, slim forearm, otherwise similar to 39A. Mfg. 1953-1957.

	$475	$400	$350	$300	$250	$200	$175	

* ***Model 39A "MOUNTIE" with K prefix*** – 24 in. barrel and slender forearm. 4,335 mfg. 1953 only.

	$795	$675	$550	$475	$425	$350	$300	

GOLDEN 39A MOUNTIE – mfg. 1957-1972.

	$495	$425	$350	$300	$250	$200	$175	

90TH ANNIVERSARY 39A RIFLE – 24 in. chrome barrel and action, select checkered walnut stock, carved squirrel on side of buttstock. 500 mfg. in 1960.

	$1,550	$1,400	$1,100	$825	$500	$425	$350	*$100*

90TH ANNIVERSARY MODEL 39M MOUNTIE CARBINE – similar to 90th Anniversary Model 39A, except 20 in. barrel, straight stock. 500 mfg. in 1960.

	$1,550	$1,400	$1,100	$825	$500	$425	$350	*$100*

Add $50-$75 for original box and papers.

MODEL 39AWL – special model made exclusively for Wal-Mart, supporting the Wildlife Management Institution and Wildlife Forever, features similar to Marlin 1897CL CLassic, 24 in. half-round, half-octagon barrel, half mag., checkered black American walnut pistol grip stock, adj. semi-buckhorn rear sight, engraved receiver with scroll and "Wildlife for Tomorrow" and "Sportsmen Supporting Conservation". 2,000 mfg. 1997 only.

	$850	$750	$550	$500	$450	$400	$350	*$729*

MODEL 39A-DL – similar to 90th Anniversary, with blue barrel and action, regular production. Mfg. 1961-1963.

	$1,150	$975	$825	$750	$500	$400	$300	

This model is also known as the "Marlin 39A Squirrel Gun."

MODEL 39 PRESENTATION – .22 cal., one of the pair in the "Brace of 1,000," engraved receiver, 20 in. tapered octagon barrel, select fancy walnut straight grip stock and forend. Mfg. 1970 only.

	$1,175	$950	$825	$700	$575	$450	$375	

Add 10%-20% for extra fancy walnut.

GRADING - PPGS™	100%	98%	95%	90%	80%	70%	60%	LAST MSR

MODEL 39A OCTAGON – similar to Golden 39A, with octagon barrel, no pistol grip cap, 2,551 rifles and 2,140 carbines were produced. Mfg. 1973.

	$775	$675	$575	$475	$425	$360	$295	

MODEL 39 CARBINE – similar to 39M, with light barrel, 3/4 tube mag. 9,695 mfg. 1963-67.

	$500	$450	$400	$325	$275	$200	$150	

MODEL 39D – similar to 39M, with pistol grip stock. Mfg. 1971-73.

	$395	$350	$300	$250	$150	$125	$100	

MODEL 39A/AS – .22 LR cal., current production model, lever action, 19-26 shot tube mag., 24 in. barrel, walnut stock (cut checkering became standard 1994), open sights, gold trigger, takedown, 6 1/2 lbs.

MSR $702	$615	$475	$375	$300	$250	$200	$175	

This model was previously designated the Model 39A. In 1988, the Model 39AS became the standard production model and included a rebounding hammer and hammer block safety. In 2001, the model nomenclature was changed back to the Model 39A.

MODEL 39TDS – .22 LR cal., carbine variation of the Model 39AS, 16 1/2 in. barrel with open sights, 5 1/4 lbs. Mfg. 1988-95.

	$550	$450	$350	$200	$175	$150	$125	*$443*

MODEL 39M – carbine version of Model 39A, 20 in. lightweight barrel, 16 shot tube mag., squared finger lever, 6 lbs. Disc. 1987.

	$425	$350	$300	$275	$225	$175	$150	*$304*

MODEL 39M OCTAGON – similar to Model 39M, with octagon barrel. 2,140 mfg. 1973.

	$695	$595	$525	$475	$425	$360	$295	

MODEL 39 CENTURY LTD – Marlin Centennial 1870-1970 Commemorative, 20 in. octagon barrel, select walnut straight stock, brass forearm cap and buttplate, name plate in butt. 35,388 mfg. 1970.

	$695	$525	$425	N/A	N/A	N/A	N/A	

This model should have the original box for 100% values.

MODEL 39A ARTICLE II – NRA Centennial Commemorative 1871-1971, "Right to Bear Arms" medallion in receiver, 24 in. octagon barrel, fancy pistol grip stock, brass buttplate and forearm cap. 6,244 mfg. 1971.

	$575	$495	$425	$375	N/A	N/A	N/A	

MODEL 39M ARTICLE II CARBINE – similar to 39A Article II, with 20 in. barrel, straight grip stock. Mfg. 3,824.

	$575	$495	$425	$375	$350	$295	$250	

MODEL 56 – similar to Model 57 Levermatic, 22 or 24 in. barrel, with mag. Mfg. 1955-64.

	$300	$250	$200	$150	$125	$100	$85	

MODEL 57 LEVERMATIC – .22 S, L, or LR cal., tube mag., 22 in. barrel, open sight, Monte Carlo pistol grip stock. Mfg. 1959-65.

	$375	$350	$300	$250	$200	$150	$125	

MODEL 57M – .22 WMR cal., similar to Model 57 Levermatic, except has 24 in. barrel.

	$400	$350	$300	$250	$200	$150	$110	

MODEL 1894M (.22 WMR) – .22 WMR cal., with 20 in. barrel, 11 shot tube mag., straight grip walnut stock and forearm, 6 1/4 lbs. Mfg. 1983-1989.

	$450	$395	$350	$250	$200	$175	$150	*$358*

MODEL 1897 COWBOY – .22 S, L, or LR cal., takedown action, 19 shot (.22 LR cal.), tube mag., rebounding hammer with block safety, 24 in. tapered octagon barrel with Micro-Groove (16 grooves) rifling, cut checkered walnut stock and forearm, adj. Marble semi-buckhorn rear and carbine front sight with brass bead, high polish blue, 6 1/2 lbs. Mfg. 1999-2001.

	$575	$495	$400	$350	$295	$265	$235	*$708*

GRADING - PPGS™	100%	98%	95%	90%	80%	70%	60%	LAST MSR

MODEL 1897T – .22 S, L, or LR cal., 14-21 shot mag., 20 in. tapered octagon barrel, hammer block safety, Marble front and rear sights, 6 lbs. Mfg. 2002-2003.

	$585	$430	$365	$330	$285	$240	$195	*$748*

MODEL 1897 CENTURY LIMITED LEVER ACTION – .22 LR cal., 100th anniversary of the Model 1897, features extensive receiver engraving and gold accenting, 24 in. half round/half octagon barrel with open sights, checkered fancy walnut stock and forearm. Limited mfg. 1997 only, limited quantities remained through 1999.

	$975	$850	$700	$625	$540	$465	$385	*$1,055*

* ***Model 1897 Century Limited Lever Action Employee Edition*** – .22 LR cal., features gold scroll work on lever, less than 100 mfg. 1997 only in ser. no. range 1-100.

	$1,725	$1,550	$1,275	N/A	N/A	N/A	N/A	

MODEL 1897 ANNIE OAKLEY – .22 LR cal., features 18 1/2 in. tapered octagon barrel with marble sights, blue receiver with rolled scroll engraving featuring gold Annie Oakley etched name on bolt, deluxe checkered walnut stock and forearm. Mfg. 1998 only.

	$950	$825	$725	$625	$525	$450	$375	*$1,054*

Add $100 for employee variation.

An employee variation of this model was made with gold inlays on finger lever, 100 mfg. total.

Rifles: .22 Cal., Slide Action

MODEL 18 – .22 S, L, or LR cal., tube mag., 20 in. round or octagon barrel, open sight, exposed hammer, plain straight grip stock. Mfg. 1906-09.

	$1,400	$1,250	$1,100	$900	$750	$600	$500	

MODEL 20 – .22 S, L, or LR cal., 24 in. octagon barrel, open sight, exposed hammer, takedown, plain straight grip stock. Mfg. 1907-22.

	$1,400	$1,250	$1,100	$900	$750	$600	$500	

MODEL 25 – .22 Short cal. and CB cap., tube mag., 23 in. barrel, open sight, exposed hammer, takedown, plain straight grip stock. Mfg. 1909-10.

	$1,550	$1,350	$1,200	$1,000	$850	$700	$600	

MODEL 29 – similar to Model 20, with 23 in. round barrel, 1/2 tube mag. Mfg. 1913-16.

	$1,300	$1,150	$1,000	$850	$700	$600	$500	

MODEL 32 – .22 S, L, or LR cal., 2/3 tube mag., 24 in. octagon barrel, open sight, plain pistol grip stock, hammerless. Mfg. 1915 only.

	$1,850	$,650	$1,500	$1,250	$1,000	$800	$700	

MODEL 37 – similar to Model 29, with 24 in. barrel, full length tube mag. Mfg. 1913-16.

	$1,250	$1,125	$1,000	$850	$700	$575	$475	

MODEL 38 – .22 S, L, or LR cal., 2/3 tube mag., 24 in. octagon barrel, open sights, hammerless, takedown, plain pistol grip stock. Mfg. 1920-30.

	$1,350	$1,200	$1,050	$900	$750	$600	$500	

Rifles: Rimfire, Semi-Auto

MODEL 60 – .22 LR cal., 14 shot (LR) tube mag., entry level rifle with 19 or 22 (disc. 2002) in. Micro-Groove barrel, blue finish, aluminum receiver, walnut finished laminated hardwood stock (laminated now standard) with pressed checkering, adj. rear sight, crossbolt safety, last shot hold open, approx. 5 1/2 lbs. New 1960.

MSR $197	$160	$125	$100	$85	$75	$65	$60	

Add $8 for 4X scope (disc. 2006).

* ***Model 60C*** – similar to Model 60, except has full coverage Mossy Oak Breakup camo stock, blue finish, 5 1/2 lbs. New 2000.

MSR $232	$175	$145	$115	$90	$80	$70	$60	

* ***Model 60DL*** – similar to Model 60, except has Walnutone walnut patterned finish. Mfg. 2004-2006.

	$175	$140	$110	$85	$75	$65	$60	*$236*

GRADING - PPGS™	100%	98%	95%	90%	80%	70%	60%	LAST MSR

* ***Model 60SN*** – features black synthetic stock, blue finish, includes sling swivel studs. New 2007.

MSR $189	$155	$125	$100	$80	$75	$65	$60	

Add $15 for 4x20mm bore sighted scope.

* ***Model 60DLX*** – .22 LR cal., 14 shot tube mag., checkered Monte Carlo walnut finished hardwood stock with full pistol grip, 19 in. barrel, engraved receiver with "50th Anniversary Edition" and gold barrel markings, swivel studs, semi-buckhorn folding rear sight, 5 1/2 lbs. New 2010.

MSR $261	$210	$175	$155	$135	$115	$100	$90	

MODEL 60SS STAINLESS – .22 LR cal., 14 shot tube mag., nickel plated aluminum receiver and other parts, laminated black/grey birch stock with Monte Carlo cheekpiece, Mar-Shield finish, 19 or 22 (disc. 2002) in. stainless barrel, most recent mfg. has adj. semi-buckhorn folding rear with high visibility post and removable cutaway Wide-scan hood front sight, 5 1/2 lbs. New 1993.

MSR $298	$245	$195	$165	$125	$110	$90	$80	

* ***Model 60SB Stainless*** – similar to Model 60SS, except has uncheckered (mfg. 1998 only) or press-checkered (new 1999) birch Monte Carlo stock, laminated hardwood became standard 2004. New 1998.

MSR $250	$220	$180	$155	$125	$85	$70	$65	

Add $17 for 4X scope (disc. 2006).

This model was previously sold to Wal-Mart only.

* ***Model 60SSK Stainless*** – similar to Model 60SS, except has black fiberglass stock with Monte Carlo cheekpiece. Mfg. 1998-2006.

	$215	$180	$140	$110	$95	$80	$70	*$269*

Add $15 for 4X scope (disc. 2001).

* ***Model 60S-CF*** – similar to Model 60SN, except features synthetic stock with carbon fiber pattern, includes sling studs. Mfg. 2007-2009.

	$195	$160	$130	$100	$85	$75	$65	*$271*

MODEL 70P (PAPOOSE) – .22 LR cal. only, semi-auto, takedown carbine with 16 1/4 in. barrel, 7 shot mag., rustproof receiver, bolt hold open, is supplied with floating nylon carrying case. Mfg. 1986-94.

	$170	$125	$90	$75	$65	$60	$55	*$225*

Subtract $25 if without 4X scope (became standard 1993).

* ***Model 70PSS*** – similar to Model 70P, except has stainless steel barrel and nickel plated parts, black checkered synthetic stock with swing swivels, last shot hold-open became standard in 1996, includes blue nylon floatable case, 3 1/4 lbs. New 1995.

MSR $329	$265	$210	$170	$135	$110	$90	$80	

* ***Model 70HC*** – .22 LR cal., semi-auto, carbine with 18 in. barrel. Mfg. 1988-95.

	$185	$155	$130	$120	$110	$100	$90	

MODEL 717M2 – .17 Mach 2 cal., 7 shot detachable mag., 18 in. sporter barrel with open sights, walnut finished hardwood stock, last shot bolt hold open, crossbolt safety, 5 1/2 lbs. Mfg. 2005-2007.

	$180	$160	$140	$120	$110	$100	$90	*$222*

MODEL 795 – .22 LR cal., 10 shot detachable mag., 18 in. barrel, black synthetic Monte Carlo stock, grooved receiver, last shot bolt hold open, approx. 5 lbs.

MSR $181	$145	$110	$90	$80	$65	$60	$55	

Add $38 for 4x20mm mounted scope and bore sighted (new 2012).

* ***Model 795SS*** – similar to Model 795, except has stainless steel barrel and nickel plated parts. New 2002.

MSR $259	$200	$160	$130	$100	$85	$70	$65	

GRADING - PPGS™	100%	98%	95%	90%	80%	70%	60%	LAST MSR

MODEL 922M – .22 WMR cal., 7 shot detachable mag., 20 1/2 in. barrel, Garand style safety, alloy receiver, hold-open device, uncheckered or checkered (became standard 1994) walnut stock with solid pad, blue steel (hard coated on receiver), 6 1/2 lbs. Mfg. 1993-2001.

	$360	$295	$240	$200	$185	$175	$165	*$454*

MODEL 990 – .22 LR cal. only, 18 shot tube mag., 22 in. barrel, last shot automatic bolt hold-open, Monte Carlo American black walnut stock with pistol grip, 5 1/2 lbs. Disc. 1987.

	$115	$90	$75	$65	$60	$55	$50	*$159*

MODEL 990L – .22 LR cal., 14 shot tube mag., 22 in. barrel, laminated two-tone brown Monte Carlo stock, gold trigger, adj. rear sight, grooved receiver, 5 3/4 lbs. Mfg. 1993-94.

	$180	$160	$145	$130	$120	$110	$100	*$223*

MODEL 995 – .22 LR cal., 7 shot mag., 18 in. barrel, Monte Carlo walnut stock, 5 lbs. Disc. 1994.

	$160	$125	$85	$70	$65	$60	$55	*$206*

* ***Model 995SS*** – .22 LR cal., stainless steel barrel and nickel-plated small parts, black fiberglass stock with molded-in checkering, adj. rear sight, last shot hold-open (new 1996), 5 lbs. Mfg. 1995-99.

	$195	$145	$110	$90	$75	$60	$50	*$255*

MODEL 7000 – .22 LR cal., 10 shot detachable mag., 18 in. heavy barrel without sights and recessed muzzle, black fiberglass synthetic stock with molded-in checkering, grooved receiver, no sights, last shot hold open, scope mounts provided, 5 1/2 lbs. Mfg. 1997-2006.

	$210	$190	$165	$140	$130	$120	$110	*$263*

* ***Model 7000T*** – .22 LR cal., target model with 18 in. heavy barrel, red, white and blue laminated hardwood stock with adj. pad, two stage target trigger with stop, aluminum forend rail with adj. stop, grooved receiver w/o sights, 7 1/2 lbs. Mfg. 1999-2001.

	$365	$300	$240	$200	$185	$175	$165	*$465*

SEMI-AUTO PROMOTIONAL MODELS

Model 50 - 1931-1935. Price Range $85 - $150.
Model 50E - 1931-1934. Price Range $85 - $165.
Model A-1 - 1936-1940. Price Range $85 - $155.
Model A-1E - 1935-1946. Price Range $85 - $160.
Model A-1C - 1941-1946. Price Range $75 - $155.
Model A-1DL - 1941-1946. Price Range $75 - $155.
Model 88-C - 1948-1956. Price Range $75 - $150.
Model 88-DL - 1953-1956. Price Range $75 - $150.
Model 89-C - 1948-1961. Price Range $75 - $150.
Model 89-DL - 1950-1961. Price Range $75 - $150.
Model 98 - 1957-1959. Price Range $75 - $150.
Model 99 - 1959-1960. Price Range $75 - $150.
Model 99C - 1961-1978. Price Range $75 - $150.
Model 99G - 1960-1965, Marlin Glenfield. Price Range $75 - $150.
Model 60 - 1960-present, Marlin Glenfield (2000 MSR $200).
Model 99DL - 1960-1964. Price Range $75 - $150.
Model 49 - 1968-1970. Price Range $75 - $150
Model 49DL - 1971-1978. Price Range $75 - $150.
Model 99M1 - 1964-1978. Price Range $75 - $150.
Model 989M2 - 1966-disc. Price Range $75 - $150.
Model 989 - 1962-1965. Price Range $75 - $150.
Model 70 (HC) - 1966-1995, Marlin Glenfield. Price Range $85 - $160.
Model 989G - 1962-1964, Marlin Glenfield. Price Range $75 - $150.
Model 990 - disc. Price Range $75 - $150.

SHOTGUNS: BOLT ACTION

MODEL 25MG GARDEN GUN – .22 WMR shot shell, features 22 in. smooth bore barrel with

GRADING - PPGS™	100%	98%	95%	90%	80%	70%	60%	LAST MSR

high visibility bead front sight only, 7 shot detachable mag., black synthetic stock, thumb safety, 6 lbs. Mfg. 1999-2002.

	$190	$155	$130	$110	$100	$90	$80	*$245*

MODEL 50 DL – 12 ga. only, upland game model, 28 in. barrel bored M, black Rynite stock with molded-in checkering, 2 shot mag., 7 1/2 lbs. Mfg. 1997-99.

	$255	$195	$150	$125	$115	$100	$90	*$330*

MODEL 55 – 12, 16, or 20 ga., 2 shot detachable mag., 26 and 28 in. full choke barrel, plain pistol grip stock. Mfg. 1950-65.

	$90	$70	$55	$40	$35	$30	$25	
With adj. choke	$100	$85	$65	$50	$45	$40	$30	

MODEL 55 GOOSE GUN – similar to Model 55, except 12 ga. only, 36 in. full choke barrel, 3 in. chamber, 2 shot mag., leather carrying strap and detachable swivels, walnut stock with rubber recoil pad, 8 lbs. Mfg. 1962-96.

	$235	$185	$145	$125	$115	$100	$90	*$308*

* ***Model 55 Goose Gun GDL*** – similar to Model 55 Goose Gun, except has black Rynite synthetic stock. Mfg. 1997-2000.

	$330	$240	$200	$180	$160	$145	$130	*$396*

MODEL 55 SWAMP GUN – similar to Model 55, 12 ga., 20 in. adj. choke barrel, 3 in. mag. Mfg. 1963-65.

	$105	$90	$70	$55	$50	$45	$35	

MODEL 55S SLUG GUN – 24 in. barrel, cylinder bore, rifle sights. Mfg. 1974-83.

	$140	$120	$110	$95	$85	$55	$40	

MODEL 59 SINGLE SHOT – .410 bore, 2 1/2 or 3 in. chamber, 24 in. barrel bored F, walnut pistol grip stock and forearm, 48,447 mfg. 1956-1965.

	$150	$125	$110	$95	$85	$55	$40	

MODEL 512 SLUGMASTER – 12 ga., 3 in. chamber, bolt action, 2 shot box mag., 21 in. rifled barrel, adj. rear sight, receiver is drilled and tapped for scope mount (included), walnut finished birch stock with pressed checkering and vent. recoil pad, 8 lbs. Mfg. 1994-99.

	$295	$220	$195	$175	$160	$145	$130	*$361*

* ***Model 512DL Slugmaster*** – similar to Model 512 Slugmaster, except has black Rynite stock, Fire Sights (with red fiberoptic inserts) became standard 1998. Disc. 1998.

	$310	$230	$200	$180	$160	$145	$130	*$372*

* ***Model 512P Slugmaster*** – 12 ga., 3 in. chamber, features 21 in. ported fully rifled barrel with front and rear Fire Sights (high visibility red and green fiberoptic inserts), 2 shot detachable box mag., black fiberglass synthetic stock with molded-in checkering, receiver is drilled and tapped, 8 lbs. Mfg. 1999-2001.

	$315	$235	$200	$180	$165	$155	$145	*$388*

MODEL 5510 – 10 ga., 3 1/2 in. mag., 2 shot mag., 34 in. barrel, leather carrying strap and detachable swivels, rubber recoil pad, marked "The Original Super Goose 10", 10 1/2 lbs. Mfg. 1976-1985.

	$220	$170	$160	$150	$140	$130	$120	*$282*

SHOTGUNS: LEVER ACTION

MODEL .410 LEVER ACTION (1929-1932 MFG.) – .410 bore, 22 or 26 in. barrel, full choke, lever action, similar to 1893, exposed hammer, plain pistol grip stock. Mfg. 1929-32 as a stockholders' promotional firearm.

	$1,800	$1,450	$1,100	$850	$750	$650	$550	

Add 20% for 22 in. barrel.

* ***Model .410 Deluxe Lever Action*** – includes deluxe checkered walnut stock and forearm.

	$2,200	$1,800	$1,600	$1,350	$1,100	$900	$800	

Deluxe forearm does not have flute in it.

GRADING - PPGS™	100%	98%	95%	90%	80%	70%	60%	LAST MSR

NEW MODEL .410 – .410 bore, 2 1/2 in. chamber, 4-5 shot tube mag., 22 in. cylinder bore barrel, hammer block safety, checkered black American walnut stock and forend, folding rear with green fiberoptic front sight, 9 1/2 lbs. Mfg. 2004-2005.

	$550	$475	$400	$365	$335	$300	$275	*$614*

SHOTGUNS: O/U

Please refer to the L.C. Smith section for currently manufactured L.C. Smith O/U shotguns.

MODEL 90 SHOTGUN – 12, 16, 20 ga., or .410 bore shotgun or combination gun configuration (12 ga. over .30/30 barrels), 26, 28, or 30 in. barrels, boxlock, extractors, checkered pistol grip stock. Mfg. 1937-1958. Guns made from 1937-49 had vent. separated barrels, after 1949, solid barrels.

* ***Model 90 Shotgun w/Double Triggers***

	$475	$425	$375	$330	$290	$265	$230
.410 bore	$1,995	$1,750	$1,550	$1,325	$1,175	$1,050	$975

Add 15% for 16 or 20 ga.
Add 20% for .410 Bore.

* ***Model 90 Shotgun w/Single Trigger***

	$625	$575	$525	$475	$440	$400	$375
.410 bore	$3,200	$2,950	$2,600	$2,300	$2,000	$1,700	$1,500

* ***Model 90 Shotgun Combination Gun*** – shotgun over .22 LR, .22 Hornet, .218 Bee, or .30-30 Win. cal., very rare, approx. 500 mfg. Mfg. 1937-1959.

	$3,200	$2,750	$2,300	$2,000	$1,800	$1,600	$1,400

SHOTGUNS: SxS

Please refer to the L.C. Smith section for both older and newly manufactured L.C. Smith SxS shotguns.

SHOTGUNS: SINGLE SHOT

MODEL 60 – 12 ga., 30 or 32 in. barrel, full choke, top lever, break open, exposed hammer, pistol grip stock. Approx. 3,000 mfg. 1923.

	$150	$135	$110	$90	$80	$70	$60

SHOTGUNS: SLIDE ACTION, 1898-1963 PRODUCTION

During 1998, Marlin issued a service bulletin recommending that slide action exposed hammer Models 1898, 16, 17, 19, 19S, 19G, 19N, 21, 24, 24G, 26, 30, 42, 49, and 49N, in addition to hammerless Models 28, 31, 43, 44, 53, and 63 should not be fired, as many of these guns are 70-100 years old, and system failures can and do happen.

MODEL 1898 – 12 ga., 5 shot tube mag., 26-32 in. barrels, various chokes, exposed hammer, pistol grip stock, grades differ in quality of wood and engraving on C and D. Mfg. 1898-1905.

Grade A	$325	$275	$225	$200	$165	$150	$140
Grade B	$580	$495	$440	$415	$360	$305	$275
Grade C	$880	$715	$635	$580	$525	$495	$440
Grade D	$1,760	$1,540	$1,320	$1,210	$1,045	$965	$880

Factory information by individual ser. no. from the Cody Firearms Museum may be available for this model in the ser. range 19,601-67,000.

MODEL 16 – 16 ga. only, 26 or 28 in. barrel, various chokes, takedown, pistol grip stock. Mfg. 1904-10.

Grade A	$325	$275	$225	$200	$165	$150	$140
Grade B	$495	$415	$360	$330	$305	$275	$250
Grade C	$635	$525	$495	$440	$415	$385	$330
Grade D	$1,320	$1,100	$990	$825	$715	$635	$550

MODEL 17 – 12 ga., 30 or 32 in. full choke barrel, solid frame, straight stock. Mfg. 1906-08.

	$335	$275	$235	$200	$165	$150	$140

GRADING - PPGS™	100%	98%	95%	90%	80%	70%	60%	LAST MSR

MODEL 17 BRUSH GUN – similar to Model 17, with 26 in. cylinder bore barrel. Mfg. 1906-08.

	$400	$325	$275	$235	$200	$175	$150	

MODEL 17 RIOT GUN – similar to Model 17, with 20 in. barrel. Mfg. 1906-08.

	$400	$325	$275	$235	$200	$175	$150	

MODEL 19 (19S, 19N, 19G, 19D) – improved lightened version of Model 1898, matte top surface on barrel. Mfg. 1906-07.

Grade A	$325	$275	$235	$200	$165	$150	$140	
Grade B	$495	$415	$360	$330	$305	$275	$250	
Grade C	$635	$525	$495	$440	$415	$385	$330	
Grade D	$1,320	$1,100	$990	$825	$715	$635	$550	

MODEL 21 – straight grip version of Model 19.

Grade A	$325	$275	$235	$200	$165	$150	$140	
Grade B	$495	$415	$360	$330	$305	$275	$250	
Grade C	$635	$525	$495	$440	$415	$385	$330	
Grade D	$1,320	$1,100	$990	$825	$715	$635	$550	

MODEL 24 – improved 21, takedown, automatic recoil lock on slide, solid matte rib. Mfg. 1908-15.

Grade G	$295	$265	$225	$195	$165	$150	$140	
Grade A	$325	$275	$235	$200	$165	$150	$140	
Grade B	$525	$440	$385	$360	$330	$305	$275	
Grade C	$660	$550	$525	$470	$440	$415	$360	
Grade D	$1,375	$1,155	$1,045	$880	$770	$660	$580	

MODEL 26 – similar to Model 24 Grade A, with solid frame, 30 or 32 in. full choke barrel. Mfg. 1909-15.

	$275	$230	$210	$195	$165	$150	$140	

MODEL 26 BRUSH GUN – 26 in. cylinder bore barrel. Mfg. 1909-15.

	$350	$295	$250	$225	$195	$165	$150	

MODEL 26 RIOT GUN – 20 in. cylinder bore barrel. Mfg. 1909-15.

	$295	$250	$195	$180	$165	$150	$140	

MODEL 28 HAMMERLESS – 12 ga., 26-32 in. barrels, various chokes, takedown, matte top barrel, pistol grip stock. Mfg. 1913-22.

Grade A	$295	$265	$235	$200	$165	$150	$140	
Grade B	$495	$415	$360	$330	$305	$275	$250	
Grade C	$635	$525	$495	$440	$415	$385	$330	
Grade D	$1,320	$1,100	$990	$825	$715	$635	$550	

MODEL 28TS TRAP GUN – similar to Model 28, with 30 in. matte rib barrel, full choke, high comb straight grip stock. Mfg. 1915.

	$415	$330	$275	$250	$220	$195	$165	

MODEL 28T – similar to Model 28TS, with fancy wood, checkering, better finish. Mfg. 1915.

	$600	$525	$495	$470	$415	$360	$300	

MODEL 30 – similar to Model 16, with automatic recoil lock on slide, also mfg. in 20 ga. 1915-1917 (Model 30-20). Mfg. 1910-14.

Grade A	$325	$275	$235	$200	$165	$150	$140	
Grade B	$495	$415	$360	$330	$305	$275	$250	
Grade C	$635	$525	$495	$440	$415	$385	$330	
Grade D	$1,320	$1,100	$990	$825	$715	$635	$550	

MODEL 30 FIELD GRADE – similar to Model 30 Grade B, with 25 in. mod. barrel, straight stock. Mfg. 1913-17.

	$335	$275	$220	$180	$160	$130	$115	

GRADING - PPGS™	100%	98%	95%	90%	80%	70%	60%	LAST MSR

MODEL 31 – scaled down small ga. (16 and 20 ga.) version of the Model 28, has 26 and 28 in. barrels, various chokes, Model 31-16 was mfg. 1914-17, Model 31-20 was mfg. 1911-23.

Grade A	$385	$305	$250	$220	$195	$165	$140	
Grade B	$495	$415	$360	$330	$305	$275	$250	
Grade C	$636	$525	$495	$440	$415	$385	$330	
Grade D	$1,320	$1,100	$990	$825	$715	$635	$550	

MODEL 31F FIELD GUN – 25 in. mod. barrel. Mfg. 1915-17.

	$395	$350	$325	$295	$265	$225	$200	

MODEL 42A – similar to Model 24, but lesser quality finishing. Mfg. 1922-34.

	$295	$250	$220	$195	$165	$140	$120	

MODEL 43 HAMMERLESS – similar to Model 28, with lesser quality finish. Mfg. 1923-30.

	$325	$275	$225	$200	$175	$150	$125	

MODEL 43TS – similar to Model 28T, lower quality.

	$525	$440	$415	$385	$360	$305	$275	

MODEL 44A – similar to Model 31 Grade A, 20 ga. only. Mfg. 1923-35.

	$350	$275	$250	$220	$195	$165	$140	

MODEL 44S – select checkered stock.

	$470	$385	$360	$330	$195	$165	$140	

MODEL 49 – lower priced version of Model 42A. They were given to purchasers of 4 shares of Marlin stock. 3,000 mfg. in 1925-28.

	$440	$360	$305	$275	$220	$195	$165	

MODEL 53 – similar to Model 43 Hammerless. Mfg. 1929-30.

	$330	$275	$250	$220	$195	$165	$140	

MODEL 63 – similar to Model 43 Hammerless, later model. Mfg. 1931-35.

	$330	$250	$220	$195	$165	$140	$110	

MODEL 63TS – similar to Model 43TS, with trap style stock.

	$385	$305	$250	$220	$195	$165	$140	

MODEL 120 MAGNUM – 12 ga., 3 in. chamber, 26-40 in. barrel, takedown, various chokes, checkered pistol grip stock. Mfg. 1971-1985.

	$300	$250	$225	$200	$195	$180	$165	*$370*

Add 10%-15% for Model 120 MXR with 40 in. barrel (mfg. 1974-75).
Subtract $35 if without VR.

MODEL 778 – 12 ga. Mag. slide action, 20-38 in. barrels, 7 3/4 lbs. Disc. 1984.

	$300	$250	$225	$200	$195	$180	$165	

PREMIER MARK I – 12 ga. only, aluminum receiver, takedown, manufactured in France for Marlin.

	$225	$190	$180	$160	$150	$140	$120	

PREMIER MARK II – similar to Mark I, except with engraved receiver and checkering. Mfg. 1960-63 in France.

	$275	$235	$200	$175	$150	$125	$100	

PREMIER MARK IV – similar to Mark II, only deluxe grade with better wood, more engraving. Mfg. 1960-63 in France.

	$300	$250	$220	$195	$165	$140	$110	
With VR	$330	$275	$250	$220	$195	$165	$140	

MAROCCHI

Current trademark established in 1922, and currently manufactured by CD Europe SRL, located in Sarezzo, Italy. Currently imported by Network Retailing LLC, located in Canby, OR. Previously imported 2005-2007 by Glenn Rea Sport Guns located in Granbury, TX, by GSI,

GRADING - PPGS™	100%	98%	95%	90%	80%	70%	60%	LAST MSR

located in Trussville, AL. Previously distributed by Precision Sales International, Inc. located in Westfield, MA.

Marocchi O/U shotguns are high quality, and currently have limited U.S. importation. Discontinued Frigon guns (manufactured by Marocchi) appear under the F section in this text.

COMBINATION GUNS

VALLEY COMBO – 12 ga. over .222 Rem. cal., 23 1/2 in. separated barrels with VR, 3 in. chamber, fold down rear sight and will accept claw scope mounts, fixed cylinder choke, DTs, engraved silver receiver, satin finish walnut Monte Carlo stock with checkering and recoil pad, 8 1/4 lbs. Disc. 1994.

$585	$480	$415	$375	$325	$295	$275	*$700*

SHOTGUNS: O/U, 1995 & EARLIER

FIELD MASTER I – 12 ga. only, 26 or 28 in. VR barrels and rib with choke tubes, engraved coin finished receiver, extractors, SNT, checkered walnut stock and forearm. Disc. 1994.

$455	$350	$295	$260	$225	$210	$190	*$530*

This model was imported exclusively by Sile Distributors.

* ***Field Master II*** – similar to Field Master I except has SST and choke tubes. Disc. 1994.

$475	$395	$325	$275	$240	$215	$200	*$550*

SKEET MODEL – 12 ga. only, 26 in. barrels bored SK/SK. Disc. 1994.

$445	$395	$325	$275	$240	$215	$200	*$520*

This model was imported exclusively by Sile Distributors.

TRAP MODEL – 12 ga. only, 30 in. barrels bored M/F, ejectors. Disc. 1994.

$560	$485	$415	$360	$300	$260	$230	*$630*

This model was imported exclusively by Sile Distributors.

AVANZA – 12 or 20 (disc. 1993) ga., 3 in. chambers, monobloc boxlock action, 26 or 28 in. vent. barrels with VR (with or without choke tubes), SST, ejectors, deluxe checkered walnut stock and forearm with vent. recoil pad, high polish bluing with gold accents, all steel lightweight mfg., 6 lbs. 5 oz.-6 lbs. 13 oz. Imported 1990-95.

$775	$675	$575	$525	$475	$425	$375	*$829*

Add $45 for 20 ga. (disc. 1993).
Subtract 10% if without choke tubes (3).
This model was imported exclusively by Precision Sales International, Inc.

* ***Avanza Sporting Clays*** – 12 ga. only, 3 in. chambers, built on 20 ga. frame, 28 in. vent. barrels with VR and choke tubes, select checkered walnut stock with deluxe recoil pad and forearm, gold-plated trigger, 7 lbs. Mfg. 1991-95.

$825	$725	$600	$550	$495	$450	$400	*$889*

Add $99 for Premier Grade (disc., included select walnut and gold etched trigger guard).
This model features a trigger that is adjustable for length and pull without special tools.

SHOTGUNS: O/U, RECENT PRODUCTION

In the U.S., Conquista shotguns are identical in specifications and features to the Marocchi Classic Doubles sold in Europe, with the exception of Classic Doubles U.S.A.

GOLDEN SNIPE III FIELD – 12 ga. only, 3 in. chambers, field configuration with 28 in. VR barrels and choke tubes. Mfg. 1998-2003.

$725	$675	$625	$575	$525	$475	$425	*$800*

GOLDEN SNIPE III SPORTING – 12 ga. only, entry level sporting clays model with 28 or 30 in. VR barrels with choke tubes, checkered walnut stock and forearm. Imported 1999-2003.

$850	$750	$675	$625	$575	$525	$450	*$950*

CONQUISTA FIELD MAGNUM GRADE I – 12 ga. only, 3 in. chambers, features 28 in. 8mm VR barrels with choke tubes, nickel finished receiver, SST, checkered walnut stock and forearm with smooth rosewood buttplate, approx. 7 1/4 lbs. Imported 1999-2001.

$1,275	$1,025	$900	$800	$700	$625	$550	*$1,490*

GRADING - PPGS™	100%	98%	95%	90%	80%	70%	60%	LAST MSR

CONQUISTA USA SPORTING – 12 ga. only, 3 in. chambers, features 30 in. vent. barrels with 10mm VR, muzzle porting, back boring, and lengthened forcing cones, blued barrels and receiver with gold accents, checkered standard or adj. walnut stock and forearm, approx. 8 lbs. Mfg. 1999-2003.

	100%	98%	95%	90%	80%	70%	60%	LAST MSR
	$1,275	$1,025	$900	$800	$700	$625	$550	$1,490

Add $100 for adj. stock.

CONQUISTA SPORTING CLAYS – 12 ga. only, boxlock action with brushed coin finish, SST, ejectors, adj. trigger, choice of 28, 30, or 32 in. 10mm VR barrels with choke tubes, right or left-hand (Grade I only) action, checkered walnut stock and forearm with recoil pad, 7 7/8 lbs. Imported 1994-2000.

* ***Conquista Sporting Clays Grade I*** – features coin finished receiver with perimeter line engraving.

	100%	98%	95%	90%	80%	70%	60%	LAST MSR
	$1,725	$1,450	$1,200	$1,000	$850	$700	$550	$1,995

Add $125 for left-hand variation.
Add $151 for adj. stock (new 1999).

* ***Conquista Sporting Clays Lady Sport*** – 12 ga. only, features lighter weight specialized stock designed to fit women, cased, 7 1/2 lbs. Mfg. 1995-99.

	100%	98%	95%	90%	80%	70%	60%	LAST MSR
	$1,800	$1,525	$1,250	$1,000	$850	$700	$550	$2,120

Add $180 for left-hand variation (Sport Spectrum only).
Add $79 for Lady Sport Spectrum (partially colored receiver).

* ***Conquista Sporting Clays Grade II*** – features better walnut and game scene engraving on receiver.

	100%	98%	95%	90%	80%	70%	60%	LAST MSR
	$1,995	$1,675	$1,425	$1,200	$1,000	$850	$700	$2,330

Add $355 for left-hand variation.

* ***Conquista Sporting Clays Grade III*** – features more elaborate game scene engraving on receiver sides and fine scrollwork throughout rest of action, includes hard gun case and stock wrench.

	100%	98%	95%	90%	80%	70%	60%	LAST MSR
	$3,225	$2,650	$2,250	$1,875	$1,650	$1,400	$1,175	$3,599

Add $396 for left-hand variation.

* ***Conquista Sporting Clays Grade IV*** – top-of-the-line Sporting Clays model. Importation began 1997. Price available by request only.

CONQUISTA TRAP MODEL – 12 ga. only, Trap configuration, 30 or 32 (disc. 1997, reintroduced 2000) in. 10mm VR barrels with fixed chokes, 8 1/4 lbs. Imported 1994-2000.

* ***Conquista Trap Model Grade I*** – features coin finished receiver with perimeter line engraving.

	100%	98%	95%	90%	80%	70%	60%	LAST MSR
	$1,725	$1,475	$1,225	$1,000	$850	$700	$550	$1,995

Add $151 for adj. stock (new 1999).

* ***Conquista Trap Model Grade II*** – features better walnut and game scene engraving on receiver.

	100%	98%	95%	90%	80%	70%	60%	LAST MSR
	$1,995	$1,675	$1,450	$1,200	$1,000	$850	$700	$2,330

* ***Conquista Trap Model Grade III*** – features more elaborate game scene engraving on receiver sides and fine scrollwork throughout rest of action, includes hard gun case and stock wrench.

	100%	98%	95%	90%	80%	70%	60%	LAST MSR
	$3,225	$2,650	$2,250	$1,875	$1,650	$1,400	$1,175	$3,599

* ***Conquista Trap Model Grade IV*** – top-of-the-line Trap model. Importation began 1997. Price available by request only.

CONQUISTA SKEET MODEL – 12 ga. only, Skeet configuration, 28 in. 10mm VR barrels with fixed Skeet chokes, 7 3/4 lbs. Imported 1994-2000.

* ***Conquista Skeet Model Grade I*** – features coin finished receiver with perimeter line engraving.

	100%	98%	95%	90%	80%	70%	60%	LAST MSR
	$1,725	$1,475	$1,225	$1,000	$850	$700	$550	$1,995

GRADING - PPGS™	100%	98%	95%	90%	80%	70%	60%	LAST MSR

* ***Conquista Skeet Model Grade II*** – features better walnut and game scene engraving on receiver.

	$1,995	$1,675	$1,450	$1,200	$1,000	$850	$700	*$2,330*

* ***Conquista Skeet Model Grade III*** – features more elaborate game scene engraving on receiver sides and fine scrollwork throughout rest of action, includes hard gun case and stock wrench.

	$3,225	$2,650	$2,250	$1,875	$1,650	$1,400	$1,175	*$3,599*

* ***Conquista Skeet Model Grade IV*** – top-of-the-line Skeet model. Importation began 1997. Price available by request only.

MODEL 03 – various gauges and barrel lengths, alloy receiver, checkered walnut stock and forearm. Importation began 2008.

MSR $1,950	$1,775	$1,525	$1,350	$1,150	$950	$750	$600	

CLASSIC DOUBLES MODEL 92 – 12 ga. only, 3 in. chambers, sporting clays configuration featuring 30 in. vented barrels with VR, back-boring, elongated forcing cones, and three screw-in chokes, low profile blued receiver, checkered walnut stock, and Schnabel forearm, adj. trigger, gold receiver accents and trigger. Imported 1996-98.

	$1,450	$1,175	$950	$850	$775	$700	$650	*$1,598*

MODEL 99 – 12 ga. only, 2 3/4 in. chambers, boxlock action with Boss locking system, silver grey receiver finish, SST, ejectors, adj. trigger, choice of 28 (Sporting or Skeet), 30, or 32 in. 10mm VR barrels with 5 extended choke tubes, choice of Sporting, Trap, or Skeet configuration, right-hand action only, deluxe checkered walnut stock and Schnabel forearm with recoil pad, approx. 7 1/2-8 lbs. New 2000.

* ***Model 99 Grade I***

MSR $2,950	$2,750	$2,475	$2,050	$1,750	$1,500	$1,250	$1,000	

* ***Model 99 Grade II*** – features better walnut and engraving on receiver. Disc. 2003.

	$2,475	$2,125	$1,725	$1,400	$1,100	$925	$800	*$2,870*

Add $155 for gold inlays.

* ***Model 99 Grade III*** – features more elaborate engraving with gold inlays and wood upgrade, flush choke tubes.

	$3,950	$3,500	$3,000	$2,500	$2,100	$1,700	$1,525	

Subtract approx. $250 if w/o gold inlays.

MODEL 99 CUSTOM GRADES – 12 ga. only, 2 3/4 in. chambers, available in either Sporting, Trap, or Skeet configuration, deluxe Model 99 with best quality walnut and elaborate engraving options per model - base model is the Blackgold (non-engraved with gold line frame accents), 28, 30, or 32 in. barrels. Importation began 2000.

Please contact the company directly for more information regarding available options and pricing for the Maroccchi custom shop.

MODEL 100 CLASSIC – available in Trap or Sporting configurations, blue receiver with light scroll engraving and gold inlays, checkered walnut stock and forearm. Importation began 2008.

MSR $3,100	$2,795	$2,400	$2,100	$1,800	$1,500	$1,200	$1,000	

SHOTGUNS: SINGLE SHOT

MODEL 2000 – 12 ga. only, 3 in. chamber, hammer, 28 in. barrel, ejector, lightly engraved receiver. Importation disc. 1991.

	$80	$70	$60	$50	$45	$40	$35	*$94*

SHOTGUNS: SEMI-AUTO

SI 12 SERIES – 12 ga. only, 3 in. chamber, various configurations include a Basic, Slug, Grade I, and Grade II models, inertia mechanism using kinetic energy, walnut or synthetic stock and forearm, approx. 6 1/2 lbs. New 2010.

Please contact the company directly for pricing and availability on this model.

GRADING - PPGS™	100%	98%	95%	90%	80%	70%	60%	LAST MSR

MARTIN, ALEX

Current trademark owned and manufactured by Dickson & MacNaughton, located in Edinburgh, Scotland.

Please contact Dickson & MacNaughton directly for more information regarding this trademark, including current availability and pricing.

MARTINI

Please refer to individual listings in the BSA Guns, Ltd. listing in the B section.

MASTERPIECE ARMS

Current pistol and rifle manufacturer located in Carrollton, GA, previously located in Braselton, GA. Dealer sales only.

CARBINES: SEMI-AUTO

MPA manufactures a line of paramilitary style semi-auto carbines patterned after the MAC Series with 30 or 35 shot mags. (interchangable with its pistols).

IMPORTANT NOTE: On model(s) where *N/A has replaced the normal 100% value, it indicates current market conditions are too unstable to accurately ascertain 100%-60% values. Factory retail prices (MSRs) reflect most recent updates. For more up-to-date information on current pricing trends and additional useful information, please visit www.bluebookofgunvalues.com, select "Information & Services" from the menu, and click on "Additional Book Information".

SIDE COCKING CARBINE – 9mm Para. or .45 ACP cal., 16 in. threaded barrel, 30 or 35 shot mag., black skeletonized stock, with or w/o scope mount.

MSR $795	*N/A	$595	$500	$450	$375	$300	$235	

Add $17 for .45 ACP cal. Add $259 for scope mount, Intrafuse handguard, holosight, flashlight and muzzle brake.

Subtract $50-$70 if w/o side cocker.

TOP COCKING CARBINE – 9mm Para. (MPA20T-A) or .45 ACP (MPA1T-A) cal., 16 in. threaded barrel, black skeletonized stock, 30 shot mag. Disc. 2010.

	*N/A	$425	$360	$325	$265	$215	$170	*$530*

Add $30 for .45 ACP cal.

MPA460 CARBINE – .460 Rowland cal., 16 in. threaded barrel, 30 shot mag., side cocking, muzzle brake, black finish, with or w/o .45 ACP upper. Mfg. 2010 only.

	*N/A	$650	$575	$500	$425	$375	$325	*$800*

Add $54 for scope mount, hand guard, and Mark III tactical scope.

MPA MINI TACTICAL CARBINE – 9mm Para. cal., 16 in. threaded barrel with birdcase muzzle brake, aluminum quad rail, multi-reticle hollow sight, MPA lightweight stock. New 2011.

MSR $795	*N/A	$595	$500	$450	$375	$300	$235	

MPA TACTICAL CARBINE – 9mm Para. or .45 ACP cal., side charger, 16 in. threaded barrel, scope mount, 30 (.45 ACP cal.) or 35 (9mm Para. cal.) shot mag., Intrafuse handguard and vertical grip, Defender stock, multi-reticle hollow sight. Mfg. 2011-2012.

	*N/A	$750	$650	$575	$500	$425	$375	*$956*

Add $16 for .45 ACP cal.

PISTOLS: SEMI-AUTO

MPA manufactures a line of paramilitary style pistols patterned after the original MAC Series from Ingram.

SIDE COCKING MODEL – 9mm Para. or .45 ACP cal., paramilitary style pistol patterned after the original MAC Series from Ingram, 30 (.45 ACP cal.) or 35 (9mm Para. cal.) shot mag., 6 or 10 (disc.) in. threaded barrels.

MSR $570	$495	$425	$375	$325	$275	$225	$195	

Add $50 for scope mount.

Add $180 for holosight, flashlight, upper Picatinny rail, and safety extension with 6 in. barrel or $254 if w/10 in. barrel.

GRADING - PPGS™	100%	98%	95%	90%	80%	70%	60%	LAST MSR

Subtract $30-$80 if w/o side charger.

TOP COCKING MODEL – 9mm Para. or .45 ACP cal., similar to side cocking model, except is top cocking.

MSR $489	$375	$325	$275	$225	$200	$175	$150	

Add $80 for 10 in. barrel and AR-15 hand guard (disc.).

MPA22T MINI PISTOL – .22 LR cal., 5 in. threaded barrel, 30 shot mag., top cocker or side cocker with scope mount, black finish. Mfg. 2010-2012.

	$385	$350	$315	$275	$250	$225	$195	*$440*

Add $85 for side cocker with scope mount.

MPA930 MINI PISTOL – 9mm Para. cal., 3 1/2 in. threaded barrel, 35 shot mag., optional scope mount, black finish.

MSR $489	$375	$325	$275	$225	$200	$175	$150	

Add $81 for side cocker with scope mount.

Add $180 for holosight, flashlight, pressure switch, upper Picatinny rail, and safety extension (disc.).

MPA460 PISTOL – .460 Rowland cal., 6 or 10 in. threaded barrel, 30 shot mag., side cocker, scope mount, muzzle brake, black finish. Mfg. 2009-2010.

	$495	$450	$395	$365	$335	$300	$275	*$580*

Add $90 for .45 ASP upper.

Add $96 for 10 in. barrel.

MPA TACTICAL PISTOL – 9mm Para. or .45 ACP cal., side cocker, 6 in. threaded barrel, 30 or 35 shot mag., multi-reticle hollow sight, includes Picatinny rail, flash light and pressure switch. New 2011.

MSR $688	$595	$525	$450	$400	$350	$300	$275	

MPA MINI TACTICAL PISTOL – .22 LR (disc. 2012) or 9mm Para. cal., side cocker, 3 1/2 (9mm Para. cal.) or 5 (.22 LR cal.) in. threaded barrel, 30 (.22 LR cal.) or 35 (9mm Para. cal.) shot mag., multi-reticle hollow sight, includes flash light, ring rail, and safety extension. New 2011.

MSR $688	$595	$525	$450	$400	$350	$300	$275	

Add $36 for 9mm Para. cal.

MPA SUB-COMPACT – .32 ACP or .380 ACP cal., DA only, 2 1/4 in. barrel, sub-compact design, 6 shot mag., solid steel construction, black or two-tone finish, black synthetic grips, 11.8 oz. Mfg. 2011-2012.

	$275	$250	$225	$195	$175	$150	$135	*$323*

Add $23 for two-tone finish.

MASTERPIECE ARMS, INC.

Previous manufacturer of derringers located in Carrollton, GA from 2000-2004.

Masterpiece Arms manufactured derringers in both steel and stainless steel configuration.

MASQUELIER S.A.

Previous manufacturer located in Belgium. Previously distributed (until 1986) by Ambel Ltd., Inc. located in Sugarland, TX.

RIFLES: SxS

CARPATHE – .243 Win., .270 Win., .30-06, 7x57R, or 7x65R cal., single shot, hair trigger, push-down cocking system. Importation disc. 1986.

	$3,500	$3,200	$2,900	$2,600	$2,300	$2,100	$1,850	*$3,850*

EXPRESS – .270 Win., .30-06, 8x57JRS, or 9.3x74R cal., O/U configuration, SST, ejectors. Add $800 for extra set of 20 ga. barrels. Importation disc. 1986.

	$3,300	$3,000	$2,800	$2,600	$2,300	$2,100	$1,850	*$3,600*

ARDENNES MODEL – top-of-the-line model, custom order only. Importation disc. 1986.

	$6,600	$6,000	$5,400	$4,800	$4,300	$3,900	$3,450	*$7,250*

GRADING - PPGS™	100%	98%	95%	90%	80%	70%	60%	LAST MSR

SHOTGUNS: SxS

BOXLOCK – 12 ga. only, 2 3/4 in. chambers, Anson & Deeley boxlock action, ejectors, fine scroll engraving with French walnut stock. Importation disc. 1986.

	$4,400	$4,000	$3,650	$3,300	$2,995	$2,600	$2,200	*$4,780*

SIDELOCK – 12 ga. only, 2 3/4 in. chambers, H&H style sidelocks, auto ejectors, English style fine scroll engraving with French walnut. Importation disc. 1986.

	$12,500	$10,000	$8,750	$7,600	$6,700	$5,800	$5,000	*$15,850*

MATCHGUNS srl

Current manufacturer established during 2001, and located in Parma, Italy. No current U.S. importation. Distributed by Gehmann, located in Karlsruhe, Germany.

During 2001, Cesare Morini left Morini Competition Arm S.A. of Switzerland and started a new company, Matchguns srl, with headquarters in Parma, Italy. For more information and current pricing on both new and used Matchguns airguns, please refer to the *Blue Book of Airguns* by Dr. Robert Beeman & John Allen.

PISTOLS

MG2/MG2E – .22 LR cal., innovative new semi-auto action with patented compact mechanism allowing recoil reduction of up to 50% w/o the use of counterweights or muzzle brakes, 6 in. barrel, fully adj. rear sight, fully adj. anatomical walnut grips, 5 shot horizontal mag. below frame, open trigger guard, blue only, adj. mechanical trigger from 60 grams - 950 grams, or electric (MG2E) trigger, includes case and tools, available in standard or rapid fire configuration, approx. 2 lbs. New mid-2002.

MSR N/A	$1,295	$1,125	$975	$850	$725	$650	$575

MG3 – .22 Short cal., otherwise similar to MG2. Mfg. 2004-2009.

	$1,295	$1,125	$975	$850	$725	$650	$575

MG4 – .32 S&W Wadcutter cal., 6 in. barrel, unique 5 shot horizontal magazine runs paralell to lower frame and is released by lever in front of open trigger guard, fully adj. anatomical walnut grips, fully adj. rear sight and trigger, equipped with safety pin and dry fire mechanism, blue cover on top of slide assembly, approx. 2.1 lbs. New 2005.

Please contact the company directly for pricing on this model.

MG5 – .22 LR cal., free pistol, single shot, carbon fiber stabilizer rods with steel adjustable weights, mechanical or electronic trigger, 11 1/2 in. barrel length, adj. sights, adj. anatomical grip. Importation began 2004.

Please contact the company directly for current pricing on this model.

MATCH GRADE ARMS & AMMUNITION

Please refer to MG Arms, Inc. listing.

MATEBA

Current trademark manufactured in Italy. Currently distributed by AWA USA, located in Hialeah, FL. Previously located in Pavia, Italy. Limited U.S. importation and distribution until 2004 by American Western Arms, located in Delray Beach, FL. Previously imported 2000-2001 by Keisler's Wholesale, located in Jeffersonville, IN, and by American Arms, Inc. until late 1999. Previously manufactured by Macchine Termo Balistiche located in Italy. Older mfg. has had little domestic importation.

PISTOLS: SEMI-AUTO

MATEBA M1911 – .45 ACP cal., choice of dual tone blue or hard chrome, 8 shot mag. Mfg. 2003-2008.

	$1,375	$1,150	$895	$800	$675	$525	$450

REVOLVERS

MATEBA REVOLVER – various cals. (older mfg.), most recent mfg. is .357 Mag./.38 Spl., .44 Mag., or .454 Casull cal., combination semi-auto pistol and revolver, action allows cylinder and slide assembly to move back when fired, causing the cylinder to rotate, unique design

GRADING - PPGS™	100%	98%	95%	90%	80%	70%	60%	LAST MSR

permits barrel to fire lowest shell in cylinder (6 o'clock position), mechanism to rear of cylinder, single or double action, 6, 7 (older mfg.), or 8 (older mfg.) shot, 3, 4, 6, or 8 in. barrel, steel/alloy frame, blue finish, flared ergonomic walnut grips, interchangeable barrels, 2 3/4 lbs.

MSR $1,800 $1,625 $1,325 $1,125 $950 $825 $700 $550

Add $100 for frame mounted scope mount.

Add $100 for .454 Casull cal.

Add $170 for polished nickel finish.

A carbine variation with 18 in. barrel is also available in this model. Price is the same as the revolver.

MATHELON ARMES

Current SxS rifle and drilling manufacturer located in Rumilly, France. Currently imported by Kebco, LLC, located in Hanover, PA. Previously imported by Rocky Mountain Armoury, located in Silverthorne, CO.

Mathelon Armes manufactures high quality drillings, double rifles, and stalking rifles. Current models include the MX and MX Express double rifles, the MD, MXD, MXDL, and MXT drillings, and the MXDK Kipplauf stalking rifle. Please contact the importer directly for more information and current pricing (see Trademark Index).

MATRA MANURHIN DEFENSE

Please refer to the Manurhin heading in this section.

MAUNZ MATCH RIFLES LLC (MAUNZ, KARL)

Current manufacturer located in Grand Rapids, OH. Previously located in Toledo and Maumee, OH circa 1960s-1987.

RIFLES: BOLT ACTION

MODEL 47 – .30-06, .308 Win., or other custom order calibers, right or left hand action, modeled after the Winchster Model 54 and the Springfield 1903, checkered pistol grip wood stock.

1,250 $1,100 $1,000 $900 $800 $700 $600

RIFLES: SEMI-AUTO

Maunz Rifles were manufactured in Toledo and Maumee Ohio from 1960's until 1987 by Karl Maunz for high-end military, law enforcement and competition. Models included the Model 87 Maunz Match Rifle, Model 77 Service Match Rifle, Model 67 Match Grade for practice, Model 67 Sniper Rifle, Model 57 and the Model 47 rifle. All models made on or prior to 2011 are custom order only.

MODEL 57 M1A – various cals. including .30-06, .308 Win., .276 Maunz or.45 Maunz (rare), other custom calibers were available, utilizes M1 Garand receiver with M14 parts, National Match barrel, custom-built glass bedded stock.

$1,800 $1,600 $1,350 $1,125 $900 $775 $625

MODEL 66 MATCH SERVICE RIFLE – .308 Win. cal., 22 in. barrel, M1A configuration with M1 and M14 G.I. parts, fiberglass stock, NM sights, M1 trigger assembly, 10 lbs., approx. 200 mfg.

$2,500 $2,250 $2,000 $1,800 $1,500 $1,250 $1,050

MODEL 67 MATCH GRADE PRACTICE RIFLE – 7.62 NATO/.308 Win. (.308x224, .308x244, .308x264), 6.30 Maunz, .338 Maunz (ltd. mfg.), or .45 Maunz (ltd. mfg.) cal., other custom calibers were available, M1A configuration with combination of M1 Garand and M14 parts, not allowed for service rifle competition.

$2,000 $1,775 $1,525 $1,250 $1,000 $875 $700

MODEL 67 ASSAULT SNIPER RIFLE – 7.62 NATO/.308 Win. (.308x224, .308x244, .308x264), or 6.30 Maunz cal., 22 in. barrel standard, medium and heavy barrels were also available, M14 sights standard, 5, 10, 20, or 30 shot mag.

$2,000 $1,775 $1,525 $1,250 $1,000 $875 $700

GRADING - PPGS™	100%	98%	95%	90%	80%	70%	60%	LAST MSR

MODEL 77 – .308 Win. cal., utilized M1A Springfield receiver initially, followed by Valley Ordnance mfg., receiver has removable lug under the barrel, red, white and blue laminated stock, ser. no. 000011-005040.

$2,100 $1,800 $1,500 $1,250 $1,050 $925 $800

MODEL 77 SERVICE MATCH RIFLE – 7.62 NATO/.308 Win. cal., custom calibers were also available, 22 in. barrel standard, medium and heavy barrels were also available, 5, 10, or 20 shot mag., NM/2A sights, special removable front globe sight, charcoal grey parkerized finish, heavyweight Kevlar or graphite/fiberglass stock with black gel coat, red/white/blue stocks also available.

$2,850 $2,500 $2,250 $1,975 $1,700 $1,350 $1,075

MODEL 87 – various cals., 26 in. medium weight barrel, synthetic stock, G.I. parts with TRW bolts, satin black finish, open sights, ser. nos. 00001-03030, 11 lbs. Mfg. 1985-89.

$2,300 $2,100 $1,800 $1,500 $1,250 $1,050 $925

MODEL 87 MATCH RIFLE – 7.62 NATO/.308 Win. (.308x224, .308x244, .308x264), 6.30 Maunz, .338 Maunz (ltd. mfg.), or .45 Maunz (ltd. mfg.) cal., other custom calibers were available, charcoal grey parkerized finish, heavyweight Kevlar or graphite/fiberglass stock with black gel coat, red/white/blue stocks also available.

$2,500 $2,250 $1,925 $1,675 $1,350 $1,125 $975

MODEL 007 – .30 Custom, 6.30 Maunz, or .45 Maunz cal., accuracy metal full lined bedded with long action to accept the M1 Garand bolt, modified M14 type gas system, stainless steel or metal receiver, scope mount, classic wood, heavyweight Kevlar, or graphite/fiberglass stock covered in black gel coat, accepts many different type of magazines, custom weight barrels available.

MSR $1,650 $1,495 $1,300 $1,100 $950 $825 $700 $600

MODEL 007 NRA MATCH RIFLE – chambered in 6.30 in. diameter with die sets for 6mm, 6.5mm, 7mm, 7.62x51mm, and .30-06 cal., 50 mfg. - one for each state, custom fit to the shooter and using his chosen serial number.

$1,650 $1,450 $1,250 $1,050 $925 $800 $700

MODEL 97 MATCH/VARMINT RIFLE – chambered for custom calibers, modeled after the US M16/AR-15, custom weight barrels, fiberglass stock, custom color stock or classic wood stock.

MSR $1,250 $1,100 $975 $850 $725 $600 $500 $400

MODEL 97 SERVICE RIFLE – 5.56 NATO or .223 Rem. cal., modeled after the US M16/AR-15, black gel coated GI fiberglass stock.

MSR $650 $575 $500 $450 $400 $350 $300 $275

MODEL M14SA – service Standard grade rifle modeled after the M14.

Previous MSR on this model was $1,400.

MODEL M16SA – Service Standard grade rifle modeled after the M16.

Previous MSR on this model was $650.

MAURITZ WIDFORSS AB

Current manufacturer, retailer, and auction house established in 1729, and located in Stockholm, Sweden.

Widforss specializes in custom order long guns, hunting equipment and accessories, and holds several annual auctions. Please visit their website or contact the company directly for more information, including product availability and pricing (see Trademark Index).

MAUSER JAGDWAFFEN GmbH

Current trademark established during 1871, and currently owned by SIG Arms AG beginning late 2000. Mauser Model 98 Magnum bolt action rifles are currently manufactured by Mauser Jagdwaffen GmbH, located in Isny, Germany. Currently imported beginning 2009 by Mauser USA, located in San Antonio, TX.

GRADING - PPGS™	100%	98%	95%	90%	80%	70%	60%	LAST MSR

In late 2000, SIG Arms AG, the firearms portion of SIG, was purchased by two Germans named Michael Lüke and Thomas Ortmeier, who have a background in textiles. Today the Lüke & Ortmeier group includes independently operational companies such as Blaser Jadgwaffen GmbH, Mauser Jagdwaffen GmbH, J.P. Sauer & Sohn GmbH, SIG-Sauer Inc., SIG-Sauer GmbH and SAN Swiss Arms AG.

From late March, 2006-2009, Models 98 and 03 were distributed exclusively by Briley Manufacturing, located in Houston, TX. The former transition name was Mauser Jagd- und Sportwaffen GmbH. On January 1, 1999, Mauser transferred all production and distribution rights of both hunting and sporting weapons to SIG-Blaser. Mauser-Werke Oberndorf Waffensysteme GmbH continues to manufacture military defense contracts (including making small bore barrel liners for tanks), in addition to other industrial machinery.

Previously imported exclusively by Brolin Arms, located in Pomona, CA during 1997-98 only. During 1998, the company name was changed from Mauser-Werke Oberndorf Waffensysteme GmbH. During 1994, the name was changed from Mauser-Werke to Mauser-Werke Oberndorf Waffensysteme GmbH. Previously imported by GSI located in Trussville, AL, until 1997, Gibb's Rifle Co., Inc. until 1995, Precision Imports, Inc. located in San Antonio, TX until 1993, and KDF located in Seguin, TX (1987-89).

HANDGUNS: EARLY PRODUCTION

MODEL 1877 SINGLE SHOT – 9mm cal., single shot, barrel release in usual hammer position and safety on left side, examples are rare.

	N/A	$15,000	$12,500	$10,000	$7,500	$5,000	$4,000

MODEL 1878 "ZIG-ZAG" REVOLVER – 7.6mm, 9mm (most common) or 10.6mm cal., Zig-Zag refers to Z-pattern grooves cut into cylinder, earliest revolvers were solid frame, gate loaded, and chambered in 9mm, most were designed with a hinged frame, third and last version had an "improved" sliding release on the forward frame, most revolvers had a rust blue frame and barrel complementing a fire blue cylinder, grips were checkered or hard rubber with a floral pattern.

7.6mm cal.	N/A	$6,500	$5,000	$4,000	$3,000	$2,500	$2,000
9mm cal.	$7,500	$7,000	$6,500	$6,000	$5,000	$4,000	$3,500
10.8mm cal.	N/A	$10,000	$8,500	$7,000	$5,500	$4,500	$3,500

Add 10% for earliest pistols with "midnight blue" finish. Premiums exist for solid frame, late improved model, and factory cased guns.

PISTOLS: SEMI-AUTO, DISC.

The Models 1906-08, 1912-14, and HSv are very rare and only infrequently encountered. A competent appraisal is advisable before buying or selling these models.

MODEL 1906-08 – 9mm Export (9x25mm) cal., detachable mag., incorporates features of both the pocket pistols and Model 1896 Broomhandle. Ser. range 1-100 (est.).

N/A	$60,000	$52,500	$45,000	$37,500	$30,000	$25,000

MODEL 1912-14 – generally chambered for 9mm Para. cal., similar to pocket pistol configuration, but considerably larger, earliest specimens have inscribed slide legend. Those under serial number 100 (approx.) are not slotted for shoulder stock while those over 100 are generally slotted. Ser. range 1-175 (est.).

N/A	$40,000	$35,000	$30,000	$25,000	$20,000	$15,000

Add 50% if slotted with matching shoulder stock.

This variation is very rare in .45 ACP cal. or with a tangent rear sight.

WTP MODEL I VEST POCKET AUTOMATIC – 6.35mm cal., 6 shot, 2 1/2 in. barrel, blue, rubber grips. Mfg. 1922-37.

$750	$655	$565	$510	$415	$340	$265

WTP MODEL II – similar to Model I, but 2 in. barrel. Mfg. 1938-40.

$1,350	$1,180	$1,015	$920	$745	$610	$475

Add 20% for brown grips or French contract.

GRADING - PPGS™	100%	98%	95%	90%	80%	70%	60%	LAST MSR

POCKET MODEL 1910 – 6.35mm or 7.65mm cal., 9 shot, 3 in. barrel, blue fixed sights, checkered walnut or hard rubber grips. Mfg. 1910-34.

	$650	$570	$490	$440	$360	$295	$230

Add 30% for sidelatch variation.

POCKET MODEL 1914 – similar to Model 1910, but 7.65mm cal., 3.4 in. barrel. Mfg. 1914-34.

	$650	$570	$490	$440	$360	$295	$230
Humpback Model	$4,000	$3,500	$3,000	$2,720	$2,200	$1,800	$1,400

Add 10% for military acceptance crown D proof by rear sight and/or Prussian eagle on trigger guard.

POCKET MODEL 1934 – similar to Model 1914, but reshaped grip. Mfg. 1934-1939.

	$750	$655	$565	$510	$415	$340	$265
Waffenamt	$1,500	$1,315	$1,125	$1,020	$825	$675	$525
Nazi Police	$1,125	$985	$845	$765	$620	$505	$395
Nazi Navy marked	$1,875	$1,640	$1,405	$1,275	$1,030	$845	$655

MODEL HSv – 9mm Para. cal., only 2 or 3 known, similar features to Model HSc, except has larger dimensions.

Extreme rarity precludes accurate pricing on this model.

Mauser Pistols: HSc Models

MODEL HSc DOUBLE ACTION – 7.65mm (8 shot) or .380 ACP (7 shot) cal., 3.4 in. barrel, blue or nickel, fixed sights, checkered walnut grips. Mfg. 1938-disc. (most recent mfg. was by R. Gamba in Italy circa 1996).

Mauser Pistols: HSc WWII Military Mfg.

* ***HSc WWII Military Mfg. Low Grip Screw*** – very rare, first variation with ser. numbers starting at 700,000, less than 2,000 mfg.

N/A	$6,000	$5,000	$4,000	$3,000	$2,000	$1,500

Add 20% if Navy marked.

* ***HSc WWII Military Mfg. Early Nazi Army*** – proofed 655 and 135.

N/A	$750	$550	$350	$300	$250	$200

Add 100% for small 655 additionally test-proofed on left tang.

* ***HSc WWII Military Mfg. Early Nazi Navy*** – marked on front grip strap.

N/A	$1,500	$1,200	$900	$600	$500	$400

* ***HSc WWII Military Mfg. Early Nazi Police*** – Eagle L proof only.

N/A	$650	$500	$400	$350	$300	$250

* ***HSc WWII Military Mfg. Wartime Nazi Army*** – proof 135 and WaA 135. Eagle N proofed also.

N/A	$600	$475	$350	$275	$250	$200

* ***HSc WWII Military Mfg. Wartime Nazi Navy*** – proofed on left side of trigger guard.

N/A	$1,200	$1,000	$800	$700	$600	$500

* ***HSc WWII Military Mfg. Wartime Nazi Police*** – proofed Eagle L.

N/A	$550	$450	$350	$325	$285	$245

Add 10% if Eagle F.

* ***HSc WWII Military Mfg. Wartime Commercial*** – standard WWII Commercial Model.

N/A	$450	$350	$300	$275	$250	$225

* ***HSc WWII Military Mfg. Swiss Commercial*** – ser. range 800,000-900,000. Very rare.

N/A	$1,400	$1,250	$1,125	$995	$900	$850

* ***HSc WWII Military Mfg. Cutaways*** – mfg. to visibly show mechanism. Should not be proofed.

N/A	$1,750	$1,250	$950	$850	$800	$750

GRADING - PPGS™	100%	98%	95%	90%	80%	70%	60%	LAST MSR

Mauser Pistols: HSc Post-WWII Mfg.

* ***HSc Post-WWII Mfg. French Manufacture*** – frequently encountered in poor condition - post-WWII production.

	N/A	$400	$350	$300	$250	$200	$175	

* ***HSc Post-WWII Mfg. Mauser Production*** – .32 or .380 cal., 15 shot, mfg. 1968-1981.

	$450	$400	$350	$300	$250	$200	$175	

Subtract 20% if not boxed or in .32 cal.

* ***HSc Post-WWII Mfg. Interarms Import*** – imported by Interarms from 1983-1985 (Mauser and Italian mfg. by Gamba).

	$350	$300	$250	$220	$180	$150	$125	*$415*

* ***HSc Post-WWII Mfg. One of Five Thousand Edition*** – American Eagle edition (marked on gun), 5,000 total mfg. (serial numbered 1-5000).

	$450	$400	$350	$300	$240	$210	$180	

* ***HSc Post-WWII Mfg. Armes De Chasse Import*** – previously imported by Armes De Chasse located in Chadds Ford, PA on a limited basis.

	$475	$425	$330	$300	$260	$240	$220	*$695*

Add $195 for Limited Series.
Add $58 For G15 variation (9 shot).

* ***HSc Post-WWII Mfg. E.A.A. Import*** – imported by European American Armory, distributed by RSR Wholesale.

	$265	$225	$195	$175	$150	$125	$110	

* ***HSc Post-WWII Mfg. Recent Gamba Mfg.*** – .32 ACP or .380 ACP cal., steel construction, double action, double safety, stippled walnut grips, recently imported by Gamba, USA until approx. 1996, and reintroduced during 2005-circa 2006.

	$395	$350	$295	$265	$240	$220	$200	

Mauser Pistols: Luger Mfg.

Both pre-war and post-war Mauser manufactured Lugers will be found in the Luger section of this book.

Mauser Pistols: P.38 Mfg.

Please refer to the P.38 entries under the P alphabetical heading.

PISTOLS: SEMI-AUTO, RECENT IMPORTATION

MODEL 80 SA – .380 ACP or 9mm Para. cal., semi-auto single action patterned after the Browning Hi-power, 4 2/3 in. barrel, blue finish with checkered walnut grips, round hammer, steel construction, 10 (C/B 1994) or 13* shot mag., 1.95 lbs. Mfg. by FEG in Hungary, imported 1992-96.

	$450	$325	$275	$240	$215	$185	$165	*$520*

MODEL 90 DA – similar to Model 80 SA, except is double action, spur hammer, and has 10 (C/B 1994) or 14* shot mag., 2.15 lbs. Mfg. by FEG, imported 1992-96.

	$445	$325	$275	$240	$215	$185	$165	*$516*

* ***Model 90 DAC*** – similar to Model 90 DA, except is compact model with 4 1/8 in. barrel, 2.05 lbs. Imported 1992-96.

	$450	$325	$275	$240	$215	$185	$165	*$520*

M-2 – .357 SIG (disc. 2001), .40 S&W, or .45 ACP cal., short recoil operation, striker fired operating system, rotating 3.54 in. barrel lockup, manual safety, 8 (.45 ACP) or 10 shot, DAO, hammerless, aluminum alloy frame with nickel chromium steel slide, black finish, includes case and trigger lock, approx. 29 or 32 1/2 oz. Mfg. by SIG in Europe, limited importation 2000-04.

	$450	$400	$350	$300	$275	$250	$225	

PISTOLS: SEMI-AUTO, MODEL 1896 BROOMHANDLES

Note: Manufactured in Oberndorf, Germany between 1897 & 1938.

GRADING - PPGS™	100%	98%	95%	90%	80%	70%	60%	LAST MSR

While many variations of the famous 1896 Broomhandle exist, most common Broomhandles are pre-war Commercials, Model 1930 Commercials, Red 9s, and Bolos. They can be found in chronological order in this section. Holster stocks are a very popular accessory in this model. Commercial stocks may be matching or may not be serial numbered to gun (proper stock).

In 1984, Federal legislation once again allowed importation of non-domestic WWI and WWII military handguns. While many of these newer imports would make workable shooters, they have in no way lowered prices on 90%+ condition specimens due to normal collector activity in top quality only pistols. Recently imported Broomhandles should have the importer's name visibly stamped on an exterior surface.

Mauser Broomhandles: Conehammer Variations

STANDARD CONEHAMMER – 7.63 Mauser cal., distinguishable by circular machined upper hammer with concentric rings. 5 1/2 in. barrel, 23 groove wooden grips, rear adjustable sight available in 1-10, 50-500, 100-300, 50-300, 50-700 meter configurations, 10 shot mag.

N/A $4,500 $3,250 $2,500 $2,000 $1,500 $1,250

Add 40% for matching stock.

FIXED SIGHT CONEHAMMER – 7.63 Mauser cal., similar to Standard Conehammer, except has fixed rear sight.

N/A $6,000 $5,000 $4,000 $3,000 $2,500 $2,000

6 SHOT CONEHAMMER - FIXED SIGHT – 7.63 Mauser cal., 4 3/4 in. barrel, 6 shot mag., rare.

N/A $9,500 $7,500 $5,500 $4,000 $3,000 $2,500

* ***6 Shot Conehammer - Adjustable Sight*** – 7.63 Mauser cal., 5 1/2 in. barrel, very rare.

N/A $13,500 $10,000 $7,500 $5,000 $3,500 $2,500

Sales of this variation are extremely limited.

TURKISH CONEHAMMER – 7.63 Mauser cal., 5 1/2 in. barrel, 10 shot mag. Approx. 1,000 mfg. for Turkey in 1898, Farsi serial numbers.

N/A $9,500 $7,000 $4,500 $3,500 $2,750 $2,250

"SYSTEM MAUSER" CONEHAMMER – 7.63 Mauser cal., "SYSTEM MAUSER" marked on top of chamber, improved 5 1/2 in. tapered barrel, 10 shot mag.

N/A $19,500 $15,000 $12,500 $9,000 $6,500 $4,500

* ***System Mauser Conehammer Stepped barrel variation*** – similar to System Mauser variation, except has older 5 1/2 in. stepped barrel with no taper.

N/A $29,500 $23,500 $15,000 $10,000 $9,000 $8,000

Add 40% for "SYSTEM MAUSER" stock or 6 shot variation.

20 SHOT CONEHAMMER – 7.63 Mauser cal., 20 shot non-detachable mag., frame can either be flatside or have milled panels, 5 1/2 in. tapered barrel, extremely rare.

N/A $50,000 $35,000 $28,500 $17,500 $12,000 $9,000

Add 20% for milled panel variation.
Add 40% for matching stock cut for 20 shot mag.

Many fake 20 shot pistols (especially flatsides with fake stocks) have surfaced over the last few years. Use extreme caution when considering purchase.

EARLY TRANSITIONAL LARGE RING HAMMER – 7.63 Mauser cal., distinguishable by large, open centered ring, 10 shot mag., 5 1/2 in. barrel.

N/A $3,250 $2,750 $2,250 $1,700 $1,450 $1,200

This variation is normally found in the 12,000-15,000 serial range only.

Mauser Broomhandles: Flatside Variations

Add approx. $750-$1,000 for matching shoulder stock, $500-$600 for non-matching stock.

ITALIAN CONTRACT FLATSIDE – 7.63 Mauser cal., distinguishable by flatside frame and DV/AV proofmarks, 10 shot mag., 5 1/2 in. barrel.

N/A $4,500 $3,000 $2,750 $2,250 $1,750 $1,250

This variation is found in the 1-5,000 serial range only.

GRADING - PPGS™	100%	98%	95%	90%	80%	70%	60%	LAST MSR

FLATSIDE COMMERCIAL – 7.63 Mauser cal., 5 1/2 in. barrel, 23 groove walnut grips, adj. rear sight typically marked 1-10 or 50-1,000.

	N/A	$3,500	$2,650	$2,000	$1,750	$1,250	$1,000	

Add 20% for pinned sight.

Early specimens may have pinned rear sights. Found in serial range 20,000-30,000.

Mauser Broomhandles: Post-1900 Variations

Add approximately $1,000-$1,500 for a matching shoulder stock on the following models, $400-$550 for non-matching, depending on the original condition. Some exceptions are noted.

PRE-WAR LARGE RING BOLO – 7.63 Mauser cal., 3.9 in. barrel, floral grips, usually found in 29,000 and 40,000 serial range.

	N/A	$3,750	$2,500	$2,000	$1,500	$1,250	$1,000	

Add $1,000 for short pre-war bolo stock, $1,750 if stock matches pistol.

LARGE RING SHALLOW MILLING – 7.63 Mauser cal., 5 1/2 in. barrel, 23 groove walnut or hard rubber grips, normally found in the 30,000-33,000 ser. range.

	N/A	$2,750	$2,250	$1,500	$1,000	$750	$500	

Add $750 for pre-war stock, $1,500 if stock matches pistol.

LARGE RING DEEP MILLING – 7.63 Mauser cal., 5 1/2 in. barrel, 35 groove walnut or hard rubber grips, normally found in the 34,000 ser. range.

	N/A	$3,000	$2,250	$1,500	$1,000	$750	$500	

Add $750 for pre-war stock, $1,500 if stock matches pistol.

PRE-WAR SMALL RING BOLO – 7.63 Mauser cal., 3.9 in. barrel, floral/checkered rubber or 31-36 groove walnut grips, usually found in 40,000-44,000 serial range.

	N/A	$3,000	$2,250	$1,500	$1,000	$750	$500	

Add $1,000 for short pre-war bolo stock, $1,750 if stock matches pistol.

6-SHOT BOLO – 7.63 Mauser cal., distinctive 6 shot mag., 3.9 in. barrel, either fixed rear sight (more common) or adjustable, could have either large ring or small ring hammer.

	N/A	$6,500	$5,000	$4,000	$3,000	$2,500	$2,000	

Add $1,000-$1,250 for short pre-war bolo stock, $1,500-$2,000 if stock matches pistol, depending on original condition.

STANDARD PRE-WAR COMMERCIAL – 7.63 Mauser cal., 5 1/2 in. barrel, 10 shot mag., 34 groove walnut or checkered black rubber grips, typically 50-1,000 meter adj. rear sight.

	N/A	$2,250	$1,850	$1,500	$1,000	$775	$650	

Original condition on this model is usually under 60% and prices usually start in the $400 range.

Add $1,000-$1,500 for matching stock, $400-$550 for non-matching, depending on original condition.

This variation is the most commonly encountered of all M1896 broomhandles. It can be encountered in the 39,000-274,000 serial range. Early guns below serial no. 100,000 are often Von Lengerke and Detmold marked and can be encountered with hard rubber grips. Rifling changed from 4 groove to 6 groove at approx. serial no. 100,000.

Note: This model is once again being imported by domestic distributors/dealers. These specimens usually have been reblued in addition to other reworking because the original condition has generally been very poor.

MAUSER BANNER CHAMBER MARKED – 7.63 Mauser or 9mm Export/9mm Mauser (rare) cal., 5 1/2 in. barrel, distinguishable by Mauser banner trademark on top of chamber, 32 groove walnut grips. Approx. 10,000 mfg. in serial range 84,000-94,000.

	N/A	$3,500	$2,250	$1,750	$1,250	$750	$500	

This model is very similar in appearance to the Pre-War Commercial.

PERSIAN CONTRACT – 7.63 Mauser cal., 5 1/2 in. barrel, distinguished by Persian lion crest in left rear frame panel, must be in the 154,000 serial range, 50-1,000 meter adj. rear sight.

	N/A	$4,500	$3,500	$2,500	$2,000	$1,500	$1,000	

This variation is frequently faked - pay close attention to serial no. and Persian crest.

GRADING - PPGS™	100%	98%	95%	90%	80%	70%	60%	LAST MSR

STANDARD WARTIME COMMERCIAL – 7.63 Mauser cal., 5 1/2 in. barrel, 10 shot mag., 30 groove walnut grips, adj. 50-1,000 meter rear sight.

N/A	$1,875	$1,550	$1,250	$875	$700	$600	

Condition is somewhat poor, and prices usually start in the $250 range.

This variation is encountered almost as frequently as the Standard Pre-War Commercial. It is usually found in the 290,000-440,000 serial range. It was the first model to utilize the "new safety" design, and can be noticed by the "NS" marking on the back of hammer. Similar features as the Pre-War Commercial, except finish and polishing exhibit more machine and tooling marks.

Note: This model is once again being imported by domestic distributors/dealers. These specimens usually have been reblued in addition to other reworking because the original condition has generally been very poor.

RED-9 ADJ. SIGHT – 9mm Para. cal., 5 1/2 in. barrel, 10 shot mag., 24 groove walnut grips usually marked with large red no. 9, adj. 50-500 meter rear sight, standard WWI military contract model with separate serial range 1-150,000, generally poorly finished. Mfg. 1916-1918.

N/A	$3,250	$2,750	$2,250	$1,750	$1,250	$850	

Add $450 for original leather.

Add 10% if Prussian Eagle proofed on front of magazine well.

Add $1,000-$1,500 for matching stock, $400-$550 for non-matching, depending on original condition.

The Red-9 may be the most popular Commercial Broomhandle whose value far outstrips its rarity.

Note: Be cautious for originality since metal refinishing is prevalent in this model. The last 10,000 guns of this German military contract are not military proofed, are better polished, and will command a slight premium.

RED-9 FIXED SIGHT – 9mm Para. cal., 3.9 in. barrel, this is a 1920 commercial rework of the Red-9 military, may be dated 1920 and/or have police markings on front grip strap.

N/A	$1,750	$1,500	$1,250	$1,000	$750	$500	

Because of the Treaty of Versailles following WWI, barrels had to be shortened to less than 4 inches and the adj. rear sight removed.

FRENCH GENDARME – 7.63 Mauser cal., 3.9 in. barrel, distinguished by Bolo barrel length on large frame, hard rubber or walnut (rare) grips, found in the serial range 431,000-434,000, adj. 50-500 meter rear sight.

N/A	$3,000	$2,250	$1,750	$1,250	$750	$500	

EARLY POST-WAR BOLO – 7.63 Mauser cal., 3.9 in. barrel, short extractor, small ring hammer, usually found in the 440,000-500,000 serial range. Fit with full-size stock.

N/A	$2,250	$1,750	$1,100	$725	$600	$500	

Add 50% for long barrel Bolos in approx. the 475,000 serial range.

LATE POST-WAR BOLO – 7.63 Mauser cal., 3.9 in. barrel, similar features of Early Post-War Bolo except has Mauser banner trademark on left rear frame panel, usually encountered in the 500,000-700,000+ serial range. Fit with full-size stock.

N/A	$2,750	$2,000	$1,500	$1,000	$800	$600	

Add 10% for late pistols with high polish salt blue finish.

Mauser Broomhandles: Post-1930 Variations

EARLY MODEL 1930 COMMERCIAL – 7.63 Mauser cal., 5.2 (common) or 5 1/2 in. stepped barrel, 12 groove walnut grips, adj. 50-1,000 meter rear sight, usually found in the 800,000-890,000 serial range.

N/A	$3,000	$2,300	$1,750	$1,450	$1,050	$850	

Add approximately $1,000-$1,500 for Mauser banner marked stock, depending on original condition (should match the gun). These late stocks were not marked with a serial number.

This broomhandle variation had a high polish, salt blue finish. Small parts are still fire blue and milling grooves were machined in receiver rails.

GRADING - PPGS™	100%	98%	95%	90%	80%	70%	60%	LAST MSR

LATE MODEL 1930 COMMERCIAL – 7.63 Mauser cal., 5 1/2 in. stepped barrel, similar appearance to early 1930 Commercial except has solid receiver rails and various small parts are salt blued. Ser. range 890,000-921,000 with production ending in late 1930s.

	100%	98%	95%	90%	80%	70%	60%
	N/A	$2,850	$2,300	$1,750	$1,450	$1,050	$850

Add approximately $1,000-$1,500 for Mauser banner marked stock, depending on original condition (should match the gun). These late stocks were not marked with a serial number.

This model is serial numbered on rear top of barrel extension assembly.

MODEL 1930 REMOVABLE MAG. – 7.63 Mauser cal., 5 1/2 in. stepped barrel, 12 groove walnut grips, adj. 50-1,000 meter rear sight, very rare.

	100%	98%	95%	90%	80%	70%	60%
	N/A	$18,000	$15,000	$9,000	$5,000	$4,000	$3,200

Original specimens of this variation have frames without the extra cuts required for the selector switch. Fakes are usually welded up Schnellfeuers made to look original. Only a very few are known in the 84,000-88,000 serial range.

SCHNELLFEUER (MODEL 712) – 7.63 Mauser cal., 5 1/2 in. stepped barrel, 12 groove walnut grips, adj. 50-1,000 meter rear sight, switchable full auto variation generally with selector switch, separate serial range 1-100,000, 10 or 20 shot detachable mag. 712 stock is internally grooved for selector switch.

	100%	98%	95%	90%	80%	70%	60%
	N/A	$8,000	$6,000	$4,000	$3,000	$2,000	$1,500

Add $750-$1,500 for correct stock.

The Model 712 is classified as a machine gun and is subject to registration and payment of a $200 transfer tax.

Broomhandle Carbines

CONE HAMMER – 7.63mm cal., 11 3/4 in. barrel, experimental variation.

	100%	98%	95%	90%	80%	70%	60%
	N/A	$22,000	$15,000	$10,000	$7,500	$6,000	$5,000

FLATSIDE TRANSITIONAL – 7.63mm cal., 11 3/4 in. barrel.

	100%	98%	95%	90%	80%	70%	60%
	N/A	$17,500	$13,750	$10,000	$7,000	$6,000	$5,000

LARGE RING HAMMER TRANSITIONAL – 7.63mm cal., 11 3/4 in. barrel.

	100%	98%	95%	90%	80%	70%	60%
	N/A	$18,500	$15,000	$12,500	$10,000	$8,500	$7,500

LARGE RING HAMMER 7.63mm cal., 14 1/2 in. barrel.

	100%	98%	95%	90%	80%	70%	60%
	N/A	$15,000	$13,000	$10,000	$8,500	$7,500	$6,500

SMALL RING HAMMER – 7.63mm cal., 14 1/2 in. barrel.

	100%	98%	95%	90%	80%	70%	60%
	N/A	$16,000	$13,000	$10,000	$8,500	$7,500	$6,500

Broomhandles: Copies from Other Countries

These pistols are Chinese manufactured copies of the original German design.

HAND-MADE MAUSER CHINESE MARKED AND OTHERS – 9mm Para. or .45 ACP cal., copies of the Mauser Broomhandle, many thousands made, fixed (.45 ACP cal.) or detachable (9mm Para.) mag., quality can vary significantly, recent imports will have import markings. IAR, Inc. imported these recently.

	100%	98%	95%	90%	80%	70%	60%
9mm Para. cal.	N/A	$750	$600	$500	$400	$325	$275
.45 ACP cal.	N/A	$1,750	$1,250	$1,000	$900	$800	$700

Add $150 for reproduction shoulder stock holster (with or w/o leather).
Subtract 25% for poor quality (QC with slave labor only goes so far).

HAND-MADE UNMARKED – poor quality.

	100%	98%	95%	90%	80%	70%	60%
	N/A	$800	$700	$600	$500	$450	$400

ASIATIC FLATSIDE UNMARKED – better quality, not exceedingly rare.

	100%	98%	95%	90%	80%	70%	60%
	N/A	$2,500	$1,800	$1,550	$1,250	$750	$500

TAKU-NAVAL DOCKYARD FLATSIDE – machine-made, better quality, approx. 6,000 mfg.

	100%	98%	95%	90%	80%	70%	60%
	N/A	$2,750	$2,200	$1,700	$1,350	$1,000	$750

Add 30% if with correct stock.

GRADING - PPGS™	100%	98%	95%	90%	80%	70%	60%	LAST MSR

SHANSEI ARSENAL .45 CAL. – .45 ACP cal., approx. 8,500 mfg., scarce and desirable in excellent condition, as most remaining original pistols are in rough condition, original stripper clips for this model are rare.

	100%	98%	95%	90%	80%	70%	60%
	N/A	$6,500	$5,000	$3,500	$2,500	$2,000	$1,500

Newly made Shansei 45s are currently priced in the $1,500-$2,200 range.

Recently, a small number of currently manufactured pistols have been marketed as "restorations." Buyer beware! Also, fake stocks have recently surfaced.

Broomhandles: Spanish Copies

VERY EARLY ASTRA-900 – Bolo grips, frame has single-line address, approx. 1,200 mfg.

	100%	98%	95%	90%	80%	70%	60%
	N/A	$3,000	$2,500	$2,250	$1,750	$1,600	$1,475

EARLY ASTRA-900 – single-line address, approx. ser. range 1,200-12,000.

	100%	98%	95%	90%	80%	70%	60%
	N/A	$2,500	$1,650	$1,200	$800	$700	$525

LATE ASTRA-900 – two and three-line address, two-line address ser. range is approx. 12,000-20,000, three-line address ser. range is approx. 20,000-34,400.

	100%	98%	95%	90%	80%	70%	60%
	N/A	$2,250	$1,650	$1,200	$800	$700	$525

Add 20% for Chinese character variation in the 27,000 serial range or 50% if in Nazi procurement range.

ROYAL SEMI-AUTO – early Royals are mostly seen in semi-auto with round bolts.

	100%	98%	95%	90%	80%	70%	60%
	N/A	$3,500	$2,700	$2,000	$1,500	$1,000	$750

There were many variations of the Royals and values assume standard variation.

ROYAL SELECTIVE FIRE – 7.63mm cal., most of approx. 33,000 Royals manufactured were selective fire, several variations, Class III transferable only.

	100%	98%	95%	90%	80%	70%	60%
Class III	N/A	$7,500	$5,000	$3,500	$2,500	$2,000	$1,750

Add 20% if detachable mag.

Add 100% if MM34 with pneumatic rate retarder (production under 1,000 pistols).

This model had either a fixed mag. or detachable mag. May have been fit with pneumatic rate retarder.

RIFLES: MILITARY PRODUCTION

As there were quite a few different manufacturers within Germany that produced the K98 military rifles and carbines, they have been listed by country in alphabetical order in this section. Most of the produced military contracts will be found under Mauser Mfg. - Oberndorf.

Add 20%-25% if with matching bayonet.

Subtract 50%-60% if bolt is not matching or contract crests have been removed, depending on remaining condition.

ARGENTINA

	100%	98%	95%	90%	80%	70%	60%
Model 1891 Rifle Argentine pattern	$800	$775	$750	$550	$500	$400	$275
Model 1891 Carbine	$750	$725	$700	$550	$450	$300	$200
Model 1909 Rifle	$900	$850	$750	$675	$550	$400	$300
Model 1909 Sniper Rifle w/scope	$2,300	$2,100	$1,800	$1,600	$1,525	$1,200	$1,000
Model 1909 Cavalry Carbine	$800	$700	$600	$550	$475	$400	$300
Model 1909 Mountain Carbine	$800	$700	$600	$550	$475	$400	$300
Model 1933 Mauser Banner	$700	$650	$550	$450	$400	$300	$250
Model 1935 Mauser Banner	$700	$650	$550	$450	$400	$300	$250

AUSTRIA

	100%	98%	95%	90%	80%	70%	60%
Model 1914 Rifle	N/A	N/A	$2,000	$1,750	$1,500	$1,000	$600

GRADING - PPGS™	100%	98%	95%	90%	80%	70%	60%	LAST MSR
BELGIUM								
Model 1889 Rifle FN mfg.	N/A	$1,750	$1,300	$950	$800	$750	$650	
Model 1889 Rifle Hopkins & Allen or Birmingham	$1,750	$1,600	$1,500	$950	$800	$750	$600	
Model 1889 Carbine (all pre-WWI)	$1,000	$900	$800	$650	$575	$500	$450	
Model 1916 Carbine (all WWI makes)	$700	$650	$600	$475	$400	$350	$300	
Model 1935 Short Rifle (FN receiver)	$700	$650	$550	$475	$425	$375	$350	
Model 1889/36 Short rifle	$600	$500	$425	$375	$300	$250	$200	
Model 50 "L" Crest	$600	$525	$475	$425	$350	$300	$225	
Model 50 "B" Crest	$575	$500	$450	$400	$325	$275	$200	
Model 50 Belgian Congo "FP" Crest	$1,200	$950	$850	$750	$600	$475	$375	
Model 50 .22 cal. Single shot trainer "B" Crest	$1,650	$1,300	$1,100	$950	$800	$750	$550	
Model 50 .22 cal. Single Shot Congo trainer "FP" crest	$1,900	$1,600	$1,400	$1,200	$1,000	$900	$700	

Add 25% for WWI German captured Belgian Mausers (rifles & carbines) converted by the Germans to 7.92mm cal. and marked with Imperial German proofs.

Post-war arsenal refinished rifles in grey paint do not command a premium.

GRADING - PPGS™	100%	98%	95%	90%	80%	70%	60%	LAST MSR
BOLIVIA								
Model 1895 Rifle (Argentine M1891 Rifle)	$600	$550	$450	$350	$250	$200	$125	
Model 1907 Rifle	$800	$750	$700	$600	$500	$400	$275	
Model 1907 Short Rifle	$800	$750	$700	$600	$500	$400	$275	
Czech marked Model VZ24 Short Rifle	$800	$750	$700	$600	$500	$400	$275	
Standard Model Mauser Banner Short Rifle	$700	$650	$550	$425	$350	$275	$150	
Model 1950 Rifle Series B-50	$700	$650	$550	$425	$350	$275	$150	
BRAZIL								
Model 1894 Rifle, Loewe mfg.	$800	$650	$550	$450	$400	$300	$250	
Model 1894 Rifle, FN mfg.	$1,000	$850	$650	$550	$450	$400	$350	
Model 1894 Carbine	$1,000	$850	$650	$550	$450	$400	$350	
Model 1904 Mauser Vergueiro Rifle	$600	$500	$400	$300	$225	$175	$100	
Model 1907 Rifle	$600	$500	$400	$300	$225	$175	$100	
Model 1907 Carbine	$600	$500	$400	$300	$200	$175	$100	
Model 1908 Rifle	$1,100	$1,000	$900	$800	$600	$400	$200	
Model 1908 Short Rifle	$825	$775	$650	$500	$375	$250	$100	
FN Mle. 1922 Carbine	$750	$650	$550	$400	$300	$225	$125	
Model 1924 VZ 24 Carbine	$800	$675	$575	$450	$300	$225	$100	

GRADING - PPGS™	100%	98%	95%	90%	80%	70%	60%	LAST MSR
Model 1924/34 Czech Carbine	$800	$675	$575	$450	$300	$225	$100	
Model 1908/34 Rifle .30-06 cal.	$800	$675	$575	$450	$300	$225	$100	
Model 1935 Mauser Banner Rifle	$1,100	$1,000	$900	$800	$600	$400	$200	
Model 1935 Mauser Banner Carbine	$1,100	$1,000	$900	$800	$600	$400	$200	
Model M954 Rifle .30-06 cal.	$800	$650	$500	$375	$200	$150	$100	

CHILE

Model 1893 Rifle - Bent bolt handle	$700	$650	$575	$475	$375	$300	$175	
Model 1895 Rifle - Army	$700	$650	$590	$475	$325	$225	$100	
Model 1895 Rifle - Anchor crest	$700	$650	$590	$475	$325	$225	$100	
Model 1895 Short Rifle	$650	$600	$550	$425	$275	$175	$80	
Model 1895 Carbine	$600	$550	$450	$325	$250	$195	$100	
Model 1912 Rifle	$700	$650	$575	$495	$375	$250	$125	
Model 1912 Rifle (7.62 NATO)	$700	$650	$575	$495	$375	$250	$125	
Model 1912 Short Rifle	$700	$650	$575	$495	$375	$250	$125	
Model 1912 Short Rifle (7.62 NATO)	$700	$650	$575	$495	$375	$250	$125	
Model 1935 Carbine (7.62 NATO)	$650	$600	$550	$425	$275	$175	$80	
Mauser Banner	$900	$850	$775	$650	$550	$375	$250	

CHINA

Gew 1871 Rifle - Chinese marked	$1,100	$1,050	$925	$850	$700	$550	$300	
Kar 1871 Rifle - Chinese marked	$1,100	$1,050	$925	$850	$700	$550	$300	
Kar 98a Carbine	$800	$750	$700	$550	$400	$275	$225	
Model 1907 Rifle - China contract	$1,000	$950	$900	$750	$500	$400	$300	
Model 1907 Carbine	$1,000	$950	$900	$750	$500	$400	$300	
Model 98/22 Rifle	$700	$650	$600	$475	$325	$250	$150	
FN Mle. 1924 or 1930 Short rifles	$700	$650	$600	$475	$325	$250	$150	
Model 21 Chinese-made VZ 24	$700	$650	$500	$400	$350	$250	$125	
Std. Model 1933 Mauser Banner Rifle	$900	$850	$800	$675	$550	$425	$300	
Std. Model 1933 Mauser Banner Carbine	$950	$875	$800	$675	$525	$350	$275	
Chiang Kai-Shek Rifle - Chinese copy	$800	$750	$675	$550	$400	$300	$175	
Chinese VZ 24 P prefix - "1937" SH. Rifle	$650	$550	$495	$350	$275	$175	$100	
Chinese copy VZ 24w/Jap. folding byt.	$1,000	$925	$800	$700	$550	$400	$300	

GRADING - PPGS™	100%	98%	95%	90%	80%	70%	60%	LAST MSR
COLOMBIA								
Model 1891 Rifle - Argentine pattern	$800	$750	$700	$600	$450	$300	$195	
Model 1912 Rifle - Steyr	$700	$600	$400	$250	$185	$150	$100	
Model 1912 Short Rifle - Steyr	$700	$600	$400	$250	$185	$150	$100	
Model VZ 24 Short Rifle	$700	$600	$400	$250	$185	$150	$100	
Model 29 Short Rifle - Steyr	$800	$700	$550	$425	$325	$225	$175	
FN Mle. 1930 Carbine	$850	$750	$700	$600	$500	$400	$350	
FN Mle. 1930 Short Rifle	$600	$500	$400	$300	$275	$225	$175	
FN Mle. 1950 Short Rifle (.30-06 cal.)	$600	$500	$400	$300	$275	$225	$150	
COSTA RICA								
Model 1895 Rifle	$800	$700	$575	$425	$350	$250	$125	
Model 1910 Rifle	$700	$600	$495	$375	$295	$175	$100	
FN Mle. 1924/1930 Short Rifle	$750	$700	$600	$500	$450	$400	$375	
CZECHOSLOVAKIA								
Model 1919 Mauser - Jelen Rifle	N/A	N/A	$4,000	$3,500	$2,800	$1,900	$1,700	
Model 1921 Mauser - Jelen Rifle	N/A	N/A	$3,500	$3,000	$2,400	$1,800	$1,500	
Model 98/22 Rifle	$600	$500	$400	$295	$200	$150	$90	
Model VZ 23 Short Rifle	$600	$500	$400	$290	$200	$150	$100	
Model VZ 23A Short Rifle	$600	$500	$400	$290	$200	$150	$100	
Model VZ 24 Short Rifle	$600	$575	$500	$450	$325	$200	$100	
Model 98/29 Rifle	$600	$500	$400	$275	$200	$125	$90	
Model VZ 08/33 Carbine	$600	$550	$500	$450	$350	$250	$150	
Model VZ 12/33 Carbine - Light VZ 24	$700	$600	$500	$400	$290	$190	$125	
Model VZ 16/33	$800	$700	$550	$450	$325	$250	$175	
Model "JC" Short Rifle	$800	$700	$500	$400	$350	$300	$250	
Model "L" SH. Rifle cal., .303, Lithuania	N/A	$1,600	$1,300	$1,000	$800	$700	$600	
DOMINICAN REPUBLIC								
M1953 Rifle - Ex-Brazil M1908	$600	$475	$275	$175	$150	$100	$75	
M1953 SH. Rifle - Ex-Brazil M1908 SHR.	$600	$475	$275	$175	$150	$100	$75	
ECUADOR								
Model 71/84 Rifle	$600	$550	$350	$200	$150	$125	$900	
Model 1891 Rifle - Argentine pattern	$550	$495	$400	$275	$190	$125	$85	

GRADING - PPGS™	100%	98%	95%	90%	80%	70%	60%	LAST MSR
Model 1907 Rifle	$600	$500	$400	$325	$250	$190	$150	
Model VZ 23 Short Rifle	$500	$425	$325	$275	$190	$150	$90	
Model VZ 24 Short Rifle	$500	$425	$325	$275	$190	$150	$90	
Model VZ 12/33 Short Rifle	$500	$425	$325	$275	$190	$150	$90	
FN Mle. 1930 Short Rifle	$750	$700	$600	$500	$450	$400	$375	
EL SALVADOR								
Model 1895 Rifle - Chilean pattern	$600	$550	$500	$400	$300	$180	$90	
Model VZ 12/33 Carbine	$500	$450	$400	$300	$200	$125	$90	
Standard Model 1935 Export	$500	$450	$350	$290	$250	$150	$90	
FN M50 Israeli Short Rifle	$500	$450	$320	$260	$200	$125	$90	
ESTONIA								
Czech Model "L" Short Rifle - .303 cal.	N/A	N/A	$1,000	$825	$700	$595	$475	
ETHIOPIA								
FN Mle. 1930 Short Rifle	N/A	$2,300	$2,000	$1,750	$1,100	$800	$700	
FN Mle. 1930 Carbine	N/A	$2,750	$2,300	$1,900	$1,600	$1,000	$900	
Model 1933 Standard Model Rifle	N/A	$2,500	$2,200	$1,800	$1,500	$900	$800	

Values assume original configuration with original parts.

svw MB | **FRANCE**

GRADING - PPGS™	100%	98%	95%	90%	80%	70%	60%	LAST MSR
Modified 98K Carbine - Hex. stacking rod	$600	$500	$400	$325	$250	$200	$150	
GERMANY								
Model 1871 Rifle - Gew 71	N/A	$1,200	$1,100	$1,000	$800	$600	$400	
Model 1871 Carbine - Kar 71	N/A	$1,200	$1,100	$1,000	$800	$600	$400	
Model 1871 Short Rifle - Jaeger 71	N/A	$1,400	$1,300	$1,200	$950	$700	$550	
Model 1871/84 Rifle	N/A	$1,200	$1,100	$1,000	$800	$600	$400	
Model 1888 Commission Rifle	N/A	$900	$850	$750	$600	$400	$275	
Model 1888/05 Commission Rifle	N/A	$900	$850	$750	$600	$400	$275	
Model 1888/14 Commission Rifle	N/A	$900	$850	$750	$600	$400	$275	
Model 1888 Commission Carbine	N/A	$900	$850	$750	$600	$400	$300	
Model 1891 Comm. Carbine w/stacking hook	N/A	$900	$850	$750	$600	$400	$300	
Model 1888/97 Rifle	N/A	N/A	N/A	$6,000	$5,000	$3,800	$3,000	

GRADING - PPGS™	100%	98%	95%	90%	80%	70%	60%	LAST MSR
Model 1898 Rifle - Gew 98	N/A	$900	$800	$700	$600	$375	$250	
Model 1898 Carbine - Kar. 98, 16.9 in. bbl.	N/A	$6,000	$5,000	$4,200	$3,700	$3,200	$2,500	
Model 1898/17 Rifle Exp.	N/A	N/A	N/A	$5,000	$4,200	$3,200	$2,500	
Model 1898/18 Rifle Exp.	N/A	N/A	N/A	$5,000	$4,200	$3,200	$2,500	
Model 1909 Self Loading Carbine	N/A	$7,500	$5,500	$4,500	$4,000	$3,500	$2,800	
Model 1898A Carbine	N/A	$800	$725	$700	$600	$450	$250	
Model 1898AZ Carbine (also Model 98a)	N/A	$800	$725	$700	$600	$450	$250	
Model 1898b Carbine	N/A	$1,000	$950	$800	$600	$500	$350	
Model Gew. 98 (Transitional)	N/A	$700	$625	$550	$450	$325	$200	
Model 33/40 Carbine ("945" 1940)	N/A	$2,500	$2,000	$1,800	$1,500	$1,200	$800	
Model 33/40 Carbine ("DOT" 1941-43)	N/A	$2,500	$2,000	$1,800	$1,500	$1,200	$800	
Model 24 (T) Rifle	N/A	$875	$800	$725	$600	$450	$300	
Model 98/40	N/A	$775	$700	$625	$500	$350	$250	
Model VG-1	N/A	N/A	N/A	$3,000	$2,500	$2,000	$1,800	
G 41M Semi-Auto Rifle	N/A	$20,000	$18,750	$17,500	$12,000	$9,000	$7,000	
G 41W Semi-Auto Rifle	N/A	$8,000	$7,000	$6,000	$5,000	$4,000	$2,750	
G/K 43 Sniper Rifle	N/A	$8,500	$7,900	$7,400	$6,800	$5,200	$3,750	
G/K 43 Semi-Auto Rifle	N/A	$3,500	$3,000	$2,500	$2,000	$1,500	$1,250	
Model 29/40 Rifle L/W issue	N/A	$1,000	$900	$800	$675	$550	$400	
Model 29/0 Rifle L/W Issue	N/A	N/A	N/A	$3,500	$3,000	$2,500	$2,150	
Model K98k "Para-troop Model"	N/A	$5,500	$4,900	$4,200	$3,800	$3,000	$2,700	

Many configurations and variants of the G/K 43 Sniper Rifle are serious fakes - consult a qualified expert before buying/selling/trading.

GREECE

FN Mle. 1930 Short Rifle	$750	$700	$600	$500	$400	$300	$200	

GUATEMALA

Czech VZ 24 Short Rifle	$700	$675	$600	$425	$350	$275	$75	
M1895 Rifle	$500	$450	$400	$275	$200	$125	$75	

HAITI

FN Mle. 1950 Short Rifle	$700	$650	$575	$450	$300	$175	$100	

IRAN (PERSIA)

Model 1895 Rifle	$600	$550	$500	$300	$200	$175	$125	
Model 98/29 Rifle	$900	$850	$800	$650	$500	$500	$300	$195

GRADING - PPGS™	100%	98%	95%	90%	80%	70%	60%	LAST MSR
Model 98/29 Short Rifle	$875	$825	$775	$475	$360	$295	$175	
Model 49 Carbine	$800	$700	$550	$400	$300	$250	$195	
FN Mle. 1924 Short Rifle	$1,200	$1,100	$950	$800	$700	$600	$500	
VZ 24 Short Rifle	$900	$800	$700	$500	$375	$275	$200	
IRAQ								
Model 1948 98k Carbine	$600	$500	$400	$300	$250	$195	$100	
ISRAEL								
German 98k with Israeli marks	$600	$500	$400	$300	$200	$150	$90	
Czech 98k w/ large triggerguard	$600	$550	$450	$275	$200	$120	$80	
FN Mle. 1950 Short Rifle	$600	$550	$450	$425	$375	$325	$275	
FN Mle. 1950 .22 Single Shot Trainer	$1,100	$950	$750	$650	$550	$450	$400	
Model 1954 Short Rifle	$625	$575	$450	$350	$250	$180	$125	
LATVIA								
Czech VZ 24 Short Rifle	$800	$750	$650	$500	$275	$225	$150	
LIBERIA								
FN Mle. 1930 Short Rifle	N/A	N/A	$850	$750	$650	$500	$400	
LITHUANIA								
Czech "L" Model Short Rifle (.303)	N/A	N/A	$900	$700	$600	$500	$425	
Model VZ 24 Short Rifle	N/A	N/A	$900	$800	$600	$450	$325	
FN Mle. 1930 Short Rifle	N/A	$1,800	$1,700	$1,500	$1,200	$900	$750	
Model 1900 Rifle	$800	$700	$600	$400	$325	$275	$190	
MANCHURIA								
Mukden Arsenal Rifle	$1,500	$1,400	$1,200	$950	$800	$650	$400	
MEXICO								
Model 1895 Rifle	$550	$475	$400	$250	$190	$125	$80	
Model 1895 Carbine	$550	$475	$400	$250	$190	$125	$80	
Model 1902 Rifle	$1,500	$1,400	$1,300	$1,050	$925	$800	$500	
Model 1907 Rifle	$600	$500	$450	$375	$300	$250	$125	
Model 1910 Rifle	$500	$400	$300	$200	$175	$125	$90	
Model 1910 Carbine	$500	$400	$300	$200	$175	$125	$90	
Model 1912 Rifle	$700	$600	$500	$325	$275	$225	$175	
Model 1912 Short Rifle	$700	$600	$500	$325	$275	$225	$175	
Model 1924 Short Rifle	$700	$650	$600	$475	$300	$250	$175	
Model 1924 Carbine	$700	$600	$500	$325	$275	$225	$175	

GRADING - PPGS™	100%	98%	95%	90%	80%	70%	60%	LAST MSR
Model 1936 Short Rifle	$700	$675	$600	$475	$400	$275	$195	
Model 1954 Short Rifle	$675	$650	$600	$475	$425	$300	$225	
MOROCCO								
FN Mle. 1950 Carbine	$650	$550	$475	$400	$350	$300	$250	
w/threaded barrel for grenade launcher	$700	$650	$600	$500	$450	$375	$300	
NETHERLANDS								
FN Mle. 1950 Carbine "W" crest	$900	$800	$700	$600	$500	$450	$375	
FN Mle. 1950 Carbine "J" crest	$850	$750	$650	$550	$450	$400	$350	
NICARAGUA								
Model VZ 12/33 Short Rifle	$700	$675	$625	$500	$400	$300	$195	
Model VZ 24 Short Rifle	$600	$550	$500	$400	$300	$195	$125	
ORANGE FREE STATE								
Model 1896 Rifle(OVS marked), DWM	$1,100	$1,000	$950	$825	$675	$525	$400	
Model 1896 Rifle (OVS marked), Loewe & Sons	$1,000	$900	$800	$650	$525	$400	$250	
Model 1896 Rifle, Chile overmark	$700	$625	$550	$425	$375	$300	$200	
Model 1895 Short Rifle	$700	$650	$550	$425	$350	$275	$195	
Model 1895 Carbine	$700	$650	$550	$425	$350	$275	$195	
PARAGUAY								
Model 1895 Rifle	$500	$425	$295	$200	$150	$110	$75	
Model 1907 Rifle (DWM)	$600	$425	$295	$200	$150	$110	$75	
Model 1907 Carbine (Full-stocked)	$600	$425	$295	$200	$150	$110	$75	
Model 1927 Rifle (Oviedo)	$495	$400	$275	$200	$150	$100	$80	
Model 1927 Short Rifle	$495	$400	$275	$200	$150	$100	$80	
Model 1927 Carbine (Full-stocked)	$495	$400	$275	$200	$150	$125	$90	
FN Mle. 1930 Short Rifle	$850	$750	$650	$550	$450	$400	$350	
Model 1933 Standard Model Rifle	$550	$450	$380	$320	$260	$190	$120	
PERU								
Model 1891 Rifle (Lange sight)	$495	$450	$400	$300	$225	$150	$90	
Model 1891 Carbine (Lange sight)	$495	$450	$400	$300	$225	$150	$90	
Model 1909 Rifle	$1,750	$1,350	$1,000	$850	$725	$675	$500	

GRADING - PPGS™	100%	98%	95%	90%	80%	70%	60%	LAST MSR
Model VZ 24 Short Rifle	$600	$550	$500	$395	$350	$295	$195	
Model VZ 32 Short Rifle (Model 32)	$700	$650	$600	$495	$375	$325	$225	
FN Short Rifle Modelo 1935	$700	$650	$600	$495	$375	$325	$225	
FN Carbine Modelo 1935	$900	$850	$775	$700	$550	$400	$295	
POLAND								
Model 1898 Rifle	$600	$550	$500	$395	$325	$275	$195	
Model 1898 Carbine (Kar 98a)	$600	$550	$500	$395	$325	$275	$195	
Model 1929 Short Rifle (Wz 29)	$800	$750	$700	$495	$425	$280	$175	
PORTUGAL								
Model 1904 Mauser-Verguiero Rifle	$700	$675	$600	$500	$425	$275	$180	
Model 1937 Short Rifle	$700	$675	$600	$475	$375	$250	$175	
Model 1937a Short Rifle	$700	$650	$600	$475	$375	$250	$180	
Model 1941 Short Rifle	$900	$850	$800	$650	$525	$300	$200	
ROMANIA								
Model VZ 24 Short Rifle, "M" or "C" Crest	$800	$750	$650	$550	$400	$250	$125	
SAUDI ARABIA								
FN Mle. 1950 Short Rifle	N/A	N/A	$1,100	$950	$800	$700	$600	
SERBIA/YUGOSLAVIA								
Model 1878/80 Rifle	$1,400	$1,300	$1,150	$900	$750	$600	$300	
Model 1885 Cavalry Carbine	$1,250	$1,175	$1,050	$900	$750	$600	$300	
Model 1886/6C and 1880/7C	$1,200	$1,100	$1,000	$850	$750	$600	$300	
Model 1899 Rifle	$650	$575	$500	$400	$275	$200	$110	
Model 1889/07 Rifle	$600	$525	$430	$325	$250	$125	$90	
Model 1899/08 Rifle	$600	$525	$430	$325	$250	$125	$90	
Model 1899C Short Rifle	$600	$525	$430	$325	$250	$125	$80	
Model 1899/08 Carbine	$900	$800	$700	$600	$400	$300	$195	
Model 1910 Rifle	$525	$450	$390	$300	$225	$160	$125	
Model 1924 Short Rifle	$575	$500	$450	$400	$350	$300	$250	
Model 1924 Carbine	$850	$700	$650	$550	$450	$400	$350	
FN Mle 1924 Short Rifle	$600	$550	$450	$375	$295	$225	$160	
FN Mle 1924 Carbine	$700	$650	$600	$475	$395	$295	$195	

GRADING - PPGS™	100%	98%	95%	90%	80%	70%	60%	LAST MSR
Czech VZ 24 Short Rifle	$600	$550	$450	$375	$250	$175	$115	
Model 1924 Short Rifle (Kragujevac)	$600	$550	$450	$375	$250	$175	$115	
M90T Short Rifle (ex-Turkish M1890)	N/A	$800	$700	$500	$400	$250	$150	
Model M24B Rifle (ex-Mexican M1912)	N/A	$800	$700	$500	$400	$250	$150	
Model 1948 Carbine (ex-German)	$900	$800	$750	$700	$600	$500	$300	
Model 1948 Carbine (Kragujevac)	$900	$800	$750	$700	$600	$500	$300	
SIAM (THAILAND)								
Model 1902 Rifle (Type 45)	$550	$450	$400	$390	$270	$195	$100	
Model 1923 Short Rifle (Type 66)	$550	$450	$400	$390	$270	$195	$100	
SLOVAK REPUBLIC								
Model VZ 24 Short Rifle	$800	$700	$600	$500	$375	$300	$180	
SOUTH AFRICAN REPUBLIC								
Model 1896 Rifle "ZAR" marked	$1,100	$1,025	$950	$775	$600	$400	$195	
SPAIN								
Model 1891 Rifle	$800	$750	$700	$550	$400	$300	$250	
Model 1892 Rifle	$1,300	$1,225	$1,100	$950	$800	$650	$500	
Model 1892 Carbine	$750	$700	$600	$500	$375	$295	$195	
Model 1893 Rifle	$750	$700	$600	$500	$375	$295	$195	
Model 1895 Carbine (Full-stocked)	$700	$625	$575	$495	$375	$295	$195	
Model 1916 Short Rifle	$600	$525	$475	$400	$325	$225	$180	
Model 1916 Experimental 8mm	$750	$700	$625	$450	$375	$295	$190	
Model 1943 Short Rifle	$500	$425	$350	$275	$195	$125	$75	
SWEDEN								
Model 1894 Carbine	$750	$700	$650	$600	$480	$390	$275	
Model 1896 Rifle	$600	$500	$400	$300	$220	$185	$120	
Model 1938 Short Rifle	$600	$500	$400	$300	$200	$125	$80	
Model 1940 Short Rifle (8mm)	$800	$700	$650	$500	$375	$295	$225	
Model 41 (1955) Sniper	$3,000	$2,500	$2,000	$1,750	$1,575	$1,325	$1,100	
SYRIA								
Model 1948 Carbine	$500	$400	$325	$275	$200	$120	$80	
TURKEY								
Model 1887 Rifle	$1,500	$1,400	$1,300	$1,100	$900	$700	$500	
Model 1887 Carbine	$1,500	$1,400	$1,300	$1,100	$900	$700	$500	
Model 1890 Rifle	$1,200	$1,150	$1,000	$900	$775	$625	$500	

GRADING - PPGS™	100%	98%	95%	90%	80%	70%	60%	LAST MSR
Model 1893 Rifle	$1,300	$1,225	$1,050	$900	$775	$675	$500	
Model 1903 Rifle 7.65mm	$1,200	$1,150	$1,000	$900	$700	$550	$400	
Model 1905 Carbine	$1,200	$1,150	$1,000	$900	$700	$500	$350	
Model VZ 98/22 Rifle	$600	$500	$400	$250	$190	$125	$90	
Model 1888 Rifle (Turkish marked)	$500	$400	$250	$200	$140	$90	$70	
Model 1888/38 Rifle (Improved)	$500	$400	$250	$200	$140	$90	$70	
Model 1938 Rifle 8mm	$500	$400	$250	$200	$140	$90	$60	
Model 1938 Short Rifle	$500	$400	$250	$200	$140	$90	$60	
URUGUAY								
FN Mle. 1895 Rifle	$900	$850	$775	$600	$400	$250	$125	
Model 1904 Rifle	$700	$625	$550	$400	$325	$260	$200	
Model 1908 Rifle	$800	$700	$600	$450	$400	$300	$200	
Model 1908 Short Rifle	$700	$600	$500	$450	$400	$300	$200	
Czech VZ 32 Short Rifle (Model 1934)	$800	$700	$600	$500	$290	$200	$120	
Czech VZ 24 Short Rifle (Model 1934)	$800	$700	$600	$500	$390	$275	$195	
FN Mle. 1930 Short Rifle	$675	$575	$500	$450	$400	$350	$300	
VENEZUELA								
Model 1910 Rifle	$500	$425	$350	$290	$240	$130	$90	
Czech VZ 24/26 Short Rifle	$600	$500	$450	$375	$300	$225	$160	
FN Mle. 1930 or 1950 Short Rifle	$1,000	$800	$600	$500	$400	$300	$200	
FN Mle. 1930 or 1950 Carbine	$975	$850	$600	$500	$400	$300	$225	
YEMEN								
FN Mle 1930 Short Rifle	N/A	N/A	$900	$800	$650	$550	$450	

YUGOSLAVIA – Please refer to listings under Serbia/Yugoslavia.

RIFLES: MILITARY PRODUCTION, K98k (KARBINE)

The following model listings represent the various manufacturers of K98k military carbines in Germany between 1934-1945. Codes following the year can be found on the guns, and will help in identification. *Backbone of the Wehrmacht: The German K98k Rifle* by Richard D. Law is an invaluable resource that lists all the codes and the placement.

The author wishes to express thanks to Wolf von Baumbach for making the following information available.

Add 15% for rifles marked M Marine (Navy) and L Luftwaffe (Air Force).

Add 100% for SS markings - beware of fakes and spurious markings.

MAUSER WERKE AG, OBERNDORF A/N

GRADING - PPGS™	100%	98%	95%	90%	80%	70%	60%
1934 - S/42 K	N/A	$9,500	$7,500	$6,000	$4,500	$3,000	$2,000
1935 - S/42 G	N/A	$8,500	$6,500	$4,500	$2,500	$1,800	$1,000
1936 - S/42 1936	N/A	$6,000	$5,000	$4,000	$3,000	$1,800	$1,000
1937 - S/42 1937	N/A	$5,000	$4,500	$3,500	$2,500	$1,800	$1,000

GRADING - PPGS™	100%	98%	95%	90%	80%	70%	60%	LAST MSR
1938 - E Code S/42 1938	N/A	$2,200	$1,800	$1,400	$1,000	$800	$600	
1938 - L Code 42 1938	N/A	$2,200	$1,800	$1,400	$1,000	$800	$600	
1939 - 42 1939	N/A	$2,000	$1,650	$1,300	$900	$700	$525	
1940 - 42 1940	N/A	$2,000	$1,650	$1,300	$900	$700	$525	
1941 - BYF 41	N/A	$2,000	$1,650	$1,300	$900	$700	$525	
1942 - BYF 42	N/A	$1,800	$1,450	$1,100	$700	$550	$425	
1943 - BYF 43	N/A	$1,800	$1,450	$1,100	$700	$550	$425	
1944 - BYF 44	N/A	$1,700	$1,375	$1,050	$675	$525	$400	
1945 - Mod. 98 BYF 45	N/A	$2,000	$1,650	$1,300	$900	$700	$525	
1945 - Mod. 98 SVW	N/A	$2,000	$1,650	$1,300	$900	$700	$525	
1945 - Mod. 98 SVW MB	N/A	$3,000	$2,800	$2,300	$1,800	$1,500	$900	
J.P. SAUER UND SOHN GEWEHRFABRIK, SUHL								
1934 - S/147K	N/A	$9,000	$7,000	$5,500	$4.500	$2,500	$2,000	
1935 - S/147G	N/A	$8,000	$6,000	$4,000	$2,000	$1,800	$1,500	
1936 - S/147 1936	N/A	$5,000	$4,000	$3,000	$1,800	$1,300	$800	
1937 - S/147 1937	N/A	$4,000	$2,600	$2,150	$1,600	$1,100	$750	
1938 - E Code S/147	N/A	$2,200	$1,800	$1,400	$1,000	$800	$600	
1938 - L Code 147 1938	N/A	$2,200	$1,800	$1,400	$1,000	$800	$600	
1939 - 147 1939	N/A	$2,200	$1,800	$1,400	$1,000	$800	$600	
1940 - 147 1940	N/A	$2,000	$1,650	$1,300	$900	$700	$525	
1941 - CE 41	N/A	$2,000	$1,650	$1,300	$900	$700	$525	
1942 - CE 42	N/A	$1,800	$1,450	$1,100	$700	$550	$425	
1943 - CE 43	N/A	$1,800	$1,450	$1,100	$700	$550	$425	
1944 - CE 44	N/A	$1,700	$1,375	$1,050	$675	$525	$400	
ERMA (ERFURTER MASCHINENFABRIK), ERFURT								
1935 - S/27 G	N/A	$3,500	$3,000	$2,500	$1,950	$1,450	$850	
1936 - S/27 1936	N/A	$3,300	$2,800	$2,350	$1,800	$1,300	$800	
1937 - S/27 1937	N/A	$3,000	$2,600	$2,150	$1,600	$1,100	$750	
1938 - S/27 or 27 1938	N/A	$2,200	$1,800	$1,400	$1,000	$800	$600	
1939 - 27 1939	N/A	$2,200	$1,800	$1,400	$1,000	$800	$600	
1940 - E Code 27 1940	N/A	$2,000	$1,650	$1,300	$900	$700	$525	
1940 - L Code AX 1940	N/A	$2,000	$1,650	$1,300	$900	$700	$525	
1941 - AX 41	N/A	$2,000	$1,650	$1,300	$900	$700	$525	
MAUSER WERKE AG, BORSIGWALDE								
1935 - S/243 G	N/A	$3,500	$3,000	$2,500	$1,950	$1,450	$850	
1936 - S/243 1936	N/A	$3,300	$2,800	$2,350	$1,800	$1,300	$800	
1937 - S/243 1937	N/A	$3,000	$2,600	$2,150	$1,600	$1,100	$750	
1938 - E Code S/243 1938	N/A	$2,200	$1,800	$1,400	$1,000	$800	$600	
1938 - L Code 243 1938	N/A	$2,200	$1,800	$1,400	$1,000	$800	$600	
1939 - 243 1939	N/A	$2,200	$1,800	$1,400	$1,000	$800	$600	
1940 - 243 1940	N/A	$2,000	$1,650	$1,300	$900	$700	$525	

GRADING - PPGS™	100%	98%	95%	90%	80%	70%	60%	LAST MSR
1941 - AR 41	N/A	$2,000	$1,650	$1,300	$900	$700	$525	
1942 - AR 42	N/A	$1,800	$1,450	$1,100	$700	$550	$425	
1943 - AR 43	N/A	$1,800	$1,450	$1,100	$700	$550	$425	
1944 - AR 44	N/A	$1,700	$1,375	$1,050	$675	$525	$400	
BERLIN-LÜBECKER MASCHINENFABRIK, LÜBECK								
1936 - S/237 1936	N/A	$3,300	$2,800	$2,350	$1,800	$1,300	$800	
1937 - S/237 1937	N/A	$3,000	$2,600	$2,150	$1,600	$1,100	$750	
1938 - E Code S/237 1938	N/A	$2,200	$1,800	$1,400	$1,000	$800	$600	
1938 - L Code 237 1938	N/A	$2,200	$1,800	$1,400	$1,000	$800	$600	
1939 - 237 1939	N/A	$2,200	$1,800	$1,400	$1,000	$800	$600	
1940 - E Code 237 1940	N/A	$2,000	$1,650	$1,300	$900	$700	$525	
1940 - L Code DUV 1940	N/A	$2,000	$1,650	$1,300	$900	$700	$525	
1941 - DUV 41	N/A	$2,000	$1,650	$1,300	$900	$700	$525	
1942 - DUV 42	N/A	$1,800	$1,450	$1,100	$700	$550	$425	
BERLIN-SUHLER-WAFFEN UND FAHRZEUGWERKE, (BSW)								
1937 - BSW 1937	N/A	$3,000	$2,600	$2,150	$1,600	$1,100	$750	
1938 - BSW 1938	N/A	$2,200	$1,800	$1,400	$1,000	$800	$600	
1939 - BSW 1939	N/A	$2,200	$1,800	$1,400	$1,000	$800	$600	
STEYR-DAIMLER-PUCH AG, STEYR								
1939 - 660 1939	N/A	$2,000	$1,650	$1,300	$900	$700	$525	
1940 - E Code 660 1940	N/A	$2,000	$1,650	$1,300	$900	$700	$525	
1940 - L Code BNZ 40	N/A	$2,000	$1,650	$1,300	$900	$700	$525	
1941 - BNZ 41	N/A	$2,000	$1,650	$1,300	$900	$700	$525	
1942 - BNZ 42	N/A	$1,800	$1,450	$1,100	$700	$550	$425	
1943 - BNZ 43	N/A	$1,800	$1,450	$1,100	$700	$550	$425	
1943 - BNZ S 43	N/A	$3,500	$3,000	$2,500	$1,950	$1,450	$850	
1944 - BNZ 44	N/A	$1,800	$1,450	$1,100	$700	$550	$425	
1944 - BNZ 4	N/A	$2,000	$1,650	$1,300	$900	$700	$525	
1944 - BNZ S 4	N/A	$3,500	$3,000	$2,500	$1,950	$1,450	$850	
1945 - Mod 98 BNZ 45	N/A	$2,000	$1,650	$1,300	$900	$700	$525	
1945 - SWJ XE 45	N/A	$7,000	$6,500	$5,500	$4,500	$3,500	$2,500	
GUSTLOFF WERKE, WEIMAR								
1940 - BSW 1940	N/A	$3,000	$2,500	$2,000	$1,800	$1,500	$1,200	
1940 - 337 1940	N/A	$2,000	$1,650	$1,300	$900	$700	$525	
1941 - BCD 41	N/A	$2,000	$1,650	$1,300	$900	$700	$525	
1942 - BCD 42	N/A	$1,800	$1,450	$1,100	$700	$550	$425	
1943 - BCD 43	N/A	$1,800	$1,450	$1,100	$700	$550	$425	
1944 - BCD 4	N/A	$1,800	$1,450	$1,100	$700	$550	$425	
1945 - BCD 45	N/A	$2,200	$1,800	$1,600	$900	$700	$500	
WAFFEN WERKE BRÜNN AG, BYSTRICA								
1942 - DOU 42	N/A	$1,800	$1,450	$1,100	$700	$550	$425	
1943 - DOU 43	N/A	$1,800	$1,450	$1,100	$700	$550	$425	
1944 - DOU 44	N/A	$1,700	$1,375	$1,050	$675	$525	$400	

GRADING - PPGS™	100%	98%	95%	90%	80%	70%	60%	LAST MSR
1945 - Mod 98 DOU 45	N/A	$1,800	$1,450	$1,100	$700	$550	$425	
WAFFEN WERKE BRÜNN AG, BRÜNN								
1943 - DOT 43	N/A	$1,800	$1,450	$1,100	$700	$550	$425	
1944 - DOT 1944	N/A	$1,800	$1,450	$1,100	$700	$550	$425	
1945 - Mod 98 SWP 45	N/A	$2,000	$1,650	$1,300	$900	$700	$525	
DOUBLE CODES								
* ***Berlin Suhl/Gustloff Werke***								
1939 - 357/1939	N/A	$1,800	$1,450	$1,100	$700	$550	$425	
* ***Erma/Mauser Borsigwalde***								
1941 - AX/AR 41	N/A	$1,800	$1,450	$1,100	$700	$550	$425	
* ***Gustloff Werke/Mauser***								
1942 - BCD/AR 42	N/A	$1,900	$1,500	$1,100	$700	$550	$425	
1943 - BCD/AR 43	N/A	$1,800	$1,450	$1,100	$700	$550	$425	
* ***Gustloff Werke/Steyr-Daimler Puch***								
1944 - BCD/BNZ 4	N/A	$1,800	$1,450	$1,100	$700	$550	$425	

RIFLES: BOLT ACTION, 1898-1946 COMMERCIAL MFG.

Approx. 125,000 commercial sporting Mausers were built between 1898 and 1946. Three action lengths; overall measurements: Short (Kurz) 8 1/4 in., Standard 8 3/4 in., and Magnum 9 1/4 in. Optional squarebridge receiver rings for custom sight mounting. Innumerable variations of triggers, barrels, sights and checkering.

Add 50% for single square bridge action.
Add 100% for double square bridge action.
Add 100% for Short (Kurz) action, except on Type K below.
Add 100% for Magnum action, except on African Type below.

SPECIAL RIFLE, TYPE A – expressly made for English market, superior finish, with round tapered barrel, silver-bead front sight on sleeved-on block with matted surface, hinged floorplate, pear shaped bolt knob, horn forend tip and PG cap, sling eyes.

N/A $7,000 $6,000 $5,000 $4,000 $3,000 $2,500

NORMAL RIFLE, TYPE B – 24 in. barrel, steel-capped PG, Schnabel forend, sling swivels, pear shaped bolt knob, hinged floorplate.

N/A $5,000 $4,500 $3,750 $3,000 $2,250 $1,750

LIGHT SHORT RIFLE, TYPE K – 6.5x54 Mauser, 8x51mm, or .250-3000 Savage cal., short action, 22 in. barrel, steel PG cap, sling swivels, pear shaped bolt knob, hinged floorplate, hard rubber buttplate.

N/A $8,000 $7,000 $6,000 $5,000 $4,250 $4,000

CARBINE, TYPE S – 20 or 24 in. barrel stocked to muzzle, steel PG cap, horn buttplate, sling swivels, pear shaped bolt knob, hinged floorplate.

N/A $6,000 $5,000 $4,000 $3,500 $3,000 $2,000

CARBINE, TYPE M – 20 in. barrel stocked to muzzle with steel forend cap, steel PG cap, trapdoor steel buttplate holding sectional cleaning rod, butterknife bolt handle, hinged floorplate.

N/A $6,000 $5,000 $4,000 $3,500 $3,000 $2,000

MILITARY SPORTING RIFLE, TYPE C – stepped round barrel, spherical bolt knob, half grip, banner Mauser imprint in side of buttstock.

N/A $2,500 $2,000 $1,750 $1,500 $1,250 $1,000

AFRICAN TYPE – 28 in. round barrel, stocked to 4 in. from muzzle, Magnum action, pear shaped bolt knob.

N/A $10,000 $8,000 $6,000 $4,500 $4,000 $4,000

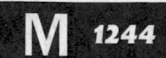

GRADING - PPGS™	100%	98%	95%	90%	80%	70%	60%	LAST MSR

EL-24 CONVERSION KIT – converts 8mm Mauser to .22 LR, includes subcaliber barrel insert, .22 cal. barrel was joined to a special bolt action breech mechanism, also available as repeating version with 5 shot mag., mfg. by Erma between the World Wars.

	N/A	$1,375	$1,200	$1,050	$900	$750	$600

* ***EL Conversion Repeating*** – includes two matching mags., ser. numbered to unit, tool, and case.

	N/A	$1,450	$1,250	$1,000	$850	$775	$695

RIFLES: BOLT ACTION, RECENT PRODUCTION

Values on currently manufactured models include single rifle case, scope mount, and matching sling.
Add $620-$815 for left-hand action, depending on model. Add $1,287 per interchangeable standard cal. barrel. Add $675 per bolt assembly, and/or $211 per bolt head. Add $996 for barrel fluting (standard cals. only). Beginning late 2006, Mauser began grading wood between grades 2-11. Grade 2 is standard wood, and the following additional charges apply to the additional wood upgrades (2011 MSRs): Grade 3 - $300, N/A domestically, Grade 4 - $480, Grade 5 - $969, Grade 6 - $1,939, Grade 7 - $2,905, Grade 8 - $4,063, Grade 9 - $5,227, Grade 10 - $6,772, Grade 11 - from $8,708.

MODEL 03 – various cals. between .222 Rem. - .375 H&H, Mauser square bridge action with safety/cocking lever on rear of breech bolt, interchangeable barrels, manual cocking, Combi-trigger can be used as single stage or set trigger, synthetic (Grey/PH Khaki) or wood stock (Grades 2-11, 2 is standard, 3 is standard in U.S.), 60 degree bolt lift, detachable mag., open sights standard (elevated rear sight at mid-barrel), Mauser double square bridge scope mount, approx. 7 3/4 lbs. New 2005. Mfg. by Blaser in Isny, Germany.

MSR $4,476	$4,050	$3,575	$3,200	$2,750	$2,300	$1,950	$1,500

Add $553 for Grade 3 checkered walnut stock.
Add $1,460 (MSR is $5,936) for Arabesque model (features coin finished receiver, Arabesque engraving, Mauser logo on floorplate and Grade 4 wood).
Add $2,957 (MSR is $7,433) for De Luxe model (features coin finished receiver with game scene engraving and Grade 5 wood).
Add $4,325 (MSR is $8,801) for Old Classic Model (features case colored receiver with gold line accents and trigger and Grade 6 wood).

* ***Model 03 Trail Extreme*** – various standard and metric cals., features black synthetic stock with patterned elastomer inlays in both forend and pistol grip, open sights with mid-barrel rear sight, 23 in. barrel, approx. 7 3/4 lbs. New 2010.

MSR $5,310	$4,875	$4,250	$3,650	$3,125	$2,550	$2,000	$1,650

* ***Model 03 Africa*** – various dangerous game cals., 23 or 25 in. barrel, Grey/Khaki (Extreme), Khaki colored synthetic (Africa PH, new 2012), or checkered Grade 4 Turkish walnut stock with installed kick stop, buckhorn rear sight, adj. front sight, sling swivels, approx. 9 3/4 lbs.

MSR $5,980	$5,500	$5,000	$4,500	$4,000	$3,500	$3,000	$2,350

Add $755 for checkered Grade 4 Turkish walnut stock.
Add $635 for Africa PH with Khaki colored synthetic stock.
Add $1,460 (MSR is $7,440) for Arabesque model (features coin finished receiver, Arabesque engraving, Mauser logo on floorplate and Grade 4 wood).
Add $2,959 (MSR is $8,939) for De Luxe model (features coin finished receiver with game scene engraving and Grade 5 wood).
Add $4,325 (MSR is $10,305) for Old Classic Model (features case colored receiver with gold line accents and trigger and Grade 6 wood).

* ***Model 03 Solid*** – various cals., 23 or 25 in. barrel (shorter lengths available upon request), thick barrel profile, adj. open sights, Grey/Khaki synthetic (Extreme) or checkered walnut stock and forearm, approx. 8 1/8 lbs.

MSR $4,960	$4,550	$4,000	$3,600	$3,200	$2,850	$2,350	$1,950

Add $553 for checkered walnut stock and forearm.
Add $1,460 (MSR is $6,420) for Arabesque model (features coin finished receiver, Arabesque engraving, Mauser logo on floorplate and Grade 4 wood).
Add $2,957 (MSR is $7,917) for De Luxe model (features coin finished receiver with game scene engraving and Grade 5 wood).

GRADING - PPGS™	100%	98%	95%	90%	80%	70%	60%	LAST MSR

Add $4,325 (MSR is $9,285) for Old Classic Model (features case colored receiver with gold line accents and trigger and Grade 6 wood).

* ***Model 03 Jagdmatch*** – .222 Rem., .22-250 Rem., .308 Win., or .300 Win. Mag. cal., 23 or 25 in. barrel with or w/o fluting, Grey/Khaki synthetic (Extreme) or checkered Grade 3 walnut stock and forearm, approx. 8 1/2 lbs.

MSR $4,910	$4,500	$4,000	$3,600	$3,200	$2,850	$2,350	$1,950	

Add $593 for checkered Grade 3 walnut stock and forearm.

Add $1,500 (MSR is $6,410) for Arabesque model. Add $2,997 (MSR is $7,907) for Deluxe model, and add $4,365 (MSR is $9,275) for the Old Classic model.

* ***Model 03 Alpine*** – various cals., 23 or 25 in. barrel, Grade 2 (disc. 2011) or Grade 5 checkered walnut stock and forearm, steel sights, 7 3/4 lbs.

MSR $6,304	$5,850	$5,200	$4,650	$4,100	$3,600	$3,100	$2,450	

Add $1,636 (MSR is $7,940) for Africa model. Add $624 (MSR is $6,920) for Solid model. Add $574 (MSR is $6,870) for Match model.

* ***Model 03 Stutzen*** – various cals., 23 or 25 in. barrel, full length Grade 5 checkered walnut stock and forearm with pistol grip cap, double fold Bavarian cheekpiece, front sling swivel, approx. 7 1/4 lbs.

MSR $7,627	$7,100	$6,100	$5,200	$4,500	$3,875	$3,100	$2,550	

Add $1,668 (MSR is $9,295) for De Luxe model (features coin finished receiver with game scene engraving and Grade 5 wood).

Add $3,035 (MSR is $10,662) for Old Classic Model (features case colored receiver with gold line accents and trigger and Grade 6 wood).

MODEL 66A – similar to Model 66S except has American configured laminate stock (wood grain), cals., action, and features are the same as the Model 66S. Imported 1988-89 only.

* ***Model 66A Standard Calibers***

	$1,900	$1,425	$1,150	$925	$800	$700	$650	*$2,100*

Add $630 per interchangeable barrel.

The "A" suffix on this model denotes American.

* ***Model 66A Magnum Calibers*** – includes Weatherby Mag. cals. also.

	$2,050	$1,500	$1,200	$975	$825	$700	$650	*$2,270*

Add $670 per interchangeable barrel.

* ***Model 66A Big Game Calibers*** – includes most popular Mag. cals. up to .458 Win. Mag.

	$2,350	$1,900	$1,425	$1,150	$950	$825	$750	*$2,700*

MODEL 66S STANDARD – telescoping short action, 5.6x57mm, 6.5x57mm, 7x57mm Mauser (disc. 1992), 7x64mm, 9.3x62mm, .243 Win., .270 Win., .30-06, or .308 Win. cal., 24 in. barrel, standard interchangeable barrels, single or double set triggers, adj. and detachable sights, Monte Carlo walnut stock with checkering, swivels, new safety, rosewood tipped forearm and pistol grip, rubber recoil pad, 7 1/2 lbs. Mfg. 1974-95.

	$2,350	$1,275	$995	$875	$775	$695	$625	*$2,722*

* ***Model 66 Standard Magnum*** – 28 in. barrel, 6.5x68mm, 8x68S, 9.3x64mm, 7mm Rem. Mag., .300 Win. Mag., or .300 Wby. Mag. cal., 7.9 lbs. Disc. 1995.

	$2,500	$1,325	$1,050	$900	$795	$695	$625	*$2,925*

* ***Model 66 Standard Carbine (Stutzen-Mannlicher)*** – .243 Win., .270 Win., .30-06, 7x64mm, or 9.3x62mm cal., 21 in. barrel, full-stock (Mannlicher only) and half-stock (disc. in 1989), double or single triggers, 7 1/2 lbs. Disc. 1995.

	$2,500	$1,325	$1,050	$900	$795	$695	$625	*$2,925*

This model was available in a half-stock "Ultra" variation until 1989. Values are similar to those listed.

* ***Model 66S Standard Diplomat*** – similar cals. as the Model 66S Standard, except not available in 5.6x57mm, similar features, except includes selected walnut and special engraving including deer and wild boar game scenes. Disc. 1995.

	$4,650	$3,850	$3,350	$2,750	$2,250	$1,850	$1,400	*$5,317*

Add $390 for Mag. cals. (similar to Model 66S Magnum).

GRADING - PPGS™	100%	98%	95%	90%	80%	70%	60%	LAST MSR

* ***Model 66 Standard Safari/Big Game*** – .375 H&H or .458 Win. Mag. cal., single trigger, 9.3 lbs. Disc. 1995.

	$2,950	$1,850	$1,350	$1,025	$875	$775	$650	*$3,487*

MODEL 66SM – telescoping short action, .243 Win. (disc.), .270 Win., 7x57mm Mauser (disc.), 7x64mm, .308 Win., .30-06, or 6.5x57mm cal. (disc.), 24 in. barrel, standard interchangeable barrels, set trigger, adj. and detachable sights, Monte Carlo walnut stock with checkering, swivels, new safety, anatomical gripped select walnut stock with Mauser-nose, cocking lever on tang, rubber recoil pad, 7 1/4 lbs. Importation 1981-95.

	$2,875	$1,800	$1,325	$1,025	$875	$775	$650	*$3,398*

* ***Model 66SM Ultra*** – all standard cals., 21 in. barrel, 7 1/4 lbs.

	$1,625	$1,325	$1,140	$920	$760	$650	$550	*$1,903*

* ***Model 66SM Magnum*** – cals. similar to Model 66S Magnum, except not available in 9.3x64mm cal., 26 in. barrel, 8.4 lbs. Disc. 1995.

	$3,025	$1,925	$1,375	$1,025	$875	$775	$650	*$3,578*

* ***Model 66SM Diplomat*** – similar cals. as the Model 66SM Standard, similar features, except includes selected walnut and special engraving including deer and wild boar game scenes. Disc. 1995.

	$5,075	$3,975	$3,450	$2,775	$2,250	$1,850	$1,400	*$5,943*

Add $382 for Mag. cals. (similar to Model 66SM Magnum).

* ***Model 66SM Carbine (Mannlicher type full stock)*** – .30-06 cal., 21 in. barrel, 7 lbs. Disc. 1995.

	$3,025	$1,925	$1,375	$1,025	$875	$775	$650	*$3,578*

These models were previously available on a custom order only basis through KDF, Inc. located in Seguin, TX.

MODEL 66SL – similar to Model 66SM, except features extra select walnut with special graining, 7 1/4 lbs. Disc. 1985.

	$1,370	$1,275	$890	$720	$580	$475	$420	*$1,470*

* ***Model 66SL Ultra*** – 7x64mm or .30-06 cal., 21 in. barrel, 7 1/4 lbs. Disc. 1985.

	$1,475	$1,325	$940	$750	$600	$450	$400	*$1,520*

* ***Model 66SL Magnum Calibers*** – similar to Model 66 S, 8.4 lbs. Disc. 1985.

	$1,475	$1,325	$940	$750	$600	$450	$400	*$1,520*

* ***Model 66SL Mannlicher Type Full Stock*** – 21 in. barrel, 7 lbs. Disc. 1985.

	$1,475	$1,325	$940	$750	$600	$450	$400	*$1,520*

MODEL 66SL DIPLOMAT – same specifications as Model 66SM, except includes selected walnut and special engraving including deer and wild boar game scenes.

Add $93 for Mannlicher full-stock (21 in. barrel). Add $387 for Mag. cals.

The last published retail price (1988) for a standard model without options was $3,167.

This model was available on an individual custom order basis only.

MODEL 660 – U.S. designation of 66S. Imported 1971-73.

	$925	$820	$720	$600	$500	$450	$400	

MODEL 66S DELUXE – special order engraved and inlaid, select wood. Priced per individual customer order. All guns are custom made only.

MODEL 66P – imported 1995 only.

	$4,250	$3,575	$3,075	$2,600	$2,075	$1,700	$1,375	*$4,888*

MODEL 66SP SUPER MATCH – .300 Win. Mag. or .308 Win. cal., telescoping short action, 27 1/2 in. heavy barrel with muzzle brake, no sights, match trigger, 3 shot mag., select European walnut stock with stippling and thumbhole, adj. cheekpiece and buttplate, includes premium scope, 12 lbs. Never imported domestically.

	$4,150	$3,500	$3,050	$2,600	$2,075	$1,700	$1,375	*$4,737*

GRADING - PPGS™	100%	98%	95%	90%	80%	70%	60%	LAST MSR

MODEL 77 – .243 Win., .270 Win., 6.5x57mm, 7x64mm, .308 Win., or .30-06 cal., 24 in. barrel, set trigger on tang, adj. and detachable sights, walnut stock with European cheekpiece and hand checkering, swivels, new safety, steel detachable box mag., rubber recoil pad, 7 1/4 lbs. Disc.

$1,130	$950	$875	$810	$750	$675	$595	*$1,331*

* ***Model 77 Ultra*** – 6.5x57mm, 7x64mm or .30-06 cal., 20 in. barrel, 7.7 lbs. Disc.

$1,175	$975	$895	$835	$760	$675	$595	*$1,394*

* ***Model 77 Magnum Calibers*** – similar to Model 66S, 8 1/8 lbs. Disc.

$1,175	$975	$895	$835	$760	$675	$595	*$1,394*

* ***Model 77 Mannlicher type full stock*** – 20 in. barrel, Mauser-set trigger, 7.7 lbs. Disc.

$1,175	$975	$895	$835	$760	$675	$595	*$1,394*

* ***Model 77 Big Game Model*** – .375 H&H cal., 26 in. barrel, 8 1/8 lbs. Disc.

$1,075	$1,000	$900	$795	$675	$575	$475	*$1,150*

MODEL 77 SPORTSMAN – .243 Win. or .308 Win. cal., sports version of the Model 77, set trigger on tang, no sights, 24 in. barrel, 9 lbs. Disc.

$1,495	$1,230	$1,075	$985	$895	$820	$740	*$1,754*

Add $430 for Zeiss 2 1/2-10X scope and mounts.

MODEL 83 MATCH SINGLE SHOT – .308 Win. cal. only, cylinder locking action with 3 locking lugs in rear, match trigger, anatomical match stock with select walnut, adj. comb and buttplate. Disc.

$2,170	$1,815	$1,660	$1,545	$1,400	$1,195	$925	*$2,594*

This model is a UIT standard rifle for 300-meter competition.

MODEL 83 MATCH UIT FREE RIFLE – .308 Win. cal. only, cylinder locking action with 3 locking lugs in rear, match trigger, anatomical match stock with select walnut, adj. comb and buttplate. Disc.

$2,320	$1,940	$1,760	$1,600	$1,430	$1,195	$925	*$2,771*

MODEL 83 STANDARD RIFLE – similar to Model 83 Match, except has removable 10 shot steel mag., 26 in. barrel. Disc.

$2,320	$1,950	$1,800	$1,625	$1,460	$1,250	$1,000	*$2,766*

MODEL 86 LAMINATED/FIBERGLASS (SR) – .308 Win. cal., updated version of the Model 83 action, 25.6 (disc.) or 28 3/4 (new 1997) in. fluted barrel with muzzle brake, black laminate wood (with thumbhole) or fiberglass (disc.) stock with rail in forearm, adj. trigger, 9 shot detachable mag., cased, 10.8 lbs. Imported 1989-1996, recent mfg. included a 2 1/2-10X power Zeiss tactical scope with detachable mount.

$10,750	$8,900	$7,700	$6,500	$5,500	$4,500	$3,500	*$11,795*

MODEL SR 93 – .300 Win. Mag. cal., precision rifle employing skeletonized cast magnesium/aluminum stock, combination right-hand/left-hand bolt, adj. ergonomics, 27 in. fluted barrel with muzzle brake, integrated bipod, 4 or 5 shot mag., approx. 13 lbs. without accessories. Disc. 1996.

$20,000	$17,250	$14,750	$11,950	$8,700	$6,500	$5,000	*$21,995*

MODEL 94 – .243 Win., .270 Win., .30-06, .308 Win., .300 Win. Mag., 7x64mm, 7mm Rem. Mag., 8x68S (disc. 1996), or 9.3x62 Mag. cal., 22 or 24 in. interchangeable barrel, aluminum block in stock bedding system, 60 degree bolt, 6 lug locking system, checkered walnut stock and forearm, 3 or 4 shot mag., lateral slide safety, approx. 7 1/4 lbs. Mfg. began 1994, U.S. importation was disc. 1995, resumed 1997 only.

$1,925	$1,550	$1,325	$1,100	$925	$850	$775	*$2,295*

Add $799 per interchangeable barrel assembly.

MODEL 96 – .25-06 Rem. (new 1997), .270 Win., .30-06, .308 Win. (new 1997), 7x64mm (new 1997), .300 Win. Mag. (new 1997), or 7mm Rem. Mag. (new 1997) cal., 16 lug bolt slides straight back allowing for low scope mounts, 22 or 24 (Mag. cals., new 1997) in. barrel, safety mechanism in bolt in addition to rear 3-position tang safety, checkered

GRADING - PPGS™	100%	98%	95%	90%	80%	70%	60%	LAST MSR

walnut stock, 4 (Mag. cals., new 1997) or 5 shot top loading mag., w/o sights, 6 1/4 lbs. Imported 1996-97.

	$625	$550	$500	$450	$400	$360	$330	*$699*

MODEL 98 COMMERCIAL – various cals., features original breech mechanisms refurbished to new condition, barrel, trigger system, and stock are new from factory.

This model was mostly distributed in Europe with no domestic MSR.

MODEL 1898 COMMEMORATIVE – 8x57mm Mauser cal., special limited edition model mfg. to commemorate the 100th anniversary of the original M-98, bright royal blue on most major metal parts, bolt and receiver have silver satin finish, checkered select European walnut. 1,998 mfg. 1998 only.

	$2,175	$1,775	$1,500	N/A	N/A	N/A	N/A	*$2,300*

MODEL 98 STANDARD/MAGNUM SAFARI – various cals. from .22-250 Rem-9.3x64mm, Safari cals include .375 H&H (disc. 2002, reintroduced 2004), .338 Lapua (new 2004), .416 Rigby, .450 Dakota (new 2001), .458 Lott (new 2001), or .500 Jeffery (new 2001) cal., 3-5 shot mag., original M-98 Magnum square bridge action with 3 lugs, Model 70 style wing safety, folding express sights (Safari model only), 24 in. barrel, features custom workmanship, extra select checkered walnut stock, 8.8 lbs., delivery time is approx. 8-12 months. Limited mfg. beginning 1998.

MSR N/A	$10,800	$9,000	$7,750	$5,850	$4,500	$3,750	$3,000	

Add $1,400 for Magnum Safari, or $2,400 for Magnum Safari in .500 Jeffery cal.

MODEL 99 – 5.6x57mm, 6.5x57mm, 7x57mm, 7x64mm, .243 Win., .25-06 Rem., .270 Win., .30- 06 or .308 Win. cal., bolt action with 60 degree throw, 24 in. free-floating barrel, jeweled bolt, available in either hand-rubbed oil or high-luster lacquer finish for stock, mini-claw extractor, adj. single stage trigger, 4 shot detachable mag., no sights, 8 lbs. Imported 1989-disc.

* ***Model 99 Classic Lacquer Finish*** – high-luster lacquer finish for stock.

	$1,110	$925	$850	$775	$700	$625	$550	*$1,272*

This model was available with either a Schnabel forearm with regular stock or rosewood capped forearm with American Monte Carlo stock.

* ***Model 99 Classic Oil Finish*** – hand rubbed oil finish for stock. Disc.

	$1,130	$995	$875	$775	$700	$625	$550	*$1,130*

This model was available with either a Schnabel forearm with regular stock or rosewood capped forearm with American Monte Carlo stock.

MODEL 99 MAGNUM – 8x68S, 9.3x64mm, 7mm Rem. Mag., .257 Wby. Mag., .270 Wby. Mag., .300 Wby. Mag., .300 Win. Mag., .338 Win. Mag., or .375 H&H cal., similar specifications as Model 99, except has 26 in. barrel and 3 shot mag. Imported 1989-disc.

* ***Model 99 Magnum Classic Lacquer Finish*** – high-luster lacquer finish for stock.

	$1,135	$950	$875	$775	$700	$625	$550	*$1,322*

This model was available with either a Schnabel forearm with regular stock or rosewood capped forearm with American Monte Carlo stock.

* ***Model 99 Magnum Classic Oil Finish*** – hand-rubbed oil finish for stock.

	$1,025	$895	$795	$725	$625	$550	$495	*$1,180*

This model is available with either a Schnabel forearm with regular stock or rosewood capped forearm with American Monte Carlo stock.

MODEL 225 – available in 13 cals. between .243 Win. and .300 Wby. Mag., bolt action, 60 degree bolt lift with 3 locking lugs, ultra fast lock time, adj. trigger, 24 or 26 (Mag. only) in. barrel, 3 or 5 shot mag., no sights, guaranteed 1/2 in. accuracy at 100 yards, many stock options available at an extra cost.

* ***Model 225 Deluxe Standard Sporter*** – standard model available in 6 regular cals. and 9 Mag. cals. Importation disc. 1989.

	$1,275	$1,000	$875	$750	$625	$550	$495	*$1,400*

GRADING - PPGS™	100%	98%	95%	90%	80%	70%	60%	LAST MSR

Add $90 for Mag. cals.

This model was formerly the KDF Model K-15.

MODEL 226 – left-handed variation of the Model 225 with slight changes. Disc. 1989.

	$1,275	$1,000	$875	$750	$625	$550	$495	*$1,400*

MODEL 2000 (DISC.) – .270 Win., .308 Win., or .30-06 cal., 5 shot mag., 24 in. barrel, leaf rear sight, checkered walnut stock. Mfg. by F.W. Heym for Mauser, 1969-71.

	$495	$475	$450	$400	$375	$350	$325	

MODEL 2000 CLASSIC – .270 Win., .30-06, .308 Win., .300 Win. Mag., or 7mm Rem. Mag. cal., features new design allowing interchangeable calibers from standard to standard and Magnum to Magnum models, bolt locks directly into barrel, detachable mag., deluxe walnut stock with checkering and rosewood forend, double function set trigger, high polish blue, includes studs. Limited importation 1998 only.

	$1,595	$1,375	$1,125	$950	$825	$700	$575	*$1,800*

* ***Model 2000 Classic Varmint*** – .22-250 Rem. or .243 Win. cal., choice of black synthetic or special varmint wood stock with accessory rail, heavy fluted barrel. Limited importation 1998 only.

	$1,900	$1,550	$1,350	$1,100	$900	$775	$650	*$2,200*

* ***Model 2000 Classic Sniper*** – .300 Win. Mag. or .308 Win. cal., features heavy fluted barrel, special set trigger system, bipod rail, and other special shooting performance features, satin blue metal finish, custom built with individual certificate. Limited importation 1998 only.

	$1,900	$1,550	$1,350	$1,100	$900	$775	$650	*$2,200*

* ***Model 2000 Classic Professional*** – .300 Win. Mag. or .308 Win. cal., features recoil reduction compensator, camo all-weather special pistol grip stock, satin blue metal finish, custom built with individual certificate. Limited importation 1998 only.

	$3,175	$2,725	$2,400	$2,100	$1,800	$1,500	$1,250	*$3,500*

MODEL 3000 – .243 Win., .270 Win., .308 Win., or .30-06 cal., 5 shot mag., 22 in. barrel, no sights, walnut Monte Carlo style stock, rosewood forearm and pistol grip, skipline checkering, recoil pad and swivels. Mfg. 1971-74.

	$525	$475	$450	$425	$395	$335	$285	

MODEL 3000 MAGNUM – similar to 3000, except 7mm Rem. Mag., .300 Win. Mag., or .375 H&H cal., 3 shot mag., 26 in. barrel.

	$575	$525	$475	$450	$415	$350	$295	

This model was mfg. by Heym for Mauser.

MODEL 4000 VARMINT RIFLE – similar to 3000, except smaller action, .222 Rem. or .223 Rem. cal., folding leaf rear sight, rubber buttplate.

	$425	$400	$375	$350	$300	$260	$225	

This model was mfg. by Heym for Mauser.

LIGHTNING MODEL – .308 Win. or 7.62x39mm cal., slide-bolt action, locking bolt similar to M-16 enabling locking directly onto free floating short barrel, fixed internal mag., specially bedded receiver, satin blue finish or stainless steel, open sights, synthetic stock available in black, light grey, blue, or NATO green. Limited importation 1998 only.

	$495	$425	$375	$325	$295	$275	$250	*$550*

LIGHTNING HUNTER MODEL – .243 Win., .270 Win., .30-06, .308 Win., .300 Win. Mag., or 7mm Rem. Mag. cal., slide-bolt mechanism, detachable mag., choice of satin blue or bright blue metal finish, checkered satin or high gloss walnut stock, with or w/o sights, free floating barrel, bedded receiver. Limited importation 1998 only.

	$650	$575	$500	$450	$400	$360	$330	*$730*

Add $50 for open sights.

Add $20 for bright blue metal finish with high gloss stock.

GRADING - PPGS™	100%	98%	95%	90%	80%	70%	60%	LAST MSR

* ***Lightning Hunter Model Stainless Steel*** – similar to Lightning Hunter Model, except has satin finish stainless steel receiver and barrel, checkered satin finished walnut stock. Limited importation 1998 only.

	$665	$585	$500	$430	$375	$315	$270	*$750*

Add $50 for open sights.

LIGHTNING HUNTER ALL-WEATHER MODEL – similar to Lightning Hunter, except has black synthetic stock, satin blue metal finish, scope mounts included, with or w/o sights. Limited importation 1998 only.

	$625	$550	$475	$400	$350	$325	$295	*$700*

Add $50 for open sights.

* ***Lightning Hunter All-Weather Model Stainless Steel*** – similar to Lightning Hunter All-Weather Model, except is satin stainless steel. Limited importation 1998 only.

	$650	$575	$500	$425	$375	$325	$295	*$730*

Add $50 for open sights.

LIGHTNING VARMINT MODEL – .22-250 Rem. or .243 Win., features slide-bolt action, free floating heavy fluted barrel, satin blue metal finish, choice of special varmint wood or synthetic stock. Limited importation 1998 only.

	$895	$775	$675	$600	$525	$475	$425	*$1,000*

* ***Lightning Varmint Model Stainless*** – similar to Lightning Varmint Model, except is satin stainless steel. Limited importation 1998 only.

	$895	$775	$675	$600	$525	$475	$425	*$1,000*

LIGHTNING SNIPER MODEL – .300 Win. Mag. or .308 Win. cal., slide-bolt action, features free floating heavy fluted barrel w/o sights, special wood or synthetic stock with built-in bipod rail, detachable mag., satin blue metal finish. Limited importation 1998 only.

	$895	$775	$675	$600	$525	$475	$425	*$1,000*

* ***Lightning Sniper Model Stainless*** – similar to Lightning Sniper Model, except is satin stainless steel. Limited importation 1998 only.

	$895	$775	$675	$600	$525	$475	$425	*$1,000*

LIGHTNING PROFESSIONAL MODEL – .300 Win. Mag. or .308 Win. cal., slide-bolt action, features special black or camo synthetic adj. stock with pistol grip, special tuned trigger system, free floating heavy fluted barrel, recoil reduction compensator. Limited importation 1998 only.

	$1,595	$1,375	$1,125	$950	$825	$700	$575	*$1,800*

RIFLES: BOLT ACTION, .22 CAL.

MODEL 20/22 – .22 LR or .22 WMR cal., bolt action, features free floating barrel, precision trigger, standard or deluxe checkered walnut stock. Limited importation 1998 only.

	$625	$550	$475	$400	$350	$325	$295	*$700*

Add $100 for Deluxe Model.

MODEL 107 STANDARD – .22 LR cal. only, bolt action, 19 1/2 in. barrel, 5 shot mag., adj. iron sights, 6 lbs. Imported 1988-89, reintroduced 1993 only.

	$300	$260	$215	$185	$170	$155	$140	*$356*

This model is the same as KDF's previous Model 2107 mfg. by Voere.

* ***Model 107 Standard Deluxe*** – .22 LR or .22 WMR cal., similar to Model 107, except has deluxe checkered walnut. Imported 1988-89 only.

	$290	$240	$210	$175	$150	$135	$120	*$320*

Add $90 for .22 WMR cal.

This model is the same as KDF's previous Model 2107 Deluxe mfg. by Voere.

MODEL 201 – .22 LR or .22 WMR cal., bolt action, free-floating 21 in. barrel, 5 shot mag., adj. trigger, scaled-down version of the K-15, unusual action incorporates two front-located

GRADING - PPGS™	100%	98%	95%	90%	80%	70%	60%	LAST MSR

locking lugs on bolt face that engage Stellite inserts on the front receiver portion, blue only, no sights, beechwood stock with cheekpiece, 6 1/2 lbs. Disc. 1997.

$635 $515 $465 $415 $365 $315 $260 *$716*

Add $19 for sights (disc.).
Add $77 for .22 WMR cal. (Model 201-SM).

This model is the same as KDF's disc. Model K-22 mfg. by Voere. Before 1989, this model came standard with a walnut stock.

* ***Model 201 Luxus*** – similar to the Model 201 except has walnut stock with rosewood forend. Disc. 1997.

$710 $650 $550 $475 $425 $375 $295 *$809*

Add $27 for sights (disc.).
Add $67 for .22 WMR cal.

This model is the same as KDF's previous Model K-22 Deluxe mfg. by Voere.

MODEL DSM34 (DEUTSCHES SPORTMODELL) – .22 LR cal., bolt action, 25.98 in. barrel. "Deutsches Sportmodell" lightweight trainer, side sling, no bayonet lug.

$3,000 $2,500 $1,750 $1,000 $750 $550 $475

MODEL MS 420B – .22 LR Sporter cal., bolt action, pre-war, 5 shot mag.

$1,425 $875 $725 $625 $525 $450 $395

Add 15%-25% for double set triggers (rare).

MODEL ES340 – .22 LR cal., single shot, bolt action, 25 1/2 in. barrel, adj. sights, checkered pistol grip, grooved forearm, pre-1935.

$725 $425 $350 $325 $295 $260 $230

MODEL ES350 – .22 LR cal., single shot, bolt action, 27 1/2 in. barrel, championship rifle, micrometer rear sight, ramp front sight, checkered full target stock, swivels, pre-1935.

$925 $550 $500 $460 $430 $400 $375

Add 15%-25% for double set triggers (rare).

MODEL EN310 – .22 LR cal., single shot, bolt action, 19 3/4 in. barrel, fixed sights, plain pistol grip stock, pre-1935.

$625 $365 $315 $280 $260 $225 $200

MODEL EL320 – .22 LR cal., single shot, bolt action, 23 1/2 in. barrel, fixed sights, checkered pistol grip stock.

$695 $395 $330 $295 $275 $250 $225

MODEL KKW – .22 LR cal., single shot, bolt action, target, 26 in. barrel, tangent rear sight, military style stock with bayonet lug. This weapon was also produced by Walther, Gustloff, and Anschütz. It was used as a training rifle in addition to commercial sales. Deduct 15% for 4mm KKW Models.

$900 $800 $700 $600 $500 $400 $300

MODEL MS350B – .22 LR cal., bolt action, repeating, 5 shot mag., 26 3/4 in. barrel, grooved receiver for scope or sight, micrometer rear sight, ramp front sight, target stock, checkered pistol grip and forearm, swivels.

$3,000 $2,000 $1,500 $1,100 $825 $675 $550

MODEL ES350B CHAMPIONSHIP RIFLE – .22 LR cal., bolt action, single shot, 26 3/4 in. barrel, grooved receiver for scope or sight, micrometer rear sight, ramp front sight, target stock, checkered pistol grip and forearm, swivels.

$4,500 $4,000 $3,000 $2,500 $1,500 $1,100 $750

MODEL ES340B – .22 LR cal., bolt action, single shot, 26 3/4 in. barrel, adj. sight, plain pistol grip stock.

$2,000 $1,750 $1,500 $1,250 $900 $675 $475

MODEL MM410B – .22 LR cal., bolt action sporter, 5 shot mag., 23 1/2 in. barrel, adj. sights, lightweight stock, checkered pistol grip, swivels.

$4,000 $3,000 $2,250 $1,750 $1,350 $875 $675

GRADING - PPGS™	100%	98%	95%	90%	80%	70%	60%	LAST MSR

MODEL MS420B – .22 LR cal., bolt action target, 5 shot mag., 26 3/4 in. barrel, adj. sights, target style stock, checkered pistol grip, swivels.

	$3,000	$2,500	$2,000	$1,600	$1,250	$1,000	$750	

RIFLES: SEMI-AUTO, .22 LR

MODEL 105 STANDARD – .22 LR cal. only, 10 shot mag., approx. 5 lbs. Imported 1995-97.

	$285	$250	$205	$180	$170	$155	$140	*$330*

SHOTGUNS

Mauser shotguns were sub-contracted to various European firms and were made in various O/U (including field and target), SxS (both boxlock and sidelock), and single shot configurations. While they are relatively rare (these shotguns had limited importation into the U.S. by Bauer located in Michigan - models included the 496 single shot, 496 SxS, 580 SxS, 610 O/U, 620 O/U, 71E O/U, and others), collectability to date has been minimal. Values will depend on the grade, configuration, features, engraving, and overall desirability. Pricing guidelines are as follows: $95 - $175 for the Model 496 single shot, $300 - $650 for the Model 496, $995 - $3,500 for the 580 SxS (mfg. by R. Gamba - same as Ambassador model), and $475 - $1,350 for the boxlock O/U models, depending on configuration, features, and original condition.

MAVERICK ARMS, INC.

Currently manufactured by Maverick Arms, Inc. located in Eagle Pass, TX. Administrative offices are at O.F. Mossberg & Sons, located in North Haven, CT. Distributor sales only.

MAVERICK® BY MOSSBERG®

RIFLES: BOLT ACTION

ALL PURPOSE SHORT/LONG ACTION – .243 Win., .270 Win., .30-06, or .308 Win. cal., short or long action, 22 in. barrel, matte blue finish, synthetic stock, Weaver style base, top load magazine. Disc. 2011.

	$275	$250	$215	$195	$155	$130	$100	*$345*

SUPER BANTAM ALL PURPOSE SHORT ACTION – .243 Win. cal., 20 in. barrel, matte blue finish, synthetic stock, Weaver style base, top load magazine. Disc. 2011.

	$275	$250	$215	$195	$155	$130	$100	*$345*

SHOTGUNS

Beginning 1992, all Maverick slide action shotguns incorporate twin slide rails in the operating mechanism.

MODEL 60 SEMI-AUTO – while advertised, this model was never manufactured.

MODEL 88 FIELD SLIDE ACTION – 12 or 20 ga., 3 in. chamber, 24 (Deer Model with iron sights), 26 (20 ga. only), 28 (12 ga. only), or 30 (disc.) in. plain (disc.) or VR barrel, wood (disc.) or black synthetic stock and forearm with recoil pad, fixed or Accu-chokes (disc. 1997, reintroduced 2002), 6 shot (w/two 3/4 in. shot shells), aluminum alloy receiver, crossbolt safety, approx. 7 1/4 lbs. New 1989.

MSR $289	$200	$175	$150	$125	$100	$85	$65	

Add $20 for adj. sights.
Add $14 for Deer Model (24 in. cyl. bore barrel, disc. 1996).
Subtract 10% if w/o Accu-choke barrel.

Maverick 88 barrels are interchangeable with Mossberg Model 500 barrels within gauge and mag. capacity.

* ***Model 88 Field Slide Action Slug*** – 12 ga., 3 in. chamber, 24 in. fully rifled or cylinder bore barrel with adj. rifle sights, blue finish, black synthetic stock and forearm.

	$190	$160	$140	$125	$100	$85	$65	*$240*

Add $17 for fully rifled barrel.

GRADING - PPGS™	100%	98%	95%	90%	80%	70%	60%	LAST MSR

* ***Model 88 Field Slide Action Deer Combos*** – includes various combinations of extra Deer barrels with rifle sights, 28 in. plain or VR barrel, or extra 18 1/2 in. cyl. bore barrel. Mfg. 1990-95.

	$245	$215	$185	$165	$135	$110	$85	*$294*

Add $10 for VR barrel.
Add $17 for Accu-choke barrel.
Add $29 for wood stock and forearm (mfg. 1992 only).

* ***Model 88 Field Slide Action Security*** – 12 ga., 18 1/2 (6 shot) or 20 (8 shot) in. barrel with cyl. bore fixed choke, regular or pistol grip (disc. 1997) synthetic stock, 6 or 8 shot, plain synthetic forearm, 7 lbs. New 1993.

MSR $289	$200	$175	$150	$125	$100	$85	$65	

Add $7 for 8 shot model with 20 in. barrel (disc. 2009).
Add $98 for Bullpup configuration (6 or 9 shot) (disc. 1994).
Add $47-$65 for combo package (disc.).

* ***Model 88 Field Slide Action Combat*** – 12 ga. only, combat design featuring pistol grip stock and forearm, black synthetic stock is extension of receiver, 18 1/2 in. cyl. bore barrel with vented shroud with built-in carrying handle, open sights. Mfg. 1990-92.

	$375	$330	$280	$255	$205	$170	$130	*$282*

MODEL 91 SLIDE ACTION – 12 ga. only, 3 1/2 in. chamber, 18 1/2 cyl. bore or 28 in. VR barrel with 1 choke tube, otherwise similar to Model 88. Mfg. 1991-95.

	$230	$200	$170	$155	$125	$105	$80	*$269*

Add $2 for VR barrel.

MODEL 95 BOLT ACTION – 12 ga. only, 3 in. chamber, synthetic stock with recoil pad, 25 in. barrel bored mod., cross-bolt trigger guard safety. Mfg. 1995-97.

	$155	$135	$115	$105	$85	$70	$55	*$184*

MODEL HS-12 TACTICAL O/U – 12 ga., 2 3/4 or 3 in. chambers, 18 1/2 in. barrels cylinder bore or Imp. Mod chokes, matte black finish, synthetic stock, rear slot sight with fiber optic front sight, no under barrel mounted Picatinny rail beginning 2012. New 2011.

MSR $531	$450	$395	$340	$300	$250	$200	$160	

Add $16 for choke tubes.
Add $18 for Thunder Ranch model with left and right side Picatinny rails and neoprene stock shell holder (new 2013).

MODEL HUNTER FIELD O/U – 12 ga., 2 3/4 or 3 in. chambers, 28 in. barrels with Imp. Mod chokes, matte black finish, synthetic stock, vent. rib, front bead sight. New 2010.

MSR $488	$395	$325	$275	$245	$200	$160	$125	

MAWHINNEY, CHUCK

Current trademark of sniper rifles manufactured by Rifle Craft, Ltd. located in the United Kingdom.

RIFLES: BOLT ACTION

M40 SNIPER – .308 Win. cal., based on the M700 Remington action, 24 in. matte black pillar bedded free floating barrel, walnut stock, engraved aluminum floorplate with Chuck Mawhinney's signature (former sniper for the Marines), includes 3-9x40mm Leupold scope. Serial numbered 1-103. New 2012.

MSR $5,000	$5,000	$4,400	$3,750	$3,150	$2,500	$2,000	$1,650	

MAXIMUS ARMS, LLC

Current pistol manufacturer, gunsmith, and customizer established in 1991 and located in Gallatin, TN. Consumer and dealer sales.

While Maximus Arms LLC has been in gunsmithing business for more than 20 years, the company started manufacturing its own guns during 2010. The company has its own foundry, and uses 17-4PH stainless steel for all its custom guns.

GRADING - PPGS™	100%	98%	95%	90%	80%	70%	60%	LAST MSR

PISTOLS: SEMI-AUTO

Maximus Arms, LLC makes 4 basic 1911-style models, but also customizes guns. All models are full-size semi-autos with checkered wood grips, match grade barrels, high rise beavertail safety, flared mag well, front and rear slide serrations, adj. trigger, polished feed ramp, lowered and flared ejection ports, two magazines and an airline approved gun case. Models include the Centurion (MSR $1,572), Gladiator (MSR $1,633), Spartacus ($1,662), and Caesar ($2,997). Please contact the company directly for more information, including options and availability (see Trademark Index).

McCANN INDUSTRIES

Current rifle and accessories manufacturer located in Spanaway, WA.

McCann Industries manufactures new Garand semi-auto rifles with design improvements that utilize a .338 or .458 Mag cal. cartridge (not Win. Mag.), in addition to a .300 Win. Mag. bolt action pistol. For more information, including pricing and availability, contact the company directly (see Trademark Index).

McMILLAN BROS. RIFLE CO.

Previous division of McMillan Group International, located in Phoenix, AZ. Dealer and consumer direct sales. During 1998, the company name changed from McBros Rifles to McMillan Bros. Rifle Co. The company name changed again during 2007 to McMillian Firearms Manufacturing. Please refer to McMillian Firearms Manufacturing LLC listing.

RIFLES: BOLT ACTION

AMERICAN HUNTER – available in 16 cals. between .22-250 Rem. and .416 Rem. Mag. (disc. 1997), camoflauged fiberglass stock, match grade stainless steel barrel, choice of MCRT (Rem. Model 700 custom type action mfg. to aerospace standards) or MCR (disc., Rem. Model 700 BDL action that has been trued). Mfg. 1993-2007

$3,050 $2,550 $2,100 $1,825 $1,550 $1,375 $1,100 *$3,500*

* ***American Hunter Yukon Hunter*** – available in 6 Mag. cals. between .300 Wby. Mag. and .458 Win. Mag., built to aerospace tolerances for any hunting situation, barrel band sling swivel, folding leaf sight, black synthetic stock. Mfg. 1993-2005.

$3,350 $2,800 $2,400 $2,050 $1,775 $1,500 $1,350 *$3,700*

* ***American Hunter Outdoorsman*** – .30-378 Wby. Mag., .338 Lapua (new 2004), or .338-378 Wby. Mag. (disc. 1997) cal., RT action only. Mfg. 1996-2008.

$3,350 $2,800 $2,400 $2,050 $1,775 $1,500 $1,350 *$3,700*

MCR TACTICAL – .308 Win. or .300 Win. Mag. cal. Mfg. 1993-2007.

$2,950 $2,400 $1,900 $1,500 $1,250 $1,050 $925 *$3,300*

This model was formerly designated the MCR Sniper Model.

* ***MCRT Tactical*** – .300 Win. Mag. or .338 Lapua (new 1998), similar to MCR Tactical. Mfg. 1993-2007.

$3,050 $2,550 $2,100 $1,825 $1,550 $1,375 $1,100 *$3,500*

Add $500 for .338 Lapua Mag (muzzle brake is standard).

This model was formerly designated the MCRT Sniper Model.

BENCHREST COMPETITOR – .222 Rem., 6mm PPC, 6mm BR, 7mm BR, or .308 Win. cal., benchrest configuration. Mfg. 1993-99.

$2,400 $1,925 $1,575 $1,275 $1,050 $900 $775 *$2,800*

1000 YARD BENCHREST (NATIONAL MATCH COMPETITOR) – .300 Win. Mag. (new 1996), .30-378 Wby. Mag. (new 1996), 7.82 Warbird (new 1996), .308 Win. (disc. 1995) or .338-378 Wby. Mag. (mfg. 1996-97) cal. Mfg. 1993-99.

$2,450 $1,950 $1,575 $1,275 $1,050 $900 $775 *$2,875*

GRADING - PPGS™	100%	98%	95%	90%	80%	70%	60%	LAST MSR

TUBB 2000 – .243 Win., .260 Rem., 7mm-08 Rem., 6mm, or .308 Win. cal., target rifle featuring metal 4 way adj. stock, Picatinny rail, hand lapped Schneider match barrel, Anschütz 2 stage trigger, state-of-the-art action, vent. handguard, 12 lbs. Mfg. 2000-2007.

	$2,875	$2,475	$2,000	$1,550	$1,250	$1,025	$875	*$3,150*

Add $400 for Tubb 2000 C (includes four 10 shot mags., cleaning rod guide, etc.).
Add $550 for Schneider custom stainless steel match barrel.

BIG MAC/BOOMER – .50 BMG cal., available as either single shot sporter, repeater sporter, light benchrest, or heavy benchrest variation. Mfg. 1993-2007.

	$4,450	$3,850	$3,250	$2,700	$2,225	$1,825	$1,525	*$4,900*

Add $300 for repeating action.
Add $500 for Tactical 50 variation.
Add $100 for Tactical single shot.
Add $100 for heavy benchrest variation.

McMILLAN FIREARMS MANUFACTURING, LLC

Current manufacturer located in Phoenix, AZ beginning 2007.

McMillan Group International is a group of McMillan family companies: McMillan Fiberglass Stocks, McMillan Firearms Manufacturing, and McMillan Machine Company.

RIFLES: BOLT ACTION, BENCH REST SERIES

50 LBR (LIGHT BENCH REST) – .50 BMG cal., single shot action, 32 in. match grade light target contoured barrel, matte black finish, BR muzzle brake with precision target crown, red/black competition stock, Jewell trigger, 28 lbs. New 2011.

MSR $9,450	$8,025	$7,025	$6,025	$5,450	$4,425	$3,615	$2,815

TUBB 2000 – various cals., benchrest rifle featuring metal 4 way adj. stock, 10 or 20 box mag., Picatinny rail, hand lapped Schneider match barrel, Anschütz 2 stage trigger, state-of-the-art action, vent. handguard, 12 lbs. Mfg. 2009-2012.

	$4,750	$4,250	$3,750	$3,350	$2,950	$2,675	$2,400	*$5,000*

RIFLES: BOLT ACTION, HUNTING SERIES

DYNASTY – .270 WSM, .300 WSM, 7mm Rem. Mag., .300 Win. Mag. or .338 Win. Mag. cal., 24 in. stainless steel match grade free floating barrel, target crown, drilled and tapped, McMillan G30 long action, black ultralight graphite Dynasty EDGE stock with pillar glass bedding and Pachmayr Decelerator pad, one piece machined aluminum hinged floorplate, sling swivels, 6 lbs., 12 oz. - 7 lbs.

MSR $6,235	$5,300	$4,650	$3,975	$3,600	$2,915	$2,385	$1,850

HERITAGE – .375 H&H or .416 Rem. Mag. cal., 24 in. stainless steel match grade free floating barrel, target crown, drilled and tapped, McMillan G30 long action, black Heritage synthetic stock with pillar glass bedding and Pachmayr Decelerator pad, drop belly extended capacity one piece hinged floorplate, 8 lbs., 4 oz.

MSR $6,370	$5,400	$4,725	$4,050	$3,675	$2,975	$2,425	$1,895

LEGACY – .270 Win., .30-06, .308 Win., or .300 Win. Mag. cal., 22 (.308 Win. cal. only) or 24 in. match grade stainless steel barrel, target crown, McMillan G30 short or long action, one piece aluminum hinged floorplate, drilled and tapped, black ultralight graphite classic sporter stock with pillar glass bedding and Pachmayr Decelerator pad, sling swivels, 6 lbs., 10 oz - 7 lbs.

MSR $6,235	$5,300	$4,650	$3,975	$3,600	$2,915	$2,385	$1,850

LONG RANGE HUNTER (LRH) – .243 Win., .308 Win., 7mm Rem. Mag., 7mm Rem. Ultra Mag., .300 Win. Mag., or .338 Lapua cal., G30 short or long action, 24, 26, or 27 in. stainless steel match grade medium heavy contour barrel with polygon rifling, McMillan A3 stock, fixed recoil pad, one-piece floorplate, optional box mag., matte black receiver or Duracoat metal finish in olive, gray, tan or Dark Earth, includes travel case, 9 1/2 - 10 lbs. New 2011.

MSR $6,775	$5,750	$5,025	$4,325	$3,900	$3,175	$2,595	$2,000

GRADING - PPGS™	100%	98%	95%	90%	80%	70%	60%	LAST MSR

OUTDOORSMAN – .300 Rem. Ultra Mag. or .30-378 Wby. Mag. cal., 28 in. fluted stainless steel match grade free floating barrel, muzzle brake, target crown, drilled and tapped, McMillan G30 long action, black McMillan Hunter EDGE ultralight graphite synthetic stock with pillar glass bedding and Pachmayr Decelerator pad, machined one piece aluminum hinged floorplate, sling swivels, 7 lbs., 11 oz.

MSR $6,450	$5,475	$4,795	$4,100	$3,725	$3,000	$2,475	$1,900	

PRESTIGE – .375 H&H or .416 Rem. Mag. cal., 24 in. match grade free floating chrome moly barrel, target crown, integral barrel band with one inch sling sloop, integral express quarter rib and front sight, McMillan G30 control round feed long action, black Prestige synthetic stock with pillar glass bedding and Pachmayr Decelerator pad, drop belly extended capacity one piece stainless floorplate, express style iron sights, 8 lbs., 4 oz.

MSR $7,495	$6,375	$5,575	$4,775	$4,325	$3,500	$2,875	$2,225	

PRODIGY – 30-06, .270 WSM, .300 WSM, 7mm Rem. Mag., .308 Win., or .300 Win. Mag. cal., 22 (.308 Win. cal. only) or 24 in. stainless steel match grade free floating barrel, target crown, drilled and tapped, McMillan G30 long or short action, black ultralight graphite Hunters EDGE stock with pillar glass bedding and Pachmayr Decelerator pad, one piece machined aluminum hinged floorplate, sling swivels, 6 lbs., 12 oz. - 7 lbs.

MSR $6,235	$5,300	$4,650	$3,975	$3,600	$2,915	$2,385	$1,850	

TACTICAL HUNTER – .243 Win., 7mm Rem. Mag., .308 Win. or .300 Win. Mag. cal., 22 or 24 in. fluted stainless steel match grade free floating barrel with #5 taper, target crown, drilled and tapped, McMillan G30 short or long action, black ultralight graphite Tactical Hunter EDGE stock with pillar glass bedding and Pachmayr Decelerator pad, one piece machined aluminum hinged floorplate, sling swivels, approx. 7 lbs.

MSR $6,415	$5,450	$4,775	$4,095	$3,700	$3,000	$2,450	$1,915	

EOL SERIES – .300 EOL Mag., .30-378 EOL Mag., 7mm EOL Mag., or .338 Lapua mag. cal., features McMillan G30 short or long action, 26 in. Schneider fluted match grade stainless steel barrel with polygon rifling, hinged floorplate or optional box mag., stock configurations include McMillan Hunter (EOL Outdoorsman), Tactical Hunter (EOL LRH-Light), or A-3LRH (EOL LRH), receiver is equipped with Picatinny rail, 8-9 1/2 lbs. Limited mfg. 2012.

	$5,150	$4,375	$3,775	$3,200	$2,600	$2,000	$1,650	*$5,670*

Add $794 for EOL LRH configuration.
Add approx. $2,350 for night force scope.

* ***EOL Series Mountain Extreme*** – 6.5x284 Norma (Alpine model only), 7mm EOL Mag., 7mm Rem. Ultra Mag., .300 EAOL Mag., .300 Rem. Ultra Mag., .338 EOL Mag., or .338 Lapua cal., 26, 27, or 28 in. match grade stainless steel fluted barrel, standard hinged floorplate, Edge Outdoorsman (Yukon), adj. A3-5 (Denali), or McMillan Dynasty (Alpine) khaki stock with gray and brown specks, sling swivels, matte black barrel finish, NP3 muzzle brake bolt stop and cocking piece housing, includes hard case. New 2013.

MSR $6,775	$5,750	$5,025	$4,300	$3,915	$3,175	$2,595	$2,000	

Add $120 for Denali model.
Add $2,339-$2,405 for scope package.

RIFLES: BOLT ACTION, TACTICAL SERIES

TAC-300 – .300 Win. Mag. cal., 26 in. medium heavy free floating contoured threaded barrel with cap and polygon rifling, detachable 5 shot box mag. or hinged floorplate, drilled and tapped, McMillan G30 long action, A-5 fiberglass buttstock, black, olive, gray, dark earth, or tan finish, adj. cheekpiece, two sling swivels, 11 lbs.

MSR $6,750	$5,725	$5,000	$4,295	$3,895	$3,150	$2,575	$2,000	

TAC-308 – .308 Win. cal., 20 or 24 in. match grade stainless steel medium heavy contoured threaded barrel with cap, detachable 5 shot box mag. or hinged floorplate, drilled and tapped, McMillan G30 short action, A-3 fiberglass buttstock, black, olive, gray, dark earth, or tan finish, adj. cheekpiece, two sling swivels.

MSR $6,495	$5,525	$4,825	$4,150	$3,750	$3,050	$2,475	$1,925	

GRADING - PPGS™	100%	98%	95%	90%	80%	70%	60%	LAST MSR

TAC-338 - .338 Lapua cal., 26 1/2 in. match grade stainless steel medium heavy contoured threaded barrel with muzzle brake, detachable 5 shot box mag. or hinged floorplate, drilled and tapped, McMillan G30 short action, A-5 fiberglass buttstock, black, olive, gray, dark earth, or tan finish, adj. cheekpiece, 6 flushmount cups with sling loops.

MSR $6,895	**$5,850**	**$5,125**	**$4,395**	**$3,975**	**$3,225**	**$2,625**	**$2,050**	

TAC-416 R/SS - .416 Barrett cal., single shot action, 29 in. match grade Navy contour or 30 in. light contour fluted threaded barrel with muzzle brake, drilled and tapped, McMillan synthetic stock with butthook and adj. saddle style cheekpiece, six flushmount cups with sling loops, bipod, decelerator pad, spacer system, adj. trigger, black, olive, gray, tan, or dark earth finish, adj. trigger. New 2013.

MSR $9,990	**$8,495**	**$7,425**	**$6,375**	**$5,775**	**$4,675**	**$3,825**	**$2,975**	

TAC-50 A1 - .50 BMG cal., 29 in. match grade Navy contour fluted threaded barrel with muzzle brake, drilled and tapped, detachable box mag., McMillan synthetic stock with butthook and adj. saddle style cheekpiece, four flushmount cups with sling loops, bipod, black, olive, gray, tan, or dark earth finish, adj. trigger.

MSR $9,990	**$8,495**	**$7,425**	**$6,375**	**$5,775**	**$4,675**	**$3,825**	**$2,975**	

TAC-50 A1-R2 - .50 BMG cal., similar to Tac-50 A1, except has McMillan Tac-50 A1-R2 stock and R2 recoil mitigation system. New 2013.

MSR $11,990	**$10,195**	**$8,925**	**$7,650**	**$6,925**	**$5,600**	**$4,595**	**$3,575**	

ALIAS STAR - 6.5x47 Lapua, 6.5 Creedmoor, or .308 Win. cal., 18 to 24 in. stainless steel match grade barrel, threaded muzzle with thread cap, detachable 10 or 20 shot mag., tactical pistol grip, matte black finish, tube or quad rail forend, Anschutz trigger, includes case, 11.6 lbs. New 2013.

MSR $8,300	**$6,875**	**$6,000**	**$5,150**	**$4,675**	**$3,775**	**$3,095**	**$2,400**	

ALIAS TARGET - .260 Rem., 6.5x47 Lapua, 6.5 Creedmoor, .308 Win., .308 Palma, or 6XC cal., 24 to 30 in. barrel, includes two detachable 10 shot mags. and one single shot loading block, competition pistol grip, matte black finish, competition buttstock and forend, Anschutz trigger, 12 lbs. New 2013.

MSR $8,300	**$6,875**	**$6,000**	**$5,150**	**$4,675**	**$3,775**	**$3,095**	**$2,400**	

RIFLES: SEMI-AUTO

IMPORTANT NOTE: On model(s) where *N/A has replaced the normal 100% value, it indicates current market conditions are too unstable to accurately ascertain 100%-60% values. Factory retail prices (MSRs) reflect most recent updates. For more up-to-date information on current pricing trends and additional useful information, please visit www.bluebookofgunvalues.com, select "Information & Services" from the menu, and click on "Additional Book Information".

M1A - .308 Win. cal., 18 or 20 in. barrel, 10 shot mag., McMillan MFS-14 modular tactical system, SOCOM five position adj. buttstock, pistol grip with finger groove, M3A fiberglass stock with saddle type cheekpiece, Picatinny style side and bottom rails, four flushmount cups with sling swivels, two-stage military trigger, many other options available.

	***N/A**	**$2,750**	**$2,450**	**$2,125**	**$1,800**	**$1,525**	**$1,300**	***$3,399***

Add $200 for compact model with 18 in. barrel.

M3A - .308 Win. cal., features McMillan M3A fiberglass stock with adj. cheekpiece, standard or full length upper handguard tactical rail. Mfg. 2011-2012.

Retail pricing was not obtainable for this model.

McMILLAN, G. & CO., INC.

Previous trademark established circa 1988, located in Phoenix, AZ.

G. McMillan & Co., Inc. had various barrel markings from 1988-1995 including G. McMillan, Harris - McMillan, and Harris Gunworks.

HANDGUNS

WOLVERINE - available in 9mm Para., 10mm, .38 Super, .38 Wad Cutter, .40 S&W, .45 ACP, or .45 Italian cal., interchangeable barrels, competition ready handgun patterned after the Colt 1911. Imported 1992-95.

GRADING - PPGS™	100%	98%	95%	90%	80%	70%	60%	LAST MSR

* ***Wolverine Combat*** – combat features including 5 1/2 in. compensated barrel.

$1,600 $1,350 $1,025 $875 $750 $625 $550 *$1,700*

* ***Wolverine Competition Match*** – competition features including 6 in. non-compensated barrel.

$1,600 $1,350 $1,025 $875 $750 $625 $550 *$1,700*

SIGNATURE JR. BOLT ACTION – available in a variety of cals., utilizes Signature benchrest short action, choice of stainless steel barrel lengths, right or left-hand action, single shot or repeater, McMillan design fiberglass stock, choice of electroless nickel or Teflon finish, 5 lbs. Mfg. 1992-95.

$2,175 $1,775 $1,350 $995 $895 $800 $700 *$2,400*

This model was also available in all titanium.

RIFLES: BOLT ACTION

The models listed were also available with custom wood stocks at varying prices. McMillan also manufactured a custom rifle from a supplied action. Features included new barreling, a fiberglass stock, matte black finish, and range testing to guarantee 3/4 M.O.A. Prices started at $1,400.

Add $150 for stainless steel receiver on most models.

TALON SPORTER – available in various cals. between .22-250 Rem. and .416 Rem., receiver available in either 4340 chrome molybdenum or 17-4 stainless steel, drilled and tapped, match grade barrel. Mfg. 1992-95.

$2,375 $1,950 $1,650 $1,325 $1,000 $895 $800 *$2,600*

The Talon action was patterned after the Winchester pre-64 Model 70. It features a cone breech, controlled feed, claw extractor, and 3 position safety.

SIGNATURE CLASSIC SPORTER – various cals. available between .22-250 Rem. and .416 Rem., premium wood stock, matte metal finish, 22 or 24 in. stainless steel barrel with button rifling, McMillan action made from 4340 chrome moly steel (either left- or right-handed), 3 or 4 shot mag. supplied with 5 shot test target. Mfg. 1988-95.

$2,250 $1,850 $1,350 $950 $850 $750 $675 *$2,400*

SIGNATURE VARMINTER – similar to Signature Model, except is available in 10 cals. between .22-250 Rem. and .350 Rem. Mag., hand bedded fiberglass stock, adj. trigger, 26 in. heavy contour barrel. Mfg. 1988-95.

$2,250 $1,850 $1,350 $995 $895 $800 $700 *$2,400*

SIGNATURE TITANIUM MOUNTAIN RIFLE – .270 Win., .280 Rem., .30-06, .300 Win. Mag., .338 Win. Mag., or 7mm Rem. Mag. cal., lighter weight variation with shorter barrel. Mfg. 1990-95.

$2,750 $2,195 $1,850 $1,450 $1,100 $925 $825 *$3,000*

Add $605 for titanium alloy light contour match grade barrel.

SIGNATURE ALASKAN – available in 11 cals. between .270 Win. and .416 Rem. Mfg. 1990-95.

$3,050 $2,475 $2,100 $1,575 $1,200 $1,000 $900 *$3,300*

TALON SAFARI – available in 15 cals. between .300 Win. Mag. and .460 Weatherby, hand-bedded fiberglass stock, 4 shot mag., 24 in. stainless steel barrel, matte black finish, 9 1/2 lbs. Mfg. 1988-95.

$3,275 $2,675 $2,300 $1,675 $1,300 $1,100 $950 *$3,600*

Add $600 for .300 Phoenix, .338 Lapua, .378 Wby. Mag., .416 Wby. Mag. or Rigby, or .460 Wby. Mag. cal.

The Talon action was patterned after the Winchester pre-64 Model 70. It featured a cone breech, controlled feed, claw extractor, and 3-position safety. Older Signature action rifles did not have this new Talon action.

M-40 SNIPER RIFLE – .308 Win. cal., Remington action with McMillan match grade heavy contour barrel, fiberglass stock with recoil pad, 4 shot mag., 9 lbs. Mfg. 1990-95.

$1,775 $1,475 $1,150 $925 $825 $725 $625 *$1,800*

M-86 SNIPER RIFLE – .300 Phoenix, .30-06 (new 1989), .300 Win. Mag. or .308 Win. cal., fiberglass stock, variety of optical sights. Mfg. 1988-95.

$1,825 $1,500 $1,150 $975 $85 $775 $675 *$1,900*

Add $550 for .300 Phoenix cal.

Add $200 for takedown feature (new 1993).

GRADING - PPGS™	100%	98%	95%	90%	80%	70%	60%	LAST MSR

* ***M-86 Sniper Rifle System*** – includes Model 86 Sniper Rifle, bipod, Ultra scope, rings, and bases. Cased. Mfg. 1988-92.

	$2,460	$2,050	$1,825	$1,600	$1,350	$1,100	$950	*$2,665*

M-87 LONG RANGE SNIPER RIFLE – .50 BMG cal., stainless steel bolt action, 29 in. barrel with muzzle brake, single shot, camo synthetic stock, accurate to 1500 meters, 21 lbs. Mfg. 1988-95.

	$3,650	$2,950	$2,500	$2,150	$1,900	$1,700	$1,575	*$3,735*

* ***M-87 Long Range Sniper Rifle System*** – includes Model 87 Sniper Rifle, bipod, 20X Ultra scope, rings, and bases. Cased. Mfg. 1988-92.

	$4,200	$3,400	$2,875	$2,550	$2,250	$2,100	$1,800	*$4,200*

* ***M-87R Long Range Sniper Rifle*** – same specs. as Model 87, except has 5 shot fixed box mag. Mfg. 1990-95.

	$3,995	$3,300	$2,700	$2,300	$2,000	$1,850	$1,700	*$4,000*

Add $300 for Combo option.

M-89 SNIPER RIFLE – .308 Win. cal., 28 in. barrel with suppressor (also available without), fiberglass stock adj. for length and recoil pad, 15 1/4 lbs. Mfg. 1990-95.

	$2,200	$1,825	$1,575	$1,250	$1,050	$875	$750	*$2,300*

Add $425 for muzzle suppressor.

M-92 BULLPUP – .50 BMG cal., bullpup configuration with shorter barrel. Mfg. 1993-95.

	$3,750	$2,950	$2,550	$2,200	$2,000	$1,850	$1,700	*$4,000*

M-93SN – .50 BMG cal., similar to M-87, except has folding stock and detachable 5 or 10 shot box mag. Mfg. 1993-95.

	$3,950	$3,250	$2,750	$2,300	$2,000	$1,850	$1,700	*$4,300*

.300 PHOENIX LONG RANGE RIFLE – .300 Phoenix cal., special fiberglass stock featuring adj. cheekpieces to accommodate night vision optics, adj. buttplate, 29 in. barrel, conventional box mag., 12 1/2 lbs. Mfg. 1992 only.

	$2,700	$2,195	$1,850	$1,450	$1,100	$925	$825	*$3,000*

.300 Phoenix was a cartridge developed to function at ranges in excess of 800 yards. It produced muzzle velocities of 3100 ft. per second with a 250 grain bullet.

COMPETITION MODELS – available in Metallic Silhouette (.308 Win. or 7mm-08 Rem. cal. - disc. 1989), National Match (.308 Win. cal. only), Long Range (.300 Win. Mag. only), or Bench Rest (shooter's choice). Each model made specifically for individual competition events. Mfg. 1988-95.

	$2,325	$1,775	$1,450	$1,100	$895	$800	$700	*$2,600*

Add $200 for Benchrest Model.
Subtract $300 for Metallic Silhouette model (disc. 1989).

MCREES PRECISION

Current manufacturer of tactical bolt action rifles located in Lesterville, MO. McRees Precision is a division of McRees Multi Services. Consumer sales through FFL dealers.

McRees Precision manufactures a bolt action rifle in various calibers with a 22 in. barrel. All rifles are guaranteed at least 1/2 MOA at 100 yards. Please contact the manufacturer directly for availabilty and pricing (see Trademark Index).

MEACHAM TOOL & HARDWARE, INC.

Current custom rifle manufacturer located Peck, ID. Consumer direct sales through FFL.

Meacham Tool & Hardware, Inc. manufactures a High Wall single shot rifle in a variety of calibers and options. Current MSR is $5,787. Please contact the company directly for availability, options, and an individual price quotation (see Trademark Index).

MEDWELL & PERRETT LIMITED

Previous long gun manufacturer located in Suffolk, England.

Medwell & Perrett manufactured best quality bolt action and double rifles, in addition to O/U shotguns.

GRADING - PPGS™	100%	98%	95%	90%	80%	70%	60%	LAST MSR

RIFLES

MEDWELL & PERRETT BOLT ACTION – various cals. up to .505 Gibbs, Medwell & Perrett action, Timney adj. trigger, select checkered walnut stock and forend, custom order only.

	$9,480	$8,600	$7,500	$6,500	$5,500	$4,500	$3,500	

Add $820 for Mag. length action.
Add $2,340 for .500 Jeffery or .505 Gibbs cal.
Add $1,770 for takedown action.

MEDWELL & PERRETT SQUARE BRIDGE BOLT ACTION – various cals. up to .505 Gibbs, square bridge action, integral telescopic mount system, barrel quarter rib, adj. trigger, deluxe checkered walnut stock and forend.

	$15,320	$12,950	$9,950	$8,500	$7,250	$6,000	$5,500	

Add $815 for Mag. length action.
Add $1,530 for .500 Jeffery or .505 Gibbs cal.

DOUBLE RIFLE SxS – most cals. up to .600 NE, back action, sidelock, ejectors, reinforced bolsters, DT, 22-26 in. chopper lump barrels with folding express sights, oil finished checkered walnut stock and forearm, 8 lbs. 14 oz.-14 lbs. 4 oz.

	$42,000	$38,000	$32,000	$26,500	$21,000	$16,000	$12,000	

Add $525 for detachable sidelocks.
Add $3,750 for cals over .375 H&H - .470 NE.
Add $9,180 for cals. over .470 NE - .577 NE.
Add $12,500 for .600 NE cal.

SHOTGUNS

O/U SIDELOCK – 12, 16, 20, 28 ga. or .410 bore, back action, sidelock, ejectors, ST, 25-30 in. barrels, oil finished deluxe walnut stock and forearm, house engraving pattern is standard, 5 lbs., 6 oz.-7 lbs., 4 oz.

	$39,420	$35,000	$30,000	$25,000	$20,000	$16,000	$13,500	

Add $4,560 for 28 ga. or .410 bore.
Add $7,200 for an extra set of interchangeable barrels (if ordered with new gun).
Add $630 for Teague choke tubes.

SxS SIDELOCK – 12, 16, 20, 28 ga. or .410 bore, ejectors, best quality SxS. New 2001.

	$34,750	$31,000	$26,000	$22,000	$18,000	$14,000	$11,000	

Add $4,440 for 28 ga. or .410 bore.

MENZ, AUGUST

Previous manufacturer located in Suhl, Germany.

Please refer to listings in the Liliput section of this text.

MERCURY (PISTOLS)

Previous manufacturer located in Belgium. Previously imported 1962-68 by Tradewinds, Inc. located in Tacoma, WA.

PISTOLS: SEMI-AUTO

MERCURY MODEL – .22 LR cal., 7 shot mag., steel frame, fixed sights.

	$400	$375	$325	$300	$275	$225	$200	

MERCURY (SHOTGUNS)

Previous importer of Spanish manufactured shotguns.

SHOTGUNS: SxS

MAGNUM MODEL – 10, 12, or 20 ga. Mag., 28 and 32 in. barrels, full and mod., boxlock, extractors, double triggers, engraved frame, checkered pistol grip stock.

12 or 20 ga.	$300	$275	$250	$225	$200	$180	$150	
10 ga.	$400	$375	$325	$300	$275	$225	$200	

MERKEL

Current trademark manufactured by Suhler Jagd-und Sportwaffen GmbH located in Suhl, Germany since circa 1898. Currently imported and distributed exclusively beginning 2010 by Steyr Arms, Inc., located in Trussville, AL. Previously imported and distributed beginning 2005-2010 by Merkel USA (previously GSI), located in Trussville, AL. Merkel USA was aquired by Steyr Arms during 2009. Previously imported during 2004 by Heckler & Koch, located in Sterling, VA, and by GSI located in Trussville, AL circa 1992-2003. Previously imported until 1992 by Armes De Chasse located in Chadds Ford, PA.

MERKEL HISTORY

During the course of its existence, Merkel has been traded under a variety of names, including E.A. Merkel, Merco, Abesser & Merkel, B. Merkel, and Gebrüder Merkel. Most of these names were used by descendants of the family patriarch, Friedrich Ernst Ferdinand Merkel.

At the end of WWII, the Merkel company was initially taken over by American troops, but then after approx. 3 months, it was turned over to the Russians for the duration of their occupation. Once the communist German government was established, the factory was owned by the government until Germany was reunited. The East German economy, like that of most former Soviet bloc countries, suffered due to lack of capitalization and from very restrictive gun laws.

Merkel was first managed by the "Treuhand", the government trustee that tried to find new owners for all East German commerce and industry. Among the applicants who had an interest in taking over the remaining Suhl gun industry was Sturm, Ruger & Co., together with members of the Simson family, who owned the biggest gun factory in Suhl before the Nazis came to power. Their offer was rejected in favor of a group of investors who enriched themselves, and went out of business after only one year.

The "Treuhand" then turned the company over to a bank and the Austrian Steyr-Mannlicher Company circa 2001. A few years later, H&K took over the company and expanded it. They had 126 employees in 2003, and are now at 171 employees. Because of H&K's engineering and marketing, Merkel became profitable again and expanded into the Eastern Europe and US marketplaces. The company went back to the original name Merkel, and bought the business and facilities of GSI, located in Trussville, AL.

During 2007, Merkel was sold to Caracal International LLC, located in the United Arab Emirates.

For many years Merkel shotguns were unfairly disadvantaged in this country because of the politics of importing firearms from communist bloc countries (goods were subject to a 65% non-favored nation tax). With the reunification of Germany in 1991, this trademark became more competitive domestically. Merkel continues to manufacture high quality guns in Suhl, Germany.

Beginning in 1995, Merkel serialization employed an alphanumeric date code for year of manufacture, making it difficult to determine year of manufacture by serial number. Higher grade models (including the 300 Series) continue to be manufactured one at a time by hand, with less than 30 being mfg. annually.

Many Merkel collectors are now categorizing older production guns into three different categories. The first is guns made before 1962, when the Berlin Wall was created. The second is the GDR guns (German Democratic Republic). The last is after the Berlin wall came down (post-1991). Premiums are paid on pre-WWII manufacture and some GDR guns. All pre-war guns may have different actions such as square, half round, and square reinforced, etc. These older production models should be appraised by a knowledgeable person, since there are a lot of things to consider when evaluating these earlier Merkels. Some guns made up for the Nürnberg and Leipzig trade shows have top quality workmanship, especially the engraving.

The engraver's signature will appear on all factory engraved Merkels manufactured since 1992.

COMBINATION GUNS

O/U MODEL – 12, 16, or 20 ga. (2 3/4 in. chamber) over 5.6x50R, 5.6x52R, 6.5x55mm, 6.5x57R, 7x57R, 7x65R, 8x57JRS, 9.3x74R, .22 Hornet (disc. 1997), .222 Rem., .243 Win., .30-06, .308 Win., or .375 H&H (disc. 1994) cal., 25.6 in. barrels, various chokes. Disc. 1999.

GRADING - PPGS™	100%	98%	95%	90%	80%	70%	60%	LAST MSR
*** Model 210E**	$5,700	$4,600	$3,700	$3,150	$2,600	$2,100	$1,800	$6,195
*** Model 211E**	$6,650	$4,750	$3,900	$3,300	$2,775	$2,275	$1,925	$7,495
*** Model 213E** – disc. 1997.	$13,000	$10,750	$8,250	$6,975	$5,825	$4,600	$3,550	$14,795
*** Model 240E-1** – 20 ga. over .22 Rem., 7x57R, or .30-06 cal. Imported 2003-2005.	$6,175	$5,150	$3,900	$3,400	$2,900	$2,400	$2,125	$7,195
*** Model 313E** – disc. 1997.	$19,350	$14,950	$12,500	$9,950	$8,350	$7,100	$5,900	$22,795

MODEL 314 – 12 ga. over 7mm-.470 NE cal., detachable H&H sidelock system, elaborate scroll engraving. Disc. pre-WWII.

	$21,250	$15,750	$13,000	$10,000	$8,500	$7,200	$6,200

SxS MODEL – similar gauges and cals. to O/U Combination Gun, boxlock models included 8EI and 9EI, 10EI is a sidelock, boxlock models ranged in MSRs from $5,500-$7,000 and the Model 10EI MSR was $9,500. Importation disc. 1990.

DRILLINGS

Previously, the Drilling Models 90 (disc. 1994), 90S (disc. 1997), 90K (disc. 1997), 95 (disc. 1994), 95K (disc. 1998), and 95S (disc. 1997) were also imported. Models differ in the amount of engraving, cocking systems, and quality of wood.

MODEL 96K – choice of 12, 16 (disc. 2005), or 20 ga., with the rifle barrel being bored in most popular U.S. and metric cals. between .22 Hornet and 9.3x74R (current standard cals. are .30-06 or 9.3x74R), 23.6 in. barrels, current models are boxlocks with Greener crossbolt and double under barrel locking lugs, extractors, tang mounted cocking for rifle, case hardened receiver with arabesque scroll engraving, DT, fitted leather case.

MSR $8,495	$7,950	$7,325	$5,900	$4,750	$3,650	$3,000	$2,500

Add $1,300 for hunting scene engraving (Model 96K Engraved).

MERKEL ANSON – 12, 16, or 20 ga., calibers 7x57R, 8x57JR, and 9.3x74R cals. most common, others noted, usually 2 shotguns over rifle, although 2 rifles over shotgun have been noted, 25.6 in. or 21.6 in. barrels, boxlock, Anson & Deeley system, double triggers, extractors, checkered pistol grip stock, pre-WWII.

Engraved Model 142	$5,000	$4,000	$3,000	$2,750	$2,500	$2,200	$2,000
Less Engraved Model 142	$4,000	$3,500	$3,000	$2,500	$2,250	$2,100	$2,000
Model 145 (least engraving)	$3,000	$2,800	$2,700	$2,600	$2,500	$2,100	$1,900

MODEL 961L – 20 ga. only over .30-06 or 9.3x74R cal., similar to Model 96K, except does not have tang mounted cocking slide, 21.6 in. barrels, standard engraving is Arabesque scroll. Importation began 2008.

MSR $8,995	$7,775	$6,500	$5,250	$4,500	$3,750	$3,000	$2,750

Add $2,000 for silver finished receiver with fine hunting scenes.

*** Model 961LS** – similar to Model 961L, except has elaborately engraved sideplates.

MSR $12,995	$11,250	$9,000	$7,750	$6,750	$5,750	$5,000	$4,250

RIFLES: BOLT ACTION

MODEL 190 – various cals., Mauser M-98 system, checkered walnut stock and extended forend, values depend on caliber and action size. Disc. pre-WWII.

	$7,500	$6,500	$5,275	$4,200	$3,200	$2,350	$1,500

Premiums exist for Magnum or Kurz (short) action.

MODEL KR1 PREMIUM – .243 Win., .270 Win., .30-06, 7mm-08, .308 Win., 7mm Rem. Mag., .300 Win. Mag., .270 WSM, or .300 WSM cal., modular design allows changing a different cal. barrel, short lock and bolt movement, three position safety, two or three

GRADING - PPGS™	100%	98%	95%	90%	80%	70%	60%	LAST MSR

shot detachable mag., fine trigger with set feature, six locking lugs, quick release mount system, pistol grip stock with cheekpiece and swivels, approx. 6.4 lbs. Importation began 2006, limited importation began 2012.

MSR $1,995	$1,750	$1,500	$1,300	$1,100	$900	$800	$700	

Add $500 for left-hand action.
Add $695 per interchangable barrel, $295 for scope mounts or $225 per individual bolt group.
Pricing may be higher on models ordered after 2012.

* ***Model KR1 Premium Stutzen Antique Carbine*** – .243 Win., .270 Win., .30-06, 7mm-08, .308 Win., or 9.3x62mm (new 2007) cal., similar to KR1 Premium, except has 20 1/4 in. barrel and full Mannlicher stock with fishscale carving. Importation began 2006.

MSR $3,395	$2,950	$2,600	$2,250	$1,850	$1,500	$1,250	$1,075	

Add $500 for left-hand action.

* ***Model KR1 Premium Weimar Luxury*** – .243 Win., .270 Win., .30-06, 7mm-08, .308 Win., 7mm Rem. Mag., .300 Win. Mag., .270 WSM, or .300 WSM cal., similar to KR1 Premium, except has deep relief hand engraved hunting scenes on silver-grey receiver, high grade stock with rosewood forearm tip, double fold Bavarian cheekpiece with modified Kaiser grip, gold plated trigger and bolt head. Limited importation 2006.

	$8,850	$7,500	$6,250	$5,000	$4,000	$3,250	$2,500	*$9,995*

Add $200 for Mag. cals.

RIFLES: DOUBLE

O/U MODEL – same cals. as the O/U Combination Gun, various actions, engraving options, and other special orders.

* ***Model 220E Boxlock*** – boxlock Blitz action, scroll engraved case hardened receiver, DTs, pistol grip with cheekpiece. Importation disc. 1994.

	$9,575	$8,250	$7,150	$6,100	$5,100	$4,250	$3,500	*$10,795*

* ***Model 221E Boxlock*** – similar to 220E, except has silver-grey receiver with hunting scene engraving. Disc. 1998.

	$12,500	$10,935	$9,375	$8,500	$6,875	$5,625	$4,375	*$10,895*

* ***Model 223E Sidelock*** – sidelock action with scroll or game scenes, removed without tools. Disc. 1997.

	$22,500	$19,685	$16,875	$15,300	$12,375	$10,125	$7,875	*$17,895*

* ***Model 323E Sidelock*** – similar to 223E Sidelock, except has scrollwork or game scene engraving, top-of-the-line O/U double rifle. Disc. 1997.

	$29,500	$26,750	$23,300	$20,000	$17,500	$13,500	$11,250	*$27,195*

MODEL 324 O/U – 6.5x55mm - .470 NE cal., premium quality pre-WWII double rifle, elaborate scroll engraving and best quality walnut. Disc. pre-WWII.

	$26,500	$23,000	$20,000	$17,500	$13,500	$11,250	$9,750	

B3 JAGD O/U BOXLOCK – .30-06 or 9.3x74R cal., boxlock action, 21.6 in. barrels, checkered walnut pistol grip stock and forearm, single trigger, standard Jagd configuration or deluxe with extra engraving. Importation began 2007.

MSR $5,495	$4,750	$4,155	$3,560	$3,230	$2,610	$2,135	$1,660	

Add $1,000 for B3 Deluxe with fishscale wood carving and better engraving.

SxS MODELS – same cals. as listed for the O/U Combination Gun.

* ***Model 128*** – various cals., scalloped Anson & Deeley action featuring engine turned removable locks and hinged floorplate, elaborate scroll and game scene engraving (on barrels), deluxe checkered walnut stock and forearm, pre-WWII mfg.

	N/A	$25,000	$21,250	$19,750	$15,750	$13,000	$10,000	

* ***Model 132*** – various cals., boxlock action with triple Greener cross bolt system, barrels, mfg. from Bohler steel, extractors (Model 132) or H&H system ejectors (Model 132E), DT, elaborate engraving and premium checkered walnut stock and forearm, pre-WWII mfg.

	$12,000	$10,500	$9,000	$8,160	$6,600	$5,400	$4,200	

Add 20% for ejectors (Model 132E).

GRADING - PPGS™	100%	98%	95%	90%	80%	70%	60%	LAST MSR

* ***Model 140-1*** – Anson & Deeley boxlock action with cocking indicators, double triggers, engraved case hardened receiver. Imported 1994-2005.

	$6,100	**$5,335**	**$4,575**	**$4,150**	**$3,355**	**$2,745**	**$2,135**	***$7,195***

Subtract approx. $400 if w/o H&H ejectors (pre-2002).
Add approx. $200 for set front trigger.
Add $1,100 for engraved hunting scenes on silver/grey receiver (Model 140-1.1).

* ***Model 140-2*** – .375 H&H, .416 Rigby, .470 NE, or .500 NE (new 2006) cal., similar to Model 140-1, except has scroll engraved silver grey receiver and positive extractors or ejectors, includes fitted leather luggage case. Importation began 2000.

MSR $11,995	**$10,500**	**$9,185**	**$7,875**	**$7,140**	**$5,775**	**$4,725**	**$3,675**	

Add $600 for ejectors.

» **Model 140-2.1** – similar to Model 140-2, except has Africa game scene engraving. Importation began 2000.

MSR $13,495	**$11,750**	**$10,280**	**$8,810**	**$7,990**	**$6,460**	**$5,285**	**$4,110**	

Add $500 for ejectors.

» **Model 140-2.2** – .375 H&H, .470 NE or .500 NE cal., similar to Model 140 2.1, except has more engraving. Importation began 2007.

MSR $18,995	**$17,000**	**$14,875**	**$12,750**	**$11,560**	**$9,350**	**$7,650**	**$5,950**	

* ***Model 141-1*** – .30-06, .308 Win. (disc.), 7x57R (new 2007), or 9.3x74R cal., Greener crossbolt Anson & Deeley boxlock action with double underbarrel locking lugs, petite frame, scroll engraved silver grey finish, ejectors, DT, deluxe checkered pistol grip walnut stock with cheekpiece and forearm, includes fitted leather case, 6.6 lbs. Importation began 2004.

MSR $8,195	**$7,500**	**$6,560**	**$5,625**	**$5,100**	**$4,125**	**$3,375**	**$2,625**	

» **Model 141-1.1 Engraved** – similar to Model 141-1, except has hunting scene engraving and single non-selective trigger. Importation began 2004.

MSR $9,495	**$8,450**	**$7,395**	**$6,335**	**$5,745**	**$4,645**	**$3,800**	**$2,955**	

Add $1,700 for Leupold scope combo (mfg. 2005-2007).

* ***Model 150-1*** – Anson & Deeley boxlock action with cocking indicators and sideplates, double triggers, silver grayed receiver with arabesque engraving. Imported 1994-98.

	$6,500	**$5,685**	**$4,875**	**$4,420**	**$3,575**	**$2,925**	**$2,275**	***$7,495***

Add $385 for H&H ejectors.
Add approx. $200 for set front trigger.

» **Model 150-1.1** – similiar to Model 150-1, except has elaborate hunting scene engraving. Importation disc. 2000.

	$7,750	**$6,780**	**$5,810**	**$5,270**	**$4,260**	**$3,485**	**$2,710**	***$8,995***

* ***Model 160S-1*** – sidelock action with Greener crossbolt featuring fine arabesque engraving, H&H ejectors, DTs, pistol grip stock with cheekpiece. Disc. 1998.

	$11,400	**$9,975**	**$8,550**	**$7,750**	**$6,270**	**$5,130**	**$3,990**	***$13,295***

Add $415 for H&H ejectors.
Add approx. $500 for set front trigger.
Add approx. $1,000 for single non-selective trigger.

» **Model 160-1.1** – similiar to Model 150-1, except has elaborate hunting scene engraving on silver-grey receiver. Importation disc. 2000.

	$13,250	**$11,595**	**$9,935**	**$9,010**	**$7,285**	**$5,960**	**$4,635**	***$14,995***

» **Model 160-2.1** – .375 H&H, .416 Rigby, .470 NE, or .500 NE (new 2006) cal., features octagon barrels, African game scene engraving with gold wire inlays on silver receiver, includes fitted leather luggage case, special order only. Imported 2002-2006.

	$20,400	**$17,850**	**$15,300**	**$13,870**	**$11,220**	**$9,180**	**$7,140**	***$23,995***

GRADING - PPGS™	100%	98%	95%	90%	80%	70%	60%	LAST MSR

* ***Model 161-1.1*** – 7x57R, .30-06, or 9.3x74R cal., sidelock action built on 28 ga. frame, 21.65 in. barrels, Greener crossbolt with double barrel locking lugs, fine engraved hunting scenes with silver grey sidelocks, H&H ejectors, DT, high grade Turkish walnut pistol grip stock with cheekpiece and semi-beavertail forend, 6.6 lbs. Imported 2006.

	100%	98%	95%	90%	80%	70%	60%	LAST MSR
	$13,850	$12,120	$10,385	$9,420	$7,615	$6,230	$4,845	*$15,995*

RIFLES: SEMI-AUTO

SR1 – .30-06, .308 Win., .300 Win. Mag., 9.3x62, 7x64 (European only), or 8x57 (European only) cal., 19.7 or 20.8 (.300 Win. Mag. cal. only) in. free-floating precision barrel, gas operated, 2 or 5 shot mag., solid rotary bolt head with 2x3 locking lugs, trigger safety, checkered walnut stock and forearm, rubber recoil pad, Battue rib sight with contrast line, adj. front sight, approx. 7 lbs. Imported 2007-2011.

	100%	98%	95%	90%	80%	70%	60%	LAST MSR
	$1,350	$1,175	$1,000	$875	$750	$625	$525	*$1,595*

RIFLES: SINGLE SHOT

MODEL K3 JAGD (K1 JAGD) STALKING RIFLE – available in 11 cals. between .243 Win. - 9.3x74R, Franz Jaeger break open action, cocking/uncocking slide type safety, matte silver receiver, adj. trigger pull, 23.6 or 25.6 (Wby. Mag. cals. only) in. barrel, pistol grip, includes 1 in. or 30mm quick detachable mounts, silver border engraving is standard, 5 lbs., 5 oz. Importation began 2002.

	100%	98%	95%	90%	80%	70%	60%	LAST MSR
MSR $3,795	$3,350	$2,900	$2,375	$1,925	$1,600	$1,300	$1,100	

Add $300 for Premium Model with light arabesque scroll engraving (disc.).
Add $1,195 per extra barrel.
Add $944 for Swarovski scope combo (mfg. 2005-2007).

During 2012, this model's nomenclature changed from K1 Jagd to K3 Jagd.

* ***Model K3 Jagd (K1 Jagd) Stalking Rifle Stutzen Carbine*** – .243 Win., .270 Win., 7x57R, .308 Win., 7mm-08 or .30-06 cal., similar to K1 Jagd Stalking Rifle, except has 19.7 in. barrel with Mannlicher full stock. Importation began 2006.

	100%	98%	95%	90%	80%	70%	60%	LAST MSR
MSR $4,195	$3,675	$3,000	$2,475	$2,050	$1,650	$1,325	$1,100	

During 2012, this model's nomenclature changed from K1 Jagd to K3 Jagd.

MODEL K-2/K-4 STALKING RIFLE – .243 Win., .270 Win., 7x57R, .308 Win., .30-06 cal., 7mm Rem. Mag., .300 Win. Mag., or 9.3x74R cal., Franz Jager single shot break open action, cocking/uncocking slide safety, octagon barrel, submodels vary in type and amount of engraving, includes best quality wood with stock carving. Importation began 2005.

* ***Model K-4 (K-2) Weimar Stalking Rifle*** – .30-06, .308 Win., .300 Win. Mag. or 7mm Rem. Mag. cal., features deep relief hand engraved hunting scenes.

	100%	98%	95%	90%	80%	70%	60%	LAST MSR
MSR $15,995	$13,750	$11,250	$9,000	$7,500	$6,250	$5,000	$4,150	

During 2012, this model's nomenclature changed from K-2 to K-4.

* ***Model K-2 Erfurt Stalking Rifle*** – features deep relief engraving on ornamental sideplates and silver pistol grip monogram. Limited importation 2005-2006.

	100%	98%	95%	90%	80%	70%	60%	LAST MSR
	$18,350	$14,995	$12,500	$10,000	$8,250	$7,000	$5,750	*$20,995*

* ***Model K-2 Suhl Luxury Stalking Rifle*** – features deep relief engraving on ornamental sideplates, gold inlays, gold gilded trigger, and silver pistol grip monogram. Limited importation 2005-2006.

	100%	98%	95%	90%	80%	70%	60%	LAST MSR
	$24,000	$20,000	$16,000	$13,000	$10,000	$8,500	$7,700	*$26,995*

MODEL 180 – various cals., with (Model 180E) or w/o ejector, double triggers, checkered walnut stock and extended forend, values depend on caliber and action size. Disc. pre-WWII.

	100%	98%	95%	90%	80%	70%	60%	LAST MSR
	$8,500	$7,250	$5,775	$4,600	$3,750	$3,000	$2,500	

MODEL 183E – various cals., sidelock, top-of-the-line rifle with elaborate engraving. Disc. pre-WWII.

	100%	98%	95%	90%	80%	70%	60%	LAST MSR
	$12,500	$10,750	$8,250	$6,975	$5,825	$4,600	$3,550	

GRADING - PPGS™	100%	98%	95%	90%	80%	70%	60%	LAST MSR

SHOTGUNS: O/U, DISC.

MODEL 100 – 12, 16, or 20 ga., various barrel lengths and chokes, boxlock, Greener cross bolt, double triggers, extractors, checkered pistol grip or English style stock, pre-WWII.

Plain	$1,850	$1,675	$1,450	$1,250	$1,000	$925	$850	
Ribbed	$1,950	$1,775	$1,550	$1,300	$1,050	$950	$875	

MODEL 101 – similar to 100, except selective extractors, rib barrel, some English style scroll engraving, pre-WWII.

$2,050 $1,850 $1,600 $1,325 $1,100 $1,000 $900

MODEL 101E – similar to 100, except auto ejectors, pre-WWII.

$2,200 $2,000 $1,750 $1,425 $1,250 $1,150 $1,000

MODEL 400 – similar to 101, except arabesque engraving and Kersten double cross bolt, pre-WWII.

$2,075 $1,875 $1,650 $1,350 $1,200 $1,100 $975

MODEL 400E – similar to 400, except auto ejector, pre-WWII.

$2,250 $2,050 $1,800 $1,450 $1,325 $1,175 $1,025

MODEL 410 – similar to 400, except more engraving and fancier wood, pre-WWII.

$2,200 $2,000 $1,750 $1,425 $1,250 $1,150 $1,000

MODEL 410E – similar to 410, except auto ejectors, pre-WWII.

$2,325 $2,175 $1,900 $1,600 $1,450 $1,225 $1,100

MODEL 200 – 12, 16, 20, 24, 28, or 32 ga., ribbed barrels in various lengths, Kersten double cross bolt, scalloped frame, boxlock, double triggers, extractors, cocking indicators, either pistol grip or English style checkered stock.

$2,750 $2,475 $2,225 $2,000 $1,750 $1,400 $1,175

Add 10%-15% for 28 ga., depending on condition.

MODEL 210 – similar to 200, except engraved and better grade wood, pre-WWII.

$3,000 $2,750 $2,475 $2,250 $2,000 $1,650 $1,325

Add 10%-15% for 28 ga., depending on condition.

MODEL 201 – 12, 16, or 20 ga., Greener crossbolt, hunting engraving or fine arabesque, dark walnut.

$3,250 $3,000 $2,625 $2,400 $2,200 $1,825 $1,500

MODEL 201E (PRE-WAR) – similar to 201, except with auto ejectors, pre-WWII.

$7,000 $6,250 $5,500 $4,950 $4,400 $3,750 $3,300

MODEL 202 (PRE-WAR) – similar to 201, except with false sideplates, higher quality wood, more profuse engraving, pre-WWII.

$8,000 $7,000 $6,250 $5,500 $4,950 $4,400 $3,750

MODEL 202E (PRE-WAR) – similar to 202, with auto ejectors, pre-WWII.

$8,000 $7,000 $6,250 $5,500 $4,950 $4,400 $3,750

MODEL 203E (PRE-WAR) – sidelock, similar to 202E, except better engraving and wood.

$8,000 $7,000 $6,250 $5,500 $4,950 $4,400 $3,750

MODEL 204E (PRE-WAR) – similar to 203E, but fine English scroll engraving and Merkel sidelocks, ejectors, scarce variation, pre-WWII.

$8,500 $7,750 $6,750 $5,750 $4,950 $4,400 $3,750

MODEL 300 – 12, 16, 20, 24, 28, 32 ga. or .410 bore, various lengths and choke ribbed barrels, Merkel-Anson boxlock, Kersten double cross bolt, two underlugs, scalloped frame, either English or pistol grip style stock, cocking indicators, pre-WWII.

$5,150 $4,600 $4,100 $3,600 $3,100 $2,650 $2,400

Add 10%-15% for 28 ga.

MODEL 300E – similar to Model 300, with auto ejectors, pre-WWII.

$5,750 $5,150 $4,600 $4,100 $3,600 $3,100 $2,650

This model is usually encountered without engraving and has standard wood.

GRADING - PPGS™	100%	98%	95%	90%	80%	70%	60%	LAST MSR

MODEL 301 – similar to Model 300, but more profusely engraved and better grade wood, pre-WWII.

	$6,750	$6,100	$5,250	$4,250	$3,995	$3,500	$3,000	

MODEL 310E – similar to Model 300, with auto ejectors, pre-WWII.

	$7,950	$7,200	$6,250	$5,300	$4,450	$3,900	$3,400	

MODEL 302 – similar to Model 301, but has auto ejectors and more elaborate ornamentation, false sideplates and better grade wood.

	$14,000	$12,000	$10,500	$8,500	$6,500	$5,750	$4,900	

MODEL 304E – special order version of Model 303E, higher quality and more ornamentation, very fine scroll engraving similar to Model 303 EL Luxus, top of Merkel O/U line.

	$22,500	$18,750	$15,750	$12,000	$10,500	$8,750	$7,500	

SHOTGUNS: O/U, RECENT PRODUCTION

MODEL 200E BOXLOCK – 12, 16, or 20 ga., case hardened scalloped boxlock action with minor scroll engraving, 26 (disc.), 26 3/4, or 28 in. barrels, checkered European walnut stock and forearm, ejectors, SST or DT, pistol grip or English style stock, solid rib, 6-7 lbs. Importation disc. 1994, quantities remained until 1998.

	$3,600	$3,150	$2,700	$2,450	$1,980	$1,620	$1,260	*$3,995*

* ***Model 200ES Boxlock Skeet*** – 12 ga. only, 26 3/4 in. VR barrels bored skeet/skeet. Imported 1993-94.

	$4,550	$3,950	$3,500	$3,000	$2,500	$2,100	$1,625	*$4,995*

* ***Model 200ET Boxlock Trap*** – 12 ga. only, 30 in. VR barrels bored full/full (other choke configurations available upon request). Importation disc. 1994.

	$4,400	$3,750	$3,300	$2,800	$2,300	$2,000	$1,550	*$5,195*

MODEL 2000CL – 12, 20, or 28 ga., 28 in. barrels with fixed IC/M chokes, Kersten double crossbolt lock, scroll engraved case hardened receiver, scalloped boxlock frame, modified Anson & Deely boxlock action, selectable ejectors, round knob, SST, high grade wood stock with semi-pistol grip or straight English style, three piece forearm, approx. 6.8 lbs. Importation began 2006.

MSR $8,495	$7,500	$6,560	$5,625	$5,100	$4,125	$3,375	$2,625	

* ***Model 2000CL Sporter*** – 12, 20, or 28 ga., similar to Model 2000CL, except chokes are SK/IC only. Limited importation 2006.

	$6,350	$5,400	$4,800	$4,200	$3,600	$3,000	$2,500	*$7,195*

MODEL 2000EL – 12, 20, 28 (new 1999) ga. or .410 bore (new 2004), Kersten double cross-bolt lock, scroll engraved, silver receiver, modified Anson & Deeley boxlock action, 26 or 28 in. fixed choke barrels, ejectors, ST or DT, select checkered walnut with pistol grip or English style stock, 3 piece forearm, 6.4-7 lbs. Imported 1998-2005.

	$5,700	$4,985	$4,275	$3,875	$3,135	$2,565	$1,995	*$6,495*

* ***Model 2000EL Sporter*** – 12, 20, or 28 ga., similar to Model 2000EL, except chokes are SK/IC only. Imported 1999-2005.

	$5,700	$4,985	$4,275	$3,875	$3,135	$2,565	$1,995	*$6,495*

MODEL 2001EL (201E) – 12, 16 (disc. 1997), 20, 28 (new 1995) ga. or .410 bore (mfg. 2004-2005), similar to Model 200E, except has coin finished action with light game scene engraving, fixed IC/MOD chokes, three piece forearm, current mfg. includes fitted luggage case.

MSR $9,995	$8,850	$7,745	$6,635	$6,020	$4,865	$3,980	$3,095	

This model's nomenclature was changed from 201E to 2001EL during 1998.

* ***Model 2001EL Sporter*** – 12, 20, or 28 ga., similar to Model 2001EL, except chokes are SK/IC only. Importation began 1999.

MSR $9,995	$8,850	$7,745	$6,635	$6,020	$4,865	$3,980	$3,095	

GRADING - PPGS™	100%	98%	95%	90%	80%	70%	60%	LAST MSR

* ***Model 201ES Skeet*** – 12 ga. only, 26 3/4 in. VR barrels bored skeet/skeet. Imported 1993-97.

	$7,850	$6,870	$5,885	$5,340	$4,315	$3,530	$2,745	*$8,495*

* ***Model 201ET Trap*** – 12 ga. only, 30 in. VR barrels bored full/full (other choke configurations available upon request). Importation disc. 1997.

	$7,850	$6,870	$5,885	$5,340	$4,315	$3,530	$2,745	*$8,495*

MODEL 2002EL (202E) – similar to Model 201E/2001EL, except has fine hunting scenes with arabesque engraving on silver false sideplates, 3 piece forearm, choice of pistol grip or English straight grip stock, includes fitted luggage case. Imported 1993-2003.

	$10,625	$9,295	$7,970	$7,225	$5,845	$4,780	$3,720	*$12,395*

This model's nomenclature was changed from 202E to 2002EL during 1998.

MODEL 203E SIDELOCK – 12, 16 (disc. 1997), or 20 ga. (24, 28, and 32 gauges were once available but are now disc.), 26 (disc.), 26 3/4, or 28 in. barrels, VR, H&H ejectors, SST (current) or DT, elaborate scroll engraving on coin finished receiver, sidelock screws are H&H style but the removable sidelocks are not, choice of English or pistol grip stock, 6-7 lbs. Disc. 1998.

	$9,750	$8,530	$7,310	$6,630	$5,360	$4,385	$3,410	*$11,995*

* ***Model 203ES Sidelock Skeet*** – 12 ga. only, 26 3/4 in. VR barrels bored SK/SK. Imported 1993-1997.

	$12,050	$10,545	$9,035	$8,195	$6,625	$5,420	$4,215	*$14,595*

* ***Model 203ET Sidelock Trap*** – 12 ga. only, 30 in. VR barrels bored full/full (other choke configurations available upon request). Importation disc. 1997.

	$12,050	$10,545	$9,035	$8,195	$6,625	$5,420	$4,215	*$14,595*

MODEL 2016CL – similar to 2000CL, except is 16 ga., 28 in. barrels with fixed IC/Mod. chokes, approx. 6.8 lbs. Importation began 2006.

MSR $8,495	$7,750	$6,780	$5,810	$5,270	$4,260	$3,485	$2,710	

Add $4,500 for two barrel set (16 and 20 ga., bored IC/Mod.).

MODEL 2016EL SIDELOCK – 16 ga., scroll engraved case hardened receiver, action similar to Model 2001EL, three piece forearm. Imported 2004-2005.

	$5,700	$4,985	$4,275	$3,875	$3,135	$2,565	$1,995	*$6,495*

Add $3,200 for 2 barrel set (16 and 20 ga. bored IC/Mod.).

MODEL 2116EL SIDELOCK – 16 ga., similar to Model 2016EL, except has upgraded wood and more engraving. Importation began 2004.

MSR $9,995	$8,850	$7,745	$6,635	$6,020	$4,865	$3,980	$3,095	

Add $4,200 for 2 barrel set (16 and 20 ga. bored IC/Mod.).

MODEL 303EL (LUXUS) – 12, 20, or 28 (new 1998) ga., similar to Model 203EL, except has H&H type sidelock action with hidden thumbnail detachable sidelocks, double underlugs, more ornamentation and better wood, DT with articulated front. Importation disc. 2006.

	$26,500	$23,500	$19,000	$16,000	$13,000	$11,000	$8,950	*$23,995*

Luxus variations are also encountered in the 201 and 203 series in addition to older pre-war models.

SHOTGUNS: SxS, PRE-WWII PRODUCTION

Merkel began manufacturing SxS shotguns during 1914.

MODEL 126E – 12, 16, or 20 ga., similar action as the Model 127, except features game scene and other engraving patterns, H&H style system ejectors, pre-WWII mfg.

	N/A	$24,725	$21,500	$16,500	$12,500	$10,000	$8,800	

MODEL 127E – 12, 16, or 20 ga., various barrel lengths and chokes, H&H style hand detachable sidelocks, auto ejectors, double triggers, pistol or English style stock, elaborate scroll engraving only, this is a best grade gun, pre-WWII mfg.

	N/A	$24,725	$21,500	$16,500	$12,500	$10,000	$8,800	

MODEL 128E – 12, 16, or 20 ga., scalloped Anson & Deeley action featuring engine turned removable locks and hinged floorplate, DT, H&H system ejectors, elaborate scroll and

GRADING - PPGS™	100%	98%	95%	90%	80%	70%	60%	LAST MSR

game scene engraving (including scroll work on barrels), deluxe checkered walnut stock and forearm, pre-WWII mfg.

	N/A	$28,000	$24,000	$20,000	$16,500	$14,000	$12,000	

MODEL 130 – 12, 16, or 20 ga., various barrel lengths and chokes, Anson & Deeley action with false side plates, boxlock, auto ejectors, English style or pistol grip stock, elaborate game scenes and arabesque engraving, pre-WWII mfg.

	N/A	$20,000	$16,500	$12,500	$9,500	$7,500	$6,350	

SHOTGUNS: SxS, RECENT PRODUCTION

Left-hand stocks are also available on some of the models in this category. Please contact Merkel USA directly for a price quotation.

MODEL 8 – 12, 16 (disc.), or 20 ga., case hardened scalloped boxlock action with light engraving, Greener crossbolt with chopper lump extension, extractors, SST (current) or DT, standard walnut with checkering, pistol grip or English style stock, sling swivels (disc. 1992). Disc. 1994.

	$1,150	$1,005	$860	$780	$630	$515	$400	*$1,695*

MODEL 47E – 12, 16 (disc. 2001), or 20 ga., case hardened scalloped boxlock action with chopper lump extension and Greener crossbolt, 26 (disc.), 26 3/4, or 28 in. barrels with fixed chokes, SST (current) or DT, ejectors, deluxe checkered walnut, pistol grip or English style stock, sling swivels (disc. 1992), 5.9-6.8 lbs.

MSR $4,595	$4,000	$3,500	$3,000	$2,720	$2,200	$1,800	$1,400	

* ***Model 47EL Custom Ltd. Ed.*** – 20 ga. only, 28 in. VR barrels with IC/Mod. fixed chokes, features luxury grade wood with English straight grip stock with medallion and DTs. Importation began 2008.

MSR $5,795	$5,150	$4,505	$3,860	$3,500	$2,830	$2,315	$1,800	

MODEL 47SL – 12, 16 (disc. 2001), 20, 28 (disc.) ga., or .410 (disc.) bore, coin finished sidelock action with scroll engraving, Greener crossbolt, ST (current) or DT, deluxe walnut stock (with cheekpiece) and forearm, sling swivels (disc. 1992).

MSR $8,995	$8,000	$7,000	$6,000	$5,440	$4,400	$3,600	$2,800	

Add approx. $600 for 28 ga. or .410 bore (mfg. 1992 only).

MODEL 76E – top-of-the-line boxlock shotgun. Importation disc. 1992.

	$2,600	$2,275	$1,950	$1,770	$1,430	$1,170	$910	*$3,500*

MODEL 122 – 12, 16, or 20 ga., Anson & Deeley boxlock action with silver greyed false sideplates, H&H ejectors, SST or DT, fine hunting scenes with arabesque engraving, pistol grip or English style stock. Imported 1993-99.

	$3,750	$3,280	$2,810	$2,550	$2,060	$1,685	$1,310	*$4,495*

MODEL 122E – 12, 16, or 20 ga., coin finished boxlock action with Greener crossbolt and chopper lump extension, cocking indicators, ejectors, DTs, deluxe game scene engraving. Importation disc. 1991.

	$4,100	$3,585	$3,075	$2,790	$2,255	$1,845	$1,435	*$3,500*

MODEL 147 – 12, 16, 20, or 28 (new 1995, 147E only) ga., 26 3/4 or 28 in. barrels, Anson & Deeley boxlock, any choke, SST (current) or DT, extractors, straight or pistol grip stock, hunting scene engraved. Disc. 1998, some inventory remained until 1999.

	$2,400	$2,100	$1,800	$1,630	$1,320	$1,080	$840	*$2,995*

* ***Model 147E*** – 12 or 20 ga., similar to Model 147, except has ejectors, fixed choke barrels, 5.8-6.8 lbs.

MSR $5,795	$5,150	$4,505	$3,860	$3,500	$2,830	$2,315	$1,800	

* ***Model 147EL*** – similar to Model 147E, except has luxury grade wood upgrade, fixed choke barrels. Importation began 1999.

MSR $7,195	$6,500	$5,685	$4,875	$4,420	$3,575	$2,925	$2,275	

Add $500 for Model 147EL Custom Ltd. Ed. with English straight grip stock medallion and DTs (new 2008).

GRADING - PPGS™	100%	98%	95%	90%	80%	70%	60%	LAST MSR

» **Model 147EL Sporter** – similar to Model 147EL, except available in 30 in. barrels with skeet chokes. Limited importation 2006, reintroduced 2008.

MSR $7,195	$6,500	$5,685	$4,875	$4,420	$3,575	$2,925	$2,275	

MODEL 147SL – 12, 16 (disc. 2001), 20, 28 ga. (disc. 2003), or .410 (mfg. 1992 only) bore, coin finished sidelock action with Greener crossbolt and chopper lump extension, 25 1/2 (disc.), 26 (disc.), 26 3/4, or 28 in. fixed choke barrels, ejectors, ST (current) or DT, deluxe game scene engraving, 6-7 lbs.

MSR $10,995	$9,995	$8,745	$7,495	$6,795	$5,495	$4,500	$3,500	

Add $750 for .410 bore (mfg. 1992 only).

* ***Model 147SSL*** – similar to Model 147SL, except has luxury wood upgrade. Imported 1999-2003.

	$8,600	$7,525	$6,450	$5,850	$4,730	$3,870	$3,010	*$9,995*

28 ga. had limited availability during 2001.

MODEL 247SL – 12, 16 (disc. 2001), 20, or 28 ga., similar to Model 147SL, except has deluxe scroll engraving. Importation disc. 1991, resumed 1993-2003.

	$7,700	$6,735	$5,775	$5,235	$4,235	$3,465	$2,695	*$8,995*

MODEL 280 PETITE FRAME – 28 ga. only, Anson & Deeley boxlock action with Greener crossbolt and double under barrel locking lugs, scroll engraving, case hardened receiver, H&H ejectors, DT, English style stock, 28 in. barrels bored IC/M, includes fitted luggage case. Importation began 2002.

MSR $4,995	$4,500	$3,935	$3,375	$3,060	$2,475	$2,025	$1,575	

* ***Model 280/360 2 Barrel Set*** – includes 28 in. 28 ga. and .410 bore barrels bored IC/M. Importation began 2002.

MSR $7,695	$6,995	$6,120	$5,245	$4,755	$3,845	$3,150	$2,450	

MODEL 280E PETITE FRAME – similar to Model 280 Petite Frame, except has fine hunting scenes engraved on silver receiver. Importation began 2002.

MSR $5,995	$5,495	$4,810	$4,120	$3,735	$3,020	$2,475	$1,925	

MODEL 280EL PETITE FRAME – 28 ga. only, Anson & Deeley boxlock action with Greener crossbolt and double underbarrel locking lugs, fine hunting scene engraving, ejectors, DT, pistol grip or English style stock, 28 in. barrels bored IC/M, includes fitted luggage case, 5.2 lbs. Importation began 2000.

MSR $7,695	$6,950	$6,080	$5,210	$4,725	$3,820	$3,125	$2,430	

Add $700 for Model 280EL Custom Ltd. Ed. with luxury wood Enlish style stock and DTs (new 2008).

* ***Model 280EL/360EL 2 Barrel Set*** – consists of both 28 ga. and .410 bore barrels with fitted luggage case. Importation began 2000.

MSR $11,195	$10,000	$8,750	$7,500	$6,800	$5,500	$4,500	$3,500	

The Model 360EL was discontinued during 2005.

MODEL 280SL PETITE FRAME – 28 ga. only, H&H style sidelock action with Greener crossbolt and double under barrel locking lugs, English style arabesque engraving featuring small scrolls, ejectors, DT, pistol grip or English style stock, 28 in. barrels bored IC/M, includes fitted luggage case, 5.2 lbs. Importation began 2000.

MSR $11,595	$10,000	$8,750	$7,500	$6,800	$5,500	$4,500	$3,500	

* ***Model 280SSL Petite Frame*** – similar to Model 280SL Petite Frame, except has quick detachable sideplates. Imported 2002-2003.

	$8,900	$7,785	$6,675	$6,050	$4,895	$4,005	$3,115	*$10,495*

MODEL 347SL – 12, 16, or 20 ga., similar to Model 247S, except has more elaborate engraving and better walnut. Importation disc. 1991, resumed 1993-97.

	$7,000	$6,125	$5,250	$4,760	$3,850	$3,150	$2,450	*$7,895*

MODEL 360 PETITE FRAME – .410 bore, 28 in. barrels bored IC/F, otherwise similar to Model 280 Petite Frame. Importation began 2002.

MSR $4,995	$4,500	$3,935	$3,375	$3,060	$2,475	$2,025	$1,575	

GRADING - PPGS™	100%	98%	95%	90%	80%	70%	60%	LAST MSR

MODEL 360E PETITE FRAME – similar to Model 360 Petite Frame, except has fine hunting scenes engraved on silver receiver. Imported 2002-2006.

	$4,750	$4,155	$3,560	$3,230	$2,610	$2,135	$1,660	*$5,495*

MODEL 360EL PETITE FRAME – .410 bore, otherwise similar to Model 280EL, 5 1/2 lbs. Importation began 2000.

MSR $7,695	$6,995	$6,120	$5,245	$4,755	$3,845	$3,150	$2,450	

MODEL 360SL PETITE FRAME – .410 bore, otherwise similar to Model 280SL, 5 1/2 lbs. Importation began 2000.

MSR $11,595	$10,000	$8,750	$7,500	$6,800	$5,500	$4,500	$3,500	

* ***Model 360SSL Petite Frame*** – similar to Model 360SL Petite Frame, except has quick detachable sideplates. Imported 2002-2003.

	$8,950	$7,830	$6,710	$6,085	$4,920	$4,025	$3,130	*$10,495*

MODEL 280SL/360SL 2 BARREL SET – consists of both 28 ga. and .410 bore barrels with fitted luggage case. New 2000.

MSR $15,995	$13,750	$12,030	$10,310	$9,350	$7,560	$6,185	$4,810	

The Model 360SL was discontinued during 2005.

MODEL 280SSL/360SSL 2 BARREL SET – similar to 280SL/360SL 2 barrel set, except has quick detachable sideplates. Imported 2002-2003.

	$12,450	$10,895	$9,335	$8,465	$6,845	$5,600	$4,355	*$14,395*

MODEL 447SL – similar to Model 347S, except is also available in 28 ga. and has more delicate scroll engraving. Importation disc. 1991, resumed 1993-2003.

	$9,250	$8,095	$6,935	$6,290	$5,085	$4,160	$3,235	*$10,995*

MODEL 1620 – 16 ga. only, Anson & Deely boxlock action, Greener crossbolt with double underbarrel locking lugs, 28 in. barrels with IC/Mod. fixed chokes, case hardened receiver with scroll engraving, H&H style ejectors, DT, English straight grip stock, includes fitted luggage case. Importation began 2002.

MSR $4,995	$4,500	$3,935	$3,375	$3,060	$2,475	$2,025	$1,575	

* ***Model 1620 2 Barrel Set*** – includes 28 in. 16 and 20 ga. barrels bored IC/M. Importation began 2002.

MSR $7,695	$6,995	$6,120	$5,245	$4,755	$3,845	$3,150	$2,450	

MODEL 1620E – 16 ga., similar to Model 1620, except has fine engraved hunting scenes on silver receiver. Importation began 2006.

MSR $5,995	$5,450	$4,770	$4,085	$3,705	$2,995	$2,450	$1,905	

MODEL 1620EL – similar to Model 1620, except has finely engraved hunting scenes on silver receiver and luxury wood upgrade. Importation began 2002.

MSR $7,695	$6,995	$6,120	$5,245	$4,755	$3,845	$3,150	$2,450	

* ***Model 1620EL 2 Barrel Set*** – includes 28 in. 16 and 20 ga. barrels bored IC/M. Importation began 2002.

MSR $11,195	$10,000	$8,750	$7,500	$6,800	$5,500	$4,500	$3,500	

MODEL 1620SL – similar to Model 1620EL, except has sidelock action. Importation began 2002.

MSR $11,595	$10,250	$8,970	$7,685	$6,970	$5,635	$4,610	$3,585	

* ***Model 1620SL 2 Barrel Set*** – includes 28 in. 16 and 20 ga. barrels bored IC/M. Importation began 2002.

MSR $15,995	$13,750	$12,030	$10,310	$9,350	$7,560	$6,185	$4,810	

MODEL 1622 – 16 ga., 28 in. barrels, Greener crossbolt, double barrel under-barrel locking lugs, case hardened receiver with cocking indicators, Anson & Deely boxlock action with full sideplates, H&H ejectors, SST or DT, pistol grip or English style stock, 6.3 lbs. Imported 2006-2007.

	$4,750	$4,155	$3,560	$3,230	$2,610	$2,135	$1,660	*$5,495*

GRADING - PPGS™	100%	98%	95%	90%	80%	70%	60%	LAST MSR

* ***Model 1622 2 Barrel Set*** – includes 28 in. 16 and 20 ga. barrels bored IC/M. Imported 2006-2007.

	$7,375	$6,100	$5,500	$4,900	$4,250	$3,450	$2,750	*$8,295*

* ***Model 1622E*** – similar to Model 1622, except had hand engraved game scenes on silver finished receiver. Imported 2006-2007.

	$5,975	$4,950	$4,400	$3,875	$3,400	$2,950	$2,300	*$6,895*

* ***Model 1622EL*** – similar to Model 1622E, except has luxury grade wood. Imported 2006-2007.

	$8,000	$7,000	$6,000	$5,440	$4,400	$3,600	$2,800	*$9,195*

* ***Model 1622EL 2 Barrel Set*** – includes 28 in. 16 and 20 ga. barrels bored IC/M. Imported 2006-2007.

	$10,400	$9,100	$7,800	$7,070	$5,720	$4,680	$3,640	*$11,995*

SHOTGUNS: SPORTING CLAYS

MODEL 47LSC SxS SPORTING CLAYS – 12 ga. only, features Anson & Deeley boxlock action with scroll engraved case hardened receiver, 28 in. barrels with Briley screw-in chokes, H&H style ejectors, SST adj. for length of pull, select grade checkered walnut stock with pistol grip and beavertail forearm, competition recoil pad. Disc. 1994.

	$2,725	$2,400	$2,050	$1,725	$1,450	$1,125	$925	*$2,995*

MODEL 200SC O/U SPORTING CLAYS – 12 ga. only, 3 in. chambers, 30 in. VR fixed choke barrels with lengthened forcing cones, Kersten double cross-bolt lock, color case hardened receiver, Blitz action, SST, fitted luggage case. Imported 1995-96.

	$6,750	$4,600	$3,750	$3,200	$2,625	$2,175	$1,850	*$7,495*

Add $500 for Briley choke tubes (5 total).

MERRILL

Previous manufacturer located in Tucson, AZ. This original pistol design was by Rex Merrill.

A newer variation of the Sportsman, now designated the XL and Hunter Model XL was offered by R.P.M. Please refer to the R.P.M. listing for more information.

PISTOLS: SINGLE SHOT

SPORTSMAN MODEL – .17 Hornet, .22 S, L, or LR, .22 WMR, .22 Rem. Jet., .22 Hornet, .30 Herrett, .30 Merrill, .38 Spl., .357 Mag., .357 Herrett, 7mm Merrill, 7mm Rocket, .256 Win. Mag., .45 LC, .44 Mag., or .30-30 Win. cal., 9, 10 3/4, or 14 in. barrel, hinged break open action, smooth walnut grips.

	$650	$575	$525	$450	$395	$350	$300	

Add $70 for interchangeable barrels.
Add $25 for wrist support.

MERWIN HULBERT & CO.

Previous company with headquarters located in New York, NY circa 1874-1891.

Merwin Hulbert offered very high quality revolvers which were serious competitors with the Colt, Smith & Wesson, and Remington large frame single actions during this era. Their guns are believed to have been manufactured in a separate section of the Hopkins & Allen plant. Most will have both Merwin Hulbert and Hopkins & Allen markings on the barrel.

Merwin revolvers have a unique twist-open mechanism. The latch on the bottom of the frame is pushed toward the rear, while barrel & cylinder are twisted clockwise and pulled forward. This design was intended to allow selective ejection of empty cases while leaving unfired cartridges in the cylinder.

A unique and highly desirable feature of Merwin revolvers is "suction". Due to the exceptionally tight machining tolerances of these revolvers, when the barrel and cylinder were twisted to the right, drawn forward, and let go of, they would return to an almost fully closed position on the frame due to the "suction" created by these tight tolerances. Merwins with extremely good "suction" will bring a 10-20% premium.

100%	98%	95%	90%	80%	70%	60%	50%	40%	30%	20%	10%

Merwins will often be found with a distinctive and unusual "punch dot" style factory engraving, often with some sort of simple panel scene (animal, bird, flowers, etc.) on one or (rare) both sides of the frame. These will usually bring perhaps a 50% premium in lower grades, while in higher condition may bring double or triple what an undecorated gun will bring. The highest quality factory Exhibition/Presentation grade guns may bring four to five times what an undecorated gun will bring. These are exceptionally rare!

REVOLVERS: LARGE FRAME

All chambered for either .44 Merwin Hulbert (usually no caliber markings), .44 Russian (usually marked "Russian Model"), or .44-40 (marked "Calibre Winchester 1873").

The Merwin Hulbert system was copied by various Spanish, Belgium, and possibly other makers. These foreign copies will bring significantly less than original Merwins.

Add 20%-25% for blue finish (rare, used on only about 5% of all Merwins). Add 10% for a rounded or "humpback" hammer that can be found on many of the earlier Merwins.

FIRST MODEL FRONTIER ARMY SA – .44 cal., square butt, open-top, scoop flutes on cylinder, 7 in. barrel, two screws above trigger guard.

100%	98%	95%	90%	80%	70%	60%	50%	40%	30%	20%	10%
$9,600	$7,200	$4,200	$3,300	$2,100	$1,850	$1,600	$1,400	$1,150	$1,050	$975	$825

SECOND MODEL FRONTIER ARMY SA – similar to First Model, except has only one screw above trigger guard.

100%	98%	95%	90%	80%	70%	60%	50%	40%	30%	20%	10%
$8,500	$7,000	$4,100	$2,800	$1,900	$1,700	$1,550	$1,400	$1,200	$1,000	$900	$800

SECOND MODEL POCKET ARMY SA – similar to Second Model Frontier Army, except has birdshead butt instead of square butt, 3 1/2 in. or 7 (scarce) in. barrel, may be marked "POCKET ARMY".

100%	98%	95%	90%	80%	70%	60%	50%	40%	30%	20%	10%
$7,500	$6,750	$4,000	$3,000	$2,500	$2,100	$1,750	$1,500	$1,250	$1,000	$800	$700

Add 10% for 7 in. barrel.

There are no First Model Pocket Army models.

THIRD MODEL FRONTIER ARMY SA – .44 cal., square butt, top strap, usually has conventional fluting on cylinder, but some have scoop flutes, 7 in. round barrel with no rib.

100%	98%	95%	90%	80%	70%	60%	50%	40%	30%	20%	10%
$7,000	$6,250	$3,750	$2,750	$2,250	$2,000	$1,500	$1,250	$1,000	$900	$750	$650

THIRD MODEL FRONTIER ARMY DA – similar to Third Model Frontier Army SA, except is double action.

100%	98%	95%	90%	80%	70%	60%	50%	40%	30%	20%	10%
$6,500	$3,500	$2,500	$2,00	$1,750	$1,500	$1,200	$1,000	$900	$825	$650	$550

There are no First or Second Model Army double action models.

THIRD MODEL POCKET ARMY SA – .44 cal., single action, birdshead butt, top strap, 3 1/2 in. or 7 in. round barrel with no rib., available with interchangeable 3 1/2 or 7 in. barrels.

100%	98%	95%	90%	80%	70%	60%	50%	40%	30%	20%	10%
$7,500	$4,750	$3,000	$2,500	$1,600	$1,400	$1,200	$1,000	$900	$750	$650	$550

Add 20% if barrels are numbered to the gun.

THIRD MODEL POCKET ARMY DA – similar to Third Model Pocket Army SA, except is double action, available with interchangeable 3 1/2 or 7 in. barrels.

100%	98%	95%	90%	80%	70%	60%	50%	40%	30%	20%	10%
$6,500	$5,000	$4,500	$3,000	$2,500	$2,000	$1,500	$1,200	$1,000	$900	$750	$600

Add 20% if barrels are numbered to the gun.

FOURTH MODEL FRONTIER ARMY SA – .44 cal., 3 1/2, 5 (most common), or 7 in. unique ribbed barrel, square butt, top strap, conventional flutes.

100%	98%	95%	90%	80%	70%	60%	50%	40%	30%	20%	10%
$9,000	$7,750	$6,000	$5,500	$4,500	$3,000	$2,500	$2,000	$1,550	$1,350	$1,150	$950

FOURTH MODEL FRONTIER ARMY DA – similar to Fourth Model Frontier Army SA, except is double action.

100%	98%	95%	90%	80%	70%	60%	50%	40%	30%	20%	10%
$8,000	$6,500	$5,500	$4,500	$3,750	$2,650	$2,250	$1,750	$1,500	$1,300	$1,100	$900

FOREIGN COPIES OF LARGE FRAME REVOLVERS – .44 cal.

These models may be based on any configuration, but 2nd & 3rd Frontier Army styles are probably the most commonly found. The words "Merwin Hulbert" (such as "Sistema Merwin Hulbert") may appear somewhere on the revolver, but are rarely, if ever, found with the Hopkins & Allen marking. These will usually bring half or less what a comparable genuine Merwin will bring.

100%	98%	95%	90%	80%	70%	60%	50%	40%	30%	20%	10%

REVOLVERS: MEDIUM & SMALL FRAME

Medium frame revolvers were usually 5 shot in .38 cal., or 7 shot in .32 cal. The .32 Long caliber 7 shot barrel and cylinder were adapted to fit the 5 shot .38 cal. medium frames. The small frame was a 5 shot in .32 cal. Models chambered for .38 MH or .32 MH cal. are very similar to the black powder loadings of the .38 S&W and .32 S&W cal. Folding hammer spurs may bring a 10-20% premium.

FIRST POCKET MODEL SA – .38 cal., 5 shot, spur-trigger, w/cyl. pin exposed at the front of the frame, distinguishing feature is round loading hole in recoil shield, with no loading gate.

$2,250	$2,000	$1,600	$1,225	$1,000	$900	$800	$700	$600	$500	$400	$350

SECOND POCKET MODEL SA – .38 cal., 5 shot, similar to First Model, except has sliding loading gate.

$1,800	$1,500	$1,250	$800	$700	$600	$500	$450	$400	$350	$300	$275

THIRD POCKET MODEL SA – .38 cal., 5 shot, similar to First Model, except has enclosed cylinder pin.

$1,600	$1,300	$900	$750	$675	$550	$475	$425	$375	$325	$275	$250

THIRD POCKET MODEL SA WITH TRIGGERGUARD – .38 cal., 5 shot, similar to Third Pocket Model, except has conventional trigger guard.

$1,500	$1,200	$900	$750	$600	$500	$450	$425	$375	$325	$275	$250

THIRD POCKET MODEL DA .38 – .38 cal., 5 shot, double action, may have folding hammer spur.

$1,350	$1,200	$1,000	$750	$600	$550	$500	$450	$400	$350	$325	$300

Add 10% for folding hammer spur.

THIRD POCKET MODEL DA .32 – .32 cal., 7 shot, double action.

$1,500	$1,200	$975	$825	$750	$650	$550	$450	$400	$300	$275	$250

SMALL FRAME DA POCKET MODEL – .32 cal., 5 shot, double action.

$1,200	$1,000	$750	$650	$575	$500	$450	$400	$350	$300	$275	$250

TIP-UP .22 MODEL – .22 rimfire cal., 7 shot, spur trigger, closely patterned after the S&W Model One. Very scarce.

$1,500	$1,250	$1,100	$950	$850	$750	$650	$550	$450	$400	$350	$300

RIFLES: SINGLE SHOT

These rifles were generally patterned after the Hopkins & Allen single shots. The Merwin Hulbert & Co. name marking may bring a 25-50% price increase over models that do not have this marking. A Merwin, Hulbert & Co. marked speciman in 90% or better condition may bring a 100% price increase over a similar Hopkins & Allen rifle.

MERWIN HULBERT & CO. (NEW MFG.)

Current trademark established in 2010. While the company secured a manufacturing facility located in Glenrock, WY, only a few prototypes were manufactured. Merwin Hulbert & Co. was a division of Sharps Rifle Co. located in Chamberlain, SD.

While Merwin Hulbert & Co. planned to begin the manufacture of the Merwin Hulbert revolvers based on the original specifications during 2010, only a few prototypes were produced. They included the 1878 Pocket Army, 1879 New Army, 1882 Pocket Army, and the 1883 New Army.

METROARMS CORPORATION

Current manufacturer of American Classic trademarked 1911 style semi-auto pistols imported and distributed by Eagle Imports, located in Wanamassa, NJ.

MetroArms Corporation was established in late 2011 under the expertise of former competitive shooter Hector Rodriquez.

GRADING - PPGS™	100%	98%	95%	90%	80%	70%	60%	LAST MSR

PISTOLS: SEMI-AUTO: AMERICAN CLASSIC SERIES

AMERICAN CLASSIC GOV'T MODEL – .45 ACP cal., single action, 8 shot, 1911 Govt. style frame, matte blue or hard chrome (mfg. 2010-2011) finish, checkered wood grips, 36 oz. New 2007.

MSR $579	$495	$425	$365	$325	$295	$275	$250	

Add $100 for hard chrome finish (disc. 2011).

AMERICAN CLASSIC GOV'T II MODEL – 9mm Para. (new 2013), .45 ACP cal., 8 (.45 ACP) or 9 shot mag., similar to Govt. model, except has deluxe blue, hard chrome (new 2010), or duo-tone (new 2012) finish, 36 oz. New 2007.

MSR $600	$500	$435	$365	$325	$295	$275	$250	

Add $91 for hard chrome finish. Add $61 for duo-tone (new 2012).

AMERICAN CLASSIC COMMANDER MODEL – 9mm Para. (new 2013) or .45 ACP cal., 4 1/4 in. barrel, 8 shot mag., blue, chrome, or duo-tone (new 2012) finish, steel frame and slide, SA, Novak rear sight, dovetail front sight, flared and lowered ejection port, extended slide stop, beavertail grip safety, combat hammer, combat trigger, rear slide serrations, diamond cut checkered mahogany grips, approx. 36 oz. New 2010.

MSR $616	$515	$450	$375	$335	$295	$275	$250	

Add $98 for hard chrome finish.
Add $75 for duo-tone finish (new 2012).

AMERICAN CLASSIC AMIGO MODEL – .45 ACP cal., Officer's Model configuration with 3 1/2 in. barrel, otherwise similar to Commander Model, 7 shot mag., deep blue, hard chrome, or duo-tone (new 2012) finish, approx. 32 1/2 oz. New 2011.

MSR $706	$600	$500	$425	$365	$325	$285	$250	

Add $90 for hard chrome finish.
Add $61 for duo-tone finish (new 2012).

AMERICAN CLASSIC TROPHY MODEL – .45 ACP cal., 5 in. barrel, 8 shot mag., hard chrome finish, steel frame and slide, SA, dovetail fiber optic front sight, adj. Novak rear sight, flared and lowered ejection port, ambidextrous thumb safety, reverse plug recoil system with full length guide rod, beveled mag well, combat hammer and trigger, front and rear slide serrations, diamond cut checkered mahogany grips, checkered main spring housing, approx. 38 oz. New 2010.

MSR $811	$700	$625	$575	$495	$450	$425	$375	

AMERICAN CLASSIC 22 MODEL – .22 LR cal., patterned after the Colt ACE, 5 in. barrel, checkered walnut diamond grips, mil spec sights, 10 shot mag., matte blue finish, 33 oz. Limited mfg. 2011 only.

	$325	$295	$275	$250	$225	$185	$170	*$365*

PISTOLS: SEMI-AUTO, MAC SERIES

MAC 1911 BOBCUT – .45 ACP cal., blue or hard chrome finish, 8 shot mag., 4 1/4 in. barrel, SA, steel frame, hammer forged steel slide, fully adj. Novak style rear sight, dovetail fiber optic front sight, custom hard wood grips with MAC logo, approx. 35 oz. New 2013.

MSR $902	$765	$675	$575	$525	$425	$350	$275	

Add $76 for hard chrome finish.

MAC 1911 CLASSIC – .45 ACP cal., blue or hard chrome finish, 8 shot mag., 5 in. ramped match bull barrel, SA, steel frame, hammer forged steel slide, fully adj. Bomar style rear sight, dovetail fiber optic front sight, flared and lowered ejection port, standard slide stop, enhanced beavertail grip safety, skeletal hammer, combat trigger, wide front and rear slide serrations, ambidextrous thumb safety, custom hard wood grips with MAC logo, wide magwell, approx. 41 oz. New 2013.

MSR $1,038	$875	$775	$65	$595	$475	$395	$300	

Add $75 for hard chrome finish.

MAC 1911 BULLSEYE – .45 ACP cal., blue or hard chrome finish, 8 shot mag., similar to Mac 1911 Classic model, except has 6 in. ramped match bull barrel, approx. 47 oz. New 2013.

MSR $1,204	$1,025	$895	$775	$695	$575	$450	$350	

Add $75 for hard chrome finish.

GRADING - PPGS™	100%	98%	95%	90%	80%	70%	60%	LAST MSR

MAC 3011 SSD – .45 ACP cal., black (Tactical model only), blue or hard chrome finish, 14 shot mag., 5 in. ramped match bull barrel, SA, steel frame, hammer forged steel slide, fully adj. Bomar style rear sight, dovetail fiber optic front sight, flared and lowered ejection port, standard slide stop, enhanced beavertail grip safety, skeletal hammer, combat trigger, wide front and rear slide serrations, ambidextrous thumb safety, aluminum grips with MAC logo, wide magwell, approx. 46 oz. New 2013.

MSR $1,128	$960	$850	$725	$650	$525	$425	$325

Add $76 for hard chrome finish or Tactical model with rail.

PISTOLS: SEMI-AUTO, SPS SERIES

SPS Series pistols are manufactured by S.P.S. in Spain, then assembled in the U.S.

SPS PANTERA – .45 ACP cal., black chrome finish, 12 shot mag., 5 in. ramped match bull barrel, SA, steel frame, hammer forged steel slide, fully adj. Bomar style rear sight, dovetail fiber optic front sight, flared and lowered ejection port, standard slide stop, enhanced beavertail grip safety, skeletal hammer, lightweight polymer trigger, wide front and rear slide serrations, ambidextrous thumb safety, glass filled nylon polymer grips with S.P.S. logo, wide magwell, approx. 37 oz. New 2013.

MSR $1,895	$1,600	$1,400	$1,200	$1,095	$875	$725	$550

SPS VISTA – 9mm (Vista Short) or .38 Super (Vista Long) cal., black chrome finish, 21 shot mag., 5 1/2 in. ramped match threaded barrel, SA, steel frame, hammer forged steel slide, scope mount, flared and lowered ejection port, standard slide stop, enhanced beavertail grip safety, skeletal hammer, lightweight polymer trigger, wide front and rear slide serrations, ambidextrous thumb safety, glass filled nylon polymer grips with S.P.S. logo, wide magwell, approx. 42-43 oz. New 2013.

MSR $2,450	$2,175	$1,900	$1,625	$1,475	$1,195	$975	$750

MICHIGAN ARMS

Previous manufacturer located in Michigan until circa 1981.

PISTOLS: SEMI-AUTO

GUARDIAN - SS – .380 ACP cal., patterned after the Walther PPK, bears close resemblance to the Indian Arms .380 semi-auto, 3 1/4 in. barrel, checkered walnut grips with medallion, 6 shot finger extension mag., fixed sights. Limited mfg.

	$375	$295	$225	$210	$190	$170	$150

This model was mfg. by using Indian Arms tooling.

M1911 A1 – .45 ACP cal., patterned after the Colt M1911 A1, fixed sights, 7 shot mag. Disc.

	$450	$395	$350	$275	$225	$210	$190

MICOR DEFENSE, INC.

Current manufacturer established in 1999 and located in Decatur, AL.

Micor manufactures a line of defense products available to the general public, as well as custom weapons and products for the defense and other related industries. Micor consists of two companies - Micor Industries, Inc. and Micor Defense, Inc. The company manufactures the Leader 416 semi-auto bullpup rifle, Leader T2 semi-auto rifle, and the Leader 338 Bullpup rifle. Additionally, Micor offers the Leader 50, a lightweight .50 BMG cal. rifle. All models were designed by Charles St. George, original designer of the Bushmaster M17 bullpup rifle. Please contact the company directly for pricing, availability, and options (see Trademark Index).

MICROTECH SMALL ARMS RESEARCH, INC. (MSAR)

Current rifle manufacturer located in Bradford, PA.

CARBINES/RIFLES: SEMI-AUTO

MSAR manufactures American-made semi-auto bullpup carbines and rifles, patterned after the Steyr AUG.

IMPORTANT NOTE: On model(s) where *N/A has replaced the normal 100% value, it indicates current market conditions are too unstable to accurately ascertain 100%-60% values. Factory retail

GRADING - PPGS™	100%	98%	95%	90%	80%	70%	60%	LAST MSR

prices (MSRs) reflect most recent updates. For more up-to-date information on current pricing trends and additional useful information, please visit www.bluebookofgunvalues.com, select "Information & Services " from the menu, and click on "Additional Book Information".

STG-556 – .223 Rem. cal., 16 or 20 in. chrome lined barrel, gas operated rotating bolt, short piston drive, 10, 20, 30, or 42 shot mag., black, tan, or OD Green finish, with or w/o 9 inch Picatinny rail, right or left hand ejection, synthetic stock, 7.2 lbs.

MSR $1,839	*N/A	$1,575	$1,395	$1,275	$1,150	$995	$825

Add $156 for 1.5x Optic.

* ***STG-556 Gebirgsjager Limited Edition*** – similar to STG-556, engraved Edelweiss flower insignia, except includes all OD Green finish, 1.5x CQB optical sight, 6 in. Picatinny side rail, three 30 shot mags., OD Green Currahee knife with nylon sheath, Giles sling with Uncle Mike's sling swivels, custom Pelican 1700 green case, and certificate of authenticity.

$3,495	$3,100	$2,750	$2,525	$2,300	$2,100	$1,875

STG-680 – 6.8mm Rem. cal., 16 or 20 in. chrome lined barrel, 10, 20, 30, or 42 shot mag., black , tan, or OD Green synthetic stock, with or w/o 9 inch Picatinny rail, right or left hand action, 7.2 lbs.

$1,725	$1,575	$1,395	$1,275	$1,150	$995	$825

Add $156 for 1.5x Optic.

MIDLAND RIFLES

Previous trademark of rifles manufactured by Gibbs Rifle Co. (please refer to the G section for previous models and pricing) and older models mfg. by Parker-Hale, Ltd. (please refer to the P section).

MIIDA

Previously manufactured by Nikko Firearms, Ltd. in Tochigi, Japan. Previously imported by Marubeni America Corp. located in New York, NY circa 1972-1974.

SHOTGUNS: O/U

MODEL 612 FIELD – 12 ga., 26 or 28 in. barrels, VR, various chokes, boxlock, auto ejectors, single selective trigger, checkered pistol grip stock. Mfg. 1972-1974.

$800	$725	$650	$575	$510	$440	$400

MODEL 2100 SKEET GUN – similar to Model 612, with 27 in. VR, skeet bore barrels, more elaborate engraving. Mfg. 1972-1974.

$875	$775	$700	$615	$550	$465	$425

MODEL 2200T TRAP GUN – similar to Model 2100, except with 29 3/4 in. imp. mod. and full choke barrels, wide VR, 60% engraved coverage and select wood. Mfg. 1972-1974.

$925	$825	$750	$665	$595	$500	$450

MODEL 2200S SKEET GUN – similar to Model 2200T, except with 27 in. skeet bore barrels.

$925	$825	$750	$665	$595	$500	$450

MODEL 2300 SERIES TRAP OR SKEET – similar to Model 2200 Trap/Skeet but with more engraving. Mfg. 1972-1974.

$975	$875	$800	$715	$630	$550	$500

MODEL GRT GRANDEE TRAP GUN – 12 ga., 29 3/4 in. full choke barrels, single selective trigger, auto ejector, boxlock with side plates, receiver fully engraved as well as breech ends of barrel, trigger guard and locking lever, gold inlaid, extensive silver line inlays, high grade select walnut stock. Mfg. 1972-1974.

$2,500	$2,200	$1,900	$1,575	$1,250	$1,000	$850

MODEL GRS GRANDEE SKEET GUN – similar to Model GRT, with 27 in. skeet bored barrels.

$2,500	$2,200	$1,900	$1,575	$1,250	$1,000	$850

GRADING - PPGS™	100%	98%	95%	90%	80%	70%	60%	LAST MSR

MILLER ARMS

Current trademark owned by Remington Arms Company, located in Madison, NC. Previously owned by Dakota Arms, located in Sturgis, SD, until June 5, 2009.

RIFLES: LEVER ACTION

SINGLE SHOT RIFLE – various cals. between .17 Dakota - .416 Rem. Mag., XXX English style checkered walnut stock and Schnabel forend, falling block action. New 2004.

* ***Single Shot Classic*** – various centerfire cals. up to .375 H&H, 24 in. round barrel, Hi-Wall falling block action with curved Farquharson lever, plain matte receiver, 7 1/2 lbs.

MSR $5,590	$4,950	$4,500	$3,900	$3,400	$2,925	$2,475	$1,950	

Add $100 for stainless steel action (disc. 2010).

* ***Single Shot Low Boy*** – various centerfire cals., 24 in. half round, half octagon barrel, falling block action, case colored receiver with gold Miller banner, jeweled block, 7 lbs.

MSR $5,590	$4,950	$4,500	$3,900	$3,400	$2,925	$2,475	$1,950	

Add $100 for stainless steel action (disc. 2010).

* ***Single Shot Model F*** – various centerfire cals. up to .45-110, 26 in. octagon barrel, lever style falling block action, perch belly buttstock, Queen Anne grip, cheekpiece, stainless steel receiver, tang sight with front globe, checkered steel buttplate or black recoil pad, 6 lbs.

	$5,650	$4,900	$4,100	$3,550	$3,100	$2,750	$2,250	*$6,095*

MILLER, DAVID CO.

See David Miller Co. listing in the D section.

MIL-SPEC INDUSTRIES CORP.

Previous pistol manufacturer and current components supplier located in Roslyn Heights, NY since 1996.

PISTOLS: SEMI-AUTO

MIL-SPEC 1911 A1 – 9mm Para., 9x21mm, 9x22mm, .40 S&W, .45 HP, or .45 ACP cal., high tech polymer and stainless steel frame, beavertail grip safety, aluminum trigger, 10 shot mag., 3 15/16 (Compact), 5 5/16 (Combat with compensator), or 5 (Government) in. barrel, choice of wood, plastic, or rubber grips, 39 1/2-46 oz. Mfg. late 1996-2006.

	$625	$550	$500	$450	$400	$360	$330	*$690*

Add $5 for parkerized finish.
Add $45 for electroless nickel finish.
Add $50 for hard chrome finish.

MILTEX, INC.

Previous handgun importer located in La Plata, MD. Miltex imported commercial Makarovs until approx. 2000.

MIROKU, B.C.

Current manufacturer established during 1893 and located in Kochi, Japan. Miroku currently manufactures long arms for Browning and Winchester (please refer to individual sections), in addition to their own line of firearms mostly distributed in Europe.

Shotguns marked Miroku only without another trademark listing represent that period of manufacture before Miroku began manufacturing shotguns for other companies (i.e. Charles Daly, Browning, and others). Most guns marked Miroku only were made on a limited basis and although somewhat rare, collector desirability to date has been minimal. Since model notations were not specified in most instances (many shotguns were made to test market demand), a model rundown is virtually impossible. Values can be approx. ascertained by comparing a Miroku shotgun of similar gauge, features, engraving/wood, and condition to an equivalent Japanese Charles Daly model. Miroku also manufactured revolvers up until approx. 1964 which may be designated Liberty Chief - limited importation into the U.S.

GRADING - PPGS™	100%	98%	95%	90%	80%	70%	60%	LAST MSR

MITCHELL ARMS, INC.

Previous manufacturer, importer, and distributor located in Fountain Valley, CA.

DERRINGERS: O/U

GUARDIAN ANGEL – .22 LR or .22 WMR cal., double action, hammerless, choice of blue, satin, nickel, or gold finish. Mfg. 1996-97.

$125 $105 $95 $85 $80 $75 $70 ***$150***

Add $10 for .22 WMR cal.
Add $20 for blue or nickel finish.
Add $40 for gold finish.
Add $10 for Deluxe Model with case and angel charm.

PISTOLS: SEMI-AUTO

AMERICAN EAGLE LUGER – 9mm Para. cal., 4 in. barrel, stainless steel with toggle action, checkered American walnut grips, American Eagle version, contoured front grip strap. Mfg. by Aimco. Disc. 1994.

$850 $725 $600 $500 $400 $300 $250 ***$695***

MITCHELL DA – 9mm Para. cal., patterned after the Sig 226, early mfg. had blue-gray finish, later mfg. had hard chrome, mfg. by Tressitu in South Africa, less than 100 mfg.

$600 $550 $475 $425 $350 $295 $250

Mitchell .22 Cal. Target Pistols

Mitchell Arms manufactured High Standard marked pistols during 1993-94. Due to litigation, the High Standard logo was dropped in 1994, and High Standard model nomenclature was dropped in 1996. These guns feature push button barrel takedown and usually, a choice between stainless steel or royal blue steel construction. Mitchell Arms is not responsible for the older High Standard pistols manufactured in New Haven and East Hartford, CT, even though Mitchell parts are interchangeable with original High Standard pistols.

MONARCH (CITATION II) – .22 LR cal., 5 1/2 bull or 7 1/4 in. fluted barrel, frame mounted bridge rear sight, checkered walnut grips with thumbrest, push button takedown, stippled front and rear grip straps, adj. trigger, travel, and weight, stainless steel or royal blue finish. Mfg. 1993-2000.

$395 $295 $245 $215 $190 $170 $150 ***$490***

MEDALIST (OLYMPIC I.S.U.) – .22 S or LR (new 1994) cal., military grip style, 6 3/4 in. special barrel with internal stabilizer, adj. barrel weights, other features similar to Citation II, stainless steel or blue finish. Mfg. 1993-2000.

$625 $550 $425 $375 $325 $275 $22 ***$700***

BARON (SHARPSHOOTER II) – .22 LR cal., 5 1/2 in. bull barrel, standard trigger, adj. rear sight, smooth grip frame, stainless steel or blue (disc.) finish. Mfg. 1993-2000.

$320 $280 $240 $210 $185 $160 $135 ***$400***

SPORTSTER (SPORT KING II) – .22 LR cal., 4 1/2 or 6 3/4 in. tapered barrel, military black checkered plastic grips, stainless steel only, adj. rear sight. Mfg. 1993-2000.

$270 $220 $185 $160 $135 $120 $110 ***$330***

MEDALLION (TROPHY II) – .22 LR cal., 5 1/2 in. bull or 7 1/4 in. fluted barrel, military grips with full checkering and thumbrest, bridge rear sight, gold-plated trigger safety and mag. release, stippled front and rear grip straps, stainless steel or royal blue (disc. 1997) finish. Mfg. 1993-2000.

$425 $350 $275 $225 $190 $170 $150 ***$500***

SOVEREIGN (VICTOR II) – .22 LR cal., 4 1/2 or 5 1/2 in. full length VR or black rib barrel, checkered walnut grips with thumbrest, stainless steel became standard 1998, gold-plated trigger, safety, mag. release, and slide lock, rib mounted sights. Mfg. 1993-2000.

$500 $425 $375 $325 $275 $225 $195 ***$600***

Add $80 for Weaver style base built into VR.

GRADING - PPGS™	100%	98%	95%	90%	80%	70%	60%	LAST MSR

HIGH STANDARD COLLECTORS ASSOCIATION SPECIAL EDITIONS

* ***HSCA-SE Trophy II*** – .22 LR cal., 100 mfg. 1993 only, cased.

$450 $375 $300 $240 $210 $180 $155

* ***HSCA-SE Victor II***

$495 $400 $325 $265 $230 $195 $170

* ***HSCA-SE Citation II***

$435 $365 $285 $225 $195 $165 $140

* ***HSCA-SE Three Gun Set*** – includes Trophy II, Olympic II, and Victor II.

$1,495 $1,295 $1,050 $935 $755 $640 $535

* ***HSCA-SE Six Gun Set*** – includes 6 3/4 in. I.S.U. Olympic (.22 Short), 4 1/2 in. Victor, 7 1/4 in. Citation, 5 1/2 in. Sharpshooter, 4 1/2 in. Sport King, and Trophy Model. Special engraving, cased, HSCA prefix with 2-digit serial number, 19 sets total mfg. 1994 only.

$2,650 $2,100 $1,675 $1,475 $1,210 $1,015 $845 ***$2,995***

Mitchell Centerfire Pistols

MODEL 57A (TOKAREV DESIGN) – .30 Mauser cal., single action semi-auto, 9 shot mag., hammer block and mag. safety, all steel construction. Imported from Yugoslavia 1990 only.

$240 $215 $180 $160 $145 $135 $120 ***$280***

MODEL 70A (TOKAREV DESIGN) – 9mm Para. cal., otherwise similar to Model 57A. Imported from Yugoslavia 1990 only.

$240 $215 $180 $160 $145 $135 $120 ***$280***

88A OFFICERS MODEL (TOKAREV DESIGN) – 9mm Para. cal., newer slenderized variation issued to the Officers Corps., short slide and frame, finger extension mag. Imported from Yugoslavia 1990 only.

$255 $225 $190 $165 $145 $135 $120 ***$300***

SKORPION – while advertised during 1987, this model never went into production.

SPECTRE – while advertised during 1987, this model never went into production.

1911 GOLD/SIGNATURE SERIES (STANDARD) – .45 ACP cal., features new tapered barrel slide lock-up, wide body frame, double stack mag., full length guide rod recoil buffer assembly, beveled mag. well, blue (disc. 1995) or stainless steel, 8 shot mag., walnut checkered grips, fixed or adj. sights. New 1994-disc.

* ***1911 Gold/Signature Series (Standard) Blue Finish***

$465 $395 $350 $325 $295 $270 $250 ***$535***

* ***1911 Gold/Signature Series (Standard) Stainless Steel*** – disc. 1997.

$675 $585 $525 $440 $385 $325 $280 ***$675***

* ***1911 Gold/Signature Series (Standard) Tactical Model*** – stainless steel, features elongated grip safety and serrated front slide, fixed or adj. rear sight. Mfg. 1996-97.

$640 $550 $500 $430 $375 $315 $270 ***$735***

Add $40 for adj. rear sight.

* ***1911 Gold/Signature Series (Standard) Bullseye Model*** – similar to Tactical Model, except has fully adj. rear sight. Mfg. 1996-97.

$850 $700 $575 $480 $410 $350 $295 ***$950***

* ***1911 Gold/Signature Series (Standard) IPSC Limited Model*** – choice of ghost ring or adj. rear sight. Mfg. 1996-97.

$1,075 $875 $675 $565 $480 $400 $350 ***$1,195***

Add $45 for ghost ring sight.

1911 GOLD/SIGNATURE SERIES (WIDE BODY) – .45 ACP cal., features new tapered barrel slide lock-up, full length guide rod recoil buffer assembly, beveled mag. well, blue (disc.

GRADING - PPGS™	100%	98%	95%	90%	80%	70%	60%	LAST MSR

1995) or stainless steel, 10 (C/B 1994) or 13* shot mag., walnut checkered grips, fixed or adj. sights. Mfg. 1994-97.

* ***1911 Gold/Signature Series (Wide Body) Blue Finish***

$595	$525	$475	$425	$375	$335	$295	*$685*

* ***1911 Gold/Signature Series (Wide Body) Standard Model*** – stainless steel, fixed sights, smooth grips. Mfg. 1996-97.

$765	$650	$550	$460	$395	$335	$285	*$840*

* ***1911 Gold/Signature Series (Wide Body) Tactical Model*** – stainless steel, features elongated grip safety and serrated front slide, adj. rear sight. Mfg. 1996-97.

$795	$675	$575	$480	$410	$350	$295	*$895*

MITCHELL .44 – .44 Mag. cal., 5 1/2 in. barrel, blue finish, 7 shot mag., checkered walnut grips, adj. rear sight. Mfg. 1996-97.

$1,050	$900	$800	$725	$650	$575	$495	*$1,190*

JEFF COOPER SIGNATURE/COMMEMORATIVE MODEL – .45 ACP cal., blue finish. Mfg. 1996-97.

* ***Jeff Cooper Signature Model***

$725	$625	$560	N/A	N/A	N/A	N/A	*$795*

* ***Jeff Cooper Commemorative Model*** – 1,000 mfg. 1996-97.

$1,650	$1,400	$1,200	N/A	N/A	N/A	N/A	*$1,895*

ALPHA SERIES – while advertised in 1995, this model never went into production.

PISTOLS: SINGLE SHOT

ROLLING BLOCK PISTOL – .22 LR, .22 WMR, .223 Rem., .357 Mag., or .45 LC cal., reproduction of the Remington Rolling Block design, 10 in. barrel. Mfg. 1991-92 only.

$340	$285	$240	$210	$185	$170	$150	*$395*

REVOLVERS: SINGLE ACTION

SINGLE ACTION ARMY – .22 LR (disc.), .357 Mag., .44-40 WCF (new 1998), .44 Mag. (disc.), .45 ACP (disc.), or .45 LC cal., 4 3/4, 5 1/2, 6 (disc. 1993), or 7 1/2 in. barrel lengths, hammer block safety mechanism, steel construction, case hardened frame, one-piece walnut stock. Imported 1986-94, re-introduced 1997. Disc.

* ***SAA Cowboy Model*** – .357 Mag., .44-40 WCF, .45 ACP (disc.), or .45 LC cal., 4 3/4 in. barrel.

$395	$350	$315	$275	$260	$245	$230	*$450*

Add $50 for nickel finish.
Add $50 for adj. rear sight (disc.).
Add $150 for dual cylinder (.357 Mag./9mm Para., .45 LC/.45 ACP, or .44-40 WCF/.44 Spl.).
Add $95 for steel back strap and trigger guard (disc.).

This model is also available in a Bat Masterson variation.

* ***SAA U.S. Army Model*** – similar to Cowboy Model, except has 5 1/2 in. barrel.

$395	$350	$315	$275	$260	$245	$230	*$450*

Add $50 for nickel finish.
Add $150 for dual cylinder (.357 Mag./9mm Para., .45 LC/.45 ACP, or .44-40 WCF/.44 Spl.).

* ***SAA U.S. Cavalry Model*** – similar to Cowboy Model, except has 7 1/2 in. barrel.

$395	$350	$315	$275	$260	$245	$230	*$450*

Add $150 for dual cylinder (.357 Mag./9mm Para., .45 LC/.45 ACP, or .44-40 WCF/.44 Spl.).
Add $50 for nickel finish.

* ***SAA .44 Mag.*** – .44 Mag. cal., fully adj. target sights. Disc. 1992.

$425	$350	$295	$250	$200	$180	$165	*$495*

* ***SAA Rimfire Model*** – .22 LR cal. Importation disc. 1989.

$230	$200	$180	$160	$145	$130	$120	*$280*

Add $30 for adj. rear sight.

GRADING - PPGS™	100%	98%	95%	90%	80%	70%	60%	LAST MSR

* ***SAA Silhouette Model*** – available with 10, 12, or 18 in. barrel in .44 Mag. or .45 LC cal. Importation disc. 1991.

	$395	$325	$260	$220	$195	$170	$155	$450

Add $175 for shoulder stock (available with 18 in. barrel only).

The shoulder stock was available with .44 Mag./.44-40 WCF cals. only.

* ***SAA Dual Cylinder*** – available in either .22 LR/.22 WMR (disc.), .22 LR/.22 WMR stainless (disc. 1988), .357 Mag./9mm Para. (disc. 1993), .44 Mag./.44-40 WCF (disc. 1991), or .45 LC/.45 ACP (new 1990) cal. Imported 1986-94.

	$475	$415	$365	$335	$300	$275	$250	$549

Add $50 for adj. rear sight (disc.).
Add $39 for nickel finish.
Add $93 for for steel backstrap.

* ***SAA Stainless Model*** – available in .22 LR or .357 Mag. (disc. 1987) cal. only, adj. sights. Imported 1986-88 only.

	$260	$225	$195	$145	$120	$105	$90	$301

Add $25 for .357 Mag.

BAT MASTERSON MODEL – .45 LC cal., 4 3/4 , 5 1/2, or 7 1/2 in. barrel with full ejector rod housing, nickel-plated, one-piece walnut stocks, hammer-block safety, rear sight is square notch in frame, two-piece backstrap. Imported 1989-94.

	$375	$285	$240	$210	$185	$170	$150	$450

Add $156 for extra .45 ACP cylinder.

MODEL 1875 REMINGTON – .357 Mag. or .45 LC cal., royal blue finish with color case hardened frame, walnut grips. Imported 1990-91.

	$345	$285	$245	$210	$185	$170	$150	$399

Add $76 for nickel finish.
Add $51 for extra convertible .45 ACP cylinder.

REVOLVERS: DOUBLE ACTION

TITAN II – .357 Mag. cal., 6 shot, 2, 4, or 6 in. barrel, blue or stainless, fixed sights, shrouded ejector rod, target hammer. Mfg. 1995 only.

	$285	$250	$220	$190	$170	$150	$135	$339

TITAN III – similar to Titan II, except has adj. rear sight. Mfg. 1995 only.

	$340	$285	$245	$200	$175	$150	$135	$429

GUARDIAN II – .38 Spl. cal., 6 shot, 3 or 4 in. barrel, fixed sights, blue only, target or combat grips. Mfg. 1995 only.

	$240	$215	$185	$165	$145	$130	$120	$275

GUARDIAN III – similar to Guardian II, except has adj. rear sight, and 6 in. barrel. Mfg. 1995 only.

	$260	$230	$195	$175	$155	$140	$130	$305

RIFLES: DISC.

MODEL 15/22 OR 20/22 SEMI-AUTO CARBINE – .22 LR cal., American walnut stock, high polish blue, detachable 10 shot mag. Mfg. 1994-95.

	$225	$195	$175	$150	$125	$100	$85	$179

Subtract $40 for 20/22 Special.
Add 30% for Deluxe model (includes deluxe walnut, rosewood accents, and fine line checkering).

LW22 SEMI-AUTO – .22 LR cal., 10 shot mag., composite or skeleton stock, patterned after Feather Industries semi-auto. Limited mfg. 1996-97.

	$300	$265	$240	$220	$195	$175	$160	$275

Add $30 for composite stock.

LW9 SEMI-AUTO – 9mm Para. cal., semi-auto, blowback action, composite or skeleton stock, patterned after Feather Industries 9mm Para. semi-auto. Limited mfg. 1996-97.

	$550	$495	$450	$395	$365	$335	$295	$500

Add $35 for composite stock.

GRADING - PPGS™	100%	98%	95%	90%	80%	70%	60%	LAST MSR

MODEL 9303/9304/9305 STANDARD BOLT ACTION – .22 LR (9303) or .22 WMR (9304, new 1995) cal., standard or deluxe variation, 10 shot mag. Mfg. 1994-95.

	$275	$235	$195	$180	$160	$145	$130	$275

Add $14 for .22 WMR cal.
Subtract $76 for special bolt action (9305).

MODEL 9301/9302 DELUXE BOLT ACTION – similar to 9304/9305, except includes deluxe walnut, rosewood accents, and fine line checkering. Mfg. 1994-95.

	$300	$265	$225	$190	$170	$150	$135	$313

Add $12 for .22 WMR cal.

M-16A3 – .22 LR, .22 WMR (disc. 1987), or .32 ACP cal., patterned after Colt's AR-15. Mfg. 1987-94.

	$450	$395	$350	$300	$275	$250	$225	$266

Add 20% for .22 WMR cal. or .32 ACP (disc. 1988).

CAR-15/22 – .22 LR cal., carbine variation of M-16 with shorter barrel and collapsible stock. Mfg. 1990-94.

	$495	$450	$395	$350	$300	$275	$250	$266

GALIL – .22 LR or .22 WMR cal., patterned after Galil semi-auto paramilitary design rifle, choice of wood stock or folding stock (new 1992). Mfg. 1987-93.

	$395	$350	$295	$265	$230	$200	$185	$359

MAS – .22 LR or .22 WMR cal., patterned after French MAS rifle. Mfg. 1987-93.

	$395	$350	$295	$265	$230	$200	$185	$359

Add $75 for .22 WMR cal. (disc. 1988).

PPS-30/50 – .22 LR cal., patterned after the Russian WWII PPS military rifle, full length barrel shroud, 20 shot banana mag., adj. rear sight, walnut stock. Mfg. 1989-94.

	$325	$275	$250	$225	$200	$185	$170	$266

Add $150 for 50 shot drum magazine.

SPECTRE CARBINE – while advertised during 1987, this model never went into production.

AK-22 – .22 LR or .22 WMR (new 1988) cal., copy of the famous Russian AK-47, fully adj. sights, built-in cleaning rod, high quality European walnut or folding stock, 20 shot mag. Mfg. 1985-94.

	$325	$275	$250	$225	$200	$185	$170	$266

Add $40 for folding stock.

AK-47 – 7.62x39mm cal., copy of the original Kalashnikov AK-47, semi-auto, teak stock and forend, 30 shot steel mag., last shot hold open. Mfg. in Yugoslavia. Imported 1986-89.

	$1,895	$1,700	$1,550	$1,400	$1,300	$1,200	$1,100	$675

Add $100 for steel folding buttstock.
Add $200 for 75 shot steel drum mag.

.308 WIN. NATO AK-47 (M77B1) – .308 Win. cal., milled receiver, adj. gas port, otherwise similar to AK-47 except has scope rail, day/night Tritium sights, and 20 shot mag. Imported 1989 only.

	$1,895	$1,700	$1,550	$1,400	$1,300	$1,200	$1,100	$775

Add $600 for military issue sniper scope and rings.

M76 – 7.92mm cal., similar to AK-47, except has longer barrel and frame set up for scope mount, counter sniper design, 10 shot mag., mfg. to mil. specs. Imported 1986-1989.

	$2,000	$1,875	$1,650	$1,475	$1,200	$950	$850	$1,995

SKS-M59 – 7.62x39mm cal., copy of the SKS-M59 standard rifle, full walnut stock, fully adj. sights, gas operated. Mfg. in Yugoslavia. Imported 1986-1989.

	$775	$675	$550	$450	$400	$350	$300	$699

R.P.K. – 7.62x39mm or .308 Win. cal., forged heavy barrel with cooling fins, teak stock, detachable bipod, mil. specs. Importation disc. 1992.

	$1,300	$1,100	$975	$850	$750	$650	$550	$1,150

Add $845 for .308 Win. cal.

GRADING - PPGS™	100%	98%	95%	90%	80%	70%	60%	LAST MSR

MODEL M-90 – 7.62x39mm or .308 Win. cal., AK-47 type action, in various configurations (heavy barrel, folding or fixed stock, finned barrel, etc.), plastic thumbhole stock, 5 shot mag., limited importation from Yugoslavia 1991-92.

$1,100	$900	$800	$700	$650	$600	$550	*$829*

Add 20% for folding stock.
Add 10% for .308 Win. cal. (wood stock only).

This model was subjected to modification due to ATF regulations after arrival in the U.S.

RIFLES: REPRODUCTIONS

HENRY RIFLE – .44-40 WCF cal., polished brass frame, octagonal barrel, original loading system. Imported 1990.

$840	$650	$585	$520	$465	$415	$375	*$999*

Iron frame also available at extra charge.

MODEL 1866 – .22 LR (disc.), .38 Spl. (disc.), or .44-40 WCF cal., patterned after the Winchester Model 1866 rifle, solid brass frame, octagon barrel. Imported 1990-93.

$715	$535	$465	$415	$375	$335	$295	*$829*

This model was also available in a carbine variation.

MODEL 1873 – .22 LR (disc.), .38 Spl.(disc), .357 Mag. (disc.), .44-40 WCF (disc.), or .45 LC cal., patterned after the Winchester 1873 rifle, octagon barrel, solid steel frame. Imported 1990-93.

$810	$640	$550	$515	$465	$415	$375	*$950*

This model was also available in a carbine variation until 1992.

SHOTGUNS: SLIDE ACTION

MODEL 9104/9105 – 12 ga. only, features 20 in. barrel with bead sights, 5 shot mag. tube, uncheckered walnut stock and forearm. Mfg. 1994-96.

$240	$195	$175	$160	$145	$130	$120	*$279*

Add $20 for adj. rear rifle sight (Model 9105).
Add $20 for interchangeable choke tube (Model 9104 only).

MODEL 9108/9109 – 12 ga. only, all-purpose self-defense model featuring 20 in. barrel with 7 shot mag., choice of military green (special order), brown walnut, or black regular or pistol grip stock and forearm. Mfg. 1994-96.

$240	$195	$175	$160	$145	$130	$120	*$279*

Add $20 for adj. rear rifle sight (Model 9109).
Add $20 for interchangeable choke tube (Model 9108 only).

MODEL 9111/9113 – 12 ga. only, 18 1/2 in. barrel with bead sights, 6 shot mag., choice of brown or green synthetic (special order), brown walnut or black regular or pistol grip stock and forearm. Mfg. 1994-96.

$240	$195	$175	$160	$145	$130	$120	*$279*

Add $20 for adj. rear rifle sight (Model 9113).
Add $20 for interchangeable choke tube (Model 9111 only).

MODEL 9114 – 12 ga. only, designed for police and riot control, choice of synthetic pistol grip or top folding (disc. 1994) buttstock, 20 in. barrel with iron sights, 6 shot mag. Mfg. 1994-96.

$295	$255	$210	$180	$160	$145	$130	*$349*

MODEL 9115 – 12 ga. only, design based on Special Air Services riot gun, 18 1/2 in. barrel with vent. heat shield, parkerized finish, 6 shot mag., stealth grey stock featuring 4 shell storage. Mfg. 1994-96.

$295	$255	$210	$180	$160	$145	$130	*$349*

Add $20 for interchangeable choke tube.

MITCHELL'S MAUSERS

Current importer located in Fountain Valley, CA.

Please refer to the Escalade and Sabre sections for previously imported semi-auto and slide action shotguns.

GRADING - PPGS™	100%	98%	95%	90%	80%	70%	60%	LAST MSR

PISTOLS: SEMI-AUTO

Mitchell's Mausers previously imported older Luger pistols in many variations. Last MSRs circa 2010 on the following models were: P08 WWI 4 in. $4,995, P08 WWII 4 in. $4,495, Navy Model 6 in. $6,495, Artillery Model 8 in. $7,995, P08 Treaty of Versailles $5,995, and $9,995 for Carbine w/stock. All were restored and were cased with accessories. Additionally, the company also imported a restored WWII P.38, cased with accessories - last MSR was $1,295.

GOLD SERIES – 9mm Para., .40 S&W, or .45 ACP cal., M1911 design, blue finish or stainless steel construction, front and rear slide serrations, extended thumb and grip safeties, adj. rear sight, checkered walnut grips. Disc. 2006.

	$875	$725	$650	$550	$495	$450	$400	*$995*

WHITE LIGHTNING – .17 Mach 2, .17 HMR, .22 LR, or .22 WMR cal., black synthetic frame with stainless steel barrel/slide, 8 1/2 in. barrel with Picatinny black synthetic rail and barrel rib, 9 shot mag. Mfg. 2006-2007.

	$535	$465	$435	$395	$360	$330	$295	*$595*

FALCON SERIES – 9mm Para., .40 S&W, or .45 ACP cal., DA/SA operation, Browning locking system operation, 3.9 (semi-compact) or 4 1/4 (compact) in. barrel, low profile sights, aluminum frame with steel frame and barrel, 12, 16, or 20 shot mag., loaded chamber indicator, approx. 32 oz. Mfg. in Serbia. Importation began late 2011.

MSR $795	$725	$650	$575	$495	$425	$350	$295	

REVOLVERS

CENTURION – .357 Mag. cal., blue finish or stainless steel construction, 6 shot, target trigger, hammer and grips, adj. rear sight, laminated one piece wood grip with medallion. Limited importation.

	$625	$550	$500	$450	$400	$350	$300	*$695*

VALKYRIE – .44 Mag. cal., red ramp front sight, laminated one piece wood grip with medallion. Limited importation.

	$775	$650	$575	$500	$450	$400	$350	*$895*

RIFLES: BOLT ACTION

Beginning 1999, Mitchell's Mausers imported a sizeable quantity of WWII Mauser 98Ks manufactured in Yugoslavia during/after WWII. These guns are basically in new condition, having been only test fired over the past 50 years. They are supplied with bayonet and scabbard, military leather sling, original field cleaning kit, and leather ammo pouch. Caliber is 8mm Mauser (7.9x57mm), and all parts numbers match on these rifles.

MODEL M48 – 8mm Mauser cal., original Mauser 98K rifle manufactured with German technology in Serbia, various grades, matching serial numbers on all parts. Limited importation 2006.

	$450	$395	$375	$345	$295	$265	$235	*$499*

The above price is for the Premium grade rifle without accessories. A special Museum Grade with bayonet, scabbard, belt hanger, and other accessories for $1,000. The Collector Grade was also available for $299 MSR.

TANKER MAUSER M63 (MODEL M48) – .243 Win., .270 Win., .30-06, 8mm Mauser, or .308 Win. cal., similar to Model 48, except the barrel length is 17.4 in., 5 shot internal mag., 1400m adj. rear sight, hardwood stock with semi-gloss finish, 7.4 lbs. Imported 2006-approx. 2010.

	$450	$395	$375	$345	$295	$265	$235	*$495*

G98 REPLICA – various standard and mag. cals., K98 design, configurations include hunting and sport tactical, 3 or 5 shot mag., approx. 7 lbs. New mfg. from Serbia late 2011.

MSR $495	$450	$400	$360	$330	$300	$275	$250	

NEW K98 – 8mm Mauser cal., original WWII Mauser mfg., all matching parts, various configurations available, including Souvenir, Collector, and Premium Grades.

MSR $789	$725	$625	$525	$450	$395	$350	$295	

GRADING - PPGS™	100%	98%	95%	90%	80%	70%	60%	LAST MSR

MAUSER SPORTERS (K98/M98) – 8mm Mauser cal., sporterized military Mauser action with choice of black laminate, brown laminate or American walnut stock with rollover cheekpiece and recoil pad, adj. rear sight, adj. trigger, controlled round feeding. Importation began 2003.

	$440	$395	$375	$345	$295	$265	$235	*$495*

The above price was for the Premium rifle, with bayonet, scabbard, belt hanger and other accessories. Other grades included the Collector Grade - $295 MSR (includes bayonet and accessories), Service Grade - $175 MSR, Trucker Grade - $149 MSR.

* ***Model K98 Souvenir Grade***

MSR $399	$360	$320	$285	$260	$240	$220	$200

* ***Model K98 Collector Grade***

MSR $499	$450	$395	$365	$335	$295	$260	$230

* ***Model K98 Premium Grade***

MSR $795	$725	$650	$550	$475	$400	$350	$295

* ***Model K98 Battle Anniversary Series*** – 8mm Mauser cal., various configurations and dates for important battles during WWII, plus the start and end of WWII. Disc. approx. circa 2010. Please contact Mitchell's Mausers for more information on this model.

MODEL 98 NORTH AMERICAN – .270 Win., .270 WSM, .30-06, .308 Win., .300 Rem. Ultra Mag., .300 Win. Mag., or 7mm Rem. Mag. cal., Mauser 98 double square bridge receiver. Imported 2003-approx. 2010.

	$7,400	$6,500	$5,500	$4,500	$3,500	$3,000	$2,500	*$7,900*

MODEL 98 VARMINTER – .220 Swift, .22-250 Rem., .223 Rem., or .223 WSM cal., features double square bridge receiver, varmint stock with Turkish walnut and fluted barrel, fully adj. trigger, 3 position side safety. Imported 2003-2006.

	$5,950	$5,250	$4,500	$3,750	$3,000	$2,250	$1,500	*$6,500*

MAUSER MAGNUM M98 – various big game cals. from .375 H&H - .500 Jeffery, double square bridge, magnum receiver, deluxe checkered walnut stock with forend cap, folding iron sights. Imported 2003-2010.

	$8,200	$7,400	$6,500	$5,500	$4,500	$3,500	$3,000	*$8,900*

Add $2,000 for .500 Jeffery cal.

BLACK ARROW – 50 BMG cal., Mauser action, 5 shot detachable box mag., fluted and compensated barrel, includes bipod and quick detachable scope mount, shock absorbing buttstock. Imported 2003-2006.

	$5,750	$4,950	$4,275	$3,600	$3,000	$2,400	$2,150	*$6,500*

SOVIET MOSIN-NAGANT – various cals., original gun dated 1942 to commemorate the battle of Stalingrad. Limited importation 2009.

U.S. pricing was not available on this model.

RIFLES: SEMI-AUTO

BLACK LIGHTNING – .17 Mach 2, .17 HMR, .22 LR, or .22 WMR cal., black synthetic thumbhole stock with full length aluminum shroud and Picatinny rail, 18 in. stainless steel barrel/action, 9 shot mag. New 2006.

MSR $595	$525	$450	$400	$350	$300	$275	$250

PPS50/22 – .22 LR cal., patterned after the Russian PPSh-41, features solid wood stock, full length perforated barrel heat shield, fixed sights, 10 or 50 shot detachable drum magazine. Importation began 2012.

MSR $495	$450	$400	$350	$300	$275	$250	$225

Add $150 for 50 shot detachable drum mag.

MODULO MASTERPIECE

Previous manufacturer located in Torino, Italy.

Modulo Masterpiece manufactured high quality pistols and rifles. These models had very little importation into the U.S.

MOLL, M.F.

Previous custom rifle manufacturer and gunsmith located in Moenchengladbach, Germany.

M.F. Moll manufactured high quality reproductions of the Sharps Model 1874 rifle. He also provided many gunsmithing services, including his own proprietary color case hardening process.

MOLOT

Current manufacturer established during 1941, and located in Vyatskie Polyany, Kirov region, Russia.

. Currently manufactured trademarks include: Vepr. rifles and shotguns, a SKS semi-auto rifle line, several models of bolt action rifles, including target models, in addition to Becas slide action and semi-auto shotguns. Please refer to these sections for more information.

MONTANA ARMORY, INC.

Current distributor of C. Sharps Arms Co., Inc. rifles located in Big Timber, MT. Please refer to the C. Sharps Arms Co. listing in the S section for more information.

MONTANA RIFLE COMPANY

Current rifle manufacturer located in Kalispell, MT.

RIFLES: BOLT ACTION

The Montana Rifle Company manufactures three different series of bolt action rifles, featuring its Model 1899 action, which is a hybrid between the Model 70 and the Mauser 98. This action utilizes a Model 70 trigger and three position safety, but also incorporates the Mauser 98 breeching system with the cone breech C-ring and large claw extractor. It also has a five point gas venting system and a new style bolt release knob.

The High Country Series includes the Alpine ($2,999 MSR), Ridgeline ($2,999 MSR), Timberline ($2,999 MSR), Summit ($2,817), Summit Youth ($2,649 MSR), and Summit Alaskan ($3,999 MSR). The Classic Series includes the Woodland ($2,199 MSR), the Wilderness ($3,099 MSR), Wilderness Supreme ($5,999 MSR), Ultra lite ($2,649 MSR), Princess ($2,999 MSR), Safari ($4,399 MSR), and the Safari Supreme ($9,999 MSR). The Tactical Series includes the Marksman ($3,099 MSR), the Sniper/Scout ($3,999 MSR), and the NATO ($4,599 MSR).

During 2011, a line of non-custom, production rifles was introduced in various standard and mag. cals. with either right or left hand action. These models include: American Standard Rifle, ASR ($1,099 MSR or $1,129 for stainless steel), Xtreme Weather Rifle, XWR ($1,199 MSR or $1,299 for stainless steel), the XVR stainless (MSR $1,399), or the Dangerous Game Rifle, DGR ($2,399 MSR or $2,499 for stainless steel), SCR ($2,499 MSR or $2,599 for stainless steel).

Please contact the company directly for more information, including available options and delivery time (see Trademark Index).

MONTGOMERY WARD

Catalog sales/retailer that has subcontracted various domestic and international manufacturers to private label various brand names under the Montgomery Ward conglomerate.

Montgomery Ward shotguns and rifles have appeared under various labels and endorsers, including Western Field and others. There have literally been hundreds of various models (shotguns and rifles) sold through the Montgomery Ward retail network. Most of these models were manufactured through subcontracts with both domestic and international firearms manufacturers. Typically, they were "spec." guns made to sell at a specific price to undersell the competition. Most of these models were derivatives of existing factory models with less expensive wood and perhaps missing the features found on those models from which they were derived. Please refer to the Store Brand Crossover Section in the back of this book under Western Field for converting Montgomery Ward models to the respective manufacturer.

To date, there has been very little interest in collecting Montgomery Ward guns, regardless of rarity. Rather than list Montgomery Ward models, a general guideline is that values generally are under those of their "1st generation relatives." As a result, prices are ascertained by the shooting value of the gun, rather than its collector value.

GRADING - PPGS™	100%	98%	95%	90%	80%	70%	60%	LAST MSR

MORINI COMPETITION ARM SA

Current target pistol manufacturer located in Bedano, Switzerland. Currently imported by Pilkington Competition Equipment, LLC, located in Monteagle, TN. Previously imported and distributed by Nygord Precision Products located in Prescott, AZ, and by Osborne's, located in Cheboygan, MI.

For more information and current pricing on both new and used Morini airguns, please refer to the *Blue Book of Airguns* by Dr. Robert Beeman & John Allen (also online).

PISTOLS: TARGET

Morini was one of the first companies to develop a sophisticated anatomical grip for handgun target shooting, and continues to be a leader in grip design.

CM-22 SEMI-AUTO – .22 LR cal., design for NRA or ISSF "standard pistol" competition, split trigger guard, direct cartridge feed, fully adj. rear sight and trigger, 6 shot mag., 5.1 in. barrel, alloy and steel construction, adj. anatomical wood grips. New 2000.

	100%	98%	95%	90%	80%	70%	60%	LAST MSR
NO MSR	$1,840	$1,525	$1,325	$1,150	$925	$825	$725	

CM-32 SEMI-AUTO – .32 S&W Wadcutter cal., otherwise similar to CM-22. Mfg. 2000-2011.

	100%	98%	95%	90%	80%	70%	60%	LAST MSR
MSR N/A	$1,875	$1,550	$1,395	$1,225	$995	$875	$775	

CM-80 STANDARD SINGLE SHOT – .22 LR cal. only, adj. grips, frame, and sights. Importation disc. 1989.

	100%	98%	95%	90%	80%	70%	60%	LAST MSR
	$925	$825	$725	$650	$585	$520	$465	*$1,015*

Add $50 for left-hand model.

* ***CM-80 Standard Single Shot Super Competition*** – .22 LR cal., similar to CM-80 Standard, except has deluxe finish, and unique plexiglass front sighting system. Importation disc. 1989.

	100%	98%	95%	90%	80%	70%	60%	LAST MSR
	$1,085	$920	$800	$690	$590	$520	$450	*$1,196*

Add $50 for left-hand model.

CM-84E FREE PISTOL – .22 LR cal., single shot, anatomical grips, unique electronic trigger features optic beam safety, cased.

	100%	98%	95%	90%	80%	70%	60%	LAST MSR
NO MSR	$1,925	$1,650	$1,325	$1,100	$925	$800	$675	

MODEL CM-102E SEMI-AUTO – .22 LR cal., advanced rapid fire competition pistol featuring updated ergonomic grips and flared trigger guard, first target pistol to utilize an electronic trigger. Mfg. 1992-97.

	100%	98%	95%	90%	80%	70%	60%	LAST MSR
	$1,525	$1,250	$995	$895	$795	$695	$595	*$1,695*

MORTIMER, THOMAS

Current trademark owned and manufactured by Dickson & MacNaughton, located in Edinburgh, Scotland.

Please contact Dickson & MacNaughton directly for more information regarding this trademark, including current availability and pricing.

MOSIN-NAGANT

Please refer to Russian Service Pistols and Rifles section.

MOSSBERG, O.F. & SONS, INC.

Current manufacturer located in North Haven, CT, 1962-present and New Haven, CT, 1919-1962.

Oscar Mossberg developed an early reputation as a designer and inventor for the Iver Johnson, Marlin-Rockwell, Stevens, and Shattuck Arms companies. In 1915, he began producing a 4-shot, .22 LR cal. palm pistol known as the "Novelty," with revolving firing pin. After producing approx. 600 of these pistols, he sold the patent to C.S. Shattuck, which continued to manufacture guns under the name "Unique." The first 600 had no markings except serial numbers, and were destined for export to South America. Very few of these original "Novelty" pistols survived in this country, and they are extremely rare specimens.

GRADING - PPGS™	100%	98%	95%	90%	80%	70%	60%	LAST MSR

Mossberg acquired Advanced Ordnance Corp. during 1996, a high quality manufacturer utilizing state-of-the-art CNC machinery.

DERRINGERS

BROWNIE – .22 LR cal., top break action, rotating firing pin, 4-barrel, double action, 4 shot, approx. 32,000 mfg. 1919-1932.

$800	$500	$400	$300	$250	$225	$200

RIFLES: DISC.

The models listed appear alphabetically first, followed by numerical models in sequence. Mossberg also has made several .22 bolt action and semi-auto sporters that are in the $115-$130 price range. While they are good shooting models, they are not covered in this section, as they are not collectible.

MODEL K – .22 S, L, or LR cal., tube mag., hammerless, 22 in. bbl., takedown, open sights, plain straight stock. Mfg. 1922-31.

$500	$350	$300	$200	$150	$100	$85

MODEL M – similar to Model K, except has 24 in. octagonal bbl. Mfg. 1928-31.

$500	$350	$300	$200	$150	$100	$85

MODEL S – similar to Model K, except has shorter mag. tube and 19 3/4 in. bbl., very rare. Mfg. 1927-31.

$1,500	$1,200	$1,000	$800	$700	$600	$500

MODEL L – .22 S, L, or LR cal., falling block action, single shot, 24 in. takedown bbl., open sights, pistol grip stock. Mfg. 1929-32.

$800	$600	$450	$400	$350	$300	$250

MODEL L-1 – rare target version of Model L with Lyman 2A tang sight and factory sling.

Add $200 to Model L values.

MODEL R – .22 S, L ,and LR cal., bolt action, 24 In. round bbl., first tube feed, ivory bead front sight, open sporting bbl. sight. Mfg. 1930-32.

$350	$300	$250	$200	$150	$100	$85

MODEL RM-7 – .30 06 or 7mm Rem. Mag. cal., bolt action, 22 inch (.30-06) or 24 inch (7mm Rem. Mag.) round barrel, three-position safety, folding leaf rear sight, gold bead front sight, hand-checkered American walnut with grip cap, built on imported Swedish rotary magazine action, cartridge release lever for unloading magazine from top. 3 (7mm Rem. Mag.) or 4 (.30-06) shot mag. Mfg. approx. 1979-80.

$400	$325	$265	$245	$230	$215	$200

MODEL B – .22 S, L, or LR cal., single shot, bolt action, 22 in. round tapered bbl. Mfg. 1930-32.

$300	$200	$175	$150	$125	$100	$75

MODEL C – .22 S, L and LR cal., single shot, 24 in. bbl., ivory bead front sight, open sporting rear sight. Mfg. 1931-32.

$300	$200	$175	$150	$125	$100	$75

MODEL C-1 – target version of Model C, Lyman front and rear sights, leather sling and swivels, special walnut stock, rare.

Add $200 to Model C values.

MODELS 10, 14, 20, 21, 25, 25A, 125 – .22 S, L, or LR cal., single shot models. Mfg. 1933-38.

$300	$200	$150	$125	$100	$75	$50

Add 25% to prices for models equipped with aperture sights.

MODEL 26B – .22 S, L, or LR cal., entirely new design in single shot rifles, easily identified by bolt handle at extreme rear of bolt, 26 in. tapered barrel, hooded ramp front sight, No. 4 rear aperture and open bbl. sight, swivels. Mfg. 1938-1941.

$300	$200	$150	$125	$100	$75	$50

GRADING - PPGS™	100%	98%	95%	90%	80%	70%	60%	LAST MSR

MODEL 26-C – similar to Model 26B with less expensive sights. Mfg. 1938-41.

$250 $200 $150 $125 $100 $75 $50

MODEL 26M (OR B26M) – rare version of 26 series model with two-piece Mannlicher-style stock. Mfg. 1938.

$600 $500 $400 $300 $250 $200 $150

MODEL 30 – .22 S, L, or LR cal., single shot, 24 in. bbl., rear peep and ramp front sights, swivels. Mfg. 1933-35.

$300 $250 $200 $150 $100 $75 $50

MODEL 34 – similar to Model 30, except with heavy stock, target style. Mfg. 1934-35.

$300 $225 $150 $100 $70 $55 $45

MODEL 35 – .22 S, L, or LR cal., single shot, first full target model, 26 in. heavy target bbl., walnut stock, hooded front ramp and No. 4 rear peep with adj. aperture sight, approx. 9 1/2 lbs. Mfg. 1935-1937.

$400 $300 $275 $225 $200 $150 $125

MODEL 35A – revised version of Model 35, with all-new "master action," approx. 8 1/4 lbs. Mfg. 1937.

$400 $300 $275 $225 $200 $150 $125

Add 50% for Model 35A-LS with Lyman sights.

MODEL 40 – .22 S, L, or LR cal., repeater with tube mag., 16 shot, 24 in. bbl., No. 3 Mossberg aperture rear sight, hooded ramp front sight, swivels, approx. 5 lbs. Mfg. 1933-1935.

$300 $200 $150 $90 $70 $65 $60

MODEL 44 – similar to Model 40, but with heavier target stock, approx. 6 lbs. Mfg. 1934-35.

$400 $300 $275 $225 $175 $135 $75

MODEL 42 – .22 S, L, or LR cal., first model with 7 rd. magazine, 24 in. bbl., front ramp, sporting bbl., and rear aperture sights, 42 in. overall length, approx. 5 lbs. Mfg. 1935-1937.

$250 $200 $125 $100 $70 $65 $60

MODEL 42A – redesign of Model 42, new master action with shorter bolt and receiver. Mfg. 1937-38.

$250 $200 $125 $100 $70 $65 $60

MODEL 42B – same basic specs. as Model 42A, approx. 6 lbs. Mfg. 1938-41.

$250 $200 $125 $100 $70 $65 $60

MODEL 42C – similar to Model 42B, with open bbl. and bead front sights. Mfg. 1938-41.

$200 $150 $100 $90 $80 $70 $65

MODEL 42M – .22 S, L, or LR cal., 7 shot magazine, bolt action, two-piece Mannlicher-style stock, 23 in. barrel, 40 in. overall length, front ramp, open bbl., and receiver aperture sights, trapdoor buttplate for extra mag. in buttstock, 6 3/4 lbs. Mfg. 1940-1944.

$300 $250 $200 $150 $100 $75 $50

Add $40 for extra magazine in buttstock.

MODELS 42M(a), 42M(b), 42M(c) – similar to Model 42M with minor changes in extractors and sights. Mfg. 1944-50.

$300 $250 $200 $150 $100 $75 $50

MODEL 42MB – military version of the Model 42M, approx. 50,000 mfg. for U.S. and British troops as a training rifle. "US Property" marked with serial number, usually found w/o bbl. sight. Mfg. 1942-43.

$350 $250 $200 $150 $110 $100 $75

Add $50 for Lend-Lease models with British proofs.

GRADING - PPGS™	100%	98%	95%	90%	80%	70%	60%	LAST MSR

MODEL L42A – left-handed version of Model 42A with true left-handed aperture sight, walnut stock, 1 1/4 in. swivels. Mfg. 1937-1938.

$750 $600 $500 $400 $300 $200 $175

MODEL 43 – .22 S, L, or LR cal., target rifle, 7-round magazine, external trigger adjustment, 13/16 in. diameter barrel, 26 in. long walnut stock with four-position 1 1/4 in. swivels in front, Lyman 17A front sight, Lyman 57 MS receiver peep sight, rare. Mfg. 1937-38.

$350 $300 $250 $200 $175 $150 $135

Add $100 for 43S Model and $100 for 43SS Model.

MODEL L43 – left-handed version of Model 43 target rifle with left-handed Lyman 57 MS rear aperture sight, rare. Mfg. 1937-38.

$750 $600 $500 $400 $300 $225 $200

Add $100 for models with true left-handed Mossberg scope.

MODEL 43B – similar to Model 44B.

$350 $300 $250 $200 $175 $150 $135

MODEL 44B – .22 S, L, LR cal. target model, mag. fed, 26 in. heavy bbl., front ramp and No. 4 receiver aperture sights, four-position front swivels, walnut stock, 43 in. overall length, approx. 8 lbs. Mfg. 1938-41.

$350 $300 $250 $200 $185 $175 $150

MODEL 44US – .22 S, L, or LR cal. target model, 7 round magazine, bolt action, 26 in. heavy bbl., overall length 43 in., approx. 8 1/2 lbs., ramp front sight with hood, rear aperture sight, detachable swivels. Mfg. 1943-45.

$350 $275 $200 $165 $150 $135 $125

MODEL 44US (US PROPERTY MARKED) – used by all branches of military for target training, approx. 53,000 mfg. 1943-44.

$350 $300 $250 $175 $150 $125 $100

MODELS 44US(a), 44US(b), 44US(c), 44US(d) – same rifle as 44US with minor changes in sights and extractors. Mfg. 1944-49.

$300 $250 $200 $175 $150 $135 $125

MODEL 45 – .22 S, L, or LR cal., tube fed, bolt action, 24 in. heavy target bbl., hooded front, sporting barrel, and receiver aperture sights, overall length 42 1/2 in., approx. 6 3/4 lbs. Mfg. 1935-1937.

$250 $200 $150 $125 $100 $85 $65

MODEL 45-A – similar to Model 45 with newer, master action. Mfg. 1937-38.

$250 $200 $150 $135 $125 $100 $85

MODEL L45-A – similar to Model 45-A, true left-handed version. Mfg. 1937-1938.

$750 $500 $400 $300 $200 $150 $100

MODEL 46 – .22 S, L, or LR cal., tube fed, bolt action, 26 in. heavy bbl., overall 44 1/2 in., beavertail walnut stock, hooded ramp front, and rear aperture sight, 7 1/2 lbs. Mfg. 1935-1937.

$300 $250 $175 $135 $125 $100 $85

MODEL 46T – similar to Model 46 with heavier bbl. and stock. Mfg. 1936-37.

$500 $400 $350 $250 $200 $150 $100

MODEL 46A – similar to Model 46 with master action. Mfg. 1937-38.

$300 $200 $150 $135 $125 $100 $85

MODEL 46-ALS – similar to Model 46-A with Lyman 17A front and 57 MS rear aperture sights, rare. Mfg. 1937-1938.

$350 $300 $250 $225 $200 $175 $150

MODEL L46-ALS – similar to Model 46-ALS with true left-handed action and left-handed Lyman rear sight, very rare. Mfg. 1937-1938.

$750 $500 $400 $300 $225 $200 $175

GRADING - PPGS™	100%	98%	95%	90%	80%	70%	60%	LAST MSR

MODEL 46B – .22 S, L, or LR cal., tube fed, new streamlined design, 43 1/3 in. overall, walnut stock, 7 lbs. Mfg. 1938-45.

$250 $200 $150 $110 $100 $85 $75

MODEL 46B-T – heavy barrel and stock, target version of Model 46-B, rare. Mfg. 1938.

$450 $300 $250 $200 $150 $110 $95

MODEL 46M – .22 S, L, or LR cal., bolt action, tube fed, with two-piece Mannlicher-style walnut stock, 23 in. bbl., overall 40 in., hooded front, sporting bbl., and rear aperture sights, 7 lbs. Mfg. 1940-1945.

$350 $300 $250 $200 $150 $110 $95

MODELS 46M(a), 46M(b) – similar to Model 46M with minor changes in sights. Mfg. 1945-1952.

$350 $300 $250 $200 $150 $110 $95

MODEL 50 – .22 S, L, or LR cal., semi-auto, tube fed through buttstock, 24 in. bbl., overall 43 3/4 in., hooded front sight and open bbl. sights, no swivels, 6 3/4 lbs. Mfg. 1939-1942.

$250 $200 $150 $135 $125 $110 $85

MODEL 51 – similar to Model 50 with receiver aperture sight, heavier, beavertail stock, QD swivels, 7 1/4 lbs. Mfg. 1939.

$250 $200 $150 $125 $110 $85 $65

MODEL 51M – similar to Model 51 with two-piece Mannlicher style walnut stock, 20 in. bbl, 40 in. overall, front ramp, rear aperture, sporting bbl. sights, 7 lbs. Mfg. 1939-46.

$300 $250 $175 $150 $125 $110 $95

MODEL 140B – .22 S, L, or LR cal., bolt action, mag. fed, 24 1/2 in. bbl., 42 in. overall, walnut stock, front ramp, sporting bbl., and rear aperture sight, 5 3/4 lbs. Mfg. 1957-1958.

$200 $150 $135 $125 $110 $85 $65

MODEL 140K – similar to Model 140B with post front and no rear aperture sight. Mfg. 1955-1958.

$200 $150 $125 $80 $70 $60 $50

MODEL 142A – .22 S, L, or LR cal., bolt action, 7 round mag., carbine model with fold down forearm, walnut stock with sling, 18 in. bbl., 27 in. overall length, rear aperture sight and military front sight, no bbl. sight, early models had "T" shaped bolt handles and wood forearms, later models had round knob bolt handle and black plastic forearm, 5 lbs. Mfg. 1949-1957.

$300 $200 $150 $125 $110 $85 $65

MODEL 142K – similar to Model 142A with less expensive sporting barrel and post front type sights, no aperture sight. Mfg. 1953-1957.

$300 $200 $150 $100 $80 $75 $55

MODEL 144 – .22 S, L, or LR cal., full target rifle, heavy 26 in. bbl., 43 in. overall length, 8 lbs., QD swivels, four-position front swivels, rear aperture, front ramp sights, "T" shaped bolt handle. Mfg. 1949-1954.

$350 $250 $200 $165 $150 $135 $125

MODEL 144LS – similar to Model 144, with round knob handle, Lyman 57 MS rear aperture and 17A front sight. Mfg. 1954-60.

$350 $300 $275 $250 $200 $185 $165

MODEL 144LS-A – similar to Model 144LS, with Mossberg S 130 rear aperture in place of Lyman 57 MS sight. Mfg. 1960-1979.

$350 $275 $250 $225 $185 $165 $150

MODEL 144LS-B – last generation of 144 series, 27 in. bbl., 15/16 in. diameter, 44 in. overall length, new Mossberg S 331 aperture, Lyman 17A front sight, 8 1/2 lbs. Mfg. 1979-85.

$350 $275 $250 $210 $190 $175 $165

GRADING - PPGS™	100%	98%	95%	90%	80%	70%	60%	LAST MSR

MODEL 146-B – .22 S, L, or LR cal., bolt action, tube fed, capacity of 30S, 23L, 20LR, 26 in. bbl., overall length 43 1/4 in., ramp front, leaf bbl. and rear aperture sights, walnut Monte Carlo stock with cheekpiece, QD swivels, adj. trigger, Schnabel forend, 7 lbs. Mfg. 1949-1954.

$300	$250	$175	$125	$100	$85	$65	

MODEL 146B-A – similar to Model 146-B, with different bbl. sight. Mfg. 1954-58.

$300	$250	$175	$125	$100	$85	$65	

MODEL 151-K – .22 S, L, or LR cal., semi-auto, butt fed, 24 in. bbl., overall 44 in., open sights, walnut Monte Carlo stock with cheekpiece and Schnabel forend, 6 lbs. Mfg. 1950-51.

$250	$175	$135	$100	$80	$70	$60	

MODEL 151(M) – .22 S, L, or LR cal., semi-auto butt fed, capacity 15LR, 20 in. bbl., overall 40 in., two-piece Mannlicher-style walnut stock, QD swivels, steel buttplate, hooded ramp front, sporting rear, micro-click aperture sights, 7 lbs. Mfg. 1946-47.

$300	$250	$175	$135	$125	$100	$85	

MODELS 151M(a), 151M(b), 151M(c) – similar to Model 151M with minor changes in buttplate and sights. Mfg. 1947-58.

$300	$250	$175	$135	$125	$100	$85	

MODEL 152 – .22 S, L, or LR cal., semi-auto, mag. fed with 7 round capacity, carbine model with hinged, fold-down forend, Monte Carlo stock with adj. sling, 18 in. bbl., 27 in. overall, receiver aperture and military post front sights, 5 lbs. Mfg. 1948-1952.

$300	$200	$150	$125	$100	$85	$65	

MODEL 152K – similar to Model 152 with open sights. Mfg. 1950-57.

$200	$150	$110	$100	$90	$75	$50	

MODEL 320B – .22 S, L, or LR cal., single shot, junior target model, bolt action, new closed breech design, 24 in. bbl., overall 43 1/2 in., 5 3/4 lbs., walnut finish Monte Carlo stock with swivels and pistol grip, front ramp, rear aperture and sporting bbl. sights. Mfg. 1960-71.

$200	$150	$125	$110	$85	$75	$55	

MODELS 320K, 320K-A – similar to Model 320B with open sights, no swivels, later models marked 321, 321K. Mfg. 1960-80.

$200	$150	$100	$70	$60	$55	$50	

MODEL 333 – .22 LR cal., semi-auto, 20 in. barrel with full mag., checkered Monte Carlo pistol grip stock and forearm with sling swivels, blue finish, gold trigger, 6 1/4 lbs. Mfg. 1972 - disc.

$225	$175	$145	$125	$100	$85	$65	

MODELS 340B, 340B-A – .22 S, L, or LR cal., bolt action, 7 round magazine, 24 in. sporting barrel, 43 1/2 in. overall length, walnut, Monte Carlo stock with cheekpiece and pistol grip, front ramp, rear aperture sights, 6 1/2 lbs. Mfg. 1958-1980.

$200	$150	$125	$110	$85	$75	$55	

At least one example of a Model 340B smoothbore gun is known. This particular specimen was factory fitted with a stock that lacked a magazine cut-out, so the gun could only be fired as a single shot. The muzzle was not threaded to accept any sort of barrel adaptor.

MODELS 340K, 340K-A – similar to Model 340B with open sights, later models marked 341. Mfg. 1958-80.

$200	$150	$125	$100	$70	$60	$55	

MODEL 340M – .22 S, L, or LR cal. bolt action, mag. fed, same operating design as other 340 series, with one-piece, walnut Mannlicher-style Monte Carlo stock with pistol grip and swivels, 18 1/2 in. bbl., 38 1/2 in. overall, open rear and bead front sights, rare, 5 1/4 lbs. Mfg. 1970-72.

$650	$500	$350	$250	$185	$175	$165	

GRADING - PPGS™	100%	98%	95%	90%	80%	70%	60%	LAST MSR

MODEL 342 – .22 S, L, or LR cal., bolt action, mag. fed, carbine model with hinged, black plastic, fold-down forend, walnut Monte Carlo stock with swivels and sling, 18 in. bbl., 38 in. overall length, military post front and rear aperture sights, 5 lbs. Mfg. 1957-1959.

$300 $200 $150 $110 $85 $75 $55

MODELS 342K, 342K-A – similar to Model 342 with open sights. Mfg. 1958-71.

$200 $175 $150 $100 $75 $55 $50

MODELS 344, 344K – .22 S, L, or LR cal., bolt action, mag. fed, walnut finish, checkered stock, 344K is carbine length. Mfg. 1985.

$300 $200 $150 $125 $85 $75 $55

MODEL 346B – .22 S, L, or LR cal., bolt action tube feed, closed-breech design, walnut Monte Carlo stock with cheekpiece, QD swivels, capacity 25S, 20L, 18LR, 24 in. bbl., 42 1/2 in. overall length, rear aperture, sporting bbl., hooded front ramp sights, 6 1/2 lbs. Mfg. 1958-1960.

$300 $250 $200 $150 $125 $85 $75

MODELS 346K, 346K-A – similar to Model 346B w/open sights. Mfg. 1958-68.

$200 $175 $150 $125 $80 $70 $55

MODEL 350K – .22 LR cal., semi-auto, LR only, mag. fed, walnut Monte Carlo stock with pistol grip and cheekpiece, 23 1/2 in. bbl., overall length 43 1/2 in., open sights, 6 lbs. Mfg. 1958-1960.

$300 $200 $150 $125 $60 $50 $40

MODEL 350 K-A – similar to Model 350K with dovetail bbl. sight. Mfg. 1960-1968.

$300 $200 $150 $100 $60 $50 $40

MODEL 351K – .22 LR cal., semi-auto, tube fed through stock, walnut Monte Carlo stock with pistol grip, 24 in. bbl., 43 in. overall length, 6 lbs. Mfg. 1958-1960.

$300 $200 $150 $100 $60 $50 $40

MODEL 351K-A – similar to Model 351K with dovetail bbl. sight. Mfg. 1960-1968.

$300 $200 $150 $100 $60 $50 $40

MODEL 352 – .22 LR cal., mag. fed, carbine model with fold-down black plastic forend, walnut Monte Carlo stock, pistol grip, swivels, web strap, 18 in. bbl., overall length 38 in., rear peep, post front sights, 5 lbs. Mfg. 1957-1959.

$300 $200 $150 $100 $75 $65 $55

MODELS 352K, 352 K-A, 352K-B – similar to Model 352 with open sights. Mfg. 1960-71.

$200 $175 $150 $100 $70 $65 $55

MODEL 353 – similar to Model 352K-A, except has front ramp and open rear sights, w/o swivels, 5 lbs. Mfg. 1972-1985.

$300 $200 $150 $100 $70 $65 $55

MODEL 354 – similar to Model 353, except stock configuration was altered. Mfg. 1985 - disc.

$250 $200 $150 $100 $70 $65 $55

MODEL 377, "PLINKSTER" – .22 LR cal., semi-auto, tube fed, synthetic stock with thumbhole, capacity 15 rds., 20 in. bbl., overall length 40 in., 6 1/4 lbs., equipped with 4X scope. Mfg. 1977-1979.

$300 $250 $200 $150 $100 $85 $75

MODELS 380, 380S – same basic design as Model 377, only with solid wood stock, open sights. Model 480 same in 1985. Mfg. 1980-85.

$250 $200 $150 $100 $75 $65 $55

MODEL 400 "PALAMINO" – .22 S, L, and LR cal., lever action, tube fed, walnut, beavertail stock and forearm, crossbolt safety, 24 in. bbl., overall length, 41 in., bead front, open rear sights, 5 1/2 lbs. Mfg. 1959-64.

$350 $300 $250 $200 $150 $135 $100

Model 400-A similar to in specs and value, dovetail.

GRADING - PPGS™	100%	98%	95%	90%	80%	70%	60%	LAST MSR

MODEL 402 "PALAMINO" – carbine version of Model 400, 20 in. barrel. Mfg. 1961-71.

$350	$300	$250	$200	$150	$135	$100	

MODEL 430 – .22 LR cal., semi-auto, tubular mag. under bbl. with capacity of 18 LR, walnut checkered Monte Carlo stock and checkered forend, 24 in. bbl., overall length 43 1/2 in., open sights, 6 1/4 lbs. Mfg. 1970-1971.

$300	$250	$175	$100	$75	$65	$55	

MODEL 432 – similar to Model 430 with 20 in. bbl., straight grip, smooth stock and forend, walnut finish. Mfg. 1970-71.

$300	$250	$175	$100	$65	$60	$50	

MODEL 472 CARBINE – .30-30 Win. or .35 Rem. cal., lever action carbine, 20 in. barrel, open sights, pistol grip or straight stock, saddle ring on straight model. Mfg. 1972-disc.

$300	$250	$200	$150	$130	$120	$110	

MODEL 472 RIFLE – similar to Carbine, except 24 in. barrel, pistol grip stock. Mfg. 1974-76.

$300	$250	$200	$155	$145	$130	$120	

MODEL 472 BRUSH GUN – similar to Carbine, except 18 in. barrel, straight stock only. Mfg. 1974-76.

$300	$250	$200	$150	$130	$120	$100	

MODEL 472 ONE IN FIVE THOUSAND – similar to Brush Gun, except Indian scene etched on receiver, brass buttplate, saddle ring and barrel bands, select stock, only 5,000 mfg., 1974.

$700	$450	$300	$200	$165	$145	$120	

MODEL 479 PCA – .30-30 Win. cal., lever action, 20 in. barrel, 6 shot capacity.

$300	$250	$200	$150	$130	$120	$100	

MODEL 479 RR – limited edition "Roy Rogers" signature model, gold trigger, barrel bands, 5,000 total mfg. New 1983.

$700	$450	$300	$200	$165	$145	$120	

MODEL 479 – .30-30 Win. cal. only, lever action, 6 shot tube mag., 20 in. barrel with adj. sights, 7 lbs. Mfg. 1985 only.

$300	$250	$200	$160	$150	$145	$140	*$232*

MODEL 480 – similar to Models 380 and 380S.

$300	$250	$200	$150	$130	$120	$100	

MODEL 620K – .22 WMR cal., single shot, bolt action, walnut Monte Carlo stock, pistol grip, cheekpiece, sling swivels, 24 in. bbl., overall 44 3/4 in., open rear, post front sights, 6 lbs. Mfg. 1959-60.

$250	$200	$150	$115	$100	$85	$75	

MODEL 620K-A – similar to Model 620K with change in bbl. sight. Mfg. 1960-68.

$250	$200	$150	$115	$100	$85	$75	

MODELS 640K, 640K-S – similar to 620 series, but 5 shot mag. repeater. Mfg. 1959-84.

$300	$250	$200	$150	$125	$105	$90	

MODEL 640KS – similar to Model 640K with deluxe checkered stock and gold trigger. Mfg. 1960-68.

$300	$250	$200	$150	$135	$120	$110	

MODEL 640M – full length, Mannlicher-styled stock, version of 640, checkered Monte Carlo cheekpiece, pistol grip, swivels and leather strap, heavy receiver, jeweled bolt, 20 in. bbl., overall 40 3/4 in., open rear and bead front sights, 6 lbs. Mfg. 1971.

$650	$500	$400	$300	$200	$165	$150	

MODEL 642K – .22 WMR cal., carbine style, bolt action, 5 rd. mag., fold-down forend, walnut stock with web sling, 18 in. bbl., overall 38 1/4 in., open bbl. and bead front sights, 5 lbs. Mfg. 1960-1968.

$400	$350	$300	$250	$200	$150	$125	

GRADING - PPGS™	100%	98%	95%	90%	80%	70%	60%	LAST MSR

MODEL 800A/B/C/F – .222 Rem. (800F), .22-250 Rem. (800C), .243 Win. (800B), or .308 Win. (800A) cal., bolt action, 22 in. barrel, folding sight, checkered pistol grip stock. Mfg. 1967-disc.

	$500	$400	$325	$300	$275	$225	$150	

MODEL 800VT – similar to 800, except .222 Rem., .22-250 Rem., or .243 Win. cal., 24 in. heavy barrel, no sights. Mfg. 1968-disc.

	$500	$400	$325	$300	$275	$225	$150	

MODEL 800D – 6.5mm Mag., .22-250 Rem., .243 Rem., or .308 Win. cal., similar to 800, with roll-over combination and cheekpiece, checkered stock with rosewood forearm tip and pistol cap, no .222 Rem. available. Mfg. 1970 only.

	$500	$400	$325	$300	$275	$225	$150	

MODEL 800E – .350 Rem. Mag. cal., 4 shot mag., approx. 53 mfg. 1970 only.

	$850	$775	$700	$625	$550	$500	$450	

MODEL 800M – .22-250, .243 Win., or .308 Win. cal., similar to 800, except 20 in. barrel, full length stock, spoon bolt handle. Mfg. 1969-1972.

	$750	$500	$400	$300	$200	$160	$145	

MODEL 810 – .270 Win., .30-06, 6.5mm Rem. Mag., or .338 Win. Mag. cal., bolt action, 22 or 24 in. barrel, rear leaf sight, checkered Monte Carlo stock. Mfg. 1970-disc.

	$500	$400	$325	$300	$275	$225	$150	

MODEL 1500 MOUNTAINEER GRADE I – .223 Rem., .243 Win., .270 Win., .30-06, or 7mm Rem. Mag. cal., bolt action, 22 or 24 (7mm Rem. Mag. only) in. barrel, 5 or 6 shot mag., available with or without sights, hardwood stock is satin finished, blued finish, about 7 lbs. 10 oz. Imported 1986-87 only.

	$325	$275	$240	$195	$180	$165	$150	*$335*

Add $15 for 7mm Rem. Mag. cal., $25 for iron sights.

In 1985, Mossberg purchased the parts inventory and importing rights for those Model 1500 rifles that Smith & Wesson imported from Howa of Japan. These models were identical to those models which S&W disc.

* ***Model 1500 Mountaineer Grade I Varmint*** – .22-250 Rem., .223 Rem., or .308 Win. cal., similar to Model 1500 Grade I, except has 24 in. heavy barrel only, Monte Carlo stock. Imported 1986-87 only.

	$385	$325	$300	$250	$205	$190	$175	*$457*

Add $10 for parkerized finish (oil finished stock with swivels - not available in .22-250 Rem. cal.).

Blue finish and high gloss wood finish available with .22-250 Rem. or .223 Rem. cal. only. Parkerized variation is available in .223 Rem. or .308 Win. cal. only (matte wood finish, includes swivels).

MODEL 1500 MOUNTAINEER GRADE II – similar to Grade I Mountaineer, except has select checkered American walnut stock. Also available in .300 Win. Mag. or .338 Win. Mag. cal. Imported 1986-87 only.

	$350	$295	$260	$205	$190	$175	$160	*$368*

Add $15 for Mag. cals.
Add $25 for iron sights.

MODEL 1550 – similar to Model 1500, except has detachable mag. and available in standard cals. (.243 Win., .270 Win., or .30-06), with or without sights. Imported 1986-87 only.

	$365	$305	$275	$225	$190	$175	$160	*$391*

Add $24 for iron sights.

MODEL 1700 LS – .243 Win., .270 Win., or .30-06 cal., no sights, jeweled bolt body and knurled bolt handle, detachable mag., Schnabel forend, deluxe checkering, 7 lbs. Imported 1986-87 only.

	$450	$400	$350	$275	$225	$200	$190	*$492*

Mossberg "Targo" Smoothbore Models

These dual-purpose smoothbore rifles were designed to fire both .22 RF bullets and shotshell ammunition. Targo barrels are threaded either externally (Models 26T, 42TR, 42T, B42T)

GRADING - PPGS™	100%	98%	95%	90%	80%	70%	60%	LAST MSR

or internally (Models 320TR, 340TR) at the muzzle for attachment of rifled and smoothbore adapters which enable the shooter to use the gun as a standard rifle, or (with the smoothbore adapter installed) as a miniature shotgun. Mossberg produced a line of Targo accessories including a barrel-mounted miniature clay target launcher, a pistol grip hand trap frame, a hand thrower (three known variations), a target carrier, clay targets, hard rubber "practice" targets, and a target catching net. The presence of one or more of these accessories augments the value of any model Targo gun. Prices quoted are for guns with all listed features exclusive of Targo accessories.

MODEL 26-T SINGLE SHOT – .22 RF/shotshell cal., bolt action, thumb lever safety located at rear of bolt, black plastic buttplate and contoured black plastic trigger guard (#R413), rifle-style open rear sight with screw adjustments for windage and elevation, shotgun style elevated front bead sight with removable sight hood, smoothbore and rifled screw-on barrel adapters and spanner wrench for adapter removal and installation, stock generally provided with sling swivels, forend necks down toward muzzle, takedown screw has retaining bail to facilitate removal by hand. Mfg. 1940-42 (only 873 mfg.).

$600 $450 $375 $335 $280 $245 $220

100% price is estimated since an example would be extremely rare.

MODEL 42T BOLT ACTION REPEATER – .22 RF/shotshell cal., box magazine (7- round) fitted with adapter screw to enable firing of .22 Short cartridges, same safety, buttplate, optional stock swivels, and shotgun style front sight as Model 26T, #R145 contoured black plastic trigger guard, supplied with the smoothbore barrel adapter only (rifled adapter, open rear sight, and front sight hood were not provided), produced 1940-42 (906 guns made), examples in 95% or better condition are uncommon.

$500 $325 $310 $295 $260 $235 $200

MODEL 42TR BOLT ACTION REPEATER – .22 RF/shotshell cal., produced before and after WWII until roughly 1949. Pre-war (1940-42) guns identical to Model 42T except rifled adapter, open rear sight, and front sight hood were provided, and no stock swivels. The earliest pre-war 42TRs were marked using a 42T barrel stamp and a separate "R" (stamped to the right of the "T"). Post-war (1946-49) guns have slotted takedown screw, magazine plate, shorter unnecked forend, and (frequently) a blue bolt knob. The most common of all Targo guns. A total of 6,577 guns were produced during the period 1940-42 (post-war production figures are not available). Both early and late versions of this model are comparably priced.

$650 $400 $325 $280 $245 $190 $175

Add $250 for cased gun with clay targets and Targo accessories.
Cased Targo guns with all accessories have been seen for $1,000+.

Note: A very small number of 42TRs were supplied with fitted cases and Targo accessories and may have been used as dealer displays. Several variations in the internal compartmentalization of these cases have been noted. The pre-war 42TR display guns came in a hard (plywood) luggage case. The post-war guns were supplied in a semi-hard (fiberboard) luggage case.

MODEL B42T BOLT ACTION REPEATER – .22 RF/shotshell cal., identical to the Model 42TR, except stock has sling swivels and metal buttplate with trapdoor for magazine storage. Gun was supplied with extended 15-round box magazine in addition to the standard 7-round mag. A comparatively scarce model marketed exclusively through mail order stores (e.g., Spiegel) in the early 1940s. According to factory records, only 250 guns were made, all in 1940.

$600 $465 $385 $350 $325 $285 $250

The 15 round magazine originally supplied with this model is scarce - good specimens are currently selling for approx. $85-$120 (may exceed legal capacity limits, depending on state).

MODEL 320TR SINGLE SHOT BOLT ACTION – .22 RF/shotshell, automatic safety with thumb lever located on right side of receiver, black plastic buttplate and contoured black plastic trigger guard. Rifle-style ("U" notch) rear sight adjustable for elevation (via sliding wedge) and windage (by deflecting sight arm laterally by hand). Sporting type vertical blade front sight. Gun supplied with rifled and smoothbore screw-in barrel adapters. A wire target carrier and a hand thrower for launching miniature clay targets were included with each gun. Limited mfg. 1961-62.

$500 $300 $275 $190 $150 $135 $115

Factory records indicate that only 962 guns were sold during the production period.

GRADING - PPGS™	100%	98%	95%	90%	80%	70%	60%	LAST MSR

MODEL 340TR BOLT ACTION REPEATER – .22 RF/shotshell cal., 7-round box magazine featuring adjustable top bar to accommodate feeding of .22 S, L, or LR cartridges. Two known variations of thumb lever safety markings (words "OFF"/"ON" and red dot). Other features identical to Model 320TR. Limited mfg. 1961-62.

	$500	$300	$275	$215	$165	$145	$125	

Factory records indicate that only 2,026 guns were sold during the production period.

RIFLES: BOLT ACTION, CURRENT PRODUCTION

4x4 RIFLE – .22-250 Rem. (new 2011), .25-06 Rem., .243 Win. (new 2011), .270 Win., .30-06, .270 WSM (new 2010), 7mm-08 Rem., 7mm WSM (new 2010), 7mm Rem. Mag. (disc. 2012), .300 Win. Mag., .300 WSM (new 2010), .308 Win. (new 2011), or .338 Win. Mag. cal., short or long action, 22 in. non-fluted or 24 in. fluted barrel with muzzle brake became standard in 2010, long action with 24 in. fluted barrel and no muzzlebrake became available during mid-2011, 4 or 5 shot detachable box mag., matte blue or Marinecote finish, sculpted walnut, Monte Carlo grey or brown laminate (Marinecote only), black Classic (new 2010), skeletonized synthetic, or Classic (new 2009) stock, vent. forearm, Weaver style scope base, rifle sights (.30-06, .300 Win. Mag., or .338 Win. Mag. only), 6.7 - 7.8 lbs. New 2007.

MSR $485	$415	$375	$325	$300	$250	$225	$195	

Add $208 for laminate or $158 for walnut stock.
Add $158 for WSM cals.
Add $49 for Marinecote finish.
Add $186 for 22 in. non-fluted barrel (select cals. only).
Add $49 for scope package (3-9x40mm, not available in .25-06 or .338 Win. mag. cal).

In 2009, a LBA (lightning bolt action) adjustable trigger became standard.

ATR (ALL TERRAIN RIFLE/MODEL 100) – .243 Win. (new 2006), .270 Win., .30-06, 7mm-08 Rem. (new 2011), or .308 Win. (new 2006) cal., 22 in. free floating non-fluted or fluted (new 2010) barrel, short or long action, matte blue or Marinecote (.270 Win. or .30-06), walnut (new 2006), black synthetic, Dura-Wood synthetic (disc. 2009) or 100% Realtree AP (disc. 2012), Realtree Xtra (new 2013), Mossy Oak Brush, Mossy Oak Break Up Infinity (new 2011), or Mossy Oak New Break-Up camo coverage stock with recoil pad, 3 shot top loading magazine, approx. 7 lbs. New 2005.

MSR $366	$310	$275	$235	$210	$175	$140	$110	

Add $50 for walnut or camo stock.
Add $38 for Dura-Wood synthetic stock (long action only, disc. 2009).
Add $47 for Marinecote (long action only, disc. 2011).
Add $38 for rifle sights and 22. in. non-fluted barrel (new 2007).
Add $38 for 3-9x40mm scope (new 2006).
Add $110 for Deer Thug Model with Mossy Oak Break Up Infinity camo, sling, fluted barrel, scope and engraved stock.

In 2009, a LBA (lightning bolt action) adjustable trigger became standard.

* ***ATR Bantam/Super Bantam (Model 100)*** – .243 Win., 7mm-08 Rem., .308 Win. cal., short action, 20 in. barrel, 5 shot, Weaver type base, matte blue metal, choice of black synthetic (Super Bantam) or walnut (Bantam) stock and forearm, Super Bantam has adj. 12-13 in. LOP, Bantam has fixed 12 in. LOP, 6 1/2 - 7 3/4 lbs. New 2007.

MSR $366	$310	$275	$235	$210	$175	$140	$110	

Add $38 for 3-9x40mm scope (Super Bantam only).
Add $50 for walnut stock.

* ***Model 100 ATR Night Train Special*** – .308 Win. cal., 22 in. fluted barrel, short action, matte blue, Multi Cam camo (new 2013), or digital green camo finish, synthetic stock, Picatinny rail, top load magazine, adj. LBA trigger, available with 4-16x50mm scope w/sun shade, flip open lens protector and bipod, or Barska 6-24x60mm illuminated reticle scope and Harris bipod. New 2010.

MSR $606	$510	$450	$385	$325	$295	$275	$250	

Add $267 for Barska scope and Harris bipod (Night Train 2 or IV).
Add $39 for 4-16x50mm scope, bipod, and digital green camo (Night Train III).

GRADING - PPGS™	100%	98%	95%	90%	80%	70%	60%	LAST MSR

MODEL 801 HALF-PINT PLINKSTER – .22 LR cal., 16 in. free floating tapered barrel, 12 1/4 LOP, single shot, crossbolt safety, adj. rifle sights, pistol grip uncheckered hardwood stock, 4 lbs.

MSR $216	$175	$150	$125	$110	$90	$75	$60

MODEL 802 PLINKSTER – .22 LR cal., 18 or 21 in. barrel with adj. iron sights, aluminum alloy receiver, blue or brushed chrome (new 2007) finish, wood, black or pink marble synthetic stock with (disc. 2012) or w/o thumbhole, Sport Grip skeletonized stock became optional mid-2012, 10 shot mag., approx. 4 lbs. New 2006.

MSR $176	$150	$125	$100	$95	$75	$65	$50

Add $8 for 4x scope (disc. 2012).
Add $19 for brushed chrome finish (new 2007).
Add $40 for Varmint model, wood stock, pink, or thumbhole stock with fold down forend (disc. 2012, black synthetic stock only).

* ***Model 802 Bantam Plinkster*** – .22 LR cal., 18 in. barrel with adj. iron sights, aluminum alloy receiver, blue or brushed chrome (mfg. 2010-2012) finish, black or pink marble synthetic stock with (mfg. 2010-2013) or w/o thumbhole, Sports Grip skeletonized stock became optional mid-2012, 10 shot mag., with or w/o Roadblocker muzzle brake (mfg. 2010-2012), scope became standard 2013, approx. 4 lbs.

MSR $184	$150	$125	$100	$95	$75	$65	$50

Add $32 for Sports Grip skeletonized stock (new 2013).
Add $38 for pink or thumbhole stock (disc. 2012).
Add $19 for brushed chrome finish (thumbhole stock only, disc. 2012).
Add $124 for Roadblocker muzzle brake (disc. 2012).

MODEL 817 – .17 HMR cal., similar to 802 Plinkster, except not available in 18 in. barrel, and 5 shot mag., black synthetic, wood, thumbhole (tip-down forend became standard with thumbhole during 2009, disc. 2012) or Sports Grip skeletonized (new mid-2012) stock, approx. 4 1/2 - 5 lbs. New 2007.

MSR $205	$175	$145	$125	$110	$90	$70	$55

Add $40 for wood or thumbhole stock.
Add $15 for brushed chrome finish (new 2007).
Add $40 for Varmint model.
Add $82 for Roadblocker muzzle brake (mfg. 2010-2012).
Add $14 for 3-9x40mm scope or $55 for 3-16x50mm scope with bipod (with Roadblocker muzzle brake only, mfg. 2010-2012).

MVP (MOSSBERG VARMINT PREDATOR) – .223 Rem. or 7.62 NATO (new 2013) cal., 18 1/2 (Predator, new 2013), 20 (Predator, new 2013), or 24 (Varmint only) in. button rifled fluted medium bull or sporter (new 2013) barrel, with or w/o threading, 5 or 10 shot mag., grey laminate benchrest stock with ergonomic pistol grip and palm swell, sling swivels, Weaver style base, LBA trigger system, approx. 7 1/2 lbs. New mid-2011.

MSR $681	$575	$500	$425	$395	$315	$285	$260

Add $21 for Varmint model.
Add $48 for 3-9x40mm scope w/rings (new 2013).
Add $159 for combo package with 4-16x50mm scope and bipod.

MVP PATROL – 5.56mm, 7.62 NATO, or .300 ACC Blackout cal., 16 1/4 in. medium bull threaded or non-threaded barrel, matte blue finish, black synthetic stock, 10 shot mag., no sights or rifle sights, 6 3/4 - 7 1/2 lbs. New 2013.

MSR $681	$575	$500	$425	$395	$315	$285	$260

Add $17 for threaded barrel.
Add $132 for 3-9x32mm lighted recticle scope.

MVP FLEX – 5.56mm or 7.62 NATO cal., 18 1/2 or 20 in. threaded or non-threaded sporter or medium bull barrel, 10 shot mag., matte blue finish, six position tactical Flex stock. New 2013.

MSR $928	$785	$675	$595	$535	$425	$350	$275

Add $21 for threaded barrel.
Add $170 for 3-9x32mm lighted reticle scope.

This model is also available in a youth configuration (12 in. LOP) at no extra charge.

GRADING - PPGS™	100%	98%	95%	90%	80%	70%	60%	LAST MSR

MVP THUNDER RANCH – 5.56 NATO cal., 18 1/2 in. medium bull threaded barrel, 10 shot mag., olive drab or matte blue finish, wood stock. New 2013.

MSR $934	$795	$695	$595	$550	$425	$350	$275	

RIFLES: LEVER ACTION

MODEL SSi-ONE INTERCHANGEABLE RIFLE/SHOTGUN – .22-250 Rem., .223 Rem., .243 Win., .270 Win., .30-06, or .308 Win. cal., also available in 12 ga., design allows interchangeable rifle/shotgun barrels, single shot, satin finished or Mossy Oak Breakup camo (new 2003, available in shotgun configuration only) checkered walnut stock and forearm, matte blue metal, 24 in. regular or heavy (.22-250 Rem. or .223 Rem. cal.) rifle barrel with ejector or 12 ga. (3 in. chamber with rifled bore for Slug, 3 1/2 in. chamber for Turkey) ported barrel, break open action, cocking indicator, drilled and tapped integral scope base, automatic safety, approx. 8 (regular) or 10 (heavy) lbs. Mfg. 2001-2004.

	$400	$350	$300	$270	$220	$180	$140	*$483*

Add $240 per interchangeable rifle barrel and $298 for SSi-One Slug Model barrel.
Add $55 for Mossy Oak Breakup stock and forearm (Turkey Model) or $77 for Mossy Oak Breakup stock and forearm (Slug Model).
Add $22 for heavy bull barrel or 12 ga. Slug (fully rifled bore) variation.

MODEL 464 – .22 LR (new mid-2009) or .30-30 Win. cal., 18 (.22 LR cal.) or 20 (.30-30 Win. cal.) in. blue barrel, 7 or 14 shot tube mag., top tang safety, uncheckered straight or pistol grip hardwood stock, drilled and tapped, side ejection, rubber buttpad, 5.6 - 6.7 lbs. New mid-2008.

MSR $497	$425	$375	$325	$295	$235	$190	$150	

Add $38 for Marinecote finish with pistol grip stock.
Add $38 for pistol grip (.30-30 Win. cal. only).
Subtract $29 for .22 LR cal. with 18 in. barrel.

MODEL 464 SPX – .22 LR or .30-30 Win. cal., 16 1/4 or 18 1/2 in. barrel, 6 (.30-30 Win. cal.) or 14 shot mag., matte black finish, six position adj. tactical stock with elevated comb, tri-rail forearm with ladder rail covers, rifle sights, 6 (.22 LR cal.) or 7 (.30-30 Win. cal.) lbs. New 2012.

MSR $497	$415	$360	$315	$285	$235	$190	$150	

Add $7 for muzzle brake.
Add $38 for 16 1/4 in. barrel with flash supressor.
Add $30 for 16 1/4 in. barrel in .30-30 Win. cal.

MODEL 464 ZMB – .30-30 Win. cal., 6 shot mag., compact 16 1/4 in. barrel with removable A2 flash suppressor, matte blue finish, six position adj. tactical stock, tri-rail forend with rail covers, 3-dot adj. fiber optic or rifle sights, drilled and tapped, sling swivel studs, 7 lbs. New 2012.

MSR $563	$465	$395	$345	$300	$250	$210	$175	

RIFLES: SEMI-AUTO

IMPORTANT NOTE: On model(s) where *N/A has replaced the normal 100% value, it indicates current market conditions are too unstable to accurately ascertain 100%-60% values. Factory retail prices (MSRs) reflect most recent updates. For more up-to-date information on current pricing trends and additional useful information, please visit www.bluebookofgunvalues.com, select "Information & Services" from the menu, and click on "Additional Book Information".

MODEL 702 PLINKSTER – .22 LR cal., 18 or 21 (chrome finish only) in. barrel with open sights, blue or brushed chrome metal finish, choice of wood, black or pink synthetic, Mossy Oak New Break-Up (disc. 2011) or Mossy Oak Break-Up Infinity (new 2012) camo, tiger maple Dura-Wood, pink, pink marbled, carbon fiber (disc. 2011) synthetic, or thumbhole synthetic stock, 10 or 25 (new 2013) detachable shot mag., aluminum alloy receiver, crossbolt safety, approx. 4 lbs. New 2006.

MSR $183	$155	$125	$110	$100	$80	$65	$50	

Add $1 for scope (available in Bantam configuration also).
Add $38 for any stock except synthetic.
Add $12 for chrome finish (21 in. barrel only).

GRADING - PPGS™	100%	98%	95%	90%	80%	70%	60%	LAST MSR

Add $33 for synthetic thumbhole stock with tip-down forend.
Add $109 for Roadblocker muzzle brake (mfg. 2010-2011).
Subtract $7 for Bantam configuration.

MODEL 715T TACTICAL CARRY – .22 LR cal., AR-15 style, 18 in. barrel, matte black finish, 10 or 25 shot mag., synthetic fixed or six-position adj. stock, front post sight, adj. rifle sights, Picatinny quad-rail forend, handle mounted top rail, acessory mag. loader, integrated A2 style carry handle, 5 1/4 lbs. New 2011.

MSR $298	$250	$215	$175	$150	$125	$100	$95

MODEL 715T FLAT-TOP – .22 LR cal., 16 1/4 in. barrel, similar to Model 715T Tactical Carry, except has flat-top with full length top rail, optional red dot sights, A2 style muzzle brake and is also available in Mossy Oak Brush camo, 5 1/2 - 5 3/4 lbs. New 2012.

MSR $355	$295	$255	$230	$200	$175	$150	$125

Add $9 for removable A2 style Picatinny mounted front and rear sights.
Add $66 for Mossy Oak Brush camo finish.

MMR HUNTER – .223 Rem. cal., 20 in. carbon steel barrel with black phosphate metal finish, 5 shot mag., anodized aluminum receiver, A2 black synthetic stock, Mossy Oak Treestand or Mossy Oak Brush camo finish, no sights, 7 1/2 lbs. New mid-2011.

MSR $978	*N/A	$700	$600	$500	$400	$350	$300

Add $94 for camo.

MMR TACTICAL – .223 Rem. cal., 16 1/4 in. carbon steel barrel with black phosphate metal finish, 10 or 30 shot mag., anodized aluminum receiver, black synthetic fixed or six-position collapsible stock, A2 style muzzle brake, no sights or removable Picatinny rail, Stark SE-1 deluxe pistol grip, quad rail forend, approx. 7 - 7 1/2 lbs. New mid 2011.

MSR $940	*N/A	$675	$575	$475	$400	$350	$300

Add $38 for Picatinny rail.

SHOTGUNS: BOLT ACTION - DISC.

MODELS G-4, 70, 73, 73B – .410 bore, single shot, mfg. 1932-40.

$150	$100	$85	$70	$60	$50	$40

MODELS 80, 83, 83B, 83D – .410 bore, 3 or 4 shot, internal top-loading mag., mfg. 1933-46.

$150	$110	$95	$75	$60	$50	$40

MODELS 75, 75A, 75B – 20 ga., bolt action, single shot, mfg. 1933-40.

$150	$100	$85	$70	$60	$50	$40

MODELS 85, 85A, 85B, 85D – 20 ga., 2 or 3 shot mag., mfg. 1934-40.

$150	$100	$85	$70	$60	$50	$40

MODELS 173, 173A, 173Y – .410 bore, single shot, "Y" designates youth model, mfg. 1957-73.

$150	$100	$85	$70	$60	$50	$40

MODELS 183, 183D, 283D(a), 183D-B, 183D-C, 183D-D, 183D-E, 183D-F, 183K, 183K-B, 183K-C, 183T, 184T, 184TY, 283T, 284T, 284TY – .410 bore, bolt action shotgun, 2 or 3 shot mag., various screw-on or C-Lect choke on some models, mfg. 1948-1985.

$175	$150	$135	$110	$95	$85	$75

MODELS 185, 185D, 185D-A, 185D-B, 185D-C, 185K, 185K-A, 185K-B – 20 ga., 2 shot 2 3/4 in. mag., various screw-on or C-Lect chokes, mfg. 1947-59.

$175	$150	$135	$110	$95	$85	$75

MODELS 190, 190D, 190D-A, 190K-A, 190K-B – 16 ga., bolt action, 2 shot 2 3/4 in. mag., various screw-on or C-Lect choke, mfg. 1955-58.

$175	$150	$135	$110	$95	$85	$75

MODELS 195, 195A, 195K-A, 195D – same as model 185 Series, only 12 ga. version, mfg. 1954-68.

$175	$150	$135	$110	$95	$85	$75

GRADING - PPGS™	100%	98%	95%	90%	80%	70%	60%	LAST MSR

MODELS 385, 385K, 385KA, 385T, 485A, 485B – 20 ga., bolt action, 3 in. chamber, detachable box mag., mfg. 1960-86.

	$175	$150	$135	$110	$95	$85	$75	

MODELS 390, 390K-A, 390K-B, 490A – 16 ga., 3 in. chamber, detachable box mag., mfg. 1971-76.

	$175	$150	$135	$110	$95	$85	$75	

MODELS 395, 395K, 395KA, 395S, 395 SPL., 495A, 495B – 12 ga., 3 in. chamber, detachable box mag., mfg. 1963-83.

	$175	$150	$135	$110	$95	$85	$75	

Add $40 for slug barrel ("S" designation) or 38 in. barrel (Spl.).

MODELS 595, 595K – 12 ga., bolt action, special police stock, 4 shot mag., mfg. 1983-85.

	$175	$150	$135	$110	$95	$85	$75	

Add $40 for 38 in. barrel (Spl.).

MODEL 695 BOLT ACTION – 12 ga. only, with detachable 2 shot mag., 3 in. chamber, 22 in. barrel with fully rifled and ported (new 1999) or Accu-choke (disc. 1998) barrel, black synthetic or Woodlands camo (with bead sights, disc. 2001) on stock and forearm, rifle or Truglo fiberoptic sights, 7 1/2 lbs. Mfg. 1996-2002.

	$275	$220	$185	$150	$135	$120	$115	*$345*

Subtract approx. $50 for Accu-choke barrel.

Add $22 for Truglo fiberoptic sights (new 1998).

Add $52 for Truglo fiberoptic sights and Woodlands camo finish (disc. 2001).

SHOTGUNS: O/U, RECENT PRODUCTION

SILVER RESERVE FIELD – 12, 20, 28 ga., or .410 bore, boxlock action with dual locking lugs, 26 or 28 in. barrels with extractors, features detailed gold inlaid game scenes engraved on silver receiver, ST, Sporting models (12 ga. only) have ported barrels with 10mm rib, wide rib, scroll engraving on silver or blue receiver, Bantam Model has 26 in. barrels and short LOP, mfg. by Khan in Turkey, 6 - 7.7 lbs. Mfg. 2005-2012.

	$595	$500	$450	$395	$360	$330	$295	*$693*

Add $349 for 12/20 ga. combo (new 2007).

SILVER RESERVE SPORTING – 12 ga. only, 3 in. chambers, 28 in. ported VR barrel with 10mm rib and front/mid bead sights, blue receiver with scroll engraving, checkered walnut stock and forearm, SST, extractors, five interchangeable choke tubes, 7.7 lbs. Disc. 2012.

	$750	$675	$575	$500	$450	$400	$365	*$851*

ONYX RESERVE SPORTING – 12 ga. only, 2 3/4 or 3 in. chambers, 28 in. ported VR barrel with 10mm rib and front/mid bead sights, 5 chokes, blue receiver with scroll engraving, checkered walnut stock and forearm. Mfg. 2010-2012.

	$750	$675	$575	$500	$450	$400	$365	*$851*

SILVER RESERVE II FIELD – 12. 20, 28 ga. or .410 bore, 2 3/4 or 3 in. chambers, 26 or 28 in. barrels with chokes, extractors or ejectors, blue finish, front bead sight, silver receiver with scroll engraving, satin finished select black walnut stock. New mid-2012.

MSR $714	$600	$525	$450	$410	$325	$275	$210	

Add $85 for ejectors.

Add $360 for 12/20 ga. 2-barrel set.

SILVER RESERVE II SPORT – 12 ga., 26 in. ported barrels, vent. rib, extended Skeet chokes, blue finish, front and mid-bead sights, silver receiver with scroll engraving, walnut stock and forearm, extractors or ejectors. New mid-2012.

MSR $877	$750	$650	$575	$500	$415	$340	$265	

Add $112 for ejectors.

SILVER RESERVE II SUPER SPORT – 12 ga., 3o or 32 in. ported barrels with extra wide high rib and 5 extended Skeet chokes, blue finish, dual bead sights, silver receiver with scroll engraving, satin finished select black walnut stock with or w/o adj. comb. New mid-2012.

MSR $1,075	$915	$800	$685	$625	$500	$410	$325	

Add $105 for adj. comb.

GRADING - PPGS™	100%	98%	95%	90%	80%	70%	60%	LAST MSR

SHOTGUNS: SxS, RECENT PRODUCTION

SILVER RESERVE FIELD – 12, 20, 28 ga., or .410 bore (limited mfg.), 3 in. chambers, boxlock action, 26 or 28 in. VR barrels, SST, silver or blue receiver with scroll engraving, checkered black walnut stock and forearm with pistol grip, ambidextrous thumb safety, dual locking lugs, chrome plated chambers and bores, extractors, Sporting models (12 ga. only, disc. 2008) have ported barrels with 10mm rib, wide rib, Bantam model has 26 in. barrels and short LOP, 6 1/2 - 7.2 lbs. Mfg. 2008-2012.

	$850	$775	$635	$525	$425	$375	$325	*$1,005*

Add $140 for Sporting Model (disc. 2008).
Add $311 for 12/20 or 20/28 ga. combo (disc. 2008).

ONYX RESERVE SPORTING – 12 ga., similar to Silver Reserve Sporting Model, except has onyx colored metal finish. Disc. 2012.

	$850	$775	$635	$525	$425	$375	$325	*$1,005*

SILVER RESERVE II FIELD – 12 or 20 ga., 26 or 28 in. barrels with standard 5 choke set, blue finish, silver receiver with scroll engraving, satin finished select black walnut stock and forearm. New mid-2012.

MSR $1,035	$875	$765	$650	$595	$475	$395	$300	

SHOTGUNS: SEMI-AUTO & SLIDE ACTION, RECENT PRODUCTION

In 1985, Mossberg purchased the parts inventory and manufacturing rights for the shotguns that Smith & Wesson discontinued in 1984. These 1000 and 3000 Series models (manufactured in Japan) are identical to those models which S&W discontinued. Parts and warranties are not interchangeable.

Beginning 1989, all Mossbergs sold in the U.S. and Canada have been provided with a Cablelock which goes through the ejection port, making the gun's action inoperable.

To celebrate its 75th anniversary, Mossberg released a new Crown Grade variation within most models during 1994, including the slide action 500 and 835 Series. These can be differentiated from previous manufacture by cut checkering, redesigned walnut or American hardwood stocks and forearms, screw-in choke tubes, and 4 different camo patterns. The Crown Grade was discontinued in 2000.

In 2013, Mossberg manufactured its 10 millionth Mossberg 500 model.

MODEL 200K SLIDE ACTION – slide action shotgun, 12 ga., 28 in., select choke, plain pistol grip stock, black nylon slide handle. Mfg. 1955-59.

	$275	$220	$185	$170	$135	$110	$85	

MODEL 200D – similar to 200K, except interchangeable choke tubes (2). Mfg. 1955-59.

	$275	$220	$185	$170	$135	$110	$85	

MODEL 500 SLIDE ACTION FIELD (1962-1998 MFG.) – 12, 20 ga., or .410 bore, slide action, 24 in. (with rifle sights) or 20-28 in. barrel (with various chokes), upper receiver slide safety, C-Lect (disc.) & Accu-choke (became standard 1994) choke system, checkered hardwood pistol grip stock after 1973. Mfg. 1962-98.

	$250	$220	$185	$170	$135	$110	$85	*$309*

Subtract 10% if without VR (disc.).
Subtract 10% for fixed choke barrel in 12 or 20 ga.

For recent Model 500 information and values, please refer to Model 500 Field - Current Mfg. later in this section.

* ***Model 500 Slide Action Field Slugster*** – 12, 16, or 20 (disc. 1997) ga., 24 in. cyl. (disc. 1997) or rifled bore (became standard 1998) barrel, barrel porting became standard in 1998, choice of sights, walnut finished hardwood stock and forearm. Disc. 1998.

	$270	$235	$200	$185	$150	$120	$95	*$336*

Subtract $75 if w/o barrel porting or rifled bore.

* ***Model 500 Slide Action Field Bantam*** – 20 ga. or .410 bore (new 1991) only, 22 in. (20 ga.), 24 in. fixed choke barrel (.410 bore), or 26 in. VR barrel with Accu-choke(s), blue or

GRADING - PPGS™	100%	98%	95%	90%	80%	70%	60%	LAST MSR

blue matte (disc.), Bantam Jake with Realtree Camo finish in 20 ga./22 in. VR barrel only (disc.), 20 ga. has walnut finish stock and .410 bore has synthetic stock (both stocks are tailored for youth dimensions), 6.9 lbs. Mfg. 1990-96, reintroduced 1998 only.

	$200	$175	$150	$135	$110	$90	$70	*$312*

Subtract $12 for .410 bore.
Add $45 for Bantam Jake configuration (disc. 1993).

* ***Model 500 Slide Action Field Turkey*** – 12 or 20 (new 1995) ga., 22 (20 ga. only), or 24 in. barrel, Woodlands metal/wood camo finish. Disc. 1997.

	$265	$230	$200	$180	$145	$120	$95	*$324*

Subtract $15 for 20 ga.
Add $60 for 24 in. VR barrel with Ghost Ring Sight (12 ga. only).

* ***Model 500 Slide Action Field Muzzleloader Combo*** – 12 ga. only, includes 24 in. (rifled bore only, new 1993) or 28 in. VR Accu-choke barrel and additional 24 in. .50 cal. muzzleloader conversion barrel with rifled bore and iron sights, walnut finished hardwood stock and forearm, 7.2 lbs. Mfg. 1991-96.

	$335	$295	$250	$225	$185	$150	$115	*$385*

* ***Model 500 Slide Action Field Quail Unlimited*** – 20 ga. only, 26 in. VR barrel with Accu-II chokes (3), engraved receiver and hand selected stock and forearm, 3,500 mfg. in 1991 to commemorate the 10th anniversary of Quail Unlimited.

	$350	$305	$260	$240	$190	$155	$120	*$359*

* ***Model 500 Slide Action Field Sporting Steel Shot*** – 12 ga. only, 3 in. chamber, 28 in. VR Accu-choke barrel with special Accu-steel tube for shooting steel shot. Mfg. 1987-90.

	$250	$220	$185	$170	$135	$110	$85	*$295*

Add $29 for camo stock (disc. 1989).

This model was phased out of production in 1990 since all Mossberg shotguns currently manufactured are capable of shooting steel shot safely.

MODEL 500 REGAL SERIES – 12 or 20 ga., slide action, 26 or 28 in. barrel, select checkered walnut, VR. Disc. 1987.

	$240	$210	$180	$165	$130	$110	$85	*$286*

Add $39 for Combo pack (includes 1 extra 24 in. slugster barrel).
Add $19 for Accu-choke.

MODEL 500 CAMPER – 12, 20 ga., or .410 bore only, 18 1/2 in. barrel, synthetic pistol grip (no stock), camo carrying case optional, blued finish. Mfg. 1986-90 only.

	$250	$220	$185	$170	$135	$110	$85	*$276*

Add $25 for .410 bore.
Add $30 for camo case.

MODEL 500 HI-RIB TRAP – 12 ga. only, high post trap rib, 28 or 30 in. barrel. Disc. 1986.

	$375	$330	$280	$255	$205	$170	$130	*$334*

Add $20 for Accu-choke.

MODEL 500 SUPER GRADE – similar to Model 500 Field, except VR and checkered, no 16 ga. Mfg. 1965-76.

	$250	$220	$185	$170	$135	$110	$85	

MODEL 500 ATR SUPER GRADE – similar to Model 500 Field, except 12 ga., VR, 30 in. full, checkered Monte Carlo. Mfg. 1968-71.

	$350	$305	$260	$240	$190	$155	$120	

MODEL 500 APR PIGEON GRADE – similar to 500 Super Grade, except etched and scroll engraving, select wood, floating VR. Mfg. 1971-75.

	$385	$335	$290	$260	$210	$175	$135	

MODEL 500 APTR PIGEON GRADE TRAP – similar to 500 ATR, except trap style stock. Mfg. 1971-75.

	$440	$385	$330	$300	$240	$200	$155	

GRADING - PPGS™	100%	98%	95%	90%	80%	70%	60%	LAST MSR

MODEL 500 DSPR DUCK STAMP COMMEMORATIVE – similar to Pigeon Grade, except wood duck etching. 1,000 mfg. 1975.

	$525	$460	$395	$355	$290	$235	$185	

MODEL 500AA 50th ANNIVERSARY – 12 ga., Pigeon grade, trap, field, and skeet configuration, hand checkered walnut stock, red bead front and middle sights, left side of receiver engraved with 50th Anniversary emblem in gold, 50th Anniversary on pistol grip cap, limited mfg. 1969 only.

	$650	$500	$435	N/A	N/A	N/A	N/A	

MODEL 500L SERIES – similar to 500 Field Grade, except no 16 ga., etched receiver, new style stock and slide. Mfg. 1977-83.

	$250	$220	$185	$170	$135	$110	$85	

MODEL 500 BULLPUP – 12 ga., 18 1/2 (6 shot) or 20 (9 shot) in. barrel, bullpup configuration, 6 or 9 shot mag., includes shrouded barrel, carrying handle, ejection port in stock, employs high impact materials. Mfg. 1986-90.

	$650	$525	$450	$415	$325	$275	$215	*$425*

Add $15 for 8 shot mag. (disc.).

MODEL 500 SPECIAL HUNTER – 12 or 20 ga., 3 in. chamber, 26 or 28 in. VR barrel with or w/o porting and Accu-chokes set, parkerized metal finish, black synthetic stock and forearm. Mfg. 1999-2002.

	$260	$225	$195	$175	$145	$115	$90	*$327*

MODEL 500 VIKING – 12 or 20 ga., 24 (12 ga. only, with rifled barrel and sights, porting became standard in 1997), 26 (20 ga. only) or 28 (12 ga. only, porting became standard in 1997) in. ported (new 1997, 12 ga. only) or unported VR barrel with one Accu-choke and twin bead sights, matte finish with green synthetic stock and forearm, approx. 7 lbs. Mfg. 1996-98.

	$230	$200	$170	$155	$125	$105	$80	*$287*

Add $40 for 12 ga. rifled barrel.
Add $108 for Slug Shooting System with ported barrel.

* ***Model 500 Viking Turkey*** – 12 ga. only, 24 in. ported VR barrel, green synthetic stock, matte finish, Accu-choke. Mfg. 1997-98.

	$230	$200	$170	$155	$125	$105	$80	*$286*

MODEL 500 CLASSIC – 12 ga., 28 in. ported barrel, vent. rib, Accu-Set choke, gold trigger, finely checkered high gloss walnut stock and forearm, jeweled bolt, red recoil pad with white Pachmayr spacer.

MSR $462	$395	$350	$295	$275	$215	$180	$140	

MODEL 500 FIELD - CURRENT MFG. – 12, 20 ga., or .410 bore, 2 3/4 or 3 in. chamber, 24, 26, or 28 in. ported (new 1997, 12 ga. only, 26 or 28 in. barrel) or unported VR (unless with rifle sights) barrel, Slug model offers choice of 12 ga. with 24 in. ported barrel and rifle sights (mfg. 2001-2004) or .410 bore (new 2003) with adj. fiber optic sights and vent. rib, matte (12 or 20 ga. only, new 2005), Mossy Oak New Break-Up (disc. 2011) or Infinity (new 2012) camo, or blue finish, walnut finished or synthetic (.410 bore only) stock, safety on back of receiver top, Accu-chokes except for Slug Model and .410 bore, supplied with 1 Accu-choke, 6-7 1/2 lbs.

MSR $401	$340	$300	$250	$230	$185	$150	$125	

Add $65 for camo.
Add $14 for Slug Model in .410 bore with adj. fiber optic sights and VR barrel (disc. 2004).
Add approx. $43-$167 for various combo packages, depending on configuration.

This model also includes the Crown Grade, manufactured 1994-2000.

* ***Model 500 Field Bantam*** – 12 (new 2001), 20 ga. or .410 bore (synthetic stock only), 3 in. chamber, similar to Model 500 Field, except has shortened, specially contoured stock and forearm (13 in. LOP), and 22 (20 ga. only) or 24 in. ported (12 ga. only, with VR) or unported barrel, 6 - 7 1/4 lbs.

MSR $401	$340	$300	$250	$230	$185	$150	$125	

Add $55 for Field combo w/24 in. fully rifled deer barrel (20 ga. only).

GRADING - PPGS™	100%	98%	95%	90%	80%	70%	60%	LAST MSR

* ***Model 500 Field Super Bantam*** – 20 ga. only, 22 (Accu-Set or X-full chokes) or 24 (fully rifled bore with porting) in. barrel, adj. 12-13 in. LOP synthetic stock and forearm, matte blue finish (pink marble stock only beginning 2010) or 100% Mossy Oak New Break-Up (disc. 2008, Slug model only) Mossy Oak Break Up Infinity (new 2011), Mossy Oak Obsession (new 2013), Realtree Xtra (new 2013), or Realtree Hardwoods HD Green camo coverage. New 2005.

MSR $401	$340	$300	$250	$230	$185	$150	$125	

Add $65 for Turkey model or Slug model with camo finish.
Add $55 for Super Bantam combo w/Field and rifled deer barrel, or $117 for combo with Mossy Oak New Break Up or Realtree camo.
Add $39 for pink marble stock.

* ***Model 500 Field Slugster*** – 12 or 20 ga., 24 in. ported (standard 1997) or unported (disc. 1996) fluted (new 2011) or non-fluted barrel with choice of cyl. (disc. 2000) or rifled (standard 2001) bore, blue or Marinecote (mfg. 1995-97) finish, choice of rifle (Bantam Model in 20 ga.), Truglo fiberoptic sights (12 ga. only, disc. 2004), or Trophy Slugster integral scope base, synthetic, or press checkered hardwood stock and forearm or 100% camo coverage (new 2004), 6 1/2 -7 1/4 lbs.

MSR $443	$375	$325	$275	$250	$200	$175	$125	

Add $23 for Truglo fiberoptic sights (mfg. 1998-2004).
Add $92 for dual comb stock and integral scope base (new 2003, includes extra synthetic cheekpiece).
Add $58-$64 for 100% camo coverage (new 2004).
Add $125 for Marinecote finish (with synthetic stock, disc.).

This model also includes the Crown Grade Slugster, manufactured 1994-2000.

* ***Model 500 Field Synthetic*** – 12, 20 ga. or .410 bore, 3 in. chamber, 24 (slug model with ported barrel with cylinder bore choke and adj. rifle sights, new 2001), 26 (20 ga. only), or 28 (12 ga. ported only) in. VR barrel, black parkerized metal finish, black synthetic stock and forearm, 7-7 1/2 lbs. Disc. 2004.

	$255	$225	$190	$175	$140	$115	$90	*$316*

Add $14 for .410 bore Bantam Slug Model.

* ***Model 500 Turkey Synthetic Thumbhole*** – 12 ga. only, matte blue finish, 100% Mossy Oak New Break-Up (disc. 2011), Realtree Xtra Green (new 2013), Realtree Hardwoods HD Green (disc. 2012), or Infinity (new 2012) camo coverage, features synthetic thumbhole stock and 20 in. barrel with X-factor turkey tube, 7 lbs. New 2007.

MSR $469	$400	$350	$300	$275	$225	$180	$140	

Add $58 for camo.

MODEL 500 50TH ANNIVERSARY – 12 ga. only, 28 in. ported barrel with vent. rib., blue finish, high gloss walnut with classic style red buttpad, white Pachmayr spacer, gold trigger, jeweled bolt, 50th Anniversary logo engraved on receiver. Limited mfg. 2011.

	$360	$300	$250	$225	$185	$150	$115	*$448*

MODEL 500 CAMO – 12 or 20 ga., 100% camo includes parkerized camo (disc.), OFM Camo (standard, mfg. 1991-96), Woodlands (mfg. 1995-2003), and various other camo finishes, metal and synthetic stock coverage, 24 (disc.), 26 (disc.), 28, or 30 (disc.) in. ported (standard 1997) or unported (disc. 2000) VR barrel (choice of cylinder bore with rifle sights or Accu-II chokes), front fiberoptic sight, includes swivels, camo sling, and drilled and tapped receiver, older Speedfeed stock (disc. 1990) holds 4 extra shells, 7 1/2 lbs. New 1986.

Subtract 10% if without Accu-II choke system.
Add $30 for Speedfeed in synthetic stock (disc. 1990).

Accu-chokes became standard in 1991. Current models are supplied with 2 choke tubes.

* ***Model 500 Camo All Purpose*** – 12 or 20 ga. (disc. 2004), 26 in. barrel, fiber optic sights, 100% Mossy Oak New Break Up (12 ga. only) or Mossy Oak Shadowgrass (20 ga. only) camo coverage. Disc. 2010.

	$345	$300	$250	$225	$185	$150	$115	*$422*

GRADING - PPGS™	100%	98%	95%	90%	80%	70%	60%	LAST MSR

* ***Model 500 Camo Waterfowl*** – 12 ga. only, 28 in. VR ported barrel with Accu-Set choke tubes, synthetic stock and forearm, 100% Woodlands (disc.), Mossy Oak Duck Blind (mfg. 2007-2012), Advantage Max-4 (new 2004), Mossy Oak Shadowgrass Blades (new 2013), or Mossy Oak Shadowgrass (mfg. 2004-2007) camo coverage.

MSR $466	$395	$350	$295	$275	$215	$180	$140	

* ***Model 500 Camo Flyway Series Waterfowl*** – 12 ga. only, 3 in. chamber, 28 in. VR barrel with X-factor ported barrel and choke tube, fiberoptic front sight, synthetic stock and forearm with Advantage Max-4 camo, includes padded sling and embossed logo, 7 1/2 lbs. New 2005.

MSR $537	$450	$395	$340	$300	$250	$200	$160	

* ***Model 500 Camo Turkey*** – 12 or 20 ga., 20 (features ported turkey tube, new 2004) or 24 in. ported barrel with fiber optic sights and XX-full choke tube only, choice of thumbhole, adj. tactical synthetic (new 2006) or synthetic stock and forearm with Woodlands (disc. 2003), Realtree Hardwoods HD Green (new 2004), Mossy Oak New Break Up (mfg. 2004-2011), Mossy Oak Infinity (new 2012) or Mossy Oak Obsession (mfg. 2004, reintroduced 2007) camo treatment, 7 1/4 - 7 1/2 lbs. New 1999.

MSR $466	$395	$350	$295	$275	$215	$180	$140	

Add $13 for Grand Slam Turkey model with X-factor ported turkey tube.
Add $133 for tactical synthetic stock and X-factor choke tube (new 2006), or $174 for tactical stock (new 2011).
Add $56 for thumbhole stock (disc. 2011).
Subtract $28 for Turkey Thug model w/engraved receiver.
Add $88 for Turkey/Deer combo with rifled bore barrel.
Add $92 for Thug Series Turkey/Deer combo with engraved receiver (new 2011).
Add $205 for Thug Series Turkey/Deer Tactical combo with engraved receiver (new 2011).

» ***Model 500 Camo Turkey Bantam*** – 20 ga. only, 22 in. VR barrel with fiberoptic sights and Accu-II X-full choke only, available in Woodlands (100% coverage), Mossy Oak Realtree Hardwoods HD Green (new 2004) or Mossy Oak Treestand camo (mfg. 2003 only) stock and forearm only, 6 1/2 lbs. Mfg. 1997-2004.

	$290	$255	$215	$195	$160	$130	$100	*$364*

* ***Model 500 Camo Combo*** – 12 or 20 ga., includes a wide variety of extra barrel combinations including slug barrel options, prices vary slightly depending on the configuration (gauge/barrel/choke set-up). Rifled bores, VR barrels, and Accu-chokes became standard in the combo package late 1994. Disc. 1998.

	$375	$330	$280	$255	$205	$170	$130	*$434*

MODEL 500 HOME SECURITY – 20 (1996 only) ga. or .410 bore, 3 in. chamber, 18 1/2 in. barrel with spreader choke, Model 500 slide-action, 5 shot mag., blue metal finish, synthetic field stock with pistol grip forearm, 6 1/4 lbs. New 1990.

MSR $459	$395	$345	$295	$275	$215	$180	$140	

* ***Model 500 Home Security Laser .410*** – includes laser sighting device in right front of forearm. Mfg. 1990-93.

	$400	$350	$300	$270	$220	$180	$140	*$451*

MODEL 500 PERSUADER – 12 or 20 (new 1995) ga., 6 or 8 shot, 18 1/2 in. plain barrel, cyl. bore or Accu-chokes (new 1995), optional rifle (12 ga./20 in. cyl. bore barrel only) or ghost ring (new 1999) sights, blue, matte (new 2006, 12 ga. only), or parkerized (12 ga. with ghost ring sights only) finish, Speedfeed stock was disc. 1990, optional bayonet lug, plain pistol grip wood (disc. 2004) or synthetic stock, approx. 6 3/4 lbs.

MSR $447	$380	$335	$285	$260	$210	$175	$135	

Add $18 for tri-rail Picatinny forend (new 2011).
Add $14 for pistol grip.
Add $159 for ghost ring sights (new 2013).
Add $146 for tactical light forend (blue finish only, new 2013).
Add $46 for 20 ga. with 18 1/2 in. stand off barrel (new 2009).
Add $38 for 20 ga. Bantam Model w/ghost ring sights (new 2013).

GRADING - PPGS™	100%	98%	95%	90%	80%	70%	60%	LAST MSR

Add $127 for parkerized finish and ghost ring sights (disc. 2004).
Add $40 for combo with pistol grip (disc.).
Add $23 for rifle sights (disc., 12 ga. only).

* ***Model 500 Persuader ZMB*** – 12 ga., 3 in. chamber, 8 shot extended tube mag., 20 in. cylinder bore barrel, bead sight, matte black finish, black synthetic stock with pistol grip, tactical tri-rail forend, drilled and tapped, sling swivels, includes black padded sling. New 2012.

MSR $460	$375	$300	$275	$250	$200	$150	$125	

* ***Model 500 Persuader Night Special Edition*** – 12 ga. only, includes synthetic stock and factory installed Mepro-Light night sight bead sight, only 300 mfg. for Lew Horton Distributing in 1990 only.

	$350	$260	$225	$200	$160	$135	$115	*$296*

MODEL 500 TACTICAL – 12 ga. only, 3 in. chamber, 18 1/2 in. cylinder bore barrel, 6 or 8 shot, adj. tactical synthetic stock, choice of matte blue or Marinecoate finish, optional tri-rail forend with removable side rails and integral bottom rail new 2011, approx. 6 3/4 lbs. New 2006.

MSR $578	$500	$395	$335	$300	$245	$200	$155	

Add $148 for Marinecote finish.
Add $15 for tri-rail forend (new 2011) or $53 for tri-rail and ghost ring sights.

MODEL 500 CHAINSAW – 12 ga., 3 in. chamber, 18 1/2 in. stand-off barrel with cyl. bore choke, 5 shot mag., pistol grip synthetic stock, matte black finish, easily removable unique "chainsaw" forend grip provides muzzle control and stability, drilled and tapped, tri-rail forend, white dot sights, 6 lbs. New 2011.

MSR $525	$450	$395	$340	$300	$250	$200	$160	

Add $106 for Model 500 Chainsaw ZMB with light and laser combo and ZMB engraved logo on receiver (new 2012).

MODEL 500 CHAINSAW ZMB – 12 ga., 3 in. chamber, 18 1/2 in. stand-off barrel with cyl. bore choke, 6 shot mag., pistol grip synthetic stock, matte black finish, easily removable unique "chainsaw" forend grip provides muzzle control and stability, drilled and tapped, tri-rail forend, white dot sights, includes light and laser combo, ZMB engraved logo on receiver, 6 lbs. New 2012.

MSR $614	$500	$425	$335	$280	$230	$185	$145	

MODEL 500 SPX SPECIAL PURPOSE – 12 ga. only, 18 1/2 in. ported barrel with M16 style front sight, LPA ghost ring rear sight, Picatinny rail, adj. tactical black synthetic stock with pistol grip, 6 3/4 lbs. New 2009.

MSR $704	$600	$525	$450	$410	$325	$275	$210	

MODEL 500 SPECIAL PURPOSE ROAD BLOCKER – 12 ga. only, features pistol grip (no stock), 18 1/2 in. barrel with heat shield and large muzzle brake, 6 lbs. New 2009.

MSR $544	$460	$400	$350	$315	$250	$200	$160	

MODEL 500 SPECIAL PURPOSE – 12 ga. only, 18 in. cylinder bored barrel, choice of blue or parkerized finish, synthetic stock with or without Speedfeed. Disc. 1996.

	$350	$295	$250	$225	$200	$175	$160	*$378*

Add $21 for Speedfeed stock.
Add $76 for ghost ring sight (parkerized finish only).

MODEL 500 SPECIAL PURPOSE (CURRENT MFG.) – 12 ga., 2 3/4 or 3 in. chamber, 18 1/2 in. cylinder bore barrel, 6 shot, matte blue finish, synthetic stock, plain bead sight, recoil reduction system. New 2013.

MSR $493	$425	$375	$325	$295	$235	$195	$150	

MODEL 500 THUNDER RANCH – 12 ga., 3 in. chamber, 18 1/2 in. cylinder bore barrel, 5 shot mag., matte black synthetic stock with 12 3/4 in. LOP, white dot sights, tri-rail Picatinny forend, non-glare matte blue metal finish, sling swivel studs, Thunder Ranch logo engraved on receiver, includes black padded sling. New mid-2011.

MSR $493	$425	$375	$325	$295	$235	$195	$150	

GRADING - PPGS™	100%	98%	95%	90%	80%	70%	60%	LAST MSR

MODEL 500 CRUISER – 12, 20, or .410 (new 1993) ga., 14 (12 ga. only, Law Enforcement Model, disc. 1995), 18 1/2, 20, or 21 (20 ga. only - mfg. 1995-2002) in. cylinder bore barrel, shroud is available in 12 ga. only, 6 or 8 (12 ga. only) shot mag., pistol grip forearm only, 5 3/4 - 7 lbs. New 1989.

MSR $447	$380	$335	$285	$260	$210	$175	$135	

Add $17 for heat shield around barrel (12 ga. only).
Add $44 for tactical Cruiser with matte blue metal finish, bead sight, and pistol grip stock.
Add $96 for 14 in. barrel (disc.).
Add approx. $34 for camper case (1993-1996).
Add $14 for 8 shot (20 in. barrel, 12 ga. only).
Add $90 for Rolling Thunder model with heat shield and large barrel stabilizer (new 2009).

* ***Model 500 Cruiser Mil-Spec*** – 12 ga. only, 20 in. cylinder bored barrel with bead sights, built to Mil-Specs., parkerized finish. Mfg. 1997 only.

	$395	$345	$295	$270	$215	$180	$140	*$478*

* ***Model 500 Crusier Blackwater Series*** – 12 ga., 3 in. chamber, 18 1/2 in. cylinder bore barrel, synthetic pistol grip, matte black finish, white dot front sight, ported stand off door breacher at muzzle, 6 shot, half-round ribbed forearm with nylon web strap, Blackwater logo on right side of receiver, approx. 6 lbs. New 2011.

MSR $478	$400	$350	$300	$275	$225	$180	$140	

MODEL 500 GHOST RING SIGHT – 12 ga. only, 3 in. chamber, 18 1/2 or 20 in. cyl. bore or Accu-choke (20 in. only - new 1995) barrel, 6 or 9 shot tube mag., blue or parkerized finish, synthetic field stock, includes ghost ring sighting device. Mfg. 1990-97.

	$270	$235	$200	$185	$150	$120	$95	*$332*

Add $53 for parkerized finish.
Add $49 for 9 shot mag. (20 in. barrel only).
Add $123 for Accu-choke barrel (parkerized finish only).
Add $134 for Speedfeed stock (new 1994 - 9 shot, 20 in. barrel only).

MODEL 500 MARINER – 12 ga. only, 3 in. chamber, 18 1/2 or 20 in. cyl. bore barrel, 6 or 9 (disc. 2008) shot, Marinecote finish on all metal parts (more rust-resistant than stainless steel), pistol grip black synthetic stock and forearm, fixed or ghost ring (mfg. 1995-99) sights, approx. 6 3/4 lbs.

MSR $611	$525	$460	$395	$350	$295	$235	$185	

Add $51 for 9 shot model with 20 in. barrel (disc. 2008).
Add $68 for ghost ring rear sight (disc. 1999).
Add $23 for Speedfeed stock (mini-combo only - disc.).

MODEL 500 J.I.C. (JUST IN CASE) – 12 ga., 3 in. chamber, 18 in. cyl. bore barrel, 6 or 8 (new 2013) shot, comes with pistol grip, impact resistant tube and strap, available in four configurations: 5.11 Pack (w/takedown 500 and tools), Crusier (survival kit in a can, blue metal, OD Green tube), Mariner (multi-tool and knife, Orange tube, Marinecote finish), Sandstorm (Desert camo tube and finish), or Black (8 shot only, new 2013), 5 1/2 lbs. New 2007.

MSR $435	$375	$330	$280	$250	$200	$170	$130	

Add $44 for Cruiser or Black, $105 for Sandstorm or $142 for Marinecote.

MODEL 500 FLEX HUNTING – 12 ga., 24 or 28 in. matte blue barrel, X-Factor ported, Accu-Set, or XX full choke, TLS tooless locking system, adj. fiber optic sight, LPA trigger, standard synthetic or adj. synthetic stock with Mossy Oak Break Up Infinity or Realtree Advantage Max 4 camo, OD Green, or tan finish. New mid-2012.

MSR $698	$595	$525	$450	$400	$325	$275	$210	

Add $49 for OD Green finish or XX-full choke.
Add $156 for adj. stock.

MODEL 500 FLEX TACTICAL – 12 ga., 18 1/2 or 20 in. cylinder bore barrel, matte blue, OD Green, or tan finish, white dot, XS ghost ring, or plain bead sight, Picatinny rail, black pistol grip, standard, or six position adj. synthetic stock, TLS tooless locking system. New mid-2012.

MSR $730	$625	$550	$475	$425	$350	$275	$225	

Add $89 for XS ghost ring sight. Add $121 for six position adj. stock.

GRADING - PPGS™	100%	98%	95%	90%	80%	70%	60%	LAST MSR

MODEL 500 FLEX ALL PURPOSE – 12 ga., 28 in. ported barrel, Accu-Set choke, matte blue or Marinecote finish, black synthetic stock, vent. rib, twin bead sights, optional LPA trigger, TLS tooless locking system. New mid-2012.

MSR $611	$525	$450	$395	$350	$295	$235	$185	

Add $50 for LPA trigger.
Add $55 for Marinecote finish.

MODEL 505 YOUTH ALL PURPOSE FIELD SLIDE ACTION – 20 ga. or .410 bore, 3 in. chamber, 20 in. barrel with Accu-Set or fixed Mod. choke, vent. rib, brass mid-bead and white front bead sights, wood stock, blue metal finish, short 12 in. LOP, 5 1/4 lbs. New 2005.

MSR $401	$340	$300	$250	$225	$185	$150	$120	

Model 505 Youth barrels are not interchangeble with any Mossberg slide action shotgun.

MODEL 510 MINI SUPER BANTAM SLIDE ACTION – 20 ga. or .410 bore, 18 1/2 in. vent. rib barrel, blue finish, or Mossy Oak Break-Up Infinity or Obession (Thug Model only) camo coverage, 10 1/2 or 11 1/2 LOP, Accu-Set or fixed choke, dual bead sights, adj. synthetic stock. New 2010.

MSR $401	$340	$300	$250	$225	$185	$150	$120	

Add $50 for camo.
Add $83 for Turkey Thug Model with Mossy Oak Obession camo coverage, sling, and engraved receiver (new 2012).

Model 510 barrels are not interchangeble with any Mossberg shotgun.

MODEL 535 ATS SLIDE ACTION (ALL TERRAIN SHOTGUN) – 12 ga. only, 3 in. chamber, features safety on rear of receiver, various configurations, 6 1/2 - 7 lbs. New 2005.

Model 535 barrels are not interchangeble with other Mossberg slide action shotgun models.

* ***Model 535 Slide Action ATS All Purpose Field*** – 12 ga. only, 28 in. barrel with Accu-set chokes, vent. rib, blue metal, walnut stock, white bead front sight. New 2005.

MSR $426	$360	$315	$275	$245	$200	$160	$125	

Add $47 for Field/Deer combo.

* ***Model 535 Slide Action ATS Turkey*** – 12 ga. only, 20 (includes X-factor ported choke tube, new 2006), 22, or 24 in. fluted or non-fluted barrel with XX-Full choke, vent. rib, fiber optic sights, matte blue (disc. 2007), Mossy Oak New Break-Up (disc. 2011), Mossy Oak Obsession (new 2007), Mossy Oak Break Up Infinity (new 2011), or Realtree Hardwoods HD Green (disc. 2012) finish, standard or tactical (new 2006) synthetic stock. New 2005.

MSR $497	$425	$375	$325	$295	$235	$190	$150	

Add $159 for "Turkey Thug" Series with Picatinny rail, Mossy Oak Break-Up camo, X-factor Turkey tube, and LPA adj. trigger or $221 for Turkey Thug Series with TruGlo red dot sight (new 2011).
Add $41 for camo and LPA adj. trigger (new 2011).
Add $50 for Turkey/Deer combo or $92 for combo with LDA adj. trigger (new 2011).
Subtract approx. $60 for matte blue finish (disc. 2007).
Add $130 for tactical synthetic stock with X-factor ported choke tube (new 2006).

* ***Model 535 Slide Action ATS Thumbhole Turkey*** – similar to Turkey model, except has synthetic thumbhole stock and 20 in. barrel with X-factor ported choke tube, not available in Mossy Oak Obsession. New 2007.

MSR $488	$415	$365	$315	$275	$225	$185	$145	

Add $71 for 100% camo coverage.

* ***Model 535 Slide Action ATS Waterfowl*** – 12 ga. only, 3 in. chamber, 28 in. barrel with Accu-set choke, vent. rib, synthetic stock, matte blue, Mossy Oak New Break-Up (disc. 2008), Mossy Oak Duck Blind (new 2007), or Advantage Max-4 camo, fiber optic sights, approx. 7 1/2 lbs. New 2005.

MSR $426	$360	$315	$275	$245	$200	$160	$125	

Add $68 for 100% camo coverage.
Add $117 for Turkey/Waterfowl combo package.

GRADING - PPGS™	100%	98%	95%	90%	80%	70%	60%	LAST MSR

* ***Model 535 Slide Action ATS Slugster*** – 12 ga. only, 24 in. fully rifled bore fluted or non-fluted barrel, synthetic stock, rifle sights or integral scope base, matte blue metal, Realtree AP (new 2007), Realtree Xtra (new 2013), or Mossy Oak New Break-Up (disc. 2007) camo. New 2005.

MSR $426	$360	$315	$275	$245	$200	$160	$125	

Add $61 for 100% Realtree AP camo coverage w/o integral scope base (disc. 2008).
Add $143 for integral scope base and LDA adj. trigger (new 2011).

MODEL 500/590 INTIMIDATOR LASER – 12 ga. only, 3 in. chamber, 18 1/2 (Model 500) or 20 (Model 590) in. cyl. bore barrel, 6 (Model 500) or 9 (Model 590) shot tube mag., blue or parkerized finish, synthetic field stock, includes laser sighting device. Mfg. 1990-93.

* ***Model 500 Intimidator***

	$500	$385	$340	$300	$265	$230	$195	*$505*

Add $22 for parkerized finish.

* ***Model 590 Intimidator***

	$550	$495	$440	$375	$340	$295	$260	*$556*

Add $45 for parkerized finish.

MODEL 590 SPECIAL PURPOSE SLIDE ACTION – 12 ga., 3 in. chamber, similar to Model 500, except has 9 shot mag., 20 in. cyl. bore barrel with or w/o 3/4 shroud, and bayonet lug, blue or parkerized finish, regular black synthetic stock, with or w/o Speedfeed, 7 1/4 lbs. New 1987.

MSR $537	$450	$395	$340	$300	$250	$200	$160	

Add $103 for tri-rail Picatinny forend and Speedfeed stock (new 2011).
Add $140 for tactical light forend in blue finish with heat shield.
Add $38 for parkerized finish.
Add $75 for heavy barrel with ghost ring sights, metal trigger guard and safety (disc. 2011).
Add $80 for ghost ring sights (parkerized finish only).
Add $33 for Speedfeed (blue, disc. 1999) or $90 for Speedfeed (parkerized) stock.

* ***Model 590 Special Purpose Slide Action Mariner*** – similar to Model 500 Mariner except is 9 shot and has 20 in. barrel, 7 lbs. Mfg. 1989-1993, reintroduced 2009.

MSR $671	$575	$500	$425	$395	$315	$260	$200	

Add 5% for Speedfeed stock (disc. 1990).
Subtract 10% if w/o pistol grip adapter (disc.)

* ***Model 590 Special Purpose Slide Action Bullpup*** – similar to Model 500 Bullpup except is 9 shot and has 20 in. barrel. Mfg. 1989-90 only.

	$650	$525	$450	$410	$325	$275	$210	*$497*

* ***Model 590 Special Purpose Slide Action Double Action*** – 12 ga. only, 3 in. chamber, world's first double action shotgun (long trigger pull), 18 1/2 or 20 in. barrel, 6 or 9 shot, bead or ghost ring sights, black synthetic stock and forearm, top tang safety, parkerized metal finish, 7-7 1/4 lbs. Mfg. 2000-2003.

	$450	$395	$335	$305	$245	$200	$155	*$510*

Add $31 for 9 shot capacity.
Add $48 for ghost ring sights.
Add $124 for Speedfeed stock (20 in. barrel with ghost ring sights only).

* ***Model 590 Special Purpose Slide Action Line Launcher*** – special purpose Marine and rescue shotgun with blaze orange synthetic stock, line dispensing canister, floating and distance heads, nylon and spectra line refills, includes case and two boxes of launching loads.

	$850	$745	$635	$580	$465	$380	$295	*$927*

MODEL 590 FLEX TACTICAL – 12 ga., 20 in. cylinder bore barrel, matte blue finish, bead sight, six position adj. baclk synthetic stock with rail. New mid-2012.

MSR $842	$715	$625	$535	$485	$395	$325	$250	

GRADING - PPGS™	100%	98%	95%	90%	80%	70%	60%	LAST MSR

MODEL 590A1 SLIDE ACTION – 12 ga., 3 in. chamber, 6 or 9 shot mag., 18 1/2 or 20 (new 2010) in. fluted or non-fluted cylinder bore heavy barrel, parkerized finish, metal trigger guard and top safety, black synthetic stock, optional Speedfeed or six position aluminum tube adj. stock, choice of 3-dot, bead, or ghost ring sights, approx. 7 1/2 lbs. New 2009.

MSR $581	$495	$435	$375	$335	$275	$225	$175	

Add $40 for fluted barrel and LDA adj. trigger (new 2011).
Add $39 for ghost ring sights.
Add $53 for Speedfeed stock.
Add $35 for choice of 3-dot or ghost rings sights with Speedfeed stock.
Add $89 for Bantam Model with shortened LOP and ghost ring sights (6 shot only, limited mfg.).
Add $69 for 9 shot.

* ***Model 590A1 Adj. Stock Slide Action*** – 12 ga. only, similar to Model 590A1, except has six position adj. aluminum stock with pistol grip, 9 shot model has 20 in. barrel, 3 dot (6 shot) or ghost ring (9 shot) sights, 7 1/2 lbs. New 2009.

MSR $789	$675	$595	$500	$460	$375	$300	$235	

Add $50 for 6 shot model with 3 dot sights.
Add $56 for tri-rail Picatinny forend (new 2011).

* ***Model 590A1 Special Purpose Slide Action (Disc.)*** – 12 ga., marked 590A1 on receiver, parkerized, ghost ring rear sight, synthetic stock and forend, ramp front sight. Disc. 1997.

	$550	$480	$410	$375	$300	$245	$190	

* ***Model 590A1 Special Purpose Slide Action Blackwater Series*** – 12 ga., 3 in. chamber, 20 in. heavy wall cylinder bore barrel, 9 shot extended mag., military trigger guard, bayonet lug, parkerized metal finish, matte black furniture, Blackwater logo on right side of receiver, top Picatinny rail, integral adj. ghost ring rear sight, white post front sight, half-round ribbed forearm with three Picatinny rails, Speedfeed buttstock with two spare shell holders on each side, rubber buttpad, 7 1/4 lbs. New 2011.

MSR $732	$625	$550	$475	$425	$345	$280	$220	

* ***Model 590A1 Mariner Slide Action*** – 12 ga. only, 18 1/2 in. cyl. bore barrel with bead sights, Marinecote finish, black synthetic stock and forearm, 6 shot only, 6 3/4 lbs. New 2009.

MSR $727	$615	$540	$460	$425	$340	$275	$215	

* ***Model 590A1 SPX Slide Action*** – 12 ga. only, 20 in. cyl. bore barrel with ghost ring sights, parkerized finish, black synthetic stock and forearm, 9 shot, includes M9 bayonet and scabbard, receiver Picatinny rail, fiber optic front sight, 7 1/4 lbs. New 2009.

MSR $867	$735	$645	$550	$500	$400	$330	$250	

MODEL 590A1 SLIDE ACTION CLASS III RESTRICTED – 12 ga. only, law enforcement/military use only with 14 in. barrel, 6 shot, seven different configurations, plus X12 model designed to use Taser International products.

Retail pricing is not available on these models.

MODEL 712 SEMI-AUTO – 12 ga. only, gas operated, shoots 2 3/4 and 3 in. shells interchangeably, plain barrel or VR, top of receiver safety, checkered hardwood stock, rubber recoil pad, fixed or Accu-choke II choking. Mfg. 1986-88 only.

	$450	$395	$335	$305	$245	$200	$155	*$345*

Subtract $25 without Accu-II choking.
Add $90 for combo pack (includes 1 extra 24 in. slugster barrel).

* ***Model 712 Semi-Auto Steel Shot*** – similar to Model 712, except has Accu-steel choking system for steel shot, 28 in. VR barrel. Mfg. 1988 only.

	$450	$395	$335	$305	$245	$200	$155	*$349*

* ***Model 712 Semi-Auto Camo/Speedfeed*** – 12 ga. only, similar to Model 712, except has camo finished metal parts, stock, and forearm, 24 or 28 in. barrel. Mfg. 1986-87 only.

	$450	$395	$335	$305	$245	$200	$155	*$390*

Add $20 for Accu-II choke.

GRADING - PPGS™	100%	98%	95%	90%	80%	70%	60%	LAST MSR

MODEL 712 REGAL SEMI-AUTO – 12 or 20 ga., action same as Model 712, special bright bluing, VR only, deluxe checkered walnut stock and forearm, gold trigger, inlaid medallion on receiver, top of receiver safety. Mfg. 1986-87 only.

	$310	$270	$230	$210	$170	$140	$110	*$366*

Add $20 for Accu-II choke.

NEW HAVEN BRAND – trademark used on previous models, plainer finish. Disc.

Values are 20% less per similar model.

MODEL 835 ULTI-MAG SLIDE ACTION – 12 ga. with 3 1/2 in. chamber (new 1988), slide action, 24 (Turkey Model - new 1990) or 28 in. VR barrel with Accu-mag choke tubes, 6 shot mag., safety on top rear of receiver, choice of camo synthetic or checkered hardwood stock. Introduced late 1988, disc. 1991.

	$375	$330	$280	$255	$205	$170	$130	*$430*

Add $30 for synthetic camo field stock.

Various Combo packages were available in this model with prices ranging from $469-$534 depending on barrel chokings and scope base options.

This model was followed by the 835 Regal Series introduced in late 1991.

MODEL 835 ULTI-MAG FIELD GRADE SLIDE ACTION – 12 ga. only, 3 1/2 in. chamber, 24 in. cyl. bore (disc.), 24 in. VR (Turkey Special, disc. 1993), or 28 in. ported (new 1997) or unported VR barrel with 1 Accu-mag choke, walnut finish stock and forearm (pressed checkering became standard 1994), blue finish, approx. 7 1/2 lbs. Disc. 1998.

	$270	$235	$200	$185	$150	$120	$95	*$331*

Add $40 for combo package (disc. 1993).

MODEL 835 ULTI-MAG SYNTHETIC (SPECIAL HUNTER) – 12 ga. only, 3 1/2 in. chamber, 26 (disc. 1999, reintroduced 2004) or 28 in. VR ported barrel with mod. Accu-mag choke, parkerized finish, black synthetic stock, 7 3/4 lbs. Mfg. 1998-2005.

	$315	$275	$235	$215	$175	$140	$110	*$394*

MODEL 835 ULTI-MAG FIELD (CROWN GRADE) – similar to Field Grade, except has gold trigger and cut checkering on walnut finished hardwood stock, blue or OFM Woodland camo (24 in. Turkey only) finish, ported (standard 1997) or unported (disc.) VR barrel, 7 3/4 lbs. Mfg. 1994-2005.

	$315	$275	$235	$215	$175	$140	$110	*$394*

* ***Model 835 Ulti-Mag Field Turkey*** – 12 ga. only, 24 in. ported VR barrel, parkerized finish, walnut finished stock and forearm. Mfg. 1997-2000.

	$320	$280	$240	$215	$175	$145	$110	*$378*

* ***Model 835 Ulti-Mag Field New Turkey*** – 12 ga. only, 24 in. ported barrel with Ulti-full choke only, choice of Realtree Advantage Timber (new 2001), Realtree Hardwoods (mfg. 2000 only), Realtree Xtra brown (disc. 1999) or Woodlands (disc. 1999) 100% camo finish, fiberoptic sights, 7 1/2 lbs. Mfg. 1999-2001.

	$450	$395	$335	$305	$245	$200	$155	*$525*

* ***Model 835 Ulti-Mag Field Crown Grade*** – 12 ga. only, 3 1/2 in. chamber, 28 in. VR ported (standard 1997) or unported barrel, walnut stock and forearm, Accu-mag choke. Disc. 1998.

	$365	$320	$275	$250	$200	$165	$130	*$421*

Add $7 for duo-comb stock.

MODEL 835 VIKING – 12 ga. only, 28 in. VR ported (standard 1997) or unported (1996 only) barrel with one Accu-Choke and twin bead sights, matte blue finish with green synthetic stock and forearm, 7.7 lbs. Mfg. 1996-98.

	$260	$225	$195	$175	$145	$115	$90	*$316*

MODEL 835 ULTI-MAG CAMO TURKEY & WATERFOWL – 12 ga. only, 3 1/2 in. chamber, OFM Woodland Camo (all-purpose camo, combo. only mfg. 1997-99), Mossy Oak Break-Up Infinity (new 2011), Realtree (mfg. 1993-99), Realtree AP (all purpose grey, mfg. 1996-99), Realtree X-tra Brown (mfg. 2000-2002), Brown Leaf (disc. 1999), Woodlands (new

GRADING - PPGS™	100%	98%	95%	90%	80%	70%	60%	LAST MSR

2000), Mossy Oak Shadow Grass (mfg. 2000-2007, Waterfowl only), Realtree Hardwoods (mfg. 2002, Turkey only), Mossy Oak New Break-up (mfg. 2003-2011), Mossy Oak Forest Floor (mfg. 2003 only), Mossy Oak Obsession (mfg. 2004, reintroduced 2007), Mossy Oak Duck Blind (new 2007, Waterfowl only), Advantage Max-4 (Waterfowl only, new 2004), Realtree Hardwoods HD Green (new 2003), Advantage Timber (mfg. 2001-2002), or Mossy Oak (mfg. 1994-99) finish, 20 (Grand Slam Turkey Model with X-factor ported turkey tube, new 2004), 24 (Turkey Special), 26 (Waterfowl, new 2004) or 28 (Waterfowl only) in. VR ported (new 1997) or unported (disc. 2000) fluted (new 2011) or non-fluted barrel with 6 choke tubes, dual comb wood (Turkey/Deer combo only) or synthetic stock, approx. 7 1/2 lbs. New 1991.

MSR $547	$465	$400	$350	$315	$250	$210	$165	

Add $33 for 24 in. fluted fully rifled barrel and LPA adj. trigger with Realtree AP camo (new 2011).
Add $140 for "Turkey Thug" Series with Picatinny rail, Mossy Oak Break-Up camo, X-factor Turkey tube, LPA adj. trigger and TruGlo red dot sight (new 2011).
Add $89 for Turkey/Deer or Turkey/Waterfowl combo.
Add $127 for Turkey/Deer Combo with fluted barrel and LDA adj. trigger (new 2011).
Add $25 for any camo finish other than Woodlands.
Add $12 for synthetic thumbhole stock with camo coverage (new 2007).
Add $185 for Specialty Turkey Model with laminated thumbhole (disc. 2008).
Add $174 for tactical synthetic stock with X-factor ported choke tube and fiber optic sights (new 2006).
Add $47 for Grand Slam Turkey Model with 20 in. barrel and X-factor ported turkey choke tube (new 2004).
Add $65 for 28 in. barrel with Mossy Oak Shadow Grass and hunter set of chokes (Waterfowl Model, disc.).
Subtract $50 for Waterfowl model w/o camo finish.
Subtract $20 for synthetic thumbhole stock with matte blue.

OFM Woodland camo finish on this model included a dual comb stock.

MODEL 835 SLUGSTER – 12 ga. only, 3 1/2 in. chamber, 6 shot mag., 24 in. ported rifled fluted (new 2011) or non-fluted (disc. 2010) slug barrel, integral scope base or rifle sights, choice of wood dual comb or synthetic stock, Realtree AP camo coverage, LPA adj. trigger became standard 2011, 7 3/4 lbs. Mfg. 2007-2011, reintroduced 2013.

MSR $620	$525	$460	$395	$350	$295	$235	$185	

Add $31 for integral scope base and dual comb stock (disc. 2009).

MODEL 835 WALNUT ULTI-MAG (REGAL) – 12 ga., 3 1/2 in. chamber, 28 in. VR barrel with Accu-Mag chokes (disc. 1996) or 24 in. rifled slug barrel, single (new 1993) or dual comb (2 comb inserts are provided for the stock affording different shooting positions), aluminum receiver, back-bored barrel, double slide bars, high gloss walnut stock with recoil pad, approx. 7 1/2 lbs. Mfg. 1991-96.

	$350	$305	$260	$240	$190	$155	$120	*$404*

Add $8 for dual comb stock.
Add $30 for 24 in. slug barrel with trophy scope base and dual comb stock.
Add $72-$83 for combo package (includes extra slug barrel with choice of sights).

MODEL 835 WILD TURKEY FED. LIMITED EDITION – 12 ga. with 3 1/2 in. chamber, 24 in. VR barrel with Accu-mag. chokes, camo finish, includes camo sling, medallion in stock, and 10-pack of Federal Turkey loads. Mfg. 1989 only.

	$425	$370	$320	$290	$235	$190	$150	*$477*

MODEL 835 NWTF SPECIAL EDITION – 12 ga. only, 24 in. VR barrel with Accu-mag chokes, features Realtree camo finish, drilled and tapped receiver, 7 1/2 lbs. Mfg. 1991 only to commemorate the National Wild Turkey Federation.

	$380	$330	$285	$260	$210	$170	$135	*$436*

MODEL 835 WATERFOWL LIMITED EDITION – 12 ga. with 3 1/2 in. chamber, 28 in. VR barrel with Accu-mag. chokes, camo finish, synthetic stock, camo sling. Mfg. 1990 only.

	$425	$370	$320	$290	$235	$190	$150	*$480*

GRADING - PPGS™	100%	98%	95%	90%	80%	70%	60%	LAST MSR

MODEL 835 FLYWAY SERIES WATERFOWL – 12 ga. only, 3 1/2 in. chamber, 28 in. VR with X-factor porting barrel and choke tubes, fiber optic sights, synthetic stock and forearm with Advantage Max-4 camo, includes padded sling and embossed logo. New 2005.

MSR $642	$450	$395	$340	$300	$250	$200	$160	

MODEL 930 SEMI-AUTO – 12 ga. only, 3 in. chamber, various configurations, approx. 7 3/4 lbs. New 2005.

* ***Model 930 Semi-Auto All Purpose Field*** – 12 ga. only, 26 or 28 in. ported barrel with Accu-set chokes, vent. rib, blue metal, walnut stock, white bead front sight. New 2005.

MSR $633	$535	$475	$400	$365	$295	$240	$185	

Add $36 for Field/Security combo with 18 1/2 in. cylinder bore barrel (disc. 2009).

* ***Model 930 Semi-Auto Turkey*** – 12 ga. only, 24 in. ported barrel with XX-Full choke, vent. rib, fiber optic sights, matte blue, Mossy Oak New Break-Up (disc. 2008), Mossy Oak Obsession (new 2007), Mossy Oak Break-Up Infinity (new 2011) or Realtree Hardwoods HD Green finish, synthetic stock. New 2005.

MSR $606	$515	$450	$385	$350	$285	$230	$180	

Add $130 for 100% camo coverage.
Add $94 for full length stock with pistol grip (new 2009).

* ***Model 930 Semi-Auto Waterfowl*** – 12 ga. only, 26 or 28 in. ported barrel with Accu-set choke, vent. rib, walnut or synthetic stock, matte or matte blue (wood stock only), Mossy Oak Duck Blind (new 2007), Mossy Oak New Break-Up (disc. 2008) or Advantage Max-4 camo, fiber optic sights. New 2005.

MSR $606	$515	$450	$385	$350	$285	$230	$180	

Add $27 for walnut stock and foream with matte blue metal finish.
Add $130 for 100% camo coverage.

* ***Model 930 Semi-Auto Slugster*** – 12 ga. only, 24 in. fully rifled bore barrel, choice of walnut, synthetic (disc. 2008), or Monte Carlo synthetic stock, rifle sights or integral scope base, matte blue metal, Realtree AP (new 2007), or Mossy Oak New Break-Up camo. New 2005.

MSR $606	$515	$450	$385	$350	$285	$230	$180	

Add $27 for walnut stock/forearm and rifle sights.
Add $118 for 100% camo coverage (disc. 2010).
Add $94 for All-Purpose Combo or $66 for Waterfowl Combo (new 2006).

* ***Model 930 Semi-Auto Tactical*** – 12 ga., 18 1/2 in. cylinder bore barrel, blue finish, 5 shot, synthetic stock.

MSR $660	$550	$480	$415	$375	$300	$250	$195	

Add $23 for heat shield.

* ***Model 930 Semi-Auto Special Purpose Home Security*** – 12 ga., 3 in. chamber, 18 1/2 cylinder bore barrel, bead sights, blue finish, black synthetic stock, 7 1/2 lbs. New 2007.

MSR $612	$525	$450	$385	$350	$285	$230	$180	

Add $46 for tactical barrel in matte blue finish or $68 for tactical barrel with heat shield (new 2011).
Add $67 for Field/Security combo (new 2010).

* ***Model 930 Semi-Auto Special Purpose Roadblocker*** – similar to Home Security Model, except has 18 1/2 in. barrel with large muzzle brake, 5 shot, 7 3/4 lbs. Mfg. 2009-2011.

	$575	$495	$415	$375	$300	$245	$190	*$670*

* ***Model 930 Semi-Auto Special Purpose SPX*** – 12 ga., 3 in. chamber, features 8 shot mag., Picatinny rail, LPA ghost ring rear sight, and winged fiber optic front sight, with or w/o pistol grip stock, 7 3/4 lbs. New 2008.

MSR $787	$675	$595	$500	$460	$370	$300	$235	

Add $96 for pistol grip stock.
Add $151 for pistol grip stock with coyote tan finish.

GRADING - PPGS™	100%	98%	95%	90%	80%	70%	60%	LAST MSR

* ***Model 930 Semi-Auto Special Purpose SPX Blackwater Series*** – 12 ga., 3 in. chamber, 8 shot, XS sight system, 18 1/2 in. cylinder bore barrel, receiver mounted sliding safety, matte black finish with Blackwater logo on right side of receiver, black composite pistol grip stock, Picatinny rail with integral adj. ghost ring sight, oversized cocking handle and bolt release, 7 3/4 lbs. New 2011.

MSR $865	$700	$615	$525	$475	$385	$315	$245	

* ***Model 930 Semi-Auto Patrick Flanigan Rhythm Series*** – 12 ga., 28 matte blue ported barrel, 13 shot, blue/yellow marbled stock, extended 12 shot mag. tube, fiber optic front sight, engraved receiver, beveled loading gate, shorter forend, built to Flanigan's specifications. New 2012.

MSR $833	$700	$615	$525	$475	$385	$315	$245	

* ***Model 930 Semi-Auto JM Pro Series*** – 12 ga., 22 or 24 in. barrel, 9 or 10 shot, matte black synthetic stock, fiber optic front sight, engraved receiver, beveled loading gate, shorter forend, built to Jerry Miculek's specifications. New 2012.

MSR $730	$625	$545	$475	$425	$345	$280	$225	

MODEL 935 MAGNUM SEMI-AUTO – 12 ga. only, 3 1/2 in. chamber, choice of turkey or waterfowl configuration, 22 (Grand Slam Turkey model with X-factor ported turkey tube), 24 (turkey only), 26, or 28 VR barrel with choke tube(s) and fiber optic front sight, matte or camo metal finish, wood (disc.) or synthetic stock and forearm, choice of full coverage Mossy Oak New Break Up, Advantage Max-4, Mossy Oak Duck Blind (new 2007), Mossy Oak Shadowgrass (disc. 2007), Mossy Oak Obsession (new 2007), Mossy Oak New Break-Up Infinity (new 2011), Realtree Xtra Green (new 2013), Mossy Oak Shadowgrass Blades (new 2013), or Realtree Hardwoods HD Green camo, approx. 7 3/4 lbs. New 2004.

MSR $682	$575	$500	$425	$395	$315	$260	$200	

Add $133 for 100% camo coverage.
Add $150 for Grand Slam Turkey model with 22 in. barrel and X-factor ported turkey tube.
Add $219 for Turkey/Deer or Turkey/Waterfowl combo (new 2005).
Add $243 for pistol grip.

MODEL 935 MAGNUM SLUGSTER – 12 ga. only, 3 1/2 in. chamber, 24 in. fully rifled barrel, choice of Monte Carlo or regular synthetic stock and foream, choice of rifle sights (disc. 2008) or integral scope base, Realtree AP camo, 7 1/2 lbs. Mfg. 2007-2010.

	$640	$550	$470	$425	$345	$280	$220	*$754*

MODEL 935 FLYWAY SERIES WATERFOWL – 12 ga. only, 3 1/2 in. chamber, 28 in. VR with X-factor ported barrel and choke tubes, fiber optic sights, synthetic stock and forearm with Advantage Max-4 camo, includes padded sling and embossed logo. New 2005.

MSR $870	$735	$645	$550	$500	$400	$330	$250	

MODEL 1000 SEMI-AUTO – 12 or 20 ga., gas semi-auto, 2 3/4 in. chamber, scroll engraved aluminum alloy receiver, plain or VR barrel, also available in trap and skeet configuration, checkered walnut stock and forearm. Imported 1986-87 only. VR became standard in 1987.

	$410	$360	$305	$280	$225	$185	$145	*$472*

Add $28 for Multi-Choke II.
Deduct $50 if without VR.

Model 1000 barrels are not interchangeable with Model 1000 Super barrels.

Manufactured by Howa, Mossberg took over this series after Smith & Wesson decided to drop the line.

* ***Model 1000 Semi-Auto Junior*** – similar to Model 1000, except 20 ga. only, shortened stock, and 22 in. VR Multi-Choke barrel. Imported 1986-87 only.

	$425	$370	$320	$290	$235	$190	$150	*$499*

* ***Model 1000 Semi-Auto Slug*** – 12 or 20 ga., 22 in. barrel with rifle sights, recoil pad. Imported 1986-87 only.

	$405	$355	$305	$275	$225	$180	$140	*$464*

* ***Model 1000 Semi-Auto Skeet*** – 12 or 20 ga., steel receiver, 26 in. VR barrel bored skeet. Mfg. 1986 only.

	$395	$345	$295	$270	$215	$180	$140	*$439*

GRADING - PPGS™	100%	98%	95%	90%	80%	70%	60%	LAST MSR

MODEL 1000 SUPER SEMI-AUTO – 12 or 20 (Super 20) ga., gas semi-auto, 3 in. chambers, shoots 2 3/4 and 3 in. shells interchangeably, steel receiver, vent. recoil pad, select checkered walnut stock and forearm, Multi-Choke II is standard (except on slug barrel). Slug models are approx. the same price as values listed directly below. Imported 1986-87 only.

$495	$435	$370	$335	$270	$225	$175	*$577*

Model 1000 Super barrels are not interchangeable with Model 1000 barrels.

Manufactured by Howa, Mossberg took over this series after Smith & Wesson decided to drop the line.

* ***Model 1000 Super Semi-Auto Waterfowler*** – 12 ga. only, matte finished wood and metal, includes swivels and camouflaged sling, 28 in. Multi-Choke barrel. Imported 1986-87 only.

$510	$445	$380	$345	$280	$230	$180	*$605*

* ***Model 1000 Super Semi-Auto Skeet*** – 12 or 20 ga., 25 in. barrel, jug choking. Imported 1986-87 only.

$575	$505	$430	$390	$315	$260	$200	*$658*

* ***Model 1000 Super Semi-Auto Trap*** – 12 ga. only, 30 in. Multi-Choke II barrel with high VR, Monte Carlo stock, recoil pad. Mfg. 1986 only.

$470	$410	$350	$320	$260	$210	$165	*$560*

MODEL 3000 SLIDE ACTION – 12 or 20 ga. only, 3 in. chamber, slide action, steel receiver, double action bars, various chokes and VR barrel lengths, checkered walnut stock and forearm, vent. recoil pad. This model was introduced in 1986 and the field version was disc. in 1987.

$325	$285	$245	$220	$180	$145	$115	*$360*

Add $25 for Multi-Choke II.

* ***Model 3000 Slide Action Waterfowler*** – 12 ga. only, similar to Model 3000, except has dull matte finish on wood and metal, includes swivels and camouflaged sling, VR only. Mfg. 1986 only.

$340	$295	$265	$215	$185	$150	$120	*$386*

Add $30 for Multi-choke II option, $70 for camo/speedfeed stock.

* ***Model 3000 Slide Action Law Enforcement*** – 12 or 20 ga. only, 18 1/2 or 20 in. cylinder bore only, rifle or bead sights. Mfg. 1986-87 only.

$325	$285	$245	$220	$180	$145	$115	*$362*

Add $25 for rifle sights.
Add $33 for black speedfeed stock.

MODEL 5500 SEMI-AUTO – 12 ga., 2 3/4 or 3 in. mag., gas operated, 18 1/2 - 30 in. barrels. Disc. 1985.

$250	$220	$185	$170	$135	$110	$85	*$307*

Add $20 for VR.

* ***Model 5500 Semi-Auto Mag.*** – 12 ga. only, 3 in. chamber, 30 in. VR barrel. Disc. 1985.

$275	$240	$205	$185	$150	$125	$95	*$325*

MODEL 5500 MKII SEMI-AUTO – 12 ga. only, supplied with 2 VR barrels - 26 in. (2 3/4 in. chamber) and 28 in. (3 in. chamber) VR barrels, includes choice of Accu-II choke tubes (lead shot only) or Accu-Steel choke tubes, blue or camo finish (new 1990), checkered hardwood stock and forearm, top receiver safety, recoil pad, 7 1/2 lbs. Mfg. 1989-1992.

$260	$225	$195	$175	$145	$115	$90	*$294*

Add $10 for 24 in. rifled slug barrel.
Add $43 for camo metal finish and synthetic stock.
Add $30 for Turkey Model (24 in. barrel, camo finish, and synthetic stock).
This model was also available with different Combo options. Prices varied between $463- $484, depending on configuration of barrel choking.

* ***Model 5500 Mk II Semi-Auto U.S. Shooting Team*** – 12 ga., 2 3/4 in. chamber, 26 in. non-Mag. barrel with VR and Accu-II chokes, blue finish, checkered walnut stock and forearm, 7 1/2 lbs. Mfg. 1991-92.

$325	$285	$245	$220	$180	$145	$115	*$376*

GRADING - PPGS™	100%	98%	95%	90%	80%	70%	60%	LAST MSR

* ***Model 5500 Mk II Semi-Auto NWTF Special Edition*** – 12 ga. only, 3 in. chamber, 24 in. VR barrel with 1 choke tube, Mossy Oak Camo finish with synthetic stock and forearm, 7.3 lbs. Mfg. 1991-92.

	$365	$320	$275	$250	$200	$165	$130	$428

MODEL 6000 SEMI-AUTO – 12 ga. only, 2 3/4 or 3 in. chamber, 28 in. VR barrel with Accu-choke, economical model with walnut finish stock, blue finish, 7.7 lbs. Mfg. 1993 only.

	$280	$245	$210	$190	$155	$125	$100	$321

MODEL 9200 CROWN SEMI-AUTO – 12 ga. only, 3 in. chamber, gas operated, shoots any shell interchangeably, 18 1/2 (SP only), 22 (Bantam only), 24 in. rifled, 24 (Turkey), 26 (U.S. Shooting Team variation, new 1993), or 28 in. VR barrel with 3 Accu-chokes, engraved aluminum receiver, synthetic (18 1/2 in. barrel only) or walnut stained hardwood stock (1 in. shorter on Bantam Model) and forearm, top receiver safety, approx. 7 1/2 lbs. Mfg. 1992-2001.

	$460	$400	$345	$310	$255	$205	$160	$574

Add approx. $73-$95 for combo package.
Add $33 for Truglo fiberoptic sights (mfg. 1998 only).
Add $23 for 24 in. rifled slug barrel with trophy scope base.
Subtract $90 for synthetic stock (Special Purpose with matte blue finish, 18 1/2 in. barrel).

* ***Model 9200 Crown Semi-Auto Viking*** – 12 ga. only, 28 in. VR barrel with one Accu-Choke and twin bead sights, matte finish with green synthetic stock and forearm, 7.7 lbs. Mfg. 1996-98.

	$365	$320	$275	$250	$200	$165	$130	$429

* ***Model 9200 Crown Semi-Auto Special Hunter*** – 12 ga. only, 28 in. VR barrel with Accu-II choke set, parkerized finish, black synthetic stock. Mfg. 1998-2001.

	$425	$370	$320	$290	$235	$190	$150	$491

* ***Model 9200 Crown Semi-Auto Camo*** – 12 ga. only, similar to Model 9200, except is supplied with OFM (disc. 1996), Mossy Oak (disc. 1999), Realtree (mfg. 1994-95), Realtree AP (mfg. 1996-99) or Woodlands (new 1995) camo finish, 24 (Turkey) or 28 in. VR barrel. Mfg. 1992-99.

	$445	$390	$335	$300	$245	$200	$155	$556

Subtract approx. $40 for Turkey Model with Woodlands camo and one choke tube.

» ***Model 9200 Crown Semi-Auto Camo New Turkey*** – 12 ga. only, 24 in. VR barrel with XX-full choke tube only and fiberoptic sights, choice of 100% Woodlands or Mossy Oak Shadow Branch camo treatment. Mfg. 1999-2001.

	$415	$365	$310	$280	$230	$185	$145	$517

Add approx. $95 for Mossy Oak Shadow Branch camo coverage.

* ***Model 9200 Crown Semi-Auto Jungle Gun*** – 12 ga. only, 18 1/2 in. plain barrel with cyl. bore, parkerized metal, synthetic stock. Mfg. 1998-2001.

	$610	$535	$455	$415	$335	$275	$215	$704

MODEL SA-20 SEMI-AUTO – 20 ga., 3 in. chamber, 20 (Tactical, new 2011), 24 (Bantam only), 26, or 28 in. ported VR barrel with 5 choke tubes, gas operation, matte blue metal finish, black synthetic stock and forearm, approx. 5 1/2 - 6 lbs., mfg. by Armsan in Turkey beginning 2008.

MSR $525	$430	$375	$325	$290	$235	$195	$150	

Add $16 for 20 in. Tactical model w/ghost ring sights and upper/lower Picatinny rails, or $13 for Tactical model w/pistol grip (new 2011).
Add $70 for Turkey Thug Model with Mossy Oak Obession camo, sling, and engraved receiver (new 2012).

This model is also available in a Bantam configuration with 24 in. barrel and shorter LOP (new 2009).

GRADING - PPGS™	100%	98%	95%	90%	80%	70%	60%	LAST MSR

MOUNTAIN RIFLERY, LLC.

Current custom rifle builder located in Pocatello, ID. Consumer direct sales.

John Bolliger has been producing top quality, custom made bolt action rifles for almost 35 years, in addition to being a noted Marlin fisherman. Currently, Mountain Riflery is concentrating on 3 series of rifles: the Signature Series, the Excalibur Series, and the Crown Series. The Signature Series has a price range of $14,500-$21,000. Please contact Mountain Riflery directly for more information, including pricing and options.

MOUNTAIN RIFLES INC.

Previous rifle manufacturer located in Palmer, AK 1995-98.

RIFLES: BOLT ACTION

MOUNTAINEER – various cals., choice of M-700 Rem. or M-70 Win. action, Chrome Moly barrel with ultra muzzle brake, Timney trigger, parkerized finish, fiberglass stock with decelerator pad, 5 1/2 lbs. Limited mfg. 1995-98.

GRADING - PPGS™	100%	98%	95%	90%	80%	70%	60%	LAST MSR
	$1,825	$1,475	$1,100	$900	$750	$675	$550	*$1,995*

SUPER MOUNTAINEER – similar to the Mountaineer, except has Kevlar epoxy bedded stock with steel crossbolts on Mag. cals., 4 1/4 lbs. Limited mfg. 1995-98.

GRADING - PPGS™	100%	98%	95%	90%	80%	70%	60%	LAST MSR
	$2,575	$2,025	$1,475	$1,100	$900	$750	$675	*$2,895*

PRO MOUNTAINEER K.S. – various cals., Winchester M-70 controlled feed action, choice of fiberglass pillar epoxy bedded, Kevlar, or KSDB (Kevlar Stock Drop Box mag.) stock with decelerator pad, parkerized finish. 6 lbs. Limited mfg. 1995-98.

GRADING - PPGS™	100%	98%	95%	90%	80%	70%	60%	LAST MSR
	$2,395	$1,950	$1,425	$1,050	$875	$725	$650	*$2,695*

Add $500 for KSDB stock with drop mag.

PRO SAFARI – various cals., Winchester M-70 controlled feed action, high gloss bluing, exhibition grade English walnut with decelerator pad, 4 shot detachable mag. 7-9 lbs. Limited mfg. 1995-98.

GRADING - PPGS™	100%	98%	95%	90%	80%	70%	60%	LAST MSR
	$3,795	$3,350	$2,875	$2,350	$1,775	$1,450	$1,200	*$3,995*

ULTRA MOUNTAINEER – various cals., features stainless steel match grade barrel with black Kevlar/Graphite thumbhole stock, approx. 5 lbs. New 1997.

GRADING - PPGS™	100%	98%	95%	90%	80%	70%	60%	LAST MSR
	$2,650	$2,075	$1,500	$1,100	$900	$750	$675	*$2,995*

Add $500 for Rigby length.

MUSGRAVE

Previous manufacturer located in the Republic of South Africa.

Musgrave had very limited importation into the U.S. Newer models manufactured by Musgrave (imported into Austria and Switzerland) included the Model 90 (features Musgrave action) Standard Rifle, Model 90 Light Rifle, Mini-90, Model 90 Varmint, Model 90 De Luxe Rifle, and Magnum Rifle, in addition to the same series in the Mauser 98 action.

RIFLES: BOLT ACTION

VALIANT BOLT ACTION RIFLE – .243 Win., .270 Win., .30-06, .308 Win., or 7mm Rem. Mag. cal., 24 in. barrel, leaf sight, skipline checkered straight stock, pistol grip. Mfg. 1971-1976.

GRADING - PPGS™	100%	98%	95%	90%	80%	70%	60%	LAST MSR
	$375	$325	$275	$250	$220	$195	$175	

PREMIER – similar to Valiant, with 26 in. barrel, select Monte Carlo stock, rosewood pistol grip cap and forearm tip.

GRADING - PPGS™	100%	98%	95%	90%	80%	70%	60%	LAST MSR
	$425	$365	$315	$275	$250	$225	$200	

RSA SINGLE SHOT TARGET RIFLE – .308 Win. cal. only, 26 in. heavy barrel, target sights and stock. Mfg. 1971-1976.

GRADING - PPGS™	100%	98%	95%	90%	80%	70%	60%	LAST MSR
	$425	$365	$315	$275	$250	$225	$200	

MUSKETEER RIFLES

Previous trademark of rifles previously imported by Firearms International Company (FIC), located in Washington, D.C.

GRADING - PPGS™	100%	98%	95%	90%	80%	70%	60%	LAST MSR

RIFLES: BOLT ACTION

SPORTER – .243 Win., .25-06 Rem., .270 Win., .264 Win. Mag., .308 Win., .30-06, 7mm Rem. Mag., or .300 Win. Mag. cal., bolt action, FN Mauser action, 24 in. barrel, no sights, checkered Monte Carlo stock. Mfg. 1963-1972.

	$375	$325	$275	$250	$220	$195	$175	

SPORTER DELUXE – adj. trigger, select wood, tear drop pistol grip, skipline checkering.

	$425	$365	$315	$275	$250	$225	$200	

CARBINE – similar to Sporter, except 20 in. barrel and full length stock.

	$375	$325	$275	$250	$220	$195	$175	

NOTES

N SECTION

NS FIREARMS CORP.

Previous importer located in Atlanta, GA until 1994. NS Firearms was a division of KFS, Inc. located in Atlanta, GA. Previously manufactured in China.

GRADING - PPGS™	100%	98%	95%	90%	80%	70%	60%	LAST MSR

RIFLES: SEMI-AUTO

MODEL 522 SPORTER – .22 LR cal., 21 in. cold hammer forged barrel, 5 shot detachable mag., grooved receiver, checkered walnut stock, 7 3/4 lbs. Imported 1994 only.

	100%	98%	95%	90%	80%	70%	60%	LAST MSR
	$250	$215	$185	$165	$145	$125	$110	*$299*

NAMBU PISTOLS

Previously manufactured in Japan for the Japanese military between 1902-1945.

PISTOLS: SEMI-AUTO

Please refer to Japanese Military Pistols for the Hamada variations and the 1893 revolver.

TYPE 14 – 8mm Nambu cal., recoil operated, 4.7 in. barrel, blue, wood grips, 8 shot mag., a simply designed pistol used by Japanese armed forces from 1925-45.

Add 25% for 3.X date Tokyo.
Add 50% for 2.X date Nagoya.
Add 400% for early Taisho era pistols dated 15.11 or 15.12 from Nagoya arsenal.
Add 10% for matching mag. on models listed.

Type 14 Nambus have a 3 or 4 digit number just forward of the lanyard ring on the right side of frame (on back of grip). Earliest Taisho era pistols are dated 15.11 or 15.12 from the Nagoya arsenal - can be identified by small trigger guard and other early features. Fewer than 100 mfg. To determine year and month of manufacture for most type 14 pistols, add "1925" to the first two digits and the last number will indicate the month (i.e. code 13.3 indicates a gun built in March of 1938).

* ***Type 14 1925-1930 Mfg.***

	100%	98%	95%	90%	80%	70%	60%
	$1,500	$1,300	$1,100	$975	$895	$715	$585

* ***Type 14 1930-1939 Mfg.*** – small trigger guard.

	100%	98%	95%	90%	80%	70%	60%
	$1,100	$965	$825	$750	$600	$495	$385

* ***Type 14 1939-1945 Mfg.*** – large trigger guard.

	100%	98%	95%	90%	80%	70%	60%
	$700	$615	$525	$475	$385	$315	$245

Add 10% for strawed trigger and safety.

TYPE 94 – 8mm Nambu cal., recoil operated, 3.8 in. barrel, blue, and bakelite wood grips, 6 shot mag. Mfg. 1935-1945.

	100%	98%	95%	90%	80%	70%	60%
	$525	$465	$395	$350	$295	$235	$185
10.X date	$2,625	$2,000	$1,750	$1,500	$1,250	$1,125	$1,000
11.X date	$1,575	$1,200	$1,050	$900	$750	$675	$600
12.X date	$1,050	$925	$795	$715	$575	$475	$375
pre-WWII	$695	$610	$525	$475	$375	$315	$245
Late square back	$625	$545	$475	$425	$345	$280	$240

Add 10% for matching magazine.

HAMADA NAMBU – Please refer to Japanese Military section.

BABY NAMBU – 7mm Nambu cal., 3 1/4 in. barrel, blue, wood grips, grip safety, one of the most desirable Japanese handguns.

	100%	98%	95%	90%	80%	70%	60%
	$4,500	$3,925	$3,375	$3,050	$2,475	$2,025	$1,575

Add 10% for matching mag. Add 50% for chamber marked "TGE" (Tokyo Gas & Electric).

PAPA NAMBU (MODEL 1904) – 8mm Nambu cal., 4.7 in. barrel, wood grips, grip safety, 8 shot mag., essentially the same action as the Baby, but a larger version. Mfg. 1904-25.

	100%	98%	95%	90%	80%	70%	60%
	$3,000	$2,625	$2,250	$2,025	$1,650	$1,350	$1,050

Add 10% for matching mag. Add 50% for chamber marked "TGE" (Tokyo Gas & Electric).

GRADING - PPGS™	100%	98%	95%	90%	80%	70%	60%	LAST MSR

GRANDPA NAMBU – 8mm Nambu cal., similar to Papa Nambu, except has smaller trigger guard and fixed lanyard ring, cherry wood based mag., issued with 2 matching mags. Early Tokyo arsenal or later Thai issue, all Grandpa frames are slotted.

	$10,000	$9,000	$8,000	$7,000	$6,000	$5,000	$4,000
w/matching shoulder stock	$20,000	$17,500	$15,000	$12,500	$10,000	$9,000	$8,000

Add $8,000 for original stock.

Add 10% for second matching mag.

Original stocks are rare and expensive, check for originality carefully.

NATIONAL POSTAL METER

Previous WWII subcontractor of M1 carbines located in Rochester, NY.

Please refer to U.S. M1 Carbines/Rifles listings under U.S. Military.

NATIONAL WILD TURKEY FEDERATION (NWTF)

Current national conservation organization located in Edgefield, SC.

Although the National Wild Turkey Federation is not a manufacturer or importer, this organization has been responsible for many special and limited editions that are listed with quanities but with issue prices only as current market values, which may vary greatly from region to region. Also, many are sold at auction, making pricing difficult to determine. "NWTF" suffix after model name indicates National Wild Turkey Federation gun of the year. Some of the models (and current values) may be listed under manufacturer listings in this text.

Manufacturer/Model	Quantity	Year	Issue Price
HANDGUNS: AUCTION/TRADE EDITIONS			
KIMBER Custom II	820	2011	N/A
REMINGTON 1911R1	1,010	2012	N/A
BROWNING Hi-Power	300	2013	N/A
RIFLES: AUCTION/TRADE EDITIONS			
REMINGTON Model 700 .270 WSM	N/A	2006	N/A
WEATHERBY Vanguard Deluxe .300 Wby. Mag. Auction	2,500	2008	N/A
WINCHESTER Model 70 Featherweight	930	2011	N/A
BENELLI R1 .30-06	450	2012	N/A
WEATHERBY Vanguard Youth .243 Win.	530	2012	N/A
BROWNING A-Bolt .30-60 cal.	700	2013	N/A
SHOTGUNS: AUCTION/TRADE EDITIONS			
NAVY ARMS Black Powder 12 ga. NWTF	500	1983	$350
WINCHESTER Model 101	300	1985	$1,895
BROWNING BPS 12 ga. NWTF	500	1986	$495
AMERICAN ARMS SxS 10 ga. 3 1/2 in.	150	1985/86	$695
WINCHESTER Model 1300 Win-Cam 12 ga.	500	1987/88	$449
WINCHESTER Model 1300 12 ga. Trade Gun	N/A	N/A	$458
BERETTA Model A-303 12 ga. NWTF	500	1988/89	$695
WINCHESTER Model 1300 12 ga. Win-Cam NWTF	500	1989	$479
WINCHESTER Model 1300 12 ga. Trade Gun	N/A	N/A	$458
BROWNING Model A5 12 ga. NWTF	500	1990	$925
MOSSBERG Model 835 12 ga. Auction	500	1991	$567
MOSSBERG Model 835 12 ga. Trade Gun	N/A	N/A	$436
REMINGTON Model 11-87 12 ga. Auction	N/A	1992	N/A
REMINGTON Model 11-87 12 ga. Trade Gun	N/A	N/A	$698
WINCHESTER Model 1300 12 ga. Auction	500	1993	$671

Manufacturer/Model	Quantity	Year	Issue Price
NEW ENGLAND FIREARMS SxS 20 ga. Auction	N/A	N/A	$167
NEW ENGLAND FIREARMS SxS 12 ga. Trade Gun	N/A	N/A	$200
NEW ENGLAND FIREARMS SxS 10 ga. Trade Gun	N/A	N/A	$240
AMERICAN ARMS Model Turkey 12 ga. Auction	300	1993	N/A
MOSSBERG Model 9200 12 ga. Auction	600	1994	$690
MOSSBERG Model 9200 12 ga. Trade	N/A	1994	N/A
LUGI FRANCHI Model 610 12 ga. Auction	600	1995	N/A
FAUSTI O/U 12 ga. Auction	720	1996	N/A
NEW ENGLAND FIREARMS Topper Jr. 20 ga. Auction	N/A	1996	N/A
FAUSTI O/U 12 ga. Auction	900	1997	N/A
NEW ENGLAND FIREARMS Jakes Topper Jr. 20 ga. Auction	N/A	1997	N/A
REMINGTON Model 870 12 ga. Auction	1,200	1998	N/A
BERETTA Model AL390 12ga.	1,400	1999	N/A
ITHACA Model 37 12ga.	1,700	2000	N/A
BROWNING BPS 12 ga.	1,900	2001	N/A
WINCHESTER Super X2	2,100	2002	N/A
WINCHESTER Model 9410 .410 bore	2,200	2003	N/A
REMINGTON Model 1100 20 ga.	2,400	2004	N/A
BROWNING BPS 12 ga.	2,400	2005	N/A
BROWNING BPS 12 ga.	1,000	2007	N/A
WINCHESTER SX3 12 ga.	2,500	2009	N/A
REMINGTON Model 1100 G-3 20 ga.	2,200	2010	N/A
FAUSTI O/U 12 ga.	600	2011	N/A
BROWNING Silver Hunter 20 ga.	750	2012	N/A
BROWNING Silver 12 ga.	1,000	2013	N/A
JAKES STOEGER Condor 20 ga.	250	2013	N/A

NAVY ARMS COMPANY

Current importer established during 1958, and located in Martinsburg, WV beginning 2005. During 2012, Navy Arms temporarily suspended the importation of firearms. Previously located in Union City, NJ, 2001-2005, in Ridgefield, NJ. Navy Arms imports are fabricated by various manufacturers including the Italian companies Davide Pedersoli & Co., Pietta & Co., and A. Uberti & C. Navy Arms also owns Old Western Scrounger ammo, which markets obsolete and hard-to-find ammo. Distributor and dealer sales.

Navy Arms has also sold a wide variety of original military firearms classified as curios and replics. Handguns included the Mauser Broomhandle, Japanese Nambu, Colt 1911 Government Model, Tokarev, Browning Hi-Power, S&W Model 1917, and others. Rifles included Mauser contract models, Japanese Type 38s, Enfields, FNs, Nagants, M1 Carbines, M1 Garands, Chinese SKSs, Egyptian Rashids, French MAS Model 1936s, among others. Most of these firearms are priced in the $75-$500 price range depending on desirability of model and condition.

For information and up-to-date pricing regarding recent Navy Arms black powder models, please refer to the *Blue Book of Modern Black Powder Arms* by John Allen (also online).

Black Powder Revolvers - Reproductions & Replicas and *Black Powder Long Arms & Pistols - Reproductions & Replicas* by Dennis Adler are also invaluable sources for most black powder revolver reproductions and replicas, and include hundreds of color images on most popular makes/models, provide manufacturer/trademark histories, and up-to-date information on related items/accessories for black powder shooting - www.bluebookofgunvalues.com.

GRADING - PPGS™	100%	98%	95%	90%	80%	70%	60%	LAST MSR

PISTOLS

TU-711 MAUSER – 9mm Para. cal., patterned after Mauser 711 (semi-auto version of the Model 712 Schnellfeuer), 5 1/4 in. barrel, 712 upper receiver that has been converted to 9mm Para. and mounted on new lower receiver, supplied with 10 and 20 shot detachable mag., mfg. in China, 2 lbs. 11 oz. Imported 1992 only.

$575	$475	$425	$375	$325	$295	$275	*$650*

TT-OLYMPIA – .22 LR cal., patterned after the Walther Olympia that won 1936 Olympics, 4 5/8 in. barrel, checkered walnut grips, mfg. in China, 27 oz. Imported 1992-98.

$255	$225	$195	$175	$160	$150	$140	*$290*

TU-90 PISTOL – .30 Tokarev or 9mm Para. cal., patterned after the rare Tokagypt variation (improved TT-33 Tokarev), 4 1/2 in. barrel, single action, wraparound synthetic grips, unique forward motion safety, mfg. in China, 30 oz. Imported 1992-98.

$115	$100	$90	$80	$70	$60	$50	*$130*

Add $15 for 9mm Para. cal.
Add $40 for pistol combo (includes both cals.).

LUGER MODEL – .22 LR cal. only, 10 shot mag., Luger toggle type action, available in blue or matte finish, 4, 6, or 8 in. barrel, checkered walnut stocks. Mfg. in U.S. 1986-87 only.

$140	$120	$95	$85	$75	$70	$65	*$165*

GRAND PRIX SILHOUETTE – .30-30 Win., 7mm Spl., .44 Mag., or .45-70 Govt. cal., 13 3/4 in. barrel, non-glare matte blue finish, walnut forearm and grips, adj. heat dispersing aluminum rib, adj. target sights, 4 lbs. Mfg. 1985 only.

$320	$280	$240	$220	$195	$175	$150	*$375*

REVOLVERS: REPRODUCTIONS

1872 OPEN TOP – .38 Spl. cal., 5 1/2 or 7 1/2 in. round barrel, case colored frame with blue cylinder and barrel, silver plated brass trigger guard and backstrap, 2 1/2-2 3/4 lbs. Limited importation 2000-2001 only.

$335	$275	$220	$185	$165	$150	$135	*$400*

1873 SAA - GUNFIGHTER SERIES & VARIATIONS – .32-20 WCF (mfg. 2002, reintroduced 2007), .357 Mag. (new 1998), .44-40 WCF or .45 LC cal., reproduction of the Colt SAA, case hardened frame with blue or nickel (disc. 1998) finish, 3 (Sheriff's Model - mfg. 1992-98), 4 3/4, 5 1/2, or 7 1/2 in. barrel, the Gunfighter Series was introduced during 2003, approx. 36 oz. Disc. 2009.

$415	$335	$295	$230	$180	$160	$145	*$511*

Add $65 for nickel finish (disc.).
Add $30 for Pinched Frame Model (7 1/2 in. barrel, .45 LC, disc. 2002).
Subtract $20 for brass trigger guard and backstrap (disc.).

The Gunfighter Series, introduced in 2003, was different than previous production in that it featured a U.S. mfg. Wolff spring kit, German silver plated backstrap and trigger guard, and black checkered gunfighter grips.

* ***1873 SAA Gunfighter Series Stainless Steel Model*** – .357 Mag. or .45 LC cal., 4 3/4, 5 1/2, or 7 1/2 in. barrel, stainless steel construction. Imported 2003-2009.

$485	$375	$315	$250	$215	$185	$155	*$608*

* ***1873 SAA Gunfighter Series Deluxe Model*** – .32-20 WCF cal., deluxe model with color case hardened and charcoal blue finishes, high polish walnut grips, includes Wolff springs. Limited importation 2003.

$365	$295	$230	$200	$180	$165	$140	*$435*

This model is sold exclusively through AcuSport.

* ***1873 SAA Gunfighter Series Economy Model*** – .44-40 WCF or .45 LC cal., 3, 4 3/4, 5 1/2, or 7 1/2 in. barrel, brass trigger guard and backstrap, 2-piece walnut grips. Imported 1993-96.

$295	$230	$185	$160	$145	$130	$120	*$345*

* ***1873 SAA Gunfighter Series Deputy Model*** – .44-40 WCF or .45 LC cal., patterned after the Colt 1877 Thunderer double action, birdshead grips, 3, 3 1/2, 4, or 4 3/4 in.

GRADING - PPGS™	100%	98%	95%	90%	80%	70%	60%	LAST MSR

barrel, case colored frame. Imported 1997-1998 only.

	$350	$275	$210	$180	$160	$145	$130	*$405*

* ***1873 SAA Gunfighter Series Flattop Target Model*** – .45 LC cal. only, features flattop frame, 7 1/2 in. barrel only, adj. spring loaded front sight and dovetailed rear sight, 30 oz. Imported 1999-2006.

	$425	$350	$285	$240	$205	$175	$150	*$514*

* ***1873 SAA Gunfighter Series Shootist Model*** – .357 Mag., .44-40 WCF, or .45 LC cal., interchangeable parts with original Colt 1st and 2nd Generation SAAs, designed for Cowboy Action Shooting, 4 3/4, 5 1/2, or 7 1/2 in. barrel, case colored frame and hammer, blue cylinder barrel, trigger guard and backstrap. Limited importation 2000 only.

	$350	$275	$210	$180	$160	$145	$130	*$385*

* ***1873 SAA Gunfighter Series Bisley Model*** – .44-40 WCF or .45 LC cal., patterned after the Colt Bisley, 4 3/4, 5 1/2, or 7 1/2 in. barrel, case colored frame, spur hammer, walnut grips. Imported 1997-2009.

	$415	$335	$295	$230	$180	$160	$145	*$511*

» **1873 SAA Gunfighter Series Bisley Model Flattop Target** – .44-40 WCF or .45 LC (disc. 2006) cal., features flattop frame, adj. front sight, and dovetailed rear sight, 40 oz. Imported 1999-2009.

	$485	$375	$315	$250	$215	$185	$155	*$608*

* ***1873 SAA Gunfighter Series Cavalry Model*** – .45 LC cal. only, exact replica of the original U.S. Government issue SAA, 7 1/2 in. barrel, arsenal stampings, inspector's cartouche on walnut stocks. Disc. 2009.

	$515	$385	$335	$280	$230	$200	$175	*$594*

* ***1873 SAA Gunfighter Series Artillery Model*** – similar specifications to the Cavalry Model, except has 5 1/2 in barrel.

	$515	$385	$335	$280	$230	$200	$175	*$594*

* ***1873 SAA Gunfighter Series Scout Small Frame Model*** – .38 Spl. cal., scaled down variation of the SAA, 4 3/4 or 5 1/2 in. barrel only. Imported 2003-2009.

	$415	$335	$295	$230	$180	$160	$145	*$511*

1875 REMINGTON REVOLVER – .44-40 WCF or .45 LC cal., reproduction of the 1875 Remington revolver, 7 1/2 in. barrel, case colored frame, 41 oz. Importation disc. 1991, resumed 1994-2000.

	$360	$295	$260	$230	$200	$175	$150	*$435*

1890 REMINGTON REVOLVER – .44-40 WCF or .45 LC cal., reproduction of the 1890 Remington revolver, 5 1/2 in. barrel, brass trigger guard and lanyard loop, 39 oz. Importation disc. 1991, resumed 1994-2000.

	$370	$295	$260	$230	$200	$175	$150	*$445*

1875 SCHOFIELD SERIES – various cals., patterned after the original S&W Schofield Model, blued finish, smooth wood grips, case colored hammer, trigger guard and opening lever. Imported 1994-2003. .44-40 WCF or .45 LC cal., similar to Wells Fargo Model, except has 3 1/2 in. barrel, 34 oz. New 1999. .45 LC cal., charcoal blue barrel and cylinder, case colored receiver, backstrap, trigger guard, and trigger, 7 1/2 in. barrel, white ivory tex grips. Importation began 2003. .44-40 WCF or .45 LC cal., similar to Deluxe Schofield, except does not have gold inlays, extensive B or C coverage scroll engraving on both frame, cylinder, and barrel. Special order only beginning 1999..44-40 WCF or .45 LC cal., available in Cavalry, Wells Fargo, or Hideout configurations, with light scroll engraving on frame and cylinder with extensive frame, barrel, and cylinder gold line inlays and scroll motifs. Special order only 1999-2009.

	$615	$535	$455	$375	$325	$250	$195	*$716*

* ***1875 Schofield Series Cavalry Model*** – .38 Spl. (new 2003), .44-40 WCF, or .45 LC cal., patterned after the original Schofield Cavalry Model, 7 1/2 in. barrel, 37 oz. Imported 1994-2009.

	$715	$600	$485	$395	$335	$250	$195	*$849*

GRADING - PPGS™	100%	98%	95%	90%	80%	70%	60%	LAST MSR

* ***1875 Schofield Series Wells Fargo Model*** – .38 Spl. (new 2003), .44-40 WCF, or .45 LC cal., 5 1/2 in. barrel, 35 oz. Mfg. 1994-2009, reintroduced 2011.

MSR $899	$750	$625	$500	$400	$335	$250	$195	

* ***1875 Schofield Series Hideout Model*** – 3 1/2 in. barrel.

	$715	$600	$485	$395	$335	$250	$195	*$849*

* ***1875 Schofield Series Founders Model*** – .38 Spl. or .45 LC cal., 7 in. barrel, features charcoal blue barrel and cylinder, case colored frame, backstrap, trigger and trigger guard, "VF" serial number prefix.

	$800	$665	$515	$400	$350	$250	$195	*$946*

* ***1875 Schofield Series Engraved Model***

	$1,425	$1,225	$1,000	$875	$750	$625	$525	

Add $215 for C engraving.

* ***1875 Schofield Series Deluxe Model***

	$1,675	$1,450	$1,250	$995	$875	$750	$625	

NEW MODEL RUSSIAN – .44 Russian cal., patterned after the S&W Model 3 Russian Third Model Single Action, 6 1/2 in. barrel, blue metal with case colored trigger, trigger guard, and hammer, smooth walnut grips, 40 oz. Imported 1999-2009.

	$765	$635	$500	$400	$350	$250	$195	*$908*

REVOLVERS: REPRODUCTIONS, COLT CARTRIDGE CONVERSIONS

1851 NAVY RICHARDS-TYPE CONVERSION – .38 Spl. or .38 LC cal., patterned after the Colt 1851 Navy Conversion, 5 1/2 or 7 1/2 in. barrel, case colored frame and hammer, blue cylinder and barrel, brass back strap and trigger guard, 40 or 44 oz. Imported 1999-2001.

	$320	$255	$200	$175	$160	$145	$130	*$375*

1860 ARMY RICHARDS-TYPE CONVERSION – .38 Spl. or .38 LC cal., patterned after the Colt 1860 Army Conversion, other specifications similar to 1851 Navy Conversion. Imported 1999-2001.

	$320	$255	$200	$175	$160	$145	$130	*$375*

1861 NAVY RICHARDS-TYPE CONVERSION – .38 Spl. or .38 LC cal., patterned after the Colt 1861 Navy Conversion, other specifications similar to 1851 Navy Conversion. Imported 1999-2001.

	$320	$255	$200	$175	$160	$145	$130	*$375*

REVOLVERS: PREMIUM BLUE REPRODUCTIONS, CARTRIDGE CONVERSIONS

During 2003, Navy Arms planned to introduce its line of Premium Blue custom guns. However, these guns were never manufactured, except for a few prototypes. Models included were: 1860 Army Richards Type I ($1,995 MSR), Richards-Mason Colt Pocket Navy Model ($2,995 MSR), Richards-Mason Colt Police Model ($2,695 MSR), 1842 Paterson Conversion Model ($2,100 MSR), Remington Navy .38 Colt Cartridge Conversion, Remington Army 5 Shot Cartridge Conversion ($1,295 MSR), and the Remington 6 Shot Cartridge Conversion ($1,495 MSR).

RIFLES: REPRODUCTIONS

REVOLVING CARBINE – .357 Mag., .44-40 WCF, or .45 LC cal., 6 shot cylinder, 20 in. barrel, case hardened frame, straight stock. Mfg. 1968-1984.

	$575	$475	$425	$375	$325	$275	$225	

REMINGTON ROLLING BLOCK BUFFALO RIFLE – .444 Marlin (disc.), .45-70 Govt., or .50-70 (disc.) cal., replica of Remington Rolling Block, 26 or 30 in. heavy octagon or 1/2 round/1/2 octagon barrel (disc. 2000), open sight, straight grip stock. Mfg. 1971-2003.

	$655	$465	$350	$260	$195	$160	$140	*$850*

Brass fittings were disc. during 1998, and replaced with steel fittings.

* ***Remington Rolling Block Buffalo Carbine*** – similar to Rifle, with 18 in. barrel. Disc. 1985.

	$385	$325	$280	$230	$180	$160	$140	*$375*

GRADING - PPGS™	100%	98%	95%	90%	80%	70%	60%	LAST MSR

* ***Remington Rolling Block Buffalo Baby Rifle*** – .22 LR, .22 Hornet, .357 Mag., or .44-40 WCF cal., replica of small frame Remington, 20 in. octagon or 22 in. round barrel, open sight, straight stock. Mfg. 1968-84.

	$215	$175	$140	$110	$90	$65	$55	

REMINGTON ROLLING BLOCK BODINE RIFLE – single or double set triggers, 30 in. heavy matte finished octagon barrel, nickel or case colored finish, "Soule" target rear tang sight, and split level globe front sight, No. 2 configuration became available during 2003, 12 lbs.

MSR $1,940	$1,700	$1,425	$1,125	$950	$800	$650	$500	

REMINGTON ROLLING BLOCK #2 BODINE RIFLE – similar to Bodine model, except has double set triggers, nickel finished receiver and lightweight barrel. New 2010.

MSR $1,937	$1,700	$1,425	$1,125	$950	$800	$650	$500	

ROLLING BLOCK PLAINS RIFLE – .45-70 Govt. cal., features 30 in. tapered octagon barrel with straight grip stock, bright polished receiver with steel furniture, 9 lbs. Imported 1997-98 only.

	$650	$500	$400	$285	$195	$175	$150	*$800*

* ***Rolling Block Plains Rifle Deluxe*** – similar to Plains Rifle, except has hand engraved coin finished receiver and trigger guard, rust blue barrel with German silver forearm tip. Imported 1997-98.

	$1,475	$1,250	$1,050	$850	$725	$600	$525	*$1,625*

ROLLING BLOCK NO. 2 CREEDMOOR TARGET – similar to Buffalo Rifle, in .45-70 Govt. or .50-70 (disc.) cal., with Creedmoor tang sight, color case hardened receiver, checkered walnut.

	$1,450	$1,175	$975	$800	$650	$500	$400	*$1,754*

* ***Rolling Block No. 2 Creedmoor Target Deluxe*** – featured hand engraved coin finished receiver and trigger guard, rust blue barrel and German silver forearm tip. Imported 1997-98.

	$1,625	$1,400	$1,200	$1,000	$850	$725	$600	*$1,875*

SHARPS NO. 2 SILHOUETTE – .45-70 Govt. cal., 30 in. octagon barrel, 10 3/4 lbs. Imported 2003-2009.

	$1,450	$1,150	$995	$850	$750	$650	$575	*$1,739*

SHARPS NO. 2 HUNTER – limited importation 2003 only.

	$750	$650	$575	$525	$475	$425	$375	*$815*

1874 SHARPS PLAINS RIFLE – .45-70 Govt. cal., 32 in. octagon barrel, case hardened receiver, checkered stock and forearm, double set triggers, 9 1/2 lbs. Mfg. 1996-2002.

	$1,020	$900	$800	$725	$625	$575	$525	*$1,175*

Add $75 for vernier rear tang or $55 for globe sight.

* ***1874 Sharps Plains Rifle Engraved*** – .45-70 Govt. cal., features hand engraved coin finished receiver. Imported 1997-98.

	$2,325	$2,000	$1,800	$1,600	$1,400	$1,200	$995	*$2,500*

Add $700 for gold inlays (Deluxe Model).

1874 SHARPS BUFFALO RIFLE – .45-70 Govt. or .45-90 (disc. 2000) cal., 28 in. octagon heavy barrel, case colored receiver, checkered stock, 10 lbs. 10 oz. Mfg. 1996-2002.

	$1,035	$925	$825	$725	$625	$575	$525	*$1,200*

Add $75 for vernier rear tang or $55 for globe sight.

* ***1874 Sharps Buffalo Rifle Engraved*** – .45-70 Govt. or .45-90 cal., features hand engraved coin finished receiver. Imported 1997-98.

	$2,325	$2,000	$1,800	$1,600	$1,400	$1,200	$995	*$2,515*

Add $700 for gold inlays (Deluxe Model).

SHARPS SPORTING RIFLE – .45-70 Govt. cal., similar to Plains Rifle, except has pistol grip stock, No. 2 configuration became available during 2003. Imported 1997-2009.

	$1,450	$1,150	$995	$850	$750	$650	$575	*$1,739*

1874 SHARPS QUIGLEY – .45-70 Govt. cal., 34 in. octagon barrel, exact reproduction of rifle used in the movie *Quigley Down Under*, with patchbox. Imported 2002-2012.

	$1,625	$1,325	$1,075	$900	$725	$625	$550	*$1,981*

GRADING - PPGS™	100%	98%	95%	90%	80%	70%	60%	LAST MSR

1874 SHARPS NO. 2 CREEDMOOR – .45-70 Govt. cal., 30 in. thin tapered round barrel, polished nickel frame and action, "Soule" rear tang sight with front globe, 9 lbs. Imported 2002-2012.

$1,525	$1,200	$1,025	$850	$750	$650	$575	*$1,844*

1874 SHARPS NO. 3 LONG RANGE – .45-70 Govt. cal., 34 in. medium weight octagon barrel with globe front target sight, shotgun buttplate, double set triggers, German silver forearm cap, 10 lbs. 14 oz. Imported 2000-2012.

$1,950	$1,575	$1,300	$1,100	$925	$725	$600	*$2,379*

1874 SHARPS SNIPER/INFANTRY RIFLE – .45-70 Govt. cal., patterned after the 3-band military sniper rifle, 30 in. barrel, color case hardened frame, hammer, and furniture, ST or DST (Sniper rifle, disc. 1995). Mfg. 1994-2000.

$895	$780	$650	$475	$395	$350	$325	*$1,060*

Add $55 for DST (Sniper).

1874 SHARPS SNIPER/INFANTRY CAVALRY CARBINE – .45-70 Govt. cal., patterned after Sharps Cavalry carbine, 22 in. barrel, color case hardened frame, hammer, patchbox, and furniture. Mfg. 1994-2009.

$975	$800	$665	$475	$395	$350	$325	*$1,246*

1873 SPRINGFIELD INFANTRY RIFLE – .45-70 Govt. cal., 32 1/2 in. barrel, 8 lbs, 4 oz. Imported 1997-2000.

$840	$750	$650	$475	$395	$350	$325	*$995*

1873 SPRINGFIELD INFANTRY CAVALRY CARBINE – similar to the 1873 Springfield Rifle, except has 22 in. barrel, 1 barrel band, 7 lbs. Imported 1997-2010.

$1,325	$1,050	$900	$775	$650	$550	$450	*$1,519*

Add $324 for Springfield Officer's Model.

KODIAK MARK IV DOUBLE RIFLE – .45-70 Govt. cal., patterned after the Colt Double rifle, semi-regulated 24 in. barrels, hammers, folding leaf rear sight, color cased hardened receiver, 10 lbs. 3 oz. Mfg. 1996-2000.

$2,450	$2,250	$2,000	$1,800	$1,600	$1,400	$1,200	*$2,815*

* ***Kodiak Mark IV Double Rifle Deluxe*** – similar to Kodiak Mark IV Double rifle, except has brown barrels and hand engraved satin finished receiver. Mfg. 1996-2000.

$3,300	$2,900	$2,600	$2,375	$2,000	$1,750	$1,500	*$3,690*

HENRY RIFLE – .44-40 WCF, .44 Rimfire (disc. 1989), or .45 LC (new 1998) cal., reproduction of Winchester's famous Henry Rifle, brass or iron frame. New 1985.

* ***Henry Rifle Military*** – 24 in. barrel, brass frame, blue barrel, walnut stock, original style sling swivels, 9 1/4 lbs. Mfg. 1985-2009.

$925	$725	$575	$450	$325	$250	$225	*$1,199*

* ***Henry Rifle Union Pacific Railroad Commemorative*** – .44-40 WCF cal., only 100 mfg.

$795	$575	$475	N/A	N/A	N/A	N/A	*$695*

* ***Henry Rifle Engraved*** – limited mfg., extensive engraving on brass frame. Disc. 1988.

$1,510	$1,275	$1,100	$900	$750	$650	$550	*$1,850*

Add $100 for steel frame.

* ***Henry Carbine*** – 24 in. barrel, limited edition of 1,000 units including 50 engraved specimens, no swivels, 8 1/4 lbs. Importation disc. 2002.

$685	$540	$450	$350	$275	$225	$195	*$875*

* ***Henry Engraved Carbine*** – limited production, only 50 mfg. Disc. 1988.

$1,450	$1,225	$1,075	$900	$750	$650	$550	*$1,750*

* ***Henry Rifle Trapper Model*** – 16 1/2 in. barrel, 7 1/4 lbs., 34 1/4 in. overall length. Disc. 2000.

$685	$540	$450	$350	$275	$225	$195	*$875*

GRADING - PPGS™	100%	98%	95%	90%	80%	70%	60%	LAST MSR

* ***Henry Rifle Iron Frame Model*** – with steel frame and buttplate, 24 in. blue barrel, select walnut, 9 1/4 lbs.

	$1,000	$825	$650	$550	$450	$375	$325	*$1,258*

Add $17 for color case hardened frame.

This model was available with either blue (.44-40 WCF cal. only) or color case hardened receiver.

MODEL 1866 YELLOWBOY CARBINE/RIFLE – .22 LR (disc.), .357 Mag. (disc.), .38 Spl. (new 1998), .44-40 WCF, or .45 LC (new 1998) cal., choice of rifle (24 1/4 in. octagon barrel, disc. 2009), short rifle (20 in. octagon barrel), or carbine (19 in. round barrel), brass (disc.) or case hardened receiver, replica of the Winchester Model 1866. Mfg. 1972-1984, reintroduced until 2010.

	$800	$625	$450	$350	$250	$225	$200	*$972*

Add $43 for rifle.

* ***Model 1866 Yellowboy 100th Anniversary Indian Victory in Little Big Horn***

	$725	$625	$525	$440	$385	$325	$280	

YELLOWBOY TRAPPER – .44-40 WCF cal., 16 1/2 in. barrel. Disc.

	$675	$575	$475	$425	$375	$325	$275	

MODEL 1873 CARBINE/RIFLE – .357 Mag. (new 1998), .44-40 WCF or .45 LC cal., choice of rifle (24 in. octagon barrel) or carbine (19 in. round barrel), replica of the Winchester Model 1873.

	$950	$750	$575	$450	$350	$295	$250	*$1,132*

Add $25 for rifle variation.

* ***Model 1873 Carbine Trapper*** – .44-40 WCF cal., similar to Carbine, with 16 1/2 in. barrel. Disc.

	$700	$600	$500	$425	$375	$325	$275	

* ***Model 1873 Border Model Rifle*** – .357 Mag., .44-40 WCF, or .45 LC cal., features 20 in. short octagon rifle barrel, case hardened receiver with blue barrel, 7 lbs. 6 oz. Imported 1999-2009.

	$915	$725	$685	$450	$350	$295	$250	*$1,079*

* ***Model 1873 Deluxe Border Model Rifle*** – similar to Model 1873 Deluxe Sporting Rifle, except has 20 in. barrel. Importation began 2001.

MSR $1,241	$1,025	$825	$625	$500	$400	$300	$225	

* ***Model 1873 Deluxe Sporting Rifle*** – deluxe variation of the Model 1873 featuring case hardened receiver, lever, and hammer, checkered pistol grip stock, and choice of 24 1/4 or 30 (not available in .357 Mag. cal., disc. 2002) in. barrel, 8 lbs. 4 oz. or 8 lbs., 14 oz. Imported 1992-2009.

	$1,000	$825	$625	$500	$400	$300	$225	*$1,218*

Add $30 for 30 in. barrel (disc. 2002).

* ***Model 1873 Deluxe Sporting Rifle Long Range*** – .44-40 WCF cal., 30 in. barrel with rear tang sight. Imported 2003 only.

	$995	$800	$625	$475	$350	$300	$250	*$1,140*

* ***Model 1873 1 of 1,000*** – only 1,000 mfg., deluxe wood, special engraving.

	$1,000	$775	$550	$460	$395	$335	$285	

MODEL 1892 CARBINE/RIFLE – .357 Mag., .44-40 WCF, or .45 LC cal., features 20 (carbine, w/o forearm cap, disc. 2001) or 24 (rifle) in. octagon barrel, choice of brass (disc.), blue, or case hardened receiver and crescent buttplate, uncheckered straight grip walnut stock and forearm, 5 lbs. 14 oz. or 7 lbs. Imported 1999-2003.

	$465	$385	$335	$280	$240	$210	$185	*$561*

Subtract approx. $65 for carbine configuration (disc. 2001).

* ***Model 1892 Carbine/Rifle Stainless*** – similar to Standard Model 1892, except is stainless steel, not available in .44-40 WCF cal. Imported 2000-2003.

	$435	$360	$300	$240	$210	$180	$155	*$530*

Add $73 for rifle configuration.

GRADING - PPGS™	100%	98%	95%	90%	80%	70%	60%	LAST MSR

* ***Model 1892 Short Rifle*** – also available in .32-20 WCF cal. (new 2002), similar to Model 1892 Standard Rifle, except has 20 in. short barrel, not available with brass frame, approx. 6 1/4 lbs. Imported 1999-2003.

$465	$385	$335	$280	$240	$210	$185	$561

* ***Model 1892 Stainless Short Rifle*** – similar to Model 1892 Short Rifle, except is stainless steel. Imported 2000 only.

$485	$360	$300	$240	$210	$180	$155	$603

MODEL 1885 HIGH WALL RIFLE – .45-70 Govt. cal., available with 30 in. medium heavy octagon barrel with crescent buttplate or 28 in. round barrel with shotgun style buttplate, standard or open target sights, case hardened frame and lever, uncheckered European walnut stock and forearm, 9 1/4 or 10 lbs. Imported 1999-2009.

$975	$750	$625	$500	$400	$300	$275	$1,169

Add $117 for rear tang sight.

LIGHTNING SLIDE ACTION – replica of original Colt Lightning, 24 in. octagon barrel, redesigned ejection system, checkered straight grip walnut stock, case colored finish, gold bead front sight, semi-buckhorn rear sight, mfg. by Pedersoli. Imported 2010-2012.

$1,075	$850	$675	$550	$500	$450	$395	$1,399

RIFLES: MODERN PRODUCTION

In addition to the models listed, Navy Arms in late 1990 purchased the manufacturing rights of the English firm Parker-Hale. In 1991, Navy Arms built a manufacturing facility, Gibbs Rifle Co., located in Martinsburg, WV and produced these rifles domestically 1991-1994 (see Gibbs Rifle Co. listing for more info on models the company currently imports).

TU-KKW TRAINING RIFLE – .22 LR cal., replica of the German "KKW" Gewehr training rifle, full sized Mauser 98K action with military sights, 26 in. barrel, detachable 5 shot mag., mfg. in China, 8 lbs. Imported 1992-94.

$240	$210	$180	$150	$135	$120	$105	$310

Add $125 for 2 3/4 power Type 89 quick mount scope (Sniper Trainer).

TU-33/40 CARBINE – .22 LR or 7.62x39mm cal., based on WWII Mauser G33/40 mountain carbine, 20 3/4 in. barrel, includes sling, adj. rear sight, mfg. in China, 7 lbs. 7 oz. Imported 1992-94.

$210	$180	$150	$135	$120	$105	$90	$210

JW-15 RIFLE – .22 LR cal., sporter bolt action based on Brno Model 5 action, 24 in. barrel, detachable 5 shot mag., receiver top is dove-tailed, mfg. in China, 5 lbs. 12 oz. Imported 1992-94.

$85	$70	$60	$50	$40	$35	$30	$100

MARTINI TARGET RIFLE – .444 Marlin or .45-70 Govt. cal., single shot, 26 or 30 in. octagon barrel, tang sight, pistol grip stock. Mfg. 1972-84.

$480	$420	$350	$250	$195	$175	$150	

RPKS-74 – .223 Rem. or 7.62x39mm (new 1989) cal., semi-auto version of the Chinese RPK Squad Automatic Weapon, Kalashnikov action, 19 in. barrel, integral folding bipod, 9 1/2 lbs. Imported 1988-89 only.

$525	$445	$350	$250	$195	$175	$150	$649

MODEL 1 CARBINE/RIFLE – .45-70 Govt. cal., action is sporterized No. 1 MKIII Enfield, choice of 18 (carbine) or 22 (rifle) in. barrel with iron sights, black Zytel Monte Carlo (rifle) or straight grip walnut (carbine) stock, 7 (carbine) or 8 1/2 (rifle) lbs. Limited importation 1999 only.

$325	$255	$200	$175	$160	$145	$130	$375

MODEL 4 CARBINE/RIFLE – .45-70 Govt. cal., action is sporterized No. 4 MKI Enfield, choice of 18 (carbine) or 22 (rifle) in. barrel, blue metal, choice of checkered walnut Monte Carlo (rifle) or uncheckered straight grip (carbine, disc. 1999) stock, 7 or 8 lbs. Mfg. 1999-2001.

$325	$255	$200	$175	$160	$145	$130	$375

GRADING - PPGS™	100%	98%	95%	90%	80%	70%	60%	LAST MSR

* ***Model No. 4 Carbine/Rifle Enfield Sporter Deluxe*** – .303 British cal., synthetic Zytel Monte Carlo stock, 25 in. barrel with original military sights, approx. 8 1/2 lbs. Mfg. 1999-2001.

	$115	$95	$85	$75	$65	$55	$50	$125

2A HUNTER CARBINE/RIFLE – .308 Win. cal., action is sporterized 2A Enfield, 18 (carbine) or 22 (rifle) in. barrel with Parker-Hale style muzzle brake, includes scope mount, 12 shot mag., black enamel synthetic Zytel stock, 6 3/4 or 10 1/4 lbs. Mfg. 1999-2001.

	$240	$210	$190	$175	$160	$145	$130	$275

Add $50 for rifle variation.

* ***2A Hunter Carbine/Rifle Enfield Sporter Deluxe*** – .308 Win. cal., 25 in. barrel, black Zytel Monte Carlo stock, original 2A Enfield military sights, approx. 8 1/2 lbs. Mfg. 1999-2001.

	$130	$110	$95	$85	$75	$65	$55	$150

SHOTGUNS: O/U, RECENT IMPORTATION

Importation of the models listed was disc. in 1990.

MODEL 83 – 12 or 20 ga., manufactured in Italy by R. Luciano, 3 in. chambers, extractors, double triggers, engraved chrome receiver, vent. barrels (bored M/F or IC/M) and rib. Introduced 1985.

	$280	$240	$215	$195	$170	$160	$150	$320

MODEL 93 – 12 or 20 ga., manufactured in Italy by R. Luciano, 3 in. chambers, ejectors, double triggers, engraved chrome receiver, vent. barrels (bored M/F or IC/M) and rib. Introduced 1985.

	$325	$285	$250	$220	$200	$185	$160	$380

MODEL 95 – similar to Model 93, except with single trigger and multi-chokes (includes 5 tubes), extractors.

	$375	$330	$295	$265	$235	$210	$190	$420

MODEL 96 SPORTSMAN – 12 ga. only, 3 in. chambers, vent. barrels and rib, engraved chrome receiver, gold-plated receiver, multi-choked with 5 choke tubes, ejectors. Introduced 1985.

	$470	$425	$375	$330	$295	$260	$230	$530

MODEL 100 – 12, 20, 28 ga., or .410 bore, 3 in. chambers, 26 in. VR barrels, photo engraved hard chrome receiver, single trigger, extractors, checkered walnut stock and forearm, approx. 6 1/4 lbs. Introduced 1985.

	$225	$205	$190	$170	$160	$150	$140	$250

SHOTGUNS: SxS, RECENT IMPORTATION

MODEL 100 – 12 or 20 ga., 3 in. chambers, 27 1/2 in. barrels, checkered European walnut, double triggers, extractors, 6 1/2 or 7 lbs. Imported 1985-87 only.

	$380	$330	$290	$260	$230	$200	$170	$475

MODEL 150 – similar to Model 100, except with ejectors. Imported 1985-87 only.

	$455	$395	$350	$310	$280	$250	$220	$574

SHOTGUNS: SINGLE SHOT

MODEL 105 SINGLE BARREL – 12, 20 ga., or .410 bore, 26 or 28 in. full choke barrel only, folding action, engraved chrome receiver, checkered hardwood stock and forearm. New 1985.

	$80	$70	$65	$60	$55	$50	$45	$90

This model was designated the Model 600 before 1988.

* ***Model 105 Single Barrel Deluxe*** – similar to Model 105, except has European walnut stock and VR.

	$95	$85	$75	$65	$60	$55	$50	$105

This model was designated the Model 600 Deluxe before 1988.

GRADING - PPGS™	100%	98%	95%	90%	80%	70%	60%	LAST MSR

P.V. NELSON GUNMAKERS LTD.

Previous manufacturer located in Bucks, England.

P.V. Nelson manufactured best quality shotguns and double rifles per individual customer order. Double rifles featured back action locks, and bolsters for extra strength. Side-by-side and over/under shotguns were available in most gauges, with a choice of rounded or regular action. Guns should be appraised individually.

NEMESIS ARMS

Current rifle manufacturer located in Calimesa, CA.

RIFLES: BOLT ACTION

VANQUISH (WINDRUNNER) – .243 Win., .260 Rem., 6.5 Creedmor (new 2011), .308 Win., or .338 Federal cal., 20 in. chrome-moly steel heavy fluted barrel, steel alloy upper, steel lower, adj. stock, 5 shot mag., Weaver rail, Versapod bipod, 12 lbs.

MSR $4,450	$3,850	$3,500	$3,150	$2,725	$2,400	$2,125	$1,775	

During 2010, this model's nomenclature changed from Windrunner to the Vanquish.

NEMO (NEW EVOLUTION MILITARY ORDNANCE)

Current centerfire rifle manufacturer located in Kalispell, MT. Dealer sales.

RIFLES: SEMI-AUTO

NEMO manufactures many variations of rifles built on the AR-15 style platform. It currently sells weapon systems to the military, law enforcement, special operations, and the civilian marketplace. NEMO also makes tactical bolt action rifles per individual specifications. Current models include Tango 2, Tango 6, Tango 8, Omen (new 2012), and the Titanium Battle Rifle. Please contact the company directly for more information on its products, availability, and pricing (see Trademark Index).

NESIKA

Current trademark of actions manufactured by Nesika Bay Precision, Inc., located in Sturgis, SD. Actions are currently distributed by Dakota Arms. Nesika also manufactured rifles circa 2004-2005. Previously located in Poulsbo, WA until 2003. Dealer and consumer sales.

On June 5, 2009, Remington Arms Company purchased Dakota Arms, Inc., including the rights to Nesika.

RIFLES: BOLT ACTION

Nesika also sold its proprietary rifle actions until 2009 in Classic ($1,275 - $1,475 MSR), Round ($1,000 - $1,350 MSR), Hunter ($1,050 - $1,450 MSR), and Tactical ($1,400 - $1,700 MSR) configurations and in a variety of cals. A Model NXP bolt action single shot pistol model was also available. Last MSR was $1,100 circa 2008.

CLASSIC HUNTER – various cals., stainless Nesika action and barrel, adj. trigger, composite, laminated, or Turkish walnut stock, hinged floorplate, various options. Mfg. 2004-2005.

	$3,450	$2,950	$2,650	$2,325	$2,000	$1,600	$1,250	*$3,710*

Add $60 for Model V or $450 for Model M.

NESIKA VARMINT – various varmint cals., single shot or repeater, stainless Nesika action and helical fluted bolt, stainless barrel, composite or wood laminated stock, various options. Mfg. 2004-2005.

	$3,050	$2,650	$2,375	$2,000	$1,750	$1,500	$1,250	*$3,440*

Add $60 for Model K.

URBAN TACTICAL – various tactical cals., heavy duty receiver with Picatinny rail and fluted 24 or 28 in. barrel, detachable box mag., black synthetic stock with adj. recoil pad. Mfg. 2004-2005.

	$4,500	$4,000	$3,500	$3,000	$2,500	$2,000	$1,650	*$5,040*

Add $160 for heavy .308 Win. cal. or $520 for Lapua or Lazzeroni Warbird or Patriot cals.

NEW ADVANTAGE ARMS, INC.

Previous handgun manufacturer located in Tucson, AZ, circa mid-1990s.

GRADING - PPGS™	100%	98%	95%	90%	80%	70%	60%	LAST MSR

DERRINGERS

4 BARREL DERRINGER – .22 LR or .22 WMR cal., 4 barrel, double action with rotating hammer, 4 shot mag., high grade alloy, 2 1/2 in. barrel, blue steel alloy or stainless steel, fixed sights, walnut grips, 15 oz. Disc.

	100%	98%	95%	90%	80%	70%	60%	LAST MSR
	$175	$150	$120	$110	$100	$90	$80	

NEW DETONICS MANUFACTURING CORPORATION

Previous manufacturer located in Phoenix, AZ 1989-1992. Formerly named Detonics Firearms Industries (previous manufacturer located in Bellevue, WA 1976-1988). Detonics was sold in early 1988 to the New Detonics Manufacturing Corporation, a wholly owned subsidiary of "1045 Investors Group Limited."

Due to space considerations, information regarding this manufacturer is available online free of charge at www.bluebookofgunvalues.com.

NEW ENGLAND ARMS CORP.

Previous importer, distributor, and retailer from 1975-2004, and located in Kittery Point, ME.

New England Arms Corp. imported, distributed, or retailed the following trademarks: Arrieta, P. Arrizabalaga, Bertuzzi, Luciano Bosis, Cosmi, Henri Dumoulin, Fair Techni-Mec (I. Rizzini), Antonio Gil, Lebeau-Courally, F.lli Rizzini, B. Rizzini, Luciano Rota, S.I.A.C.E., and Fabio Zanotti. These trademarks may be found under their own headings in this text.

New England Arms Corp. should not be confused with New England Firearms.

NEW ENGLAND CUSTOM GUN SERVICE, LTD. (NECG LTD.)

Current importer of various firearms manufacturers/trademarks established during 1986 and currently located in Claremont, NH. The company previously represented custom-made guns from small makers in Germany, including Adamy-Jagdwaffen, Johannsen, Max Ern, and Prechtl Mausers.

NECG, Ltd. specializes in custom gun services including checkering, stock fitting/alterations, claw mount scope installation and repair, detachable rifle scope mounts, and other gunsmithing services. NECG is licensed for both permanent and temporary exports through both the BATFE and DOS. Please contact the company directly regarding more information on their extensive line of products and services (see Trademark Index).

NEW ENGLAND FIREARMS

Current trademark established during 1987, located and previously manufactured in Gardner, MA until Nov. 1, 2007. Beginning Nov. 1, 2007, the NEF trademark applies to imported guns only. Distributor sales.

During late Jan. of 2008, Remington acquired the Marlin Firearms Company, which had purchased the H&R, New England Firearms (NEF), and L.C. Smith brands during 2000. On May 31st, 2007, Remington Arms Co. was acquired by Cerberus Capital.

During 2000, Marlin Firearms Co. purchased the assets of H&R 1871, Inc., and the name was changed to H&R 1871, LLC. Brand names include Harrington & Richardson, New England Firearms, and Wesson & Harrington.

All NEF firearms utilize a transfer bar safety system and have a $10 service plan which guarantees lifetime warranty.

New England Firearms should not be confused with New England Arms Corp.

REVOLVERS: DOUBLE ACTION

Ultra Models listed were available in blue finish only. All Ultras were supplied with a lockable storage case beginning 1993.

STANDARD REVOLVER .22 (MODEL R92) – .22 S, L, and LR cal., 9 shot, swing out cylinder, 2 1/2 (disc. 1997), 3 (new 1998) or 4 in. barrel, blue or nickel finish, hardwood stocks, fixed rear sight, 25-28 oz. Mfg. 1988-99.

	100%	98%	95%	90%	80%	70%	60%	LAST MSR
	$125	$95	$85	$70	$60	$55	$40	*$144*

Add $10 for nickel finish.

GRADING - PPGS™	100%	98%	95%	90%	80%	70%	60%	LAST MSR

* ***Standard Revolver .32 H&R Mag. (Model R73)*** – .32 H&R Mag. cal. similar to Standard Revolver .22, except has 5 shot cylinder, 2 1/2 (disc.), 3, or 4 in. barrel, choice of blue or nickel finish (not available with 4 in. barrel), 23-26 oz. Mfg. 1988-99.

$125	$95	$85	$70	$60	$55	$40	*$144*

Add $10 for nickel finish (2 1/2 or 3 in. barrel only).

ULTRA MODEL – .22 S, L, and LR cal., 9 shot, swing-out cylinder, 4 or 6 in. solid rib target-grade barrel with rebated muzzle and fully adj. rear sight, blue finish, smooth hardwood grips, 36 oz. Disc. 1999.

$150	$115	$95	$80	$70	$60	$55	*$180*

ULTRA MAG (MODEL R22) – .22 WMR cal., 6 shot, 4 (disc. 1997) or 6 in. solid rib barrel, adj. rear sight, swing-out cylinder, blue finish, 36 oz. Mfg. 1988-99.

$150	$115	$95	$80	$70	$60	$55	*$180*

LADY ULTRA – .32 H&R Mag. cal., swing-out cylinder, 5 shot, blue finish, 3 (disc. 1997, reintroduced 1999) or 4 (mfg. 1998 only) in. barrel with rib, adj. sights, thinner contoured grips, 31 oz. Mfg. 1991-99.

$150	$115	$95	$80	$70	$60	$55	*$180*

RIFLES: SEMI-AUTO

SPORTSTER SL – .22 LR cal., 19 in. barrel, 10 shot mag., uncheckered hardwood stock, grooved steel receiver, 5 1/2 lbs. Mfg. 2004 only.

$125	$105	$90	$80	$70	$60	$55	*$157*

RIFLES: SINGLE SHOT

Beginning Nov. 1, 2007, H&R 1871 decided that all products built in the USA will carry the H&R brand name, and all imported products will be sold under the NEF brand name. The Handi-Rifle, Super Light Handi-Rifle, Sportster, and Survivor are now under the H&R brand name.

HANDI-RIFLE – .204 Ruger (new 2005), .22 Hornet, .22-250 Rem. (mfg. 1992-94, reintroduced 2004), .223 Rem., .243 Win. (new 1992), .25-06 Rem. (new 2004), .270 Win. (new 1993), .280 Rem. (new 1996), .30-30 Win., .30-06 (new 1992), .308 Win. (new 1998), .35 Whelen (new 2006), .357 Mag. (mfg. 1999-2003), .44 Rem. Mag. (new 1996), .444 Marlin (new 2007), .45-70 Govt., 7mm-08 Rem. (new 2003), .500 S&W (new 2005), 7x57mm Mauser (mfg. 1998-2003), 7.62x39mm (new 2006), or 7x64mm Brenneke (mfg. 1998-2003) cal., break open single shot action, 22 or 26 (.280 Rem. only) in. regular or bull (.223 Rem., .243 Win., or .22-250 Rem.) barrel, blue receiver, regular or Monte Carlo walnut stained hardwood stock, scope mount rail or ramp front and adj. rear sights, sling swivels, 7 lbs. Mfg. 1989-2008.

$220	$180	$145	$110	$80	$70	$60	*$270*

Add $20 for Handi-Rifle .243 Win./Huntsman .50 cal. black powder muzzleloader rifle combo (disc. 2002).

Add $39 for 3-9x32mm mounted and bore sighted scope (.223 Rem. or .243 Win. cal. only).

This model in .22-250 Rem., .223 Rem., 7.62x39mm, or .243 Win. cal. is supplied with heavy barrel, scope mount, and no sights.

* ***Handi-Rifle Synthetic*** – .22 Hornet, .223 Rem., .243 Win., .270 Win., .280 Rem., .30-30 Win. (disc. 2003), .30-06, .357 Mag. (mfg. 2002-2003, reintroduced 2008), .44 Rem. Mag. (disc. 2003, reintroduced 2008), .444 Marlin (new 2008), or .45-70 Govt. cal., 22 or 26 (.280 Rem. only) in. barrel, blue finish, features black synthetic stock and forearm, adj. sights on some cals., scope base mount only on others, 7 lbs. Mfg. 1998-2008.

$220	$180	$140	$110	$80	$70	$60	*$278*

Add $23 for Handi-Rifle combo with 20 ga. Pardner barrel (not available in all cals., disc. 2006).

Subtract $42 for .357 Mag. or .44 Mag. cal.

* ***Handi-Rifle Synthetic Stainless*** – .22-250 Rem. (new 2004), .223 Rem., .243 Win., .270 Win., or .30-06 (new 2004) cal., similar to Handi-Rifle Synthetic, features 22 in. matte stainless steel barrel with matte nickel finished receiver, 7 lbs. Mfg. 2003-2008.

$255	$200	$160	$120	$80	$70	$60	*$319*

GRADING - PPGS™	100%	98%	95%	90%	80%	70%	60%	LAST MSR

* ***Handi-Rifle Youth*** – .223 Rem., .243 Win., or 7mm-08 Rem. (new 2005) cal., features 22 in. barrel and shortened stock dimensions (13 1/2 in. LOP), blue finish, supplied with scope rail mount and hammer extension, no iron sights, approx. 7 lbs. Mfg. 1998-2006.

$235	$185	$140	$110	$85	$70	$60	$292

* ***Handi-Rifle 10th Anniversary*** – same cals. as Handi-Rifle, limited edition features scroll engraving by Ken Hurst, deep bluing on receiver, steel trigger guard and forearm spacer, select hand checkered walnut, less than 100 mfg. 1997 only.

$695	$475	$350	$285	$250	$215	$185	$750

* ***Handi-Rifle NTA Anniversary Edition*** – .223 Rem. only, 24 in. heavy barrel w/o sights, features checkered black/grey laminate stock and forearm with NTA (National Trapper's Association) medallion in stock. Limited production 1999 only.

$225	$200	$175	$160	$145	$135	$125	$272

SUPER LIGHT HANDI-RIFLE – .22 Hornet, .223 Rem., or .243 Win. cal., break open single shot, black synthetic stock and forearm, recoil pad, 20 in. special contour barrel with rebated muzzle, .22 Hornet has sights (Model SB2-SL4), .223 Rem. has scope base and hammer extension (Model SB2-SL3), approx. 5 1/2 lbs. Mfg. 1997-2008.

$220	$180	$140	$110	$80	$70	$60	$278

Add $23 for Handi-Rifle combo with 20 ga. Pardner barrel (not available in all cals., disc. 2006).
Add $31 for 3-9x32mm mounted and bore sighted scope (.243 Win. cal., Youth only, new 2007).

This model is also available as a Youth Model with shorter stock dimensions (11 3/4 in. LOP).

SPORTSTER – .17 HMR (new 2002), .17 Mach 2 (mfg. 2005-2007), .22 LR, or .22 WMR (new 2001) cal., 20 (mid-weight) or 22 (.17 HMR cal. only, heavy) in. barrel with Weaver style scope rail, no iron sights, available in either adult or youth (.22 LR cal. only) dimensions, black polymer stock and forearm. Mfg. 1999-2008.

$120	$100	$85	$75	$65	$55	$50	$148

Add $13 for .17 Mach 2 (disc.) or $29 for .17 HMR cal.

SURVIVOR – .223 Rem., .308 Win. (new 1999), .357 Mag. (disc. 1998) or .410/45 LC (new 2007) cal., similar in design to the Survivor Series shotgun, removable forearm with ammo storage, thumbhole stock with storage compartment, no iron sights, 20 (.410/45 LC cal. only) or 22 in. barrel, blue or nickel finish, .357 Mag. cal. has open sights, .223 Rem. and .308 Win. cal. have heavy barrels and scope mount rail, 6 lbs. Mfg. 1996-2008.

$230	$180	$145	$110	$80	$70	$60	$281

Add approx. $15 for nickel finish (disc. 1998, reintroduced 2007 for .410/45 LC cal. only).
Subtract $76 for .410/45 LC cal. (new 2007).

SHOTGUNS: SEMI-AUTO

EXCELL AUTO – 12 ga., 3 in. chamber, 28 in. VR barrel with screw-in choke tubes, 5 shot mag., black synthetic or walnut pistol grip stock with fluted comb, vent. recoil pad, bead front sight, approx. 7 lbs. Imported 2008-2010.

$375	$315	$265	$225	$185	$160	$140	$421

Add $34 for walnut stock.

* ***Excell Auto Turkey*** – 12 ga., 3 in. chamber, 5 shot mag., 22 in. vent. rib barrel with choke tubes and fiber optic sights, Realtree Advantage Hardwoods camo covered pistol grip stock and barrel, 7 lbs. Imported 2008-2010.

$450	$395	$345	$300	$265	$230	$195	$513

* ***Excell Auto Waterfowl*** – 12 ga., 28 in. VR barrel, 5 shot, 100% Advantage Wetlands camo coverage, 7 lbs. Imported 2008-2010.

$450	$395	$345	$300	$265	$230	$195	$513

* ***Excell Auto Combo*** – includes 24 in. rifled slug barrel and 28 in. regular barrel, synthetic stock only. Imported 2008-2010.

$495	$425	$380	$330	$290	$260	$230	$576

GRADING - PPGS™	100%	98%	95%	90%	80%	70%	60%	LAST MSR

SHOTGUNS: SINGLE SHOT

Beginning Nov. 1, 2007, H&R 1871 decided that all products built in the U.S.A. will carry the H&R brand name, and all imported products will be sold under the NEF brand name. The Pardner Series and Tracker Slug are now under the H&R brand name.

PARDNER – 12, 16 (new 1989), 20, 28 ga. (new 1991), or .410 bore, 2 3/4 or 3 in. chamber (12, 20 ga., and .410 bore), single shot, break open action, safety transfer bar mechanism on hammer, side lever release, color case hardened receiver, 14 in. LOP, 24 (disc.), 26, 28, or 32 in. barrel, fixed or mod. choke tube (12 or 20 ga. only, with black synthetic stock and forearm), extractor, walnut stained hardwood or black synthetic (12 or 20 ga. only) stock and forearm, 5-6 lbs. Mfg. 1987-2008.

$100	$85	$75	$65	$55	$45	$40	*$129*

Add $15 for 32 in. barrel (12 ga. only).
Add $22 for modified choke tube (12 or 20 ga. only).
Add $65 for Pardner 12 ga. Shotgun/Huntsman .50 cal. black powder muzzleloader combo (disc. 2002).

* ***Pardner Compact (Youth)*** – 12 (new 1998), 20, 28 ga., or .410 bore, similar to Pardner, except has 22 in. barrel and straight grip stock with recoil pad, 12 1/2 in. LOP. Disc. 2008.

$115	$95	$75	$65	$55	$45	$40	*$137*

Add $21 for Pardner Youth .22 cal. barrel/.410 bore Versa-Pack combo (disc. 2007).
Add $14 for modified choke tube (20 ga. only with black synthetic stock and forearm).

* ***Pardner Turkey Gun*** – 10 or 12 ga. only, 3 (disc.) or 3 1/2 in. chamber, 24 in. barrel with fixed or full choke tube, camo or matte black wood finish, 6 or 9 (10 ga.) lbs. Mfg. 1999-2008.

$135	$115	$90	$80	$70	$60	$50	*$176*

Add $10 for Mossy Oak Break-Up camo in 12 ga. with full choke bore.
Add $58 for 10 ga. in black matte wood finish (disc. 2007).
Add $88 for 10 ga. with camo wood finish.

* ***Pardner Youth Turkey*** – 20 ga. only, features 22 in. full choke barrel and camo painted wood. Mfg. 1999-2008.

$135	$110	$90	$80	$70	$60	$50	*$186*

* ***Pardner Waterfowl (Special Purpose)*** – 10 or 12 (mfg. 2002-2006) ga., 3 1/2 in. chamber, 28 or 32 (10 ga. only, new 1996) in. barrel, blue barrel and receiver, walnut or Mossy Oak Break Up camo (new 2002) finish on stock and forearm, recoil pad, 9 1/2 lbs. Mfg. 1988-2008.

$185	$150	$125	$100	$85	$65	$55	*$228*

Add $36 for camo.
Subtract 15% for 12 ga.

* ***Pardner NRA Foundation Youth*** – 20, 28 (disc. 2001) ga. or .410 bore, 22 in. barrel, high luster bluing, features "NRA Foundation Youth Endowment Edition" laser etched in black on stock, approx. 5 1/2 lbs. Mfg. 1999-2002.

$130	$105	$90	$75	$65	$55	$45	*$161*

* ***Pardner National Wild Turkey Federation (NWTF)*** – 10 or 20 (new 1993) ga., 22 (20 ga. only) or 24 in. barrel with full screw-in choke, full Mossy Oak camo treatment, includes swivels and sling. Mfg. 1992-96.

$190	$160	$135	$110	$95	$80	$70	*$230*

Subtract $80 for 20 ga.

This model was drilled and tapped for scope mounts.

SURVIVOR SERIES – 12 (disc. 2003), 20 ga. (disc. 2003), or .410/.45 LC (new 1995) bore, 3 in. chamber, 20 (.410/.45 LC) or 22 in. barrel with Mod. choke, blue or electroless nickel finish, synthetic thumbhole designed hollow stock with pistol grip, removable forend holds additional ammo, sling swivels, and black nylon sling, 13 1/4 in. LOP, 6 lbs. Mfg. 1992-93, reintroduced 1995-2006.

$175	$150	$120	$100	$85	$75	$65	*$219*

Add $18 for electroless nickel finish.
Subtract 20% for 12 or 20 ga.

GRADING - PPGS™	100%	98%	95%	90%	80%	70%	60%	LAST MSR

TRACKER SLUG MODEL – 10 ga. (mfg. 1994 only), 12, or 20 ga., 3 (12 or 20 ga.) or 3 1/2 (10 ga. only) in. chamber, 24 in. cylinder bore barrel, case colored receiver, includes recoil pad and adj. sights, 6 lbs. Mfg. 1992-2001.

$120	$90	$75	$60	$50	$45	$40	*$143*

* ***Tracker Slug Model II*** – 12 or 20 ga., 3 in. chamber, similar to Tracker Slug Model except has 24 in. rifled slug barrel, 14 in. LOP, 5 1/4 lbs. Mfg. 1995-2008.

$150	$120	$90	$75	$60	$50	$45	*$194*

Add $44 for Tracker II 12 ga. Slug Gun/Huntsman .50 cal. black powder muzzleloader (disc. 2002).

SHOTGUNS: SLIDE ACTION

Beginning Nov. 1, 2007, H&R 1871 decided that all products built in the U.S.A. will carry the H&R brand name, and all imported products will be sold under the NEF brand name. The Pardner Series is now under the H&R brand name.

PARDNER PUMP – 12 or 20 (new 2006) ga., 3 or 3 1/2 (mfg. 2006) in. chamber, steel receiver, crossbolt safety, double action bars, 28 in. VR barrel with choke tube, black synthetic (new 2005), synthetic with carbon fiber dip, or uncheckered walnut stock with or w/o camo (disc. 2010) coverage, recoil pad, matte black metal finish, 7 1/2 lbs. Mfg. 2004-2008.

$185	$165	$145	$115	$100	$85	$75	*$233*

Add $20 for walnut stock and forearm.
Add $20 for synthetic stock with carbon fiber dip (mfg. 2008-2009).
Add $57 for synthetic stock with 100% Realtree APG/HD camo coverage (disc. 2010).
Add $65 for 12 ga. with 3 1/2 in. chamber (disc. 2007).
Subtract $12 for 18 1/2 in. barrel with rifled cylinder bore choke.

* ***Pardner Pump Turkey*** – includes 100% Mossy Oak Breakup (disc.) or Realtree (new 2006) camo coverage, 22 in. barrel with Truglo front and rear sights, one Turkey choke tube. Mfg. 2005-2010.

$265	$235	$200	$175	$150	$135	$120	*$332*

* ***Pardner Pump Combo*** – 12 ga. only, 3 in. chamber, includes 22 in. rifled slug and 28 in. barrel with modified choke tube. Mfg. 2005-2010.

$295	$250	$220	$185	$155	$125	$115	*$349*

* ***Pardner Pump Protector*** – .12 ga., black synthetic stock, 18 1/2 in. barrel, bead front sight, matte finished metal, swivel studs, vent. recoil pad, 5 shot tube mag., crossbolt safety. Mfg. 2006-2007.

$155	$135	$115	$100	$85	$75	$65	*$186*

* ***Pardner Pump Compact (Youth)*** – 20 ga., take-down action, 21 in. barrel, black American walnut (disc. 2010) or black synthetic pistol grip stock with or w/o camo (disc. 2010), fluted comb, vent. recoil pad, bead front sight, drilled and tapped, 5 shot mag., 13 in. LOP, approx. 6 1/2 lbs. Mfg. 2006-2008.

$185	$165	$145	$115	$100	$85	$75	*$233*

Add $20 for black walnut stock and forearm (disc. 2010).
Add $57 for 100% Realtree APG/HD camo coverage (mfg. 2008-2010).

* ***Pardner Pump Slug*** – 12 or 20 ga., take-down action, 21 (20 ga.) or 22 (12 ga.) in. rifled barrel, matte metal finish, black synthetic (12 ga.) or walnut (20 ga.) pistol grip stock with fluted comb, swivel studs, vent. recoil pad, ramp front sight, adj. rear sight, drilled and tapped, 5 shot mag., crossbolt safety, approx. 6 1/2 lbs. Mfg. 2006-2008.

$250	$215	$190	$160	$140	$115	$100	*$298*

Add $33 for full cantilever scope mount (new 2009).
Add $44 for walnut stock and forearm.

NEW ULTRA LIGHT ARMS LLC

Current rifle manufacturer located in Granville, WV. Dealer sales.

RIFLES: BOLT ACTION

Add $85 for left-hand action on the following models.
Add $168 for jewell HVR trigger or $68 for stainless steel barrel.

GRADING - PPGS™	100%	98%	95%	90%	80%	70%	60%	LAST MSR

ULTRA LIGHT RIFLE – caliber to customer specs., various actions, 2-position 3-function safety in top of stock, Timney trigger, Douglas barrel, no sights, Kevlar stock reinforced with graphite, recoil pad, Dupont Imron epoxy finish, designed to customer specifications, includes hard case, 5 1/4-5 3/4 lbs.

Please contact the company directly for a price quote on this model.

MODEL 20 SERIES – various short action centerfire cals. available between .17 Rem. and .358 Win., 5 1/4 lbs.

MSR $3,040 $2,775 $2,300 $1,750 $1,300 $1,050 $925 $850

* ***Model 20 RF*** – .22 LR cal., single shot or repeater, 5 1/4 lbs.

MSR $1,500 $1,350 $1,175 $1,000 $875 $775 $650 $550

Add $50 for repeater action.

MODEL 24 – various cals. between .25-06 Rem. - .338-06 cal., long action, 5 1/4 lbs.

MSR $3,125 $2,875 $2,400 $1,900 $1,500 $1,250 $1,025 $900

MODEL 28 MAGNUM – various Mag. cals. between .264 Win. Mag. - .338 Win. Mag., 5 3/4 lbs.

MSR $3,375 $3,150 $2,775 $2,400 $2,050 $1,650 $1,300 $1,175

MODEL 32 MAGNUM – 7mm STW, .300 Wby. Mag., or .340 Wby. Mag. cal., other calibers available by request, dangerous game rifle. New 2005.

MSR $3,365 $3,150 $2,775 $2,400 $2,050 $1,650 $1,300 $1,175

MODEL 40 MAGNUM – .416 Rigby cal., other calibers available by request, otherwise similar to Model 28 Magnum.

MSR $3,365 $3,150 $2,775 $2,400 $2,050 $1,650 $1,300 $1,175

NEWTON ARMES

Current rifle manufacturer established in 2008, and located in Belgium.

While Newton Armes has advertised a "Leverbolt" straight pull/push bolt action rifle utilizing some features of the original Newton Arms Co. rifle combined with the styling of the older Mauser 98 Sporting rifles, only prototypes have been manufactured to date.

NEWTON ARMS CO.

Previous manufacturer located in Buffalo, NY and New Haven, CT 1914-1932.

RIFLES: BOLT ACTION

Rifles: Newton Arms Co. Inc. Buffalo, NY

MODEL 1914 RIFLE GROUP – .256 Newton, .30 Newton, .33 Newton, .35 Newton, and .40 Newton cal., three Grades (A, B and C) of Mauser and Sauer rifles converted to Adolph and Newton calibers, total production is unknown. Two Models (A & B) of Mauser rifles and one Model (C) full stocked carbine converted to .256 Newton comprising the only shipment of 24 rifles from Germany in 1914. Mauser rifles are of the Type B style with various patterns and features 24 in. barrels, checkered pistol grip, double set or single triggers, hunting or military rear sights and sling swivels. One Model (D) of a sporting Haenel rifle converted to .256 Newton with Marlin made barrels.

$3,500 $3,000 $2,500 $2,000 $1,500 $1,250 1,000

NEWTON SPRINGFIELD – .256 Newton cal., square cut rifled barrels, marked o-o-o before and after the barrel address and Newton style stock were assembled on a Springfield action by Newton or sold separately to be assembled by the owner of the action, customer supplied the sights. Marlin made.

$1,500 $1,250 $1,100 $1,000 $900 $800 $700

Due to the low numbered receivers and the fact that many of these barrels were customer fitted, it is not advisable to fire these rifles until a competent gunsmith has performed an inspection.

FIRST MODEL 1916 NEWTON RIFLE – .22 Newton (10-14 rifles), .256 Newton, .30-06, .30 Newton, .35 Newton, and .40 Newton (4 rifles) cal., standard features are Mauser style action, 24 in. round barrel, pistol grip, checkered stock, steel buttplate and grip cap, double set triggers that both face forward, rear and front sights on barrel bands, all rifles are takedowns

GRADING - PPGS™	100%	98%	95%	90%	80%	70%	60%	LAST MSR

by unscrewing floorplate, options included bolt peep sight, Lyman 48 long tang sight, cheek piece, serrated butt plate, long barrels, recoil pad, sling swivels and slings, barrels marked "Newton Arms Co. Inc. o-o Buffalo, N.Y. o-o." Total production about 4,000 rifles.

	100%	98%	95%	90%	80%	70%	60%	LAST MSR
	$3,200	$2,300	$1,800	$1,500	$1,300	$1,200	$1,100	

Add $100 for optional bolt peep sight.
Add $100 for figured wood or cheekpiece.

Rifles: Chas. Newton Rifle Corp., Buffalo, NY

MODEL 1922 NEWTON MAUSER – .256 Newton cal., Mauser barreled action assembled into a sporting rifle by Sauer, checkered pistol grip, spoon bolt handle, double set triggers facing each other, three leaf rear sight and Schnabel forend, barrels converted to .256 Newton after they arrived in the U.S. A. Barrel markings vary, Chas. Newton Rifle Corporation, Krupp Steel or Rustless Steel. Made in Germany, 100 rifles imported.

	100%	98%	95%	90%	80%	70%	60%	LAST MSR
	$3,500	$3,200	$3,000	$2,800	$2,500	$2,000	$1,500	

Rifles: Buffalo Newton Rifle Corp., New Haven, CT

MODEL 1924 BUFFALO NEWTON RIFLE – .256 Newton, .30 Newton, .35 Newton, and .30-06 cal., standard features are Mauser style action, 24 in. round barrel, pistol grip checkered stock, steel buttplate and grip cap, double set triggers facing each other, "dogleg" style bolt handle, cross bolt in the stock, rear sight dovetailed into the barrel, all rifles are takedowns by unscrewing the floor plate, Barrels marked "Buffalo Newton Rifle Co New Haven Conn U.S.A." ,some options include sling swivels and slings, Lyman 48 long or short tang sight. About 1,000 mfg.

* ***Meeker Rifles*** – similar to Model 1924 Buffalo Newton Rifle, except are marked "Meeker Arms Co, Model 1925, New Haven Conn." Total production is unknown although probably a low number.

	100%	98%	95%	90%	80%	70%	60%	LAST MSR
	2,000	$1,700	$1,300	$1,000	$900	$800	$700	

NEWTOWN FIREARMS

Current manufacturer located in Hangtown, CA.

CARBINES: SEMI-AUTO

NF-15/GEN 2 TACTICAL – 5.56 NATO cal., AR-15 style, choice of piston or gas operation, 16 in. match grade Vanadium steel fluted barrel with flash hider, quad Picatinny rail, black furniture, collapsible stock, sub MOA accuracy guaranteed, 10 or 20 shot mag., 8 lbs.

	100%	98%	95%	90%	80%	70%	60%	LAST MSR
MSR $2,950	$2,775	$2,300	$1,950	$1,575	$1,250	$1,000	$875	

NEXT GENERATION ARMS

Current rifle manufacturer located in Hayden, ID.

RIFLES: SEMI-AUTO

Next Generation Arms manufactures AR-15 style rifles with an emphasis on being lighter, shorter, more reliable and easier to clean. There are many configurations possible, but most use a Noveske 14 1/2 in. barrel and a Geissele trigger. These are combined with advanced design and manufacturing as well as ceramic coatings. Please contact the company directly for more information (see Trademark Index).

NIGHTHAWK CUSTOM

Current manufacturer located in Berryville, AR. since 2004. Consumer custom order sales.

NIGHTHAWK CUSTOM

PISTOLS: SEMI-AUTO

Nighthawk Custom offers a complete line of high quality 1911 style semi-auto pistols. Please contact the company directly for more information on custom pistols, a wide variety of options, gunsmithing services and availability (see Trademark Index).

All pistols are available in Perma Kote ceramic based finish in Black, Sniper Gray, Coyote Tan, Titanium Blue, Dark Earth & OD Green.

Add $200 for Crimson Trace laser grips on any applicable model (not bobtail). Add $150 for Ed Brown bobtail. Add $65 for ambidextrous safety. Add $50 for crowned barrel. Add $50 for beveled

GRADING - PPGS™	100%	98%	95%	90%	80%	70%	60%	LAST MSR

and recessed slide stop. Add $350 for Complete Hard Chrome Finish. Add $350 for Complete Diamond Black Finish.

GRP (GLOBAL RESPONSE PISTOL) – 9mm Para. (new 2012), 10mm (new 2012), or .45 ACP cal., black Perma Kote ceramic based finish, 5 in. match grade barrel, 8 shot mag., match grade trigger, front and rear cocking serrations, Heinie or Novak Extreme Duty adj. night sights, Gator Back (disc.) or Golf Ball grips, 41 oz.

MSR $2,896	$2,650	$2,225	$1,900	$1,550	$1,200	$975	$825	

Add $100 for GRP II with 4 1/4 in. barrel (disc. 2011).
Add $200 for GRP Recon Model with integrated lower rail with Surefire X300 weapon light.
Add $200 Crimson Trace laser grips.
Add $350 for the FLX high capacity double stack frame (disc. 2011).

TALON – 9mm Para., .40 S&W (disc. 2011), 10mm, or .45 ACP cal., black Perma Kote ceramic based finish, 4 1/4 (Talon II) or 5 in. match grade, lightweight aluminum match trigger, hand checkering on rear of slide with serrated top slide, front and rear slide serrations, 25 LPI checkering on front strap, Novak night sights, cocobolo, walnut, or black cristobal grips, tactical mag. release, 36-41 oz.

MSR $3.095	$2,750	$2,400	$1,975	$1,600	$1,300	$1,000	$875	

Add $100 for Recon Model with integrated lower rail.
Add $200 for anodized aluminum lightweight frame.
Add $350 for the FLX high capacity double stack frame (disc. 2011).

* ***Talon IV*** – similar to Talon, except compact model with 3.6 in. barrel, gray frame and black slide, rear slide serrations, and black grips. Disc. 2010.

	$2,225	$1,950	$1,600	$1,300	$1,050	$875	$750	*$2,425*

FALCON – 9mm Para., 10mm, or .45 ACP cal., 5 in. match grade stainless steel or carbon steel crowned barrel with chamfered bushing, one-piece fully machined mainspring/magwell combination, rear cocking serrations, Coyote Tan, Black, or OD Green finish, dimpled grips, ball radius cut slide top, Heinie ledge rear sight, 39 oz. New 2011.

MSR $3,095	$2,800	$2,525	$2,275	$1,800	$1,450	$1,225	$1,000	

DOMINATOR – .45 ACP cal., 5 in. crowned match grade barrel, stainless steel frame with black Perma Kote slide, Nighthawk Custom fully adjustable rear sights, 8 shot, hand serrated rear og slide with serrated top slide, front and rear slide serrations, 25 LPI checkering on front strap, cocobolo double diamond grips with laser engraved Nighthawk Custom logo, 40 oz.

MSR $3,250	$2,875	$2,525	$2,100	$1,700	$1,350	$1,000	$875	

Add $100 for Recon Model with integrated lower rail.
Add $350 for the FLX high capacity double stack frame (disc. 2011).

HEINIE TACTICAL CARRY – .45 ACP cal., 5 in. Heinie match grade barrel, black Perma Kote ceramic based finish, double diamond cocobolo or aluminum grips with Heinie logo, Heinie Straight Eight Slant Pro night sights, Heinie trigger, complete carry dehorned, Heinie signature magwell, flat slide top with 40 LPI serrations, done in collaboration with renowned gunsmith Richard Heinie, 40 oz.

MSR $3,895	$3,600	$3,250	$2,850	$2,450	$2,000	$1,600	$1,200	

HEINIE PDP – .45 ACP cal., 4 1/2 or 5 (full size) in. Heinie match grade barrel, cocobolo wood grips with Heinie logo, fixed sights, scalloped front strap and mainspring housing, extended combat safety, contoured for carry magwell, Heinie match hammer, sear, and disconnector, serrated rear of slide & slide top, Heinie aluminum trigger, tactical mag release, 38 oz.

MSR $3,395	$3,000	$2,600	$2,150	$1,700	$1,350	$1,000	$875	

HEINE LONG SLIDE – 10mm or .45 ACP cal., 6 in. match grade barrel, black Perma Kote ceramic based finish, cocobolo wood grips with Heinie logo, Nighthawk Custom fully adjustable rear or fixed sights, 25 LPI checkering on front strap, contoured for carry, 44 oz.

MSR $3,595	$3,175	$2,750	$2,425	$1,925	$1,550	$1,300	$1,000	

Add $100 for Recon Model with integrated lower rail.
Add $150 for extended magazine well.

GRADING - PPGS™	100%	98%	95%	90%	80%	70%	60%	LAST MSR

Add $350 for unique Nighthawk Custom camouflage finish; available in Digital, Woodland or Desert Camo (disc. 2011).

HEINE SIGNATURE SERIES – 9mm Para. cal., available in Competition, Government Recon, and Office Compact configurations, features silver Heine Signature Series engraved logo on right of slide, features same thin frame as Lady Hawk model.

* ***Heine Signature Series Competition*** – 5 in. barrel, hand signed thin grip panels, fully machined one piece mainspring housing and magwell combination that has been thinned and scalloped, red fiber optic front sights, black Heine Slant Pro rear sights, hand serrated rear of slide, slide top serrations, crowned and recessed match grade barrel, tool steel hammer and hammer strut, lightweight aluminum match grade trigger, recessed slide stop, chamfered frame, 40 oz. New 2012.

MSR $3,450	$3,050	$2,650	$2,350	$1,850	$1,500	$1,275	$1,000	

* ***Heine Signature Series RECON*** – 9mm Para. cal., 5 in. match grade barrel, similar features as the Competition, except has integrated recon light rail. X300 tactical light, and Heine Slant Pro Night Sights. New 2012.

MSR $3,550	$3,150	$2,700	$2,375	$1,850	$1,525	$1,300	$1,075	

* ***Heine Signature Series Compact*** – 9mm Para. cal., similar to the RECON and the Competition model, except has smaller officer-style frame designed for concealed carry. New 2012.

MSR $3,450	$3,050	$2,675	$2,375	$1,875	$1,500	$1,250	$1,000	

T3 – 9mm Para, .40 S&W (disc. 2011) or .45 ACP cal., 4 1/4 in. match grade stainless steel fully crowned barrel, Officer size frame, black Perma Kote finish, extended mag. well, flush forged slide stop with chamfered frame, tactical mag. release, unique Nighthawk T3 magwell, horizontally serrated no-snag mainspring housing and rear of slide, skeletonized aluminum match trigger, 38 oz.

MSR $3,250	$2,900	$2,400	$1,975	$1,650	$1,300	$1,050	$850	

Add $150 for T3 Stainless model, complete stainless steel model.
Add $200 for anodized aluminum lightweight frame.
Add $495 for T3 Comp model (.45 ACP cal. only), with Schuemann AET hybrid comp. ported barrel (new 2010).

* ***T3 Thin*** – similar to the T3, except is smaller design for concealed carry. New 2012.

MSR $3,400	$3,000	$2,625	$2,325	$1,850	$1,450	$1,225	$1,000	

LADY HAWK – 9mm Para. or .45 ACP cal., 4 1/4 in. crowned match grade barrel, ultra thin aluminum grips, Heinie Slant Pro Straight Eight sights, modified ultra thin chain link front strap and mainspring housing for reduced grip circumference, titanium blue Perma Kote finish with hard chromed controls, 36 oz.

MSR $3,450	$3,050	$2,650	$2,375	$1,850	$1,450	$1,225	$1,000	

Add $100 for Recon Model with integrated lower rail.
Add $200 for anodized aluminum lightweight frame.
Add $200 for complete stainless steel model.

10-8 – .45 ACP cal., 5 in. barrel, green or black linen micarta grips, black Perma Kote finish, 8 shot, Hilton Yam/10-8 performance designed U-notched rear and serrated front sights with tritium inserts, low profile Dawson Light Speed Rail, front/rear cocking serrations, long solid trigger with hidden fixed over travel stop, strong side only safety, 42 oz. Mfg. 2009-2010.

	$2,350	$2,025	$1,650	$1,325	$1,175	$900	$775	*$2,595*

ENFORCER – .45 ACP cal., 5 in. barrel, Novak low mount tritium or Heinie Slant Pro night sights, black Perma Kote finish, extended tactical mag. catch, aggressive no slip G10 Golf Ball grips, unique frame with integrated plunger tube and mag well, hand serrations on rear of slide with serrated top slide, front and rear slide cocking serrations, lanyard loop mainspring housing, complete de-horn and ready for carry, 39 oz.

MSR $3,395	$3,050	$2,700	$2,375	$1,850	$1,450	$1,225	$1,000	

Add $100 for Recon Model with integrated lower rail.

GRADING - PPGS™	100%	98%	95%	90%	80%	70%	60%	LAST MSR

AAC (ADVANCED ARMAMENT CORPORATION) – 9mm Para. or .45 ACP cal., 5 in. threaded barrel, stainless steel thread protector, done in collaboration with Advanced Armament Corporation, lightning cuts on the top and sides of the slide, mainspring housing and front strap that match the Advanced Armament M4-2000 suppressor, tall Heinie Slant Pro Straight eight suppressor front sights designed for use with suppressor, Perma Kote finish in black, ultra thin Nighthawk Custom Alumagrips, solid, blacked out aluminum trigger, 39 oz. New 2010.

MSR $3,295	$2,950	$2,625	$2,325	$1,825	$1,450	$1,225	$1,000	

Add $100 for Recon Model with integrated lower rail.

PREDATOR – 9mm Para., 10mm, or .45 ACP cal., 4 1/4 or 5 in. barrel, black Perma Kote ceramic based finish with black slide, double diamond cocobolo, walnut, or black cristobal checkered grips, Heinie Slant Pro Straight Eight or Novak Lo-Mount night sights, hand checkering on rear of slide with serrated top slide, front and rear slide serrations, 25 LPI checkering on front strap, unique one piece precision fit barrel designed to reduce muzzle flip and felt recoil, one inch at 25 yards guaranteed accuracy, top-of-the-line model, 32-34 oz.

MSR $3,450	$3,050	$2,650	$2,375	$1,850	$1,450	$1,225	$1,000	

Add $75 for Predator III model with Officer frame and 4 1/4 in. barrel.
Add $100 for Recon Model with integrated lower rail.
Add $350 for the FLX high capacity double stack frame. (9mm & 10mm Government size only, disc. 2011)

Also available as Predator II with 4 1/4 in. barrel.

CHRIS COSTA RECON – 9mm Para. or .45 ACP cal., 8 (.45 ACP) or 10 (9mm Para.) shot mag., fully machined slide and one piece mainspring housing, top serrations, red fiber optic or tritium dot front sights, EVERLAST recoil system, magwell with rounded butt, Jardine Tactical Hook rear sights, extreme high cut checkered front strap, integrated recon light rail, multi-faceted slide top, barrel is crowned and beveled flush with the bushing, lightweight aluminum medium solid match trigger, 10-8 Performance Hyena Brown grips, COSTA logo engraved in silver. New 2012.

MSR $3,695	$3,250	$2,800	$2,425	$1,875	$1,525	$1,300	$1,075	

* ***Chris Costa Compact*** – similar to Chris Costa Recon, except has smaller, officer-style frame, and black 10-8 Performance 5 LPI grips. New 2012.

MSR $3,695	$3,250	$2,800	$2,425	$1,875	$1,525	$1,300	$1,075	

BOB MARVEL CUSTOM 1911 – .45 ACP cal., hand stippling on top of slide, bull nose front taper, proprietary bull barrel system, fully adjustable sights, one-piece mainspring housing and magwell, high cut front strap, lightweight aluminum medium solid match trigger, Nighthawk Custom/Marvel EVERLAST recoil system. New 2012.

MSR $3,995	$3,525	$3,050	$2,600	$2,000	$1,650	$1,425	$1,250	

RIFLES: BOLT ACTION

HUNTING RIFLE – various cals., bolt action, available in Hunting, Varmint, and Bench Rest configurations, Broughton barrel, synthetic stock. Disc. 2011.

	$3,500	$3,100	$2,650	$2,250	$1,800	$1,375	$1,125	*$3,895*

TACTICAL RIFLE – .308 Win., 7mm Rem. Mag., .300 Rem. Mag., or .338 Lapua cal., with or w/o Surgeon action, with or w/o bolt on Picatinny rail with choice of 0 or 20 MOA integral elevation, Jewell trigger, Perma Kote finish in choice of Desert Sand, OD Green, Sniper Gray, Desert camo, Woodland camo, or Urban camo finish, tactical synthetic stock with adj. comb. Mfg. 2009-2011.

	$3,800	$3,350	$2,900	$2,500	$2,000	$1,500	$1,225	*$4,250*

Add $550 for short Surgeon action.
Add $595 for 100% coverage Custom woodland or digital camouflage finish.
Add $625 for Magnum Surgeon action.
Add $650 for long Surgeon action.
Add $875 for XL action in .338 Lapua cal.

GRADING - PPGS™	100%	98%	95%	90%	80%	70%	60%	LAST MSR

SHOTGUNS

TACTICAL SLIDE ACTION – 12 ga., reworked 3 in. chambered action for faster, smoother cycling, Hogue Over Molded style stock with 12 or 14 in. LOP, Big Dome large safety, 2-shot extension, fully adjustable and protected ghost ring rear sight with red fiber optic front, 4 or 6 round shell carrier. Rust-Proof ceramic finish in a variety of colors including camo.

MSR $1,350	$1,150	$995	$825	$700	$500	$450	$375	

Add $35 for Tritium front sight upgrade.
Add $75 for Picatinny rail on top of receiver.
Add $85 for magazine clamp with rail & swing swivel.
Add $125 for breaching tool.
Add $125 for Surefire Tactical light with ring mount.
Add $165 for 5-position stock.

TACTICAL SEMI-AUTO – 12 ga., 2 3/4 in. chamber, 18 in. barrel, pistol grip synthetic stock, Surefire fore end weapon light, hand tuned action, Rust-Proof ceramic finish in a variety of colors including camouflage patterns. tactical charging handle on the bolt, fully adjustable and protected ghost ring rear sight, red fiber optic front sight, 2-shot extension, 4 or 6 round shell carrier. Disc. 2011.

	$1,800	$1,550	$1,250	$1,125	$800	$675	$550	*$2,060*

Add $35 for Tritium front sight blade.
Add $75 for Picatinny rail on top of receiver.
Add $299 for Surefire forend tactical weapon light.

NIKKO FIREARMS CO., LTD.

Previous manufacturer located in Tochigi, Japan circa 1958-1989.

NIKKO HISTORY AND GENERAL INFORMATION

The publisher wishes to thank the Golden Eagle Collectors Association for providing this publication with the information listed. Please refer to the Golden Eagle heading in this text for information on Nikko manufactured Golden Eagle firearms.

Both Nikko Firearms Co., Ltd. and Nikko Arms Co., Ltd. were trade names used by the Kodensha Co., Ltd. of Tochigi, Japan on products they manufactured and distributed worldwide. Nikko is the name of the Prefecture, or district, in which Tochigi City is located, about 50 miles north of Tokyo. The word Nikko translates to English as "sunshine." Kodensha first manufactured or distributed under the Nikko name in April 1955, and exported out of Japan beginning in August 1958. Nothing is known of the origin of the Kodensha Co.

Kodensha first approached the American shotgun market in about 1958 or 1959 using the Japanese export marketing firm of Kyowa-Boeki-Bussan. They contacted various U.S. distributors, and in about 1959 or 1960, Continental Arms Co. of New York City began importing the Nikko "Grade 5." Continental imported these Nikko over/unders, in various models and configurations, until about 1972.

In 1962, the Kodensha Co., Ltd. formed a joint venture with Olin/Winchester of New Haven, CT to produce the Winchester Model 101 over/under shotgun. This venture was known as the Olin- Kodensha Co. Ltd. Added a little later was the side-by-side Model 23, and the Model 96 Xpert (a budget priced 101). The "pre-Olin" Kodensha factory was considerably outdated, and the joint venture began a complete modernization process, with the financial and technical assistance of Olin. Millions of dollars of machinery and technology were brought in, and the entire manufacturing process was upgraded to the then current standards.

One of the conditions of the joint venture was that Kodensha restrict their own products (made in the same factory, but recorded separately from the joint venture) to sale in Japan only. At the outset of the 25 years that the joint venture existed, Kodensha was probably amenable to this, as they were reaping huge financial and technical benefits from Olin. But, by the mid 1960s, when the factory was in place and running smoothly, Kodensha essentially ignored that condition of the agreement, leaving Olin at somewhat of a disadvantage, not wanting to jeopardize their investment or production source. Additionally, Olin/Winchester was allowed only two

permanent personnel, hardly enough to monitor the activities of a factory which employed up to 400 people. As an example, when walnut stock blanks arrived from France, Kodensha took first pick, and Olin got what was left over.

Kodensha converted an existing building near the manufacturing plant into an assembly area for Nikko, and other brands of guns. This building was probably the "true" Nikko Firearms Co., Ltd. Manufactured components from the Olin-Kodensha factory were carted to the Nikko plant for final assembly and fitting. This "dual-factory" arrangement continued until the mid 1980s. In 1981, for an unknown reason, the Olin-Kodensha name was changed to OK Firearms Co. Ltd. In October 1987, Olin/Winchester sold their interest in OK Firearms to Classic Doubles International, which continued making the 101 style shotgun under their own name. For reasons unknown, Classic Doubles went out of business in December 1988. Shortly thereafter, the entire factory was torn down.

During the "dual-factory" days, Nikko produced firearms for the following distributors or retailers: 1) Kanematsu Gosho of Arlington Heights, IL approx. 1974-1982 - distributed Nikko brand shotguns, Golden Eagle brand shotguns and rifles (1975 through March 1977 only); 2) Golden Eagle Firearms, Houston, TX March 1977 through early 1981 - Golden Eagle shotguns and rifles; 3) Tradewinds, Inc. of Tacoma, WA exported from Japan by Caspoll International, Tokyo January 1971 through December 1972 - Shadow Seven; Shadow Indy (Model 707); Gold, Silver, and Black Shadow over/ under shotguns; 4) Marubeni America, Inc. of New York City 1972-1974 - Miida brand over/under shotguns; 5) Winchester GMBH of West Germany, manufactured by Olin-Kodensha (dates unknown - early 1980s) - Winchester Model 777 rifle (Golden Eagle look-alike); 6) Parker Reproduction shotguns, distributed in the US by Reagent Chemical & Research, Inc. 1984-1988; 7) International Star Commerce Corp. (ISCC) of Salt Lake City, Utah approx. 1982 - distributor of Nikko brand shotguns; 8) Moore Supply Co. of Salt Lake City, UT beginning mid-1981 - distributor of Nikko brand shotguns; 9) USA Nikko, Inc. of Los Angeles, CA (factory reps and distributors of Nikko shotguns), initial date unknown, through December 1981; 10) Weatherby, Inc. of Los Angeles, CA May 1972 to 1981. Centurion semi-auto and Patrician pump shotguns, some Mark 22 rifles. Olympian O/U shotgun and possibly other O/Us from 1978-81. Model 82 semi-auto and Model 92 pump shotguns; 11) Savage Industries of Hamden, CT 1981-1982 - Savage/Fox FA-1 and FP-1 shotguns; 12) Charles Daly. "Automatic" distributed by Sloans (Japanese made only) mid-1980s; 13) Sears, Roebuck Co. Ted Williams Model 400 and possibly others; 14) Churchill semi-auto, imported by Kassnar mid-1980s; 15) High Standard of Hamden, CT 1974-75 - Supermatic Shadow Indy (Model 707, an O/U), Supermatic Shadow Seven (also O/U), and Supermatic Shadow semi-auto.

NOTE: ALL of the semi-auto shotguns used essentially the same design. Each distributor may have made a few cosmetic or dimensional embellishments to differentiate their gun. Differences exist in barrel/breech fit, magazine caps, pistol grip caps, checkering pattern, piston size, ejector location, fluted bolt. Use caution if interchanging parts. Generally, the same statement can be made about the pump versions also.

NOBLE MFG. CO.

Previous manufacturer and importer of Spanish SxS shotguns located in Haydenville, MA 1953-1971.

Noble manufactured semi-auto, lever, and slide action rifles and slide action shotguns, in addition to importing Spanish SxS shotguns. Shotgun models included the Model 420, 420 EK, and 450 E. While most models were relatively inexpensive, good working, utilitarian guns, there has been little collectibility to date and most rifles are seen priced in the $45-$150 price range while the shotguns are priced in the $75-$300 range, depending on gauge and features.

NOR-CAL PRECISION

Previous manufacturer and riflesmith circa 1989-2009 and located in American Canyon, CA.

Nor-Cal Precision manufacutured custom rifles based on the Rem. M700 action, in addition to a variety of gunsmithing services.

GRADING - PPGS™	100%	98%	95%	90%	80%	70%	60%	LAST MSR

NOREEN FIREARMS LLC

Current manufacturer located in Belgrade, MT.

RIFLES

Noreen manufactures a complete line of long range precision rifles in .338 Lapua to .50 BMG cal. A wide variety of options, configurations, and accessories are available. Please contact the company directly for more information (see Trademark Index).

IMPORTANT NOTE: On model(s) where *N/A has replaced the normal 100% value, it indicates current market conditions are too unstable to accurately ascertain 100%-60% values. Factory retail prices (MSRs) reflect most recent updates. For more up-to-date information on current pricing trends and additional useful information, please visit www.bluebookofgunvalues.com, select "Information & Services " from the menu, and click on "Additional Book Information".

BAD NEWS ULTRA LONG RANGE SEMI-AUTO (ULR) – .300 Win. Mag. or .338 Lapua cal., matte black finish, aluminum receiver, mil-spec or adj. trigger, 5 or 10 shot detachable box mag., 26 in. barrel, custom muzzle brake, one piece bolt carrier, Picatinny quad rail on handguard, Magpul PRA adj. stock.

MSR $5,995	*N/A	$4,475	$3,825	$3,475	$2,800	$2,295	$1,785	

ULTRA LONG RANGE BOLT ACTION (ULR) – .338 Lapua, .408 Cheytac, .416 Barrett, or .50 BMG cal., single shot, 34 in. button rifled chrome-moly barrel, tactical black or desert camo finish, shell holder bolt, Timney adj. trigger, Picatinny top rail, muzzle brake, folding rotating bipod, collapsible shoulder stock.

MSR $2,599	$2,200	$1,925	$1,650	$1,495	$1,210	$995	$775	

Add $300 for .338 Lapua, .408 Cheytac, or .416 Barrett cal.
Add $900 for XLR Extreme stock.

NORICA LAURONA

Current firearms and airgun manufacturer established in 1917 and located in Eibar, Spain. Norica changed its name to Norica Laurona in 2010. Norica started making airguns in 1917, and acquired the Laurona trademark in 2010. Please refer to the Laurona listing for current firearms information.

For more information and current pricing on both new and used Norica airguns, please refer to the *Blue Book of Airguns* by Dr. Robert Beeman & John Allen (also online).

NORINCO

Current division of China North Industries Corp. established in 1981, and located in Beijing, China. Norinco currently manufactures small arms and large military weapons for commerical, law enforcement, and military applications. No current U.S. importation. Distributed throughout Europe by Norconia GmbH, located in Rottendorf, Germany. Previously imported and distributed exclusively by Interstate Arms Corp., located in Billerica, MA. Previous importers have included: Norinco Sports U.S.A., located in Diamond Bar, CA, Century International Arms, Inc. located in St. Albans, VT; China Sports, Inc. located in Ontario, CA; Interarms located in Alexandria, VA; KBI, Inc. located in Harrisburg, PA; and others.

Norinco pistols, rifles, and shotguns are manufactured in the People's Republic of China by China North Industries Corp. (Norinco has over 100 factories). Currently, due to government legislation, Norinco cannot legally sell weapons in the U.S.

PISTOLS: SEMI-AUTO

MODEL 213 – 9mm Para. cal., single action, satin blue finish. Imported 1988 only.

	$225	$185	$150	$135	$125	$115	$105	*$200*

TYPE 54-1 TOKAREV STANDARD – 7.62x25mm Tokarev or .38 Super cal., single action semi-auto, 4 1/2 in. barrel, 8 shot mag., fixed sights, blue finish, 29 oz. Imported 1989-95.

	$175	$150	$125	$100	$80	$70	$65	*$145*

Add 25% for .38 Super cal.

GRADING - PPGS™	100%	98%	95%	90%	80%	70%	60%	LAST MSR

* ***Type 54-1 (213A Model) Tokarev Standard Double Column*** – similar to Standard Model, except is also available in 9mm Para. cal. and has 10 (C/B 1994) or 13* shot mag., 35 oz. Imported 1991-95.

	$250	$215	$185	$165	$135	$125	$110	*$185*

* ***Type 54-1 (213/201C/54T Model) Tokarev Standard Compact*** – .38 Super, 9mm Para., or 7.62x25mm Tokarev cal., 3.8 in. barrel, 8 shot mag., 27 oz. Imported 1991-95.

	$250	$215	$185	$165	$135	$125	$110	*$185*

TYPE 59 MAKAROV – 9x18mm Makarov or .380 ACP cal., double action semi-auto, 3 1/2 in. barrel, 8 shot bottom release mag., checkered plastic grips, PPK design with additional features, adj. rear sight, 24 oz. Imported 1989-95.

	$195	$175	$150	$135	$125	$115	$95	*$185*

TYPE 77B – 9mm Para. cal., semi-auto single action, action patterned after the older German Lignose (unique design permits one handed operation utilizing "trigger guard cocking" enabling the slide to be moved backward cocking the hammer), 5 in. barrel, 8 shot mag., adj. rear sight, 34 oz. Limited importation 1991-95.

	$425	$350	$295	$250	$225	$195	$165	*$285*

MODEL 1911 A1 – .45 ACP cal. only, patterned after the Colt 1911 A1, 5 in. barrel, 7 shot mag., fixed sights, blue or parkerized finish, wood grips, 39 oz. Imported 1991-95.

	$525	$475	$450	$400	$350	$300	$275	*$320*

RIFLES: SEMI-AUTO

TYPE 84S AKS RIFLE – .223 Rem. cal., semi-auto Kalashnikov action, 16.34 in. barrel, hardwood stock and pistol grip, 30 shot mag., 1,000 meter adj. rear sight, includes bayonet and sheath, 8.87 lbs. Imported 1988-89 only.

	$1,450	$1,250	$1,150	$1,000	$925	$875	$795	*$350*

* ***Type 84S-1 AKS Rifle*** – similar to Type 84S AKS except has under-folding metal stock. Imported 1989 only.

	$1,600	$1,500	$1,400	$1,250	$1,100	$1,000	$900	*$350*

* ***Type 84S-3 AKS Rifle*** – similar to Type 84S AKS except has composite fiber stock (1 1/2 in. longer than wood stock). Imported 1989 only.

	$1,295	$1,100	$1,000	$950	$900	$800	$750	*$365*

* ***Type 84S-5 AKS Rifle*** – similar to Type 84S AKS except has side-folding metal stock. Imported 1989 only.

	$1,600	$1,500	$1,450	$1,350	$1,200	$1,100	$1,000	*$350*

NHM-90/91 (AK-47 THUMBHOLE) – .223 Rem. or 7.62x39mm cal., features new thumbhole stock for legalized import, 5 shot mag. Imported 1991-1993, configuration was restyled and renamed NHM-90/91 in 1994.

	$750	$675	$575	$500	$450	$350	$300	*$375*

NHM-90/91 SPORT – 7.62x39mm cal., choice of 16.34 (NHM-90) or 23.27 (NHM-91) in. barrel, hardwood thumbhole stock, NHM-91 has bipod, 5 shot mag., 9-11 lbs. Imported 1994-95.

	$550	$500	$450	$425	$385	$350	$325	

The .223 Rem. cal. was also available for the Model NHM-90. Each Model NHM-90/91 was supplied with three 5 shot mags., sling, and cleaning kit.

MODEL B THUMBHOLE – 9mm Para. cal., patterned after the Uzi, features sporterized thumbhole wood stock, 10 shot mag. Importation 1995 only.

	$795	$695	$600	$550	$500	$450	$400	*$625*

R.P.K. RIFLE – 7.62x39mm cal., includes bipod. Importation disc. 1993.

	$1,200	$1,000	$900	$800	$725	$650	$600	*$600*

GRADING - PPGS™	100%	98%	95%	90%	80%	70%	60%	LAST MSR

TYPE SKS – .223 Rem. or 7.62x39mm cal., SKS action, 20.47 in. barrel, 10 (C/B 1994) or 30* shot mag., 1,000 meter adj. rear sight, hardwood stock, new design accepts standard AK mag., with or w/o folding bayonet, 8.8 lbs. Imported 1988-1989, reintroduced 1992-95 with Sporter configuration stock.

$475	$400	$350	$325	$300	$250	$225	*$150*

Add $100 for synthetic stock and bayonet.
Subtract 15% if refinished.

TYPE 81S AKS RIFLE – 7.62x39mm cal., semi-auto Kalashnikov action, 17 1/2 in. barrel, 5, 30, or 40 shot mag., 500 meter adj. rear sight, fixed wood stock, hold open device after last shot, 8 lbs. Imported 1988-1989.

$1,200	$1,000	$900	$800	$725	$650	$600	*$385*

* ***Type 81S-1 AKS Rifle*** – similar to Type 81S AKS except has under-folding metal stock. Imported 1988-89.

$1,300	$1,075	$950	$850	$750	$625	$575	*$385*

TYPE 56S-2 – 7.62x39mm cal., older Kalashnikov design with side-folding metal stock. Importation disc. 1989.

$1,500	$1,350	$1,200	$1,100	$1,000	$900	$800	*$350*

TYPE 86S-7 RPK RIFLE – 7.62x39mm cal., AK action, 23.27 in. heavy barrel with built-in bipod, in-line buttstock, 11.02 lbs. Imported 1988-1989.

$1,500	$1,275	$1,075	$950	$850	$750	$650	*$425*

TYPE 86S BULLPUP RIFLE – 7.62x39mm cal., bullpup configuration with AK action, under-folding metal stock, 17 1/4 in. barrel, ambidextrous cocking design, folding front handle, 7 lbs. Imported 1989 only.

$1,850	$1,650	$1,500	$1,250	$1,100	$1,000	$900	*$400*

DRAGUNOV (MODEL 350 NDM-86) – 7.62x54mm Russian, sniper variation of the AK-47, features 24 in. barrel with muzzle brake, special laminated skeletonized wood stock with vent. forearm, detachable 10 shot mag., 8 lbs. 9 oz. Importation disc. 1995.

$2,950	$2,650	$2,400	$2,250	$2,000	$1,850	$1,650	*$3,080*

This model was also imported by Gibbs Rifle Co. located in Martinsburg, WV.

* ***Dragunov Carbine*** – similar to Dragunov rifle, except shorter barrel, various accessories including a lighted scope were also offered, plastic furniture.

$1,200	$1,000	$875	$775	$675	$600	$550	

OFFICERS NINE – 9mm Para. cal., 16.1 in. barrel, action patterned after the IMI Uzi, 32 shot mag., black military finish, 8.4 lbs. Limited 1988-89.

$1,100	$995	$850	$725	$650	$575	$500	*$450*

RIFLES: .22 CAL.

MODEL EM-321 – .22 LR cal., slide action, 19 1/2 in. barrel, 10 shot tube mag., hardwood stock and forearm, fixed sights, 6 lbs. Importation began 1989-90, resumed 1994-disc.

$135	$115	$95	$85	$75	$65	$55	

TYPE EM-332 – .22 LR cal., bolt action, 18 1/2 in. barrel with adj. rear sight, mag. holder on stock holds two extra 5 shot mags., Monte Carlo stock with cheekpiece and recoil pad, 4 1/2 lbs. Imported 1991-93.

$225	$195	$165	$140	$120	$95	$80	

SHOTGUNS: O/U

TYPE HL12-203 – 12 ga. only, 2 3/4 in. chambers, boxlock action, ejectors, 30 in. vent. barrels and rib, single trigger, multi-chokes, checkered stock and forearm, 7 1/2 lbs. Imported 1989-1993.

$400	$350	$300	$265	$225	$200	$185	

GRADING - PPGS™	100%	98%	95%	90%	80%	70%	60%	LAST MSR

SHOTGUNS: SEMI-AUTO

MODEL 2000 FIELD – 12 ga. only, 2 3/4 in. chamber, steel receiver and aluminum alloy trigger guard, 26 or 28 in. VR barrel with M choke tube, choice of black synthetic or checkered hardwood stock and forearm, approx. 7 1/2 lbs. Limited importation 1999 only.

$260	$230	$200	$185	$170	$160	$150	*$299*

Add $8 for wood stock and forearm.

Choke tubes are interchangeable with the WinChoke system.

* ***Model 2000 Field Defense*** – 12 ga. only, 2 3/4 in. chamber, 18 1/2 in. barrel with cyl. choke tube and choice of bead, rifle, or ghost ring sights, matte black metal finish, black synthetic stock and forearm with recoil pad. Limited importation 1999 only.

$245	$225	$190	$175	$160	$155	$145	*$282*

Add $5 for rifle sights.
Add $17 for ghost ring sights.

SHOTGUNS: SLIDE ACTION

TYPE HL12-102 – 12 ga. only, 2 3/4 in. chamber, 28.4 in. barrel, 3 shot mag., crossbolt safety on rear trigger guard, fixed chokes, 9.3 lbs. Imported 1989-93.

$230	$200	$175	$165	$150	$135	$120

MODEL 98 FIELD – 12 ga. only, 3 in. chamber, 26 or 28 in. VR barrel with M choke tube, choice of black synthetic or uncheckered hardwood stock and forearm with recoil pad, approx. 7 lbs. Limited importation 1999 only.

$185	$160	$140	$125	$110	$100	$90	*$205*

Add $8 for wood stock and forearm.
Add $55 for Field Combo (includes extra 18 1/2 in. barrel) or $82 for Field Combo with 22 in. slug or turkey barrel.

* ***Model 98 Field Turkey*** – similar to Model 98 Field, except has 22 in. VR barrel with extra full choke tube, black synthetic stock and forearm only. Limited importation 1999 only.

$190	$165	$140	$125	$110	$100	$90	*$216*

* ***Model 98 Field Defense*** – 12 ga. only, 3 in. chamber, 18 1/2 in. barrel with cyl. choke tube and choice of bead, rifle, or ghost ring sights, matte black metal finish, black synthetic stock and forearm with recoil pad. Limited importation 1999 only.

$170	$150	$130	$115	$100	$90	$80	*$190*

Add $15 for ghost ring sights.

MODEL 983 – 12 ga. only, 22 in. barrel with external rifled choke tube and adj. rifle sights, synthetic black stock. Limited importation 2002 only.

$215	$170	$155	$135	$125	$105	$95	*$230*

MODEL 984/985/987 – 12 ga. only, 3 in. chamber, field series with 26 or 28 in. VR barrel and M choke tube, black synthetic or uncheckered hardwood stock and forearm, matte black metal finish. Limited importation 2001-2002.

$200	$170	$155	$135	$125	$105	$95	*$235*

Add $10 for hardwood stock (Models 985 & 987).

NORINCO USA

Previous manufacturer located in Jefferson City, MO.

Retired Marine Jon Morgan applied for the Norinco trademark circa 2007 to be used for firearms manufactured in the U.S. However, no production firearms were manufactured using the Norinco name.

NORSMAN SPORTING ARMS & OUTFITTERS LLC

Current rifle manufacturer/customizer located in Havre, MT since 1999. Previously located in Bismarck, ND until 1999. Consumer direct sales.

Norsman specializes in both wood and synthetic take-down rifles and multiple barrel/caliber configurations, in addition to a SxS double rifle and falling block rifle. Please contact the factory directly for additional information, prices, and delivery time (see Trademark Index).

GRADING - PPGS™	100%	98%	95%	90%	80%	70%	60%	LAST MSR

RIFLES: BOLT ACTION

VIKING GRADE – most standard cals., unique NSA takedown action, many options, including left-hand models, custom orders also available.

MSR $8,000	$7,500	$6,750	$5,750	$5,250	$4,500	$3,750	$3,000

Add $1,500 per interchangeable barrel.

VIKING GRADE MAGNUM – most standard Mag. cals., unique NSA takedown action, many options and custom orders available, including left-hand.

MSR $10,800	$10,250	$9,250	$8,000	$6,750	$5,500	$4,500	$3,500

Add $2,000 per interchangeable barrel.

FIELD GRADE SYNTHETIC – most standard cals., unique NSA takedown action, many options and custom orders available.

MSR $4,250	$3,850	$3,350	$2,850	$2,500	$2,100	$1,850	$1,500

Add $1,200 per interchangeable barrel.

ODIN GRADE – .223 Rem. - .505 Gibbs cal., available in right or left-hand Mauser style action, presentation grade walnut stock, match grade barrel, competition trigger, three position wing safety, quarter rib with banded ramped front sights, barrel band swivel, gold monogram stock oval, metal pistol grip cap, leather covered recoil pad, hand cut checkering, quick detachable scope bases and rings, engraving with gold inlays. New 2003.

MSR $12,500	$11,500	$10,000	$8,500	$7,750	$6,500	$5,500	$4,150

THOR GRADE – .223 Rem. - .416 Rem. cal., right or left-hand Mauser style action, extra fancy grade walnut stock, premium match grade barrel, competition trigger, three position wing safety, quarter rib with banded ramped front sights, barrel band swivel, metal pistol grip cap, rubber recoil pad, hand cut checkering, quick detachable scope bases and rings. New 2003.

MSR $10,200	$9,500	$8,500	$7,500	$6,500	$5,500	$4,500	$3,500

TYR GRADE – .223 Rem. - .416 Rem. cal., right or left-hand Mauser style action, fiber core or kevlar wrapped composite stock, premium match grade barrel, competition trigger, teflon all-weather coating on metal and stock, adj. rear and banded ramped front sights, three position wing safety, swivel studs, rubber recoil pad, quick detachable scope bases and rings. New 2003.

MSR $7,900	$7,350	$6,450	$5,600	$4,750	$3,950	$3,250	$2,400

VOYAGER GRADE – .223 Rem. - .416 Rem. cal., Mauser style titanium action, fiber core or kevlar wrapped composite stock, premium match grade barrel, competition trigger, teflon all-weather coating on metal and stock, adj. rear and banded ramped front sights, three position wing safety, swivel studs, rubber recoil pad, quick detachable scope bases and rings. New 2003.

MSR $12,500	$11,500	$10,000	$8,500	$7,750	$6,500	$5,500	$4,150

RIFLES: SxS

VIKING GRADE – most standard cals. including .30-30 WCF, .30-40 Krag, .375 Win., .444 Marlin, .45-70 Govt., as well as traditional European NE cals. up to .600 NE, built per individual custom order. New 2000.

MSR $24,500	$22,550	$19,750	$16,400	$14,000	$12,000	$10,000	$8,500

RIFLES: SINGLE SHOT

VIKING GRADE – standard cals. include .30-30 WCF, .30-40 Krag, .375 Win., .444 Marlin, or .45-70 Govt. cal., European cals. up to .600 NE also available, falling block Farquharson action, Bespoke quality, built per individual custom order. New 2011.

MSR $24,500	$22,550	$19,750	$16,400	$14,000	$12,000	$10,000	$8,500

NORTH AMERICAN ARMS, INC.

Current manufacturer established circa 1976, and currently located in Provo, UT. Distributor and dealer sales.

North American Arms was originally founded under the name Rocky Mountain Arms circa 1974-1975 by noted handgun entrepreneur Dick Casull. During 1976-1977, the company's name was changed to North American Arms, and it became part of the Tally Corp. of

GRADING - PPGS™	100%	98%	95%	90%	80%	70%	60%	LAST MSR

Newbury Park, CA. North American Arms was relocated from Salt Lake City to Provo, UT in 1978, and moved again in 1984 to Spanish Fork, UT. During 1986-1987, Teleflex Corp., an aerospace company, bought North American Arms' parent company, the Tally Corp. In 1992, Teleflex decided to sell off the gunmaking company, and North American Arms was purchased by Sandy Chisholm, a Teleflex employee. The company relocated again in 1994 to Provo, UT.

PISTOLS: SEMI-AUTO

In addition to many accessories being available for the Guardian Pistol Series, there is also a Guardian Custom Shop that offers consumers a customized Guardian model, with a wide variety of finish, slide, sight, grips, and serialization options. Please contact the company directly for more information on these custom shop special orders and options.

NAA .25 GUARDIAN – .25 ACP cal., similar to NAA .32 Guardian, except is smaller size, 15 oz. New 2006.

MSR $402	$355	$310	$265	$240	$195	$160	$125

NAA .32 GUARDIAN – .32 ACP cal., double action only, hammerless, stainless steel construction, 6 shot mag., 2 1/8 in. barrel, fixed low profile sights, dimpled black synthetic grips, 13 1/2 oz. New 1999.

MSR $402	$355	$310	$265	$240	$195	$160	$125

Add $28 for ILS (integral locking system) option.

NAA .32 NAA GUARDIAN – .32 NAA cal. (.380 ACP casing necked down to .32 cal.), double action only, larger version of the NAA .32 Guardian, 2.49 in. barrel, 6 shot mag., dimpled black grips, 18.7 oz. New 2002.

MSR $449	$385	$335	$290	$260	$210	$175	$135

NAA .380 GUARDIAN – .380 ACP cal., double action only, larger version of the NAA .32 Guardian, 2.49 in. barrel, 6 shot mag., dimpled black grips, mfg. in partnership with Kahr Arms, 18.7 oz. New 2001.

MSR $449	$385	$335	$290	$260	$210	$175	$135

Add $30 for ILS (integral locking system) option.

REVOLVERS: MINI SERIES

All NAA mini revolvers are manufactured to highest quality control standards and have half-way notches cut on the front cylinder face allowing the hammer to lock up the cylinder between cartridges. This allows the gun to be carried fully loaded without the danger of accidental discharge.

NAA .17 – .17 HMR or .17 Mach 2 cal., otherwise similar to NAA .22 Model. Mfg. 2005-2008.

	$155	$135	$115	$105	$85	$70	$55	*$193*

Add $22 for holster grip accessory.
Add $15 for .17 HMR cal.
Add $43 for .17 HMR cal. with extra .17 Mach 2 conversion cylinder.

NAA .22 S/LR – .22 Short (new 1994) or .22 LR cal., 5 shot, single action, spur trigger, 1 1/8, 1 5/8, or 2 1/2 (disc.) in. barrel with blade front and notched rear sight, stainless steel, plastic (disc.) or laminated rosewood grips, approx. 4 1/2 oz. New 1975.

MSR $209	$175	$150	$125	$100	$85	$70	$55

Add $15 for 2 1/2 in. barrel (disc.).
Add $30 for holster grip accessory.
Add $59 for quick-release belt buckle option (1 1/8 in. barrel only).

The optional holster grip allows the pistol to fold forward allowing concealability, safety, and has a clip which allows it to be attached to a belt.

NAA .22 MAGNUM – similar to .22 LR, except in .22 WMR cal., barrel porting became available during 2012, 6.5 oz.

MSR $219	$185	$160	$130	$120	$95	$80	$60

Add $20 for ported barrel (new 2012).
Add $18 for 2 1/2 in. barrel (disc.).

GRADING - PPGS™	100%	98%	95%	90%	80%	70%	60%	LAST MSR

Add $35 for revolver with extra .22 LR conversion cylinder.
Add $30 for holster grip accessory.
Add $59 for quick-release belt buckle option (1 1/8 in. barrel only).

NAA .22 MAGNUM CONVERTIBLE – similar to NAA .22 WMR cal., except has extra LR cylinder in pouch.

MSR $254	$210	$185	$160	$145	$115	$95	$75	

Add $18 for 2 1/2 in. barrel (disc.).
Add $30 for holster grip accessory.

NAA PUG – .22 WMR cal., 1 in. barrel, tritium or white dot XS sight system, oversized pebble textured rubber grips, 6.4 oz. New mid-2007.

MSR $314	$260	$225	$190	$170	$140	$115	$90	

Add $20 for tritium sights.

PORTED MAGNUM – .22 WMR cal., 5 shot, 1 5/8 in. ported barrel, bead front fixed sights, 6.5 oz. New 2012.

MSR $239	$200	$180	$160	$145	$120	$100	$80	

Add $35 for extra combo cylinder.

PORTED SNUB – .22 WMR cal., 5 shot, 1 1/8 in. ported barrel, bead front fixed sights, 6.2 oz. New 2012.

MSR $239	$200	$180	$160	$145	$120	$100	$80	

Add $35 for extra combo cylinder.

MINI-MASTER TARGET REVOLVER – .17 HMR (mfg. 2003-2009), .17 Mach 2 (mfg. 2005-2009), .22 LR, or .22 WMR cal., 5 shot, 4 in. heavy vent. barrel, unfluted bull cylinder, spur trigger, fixed or adj. white outline rear sight, oversized black rubber Mini-master grip, 10.7 oz. New 1990.

MSR $284	$240	$210	$180	$165	$130	$110	$85	

Add $35 for extra combo cylinder.
Add $30 for adj. rear sight (elevation only).

This model was also available in hot fuschia colored oversized grips.

MINI-MASTER BLACK WIDOW – .17 HMR (new 2003-disc.), 17 Mach 2 (new 2005-disc.), .22 LR or .22 WMR cal., 2 in. heavy VR barrel, full size black rubber grip, fixed or adj. rear sight, unfluted cylinder, 8.8 oz. New 1991.

MSR $274	$220	$195	$165	$150	$120	$100	$75	

Add $35 for extra combo cylinder.
Add $25 for adj. rear sight (elevation only).

This model was also available in hot fuschia colored oversized grips.

THE EARL – .22 WMR cal., 5 shot, SA, 2 1/2 (Sheriff Model, new 2012), 3, 4, or 6 (Hogleg Model, new 2012) in. heavy octagon barrel, stainless steel frame, wood grips, top strap channel, bead front sight, faux loading lever secures cylinder pin, available with or w/o .22 LR cal. conversion cylinder, approx. 9 oz. New 2009.

MSR $284	$245	$215	$185	$165	$135	$110	$85	

Add $35 for .22 LR conversion cylinder.
Add $11 for 6 in. barrel (Hogleg Model), new 2012.

THE WASP – .22 WMR cal., 1 1/8 (Wasp Snub) or 1 5/8 in. VR barrel, spur trigger, skeleton hammer, 5 shot, features black cylinder flutes and black lines on revolver, cylinder and lower shroud, stainless post front sight with notched rear, dimpled black synthetic grips, 6.4 oz. New 2011.

MSR $249	$210	$185	$160	$145	$115	$95	$75	

Add $35 for extra .22 LR conversion cylinder.

NAA RANGER – .22 WMR cal., 5 shot, spur trigger, pivoting top-break action, 1 5/8 in. barrel, half-moon fixed sights, laminated grips, 7.2 oz. Limited mfg. 2011 only.

	$425	$365	$325	$285	$250	$225	$195	*$499*

GRADING - PPGS™	100%	98%	95%	90%	80%	70%	60%	LAST MSR

NAA STANDARD SET – 3 gun set (.22 Short, .22 LR, and .22 WMR cals.) in walnut display case with matching serial numbers, high polish finish with matte contours.

MSR $749	$550	$480	$415	$375	$305	$250	$195	

NAA DELUXE SET – 3 gun set (.22 Short, .22 LR, and .22 WMR cals.) in walnut display case with matching serial numbers, high polish finish on entire gun.

MSR $893	$750	$655	$565	$510	$415	$340	$265	

CASED .22 MAG. – includes .22 WMR cal. model in walnut display case with high polish finish with matte contours.

MSR $375	$315	$265	$230	$200	$175	$150	$125	

NAA SINGLE ACTION REVOLVER – .45 Win. Mag. or .450 Mag. Express cal., polished stainless steel, transfer bar safety inside the hammer, 5 shot, 7 1/2 in. barrel, walnut grips, includes presentation case. Disc. 1984.

Matte finish	$1,200	$1,050	$900	$815	$660	$540	$420	
High polish finish	$1,400	$1,225	$1,050	$950	$770	$630	$490	
Both cylinders	$1,650	$1,445	$1,240	$1,120	$910	$745	$580	*$650*

This model was also available by special order with 10 1/2 in. barrel and optional scope. Extra cylinders were also available at $75-$100 and were fitted to the gun. A set including 2 cylinders could also be ordered. North American Arms cannot perform any repair work on .450 Mag. Express revolvers.

SIDEWINDER – .22 WMR cal., features a swing-out style cylinder assembly, 1 in. barrel, stainless steel construction, 5 shot, wood grips. New 2013.

MSR $349	$300	$265	$230	$200	$185	$170	$165	

Add $40 for .22 LR conversion cylinder assembly.

NORTH AMERICAN SAFARI EXPRESS

Previous trademark for those rifles (SxS) assembled by A. Francotte of Belgium for exclusive importation by Armes De Chasse located in Chadds Ford, PA.

NORTHERN COMPETITION

Current rifle manufacturer located in Bristol, WI. Consumer direct sales through FFL.

RIFLES: SEMI-AUTO

Northern Competition manufactures a line of AR-15 style rifles in various calibers and configurations. Current models include the Cheetah (MSR $1,869), Cougar (MSR $1,618), and Complete Service rifle (MSR $1,495). Previous models included the Predator and Ranch models. Please contact the company directly for more information, pricing, and availability (see Trademark Index).

NORTHWEST ARMS

Please refer to Wilkinson Arms listing in the W section.

NOSLER, INC.

Current rifle, ammunition, and bullet manufacturer located in Bend, OR.

John Nosler founded Nosler, Inc. in 1948, and is responsible for the development of numerous bullet designs optimized for accuracy or dangerous game hunting.

RIFLES: BOLT ACTION

MODEL 48 SERIES – various cals., features NoslerCustom push feed action, 3 or 4 shot mag., 24 in. barrel w/o sights, standard, 2, or 3 position safety, Rifle Basix or Timney trigger, various synthetic or wood stocks, Cerakote and Microslick metal coating. Guaranteed accuracy at 100 yards, available in Trophy Grade, Legacy, Professional, and Custom configurations, approx. 6 1/4 - 8 3/4 lbs. New 2005.

* ***Model 48 Custom*** – various cals., features Kevlar/Carbon fiber stock in various color Cerakote finish, various barrel lengths between 20-26 in., available in Long Range, Expedition, High Country, and Brush Country packages, 6 1/2-7 1/2 lbs.

MSR $3,195	$2,700	$2,375	$2,025	$1,825	$1,475	$1,200	$950	

GRADING - PPGS™	100%	98%	95%	90%	80%	70%	60%	LAST MSR

Add $200 for factory installed muzzle brake.
Add $100 for detachable magazine.
Add $100 for 3-position safety.

* ***Model 48 Custom Varmint*** - .204 Ruger, .223 Rem., or .22-250 Rem. cal., features Coyote tan Kevlar/Carbon fiber stock, Graphite Black or Coyote Tan Cerakote, 7 1/4 lbs. Disc. 2011.

	100%	98%	95%	90%	80%	70%	60%	LAST MSR
	$2,650	$2,200	$1,800	$1,450	$1,150	$1,000	$900	*$2,995*

* ***Model 48 Legacy*** - various cals., features deluxe checkered walnut stock, special engraved floorplate bearing the signature of John A. Nosler, no sights, Midnight Blue Cerakote finish, 7 1/2 - 8 lbs.

	100%	98%	95%	90%	80%	70%	60%
MSR $2,695	$2,295	$2,000	$1,725	$1,550	$1,250	$1,025	$800

* ***Model 48 Professional*** - various cals., features black Bell & Carlson composite stock, matte black Cerakote finish, no sights, 6 1/2 -7 1/2 lbs. New 2012.

	100%	98%	95%	90%	80%	70%	60%
MSR $2,695	$2,295	$2,000	$1,725	$1,550	$1,250	$1,025	$800

Add $100 for detachable magazine.
Add $200 for factory installed muzzle brake.

* ***Model 48 Trophy*** - various cals., features black and spiderweb gray Bell & Carlson composite stock, magnesium color Cerakote finish, blind bottom magazine, no sights, 6 1/2-7 lbs.

	100%	98%	95%	90%	80%	70%	60%
MSR $1,995	$1,800	$1,575	$1,300	$1,050	$875	$750	$625

Add $200 for factory installed muzzle brake.

* ***Model 48 Outfitter*** - various cals., features black and spiderweb gray Bell & Carlson composite stock, magnesium color Cerakote finish. New 2013

	100%	98%	95%	90%	80%	70%	60%
MSR $2,395	$2,025	$1,775	$1,525	$1,375	$1,115	$915	$715

CUSTOM LIMITED EDITION SERIES - .280 Ackley Improved (Series 2), .300 WSM (Series 1, limited quantities), or .338 Win. Mag. (Series 3) cal., features NoslerCustom barreled action with 3-position safety, integral Leupold QD scope mounts, 24 in. barrel w/o sights, fancy checkered walnut stock with forend and pistol grip caps, Pachmayr Decelerator recoil pad, only 500 of each series mfg. (ser. no. range 001-500), shipped in Kalispel Aluminum case or Pelican Polymer hard case with leather sling, 9 lbs. New 2005.

	100%	98%	95%	90%	80%	70%	60%
MSR $4,195	$3,950	$3,600	$3,200	$2,800	$2,450	$2,150	$1,750

Add $200 for Series 1 in .300 WSM cal. (limited quantities).

The Series 1 rifle comes with a Leupold VXIII 2.5-8x36 scope calibrated for the Nosler ammunition sold with the rifle.

The Series 2 rifles comes with a Leupold VXIII 2.5-8x36, VXIII 3.5-10x40, or VXIII 4.5-14x40 scope, calibrated for the Nosler ammunition sold with the rifle.

The Series 3 rifle comes with Leupold VXIII 2.5-8x36mm, VXIII 3.5-10x40, or VXIII 4.5-14x40 scope, calibrated for the Nosler ammunition sold with the rifle.

SANCTUARY EDITION SERIES - .270 WSM cal. only, 24 in. barrel w/o sights, matte black Cerakote finish, fancy grade checkered bubinga wood stock with forend and pistol grip caps, Pachmayr Decelerator recoil pad, integral Leupold QD scope mounts, only 25 mfg. (ser. no. range 001-025 w/SE prefix), shipped in Americase hard case with Leupold LPS or VX7 scope. New 2012.

	100%	98%	95%	90%	80%	70%	60%
MSR $5,495	$5,100	$4,500	$4,000	$3,450	$2,950	$2,650	$2,250

RIFLES: SEMI-AUTO

VARMAGEDDON - 5.56 NATO cal., AR-15 style, 18 in. stainless steel barrel, forged Vltor upper receiver with Picatinny rail and integrated 13 1/2 in. NSR handguard with KeyMod system, extended feed ramp, Magpul PRS stock, MOE grip, Geissele SD-E trigger. New 2013.

	100%	98%	95%	90%	80%	70%	60%
MSR $2,295	$2,100	$1,875	$1,675	$1,500	$1,325	$1,100	$925

Add $900 for package with Leupold Varmageddon scope and CDS turret.

NOWLIN MFG., INC.

Previous custom handgun manufacturer. Nowlin Guns continues to manufacture a wide variety of pistol components. The company was established in 1982, and is currently located in Claremore, OK.

PISTOLS: SEMI-AUTO

Nowlin discontinued all its pistols in late 2010. The following is a listing of its products with last MSRs. Nowlin Mfg., Inc. manufactured a complete line of high quality M1911 A1 styled competition and defense pistols, available in 9mm Para., 9x23mm, .38 Super, .40 S&W, or .45 ACP cal. Various frame types are available, including a variety of Nowlin choices. Recent models (available in blue or nickel finish) included the NRA Bianchi Cup (approx. 1997 retail was $2,750 - disc.), 007 Compact ($1,395 - disc.), Compact X2 ($1,436 - disc.), Match Classic ($1,695 - disc. 2010), Crusader ($1,999 - disc. 2010), Avenger w/STI frame ($2,279 - disc. 2010), Challenger ($2,049 - disc. 2010), World Cup PPC ($2,219 - disc. 2010), STI High Cap. Frame ($1,595 - disc. 1999), Mickey Fowler Signature Series ($2,187 - disc. 2010), Compact Carry ($1,695 - disc. 1999), Compact 4 1/4 in. ($1,750, .45 ACP, disc. 2002), Gladiator ($1,447 in .45 ACP cal., disc. 2002), Match Master ($2,795 - disc. 2010), Bianchi Cup Master Grade ($5,019, .38 Super cal., disc. 2010) and the Custom Shop Excaliber Series ($3,029 - disc. 2010).

NOTES

O SECTION

O'BRIEN RIFLE CO.

Previous bolt action rifle manufacturer located in Las Vegas, NV circa 1966-1971.

Vern O'Brien manufactured high quality bolt action rifles, many of which were chambered for proprietary calibers, including the .17 Mach 4, .17 Javelina, .17-222, .17-222 Mag., and .17-223. There were basically two grades - a Field Grade with rosewood forend tip and pistol grip, and a Presentation Grade with basket weave checkering, Javelina inlaid in the stock opposite the cheekpiece, and a diamond inlaid below the action. All rifles were based on the Sako L-461 action. Circa 1971, Vern O'Brien sold his company to H&R, which produced a rifle similar to his called the 317 Ultra Wildcat. Values are hard to predict in today's marketplace because so few are encountered. A starting price range for the Field Grade is $750-$1,400, and $1,150-$2,500 for the Presentation Grade.

O.D.I. (OMEGA DEFENSIVE INDUSTRIES)

Previous manufacturer located in Midland Park, NJ circa 1981-82.

Essex Arms, located in Island Pond, VT, acquired the remaining O.D.I. Viking inventory of parts for the Viking pistol, in addition to being a components supplier (slides and receivers) for M-1911 styled pistols. Previously, Randco Manufacturing, located in Monrovia, CA, was providing service (and had parts) for these older O.D.I. pistols.

GRADING - PPGS™	100%	98%	95%	90%	80%	70%	60%	LAST MSR

PISTOLS: SEMI-AUTO

VIKING & VIKING COMBAT – .45 ACP or 9mm Para. (advertised, but never mfg.) cal., Viking Model is Government size and the Combat Model is Commander size. All stainless steel construction, the design utilizes the Seecamp double action, teakwood grips. 4 1/4 (Viking Combat Model) or 5 in. (Viking Model) barrel, 7 shot mag., 39 oz. Approx. 200-300 Viking Combat Models were made from kits.

	100%	98%	95%	90%	80%	70%	60%	LAST MSR
	$495	$385	$295	$240	$210	$180	$155	*$579*

Add $100 for slide with crossbolt safety.

OBERLAND ARMS

Current manufacturer of paramilitary style firearms located in Huglfing, Germany. Previously located in Habach, Germany. No current U.S. importation.

FIREARMS

Oberland Arms manufactures a wide variety of high quality paramilitary style rifles, including an OA-15 series based on the AR-15 style. Oberland Arms also used to manufacture pistols. Many rifle options and configurations are available. Please contact the company directly for more information, including pricing, options, and U.S. availability (see Trademark Index).

OBREGON

Previously manufactured by Fabrica de Armas Mexico located in Mexico City, Mexico.

PISTOLS: SEMI-AUTO

OBREGON – 11.43mm cal., patterned somewhat after the Colt Model 1911A1, features tubular slide and Savage/Steyr type action, 1,000 pistols mfg. in Mexico for commercial sale during and after WWII, slide marked "Sistema Obregon Cal 11.43mm".

	100%	98%	95%	90%	80%	70%	60%
	$4,750	$4,250	$3,750	$3,250	$2,750	$2,250	$1,750

OHIO ORDNANCE WORKS, INC.

Current rifle and related components manufacturer established in 1981, and located in Chardon, OH.

Ohio Ordnance Works also manufactures machine guns, components, and accessories.

GRADING - PPGS™	100%	98%	95%	90%	80%	70%	60%	LAST MSR

RIFLES: SEMI-AUTO

MODEL BAR 1918A3 – .30-06 cal., patterned after the original Browning BAR (M1918A2) used during WWI, all steel construction utilizing original parts except for lower receiver, 24 in. barrel, original folding type rear sight, includes two 20 shot mags., matte metal and wood finish, Bakelite or American walnut stock and forearm, carrying handle, web sling, bipod, flash hider, bolt open hold device, 20 lbs.

MSR $4,300	$3,650	$3,195	$2,750	$2,475	$2,000	$1,650	$1,275	

MODEL BAR A1918 SLR – .30-06 cal., similar to Model BAR 1918A3, except does not have A3 carry handle, mfg. by Ohio Ordnance Works, Inc. 2005-2007.

	$3,100	$2,800	$2,450	$2,100	$1,800	$1,575	$1,300	*$3,350*

Add $200 for walnut stock.

MODEL 1928 BROWNING – .30-06, 7.65mm, .308 Win., or 8mm (disc.) cal., semi-auto action patterned after the 1928 Browning watercooled machine gun, blue (disc.) or parkerized finish, includes tripod, water hose, ammo can, 3 belts, and belt loader. Limited production late 2001-2007.

	$3,750	$3,400	$3,000	$2,650	$2,300	$2,100	$1,900	*$4,000*

Add $200 for .308 Win. or 8mm (disc.) cal.

Add approx. $2,000 for blue finish (limited mfg.).

MODEL M-240 SLR – 7.62 NATO cal., belt fed, gas operated, air cooled, fires from closed bolt, sling, cleaning kit, ruptured case extractor, gas regulator cleaning tool, disassembly tools, 2500 M-13 links, custom fit hard case, 24.2 lbs. New 2007.

MSR $13,918	$11,825	$10,350	$8,875	$8,040	$6,500	$5,325	$4,140	

MODEL VZ2000/VZ2000 SBR – 7.62x39mm cal., Czech VZ 58 copy, new milled receiver, original barrels, heat cured paint finish (matches original Czech finish), choice of bakelite furniture with folding stock or pistol grip with quad Picatinny rail and vertical grip (VZ2000 Tactical), includes four 30 shot mags., pouch, sling, cleaning kit, original bayonet, 6 lbs.

MSR $1,026	$875	$765	$650	$595	$475	$395	$300	

MODEL 1917A1 WATERCOOLED – .30-06 or .308 Win. cal., semi-auto copy of the military 1917A1 machine gun, various packages are available. Mfg. 2011-2012.

	$5,000	$4,650	$4,250	$3,850	$3,450	$3,150	$2,850	*$5,000*

Add $1,005 for deluxe package including 1917A1 tripod.

Add $1,500 for "The Works" package including 1917A1 tripod, water hose and can, wooden box, and linker.

MODEL 1919A4 SEMI-AUTO BELTFED – .308 Win. cal., copy of military 1919A4 machine gun, various packages available. Mfg. 2011-2012.

	$2,000	$1,800	$1,650	$1,500	$1,375	$1,250	$1,100	*$2,000*

Add $550 for Deluxe Package including M2 tripod and pintle.

Add $945 for "The Whole Enchilada" package including M2 tripod with pintle, trunnion shield, 1919A4 linker, and .30-06 barrel.

OLD-WEST GUN CO.

Previous importer and distributor that took over the inventory of Allen Firearms after they went out of business in early 1987.

Old-West Gun Co. changed their name to Cimarron Arms in late 1987. Please refer to Cimarron Arms in this text for approximate prices on similar models from Old-West Gun Co.

OLLENDORFF, PHILIPP

Current manufacturer established during 1986, and located in Scharnitz, Austria.

FIREARMS

Philipp Ollendorff manufactures best quality double rifles, O/U shotguns, stalking rifles, and other long gun configurations. All guns are made to custom order, and there are many options available. Please contact the manufacturer directly for more information, including model availability and a price quotation (see Trademark Index).

GRADING - PPGS™	100%	98%	95%	90%	80%	70%	60%	LAST MSR

OLYMPIC ARMS, INC.

Current manufacturer established during 1976, and located in Olympia, WA. Sales through Olympic dealers only.

Olympic Arms, Inc. was founded by Robert C. Schuetz, and began as Schuetzen Gun Works (SGW) in 1956, manufacturing barrels in Colorado Springs, Colorado. Prior to that Mr. Schuetz had been partnered in business with well known gunsmith P.O. Ackley. In 1975 the company moved to Olympia, Washington, and while its business in rifle barrels and barrel blanks thrived, it also began manufacturing complete custom bolt action rirfles. In 1982, Schuetzen Gun Works began to manufacture AR-15/M16 rifles and components under the trade name of Olympic Arms, Inc., while custom bolt action rifles continued to be produced under the SGW brand. In late 1987, Olympic Arms, Inc. acquired Safari Arms of Phoenix, AZ. As of Jan. 2004, the Safari Arms product name was discontinued, and all 1911 style products are now being manufactured in the Olympic Arms facility in Olympia, WA. Schuetzen Pistol Works is the in-house custom shop of Olympic Arms. Olympic Arms is one of the few AR-15 manufacturers to make every major component part in-house.

PISTOLS: SEMI-AUTO

Please refer to the Safari Arms section for previously manufactured pistols made under the Safari Arms trademark.

BIG DEUCE – .45 ACP cal., 6 in. longslide version of the MatchMaster, matte black slide with satin stainless steel frame, smooth walnut (disc.) or cocobolo grips with double diamond checkering, double slide serrations, 44 oz. Mfg. 1995-2004, reintroduced 2006.

MSR $1,164 $1,025 $900 $725 $600 $500 $400 $350

COHORT – .45 ACP cal., features Enforcer slide and MatchMaster frame, 4 in. stainless steel barrel, beavertail grip safety, extended thumb safety and slide release, commander style hammer, smooth walnut grips with laser etched Black Widow logo (disc.) or checkered walnut grips, finger grooved front grip strap, fully adj. rear sight, 37 oz. New 1995.

MSR $974 $850 $750 $650 $550 $450 $400 $350

WHITNEY WOLVERINE – .22 LR cal., patterned after original Whitney Wolverine, 4 5/8 in. barrel, features lightweight polymer frame and vent. rib, marked "Olympic Arms" on side of frame, 10 shot mag., matte black, pink (new 2011), desert tan (new 2011), or coyote brown (new 2011) finish, black checkered grips, bright pink polymer frame became an option during late 2010, 19.2 oz.

MSR $294 $260 $230 $200 $185 $170 $165 $155

Add $16 for flash suppressor.

ENFORCER – .45 ACP cal., 3.8 (disc.) or 4 in. bushingless stainless bull barrel, 6 shot mag., shortened grip, available with max hard finish aluminum frame, parkerized, electroless nickel, or lightweight (disc.) anodized finishes, Triplex counterwound self-contained spring recoil system, flat or arched mainspring housing, adj. sights, ambidextrous safety, neoprene or checkered walnut grips, finger grooved front grip strap, 27 (lightweight model) or 35 oz.

MSR $1,034 $925 $825 $675 $575 $475 $400 $350

This model was originally called the Black Widow. After Safari Arms became Schuetzen Pistol Works, this model was changed extensively to include stainless construction, beavertail grip safety, and combat style hammer.

MATCHMASTER – similar to the Enforcer, except has 5 or 6 in. barrel and 7 shot mag. rounded (R/S) or squared off trigger guard, finger grooved front grip strap, single or double (6 in. barrel) slide serrations, approx. 40 oz.

MSR $1,034 $850 $725 $600 $500 $425 $395 $375

Add $70 for 6 in. barrel.

BLAK-TAC MATCHMASTER – .45 ACP cal., 5 in. National Match barrel, 7 shot mag., widened and lowered ejection port, Blak-Tac treated frame and slide, low profile combat sights, adj. trigger, approx. 40 oz. Mfg. 2003-2008.

$875 $775 $675 $575 $500 $450 $400 ***$995***

GRADING - PPGS™	100%	98%	95%	90%	80%	70%	60%	LAST MSR

STREET DEUCE – .45 ACP cal., M1911A1 styled frame, 5.2 in. stainless steel National Match bushingless barrel, stainless frame, steel slide, lowered and widened ejection port, 7 shot mag., diamond pattern checkered rosewood (disc.) or cocobolo grips, 38 oz. New 2001, mfg. by Custom Shop.

MSR $1,294	$1,150	$1,000	$875	$775	$675	$575	$475	

JOURNEYMAN – similar to Street Deuce, except has 4.2 in. bull barrel and 7 shot mag., 35 oz. New 2001.

MSR $1,294	$1,150	$1,000	$875	$775	$675	$575	$475	

WESTERNER – .45 ACP cal., 5 in. stainless steel barrel, 7 shot mag., 100% case colored finish on frame and slide, fitted barrel bushing, wide beavertail grip safety, shaped and tensioned extractor, fully adj. LPA rear sight, dovetail front blade sight, custom made laser etched smooth holly (disc.) or Westerner icon grips, 39 oz. New 2003.

MSR $1,164	$1,025	$900	$725	$600	$500	$400	$350	

* ***Westerner Trail Boss*** – similar to Westerner, except has 6 in. barrel, dual slide serrations, 7 shot mag., laser etched Westerner icon grips, 43 oz. New 2005.

MSR $1,234	$1.050	$925	$750	$625	$500	$400	$350	

* ***Westerner Constable*** – similar to Westerner, except has 4 in. barrel, compact frame, 35 oz. New 2005.

MSR $1,164	$1,000	$875	$750	$650	$550	$450	$350	

K22 – .22 LR cal., 6 1/2 in. button rifled stainless steel barrel, forged flattop with Picatinny rails, gas block, free floating aluminum tube handguard with knurling, non-chromed bore, A2 flash suppressor, 4.3 lbs. New 2011.

MSR $896	$775	$675	$575	$475	$425	$395	$375	

K23P – 5.56 NATO cal., 6 1/2 in. chromemoly steel barrel, A2 upper w/aluminum handguard, A2 flash supressor, recoil buffer in back of frame, 5.12 lbs. New 2007.

MSR $975	$895	$825	$725	$625	$525	$450	$400	

Add $95 for A3 upper receiver (disc. 2011) or $144 for A3 upper w/Picatinny rail and Firsh handguard (disc. 2011).

OA-93 PISTOL – .223 Rem. (older mfg.), 5.56 NATO (current mfg.), or 7.62x39mm (very limited mfg., disc.) cal., gas operated without buffer tube stock, or charging handle, 6 (most common, disc.), 6 1/2 (new 2005), 9 (disc.), or 14 (disc.) in. free-floated match stainless steel threaded barrel with flash suppressor, upper receiver utilizes integral scope mount base, 30 shot mag., 4 lbs. 3 oz., approx. 500 mfg. 1993-94 before Crime Bill discontinued production, reintroduced late 2004.

MSR $1,268	$1,150	$1,050	$900	$825	$750	$700	$650	

Last MSR in 1994 was $2,700

Add 100% for 7.62x39mm cal.

OA-96 AR PISTOL – .223 Rem. cal., 6 in. barrel only, similar to OA-93 Pistol, except has pinned (fixed) 30 shot mag. and rear takedown button for rapid reloading, 5 lbs. Mfg. 1996-2000.

	$860	$775	$650	$575	$495	$450	$395	*$860*

OA-98 PISTOL – .223 Rem. cal., skeletonized, lightweight version of the OA-93/OA-96, 6 1/2 in. non-threaded barrel, 10 shot fixed (disc.) or detachable (new 2006) mag., denoted by perforated appearance, 3 lbs. Mfg. 1998-2003, reintroduced 2005-2007.

	$995	$875	$800	$750	$700	$650	$600	*$1,080*

RIFLES: BOLT ACTION

In 1993, Olympic Arms purchased the rights, jigs, fixtures, and machining templates for the Bauska Big Bore Magnum Mauser action. Please contact Olympic Arms (see Trademark Index) for more information regarding Bauska actions both with or without fluted barrels.

GRADING - PPGS™	100%	98%	95%	90%	80%	70%	60%	*LAST MSR*

ULTRA MAG BBK-01 – various cals. between .300 Win. Mag.-.505 Gibbs, custom order rifle available with many barrel options and other special order features, price on request from the factory.

This model was formerly the Bauska BBK-02.

BOLT ACTION SAKO – various cals. between .17 Rem.-.416 Rem. Mag., 26 in. fluted barrel, various stock configurations, values represent base price with no options. Disc. 2000.

	$660	**$575**	**$500**	**$450**	**$400**	**$360**	**$330**	***$660***

ULTRA CSR TACTICAL RIFLE – .308 Win. cal., Sako action, 26 in. broach cut heavy barrel, Bell & Carlson black or synthetic stock with aluminum bedding, Harris bipod, carrying case. Mfg. 1996-2000.

	$1,450	**$1,250**	**$1,100**	**$1,000**	**$800**	**$700**	**$600**	***$1,140***

COUNTER SNIPER RIFLE – .308 Win. cal., bolt action utilizing M-14 mags., 26 in. heavy barrel, camo-fiberglass stock, 10 1/2 lbs. Disc. 1987.

	$1,300	**$1,100**	**$975**	**$895**	**$750**	**$650**	**$600**	***$1,225***

SURVIVOR I CONVERSION UNIT – .223 Rem. or .45 ACP cal., converts M1911 variations into carbine, bolt action, collapsible stock, 16 1/4 in. barrel, 5 lbs.

	$275	**$225**	**$195**	**$150**	**$125**	**$110**	**$95**	

This kit was also available for S&W and Browning Hi-Power models.

RIFLES: SEMI-AUTO

Olympic Arms is currently shipping high capacity mags. with its rifles/carbines to those states where legal.

The PCR (Politically Correct Rifle) variations listed refer to those guns manufactured after the Crime Bill was implemented in September 1994 through 2004. PCR rifles have smooth barrels (no flash suppressor), a 10 shot mag., and fixed stocks. Named models refer to the original, pre-ban model nomenclature.

Olympic Arms has also made some models exclusively for distributors. They include the K30R-16-SST (Sports South, LLC), K16-SST (Sports South, LLC), and the PP FT M4 SS (Lew Horton). Please contact these distributors for more information, availability, and pricing.

Add $30 for Coyote Brown, Desert Tan, or Pink furniture on models with carbine length handguards, pistol grip, and collapsible buttstock (new 2010).

Add $142 for A3 forged flattop upper receiver with Picatinny rails and detachable carry handle.

COMPETITOR RIFLE – .22 LR cal., Ruger 10/22 action with 20 in. barrel featuring button cut rifling, Bell & Carlson thumbhole fiberglass stock, black finish and matte stainless fluted barrel, includes bipod, 6.9 lbs. Mfg. 1996-99.

	$575	**$500**	**$450**	**$400**	**$360**	**$330**	**$300**	***$575***

ULTRAMATCH/PCR-1 – .223 Rem. cal., AR-15 action with modifications, 20 or 24 in. match stainless steel barrel, Picatinny flattop upper receiver, Williams set trigger optional, scope mounts, 10 lbs. 3 oz. New 1985.

* ***Ultramatch PCR-1*** – disc. 2004.

	$950	**$850**	**$750**	**$675**	**$625**	**$575**	**$525**	***$1,074***

* ***Ultramatch PCR-1P*** – .223 Rem. cal., premium grade ultramatch rifle with many shooting enhancements, including Maxhard treated upper and lower receiver, 20 or 24 in. broach cut Ultramatch bull barrel, 1x10 in. or 1x8 in. rate of twist. Mfg. 2001-2004.

	$1,175	**$1,050**	**$925**	**$825**	**$725**	**$625**	**$550**	***$1,299***

* ***Ultramatch UM-1*** – .223 Rem. cal., 20 in. stainless Ultramatch barrel with non-chromed bore, gas block, free floating aluminum tube with knurling, approx. 8 1/2 lbs. Disc. 1994, reintroduced late 2004-2012.

	$1,250	**$1,075**	**$950**	**$825**	**$750**	**$675**	**$600**	

Last MSR in 1994 was $1,515, last MSR in 2012 was $1,329.

GRADING - PPGS™	100%	98%	95%	90%	80%	70%	60%	LAST MSR

* ***Ultramatch UM-1P*** – .223 Rem. cal., similar to UM-1 Ultramatch, except has 20 (disc. 2006) or 24 in. Ultramatch bull stainless barrel, premium grade ultramatch rifle with many shooting enhancements, 9 1/2 lbs. New 2005.

MSR $1,624	$1,495	$1,325	$1,100	$975	$825	$775	$700	

INTERCONTINENTAL – .223 Rem. cal., features synthetic wood-grained thumbhole buttstock and aluminum handguard, 20 in. Ultramatch barrel (free floating). Mfg. 1992-1993.

	$1,650	$1,350	$1,050	$875	$750	$600	$550	*$1,371*

INTERNATIONAL MATCH – .223 Rem. cal., similar to Ultramatch, except has custom aperture sights. Mfg. 1991-93.

	$1,475	$1,150	$950	$800	$675	$575	$525	*$1,240*

SERVICE MATCH/PCR SERVICE MATCH – .223 Rem. cal., AR-15 action with modifications, 20 in. SS Ultramatch barrel, carrying handle, standard trigger, choice of A1 or A2 flash suppressor (Service Match only), 8 3/4 lbs.

* ***Service Match SM-1*** – 9.7 lbs., disc. 1994, reintroduced late 2004-2012.

	$1,095	$995	$875	$775	$700	$625	$550	

Last MSR in 1994 was $1,200, last MSR in 2012 was $1,273

* ***Service Match SM-1P Premium Grade*** – .223 Rem. cal., Maxhard upper and lower receiver, 20 in. broach cut Ultramatch super heavy threaded barrel (1 turn in 8 in. is standard), flash suppressor, 2-stage CMP trigger, Blak-Tak Armour bolt carrier assembly, Bob Jones NM interchangeable rear sight system, AC4 pneumatic recoil buffer, Turner Saddlery competition sling, GI style pistol grip. Mfg. 2005-2012.

	$1,575	$1,350	$1,200	$1,025	$900	$800	$725	*$1,728*

* ***Service Match PCR*** – disc. late 2004.

	$825	$750	$675	$625	$550	$500	$450	*$1,062*

* ***Service Match PCR-SMP Premium Grade*** – .223 Rem. cal., Maxhard upper and lower receiver, 20 in. broach cut Ultramatch super heavy barrel (1 turn in 8 in. is standard), 2-stage CMP trigger, Blak-Tak Armour bolt carrier assembly, Bob Jones NM interchangeable rear sight system, AC4 pneumatic recoil buffer, Turner Saddlery competition sling, GI style pistol grip. Mfg. 2004 only.

	$1,100	$950	$800	$700	$600	$550	$475	*$1,613*

MULTIMATCH ML-1/PCR-2 – .223 Rem. cal., tactical short range rifle, 16 in. Ultramatch barrel with A2 upper receiver, aluminum collapsible (Multimatch ML-1) or fixed (PCR-2) stock, carrying handle, A2 flash suppressor (Multimatch ML-1 only). New 1991.

* ***Multimatch ML-1*** – 7.35 lbs. Disc. 2012.

	$1,050	$950	$850	$750	$675	$600	$525	

Last MSR in 1994 was $1,200, last MSR in 2012 was $1,188

* ***Multimatch PCR-2*** – disc. late 2004.

	$750	$675	$600	$525	$450	$425	$400	*$958*

MULTIMATCH ML-2/PCR-3 – .223 Rem. cal., features Picatinny flattop upper receiver with stainless steel 16 in. Ultramatch bull (new 2005) barrel, carrying handle (disc.), approx. 7 1/2 lbs. New 1991.

* ***Multimatch ML-2*** – .223 Rem. cal., tubular aluminum handguard, A2 stock, 7 1/2 lbs. Disc. 1994, reintroduced late 2004.

MSR $1,253	$1,095	$975	$850	$750	$675	$600	$525	

Last MSR in 1994 was $1,200

* ***Multimatch PCR-3*** – disc. late 2004.

	$850	$750	$650	$550	$500	$450	$350	*$958*

AR-15 MATCH/PCR-4 – .223 Rem. cal., patterned after the AR-15 with 20 in. barrel and solid synthetic stock, 8 lbs. 5 oz. Mfg. 1975-2004.

GRADING - PPGS™	100%	98%	95%	90%	80%	70%	60%	LAST MSR
* ***PCR-4***								
	$850	$750	$650	$575	$525	$475	$425	*$803*
* ***AR-15 Match***								
	$1,095	$995	$875	$775	$650	$575	$495	*$1,075*

CAR-15/PCR-5 – modified AR-15 with choice of 11 1/2 (disc. 1993) or 16 in. barrel, stowaway pistol grip and collapsible stock (CAR-15 only), 7 lbs. Mfg. 1975-1998, PCR-5 reintroduced 2000-2004.

* ***PCR-5*** – .223 Rem., 9mm Para. (new 1996), .40 S&W (new 1996), or .45 ACP (new 1996) cal. Disc. 1998, reintroduced 2000-2004.

	$950	$850	$800	$725	$650	$600	$550	*$755*

Add $45 for 9mm Para., .40 S&W, or .45 ACP cal.

* ***CAR-15*** – .223 Rem., 9mm Para., .40 S&W, .45 ACP, or 7.62x39mm cal.

	$1,050	$950	$850	$775	$650	$575	$495	*$1,030*

Add $170 for pistol cals.

PCR-6 – 7.62x39mm cal., 16 in. barrel, post-ban only, A-2 stowaway stock, carrying handle, 7 lbs. Mfg. 1995-2002.

	$895	$795	$725	$650	$500	$475	$425	*$870*

PCR-7 ELIMINATOR – .223 Rem. cal., similar to PCR-4, except has 16 in. barrel, 7 lbs. 10 oz. Mfg. 1999-2004.

	$850	$750	$675	$625	$585	$540	$510	*$844*

PCR-8 – .223 Rem. cal., same configuration as the PCR-1, except has standard 20 in. stainless steel heavy bull barrel with button rifling. Mfg. 2001-2004.

	$825	$725	$675	$640	$600	$550	$525	*$834*

* ***PCR-8 Mag.*** – .223 WSSM or .243 WSSM cal., otherwise similar to PCR-8. Mfg. 2004.

	$925	$825	$750	$675	$600	$550	$500	*$1,074*

This model was also scheduled to be available in .308 Olympic Mag. and 7mm Olympic Mag. cals.

PCR-9/10/40/45 – 9mm Para., 10mm, .40 S&W, or .45 ACP cal., similar to PCR-5 Carbine except for pistol cal., A2 upper standard, 16 in. barrel, A2 buttstock, mil spec lower receiver. Mfg. 2001-2004.

	$875	$775	$675	$600	$550	$495	$450	*$835*

PCR-16 – .223 Rem. cal., 16 in. match grade bull barrel, two-piece aluminum free-floating handguard, Picatinny receiver rail, 7 1/2 lbs. Mfg. 2003-2004.

	$825	$750	$650	$600	$565	$535	$500	*$714*

PCR-30 – .30 Carbine cal., forged aluminum receiver with matte black anodizing, parkerized steel parts, A-2 adj. rear sight, accepts standard GI M1 .30 Carbine mags., 16 in. barrel with 1 turn in 12 in. twist, 7.15 lbs. Mfg. 2004.

	$875	$825	$750	$700	$650	$600	$575	*$899*

PLINKER – .223 Rem. cal., similar to PCR-5, except has 16 in. button rifled barrel standard, A1 sights, cast upper/lower receiver, 100% standard mil spec parts, 7 lbs. Mfg. 2001-2004.

	$650	$595	$550	$500	$495	$450	$425	*$598*

PLINKER PLUS – 5.56 NATO cal., similar to Plinker, except has 16 (disc. 2009, reintroduced 2011) in. button rifled threaded chromemoly steel barrel with A2 flash suppressor, standard A1 upper or flat top with Picatinny rails (new 2012), cast upper/lower receiver, 100% standard Mil-spec parts, A2 or M4 six point collapsible stock (new 2012), 7-8.4 lbs. New 2005.

MSR $688	$600	$525	$450	$395	$350	$300	$275	

Add $26 for Plinker Plus flat top with Picatinny rails and collapsible stock (new 2012).

GRADING - PPGS™	100%	98%	95%	90%	80%	70%	60%	LAST MSR

* ***Plinker Plus 20*** – 5.56 NATO cal., similar to Plinker Plus, except has 20 in. button rifled threaded chrome moly steel barrel with A2 flash suppressor, choice of A2 configuration or flat top upper receiver with Picatinny rails, cast upper/lower receiver, 100% standard Mil-spec parts, A2 stock, 7-8.4 lbs. New 2012.

MSR $908	$900	$825	$725	$650	$600	$575	$550	

CAR-97 – .223 Rem., 9mm Para., 10mm, .40 S&W, or .45 ACP cal., similar to PCR-5, except has 16 in. button rifled barrel, A2 sights, fixed CAR stock, post-ban muzzle brake, approx. 7 lbs. Mfg. 1997-2004.

	$795	$750	$675	$600	$550	$500	$450	*$780*

Add approx. $65 for 9mm Para., .40 S&W, or .45 ACP cal.

* ***CAR-97 M4*** – .223 Rem. cal., M4 configuration with contoured barrel, fixed carbine tube stock, factory installed muzzle brake, oversized shortened handguard. Mfg. 2003-2004.

	$800	$750	$675	$600	$550	$500	$450	*$839*

Add $95 for detachable carrying handle (new 2004).

FAR-15 – .223 Rem. cal., featherweight model with A1 contour lightweight button rifled 16 in. barrel, fixed collapsible stock, 9.92 lbs. Mfg. 2001-2004.

	$775	$700	$650	$600	$550	$500	$450	*$822*

GI-16 – 5.56 NATO cal., forged aluminum receiver with black matte finish, A1 type upper receiver, parkerized steel parts, A1 adj. rear sights, 16 in. button rifled match grade barrel, M4 collapsible stock, 6.6 lbs. Mfg. 2004, reintroduced 2006-2012.

	$800	$750	$700	$625	$575	$525	$475	*$857*

GI-20 – .223 Rem. cal., similar to GI-16, except has 20 in. heavy barrel and A-2 lower receiver, 8.4 lbs. Mfg. 2004.

	$725	$650	$595	$550	$495	$450	$425	*$749*

OA-93 CARBINE – .223 Rem. cal., 16 in. threaded barrel, design based on OA-93 pistol, aluminum side folding stock, flattop receiver, round aluminum handguard, Vortex flash suppressor, 7 1/2 lbs. Mfg. 1995 - civilian sales disc. 1998, reintroduced 2004-2007.

	$1,250	$1,050	$925	$825	$750	$675	$625	

Last MSR in 1998 was $1,550.
Last MSR in 2007 was $1,074

* ***OA-93PT Carbine*** – .223 Rem. cal., aluminum forged receiver, black matte hard anodized finish, no sights, integral flattop upper receiver rail system, match grade 16 in. chrome-moly steel barrel with removable muzzle brake, push button removable stock, vertical pistol grip, 7.6 lbs. Mfg. 2004 only, reintroduced 2006-2007.

	$985	$875	$825	$750	$675	$600	$550	*$1,074*

LTF/LT-MIL4 LIGHTWEIGHT TACTICAL RIFLE – 5.56 NATO cal., available in LTF (fluted), LT-M4 (new 2011), or LT-MIL4 (disc. 2009) configuration, black matte anodized receiver, Firsh type forearms with Picatinny rails, parkerized steel parts, adj. flip-up sight system, 16 in. non-chromed fluted, M4 stainless steel (new 2011), or MIL4 threaded barrel with flash suppressor, tube style Ace FX buttstock, 6.4 lbs. New 2005.

MSR $1,240	$1,125	$975	$850	$775	$700	$650	$600	

Subtract $97 for M4 style stainless steel barrel (new 2011).
Subtract approx. 10% if w/o fluted barrel.

LTF PREDATOR – .204 Ruger (new 2012), 5.56 NATO, or 6.8 SPC (new 2012) cal., similar to LTF, except has ERGO grip and available in black or 100% camo coverage. New 2011.

MSR $1,240	$1,125	$975	$850	$775	$700	$650	$600	

K3B CARBINE – 5.56 NATO cal., 16 in. match grade chrome-moly steel threaded barrel with flash suppressor, adj. A2 rear sight, A2 (disc.) or M4 collapsible (new 2012) buttstock, adj. front post sight, A3 flattop receiver became standard 2011, 6 3/4 lbs.

MSR $1,006	$925	$800	$700	$600	$525	$475	$425	

GRADING - PPGS™	100%	98%	95%	90%	80%	70%	60%	LAST MSR

* ***K3B-FAR Carbine*** – similar to K3B Carbine, except has smaller stainless barrel diameter and is lightweight, 6 lbs. New 2005.

MSR $1,071	$975	$850	$725	$625	$550	$500	$450	

* ***K3B-M4 Carbine*** – similar to K3B Carbine, except has M4 handguard, collapsible stock, and 16 in. M4 stainless barrel, 6.3 lbs. New 2005.

MSR $1,104	$1,000	$875	$750	$650	$575	$525	$475	

* ***K3B-M4-A3-TC Carbine*** – similar to K3B-M4, except is tactical carbine version with Firsh handguard, flattop upper receiver with Picatinny rail, and detachable carry handle, 6.7 lbs. New 2005.

MSR $1,247	$1,150	$1,025	$925	$825	$775	$700	$650	

K4B/K4B68 – 5.56 NATO or 6.8 SPC (new 2010) cal., 20 in. match grade chrome-moly steel button rifled threaded barrel with flash suppressor, adj. A2 rear sight, A2 buttstock, adj. front post sight, A2 upper receiver and handguard, 8 1/2 lbs.

MSR $1,033	$950	$825	$725	$625	$550	$500	$450	

Add $65 for 6.8 SPC cal.

K4B-A4 – .223 Rem. cal., features 20 in. barrel with A2 flash suppressor, elevation adj. post front sight, bayonet lug, Firsh rifle length handguard with Picatinny rails, flattop receiver, 9 lbs. Mfg. 2006-2008.

	$850	$760	$675	$600	$550	$500	$450	*$941*

K7 ELIMINATOR – 5.56 NATO cal., 16 in. stainless steel threaded barrel with flash suppressor, adj. A2 rear sight, A2 buttstock, adj. front post sight, 6.8 lbs. New 2005.

MSR $1,039	$950	$825	$725	$625	$550	$500	$450	

K8 – .204 Ruger (new 2012), 6.8 SPC (new 2012) or 5.56 NATO cal., 20 in stainless steel button rifled bull barrel, A2 buttstock, Picatinny flattop upper receiver, gas block, free floating aluminum knurled tube, satin bead blast finish on barrel, 8 1/2 lbs. New 2005.

MSR $909	$895	$800	$700	$625	$550	$500	$450	

Add $58 for .204 Ruger cal.
Add $125 for 6.8 SPC cal.

This model is marked "Target Match" on mag. well.

* ***K8-MAG*** – similar to K8, except available in .223 WSSM, .243 WSSM, .25 WSSM, or .300 OSSM (new 2006) cals., and has 24 in. barrel, 5 shot mag., 9.4 lbs. New 2005.

MSR $1,364	$1,250	$1,125	$995	$900	$800	$700	$600	

K9/K10/K40/K45 – 9mm Para. (K9), 10mm Norma (K10), .40 S&W (K40), or .45 ACP (K45) cal., blow back action, adj. A2 rear sight, 10 shot converted Uzi (10mm, .40 S&W or .45 ACP cal.) or 32 (9mm Para.) shot converted Sten detachable mag., 16 in. threaded stainless steel barrel with flash suppressor, M4 collapsible buttstock, bayonet lug, 6.7 lbs. New 2005.

MSR $1,006	$925	$825	$700	$600	$550	$500	$450	

* ***K9GL/K40GL*** – 9mm Para. or .40 S&W cal., otherwise similar to K9 Series, lower receiver designed to accept Glock magazines, 16 in. barrel with flash suppressor, collapsible stock, does not include magazine. New 2005.

MSR $1,157	$1,050	$975	$850	$750	$650	$575	$500	

K16 – 5.56 NATO, 6.8 SPC (new 2012), 7.62x39mm (new 2012), or .300 AAC Blackout (new 2012) cal., 16 in. free floating button rifled barrel, A2 buttstock, flattop upper receiver with Picatinny rails, 7 1/2 lbs. New 2005.

MSR $829	$775	$725	$650	$600	$550	$500	$450	

Add $62 for 7.62x39mm, 6.8 SPC, or .300 AAC Blackout cal.

K22 M4 – .22 LR cal., 16 in. stainless steel barrel, M4 six-point collapsible stock, forged A2 upper, adj. rear sight, adj. post front sight with bayonet lug, A1 flash suppressor, fiberite carbine length handguard with heat shield, 6.6 lbs. Mfg. 2011-2012.

	$950	$850	$725	$625	$575	$525	$475	*$1,039*

GRADING - PPGS™	100%	98%	95%	90%	80%	70%	60%	LAST MSR

K22 RIMFIRE TARGET MATCH – .22 LR cal., 16 in. stainless steel bull barrel, A2 fixed trapdoor stock, flattop with Picatinny rails, no sights, free floating aluminum handguard tube with knurling, muzzle crown, 8.6 lbs. New 2011.

MSR $831	$775	$725	$650	$600	$550	$500	$450	

K22 SURVIVAL LIGHT – .22 LR cal., 16 in. stainless steel featherweight barrel, side folding stock, flattop with Picatinny rails, gas block, free floating slotted aluminum handguard, A1 flash suppressor, 6 lbs. Mfg. 2011-2012.

	$825	$795	$715	$625	$575	$525	$475	*$883*

K30 – .30 Carbine cal., similar to K16, except has A2 upper receiver, collapsible stock, and threaded barrel with flash suppressor, 6.6 lbs. Mfg. 2005-2006.

	$825	$700	$625	$550	$500	$450	$400	*$905*

Add $95 for A3 upper receiver.

K30R – 7.62x39mm cal., 16 in. stainless steel barrel, M4 six-point collapsible stock, A2 flash suppressor, pistol grip, matte black anodized receiver, parkerized steel parts, A2 upper with adj. rear sight, 6 3/4 lbs. New 2007.

MSR $974	$895	$795	$695	$595	$550	$500	$450	

K68 – 6.8 SPC cal., 16 or 20 (optional) in. stainless steel barrel, M4 six-position collapsible stock, A2 upper with adj. rear sight, matte black anodized receiver, parkerized steel parts, pistol grip, A2 flash suppressor, 6.62 lbs. New 2007.

MSR $1,104	$995	$875	$750	$625	$575	$525	$475	

K74 – 5.45x39mm cal., 16 in. button rifled stainless steel barrel with A2 flash suppressor, A2 upper with adj. front sight, M4 type six-position collapsible stock, 6 3/4 lbs. New 2009.

MSR $1,058	$975	$875	$775	$675	$600	$550	$495	

UMAR (ULTIMATE MAGNUM AR) – .22-250 Rem., .223 WSSM, .243 WSSM, .25 WSSM, or .300 OSSM cal., 24 in. heavy match grade stainless steel bull barrel, black matte anodized aluminum forged receiver, parkerized steel parts, flat top/gas block with Picatinny rails, sling swivel mount, A2 stock w/trapdoor, Ergo tactical deluxe pistol grip, Predator Firsch free floating handguard, 9.4 lbs. New 2012.

MSR $1,589	$1,395	$1,225	$1,075	$925	$825	$725	$625	

The upper receiver of this model will not work on standard AR-15 lowers.

GAMESTALKER/GSG2 – .204 Ruger (mfg. 2011 only), 6.8 SPC (GSG2, new 2011), 5.56 NATO (GSG2, new 2011), 7.62x39mm (GSG2, new 2011), .243 WSSM, .25 WSSM, or .300 OSSM cal., 22 in. stainless steel barrel, flattop upper receiver with Picatinny rail, free floating aluminum handguard, ACE skeleton stock with ERGO Sure Grip, 100% camo coverage, approx. 7 1/2 lbs. New 2010.

MSR $1,364	$1,250	$1,125	$995	$900	$800	$700	$600	

Subtract $130 for GSG2 Model (new 2011).

OMEGA

Previous trademark manufactured by Armero Specialistas Reunidas, located in Eibar, Spain, circa 1920s.

PISTOLS: SEMI-AUTO

SEMI AUTOMATIC PISTOL – 6.35mm or 7.65mm cal., "Eibar" type action, marked "Omega" on slide, 6 shot mag.

6.35 cal.	$275	$225	$150	$115	$70	$55	$40
7.65 cal.	$295	$235	$160	$125	$80	$70	$55

OMEGA FIREARMS

Previous manufacturer located in Flower Mound, TX circa 1965-1969.

RIFLES: BOLT ACTION

OMEGA III – various cals., 4 or 5 shot rotary mag., four triangular bolt locking lugs, premium walnut or laminated stock. Disc. late 1960s.

	$775	$650	$575	$495	$425	$360	$295

GRADING - PPGS™	100%	98%	95%	90%	80%	70%	60%	LAST MSR

OMEGA PISTOL

Previously manufactured and distributed by Springfield Armory located in Geneseo, IL. Omega conversion kits only were available until 1996 from Safari Arms located in Olympia, WA under license from Peters-Stahl in Germany.

PISTOLS: SEMI-AUTO

OMEGA - .38 Super, 10mm Norma, or .45 ACP cal., single action, ported slide, 5 or 6 in. interchangeable ported or unported barrel with polygon rifling, special lock-up system eliminates normal barrel link and bushing, Pachmayr grips, dual extractors, adj. rear sight. Mfg. 1987-90.

	$625	$560	$495	$425	$360	$295	$265	*$849*

Add $663 for interchangeable conversion units.
Add $336 for interchangeable 5 or 6 in. barrel (including factory installation).

Each conversion unit includes an entire slide assembly, one mag., 5 or 6 in barrel, recoil spring guide mechanism assembly, and factory fitting.

OMEGA RIFLES/SHOTGUNS

Previous trademark of select rifles/shotguns imported by K.B.I., Inc. located in Harrisburg, PA, until 1994.

RIFLES

To date, there has been little collector interest for Omega rifles. Values are mostly determined by the shooting value rather than collector value.

SHOTGUNS

STANDARD O/U - 12, 20 (disc.), 28 (disc.) ga., or .410 (disc) bore, boxlock action, folding design, SNT, 26 or 28 in. VR barrels, extractors, checkered walnut stock and forearm, 5 1/2-7 lbs. Disc. 1994.

	$425	$330	$295	$260	$230	$200	$180	

* ***Deluxe O/U*** - 12 ga. only, similar to Standard Model except has better walnut. Importation disc. 1990.

	$335	$290	$255	$220	$185	$160	$140	*$379*

STANDARD SxS - 20, 28 ga., or .410 bore, boxlock action, folding design, double triggers, hardwood stock and forearm, 26 in. barrels, extractors, 5 1/2 lbs. Disc. 1989.

	$190	$165	$140	$120	$110	$100	$90	*$229*

Add $40 for 28 ga. or .410 bore.

* ***Deluxe SxS*** - .410 bore only, similar to Standard Model except has better walnut. Disc. 1989.

	$200	$185	$170	$155	$140	$130	$120	*$249*

SINGLE BARREL - 12, 20 ga., or .410 bore, various barrel lengths, matte blue finish, extractor. Importation disc. 1987.

	$85	$75	$65	$55	$45	$40	$35	*$95*

STANDARD FOLDING SINGLE BARREL - 12, 16, 20, 28 ga., or .410 bore, 28 or 30 in. barrel, checkered hardwood stock, matte chrome receiver, approx. 5 1/2 lbs. Importation disc. 1987.

	$160	$135	$115	$100	$85	$70	$65	*$180*

DELUXE FOLDING SINGLE BARREL - 12, 16, 20, 28 ga., or .410 bore, similar to Standard Model, except has checkered walnut stock and forearm, blue receiver. Importation disc. 1987.

	$195	$160	$135	$115	$100	$85	$70	*$220*

OMEGA WEAPONS SYSTEMS INC.

Previous shotgun manufacturer established circa 1998, and located in Tucson, AZ. Previously distributed by Defense Technology, Inc., located in Lake Forest, CA.

SHOTGUNS: SEMI-AUTO

OMEGA SPS-12 - 12 ga. only, 2 3/4 in. chamber, features gas operation and 5 shot

GRADING - PPGS™	100%	98%	95%	90%	80%	70%	60%	LAST MSR

detachable mag., 20 in. barrel, protected ghost ring rear and front sight, synthetic stock (with or w/o pistol grip) and forearm, 9 lbs. Mfg. 1998-2005.

	$195	$180	$165	$150	$135	$125	$115	*$225*

OMNI

Previous manufacturer located in Riverside, CA 1992-1998. During 1998, Omni changed its name to E.D.M. Arms. Previously distributed by First Defense International located in CA.

RIFLES: BOLT ACTION

LONG ACTION SINGLE SHOT – .50 BMG cal., competition single shot, chrome-moly black finished receiver, 32-34 in. steel or stainless steel barrel with round muzzle brake, benchrest fiberglass stock, designed for FCSA competition shooting, 32 lbs. Mfg. 1996-98.

	$3,600	$3,200	$2,800	$2,500	$2,150	$1,800	$1,500	*$3,500*

Add $400 for painted stock (disc. 1996).

SHELL HOLDER SINGLE SHOT – similar to Long Action Single Shot, except has fiberglass field stock with bipod, 28 lbs. Mfg. 1997-98.

	$2,975	$2,750	$2,525	$2,150	$1,800	$1,500	$1,250	*$2,750*

MODEL WINDRUNNER – .50 BMG cal., long action, single shot or 3 shot mag., 1-piece I-beam, chrome-moly black finished receiver, 36 in. barrel with round muzzle brake, fiberglass tactical stock, 35 lbs. Mfg. 1997-1998.

	$6,950	$6,425	$5,875	$5,325	$4,750	$4,175	$3,500	*$7,500*

Add $750 for 3 shot repeater.

MODEL WARLOCK – .50 BMG or 20mm cal., single, 3 (20mm), or 5 (.50 BMG) shot fixed mag., fiberglass field stock, massive design chrome-moly black finished receiver, muzzle brake, 50 lbs. Mfg. 1997-1998.

	$10,750	$8,950	$7,750	$6,750	$5,500	$4,750	$3,950	*$12,000*

E.D.M. ARMS MODEL 97 – available in most cals. up to .308 Win., single shot or repeater (cals. .17 Rem. through .223 Rem. only), wire-cut one-piece receiver, black tactical stock with pillar-bedded chrome-moly barrel, black finished receiver, unique trigger with safety, 9 lbs. Mfg. 1997-98.

	$2,525	$2,150	$1,800	$1,500	$1,250	$1,100	$925	*$2,750*

E.D.M. ARMS WINDRUNNER WR50 – .50 BMG cal., sniper rifle, 5 shot mag., removable tactical adj. stock, take-down action with removable barrel, wire-cut one-piece receiver, titanium muzzle brake, blackened chrome-moly barrel, approx. 29 lbs. Mfg. 1998 only.

	$11,750	$10,250	$9,500	$8,250	$7,000	$5,750	$4,500	*$12,900*

OMNI (CURRENT MFG.)

Please refer to listings in the American Tactical section.

ONLY LONG RANGE

Please refer to Noreen Firearms LLC listing.

OPTIMA

Current trademark of O/U and single shot shotguns manufactured by Hatsan Arms Company, located in Izmir, Turkey. No current U.S. importation.

OPUS SPORTING ARMS, INC.

Previous manufacturer located in Long Beach, CA.

RIFLES: BOLT ACTION

OPUS ONE – .243 Win., .270 Win., or .30-06 cal., U.S.R.A. Co. Model 70 action, 24 in. barrel, deluxe checkered walnut stock with ebony forend cap, 6 3/4 lbs., Halliburton cased. Mfg. 1987-88 only.

	$2,350	$1,995	$1,675	$1,250	$1,000	$875	$795	*$2,700*

GRADING - PPGS™ 100% 98% 95% 90% 80% 70% 60% *LAST MSR*

OPUS TWO – similar to Opus One, except in 7mm Rem. Mag. or .300 Win. Mag. cal., 7 1/4 lbs., cased. Mfg. 1987-88 only.

$2,350 $2,050 $1,705 $1,300 $1,000 $875 $795 ***$2,700***

OPUS THREE – similar to Opus Two, except in .375 H&H or .458 Win. Mag. cal., 10 1/4 lbs., cased. Mfg. 1987-88 only.

$2,600 $2,275 $1,800 $1,375 $1,050 $900 $825 ***$2,850***

OREGON ARMS

Please refer to the Chipmunk Rifles, Inc. section.

ORTGIES PISTOLS

Previous trademark of pistols manufactured by Deutsche Werke A.G. located in Erfurt, Germany.

PISTOLS: SEMI-AUTO

VEST POCKET AUTOMATIC – .25 ACP cal., 6 shot, 2 3/4 in. barrel, blue or nickel finish, fixed sights, wood grips. Mfg. 1921-28.

$350 $250 $200 $175 $150 $125 $100

POCKET AUTOMATIC – .32 ACP cal. (8 shot) mfg. 1920-1928 or .380 ACP cal. (7 shot) mfg. 1922-1926, 3 1/4 in. barrel, blue or nickel finish, fixed sights, wood grips.

$400 $300 $200 $175 $150 $125 $100

Add 20% for .380 ACP cal. or double safety variation.

ORVIS

Current catalog retailer and importer of private label subcontracted shotguns located in Manchester, VT and many other locations.

Orvis imports various shotguns under subcontract with various international manufacturers, including Arrieta and Caesar Guerini. Typical custom order delivery time is 2-8 months. Most of these private label models will approximate the values of the equivalent model manufactured by the subcontractor unless there are additional features and/or options which will add to the value.

SHOTGUNS: O/U

The MSR of currently manufactured models in this section also includes custom fitting to individual measurements - delivery is typically within 8 weeks.

SKB GREEN MOUNTAIN UPLANDER (MODEL 555) – 12, 20, 28 ga., or .410 bore, 25-27 in. barrels, blue frame, straight stock with leather covered recoil pad. Disc.

$750 $675 $600 $550 $500 $450 $400 ***$995***

Add 15% for 28 ga. or .410 bore.

UPLANDER – 12, 20, 28 ga. or .410 bore, engraved coin finished boxlock action with sideplates, 26 (disc.) or 28 in. VR barrels with choke tubes (except 28 ga.), SST, straight (disc.) or pistol grip, select American black walnut with 26 LPI checkering, leather covered recoil pad since 1992, 6-7 lbs. Mfg. by P. Beretta of Italy.

MSR $4,795 $4,075 $3,575 $3,050 $2,775 $2,225 $1,825 $1,425

Add $1,250 for 28/20 ga. combo with case.

WATERFOWLER – 12 ga. only, 3 in. chambers, matte metal finish, 28 in. barrels with choke tubes, steel shot compatible, 7 1/2 lbs. Mfg. by P. Beretta of Italy. Disc. 2011.

$3,150 $2,725 $2,150 $1,650 $1,250 $1,025 $900

SPORTING CLAYS – 12 ga. only, 30 in. vented barrels with VR and choke tubes, adj. trigger, oil finished checkered walnut stock and forearm. Mfg. 1994-disc.

$3,750 $3,350 $2,875 $2,450 $2,100 $1,675 $1,350 ***$4,100***

This model was also available in a women's configuration in 20 ga. with lightweight frame - includes carrying case.

GRADING - PPGS™	100%	98%	95%	90%	80%	70%	60%	LAST MSR

FIELD – 12, 20, 28 ga. or .410 bore, case colored boxlock action with sideplates, ST, auto ejectors (12 and 20 ga. only), checkered Turkish walnut stock and forearm, 26 or 28 in. VR barrels with 5 choke tubes (except .410 bore), blue metal finish, mfg. in Turkey beginning 2010.

MSR $1,995	$1,825	$1,600	$1,300	$1,000	$850	$700	$550	

SUPER FIELD – 12 or 20 ga., 26 (Uplander 20 ga. only), 28 (All Rounder), or 30 (Sporting Clays) in. VR barrels, configurations include Uplander 20 ga. with straight grip stock, All Rounder 12 ga. with 28 in. barrels and pistol grip stock, and Sporting Clays 12 ga. with 30 in. barrels, wide rib, and pistol grip stock, blue receiver, choke tubes, mfg. in Italy. Limited importation 1995 only.

	$1,495	$1,250	$1,000	$875	$750	$625	$500	*$2,150*

PREMIER GRADE – 12 or 20 ga., 3 in. chambers, 20 ga. features 28 in. barrels with straight grip stock, 12 ga. features pistol grip stock, select oil-finished European stock and forearm, choke tubes, blue frame with scrolled engraving, adj. trigger, cased, mfg. in Belgium 1995-98.

	$6,450	$5,875	$5,250	$4,675	$4,000	$3,450	$2,675	*$6,450*

Add $100 for Premier Grade Sporting.

This model is also available as a 20 ga. Superlight with straight grip stock and 26 in. barrels.

ORVIS DELUXE GRADE – similar to Uplander and Waterfowler, except has engraved bird scenes and scroll work on antique coin-finished receiver, deluxe checkered walnut stock and forearm, case. Imported 1993-94 only.

	$4,250	$3,575	$2,950	$2,300	$1,900	$1,500	$1,275	*$4,950*

RUGER/ORVIS MODEL – 12 or 20 ga., 3 in. chambers, Red Label Ruger action with customized Orvis features including blue receiver and straight grip English checkered stock. Disc. 1993.

	$1,295	$975	$850	$725	$600	$495	$450	*$1,295*

KNOCKABOUT – 12, 20, 28 ga. or .410 bore, 28 in. barrels, checkered pistol grip walnut stock and forearm, rubber recoil pad, color case hardened frame, gold trigger.

MSR $3,695	$3,125	$2,725	$2,350	$2,125	$1,725	$1,400	$1,095	

This model is also available in a two and three barrel set - please contact Orvis directly for pricing (see Trademark Index).

SHOTGUNS: SxS

WATERFOWLER – 12 ga. only, 3 in. chambers, matte metal finish, 28 in. barrels with choke tubes, 7 3/4 lbs. Mfg. by P. Beretta of Italy until 1993.

	$1,950	$1,725	$1,475	$1,125	$950	$825	$700	*$1,950*

CUSTOM UPLANDER – 12, 16, 20, 28 ga., or .410 bore, traditional frame, 25 or 27 in. barrels only, case colored or blue sidelock action with light engraving, DT, custom ordered gun, mfg. by Arrieta located in Spain.

	N/A	$2,525	$2,250	$1,950	$1,650	$1,450	$1,025	

Add $950 for SNT.
Add $1,200 for extra set of barrels (same ga.).

UPLAND CLASSIC – 12, 16, 20, 28 ga. or .410 bore, sidelock, Bellota steel chrome lined barrel, ejectors, Anson-style forearm release, customer choice of stock and forearm design, barrel lengths, chokes, chamber size and rib design, hand made by Arrieta. New 2013.

MSR $5,900	$5,000	$4,375	$3,750	$3,400	$2,750	$2,250	$1,750	

FIELD GRADE – 12, 20, 28 ga. or .410 bore, case colored boxlock action with sideplates, ST, extractors, straight grip Turkish walnut stock and forearm, 26 or 28 in. VR barrels with 5 choke tubes (except .410 bore), blue metal finish, mfg. in Turkey. New 2010.

MSR $1,995	$1,825	$1,600	$1,300	$1,000	$850	$700	$550	

GRADING - PPGS™	100%	98%	95%	90%	80%	70%	60%	LAST MSR

FINE GRADE – 12, 16, 20, 28 ga., or .410 bore, custom ordered gun, custom order barrel lengths, sidelock action, DT, mfg. by Arrieta located in Spain. Disc. 1999.

	$4,650	$3,775	$3,150	$2,500	$1,995	$1,500	$1,150	*$4,650*

Add $950 for SNT.
Add $1,950 for extra set of barrels (same ga.).

ROUNDED ACTION MODEL – sidelock, chopper lump Bellota steel chrome lined barrels, hand oil finished checkered walnut stock and forearm, ejectors, 5-pin rounded action, DT, optional engraving, mfg. by Arrieta. New 2012.

MSR $10,495	$8,925	$7,800	$6,695	$6,075	$4,915	$4,000	$3,125

* ***Rounded Action Uplander*** – similar to Rounded Action, except has less engraving, blue or case hardened frame. New 2000.

	N/A	$4,450	$3,950	$3,500	$3,000	$2,500	$2,000

FEATHERLIGHT – 20 or 28 ga., barrels up to 28 in., case colored round action, DT, accent engraving, 5 1/2 to 5 3/4 lbs. New 2013.

MSR $6,300	$5,350	$4,675	$4,000	$3,625	$2,950	$2,400	$1,875

OTTOMANGUNS

Current shotgun and airgun manufacturer located in Istanbul, Turkey. Previously imported during 2011 by American Tactical Imports (ATI), located in Rochester, NY.

Ottomanguns manufactures a complete line of good quality shotguns in a variety of configurations, including O/U, SxS, semi-auto, slide action, and single barrel. The company also manufactures air rifles. Currently, only semi-auto and slide action shotguns are being imported. Please contact the importer directly for more information (see Trademark Index).

SHOTGUNS: SEMI-AUTO

SULTAN SERIES – 12 ga., 18 1/4 or 28 (walnut stock only) in. barrel, available with walnut stock and blue steel, or synthetic stock (camo, nickel or black pistol grip), 5 shot, black recoil pad. Importation disc. 2011.

$240	$215	$185	$160	$140	$125	$110	*$279*

Add $29 for synthetic pistol grip stock.
Add $44 for Marine variation with nickel finish.
Add $29 for digital camo.
Add $117 for walnut stock.

SHOTGUNS: SLIDE ACTION

GRAND VAZIR SERIES – 12 ga., 5 shot, 18 1/2 in. barrel, synthetic stock with matte black, Marine nickel, or digital camo finish. Importation disc. 2011.

$185	$160	$140	$120	$110	$100	$90	*$220*

Add $22 for Marine model with nickel finish.
Add $61 for digital camo.

OWEN, KEN

Current custom long gun manufacturer located in Moscow, TN.

RIFLES

Ken Owen specializes in building big bore double rifles and express boxlock rifles. All guns are built to customer order. Standard boxlock double rifle prices begin at $23,000 for .500 NE and 577 NE cals. Other calibers are also available. Please contact Mr. Owen directly for more information, including a price quotation, available options, and delivery time (see Trademark Index).

P SECTION

P.38 MILITARY & COMMERCIAL PISTOLS

Previously manufactured P.38s from various German companies circa 1938-1946, including Mauser (byf & svw codes), Spreewerke (cyq code), and Walther (480 & AC codes). See French military section for late war/post-war French mfg. (svw code and star proof). Also includes Walther post-war mfg. and recent conversions fabricated by John Martz.

Also See: CZ, Fabrique Nationale, Luger, Mauser, and Walther for other German military pistols.

GRADING - PPGS™	100%	98%	95%	90%	80%	70%	60%	LAST MSR

PISTOLS: SEMI-AUTO, CIRCA 1938-1946

A note on how values are affected by import marked P.38s: some of the earliest imported P.38 were discreetly marked by I.A.C. on the flat surface under the slide. A few were even marked under the grips. When lightly marked in those areas, there is little reduction in value. However, most recently imported P.38s are more visibly marked on the sides of the slide or the barrel. The more desirable the gun, the more gets subtracted for the visible markings (i.e., very few P.38 collectors are interested in an ac No Date or 480 Code if markings are visible). As a result, some P.38 values could be reduced as much as 50%, while hidden markings may lower the value only 10%-20%. It all depends on the variation and how visible the markings are.

Subtract 40%-50% on most common P.38s if recently imported and/or refinished by importer.

Add 100% for two Walther matching magazines where applicable. Beware of fakes or post-war re-numbering.

AP "ARMEE PISTOLE" – 9mm Para. cal., concealed hammer prototype from 1936, approx. 50 handmade examples, each one different in some details, walnut checkered grips.

Extreme rarity precludes accurate pricing on this model. However, examples seen at auctions have been priced at $25K-$35K.

Add 30% for dural finish.

Add 30% for matching mag.

Add 30% for slotted milling for stock.

PROTOTYPE HP "HEERES PISTOLE" & FIRST MODEL P.38 – 7.65mm or 9mm Para. cal., first experimental production, ser. numbered 1010-1050, many different configurations, some have acid etched "PRIVAT" markings on receiver, checkered takedown lever, thick safety lever, rectangular firing pin, thin rear sight.

Extreme rarity precludes accurate pricing. Auction pricing indicates $10,000 - $15,000.

Add 30% for 7.65mm cal.

Add 30% for matching mag. (rare).

Add 100% for factory short barrel (sleeved but not proofed).

Add 50% for Mod. P.38 designation.

This production range has only the short barrel variation to be authenticated (1029, 7.65mm, Mod. P.38). Most surviving prototypes are in poor condition due to GI use as a shooter after the war, and most mint examples are fakes.

HP "HEERES PISTOLE" – 9mm Para. cal., early Walther commercial production begins at ser. no. 1050, high polish until approx. 13000 ser. no. range beginning at 1050, approx. 24,000 mfg. 1938-1944.

It is recommended that early variations are evaluated and priced by an expert. Watch for fakes.

* ***HP "Heeres Pistole" Experimental "Concealed Extractor"*** – 7.65mm or 9mm Para., first experimental production ser. range 1050 - approx. 1080, handmade high polish finish, approx. 20 mfg. Rarely seen in U.S. market.

N/A	$13,000	$11,375	$10,275	$8,195	$6,750	$5,200	

Add 20% for 7.65mm Para. cal.

Add 30% for dural aluminum frame.

GRADING - PPGS™	100%	98%	95%	90%	80%	70%	60%	LAST MSR

* ***HP "Heeres Pistole" "Swedish" HP*** – experimental first production HP for Swedish trials, ser. range H1045-H2074, "H" prefix, rectangular firing pin and crown/N proofs, thin sight, thick safety lever, high polish, handmade craftsmanship.

	N/A	$3,050	$2,625	$2,375	$1,925	$1,575	$1,225	

Add 30% for rare matching magazine.

* ***HP "Heeres Pistole" Standard HP Production*** – ser. range 2080-approx. 24000, high polish finish until approx. ser. no. 13000 - then changed to military blue (1942).

	N/A	$2,375	$2,025	$1,825	$1,475	$1,200	$950	

Add 20% for Nazi eagle over 359 (E/359) military proof.
Add 20% for high polish finish.
Add 300% for alloy frame, ser. range 6850-6950.

* ***HP "Heeres Pistole" 7.65mm Para HP Production*** – 7.65mm Para. cal., single or double action, very limited mfg., rarest collector category for standard production P.38s, ser. no. range 3000-3200.

	N/A	$15,000	$13,125	$11,850	$9,450	$7,800	$6,000	

Add 100% for single action with long tang and target sights.

* ***HP "Heeres Pistole" Late War Mod. P.38 Production*** – marked "MOD P38" on left slide, rough military blue finish, some frames show heavy tool marks, ser. range 24150-25990.

	N/A	$2,800	$2,400	$2,200	$1,700	$1,400	$1,050	

Early high polish, hand-made examples have been verified 001-006 (3rd issue Zero Series development).

ZERO-SERIES – 9mm Para. cal., features Walther banner, high polish finish, black checkered grips, up to 5-digit number w/o suffix. Mfg. 1940, ser. no. range 01-013714.

* ***Zero Series - 1st Issue*** – internal extractor, square firing pin, ser. range 01-01000.

	N/A	$10,500	$9,100	$8,150	$6,600	$5,400	$4,300	

Add 50% for matching mag.
Auction prices have sold between $10,000 and $15,000.

* ***Zero Series - 2nd Issue*** – external extractor, thin slide, square firing pin, ser. range 02005-03478, more difficult to find than 1st Issue.

	N/A	$8,500	$7,450	$6,700	$5,350	$4,425	$3,400	

Add 40% for matching mag.

* ***Zero Series - 3rd Issue*** – external extractor, round firing pin, ser. no. range 03520-013714, after ser. no. 10000, some models had brown military style grips, baseline for military P.38s to follow.

	N/A	$3,200	$2750	$2,550	$2,000	$1,750	$1,300	

Add 30% for matching mag.

P.38 – 9mm Para. cal., double action, 5 in. barrel, 8 shot mag., fixed sights, brown or black composite grips, blue finish. Many variations exhibiting a variety of metal finishes and codings, 34 oz. Over 1,000,000 manufactured during WWII.

Based on the prototype "Armee Pistol" from 1936, this model was adopted as the standard service pistol of the German Military in 1938 and refined in the "Zero Series". The P.38 was manufactured by Walther - code "480" and "ac" (mfg. April 1940-1945), Mauser - code "byf" and "svw" (mfg. late 1942-1945), and Spreewerke - "cyq" and "cvq" (mfg. 1942-1945). The finish on most WWII 1942 and Later P.38s is not of the same quality as the pre-war and early war Walther guns with the Spreewerk models being the poorest. Note: The cvq stamp is currently thought to be attributed to a broken die and not to a Spreewerk code change.

* ***480 Code First Military Contract*** – 9mm Para. cal. "480" code replaces Walther banner on slide, approx. 7,200 mfg. with ser. range 1-7374, rare in any condition above 90%. Production started April 1940. "480" code changed to "ac" approx. October 1940.

	N/A	$7,000	$6,125	$5,525	$4,400	$3,650	$2,800	

Add 30% for matching mag.

GRADING - PPGS™	100%	98%	95%	90%	80%	70%	60%	LAST MSR

ac-NO DATE (UNDATED) – 9mm Para. cal., "ac" (Walther code) appears on slide without date, "ac" on left trigger guard, 2,620 mfg. with ser. range 7,384-9,912, rarest military coded P.38, rarely encountered in 90% or better original condition.

	N/A	$8,500	$7,450	$6,700	$5,350	$4,425	$3,400	

Add 30% for matching mag.

* ***ac-40 Added (Surcharge)*** – mm Para. cal., hand pantographed or stamped "40" date added underneath "ac" code after the slide was blued, ser. range. 9988-5942a, 6,000 mfg., high polish, rare in any condition above 90%.

	N/A	$3,600	$3,150	$2,850	$2,275	$1,875	$1,450	

Add 30% for matching mag.

* ***ac-40 Standard*** – 9mm Para. cal., machined stamped, "40" indicates 1940 mfg., approx. 14,000 mfg., ser. range 5942a-9965b.

	N/A	$2,800	$2,425	$2,200	$1,725	$1,400	$1,100	

Add 30% for matching mag.

* ***ac-41 1st and 2nd Variation*** – 9mm Para. cal., last military high polish P.38s, only 1st var. has "ac" on left trigger guard (ser. range 1-4833b), 2nd var. continues to serial no. 4527i.

	N/A	$2,100	$1,800	$1,650	$1,400	$1,000	$800	

Add 30% for matching mag.
Add 25% for early variation with "ac" on trigger guard (until b-block).

* ***ac-41 3rd Variation*** – 9mm Para. cal., standard (dull) military blue finish over unpolished metal surface begins, ser. range. approx. 5015i-9973j.

	N/A	$1,575	$1,350	$1,225	$995	$800	$625	

Add 30% for matching mag.

* ***ac-42 1st and 2nd Variations*** – mm Para. cal., dull military finish, serial range 1-9197k, ac-42 1st var. last P.38 to have E/359 stamped small parts and serialized magazine. Serialized mag. stop at approx. 9500c.

	N/A	$900	$800	$725	$600	$500	$400	

Add 25% for 1st variation.
Add 30% for matching mag. (First variation only).

* ***ac-43, ac-44 and ac-45 Standard Issue*** – 9mm Para. cal., dull military finish, letters are followed by two digit code corresponding to year of mfg. 1943, 44 and 45. Early two-line "stacked" codes are more desirable than later single line models, except for ac-43 3rd var. Highest P.38 production occurred in 1943 and 1944.

	N/A	$750	$650	$575	$450	$400	$325	

Add 15% for ac-43 single line code.
Add 20% for fnh marked barrel.
Add 30% for FN frame (marked with "MI" or E/140).
Add 20% for ac-45 all matching "c" block.
Add 250% for */35 or 35/* on left side of frame.
Subtract 20% for ac-45 "c" block mismatch (one E/359 slide stamp).
FN slide (ac-43 or ac-44). Extreme rarity precludes accurate pricing. Approx. 200-250 assembled.

* ***ac-45 0-Series*** – 9mm Para. cal., late war 0-Series with rough milled finish, ser. range 025960-027659. Serialized in commercial manner.

	$3,000	$2,600	$2,200	$1,940	$1,575	$1,275	$1,000	

byf-42 STANDARD ISSUE – 9mm Para. cal., "byf" (Mauser code) appears on slide, dull military finish, ser. range 1-4783a. Some very early pistols have eagle 135 (E/135) stamped on five small parts (trigger, hammer, etc.)

	N/A	$2,300	$1,850	$1,600	$1,250	$1,025	$825	

Add 40% for early E/135 proofed parts.

GRADING - PPGS™	100%	98%	95%	90%	80%	70%	60%	LAST MSR

byf-43 & byf-44 STANDARD ISSUE – 9mm Para. cal., dull military finish, byf-43 ser. range 1-approx. 6500q, byf-44 9000p-10000z, and 1-approx. 5000e (overlap with svw-45).

N/A	$750	$650	$625	$500	$400	$325	

Add 20% for mixed E/135 and E/WaA135 acceptance stamps.
Add 100% for mixed blue and phosphate finish major components, also known as "Dual Tone".
Add 120% for all gray phosphate finish.
Add 50% for Mauser assembly with FN slide (marked ac-43 or ac-44 with E/WaA135 stamps).
Add 25% for byf-44 with all E/135 acceptance stamps.
Add 40% for byf-43 with all E/WaA135 acceptance stamps.

byf-43 & byf-44 POLICE ISSUE – mm Para. cal., dull military finish, eagle over "L" (E/L) or eagle over "F" (E/F) acceptance and commercial eagle over "N" (E/N) proof stamps, unique ser. range 1-7600.

N/A	$2,100	$1,800	$1,500	$1,425	$1,175	$900	

Add 20% for byf-43 E/L.
Add 60% for FN slide (ac-43 or ac44 marked).
Add 40% for byf-44 E/F.

svw-45 STANDARD ISSUE – 9mm Para. cal., "svw" (Mauser code) appears on slide, Nazi proofed only, most with dual tone finish, few all blue (rare) or all gray.

$2,800	$2,500	$2,100	$1,825	$1,475	$1,200	$950	

Add 20% for all gray phosphate finish.

* ***svw-45 Police Issue*** – 9mm Para. cal., dull military finish, E/F acceptance and E/N proof stamps.

Extreme rarity precludes accurate pricing. It is recommended that this variation is evaluated and priced by an expert. Watch for fakes.

cyq STANDARD ISSUE – 9mm Para. cal., "cyq" (Spreewerk code) appears on slide, dull military finish, eagle over "88" (E/88) acceptance, variation typically exhibits rough machining with visible circular milling marks, ser. range 1-approx. 10,000z, no year dates were used by Spreewerk.

N/A	$700	$600	$550	$450	$375	$295	

Add 150% for E/359 small parts (very few noted during initial production).
Add 15% for early features (early frame and secondary extractor cut), ser. range 1a - approx. 1000d.
Add 150% for FN frame (marked with "MI", "m", or E/140).
Add 35% for no suffix letter, ser. range 1 - 10000.

* ***cyq Standard Issue Later Production*** – 9mm Para. cal., dull military finish, E/88 acceptance, ser. range approx. a1-approx. b5000.

N/A	$1,000	$875	$775	$575	$475	$375	

Add 25% for "b" prefix serial number.

* ***cyq Zero Series*** – 9mm Para. cal., dull military finish, E/88 acceptance, ser. range 01-approx. 08000.

$1,500	$1,300	$1,100	$1,000	$850	$700	$525	

Add 50% for Spreewerk assembly with FN slide (marked ac-43 or ac-44 with E/88 stamps).

PISTOLS: SEMI-AUTO, WALTHER POST-WAR MFG.

MODEL P38 – post-war version of P38 Military, .22 LR, .7.65mm Luger, or 9mm Para. cal., 5 in. barrel, 8 shot, alloy frame, polished blue or matte black finish, 28 oz. W. German manufacture. Mfg. began 1956, currently imported into the U.S. by Earl's Repair Service. See German WWII Military Pistols for wartime listings.

$725	$675	$500	$375	$325	$275	$225	

Add approx. $400 for .22 LR conversion kit.
Add 40% for high polish finish.

Note: Due to the release of large numbers of W. German Police and Army trade-ins of P.38 9mm Para. and PP .32 ACP cal. models, the actual value of original models in 90% or less condition has decreased somewhat. The two models most affected are the P-1 variation of the P.38, and the German PP in .32 ACP cal.

GRADING - PPGS™	100%	98%	95%	90%	80%	70%	60%	LAST MSR

* ***Model P38 Long Barrel Special Edition*** – 9mm Para. cal., steel frame, 6, 7, or 8, in. barrel, wood grips, 50 mfg. 1988.

	$4,000	$3,500	$2,900	N/A	N/A	N/A	N/A	

* ***Model P38 Steel Frame*** – .22 LR, 7.65mm Luger or 9mm Para. cal., similar to regular P.38, except has steel frame, 34 oz. Imported 1987-89 only, and in limited quantities.

	$1,750	$1,500	$1,250	$1,000	$750	$600	$450	*$1,400*

Add 30% for 7.65mm Luger cal.

* ***Model P38 in .22 LR Cal.*** – disc. 1989.

	$1,200	$950	$750	$550	$375	$325	$300	*$1,050*

MODEL P38 II – similar to the Standard P.38, except has reinforced slide.

	$725	$550	$450	$375	$325	$275	$225	

MODEL P38K – 7.65mm Luger or 9mm Para. cal., shortened 2.8 in. barrel variation of P.38, front sight on slide, adj. rear sight, 27.9 oz. 3,000 mfg. 1974-81.

	$1,500	$1,250	$1,000	$750	$650	$525	$400	

Add 30% for 7.65mm Luger cal.

Beware of fakes!

MODEL P38 SPECIAL EDITIONS/ENGRAVED

* ***Model P38 50th Year Commemorative*** – 9mm Para. cal., steel frame, carved grips, presentation engraved with deluxe walnut presentation case. Introduced 1987, inventory depleted 1992.

	$2,500	$1,850	$1,300	N/A	N/A	N/A	N/A	*$950*

* ***Model P38 HP 60th Year Commemorative*** – 9mm Para. or 7.65mm (.30 Luger) cal., special production, steel frame, high polish, wood grips, includes wood presentation case. Approx. 100 mfg. in each caliber. Mfg. 1998.

	$2,500	$1,900	$1,300	N/A	N/A	N/A	N/A	

Add 10% for 7.65mm cal.

Subtract 20% if w/o original factory walnut case and accessories.

* ***Model P38 100th Year Commemorative*** – 9mm Para. cal., alloy or steel frame with slide engraving "100 Jahre Walther 1886-1986." Imported by Interarms.

	$1,200	$950	$700	N/A	N/A	N/A	N/A	

Add 75% for steel frame.

* ***Model P38 Blue Engraved*** – .22 LR, 7.65mm Luger, or 9mm Para. cal.

9mm Para. cal.	$2,250	$1,750	$1,500	N/A	N/A	N/A	N/A	
7.65mm Luger cal.	$2,500	$2,000	$1,500	N/A	N/A	N/A	N/A	
.22 LR cal.	$2,500	$2,000	$1,500	N/A	N/A	N/A	N/A	*$1,850*

* ***Model P38 Chrome Engraved*** – .22 LR, 7.65mm Luger, or 9mm Para. cal.

	$1,950	$1,500	$1,000	N/A	N/A	N/A	N/A	*$2,125*

* ***Model P38 Silver Engraved*** – .22 LR, 7.65mm Luger, or 9mm Para. cal.

	$1,950	$1,500	$1,000	N/A	N/A	N/A	N/A	*$2,100*

* ***Model P38 Gold Engraved*** – .22 LR, 7.65mm Luger, or 9mm Para. cal.

	$2,600	$2,100	$1,550	N/A	N/A	N/A	N/A	*$2,050*

MODEL P1 – 9mm Para. and 7.65mm Luger cal., post-war commercial variation of the P.38 with steel slide and alloy frame, 5 in. barrel, 8 shot mag., blue or phosphate finish, black plastic grips. Disc.

	$675	$550	$400	$300	$250	$215	$165	
Imp. Police Trade-Ins	$375	$325	$275	$225	$200	$170	$135	

Add 50% for 7.65mm Luger.

MODEL P1A1 – 9mm Para. cal., utilizes design elements from the P5 and P38, only 10 mfg.

	$4,000	$3,600	$3,200	$2,850	$2,500	$2,150	$1,775	

GRADING - PPGS™	100%	98%	95%	90%	80%	70%	60%	LAST MSR

MODEL P4 – 9mm Para. or 7.65mm Luger cal., modernized variation of the original P.38, 4 1/2 in. barrel, 8 shot mag., updates include reinforced steel slide and alloy frame, includes decocking lever and automatic safeties, rear sight, 29 oz. Mfg. 1975-81, importation disc. 1982.

	$725	$600	$525	$425	$300	$250	$200	

Add 30% for commercial variation.
Add 50% for 7.65mm Luger.

PISTOLS: SEMI-AUTO, JOHN MARTZ CONVERSIONS

P.38 - JOHN MARTZ CONVERSIONS BABY – 9mm Para. cal., shortened barrel (3 in.) grip, and two 7 shot mags., 70 fabricated.

	$3,600	$2,950	$2,100	$1,850	$1,500	$1,300	$1,000	

P.38 - JOHN MARTZ CONVERSIONS – .38 Super (4 or 6 in. barrel, 9 fabricated) or .45 ACP (4 or 7 1/2 in. barrel, 24 fabricated) cal. Disc.

	$5,700	$3,675	$2,600	$2,200	$1,800	$1,500	$1,275	

P.38 - JOHN MARTZ CONVERSIONS CARBINE – 9mm Para. cal., 16 in. barrel, adj. rear sight, 30 fabricated w/shoulder stocks. Disc.

	$9,850	$7,500	$5,000	$4,300	$3,600	$3,200	$2,600	

P.A.F.

Previous manufacturer located in S. Africa. P.A.F. stands for Pretoria Arms Factory.

PISTOLS: SEMI-AUTO

.25 ACP PISTOL – .25 ACP cal., patterned after the Baby Browning, blue finish. Approx. 10,000 mfg.

	$300	$275	$250	$235	$225	$200	$180	

P.A.W.S., INC.

Previous manufacturer located in Salem, OR. Distributor and dealer sales. Previously distributed by Sile Distributors, Inc. located in New York, NY.

CARBINES

ZX6/ZX8 CARBINE – 9mm Para. or .45 ACP cal., semi-auto paramilitary design carbine, 16 in. barrel, 10 or 32* shot mag., folding metal stock, matte black finish, aperture rear sight, partial barrel shroud, 7 1/2 lbs. Mfg. 1989-2004.

	$715	$635	$550	$475	$375	$300	$250	

The ZX6 is chambered for 9mm Para., while the ZX8 is chambered for .45 ACP.

PGW DEFENCE TECHNOLOGIES, INC.

Current manufacturer established in 1992, and located in Winnipeg, Manitoba, Canada. Previous company name was Prairie Gun Works until 2003. Currently imported by Leroy's Big Valley Gun Works, located in Glasgow, MT.

RIFLES: BOLT ACTION

PGW manufactures approx. 50-60 guns annually. They also sell their actions separately for $400-$2,300, depending on caliber and configuration.

M-15 Ti ULTRA LITE – various cals., titanium (denoted by "Ti" model suffix) or re-machined Rem. 700 (disc.) short action, 20 in. barrel, Kevlar stock with glass bedding, matte metal finish, approx. 4 1/2-6 1/4 lbs. Mfg. 1996-2009.

	$2,650	$2,300	$2,000	$1,750	$1,750	$1,525	$1,375	

Subtract $300 for benchrest or varmint single shot.
Add $100 for tactical stainless.
Add $200 for stainless steel (disc.).
Add $120 for Ultra Lite muzzle brake (disc.).
Add $200 for teflon black finish.
Add $100 for electroless nickel plating (disc.).

This model is also available in a hunter tactical configuration (Model M-15 Ti/HT) at no extra charge.

GRADING - PPGS™	100%	98%	95%	90%	80%	70%	60%	LAST MSR

M-18 Ti ULTRA LIGHT – most long action cals. to .340 Wby. Mag., titanium or re-machined Rem. Model 700 long (disc.) action, 22 in. barrel, matte metal finish, approx. 4 3/4 lbs. Mfg. 1996-2009.

	$2,650	$2,300	$2,000	$1,750	$1,750	$1,525	$1,375	

Subtract $300 for single shot.
Add $100 for stainless steel.
Add $200 for teflon black finish.
Add $120 for Ultra Lite muzzle brake (disc.).
Add $100 for electroless nickel plating (disc.).

TIMBERWOLF – .338 Win. or .408 Chey Tac cal., titanium or stainless steel construction, adj. trigger, 5 shot mag., custom teflon finish, single shot or repeater, various barrel lengths and stock configurations.

MSR $7,000	$6,500	$5,750	$5,000	$4,250	$3,500	$2,750	$2,300	

COYOTE – .308 Win. cal., titanium or stainless steel construction, adj. trigger, 5 shot mag., custom teflon finish, single shot or repeater, match grade fluted barrel, various barrel lengths and stock configurations.

MSR $5,500	$4,995	$4,500	$4,000	$3,500	$3,000	$2,650	$2,150	

LRT-2 (PGW/GIBBS) – various large cals. starting with .378, designed for dangerous game, 4 1/2 in. mag. box, one piece bolt, Sako type extractor, choice of Safari style or A-2 stock, 10-18 lbs. Mfg. 1999-2009.

	$2,625	$2,350	$1,950	$1,750	$1,500	$1,250	$1,000	

Add $100 for A-2 stock.
Add $725 for .408 Cheyenne cal.

LRT-3 (PGW/GIBBS) – .50 BMG cal., single shot action, Big Mac stock. Mfg. 1999-2009.

	$4,150	$3,700	$3,400	$3,100	$2,800	$2,500	$2,250	

PHSADC (PAKISTAN HUNTING & SPORTING ARMS DEVELOPMENT COMPANY)

Current manufacturer located in Peshawar, Pakistan. No current U.S. importation.

FIREARMS

PHSADC manufactures a complete line of shotguns, pistols, revolvers, rifles, and replicas of vintage guns. Currently, these guns are not imported into the U.S. Please contact the company directly for more information, including pricing and availability (see Trademark Index).

PKP, INC.

Previous manufacturer and distributor located in Tempe, AZ. Dealer or consumer direct sales.

PISTOLS

POWELL KNIFE PISTOL MR-38 – .38 Spl., unique knife-pistol design allows barrel to be incorporated into the upper rear portion of the break-action blade assembly, 1 3/4 in. barrel, stainless steel with wood handles, 17 oz. Limited mfg. 1997-98.

	$415	$350	$275	$225	$195	$165	$140	*$450*

POF USA

Please refer to the Patriot Ordnance Factory listing in this section.

PPK s.r.o.

Current manufacturer located in Holice, Czech Republic. No current U.S. importation.

Zbrojovka Holice is a registered trademark of PPK. The company currently makes Drulov pistols (see Drulov listings in the D section), a Model ZP SxS shotgun and a series of bolt action rifles based on the K98 Mauser - models include the Eco, Standard, and Lux, in addition to a Brno single shot and semi-auto rifle. Please contact the company directly for more information, pricing and availability (see Trademark Index).

GRADING - PPGS™	100%	98%	95%	90%	80%	70%	60%	LAST MSR

P.S.M.G. GUN COMPANY

Previous manufacturer located in Arlington, MA.

PISTOLS: SEMI-AUTO

SIX IN ONE SUPREME – .22 LR, 7.65mm Luger, .38 Super, .38 Spl., 9mm Para., or .45 ACP cal., single action, 3 1/4, 5, or 7 1/2 in. barrel with solid cooling rib, adj. rear sight. Limited mfg. 1988-1989.

	100%	98%	95%	90%	80%	70%	60%	LAST MSR
	$700	$600	$500	$450	$400	$365	$330	*$895*

Add $20-$55 for caliber options.
Add $25 for 7 1/2 in. barrel.
Add $35 for satin nickel plating.
Add $225 per extra barrel.
Add $450 per individual conversion unit.

PTK INTERNATIONAL, INC.

Previous distributor located in Atlanta, GA.

Please refer to listing under Poly-Technologies in this section.

PTR 91, INC.

Current rifle manufacturer located in Bristol, CT. Previously located in Farmington, CT. Represented by Vincent A. Pestilli & Associates, located in Brownfield, ME. Previous company name was J.L.D. Enterprises.

PISTOLS: SEMI-AUTO

PTR-91 PDW – .308 Win. cal., 8 3/8 in. barrel with flash hider, tactical handguard, black aluminum butt cap, H&K type polymer trigger group, includes one 20 shot mag., approx. 7 1/2 lbs. New 2012.

	100%	98%	95%	90%	80%	70%	60%	LAST MSR
MSR $1,099	$975	$875	$750	$650	$550	$500	$450	

PTR-32 PDW – 7.62x39mm cal., otherwise similar to PTR-91 PDW, except has one banana shaped 30 shot mag. Limited mfg. 2012 only.

	100%	98%	95%	90%	80%	70%	60%	LAST MSR
	$1,050	$950	$800	$700	$600	$500	$450	*$1,199*

This model was also available with a picatinny rail (Model PTW-32 PDW-R), limited mfg. 2012 only.

RIFLES: SEMI-AUTO

The following rifles utilize an H&K delayed blowback action with roller bearings. PTR-91 also manufactures the SBR (Short Barrel Rifle) for military/law enforcement.

IMPORTANT NOTE: On model(s) where *N/A has replaced the normal 100% value, it indicates current market conditions are too unstable to accurately ascertain 100%-60% values. Factory retail prices (MSRs) reflect most recent updates. For more up-to-date information on current pricing trends and additional useful information, please visit www.bluebookofgunvalues.com, select "Information & Services" from the menu, and click on "Additional Book Information".

PTR-91F – .308 Win. cal., CNC machined scope mounts, H&K style hooded front blade and four position diopter rear sight, 18 in. barrel with 1:12 twist, black furniture, pre-ban H&K flash hider, or welded muzzle brake (PTR-91C), H&K Navy type polymer trigger group, 20 shot mag., one piece forged cocking handle, parkerized finish, matte black coated.

	100%	98%	95%	90%	80%	70%	60%	LAST MSR
MSR $1,245	$1,150	$1,025	$900	$800	$700	$600	$550	

Add $200 for tactical handguard, side folding stock, and pre-ban flash hider (PTR-91R, disc. 2008).
Add $200 for tactical handguard, side folding stock, and muzzle brake (PTR-91 RC, disc. 2008).

* ***PTR-91T*** – .308 Win. cal., similar to Model PTR-91, except has green furniture and original H&K flash hider. Limited mfg. 2005.

	100%	98%	95%	90%	80%	70%	60%	LAST MSR
	$895	$800	$700	$600	$500	$450	$400	*$995*

PTR-91 AI – .308 Win. cal., match grade rifle with polymer trigger group, match grade barrel, H&K style hooded front blade and four position diopter rear sight, 20 shot mag., steel bipod, steel handguard with bipod recesses, pre-ban H&K flash hider, with (PTR-91 AI C) or w/o (PTR-91 AI F) muzzle brake with match grade barrel. Mfg. 2005-2008.

	100%	98%	95%	90%	80%	70%	60%	LAST MSR
	$1,150	$925	$825	$725	$600	$500	$425	*$1,295*

GRADING - PPGS™	100%	98%	95%	90%	80%	70%	60%	LAST MSR

PTR-91 G.I. – .308 Win. cal., 18 in. H&K type profile barrel and polymer trigger group, 20 shot mag., OD Green furniture, matte parkerized finish. New 2012.

MSR $999	*N/A	$850	$725	$625	$500	$450	$425	

PTR-91 CLASSIC – .308 Win. cal., 18 in. H&K type profile barrel with flash hider, 20 shot mag., black (Classic Black) or wood (Classic Wood) furniture with slimline handguard, black powdercoated finish, H&K navy type polymer trigger group. Limited mfg. 2012 only.

	$875	$750	$625	$550	$500	$450	$395	$969

Add $30 for Classic Wood.

PTR-91 KC – .308 Win. cal., "Kurz" law enforcement carbine with 16 in. barrel, H&K style hooded front blade and four position diopter rear sight, 10 (compliant) or 20 (disc.) shot mag., tropical green (disc.) or black furniture, wide handguard with bipod recesses, pre-ban H&K flash hider or welded muzzle compensator (PTR-91KC). New 2005.

MSR $1,245	$1,150	$1,025	$900	$800	$700	$600	$550	

Add $100 for PTR-91 KFO with side folding stock and pre-ban flash hider (disc. 2006).

PTR-91 KFM4 – .308 Win. cal., "Kurz" paratrooper carbine, 16 in. barrel, H&K style hooded front blade and four position diopter rear sight, 20 shot mag., tropical green (disc.) or black furniture, wide handguard with bipod recesses and three complete rails, H&K Navy type polymer trigger group, M4 type 6 position telescoping stock and flash hider. New 2005.

MSR $1,450	$1,295	$1,095	$975	$850	$725	$600	$500	

Add $100 for welded scope mount (Model PTR-91 KFM4R, new 2011).

PTR-91 KF – .308 Win. cal., 16 in. barrel, 20 shot mag., black furniture with tactical handguard, pre-ban H&K flash hider, standard fixed stock, H&K Navy polymer trigger group.

MSR $1,245	$1,150	$1,025	$900	$800	$700	$600	$550	

PTR-91 KPF GERMAN PARATROOPER – .308 Win. cal., 16 in. barrel, 20 shot mag., black furniture, three rails, pre-ban H&K flash hider, H&K Navy polymer trigger group, original German telescoping stock.

MSR $1,915	$1,775	$1,575	$1,375	$1,150	$925	$800	$675	

Add $100 for welded scope mount (Model PTR-91 KPFR, new 2011).

PTR-MSG 91 SNIPER – .308 Win. cal., 18 in. fluted target barrel, black furniture, tactical aluminum handguard, welded Picatinny accessory rail, Harris bipod, adj. Magpul stock with cheekpiece, pre-ban H&K flash hider, with (Model PTR-MSG 91 C) or w/o (PTR-MSG 91) welded muzzle compensator.

MSR $2,125	$1,975	$1,775	$1,575	$1,375	$1,150	$900	$750	

PTR-MSG 91 SS SUPER SNIPER – .308 Win. cal., 20 in. fluted free floating match barrel, 10 shot mag., black furniture with tactical super sniper handguard, welded Picatinny accessory rail, Harris bipod, no sights, adj. Magpul stock.

MSR $2,770	$2,495	$2,250	$1,975	$1,750	$1,500	$1,225	$975	

PTR-91 SC SQUAD CARBINE – .308 Win. cal., 16 in. fluted barrel, H&K style hooded front blade and four position diopter rear sight, black furniture, tactical aluminum handguard with three rails, welded Picatinny accessory rail, 20 shot mag., standard stock, pre-ban H&K flash hider, with or w/o welded compensator (compliant model).

MSR $1,550	$1,425	$1,250	$1,050	$925	$800	$675	$550	

PTR-32 KF – 7.62x39mm cal., 16 in. barrel, H&K style hooded front blade and four position diopter rear sight, 30 shot mag., black furniture, tactical aluminum handguard, pre-ban H&K flash hider, H&K Navy type polymer trigger group, standard stock.

MSR $1,175	$1,050	$925	$825	$725	$600	$500	$450	

Add $50 for welded scope mount (Model PTR-32KFR, new 2011).

PTR-32 KC – 7.62x39mm cal., 16 in. barrel, H&K style hooded front blade and four position diopter rear sight, 10 shot mag., black furniture, tactical aluminum handguard, H&K Navy type polymer trigger group, welded muzzle compensator.

MSR $1,175	$1,050	$925	$825	$725	$600	$500	$450	

Add $50 for welded scope mount (Model PTR-32 KCR, new 2011).

GRADING - PPGS™	100%	98%	95%	90%	80%	70%	60%	LAST MSR

PTR-32 KFM4 – 7.62x39mm cal., 16 in. barrel, H&K style hooded front blade and four position diopter rear sight, 30 shot mag., black furniture, tactical aluminum handguard with three rails, pre-ban H&K flash hider, H&K Navy type polymer trigger group, M4 six position telescoping stock.

MSR $1,485	$1,325	$1,100	$975	$850	$725	$600	$500	

Add $100 for welded scope mount (model PTR-32 KFM4R, new 2011).

PTR-32 KCM4 – 7.62x39mm cal., 16 in. barrel, H&K style hooded front blade and four position diopter rear sight, 10 shot mag., black furniture, tactical aluminum handguard with three rails, H&K Navy type polymer trigger group, M4 style fixed stock, welded compensator.

MSR $1,485	$1,325	$1,100	$975	$850	$725	$600	$500	

Add $100 for welded scope mount (Model PTR-32 KCM4R, new 2011).

PTR-32 KPF – 7.62x39mm cal., 16 in. barrel, 30 shot mag., black furniture, three rails, original German telescoping stock. New 2011.

MSR $1,980	$1,825	$1,600	$1,400	$1,150	$925	$800	$675	

Add $100 for welded scope mount (Model PTR-32 KPF4).

PTR-91 MSR – .308 Win. cal., 18 in. crown tapered target barrel, 5 shot mag., H&K Navy type polymer trigger group, sling swivel, earth tone furniture with free floating handguard, 8 in. welded scope mount, black synthetic stock with adj. cheekpiece. New 2012.

MSR $1,200	$1,075	$950	$825	$700	$675	$550	$425	

P.V. NELSON, (GUNMAKERS)

Please refer to the N section for this manufacturer.

PACIFIC INTERNATIONAL

Previous manufacturer located in Sacramento, CA circa mid-1970s-1980s.

PISTOLS: SEMI-AUTO

VEGA COMBAT MATCH – .45 ACP cal., stainless steel frame, 5 in. match grade barrel, 7 shot mag., rear slide serrations, checkered wood grips, extended speed safety.

	$475	$425	$350	$325	$300	$275	$250	

MINI VEGA – .25 ACP cal., stainless steel frame, copy of the FN 1905 Browning Vest Pocket.

	$275	$235	$200	$180	$160	$140	$120	

M. PADRÓNE

Previous trademark manufactured by F.A.I.R. srl, located in Marcheno, Italy. Previously imported until 2011 by Padrone USA, located in San Antonio, TX.

M. Padróne guns were high quality round body boxlock O/U shotguns on a small action - 12 ga. was not available.

PALM PISTOL

Please refer to the Constitution Arms listing in the C section.

PALMETTO ARMS CO.

Previous manufacturer until 2007 and current retailer located in Brescia, Italy.

Palmetto Arms Co. manufactured black powder reproductions and replicas, but they produced only a small number of firearms, including the Outlaw SA revolver, Colt Root pistol, and the Lightning slide action rifle/carbine. Values are determined by each model's competitive shooting value, since there is almost no collectibility for this trademark.

PARAMOUNT

Previous trademark manufactured by Imperial Gun Co., Ltd. located in Surrey, England. Actions were previously imported by O.K. Weber, Inc. located in Eugene, OR and Olympic Arms, Inc. located in Olympia, WA.

GRADING - PPGS™	100%	98%	95%	90%	80%	70%	60%	LAST MSR

RIFLES: SINGLE SHOT

THE IMPERIAL - .308 Win. cal., single shot target rifle featuring thumbhole stock and CPE aperture rear sight, fully adj. trigger, vent. forearm. Disc. 1994.

$3,250	$2,700	$2,250	$1,850	$1,400	$1,000	$795	*$3,400*

RANGEMASTER - various cals., single shot design, steel frame, contoured walnut grips, satin chrome finish, 8 1/2 lbs. Limited importation 1992-94.

$1,600	$1,400	$1,200	$995	$895	$795	$695	*$1,800*

PARA INC., USA

Current manufacturer established in 1985, and located in Pineville, NC. Previous company name was Para-Ordnance Mfg. Inc., and was located in Scarborough, Ontario, Canada until June 2009. Previously located in Ft. Lauderdale, FL. Dealer and distributor sales.

Para-Ordnance Mfg. was founded by Ted Szabo and Thanos Polyzos. Szabo was born in Hungary and his family fled the country when the Russians invaded during the Hungarian Revolution of 1956. Polyzos was born in Greece and later emigrated to Canada.

On Jan. 30, 2012, Freedom Group, Inc. purchased the assets of Para USA, Inc. Manufacturing is scheduled to remain in Pineville, NC.

PISTOLS: SEMI-AUTO

From 1985-2009, pistols were marked "Made in Canada" with a Canadian maple leaf on the slide.

In 1999, Para-Ordnance introduced their LDA trigger system, originally standing for Lightning Double Action. During 2002, all alloy frame pistols were discontinued, and the abbreviation LDA became Light Double Action. Beginning 2003, all Para-Ordnance models were shipped with two magazines. Beginning Jan. 1, 2004, all Para-Ordnance models were replaced for the general market (except California) with the introduction of the new Power Extractor (PXT) models. The Griptor system, featuring front grip strap grasping grooves, became available during 2005, and the accessory mounting rail option became available during 2006.

Previous Para-Ordnance model nomenclature typically listed the alphabetical letter of the series, followed by a one or two digit number indicating magazine capacity, followed by the number(s) of the caliber. Hence, a Model P14.45 is a P Series model with a 14 shot mag. in .45 ACP cal., and a 7.45LDA indicates a .45 ACP cal. in Light Double Action with a 7 shot mag.

Current Para-Ordnance nomenclature typically features the configuration type on the left side of the slide. The model designation is located on the right side of the slide and underneath it on the frame the product code (new 2006)/order number (changed to product code during 2006), which is alpha-numeric, may also appear. For current product codes for the various Para-Ordnance models, please visit www.paraord.com.

Para-Ordnance offers the following finishes on its pistols: Regal (black slide, black frame w/ stainless fire controls), Midnight Blue (blue slide, blue frame w/blue fire controls), Coyote Brown, Covert Black (black slide, black frame, and black fire controls), Black Watch (black slide, green frame, green (double stack) or black (single stack) fire controls), Spec Ops (green slide, green frame w/black fire controls), or Sterling (all stainless, black slide w/polished sides), in addition to stainless steel construction.

As this edition went to press, Para Inc., USA had yet to establish 2013 U.S. prices.

6.45 LDA/LLDA - Models 6.45 LDA (changed to Para-Companion, marked Para-Companion on left side of slide and C7.45LDA on right side of slide) and 6.45 LLDA were advertised in the 2001 Para-Ordnance catalog (became the Para-Carry, marked Para-Carry on left side of slide and 6.45 LLDA on right side of frame), the 6.46 LLDA was never mfg., prototype only. Mfg. 2001-2003.

GRADING - PPGS™	100%	98%	95%	90%	80%	70%	60%	LAST MSR

C SERIES MODELS – .45 ACP cal., DAO, 3 (Carry), 3 1/2 (Companion or Companion Carry), 4 1/2 (CCW or Tac-Four), or 5 in. barrel, stainless steel only, single or double (Tac-Four only) stack mag., 6 (Carry), 7, or 10 (Tac-Four only) shot mag., approx. 30-34 oz. Mfg. 2003.

$775	$680	$580	$525	$425	$350	$270	*$939*

Add $70 for Companion Carry Model.

D SERIES MODELS – 9mm Para., .40 S&W, or .45 ACP cal., DAO, 3 1/2 or 5 in. barrel, 7 or 10 shot single stack mag., steel receiver, matte black finish or stainless steel. Mfg. 2003.

$715	$625	$535	$485	$395	$320	$250	*$859*

Add $80 for stainless steel.

P SERIES MODELS – 9mm Para. or .45 ACP cal., single action, 3 1/2, 4 1/4, or 5 in. barrel, 10 shot mag., matte black (5 in. barrel only) or stainless steel finish.

* ***P Series Model P10*** – 9mm Para. (new 1998), .40 S&W, .45 ACP, 10mm (mfg. 1998 only, stainless steel) cal., single action, super compact variation featuring 3 in. barrel and shortened grip, 10 shot double column mag., 3-dot sights, choice of alloy (matte black), steel (matte black), or stainless (duo-tone - disc. 2000, or bright finish) frame, 31 oz. with steel frame or 24 oz. with alloy frame. Mfg. 1997-2002.

$625	$545	$470	$425	$345	$280	$220	*$740*

Add $10 for steel frame.
Add $49 for stainless steel.
Add $45 for stainless steel with duo-tone finish (disc. 2000).

* ***P Series Model P12*** – .40 S&W (disc. 2002) or .45 ACP cal., compact variation of the P14 featuring 10 (C/B 1994) or 11* shot mag. and 3 1/2 in. barrel, 33 oz. with steel frame (disc. 2002) or 24 oz. with alloy frame (disc. 2002) or stainless steel (standard beginning 2003, duo-tone stainless was disc. 2000). Mfg. 1990-2003.

$750	$655	$560	$510	$410	$335	$260	*$899*

Subtract 10% for steel frame (disc. 2002).

* ***P Series Model P13*** – .40 S&W (disc. 2000) or .45 ACP cal., similar to P14, except has 10 (C/B 1994) or 12* shot mag., 4 1/4 in. barrel, 35 oz. with steel frame (disc. 2002) or 25 oz. with alloy frame (disc. 2002), stainless steel became standard 2003 (duo-tone stainless was disc. 2000). Mfg. 1993-2003.

$750	$655	$560	$510	$410	$335	$260	*$899*

* ***P Series Model P14*** – .40 S&W (mfg. 1996-2000) or .45 ACP cal., patterned after the Colt Model 1911A1 except has choice of alloy (matte black, disc. 2002), steel (matte black), or stainless steel (stainless or duo-tone finish) frame that has been widened slightly for extra shot capacity (13* shot), 10 shot (C/B 1994) mag., single action, 3-dot sight system, rounded combat hammer, 5 in. ramped barrel, 38 oz. with steel frame or 28 oz. with alloy frame (disc. 2002), duo-tone stainless steel was disc. 2000. Mfg. 1990-2003.

$685	$600	$515	$465	$375	$310	$240	*$829*

Add $70 for stainless steel.

* ***P Series Model P15*** – .40 S&W cal., otherwise similar to P13, 36 oz. with steel frame or 28 oz. with alloy frame. Mfg. 1996-99.

$625	$545	$470	$425	$345	$280	$220	*$740*

Add $10 for steel frame.
Add $59 for stainless steel.
Add $45 for stainless steel with duo-tone finish.

* ***P Series Model P16*** – .40 S&W cal., otherwise similar to P14, steel or stainless steel (new 1997) frame only. New 1995-2002.

$640	$560	$480	$435	$350	$290	$225	*$750*

Add $49 for stainless steel.
Add $35 for duo-tone stainless steel (disc. 2000).

GRADING - PPGS™	100%	98%	95%	90%	80%	70%	60%	LAST MSR

* ***P Series Model P18*** – 9mm Para. cal., 5 in. ramped barrel, stainless steel, solid barrel bushing, flared ejection port, quadruple safety, adj. rear sight, 40 oz. Mfg. 1998-2003.

	$800	$700	$600	$545	$440	$360	$280	*$960*

PXT 1911 SINGLE STACK SERIES – .38 Super or .45 ACP cal., features new power extractor design with larger claw (PXT), left slide is marked "Para 1911", right side marked with individual model names, various configurations, barrel lengths, and finishes, single action, single stack mag., spurred or spurless (light rail models only) hammer. New 2004.

* ***Slim Hawg*** – .45 ACP cal. only, 3 in. barrel, 6 shot mag., 3-dot sights, choice of stainless steel (disc. 2009) or Covert Black (new 2006) finish, 24 or 30 (stainless) oz.

MSR $949	$850	$750	$650	$595	$475	$395	$325	

Add $140 for stainless steel (disc. 2009).

* ***Super Hawg Single Stack*** – .45 ACP cal., similar to S14.45 Ltd., except has 6 in. barrel and stainless finish, 8 shot mag. Mfg. 2008-2010.

	$1,250	$1,095	$935	$850	$685	$560	$435	*$1,369*

* ***GI Expert*** – .45 ACP cal., 5 in. barrel, 8 shot mag., 3 dot sights, steel frame, black finish. New 2009.

MSR $649	$575	$495	$425	$375	$300	$245	$200	

» **GI Expert Stainless** – .45 ACP cal., 5 in. barrel, 8 shot mag., similar to GI Expert, except is weather resistant stainless steel. New 2010.

MSR $699	$615	$550	$475	$400	$350	$300	$250	

» **GI Expert ESP** – .45 ACP cal., 5 in. barrel, 8 shot mag., similar to GI Expert, except has beavertail grip safety with speed bump, lightweight match trigger with adj. overtravel, fiber optic front sight. Mfg. 2010.

	$625	$525	$450	$400	$350	$300	$250	*$699*

» **GI Expert LTC** – .45 ACP cal., 4 1/4 in. barrel, 8 shot mag., similar to GI Expert, except has compact frame, beavertail grip safety, competition trigger, fiber optic front sight, double diamond checkered wood grips, alloy receiver, black slide, black frame. New 2011.

MSR $799	$700	$625	$525	$425	$375	$325	$295	

* ***1911 Wild Bunch*** – .45 ACP cal., 7 shot mag., 5 in. barrel, black steel frame, 3-dot sights, traditional spur hammer, designed for SASS competition shooting, laser engraved SASS locking behind cocking serrations, checkered wood grips, stainless became standard during 2012. New 2011.

MSR $949	$795	$650	$525	$425	$375	$325	$275	

* ***1911 OPS*** – .45 ACP cal. only, 3 1/2 in. barrel, 7 shot mag., 3-dot sights, stainless steel construction, 32 oz. Disc. 2008.

	$975	$855	$730	$665	$535	$440	$340	*$1,099*

* ***1911 LTC*** – 9mm Para. (mfg. 2008-2010) or .45 ACP cal., 4 1/4 in. barrel, 8 or 9 (9mm Para) shot mag., 3-dot sights, steel (disc.), alloy or stainless steel (disc. 2009) construction, Covert black (9mm Para.) or Regal finish, 28 (alloy) or 35 oz.

MSR $899	$775	$675	$550	$425	$375	$325	$295	

Add $20 for steel (disc.), or $150 for stainless steel (disc. 2009).

* ***1911 SSP Series*** – .38 Super (disc. 2008) or .45 ACP cal., 5 in. barrel, 8 or 9 (.38 Super cal. only) shot mag., fiber optic (new 2011) 3-dot or Novak adj. (Tactical Duty Model only, disc.) sights, steel or stainless steel (mfg. 2006-2008) construction, Black Covert (new 2008) or Regal (disc.) finish, steel frame (new 2011), stainless (disc. 2008), or bright stainless (.38 Super cal. only), premium cocobolo (new 2011), checkered wood (disc.) or pearl (.38 Super cal.) grips, 39 oz. Disc. 2008, reintroduced 2011.

MSR $899	$775	$675	$550	$425	$375	$325	$295	

Add $230 for stainless steel.
Add $250 for .38 Super cal., or $280 for .38 Super with pearl grips.
Add $250 for Tactical Duty SSP with Novak adj. sights (disc. 2008).

GRADING - PPGS™	100%	98%	95%	90%	80%	70%	60%	LAST MSR

* ***1911 SSP Gun Rights*** – .45 ACP cal., 14 shot, 5 in. barrel, stainless steel construction, 40 oz. Mfg. mid-2009-2011.

	$1,025	$895	$775	$695	$565	$475	$375	*$1,149*

Para USA made a donation to the NRA-ILA fund for every pistol sold.

* ***1911 Black Ops/Black Ops Ltd.*** – .45 ACP cal., 5 in. barrel, 8 shot mag., fiber optic front and adj. rear sight (Black Ops Ltd.) or night sights (Black Ops), stainless steel with black finish, gold Para. emblem on checkered wood grips, adj. trigger. New 2012.

MSR $1,299	$1,150	$995	$850	$775	$625	$500	$395	

* ***1911 Limited*** – .45 ACP cal., 5 in. barrel, 8 shot mag., fiber optic front and adj. rear sight, stainless steel with Sterling finish, gold Para. emblem on checkered wood grips, adj. trigger, 39 oz. Disc. 2008, reintroduced 2011 only.

	$1,150	$995	$850	$775	$625	$500	$395	*$1,289*

* ***1911 100th Anniversary*** – .45 ACP cal., based on Browning's Government Model, includes 7 and 8 shot mag., 5 in. barrel, 3-dot sights, steel frame, black finish, smooth cocobolo grips, 100th Anniversary laser engraved on side of frame. Mfg. 2011.

	$950	$825	$700	N/A	N/A	N/A	N/A	*$1,079*

Add $1,320 for set of two pistols (1911 and 14.45 100th Anniversary) with carved walnut presentation box.

* ***1911 Nite-Tac*** – .45 ACP cal. only, 5 in. barrel, 8 shot mag., 3-dot sights, stainless steel construction, Covert Black finish or stainless, features light rail on frame, flush spurless hammer, 40 oz. Disc. 2008.

	$1,025	$875	$750	$650	$550	$450	$375	*$1,149*

* ***Todd Jarrett USPSA Limited Edition*** – .45 ACP cal., 5 in. barrel, 8 shot mag., features Novak adj. sights, steel construction, Covert Black/Sterling finish, 39 oz.

	$1,550	$1,355	$1,160	$1,055	$850	$695	$540	*$1,729*

PXT HIGH CAPACITY SERIES – 9mm Para., 40 S&W, or .45 ACP cal., single action, 10 shot or high capacity mag., various barrel lengths, construction, and finishes.

* ***Hawg 7*** – .45 ACP cal., similar to Hawg 9, except has 3 1/2 in. barrel, 7 shot mag., steel receiver, black finish, Griptor grasing grooves. New 2011.

MSR $899	$775	$675	$550	$425	$375	$325	$295	

* ***Hawg 9*** – 9mm Para. cal., compact frame, 12 shot mag., 3 in. ramped barrel with guide rod, dovetailed, low mount, 3-dot fixed sights, alloy receiver, steel slide, spurred competition hammer, match grade trigger, black polymer grips, Regal black finish, three safeties, 24 oz. Mfg. 2005-2010.

	$875	$765	$655	$595	$480	$395	$305	*$959*

* ***Lite Hawg 9*** – similar to Hawg 9, except is steel and has light rail, flush spurless hammer, Covert Black finish. Disc. 2008.

	$990	$865	$740	$675	$545	$445	$345	*$1,099*

* ***Lite Hawg .45*** – .45 ACP cal., similar to Lite Hawg 9, except has 10 shot mag., flush spurless hammer, Covert Black finish. Disc. 2008.

	$990	$865	$740	$675	$545	$445	$345	*$1,099*

* ***Warthog*** – .45 ACP cal., lightweight, compact design, 3 in. ramped barrel, alloy or stainless frame, 10 shot mag., tritium night (disc.) or 3-dot (upgraded fiber optic became standard during 2011) sights, spur competition hammer, match grade trigger, extended slide lock, beavertail grip and firing pin safeties, black polymer grips, matte black (new 2011), Covert Black (Para-Kote, disc.), or Regal (disc.) finish, or stainless steel construction, 24 or 31 oz. New 2004.

MSR $979	$885	$775	$655	$595	$480	$395	$325	

Add $60 for stainless steel.

GRADING - PPGS™	100%	98%	95%	90%	80%	70%	60%	LAST MSR

* ***Nite Hawg*** – .45 ACP cal., 3 in. barrel, 10 shot mag., tritium night sights, compact alloy frame, Covert Black finish, black plastic grips, 24 oz.

	$995	$870	$745	$675	$545	$450	$350	*$1,099*

* ***Big Hawg*** – .45 ACP cal., 5 in. barrel, 14 shot mag., 3-dot sights, alloy frame, Regal finish with chrome accents, black plastic grips, 28 oz.

	$875	$765	$655	$595	$480	$395	$305	*$959*

* ***Super Hawg High Capacity*** – .45 ACP cal., similar to S14.45 Ltd., except has 6 in. barrel and stainless finish. Mfg. 2008-2010.

	$1,250	$1,095	$935	$850	$685	$560	$435	*$1,369*

* ***P14.45*** – .45 ACP cal., 5 in. barrel, 14 shot mag., 3-dot (fiber optic became standard 2011) sights, Covert Black finish steel (new 2008) or stainless steel (disc.) construction, black synthetic grips, brushed stainless steel, 40 oz.

MSR $879	$795	$725	$625	$575	$475	$375	$295	

Add $230 for stainless steel (disc.2009).

* ***P14.45 Stainless*** – .45 ACP cal., 5 in. barrel, 14 shot mag., similar to P14.45, except is all stainless steel, 40 oz. New 2012.

MSR $899	$750	$650	$525	$425	$375	$325	$295	

Add $30 for light rail.

* ***P14.45 Gun Rights*** – .38 Super or .45 ACP cal., 8 or 9 shot, 5 in. barrel, steel or stainless steel construction, Covert Black or bright stainless, 39 oz. Mfg. mid-2009-2011.

	$1,025	$895	$775	$695	$565	$475	$375	*$1,159*

Para USA made a donation to the NRA-ILA fund for every pistol sold.

* ***P18.9*** – 9mm Para. cal., 5 in. barrel, 18 shot mag., adj. sights, stainless steel construction, black synthetic grips, brushed stainless steel, 40 oz.

	$1,025	$895	$770	$695	$565	$460	$360	*$1,139*

* ***S14.45 Limited (PXT High Capacity Limited)*** – .45 ACP cal., single action, 10 (disc.) or 14 shot mag., adj. sights, 3 1/2 (stainless steel, disc. 2005), 4 1/4 (stainless steel, disc. 2005), or 5 (steel, disc. 2005, or stainless steel) in. barrel, Covert (disc. 2005) or Sterling finish, black synthetic grips, 40 oz.

MSR $1,289	$1,150	$995	$850	$775	$625	$500	$395	

Add $110 for Long Slide Limited Model (mfg. 2011).
Add $75 for 3 1/2 or 4 1/4 in. barrel or stainless steel (disc. 2006).

* ***14.45 Black Ops*** – .45 ACP cal., 14 shot mag., 5 in. barrel, night sights, stainless steel frame, black finish. New 2012.

MSR $1,299	$1,150	$995	$850	$775	$625	$500	$395	

* ***S16.40 Limited (PXT High Capacity Limited)*** – .40 S&W cal., single action, 10 (disc.) or 16 shot mag., adj. sights, 3 1/2 (stainless steel, disc. 2005), 4 1/4 (stainless steel, disc. 2005), or 5 (steel, disc. 2005, or stainless steel) in. barrel, Covert (disc. 2005) or Sterling finish, black synthetic grips, 40 oz.

MSR $1,289	$1,150	$995	$850	$775	$625	$500	$395	

Add $75 for 3 1/2 or 4 1/4 in. barrel or stainless steel (disc. 2006).

* ***S12-45 Limited*** – .45 ACP cal., 3 1/2 in. ramped barrel, 10 or 12 shot mag., stainless steel frame with black slide, Novak adj. rear sight, spur competition hammer, checkered cocobolo grips with gold medallions, 34 oz. Mfg. 2005-2006.

	$995	$870	$745	$675	$545	$450	$350	*$1,105*

* ***18.9 Limited*** – 9mm Para. cal., 5 in. barrel, stainless steel frame, black Sterling finish, stainless slide, 10 or 18 shot mag., fiber optic front sights, adj. rear sights, includes two mags. New 2011.

MSR $1,289	$1,150	$995	$850	$775	$625	$500	$395	

GRADING - PPGS™	100%	98%	95%	90%	80%	70%	60%	LAST MSR

* ***Todd Jarrett USPSA .40 Limited Edition*** – .40 S&W cal., single action, 16 shot mag., 5 in. barrel, Novak adj. sights, steel construction, Covert Black/Sterling finish, flared magwell, black synthetic grips, 40 oz. Disc. 2008.

	$1,495	$1,310	$1,120	$1,015	$820	$675	$525	*$1,729*

14.45 TACTICAL – .45 ACP cal., 4 1/4 (disc.) or 5 in. match grade barrel, 8 shot mag., stainless steel frame, black finish, checkered front grip strap, Ed Brown National Match bushing and slide stop, Tactical II hammer, power extractor, flat checkered mainspring housing, alloy base pads, fiber optic sights. New 2011.

MSR $1,599	$1,375	$1,200	$1,025	$925	$750	$625	$475	

16.40 TT – .40 S&W cal., SA, 16 shot mag., 5 in. barrel, stainless steel frame, duo-tone finish, adj. sights, 42 oz. New 2012.

MSR $1,899	$1,695	$1,450	$1,250	$1,050	$875	$750	$650	

PXT LDA SINGLE STACK (CARRY OPTION SERIES) – 9mm Para. (new mid-2006), .45 GAP (new mid-2006) or .45 ACP cal., DAO, single stack mag., various barrel lengths and finishes, features Griptor grips (grooved front grip strap), spurless flush hammer and rounded grip safety.

* ***Carry Gap*** – .45 GAP cal., 3 in. barrel, 6 shot mag., 3-dot sights, steel frame, Covert Black finish, 30 oz. Disc. 2008.

	$975	$855	$730	$665	$535	$440	$340	*$1,079*

* ***CCO Gap*** – similar to Carry Gap, except has 7 shot mag. and 3 1/2 in. barrel, 31 oz. Mfg. 2006-2008.

	$975	$855	$730	$665	$535	$440	$340	*$1,079*

* ***Covert Black Carry*** – .45 ACP cal., 6 shot mag., 3 in. barrel, Novak adj. sights, stainless steel construction, Covert Black finish, 30 oz.

	$1,025	$895	$770	$695	$565	$460	$360	*$1,149*

* ***Carry*** – similar to Covert Black Carry, except has 3-dot sights and is brushed stainless steel.

MSR $1,149	$1,025	$895	$770	$695	$565	$460	$360	

* ***Carry 9*** – 9mm Para. cal., 8 shot mag., 3 in. barrel, 3-dot sights, alloy frame, Covert Black finish, 24 oz. Mfg. mid-2006-2011.

	$900	$785	$675	$610	$495	$405	$315	*$999*

* ***Stealth*** – .45 ACP cal., 3 in. barrel, alloy frame, black anodized finish, night sights, 24 oz. New 2012.

MSR $1,339	$1,175	$1,025	$875	$800	$650	$525	$450	

* ***PDA*** – 9mm Para cal., 3 in. barrel with fiber optic front and two-dot rear sights, alloy frame with Sterling/Covert Black finish. Mfg. 2008-2011.

	$1,125	$975	$825	$750	$605	$495	$385	*$1,249*

* ***PDA .45*** – .45 ACP cal., 3 in. barrel with three dot sights, 6 shot mag., alloy frame with stainless/Covert Black finish. Mfg. 2008-2011.

	$1,150	$995	$850	$775	$625	$500	$395	*$1,299*

* ***CCO*** – .45 ACP cal., 7 shot mag., 3 1/2 in. barrel, 3-dot sights, stainless steel construction, brushed stainless finish, 32 oz. Disc. 2008.

	$1,000	$875	$750	$680	$550	$450	$350	*$1,129*

* ***CCW*** – similar to CCO model, except has 4 1/4 in. barrel, 34 oz. Disc. 2008.

	$1,000	$875	$750	$680	$550	$450	$350	*$1,129*

* ***Companion*** – .45 ACP cal., 3 1/2 in. barrel, 7 shot mag., stainless steel frame, LDA trigger system, black finish, fiber optic front sight, 2-dot rear sight. New 2011.

MSR $999	$895	$775	$650	$595	$475	$395	$300	

GRADING - PPGS™	100%	98%	95%	90%	80%	70%	60%	LAST MSR

* ***Companion II*** – .45 ACP cal., 4 1/4 in. barrel, 8 shot mag., stainless steel frame, black finish, fiber optic sight, single stack, DA trigger system, gold trigger, checkered wood grips with gold Para logo, includes two mags. Mfg. 2011.

$750	$650	$525	$425	$375	$325	$295	*$899*

PXT LDA SINGLE STACK – .45 ACP cal., DAO, non-carry option models, spurless flush hammer, various configurations and barrel lengths.

* ***CCO Companion Black Watch*** – .45 ACP cal., 7 shot mag., 3 1/2 in. barrel, 3-dot sights, stainless steel construction, Black Watch finish, 32 oz.

$975	$855	$730	$665	$535	$440	$340	*$1,099*

* ***Tac-S*** – .45 ACP cal., 8 shot mag., 4 1/4 in. barrel, 3-dot sights, steel frame, Spec Ops finish, 35 oz.

$865	$755	$650	$590	$475	$390	$305	*$999*

* ***LDA SSP*** – .45 ACP cal., 8 shot mag., 5 in. barrel, 3-dot sights, stainless steel construction, brushed stainless finish, 39 oz. Disc. 2009.

$1,025	$895	$770	$695	$565	$460	$360	*$1,149*

* ***Covert Black Nite-Tac SS*** – .45 ACP cal., 8 shot mag., 5 in. barrel, 3-dot sights, stainless steel construction, Covert Black finish, includes light rail, checkered wood grips, 40 oz. Mfg. 2006-2007.

$1,000	$875	$750	$650	$550	$450	$375	*$1,125*

* ***Nite-Tac SS*** – .45 ACP cal., 8 shot mag., 5 in. barrel, 3-dot sights, stainless steel construction, brushed stainless finish, includes light rail, checkered wood grips, 40 oz. Mfg. 2006-2007.

$1,000	$875	$750	$650	$550	$450	$375	*$1,125*

* ***PXT LDA Limited*** – .45 ACP cal., DAO, single stack 7 shot mag., steel or stainless steel, 5 in. barrel.

$935	$800	$700	$600	$500	$400	$350	*$1,035*

Add $75 for stainless steel.

PXT LDA HIGH CAPACITY (CARRY OPTION SERIES) – 9mm Para., .40 S&W, or .45 ACP cal., spurless flush hammer, rounded grip safety, various options, barrel lengths and magazine capacity.

* ***Carry 12*** – .45 ACP cal., 12 shot mag., 3 1/2 in. barrel, low mount 3-dot tritium night sights, stainless steel construction, black synthetic grips, brushed stainless finish, 34 oz.

$1,050	$920	$785	$715	$575	$470	$365	*$1,199*

* ***Tac-Four*** – .45 ACP cal., 13 shot mag., 4 1/4 in. barrel, 3-dot sights, stainless steel construction, black synthetic grips, brushed stainless finish, 36 oz.

$960	$840	$735	$625	$525	$425	$350	*$1,099*

* ***Tac-Forty*** – .40 S&W cal., 15 shot mag., 4 1/4 in. barrel, 3-dot sights, stainless steel construction, black synthetic grips, brushed stainless finish, 36 oz. Mfg. 2007.

$925	$825	$725	$625	$525	$425	$350	*$1,049*

* ***Tac-Five*** – 9mm Para cal., 18 shot mag., 5 in. barrel, Novak adj. sights, stainless steel construction, black synthetic grips, Covert Black finish, 37 1/2 oz. Mfg. 2007.

$1,050	$920	$785	$715	$575	$470	$365	*$1,185*

This model was also available in a limited edition "Canadian Forces" model with a maple leaf on the slide.

PXT LDA HIGH CAPACITY SERIES – .45 ACP cal., DAO, 14 shot mag., 5 in. barrel, 3-dot sights, steel or stainless steel construction, spurless flush hammer, Covert Black finish or stainless steel.

* ***Covert Black Hi-Cap .45*** – steel frame, Covert Black finish. Disc. 2008.

$950	$830	$710	$645	$520	$425	$330	*$1,099*

GRADING - PPGS™	100%	98%	95%	90%	80%	70%	60%	LAST MSR

* ***Hi-Cap .45*** – stainless steel construction, brushed stainless finish. Disc. 2008.

	$955	$840	$730	$625	$525	$425	$350	*$1,099*

* ***Covert Black Nite-Tac .45*** – steel frame, Covert Black finish, includes light rail. Mfg. 2006-2008.

	$955	$840	$730	$625	$525	$425	$350	*$1,099*

* ***Coyote Brown Nite-Tac .45*** – .45 ACP cal., similar to Covert Black Nite-Tac, except has adj. fiber optic sights and Coyote Brown finish.

	$1,175	$1,030	$880	$800	$645	$530	$410	*$1,349*

* ***Nite-Tac .45*** – stainless steel construction, brushed stainless finish, includes light rail. Mfg. 2006-2008.

	$1,025	$900	$775	$650	$550	$450	$350	*$1,199*

* ***Hi-Cap Limited .45*** – adj. sights, stainless steel construction, Sterling finish. Disc. 2009.

	$1,075	$940	$805	$730	$590	$485	$375	*$1,279*

* ***Colonel*** – .45 ACP cal., 4 1/4 in. ramped barrel, low mount white 3-dot fixed sights, steel frame, 10 or 14 shot mag., spur competition hammer, LDA trigger, black polymer grips with medallions, green spec. ops. finish, 37 oz. Mfg. 2005-2006.

	$795	$695	$595	$540	$435	$360	$280	*$899*

PXT LDA HIGH CAPACITY LIMITED – 9mm Para., .40 S&W, or .45 ACP cal., DAO, 10, 14, 16, or 18 shot mag., steel or stainless steel, 5 in. barrel. Disc. 2006.

	$935	$800	$700	$600	$500	$400	$350	*$1,035*

Add $75 for stainless steel.

PXT LTC HIGH CAPACITY – .45 ACP cal., 4 1/4 in. barrel, 10 or 14 shot mag., 3-dot fixed sights, stainless steel frame, match grade trigger, black polymer grips with medallions, green spec. ops. finish, three safeties, 37 oz. Mfg. 2005-2006.

	$750	$655	$560	$510	$410	$335	$260	*$855*

S SERIES MODELS – .40 S&W or .45 ACP cal., single action, 3 1/2, 4 1/4, or 5 in. barrel, 10 shot mag., matte black (5 in. barrel only) or stainless steel finish.

* ***S Series Model S10 Limited*** – similar to P10, except has competition shooting features, including beavertail grip safety, competition hammer, tuned trigger, match grade barrel, front slide serrations, choice of steel or alloy frame with matte black finish or stainless steel, 40 oz. Mfg. 1999-2002.

	$765	$670	$575	$520	$420	$345	$270	*$865*

Add $10 for steel receiver.
Add $24 for stainless steel.

* ***S Series Model S12 Limited*** – .40 S&W (disc. 2002) or .45 ACP cal., similar to P12, except has competition shooting features, including beavertail grip safety, competition hammer, tuned trigger, match grade barrel, front slide serrations, choice of steel or alloy (disc. 2002) frame, matte black (disc. 2002) or stainless steel finish, 40 oz. Mfg. 1999-2003.

	$895	$785	$670	$610	$490	$405	$315	*$1,049*

Subtract 10% for steel frame (disc. 2002).

* ***S Series Model S13 Limited*** – .40 S&W (disc. 2002) or .45 ACP cal., similar to P13, except has competition shooting features, including beavertail grip safety, competition hammer, tuned trigger, match grade barrel, front slide serrations, choice of steel or alloy (disc. 2002) frame, matte black (disc. 2002) or stainless steel finish, 40 oz. Mfg. 1999-2003.

	$895	$785	$670	$610	$490	$405	$315	*$1,049*

* ***S Series Model S14 Limited*** – .40 S&W (disc. 2002) or .45 ACP cal., similar to P14, except has competition shooting features, including beavertail grip safety, competition hammer, tuned trigger, match grade barrel, front slide serrations, matte black or stainless steel, 40 oz. Mfg. 1998-2003.

	$850	$745	$635	$580	$465	$380	$295	*$989*

Add $60 for stainless steel.

GRADING - PPGS™	100%	98%	95%	90%	80%	70%	60%	LAST MSR

* ***S Series Model S16 Limited*** – .40 S&W cal., similar to P16, except has 5 in. barrel and competition shooting features, including beavertail grip safety, competition hammer, tuned trigger, match grade barrel, front slide serrations, matte black steel or stainless steel, 40 oz. Mfg. 1998-2003.

	$850	$745	$635	$580	$465	$380	$295	*$989*

Add $60 for stainless steel.

T SERIES MODELS – 9mm Para., .40 S&W (stainless steel only), or .45 ACP cal., DAO, 5 in. barrel, 7 (.45 ACP cal. only, single stack mag.) or 10 shot mag., steel or stainless steel, matte black finish or stainless steel. Mfg. 2003.

	$825	$720	$620	$560	$455	$370	$290	*$1,009*

Add $80 for stainless steel.

RIFLES: SEMI-AUTO

TTR SERIES – .223 Rem. cal., paramilitary design, 16 1/2 in. chrome lined barrel, DIGS (delayed impingement gas system) operation, 30 shot mag., flip up front sight and adj. flip up rear sight, flattop receiver with full length Picatinny rail, black finish, single stage trigger, available in Short Rail with fixed stock (TTR-XASF, mfg. 2009), or 5 position folding stock with Short Rail (TTR-XAS), Long Rail (TTR-XA), and Nylatron (TTR-XN, mfg. 2009) forearm configurations. Mfg. 2009-late 2011.

	$2,050	$1,800	$1,575	$1,350	$1,150	$975	$825	*$2,397*

Add $100 for Nylatron forearm (mfg. 2009).

PARDINI, ARMI S.r.l.

Current manufacturer located in Lido di Camaiore, Italy. Currently imported by Pardini USA, LLC beginning 2012 located in Tampa, FL. Previously imported until 2012 by Larry's Guns, located in Gray, ME. Previously imported until 2004 by Nygord Precision Products located in Prescott, AZ, and distributed until 1996 by Mo's Competitor Supplies & Range, Inc. located in Brookfield, CT, and until 1990 by Fiocchi of America, Inc., located in Ozark, MO.

For more information and current pricing on both new and used Pardini airguns, please refer to the *Blue Book of Airguns* by Dr. Robert Beeman & John Allen (also online).

PISTOLS: SEMI-AUTO

PC45 – .40 S&W, .45 ACP, or 9x21mm cal., single action mechanism designed for stock competition category, adj. trigger pull. Limited importation by Nygord 2000-2004.

	$1,295	$1,050	$840	$715	$575	$500	$440

Add $75 for 6 in. barrel and slide.

* ***PC45S*** – similar to PC, except has compensator and scope mount with optical sight.

	$1,500	$1,250	$1,100	$950	$850	$725	$600

* ***PCS-Open*** – similar to PCS, except w/o scope and frame mount, top-of-the-line semi-auto.

	$1,650	$1,400	$1,250	$1,100	$950	$850	$725

GT9/PC40/GT45 DEFENSE/SPORT – 9mm Para., 9x21mm (disc. 2011), .40 S&W, or .45 ACP cal. 5 or 6 in. barrel, single action, diamond wood grips, matte silver, 13 or 17 (9x21mm) shot mag., black, silver, bronze, or two-tone finish. Importation began late 2004.

MSR $1,999	$1,850	$1,625	$1,300	$1,050	$875	$775	$650

Add $150 for 6 in. barrel.
Add $100 for silver or bronze finish.
Add $50 for .40 S&W or .45 ACP cal.
Add $95 for 6 in. barrel and slide (disc.).
Add $500 for titanium finish in 9mm Para. cal. with 6 in. barrel only.
Add $999 for 9mm Para. or .40 S&W cal. conversion kit for GT45 Model.
Add $230 for GT45S Model with compensator in silver finish (disc. 2011).

GRADING - PPGS™	100%	98%	95%	90%	80%	70%	60%	LAST MSR

* **GT9/GT40 Defense Sport Inox** – 9mm Para. or .40 S&W (IPSC) cal., features 5 or 6 in. stainless steel barrel.

MSR $3,400	$3,150	$2,675	$2,300	$2,000	$1,650	$1,350	$1,250	

Add $800 for 5 in. barrel and 9mm Para. cal. or $1,100 for 9mm Para. cal. with 6 in. barrel.

PISTOLS: TARGET

Pardini pistols have always been known for their technological improvements developed from ongoing design research. During 1991, the entire Pardini pistol line was modified both internally and externally to improve function and reliability - these changes included the addition of grooves on the barrel shroud to accept scope mounts directly.

MODEL SP/MODEL SP NEW (STANDARD PISTOL) – .22 LR cal. only, semi-auto, target grips, adj. sights, 4.92 in. barrel, interchangeable grips, 5 shot detachable mag., SP features mechanical trigger, SP New features second generation electronic trigger, approx. 2.4 lbs. New 1991.

MSR $1,849	$1,675	$1,395	$1,275	$1,000	$875	$775	$650	

Add $300 for SP Rapid Fire.
Add $145 for SP Master Model (disc.).
Subtract approx. 10% for SP model with mechanical trigger.

MODEL SP1 – .22 LR cal., semi-auto, features electronic trigger, blue/silver two-tone finish, adj. anatomic target wood grips, includes six tungsten weights. New 2005.

MSR $2,249	$1,925	$1,750	$1,550	$1,350	$1,150	$1,000	$900	

MODEL SP1/SP1 NEW RAPID FIRE – .22 LR cal., semi-auto, similar to Model SP1, SP1 has second generation electronic trigger, SP1 New has mechanical trigger, developed for rapid fire discipline, includes six tungsten weights. New 2005.

MSR $2,569	$2,250	$1,925	$1,725	$1,500	$1,250	$1,000	$850	

LADIES PISTOL – similar to Model SP, except grips are suitable for smaller hands. Importation disc. 1999.

	$850	$700	$600	$520	$460	$410	$380	*$995*

MODEL GP/GP E (RAPID FIRE PISTOL) – .22 Short cal., semi-auto, features enclosed style grip assembly, adj. sights, choice of electronic (GP E, new 2004) or mechanical (GP) trigger, 5.12 in. barrel. Imported 1991-2004.

	$1,425	$1,250	$1,050	$875	$775	$675	$575	

Add $500 for "Schumann" Model (wraparound grip, special muzzle ports, sights, weights, etc.).

MODEL HP/HP E/HP NEW (CENTERFIRE PISTOL) – .32 S&W Wadcutter or .32 ACP (new 2012) cal., semi-auto, similar to Model SP Pistol, 4.92 in. barrel, beginning 2004, HP has second generation electronic trigger, HP E has electronic trigger, HP New has mechanical trigger, 5 shot mag., includes 4 (HP) or 6 (HP E & HP New) weights. New 1991.

MSR $2,099	$1,850	$1,600	$1,325	$1,125	$900	$800	$700	

Add $50 for .32 ACP cal. (new 2012).
Add $350 for HP E model with electronic trigger.
Add $999 for .22 LR cal. conversion kit (new 2012).

MODEL K22 – .22 LR cal., top-of-the-line single shot target pistol, 11.8 in. barrel, mechanical trigger, toggle bolt pushes cartridge into chamber, unique ventilated front sight assembly that also supports counterweights, cocking lever action, 38 1/2 oz. Imported 2000-2008.

	$1,770	$1,475	$1,250	$1,050	$875	$775	$675	*$1,899*

MODEL K50 (FREE PISTOL) – .22 LR cal., single shot, sliding rotating bolt, 9.06 in. barrel, tilted anatomical grip, top-of-the-line match pistol. Mfg. 1991-99.

	$925	$750	$600	$500	$450	$420	$395	*$1,050*

PARDINI/NYGORD MASTER – .22 LR cal., designed for NRA bullseye shooting, micrometer rear sight and small Adco red-dot sight, anatomical target grips. Imported 2000-2004.

	$1,325	$1,145	$875	$750	$650	$550	$450	

GRADING - PPGS™	100%	98%	95%	90%	80%	70%	60%	LAST MSR

FPM/FPE FREE PISTOL – .22 LR cal., single shot, 11 in. barrel with elevated front sight designed by Buck Rogers, compensator, with (FPE) or w/o (FPM) electronic trigger, 2 1/2 lbs. Importation began 2009.

MSR $2,099	$1,950	$1,775	$1,550	$1,325	$1,100	$950	$800	

Add $280 for electronic trigger (FPE Model).

PARDUS

Current manufacturer located in Istanbul, Turkey. No current U.S. importation.

SHOTGUNS

Pardus manufactures a complete line of good quality O/U, SxS, semi-auto, slide action and single shot shotguns, in addition to air rifles. Currently these guns are not being imported into the U.S. Please contact the company directly for more information, including pricing and availability (see Trademark Index).

PARKER BROS. MAKERS

Current manufacturer established 1999 and located in Meriden, CT.

SHOTGUNS: O/U

Parker Bros. Makers manufactures an O/U shotgun in 12 ga. Six grades are offered, and the most recent MSRs are as follows: Invincible ($125,000), A-1 Special ($90,000), AA ($65,000), B ($37,500), C ($24,500), and PA ($18,500). Although advertised beginning in 1999, very few shotguns have been manufactured to date.

PARKER BROTHERS

Previously manufactured in Meriden, CT from 1866-1934. Remington took over production in 1934, and in 1938, the plant was moved to Ilion, NY. Over 4,500 "Transition Guns" (exhibiting Meriden and Ilion characteristics) were produced in Meriden between 1934-1937 and about 1,600 Parkers were manufactured at the Ilion location before production stopped circa 1942. Total production reached approx. 242,487.

During 2006, Remington Arms Co. announced the release of a new AAHE 28 ga. Parker, manufactured in the U.S. by Connecticut Shotgun Co.

95% of the original Parkers bought and sold each year are in 30% or less condition (referring to original case colors). Percentages on following pages refer to the amount of original case colors remaining on frame.

Parker Gun Identification & Serialization was published in late 2002, and has been reprinted due to popular demand. Compiled by using records from *The Parker Story, Vols. I & II*, this title features more than 100 detailed images allowing easy visual identification on the grades, frame sizes, and other important information. Additionally, listings on over 155,000 serial numbers are provided, specifying the original configuration, including grade, action type, extra features, stock configuration, gauge, and barrel length - an invaluable asset when determining original configuration on most Parkers Brothers shotguns. The author wishes to especially thank Mr. William Mullins, in addition to Charles Price, Roy Gunther, Louis C. Parker III, and Daniel Cote for sharing the following Parker production statistics with this publication.

SHOTGUNS: MISC. FACTS

Values listed in the 95%-100% condition columns can vary a lot as there is very little supply and strong demand for these high condition "cream puffs."

Note: Values are for guns without ejectors, unless otherwise indicated. An "E" suffix indicates ejectors. Skeet models with ejectors, beavertail forearm, and single selective trigger are valued at approx. 50%-75% higher than values shown. Higher grade Parkers typically had ejectors, and ejectors typically add 25%-30% value to a Parker in all grades. Also, lower condition, high grade models sometimes have their values established by the potential gain in refurbishing these specimens. Remember, it only costs a few hundred dollars more to refinish an A1 Special compared a VH Grade.

Due to the extremely high value of Parker Guns, extreme care should be taken in their purchase. There are many upgraded and refinished guns represented as original; expert advice should always be sought. Many collectors would rather own a specimen with 30% original case colors than a refinished gun that is 100% (regardless who did the work). Many advanced collectors will discount a refinished Parker's value 40%-60% off the price for an original gun. Misrepresentation of refinished or upgraded Parkers is rampant today - especially case colors. Also, beware of fake boxes and hanging tags - if the box and Parker shotgun are an original "pair," the value is enhanced tremendously. If the box/hanging tag is fake, you could pay as much as $1,500 to learn this lesson! In other words, do your homework, be careful, shop carefully, and above all, get a receipt for exactly what it is that you are purchasing.

Frame size on Parker shotguns is determined by the number on the bottom of the rear barrel lug on breech. Frame sizes (from largest to smallest) include 7, 6, 5, 4, 3, 2, 1 1/2, 1, 1/2, 0, 00, and 000. 8 ga. guns typically are framed 6 or 7. 10 ga. guns typically are 3 or 4. 12 ga. guns typically range from 2 through 1 (more desirable). "1/2" frame 12 ga. guns are very rare and desirable. 20 and 16 gauges range from 2 through 0 (more desirable, rare in 16 ga.). 28 ga. guns are either 0 or 00 (more desirable and approx. 50% more). .410 bore shotguns are 00 or 000 (most common and most desirable). 8 and 10 ga. steel barreled shotguns are very rare, and prices can equal .410 bore values if the original condition is there. Factory original 10 ga., 3 1/2 in. Mag. guns command premium prices, as very few were made and they are extremely rare. These guns are stamped "For 3 1/2 shells" on the barrel lug and are late serial numbered (240,000 range).

The grade on Parker shotguns is a number or initials located on the water table of the frame. An alphabetical designation would indicate the grade immediately. For numerals, a "2" would indicate a GH, while an "8" would specify an A-1 Special - interpolate for the others (numbers 3 through 7). Parker shotguns manufactured by Remington will have date codes stamped on left barrel flat that correspond to the month and the year (see Remington serialization in the Serialization Section). Also, if a Parker gun was returned to Remington for repair, alteration, or refinishing, it will usually have the date code stamped with a suffix of 3 (i.e., OK3 represents some type of rework completed in either July of 1941 or 1963). There is some ambiguity with the year as the year codes repeat.

Skeleton buttplates were furnished as standard on Parker guns starting with Grade 3 or on D and higher grades over most of the years of production. They were perhaps an option on the lower grades at times, and no doubt a customer could have ordered one as a special option on a lower grade for additional cost. Since skeleton buttplates were standard on the D Grades and above, they should not be considered an added value on these grades. And even if present on lower grades, if you cannot prove factory originality, a skeleton buttplate will not add any value.

A note about Parker condition: Percentages of condition indicate the amount of original case colors remaining on the frame, but sometimes these colors are faded and the rest of the gun is excellent - hence, all the separate condition factors must be considered when determining overall condition.

A Parker IS NOT 60% if the barrel bluing and stock/forearm varnish are 60% but case colors are only 10%. Typically, a 60% case color Parker shotgun will have 90%+ blue and varnish, yet this does not mean the gun is 90% overall. Similarly, a 20% case color Parker will probably have 90% barrel bluing remaining. Strong, original case colors are the key in determining Parker condition and subsequent values. However, for shotguns under 30% condition, the overall condition of the gun should determine value.

Collectors also place value on the screws on the receiver being aligned as they left the factory and not tampered with.

The Parker Story, Vol. I was published in late 1998. This book has production statistics derived from factory records, and the quantities manufactured listed in this text for steel-barreled hammerless Parker guns are taken from this book. This publication also has more detailed production statistics on Parker guns produced from 1869-1942, including a breakdown by action type (lifter, top lever, and hammerless), grade, barrel steel, gauge, and barrel length. Some grades, gauges, etc., are fewer in number than previously estimated. All the grades are pictured in color,

100%	98%	95%	90%	80%	70%	60%	50%	40%	30%	20%	10%

including the Invincible. Parker Reproductions are also covered in detail, including production statistics. *Vol. II* was published in late 2000.

The Parker Gun Collectors Association can also provide research letters on certain Parkers. Please refer to their listing under Firearms Organizations in the back of this text for contact information.

SHOTGUNS: SxS, DAMASCUS BARRELS & PRICING

Parker damascus barreled shotguns (hammer or hammerless) are very collectible if original condition is over 40%. Specimens in 80% or better condition with strong case colors can approximate values of the steel barrel models if the bores are in excellent condition (no pitting). Values for under 40% specimens fall off rapidly and are no longer comparable to steel barrel guns. As an example, a 12 ga. steel "D" Grade (without ejectors) has a price range from $2,750 to $9,000 (10%-100%) with a rather even downward progression of values in between the high and low ranges. A 100% damascus hammer "D" Grade could have a $15,000-$18,000 price tag hanging from the trigger guard, while a 5%-15% condition specimen is typically seen priced in the $2,000-$3,000 range. A truly 95%-100% original damascus barreled, hammer Parker is more rare and desirable than a similar grade damascus hammerless Parker or a steel barreled hammerless Parker. Remember, the guns are not rare but their condition is.

Due to articles in a national firearms quarterly publication discussing the "shootability" of damascus barreled guns (Parker and other major manufacturers), and the positive results obtained, there has been a renewed interest in these guns. Prices have increased accordingly, and in some instances values for high condition guns have exceeded their steel barreled counterparts.

SHOTGUNS: SxS, FLUID STEEL BARREL MODELS & PRICING

The desirability of older Parker shotguns in today's marketplace can be greatly enhanced if the stock dimensions fit today's potential owner (typically 13 1/2 in. - 14 1/2 in. LOP), adding value due to the shootability.

Add 20% for SST.
Add 20% for beavertail forearm.
Add 40%-50% for VR (rare on smaller gauges).
Add 20% for straight English stock.
Add 20% for original skeleton steel buttplate (standard on Grade D/3 and higher).
Add 20% for short barrels (26 in. with open chokes) on 12 ga.
Add 20% for 30 or 32 in. barrels on 28 ga.
Add 50% for 28 or 30 in. barrels on .410 ga.

TROJAN – Parker's lowest-priced gun, single or double triggers, but no auto ejectors available, very rarely found in mint condition because they were used a lot, a genuine utility gun, introduced 1912-13 with approx. 33,000 total mfg.

100%	98%	95%	90%	80%	70%	60%	50%	40%	30%	20%	10%
*** Trojan 12 ga.**											
N/A	N/A	$4,000	$3,500	$3,000	$2,700	$2,200	$1,800	$1,500	$1,250	$1,000	$750
*** Trojan 16 ga.**											
N/A	N/A	$4,700	$4,200	$3,500	$3,200	$2,700	$2,200	$1,800	$1,500	$1,200	$1,000
*** Trojan 20 ga.**											
N/A	N/A	$5,200	$4,800	$4,300	$4,000	$3,500	$3,000	$2,600	$2,000	$1,800	$1,400

VH – Parker's biggest selling model, offered with all options, the most commonly found Parker. Approx. 79,000 mfg. 10 ga. is very rare in this model.

Add 25%-30% for ejectors, depending on original condition (VHE Model).

100%	98%	95%	90%	80%	70%	60%	50%	40%	30%	20%	10%
*** VH 12 ga.**											
N/A	N/A	$4,700	$4,300	$4,000	$3,750	$3,200	$3,000	$2,500	$2,250	$2,000	$1,500
*** VH 16 ga.**											
N/A	N/A	$5,200	$4,800	$4,200	$4,000	$3,750	$3,500	$3,000	$2,500	$2,250	$2,000

100%	98%	95%	90%	80%	70%	60%	50%	40%	30%	20%	10%
*** VH 20 ga.**											
N/A	N/A	$8,000	$7,500	$7,200	$6,500	$5,000	$4,500	$4,000	$3,500	$3,000	$2,750
*** VH 28 ga.**											
N/A	N/A	$25,000	$22,000	$18,000	$16,000	$14,000	$12,000	$10,000	$8,000	$7,000	$6,500
*** VH .410 bore.**											
N/A	N/A	$32,500	$27,500	$22,500	$20,000	$16,500	$15,000	$13,000	$11,000	$10,000	$9,000

PH – offered for a very short time, most had twist barrels, prices here are for fluid steel barrels only. Approx. 1,400 mfg. A very few .410 bores were mfg. 10 ga. with fluid steel barrels is very rare in this model.

Add 25%-30% for ejectors, depending on original condition (PHE Model).

100%	98%	95%	90%	80%	70%	60%	50%	40%	30%	20%	10%
*** PH 12 ga.**											
N/A	N/A	$6,000	$5,500	$5,000	$4,500	$4,000	$3,750	$3,000	$2,500	$2,250	$1,700
*** PH 16 ga.**											
N/A	N/A	$6,500	$6,000	$5,500	$5,000	$4,500	$4,000	$3,500	$3,000	$2,500	$2,200
*** PH 20 ga.**											
N/A	N/A	$10,000	$9,500	$8,500	$8,000	$7,500	$6,500	$6,000	$5,500	$4,500	$3,750

*** PH 28 ga. & .410 bore**

Extreme rarity precludes accurate pricing on this model.

GH – very popular model, barrels marked "Parker Special Steel", engraved moderately with all options available. 10 ga. with fluid steel barrels is very rare in this model, approx. 4,300 mfg.

Add 25%-30% for ejectors, depending on original condition (GHE Model).

100%	98%	95%	90%	80%	70%	60%	50%	40%	30%	20%	10%
*** GH 12 ga.**											
N/A	N/A	$7,000	$6,500	$6,000	$5,500	$5,000	$4,500	$4,000	$3,000	$2,750	$2,450
*** GH 16 ga.**											
N/A	N/A	$8,000	$7,500	$7,000	$6,500	$6,000	$5,500	$4,500	$3,500	$3,250	$2,500
*** GH 20 ga.**											
N/A	N/A	$12,000	$11,000	$10,000	$9,000	$8,000	$7,500	$7,000	$6,000	$5,500	$4,500
*** GH 28 ga.**											
N/A	N/A	$33,000	$28,000	$23,000	$21,000	$17,500	$15,000	$12,000	$10,000	$8,500	$7,500
*** GH .410 bore**											
N/A	N/A	$45,000	$40,000	$37,000	$35,000	$30,000	$25,000	$20,000	$18,000	$16,000	$15,000

DH – the most popular higher grade gun, very tastefully engraved and flawlessly finished, approx. 9,400 mfg.

Add 25%-30% for ejectors, depending on original condition (DHE Model).

100%	98%	95%	90%	80%	70%	60%	50%	40%	30%	20%	10%
*** DH 12 ga.**											
N/A	N/A	$8,500	$8,000	$7,000	$6,500	$6,000	$5,500	$5,000	$4,000	$3,500	$2,750
*** DH 16 ga.**											
N/A	N/A	$9,000	$8,500	$7,500	$7,000	$6,500	$6,000	$5,500	$4,500	$4,000	$3,250
*** DH 20 ga.**											
N/A	N/A	$14,500	$13,000	$12,000	$11,000	$10,000	$9,000	$8,000	$7,000	$6,000	$5,500
*** DH 28 ga.**											
N/A	N/A	$42,000	$37,750	$32,000	$27,250	$23,000	$20,000	$18,000	$16,000	$14,000	$12,000
*** DH .410 bore**											
N/A	N/A	$70,000	$65,000	$55,000	$50,000	$45,000	$40,000	$35,000	$30,000	$25,000	$20,000

CH – scarce because they were only slightly more decorative than the DH, Acme steel barrels. Approx. 1,100 mfg. 10 ga. is very rare in this model.

Add 25%-30% for ejectors, depending on original condition (CHE Model).

100%	98%	95%	90%	80%	70%	60%	50%	40%	30%	20%	10%

*** *CH 12 ga.***

N/A	N/A	$16,000	$15,000	$13,750	$11,750	$10,000	$9,000	$8,500	$7,500	$7,000	$6,500

*** *CH 16 ga.***

N/A	N/A	$19,000	$18,000	$15,000	$13,500	$12,000	$11,000	$9,500	$8,500	$7,500	$7,000

*** *CH 20 ga.***

N/A	N/A	$24,000	$23,000	$20,000	$19,000	$18,000	$16,000	$13,000	$11,000	$10,000	$9,000

*** *CH 28 ga.***

N/A	N/A	$70,000	$65,000	$55,000	$50,000	$45,000	$40,000	$35,000	$30,000	$25,000	$20,000

*** *CH .410 bore*** – very rare, approx. 6 are known to exist.

This model/gauge is very rare, and prices typically start in the $50,000-$100,000 range, depending on original condition.

BH – quite popular and decorative, 4 styles of engraving available, Acme steel barrels. Approx. 700 mfg. 10 ga. is very rare in this model.

Add 25%-50% for ejectors, depending on original condition (BHE Model).

*** *BH 12 ga.***

N/A	N/A	$25,000	$22,000	$20,000	$18,000	$17,000	$16,000	$13,000	$11,000	$9,000	$8,000

*** *BH 16 ga.***

N/A	N/A	$28,000	$26,000	$24,000	$21,000	$19,000	$18,000	$15,000	$12,000	$10,000	$9,000

*** *BH 20 ga.***

N/A	N/A	$35,000	$32,000	$28,000	$25,000	$22,000	$20,000	$18,000	$15,000	$12,500	$11,000

*** *BH 28 ga.***

N/A	N/A	N/A	$90,000	$80,000	$70,000	$60,000	$50,000	$48,000	$45,000	$40,000	$35,000

*** *BH .410 bore*** – only 2 guns are known in this grade.

Extreme rarity precludes accurate price evaluation, but will be VERY expensive.

AH – a scarce gun, extremely decorative and flawlessly executed, Acme steel barrels. Approx. 300 mfg. 10 ga. is very rare in this model.

Add 25%-50% for ejectors, depending on original condition (AHE Model).

*** *AH 12 ga.***

N/A	N/A	$40,000	$37,000	$35,000	$32,000	$30,000	$28,000	$25,000	$22,000	$20,000	$18,000

*** *AH 16 ga.***

N/A	N/A	$50,000	$47,000	$45,000	$37,500	$35,000	$33,000	$30,000	$28,000	$25,000	$23,000

*** *AH 20 ga.***

N/A	N/A	$65,000	$62,000	$60,000	$55,000	$50,000	$45,000	$40,000	$37,000	$35,000	$32,000

*** *AH 28 ga.***

N/A	N/A	N/A	$105,000	$95,000	$85,000	$75,000	$70,000	$60,000	$55,000	$50,000	$45,000

*** *AH .410 bore*** – it is believed that only one gun was manufactured.

Rarity precludes accurate pricing.

AAH – very elaborate model, early AAs have Whitworth barrels, late ones have Peerless. Approx. 240 mfg.

Add 25%-50% for ejectors, depending on original condition (AAHE Model).

*** *AAH 12 ga.***

N/A	N/A	$65,000	$60,000	$55,000	$50,000	$45,000	$42,500	$40,000	$35,000	$33,000	$30,000

*** *AAH 16 ga.***

N/A	N/A	$80,000	$75,000	$70,000	$60,000	$55,000	$50,000	$48,000	$45,500	$40,000	$35,000

*** *AAH 20 ga.***

N/A	N/A	$90,000	$85,000	$80,000	$75,000	$72,000	$68,000	$65,000	$60,000	$55,000	$50,000

*** AAH 28 ga.**

100%	98%	95%	90%	80%	70%	60%	50%	40%	30%	20%	10%
N/A	N/A	N/A	$125,000	$120,000	$112,000	$105,000	$100,000	$90,000	$85,000	$80,000	$75,000

AAHE (NEW MFG.) – 28 ga., available through Remington Arms Co., and made by Connecticut Shotgun, serialization continues from the last of the Parker Bros. production, limited availability beginning 2006.

The current MSR on this model is $49,000.

A-1 SPECIAL GRADE – 100% engraved, all were special ordered, each one inspected by the company president before being shipped. Approx. 80 mfg.

*** A-1 Special Grade 12 ga.**

100%	98%	95%	90%	80%	70%	60%	50%	40%	30%	20%	10%
N/A	N/A	$80,000	$75,000	$70,000	$65,000	$60,000	$55,000	$50,000	$45,000	$40,000	$35,000

*** A-1 Special Grade 16 ga.**

100%	98%	95%	90%	80%	70%	60%	50%	40%	30%	20%	10%
N/A	N/A	$110,000	$105,000	$100,000	$95,000	$90,000	$80,000	$75,000	$70,000	$60,000	$55,000

*** A-1 Special Grade 20 ga.**

100%	98%	95%	90%	80%	70%	60%	50%	40%	30%	20%	10%
N/A	N/A	N/A	$150,000	$145,000	$140,000	$130,000	$120,000	$115,000	$110,000	$100,000	$90,000

*** A-1 Special Grade 28 ga.** – extreme rarity and desirability factors preclude accurate price evaluation by condition factors. 70% original condition A-1 Specials HAVE sold for up to $200,000.

INVINCIBLE GRADE – only 3 documented mfg. $1,250 MSR circa 1930, extreme rarity and desirability factors preclude accurate price evaluation on this model. Currently, all three guns are on loan to the National Firearms Museum in Fairfax, VA.

SHOTGUNS: SINGLE BARREL TRAP

12 or 20 (rare) ga., 26 (20 ga. only, rare), 28 (very rare), 30 (rare), 32, or 34 (rare) in. barrels, any boring was available, as was stock configuration, boxlock, auto ejector. The grades differ only in engraving, checkering and wood finish.

It should be noted that single barrel trap guns cannot be compared to the SxS models, as they are not as desirable, even though they are more rare. Approximately 1,900 Parker single barrel trap guns were manufactured, mostly in SC Grade. Most SxS collectors are not that interested in single barrel trap models and very few collectors specialize in single barrels.

Add 15% for 30 or 34 in. barrel.

S.C. GRADE

100%	98%	95%	90%	80%	70%	60%	50%	40%	30%	20%	10%
N/A	N/A	$8,500	$8,000	$7,000	$6,000	$5,000	$4,000	$3,000	$2,500	$2,250	$2,000

S.B. GRADE

100%	98%	95%	90%	80%	70%	60%	50%	40%	30%	20%	10%
N/A	N/A	$10,500	$10,000	$9,000	$8,000	$7,000	$6,000	$5,000	$4,500	$3,800	$2,800

S.A. GRADE

100%	98%	95%	90%	80%	70%	60%	50%	40%	30%	20%	10%
N/A	N/A	$14,500	$14,000	$13,000	$12,000	$11,000	$10,000	$9,000	$8,500	$7,500	$6,500

S.A.A. GRADE

Extreme rarity (research indicates only one manufactured) precludes accurate pricing.

S.A.-1 SPECIAL GRADE

Extreme rarity (research indicates only four manufactured) precludes accurate pricing. One known 100% example sold in the $30,000 - $40,000 range.

PARKER GUNMAKERS

Current division of Remington, established in 2006.

28 ga. AAHE Parker guns are manufactured by Connecticut Shotgun Manufacturing Company, located in New Britain, CT. Prices begin at $49,000 and go up depending on customer specifications. Please contact the company directly for a price quotation and list of available options. Current delivery time is approx. 12 months (see Trademark Index).

PARKER PISTOLS

Refer to the Wyoming Arms listing in the W section.

GRADING - PPGS™	100%	98%	95%	90%	80%	70%	60%	LAST MSR

PARKER REPRODUCTIONS

Previously imported by the Parker Reproduction Division of Reagent Chemical & Research, Inc., located in Middlesex, NJ. Previously distributed by Parker

Reproductions located in Webb City, MO. These shotguns were manufactured at the Olin-Kodensha plant in Tochigi, Japan to original Parker specifications by Winchester until the factory closed in January, 1989.

In 1984, Winchester was contracted by Reagent Chemical & Research, Inc. to manufacture a new Parker shotgun. The new SxS was a DHE model, available in 20 and 28 ga. initially. These models were fabricated in Japan to original Parker specifications, and the reproduction was so authentic that most parts are interchangeable with the late Parkers made by Remington in Ilion, NY. In 1993, a 16/20 ga. combo was introduced in some models. On Sept. 17, 1999, a flood destroyed all remaining inventory, including parts and most of the factory records.

During 2004, Connecticut Shotgun Manufacturing Company offered a limited quantity of A1 Specials in-the-white w/o metal finish and engraving in 12 or 20 ga. only, without cases or accessories. MSRs were $5,850 for one set of barrels and $6,750 for a 2 barrel set.

SHOTGUNS: SxS

12,268 Parker Reproductions shotguns were mfg. circa 1984-1989. Because of the high quality and limited mfg. of these reproductions, they have become very collectible, as they offer the shooter the only realistic alternative to using an original Parker Bros. shotgun. Currently, higher grade Parker Reproductions in smaller gauges are very desirable, and 95%-100% values are getting harder to accurately determine.

DHE GRADE – 12 (new 1986), 20, or 28 (new 1984) ga., 26 or 28 in. barrels, boxlock action, ejectors, single selective or double triggers, beavertail or splinter forend, straight or pistol grip stock, skeleton steel buttplate, engraving in original DH style, case hardened frame, rust blue barrels. Supplied with leather trunk case, canvas and leather cover, and snap caps. Disc.

	100%	98%	95%	90%	80%	70%	60%	LAST MSR
12 ga.	$4,200	$3,600	$3,100	$2,800	$2,500	$2,200	$2,000	
20 ga.	$5,200	$4,350	$3,650	$3,100	$2,750	$2,500	$2,250	
28 ga.	$5,600	$4,750	$3,950	$3,450	$3,000	$2,750	$2,500	

Add approx. 10% for SST.
Add $150 for beavertail forend.
Add $650 for Sporting Clays Model w/choke tubes (approx. 125 mfg. in 2 barrel sets).
Add $700-$1,150 per extra set of barrels, depending on gauge, configuration, and condition.

Quantities mfg. for this model are as follows: 12 ga. - 2,137 mfg., 20 ga. - 6,050 mfg., 28 ga. - 4,203 mfg.

* ***DHE Grade Steel Shot Special*** – similar to 12 ga. D Grade, except has strengthened No. 1 1/2 barrels, 3 in. chambers, and chrome lined 28 in., 7 1/4-7 1/2 lbs. Approx. 349 mfg. 1987-89.

100%	98%	95%	90%	80%	70%	60%	LAST MSR
$5,100	$4,250	$3,400	$3,000	$2,350	$1,850	$1,700	*$3,370*

Add $100 for beavertail forend.

* ***DHE Grade Small Gauge Combo*** – available in either 28 ga./.410 bore (disc.) or 16/20 ga. (mfg. 1993-97) combo with 2 barrels and 2 forends. Less than 160 mfg. of the 28 ga./.410 bore combo. Disc.

» **DHE Grade Small Gauge Combo 28 ga./.410 bore**

100%	98%	95%	90%	80%	70%	60%	LAST MSR
$15,500	$13,000	$11,000	$9,000	$7,500	$6,500	$5,500	*$4,970*

» **DHE Grade Small Gauge Combo 16/20 ga.** – new 1994 - disc.

100%	98%	95%	90%	80%	70%	60%	LAST MSR
$8,000	$7,250	$6,000	$5,000	$4,000	$3,250	$2,850	*$4,870*

* ***DHE Grade 3-Barrel Set*** – includes two 28 ga. and one .410 bore barrels, cased. Disc.

100%	98%	95%	90%	80%	70%	60%	LAST MSR
$20,000	$17,000	$15,000	$13,000	$11,000	$9,750	$8,500	*$5,630*

GRADING - PPGS™	100%	98%	95%	90%	80%	70%	60%	LAST MSR

BHE GRADE LIMITED EDITION – 12, 20, 28 ga. or 410 bore, original Parker BH specifications, single selective or double trigger(s), 26 or 28 in. barrels, straight or pistol grip stock, engraved skeleton buttplate, bank note scroll engraving around game scenes, cased. Only 100 manufactured in 12 and 20 ga., seven in 28 ga., and nine in .410 bore during late 1987-1989. Disc.

12 ga.	$8,250	$7,500	$6,500	$5,500	$4,750	$4,000	$3,250
20 ga.	$10,000	$9,000	$7,750	$6,500	$5,500	$4,500	$3,750
28 ga.	$19,500	$17,000	$15,000	$13,000	$10,500	$8,750	$7,000
.410 bore	$21,500	$18,750	$16,750	$13,500	$11,250	$9,000	$7,250
2 barrel set (28 ga. & .410 bore)	$30,000	$26,000	$23,000	$20,000	$17,500	$15,000	$12,500

Last MSR was $3,970 (single ga.).

A 28 ga./.410 bore combo was also available with 2 forends, only two sets were made.

A-1 SPECIAL – 12, 16/20 ga. combo (introduced 1993), 20, or 28 ga., original Parker A-1 specifications, 26 or 28 in. barrels, single selective or double trigger(s), fine scroll engraving with game scenes, 32 lines/in. checkering, cased with accessories. Limited mfg. 1988-89.

12 ga.	$12,500	$11,500	$10,250	$9,000	$7,475	$4,800	$4,350
20 ga.	$13,500	$11,500	$10,000	$9,750	$8,500	$5,500	$4,750
28 ga.	$15,500	$13,000	$11,000	$9,000	$7,500	$6,500	$5,500
.410 bore	$32,500	$28,000	$24,000	$20,000	$17,500	$15,000	$13,500
2 barrel set (16 ga. & 20 ga)	$30,000	$26,000	$22,000	$18,500	$16,000	$14,500	$12,500
3 barrel set (28 ga. & .410 bore)	$50,000	$45,000	$40,000	$35,000	$30,000	$25,000	$20,000

Last MSR was $11,200 (single ga., one set of barrels).

Add $2,000 for 16 ga. barrel (splinter model only).

Approx. 350 sets were manufactured with factory engraving. Fourteen 3 barrel sets were mfg. in this grade, which included two 28 ga. barrels (26 and 28 in.) and one .410 bore barrel (26 in.).

* ***A-1 Special Custom Engraved*** – custom (per individual special order) engraving, available with two sets of barrels only, cased with accessories, approx. 300 sets mfg. during 1988-1989.

Prices started at $11,000 and went up according to individualized special features.

* ***A-1 Special Federal Duck Stamp Collector's Series*** – available in 12 or 20 ga., A-1 Special specifications, authorized by U.S. Department of Interior. Only 4 sets are known to exist in this model, two 12 ga. sets, and two 20 ga. sets (one is a cutaway gun).

12 ga. 2 barrel set	$39,500	$35,000	$31,000	$29,000	$26,500	$15,000	$13,500
20 ga. 2 barrel set	$55,500	$51,500	$46,000	$41,000	$38,500	$23,500	$18,500

Last MSR was $14,000.

This model included special case and 2 barrels per buyer's specifications.

PARKER-HALE LIMITED

Previous gun manufacturer located in Birmingham, England. Rifles were manufactured in England until 1991 when Navy Arms purchased the manufacturing rights and built a plant in West Virginia for fabrication. This new company was called Gibbs Rifle Company, Inc. and they manufactured models very similar to older Parker-Hale rifles during 1992-94. Shotguns were manufactured in Spain and imported by Precision Sports, a division of Cortland Line Company, Inc. located in Cortland, NY until 1993.

Parker was the previous trade name of the A.G. Parker Company, located in Birmingham, England, which was formed from a gun making business founded in 1890 by Alfred Gray Parker. The company became the Parker-Hale company in 1936. The company was purchased by John Rothery Wholesale circa 2000.

Parker-Hale Ltd. continues to make a wide variety of high quality firearms cleaning accessories for both rifles and shotguns, including their famous bipod.

GRADING - PPGS™	100%	98%	95%	90%	80%	70%	60%	LAST MSR

Due to space considerations, information regarding this manufacturer is available online free of charge at www.bluebookofgunvalues.com.

PATRIOT ORDNANCE FACTORY (POF)

Current rifle manufacturer located in Glendale, AZ.

CARBINES/RIFLES: SEMI-AUTO

Patriot Ordnance Factory manufactures AR-15 style paramilitary rifles and carbines, as well as upper and lower receivers and various parts. The semi-auto carbines and rifles use a unique gas piston operating system that requires no lubrication. A wide variety of options are available for each model. Please contact the company directly for more information, including option pricing (see Trademark Index).

IMPORTANT NOTE: On model(s) where *N/A has replaced the normal 100% value, it indicates current market conditions are too unstable to accurately ascertain 100%-60% values. Factory retail prices (MSRs) reflect most recent updates. For more up-to-date information on current pricing trends and additional useful information, please visit www.bluebookofgunvalues.com, select "Information & Services" from the menu, and click on "Additional Book Information".

P308 MID-LENGTH RIFLE – .308 Win. cal., 16 1/2 or 20 in. heavy contour fluted barrel, gas piston operated, 3-position gas regulation for normal, suppressed and single action modes, FMP-A3 muzzle device, corrosion resistant operating system, chrome plated mil spec bolt, optional fixed hooded front sight, optional Troy or Diamondhead flip up sights, hunter/sniper or tactical aircraft aluminum alloy modular railed receiver, nickel, black, Olive Drab (new 2013), and CeraKote Burnt Bronze (new 2013) hard coat anodized Teflon finish, oversized trigger guard, Magpul MOE pistol grip, Magpul CTR six position collapsible stock, Ergo ladder rail covers, sling, bipod mount, Magpul PMAG 20 shot mag., approx. 9 lbs.

MSR $3,220	$2,675	$2,150	$1,825	$1,600	$1,350	$1,175	$1,000

Add $100 for Olive Drab (new 2013) or Cerakote Burnt Bronze (new 2013) finish.

This model is also available with a 12 1/2 or a 14 1/2 in. barrel for military/law enforcement.

P308 HUNTING RIFLE – .243 Win or .308 Win. cal., 20 in. heavy contour fluted barrel, gas piston operated, 3-position gas regulation for normal, suppressed and single action modes, FMP-A3 muzzle device, corrosion resistant operating system, chrome plated mil spec bolt, optional fixed hooded front sight, optional Troy or Diamondhead flip up sights, hunter/sniper aircraft aluminum alloy Olive Drab Cerakote modular railed receiver, Olive Drab Cerakote finish, oversized trigger guard, Magpul MOE pistol grip, fixed polymer buttstock, Ergo ladder rail covers, sling, bipod mount, 5 shot stainless steel mag., approx. 9 lbs.

MSR $3,220	$2,675	$2,150	$1,825	$1,600	$1,350	$1,175	$1,000

P415 MID-LENGTH RIFLE – 5.56 NATO cal., 16 1/2 or 18 in. heavy contour fluted barrel, gas piston operated, 3-position gas regulation for normal, suppressed and single action modes, FMP-A3 muzzle device, corrosion resistant operating system, chrome plated mil spec bolt, optional fixed hooded front sight, optional Troy or Diamondhead flip up sights, hunter/sniper or tactical aircraft aluminum alloy modular railed receiver, nickel and black hard coat anodized Teflon finish, oversized trigger guard, Magpul MOE pistol grip, Magpul CTR six position collapsible stock, Ergo ladder rail covers, sling, bipod mount, Magpul PMAG 30 shot mag., approx. 8 lbs. New 2012.

MSR $2,320	*N/A	$1,775	$1,500	$1,325	$1,050	$875	$675

This model is also available with a 14 1/2 in. barrel for military/law enforcement.

P415 HUNTING RIFLE – 5.56 NATO cal., 18 in. heavy contour fluted barrel, gas piston operated, 3-position gas regulation for normal, suppressed and single action modes, FMP-A3 muzzle device, corrosion resistant operating system, chrome plated mil spec bolt, optional fixed hooded front sight, optional Troy or Diamondhead flip up sights, hunter/sniper aircraft aluminum alloy modular railed receiver, Olive Drab Cerakote finish, oversized trigger guard, Magpul MOE pistol grip, fixed polymer buttstock, Ergo ladder rail covers, sling, bipod mount, 5 shot stainless steel mag., approx. 8 lbs.

MSR $2,320	$1,825	$1,650	$1,425	$1,295	$1,050	$875	$675

GRADING - PPGS™	100%	98%	95%	90%	80%	70%	60%	LAST MSR

P415 SPECIAL PURPOSE RIFLE – .223 Rem. cal., 18 in. heavy contour chrome lined fluted barrel, gas piston operated, A3 muzzle device, corrosion resistant operating system, nickel plated A3 flattop upper receiver and charging handle, M4 feed ramp, nickel and black hard coat anodized Teflon finish, fixed removable hooded front sight, optional Troy flip up sight, single stage trigger, Magpul PRS or six position adj. buttstock, tactical rail handguard, approx. 9 lbs. Disc. 2011.

$1,825 $1,650 $1,425 $1,295 $1,050 $875 $675 *$1,999*

P415 RECON CARBINE – .223 Rem. cal., 16 in. heavy contour chrome lined fluted barrel, gas piston operated, A3 muzzle device, corrosion resistant operating system, nickel plated A3 flattop upper receiver and charging handle, M4 feed ramp, nickel and black hard coat anodized Teflon finish, fixed removable hooded front sight, optional Troy flip up sight, single stage trigger, oversized trigger guard, Magpul PRS or six position adj. buttstock, tactical rail handguard, approx. 8 lbs. Disc. 2011.

$1,825 $1,650 $1,425 $1,295 $1,050 $875 $675 *$1,999*

P415 CARBINE – .223 Rem. cal., 16 in. heavy contour chrome lined fluted barrel, gas piston operated, A3 muzzle device, corrosion resistant operating system, nickel plated A3 flattop upper receiver and charging handle, M4 feed ramp, nickel and black hard coat anodized Teflon finish, fixed removable hooded front sight, optional Troy flip up sight, single stage trigger, oversized trigger guard, Magpul CTR retractable six position buttstock, M4 plastic handguard or Predator P-9 tactical rail system, sling/bipod mount, approx. 7-7.4 lbs. Disc. 2011.

$1,825 $1,650 $1,425 $1,295 $1,050 $875 $675 *$1,999*

Add $300 for Predator P-9 tactical rail system.

PISTOLS: SEMI-AUTO

P308 PISTOL – .308 Win. cal., 12 1/2 in. heavy contour fluted barrel, gas piston operated, 3-position gas regulation for normal, suppressed and single action modes, FMP-A3 muzzle device, corrosion resistant operating system, chrome plated mil spec bolt, optional fixed hooded front sight, optional Troy or Diamondhead flip up sights, hunter/sniper or tactical aircraft aluminum alloy modular railed receiver, nickel and black hard coat anodized Teflon finish, oversized trigger guard, Magpul MOE pistol grip, PWS enhanced pistol buffer tube, Ergo ladder rail covers, sling, bipod mount, Magpul PMAG 20 shot mag., approx. 7 1/2 lbs.

MSR $3,220 $2,850 $2,250 $1,900 $1,650 $1,350 $1,175 $1,000

P415 PISTOL – 5.56 NATO cal., 7 1/4 or 10 1/2 in. heavy contour fluted barrel, gas piston operated, 3-position gas regulation for normal, suppressed and single action modes, FMP-A3 muzzle device, corrosion resistant operating system, chrome plated mil spec bolt, optional fixed hooded front sight, optional Troy or Diamondhead flip up sights, hunter/sniper or tactical aircraft aluminum alloy modular railed receiver, nickel and black hard coat anodized Teflon finish, oversized trigger guard, Magpul MOE pistol grip, PWS enhanced pistol buffer tube, Ergo ladder rail covers, sling, bipod mount, Magpul PMAG 30 shot mag., approx. 6 1/2 lbs.

MSR $2,320 $2,075 $1,800 $1,525 $1,375 $1,100 $900 $725

PASTUSEK INDUSTRIES

Previous manufacturer located in Fort Worth, TX 1993-2000.

PISTOLS: SEMI-AUTO

HSK (SPORT KING) – .22 LR cal., 4 1/2 or 5 1/2 in. barrel. Mfg. 1995-2000.

$275 $250 $225 $195 $175 $150 $135 *$312*

HSS (SHARPSHOOTER) – .22 LR cal., 5 1/2 in. bull barrel. Mfg. 1995-2000.

$315 $275 $240 $210 $190 $165 $150 *$379*

HSC (SUPERMATIC CITATION) – .22 LR cal., 5 1/2 bull or 7 1/4 in. fluted barrel. Mfg. 1995-2000.

$340 $295 $265 $230 $210 $180 $165 *$388*

Add $22 for 7 1/4 in. fluted barrel.

This model was also available with an 8, 10, or 12 in. bull barrel.

GRADING - PPGS™	100%	98%	95%	90%	80%	70%	60%	LAST MSR

HST (SUPERMATIC TROPHY) – .22 LR cal., 5 1/2 bull or 7 1/4 in. fluted barrel. Mfg. 1995-2000.

	$400	$340	$275	$240	$220	$180	$165	*$494*

This model was also available with an 8, 10, or 12 in. bull barrel. Left-hand ejection is also an option on this model.

HSV (VICTOR) – .22 LR cal., 3 7/8, 4 1/2, 5 1/2, 8 (optional), or 10 (optional) in. VR barrel. Mfg. 1995-2000.

	$475	$375	$300	$250	$230	$185	$165	*$569*

Add $30 for dove tail rib on 5 1/2 in. barrel only.

Add $79 for Weaver rib on 5 1/2 in. barrel only.

HSO (OLYMPIC) – .22 S or .22 LR cal., 6 3/4 in. barrel only. Mfg. 1995-2000.

	$495	$395	$325	$265	$245	$195	$170	*$599*

PAUZA SPECIALTIES

Previously manufactured by Pauza Specialties circa 1991-96, and located in Baytown, TX. Previously distributed by U.S. General Technologies, Inc. located in South San Francisco, CA.

Pauza previously manufactured the P50 semi-auto rifle for Firearms International, Inc. - please refer to that section for current information.

RIFLES

P50 SEMI-AUTO – .50 BMG cal., semi-auto, 24 (carbine) or 29 (rifle) in. match grade barrel, 5 shot detachable mag., one-piece receiver, 3-stage gas system, takedown action, all exterior parts Teflon coated, with aluminum bipod, 25 or 30 lbs. Mfg. 1992-96.

	$5,950	$5,250	$4,600	$4,100	$3,650	$3,200	$2,800	*$6,495*

PEACE RIVER CLASSICS

Previous manufacturer located in Bartow, FL until 2001. Peace River Classics was a division of Tim's Guns.

RIFLES: SEMI-AUTO

PEACE RIVER CLASSICS SEMI-AUTO – .223 Rem. or .308 Win. (new 1998, possible prototypes only) cal., available in 3 configurations including the Shadowood, the Glenwood, and the Royale, hand-built utilizing Armalite action, patterned after the AR-15, match grade parts throughout, special serialization, laminate thumbhole stock. Very limited mfg. 1997-2001.

Last MSR on the .223 Rem. cal. in 2001 was $2,695, or $2,995 for .308 Win. cal

Due to this model's rarity factor, accurate values are hard to ascertain.

PEDERSEN CUSTOM GUNS

Previously manufactured circa 1973-1975 by O.F. Mossberg located in North Haven, CT. Pedersen Custom Guns was a division of O.F. Mossberg.

Due to space considerations, information regarding this manufacturer is available online free of charge at www.bluebookofgunvalues.com.

PEDERSEN DEVICE

Please refer to listing under Springfield Armory - Model 1903 Mark I.

PEDERSOLI, DAVIDE & C. Snc.

Current manufacturer of modern, black powder, and older historically significant firearms established in 1957, and located in Brescia, Italy. Currently imported on a limited basis by IFG (Italian Firearms Group), located in Rockledge, FL, beginning 2011. Currently, full-line distributors include Cherry's Fine Guns, located in Greensboro, NC, Dixie Gun Works, Inc., located in Union City, TN, and Flintlocks, Etc., located in Richmond, MA. Current importers include Cabela's, located in Sidney, NE, Cimarron FA Co., located in Fredricksburg, TX, E.M.F., located in Santa Ana, CA, Taylor's, located in Winchester, VA, and Navy Arms, located in Martinsburg, WV.

D. Pedersoli manufactures top quality black powder replicas and other high quality firearms reproductions. During 2011 the company released a new lever action Model 1886, and a single action revolver patterned after the original model made famous by Doc Holiday. During 2012, Pedersoli took over Euroarms production of Civil War muskets. Please check with Pedersoli's importers and distributors for model availability and pricing on all D. Pedersoli firearms (see Trademark Index for listings).

For more information and up-to-date pricing regarding current Pedersoli black powder models, please refer to the *Blue Book of Modern Black Powder Arms* by John Allen.

Black Powder Revolvers - Reproductions & Replicas and *Black Powder Long Arms & Pistols - Reproductions & Replicas* by Dennis Adler are also invaluable sources for most black powder reproductions and replicas, and includes hundreds of color images on most popular makes/models, provide manufacturer/trademark histories, and up-to-date information on related items/accessories for black powder shooting - www.bluebookofgunvalues.com

RIFLES: REPRODUCTIONS

Some Pedersoli reproduction rifles may be listed separately under the various U.S. distributors and importers.

For current values on older Pedersoli manufactured reproductions, please refer to a similar newer model/configuration in the same condition factor listed under the importer's sections. The following is a complete listing of all Pedersoli rifles currently manufactured by D. Pedersoli in Italy. Most of these will be imported by the various U.S. importers and distributors, please check these listings for pricing.

Premium Model V740, Colt 1877 Thunderer "Doc Holliday" Blued Model S630-S632, and Nickel Model S631-S633, Pedersoli Lightning Sporter Model S/V/L 927, 929, 930, 931 Double Rifle, Pedersoli High Wall Sporting Model S804-S805, Pedersoli High Wall Classic Model 806-S807, Colt Kodiak Mark IV SxS, Colt Lightning slide action rifle in 3 variations (Standard, Premium, and Deluxe), Remington Mississippi Rolling Block Model S844, Rem. Rolling Block, Rem. Rolling Block Long Range Creedmoor (Standard and Deluxe), Rem. Rolling Block Silhouette, Rem. Rolling Block Target (Standard and Deluxe), Rem. Rolling Block Super Match, Rem. Rolling Block John Bodine (Standard and Deluxe), Rem. Rolling Block Creedmoor #2, Rem. Rolling Block Sporting, Rem. Rolling Block #1 Sporting rifle, Rem. Rolling Block Baby Carbine, Sharps 1859 Cavalry Model S766, Sharps 1859 Berdan Model S761, Sharps 1859 Infantry Model S760, Sharps 1863 Model S755, Sharps 1862 Confederate Carbine, Sharps 1874 Sporting Model S780 Standard, Sharps 1874 Cavalry Model S775, Sharps 1874 Sniper Model S791, Sharps 1874 Infantry Model S790, Sharps 1874 Business Model S771, Sharps 1874 Billy Dixon Model S776, Sharps 1874 Buffalo Model S774, Sharps 1874 Creedmoor #2 Model S792, Sharps 1874 Long Range Model S788, Sharps 1874 Silhouette Model S782 Standard, Sharps 1874 Quigley Sporting Model S789, Sharps 1874 Boss Model S770, Sharps 1874 Competition Model S795, Sharps 1874 Sporting Model L780 Deluxe and Model LL780 Extra Deluxe, Sharps Silhouette "PTESAN-WI" Model LL782 Extra Deluxe, Sharps Silhouette Model LX782 Deluxe, Sharps Bench Rest .22 LR Model S758, Sharps Scheibenstutzen .22 LR Model S798, Sharps Light Model S759, Sharps Light Varmint Hunter, Sharps Old West Maple Model S767, Sharps Old West Walnut Model S769, SxS "La Bohemienne", Springfield Trapdoor Officer Model S910 Standard, Model L910 Deluxe, and Model LL910 Extra Deluxe, Springfield Trapdoor Rifle Model S905 Standard, Model L905 Deluxe, and Model LL905 Extra Deluxe, Springfield Trapdoor Carbine Model S900 Standard, Model L900 Deluxe, and Model LL900 Extra Deluxe, Springfield Trapdoor Long Range Rifle Model S906, Winchester Model 1886 Lever Action Classic and Premium, Winchester Model 1886 Lever Action Wildbuster, Browning 1886 Lever Action Model S740 and Winchester Model 71 Lever Action.

SHOTGUNS: REPRODUCTIONS

Pedersoli also manufactured a limited number of O/U and SxS shotguns between 1957-1973. These guns have had little importation into the U.S. Current values for these guns would be $650-$1,250, depending on features and configurations.

GRADING - PPGS™	100%	98%	95%	90%	80%	70%	60%	LAST MSR

PEERLESS RIFLE COMPANY

Current custom riflemaker and gunsmith established in 1988 and located in Glendale, CA. Consumer direct sales.

Ray Riganian has been making quality custom bolt action rifles since 1988. Please contact him directly for current availability and more information (see Trademark Index).

RIFLES: BOLT ACTION

Values are for base rifle only. Please contact the company for a price quotation and available options.

PEERLESS I – various cals., various blueprinted actions, available in either a lightweight, long range, tactical, or varmint configuration, McMillan fiberglass stock with Pachmayr Decelerator recoil pad, various barrel lengths, matte black metal finish, custom order only.

MSR $3,500	$3,500	$3,150	$2,750	$2,400	$2,100	$1,775	$1,500	

PEERLESS II – various cals., various blueprinted actions, features California English XXX walnut stock, various barrel lengths, matte black metal finish, custom order only.

	$6,500	$5,750	$5,000	$4,300	$3,750	$3,150	$2,500	*$6,500*

Add $1,400 for .375 H&H cal.

Add $2,100 for .416 Rem., .458 Lott, or .470 Capstick.

Other calibers such as .416 Rigby, .505 Gibbs, and .500 Jeffery were quoted on an individual basis.

PEERLESS II SPORTER – various cals., Win. Mod. 70 or Mauser 98 action, features California English XXX handcheckered walnut stock, ebony forend tip, steel grip cap, and cheekpiece, various match grade barrel lengths, matte black metal finish, custom order only.

MSR $8,500	$8,500	$7,995	$7,250	$6,500	$5,750	$4,950	$4,350	

Add $500 for Mag. cals.

Add $550 for Mauser 98 action.

Add $2,000 for Peerless II Safari in .375 H&H cal. or $3,000 for .416 Rem. or .458 Lott cal. (new 2011).

PEERLESS ROYAL EXPRESS RIFLE – various cals., including .375 H&H, .416 Rem., or .458 Lott cals., similar features as the Sporter, extra deep Blackburn steel trigger guard and floorplate, 5 shot, custom made box mag. (.416 or .458 cal. only), quick detachable scope mount system, barrel band swivel base, front sight and bead, quarter rib with one standing leaf, custom order only.

MSR $12,500	$12,500	$10,500	$8,750	$7,500	$6,250	$5,000	$3,175	

Add $300-$5,000 for .375 H&H cal. and higher on Mauser 98 action.

Add $3,500-$5,000 for .375 H&H cal. and higher on Granite Mt. action.

PENTHENY de PENTHENY

Current trademark owned by Wyoming Armory beginning 2009. Previous manufacturer and gunsmith 1987-2009, and located in Santa Rosa, CA.

Currently, Wyoming Armory is not producing rifles. Please contact the company directly for more information (see Trademark Index).

RIFLES: BOLT ACTION

The rifles listed included ebony forend tips, old English style black recoil pads, steel skeleton grip caps, four panels of 22 LPI checkering, and other custom features. These models were built on a U.S.R.A. Model 70 action.

THE INVADER – small and medium bore cals., classic styled Claro walnut stock, blue finish.

	$5,400	$4,500	$3,850	$2,975	$2,400	$1,975	$1,500	*$5,400*

THE NORMAN – Mag. cals., classic styled English walnut stock, blue finish.

	$5,400	$4,500	$3,850	$2,975	$2,400	$1,975	$1,500	*$5,400*

THE CONQUEROR – large bore cals., classic styled English walnut stock, blue finish, rifle has secondary recoil lug, dual steel reinforcing bolts, and express sights including fixed and folding leaves.

	$6,300	$5,500	$4,750	$3,650	$3,000	$2,400	$1,975	*$6,300*

PERAZZI

Current manufacturer established in 1957, and located in Brescia, Italy. Imported and distributed by Perazzi USA, Inc. located in Azusa, CA. Previously located in Monrovia, CA until 2002, and in Rome, NY during the 1980s.

Ivo Fabbri and Daniel Perazzi were partners in the shotgun manufacturing business beginning in 1960 - these guns are ser. no. 5001-5339.

Note: Previously, Perazzi shotguns were imported by both Winchester and Ithaca during the 1960s and 1970s. The company now has its own distribution network and its current model line-up is extensive. Perazzi shotguns are well known for their quality control standards and reliability in clay target championships and in-field conditions.

SHOTGUNS

Perazzi shotguns have incorporated many improvements during their manufacture. One of the most important changes has been the modification of the forearm design. Basically, there have been 4 different types: Type 1 has a serial range of 30,000-33,250, Type 2 is serial numbered 33,251-35,450, Type 3 has a range of 35,451-51,242, Type 4 started at 51,243 and is still current as of this writing. Differences include changes in the forearm iron and barrel lug attachment. Because of these forearm changes (and other parts modifications), the desirability factor on a Type 4 forearm shotgun as opposed to previous types is much greater. Competition shooters prefer Type 4 as they are the current design. If a Type 1 or 2 competition gun develops problems, they are automatically retrofitted to the Type 4 design - and these modifications are expensive. For these reasons, the serial number of a Perazzi competition gun will determine its type. Since Types 1 through 3 are discontinued, they will be less desirable (and less expensive) than the values listed for Type 4.

As a final note on older Perazzi shotguns, the most collectible models will be those specimens which exhibit the highest quality and are equally rare. Older SCO grades on small frames with older style "V" springs are at the top for desirability. Also, any older SPECIAL GUNS were all custom made - usually engraved by master engravers with Angelo Galeazzi being considered one of the best.

Perazzi Shotguns Information

Until 1988 most trap guns did not have a "Special" option package which includes an adjustable trigger group (designated P4). Models listed in the following sections assume a Type 4 forearm attachment design and are serial numbered 51,243 and above. Models that are serial numbered below 51,243 are an older design and will be priced less than the newer Type 4 models.

Rather than describe all the following models individually, descriptions will appear only once and are listed. The various grades have similar features and engraving (i.e., an SCO Grade Sideplate in American Skeet would appear similar to an American Trap SCO Grade Sideplate, except for stock dimensions).

Older SHO (Type 3s) and DHO models with rebounding hammers (disc.) are perhaps the most collectible Perazzi shotguns currently.

SC3 and other higher grade models have not been listed due to space consideration. The 14th Edition *Blue Book of Gun Values* did include all pertinent information, including 1993 pricing pertaining to the Perazzi higher grade models available at the time.

Recently, some Model MX8s have been modified by adding sideplates, engraving, and other markings of the higher grade models. These upgraded shotguns usually have the original markings polished off. Perazzi can verify any gun suspected of upgrading. These upgrades need to be valued individually, and should not be confused with factory original guns. Perazzi discontinued "Mirage" model nomenclature during 1998.

Perazzi Grades and Descriptions

Due to space considerations and relative low manufacture, the higher grade Perazzis have been described but not individually priced. Please contact Perazzi, USA for more information and prices on these higher grades (see Trademark Index).

GRADES AND DESCRIPTIONS

* ***Special Model*** – introductory level model with high polished blue on barrels and receiver, normally with model name on lower frame sides in gold letters and numerals. Checkered walnut stock (interchangeable) and forearm, all have adjustable trigger assembly.
* ***Gold Outline Model*** – similar to Standard Model, except has gold line engraving around perimeter of frame, also features better grade of walnut. This configuration is very rare.
* ***SC3 Model*** – features coin finished receiver with different styles of scroll engraving and different patterns of game scene engraving (snipe, grouse, pointing bird dog, or woodcock). Better grade of walnut than the Gold Outline Model.
* ***SCO Model*** – more elaborate than SC3 Model in that it features different styles of scroll engraving (deep relief "gargoyles" or fine English scroll) and different game scene engraving patterns. Again, a better grade of walnut (in addition to finer checkering) is utilized.
* ***SCO Gold Grade Model*** – differentiated from SCO Model in that it has engraving patterns featuring multiple gold inlays on receiver sides (including different duck scenes, separate grouse scenes, woodcock, and deep relief "gargoyle").
* ***SCO Grade Sideplate Model*** – includes coin finished receiver with game scene engraved sideplates (with boxlock action). Game scene engraving choices include different duck scenes, grouse, "Chisel" relief scroll, and Diana Goddess of the Hunt pattern.
* ***SCO Gold Grade Sideplate Model*** – similar to SCO Grade Sideplate Model, except has game figures on sideplates in relief gold. Patterns include different grouse scenes, separate ducks patterns, and dogs flushing upland game. This model can also be ordered with detachment lever for sideplates.
* ***Extra Grade Model*** – denoted by top-of-the-line fine bank note style game scene engraving with elaborate scroll and relief work on metal perimeters. Game scene choices include different dog scenes, grouse, and duck. Top quality Circassian finely checkered walnut.
* ***Extra Gold Grade Model*** – top-of-the-line boxlock model that differs from Extra Grade Model in that birds/dogs are in gold relief. This model can also be ordered with detachment lever for sideplates.
* ***SHO Over & Under Model*** – features sidelock action with coin finished receiver and intricate bank note game scene engraving with choices including different duck patterns and pheasant. Top quality walnut and checkering. Type One SHOs have non-rebounding firing pins, while Type Two guns have rebounding firing pins (since 1985).

This model is individually handmade per customer's specifications. Currently, no orders are being taken for this series.

* ***SHO Gold Over & Under Model*** – similar to SHO Over & Under Model, except features game scene of wildlife in relief gold. This model is the best sidelock special order grade that Perazzi currently offers for sale.

This model is individually handmade per customer's specifications. Currently, no orders are being taken for this series.

* ***DHO SxS Models*** – top-of-the-line sidelock model in 12 ga. only for DHO and DHO Gold grades. DHO Extra and DHO Gold Extra grades have similar engraving to Extra Grade and Extra Gold Grade models and are available in all gauges. The DHO Gold Extra is the most elaborate, highly finished SxS shotgun that an individual can currently special order from any company. The DHO model is exceedingly rare, and specimens should be appraised individually.

This model is entirely handmade per customer's specifications. Currently, no orders are being taken for this series.

RIFLES: O/U

9.3x74R - .375 Flanged Magnum. Current barrel length is 24 in.

Perazzi offers the following high grade O/U Express rifles:

SCO Grade: Express SCO ($40,653 MSR), or Express SCO w/sideplates ($52,138 MSR).

GRADING - PPGS™	100%	98%	95%	90%	80%	70%	60%	LAST MSR

SCO Gold Grade: Express SCO Gold ($46,598 MSR), or Express SCO Gold w/sideplates ($58,295 MSR).

Extra Grade: Express Extra ($95,288 MSR), Express Extra Gold ($101,500 MSR), or Express Extra Super ($110,031 MSR).

EXPRESS SC2 – 9.3x74R, or .375 flanged Magnum cal., boxlock action, 24 in. barrels, non-removable trigger group, fixed stock, barrel selector on trigger guard. New 2012.

MSR $22,103	$17,750	$15,250	$13,000	$11,000	$9,000	$7,500	$6,000

EXPRESS SC3 – 9.3x74R or .375 flanged Magnum cal., 24 in. barrels, non-removable trigger group, fixed stock, barrel selector on opening lever. New 2012.

MSR $29,312	$25,000	$21,500	$18,000	$16,000	$14,000	$12,000	$9,750

SHOTGUNS: O/U, STANDARD MODELS & COMBINATIONS, RECENT MFG.

Perazzi manufactures approx. 1,500-2,400 O/U and single barrel shotguns annually, yet there are nearly 200 models and configurations! Because of this, and due to space considerations, only the Standard Grade models are listed and described individually and priced separately, with shooting discipline(s) listed also.

Higher grade Perazzi models, including the SC3 Grade, SCO Grade, SCO Gold Grade, SCO Grade w/sideplates, and SCO Gold w/sideplates have current MSRs only and are listed under the individual discipline category names.

Combination models (available in Trap, Skeet, and Sporting configurations) include an extra single barrel available in 32, 34, or 35 in. Current MSR on these combo models can be determined by adding on the MSR of the extra barrel to the MSR of the base O/U.

Throughout the years, Perazzi made many economical models: the MX-3, MX-3 Special, MX-5, MX-6, MX-7, MX-11, MX-14, MX-15, and the MX-16 models all have plain flat side, not sea shell sculpted receivers to save production costs. Among them, the MX-3, MX-5, MX-6, and the MX-7 models all have rounded monoblocs for further cost savings at the time.

In the past when the dollar was strong, some grey market Perazzis were imported into the U.S. from the U.K, and they can be ascertained by their serial numbers. These guns may not have the same warranty as the shotguns imported by Perazzi USA.

Subtract 20% for O/U receiver but with only one single barrel, and non-adj. rib, unless originally priced as a single barrel trap gun.
Subtract 20% for fixed SK/SK chokes.
Add $300 for external selectable trigger on detachable trigger group.
Add $200 for guns with older generation factory choke tube set.

MIRAGE – similar features as the MX-8, in all configurations. The Mirage model nomenclature was discontinued in 1998.

	$6,400	$5,500	$4,700	$4,000	$3,500	$3,000	$2,700

Subtract 15-20% for Type 3 guns (older Ithaca and Winchester imported models).

MT-6 – named after the 1976 Montreal Olympics, silver strips on receiver, fixed trigger group, early guns have different barrel under lug and forearm. Disc.

	$4,000	$3,800	$3,200	$2,800	$2,300	$1,800	$1,600

Add 15-20% for later production blue receiver with Type 4 forearm.

MS 80 – named after the 1980 Moscow Olympics, sculpted receiver, fixed trigger group, disc.

	$4,500	$4,200	$3,800	$3,200	$2,700	$2,100	$1,900

GRANDITALIA – plain side receiver, fixed SST, choke tubes in bottom barrel, fixed choke top. Mfg. 1980-81.

	$4,300	$4,000	$3,400	$2,900	$2,400	$1,900	$1,700

MX-1/MX-2 STANDARD – 12 ga. only, live pigeon and Olympic Trap gun, top firing first, choked tighter on bottom barrel, detachable trigger group. MX-2 disc. late 1996.

MSR $9,861	$6,000	$5,100	$4,500	$3,500	$3,000	$2,700	$2,400

GRADING - PPGS™	100%	98%	95%	90%	80%	70%	60%	LAST MSR

MX-3 – plain side receiver, detachable trigger group, top firing, choked tighter on bottom barrel, rounded monobloc, econo model. Disc.

	$4,000	$3,500	$3,000	$2,500	$2,100	$1,800	$1,600	

Add 10% for "MX-3 Special" model with adj. trigger group and square monobloc.

MX-4 – similar to the MX-3 Special, except without P4 trigger, European model, disc.

	$4,200	$3,700	$3,100	$2,600	$2,200	$1,900	$1,700	

MX-5 – plain side receiver, fixed trigger group, rounded monobloc, entry level model introduced in 1985, disc.

	$4,000	$3,400	$2,800	$2,400	$2,000	$1,700	$1,500	

MX-6 – plain side receiver, detachable trigger group, rounded monobloc, econo model, disc.

	$4,200	$3,600	$3,000	$2,600	$2,200	$1,900	$1,700	

MX-7 – plain side receiver, fixed trigger group, rounded monobloc, econo model introduced 1992, disc.

	$4,100	$3,500	$2,900	$2,500	$2,100	$1,800	$1,600	

MX-8 STANDARD – 12 or 20 ga., named after the 1968 Olympics in Mexico City, this is the current "standard" Perazzi model available in Trap, Skeet, and Sporting configurations, removable trigger group with flat or coil spring.

Subtract 15%-20% for older Type 3 guns (Ithaca and Winchester imports).

* ***MX-8 Sporting*** – 12 or 20 ga., features removable trigger group, fixed rib, chokes, and stock, has barrel selector on safety lever.

MSR $9,861	$6,000	$5,100	$4,500	$3,500	$3,000	$2,700	$2,400	

Add $2,000 for Combo set - includes extra set of barrels (12 ga. only).

* ***MX-8L Sporting*** – 12 ga. only, features lightly engraved action, removable trigger group, fixed rib, chokes, and stock.

MSR $11,944	$9,150	$7,775	$6,250	$5,500	$4,850	$4,250	$3,750	

* ***MX-8 Trap*** – 12 or 20 ga., features removable trigger group, fixed rib, chokes, and stock.

MSR $9,861	$6,000	$5,100	$4,500	$3,500	$3,000	$2,700	$2,400	

* ***MX-8L Trap*** – 12 ga. only, features lightly engraved action, removable trigger group, fixed rib, chokes, and stock.

MSR $11,944	$9,150	$7,775	$6,250	$5,500	$4,850	$4,250	$3,750	

* ***MX-8 Skeet*** – 12 or 20 ga., features removable trigger group, fixed rib, chokes, and stock.

MSR $9,861	$6,000	$5,100	$4,500	$3,500	$3,000	$2,700	$2,400	

Add $2,652 for Combo set - includes extra set of barrels (12 ga. only).

* ***MX-8L Skeet*** – 12 ga. only, features lightly engraved action, removable trigger group, fixed rib, chokes, and stock.

MSR $11,944	$9,150	$7,775	$6,250	$5,500	$4,850	$4,250	$3,750	

Add $2,652 for Combo set - includes extra set of barrels.

* ***MX-8 Special*** – similar to MX-8, except has ramped rib and adj. trigger. Disc. circa mid-1990s.

	$8,200	$6,200	$5,500	$5,000	$4,400	$3,800	$3,250	*$12,155*

* ***MX-8B*** – similar to the MX-8, except has a detachable coil spring trigger group, bottom barrel choke tubes, a promotional model at the time, limited configuration.

	$6,900	$6,000	$5,000	$4,000	$3,200	$2,900	$2,500	

MX-9 – with changeable mid sight and adj. comb for changing POI, disc.

	$6,700	$5,900	$4,900	$4,000	$3,200	$2,900	$2,500	

GRADING - PPGS™	100%	98%	95%	90%	80%	70%	60%	LAST MSR

MX-10/MX-10RS – similar to the MX-8 Trap, except has adj. rib and stock, mostly in Trap configuration, RS model has higher adj. rib for American Trap.

MSR $11,914	$8,200	$7,200	$6,200	$5,200	$4,400	$3,800	$3,200	

Add approx. $1,500 for combo model with top single barrel with adj. rib.
Add approx. $1,600 for RS combo model with unsingle barrel with adj. rib.

MX-11 – plain side receiver, square monobloc, detachable trigger group, newer entry level model.

	$5,200	$4,400	$3,600	$3,100	$2,800	$2,600	$2,200	

MX-12/3 STANDARD – 12 ga., Sporting configuration only, features non-detachable trigger group with coil springs, adj. VR with 3 notches, and adj. comb.

MSR $11,419	$7,900	$6,950	$6,000	$5,000	$4,200	$3,650	$3,000	

Add approx. $400 ($817 MSR) for factory choke tubes (Model MX-12/3C).

MX-12/MX-20 STANDARD – 12 or 20 ga., available in Sporting or Game configuration, MX-20 has a true 20 ga. frame, seashell sculpted receiver, non-detachable selective trigger, engravings on frame border, trigger guard, and forearm.

MSR $10,058	$7,900	$6,900	$5,900	$5,000	$4,200	$3,600	$3,000	

Add approx. $400 ($872 MSR) for factory choke tubes (Model MX-12C - MX-20C, Sporting configuration only).
Add $2,000 for Combo Set - includes extra set of 12 ga. O/U barrels.

MX-14 TRAP COMBO – 12 ga., American Trap combo model includes fixed rib unsingle and fixed rib O/U barrels, adj. comb, black trigger, blue or nickel frame finish, plain side receiver, current production entry level model.

MSR $13,333	$9,200	$7,400	$6,200	$5,500	$5,000	$4,450	$3,750	

Add $1,200 for MX-14 L Model with light engraving.
Subtract $2,000 for unsingle barrel only.
Subtract $1,400 for O/U barrels only.

MX-16 – 16 ga., limited production entry level model, plain side receiver, non-detachable, selective trigger with flat spring.

	$5,800	$4,800	$4,000	$3,600	$3,200	$2,800	$2,400	

Add $1,000 for combo gun with extra top single barrel.

MX-28 STANDARD – 28 ga., scaled down frame, with SC2 engraving, otherwise similar to MX-12/MX-20.

MSR $19,723	$14,000	$11,000	$8,500	$7,500	$6,600	$5,800	$5,200	

Add approx. $400 for choke tubes.

MX-28B STANDARD – 28 ga., Game configuration only, non-detachable trigger group with fixed chokes.

MSR $13,550	$9,450	$8,000	$6,800	$5,750	$4,700	$4,000	$3,400	

MX-410 STANDARD – .410 bore frame, with SC2 engraving, otherwise similar to MX-12/MX-20.

MSR $19,723	$14,000	$11,000	$8,500	$7,500	$6,600	$5,800	$5,200	

MX-410B O/U STANDARD – .410 bore, Game configuration only, non-detachable trigger group with fixed chokes.

MSR $13,550	$9,450	$8,000	$6,800	$5,750	$4,700	$4,000	$3,400	

MX-2000 O/U SERIES STANDARD – 12, 20, 28 ga., or .410 bore, choice of removable or non-removable trigger group, fixed or adj. VR, fixed or adj. comb stock, fixed chokes or choke tubes, MX-2000-style engraving and gold lettering on receiver, available in Trap (MX-2000/3 and MX-2000/8), Sporting (MX-2000 S/3), Skeet or Pigeon (MX-2000/8), or Game (MX-2000S).

Subtract 20% for top single barrel only.
Subtract 20% for fixed SK/SK choke Skeet models.
Subtract 15% for unsingle model with adj. rib.

GRADING - PPGS™	100%	98%	95%	90%	80%	70%	60%	LAST MSR

* ***MX-2000S Game*** – 12, 20, 28 (on 20 ga. frame) ga. or .410 (on 20 ga. frame) bore, features non-removable trigger group, fixed rib, chokes, and stock.

MSR $11,068 $8,600 $7,600 $6,800 $5,800 $4,800 $3,800 $3,300

» ***MX-2000S Gold Game*** – 12, 20, 28 (on 20 ga. frame) ga. or .410 (on 20 ga. frame) bore, features gold inlays on receiver, non-removable trigger group, fixed rib, chokes, and stock.

MSR $19,702 $14,000 $11,000 $8,500 $7,500 $6,600 $5,800 $5,200

* ***MX-2000S Sporting*** – 12 or 20 ga., features non-removable trigger group, fixed rib, chokes, and stock.

MSR $11,068 $8,600 $7,600 $6,800 $5,800 $4,800 $3,800 $3,300

Add $816 for seven choke tubes (Model MX-2000SC).

Add $3,993 for Combo Set - includes extra set of 12 ga. O/U barrels.

» ***MX-2000S Gold Sporting*** – 12 or 20 ga., features gold inlays on receiver, non-removable trigger group, fixed rib, chokes, and stock.

MSR $19,700 $14,000 $11,000 $8,500 $7,500 $6,600 $5,800 $5,200

Add $817 for seven interchangeable choke tubes (Model MX-2000SC Gold).

* ***MX-2000 S/3 Sporting*** – 12 ga. only, non-removable trigger group with coil springs, adj. rib with 3 notches and adj. comb.

MSR $12,428 $9,750 $8,350 $7,250 $6,200 $5,150 $4,100 $3,650

Add $817 for seven interchangeable choke tubes (Model MX-2000 S/3C).

* ***MX-2000/8 Pigeon*** – 12 ga. only, features removable trigger group, fixed rib, chokes, and stock.

MSR $11,068 $8,600 $7,600 $6,800 $5,800 $4,800 $3,800 $3,300

Add $1,360 for adj. rib with 3 notches and adj. comb. (Model MX-2000/3).

* ***MX-2000/8 Skeet*** – 12 or 20 ga., features removable trigger group, fixed rib, chokes, and stock.

MSR $11,068 $8,600 $7,600 $6,800 $5,800 $4,800 $3,800 $3,300

Add $2,728 for Combo set - includes extra set of 12 ga. O/U barrels.

* ***MX-2000/8 Sporting*** – 12 or 20 ga., features removable trigger group, fixed rib, chokes, and stock.

MSR $11,068 $8,600 $7,600 $6,800 $5,800 $4,800 $3,800 $3,300

Add $1,424 for seven choke tubes (Model MX-2000/8C).

Add $3,993 for Combo Set - includes extra set of 12 ga. O/U barrels.

* ***MX-2000/8 Trap*** – 12 ga. only, removable trigger group, fixed rib, chokes, and stock.

MSR $11,068 $8,600 $7,600 $6,800 $5,800 $4,800 $3,800 $3,300

Add $1,360 for adj. rib with three notches and adj. comb (Model MX-2000/3).

* ***MX-2000/8 Gold*** – 12 or 20 ga., features gold inlays on receiver, removable trigger group, fixed rib, chokes, and stock, manufactured for Trap, Sporting, Skeet, Pigeon, and Game configurations.

MSR $19,700 $14,000 $11,000 $8,500 $7,500 $6,600 $5,800 $5,200

Add $1,361 for adj. rib with three notches and adj. comb (Model MX-2000 Gold Adj. Rib).

MX-2005 PIGEON – 12 ga. only, features removable trigger group, adj. rib with 5 notches, adj. comb, fixed chokes.

MSR $12,428 $9,750 $8,350 $7,250 $6,200 $5,150 $4,100 $3,650

MX-2005 TRAP – 12 ga. only, Trap model with extra high adj. rib with 5 notches, adj. comb., removable trigger group, fixed chokes, unsingle or combo.

Unsingle $7,600 $6,800 $5,800 $4,800 $4,000 $3,500 $3,000

MSR $17,436 $12,750 $10,000 $7,750 $6,750 $5,750 $5,100 $4,500

* ***MX-2005 Trap Combo*** – 12 ga. only, Trap model with extra high adj. rib with 5 notches, adj. comb., removable trigger group, fixed chokes, includes extra single barrel. Disc.

$10,500 $9,500 $8,600 $7,800 $6,800 $6,000 $5,000

GRADING - PPGS™	100%	98%	95%	90%	80%	70%	60%	LAST MSR

MX-2008 TRAP – 12 ga. only, features removable trigger group, adj. rib with 5 notches, adj. comb., fixed chokes, no single barrel available.

MSR $12,428	$9,750	$8,350	$7,250	$6,200	$5,150	$4,100	$3,650

MX-2000/10 TRAP COMBO – 12 ga., American Trap combo model includes adj. rib top single and adj. rib O/U barrels, adj. comb, gold trigger, blue or nickel frame finish, marked "Perazzi MX-2000" on side of receiver.

MSR $17,436	$12,750	$10,000	$7,750	$6,750	$5,750	$5,100	$4,500

This combo set is also available with a short rib.

MX-2000/RS TRAP COMBO – similar to MX-2000/10 Trap, except has unsingle barrel with high profile adj. rib.

MSR $17,436	$12,750	$10,000	$7,750	$6,750	$5,750	$5,100	$4,500

This combo set is also available with a short rib.

SHOTGUNS: AMERICAN TRAP, SINGLE BARREL & COMBINATIONS

All guns are 12 ga., equipped with Perazzi's removable trigger group (flat or coil springs), and the VR barrel lengths are currently 32, 34, or 35 inches, unless otherwise stated. Fixed chokes are standard.

Combo models typically include an extra set of O/U barrels without extra forearm.

Add approx. $500 for four choke tubes on current models listed within this category.

MX-8 – 12 ga., top single configuration, features fixed rib chokes and stock, gold trigger, blue or nickel frame finish. Mfg. for U.S. market only.

MSR $9,199	$7,200	$6,200	$5,200	$4,200	$3,600	$2,950	$2,600

Add $4,560 for Combo Set - includes extra set of 12 ga. O/U barrels.

MX-10 – 12 ga., top single configuration, features adj. rib with 4 notches, adj. comb., blue or nickel frame finish, gold trigger. Mfg. for the U.S. marketplace only.

MSR $10,216	$8,000	$7,200	$6,200	$5,200	$4,200	$3,600	$2,950

Add $5,917 for Combo Set - includes extra set of 12 ga. O/U barrels.

* ***MX-10 RS*** – 12 ga., unsingle configuration, features high profile adj. rib with 4 notches, adj. comb., blue or nickel frame finish. Mfg. for the U.S. marketplace only.

MSR $10,216	$8,000	$7,200	$6,200	$5,200	$4,200	$3,600	$2,950

Add $5,917 for Combo Set - includes extra set of 12 ga. O/U barrels.

MX-15 – 12 ga., unsingle configuration, with adj. rib, adj. comb, plain side receiver, black trigger, blue finish only, current production entry level model.

MSR $8,395	$5,900	$4,900	$4,100	$3,600	$3,200	$2,700	$2,200

* ***MX-15L*** – 12 ga., unsingle configuration, nickel plated frame with light engraving, gold trigger, with adj. rib, adj. comb.

MSR $10,478	$6,500	$5,700	$5,100	$4,600	$4,000	$3,500	$3,000

MX-2000 – 12 ga. only, unsingle configuration with high tapered adj. rib with 5 notches, "Perazzi MX-2000" marked on receiver sides surrounded by engraving, gold trigger, blue or nickel frame finish. Mfg. for U.S. marketplace only.

MSR $11,148	$7,250	$6,250	$5,350	$4,750	$4,150	$3,600	$3,100

MX-2000/8 – 12 ga. only, top single configuration, fixed rib, chokes, and stock. Mfg. for U.S. marketplace only.

MSR $9,564	$7,450	$6,375	$5,300	$4,300	$3,650	$3,000	$2,650

Add $5,497 for Combo Set - includes extra set of 12 ga. O/U barrels.

MX-2005 – 12 ga. only, 34 in. barrel only, unsingle configuration, extra high tapered adj. rib with 5 notches, adj. comb., removable trigger group, fixed chokes, gold trigger, blue or nickel frame finish, marked "Perazzi MX-2005" on both sides of receiver surrounded by light engraving. Mfg. for U.S. marketplace only.

MSR $11,148	$7,250	$6,250	$5,350	$4,750	$4,150	$3,600	$3,100

Add $6,288 for Combo Set - includes extra set of 12 ga. barrels.

GRADING - PPGS™	100%	98%	95%	90%	80%	70%	60%	LAST MSR

TM1 – 12 ga., single barrel receiver, detachable trigger, disc.

	$2,900	$2,500	$2,100	$1,800	$1,500	$1,200	$1,100	

Add $150 for Special model with P4 adj. trigger.
Add $200 for TMS model with factory choke tubes.

TMX – 12 ga., American Trap model, newer production, similar to the TM1, except has high rib, disc.

	$3,600	$3,000	$2,500	$2,100	$1,800	$1,500	$1,200	

TM9 – 12 ga., top single configuration with non-adj. fixed VR, sculpted frame, blue or nickel frame finish, black trigger. Mfg. for U.S. marketplace only.

MSR $8,395	$6,250	$5,500	$4,750	$4,000	$3,250	$2,750	$2,250	

* ***TM9X*** – 12 ga., top single configuration, features adj. 4 notch rib, adj. comb, blue or nickel frame finish, black trigger. Mfg. for U.S. marketplace only.

MSR $9,755	$7,650	$6,500	$5,400	$4,400	$3,700	$3,000	$2,750	

SHOTGUNS: O/U, HIGH GRADE COMBO SETS (TRAP, SKEET, AND SPORTING)

Perazzi offers a wide variety of combination sets in Trap, Skeet, and Sporting configurations. These combination sets include a choice of either 29 1/2 or 31 1/2 in. O/U VR barrels with or w/o choke tubes and one VR barrel (choice of top single or bottom single) with or w/o choke tubes. There are numerous configurations available, including many engraving, rib, and stock options. All shotguns, except the MX12, are equipped with a removable trigger group and flat springs.

Currently, Perazzi offers the following Trap, Skeet, and Sporting combination sets:

SC3 Grade Models: MX8 SC3 Trap ($20,961 MSR), SC3 Trap ($23,336 MSR), MX8 SC3 Skeet ($20,961 MSR), MX8 SC3 Sporting ($20,961 MSR), and the MX12 SC3 Sporting ($20,961MSR).

SCO Grade Models: MX8 SCO Trap ($34,615 MSR), SCO Trap (36,990 MSR), MX8 SCO Skeet ($34,615 MSR), MX8 SCO Sporting ($34,615 MSR), and the MX12 SCO Sporting ($34,615 MSR).

SCO Gold Grade: MX8 SCO Gold Trap ($38,383 MSR), SCO Gold Trap ($40,758 MSR), MX8 SCO Gold Skeet ($38,383 MSR), MX8 SCO Gold Sporting ($38,383 MSR), and the MX12 SCO Gold Sporting ($38,383 MSR).

SCO Grade Models w/sideplates: MX8 SCO Trap ($49,722 MSR), SCO Trap ($52,097 MSR), MX8 SCO Skeet ($49,722 MSR), MX8 SCO Sporting ($49,722 MSR), and the MX12 Sporting ($49,722 MSR).

SCO Gold Grade Models w/sideplates: MX8 SCO Gold Trap ($55,148 MSR), SCO Gold Trap ($57,523 MSR), MX8 SCO Gold Skeet ($55,148 MSR), MX8 SCO Gold Sporting ($55,148 MSR), and the MX12 SCO Gold Sporting ($55,148 MSR).

Previous models included: MX-2005 ($20,964 last MSR), DB81 Trap ($16,023 last MSR), MX2000/8 Gold Trap ($26,467 last MSR), MX2000 Gold Trap ($24,4000 last MSR), MX2000/8 Gold Skeet ($23,701 last MSR), and the MX2000S Gold Sporting ($21,296 last MSR).

SHOTGUNS: O/U, TRAP, HIGHER GRADES

12 or 20 ga. Current barrel lengths include 29 1/2, 30 3/4, or 31 1/2 in.

Perazzi offers the following high grade trap shotguns:

SC2 Grade: MX8 SC2 ($13,592 MSR).

SC3 Grade: MX8 SC3 ($16,732 MSR), MX8/20 SC3 (last MSR in 2011 was $22,716), an SC3 Adj. Rib ($18,093 MSR).

SCO Grade: MX8 SCO ($28,448 MSR), and SCO Adj. Rib ($29,809 MSR).

SCO Gold Grade: MX8 SCO Gold ($32,143 MSR), SCO Gold Adj. Rib ($33,504 MSR).

SCO Grade w/sideplates: MX8 SCO ($43,633 MSR), and SCO Adj. Rib ($44,994 SR).

SCO Gold Grade w/sideplates: MX8 SCO Gold ($49,247 MSR), and SCO GOld Adj. Rib

GRADING - PPGS™	100%	98%	95%	90%	80%	70%	60%	LAST MSR

($50,608 MSR).

Extra Grade: Extra ($83,038 MSR), Extra Gold ($89,250 MSR), and Extra Super ($97,825 MSR).

SHOTGUNS: O/U, SKEET HIGHER GRADES

12 or 20 ga., 26 3/4, 27 9/16, 28 3/8, 29 1/2, or 34 in. barrels.

Perazzi offers a wide variety of competition style shotguns.

SC2 Grade: MX8 SC2 ($13,592 MSR).

SC3 Grade: MX8 SC3 ($16,732 MSR) and the MX8/20 SC3 ($16,732 MSR).

SCO Grade: MX8 SCO and the MX8/20 SCO ($28,448 MSR).

SCO Gold Grade: MX8 SCO Gold and the MX8/20 Gold ($32,143 MSR).

SCO Grade w/sideplates: MX8 SCO and the MX8/20 SCO ($43,633 MSR).

SCO Gold Grade w/sideplates: MX8 SCO Gold and the MX8/20 SCO Gold ($49,247 MSR).

Extra Grade: Extra ($83,038 MSR), Extra Gold ($89,250 MSR), and Extra Super ($97,825 MSR).

Subtract $250-$500 on older Mirage Models (without the "Special" designation) that do not have the adjustable 4 position trigger.

SHOTGUNS: O/U, 4-GAUGE SKEET SETS

STANDARD GRADE MODELS

* ***Standard Grade Model MX3 Special***

$5,200	$4,875	$4,650	$4,500	$4,150	$3,650	$3,150	*$15,400*

* ***Standard Grade Model Mirage Special*** – disc. 1994.

$5,850	$5,500	$4,850	$4,600	$4,200	$3,700	$3,200	*$17,500*

SHOTGUNS: O/U, SPORTING HIGHER GRADES

12 or 20 ga.

Perazzi offers a wide variety of competition style shotguns. Current Sporting models include:

SC2 Grade: SC2 Adj. Rib ($14,953 MSR), MX8 SC2 ($13,592 MSR), MX8C SC2 ($15,016 MSR), MX12 SC2 ($15,016 MSR), and MX12C SC2 ($14,408 MSR).

SC3 Grade: MX8 SC3 ($16,732 MSR), MX8/20 SC3 ($16,732 MSR), MX8C SC3 and MX8/20C SC 3 ($18,156 MSR), MX12 SC3 and MX20 SC3 ($16,732 MSR), and the MX12C SC3 and MX20C SC3 ($17,548 MSR).

SCO Grade: MX8 SCO ($28,448 MSR), MX8/20 SCO ($28,448 MSR), MX8C SCO and MX8/20C SCO ($29,873 MSR), MX12 SCO and MX20 SCO ($28,448 MSR), and the MX12C SCO and MX20C SCO ($29,265 MSR).

SCO Gold Grade: MX8 SCO Gold and MX8/20 Gold ($32,143 MSR), MX8C SCO Gold and MX8/20 C Gold ($33,568 MSR), MX12 SCO Gold and MX20 SCO Gold ($32,143 MSR), MX12C SCO Gold and the MX20 SCO Gold ($32,960 MSR).

SCO Grade w/sideplates: MX8 SCO and MX8/20 SCO ($43,633 MSR), MX8C SCO and MX8/20 C SCO ($45,058 MSR), MX12 SCO and MX20 SCO ($43,633 MSR) and the MX12C SCO and MX20C SCO ($44,450 MSR).

SCO Gold Grade w/sideplates: MX8 SCO Gold and MX8/20 SCO Gold ($49,247 MSR), MX8C SCO Gold and MX8/20 C SCO Gold ($50,671 MSR), MX12 SCO Gold and MX20 SCO Gold ($49,247 MSR), and the MX12C SCO Gold and the MX20C SCO Gold ($50,063 MSR).

Extra Grade: Extra ($83,038 MSR), Extra Gold ($89,250 MSR), and Extra Super ($97,825 MSR).

SHOTGUNS: O/U, PIGEON-ELECTROCIBLES HIGHER GRADE

Perazzi offers a wide variety of Pigeon shotguns.

Current models include:

SC2 Grade: MX8 SC2 ($13,592 MSR).

SC3 Grade: MX8 SC3 ($16,732 MSR).

SCO Grade: MX8 SCO ($28,448 MSR).

GRADING - PPGS™	100%	98%	95%	90%	80%	70%	60%	LAST MSR

SCO Gold Grade: MX8 SCO Gold ($32,143 MSR).

SCO Grade w/sideplates: MX8 SCO ($43,633 MSR).

SCO Gold Grade w/sideplates: MX8 SCO Gold ($49,247 MSR).

Extra Grade: Extra ($83,038 MSR), Extra Gold ($89,250 MSR), and Extra Super ($97,825 MSR).

SHOTGUNS: O/U, GAME/HUNTING - BOXLOCK ACTION

Available in 12, 20, 28 ga., or .410 bore, 26 (disc. on MX8/12 ga. and MX12 1994), 26 3/4, 27 9/16, 28 3/8, or 29 1/2 in. barrels. Perazzi offers a wide variety of game/hunting configurations. Current models include:

SC2 Grade Models: MX12 SC2 ($13,592 MSR) or MX20 SC2 ($13,592 MSR).

SC3 Grade Models: MX12 SC3 and MX20 SC3 ($16,732 MSR), MX28 SC3 and MX410 SC3 ($26,552 MSR).

SCO Grade Models: MX12 SCO and MX20 SCO ($28,448 MSR), MX28 SCO and MX410 SCO ($38,383 MSR).

SCO Gold Grade: MX12 SCO Gold and MX20 SCO Gold ($32,143 MSR), MX28 SCO Gold and MX410 SCO Gold ($41,975 MSR).

SCO Grade w/sideplates: MX12 SCO and MX20 SCO ($43,633 MSR), and the MX28 and MX410 SCO ($53,569 MSR).

SCO Gold Grade w/sideplates: MX12 SCO Gold and MX20 SCO Gold ($49,247 MSR), MX28 SCO and MX410 SCO Gold ($58,833 MSR).

Extra Models: Extra ($83,038 MSR), Extra Gold ($89,250 MSR), and the Extra Super ($97,825 MSR).

Four Game Shotgun Sets includes 12, 20, 28 ga. and .410 bore shotguns: SC2 ($71,167 MSR), SC3 ($87,000 MSR), SCO ($147,917 MSR), SCO w/sideplates ($226,917 MSR), Extra ($332,083 MSR), Extra Gold ($357,000 MSR), or Extra Super ($391,250 MSR).

SHOTGUNS: O/U, SIDELOCK MODELS

All Perazzi sidelock O/U models were discontinued in 1992. The most desirable configurations in this model are the Skeet, Pigeon, and Sporting variations (pricing follows new SHO Gold values).

O/U SIDELOCK TRAP MODELS – older models without rebounding hammers are not as desirable. The most desirable configurations in this model are the Skeet, Pigeon, and Sporting variations (pricing follows new SHO Gold values). All SHO sidelock models were disc. 1992.

Model	100%	98%	95%	90%	80%	70%	60%	LAST MSR
* ***Sidelock Trap Model SHO Older Mfg.***	$12,000	$11,000	$10,000	$9,000	$8,500	$7,600	$6,800	

Add $6,000 for game scene engraving.

Model	100%	98%	95%	90%	80%	70%	60%	LAST MSR
* ***Sidelock Trap Model SHO Newer Mfg.***	$28,500	$25,000	$21,500	$18,000	$16,500	$14,000	$12,000	*$43,000*
* ***Sidelock Trap Model SHO Gold Older Mfg.***	$17,000	$15,000	$13,000	$11,000	$9,950	$8,750	$7,000	
* ***Sidelock Trap Model SHO Gold Newer Mfg.***	$34,000	$29,500	$25,000	$21,250	$17,750	$14,000	$12,000	*$48,000*

* ***Sidelock Trap Model SHO Extra*** – while advertised, none were sold.
Last MSR was $80,000

* ***Sidelock Trap Model SHO Gold Extra*** – while advertised, none were sold.
Last MSR was $86,000

O/U SIDELOCK SKEET MODELS – older models without rebounding hammers are not as desirable.

Model	100%	98%	95%	90%	80%	70%	60%	LAST MSR
* ***Sidelock Skeet Model SHO Older Mfg.***	$15,000	$12,000	$9,500	$8,500	$7,600	$6,800	$5,900	

GRADING - PPGS™	100%	98%	95%	90%	80%	70%	60%	LAST MSR

* ***Sidelock Skeet Model SHO Newer Mfg.***

$35,850	$30,000	$25,000	$20,000	$17,000	$14,500	$12,750	*$43,000*

* ***Sidelock Skeet Model SHO Gold Older Mfg.***

$18,000	$15,750	$12,000	$9,500	$8,500	$7,600	$6,800	

* ***Sidelock Skeet Model SHO Gold Newer Mfg.***

$45,000	$34,500	$27,250	$22,000	$18,500	$15,950	$13,750	*$48,000*

* ***Sidelock Skeet Model SHO Extra*** – imported 1985-92.

$68,750	$54,700	$38,100	$32,000	$26,500	$21,250	$18,000	*$80,000*

* ***Sidelock Skeet Model SHO Gold Extra*** – similar to SHO Extra, except has gold inlays. Imported 1992 only.

$72,750	$56,500	$39,500	$33,000	$27,000	$22,000	$18,500	*$86,000*

Subtract $20,000 if not signed by a known engraver.

SHO HUNTING MODELS – all SHO Hunting models should be evaluated and possibly appraised by someone who has a great deal of knowledge of both newer and older higher grade Perazzi shotguns. There are many variables that can come into play for price consideration, therefore an expert opinion is encouraged before buying, selling or trading the following models.

* ***SHO Hunting Model Older Mfg.*** – older models without rebounding hammers are not as desirable.

$12,000	$9,500	$8,500	$7,600	$6,800	$5,950	$5,150	

* ***SHO Hunting Model Newer Mfg.*** – 12 ga. only, introductory sidelock O/U model with bank note game scene engraving on coin finished receiver.

$29,950	$25,000	$20,000	$17,000	$14,500	$12,750	$10,250	*$43,000*

* ***SHO Hunting Model Gold Older Mfg.*** – older models without rebounding hammers are not as desirable.

$18,000	$15,750	$12,000	$9,500	$8,500	$7,600	$6,800	

* ***SHO Hunting Model Gold Newer Mfg.*** – similar to SHO, except has game scenes in gold relief.

$38,650	$31,500	$26,500	$21,250	$18,000	$15,500	$13,750	*$48,000*

* ***SHO Hunting Model Extra*** – importation began 1992.

$68,750	$54,700	$38,100	$32,000	$26,500	$21,250	$18,000	*$80,000*

* ***SHO Hunting Model Gold Extra*** – similar to SHO Extra, except has gold inlays. Importation began 1992.

$72,750	$56,500	$39,500	$33,000	$27,000	$22,000	$18,500	*$86,000*

SHOTGUNS: SxS, HUNTING - SIDELOCK MODELS

DHO Models have not been included within the scope of this text due to the extreme rarity factor. Please contact Perazzi USA for more information on these models and current pricing.

Subtract 40% without rebounding hammers on older DHO models.

SHOTGUNS: SxS GAME SHOTGUNS

12, 20, 28, or .410 bore. Current barrel lengths include 26 3/4, 27 9/16, 28 3/8, or 29 1/2 in.

Perazzi offers the following high grade SxS Game shotguns:

SC2 Grade: DC SC2 ($18,639 MSR)

SC3 Grade: DC SC3 ($21,781 MSR)

SCO Grade: DC SCO ($33,495 MSR), DC SCO w/sideplates ($48,685 MSR).

SCO Gold Grade: DC SCO Gold ($37,195 MSR), DC SCO Gold w/sideplates ($54,297 MSR).

DC Extra Grade: DC Extra ($88,083 MSR), DC Extra Gold ($94,300 MSR), and the DC Extra Super ($102,875 MSR).

GRADING - PPGS™	100%	98%	95%	90%	80%	70%	60%	LAST MSR

DC STANDARD – 12, 20, 28 ga., or .410 bore, boxlock action, features removable trigger group, fixed rib chokes and stock. New 2012.

MSR $14,912 $11,250 $9,000 $8,000 $7,000 $6,000 $5,250 $4,500

PEREGRINE INDUSTRIES, INC.

Previous company located in Huntington Beach, CA circa 1991.

While advertised, Peregrine Industries, Inc. never manufactured the Falcon Model.

PERODEAU, J.J.

Current custom long gun maker located in Enid, OK.

J.J. Perodeau makes high quality custom SxS rifles and shotguns. Please contact the company directly for more information, availability and pricing (see Trademark Index). J.J. Perodeau is also an agent for George Granger.

PERUGINI-VISINI

Current manufacturer established during 1968 and located in Nuvolera, Brescia, Italy. Currently imported by P&V USA LLC, lcoated in Lakeland, FL. Previously imported 2002-2004 by Old Friends Hunting & Shooting Co., located in Livingston, MT. Rifles were previously imported and distributed until 1992 by William Larkin Moore & Co., previously located in Westlake Village, CA. All other models listed were previously imported and distributed by Armes De Chasse located in Chadds Ford, PA until 1988.

Perugini-Visini are manufacturers of best quality shotguns and rifles. Action types include side lock, boxlock, bolt action, and single shot. All Perugini-Visini guns are manufactured on a custom order basis only. Annual production is approx. 60 guns. Please contact the importer directly for more information and current pricing (see listing in Trademark Index). All pricing FOB Italy and subject to change due to Euro currency conversion rates.

RIFLES

STANDARD MODEL: BOLT ACTION – available in most U.S. and metric cals., Mauser 98K action, 24 or 26 in. barrel, 3 shot mag. (non-detachable), matte finished European walnut, high polish bluing, no sights. Importation disc. 1987.

$4,250 $3,800 $3,400 $2,950 $2,500 $2,000 $1,800 ***$4,250***

DELUXE MODEL: BOLT ACTION – similar to Standard Model, except has finely checkered oil finished walnut stock, sights, knurled bolt handle, and is cased. Importation disc. 1987.

$4,250 $3,800 $3,400 $2,950 $2,500 $2,000 $1,800 ***$4,250***

MODEL EAGLE SINGLE SHOT – available in most U.S. and metric cals., Anson & Deeley type action, ejector, sights, adj. trigger, oil finished finely checkered European walnut stock, 24 or 26 in. Hämmerli barrel. Importation disc. 1987.

$5,255 $4,500 $3,800 $3,400 $2,950 $2,500 $2,000 ***$5,255***

EAGLE MODEL SINGLE SHOT (CURRENT MFG.) – best quality single shot built on Perugini-Visini patented action with optional sideplates. Available in many traditional U.S. and European calibers. Options include Perugini-Visini claw mounts, optics, set trigger, and custom engraving.

Prices start at $27,000.

"PROFESSIONAL" BOLT ACTION MAGAZINE RIFLE – dedicated Perugini & Visini Mauser action for cals. up to .375 H&H, includes express sights, sling swivels, and quarter rib. Claw mounts, optics, and ornamental engraving are optional.

MSR $32,000 $28,750 $23,000 $18,750 $15,250 $12,650 $10,250 $8,750

"PROFESSIONAL" BOLT ACTION MAGNUM RIFLE – best quality big game and Safari rifle built on a dedicated Perugini-Visini Magnum Mauser action. Available in all calibers. Long tang, quarter rib, and express sights are standard. Options include Perugini-Visini claw mounts, optics, and custom engraving.

MSR $32,000 $28,750 $23,000 $18,750 $15,250 $12,650 $10,250 $8,750

GRADING - PPGS™	100%	98%	95%	90%	80%	70%	60%	LAST MSR

"SELOUS" EXPRESS SxS DOUBLE RIFLE – best quality back-action sidelock rifle available in all calibers up to .600 NE. Chopper lump barrel with patented ejectors and Zanatti triple compass bolting. Express sights and rib, fine rose, and scroll engraving are standard. Options include Perugini-Visini claw mounts, optics, and custom engraving.

Prices start at $95,000.

* ***"Selous" Express SxS Double Rifle*** – 9.3x74R, .375 H&H, .458 Win. Mag., .470 NE, or .500 3 in. NE cal., H&H style detachable sidelock action, ejectors, folding leaf rear sight, border engraving with best quality checkered walnut, top-of-the-line model, leather cased. Importation disc. 1992.

$23,000	**$18,500**	**$15,000**	**$12,000**	**$10,000**	**$9,000**	**$8,150**	***$26,000***

* ***"Selous" Express SxS Double Rifle Sidelock Super Express*** – choice of 9 different cals. including .470 Nitro Express, H&H patterned sidelocks, chopper lump barrels, third lever fastener, multi-leaf express sights, coin finished or case hardened receiver, engraving patterns optional. Importation disc. 1989.

$9,500	**$8,400**	**$7,400**	**$6,850**	**$6,100**	**$5,600**	**$5,000**	***$10,500***

VICTORIA MODEL D EXPRESS SxS DOUBLE RIFLE – best quality Anson and Deeley boxlock with chopper lump or mono bloc barrels and Zanatti bolting, patented ejectors, available in all traditional express calibers up to .500 NE, express sights and rib are standard. Options include claw mounts, optics, and custom engraving.

Prices start at $48,200.

* ***Victoria Model D Express SxS Double Rifle Mag.*** – similar to Model Victoria, except in .375 H&H, .458 Win., .470 NE, or .500-3 in. NE cal., demi-bloc barrels, and has elaborate engraving. Importation disc. 1992.

$10,950	**$9,150**	**$8,200**	**$7,400**	**$6,600**	**$5,800**	**$5,100**	***$13,750***

VICTORIA MODEL M EXPRESS SxS DOUBLE RIFLE – similar to the Victoria Model D Express SxS Double Rifle, except has monobloc barrel construction, available in all calibers up to 9.3x74R cal.

Prices start at $25,900.

* ***Victoria Model M Express SxS Double Rifle*** – .30-06, 7x57R, 7x65R or 9.3x74R cal., Anson & Deeley boxlock action, border engraving, ejectors, folding leaf rear sight, DT, 24 or 26 in. monobloc barrels with chopper lumps, leather cased. Importation disc. 1992.

$7,000	**$5,700**	**$4,600**	**$3,500**	**$2,950**	**$2,500**	**$2,000**

PRINCESS MODEL D EXPRESS O/U DOUBLE RIFLE – best quality Boss-style boxlock available in all calibers including traditional express calibers, chopper lump barrels with patented ejectors, quarter rib, and expres sights are standard. Options include claw mounts, optics, sideplates, and custom engraving.

MSR $48,200	**$44,000**	**$38,000**	**$32,000**	**$27,000**	**$23,000**	**$18,500**	**$15,500**

PRINCESS MODEL M EXPRESS O/U DOUBLE RIFLE – similar to the Princess Model D Express O/U Double Rifle, except has monobloc barrel construction and available in all calibers up to 9.3x74 cal.

$24,000	**$20,500**	**$17,000**	**$14,000**	**$11,000**	**$9,000**	**$7,000**	***$26,900***

RENAISSANCE DOUBLE RIFLE – .375 H&H cal., demi-bloc barrels, Anson & Deeley boxlock action, includes scroll engraving with game scene on trigger plate.

This model has a current MSR of $24,950.

BOXLOCK EXPRESS SxS – .444 Marlin or 9.3x74R cal., Anson & Deeley boxlock action, ejectors, color case hardened frame, iron sights. Importation disc. 1989.

$3,150	**$2,800**	**$2,500**	**$2,200**	**$1,950**	**$1,700**	**$1,475**	***$3,500***

BOXLOCK MAGNUM O/U – .270 Win., .375 H&H, or .458 Win. Mag. cal., Anson & Deeley boxlock action, ejectors, monobloc barrels, select walnut. Importation disc. 1989.

$5,500	**$4,900**	**$4,300**	**$3,750**	**$3,100**	**$2,600**	**$2,200**	***$6,100***

GRADING - PPGS™	100%	98%	95%	90%	80%	70%	60%	LAST MSR

MODEL CARBINE – available in many calibers, deluxe gun with game scene engraved floor plate, case hardened engraved receiver, Mauser action, quick detachable claw mounts, includes Swarovski or Zeiss scope and case.

The Standard Model has a MSR of $15,000.

The Deluxe Model has a MSR of $30,000.

SHOTGUNS

AUSONIA SxS – 12 or 20 ga., exposed hammers with double Purdey type sidelock action, various engraving options, chopper lump barrels.

MSR $34,950	$31,000	$25,000	$20,000	$17,000	$14,000	$12,000	$9,950	

LIBERTY MODEL SxS – Anson and Deeley boxlock, chopper lump or mono bloc barrels, Zanatti triple compass bolting, available in all gauges and configurations.

MSR $28,250	$25,000	$22,000	$18,750	$15,000	$12,000	$10,000	$7,950	

CLASSIC MODEL SxS – best quality H&H sidelock ejector with chopper lump or mono bloc barrels and Zanatti bolting, available in all gauges and configurations.

MSR $44,980	$39,950	$35,000	$30,000	$25,000	$20,000	$16,250	$14,000	

REGINA MODEL SxS – 12 ga., heavy frame competition and hunting model, features removable trigger group with chopper lump barrel construction, border engraving is standard, supplied with extra trigger group and Nasco case, engraving upgrade and sideplates optional.

	N/A	$11,500	$9,950	$8,700	$7,600	$6,500	$5,150	

ROMAGNA HAMMER GUN – best quality external hammer bar action, chopper lump barrels with Zanatti bolting, available in all gauges and configurations, and heavy competiton model optional.

	$25,000	$20,500	$15,000	$10,000	$7,500	$5,000	$3,750	*$27,600*

Add $2,900 for ejectors and self-cocking mechanism.

MAESTRO O/U – 12 or 20 ga., Boss style scalloped receiver with removable trigger group, monobloc barrels are standard, chopper lump barrels optional, sideplated versions available in various models, forend types include standard release or optional Anson release, custom stock dimension standard.

Base price for 12 ga. is $19,600 and $24,700 for 20 ga.

Perugini-Visini utilizes advanced CNC manufacturing processes along with meticulous hand fitting and finishing with all Maestro models. Maestro models are available with any combination of barrel sets including 16 ga., 28 ga., and .410 bore.

* ***Maestro O/U Standard/Traveling Hunter Model*** – available in either competition or hunting configuration in 12 ga. or 20 ga., UM8 monobloc barrels and removable trigger, wood upgrade and custom engraving were optional.

	$10,950	$9,750	$8,600	$7,600	$6,700	$5,800	$4,350	*$12,000*

* ***Maestro O/U Lusso Model*** – sideplated version including exhibition walnut stock and choice of traditional rose and scroll or bulino game scene engraving, options included ornamental engraving.

	$23,750	$19,000	$16,500	$13,750	$11,000	$9,000	$8,250	*$26,500*

* ***Maestro O/U Reale Piccione Model*** – best quality sideplated removable trigger group competition or hunting O/U. This O/U is designed and fabricated with particular MOI for flyer and helice shooting. Standard features include adj. trigger, monobloc barrels with Boss side ribs, Anson plunger release, maker's forearm crest, gold oval, gold pigeon inlayed in forearm. Standard or choice of rose and scroll or bulino game scene engraving. Optional ornamental engraving was available.

	$29,500	$25,000	$21,000	$17,000	$13,750	$11,750	$9,475	*$33,750*

NOVA O/U/PERUGINI-VISINI BOSS – best quality Boss pattern sidelock O/U with back action locks and chopper lump barrels, Optional Boss-style forend iron and barrel bolsters, English rose and scroll engraving standard, ornamental engraving optional.

Current MSR on this model is $57,000.

GRADING - PPGS™	100%	98%	95%	90%	80%	70%	60%	LAST MSR

MICHELANGELO O/U – all gauges, sidelock or boxlock, chopper lumps or mono bloc barrels, for competition and game shooting.

MSR $57,000	$52,500	$46,000	$41,000	$35,000	$30,000	$25,000	$19,500	

PETERS STAHL GmbH

Previous pistol manufacturer located in Paderborn, Germany until 2010. Previously imported until 2009 by Euro-Imports, located in Yoakum, TX. Previously distributed by Swiss Trading GmbH, located in Bozeman, MT. Previously imported 1998-1999 by Peters Stahl, U.S.A. located in Delta, UT, and by Franzen International Inc. located in Oakland, NJ until 1998.

PISTOLS: SEMI-AUTO

Peters Stahl manufactured high quality semi-auto pistols based on the Model 1911 design, but had limited U.S. importation. Models include the Multicaliber, 92-Sport, O7-Sport, HC-Champion and variations, 1911-Tactical/Classic, PLS, and a .22 LR. Peters-Stahl also manufactures multicaliber conversion kits of the highest quality. Recent models previously imported (until 2000) included the Model Millennium (MSR was $2,195), Match 22 LR (MSR was $1,995), Trophy Master (MSR was $1,995), Omega Match (MSR was $1,995), High Capacity Trophy Master (MSR was $1,695), O7 Multicaliber (MSR was $1,995), and the 92 Multicaliber (MSR was $2,610-$2,720). In the past, Peters Stahl has manufactured guns for Federal Ordnance, Omega, Schuetzen Pistol Works, and Springfield Armory.

PFEIFER-WAFFEN

Current manufacturer located in Feldkirch, Austria. No current U.S. importation.

FIREARMS

Pfeifer-Waffen manufactures the unique "safety-rifle" in four configurations, the SR2, SR2 Magnum, SR2 Afrika, and the SR3 (base price begins at €2,548), an SR-Sport (base price begins at €3,337), a Liliput youth rifle in .22 Hornet, a repeating rifle, and a Zeliska revolver in .458 Win. Mag. or .600 NE cal. Please contact the company directly for more information, including pricing and availability (see Trademark Index).

PHELPS MFG. CO.

Previous manufacturer located in Evansville, IN circa 1978-1996.

Phelps Manufacturing Company began shipping guns in early 1978. Phelps guns were investment cast in 4140 steel, with basic single action simplicity, and a transfer bar safety.

REVOLVERS

HERITAGE I – .45-70 cal., single action revolver, incorporates transfer bar hammer safety, blue finish (standard), nickel (optional), adj. rear sight, 8 in. barrel standard, other barrel lengths up to 20 in. available, 6 lbs. Disc. 1996.

	$2,500	$2,000	$1,675	$1,425	$1,255	$1,020	$885	*$2,250*

Add $20 for each additional in. of barrel.

EAGLE I – .444 Marlin cal., single action revolver, blue finish, adj. rear sight, barrel options same as Heritage I, 6 lbs. Disc. 1996.

	$2,050	$1,675	$1,425	$1,255	$1,020	$885	$715	*$2,250*

PATRIOT – .375 Win. cal., single action revolver, blue finish, adj. rear sight, barrel options are the same as Heritage I. Limited mfg. 1993-94.

	$1,925	$1,550	$1,350	$1,185	$965	$840	$670	*$2,225*

GRIZZLY .50-70 – .50-70 cal., otherwise similar to Heritage I. Mfg. 1992-96.

	$2,300	$1,875	$1,500	$1,325	$1,085	$930	$750	*$2,580*

Add $20 for each additional in. of barrel.

GRADING - PPGS™	100%	98%	95%	90%	80%	70%	60%	LAST MSR

PHILLIPS & ROGERS, INC.

Previous manufacturer 1992-2003, and located in Huntsville, TX since 1997. Previously located in Conroe, TX circa 1992-1997.

In addition to manufacturing the firearms listed, Phillips & Rogers also made a multi-caliber conversion cylinder for all Ruger .357 Mag., new model Blackhawk revolvers (disc. 1996) - the retail price was $145. Multi-caliber conversion cylinders were also available for the Ruger new Model Blackhawk (allows shooting .45 LC, .45 Win. Mag., or .45 ACP - retail price was $185) and the Ruger Super Blackhawk (converts .44 Mag. to .50 AE w/barrel change - $550). A new version of the Ruger .50 AE conversion was also available for $995.

REVOLVERS

MEDUSA MODEL 47 REVOLVER – multi-caliber, over 25 cals. in the .355 - .380 diameter range (including .357 Mag., .38 Super, .38 Spl., 9mm Para., etc.), unique design does not utilize half-moon clips or cylinder/barrel changes, 2 1/2, 4, 5, 6, or 8 in. barrel, 6 shot, double action, matte blue finish, rubber or wood grips. Mfg. 1993-2003.

	100%	98%	95%	90%	80%	70%	60%	LAST MSR
	$750	$675	$575	$475	$400	$350	$325	*$599*

Add $95 for 8 in. barrel.

RIFLES: BOLT ACTION

WILDERNESS EXPLORER – .218 Bee, .22 Hornet, .44 Mag., or .50 AE cal., bolt action, features 18 in. match grade barrel, quick change bolt face and barrel allowing interchangeable calibers, white speckled black synthetic stock, side safety, 5 1/2 lbs. Mfg. 1997 only.

	100%	98%	95%	90%	80%	70%	60%	LAST MSR
	$925	$825	$725	$650	$575	$500	$425	*$995*

PHOENIX ARMS

Current manufacturer located in Ontario, CA since 1992. Distributor sales only.

PISTOLS: SEMI-AUTO

RAVEN – .25 ACP cal., single action, 2 7/16 in. barrel, 6 shot mag., alloy frame, choice of finishes and grips. Disc. 1998.

	100%	98%	95%	90%	80%	70%	60%	LAST MSR
	$70	$50	$45	$40	$35	$30	$25	*$79*

This model was supplied with a magazine disconnect lock.

HP MODEL – .22 LR or .25 ACP cal., single action, 3 in. VR barrel, 10 (.25 ACP), 10 (C/B 1994), or 11* (.22 LR) shot staggered mag., alloy frame, firing pin block safety, adj. rear sight, choice of polished blue or satin nickel finish, keyed mag. lock and safety cable lanyard, 20 oz. New 1994.

	100%	98%	95%	90%	80%	70%	60%
MSR $145	$120	$100	$80	$70	$60	$50	$45

Add $99 for laser sight and mount (new 1998).
Add $45 for 2-in-1 target barrel and magazine conversion kit.

* ***HP Model Range Kit*** – includes HP Model in .22 LR with 5 in. extended barrel, extended mag., locking plastic storage case (compartmentalized during 2000), and cleaning kit. New 1998.

	100%	98%	95%	90%	80%	70%	60%
MSR $188	$150	$120	$100	$90	$75	$65	$55

* ***HP Model Deluxe Range Kit*** – similar to HP Range Kit, except has 3 and 5 in. barrels and extended mag. New 1999.

	100%	98%	95%	90%	80%	70%	60%
MSR $224	$185	$165	$135	$110	$100	$90	$80

PHOENIX ARMS CO.

Previous importer located in Lowell, MA.

PISTOLS: SEMI-AUTO

PHOENIX – .25 ACP cal., Belgian semi-auto, previously manufactured by Robar et DeKerkhove located in Liege, Belgium.

	100%	98%	95%	90%	80%	70%	60%
	$495	$450	$400	$350	$300	$250	$200

GRADING - PPGS™	100%	98%	95%	90%	80%	70%	60%	LAST MSR

PIETTA, F.LLI

Current firearms, black powder, replica firearms and accessories manufacturer established in 1962 by Knight Giuseppe Pietta and located in Gussago, Italy. Pietta single action revolvers are currently imported and distributed by Cabela's, located in Sidney, NE, Cimarron F.A. Co., located in Fredericksburg, TX, Dixie Gun Works, located in Union City, TN, E.M.F., located in Santa Ana, CA, Heritage, located in Miami, FL, Navy Arms, located in Martinsburg, WV, Taylor's & Co, located in Winchester, VA, Legacy Sports International (shotguns too), located in Reno, NV, and Traditions, located in Old Saybrook, CT. Importers also stamp their own brand names on Pietta firearms, but all guns have Pietta listed as a manufacturer.

The company introduced a modern SAA revolver during 2003, in cals. .357 Mag., .44-40 WCF, and .45 LC, and it was awarded Best Gun of the Year from SASS twice. During 2005, Pietta introduced the Challenge semi-auto shotgun line, which included the Mistral and the Zephyrus, and production began in 2006 (mostly European sales). These were followed by the Superior and Ghibley models, in addition to a line of tactical slide action shotguns.

Semi-auto shotguns were previously imported under the Verona name into the U.S. by Legacy Sports International in 12 and 20 gauge until 2010. Please refer to the Verona section for these older models.

During 2010, Pietta introduced the PPS50 carbine in .22 LR cal. with shrouded barrel, in addition to the MK85 .22 LR cal. pistol with shrouded barrel and side mounted magazine.

For more information and up-to-date pricing regarding current Pietta black powder models, please refer to the *Blue Book of Modern Black Powder Arms* by John Allen.

Black Powder Revolvers - Reproductions & Replicas and *Black Powder Long Arms & Pistols - Reproductions & Replicas* by Dennis Adler are also invaluable sources for most black powder reproductions and replicas, and includes hundreds of color images on most popular makes/models, provide manufacturer/trademark histories, and up-to-date information on related items/accessories for black powder shooting - www.bluebookofgunvalues.com.

Pietta firearms may be listed separately under the importers - please refer to the individual listings.

REVOLVERS: REPRODUCTIONS, SAA & VARIATIONS

Factory engraving and other embellishments or finished (white steel, nickel, etc.) may be special ordered by contacting the importers directly.

Add $80 for antique patina finish. Add $125 for silver plating. Add $45 for white finish. Add $220 for Pietta S.A. photo engraving. Add $980 for Pietta S.A. full deep laser engraving. Add $105 for gold inlay initials. Add $60 for checkered grips. Add $22 for white plastic one-piece grips. Add $170 for nickel plating. Add $90 for action job.

1873 PIETTA SAA & VARIATIONS – .22 LR, .357 Mag., .44-40 WCF, .44 Win. Mag., or .45 LC cal., 3 3/4, 4 3/4, 5 1/2, 7 1/2, 10, or 12 in. forged hammer barrel, brass or steel backstrap and trigger guard, 4140 steel or stainless steel, New Model cross pin frame (w/ plunger), case colored frame or blue finish, bevelled cylinder, original hammer design with transfer bar safety (.22 LR cal. only), one-piece European walnut grips.

*** *1873 Pietta SAA w/Steel Backstrap & Triggerguard***

MSR	100%	98%	95%	90%	80%	70%	60%
MSR $510	$425	$365	$335	$300	$275	$250	$225

Add $260 for stainless steel.

*** *1873 Pietta SAA w/Brass Backstrap & Triggerguard***

MSR	100%	98%	95%	90%	80%	70%	60%
MSR $480	$425	$375	$325	$300	$275	$250	$225

Add $260 for stainless steel.

*** *1873 Pietta Millenium SAA*** – .357 Mag. or .45 LC cal., 4 3/4 or 5 1/2 in. barrel, matte blue finish, brass backstrap and trigger guard.

MSR	100%	98%	95%	90%	80%	70%	60%
MSR $380	$325	$295	$265	$235	$200	$185	$160

*** *1873 Pietta Bird's Head SAA***

MSR	100%	98%	95%	90%	80%	70%	60%
MSR $510	$425	$365	$335	$300	$275	$250	$225

Add $260 for stainless steel.

GRADING - PPGS™	100%	98%	95%	90%	80%	70%	60%	LAST MSR

* ***1873 Pietta SAA Model "T"***

MSR $540	$450	$395	$350	$300	$275	$250	$225	

Add $230 for stainless steel.

* ***1873 Pietta Buntline SAA*** – .45 LC cal., 12 in. barrel, blue finish, New Model frame with steel backstrap.

MSR $575	$495	$450	$400	$365	$335	$300	$275	

Add $125 for Antique blue finish.
Add $225 for nickel plating.

* ***1873 Pietta .22 Cal. SAA***

MSR $380	$325	$295	$265	$235	$200	$185	$160	

SHOTGUNS

Pietta currently manufactures a Challenge semi-auto shotgun line including the Superior I, II, and III, the Ghibli, Gold Series, and Mistral models. The company also manufactures a slide action shotgun in both sporting and tactical configurations. Please contact the company directly for more information on U.S. availability and pricing.

PIONEER ARMS CORP.

Current manufacturer located in Radom, Poland. Currently imported by Pioneer Arms, located in North Bennington, VT. Previously located in Moline, IL.

Pioneer manufactures a line of SxS hammer coach guns with 18 1/2 in. barrels and 3 in. chambers. Current MSR is $2,500. Please contact the importer directly for more information, including options and availability (see Trademark Index).

PIOTTI

Current manufacturer established circa 1955, and located in Brescia, Italy. Currently imported and distributed exclusively by William Larkin Moore & Co. located in Scottsdale, AZ.

Fratelli Piotti is one of the world's premier gunmakers. These long guns meet the highest standards of craftsmanship and are made to customer specifications. A variety of gauges, engraving, styles, chokes, etc. are available. Fratelli Piotti manufactures approx. 65-70 guns per year.

RIFLES: CUSTOM

Piotti also manufactures a custom SxS double rifle on a very limited basis.

Current MSR on this model w/o engraving starts at $91,000.

SHOTGUNS: O/U

PIOTTI BOSS – 12, 16, 20, or 28 ga., 26-32 in. barrels, single or double triggers, standard with King 2 engraving, Turkish Circassian walnut, various engraving patterns available, 6 - 7 1/2 lbs. New 1995.

MSR $73,900	$67,500	$61,000	$54,000	$40,000	$31,000	$25,000	$21,000	

Add $3,925 for single trigger.
Add $5,100 for 16 or $4,125 for 20 ga.
Add $10,700 for 28 ga.

SHOTGUNS: SxS

For the following models - add $3,2750 for single trigger, $12,450 for H&H type self-opening mechanism, $1,355 - $2,200 for hand-detachable locks, $1,125 for pinless action or $800 for rounded action, approx. $1,775 - $3,550 for leather case, 10 ga. (disc., last MSR was $7,125), $1,225 for 16 or 20 ga., $1,675 for 28 ga. or .410 bore boxlock, and $3,225 for 28 ga. or .410 bore sidelock.

HAMMER GUN – 12 ga. only, self cocking ejector model, DT, exposed hammers, back action with fine scroll engraving. Importation began 2001.

MSR $46,500	$41,000	$35,750	$31,000	$24,500	$19,500	$13,000	$10,000	

Add $4,700 for ejectors and self-cocking mechanism.

GRADING - PPGS™	100%	98%	95%	90%	80%	70%	60%	LAST MSR

PIUMA (BSEE) – 10, 12, 16, 20, 28 ga., or .410 bore, Anson & Deeley boxlock ejector double with chopper lump barrels, level file-cut rib, light scroll and rosette engraving, scalloped frame.

MSR $20,300	$18,000	$13,000	$10,250	$8,500	$7,000	$5,750	$4,500	

WESTLAKE – 12, 16, 20, 28 ga., or .410 bore, H&H sidelock action, moderate scroll engraving. Mfg. disc. 1989.

	$8,500	$7,500	$6,050	$5,300	$4,700	$4,200	$3,750	*$8,400*

MONTE CARLO – 12, 16, 20, 28 ga., or .410 bore, best-quality H&H pattern sidelock ejector double with chopper lump barrels, Purdey style scroll and rosette engraving. Importation disc. 1990.

	$10,500	$9,250	$8,200	$7,100	$6,000	$5,000	$4,500	*$11,400*

KING NUMBER 1 – 12, 16, 20, 28 ga., or .410 bore, best-quality H&H pattern sidelock ejector double with chopper lump barrels, level file-cut rib, very fine full coverage scroll engraving with small floral bouquets, gold crest in forearm, gold crown in top lever, name in gold, and finely figured wood.

MSR $39,900	$36,500	$25,500	$20,000	$14,500	$10,250	$7,750	$6,600	

KING EXTRA – 12, 16, 20, 28 ga., or .410 bore, best-quality H&H pattern sidelock ejector double with chopper lump barrels, level file-cut rib, choice of either Bulino game scene engraving or standard cameo game scene engraving with gold inlays, engraved and signed by a master engraver, exhibition grade wood.

Please contact the importer directly for a price quotation on this model.

LUNIK – 12, 16, 20, 28 ga., or .410 bore, best-quality H&H pattern sidelock ejector double with lump (demi-bloc) barrels, level file-cut rib, Renaissance style large scroll engraving in relief, gold crown in top lever, gold name, gold crest in forearm, finely figured wood.

MSR $42,800	$37,250	$26,000	$21,000	$15,500	$11,500	$8,700	$6,950	

MONACO NUMBER 1 OR 2 – 12, 16, 20, 28 ga., or .410 bore, best-quality H&H pattern sidelock ejector double with lump (demi-bloc) barrels, level file-cut rib, Renaissance style large scroll engraving in relief, gold crown in top lever, gold name, gold crest in forearm, finely figured wood.

MSR $52,500	$47,000	$38,000	$31,500	$25,000	$20,000	$18,000	$16,000	

MONACO NUMBER 3 – next to top-of-the-line model.

Current MSR on this model is $55,700.

MONACO NUMBER 4 – top-of-the-line model with every refinement incorporated. Custom order only and extremely rare.

Current MSR on this model is $76,000.

PIRANHA

Previous trademark of a recoilless semi-auto 9mm Para. cal. pistol that was advertised circa 1996, but never manufactured by Recoilless Tech, Inc. located in Glendale and Phoenix, AZ. While advertised, Piranha pistols were never manufactured (except a few prototypes).

R.T.I. tried to develop its manufacturing capability for the semi-auto Piranha Recoilless Pistol, utilizing hesition lock bi-angular springs to reduce 85% of the recoil, and which also allowed changing calibers by changing the barrel.

PISTOL DYNAMICS

Current semi-auto pistol manufacturer located in Palm Bay, FL.

PISTOLS: SEMI-AUTO

Pistol Dynamics manufactures high quality 1911-style semi-auto pistols. Series include the Signature (base price $3,800 MSR), Combat Special Evolution (base price $3,600 MSR), Combat Special Classic (base price $4,600 MSR), Scout (base price $2,900 MSR), and the X-O (base price $2,400 MSR). Options and delivery times vary from each model. Please contact the company directly for availability and pricing (see Trademark Index).

PLAINS RIFLE

A Plains rifle is a modification of the Kentucky rifle. Its original purpose was for use

GRADING - PPGS™	100%	98%	95%	90%	80%	70%	60%	LAST MSR

on the western frontier.

The Plains rifle is often referred to as a half stock, and first appeared around the end of the first quarter of the 19th century, with production ending by 1880. There was a demand for shorter rifles to be carried on horseback and larger bores for bigger game. Bores ranged from .50 to .60 caliber, and barrel lengths were 36 to 40 inches. Plains rifles are generally found with percussion ignition systems.

Like the Kentucky rifle, Plains rifles were all handmade. Jacob and Samuel Hawken are considered the originators of the Plains rifle. They were the sons of Christian Hawken, Kentucky rifle maker of Hagerstown, MD. The popularity of Jacob and Samuel's guns spread rapidly. Gunmakers from across the country began to copy the Plains style rifle. In addition to the Hawken brothers, other well-known makers were Horace Dimick, J.P. Gemmer, James Henry, and Henry Leman. Like Kentucky rifles, values for Plains rifles differ greatly, depending on the maker, condition, and style. Values can range anywhere from $500-$50,000! Flintlock Plains rifles are scarce.

The publisher would like to thank Mr. Jim Buelow for making the above information available to the *Blue Book of Gun Values*.

POINTER

Previous trademark of shotguns imported until 2008 by Legacy Sports International, located in Reno, NV. Previously located in Alexandria, VA.

SHOTGUNS: O/U

POINTER TURKISH SPORTING/FIELD - 12 ga., 3 in. chambers, 28 in. barrels, blue (disc.) or electroless nickel finish with floral engraving, five multi-chokes, select walnut stock and forearm, Kickeez buttpad, Truglo sight, extractors, gold trigger, 7.7 lbs. Mfg. by Zafer Arms Co. in Turkey. Limited importation 2006-2007.

$525	**$460**	**$415**	**$350**	**$300**	**$260**	**$220**	***$599***

POINTER ITALIAN SPORTING/FIELD - 12, 20, 28 ga., or .410 bore, 3 in. chambers, 28 in. barrels, blue/nickel finish, fixed or multi-chokes, select walnut stock and forearm, ejectors, 6.1-7.4 lbs. Imported 2007-2008.

$1,150	**$995**	**$875**	**$750**	**$625**	**$525**	**$450**	***$1,299***

Add $200 for 28 ga. or .410 bore.

POINTER ITALIAN SPORTING CLAYS - 12 ga., 3 in. chambers, 28 in. barrels, blue/nickel finish, multi-chokes, select walnut stock and forearm, ejectors, 7.6 lbs. Imported 2007-2008.

$1,150	**$995**	**$875**	**$750**	**$625**	**$525**	**$450**	***$1,299***

POLI, ARMI F.LLI

Current manufacturer established in 1966, and located in Gardone, Italy. Currently imported by Deep River Sporting Clays, located in Sanford, NC. Previously imported by Cole Gunsmithing, located in Harpswell, ME, and by Anglo American Sporting Agency, located in Corona Del Mar, CA..

Armi F.lli Poli manufactures high quality, SxS and single barrel hammer shotguns in 12, 16, 20, 28 ga., or .410 bore. Current models include the Ivory (hammerless, boxlock action), Opal (hammerless, boxlock action with sideplates), Lapis (lightweight, scalloped boxlock action, hammerless), Onix (scalloped boxlock action, hammerless), Coral (sidelock back action w/hammers), Ruby (petite sidelock back action w/hammers), Emerald (sidelock back action w/hammers), Amethyst (sidelock, hammerless), Sapphire, Kristal, Zircon, and Zircon Deluxe. Please contact the importer for more information, including pricing and availability (see Trademark Index).

POLI NICOLETTA & C. snc.

Current manufacturer established in 1975, and located in Brescia, Italy. No current U.S. importation.

Poli Nicoletta manufactures good quality lightweight hunting rifles and shotguns, in addition to choke tubes and scope mounts. Please contact the company directly for more information, including pricing (includes freight) and availability (see Trademark Index).

GRADING - PPGS™	100%	98%	95%	90%	80%	70%	60%	LAST MSR

POLY TECHNOLOGIES, INC.

Previously distributed by PTK International, Inc. located in Atlanta, GA. Previously imported by Keng's Firearms Specialty, Inc., located in Riverdale, GA. Manufactured in China by Poly Technologies, Inc.

Poly Technologies commercial firearms are made to Chinese military specifications and have excellent quality control.

These models were banned from domestic importation due to 1989 Federal legislation.

RIFLES: SEMI-AUTO

Add 10% for NIB.

AKS-762 – 7.62x39mm or .223 Rem. cal., 16 1/4 in. barrel, semi-auto version of the Chinese AKM (Type 56) paramilitary design rifle, 8.4 lbs., wood stock. Imported 1988-89.

$1,495	$1,325	$1,100	$975	$875	$795	$750	*$400*

Add $100 for side-fold plastic stock.

This model was also available with a downward folding stock at no extra charge.

SKS – 7.62x39mm cal., 20 9/20 in. barrel, full wood stock, machined steel parts to Chinese military specifications, 7.9 lbs. Imported 1988-89.

$550	$475	$400	$350	$300	$275	$250	*$200*

AK-47/S (LEGEND) – 7.62x39mm cal., 16 3/8 in. barrel, semi-auto configuration of the original AK-47, fixed, side-folding, or under-folding stock, with or w/o spike bayonet, 8.2 lbs. Imported 1988-89.

$2,000	$1,800	$1,600	$1,350	$1,200	$1,000	$925	*$550*

Add 10% for folding stock.

The "S" suffix in this variation designates third model specifications.

* ***AK-47/S National Match Legend*** – utilizes match parts in fabrication.

$1,950	$1,750	$1,550	$1,275	$1,050	$975	$900

RPK – 7.62x39mm cal. Disc.

$1,475	$1,300	$1,150	$1,025	$925	$850	$775

M-14/S – .308 Win. cal., 22 in. barrel, forged receiver, patterned after the famous M-14, 9.2 lbs. Imported 1988-89.

$1,100	$950	$850	$775	$725	$650	$575	*$700*

POWELL, WILLIAM & SON (GUNMAKERS) LTD.

Please refer to the W Section for this trademark.

PRAIRIE GUN WORKS

Please refer to PGW Defence Technologies listing.

PRANDELLI-GASPERINI

Previous manufacturer located in Brescia, Italy. Previously imported by Richland Arms located in Blissfield, MI.

Prandelli-Gasperini made both O/U and SxS shotguns in either sidelock or boxlock. Currently, values for the older boxlock models are in the $475-$675 range (assuming 80% or better original condition). Sidelock models in similar condition are usually valued in the $1,350 - $2,100 range, depending on gauge, embellishments, and condition.

Approx. 250 specimens of this trademark were imported during Richland Arms importation.

PRECHTL, WAFFEN

Please refer to Waffen, Prechtl in the W section.

PRECISION FIREARMS LLC

Current firearms manufacturer located in Hagerstown, MD. Dealer and consumer sales through FFL.

Precision Firearms manufactures high quality AR-15 style rifles and upper assemblies. Calibers currently include .17 Rem., .204 Ruger, .223 Wylde, 5.56 NATO, 6.5 Grendel,

GRADING - PPGS™	100%	98%	95%	90%	80%	70%	60%	LAST MSR

.264 LBC, 6.8 SPC II, and .308 Win. Please contact the manufacturer directly for more information, availability, and pricing (see Trademark Index).

PRECISION SMALL ARMS, INC. (PSA)

Current manufacturer established in 1984, and made under license from Fabrique Nationale, Herstal, Belgium in Aspen, CO, since 2007. Previously manufactured in Montrose, CO during 2006 and in Charlottesville, VA until 1995.

PISTOLS: SEMI-AUTO

The PSP pistol was not in production from 1995-2006, but approx. 1,000 nickel plated units were sold to various dealers between 1995-2006 from inventory. The handgun business of Precision Small Parts Ltd (PSP) was put into a new entity called Precision Small Arms, Inc. (PSA) in 1997, although the pistol has been marketed as the PSA-25 since 1995. Beginning mid-2010, all pistols are machined from billet, engraved variations are performed by Master Engraver Angelo Bee.

(PSP) PSA-25 TRADITIONAL - .25 ACP (6.35mm), single action, stricker fired, blow back mechanism, 2 1/8 in. barrel, 6 shot mag., checkered black polymer grips, all steel construction with choice of high polished blue (new 1990), black oxide (disc. 1998), brushed satin nickel (Nouveau Satin), high polished nickel finish (Nouveau Mirror), or "1911 Hot Blue" glass/zircon bead blasted finish (new 2008), triple safety system, 7 1/4 - 9 1/2 oz. Mfg. 1984-1995, reintroduced 2006.

MSR	100%	98%	95%	90%	80%	70%	60%	LAST MSR
MSR $650	$550	$475	$415	$375	$300	$250	$195	

Add $100 for Nouveau Mirror or Traditional HP Model.

* ***PSA-25 Stainless Steel*** – features 303 stainless steel construction, satin, high polish or vacuum deposition coated black finish. Introduced 2010.

MSR	100%	98%	95%	90%	80%	70%	60%	LAST MSR
MSR $775	$650	$575	$495	$440	$360	$295	$230	

Add $15 for Nouveau Mirror finish (disc. 2011).
Add $35 for non-polished (disc. 2011) or $60 for black finish.

* ***PSA-25 Bone & Charcoal*** – bone and charcoal color case hardening by Shiloh Sharps, Turkish walnut burl grips. New 2012.

MSR	100%	98%	95%	90%	80%	70%	60%	LAST MSR
MSR $1,004	$850	$750	$625	$575	$475	$385	$300	

* ***PSA-25 Featherweight*** – features 7075 T652 aircraft aluminum frame with high polish chrome over nickel steel slide and mag., gold-plated trigger, aluminum two tier serial numbered case and original 1931 FN style grips. Introduced 2010.

MSR	100%	98%	95%	90%	80%	70%	60%	LAST MSR
MSR $1,031	$875	$775	$650	$595	$475	$395	$300	

Add $190 for stainless steel slide (S Model) or $696 stainless steel slide and Grade 5 titanium skeletonized trigger (T Model).

* ***PSA-25 Diplomat*** – features blued, high polish frame and slide, 24Kt. gold plated external components, ivory grips. New 1999.

MSR	100%	98%	95%	90%	80%	70%	60%	LAST MSR
MSR $1,086	$925	$815	$695	$625	$515	$415	$325	

* ***PSA-25 Beauxart Stainless*** – high polish chrome over nickel plated finish, silver nickel grips with mother-of-pearl inlay, metal mag. catch and trigger. Introduced 2011.

MSR	100%	98%	95%	90%	80%	70%	60%	LAST MSR
MSR $950	$800	$700	$600	$550	$440	$360	$280	

* ***PSA-25 Case Colored*** – .25 cal., 6 shot, walnut burl grips, 24 KT gold plated trigger, two nickel plated magazines, ships with its own black or brown hand crafted Swedish leather zippered pouch. Only 500 to be mfg. mid-2012.

MSR	100%	98%	95%	90%	80%	70%	60%	LAST MSR
MSR $923	$825	$725	$600	$550	$475	$400	$325	

* ***PSA-25 Montreux*** – high polish 18 Kt. (rose gold) or high polish 24 Kt. (yellow gold) gold plated frame, slide, and external components, ivory grips. Yellow Gold introduced 1999, Rose Gold introduced 2010.

MSR	100%	98%	95%	90%	80%	70%	60%	LAST MSR
MSR $1,086	$925	$815	$695	$625	$515	$415	$325	

Add $108 for Rose Gold.

* ***PSA-25 Sterling*** – high polish sterling silver plated finish, 7 gram solid silver trigger, metal mag. catch, silver nickel grips with carbon fiber inlay. Mfg. 2010-2012.

	100%	98%	95%	90%	80%	70%	60%	LAST MSR
	$1,095	$900	$825	$725	$625	$550	$495	*$1,250*

GRADING - PPGS™	100%	98%	95%	90%	80%	70%	60%	LAST MSR

* ***PSA-25 Presidential*** – features high polished 24Kt. gold plated slide, frame, magazine, and trigger, Dendrite ivory grips. Disc. 1999.

	$600	$475	$375	$315	$270	$230	$200	*$725*

* ***PSA-25 Renaissance Series*** – available in High Polish (nickel plated, engraved), French Blue (330 grit finish, engraved), and Coin (glass/Zircon bead blasted nickel finish), ivory grips, 24 Kt. gold plated grip screw, nut, trigger, mag. catch and trigger.

MSR $2,876	$2,450	$2,150	$1,825	$1,675	$1,350	$1,100	$850	

* ***PSA-25 Imperiale*** – features hand inlaid 24 kt. gold scroll pattern on frame and slide by Angelo Bee, high polish black oxide finish, ivory grips. Introduced 1997. Limited ed.

MSR $3,527	$3,195	$2,775	$2,350	$1,950	$1,650	$1,350	$1,150	

* ***PSA-25 Signature Editions*** – similar to Imperiale, except has "Michael B. Kassnar" signature on left slide top in gold. Mfg. 1989-91.

	$325	$295	$260	$230	$200	$175	$160	*$385*

There were also two Limited Signature Editions (less than 10 mfg.) which retailed for $1,458 and approx. $2,150.

* ***PSA-25 Grand Exhibition No. 1*** – features hand inlaid 24 Kt. orange, yellow and green gold scroll pattern with rosettes on frame and slide high polish blue finish, ivory grips. Introduced 2009. Limited ed.

MSR $5,281	$4,475	$3,915	$3,350	$3,050	$2,450	$2,000	$1,550	

PREDATOR TACTICAL LLC

Current manufacturer located in Tempe, AZ.

Predator Tactical LLC was founded by champion competition shooter Matt Burkett. The company manufactures best quality high capacity semi-auto pistols based on STI frames (MSRs start at $3,525), as well as the 1911 Shrike Series (MSRs start at $2,800), based on Caspian Arms frames. Predator Tactical also offers customized rifles and shotguns. Please contact the company for more information, including pricing and availability (see Trademark Index).

PREMIER

Previous trademark manufactured in Italy and Spain by various companies.

SHOTGUNS: SxS

Note: Premier is a trade name for guns that have been produced in both Spain and Italy for various importers.

REGENT MODEL – 12, 16, 20, 28 ga., or .410 bore, 26, 28, or 30 in. barrels, various chokes, checkered pistol grip stock and beavertail forearm. Mfg. 1955-disc.

	$325	$275	$250	$220	$195	$140	$110	

Add 33% for 28 ga. or .410 bore.

REGENT MAGNUM EXPRESS – 12 ga., 3 in. chambers only, 30 in. full barrel, recoil pad. Mfg. 1957-disc.

	$375	$325	$275	$250	$220	$165	$140	

REGENT 10 GAUGE MAGNUM – similar to 12 ga. Mag., but 10 ga., 3 1/2 in. chamber, 32 in. full and full barrel. Mfg. 1975-disc.

	$550	$495	$450	$375	$325	$250	$195	

BRUSH KING – 12 or 20 ga., 22 in. imp. cyl. and mod. barrels, straight grip stock. Mfg. 1959-disc.

	$325	$275	$250	$220	$195	$140	$110	

MONARCH SUPREME GRADE – 12 or 20 ga., 26 or 28 in. barrels, various chokes, boxlock, auto ejectors, select stock. Mfg. 1959-disc.

	$575	$500	$450	$385	$360	$330	$275	

PRESENTATION CUSTOM GRADE – custom-made, gold and silver game scene. Mfg. 1959-disc.

	$1,350	$1,100	$990	$880	$825	$715	$605	

GRADING - PPGS™	100%	98%	95%	90%	80%	70%	60%	LAST MSR

AMBASSADOR MODEL – 12, 16, 20 ga., or .410 bore, 26 or 28 in. barrels, mod. and full choke, checkered pistol grip stock. Mfg. 1957-disc.

	$440	$385	$360	$330	$305	$250	$220	

Add 33% for .410 bore.

PRIMARY WEAPONS SYSTEMS

Current manufacturer located in Boise, ID.

Primary Weapons Systems manufactures a series of AR-15 style semi-auto pistols, rifles, and bolt action rifles, as well as SBR models for law enforcement and military.

PISTOLS: SEMI-AUTO

MK107 SERIES – .223 Wylde (new 2013), 5.56 NATO (disc. 2012), 7.62x39mm (disc. 2012) cal., 30 shot mag., 7 1/2 in. Isonite QPQ treated, 1:8 twist button rifled barrel. Mil-Spec upper and lower receiver, ALG Defense QMS trigger, enhanced bolt carrier group, PWS KeyMod rail system, BCMGUNFIGHTER charging handle, Magpul MOE furniture and sights.

MSR $1,750	$1,475	$1,295	$1,100	$1,000	$815	$675	$525	

MK109 SERIES – .300 BLK cal., 9 3/4 in. stainless steel, 30 shot polymer mag., Isonite QPD treated, button rifled barrel, mil-spec upper and lower receiver, quad rail, available in matte black or flat dark earth finish, enhanced charging handle and bolt carrier group, Micro-slicked Internals, Magpul XT rail panels, Magpul MOE grip, MBUS sights, approx. 5 1/5 lbs. Disc. 2012.

	$1,525	$1,300	$1,100	$925	$750	$675	$575	*$1,700*

Add $200 for Flat Dark Earth finish.

RIFLES: BOLT ACTION

MK3 SERIES – .300 Win. Mag., 21 3/4 in. stainless steel barrel, 30 shot mag., Isonite QPQ treated barrel and receiver, Jewell trigger, PRC muzzle device, 5 shot mag., KRG Whisky-3 folding chassis, AI mag. compatibility, 11 1/2 lbs. New 2012.

MSR $6,496	$5,525	$4,825	$4,150	$3,750	$3,0050	$2,495	$1,925	

T3 RIMFIRE SERIES – .22 LR cal., 21 1/2 in. barrel, choice of stock, Summit 10/22 action, 30 shot mag., approx. 4 lbs.

MSR $800	$675	$595	$500	$450	$375	$300	$235	

RIFLES: SEMI-AUTO

IMPORTANT NOTE: On model(s) where *N/A has replaced the normal 100% value, it indicates current market conditions are too unstable to accurately ascertain 100%-60% values. Factory retail prices (MSRs) reflect most recent updates. For more up-to-date information on current pricing trends and additional useful information, please visit www.bluebookofgunvalues.com, select "Information & Services" from the menu, and click on "Additional Book Information".

MK1 SERIES – .223 Wylde (new 2013), 5.56 NATO (disc. 2012), or .300 BLK cal., 16 in. stainless steel, Isonite QPD treated, button rifled barrel, 30 shot polymer mag., mil-spec upper and lower receiver, quad rail, available in matte black or flat dark earth finish, enhanced bolt carrier group, Micro-slicked Internals, Magpul XT rail panels, Magpul MOE grip, MBUS sights, Triad 30 flash suppressor, ALG Defense QMS trigger, PWS KeyMod rail system, BCMGUNFIGHTER charging handle, approx. 7 lbs.

MSR $1,750	*N/A	$1,295	$1,100	$1,000	$815	$675	$525	

This series is also available with 7, 9 1/2, 10 1/2 or 14 1/2 in. barrels for military/law enforcement.

MK2 SERIES – .308 Win. cal., SR-25 platform, 16.1 in, Isonite QPD treated button rifled barrel, 30 shot polymer mag., mil-spec upper and lower receiver, quad rail, available in matte black or flat dark earth finish, enhanced bolt carrier group, Micro-slicked Internals, Magpul XT rail panels, Magpul MOE grip, MBUS sights, ALG Defense QMS trigger, PWS KeyMod rail system, BCMGUNFIGHTER charging handle, 8 lbs., 12 oz.

MSR $2,600	*N/A	$2,225	$1,925	$1,725	$1,400	$1,150	$895	

Add $200 for Flat Dark Earth finish.

This series is also available with 12 1/2 or 14 1/2 barrels for military/law enforcement.

GRADING - PPGS™	100%	98%	95%	90%	80%	70%	60%	LAST MSR

WOODLAND SPORTING RIFLE – .223 Wylde or .300 BLK cal., 16.1 or 18 in. free floating stainless steel, Isonite QPQ treated, button rifled barrel, enhanced charging handle, PWS Mil Spec upper and lower receiver, enhanced DI carrier, black olive (disc.) or walnut stock, 30 shot polymer mag. approx. 7 1/2 - 8 lbs. New 2012.

MSR $1,500	*N/A	$1,125	$950	$875	$700	$575	$450	

WRAITH 3GUN COMPETITION RIFLE – .223 Wylde cal., 18 in. free floating stainless steel, Isonite QPQ treated, button rifled barrel, enhanced charging handle, PWS mil-spec upper and lower receiver, enhanced DI carrier, black olive or walnut stock, 30 shot polymer mag., Daniel Defense free float handguard, JP Tactical EZ trigger, 7 lbs., 14 oz. Mfg. 2012.

	*N/A	$1,575	$1,275	$1,025	$900	$775	$675	*$2,000*

PRINZ

Previous manufacturer of bolt action rifles, single shot rifles, and combination guns. Previously imported and distributed by Helmut Hofmann Inc. located in Placitas, NM.

RIFLES

GRADE 1 BOLT ACTION – .243 Win., .30-06, .308 Win., .300 Win. Mag., or 7mm Rem. Mag. cal., single or double set trigger(s), oil finished walnut stock.

	$495	$440	$385	$360	$330	$275	$250	

* ***Grade 1 Bolt Action Carbine*** – similar to Grade 1 except has carbine barrel.

	$570	$495	$435	$390	$360	$330	$275	

GRADE 2 BOLT ACTION – similar to Grade 1 except has rosewood forend cap.

	$545	$485	$425	$385	$360	$330	$275	

TIP-UP RIFLE – available in 8 cals. between .222 Rem. and .30-06, high quality and limited mfg. Importation began 1989.

	$2,175	$1,900	$1,675	$1,375	$1,100	$950	$775	

PRINCESS MODEL 85 – combination gun available in 12 ga. (2 3/4 in. chamber) and choice of 8 cals. between .222 Rem. and .30-06.

	$1,450	$1,275	$1,100	$925	$800	$775	$650	

This model came standard with a leather case.

PROFESSIONAL ORDNANCE, INC.

Previous manufacturer located in Lake Havasu City, AZ 1998-2003. Previously manufactured in Ontario, CA circa 1996-1997. Distributor sales only.

During 2003, Bushmaster bought Professional Ordnance and the Carbon 15 trademark. Please refer to the Bushmaster section for currently manufactured Carbon 15 rifles and pistols (still manufactured in Lake Havasu City).

PISTOLS: SEMI-AUTO

CARBON-15 TYPE 20 – .223 Rem. cal., Stoner type operating system with recoil reducing buffer assembly, carbon fiber upper and lower receiver, hard chromed bolt carrier, 7 1/4 in. unfluted stainless steel barrel with ghost ring sights, 30 shot mag. (supplies were limited), also accepts AR-15 type mags., 40 oz. Mfg. 1999-2000.

	$950	$800	$725	$650	$575	$525	$475	*$1,500*

CARBON-15 TYPE 21 – .223 Rem cal., ultra lightweight carbon fiber upper and lower receivers, 7 1/4 in. "Profile" stainless steel barrel, quick detachable muzzle compensator, ghost ring sights, 10 shot mag., also accepts AR-15 type mags., Stoner type operating sytem, tool steel bolt, extractor and carrier, 40 oz. Mfg. 2001-2003.

	$850	$750	$675	$600	$550	$500	$450	*$899*

CARBON-15 TYPE 97 – similar to Carbon 15 Type 20, except has fluted barrel and quick detachable compensator, 46 oz. Mfg. 1996-2003.

	$925	$800	$725	$625	$575	$525	$475	*$964*

GRADING - PPGS™	100%	98%	95%	90%	80%	70%	60%	LAST MSR

RIFLES: SEMI-AUTO

CARBON-15 TYPE 20 – .223 Rem. cal., same operating system as the Carbon-15 pistol, 16 in. unfluted stainless steel barrel, carbon fiber buttstock and forearm, includes mil spec optics mounting base, 3.9 lbs. Mfg. 1998-2000.

	$975	$850	$795	$725	$650	$550	$475	*$1,550*

CARBON-15 TYPE 21 – .223 Rem. cal., ultra light weight carbon fiber upper and lower receivers, 16 in. "Profile" stainless steel barrel, quick detachable muzzle compensator, Stoner type operating system, tool steel bolt, extractor and carrier, optics mounting base, quick detachable stock, 10 shot mag., also accepts AR-15 type mags., 3.9 lbs. Mfg. 2001-2003.

	$975	$850	$795	$725	$650	$550	$475	*$988*

CARBON-15 TYPE 97/97S – .223 Rem. cal., ultra lighweight carbon fiber upper and lower receivers, Stoner type operating system, hard chromed tool steel bolt, extractor and carrier, 16 in. fluted stainless steel barrel, quick detachable muzzle compensator, optics mounting base, quick detachable stock, 30 shot mag., also accepts AR-15 type mags., 3.9 lbs. Mfg. 2001-2003.

	$1,075	$900	$825	$750	$675	$600	$550	*$1,120*

Add $165 for Model 97S (includes Picatinny rail and "Scout" extension, double walled heat shield forearm, ambidextrous safety, and multi-point silent carry).

PROOF RESEARCH

Current rifle manufacturer located in Columbia Falls, MT. Consumer sales through FFL dealers.

Proof Research manufactures AR-15 style rifles in calibers from .204 Ruger - 6.8 SPC. Its AR-10 quad rail rifle features a Magpul PRS stock and carbon fiber wrapped barrel. Please contact the company directly for more information on availability and pricing (see Trademark Index).

PUMA

Current trademark of firearms imported by Legacy Sports International LLC, located in Reno, NV. Previously located in Alexandria, VA.

HANDGUNS: LEVER ACTION

MODEL 92 BOUNTY HUNTER – .44-40 WCF, .44 Mag., .45 LC cal., 12 in. barrel with elevated post front and adj. rear sight, 6 shot full length mag. tube with one barrel band on forearm, shortened Italian walnut stock with large loop lever, 24 in. overall length, case colored frame, hammer, and lever. Mfg. in Italy by Chiappa Firearms. New 2009.

MSR $1,253	$1,025	$900	$800	$700	$625	$550	$425	

PISTOLS: SEMI-AUTO

MODEL 1911-22 – .22 LR cal., 4 3/4 in. barrel, black finish, 10 shot mag., SA, checkered walnut grips, fixed sights, manual safety, 39 oz. Mfg. 2010-2011.

	$275	$225	$200	$185	$170	$160	$150	*$323*

REVOLVERS: SINGLE ACTION

Recent manufacture is by Pietta, except for the Model 1873.

WESTERNER – .357 Mag., .44-40 WCF, or .45 LC cal., 4 3/4, 5 1/2, or 7 1/2 in. barrel, case colored frame/blue barrel or nickel finish, choice of all steel or brass trigger guard and gripstraps, choice of one-piece smooth walnut or synthetic ivory (nickel finish) grips, developed for cowboy action shooting, mfg. in Italy by Pietta. Mfg. 2009-2010.

	$525	$465	$385	$335	$300	$275	$250	*$589*

Add $70 for nickel finish with white synthetic ivory or walnut Birdshead grips.
Add $10 for steel frame.
Add $100 for factory tuned model (not available in .44-40 WCF or 7 1/2 in. barrel).

* ***Westerner Stainless*** – .357 Mag. or .45 LC cal., otherwise similar to Westerner with white one-piece synthetic grips. Mfg. 2009-2010.

	$750	$675	$600	$550	$495	$450	$395	*$829*

GRADING - PPGS™	100%	98%	95%	90%	80%	70%	60%	LAST MSR

MODEL 1873 – .22 LR cal., black oxide finish, 4 3/4, 5 1/2 (new 2011), or 7 1/2 (new 2011) in. barrel, 6 shot, black or antique finish, plain walnut or black synthetic (new 2011) grips with medallions, includes key operated hammer block safety on left recoil shield, fixed sights. New 2010.

MSR $189	$165	$150	$130	$120	$110	$100	$90	

Add $96 for 5 1/2 or 7 1/2 in. barrel (new 2011), includes extra cylinder.
Add $55 for .22 WMR cylinder only (new 2011).

RIFLES: LEVER ACTION

MODEL 1886 – .45-70 Govt. cal., patterned after the Winchester Model 1886, choice of 22 in. round or 26 in. octagon rifle barrel carbine with forearm barrel band, crescent buttplate, open sights, case colored frame with blued barrel and mag. tube, Italian walnut stock, standard loop lever, 7 or 8 shot mag., 8-9 lbs. Mfg. in Italy by Chiappa. New 2009.

MSR $1,390	$1,250	$1,025	$875	$775	$700	$625	$550	

MODEL 92 – .357 Mag./.38 Spl., .44 Mag., .45 LC, .454 Casull (new 2002, carbine only), or .480 Ruger (new 2004) cal., 9 (.454 Casull) or 10 shot tube mag., 20 in. round or 24 in. octagon barrel, choice of blue, brass (disc. 2008), case colored frame, or stainless steel (disc. 2008) receiver and barrel, regular or large loop (.357 Mag. or .45 LC cal. only, new 2005), uncheckered walnut stock and forearm. Mfg. by Rossi (2001-2008) and Chiappa Firearms (beginning 2009). Importation began 2001.

* ***Model 92 Round Barrel Carbine*** – .357 Mag./.38 Spl., 44-40 WCF (new 2009), .44 Mag., .45 LC, .454 Casull (mfg. 2002-08), or .480 Ruger (mfg. 2004-08) cal., blue, brass (disc. 2008) case colored, or stainless steel (disc. 2008), 16, 18 (disc. 2010), or 20 in. ported (.44 Mag. or .454 Casull cal. only, new 2005) or unported barrel, 8 or 10 shot mag., with or w/o large loop lever (16 in. barrel only), 6.1 lbs.

MSR $1,053	$925	$800	$700	$600	$525	$450	$400	

Add $41 for large loop lever model.
Add $87 for stainless steel construction (disc. 2008).
Add $30 for HiViz sights and ported barrel (not available on .357 Mag. or .45 LC cal., disc. 2008).
Add $31 for .454 Casull (last MSR was $642) or $47 for .480 Ruger cal. (disc. 2008, last MSR was $660).
Subtract approx. 20% for Rossi mfg. (disc. 2008), except for .454 Casull or .480 Ruger cal.

* ***Model 92 Octagon Barrel Rifle*** – .357 Mag./.38 Spl., .44 Mag., or .45 LC cal., choice of blue/case colored, stainless steel (disc.) or stainless steel/brass (not available in .44 Mag. cal., disc.), 20 (new 2007) or 24 in. octagon barrel, 10 or 12 shot mag., 7.7 lbs.

MSR $1,053	$925	$800	$700	$600	$525	$450	$400	

Add $41 for brass (disc. 2008).
Add $93 for buckhorn sights and saddle ring (mfg. 2002-08).
Add $55 for stainless steel construction (disc. 2008).
Subtract approx. 40% for older Rossi mfg. (disc. 2008).

* ***Model 92 Chuck Connors Commemorative*** – .44-40 WCF cal., patterned after the rifle Chuck Connors used in "*The Rifleman*" TV Series, features include commemorative medallion in stock, signature engraved on left side of receiver, signature laser etched into right side of the stock, case colored frame, 1,000 to be mfg. sequentially. Mfg. 2009-2010.

	$1,150	$975	$850	$775	$700	$625	$550	*$1,299*

RIFLES: SEMI-AUTO

PPS/22 – .22 LR cal., 16 in. shrouded barrel with open sights, choice of uncheckered wood or black, green, or sand colored synthetic or Wildcat tactical adj. stock, 10 (clip), 30 (clip or drum) or 50 shot drum mag., Wildcat stock includes optional Picatinny rail, pistol grip, and vertical forend grip, mfg. by Pietta. Mfg. 2009-2010.

	$475	$425	$375	$325	$295	$275	$250	*$519*

Add $40 for 50 shot drum mag or wood stock.
Add $50 for black, green, or sand colored, or Wildcat synthetic stock.

GRADING - PPGS™	100%	98%	95%	90%	80%	70%	60%	LAST MSR

SHOTGUNS: LEVER ACTION

MODEL 1887 – 12 ga., 2 3/4 in. chamber, patterned after the Winchester Model 1887, 22 or 28 in. barrel, case colored frame, blued barrel and mag tube, uncheckered pistol grip walnut stock and forearm, 5 shot mag. with FastLoad variation (22 in. barrel only) allows breech to accept 2 rounds, 7 1/2 lbs. Mfg. in Italy by Chiappa. New 2009.

MSR $1,179	$975	$825	$775	$650	$550	$475	$375

Add $45 for 28 in. barrel.

PURDEY, JAMES & SONS, LTD.

Current manufacturer established in 1814, and located in London, England. Annual production is approximately 75 guns.

Purdey guns have long been regarded as among the finest in the world. They have typically been made to customer specifications, and as such, should be appraised individually for purposes of evaluation. Values vary with gauge, barrel length, chamber length and age. Listed are the modern models and approximate values for reference purposes.

Prices indicated for manufacturer's suggested retail and 100% condition factors are listed in English pounds. All new prices do not include VAT (approx. 20%). Values for used guns in 98%-60% condition factors are priced in U.S. dollars.

RIFLES: CUSTOM ORDER & OLDER PRODUCTION

New rifle prices represent the base price with standard fine scroll and bouquet engraving.

PURDEY DOUBLE RIFLE CURRENT MFG. – various English Nitro Express cals., 25 1/2 in. barrels, folding leaf sight, checkered pistol grip stock, recoil pad, sidelock, auto ejectors.

* ***Purdey Double Rifle Smaller Calibers*** – .300 H&H or .375 H&H cal.

MSR £102,000	£102,000	$97,500	$85,000	$70,000	$55,000	$47,500	$40,000

* ***Purdey Double Rifle .416 Rigby - .500 NE***

MSR £98,900	N/A	N/A	$80,000	$70,000	$62,500	$56,000	$50,000

* ***Purdey Double Rifle .577 NE & .600 NE***

MSR £108,000	N/A	N/A	$97,500	$85,000	$77,500	$72,000	$66,000

The values represent base price only.

Since each Purdey is basically a special order, new gun pricing is calculated per individual customer work order.

PURDEY DOUBLE RIFLE OLDER MFG.

.300 H&H cal. or less	N/A	$57,500	$52,250	$46,000	$42,000	$37,000	$32,000
Up to .375 H&H cal.	N/A	$70,000	$59,500	$51,000	$45,000	$40,000	$35,000
Up to .470 NE cal.	N/A	$92,500	$80,000	$72,500	$65,000	$57,500	$50,000
Up to .600 NE cal.	N/A	$100,000	$90,000	$80,000	$70,000	$60,000	$55,000

Add 30% for self-opening action.
Subtract 15% if w/o ejectors.

MAGAZINE RIFLE – cals. up to .375 H&H are built on Mauser action, 24 in. barrel, folding leaf sight, checkered best quality walnut pistol grip stock, individually built per customer specifications.

MSR £28,000	£28,000	$28,000	$24,500	$18,250	$14,500	$10,000	$8,500

MAGNUM MAGAZINE RIFLE – .375 H&H, .416/450, and .500 cal., built on modern Magnum action, individually built per customer's specifications.

MSR £25,500	N/A	N/A	$21,500	$16,500	$13,000	$10,000	$8,750

SHOTGUNS: CUSTOM ORDER & OLDER PRODUCTION

New shotgun prices represent the base price with standard fine scroll and bouquet engraving.

BEST QUALITY GAME GUN SxS – 10, 12, 16, 20, 28 ga., or .410 bore, best quality sidelock action. 26-30 in. barrels, any choke and style of rib, checkered straight or pistol grip stock,

GRADING - PPGS™	100%	98%	95%	90%	80%	70%	60%	LAST MSR

auto ejector gun, best quality only, includes leather case. Mfg. since 1880.

MSR £71,000	£71,000	$70,000	$60,000	$46,000	$35,000	$25,000	$20,000	

Add £1,750 for 28 ga., or £4,500 for .410 bore or 10 ga. on new mfg.
Add £11,000 for extra set of barrels.
Add £5,500 for damascus steel barrels (limited mfg.).

* ***Best Quality Game Gun SxS Damascus*** – both frame and barrels are made from 100% damascus steel. New 2009.

Base price for this model is £76,000.

* ***Best Quality Game Gun Older Mfg.***

	$38,500	$32,500	$27,500	$21,500	$17,750	$15,250	$12,750	

* ***Best Quality Heavy Duck Gun***

	$20,500	$17,000	$14,000	$11,000	$9,500	$8,750	$7,500	

Add 50% for 20 ga.
Add 100% for 28 ga. or .410 bore, depending on condition.
Subtract 10%-15% if not cased with accessories.
Add $1,000 for SST.

O/U GUN – 12, 16, 20, 28 ga., or .410 bore best quality sidelock action. 26-30 in. barrels, any choke, auto ejectors, ST, checkered straight or pistol grip stock, includes leather case. Since WWII, Purdey has taken over the Woodward Company, and later guns have the Woodward O/U action. Very few early actions.

MSR £79,000	£79,000	$80,000	$60,000	$40,000	$35,000	$28,000	$25,000	

Add £4,000 for 28 ga. or £5,500 for .410 bore.
Add £16,000 (same ga.) or £19,000 (different ga.) for extra set of barrels.
Add £5,500 for damascus steel barrels (limited mfg.).

* ***O/U Gun Damascus*** – both frame and barrels are made from 100% damascus steel. New 2009.

Base price for this model is £89,000 (limited mfg.).

* ***O/U Gun Older mfg.***

	$47,500	$41,750	$37,500	$33,000	$29,950	$27,00	$25,000	
28 ga.	$107,500	$95,000	$85,000	$75,000	$68,750	$59,950	$55,000	

Add $3,000 for Woodward action.
Add 50% for 20 ga.
Add 100% for 28 ga.
Add 10% for SST.

PURDEY SPORTER O/U – 12 or 20 ga., 28 - 32 in. barrels, trigger plate action, solid or vent. rib, detachable single or double trigger, includes Sporter pattern large scroll engraving, major parts mfg. by Purdey and sent to Italy for assembly by Perugini & Visini. New 2008.

MSR £31,000	£31,000	$37,500	$30,000	$24,000	$18,000	$15,000	$12,500	

Add £4,200 for 28 ga. barrels (20 ga. frame only).

HAMMER EJECTOR GAME GUN – 12 or 20 ga., ejectors, top tang safety, special order only, case colored receiver, traditional fine scroll engraving, checkered straight grip English stock and splinter forearm. New 2002, first importation in U.S. during 2008.

MSR £74,000	£74,000	$65,000	$52,000	$32,500	$20,000	$16,500	$12,500	

Griffin & Howe is the exclusive U.S. agent for this model.

SINGLE BARREL TRAP GUN – 12 ga. Purdey action only, similar to O/U specifications. Mfg. prior to WWII.

	$11,250	$10,000	$8,750	$7,900	$7,200	$6,750	$5,950	

PUSKARSTVO SPENDAL d.o.o.

Current custom long arm manufacturer located in Slovenija, Slovakia.

Puskarstvo Spendal manufactures high quality shotguns and rifles in various configurations by custom order only. Please contact the company directly for more information including U.S. availability and pricing (see Trademark Index).

Q SECTION

Q.S. ARMI

Current pistol and ammunition manufacturer located in Lecco, Italy. No current U.S. importation. Previous company name was Q.S. Progetto Meccanica s.a.s.

Q.S. Armi manufactures a line of M1911-style semi-auto pistols. Current models include the 2011 Tex, Hawk, 120 FS, 102 KP, 102 AM, 94CC, and the 94AM. The 120 FS, 102 KP, 94CC, and 94AM are available in Q.S. Armi's proprietary 7penna centerfire ammunition (7x23mm), as well as 9mm Para. For more information regarding these models and ammunition, please contact the company directly (see Trademark Index).

QFI (QUALITY FIREARMS INC.)

Previous manufacturer located in Opa Locka, FL circa December 1990-1992.

GRADING - PPGS™	100%	98%	95%	90%	80%	70%	60%	LAST MSR

PISTOLS: SEMI-AUTO

MODEL LA380 – .380 ACP cal., single action, 6 shot, magazine disconnect, hammer, trigger, and firing pin block safeties, 3 1/4 in. barrel, blue or chrome finish. Mfg. 1991-92.

	100%	98%	95%	90%	80%	70%	60%	LAST MSR
	$125	$100	$90	$80	$70	$60	$55	*$147*

Add $23 for chrome finish.

* ***Model LA380SS*** – stainless steel variation of the Model LA380. Mfg. 1992 only.

	100%	98%	95%	90%	80%	70%	60%	LAST MSR
	$195	$165	$135	$110	$95	$75	$70	*$220*

MODEL SA 25 – .25 ACP cal., single action, 2 1/2 in. barrel, 6 shot, includes inertial firing pin, external exposed hammer with half cock, and trigger blocking thumb safety, blue, Dynachrome, or blue/gold finish, smooth walnut grips. Mfg. 1991 only.

	100%	98%	95%	90%	80%	70%	60%	LAST MSR
	$55	$45	$40	$35	$30	$25	$25	*$55*

Add $50 for blue/gold finish.
Add $10 for chrome finish with pearlite plastic grips.

TIGRESS MODEL – .25 ACP or .380 ACP cal., single action, 2 1/2 (.25 ACP) or 3 1/4 (.380 ACP) in. barrel, blue frame with gold-plated slide, 6 shot with finger extension on mag., white polymer grips with a red rose scrimshawed on both sides, designed for women, supplied with zippered gold pouch, 14 or 25 oz. Mfg. 1991 only.

	100%	98%	95%	90%	80%	70%	60%	LAST MSR
	$130	$100	$90	$80	$70	$60	$55	*$155*

Add $85 for .380 ACP cal.

REVOLVERS: DOUBLE ACTION

All revolvers under this heading are 6-shot.

RP SERIES STANDARD REVOLVER – .22 LR, .22 WMR, .32 S&W Long, .32 H&R Mag or .38 Spl. cal., 2 or 4 in. barrel, blue or chrome finish, fixed sights, hammer block safety, without ejector assembly, composition grips. Mfg. in U.S. 1990-disc.

	100%	98%	95%	90%	80%	70%	60%	LAST MSR
	$85	$70	$65	$60	$55	$50	$45	*$105*

Add $15-20 for chrome finish.
Add approx. $5 for 4 in. barrel.

MODEL SO 38 – .38 Spl. cal., swing out cylinder, 6 shot, 2 in. SR or 4 in. VR barrel, hammer block safety, composition grips. Mfg. 1991 only.

	100%	98%	95%	90%	80%	70%	60%	LAST MSR
	$175	$135	$115	$95	$80	$75	$65	*$175*

REVOLVERS: SINGLE ACTION

SAA WESTERN RANGER – .22 LR cal., 6 shot, 3, 4 (disc. 1991), 4 3/4 (new 1992), 6 (disc. 1991), 6 1/2 (new 1992), 7 (disc. 1991), or 9 in. barrel, blue finish with gold accenting, walnut grips. Mfg. 1991-92.

	100%	98%	95%	90%	80%	70%	60%	LAST MSR
	$85	$70	$65	$60	$55	$50	$45	*$105*

Add approx. $5 for 7 (disc.) or $7 for 9 in. barrel.
Add approx. $15-$35 for .22 WMR extra cylinder (combo).

GRADING - PPGS™	100%	98%	95%	90%	80%	70%	60%	LAST MSR

SAA PLAINS RIDER – similar to Western Ranger, except has black composition grips and no gold accenting. Mfg. 1991-92.

	$80	$65	$55	$50	$45	$40	$35	*$100*

Add $11 for 9 in. barrel.
Add approx. $26 for .22 WMR extra cylinder (combo).

SAA HORSEMAN SERIES – .357 Mag., .44 Mag., or .45 LC cal., 6 shot, 6 1/2 or 7 1/2 in. barrel, color case hardened or blue (Dark Horseman only) finish, walnut or black composition grips, hammer block safety. Mfg. 1991 only.

	$250	$220	$190	$170	$150	$130	$115	*$250*

The Dark Horseman had an extended grip frame with black composition grips and an adj. rear sight.

QIQIHAR HAWK INDUSTRIES CO., LTD.

Current manufacturer established during 1956, and located in Heilongjiang Province, China. No current U.S. importation.

Qiqihar manufactures good quality O/U, SxS, slide action, and semi-auto shotguns. Please contact the company directly for more information, including pricing and domestic availability (see Trademark Index).

QUACKENBUSH, H.M.

Previous rifle manufacturer circa 1886-1922, and located in Herkimer, NY. Quackenbush also manufactured airguns 1871-1943.

For more information on Quackenbush airguns, including the combination rimfire/airgun, please refer to the *Blue Book of Airguns,* by Dr. Robert Beeman & John Allen (also online).

RIFLES: .22 CAL., RIMFIRE

Only one breech mechanism was used on all H.M. Quackenbush rimfire rifles, the company's only rifle configuration was a swinging breech single shot. The breech pivots to the right of the gun. All Quackenbush guns were .22 caliber rimfire because the action was not strong enough for more powerful cartridges. These models were supplied in several different boxes, and often came with a cleaning rod, catalog, and paper targets. These and other accessories will significantly add to the value of the firearms prices listed. No serial numbers were applied to Quackenbush guns. Many variations of these models are encountered, which can also add premiums to the values listed, and can be used to estimate date of manufacture. Quackenbush also manufactured heavy metal targets for these rifles 1884-1931.

SAFETY RIFLE – single shot, swinging breech, walnut stock, 18 (most common) or 22 in. barrel. Mfg. 1886-1922.

	$800	$700	$600	$400	$350	$300	$200	

Add 10% for each of the following: heavy cast iron buttplate, original factory blue finish, optional Town & Country combination rear and front sights, barrel and optional sights where rear sight is approx. 1 in. forward of the breech end of the barrel, and for factory walnut forearm.
Add 20% for a raised single line curved knurl ring around the barrel in front of the receiver.
Add 30% for original box.

JUNIOR SAFETY RIFLE – similar to Safety Model, except smaller and has tubular receiver, wire stocked, swinging breech, 18 in. barrel only. Approx. 8,000 mfg. 1890-1920.

	$900	$800	$700	$500	$400	$375	$350	

Add 10% for original factory blue finish.
Add 30% for original box.

BYCYCLE RIFLE – similar to Safety Model, retractable wire stock, and a wire pistol grip, fixed rear sight, nickel finish, 12 in. barrel. Only 4,321 were sold during 1896-1919.

	$1,800	$1,750	$1,550	$1,300	$1,150	$900	$600	

Add 10% for original factory blue finish.
Add 30% for original box.
Subtract 50% if retractable shoulder stock is missing.

Manufacturer/Model	Quantity	Year	Issue Price

QUAIL UNLIMITED, INC.

Current national conservation organization with national headquarters located in Albany, GA. Previously located in Edgefield, SC.

Although Quail Unlimited, Inc. is not a manufacturer or importer, this organization has been responsible for many special and limited editions. These are listed below with quantities, but without secondary market prices, since they may vary greatly from region to region. Some of the models (and current values) may be listed under manufacturer listings in this text. Because of the relatively low quantities involved with these special editions, most of the models listed below have premiums currently being asked over issue prices, and the amount will vary with the region and acceptance by Quail Unlimited members. Quail Unlimited designated their special editions as follows: 1986 - Grand Slam I - Bobwhite Edition, 1987 - Grand Slam II - California Edition, 1988 - Grand Slam III - Gambel Edition, 1989 - Grand Slam IV - Mountain Quail Edition, 1990 - Grand Slam V - Scaled Quail Edition, 1992 - Gun Dog I - Pointer Edition, 1993 - Gun Dog II - Setter Edition, 1994 - Gun Dog III - Brittany Edition, 1995 - Gun Dog IV - German Shorthair Edition, 1996 - Gun Dog V - Belgian Edition. 1994 - Golden Covey I - Full Covey Edition, 1995 - Golden Covey II - Bobwhite Edition, 1997 - Upland I - Ruffed Grouse Edition.

SPECIAL/LIMITED EDITIONS

Quail Unlimited has not done a special/limited edition since 2008.

Manufacturer/Model	Quantity	Year	Issue Price
BROWNING Superposed 20 ga.	100	1986	$2,850
WINCHESTER Model 101 28 ga.	100	1987	$2,195
BROWNING Sweet 16 16 ga.	100	1988	$1,895
WINCHESTER Model 23 12 ga.	100	1989	$2,885
BROWNING Citori Lightning .410 bore	100	1990	$2,295
Add $500 to issue price for silver finish (standard finish was nickel).			
Add $700 to issue price for gold finish (standard finish was nickel).			
BROWNING Model A-5 20 ga.	100	1992	$1,795
BROWNING Citori Lightning 28 ga.	100	1993	$2,395
BROWNING Model A-5 20 ga.	100	1993	$1,795
BROWNING Citori Lightning .410 bore	100	1994	$2,395
BROWNING Citori Lightning German Shorthair 20 ga.	100	1995	$2,395
BELGIAN BROWNING Model A-5 20 ga. 3 in. GRIII (15th Anniv.)	75	1996	$2,195
BELGIAN BROWNING Model A-5 20 ga. 3 in. GRV (15th Anniv.)	25	1996	$3,995
RIZZINI SxS 20 ga. (15th Anniv.)	34	1996	$2,850
RIZZINI SxS 20 ga. (Gold) (15th Anniv.)	15	1996	$4,250
BROWNING Citori Superlight 20 ga.	100	1997	$2,495
WINCHESTER Model 12 20 ga.	100	1997	$995
WINCHESTER Model 12 20 ga.Chevy/QU Exclusive	298	1997	$995
BROWNING Citori Superlight 28 ga.	100	1998	$2,495
BROWNING Model A-5 Chevrolet	299	1998	$1,495
FRANCHI 620 VS 20 ga.	100	1999	$1,195
BROWNING Citori Upland 12 ga.	100	1999	$2,495
BERETTA Whitewing TWRA Executive Ed. 12 or 20	72	1999	$1,595
BERETTA AL390 TWRA Reg. Ed. 12 or 20 ga.	40	1999	$995
BERETTA AL390 TWRA Youth Ed. 12 or 20 ga.	25	1999	$995
BROWNING Citori Superlight 20 ga.	100	2000	$2,495
STURM RUGER Red Label 28 ga. Chevrolet	259	2000	$1,995

Manufacturer/Model	Quantity	Year	Issue Price
FRANCHI Feniche 28 ga. 20th Anniversary	125	2000	$1,195
ITHACA GUN Model 37 16 ga. 20th Anniversary	150	2000	$995
FRANCHI 620 VS 20 ga. Chevrolet Franchi	400	2001	$1,395
BROWNING Citori Superlight .410 bore	100	2001	$2,495
FRANCHI Feniche 28 ga. Encore	100	2001	$1,295
FRANCHI 620VS 20 ga. Chevrolet	252	2001	$1,395
BROWNING Triton Upland Special 20 ga.	50	2002	$1,695
BROWNING Citori Feather 20 ga.	100	2002	$2,595
BROWNING Gold Auto 20 ga. Heritage I Ed. (GR2)	75	2002	$1,895
BROWNING Gold Auto 20 ga., Heritage I Ed. (GR3)	25	2002	$2,195
CHARLES DALY Superior Hunter 20 ga. 20th Anniversary	100	2002	$789
BROWNING Gold Auto 12 ga. Heritage I Ed. (GR2)	75	2003	$1,895
BROWNING Gold Auto 12 ga., Heritage I Ed. (GR3)	25	2003	$2,195
FRANCHI 620VS 20 ga. Dinner Gun	150	2003	$1,295
CHARLES DALY Superior Hunter II 28 ga.	50	2003	$799
CHARLES DALY Superior Hunter II 12 ga.	50	2004	$789
BROWNING Citori Feather 16 ga. Heritage III (GR2)	75	2004	$2,695
BROWNING Citori Feather 16 ga. Heritage III (GR3)	25	2004	$2,995
FRANCHI 48AL Dlx 28 ga. Dinner Gun	150	2005	$1,395
BROWNING 525 Citori 28 ga. Heritage IV (GR2)	75	2005	$2,699
BROWNING 525 Citori 28 ga. Heritage IV (GR3)	25	2005	$2,899
REMINGTON 11-87 20 ga. 25th Anniversary	150	2006	$1,395
BROWNING 525 Citori .410 Bore Heritage V (GR2)	75	2006	$2,599
BROWNING 525 Citori .410 Bore Heritage V (GR3)	25	2006	$2,999
BROWNING Gold 25th Anniversary 20 ga.	25	2006	$1,595
BROWNING Citori Gran Lightning	1	2007	$6,000
BROWNING 525 Citori .410 Bore Heritage V (GR2)	75	2008	$2,599
BROWNING 525 Citori .410 Bore Heritage V (GR3)	25	2008	$2,899

QUALITY PARTS CO./BUSHMASTER

Quality Parts Co. was a division of Bushmaster Firearms, Inc. located in Windham, ME that manufactured AR-15 type paramilitary rifles and various components and accessories for Bushmaster. Please refer to the Bushmaster listing in the B section for current model listings and values.

R SECTION

R GUNS

Current manufacturer, importer, and dealer located in Carpentersville, IL.

R Guns offers a line of AR-15 style rifles and carbines in various configurations, upper and lower receivers, accessories, and related components. Please contact the company directly for more information on its various models, availability, and pricing (see Trademark Index).

RAAC

Current importer located in Scottsburg, IN.

GRADING - PPGS™	100%	98%	95%	90%	80%	70%	60%	LAST MSR

RIFLES AND SHOTGUNS

Russian American Armory Company is an import company for Molot, located in Russia. Current product/model lines include Vepr. rifles, in addition to a line of bolt action rifles, including the LOS/BAR Series, CM-2 Target rifle, Korshun, and Sobol hunting model. Please check individual heading listings for current information, including U.S. availability and pricing. Please contact the company directly for current offerings (see Trademark Index).

MKA 1919 – 12 ga., 3 in. chamber, AR-15 style, 18 1/2 in. barrel with three choke tubes, 5 shot box mag., self adjusting gas system, A2 configuration with carry handle and front sight, Picatinny rail, bolt hold open after last round, choice of matte black or 100% camo coverage. Mfg. by Ücyildyz Arms Ind. Co. Ltd. located in Turkey.

MSR	100%	98%	95%	90%	80%	70%	60%
MSR $700	$650	$575	$525	$475	$435	$400	$375

Add $100 for 100% camo coverage.
Add $500 for flat top receiver and adj. stock.

RAF

Previous manufacturer of shotguns and rifles located in St. Etienne, France circa 1994-96.

RAF manufactured superposed rifles, shotguns, combination guns, and semi-auto rimfire rifles.

RBA

Previous competition pistol manufacturer located in Granarolo Emilia, Italy.

PISTOLS: SEMI-AUTO

Renzo Bonora Armi (RBA) manufactured high quality competition pistols in both .22 LR and .32 S&W Wadcutter. These pistols had little, if any, importation into the U.S.

R.F.M.

Current long arm manufacturer located in Sarezzo, Italy.

SHOTGUNS

R.F.M. manufactures good quality shotguns, including the SK Series, Zeus SxS Series, Mythos SxS, Forest SxS (camo, divergent barrels), and the Canard.

R.G. INDUSTRIES

Previous importer located in Miami, FL. Operations ceased in January of 1986.

HANDGUNS

R.G. Industries manufactured and imported plain utilitarian revolvers and semi-auto pistols. Unfortunately, because of a product liability situation, R.G. Industries was litigated out of business during 1986. Although their models represent good values, they are not collectible, and so a generalized listing is provided.

RG 14 S, RG 23, RG 31

	100%	98%	95%	90%	80%	70%	60%
	$95	$80	$70	$60	$55	$50	$45

RG 40, RG 74, & HIGHNOON S.A.

	100%	98%	95%	90%	80%	70%	60%
	$125	$115	$95	$80	$70	$60	$55

GRADING - PPGS™	100%	98%	95%	90%	80%	70%	60%	LAST MSR

RG 26 SEMI-AUTO – .25 ACP cal., 6 shot mag., 2 1/4 in. barrel, plastic grips, single action, 12 oz.

	$65	$55	$50	$40	$35	$30	$25	*$66*

RGS LLC

Current rifle manufacturer located in Casper, WY.

RGS LLC is owned and operated by Robert J. Stone, who studied for 11 years under Dale Storey of DGS, Inc. Stone is a master machinist and offers custom rifles in a variety of configurations, including tactical, long range, big game, and modern plains rifles. Many options are available. Please contact him directly for more information, including available options, pricing, and delivery time (see Trademark Index).

RND MANUFACTURING

Current manufacturer located in Longmont, CO. Previously distributed by Mesa Sportsmen's Association, L.L.C. located in Delta, CO. Dealer or consumer direct sales.

PISTOLS: SEMI-AUTO

RND PISTOL – 5.56 NATO cal., AR-15 style, round shrouded handguard, 7 1/2 in. barrel with muzzle brake, pistol grip, full length vent. Picatinny rail, 9 1/2 lbs. New 2010.

MSR $2,000	$2,000	$1,800	$1,600	$1,350	$1,100	$900	$700

RIFLES: SEMI-AUTO

RND EDGE SERIES – .223 Rem. (RND 400), .300 WSM (RND 1000, new 2003), .300 Ultra (RND 2100, new 2003), .308 Win. (RND 800, new 2010), .338 Lapua Mag. (RND 2000, new 1999), .375 Super Mag. (RND 2600), .408 Cheytac (RND 2500) or 7.62x39mm (disc.) cal., patterned after the AR-15 style, CNC machined, 18, 20, or 24 in. barrel, choice of synthetic (Grade I), built to individual custom order, handmade laminated thumbhole (Grade II, disc. 1998), or custom laminated thumbhole stock with fluted barrel (Grade III, disc. 1998), vented aluminum shroud, many options and accessories available, approx. 11 1/2-16 lbs., custom order only, values represent base model. New 1996.

MSR $2,295	$2,295	$2,000	$1,750	$1,300	$1,050	$850	$725

Add $1,500 for .308 Win. cal. (new 2010). Add $1,600 for .300 WSM cal. Add $2,500 for .338 Lapua Mag. cal. Add $2,500 for .300 Ultra (RND 2100). Add $8,205 for .375 Super Mag. (RND 2600) or .408 Cheytac (RND 2500) cal. Add $355 for Grade II or $605 for Grade III (disc.).

RND 3000/3100 – .50 BMG or .416 Rem. Mag. (RND 3100) cal., semi-auto, 26 in. barrel with muzzle brake, piston driven operation, fully adj. stock, full lenth integrated Picatinny rail, fully adj. stock, double stock mag., includes optics 3.2x17mm scope, black or various camo colors, includes bipod, 28 lbs.

MSR $11,500	$11,500	$10,000	$9,000	$8,250	$7,500	$6,750	$6,000

RPA INTERNATIONAL LTD.

Current rifle manufacturer located in Kent, England. No current U.S. importation.

RIFLES

RPA International Ltd. manufactures high quality bolt action rifles, including a tactical long range sniper model, the Rangemaster 7.62 STBY (£4,167 MSR), Rangemaster 7.62 (£4,167 MSR), Rangemaster 338 (£5,040 MSR), and the Rangemaster 50 (£5,833 MSR). The Rangemaster Series includes a folding stock, stainless steel barrel and muzzle brake, Picatinny rails and tactical bipod. The Interceptor is available in a single shot (£2,154 MSR) and a Repeater (£2,200 MSR) version. The Hunter rifle comes with or w/o a thumbhole stock (£2,166 base MSR), Highland Stalker (£2,166 MSR), Woodland Stalker (£2,083 MSR). The Target Rifle Series includes the Elite Single Shot (£2,450 MSR), and the Ranger (£2,375 MSR). The G2 Series is a high performance tactical rifle in 7.62x51mm caliber with a 26 in. (G2 7.62) or 16 in. (G2 7.62 STBY) steel fluted barrel, muzzle brake and integral Picatinny rail. Both models are £4,333 MSR. Additionally, the company makes custom rifles and actions. Please contact the company directly for pricing, U.S. availability and options (see Trademark Index).

GRADING - PPGS™	100%	98%	95%	90%	80%	70%	60%	LAST MSR

RPB INDUSTRIES

Previous company located in Avondale, GA. RPB Industries' guns were made by Masterpiece Arms.

CARBINES: SEMI-AUTO

RPB CARBINE – .45 ACP cal., closed bolt blowback action, 16 1/4 in. barrel, fixed skeletonized stock and forearm pistol grip, accepts M-3 military submachine gun mags., black finish, 9 1/2 lbs. Mfg. 2000-2004.

	100%	98%	95%	90%	80%	70%	60%	LAST MSR
	$450	$375	$325	$285	$260	$235	$210	

Add $75 for Deluxe Model with EZ cocker and installed scope mount.

RPM

Current manufacturer located in Tucson, AZ, and previously located in Afton, MO 2002-2003.

During 2004, RPM changed the name of the company to Gateway Precision Arms. During 2008, the company name was changed back to RPM.

PISTOLS: SINGLE SHOT

XL PISTOL – many cals. available, tip-up action, 8, 10 3/4, 12, or 14 in. barrel, positive thumb safety, steel frame, cocking indicator, right or left-hand action. Disc.

	100%	98%	95%	90%	80%	70%	60%	LAST MSR
	$785	$675	$600	$550	$500	$450	$395	*$858*

XL HUNTER – over 40 cals., tip-up action, stainless steel frame, 5 1/16 in. under-lug, 12 or 14 in. Douglas chrome-moly (new 2004) or stainless steel barrel, ISGW rear and Patridge or hooded front sights, with (became standard 2000) or w/o external positive extractor. New 1995.

	100%	98%	95%	90%	80%	70%	60%	LAST MSR
MSR $1,235	$1,125	$975	$875	$725	$625	$525	$450	

Add $250 for stainless steel barrel.
Add $160 for integral muzzle brake.
Add $50 for left-hand action.
Add $390 or $440 per extra barrel, depending on length.

RWC (RUSSIAN WEAPON COMPANY)

Current importer located in Tullytown, PA.

RWC is an exclusive importer for Izhmash and Saiga rifles, in addition to also importing a line of tactical rifle accessories. Please refer to Izhmash and Saiga sections for current models, or contact the company for more information on model availability and pricing (see Trademark Index).

RWS

Current trademark of airguns and ammunition manufactured by Dynamit Nobel GmbH which has been manufacturing firearms and airguns in Nuremberg, Stadeln, and Troisdorf, Germany since 1865. RWS became part of Dynamit Nobel in 1931. Dynamit Nobel is now a division of RUAG AmmoTec GmbH, located in Furth, Germany. RWS firearms were imported until 1995 by Dynamit Nobel of America, Inc. located in Closter, NJ. Other trademarks (including Rottweil) by Dynamit Nobel can be located under individual heading names in this text.

For more information and current pricing on both new and used RWS airguns produced by Dianawerk, Mayer, and Grammelspacher, please refer to the *Blue Book of Airguns* by Dr. Robert Beeman & John Allen (also online).

RIFLES: BOLT ACTION, TARGET

MODEL 820 L – .22 LR cal. only, 24 (disc.) or 26 in. barrel, no. 100 aperture sight, oil polished stock for 3 position match, stippled pistol grip and forearm, recoil pad, adj. trigger, 10.6 lbs. Disc. 1994.

	100%	98%	95%	90%	80%	70%	60%	LAST MSR
	$1,275	$1,000	$850	$700	$575	$475	$400	*$1,500*

Previous to 1986 this model was designated the 820 S and was supplied with a no. 75 aperture rear sight.

GRADING - PPGS™	100%	98%	95%	90%	80%	70%	60%	LAST MSR

* ***Model 820 S*** – with Model 82 aperture sight.

	$1,100	$895	$795	$650	$560	$480	$420	*$995*

MODEL 820 F MATCH – similar to Model 820 L, except has heavy match barrel, 15.4 lbs. Disc. 1994.

	$1,750	$1,400	$1,275	$1,000	$850	$700	$575	*$2,000*

* ***Model 820 SF Match*** – with Model 820 L aperture sight. Disc.

	$1,125	$900	$795	$650	$560	$480	$420	*$1,010*

MODEL 820 K – .22 LR cal. only, made for running boar competition, 24 in. barrel, stock similar to Model 820 SF, no sights, 9 1/2 lbs. without barrel weight or scope. Importation disc. 1986.

	$900	$775	$695	$615	$540	$470	$420	*$870*

RADOM

Current trademark manufactured by Fabryka Broni, Lucznik - Radom Sp. z o.o., located in Radom, Poland. No current U.S. importation. Previously manufactured 1925-1945 by the Polish Arsenal located in Radom, Poland & Steyr, Austria. Post WWII also manufactured by Z.M. Lucznik (Radom Factory) in Radom, Poland. Recent importation was by Dalvar of U.S.A., located in Seligman, AZ. Previously located in Richardson, TX and Henderson, NV.

REVOLVERS

RADOM REVOLVER – Nagant design, dated 1931-36.

	$2,500	$1,900	$1,500	$1,000	$800	$600	$500	

PISTOLS: CURRENT MFG.

VIS WZ.35 – 9mm Para. cal., patterned after the WWII Radom pistol, supplied with case. New 2011.

This model is currently not being imported into the U.S.

PISTOLS: SEMI-AUTO, 1935-1939 PRODUCTION

Serial number ranges use #### for the no alphabetical prefix series, 1#### for the first alphabetical prefix series, and 2#### for the second alphabetical prefix series. Mill marks are more prominent as the war progressed.

P-35 AUTOMATIC – 9mm Para. cal., 8 shot, blue finish, 4 3/4 in. barrel, fixed sights, black VIS/FB plastic grips. Mfg. 1935 through WWII.

* ***wz.35 VIS Polish Eagle*** – eagle logo, unblued barrel, rust blue, lanyard loop, ser. no. 01-49,000, dated 1936, 1937 (rarest date), 1938, or 1939.

	$4,500	$3,500	$3,000	$2,500	$2,000	$1,500	$1,000	

Add 50% for 1937 mfg. if in 95%+ condition, otherwise, add 15%.
Add 25% for 1936 mfg. if in 95%+ condition, otherwise, add 10%.

PISTOLS: SEMI-AUTO, LATE 1939-1945 PRODUCTION

Serial number ranges use #### for the no alphabetical prefix series, 1#### for the first alphabetical prefix series, and 2#### for the second alphabetical prefix series. Mill marks are more prominent as the war progressed.

P.35 VIS POLISH EAGLE NAZI CAPTURE – eagle logo and WaA marks, rust blue, all 3 levers, lanyard loop, many small parts serial numbered, ser. no. range 49,400-52,500.

	N/A	$3,150	$2,500	$2,000	$1,600	$1,200	$850	

Beware of fakes!

P.35 NAZI RADOM TYPE 1 - 3 LEVER & SLOT – rust blue, unblued barrel, lanyard loop, black VIS/FB plastic grips, many small parts ser. numbered, ser. nos. 01-12,500 & 1/A0001-1/E8000 (1st Series) prefix.

	$1,600	$1,150	$925	$725	$575	$500	$425	

Add 100% for Navy characteristics: Kreigsmarine Eagle/M marked, blued barrel, may/may not be "N"/"O" grip strap marked.

GRADING - PPGS™	100%	98%	95%	90%	80%	70%	60%	LAST MSR

Add 50% for S/N Range 01-12,500, early characteristics: blued barrel, early slide/logo position, no P.35(p), no lanyard loop.

Beware of fakes!

P.35 NAZI RADOM TYPE II - 3 LEVER & NO SLOT – salt blue, lanyard loop, early e/WaA77 on left frame and slide changes to later e/77, some brown VIS/FB plastic grips, a few with pressed VIS/FB wood grips, serial numbered 1/E8001-1/Z1000 (1st Series) prefix.

$1,250 $1,000 $800 $600 $500 $350 $300

Add 30% if P.35(p) marked if in 95%+ condition, otherwise add 15%.

P.35 NAZI RADOM TYPE III - 2 LEVER & NO SLOT – lanyard loop, salt blue, e/77 on left side of slide and frame, brown plastic VIS/FBN grips common, pressed VIS/FB wood grips rarely seen, serial numbered 1/Z1001-2/H8900.

$925 $800 $675 $525 $425 $325 $275

Certain Radoms w/German acceptance marks will bring a premium.

* ***P.35 Nazi Steyr Type III - 2 Lever & No Slot*** – salt blued or phosphate exterior with blued small parts also on phosphate models, serial numbered in late 2/A or 2/B with e/77 on left side of slide and frame and 2/H8901 through 2/K w/o e/77 on left side of slide and frame, e/623 on front left side of trigger guard, many with grooved wood grips, mostly all Steyr mfg.

  $2,250 $1,950 $1,750 $1,500 $1,100 $900 $750

* ***P.35 Nazi Steyr Type III - 2 Lever & No Slot "bnz" Slide*** – rough milled phosphate exterior, some "blank" slides noted, wood grips, serial numbered 2/K1440-2/K2400, mostly all Steyr mfg.

  $4,750 $3,750 $3,000 $2,450 $2,100 $1,750 $1,500

PISTOLS: SEMI-AUTO, RECENT PRODUCTION

VIS P-35 – 9mm Para. cal., patterned after the 1937 P-35, large Polish eagle stamped on left side of slide, with or w/o slotted rear grip strap for shoulder stock, 4 1/2 in. barrel, 36 oz. Limited mfg. 1997 only.

$2,600 $1,425 $1,215 $1,015 $925 $825 $750 *$2,999*

MODEL 64 – PPK sized pistol chambered for the 9x18mm Makarov cartridge. Rare.

$250 $150 $125 $100 $95 $85 $80

TOKAREV (PISTOLET TT) – Polish copy w/manual safety, well made.

$500 $400 $350 $325 $300 $250 $200

* ***TT-33 (FB Radom)*** – 7.62x25 cal., includes two mags. and cleaning rod, mfg. FB Radom, Poland 1947-1950.

  $275 $230 $200 $180 $165 $150 $140

* ***TT-33 (Radom)*** – 7.62x25 cal., inlcudes two mags. and cleaning rod, mfg. by Radom in Poland 1950-1954.

  $275 $230 $200 $180 $165 $150 $140

VANAD P-83 – 9x18mm Makarov cal., 8 shot mag., available in Standard Military Issue or Special Eagle Limited Edition, loaded chamber indicator, firing pin block safety, steel receiver with external hammer, 3 1/2 in. barrel, drift adj. target sights, checkered composition grips, 26 oz. Imported 1994 (Standard Military Issue), 1997-circa 2008.

$350 $290 $265 $235 $210 $190 $170

Add $46 for Standard Military Issue.

* ***Vanad P-93 9mm*** – 9mm Makarov cal., similar to the Vanad P-83, except decocking lever is on the frame instead of the slide, black oxide finish, 3.9 in. barrel.

  $350 $250 $225 $200 $175 $150 $125

MAG 95 – 9mm Para. cal., single or double action with firing pin block, external hammer, ambidextrous hammer drop safety, 4 1/2 in. barrel, two matching number mags., 37 oz. Limited importation 1997 only.

$650 $550 $450 $400 $350 $300 $275 *$749*

GRADING - PPGS™	100%	98%	95%	90%	80%	70%	60%	LAST MSR

MAG 98 – 9mm Para. cal., similar to Mag 95, except has two matching mags., holster, and cleaning rod. Most of these are police/military trade-ins.

	$550	$450	$400	$350	$300	$275	$250	

RIFLES: SEMI-AUTO

Fabryka Broni Lucznik currently manufactures a variety of semi-auto rifles and carbines designed after the Model 96 Beryl assault rifle. Please contact the company directly for U.S. availability and pricing (see Trademark Index).

RAM-LINE, INC.

Previous manufacturer located in Grand Junction, CO until 1995.

In addition to the Ram-Tech pistol, Ram-Line, Inc. also manufactured a complete line of synthetic and wood stocks for a variety of firearms. Ram-Line continues to manufacture a complete line of magazines for most popular pistols and rifles.

PISTOLS: SEMI-AUTO

EXACTOR PISTOL – .22 LR cal., single action, aircraft alloy receiver with 5 1/2 in. polymer VR barrel and steel liner, unique two-motion safety blocks hammer, trigger, and sear, 15 shot mag., matte finish, easy disassembly, injected molded grip, fixed sight, 20.3 oz., supplied with case. Mfg. 1990-93.

	$195	$165	$135	$110	$95	$75	$70	*$225*

* ***Exactor Pistol Target*** – similar to above, except has 7 1/2 in. barrel, 23 oz. Disc. 1993.

	$265	$230	$195	$150	$125	$110	$95	*$300*

RAM-TECH PISTOL – similar to Exactor pistol, except 4 1/2 in. barrel w/o VR. Mfg. 1994-95.

	$175	$145	$125	$100	$85	$70	$65	*$200*

RAMIREZ, TODD

Current custom rifle manufacturer located in Alba, TX.

Todd Ramirez manufactures custom order bolt action rifles. Each gun is built per individual customer specifications, and a variety of options are available. Synthetic rifles include the Tac-Hunter (starts at $12,000) and the Syn-Fle (starts at $15,000). Premium signature wood rifle starts at $28,000. Premium Wood rifle starts at $30,000. He also offers gunsmithing, gun fitting, restoration, metal work, and other services. Please contact him directly for more information, including an indivdualized price quotation, available options, and delivery time (see Trademark Index).

RAMO DEFENSE SYSTEMS

Previous rifle manufacturer 1999-2003 and located in Nashville, TN.

RIFLES: BOLT ACTION

TACTICAL .308 – .308 Win. cal., Rem. M-700 long action, match grade stainless steel barrel, skeletonized black synthetic stock with cheekpad, matte black metal finish, 4 shot mag., 16 lbs. Mfg. 1999-2003.

	$2,495	$2,100	$1,850	$1,600	$1,400	$1,200	$995	*$2,495*

M91/M91A2 – .308 Win. or .300 Win. Mag. cal., Rem. M-700 long action, black Kevlar and fiberglass stock, matte black metal finish, 4 shot mag., 14 lbs. Mfg. 1999-2003.

	$2,695	$2,250	$1,950	$1,675	$1,475	$1,250	$995	*$2,695*

Add $200 for .300 Win. Mag. cal.

M600 SINGLE SHOT – .50 BMG cal., single shot, twin tube skeletonized stock with pistol grip and cheekpiece, 32 in. barrel with fins at breech and muzzle brake, 23 lbs. Mfg. 1999-2003.

	$4,195	$3,700	$3,200	$2,750	$2,250	$1,950	$1,675	*$4,195*

M650 REPEATER – .50 BMG cal., repeater action with 6 shot detachable rotary mag., stock and barrel (30 in.) similar to M600, approx. 30 lbs. Mfg. 1999-2003.

	$6,395	$5,750	$5,150	$4,500	$3,750	$3,000	$2,250	*$6,395*

GRADING - PPGS™	100%	98%	95%	90%	80%	70%	60%	LAST MSR

RANDALL FIREARMS COMPANY

Previously manufactured in Sun Valley, CA. Manufactured between June 7, 1983 and December 15, 1984 - final plant closing was June 15, 1985.

Before manufacturing ceased in May of 1985, 24 models with 12 variations in 3 different calibers had been produced. In some instances, production on certain models was very limited and premiums for these low volume niches are starting to develop. Between June of 1983 and May of 1984, 9,968 handguns were manufactured with 75% of all 9mm Para. pistols being exported to Europe and 35% of 9mm Para. production employing a 10 groove barrel. Models manufactured after 1984 came equipped with an extended slide stop, long trigger, and beavertail grip safety. Production ser. nos. started at 02000 for right-hand models and 02100 for left-hand models. All but the first 200 (approx.) serial numbers started with "RF" and ended with "C" or "W." A few rare mis-marks are in circulation. Total mfg. for all models and variations was 9,968. Randall prototype serialization starts with a "T" - less than 45 were manufactured and these specimens command up to a 50% premium. In addition, 78 serial numbers under 2,000 were manufactured by special order.

Models listed are generally described with values per specific variations listed afterward.

Due to space considerations, information regarding this manufacturer is available online free of charge www.bluebookofgunvalues.com.

RANGER ARMS INC.

Previous manufacturer located in Gainesville, TX until the early 1970s.

Ranger Arms Inc. manufactured good quality, bolt action rifles in various calibers and configurations. Although somewhat rare in that there were not a large number manufactured, collectibility to date has been limited with specimens in 90%+ condition, typically priced in the $375-$500 range.

RAPTOR ARMS CO., INC.

Previous rifle manufacturer located in Shelton, CT, approx. 1997-mid 1999. Previously distributed by Davidson's and Jerry's Sport Centers.

RIFLES: BOLT ACTION

RAPTOR SPORTING RIFLE – .243 Win., .25-06 Rem., .270 Rem., .30-06, or .308 Win. cal., features "Taloncote" or blue (mfg. 1998 only) finished or stainless steel (new 1999) barreled action, black checkered fiberglass reinforced synthetic stock, adj. trigger, with or w/o sights. Mfg. 1997-99.

$230 $195 $175 $160 $150 $140 $130 ***$259***

Add $30 for sights (disc.).
Add $15 for blue finish (disc.).
Add $36 for heavy barrel.
Add $50 for stainless steel barreled action with sights (new 1999).

* ***Raptor Sporting Rifle Peregrine Deluxe*** – similar to Raptor Sporting Rifle, except has deluxe checkered or plain hardwood stock. Mfg. 1998 only.

$265 $225 $195 $175 $160 $150 $140 ***$309***

Subtract $10 for plain hardwood stock and no sights (blue finish only).

RASHEED (RASHID)

Previous Egyptian military rifle mfg. circa mid-1960s.

RIFLES: SEMI-AUTO

RASHEED – 7.62x39mm cal., gas operated mechanism with tilting bolt, 20 1/2 in. barrel with folding bayonet, bolt cocking is by separate bolt handle installed on right side of receiver, detachable 10 shot mag., open type sights, hardwood stock with vent. forend, approx. 8,000 mfg. circa mid-1960s.

$650 $575 $475 $425 $350 $275 $200

GRADING - PPGS™	100%	98%	95%	90%	80%	70%	60%	LAST MSR

RAVELL

Previous manufacturer located in Barcelona, Spain.

RIFLES: SxS

MAXIM DOUBLE RIFLE – .375 H&H or 9.3x74R cal., H&H type sidelock action with automatic ejectors, Purdey scroll engraving, 23 in. barrels, deluxe walnut with full pistol grip and rubber buttplate, double articulated triggers. Importation disc. circa 1998.

	100%	98%	95%	90%	80%	70%	60%	LAST MSR
	$6,600	$6,100	$5,000	$4,000	$3,500	$2,950	$2,600	*$7,000*

Add 10% for .375 H&H cal.

RAVEN ARMS

Previous manufacturer located in Industry, CA circa 1970-1991. Approximately 2 million were mfg.

PISTOLS: SEMI-AUTO

P-25 – .25 ACP cal., single action, 2 7/16 in. barrel, 6 shot mag., walnut grips, available in nickel, blue, or chrome finish, 15 oz. Disc. 1984.

	100%	98%	95%	90%	80%	70%	60%	LAST MSR
	$70	$60	$50	$40	$30	$25	$25	

MP-25 – similar to Model P-25, except die-cast slide serrations are slightly different. Disc. 1992.

	100%	98%	95%	90%	80%	70%	60%	LAST MSR
	$60	$50	$45	$40	$35	$30	$25	*$70*

Walnut, slotted plastic, or ivory colored grips were available for this model. From 1987 on, a sear blocking safety was added to the MP-25.

RECORD-MATCH

Previously manufactured by Anschütz, located in Zella-Mehlis, Germany circa pre-WWII.

PISTOLS: SINGLE SHOT, TARGET

MODEL 210 FREE PISTOL - .22 LR cal., Martini action, 11 in. barrel, single shot, blue, carved and checkered walnut grips and forearm, set trigger (button release), micrometer rear sight, deluxe target pistol, pre-WWII.

	100%	98%	95%	90%	80%	70%	60%	LAST MSR
	$1,320	$1,265	$1,210	$1,100	$880	$745	$550	

MODEL 210A – similar to Model 210, except alloy frame.

	100%	98%	95%	90%	80%	70%	60%	LAST MSR
	$1,265	$1,210	$1,155	$1,045	$825	$690	$495	

MODEL 200 FREE PISTOL - similar to Model 210, except less deluxe features and spur trigger guard, pre-WWII.

	100%	98%	95%	90%	80%	70%	60%	LAST MSR
	$990	$935	$770	$660	$525	$440	$360	

RED ROCK ARMS

Current manufacturer established April 2003 and located in Mesa, AZ. During late 2006, the company name was changed from Bobcat Weapons, Inc. to Red Rock Arms.

PISTOLS: SEMI-AUTO

BWA5 FSA – 9mm Para. cal., H&K paramilitary design, roller locked delayed blowback action, 8.9 in. stainless steel barrel, black Duracoat finished stock, pistol grip, and forearm, 10, 30, or 40 shot mag., approx. 5.3 lbs. Mfg. 2007-2008.

	100%	98%	95%	90%	80%	70%	60%	LAST MSR
	$1,525	$1,350	$1,125	$900	$775	$650	$550	*$1,700*

RIFLES: SEMI-AUTO

ATR-1 CARBINE - .223 Rem. cal., H&K paramilitary design, 16 1/4 in. barrel, adj. front and rear sight, black furniture, 30 shot AR-15 style mag., available with or w/o flash suppressor, 8 lbs. New 2007.

	100%	98%	95%	90%	80%	70%	60%	LAST MSR
MSR $1,400	$1,250	$1,075	$925	$825	$750	$650	$575	

GRADING - PPGS™	100%	98%	95%	90%	80%	70%	60%	LAST MSR

BW5 FSA – 9mm Para. cal., H&K paramilitary design, stamped steel lower receiver, roller locked delayed blowback action, 16 1/2 in. stainless steel barrel (3-lug barrel and 9 in. fake suppressor), black Duracoat finished stock, pistol grip, and forearm, 10, 30, or 40 shot mag., approx. 6.7 lbs. Mfg. 2006-2008.

	$1,525	$1,350	$1,125	$900	$775	$650	$550	*$1,700*

REDOLFI F.LLI S.N.C.

Current long gun manufacturer and retail gun shop located in Brescia, Italy. No current U.S. importation.

Redolfi F.lli manufactures good quality rifles and shotguns. Many custom options are available. Please contact the company directly for more information, including pricing, U.S. availability and delivery time (see Trademark Index).

GARY REEDER CUSTOM GUNS

Current custom manufacturer located in Flagstaff, AZ. Consumer direct sales.

HANDGUNS

For over 30 years, Gary Reeder has specialized in customizing revolvers from various manufacturers, and is now building several series of custom revolvers on his own frames, in addition to customizing customer supplied handguns. Gary's son Kase also manufactures several series of Model 1911 style pistols built to customers specifications in .45 ACP and 10mm. Reeder currently produces well over 60 different series of custom hunting handguns, cowboy guns, custom 1911s, and large caliber hunting rifles. For more information on his extensive range of custom guns, please contact the factory directly (see Trademark Index).

REGENT

Current trademark of semi-auto pistols manufactured by Trabzon Gun Industry Corp., located in Turkey, and imported by Umarex USA, Inc.

PISTOLS: SEMI-AUTO

R100 1911-A1 – .45 ACP cal., patterned after the Govt. M1911-A1, black steel frame, SA, 7 shot mag., 5 in. barrel, bar stock slide, low cut ejection port, wide spur hammer, brown checkered synthetic grips, serrated ramp front sight, fixed notch rear sight, blue finish, accepts most aftermarket M1911 style parts, approx. 40 oz. New 2011.

MSR $499	$425	$365	$325	$285	$260	$240	$200

R200S – .45 ACP cal., 5 in. barrel, 7 shot mag., satin nickel finished frame and slide with double serrations, skeletonized trigger and bobbed hammer, combat style sights, double diamond checkered synthetic grips, 40 oz. New 2012.

MSR $620	$550	$495	$450	$395	$350	$325	$295

R350CR – .45 ACP cal., 4 in. barrel, 7 shot mag., lower Picatinny rail, bobbed hammer and skeletonized trigger, checkered front grip strap, double diamond checkered Hogue synthetic grips, 35 oz. New 2012.

MSR $549	$450	$400	$365	$335	$300	$275	$250

REISING ARMS COMPANY

Previous manufacturer originally located in Hartford, CT and later in New York, NY.

PISTOLS: SEMI-AUTO

TARGET AUTOMATIC PISTOL – .22 LR cal., 12 shot, 6 3/4 in. barrel, blue, brown hard rubber grips, hinged frame, outside hammer. Mfg. 1921-24.

$1,000	$900	$800	$675	$575	$475	$375

This model was mfg. in Hartford, CT from serial number 1,001-4,000. The New York, NY address occurs in the serial range 10,000-12,000.

Warning: This pistol's slide may crack if modern high speed .22 LR ammo is used extensively.

100%	98%	95%	90%	80%	70%	60%	50%	40%	30%	20%	10%

REMINGTON ARMS COMPANY, INC.

Current manufacturer and trademark established in 1816, with factories currently located in Ilion, NY, Lonoke, AR, and Mayfield, KY.

Founded by Eliphalet Remington II and originally located in Litchfield, Herkimer County, NY circa 1816-1828. Remington established a factory in Ilion, NY next to the Erie Canal in 1828, and together with his sons Philo, Samuel, and Eliphalet III pioneered many improvements in firearms manufacture. Corporate offices were moved to Madison, NC in 1996. DuPont owned a controlling interest in Remington from 1933-1993, when the company was sold to Clayton, Dubilier & Rice, a New York City based finance company. The Mayfield, KY plant opened in 1997. On May 31st, 2007, a controlling interest in the company was sold to Cerberus Capital. Currently, Remington employs 2,500 workers in the U.S., including 1,000 in its Ilion, NY plant alone. Recently, Remington has acquired Harrington & Richardson Firearms (H & R), and Marlin Firearms. The company has moved manufacturing to their Remington plant in Ilion, New York. Remington management has every intention of keeping all three product identities separate.

For recent information on long guns imported by Spartan Gun Works, a Remington subsidiary, please refer to the Spartan Gun Works listing in the S section.

As this edition went to press, Remington had yet to establish its pricing for 2013.

REMINGTON TRADEMARKS - 1816-PRESENT

1816-1847 - Remington (company manufactured and distributed rifle barrels to gunsmiths throughout America)
1847-1853 - E. Remington & Son
1854-1888 - E. Remington & Sons
1888-1914 - Remington Arms Company
1914-1916 - Remington Arms & Ammunition Company, Inc.
1916-1920 - Remington Arms - Union Metallic Cartridge Co., Inc.
1920 to date - Remington Arms Company, Inc.

HANDGUNS: 1857-1945 PRODUCTION

BEALS' FIRST MODEL POCKET REVOLVER – percussion .31 cal., 5 shot, smooth cylinder, 3 in. octagon barrel, blue finish, one-piece Gutta Percha grip, brass or iron trigger guard. Approx. 3,000 produced, 1857-58.

N/A	$4,500	$4,000	$3,500	$2,500	$2,000	$1,500	$1,000	$800	$600	$500	$400

Add 75% for original pasteboard box and accessories.

BEALS' SECOND MODEL POCKET REVOLVER – percussion .31 cal., 5 shot, smooth cylinder, 3 in. octagon barrel, blue finish, 2-piece hard rubber grips, spur trigger. Less than 1,000 produced 1858-1859. Quite rare.

N/A	$6,000	$5,500	$4,500	$3,500	$2,250	$2,000	$1,500	$1,250	$1,000	$900	$800

BEALS' THIRD MODEL POCKET REVOLVER – percussion .31 cal., 5 shot, smooth cylinder, 4 in. octagon barrel, blue finish, 2-piece hard rubber grips, spur trigger, first Remington revolver with loading lever. Less than 1,000 mfg. 1859-1860.

N/A	$4,500	$4,000	$3,500	$2,500	$2,000	$1,500	$1,000	$800	$600	$500	$400

BEALS' NAVY REVOLVER – percussion .36 cal., 6 shot, smooth cylinder, 7 1/2 in. octagon barrel, blue finish, 2-piece walnut grips, some martially marked with inspector's initials and cartouche on grips. Approx. 15,000 produced, 1861-62. Barrel address is "Beals' Patent, Sept. 14, 1858 - Manufactured by Remingtons', Ilion, N.Y."

* ***Beals' Navy Revolver Martial/Commercial Model*** – single wing base pin (very rare), less than 400 mfg. Serial range under 400, very desirable.

N/A	$7,500	$6,500	$5,500	$5,000	$4,250	$3,500	$3,000	$2,500	$2,000	$1,500	$1,250

* ***Beals' Navy Revolver Martial/Commercial Model*** – several variations with approx. serialization 1-15,500, most were purchased by military but were not inspected.

N/A	$7,000	$6,000	$5,250	$4,500	$4,000	$3,000	$2,500	$2,250	$1,750	$1,250	$1,000

Subtract 20% for cartridge conversion.

100%	98%	95%	90%	80%	70%	60%	50%	40%	30%	20%	10%

* ***Beals' Navy Revolver Martially marked*** – serial range 13,500 to approx. 16,000. Approx. 500 mfg.

N/A	$8,000	$7,000	$6,000	$5,250	$4,500	$3,750	$3,250	$2,750	$2,250	$1,750	$1,500

BEALS' ARMY REVOLVER

Subtract 20% for cartridge conversions.

* ***Beal's Army Revolver Martial/Commercially Model*** – percussion .44 cal., 6 shot, smooth cylinder, 8 in. octagon barrel, blue finish, 2-piece walnut grips. Barrel address is "Beals' Patent, Sept. 14, 1858 - Manufactured by Remingtons', Ilion, N.Y."

N/A	$7,000	6,000	$5,500	$4,500	$4,000	$3,000	$2,500	$2,250	$1,750	$1,250	$1,000

Subtract 20% for cartridge conversions.

* ***Beals' Army Revolver Martially marked*** – serial range is approx. 850-1,900 inspected by "WAT" or "CGC", very desirable. Approx. 1,000 mfg.

N/A	$8,000	$7,000	$6,000	$5,250	$4,500	$3,750	$3,250	$2,750	$2,250	$1,750	$1,500

RIDER'S DOUBLE-ACTION POCKET REVOLVER – percussion .31 cal., 5 shot, unusual "mushroom-shaped" cylinder, 3 in. octagon barrel, blue finish, 2-piece hard rubber grips, brass trigger guard, no loading lever. One of the earliest double action handguns produced. Approx. 20,000 produced, 1860-70.

N/A	$3,000	$2,500	$2,000	$1,500	$1,250	$1,000	$800	$700	$600	$500	$400

Subtract 20% for conversion to cartridge.

RIDER'S SINGLE-SHOT BRASS PARLOR PISTOL – percussion .17 cal., all brass construction, grips included. Fewer than 1,000 produced, 1859-1860. MANY FAKES, caveat emptor.

N/A	$10,000	$9,000	$8,000	$7,000	$5,000	$4,500	$4,000	$3,500	$3,000	$2,500	$2,000

MODEL 1861 (ELLIOT'S PATENT) NAVY REVOLVER – percussion .36 cal., 6 shot, unfluted cylinder, 7 1/2 in. octagon barrel, blue finish, 2-piece walnut grips. Loading lever has slot allowing cylinder pin to be pulled forward without lowering lever. Approx. 6,000 produced 1862-63 in serial range approx. 15,000-21,000. Barrel address "Patented Dec. 17, 1861, 1858 - Manufactured by Remingtons', Ilion, N.Y."

* ***Model 1861 Navy Revolver Martial/Commercial Model***

N/A	$6,500	$5,750	$5,250	$4,500	$4,000	$3,000	$2,500	$2,250	$1,750	$1,250	$1,000

Subtract 20% for cartridge conversion.

* ***Model 1861 Navy Revolver Martially marked*** – over 4,000 martially inspected "CGC".

N/A	$7,500	$6,750	$6,000	$5,250	$4,500	$3,750	$3,250	$2,750	$2,250	$1,750	$1,500

MODEL 1861 (ELLIOT'S PATENT) ARMY REVOLVER – percussion .44 cal., 6 shot, unfluted cylinder, 8 in. octagon barrel, blue finish, 2-piece walnut grips. Majority are martially inspected "CGC". Loading lever has slot allowing cylinder pin to be pulled forward without lowering lever. Approx. 10,000 produced 1862-63 in approx. serial range 1,900-12,000. Barrel address "Patented Dec. 17, 1861, 1858 - Manufactured by Remingtons', Ilion, N.Y."

N/A	$7,500	$7,000	$5,000	$4,000	$2,500	$2,000	$1,800	$1,500	$1,250	$1,000	$750

Subtract 20% for cartridge conversion.

NEW MODEL ARMY REVOLVER – percussion .44 cal., 6 shot, unfluted cylinder, 8 in. octagon barrel, blue finish, 2-piece walnut grips. Approx. 135,000 produced 1863-1888 in serial range 12,000-148,000. Barrel address "Patented Sept. 14, 1858 - Manufactured by Remingtons', Ilion, N.Y. - New Model." Early models lack "New Model" markings on barrel and have transition features from "1861" model. Erroneously called the "Remington Model 1858 Revolver."

N/A	$7,500	$7,000	$5,000	$4,000	$2,500	$2,000	$1,800	$1,500	$1,250	$1,000	$750

Subtract 20% for cartridge conversion (most are in .46 rimfire). Subtract 15% if not martially inspected and cartouched.

NEW MODEL NAVY REVOLVER – percussion .36 cal., 6 shot, unfluted cylinder, 7 1/2 in. octagon barrel, blue finish, 2-piece walnut grips. Approx. 18,000 produced in percussion from 1863-1878 with serial range 21,000-48,000. None were martially marked at time of mfg. Approx. 4,000 were purchased by U.S. Navy during 1863-65 in serial range

100%	98%	95%	90%	80%	70%	60%	50%	40%	30%	20%	10%

21,000-32,000. Barrel address "Patented Sept. 14, 1858 - Manufactured by Remingtons', Ilion, N.Y. - New Model." Early specimens lack "New Model" markings on barrel and have transition features from "1861" model.

100%	98%	95%	90%	80%	70%	60%	50%	40%	30%	20%	10%
N/A	$7,000	$6,750	$4,750	$3,750	$2,250	$1,800	$1,500	$1,400	$1,200	$900	$750

Subtract 20% for cartridge conversion (most are in .38 rimfire). Subtract 15% if not martially inspected and cartouched.

NEW MODEL BELT REVOLVER, SINGLE ACTION – percussion .36 cal., 6 shot, unfluted or fluted cylinder, 6 1/2 in. octagon barrel, blue or nickel finish, 2-piece walnut grips. Approx. 5,000 produced 1863-72.

100%	98%	95%	90%	80%	70%	60%	50%	40%	30%	20%	10%
N/A	$5,000	$4,500	$4,000	$3,000	$2,250	$1,900	$1,500	$1,300	$1,100	$900	$800

Add 30% for fluted cylinder (cylinder numbered to the gun).
Subtract 20% for cartridge conversion (mfg. 1870-1886).

NEW MODEL BELT REVOLVER, DOUBLE ACTION – percussion .36 cal., 6 shot, smooth or fluted cylinder, 6 1/2 in. octagon barrel, blue or nickel finish, 2-piece walnut grips. Approx. 2,500 produced 1863-72.

100%	98%	95%	90%	80%	70%	60%	50%	40%	30%	20%	10%
N/A	$5,000	$4,500	$4,000	$3,000	$2,250	$1,900	$1,500	$1,300	$1,100	$900	$800

Add 30% for fluted cylinder (most not numbered to the gun).
Subtract 20% for cartridge conversion.

NEW MODEL POLICE REVOLVER – percussion .36 cal., 5 shot, smooth cylinder, 3 to 6 1/2 in. octagon barrels, blue or nickel finish, 2-piece walnut grips. Approx. 18,000 produced 1863-1872.

100%	98%	95%	90%	80%	70%	60%	50%	40%	30%	20%	10%
N/A	$4,800	$4,400	$3,750	$2,750	$2,000	$1,750	$1,400	$1,200	$1,000	$850	$750

Add 10% for 6 1/2 in. barrel.
Subtract 20% for cartridge conversion.

NEW MODEL POCKET REVOLVER – percussion .31 cal., 5 shot, smooth cylinder, spur trigger, 3 to 4 1/2 in. octagon barrel, blue or nickel finish, two-piece walnut grips. Approx. 25,000 produced, 1863-1888.

100%	98%	95%	90%	80%	70%	60%	50%	40%	30%	20%	10%
N/A	$4,800	$4,400	$3,750	$2,750	$2,000	$1,750	$1,400	$1,200	$1,000	$850	$750

Add 25% for brass frame.
Subtract 20% for cartridge conversion.

ELLIOT'S ZIG-ZAG DERRINGER – .22 short rimfire cartridge, 6 shot, 6 barrel cluster (rotating), ring trigger, 3 in. barrel cluster, blue finish, 2-piece hard rubber grips. Fewer than 1,000 produced, 1861-63. Reputed to be Remington's first cartridge handgun. William Elliot's patent, desirable.

100%	98%	95%	90%	80%	70%	60%	50%	40%	30%	20%	10%
N/A	$6,000	$5,000	$4,000	$3,000	$2,400	$2,200	$2,000	$1,800	$1,500	$1,250	$1,000

ELLIOT'S FIVE SHOT "RING TRIGGER" DERRINGER – .22 short rimfire cartridge, 5 shot, 5 barrel cluster (fixed), 3 in. barrel cluster, blue finish, 2-piece hard rubber, walnut, ivory or pearl grips, ring trigger. Approx. 10,000 produced (combined production total with .32 cal.).

100%	98%	95%	90%	80%	70%	60%	50%	40%	30%	20%	10%
N/A	$5,000	$4,750	$3,500	$2,500	$2,250	$2,000	$1,750	$1,500	$1,400	$1,200	$950

ELLIOT'S FOUR SHOT "RING TRIGGER" DERRINGER – cartridge .32 rimfire cal., 4 shot, 4 barrel cluster (fixed), ring trigger, 3 3/8 in. barrel cluster, blue finish, 2-piece hard rubber, walnut, ivory or pearl grips. Approx. 10,000 produced (combined production with .22 cal.).

100%	98%	95%	90%	80%	70%	60%	50%	40%	30%	20%	10%
N/A	$5,000	$4,750	$3,500	$2,500	$2,250	$2,000	$1,750	$1,500	$1,400	$1,200	$950

VEST POCKET PISTOL – rimfire cartridge .22, .30, .32, or .41 cal., single shot, various barrel lengths, blue or nickel (post 1870) finish, 2-piece walnut grips, spur trigger. Rider's patent.

* ***Vest Pocket Pistol .22 Rimfire*** – approx. 25,000 produced, 1865-1888. Copied by European gunmakers.

100%	98%	95%	90%	80%	70%	60%	50%	40%	30%	20%	10%
N/A	$3,200	$2,800	$2,150	$1,600	$1,100	$950	$850	$650	$525	$425	$325

Subtract 25% for guns lacking company name.

* ***Vest Pocket Pistol .30 or .32 Rimfire*** – approx. 18,000 mfg. 1865-1888. Copied by European gunmakers.

100%	98%	95%	90%	80%	70%	60%	50%	40%	30%	20%	10%
N/A	$3,500	$3,000	$2,200	$1,700	$1,200	$1,000	$800	$700	$600	$500	$400

100%	98%	95%	90%	80%	70%	60%	50%	40%	30%	20%	10%

* ***Vest Pocket Pistol .41 Rimfire*** – approx. 25,000 produced, 1865-1888. Copied by European gunmakers.

N/A	$3,100	$2,800	$2,100	$1,600	$1,100	$1,000	$900	$700	$600	$500	$400

ELLIOT'S O/U DERRINGER – cartridge .41 Rimfire cal., 2 shot, 3 in. superimposed barrels, oscillating firing pin, spur trigger, many finishes, hard rubber, rosewood, walnut, ivory, pearl, or other 2-piece grips. Approx. 112,000 produced between 1867-1935. William Elliot's patent.

The dates on the following sub-models are estimates calculated after examining original sales receipts found with guns in factory boxes which were then compared to the numbers of guns manufactured each year.

Subtract 50% if barrel hinge is cracked.

* ***E. Remington & Sons Production 1867-1888*** – first 100 made with side address: "MANUFACTURED BY E. REMINGTON & SONS ILION, NY", maker's name and patent data stamped between the barrels, no extractor, made for patent holder William H. Elliot, and sold independently from the manufacturer.

» **"Manufactured by E. Remington & Sons Ilion NY" Side Address** – first 100 made with side address for patent holder William H. Elliot, and sold independently from the manufacturer. Extremely hard to find in any condition. Maker's name and patent data stamped between the barrels, w/o extractor.

N/A	N/A	$12,000	$8,500	$7,000	$5,500	$4,250	$4,000	$3,750	$3,500	$3,250	$3,000

» **"E. Remington & Sons. Ilion. N.Y." Side Address (1868-1869)** – maker's name and patent data stamped between the barrels, made without an extractor (about 1,600 produced).

N/A	N/A	$5,500	$4,250	$3,750	$3,250	$2,750	$2,250	$1,750	$1,500	$1,100	$1,000

» **"E. Remington & Sons. Ilion. N.Y." Side Address (1868-1869)** – made with extractor (probably more than 300 made).

N/A	N/A	$6,500	$5,500	$4,500	$4,000	$3,600	$3,200	$3,000	$2,600	$2,200	$1,800

» **"Remingtons Ilion N.Y. U.S.A." Side Address (1868-1869)** – made without an extractor (around 20 mfg.), very rare.

N/A	N/A	$15,000	$12,000	$9,000	$7,500	$6,500	$5,500	$5,000	$4,500	$4,000	$3,500

» **"Remington Ilion N.Y. U.S.A." Side Address (1868-1869)** – made with extractor (perhaps 130 made).

N/A	N/A	$11,000	$8,000	$7,000	$6,000	$5,000	$4,000	$3,500	$3,000	$2,500	$2,000

* ***"E. Remington & Sons. Ilion. N.Y. Elliot's Patent Dec. 12th 1865" Two Line Address (Top of Barrel, 1870-1888)*** – made with extractor (12,000 to 18,000 produced between 1870 and 1888), sequential numbering ended within this address.

N/A	N/A	$5,000	$4,000	$3,500	$3,000	$2,750	$2,500	$1,600	$1,200	$900	$600

* ***Remington Arms Company Production (1889-1910)*** – there are six address variations during this production period. All are batch numbered.

Add 25% for slant-line gap (very scarce).

Add 25% for original cardboard box.

» **"Remington Arms Co. Ilion. N.Y." Side Address (1889-1893)** – first address, short line, all are batch numbered, estimated production of 8,000.

N/A	N/A	$,500	$3,750	$3,000	$2,000	$1,600	$1,300	$1,000	$800	$600	$400

» **"Remington Arms Co. Ilion. N.Y." Side Address (1894-1898)** – second address, slant line, estimated production of 14,500.

N/A	N/A	$5,625	$4,675	$3,750	$2,500	$2,000	$1,625	$1,250	$1,000	$750	$500

» **"Remington Arms C O. Ilion, N.Y." Side Address (1899)** – third address, slant line (C O gap), estimated production of 2,200.

N/A	N/A	$5,625	$4,675	$3,750	$2,500	$2,000	$1,625	$1,250	$1,000	$750	$500

100%	98%	95%	90%	80%	70%	60%	50%	40%	30%	20%	10%

» **"Remington Arms Co. Ilion, N.Y." Side Address (1900-1903)** – fourth address, (big C, little o), estimated production of 12,000.

N/A	N/A	$5,625	$4,675	$3,750	$2,500	$2,000	$1,625	$1,250	$1,000	$750	$500

» **"Remington Arms Co. Ilion. N.Y." Side Address (1904-1910)** – fifth address, (48mm long), estimated production of 8,000.

N/A	N/A	$5,625	$4,675	$3,750	$2,500	$2,000	$1,625	$1,250	$1,000	$750	$500

» **"Remington Arms Co. Ilion, N. Y." Side Address (1904-1910)** – sixth address, (50mm gaps), estimated production is unknown.

N/A	N/A	$5,625	$4,675	$3,750	$2,500	$2,000	$1,625	$1,250	$1,000	$750	$500

* ***"Remington Arms - U.M.C. CO. Ilion, N.Y." (1911-1935)*** – sequential numbering resumes.

Add 25% for original cardboard box.

» **"Remington Arms - - U.M.C.CO.Ilion, N.Y." First Variation (1911)** – no "L" serial number prefix, numbered 1-3000.

N/A	N/A	$5,000	$4,000	$3,500	$2,750	$2,500	$1,800	$1,200	$900	$600	$400

» **"Remington Arms - - U.M.C.CO. Ilion, N.Y." Second Variation 1911-1935** – "L" serial number prefix, numbered in two series from L90XXX-L99999 and the later group L75XXX-L76XXX, these are guns with the rib between the barrels, approx. 27,000 mfg.

N/A	N/A	$3,500	$2,500	$2,000	$1,500	$1,200	$900	$700	$600	$500	$400

» **"Remington Arms - - U.M.C.CO.Ilion, N.Y. Third Variation Monoblocks (1929-1935)** – these are among the last produced Remington Double Deringers and do NOT have ribs between the barrels, the rib area formerly now has been "fluted" with smooth contouring. Approx. 500 mfg.

N/A	N/A	$5,000	$4,000	$3,500	$2,750	$2,500	$2,000	$1,500	$1,300	$1,100	$1,000

MODEL 1866 NAVY ROLLING BLOCK PISTOL – cartridge .50 rimfire cal., single shot, 8 1/2 in. round barrel, spur trigger, walnut grip and forearm, blue finish. Approx. 6,500 produced, 1866-67. Erroneously designated as, "Model of 1865 Navy".

* ***Model 1866 Navy Rolling Block Pistol Martially Marked***

N/A	N/A	$6,000	$5,250	$4,500	$4,000	$3,500	$3,000	$2,500	$2,000	$1,750	$1,500

Subtract 30% if not martially marked (Commercial Model mfg. 1866 - 1868).

Subtract 25% for centerfire breech block.

Fewer than 150 remain in original condition. Martially marked specimens are very rarely encountered.

COMBINATION PISTOL-SHOTGUN – 20 ga., 11 3/4 in. single barrel with smooth bore, rolling block action, designed as a pistol or shotgun (with detachable shoulder stock). Mfg. circa mid-1920s by an unknown manufacturer (possibly Bannerman's). Rolling block receivers appear to have been from foreign made military rifles.

Extreme rarity factor precludes accurate pricing information.

In either configuration, this model is an NFA firearm that cannot be legally owned unless registered with the BATFE.

MODEL 1870 NAVY ROLLING BLOCK PISTOL – cartridge .50 centerfire cal., single shot, 7 in. round barrel, standard trigger with trigger guard, walnut grip and forearm, blue finish. Approx. 6,400 produced 1870-75. Modified by Remington for the Navy from Model 1866 pistols.

N/A	N/A	$4,000	$3,000	$2,500	$1,800	$1,500	$1,300	$1,200	$1,100	$1,000	$900

Add approx. 20% for 8 in. commercial version (approx. 200-400 mfg.) without inspector's marks.

MODEL 1871 ARMY ROLLING BLOCK PISTOL – cartridge .50 centerfire cal., single shot, 8 in. round barrel, standard trigger with trigger guard, walnut grip and forearm, blue finish. Approx. 5,000 produced, 1871-72.

N/A	$4,000	$3,500	$3,000	$2,500	$2,000	$1,750	$1,500	$1,400	$1,100	$1,000	$900

Subtract 10% for Commercial Model w/o military markings and cartouche.

Smooth bored version was authorized by the U.S. Ordnance Department.

100%	98%	95%	90%	80%	70%	60%	50%	40%	30%	20%	10%

MODEL OF 1887 PLINKER ROLLING BLOCK PISTOL – cartridge .22, .25 rimfire and .32, .50 centerfire cals., single shot, utilizing surplus M-1871 Army rolling block frames, 8 in. round barrel, standard trigger with trigger guard, walnut grip and forearm, blue finish. Approx. 800 mfg. 1887-91.

N/A	$3,000	$2,500	$2,000	$1,750	$1,500	$1,250	$1,000	$900	$800	$700	$600

Add 10% for Navy rolling block framed.

Navy framed 1887s are discernible by military proofs on right side of frame, Remington altered from original Navy Model 1870. Estimated mfg. of 100.

MODEL 1891 TARGET MODEL ROLLING BLOCK PISTOL – cartridge .22, .25 rimfire and .32 centerfire cals., single shot, 10 in. part octagon, part round barrel, standard trigger with trigger guard, smooth walnut grip and forearm, blue finish. Limited mfg. of 116 between 1891-1900.

N/A	$3,000	$2,500	$2,000	$1,750	$1,500	$1,250	$1,000	$900	$800	$700	$600

Removing the grips on this model may reveal a 4-digit number, indicating the refurbished military action.

MODEL 1901 TARGET ROLLING BLOCK PISTOL – cartridge .22 S and L, .25 rimfire, .32 centerfire, or .44 S&W Russian cal., single shot, 10 in. part octagon, part round barrel, standard trigger with trigger guard, checkered walnut grip and forearm, blue finish. Limited mfg. of only 734 sold between 1901-1909.

N/A	$3,500	$3,000	$2,500	$2,000	$1,500	$1,250	$1,000	$900	$800	$700	$600

Add $200 for .44 S&W Russian cal.

Removing the grips on this model may reveal a 4-digit number, indicating the refurbished military action.

REMINGTON-RIDER'S MAGAZINE PISTOL – .32 rimfire cal., 5 shot, 3 in. octagonal barrel, spur trigger, walnut, rosewood, ivory or pearl grips. Limited mfg. 1871-1888.

N/A	$3,500	$3,000	$2,500	$1,750	$1,400	$1,200	$1,000	$850	$750	$650	$500

Add 75% for original case hardened receiver and blued barrel.

Beware of faked blued finish. Most of this model were engraved, and a non-engraved specimen, while rare, is not necessarily more desirable.

ELLIOT'S SINGLE SHOT DERRINGER – .41 rimfire cartridge cal., single shot, 2 1/2 in. round barrel, spur trigger, walnut 2-piece grips, blue and/or nickel finish. Approx. 10,000 produced, 1867-1888. Also known as the "Mississippi Derringer."

N/A	$3,500	$3,100	$2,600	$2,200	$1,600	$1,500	$1,300	$1,100	$1,000	$800	$700

NO. 1 (SMOOT PATENT) REVOLVER – cartridge .30 Rimfire cal., 5 shot, 2 3/4 in. octagon barrel, spur trigger, walnut, hard rubber, pearl or ivory two-piece grips. Number produced debatable, 1873-1888.

N/A	$2,000	$1,800	$1,300	$900	$800	$600	$500	$400	$380	$350	$300

Add 30% on early No. 1s with revolving recoil shield.

Add 75% for original pasteboard box with label.

Nearly all were nickel plated. Beware of fake blue finish - a number have come on the market in the past few years.

On Number 1 through Number 4 Revolvers, ivory grips refer to Remington Celluloid, not genuine ivory. Only in rare instances does ivory appear.

NO. 2 (SMOOT PATENT) REVOLVER – cartridge .30 or .32 Rimfire cal., 5 shot, 2 3/4 in. octagon barrel, spur trigger, hard rubber, pearl or ivory two-piece grips. Number produced debatable, 1873-1888.

N/A	$2,000	$1,800	$1,300	$900	$800	$600	$500	$400	$380	$350	$300

Add 75% for original pasteboard box with label.

Nearly all were nickel plated. Beware of fake blue finish. A number have come on the market in the past few years.

100%	98%	95%	90%	80%	70%	60%	50%	40%	30%	20%	10%

NO. 3 (SMOOT PATENT) REVOLVER – cartridge .38 Rimfire or Centerfire cal., 3 3/4 in. octagon barrel with or without barrel rib, spur trigger, hard rubber, ivory or pearl 2-piece grips, "Bird-Head and Saw Handle" grip frame with Remington logo "R" on the "saw handle" hard rubber grips, Bird-Head referred to models with or without a barrel rib. Number produced debatable, 1875-1888.

N/A	$2,000	$1,800	$1,300	$900	$800	$600	$500	$400	$380	$350	$300

Add a small premium for centerfire calibers.
Add 75% for original pasteboard box with label.

Nearly all were nickel plated. Beware of fake blue finish. A number have come on the market in the past few years.

NO. 4 REVOLVER – cartridge .38 and .41 Rimfire or Centerfire cals., 5 shot, 2 1/2 in. round barrel, hard rubber, pearl or ivory 2-piece grips. Number produced debatable, 1877-88.

N/A	$2,000	$1,800	$1,300	$900	$800	$600	$500	$400	$380	$350	$300

Add a small premium for centerfire calibers.
Add 25% for original pasteboard box with label.

Nearly all were nickel plated. Beware of fake blue finish. A number have come on the market in the past few years.

IROQUOIS REVOLVER – .22 rimfire cartridge cal., 7 shot, 2 1/4 in. round barrel, spur trigger, hard rubber, pearl, or ivory 2-piece grips, nickel finish, fluted or non-fluted cylinder. Approx. 10,000 produced 1878-1888.

N/A	$2,200	$2,000	$1,800	$1,500	$1,300	$1,000	$850	$750	$600	$450	$375

Subtract 25% if unmarked.
Add 25% for fluted cylinder.
Add 75% for original pasteboard box with label.
Add 50% for original factory engraving.

Nearly all were nickel plated. Beware of fake blue finish.

MODEL 1875 SINGLE ACTION REVOLVER – .44 Rem., .44-40 Win., or .45 Colt centerfire cal., 6 shot, 7 1/2 or 5 3/4 (scarce) in. round barrel, standard trigger with trigger guard, blue or nickel finish, walnut, ivory, or pearl 2-piece grips, serial numbered in at least two batches. Approx. 30,000-40,000 produced, 1875-1888.

N/A	$15,000	$14,000	$10,000	$6,000	$4,000	$3,000	$2,400	$2,200	$2,000	$1,750	$1,500

Add 25% for blue finish.
Add 50% for U.S.I.D. "Indian Police" markings (beware of fakes).
Add 10% for .45 cal.

There is some debate over originality of the 5 3/4 in. barrel - some are known, but many were altered post-factory. Never cataloged.

MODEL 1888 SINGLE ACTION REVOLVER – cartridge .44 Centerfire cal., resembles 1890 SA, has "E. Remington & Sons" barrel address, 5 3/4 in. barrel, nickel finish with walnut grips, very desirable and little known.

N/A	$12,000	$11,000	$9,000	$5,000	$3,500	$3,000	$2,400	$2,200	$2,000	$1,750	$1,500

This model was never listed in a Remington catalog nor price list. Rather, it first appeared in a Hartley & Graham ad in late 1888. This revolver was made from parts of Models 1875 & 1890 pistols. Model nomenclature was created by collectors, not the factory.

MODEL 1890 SINGLE ACTION REVOLVER – .44-40 WCF cal., 6 shot, 7 1/2 or 5 3/4 in. round barrel, standard trigger with trigger guard, hard rubber 2-piece grips with Remington monogram, ivory or pearl grips on special order, blue or nickel finish. Approx. 2,000 produced, 1891-94.

N/A	$15,000	$14,000	$10,000	$6,000	$4,000	$3,000	$2,000	$1,500	$1,000	$900	$700

Add 25% for blue finish.
Add 50% for original pasteboard box.

MODEL 51 SEMI-AUTO – .32 ACP or .380 ACP cal., 8 shot (7 in mag., 1 in chamber), hard rubber 2-piece grips with company's name, black finish. Approx. 65,000 mfg. 1918-1926.

$800	$750	$650	$500	$375	$350	$300	$250	$225	$200	$175	$160

100%	98%	95%	90%	80%	70%	60%	50%	40%	30%	20%	10%

Add $250 for original box, brochure, oiler, and cleaning rod.

Although the .380 ACP cal. is much more common than .32 ACP cal., it commands a slight premium.

MODEL 1911 REMINGTON - UMC – .45 ACP cal., WWI M1911 military contract, over 21,500 mfg. (ser. numbered 1-21,676) in 1918-19 only, blue finish.

N/A	$6,950	$5,550	$4,000	$3,000	$2,500	$2,000	$1,900	$1,600	$1,400	$1,200	$1,000

Many 98%-100% specimens encountered in this model have been refinished - be careful.

MODEL 1911A1 REMINGTON RAND – approx. 1,086,624 mfg. 1943-1945 in Syracuse, NY, ser. no. ranges 916,405-1,041,404, 1,279,649-1,441,430, 1,471,431-1,609,528, 1,743,847-1,816,641, 1,890,504-2,075,103, 2,134,404-2,244,803, and 2,380,014-2,619,013, parkerized finish. Mfg. during WWII by Remington Rand Corp. These pistols were not made by Remington Arms Company during the war - Remington Rand was originally the Remington Standard Typewriter Company which was sold by E. Remington & Sons in 1884.

$2,500	$2,100	$1,900	$1,500	$1,200	$1,000	$900	$750	$650	$550	$450	$375

Add 20% with original shipping carton (watch for fakes).

MARK III SIGNAL PISTOL – 10 ga., single shot, brass frame, 9 in. round steel barrel, spur trigger, walnut 2-piece grips. Approx. 25,000 produced, 1915-18.

N/A	$600	$525	$400	$325	$275	$250	$225	$200	$180	$160	$150

Add $250 for original WWI web belt, cloth holster, and cloth cartridge pouch.

GRADING - PPGS™	100%	98%	95%	90%	80%	70%	60%	LAST MSR

HANDGUNS: POST-WWII PRODUCTION

MODEL 1911 R1 – .45 ACP cal., 5 in. satin stainless steel barrel, high polish blue slide and frame, checkered double diamond walnut grips, 7 shot mag., rear slide serrations, fixed sights, Remington logo on left side of slide, and 1911 R1 on right side of slide, 38 1/2 oz. Mfg. in USA. New mid-2010.

MSR $699	$625	$550	$495	$450	$395	$350	$300	

Model XP-100 & Variations

Manufacture stopped on the XP-100 at the end of 1994, and resumed briefly during 1998-99 (Model XP-100R).

MODEL XP-100 – .221 Rem. Fireball cal., single shot bolt action pistol, one-piece Dupont Zytel (nylon) pistol grip stock, adj. sights, drilled and tapped for receiver sight and scope, 4-digit ser. no., 3 3/4 lbs. Mfg. 1963-1985.

	$900	$850	$750	$600	$400	$300	$250	

MODEL XP-100 CUSTOM – .22-250 Rem. (new 1992), .223 Rem., .250 Savage, 6mm BR Rem., 7mm BR Rem., .308 Win. (new 1992), .35 Rem., or 7mm-08 Rem. cal., choice of standard or heavy barrel, available through custom gun shop only, choice of right or left-hand action, wood stock with contoured pistol grip, without sights. Mfg. by Custom Shop 1986-94.

	$1,000	$925	$800	$700	$600	$500	$400	*$945*

MODEL XP-100 HUNTER – .223 Rem., 7mm BR Rem., 7mm-.08 Rem., or .35 Rem. cal., 14 1/2 in. barrel, drilled and tapped for sights, laminated wood stock, 4 3/8 lbs. Mfg. 1993-1994.

	$900	$850	$750	$600	$400	$300	$250	*$548*

MODEL XP-100 VARMINT SPECIAL – single shot bolt action pistol, .223 Rem. (new 1986) cal., 14 1/2 in. barrel, drilled and tapped for receiver sights and scope, one-piece pistol grip nylon stock, 4 1/8 lbs. Mfg. 1986-1992.

	$900	$850	$750	$600	$400	$300	$250	*$419*

Add $100 for original hard zipper case.

MODEL XP-100 WALNUT – 7mm BR Rem. cal., 10 1/2 in. barrel, solid American walnut stock and target sights, 3 7/8 lbs. Mfg. 1993-94.

	$900	$850	$750	$600	$400	$300	$250	*$625*

GRADING - PPGS™	100%	98%	95%	90%	80%	70%	60%	LAST MSR

MODEL XP-100R – .22-250 Rem., .223 Rem., .260 Rem., or .35 Rem. cal., right-hand repeater with 4 or 5 shot blind mag., fiberglass composite stock, 14 1/2 in. barrel, drilled and tapped receiver, approx. 4 1/2 lbs. Mfg. 1998-99.

	$900	$850	$750	$600	$400	$300	$250	*$665*

MODEL XP-100R KS – .22-250 Rem. (new 1992), .223 Rem., .250 Savage (new 1991), 7mm-08 Rem., .308 Win. (new 1992), .35 Rem., or .350 Rem. Mag. (new 1991) cal., repeater variation, Kevlar synthetic stock, right-hand action only, open sights (except for .223 Rem. and .250 Savage) 4 1/8 lbs. Mfg. 1990-94.

	$950	$875	$775	$675	$595	$495	$400	*$840*

This model was available through Remington's Custom Shop only.

MODEL XP-SILHOUETTE – .35 Rem. (mfg. 1987-92) or 7mm BR Rem. (mfg. 1980-92) cal., bench rest model, 14 1/2 in. barrel, drilled and tapped, nylon (disc. 1992) or walnut (new 1992) stock, 3 7/8 lbs. Disc. 1992.

	$900	$850	$750	$600	$400	$300	$250	*$427*

Add $15 for .35 Rem. cal.

100%	98%	95%	90%	80%	70%	60%	50%	40%	30%	20%	10%

RIFLES: DISC.

REVOLVING PERCUSSION RIFLE – .36 or .44 (rare) cal., 6 shot unfluted cylinder, 24 or 28 in. octagon barrel, walnut stock with crescent butt, scroll trigger guard, blue with case hardened frame. Fewer than 1,000 mfg. 1866-1872.

N/A	N/A	$20,000	$14,000	$7,000	$5,500	$4,500	$3,500	$3,000	$2,500	$2,250	$2,000

Add 50% for factory engraved examples (only one known currently).

Frames were made especially for this model, and are not altered New Model revolvers. .38 R.F. factory conversions will be serial numbered on the recoil plate and cylinder. The ultimate in rarity in Remington Revolving Rifles is the .46 rimfire cal. Only five of this model are presently known.

MODEL 1862 "ZOUAVE RIFLE" – .58 cal., muzzle loading percussion, 33 in. round blue barrel, two barrel bands, case hardened lock, brass furniture. Mfg. 12,501, 1862-1865.

N/A	$6,000	$5,000	$4,000	$2,750	$2,500	$2,100	$2,000	$1,750	$1,500	$1,250	$1,000

Add $450 for correct sword type bayonet and scabbard in excellent condition.

Most models are in excellent condition, as few, if any, were distributed to the troops during the Civil War.

U.S. MILITARY MUSKET - PATTERN 1863 – .58 cal., muzzle loading percussion, 40 in. round barrel, three barrel bands, blue barrel, case hardened lock, iron furniture. 40,000 Mfg. in 1864.

N/A	$5,000	$4,500	$4,000	$3,000	$2,000	$1,500	$1,250	$1,000	$800	$700	$600

U.S. NAVY M1867 ROLLING BLOCK CARBINE – .50-45 centerfire cal., 23 1/4 in. barrel, open sight, blue with case hardened frame, bar and ring on frame, walnut straight grip stock. 5,000 mfg. 1868-1869 by Springfield Armory from receivers made by E. Remington & Sons in Ilion, NY.

N/A	N/A	$4,500	$4,000	$2,500	$2,000	$1,750	$1,500	$1,250	$1,000	$750	$500

U.S. NAVY "ANNAPOLIS CADET" MILITARY RIFLE – .50-45 centerfire cal., Mfg. by Springfield Armory utilizing rolling block receivers supplied by E. Remington & Sons in Ilion, NY. Mfg. 1868.

N/A	N/A	$4,500	$4,000	$2,950	$2,000	$1,750	$1,500	$1,250	$1,000	$750	$500

Add $150 for correct angular bayonet in excellent condition.

U.S. ARMY MODEL 1870 "EXPERIMENTAL" TRIALS REMINGTON ROLLING BLOCK MILITARY CARBINE – .50-70 Govt. cal., single shot, rolling block action with sling ring on left side of receiver, mfg. by Springfield Armory under license from E. Remington & Sons. 331 mfg. 1870.

N/A	N/A	N/A	$14,000	$12,000	$10,000	$9,000	$8,000	$7,000	$6,000	$5,000	$4,000

This model is extremely rare, and fewer than six are known to be in private hands. Disposition after the military trials is not known.

100%	98%	95%	90%	80%	70%	60%	50%	40%	30%	20%	10%

U.S. ARMY MODEL 1870 "EXPERIMENTAL" TRIALS REMINGTON ROLLING BLOCK MILITARY RIFLE – .50-70 Govt. cal., single shot, rolling block action, mfg. by Springfield Armory under license from E. Remington & Sons. Mfg. 1870.

N/A	N/A	$6,000	$5,500	$5,000	$4,500	$4,000	$2,750	$2,250	$1,750	$1,250	$1,000

Approx. 1,041 were mfg. 1870 and issued to infantry troops on the frontier for trial. This is a rarely encountered Springfield firearm.

U.S. NAVY MODEL 1870 (TYPES 1 & 2) MILITARY RIFLE – mfg. by Springfield Armory under license from E. Remington & Sons. Mfg. 1870.

N/A	$5,000	$4,500	$4,000	$3,000	$2,000	$1,500	$1,250	$1,000	$800	$1,000	$600

Add $300-$600 for correct Ames sword bayonet and scabbard. Beware of modern copies.

10,000 of these models were mfg. in 1870, but were not accepted by the U.S. Navy, reputedly because of the "unsafe" location of the rear sight (too close to the chamber). These "Type 1" Navy rifles were sold to Poultney & Trimble, who sold them to France. Springfield Armory subsequently manufactured 14,000 "Type 2" rifles with the rear sight moved up the barrel, and these models were accepted by the U.S. Navy. Values are the same for both types.

U.S. ARMY MODEL 1871 MILITARY RIFLE – .50-70 Govt. cal., single shot, rolling block action, mfg. by Springfield Armory under license from E. Remington & Sons. Mfg. 1872.

N/A	$3,500	$3,250	$2,750	$2,000	$1,750	$1,500	$1,200	$900	$700	$500	$400

10,101 of these models were mfg., but there is no evidence to suggest that they were ever issued to the troops. As a result, many of these models can be found in excellent or above average condition.

NO. 1 LONG RANGE "CREEDMOOR" TARGET RIFLE – .44-77, .44-90, or .44-100 cal., rolling block, 1/3 octagon barrel, case hardened receiver, long range tang sight, globe front sight, checkered pistol grip stock, blue. Approx. 500 mfg., 1873-1878.

N/A	$14,000	$13,000	$10,000	$8,000	$6,000	$5,000	$4,000	$3,000	$2,500	$2,200	$2,000

Add premiums for higher grade guns with select wood, additional checkering, and other deluxe features.

Add 25%+ for factory cased guns.

Factory cased guns are rarely encountered. Buyers beware of post-factory cases.

NO. 1 SPORTING RIFLE – rolling block, .40-50, .40-70, .44-70, .44-77, .45-70, .50-45, or .50-70 centerfire, .38 or .46 rimfire cal., 28 or 30 in. octagon barrels, folding leaf sight, straight grip stock. Approx. 10,000 mfg., 1868-86.

N/A	$6,000	$5,000	$3,500	$3,000	$2,500	$2,000	$1,500	$1,000	$750	$500	$300

Subtract 25% for rimfire cals.

Add 20% for .44-77, .45-70, or .50-70 cal. (primary buffalo hunting cals.).

NO. 1 1/2 SPORTING RIFLE – .22, .25 Stevens, .25 Long, .32, and .38 Long & Extra Long rimfire cal., also in .32-20 WCF, .38-40 WCF, and .44-40 WCF, 24-28 in. octagon medium weight barrel, straight grip walnut stock, somewhat lighter than the No. 1 Sporting. Several thousand mfg., 1888-97.

N/A	$4,000	$3,500	$2,750	$1,750	$1,250	$900	$800	$650	$550	$450	$300

Add 20% for centerfire cals.

NO. 2 SPORTING RIFLE – available in many rimfire cals. between .22 and .38 as well as several centerfire cals. between .22 and .38-40 WCF, blue barrel finish with case hardened frame, perch belly style walnut stock, many special orders available, smaller size action than the No. 1 and rear of frame is curved. Mfg. 1873-1909.

N/A	$3,500	$3,000	$2,250	$1,250	$750	$700	$600	$400	$300	$200	$150

LIGHT BABY CARBINE – .44-40 WCF cal., rolling block, 20 in. lightweight round blue barrel with band, straight stock, nickel or case colored receiver. Several thousand mfg., 1884-1902, a few early carbines are known to exist in .44 Long rimfire cal.

N/A	$7,000	$6,000	$5,000	$3,500	$2,750	$2,250	$1,750	$1,500	$1,000	$750	$600

Add 25% for blue barrel with color case hardened receiver.

Most made with nickel-plated receivers.

100%	98%	95%	90%	80%	70%	60%	50%	40%	30%	20%	10%

REMINGTON - HEPBURN NO. 3 SPORTING & TARGET RIFLES – falling block, single shot, side lever actuated, blued barrel, case hardened actions, patented 1879, first introduced 1880, many custom features were offered, variations as follows:

* ***Remington - Hepburn No. 3 Sporting & Target*** – various cals. from .22 rimfire to .50-90 Sharps, 26, 28, or 30 in. round or octagon barrel, open sight, semi-pistol grip stock. Mfg. 1880-1907.

N/A $9,000 $8,500 $6,000 $4,000 $2,500 $2,250 $2,000 $1,500 $1,250 $1,000 $800

.22 rimfire caliber versions of this model are exceedingly rare.

* ***Remington - Hepburn No. 3 Match Rifle A Quality*** – similar to Sporting and Target, with target match sights (tang), and Schuetzen stock w/o cheekpiece. Fewer than 1,000 mfg., 1883-1907.

N/A $12,000 $9,500 $6,000 $4,000 $2,500 $2,250 $2,000 $1,500 $1,250 $1,000 $800

» **Remington - Hepburn No. 3 Match Rifle B Quality** – select grade wood and vernier rear tang sight, checkered at wrist and forearm, buttstock w/cheekpiece.

N/A $12,000 $9,500 $6,000 $4,000 $2,500 $2,250 $2,000 $1,500 $1,250 $1,000 $800

* ***Remington - Hepburn No. 3 Long Range Creedmoor*** – .44-77, .44-90, or .44-105 centerfire cal., 32 or 34 in. barrel, target sight, often with heel sight, stock with shotgun butt. A few hundred mfg., 1880-1907.

N/A $16,500 $12,000 $8,825 $6,250 $4,475 $3,875 $3,175 $2,700 $2,475 $2,150 $1,800

* ***Remington - Hepburn No. 3 Mid Range Creedmoor*** – similar to Long Range, in .40-65 WCF, rarely other cals., 28 in. barrel.

N/A $11,000 $9,500 $7,000 $5,000 $3,500 $2,750 $2,500 $2,000 $1,750 $1,500 $1,000

* ***Remington - Hepburn No. 3 Long Range Military*** – similar to Creedmoor, with 34 in. full musket stock, in .44-75-520 Rem. cal., military sights, rarely encountered. Mfg. circa 1880s.

N/A $12,000 $10,000 $9,000 $6,250 $4,475 $3,875 $3,175 $2,700 $2,475 $2,150 $1,800

* ***Remington - Hepburn No. 3 Walker-Hepburn Schuetzen Match*** – under-lever action, 30 or 32 in. barrel, tang sight, palm rest, special Schuetzen stock, approx. 23 mfg. in 1903-1904, perhaps the rarest single shot American rifle.

Extreme rarity factor precludes accurate price evaluation but a few have been observed with price tags in the $30,000 - $75,000+ range, depending on condition.

* ***Remington - Hepburn No. 3 Walker-Hepburn Schuetzen Match With False Muzzle***

Add a premium according to condition - very rare.

NO. 4 ROLLING BLOCK RIFLE – .22 S-L-LR, .25 Stevens (barrels marked "25-10"), or .32 Short or Long cal. rimfire, 22 1/2 in. octagon barrel standard with round barrels available late in the series, smooth bore barrel was introduced approx. 1911, blue finish with case hardened frame, solid frame initially followed by takedown in 2 different types (lever release introduced approx. 1901, screw in approx. 1924), this model was Remington's smallest rolling block. Approx. 350,000 mfg. 1890-1933.

N/A $1,500 $1,300 $1,000 $700 $600 $500 $450 $400 $375 $300 $250

Solid frame variations will command a slight premium, especially if over 90% original condition.

* ***No. 4 Rolling Block Rifle Cadet Model*** – similar to Boy Scout, 28 in. barrel, lever takedown, tapered forend, no handguard, no barrel band or bayonet lug, frame unmarked, predates the Boy Scout Model. Mfg. 1911-1912, exceedingly rare.

N/A $4,000 $3,000 $2,000 $2,000 $1,750 $1,500 $1,200 $1,110 $1,000 $900 $800

The existence of this No. 4 variation has only recently been discovered. Almost unknown to even advanced collectors.

* ***No. 4-S Rolling Block Rifle "Boy Scout"***

N/A $3,500 $3,000 $2,500 $2,000 $1,600 $1,300 $1,000 $900 $800 $700 $600

* ***No. 4-S Rolling Block Rifle Military*** – .22 S-L-LR cal., either marked "MILITARY MODEL" (most common) or "AMERICAN BOY SCOUT" (rare), 28 in. round barrel with musket

100%	98%	95%	90%	80%	70%	60%	50%	40%	30%	20%	10%

type forend (1 barrel band), thought to have been used by military academies to train their young cadets.

100%	98%	95%	90%	80%	70%	60%	50%	40%	30%	20%	10%
N/A	$2,500	$2,250	$1,800	$1,700	$1,500	$1,200	$1,000	$900	$800	$700	$600

Original pot-metal bayonets for No. 4-S rifles are exceedingly rare and one in excellent condition may bring $1,250+. A correct leather scabbard can bring an additional $500.

NO. 5 HIGH-POWER, ROLLING BLOCK SPORTING & TARGET RIFLE – various centerfire calibers, including .30-40 Govt, .303 British, etc., round barrel. Manufactured in the early 20th century. Very few made - possibly only 300.

100%	98%	95%	90%	80%	70%	60%	50%	40%	30%	20%	10%
N/A	$7,000	$6,000	$5,000	$3,000	$2,000	$1,500	$1,250	$1,000	$900	$800	$700

NO. 6 FALLING BLOCK RIFLE – .22 S-L-LR or .32 short or long rimfire cal., 20 in. round barrel, boy's gun with small dimensions, takedown action, case hardened (early mfg.) or blue finish, also available in smooth bore, 497,000 mfg. 1901-33.

100%	98%	95%	90%	80%	70%	60%	50%	40%	30%	20%	10%
N/A	$650	$600	$500	$350	$300	$250	$225	$200	$180	$170	$150

Add 10% for smooth bore barrel.

Original case colors will bring a premium on this model.

Improved Model 6 became available circa 1905, and featured a blue frame in 24 in. barrel.

NO. 7 ROLLING BLOCK RIFLE – .22 S, .22 LR, or .25-10 Stev. rimfire cal., constructed on Rem. Model 1871 SS pistol action frame, 24, 26, or 28 in. 1/2 round, 1/2 octagon tapered barrels, marked "REMINGTON ARMS CO. ILION, NY USA" on barrel top flat, distinctive long tang pistol grip stock, checkered pistol grip and forearm, hard rubber buttplate, available in Target or Sporting configurations, with or w/o special Lyman tang mounted sight, ser. no. range 300,000. Last of the Rolling Block Rifles, very desirable. Approx. 350 mfg. 1903-10.

100%	98%	95%	90%	80%	70%	60%	50%	40%	30%	20%	10%
N/A	$9,000	$8,000	$7,000	$5,500	$4,900	$4,300	$3,700	$3,100	$2,650	$2,250	$1,750

REMINGTON KEENE MAGAZINE BOLT ACTION RIFLE – .45-70 Govt., .40, or .43 cal. Approx. 5,000 mfg. 1880-1888.

* ***Remington Keene Magazine Bolt Action Rifle Frontier Model*** – those made for U.S. Dept. of Interior (Indian Police), marked U.S.I.D. will command a 75% premium.

100%	98%	95%	90%	80%	70%	60%	50%	40%	30%	20%	10%
N/A	N/A	$5,000	$4,000	$3,000	$2,225	$1,750	$1,500	$1,000	$900	$800	$700

* ***Remington Keene Magazine Bolt Action Rifle Full Stock Carbine Model*** – 22 in. barrel, full stock.

100%	98%	95%	90%	80%	70%	60%	50%	40%	30%	20%	10%
N/A	N/A	$5,500	$4,500	$3,000	$2,225	$1,750	$1,500	$1,000	$900	$800	$700

* ***Remington Keene Magazine Bolt Action Rifle Carbine Model*** – 20 In. barrel, half stock, very limited mfg.

Rarity precludes accurate pricing.

* ***Remington Keene Magazine Bolt Action Army Rifle*** – 32 1/2 in. barrel, full stock.

100%	98%	95%	90%	80%	70%	60%	50%	40%	30%	20%	10%
N/A	N/A	$5,000	$4,000	$3,000	$2,225	$1,750	$1,500	$1,000	$900	$800	$700

* ***Remington Keene Magazine Bolt Action Sporting Rifle*** – 1/2 oct. barrel, full or "BUTTON" mag. Add for pistol grip and select wood variations.

100%	98%	95%	90%	80%	70%	60%	50%	40%	30%	20%	10%
N/A	N/A	$5,000	$4,000	$3,000	$2,225	$1,750	$1,500	$1,000	$900	$800	$700

* ***Remington Keene Magazine Bolt Action Navy Rifle*** – 29 1/2 in. barrel, full stock.

100%	98%	95%	90%	80%	70%	60%	50%	40%	30%	20%	10%
N/A	N/A	$5,000	$4,000	$3,000	$2,225	$1,750	$1,500	$1,000	$900	$800	$700

REMINGTON-LEE MAGAZINE BOLT ACTION RIFLE (MODEL 1879) – marked "Lee Arms Co., Bridgeport, Conn, USA, patented Nov. 4th, 1879" on upper left flat of receiver but all rifles were made at E. Remington & Sons, Ilion, NY. Remington, on April 1, 1881, acquired all the materials, fixtures and tooling from Sharps to complete the US Navy contract, and used the Lee-Borchardt projected nose magazine or the Lee-Cook magazine with the sliding detent on the side.

* ***U.S. Navy First Contract*** – .45-70 Govt. cal., 29 in. barrel, one piece bolt, bolt handle is forward and part of the right locking lug, serial numbers 1-300, US Navy Insp. WWK & HN, 300 delivered January 1882.

100%	98%	95%	90%	80%	70%	60%	50%	40%	30%	20%	10%
N/A	$5,000	$4,000	$3,500	$3,000	$2,500	$2,000	$1,600	$1,100	$700	$400	$250

100%	98%	95%	90%	80%	70%	60%	50%	40%	30%	20%	10%

* ***U.S. Navy Non-Contract*** – .45-70 Govt. cal., 29 in. barrel, Remington Rolling Block front and rear sights, bolt handle is forward and part of the right locking lug, serial number range 301 - 1300, US Navy Insp. WMF, 700 delivered late 1884.

N/A	N/A	$3,800	$3,300	$2,800	$2,300	$1,800	$1,400	$900	$600	$300	$250

* ***Military Non-Contract*** – .43 Spanish cal., 29 or 32 in. barrel, one piece bolt with the bolt handle moved to the classic Lee bent down position behind the right receiver wall, serial numbers 1301 - 7000, over 3,900 were sold to the Chinese Govt. in June 1884.

N/A	N/A	$3,500	$3,000	$2,500	$2,000	$1,500	$1,100	$800	$500	$300	$250

REMINGTON LEE MAGAZINE RIFLE (MODEL 1882) – marked "Lee Arms Co., Bridgeport, Conn, USA, Patented Nov. 4th, 1879" on upper left flat of receiver and "E. Remington & Sons, Ilion, NY, USA, Sole Manufacturers and Agents" on the left receiver side wall, uses the Lee-Diss box magazine with two grooves on the side, one-piece bolt with the bolt handle bent down and back of the right receiver wall.

* ***U.S. Army Trials*** – .45-70 Govt. cal., 32 1/2 in. barrel, serial number range 8800 - 9800, 750 were delivered September 1884 to the US Army, US Army Insp. DFC stamped on receiver, barrel and in a boxed script on the buttstock, field tested in 1885, withdrawn, declared surplus and about 400 were sold to a Boston arms dealer, these were later sold to the Massachusetts Naval Brigade and had stamped or painted unit markings applied to the buttstock. Front and rear sights are of the US Springfield pattern.

N/A	$5,00	$4,000	$3,500	$3,000	$2,500	$2,000	$1,600	$1,100	$700	$400	$250

* ***Chinese Contract*** – .45-70 Govt. or .43 Spanish cal., 20 1/2 (carbine), 28, 29, or 32 in. barrel, serial number range est. 11000 - 25000, over 14,000 produced starting in late 1884, around serial number 14000 the Lee Arms Co. markings were discontinued and the E. Remington & Sons markings moved to the upper left flat on the receiver, Chinese ideograms stamped on receiver ring. The Chinese defaulted on the contract in mid 1885, Remington resold the rifles after removing the Chinese markings, some rifles were fitted with a bayonet lug on the side of the barrel for a saber bayonet, front and rear sights are of the rolling block pattern.

N/A	N/A	$4,000	$3,500	$3,000	$2,500	$2,000	$1,600	$1,100	$700	$400	$250

Add 25% for carbine. Add 50% for conversion Model 1882 or 1885 (120 rifles and 100 carbines were inventoried with "altered bolts" in 1888).
Subtract 10% for .43 Spanish cal.

REMINGTON LEE MAGAZINE RIFLE (MODEL 1885) – 32 in. barrel, marked "E. Remington & Sons, Ilion, NY, USA, Sole Manufacturers and Agents, Patented Nov. 4th, 1879", serial number range 41000 - 47000, action revised to accept the new two piece bolt with separate bolt head, uses the Lee-Diss box magazine with two grooves on the side. Mfg. after the 1886 bankruptcy and 1888 reorganization of E. Remington & Sons.

N/A	$3,800	$3,200	$2,700	$2,300	$1,900	$1,500	$1,100	$800	$500	$300	$250

Add 100% for New Zealand purchase, distinctively marked NZ with broad arrows over 87 on receiver ring. 500 sold to New Zealand in 1887.
Add 200% for British Trials rifle, 300 purchased January 1887, marked WD under board arrow on buttstock and fitted with cutoff on right side of action.

* ***U.S. Navy Contract*** – .45-70 Govt. cal., 32 1/2 in. barrel, serial number range 50001 - 54000, front and rear sights are of the US Springfield pattern, over 3,400 were accepted by the US Navy from 1888 to 1894, marked on the receiver ring - USN over anchor over Navy serial number over US Navy inspector, the Naval serial numbers range from 1001 to over 4000, the Navy inspectors are: WWK, HHE, ACD, CEC, HE, and SWV, a few rifles were issued without being inspected.

N/A	$4,500	$4,000	$3,500	$3,000	$2,500	$2,000	$1,600	$1,100	$700	$400	$250

Add 50% for documented Hawaiian National Guard Purchase, NGH stamped on buttstock, no USN proofs. 350+ purchased in 1893 by Provisional Government of Hawaii.

REMINGTON LEE SMALL BORE MAGAZINE RIFLE (MODEL 1899) – marked "Remington Arms Company, Ilion, NY, USA, Patented Aug, 26th, 1884, Sept. 9th, 1884, March 17th, 1885, Jan. 18th 1887", two-piece bolt with two locking lugs on the bolt head, uses the Lee-Diss box magazine with three grooves on the side.

100%	98%	95%	90%	80%	70%	60%	50%	40%	30%	20%	10%

* ***Michigan National Guard Contract*** – .30-40 Govt. cal., 29 1/2 in. barrel, serial number range 100001 - 102200. 1,001 shipped in 1898 and 1,000 in 1899.

N/A	$3,800	$3,200	$2,700	$2,300	$1,900	$1,500	$1,100	$800	$500	$300	$250

* ***Cuban Contract*** – .30-40 Govt. cal., 20 (carbine) or 29 1/2 (rifle) in. barrel, serial number range 1 - 3000. 2,600 carbines and 400 rifles shipped to Cuba in 1905, the Cuban Coat of Arms and serial number are stamped on the receiver ring, in 1914 a number of the carbines and rifles were returned to Remington, the Cuban crest polished off, reblued and, in 1915, 1,153 carbines sold to the French Army for their Automobile Corps.

N/A	$3,800	$3,200	$2,700	$2,300	$1,900	$1,500	$1,100	$800	$500	$300	$250

Add 25% for carbine.

REMINGTON LEE SPORTING & TARGET RIFLES – The original 1879 Lee Arms catalog advertised a sporting rifle "to be made in the ensuing season". Only a few handmade, tool room model sporters were made at Sharps and at least one of these has the turned down bolt handle, a search of period E. Remington & Sons advertising from 1881 to 1888 has not turned up any mention of Remington Lee sporters, the Keene sporter apparently met the need for a bolt action sporter and any factory Remington Lee sporter from this period should be considered a tool room model.

* ***Remington Lee M1885*** – .43 Spanish, .44-77, .45-70 Govt., or .45-90 cal., 26 in. round barrel, the 1904-05 Remington Arms catalog advertised Remington Lee sporters, based on the US Navy M1885 action, checkered half pistol grip stock with rifle buttplate and two points facing the action, serial number range 54000.

N/A	N/A	$3,100	$2,500	$2,300	$1,900	$1,500	$1,100	$800	$500	$350	$300

* ***Remington Lee M1899*** – 6mm USN, 7mm Spanish Mauser, 7.65 Belgian Mauser, .30-30 Win., .30-40 Krag, .303 British, .32 Win. Spl., .32-40 B&W High Power, .35 Win., .38-55 High Power, .38-72 or .405 Win. cal., the Standard Grade sporter has 24, 26 (standard), or 28 in. round barrel, checkered half pistol grip stock with rifle buttplate and two points facing the action, Standard Grade, Heavy Weight sporter has 24 and 26 in. heavy barrel, express sights, checkered half pistol grip stock with shotgun buttplate and three points facing the action, Special Remington Lee Sporter is high grade, 26 in. half round, half octagon barrel, select extra fine checkered English walnut stock, shotgun butt with center grain exposed and heel and toe steel tips and five points facing the action, wind gauge front Lyman sight and aperture rear sight, the standard three grooves on the side Lee-Diss magazine was used, to accommodate the shorter cartridges the .30-30, .32 Win. and .32-40 B&W magazines have a rear spacer while the .38-55 magazine has a front spacer. Serial number range 75001-76446. A total of 1,446 factory sporters were shipped from 1899 to 1909.

N/A	$3,500	$2,700	$2,100	$1,600	$1,100	$900	$750	$600	$450	$300	$250

Add 100% for Special Remington Lee Sporter.

Add 200-300% for documented Military or Sporting Target Rifle.

Original retail price for the Standard Grade Sporter was $25 in 1905. Original retail price for the Special Remington Lee Sporter was $60 in 1905.

MODEL 1903-A3 MAGAZINE BOLT RIFLE – please refer to listing under Springfield Armory.

MODEL 1917 ENFIELD (REMINGTON MFG.) – mostly mfg. by the Remington plants in Eddystone, PA and Ilion, NY. Please refer to listings under Enfield.

REMINGTON-BEALS SPORTING RIFLE – .32 Long Rimfire or .38 Long Rimfire cal., Fordyce Beals invented a single-shot, breechloading rifle that would bear his name--the Remington-Beals Single-Shot Rifle. The breech of this rifle is opened by lowering the under-lever, which slides the barrel forward. Two chamberings of this rifle were made between 1866 and 1872. Both iron (early production) and brass-framed receivers were made. The under-powered rifle was not very popular, as fewer than 900 were made in seven years of production.

N/A	N/A	$2,500	$2,000	$1,200	$1,000	$900	$800	$700	$600	$500	$400

RIFLES: CANE VARIATIONS

Patented by John F. Thomas on February 9, 1858. Manufactured by E. Remington & Sons from 1858 through 1886, in percussion (1858 - 1861), and later in rimfire (1866 to 1886).

REMINGTON RIFLE CANES - .31 PERCUSSION – different handle configurations include right angle, bulbous head, ball and claw (exceedingly rare), large dog's head, full curve with short and long upper shaft, other non-factory handle configurations (ivory, silver, gold) are known, cane coverings are black gutta percha, black rifle cane coverings frequently turn brown with age and exposure to sunlight. Only about 300 percussion cane guns were made prior to the Civil War. Initially called Remington's New Patent Gun Cane.

100%	98%	95%	90%	80%	70%	60%	50%	40%	30%	20%	10%
N/A	$9,500	$8,500	$7,500	$7,000	$6,000	$5,500	$5,000	$4,500	$3,500	$3,000	$2,500

Add 20% for "dog's head".
Add 50% for "right angle", or "ball and claw", or "bulbous" handle.
Subtract 30% for after market or custom handles

Percussion rifle canes converted to .32 centerfire have been observed, but cannot be verified as factory conversions.

REMINGTON RIFLE CANES - .22 SHORT AND .32 LONG RIMFIRE – Remington No.1 Rifle Cane in .22 short RF - handle configurations include the small dog's head and two variations of curved handles (short shaft and long shaft). Remington No.2 Rifle Cane in .32 short rimfire - handle configurations include the large dog's head and two variations of curved handles (short shaft and long shaft). Cane coverings are black gutta percha, many different handle, barrel, shaft and overall lengths (33 1/2" to 36 1/2" known) were made. A number of after-market handles are known. Remington's rimfire cane guns were first made with internal hammers, but were improved with a rod driving the firing pin. At least 1,750 rimfire rifle canes were made after the Civil War and prior to 1886.

100%	98%	95%	90%	80%	70%	60%	50%	40%	30%	20%	10%
N/A	$8,000	$7,500	$7,000	$6,500	$6,000	$5,500	$4,000	$3,500	$3,000	$2,500	$2,000

Add 30% for "dog's head".
Subtract 30% for after market or non-factory custom handles.

Factory special order canes such as coral colored gutta percha (.32 long rimfire cal.) or takedown canes are too rare to be priced. During 2010, a fourth example of a coral colored cane rifle in .32 cal. and standard curved handle was discovered.

RIFLES: ROLLING BLOCK, RECENT MFG.

The following models are manufactured in limited quantities by the Remington Custom Shop.

NO. 1 ROLLING BLOCK CREEDMOOR MID-RANGE TARGET – .45-70 Govt. cal., rolling block action, patterned after the original Remington No. 1 mid-range Creedmoor-style configuration, 30 in. half-round half-octagon tapered barrel, includes rear tang aperture and front globe sight with four interchangeable inserts, checkered walnut stock and forearm, SST, case colored receiver, cased, 9 7/8 lbs. Mfg. 1997-98.

GRADING - PPGS™	100%	98%	95%	90%	80%	70%	60%	LAST MSR
	$2,800	$2,500	$1,900	$1,665	$1,415	$1,140	$950	$2,799

Subtract $750 if w/o original case.

NO. 1 ROLLING BLOCK MID-RANGE SPORTING – .45-70 Govt. cal., 30 in. round barrel, checkered pistol grip sporter stock and forearm, blue barrel and receiver, adj. buckhorn rear sight, 8 3/4 lbs. Mfg. 1998-2011.

GRADING - PPGS™	100%	98%	95%	90%	80%	70%	60%	LAST MSR
	$2,575	$2,275	$1,850	$1,600	$1,375	$1,100	$900	$2,992

NO. 1 ROLLING BLOCK SILHOUETTE – .45-70 Govt. cal., meets BPCR silhouette requirements, similar to No. 1 Rolling Block Mid-Range Sporter, except has 30 in. round heavy barrel w/o sights and single set or double triggers, blue or case colored receiver. Mfg. 2000-2011.

GRADING - PPGS™	100%	98%	95%	90%	80%	70%	60%	LAST MSR
	$2,925	$2,450	$1,975	$1,700	$1,425	$1,125	$925	$3,441

Add $450 for case colored receiver.
Add $300 for single set trigger.

GRADING - PPGS™	100%	98%	95%	90%	80%	70%	60%	LAST MSR

RIFLES: SEMI-AUTO - CENTERFIRE

The models have been listed in numerical sequence for quick reference.

IMPORTANT NOTE: On model(s) where *N/A has replaced the normal 100% value, it indicates current market conditions are too unstable to accurately ascertain 100%-60% values. Factory retail prices (MSRs) reflect most recent updates. For more up-to-date information on current pricing trends and additional useful information, please visit www.bluebookofgunvalues.com, select "Information & Services " from the menu, and click on "Additional Book Information".

MODEL FOUR - 6mm Rem., .243 Win., .270 Win., .280 Rem. (mfg. 1984-87), .30-06, .308 Win. (disc. 1984), or 7mm Express (mfg. 1981-83) cal., cartridge "head" imbedded in bottom of receiver, gas operation with metering system, 22 in. barrel, 4 shot detachable mag., deluxe Monte Carlo stock and forend, detachable sights. Mfg. 1981-87.

$650	$550	$450	$375	$275	$225	$200	*$475*

* ***Model Four Special Diamond Anniversary*** - .30-06 cal. only, commemorates the 75th anniversary of the Model 8, laser engraved with gold and premium checkered walnut stock and forearm. One grade only, approx. 1,400 shipped from 1982-1988, final 100 shipped in 1994 using Model 7400 stocks.

$1,300	$1,200	$1,000	N/A	N/A	N/A	N/A

* ***Model Four High Grades*** - only two mfg.

Extreme rarity precludes accurate pricing.

MODEL 5 - .30 Carbine cal., recoiling barrel, approx. 300 mfg.

$1,750	$1,550	$1,350	$1,150	$950	$750	$600

MODEL 8 - .25 Rem., .30 Rem., .32 Rem., or .35 Rem. cal., 22 in. barrel, open sights, 5 shot non-detachable box mag., plain stock. Approx. 60,000 mfg. 1906-1936.

$1,500	$1,300	$1,100	$950	$750	$600	$500

Add 35% for .25 Rem. cal.
Add 75% for C grades.
Add substantial premiums for higher grades D, E, and F.
Add substantial premiums for Military Trials Rifles and POE modified police extended detachable magazine models.

MODEL 74 SPORTSMAN - .280 Rem. (European special order only) or .30-06 cal., 22 in. barrel, 4 shot mag., uncheckered hardwood stock and forearm, open sights, 7 1/2 lbs. Mfg. 1984-87.

$350	$325	$300	$250	$225	$200	$150	*$353*

MODEL 81 WOODSMASTER - .30 Rem., .32 Rem., .35 Rem., or .300 Savage cal., takedown action, 5 shot, non-detachable box mag., 22 in. round barrel, notched elevator rear sight. An improvement of the Model 8; was available in 5 grades. 56,091 mfg. 1936-1950.

$1,350	$1,200	$1,000	$850	$700	$550	$425

Add 15% for early mfg. with beavertail forearm.
Add 75% for stamped B and C grades.
Add substantial premiums for higher grades D, E, and F.
Add substantial premiums for FBI "Special Police" rifle and "Special Police" rifle with extended detachable magazine.

The .32 Rem. cal. was dropped after WWII and the .300 Savage was added in 1940. A few specimens have been observed in .25 Rem. cal., which was advertised only the first year as a production model and were made as original factory models until remaining .25 Rem. barrels from Model 8 stock was depleted. Therefore, original factory production in .25 Rem. cal. would only be found in the first few years of model production.

MODEL 740 WOODSMASTER - .244 Rem. (mfg. 1957-59), .280 Rem. (mfg. 1957-59), .30-06 (first caliber, introduced 1955) or .308 Win. (introduced 1956) cal., 22 in. barrel, open sight, box mag., gas operated, plain pistol grip stock. Mfg. 1955-1959.

$325	$275	$225	$210	$200	$190	$180

GRADING - PPGS™	100%	98%	95%	90%	80%	70%	60%	LAST MSR

MODEL 740ADL – similar to 740A, with checkered stock, grip cap and sling swivels. Mfg. 1955-1959.

.244 Rem. or .30-06 cal.	$375	$325	$280	$250	$225	$200	$180	
.280 Rem. or .308 Win. cal.	$415	$350	$300	$275	$250	$225	$200	

MODEL 740BDL – similar to 740ADL, with select wood. Mfg. 1955-1957.

.244 Rem. or .30-06 cal.	$395	$340	$295	$250	$225	$200	$180	
.308 Win. cal.	$425	$375	$350	$325	$275	$225	$200	

BDLs were not listed in the 1958 or 1959 Remington price list.

MODEL 740D PEERLESS GRADE – similar to Model 740, with scroll engraving and fancy wood. Mfg. 1955-1960.

$3,000 $2,000 $1,275 N/A N/A N/A N/A

MODEL 740F PREMIER GRADE – similar to Model 740, with extensive hand engraved game scenes and scroll work, best grade wood.

$6,000 $4,500 $2,750 N/A N/A N/A N/A

* ***Model 740F Premier Grade w/Inlays*** – similar to Model 740F Premier Grade, except has game scenes inlayed with gold.

$8,000 $6,750 $4,150 N/A N/A N/A N/A

MODEL 742 (A) WOODSMASTER – 6mm Rem. (mfg. 1963), .243 Win. (mfg. 1968), .280 Rem. (marked 7mm Express 1979-1980), .30-06, or .308 Win. cal., 22 in. barrel, open sights, 4 shot box mag., gas operated, checkered pistol grip stock. Mfg. 1960-80.

$325 $290 $275 $250 $235 $210 $185

Add 10% for .280 Rem. cal.

MODEL 742ADL DELUXE – similar to the Model 742, except has fine checkering, sling swivels and roll engraved game scenes on receiver.

$350 $300 $275 $260 $235 $215 $195

MODEL 742BDL DELUXE – similar to Model 742ADL, except .30-06 or .308 Win. cal., step receiver, right-hand action with choice of right-hand or left-hand cheekpiece, Monte Carlo basket weave checkered stock and forend, black pistol grip cap and forend tip. Mfg. 1966-1980.

$400 $350 $300 $260 $235 $215 $195

MODEL 742C CARBINE – similar to 742, except .280 Rem., .30-06, or .308 Win. cal. only, 18 1/2 in. barrel. Mfg. 1961-80.

$450 $400 $350 $300 $275 $260 $235

* ***Model 742CDL Deluxe Carbine*** – similar to Model 742C carbine, except has fine checkering, sling swivels and roll engraved game scenes on receiver. Mfg. 1961-1963.

$475 $425 $375 $325 $300 $275 $250

MODEL 742D PEERLESS GRADE – similar to Model 742ADL, with scroll engraving and fancy wood. Mfg. 1961-1980.

$3,000 $2,000 $1,250 N/A N/A N/A N/A

MODEL 742F PREMIER GRADE – similar to Model 742ADL, with extensive hand engraved game scenes and scroll work, best grade wood.

$6,000 $4,500 $2,750 N/A N/A N/A N/A

* ***Model 742F Premier Grade w/Inlays*** – similar to Model 742F Premier Grade, except has game scenes inlayed in gold.

$8,000 $6,750 $4,200 N/A N/A N/A N/A

MODEL 742 150TH YEAR ANNIVERSARY – .30-06 cal. only, 11,412 mfg. 1966 only.

$425 $325 $300 N/A N/A N/A N/A

GRADING - PPGS™	100%	98%	95%	90%	80%	70%	60%	LAST MSR

MODEL 742 CANADIAN CENTENNIAL – 1,968 mfg. in 1967. Issue price was $200.

	$525	$475	$425	N/A	N/A	N/A	N/A	

REMINGTON/RUGER CANADIAN CENTENNIAL SET – please refer to the Sturm Ruger section of this text.

MODEL 742 BICENTENNIAL – similar to 742ADL, with inscription on receiver. 10,108 mfg. 1976 only.

	$425	$325	$300	$275	$225	$200	$185	

MODEL 750 – .243 Win., .30-06, or .308 Win. cal., 18 1/2 (not avail. in .243 Win.) or 22 in. barrel with iron sights, replaces the wood stocked Model 7400, and features improved gas system, lower profile, rotary bolt lockup, redesigned black synthetic stock and forearm, sling swivels became standard 2007, R3 recoil pad, 7 1/2 lbs. New 2006.

MSR $884	$725	$575	$475	$400	$350	$295	$265	

MODEL 750 WOODMASTER – .243 Win., .270 Win., .30-06, .308 Win., or .35 Whelen (disc.) cal., 18 1/2 or 22 in. barrel with iron sights, replaces the wood stocked Model 7400, and features improved gas system, lower profile, rotary bolt lockup, checkered walnut stock and forearm, sling swivels became standard 2007, R3 recoil pad, 7 1/2 lbs. New 2006.

MSR $1,004	$825	$700	$600	$500	$400	$350	$295	

Carbine variation is available in .30-06, or .308 Win. cal. only.

MODEL 7400 – 6mm Rem. (disc. 1987), .243 Win., .270 Win., 7mm Express (mfg. 1981-83), .280 Rem. (introduced 1984, disc. 2000), .30-06, .308 Win., or .35 Whelen (mfg. 1993-95) cal., modified Model 742 action, gas operation, 22 in. barrel, 4 shot detachable mag., pressed checkered Monte Carlo walnut stock, 7 1/2 lbs. Mfg. 1981-2005.

	$515	$410	$325	$260	$230	$210	$185	*$651*

Add 15% for .35 Whelen cal.

Beginning in 1991, a high gloss wood finish became available in cals. .270 Win. and .30-06 (Model 7400 High Gloss). From 1998-2003, receiver panels had fine line rolled game scene engraving.

* ***Model 7400 Carbine*** – .30-06 cal. only, similar to Model 7400 Rifle, except has 18 1/2 in. barrel, 7 1/4 lbs. Mfg. 1988-2005.

	$515	$410	$325	$260	$230	$210	$185	*$651*

* ***Model 7400 SP (Special Purpose)*** – .270 Win. or .30-06 cal., similar to Model 7400, except has non-reflective matte finish on both wood and metalwork. Mfg. 1993-94.

	$435	$370	$300	$255	$230	$210	$185	*$524*

* ***Model 7400 Weathermaster*** – .270 Win. or .30-06 cal., features matte nickel plated receiver, barrel, and magazine, black synthetic stock and forearm, 22 in. barrel with open sights, 7 1/2 lbs. Mfg. 2003-2004.

	$495	$400	$315	$255	$230	$210	$185	*$624*

* ***Model 7400 Synthetic*** – same cals. as Model 7400, features black fiberglass reinforced synthetic stock and forend, matte black metal finish, 22 in. barrel only. Mfg. 1998-2006.

	$465	$385	$330	$285	$265	$240	$220	*$589*

» ***Model 7400 Synthetic Carbine*** – .30-06 cal., similar to Model 7400 Synthetic, except has 18 1/2 in. barrel. 7 1/4 lbs. Mfg. 1998-2006.

	$465	$385	$330	$285	$265	$240	$220	*$589*

* ***Model 7400 175th Anniversary*** – .30-06 cal. only, Anniversary Model with roll engraving and high gloss finish. 5,000 mfg. in 1991 only.

	$475	$400	$300	N/A	N/A	N/A	N/A	*$515*

A limited quantity of .270 Win. cal. were specially made in this 175th Anniversary Model for distributor Bill Hicks in MN. Pricing varies, since these rifles are a special edition.

* ***Model 7400 ADF Limited Edition*** – .30-06 cal. only, special edition 1997 only featuring Buckmaster's American Deer Foundation, special ADF engraving. Approx. 800 mfg. 1997 only.

	$495	$400	$315	N/A	N/A	N/A	N/A	*$600*

GRADING - PPGS™	100%	98%	95%	90%	80%	70%	60%	LAST MSR

MODEL 7400 ENGRAVED – the engraved Model 7400s were introduced 1988.

* ***Model 7400 D Grade (Peerless)*** – scroll engraving and fancy wood.

	N/A	$2,900	$2,075	N/A	N/A	N/A	N/A	$4,532

* ***Model 7400 F Grade (Premier)*** – extensive hand engraved game scenes and scroll work, best grade wood.

	N/A	$6,000	$4,400	N/A	N/A	N/A	N/A	$8,799

* ***Model 7400 F Grade with gold inlays (Premier Gold)*** – with game scenes inlayed in gold.

	N/A	$7,500	$6,000	N/A	N/A	N/A	N/A	$11,999

MODEL R-15 VTR (VARMINT TARGET RIFLE) PREDATOR – .204 Ruger or .223 Rem. cal., 18 (carbine, .204 Ruger disc. 2009) or 22 in. free floating chrome-moly fluted barrel, fixed or telestock (Carbine CS) with pistol grip, 5 shot fixed (new 2012, .223 Rem. cal. only) or detachable mag. (compatible with AR-15 style mags.), R-15 marked on magwell, single stage trigger, flattop receiver with Picatinny rail, no sights, round vent. forearm, 100% Advantage Max-1 HD camo coverage except for barrel, includes lockable hard case, mfg. by Bushmaster in Windham, ME 2008-2011, and in Ilion, NY beginning 2011, 6 3/4 - 7 3/4 lbs. New 2008.

MSR $1,327	$1,150	$1,000	$900	$775	$700	$625	$550	

* ***Model R-15 VTR Stainless*** – .223 Rem. cal., similar to Predator, except has 24 in. stainless triangular barrel, OD Green (disc.) or Advantage Max-1 HD camo, fixed stock, pistol grip, and tubed forearm, 7 3/4 lbs. New 2009.

MSR $1,529	$1,300	$1,150	$1,050	$900	$775	$700	$625	

* ***Model R-15 VTR Thumbhole*** – .223 Rem. cal., similar to VTR Stainless, except has 24 in. fluted barrel, OD Green camo thumbhole stock. Mfg. 2009-2010.

	$1,275	$1,125	$1,000	$900	$800	$700	$625	$1,470

* ***Model R-15 VTR Byron South Signature Edition*** – .223 Rem. cal., 18 in. barrel, Advantage Max-1 HD camo pistol grip stock. Mfg. mid-2008-2011.

	$1,625	$1,400	$1,225	$1,050	$900	$800	$700	$1,845

MODEL R-15 – .30 Rem. AR or .450 Bushmaster (disc. 2011) cal., 18 (.450 Bushmaster cal., mfg. 2010-2011) or 22 (.30 Rem. cal.) in. fluted barrel, similar to R-15 VTR Predator, except has 4 shot detachable mag., 100% Realtree AP HD camo coverage, approx. 7 3/4 lbs. New 2009.

MSR $1,327	*N/A	$1,000	$900	$775	$700	$625	$550	

Add $355 for .450 Bushmaster cal. (disc. 2011)..

MODEL R-25 – .243 Win., 7mm-08 Rem., or .308 Win. cal., 20 in. free floating fluted chrome-moly barrel, single-stage trigger, ergonomic pistol grip fixed stock with 100% Mossy Oak Treestand camo coverage, front and rear sling swivels, 4 shot fixed (.308 Win. cal. only, new 2012) or detachable mag., R-25 marked on magwell, includes hard case, 7 3/4 lbs. New 2009.

MSR $1,697	*N/A	$1,225	$1,075	$950	$850	$750	$650	

RIFLES: SLIDE ACTION, CENTERFIRE

MODEL SIX – 6mm Rem. (disc. 1985), .243 Win., .270 Win., .30-06, or .308 Win. (disc. 1984) cal., cartridge "head" imbedded in bottom of receiver, 4 shot mag. Mfg. 1981-1987.

	$650	$550	$450	$375	$275	$225	$200	$439

Add 40% for 6mm Rem. cal.
Add 20% for .243 and .308 cals.

* ***Model Six High Grades***

Extreme rarity precludes accurate pricing.

Only three high grade Model Sixes were manufactured.

MODEL 14/14A RIFLE – .25 Rem., .30 Rem., .32 Rem., or .35 Rem. cal., 22 in. barrel, 5 shot mag., open sights, plain pistol grip stock, 6 lbs. Mfg. 1912-1935.

	N/A	$1,000	$900	$750	$500	$300	$250	

GRADING - PPGS™	100%	98%	95%	90%	80%	70%	60%	LAST MSR

Add 30% for "thumbnail" safety on bolt (introduced in 1919).
Add 15% for .25 Rem.

Model 14 was used up to 1919 at which time Model 14A was stamped on new barrels. After 1924 "Model 14" was stamped on all receivers including those of the Model 14 1/2, and new barrels were no longer stamped with the Model. Exceptions will be found. This model was also manufactured in higher grades, including C, D, and F. Premiums vary according to originality and condition.

MODEL 14R CARBINE – similar to 14A, with 18 1/2 in. barrel, straight grip stock.

N/A	$1,200	$1,100	$900	$600	$400	$350

Add 25% for .25 Rem. cal.
Add 10% for .35 Rem. cal.

MODEL 14 1/2 RIFLE – .38-40 WCF or .44-40 WCF cal., similar to 14A, with 10 shot mag., 22 1/2 in. barrel. Mfg. began Dec. 5, 1913-34.

N/A	$1,600	$1,400	$1,050	$950	$850	$700

Add 10% for .44-40 WCF cal.

Quantities mfg. of this model are unknown, as serial numbers were intermixed with the Model 14. Rifles and carbines made after 1924 are marked Model 14 on the receiver.

This model was also manufactured in higher grades, including C, D, and F. Premiums vary according to originality and condition.

MODEL 14 1/2 R CARBINE – similar to 14 1/2 Rifle, with 8 shot mag. and 18 1/2 in. barrel.

N/A	$2,800	$2,400	$2,000	$1,600	$1,200	$1,000

Add 30% for "thumbnail" safety on bolt (introduced in 1919).

MODEL 25/25A RIFLE – .25-20 WCF or .32-20 WCF cal., 24 in. barrel, open sights, tube mag., plain pistol grip stock. Mfg. 1923-35.

N/A	$1,250	$1,100	$900	$750	$675	$500

MODEL 25R CARBINE – similar to 25A, with 18 in. barrel (18 1/2 in. standard after 1934), and straight stock, sling eyes and shielded rear sight.

N/A	$3,000	$2,600	$2,200	$2,000	$1,750	$1,400

MODEL 76 SPORTSMAN – .30-06 cal. only, 22 in. barrel, 4 shot mag., uncheckered hardwood stock and forearm, open sights, 7 1/2 lbs. Mfg. 1984-87.

$300	$275	$250	$200	$170	$160	$150	*$319*

MODEL 141/141A – .25 Rem. (very few mfg. during 1936 only), .30 Rem., .32 Rem., or .35 Rem. cal., 24 in. barrel, takedown, open sights, plain pistol grip stock. Mfg. 1936-1950.

$800	$700	$600	$500	$450	$400	$300

Add 60% for .25 Rem. cal.

MODEL 141B/141C SPECIAL GRADE – similar to Model 141/141A, except has checkered fancy wood stock and forearm. Early models were marked 141C.

$1,750	$1,600	$1,400	$1,050	$950	$850	$700

Subtract 30% for plain forearm.

MODEL 141D PEERLESS GRADE – similar to Model 141/141B Special, except light engraving.

$6,000	$5,250	$4,600	$4,000	$3,400	$2,650	$2,000

MODEL 141F PREMIER GRADE – similar to Model 141/141 D Peerless Grade, except has extra fancy wood stock and heavy engraving.

$7,500	$6,500	$5,750	$5,250	$4,500	$3,750	$3,000

MODEL 141R CARBINE – plain stock and forearm, 18 1/2 in. barrel. Mfg. 1936-1942.

$1,800	$1,600	$1,400	$1,050	$950	$850	$700

Add 10% for .35 cal.

GRADING - PPGS™	100%	98%	95%	90%	80%	70%	60%	LAST MSR

MODEL 760 GAMEMASTER – .222 Rem. (mfg. 1958-61), .223 Rem. (limited mfg. 1964-69), 6mm Rem. (introduced 1969), .243 Win. (introduced 1968), .244 (mfg. 1956-59), .257 Roberts (mfg. 1955-58), .270 Win., .280 Rem. (mfg. 1958-1967), .30-06, .300 Sav. (disc. 1958), .308 Win., or .35 Rem. (mfg. 1952-67, and 1980) cal., 22 in. barrel, detachable mag., uncheckered or checkered (new 1964) pistol grip stock. Mfg. 1952-1980.

	$500	$400	$350	$300	$275	$250	$225	
.222 Rem. cal.	$1,150	$900	$800	$725	$650	$575	$500	
.223 Rem. cal.	$1,350	$995	$850	$775	$700	$625	$575	
.257, .244, & .280 cal.	$850	$695	$575	$450	$400	$350	$300	

Subtract 20% for .30-06 and .270 cal.

MODEL 760C CARBINE – .270 Win., .280 Win., .30-06, .308 Win., or .35 Rem. cal., 18 1/2 in. barrel.

	$600	$550	$500	$400	$300	$275	$250	

Subtract 10% for .30-06 cal.
Add 50% for .280 and .35 cals.

MODEL 760 (CDL) CARBINE (FIVE DIAMOND) – similar to Model 760C Carbine, except has checkered stock, pistol grip cap and sling swivels. Mfg. 1961-1963.

	$650	$600	$550	$450	$350	$300	$275	

Add 50% for .280 Rem. cal.

MODEL 760D PEERLESS GRADE – similar to 760, with scroll engraving and fancy wood. Mfg. 1953-1980.

	$3,000	$2,000	$1,200	N/A	N/A	N/A	N/A	

MODEL 760F PREMIER GRADE – similar to Model 760 Peerless, with extensive hand engraved game scenes, and scroll work, best grade wood.

	$6,000	$4,500	$2,600	N/A	N/A	N/A	N/A	

* ***Model 760F Premier w/Inlays*** – similar to Model 760F Premier Grade, except has game scenes inlaid in gold.

	$8,000	$6,750	$4,100	N/A	N/A	N/A	N/A	

MODEL 760 150 YEAR ANNIVERSARY – .30-06 cal. only, similar to Model 760, except has commemorative inscription roll engraved on receiver. 4,610 mfg. 1966 only.

	$495	$425	$350	N/A	N/A	N/A	N/A	

MODEL 760 BICENTENNIAL – .30-06 cal. only, similar to Model 760, with commemorative inscription, roll engraved on receiver. 3,804 mfg. 1976 only.

	$495	$425	$350	$300	$275	$250	$225	

MODEL 760ADL – similar to Model 760, except with checkered stock, grip cap, sling swivels. Mfg. 1953-1963.

	$600	$500	$400	$300	$275	$250	$225	

Add 100% for .222 and .223 cals.
Add 50% for .244, .257, and .280 cals.

MODEL 760BDL – similar to Model 760ADL, except has select grade wood. Mfg. 1953-1957.

	$650	$525	$475	$425	$400	$375	$325	

Only a few BDL grade rifles have been observed with the grade marked on the receiver. Flawed BDL grade stocks were downgraded and fitted to ADL grade rifles.

MODEL 760BDL DELUXE – similar to Model 760, except .270 Win., .30-06, or .308 Win. cal. only, step receiver, available with right or left-hand cheekpiece on Monte Carlo stock, basket weave checkering pattern, black pistol grip and forend tip. Mfg. 1966-1980.

	$600	$450	$350	$300	$275	$250	$225	

Add 20% for .308 Win. cal.
Add 10% for left-hand.

GRADING - PPGS™	100%	98%	95%	90%	80%	70%	60%	LAST MSR

MODEL 7600 – 6mm Rem. (disc. 1984), .243 Win., .270 Win., .280 Rem. (mfg. 1988-2000), .30-06, .308 Win., or .35 Whelen (mfg. 1988-96) cal., modified 760 action, 22 in. barrel, 4 shot detachable mag., pressed checkered pistol grip stock and forearm, 7 1/2 lbs. New 1981.

MSR $900	$700	$550	$415	$340	$265	$230	$195	

Add 10% for .35 Whelen cal. (disc.)

Depending on overall desirability, typical NIB asking prices for Grice Wholesale guns listed below will be 10%-15% higher than standard production.

In addition, walnut stocked rifles in .35 Whelan and carbines in .35 Rem. cal. were offered.

Beginning in 1990, a high gloss wood finish became available in cals. .270 Win. and .30-06 (Model 7600 High Gloss). From 1996-2003 receiver panels have fine line rolled game scene engraving.

A Pennsylvania distributor, Grice Wholesale, has offered a wide variety of special order, non-cataloged Model 7600s since 1990. The initial 1990 order was for 500 Model 7600s in 7mm-08 cal., followed by 1,000 7mm-08 cal. 175th Anniversary roll marked rifles in 1991. In 1992, the Deer Hunter Special, with a roll marked, gold filled deer scene was offered. This model was repeated in 1993 with a cabin and game scene engraving - 500 in .270 Win., 500 in .30-06, and 1,000 in 7mm-08 cal. were offered each year.

Over the years, Grice has also offered non-cataloged calibers such as 6mm Rem., .257 Roberts, .25-06 Rem., .260 Rem., .35 Rem. and .35 Whelen. Black and brown laminate stocks have also been offered.

The 2005 special orders were Model 7600s with maple stocks in 6mm Rem., .25-06 Rem., and 7mm-08 cal. 500 rifles were offered in .30-06 with a special roll marking commemorating the 100th anniversary of the .30-06, also with maple stocks.

In late 2006, Grice offered several Model 7600s with black laminated stocks - 7mm-08 cal., .30-06 cal. with a laser engraved "ONE OF 250 .30-06 100TH ANNIVERSARY 1906-2006" logo on the buttstock, and a Model 7615 in .223 Rem. cal. with a 22 in. barrel. Additionally, 300 walnut stocked Model 7600s in .300 Sav. cal. were also offered.

The 2007 Grice Special Run was in .280 Rem. with commemorative roll markings on the receiver and laser engraved "One of 500 280 Rem 50th Anniversary 1957 - 2007" on the high gloss finish walnut stock.

* ***Model 7600 Carbine*** – .30-06 cal. only, similar to Model 7600 Rifle, except has 18 1/2 in. barrel, 7 1/4 lbs.

MSR $900	$700	$550	$415	$340	$265	$230	$195	

A total of 170 Larry Benoit Commemorative carbines were manufactured in 1999 and 2000 for Wilderness Trading and Supply Co. in VT. MSR was $995. Pricing varies on these models, since these guns were a limited special order.

* ***Model 7600P Patrol Rifle*** – .308 Win. cal., 16 1/2 in. barrel, synthetic stock, parkerized finish, Wilson Combat ghost ring sights, designed for police/law enforcement only.

Remington does not publish consumer retail pricing for this police/law enforcement model. Secondary prices for this model will be slightly higher than for current pricing on the Model 7600 Synthetic.

* ***Model 7600 SP (Special Purpose)*** – .270 Win. or .30-06 cal., similar to Model 7600, except has non-reflective matte finish on wood and metalwork. Mfg. 1993-94.

	$420	$360	$280	$230	$205	$185	$165	*$496*

* ***Model 7600 Synthetic*** – same cals. as Model 7600, features black fiberglass reinforced synthetic stock and forend, matte black metal finish, 22 in. barrel only, SuperCell recoil pad became standard 2011, 7 1/2 lbs. New 1998.

MSR $756	$595	$475	$385	$315	$265	$240	$225	

During 2007, Grice offered 500 Model 7600 QWAC (Quick Woods Action Carbine) in .308 Win. cal. with 18 1/2 in. barrels, Realtree AP camo synthetic stocks and fiber optic front and rear sights.

» **Model 7600 Synthetic Carbine** – .30-06 cal., similar to Model 7600 Synthetic, except has 18 1/2 in. barrel, SuperCell recoil pad became standard in 2011, 7 1/4 lbs. New 1998.

MSR $756	$595	$475	$385	$315	$265	$240	$225	

GRADING - PPGS™	100%	98%	95%	90%	80%	70%	60%	LAST MSR

* ***Model 7600 175th Anniversary*** – also available in 7mm-08 Rem. cal., 1,000 mfg. 1991 only.

	$625	$525	$375	N/A	N/A	N/A	N/A	

* ***Model 7600 ADF Limited Edition*** – .30-06 cal. only, special edition 1997 only featuring Buckmaster's American Deer Foundation, special ADF engraving. Approx. 800 mfg. 1997 only.

	$500	$425	$325	N/A	N/A	N/A	N/A	*$567*

MODEL 7600 ENGRAVED – hand engraved Model 7600s were introduced 1988.

* ***Model 7600 D Grade (Peerless)*** – features scroll engraving and fancy wood.

MSR POR	N/A	$2,900	$2,075	N/A	N/A	N/A	N/A	

Last published MSR was $4,532 (2007)

* ***Model 7600 F Grade (Premier)*** – features extensive hand engraved game scenes and scroll work and best grade wood.

MSR POR	N/A	$6,000	$4,400	N/A	N/A	N/A	N/A	

Last published MSR was $8,799 (2007)

* ***Model 7600 F Premier Grade w/Inlays*** – top-of-the-line custom shop model with game scenes inlaid in gold.

MSR POR	N/A	$7,500	$6,000	N/A	N/A	N/A	N/A	

Last published MSR was $11,999 (2007)

MODEL 7615 – .223 Rem., 10 shot AR-15 compatible detachable box mag., accepts AR-15 and M16 style magazines, 16 1/2 (tactical model with pistol grip and non-collapsible tube stock and Knoxx Special Ops NRS recoil suppressor), 18 1/2 (ranch rifle, walnut stock and forearm), or 22 (camo hunter, 100% Mossy Oak Brush camo coverage) in. barrel w/o sights, synthetic or walnut (ranch carbine) stock and forearm, drilled and tapped, approx. 7 lbs. Mfg. 2007-2008, mfg. in Ilion, NY.

	$790	$685	$575	$500	$450	$400	$350	*$955*

Add $54 for Camo Hunter with 100% camo coverage.

MODEL 7615P PATROL RIFLE – .223 Rem. cal., 16 1/2 in. barrel, 10 shot or extended mag., synthetic stock, parkerized finish, accepts AR-15 and M16 style magazines, Wilson Combat ghost ring sights, designed for police/law enforcement, 7 lbs.

Remington does not publish consumer retail pricing for this police/law enforcement model. Secondary prices for this model will be slightly higher than for current pricing on the Model 7600 Carbine.

MODEL 7615 SPS – .223 Rem. cal., 16 1/2 in. blue barrel, Picatinny rail, action, slide release and safety based on the Model 870, 10 shot mag, accepts AR-15 and M16 style mags., black pistol grip synthetic stock. Mfg. 2008.

	$695	$625	$550	$500	$450	$400	$350	*$805*

This model was available through Remington Premier dealers only.

RIFLES: RIMFIRE, BOLT ACTION

From 1930-1960 Remington produced a number of bolt action .22 cal. Rimfire rifles, both single shot and repeaters. They were good quality, serviceable weapons with many slight variations upon a basic design. Whenever possible, models have been listed in numerical sequence.

On factory engraved E & F grade rifles, the ser. no. is usually engraved instead of stamped, and there is no standard factory engraving pattern on these grades.

MODEL FIVE – .17 HMR (new 2008), .22 LR, or .22 WMR cal., 22 in. barrel with adj. flip-up rear sight, blued finish, 5 shot detachable mag., checkered satin finished brown laminated or European walnut (.22 LR only, mfg. 2008) stock and forend, grooved steel receiver, safety located next to bolt, includes sling swivels, 6 3/4 lbs., mfg. in Serbia. Mfg. 2006-2009.

	$175	$150	$135	$120	$100	$85	$70	*$203*

Add 30% for walnut stock (disc. 2008, last MSR was $349).

GRADING - PPGS™	100%	98%	95%	90%	80%	70%	60%	LAST MSR
* ***Model Five Youth*** – .22 LR cal., 16 1/2 in. barrel with open sights, shortened LOP, hardwood stock, 5 shot detachable mag. with single shot adapter. Mfg. 2008-2009.	$140	$125	$105	$95	$75	$65	$50	$167
MODEL 33	$250	$225	$195	$175	$150	$115	$90	
MODEL 33 NRA	$525	$475	$375	$350	$275	$225	$175	
MODEL 33-P	$325	$300	$250	$210	$190	$140	$110	
MODEL 33 SB	$400	$350	$325	$300	$250	$225	$175	

263,557 of the Model 33 were mfg. 1932-35.

MODEL 34	$325	$300	$275	$250	$200	$175	$150	
MODEL 34 NRA	$500	$475	$395	$350	$295	$235	$185	

162,941 of the Model 34 were mfg. 1932-36.

MODEL 34-P	$375	$325	$285	$260	$210	$185	$160	
MODEL 37 "RANGEMASTER" TARGET RIFLE – .22 LR cal., 5 shot mag. with single shot adapter, 28 in. barrel, target sights and scope bases, target stock, 12 1/2 lbs. Mfg. 1937-40.	$1,300	$1,200	$1,000	$850	$700	$550	$425	
w/original bbl band on stock	$2,200	$1,925	$1,650	$1,495	$1,210	$990	$770	
MODEL 37 - 1940 – improved trigger and stock design. Mfg. 1940-54.	$1,200	$1,050	$1,000	$850	$700	$550	$425	

Total manufacture of the Model 37 was 12,198.

MODEL 341 A	$300	$275	$250	$195	$160	$135	$100	
MODEL 341 P	$350	$300	$275	$250	$200	$160	$125	
MODEL 341 SB	$500	$440	$375	$340	$275	$225	$175	

131,604 of the Model 341 "Sportsmaster" were mfg. 1936-40.

MODEL 41 A	$250	$225	$190	$170	$140	$115	$90	
MODEL 41 AS (.22 REM. SPEC. CAL.)	$390	$340	$295	$265	$225	$185	$150	
MODEL 41 P	$300	$260	$225	$200	$170	$140	$100	
MODEL 41 SB	$400	$350	$300	$270	$220	$180	$140	

306,880 of the Model 41 "Targetmaster" were produced 1936-39.

MODEL 411	$600	$525	$450	$410	$330	$270	$210	

Add 50% premium for .22 Short.

The Model 411 is similar to the Model 41 single shot, but in CB Cap or .22 Short and without safety on rear of bolt. Eye screw for gallery use. 1,316 mfg. 1937-39 (although never cataloged).

GRADING - PPGS™	100%	98%	95%	90%	80%	70%	60%	LAST MSR

MODEL 412 YOUTH BOLT ACTION – .22 LR cal., single shot with second shot holder, 19 3/4 in. barrel with adj. sights, automatic safety, uncheckered hardwood stock, blue finish, 4 1/2 lbs. Limited mfg. 2006.

While advertised with a MSR of $136, these rifles were mfg. in Mexico, but were not shipped to Remington.

MODEL 504 – .17 Mach 2 (new 2005) or .22 LR cal., bolt action, drilled and tapped solid steel receiver, 20 in. barrel w/o sights, matte metal finish, features 5-R button rifling (same as the Model 40-XR), dual bedding points, fully adj. trigger group, dual extractors, 6 shot detachable mag., checkered American walnut stock, cocking indicator, approx. 6 lbs. Mfg. 2004-2006 in Ilion, NY.

	100%	98%	95%	90%	80%	70%	60%	LAST MSR
	$615	$540	$460	$420	$340	$275	$215	*$738*

* ***Model 504-T*** – .17 HMR or .22 LR cal., similar to Model 504, except has 20 in. heavy free floating barrel, Eley match chamber, 5 (.17 HMR) or 6 shot mag., brown laminate Monte Carlo stock with palm swell and beavertail forend, satin blue metal, approx. 6 1/2 lbs. Mfg. 2005-2006.

	100%	98%	95%	90%	80%	70%	60%	LAST MSR
	$695	$610	$520	$475	$380	$315	$245	*$839*

Add $26 for .17 HMR cal.

MODEL 504 CUSTOM C GRADE – .22 LR cal., bolt action, 24 in. carbon steel blue barrel, "C" grade fancy semi-gloss American walnut stock with rosewood pistol grip and forend caps, 6 1/2 lbs., limited mfg. 2006-2008.

	100%	98%	95%	90%	80%	70%	60%	LAST MSR
	$1,495	$1,310	$1,120	$1,015	$820	$675	$525	*$1,836*

	100%	98%	95%	90%	80%	70%	60%
MODEL 510 A	$220	$195	$175	$150	$120	$110	$100
MODEL 510 C (CARBINE)	$375	$325	$275	$250	$200	$190	$175
MODEL 510 P	$280	$250	$225	$200	$165	$150	$130
MODEL 510 ROUTLEDGE/SMOOTHBORE	$375	$325	$285	$260	$210	$195	$175

Add 15% for Mo-Skeet-O Bore.

These models were mfg. 1939-62. Approx. 545,000 were mfg.

	100%	98%	95%	90%	80%	70%	60%
MODEL 510-X	$230	$195	$175	$155	$125	$110	$100
MODEL 510-X SB	$350	$300	$265	$240	$195	$160	$125
MODEL 511 A	$250	$225	$195	$175	$150	$120	$110

Add 50% for smooth bore.

	100%	98%	95%	90%	80%	70%	60%
MODEL 511 P	$285	$255	$225	$195	$160	$150	$125

These models were mfg. 1939-1962. Approx. 375,000 mfg.

	100%	98%	95%	90%	80%	70%	60%
MODEL 511-X (29,120 MFG.)	$250	$225	$195	$175	$150	$125	$110
MODEL 512 A	$250	$225	$195	$175	$150	$120	$90

Add 50% for smooth bore.

	100%	98%	95%	90%	80%	70%	60%
MODEL 512 P	$295	$255	$225	$195	$160	$150	$125

These models were mfg. 1940-1962. Approx. 395,000 mfg.

GRADING - PPGS™	100%	98%	95%	90%	80%	70%	60%	LAST MSR

MODEL 512-X (30,670 MFG.)

	$250	$225	$195	$175	$150	$125	$110

These models were mfg. 1964-1966. 19,901 Model 510-Xs were mfg. and mixed with the Model 511-X and 512-X.

MODEL 513S/513SA SPORTER "MATCHMASTER" – .22 LR cal., sporting variation of the Model 513T, with open sights and checkered sporter stock. 13,677 were mfg. 1940-1957 (including the Model 513SP).

	$850	$745	$640	$580	$470	$385	$300

Add 15% for select figured or hand rubbed oil finished walnut stock.

The Model 513S Sporting Rifle designates either the 513SA or 513SP Model. Both guns were designated "Matchmaster", along with the Model 513T.

MODEL 513SP SPORTER "MATCHMASTER" – .22 LR cal., similar to Model 513SA, except has Remington Point-Crometer receiver aperture sight. Mfg. 1942-1950.

	$925	$775	$675	$600	$500	$400	$325

Add 15% for select figured or hand rubbed oil finished walnut stock.

MODEL 513T (TARGET) "MATCHMASTER" – .22 LR cal., 27 in. tapered barrel, raked bolt handle, Redfield aperture rear sight, target stock, 6 shot, sling swivels. Approx. 166,000 were mfg. 1940-1968.

	$450	$395	$340	$300	$250	$205	$160

A "TR" suffix on this gun indicated with sights, a "TX" indicated w/o sights, a "TS" indicated sporter. Most 513s are marked either 513T (Target) or 513S (Sporter).

MODEL 514 (1948-1970)

	$180	$160	$140	$130	$100	$90	$85

MODEL 514 P (1952-1971)

	$225	$200	$175	$155	$130	$120	$100

MODEL 514 BOY'S RIFLE (1961-1970)

	$225	$200	$170	$155	$120	$95	$80

MODEL 514 ROUTLEDGE/SMOOTHBORE

	$300	$265	$225	$200	$175	$165	$150

The Routledge/Smoothbore was mfg. 1951-1969 - 5,557 were mfg.

Serialization began in 1968, approx. 780,000 mfg.

MODEL 521T/TL JR. – .22 LR cal., 25 in. barrel, Lyman target sights, takedown, 6 shot mag., target stock, approx. 67,000 were mfg. 1947-68.

	$395	$350	$300	$250	$200	$175	$150

These models had no ser. no. until 1954. This model's nomenclature changed to 521T in 1959.

MODEL 540X RIMFIRE – .22 LR cal., single shot bolt action, 26 in. heavy barrel, no sights, target stock, adj. butt, approx. 5,115. Mfg. 1969-74.

	$425	$370	$320	$290	$235	$190	$150

MODEL 540XR – similar to Model 540X, with large position style stock with adj. buttplate. Mfg. 1974-1983.

	$475	$425	$400	$350	$300	$250	$200

Add 15% for original sights.

* ***Model 540XR JR*** – similar to Model 540X, except 1 1/2 in. shorter stock. Mfg. 1974-1983.

	$425	$375	$325	$275	$220	$195	$150

MODEL 541S CUSTOM – .22 S, L, or LR cal., bolt action, 24 in. barrel, drilled and tapped, 5 shot mag., adj. match trigger, scroll engraved receiver and trigger guard, checkered walnut stock with rosewood pistol grip cap, buttplate, and forend tip. Mfg. 1972-1984.

	$800	$750	$700	$600	$500	$375	$275

GRADING - PPGS™	100%	98%	95%	90%	80%	70%	60%	LAST MSR

MODEL 541T – .22 LR cal. only, 5 shot mag., 24 in. standard or heavy (new 1993) barrel, checkered American walnut stock with satin finish, barrel is drilled and tapped, 5 7/8 lbs. Mfg. 1986-1999.

	$500	$440	$375	$340	$275	$225	$175	*$465*

Add $50 for heavy barrel.
Add 50% for maple stock.

MODEL 541X – .22 LR cal. only, bolt action, U.S. military training rifle, 27 in. barrel, 5 shot mag., ser. no. inscribed by hand on bolt, 9,077 mfg. 1984-86.

	$475	$400	$375	$350	$300	$250	$195

MODEL 547 CUSTOM CLASSIC – .17 HMR or .22 LR cal., Model 700 style action and bolt handle, high polished 22 in. Shilen custom barrel w/o sights, classic walnut stock with rosewood forend tip, 3 lbs. trigger pull, guaranteed 1/2 in. 5 shot groups at 50 yards, mfg. by custom shop. New 2008.

MSR $1,313	$1,095	$925	$825	$725	$625	$525	$450

This model is also available in .17 Mach 2 or .22 WMR cal. on special request.

* ***Model 547-T Custom Classic*** – .17 HMR or .22 LR cal., similar to Model 547 Classic, except has 18 1/4 in. stainless steel heavy target barrel, mfg. by custom shop. New 2009.

MSR $1,558	$1,325	$1,075	$925	$800	$700	$600	$550

* ***Model 547-C Custom Classic*** – .17 HMR or .22 LR cal., similar to Model 547 Classic , except has 22 in. medium contour barrel, C Grade stock with rosewood forend tip and pistol grip cap, mfg. by custom shop. New 2009.

MSR $1,984	$1,750	$1,500	$1,250	$1,025	$900	$775	$650

MODEL 580 SINGLE SHOT – .22 S, L, or LR cal., bolt action, 24 in. barrel, open sights, Monte Carlo stock. Mfg. 1967-78.

	$200	$180	$160	$130	$100	$90	$70

Add 50% for smooth bore (Model 580SB).

MODEL 580BR – Boy's Model, 1 in. shorter stock. Mfg. 1971-78.

	$195	$170	$150	$135	$110	$95	$75

MODEL 581 – .22 LR cal., bolt action, 6 shot mag., converts to single shot. Mfg. 1967-83.

	$225	$195	$170	$155	$125	$100	$80

Add 25% for smooth bore.

MODEL 581 SPORTSMAN – .22 LR cal., bolt action, 5 shot mag., 24 in. barrel, hardwood uncheckered stock, 4 3/4 lbs. Mfg. 1986-99.

	$225	$200	$180	$160	$110	$90	$70	*$239*

MODEL 582 – similar to 581, with tube mag. Mfg. 1967-83.

	$225	$195	$170	$155	$125	$100	$80

MODEL 591 – 5mm Rimfire Mag. cal., 24 in. barrel, open sight, 5 shot mag., Monte Carlo stock. Approx. 27,000 mfg. 1970-1974.

	$350	$310	$275	$250	$200	$175	$120

MODEL 592 – similar to 591, with tube mag. Approx. 25,000 mfg. 1970-1974.

	$350	$310	$275	$250	$200	$175	$120

RIFLES: RIMFIRE, "NYLON SERIES"

These models can be identified by the markings on the grip cap.

NYLON 10 SINGLE SHOT – .22 S, L, or LR cal., bolt action, automatic safety, 19 5/8 or 24 (mfg. 1964 only) in. barrel, Mohawk Brown nylon stock, approx. 4 lbs. 8,606 were mfg. 1962-1964.

19 5/8 in. bbl.	$575	$500	$450	$400	$300	$275	$250

Add 50% for 24 in. barrel.

GRADING - PPGS™	100%	98%	95%	90%	80%	70%	60%	LAST MSR

* ***Nylon 10-SB Single Shot*** – .22 shot cal., similar to Nylon 10, except has 19 5/8 (2,064 mfg.) or 24 (rare, quantity unknown) in. smooth bore barrel used for .22 shot cartridges.

19 5/8 in. barrel	$1,200	$1,100	$995	$850	$700	$600	$450

Nylon 10s with 24 in. barrels are very rare, and accurate pricing is hard to ascertain. Some specimens have sold in the $1,350-$8,000 range, depending on original condition.

MOHAWK 10-C – similar to Model Nylon 77, renamed after changing to a 10 shot box mag, approx. 129,000 were mfg. 1971-78.

	$295	$250	$200	$175	$125	$115	$110

MODEL 11 NYLON – .22 S, L, or LR cal., bolt action repeater, 6 or 10 shot detachable box mag., 19 5/8 or 24 (mfg. 1964 only) in. barrel, 4 1/2 lbs. 22,423 were mfg. 1962-1964.

19 5/8 in. barrel	$450	$400	$350	$275	$250	$200	$150
24 in. barrel	$1,000	$900	$775	$625	$500	$375	$250

MODEL 12 NYLON – similar to Model 11 Nylon, with 15 shot tube mag., 19 5/8 or 24 (mfg. 1964 only) in. barrel. 27,551 were mfg. 1962-1964.

19 5/8 in. bbl.	$500	$425	$350	$250	$175	$150	$125

Add 50% for 24 in. barrel.

NYLON 66 AUTOLOADER – .22 LR cal., 19 5/8 in. barrel, open sights, 14 shot buttstock tube mag., 4 lbs. Stock, receiver, and forearm made from Zytel plastic in black, brown, or green, metal receiver cover. 1,050,336 were mfg. 1959-90.

Mohawk Brown	$400	$350	$300	$260	$230	$200	$175
Black Diamond	$500	$450	$400	$350	$300	$260	$230
Apache Black/Chrome	$575	$525	$450	$400	$350	$300	$250
Seneca Green	$625	$550	$475	$425	$350	$300	$260
Gallery Special (.22 Short cal. only)	$850	$775	$700	$625	$525	$425	$325

Last MSR was $124.

Approx. 56,000 Black Diamond models were mfg., approx. 221,000 Apache Black/Chrome models were mfg., and approx. 45,000 Seneca Green were mfg.

NYLON 66 150TH ANNIVERSARY – 3,792 mfg. in 1966 only with 150th Anniversary Remington logo on receiver cover.

	$600	$500	$475	$425	$350	$275	$200

NYLON 66 BICENTENNIAL – inscription on receiver cover, 10,268 mfg. 1976 only, Mohawk brown nylon stock only.

	$550	$450	$425	$350	$300	$250	$175

NYLON 76 LEVER ACTION – similar to Nylon 66, except short throw lever action, 25,312 mfg. in standard with Apache Black/Chrome finish, 1,615 mfg. in black chrome finish 1962-64 only.

Standard finish	$800	$700	$600	$500	$400	$350	$275
Apache Black/Chrome	$1,500	$1,325	$1,100	$850	$700	$575	$450

The Nylon 76 "Trail Rider" is the only lever action repeating rifle ever mfg. by Remington.

NYLON 77 – .22 LR cal., 19 5/8 in. barrel, open sights, 5 shot box mag., otherwise similar to Nylon 66. 15,327 were mfg. 1970-71 only.

	$350	$300	$275	$225	$195	$175	$150

NYLON APACHE 77 – similar to Model 10-C, but black painted external metal and dark olive green stock/receiver. Mfg. for K-Mart in 1987-89.

	$200	$175	$150	$125	$100	$85	$75

RIFLES: RIMFIRE, SEMI-AUTO

Please note: Model 597 rifles in .17 HMR caliber have been recalled by Remington - please visit Remington's website for more information: www.remington.com, or call 1-800-243-9700, #3.

GRADING - PPGS™	100%	98%	95%	90%	80%	70%	60%	LAST MSR

MODEL 16/16A AUTOLOADING RIFLE – .22 Rem. Autoloading cal., 22 in. barrel, open sights, tube mag. in buttstock, straight stock. 17,738 mfg. 1914-28.

	$1,200	$950	$800	$700	$600	$500	$400

* ***Model 16/16A Autoloading Rifle C Special Grade*** – similar to Model 16/16A, except has select checkered walnut stock and forearm.

	$1,750	$1,500	$1,250	$1,000	$900	$750	$600

* ***Model 16/16A Autoloading Rifle D Peerless Grade*** – similar to Model 16/16A C Special Grade, except has lightly scroll engraved receiver and barrel, hand honed internal parts.

	$6,000	$5,500	$5,000	$4,000	$3,500	$3,000	$2,500

* ***Model 16/16A Autoloading Rifle F Premier Grade*** – top-of-the-line model with best quality checkered walnut stock, fully engraved receiver featuring rabbits or squirrels, gold nameplate on stock.

	$10,000	$8,000	$7,000	$6,000	$5,250	$4,500	$3,500

MODEL 24/24A AUTOLOADING RIFLE – .22 S or LR cal., 19 in. barrel, open sights, Browning semi-auto design, bottom ejection, tube mag. through buttstock, takedown, plain pistol grip stock. Approx. 131,000 mfg. 1922-35.

	$1,250	$950	$800	$700	$600	$500	$400

* ***Model 24/24A Autoloading Rifle C Special Grade*** – similar to Model 24/24A, except has select checkered walnut stock and forearm.

	$1,750	$1,500	$1,250	$1,000	$900	$750	$600

* ***Model 24/24A Autoloading Rifle D Peerless Grade*** – similar to Model 24/24A C Special Grade, except has lightly scroll engraved receiver and barrel, hand honed internal parts.

	$6,000	$5,500	$5,000	$4,000	$3,500	$3,000	$2,500

Add a 20% premium for .22 Short cal.

* ***Model 24/24A Autoloading Rifle E Expert Grade*** – similar to Model 24/24A D Peerless Grade, except has silver nameplate inlaid in stock.

	$7,000	$6,000	$5,250	$4,250	$3,500	$3,250	$2,750

* ***Model 24/24A Autoloading Rifle F Premier Grade*** – top-of-the-line model with best quality checkered walnut stock, fully engraved receiver featuring rabbits or squirrels, gold nameplate on stock.

	$10,000	$8,000	$7,000	$6,000	$5,250	$4,500	$3,500

MODEL 241A (LA/SA) SPEEDMASTER – .22 S (Model 241 SA) or LR (Model 241 LA) cal., 24 in. barrel, replaced the Browning designed Model 24, open sights, takedown (button located on left side of receiver), blue (most common) or chrome plated (either full plating or receiver and trigger plate only, scarce), 10 (.22 LR cal.) or 15 (.22 Short cal.) shot tube mag. in buttstock, non-checkered walnut stock and forearm, model name and ser. no. stamped on left side of receiver, "Speedmaster" and the Remington logo added during 1936, approx. 6 lbs. Approx. 107,000 mfg. 1935-1951, with serialization ending at approx. 132,000 (after 1946, serialization and dates became inaccurate).

	$1,000	$750	$650	$600	$550	$425	$350

Add a 20% premium for .22 Short cal.

The B Grade was introduced in early 1940. Approx. 7,600 Model 241s were manufactured for the U.S. Government between 1942-1945. An unknown quantity was also sold to the U.S. Navy for training in 1944-1945.

* ***Model 241A Speedmaster C Special Grade*** – similar to Model 241A Speedmaster, except has select checkered walnut stock and forearm.

	$1,500	$1,300	$1,100	$900	$800	$650	$500

* ***Model 241A Speedmaster D Peerless Grade*** – similar to Model 241A Speedmaster C Special Grade, except has lightly scroll engraved receiver and barrel, hand honed internal parts.

	$6,000	$5,250	$4,600	$4,000	$3,400	$2,650	$2,000

GRADING - PPGS™	100%	98%	95%	90%	80%	70%	60%	LAST MSR

* ***Model 241A Speedmaster E Expert Grade*** – similar to Model 241A Speedmaster D Peerless Grade, except has silver nameplate inlaid in stock.

	$7,000	$6,000	$5,200	$4,250	$3,550	$2,850	$2,500	

* ***Model 241A Speedmaster F Premier Grade*** – top-of-the-line model with best quality checkered walnut stock, fully engraved receiver featuring rabbits or squirrels, gold nameplate on stock.

	$7,500	$6,500	$5,750	$5,150	$4,400	$3,650	$3,000	

MODEL 522 VIPER – .22 LR cal., semi-auto blowback action, 20 in. barrel, full-length black synthetic resin stock with beavertail forend, 10 shot mag., cocking indicator, adj. rear sight, grooved synthetic receiver, 4 5/8 lbs. Mfg. 1993-97.

	$125	$110	$95	$85	$70	$60	$50	*$152*

MODEL 550A – .22 S, L, or LR cal., 24 in. barrel, open sights, shell deflector, dual extractors, tube mag., plain one piece pistol stock. 34,577 mfg. 1941-46.

	$275	$240	$200	$185	$150	$125	$95	

Add 100% if w/o shell deflector (not tapped).

MODEL 550-1 – similar to Model 550A, except has single extractor. Approx. 730,000 mfg. 1946-1970.

	$250	$220	$190	$170	$140	$115	$90	

MODEL 550P – similar to Model 550-1, with aperture rear sight.

	$300	$265	$225	$200	$165	$135	$100	

MODEL 550-2G – .22 Short cal., similar to Model 550-1, except 22 in. barrel and eye screw for counter chain in shooting gallery.

	$350	$305	$265	$240	$195	$160	$125	

MODEL 552A SPEEDMASTER – .22 S, L, or LR cal., 23 in. barrel, semi-auto, open sights, tube mag., pistol grip stock. Mfg. 1957-disc.

	$275	$240	$205	$185	$150	$125	$95	

This model was also mfg. in a 150th Anniversary Model (1966 only, approx. 6,565 mfg.) and a 175th Anniversary (1991 only). Slight premiums are being asked if condition is 98% or better.

MODEL 552C similar to Model 552A, with 21 in. barrel. Mfg. 1961-1977.

	$275	$240	$200	$185	$150	$125	$95	

MODEL 552 BDL DELUXE SPEEDMASTER – .22 S, L, or LR cal., similar to Model 552C, except checkered gloss finished walnut Monte Carlo stock and forearm, 21 in. barrel, approx. 5 1/2 lbs. New 1966.

MSR $667	$515	$380	$300	$240	$210	$180	$165	

* ***Model 552 BDL Deluxe Fieldmaster NRA Edition*** – features laser etched "NRA" on both sides of receiver. Limited mfg. 2006-2007.

	$400	$350	$300	$270	$220	$180	$140	*$532*

MODEL 552 175th ANNIVERSARY – 1,000 mfg. 1991 only.

	$500	$440	$375	$340	$275	$225	$175	

MODEL 597 – .22 LR cal., alloy receiver with nickel plated bolt, matte black metal finish, one-piece dark grey smooth synthetic stock, 20 in. free-floating barrel, 10 shot staggered detachable mag., adj. iron sights, new trigger design, 5 1/2 lbs. New 1997, mfg. in Mayfield, KY.

MSR $208	$165	$130	$115	$100	$85	$70	$55	

Add $44 for 3-9x32mm scope combo (new 2007).

This model has also been available in several limited production runs. Prices are usually slightly higher than the standard pricing listed above.

* ***Model 597 Sporter*** – .22 LR cal., similar to Model 597 Semi-Auto, except has hardwood stock, includes sling swivel studs. Mfg. 1998-2000.

	$160	$140	$120	$110	$90	$70	$55	*$199*

GRADING - PPGS™	100%	98%	95%	90%	80%	70%	60%	LAST MSR

* ***Model 597 Stainless Sporter*** – .22 LR cal., similar to Model 597 Sporter, except has stainless steel barrel and hardwood stock. Mfg. 2000 only.

	$190	$165	$145	$130	$105	$85	$65	*$239*

* ***Model 597 SS*** – .22 LR cal., similar to Model 597 Semi-Auto, except has stainless steel with satin finished receiver and barrel, and synthetic stock and beavertail style forend. Mfg. 1998-2007.

	$220	$195	$165	$150	$120	$100	$75	*$283*

* ***Model 597 LSS*** – .22 LR cal., similar to Model 597 Semi-Auto, except has stainless steel barrel with matching finish alloy receiver, and satin finished brown wood laminate stock, 5 1/2 lbs. Mfg. 1997-2007.

	$285	$250	$215	$195	$155	$130	$100	*$348*

* ***Model 597 HB LS*** – .22 LR cal., similar to Model 597 LSS, except has 20 in. heavy steel barrel. Mfg. 2001-2007.

	$275	$240	$205	$185	$150	$125	$95	*$337*

* ***Model 597 Camo*** – .22 LR cal., similar to Model 597 Semi-Auto, except features Truglo fiber optic sights and Mossy Oak blaze orange or pink camo stock, 5 1/2 lbs. New 2008.

MSR $300	$240	$195	$175	$145	$120	$95	$75	

* ***Model 597 FLX*** – .22 LR cal., similar to Model 597 Semi-Auto, except has 20 in. carbon steel barrel, 10 shot mag., Next digital FLX camo synthetic stock. New 2009.

MSR $300	$240	$195	$175	$145	$120	$95	$75	

* ***Model 597 AAC-SD*** – .22 LR cal., black synthetic stock, 16 1/2 in. threaded barrel with thread protector, includes scope rail, 10 shot mag., no sights, 5 1/2 lbs. New 2011.

MSR $252	$195	$155	$125	$110	$100	$85	$75	

MODEL 597 TVP (Target Varmint Plinker) – .22 LR cal., stainless action and 20 in. heavy stainless barrel, bolt guidance system with twin steel guide rails, non-glare matte finish metal, ambidextrous laminated thumbhole stock with scalloped forend, 10 shot mag., includes scope mounting rail, 5 1/2 lbs. New 2008.

MSR $595	$475	$380	$310	$260	$215	$200	$155	

MODEL 597 CUSTOM TARGET – .22 LR cal., 20 in. custom contoured satin finish heavy stainless free floating barrel w/o sights, match chamber, special green laminated stock with Monte Carlo profile and beavertail forend. Mfg. 1998-2000.

	$500	$440	$375	$340	$275	$225	$175	*$599*

* ***Model 597 Custom Target .22 Mag.*** – .22 WMR cal., otherwise similar to Model 597 Custom Target. Disc. 2000.

	$600	$525	$450	$410	$330	$270	$210	*$745*

MODEL 597 MAGNUM SYNTHETIC – .17 HMR (mfg. 2003-2007) or .22 WMR cal., similar in appearance to Model 597, 8 shot mag., 20 in. barrel, black synthetic stock with sling swivel studs, 6 lbs. New 1997.

MSR $531	$415	$330	$260	$220	$195	$175	$135	

* ***Model 597 Magnum Synthetic LS*** – .17 HMR (mfg. 2002-2003 only) or .22 WMR cal., similar to Model 597 Magnum Synthetic, except features brown laminate stock with sling swivel studs and steel barrel. Mfg. 1998-2003.

	$315	$275	$235	$215	$175	$140	$110	*$377*

* ***Model 597 Magnum Synthetic LS Heavy Barrel*** – .17 HMR (disc. 2007) or .22 WMR cal., similar to Model 597 Magnum LS, except has 20 in. heavy barrel, 6 lbs. New 2001.

MSR $633	$495	$410	$330	$285	$245	$210	$185	

MODEL 597 VTR (VARMINT TARGET RIFLE) – .22 LR or .22 WMR cal., 16 in. heavy barrel, 10 or 30 shot mag., Picatinny top rail, fixed A2 or Pardus collapsible stock with pistol grip, with (collapsible stock only) or w/o free-floating Quad rail, choice of matte black or A-TACS digital camo finish, nickel Teflon plating, 5 1/2 lbs. Mfg. 2010-2011.

	$415	$375	$330	$300	$275	$250	$225	*$465*

GRADING - PPGS™	100%	98%	95%	90%	80%	70%	60%	LAST MSR

Add $26 for .22 WMR cal. (fixed A-2 stock only).
Add $153 for A-TACS overmolded stock or free-floating Quad Rail system.

MODEL 597 TARGET RIFLE – .22 LR cal., heavy barrel, black, grey and yellow ShurShot target laminated skeletonized stock, scope rail, 10 shot detachable mag., last shot hold open, twin steel guide rails. Mfg. 2008.

	$425	$370	$320	$290	$235	$190	$150	*$505*

This model was available through Remington Premier dealers only.

* ***Model 597 Heavy Barrel*** – .22 LR cal., features 16 1/2 in. heavy barrel w/o sights, scope rail installed, OD Green or A-TACS digital camo synthetic stock, 5 3/4 lbs. New 2012.

MSR $249	$200	$160	$130	$110	$100	$85	$75

Add $100 for A-TACS Digital camo stock.

RIFLES: RIMFIRE, SLIDE ACTION

MODEL 12A – .22 S, L, and LR cal., hammerless, 22 in. round or octagon barrel, open sights, tube mag., plain grip stock, approx. 840,000 (all variations) were mfg. 1909-1936.

$1,100	$975	$850	$750	$650	$550	$450

Originally this model was designated "The New .22 Repeater," and did not have a model number. In 1913, the model nomenclature changed from Grades 1-6 to Grades A-F.

MODEL 12B (GALLERY SPECIAL) – .22 Short cal., 24 in. octagon barrels, 15 shot mag., hammerless, open sights, half pistol grip (common) or straight grip (approx. 10%) stock.

$1,600	$1,350	$1,100	$950	$795	$675	$550

Add 15% for extended mag. tube.

MODEL 12C (NO. 3) – .22 S, L, and LR cal., 24 in. octagon barrel, half pistol grip (common) or straight grip (approx. 10%) stock, hammerless, open sights, tube mag.

$1,300	$1,100	$1,000	$975	$760	$650	$500

* ***Model 12C D Peerless Grade*** – 24 in. octagon barrel, fine scroll engraving on receiver with small game scenes, checkered English walnut stock with pistol grip, grooved forearm.

$6,500	$5,750	$5,100	$4,500	$4,000	$3,000	$2,500

* ***Model 12C E Expert Grade*** – similar to Model 12 C Peerless Grade, except has upgraded wood, checkered forearm, and hand polished parts.

$8,000	$7,000	$6,200	$5,250	$4,650	$3,850	$3,500

* ***Model 12C F Premier Grade*** – top-of-the-line model with best quality checkered walnut stock, fully engraved receiver featuring rabbits and squirrels, very limited mfg.

$10,000	$8,000	$7,000	$6,000	$5,500	$4,500	$3,500

MODEL 12C NRA TARGET – .22 S, L, or LR cal., features 24 in. octagon barrel and extended Lyman aperture rear sight and globe front sight, no barrel dovetails, designed for NRA sponsored smallbore rifle matches, limited manufacture beginning 1917.

$1,750	$1,500	$1,400	$1,200	$950	$850	$650

MODEL 12CS – similar to Model 12C, chambered for .22 Rem. Spl. (.22 WRF) cal.

$1,350	$1,200	$1,000	$900	$800	$650	$550

MODEL 121A – .22 S, L, or LR cal., 24 in. round barrel, hammerless, tube mag., plain pistol grip stock. 201,000 were mfg. 1936-1954.

$800	$725	$625	$575	$475	$415	$375

Originally designated Model 121.

* ***Model 121A D Peerless Grade*** – 24 in. octagon barrel, fine scroll engraving on receiver with small game scenes, checkered English walnut stock with pistol grip, grooved forearm.

$6,500	$5,750	$5,100	$4,500	$3,900	$3,150	$2,500

GRADING - PPGS™	100%	98%	95%	90%	80%	70%	60%	LAST MSR

* ***Model 121A E Expert Grade*** – similar to Model 121A Peerless Grade, except has upgraded wood, checkered forearm, and hand polished parts.

	$7,500	$6,500	$5,700	$4,750	$4,000	$3,250	$3,000	

* ***Model 121A F Premier Grade*** – top-of-the-line model with best quality checkered walnut stock, fully engraved receiver featuring rabbits and squirrels, very limited mfg.

	$8,500	$7,500	$6,500	$5,650	$5,000	$4,150	$3,500	

MODEL 121S – similar to Model 121A, except chambered for .22 Rem. Spl. (rare) cal.

	$1,350	$1,200	$900	$850	$700	$600	$500	

MODEL 121SB/ROUTLEDGE – similar to Model 121A, except smooth bore for .22 shot, at least 5 different chamberings and barrel markings. Approx. 3,000 were mfg. pre-WWII-1952.

	$1,500	$1,300	$1,050	$950	$795	$675	$550	

MODEL 572/572A LIGHTWEIGHT – .22 S, L, LR cal., slide action, anodized alloy receiver and barrel sleeve, steel barrel, checkered "Sun-Grain" stock and forend, 4 lbs. Offered in 3 colors. Approx. 34,785 mfg., 1958-62.

Buckskin Tan	$400	$375	$325	$300	$250	$200	$150	
Crow-Wing Black	$450	$395	$350	$325	$275	$225	$175	
Teal-Wing Blue	$800	$700	$600	$545	$440	$360	$280	

MODEL 572SB/ROUTLEDGE – similar to Model 572A, except smooth bore.

	$675	$550	$450	$395	$340	$305	$250	

MODEL 572 FIELDMASTER – .22 S, L, or LR cal., slide action, 21 in. barrel, walnut stock and forearm, tube mag., 5 1/2 lbs. Mfg. 1955-88.

	$325	$300	$275	$225	$175	$150	$125	*$176*

This model was also mfg. in a 150th Anniversary Model (1966 only). 20% premiums if condition is 98% or better.

MODEL 572 BDL DELUXE FIELDMASTER – similar to Model 572 Fieldmaster, except is also available in .22 Smoothbore (mfg. 2007-2009), checkered gloss finished walnut Monte Carlo stock and forearm. New 1966.

MSR $682	$525	$375	$275	$225	$185	$160	$140	

Add 15% for .22 Smoothbore (Model 572SB, disc. 2009, last MSR was $659).

This model has also been available in several limited production runs. Prices are usually slightly higher than the standard pricing listed above.

MODEL 572 175th ANNIVERSARY – 300 mfg. 1991 only.

	$500	$440	$375	$340	$275	$225	$175	

RIFLES: BOLT ACTION, CENTERFIRE

The models in this section have been listed in numerical sequence for quick reference.

Remington has manufactured many limited production runs for various distributors and wholesalers over the years. These rifles are usually built to a specific configuration (caliber, stock, barrel length, finish, etc.), and are usually available until supplies run out. While these models are not included in this section, pricing in most cases will be similar to the base models from which they were derived.

MODEL SEVEN LIGHTWEIGHT – .17 Rem. (mfg. 1993-95), .222 Rem. (disc. 1984), .223 Rem. (new 1984), .243 Win., .260 Rem. (new 1997), 6mm Rem. (disc. 1994), 7mm-08 Rem., or .308 Win. cal., short action, 18 1/2 in. barrel, 4 or 5 shot mag., individually test fired, shortened LOP, oil finished American walnut stock, adj. rear and ramp front sight (w/o sights on .17 Rem.), 6 1/4 lbs. Mfg. 1983-1999.

	$525	$410	$295	$260	$210	$180	$165	*$585*

Add 5%-10% for .17 Rem. cal.

Add 10% for .222 Rem. cal.

All steel Model Sevens (including floor plate and trigger guard) are currently commanding a small premium.

GRADING - PPGS™	100%	98%	95%	90%	80%	70%	60%	LAST MSR

* ***Model Seven Lightweight LS*** – .223 Rem., .243 Win., .260 Rem. (disc. 2001), .308 Win., or 7mm-08 Rem. cal., features brown laminated stock, 20 in. steel barrel, matte barrel and satin wood finish, 6 1/2 lbs. Mfg. 2000-2005.

	$590	$455	$325	$260	$225	$200	$180	$735

* ***Model Seven Lightweight LS Magnum*** – .300 Rem. SAUM or 7mm Rem. SAUM cal., short action, 22 in. barrel, blue action and barrel, 3 shot mag. with detachable floor plate, brown laminated stock, sling swivel studs, 7 1/8 lbs. Mfg. 2002-2005.

	$615	$455	$350	$285	$250	$215	$185	$775

* ***Model Seven Lightweight LSS*** – .22-250 Rem., .243 Win. (disc. 2001), or 7mm-08 Rem. cal., similar to Model Seven LS, except has stainless steel barrel w/o sights. Mfg. 2000-2003.

	$610	$445	$325	$265	$230	$195	$170	$770

* ***Model Seven Lightweight SS*** – .223 Rem. (mfg. 1997-2002), .243 Win., .260 Rem. (new 1997), .308 Win., 6.8mm Rem. SPC (new 2006), or 7mm-08 Rem. cal., features stainless steel construction, 20 in. barrel w/o sights, and synthetic stock, 6 1/4 lbs. Mfg. 1994-2006.

	$650	$475	$350	$260	$225	$195	$170	$825

* ***Model Seven Lightweight SS Magnum*** – .300 Rem. SAUM or 7mm Rem. SAUM cal., short action, satin finished stainless steel action and 22 in. barrel, 3 shot mag. with detachable floor plate, black synthetic stock, sling swivel studs, 7 1/8 lbs. Mfg. 2002-2006.

	$675	$500	$375	$295	$255	$220	$185	$852

* ***Model Seven Lightweight Youth*** – .204 Ruger (limited mfg. 2004 only), .223 Rem. (new 2000), .243 Win., 6mm Rem. (disc. 1994), .260 Rem. (new 1998), .308 Win. (disc.), 6.8mm Rem. SPC (mfg. 2006), or 7mm-08 Rem. (new 1994) cal., also available in 20 in. barrel beginning 2000, uncheckered hardwood (.260 Rem. cal.) or synthetic (new 2004) stock shortened 1 in., 6 lbs. Mfg. 1993-2007.

	$525	$425	$335	$275	$230	$200	$185	$684

Subtract $33 for limited edition synthetic stock model in .204 Ruger cal.

* ***Model Seven Lightweight FS*** – .243 Win., 7mm-08 Rem., or .308 Win. cal., 18 1/2 in. parkerized blue barrel, grey or grey camo Kevlar fiberglass stock, adj. rear sight, 5 1/4 lbs. Mfg. 1987-89 only.

	$525	$455	$415	$375	$335	$310	$285	$600

* ***Model Seven XCR Camo*** – .243 Rem., .270 WSM, .300 WSM, .308 Win., or 7mm-08 Rem. cal., 20 in. fluted stainless steel barrel, stainless steel action utilizing TriNyte corrosion protection, Realtree AP HD camo stock with R3 recoil pad, 3-4 shot non-detachable mag., approx. 7 lbs. Mfg. 2007 only.

	$925	$825	$725	$625	$550	$475	$400	$1,080

Add 10% for WSM cals.

* ***Model Seven Synthetic*** – .223 Rem., .243 Win., .260 Win., .308 Win., or 7mm-08 cal., 18 1/2 (Youth only .243 Win. or 7mm-08 cal.) or 20 in. barrel w/o sights, features black synthetic stock with SuperCell recoil pad, matte blue metal finish, X-Mark Pro adj. trigger, hinged floorplate, externally adj. trigger, approx. 6 1/2 lbs. New 2011.

MSR $709	$575	$485	$430	$385	$350	$325	$295

* ***Model Seven Predator*** – .17 Rem. Fireball (disc. 2010), .204 Ruger (disc. 2010), .223 Rem., .22-250 Rem., or .243 Win. cal., Model 700 BDL action, 22 in. fluted barrel w/o sights, 100% Mossy Oak Brush camo coverage, 2 3/4 in. shorter than normal Model 700, SuperCell recoil pad became standard 2011, designed for smaller shooters, 7 lbs. New 2008.

MSR $886	$760	$675	$575	$475	$400	$350	$295

GRADING - PPGS™	100%	98%	95%	90%	80%	70%	60%	LAST MSR

* ***Model Seven Lightweight CDL (Classic Deluxe)*** – .17 Rem. Fireball (mfg. 2007-2010), .204 Ruger (disc. 2007), .223 Rem. (disc. 2007), .22-250 Rem. (disc. 2007), .243 Win., .260 Rem., 6.8mm Rem. SPC (mfg. 2006), 7mm-08 Rem., or .308 Win. cal., 20 or 22 in. barrel, no sights, checkered deluxe walnut stock and forearm with R3 (disc.) or SuperCell (new 2010) recoil pad, X-Mark Pro adj. trigger, 6 1/2 lbs. New 2006.

MSR $1,029	**$815**	**$650**	**$525**	**$425**	**$350**	**$300**	**$265**	

* ***Model Seven Lightweight CDL Magnum*** – .270 WSM, 7mm RSAUM (disc. 2007), .300 RSAUM (disc. 2007), .300 WSM (disc. 2010), or .350 Rem. Mag. (disc. 2010) cal., 22 in. barrel, no sights except for .350 Rem. Mag., checkered deluxe walnut stock and forearm, R3 (disc. 2010) or SuperCell (new 2011) recoil pad, 7 3/8 lbs. Mfg. 2006-2011.

	$865	**$725**	**$600**	**$500**	**$400**	**$350**	**$300**	***$1,054***

Subtract $28 for .350 Rem. Mag. cal. (disc. 2010).

* ***Model Seven Lightweight Custom MS (Mannlicher Stock)*** – .222 Rem., .22-250 Rem., .223 Rem., .243 Win., .250 Savage, .257 Roberts, .260 Rem. (new 1997), .308 Win., .35 Rem., .350 Rem. Mag., 6mm Rem., or 7mm-08 Rem. cal., features 4 or 6 shot mag., 20 in. custom shop barrel with Model 7 action bedded to a Mannlicher style two-tone brown laminate full stock, hinged floorplate, 6 1/2 lbs. Mfg. 1993-2011.

	$2,575	**$2,200**	**$1,900**	**$1,600**	**$1,300**	**$1,100**	**$900**	***$2,992***

This model was available from the Custom Shop only (special order).

* ***Model Seven Lightweight Custom KS*** – .223 Rem. (new 1989), .260 Rem. (new 1998), 7mm BR Rem. (mfg. 1989-1990), 7mm-08 Rem. (new 1989), .308 Win. (new 1991), .35 Rem., or .350 Rem. Mag. cal., 20 in. barrel with (.35 Rem. or .350 Rem. Mag.) or w/o sights, Aramid/Kevlar fiberglass synthetic stock with solid recoil pad, 5 3/4 lbs. Mfg. 1987-2011.

	$2,225	**$1,900**	**$1,650**	**$1,400**	**$1,150**	**$925**	**$775**	***$2,542***

This model is available from the Custom Shop only (special order).

* ***Model Seven Lightweight AWR (Alaskan Wilderness Rifle)*** – 6.8mm Rem. SPC (mfg. 2005-2007), .300 Rem. SAUM, or 7mm Rem. SAUM cal., short action, stainless steel action and 22 in. barrel with matte black Teflon satin finish, 3 shot detachable mag., fiberglass matte black stock, sling swivel studs, 6 1/8 lbs. Mfg. 2002-2008.

	$2,495	**$2,150**	**$1,850**	**$1,550**	**$1,250**	**$1,000**	**$775**	***$2,927***

This model was available from the Custom Shop only (special order).

* ***Model Seven Lightweight AWR II*** – .260 Rem. (disc. 2009), .270 WSM (disc. 2009), .300 WSM (disc. 2009), 7mm-08 Rem. (disc. 2009), .308 Win. (disc. 2009), 7mm RSAUM, .300 RSAUM, or .350 Rem. Mag. (disc. 2009) cal., 20 or 22 in. stainless steel black TriNyte coated barrel, Bell & Carlson reinforced olive green fiberglass stock, hinged floorplate, no sights, mfg. by custom shop, 6 1/8 lbs. Mfg. mid-2008-2011.

	$2,575	**$2,200**	**$1,900**	**$1,600**	**$1,300**	**$1,100**	**$900**	***$2,992***

Additional calibers were available by request.

* ***Model Seven 25th Anniversary Ltd. Ed.*** – 7mm-08 Rem. cal., 20 in. barrel, Classic Deluxe style American walnut stock laser engraved with "Model Seven 25th Anniversary" 25th Anniversary medallion inletted in pistol grip cap, high lustre blue with jeweled bolt, X-Mark Pro trigger, 6 1/2 lbs. Mfg. 2008 only.

	$775	**$650**	**$550**	**$450**	**$395**	**$350**	**$295**	***$969***

MODEL 30A RIFLE – .25 Rem., .30 Rem., .30-06 (original cal.), .32 Rem., .35 Rem., or 7x57mm Mauser (introduced 1931) cal., Enfield M/1917 type action, 22 in. barrel, checkered pistol grip stock. Mfg. 1921-40.

	$700	**$640**	**$550**	**$500**	**$400**	**$325**	**$260**	

MODEL 30R CARBINE – .25 Rem., .30 Rem., .32 Rem., .35 Rem., or .30-06 cal., similar to Model 30A, with 20 in. barrel. Introduced 1927.

	$750	**$625**	**$575**	**$500**	**$400**	**$325**	**$275**	

GRADING - PPGS™	100%	98%	95%	90%	80%	70%	60%	LAST MSR

MODEL 30 EXPRESS – .25 Rem., .30 Rem., .32 Rem., .35 Rem., or .30-06 cal. Introduced 1926.

	$700	$640	$550	$500	$400	$325	$260	

MODEL 30S (SPECIAL GRADE) – .25 Rem. Rimless (introduced 1931), .257 Roberts (new 1934), 7x57mm Mauser (introduced 1931), or .30-06 (original cal.) cal., deluxe version of Model 30A, 22 or 24 in. barrel, Lyman receiver sight, special stock, 7 1/2 lbs. Mfg. 1930-40.

	$800	$725	$650	$575	$500	$375	$300	

The Model 30S Express Rifle was introduced in 1934 in .257 Roberts cal.

MODEL 78 SPORTSMAN – .223 Rem., .243 Win., .270 Win., .30-06, or .308 Win. cal., 22 in. barrel, 4 shot mag., uncheckered hardwood stock, open sights, 7 lbs. Mfg. 1984-89.

	$400	$350	$275	$225	$200	$160	$150	*$333*

MODEL XR-100 RANGEMASTER – .204 Ruger, .22-250 Rem., or .223 Rem. cal., features XP-100 single shot target pistol action with Model 40-XP target adj. trigger, 26 in. barrel, laminate thumbhole stock with vent. beavertail forend, 9 1/8 lbs. Mfg. 2005-2007.

	$875	$725	$625	$525	$450	$400	$375	*$1,057*

MODEL 600 – .222 Rem., .223 Rem. (very rare), 6mm Rem., .243 Win., .308 Win., or .35 Rem. cal., 18 1/2 in. VR barrel, dog leg bolt handle, checkered pistol grip stock. 94,086 were mfg. 1964-68.

Reg. cals.	$475	$365	$290	$220	$200	$180	$160	
.35 Rem. cal.	$850	$700	$600	$450	$350	$300	$260	
.222 Rem. cal.	$550	$500	$450	$400	$365	$340	$300	
.223 Rem. cal.	$1,500	$1,200	$1,000	$750	$550	$450	$350	

315 Model 600s in .223 Rem. cal. were mfg.

* ***Model 600 Montana Centennial*** – 6mm Rem. cal., 1,020 mfg. in 1964 only.

	$1,600	$1,300	$1,000	N/A	N/A	N/A	N/A	*$125*

MODEL 600 MAGNUM – 6.5mm Rem. Mag. or .350 Rem. Mag. cal., laminated walnut/beech stock with or without recoil pad (early mfg. walnut stocks did not have recoil pad). Mfg. 1965-1968.

	$1,050	$925	$825	$725	$600	$500	$425	

MODEL 600 MOHAWK – .222 Rem., 6mm Rem., .243 Win., or .308 Win. cal., this variation was a promotional model, 18 1/2 in. barrel with no rib. 94,920 were mfg. 1971-79.

	$420	$340	$300	$285	$255	$235	$210	

MODEL 660 STANDARD – .222 Rem., 6mm Rem., .243 Win., or .308 Win. cal., 20 in. barrel, open sights, dog leg bolt handle, checkered pistol grip stock, black pistol grip cap and forend tip. 50,536 were mfg. 1968-71.

	$550	$500	$450	$400	$365	$340	$310	

Add 10% for .222 Rem. cal.

* ***Model 660 Standard .223 Rem. cal.*** – 227 total mfg. This cal. was never listed in a Remington catalog.

	$1,600	$1,250	$750	$600	$500	$400	$350	

MODEL 660 MAGNUM – 6.5mm Rem. Mag. or .350 Rem. Mag. cal., laminated stock and recoil pad.

	$1,100	$950	$825	$725	$600	$500	$375	

MODEL 673 GUIDE RIFLE – .243 Win., .300 Rem. Ultra Mag., .350 Rem. Mag., 6.5mm Rem. Mag. (new 2004) or .308 Win. (new 2004) cal., patterned after the Model 600 Magnum and features the Model Seven action, 22 in. contoured barrel with VR and open sights, drilled and tapped, two-tone tan wide striped checkered laminate stock with solid recoil pad, 3 shot hidden mag., polished blue metal, 7 1/2 lbs. Mfg. 2003-2006.

	$800	$675	$600	$510	$450	$395	$365	*$893*

GRADING - PPGS™	100%	98%	95%	90%	80%	70%	60%	LAST MSR

MODEL 710 SPORTSMAN – .270 Win., .243 Win. (new 2006), .30-06, 7mm Rem. Mag. (new 2004) or .300 Win. Mag. (new 2004) cal., unique bolt to barrel lockup design utilizing 3 locking lugs on bolt face that lock directly in an integrated rear barrel extension (as opposed to locking into the receiver), long action, steel (became standard 2005) or polymer receiver sleeve (disc. 2004), adj. trigger, detachable 4 shot box mag, 60 degree bolt throw, 22 in. ordnance grade steel barrel with matte finish, grey synthetic stock with solid pad, supplied with bore sighted 3-9x40mm Bushnell Sharpshooter scope and mounts, ISS (Integrated Security System) bolt locking safety, 7 1/8 lbs. Mfg. 2001-2006.

	$360	$320	$295	$265	$250	$240	$230	*$439*

Add $39 for limited edition Skyline Excel camo (mfg. 2004 only).

This model was also available in a Youth Model (.243 Win. cal. only, shortened LOP - includes scope, new 2006) at no extra charge.

MODEL 715 SPORTSMAN – .243 Win., .270 Win., .30-06, 7mm-08 Rem., 7mm Rem. Mag., or .300 Win. mag. cal., 22 or 24 in. blue ordnance grade barrel, black synthetic stock with molded sling swivel studs, 60 degree bolt lift, updated magazine latch, detachable 3-4 shot mag., no sights, Picatinny rail. Mfg. 2008.

	$295	$265	$235	$215	$190	$170	$150	*$349*

This model was available through Remington Premier dealers only.

MODEL 720A – Enfield type action, .257 Roberts, .270 Win., or .30 - 06 cal., 22 in. barrel, open sights, 5 shot, checkered pistol grip stock, 2,500 mfg. 1941-44.

	$1,600	$1,400	$1,200	$1,000	$700	$550	$450

Add 50%+ for .270 Win. cal.

Add 100%+ for .257 Roberts cal.

Most of this model was chambered for .30-06 cal.

MODEL 720 MILITARY – .257 Roberts, .270 Win., or .30-06 cal., purchased by the Dept. of Navy during 1942 and used for trophies, discernible by crossed cannon proofs on wood, approx. 100 were chambered for .270 Win. and 20 or less were chambered for the .257 Roberts. 920-1,000 mfg. 1942 only.

.30-06 cal.	$2,400	$2,150	$1,800	$1,575	$1,225	$1,000	$850
.270 Win. cal.	$2,800	$2,400	$2,150	$1,800	$1,575	$1,225	$1,000
.257 Roberts cal.	$3,650	$3,300	$2,875	$2,450	$2,150	$1,800	$1,575

MODEL 720R – similar to 720A, except with 20 in. barrel.

	$1,800	$1,500	$1,200	$1,000	$700	$575	$475

This is the rarest variation in the Model 720 Series.

MODEL 720S – similar to 720A, except with 24 in. barrel.

	$1,600	$1,400	$1,200	$1,000	$700	$525	$425

MODEL 721 – .264 Win. Mag., .270 Win., .280 Rem. (new 1960), or .30-06 cal., 24 in. barrel, open sights, 4 shot, plain pistol grip stock. Mfg. 1948-1962.

	$500	$450	$400	$325	$275	$250	$175

.280 Rem. (688 mfg.) and .264 Win. Mag. (1,115 mfg.) are rare in this model. 100% condition on these calibers could bring $700+.

MODEL 721ADL – similar to Model 721A, except has deluxe checkered stock.

	$525	$475	$400	$350	$300	$260	$210

This model's suffix does not appear on the gun. ADL features will determine the model.

MODEL 721BDL – similar to Model 721ADL, except has extra select wood.

	$650	$500	$475	$425	$350	$315	$295

This model's suffix does not appear on the gun. BDL features will determine the model.

MODEL 721A MAGNUM – .264 Win. Mag. or .300 H&H cal., 26 in. heavy barrel, recoil pad, 3 shot mag., 8 1/4 lbs.

	$700	$600	$550	$500	$450	$400	$350

Add 15% for .264 Win. Mag. cal.

GRADING - PPGS™	100%	98%	95%	90%	80%	70%	60%	LAST MSR

MODEL 721ADL MAGNUM – .264 Win. Mag. cal., similar to Model 721A Magnum, checkered. 1,115 mfg. 1961-1962, not cataloged.

	$800	$700	$650	$575	$500	$450	$400

MODEL 721BDL MAGNUM – similar to Model 721ADL Magnum, select wood.

	$850	$750	$700	$600	$500	$450	$400

MODEL 722(A) – short action version of 721A, .222 Rem. (mfg. 1950-62), .222 Rem. Mag. (mfg. 1958-62), .243 Win. (mfg. 1960-62), .244 Rem. (mfg. 1957-62), .257 Roberts (disc. 1960), .300 Savage (disc. 1959), or .308 Win. (mfg. 1956-62) cal., 7 lbs. Mfg. 1948-1962.

	$525	$475	$400	$350	$300	$260	$200

Subtract 10% for .300 Savage cal.
Add 20% for .257 Roberts or .308 Win. cal.

.222 Rem. Mag. (3,803 mfg.) and .243 Win. (2,186 mfg.) are rare in this model. Add approx. 25% to values for these cals.

MODEL 722ADL – similar to Model 722(A), except with deluxe checkered wood.

	$525	$500	$400	$350	$300	$275	$200

This model's suffix does not appear on the gun. ADL features will determine the model.

MODEL 722BDL – similar to Model 722ADL, except features extra select wood.

	$795	$750	$700	$600	$500	$450	$400

This model's suffix does not appear on the gun. BDL features will determine the model.

MODEL 725ADL – .222 Rem., .243 Win., .244 Rem., .270 Win., .280 Rem., or .30-06 cal., 22 in. barrel, open sights, 4 shot mag., checkered Monte Carlo stock. 16,635 mfg. 1958-61.

.30-06 cal.	$650	$600	$550	$450	$400	$375	$350
.270 Win. cal.	$750	$600	$550	$500	$375	$350	$325
.280 Rem. cal.	$1,050	$900	$650	$550	$400	$350	$325
.222 Rem. cal.	$900	$700	$600	$500	$400	$350	$325
.244 Rem. cal.	$900	$700	$600	$500	$400	$350	$325
.243 Win. cal.	$900	$700	$600	$500	$400	$350	$325

NIB will bring a 30%-50% premium.

Caliber mfg. breakdown is as follows: 7,657 in .30-06; 2,784 in .280 Rem.; 2,818 in .270 Win.; 840 in .244 Rem.; 1,478 in .222 Rem.; 998 in .243 Win.

MODEL 725 KODIAK – .375 H&H Mag. or .458 Win. Mag. cal., 26 in. barrel, 3 shot mag., recoil reducer in muzzle, deluxe checkered Monte Carlo stock, black pistol grip cap and forend tip. 52 mfg. 1961 only.

	$6,000	$4,000	$3,250	$2,700	$2,200	$1,900	$1,650

Only 24 rifles in .458 Win. Mag. were mfg. and 28 rifles in .375 H&H Mag.

MODEL 770 – .243 Win., .270 Win., .30-06, .308 Win., .300 Win. Mag., 7mm-08 Rem., or 7mm Rem. Mag. cal., matte black metal finish, Picatinny rail, 3 or 4 shot detachable mag., black synthetic stock with raised cheekpiece, includes factory mounted and bore sighted 3-9x40mm Bushnell scope, 20 (Youth Model only), 22 or 24 in. barrel, Model 700 based action with 60 degree bolt lift, "R" on pistol grip cap, also available in Youth model with short LOP (.243 Win. cal. only), 8 1/2 lbs. New 2007, mfg. in Mayfield, KY.

MSR $375	$325	$260	$230	$200	$185	$170	$165

* ***Model 770 Stainless*** – .270 Win., .30-06, 7mm Rem. Mag., or .300 Win. Mag. cal., similar to Model 770, except has 22 or 24 in. stainless steel barrel and Realtree AP HD camo stock, 8 1/2 lbs. New 2008.

MSR $458	$385	$340	$295	$260	$225	$200	$185

MODEL 788 – .222 Rem. (disc. 1979, reintroduced 1982-83), .22-250 Rem., .223 Rem. (new 1975), 6mm Rem. (mfg. 1969-1979), .243 Win. (new 1969), .308 Win. (new 1969), .30-30 Win. (disc. 1972), 7mm-08 Rem. (new 1980), or .44 Mag. (disc. 1970) cal., 18 1/2 (Carbine, .243 Win., .308 Win., or 7mm-08 Rem. cal.), 22 (6mm Rem., .243 Win.,

GRADING - PPGS™	100%	98%	95%	90%	80%	70%	60%	LAST MSR

and .308 Win. cal.), or 24 (.222 Rem., .22-250 Rem., .223 Rem. cal. 1967-1979, .223 Rem. and .22-250 Rem. cal. 1980-83) in. barrel, short action, open sights, plain pistol grip Monte Carlo stock. Mfg. 1967-1983.

$550 $425 $400 $350 $275 $250 $225

Add 10% for .30-30 Win. cal.
Add 15% for 7mm-08 Rem. cal.
Add 30% for .44 Mag. cal.
Add 10% for left-hand action (6mm Rem. and .308 Win. cal. only, mfg. 1969-1979).

In 1970, this gun was also manufactured with a 4X scope as a promotion, but was a non-Remington catalog item.

MODEL 798 – various cals. between .243 Win. - .458 Win. Mag., features square bridge Mauser 98 long action, 22 or 24 in. steel or stainless steel (green laminate stock only) barrel w/o sights, polished blue finish, hinged floorplate, black synthetic (Model 798 SPS, new 2008), satin walnut, Realwood walnut (Safari Grade only, new 2008), or brown or green (mfg. 2007) laminate stock, controlled round feeding with claw extractor, sporter style two position safety, 7 lbs. Importation from Zastava 2006-2008.

$450 $415 $375 $350 $325 $300 $285 *$527*

Add $43 for .300 Win. Mag. or 7mm Rem. Mag. cal.
Add $443 for .375 H&H or $513 for .458 Win. Mag. cal. (26 in. barrel only).
Add $121 for satin walnut stock.

* ***Model 798 Safari Grade*** – .375 H&H or .458 Win. Mag. cal., 22 in. heavy barrel with adj. open sights, Realwood laminated stock, front barrel band with sling swivel, drilled and tapped, 8 1/4 lbs. Mfg. 2008.

$950 $850 $750 $650 $575 $500 $450 *$1,141*

Add $72 for .458 Win. Mag. cal.

MODEL 799 – .22 Hornet (detachable mag.), .22-250 Rem., .222 Rem., .223 Rem., or 7.62x39mm cal., features Mauser 98 short action, brown laminate stock, 20 in. barrel w/o sights, otherwise similar to Model 798. Imported 2006-2008.

$550 $475 $425 $375 $335 $295 $275 *$648*

RIFLES: BOLT ACTION, MODEL 700 & VARIATIONS

MODEL 700 TITANIUM ULTIMATE LIGHTWEIGHT – .260 Rem., .270 Win., .30-06, .300 Rem. SAUM (new 2004), .308 Win. (new 2002), 7mm Rem. SAUM (new 2004), or 7mm-08 Rem cal., titanium receiver (drilled and tapped), spiral cut breech bolt with flutes and skeleton handle, 22 in. stainless steel barrel, satin stainless finish on receiver and barrel, ultra lightweight carbon-fiber matte finished Kevlar reinforced stock, 3-4 shot fixed mag., sling swivel studs, 5 1/4 - 5 1/2 lbs. Mfg. 2001-2006.

$1,200 $1,050 $850 $775 $600 $500 $450 *$1,412*

Add $40 for Rem. SAUM cals.

MODEL 700 AS – .22-250 Rem., .243 Win., .270 Win., .280 Rem., .30-06, .308 Win., 7mm Rem. Mag., or .300 Wby. Mag. cal., synthetic stock is made from Arylon resin, matte black finished stock and metal, 22 or 24 in. barrel, 6 1/2 lbs. Mfg. 1989-91 only.

$550 $400 $360 $300 $260 $220 $195 *$528*

Add $21 for 7mm Rem. Mag. or .300 Wby. Mag. cal.

MODEL 700 FS – .243 Win., .270 Win., .30-06, .308 Win., or 7mm Rem. Mag. cal., 22 in. polished blue barrel, grey or grey camo Kevlar fiberglass stock with solid recoil pad, open sights, 6 1/4 lbs. Mfg. 1987-88 only.

$600 $500 $415 $375 $335 $310 $285 *$613*

Add $20 for 7mm Rem. Mag. cal. (24 in. barrel).

MODEL 700 TACTICAL – 6.8mm SPC cal., 20 in. parkerized barrel, synthetic stock, approx. 9 lbs. Limited availability 2005-2006.

$800 $650 $550 $450 $400 $300 $275 *$990*

GRADING - PPGS™	100%	98%	95%	90%	80%	70%	60%	LAST MSR

MODEL 700 TARGET TACTICAL – .308 Win. cal., 26 in. triangular contour barrel with 5-R tactical rifling, steel trigger guard and floorplate, X-Mark Pro adj. trigger, Bell & Carlson Medalist adj. stock, tactical bolt handle, OD Green finish, 11 3/4 lbs. New 2009.

MSR $2,117	$1, 850	$1,600	$1,375	$1,150	$950	$825	$700	

MODEL 700P & VARIATIONS – various cals., long or short action, various barrel lengths, designed for police/law enforcement and military, current configurations include: 700P, 700P TWS (Tactical Weapons System, includes scope, bipod and case), 700P LTR (Light Tactical Rifle), 700P LTR TWS (Light Tactical Rifle/Tactical Weapons System, includes scope, bipod, and case), 700P USR (Urban Sniper Rifle), Model M24/M24A2/M24A3 Sniper Weapon System (combination of Model 700 and Model 40-XB design, with scope, case, and bipod), and from the Remington Custom Shop Model 40-XS Tactical Rifle System, Model 40-XB Tactical, and the Model 40-XS 338 Tactical.

Remington does not publish consumer retail pricing for these police/law enforcement models. Secondary prices for base models w/o scopes and other options will be slightly higher than for current pricing on the Model 700BDL Custom Deluxe. Prices for rifles with scopes and other features will be determined by how much the individual options and accessories add to the base value.

MODEL 700 RS – .270 Win., .280 Rem., or .30-06 cal., 22 in. matte finished barrel and action, grey or grey camo DuPont Rynite synthetic stock with smooth cheekpiece and solid recoil pad, open sights, 7 1/4 lbs. Mfg. 1987-88 only.

$650	$550	$500	$425	$360	$310	$285	*$547*

Add 30% for .280 Rem. cal.

In 1987 less than 500 rifles were dual barrel marked - 7mm EXP REM .280 REM. These specimens will command a 40% premium.

MODEL 700 CAMO SYNTHETIC – .22-250 Rem. (disc. 1993), .243 Win., .270 Win. (disc. 1993), .280 Rem. (disc. 1993), 7mm-08 Rem. (disc. 1993), 7mm Rem. Mag., .30-06, .308 Win. (disc. 1993), or .300 Wby. Mag. (disc. 1993) cal., 22 or 24 (Mag. only) in. barrel, features synthetic stock and is fully camouflaged in Mossy Oak Bottomland pattern, open sights, approx. 7 1/4 lbs. Mfg. 1992-94.

$550	$450	$350	$315	$285	$265	$250	*$581*

Add $27 for Mag. cals.

MODEL 700ADL DELUXE RIFLE/CARBINE – .22-250 Rem. (disc. 1991), .222 Rem. (disc.), .222 Rem. Mag. (disc.), .25-06 Rem. (disc. 1991), 6mm Rem. (disc.), .243 Win. (disc. 1997), .270 Win., .280 Rem. (disc. 1997 - marked 7mm Express 1979-82), .30-06, .308 Win. (disc. 2001), or 7mm Rem. Mag. (disc. 2002) cal., 20 (carbine mfg. 1962-1963), 22, or 24 in. barrel, open sights, 4 shot mag., checkered Monte Carlo stock or brown laminated stock (new 1988). Mfg. 1962-2005.

$475	$375	$295	$250	$215	$185	$165	*$580*

Add 5% for 7mm Rem. Mag. cal. (disc. 2002).

Add 60% for carbine with 20 in. barrel (mfg. 1962-63).

Add 50% for .222 Rem. Mag. or .280 Rem. cal. 20 in barrel.

Add 15% for 7mm Rem. Mag., .264 Win. Mag., or .300 Win. Mag. cal. with stainless steel barrel (mfg. 1962-1970).

During 1962-63, the 20 in. barrel was standard on .222 Rem., .222 Rem. Mag., .243 Win., .270 Win., .280 Rem., .30-06, or .308 Win. cal. In 1964, these cals. had a standard barrel length of 22 in.; 24 in. barrels were standard on 7mm Rem. Mag. and .264 Win. Mag. cal.

During 1984, Remington began stamping a safety warning on the barrel.

In 1987-89, Remington introduced a Model 700 Gun Kit that enabled the owner to assemble the stock to the barreled action. All metal work was completely finished and wood finishing was all that is required. This kit was available in most popular cals. - last MSR price was $333 (1989).

* ***Model 700ADL Deluxe Rifle Synthetic*** – .22-250 Rem. (new 1999), .223 Rem., .243 Win., .270 Win., .30-06, .308 Win., .300 Win. Mag. (new 1999), or 7mm Rem. Mag., features fiberglass reinforced synthetic stock with positive checkering, black matte finish on metal, open sights, approx. 7 3/8 lbs. Mfg. 1996-2005.

$395	$315	$260	$215	$185	$170	$155	*$500*

Add $27 for .300 Win. Mag. or 7mm Rem. Mag. cal.

GRADING - PPGS™	100%	98%	95%	90%	80%	70%	60%	LAST MSR

* ***Model 700ADL Deluxe Rifle Synthetic Youth*** – .243 Win., .270 Win. (new 2004), .30-06 (new 2004), or .308 Win. cal., similar to Model 700ADL Synthetic, except has 20 in. barrel and 1 in. shorter LOP. Disc. 2005.

	$395	$315	$260	$215	$185	$170	$155	*$500*

* ***Model 700ADL/LS Deluxe Rifle*** – .243 Win. (mfg. 1989-1993), .270 Win. (new 1989), .30-06, or 7mm Rem. Mag. (mfg. 1988-1993) cal., brown laminate stock with checkering. Mfg. 1988-1993, reintroduced 2002-2004.

	$460	$360	$280	$230	$175	$165	$155	*$580*

Add $27 for 7mm Rem. Mag. cal. (disc.).

This model was available through selected distributors only.

MODEL 700BDL CUSTOM DELUXE – .17 Rem. (disc. 2007), .22-250 Rem. (disc. 2007), .222 Rem. (disc. 2007), .223 Rem. (disc. 2007), .243 Win., .25-06 Rem. (disc. 2007), .264 Win. Mag. (disc.), .270 Win., .280 Rem. (mfg. 1992-95, resumed 2000-2002), .300 Savage (mfg. 1992 only), .30-06, .308 Win. (disc. 1995), .35 Whelen (mfg. 1989-94), 6mm Rem. (disc. 1994), 7mm-08 Rem. (disc. 1994, reintroduced 2000-2002), 7mm Rem. Mag., 7mm-06 Rem. (designated 7mm-Exp Rem., approx. 200-300 mfg., disc.) .308 Win. (left-hand only, disc. 2004), .300 Win. Mag. (disc. 2007), .300 Rem. Ultra Mag (new 1999), .338 Win. Mag. (mfg. 1988-94, resumed 1997-2002), .338 Rem. Ultra Mag. (mfg. 2000-2002, mfg. 2004 in left-hand only), .375 Rem. Ultra Mag. (mfg. 2001-2002), 7mm Rem. Ultra Mag. (mfg. 2001-2007), or 8mm Mag. (disc.) cal., 22, 24 (Magnum), or 26 (SAUM cals.) in. barrel, similar to 700ADL Deluxe, except with hinged floorplate, cut skipline checkering, black pistol grip cap and forend tip, receiver and floorplate fine line engraving was standard 1997-2001, non-embellished beginning 2002, supplied with open sights first year, hooded ramp front sight and adj. rear sight then became standard, R3 recoil pad supplied on Mag. cals., X-Mark Pro adj. trigger became standard 2008, approx. 7 1/4-7 5/8 lbs.

MSR $985	$785	$600	$460	$350	$300	$280	$260
.222 Rem. Mag. cal.	$800	$725	$550	$350	$325	$300	$275
.350 Rem. Mag. cal.	$1,000	$800	$550	$350	$325	$300	$275
6.5mm Rem. Mag. cal.	$1,000	$800	$550	$350	$325	$300	$275

Add $30 for 7mm Rem. Mag., or .300 Rem. Ultra Mag. (currently mfg. Mag. cals.).

Add $27-$67 for left-hand model (available in certain cals. only, short action .22-250 Rem. and .243 Win. cals. are scarce in left-hand, disc. 2004).

Add 15% for 7mm Rem. Mag., .264 Win. Mag., or .300 Win. Mag. cal. with stainless steel barrel (mfg. 1962-1970).

In 1962, the 20 in. barrel was standard on .222 Rem., .222 Rem. Mag., .243 Win., .270 Win., .280 Rem., .30-06, or .308 Win. cal. In 1964, these cals. had a standard barrel length of 22 in. 24 in. barrels were standard on 7mm Rem. Mag. and .264 Win. Mag. cals.

Remington mfg. the Model 700BDL in .350 Rem. Mag. and 6.5mm Rem. Mag. (1,584 mfg. between 1969-75). 1,558 were assembled in 1969, and sold through 1975. The .350 Rem. Mag. mfg. in 1969 is 3 times rarer than the 1985 Model 700 Classic chambered for .350 Rem. Mag.

During 1984, Remington began stamping a safety warning on the barrel.

MODEL 700BDL 200th ANNIVERSARY SPECIAL EDITION – .30-06 cal., features curly maple stock with ebony forend cap and pistol grip, 200th Anniversary and Remington cameo/caption laser etched on floorplate. Limited mfg. 1993 only.

	$725	$650	$575	$500	$400	$300	$200

MODEL 700 BDL 50TH ANNIVERSARY EDITION – 7mm Rem. Mag. cal., includes original features such as satin finish, B Grade walnut stock with cut fleur-de-lis checkering, 24 in. blued steel barreled action, black vent recoil pad, white line spacers, open sights, X-Mark Pro trigger, hinged floorplate features commemorative laser engraving, approx. 7 1/2 lbs. New 2012.

MSR $1,399	$1,175	$1,050	$875	$775	$675	$575	$475

MODEL 700 CLASSIC (LTD EDITION) – similar to 700BDL, except has classic straight stock, high polish bluing, has been offered in .17 Rem., .220 Swift, .221 Fireball (new 2002),

GRADING - PPGS™	100%	98%	95%	90%	80%	70%	60%	LAST MSR

.222 Rem., .22-250 Rem. (Classic only), .223 Rem., .250 Savage (250/3000), 6.5x55mm Swedish, 6mm Rem. (Classic only), 7x57mm Mauser, 8mm Rem. Mag., 8mm Mauser, .243 Win. (Classic only), .25-06 Rem., .257 Roberts, .264 Win. Mag., .270 Win. (Classic only), .280 Rem., .300 Savage (new 2003), .300 Win. Mag., .300 Wby. Mag., .30-06 (Classic only), .308 Win. (new 2005), 7mm-08 Rem., 7mm Wby. Mag., .338 Win. Mag., .350 Rem. Mag., .35 Whelen, .300 H&H, or .375 H&H cal. The original Model 700 Classic was mfg. 1978-1985. Limited edition calibers were introduced during 1981 (see listings), and continued to be produced annually until 2005.

$750	$675	$575	$475	$375	$325	$275	*$716*

Add 25% for 7x57mm Mauser, .220 Swift, .338 Win. Mag., .350 Rem. Mag., .250 Savage, .257 Roberts, .300 H&H, or .35 Whelen cal.

The Model 700 Classic was originally introduced in 1978 in .22-250 Rem., 6mm Rem., .243 Win., .270 Win., .30-06, and 7mm Rem. Mag., and was part of the standard Remington product lineup until 1985. Limited editions were introduced during 1981.

This model is produced in limited quantities of a different caliber each year. Add premiums for several calibers in NIB condition only (including 7x57mm Mauser, .257 Roberts, .300 H&H, and .375 H&H).

The following is a list of annual Limited Classic calibers offered previously with year of manufacture: 7x57mm Mauser (1981), .257 Roberts (1982), .300 H&H (1983), .250 Savage (1984), .350 Rem. Mag. (1985), .264 Win. Mag. (1986), .338 Win. Mag. (1987), .35 Whelen (1988), .300 Wby. Mag. (1989), .25-06 Rem. (1990), 7mm Wby. Mag. (1991), .220 Swift (1992), .222 Rem. (1993), 6.5x55mm Swedish (new 1994), .300 Win. Mag. (1995), .375 H&H Mag. (1996), .280 Rem. (1997), 8mm Rem. Mag. (1998), .17 Rem. (1999), .223 Rem. (2000), 7mm-08 Rem. (2001), .221 Fireball (2002), .300 Savage (2003), 8mm Mauser (2004), and .308 Win. (2005).

MODEL 700BDL DM (DETACHABLE MAG.) – .243 Win. (disc. 1999), .25-06 Rem. (disc. 1997), .260 Rem., .270 Win., .280 Rem. (disc. 1999), 6mm Rem. (disc. 1996), 7mm Rem. Mag., 7mm-08 Rem. (disc. 1999), .30-06, .308 Win. (disc. 1996), .300 Win. Mag. (disc. 2002), or .338 Win. Mag. (disc. 1996) cal., 22 or 24 in. barrel, Monte Carlo walnut stock with 20 LPI skip-line checkering, high polish bluing, black forend cap, receiver and floorplate fine line engraving was standard 1997-2001, open sights, 3-4 shot detachable mag. Mfg. 1995-2004.

$775	$595	$460	$350	$325	$300	$275	*$749*

Add $27 for .300 Win. Mag. and 7mm Rem. Mag. cals.

Left-hand actions on this model were disc. in 1999. Their last retail prices ranged from $665 - $692, depending on caliber.

* ***Model 700BDL Lew Horton Special Edition*** – .257 Roberts cal., 500 mfg. in 1990 only, first time the 700BDL has been offered in .257 Roberts cal.

$735	$595	$460	$395	$360	$325	$280	*$580*

MODEL 700BDL SS (STAINLESS SYNTHETIC) – .223 Rem. (mfg. 1993-94), .243 Win. (mfg. 1993-94), .25-06 Rem. (disc. 1994), .270 Win., .280 Rem. (disc. 1995), .30-06, .308 Win. (disc. 1994), 7mm Rem. (mfg. 1993-94), 7mm-08 Rem. (mfg. 1993-94), .300 Win. Mag. (new 1993), .300 Rem. Ultra Mag. (new 1999), .300 Rem. SA Ultra Mag. (new 2003), .300 Wby. Mag. (mfg. 1993-94), .338 Win. Mag. (mfg. 1993-94, resumed 1997-2002), .338 Rem. Ultra Mag. (new 2000), 7mm Rem. Mag., 7mm Rem. Ultra Mag. (new 2001), 7mm Rem. SA Ultra Mag. (new 2003), 7mm Wby. Mag. (scarce, disc. 1994), .375 Rem. Ultra Mag. (mfg. 2001-2002), or .375 H&H (mfg. 1997-2002) cal., features matte finished 416 stainless steel barrel, receiver, and bolt, black synthetic stock with checkering, R3 recoil pad became standard during 2004, drilled and tapped, hinged floorplate mag., 24 or 26 (Rem. Ultra Mag. cals.) in. barrel, no sights, 6.25-7 lbs. Mfg. 1992-2004.

$775	$595	$460	$350	$325	$300	$275	*$735*

Add $26 for Mag. cals., except 7mm Rem. Mag.
Add $40 for Ultra Mag. or SA Ultra Mag. cals.
Add approx. $100 for .223 Rem. cal., $150 for 7mm Wby. Mag. cal.

GRADING - PPGS™	100%	98%	95%	90%	80%	70%	60%	LAST MSR

* ***Model 700BDL LSS*** – .270 Win. (left-hand only, disc. 2000), .300 Win. Mag., .300 Rem. Ultra Mag. (new 1999), .338 Rem. Ultra Mag. (new 2000), .30-06 (left-hand only, disc. 2000), 7mm Rem. Ultra Mag., 7mm Rem. Mag., or .375 Rem. Ultra Mag. cal., stainless steel barreled action, grey tinted laminate Monte Carlo wood stock, 24 or 26 (Rem. Ultra Mag. cals.) in. barrel, w/o sights, 7 1/2 lbs. Mfg. 1996-2004.

	$800	**$650**	**$600**	**$500**	**$400**	**$300**	**$275**	***$827***

Add $13 for Rem. Ultra Mag. cal.

Add $40 for Mag. cals. in left-hand action.

* ***Model 700BDL SS DM (Detachable Mag.)*** – .243 Win. (disc. 1997), .25-06 Rem. (disc. 2002), .260 Rem. (mfg. 1997-2000), .270 Win., .280 Rem. (disc. 2002), 6mm Rem. (disc. 1995), 7mm Rem. Mag., 7mm-08 Rem. (disc. 1998, resumed 2000-2001), .30-06, .308 Win. (disc. 1999), .300 Win. Mag., .300 Wby. Mag. (disc. 2000), or .338 Win. Mag. (disc. 1996) cal., features 3-4 shot detachable mag., stainless steel, 24 in. barrel, satin finish metalwork, R3 recoil pad became standard during 2004, black non-reflective stock with checkering, receiver and floorplate fine line engraving was standard in 1997-2001, w/o sights, 7 3/8 lbs. Mfg. 1995-2004.

	$800	**$650**	**$600**	**$500**	**$400**	**$300**	**$275**	***$801***

Add $27 for Mag. cals.

Add $89 for muzzle brake (Model 700BDL SS DM-B, mfg. 1996-2001, available in 7mm STW, 7mm Rem. Mag. [disc. 1999] or .300 Win. Mag. cals. only).

MODEL 700BDL VARMINT SPECIAL – .22-250 Rem., .222 Rem., .223 Rem., .25-06 Rem. (disc.), 6mm Rem., .243 Win., .308 Win., or 7mm-08 Rem. cal., 24 in. heavy barrel, checkered walnut stock, no sights. Mfg. 1967-94.

	$850	**$750**	**$625**	**$500**	**$450**	**$400**	**$350**	***$565***

* ***Model 700VS (Varmint Synthetic)*** – .220 Swift (disc. 1996), .22-250 Rem., .223 Rem., .243 Win. (mfg. 1997-98), or .308 Win. cal., short action, composite textured black and grey synthetic stock features Kevlar, fiberglass, and graphite, matte metal finish, 26 in. heavy barrel w/o sights, 9 1/8 lbs. Mfg. 1992-2004.

	$650	**$470**	**$410**	**$330**	**$295**	**$265**	**$250**	***$811***

Add $26 for left-hand action.

The right-hand model was disc. 1998, but resumed in 2000.

* ***Model 700VSF Varmint Special*** – .17 Rem. Fireball (new 2007), .22-250 Rem., .223 Rem., or .308 Win. cal., updated Model 700VS with VS SFII stock design in desert tan with black webbing and R3 recoil pad, 26 in. fluted heavy blue barrel, blue receiver, available in right or left-hand action, 9 lbs. Mfg. 2005-2007.

	$925	**$825**	**$700**	**$600**	**$525**	**$450**	**$400**	***$1,159***

Add $26 for left-hand action.

* ***Model 700VS SF/SF-P (Varmint Synthetic Stainless Fluted/Ported)*** – .220 Swift (ported barrel only until 2000), .22-250 Rem., .223 Rem. (w/o porting), .308 Win. (ported barrel only, disc. 1999) or .338 Rem. Ultra Mag. (mfg. 2000 only) cal., stainless steel action with 26 in. barrel with flutes, 2 barrel ports became an option in some cals. during 1998-99 only (Model SF-P), 8 1/2 lbs. Mfg. 1994-2004.

	$820	**$600**	**$475**	**$415**	**$360**	**$300**	**$255**	***$976***

Add 5% for ported barrel (Model 700VS SF-P, disc. 1999).

* ***Model 700VS SF-II Varmint Special (Varmint Synthetic Stainless Fluted)*** – .17 Rem. Fireball (mfg. 2008-2010), .204 Ruger (disc. 2010), .220 Swift, .22-250 Rem., or .223 Rem. cal., updated Model 700 VS SF with reconfigured H-S Precision composite stock, palm swell and contoured beavertail forend, 26 in. heavy barrel with black fluting, black synthetic stock with spruce green webbing, X-Mark Pro adj. trigger became standard 2007, 8 1/2 lbs. Mfg. 2005-2011.

	$1,150	**$975**	**$825**	**$725**	**$625**	**$525**	**$450**	***$1,387***

* ***Model 700VLS (Varmint Laminated Stock)*** – .204 Ruger (new 2005), .222 Rem. (mfg. 1995 only), .22-250 Rem., .223 Rem., .243 Win., 6mm Rem. (mfg. 1998-2007), .260

GRADING - PPGS™	100%	98%	95%	90%	80%	70%	60%	LAST MSR

Rem. (disc. 1999), .308 Win., or 7mm-08 Rem. (mfg. 1997-99) cal., 26 in. heavy barrel w/o sights, blue metalwork, brown laminated stock with (disc. 2001) or w/o skip line checkering, beavertail shaped forend became standard 1998, X-Mark Pro adj. trigger became standard 2007, 9 3/8 lbs. New 1995.

MSR $1,045	$840	$715	$600	$525	$450	$400	$350	

* ***Model 700LV SF (Light Varmint Stainless Fluted)*** – .204 Ruger (new 2005), .17 Rem., .221 Rem. Fireball, .223 Rem., or .22-250 Rem. cal., short action, 22 in. fluted barrel w/o sights, black composite stock with R3 recoil pad, stainless action and barrel, jeweled bolt, blind box mag., 6 3/4 lbs. Mfg. 2004-2007.

	$835	$650	$525	$425	$365	$335	$295	*$1,040*

* ***Model 700VL SS TH (Thumbhole)*** – .204 Ruger, .22-250 Rem., or .223 Rem. cal., stainless action with 26 in. heavy stainless barrel w/o sights, 4 or 5 shot mag., brown laminated thumbhole stock with vent. beavertail forend, X-Mark Pro adj. trigger became standard 2007, 9 1/4 lbs. Mfg. 2007-2011.

	$950	$800	$675	$575	$500	$425	$375	*$1,130*

MODEL 700 VTR – .17 Rem. Fireball (mfg. 2009-2010), .204 Ruger (disc. 2010), .223 Rem., .22-250 Rem., .243 Win. (new 2009), or .308 Win. cal., 22 in. barrel, OD Green, desert camo (mfg. 2009), or A-TACS digital camo (new 2010) overmolded stock, integrated muzzle brake design, triangular shaped barrel contour, X-Mark Pro adj. trigger, approx. 7 1/2 lbs. New 2008.

MSR $908	$725	$585	$480	$400	$350	$300	$275	

Add $51 for A-TACS stock (.223 Rem. or .308 Win. cal. only).

MODEL 700VS COMPOSITE – .22-250 Rem., .223 Rem., or .308 Win. cal., similar to Model 700 Sendero Composite, except is available in short action only. Mfg. by Custom Shop 1999-2000.

	$1,550	$1,225	$825	$700	$600	$550	$500	*$1,912*

MODEL 700BDL SS CAMO RMEF – .300 Rem SA Ultra Mag. (mfg. 2003), .300 Rem. Ultra Mag. (mfg. 2001), .300 Win. Mag. (new 2004), or 7mm Rem. Ultra Mag. (mfg. 2002) cal., Realtree Hardwoods camo stock treatment, satin finished receiver and round barrel, laser engraved floorplate including RMEF logo, limited special edition for the Rocky Mountain Elk Foundation, approx. 7 1/2 lbs. New 2001-2004.

	$680	$525	$405	N/A	N/A	N/A	N/A	*$835*

MODEL 700BDL DALE EARNHARDT JR. – .30-06 cal., 22 in. blue barrel, 4 shot mag., synthetic stock with Dale Earnhardt Jr. signature #8 logo, special ser. no. (DEJ8xxx), R3 recoil pad, no sights, drilled and tapped. Limited mfg. 2004 only.

	$675	$525	$425	N/A	N/A	N/A	N/A	*$735*

MODEL 700 VARMINT SF – .17 Rem. Fireball (disc. 2010), .204 Ruger (disc. 2010), .220 Swift, .223 Rem., .22-250 Rem., or .308 Win. cal., 26 in. heavy stainless barrel, synthetic stock with Hogue overmolded grip panels, vent. forend, X-Mark Pro adj. trigger, approx. 8 1/2 lbs. New 2009.

MSR $981	$785	$615	$500	$400	$325	$275	$260	

MODEL 700 MOUNTAIN RIFLE DM (DETACHABLE MAG.) – .243 Win. (disc. 1997), .260 Rem. (new 1998), .25-06 Rem. (disc. 2002), .270 Win., .280 Rem., 7mm-08 Rem., or .30-06 cal., detachable mag., 22 in. barrel, satin finished American walnut stock, R3 recoil pad became standard on Mag. cals. during 2004, satin bluing, without sights, approx. 6 1/2 lbs. Mfg. 1995-2006.

	$685	$550	$425	$350	$300	$265	$250	*$841*

* ***Model 700 Mountain Rifle LSS (Laminated Stock Stainless)*** – .260 Rem. (disc. 2007), .270 Win., .280 Rem. (new 2007), .30-06, or 7mm-08 Rem. cal., features stainless action and 22 in. barrel w/o sights, brown laminate stock, X-Mark Pro adj. trigger became standard 2008, approx. 6 1/2 lbs. Mfg. 1999-2010.

	$900	$800	$700	$600	$500	$400	$350	*$1,095*

GRADING - PPGS™	100%	98%	95%	90%	80%	70%	60%	LAST MSR

MODEL 700BDL MOUNTAIN RIFLE (FIXED MAG.) – .243 Win. (new 1988), .25-06 Rem. (new 1992), .257 Roberts (new 1991), .270 Win., 7mm-08 Rem. (new 1988), .280 Rem., .30-06, .308 Win. (new 1988), or 7x57mm Mauser (new 1990) cal., 22 in. tapered barrel, checkered satin finished American walnut stock with cheekpiece and ebony forend, 4 shot mag., without sights, 6 3/4 lbs. Mfg. 1986-94.

	$445	$380	$315	$275	$250	$220	$195	*$532*

Add 20% for .257 Roberts or 7x57mm Mauser cal.

MODEL 700 MOUNTAIN SS – .25-06 rem., .270 Win., .280 Rem., .30-06, .308 Win., or 7mm-08 Rem. cal., 22 in. stainless steel barrel with satin stainless finish, Bell & Carlson adj. stock, X-Mark Pro trigger, 6 1/2 lbs. New 2012.

MSR $1,123	$925	$800	$700	$600	$525	$450	$375	

* ***Model 700BDL Mountain Rifle Stainless*** – .25-06 Rem., .270 Win., .280 Rem., or .30-06 cal., 22 in. barrel, black synthetic stock with pressed checkering, blind mag., 7 1/4 lbs. Mfg. 1993 only.

	$450	$385	$315	$275	$250	$220	$195	*$532*

MODEL 700BDL EUROPEAN – .243 Win., .270 Win., .280 Rem., 7mm-08 Rem., 7mm Rem. Mag., .30-06, or .308 Win. cal., Monte Carlo stock with hand-rubbed oil finish, 22 or 24 (Mag. cals. only) in. barrel, hinged floorplate, iron sights, approx. 7 1/4 lbs. Disc. 1994.

	$445	$375	$325	$280	$250	$220	$195	*$532*

Add $27 for 7mm Rem. Mag. cal.

MODEL 700CDL CLASSIC DELUXE – various cals. between .223 Rem. - .35 Whelen, classic style checkered walnut stock with satin finish, black forend tip and pistol grip cap, satin blue or high polish (new 2008, select cals. only) metal finish, SuperCell became standard 2010 or R3 (disc. 2009) recoil pad, 24 or 26 (Mag. cals.) in. barrel w/o sights, integral extractor, hinged floorplate, 3-5 shot mag., X-Mark Pro adj. trigger, approx. 7 1/2 lbs. New 2004.

MSR $1,019	$865	$700	$600	$500	$450	$400	$335	

Add $29 for Mag. cals.

Add $29 for left-hand action (select cals. only, new 2005).

This model was also manufactured in .204 Ruger cal. as part of a Friends of NRA limited edition - 1,050 were manufactured. Values can vary significantly depending on locality and perceived desirability.

* ***Model 700CDL Classic Deluxe Detachable Mag*** – .243 Win., .270 Win., .30-06, .300 Win. Mag., 7mm-08 Rem., or 7mm Rem. Mag. cal., features detachable box mag., 24 or 26 in. barrel, satin finished blued action and barrel, X-Mark Pro adj. trigger, straight comb walnut stock with cheekpiece. New 2011.

MSR $1,041	$885	$730	$625	$525	$450	$400	$350	

Add $29 for Mag. cals. (26 in. barrel only).

* ***Model 700CDL SF Limited Edition*** – .17 Rem. Fireball (mfg. 2007), .257 Roberts (mfg. 2009), .260 Rem. (mfg. 2008) .280 Rem. (new 2010), .30-06 (mfg. 2006) or 6mm Rem. (mfg. 2011 only), 7mm Rem. Mag. (new 2012) cal., 24 in. stainless fluted barrel, checked satin finished walnut stock, black forend tip and pistol grip cap, engraved floorplate, drilled and tapped, X-Mark Pro adj. trigger became standard 2007. Limited mfg. by caliber beginning 2006.

MSR $1,214	$995	$825	$700	$600	$525	$450	$395	

The 7mm Rem. Mag. cal. released in 2012 features a 50th Anniversary commemorative floorplate.

MODEL 700 CDL 100TH ANNIVERSARY – .375 H&H cal., 22 in. barrel with open sights, satin checkered American walnut stock and forearm, Supercell recoil pad and X-Mark Pro adj. trigger, approx. 7 1/2 lbs. New 2012.

MSR $1,450	$1,195	$1,025	$875	$775	$675	$575	$475	

* ***Model 700CDL SF (Stainless Fluted)*** – .17 Rem. Fireball (disc. 2009), .257 Wby. Mag. (new 2008), .270 Win., .270 WSM, 7mm-08 Rem., 7mm Rem. Mag., .30-06, or .300

GRADING - PPGS™	100%	98%	95%	90%	80%	70%	60%	LAST MSR

WSM cal., 3-4 shot mag., 24 or 26 (.30-06 cal. only) in. stainless fluted barrel, satin finished checkered walnut stock and forearm, R3 (disc. 2009) or SuperCell became standard 2010 recoil pad, X-Mark Pro adj. trigger, approx. 7 1/2 lbs. New 2007.

MSR $1,169	$975	$825	$700	$600	$525	$450	$395	

Add $28 for Mag. cals. or $89 for WSM cals.

*** *Model 700 CDL "Boone & Crockett" Series*** – .243 Win., .270 Win., .270 WSM, .30-06, 7mm-08 Rem., 7mm Rem. Mag., .300 WSM, or .300 Win. Mag. cal., 24 or 26 in. fluted blue barrel, brown laminate stock, "Boone & Crockett" medallion insert on grip cap, "Boone & Crockett" laser engraved on barrel, X-Mark Pro adj. trigger. Mfg. 2008.

	$800	$725	$650	$575	$525	$450	$375	*$959*

Add 10% for regular Mag. cals. or 15% for WSM cals.

This model was offered through Remington Premier dealers only.

MODEL 700 SENDERO – .25-06 Rem., .270 Win. (disc. 2001), .300 Win. Mag., or 7mm Rem. Mag. cal., similar to Model 700 VS, except has long action for Mag. cals., 24 (non-cataloged) or 26 in. barrel, 9 lbs. Mfg. 1994-2002.

	$635	$510	$420	$335	$295	$265	$250	*$788*

Add $27 for Mag. cals.

Add approx. $100 for fluted barrel (not cataloged).

*** *Model 700 Sendero Special SF (Stainless Fluted)*** – .25-06 Rem. (disc. 2002), .300 Win. Mag., .300 Wby. Mag. (mfg. 1997-2001), .300 Rem. Ultra Mag. (new 1999), .300 Rem SA Ultra Mag. (new 2003), .338 Rem. Ultra Mag. (new 2000), 7mm STW (mfg. 1997-2002), 7mm Rem. Mag., 7mm Rem. Ultra Mag. (new 2001), or 7mm Rem. SA Ultra Mag. (new 2003) cal., 26 in. varmint type fluted barrel, approx. 8 1/2 lbs. Mfg. 1996-2004.

	$835	$640	$475	$415	$360	$300	$255	*$1,003*

*** *Model 700 Sendero Special SF-II*** – .264 Win. Mag. (disc. 2011), .300 Win. Mag., .300 Rem. Ultra Mag., 7mm Rem. Mag., or 7mm Rem. Ultra Mag. (disc. 2011) cal., 3-4 shot mag., stainless steel action and 24 or 26 in. fluted heavy barrel, black H-S Precision synthetic stock with grey webbing and full length aluminum bedding, X-Mark Pro adj. trigger became standard 2007, 8 1/2 lbs. New 2006.

MSR $1,451	$1,175	$995	$875	$750	$650	$550	$475	

MODEL 700 SENDERO CUSTOM – various cals., 26 in. heavy barrel, features blue printed Model 700 stainless steel action, machined steel trigger guard with engraved floor plate, 40X adj. trigger, composite stock with cheekpiece. New 2012.

MSR $3,535	$2,925	$2,500	$2,075	$1,650	$1,450	$1,225	$1,050	

MODEL 700 SENDERO COMPOSITE – .25-06 Rem., .300 Win. Mag., or 7mm STW cal., features 26 in. composite barrel, matte black finished steel action, Kevlar reinforced black synthetic stock, 7 7/8 lbs. Mfg. 1999 only.

	$1,395	$1,125	$750	$650	$575	$525	$475	*$1,665*

MODEL 700 LSS – .257 Wby. Mag. cal., 26 in. stainless steel barrel, black laminate stock, X-Mark Pro adj. trigger, SuperCell recoil pad. Mfg. 2008.

	$840	$735	$650	$575	$525	$450	$375	*$972*

This model was available through Remington Premier dealers only.

MODEL 700 ALASKAN Ti – .25-06 Rem., .270 Win., .270 WSM, .280 Rem., 7mm-08 Rem., 7mm Rem. Mag., .30-06, .300 WSM, .300 Win. Mag., or .308 Win. (disc. 2007) cal., titanium receiver with spiral cut fluted bolt with skeletonized bolt handle, lightweight fluted stainless 24 in. barrel w/o sights, black pillar bedded Bell & Carlson synthetic stock with MaxxGuard finish and R3 recoil pad, X-Mark Pro adj. trigger, 3-4 shot mag., hinged floorplate, approx. 6 1/4 lbs. Mfg. 2007-2009.

	$1,775	$1,500	$1,250	$1,000	$875	$800	$725	*$2,225*

Add $27 for 7mm Rem. Mag. and .300 Win. Mag., or $124 for WSM cals.

GRADING - PPGS™	100%	98%	95%	90%	80%	70%	60%	LAST MSR

MODEL 700 ETRONX VS SF – .220 Swift (electronic primer), .22-250 Rem. (electronic primer), or .243 Win. (electronic primer) cal., features patented Etronx technology utilizing an electronic discharge for virtually instant cartridge ignition, CPU located in stock incorporates standard 9V battery, and allows electric signal to be passed through a ceramic coated firing pin, which in turn activates the specially designed electronic primer. There are no moving parts in this system, and therefore, nothing to delay ignition. Electronic trigger mechanism enables almost zero lock time. LED on top of grip indicates system status (fire or safe mode), chamber status (loaded or not loaded), low battery indicator, and any possible system malfunction. 26 in. heavy stainless steel barrel with black flutes, alumiunum bedding, Kevlar reinforced composite stock with matte black finish, 8 7/8 lbs. Mfg. late 1999-2003.

	$1,150	$950	$750	$640	$535	$450	$390	*$1,332*

This model can fire only Etronx ammunition which used an electronic primer. Remington still manufactures Etronx ammunition in .22-250 Rem. and .220 Swift only.

Because the Etronx ignition system used an electronic primer the same size as a standard rifle primer, reloading was no different than using standard cases, powder, and bullets. The only thing that changed was the electronic primer. Ammunition is now scarce, but Etronx primers are still available from Remington.

MODEL 700 SPS (SPECIAL PURPOSE SYNTHETIC) – various cals., 20 (Youth Model), 24 or 26 in. barrel, standard or Youth synthetic stock with SuperCell (became standard 2010, except on Youth Model) or R3 (disc. 2009) recoil pad, X-Mark Pro adj. trigger standard, except on Youth model, approx. 7 3/8 lbs. New 2005, mfg. in Ilion, NY.

MSR $709	$565	$475	$415	$350	$310	$270	$230	

This model is available in a Youth variation in cals. .243 Win., .270 Win. (disc.), 7mm-08 Rem., .30-06 (disc.) or .308 Win. (disc.) at no extra charge.

This model is also available in left-hand action at no extra charge - calibers are .270 Win., .30-06, .300 Win. Mag., or 7mm Rem. Mag. (new 2009).

* ***Model 700 SPS DM*** – .243 Win., .270 Win., .30-06, 7mm-08 Rem., 7mm Rem. Mag. or .300 Win. Mag. cal., features detachable mag., X-Mark Pro trigger, otherwise similar to Model 700 SPS. Mfg. 2005-2010.

	$575	$495	$435	$375	$335	$295	$260	*$717*

* ***Model 700 SPS Camo*** – .223 Rem., .243 Win., .270 Win., .300 Win., .30-06, 7mm-08 Rem., or 7mm Rem. Mag. cal., 20, 22, or 24 in. barrel, matte blued finish, hinged floor plate, X-Mark Pro adj. trigger, Mossy Oak Break Up Infinity camo synthetic stock, 7- 7 1/2 lbs. New 2011.

MSR $785	$625	$540	$485	$425	$395	$350	$300	

* ***Model 700 SPS Stainless*** – various cals., features stainless steel barreled action, 24 or 26 in. barrel w/o sights, synthetic stock with R3 (disc. 2007) or SuperCell (new 2008) recoil pad, X-Mark Pro adj. trigger standard 2008, approx. 7 1/4 lbs. New 2005.

MSR $813	$640	$535	$465	$400	$350	$300	$275	

Add $39 for WSM cals.

* ***Model 700 SPS Varmint*** – .17 Rem. Fireball (disc. 2011) .204 Ruger, .22-250 Rem., .223 Rem., .243 Win. or .308 Win. cal., features 26 in. heavy barrel, matte blue metal finish, black synthetic stock with vent. beavertail forend, X-Mark Pro adj. trigger, approx. 8 1/2 lbs. New 2007.

MSR $739	$595	$485	$420	$365	$330	$300	$265	

Add $30 for left-hand action (new 2008, not available in .204 Ruger).

MODEL 700 SPS LONG RANGE – .25-06, .300 Win. Mag., .300 Rem. Ultra Mag., or 7mm Rem. Mag. cal., 26 in. barrel w/o sights, black synthetic w/grey overmolded varmint stock, 8 3/4 lbs. New 2012.

MSR $739	$595	$485	$420	$365	$330	$300	$265	

GRADING - PPGS™	100%	98%	95%	90%	80%	70%	60%	LAST MSR

* ***Model 700 SPS Buckmasters Edition*** – .243 Win., .270 Win., .30-06, .300 Win. Mag., 7mm-08 Rem., or 7mm Rem. Mag. cal., 3 or 4 shot mag., 20-26 in. barrel, engraved floorplate with Buckmasters logo, Realtree Hardwoods camo stock, also available in Youth (Youngbucks edition with 20 in. barrel), R3 recoil pad, approx. 7 1/8 lbs. Mfg. 2007-2010.

	$595	$500	$425	$365	$330	$300	$260	*$754*

* ***Model 700 SPS Tactical*** – .223 Rem. or .308 Win. cal., 20 in. heavy contour barrel, black oxide finish, black synthetic overmolded Hogue stock, laser engraved "Tactical" on barrel, X-Mark Pro adj. trigger, matte black finish, 7 1/2 lbs. Mfg. 2008, reintroduced 2010.

MSR $765	$615	$515	$450	$385	$335	$295	$250	

This model was available through Remington Premier dealers only in 2008.

* ***Model 700 SPS Tactical AAC-SD*** – .308 Win. cal., features 20 in. heavy barrel with threaded muzzle, Hogue overmold Ghillie Green Pillar bedded stock, X-Mark Pro adj. trigger. New 2011.

MSR $817	$645	$550	$460	$400	$350	$295	$250	

* ***MODEL 700 SPS Tactical Blackhawk*** – .223 Rem. or .308 Win. cal., 20 in. triangular contoured barrel, Bell & Carlson Metalist adj. stock, pistol grip cap, steel floorplate and triggerguard, X-Mark Pro trigger, synthetic stock, tactical bolt handle, 8 1/2 lbs. New 2012.

MSR $850	$695	$625	$560	$520	$485	$435	$395	

MODEL 700 XCR (XTREME CONDITIONS RIFLE) – .25-06 Rem. (new 2007), .270 Win., .270 WSM, .30-06, 7mm Rem. Mag., .300 WSM, .300 Win. Mag., 7mm Rem. Ultra Mag., 7mm-08 Rem. (new 2007), .300 Rem. Ultra Mag., .338 Rem. Ultra Mag., .338 Win. Mag., .375 H&H, or .375 Rem. Ultra Mag. cal., 24 or 26 in. stainless steel barrel with TriNyte corrosion control, patented black Hogue overmolded stock with R3 recoil pad, X-Mark Pro adj. trigger, approx. 7 1/2 lbs. Mfg. 2005-2009.

	$865	$665	$560	$500	$450	$400	$350	*$1,065*

Add $27 for Mag. cals. or $76 for WSM cals.

Add 10% for left-hand action (available in .270 Win., .30-06, .300 Rem. Mag., or .300 Rem. Ultra Mag., mfg. 2008).

* ***Model 700 XCR RMEF*** – .30-06 (mfg. 2009), 7mm Rem. Mag. (disc.), 7mm Rem. Ultra Mag. (mfg. 2008), .300 Rem. Ultra Mag. (mfg. 2007, again in 2010) or .300 WSM (mfg. 2006) cal., features RMEF camo Realtree Hardwood HD (disc. 2006) or AP (new 2007) camo overmolded stock with R3 recoil pad, X-Mark Pro adj. trigger became standard 2007. Mfg. 2005-2010.

	$950	$825	$675	$575	$500	$425	$375	*$1,199*

Subtract approx. 10% for 7mm Rem. Mag. cal.

MODEL 700 XCR TACTICAL – .223 Rem., .308 Win. or .300 Win. Mag. cal., 3-5 shot mag., features 26 in. stainless steel receiver/barrel with black TriNyte PVD coating, tactical Bell & Carlson OD Green stock with full length aluminum bedding, X-Mark Pro adj. trigger, 9 1/8 lbs. New 2007.

MSR $1,510	$1,250	$1,050	$925	$825	$725	$625	$500	

* ***Model 700 XCR Tactical .338 Lapua*** – .338 Lapua cal., similar to Model 700 XCR Tactical, except has 5 round detachable mag. box, steel trigger guard, and AAC muzzle brake. New 2011.

MSR $2,468	$2,075	$1,825	$1,575	$1,325	$1,100	$925	$775	

* ***Model 700 XCR Compact Tactical*** – .223 Rem. or .308 Win. cal., similar to Model 700 XCR, except has 20 in. fluted varmint contour barrel, compact dimensions, 7 1/2 lbs. New 2008.

MSR $1,510	$1,250	$1,050	$925	$825	$725	$625	$500	

GRADING - PPGS™	100%	98%	95%	90%	80%	70%	60%	LAST MSR

MODEL 700 XCR II (XTREME CONDITIONS RIFLE) – various cals., 24 or 26 in. barrel, stainless steel barrel and receiver with matte black TriNyte finish, Hogue OD green synthetic stock with overmolding in grip and forend areas, SuperCell recoil pad, X-Mark Pro adj. trigger, hinged floorplate, approx. 7 1/2 lbs. New 2010.

MSR $1,005	$800	$615	$475	$350	$300	$280	$260	

Add $29 for standard Mag. cals.
Add $80 for .300 WSM cal.

* ***Model 700 XCR II Camo Bone Collector Edition*** – .30-06 cal., 24 in. barrel, "Bone Collector" with logo engraved on floorplate, Realtree AP HD camo stock, TriNyte metal finish, X-Mark Pro adj. trigger, overmolded stock. Mfg. 2010-2011.

	$875	$765	$575	$500	$450	$400	$350	*$1,063*

* ***Model 700 XCR II Camo RMEF Edition*** – .25-06 Rem. (new 2012) or .300 Win. Mag. cal., similar to Model 700 XCR II Camo Bone Collector, except does not have Bone Collector engraved floorplate, Realtree AP camo synthetic overmolded stock, 7 1/2 lbs. Limited edition beginning 2011.

MSR $1,134	$925	$795	$600	$525	$450	$400	$350	

MODEL 700 XHR (XTREME HUNTING RIFLE) – .243 Win., .25-06 Rem., .270 Win., 7mm-08 Rem., .30-06, 7mm Rem. Mag., .300 Win. Mag., 7mm Rem. Ultra Mag., or .300 Rem. Ultra Mag. cal., 24 or 26 (Mag. cals.) in. triangular barrel with satin black oxide metal finish, hinged floorplate, X-Mark Pro adj. adj. trigger, Hogue overmolded synthetic stock with Realtree AP HD camo, jeweled bolt, front and rear swivel studs, SuperCell recoil pad. Mfg. 2009-2010.

	$750	$650	$550	$450	$400	$350	$300	*$915*

Add $28 for Mag. cals.

MODEL 700 CUSTOM KS MOUNTAIN RIFLE – .270 Win., .280 Rem., .300 Win. Mag., .300 Wby. Mag. (new 1989), .300 Rem. Ultra Mag. (new 1999), .30-06, .338 Win. Mag. (new 1986), .338 Rem. Ultra Mag. (new 2000), .35 Whelen (new 1989), 7mm STW (new 1999), 7mm Rem. Mag., 7mm Rem. Ultra Mag. (new 2001), 8mm Rem. Mag. (new 1986), .375 Rem. Ultra Mag. (new 2001), or .375 H&H cal., 22 (disc.), 24 or 26 (Ultra Mag. cals. only) in. carbon steel barrel, no sights, features extra lightweight Kevlar fiber-reinforced stock, available in either right or left-hand action, 6 3/8 - 7 lbs. Mfg. 1986-2004, reintroduced 2006-2008.

	$1,800	$1,525	$1,250	$1,000	$875	$800	$725	*$2,265*

Add $80 for left-hand action.

This model was available from the Custom Shop only (special order).

* ***Model 700 Custom KS Mountain Rifle Stainless*** – similar to Model 700 Custom KS Mountain Rifle, except has stainless steel action and barrel. Mfg. 1995-2004, reintroduced 2006.

	$1,950	$1,650	$1,325	$1,050	$900	$825	$750	*$2,465*

Add $80 for left-hand action.

* ***Model 700 Custom KS Mountain Rifle Wood Grained Kevlar*** – similar to Model 700 Custom KS Safari Grade, except has wood grained Kevlar stock. Mfg. 1992-93.

	$1,000	$875	$750	$650	$550	$485	$430	*$1,109*

Add $63 for left-hand action.

MODEL 700 SAFARI GRADE – .375 H&H, 8mm Rem. Mag. (new 1986), .416 Rem. Mag. (new 1989), or .458 Win. Mag. cal., heavier 700BDL barrel, 3 shot mag., 24 in. barrel, available with either Classic or Monte Carlo stock configuration, custom shop special order only, 9 lbs. Mfg. 1962-2000.

	$1,395	$1,225	$1,000	$850	$700	$600	$500	*$1,225*

Add $73 for left-hand model (Classic stock only).

* ***Model 700 Safari Grade Custom KS*** – 8mm Rem. Mag., .375 H&H, .416 Rem. Mag., or .458 Win. Mag. cal., stock made from Aramid fiber or Kevlar (disc.) and fiberglass, 24 in. barrel with barrel band, including sling swivel, adj. safari sights, blind 3 shot mag., 9 lbs. Mfg. 1989-2004, reintroduced 2006-2011.

	$2,400	$2,050	$1,775	$1,500	$1,250	$1,050	$900	*$2,841*

This model was also available in left-hand action at no extra charge.

GRADING - PPGS™	100%	98%	95%	90%	80%	70%	60%	LAST MSR

* ***Model 700 Safari Grade Custom KS Stainless*** – .375 H&H, .416 Rem. Mag., or .458 Win. Mag. cal., features fiberglass and Aramid or Kevlar (disc.) stock and stainless steel action. Mfg. 1993-2004, reintroduced 2006-2011.

	$2,575	$2,150	$1,850	$1,550	$1,300	$1,050	$900	*$3,067*

MODEL 700 ABG (AFRICAN BIG GAME) – .375 H&H, .375 Rem. Ultra Mag., .416 Rem. Mag., or .458 Win. Mag. cal., straight line 3 shot detachable box mag., checkered brown laminate stock with right-hand cheekpiece, open sights, matte blue finished steel receiver, 26 in. barrel with barrel band and safari sights, custom shop special order only, 9 1/2 lbs. Mfg. 2001-2004, reintroduced 2006.

MSR $3,217	$2,700	$2,225	$1,875	$1,550	$1,325	$1,100	$975	

MODEL 700 APR (AFRICAN PLAINS RIFLE II) – .300 Win. Mag., .300 Wby. Mag., .300 Rem. Ultra Mag. (new 1999), .338 Win. Mag., .338 Rem. Ultra Mag. (new 2000), .375 H&H, 7mm Rem. Mag, 7mm STW (by request only, ltd. mfg.), 7mm Rem. Ultra Mag. (new 2001), or .375 Rem. Ultra Mag. (new 2001) cal., 3 shot, custom shop variation with 26 in. custom shop barrel, satin finish metal and brown, pressure laminated, checkered wood stock with satin finish and buttpad, machined steel trigger guard and floor plate, 7 3/4 lbs. Mfg. 1994-2004, reintroduced 2006-2011.

	$2,400	$2,050	$1,775	$1,500	$1,250	$1,050	$900	*$2,841*

MODEL 700 AWR (ALASKAN WILDERNESS RIFLE) – .300 Win. Mag., .300 Wby. Mag., .300 Rem. Ultra Mag. (new 1999), .338 Win. Mag., .338 Rem. Ultra Mag. (new 2000), .375 H&H, 7mm STW (new 1998), 7mm Rem. Mag., 7mm Rem. Ultra Mag. (new 2001), or .375 Rem. Ultra Mag. (new 2001) cal., black synthetic fiberglass with Kevlar stock, black stainless steel action with Teflon coating, approx. 7 lbs. Mfg. 1994-2004, reintroduced 2006-2007.

	$1,475	$1,250	$1,000	$875	$750	$650	$550	*$1,761*

Add $80 for left-hand action.

MODEL 700 AWR II (ALASKAN WILDERNESS RIFLE) various cals., black TriNyte full length stock with aluminum bedding block, adj. Model 40-X trigger, machined stainless steel trigger guard and floorplate, fluted barrel, 7 1/2 lbs. New 2008.

MSR $3,504	$2,925	$2,450	$2,050	$1,650	$1,450	$1,225	$1,050	

This model is also available in left hand action at no extra charge.

MODEL 700 NORTH AMERICAN CUSTOM – various cals., short or long action, blue steel or stainless steel fluted barrel, composite stock with full length aluminum bedding block, Model 40-X adj. trigger, machined steel trigger guard and floorplate, 7 1/2 lbs. New 2008.

MSR $2,919	$2,450	$2,100	$1,800	$1,500	$1,250	$1,050	$900	

Add $218 for stainless steel action and barrel.

This model is also available in left hand action at no extra charge.

MODEL 700C GRADE (CUSTOM SHOP) – various standard and Mag. cals., from custom shop, no engraving, deluxe checkered Monte Carlo C grade wood stock with rosewood forearm cap, high polish finish, BDL style trigger guard and hinged floorplate, 24 or 26 in. steel barrel, blued high polished action, 7 1/2 lbs. Mfg. 1964-1983, 2003-2004, reintroduced 2006.

MSR $3,212	$2,700	$2,225	$1,825	$1,575	$1,325	$1,100	$975	

MODEL 700D PEERLESS GRADE (CUSTOM SHOP) – scroll engraving, best wood. Mfg. 1962-83.

	$2,000	$1,625	$1,400	$1,175	$900	$800	$700	

MODEL 700F PREMIER GRADE (CUSTOM SHOP) – elaborate engraving, best wood. Mfg. 1962-83.

	$3,450	$2,850	$2,500	$2,200	$2,035	$1,870	$1,760	

MODEL 700 CUSTOM GRADE – special order only, grades differ in amount of engraving and type of walnut. Available as a custom order only through Remington. Values reflect 1991 information. The Remington Custom Shop should be contacted for a current price quotation and the availability of options.

Special order Model 700s mfg. between early '60s-1982 were designated C Grade, D Grade, or F Grade. Values will approximate Custom Grade Models I-III listed. In 1991, Remington discontinued Custom Grade Model designations.

GRADING - PPGS™	100%	98%	95%	90%	80%	70%	60%	LAST MSR

* ***Model 700 Custom Grade Model I*** – mfg. 1983-91.

	$1,400	$1,100	$900	$750	$585	$485	$415	*$1,314*

* ***Model 700 Custom Grade Model II*** – mfg. 1983-91.

	$2,300	$1,900	$1,500	$1,200	$925	$825	$650	*$2,335*

* ***Model 700 Custom Grade Model III*** – mfg. 1983-91.

	$2,900	$2,150	$1,750	$1,540	$1,265	$1,055	$875	*$3,650*

* ***Model 700 Custom Grade Model IV*** – mfg. 1983-91.

	$4,875	$4,100	$2,950	N/A	N/A	N/A	N/A	*$5,695*

MODEL 700 CUSTOM RIFLE – the Remington Custom Shop should be contacted directly (see Trademark Index) for current information regarding this model. New 1992.

MSR POR	N/A	$3,000	$2,500	$1,500	$1,000	$850	$725

Last published MSR was $3,999 (2007)

Beginning 1992, Remington stopped Custom Grade Model designations in favor of individualized quotations per work order.

RIFLES: BOLT ACTION, MODEL 40X & VARIATIONS

MODEL 40X SPORTER – .22 LR cal. only, sporterized version of the Model 40X Target Rifle, 5 shot mag., custom 700 stock, a special order only gun from the factory. Rare, less than 700 mfg. 1969-77, parts clean-up to 1980.

	$3,800	$3,000	$2,600	$2,200	$1,800	$1,575	$1,325

Add 10% if NIB.

This model was last listed in the 1977 Remington catalog - retail was $525.

MODEL 40X TARGET RIFLE (RANGEMASTER) – .22 LR cal., 28 in. heavy barrel, Redfield Olympic sights, scope bases, target stock, rubber butt, first production rifle with built in bedding device and adjustment screws, 12 3/4 lbs. Mfg. 1956-64.

	$850	$750	$650	$550	$450	$375	$325
No sights	$750	$650	$550	$475	$400	$350	$300

MODEL 40X STANDARD BARREL (RANGEMASTER) – similar to Model 40X Target Rifle, with lighter barrel, 10 3/4 lbs.

	$750	$650	$550	$500	$450	$400	$375
No sights	$650	$550	$450	$400	$375	$350	$325

MODEL 40X CENTERFIRE (RANGEMASTER) – similar to Model 40X Rim Fire, except in .222 Rem., .222 Rem. Mag., .30-06, or .308 Win. cal. Mfg. 1961-64.

	$550	$475	$380	$310	$250	$220	$190
No sights	$495	$450	$360	$295	$240	$200	$180

MODEL 40X INTERNATIONAL FREE RIFLE – .22 LR cal., top-of-the-line rimfire target rifle with heavy barrel, finished or unfinished laminated thumbhole stock with finger grooves, adj. palm rest, buttplate, and front sling swivel, choice of half-ounce set trigger, or 2 oz. target trigger, no sights, right or left hand stock, 15 lbs. 123 mfg. 1960-1973.

	$925	$850	$725	$600	$500	$425	$350

MODEL 40-XB RANGEMASTER RIMFIRE – .22 LR cal., bolt action single shot, 28 in. light or heavy barrel, no sights, target stock with guide rail, rubber buttplate. Mfg. 1964-1974.

	$775	$675	$575	$525	$420	$335	$275

MODEL 40-XB RANGEMASTER CENTERFIRE – available in 18 cals. between .22 BR Rem. and .300 Rem. Ultra Mag., custom made, 27 1/4 in. barrel (current production is stainless steel action and barrel), single shot or repeater (5 shot mag.), walnut stock, test fired, right or left-hand action, 10 1/2 -11 1/4 lbs. Mfg. by Custom Shop. New 1964.

MSR $2,561	$2,125	$1,800	$1,525	$1,250	$995	$750	$600

Add $152 for repeater model.
Add $302 for left-hand action.

An International Free Rifle was also offered - only 107 were mfg. with premiums being paid.

GRADING - PPGS™	100%	98%	95%	90%	80%	70%	60%	LAST MSR

MODEL 40-XBBR – similar to Model 40-XB Rangemaster Centerfire, except single shot only, 20 or 24 in. barrel.

	$1,300	$1,150	$975	$800	$650	$500	$450	

Add $125 for 2 oz. trigger.

MODEL 40-XB KS (KEVLAR STOCK) – 18 short action cals. between .22 BR Rem. - .300 Rem. Ultra Mag., 27 1/4 in. bright finished stainless steel barrel w/o sights, drilled and tapped, single shot or repeater, black finish Aramid fiber/Kevlar stock w/cheekpiece, right or left-hand action, no sights, 9 3/4 - 10 1/4 lbs. Mfg. by Custom Shop. Mfg. 1987-2005, reintroduced 2007.

MSR $2,863	$2,425	$2,050	$1,725	$1,500	$1,200	$975	$775	

Add $151 for repeater model.
Add $300 for 2 oz. trigger.

MODEL 40-XBBR KS – similar to Model 40-XB KS, except is bench rest model and single shot, 10 1/2 lbs. Mfg. by Custom Shop. New 1987.

MSR $3,920	$3,400	$2,975	$2,250	$1,825	$1,400	$1,100	$900	

MODEL 40-XC KS – .223 Rem. (mfg. 1995-99) or .308 Win. cal., 24 in. stainless steel barrel w/o sights, National Match Course 5 shot repeater rifle, adj. trigger pull, adj. comb, drilled and tapped, wood (disc. 1989) or fiberglass with Kevlar (standard 1990) stock, 11 lbs. Disc. 2004, reintroduced 2006.

MSR $3,067	$2,625	$2,225	$1,800	$1,450	$1,150	$925	$800	

Subtract approx. $120 for wood stock.

MODEL 40-XB TACTICAL – .308 Win. cal., repeater action with adj. 40-X trigger, aluminum bedding block, 27 1/4 in. button rifled fluted stainless barrel, Teflon coated metal, matte black H-S Precision synthetic tactical stock with vertical pistol grip, 10 1/4 lbs. New 2004.

MSR $2,992	$2,550	$2,200	$1,800	$1,450	$1,200	$925	$800	

MODEL 40-XB TDR/TIR (TARGET DEPLOYMENT/INTERDICTION RIFLE) – .308 Win. cal., super match stainless steel hand lapped barrel, BCS 1000 (TDR) or H-S PST25 tactical/vertical pistol grip stock (TIR), custom tuned match trigger, one-piece heavy duty steel trigger guard, heavy stainless recoil lug, integral mounting system with #8 screws, Picatinny rail, double pinned bolt handle, muzzle brake, MOA accuracy guaranteed to 600 yards, includes hard carrying case, mfg. by Custom Shop.

These models are POR.

MODEL 40-XB – .308 Win. cal., 27 1/4 in. stainless steel barrel, repeater action, Teflon coated synthetic H-S Precision stock, mfg. by the Custom Shop.

Remington does not publish consumer retail pricing for this police/law enforcement model. Secondary prices for base models w/o scopes and other options will be similar to the Model 40-XB Tactical listed above. Prices for rifles with scopes and other features will be determined by how much the individual options and accessories add to the base value.

MODEL 40-XS TACTICAL – .308 Win. or .338 Lapua cal., stainless steel action and barrel, adj. trigger, non-reflective black polymer coating, titanium bedded McMillan A5 adj. stock, AR type extractor, detachable mag., muzzle brake (.338 Lapua cal.), steel trigger guard and floorplate, mfg. by custom shop.

MSR $4,400	$3,675	$3,050	$2,500	$2,000	$1,650	$1,350	$1,175	

Add $550 for .338 Lapua cal.
Add $2,731 for Model 40-XS Tactical Weapons System with Harris bipod, Picatinny rail, Leupold Mark IV 3.5-10x40mm long range M1 scope, Turner AWS tactical sling, and military grade hard case.

MODEL 40-X TDR – .308 Win. cal., repeater action, 20 in. barrel, features various stock/receiver colors, including black, OD Green, tan and flat dark earth. Limited mfg. 2011 only.

	$2,775	$2,300	$1,875	$1,500	$1,200	$995	$825	*$3,170*

MODEL 40-X TIR – .308 Win. cal., repeater action, 20 in. barrel, stock/slash receiver colors include black/black, black/OD Green, or black/tan. Limited mfg. 2011 only.

	$3,600	$3,100	$2,400	$1,925	$1,500	$1,250	$1,000	*$4,087*

GRADING - PPGS™	100%	98%	95%	90%	80%	70%	60%	LAST MSR

MODEL 40-X TACTICAL MOD – .308 Win. cal., 20 in. barrel, barreled action colors include flat dark earth (FDE), OD Green, or black. Limited mfg. 2011 only.

	$4,300	$3,600	$3,000	$2,300	$1,875	$1,500	$1,325	*$4,850*

MODEL 40-XRBR KS RIMFIRE SINGLE SHOT – .22 LR cal., 24 in. heavy stainless barrel, no sights, adj. buttplate and palm stop, target wood (disc. 1989) or fiberglass with Kevlar (became standard 1990, and was available only in benchrest configuration) stock, Remington green stock became standard beginning 2007, approx. 9 3/4 lbs. Mfg. 1974-2004, reintroduced 2007-2011.

	$2,550	$2,200	$1,800	$1,450	$1,200	$925	$800	*$2,992*

Subtract 20% for wood stock.

MODEL 40-XR KS SPORTER – .22 LR or .22 WMR cal., Model 40-XR action, match chambered, custom sporter contoured 24 in. barrel, fiberglass with Kevlar stock, drilled and tapped receiver, w/o sights, special order. Mfg. 1994-99.

	$1,375	$1,100	$750	$625	$550	$500	$450	*$1,638*

MODEL 40-XB THUMBHOLE – available in 18 centerfire cals. between .22 BR Rem. - .300 Rem. Ultra Mag, 27 1/4 in. heavy stainless barrel w/o sights, single shot or repeater action, drilled and tapped, two-tone laminated satin finished thumbhole stock with rollover cheekpiece, 11 3/4 lbs. New 1999.

MSR $2,863	$2,425	$2,050	$1,725	$1,475	$1,200	$975	$775	

Add $151 for repeater action (new 2000).

MODEL 40-XR CUSTOM SPORTER – .22 LR or .22 WMR (new 2000) cal., repeater action, top-of-the-line sporter from the custom shop, individually made per customer's specifications. Disc. 2006, reintroduced 2008.

MSR $4,489	$3,850	$3,150	$2,550	$2,000	$1,625	$1,325	$1,100	

MODEL 40-XR CUSTOM SPORTER HIGH GRADES – .22 LR cal. only, single shot, available on special order from Remington's Custom Shop only, Grades I-IV (disc. 1991) increase by amount of engraving, quality of wood, and other special order options and features. Mfg. 1986-1991.

Values for Custom Grades listed reflect 1991 (the year of discontinuance) price information. The Remington Custom Shop should be contacted directly regarding current values and options.

* ***Model 40-XR Custom Sporter High Grade Model I*** – mfg. 1986-91.

	$1,100	$925	$795	$690	$580	$485	$415	*$1,314*

* ***Model 40-XR Custom Sporter High Grade Model II*** – mfg. 1986-91.

	$1,995	$1,675	$1,295	$1,150	$935	$815	$650	*$2,335*

* ***Model 40-XR Custom Sporter High Grade Model III*** – mfg. 1986-91.

	$2,900	$2,150	$1,750	$1,540	$1,265	$1,055	$875	*$3,650*

* ***Model 40-XR Custom Sporter High Grade Model IV*** – mfg. 1986-91.

	$4,875	$4,100	$2,950	$2,650	$2,350	$2,000	$1,750	*$5,695*

MODEL 40-SSA SPECIAL LIMITED EDITION – .308 Win. cal., 24 in. barrel, re-creation of the 1966 Model 700 M40 to the U.S.M.C. specification of 1966, wood stock, endorsed and authenticated by the U.S. Marine Corps Scout/Sniper Association. 1,000 mfg. 2006-2007.

	$2,000	$1,750	$1,500	N/A	N/A	N/A	N/A	

MODEL XM3 TACTICAL – .308 Win. cal., choice of steel or titanium action, match grade 18 1/2 in. stainless threaded barrel, Model 40-X action, custom bedded McMillan stock with adjustable LOP, Harris bipod, steel trigger guard, Nightfore NXS 3.5-15x50mm mil dot scope, guaranteed MOA accuracy to 1,000 yards, Hardigg Storm case with all tools and maintenance equipment, mfg. by Custom Shop. Mfg. 2009-2011.

	$9,250	$8,000	$7,000	$6,000	$5,000	$4,000	$3,500	*$10,281*

Add $2,128 for steel action.

SHOTGUNS: O/U

100% values listed for Model 3200s assume NIB condition - subtract 10%-15% if without box, warranty card, and original shipping container (with packing materials).

GRADING - PPGS™	100%	98%	95%	90%	80%	70%	60%	LAST MSR

MODEL 32 – 12 ga., double lock action, DT (early mfg.) or SST (standard 1938), separated barrels, 26, 28, or 30 in. barrels without rib, SR, or VR. Approx. 6,050 mfg. (ser. range approx. 0001-5,053) 1931-1947. There is a discrepancy as to when serialization started on this model.

	100%	98%	95%	90%	80%	70%	60%	LAST MSR
	N/A	$2,000	$1,800	$1,500	$1,000	$800	$700	

Add 10% for SST.
Add 10% for vent. or solid rib.
Add 20% for VR on 28 in. barrels.

Model 32 serialization is as follows: 1932 - 1-903; 1933 - 904-948; 1934 - 949-1,727; 1935 - 1,728-2,610; 1936 - 2,611-3,259; 1937 - 3,260 - 3,755; 1938 - 3,756-3,958; 1939 - 3,959-4,202; 1940 - 4,203-4,425; 1941 - 4,426-4,741; 1942 - 4,742 - 5,020; 1943 - 5,021-5,031; 1944 - 5,032-5,049; 1945 to 1947 - 5,050-5,053.

MODEL 32D TOURNAMENT

	100%	98%	95%	90%	80%	70%	60%	LAST MSR
	$3,750	$3,000	$2,500	$2,000	$1,750	$1,400	$1,175	

MODEL 32E EXPERT – less than 35 mfg.

	100%	98%	95%	90%	80%	70%	60%	LAST MSR
	$4,500	$3,950	$3,500	$2,975	$2,650	$2,200	$1,875	

MODEL 32F PREMIER

	100%	98%	95%	90%	80%	70%	60%	LAST MSR
	$6,500	$5,500	$5,000	$4,500	$3,520	$2,750	$2,300	

Note: Grades differ in quality, grade of wood, and amount of engraving.

MODEL 32 SKEET – similar to 32A, with 26 or 28 (more desirable) in. skeet bored barrels, SST. Mfg. 1932-42.

	100%	98%	95%	90%	80%	70%	60%	LAST MSR
	N/A	$2,000	$1,800	$1,500	$1,000	$800	$700	

Add 10% for VR.
Add 10%-15% for 28 in. barrels.

MODEL 32TC TARGET – similar to 32A, with 30 or 32 in. VR full choke barrels, trap style stock. Mfg. 1932-42.

	100%	98%	95%	90%	80%	70%	60%	LAST MSR
	$3,000	$2,300	$1,800	$1,700	$1,600	$1,475	$1,300	

Add 10% for 30 in. VR barrels.

MODEL 300 IDEAL – 12 ga. only, 3 in. chambers, boxlock action, features unique forearm latching system that Incorporates barrel selector switch, 26, 28, or 30 in. 8mm VR barrels with twin beads and Rem. chokes (3), engraved receiver sides, gold SST, high polish blue, checkered satin finished American walnut stock and forearm with English style solid recoil pad, 7 3/8 - 7 7/8 lbs. Mfg. 2000-2001.

	100%	98%	95%	90%	80%	70%	60%	LAST MSR
	$1,150	$995	$875	$800	$750	$700	$650	*$1,332*

MODEL 332 – 12 ga. only, 3 in. chambers, new modified boxlock action with underlock, designed by custom shop, low profile receiver with Model 32 type styling, engraved frame panels, 26, 28, or 30 in. 8mm VR light contour monobloc barrels with Remchokes, glass-bead blasted black oxide metal finish which resembles Model 32 rust bluing, high gloss finished checkered walnut stock and slim forearm with solid rubber recoil pad, mechanical SST, ejectors, 7 1/2 - 8 lbs. Mfg. in Ilion late 2001-2006.

	100%	98%	95%	90%	80%	70%	60%	LAST MSR
	$1,425	$1,075	$925	$775	$625	$550	$475	*$1,759*

* ***Model 332 Engraved*** – introduced 2004.

» **Model 332 D Grade (Peerless)**

	100%	98%	95%	90%	80%	70%	60%	LAST MSR
	$3,150	$2,200	$1,500	N/A	N/A	N/A	N/A	*$4,184*

» **Model 332 F Grade (Premier)**

	100%	98%	95%	90%	80%	70%	60%	LAST MSR
	$6,300	$4,550	$2,975	N/A	N/A	N/A	N/A	*$7,706*

» **Model 332 F Grade w/gold inlays (Premier Gold)** – top-of-the-line Custom Shop model.

	100%	98%	95%	90%	80%	70%	60%	LAST MSR
	$9,375	$5,300	$3,575	N/A	N/A	N/A	N/A	*$11,122*

GRADING - PPGS™	100%	98%	95%	90%	80%	70%	60%	LAST MSR

MODEL 396 SKEET/SPORTING CLAYS – 12 ga. only, satin finished boxlock action with engraved sideplates, 28 or 30 in. barrels with 10mm VR and Rem. chokes, select checkered walnut stock and target style forend, Sporting Clays Model has ported barrels, SST, ejectors, approx. 7 1/2 lbs. Mfg. 1996-98.

*** *Model 396 Skeet***

	$1,750	$1,475	$1,250	$1,075	$925	$800	$700	*$1,993*

*** *Model 396 Sporting Clays***

	$1,875	$1,575	$1,300	$1,100	$950	$825	$725	*$2,126*

MODEL 3200 FIELD – 12 ga., 26, 28, or 30 in. barrels, VR, various chokes, boxlock, auto ejectors, single selective trigger, checkered pistol grip stock, separated barrels. Mfg. 1973-77.

	$1,250	$1,050	$975	$900	$850	$800	$750

During 1998-2000, the custom shop once again manufactured a limited amount of the Model 3200 from existing parts (parts cleanup).

Model 3200s with shorter barrels (26 or 28 in.) and open choking are more desirable than 30 in. tubes bored F/M.

Model 3200 serialization is as follows: 1973 - 4,200-16,667; 1974 - 16,668-27,393; 1975 - 27,394-35,303; 1976 - 35,304-39,216; 1977 - 39,217-41,432; 1978 - 41,433-42,813; 1979 - 42,814-44,278; 1980 - 44,279-45,504; 1981 - 45,505-45,974; 1982 - 45,975-47,200; 1983 - 47,201-47,308.

MODEL 3200 MAGNUM – 12 ga., 3 in. chambers, 30 in. heavy wall barrels (steel shot compatible), less than 1,000 mfg. 1975-77.

	$1,695	$1,575	$1,475	$1,200	$1,050	$950	$850

MODEL 3200 SKEET – similar to 3200 Field, with 26 or 28 in. skeet bored barrels, skeet style stock. Mfg. 1973-80.

	$1,375	$1,125	$995	$850	$750	$650	$575

28 in. barrels will command a premium on this model.

This model was also mfg. in a 28 in. IM/F configuration with gold pigeon on bottom for live pigeon shooting. Since less than 300 were mfg., prices in the $2,700 range are being asked if NIB condition. This model generally had a trap style rib, but there have been some field ribs as well. Originally, it was called the "Competition Live Pigeon" and was mfg. with a competition receiver and trap grade style wood.

*** *Model 3200 Skeet Competition Four Ga. Set*** – includes 12, 20, 28 ga., or .410 bore, cased. Mfg. 1980-83.

	$5,500	$5,000	$4,600	$4,200	$4,000	$3,800	$3,500

Add 10%-15% for 28 in. barrels.

MODEL 3200 COMPETITION SKEET – similar to 3200 Skeet, with scroll engraved frame and trigger guard, select wood. Mfg. 1976-83.

	$1,700	$1,450	$1,250	$995	$950	$850	$750

Add 10%-15% for 28 in. VR barrels.

MODEL 3200 TRAP – similar to Model 3200 Field, with 30 or 32 in. barrels choked IM/F or F/F, stock and rib. Mfg. 1973-77.

	$1,375	$1,100	$950	$875	$800	$750	$700

30 in. barrels are more desirable than 32 in.

MODEL 3200 SPECIAL TRAP – similar to 3200 Trap, except fancy wood. Mfg. 1973-80.

	$1,450	$1,300	$1,200	$1,000	$875	$800	$750

MODEL 3200 COMPETITION TRAP – similar to 3200 Trap, with scroll engraving. Mfg. 1976-83.

	$1,950	$1,800	$1,675	$1,450	$1,200	$950	$875
Pigeon Grade	$2,450	$2,150	$1,850	$1,500	$1,250	$995	$900

The Pigeon Grade featured a gold pigeon on receiver bottom - approx. 250 mfg. 1979-83.

There was a special production of this model during 1991-92 which was limited to approx. 100 guns.

GRADING - PPGS™	100%	98%	95%	90%	80%	70%	60%	LAST MSR

MODEL 3200 PREMIER – 12 ga., sold through Remington's International Division, 500 mfg. 1975 only, patterned after "One of 1000" series, regular or Monte Carlo stock.

	$2,900	$2,500	$2,150	$1,800	$1,500	$1,200	$1,025	

Add 125% for engraving (only 116 mfg., engraving was done in Belgium).

MODEL 3200 "ONE OF 1000" – limited edition, elaborate engraving, fancy wood, supplied with hard case, made in both skeet and trap models. Mfg. 1,000 each model: 1973 (Trap) and 1974 (Skeet).

Trap (30 IM/F or F/F)	$2,150	$1,750	$1,475	$1,325	$1,200	$1,075	$875	
Skeet (26 or 28 in. SK/SK)	$1,925	$1,675	$1,475	$1,325	$1,200	$1,075	$875	

Add 10% for 28 in. barrels on the Skeet Model.

PEERLESS FIELD GRADE – 12 ga. only, 3 in. chambers, 26, 28, or 30 in. VR barrels with Rem. chokes, boxlock with engraved sideplates, SST, ejectors, high-gloss checkered walnut stock and forearm with vent. recoil pad, 3.28 milliseconds lock time, blue metal, approx. 7 1/2 lbs. Mfg. 1993-98.

	$1,000	$900	$850	$800	$750	$700	$650	*$1,172*

This model is an entirely new design not sharing any parts with either the Models 32 or 3200.

PREMIER FIELD MODEL – 12, 20, or 28 ga., 3 in. chambers, 26 or 28 in. 7mm VR barrels with Pro-Bore chokes, nickel finished receiver with game scene engraving, boxlock action, gold trigger, satin finished deluxe walnut stock with Schnabel forearm, solid recoil pad, SST, ejectors, includes hard case, 6 1/2 - 7 3/4 lbs. Previously imported 2006-2009 from Italy.

	$1,850	$1,575	$1,325	$1,125	$975	$850	$725	*$2,086*

Add $42 for 28 ga.

* ***Premier Model Competition STS*** – 12 ga., similar to Premier Model, 28, 30, or 32 (new 2008) in. barrels, titanium PVD finished receiver, 10mm target type VR, five extended choke tubes, high gloss wood finish, barrel selector on tang safety, approx. 7 1/2 lbs. Mfg. 2006-2009.

	$2,200	$1,925	$1,650	$1,450	$1,275	$1,050	$850	*$2,540*

Add $350 for adj. comb (new 2007).

* ***Premier Model Upland Special*** – similar to Premier Field Model, except has color case hardened receiver with gold game scene engraving and oil finished wood. Mfg. 2006-2010.

	$1,950	$1,650	$1,375	$1,125	$975	$850	$725	*$2,226*

Add $42 for 28 ga.

* ***Premier Ruffed Grouse*** – 20 ga., 3 in. chambers, 26 in. vent. rib blue barrels, features two 14 Kt. ruffed grouse gold inlays on each side of frame, oil finished straight grip walnut stock, 6 3/4 lbs. Mfg. 2006-2009.

	$2,050	$1,700	$1,400	$1,125	$975	$850	$725	*$2,380*

SHOTGUNS: SxS

The author wishes to express thanks to Charles Semmer for once again updating the following section on older Remington SxS Shotguns.

Because E. Remington & Sons shotguns are classified as antique, it may be helpful to consult the "NRA Antique Condition Standards" section in the front of this text to convert to the Percentage Grading System listed.

For Remington serialization, please refer to the Serialization section.

MODEL 1873 "HAMMER LIFTER" – 10 or 12 ga., also known as Whitmore Hammer Lifter, 28 or 30 in. decarbonized, twist, or damascus barrels, top "thumb lever" action activated by pushing upward to open, rib top marked "E. REMINGTON & SONS, ILION, N.Y.", patented "AUG. 8, 1871, APRIL 16, 1872", steel buttplate, pistol grip was optional, grades above 3 were made to order. Approx. 5,000 mfg. from 1873-78, starting with ser. no. 1.

100%	98%	95%	90%	80%	70%	60%	50%	40%	30%	20%	10%

* ***Model 1873 "Hammer Lifter" Grade 1*** – decarbonized steel barrels, no checkering or engraving.

$2,300	$2,000	$1,600	$1,300	$1,200	$900	$700	$575	$425	$300	$250	$225

* ***Model 1873 "Hammer Lifter" Grade 2*** – twist steel barrels, checkering, no engraving.

$3,200	$2,800	$2,500	$1,900	$1,600	$1,200	$1,075	$875	$750	$550	$350	$275

* ***Model 1873 "Hammer Lifter" Grade 3*** – twist or damascus steel barrels, checkering and engraving.

$4,800	$4,600	$4,000	$3,000	$1,900	$1,500	$1,400	$1,200	$875	$650	$450	$350

Add 20% to Grade 3 prices for higher grades (extra fine engraving).

MODEL 1875 AND 1876 "LIFTER" (WHITMORE LIFTER) – 10 or 12 ga., 28 or 30 in. decarbonized, twist, or damascus barrels, top "thumb lever" action activated by pushing upward to open, rib top marked "E. REMINGTON & SONS, ILION, N.Y.", patented "AUG. 8, 1871, APRIL 16, 1872", steel buttplate, pistol grip was optional, the Model 1875 started with ser. no. 1, and went to approx. 3,350, the Model 1876 started with ser. no. 3,350 and went to approx. 5,900. Approx. 5,900 Model 1875s and 1876s were mfg. 1875-1882.

* ***Model 1875/1876 "Lifter" Grade 1*** – decarbonized steel barrels, no checkering or engraving.

$2,300	$2,000	$1,600	$1,300	$1,200	$900	$700	$575	$425	$300	$250	$225

* ***Model 1875/1876 "Lifter" Grade 2*** – twist steel barrels, checkering, no engraving.

$2,600	$2,400	$1,900	$1,600	$1,300	$1,100	$900	$750	$650	$500	$350	$275

* ***Model 1875/1876 "Lifter" Grade 3*** – twist or damascus steel barrels, checkered and engraving.

$4,500	$4,200	$3,600	$3,200	$1,800	$1,400	$1,100	$1,000	$750	$600	$500	$400

* ***Model 1875/1876 "Lifter" Grade 4*** – twist or damascus steel barrels, checkered and extra fine engraving.

$5,500	$5,000	$4,000	$3,600	$3,100	$2,400	$1,500	$1,200	$1,000	$700	$600	$450

* ***Model 1875/1876 "Lifter" Grade 5*** – damascus steel barrels, checkered and superior engraving.

$6,000	$5,500	$4,500	$3,800	$3,200	$2,700	$1,800	$1,400	$1,150	$900	$700	$500

Add 50% to the few Model 1873s and 1875s that are rib marked "NEW YORK & LONDON" (approx. 12 known), and higher premiums if Birmingham proofed.

Add 100% for double rifles and combination guns in Models 1873, 1875, and 1876.

There were very few double rifles and combination guns made in Models 1873, 1875, and 1876 - they are very rare, and be aware of fake double rifles.

MODEL 1878 HAMMER (HEAVY DUCK GUN) – 10 ga., called the Heavy Duck Gun, 30-32 in., 9 3/4 and 10 lbs., "thumb-lever" action, thick bolsters, top extension rib, no flash fences, steel buttplate. Approx. 2,500 mfg. from 1878-82, starting with ser. no. 1.

* ***Model 1878 Hammer Grade 1*** – decarbonized steel barrels, no checkering, no engraving.

$2,300	$2,000	$1,600	$1,300	$1,200	$900	$700	$575	$425	$300	$250	$250

* ***Model 1878 Hammer Grade 2*** – twist steel barrels, checkered, no engraving.

$2,600	$2,400	$1,900	$1,600	$1,300	$1,100	$900	$750	$650	$500	$375	$300

* ***Model 1878 Hammer Grade 3*** – laminated steel barrels, checkered, engraved.

$4,500	$4,200	$3,800	$3,200	$1,800	$1,400	$1,100	$1,000	$750	$600	$500	$400

* ***Model 1878 Hammer Grade 4*** – damascus steel barrels, checkered, extra fine engraving.

$6,000	$5,300	$4,500	$3,800	$3,200	$2,700	$1,800	$1,400	$1,150	$900	$650	$600

MODEL 1879 SxS HAMMER – some 10 ga., usually 12 ga., top extension rib, no flash fences, steel buttplate, only Whitmore model with Deeley & Edge forend catch, but there are some with wedge pin forends (look for extension rib). Ser. nos. within the Model 1878.

Add 40% for this scarce variation to Model 1878 listed prices.

100%	98%	95%	90%	80%	70%	60%	50%	40%	30%	20%	10%

MODEL 1882 SxS HAMMER – (includes the unique Model 1883), 10 or 12 ga., 30 or 32 in. decarbonized, twist or damascus steel barrels, rib marked "E. REMINGTON & SONS, ILION, N.Y.", typical top lever, all grades have checkered pistol grip and forend with various designs according to grade. All contain Deeley & Edge forend catch. Approx. 16,000 Model 1882s, possibly 1,000 Model 1883s were mfg. from 1882-88. Started with ser. no. 1,000.

* ***Model 1882 SxS Hammer Grade 1*** – decarbonized steel barrels, no engraving, steel buttplate.

$1,900 $1,700 $1,400 $1,200 $1,100 $900 $700 $600 $450 $300 $250 $200

* ***Model 1882 SxS Hammer Grade 2*** – twist steel barrels, no engraving, steel buttplate.

$2,000 $1,800 $1,600 $1,300 $1,200 $1,000 $800 $675 $550 $375 $275 $225

* ***Model 1882 SxS Hammer Grade 3*** – laminated steel barrels, engraved, steel buttplate.

$2,500 $2,300 $1,800 $1,600 $1,300 $1,200 $900 $750 $650 $450 $350 $250

* ***Model 1882 SxS Hammer Grade 4*** – damascus steel barrels, engraved, steel buttplate.

$3,400 $3,100 $2,700 $2,100 $1,800 $1,400 $1,000 $850 $700 $550 $400 $300

* ***Model 1882 SxS Hammer Grade 5*** – fine damascus steel barrels, finely engraved, superior rubber or steel buttplate.

$5,000 $4,500 $3,800 $3,300 $3,000 $2,600 $1,700 $1,400 $1,100 $900 $650 $500

* ***Model 1882 SxS Hammer Grade 6*** – extra fine damascus steel barrels, fine scroll engraved, superior rubber buttplate.

$8,000 $7,200 $6,000 $5,000 $4,400 $3,800 $3,100 $2,700 $2,000 $1,300 $1,100 $900

Add 25% for optional auxiliary rifle barrel insert.

MODEL 1883 – identified by its hammer shape which is slightly different than the Model 1882, other than that, the guns are identical.

Add 50% to Model 1882 values for this model.

MODEL 1885/1887 SxS HAMMER – 10, 12, or 16 ga., different hammer style variation of the Model 1882, 28, 30, or 32 in. decarbonized, twist or damascus steel barrels, rib marked "E. REMINGTON & SONS, ILION, N.Y.", top lever, all grades are checkered pistol grip and forend with various designs according to grade, Deeley & Edge forend catch, rubber buttplate with ERS logo. Approx. 7,000 mfg. from 1885-88. Ser. nos. started at 16,700. Guns before ser. no. 20,200 are considered Model 1885s, ser. nos. after are considered Model 1887s.

* ***Model 1885/1887 SxS Hammer Grade 1*** – decarbonized steel barrels, no engraving.

$1,900 $1,700 $1,400 $1,200 $1,100 $900 $700 $600 $450 $300 $250 $200

* ***Model 1885/1887 SxS Hammer Grade 2*** – twist steel barrels, no engraving.

$2,000 $1,800 $1,600 $1,300 $1,200 $1,000 $800 $675 $550 $375 $300 $225

* ***Model 1885/1887 SxS Hammer Grade 3*** – damascus steel barrels, no engraving.

$2,300 $2,100 $1,800 $1,600 $1,300 $1,200 $900 $750 $650 $450 $350 $250

* ***Model 1885/1887 SxS Hammer Grade 4*** – damascus steel barrels, engraved.

$3,400 $3,100 $2,700 $2,100 $1,800 $1,400 $1,100 $900 $800 $675 $500 $400

* ***Model 1885/1887 SxS Hammer Grade 5*** – fine damascus steel barrels, finely engraved.

$4,500 $4,200 $3,800 $3,300 $3,000 $2,600 $2,000 $1,500 $1,000 $700 $600 $500

* ***Model 1885/1887 SxS Hammer Grade 6*** – extra fine damascus steel barrels, fine scroll engraved.

$8,000 $7,200 $6,000 $5,800 $5,000 $4,500 $3,500 $2,800 $2,000 $1,500 $1,200 $900

* ***Model 1885/1887 SxS Hammer Grade 7*** – superior damascus steel barrels, extra fine scroll engraved, game scene.

$12,000 $11,500 $10,000 $9,000 $8,500 $7,800 $6,600 $4,800 $4,200 $3,400 $2,000 $1,000

Add 25% for optional auxiliary rifle barrel insert.
Add 33% for 16 ga.

100%	98%	95%	90%	80%	70%	60%	50%	40%	30%	20%	10%

MODEL 1889 SxS HAMMER – 10, 12, or 16 ga., 26 (a few known to exis), 28, 30, or 32 in. decarbonized, twist, or damascus barrels, exposed "circular" hammers, rib marked "REMINGTON ARMS CO. ILION, N.Y. U.S.A.", top lever, all grades have checkered pistol grip and forend with various designs according to grade, Deeley & Edge forend catch. Grade number is stamped on water table left of the ser. no. Rubber buttplate with RACo logo. 134,200 mfg. 1889-1908. Ser. range from 30,000 to 100,000. After the year 1900, ser. nos. are in the 200,000 range.

Add 50%-100% for lightweight 12 gauge model, depending on condition.

* ***Model 1889 SxS Hammer Grade 1*** – decarbonized steel barrels, no engraving.

$2,000	$1,800	$1,600	$1,300	$1,200	$1,000	$800	$675	$550	$375	$275	$225

* ***Model 1889 SxS Hammer Grade 2*** – twist steel barrels, no engraving.

$2,300	$2,100	$1,800	$1,600	$1,300	$1,200	$900	$750	$650	$450	$350	$250

* ***Model 1889 SxS Hammer Grade 3*** – damascus steel barrels, no engraving.

$2,500	$2,300	$2,000	$1,800	$1,500	$1,300	$1,000	$850	$750	$550	$400	$300

* ***Model 1889 SxS Hammer Grade 4*** – damascus steel barrels, engraved.

$5,000	$4,500	$3,800	$3,200	$2,600	$2,200	$1,700	$1,400	$1,100	$900	$650	$500

* ***Model 1889 SxS Hammer Grade 5*** – damascus steel barrels, finely engraved.

$8,000	$7,500	$6,000	$5,000	$4,400	$3,800	$3,100	$2,700	$2,000	$1,300	$1,100	$900

* ***Model 1889 SxS Hammer Grade 6*** – extra fine damascus steel barrels, fine scroll engraved.

$11,000	$10,500	$9,800	$9,000	$8,500	$7,800	$6,500	$4,800	$4,200	$3,400	$2,200	$1,100

* ***Model 1889 SxS Hammer Grade 7*** – superior damascus steel barrels, extra fine scroll engraved, game scene.

$24,000	$21,000	$18,000	$12,000	$11,000	$9,500	$7,300	$6,000	$4,800	$3,850	$2,750	$1,600

Add 33% for 16 ga.

Grades 4 through 7 may command higher values. To date, there are only 24 examples known of these engraved Model 1889 hammer guns - nine Grade 4s, six Grade 5s, five Grade 6s, and four Grade 7s.

MODEL 1894 SxS HAMMERLESS – 10, 12, or 16 ga., 26 to 32 in. "Remington", "Ordnance", or damascus steel barrels, auto ejectors, boxlock, double triggers, checkered pistol grip or straight stock, Purdey forend snap. Grades A, B, F, and C have RACo hard rubber butt, Grade D, horn butt, Grade E, horn on heel and toe plates, push button forearm release. Grade is usually stamped on the water table. 16 and especially 10 ga., are considered scarce and will command a higher value. 41,194 mfg. between 1894-1910 in the 100,000 block serial range.

* ***Model 1894 SxS Hammerless Grade AE*** – no engraving.

$2,000	$1,800	$1,600	$1,300	$1,200	$1,000	$800	$675	$550	$400	$300	$250

* ***Model 1894 SxS Hammerless Grade BE*** – scroll and line engraving.

$4,000	$3,700	$3,200	$2,900	$2,600	$2,200	$1,700	$1,200	$900	$600	$500	$375

* ***Model 1894 SxS Hammerless Grade FE Trap*** – scroll and line engraving.

$4,000	$3,700	$3,200	$2,900	$2,600	$2,200	$1,700	$1,200	$900	$600	$500	$375

* ***Model 1894 SxS Hammerless Grade CE*** – extra scroll engraving, silver name plate.

$6,000	$5,700	$5,200	$4,800	$4,300	$3,800	$3,000	$2,400	$1,800	$1,100	$700	$600

* ***Model 1894 SxS Hammerless Grade DE*** – fine scroll and game engraving, silver name plate.

$13,000	$12,000	$10,000	$9,500	$8,000	$7,500	$6,000	$4,800	$3,600	$2,200	$1,800	$1,100

* ***Model 1894 SxS Hammerless Grade EE*** – finest quality scroll, bird and game engraving, gold name plate.

$25,000	$23,000	$20,000	$16,000	$13,000	$10,000	$8,400	$7,800	$6,000	$3,850	$2,750	$2,300

Add 33% for 10 or 16 ga.

100%	98%	95%	90%	80%	70%	60%	50%	40%	30%	20%	10%

Add 15% to CE and BE guns that are extractor only, which are called B and C grade.
Add 25% for "Ordnance" barrels.

A few Remington Model 1894 SPECIAL grade guns were produced; they are so rare, it is not practical to attempt a value.

MODEL 1900 SxS HAMMERLESS – 12 or 16 ga., 28 or 30 in. "Remington" or damascus steel barrels, lower priced gun to meet market competition, quality a cut below the Model 1894, but mechanically the same, snap forearm. No engraving was offered on this model. 98,475 mfg. between 1900-10 in the 300,000 block serial range.

* ***Model 1900 SxS Hammerless Grade K and KD*** – Remington or Damascus steel barrels, non-ejector.

$1,800	$1,600	$1,400	$1,200	$1,050	$900	$750	$650	$500	$375	$250	$200

* ***Model 1900 SxS Hammerless Grade KE and KED*** – Remington or damascus steel barrels, ejectors.

$2,000	$1,800	$1,600	$1,300	$1,200	$1,000	$875	$750	$650	$500	$350	$250

PARKER AHE – while advertised, the Remington re-issue of the original Parker AHE Model was never mfg. due to product liability considerations. Older Remington manufactured Parkers may be found in the Parker section.

PARKER AAHE – please refer to the Parker Brothers section.

GRADING - PPGS™	100%	98%	95%	90%	80%	70%	60%	LAST MSR

PREMIER – 12, 20, 28 ga. or .410 bore, 2 3/4 (28 ga.) or 3 in. chambers, Anson & Deeley boxlock action, ejectors, gold SST, 27 (28 ga. or .410 bore) or 28 in. polished blue barrels with choke tubes, single bead sight, case colored receiver, oil finished walnut stock, semi beavertail forend, Remington "R" logo in gold on bottom of frame, gold woodcock inlaid on each side of receiver, three different frame sizes, 6 1/2 - 7 1/2 lbs. Limited mfg. 2007, imported from Spain.

	100%	98%	95%	90%	80%	70%	60%	LAST MSR
	$1,850	$1,575	$1,325	$1,125	$975	$850	$725	*$2,086*

Subtract $56 for 12 or 20 ga.

* ***Premier Upland Special*** – 28 ga. or .410 bore, features 27 in. polished blue barrels with RemChokes, similar to Premier, except has straight grip English style stock, 6 1/2 lbs. Limited mfg. 2007.

	100%	98%	95%	90%	80%	70%	60%	LAST MSR
	$1,850	$1,575	$1,325	$1,125	$975	$850	$725	*$2,086*

SHOTGUNS: SEMI-AUTO, DISC.

REMINGTON AUTOLOADING SHOTGUN (PRE-MODEL 11) – 12 ga. only, 28 in. barrel, Full choke, Modified choke or Cylinder bore, chambered for cartridge up to 2 3/4 in., walnut stock with plain rounded pistol grip. Approx. 92,000 mfg.

	100%	98%	95%	90%	80%	70%	60%
	$1,000	$900	$800	$700	$600	$500	$450

Also manufactured in: Special Grade; Trap Grade; Tournament Grade; Expert Grade; Premier Grade & Riot Gun. These higher grades command pricing premiums similar to Model 11 special grades.

MODEL 11A AUTOLOADER 5-SHOT – 12, 16 and 20 ga., walnut, American walnut (new 1925), or A Grade American walnut checkered (new 1940) stock. Number of Model 11's produced (to include the Sportsman) 837,328.

	100%	98%	95%	90%	80%	70%	60%
Plain barrel	$800	$700	$600	$500	$400	$300	$225
Solid rib	$900	$800	$700	$600	$500	$400	$300
Vent. rib	$1,000	$900	$800	$700	$550	$450	$350

Add 35% for barrels marked "Long Range" - beware of fakes.

This model was mfg. under patent agreement with John Browning.

MODEL 11B SPECIAL – select figured walnut hand checkered stock and forearm.

	100%	98%	95%	90%	80%	70%	60%
Plain barrel	$1,500	$1,300	$1,100	$900	$700	$500	$400

Solid and vent. rib models will bring additional premiums.

GRADING - PPGS™	100%	98%	95%	90%	80%	70%	60%	LAST MSR

MODEL 11C TRAP GRADE – select figured walnut hand checkered straight grip stock and forearm.

Plain barrel	$1,700	$1,500	$1,300	$1,100	$850	$600	$500	

Solid and vent. rib models will bring additional premiums.

MODEL 11D TOURNAMENT – fine English or American Walnut stock and forearm with fine hand checkering, scroll engraving left and right side of receiver and barrel.

	$2,500	$2,300	$2,000	$1,700	$1,200	$1,000	$800	

Solid and vent. rib models will bring additional premiums.

MODEL 11E EXPERT – best English or American Walnut hand checkered stock and forearm, scroll engraving on receiver and barrel with game panel scenes.

	$5,000	$4,500	$4,000	$3,500	$2,750	$2,000	$1,800	

Solid and vent. rib models will bring additional premiums.

MODEL 11F PREMIER – finest Circassian or figured American walnut elaborate hand checkered stock and forearm, extensive engraving of game scenes and fine scroll on receiver and barrel.

	$8,000	$7,000	$6,000	$5,000	$4,000	$3,000	$2,500	

Solid and vent. rib models will bring additional premiums.

Note: Grades differ in quality, grade of wood, and amount of engraving.

MODEL 11R – 12 ga. only, plain walnut stock.

	$1,200	$1,000	$800	$700	$500	$400	$275	

SPORTSMAN MODEL – 12, 16, or 20 ga., 26 (3 shot only) in. barrel, skeet choke, beavertail forend, manufactured in Field, Riot, and Skeet configurations. Mfg. 1931-1949.

Plain barrel	$500	$450	$400	$350	$300	$225	$200	
Solid rib	$600	$550	$500	$450	$375	$300	$250	
Vent. rib	$1,000	$900	$800	$700	$550	$450	$350	

Add a premium for Riot and Skeet configurations.

MODEL 48 MOHAWK (SPORTSMAN) – 12, 16, or 20 ga., 26, 28, or 32 in. barrels, 3 shot, mechanical (solid breech) ejection system, various chokes, rounded receiver, checkered pistol grip stock with cap. Approx. 275,000 mfg., 1949-60.

Plain barrel	$300	$225	$200	$185	$175	$165	$140	
VR barrel	$325	$275	$250	$200	$175	$165	$140	

MODEL 48B SELECT

	$420	$360	$310	$290	$245	$220	$195	

MODEL 48D TOURNAMENT

	$1,500	$1,300	$1,100	$950	$825	$700	$650	

MODEL 48F PREMIER

	$5,750	$5,250	$4,750	$3,500	$3,000	$2,500	$2,000	

MODEL 48A RIOT GUN – 12 ga. only, 20 in. plain barrel.

	$275	$220	$195	$165	$150	$140	$110	

MODEL 48SA SKEET – 26 in. barrel, skeet bore, ivory bead. Mfg. 1949-60.

Plain barrel	$305	$275	$255	$230	$210	$195	$165	
With VR barrel	$395	$350	$300	$260	$230	$210	$195	

MODEL 48SC SKEET – "C" suffix designates C-grade wood.

	$495	$450	$375	$325	$285	$250	$225	

MODEL 48SD TOURNAMENT – custom shop engraved.

	$1,500	$1,300	$1,100	$950	$825	$700	$650	

MODEL 48SF PREMIER – custom shop engraved.

	$5,750	$5,250	$4,750	$3,500	$3,000	$2,500	$2,000	

GRADING - PPGS™	100%	98%	95%	90%	80%	70%	60%	LAST MSR

MODEL 11-48 – 12, 16, 20, 28 (introduced 1952) ga., or .410 (introduced 1954) bore, recoil operated action, walnut stock. Approx. 429,000 mfg., 1949-1968.

	100%	98%	95%	90%	80%	70%	60%	LAST MSR
Plain barrel (12 or 16 ga.)	$300	$250	$225	$195	$175	$165	$140	
Plain barrel (20 ga.)	$350	$300	$265	$230	$200	$175	$150	
Plain barrel (28 ga.)	$675	$600	$525	$450	$375	$300	$250	
Plain barrel (.410 bore)	$725	$650	$550	$450	$375	$300	$250	

Add 10%-20% for VR barrel, depending on original condition.

MODEL 58ADL "SPORTSMAN - 58" – 12, 16, or 20 ga., 26, 28, or 30 in. barrel, gas operation, various chokes, 3 shot, checkered pistol grip stock, scroll game scene engraved. Approx. 271,000 mfg., 1956-63.

	100%	98%	95%	90%	80%	70%	60%	LAST MSR
Plain barrel	$275	$250	$220	$195	$140	$120	$110	
VR barrel	$360	$305	$275	$250	$220	$165	$140	

Add 5% for Magnum in 12 ga.

MODEL 58 X-SERIES (SUNGRAIN) – similar to Model 58ADL semi-auto, except has blonde stock, available in Field (special order only), Skeet, or Trap configuration.

	100%	98%	95%	90%	80%	70%	60%	LAST MSR
	$395	$350	$300	$250	$175	$160	$140	

MODEL 58BDL – similar to 58ADL, with select wood.

	100%	98%	95%	90%	80%	70%	60%	LAST MSR
Plain barrel	$325	$275	$250	$225	$210	$195	$165	
VR barrel	$385	$340	$300	$275	$250	$200	$175	

MODEL 58SA SKEET GUN – similar to 58ADL, with 26 in. skeet bore VR barrel, skeet stock.

	100%	98%	95%	90%	80%	70%	60%	LAST MSR
	$450	$400	$350	$300	$275	$250	$200	

MODEL 58SC SKEET – "C" suffix designates C-grade wood.

	100%	98%	95%	90%	80%	70%	60%	LAST MSR
	$550	$500	$440	$415	$385	$330	$305	

MODEL 58D TOURNAMENT – custom shop engraved.

	100%	98%	95%	90%	80%	70%	60%	LAST MSR
	$1,500	$1,300	$1,100	$950	$825	$700	$650	

MODEL 58F PREMIER – custom shop engraved.

	100%	98%	95%	90%	80%	70%	60%	LAST MSR
	$5,750	$5,250	$4,750	$3,500	$3,000	$2,500	$2,000	

Note: Models differ in grade of wood, amount of engraving, and gold inlays.

MODEL 878A "AUTOMASTER" – 12 ga. gas operated semi-auto, 26, 28, or 30 in. barrels, action similar to Model 58. Approx. 62,000 mfg., 1959-1962.

	100%	98%	95%	90%	80%	70%	60%	LAST MSR
	$265	$235	$200	$185	$170	$160	$150	

Add 10% for VR.

Barrels on this model are interchangeable with those on the Model 58.

SHOTGUNS: SEMI-AUTO, CURRENT/RECENT PRODUCTION

MODEL SP-10 – 10 ga., 3 1/2 in. chamber, semi-auto stainless steel gas system operation, lighter recoil than most 12 ga. mags., 30 in. barrel with 3/8 in. VR and Rem chokes (2), checkered stock and forearm with low gloss satin finish, matte metal finish, crossbolt safety, R3 recoil pad became standard 2004, supplied with camo sling, approx. 11 lbs. Mfg. 1989-2010.

	100%	98%	95%	90%	80%	70%	60%	LAST MSR
	$1,475	$1,200	$1,050	$925	$825	$725	$625	*$1,845*

The first 5,000 SP-10s were assigned special serialization (LE89 prefix) - no premiums exist at this time, however.

This model is NOT a re-designed Ithaca Mag-10 and the parts are NOT interchangeable. The SP-10 is a newer design.

* ***Model SP-10 Magnum Camo*** – 10 ga., 23 (Turkey Model, mfg. 1999-2000, reintroduced 2007 with Williams Firesights), or 26 in. VR barrel, choice of Mossy Oak (disc. 1996), full coverage Mossy Oak Break-Up (mfg. 1997-2004), full coverage Mossy Oak

GRADING - PPGS™	100%	98%	95%	90%	80%	70%	60%	LAST MSR

Obsession or Duck Blind (new 2007), regular or thumbhole (Turkey only) stock, R3 recoil pad (became standard 2005), or Bottomland (mfg. 1994-96) camo finish. Mfg. 1993-2010.

	$1,550	$1,200	$1,000	$900	$800	$700	$625	*$2,012*

Add $14 for Magnum Waterfowl with 100% Mossy Oak Duck Blind camo and special waterfowl choke tubes (new 2007).

Add $125 for Turkey Magnum with 100% Mossy Oak Obsession camo and thumbhole stock (new 2007).

Subtract 10% for disc. camo finishes.

* ***Model SP-10 Magnum Synthetic*** – 10 ga., features lightweight black synthetic stock and forearm, matte non-reflective metal finish, 26 in. barrel only, 10 3/4 lbs. Mfg. 2000-2004.

	$995	$875	$785	$675	$575	$550	$475	*$1,331*

* ***Model SP-10 Turkey Camo NWTF 25th Anniversary*** – 12 ga., limited mfg. to commemorate the 25th Anniversary of the NWTF during 1998, Truglo fiberoptic sights. Mfg. 1998 only.

	$1,050	$925	$775	N/A	N/A	N/A	N/A	*$1,225*

* ***Model SP-10 Turkey Combo*** – includes choice of either 26 or 30 in. VR regular barrel and extra 22 in. deer barrel with rifle sights. Mfg. 1991-94.

	$1,295	$1,125	$925	$775	$700	$650	$625	*$1,132*

MODEL 11-96 EURO LIGHTWEIGHT – 12 ga. only, steel receiver with distinctive slight hump over chamber, 26 or 28 in. 6mm VR Rem Choke barrel, checkered walnut stock and forearm, receiver panel engraving, approx. 7 lbs. Mfg. 1996 only.

	$715	$615	$550	$475	$395	$335	$295	*$852*

MODEL 105 CTi – 12 ga. only, 3 in. chamber, skeletonized titanium receiver with carbon fiber shell, gas operated, 4 shot mag., TriNyte receiver coating, bottom feed and ejection, overbored 26 or 28 in. carbon fiber VR barrel with three ProBore chokes, rotary bolt lock-up, checkered walnut stock with bolt speed rate reducer (results in up to 50% recoil energy reduction), target grade roller sear trigger, R3 recoil pad, utilizing oil filled cylinder in stock, includes hardshell case, 7 lbs. Mfg. 2006-2008.

	$1,225	$1,000	$875	$775	$675	$600	$525	*$1,548*

MODEL 105 CTi-II – 12 ga. only, 26 or 28 in. barrel, improved variation of the original Model 105 CTi, with changes in the gas valve, bolt release/head, and other engineering improvements, including an adj. LOP kit. Limited mfg. 2009.

	$1,225	$1,000	$875	$775	$675	$600	$525	*$1,559*

VERSA-MAX – 12 ga., 3 1/2 in. chamber, self-cleaning Versaport gas system regulates cycling pressure based on shell length (2 3/4-3 1/2 in.), 26 or 28 in. VR barrel with 4 (Waterfowl) or 5 Pro Bore flush (synthetic only) or extended choke tubes, overmolded black or camo synthetic stock/forearm with grey or black checkered insert panels, Soft-Touch matte black, Mossy Oak Duck Blind or Realtree AP HD 100% camo finish, adj. stock with SuperCell recoil pad, 7 3/4 lbs. New late 2010.

MSR $1,399	$1,195	$1,050	$900	$775	$650	$525	$425	

Add $200 for Waterfowl model with 100% camo finish.

Remington has found that a limited number of its Versa Max shotguns may have hammers out of specification. This condition may result in inconsistent firearm performance. Inconsistent firearm performance may result in property damage, serious personal injury or death.

If you have a Remington Versa Max shotgun, immediately discontinue use of the shotgun and contact Remington at 1-800-243-9700, Prompt #4. Remington will arrange for the return shipment of your Versa Max shotgun and upon receipt will immediately inspect and retrofit your Versa Max shotgun and return it to you at no cost to you. All Versa Max shotguns that have the hammer enhancement will contain a "V" stamped that can be seen by looking in the ejection port or through the carrier.

GRADING - PPGS™	100%	98%	95%	90%	80%	70%	60%	LAST MSR

VERSA MAX TACTICAL - 12 ga., 3 1/2 in. chamber, 22 in. VR barrel with HiViz sights, extended mag tube, includes Picatinny rail, black synthetic stock with overmolded grips, SuperCell recoil pad, 7 3/4 lbs. New 2012.

MSR $1,399	$1,195	$1,050	$900	$775	$650	$525	$425	

Shotguns: Semi-Auto, Model 1100 & Variations

3 in. shells (12 or 20 ga.) may be shot in Magnum receivers only, regardless of what the barrel markings may indicate (the ejection port is larger in these Magnum models with "M" suffix serialization).

Model 1100 serial numbers on the receiver started with the number 1001. All but the early guns also have a prefix letter. All Model 1100 Remington shotguns were serial numbered in blocks of numbers. Each serial number has a suffix and the following indicates the meaning: V = 12 ga. standard, M = 12 ga. Mag., W = 16 ga., X = 20 ga., N = 20 ga. Mag., K = 20 ga. lightweight, U = 20 ga. lightweight Mag., J = 28 ga., H = .410 bore.

Add $877 for custom shop Etchen stock and forearm installed on new Model 1100s (mfg. 2000-circa 2010).

SPORTSMAN 12 AUTO - 12 ga. only, 2 3/4 in. chamber, 28 or 30 in. VR barrel, similar to Model 1100 action, hardwood stock and forearm, 7 3/4 lbs. Mfg. 1985-86 only.

$300	$260	$220	$195	$170	$160	$150	*$405*

Add 10% for Rem. chokes (mfg. 1986 only).

MODEL 1100 FIELD - 12 (disc. 1987), 16 (mfg. 1964-1980), or 20 (new 1964) ga., 26, 28, or 30 in. barrels, various chokes, gas operated, checkered pistol grip stock and forearm, "cut" checkering and receiver scroll markings became standard in 1979, Rem Chokes became standard 1987 (introduced 1986 as $40 option), VRs became standard in 1985 on this model, 20 ga. lightweight frame became standard 1972, prices assume VR and Rem Chokes. Mfg. 1963-1988.

$350	$295	$265	$225	$200	$185	$170	*$545*

Add 25% for 16 ga.
Add 75%-100% for left hand ejection port in 20 ga. only, if in 95%+ original condition.
Subtract $40 if without VR.
Subtract $45 if without Rem. chokes.

The Model 1100 20 ga. Standard (12 ga. frame) was disc. in 1969 (mahogany wood stock and forearm - advertised as a Lightweight), except for Skeet A & B grades. This model was produced only in a Lightweight or Mag. 20 (3 in. chamber), 28 ga., or .410 bore, before the release of the Model 11-87.

The Model 1100 left-hand, with the ejection port on the left side of the receiver was introduced in 1972 in both 20 and 12 ga., with either VR or plain barrels. The 20 ga. left-hand model was disc. in 1977.

MODEL 1100 SPECIAL FIELD - 12, 20 ga., or .410 (limited mfg., disc.) bore, 21 (disc. 1993) or 23 (new 1994) in. VR barrel, various chokes, gas operated, checkered straight grip stock, VR standard, high gloss wood finish (1991 only) or satin wood finish. Rem. chokes became standard in 1987. Mfg. 1983-1999.

$510	$415	$325	$265	$230	$210	$180	*$665*

Subtract 10% if without Rem. chokes.
Add 15%-20% for .410 bore.

Two hundred .410 bore models were mfg. for National Shooting Supplies in Houston, TX.

MODEL 1100 SAM WALTON SPECIAL EDITION - 12 or 20 ga., manufactured for Wal-Mart stores at a lower price point with standard features and wood, 5,000 mfg. in both 12 and 20 ga., serialization was almost matching with the exception of the 12 or 20 after the prefix being different (an example being SMW12134 and SMW201234). Mfg. late 2001 only.

$395	$350	$300	$260	$230	$200	$175

MODEL 1100 CLASSIC FIELD - 12 (new 2006), 16, 20 (new 2004), 28 (new 2006) ga. or .410 bore (new 2006), 2 3/4 in. chamber, 25 (.410 bore or 28 ga. only), 26 or 28 in. VR light contoured barrel with Rem Choke, non-embellished receiver with blue finish, satin (disc.) or gloss finished American walnut stock and forearm, 7 lbs. Mfg. 2003-2006.

$675	$550	$475	$400	$350	$300	$275	*$834*

Add $34 for 28 ga. or .410 bore.

GRADING - PPGS™	100%	98%	95%	90%	80%	70%	60%	LAST MSR

MODEL 1100 "1 OF 3,000" FIELD – 12 ga. only, limited edition, serial numbered 1-3,000, deluxe walnut, gold washed etched hunting scenes on receiver, 28 in. modified VR barrel. Mfg. 1980.

	$1,100	$900	$600	$500	$425	$350	$300	

MODEL 1100 SMALL GAUGE – 28 ga. or .410 bore, 25 in. barrel, scaled down receiver, skeet and field fixed choke, VR standard. Mfg. 1969-94.

	$550	$475	$425	$365	$300	$275	$250	*$647*

MODEL 1100 LW-20 (LIGHTWEIGHT) – 20 ga. only, 2 3/4 in. chamber, lightweight scaled down receiver, mag. tube, and barrel, similar to 28 ga./.410 bore frame, standard length ejection port, with mahogany stock, 26 or 28 in. barrel, 6 1/2 lbs. Mfg. 1970-76.

	$510	$415	$325	$265	$230	$210	$180	

Subtract 10% if w/o VR.

Remington introduced a lightweight 20 ga. Model 1100 in 1961, with standard frame, mahogany stock and forearm. This model was disc. in Dec., 1969.

MODEL 1100 LT-20 – 20 ga. only, variation of Model 1100 LW-20, 2 3/4 in. chamber, has opened ejection port and barrel extension similar to 12 ga. (long), lightened receiver, 23, 26 (disc., gloss wood only) or 28 (disc., satin wood only) in. barrel, VR became standard 1985, hi-gloss (disc.) or satin finish walnut stock and forearm, 6 1/2 lbs. Mfg. 1977-95.

	$600	$450	$325	$265	$230	$210	$180	*$665*

Subtract 10% if without VR.
Subtract $34 for gloss walnut.

Rolled scroll receiver engraving became standard on 20 ga. in 1998.

MODEL 1100 LT-20 YOUTH – 20 ga. only, similar to Model 1100 Lightweight, except stock is 1 in. shorter and 21 in. barrel only. Disc. 1998.

	$500	$415	$325	$265	$230	$210	$180	*$659*

* ***Model 1100 LT-20 Youth Camo NWTG*** – 20 ga. only, features 100% Mossy Oak Break-up camo finish, Truglo fiberoptic sights, 6 1/2 lbs. Mfg. 1998 only.

	$495	$415	$325	$265	$230	$210	$180	*$652*

MODEL 1100 LT-20 MAG. (LIGHTWEIGHT MAGNUM) – chambered for 3 in. 20 ga. Mag., 20 (disc.), 26 (disc.), or 28 in. barrel, Rem Chokes became standard 1987. Introduced 1977, disc. 1998.

	$500	$415	$325	$265	$230	$210	$180	*$659*

Subtract 10% if without VR.

MODEL 1100 MAGNUM DUCK GUN – similar to 1100, in 12 (disc. 1987) or 20 ga., 3 in. chamber, recoil pad, VR became standard 1984, Rem. chokes became standard 1987. Mfg. 1963-88.

	$400	$325	$280	$260	$220	$200	$180	*$533*

Add $80 for left-hand model (disc. 1986).
Subtract $40 if without VR.
Subtract $45 if without Rem. chokes.

* ***Model 1100 Magnum Duck Gun Special Purpose (SP)*** – 12 ga. only, low luster finish on stock and forearm, sand blasted metal parts. Mfg. 1985-86 only.

	$395	$350	$295	$265	$235	$200	$180	*$550*

Add $40 for Rem. chokes

MODEL 1100 DEER GUN – 12 (disc. 1987) or 20 ga., 20 (disc.), 21 in. (20 ga. only) or 22 (disc.) in. imp. cyl. barrel with rifle sights. Disc. 1996.

	$435	$345	$270	$225	$200	$185	$165	*$584*

Add $80 for left-hand model (disc. 1986).
Add $117 for 21 in. fully rifled cantilever deer barrel.

* ***Model 1100 Deer Gun Special Purpose (SP)*** – similar to Model 1100 Deer Gun, except has low luster finish on stock and forearm, sandblasted metal parts. Mfg. 1986 only.

	$335	$295	$275	$255	$220	$200	$180	*$495*

GRADING - PPGS™	100%	98%	95%	90%	80%	70%	60%	LAST MSR

MODEL 1100 SYNTHETIC (INCLUDING LT-20) – 12, 16 (new 2003), or 20 (LT-20) ga., 2 3/4 in. chamber, 26 (20 ga. only) or 28 (12 ga. only) in. VR barrel with Rem. choke, checkered black synthetic stock and forearm, matte metal finish, 7-7 1/2 lbs. Mfg. 1996-2004.

	$430	$340	$275	$225	$195	$165	$140	*$549*

Add $157-$296 (factory MSR) per extra barrel (2 3/4 in. chamber only), depending on configuration.

* ***Model 1100 Synthetic Deer*** – 12 or 20 (LT-20) ga., 21 in. fully rifled barrel with choice of cantilever scope mount (12 ga. only, became standard 2004 in 12 ga.) or rifle sight (20 ga. only), 7 or 7 1/2 lbs. New 1997-2004.

	$495	$375	$300	$240	$210	$180	$155	*$629*

Subtract approx. $50 for rifle sights.

* ***Model 1100 LT-20 Synthetic Youth*** – features 21 in. VR barrel, matte black synthetic stock and forearm. Mfg. 1999-2004.

	$430	$340	$275	$225	$195	$165	$140	*$549*

Add $63 for Youth Turkey Camo - includes 3 in. chamber and 100% Realtree Advantage or Skyline Excel (new 2003) camo on stock and forearm.

MODEL 1100 TACTICAL – 12 ga. only, 3 in. chamber, choice of Speedfeed IV pistol grip or black synthetic stock and forearm, 6 (Speedfeed IV) or 8 (22 in. barrel only) shot mag., 18 (Speedfeed IV with fixed IC choke) or 22 (synthetic with Rem Chokes and HiViz sights) in. VR barrel, OD Green metal finish, R3 recoil pad, approx. 7 1/2 lbs. Disc. 2006.

	$640	$575	$515	$450	$400	$350	$295	*$759*

Add $40 for 22 in. barrel.

MODEL 1100 TAC-2/TAC-4 – 12 ga., 2 3/4 in. chamber, 18 (bead sight) or 22 in. VR barrel, Hi-Viz sights, bead blasted black oxide metal finish, black synthetic stock with (Tac-2 with SFIV stock) or w/o (Tac-4) pistol grip, fixed (18 in.) or Rem Chokes, 6 or 8 shot mag., sling swivels, R3 recoil pad, 7 1/2 - 7 3/4 lbs. New 2007.

MSR $943	$795	$675	$575	$500	$450	$400	$350	

Add $72 for Tac-4 with 4 shot mag. and 22 in. VR barrel.

MODEL 1100 G3 – 12 or 20 ga., 3 in. chamber, steel receiver with titanium PVD coating, all internal operating parts feature a nickel/Teflon coating, pressure compensated overbored 26 or 28 in. VR barrel with five ProBore chokes, two-piece RealWood semi-fancy carbon fiber laminated wood stock and forearm with high gloss finish and machine cut checkering, "R" insignia on pistol grip cap, R3 recoil pad, satin finished receiver, includes high grade travel case, 6 3/4 - 7 5/8 lbs. Mfg. 2006-2008.

	$1,045	$915	$775	$675	$575	$500	$450	*$1,239*

Add $90 for left-hand action (new 2008).

MODEL 1100 COMPETITION – 12 ga. only, 2 3/4 in. chamber with .735 bore diameter, 30 in. barrel with 10mm target style rib and five ProBore choke tubes, receiver and internal parts are nickel/Teflon finished, high gloss semi-fancy adj. or non-adj. American walnut (disc. 2011) or black synthetic (new 2011) stock and forearm, R3 recoil pad, 8 lbs. New 2006.

MSR $1,242	$1,050	$900	$775	$650	$525	$450	$375	

Add approx. 15% for walnut stock and forearm (disc. 2011).

MODEL 1100 COMPETITION MASTER – 12 ga. only, 2 3/4 in. chamber, designed for 3 gun matches in practical shooting, 22 in. VR barrel with fiberoptic front sight and Rem Choke, 8 shot mag., grey synthetic stock and forearm, features R3 recoil pad, matte black finish, 8 lbs. Mfg. 2003-2004.

	$775	$600	$525	$465	$435	$395	$350	*$932*

MODEL 1100 TOURNAMENT SKEET – 12 or 20 (LT-20 variation disc. 1995) ga., 26 in. skeet bored or Rem Choke barrel, optional Cutts Compensator available from Jan. 1964 to Dec. 1976, 8 lbs. Mfg. 1963-1994, 1996-97, reintroduced 2003 in 12 ga. only. Disc. 2008.

	$895	$675	$550	$475	$400	$350	$300	*$1,084*

Add 5% for left-hand model (disc. 1986).

GRADING - PPGS™	100%	98%	95%	90%	80%	70%	60%	LAST MSR

MODEL 1100 SMALL GAUGE SKEET – 28 ga. or .410 bore, 25 or 26 (disc.) in. VR barrel, 6 1/2-7 1/4 lbs. Mfg. 1969-94.

	100%	98%	95%	90%	80%	70%	60%	LAST MSR
	$550	$450	$415	$375	$300	$265	$230	$692

2 1/2 in. chamber is standard on the .410 bore (Skeet only).

MODEL 1100 SKEET MATCHED PAIR – 28 ga. and .410 bore, walnut stock and forearm. 5,067 cased Skeet sets were mfg. 1969 and 1970 only.

	100%	98%	95%	90%	80%	70%	60%	LAST MSR
	$1,250	$995	$875	$765	$635	$530	$455	

MODEL 1100 SPORTING – 12 (new 2000), 20 (new 1998, LT variation new 2006), 28 ga., or .410 bore (new 2004), 25 (28 ga. only, disc. 2003), 27 (small gauge only, new 2004) or 28 (20 ga. only) in. VR Rem Choke barrel with 4 extended Briley choke tubes, 12 ga. has lightweight 28 in. VR target barrel, high gloss checkered deluxe walnut stock and forearm, 6 1/2 - 8 lbs. New 1996.

	100%	98%	95%	90%	80%	70%	60%	LAST MSR
MSR $1,211	$975	$775	$650	$550	$450	$395	$350	

Add $56 for 28 ga. or .410 bore.

MODEL 1100 PREMIER SPORTING – 12, 20, 28 ga., or .410 bore, 2 3/4 in. chamber, 27 or 28 in. VR barrel with 4 Briley extended choke tubes, nickel finished receiver with gold trigger and receiver inlays, high gloss finish select walnut stock and forearm, includes travel case, 6 1/2 - 8 lbs. Mfg. 2008-2011.

	100%	98%	95%	90%	80%	70%	60%	LAST MSR
	$1,195	$1,000	$825	$725	$625	$525	$475	$1,415

Add $56 for 28 ga. or .410 bore.

MODEL 1100 TA TRAP – 12 ga., 30 in. barrel, recoil pad on regular stock, available in left or right-hand. Mfg. 1979-86.

	100%	98%	95%	90%	80%	70%	60%	LAST MSR
	$410	$330	$295	$270	$230	$210	$190	$570

Add 5% for Monte Carlo stock.
Add $50 for left-hand model.

MODEL 1100 TB TRAP – 12 ga., 30 in. VR full choke barrel, special trap stock, select wood, right or left side ejection port. Mfg. 1963-1981.

	100%	98%	95%	90%	80%	70%	60%	LAST MSR
	$475	$400	$325	$300	$245	$210	$190	
Monte Carlo stock	$495	$415	$340	$310	$280	$235	$220	

Some left-handed trap shooters may pay a premium for the left side ejection port.

MODEL 1100 TD TOURNAMENT TRAP – 12 ga., 30 in. VR full choke barrel, special trap stock, extra select wood. Mfg. 1979-86.

	100%	98%	95%	90%	80%	70%	60%	LAST MSR
	$550	$495	$425	$365	$325	$285	$250	$675

Add 5% for Monte Carlo stock.

MODEL 1100 CLASSIC TRAP – 12 ga. only, features 30 in. VR light contour target barrel, high gloss checkered walnut Monte Carlo stock and forearm, high polish blue, receiver features fine line engraving and gold inlays, 8 1/4 lbs. New 2000.

	100%	98%	95%	90%	80%	70%	60%	LAST MSR
MSR $1,270	$995	$775	$640	$525	$425	$350	$300	

MODEL 1100 150TH ANNIVERSARY – limited mfg. in 1966 only.

	100%	98%	95%	90%	80%	70%	60%	LAST MSR
	$400	$340	$290	N/A	N/A	N/A	N/A	

MODEL 1100 BICENTENNIAL – 12 ga. only, configurations include Trap, Skeet, and Trade, mfg. to commemorate U.S. Bicentennial (1776-1976).

	100%	98%	95%	90%	80%	70%	60%	LAST MSR
Trap or Skeet	$450	$375	$325	N/A	N/A	N/A	N/A	
Trade	$375	$295	$225	N/A	N/A	N/A	N/A	

In 1976, the 1100 Bicentennial Trap retailed for $320 ($330 w/Monte Carlo stock), the Skeet retailed for $285, and the Trade retailed for $270.

MODEL 1100 DUCKS UNLIMITED – for individual listings, including chapter dinner guns and special/limited editions, please refer to Ducks Unlimited section.

There are two main variations of Model 1100 DU shotguns. The most desirable are those guns specifically manufactured for DU individual chapters, which are auctioned off at each chapter's annual banquet. These shotguns are referred to as "dinner guns", and since they are individually

GRADING - PPGS™	100%	98%	95%	90%	80%	70%	60%	LAST MSR

auctioned off at each chapter, prices can vary considerably from one chapter location to another. Please refer to individual listings in the Ducks Unlimited section for Model 1100 DU dinner guns and current values.

The second Model 1100 DU variation is a special/limited edition which is typically not auctioned off at the individual DU chapters. These limited/special editions are usually sold through normal firearms distribution, which includes both distributors and dealers. Values for these Model 1100 DU special/limited editions generally command a small premium above normal Model 1100 prices, if condition is NIB.

MODEL 1100 D-GRADE (TOURNAMENT) – custom order only, any gauge. New 1963.

MSR POR	N/A	$2,900	$2,075	N/A	N/A	N/A	N/A

Last published MSR was $4,532 (2007)

MODEL 1100 F-GRADE (PREMIER) – custom order only, any gauge. New 1963.

MSR POR	N/A	$6,000	$4,400	N/A	N/A	N/A	N/A

Last published MSR was $8,799 (2007)

MODEL 1100 F-GRADE W/GOLD (GOLD PREMIER) – with gold inlay, custom order only. New 1963.

MSR POR	N/A	$5,550	$3,600	N/A	N/A	N/A	N/A

Last published MSR was $11,999 (2007)

Shotguns: Semi-Auto, Model 11-87 & Variations

Model 11-87 barrels will not fit the Model 1100 or Model 11-87 Super Magnum models.

Remington MSRs on extra barrels (3 in. chamber standard) for the following currently manufactured models range from $282-$336 per barrel, depending on configuration. Many options are available from the custom shop, and are POR.

MODEL 11-87 SPORTSMAN SYNTHETIC/CAMO – 12 or 20 ga., 3 in. chamber, gas operated, choice of black synthetic stock and forearm or 100% Mossy Oak New Break-Up camo finish, 20 (fully rifled with cantilever scope rail, 20 ga. only), 21 (fully rifled with cantilever, 12 ga. only), 26 or 28 in. VR barrel with Rem Chokes, 7 1/4 - 8 1/4 lbs. New 2005.

MSR $804	$665	$550	$450	$350	$295	$250	$225

Add $125 for 20 or 21 in. fully rifled barrel with cantilever scope mount.
Add $111 for 100% Mossy Oak New Break-Up camo.
Add $13 for NRA Edition with Mossy Oak New Break-Up on stock and forearm (12 ga. only, disc. 2006).

* ***Model 11-87 Sportsman Synthetic ShurShot*** – 12 ga., synthetic ShurShot Realtree Hardwoods HD camo stock, 21 in. fully rifled barrel, otherwise similar to Model 11-87 Sportsman Synthetic/Camo. New 2008.

MSR $1,012	$875	$775	$675	$575	$500	$425	$350

* ***Model 11-87 Sportsman Field*** – 12 or 20 ga., 3 in. chamber, features satin finish, walnut stock and forearm with pressed checkering, matte metal finish, 26 or 28 in. VR barrel with Rem chokes, 7 1/4 or 8 1/4 lbs. New 2010.

MSR $845	$695	$575	$465	$365	$315	$265	$225

* ***Model 11-87 Sportsman Youth*** – 20 ga., 3 in. chamber, 21 in. VR barrel with Remchokes, features 13 in. LOP, Mossy Oak New Break-Up 100% camo coverage. Mfg. 2008.

	$725	$625	$550	$475	$400	$350	$295	*$818*

This model was available through Remington Premier dealers only.

* ***Model 11-87 Compact Sportsman*** – 20 ga., 3 in. chamber, 21 in. VR barrel with Rem Choke, black synthetic or 100% Mossy Oak Break-Up camo stock, adj. LOP allows up to 1 in. of adjustment with three spacers, SuperCell recoil pad, compact features, 6 1/2 lbs. New 2009.

MSR $804	$665	$550	$450	$350	$295	$250	$225

Add $111 for 100% camo finish.

GRADING - PPGS™	100%	98%	95%	90%	80%	70%	60%	LAST MSR

MODEL 11-87 PREMIER – 12 or 20 (new 1999, LT-20) ga. (3 in. chamber), 26, 28, 30 (12 ga. only, new 2000) or 32 (disc. 1996) in. VR Rem. choked barrel, successor to Model 1100, gas compensating action adaptable to all loads, stainless steel magazine tube, polished blue finish, high gloss or satin (current mfg. is in 12 ga./28 in. barrel only) finished and checkered walnut stock and forearm, a high gloss wood finish option became available in 1991 at N/C, and is now standard, fine line receiver engraving (referred to as embellished receiver) became standard during 1999, solid recoil pad, 8 1/8 - 8 3/8 lbs. Mfg. 1987-2006.

$685 $525 $435 $375 $315 $275 $250 *$860*

Add $84 for 21 in. fully rifled cantilever deer barrel.
Add $67 for left-hand action (12 ga. only).

Note: Model 11-87 Premier barrels are not interchangeable with Model 1100 barrels.

* ***Model 11-87 Premier Upland Special*** – 12 or 20 ga., 3 in. chamber, 23 in. (light contour barrel on 12 ga.) VR barrel, straight grip satin finished checkered walnut stock and forearm, high polish metal with engraving, 6 1/2 or 7 1/4 lbs. Mfg. 2000-2006.

$685 $525 $435 $375 $315 $275 $250 *$860*

MODEL 11-87 PREMIER 3 1/2 IN. SUPER MAGNUM – 12 ga. only, 3 1/2 in. chamber, 28 in. VR barrel with Rem. chokes, blue high polish non-embellished receiver and barrel, checkered high gloss walnut stock and forearm or 100% Mossy Oak Break-Up camo (disc. 2004) coverage, 8 1/4 lbs. Mfg. 2001-2006.

$750 $600 $525 $450 $375 $325 $275 *$932*

Add approx. 10% for camo (disc. 2004).

MODEL 11-87 SP (SPECIAL PURPOSE) – 12 ga. only, 3 in. chamber, 26, 28, or 30 (disc.) in. VR Rem. choked barrel, parkerized metal with satin finish wood stock and forearm, vent. recoil pad, camouflaged nylon sling, 8 1/4 lbs. Mfg. 1987-2003.

$590 $465 $395 $350 $315 $275 $250 *$765*

MODEL 11-87 SP (SPECIAL PURPOSE) 3 1/2 IN. SUPER MAGNUM – 12 ga. only, 3 1/2 in. chamber, non-reflective black matte finish on barrel and receiver, 26 or 28 in. VR barrel with Rem. choke, satin finished stock and forearm, approx. 8 1/8 lbs. Mfg. 2000-2005.

$725 $525 $450 $375 $325 $300 $280 *$912*

MODEL 11-87 P (POLICE) – 12 ga. only, 18 in. barrel, improved cylinder choke, synthetic stock, parkerized finish, choice of bead or rifle sights, 7 shot extended mag., designed for police/law enforcement.

Remington does not publish consumer retail pricing for this police/law enforcement model. Secondary prices for this model will be slightly higher than for current pricing on the Model 11-87 SPS.

MODEL 11-87 SPS (SPECIAL PURPOSE SYNTHETIC) – see individual sub-models listed below.

* ***Model 11-87 SPS 3 in. Magnum*** – similar to Model 11-87 SP 3 in. Mag., except is supplied with black synthetic stock and forearm. Disc. 2004.

$610 $475 $400 $360 $315 $275 $250 *$791*

* ***Model 11-87 SPS Camo (Special Purpose Synthetic Camo)*** – 12 ga. only, 3 in. chamber, 21 (mfg. 1999-2005), 26 or 28 (disc. 1998) in. VR barrel with Rem Choke, available in Mossy Oak Bottomland (disc. 1996), Mossy Oak Obsession (new 2006) or Mossy Oak Break-Up (mfg. 1997-2005) finish. Mfg. 1994-2006.

$765 $575 $450 $375 $325 $300 $280 *$963*

* ***Model 11-87 SPS Waterfowl*** – 12 ga., 3 in. chamber, 100% Mossy Oak New Shadow Grass camo coverage, 28 in. VR barrel with HiViz front sight (interchangeable), includes sling and swivels, 8 1/4 lbs. Mfg. 2004-2006.

$825 $625 $525 $450 $400 $350 $300 *$999*

GRADING - PPGS™	100%	98%	95%	90%	80%	70%	60%	LAST MSR

* ***Model 11-87 SPS-BG Camo (Special Purpose Synthetic Big Game)*** – 12 ga. only, 21 in. plain barrel with rifle sights and Rem Choke. Mfg. 1994 only.

	$555	$425	$350	$290	$250	$225	$200	*$692*

* ***Model 11-87 SP/SPS (Special Purpose Deer Gun)*** – 12 ga. only, 3 in. chamber, 21 in. IC or Rem Choke (Model SP, mfg. 1989-2003) or fully rifled (new 1993, became standard 2004) barrel with rifle sights, parkerized metal with matte finished wood or black synthetic (Model SPS, new 1993) stock and forearm, vent. recoil pad, includes camouflaged nylon sling, 7 1/4 lbs. Mfg. 1987-2005.

	$695	$525	$450	$395	$350	$300	$250	*$908*

Subtract 10% for fixed choke barrel or if w/o cantilever (became standard 2005) scope mount.

Rem Chokes were standard on this model between 1989-1992.

* ***Model 11-87 SP Thumbhole Deer Gun*** – 12 ga., features grey laminate thumbhole wood stock and forearm, 21 in. rifled barrel with cantilever scope mount, 8 lbs. Mfg. 2006-2007.

	$925	$825	$725	$625	$550	$500	$425	*$1,135*

* ***Model 11-87 SPS-T (Special Purpose Turkey)*** – 12 ga. only, 3 in. chamber, 21 in. VR barrel with Rem Choke, available in flat black (disc. 2000) or 100% camo treatment in Mossy Oak (disc. 1996), Mossy Oak Break Up (new 1999), Realtree X-tra Brown (mfg. 1997 only), or Greenleaf (disc. 1996), TruGlo rifle sights became standard in 2002 (Model SPS-T Turkey Gun RS/TG). Disc. 2003.

	$765	$550	$460	$385	$335	$300	$280	*$963*

Add $324 for Leupold Gilmore red dot sights, Monte Carlo stock and superfull choke tube (mfg. 2000 only).

Subtract approx. $20 if w/o TruGlo rifle sights.

» **Model 11-87 SPS Turkey Camo NWTF** – 20 ga. only, features 100% Mossy Oak Break-Up camo finish, TruGlo fiberoptic sights, 6 1/2 lbs. Mfg. 1998 only.

	$675	$575	$450	$395	$325	$290	$265	*$832*

MODEL 11-87 SPS 3 1/2 IN. SUPER MAGNUM – choice of 26 or 28 in. VR barrel with Rem Choke, black synthetic or 100% Mossy Oak Break-Up (disc. 2005) or Mossy Oak Obsession (new 2006) camo covered stock and forearm, approx. 8 1/8 lbs. Mfg. 2000-2007.

	$950	$825	$725	$575	$475	$400	$350	*$1,076*

Add $99 for camo coverage.

* ***Model 11-87 SPS-T 3 1/2 in. Super Magnum Turkey Camo*** – 12 ga. only, 3 1/2 in. chamber, full coverage Mossy Oak Break-Up (disc. 2003) or Obsession (new 2005) camo treatment, 23 in. barrel with TruGlo rifle sights and Rem Choke tube, thumbhole stock became optional 2006, 8 1/8 lbs. Mfg. 2001-2007.

	$1,000	$875	$775	$675	$600	$525	$450	*$1,175*

Add $66 for thumbhole stock (new 2006).

* ***Model 11-87 SPS 3 1/2 in. Waterfowl*** – 12 ga., 30 in. barrel with HiViz sight system and Rem Chokes, 100% Mossy Oak Duck Blind camo coverage, Speedfeed synthetic stock, 8 1/4 lbs. Mfg. 2007.

	$1,025	$875	$775	$675	$600	$525	$450	*$1,199*

MODEL 11-87 3 1/2 IN. SPORTSMAN SUPER MAG – 12 ga. only, 28 in. VR barrel with Rem Chokes and HiViz sights, 3 lbs. trigger pull, black synthetic stock and forearm with SuperCell recoil pad, overmolded grips became standard 2010, 8 1/4 lbs. New 2008.

MSR $859	$750	$675	$575	$500	$450	$400	$375	

Subtract 5% if w/o overmolded grips.

* ***Model 11-87 3 1/2 in. Sportsman ShurShot Turkey*** – 12 ga., features 100% RealTree AP Green HD camo coverage with skeletonized ShurShot stock, elevated HiViz sights, extended choke tubes, SuperCell recoil pad, overmolded grips became standard 2010, 7 5/8 lbs. New 2008.

MSR $998	$885	$750	$650	$575	$500	$450	$395	

GRADING - PPGS™	100%	98%	95%	90%	80%	70%	60%	LAST MSR

* ***Model 11-87 3 1/2 In. Sportsman Super Mag Waterfowl*** – 12 ga., features 100% Mossy Oak Duck Blind camo coverage, Speedfeed stock with SuperCell recoil pad, HiViz sights, overmolded grips became standard 2010, 8 1/4 lbs. New 2008.

MSR $998	$885	$750	$650	$575	$500	$450	$395	

MODEL 11-87 3 1/2 IN. SUPER MAGNUM XCS (XTREME CONDITIONS) – 12 ga., 28 in. VR barrel with Remchokes, features choice of black synthetic Speedfeed stock and forearm, or Mossy Oak Duck Blind camo coverage, grey TriNyte PVD coating on receiver and barrel, nickel plated internal components. Mfg. 2008.

	$1,000	$875	$775	$675	$600	$525	$450	$1,188

Add $40 for Mossy Oak Duck Blind stock and forearm camo coverage.

This model was available from Remington Premier dealers only.

MODEL 11-87 SPORTING CLAYS – 12 ga. only, 26 (disc. 1996) or 28 in. VR barrel with extended Rem Choke (knurled extension chokes allow for no-wrench field changes), specially balanced, satin finished walnut, top metal surfaces have fine matte finish, radiused recoil pad, twin bead sights on 5/16 wide VR, 7 1/2 lbs. Mfg. 1992-1999.

	$675	$575	$450	$395	$325	$290	$265	$833

* ***Model 11-87 Sporting Clays NP*** – 12 ga. only, features matte nickel plated receiver with engraving, satin finished checkered stock and forearm, 28 (new 1998) or 30 in. VR ported barrel with extended choke tubes, 7 3/4 lbs. Mfg. 1997-2001.

	$775	$650	$525	$450	$375	$325	$295	$948

MODEL 11-87 PREMIER SKEET – 12 ga. only, 26 in. VR Rem Choke barrel, deluxe walnut with quality cut checkering, 7 3/4 lbs. Mfg. 1987-1999.

	$650	$550	$475	$425	$375	$325	$275	$799

Add approx. $70 for left-hand action.

Subtract 10% if without Rem. chokes.

MODEL 11-87 PREMIER TRAP – 12 ga. only, 30 in. raised VR Rem Choke barrel, deluxe walnut stock (Monte Carlo became standard in 1996) with quality cut checkering, 8 1/4 lbs. Mfg. 1987-1999.

	$660	$565	$440	$385	$300	$275	$260	$833

Subtract $30 if without Monte Carlo stock.

Add approx. $40 for left-hand action (disc. 1994).

Subtract 10% if without Rem Chokes.

MODEL 11-87 175TH ANNIVERSARY – 12 ga. only, 28 in. barrel with Rem Choke, 175th Anniversary Model (1816-1991) with light engraving and high gloss wood finish. 4,606 mfg. 1991 only.

	$515	$425	$335	N/A	N/A	N/A	N/A	$618

MODEL 11-87 DALE EARNHARDT COMMEMORATIVE – 12 or 20 ga., features "7 Time Winston Cup Champion" tributary banner on right side with gold letters, 28 in. light contoured VR barrel, select checkered American walnut stock and forearm, serialization starts with DE, 7 3/4 lbs. Mfg. 2003-2004.

	$800	$650	$575	N/A	N/A	N/A	N/A	$972

MODEL 11-87 D-GRADE (TOURNAMENT) – custom order only, any gauge. New 1987.

MSR POR	N/A	$2,900	$2,075	N/A	N/A	N/A	N/A	

Last published MSR was $4,532 (2007)

MODEL 11-87 F-GRADE (PREMIER) – custom order only, any gauge. New 1987.

MSR POR	N/A	$6,000	$4,400	N/A	N/A	N/A	N/A	

Last published MSR was $8,799 (2007)

MODEL 11-87 F-GRADE W/GOLD (GOLD PREMIER) – with gold inlay, custom order only. New 1987.

MSR POR	N/A	$5,550	$3,600	N/A	N/A	N/A	N/A	

Last published MSR was $11,999 (2007)

100%	98%	95%	90%	80%	70%	60%	50%	40%	30%	20%	10%

SHOTGUNS: SINGLE BARREL

MODEL NO. 3 RIDER SINGLE BARREL – 12 ga., single barrel, 30 or 32 in. barrels, top lever break open, button release forend, plain pistol grip stock. Approx. 87,850 mfg. 1893-1903.

100%	98%	95%	90%	80%	70%	60%	50%	40%	30%	20%	10%
N/A	$450	$400	$300	$260	$200	$150	$130	$110	$90	$75	$65

MODEL NO. 9 RIDER SINGLE BARREL – similar to No. 3, screw release forend, auto ejector. 65,698 mfg. 1902-10.

100%	98%	95%	90%	80%	70%	60%	50%	40%	30%	20%	10%
N/A	$450	$400	$300	$260	$200	$150	$130	$110	$90	$75	$65

GRADING - PPGS™	100%	98%	95%	90%	80%	70%	60%	LAST MSR

MODEL 90-T (TRAP) – 12 ga., 32 (disc. 1993) or 34 in. VR barrel with fixed full choke, matte black receiver and wood around tang area, deluxe checkered stock and forearm, short throw top-lever release, elongated forcing cone, approx. 8 3/4 lbs. Mfg. 1992-97.

	100%	98%	95%	90%	80%	70%	60%	LAST MSR
	$1,850	$1,550	$1,375	$1,175	$1,025	$925	$850	*$3,199*

Add $50 for factory porting.

* ***Model 90-T HPAR (High Post w/adj. Rib)*** – features high post, adj. rib. Mfg. 1994-97.

	100%	98%	95%	90%	80%	70%	60%	LAST MSR
	$2,300	$1,875	$1,700	$1,550	$1,450	$1,325	$1,075	*$3,992*

MODEL 310 SKEET – .32 Rimfire case loaded with No. 12 leadshot, break open single shot, .310 bore shotgun, used in conjunction with a self-operated trap set which threw half-size clay targets, entire set-up included gun, shooting booth, ammunition, and trap thrower, 5 1/2 lbs., mfg. circa late 1960s.

	100%	98%	95%	90%	80%	70%	60%
Gun only	$425	$350	$300	$250	$195	$175	$150

Add 25%-75% depending on the amount of original accessories included.

This model was mfg. by CBC in Brazil, and imported into the U.S. as the .310 Skeet. This model was never mass produced, but test marketed for approx. 5 years in CT, NJ, PA, and TX primarily at amusement parks. It failed commercially due to lack of sales.

SHOTGUNS: SLIDE ACTION, DISC.

REMINGTON REPEATING SHOTGUN – 12 ga., hammerless, bottom ejection, takedown, plain barrel only, blue finish, sight notch on receiver top, marked "REMINGTON ARMS CO." with February 3rd, 1903 and May 18th, 1905 patent dates, walnut pistol grip stock and short forearm, hard rubber buttplate, 7 1/2 lbs., approx. 10,000 mfg. 1908-10.

	100%	98%	95%	90%	80%	70%	60%
	$295	$225	$200	$175	$150	$125	$110

Add 10% for 32 in. barrel.

There were 7 grades of this model (Numbers 0-6) that were originally priced from $27 to approx. $140. This model was renamed the Model 10 in 1911.

MODEL 10A – 12 ga., 26-32 in. barrels, various chokes, takedown, plain pistol grip stock. Mfg. 1911-29.

	100%	98%	95%	90%	80%	70%	60%
	$300	$275	$200	$175	$150	$125	$110

Add 10% for 32 in. full choke barrel.
Add 35% for guns marked "Long Range" - beware of fakes.

MODEL 17A – 20 ga., 26-32 in. barrel, various chokes, takedown, bottom ejection, 4 shot mag., plain grip stock. Approx. 48,000 mfg., 1917-33.

	100%	98%	95%	90%	80%	70%	60%
Plain barrel	$350	$275	$220	$195	$165	$140	$110
Solid. rib	$450	$375	$325	$290	$270	$250	$210

Grades range from "A" - "F" in suffix form, "F" being the highest. Large premiums are paid for mint condition, higher grade models.

MODEL 17R – 20 ga. only, security configuration, 20 in. cylinder bore barrel, 4 shot mag. Mfg. circa 1920s.

	100%	98%	95%	90%	80%	70%	60%
	$325	$265	$235	$200	$150	$120	$100

MODEL 29A – 12 ga., 26-32 in. barrel, bottom ejection, various chokes, takedown, 5 shot mag., checkered pistol grip stock. Approx. 24,000 mfg., 1929-33.

	100%	98%	95%	90%	80%	70%	60%
	$325	$265	$235	$200	$150	$120	$100

Add 15% for solid rib, 25% for VR.

GRADING - PPGS™	100%	98%	95%	90%	80%	70%	60%	LAST MSR

* ***Model 29A 32 in. Long Range barrel*** – should be marked "Long Range" - beware of fakes.

	$525	$475	$425	$350	$250	$200	$180	

Grades range from A - C and TA - TF, lowest to highest. Premiums exist for finer condition upper grades. The Model 29 was similar in appearance to the Model 10.

MODEL 29R – 12 ga. only, security configuration, 20 in. cylinder bore barrel, 5 shot mag. Mfg. circa 1920s.

	$375	$325	$265	$235	$200	$150	$120	

MODEL 29S – "Trap Special" with trap style straight grip stock, matted or VR rib.

	$500	$450	$425	$375	$350	$325	$300	

Add 20% for VR rib.

MODEL 31A – 12, 16, or 20 ga., side ejection, 2 or 4 shot mag., 26-32 in. barrels, various chokes, takedown, pistol grip stock. Approx. 160,000 mfg., 1931-49.

Plain barrel	$395	$345	$300	$265	$225	$185	$150	
Solid rib	$455	$385	$345	$300	$270	$230	$190	
Vent. rib	$475	$415	$375	$320	$290	$250	$210	

Add 15% for 20 ga.

Grades range from A - F suffixes. Higher grades will bring considerable premiums in excellent condition.

Early models will command a small premium in this model.

TC suffix is Target Model.

MODEL 31B "SPECIAL" – higher grade wood and hand checkered pistol grip stock and forearm.

	$650	$550	$440	$385	$360	$305	$275	

MODEL 31R "RIOT" GRADE – features shortened barrel.

	$425	$365	$325	$295	$270	$230	$190	

MODEL 31D TOURNAMENT – features scroll engraving.

	$1,600	$1,350	$1,100	$880	$715	$580	$525	

MODEL 31E EXPERT – features scroll engraving with game scene on left side of receiver.

	$1,750	$1,500	$1,325	$1,100	$935	$880	$770	

MODEL 31F PREMIER – features scroll engraving and game scenes on both sides of receiver. Introduced 1942.

	$2,950	$2,550	$2,200	$1,875	$1,600	$1,500	$1,300	

Add 20% for 20 ga.

Note: Grades differ in quality, grade of wood, and amount of engraving.

This model was also available with a Cutts compensator 1940-49, or a Poly Choke on special order from 1941-49.

MODEL 31TC TRAP – similar to 31A, with 12 ga. only, 30 or 32 in. VR barrel milled out of one piece of steel, full choke, trap stock and beavertail forend, pad.

	$875	$795	$675	$575	$450	$375	$300	

Subtract 10% for lightweight receiver.

TC stands for Trap with C Grade wood.

MODEL 31S TRAP SPECIAL – solid rib barrel, plainer wood.

	$550	$500	$450	$400	$365	$345	$325	

MODEL 31H HUNTER – similar to 31S, with sporter stock. Mfg. 1941-disc.

	$395	$350	$300	$275	$250	$220	$195	

MODEL 31L LIGHTWEIGHT – features an alloy receiver, available in both field and skeet. Mfg. 1941-1950.

	$350	$325	$300	$275	$250	$225	$200	

GRADING - PPGS™	100%	98%	95%	90%	80%	70%	60%	LAST MSR

MODEL 31 SKEET – similar to 31A, with 26 in. skeet bored barrel, standard solid rib, beavertail forend.

Plain barrel	$495	$450	$395	$365	$335	$265	$220	
Vent. rib	$650	$550	$495	$425	$375	$340	$295	

Subtract 10% for lightweight receiver.
Add 20% for 20 ga. with VR barrel.

SHOTGUNS: SLIDE ACTION, MODEL 870 & RECENT VARIATIONS

3 in. shells (12 or 20 ga.) may be shot in Magnum receivers only regardless of what the barrel markings may indicate (the ejection port is larger in these Magnum models with M suffix serialization).

Remington has manufactured many limited production runs for various distributors and wholesalers over the years. These shotguns are usually built to a specific configuration (gauge, stock, barrel length, finish, etc.), and are usually available until supplies run out. While these models are not included in this section, pricing in most cases will be similar to the base models from which they were derived.

In April 2009, Remington made its 10 millionth Model 870 slide action shotgun, making it the most manufactured shotgun in firearms history.

Many custom shop options are available, all are POR.
Add 25%-35% for 16 ga. on older mfg., if original condition is 95%+.
Remington MSRs on extra barrels (3 in. chamber is standard, except for Skeet barrel) for the following currently manufactured models range from $124-$327 per barrel, depending on configuration.

MODEL 870AP – "Wingmaster," 12, 16, or 20 ga., 26, 28, or 30 in. barrel, 5 shot, various chokes, plain pistol grip stock. Mfg. 1950-63.

Plain barrel	$220	$195	$175	$165	$140	$120	$110	
Vent. rib	$250	$220	$200	$195	$165	$150	$140	

Add 15% for "Sungrain" blonde maple wood (mfg. 1959-1961).

MODEL 870ADL – deluxe checkered version of 870AP. Mfg. 1950-63.

Plain barrel	$250	$220	$200	$180	$165	$140	$120	
Matted top barrel	$275	$250	$220	$210	$195	$165	$140	
Vent. rib	$300	$275	$250	$225	$200	$175	$150	

MODEL 870BDL – select walnut stock.

Plain barrel	$275	$250	$220	$200	$180	$165	$140	
Vent. rib	$315	$290	$260	$240	$210	$195	$165	

SPORTSMAN 12 PUMP – 12 ga. only (3 in. chamber), 28 or 30 in. barrel, recoil pad, VR standard, hardwood stock and forearm, Model 870 type action, 7 1/2 lbs. Mfg. 1984-86.

	$275	$235	$195	$175	$160	$150	$140	*$270*

Add $35 for Rem. chokes.

MODEL 870 EXPRESS – 12, 16 (mfg. 2002-2006), 20 (new 1991), 28 ga. (disc., reintroduced 2002-2004), or .410 bore (disc., reintroduced 2002-2004), 2 3/4 or 3 in. chamber, 20, 25 (28 ga. or .410 bore only), 26, or 28 in. VR Rem Choke (12 or 20 ga., supplied with Mod. Rem Choke) barrel, parkerized metal, matte finished hardwood stock and forearm, solid recoil pad, 6 - 7 1/4 lbs. New 1987.

MSR $411	$335	$270	$220	$190	$170	$155	$135	

Add 15% for 28 ga. or .410 bore (disc.).
Add $28 for left-hand action (12 ga., 28 in. barrel only, new 1998).
Various combination packages (includes regular and deer barrels) are available in both 12 and 20 ga. Retail prices range from $597-$657.

* ***Model 870 Express Synthetic*** – 12 or 16 ga. (disc. 2005), 26 or 28 in. VR barrel with one Rem Choke, features black synthetic stock and forearm. New 1994.

MSR $411	$335	$270	$220	$190	$170	$155	$135	

GRADING - PPGS™	100%	98%	95%	90%	80%	70%	60%	LAST MSR

» **Model 870 Express Synthetic Deer** – 12 or 20 (disc. 2010) ga., features 20 in. fully rifled barrel with rifle sights. New 2002.

MSR $457	$375	$280	$230	$190	$170	$150	$135	

* ***Model 870 Express Deer Gun*** – 12 or 20 ga., 20 in. IC choked barrel or fully rifled barrel with rifle sights, Monte Carlo stock. Introduced in 1991.

MSR $411	$335	$270	$220	$190	$170	$155	$135	

Add $46 for fully rifled barrel with rifle sights.
Add $122 for fully rifled barrel with cantilever scope mount in 12 (23 in. barrel) or 20 (18 1/2 in. barrel) ga. (disc. 2011).
Add $87 for fully rifled barrel with cantilever scope mount and Bushnell scope (12 or 20 ga., mfg. 2005).
Add $78 for cantilever scope mount and IC Rem Choke (disc. 1991).

* ***Model 870 Express Magnum ShurShot Deer*** – 12 or 20 ga., 23 in. fully rifled barrel with cantilever scope mount, features black thumbhole ShurShot synthetic stock and forearm. New 2008.

MSR $571	$440	$370	$315	$265	$230	$200	$180	

* ***Model 870 Express Turkey*** – 12 ga. only, choice of wood with flat finish (disc. 2008), Realtree Advantage (mfg. 1998-2005), Skyline Excel (mfg. 2003-2005), or Mossy Oak Break-Up (new 2006) camo stock and forearm, 21 in. plain or VR barrel with Rem. turkey choke, 7 1/4 lbs.

MSR $485	$395	$335	$285	$245	$210	$185	$160	

Add $43 for ShurShot skeletonized stock with Mossy Oak Obsession camo stock and forearm with 21 in. VR barrel.
Subtract approx. 10% for wood stock and forearm.

* ***Model 870 Express Compact Synthetic*** – 20 ga., 21 in. VR barrel with RemChoke, 13 in. LOP and adj. LOP kit, SuperCell recoil pad, black synthetic stock and forearm, 6 lbs. New 2009.

MSR $411	$335	$270	$220	$190	$170	$155	$135	

* ***Model 870 Express Compact Camo*** – 20 ga., 21 in. barrel with RemChoke, 13 in. LOP and adj. LOP kit, SuperCell recoil pad, synthetic stock and forearm with RealTree Hardwoods or Mossy Oak Pink Blaze camo coverage. New 2009.

MSR $461	$375	$300	$255	$215	$185	$165	$150	

* ***Model 870 Express Jr. Compact*** – 20 ga., 18 3/4 in. barrel with RemChoke, 12 in. LOP and adj. LOP kit, SuperCell recoil pad, black synthetic stock and forearm. New 2009.

MSR $411	$335	$270	$220	$190	$170	$155	$135	

* ***Model 870 Express Compact (Youth)*** – 16 (mfg. 2004-2005) or 20 ga. only, 21 in. VR barrel with Rem. choke, 13 in. LOP with recoil pad, choice of RealTree Advantage (mfg. 1998-2005), Mossy Oak Break-Up (new 2006), or Skyline Excel (mfg. 2003-2005) camo or regular wood finish on stock and forearm, 6 lbs.

MSR $411	$335	$270	$220	$190	$170	$155	$135	

Add $43 for Youth Deer Gun (fully rifled 20 in. barrel, mfg. 1994-2008).
Add $87 for Youth Turkey with choice of NWTF Jake's Skyline Excel camo (disc. 2005).
Add $72 for Youth Turkey with camo (disc. 2006, reintroduced 2008-2009).

* ***Model 870 Express Junior*** – 20 ga., 18 3/4 in. VR barrel, features Mossy Oak Break-Up camo finish on stock and forearm, matte metal finish, 6 lbs. Mfg. 2006-2008.

	$360	$310	$270	$235	$200	$180	$160	*$445*

* ***Model 870 Express Synthetic Tactical (HD, Home Defense)*** – 12 or 20 (new 2007, 7 shot mag. only) ga., 18 in. cyl. choked barrel with bead front sight, black synthetic stock and forend. New 1991.

MSR $407	$315	$265	$230	$200	$175	$150	$125	

Add $30 for 12 ga. 7 shot tube mag. or $38 for 20 ga. 7 shot tube mag.
Add $176 for ghost ring sights with Rem chokes.

GRADING - PPGS™	100%	98%	95%	90%	80%	70%	60%	LAST MSR

* ***Model 870 Express Tactical 20 Ga.*** – 20 ga., features black Knoxx Spec-Ops stock with 7 shot mag., 18 1/2 in. barrel with fixed cyl. choke, black synthetic stock, matte black finish, drilled and tapped, 6 lbs. New 2009.

MSR $539 $445 $375 $320 $280 $240 $210 $180

» **Model 870 Express Tactical Camo** – 12 ga., 6 shot mag. with 2 shot mag. extension, 18 1/2 in. barrel with Rem choke, XS Ghost Ring Sight Rail and XSR Ghost Ring sights, synthetic stock with A-TACS camo coverage, 7 1/2 lbs. New 2010.

MSR $699 $575 $485 $435 $380 $325 $275 $225

* ***Model 870 Express Combo*** – 12 ga., includes 23 in. cantilever fully rifled and 28 in. Rem Choke barrels with vent. rib, black synthetic stock. Mfg. 2008.

$460 $360 $275 $225 $185 $160 $145 *$585*

This model was available through Remington Premier dealers only.

* ***Model 870 Express Specialty*** – 12 or 20 ga., 18 in. cylinder bore or Rem Choke barrel, folding or Knoxx Spec-Ops pistol grip stock, 2 or 7 shot mag extension. Mfg. 2008.

$365 $315 $270 $235 $200 $180 $160 *$452*

Add $27 for 2 shot mag. extension with Knoxx Spec-Ops stock.

Add $53 for synthetic folding stock with 7 shot mag extension.

This model was available through Remington Premier dealers only.

MODEL 870 EXPRESS SUPER MAGNUM – 12 ga., 3 1/2 in. chamber, choice of checkered natural hardwood, black synthetic, or 100% camo stock and forearm (disc.), 23 (disc.), 26 (synthetic only), 28 or 30 (2007-disc) in. VR barrel, recoil pad, approx. 7 1/2 lbs. New 1998.

MSR $462 $380 $320 $280 $240 $210 $190 $170

Add $15 for synthetic non-camo Turkey Model with 23 in. barrel (mfg. 1999-2007).

Add $124 for 100% Skyline Fall Flight camo coverage (mfg. 2005).

Add $158 for combo package (hardwood only, includes 26 in. regular and 20 in. fully rifled deer barrel).

* ***Model 870 Express Super Magnum Turkey Camo*** – features Mossy Oak Break-Up (new 2006), 100% RealTree Advantage (disc. 2005) or Skyline Excel (mfg. 2003-2005) camo on metal and stock/forearm, 23 in. VR barrel only with Turkey extra full Rem Choke, 7 1/4 lbs. Mfg. 1998-2010.

$475 $415 $360 $325 $280 $250 $225 *$587*

* ***Model 870 Express Super Magnum Turkey/Waterfowl*** – 12 ga., features 100% Mossy Oak Bottom Land camo coverage, 26 in. barrel with Rem choke and Hi-Viz sights, includes sling, 8 1/4 lbs. New 2010.

MSR $620 $500 $430 $375 $325 $285 $250 $225

* ***Model 870 Express Super Magnum Synthetic Camo*** – 12 ga., 3 1/2 in. chamber, 23 or 26 in. VR barrel with Rem Choke, 100% Mossy Oak Break-Up camo coverage, wood or synthetic stock and forearm. Mfg. 1999 only.

$385 $320 $265 $240 $220 $200 $180 *$532*

* ***Model 870 Express Super Magnum Camo*** – 12 ga., 26 in. vent. rib. barrel, Rem Choke, 100% Mossy Oak Break-Up camo coverage, sling swivels, HiViz sights, camo sling. Mfg. 2008.

$430 $340 $275 $225 $185 $160 $145 *$545*

This model was available through Remington Premier dealers only.

MODEL 870 SPS SUPER MAG PREDATOR – 12 ga., 3 1/2 in. chamber, 20 in. barrel, Rem Chokes, TruGlo red dot sights, 100% Mossy Oak Obsession camo coverage, includes scope and overmolded grips, 7 1/8 lbs. New 2010.

MSR $700 $575 $470 $415 $365 $325 $295 $260

MODEL 870 SPS SUPER MAG TURKEY – 12 ga., 3 1/2 in. chamber, 23 in. rifle sighted barrel, 100% RealTree AP HD camo coverage with ShurShot thumbhole stock and SuperCell recoil pad, Wingmaster HD extended Rem Choke, black sling, sling swivels, TruGlo fiber optic sights. New 2008.

MSR $671 $565 $470 $420 $365 $325 $295 $260

GRADING - PPGS™	100%	98%	95%	90%	80%	70%	60%	LAST MSR

MODEL 870 SPS SUPER MAG. MAX GOBBLER – 12 ga., 23 in. rifle sighted barrel, 100% RealTree APG HD camo Knoxx Spec-Ops stock, drilled and tapped, Williams Fire Sight fiber optic sights, R3 recoil pad, sling, Rem Chokes. Mfg. 2008.

	100%	98%	95%	90%	80%	70%	60%	LAST MSR
	$675	$550	$450	$350	$315	$275	$250	$819

MODEL 870 SPS SUPER SLUG – 12 ga., 3 in. chamber, 25 1/2 in. extra heavy fully rifled barrel, ShurShot pistol grip stock with Mossy Oak Treestand camo coverage, drilled and tapped, Weaver rail, sling swivels, SuperCell recoil pad, 7 7/8 lbs. New 2009.

	100%	98%	95%	90%	80%	70%	60%	LAST MSR
MSR $829	$665	$560	$460	$400	$350	$300	$250	

MODEL 870 SPECIAL PURPOSE MARINE MAGNUM – 12 ga. only, 3 in. chamber, 18 in. plain barrel bored cyl., electroless nickel plated metal finish, 6 or 7 shot mag., R3 recoil pad became standard during 2004, sling swivels and Cordura sling, 7 1/2 lbs.

	100%	98%	95%	90%	80%	70%	60%	LAST MSR
MSR $829	$665	$560	$460	$400	$350	$300	$250	

Add $117 for XCS Marine Model with black TriNyte metal coating (mfg. 2007-2008).

MODEL 870 WINGMASTER – 12 or 20 ga., 26 or 28 in. vent. rib. barrel, Rem Chokes, high gloss semi-fancy Claro walnut stock, engraved receiver with pheasant and duck scenes, gold trigger, silver grip cap with raised Remington "R" logo. Mfg. 2008.

	100%	98%	95%	90%	80%	70%	60%	LAST MSR
	$795	$725	$650	$575	$500	$450	$395	$955

This model was available through Remington Premier dealers only.

MODEL 870 FIELD WINGMASTER – 12, 16 (disc. 1980, reintroduced late 2001), 20 (LW-20), 28 (disc. late 1994, reintroduced 1999) ga., or .410 (disc. late 1994, reintroduced 1999) bore, various barrel lengths (26, 28, and 30 are current mfg.), incorporates twin slide rails, 3 in. chamber in 12 ga. became standard in 1985, Rem Chokes became standard in 1987, lightweight frame on 20 ga. was introduced 1972, checkered walnut stock and forearm, a choice of high gloss or satin (28 in. barrel only) wood finish became available in 1991, approx. 6 1/2 - 7 1/4 lbs. New 1964.

	100%	98%	95%	90%	80%	70%	60%	LAST MSR
Plain barrel (disc. 1984)	$250	$225	$205	$190	$175	$160	$150	

* ***Model 870 Field Wingmaster with Vent. rib*** – 12, 16 (disc.), or 20 (LW-20) ga., 26 or 28 in. VR barrel (became standard in 1985).

	100%	98%	95%	90%	80%	70%	60%	LAST MSR
MSR $818	$600	$475	$385	$315	$265	$215	$190	

Subtract 10% without Rem Chokes.
Add $48 for left-hand model (12 ga. only, disc. 1994).
Add $80 for 20 in. fully rifled deer barrel with cantilever scope mount (12 ga. - mfg. 1992-1999 or 20 ga. - mfg. 1992-1995).

Beginning 1998, rolled scroll engraving started to appear on 20 ga. guns only. During 2005, a Wingmaster Jr. was released in a LW-20 in 20 ga. with 12 in. LOP and 18 3/4 in. barrel at no extra charge.

* ***Model 870 Field Wingmaster Small Gauge*** – 28 ga. or .410 bore, scaled down 870 on lightweight smaller frame, 25 in. fixed (F or M, .410 bore only) or Rem Choke (28 ga. only, new 1999) barrel, VR became standard 1984, satin finished wood, 6-6 1/2 lbs. Mfg. 1969-94, reintroduced 1999.

	100%	98%	95%	90%	80%	70%	60%	LAST MSR
MSR $873	$715	$575	$450	$350	$315	$275	$250	

Add $56 for 28 ga.
Subtract 15% if w/o VR.

* ***Model 870 Field Wingmaster 50th Anniversary Classic Trap*** – 12 ga. only, 2 3/4 in. chamber, features high polish blue fine line embellished receiver with gold inlays, 30 in. low profile light contour barrel, checkered high gloss semi-fancy walnut stock and forearm with cut checkering, 8 lbs. New 2000.

	100%	98%	95%	90%	80%	70%	60%	LAST MSR
MSR $1,081	$875	$725	$625	$525	$425	$350	$300	

* ***Model 870 Field Wingmaster 100th Anniversary*** – 12 ga., features "100th Anniversary of Pump Action Shotguns" embellished on left side of receiver with gold banners, fleur-de-lis laser engraved checkering on high gloss walnut stock and forearm. Mfg. 2008.

	100%	98%	95%	90%	80%	70%	60%	LAST MSR
	$830	$665	$500	$400	$350	$300	$285	$1,035

This model was available through Remington Premier dealers only.

GRADING - PPGS™	100%	98%	95%	90%	80%	70%	60%	LAST MSR

* ***Model 870 Field Wingmaster Dale Earnhardt Tribute*** – 12 (mfg. 2005) or 20 (new 2006) ga., 28 in. VR barrel with Rem Chokes, special embellishments featuring Dale Earnhardt. Mfg. 2005-2006.

$710	$575	$475	$400	$345	$300	$265	*$820*

* ***Model 870 Field Wingmaster NRA Edition*** – 12 ga., 28 in. VR barrel, features NRA Heritage logo on receiver. Mfg. 2006.

$495	$395	$325	$275	$220	$195	$175	*$685*

MODEL 870 WINGMASTER 3 1/2 IN. SUPER MAGNUM – 12 ga. only, 28 in. VR barrel with choke tubes, high polish blue with receiver engraving, high gloss walnut stock and forearm with cut checkering, 7 1/2 lbs. Mfg. 2000-2006.

$610	$500	$410	$355	$300	$265	$250	*$732*

MODEL 870 MAGNUM DUCK GUN – 3 in. chamber, 12 or 20 ga., 26, 28, or 30 in. full or mod. barrel, recoil pad, 3 in. chambers became standard on all Model 870s starting in 1985. Rem Chokes became standard 1987 (introduced 1986 as $40 option). New 1964.

Please refer to Model 870 Field Wingmaster prices.

MODEL 870 SPECIAL PURPOSE – 12 ga. only, differs only in that metal parts are sand blasted, choice of Mossy Oak Camo (new 1992), black synthetic, or checkered wood stock with low luster finish, 21 (Turkey barrel), 26, or 28 in. VR barrel. Rem Chokes were introduced 1986.

Add $75 for wood stock and forearm (disc. 1992).

Subtract 10% without Rem Chokes.

* ***Model 870 Special Purpose Super Magnum Synthetic Camo*** – 12 ga. only, 3 1/2 in. chamber, 26 or 28 in. VR barrel with Rem Choke, available in either Mossy Oak (disc. 1995), Bottomland (disc. 1996), full coverage Mossy Oak Break-Up (mfg. 1997-2005) or Mossy Oak Obsession (new 2006) finish. Mfg. 1994-2007.

$575	$475	$375	$300	$265	$225	$190	*$741*

* ***Model 870 Special Purpose SPS-T (Turkey) Super Magnum*** – 12 ga. only, features 3 1/2 in. chamber, choice of 23, 26 (disc. 2004), or 28 (mfg. 2001-2004) in. VR barrel with Rem Chokes, fully camouflaged in Mossy Oak Break-Up (disc. 2005) or Obsession (new 2005) pattern, choice of standard wood, thumbhole (new 2005), or synthetic (26 in. barrel only) stock. Mfg. 2000-2007.

$575	$475	$375	$300	$265	$225	$190	*$741*

Add $58 for TruGlo rifle sights thumbhole stock and with 100% Mossy Oak Obsession coverage (new 2005).

Add $18 for cantilever scope mount (mfg. 2001-2005) with Turkey super full choke tube.

Add approx. $330 if with Leupold Gilmore red dot sights and Turkey super full choke tube - 23 in. barrel only (mfg. 2000 only).

Add $58 for Maxx Gobbler model with 100% RealTree APG HD camo coverage, Knoxx Special Ops stock, and Williams Fire Sights (new 2007).

* ***Model 870 Special Purpose SPS-BG Camo (Special Purpose Synthetic Big Game)*** – 12 ga. only, 20 in. plain barrel with rifle sights and Rem. choke. Mfg. 1994 only.

$350	$285	$235	$200	$170	$150	$130	*$442*

* ***Model 870 Special Purpose Deer*** – 12 ga., 3 in. chamber, grey laminate thumbhole stock and forearm with R3 recoil pad, 23 in. fully rifled barrel with cantilever scope mount, 8 1/8 lbs. Mfg. 2006-2007.

$650	$575	$525	$450	$400	$365	$335	*$799*

* ***Model 870 Special Purpose Synthetic ShurShot*** – 12 ga., features 23 in. fully rifled barrel with cantilever scope mount, 3 lbs. trigger pull, ShurShot thumbhole stock with SuperCell recoil pad and extended forearm grip, RealTree Hardwoods HD camo on stock and forend. Mfg. 2008-2009.

$525	$475	$425	$365	$325	$275	$235	*$652*

GRADING - PPGS™	100%	98%	95%	90%	80%	70%	60%	LAST MSR

* ***Model 870 Special Purpose Turkey (SPS-T)*** – 12 (disc. 2004) or 20 ga., 20 (new 2002) or 21 in. VR barrel with Rem Choke, available in flat black, Mossy Oak (disc. 1996, reintroduced 2002), Greenleaf (disc. 1996), or Realtree X-tra Brown (full SPS-T-camo, mfg. 1997 only) finish. Disc. 1999, reintroduced 2002-2005.

	$460	$365	$285	$250	$215	$180	$170	*$621*

This model was also available 2002-2003 in a Youth Model with 1 in. shorter LOP.

* ***Model 870 Special Purpose Deer Gun (SPS-Deer)*** – 12 ga. only, 3 in. chamber, 20 in. Rem Choke barrel (disc. 1992) or fully rifled barrel with rifle sights (new 1993), satin finished (disc. 1992) or black synthetic (new 1993) stock and forearm, matte black metal, 7 1/4 lbs. Mfg. 1989-1999.

	$345	$275	$225	$195	$175	$160	$145	*$436*

Add $28 for deer barrel with Rem Choke and cantilever scope mount (disc. 1996).
Add $60 for fully rifled deer barrel with cantilever scope mount.
Add $65 for cantilever scope mount system (disc. 1992).

* ***Model 870 Special Purpose Super Slug Deer (SPS Super Slug Deer)*** – 12 or 20 (new 2004) ga., 3 in. chamber, 23 in. fully rifled barrel with cantilever scope mount, matte black metal finish, black synthetic Monte Carlo stock and forearm, approx. 8 lbs. Mfg. 1999-2004.

	$470	$375	$310	$255	$225	$195	$175	*$580*

MODEL 870 XCR (XTREME CONDITIONS) – 12 ga., 28 in. vent. rib. barrel, black synthetic or Mossy Oak Duck Blind (Waterfowl) camo coverage, Rem Choke, TriNyte PVD coating, Speedfeed stock, nickel plated internal parts. Mfg. 2008.

	$675	$550	$425	$350	$315	$275	$250	*$899*

Add $56 for Waterfowl model with camo.

This model was available through Remington Premier dealers only.

MODEL 870 LIGHTWEIGHT – 20 ga. only, lighter and shorter mahogany stock than magnum model, 23 in. barrel. Mfg. 1972-83.

	$270	$230	$210	$190	$175	$165	$155	

Add $30 for VR.

MODEL 870 LIGHTWEIGHT (MAGNUM) – 20 ga., 3 in. chamber, 26 or 28 in. barrel, Rem Chokes became standard 1987, 6 lbs. Mfg. 1972-1994.

	$365	$320	$260	$225	$200	$175	$160	*$460*

Subtract 10% without Rem Chokes.
Subtract $40 without VR.

MODEL 870 SPECIAL FIELD – 12 or 20 (LW-20) ga., lighter straight grip stock with solid recoil pad, 21 (disc. 1993) or 23 (new 1994) in. VR barrel, Rem Chokes became standard 1987 (introduced 1986 as $40 option), 6 1/4 or 7 lbs. Mfg. 1984-1995.

	$380	$320	$265	$230	$210	$190	$175	*$473*

Subtract 10% without Rem Chokes.

MODEL 870 BRUSHMASTER – 12 or 20 (disc.) ga., 20 in. barrel with imp. cyl. (disc.) or Rem Choke and rifle sights, 3 in. chamber standard for 1985, normal bluing with satin finished wood. Disc. 1994.

	$355	$310	$255	$225	$200	$175	$160	*$452*

Add $43 for left-hand model.

MODEL 870 POLICE – 12 ga. only, 18 or 20 in. plain barrel, choice of blue or parkerized finish, bead or rifle (disc. 1995, 20 in. barrel only) sights, Police cylinder (disc.) or IC choke. Mfg. 1994-2006 (last year of civilan sales).

	$385	$315	$250	$200	$175	$160	$145	*$492*

Add $13 for parkerized finish.
Add $44 for rifle sights (disc. 1995).

Remington also offers a Model 870P, 870P MAX ,870MCS, and 870P Synthetic for police/law enforcement, featuring extended capacity magazines, improved cylinder chokes, collapsible stocks, with some models having shorter than 18 in. barrels. While Remington does not publish

GRADING - PPGS™	100%	98%	95%	90%	80%	70%	60%	LAST MSR

consumer retail pricing for these police/law enforcement models, secondary prices for these guns will be slightly higher than for current pricing on the Model 870 Police.

MODEL 870 TACTICAL – 12 ga. only, 3 in. chamber, 18 or 20 in. fixed IC choke barrel, 6 or 7 (20 in. barrel only) shot mag., OD Green metal finish, black synthetic tactical or Knoxx Spec-Ops adj. recoil absorbing stock with pistol grip, open sights, approx. 7 1/2 lbs. Mfg. 2006.

	100%	98%	95%	90%	80%	70%	60%	LAST MSR
	$515	$465	$425	$385	$350	$320	$290	*$599*

Add $26 for SpecOps adj. stock.

MODEL 870 TAC-2/TAC-3 – 12 ga., 3 in. chamber, 18 or 20 (disc) in. cyl. bore barrel, black oxide metal finish, black synthetic stock and forearm, pistol grip with choice of Knoxx Spec-Ops folding stock (Tac-2 FS), Knoxx Spec-Ops tube stock or regular synthetic (disc. 2008) stock, 6 (Tac-2 w/18 in. barrel) or 8 (Tac-3 w/20 in. barrel, disc. 2008) shot mag., bead sights, R3 recoil pad on fixed stock, approx. 7 lbs. New 2007.

	100%	98%	95%	90%	80%	70%	60%	LAST MSR
MSR $750	$615	$535	$470	$415	$380	$340	$300	

MODEL 870 TACTICAL BLACKHAWK – 12 ga. only, 3 in. chamber, 18 in. barrel with fixed cyl. choke, grooved pistol grip with Blackhawk Spec Ops adj. stock, 7 lbs. New 2012.

	100%	98%	95%	90%	80%	70%	60%	LAST MSR
MSR $638	$550	$465	$415	$365	$325	$295	$260	

MODEL 870 TACTICAL DESERT RECON – 12 ga., 18 or 20 in. barrel, Digital Tiger TSP Desert Camo stock and forend, special ported tactical extended Rem Choke tube, Speedfeed stock with 2 or 3 shot carrier. Mfg. 2008-2009.

	100%	98%	95%	90%	80%	70%	60%	LAST MSR
	$575	$500	$450	$400	$365	$335	$295	*$692*

Add $67 for 20 in. barrel.

MODEL 870 RIOT – 12 ga. only, 18 or 20 in. barrel, choice of blue or parkerized metal finish. Disc. 1991.

	100%	98%	95%	90%	80%	70%	60%	LAST MSR
	$295	$265	$225	$200	$170	$150	$130	*$355*

Add $40 for police rifle sights (20 in. barrel only).

MODEL 870 D-GRADE (TOURNAMENT) – custom order only, any gauge. New 1950.

	100%	98%	95%	90%	80%	70%	60%	LAST MSR
MSR POR	N/A	$2,900	$2,075	N/A	N/A	N/A	N/A	

Last published MSR was $4,532 (2007)

MODEL 870 F-GRADE (PREMIER) – custom order only, any gauge. New 1950.

	100%	98%	95%	90%	80%	70%	60%	LAST MSR
MSR POR	N/A	$6,000	$4,400	N/A	N/A	N/A	N/A	

Last published MSR was $8,799 (2007)

MODEL 870 F-GRADE W/GOLD (GOLD PREMIER) – with gold inlays, custom order only. New 1950.

	100%	98%	95%	90%	80%	70%	60%	LAST MSR
MSR POR	N/A	$5,550	$3,600	N/A	N/A	N/A	N/A	

Last published MSR was $11,999 (2007)

MODEL 870 DUCKS UNLIMITED – for DU individual chapter dinner guns, please refer to listings in the Ducks Unlimited section, "DU" in serial number, disc.

There are two main variations of Model 870 DU shotguns. The most desirable are those guns specifically manufactured for DU individual chapters, which are auctioned off at each chapter's annual banquet. These shotguns are referred to as "dinner guns", and since they are individually auctioned off at each chapter, prices can vary considerably from one chapter location to another. Please refer to individual listings in the Ducks Unlimited section for Model 870 DU dinner guns and current values.

The second Model 870 DU variation is a special/limited edition which is typically not auctioned off at the individual DU chapters. These limited/special editions are usually sold through normal firearms distribution, which includes both distributors and dealers. Values for these Model 870 DU special/limited editions generally command a small premium above normal Model 870 prices, if condition is NIB.

MODEL 870 "WILDLIFE FOR TOMORROW" – 12 ga. only, side panels fine line laser etched with gold engraving, special wood, 2,000 mfg. for Wildlife Forever fundraiser 1996.

	100%	98%	95%	90%	80%	70%	60%	LAST MSR
	$325	$250	$175	N/A	N/A	N/A	N/A	

GRADING - PPGS™	100%	98%	95%	90%	80%	70%	60%	LAST MSR

MODEL 870 150TH ANNIVERSARY – 12 ga. only, 2,534 mfg. 1966 only.

	$400	$325	$275	N/A	N/A	N/A	N/A	

MODEL 870 BICENTENNIAL – 12 ga. only, configurations include Trap, Skeet, and Trade, mfg. to commemorate U.S. Bicentennial (1776-1976).

Trap or Skeet	$425	$350	$295	N/A	N/A	N/A	N/A	
Trade	$375	$295	$225	N/A	N/A	N/A	N/A	

In 1976, the 870 Bicentennial Trap retailed for $255 ($265 w/Monte Carlo stock), and the Skeet retailed for $220.

MODEL 870 SC SKEET – 12, 16 (disc. 1960), or 20 ga., 26 in. VR skeet bore barrel, C grade hand checkered wood stock. Mfg. 1950-79.

	$600	$445	$365	$280	$245	$210	$185	

MODEL 870 SKEET MATCHED PAIR – includes .410 bore and 28 ga., 1,503 cased sets mfg. 1969 only.

	$1,150	$995	$895	$785	$655	$550	$465	

MODEL 870 TA TRAP – 12 ga. trap model, deluxe walnut, VR. Add $15 for Monte Carlo stock. Mfg. 1978-86.

	$425	$375	$325	$275	$250	$225	$200	*$430*

MODEL 870 TB TRAP – similar to 870, with 28 or 30 in. VR full choke barrel, trap stock, recoil pad. Mfg. 1950-81.

	$425	$375	$325	$275	$250	$225	$200	

MODEL 870 TC TRAP – higher grade walnut and special VR, Rem Chokes became standard 1987. Mfg. 1950-1979, reintroduced 1996-1999.

	$600	$475	$400	$350	$275	$240	$220	*$680*

Subtract 5% if w/o Monte Carlo stock.
Add 20% for early Model 870 TC Trap guns with hand cut checkering.

MODEL 870 COMPETITION TRAP – 12 ga. single shot competition model, reduced recoil, competition walnut stock with cut checkering, VR. 5,300 mfg. 1980-86.

	$550	$475	$395	$350	$315	$275	$250	*$680*

MODEL 870 ALL AMERICAN TRAP – 30 in. full choke barrel, engraved receiver, trigger guard and barrel, deluxe trap stock. Approx. 1,000 mfg. 1972-76.

	$795	$700	$650	$605	$495	$440	$385	

MODEL 887 NITRO MAG SPS – 12 ga., 3 1/2 in. chamber, action design based on Model 870, features Armorlokt coating on all exterior metal surfaces which eliminates rust, matte black finish, 26 or 28 in. VR barrel with Rem Choke, steel liner is encased in thick polymer jacket, SuperCell recoil system, HiViz front sight, synthetic stock and forearm with specially contoured grip panels, push button trigger guard safety, approx. 7 1/2 lbs. New 2009.

MSR $436	$370	$315	$280	$250	$225	$200	$180	

* ***Model 887 Nitro Mag Waterfowl Camo*** – 12 ga., 3 1/2 in. chamber, similar to Model 887 Nitro Mag SPS, except features 100% RealTree Advantage Max-4 HD camo coverage. New 2009.

MSR $582	$480	$430	$365	$325	$295	$265	$240	

Add $145 for combo package with Mossy Oak Break Up camo and extra 22 in. turkey barrel.

* ***Model 887 SPS Bone Collector*** – 12 ga., 3 in. chamber, 26 in. vent. rib barrel, Rem Choke, 100% AP HD camo coverage, features "Bone Collector" logo, otherwise similar to Model 887 Nitro Mag SPS, 7 1/4 lbs. Mfg. 2010-2011.

	$525	$475	$425	$365	$325	$285	$240	*$642*

MODEL 887 NITRO MAG TACTICAL – 12 ga., 3 in. chamber, 18 1/2 in. barrel with Rem Choke and Hi-Viz front sight, black synthetic stock and forearm, 4 shot mag. and 2 shot extension with mag. tube hanger bracket, Picatinny rail, SuperCell recoil pad, ArmorLokt coated metal finish, 6 7/8 lbs. New 2010.

MSR $524	$425	$380	$335	$295	$260	$230	$195	

GRADING - PPGS™	100%	98%	95%	90%	80%	70%	60%	LAST MSR

RENATO GAMBA

Please refer to the Gamba listing in the G section.

RENETTE, GASTINNE

Please refer to the Gastinne Renette listing in the G section.

REPUBLIC ARMS, INC.

Previous manufacturer 1997-2001, and located in Chino, CA.

PISTOLS: SEMI-AUTO

THE PATRIOT – .45 ACP cal., double action only, ultra compact with 3 in. barrel, 6 shot mag., ultra compact black polymer frame and stainless steel slide (either brushed or with black Melonite coating, new 2000), locked breech action, checkered grips, 20 oz. New 1997.

$265 $230 $210 $185 $175 $165 $155 *$299*

REPUBLIC ARMS OF SOUTH AFRICA

Previous manufacturer located in Jeppestown, Union of South Africa. Previously imported until 2002 by TSF Ltd., located in Fairfax, VA.

PISTOLS: SEMI-AUTO

RAP 401 – 9mm Para. cal., 8 shot mag., otherwise similar to Rap-440. Importation 1999-circa 2002.

$495 $425 $375 $350 $325 $300 $275

RAP-440 – .40 S&W cal., compact double action, 3 1/2 in. barrel with high contrast 3-dot sights, last shot hold open, hammer drop safety/decocking lever, firing pin block safety, 7 shot mag., all steel construction, 31 1/2 oz., includes case, spare magazine, and lock. Imported 1998-circa 2002.

$545 $475 $425 $395 $375 $330 $300

Add $50 for Trilux tritium night sights.

SHOTGUNS: SLIDE ACTION

MUSLER MODEL – 12 ga., lightweight shotgun, polymer reinforced stock and forearm, action opening release lever, action locks open after the last round. Imported 1998-circa 2002.

$549 $475 $425 $395 $375 $330 $300

RETAY ARMS CORP.

Current manufacturer located in Konya, Turkey. No current U.S. importation.

Retay Arms Corp. manufactures a line of good quality semi-auto shotguns. The company also manufactures a complete lineup of blank pistols, air rifles, and spear guns. Please contact the company directly for more information, including pricing and domestic availability (see Trademark Index).

REXIO

Previous trademark of guns manufactured in Argentina beginning late 1999. Previously imported and distributed until 2002 by VAM Distribution Company, LLC, located in Wooster, OH.

PISTOLS: SINGLE SHOT

OUTFITTER RC-SERIES – various cals., including .45 LC/.410 bore, tip-up action, 6 or 10 in. barrel, synthetic SAA style grip and full forearm, opening release lever in front of trigger guard, transfer bar safety, with or w/o (.45 LC/.410 bore only) sights, manual locking safety, 2.2-3 lbs. Imported 2000-2002.

$185 $165 $145 $130 $120 $110 $100 *$205*

REVOLVERS

RJ-22 SERIES – .22 LR cal., 9 shot, 4 or 6 in. VR barrel with full shroud, choice of wood or synthetic grips with finger grooves, adj. sights, 2.1-2.6 lbs. Imported 2000-2002.

$150 $135 $125 $115 $105 $100 $95 *$170*

GRADING - PPGS™	100%	98%	95%	90%	80%	70%	60%	LAST MSR

RJ-38 SERIES – .38 Spl. cal., 6 shot, 3 or 4 in. VR barrel with full shroud, choice of wood or synthetic grips with finger grooves, 1.8-2 lbs. Imported 2000-2002.

	$150	$140	$125	$115	$110	$105	$100	*$170*

RS-22 SERIES – .22 LR or .22 WMR cal., 8 (.22 WMR) or 9 (.22 LR) shot, alloy or steel frame, blue finish, rubber grips with finger grooves, 4 or 6 in. VR barrel with full shroud, fixed or adj. sights, supplied with plastic case. Imported 2000-2002.

	$155	$140	$125	$115	$110	$105	$100	*$175*

Add $12 for adj. sights.

* ***RS-22 Series Stainless*** – similar to RS-22 Series, except is stainless steel. Imported 2000-2002.

	$175	$150	$130	$120	$115	$110	$105	*$200*

Add $12 for adj. sights.

RS-357 SERIES – .357 Mag. cal., 6 shot, alloy or steel frame, 3, 4, or 6 in. VR barrel with full shroud, fixed or adj. sights, supplied with plastic case. Imported 2000-2002.

	$155	$140	$125	$115	$110	$105	$100	*$175*

Add $12 for adj. sights.

* ***RS-357 Series Stainless*** – similar to RS-357 Series, except is stainless steel. Imported 2000-2002.

	$175	$150	$130	$120	$115	$110	$105	*$200*

Add $12 for adj. sights.

RHINO ARMS

Current rifle manufacturer located in Washington, MO.

RIFLES: SEMI-AUTO

Rhino Arms manufactures a complete line of AR-15 style carbines/rifles.

IMPORTANT NOTE: On model(s) where *N/A has replaced the normal 100% value, it indicates current market conditions are too unstable to accurately ascertain 100%-60% values. Factory retail prices (MSRs) reflect most recent updates. For more up-to-date information on current pricing trends and additional useful information, please visit www.bluebookofgunvalues.com, select "Information & Services" from the menu, and click on "Additional Book Information".

Add $45 for Magpul ACS stock, $155 for Magpul PRS stock, or $165 for Magpul UBR stock.

RA-4B SERIES – .223 Rem. cal., 16 or 20 (RA-4BV only) in. chrome-moly heavy barrel, aluminum lower receiver, flattop upper, A2 flash hider, choice of A2 buttstock (RA-4B or RA-4BV) or M4 buttstock (RA-4BG or RA-4BT), 10 or 30 shot mag., anti-walk receiver retaining pins. Disc. 2010.

	*N/A	$825	$750	$675	$595	$550	$495	*$978*

Add $44 for RA-4BG model with rail gas block and M4 buttstock.
Add $248 for RA-BT model with four rail handguard and M4 buttstock.
Add $119 for RA-4BV model with 20 in. barrel, free float tube and A2 buttstock.

RA-4P SERIES – .223 Rem. cal., 16 or 20 (RA-4PV) in. chrome-moly steel barrel, flattop upper, aluminum lower, A2 or Rhino flash hider, 10 or 30 shot mag., ERGO grip, Magpul CTR or PRS buttstock, anti-walk receiver retaining pins. Disc. 2010.

	*N/A	$1,000	$875	$750	$625	$550	$500	*$1,243*

Add $35 for RA-4PG model with four rail gas block, CAR handguard, and CTR buttstock.
Add $185 for RA-4PT model with four rail gas block, four rail handguard, and CTR buttstock.
Add $247 for RA-PV model with four rail gas block, free float tube, and PRS buttstock.

STANDARD 5.56/.300 BLACKOUT – 5.56 NATO or .300 Blackout cal., 16 in. chromemoly barrel, machined aluminum receiver, gas block with integrated Picatinny rail, free floating carbon fiber handguard, Ergo grip, Magpul CTR stock, 7.6 (5.56 NATO) or 8.1 lbs.

MSR $2,405	*N/A	$1,795	$1,550	$1,395	$1,125	$925	$725

Add $270 for .300 Blackout cal.

GRADING - PPGS™	100%	98%	95%	90%	80%	70%	60%	LAST MSR

STANDARD 308 (RA-5D) – .308 Win. cal., 18 in. chromemoly heavy barrel, aluminum upper and lower receiver, rail gas block, 10 or 20 shot mag., Rhino flash hider, free float tube, Magpul UBR or CTR stock, ERGO grip, anti-walk receiver retaining pins, 8.8 lbs.

MSR $3,015	*N/A	$2,225	$1,925	$1,725	$1,400	$1,150	$895	

RHODE ISLAND ARMS COMPANY

Previous manufacturer located in Hope Valley, RI.

SHOTGUNS: O/U

MORRONE MODEL – 12 or 20 ga., 26 or 28 in. plain barrels, boxlock, extractors, single trigger, checkered straight or pistol grip stock. Mfg. 1949-1953, only 500 of these guns were mfg., 450 in 12 ga., and 50 in 20 ga., very few with VR, they are quite rare although collector interest is not overwhelming.

	$1,100	$880	$770	$660	$550	$495	$440	

Add 20% for 20 gauge.
Add 20% for VR.

RIB MOUNTAIN ARMS, INC.

Previous rifle manufacturer circa 1992-2000, and located in Beresford and Sturgis, SD.

RIFLES: BOLT ACTION

MODEL 92 – .50 BMG cal., match grade barrel with muzzle brake, long action, walnut thumbhole stock, Timney trigger, approx. 28 lbs. Mfg. 1997-2000.

	$3,175	$2,725	$2,275	$2,000	$1,750	$1,575	$1,300	*$3,475*

MODEL 93 – similar to Model 92, except has short action with removable shell holder bolt, approx. 25 lbs. Mfg. 1997-2000.

	$3,175	$2,725	$2,275	$2,000	$1,750	$1,575	$1,300	*$3,475*

RICHLAND ARMS COMPANY

Previous importer (until 1986) located in Blissfield, MI. The models listed were made by various manufacturers located in either Italy or Spain.

SHOTGUNS

MODEL 80 LS SINGLE SHOT – 12, 20 ga., or .410 bore, 26 or 28 in. full choke barrel. Mfg. 1986 only.

	$140	$120	$110	$100	$90	$80	$70	*$162*

MODEL 711 MAGNUM SxS – 10 ga., 3 1/2 in. chamber, 12 ga., 3 in. chamber, 32 in. full and full, 30 in. full and full, 20, 28 ga., and .410 bore also available on special order, hammerless, boxlock, extractors, checkered walnut stock, recoil pad. Mfg. 1963-1985 in Spain.

10 gauge	$400	$325	$275	$250	$230	$210	$190	
12 gauge	$340	$295	$265	$250	$230	$210	$190	
20 gauge	$450	$340	$295	$260	$230	$210	$195	

MODEL 707 DELUXE SxS – 12 or 20 ga., 3 in. chambers, 26, 28, or 30 in. barrels, various chokes, boxlock, extractors, double triggers, checkered stock and forend. Mfg. 1963-1972 in Spain.

	$330	$300	$275	$250	$230	$210	$190	

MODEL 200 FIELD GRADE SxS – 12, 16, 20, 28 ga., or .410 bore, 22, 26, and 28 in. barrels, various chokes, Anson & Deeley boxlock, extractors, double triggers, checkered stock, 6 lbs. 2 oz. - 7 lbs. 4 oz. Mfg. 1963-85 in Spain.

	$330	$300	$275	$250	$230	$210	$190	*$379*

Add 20% for 20 ga., or 50% for 28 ga. or .410 bore.

MODEL 202 ALL PURPOSE SxS – similar to Field, except 2 sets of barrels, 12 and 20 ga. only. Mfg. 1963-disc. in Spain.

	$450	$400	$350	$300	$275	$250	$225	

Add 20% for 20 ga., or 50% for 28 ga. or .410 bore.

GRADING - PPGS™	100%	98%	95%	90%	80%	70%	60%	LAST MSR

MODEL 41 ULTRA O/U – 20, 28 ga., or .410 bore, 3 in. chambers (.410 bore only), single non-selective trigger, 26 or 28 in. barrels, extractors, VR, engraved silver finished receiver, select checkered walnut stock and forearm, 6 lbs. 2 oz. Importation disc. 1986.

	100%	98%	95%	90%	80%	70%	60%	LAST MSR
	$395	$350	$300	$260	$230	$200	$180	*$298*

MODEL 747 O/U – 12 or 20 ga. only, 3 in. chambers, Greener crossbolt, boxlock action, VR and barrels, SST, extractors. Importation disc. 1986.

	100%	98%	95%	90%	80%	70%	60%	LAST MSR
	$475	$425	$350	$325	$310	$295	$280	*$464*

MODEL 757 O/U – 12 ga., 3 in. chambers, boxlock action with Greener crossbolt, vent. barrels and rib, double triggers, extractors, walnut stock and forearm, 7 lbs. 4 oz. New 1986. Importation disc. 1986.

	100%	98%	95%	90%	80%	70%	60%	LAST MSR
	$325	$275	$225	$200	$185	$170	$155	*$325*

Add 20% for multi-chokes (Model 7570).

MODEL 787 O/U – 12 ga. only, 3 in. chambers, boxlock action with silver finish, single trigger, vent. barrels and rib, extractors, walnut stock with recoil pad, is supplied with 5 interchangeable choke tubes, 7 1/4 lbs. Made 1986 only.

	100%	98%	95%	90%	80%	70%	60%	LAST MSR
	$495	$440	$380	$340	$310	$280	$250	*$471*

MODEL 808 O/U – 12 ga., 26, 28, or 30 in. barrels, various chokes, boxlock, extractors, checkered stock. Mfg. 1963-1968 in Italy.

	100%	98%	95%	90%	80%	70%	60%	LAST MSR
	$425	$375	$330	$315	$290	$270	$230	

MODEL 810 O/U – 10 ga., 3 1/2 in. chambers, ST, extractors.

	100%	98%	95%	90%	80%	70%	60%	LAST MSR
	$600	$550	$500	$460	$430	$395	$360	

MODEL 828 O/U – 28 ga., single non-selective trigger, extractors, engraved, only 250 imported.

	100%	98%	95%	90%	80%	70%	60%	LAST MSR
	$650	$550	$500	$450	$400	$350	$325	

RIEDL RIFLE COMPANY

Previous single shot rifle manufacturer.

RIFLES: SINGLE SHOT

SINGLE SHOT RIFLE – many cals., 22-30 in. barrel, rack and pinion action, operated by trigger guard/lever, fully adj. trigger, select walnut stock, basically custom made.

	100%	98%	95%	90%	80%	70%	60%	LAST MSR
	$495	$470	$440	$415	$385	$330	$305	

* ***Single Shot Rifle Stainless Barrel***

	100%	98%	95%	90%	80%	70%	60%	LAST MSR
	$560	$535	$505	$480	$450	$395	$370	

RIFLES, INC.

Current custom rifle manufacturer located in Pleasanton, TX. Previously located in Cedar City, UT. Dealer or direct consumer sales.

Riflemaker and custom gunsmith Lex Webernick has been manufacturing lightweight sporting rifles for more than 20 years.

RIFLES: BOLT ACTION

On the following models, the customer must provide a Remington or Winchester action.

Add $175 for muzzlebrake (stainless quiet Slimbrake II) on Classic and Master Series.

CLASSIC – various cals., features stainless lapped barrel, matte stainless finish, laminated fiberglass stock with pillar glass bedding, approx. 6 1/2 lbs. New 1996.

	100%	98%	95%	90%	80%	70%	60%	LAST MSR
MSR $2,600	$2,350	$2,125	$1,650	$1,225	$1,085	$870	$765	

Add $100 for left-hand action.

LIGHTWEIGHT STRATA STAINLESS – various cals., lightened stainless Remington action, match grade barrel with Slimbrake, matte stainless finish, 5 lbs. New 1996.

	100%	98%	95%	90%	80%	70%	60%	LAST MSR
MSR $2,900	$2,650	$2,400	$2,025	$1,650	$1,450	$1,195	$1,000	

Add $150 for left-hand action.

GRADING - PPGS™	100%	98%	95%	90%	80%	70%	60%	LAST MSR

LIGHTWEIGHT 70 – most cals. up to .375 H&H, features Winchester Model 70 stainless controlled round feeding blue printed action, match grade stainless steel barrel with muzzle brake, matte stainless finish, laminated Kevlar/boron/graphite stock with glass bedding, approx. 5 1/2 lbs. New 1997.

MSR $2,800 $2,550 $2,300 $1,950 $1,600 $1,410 $1,160 $980

Add $150 for left-hand action.

TITANIUM STRATA – various cals., based on lightened and blue printed Rem. 700 action, titanium receiver, 4 1/2 lbs. New 2002.

MSR $3,500 $3,150 $2,650 $2,100 $1,775 $1,500 $1,215 $1,000

VARMINT/TARGET – similar to Classic, except has different stock design and dimensions, different barrel contour. Mfg. 1998-99.

$1,800 $1,375 $1,075 $960 $775 $655 $550 *$1,900*

Add $250 for Varmint brake.

MASTER SERIES – various cals. up to .300 Wby. Mag., designed for long range accuracy, blue printed Rem. Model 700 action, fiberglass stock, guaranteed 1/2 MOA accuracy, 7 3/4 lbs. New 1998.

MSR $2,900 $2,650 $2,150 $1,700 $1,450 $1,195 $1,000 $825

CANYON – various cals., designed for long range shooting, synthetic stock with adj. cheekpiece available in 6 colors, stainless steel action/barrel with muzzle brake, 10 lbs. New 2011.

MSR $3,500 $3,150 $2,650 $2,100 $1,775 $1,500 $1,215 $1,000

SIGNATURE SERIES – .300 Rem. Ultra Mag. cal., blue printed, Rem. M-700 stainless receiver, honed trigger assembly, 27 in. fluted match grade stainless steel barrel with matte finish, w/o sights, synthetic McMillan sporter stock, each gun is signed by Lex Webernick on the floorplate, guaranteed 1/2 MOA accuracy. Limited mfg. 2000-2006.

$2,600 $2,050 $1,700 $1,500 $1,235 $1,030 $855 *$2,800*

Add $175 for Slimbrake.
Add $150 for left-hand action.

SAFARI – .375 H&H, .416 Rem., or .458 Lott cal., Win. Model 70 action, features match grade barrel with Slimbrake, matte stainless or black Teflon finish, various options are available, 8 1/2 lbs. New 1996.

MSR $3,200 $2,950 $2,625 $2,100 $1,700 $1,450 $1,195 $1,010

PEAR FLAT LTD. ED. – 6.5-284 cal., features distinctive skip fluting pattern on barrel, bolt, and shroud, barb wire camo synthetic stock, pear flat engraved on floor plate. Only 100 to be mfg. beginning 2009. Disc. 2010.

$2,950 $2,550 $2,000 $1,740 $1,495 $1,215 $1,000 *$3,250*

RIGANIAN, RAY (RIFLEMAKER)

Please refer to the Peerless Rifle Company listing in the P section.

RIGBY, JOHN & CO. (GUNMAKERS), INC.

Current trademark established during 1735, and currently manufactured in Paso Robles, CA since 1997. Previously manufactured in Dublin, Ireland from 1735-1897. Previously manufactured in London, England 1865-1996. Currently distributed domestically by John Rigby & Co. (Gunmakers), Inc., located in Paso Robles, CA. Previously imported by Griffin & Howe until 1998.

Original trade name was W. & J. Rigby circa 1820-1865, during the percussion era. Rigby has always been well-known for its dueling pistols. The first London Branch of J. Rigby was opened in 1865, and the Dublin Premises were closed during 1897. John Rigby became superintendent of the small arms factory at Enfield circa 1880, and was in charge of development for the .303 caliber rifle. The firm became a company in 1900, and has been responsible for many of the large caliber developments in both rifles and ammunition. During 1997, Rigby was acquired by an American investment group located

GRADING - PPGS™	100%	98%	95%	90%	80%	70%	60%	LAST MSR

in Paso Robles, CA.

Rigby is one of the world's finest gunmakers. A good portion of the guns they manufactured were custom built to customer specifications. They were chambered for the large black powder express cartridges used for dangerous game in Africa and Asia. The modern Rigby guns follow this same tradition.

Please contact the company directly for more information on the currently manufactured models listed, including delivery time.

We will list the modern Rigby Guns with approximate values but strongly urge that if purchase or sale is contemplated, a professional appraisal be utilized.

RIFLES

Current delivery time on the current rifles is approx. 10-12 months on sidelocks, and 6 months on boxlocks.

SINGLE SHOT RIFLE – .30-06, .308 Win., .300 H&H cal., other calibers available by request, 22-28 in. barrel, falling block Hagen style action, color case hardened action and finish, exhibition grade English walnut, Pachmayer Decelerator pad, Rigby scroll patterned engraving with three initials on trigger guard, approx. 4-6 month delivery time. New 2010.

Current MSR on this model is $16,500.

Many options include wood upgrades, engraving, express sights, telescopic sight, case, or other details.

SINGLE SHOT STALKING RIFLE – .22 Hornet - .500 NE cals., Farquharson lever actuated falling block action, 24 in. barrel, extractor, checkered pistol grip stock, deluxe finish and engraving. Reintroduced 2000-2003.

	$9,250	$8,500	$7,500	$6,500	$5,500	$4,500	$3,500	*$9,750*

.350 MAGNUM MAGAZINE RIFLE – .350 Magnum cal. originally, most were rechambered to .375 H&H Mag. cal.

	$3,995	$3,400	$2,950	$2,600	$2,300	$2,000	$1,700	

AFRICAN (HEAVY) EXPRESS MAGAZINE RIFLE – various dangerous game cals., new double square bridge Mauser action (pre-1939), claw extraction bolt action, 3-5 shot mag., 20-28 in. barrel, exhibition grade checkered walnut, full pistol grip stock.

Current MSR on this model is $33,500.

Many options include wood upgrades, engraving, express sights, telescopic sight, case, or other details.

LIGHT STANDARD MAGAZINE RIFLE – similar to Heavy Express Magazine rifle, except in smaller calibers.

Current MSR on this model is $18,500.

Many options include wood upgrades, engraving, express sights, telescopic sight, case, or other details.

BEST QUALITY STANDARD GRADE SIDELOCK EJECTOR DOUBLE RIFLE – currently mfg. cals. include .375 H&H Flanged, .416/500 Flanged, .470 NE, .500 NE, or .577 NE, 3 leaf express sights, older mfg. has included .22 LR, .275 Mag., .350 Mag., .416 Rigby, .458 Win. Mag., .465, or .470 NE cal., 24-28 in. barrels, case colored contoured and reinforced Greener sidelock action with cross bolt, deluxe finish and engraving.

Base price on this model is $49,500 with scroll engraving.

Many options include wood upgrades, engraving, express sights, telescopic sight, case, or other details.

REGENT GRADE SIDELOCK EJECTOR DOUBLE RIFLE – various cals., top-of-the-line model with choice of game scenes or elaborate scroll engraving.

Base price on this model is $85,000.

BEST QUALITY BOXLOCK EJECTOR DOUBLE RIFLE – current production includes .375 H&H Flanged, .416/500 Flanged, .470 NE, .500 NE, or .577 NE cal., 22-26 in. barrels, Greener cross bolt, Anson & Deeley action.

Add $3,500 for .500 NE cal.
Add $7,500 for .577 NE cal.
Current MSR on this model is $32,500.

GRADING - PPGS™	100%	98%	95%	90%	80%	70%	60%	LAST MSR

SECOND QUALITY BOXLOCK EJECTOR DOUBLE RIFLE – similar to Best Quality, with less select wood and engraving. Disc.

	$12,750	$10,750	$9,750	$8,750	$7,350	$6,350	$5,000	

Subtract 35% without ejectors.

Values are for larger calibers, smaller cals. could have less value than listed.

SHOTGUNS: O/U

LINEAR LOCK (SIDELOCK) – 12, 16 (new 2006), 20, 28 ga. or .410 bore, true sidelock action with double safety sears, configured for clay pigeon sports, live bird, or field use, all working parts are titanium nitride coated, various length vent. barrels with VR, exhibition grade English walnut and various stock configurations, case colored, rust blue, or coin finished is standard, 100% small English scroll engraved. New 2000.

Base price on this model is $47,500.

REGENT GRADE LINEAR LOCK (SIDELOCK) – top-of-the-line model utilizing linear locks, choice of game scene or elaborate scroll engraving.

Current MSR on this model is $89,500.

SHOTGUNS: SxS

HAMMER SHOTGUN – 12, 16, 20, 28 ga. or 410 bore, manual cocking hammers, rebounding firing pins and hammers, extractors only, exhibition grade English walnut, 70% English scroll engraving coverage, special order only.

This model is POR - please contact the company directly for a price quotation.

BOXLOCK SHOTGUN – all gauges, barrel lengths and chokes to order, checkered stock to order, auto ejectors, double triggers.

* ***Boxlock Shotgun Chatsworth Grade***

	$4,500	$3,500	$3,000	$2,500	$2,000	$1,600	$1,200	

* ***Boxlock Shotgun Sackville Grade*** – deluxe engraved.

	$5,900	$5,000	$4,500	$3,750	$3,100	$2,650	$2,200	

Add 20% for 20 ga.
Add 40% for 28 ga.
Add 60% for .410 bore.

SIDELOCK SHOTGUN - PRE-1997 PRODUCTION – all gauges, barrel lengths and chokes to specifications, double triggers, auto ejectors, stocked to order.

* ***Sidelock Shotgun - Pre-1997 Production Sandringham Grade***

	$9,500	$7,500	$6,000	$5,000	$4,450	$3,775	$2,950	

* ***Sidelock Shotgun - Pre-1997 Production Regal Grade*** – deluxe engraved.

	$12,500	$10,000	$8,750	$7,500	$6,400	$5,250	$4,250	

Add 20% for 20 ga.
Add 40% for 28 ga.
Add 60% for .410 bore.

BEST QUALITY SIDELOCK - CURRENT MFG. - 12, 16 (disc.), 20, 28 ga. or 410 bore, case colored or coin finished contoured hand detachable sidelock action, Krupp steel barrels, current engraving includes fine frame and border English scroll, also available with optional game scene engraving on both sidelocks.

Current MSR on this model is $39,950.

REGENT GRADE SIDELOCK – top-of-the-line sidelock shotgun with choice of game scene or elaborate scroll engraving.

Current MSR on this model is $72,000.

RIZZINI & TANFOGLIO srl

Previous longarm manufacturer established 2005-early 2010 and located in Gardone, Italy.

GRADING - PPGS™	100%	98%	95%	90%	80%	70%	60%	LAST MSR

Rizzini & Tanfoglio combined two great names of Italian gunmaking into one company. Rizzini & Tanfoglio manufactured best quality shotguns and rifles, utilizing some of Europe's top engravers. Prices varied depending on custom order features. For current models, please refer to Battista Rizzini listing.

RIFLES

Calibers .375 H&H, .470 NE, .500 NE, and .600 NE were POR on the following models.

BOXLOCK SxS – various cals., choice of traditional or round body action, express sights, engraving quoted separately, custom order only.

Base price on this model was €26,240, including IVT tax.
Add €1,830 for round body action.

SIDELOCK SxS – various cals., traditional action only, express sights, engraving quoted separately, custom order only.

Base price on this model was €36,612, including IVT tax.

SHOTGUNS

Add 10% for 28 ga. or .410 bore.

HAMMER SxS – various gauges, choice of round or RT style round body action, rose and scroll engraving, custom order only.

Base price on this model was €21,967, including IVT tax.
Add €1,221 for RT style round body action.

BOXLOCK SxS – various gauges, choice of traditional English style or round body action, rose and scroll engraving, custom order only.

Base price on this model was €12,814, including IVT tax.
Add €4,882 for round body action.

401 SIDELOCK O/U – various gauges, Boss type locking system, chopper lump barrels, ST, best quality wood, engraving quoted separately, custom order only.

Base price on this model was €35,736, including IVT tax.

SIDELOCK SxS – various gauges, choice of English, special RT style, or round body action, engraving quoted separately, custom order only.

Base price on this model ranged approx. €29,900, including IVT tax.
Add €3,662 for special RT style action.
Add €4,882 for round body action.

RIZZINI, BATTISTA

Current manufacturer established during 1965, and located in Marcheno, Italy. Currently imported and distributed beginning 2012 by Fierce Products, located in Gunnison, UT, and by William Larkin Moore, located in Scottsdale, AZ. Previously imported 2008-2011 by Rizzini USA, located in New Britain, CT, previously located in West Chester, PA. Previously imported in the U.S. 2002-2003 by SIG Arms, located in Exeter, NH, and by New England Arms Corp. located in Kittery Point, ME. Dealer direct sales.

RIFLES: O/U

The models listed are available in 7x65 JRS, 8x57 JRS, 9.3x74R, .30-06, .308 Win., .444 Marlin, or .30R Blaser cal.

EXPRESS 90L – 23 1/2 in. barrels, ST, ejectors, deluxe wood and features, standard dimensions, includes case, 7 3/4 lbs.

MSR $5,995	$5,275	$4,615	$3,955	$3,585	$2,900	$2,375	$1,845

EXPRESS 92EL – similar to Express 90, except has sideplates with more elaborate engraving, includes Nizzoli case, custom dimensions available, 7 3/4 lbs.

MSR $12,548	$11,500	$9,950	$9,000	$8,100	$7,200	$6,300	$5,400

GRADING - PPGS™	100%	98%	95%	90%	80%	70%	60%	LAST MSR

WILD EXPRESS – various cals., low profile boxlock action, ejectors, ST, coin finished receiver with relief game scene engraving, oil finished, hand checkered pistol grip select walnut stock with cheekpiece and Schnabel forend. Imported 2004-2012.

	$5,250	$4,500	$3,950	$3,250	$2,750	$2,300	$1,950	*$5,754*

SHOTGUNS: O/U

During 2012, Rizzini upgraded the wood and the engraving on its currently manufactured models.

INVERNESS ROUND BODY DELUXE (ROUND BODY EL) – all gauges, 26, 28, 29 or 30 in. solid rib barrels, ejectors, SST, coin finished or case colored steel frame, two frame sizes, fancy Turkish checkered walnut stock and forearm, five screw-in flush chokes, scroll engraving, cased, approx. 6 lbs. Importation disc. 2012.

	$5,500	$4,950	$4,400	$3,850	$3,300	$2,600	$2,150	*$6,078*

Add $607 for 28 ga. or .410 bore (small frame).

INVERNESS ROUND BODY DELUXE (ROUND BODY EM) – all gauges, 26, 28, 29 or 30 in. vent. rib barrels, ejectors, SST, coin finished or case colored steel receiver, two frame sizes, fancy Turkish checkered walnut stock and forearm, five screw-in flush chokes, scroll engraving, approx. 6 lbs. Mfg. 2007-2012.

	$4,500	$3,750	$3,300	$2,850	$2,400	$2,000	$1,650	*$4,985*

Add $644 for 28 ga. or .410 bore (small frame).

OMNIUM EM – all gauges, blued frame with basic scroll engraving, two frame sizes, SST, ejectors, 24 1/2 - 30 in. VR barrels with choke tubes, cased, approx. 6 3/4 lbs. New 2004.

MSR $2,450	$2,295	$1,925	$1,650	$1,495	$1,210	$990	$770	

AURUM CLASSIC – 12, 16, 20, 28 ga. or .410 bore, boxlock action, three frame sizes, SST, ejectors, 24 1/2 - 30 in. VR barrels with choke tubes (except 16 ga.), case hardened receiver with light engraving, cased. New 1996.

MSR $3,495	$3,195	$2,795	$2,395	$2,175	$1,755	$1,440	$1,120	

Add $464 for Aurum small action in 28 ga. or .410 bore.
Add $1,635 for Aurum small action combo (28 ga. & .410 bore).
Add $1,143 for Aurum Classic 20/28 ga. combo.

* ***Aurum Classic Light*** – 12 or 16 ga., nickel plated alloy frame, scroll engraving with gold inlays, cased, approx. 6 1/4 lbs. Imported 2000-2004, reintroduced 2007.

MSR $3,695	$3,395	$2,970	$2,545	$2,310	$1,865	$1,530	$1,190	

* ***Aurum Classic Teutonic*** – all gauges, 24 1/2 - 30 in. VR barrels with five screw-in flush choke tubes, boxlock action, hand finished relief game scene engraving, oil finished checkered pistol grip stock and Schnabel forend, cased. Imported 2004-2011.

	$2,825	$2,350	$1,850	$1,525	$1,250	$1,025	$950	*$3,194*

ARTEMIS CLASSIC – all gauges, 24 1/2 - 30 in. VR barrels with five flush choke tubes, case hardened boxlock action with three frame sizes, hand finished game scene engraved sideplates with gold inlays, ejectors, SST, oil finished checkered select walnut pistol grip stock and Schnabel forend, approx. 6 3/4 lbs. New 1996.

MSR $3,995	$3,650	$3,195	$2,740	$2,480	$2,010	$1,645	$1,280	

Add $675 for Artemis small action in 28 ga. or .410 bore.
Add $1,845 for small action combo with 28 ga. and .410 bore barrels.

ARTEMIS DELUXE FIELD – all gauges, 24 1/2 - 30 in. VR barrels, engraved coin finished frame with sideplates, boxlock action in three frame sizes, ejectors, SST, oil finished hand checkered pistol grip select walnut stock with Schnabel forend, approx. 6 3/4 lbs.

MSR $7,495	$6,695	$5,860	$5,020	$4,555	$3,680	$3,015	$2,345	

Add $450 for Aurum small action in 28 ga. or .410 bore.

ARTEMIS DELUXE SPORTING – 12 ga., coin finished action, sideplates with hand finished game scenes, SST, ejectors, extra select walnut stock, 28, 29 1/2, 30, or 32 in. barrels, 10mm rib, 5 extended chokes, cased. Importation began 2004.

MSR $7,679	$6,950	$5,750	$4,500	$3,650	$3,150	$2,750	$2,450	

GRADING - PPGS™	100%	98%	95%	90%	80%	70%	60%	LAST MSR

ARTEMIS EL – top-of-the-line gun with hand engraving, three frame sizes. Importation disc. 2000, reintroduced 2004-2012.

	$16,500	$14,250	$11,250	$9,500	$8,350	$7,100	$6,250	*$18,750*

Add $3,750 for small action in 28 ga. or .410 bore.

MODEL BR 320 COMPETITION – 12 or 20 ga., 2 3/4 or 3 in. chambers, 28-34 in. barrels, fixed chokes, 10mm rib, color case hardened boxlock action, light engraving with Rizzini name in gold, SST, pistol grip stock with palm swell and round forend. New 2007.

MSR $3,795	$3,395	$2,970	$2,545	$2,310	$1,865	$1,530	$1,190	

MODEL BR 440/440 EL COMPETITION – 12 or 20 ga., 28-32 in. barrels with 5 chokes, removable trigger group, SST, blue frame, scroll (440) or hand (440 EL) engraving, checkered pistol grip select (440) or fancy (EL) walnut stock and forearm. New 2007.

MSR $7,950	$7,195	$6,295	$5,395	$4,895	$3,955	$3,240	$2,520	

Add $3,562 for Model BR 440 EL.

780 FIELD SERIES – 10, 12, or 16 ga., boxlock action, DTs, extractors, checkered walnut stock and forearm. Importation disc. 1998.

	$1,075	$875	$750	$675	$595	$525	$450	*$1,225*

Add $550 for 10 ga.
Add $150 for ejectors (Model S780 E).
Add $200 for SST with ejectors (Model S780 EM).
Add $350 for SST, ejectors, and upgraded wood (Model S780 EML).
A Model S780 EMEL was also available that is entirely hand-finished and engraved for $5,995.

* ***780 Field Series Competition*** – includes Skeet, Trap, and Sporting Clays configuration. Importation disc. 1998.

	$1,375	$1,050	$925	$825	$725	$625	$525	*$1,600*

* ***780 Field Series Small Gauge*** – includes 20, 28, or 36 (.410 bore) ga., DTs, ejectors. Importation disc. 1998.

	$1,275	$975	$875	$800	$725	$625	$525	*$1,500*

Add $50 for SST (Model 780 EM).

S 780 EMEL FIELD – 12, 16, 20, 28 ga. or .410 bore, highly polished coin finish, 28 or 29 1/2 in. barrels, hand engraved ornamental motifs and game scenes, SST, ejectors, extra select hand checkered and polished walnut stock, includes Nizzoli case. Disc. 2012.

	$13,000	$11,000	$9,250	$7,800	$6,800	$5,350	$4,850	*$14,470*

Add $2,896 for small frame in 28 ga. or .410 bore.

782 EM FIELD SERIES – 12 or 16 ga., boxlock action with sideplates, SST ejectors, extractors, checkered walnut stock and forearm. Importation disc. 1998.

	$1,450	$1,150	$995	$875	$750	$675	$550	*$1,700*

Add $450 for Slug variation (Model 782 EM Slug).
Add $350 for better engraving and wood (Model 782 EML).
A Model S7820 EMEL was also available that was entirely hand-finished and engraved for $12,000.

* ***S 782 EMEL Field Series Deluxe*** – all gauges, individually made per customer specifications, 27 1/2 in. VR barrels with choke tubes (except .410 bore), coin finished receiver with side plates featuring elaborate Bulino game scene engraving with gold inlays and fine scroll borders, deluxe English walnut, Nizzoli best leather case. Imported 1994-2012.

	$13,995	$11,850	$10,350	$8,900	$7,500	$6,250	$5,200	*$15,565*

Add $3,110 for small action in 28 ga. or .410 bore.

790 SERIES COMPETITION – 12 or 20 ga., choice of Trap, Skeet, or Sporting Clays configuration, features black frame outlined with gold line engraving. Importation disc. 1999.

	$1,725	$1,475	$1,300	$1,050	$925	$825	$695	*$2,275*

Subtract $150 for 20 ga. Trap.
Subtract $50 for 20 ga. Skeet.
Add $1,050 for 20 ga. Sporting (includes sideplates and quick detachable stock).

GRADING - PPGS™	100%	98%	95%	90%	80%	70%	60%	LAST MSR

A Model 790 Trap EL was also available that was entirely hand-finished with 18Kt. gold and hand engraving - prices began at $5,650 in 12 ga., $5,200 in 20 ga.

*** *790 Series Competition Small Gauge*** – similar to 790 Competition Series, except in 20, 28, or 36 (.410 bore) ga., SST and ejectors standard. Importation disc. 2000.

	100%	98%	95%	90%	80%	70%	60%	LAST MSR
	$1,375	$1,150	$995	$875	$750	$675	$550	*$1,750*

A Model 790 EMEL was also available that was entirely hand-finished with 18 Kt. gold and hand engraving - prices began at $9,600.

*** *S 790 EL Series Competition Sporting*** – includes multi-chokes and case. Importation disc. 2000, reintroduced 2004-2012 by special order only.

	100%	98%	95%	90%	80%	70%	60%	LAST MSR
	$7,000	$6,000	$5,000	$4,000	$3,500	$2,950	$2,650	*$7,885*

S 790 EMEL SERIES FIELD – all gauges, individually made per customer specifications, 27 1/2 in. VR barrels with choke tubes (except .410 bore), color case hardened or coin finished receiver with ornate ornamental engraving and Rizzini crest, deluxe English walnut, Nizzoli best leather case. Imported 1994-2012.

	100%	98%	95%	90%	80%	70%	60%	LAST MSR
	$10,000	$8,500	$7,000	$6,000	$5,000	$4,250	$3,625	*$11,875*

Add $2,375 for small action in 28 ga. or .410 bore.

792 SMALL GAUGE MAG. SERIES – 20, 28, or 36 (.410 bore) ga., Mag. chambers, SST, ejectors, includes engraved sideplates. Importation disc. 1998.

	100%	98%	95%	90%	80%	70%	60%	LAST MSR
	$1,675	$1,325	$1,100	$895	$750	$675	$595	*$2,000*

A Model 792 EMEL was also available that was entirely hand finished with 18Kt. gold and hand engraving - prices begin at $8,250.

S 792 EMEL FIELD – all gauges, individually made per customer specifications, 27 1/2 in. VR barrels with choke tubes (except .410 bore), coin finished receiver with side plates featuring upgraded Bulino game scene engraving and fine scroll borders, deluxe English walnut, Nizzoli leather case. Imported 1994-2012.

	100%	98%	95%	90%	80%	70%	60%	LAST MSR
	$10,650	$9,500	$8,250	$7,000	$6,000	$5,000	$4,150	*$12,485*

Add $2,496 for small action in 28 ga. or .410 bore.

MODEL 2000 TRAP – 12 ga. only, includes nickel finished receiver with sideplates, gold trigger, VR barrels and rib. Importation disc. 1998.

	100%	98%	95%	90%	80%	70%	60%	LAST MSR
	$1,675	$1,375	$1,275	$1,025	$925	$825	$695	*$2,200*

A Model 2000 Trap EL was also available that was entirely hand finished with 18Kt. gold and hand engraving - prices began at $5,290.

MODEL 2000-SP – 12 ga. only, 26, 28, 30, or 32 in. overbored barrels with choke tubes, includes engraved sideplates, semi-fancy select walnut with quick detachable stock, cased. Imported 1994-98.

	100%	98%	95%	90%	80%	70%	60%	LAST MSR
	$3,000	$2,700	$2,400	$1,975	$1,600	$1,300	$1,000	*$3,650*

PREMIER SPORTING – 12 or 20 ga., 28, 29 1/2, 30, 32 or 34 in. multi-choke (5 extended chokes) barrels, hard cased, custom dimensions upon application. Imported 1994-2006.

	100%	98%	95%	90%	80%	70%	60%	LAST MSR
	$2,600	$2,050	$1,650	$1,375	$1,100	$900	$750	*$2,995*

PREMIER II – similar to Premier Sporting, except has blued receiver, European target style stock and beavertail foream, extra select walnut. Limited importation 2004 only.

	100%	98%	95%	90%	80%	70%	60%	LAST MSR
	$2,950	$2,800	$2,275	$1,775	$1,450	$1,300	$1,075	*$4,050*

VERTEX SPORTING – 12 ga., chromium finished (disc.), or matte black finished action, light border and scroll engraving (disc.), ejectors, ST or SST, hand checkered oil finished select walnut pistol grip stock and forend, 28 - 32 in. barrels, long forcing cones, 5 extended chokes, cased. Importation began 2004.

	100%	98%	95%	90%	80%	70%	60%	LAST MSR
MSR $2,475	$2,295	$2,010	$1,720	$1,560	$1,260	$1,035	$800	

S 2000 SPORTING – 12 ga., chromium finished action, 28 - 32 in. VR barrels, ejectors, SST, 10mm rib, long forcing cones, 5 extended chokes, sideplates with English scroll and border engraving, extra select walnut checkered pistol grip stock with palm swell, cased. Importation began 2004.

	100%	98%	95%	90%	80%	70%	60%	LAST MSR
MSR $5,595	$5,295	$4,635	$3,970	$3,600	$2,910	$2,385	$1,855	

GRADING - PPGS™	100%	98%	95%	90%	80%	70%	60%	LAST MSR

SPORTING EL – includes multi-chokes and case. Importation disc. 2000.

	$2,975	$2,850	$2,500	$2,225	$1,950	$1,675	$1,500	*$3,750*

UPLAND EL – all gauges, 27 1/2 in. VR barrels with choke tubes (except .410 bore), case hardened receiver, deluxe walnut, hard case. Imported 1994-2003.

	$2,625	$2,400	$2,100	$1,800	$1,500	$1,200	$995	*$2,800*

SHOTGUNS SxS

BR550 – 20 ga., scalloped boxlock action with coin finish or case colors, 26 1/2, 28, or 29 1/8 in. barrels, DT or SST, ejectors, fixed chokes, floral scroll engraving, checkered straight grip English style walnut stock. Importation began 2006.

MSR $4,495	$4,195	$3,670	$3,145	$2,855	$2,300	$1,890	$1,470	

BR 552 – 20 ga., engraved boxlock action with sideplates, 26 1/2, 28, or 29 1/8 in. barrels, DT or SST, ejectors, fixed chokes, extensive floral scroll engraving, checkered walnut pistol grip stock. Imported 2006-2012.

	$3,650	$3,395	$2,800	$2,500	$2,150	$1,750	$1,500	*$4,100*

UPLAND EL – various gauges, standard dimensions only, deluxe engraving with premium grade checkered walnut straight grip stock and forearm. Disc. 2012.

	$4,350	$3,950	$3,500	$2,950	$2,400	$1,850	$1,500	*$4,700*

RIZZINI, EMILIO

Current trademark owned by Fausti Stefano srl. since 1999. Previous shotgun manufacturer established circa 1974-1999, and located in Brescia, Italy. No current U.S. importation. Previously imported by Tristar Sporting Arms, Ltd., located in N. Kansas City, MO, and by Traditions, located in Old Saybrook, CT. (see Traditions section for listings). Some models were also previously imported by Armsport, Inc, located in Miami, FL.

Fausti Stefano srl acquired Emilio Rizzini in 1999. All Emilio Rizzini shotguns were equipped with a patented Four Locks locking system. Models listed were introduced during 1999. Most Emilio Rizzini field shotguns were available with fixed or interchangeable choke tubes.

Due to space considerations, information regarding this manufacturer is available online free of charge at www.bluebookofgunvalues.com.

RIZZINI, F.LLI

Current manufacturer located in Magno V.T., Italy. Consumer direct sales through FFL dealer. Some models were previously imported by New England Arms Corp. located in Kittery Point, ME, and by L. Michael Weatherby, located in Laguna Niguel, CA. Please contact the company directly for more information, including an individualized quotation and delivery time (see Trademark Index).

F.lli Rizzini manufactures some of the most technologically advanced rifles and shotguns in the world, approx. 11 guns per year.

RIFLES: SxS, CUSTOM

R1-E SAFARI SIDELOCK EJECTOR – 8x57 JRS, 9.3x74R, .375 H&H or .470 NE cal., every possible refinement, best quality double rifle, includes Purdey English scroll engraving and case. New 2005.

This model has a MSR of €88,000 for metric cals., €95,000 for dangerous game cals.

Delivery time on this model is approx. 2-4 years, depending on the engraver and amount of engraving.

R3-E SAFARI BOXLOCK – 8x57 JRS, 9.3x74R, or .444 Marlin cal. only, best quality boxlock double rifle, includes Purdey English scroll engraving and case. New 2005.

This model has a current MSR of €68,000.

Add €5,000 for patented scope mount.

Delivery time on this model is approx. 2-4 years, depending on the engraver and amount of engraving.

GRADING - PPGS™	100%	98%	95%	90%	80%	70%	60%	LAST MSR

SHOTGUNS: O/U, OLDER MFG.

In the past the Rizzini brothers collaborated with Rinaldo Zoli to make boxlock shotguns that were usually imported by Abercrombie & Fitch. These guns are normally marked on the water table "Zoli Rizzini". The Zoli Rizzini gun factory closed in 1971.

Zoli Rizzini manufactured an O/U boxlock with sideplates in most gauges, including 28 ga. and .410 bore. They were available with or w/o ejectors, and single or double triggers. Prices can range from $1,250 - $3,750, depending on gauge and configuration, with the smaller gauges being worth more than the 12 or 20.

SHOTGUNS: SxS, CUSTOM, OLDER MFG.

Zoli Rizzini guns are not to be confused with the quality of current Rizzini F.lli mfg. Normally these older Field Grade models (non-ejector, boxlock action in 12, 16, 20, 28 ga. or .410 bore) sell in the $500-$1,200 range, with a 25% premium for 28 ga. or .410 bore. Deluxe Field Models with scalloped boxlock action ad ejectors are currently valued in the $1,500-$2,500 range with a 30% premium for 28 ga. or .410 bore. The Extra Lusso Model (top-of-the-line) currently sells in the $3,500 range in 12 ga., $4,750 in 28 ga., and $4,250 in .410 bore.

SHOTGUNS: SxS, CUSTOM, RECENT MFG.

Today's F.lli Rizzini shotguns are made to individual custom order only. Prices do not include engraving, and prices will be substantially more for famous name engravers such as Pedersoli, Fracassi and Torcoli. F.lli Rizzini makes their own barrels in-house, and use their patented mechanisms.

Please contact the manufacturer directly for a quotation on special engraving options.

R1-E SIDELOCK EJECTOR – 12, 16, 20, 28 ga., or .410 bore, F.lli Rizzini patented sidelocks, select Circassian walnut, various barrel lengths, without engraving.

Current MSR on this model is €65,000.
Add €5,000 for 28 ga. or .410 bore. Add €16,000 for extra barrels (same ga.).
Current MSR on a pair of 12 & 20 ga. is €156,000 and €168,000 for a pair of 28 ga. and .410 bore.

Engraving on this model is quoted on a special order basis. Estimates may only be given at time of order. Only the best quality engravers are used for this model.

R2-E BOXLOCK EJECTOR – 12, 16, or 20 ga., select walnut, detachable bottom inspection plate, various barrel lengths, without engraving. Disc. 1995.

$10,500	$9,000	$8,000	$7,000	$6,200	$5,500	$4,750	*$25,000*

* ***R2-E Boxlock Ejector 28 ga. or .410 bore.*** – otherwise similar to above. Disc. 1995.

$12,750	$11,500	$10,000	$8,750	$7,500	$6,250	$5,000	*$27,500*

R3-E BOXLOCK EJECTOR – best quality patented boxlock ejector model w/o engraving, Importation began 2000.

Current MSR on this model is €48,000.
Add €5,000 for 28 ga. or .410 bore.
Add €16,000 per extra barrels (same ga.).

Delivery time on this model is approx. 2-4 years, depending on engraver and amount of engraving.

RIZZINI, I. (ISIDORA)

Please refer to the Fair Tecni-Mec listing in the F section.

THE ROBAR COMPANIES, INC.

Current customizer established during 1986, and located in Phoenix, AZ.

Robar is a leader in custom metal finishing, including combination finishes. These include the Roguard black finish, NP3 surface treatment, and additional finishes including bluing, electroless nickel, Polymax camoflauge, and Polymax finish. Please contact Robar directly (see Trademark Index) for more information, including current prices on their lineup of firearms, custom metal and wood finishes, and customizing services, including shotguns.

GRADING - PPGS™	100%	98%	95%	90%	80%	70%	60%	LAST MSR

ROBERT HISSERICH COMPANY

Previous gunsmith and previous custom rifle manufacturer located in Mesa, AZ. Previous company name was Stockworks.

RIFLES: BOLT ACTION

ROBERT HISSERICH BOLT GUN – various cals., features Weatherby Vanguard action, Pac-Nor stainless steel barrel, Pachmayr decelerator pad, hinged floor plate, black synthetic stock. Mfg. 2003 - disc.

	100%	98%	95%	90%	80%	70%	60%	LAST MSR
	$1,795	$1,500	$1,250	$1,050	$875	$750	$625	

LIGHTWEIGHT RIFLES SLR – various cals., Rem. long or short action, Kevlar/fiberglass MPI stock, match grade Pac-Nor barrel, straight flutes in bolt body, Timney trigger, straight line muzzle brake, pillar bedded action, free floating barrel, "window" cuts in action for lightening, black oxide finish on carbon or stainless steel, English or Claro walnut deluxe checkered stock, custom order only - allow 3-4 months. Approx. 4 3/4-5 lbs.

	100%	98%	95%	90%	80%	70%	60%	LAST MSR
	$2,600	$2,300	$2,000	$1,800	$1,600	$1,400	$1,200	

Add $200 for stainless steel.

SHARPSHOOTER – various cals., Win. Model 70 action with controlled feeding, precision long range hunting rifle with Schnieder stainless steel fluted barrel, laminated stock with ebony forend tip, titanium firing pin, pillar glass bedded with free floating barrel, includes Leupold 6.5-20x40mm scope, custom order only.

	100%	98%	95%	90%	80%	70%	60%	LAST MSR
	$5,950	$5,100	$4,500	$3,900	$3,400	$2,850	$2,150	

ROBERTS, J & SON (GUNMAKERS) LTD.

Please refer to the J. Roberts & Son (Gunmakers) Ltd. listing in the J section.

ROBERTSON

Current trademark manufactured by Boss & Co., Ltd. in Birmingham, England.

Please refer to the individual listings in the Boss section for this trademark.

ROBINSON ARMAMENT CO.

Current rifle manufacturer located in Salt Lake City, UT. Currently distributed by ZDF Import/Export, Inc., located in Salt Lake City, UT. Dealer and consumer direct sales.

PISTOLS: SEMI-AUTO

XCR-L MICRO PISTOL – 5.56 NATO, 6.8 SPC, or 7.62x39mm cal., 7 or 7 1/2 in. chrome lined barrel, upper, side, and lower rails, two stage trigger, accepts M-16 magazines, left side charging handle, various sight options, approx. 5 lbs. New 2010.

	100%	98%	95%	90%	80%	70%	60%	LAST MSR
MSR $1,550	$1,425	$1,225	$1,000	$800	$725	$600	$500	

XCR-M – various cals., gas piston operating system, various options available. New 2012.

	100%	98%	95%	90%	80%	70%	60%	LAST MSR
MSR $2,175	$1,900	$1,650	$1,400	$1,175	$950	$825	$725	

RIFLES: SEMI-AUTO

M96 EXPEDITIONARY RIFLE/CARBINE – .223 Rem. cal., tactical modular design, unique action allows accessory kit (new 2000) to convert loading from bottom to top of receiver, 16.2 (Recon Model, new 2001), 17 1/4 (carbine, new 2000) or 20 1/4 in. barrel with muzzle brake, stainless steel receiver and barrel, matte black finish metal, black synthetic stock and forearm, adj. sights, gas operated with adjustment knob, last shot hold open, rotating bolt assembly, 8 1/2 lbs. Mfg. 1999-2006.

	100%	98%	95%	90%	80%	70%	60%	LAST MSR
	$1,495	$1,300	$1,100	$925	$850	$775	$700	

Add $750 for rifle/carbine with top feed.

XCR-L MODEL – .223 Rem., 6.8mm SPC, or .308 Win. (new 2008) cal., tactical design, 16 in. full floating barrel, handguard with 8 in. side and bottom Picatinny rails, open sights, quick change barrel system, bolt hold open, side folding stock standard until 2008, stock configuration optional beginning 2009, two-stage trigger, uses M16 mags., 7 1/2 lbs. New 2006.

	100%	98%	95%	90%	80%	70%	60%	LAST MSR
MSR $1,550	$1,425	$1,225	$1,000	$850	$725	$600	$500	

Add $500-$550 for conversion kit, depending on caliber (includes barrel, bolt, and 25 shot mag.).

GRADING - PPGS™	100%	98%	95%	90%	80%	70%	60%	LAST MSR

Add $200 for 6.8mm SPC or .308 Win. cal.
Add $150-$250 for stock option, depending on configuration.
Add $50 for 16 in. heavy barrel or $75 for 18 in. heavy barrel.

The model nomenclature was changed from XCR to XCR-L (lightweight) during 2008.

XCR-M – .260 Rem. or .308 Win. cal., 18.6 in. stainless steel barrel, approx. 8 lbs. New 2012.

MSR $2,400	$2,150	$1,800	$1,500	$1,200	$1,000	$900	$800

ROCHE, CHRISTIAN

Current manufacturer located in Veauche, France.

Christian Roche manufactures quality SxS shotguns and double rifles. Since all orders are per individual specifications, the factory must be contacted directly to obtain a current price quotation and information (see Trademark Index).

ROCK ISLAND ARMORY

Previous WWII Springfield Model 1903 rifle subcontractor located in Rock Island, IL. Please refer to Springfield Armory listing for more information.

ROCK ISLAND ARMORY (CURRENT MFG.)

Current trademark manufactured by Arms Corp. of the Philippines. Currently imported by Armscor Precision International, located in Pahrump, NV.

PISTOLS: SEMI-AUTO

M1911-A1 CSP – .45 ACP cal., officer's configuration with 3 1/2 in. barrel, checkered hardwood grips, 2.16 lbs. Importation began 2002.

No MSR	$415	$375	$325	$300	$280	$260	$220

Add $52 for two-tone finish (disc. 2011).
Add $105 for stainless steel (disc. 2011).
Add $58 for Model 1911-A1 CS RIA Tactical.

M1911-A1 FSP – 9mm Para. (new 2011), .38 Super or .45 ACP cal., patterned after the Colt Govt. Model, 7 shot mag. (2 provided), 5 in. barrel, parkerized (disc. 2001), nickel, blue (new 2002), two-tone (new 2002), or stainless steel (new 2002), skeletonized combat hammer and trigger, front and rear slide serrations, hard rubber grips, 38 oz. Imported 1996-97, reintroduced 2001.

No MSR	$395	$360	$320	$295	$280	$260	$240

Add $10 for MSP Model or for .38 Super cal.
Add $18 for Duracoat finish.
Add $34 for two-tone finish.
Add $100 for stainless steel (disc. 2011)
Add $60 for a high capacity configuration (Model 1911-A2 HC, 13 shot mag., disc. 2009).
Add $60 for Model 1911-A1 FS RIA Tactical (.45 ACP cal. only) or $84 for FS RIA Tactical with Duracoat (new 2012).
Add $205 for Model 1911-A2 FS RIA Match Model (.45 ACP cal. only).
Add $55 for nickel finish (Model 1911-A1 FSNP).
Add $100 for night sights (new 2012).

M1911-A1 FS MATCH – .45 ACP cal., 5 or 6 in. barrel, features fiber optic front sight and LPA rear sight, skeletonized trigger and bobbed hammer, double diamond checkered walnut grips, parkerized finish, 8 shot mag. New 2011.

No MSR	$650	$575	$500	$450	$400	$350	$300

M1911-A1 FS TACTICAL – .45 ACP cal., features skeletonized trigger, bobbed hammer, and lower Picatinny rail, diamond checkered walnut or VZ (new 2013) grips, parkerized finish, 8 shot mag., standard or Meprolite night sights. New 2011.

No MSR	$525	$450	$400	$365	$335	$300	$275

Add $100 for Meprolite night sights.

GRADING - PPGS™	100%	98%	95%	90%	80%	70%	60%	LAST MSR

M1911-A1 MAP/MAPP SERIES – 9mm Para. cal., SA/DA operation, MAP 1 Series is standard configuration, while MAPP 1 Series is tactical with lower Picatinny rail, 3 1/2 (MAPP 1), or 4 (MAP 1) in. barrel, fixed front and adj. rear sight, double slide serrations, ambidextrous safety, 16 shot mag., synthetic grip frame with steel slide. New 2010.

No MSR	$450	$400	$350	$300	$275	$250	$225	

M1911-A1 MICRO MAG – .22 TCM and 9mm Para. cals., supplied with 2 barrels and 2 mags., 22 shot mag., features an appearance similar to M1911-A1 FS Tactical. New 2011.

No MSR	$575	$500	$425	$375	$325	$300	$275	

Add $45 for Micro Mag Target Model (new 2012).

XT22 – .22 LR cal., 5 in. barrel, skeletonized trigger, bobbed hammer, checkered synthetic grips, parkerized finish, 15 shot mag., 38 oz. New 2011.

No MSR	$470	$425	$350	$300	$250	$200	$175	

TCM SERIES – .22 TCM or 9mm TCM cal., available in MicroMag, Target, Midsize Standard, VZ Midsize, or VZ Fullsize configurations, SA, dovetail ramp tactical or target dj. sights, parkerized finish, black checkered synthetic grips, 17 shot mag., combat hammer, skeletonized trigger, includes extra 9mm barrel. New 2013.

No MSR	$742	$650	$550	$500	$410	$335	$260	

ROCK-OLA MANUFACTURING CO.

Previous WWII M1 carbine subcontractor located in Chicago, IL. Please refer to US M1 carbines/rifles under U.S. Military listing for more information.

ROCK RIVER ARMS, INC.

Current handgun and rifle manufacturer established in 1996 and located in Colona, IL beginning 2004. Previously located in Cleveland, IL until 2003. Dealer and consumer direct sales.

PISTOLS: SEMI-AUTO

Rock River Arms made a variety of high quality M-1911 based semi-autos through 2011. They specialized in manufacturing their own National Match frames and slides. Previous models included: the Standard Match (disc. 2003, last MSR was $1,150), Ultimate Match Achiever (disc. 2003, last MSR was $2,255), Matchmaster Steel (disc. 2001, last MSR was $2,355), Elite Commando (disc. 2005, last MSR was $1,725), Hi-Cap Basic Limited (disc. 2003, last MSR was $1,895), and the Doug Koenig Signature Series (disc. 2003, last MSR was $5,000, .38 Super cal.). Rock River Arms still offers parts.

BASIC LIMITED MATCH – 9mm Para., .38 Super, .40 S&W, or .45 ACP cal., blue, hard chrome, black "T", or black/green "T" duotone finish, 4 1/4, 5, or 6 in. barrel, National Match frame and slide with low mount Bo-Mar hidden leaf rear sight, beveled mag well and choice of 20, 25, or 30 LPI checkered front strap, match Commander hammer and match sear, tuned and polished extractor and extended ejector, lowered and flared ejection port, beavertail grip safety, aluminum speed trigger, two piece recoil guide rod and polished feed ramp, RRA dovetail front sight, serrated slide stop and ambidextrous safety, deluxe checkered grips. Disc. 2010.

	$1,675	$1,465	$1,255	$1,140	$920	$755	$585	*$1,840*

LIMITED MATCH – 9mm Para., .38 Super, .40 S&W, or .45 ACP cal., blue, hard chrome, black "T" or black/green duotone finish, National match frame with beveled mag well and choice of 20, 25, or 30 LPI checkered front and rear strap, 4 1/4, 5, or 6 in. barrel with double slide serrations and RRA borders, low mount Bo-Mar hidden leaf rear sight, RRA dovetail front sight, 40 LPI checkering under trigger guard, Match Commander hammer and match sear, aluminum speed trigger, beavertail grip safety with raised pad, extended mag. release button, tuned and polished feed ramp, deluxe checkered grips, two-piece recoil guide rod. Disc. 2010.

	$1,975	$1,700	$1,500	$1,300	$1,100	$900	$750	*$2,185*

GRADING - PPGS™	100%	98%	95%	90%	80%	70%	60%	LAST MSR

NATIONAL MATCH HARDBALL – 9mm Para., .38 Super, .40 S&W, or .45 ACP cal., blue, hard chrome, black "T" or black/green "T" duotone finish, forged National Match frame with 4 1/4, 5, or 6 in. barrel, beveled mag well, choice of 20, 25, or 30 LPI checkered front strap, choice of rear or double slide serrations, aluminum speed trigger, milled in Bo-Mar rear sight with hidden rear leaf, lowered and flared ejection port, polished feed ramp, tuned and polished extractor and extended ejector, checkered rosewood grips. Disc. 2011.

	$1,400	$1,225	$1,050	$950	$770	$630	$490	*$1,550*

BULLSEYE WADCUTTER – 9mm Para., .38 Super, .40 S&W, or .45 ACP cal., blue, hard chrome, black "T" or black/green "T" duotone finish, 7 shot mag., 4 1/4, 5, or 6 in. barrel, National Match frame with choice of RRR Slide mount, Bo-Mar rib, Caspian frame mount sights, or Weigand 3rd Gen. frame mount, double slide serrations, choice of 20, 25, or 30 LPI checkered front strap, beavertail grip safety with raised pad, lowered and flared ejection port, Commander hammer and match sear, aluminum speed trigger, checkered rosewood grips. Disc. 2011.

	$1,550	$1,355	$1,160	$1,055	$850	$695	$540	*$1,715*

Add $35 for Caspian frame mount or Bo-Mar rib.

TACTICAL PISTOL – 9mm Para., .38 Super, .40 S&W, .45 ACP cal., blue, hard chrome, black "T" or black/green "T" duotone finish, 5 in. barrel with double slide serrations, RRA bar stock frame with integral light rail, choice of 20, 25, or 30 LPI checkered front strap, lowered and flared ejection port, RRA dovetail front sight with tritium inserts, Heinie rear sight with tritium inserts, optional Novak rear sight, aluminum speed trigger, tuned and polished extractor, extended ejector, beavertail grip safety, tactical mag. catch and safety, standard recoil system, completely dehorned for carry, checkered rosewood grips, optional ambidextrous safety, optional Smith & Alexander magwell. Disc. 2011.

	$1,850	$1,620	$1,385	$1,260	$1,015	$830	$645	*$2,040*

BASIC CARRY – .45 ACP cal., 5 in. National Match barrel with double slide serrations, parkerized finish, checkered rosewood grips, RRA forged National Match frame, choice of 20, 25, or 30 LPI checkered front strap, lowered and flared ejection port, RRA dovetail front sight, Heinie rear sight, Match Commander hammer and match sear, aluminum speed trigger, beavertail grip safety, standard mag. catch, safety, and standard recoil system. Disc. 2010.

	$1,450	$1,270	$1,085	$985	$795	$650	$505	*$1,600*

RRA PRO CARRY – 9mm Para., .38 Super, .40 S&W, or .45 ACP cal. 4 1/4, 5, or 6 in. barrel with slide serrations, RRA National Match frame with choice of 20, 25, or 30 LPI checkered front strap, lowered and flared ejection port, RRA dovetail front sight with tritium inserts, Match Commander hammer, aluminum speed trigger, tuned and polished extractor, extended ejector, deluxe rosewood grips, choice of Heinie or Novak rear sight with tritium inserts, beavertail grip safety. Disc. 2010.

	$1,675	$1,465	$1,255	$1,140	$920	$755	$585	*$1,920*

RRA SERVICE AUTO – 9mm Para. cal., similar to RRA Pro Carry, except with 5 in. barrel and double slide serrations. Mfg. 2009-2010.

	$1,575	$1,380	$1,180	$1,070	$865	$710	$550	*$1,790*

LIMITED POLICE COMPETITION – 9mm Para. cal., 5 in. National Match barrel, blue, hard chrome, black "T", or black/green "T" duotone finish, RRA forged National Match frame with beveled mag well with choice of 20, 25, or 30 LPI checkered front strap, double slide serrations, 3-position rear sight, choice of wide or narrow blade, RRA dovetail front sight, tall, thinned, and relieved for PPC, Smith & Alexander flared mag well, lowered and flared ejection port, Match Commander hammer and match sear, tuned and polished extractor and extended ejector, beavertail grip safety and flat checkered mainspring housing, deluxe checkered grips, ambidextrous safety, tuned and polished feed ramp, two-piece recoil spring guide rod. Disc. 2010.

	$2,095	$1,825	$1,600	$1,375	$1,250	$1,000	$775	*$2,375*

GRADING - PPGS™	100%	98%	95%	90%	80%	70%	60%	LAST MSR

UNLIMITED POLICE COMPETITION – 9mm Para. cal., forged 6 in. National Match barrel, RRA forged National Match frame with beveled mag well, choice of 20, 25, or 30 LPI checkered front strap, double slide serrations, similar configuration as Limited Police Competition. Disc. 2010.

	$2,095	$1,825	$1,600	$1,375	$1,250	$1,000	$775	*$2,375*

LAR-15 – .223 Rem. cal., 7 or 10 1/2 in. barrel, A2 or A4 configuration, A2 flash hider, single stage trigger, Hogue rubber pistol grip, approx. 5 lbs.

MSR $945	$850	$740	$625	$560	$455	$370	$290	

Add $10 for aluminum free floating forearm or $45 for gas block sight base.

LAR-9 – similar to LAR-15, except is 9mm Para. cal., A1 flash hider, 4.8 - 5.2 lbs.

MSR $1,080	$995	$865	$750	$650	$550	$450	$350	

Add $10 for A4 upper, $45 for aluminum free floating forearm with A2 front sight, or $60 for aluminum free floating handguard with gas block sight base.

LAR-40 – .40 S&W cal., 7 or 10 1/2 in. barrel, forged lower receiver with integral magwell, A2 or A4 upper, single stage trigger, Hogue rubber pistol grip, approx. 5 lbs. Mfg. 2010-2011.

	$1,050	$900	$800	$700	$600	$500	$400	*$1,120*

Add $45 for 7 in. barrel and free float tube handguard.
Add $10-$15 for gas block sight base.

PDS PISTOL (PISTON DRIVEN SYSTEM) – .223 Rem. cal., 8 in. barrel, features full length upper and partial lower Picatinny rails, and performance piston system with adj. gas piston, Hogue rubber pistol grip, ribbed forend, single stage trigger, injection molded ribbed handguard, folding ambidextrous non-reciprocating charging handles, two-position regulator, approx. 5 lbs. New 2010.

MSR $1,335	$1,225	$1,100	$950	$875	$800	$725	$650	

Add $150 for aluminum tri-rail handguard.

RIFLES: SEMI-AUTO

Rock River Arms makes a variety of AR-15 style rifles/carbines in .223 Rem. cal. Previous models include the CAR UTE (disc. 2004, last MSR was $850), Tactical Carbine A2, M4 Entry (disc. 2003, last MSR was $875), and NM A2-DCM Legal (disc. 2005, last MSR was $1,265).

Beginning 2006, Rock River Arms released a series of paramilitary style rifles in 9mm Para. cal. Also during 2006, the company released a series of paramilitary style rifles in .308 Win. cal.

A wide variety of options are available for each rifle. Base model assumes black furniture.

LAR-15 STANDARD A2 – .223 Rem. cal., forged A2 upper receiver, 20 in. Wilson chrome-moly barrel, A2 flash hider, two-stage match trigger, A2 pistol grip, handguard, and buttstock, 8.6 lbs.

MSR $980	$900	$775	$650	$595	$475	$395	$300	

LAR-15 STANDARD A4 – similar to Standard A2 model, except has forged A4 upper receiver, 8.2 lbs.

MSR $940	$850	$715	$600	$525	$465	$395	$295	

LAR-15 NATIONAL MATCH A2 – .223 Rem. cal., forged A2 upper receiver, 20 in. Wilson heavy match stainless barrel, 20 shot mag., two-stage match trigger, A2 flash hider, A2 pistol grip and buttstock, free floating handguard, 9.7 lbs.

MSR $1,250	$1,095	$925	$775	$675	$575	$500	$415	

LAR-15 NATIONAL MATCH A4 – .223 Rem. cal., similar to National Match A2 model, except has forged A4 upper receiver with NM carry handle, 9.7 lbs.

MSR $1,345	$1,195	$1,025	$850	$750	$600	$495	$385	

LAR-15 CAR A2 – .223 Rem. cal., forged A2 upper receiver, 16 in. Wilson chrome-moly barrel, A2 flash hider, two-stage match trigger, CAR length handguard, A2 pistol grip, fixed or tactical CAR stock, 7 1/2 lbs.

MSR $960	$875	$750	$635	$580	$465	$380	$295	

Add $15 for six-position tactical stock.

GRADING - PPGS™	100%	98%	95%	90%	80%	70%	60%	LAST MSR

Add $175 for tactical carry handle.
Add $145 for quad rail and tactical CAR stock.

LAR-15 CAR A4 – .223 Rem. cal., similar to CAR A2, except has forged A4 upper receiver, 7.1 lbs.

MSR $925	$850	$715	$600	$525	$465	$395	$295	

Add $15 for six-position tactical stock.
Add $145 for quad rail and tactical stock.
Add $175 for tactical carry handle.

LAR-15 MID-LENGTH A2 – .223 Rem. cal., forged A2 upper receiver, 16 in. Wilson chrome-moly barrel, two-stage match trigger, mid-length handguard, A2 pistol grips and buttstock, 7 1/2 lbs.

MSR $960	$875	$750	$625	$575	$465	$375	$295	

Add $15 for six-position tactical stock.

LAR-15 MID-LENGTH A4 – .223 Rem. cal., similar to Mid-Length A2 model, except has forged A4 upper receiver, 7.1 lbs.

MSR $925	$850	$715	$600	$525	$465	$395	$295	

Add $15 for six-position tactical stock.
Add $170 for quad rail and tactical stock.
Add $175 for tactical carry handle.

LAR-15 TACTICAL CAR A4 – .223 Rem. cal., forged A4 upper receiver, detachable tactical carry handle, 16 in. Wilson chrome-moly barrel, A2 flash hider, two-stage match trigger, Hogue rubber pistol grip, R-4 handguard, six-position tactical CAR stock, 7 1/2 lbs.

MSR $995	$925	$810	$695	$630	$510	$415	$325	

Add $40 for chrome lined barrel.
Add $45 for A2 carry handle or $80 for tactical carry handle.

LAR-15 ELITE CAR A4 – .223 Rem. cal., similar to Tactical CAR A4, except has mid-length handguard, 7.7 lbs.

MSR $995	$925	$810	$695	$630	$510	$415	$325	

Add $40 for chrome lined barrel.
Add $45 for A2 carry handle or $80 for tactical carry handle.

LAR-15 ELITE COMP – .223 Rem. cal., 16 in. barrel with tactical muzzle brake, MagPul CTR stock, features free floating half-round, half-quad handguard, Pads flip up rear sight, pistol grip, 8.4 lbs. New 2008.

MSR $1,445	$1,375	$1,200	$1,025	$925	$750	$625	$475	

LAR-15 TACTICAL CAR UTE2 – .223 Rem. cal., forged Universal Tactical Entry 2 upper receiver, 16 in. Wilson chrome-moly barrel, A2 flash hider, two-stage match trigger, Hogue rubber pistol grip, R-4 handguard, six-position tactical CAR stock, 7 1/2 lbs.

MSR $1,060	$965	$825	$700	$625	$510	$415	$325	

LAR-15 ELITE CAR UTE2 – .223 Rem. cal., similar to Tactical CAR UTE2, except has mid-length handguard, 7.7 lbs.

MSR $1,060	$965	$825	$700	$625	$510	$415	$325	

LAR-15 ENTRY TACTICAL – .223 Rem. cal., forged A4 upper receiver, 16 in. Wilson chrome-moly R-4 heavy barrel, detachable tactical carry handle, A2 flash hider, two-stage match trigger, Hogue rubber pistol grip, R-4 handguard with double heat shields, six-position tactical CAR stock, 7 1/2 lbs.

MSR $995	$925	$810	$695	$625	$510	$415	$325	

Add $40 for chrome lined barrel.
Add $45 for A2 carry handle or $80 for tactical carry handle.

LAR-15 PRO-SERIES GOVERNMENT – .223 Rem. cal., forged A4 upper receiver, 16 in. chrome lined Wilson chrome-moly barrel, A2 flash hider, two-stage match trigger, flip-up rear sight, Hogue rubber pistol grip, six-position tactical CAR stock, Surefire M73 quad

GRADING - PPGS™	100%	98%	95%	90%	80%	70%	60%	LAST MSR

rail handguard, Surefire M951 WeaponLight light system, EOTech 552 Holosight red-dot optical sight, side mount sling swivel, 8.2 lbs.

MSR $2,375	$2,150	$1,850	$1,575	$1,425	$1,150	$950	$725	

LAR-15 PRO-SERIES ELITE – .223 Rem. cal., forged A4 upper receiver, chrome lined 16 in. Wilson chrome-moly barrel, RRA tactical muzzle brake, flip front sight and gas block assembly, two-stage match trigger, Winter trigger guard, Badger tactical charging handle latch, A.R.M.S. #40L low profile flip-up rear sight, ERGO sure-grip pistol grip, six-position tactical CAR stock, MWI front sling adapter, MWI CAR stock end plate adapter loop rear sling mount, Daniel Defense 12.0 FSPM quad rail handguard, SureFire M910A-WH vertical foregrip weaponlight, Aimpoint Comp M2 red dot optical sight and QRP mount with spacer, 9 1/2 lbs.

MSR $2,750	$2,500	$2,175	$1,975	$1,595	$1,300	$1,025	$975	

LAR-15 VARMINT EOP (ELEVATED OPTICAL PLATFORM) – .223 Rem. cal., forged EOP upper receiver, 16, 18, 20, or 24 in. Wilson air gauged stainless steel bull barrel, Weaver style light varmint gas block with sight rail, two-stage match trigger, Winter trigger guard, knurled and fluted free floating aluminum tube handguard, Hogue rubber pistol grip, A2 buttstock, approx. 8.2 - 10 lbs.

MSR $1,140	$1,025	$875	$725	$675	$525	$450	$350	

Add $10 for 18, $20 for 20, or $30 for 24 in. barrel.

LAR-15 VARMINT A4 – .223 Rem. or .308 Win. (mfg. 2010-2011) cal., similar to Varmint EOP, except has forged A4 upper receiver., 7.9 - 11.6 lbs.

MSR $1,105	$995	$850	$725	$650	$525	$425	$350	

Add $10 for 18, $20 for 20, or $30 for 24 in. barrel.
Add $395 for .308 Win. cal. (mfg. 2010-2011).

LAR-15 PREDATOR PURSUIT RIFLE – .223 Rem. cal., similar to Varmint A4, except has 16 (Predator Mid-Length, new 2011) or 20 in. Wilson heavy match stainless steel barrel, 8.1 lbs.

MSR $1,125	$1,000	$875	$725	$675	$525	$450	$350	

FRED EICHLER SERIES PREDATOR RIFLE – .223 Rem. cal., 16 in. mid-length stainless steel cryogenically treated barrel, low profile hidden gas block, chrome RRA National Match two-stage trigger with parkerized finish on trigger shoe, RRA winter trigger guard, RRA free-floating handguard with full length Picatinny top rail and 2 1/2 in. rails at 3, 6, and 9 o'clock positions, over molded pistol grip, RRA six position or Operator stock, 20 shot mag., forged A4 upper flattop, custom muzzle break, two-tone black/tan finish, includes hard case. New 2012.

MSR $1,395	$1,225	$1,050	$875	$775	$625	$525	$450	

LAR-15 COYOTE – .223 Rem. cal., forged A4 upper receiver, 16 or 20 in. Wilson chrome-moly HBar barrel, Smith Vortex flash hider, Weaver style light varmint gas block with sight rail, two-stage match trigger, Winter trigger guard, Hogue rubber pistol grip, Hogue overmolded free float tube handguard, ACE ARFX skeleton stock, 8.4 lbs.

MSR $1,190	$1,075	$925	$775	$695	$575	$450	$350	

Add $15 for 20 in. barrel.

LAR-15 OPERATOR SERIES – .223 Rem. cal., 16 in. chrome-moly barrel, tactical muzzle brake, forged LAR-15 lower, forged A4 upper receiver, upper Picatinny rail, Operator CAR stock, matte black finish, two-stage trigger, winter trigger guard, ERGO SureGrip, configurations include the Entry (R-4 handguard and barrel profile), the Tactical (R-4 handguard), and the Elite (half-quad free float handguard with mid-length gas system), designed for left-handed shooters, 7.2-8 lbs. New 2011.

MSR $1,050	*N/A	$875	$750	$675	$535	$440	$340	

IMPORTANT NOTE: On model(s) where *N/A has replaced the normal 100% value, it indicates current market conditions are too unstable to accurately ascertain 100%-60% values. Factory retail prices (MSRs) reflect most recent updates. For more up-to-date information on current pricing trends and additional useful information, please visit www.bluebookofgunvalues.com, select "Information & Services " from the menu, and click on "Additional Book Information".

GRADING - PPGS™	100%	98%	95%	90%	80%	70%	60%	LAST MSR

LAR-15 ATH (ADVANCED TACTICAL HUNTER) CARBINE – .223 Rem. cal., forged A4 upper and LAR-15 lower receiver, 18 in. heavy match cryo treated stainless steel barrel, muzzle brake, matte black finish, low profile gas block, two-stage trigger, winter trigger guard, ERGO Sure Grip pistol grip, half-quad free float handguard with three rail covers, Operator CAR stock, 7.7 lbs. New 2011.

MSR $1,300	$1,150	$975	$825	$750	$600	$495	$385	

LAR-15 9.11 COMMEMORATIVE – .5.56 NATO or .223 Rem. cal., 16 in. lightweight chrome moly barrel, forged A4 upper receiver, mid-length gas system with low profile gas block, chromed bolt carrier group, RRA tactical muzzle brake, two-stage chrome trigger group, winter trigger guard, star safety, overmolded pistol grip, Hogue free float tube handguard, non-collapsible or six position tactical CAR stock, flat black finish with American flag, and "9*11 Tenth Year Commemoration" engraved on receiver. Limited mfg. mid-2011.

	$995	$850	$725	N/A	N/A	N/A	N/A	*$1,011*

Add $25 for non-collapsible stock, pinned/welded tactical muzzle brake, and 10 shot mag.

LAR-15 HUNTER – .223 Rem. cal., 16 in. chromemoly barrel, forged A4 upper receiver, tactical muzzle brake, low profile gas block, two-stage trigger, winter trigger guard, half-quad free float mid-length handguard with three rail covers, Operator CAR stock, Hogue rubber pistol grip, WYL-Ehide or PRK-Ehide anodized camo finish, 7.6 lbs. New 2012.

MSR $1,480	$1,395	$1,200	$1,000	$925	$750	$625	$475	

PDS CARBINE (PISTON DRIVEN SYSTEM) – .223 Rem. cal., 16 in. chrome moly barrel, A2 flash hider, black finish, full length upper and partial lower Picatinny rails, and performance piston system with adj. gas piston, Hogue rubber pistol grip, ribbed forend, two stage trigger, injection molded ribbed or tri-rail handguard, folding ambidextrous non-reciprocating charging handles, two-position regulator, side folding six-position tactical stock with receiver extension storage compartment, approx. 7.4 lbs. New 2011.

MSR $1,685	$1,550	$1,300	$1,100	$900	$700	$600	$550	

Add $155 for tri-rail handguard.

LAR-6.8 A2/A4 – .6.8mm Rem. SPC cal., forged A2 or A4 upper receiver, 16 in. Wilson chrome-moly barrel, A2 flash hider, two-stage match trigger, A2 pistol grip and buttstock, choice of CAR length or mid-length handguard, 7 1/2 lbs.

MSR $960	$875	$725	$625	$525	$475	$395	$295	

Add $15 for A4 with six-position stock.
Add $35 for A2 buttstock.

LAR-6.8 COYOTE – 6.8mmSPC cal., forged A4 upper receiver, 16 in. Wilson chrome-moly HBar barrel, Smith Vortex flash hider, Weaver style light varmint gas block with sight rail, two-stage match trigger, Winter trigger guard, Hogue rubber pistol grip, Hogue overmolded free float tube handguard, A2 stock, 7 lbs.

MSR $1,200	$1,095	$925	$775	$695	$575	$450	$350	

LAR-458 CAR A4 – .458 SOCOM cal., forged A4 upper receiver, 16 in. Wilson chrome-moly bull barrel, A2 flash hider, Weaver style varmint gas block with sight rail, two-stage match trigger, knurled and fluted free floating aluminum tube handguard, A2 buttstock and pistol grip, 7.6 lbs.

MSR $1,150	$1,025	$875	$750	$675	$550	$440	$340	

Add $280 for Operator model with half quad free float with full length top rail and CAR stock (new 2010)

LAR-458 MID-LENGTH A4 – .458 SOCOM cal., forged A4 upper receiver, 16 in. chrome-moly bull barrel, A2 flash hider, gas block with sight rail, two-stage match trigger, knurled and fluted free floating aluminum tube handguard, A2 buttstock and pistol grip, 7.8 lbs. New 2010.

MSR $1,150	$1,025	$875	$750	$675	$550	$440	$340	

Add $290 for Operator model with half quad free float with full length top rail, Vortex flash hider and CAR stock (new 2010).

GRADING - PPGS™	100%	98%	95%	90%	80%	70%	60%	LAST MSR

LAR-8 MID LENGTH A2/A4 – .308 Win. cal., 16 in. barrel with A2 flash hider, CAR buttstock, gas block sight base, Hogue rubber grip, two stage trigger, forged A2 or A4 upper receiver, mid-length handguard, approx. 8 lbs. New 2010.

MSR $1,265	$1,125	$975	$825	$750	$600	$495	$385	

Add $110 for A4 configuration.

LAR-8 ELITE OPERATOR – .308 Win. cal. 16 in. barrel, similar to Mid-length A4, except has advanced half quad rail, flip front sight, gas block sight base, Operator stock and Smith Vortex flash hider. New 2010.

MSR $1,670	$1,525	$1,300	$1,100	$900	$700	$600	$550	

LAR-8 STANDARD A2/A4 – .308 Win. cal., forged lower and A2 or A4 upper receiver, 20 in. chrome-moly barrel, A2 flash hider, gas block sight base, two stage trigger, A2 buttstock, A2 handguard, Hogue rubber pistol grip, approx. 9 lbs. New 2010.

MSR $1,300	$1,150	$975	$825	$750	$600	$495	$385	

Add $100 for A2 configuration.

LAR-8 STANDARD OPERATOR – .308 Win. cal. 16 in. barrel, similar to LAR-8 Standard A4, except has advanced half quad rail, flip front sight, gas block sight base, Operator stock and Smith Vortex flash hider. New 2010.

MSR $1,720	$1,550	$1,315	$1,100	$900	$700	$600	$550	

LAR-8 PREDATOR HP – .308 Win. cal., forged lower and upper receiver, 20 in. bead blasted lightweight stainless steel barrel, gas block sight base, two stage trigger, A2 buttstock, free float tube handguard, Hogue rubber pistol grip, approx. 8.6 lbs. New 2010.

MSR $1,535	$1,425	$1,225	$1,030	$925	$750	$625	$475	

Add $50 for Operator A2 stock.

LAR-8 VARMINT A4 – .308 Win. cal., forged LAR-8 lower, forged A4 upper receiver with forward assist and port door, 20 or 26 in. cryo treated stainless steel bull barrel, varmint gas block with sight rail, two-stage trigger, winter trigger guard, Hogue rubber pistol grip, A2 buttstock, aluminum free float tube handguard, 10.4-11.6 lbs. New 2011.

MSR $1,500	$1,400	$1,200	$1,000	$925	$750	$625	$475	

Add $5 for 26 in. barrel.
Add $110 for quad rail.

LAR-9 CAR A2/A4 – 9mm Para. cal., forged A2 or A4 upper receiver, 16 in. Wilson chrome-moly barrel, A1 flash hider, standard single stage trigger, CAR length handguard, A2 pistol grip, six-position tactical CAR stock, approx. 7 lbs.

MSR $1,085	$995	$875	$750	$675	$525	$450	$350	

Add $25 for A2 buttstock.

LAR-10 VARMINT A4 – .308 Win. cal., forged A4 upper reciever with forward assist and port door, 26 in. Wilson stainless steel bull barrel, Weaver type sight base gas block, two-stage match trigger, knurled and fluted free floating aluminum tube handguard, Hogue pistol grip, A2 buttstock, 11.6 lbs. Disc. 2010.

	$1,225	$1,070	$925	$825	$675	$550	$425	*$1,350*

LAR-10 MID-LENGTH A2/A4 – .308 Win. cal., forged A2 or A4 upper receiver with forward assist and ejection port door, 16 in. Wilson chrome-moly barrel, A2 flash hider, A2 front sight or A4 gas block with sight base, two-stage match trigger, mid-length handguard, Hogue rubber pistol grip, six-position tactical CAR stock, approx. 8 lbs. Disc. 2009.

	$1,000	$875	$750	$675	$550	$450	$350	*$1,100*

Add $50 for A2 sights.

LAR-10 STANDARD A2/A4 – .308 Win. cal., forged A2 or A4 upper receiver, with forward assist and port door, 20 in. Wilson chrome-moly barrel, A2 flash hider, A2 front sight or A4 gas block sight base, two-stage match trigger, A2 handguard, Hogue rubber pistol grip, A2 buttstock, 9.3 lbs. Disc. 2009.

	$1,000	$875	$750	$675	$550	$450	$350	*$1,100*

Add $45 for A2 sights.

GRADING - PPGS™	100%	98%	95%	90%	80%	70%	60%	LAST MSR

LAR-40 MID-LENGTH A2/A4 – .40 S&W cal., forged A2 upper, 16 in. chrome-moly barrel, A2 flash hider, two-stage match trigger, mid-length handguard, Hogue rubber pistol grip, six-position tactical CAR stock, approx. 7 lbs. Mfg. 2010-2011.

	$1,000	$875	$725	$675	$525	$450	$350	*$1,125*

Add $15 for A2 configuration.

LAR-40 CAR A2/A4 – .40 S&W cal., forged A2 or A4 upper receiver, 16 in. chrome-moly barrel, A2 flash hider, single stage trigger, R-4 handguard, six-position tactical CAR stock with Hogue pistol grip, approx. 7 lbs. Disc. 2011.

	$1,000	$875	$725	$675	$525	$450	$350	*$1,125*

Add $25 for A2 buttstock.

TASC RIFLE – .223 Rem. cal., forged A2 upper receiver with lockable windage and elevation adj. rear sight, 16 in. Wilson chrome-moly barrel, A2 flash hider, two-stage match trigger, Hogue rubber pistol grip, A2 buttstock or six-position CAR tactical buttstock, choice of R-4 or mid-length handguard, approx. 7 1/2 lbs. Disc. 2009.

	$875	$765	$655	$595	$475	$395	$300	*$950*

Add $15 for six-position collapsible stock.

PRO-SERIES TASC – .223 Rem. cal., forged A2 upper reciever, chrome lined 16 in. Wilson chrome-moly barrel, Smith Vortex flash hider, two-stage match trigger, oversize winter trigger guard, A2 rear sight with lockable windage and elevation, Hogue rubber pistol grip, six-position tactical CAR stock, Surefire M85 mid-length quad rail, graphite fore grip, EOTech 511 Holosight, Midwest Industries A2 adj. cantilever sight mount, 8.7 lbs. Disc. 2009.

	$1,850	$1,600	$1,400	$1,200	$1,000	$800	$675	*$2,000*

ROCKY MOUNTAIN ARMS CORP.

Previous manufacturer of mini revolvers circa mid-1960s, and located in Salt Lake City, UT.

REVOLVERS

MINI REVOLVER – .22 Short cal., 5 shot, stainless steel, locking bolt is in top strap, bolt cam on left side of hammer, supplied with black velveteen case.

	$275	$225	$150	$120	$105	$90	$80	

When RMAC went out of business, production was resumed by North American Arms Corp., then after another company change, Freedom Arms started production.

ROCKY MOUNTAIN ARMS, INC.

Current firearms manufacturer located in Longmont, CO since 1991.

Rocky Mountain Arms is a quality specialty manufacturer of rifles and pistols. All firearms are finished in a Dupont Teflon-S industrial coating called "Bear Coat".

PISTOLS: SEMI-AUTO

BAP (BOLT ACTION PISTOL) – .308 Win., 7.62x39mm, or 10mm Rocky Mountain Thunderer (10x51mm) cal., features 14 in. heavy fluted Douglas Match barrel, Kevlar/graphite pistol grip stock, supplied with Harris bipod and black nylon case. Mfg. 1993 only.

	$1,425	$1,275	$1,100	$950	$825	$700	$575	*$1,595*

1911A1-LH – .40 S&W or .45 ACP cal., specifically designed for left-handed shooters, featuring left side ejection port and right side controls, gold cup size, stainless steel construction, hand fitted parts, integral ramp barrel, Millett adj. sights, test target. Mfg. 1991-93.

	$1,295	$995	$750	$640	$535	$450	$390	*$1,395*

Add $100 for Bo-Mar sights.

BACKUP PLUS – .45 ACP cal., hand tuned AMT Back-up pistol, black DuPont Teflon-S finish, Tritium front night sight. Mfg. 1995-97.

	$575	$515	$450	$400	$360	$330	$300	*$650*

GRADING - PPGS™	100%	98%	95%	90%	80%	70%	60%	LAST MSR

22K PISTOLS – .22 LR cal., AR style pistols featuring 7 in. barrel, choice of matte black or NATO Green Teflon-S finish, will use Colt conversion kit, choice of carrying handle or flattop upper receiver, 10 or 30 shot mag., includes black nylon case. Mfg. 1993 only.

	$475	$425	$375	$350	$325	$295	$275	*$525*

Add $50 for flattop receiver with Weaver style bases.

PATRIOT PISTOL – .223 Rem. cal., AR-15 style pistol featuring 7 in. match barrel with integral Max Dynamic muzzle brake, 21 in. overall, available with either carrying handle upper receiver and fixed sights or flattop receiver with Weaver style bases, fluted upper receiver became an option in 1994, accepts standard AR-15 mags, 5 lbs. Mfg. 1993-94 (per C/B), reintroduced 2005.

MSR $3,000	$2,850	$2,500	$2,250	$2,000	$1,750	$1,500	$1,250	

KOMRADE – 7.62x39mm cal., includes carrying handle upper receiver with fixed sights, floating 7 in. barrel, Teflon red or black finish, 5 lbs., 5 shot mag. Mfg. 1994-95.

	$1,825	$1,650	$1,425	$1,200	$975	$850	$775	*$1,995*

RIFLES: BOLT ACTION

PROFESSIONAL SERIES – .223 Rem., .30-06, .308 Win., or .300 Win. Mag. cal., bolt action rifle utilizing modified Mauser action, fluted 26 in. Douglas premium heavy match barrel with integral muzzle brake, custom Kevlar-Graphite stock with off-set thumbhole, test target. Mfg. 1991-95.

	$2,050	$1,650	$1,275	$995	$850	$725	$600	*$2,200*

Add $100 for .300 Win. Mag. cal.
Add $300 for left-hand action.

PRAIRIE STALKER – .223 Rem., .22-250 Rem., .30-06, .308 Win., or .300 Win. Mag. cal., choice of Remington, Savage, or Winchester barreled action, includes Choate ultimate sniper stock, lapped bolt and match crown, "Bear Coat" all-weather finish, includes factory test target. Limited mfg. 1998 only.

	$1,595	$1,350	$1,150	$950	$875	$775	$675	*$1,795*

* ***Prairie Stalker Ultimate*** – similar to Prairie Stalker, except custom barrel and caliber specifications are customer's choice. Limited mfg. 1998 only.

	$2,200	$1,875	$1,625	$1,400	$1,200	$1,000	$895	*$2,495*

PRO-VARMINT – .22-250 Rem., or .223 Rem. cal., RMA action, 22 in. heavy match barrel with recessed crown, "Bear Coat" metal finish, Choate stock with aluminum bedding. Mfg. 1999-2002.

	$995	$875	$800	$725	$650	$575	$450	*$1,095*

POLICE MARKSMAN – .308 Win. or .300 Win. Mag. cal., similar to Professional Series, except has 40X-C stock featuring adj. cheekpiece and buttplate, target rail, Buehler micro-dial scope mounting system. Mfg. 1991-95.

	$2,325	$1,995	$1,650	$1,325	$1,100	$900	$700	*$2,500*

Add $100 for .300 Win. Mag. cal.
Add $400 for left-hand action.
Add $400 for illuminated dot scope (4-12x56mm).

* ***Police Marksman II*** – .308 Win. cal., RMA action, 22 in. heavy match barrel with recessed crown, "Bear Coat" metal finish, Choate stock with aluminum bedding. Mfg. 1999-2002.

	$995	$875	$800	$725	$650	$575	$450	*$1,095*

PRO-GUIDE – .280 Rem., .35 Whelen, .308 Win., 7x57mm Mauser, or 7mm-08 Rem. cal., Scout Rifle design with 17 in. Shilen barrel, "Bear Coat" finish, approx. 7 lbs. Mfg. 1999-2002.

	$2,025	$1,800	$1,600	$1,425	$1,200	$1,000	$825	*$2,295*

NINJA SCOUT RIFLE – .22 WMR cal., takedown rifle based on Marlin action, black stock, 16 1/2 in. match grade crowned barrel, forward mounted Weaver style scope base, adj. rear sight, 7 shot mag. Mfg. 1991-95.

	$640	$575	$525	$460	$430	$390	$360	*$695*

Add $200 for illuminated dot scope (1.5-4X) w/extended eye relief.

GRADING - PPGS™	100%	98%	95%	90%	80%	70%	60%	LAST MSR

SCOUT SEMI-AUTO – .22 WMR cal., patterned after Marlin action. Mfg. 1993-95.

	$650	$575	$495	$395	$350	$295	$260	*$725*

Add $200 for illuminated dot scope (1.5-4X) w/extended eye relief.

RIFLES: SEMI-AUTO

M-SHORTEEN – .308 Win. cal., compact highly modified M1-A featuring 17" match crowned barrel, custom front sight, mod. gas system, hand honed action and trigger, custom muzzle brake. Mfg. 1991-94.

	$1,650	$1,425	$1,175	$995	$850	$725	$600	*$1,895*

Add $200 for Woodland/Desert camo.

VARMINTER – .223 Rem. cal. only, AR-15 style rifle with 20 in. fluted heavy match barrel, flattop receiver with Weaver style bases, round metal National Match hand guard, free float barrel, choice of NATO green or matte black Teflon-S finish, supplied with case and factory test target (sub-MOA accuracy). Mfg. 1993-94.

	$2,195	$1,800	$1,600	$1,400	$1,200	$1,000	$875	*$2,495*

PATRIOT MATCH RIFLE – .223 Rem. cal., AR-15 style, 20 in. Bull Match barrel, regular or milled upper and lower receivers, two-piece machined aluminum hand guard, choice of DuPont Teflon finish in black or NATO green, 1/2 MOA accuracy, hard case. Mfg. 1995-97, reintroduced 2005.

MSR $2,500	$2,350	$2,050	$1,700	$1,425	$1,200	$1,000	$895	

SHOTGUNS: SLIDE ACTION

870 COMPETITOR – 12 ga., 3 in. chamber, security configuration with synthetic stock, hand-honed action, ghost ring adj. sights, "Bear Coat" finish, high visibility follower. Mfg. 1996-97.

	$695	$625	$550	$500	$450	$400	$360	*$795*

ROCKY MOUNTAIN ELK FOUNDATION

Current national conservation organization with national headquarters located in Missoula, MT.

RIFLES: BOLT ACTION

RUGER NO. 1-A LIGHT SPORTER – .35 Whelen cal., features gold inlaid elk on right side of receiver and mountain scene with gold accents on left side, engraved by Adams & Son, blue finish, deluxe wood, 50 mfg. 1995 only.

	$2,395	$1,850	$1,475	N/A	N/A	N/A	N/A	*$2,395*

SAUER MODEL 90 – .270 Win. or .30-06 cal., banquet offering only, total mfg. unknown.

	$1,375	$1,100	$925	N/A	N/A	N/A	N/A	

ROEDALE PRECISION

Current custom rifle manufacturer located in Hasbergen, Germany. No current U.S. importation.

Pete Lincoln custom makes precision a Viper series of bolt action rifles, in addition to related components. Please contact the company directly for more information, pricing, and current availability (see Trademark Index).

ROGAK

Please refer to the L E S Incorporated listing in the L section for more information on the Rogak Pistol.

ROGUE RIVER RIFLEWORKS

Current manufacturer located in Paso Robles, CA. Rogue River Rifleworks currently manufactures the John Rigby line of rifle and shotguns, but is no longer manufacturing the models listed here.

GRADING - PPGS™	100%	98%	95%	90%	80%	70%	60%	LAST MSR

RIFLES

BOLT ACTION MODEL – 7mm STW, .300 Win. Mag., .30-378 Wby. Mag., 8mm Rem. Mag., .375 H&H, .416 Rem. Mag., or .458 Win. Mag. cal., choice of Remington M-700 or Winchester M-70 action, Pac-Nor match grade barrel (with cryogenic treatment), engraved receiver, floorplate, and grip cap, jewelled bolt, exhibition grade checkered walnut stock with ebony forend cap. Limited mfg. 1998-2004.

	100%	98%	95%	90%	80%	70%	60%	LAST MSR
	$7,250	$6,250	$5,400	$4,500	$3,500	$2,750	$1,925	*$10,500*

LEVER ACTION MODEL – .243 Win., .260 Rem., 7mm-08 Rem., .308 Win., or .358 Win. cal., features rebuilt Winchester Model 88 action, match grade chrome moly barrel, exhibition grade walnut, choice of American classic or Mannlicher stock design. Limited mfg. 1998-2004.

	100%	98%	95%	90%	80%	70%	60%	LAST MSR
	$3,500	$3,100	$2,600	$2,000	$1,400	$950	$600	*$5,100*

SxS MODEL – .470 NE, .500 NE, or .577 NE cal., Anson & Deeley action, Purdey double locking lugs, Greener crossbolt, Southgate selective ejectors, quarter rib with rear sights, exhibition grade wood, case colored or coin finished receiver. Limited mfg. 1998-2000.

Prices started at $12,500 for .470 NE cal. A 12, 16, or 20 ga. shotgun barrel conversion kit was also available for $3,800.

RÖHM

Previous firearms manufacturer located in Sontheim an der Brenz, Germany. Limited importation into the U.S. Röhm still manufactures gas alarm pistols, mostly for European sales.

Röhm produced inexpensive revolvers for the U.S. marketplace during the late 1960s-1970s. Most of these guns were built as sub-contracts for U.S. companies and/or distributors (i.e., Hy-Score, a previous distributor located in Brooklyn, NY). Some of the models included are RG-7 through RG-88 (21 variations), Romo, Thalco, Valor, Vestpocket, Western Style, Zephyr, and others. Röhm also manufactured a few semi-auto pistols (RG-25 and RG-26) at approx. the same time. Currently, these guns are seen priced in the $35-$125 range, as the shooting value determines the price tag, not collector interest.

DERRINGERS

DERRINGER – .22 LR cal., blue, copy of Remington O/U derringer. Excellently made, but half-cock safety is old design and could fail if dropped.

	100%	98%	95%	90%	80%	70%	60%	LAST MSR
	$150	$115	$95	$85	$75	$65	$55	

ROHRBAUGH FIREARMS CORP.

Current manufacturer located in Bayport, NY, previously located in Deer Park, NY.

PISTOLS: SEMI-AUTO

R-9 – 9mm Para. or .380 ACP (new 2007) cal., DAO, 2.9 in. barrel, free bored to reduce felt recoil, frame is 7075-T651 aluminum, stainless steel or black Stealth slide, 6 shot mag., parts cut from solid billets, all internal parts are stainless, short recoil locked breech with cam operated tilting barrel locking system, recessed hammer, carbon fiber (disc.) or G10 grips, no sights, 12.8 (carbon fiber grips) or 13 1/2 (G10 grips) oz. New 2003.

	100%	98%	95%	90%	80%	70%	60%	LAST MSR
MSR $1,150	$1,000	$875	$750	$680	$550	$450	$350	

Add $45 for black Stealth slide.

* ***R9S Model*** – similar to Model R-9, except has fixed open sights, 9mm Para. cal. variations include Tribute (silver gun with black/blue CF grips, new 2012), Coyote (Coyote Tan metal finish, new 2012), and Covert (black with sights, new 2012). New 2004.

	100%	98%	95%	90%	80%	70%	60%	LAST MSR
MSR $1,150	$1,000	$875	$750	$680	$550	$450	$350	

Add $45 for black Stealth slide.
Add $200 R9S Tribute (new 2012). Add $600 for R9S Coyote or Covert (new 2012).
Add $45 for Elite Custom Model (Model R9SE, disc.).

ROHRBAUGH ROBAR R9 SERIES – similar to original R9, except frame, barrel, slide and trigger are treated with Robar Industries NP3 coating (corrosion resistant and self lubricating), polished stainless steel, limited lifetime warranty. Mfg. 2010 only.

	100%	98%	95%	90%	80%	70%	60%	LAST MSR
	$1,500	$1,315	$1,125	$1,020	$825	$675	$525	*$1,795*

ROPER

Previously manufactured revolving rifles and shotguns made circa 1866-1876 in Amherst, MA and Hartford, CT.

Sylvester Roper manufactured revolving rifles and shotguns in Amherst, MA beginning circa 1866 under the name Roper Repeating Rifle Company. Production was later moved to Hartford, CT circa 1869, and the company name was changed to Roper Sporting Arms Company.

Guns should be evaluated individually to determine value.

ROSS RIFLE COMPANY

Previous manufacturer located Quebec City, Canada circa 1900-1917.

The Ross rifle was the design of Sir Charles Henry Augustus Frederick Lockhart Ross (1872-1942), 9th Baronet of Balnagown, born in Scotland. He came to Canada in 1897, and left in 1917, following government expropriation of his plant.

While still a student at England's Eton College in 1893, Ross patented his first rifle design, which never left the drawing board. His patent of 1897 was more practical, and reached limited production first in Hartford, CT, then shortly after by the Chas. Lancaster firm in England. Ross worked with J.A. Bennett in Hartford until 1905, and apparently supplied components to Charles Lancaster in London, England until just before WWI began in 1914. By 1903, the new Ross Plant in Quebec City had begun production of early commercial rifles.

Ross was responsible for developing the first commercially available high velocity round in 1906, the .280 Ross, which developed a muzzle velocity in excess of 3,000 FPS, supplied initially as the 1907 Scotch Deerstalker Model. Patterns were sent to Eley in England, who produced the early ammunition for Ross.

While early Ross Commercial Sporting Rifles could almost be considered to be "custom" rifles with many available variations, it would appear the military rifle production was considered to be the "bread and butter" for the Ross Plant in Canada.

It must be recognized that while Ross provided the basic military designs for the MK I, MK II, and MK III variations, on-going military production was entirely at the mercy of a multitude of Canadian government inspectors, insisting upon almost daily alterations at several points. Overall lengths, weights, and even sights were decided by others. Politically, it was found expedient to lay all the blame for any and all faults real or imagined squarely upon Sir Charles himself.

Unfortunately, the Ross MK III was saddled with a Crown of Thorns similar to low-numbered Springfield 1903 receivers. The reality was (and still is) that with considerable difficulty, a MK III bolt can be reversed 180 degrees in its sleeve, then with added brute force and ignorance, can be partially inserted in its receiver and fired, with highly unpleasant results. A complete mechanical inspection by a competent gunsmith who is familiar with Ross rifles is urged before firing one of these guns, but verifying that the gas escape port in the bolt-head is visible with the bolt pulled back provides confirmation that all is as it should be.

The author wishes to express his thanks to Mr. Barry DeLong & Mr. Steve Engleson for making the following information available.

Further information on Ross Rifle Co. products can now be found on the Internet at RossRifle.com . All new and/or unusual findings can be offered for review and discussion, and any questions regarding Ross can likely be intelligently answered.

RIFLES: BOLT ACTION

The values listed are for specimens that have been unaltered except where noted.

MODEL 1897 SPORTER – .303 Brit. cal., 26 inch barrel, 5 round magazine, known as the "hammer model" because the bolt cocked the hammer as it traveled over it, clip loaded Mannlicher type magazine, bolt head design of solid opposing locking lugs with vertical travel and horizontal locking. Hartford, CT version has checkered walnut straight stock and a two leaf rear sight, Lancaster version has checkered walnut pistol grip stock, V notch rear sight and tang mounted peep sight. Mfg. 1897-1900.

This variation is encountered with such low frequency that consistent market pricing cannot be established.

GRADING - PPGS™	100%	98%	95%	90%	80%	70%	60%	LAST MSR

MODEL 1900 SPORTER – similar to the Model 1897, except has no hammer and a coil mainspring and internal bolt striker. Mfg. 1900-01.

This variation is encountered with such low frequency that consistent market pricing cannot be established.

RIFLES: BOLT ACTION, CANADIAN PRODUCTION

Canadian production of Ross Rifles consisted of three basic centerfire actions and one rimfire. All four were produced in sporting and military configurations. Commerical rifles typically have a serial number on the left side of the barrel immediately ahead of the receiver. Military rifles are numbered on the right side of the stock - a three digit number from 1-999 over the year manufactured/accepted, followed initially by one letter, then two letters. The Military Contract Cadets are numbered similarly, but the letter is ahead of the number over the date.

MARK I (MILITARY)/MODEL 1903 (SPORTING) – a modification of the Model 1900, "Patented 1903" on left side of receiver, slide button safety, slimmed and completely knurled bolt cocking-piece and thumbpiece mag. lifter, enclosed mag.

* ***Mark I*** – .303 Brit. cal., 28 in. barrel, walnut stock, overall length of 45 and 5/8th inches, H-type hinged rear sight adjustable to 2,200 yards with adjustments for windage and elevation. These will normally be found with a modified Ross MkI sight, referred to as the MkI* sight. The original sights are extremely scarce.

$2,500	**$2,000**	**$1,750**	**$1,500**	**$1,200**	**$900**	**$800**	

Those models with the original Mk I or Mk I* sight and original nosecap would bring a premium with values up to $3,500 for a top condition specimen.

In 1905, the first 1,000 rifles were delivered to the Royal Northwest Mounted Police in Regina, Saskatchewan. The early Mk Is used the Ross Mk I and Mk I* rear sight. Most were retrofitted with the Ross Mk II sight. The early nosecaps were formed from sheet metal.

* ***Model 1903 Sporter*** – .303 British (most common), .256 Mannlicher, or .370 Express cal., 26 or 28 in. barrel, walnut checkered stock, two leaf English style rear sight, 5 round magazine. Very scarce with manufacture in Hartford, CT, USA and Quebec City, Canada. Slight variations based on manufacture location.

$3,300	**$2,800**	**$2,300**	**$1,800**	**$1,500**	**$1,200**	**$1,000**	

Add 50% for .256 Mannlicher cal.
Add 50% for .370 Express cal.

MARK II (MILITARY)/MODEL 1905 (SPORTING) – "1905 Patented" on left side of receiver, action is cocked on opening, bolt action camming to initiate cartridge extraction, did not have bolt knurled thumbpiece, improved extractor added to later Model 1905 variations. Mfg. beginning 1906.

* ***Mark II Original (No Star and slightly modified MkII*)*** – .303 Brit. cal., Ross MKII or MKIII sight, early model with flat buttplate and "stepped" nosecap (similar to MKI rifles), fitted with the Ross MkII sight (aka "ski-jump" sight). Mfg. 1906.

$2,000	**$1,750**	**$1,500**	**$1,000**	**$750**	**$550**	**$500**	

The seldom-found "MkII with the MkIII rear sight" (flat-top" and fragile sight) produced in 1907 variant is at least as scarce as this one, and can be considered to be of comparable value.

* ***Mark II 2**** – .303 Brit. cal., 30 1/2 in. heavy barrel, military issue, but primarily a target rifle. Hindsight determined that this was likely the best Military rifle that Ross had ever produced. Scarce variation and seldom seen today. There are four basic variants: (1) Sutherland sight on barrel, no receiver base or sight, and extended sword bar to fit the MkII bayo (2) Sutherland sight on barrel, stamped receiver base and full-length wood so the new MkII bayonet now fits (3) Sutherland sight on barrel, milled base on receiver with MkIII Battlesight and (4) One-piece top wood (no barrel sight) and milled base on receiver with MkIII Battlesight.

$2,500	**$2,000**	**$1,750**	**$1,500**	**$1,200**	**$900**	**$800**	

NOTE:- This variant really shares very little with the other MkII rifles. When it was first introduced in 1908, both Ross and the Canadian Government referred to it as the "Rifle, Ross

GRADING - PPGS™	100%	98%	95%	90%	80%	70%	60%	LAST MSR

MkIII". This continued until what is now known as the MkIII was later introduced in 1910, and at that time, it was decided to call it the MkII.**

* ***Mark II 3**** – .303 Brit. cal., 28 in. barrel, most commonly encountered example, includes 20,000 sold to U.S. with flaming bomb proofmark added, found with the Canada Tool barrel sight, U.S. contract rifles were fitted with a "Kerr NOBUCKL" sling in the U.S.

$1,500	**$1,250**	**$900**	**$800**	**$700**	**$600**	**$550**	

The scarce U.S. sub-variation was shortened by approx. 7/8 in. and has a rechambered barrel. This model is seldom seen and commands a premium, particularly if still fitted with the unique MkI bayonet with the "cranked" crossguard. Suspicions are that a small run was modified and then used by rifle teams.

* ***Mark II 4**** – .303 Brit. cal., 28 in. barrel, similar to MKII 3*, except that reportedly, it was initially fitted with the earlier Ross MKIII sight (flat-top) then later were converted to MkII 3* condition, using the Canada Tool ladder sight.

$1,500	**$1,250**	**$900**	**$800**	**$700**	**$600**	**$550**	

* ***Mark II 5**** – .303 Brit. cal., 28 in. barrel. A relatively seldom encountered variant that has the Sutherland "H" type sight variation fitted. Several of these, as well as MkII 4*'s converted back to MkII 3* status have surfaced with US acceptance marks.

$1,500	**$1,250**	**$900**	**$800**	**$700**	**$600**	**$550**	

* ***Model 1905 M Sporter*** – .303 Brit. cal., 28 in. barrel, illustrated in 1906 catalog only, Enfield barrel sight. Very few known.

$1,500	**$1,200**	**$1,000**	**$850**	**$600**	**$550**	**$500**	

Note: this model is basically a sporterized military rifle done by the factory. Rifles have been altered after leaving the factory and can appear similar to an original specimen.

* ***Model 1905 R Sporter*** – .303 Brit. cal., 26 or 28 in. barrel, no checkering on stock, originally fitted with Winchester semi-buckhorn sight. The Military short MkII barrel with the coarse LH threads were used.

$1,000	**$800**	**$700**	**$650**	**$600**	**$550**	**$500**	

* ***Model 1905 E Sporter*** – .303 Brit. or .35 WCF cal., 22, 24, 26 or 28 in. barrel, built up on MKII** receiver, fine-thread heavy barrel, checkered pistol grip wood, found with or without the Harris lever, several different multi-leaf "express" sights found on this model. Can almost be considered a "Factory Custom" model.

$2,000	**$1,700**	**$1,300**	**$1,100**	**$825**	**$750**	**$600**	

Add 25% for .35 WCF cal.

Add $500 if fitted with a Lyman 50 sight (catalog option).

* ***Mark II** Commercial Target Model*** – .303 Brit. cal., 30 1/2 in. barrel, identical to the Military 2* rifle but typically found with commercial finish on wood and no sling swivels, target sight on bridge over receiver and serial number on barrel.

$2,500	**$2,350**	**$2,000**	**$1,800**	**$1,500**	**$1,250**	**$1,000**	

Add $500 for Presentation Target Rifle w/o inscription.

Values increase for a model with an engraved inscription, depending on documentation.

With the multitude of commercially available sights that were acceptable for official Matches in Canada, Britain and the USA, the prices above reflect no sights, and sight values should be added.

This model won almost all rifle matches from 1908 to 1913. A Presentation Target Rifle with deluxe wood and finish, and with a sterling silver medallion in stock was offered in several catalogs, but is seldom encountered.

MODEL 1907 & 1905/1910 MATCH TARGET RIFLE – between the MkII (1905) and the MkIII (1910), two important and scarce rifles were built and sold on a modified MkII action with threaded, not solid, locking lugs.

GRADING - PPGS™	100%	98%	95%	90%	80%	70%	60%	LAST MSR

* ***Model 1907 "Scotch Deer Rifle Stalking Pattern"*** – .280 Ross cal., 26 or 28 in. barrel, 4 shot mag., walnut pistol grip checkered stock, finely finished for Canadian/U.S. market, usually fitted with steel buttplate. For the British and Colonial market, it appears that major components were supplied by Ross "in the white" to British gunmakers for completion, usually found U.K. proofed, finer finish on steel and wood with checkered walnut butt.

	$3,300	$3,000	$2,500	$2,000	$1,750	$1,500	$1,250	

Add $500+ if English customized and cased.

These variants are definitely considered to be Custom Rifles, and should be priced based upon the Maker's reputation along with the individual rifle's features and overall current condition.

This model was a favorite in England circa 1908-1912 for use in both India and Africa. English gunmakers such as Cogswell & Harrison, Gibbs, Westley Richards and others offered this model and the Model 1910 in their catalogs. The majority of British Makers catalogues show both the Standard Factory Ross Sporters as well as "custom" rifles available.

* ***Model 1905/Model 1910 Match Target Model*** – .280 Ross cal., single-shot with 30 1/2 in. barrel, tangent rear sight on heel of butt and optical hooded front sight, free-floated barrel, can be found in early (tapered forend) and later (deep forend with finger grooves) versions. Very scarce and none found blued (left in the white). If found with barrel-weight marked in grains on the barrel, this is usually an indication of Bisley use.

	$4,200	$3,900	$3,400	$3,000	$2,600	$2,200	$1,900	

MKIII (MILITARY)/MODEL 1910 (SPORTER) RIFLE – replaced the previously used solid lugs which traveled vertically, has the "triple thread, interrupted-screw, double-bearing cam bolt" with the bolt head traveling horizontally.

It must be noted here that ALL rifles Military and Commercial that Ross built on the basic 1910 receiver have either M-10 or M-1910 roll-engraved on the receiver ring. This being the case ONLY the .280 Commercial Sporter is correctly referred to as an M-10. All other variants have their own designation, and are clearly not M-10's. This has increasingly been used, usually deliberately to the seller's advantage, on Internet Auctions over the last few years, and amounts to deliberate misrepresentation.

The newly-designed bolt replaced the previously used solid lugs which traveled vertically, and has the "triple thread, interrupted-screw, double-bearing cam bolt-head" with the bolt head traveling with its lugs horizontal, rather than vertically, as with the two previous designs.

It is these models where the report of "bolt blowbacks" have occurred. The bolt on these models, could, with some difficulty be rotated 180 degrees and hence not close completely. If fired in this situation, the bolt could blow back and potentially injure the shooter. Sporters were produced in three grades: R (economy), E (military box magazine and checkered wood) and the top of the line - the M-10.

* ***MKIII/MKIII B Military*** – .303 Brit. cal., 30 1/2 in. barrel, slight changes only through the production run, early models had stamped sheet metal nosecaps, later ones were forged. Models found with British proofs were likely in the trenches in France and later used by WWII British Homeguard. For the MkIII B, the only change from Canadian issue is the front and rear sights, plus the lack of expected identification and acceptance marks stamped in the buttstock.

	$2,000	$1,850	$1,500	$1,250	$1,000	$750	$650	

* ***Military Match Target Model*** – .280 Ross cal., 26 in. barrel, box mag. (same as M-10 Sporter with flat floorplate), light walnut stocks with a commercial finish and a Ross MkIII battle sight, recalibrated for .280 Ross cal. Mfg. circa 1913. Extremely scarce.

	$10,000	$7,500	$6,500	$5,000	$3,500	$2,500	$2,000	

While originally thought to have been produced in 1912, recent information points to a manufacture date in late 1913. Ross considered this model to be the perfect military rifle. A suspected total of 25 rifles were built on the commercial line and all known examples are serial numbered in the 10,200 range. The large majority of these were reported as destroyed in Quebec post-WWII.

GRADING - PPGS™	100%	98%	95%	90%	80%	70%	60%	LAST MSR

* ***Model R-10*** – .303 Brit. cal., 26 or 28 in. barrel, no checkering, Winchester semi-buckhorn rear sight, military five shot box mag., plain steel uncheckered rifle buttplate.

$1,500	$1,250	$1,000	$750	$600	$550	$500	

There is the possibility that Ross used previously rejected military components in these rifles. This is a fairly plain rifle, but seldom encountered.

* ***Model E-10*** – .303 Brit. or .35 WCF cal., 26 or 28 in. barrel, checkered straight grain walnut stock, M-10 pattern checkering on bottom of pistol grip, military box mag, several different express sights can be found on this model. Scarce.

$1,700	$1,350	$1,000	$800	$700	$600	$550	

Add 25% for .35 WCF cal.

Add $200-$300 for Lyman "long-staff" 48 rear sight (catalog option).

* ***Model M-10*** – .280 Ross cal., 24, 26 or 28 in. barrel, enclosed four shot double row mag., beautifully finished, checkered walnut pistol grip stock, grip cap screwed to pistol grip, flat floorplate, 0 to 500 yard sight on barrel, some are equipped with Porter "pop up" sight on the rear receiver bridge.

$2,000	$1,750	$1,500	$1,000	$700	$600	$500	

Add $200-$250 for rifles with Porter aperture sight or factory Catalog option Lyman 48S sight.

Facory-custom features like a cheekpiece also add at least 25%.

* ***Mark III Homeguard Model*** – .303 Brit. cal., identical to the Canadian issued Mk III Military Model but appears to have superior finish and fit on wood and metal, serial number will be found on the barrel just ahead of the receiver, issue stamps may (or may not) be stamped in the stock, considered to be commercial, not military. Less than 1,000 mfg. The serial number always shows a prefix of "HG".

$3,000	$2,700	$2,300	$1,700	$1,500	$1,250	$1,000	

MODEL 1912 CADET

* ***Model 1912 Cadet Commercial*** – serial number on the left side of the barrel, ahead of the receiver, usually found stocked with fine-grain light walnut, with a semi-gloss finish very similar to the commercial centerfire Sporters, as opposed to the open-grain dark walnut of the Military Cadets.

$800	$750	$550	$450	$375	$350	$300	

* ***Model 1912 Cadet Military*** – serial number stamped in stock over year of acceptance, preceeded by a letter, usually multiple "CC" (Cadet Corps) stamps also.

$800	$725	$525	$425	$375	$350	$300	

The Canadian government through the Dept. of Militia and Defence (M&D) ordered 10,000 Cadets, of which only approx. 6,000 were delivered beginning in 1913 and ending in 1916. The majority of these military Cadets were destroyed by the Canadian government. Any military accepted Cadets from the four contract years are scarce.

When the Ross Plant was expropriated in 1917 by the Canadian Government, a large quantity of unfinished Ross Cadet components remained. These were later assembled and sold on the Commercial Market in Canada, and are now referred to as "Clean-Up Run" Cadets. These Cadets appear to be the same as the Military version, with open-grain walnut stocks, rather than the much better-finished light walnut Commercial stocks. No serials or proof-stamps in either wood or steel are usually found, but occasionally, light inspectors stamps have been noted stamped on the bottom of the wrist. Also, it appears that Canada's authorities have stamped their own identification numbers and/or letters on some. This has likely only been done relatively recently.

* ***Model 1912 Cadet Carbine*** – This unique Cadet Model first appeared in the commercial catalog issued in early 1913. The same catalog, destined for the U.S. market, serviced by Post & Floto in New York City was essentially the same catalog, but all prices were manually over-stamped with red ink. The page illustrating and describing this new half-stock Cadet addition shows "For Canada Trade Only". For many years, it was considered that this Model wasn't produced, but was only "floated" in the catalogs to gauge the potential market. Over the last few years, extensive searches

GRADING - PPGS™	100%	98%	95%	90%	80%	70%	60%	LAST MSR

and correspondence with other collectors found that currently, at least four identical specimens survived in advanced Ross Collections. For whatever reason, Ross offered it with a unique forged buttplate, rather than the early MkIII Military buttplate with the brass trap-door used for all the other Cadets. The stocks on all four examples seen to date appear to have used the same grade of light straight-grain walnut used for the Commercial MkII** Target rifles and finished similarly as well.

	100%	98%	95%	90%	80%	70%	60%	LAST MSR
	$1,500	$1,200	$1,000	$850	$600	$550	$500	

ROSSI

Current trademark manufactured by Amadeo Rossi S.A., established in 1889 and located in Sao Leopoldo, Brazil. Currently imported exclusively by BrazTech, International beginning late 1998, located in Miami, FL. Previously imported by Interarms, located in Alexandria, VA.

PISTOLS: LEVER ACTION

RANCH HAND – .357 Mag., .44 Mag., or .45 LC cal., 12 in. barrel, "mare's leg" style with large loop lever, blue steel or case colored (.45 LC cal. only) receiver, adj. buckhorn rear sights, milled front post sights, uncheckered Brazilian hardwood stock and forearm, single stage trigger, 6 shot shortened mag. tube, saddle ring with leather strap, steel buttplate, includes Taurus Security System safety, 4.9 lbs. New mid-2010.

	100%	98%	95%	90%	80%	70%	60%	LAST MSR
MSR $595	$500	$440	$375	$340	$275	$225	$175	

Add $81 for case colored receiver (.45 LC cal. only).

PISTOLS: SINGLE SHOT

ROCKET SINGLE SHOT – .22 LR, .22 Hornet, .22-250 Rem., .220 Swift, .223 Rem., .30-30 Win., .357 Mag., .44 Mag., or .45 LC cal., break open single shot action. Limited importation 2000 only.

	100%	98%	95%	90%	80%	70%	60%	LAST MSR
	$135	$120	$110	$100	$90	$80	$75	*$149*

Add $36 for stainless steel.
Add 25% for Centerfire calibers.

MATCHED PAIR PISTOL – includes .22 LR barrel and extra .45 LC/.410 bore (2 1/2 in. chamber) barrels with fiber optic sights, 11 in. barrels, blue finish only, combat style wrap-around rubber grips with red insert, Taurus security system. New 2012.

	100%	98%	95%	90%	80%	70%	60%	LAST MSR
MSR $367	$300	$265	$225	$200	$165	$135	$100	

REVOLVERS: DOUBLE ACTION

All discontinued models in this section were only imported by Interarms only, not Braztech. Braztech is the exclusive North American importer for Rossi firearms starting late 1998.
All currently manufactured Rossi firearms incorporate the Taurus Security System safety.

MODEL 31 – .38 Spl. cal., 5 shot, 4 in. medium barrel, target trigger and hammer, 22 oz. Disc. 1985.

	100%	98%	95%	90%	80%	70%	60%	LAST MSR
	$120	$105	$95	$85	$75	$70	$65	*$139*

Add $5 for nickel.

MODEL 51 – .22 LR cal., 6 shot, 6 in. barrel, blue only, adj. sights. Disc. 1985.

	100%	98%	95%	90%	80%	70%	60%	LAST MSR
	$125	$110	$100	$90	$85	$80	$75	*$149*

* ***Model 51 Sportsman 511 Stainless*** – .22 LR cal. only, stainless steel, 4 in. barrel with matted rib, adj. rear sight, 6 shot, hardwood stocks, 30 oz. Imported 1986-90 only.

	100%	98%	95%	90%	80%	70%	60%	LAST MSR
	$190	$160	$125	$100	$85	$70	$65	*$235*

MODEL 68 – .38 Spl. cal., 5 shot, 2 or 3 in. barrel, blue or nickel (3 in. barrel only), choice of wood or rubber grips with 2 in. barrel. Disc. 1998.

	100%	98%	95%	90%	80%	70%	60%	LAST MSR
	$165	$135	$100	$90	$80	$70	$65	*$225*

MODEL 69 – .32 S&W cal., 6 shot, 3 in. barrel, walnut grips. Disc. 1985.

	100%	98%	95%	90%	80%	70%	60%	LAST MSR
	$120	$105	$95	$85	$75	$70	$65	*$139*

Add $5 for nickel finish.

GRADING - PPGS™	100%	98%	95%	90%	80%	70%	60%	LAST MSR

MODEL 70 – .22 LR cal., 6 shot, 3 in. barrel. Disc. 1985.

$120 $105 $95 $85 $75 $70 $65 *$139*

Add $5 for nickel finish.

MODEL 84 STAINLESS – .38 Spl. cal., 6 shot, 3 or 4 in. solid raised rib barrel, standard service sights, checkered hardwood grips, 27 1/2 oz. Imported 1985-86 only.

$190 $155 $125 $100 $85 $70 $65 *$205*

MODEL 85 STAINLESS – please refer to Model 851 Stainless.

MODEL 88 STAINLESS – .38 Spl. cal., 5 shot, stainless steel construction, 2 or 3 in. barrel, hardwood or rubber (2 in. barrel only) grips, 21 oz. Disc. 1998.

$195 $145 $110 $90 $75 $70 $65 *$255*

* ***Model 88 Stainless Lady Rossi*** – .38 Spl. cal., 2 in. barrel, stainless steel, slim round grips. Imported 1995-1998.

$215 $175 $150 $120 $105 $90 $80 *$285*

MODEL 89 STAINLESS – .32 S&W cal. only, 6 shot, 3 in. barrel. Imported 1985-86. Reintroduced 1989-90.

$175 $135 $115 $90 $75 $60 $55 *$215*

MODEL 94 – .38 Spl. cal., 6 shot, 3 or 4 in. barrel, blue finish only, 27 1/2 oz. Imported 1985-1988.

$160 $140 $120 $110 $95 $85 $75 *$185*

MODEL 95 – please refer to Model 951.

MODEL R351 – .38 Spl.+P cal., 5 shot, 2 or 4 (VR) in. barrel, blue finish, combat rubber grips, supplied with key lock, 24 oz. Importation began 1999.

MSR $401 $340 $300 $250 $225 $185 $150 $125

MODEL R352 – similar to Model R351, except is stainless steel. Importation began 1999.

MSR $465 $395 $350 $295 $275 $215 $180 $140

MODEL R461 – .357 Mag.+P cal., 6 shot, 2 in. barrel, blue finish, combat rubber grips, supplied with key lock, 26 oz. Importation began 1999.

MSR $401 $340 $300 $250 $225 $185 $150 $125

MODEL R462 – similar to Model R461, except is stainless steel. Importation began 1999.

MSR $465 $395 $350 $295 $275 $215 $180 $140

MODEL 515(M) STAINLESS – .22 LR or .22 WMR (Model 515M) cal., double action, 6 shot, classic kit gun design, stainless steel with shrouded ejector rod, adj. rear sight, checkered custom wood grips, 4 in. barrel, 30 oz. Imported 1992 only.

$195 $145 $110 $90 $75 $70 $65 *$248*

MODEL 515 STAINLESS – .22 WMR cal., similar to 515(M), supplied with 2 pairs of grips (checkered wood and rubber wraparound). Imported 1994-98.

$210 $165 $140 $110 $95 $85 $75 *$270*

MODEL 518 STAINLESS – .22 LR cal., otherwise similar to Model 515 Stainless. Disc. 1998.

$195 $155 $135 $110 $95 $80 $75 *$255*

MODEL 677 FS – .357 Mag. cal., 6 shot, 2 in. heavy barrel, enclosed ejector rod, rubber combat grips, matte blue finish, 26 oz. Imported 1997-98.

$215 $160 $135 $110 $95 $80 $70 *$260*

MODEL 720 STAINLESS – .44 Spl. cal., choice of hammer or hammerless (new 1994) design, 3 in. ribbed barrel, double action, 5 shot with fluted or unfluted cylinder, full ejector rod shroud, adj. rear sight, rubber combat grips, stainless, 27 1/2 oz. Imported 1992-98.

$220 $180 $155 $125 $110 $90 $80 *$290*

* ***Model 720C Stainless*** – similar to Model 720 Stainless, except hammerless.

$220 $180 $155 $125 $110 $90 $80 *$290*

GRADING - PPGS™	100%	98%	95%	90%	80%	70%	60%	LAST MSR

MODEL 851 – .38 Spl.+P cal., 4 in. VR barrel, 6 shot, integral key lock, checkered combat rubber grips, blue finish, 32 oz. Importation began 2001.

MSR $401	$340	$300	$250	$225	$185	$150	$125	

MODEL 851 STAINLESS – .38 Spl. cal., 3 (disc. 1994) or 4 in. VR barrel, 6 shot, walnut grips, adj. rear sight, 27 1/2 oz. Mfg. 1985-98.

	$195	$155	$135	$110	$95	$80	$75	$255

MODEL 877 FS STAINLESS – .357 Mag. cal., 6 shot, small frame, 2 in. barrel with full ejector rod housing, rubber combat grips, 26 oz. Mfg. 1996-98.

	$220	$175	$150	$120	$105	$90	$80	$290

MODEL 951 – .38 Spl. cal., 6 shot, 3 or 4 in. VR barrel, blue finish only, 27 1/2 oz. Imported 1985-90.

	$190	$155	$135	$120	$110	$100	$90	$233

MODEL 971 – .357 Mag. cal., 4 in. solid rib barrel with ejector rod, 6 shot, adj. rear sight, blue only, hardwood grips, 36 oz. Imported 1988-98.

	$200	$160	$145	$135	$125	$115	$105	$255

* ***Model 971 Stainless*** – .357 Mag. cal., 2 1/2 (new 1992), 4, or 6 in. solid rib barrel with full ejector rod shroud, 6 shot, combat style rubber grips, adj. rear sight, 35.4 - 40 1/2 oz. Imported 1989-98.

	$220	$175	$145	$135	$125	$115	$105	$290

* ***Model 971 Compensated*** – .357 Mag. cal., stainless steel, 3 1/4 in. compensated barrel, 32 oz. Imported 1993-98.

	$220	$175	$145	$135	$125	$115	$105	$290

MODEL 971 VRC STAINLESS – .357 Mag. cal., stainless steel, 6 shot, choice of 2 1/2, 4, or 6 in. barrel with 8-port compensator and full-length ejector shroud, combat rubber grips, adj. rear sight, 30-39 oz. Mfg. 1996-98.

	$295	$220	$175	$135	$115	$100	$85	$340

MODEL 971 (NEW MFG.) – .357 Mag. cal., 4 in. barrel with solid rib and full ejector shroud, 6 shot, checkered combat rubber grips, adj. rear sight, integral key lock, 32 oz. Importation began 2001.

MSR $465	$395	$350	$295	$275	$215	$180	$140	

MODEL 972 – similar to Model 971, except is stainless steel, 6 in. barrel only. Importation began 2001.

MSR $523	$450	$395	$340	$300	$250	$200	$160	

MODEL R981 – .22 LR cal., 2, 4, or 6 in. barrel, 8 shot, blue finish, ribber grips, DA/SA, fiber optic front sight, adj. rear sight. New 2013.

MSR $417	$350	$300	$265	$240	$195	$160	$125	

CYCLOPS (MODEL 988 STAINLESS) – .357 Mag. cal., 6 or 8 shot, 8 or 10 3/4 (ported or unported, new 1998) in. full shroud barrel with 8 compensation ports, black rubber grips, 51 oz. Imported 1997-98.

	$385	$300	$230	$175	$140	$125	$105	$429

Add $50 for unported 10 3/4 in. barrel.
Add $60 for ported 10 3/4 in. barrel.

RIFLES

For previous information on Rossi mfg. Puma rifles imported by Legacy, please refer to the Puma section.

CIRCUIT JUDGE .22 REVOLVING CYLINDER – .22 LR/.22 WMR cal., includes interchangeable cylinders, SA/DA, 9 shot, 18 1/2 in. barrel, adj. rear and fiber optic front sight, black synthetic thumbhole stock, lower Picatinny rail on forearm, includes scope mount base and hammer extension, blue finish, Taurus Security System, 5 1/2 lbs. New mid-2012.

MSR $732	$625	$550	$475	$425	$350	$275	$225	

GRADING - PPGS™	100%	98%	95%	90%	80%	70%	60%	LAST MSR

CIRCUIT JUDGE .44 MAG. REVOLVING CYLINDER – .44 Mag. cal., 5 shot revolving cylinder, SA/DA operation, 18 1/2 in. barrel with cushioned recoil pad with spacer, fiber optic front, uncheckered Monte Carlo wood stock with recoil pad and forearm, blue finish, includes scope mount base and hammer extention, Taurus Security System, 5.2-5.6 lbs. New 2011.

MSR $684	$575	$500	$425	$395	$315	$260	$200	

FIELD GRADE SINGLE SHOT RIMFIRE – .17 HMR (new 2003), .22 LR (disc. 2003), or .22 WMR (disc. 2003) cal. , 23 in. matte finished blue or stainless steel barrel, natural (matte blue) or black (stainless steel) finished wood, adj. sights, ejector, 4 3/4-6 1/4 lbs. Disc. 2006.

	$140	$115	$95	$80	$70	$60	$60	*$175*

Add $47 for stainless steel.

FIELD GRADE FULL SIZE SINGLE SHOT CENTERFIRE – .22-250 (mfg. 2005-disc.), .223 Rem. (new 2002), .243 Win. (new 2002), .270 Win. (mfg. 2004-disc.), .30-06 (mfg. 2004-disc.), .308 Win. (new 2004-disc.), .357 Mag./.38 Spl. (disc. 2003), .44 Mag., 7.62x39mm (mfg. 2005-disc.), or .410/45 LC (disc. 2003) cal., 23 in. standard or heavy (new 2005, w/o sights) barrel, choice of matte blue or matte stainless steel (disc. 2004), Monte Carlo stock became an option in 2002 (disc.), black synthetic stock with recoil pad, removable cheekpiece, blue finish, extra wide extractor, ejector, adj. rear sight, Taurus Security System safety, includes scope mount base, 6 1/4 lbs. Importation began 2001.

MSR $314	$265	$225	$200	$180	$145	$120	$95	

Add $6 for heavy barrel.

FIELD GRADE YOUTH SIZE SINGLE SHOT CENTERFIRE – .223 Rem. or .243 Win. cal., 22 in. button rifled barrel, black synthetic stock with recoil pad, removable cheekpiece, blue finish, fiber optic front sight, scope mount base and hammer extension, Taurus Security System safety, 6 1/4 lbs., includes carrying case. Importation began 2001.

MSR $314	$265	$225	$200	$180	$145	$120	$95	

MODEL 59 LEVER ACTION – .22 WMR cal. version of Model 62 SA, 10 shot mag., 5 1/2 lbs. Importation disc. 1998.

	$220	$170	$130	$120	$110	$100	$90	*$280*

MODEL 62 SA SLIDE ACTION – .22 LR cal., copy of Win. 1890 "Gallery" model, rifle (23 in. barrel) or carbine (16 1/2 in. barrel) available, takedown action, blue or nickel finish, round or octagon barrel, 12 or 13 shot tube mag. Importation disc. 1998.

	$185	$145	$115	$95	$85	$80	$75	*$240*

Add $10 for nickel finish.
Add $10 for octagon barrel.

* ***Model 62 SA Slide Action Stainless*** – similar to regular model, except is stainless steel. Imported 1986 only.

	$165	$145	$120	$100	$85	$70	$65	*$192*

MODEL 62 SAC CARBINE LEVER ACTION – similar to Model 62 SA, except has 16 1/2 in. carbine barrel with full length mag. tube (12 shot), 4 1/4 lbs. Imported 1988-98.

	$185	$145	$115	$95	$85	$80	$75	*$240*

Add $10 for nickel finish.

* ***Model 62 SAC Carbine Stainless Lever Action*** – similar to Model 62 SAC Carbine, except is stainless steel. Imported 1998 only.

	$215	$165	$125	$100	$85	$70	$65	*$280*

MODEL 65/92 SRC LEVER ACTION – .38 Spl./.357 Mag., .44 Spl./.44 Mag., .44-40 WCF (mfg. 1995-98), or .45 LC (mfg. 1995-98) cal., patterned after Win. Model 92, 16 (.38 Spl./.357 Mag. only), 20 (blue or stainless) or 24 (new 1997, half round/half octagon) in. barrel, 5-5 3/4 lbs. Importation disc. 1998.

	$285	$220	$165	$125	$110	$100	$90	*$360*

Add approx. $70 for 24 in. half-round, half-octagon barrel.

This model in .44 Spl./.44 Mag., .44-40 WCF, or .45 LC cal. is sometimes known as the Model 65. This model was also available in matte blue finish at no extra charge.

GRADING - PPGS™	100%	98%	95%	90%	80%	70%	60%	LAST MSR

MODEL 92 EL JEFE OCTAGON BARREL LEVER ACTION – .357 Mag./.38 Spl., .44 Mag., or .45 LC cal., 20 or 24 in. octagon barrel, blued barrel with choice of blue, blue/case colored, stainless, and blue/brass finish, 10 or 12 shot tube mag., open sights, uncheckered walnut stock with curved buttplate and forearm, regular lever loop, includes Taurus security system, 7 lbs. New 2009.

MSR $642	$550	$475	$415	$375	$300	$250	$195	

Add $42 for stainless steel frame and barrel.
Add $63 for brass frame with 24 in. barrel (.45 LC cal. only).

MODEL 92 EL JEFE ROUND BARREL LEVER ACTION – .357 Mag./.38 Spl., .44 Mag., .45 LC, or .454 Casull cal., 8 or 10 shot tube mag., 16 or 20 in. round barrel, blue or stainless steel (.44 Mag. cal. only) finish, uncheckered walnut stock with crescent butt plates, open sights, Taurus Security System safety, regular or large loop lever, 4.8-5 lbs. New 2009.

MSR $559	$485	$430	$370	$335	$295	$260	$230	

Add $36 for scope mount, base and rings.
Add $40 for stainless steel (.44 Mag. cal. only).
Add $10 for large loop lever (.357 Mag., or .45 LC cal. only, disc. 2009, reintroduced 2011).
Add $40 for .454 Casull cal.

PICK 4 YOUTH GUN – includes .22 LR barrel with fiber optic adj. sight, .243 Win. with fixed fiber optic sight, 20 ga. and .410 barrel with brass bead front sights, blue finish, barrels change w/o screw, removable cheekpiece, Taurus security system, break-open design, black synthetic or hi-def green (disc. 2011) stock, includes softside custom carry case, approx. 7 lbs. New 2011.

MSR $547	$465	$400	$350	$315	$250	$210	$165	

RIO GRANDE LEVER ACTION – .30-30 Win. or .45-70 Govt. (new 2012) cal., 20 in. barrel, blue or stainless, 6 shot, adj. buckhorn rear sight, post front, Brazilian hardwood stock or Realtree APG camo with recoil pad, 7 lbs. New mid-2010.

MSR $541	$485	$415	$365	$315	$280	$250	$225	

Add $59 for stainless steel or camo.
Add $79 for .45-70 Govt. cal. with large loop lever.

ROCKET SINGLE SHOT – .22 LR, .22 Hornet, .22-250 Rem., .220 Swift, .223 Rem., .30-30 Win., .357 Mag., .44 Mag., or .45 LC cal., action and other specifications similar to Model S12 shotgun. Limited importation 2000 only.

	$160	$145	$130	$115	$100	$90	$80	*$179*

Add $30 for stainless steel.
Add 15% for Centerfire cals.

TRIFECTA YOUTH GUN – includes .22 LR barrel with fiber optic adj. sight, choice of .243 Win. or .44 Mag. barrel with fixed fiber optic sight, 20 ga. barrel with brass bead front sights, blue finish, barrels change w/o screw, removable cheekpiece, Taurus security system, break-open design, black synthetic stock, includes softside custom carry case, 6.3 lbs. New 2011.

MSR $465	$395	$350	$295	$275	$215	$180	$140	

WIZARD SINGLE SHOT – .22-250, .223 Rem., .243 Win., .270 Win., .30-06, or .308 Win. cal., 23 in. carbon steel barrel with fiber optic front sight and adj. rear sight, break open single shot, blue or nickel (.243 cal. only, disc. 2012) finish, button rifled, Brazilian hardwood Monte Carlo stock, Realtree APG (disc.), or Green camo (disc. 2012) with vent. recoil pad, includes Weaver scope base, single stage trigger, transfer bar, manual safety and Taurus Security System, interchangeable barrels, approx. 7 lbs. New 2010.

MSR $378	$315	$275	$235	$215	$175	$140	$110	

Add $10 for nickel finish (.243 Win. cal. only, disc. 2012).
Add $50 for Realtree APG (disc.), or Green (disc. 2012) camo.

* ***Wizard Single Shot Youth Model*** – .223 Rem., .243 Win., or .308 Win. cal., 22 in. carbon steel barrel with fiber optic front sight and adj. rear sight, break open single shot, blue finish, button rifled, Brazilian hardwood Monte Carlo stock, Realtree APG (disc.),

GRADING - PPGS™	100%	98%	95%	90%	80%	70%	60%	LAST MSR

or Green (disc. 2012) camo with vent. recoil pad, includes Weaver scope base, single stage trigger, transfer bar, manual safety and Taurus Security System, interchangeable barrels, 13 1/4 in. LOP stock, 6 1/4 lbs. New 2010.

MSR $378	$315	$275	$235	$215	$175	$140	$110	

Add $55 for camo (disc.).

SHOTGUNS: LEVER ACTION

RIO GRANDE – .410 bore (2 1/2 in. chamber), 20 in. smoothbore barrel, blue finish or stainless steel, uncheckered hardwood stock with vent. recoil pad and forearm, side ejection, adj. buckhorn sights, includes scope mount base, Taurus Security System, 5.8 lbs. New 2012.

MSR $579	$495	$425	$375	$325	$275	$225	$175	

Add $65 for stainless steel.

SHOTGUNS: REVOLVING

Add approx. $60 for .22 LR/.22 Mag. convertible cylinder.

CIRCUIT JUDGE – .45 LC/.410 bore or 28 ga. (prototypes only), 5 shot revolving cylinder, SA/DA operation, 18 1/2 in. barrel with fiber optic sights (.410 bore only) or bead front sight only (28 ga.), uncheckered Monte Carlo wood stock with recoil pad with spacer, blue (28 ga.) or stainless (.410 ga.) finish, includes scope mount base and hammer extention, Taurus Security System, 5.2-5.6 lbs. New 2011.

MSR $684	$575	$500	$425	$395	$315	$260	$200	

Add $48 for stainless finish.

CIRCUIT JUDGE TUFFY – .45 LC/.410 bore (3 in. chamber), SA/DA, 18 1/2 in. barrel with fiber optic sights, 5 shot, matte black finish, black synthetic thumbhole stock with buttstock indicator and lower Picatinny rail on forearm, includes scope mount base, hammer extension, threadguard, straight rifled choke and choke tube wrench, Taurus Security System, 4.6 lbs. New mid-2012.

MSR $684	$575	$500	$425	$395	$315	$260	$200	

CIRCUIT JUDGE LEVER ACTION – .410 bore/.45 LC cal., shoots .410 bore (3 in. chamber), or .45 LC cal. ammunition, 5 shot revolving cylinder, lever action operation, 18 1/2 in. barrel with iron sights, Monte Carlo wood stock and forearm with recoil pad, stainless steel (mfg. 2011 only) or blue finish, shrouded low profile hammer, SA trigger, includes scope mount base, thread guard, straight rifled choke, and choke tube wrench, 5.2 lbs. New 2011.

MSR $684	$575	$500	$425	$395	$315	$260	$200	

SHOTGUNS: SxS

OVERLUND – 12, 20 ga., or .410 bore, exposed hammers, 20 (Coach Model), 26, or 28 in. barrels, double triggers. Importation disc. 1988.

	$275	$230	$185	$155	$140	$125	$115	*$332*

SQUIRE – 12, 20 ga., or .410 bore, hammerless, 20, 26 or 28 in. barrels, double triggers, raised matted rib, beavertail forearm, pistol grip, hardwood stock, 3 in. chambers. Imported 1985-90.

	$300	$245	$195	$160	$150	$140	$130	*$350*

SHOTGUNS: SINGLE SHOT

MODEL S12/S20/S41 – 12, 20 ga., or .410 bore, 3 in. chamber, 22 (Youth) or 28 (Standard) in. barrel, lightweight break open action with external hammer, ejector, uncheckered hardwood (disc. 2011), or black synthetic (new 2012) stock and forearm with sling swivels, blue finish, supplied with trigger lock, approx. 5 lbs. Importation began 1999.

MSR $175	$150	$125	$115	$100	$85	$70	$55	

Add $155 for 12 or 20 ga. Slug gun with 23 in. fully rifled barrel with adj. TruGlo sights (new 2004).
Add $57 for 12 ga. Turkey Model w/3 1/2 in. chamber, fiber optic sights and removable choke (mfg. 2007-2011).

This model is also available as a Youth Model in 20 ga. or .410 bore (.410 bore weighs approx. 4 lbs.) - prices are the same as listed.

GRADING - PPGS™	100%	98%	95%	90%	80%	70%	60%	LAST MSR

MATCHED PAIR RIMFIRE RIFLE/SHOTGUN – includes choice of .17 HMR, .22 LR, or .22 Mag. cal. rifle 23 in. barrel and interchangeable 12 or 20 ga. shotgun 28 in. barrel, rifle barrel has standard (disc.) or fiber optic front sights, black synthetic stock and forearm, blue finish, Taurus Security System, current mfg. includes scope mount base on rifle barrel, and matched pair carrying case, 5 1/4 or 6 1/4 lbs. Importation began 2000.

MSR $298 $250 $225 $195 $175 $140 $115 $90

Add $39 for .17 HMR cal.
Add $65 for 23 in. barrel.
Add $83 for stainless steel (.410 bore and .22 LR or .17 HMR cal. only, disc. 2009).
Add approx. $95 for pink, black, or green/brown laminate stock (20 ga. or .410 bore only, disc. 2012).
Add $20 for nickel.

* ***Matched Pair Rimfire Rifle/Shotgun Youth*** – similar to Matched Pair Rimfire Rifle/Shotgun, except is Youth model with same 13 1/4 in. LOP, choice of .17 HMR or .22 LR rifle barrel (18 1/2 in.) or 20 ga. or .410 bore shotgun barrel (22 in.), fiber optic sights on rifle barrel, blue or nickel finish, black synthetic stock and forearm, Taurus Security System, current mfg. includes matched pair carrying case, 3 1/4-5 3/4 lbs. Importation began 2000.

MSR $233 $195 $175 $145 $135 $100 $90 $70

Add $47 for .17 HMR cal.
Add $83 for stainless steel (.410 bore and .22 LR or .17 HMR cal. only, disc. 2009).
Add $9 for fiber optic sights (20 ga./.22 LR only).
Add approx. $95 for pink, black, or green/brown laminate stock (20 ga. or .410 bore only).
Add $45 for .410 bore and .17 HMR rifle barrel.
Add $37 for nickel.

TRIFECTA YOUTH GUN – includes .22 LR barrel with fiber optic adj. sight, choice of .243 Win. or .44 Mag. barrel with fixed fiber optic sight, 20 ga. barrel with brass bead front sights, blue finish, barrels change w/o screw, removable cheekpiece, Taurus security system, break-open design, black synthetic stock, includes softside custom carry case, 6.3 lbs. Mfg. 2007-2012.

$375 $335 $300 $265 $230 $200 $175 ***$449***

Add $86 for pink/black, black, or green/brown laminate stock (disc.).
Add $54 for high definition green camo stock (disc.).

MATCHED PAIR CENTERFIRE RIFLE/SHOTGUN – includes 12 or 20 ga. barrel and choice of .223 Rem., .243 Win., .270 Win. (disc.), .30-06 (disc.) , or .308 Win. (disc.) cal., 28 in. shotgun barrel, or 23 in. rifle barrel with fiber optic sights, Taurus Security System, current mfg. includes matched pair carrying case, 5-6 1/4 lbs. Importation began 2000.

MSR $352 $300 $265 $225 $200 $165 $135 $100

* ***Matched Pair Centerfire Rifle/Shotgun Youth*** – includes 20 ga. barrel and choice of .22-250 Rem. (mfg. 2005-disc.), .223 Rem., .243 Win., .270 Win. (disc.), .30-06 (disc.), .308 Win. (disc.), .44 Mag. cal., 22 in. shotgun and rifle barrel, 5 1/4 lbs.

MSR $352 $300 $265 $225 $200 $165 $135 $100

TUFFY – .410 bore, break open single shot with safety mounted on left side of receiver, 18 1/2 in. barrel with brass bead front sight, black synthetic sculpted thumbhole stock with 4 shell storage capacity, ejector, blue or nickel finish, transfer bar safety, 3 lbs. New 2009.

MSR $209 $175 $150 $125 $110 $95 $85 $75

Add $8 for nickel finish.

ROSSLER WAFFEN GmbH

Current bolt action rifle manufacturer located in Kufstein, Austria. No current U.S. importation.

RIFLES: BOLT ACTION

TITAN – various centerfire cals., 16 in. barrel, available with traditional checkered walnut or black synthetic stock, right or left hand action, various configurations include the Standard,

GRADING - PPGS™	100%	98%	95%	90%	80%	70%	60%	LAST MSR

Luxury Excusive, Allround (synthetic stock only), or Stutzen (Mannliciher full stock), top tang safety, approx. 6.6 lbs. New 2012.

Base price on this model begins at €1,362.

Please contact the factory directly for more information, including current U.S. availability, delivery time, and list of available options (see Trademark Index).

ROTA, LUCIANO

Previous manufacturer located in Brescia, Italy until 2009. Previously imported and distributed 2002-2005 by Tristar, located in N. Kansas City, MO, and by New England Arms Corp., located in Kittery Point, ME.

SHOTGUNS: SxS

The Models 105 and 106 were imported exclusively by New England Arms, and the Model 411 was imported exclusively by Tristar.

MODEL 105 – most gauges, 26-32 in. barrels, boxlock action with sideplates, floral scroll engraving, choice of case colored or coin finished receiver, fixed chokes (any combination), extractors, Circassian checkered walnut stock and forearm. Importation disc. 2004.

$1,325	$1,075	$875	$750	$650	$550	$500	*$1,595*

Add $100 for 28 ga. or .410 bore.
Add $50 for ST, or $175 for multichokes.
Add $500 for hand engraving.

MODEL 106 – all gauges, Anson & Deeley type engraved boxlock action, DT or ST, ejectors, extractors, Circassian checkered walnut stock and forearm, case colored action. Importation disc. 2004.

$1,225	$950	$775	$675	$550	$500	$450	*$1,395*

Add $100 for 28 ga. or .410 bore.
Add $155 for 10 ga.
Add $50 for ST, or $175 for multichokes.
Add $300 for hand engraving.

* ***Model 106 Slug Gun*** – 12 or 20 ga., similar to Model 106, except has 25 in. barrels with express rib and folding leaf rear sight, with or w/o sideplates, tapered front ramp sight, choke tubes. Importation disc. 2004.

$1,325	$1,075	$875	$750	$650	$550	$500	*$1,595*

Add $200 for hand engraving.
Add $400 for sideplates.

MODEL 411 SERIES – various configurations, all models include boxlock action, checkered walnut stock and forearm, and have either color case hardened or coin finished frame. Importation by Tristar began 2003.

* ***Model 411 Series Field*** – 12, 16, 20, 28 ga., or .410 bore, DTs, splinter forearm, 3 choke tubes included except for fixed chokes on 16, 28 ga., and .410 bore, extractors, 6 1/4-7 1/4 lbs.

$775	$675	$550	$500	$450	$400	$350	*$849*

* ***Model 411 Series D Field*** – 12, 20, 28 ga., or .410 bore, straight grip English stock with ST, ejectors, 6 1/4-7 1/4 lbs.

$995	$875	$775	$650	$525	$400	$350	*$1,110*

* ***Model 411 Series F Field*** – 12, 20, 28 ga. or .410 bore, engraved coin finished action with sideplates, gold ST, ejectors, straight grip English stock, 6 1/4-7 1/4 lbs.

$1,475	$1,250	$995	$875	$775	$650	$525	*$1,608*

* ***Model 411 Series R Field*** – 12 or 20 ga., 20 in. fixed choke barrels bored cyl./cyl., DTs, extractors, designed for cowboy competition, approx. 6 1/2 lbs. Disc. 2003.

$675	$550	$500	$450	$400	$350	$295	*$745*

GRADING - PPGS™	100%	98%	95%	90%	80%	70%	60%	LAST MSR

ROTTWEIL

Previous firearms manufacturer located in Rottweil, Germany. Previously imported on a limited basis by RUAG Ammotec, USA located in Closter, NJ, and by Rottweil Competition, located in Orange, CA.

SHOTGUNS

PARAGON – 12 ga. only, new design featuring boxlock action, 11 different stock configurations, detachable and interchangeable trigger group, trigger and sear safety, ejectors (switchable to extractors), various barrel lengths (30 in. standard) and rib combinations, cased. Limited importation 1993-99.

$6,950	$6,500	$5,750	$4,850	$3,950	$3,000	$2,500	*$7,500*

Add $850 for Trap Model.
Add $3,150 per extra set of barrels.

* ***Paragon Sporting Clays Deluxe*** – 30 in. barrels only, features better quality wood and engraving. Limited importation.

$6,950	$6,500	$5,750	$4,850	$3,950	$3,000	$2,500	*$7,500*

MODEL 650 FIELD O/U – 12 ga. only, 28 in. barrels with VR, ejectors, single trigger, select checkered walnut, multi-choked with 6 choke tubes, lightly engraved, coin finished receiver. Importation disc. 1986.

$750	$650	$595	$550	$500	$460	$435	*$850*

MODEL 72 FIELD O/U – 12 ga. only, 28 in. vent. barrels and rib, sand blasted receiver, select walnut checkered stock and forearm, single trigger, ejectors. Importation disc. 1987.

$1,850	$1,650	$1,450	$1,200	$1,000	$850	$700	*$2,295*

MODEL 72 AMERICAN SKEET O/U – 12 ga. only, 26 3/4 in. barrels, VR, ejectors, select French walnut stock and forearm, marginal engraving on sand blasted receiver, single trigger, 7 1/2 lbs. Importation disc. 1987.

$1,850	$1,650	$1,450	$1,200	$1,000	$850	$700	*$2,295*

This model was distributed exclusively by Paxton Arms, located in Dallas, TX.

MODEL 72 AAT SINGLE BARREL TRAP – 12 ga. only, adj. American trap (AAT), barrel features adj. point of impact, 34 in. barrel bored full, high VR. Importation disc. 1986.

$1,400	$1,200	$1,000	$850	$700	$650	$600	*$2,295*

MODEL 72 AT O/U – 12 ga. only, 32 in. IM & F barrels, VR, sand blasted receiver, checkered select walnut stock and forearm, non-adj. point of impact, single trigger, ejectors. Importation disc. 1987.

$1,850	$1,650	$1,450	$1,200	$1,000	$850	$700	*$2,295*

MODEL 72 AAT COMBINATION – 12 ga. only, comes with 2 single barrels (32 and 34 in.) each with impact point adjustment. Importation disc. 1986.

$2,450	$2,100	$1,850	$1,600	$1,450	$1,250	$995	*$2,850*

* ***Model 72 AAT Combination*** – supplied with 1 single adj. barrel and 32 in. O/U barrels.

$2,450	$2,100	$1,850	$1,600	$1,450	$1,250	$995	*$2,850*

MODEL 72 AAT 3-BARREL SET – 12 ga. only, supplied with 2 single barrels (32 and 34 in.) with impact point adjustment, and 1 set of 32 in. O/U barrels bored IM & F. Importation disc. 1986.

$2,850	$2,600	$2,300	$2,000	$1,800	$1,600	$1,400	*$3,250*

MODEL 72 INTERNATIONAL TRAP – 12 ga. only, O/U 30 in. barrels bored IM & F with extra high rib. Importation disc. 1987.

$1,850	$1,650	$1,450	$1,200	$1,000	$850	$700	*$2,295*

MODEL 72 INTERNATIONAL SKEET – 12 ga. only, 26 3/4 in. barrels, VR, select walnut stock and forearm. Importation disc. 1987.

$1,850	$1,650	$1,450	$1,200	$1,000	$850	$700	*$2,295*

GRADING - PPGS™	100%	98%	95%	90%	80%	70%	60%	LAST MSR

ROYAL AMERICAN SHOTGUNS

Previously imported by Royal Arms International, located in Woodland Hills, CA circa 1985-87.

SHOTGUNS

MODEL 100 O/U – 12 or 20 ga., 2 3/4 in. chambers, double triggers, extractors, vent. rib and barrels. Imported 1985-87 only.

	100%	98%	95%	90%	80%	70%	60%	LAST MSR
	$325	$265	$240	$220	$200	$180	$170	*$390*

Add $40 for 3 in. chambers, single trigger, and auto ejectors.

MODEL 600 BOXLOCK SxS – 12, 20, 28 ga., or .410 bore, sideplates, silver finished receiver, 3 in. chambers, single trigger, auto ejectors. Imported 1985-87 only.

	100%	98%	95%	90%	80%	70%	60%	LAST MSR
	$365	$295	$265	$235	$210	$195	$180	*$420*

Subtract 25% for double triggers and 2 3/4 in. chambers.

MODEL 800 SIDELOCK SxS – 12, 20, 28 ga., or .410 bore, sidelock with sideplates, silver finished receiver, 3 in. chambers, single trigger, checkered select walnut straight grip stock, auto ejectors. Imported 1985-87 only.

	100%	98%	95%	90%	80%	70%	60%	LAST MSR
	$775	$650	$595	$550	$500	$460	$435	*$899*

RUBY

Previous trademark manufactured by Gabilondo, located in Eibar, Spain.

RUGER

See the Sturm, Ruger, & Co. listing in the S section.

RUKO SPORTING GOODS, INC.

Previous importer (non-exclusive) located in Buffalo, NY that imported Arms Corp. of the Philippines firearms circa 1990-95. Ruko Sporting Goods, Inc. (previously Ruko Products) firearms were manufactured by the Arms Corporation of the Philippines. In 1991, Ruko Products, Inc. became the exclusive domestic importer for arms manufactured by Arms Corp. of the Philippines. These firearms were marked "Ruko-Armscor" on the barrels.

Please refer to the Armscor section for current importation, as well as previous importation by Armscorp Precision, Inc. and Ruko Products, Inc.

RUSSIAN AMERICAN ARMORY COMPANY

See RAAC listing.

RUSSIAN SERVICE PISTOLS AND RIFLES

Previously manufactured at various Russian military arsenals (including Tula).

HANDGUNS

MODEL TT30 & TT33 TOKAREV AUTOMATIC – 7.62mm Tokarev cal., modified Colt 1911 design, Petter-type unitized trigger/hammer assembly, 8 shot, 4 1/2 in. barrel, blue finish. Mfg. 1930-1954.

	100%	98%	95%	90%	80%	70%	60%	LAST MSR
1930-1945 Mfg.	$1,200	$1,050	$900	$815	$660	$540	$420	
TT30 Model	$2,400	$2,100	$1,800	$1,630	$1,320	$1,080	$840	

Add 20% for matching mag.

Subtract 30% for post-war version mfg. 1946-1954.

Values listed assume original condition - no recent imports with importer markings.

* ***Model TT Tokarev Automatic Recent Import*** – 7.62x25mm Tokarev cal., must be stamped by importer, most modified by addition of a thumb safety, Russian Arsenal mfg., currently imported by Century Arms International, Inc. and others.

	100%	98%	95%	90%	80%	70%	60%	LAST MSR
No MSR	$225	$195	$170	$155	$125	$100	$80	

Add 50% if w/o thumb safety.

GRADING - PPGS™	100%	98%	95%	90%	80%	70%	60%	LAST MSR

NAGANT REVOLVER – 7 shot, cylinder comes forward to seal barrel.

	$260	$225	$185	$165	$135	$115	$100	

Add 10% for pre-communist Imperial marked.

"GRU" marked gun (Armed Forces Intelligence) has shorter barrel and grip frame. While rarer, there is a slight premium being asked.

MAKAROV MD – 9mm Makarov (9x18mm) cal., 8 shot mag. double action, 3.7 in. barrel, mfg. circa 1952, standard Russian Service pistol 1957-2003.

	$450	$400	$350	$300	$250	$200	$150	

Add approx. 50% for one matching mag., or 100% for two matching mags.

Subtract 50% for pistols with recent import markings.

Recent commercial models with adj. rear sight are currently selling in the $150-$175 range.

MODEL PSM – 5.45x18mm Soviet cal., based on the Walther PPK design, with steel penetrator cored bullet designed to defeat Kevlar body armor, usually found with thin brown holster and extra mag., configurations include: military with black anodized aluminum grips, and the commercial with grey ribbed plastic grips.

Military	$3,500	$3,050	$2,625	$2,375	$1,925	$1,575	$1,225	
Commercial	$3,000	$2,625	$2,250	$2,050	$1,650	$1,350	$1,050	

These models are usually encountered in high condition.

RIFLES

Original Soviet Mosin-Nagant bolt action rifles/carbines include: M1891 rifle, M1891 Dragoon, M1891/30 Rifle, M1891/30 Sniper Model, M1910 Carbine, M1938 Carbine, and the M1944 Carbine. Values for these older original military configurations will approximate values listed for the original mfg. Mosin-Nagant.

TOKAREV M1938 & M1940 (SVT) SEMI-AUTO – 7.62x54R cal., SVT M40 is the more common variation, while the SVT M38 sniper is very rare, 10 shot mag., first Russian military semi-auto, large quantities manufactured beginning 1938, but original surviving specimens in excellent condition are now very scarce.

SVT M38	$4,500	$4,000	$3,500	$3,000	$2,500	$2,000	$1,500	
SVT M40	$1,800	$1,500	$1,200	$1,000	$800	$700	$600	

MOSIN-NAGANT BOLT ACTION – various cals., bolt action, many produced under various military contracts, including Remington, New England Westinghouse, and Sako, prices assume recent importation.

Original mfg.	$395	$350	$300	$275	$250	$225	$200	
Recent imports	$200	$180	$160	$140	$120	$100	$95	

Add $40% for laminate stock.

RPD SEMI-AUTO – 7.62x39mm cal., converted from belt fed to semi-auto only, fired from closed bolt, milled receiver, includes 50 shot mag., recent importation.

	$3,795	$3,495	$2,950	$2,600	$2,300	$2,000	$1,750	

RUTTEN HERSTAL

Previous firearms manufacturer of O/U shotguns located in Herstal, Belgium. Previously imported by Labanu, Inc. located in Ronkonkoma, NY.

For more information and current pricing on both new and used Rutten airguns, please refer to the *Blue Book of Airguns* by Dr. Robert Beeman & John Allen (also available online).

SHOTGUNS: O/U

MODEL RM 100 – 12 ga., 3 in. chambers, VR multi-choke barrels, ejectors, checkered walnut stock and forearm, hard case. Imported 1995-98.

	$875	$775	$675	$575	$500	$450	$400	*$1,095*

MODEL RM 285 – similar to Model RM 100, except has engraved side plates and silver engraved receiver, select walnut with Schnabel forearm, hard case. Imported 1995-98.

	$1,025	$850	$725	$600	$500	$450	$400	*$1,295*

S SECTION

S.A.C.M.

Previous company located in Cholet, France. S.A.C.M. stands for Societe Alsacienne de Construction Mechanique.

GRADING - PPGS™	100%	98%	95%	90%	80%	70%	60%	LAST MSR

PISTOLS: SEMI-AUTO

FRENCH MODEL 1935A – 7.65mm Long cal., 8 shot, 4.3 in. barrel, blue, fixed sights, checkered stocks, used by French troops in WWII and Indochina 1945-1954. Mfg. 1935-45.

	$250	$220	$205	$180	$165	$150	$140	

Add 50% for Nazi WWII mfg. (Waffenamt proofed).

S.A.M.

Please refer to Shooter Arms Manufacturing Incorporated.

S.I.A.C.E.

Current shotgun and rifle manufacturer located in Gardone V.T., Italy. S.I.A.C.E. also offers an extensive variety of gunsmithing services. Currently imported by Cherry's Fine Guns, located in Greensboro, NC, Kebco LLC, located in Hanover, PA, British Sporting Arms, located in Millbrook, NY, Briley Mfg., located in Houston, TX, and Cabela's. Previously imported on a private label basis by Dakota Arms, located in Sturgis, SD, Luxus Arms, located in Millford, OH, and by New England Arms Corp., located in Kittery Point, ME.

RIFLES: SxS

Add 40% per set of small gauge shotgun barrels with additional forearm.

MODEL ALASKA – 7x65R, 9.3x74R, .30-06, .45-70 Govt., .30R Blaser (new 2012), or 8x57JRS (new 2012), or .444 Marlin cal., rounded scalloped boxlock with hand engraving, sideplates, figured Turkish walnut with skipline checkering, extractors and DT. Limited importation beginning 2002.

Current MSR on this model is €3,960.
Add €1,370 for the Alaska Lusso model or €3,060 for Alaska Lusso EL model with sideplates.
Add €450 for ejectors or single trigger.

MODEL YUKON – 8x57JRS, .30-06, .45-70 Govt., or .444 Marlin cal., exposed hammers, sidelock action, Bulino style hand engraving, figured Turkish walnut. Limited importation beginning 2002.

Current MSR on this model is €4,090.
Add €1,370 for the Yukon Lusso model.

EXPRESS BIG HUNTER – .375 Flanged Mag. NE, .375 H&H, .416 Rigby, .450 NE, .450/400 NE, .450/400 Mag., .470 NE, .500/416 NE, or .500 NE cal., 23 5/8 or 25 5/8 in. chrome/steel monobloc barrels, nickel/chrome action, case hardened or French gray receiver, extrators or ejectors, double triggers, best quality high grade walnut with custom dimensions and beavertail forend. New 2012.

Current MSR on this model is €10,500.
Many options and upgrades are available - please contact the importer for a price quotation.

SHOTGUNS: O/U

600T LUSSO EL – 12, 20, 24, 28, 32 ga. or .410 bore, ST or DT, sideplates with fine hand engraving, high grade walnut stock made to customer's specifications.

Current MSR on this model is €6,040.
Add €360 for multichokes (12, 20, or 28 ga.).

EVOLUTION – 12 or 20 ga., Boss type locking system, detachable trigger group, scroll engraving, high grade walnut stock made to customer's specifications.

Current MSR on this model is €13,650.
Special engraving is available on request for an additional charge.

GRADING - PPGS™	100%	98%	95%	90%	80%	70%	60%	LAST MSR

VICTORY – 12, 20, or 28 ga., scalloped round body action, double safety sears, all metal from one piece of solid nickel/chrome steel, monoblock barrels, ejectors, single trigger, high grade walnut stock made to customer's specifications, long trigger guard. New 2009.

Base price on this model is €8,600.

Special engraving, mobilchokes, and beavertail forend are available upon request for additional charge.

SHOTGUNS: SxS

MODEL GARDONE HAMMER GUN – 12, 16, 20, 28 ga., or .410 bore, scalloped boxlock with different round frame sizes for each gauge, ejectors, DT, full coverage best hand engraving, checkered deluxe Turkish walnut and custom dimensions. Imported 2000-2004.

	100%	98%	95%	90%	80%	70%	60%	LAST MSR
	$3,650	$3,125	$2,700	$2,250	$1,850	$1,450	$1,250	*$3,995*

This model was imported by New England Arms only.

MODEL VINTAGE HAMMER GUN – 12, 16, or 20 ga., sidelock, case hardened or coin finished receiver with border edged engraving, top tang safety, DT, extractors, monobloc barrels.

	100%	98%	95%	90%	80%	70%	60%	LAST MSR
	$2,625	$2,000	$1,425	$1,100	$850	$700	$550	*$2,950*

This model was only imported by New England Arms.

MODEL ETON HAMMER GUN – 12, 16, 20, 28 ga., or .410 bore, 2 3/4 in. chambers standard, DT, extractors, monobloc barrels, case colored or coin finished receiver with scroll engraving, Turkish walnut, straight or pistol grip stock with splinter or semi-beavertail forearm. Imported 2000-2004.

	100%	98%	95%	90%	80%	70%	60%	LAST MSR
	$3,650	$3,125	$2,700	$2,250	$1,850	$1,450	$1,250	*$3,995*

Add $1,250 for ejectors and self cocking system (Model Eton Deluxe).

This model was only imported by New England Arms.

MODEL 350G LUSSO/SUPER LUSSO HAMMER GUN (AURORA) – 12, 20, 24 (disc.), 28, 32 (disc.) ga., or .410 bore, back action sidelock, case hardened or coin finished receiver with finely engraved rose and scroll patterns, DT, extractors (Lusso) or ejectors (Super Lusso), top tang safety.

Current MSR on the Model 350G Lusso Model is €6,170.

Current MSR on the Model 350G Super Lusso Model is €7,990.

Add €3,640 for 28 ga. or .410 bore.

Add €900 for ST, €390 for beavertail forearm, or €360 for multichokes (12, 20, and 28 ga.).

This model became part of the Juno Series.

MODEL 370B HAMMER GUN (CONCORDIA) – 12, 16 (disc.), 20, 24 (disc.), 28 or 32 (disc.) ga., or .410 bore, scalloped frame back action sidelock, silver or case hardened receiver with fine scroll engraving, top tang safety, select checkered Turkish walnut, prices include custom dimensions.

Current MSR on this model is €7,600.

Add €3,640 for 28 ga. or .410 bore.

MODEL 371Q JUNO HAMMER GUN – 12, 16, 20, 24, 28, 32 ga., or .410 bore, sidelock, available with self cocking and ejectors, silver or case colored receiver, best quality rose and scroll engraving, DT or ST, top tang safety, select checkered Turkish walnut, prices include custom dimensions.

	100%	98%	95%	90%	80%	70%	60%	LAST MSR
	$5,525	$4,750	$3,950	$3,150	$2,450	$1,875	$1,450	

This model was only imported by New England Arms.

MODEL 475P BIS EL – 12, 20, 28 ga. or .410 bore, hammerless, Anson & Deely boxlock with sideplates and pins, ST or DT, ejectors, straight grip checkered walnut stock, coin finished receiver with light scroll scene engraving.

Current MSR on this model is €4,000.

Add €830 for .410 bore.

Add €450 for ST.

GRADING - PPGS™	100%	98%	95%	90%	80%	70%	60%	LAST MSR

MODEL 475P SUPERLIGHT – 12, 20, 28 ga. or .410 bore, hammerless, scalloped boxlock action with scroll engraving, ejectors, DT, checkered straight grip English stock with splinter forearm, 5.4 - 6 lbs.

Current MSR on this model is €4,420. Superlight EL Model (sideplates) is €5,270.
Add €800 for .410 bore.

MODEL 900 HAMMERLESS – 12 or 20 ga., deluxe hammerless model with H&H style sidelock action, ejectors, demibloc barrels, DT or ST, briar walnut stock and forend.

Current MSR on this model is €13,000, w/o engraving.

This model is available in other gauges by request.

S.P.S.

Current handgun manufacturer established circa 1997, and located in Ripollet, Barcelona, Spain. Currently assembled beginning 2013 in the U.S. by MetroArms Corporation and imported by Eagle Imports, located in Wanamassa, NJ.

S.P.S. manufactures a variety of semi-auto pistols based on the M1911 design, and many configurations are available, including competition, standard, and compact models in 9mm Para., .38 Super, .40 S&W and .45 ACP cal. Please refer to MetroArms listing for currently imported models.

S.W.D., INC.

Previous manufacturer located in Atlanta, GA.

Similar models have previously been manufactured by R.P.B. Industries, Inc. (1979-82), and met with BATF disapproval because of convertibility into fully automatic operation. "Cobray" is a trademark for the M11/9 semiautomatic pistol.

CARBINES

SEMI-AUTO CARBINE – 9mm Para. cal., same mechanism as M11, 16 1/4 in. shrouded barrel, telescoping stock.

GRADING - PPGS™	100%	98%	95%	90%	80%	70%	60%	LAST MSR
	$550	$495	$450	$400	$325	$275	$235	

PISTOLS: SEMI-AUTO

COBRAY M-11/NINE mm – 9mm Para. cal., fires from closed bolt, 3rd generation design, stamped steel frame, 32 shot mag., parkerized finish, similar in appearance to Ingram Mac 10.

GRADING - PPGS™	100%	98%	95%	90%	80%	70%	60%	LAST MSR
	$475	$395	$350	$300	$295	$275	$250	

This model was also available in a fully-auto variation, Class III transferable only.

REVOLVERS

LADIES HOME COMPANION – .45-70 Govt. cal., double action design utilizing spring wound 12 shot rotary mag., 12 in. barrel, steel barrel and frame, 9 lbs. 6 oz. Mfg. 1990-94.

GRADING - PPGS™	100%	98%	95%	90%	80%	70%	60%	LAST MSR
	$650	$525	$400	$360	$335	$310	$290	

SHOTGUNS: SINGLE SHOT

TERMINATOR – 12 or 20 ga., tactical design shotgun with 18 in. cylinder bore barrel, parkerized finish, ejector. Mfg. 1986-88 only.

GRADING - PPGS™	100%	98%	95%	90%	80%	70%	60%	LAST MSR
	$150	$125	$95	$80	$70	$60	$55	*$110*

SAE

Previous importer located in Miami, FL. SAE stands for Spain America Enterprises Inc. SAE imported Felix Sarasqueta shotguns from Spain until circa 1988.

SHOTGUNS: O/U

MODEL 70 – 12 or 20 ga., 3 in. chambers, boxlock action, single trigger, ejectors, 26 in. VR barrel, European checkered walnut stock and forearm, standard finish is blue, Model 70 multi-choke has silver finished action with Florentine engraving and low gloss stock finish. Imported 1988 only.

GRADING - PPGS™	100%	98%	95%	90%	80%	70%	60%	LAST MSR
	$400	$275	$260	$245	$230	$215	$195	*$598*

Add $120 for multi-chokes (27 in. barrel).

GRADING - PPGS™	100%	98%	95%	90%	80%	70%	60%	LAST MSR

MODEL 66C – 12 ga. only, 26 in. Skeet or 30 in. F&M VR barrels, boxlock with engraved sideplates including 24Kt. gold inlays, Monte Carlo deluxe stock and beavertail forearm. Imported 1988 only.

	$950	$725	$650	$575	$495	$450	$395	$1,544

SHOTGUNS: SxS

MODEL 210S – 12, 20 ga., or .410 bore, 3 in. chambers, boxlock action, double triggers, extractors, silver finished receiver with light engraving, approx. 7 lbs. Imported 1988 only.

	$420	$280	$260	$245	$230	$215	$195	$638

MODEL 340X – 12 or 20 ga., sidelock action, 26 in. barrels with 2 3/4 in. chambers, H&H boxlock action, case hardened finish with moderate scroll engraving, straight grip select walnut stock and forearm with high gloss finish. Imported 1988 only.

	$700	$550	$495	$460	$430	$395	$375	$1,170

MODEL 209E – 12, 20 ga., or .410 bore, H&H type sidelock action, 26 or 28 in. barrels with 2 3/4 in. chambers, hand engraved coin finished receiver, select checkered walnut stock and forearm, double triggers. Imported 1988 only.

	$925	$700	$650	$575	$495	$450	$395	$1,490

SCCY INDUSTRIES

Current pistol manufacturer located in Daytona Beach, FL. Previously located in South Daytona, FL.

PISTOLS: SEMI-AUTO

SCCY offers a lifetime guarantee on all its pistols.

Add $25 for nickel boron slide.

CPX-1 – 9mm Para. cal., 3.1 in. stainless steel barrel, DAO, lightweight compact polymer frame with stainless steel slide, natural, black carbon or two-tone finish, 10 shot mag., 3 dot sights, includes two 10 shot double stack mags., lock, finger extensions and flat bases, 15 oz.

MSR $319	$265	$235	$215	$185	$170	$160	$150

Add $20 for two-tone finish.

CPX-2 – similar to CPX-1, except has no manual safety. New 2011.

MSR $299	$265	$230	$210	$190	$180	$170	$155

Add $20 for two-tone finish.

SI DEFENSE, INC.

Current AR-15 style carbine/rifle manufaturer located in Kalispell, MT.

SI Defense makes a line of AR-15 style carbines/rifles in 14 calibers between .204 Ruger-.338 RCM. Many variations and features are available. MSRs start at $1,200. Please contact the company directly for current model availability, options, delivery time, and pricing (see Trademark Index).

SKB SHOTGUNS

Previously manufactured by the SKB Arms Company located in Tokyo, Japan from 1855-until December, 2009. Limited remaining inventory is currently distributed by G.U. Inc. located in Omaha, NE. Dealer sales.

SKB Arms Company exported its first shotguns into the U.S. during 1966. SKB also manufactured shotguns for Browning, Weatherby, and Birmingham Small Arms (BSA). In 1986 SKB had produced its one millionth shotgun. In 1987, importation resumed on most SKB models. While the model numbers have changed, quality is similar to those models imported previously by Ithaca. In most cases, the newer models are derived closely from their previous counterparts. Listings in this section will differentiate older, disc. models from more recently imported models. Ithaca imported from 1968 to 1978, Mitsui and Co. Chicago, IL from 1980 to 1983, and G.U. Inc from 1987 to 2010.

GRADING - PPGS™	100%	98%	95%	90%	80%	70%	60%	LAST MSR

Early in 2010, the owners made the difficult decision to close the SKB Shotguns factory and negotiated the sale of the brand name, mechanical drawings and all of the remaining parts to G.U. Inc.

SKB also manufactured other models and variations of O/Us and semi-autos (Models 1900 and 3000 Field) shotguns that were not imported into the U.S.

SHOTGUNS: O/U

Although the manufacture of SKB O/U shotguns was discontinued in December of 2009, G.U., Inc. still has remaining inventory of the GC 7 Series and the Model 85TTR, and the most recent MSRs have been included.

MODEL 85 TARGET SUPER SPORT (TSS) – 12, 20, 28 ga. or .410 bore, monobloc barrel construction, 2 different frame sizes, Greener crossbolt, non-detachable trigger assembly, silver nitride receiver finish, polished blue barrels, available in Sporting Clays, Skeet, or Trap configuration (including sets), Mag-na-ported barrels, Hi-Viz competition front sight, available with or w/o adj. comb stock (Graco CTS systems), matte wood finish. New 2002.

* ***Model 85 TSS Sporting Clays*** – choice of fixed or adj. comb stock, 28, 30, or 32 in. VR barrels, 8.5mm (28 ga. or .410 bore) or 12mm (12 or 20 ga.) stepped VR, 7 1/2-8 1/2 lbs. Mfg. 2002-2008.

$1,850	$1,525	$1,225	$950	$875	$800	$725	*$2,199*

Add $90 for .410 bore and 28 ga.
Add $230 for adj. comb on stock.
Add $190 for pigeon porting by Mag-na-port.
Add $400 for high grade wood (limited availability, new 2003).

» ***Model 85 TSS Sporting Clays 2 Gauge Set*** – includes 2 sets of barrels in different gauges. Mfg. 2002-2008.

$3,000	$2,525	$2,050	$1,800	$1,600	$1,400	$1,200	*$3,549*

Add $230 for adj. comb on stock.
Add $380 for pigeon porting by Mag-na-port.
Add $470 for high grade wood (limited availability).

» ***Model 85 TSS Sporting Clays 3 Gauge Set*** – includes 20 ga., 28 ga. and .410 bore and 30 in. barrels, includes aluminum case. Mfg. 2002-2008.

$4,800	$4,200	$3,600	$3,265	$2,640	$2,160	$1,680	*$5,349*

Add $230 for adj. comb on stock.
Add $550 for high grade wood (limited availability, new 2004).

* ***Model 85 TSS Skeet*** – choice of fixed or adj. comb stock, 28, 30, or 32 in. VR barrels, 8.5mm (28 ga. or .410 bore) or 9.5mm (12 ga.) sloped VR, 7 lbs. 6 oz.-8 lbs. 6 oz. Mfg. 2002-2008.

$1,850	$1,525	$1,225	$950	$875	$800	$725	*$2,199*

Add $90 for .410 bore and 28 ga.
Add $230 for adj. comb on stock.
Add $400 for high grade wood (limited availability, new 2003).

» ***Model 85 TSS Skeet 3 Gauge Set*** – includes 20 ga., 28 ga. and .410 bore and 28 in. barrels, includes aluminum case. Mfg. 2002-2008.

$4,800	$4,200	$3,600	$3,265	$2,640	$2,160	$1,680	*$5,349*

Add $230 for adj. comb on stock.
Add $550 for high grade wood (limited availability, new 2004).

* ***Model 85 TSS Trap*** – choice of 30 or 32 in. barrels, fixed or adj. comb standard or Monte Carlo stock, 8 3/4 lbs. Mfg. 2002-2008.

$1,850	$1,525	$1,225	$950	$875	$800	$725	*$2,199*

Add $230 for adj. comb.
Add $190 for pigeon porting by Mag-na-port.

GRADING - PPGS™	100%	98%	95%	90%	80%	70%	60%	LAST MSR

* ***Model 85 TSS Trap Un-Single*** – 12 ga. only, bottom un-single, 32 or 34 in. barrel with adj. rib, fixed or adj. comb stock, standard or Monte Carlo stock, 8 3/4 lbs. Mfg. 2002-2008.

$2,100 $1,750 $1,375 $1,050 $975 $850 $750 *$2,499*

Add $230 for adj. comb on stock.
Add $400 for high grade wood (limited availability, new 2003).
Add $114 for pigeon porting by Mag-na-port.

» **Model 85 TSS Un-Single Combo** – includes bottom un-single barrel and extra 30 or 32 in. VR O/U barrels. Mfg. 2002-2008.

$2,975 $2,450 $2,000 $1,750 $1,500 $1,250 $1,000 *$3,489*

Add $230 for adj. comb on stock.
Add $400 for high grade wood (limited availability, new 2003).
Add $300 for pigeon porting by Mag-na-port.
Add $210 for combo with 13 1/2 in. LOP stock (adj. comb only).

MODEL 85TTR TRAP SERIES – 12 ga., 3 in. chambers, 30, 32, or 34 in. barrels, low profile boxlock action, ejectors, Greener crossbolt, silver nitride finish receiver with scroll engraving, fixed or adj. Grade II/III American black walnut checkered stock with matte finish, 9mm tapered top rib, competition choke tubes, HiViz comp. sight, SST, Pachmayr XLT recoil pad. Mfg. 2009-2010.

$2,050 $1,750 $1,425 $1,100 $875 $775 $650 *$2,329*

Add $230 for adj. comb.
Add $570 for high grade deluxe wood.

* ***Model 85TTR Un-Single*** – 32 or 34 in. barrels, fixed or adj. comb stock. Disc. 2010.

$2,400 $2,150 $1,825 $1,600 $1,350 $1,100 $895 *$2,799*

Add $230 for adj. comb.
Add $400 for high grade deluxe wood.

* ***Model 85TTR Combo*** – includes choice of 30, 32, or 34 in. barrels, adj. comb stock, also available in short (13 1/2 in.) LOP. Disc. 2010.

$3,625 $3,250 $2,825 $2,400 $2,000 $1,650 $1,350 *$4,049*

Add $400 for high grade deluxe wood.

MODEL 500 – 12, 20, 28 ga., or .410 bore, field grade, selective ejectors, VR, SST, 26 in. imp. cyl. and mod., 28 in. full and mod., and 30 in. full and mod. barrels, checkered stock. Prices below assume 50% engraving coverage and gold SST. Mfg. in Japan by SKB 1966-1979, imported by Ithaca.

$1,000 $875 $750 $680 $550 $450 $350

Add 10% for 28 ga. or .410 bore.
Add 10%-15% for fully engraved frame with pheasant, or duck/quail and dog game scene if in 98%+ condition.

The Model 500 varied quite a bit during the course of production in the amount of factory engraving (engraved animals or not), the quality of wood, style of checkering, and also had either silver or gold trigger. This model should also be checked carefully for hairline cracks in the buttstock, where it joins the receiver. Also, beware of bluing wear on frame bottom, and on the front and back of the trigger guard.

* ***Model 500 Magnum*** – 12 ga., 3 in. Mag., field grade, similar to Model 500, except 3 in. Mag. chambers.

$1,000 $875 $750 $680 $550 $450 $350

MODEL 505 FIELD – 12, 20, 28 ga. or .410 bore, blue (new 1998) or silver nitride engraved frame (disc. 1997), 3 in. chambers, 26 or 28 in. barrels (supplied with choke tubes), single selective trigger, ejectors, matte finished (new 2006) or high gloss (disc. 2005) checkered walnut stock with recoil pad and forearm, 6 3/4 - 7 3/4 lbs.

$1,225 $975 $800 $700 $550 $500 $450 *$1,429*

Add $500 for combo package.
Add 10% for 28 ga. or .410 bore.

GRADING - PPGS™	100%	98%	95%	90%	80%	70%	60%	LAST MSR

The combo package included either 12/20 ga. barrels with Inter-chokes or 28 ga./.410 bore barrels.

* ***Model 505 Sporting Clays*** – 28 or 30 in. multi-choke barrels, blue frame with light engraving, dimensioned for Sporting Clays competition, 1997 importation features Schnabel forearm, semi-wide channeled rib, and lengthened forcing cones, approx. 8 1/4 lbs. Older importation, in addition to new model imported 1997-2002.

$1,100 $975 $825 $750 $600 $495 $385 ***$1,299***

* ***Model 505 Trap*** – 12 ga., 30 or 32 in. choke tube barrels with or without Monte Carlo stock, high rib.

$1,100 $975 $825 $750 $600 $495 $385 ***$995***

Add $400 for O/U Trap Combo.

The above Combo includes one set of O/U Trap barrels and a top single Trap barrel.

* ***Model 505 Skeet*** – 12, 20, 28 ga., or .410 bore, 28 in. barrels with multi-chokes.

$1,100 $975 $825 $750 $600 $495 $385 ***$995***

Add 10% for 28 ga. or .410 bore.

* ***Model 505 3-Ga. Skeet Set*** – includes 20, 28 ga., and .410 bore fitted 28 in. barrel sets with Individual forends, aluminum case.

$2,800 $2,450 $2,100 $1,900 $1,525 $1,250 $975 ***$2,195***

MODEL 585 FIELD – 12, 20, 28 ga., or .410 (new 1995) bore, silver nitride engraved receiver, 3 in. chambers, 26 or 28 in. barrels (supplied with choke tubes), similar to 505 Series, except has .735 in. diameter bore on 12 ga. models and includes lengthened forcing cones with extended length "Competition Series" Inter-Choke System designed to improve shot patterns and reduce recoil, SST, ejectors, high gloss (disc. 2005), matte finished (new 2006), or checkered walnut stock with recoil pad and forearm (Youth/Ladies model is also available with 13 1/2 LOP), 6 lbs. 10 oz.-7 lbs. 11 oz. Imported 1992-2008.

$1,425 $1,200 $1,000 $850 $725 $600 $550 ***$1,699***

Add 10% for 28 ga. or .410 bore.

Add $200 for Gold Package featuring choice of silver or blue receiver, gold plated trigger, and 2 gold game scenes with Schnabel forearm - new 1998.

* ***Model 585 Field Set*** – includes 12/20 ga., 20/28 ga., 28 ga./.410 bore, 26 or 28 (new 1994) in. VR barrels with SKB Inter-choke system, silver nitride receiver with finely engraved scroll game scenes, low profile receiver, crossbolt locking system, SST, ejectors, manual safety, checkered high gloss (disc. 2005) or matte finish (new 2006) American walnut stock and forearm. Disc. 2008.

$2,375 $2,000 $1,700 $1,350 $1,100 $975 $850 ***$2,749***

Add $80 for 20/28 ga. set or 28 ga./.410 bore set.

Add approx. $340 for Gold Package featuring choice of silver or blue (disc. 2004) receiver, gold plated trigger, and 2 gold game scenes with Schnabel forearm - new 1998.

* ***Model 585 Medallion*** – 12 or 20 ga., 3 in. chambers, features two inlaid medallions in gold or bronze finish (medallion artwork by Ron Van Gilder and Rocky Capece), very limited production. Mfg. 2000-2005.

$1,610 $1,275 $1,025 $900 $800 $700 $600 ***$1,819***

* ***Model 585 Upland*** – 12, 20, or 28 ga., 3 in. chambers for 12 and 20 ga., features straight grip stock with recoil pad and 26 in. VR barrels, Schnabel forearm, 6 lbs. 10 oz.-7 lbs. 10 oz. Mfg. 1997-2005.

$1,425 $1,250 $1,075 $975 $785 $640 $500 ***$1,549***

Add 10% for 28 ga.

Add $200 for Gold Package featuring choice of silver or blue receiver, gold plated trigger, and 2 gold game scenes with Schnabel forearm - mfg. 1998-2005.

GRADING - PPGS™	100%	98%	95%	90%	80%	70%	60%	LAST MSR

* ***Model 585 Trap*** – 12 ga., 30 or 32 in. choke tube barrels with or w/o Monte Carlo stock, high rib. Disc. 2002.

$1,425	$1,250	$1,075	$975	$785	$640	$500	*$1,619*

Add $200 for Gold Package featuring choice of silver or blue receiver, gold plated trigger, and 2 gold game scenes with Schnabel forearm - mfg. 1998-2002.

Add $800 for O/U Trap Combo or $1,100 for O/U Trap Combo with Gold Package.

The above Combo includes one set of O/U Trap barrels and a top single Trap barrel.

* ***Model 585 Skeet*** – 12, 20, 28 ga., or .410 bore, 28 or 30 (12 ga. only - new 1994) in. barrels with multi-chokes. Disc. 2002.

$1,425	$1,250	$1,075	$975	$785	$640	$500	*$1,619*

Add 10% for 28 ga. or .410 bore.

Add $200 for Gold Package featuring choice of silver or blue receiver, gold plated trigger, and 2 gold game scenes with Schnabel forearm - mfg. 1998-2002.

* ***Model 585 3-Ga. Skeet Set*** – includes 20, 28 ga., and .410 bore fitted 28 in. barrel sets with individual forend, aluminum case. Disc. 2002.

$3,175	$2,550	$2,000	$1,700	$1,525	$1,400	$1,300	*$3,779*

Add $450 for Gold Package featuring choice of silver or blue receiver, gold plated trigger, and 2 gold game scenes with Schnabel forearm - mfg. 1998-2002.

* ***Model 585 Sporting Clays*** – 12, 20, 28 ga. or .410 bore, 3 in. chambers (12 and 20 ga.), 28 or 30 in. multi-choke barrels, dimensioned for Sporting Clays competition, narrow rib (3/8 in.) became available 1994. Disc. 2002.

$1,425	$1,250	$1,075	$975	$785	$640	$500	*$1,679*

Add 10% for 28 ga. or .410 bore.

Add $200 for Gold Package featuring choice of silver or blue receiver, gold plated trigger, and 2 gold game scenes with Schnabel forearm - mfg. 1998-2002.

» **Model 585 Sporting Clays Set** – includes 2 sets of barrels (12 ga. - 30 in., 20 ga. - 28 in.). Mfg. 1996-2002.

$2,135	$1,775	$1,495	$1,200	$1,050	$925	$825	*$2,419*

Add $300 for Gold Package featuring choice of silver or blue receiver, gold plated trigger, and 2 gold game scenes with Schnabel forearm - mfg. 1998-2002.

* ***Model 585 Waterfowler*** – 12 ga. only, 3 in. chambers, oil finished stock and forearm, matte finished barrel and receiver. Imported 1995-2000, reintroduced 2005.

$1,425	$1,250	$1,075	$975	$785	$640	$500	*$1,549*

* ***Model 585 Youth/Ladies*** – 12 or 20 ga., 26 or 28 (12 ga. only) in. VR barrels, features 13 1/2 in. LOP, barrels have .735 in. bores with lengthened forcing cones. Imported 1994-2008.

$1,425	$1,200	$975	$850	$725	$600	$550	*$1,699*

Add $200 for Gold Package featuring choice of silver or blue receiver, gold plated trigger, and 2 gold game scenes with Schnabel forearm - new 1998.

MODEL 585 150th ANNIVERSARY – 12 or 20 ga., 3 in. chambers, silver nitride engraved receiver with gold game scenes, matte finished metal, 26 or 28 in. barrels, matte finish high grade black American walnut stock with finger groove forend, 6 lbs. 12 oz. - 7 lbs. 14 oz. 150 mfg. 2005 only.

$2,100	$1,825	$1,575	N/A	N/A	N/A	N/A	*$1,999*

A total of 150 of this model was manufactured - 70 in 12 ga. w/28 in. barrels, 25 in 12 ga. w/26 in. barrels, 30 in 20 ga. w/28 in. barrels, and 25 in 20 ga. w/26 in. barrels.

MODEL 600 FIELD GRADE – similar to Model 500, except silver-plated frame and select wood and fully engraved.

$1,200	$1,050	$900	$815	$650	$550	$425	

Add 10% for 28 ga. or .410 bore.

An unknown quantity of Model 600s were mfg. with hand engraved blue receivers - a small premium may be asked.

GRADING - PPGS™	100%	98%	95%	90%	80%	70%	60%	LAST MSR

MODEL 600 MAGNUM – similar to Model 600 Field, except chambered for 3 in. Mag., 12 ga. Mfg. 1969-72 by SKB.

$1,200 $1,050 $900 $815 $650 $550 $425

MODEL 600 TRAP GRADE – similar to Model 600 Field Grade, except 12 ga. only, trap stock, recoil pad, select wood.

$1,200 $1,050 $900 $815 $650 $550 $425

MODEL 600 DOUBLES GUN – similar to Model 600 Trap, except choked for 21 yd. and 30 yd. targets. Mfg. 1973-75.

$1,200 $1,050 $900 $815 $650 $550 $425

MODEL 600 SKEET GRADE – 12, 20, 28 ga., or .410 bore, 26 or 28 in. barrels, bored S&S, otherwise similar to Model 600 Trap.

$1,200 $1,050 $900 $815 $650 $550 $425

Add 10% for 28 ga. or .410 bore.

MODEL 600 SKEET GRADE COMBO SET – similar to Model 600 Skeet, except fitted with matched set of 20, 28 ga., and .410 bore barrels, in fitted case.

$2,650 $2,250 $1,875 $1,550 $1,325 $1,175 $1,025

MODEL 605 FIELD – similar to Model 505 Deluxe Field except has silver finished engraved receiver with better walnut. Importation disc. 1992.

$1,275 $1,125 $950 $875 $700 $575 $450 ***$1,195***

Add $500 for extra set of barrels (Combo).
Add 10% for 28 ga. or .410 bore.

* ***Model 605 Trap*** – 12 ga., 30 or 32 in. choke tube barrel with or without Monte Carlo stock, high rib.

$1,275 $1,125 $950 $875 $700 $575 $450 ***$1,195***

Add $400 for O/U Trap Combo.

The above Combo includes one set of O/U Trap barrels and a top single Trap barrel.

* ***Model 605 Skeet*** – 12, 20, 28 ga., or .410 bore, 28 in. barrels with multi-chokes.

$1,275 $1,125 $950 $875 $700 $575 $450 ***$1,195***

Add 10% for 28 ga. or .410 bore.

* ***Model 605 3-Ga. Skeet Set*** – includes 20, 28 ga., and .410 bore fitted 28 in. barrel sets with individual forends, aluminum case.

$2,900 $2,550 $2,175 $1,975 $1,595 $1,300 $1,000 ***$2,395***

* ***Model 605 Sporting Clay*** – 28 or 30 in. multi-choke barrels, dimensioned for Sporting Clay competition.

$1,275 $1,125 $950 $875 $700 $575 $450 ***$1,245***

* ***Model 605 DU Sponsor Gun*** – mfg. for DU chapters - dinner auction gun, 850 mfg. in 12 ga. (1990) and 850 mfg. in 20 ga. (1991). Features gold inlays and presentation case.

Currently, prices seem to range between $1,200-$1,400.

DU sponsor gun values are usually hard to ascertain in the secondary marketplace.

MODEL 680 ENGLISH – similar to Model 600 Field, except English style stock, select walnut and fine scroll engraving. Mfg. 1973-76.

$1,300 $1,150 $975 $850 $725 $650 $600

Add 10% for 20 ga.

MODEL 685 FIELD – similar to Model 585 Deluxe Field, except has silver finished engraved receiver with gold inlays and better walnut, engine turned monobloc. Imported 1992-1995.

$1,525 $1,325 $1,150 $1,025 $850 $675 $525 ***$1,549***

Add 10% for 28 ga. or .410 bore.

GRADING - PPGS™	100%	98%	95%	90%	80%	70%	60%	LAST MSR

* ***Model 685 Field Set*** – includes 12/20, 20/28 ga., 28 ga./.410 bore 26 or 28 (new 1994) in. VR barrels with SKB Inter-choke system (on 12, 20, and 28 ga.), silver nitride receiver with finely engraved scroll game scenes, low profile receiver, crossbolt locking system, SST, ejectors, manual safety, checkered high gloss American walnut stock and forearm.

$2,225	$1,950	$1,675	$1,500	$1,225	$1,000	$775	*$2,149*

* ***Model 685 Trap*** – 12 ga., 30 or 32 in. choke tube barrels with or w/o Monte Carlo stock, high rib.

$1,525	$1,325	$1,150	$1,025	$850	$675	$525	*$1,595*

Add $600 for O/U Trap Combo.

The above Combo includes one set of O/U Trap barrels and a top single Trap barrel.

* ***Model 685 Skeet*** – 12, 20, 28 ga., or .410 bore, 28 or 30 (12 ga. only - new 1994) in. barrels with multi-chokes.

$1,525	$1,325	$1,150	$1,025	$850	$675	$525	*$1,595*

Add 10% for 28 ga. or .410 bore.

* ***Model 685 3-Ga. Skeet Set*** – includes 20, 28 ga., and .410 bore fitted 28 in. barrels sets with individual forends, aluminum case.

$3,300	$2,895	$2,475	$2,250	$1,800	$1,475	$1,150	*$2,949*

* ***Model 685 Sporting Clays*** – 28 (all gauges), 30 (12 ga. only), or 32 (12 ga. only) in. multi-choke barrels, dimensioned for Sporting Clays competition, 3/8 in. narrow rib became available 1994. Importation disc. 1995.

$1,525	$1,325	$1,150	$1,025	$850	$675	$525	*$1,595*

Add 10% for 28 ga.

* ***Model 685 Sporting Clays Set*** – includes one set of 12 ga. (28, 30, or 32 in. VR barrels) and 20 ga. (28 in. only) or one set of 32 and 28 in. barrels in 12 ga only. Imported 1994-95.

$2,225	$1,950	$1,675	$1,500	$1,225	$1,000	$775	*$2,295*

MODEL 700 TRAP GRADE – 12 ga., similar to Model 600 Trap, except more engraving, better grade wood, wide rib. Mfg. 1969-75.

$1,300	$1,125	$975	$875	$715	$585	$450	

MODEL 700 DOUBLES GUN – 12 ga., similar to Model 700 Trap, except choked for 21 yd. and 30 yd. targets. Mfg. 1973-75.

$1,300	$1,125	$975	$875	$715	$585	$450	

MODEL 700 SKEET GRADE – similar to Model 700 Doubles, only bored S&S, available in 12 or 20 ga.

$1,300	$1,125	$975	$875	$715	$585	$450	

MODEL 785 FIELD – 12, 20, 28 ga., or .410 bore, silver nitride engraved receiver, 3 in. chambers, 26 or 28 in. barrels (supplied with choke tubes), similar to 585 Series, except has chrome lined bores on all models and also includes lengthened forcing cones with extended length "Competition Series" Inter-Choke System designed to improve shot patterns and reduce recoil, SST, ejectors, checkered walnut stock with recoil pad and forearm, 6 lbs. 10 oz.-7 lbs. 11 oz. Imported 1995-2002.

$1,900	$1,650	$1,400	$1,150	$1,000	$900	$800	*$2,119*

Add 10% for 28 ga. or .410 bore.

* ***Model 785 Field Set*** – includes 12/20, 20/28 ga., 28 ga./.410 bore, 26 or 28 in. VR barrels with SKB Inter-Choke system (on 12 and 20 ga.), silver nitride receiver with finely engraved scroll game scenes, low profile receiver, crossbolt locking system, SST, ejectors, manual safety, checkered high gloss American walnut stock and forearm. Importation disc. 2002.

$2,680	$2,300	$1,925	$1,600	$1,500	$1,375	$1,275	*$3,019*

Add $100 for 20/28 ga. set or 28 ga./.410 bore set.

GRADING - PPGS™	100%	98%	95%	90%	80%	70%	60%	LAST MSR

* ***Model 785 Medallion*** – 12, 20, or 28 ga., 3 in. chambers, features inlaid medallions in gold or bronze finish (medallion artwork by Ron Van Gilder and Rocky Capece), very limited production. Mfg. 2000-2005.

	$2,075	$1,750	$1,450	$1,175	$1,050	$925	$825	*$2,389*

Add 10% for 28 ga.

* ***Model 785 Trap*** – 12 ga., 30 or 32 in. choke tube barrels with or w/o Monte Carlo stock, high rib. Importation disc. 2002.

	$1,940	$1,625	$1,365	$1,125	$995	$895	$800	*$2,199*

Add $880 for O/U Trap Combo.

The above Combo includes one set of O/U Trap barrels and a top single Trap barrel.

* ***Model 785 Skeet*** – 12, 20, 28 ga., or .410 bore, 28 or 30 (12 ga. only) in. barrels with multi-chokes. Importation disc. 2002.

	$1,940	$1,625	$1,365	$1,125	$995	$895	$800	*$2,199*

Add 10% for 28 ga. or .410 bore.

* ***Model 785 3-Ga. Skeet Set*** – includes 20, 28 ga., and .410 bore fitted 28 in. barrel sets with individual forends, aluminum case. Importation disc. 2002.

	$3,835	$2,975	$2,350	$2,000	$1,600	$1,400	$1,295	*$4,439*

* ***Model 785 Sporting Clays*** – 12, 20, or 28 ga., 28 in. (all gauges), 30 in. (12 ga. only), or 32 in. (12 ga. only) multi-choke barrels, dimensioned for Sporting Clays competition with 12mm narrow rib. Importation disc. 2002.

	$2,000	$1,675	$1,375	$1,150	$995	$895	$800	*$2,269*

Add 10% for 28 ga.

» **Model 785 Sporting Clays Set** – includes 2 sets of barrels (12 ga. - 30 in., 20 ga. - 28 in.). Imported 1996-2002.

	$2,775	$2,450	$2,125	$1,825	$1,625	$1,400	$1,200	*$3,149*

MODEL 800 TRAP GRADE – 12 ga., similar to Model 700 Trap, except more engraving, better grade wood, wide rib. Limited mfg. 1969-1975.

	$1,500	$1,300	$1,125	$1,025	$825	$675	$525

MODEL 800 SKEET GRADE – 12 or 20 ga., skeet chokes. Mfg. 1969-1975.

	$1,500	$1,300	$1,125	$1,025	$825	$675	$525

MODEL 880 CROWN GRADE – 12, 20, 28 ga., or .410 bore, coin finished receiver, extensively engraved with sideplates, SST, ejectors, select walnut with fleur-de-lis scroll style checkering, double crossbolt action. Limited mfg. Disc. 1980.

	$2,000	$1,825	$1,625	$1,300	$1,150	$975	$890

Add 25% for 28 ga. or .410 bore (extremely rare).

MODEL 885 – available in either Field, Skeet, or Trap configuration, coin finished receiver featuring fine scroll engraving with game scenes, boxlock action with sideplates, beginning 1992, the 885 Series in 12 ga. features lengthened forcing cones, .735 bore, and a competition series of extended length multi-chokes. Imported 1988-94.

* ***Model 885 Field*** – 12, 20, 28 ga., or .410 bore, field dimensions, 26 or 28 in. barrels include choke tubes. Imported 1989-94.

	$2,100	$1,825	$1,575	$1,425	$1,150	$950	$725	*$1,895*

Add 10% for 28 ga. or .410 bore.

* ***Model 885 Trap*** – 12 ga., 30 or 32 in. barrels with multi-chokes, standard or Monte Carlo stock.

	$2,100	$1,825	$1,575	$1,425	$1,150	$950	$725	*$1,949*

Add $700 for O/U Trap Combo.

The above Combo includes one set of O/U Trap barrels and a top single Trap barrel.

GRADING - PPGS™	100%	98%	95%	90%	80%	70%	60%	LAST MSR

* ***Model 885 Skeet*** – 12, 20, 28 ga., or .410 bore, 28 or 30 (12 ga. only - new 1994) in. barrels with multi-chokes.

$2,100 $1,825 $1,575 $1,425 $1,150 $950 $725 *$1,949*

Add 10% for 28 ga. or .410 bore.

* ***Model 885 Field Set*** – includes 12/20, 20/28 ga., 28 ga./.410 bore 26 or 28 (new 1994) in. VR barrels with SKB Inter-Choke system (on 12 and 20 ga.), silver nitride receiver with finely engraved scroll game scenes, low profile receiver, crossbolt locking system, SST, ejectors, manual safety, checkered high gloss American walnut stock and forearm.

$2,800 $2,450 $2,100 $1,900 $1,525 $1,250 $975

* ***Model 885 3-Ga. Skeet Set*** – includes 20, 28 ga., and .410 bore fitted 28 in. barrel sets with individual forends, aluminum case.

$4,000 $3,500 $3,000 $2,725 $2,200 $1,800 $1,400 *$3,595*

* ***Model 885 Sporting Clays*** – 28 (all gauges), 30 (12 ga. only), or 32 (12 ga. only) in. multi-choke barrels, dimensioned for Sporting Clays competition, 3/8 in. narrow rib became available 1994.

$2,100 $1,825 $1,575 $1,425 $1,150 $950 $725 *$1,949*

MODEL 5600 – 12 ga. only 26, 28 and 30 inch barrels available as Trap or Skeet only, boxlock action, VR and ventilated barrels, ejectors, mechanical trigger, no barrel selector, blued receiver no engraving select walnut. Imported 1980 -1981.

$1,200 $1,050 $900 $815 $650 $550 $425

MODEL 5700 – 12 ga. only, 26, 28 and 30 inch barrels available as Trap or Skeet only, boxlock action, VR and ventilated barrels, ejectors, mechanical trigger, no barrel selector, The receiver has a nitride case hardened finish with hand engraved game scene and scroll engraving, select walnut. Imported 1980 -1981.

$1,600 $1,400 $1,200 $1,095 $875 $725 $550

MODEL 5800 – 12 ga. only 26, 28 and 30 inch barrels available as Trap or Skeet only, boxlock action, VR and ventilated barrels, ejectors, mechanical trigger, no barrel selector, receiver has a nitride case hardened finish with a lavish hand engraved scroll patten, select walnut with ivory grip cap. Imported 1980 -1981.

$2,500 $2,195 $1,875 $1,700 $1,375 $1,125 $875

* ***Model 5800 Custom Deluxe*** – 12 ga. only, 26, 28 and 30 inch barrels available as Trap or Skeet only, boxlock action, VR, and ventilated barrels, ejectors, mechanical trigger, no barrel selector, receiver has a nitride case hardened or blue finish with a lavish hand engraved scroll and 24kt gold game scene inlays in pattern, select walnut with ivory. Very limited importation 1984.

$5,000 $4,375 $3,750 $3,400 $2,750 $2,250 $1,750

GC 7 GAME BIRD SERIES – 12, 20, 28 ga., or .410 bore, 3 in. chambers (except 28 ga.), low profile boxlock action, Greener crossbolt, silver nitride finished receiver with scroll engraving, 26 or 28 in. monobloc barrels, lengthened forcing cones, Briley F2 choke tubes, top vent. rib, SST, inertia (12 or 20 ga.), or mechanical (28 ga. or .410 bore) trigger, Grade I, II, or III checkered American black walnut stock and forearm, black Pachmayr or plastic recoil pad. Mfg. 2009-2010.

$1,395 $1,200 $995 $850 $700 $600 $525 *$1,569*

Add $90 for 28 ga. or .410 bore.
Add $250 for Grade II.
Add $630 for Grade III.

* ***GC 7 Game Bird Youth & Ladies*** – 12 or 20 ga., 3 in. chambers, low profile boxlock action, Greener crossbolt, silver nitride finished receiver with scroll engraving, 26 or 28 in. monobloc barrels, lengthened forcing cones, Briley F2 choke tubes, top vent. rib, SST, inertia (12 or 20 ga.) trigger, standard or deluxe checkered American black walnut stock and forearm, black Pachmayr or plastic recoil pad. Mfg. 2009-2010.

$1,395 $1,200 $995 $850 $700 $600 $525 *$1,569*

Add $250 for Grade II.
Add $630 for Grade III.

GRADING - PPGS™	100%	98%	95%	90%	80%	70%	60%	LAST MSR

* ***GC 7 Game Bird Multi-Gauge Set*** – includes 12 and 20 ga., 20 and 28 ga., or 28 ga. and .410 bore 28 in. barrel sets. Disc. 2010.

$2,375	$2,100	$1,800	$1,500	$1,250	$1,000	$850	*$2,629*

Add $300 for Grade II.
Add $820 for Grade III.
Add $90 for 28 ga. or .410 bore.

GC 7 CLAYS SERIES – 12, 20, 28 ga., or .410 bore, 3 in. chambers (except 28 ga.), low profile boxlock action, ejectors, Greener crossbolt, silver nitride finished receiver with game scene engraving, 28, 30, or 32 in. monobloc barrels, lengthened forcing cones, Briley F2 choke tubes, top vent. rib, SST, inertia (12 or 20 ga.), or mechanical (28 ga. or .410 bore) trigger, fixed or adj. comb Grade I, II, or III checkered American black walnut stock and forearm, black Pachmayr recoil pad. Mfg. 2009-2010.

$1,495	$1,275	$1,050	$850	$725	$600	$550	*$1,679*

Add $100 for 28 ga.
Add $420 for adj. comb.
Add $600 for Grade II.
Add $870 for Grade III.

* ***GC 7 Clays 2 Barrel Set*** – includes 12 and 20 ga., 20 and 28 ga., or 28 ga. and .410 bore 30 in. barrel sets. Disc. 2010.

$3,150	$2,800	$2,475	$2,150	$1,800	$1,500	$1,250	*$3,449*

Add $100 for 20 and 28 ga. or 28 ga. and .410 bore.
Add $450 for Grade II.
Add $600 for Grade III.

* ***GC 7 Clays 3 Barrel Set*** – includes 20, 28 ga. and .410 bore with choice of 28 or 30 in. barrel sets. Disc. 2010.

$4,800	$4,200	$3,600	$3,265	$2,625	$2,150	$1,675	*$4,999*

Add $200 for adj. comb.
Add $400 for Grade III.

GC 7 TRAP SERIES – 12 ga., 30, 32, or 34 in. barrels, Briley X2 extended choke tubes, top vent. rib, fixed or adj. comb Grade II or III checkered American black walnut stock and forearm, black Pachmayr XLT recoil pad. Mfg. 2009-2010.

* ***GC 7 Trap Top Single*** – 32 in. barrels, 13 1/2 in. LOP, adj. comb Grade I stock. Disc. 2010.

$1,425	$1,200	$1,000	$825	$700	$575	$475	*$1,599*

* ***GC 7 Trap Un-Single*** – 32 or 34 in. barrels, fixed or adj. comb Grade II/III stock. Disc. 2010.

$2,450	$2,125	$1,800	$1,500	$1,250	$995	$850	*$2,799*

Add $200 for adj. comb.
Add $400 for Grade III.

* ***GC 7 Trap Un-Single Combo*** – includes 30, 32, or 34 in. barrels, adj. comb Grade II/III stock. Disc. 2010.

$3,650	$3,300	$2,950	$2,600	$2,200	$1,800	$1,475	*$4,049*

Add $400 for Grade III.

SHOTGUNS: O/U, DETACHABLE TRIGGER MODELS

SKB began producing the detachable trigger models in 1984 with very limited importation into the U.S. market These Models included the 4000, 5100, 5500, 5700D, 5800D 5900D 5000, 6000, 8000 and the Medalist. These models and the MJ series were Primarily exported to Europe.

MEDALIST – 12 ga. onl, 30 and 32 inch barrels, choke tube barrels available as Sporting Clays only, boxlock action, VR, ejectors, and ventilated barrels, mechanical trigger, no barrel selector, silver nitride finished receiver, hand engraved scroll, detachable trigger, select walnut. Only eight pieces imported in 2009.

$4,000	$3,500	$3,000	$2,725	$2,200	$1,800	$1,400	*$4,200*

Add $300 for additional trigger group.

GRADING - PPGS™	100%	98%	95%	90%	80%	70%	60%	LAST MSR

MODEL 4000 – 12 ga. only, 26, 28 and 30 inch barrels, fixed choke, available as Trap or Skeet only, boxlock action, VR, ejectors, and ventilated barrels, mechanical trigger, no barrel selector, Silver nitride finished receiver, hand engraved scroll, detachable trigger select walnut. Very limited importation.

	$3,200	$2,800	$2,400	$2,175	$1,750	$1,425	$1,125	*$3,500*

Add $300 for additional trigger group.
Add $200 for choke tube barrels.

MODEL 5000 – 12 ga. only, 26, 28 and 30 inch barrels available as Trap, Skeet and Sporting Clays, side plated boxlock action, VR and ventilated barrels, mechanical trigger, no barrel selector, Silver nitride finished receiver, hand engraved scroll, detachable trigger, select walnut. Very limited importation.

	$5,000	$4,375	$3,750	$3,400	$2,750	$2,250	$1,750	*$5,500*

Add $300 for additional trigger group.
Add $200 for choke tube barrels.

MODEL 5100 – 12 ga. only, 26, 28 and 30 inch barrels available as Trap or Skeet only, boxlock action, VR and ventilated barrels, ejectors, mechanical trigger, no barrel selector, Silver nitride finished receiver, hand engraved scroll, detachable trigger select walnut. Very limited importation.

	$3,200	$2,800	$2,400	$2,175	$1,750	$1,425	$1,125	*$3,500*

Add $300 for additional trigger group.
Add $200 for choke tube barrels.

SHOTGUNS: SxS

Ithaca Gun Company imported the Models 100, 150, 200E, and 280 from 1967 to 1977. These SxS were available in 12 and 20 ga only and featured 25 to 30 in. barrels with fixed chokes, and all were boxlock actions. The more expensive models differ in the amount of engraving, grade of walnut, style of checkering.

Mitsui Trading Company imported the Models 100, 200, 280, 300, 400 and 480 from 1979 to 1981.

G. U. Inc. imported the Model 200, 200E, 400, 400E, 385 and 485 from 1989 to 2004. These SXS models all had silver nitride (coin) finished receiver and choke tube barrels. The Model 200, 200E, 400 and 400E were produced in 1989 only. The 385 and 485 were produced from 1996 -2004.

Add approx. 10% for NIB condition on the following models.

ROYAL DELUXE – 12 ga., 2 3/4 in. chamber, 26, 28 or 30 in. barrels with fixed chokes and swamped rib, the base model was fitted with ejectors, double triggers, beavertail forend and pistol grip stock, receiver was hand engraved with a game scene. Special Order models included: Trap and Skeet and Heavy Duck with 3 in. chamber. Imported by Stoeger Arms Corporation 1960-1961.

	$1,400	$1,225	$1,050	$950	$775	$625	$495	

Add 15% for ejectors.
Add 15% for SST.
Add 15% for solid VR.
Add 15% for floating VR.
Add 10% for custom engraving.

MODEL 100 – 12 or 20 ga, SST, extractors, chrome barrels and splinter forend and pistol grip stock, and light scroll engraving. The Mitsui imports had a game scene engraving pattern and beavertail forends.

	$1,050	$925	$795	$715	$575	$475	$375	

Add 20% for 20 ga.
Add 10% for NIB condition.
Add 10% for fully engraved receiver with pheasant, or duck/quail and dog game scene if in 98%+ condition.

GRADING - PPGS™	100%	98%	95%	90%	80%	70%	60%	LAST MSR

MODEL 150 – 12 or 20 ga, SST, extractors, chrome barrels and beavertail forend, pistol grip stock, and scroll engraving. Mfg. from 1972-1974.

	$1,050	$925	$795	$715	$575	$475	$375	

Add 20% for 20 ga.
Add 10% for NIB condition.

MODEL 200/200E – 12 or 20 ga, gold SST, ejectors, chrome barrels and beavertail forend and pistol grip stock. The early models had a blued receiver with hand cut scroll engraving, the later models were acid etched engraved with German silver plating. The Mitsui models were similar to the later Ithaca models.

	$1,400	$1,225	$1,050	$950	$775	$625	$495	

Add 20% for 20 ga.
Add 10% for NIB condition.

MODEL 200/200E (RECENT MFG.) – 12 or 20 ga, scalloped boxlock action with silver nitride (coin) finished with a game scene engraving pattern, gold SST, ejectors, and beavertail forend. Model 200 featured a pistol grip stock, the Model 200E had an English straight stock, choke tube barrels. Very limited production, imported by G.U. Inc. in 1989.

	$1,750	$1,525	$1,300	$1,195	$950	$795	$600	*$895*

Add 10% for NIB condition.
Add 20% for 20 ga models.

MODEL 280 – 12 or 20 ga, gold SST, ejectors, chrome barrels and beavertail forend, English straight grip stock, blued receiver with hand cut game scene with scroll engraving wrapping around receiver. The Mitsui models were similar to the later Ithaca models.

	$1,400	$1,225	$1,050	$950	$775	$625	$495	

Add 20% for 20 ga.
Add 10% for NIB condition.

MODEL 300 – 12 or 20 ga, gold SST, ejectors, chrome barrels and beavertail forend and pistol grip stock, receivers are etched with a florentine scroll pattern plated with German silver, barrel monobloc is engraved with scroll.

	$1,450	$1,275	$1,095	$975	$800	$650	$500	

Add 20% for 20 ga.
Add 10% for NIB condition.

MODEL 385 FIELD – 12 (new 1998), 20 or 28 ga., scalloped boxlock action with silver nitride receiver, engraved scroll and game scene designs, SST, ejectors, automatic safety, semi-fancy gloss or matte finished American walnut, English or pistol grip stock, beavertail or satin finished splinter forearm. Imported 1992-2004.

	$2,200	$1,925	$1,650	$1,495	$1,200	$995	$775	*$2,049*

* ***Model 385 Field Set*** – includes a pair of 20 and 28 ga., 26 or 28 in. barrels, choice of pistol grip or English straight stock with high gloss or matte finish, beavertail or splinter forearm. Imported 1992-2004.

	$3,200	$2,800	$2,400	$2,175	$1,750	$1,425	$1,125	*$2,929*

* ***Model 385 Field DU Commemorative*** – features gold inlaid mallards on both receiver sides and gold inlaid DU duck head on receiver bottom, includes hard shell case, and signed letter from SKB president, DU serial number, includes pair of 20 and 28 ga. 26 in. barrels, pistol grip stock, beavertail forearm, high gloss finish. Imported 1992.

	$4,200	$3,675	$3,150	N/A	N/A	N/A	N/A	*$5,000*

This model was a DU "Collectors Series" gun.

* ***Model 385 Field Sporting Clays*** – 12, 20 (new 2000), or 28 (new 2000) ga., 3 in. chambers (12 ga.), 28 or 30 (new 2003) in. barrels with raised VR and double bead sights, pistol grip stock, beavertail forearm, approx. 7 1/2 lbs. Imported 1998-2004.

	$2,300	$2,000	$1,725	$1,550	$1,250	$1,025	$800	*$2,159*

GRADING - PPGS™	100%	98%	95%	90%	80%	70%	60%	LAST MSR

» **Model 385 Field Sporting Clays Set** – includes a pair of 20 and 28 ga., 28 or 30 (new 2003) in. barrels. pistol grip stock, beavertail forearm, high gloss or matte finish. Imported 1992-2004.

	$3,200	$2,800	$2,400	$2,175	$1,750	$1,425	$1,125	*$3,059*

MODEL 400 – 12 or 20 ga, gold SST, ejectors, chrome barrels and beavertail forend and pistol grip stock, receivers are etched with a Florentine scroll pattern plated with German silver, barrel monobloc is extensively engraved with matching scroll, presentation grade walnut with 24 line checkering.

	$1,800	$1,575	$1,350	$1,225	$995	$800	$625	

Add 20% for 20 ga.
Add 10% for NIB condition.

MODEL 400/400E (RECENT MFG.) – 12 or 20 ga, boxlock action with side plates, silver nitride (coin) finished with a game scene engraving patterns, gold SST, ejectors, and beavertail forend, choke tube barrels. Model 400 featured a pistol grip stock, the Model 400E had an English straight stock. Very limited production, imported by G.U. Inc. in 1989.

	$2,000	$1,750	$1,500	$1,350	$1,100	$900	$700	*$1,195*

Add 10% for NIB condition.
Add 20% for 20 ga. models.

MODEL 480 – 12 or 20 ga, gold SST, ejectors, English straight stock, floor plate, trigger guard and top lever were a black chrome finish.

	$1,800	$1,575	$1,350	$1,225	$995	$800	$625	

Add 20% for 20 ga.
Add 10% for NIB condition.

MODEL 485 FIELD – 12 (new 1998), 20 or 28 ga., sideplate boxlock action with silver nitride finish, engraved upland game scene designs, 26 or 28" barrels with raised VR rib SST, ejectors, automatic safety, semi-fancy American walnut in either high gloss or matte finish (new 2002), English or pistol grip stock, beavertail or splinter forearm. Imported 1997 - 2004.

	$2,900	$2,525	$2,175	$1,975	$1,595	$1,300	$1,000	*$2,769*

* ***Model 485 Field Set*** – includes a pair of 20 and 28 ga., 26 or 28 in. barrels, choice of pistol grip or English straight stock, beavertail or splinter forearm, high gloss or matte finish, very limited production. Imported 1998-2004.

	$4,200	$3,675	$3,150	$2,850	$2,300	$1,895	$1,475	*$3,949*

SHOTGUNS: SEMI-AUTO

MODEL 300 STANDARD – 12 or 20 ga., 3 in. chamber, recoil operated, 26 in. imp. cyl., 28 in. mod. or full plain barrel, 30 in. full, checkered pistol grip stock. Mfg. 1968-72.

	$350	$300	$265	$240	$195	$160	$125	

MODEL XL 300 – 12 or 20 ga., 2 3/4 (12 ga.) or 3 (20 ga.) in. chamber, gas operated, white alloy receiver with light game scene etching, 4 shot mag., 26-30 in. plain barrel.

	$375	$325	$275	$250	$200	$175	$125	

MODEL 1300 UPLAND – 12 or 20 ga., 3 in. chamber, 22, 26, or 28 in. VR barrel with multi-chokes, matte black receiver, checkered walnut stock and forearm. Importation resumed 1988-96.

	$550	$475	$415	$375	$300	$250	$195	*$495*

This model was previously designated the Model XL-300. The new Model 1300 was available in Slug configuration with 22 in. barrel/iron sights at no extra charge. Recent Model 1300s have a magazine cutoff system on front left side of frame.

MODEL 900 STANDARD – 12 or 20 ga., 3 in. chamber, similar to Model 300 standard, except has vent. rib. barrel. Mfg. 1968-1972.

	$350	$300	$265	$240	$195	$160	$125	

GRADING - PPGS™	100%	98%	95%	90%	80%	70%	60%	LAST MSR

XL 900 – similar to XL 300, except has vent. rib barrel and no recoil pad, 6 1/4 lbs.

$400 $350 $300 $275 $225 $180 $140

XL 900 MR – 12 ga. only, gas operated, 26-30 in. barrel, 5 shot, alloy receiver, engraved game bird scroll work on receiver, shoots both 2 3/4 and 3 in. shells by interchanging barrels. Disc. 1980.

$400 $350 $300 $275 $225 $180 $140

XL 900 TRAP GRADE – similar to XL 900 MR, 12 ga. only, scroll engraved black chrome receiver, 30 in. imp. mod. or full barrel, trap style stock, straight or Monte Carlo, recoil pad. Mfg. 1980-disc.

$400 $350 $300 $275 $225 $180 $140

XL 900 SKEET GRADE – similar to XL 900 MR, except scroll engraved black chrome receiver, 26 in. barrel, skeet stock. Mfg. 1972-disc.

$400 $350 $300 $275 $225 $180 $140

XL 900 SLUG GUN – similar to XL 900 MR, except 24 in. slug barrel, rifle sights, no rib. Mfg. 1972-disc.

$400 $350 $300 $275 $225 $180 $140

MODEL 1900 – 12 or 20 ga., 3 in. chamber, 22, 26, or 28 in. VR barrel with multi-chokes, deluxe outdoor field scene etched on receiver, gold trigger, approx. 1,000-2,000 mfg. per year. Importation disc. 1996.

$585 $510 $440 $400 $325 $265 $200 *$545*

This model was previously designated the Model XL 900. The Model 1900 was available in Slug configuration with 22 in. barrel and iron sights or Trap Model at no extra charge. Recent Model 1900s have a magazine cutoff system on front left side of frame.

MODEL 3000 – 12 or 20 ga., 3 in. chamber, gas operated, (shoots both 2 3/4 and 3 in. shells interchangeably) with semi-squareback styling, elaborate game scenes etched on both sides of receiver, deluxe checkered walnut stock and forearm. Imported 1988-90.

$650 $575 $490-5 $440 $360 $295 $225 *$597*

Add $50 for Trap model (2 3/4 in. chamber).

This model has not previously been imported in this configuration.

SHOTGUNS: SINGLE BARREL, TRAP

MODEL 505 TRAP – 12 ga., 32 or 34 in. barrel with multi-chokes, regular or Monte Carlo stock.

$875 $725 $650 $525 $475 $430 $395 *$995*

MODEL 605 TRAP – 12 ga., 32 or 34 in. barrel with multi-chokes.

$1,075 $850 $750 $675 $575 $500 $450 *$1,195*

CENTURY TRAP – 12 ga., 32 or 34 in. VR barrel, engraved, auto ejector, full choke, checkered walnut stock. Mfg. 1973 and 1976.

$550 $525 $470 $440 $385 $360 $320

This model was imported by Ithaca.

CENTURY II TRAP – improved trap stock version of Century, Monte Carlo stock.

$600 $550 $495 $470 $415 $385 $350

This model was imported by Ithaca.

SHOTGUNS: SLIDE ACTION

MODEL 7300 – 12 or 20 ga., 2 3/4 or 3 in. chambers, blue only, French walnut stock-hand checkered, twin action slide bars. Disc. 1980.

$350 $300 $265 $240 $195 $160 $125

MODEL 7900 – trap or skeet variation of the Model 7300.

$350 $300 $265 $240 $195 $160 $125

SKS

SKS designates a semi-auto rifle design originally developed by the Russian military, and manufactured in Russia by both Tula Arsenal (1949-1956) and by Izhevsk Arsenal from 1953-1954. Currently manufactured in Russia, China, and many other countries. Previously manufactured in Russia, China (largest quantity), N. Korea, East Germany, Romania, Albania, Yugoslavia, and North Vietnam.

SKS DEVELOPMENT & HISTORY

SKS (Samozaryadnyi Karabin Simonova) - developed by Sergei Gavrilovich Simonov in the late 1940s to use the 7.62 cartridge of 1943 (7.62x39mm). The SKS is actually based on an earlier design developed by Simonov in 1936 as a prototype self-loading military rifle. The SKS was adopted by the Soviet military in 1949, two years after the AK-47, and was originally intended as a complement to the AK-47s select-fire capability. It served in this role until the mid-to-late 1950s, when it was withdrawn from active issue and sent to reserve units and Soviet Youth "Pioneer" programs. It was also released for use in military assistance programs to Soviet Bloc countries and other "friendly" governments. Much of the original SKS manufacturing equipment was shipped to Communist China prior to 1960. Since then, most of the SKS carbines produced, including those used by the Viet Cong in Vietnam, have come from China.

Like the AK-47, the Simonov carbine is a robust military rifle. It, too, was designed to be used by troops with very little formal education or training. It will operate reliably in the harshest climatic conditions, from the Russian arctic to the steamy jungles of Southeast Asia. Its chrome-lined bore is impervious to the corrosive effects of fulminate of mercury primers and the action is easily disassembled for cleaning and maintenance.

The SKS and a modified sporter called the OP-SKS (OP stands for Okhotnichnyi Patron) are the standard hunting rifles for a majority of Russian hunters. It is routinely used to take everything from the Russian saiga antelope up to and including moose, boar, and brown bear. The main difference between the regular SKS and the OP variant is in the chamber dimensions and the rate of rifling. The OP starts as a regular SKS, then has the barrel removed and replaced with one designed to specifically handle a slightly longer and heavier bullet.

Prior to the "assault weapons" ban, hundreds of thousands of SKS carbines were imported into the U.S. The SKS was rapidly becoming one of the favorites of American hunters and shooters. Its low cost and durability made it a popular "truck gun" for those shooters who spend a lot of time in the woods, whether they are ranchers, farmers, or plinkers. While the Russian made SKS is a bonafide curio and relic firearm and legal for importation, the Clinton administration suspended all import permits for firearms having a rifled bore and ammunition from the former Soviet Union in early 1994. In order to get the ban lifted, the Russian government signed a trade agreement, wherein they agreed to deny export licenses to any American company seeking SKS rifles and a variety of other firearms and ammunition deemed politically incorrect by Clinton & Gore. The BATF then used this agreement as a reason to deny import licenses for any SKS from any country.

Most of the SKS carbines imported into the U.S. came from the Peoples Republic of China. They were a mix of refurbished military issue, straight military surplus, and even some new manufacture. Quality was rather poor. Compared to the SKS Chinese carbines, only a few Russian made SKSs ever made it into the U.S. All are from military stockpiles and were refurbished at the Tula Arms Works, probably the oldest continuously operating armory in the world. Recently, more SKS carbines have been imported from the former Yugoslavia by Century International Arms. These carbines carry the former Soviet Bloc designation of "Type 58" and feature milled receivers. Quality is generally good, and values are comparable to other Russian/European SKS imports. Values for unmodified Russian and Eastern European made SKS carbines (those with the original magazines and stock) are higher than the Chinese copies.

The most collectible SKS is East German mfg., and SKS rifles mfg. in N. Korea and N. Vietnam are also quite rare in the U.S.

GRADING - PPGS™	100%	98%	95%	90%	80%	70%	60%	LAST MSR

Over 600 million SKS carbines have been manufactured in China alone, by over 45 different manufacturers, in addition to the millions manufactured in other former Soviet Bloc countries. The Simonov carbine was the best selling semi-auto rifle in America (and other countries) during 1993-94, and remains a popular choice for plinking, hunting, and protection in the new millennium.

RIFLES: SEMI-AUTO

SKS – 7.62x39mm Russian cal., Soviet designed, original Soviet mfg. as well as copies mfg. in China, Russia, Yugoslavia, and many other countries, gas operated weapon, 10 shot fixed mag., wood stock (thumbhole design on newer mfg.), with or w/o (newer mfg.) permanently attached folding bayonet, tangent rear and hooded front sight, no current importation from China, Russia, or the former Yugoslavia.

Please refer to individual importers for other SKS listings, including Norinco, Poly-Technologies, and Mitchell Arms.

*** *SKS Mfg. in Russia, Yugoslavia, Romania***

	100%	98%	95%	90%	80%	70%	60%	LAST MSR
	$395	$365	$325	$295	$275	$235	$195	

*** *SKS Chinese Recent Mfg. w/Thumbhole Stock***

	100%	98%	95%	90%	80%	70%	60%	LAST MSR
	$295	$275	$250	$225	$200	$185	$165	

SRM ARMS

Current shotgun manufacturer located in Meridan, ID. Exclusively distributed by GSA Direct LLC located in Boise, ID. Dealer sales.

SHOTGUNS: SEMI-AUTO

SRM Arms also manufactures a 10 (Model 1208) or 13 (Model 1212) in. barrel shotgun for military/law enforcement.

MODEL 1216 – 12 ga., 3 in. chamber, 18 1/2 in. barrel with fixed choke, bullpup with pistol grip configuration, semi-auto roller-locked delayed blowback system, matte black finish, features a rotating detachable 16 shot mag with four separate tubes, ambidextrous receiver with tip up action, full length top Picatinny rail and three handguard rails, ghost rear and post front sights, 34 1/2 in. OAL, 7 1/4 lbs. New late 2011.

	100%	98%	95%	90%	80%	70%	60%	LAST MSR
MSR $2,399	$2,175	$1,875	$1,575	$1,300	$1,150	$925	$800	

The concept of the SRM shotgun began in the early 2000's when special forces personnel described their dream shotgun to the SRM developers. The first model was previewed in 2008, with final versions arriving late 2011.

SSK INDUSTRIES

Current customizer and Class II manufacturer located in Wintersville, OH.

SSK Industries manufactures complete guns, and furnishes a wide variety of gunsmithing services.

SSK Industries manufactures complete rifles and suppressors for police, military, and civilian use (where legal in accord with BATFE regulations). Their custom shop works on virtually anything 20mm or smaller.

SSK Industries used Thompson Center flatside frames and applied an industrial hard chrome finish prior to the introduction of stainless steel receivers. Most SSK handguns and rifles are extensively customized in exotic calibers, finishes, and various engraving options. Receivers and barrels could be purchased separately - values below are for complete assembled pistols.

SSK has also manufactured various limited editions including the Handgun Hunters International (HHI) Models 1, 2, and 3. Issue prices on these guns were $1,100 (Model 3), $1,200 (Model 2), and $1,300 (Model 1). Only 50 were mfg. total in 1987. SSK also customized a Ruger Super Redhawk (.44 Mag. or .45 LC cal.). This variation came with either a scoped 7 1/2 in. octagon barrel (Beauty Model) or a 6 in. bull barrel with muzzle brake (Beast Model). Prices started at $1,430 - add $245 extra for .45 LC cal.

GRADING - PPGS™	100%	98%	95%	90%	80%	70%	60%	LAST MSR

PISTOLS: SINGLE SHOT

Values listed are for basic models with no options or special features.

SSK-CONTENDER – over 150 cals. available from .17 Bee to .50-70, various custom barrels available, basically, this is a custom order only gun.

	$1,500	$1,375	$1,250	$1,125	$1,000	$900	$825	

Individual barrels were available starting at $268.

An arrestor muzzle brake was available on special order.

This model included barrel, frame, stocks, and sights as standard equipment.

SSK-XP100 – various cals. between .17 and .50, includes TSOB mount and rings.

	$1,700	$1,500	$1,300	$1,150	$1,025	$925	$850	*$1,700*

The .50 cal. XP100 (12.9 X 50.8 JDJ) came with SSK muzzle brake, scope, dies, and new reinforced fiberglass stock.

SSK ENCORE – over 400 calibers available with plain, fluted, and heavy barrels.

Please contact the company directly for pricing on this model.

RIFLES

Values listed are for basic models with no options or special features. In addition, SSK custom manufactures a bolt action rifle available in almost any caliber and configuration - prices started at approx. $2,000 and can go as high as $6,000, depending on the customer's individual special orders. SSK also has developed a 6.5mm, 7mm, or .30 cal. upper unit conversion for AR-15s and M-16s utilizing heavy sub-sonic "whisper" ammunition. SSK also manufactures a line of .50 cal. rifles, and a complete AR-15 starts at $1,500.

SSK TCR 87 – .14 through .500 cals., Nitro Express cals. are also available, features Thompson Center TRC 87 receiver, and SSK custom barrels, muzzle brakes, and exotic finishes were available at extra cost.

	$1,700	$1,500	$1,300	$1,150	$1,025	$925	$850	

SSK RUGER NO. 1 – many cals. including .577 NE (optional), custom order rifle based on a Ruger No. 1 frame.

	$2,000	$1,800	$1,600	$1,400	$1,250	$1,100	$1,000	

SSK BOLT ACTION – various cals., ground up custom order rifle.

	$2,500	$2,250	$1,800	$1,600	$1,400	$1,250	$1,100	

STI INTERNATIONAL

Current manufacturer established during 1993, and located in Georgetown, TX. Distributor and dealer sales.

In addition to manufacturing the pistols listed, STI International also makes frame kits in steel, stainless steel, aluminum, or titanium - prices range between $204-$690.

PISTOLS: SEMI-AUTO

The beginning numerals on all STI pistols designate the barrel length, and most of the following models are listed in numerical sequence.

2.5 NEMESIS – 7mm cal., 2 1/2 in. barrel. Mfg. 2010.

	$840	$725	$625	$525	$450	$400	$350	*$870*

3.0 TOTAL ECLIPSE – 9mm Para., .40 S&W, or .45 ACP cal., 3 in. barrel, skeletonized trigger, aluminum frame, polymer grips, beavertail safety, fixed 2-dot tritium sights, blue finish, 23.1 oz. New 2011.

MSR $1,843	$1,700	$1,450	$1,250	$1,050	$925	$800	$675	

3.0 SHADOW – 9mm Para., .40 S&W, or .45 ACP cal., 3 in. bull barrel, matte black KG coated finish, forged aluminum frame, undercut trigger guard, stippled front strap, ultra thin G-10 grips with STI logo, rear cocking serrations, curved trigger, beavertail grip safety, fixed tritium 2 dot sights, 23.4 oz. New 2010.

MSR $1,383	$1,200	$1,000	$875	$725	$625	$525	$450	

GRADING - PPGS™	100%	98%	95%	90%	80%	70%	60%	LAST MSR

3.0 ELEKTRA – 9mm Para., .40 S&W, or .45 ACP cal., forged aluminum frame, 3 in. bull barrel, stainless steel slide, rear cocking serrations, beavertail grip safety, fixed tritium 2 dot sights. New 2010.

MSR $1,383	$1,200	$1,000	$875	$725	$625	$525	$450	

3.0 ROGUE – 9mm Para. cal., 3 in. bull barrel, forged aluminum compact frame, STI stippled front strap, undercut trigger guard, blued slide with Duracoated frame, intergral sights, 21 oz. Mfg. 2009.

	$925	$825	$725	$650	$575	$500	$425	*$1,024*

3.0 ESCORT – 9mm Para. or .45 ACP cal., 3 in. bull barrel, checkered cocobolo grips, round top slide with rear cocking serrations, adj. 3-dot sights, blue slide with Duracoated frame, stippled front strap, 22.8 oz. New 2009.

MSR $1,166	$1,025	$925	$825	$725	$650	$575	$500	

3.0 OFF DUTY – 9mm Para. or .45 ACP cal., compact frame, blued or hard chrome matte finish, 3 in. barrel with blue slide, checkered cocobolo grips, stippled front strap, competition front sight, tactical rear sight, 31.3 oz. New 2009.

MSR $1,243	$1,075	$950	$825	$700	$600	$525	$450	

3.0 SPARTAN – 9mm Para. or .45 ACP cal., 1911 Commander steel frame, parkerized finish, bald front strap, hand checkered double diamond mahogany grips, rear slide serrations, STI long curved trigger, 3.24 in. chrome non-ramped bushing barrel, STI high ride beavertail grip safety, competition front sights, fixed rear sights, 32.7 oz. New 2012.

MSR $706	$650	$575	$500	$450	$400	$375	$350	

3.0 LAWMAN – 9mm Para. or .45 ACP cal., 3.24 in. STI ramped bushing barrel, polished blue finish, forged steel frame with 30 LPI front strap checkering, undercut trigger guard, G10 grip panels, front and rear slide cocking serrations, long curved aluminum trigger, high-ride beavertail safety, recoil master guide rod, ramped front sight, tactical adj. rear sight, single sided thumb safety, 24.8 oz. New 2012.

MSR $1,433	$1,225	$995	$850	$725	$575	$500	$450	

3.25 GP5 – 9mm Para. cal., 3 1/4 in. barrel, DAO, blue finish, chrome-moly steel frame with integral tactical rail, textured polymer grips, double slide serrations, ambidextrous safety, internal extractor, adj. sights, 24.2 oz. Mfg. by Grand Power, Ltd. 2010-2011.

	$595	$550	$500	$450	$400	$375	$350	*$663*

3.4 BLS9/BLS40 – 9mm Para. or .40 S&W cal., blue finish, Govt. length grips, Heinie low mounted sights, single stack mag., 30 oz. Mfg. 1999-2005.

	$765	$650	$565	$460	$400	$360	$330	*$889*

3.4 LS9/LS40 – 9mm Para. or .40 S&W (disc. 2008) cal., blue finish, Commander length grips, single stack mag., Heinie low mount rear sight, slide integral front sight, 28 oz. New 1999.

MSR $1,002	$925	$750	$625	$525	$450	$400	$350	

3.4 ESCORT – 9mm Para. or .45 ACP cal., 1911 forged aluminum Commander style frame, 3.4 in. ramped bull barrel, slide with rear cocking serrations, Duracoat finish with blue slide, undercut trigger guard, stippled front strap, rosewood grips, STI hi-ride beavertail grip safety, fixed Novak style 3-dot sights, 22.8 oz. Mfg. 2007-2008.

	$925	$825	$725	$650	$575	$500	$425	*$1,024*

3.9 FALCON – .38 Super, .40 S&W, or .45 ACP cal., STI standard frame, 3.9 in. barrel, size is comparable to Officers Model, adj. rear sight. Limited mfg. 1993-98.

	$1,875	$1,375	$1,175	$925	$850	$775	$675	*$2,136*

3.9 STINGER – 9mm Para. or .38 Super cal., black frame, designed for IPSC and USPSA competition, 38 oz. Mfg. 2005-2008.

	$2,500	$2,225	$1,975	$1,750	$1,575	$1,375	$1,150	*$2,773*

GRADING - PPGS™	100%	98%	95%	90%	80%	70%	60%	LAST MSR

3.9 V.I.P. – 9mm Para. (new 2009), .40 S&W (new 2009), or .45 ACP cal. only, aluminum frame, STi modular polymer frame, stainless steel slide, 3.9 in. barrel with STi Recoilmaster muzzle brake, 10 shot double stack mag., STI fixed sights, 25 oz. Mfg. 2001-2006, reintroduced 2009.

MSR $1,662	$1,425	$1,275	$1,025	$950	$850	$750	$650	

3.9 GUARDIAN – 9mm Para. (new 2009) or .45 ACP cal., 1911 Commander style blue frame, 3.9 in. ramped bull barrel, stainless slide with polished sides, stippled front strap, undercut trigger guard, rosewood grips, fixed 3-dot sights, 32.4 oz. New 2007.

MSR $1,121	$1,000	$850	$750	$650	$575	$500	$425	

3.9 TACTICAL – 9mm Para., .40 S&W, or .45 ACP cal., matte blue finish, 3.9 in. bull barrel, modular steel frame with integral tactical rail, flat top slide with rear cocking serrations, black glass filled nylon polymer grips, long curved trigger, high ride beavertail grip safety, fixed rear sight, ramped front sight, 34 oz. New 2012.

MSR $2,019	$1,775	$1,500	$1,250	$1,000	$875	$800	$675	

4.0 SPARTAN – 9mm Para. or .45 ACP cal., 1911 Commander steel frame, parkerized finish, bald front strap, hand checkered double diamond mahogany grips, rear slide serrations, STI long curved trigger, 4.26 in. chrome non-ramped bushing barrel, STI high ride beavertail grip safety, competition front sights, fixed rear sights, 34.3 oz. New 2012.

MSR $706	$650	$575	$500	$450	$400	$375	$350	

4.0 LAWMAN – 9mm Para. or .45 ACP cal., 4.26 in. STI ramped bushing barrel, polished blue finish, forged steel frame with 30 LPI front strap checkering, undercut trigger guard, G10 grip panels, front and rear slide cocking serrations, long curved aluminum trigger, high-ride beavertail safety, recoil master guide rod, ramped front sight, tactical adj. rear sight, single sided thumb safety, 37.3 oz. New 2012.

MSR $1,433	$1,225	$995	$850	$725	$575	$500	$450	

4.15 TACTICAL – 9mm Para., .40 S&W, or .45 ACP cal., blue steel, fixed sights, short trigger, ambidextrous safety, 34 1/2 oz. New 2004.

MSR $2,019	$1,775	$1,500	$1,250	$1,000	$875	$800	$675	

4.15 RANGER II (3.9 RANGER) – 9mm Para. (new 2009), .40 S&W (new 2009), or .45 ACP cal. only, Officer's Model with 3.9 (Ranger, disc. 2004) or 4.15 (Ranger II, new 2005) in. barrel and 1/2 in. shortened grip frame, 6 shot mag., blue steel frame with stainless steel slide, single stack mag., low mount STI/Heinie sights, 29 oz. New 2001.

MSR $1,121	$1,000	$850	$750	$650	$575	$500	$425	

Add $192 for Ranger III configuration (new 2010).

4.15 DUTY CT – 9mm Para., .40 S&W or .45 ACP cal., 5 in. bull barrel, matte blue finish, integral tactical rail, flat-top slide with rear cocking serrations, ramped front sight, fixed rear sight, 36.6 oz. Mfg. 2006-2008.

	$1,100	$950	$825	$700	$600	$525	$450	*$1,286*

4.15 STEELMASTER – 9mm Para. cal., 4.15 in. Trubore barrel, blue finish with polished classic slide, sabertooth cocking serrations, C-More red dot scope with blast shield and thumbrest, black glass filled nylon polymer grips with aluminum magwell, 38.9 oz. New 2009.

MSR $2,893	$2,500	$2,050	$1,750	$1,450	$1,200	$995	$875	

4.15 MATCHMASTER – .38 Super cal., 4.15 in. Trubore barrel, blue finished with polished classic slide, sabertooth front and rear cocking serrations, black glass filled nylon polymer grips with aluminum magwell, drilled and tapped, C-More red dot scope with blast shield and thumb rest, 38.9 oz. New 2009.

MSR $3,029	$2,625	$2,200	$1,850	$1,500	$1,250	$995	$875	

4.25 GP6 – 9mm Para. cal., 4 1/4 in. barrel, DA/SA, blue finish, chrome-moly steel frame with integral tactical rail, textured polymer grips, double slide serrations, ambidextrous safety, internal extractor, adj. sights, 26.1 oz. Mfg. by Grand Power, Ltd. New 2009.

MSR $663	$595	$550	$500	$450	$400	$375	$350	

Add $34 for GP6-C model with fiber optic front sight and adj. rear sight (mfg. 2010-2011).

GRADING - PPGS™	100%	98%	95%	90%	80%	70%	60%	LAST MSR

4.25 EL COMMANDANTE – 9mm Para. cal., blue matte finish, Government steel frame, 4.25 in. non-ramped bushing barrel, beavertail grip safety, steel trigger, single sided thumb safety, one-piece original GI style guide rod, GI steel sights, smooth wood grips, rear slide cocking serrations, 34 1/2 oz. Mfg. 2011 only.

	100%	98%	95%	90%	80%	70%	60%	LAST MSR
	$895	$725	$625	$525	$450	$400	$350	*$942*

4.3 HAWK – various cals., 4.3 in. barrel, STI standard frame (choice of steel or aluminum), 27 or 31 oz. Mfg. 1993-1999.

	100%	98%	95%	90%	80%	70%	60%	LAST MSR
	$1,725	$1,275	$1,075	$875	$800	$700	$600	*$1,975*

4.3 NIGHT HAWK – .45 ACP cal., 4.3 in. barrel, STI wide extended frame, blue finish, 33 oz. Limited mfg. 1997-99.

	100%	98%	95%	90%	80%	70%	60%	LAST MSR
	$1,875	$1,375	$1,175	$925	$850	$775	$675	*$2,136*

5.0 G.I. – .45 ACP cal., 5 in. non-ramped bushing barrel, matte blue finish, steel frame and trigger, beavertail grip safety, matte blue slide with rear cocking serrations, smooth wood grips, GI steel sights, 35.3 oz. New 2010.

	100%	98%	95%	90%	80%	70%	60%	LAST MSR
MSR $831	$775	$700	$625	$550	$500	$450	$395	

5.0 FB7 – 7mm or 9mm Para. cal., 5 in. barrel. Mfg. 2010-2011.

	100%	98%	95%	90%	80%	70%	60%	LAST MSR
	$1,750	$1,500	$1,250	$1,000	$875	$800	$675	*$1,940*

5.0 SPARROW – .22 LR cal. only, unlocked blowback action, STI standard extended frame, 5.1 in. ramped bull barrel, fixed sights, blue finish, 30 oz. Limited mfg. 1998-1999 only.

	100%	98%	95%	90%	80%	70%	60%	LAST MSR
	$1,025	$900	$800	$700	$600	$500	$400	*$1,090*

5.0 EDGE – 9mm Para., 10mm Norma (disc. 2008), .40 S&W, or .45 ACP cal., designed for limited/standard IPSC competition, STI extended wide body frame, double stack mag., blue finish, 39 oz. New 1998.

	100%	98%	95%	90%	80%	70%	60%	LAST MSR
MSR $2,014	$1,775	$1,500	$1,250	$1,000	$875	$800	$675	

5.0 DUTY ONE – 9mm Para., .40 S&W, or .45 ACP cal., ramped bull barrel, checkered wood grips, 38 oz. New 2005.

	100%	98%	95%	90%	80%	70%	60%	LAST MSR
MSR $1,312	$1,125	$950	$825	$700	$600	$525	$450	

5.0 SENTRY – 9mm Para., .40 S&W, or .45 ACP cal., 5 in. ramped barrel with bushing, classic polished flat-top slide with front and rear cocking serrations, checkered cocobolo grips, blue finish, competition front and adj. rear sights, 35.3 oz. New 2009.

	100%	98%	95%	90%	80%	70%	60%	LAST MSR
MSR $1,614	$1,395	$1,150	$1,000	$875	$750	$625	$500	

5.0 APEIRO – 9mm Para., .40 S&W, or .45 ACP cal., 5 in. Schuemann Island style barrel, long wide steel frame, stainless steel slide, blue finish, black glass filled nylon polymer grips, stainless magwell, Dawson fiber optic front and adj. rear sights, 38 oz. New 2010.

	100%	98%	95%	90%	80%	70%	60%	LAST MSR
MSR $2,717	$2,350	$1,950	$1,725	$1,450	$1,200	$1,000	$900	

5.0 EXECUTIVE – .40 S&W cal. only, STi long/wide frame, 10 shot double stack mag., stainless construction, grey nylon polymer grips and square trigger guard, hard chrome finish with black inlays, fiberoptic front and STI adj. rear sights, approved for IPSC standard and USPSA limited edition, 38 oz. New 2001.

	100%	98%	95%	90%	80%	70%	60%	LAST MSR
MSR $2,489	$2,175	$1,825	$1,525	$1,300	$1,050	$900	$800	

* ***5.0 Executive IPSC 30th Commemorative*** – 9mm Para., .40 S&W, or .45 ACP cal., ramped bull barrel, two-tone hard chrome finish, special engraved slide with "IPSC 30th Anniversary" on side, 39 oz. Mfg. 2005-2006.

	100%	98%	95%	90%	80%	70%	60%	LAST MSR
	$2,500	$2,225	$1,975	N/A	N/A	N/A	N/A	*$2,775*

* ***5.0 Executive Special Edition*** – 9mm Para., .40 S&W, or .45 ACP cal., ramped bull barrel, 24Kt. gold on all steel surfaces, checkered black grips, "Special Edition" engraved on slide, 39 oz. Mfg. 2005-2006.

	100%	98%	95%	90%	80%	70%	60%	LAST MSR
	$2,625	$2,325	$2,000	N/A	N/A	N/A	N/A	*$2,930*

GRADING - PPGS™	100%	98%	95%	90%	80%	70%	60%	LAST MSR

5.0 STI 20TH ANNIVERSARY – 9mm Para., .40 S&W, or .45 ACP cal., 5 in. bull barrel, steel frame, PVD and TIN (titanium nitride) finish, black glass filled nylon polymer filled grips, TIN coated magwell, beavertail grip safety, Dawson fiber optic front and STI adj. rear sight, 38 oz. Limited edition of 200 during 2010.

	$3,300	$2,950	$2,600	N/A	N/A	N/A	N/A	*$3,623*

5.0 100TH ANNIVERSARY SPECIAL EDITION – .45 ACP cal., consists of 2 pistols - one is traditional GI style 1911, and the other gun is built on STI's patented high capacity modular frame, boxed with 2011 STI "challenge" coin, 500 sets mfg. beginning 2011.

MSR $4,154	$3,875	$3,400	$2,900	$2,400	$2,100	$1,950	$1,700	

5.0 TROJAN – 9mm Para., .40 S&W, .38 Super, or .45 ACP, standard Govt. length grips, single stack mag., stainless steel available 2006, 36 oz. New 1999.

MSR $1,121	$1,000	$850	$750	$650	$575	$500	$425	

Add $288 for .38 Super with .45 ACP conversion kit (disc. 2011).
Add $412 for stainless steel (disc. 2011).

5.0 TRUBOR (COMPETITOR) – 9mm Para. or .38 Super cal. only, standard frame, classic slide with front and rear serrations, square hammer, compensator, double stack mag., match sear, STI "Alchin" style blast deflector mount, TruBor compensator became standard 2005, C-More rail scope, wide ambidextrous and grip safeties, 41.3 oz. Mfg. 1999-2011.

	$2,475	$2,050	$1,750	$1,450	$1,200	$995	$875	*$2,864*

5.0 TRUBOR GM – 9mm Para. or .38 Super cal., 5 in. TruBor bull barrel, hard chrome finish with blue color inlays, classic flat-top slide, sabertooth cocking serrations, blue glass filled nylon polymer grips with stainless steel magwell, drilled and tapped, C-More gray scope, 44.6 oz. Mfg. 2009-2011.

	$3,350	$3,000	$2,700	$2,250	$1,800	$1,400	$1,175	*$3,655*

5.0 SPARTAN – .45 ACP cal., 1911 Govt. steel frame, parkerized finish, bald front strap, hand checkered double diamond wood grips, front and rear slide serrations, STI long curved trigger, 5 in. chrome ramped bushing barrel, STI high ride beavertail grip safety, fiber optic front sights, adj. rear sights, 35.3 oz. New 2007.

MSR $706	$650	$575	$500	$450	$400	$375	$350	

5.0 USPSA SINGLE STACK – 9mm Para., .40 S&W, or .45 ACP cal., 5 in. stainless steel barrel, tri-top two-tone slide with sabertooth cocking serrations, blue frame, 30 LPI front strap checkering, checkered steel D&T mainspring housing and magwell, competition front and adj. rear sight, 38.3 oz. New 2009.

MSR $1,814	$1,525	$1,225	$950	$800	$675	$550	$475	

5.0 USPSA DOUBLE STACK – 9mm Para., .40 S&W, or .45 ACP cal., 5 in. stainless steel barrel, tri-top two-tone slide with sabertooth cocking serrations, blue frame, 30 LPI front strap checkering, checkered steel D&T mainspring housing and magwell, competition front and adj. rear sight, 38.3 oz. New 2009.

MSR $2,818	$2,425	$2,000	$1,750	$1,450	$1,200	$1,000	$900	

5.0 IPSC DOUBLE STACK – 9mm Para., .40 S&W, or .45 ACP cal., 5 in. bull barrel, blue frame, two-tone hard chrome slide with sabertooth cocking serrations, Dawson fiber optic front and adj. rear sights, black glass filled nylon polymer grips with stainless steel magwell, 38 oz. New 2009.

MSR $2,818	$2,425	$2,000	$1,750	$1,450	$1,200	$1,000	$900	

5.0 RANGEMASTER – 9mm Para. or .45 ACP cal., black frame, ramped bull barrel, STI Recoilmaster guide rod, 38 oz. New 2005.

MSR $1,536	$1,350	$1,100	$900	$775	$625	$525	$475	

5.0 RANGEMASTER II – similar to Rangemaster, except does not have extended frame dust cover. Mfg. 2006.

	$1,175	$965	$850	$725	$625	$525	$475	*$1,344*

GRADING - PPGS™	100%	98%	95%	90%	80%	70%	60%	LAST MSR

5.0 EAGLE – 9mm Para., .357 SIG, .38 Super, .40 S&W, or .45 ACP cal., 5.1 in. barrel, STI standard full size wide body govt. model frame (choice of steel or aluminum), double stack mag., adj. rear sight, polished blue finish, high ride beavertail grip safety, black glass filled nylon polymer grips, 31 or 35 oz.

MSR $1,964	$1,775	$1,500	$1,250	$1,000	$875	$800	$675	

Add $266 for .38 Super with .45 ACP conversion kit (disc. 2011).

5.0 TACTICAL – 9mm Para., .40 S&W, or .45 ACP cal., blue steel, fixed sights, short trigger, ambidextrous safety, 39 oz. New 2004.

MSR $2,019	$1,775	$1,500	$1,250	$1,000	$875	$800	$675	

* ***5.0 Tactical Lite*** – similar to 5.0 Tactical, except stainless slide, alloy frame, fixed sights, 34 1/2 oz. Mfg. 2004-2005.

	$1,800	$1,525	$1,300	$1,050	$900	$825	$700	*$2,002*

5.0 TRUSIGHT – 9mm Para., .40 S&W, or .45 ACP (disc. 2008) cal., 5 in. ramped bull barrel with expansion chamber, black glass filled nylon polymer grip with aluminum magwell, Dawson fiber optic front sight, adj. rear sight, blue finish with polished slide, 39 oz. Mfg. 2006-2009.

	$1,795	$1,525	$1,275	$1,050	$900	$825	$700	*$1,985*

5.0 LEGEND – 9mm Para., .40 S&W, or .45 ACP cal., STI modular steel long wide frame, Tri-top forged slide with sabertooth cocking serrations and hard chrome with black inlay and polished sides, blue frame, black glass filled nylon polymer grips with hard chrome magwell, Dawson fiber optic front sights, adj. rear sight, 38 oz. New 2007.

MSR $2,697	$2,325	$1,950	$1,725	$1,450	$1,200	$1,000	$900	

LEGACY MODEL – 45 ACP cal., 5 in. ramped STI bushing barrel, PVD finish, polished flat top black slide, rear cocking serrations, front strap checkering, custom cocobolo grips, ambidextrous thumb safety, ramped front sight, 36 oz. Mfg. 2006-2008.

	$1,750	$1,500	$1,250	$1,000	$900	$825	$700	*$1,929*

5.0 LAWMAN (LSA) – .45 ACP cal., 1911 Govt. style, 5 in. barrel, hammer forged carbon steel frame, designed for duty, self-defense, IPSC, USPSA, and IDPA competition, 36 oz. New 2005.

MSR $1,433	$1,225	$995	$850	$725	$575	$500	$450	

5.0 SENTINEL – 9mm Para., .40 S&W, or .45 ACP cal., 1911 Govt. forged frame, 5 in. barrel, flat-top slide with rear cocking serrations, matte blue finish, front strap 30 LPI checkering, checkered steel D&T mainspring housing and flared magwell, STI competition front sights, adj. rear sight, thick rosewood grips, 38.3 oz. Mfg. 2007-2008.

	$1,395	$1,200	$1,025	$875	$750	$625	$550	*$1,598*

5.0 SENTINEL PREMIER – .45 ACP cal., 1911 Govt. forged frame, 5 in. barrel with bushing, polished slide with rear cocking serrations, hard chrome finish, front strap 30 LPI checkering, checkered steel D&T mainspring housing and flared magwell, tritium sights, 36.7 oz. New 2009.

MSR $1,963	$1,725	$1,575	$1,225	$1,000	$875	$800	$675	

5.1 LIMITED – while advertised during 1998, this model never went into production.

Last MSR was $1,699

5.5 EAGLE – various cals., features STI standard frame, 5 1/2 in. compensated barrel, 44 oz. Limited mfg. 1994-98.

	$2,100	$1,750	$1,475	$1,200	$995	$895	$775	*$2,399*

5.5 GRANDMASTER – .38 Super cal. standard, custom order gun with any variety of options available, double stack mag., 42 oz. Mfg. 2001-2008.

	$3,075	$2,650	$2,275	$1,900	$1,650	$1,425	$1,200	*$3,371*

5.5 TRUBORE – 9mm Para. or .38 Super cal., modular steel frame, 5.5 in. Trubor barrel, polished blue finish, black glass filled nylon polymer grips with aluminum magwell, lightened slide with front and rear cocking serrations, two inch integral compensator, C-More scope

GRADING - PPGS™	100%	98%	95%	90%	80%	70%	60%	LAST MSR

sights, ambidextrous thumb safety, 41 oz. New 2012.

MSR $2,893	$2,495	$2,050	$1,750	$1,450	$1,200	$995	$875	

5.5 STI GM – 9mm Para. or .38 Super cal., modular steel frame, 5.5 Trubor bull barrel with two inch integral compensator, hard chrome finish with blue inlay, C-More scope sight, blue glass filled polymer grips with stainless magwell and drilled and tapped mag. release, lightened slide with sabertooth cocking serrations, high ride beavertail grip safety, ambidextrous thumb safety, 44.6 oz. New 2012.

MSR $3,692	$3,375	$3,000	$2,700	$2,250	$1,800	$1,400	$1,175	

6.0 HUNTER – 10mm cal. only, 6 in. barrel, STI super extended heavy frame with single stack mag., blue finish, 51 oz. Only 2 mfg. 1998, disc. 2000.

	$2,250	$1,875	$1,650	$1,425	$1,200	$995	$895	*$2,485*

Add $350 for Leupold 2X scope with terminator mount.

6.0 EAGLE – 9mm Para., .40 S&W, or .45 ACP cal., features STI super extended heavy frame, 6 in. barrel, blue finish, wide body with double stack mag., 42 oz. New 1998.

MSR $2,070	$1,795	$1,500	$1,300	$1,050	$875	$800	$725	

Add $267 for .38 Super with .45 ACP conversion kit (disc. 2008).

6.0 TROJAN – similar to Trojan 5.0, except has 6 in. barrel and single stack mag., 36 oz. New 2000.

MSR $1,434	$1,225	$995	$850	$725	$575	$500	$450	

Add $143 for .38 Super with .45 ACP conversion kit (disc. 2008).

6.0 PERFECT 10 – 10mm Norma cal., 6 in. bull barrel, blue finish with polished classic flat-top slide, front and rear cocking serrations, ramped front and Heinie fixed rear sights, 6 inch integral tactical rail, black glass filled nylon polymer grips with aluminum magwell, 37 1/2 oz. New 2009.

MSR $2,483	$2,175	$1,825	$1,525	$1,300	$1,050	$900	$800	

6.0 TARGETMASTER – 9mm Para. or .45 ACP cal., black frame, ramped bull barrel, two piece steel guide rod, 40 oz. New 2005.

MSR $1,712	$1,475	$1,175	$925	$800	$675	$550	$475	

6.0 .450 XCALIBER – .450 cal., single stack mag., V-10 barrel and slide porting, stainless grip and thumb safeties, adj. rear sight. Limited mfg. 2000-2002.

	$1,000	$850	$750	$650	$525	$450	$395	*$1,122*

6.0 .450+ XCALIBER – .450+ cal., otherwise similar to Xcaliber 6.0 .450, except has 6 in. frame with patented polymer grip and double stack mag. Limited mfg. 2000-2002.

	$1,775	$1,575	$1,350	$1,175	$995	$875	$775	*$1,998*

REVOLVERS

TEXICAN SAA – .45 LC cal., blue finish, color case hardened frame and hammer, 5 1/2 in. barrel, 6 shot, hard rubber grips with STI logo, floating firing pin, fixed sights, 36 oz. Mfg. 2007-2010.

	$1,195	$1,000	$875	$750	$600	$500	$400	*$1,344*

RIFLES/CARBINES: SEMI-AUTO

STi 10/22 FORCE – .22 LR cal., aluminum receiver, 21 in. Lothar Walther barrel, black synthetic Hogue stock, 7 lbs. Mfg. 2003-2006.

	$975	$850	$725	$625	$500	$400	$350	*$1,103*

STI SPORT 10-22 RIFLE/CARBINE – .22 LR cal., 16 in. lined aluminum barrel or 20 in. stainless steel bull barrel. Mfg. 2010-2011.

	$895	$825	$750	$675	$600	$525	$450	*$978*

STI SPORTING/TACTICAL CARBINE – .223 Rem. cal., 16 in. stainless steel barrel, JP trigger group, gas block, Valkyrie handguard, tactical compensator, black Teflon coating, fixed A2 or collapsible buttstock, optional rails, approx. 7 lbs. New 2010.

MSR $1,342	$1,225	$1,075	$925	$800	$675	$550	$475	

GRADING - PPGS™	100%	98%	95%	90%	80%	70%	60%	LAST MSR

STL

Current bolt action rifle manufacturer located in Heiligkreuzsteinach, Germany.

STL manufactures both hunting and match rifles in calibers from .222 Rem.-.50 BMG. Many configurations and options are available. Please contact the manufacturer directly for more information, including U.S. availability and pricing (see Trademark Index).

SWS 2000

Previous rifle manufacturer located in Krefeld, Germany until 2010. Previously imported until 2009 by Euro-Imports, located in Yoakum, TX.

RIFLES

SWS 2000 manufactured a variety of sporting and tactical style rifles in a variety of configurations.

Prices ranged from €2,600-€3,759 for sporting and hunting models, and €6,162-€7,910 for tactical rifles.

SABATTI s.p.a.

Current manufacturer located in Gardone, Italy with history tracing back to 1674. Select rifles and combination guns are currently imported by the Italian Firearms Group (IFG), located in Rockledge, FL. SxS double rifles are also imported by EAA, located in Rockledge, FL. Sabatti sub-contracts some of its models for private label sales.

In 1960, the sons of Antonio Sabatti formed the current company, and manufacture currently includes good quality O/U and SxS shotguns, O/U combination and double rifles, bolt action and semi-auto rifles, and slide action and single shot shotguns. Sabatti should be contacted directly (see Trademark Index) regarding more information and domestic availability on their extensive firearms lineup.

RIFLES: SxS

SAB92SF – .45-70 Govt. or 9.3x74R (new 2010) cal., 24 in. barrels, scalloped boxlock action, extractors, drilled and tapped, walnut stock, nickel (disc.) or case colored receiver. This model is sold exclusively by Cabela's. Imported 2009-2011.

	100%	98%	95%	90%	80%	70%	60%	LAST MSR
	$3,200	**$2,800**	**$2,500**	**$2,100**	**$1,875**	**$1,650**	**$1,500**	***$3,432***

* ***SAB92SF Deluxe*** – .375 H&H (disc. 2011), .416 Rigby, .450 NE, .458 Win. Mag. (disc. 2011), .45-70 Govt., .470 NE, .500 NE, or .600 NE (limited mfg. only) cal., 24 in. barrels, scalloped engraved boxlock action, ejectors or extractors, drilled and tapped, deluxe checkered walnut stock, nickel receiver, beavertail forend, this model is sold exclusively by Cabela's. Importation began 2009.

	100%	98%	95%	90%	80%	70%	60%	LAST MSR
MSR $6,482	**$5,975**	**$5,300**	**$4,700**	**$4,150**	**$3,600**	**$3,050**	**$2,500**	

Add $492 for ejectors.

Subtract $1,282 for .45-70 Govt. cal.

SABRE

Previous trademark of shotguns previously imported by Mitchell's Mausers, located in Fountain Valley, CA.

SHOTGUNS: SEMI-AUTO

SABRE – 12 ga. only, gas operated, 18 1/2 (w/o VR), 22, or 28 in. VR barrel with choke tubes, choice of black fiberglass or checkered walnut stock and forearm, configurations include Hunting, Turkey, Deer Hunter, and Police, mfg. in Turkey. Importation disc. 2007.

	100%	98%	95%	90%	80%	70%	60%	LAST MSR
	$435	**$375**	**$325**	**$275**	**$235**	**$210**	**$190**	***$495***

Add $50 for Police model.

SABRE DEFENCE INDUSTRIES LLC.

Previous manufacturer from 2002-2010, with production headquarters located in Nashville, TN, and sales offices located in Middlesex, U.K. This company was previously known as Ramo Mfg., Inc., which was founded in 1977. Sabre Defence was

GRADING - PPGS™	100%	98%	95%	90%	80%	70%	60%	LAST MSR

also the U.S. distributor for Sphinx pistols until 2009.

CARBINES/RIFLES: SEMI-AUTO

Sabre Defence Industries manufactured many variations of the XR15 line of tactical design carbines and rifles for civilians, law enforcement, and military.

XR15A3 COMPETITION EXTREME – .223 Rem. cal., 16, 18, or 20 in. stainless steel fluted barrel, 30 shot mag., A3 upper and matched lower, black anodized finish, CTR six position retractable stock, free float handguard, Ergo grip, match trigger, flip up sights, mid-length barrel assembly, M4 feed ramp, includes two mags., cleaning kit, and tactical case. Disc. 2010.

$1,950	$1,700	$1,450	$1,275	$1,025	$850	$750	*$2,189*

XR15A3 COMPETITION SPECIAL – .223 Rem. or 6.5 Grendel cal., 16 (.223 Rem. cal. only), 18, or 20 in. stainless steel fluted barrel, 30 shot mag., A3 upper and matched lower, black anodized finish, A2 fixed stock, tubular free float handguard, Ergo grip, match trigger, mid-length barrel assembly, M4 feed ramp, includes two mags., cleaning kit, and tactical case. Disc. 2010.

$1,700	$1,475	$1,250	$1,125	$895	$725	$575	*$1,899*

Add $200 for 6.5 Grendel cal.

XR15A3 COMPETITION DELUXE – .223 Rem. or 6.5 Grendel cal., 16, 18, or 20 in. stainless or vanadium steel fluted barrel, 25 (6.5 Grendel cal.) or 30 shot mag., A3 upper and matched lower, black anodized finish, five position retractable stock, tactical handguard, Ergo grip, match trigger, flip up sights, competition Gill-brake, fluted mid-length barrel assembly, M4 feed ramp, includes two mags., cleaning kit, and tactical case. Disc. 2010.

$2,075	$1,815	$1,555	$1,415	$1,150	$950	$725	*$2,299*

Add $200 for 6.5 Grendel cal.
Add $300 for piston system upgrade (Competition Deluxe Piston, new 2010).

XR15A3 SPR – .223 Rem. or 6.5 Grendel cal., 16, 18, or 20 in. stainless or vanadium steel fluted barrel, 25 (6.5 Grendel cal.) or 30 shot mag., A3 upper and matched lower, black anodized finish, five position retractable stock, tactical handguard, Ergo grip, match trigger, flip up sights, bipod, fluted mid-length barrel assembly, M4 feed ramp, includes two mags., cleaning kit, and tactical case, 8.7 lbs. Disc. 2010.

$2,250	$1,975	$1,695	$1,525	$1,225	$1,015	$785	*$2,499*

Add $200 for 6.5 Grendel cal.

XR15A3 M4 FLAT TOP – .223 Rem., 6.5 Grendel, or 7.62x39mm (disc. 2009) cal., 16 in. vanadium contoured barrel, 25 (6.5 Grendel cal. only) or 30 shot mag., A3 upper and matched lower, M4 oval handguard, flip up sights, black anodized finish, A2 grip, single stage trigger, six position collapsible stock, M4 feed ramp, A2 flash hider, includes two mags., cleaning kit, and tactical case, 6.4 lbs. Disc. 2010.

$1,350	$1,150	$995	$875	$750	$650	$525	*$1,507*

Add $70 for 7.62x39mm cal. (disc. 2009).
Add $34 for chrome lined barrel.
Add $193 for 6.5 Grendel cal.

XR15A3 M5 FLAT TOP – .223 Rem. or 6.5 Grendel cal., 16 in. vanadium contoured mid-length barrel, 25 (6.5 Grendel cal. only) or 30 shot mag., black anodized finish, A3 upper and matched lower, flip up sights, single stage trigger, six position collapsible stock, M4 feed ramp, A2 flash hider, mid-length handguard, Ergo grip, includes two mags., cleaning kit, and tactical case, 6 1/2 lbs. Disc. 2010.

$1,350	$1,150	$995	$875	$750	$650	$525	*$1,504*

Add $195 for 6.5 Grendel cal.
Add $33 for chrome lined barrel.

XR15A3 M4 CARBINE – .223 Rem., 6.5 Grendel, or 7.62x39mm (disc. 2009) cal., 16 in. vanadium contoured alloy barrel, 25 (6.5 Grendel cal. only) or 30 shot mag., black anodized finish, A3 upper and matched lower, M4 oval handguard, forged front sight, no

GRADING - PPGS™	100%	98%	95%	90%	80%	70%	60%	LAST MSR

rear sight, A2 grip, single stage trigger, six position collapsible stock, M4 feed ramp, A2 flash hider, includes two mags., cleaning kit, and tactical case, 6.3 lbs. Disc. 2010.

	$1,195	$1,050	$875	$775	$650	$550	$450	$1,344

Add $100 for 7.62x39mm cal. (disc. 2009).
Add $33 for chrome lined barrel.
Add $205 for 6.5 Grendel cal.

XR15A3 PRECISION MARKSMAN RIFLE – .223 Rem. or 6.5 Grendel cal., 20 or 24 in. stainless steel barrel, 25 (6.5 Grendel cal.) or 30 shot mag., A3 upper and match lower, mid-length gas system, rail handguards, Ergo tactical deluxe grip with palm rest, match trigger, fluted mid-length barrel assembly, black anodized finish, M4 feed ramp, Magpul PRS adj. stock, includes Leupold 6.5-20x50 Mark IV scope (standard through 2009), two mags., cleaning kit and tactical case, approx. 10 lbs. Disc. 2010.

	$2,200	$1,950	$1,700	$1,475	$1,225	$1,000	$800	$2,415

Add $126 for 6.5 Grendel cal.
Add $1,185 for Leupold scope.

XR15A3 M4 TACTICAL – .223 Rem., 6.5 Grendel, or 7.62x39mm (disc. 2009) cal., 16 in. vanadium chrome lined contoured barrel, 25 (6.5 Grendel cal. only) or 30 shot mag., A3 upper and matched lower, multi-rail handguards, flip up sights, black anodized finish, Ergo grip, single stage trigger, six position collapsible stock, M4 feed ramp, A2 flash hider, tactical Gill-brake, includes two mags., cleaning kit, and tactical case, approx. 7 lbs. Disc. 2010.

	$1,825	$1,625	$1,400	$1,225	$975	$800	$650	$1,993

Add $40 for 7.62x39mm cal. (disc. 2009).
Add $176 for 6.5 Grendel cal.

* ***M4 Tactical Piston Carbine*** – .223 Rem. cal., 16 in. chrome-moly steel barrel, 30 shot mag., similar to M4 Tactical, except has mid-length gas piston system, 7 lbs. Mfg. 2010 only.

	$2,250	$1,975	$1,695	$1,525	$1,225	$1,015	$785	$2,499

XR15A3 M5 CARBINE – .223 Rem., 6.5 Grendel, or 7.62x39mm (disc. 2009) cal., 16 in. vanadium contoured barrel, 25 (6.5 Grendel cal. only) or 30 shot mag., A3 upper and matched lower, mid-length handguards, black anodized finish, forged front sight, Ergo grip, single stage trigger, six position collapsible stock, M4 feed ramp, A2 flash hider, includes two mags., cleaning kit, and tactical case, 6.4 lbs. Disc. 2010.

	$1,195	$1,050	$875	$775	$650	$550	$450	$1,341

Add $30 for 7.62x39mm cal. (disc. 2009).
Add $33 for chrome lined barrel.
Add $208 for 6.5 Grendel cal.

M5 TACTICAL CARBINE – .223 Rem. or 6.5 Grendel cal., 16 in. chrome-moly chrome lined barrel, 25 or 30 shot mag., mid-length gas system, free float quadrail handguards, flip up front and rear sights, collapsible buttstock, single stage Mil Spec trigger, ergonomic pistol grip, trigger lock, sling, cleaning kit, and case, approx. 7 lbs. Mfg. 2009-2010.

	$1,925	$1,700	$1,475	$1,250	$1,025	$875	$725	$2,117

Add $235 for 6.5 Grendel cal.

* ***M5 Tactical Piston Carbine*** – .223 Rem. cal., 16 in. chrome-moly steel barrel, 30 shot mag., similar to M5 Tactical, except has mid-length gas piston system, 7.3 lbs. Mfg. 2010.

	$2,250	$1,975	$1,695	$1,525	$1,225	$1,015	$785	$2,499

XR15A3 A4 RIFLE – .223 Rem. cal., 20 in. vanadium govt. contour barrel, 30 shot mag., black anodized finish, A3 upper and matched lower, A2 round handguard, forged front sight, A2 grip, single stage trigger, fixed A2 stock, M4 feed ramp, A2 flash hider, includes two mags., approx. 7.2 lbs. Disc. 2010.

	$1,215	$1,075	$895	$775	$650	$550	$450	$1,384

Add $34 for chrome lined barrel.

GRADING - PPGS™	100%	98%	95%	90%	80%	70%	60%	LAST MSR

XR15A3 A2 NATIONAL MATCH – .223 Rem. cal., 20 in. stainless steel matte finished H-Bar barrel, 30 shot mag., black anodized finish, A3 upper and matched lower, NM handguards, forged front sights, NM rear sight, A2 grip, two-stage trigger, fixed A2 stock, M4 feed ramp, A2 flash hider, includes two mags. Disc. 2009.

	$1,525	$1,335	$1,150	$1,050	$850	$695	$550	*$1,699*

XR15A3 FLAT TOP CARBINE – .223 Rem. cal., 16 in. vanadium barrel, 30 shot mag., A3 upper and matched lower, black anodized finish, CAR round handguards, flip up sights, Ergo grip, single stage trigger, six position collapsible stock, M4 feed ramp, A2 flash hider, includes two mags. Disc. 2009.

	$1,200	$1,050	$895	$825	$675	$550	$425	*$1,319*

Add $40 for chrome lined barrel.

XR15A3 HEAVY BENCH TARGET – .204 Ruger, .223 Rem., or 6.5 Grendel cal., 24 in. fluted match grade stainless steel heavy barrel, 4 (6.5 Grendel, disc. 2009), 10, or 25 (6.5 Grendel) shot mag., black anodized finish, A3 upper and matched lower, tubular free float handguards, flip up sights, Ergo grip, single stage adj. trigger, fixed A2 stock, sling swivel stud and bipod, includes two mags., cleaning kit, and tactical case, 9.3 lbs. Disc. 2010.

	$1,700	$1,475	$1,275	$1,125	$900	$750	$600	*$1,889*

Add $200 for 6.5 Grendel cal.

XR15A3 VARMINT – .223 Rem. cal., 20 in. fluted match grade stainless steel heavy barrel, 10 shot mag., A3 upper and matched lower, black anodized finish, tubular free float handguards, Ergo grip, match trigger, fixed A2 stock, sling swivel stud, includes two mags., cleaning kit, and tactical case. Disc. 2009.

	$1,550	$1,350	$1,175	$1,050	$850	$695	$550	*$1,709*

LIGHT SABRE – .223 Rem. cal., 16 in. chrome-moly barrel, 30 shot mag., mid-length gas system, M5 carbine upper, forged front sight, one piece polymer lower assembly, single stage Mil Spec trigger, 5.9 lbs. Mfg. 2009-2010.

	$1,100	$1,075	$925	$800	$675	$550	$425	*$1,229*

SACO DEFENSE INC.

Previous firearms manufacturer located in Saco, ME. Saco Defense was purchased by General Dynamics in July of 2000, and continues to produce guns for military defense contracts. This company was previously owned by Colt's Manufacturing Company, Inc. during late 1998-2000.

In the past, Saco Defense utilized their high-tech manufacturing facility to produce guns for Magnum Research, Weatherby (contract ended Sept., 2001), and others.

SAFARI ARMS

Previous trademark manufactured in Olympia, WA. M-S Safari Arms, located in Phoenix, AZ, was started in 1978 as a division of M-S Safari Outfitters. In 1987, Safari Arms was absorbed by Olympic Arms. Safari Arms manufactured 1911 style pistols since the acquisition of M-S Safari Arms in 1987. In Jan. 2004, the Safari Arms name was discontinued and all 1911 style pistols are now being manufactured by Olympic Arms. Please refer to the Olympic Arms section for currently manufactured models.

Safari Arms previously made the Phoenix, Special Forces, Camp Perry, and Royal Order of Jesters commemoratives in various configurations and quantities. Prices average in the $1,500 range except for the Royal Order of Jesters ($2,000).

SCHUETZEN PISTOL WORKS

Schuetzen Pistol Works is the current custom shop of Olympic Arms. Some of the pistols made by Safari Arms had the "Schuetzen Pistol Works" name on them (c. 1994-96). Until Jan. 2004, all pistols were are marked with the Safari Arms slide marking. All pistols, however, have been marked "Safari Arms" on the frame. The pistols formerly in this section have been moved to the PISTOLS: SEMI-AUTO category.

GRADING - PPGS™	100%	98%	95%	90%	80%	70%	60%	LAST MSR

PISTOLS: SEMI-AUTO

Safari Arms manufactured mostly single action, semi-auto pistols derived from the Browning M1911 design with modifications. Please refer to Olympic Arms listing for currently manufactured pistols.

GI SAFARI – .45 ACP cal., patterned after the Colt Model 1911, Safari frame, beavertail grip safety and commander hammer, parkerized matte black finish, 39.9 oz. Mfg. 1991-2000.

	$500	$455	$395	$350	$295	$275	$250	*$550*

CARRYCOMP – similar to MatchMaster, except utilizes W. Schuemann designed hybrid compensator system, 5 in. barrel, available in stainless steel or steel, 38 oz. Mfg. 1993-99.

	$1,030	$875	$750	$600	$500	$425	$375	*$1,160*

* ***CarryComp Enforcer*** – similar to Enforcer, except utilizes W. Schuemann designed hybrid compensator system, available in stainless steel or steel, 36 oz. Mfg. 1993-96.

	$1,175	$1,025	$875	$750	$600	$500	$425	*$1,300*

CARRIER – .45 ACP cal. only, reproduction of the original Detonics ScoreMaster, except has upgraded sights, custom made by Richard Niemer from the Custom Shop. New 1999-2001.

	$750	$625	$575	$500	$450	$400	$350	*$750*

RENEGADE – .45 ACP cal., left-hand action (port on left side), 4 1/2 (4-star, disc. 1996) or 5 (new 1994) in. barrel, 6 shot mag., adj. sights, stainless steel construction, 36-39 oz. Mfg. 1993-98.

	$955	$800	$700	$600	$525	$450	$395	*$1,085*

Add $50 for 4-star (4 1/2 in. barrel, disc.).

RELIABLE – similar to Renegade, except has right-hand action. Mfg. 1993-98.

	$730	$620	$525	$450	$425	$400	$375	*$825*

Add $60 for 4-star (4 1/2 in. barrel, disc.).

GRIFFON PISTOL – .45 ACP cal., 5 in. stainless steel barrel, 10 shot mag., standard govt. size with beavertail grip safety, full-length recoil spring guide, commander style hammer, smooth walnut grips, 40 1/2 oz. Disc. 1998.

	$855	$725	$650	$575	$500	$450	$395	*$920*

BLACK WIDOW – .45 ACP cal., 3.9 in. barrel, hand contoured front gripstrap, schrimshawed ivory Micarta grips with Black Widow emblem, 6 shot mag., 27 oz. Inventory was depleted 1988.

	$565	$510	$460	$430	$400	$375	$350	*$595*

BILL OF RIGHTS BICENTENNIAL MATCHED SET – includes the MatchMaster Pistol and ServiceMatch Rifle, features beryllium receivers and special engraving. Disc.

	$8,950	$6,500	$4,750	N/A	N/A	N/A	N/A	*$7,400*

PARTNER – .22 LR cal., formerly the Whitney Wolverine, 8 shot mag., black plastic grips, non-adj. sights. Advertised beginning late 1997.

While advertised since 1997, this gun was not manufactured commercially.

MODEL 81 TARGET PISTOL – .38 Spl. or .45 ACP cal., 5 in. barrel, hand contoured front gripstrap, 2 lbs. 10 oz. Disc. 1987.

	$775	$695	$550	$440	$410	$375	$350	*$875*

Add $50 for Deluxe Model (with Herrett adj. grips).

* ***Model 81L Target Pistol*** – .38 Spl. or .45 ACP, 6 in. barrel, 2 lbs. 13 oz. Disc. 1987.

	$850	$775	$695	$550	$440	$410	$375	*$975*

Add $50 for Deluxe Model (with Herrett adj. grips).

* ***Model 81 NM Target Pistol*** – .38 Spl. or .45 ACP cal., similar frame as Model 81, except has flat front gripstrap, 5 in. barrel, 2 lbs. 5 oz. Disc. 1987.

	$775	$695	$550	$440	$410	$375	$350	*$875*

* ***Model 81BP Target Pistol*** – .38 Spl. or .45 ACP cal., 6 in barrel, contoured front gripstrap, faster cycle time, 2 lbs. 9 oz. Disc. 1987.

	$875	$775	$695	$550	$440	$410	$375	*$995*

GRADING - PPGS™	100%	98%	95%	90%	80%	70%	60%	LAST MSR

* ***Model 81 Target Pistol Silueta*** – .45 ACP or .38/.45 Wildcat cal., 10 in. extended barrel, designed for silhouette shooting, 2 lbs. 14 oz. Disc. 1987.

	$875	$775	$695	$550	$440	$410	$375	*$1,050*

PISTOLS: SINGLE SHOT

ULTIMATE/UNLIMITED – various cals., bolt action target pistol, 14 15/16 in. barrel, black finished metal, laminated stock. Disc. 1987.

	$850	$775	$695	$550	$440	$410	$375	*$975*

SAFARI CLUB INTERNATIONAL

SCI is an international hunting and conservation organization with headquarters located in Tucson, AZ.

Although Safari Club International (SCI) is not a manufacturer or importer, this organization is responsible for special and limited editions similar to the one listed. Additionally, SCI also has one custom-built rifle manufactured for each annual SCI convention with an auction determining the price of the rifle.

Manufacturer/Model	Quantity	Year	Issue Price
SPECIAL/LIMITED EDITIONS			
WINCHESTER Super Grade 25th Anniversary	200	1997	$1,395

SAFETY HARBOR FIREARMS, INC.

Current manufacturer located in Safety Harbor, FL.

Safety Harbor Firearms also manufactures a line of KEG (Kompact Entry Gun) slide action shotguns (12 and 20 ga.), in short barrel lengths that are classified as NFA weapons. Please contact the manufacturer directly for more information, availability and pricing for these models (see Trademark Index).

GRADING - PPGS™	100%	98%	95%	90%	80%	70%	60%

RIFLES: BOLT ACTION

SHF R50 – .50 BMG cal., 18, 22, or 29 in. barrel, side mounted 3 (disc. 2009) or 5 shot mag., black reinforced fixed tube stock with vent. recoil pad, partially shrouded barrel with muzzle brake, Picatinny rails, 17 1/2 lbs.

MSR $2,450	$2,325	$2,100	$1,825	$1,675	$1,350	$1,100	$850

SHF S50 – .50 BMG cal., single shot, 18, 22, or 29 in. barrel, similar stock and handguard as the SHF R50. New mid-2009.

MSR $1,950	$1,800	$1,650	$1,475	$1,325	$1,075	$875	$775

SAIGA

Current trademark manufactured by Izhmash, located in Izhevsk, Russia. Currently distributed exclusively beginning 2012 by RWC Group LLC, located in Tullytown, PA. Currently imported beginning late 2011 by US Sporting Goods, Inc., located in Rockledge, FL, RAAC (Russian American Armory Company), located in Scottsburg, IN, and K-VAR Corp., located in Las Vegas, NV. Previously imported by European American Armory Corp., located in Sharpes, FL.

CARBINES/RIFLES: SEMI-AUTO

SAIGA RIFLE – .223 Rem. (Model IZ-114), 5.45x39mm (Model IZ-240), or .308 Win. (Model IZ-139) cal., Kalashnikov type action, black synthetic or hardwood (new 2003, only available in .308 Win. cal.) stock and forearm, 16, 20, or 21 (.308 Win. cal. only) in. barrel length, matte black metal, 7-8 1/2 lbs. Imported 2002-2004, reintroduced 2006.

MSR $560	$475	$415	$350	$325	$260	$215	$175

Add $20 for 20 in. barrel or 16 in. barrel with adj. cheekpiece.
Add $275 for .308 Win. cal.
Add $80 for 5.45x39mm cal. with AK-style forend and handguard.

GRADING - PPGS™	100%	98%	95%	90%	80%	70%	60%	LAST MSR

* ***Saiga Rifle 7.62x39mm Cal.*** – 7.62x39mm (Model IZ-132) cal., 16.3 or 20 in barrel, 10 shot mag., otherwise similar to Saiga Rifle. Imported 2002-2004, reintroduced 2006.

MSR $535	$450	$395	$350	$300	$250	$200	$160	

Add $45 for 20 in. barrel or for 16 in. barrel with adj. cheekpiece.
Add $105 for 16 in. barrel with AK-47 style forend and handguard.

SAIGA 100 – .223 Rem., .30-06, .308 Win., or 7.62x39mm cal., hunting configuration with black synthetic stock, 3 or 10 shot mag., 22 in. barrel with open sights, 7.7 lbs. Imported 2006-disc.

	$650	$595	$550	$495	$450	$400	$350	

Add 15% for .308 Win. cal.

SAIGA CARBINE CONVERSION – 7.62x39mm cal., AK-style carbine, polymer furniture. New 2012.

MSR $900	$775	$675	$575	$525	$425	$350	$275	

Add $20 for Tuning B Model (CBS collapsible stock, RS47SET polymer forward handguard, four rails and G47 pistol grip).
Add $525 for Tuning C Model (ARSNL fully adj. stock, XRS47 aluminum 5 rails handguard, UPG47 pistol grip w/interchangeable finger grooves and backstraps).

SHOTGUNS: SEMI-AUTO

SAIGA MODEL – 12 or 20 ga., 3 in. chamber, 5 shot detachable box mag., Kalashnikov type action, black synthetic stock and forearm, 19-22 in. barrel length, matte black metal, with or w/o side rail, optional adj. leaf sight or notch rear sight 6.7-10 lbs. Imported 2002-2004, reintroduced 2006.

MSR $780	$675	$595	$500	$450	$375	$300	$235	

Add $25 for adj. leaf sight or $13 for notch rear sights.
Add $94 for 20 ga.
Add $40 for RPK handguard (disc.).
Add 10% for choke tubes (12 ga. only, disc.).

* ***Saiga Model .410 Bore*** – .410 bore, 19 or 21 in barrel, 4 or 10 (disc.) shot detachable box mag., NATO or Warsaw buttstock, with or w/o side scope rail, otherwise similar to Saiga Shotgun, approx. 6.6 lbs. Imported 2002-2004, reintroduced 2006.

MSR $646	$500	$475	$415	$375	$300	$250	$195	

* ***Saiga Skeletonized Stock*** – 12 ga. only, 19 in. barrel, plastic or laminated skeletonized stock, Picatinny rail, with or w/o magwell, 4 or 5 shot mag., AK sights. New 2012.

MSR $994	$850	$750	$650	$575	$475	$375	$300	

Add $81 for laminated stock.

* ***Saiga Hunting Model*** – 12 ga. only, 19 in. barrel, wooden or plastic Monte Carlo or hunting style stock, with or w/o mag well, Picatinny rail, optional leaf or AK sights, 4 or 5 shot mag. New 2012.

MSR $885	$750	$650	$575	$500	$415	$350	$275	

Add $45 for wooden stock.
Add $144 for optional leaf sight.
Add $80 for hunting stock.

SAKO, LTD.

Current rifle manufacturer established circa 1921 and located in Riihimäki, Finland. Current models are presently being imported by Beretta USA, located in Accokeek, MD. Previously imported by Stoeger Industries, Inc. located in Wayne, NJ, Garcia, and Rymac.

During 2000, Sako, Ltd. was purchased by Beretta Holding of Italy. All currently produced Sakos are imported by Beretta USA Corp. located in Accokeek, MD.

Beginning 2000, most Sako rifles (except the Action I in .223 Rem. cal.) are shipped with a Key Concept locking device. This patented system uses a separate key to activate an almost invisible lock which totally blocks the firing pin and prevents bolt movement.

GRADING - PPGS™	100%	98%	95%	90%	80%	70%	60%	LAST MSR

PISTOLS: SEMI-AUTO

Less than 200 Triace pistols were imported into the United States.

TRIACE – .22 Short, .22 LR, or .32 S&W Wadcutter cal., target pistol incorporating unique action, competition walnut grips with thumbrest and adj. heel, blue finish with chrome accents. Imported 1985-86 only.

$1,300 $1,150 $950 $825 $700 $600 $500 *$1,395*

* ***Triace Pistol Kit*** – consists of Triace frame, .22 Short, .22 LR, and .32 S&W barrels. Cased with accessories. Imported 1985-86 only.

$2,500 $2,200 $2,000 $1,500 $1,300 $1,175 $1,025 *$2,385*

RIFLES: BOLT ACTION, DISC.

Sako used FN Mauser-style long actions under the Sako name circa 1951-1960. Serial numbers started with 100,001. During 1962, Sako introduced its L61R action, but older FN long actions remained at the factory. Sako also manufactured commercial Mauser actioned rifles for Weatherby and others. Previous importation for these FN actioned Sakos included Firearms International. Note: Prices are for pre-1972 Sako rifles, unless stated otherwise. Pre-1972 Sakos utilize the L-46, L-461, L-469, L-579, L-591, L-57, and L-61 R actions.

Model names on previous imported Sako rifles from Garcia are located on the bottom of the barrel in front of the forend.

Add 10%-15% for popular Mag. cals. on rifles listed.
Subtract approx. 25% for post-1972 models.

DELUXE – various cals., Monte Carlo stock, skipline checkering, long, medium, or short actions, contrasting pistol grip cap and forend tip, engraved floorplate.

$1,045 $925 $775 $625 $450 $425 $385

STANDARD SPORTER – long, medium, and short actions.

$850 $725 $625 $500 $450 $410 $375

HEAVY BARREL MODEL – long, medium, and short actions.

$725 $625 $500 $450 $410 $375 $300

FINNBEAR MODEL SPORTER – .25-06 Rem., .264 Win., .270 Win., .30-06, .300 Win. Mag., .338 Win. Mag., 7mm Rem. Mag., or .375 H&H cal., long L-61 R action, 24 in. barrel, half stock.

$1,100 $975 $800 $725 $550 $475 $425

FINNBEAR MODEL MANNLICHER CARBINE – .25-06 Rem., .264 Win., .270 Win., .30-06, .300 Win. Mag., .338 Win. Mag., 7mm Rem. Mag., or .375 H&H cal., similar to Finnbear Sporter, except has 20 in. barrel and Mannlicher stock.

$1,300 $1,100 $975 $800 $725 $550 $475

FORESTER MODEL SPORTER – .22-250 Rem., .243 Win., or .308 Win. cal., 23 in. barrel, medium L-579 action, sporter half stock.

$1,050 $925 $775 $700 $525 $450 $400

FORESTER MODEL MANNLICHER CARBINE – .22-250 Rem., .243 Win., or .308 Win. cal., 20 in. barrel, medium L-579 action, Mannlicher stock.

$1,300 $1,100 $975 $800 $725 $550 $475

VIXEN MODEL SPORTER – .222 Rem., .222 Rem. Mag., or .223 Rem. cal., short L-461 action, 23 1/2 in. barrel, sported half stock.

$1,050 $925 $775 $700 $525 $450 $400

L-46 action pre-Vixen Sakos had detachable mags.

VIXEN MODEL HEAVY BARREL SPORTER – .222 Rem., .222 Rem. Mag., or .223 Rem. cal., short L-461 action, similar to the Vixen Model Sporter, except has 23 1/2 in. heavy barrel.

$1,050 $925 $775 $700 $525 $450 $400

L-46 action pre-Vixen Sakos had detachable mags.

GRADING - PPGS™	100%	98%	95%	90%	80%	70%	60%	LAST MSR

VIXEN MODEL MANNLICHER CARBINE – .222 Rem., .222 Rem. Mag., or .223 Rem. cal., short action, 20 in. barrel, Mannlicher stock.

	$1,300	$1,100	$975	$800	$725	$550	$475	

MAUSER ACTION (FN) – .270 Win. or .30-06 cal., long action. Mfg. 1950-57.

	$695	$500	$400	$345	$310	$280	$260	

MAGNUM MAUSER (FN) – 8x60S, 8.2x57mm, .300 H&H, or .375 H&H cal.

	$745	$635	$580	$495	$450	$410	$375	

MODEL 74 – various cals.

	$650	$575	$450	$375	$340	$320	$290	

MODEL 78 – .22 LR, .22 WMR, or .22 Hornet cal., detachable mag., same size as short action Standard Model. Importation disc. 1986.

	$480	$395	$340	$310	$280	$265	$250	*$647*

Add $30 for .22 Hornet cal.

FINNSPORT MODEL 2700 – available in long (AIII) action only, .270 Win., .300 Win. Mag. cals., select checkered walnut. Disc. 1985.

	$750	$675	$600	$560	$510	$475	$430	*$910*

ANNIVERSARY MODEL – 7mm Rem. Mag. cal. only, 1,000 mfg.

	$2,750	$1,625	$975	N/A	N/A	N/A	N/A	

The 100% value on this model refers to NIB unfired condition with factory papers.

RIFLES: BOLT ACTION, RECENT PRODUCTION

Beginning late 2001, Sako established a custom shop, which allows the consumer to select from a wide variety of finishes, options, and special orders, including individual stock dimensions. Please contact Beretta USA for more information regarding the Sako custom shop.

All Sako left-handed models are available in medium or long action only.

Some older model TRG rifles (Models TRG-S, TRG-22, and TRG-42) have experienced firing pin breakage. Ser. no. ranges on these U.S. distributed rifles are 202238 - 275255 and 973815 - 998594. Please contact Beretta USA directly (str@berettausa.com or 800-803-8869) for a replacement firing pin assembly if you have a rifle within these serial number ranges.

FINNFIRE – .22 LR cal., 22 in. regular or heavy (new 1996) or 23 (Sporter/Varmint and Target) in. cold-hammer forged free-floating barrel, M-P94S action, single stage adj. trigger, 50 degree bolt lift, 2 position safety, European walnut pistol grip or adj. Target competition (new 2003) stock, cocking indicator, available in Hunter, Target (new 2003)/ Sporter (new 1999), or Varmint configuration, 5 or 10 shot mag., integral 11mm dovetail (for scope mounting), with (new 1996) or w/o open sights, 5 3/4 (Target/Sporter) lbs. Imported 1994-2005.

	$850	$725	$625	$525	$450	$400	$350	*$1,044*

Add $45 for Varmint Model with heavy barrel.
Add $125 for Target/Sporter Model with 10 shot mag. and adj. competition stock.

QUAD – .17 HMR, .17 Mach 2, .22 LR, or .22 WMR cal., 22 in. barrel, black synthetic stock with ambidextrous palm swell and adj. buttpad, interchangeable rimfire barrels, 50 degree bolt lift, blued finish, 5 shot mag., no sights, 5 3/4 lbs. Mfg. 2005-2007.

	$760	$650	$575	$500	$425	$375	$325	*$925*

* ***Quad 2-Barrel Combo*** – .17 HMR and .22 LR cal., includes two interchangeable barrels, fitted aluminum case. Limited importation 2008.

	$1,500	$1,250	$1,000	$875	$775	$700	$625	*$1,750*

* ***Quad 4-Barrel Combo*** – includes four interchangeable 22 in. rimfire barrels in cals. .17 HMR, .17 Mach 2, .22 LR, and .22 WMR, barrels are color coded to indicate caliber and change quickly with barrel tool, choice of oil finished walnut or black synthetic (new 2008) stock, single stage trigger, detachable 5 shot mag., approx. 6.1-7.7 lbs. Mfg. 2005-circa 2010.

	$1,475	$1,275	$1,050	$900	$800	$700	$650	*$1,700*

Add $275 for wood stock.

GRADING - PPGS™	100%	98%	95%	90%	80%	70%	60%	LAST MSR

HUNTER LIGHTWEIGHT RIFLE – available in short action (AI) in .17 Rem., .222 Rem., or .223 Rem. cal., medium action (AII) in .22-250 Rem., .243 Win., .308 Win., or 7mm-08 Rem. cal., or long action (AIII) in .25-06 Rem., .270 Win., .280 Rem., .30 - 06, .270 Wby. Mag. (disc. 1996), 7mm Wby. Mag. (disc. 1996), 7mm Rem. Mag., .300 Win. Mag., .300 Wby. Mag., .338 Win. Mag., .340 Wby. Mag. (disc. 1996), .375 H&H, or .416 Rem. Mag. (new 1991) cal., 21 1/4, 21 3/4, or 22 in. barrel, classic styled stock with choice of oil (disc. 1996) or matte lacquer finish, finely checkered French walnut. Disc. 1997.

$850	$685	$550	$490	$460	$430	$410	*$1,050*

Add $35 for long action.
Add $50-$70 for Mag. cals.
Add approx. $80 for left-hand action (available in all Mag. cals. - mfg. 1994-96).

* ***Hunter Lightweight Rifle Carbine (Handy)*** – available in medium action in .22-250 Rem. (disc. 1990), .243 Win. (new 1991), .308 Win. (new 1991) cal. or long action in .25-06 Rem. (disc. 1990), 7mm Rem. Mag. (disc. 1990), .338 Win. Mag. cal., or .375 H&H (new 1990) cal., 18 1/2 in. barrel with iron sights, oil or lacquer finished deluxe walnut stock with checkering, approx. 7 lbs. Mfg. 1986-91.

$725	$650	$600	$490	$460	$430	$410	*$945*

Add $50-$65 for long action (Mag. cals.).

LONG RANGE HUNTING MODEL – available in long action in .25-06 Rem., .270 Win., .300 Win. Mag., or 7mm Rem. Mag. cal., 26 in. heavy barrel only w/o sights. Mfg. 1996-97.

$1,030	$785	$625	$545	$495	$465	$440	*$1,275*

Add $15 for Mag. cals.

FIBERCLASS MODEL – available in medium action (disc. 1992) in .22-250 Rem., .243 Win., .308 Win., or 7mm-08 cal., or long action in .25-06 Rem., .270 Win., .280 Rem., .30-06, 7mm Rem. Mag., .300 Win. Mag., .338 Win. Mag., .375 H&H, or .416 Rem. Mag. (new 1991) cal., has black fiberglass stock. Disc. 1996.

$1,170	$930	$785	$725	$630	$560	$510	*$1,388*

Add $17-$37 for Mag. cals.
Subtract $40 for medium action cals. (disc. 1992).
Add $80 for left-hand action (disc. 1989).

* ***FiberClass Model Carbine (Handy)*** – available in medium action in .243 Win. or .308 Win. cal. and long action in .25-06 Rem. (disc.), .270 Win. (disc.), .30-06, 7mm Rem. Mag. (disc.), .300 Win. Mag. (disc.), .338 Win. Mag., or .375 H&H (new 1991) cal., 18 1/2 in. barrel with fiberglass stock. Mfg. 1986-91.

$995	$895	$775	$725	$630	$560	$510	*$1,239*

Add $50-$65 for Mag. cals.

LAMINATED RIFLE – available in short action (disc. 1989), medium action in .22-250 Rem., .243 Win., .308 Win., or 7mm-08 Rem. cal., or long action in .25-06 Rem., .270 Win., .280 Rem., .30-06, 7mm Rem. Mag., .300 Win. Mag., .338 Win. Mag., .375 H&H, or .416 Rem. Mag. (new 1991) cal., features laminated wood stock. Mfg. 1988-95.

$985	$790	$635	$550	$495	$460	$430	*$1,200*

Add $35 for short action.
Add $55 for long action.
Add $75-$95 for Mag. cals.
Add approx. $100 for left-hand action (disc.).

The left-hand action was available in .270 Win., .280 Rem., .30-06, 7mm Rem. Mag., .300 Win. Mag., .338 Win. Mag., .375 H&H, or .416 Rem. Mag. cal.

MODEL TRG-21 – .308 Win. cal., bolt action, 25 3/4 in. barrel, new design features modular synthetic stock construction with adj. cheekpiece and buttplate, stainless steel barrel, cold hammer forged receiver, and resistance free bolt, 10 shot detachable mag., 10 1/2 lbs. Imported 1993-99.

$2,300	$2,000	$1,800	$1,600	$1,400	$1,200	$975	*$2,699*

GRADING - PPGS™	100%	98%	95%	90%	80%	70%	60%	LAST MSR

MODEL TRG-22 – .308 Win. cal., bolt action, 20 or 26 in. barrel, updated TRG-21 design featuring adj. modular synthetic stock (green, desert tan, or all black) construction with adj. cheekpiece and buttplate, competition trigger, Picatinny rail became standard circa 2011, choice of blue (disc. 2002) or phosphate (new 2002) metal finish, stainless steel barrel, cold hammer forged receiver, and resistance free bolt, 10 shot detachable mag., approx. 10 1/4 lbs. Importation began 2000.

MSR $3,450	$2,950	$2,450	$1,975	$1,750	$1,500	$1,250	$1,000	

Add $2,375 for folding stock.
Add $1,710 for folding stock in green finish.
Subtract approx. 10% if without Picatinny rail.

MODEL TRG-41 – .338 Lapua Mag. cal., similar to Model TRG-21, except has long action and 27 1/8 in. barrel, 7 3/4 lbs. Imported 1994-99.

	$2,700	$2,425	$2,150	$1,850	$1,625	$1,400	$1,200	*$3,099*

MODEL TRG-42 – .300 Win. Mag. (disc. 2012) or .338 Lapua Mag. cal., updated TRG-41 design featuring long action and 27 1/8 in. barrel, Picatinny rail became standard during 2011, choice of black composite/blue finish, desert tan, or green composite/phosphate (new 2002) finish, 5 shot mag., 11 1/4 lbs. Importation began 2000.

MSR $4,400	$3,995	$3,500	$3,150	$2,775	$2,325	$1,925	$1,750	

Add $2,400 for folding stock with Picatinny rail.
Subtract approx. $775 if without Picatinny rail (desert tan stock only).

MODEL TRG-S – available in medium action (disc. 1993) in .243 Win. or 7mm-08 cal., or long action in .25-06 Rem. (Mfg. 1994-98), .270 Win. (disc. 2000), 6.5x55mm Swedish (disc. 1998), .30-06 (disc.), .308 Win. (disc. 1995), .270 Wby. Mag. (disc. 1998), 7mm Wby. Mag. (Mfg. 1998), 7mm Rem. Mag. (disc.), .300 Win. Mag. (disc.), .300 Wby. Mag. (mfg. 1994-99), .30-378 Wby. Mag. (new 1998, 26 in. barrel only), .338 Win. Mag. (disc. 1999), .338 Lapua Mag. (new 1994), .340 Wby. Mag. (disc. 1998), 7mm STW (26 in. barrel only, disc. 1999), .375 H&H (disc. 1998), or .416 Rem. Mag. (disc. 1998) cal., black synthetic stock, Sporter variation derived from the Model TRG-21, 22 (disc.), 24 (Mag. cals. only, disc.), or 26 in. barrel, 3 or 5 shot detachable mag., fully adj. trigger, 60 degree bolt lift, matte finish, 8 1/8 lbs. Imported 1993-2004.

	$775	$650	$525	$475	$440	$415	$380	*$896*

MANNLICHER CARBINE – available in short action (disc. 1989), medium action in .243 Win. or .308 Win. cal., or long action in .25-06 Rem. (disc. 1991), .270 Win., .30 - 06, 7mm Rem. Mag. (disc. 1991), .300 Win. Mag. (disc. 1991), .338 Win. Mag., or .375 H&H cal., 18 1/2 in. barrel, two-piece full Mannlicher style stock, open sights. Disc. 1996.

	$1,050	$825	$650	$550	$500	$465	$440	*$1,275*

Add approx. 5% for long action.
Add $60-$75 for Mag. cals.

PPC MODEL – 22 PPC or 6 mm PPC cal., 21 3/4 or 23 3/4 (Benchrest Model) in. barrel, single shot in Benchrest Model, 4 shot mag. in Hunter or Deluxe Model, checkered walnut stock, Deluxe Model has rosewood pistol grip and forearm caps plus skip line checkering, matte lacquer finish on Hunter and Deluxe, oiled finish on Benchrest, 6 1/4 or 8 3/4 (Benchrest Model with heavy barrel) lbs. Imported 1989-97.

	$1,250	$950	$750	$650	$600	$540	$500	*$1,535*

Add $320 for Deluxe Hunter Model (disc. 1993).
Add $85 for Benchrest Model (disc. 1993).

VARMINT RIFLE – available in short action (AI) in .17 Rem., .222 Rem., or .223 Rem., and medium action (AII) .22-250 Rem., .243 Win., .308 Win., or 7mm-08 cal., 22 3/4 in. heavy barrel, no sights. Disc. 1997.

	$1,025	$795	$615	$545	$475	$430	$400	*$1,240*

CLASSIC GRADE – .243 Win., .270 Win., .30-06, or 7mm Rem. Mag. cal., short (AI, disc. 1992), medium (AII), or long (AIII) action, classic styled stock, finely checkered French

GRADING - PPGS™	100%	98%	95%	90%	80%	70%	60%	LAST MSR

walnut with matte lacquer finish. Disc. 1985, reintroduced 1992-97.

	$895	$745	$600	$545	$475	$430	$400	$1,050

Add $50 for Mag. cal.
Add $35 for long action.
Add $120-$135 for left-hand action (disc. 1994) (.270 Win. or 7mm Rem. Mag cal. only).

In 1992, the Classic Grade was once again imported into the U.S. in .243 Win., .270 Win., .30-06, or 7mm Rem. Mag. cal.

DELUXE LIGHTWEIGHT RIFLE – available in short action (AI) in .17 Rem., .222 Rem., or .223 Rem. cal., medium action (AII) in .22-250 Rem., .243 Win., .308 Win., or 7mm-08 Rem. cal., or long action (AIII) in .25-06 Rem., .270 Win., .280 Rem., .30 - 06, 7mm Rem. Mag., .300 Win. Mag., .300 Wby. Mag., .338 Win. Mag., .375 H&H, or .416 Rem. Mag. (new 1991) cal., 21 1/4, 21 3/4, or 22 in. barrel, deluxe quality skipline checkered walnut stock with rosewood forend tip. Disc. 1997.

	$1,185	$965	$750	$650	$595	$540	$500	$1,475

Add $35 for long action.
Add $50-$70 for Mag. cals.
Add $150-$175 for left-hand action (disc. 1994, available in long action only).

SAFARI GRADE – available in long (AIII) action only, .300 Win. Mag. (disc. 1989), .338 Win. Mag., .375 H&H, or .416 Rem. Mag. (new 1991) cal., deluxe walnut with sculptured cheekpiece, 22 in. barrel, 4 shot mag., open sights, sling swivels. Disc. 1996.

	$2,235	$1,785	$1,475	$1,250	$1,050	$900	$795	$2,765

SUPER DELUXE – a limited edition rifle available on special order only, various cals. are available in the short (AI), medium (AII), and long (AIII) actions, presentation grade walnut with both checkering and carving, rosewood forend tip. Disc. 1997.

	$2,400	$1,825	$1,475	$1,250	$1,050	$900	$795	$3,100

SAKO 75 HUNTER – available in 5 action sizes, .17 Rem. (mfg. 1998-2002), .222 Rem. (mfg. 1998-2002), .223 Rem. (new 1998), .22-250 Rem., .243 Win., .308 Win., 7mm-08 Rem., .25-06 Rem., .260 Rem. (new 2005), .270 Win., .270 WSM (new 2004), .280 Rem. (disc. 2004), .30-06, .270 Wby. Mag. (disc. 2001), 6.5x55mm (new 2005), 7mm Rem. Ultra Mag. (mfg. 2002-2003), 7mm Wby. Mag. (disc. 2003), 7mm STW (disc. 2003), 7mm WSM (new 2005), 7mm Rem. Mag., .300 WSM (new 2004), .300 Win. Mag., .300 Wby. Mag. (disc. 2003), .300 Rem. Ultra Mag. (mfg. 2000-2003), .338 Win. Mag., .340 Wby. Mag. (disc. 2003), .375 H&H, or .416 Rem. Mag. (disc. 2001) cal., hammer forged 22-24 3/8 in. barrel, utilizes 3 locking lugs, mechanical ejector, 5 bolt sliding guides with 70 degree bolt lift, 3-position rear tang safety, available with top loading fixed mag. (hinged floorplate, .300 Rem. Ultra Mag., .416 Rem. Mag., and 7mm Rem. Ultra mag. cals. only), or detachable staggered 4-6 shot mag., checkered walnut stock, no sights, approx. 7 3/4 lbs. Mfg. 1997-2007.

	$1,125	$900	$725	$625	$550	$500	$450	$1,375

Add $100 for .375 H&H cal.

This model was also available in left-hand action in .270 Win. or .30-06 cal. at no extra charge.

SAKO 75 DELUXE – similar cals. as Sako 75 Hunter, features hinged floorplate and deluxe walnut stock with gloss finish, skipline checkering, and rosewood forend and pistol grip caps, custom stock bedding and iron sights available on .375 H&H or .416 Rem. Mag. cals., approx. 7 3/4 lbs. Mfg. 1997-2007.

	$1,700	$1,450	$1,200	$925	$750	$625	$550	$2,050

Add $125 for .416 Rem. Mag.

SAKO 75 KING RANCH – .270 Win., .30-06, or .300 WSM cal., 22 7/8 or 24 3/8 (.300 WSM cal. only) in. barrel, similar to Sako 75 Deluxe, except has King Ranch "W" stock checkering and gold-filled "W" emblem on floorplate. Mfg. 2006-2007.

	$2,050	$1,650	$1,325	$1,050	$875	$750	$625	$2,475

GRADING - PPGS™	100%	98%	95%	90%	80%	70%	60%	LAST MSR

SAKO 75 STAINLESS SYNTHETIC – available in .22-250 Rem., .243 Win., .25-06 Rem., .260 Rem. (new 2005), .270 Win., .270 WSM (new 2004), .30-06, .308 Win., .300 Win. Mag., .300 Wby. Mag. (mfg. 1999-2003), .300 WSM (new 2004), .300 Rem. Ultra Mag. (mfg. 2000-2003), 7mm-08 Rem. (new 1998), 7mm STW (mfg. 1998-2003), 7mm WSM (new 2006), 7mm Rem. Mag., 7mm Rem. Ultra Mag. (mfg. 2002-2003), .338 Win. Mag., or .375 H&H cal., 3-4 shot detachable mag. (except for floorplate with Rem. Ultra Mag. cals.), features black composite stock with soft rubber grip inserts in pistol grip and forearm area, matte stainless steel metal, 7 3/4 lbs. Mfg. 1997-2007.

$1,150	$900	$750	$640	$535	$450	$390	*$1,425*

SAKO 75 STAINLESS WALNUT – .270 Win., .30-06, .300 Win. Mag., .300 Wby. Mag., .338 Win. Mag., 7mm STW, or 7mm Rem. Mag. cal., features checkered walnut stock and forearm. Imported 1999-2002.

$1,050	$840	$685	$575	$485	$400	$350	*$1,239*

Add $35 for Mag. cals.

SAKO 75 GREY WOLF – .22-250 Rem., .223 Rem., .243 Win., .25-06 Rem., .260 Rem., .270 Win., .30-06, .308 Win., .270 WSM, .300 WSM, 7mm WSM, or 7mm-08 Rem. cal., available in 4 frame sizes and 3 barrel lengths. Mfg. 2005-2007.

$1,225	$925	$800	$700	$600	$525	$450	*$1,550*

SAKO 75 VARMINT – .17 Rem. (disc. 2003), .22-250 Rem., .222 Rem. (disc. 2002), .223 Rem., .22 PPC (mfg. 1999-2003), or 6mm PPC (mfg. 1999-2003) cal., 23 5/8 in. heavy barrel w/o sights and beavertail forend, 5 or 6 shot detachable mag., 8 5/8 lbs. Mfg. 1998-2005.

$1,400	$1,000	$850	$725	$650	$575	$500	*$1,628*

SAKO 75 VARMINT W/SET TRIGGER – similar to Sako 75 Varmint, except is also available in .204 Ruger, .243 Win., .260 Rem., or .308 Win. cal., set trigger. Mfg. 2005-2007.

$1,575	$1,275	$975	$800	$700	$600	$500	*$1,850*

SAKO 75 STAINLESS VARMINT LAMINATED – .22-250 Rem., .222 Rem. (disc. 2002), .223 Rem., .22 PPC (disc. 2003), 6mm PPC (disc. 2003), or 7mm-08 Rem. (new 2002) cal., similar to Sako 75 Varmint, features stainless steel action and barrel, brown laminated wood stock, 9 lbs. Mfg. 1999-2005.

$1,475	$1,175	$875	$765	$635	$530	$455	*$1,794*

SAKO 75 STAINLESS VARMINT LAMINATED W/SET TRIGGER – similar to Sako 75 Stainless Varmint Laminated, except is also available in .204 Ruger, .243 Win., .260 Rem., or .308 Win. cal., set trigger. Mfg. 2005-2007.

$1,675	$1,375	$1,025	$850	$725	$600	$500	*$1,950*

SAKO 75 CUSTOM DELUXE – .270 Win. or .30-06 cal., extra grade deluxe oil finished walnut stock with rosewood forend tip and pistol grip cap, 7 3/4 lbs. Imported late 2003-2007.

$3,750	$3,250	$2,575	$2,175	$1,850	$1,550	$1,350	*$4,325*

This model was available through Sako showcase dealers only.

SAKO 75 SINGLE SHOT – .22-250 Rem. (disc. 2005), .243 Win. (disc. 2005), 7mm-08 Rem. (disc. 2005), 6mm PPC (disc. 2005), or .308 Win. cal., medium III action, stainless steel action and barrel, heavy free floating fluted barrel w/o sights, 9 lbs. Mfg. 2004-2007.

$2,850	$2,375	$2,125	$1,850	$1,550	$1,350	$1,150	*$3,450*

SAKO 75 80TH ANNIVERSARY – .375 H&H cal., limited edition rifle featuring Mauser style claw extractor, premium grade checkered walnut with ebony forend tip, cold hammer forged match grade barrel has 1/4 rib with open sights, 5 shot internal mag. with hinged floorplate, includes Swarovski PV-1 scope and case, only 80 rifles (serial numbered 200101-200180) mfg. 2001-2007.

$16,500	$14,000	$11,000	$9,000	N/A	N/A	N/A	*$19,550*

SAKO 75 SUPER DELUXE – a limited edition rifle available special order only, presentation grade walnut with both checkering and carving, rosewood forend tip.

Limited availability precludes accurate pricing on this model.

GRADING - PPGS™	100%	98%	95%	90%	80%	70%	60%	LAST MSR

SAKO 85 FINNLIGHT ST (FINNLIGHT) – .22-250 Rem. (new 2010), .243 Win, .25-06 Rem., .260 Rem. (mfg. 2006-2008), .270 Win., .270 WSM (new 2004), .280 Rem. (disc. 2007), .30-06, .308 Win., .300 Win. Mag., .300 WSM (new 2003), .338 Win. Mag. (disc. 2008), 6.5x55mm, 7mm-08 Rem., 7mm WSM (mfg. 2005-2007), or 7mm Rem. Mag. cal., stainless steel action with four sizes, 20 1/4, 20 7/8, or 24 3/8 in. stainless steel free-floating fluted barrel, alloy trigger guard/mag. bottom, black synthetic stock, 4 or 5 shot detachable mag., no sights, 6 1/2 lbs. Importation began 2001.

MSR $1,650	$1,400	$1,150	$900	$800	$700	$625	$550	

Add $50 for WSM cals.

SAKO 85 HUNTER – various cals. between .22-250 - .375 H&H, 3 lug bolt, available in 5 action sizes, checkered walnut stock and forearm, 22 1/2 or 24 3/8 in. blue barrel, blue action, 4-5 shot detachable mag., short claw extractor on bolt, two-position safety, adj. trigger, guaranteed 1 MOA 5 shot groups, approx. 7 1/2 lbs., mfg. to celebrate Sako's 85th anniversary during 2006. Importation 2006-2008.

	$1,400	$1,100	$875	$775	$675	$575	$525	*$1,700*

Add $50 for .370 Sako Mag., .375 H&H, or WSM cals.

SAKO 85 CLASSIC – .25-06 Rem., .270 Win., .30-06, .308 Win. (new 2010), .300 Win. Mag., .338 Win. Mag., .370 Sako Mag. (limited mfg., disc.), .375 H&H, .270 WSM, .300 WSM, or 7mm Rem. Mag. cal., available in four action sizes, 22 7/16 or 24 3/8 in. barrel, 5 or 6 shot detachable mag., single stage trigger, pistol grip checkered walnut stock with rosewood forend and pistol grip cap., open sights, approx. 7 lbs. New 2009.

MSR $2,200	$1,925	$1,650	$1,350	$975	$875	$775	$675	

Add $50 for WSM cals.

SAKO 85 STAINLESS SYNTHETIC – similar to Sako 85 Hunter, except has black synthetic stock with overmolded grips and matte stainless steel barrel/action, FinSoft recoil reduction system. Imported 2007-2008.

	$1,275	$975	$775	$675	$575	$525	$475	*$1,575*

Add $50 for WSM cals.

SAKO 85 GREY WOLF – .270 Win., .270 WSM, .30-06, .300 Win. Mag., .300 WSM, or 7mm Rem. Mag. cal., similar to Sako 85 Stainless Synthetic, except has checkered grey laminate stock, no recoil pad. Importation began 2007.

MSR $1,600	$1,375	$1,100	$900	$800	$700	$625	$550	

Add $50 for WSM cals.

SAKO 85 VARMINT – .204 Ruger, .22-250 Rem., .223 Rem., .243 Win., or .308 Win. cal., two action sizes, 23 5/8 in. heavy blue (walnut stock, disc.) or stainless barrel w/o sights, set trigger, uncheckered walnut (disc.) or laminate stock (standard w/stainless barrel beginning 2009). Importation began 2008.

MSR $2,000	$1,750	$1,525	$1,200	$1,000	$925	$800	$700	

Subtract approx. 10% for uncheckered walnut stock (disc. 2008).

SAKO 85 BAVARIAN – .270 Win., .270 WSM, .30-06, .300 Win. Mag., .300 WSM, .308 Win., 6.5x55 Swede, 7mm-08 Rem., or 7mm Rem. Mag. cal., four action sizes, 22 7/16 or 24 3/8 in. barrel, features high grade checkered European walnut stock with Bavarian cheekpiece and rosewood pistol grip cap, open sights, set trigger, 4-6 shot detachable mag., 7-7 3/4 lbs. New 2009.

MSR $2,200	$1,950	$1,625	$1,325	$995	$875	$800	$700	

Add $50 for WSM cals.

SAKO 85 KODIAK – .338 Win. Mag. or .375 H&H cal., stainless steel action and barrel with special matte coating, long action, 21 1/4 in. barrel with band, 4 shot detachable mag., grey laminated reinforced hardwood stock with two crossbolts and checkering, adj. open sights, 8 lbs. New 2009.

MSR $1,925	$1,675	$1,300	$1,050	$925	$825	$725	$650	

SAKO A-7 – various short and medium action cals. between .22-250 Rem. - 300 Win. Mag., 22 7/16 or 24 3/8 in. hammer forged match grade barrel, adj. trigger, lightweight

GRADING - PPGS™	100%	98%	95%	90%	80%	70%	60%	LAST MSR

synthetic stock with recoil lugs, detachable top loading magazine, Weaver style scope base, two position safety. Mfg. 2009-2011.

	$825	$700	$600	$550	$500	$450	$400	*$935*

Add $45 for WSM cals.

* ***Sako A-7 Stainless*** – current cals. are .270 WSM, and .300 WSM, previously avail. in various cals. between .22-250 Rem. and .300 Win. Mag., similar to A-7, except has 24 3/8 in. stainless steel action and barrel. New 2009.

MSR $1,375	$1,200	$1,050	$875	$750	$625	$500	$400	

Subtract approx. $350 if without Tecomate finish.

Subtract approx. $50 for non-WSM cals.

RIFLES: LEVER ACTION

FINNWOLF – .243 Win. or .308 Win. cal., lever action, LV63 action, 4 shot mag. early model, 3 shot mag. later model. Mfg. 1962-1974.

	$895	$775	$550	$500	$440	$410	$375	

Add 15% for early model with 4 shot mag.

* ***Finnwolf Sako Collectors Association*** – .243 Win. or .308 Win. cal., gold lettering on left side of breech, approx. 175 mfg. in 1982.

	$2,995	$1,750	$1,050	N/A	N/A	N/A	N/A	

The 100% value on this model refers to NIB unfired condition with factory papers.

SALERI, W.R. di SALERI WILLIAM & C. snc

Current long gun manufacturer established in 1998 located in Gardone, Italy. No current U.S. importation. Previously imported by Kevin's Fine Outdoor Gear & Apparel, located in Thomasville, GA, by MacGregor Wing and Clay, located in Cary, NC, and by S.R. Lamboy, located in Victor, NY.

RIFLES AND SHOTGUNS

W.R. Saleri manufactures high quality boxlock O/U and SxS shotguns, Express SxS rifles, and single barrel shotguns and rifles. Saleri offers square frame and round body models. Please contact the company directly for more information, including pricing, delivery time, and availability (see Trademark Index).

SAMCO GLOBAL ARMS, INC.

Current importer and distributor located in Miami, FL. Dealer sales.

Samco Global Arms purchased the Charles Daly trademark in late 2012, and is currently importing a variety of Charles Daly shotgun configurations (see Charles Daly in the D section). Samco also imports Akkar shotguns from Turkey, as well as a variety of foreign and domestic surplus military rifles, including various contract Mausers, Loewe, Steyr, Czech, Lee Enfield, Mosin-Nagant, etc. Samco also imports European surplus pistols. Most of these guns offer excellent values to both shooters and collectors. Please contact the company directly for current availability and pricing, as its inventory changes weekly (see Trademark Index).

SAN SWISS ARMS AG

Current company established during late 2000, with headquarters located in Neuhausen, Switzerland.

In late 2000, SIG Arms AG, the firearms portion of SIG, was purchased by two Germans named Michael Lüke and Thomas Ortmeier, who have a background in textiles. Today the Lüke & Ortmeier group includes independently operational companies such as Blaser Jagdwaffen GmbH, Mauser Jagdwaffen GmbH, J.P. Sauer & Sohn GmbH, SIG-Sauer Inc., SIG-Sauer GmbH and SAN Swiss Arms AG. Please refer to individual listings.

SARASQUETA, FELIX

Previous manufacturer located in Eibar, Spain. Previously imported and distributed by SAE (Spain America Enterprises), Inc. located in Miami, FL.

GRADING - PPGS™	100%	98%	95%	90%	80%	70%	60%	LAST MSR

SHOTGUNS: O/U

MODEL MERKE – 12 ga. only, boxlock action, 22 or 27 in. separated barrels, single non-selective trigger, blue only, extractors, recoil pad. Imported 1986 only.

$255 $215 $200 $190 $180 $170 $160 *$291*

SAR ARMS

Sar Arms is a member of the Sar Arms International (Sarsilmaz) Firearms Group, which is one of the largest firearms manufacturers in the world. Please refer to the Sarsilmaz listing in this section.

SARASQUETA, J.J.

Previous manufacturer located in Eibar, Spain. Imported until 1984 by American Arms, Inc. located in Overland Park, KS.

SHOTGUNS: SxS

MODEL 107 E – 12, 16, or 20 ga., ejectors, various barrel lengths, checkered walnut stock and forearm, double triggers.

$360 $290 $270 $255 $240 $215 $200 *$435*

MODELS 119E-132E-1882E – more deluxe versions of Model 107E.

$470 $375 $340 $315 $285 $255 $230 *$570*

MODEL 130 E – more deluxe version of Model 119 E.

$800 $635 $590 $555 $515 $480 $450 *$960*

MODEL 131 E – action similar to Model 107 E, except has deluxe engraving.

$1,050 $845 $770 $710 $665 $620 $585 *$1,250*

MODEL 1882 E LUXE – double triggers, moderate engraving, otherwise similar to Model 107 E.

$825 $660 $615 $565 $520 $480 $450 *$990*

* ***Model 1882 E Luxe w/gold inlays*** – SST, extensive engraving.

$1,120 $920 $850 $790 $740 $695 $650 *$1,320*

* ***Model 1882 E Luxe w/silver inlays*** – SST, extensive engraving.

$1,055 $855 $795 $740 $700 $660 $630 *$1,260*

MODEL 150 E – 12 or 16 ga., single trigger, ejectors, select walnut and extensive engraving.

$1,285 $1,035 $960 $895 $835 $770 $695 *$1,500*

* ***Model 150 E Trap*** – similar to Model 150 E, except trap dimensions on stock.

$1,360 $1,125 $1,010 $940 $875 $790 $720 *$1,600*

SARASQUETA, VICTOR

Previous manufacturer located in Eibar, Spain. Trademark was sold to Diarm S.A. circa 1986.

SHOTGUNS:SxS

MODEL 3 BOXLOCK – 12, 16, or 20 ga., all standard barrel lengths and chokes, boxlock, double triggers, checkered English style stock and forearm.

Extractors $445 $395 $350 $295 $250 $215 $185

Auto ejectors $575 $515 $450 $375 $300 $250 $225

HAMMERLESS SIDELOCK – 12, 16, 20, 28 ga., or .410 bore, SxS, barrel length and choke to order, straight English style stock, models differ as to amount of engraving, grade of wood, and overall quality as follows:

Add 25% for 28 ga.

Add 30% for .410 bore.

MODEL 4 – extractors.

$995 $850 $750 $625 $550 $500 $450

GRADING - PPGS™	100%	98%	95%	90%	80%	70%	60%	LAST MSR
MODEL 4E – auto ejectors.								
	$1,350	$1,150	$875	$725	$600	$525	$475	
MODEL 203 – extractors.								
	$1,100	$925	$800	$675	$575	$525	$475	
MODEL 203E – auto ejectors.								
	$1,450	$1,225	$950	$825	$700	$600	$525	
MODEL 6E								
	$1,800	$1,500	$1,200	$995	$800	$725	$650	
MODEL 7E								
	$1,950	$1,625	$1,300	$1,100	$900	$800	$700	
MODEL 10E								
	$3,250	$2,850	$2,450	$2,150	$1,775	$1,500	$1,200	
MODEL 11E								
	$3,500	$3,125	$2,650	$2,325	$1,900	$1,575	$1,250	
MODEL 12E								
	$3,700	$3,275	$2,800	$2,450	$1,975	$1,625	$1,300	

SARCO, INC.

Current importer and wholesaler located in Stirling, NJ.

Sarco Inc. imports a wide variety of foreign and domestic surplus military style rifles and shotguns that offer excellent values for the shooter. Please contact the company directly, as inventory changes constantly (see Trademark Index).

SARDIUS

Please refer to the Sirkis Industries section in this text.

SARRIUGARTE, FRANCISO S.A.

Previous manufacturer located in Elgoibar, Spain. Previously part of the Diarm S.A. Group which was imported and distributed by American Arms, Inc. located in North Kansas City, MO.

SARSILMAZ (SAR ARMS)

Current manufacturer established during 1880, and located in Istanbul, Turkey. Pistols currently imported under private label by Armalite, Inc., located in Geneseo, IL (refer to listings in Armalite section), and by European American Armory, located in Rockledge, FL. Select slide action shotguns currently imported by US Sporting Goods Inc. located in Rockledge, FL. Previously distributed 2000-2003 by PMC, located in Boulder City, NV. Previously imported and distributed until 2000 by Armsport, Inc. located in Miami, FL.

PISTOLS: SEMI-AUTO

Sarsilmaz manufactures a wide variety of semi-auto pistols in many configurations. Current models include the K10, K12, Kilinc 2000, B6, V8, CM9, P6, P8 Series, and the ST10. These models/series are not currently imported into the U.S. Please refer to the Armalite and European American Armory sections for current importation.

Please contact Sarsilmaz directly for more information, including pricing on its line of non-imported semi-auto pistols (see Trademark Index).

SHOTGUNS

Sarsilmaz manufactures a variety of shotguns in O/U, semi-auto, and slide action configurations. Some of these models have been imported in the past in limited quantities. Currently, Sarsilmaz is manufacturing select models for US Sporting Goods Inc. (see listings here) and some models for Bernardelli.

GRADING - PPGS™	100%	98%	95%	90%	80%	70%	60%	LAST MSR

SAR SEMI-AUTO SHOTGUN/SARSA – 12, 20, or 28 ga., 3 in. chamber (12 and 20 ga.), inertia/recoil operation, dual action bars, 22, 26, or 28 in. VR barrel with Benelli style choke tubes, aluminum receiver, steel bolt, polymer stock and forearm, choice of matte black or 100% camo finish, recoil pad, various configurations, 5.5-6.1 lbs. Importation began 2011.

MSR $424	$365	$315	$285	$260	$235	$210	$190	

Add $56 for 100% camo coverage (not available in 28 ga.).

SAR SLIDE ACTION – 12, 20, or 28 (disc. late 2011) ga., 2 3/4, 3 or 3 1/2 in. (12 ga. only) chamber, dual action bars, 22, 26, or 28 in. VR barrel with Benelli style choke tube, aluminum receiver, polymer stock and forearm, choice of matte black or 100% camo coverage, various configurations, 5.7-6.2 lbs. Importation began 2011.

MSR $290	$240	$200	$175	$160	$150	$140	$130	

Add $56 for 100% camo coverage.
Add $67 for combo package with extra barrel (3 1/2 in. chamber only).

SAR SLIDE ACTION SPECIAL PURPOSE – 12 ga., 3 in. chamber, tactical configuration with black polymer pistol grip stock and extended grooved forearm, dual action bars, 18 1/2 in. fixed or screw in choke barrel with muzzle brake, aluminum receiver, optional Picatinny rail with Ghost Ring sight, 5 3/4 lbs. Importation began 2011.

MSR $346	$300	$275	$250	$230	$210	$190	$175	

Add $23 for Picatinny rail.
Subtract $67 for bead sights.

SATTERLEE ARMS, LLC

Current custom rifle manufacturer located in Deadwood, SD.

RIFLES: BOLT ACTION, CUSTOM

Stuart Satterlee builds a series of bolt action custom rifles utilizing a Mauser style action. Series include: North American, Ultimate Mountain Rifle, British Express Rifle, and the African. Please contact him directly for more information, including available options, pricing, and delivery time (see Trademark Index).

SAUER, J.P., & SOHN

Current manufacturer located in Eckernförde, Germany since 1751 (originally Prussia). Currently imported by Sauer USA, located in San Antonio, TX. Previously manufactured in Suhl pre-WWII. Previously imported and warehoused 1995-2007 by SIG Arms, located in Exeter, NH. Rifles were previously imported until 1995 by the Paul Company Inc. located in Wellsville, KS and until 1994 by G.U., Inc. located in Omaha, NE.

In 1972, J.P. Sauer & Sohn entered into a cooperative agreement with SIG. During 2000, SAN Swiss Arms AG purchased SIG Arms AG, including the J.P. Sauer & Sohn trademark. Production remains in Eckernförde, Germany.

DRILLINGS & COMBINATION GUNS

COMBO BBF 54 O/U – standard grade combination gun, 16 ga./.222 Rem., .243 Win., 6.5x57R, 7x57R, 7x65R, or .30-06 cals., ejectors, double triggers with front set trigger, moderate engraving on coin finished receiver, Greener crossbolt with double barrel lugs, 6 lbs. Importation disc. 1986.

	$2,200	$2,060	$1,760	$1,565	$1,380	$1,250	$1,125	*$2,495*

* ***Combo BBF 54 O/U Luxury Grade*** – similar to Combo BBF 54, except game scene engraved and deluxe crotch walnut.

	$2,450	$2,200	$2,000	$1,785	$1,600	$1,475	$1,300	*$2,745*

SAUER COMBINATION GUN – 20 ga. over 7x57R, 7x65R, 8x57IRS, or 9.3x74R cal., double underlug, Greener crossbolt, 23.6 in. barrels, express sight, brass foresight bead, gold DT, silver nitride receiver with game scene and fine arabesque scroll engraving, best quality checkered walnut stock and forearm with German cheekpiece, silver pistol grip cap. New 2012.

This model has a current MSR of $67,461.

This model is also available with larger sideplates and interchangeable barrels - please contact the importer for information and pricing (see Trademark Index).

GRADING - PPGS™	100%	98%	95%	90%	80%	70%	60%	LAST MSR

SAUER MODEL 3000 DRILLING – available in either 16 ga./.30-06, 6.5x57R, 7x57R, 7x65R, or 12 ga./.222 Rem. (disc.), .243 Win., .30-06, 6.5x57R, 7x57R, 7x65R, or 9.3x74R cal., Greener crossbolt and double barrel lug locking, cocking indicators, front set trigger, automatic safety, walnut pistol grip stock with hog-back and cheekpiece, Grade III scroll engraving, 7 1/4 lbs. Importation disc. 1999.

	$4,300	$3,600	$3,100	$2,675	$2,200	$1,800	$1,400	*$4,600*

This model was also previously imported by Weatherby and Colt - please refer to separate listings for more information.

* ***Sauer Model 3000 Drilling Luxury Grade*** – similar to Model 3000 standard, except select root timber and extensive engraving featuring two animals. Importation disc. 1999.

	$5,550	$4,875	$4,400	$3,875	$3,475	$3,000	$2,575	*$6,100*

LUFTWAFFE M30 SURVIVAL DRILLING – 12 or 16 ga. (65mm) SxS over 9.3x74R, 28 in. barrels, large eagle and swastika on stock and breech end of right barrel. Originally mfg. for Luftwaffe pilots during WWII. approx. 2,450 mfg. 1941-1942.

	$20,000	$17,500	$15,000	$13,000	$11,000	$8,000	$7,000	

Subtract 40% if w/o original aluminum case or accessories.

SAUER MODEL 3000E DRILLING – see listing under Colt Sauer Drilling.

PISTOLS: SEMI-AUTO

MODEL 1913 POCKET AUTOMATIC – .32 ACP cal., 7 shot, 3 in. barrel, fixed sights, blue, black rubber grips. Mfg. 1913-30.

	$295	$225	$185	$165	$155	$145	$135	

MODEL 1913 25 AUTOMATIC – .25 ACP cal., 7 shot, 2 1/2 in. barrel, fixed sights, blue, black rubber grips. Mfg. 1913-30.

	$350	$300	$250	$200	$175	$150	$135	

MODEL 28 – .25 ACP cal., 7 shot, 3 in. barrel, fixed sights, blue, black rubber grips. Mfg. 1930-38.

	$325	$285	$250	$200	$175	$150	$135	

BEHÖRDEN "AUTHORITY" M1930 MODEL – .32 ACP cal., 3 in. barrel, blue, black lacquer, or white, black plastic grips.

	$450	$350	$275	$225	$175	$150	$135	

Very rare alloy frame and slide examples can sell in the $3,500-$5,500.

MODEL 38 H DOUBLE ACTION AUTOMATIC – .22 LR (extremely rare), .32 ACP, or .380 ACP (rare) cal., 3 1/4 in. barrel, fixed sights, blue, plastic grips. Mfg. 1938-45.

.32 ACP cal.	$600	$450	$375	$325	$275	$250	$225	

Add 100% for early high polish guns.
Add 10% for Waffenamt proofing.
Add 15%-25% for police markings.
Add 60% for alloy frame.
Rarity precludes accurate pricing on the .22 LR and .380 ACP cal. models, but it is estimated these can sell in the $2,500-$7,500 range.

REVOLVERS: SA/DA

Sauer manufactured .38 cal. double action revolvers circa 1960-1985, and also licensed other manufacturers, including Armi San Paolo. Most had blue finish and walnut grips. Current values range from $150-$295, depending on condition.

RIFLES: BOLT ACTION

Add $1,081-$2,156 per interchangeable barrel depending on rifle configuration on the following models where applicable.
Add $631-$677 per spare bolt, depending on rifle configuration.
Add $683 for left-hand.
Add $1,763 for Model 202 conversion kit or $1,917-$2,776 for Model 202 takedown conversion kit, depending on caliber.

GRADING - PPGS™	100%	98%	95%	90%	80%	70%	60%	LAST MSR

SAUER PRE-WWII BOLT ACTION RIFLE – most popular European cals. and .30 - 06, 22 or 24 in. barrel, raised solid rib, Krupp steel, double-set triggers, folding 3 leaf express sight, checkered sporter stock. Mfg. pre-WWII.

	$1,395	$1,250	$1,050	$875	$750	$625	$550	

MODEL 90 STANDARD – .22-250 Rem., .222 Rem. (only 3 mfg.), .243 Win., .25-06 Rem., 6.5x55mm, .270 Win., .30-06, .308 Win. (late mfg.), .300 Win. Mag., .300 Wby. Mag., 7mm Rem. Mag., .375 H&H, or .458 Win. Mag. cal., 24 in. barrel, 3 or 4 shot detachable mag., satin, oil finished checkered walnut stock with Monte Carlo cheekpiece and rosewood forend cap, 2 stage set trigger, free floated barrel, approx. 7 1/2 lbs. Importation disc.

	$1,000	$875	$750	$625	$550	$500	$450	*$1,175*

Early importation rifles came standard with a half stock and barrel band, and also had European sling swivels with milled stops. In 1989, this model's design changed to look more like the Colt Sauer rifle (w/o sights, gloss finished stock and set trigger was removed). During 1985-1989, Sauer exported to Sigarms 2,300 Model 90 rifles, 1,100 of these were in Mag. cals.

* ***Model 90 Standard Stutzen*** – .22-250 Rem., .222 Rem. (3 mfg.), or .243 Win., Mannlicher style full stock, not available in European or Mag. cals. Importation disc. 1989.

	$1,200	$995	$850	$750	$650	$475	$500	*$1,225*

* ***Model 90 Standard Safari*** – .458 Win. Mag cal., 23.62 in. barrel, 10 1/2 lbs. Imported 1986-88 only.

	$1,250	$950	$850	$750	$650	$575	$500	*$1,675*

MODEL 90 SUPREME (LUX) – .243 Win., .25-06 Rem., 6.5x55 Swedish, .270 Win., .30 - 06, .300 Win. Mag., .300 Wby. Mag., 7mm Rem. Mag., .338 Win. Mag., or .375 H&H cal., similar to Model 90, satin finished deluxe stock with Monte Carlo cheekpiece and rosewood forearm and pistol grip caps, gold trigger, no sights, 7.1-7.7 lbs. Importation 1987-98.

	$1,995	$1,750	$1,500	$1,300	$1,050	$875	$775	*$1,350*

Add approx. 60% for Grade I engraving, 100% for Grade II, 125% for Grade III, and 160% for Grade IV.

* ***Model 90 Supreme (Lux) Safari***

While advertised, this model had limited importation. MSR was set at $1,795.

* ***Model 90 Supreme (Lux) Stutzen***

While advertised, this model had little importation. MSR was set at $1,200.

MODEL 200 BOLT ACTION – available in 15 cals. between .243 Win. and .375 H&H, short and medium actions only, 23.62 in. unique interchangeable barrels, 6 lug bolt, easily detachable stock and forearm, optional set trigger, detachable mag. with hidden release button, 7.7 lbs. Production disc. 1993.

	$1,225	$925	$800	$700	$600	$525	$450	*$1,395*

Add $100 for 7mm Rem. Mag. or .300 Win. Mag. cal.
Add $300 for extra interchangeable barrel.

During 1986-89, Sauer exported to Sigarms 4,170 Model 200 rifles, 1,370 of these were in Mag. cals.

* ***Model 200 Bolt Action Lightweight*** – similar to Model 200, only with alloy receiver, 6.6 lbs.

	$1,225	$925	$800	$700	$600	$525	$450	*$1,395*

Add $150 for left-hand version.

* ***Model 200 Bolt Action Lux*** – similar to Model 200, except has deluxe walnut, rosewood forend tip and pistol grip cap, marmorized bolt and gold trigger.

	$1,395	$1,175	$925	$800	$700	$600	$525	*$1,595*

* ***Model 200 Bolt Action Lux American*** – similar to Model 200 Lux, except has high gloss Monte Carlo stock, 24 in. barrel, jeweled bolt, and gold trigger.

	$1,395	$1,175	$925	$800	$700	$600	$525	*$1,595*

Add $150 for left-hand version.

GRADING - PPGS™	100%	98%	95%	90%	80%	70%	60%	LAST MSR

* ***Model 200 Bolt Action Lux European*** – similar to Model 200 Lux, except has European configured stock with Schnabel forearm, 26 in. barrel.

	$1,395	$1,175	$925	$800	$700	$600	$525	*$1,595*

Add $95 for left-hand version.

* ***Model 200 Bolt Action Carbon Fiber*** – similar to Model 200, except has carbon fiber stock. Imported 1987-88 only.

	$800	$700	$625	$565	$500	$465	$430	*$1,200*

MODEL 202 SUPREME (LUX) – .22-250 Rem. (new 2001), .243 Win. (disc. 1998, resumed 2000), .25-06 Rem., .270 Win., .30-06, .308 Win., 6.5x55mm Swedish (disc. 2000), or 7x64mm (disc. 1997) cal., steel receiver, modular design allowing barrel change within 2 minutes, dual safety, 2 piece figured walnut stock, cocking indicator, detachable 3-5 shot mag., takedown with interchangeable barrels, right or left-hand action, 7 1/2 lbs. Imported 1994-2004.

	$2,500	$2,250	$2,000	$1,750	$1,500	$1,300	$1,050	*$3,400*

Add $300 for left-hand action (.30-06 cal. only).
Add $900 per extra barrel in non-Mag. cals.
Also available in left-hand action in .270 Win. (disc. 2000) or .30-06 cal.

* ***Model 202 Supreme (Lux) Magnum*** – .300 Win. Mag., .300 Wby. Mag., .338 Win. Mag. (disc. 1997), .375 H&H, 7mm Rem. Mag., 6.5x68mm (importation disc. 1997), or 8x68mm (importation disc. 1997) cal., converts to 7 cals., 7.7 lbs. Imported 1994-2004.

	$2,750	$2,350	$2,100	$1,800	$1,550	$1,350	$1,150	*$3,600*

Add $200 for .375 H&H cal.
Was also available until 2000 in left-hand action in .300 Win. Mag. or 7mm Rem. Mag. cal.

MODEL 202 CLASSIC – various cals., choice of aluminum or steel receiver, Classic styling with Monte Carlo walnut checkered Grade 2 stock and forearm with ebony forend tip, iron sights on barrel, includes sling swivels, round bolt handle, right or left hand action, 2-3 shot mag., black Ilaflon metal finish. New 2012.

MSR $3,509	$3,200	$2,850	$2,400	$2,000	$1,750	$1,500	$1,250	

MODEL 202 CLASSIC XT (STANDARD) – similar to Model 202 Synthetic, except has checkered walnut stock and forearm, 7.7 lbs. Importation began 2001.

MSR $2,995	$2,695	$2,350	$2,100	$1,450	$1,050	$900	$775	

MODEL 202 ELEGANCE – various cals., features Grade 4 walnut Monte Carlo stock with ebony forend tip and pistol grip cap, jeweled bolt, swept back bolt handle, detachable mag., 23 1/2 or 25 1/2 in. barrel with iron sights.

MSR $4,495	$4,050	$3,500	$3,050	$2,600	$2,400	$2,000	$1,500	

MODEL 202 SYNTHETIC – .22-250 Rem. (new 2001), .243 Win. (new 2001), .25-06 Rem., .270 Win., .30-06, .308 Win., .300 Win. Mag., 7mm Rem. Mag. (new 2000), .300 Wby. Mag., .375 H&H (disc. 2005), or 6.5x55mm Swedish (disc. 2000) cal., features black synthetic stock, 24 or 26 in. barrel w/o sights, 7.7 lbs. Imported 1999-2008.

	$1,750	$1,200	$995	$875	$750	$675	$600	

Add $200 for Mag. cals., $400 for .375 H&H cal.
Add $900 for interchangeable standard cal. barrel, or $1,000 for Mag. cal. barrel.

MODEL 202 OUTBACK – various cals., 22 in. black Ilaflon fluted barrel, 3 shot mag., aluminum receiver, flat bolt handle, set trigger, steel front sight, synthetic Monte Carlo stock with Soft Touch, synthetic mag. floorplate, drilled and tapped, 6.4 lbs. New 2009.

MSR $3,719	$3,325	$2,850	$2,100	$1,825	$1,600	$1,400	$1,225	

MODEL 202 HARDWOOD – 9.3x62mm, 8x57IS, or .308 Win. cal., similar to Model 202 Outback, except has shorter 18.1 in. barrel, 5 shot detachable box mag., sling swivels, black or Realtree AP HD Blaze camo synthetic stock, not available in left hand. New late 2011.

MSR $4,029	$3,600	$3,175	$2,675	$2,100	$1,750	$1,495	$1,325	

GRADING - PPGS™	100%	98%	95%	90%	80%	70%	60%	LAST MSR

MODEL 202 YUKON – various cals., 20 or 22 in. black Ilaflon fluted barrel, 3 shot mag., steel receiver, round bolt handle, set trigger, synthetic Realtree AP HD camo Monte Carlo stock with Soft Touch, drilled and tapped. New 2009.

MSR $3,772	$3,325	$2,850	$2,325	$1,825	$1,600	$1,400	$1,225	

MODEL 202 POLAR – various cals., 20 or 22 in. silver Ilaflon fluted barrel, 3 shot mag., steel receiver, round bolt handle, set trigger, synthetic Realtree AP HD Snow camo Monte Carlo stock with Soft Touch, drilled and tapped. New 2009.

MSR $3,772	$3,325	$2,850	$2,325	$1,825	$1,600	$1,400	$1,225	

MODEL 202 LIGHTWEIGHT – .22-250 Rem., .243 Win., .25-06 Rem., .270 Win., .30-06, .308 Win., and various metric cals., 24 in. fluted barrel w/o sights, aluminum alloy receiver with integral Weaver rail, Ilaflon (disc.) or Teflon coated metal, black synthetic stock, 6 1/2 lbs. Imported 2001-2008.

	$2,600	$1,500	$1,225	$975	$800	$700	$600	

MODEL 202 VARMINTER – .22-250 Rem., .243 Win., or .25-06 Rem. cal., 24 in. match grade fluted bull barrel with no sights, 3 shot mag., matte black finish, adj. cheekpiece on checkered Turkish walnut stock, 9 1/2 lbs. Imported 2001-2005.

	$2,950	$1,500	$1,225	$975	$800	$700	$600	*$3,400*

MODEL 202 FOREST – .270 Win., 7x64, .308 Win., .30-06, 8x57, or 9.3x62 cal., 20 in. black Ilaflon barrel, 4 shot mag., aluminum receiver, round bolt handle, set trigger, forest sights, Grade 3 walnut stock and forend with cheekpiece, synthetic mag. floorplate, drilled and tapped. New 2009.

MSR $3,979	$3,625	$3,225	$2,675	$2,250	$1,825	$1,500	$1,250	

MODEL 202 HIGHLAND – various cals., 20 in. black Ilaflon fluted barrel, 3 shot mag., aluminum receiver, round bolt handle, set trigger, steel front sight, Grade 3 Monte Carlo walnut stock and Schnabel forend with cheekpiece, synthetic mag. floorplate, drilled and tapped. New 2009.

MSR $3,979	$3,625	$3,225	$2,675	$2,250	$1,825	$1,500	$1,250	

MODEL 202 STUTZEN – various cals., steel or lightweight alloy receiver, full length Grade III checkered walnut Mannlicher stock and forearm, swept back bolt handle. New 2012.

MSR $4,641	$4,100	$3,600	$3,150	$2,650	$2,150	$1,850	$1,550	

MODEL 202 SUPER GRADE

While advertised in 1994, this model was never imported. MSR was set at $1,020.

MODEL 202 HUNTER MATCH

While advertised in 1994, this model was never imported. MSR was set at $1,495.

MODEL 202 ALASKA

While advertised in 1994, this model was never imported. MSR was set at $1,335.

MODEL 202 TAKEDOWN SERIES – available in many standard and Mag. cals., 2 or 4 shot mag., takedown action allows disassembly within seconds, point of impact remains constant, open sights on .375 H&H Mag. cal., 6 bolts connect forend with action, and can be detached by pressing a button, deluxe checkered walnut (Grade 4 standard beginning 2010), round or flat bolt handle, approx. 8.8 lbs. Importation began 2003.

MSR $6,333	$5,850	$5,100	$4,450	$3,750	$3,150	$2,775	$2,125	

Add $380 for Forest model with Grade III walnut.

Add $1,258 for Elegance model with Grade IV walnut.

* ***Model 202 Takedown Hatari*** – .375 H&H, .416 Rem. Mag., or .458 Lott cal., 23.6 in. barrel with express sights with H&H style fold down front sight, blued steel receiver, Ilaflon coated metal parts, large forend, four different wood choices (Grades 3-6), 3 shot mag.

MSR $8,488	$7,825	$7,100	$6,500	$5,700	$4,900	$4,000	$3,000	

Add $268 for Grade 4 wood, $705 for Grade 5, and $1,436 for Grade 6 wood.

GRADING - PPGS™	100%	98%	95%	90%	80%	70%	60%	LAST MSR

MODEL 205 TR TARGET – 6.5x55mm or .308 Win. cal., true left-hand variation, 200 meter diopter sights, modular design allows changing single components including caliber, free floating barrel with vent. forearm, 5 shot mag., interchangeable barrel systems, 12.1 lbs. Imported 1994-97.

	$1,775	$1,575	$1,400	$1,250	$1,100	$950	$825	$1,900

SSE 3000 PRECISION RIFLE – .308 Win. cal., very accurate, law enforcement counter Sniper Rifle, built to customer specifications.

	$4,845	$3,655	$3,200	$2,850	$2,500	$2,275	$2,000	

SSG 2000 – available in .223 Rem., 7.5mm Swiss, .300 Wby. Mag., or .308 Win. (standard) cal., bolt action, 4 shot mag., no sights, deluxe sniper rifle featuring thumbhole style walnut stock with stippling and thumbwheel adj. cheekpiece, 13 lbs. Importation disc. 1986.

	$2,480	$2,260	$1,950	$1,700	$1,500	$1,300	$1,100	$2,850

This model was available in .223 Rem., .300 Wby. Mag., or 7.5mm cal. by special order only.

SSG 3000 – .223 Rem., 22 1/2 in. barrel, Parker-Hale bipod, 2-stage match trigger, includes 2 1/2-10x52mm Zeiss scope, 200 mfg. for Swiss police.

	$12,000	$10,000	$8,500	$7,000	$6,750	$5,500	$4,250	

SSG 3000 (CURRENT MFG.) – See listing under Sig-Sauer.

RIFLES: SEMI-AUTO

MODEL 303 – .30-06, .300 Win. Mag., 7x64, 8x57, or 9.3x62mm cal., gas operated, 2 shot mag., 20 or 22 in. interchangeable barrel, Classic XT black synthetic stock standard with various walnut stock upgrades including thumbhole (GTI Classic or GTI Elegance), noiseless cocking and decocking lever on back of receiver, Nitrobond metal finish, open sights with HiViz front and rear Battue rib optional, Elegance model has polished jewelled bolt, approx. 7 1/8 lbs. New 2010.

MSR $3,352	$3,000	$2,600	$2,200	$1,850	$1,575	$1,275	$1,100	

Add $483 for Classic Grade II walnut or $1,400 for Elegance Grade IV walnut stock and forearm.
Add $1,700 for Grade II walnut on GTI Classic with thumbhole stock (new 2012), or $2,988 for Grade IV walnut on GTI Elegance model with thumbhole stock (new 2012).

RIFLES: SxS

SAUER DOUBLE RIFLE – 7x57R or 9.3x74 cal., best quality walnut stock and forearm, forged steel receiver with game animals, hunting scenes and arabesque scroll engraving. New 2012.

This model has a current MSR of $67,461.

SHOTGUNS

MEISTERWERK SxS – sidelock, best quality checkered walnut stock and forearm, DT, alloy receiver with traditional pre-war English arabesque engraving standard, other engraving options available. New 2011.

The model has a current MSR of $84,327.

MODEL IX SxS – 20 ga., boxlock, 28 in. barrels with quarter and half choke, forged steel color case hardened or silver nitride receiver with light arabesque scroll engraving and scalloped borders, double underlug, Greener action, H&H style ejectors, gold DT, straight grip English style Grade 7 hand checkered walnut stock and forearm, recoil pad. New 2011.

This model has a current MSR of $45,536.

MODEL 60 SxS – various gauges, boxlock action, DT, extractors, checkered walnut stock and forearm, this model was the standard model of its period.

	$975	$875	$750	$650	$550	$450	$395	

Add 20% for 20 ga.

ROYAL MODEL SxS – 12, 16 or 20 ga., 26, 28, or 30 in. barrels, various chokes, boxlock, scalloped engraved frame, cocking indicators, SST, auto ejectors, Krupp steel barrel, checkered pistol grip stock. Mfg. 1955-77.

	$1,650	$1,375	$1,210	$1,100	$880	$770	$660	

Add 20% for 20 ga.

GRADING - PPGS™	100%	98%	95%	90%	80%	70%	60%	LAST MSR

ARTEMIS SxS – 12 ga., 28 in. barrels, mod. and full choke, H&H type sidelock, SST, auto ejector, Krupp steel, checkered pistol grip stock. Mfg. 1966-77.

* ***Artemis SxS Grade I*** – fine line engraved.

	$5,500	$4,620	$3,850	$3,520	$3,080	$2,640	$2,200	

* ***Artemis SxS Grade II*** – extensive engraving.

	$6,600	$5,500	$4,840	$4,235	$3,850	$3,300	$3,080	

GRADE 380 SxS

	$4,500	$4,000	$3,500	$3,000	$2,500	$2,200	$1,500	

GRADE F-40 SxS

Rarity factor precludes accurate price evaluation.

MODEL F-45 SxS

	$12,000	$10,500	$9,000	$8,000	$6,500	$5,000	$3,200	

MODEL F-60 SxS

	$23,000	$20,000	$17,000	$14,000	$12,000	$9,000	$5,000	

MODEL 66 O/U FIELD GUN – 12 ga., 28 in. mod. and full, Krupp steel barrels, H&H type sidelocks, SST, auto ejectors, checkered pistol grip stock, available in three grades of engraving. Mfg. 1966-75.

Grade I	$2,200	$1,760	$1,540	$1,320	$1,100	$880	$770	
Grade II	$3,080	$2,420	$1,980	$1,650	$1,430	$1,210	$990	
Grade III	$3,850	$3,300	$2,860	$2,420	$1,980	$1,650	$1,320	

MODEL 66 O/U SKEET GUN – similar to Field Gun, with 26 in. VR skeet bored barrel and vent. forearm. Mfg. 1966-1975.

	$2,300	$1,800	$1,600	$1,400	$1,150	$925	$775	

MODEL 66 O/U TRAP GUN – similar to 66 Skeet, with 30 in. barrels, full and full, or mod. and full choke, trap style stock.

Grade I	$2,090	$1,760	$1,540	$1,320	$1,100	$880	$770	
Grade II	$3,080	$2,420	$1,980	$1,650	$1,430	$1,210	$880	
Grade III	$3,850	$3,300	$2,860	$2,420	$1,980	$1,650	$1,320	

SAUER/FRANCHI STANDARD GRADE O/U – 12 ga. only, double triggers, checkered walnut stock and forearm, SST, blue finish only, sling swivels, VR. Importation disc. 1986.

	$375	$340	$315	$290	$275	$260	$245	*$785*

* ***Sauer/Franchi Standard Regent Grade O/U*** – similar to Standard grade, except has single trigger and lightly engraved silver finished receiver. Importation disc. 1986.

	$475	$395	$350	$310	$290	$275	$265	*$825*

* ***Sauer/Franchi Standard Favorit Grade O/U*** – similar to Regent Grade, except has elaborate scroll engraving on coin finished receiver, gold-plated trigger. Importation disc. 1986.

	$550	$495	$450	$420	$385	$350	$300	*$875*

* ***Sauer/Franchi Standard Diplomat Grade O/U*** – similar to Favorit Grade, except has more elaborate scroll engraving and with model name gold filled on receiver sides and barrel, extra grain French walnut, cased.

	$875	$750	$625	$550	$495	$460	$435	*$1,520*

SAUER/FRANCHI SPORTING S O/U – 12 ga. only, 28 in. barrels, ejectors, SST, select European walnut with checkered stock and forearm, 10mm VR, plain silver finished receiver with model name gold filled on both sides. Importation disc. 1986.

	$800	$700	$600	$500	$450	$420	$395	*$1,375*

SAUER/FRANCHI MODEL TRAP O/U – similar to Sporting S, except has 29 in. barrels, trap chokes and stock dimensions. Importation disc. 1986.

	$875	$750	$625	$550	$495	$460	$435	*$1,375*

GRADING - PPGS™	100%	98%	95%	90%	80%	70%	60%	LAST MSR

SAUER/FRANCHI MODEL SKEET O/U - similar to Sporting S, except has skeet chokes. Importation disc. 1986.

	$875	$750	$625	$550	$495	$460	$435	*$1,375*

SAVAGE ARMS, INC.

Current manufacturer located in Westfield, MA since 1959, with sales offices located in Suffield, CT. Previously manufactured in Utica, NY - later manufacture was in Chicopee Falls, MA. Dealer and distributor sales.

This company originally started in Utica, NY in 1894. The Model 1895 was initially manufactured by Marlin between 1895-1899. After WWI, the name was again changed to the Savage Arms Corporation. Savage moved to Chicopee Falls, MA circa 1946 (to its Stevens Arms Co. plants). In the mid-1960s the company became The Savage Arms Division of American Hardware Corp., which later became The Emhart Corporation. This division was sold in September 1981, and became Savage Industries, Inc. located in Westfield, MA (since the move in 1960). On November 1, 1989, Savage Arms Inc. acquired the majority of assets of Savage Industries, Inc.

Savage Arms, Inc. will offer service and parts on their current line of firearms only (those manufactured after Nov. 1, 1995). These models include the 24, 99, and 110 plus the imported Model 312. Warranty and repair claims for products not acquired by Savage Arms, Inc. will remain the responsibility of Savage Industries, Inc. For information regarding the repair and/or parts of Savage Industries, Inc. firearms, please refer to the Trademark Index in the back of this text. Parts for pre-1989 Savage Industries, Inc. firearms may be obtained by contacting the Numrich Gun Parts Corporation located in West Hurley, NY (listed in Trademark Index). Savage Arms, Inc. has older records/info. on pistols, the Model 24, older mfg. Model 99s, and Model 110 only. A factory letter authenticating the configuration of a particular specimen may be obtained by contacting Mr. John Callahan (see Trademark Index for listings and address). The charge for this service is $30.00 per gun, and $25.00 per gun for Models 1895, 1899, and 99 rifles. Please allow 8 weeks for an adequate response.

For more Savage model information, please refer to the Serialization section in the back of this text.

Please refer to the *Blue Book of Modern Black Powder Arms* by John Allen (also online) for more information and prices on Savage's lineup of modern black powder models. For more information and current pricing on both new and used Savage airguns, please refer to the *Blue Book of Airguns* by Dr. Robert Beeman & John Allen (also online).

Black Powder Long Arms and Pistols - Reproductions & Replicas by Dennis Adler is also an invaluable source for most black powder reproductions and replicas, and includes hundreds of color images on most popular makes/models, provides manufacturer/trademark histories, and up-to-date information on related items/accessories for black powder shooting - www.bluebookofgunvalues.com

COMBINATION GUNS

All Model 24s are under the domain of Savage Arms, Inc.

Add 20% for .22 Mag. cal. on models listed below, where applicable.

MODEL 24 O/U - .22 LR over .410 bore, open rifle sight, visible hammer, break open, plain pistol grip stock. Mfg. 1950-65.

	$525	$475	$425	$375	$335	$260	$225	

This model featured top lever opening, except on the Models 24S and 24MS.

MODEL 24B-DL - .22 LR or .22 WMR cal. over .410 bore.

	$500	$450	$375	$325	$265	$215	$165	

MODEL 24P - .22 LR over 20 ga. or .410 bore.

	$450	$375	$325	$265	$215	$165	$135	

GRADING - PPGS™	100%	98%	95%	90%	80%	70%	60%	*LAST MSR*

MODEL 24S – .22 LR cal. over 20 ga. or .410 bore barrel, similar to Model 24, side lever, dovetail for scope. Mfg. 1964-1971.

$395 $350 $315 $275 $250 $225 $190

MODEL 24MS – similar to Model 24S, with .22 WMR cal. barrel. Mfg. 1964-71.

$600 $550 $450 $400 $350 $275 $225

MODEL 24DL – .22 LR cal. over 20 ga. or .410 bore barrel, similar to Model 24S, with top lever, satin chrome frame and checkered stock. Mfg. 1962-69.

$395 $350 $315 $275 $250 $225 $190

MODEL 24MDL – similar to Model 24DL, with .22 WMR cal. barrel and chrome frame. Mfg. 1962-69.

$495 $450 $400 $350 $275 $225 $185

MODEL 24FG – similar to Model 24DL, w/o Monte Carlo stock, with top lever. Mfg. 1972-disc.

$450 $395 $325 $275 $230 $210 $180

Action was changed to under lever opening in front of trigger guard circa 1980.

MODEL 24 FIELD – .22 LR or .22 WMR over 20 ga. or .410 bore, under lever opening in front of trigger guard introduced circa 1980, lightweight field version, 24 in. separated barrels, 3 in. chambers, 6 3/4 lbs. Disc. 1989.

$395 $350 $315 $275 $250 $225 $190 ***$209***

MODEL 24F (PREDATOR) – choice of .17 HMR (new 2004), .22 Hornet, .222 Rem. (disc. 1989), .223 Rem., or .30-30 Win. (12 ga. only) cal., over 12, 20 ga., or .410 bore (mfg. 1998-2000), 3 in. chamber, 24 in. barrels, 12 ga. barrel is available either with fixed choke or choke tube, wood (disc.) or matte black Dupont Rynite synthetic stock, hammer block safety, DTs, approx. 8 lbs. Mfg. 1989-2007.

$585 $450 $345 $290 $235 $200 $180 ***$698***

Add $31 for 12 ga.
Add $55 for .410 bore adaptor (12 ga. only, disc. 2000).
Add $14 for Camo Rynite stock (disc., Model 24F-T, Turkey Model-12 ga./.22 Hornet or .223 Rem. cal. only).

MODEL 24V – similar to Model 24, in .22 Hornet (disc. 1984), .222 Rem. (new 1967), .223 Rem., .30-30 Win., .357 Max., or .357 Mag.(disc.), 20 ga., 3 in. chamber, 24 in. barrels, single trigger, 7 lbs. Mfg. 1967-1989.

$495 $425 $375 $325 $275 $250 $225

Action was changed to under lever opening in front of trigger guard circa 1980.

MODEL 24D – .22 LR or .22 WMR over .410 bore or 20 ga., black or case hardened frame, game scene decoration was eliminated in 1974, forearm not checkered after 1976. Introduced 1971.

$475 $425 $340 $275 $230 $210 $180

Action was changed to under lever opening in front of trigger guard circa 1980.

MODEL 24E – .22 LR cal. over .410 bore, case colored frame, wood stock and forearm. Disc.

$450 $395 $325 $275 $230 $210 $180

MODEL 24C CAMPER'S COMPANION – .22 LR over 20 ga., 20 in. barrel cylinder bore, buttplate opens to store ten .22 LR cartridges and one 20 ga. shell in buttstock, nickel finish, carrying case, 5 3/4 lbs. Mfg. 1972-88.

$675 $625 $575 $525 $450 $400 $325 ***$239***

Add 10% for nickel finish (Model 24CS - shipped with pistol grip stock also).

Action was changed to under lever opening in front of trigger guard circa 1980.

MODEL 24 VS – similar to Model 24CS, only .357 Mag. over 20 ga., nickel finish, accessory pistol grip stock is included.

$595 $550 $475 $400 $350 $275 $225

GRADING - PPGS™	100%	98%	95%	90%	80%	70%	60%	LAST MSR

MODEL 389 – 12 ga. with 3 in. chamber over choice of .308 Win. or .222 Rem., choke tubes standard, hammerless, double triggers, checkered walnut stock and forearm with recoil pad. Mfg. 1988-90 only.

	$850	$775	$675	$550	$450	$375	$325	*$919*

MODEL 42 – .22 LR or .22 WMR cal. over .410 bore, 3 in. chamber, 20 in. separated barrels with open sights, black synthetic stock with recoil pad and forearm with red accents, sling swivels, opening lever in front of trigger guard, 6.1 lbs. New 2013.

MSR $480	$415	$365	$335	$300	$275	$250	$225	

MODEL 2400 O/U – 12 ga. full choke barrel over .222 Rem. or .308 Win. rifle barrel, 23 1/2 in. barrels, folding leaf sight, solid rib, dovetailed for scope mount, checkered Monte Carlo stock. Mfg. by Valmet 1975-1980.

	$695	$625	$575	$525	$495	$440	$415	

PISTOLS: BOLT ACTION

MODEL 501F SPORT STRIKER – .22 LR cal., left-hand bolt, right side ejection, 10 in. button rifled barrel with scope blocks, 10 shot mag., grey fiberglass/graphite composite stock, 4 lbs. Mfg. 2000-2005.

	$235	$200	$180	$165	$145	$130	$125	*$245*

Add $46 for XP package (Model 501FXP, includes scope and mounts).

MODEL 502F SPORT STRIKER – similar to Model 501F Sport Striker, except is .22 WMR cal., and 5 shot mag. Mfg. 2000-2005.

	$295	$260	$220	$195	$180	$160	$140	*$269*

MODEL 503F SPORT STRIKER – similar to Model 501F Sport Striker, except available in .17 HMR cal., 4 lbs. Mfg. 2003-2005.

	$295	$260	$225	$185	$165	$155	$140	*$295*

* ***Model 503FSS Sport Striker*** – similar to Model 503F Sport Striker, except is stainless steel. Mfg. 2003-2004.

	$325	$285	$240	$200	$150	$125	$110	*$335*

MODEL 510F STRIKER CENTERFIRE – .22-250 Rem. (disc. 2002), .223 Rem. (new 1999), .243 Win., .260 Rem. (mfg. 1999-2000), .308 Win., or 7mm 08 Rem. cal., left-hand short bolt action with right-hand ejection, 14 in. free floating unported barrel, 2 shot internal box mag., blue barrel action, black composite stock with grooved forend and wide bottom swell, drilled and tapped, 5 lbs. Mfg. 1998-2003.

	$475	$425	$360	$325	$295	$275	$250	*$469*

MODEL 516FSS STRIKER – similar to 510F Striker, except has stainless steel barreled action. Mfg. 1998-2000.

	$495	$450	$375	$335	$300	$280	$260	*$462*

* ***Model 516FSAK Striker*** – .243 Win., .270 WSM (mfg. 2003-2004), .300 WSM (new 2003), .308 Win., 7mm WSM (disc. 2004), or 7mm-08 Rem. cal., similar to 516FSS Striker, except has adj. muzzle brake (AMB), 14 in. ported barrel. Mfg. 1998-2005.

	$650	$575	$500	$450	$400	$350	$300	*$621*

* ***Model 516FSAK Striker Camo*** – .300 WSM cal., similar to 516FSAK Striker, except has camo treatment stock. Mfg. 2002 only.

	$650	$575	$500	$450	$400	$350	$300	*$538*

MODEL 516BSAK/BSS SUPER STRIKER – similar cals. to Model 510F Striker, features dual pillar bedded short action and custom designed thumbhole laminate grey stock, stainless steel frame and fluted 14 in. barrel with adj. muzzle brake (AMB), new ESP (Engineered Step Performance) adj. two-stage trigger, approx. 5 lbs. Mfg. 1999-2001.

	$725	$650	$575	$500	$450	$400	$350	*$618*

Subtract approx. $50 if w/o muzzle brake (Model 516BSS, disc. 2000).

GRADING - PPGS™	100%	98%	95%	90%	80%	70%	60%	LAST MSR

PISTOLS: SEMI-AUTO

MODEL 1907 AUTO PISTOL – .32 ACP or .380 ACP cal., 9 (.380 ACP) or 10 (.32 ACP) shot mag., 3 13/16 (.32 ACP) or 4 5/16 (.380 ACP) in. barrel, blue, fixed sights, metal (early mfg. in .32 ACP only until ser. no. 10,980) or hard rubber grips, exposed cocking piece. Mfg. 1910-17.

.32 ACP cal.	$600	$550	$425	$300	$200	$150	$125	
.380 ACP cal.	$700	$650	$525	$400	$300	$250	$200	

Add 40% for original box with instructions (beware of recent reproductions).
Add large premiums for factory nickel, silver, or gold finish (rare).

There were three different types of pearl grips: the early variation was a snap-on with an S/A logo, screw-on with an indian head logo, and the flared 1917 with no logo. Asking prices for the grips alone are in the $250-$1,000 range (this also applied to the Model 1915 Hammerless and Model 1917 Automatic).

MODEL 1915 HAMMERLESS – similar to Model 1907, with grip safety and no visible cocking piece. Mfg. 1915-17.

.32 ACP cal.	$900	$750	$500	$400	$300	$225	$200	
.380 ACP cal.	$1,350	$1,100	$800	$650	$400	$300	$250	

Add 40% with original box and instruction manual.

MODEL 1917 AUTOMATIC – similar to Model 1907, with spur cocking piece and trapezoidal grips. Mfg. 1920-28.

.32 ACP cal.	$500	$425	$300	$200	$150	$130	$110	
.380 ACP cal.	$625	$475	$400	$350	$300	$250	$200	

Add 40% with original box and instruction manual.

M1907 U.S. ARMY TEST TRIAL .45 ACP – .45 ACP cal., large version of Model 1907, exposed hammer. Approx. 400 mfg. 1907-11 for military trials.

	$12,500	$10,000	$8,500	$7,000	$6,000	$5,000	$4,000	

Add 300% for experimental M1910 and M1911.
Add 200% if in original condition.

Most pistols were repurchased from the government, reconditioned (many reblued), and resold to the public as commercial models.

PISTOLS: SINGLE SHOT

MODEL 101 – .22 LR cal., 5 1/2 in. barrel, single action, adj. sight, swing out barrel, blue, wood grips. Mfg. 1960-68.

	$225	$200	$135	$100	$80	$70	$60	

RIFLES: LEVER ACTION, DISC.

Whenever Savage made an engineering change on a model, it was usually designated with a letter suffix after the model number. These letters were added to the basic model numbers as the changes were made. The engineering changes could be dimensional on any part, cosmetic, or a total component redesign. The letter suffixes indicated to the company what changes were incorporated into that variation. Most model suffixes are preceeded with a dash. These alphabetical suffix variations are not listed separately in this section, but values will be similar to the base model, unless denoted otherwise.

MODEL 1895 – .303 Savage cal. only, lever action, mfg. in either carbine (22 in.), rifle (26 in.), or musket (30 in.) variations, round (scarce) or octagon barrel that has Marlin proofmark under the forend, open top, solid breech, side ejecting, 6 shot rotary mag., some had unfired shots indicator. Originally mfg. by Marlin, marked "Savage Repeating Arms Co. Utica, N.Y. U.S.A. Pat. Feb. 7, 1893", approx. 6,000 mfg. 1895-99, early models had hole in top of bolt - later ones were smooth.

	N/A	$6,500	$5,300	$4,500	$3,800	$3,100	$2,600	

Values assume rifle configuration - add a 150%+ premium for the carbine (rare) and musket (rare) and for unfired shots indicator.

GRADING - PPGS™	100%	98%	95%	90%	80%	70%	60%	LAST MSR

MODEL 1895 ANNIVERSARY – a replica of the original M1895, .308 Win. cal., 24 in. octagon barrel, engraved receiver, brass-plated lever, straight stock, Schnabel forend, medallion in stock, brass crescent buttplate. Mfg. 9,999 in 1970 only, by Savage Arms, Division of Emhart to commemorate Savage's 75th year.

$550 $400 $300 N/A N/A N/A N/A *$195*

MODEL 1899 – improvement of Model 1895 with squared-off front end of breech bolt and cocking indicator as opposed to viewing hole indicator. Early Model 1899s have oblong cocking indicator located on the top of the breech bolt. In approx. 1908, this was changed to a pin on the upper tang. A wide variety of special order features were available including special length barrels (up to 30 in.), pistol grip stocks, checkering, woods, plating, grades of engraving, sights, etc., all of which can command a moderate to sizeable premium.

Add 20% for .25-35 WCF, .32-40 WCF, or .38-55 WCF cal.

Add approx. 100% for fancy checkered deluxe grade wood or 30% for checkered plain grain wood on models below that apply.

Any factory engraved Savage 99 is rare (less than 1,000 mfg. to date) with values having to be computed one gun at a time. Engraved Model 1899s range from $2,500-$75,000+, depending on the level of engraving and original condition. Values assume standard rifle with no engraving options (Grades A through G).

In 1905 Savage broadened the variety of this model and added the 1899A2, CD, BC, AB, Excelsior, Leader, Crescent, Victor, Rival, Premier, and Monarch (top-of-the-line model). Prices at the time ranged from $21 to $250 - quite a range.

All Model 1899s and 99s fall within the domain of Savage Arms, Inc.

Rifles under ser. no. 90,000 should be inspected before firing for possible receiver cracking at rear left corner.

From 1899-circa 1950, Model 1899s had serial numbers stamped on buttplate, buttstock, and forearm. A factory drilled and tapped Model 1899 has the model nomenclature moved to the left side.

* ***Model 1899A Rifle*** – .303 Savage, .30-30 Win., .25-35 WCF, .32-40 WCF, .38-55 WCF, or .300 Sav. cal., 26 in. round barrel, straight grip stock, crescent or shotgun butt with steel buttplate, takedown added 1909. Mfg. 1899-1927, Short rifle (22 in.) mfg. 1899-1922.

$1,300 $1,100 $900 $800 $700 $650 $575

* ***Model 1899B Rifle*** – .303 Savage, .30-30 Win., .25-35 WCF, .32-40 WCF, or .38-55 WCF cal., 26 in. octagon barrel, straight grip stock, crescent or shotgun butt with steel buttplate. Mfg. 1899-1915.

$1,500 $1,250 $1,050 $850 $750 $600 $550

Add 35% for .25-35 WCF, .32-40 WCF. and .38-55 WCF.

* ***Model 1899C Rifle*** – .303 Savage, .30-30 Win., .25-35 WCF, .32-40 WCF, or .38-55 WCF cal., 26 in. half octagon barrel, straight grip, crescent or shotgun butt with steel buttplate. Mfg. 1899-1915.

$1,800 $1,600 $1,350 $1,200 $1,000 $850 $750

Add 35% for .25-35 WCF, .32-40 WCF, or .38-55 WCF.

* ***Model 1899-D Military Rifle (Musket)*** – .30-30 Win. or .303 Savage cal., 28 or 30 in. round barrel with two barrel bands, straight grip stock with bayonet lug.

$8,000 $7,000 $6,000 $5,000 $4,000 $3,500 $3,000

* ***Model 1899-F Carbine*** – various cals., three cataloged variations, first variation w/small barrel band is controversial as to whether or not it exists, all variations have sling ring and carbine butt.

$2,800 $2,500 $2,200 $1,900 $1,600 $1,200 $900

Add approx. 25% for Winchester calibers. Add 10% for .30-30 Win. cal.

* ***Model 1899H Rifle*** – .22 Hi-Power, .25-35 WCF, .30-30 Win., or .303 Savage cal., 20 in. featherweight barrel, straight grip, shotgun butt with steel or hard rubber buttplate, takedown added in 1909. Mfg. 1905-1915.

$1,400 $1,200 $1,000 $750 $650 $600 $550

Add 10% for .22 Hi-Power. Add 20% for .25-35 WCF.

GRADING - PPGS™	100%	98%	95%	90%	80%	70%	60%	LAST MSR

* ***Model 1899 .250-3000 Rifle*** – takedown frame only, pistol grip checkered stocks with corrugated steel buttplate, fine cross-checkered trigger (unique to this model). Mfg. 1914-1921.

	$1,600	$1,300	$940	$850	$690	$565	$440	

MODEL 99A – .30-30 Win., .300 Sav., or .303 Sav. cal., lever action, 24 in. barrel, open sight, hammerless, straight grip stock, crescent butt. Mfg. 1920-36.

	$975	$850	$725	$625	$525	$450	$375	

MODEL 99A RECENT PRODUCTION – similar to original, with .243 Win., .250 Sav., .300 Sav., .308 Win., or .375 Win. (1981 only, approx. 1,500 mfg.) cal., 20 or 22 in. barrel, tang safety, conventional butt. Mfg. 1971-81.

	$475	$415	$355	$325	$260	$215	$165	

Add 100% for .375 Win. or 50% for .250 Sav. cal.

MODEL 99B – takedown version of original Model 99A, 24 (introduced 1926-27) or 26 (initial standard barrel length) in. barrel. Mfg. 1920-34.

	$1,200	$1,050	$900	$815	$660	$540	$420	

MODEL 99H CARBINE – .250-3000 Sav., .30-30 Win., .300 Sav. (scarce) or .303 Sav. cal., solid frame, carbine type stock. Mfg. 1923-40.

	$1,400	$1,200	$850	$775	$650	$500	$450	

Add 30% for .250 Sav. and .300 Sav. cal.

There were four variations of this model - the latter three had barrel bands. The first variation did not have a barrel band or side panels on the buttstock.

MODEL 99E – .22 Hi Power, .250-3000 Sav., .30-30 Win., .300 Sav., or .303 Sav. cal., 20, 22 or 24 in. barrel, solid frame, straight stock. Mfg. 1922-34.

	$1,200	$950	$800	$600	$500	$450	$400	

Add 35% for .22 Hi Power or .250 Sav. cal.

MODEL 99E CARBINE – .243 Win., .250 Sav., .300 Sav., or .308 Win. cal., 22 in. barrel, checkered pistol grip stock, 5 shot rotary mag. Mfg. 1960-82.

	$600	$550	$500	$450	$375	$300	$250	*$343*

Add 25% for early Schnabel forearm.

MODEL 99F FEATHERWEIGHT – similar to pre-war Model 99E, except takedown and 1/2 pound lighter, also mfg. with .410 bore shotgun barrel. Mfg. 1920-40.

	$1,400	$1,200	$950	$850	$750	$650	$600	

Add 35% for .410 bore shotgun barrel.
Add 10% for cut checkering.
Add 10% for .22 HP or .250 Sav. cal.

MODEL 99F – .243 Win., .250-3000 Sav., .284 Win., .300 Sav., .308 Win., or .358 Win. cal., solid frame, checkered pistol grip stock. Mfg. 1955-73.

	$750	$655	$565	$510	$415	$340	$265	

Add 35% for .250-3000 Sav.
Add 15% for .243 Win. or .308 Win. cal.
Add 75% for .284 Win. or .358 Win. cal.

This model, in many cases, had the receiver marked "99M".

MODEL 99G – similar to Model 99E pre-war, with checkered pistol grip stock and takedown. Mfg. 1922-41.

	$1,500	$1,200	$900	$750	$675	$575	$500	

Add 35% for .250 Sav. cal.

MODEL 99EG – similar to Model 99G, with solid frame and no checkering. Mfg. 1935-41.

	$795	$685	$600	$525	$400	$350	$300	

Add 35% for .250-3000 Sav. cal.
Add 40% for .22 HP cal.

GRADING - PPGS™	100%	98%	95%	90%	80%	70%	60%	LAST MSR

MODEL 99EG POST-WAR – .243 Win., .250 Sav., .300 Sav., .308 Win., or .358 Win. cal., checkered stock. Mfg. 1946-60.

$575 $525 $450 $395 $340 $295 $260

Add 255 for .243 Win. cal.
Add 50% for .358 Win. or .250 Sav. cal.

MODEL 99R PRE-WAR – .250-3000 Sav., .303 Sav., or .300 Sav. cal., 22 or 24 in. barrel, large pistol grip stock and forearm. Mfg. 1932-42.

$800 $625 $525 $425 $380 $325 $300

Add 35% for .250-3000 Sav. cal.

MODEL 99R POST-WAR – .250-3000 Sav., .300 Sav., .308 Win., .358 Win., or .243 Win. cal., similar to Pre-War, 24 in. barrel only, swivel studs. Mfg. 1946-60.

$600 $525 $450 $400 $350 $325 $300

Add 35% for .250-3000 Sav. or .358 Win. cal.

MODEL 99RS PRE-WAR – similar to Model 99R Pre-War, with Lyman aperture sight, swivels and sling. Mfg. 1932-42.

$950 $800 $640 $580 $470 $385 $300

MODEL 99RS POST-WAR – similar to Model 99R Post-War, with Redfield receiver sight. Mfg. 1946-58.

$700 $615 $525 $475 $385 $325 $300

MODEL 99T – 20 or 22 in. barrel, solid frame, lightweight, checkered pistol grip stock. Mfg. 1935-40.

$1,600 $1,400 $1,100 $1,000 $900 $750 $600

Add 50% for .22 HP cal.

MODEL 99K – engraved receiver and fancy wood stock, Lyman aperture sight and folding middle sight. Mfg. 1926-40.

$3,750 $3,500 $3,000 $2,750 $2,500 $2,200 $1,875

MODEL 99DL – .243 Win., .250-3000 Sav., .284 Win., .300 Sav., .308 Win., or .358 Win. cal., Monte Carlo stock and sling swivels. Post-war mfg. 1960-73.

$700 $615 $525 $475 $385 $325 $300

Add 10% for cut checkering.
Add 35% for .250-3000 Sav. cal.
Add 35% for .284 Win. or .358 Win. cal.

MODEL 99C – available in .22-250 Rem. (rare), .243 Win., .284 Win. (disc.), 7mm-08 (disc.), or .308 Win. cal., similar to Model 99F Post-War, 22 in. barrel, Monte Carlo stock with cut checkering and recoil pad, top tang safety, cocking indicator, open sights, detachable 4 shot box mag., high gloss bluing, drilled and tapped, 7 3/4 lbs. Mfg. 1965, reintroduced 1995-1997 in cals. .243 Win. or .308 Win. only.

$575 $495 $425 $375 $300 $250 $200 *$629*

Add 50% for .22-250 cal.
Add 75% for .284 Win. or 7mm-08 cal.

MODEL 99CD – similar to Model 99C, with Monte Carlo cheekpiece stock. Mfg. 1975-81.

$625 $550 $475 $425 $350 $300 $250

MODEL 99-CE (CENTENNIAL EDITION) – .300 Sav. cal. only, limited edition featuring fully engraved nickel receiver and lever, 24Kt. gold-plated receiver figures, trigger, and safety, deluxe hand checkered walnut stock and forearm, 1,000 mfg. 1996-97 only, serial numbered AS0001-AS1000.

$1,500 $1,100 $750 N/A N/A N/A N/A *$1,660*

MODEL 99-358 (BRUSH GUN) – .358 Win. cal., recoil pad. Mfg. 1977-80.

$1,300 $1,100 $900 $800 $700 $600 $550

MODEL 99-375 (BRUSH GUN) – .375 Win. cal., recoil pad, fluted forearm. Mfg. 1980 only.

$1,500 $1,300 $1,050 $950 $875 $800 $725

GRADING - PPGS™	100%	98%	95%	90%	80%	70%	60%	LAST MSR

MODEL 99PE – elaborately engraved and plated receiver, tang, and lever, fancy wood with hand cut checkering. Mfg. 1966-70.

	$1,800	$1,600	$1,400	$1,200	$1,000	$850	$700	

This model had the receiver marked "99M".

MODEL 99DE CITATION – similar to Model 99PE, except with less engraving and pressed checkering. Mfg. 1968-70.

	$1,200	$1,050	$900	$800	$700	$600	$500	

This model had the receiver marked "99M".

MODEL 99M – while the receivers on Models 99F, 99PE, and 99DE were marked "99M" this is not a model designation. Rather, the "M" barrel designation indicated Monte Carlo stock.

RIFLES: DISC., CENTERFIRE & RIMFIRE

Savage made a wide variety of inexpensive, utilitarian rifles that, to date, have attracted mostly shooting interest, but little collector interest. A listing of these models may be found in the back of this text under "Serialization."

Whenever Savage made an engineering change on a model, it was usually designated with a letter suffix after the model number. These letters were added to the basic model numbers as the changes were made. The engineering changes could be dimensional on any part, cosmetic, or a total component redesign. The letter suffixes indicated to the company what changes were incorporated into that variation. Most model suffixes are preceeded with a dash. These alphabetical suffix variations are not listed separately in this section, but values will be similar to the base model, unless denoted otherwise.

MODEL 1903 STANDARD SLIDE ACTION – .22 S, L, or LR cal., 24 in. barrel, open sights, box mag., pistol grip stock. Mfg. 1903-1922.

	$675	$590	$505	$460	$370	$305	$235	

* ***Model 1903 Standard Slide Action Grade EF*** – features "B" grade checkering on fancy English walnut stock, Savage #22B front sight, and #21B micrometer open rear sight.

	$950	$875	$655	$595	$480	$395	$305	

* ***Model 1903 Standard Slide Action Expert Grade*** – features "A" grade engraving on receiver, "B" grade checkering on fancy American walnut stock, standard sights.

	$1,950	$1,705	$1,465	$1,325	$1,075	$880	$685	

* ***Model 1903 Standard Slide Action Grade GH*** – features "A" grade checkering on plain American walnut stock, no engraving, #22B front sight, and #21B micrometer open rear sight.

	$900	$800	$600	$545	$440	$360	$280	

* ***Model 1903 Standard Slide Action Gold Medal*** – features animal ornamentation on receiver, less elaborate checkering on plain American walnut stock, standard sights.

	$1,050	$920	$790	$715	$580	$475	$370	

MODEL 1909 SLIDE ACTION – similar to Model 1903, with 20 in. round barrel. Mfg. 1909-1915.

	$750	$655	$565	$510	$415	$340	$265	

MODEL 1904 SINGLE SHOT – .22 S, L, or LR cal., bolt action, 18 in. barrel, straight stock. Mfg. 1904-17.

	$175	$155	$130	$120	$95	$80	$60	

MODEL 1905 SINGLE SHOT – similar to Model 1904, except 24 in. barrel, takedown. Mfg. 1905-19.

	$200	$155	$130	$120	$95	$80	$60	

MODEL 1911 BOLT ACTION – .22 S cal. only, bolt action, 20 shot tubular mag. in buttstock, 20 in. barrel. Limited mfg. 1911-12.

	$500	$350	$300	$270	$220	$180	$140	

GRADING - PPGS™	100%	98%	95%	90%	80%	70%	60%	LAST MSR

MODEL 1912 AUTOLOADER – .22 LR cal., semi-auto, 20 in. barrel, takedown, straight stock. Mfg. 1912-16.

	$850	$655	$565	$510	$415	$340	$265	

MODEL 1914 SLIDE ACTION – .22 S, L, and LR cal., 24 in. octagon barrel, plain pistol grip stock. Mfg. 1914-26.

	$450	$395	$340	$305	$250	$205	$160	

MODEL 19 NRA BOLT ACTION – .22 LR cal., 25 in. barrel, adj. aperture sight, 5 shot, military stock. Approx. 50,000 mfg. 1919-32.

	$275	$240	$205	$185	$150	$125	$95	

Between 1943-45 approx. 6,000 Model 19s were made under military contract - add 15%.

MODEL 19 BOLT ACTION TARGET – .22 LR cal., 25 in. barrel, speed lock, adj. aperture sight, target stock. Mfg. 1933-46.

	$300	$265	$225	$205	$165	$135	$105	

MODEL 19L – similar to Model 19, with Lyman receiver sight. Mfg. 1933-42.

	$330	$290	$250	$225	$180	$150	$115	

MODEL 19M – similar to Model 19, with 28 in. heavy barrel and scope bases. Mfg. 1933-42.

	$330	$290	$250	$225	$180	$150	$115	

MODEL 19H – similar to Model 19, except .22 Hornet cal. Mfg. 1933-42.

	$550	$480	$415	$375	$305	$250	$195	

MODEL 1920 BOLT ACTION – Mauser type action, .250-3000 Sav. or .300 Sav. cal., 22 or 24 in. barrel, open sights, 5 shot, checkered pistol grip, Schnabel forend. Mfg. 1920-31.

	$900	$775	$675	$575	$500	$450	$400	

Add 10% for .250-3000 Sav. cal.

MODEL 1920-1926 – similar to Model 1920, with 24 in. barrel, Lyman aperture sight, Mfg. 1926-31.

	$900	$775	$675	$575	$500	$450	$400	

Add 10% for .250-3000 cal.

MODEL 1922 – .22 LR cal., predecessor of the Model 23A, mfg. 1922.

	$250	$220	$190	$170	$140	$115	$90	

MODEL 23A BOLT ACTION RIFLE – .22 LR cal., 23 in. barrel, open sights, plain pistol grip stock, Schnabel forend. Mfg. 1923-33.

	$250	$220	$190	$170	$140	$115	$90	

MODEL 23AA – improved version of Model 23A, with speedlock and checkered stock. Mfg. 1933-42.

	$300	$265	$225	$205	$165	$135	$105	

MODEL 23B – .25-20 WCF cal., same configuration as Model 23A, 25 in. barrel, full forearm. Mfg. 1923-42.

	$300	$265	$225	$205	$165	$135	$105	

MODEL 23C – .32-20 WCF cal., similar to Model 23B. Mfg. 1923-42.

	$350	$305	$265	$240	$195	$160	$125	

MODEL 23D – .22 Hornet cal., similar to Model 23B. Mfg. 1933-47.

	$375	$325	$275	$240	$225	$185	$140	

MODEL 25 SLIDE ACTION – .22 S, L, or LR cal., 24 in. octagon barrel, open sights, takedown, hammerless, tube mag., plain pistol grip stock. Mfg. 1925-29.

	$350	$305	$265	$240	$195	$160	$125	

MODEL 40 BOLT ACTION RIFLE – .250-3000 Sav., .300 Sav., .30-30 Win., or .30-06 cal., 22 or 24 in. barrel, open sights, 4 shot mag., plain pistol grip stock, Schnabel forend. Mfg. 1928-40.

	$350	$305	$265	$240	$195	$160	$125	

Add 10% for .250-3000 Sav. cal.

GRADING - PPGS™	100%	98%	95%	90%	80%	70%	60%	LAST MSR

MODEL 45 SUPER – similar to Model 40, with Lyman receiver sight and checkered stock. Mfg. 1928-40.

	$385	$335	$290	$260	$210	$175	$135	

MODEL 29 SLIDE ACTION – .22 S, L, or LR cal., 22 in. barrel, octagon until 1940, round on post-WWII, open sights, checkered pistol grip stock on pre-war, plain on late model. Mfg. 1929-67.

Pre-war	$350	$305	$265	$240	$195	$160	$125	
Late model	$300	$265	$225	$205	$165	$135	$105	

MODEL 3 SINGLE SHOT – .22 S, L, or LR cal., bolt action, 26 in. barrel, 24 in. barrel on post-war, open sights, plain grip stock. Mfg. 1930-47.

	$85	$75	$65	$60	$45	$40	$30	

MODEL 3S – similar to Model 3, with aperture sight. Mfg. 1930-47.

	$100	$90	$75	$70	$55	$45	$35	

MODEL 3ST – similar to Model 3S, with swivels and sling. Mfg. 1930-47.

	$110	$95	$85	$75	$60	$50	$40	

MODEL 4 BOLT ACTION REPEATER – .22 S, L, or LR cal., 24 in. barrel, open sights, takedown, 5 shot, checkered pistol grip stock on pre-war, plain stock on post-war. Mfg. 1933-65.

Pre-war	$120	$105	$90	$80	$65	$55	$40	
Post-war	$110	$95	$85	$75	$60	$50	$40	

MODEL 4S – similar to Model 4, with aperture sight. Mfg. 1933-42.

	$120	$105	$90	$80	$65	$55	$40	

MODEL 4M – similar to Model 4, except .22 WMR cal. Mfg. 1961-65.

	$110	$95	$85	$75	$60	$50	$40	

MODEL 5 – similar to Model 4, with tubular mag. Mfg. 1938-64.

	$110	$95	$85	$75	$60	$50	$40	

MODEL 5S – similar to Model 5, with aperture sight. Mfg. 1936-42.

	$120	$105	$90	$80	$65	$55	$40	

MODEL 6 AUTOLOADER – .22 S, L, or LR cal., 24 in. barrel, tubular mag., takedown, checkered pistol grip stock on pre-war, plain stock on post-war. Mfg. 1938-68.

Pre-war	$150	$130	$115	$100	$85	$70	$55	
Post-war	$140	$125	$105	$95	$75	$65	$50	

MODEL 6S – similar to Model 6, with aperture sight. Mfg. 1938-42.

	$150	$130	$115	$100	$85	$70	$55	

MODEL 7 AUTOLOADER – similar to Model 6, with box mag. Mfg. 1939-51.

Pre-war	$150	$130	$115	$100	$85	$70	$55	
Post-war	$140	$125	$105	$95	$75	$65	$50	

MODEL 7S – similar to Model 7, with aperture sight. Mfg. 1938-42.

	$150	$130	$115	$100	$85	$70	$55	

MODEL 60 AUTOLOADER – .22 LR cal., 20 in. barrel, leaf sight, tubular mag., checkered Monte Carlo walnut stock. Mfg. 1969-72.

	$95	$85	$70	$65	$50	$45	$35	

MODEL 90 AUTOLOADING CARBINE – similar to Model 60, with 16 1/2 in. barrel, plain carbine stock, with barrel band.

	$95	$85	$70	$65	$50	$45	$35	

MODEL 88 AUTOLOADER – similar to Model 60, except has walnut finished hardwood stock. Mfg. 1969-72.

	$85	$75	$65	$60	$45	$40	$30	

GRADING - PPGS™	100%	98%	95%	90%	80%	70%	60%	LAST MSR

MODEL 63/63K SINGLE SHOT – .22 S, L, or LR cal., bolt action, 18 in. barrel, open sights, trigger locks with key (only on Model 63K), full length pistol grip walnut finished hardwood stock, Model 63s were mfg. 1964-69, Model 63Ks were mfg. 1970-72.

	$80	$70	$60	$55	$45	$35	$30	

MODEL 63KM – .22 WMR cal., similar to Model 63K.

	$115	$100	$85	$80	$65	$50	$40	

MODEL 219 SINGLE SHOT – .22 Hornet, .25-20 WCF, .32-20 WCF, or .30-30 Win. cal., 26 in. barrel, open sights, hammerless, break open, top lever, plain pistol grip stock. Mfg. 1938-65.

.30-30 Win. cal.	$195	$170	$145	$135	$105	$90	$70	

Add 15% for all other cals.

MODEL 219L – similar to Model 219, with side lever. Mfg. 1965-67.

	$135	$120	$100	$90	$75	$60	$45	

MODELS 221, 222, 223, 227, 228, AND 229 – single shot, similar to Model 219, only supplied with additional interchangeable shotgun barrel, different model numbers are for different cals., gauges, and barrel lengths, all have been disc.

	$130	$115	$100	$90	$70	$60	$45	

SAVAGE/STEVENS MODEL 65 – please refer to listing under Stevens section.

MODEL 34M – similar to Model 34, chambered for .22 WMR cal. Mfg. 1969-73.

	$90	$80	$70	$60	$50	$40	$30	

MODEL 35 – .22 LR cal., bolt action, 22 in. barrel, 5 shot detachable mag., open sights, hardwood Monte Carlo stock. Disc. 1985.

	$90	$80	$70	$60	$50	$40	$30	*$100*

MODEL 36 – .22 LR cal., single shot, otherwise similar to Model 35. Mfg. 1983-84.

	$90	$80	$70	$60	$50	$40	$30	

MODEL 46 – similar to Model 34, with tubular mag. Mfg. 1969-73.

	$90	$80	$70	$60	$50	$40	$30	

MODEL 65M – .22 WMR cal., similar to Model 65.

	$95	$85	$70	$65	$50	$45	$35	

SAVAGE/FOX MODEL FB-1 – .22 LR cal., bolt action, 24 in. barrel, hooded front sight, Williams adj. rear sight, premium walnut stock with rollover cheekpiece, rosewood tip and forend cap, fancy cut checkering. Mfg. 1981 only.

	$225	$195	$170	$155	$125	$100	$80	

SAVAGE/STEVENS MODEL 72 "CRACKSHOT" – please refer to listing under Stevens section.

SAVAGE/STEVENS MODEL 73 – similar to Model 63, w/o Monte Carlo stock. Mfg. 1964-69.

	$125	$110	$95	$85	$70	$55	$45	

SAVAGE/STEVENS MODEL 89 SINGLE SHOT – please refer to listing under Stevens section.

MODEL 340 BOLT ACTION – .22 Hornet, .222 Rem., .223 Rem., or .30-30 Win. cal., 22 and 24 in. barrel, open sights, 4 or 5 shot mag., 7 1/2 lbs., plain pistol grip stock. Mfg. 1950-85.

	$225	$195	$170	$155	$125	$100	$80	*$257*

EL 340C – similar to Model 340, with aperture sight, checkered stock, and sling swivels. Mfg. 1952-60.

	$235	$205	$175	$160	$130	$105	$80	

MODEL 340V – .225 Win. cal., varmint configuration, 24 in. barrel. Limited mfg. in late 1960s.

	$295	$260	$220	$200	$160	$135	$105	

GRADING - PPGS™	100%	98%	95%	90%	80%	70%	60%	LAST MSR

MODEL 340S DELUXE – similar to Model 340, with aperture sight, checkered stock, sling swivels. Mfg. 1952-60.

	$300	$265	$225	$205	$165	$135	$105	

MODEL 342 AND 342S – .22 Hornet cal., similar to Model 340. Mfg. 1950-55.

	$300	$265	$225	$205	$165	$135	$105	

MODEL 982DL/MDI – .22 LR (DL) or .22 WMR (MDI) cal., bolt action, 22 in. barrel, ramp front sight, folding leaf rear sight, checkered American walnut stock with Monte Carlo comb, matte receiver finish. Mfg. 1981 only.

	$195	$175	$150	$125	$100	$85	$65	

Add 20% for .22 WMR cal.

RIFLES: RIMFIRE, CURRENT PRODUCTION

Savage introduced a new line of Rimfire rifles during 1996. Recent Savage nomenclature usually involves alphabetical suffixes which mean the following: B - Brown laminated wood stock, BT - laminated thumbhole stock, C - Clip, EV - Evolution Stock, F - composite/synthetic stock, G - hardwood stock, H - hinged floorplate, K - Muzzlebrake, L - left-hand, NS - No Sights, P - Police, RD - Red Dot Sight, RJ - Royal Jacaranda Stock, SR - Suppressor Ready, S/SS - stainless steel, T - (Rimfire) peep sights, TR - Tactical Style Rimfire, TRR - Tactical Style Rimfire w/ Picatinny Rail, V - Long Range (Varmint w/heavy barrel), XP - package gun (scope, sling, and rings/base), Y - Youth/Ladies Model (shortened dimensions). Hence, the Model Mark II-GLY designates a Mark II model with hardwood stock, left-hand action in a Youth configuration. A Model 93 Series with BTVSS suffix indicates a laminated thumbole stock with heavy barrel in stainless steel.

Subtract 10% if w/o AccuTrigger (became standard on most rimfire rifles 2006, except Model 64 and Model 200).

CUB (G) – .17 Mach 2 (mfg. 2005 only), or .22 LR cal., single shot Youth Model with 16 1/8 in. barrel and shortened hardwood stock in regular or pink (new 2009) finish, traditional safety, aperture rear sight, AccuTrigger became standard 2006, 4 1/2 lbs. Mfg. 2003-2011.

	$175	$140	$110	$90	$80	$70	$60	*$227*

Add 10% for .17 Mach 2 cal. (mfg. 2005).
Add $14 for pink stock.

* ***Cub Target*** – .22 LR cal., similar to Cub Model, except has ergonomic thumbhole stock. Mfg. 2007-2011.

	$225	$175	$130	$110	$95	$85	$75	*$282*

Add $14 for pink stock (new 2008).

RASCAL SERIES – .22 LR cal., single shot, 16 in. barrel, AccuTrigger, manual safety, cocks by lifting bolt, fixed front and aperture rear sights, feed ramp, walnut hardwood or black, pink, blue, red, yellow, orange or green synthetic stock, 2.66 lbs. New 2012.

MSR $180	$155	$135	$120	$110	$100	$95	$90	

Add $45 for hardwood stock or left-hand action (hardwood only).

MARK I-G SERIES BOLT ACTION – .22 S-L-LR, or LR shot (Mark I - GSB) cal., single shot, self-cocking, 19 (Mark I-GY, Youth Model) or 20 3/4 in. barrel, checkered hardwood stock, AccuTrigger became standard 2006, approx. 5 lbs. New 1996.

MSR $255	$200	$155	$110	$90	$80	$70	$60	

Subtract $30 for Mark I-GY (Youth Model).
Add $35 for Youth Color (mfg. 2002-2005) or $31 for Camo Youth (mfg. 2002-2004).
Add $7 for scope (Model Mark I-GYXP only, mfg. 2002-2004).

This Model was also available with left-hand action (Mark I-GL, disc. 2003), Youth Model (Mark I-GY), Youth Color (Mark I-GLY, features blue/green/grey laminate stock, mfg. 2002-2009), Camo Youth (Mark I-Y Camo, mfg. 2002-2004), or with smooth bore barrel (Mark I-GSB, disc. 2009).

GRADING - PPGS™	100%	98%	95%	90%	80%	70%	60%	LAST MSR

* ***Mark I-FVT Series Bolt Action*** – similar to Mark I-G, except has black synthetic stock, 21 in. heavy barrel and aperture target sights, 5 1/4 lbs. New 2005.

MSR $445 $335 $235 $175 $140 $110 $90 $80

MARK II-F SERIES BOLT ACTION – .17 Mach 2 (new 2004) or .22 LR cal., 21 in. blue barrel, checkered black synthetic stock, 10 shot mag., AccuTrigger became standard 2006, fiber optic sights, 5 lbs. New 1998.

MSR $220 $180 $135 $100 $85 $75 $65 $60

Add $75 for .17 Mach 2 cal.

Add $7 for Mark II-FXP package (includes 4x15mm scope, disc. 2005).

* ***Mark II Series Bolt Action Camo*** – .22 LR cal. only, similar to Mark II-F, Next G1 camo stock, 5 1/2 lbs. New 2002.

MSR $270 $210 $170 $125 $95 $80 $75 $65

Add $183 for Mark II XP Camo package with 3-9x32mm scope (Mfg. 2008-disc.).

* ***Mark II Series Bolt Action FSS*** – .17 Mach 2 (mfg. 2004-2005) or .22 LR cal., 21 in. stainless steel barrel with sights, black graphite/polymer stock with checkering, dovetailed receiver, 5 lbs. New 1997.

MSR $325 $250 $195 $145 $100 $85 $75 $65

Add 10% for .17 Mach 2 cal.

* ***Mark II Series Bolt Action FV*** – .17 Mach 2 (mfg. 2004) or .22 LR cal., features 21 in. heavy barrel, no sights, AccuTrigger, black synthetic stock, 5 shot detachable mag., blued finish, Weaver style bases included, 7 1/2 lbs. New 1998.

MSR $235 $190 $140 $100 $85 $75 $65 $60

Add $90 for .17 Mach 2 cal.

Add $60 for Mark II-FVSS (stainless) in .17 Mach 2 cal. (mfg. 2005 only).

Add $55 for Mark II-FVXP package (includes 4x32mm scope, disc. 2004, reintroduced 2006 with 3-9x40 scope).

* ***Mark II Series Bolt Action FVT*** – .22 LR cal., 21 in. heavy barrel with target sights, AccuTrigger, black synthetic stock, 5 shot detachable mag., blued finish, 6 lbs. New mid-2005.

MSR $455 $440 $240 $175 $140 $110 $90 $80

* ***Mark II Series Bolt Action FV-SR*** – .22 LR cal., 16 1/2 in. threaded barrel, AccuTrigger, no sights, black synthetic stock, 5 shot detachable mag., 5 1/2 lbs. New 2011.

MSR $260 $210 $160 $110 $90 $80 $70 $60

* ***Mark II Series Bolt Action G*** – .17 Mach 2 (mfg. 2004-2005) or .22 LR cal., 21 in. barrel, detachable 10 shot mag., AccuTrigger, checkered hardwood walnut stock, open sights, 5 1/2 lbs. New 1996.

MSR $235 $185 $140 $100 $85 $75 $65 $60

Add $64 for Mark II-GV (mfg. 2005).

Add $7 for Mark II-GXP package (includes 4x15mm scope, disc. 2004).

Add $7 for Mark II-GLXP package (left-hand, includes 4x15mm scope, disc. 2004).

This Model is also available with left-hand action (Mark II-GL), Youth Model (Mark II-GY), Youth Model Left-Hand (Mark II-GLY), Varmint Left Hand (Mark II GLV, disc. 2005) at no additional charge.

* ***Mark II Series Bolt Action BRJ*** – .22 LR cal., 21 in. fluted carbon steel barrel, 5 shot detachable box mag., AccuTrigger, tri-color wood laminate stock, 7 lbs. New 2010.

MSR $500 $410 $330 $270 $220 $185 $160 $140

* ***Mark II Series Bolt Action BSEV*** – .22 LR cal., 21 in. fluted stainless steel barrel, 5 shot mag., AccuTrigger, tri-color wood laminate thumbhole stock, no sights, 6.8 lbs. New 2010.

MSR $595 $485 $410 $340 $275 $225 $175 $150

GRADING - PPGS™	100%	98%	95%	90%	80%	70%	60%	LAST MSR

* ***Mark II Series Bolt Action BV/LV*** – .17 Mach 2 (mfg. 2005) or .22 LR cal., features 21 in. blue heavy barrel, 5 shot mag., no sights, grey or brown laminated hardwood stock with (Mark II LV, disc. 2004) or w/o (Mark II BV) cut checkering, 6 1/2 lbs. New 1997.

MSR $385 $310 $240 $190 $150 $120 $105 $100

Add 10% for Mark II BVSS (stainless) in .17 Mach 2 cal. - grey finish only, mfg. 2005.

* ***Mark II Series Bolt Action BTV*** – .22 LR cal., 21 in. heavy barrel, AccuTrigger, 5 shot detachable box mag., laminate thumbhole stock, no sights, blued finish, 7 1/2 lbs. New 2009.

MSR $445 $345 $240 $180 $140 $110 $90 $80

* ***Mark II Series Bolt Action BTVS*** – .22 LR cal., 21 in. heavy stainless barrel w/o sights, 5 shot detachable box mag., features brown laminated thumbhole stock with vent. forend, stainless steel action, 7 1/2 lbs. New 2007.

MSR $495 $395 $325 $275 $220 $180 $160 $140

» **Mark II Series Bolt Action BVTLSS** – .22 LR cal., similar to Model BTVS, except has left-hand action. New 2009.

MSR $495 $395 $325 $275 $220 $180 $160 $140

* ***Mark II Series Bolt Action Classic*** – .22 LR cal., 21 (disc.) or 24 in. matte blue barrel, 5 shot detachable box mag., hinged floorplate, checkered pistol grip walnut stock, no sights. Mfg. 2007-2010.

$485 $410 $345 $285 $225 $175 $150 *$575*

Add $33 for MK Classic T with target sights (mfg. 2008).

* ***Mark II Series Bolt Action TR*** – .22 LR cal., 22 in. fluted carbon steel barrel, 5 shot detachable box mag., black wood straight comb stock, AccuTrigger, 7 1/2 lbs. New 2010.

MSR $515 $415 $335 $280 $230 $185 $160 $140

» **Mark II Series Bolt Action TRR/TRR-SR** – .22 LR cal., similar to Mark II TR Model, except has top Picatinny rail, Model TRR-SR with threaded barrel became standard 2011, 7.8 lbs. New 2010.

MSR $605 $500 $430 $350 $285 $230 $190 $170

MODEL 64 SERIES SEMI-AUTO – .22 LR cal., 20 1/4 in. barrel with adj. rear sight, 10 shot detachable mag., choice of black synthetic (Model 64F), checkered hardwood (Model 64G), or camo stock, thumb operated rotary safety, Accu-Trigger not available, 5 1/2 lbs. New 1996.

* ***Model 64G Semi-Auto*** – .22 LR cal., 21 in. barrel, AccuTrigger not available, 10 shot detachable box mag, checkered hardwood walnut stock, open sights, blued finish, 5 1/2 lbs.

MSR $215 $170 $135 $100 $75 $70 $65 $60

Add $9 for Model 64-GXP package (includes 4x15mm scope, disc. 2005).

* ***Model 64F/64FV Semi-Auto*** – .22 LR cal., similar to Model 64, except has black graphite/polymer checkered stock, 20 1/4 regular (disc. 2012) or 21 (Model 64FV, mfg. 1998-2004, in 2013 21 in. became standard) in. heavy barrel, not available w/Accu-Trigger, 5 or 6 lbs. New 1997.

MSR $175 $135 $100 $85 $75 $70 $65 $60

Add $48 for Model 64FV with heavy barrel (disc. 2004).
Add $10 for Model 64-FXP package (includes unmounted 4x15mm scope).
Add $75 for Model 64-FVXP package (includes 4x32mm scope, new 2006).
Add $61 for Model 64-FRD (Red Dot sight, mfg. 2009-2011).

* ***Model 64FSS Semi-Auto*** – similar to Model 64F, except has stainless steel barrel and action with checkered black synthetic graphite/polymer stock, 5 lbs. New 2002.

MSR $245 $185 $145 $110 $80 $70 $65 $60

GRADING - PPGS™	100%	98%	95%	90%	80%	70%	60%	LAST MSR

* ***Model 64FVSS Semi-Auto*** – similar to Model 64FSS, except has 21 in. heavy barrel, 6 lbs. Mfg. 2002-2004.

	$190	$150	$115	$100	$85	$70	$65	*$240*

* ***Model 64F Semi-Auto Camo*** – similar to Model 64F, except has Realtree Hardwoods HD (disc.) or Next G1 camo finish and 21 in. barrel, 5 lbs. New 2003.

MSR $235	$180	$140	$110	$90	$80	$70	$60	

* ***Mark 64TR-SR Semi-Auto*** – .22 LR cal., 16 1/2 in. threaded heavy barrel, 10 shot detachable box mag., no sights, matte finish, AccuTrigger is not available, scope rail, 6.6 lbs. New 2011.

MSR $335	$265	$210	$155	$110	$85	$70	$65	

* ***Model 64BTV Semi-Auto*** – .22 LR cal., 10 shot detachable box mag., 21 in. heavy barrel, laminated walnut thumbhole stock, AccuTrigger not available, rear aperture sight, 7 1/2 lbs. Mfg. 2008-2012.

	$310	$240	$180	$140	$110	$90	$80	*$381*

MODEL 93 SERIES MAGNUM BOLT ACTION – .22 WMR cal., 21 in. barrel with adj. rear sight, 5 shot detachable mag., checkered right or left-hand (Model 93 GL) hardwood Monte Carlo stock, AccuTrigger became standard 2006, 5 3/4 lbs. New 1996.

* ***Model 93 G/GL Series Magnum Bolt Action*** – .22 WMR cal., 21 in. barrel, AccuTrigger, 5 shot detachable box mag., checkered hardwood walnut stock, open sights, blued finish, right or left (Model 93GL) hand action, 5 3/4 lbs.

MSR $260	$210	$170	$125	$100	$75	$70	$65	

* ***Model 93F/FV Series Magnum Bolt Action*** – .22 WMR cal., 21 in. blue regular (F) or heavy (FV) barrel with checkered black synthetic graphite polymer stock, 5 shot detachable box mag., open (93F) or no (93FV) sights, AccuTrigger, 5 1/2-6 lbs. New 1998.

MSR $245	$190	$160	$125	$90	$75	$70	$65	

Add $70 for Model 93FV with heavy barrel (new 2006).

* ***Model 93FSS Series Magnum Bolt Action*** – .22 WMR cal., 21 in. stainless steel barrel and action with checkered black synthetic graphite/polymer stock, AccuTrigger, 5 shot detachable box mag., fiber optic (new 2013) open sights, 5 lbs. New 1997.

MSR $330	$265	$210	$155	$110	$85	$70	$65	

* ***Model 93FVSS Series Magnum Bolt Action*** – similar to Model 93FSS, except has 21 in. heavy barrel with recessed crown and button rifling, drilled and tapped, Weaver bases included, 6 lbs. New 1998.

MSR $335	$270	$220	$165	$120	$90	$70	$65	

Add $60 for Model 93FVSSXP package (includes 3-9x40mm scope and mounts).

* ***Model 93F Camo Series Magnum Bolt Action*** – similar to Model 93G, except has Realtree Hardwoods HD camo finish. Mfg. 2003-2004.

	$180	$150	$110	$90	$75	$70	$65	*$211*

* ***Model 93XP Camo*** – .22 WMR cal., 5 shot detachable box mag., 22 in. barrel, 100% Brush or Mossy Oak Camo finished stock, AccuTrigger, includes 3-9x40 scope and mounts, 5 1/4 lbs.

MSR $485	$400	$325	$270	$220	$185	$160	$140	

* ***Model 93 BRJ Series Magnum Bolt Action*** – .22 WMR cal., 21 in. carbon steel fluted barrel, 5 shot mag., AccuTrigger, tricolor wood laminate stock, no sights, 7 lbs. New 2010.

MSR $510	$425	$335	$280	$275	$225	$185	$160	

* ***Model 93 BSEV Series Magnum Bolt Action*** – .22 WMR cal., similar to Model 93 BRJ, except has oversized thumbhole stock, 6.8 lbs. New 2010.

MSR $605	$500	$425	$375	$275	$225	$175	$140	

GRADING - PPGS™	100%	98%	95%	90%	80%	70%	60%	LAST MSR

* ***Model 93 BTVS Series Magnum Bolt Action*** – similar to Model 93FVSS, except has brown laminated thumbhole stock, stainless steel action and 21 in. heavy barrel w/o sights. New 2007.

MSR $490	$410	$325	$265	$220	$185	$160	$140	

* ***Model 93 Series Classic Magnum Bolt Action*** – .22 WMR, features 24 in. regular or heavy high luster blue barrel with or w/o aperture rear sight, 5 shot detachable box mag., with (Model 93 Classic-T) or w/o sights. Mfg. 2008-2010.

	$485	$410	$345	$285	$230	$190	$170	*$582*

Add $35 for heavy barrel with aperture rear sight (Model 93 Classic-T, disc. 2008).

MODEL 93R17 SERIES BOLT ACTION – .17 HMR cal., black synthetic or hardwood stock and forearm, 20 3/4 or 21 in. barrel, otherwise similar to Model 93 Series, AccuTrigger became standard 2006, 5 lbs. New 2003.

* ***Model 93R17 BRJ Series Bolt Action*** – .17 HMR cal., 21 in. fluted carbon steel barrel, 5 shot mag., AccuTrigger, tricolor wood laminate stock, 7 lbs. New 2010.

MSR $510	$415	$340	$285	$225	$185	$160	$140	

* ***Model 93R17 BSEV Series Bolt Action*** – .17 HMR cal., similar to Model 93R17 BRJ, except has oversized thumbhole stock, 6.8 lbs. New 2010.

MSR $605	$495	$425	$360	$285	$230	$190	$170	

* ***Model 93R17 BTV Series Bolt Action*** – .17 HMR cal., 21 in. barrel, laminated hardwood thumbhole stock, no sights, 5 shot detachable mag., AccuTrigger, 7 1/2 lbs. New 2009.

MSR $415	$325	$250	$180	$130	$90	$70	$65	

* ***Model 93R17 BTVS Series Bolt Action*** – .17 HMR cal., stainless, 21 in. barrel, 5 shot detachable mag., AccuTrigger, laminated hardwood thumbhole stock, target sights, 7 1/2 lbs. New 2003.

MSR $465	$385	$295	$250	$210	$165	$140	$135	

This model is also available with left-hand action and stainless steel barrel (Model BTVLSS, new 2009) at no extra charge.

* ***Model 93R17 BV Series Bolt Action*** – .17 HMR cal., 21 in. barrel, steel action, walnut lacquer hardwood stock, 5 shot detachable mag., AccuTrigger, no sights, 7 lbs. New 2003.

MSR $385	$315	$240	$175	$125	$90	$70	$65	

* ***Model 93R17 BVSS Series Bolt Action*** – .17 HMR cal., 21 in. barrel, grey laminated hardwood stock, stainless steel action, no sights, 5 shot detachable mag., AccuTrigger, 6 lbs. New 2003.

MSR $410	$335	$270	$210	$165	$140	$120	$100	

* ***Model 93R17 Series Bolt Action Camo*** – similar to Model 93R17F, except has Realtree Hardwoods HD (disc.) or Next G1 camo finish. New 2003.

MSR $330	$265	$210	$160	$115	$85	$70	$65	

Add $155 for 93R17XP camo package (Mossy Oak, Snow, or Brush camo) with 3-9x40mm scope (new 2008).

* ***Model 93R17 F Series Bolt Action*** – .17 HMR cal., 21 in. barrel, 5 shot detachable box mag., AccuTrigger, checkered black synthetic stock, no sights, 5 lbs.

MSR $260	$215	$165	$125	$90	$75	$70	$65	

Add $60 for Model 93R17FXP package (includes 3-9x40mm scope, new 2006).

* ***Model 93R17 FSS Series Bolt Action*** – similar to Model 93R17F, except has stainless steel barrel and action with checkered black synthetic graphite/polymer stock, 5 lbs. New 2003.

MSR $315	$260	$210	$160	$115	$85	$70	$65	

* ***Model 93R17 FV Series Bolt Action*** – similar to Model 93R17F, except has 21 in. heavy barrel, 5 1/2 lbs. New 2003.

MSR $275	$230	$185	$140	$110	$90	$70	$65	

GRADING - PPGS™	100%	98%	95%	90%	80%	70%	60%	LAST MSR

* ***Model 93R17 FVSS Series Bolt Action*** – similar to Model 93FSS, except has 21 in. heavy stainless steel barrel with recessed crown and button rifling, drilled and tapped, Weaver bases included, 5 1/2 lbs. New 2003.

MSR $395	$325	$260	$180	$135	$110	$90	$75	

* ***Model 93R17 GV/GLV Series Bolt Action*** – similar to Model 93R17 F, except has checkered hardwood stock with varmint barrel, GLV is left-hand model, 5 lbs. New 2003.

MSR $290	$235	$190	$140	$100	$85	$70	$65	

Add $55 for Model 93R17GVXP package (includes 3-9x40mm scope, new 2006).

* ***Model 93R17 TR Bolt Action*** – .17 HMR cal., 22 in. fluted carbon steel barrel, 5 shot mag., black wood straight comb stock, AccuTrigger, 7 1/2 lbs. New 2010.

MSR $520	$435	$340	$290	$230	$185	$160	$140	

» ***Model 93R17 TRR/TRR-SR Bolt Action*** – .17 HMR cal., similar to Mark 93R17 TR Model, except has top Picatinny rail, TRR-SR Model with threaded barrel became standard 2011, 7.8 lbs. New 2010.

MSR $615	$515	$450	$395	$280	$225	$175	$140	

* ***Model 93R17/93R17T Classic Series Bolt Action*** – .17 HMR cal., features 24 in. high luster blue barrel, 5 shot detachable box mag., walnut stock, no sights, Model 93R17T Classic with target barrel and aperture rear sight (new 2008) became standard during 2011, 6 1/2 lbs. Mfg. 2007-2012.

	$540	$435	$350	$300	$230	$190	$170	*$659*

MODEL 900 SERIES – .22 LR cal., single (Target/Silhouette Model) or 5 shot (Biathlon Model), 21 or 25 (Target Model) in. free floated barrel, uncheckered hardwood stock, right or left-hand action, approx. 8 lbs. Mfg. 1996-2001.

* ***Model 900B Series Biathlon*** – blonde stock, supplied with five 5 shot mags., includes shooting rail and barrel snow cover, aperture rear sight. Mfg. 1996-97.

	$445	$395	$350	$300	$265	$230	$200	*$498*

This model was also available with left-hand action (Model 900B-LH, new 1997).

* ***Model 900S Series Silhouette*** – brown hardwood stock, heavy 21 in. barrel with muzzle crown, scope bases installed, w/o sights. Mfg. 1996-97.

	$300	$265	$230	$200	$180	$160	$140	*$346*

This model was also available with left-hand action (Model 900S-LH, mfg. 1997).

* ***Model 900TR Series Target*** – features aperture sights, shooting rail with hand stop, 25 in. barrel. Disc. 2001.

	$395	$325	$280	$235	$200	$180	$160	*$448*

This model was also available with left-hand action (Model 900TR-LH, new 1997).

RIFLES: CENTERFIRE, CURRENT/RECENT PRODUCTION

The 110 Series was first produced in 1958. Beginning in 1992, Savage Arms, Inc. began supplying this model with a master trigger lock, earmuffs, shooting glasses (disc. 1992), and test target.

Beginning 1994, all Savage rifles employ a laser etched bolt featuring the Savage logo. During 1996, Savage began using pillar bedded stocks for many of their rifles.

Recent Savage nomenclature usually involves alphabetical suffixes which mean the following: B - laminated wood stock, BT - laminated thumbhole stock, C - detachable box mag., EV - Evolution stock, F - composite/synthetic stock, G - hardwood stock, H - hinged floorplate, K - AccuStock or standard muzzle brake, AK - adj. muzzle brake with fluted barrel, L - left-hand, LE - Law Enforcement, NS - no sights, P - police (tactical) rifle, SB - smooth bore, SE - safari express, SR - suppressor ready, SS - stainless steel, SS-S - stainless steel single shot, T - Target (aperture rear sight), TR - tactical style rimfire, TRR - tactical style rimfire w/rail, U - high luster blue, blue metal finish and/or stock finish, V - Long Range (Varmint w/heavy barrel), XP - package gun (scope, sling, and rings/base), Y - Youth/ Ladies Model. A 2 digit model number (10) designates new short action. A 3 digit model number (110) indicates long action.

GRADING - PPGS™	100%	98%	95%	90%	80%	70%	60%	LAST MSR

Hence, the Model 111FCNS designates a 111 Series firearm with synthetic stock, detachable magazine, and no sights. Likewise, a Model 11FYCXP3 indicates a Model 11 Series with synthetic stock, youth dimensions, detachable magazine, is a packaged gun which includes scope. The Model 116FHSAK indicates a long action rifle with hinged floorplate, synthetic stock, stainless steel action/barrel with adj. muzzlebrake.

During 2003, Savage released its new patented AccuTrigger, which allows the consumer to adjust the trigger pull from the outside of the rifle from 1 1/2 lbs. - 6 lbs. using a proprietary tool. The AccuTrigger also has almost no trigger creep and is infinitely adjustable. Initially, it was released in all Varmint, LE, and heavy barrel long range rifles, and during 2004, the AccuTrigger became standard on nearly all Savage centerfire rifles, except the Model 11 and 11FCXP3 and 10/110G Package guns. During 2007, Savage began offering target actions with AccuTrigger, right bolt, and choice of left or right port ejection with .223 Rem. bolt head - MSR is $560-$595.

During 2008, Savage Arms introduced a new personal anti-recoil device (P.A.D.), which is installed in many Savage bolt action centerfire rifles. The P.A.D. reduces recoil by 45% from OEM solid and vented pads.

In 2009, Savage Arms introduced its Accustock, which incorporates a rigid aluminum rail and 3D bedding cradle that is firmly imbedded in the stock throughout the length of the rifles forend. Many Savage Centerfire rifles now incorporate the Accustock bedding system.

Also during 2009/2010, Savage introduced varmint short actions, along with both long and short sporter actions. Sporter actions had an MSR of $481, while the varmint short actions' MSR was $505. A dual port receiver, allowing left loading and right ejection was also released in 2009 - MSR was $595.

During 2010, Target actions became available in stainless steel only (in either single or dual port configuration) - MSR on the single port is $613, and $651 for the dual port.

During 2012, Savage introduced its new AXIS Series.

Whenever possible, the models within this category have been listed in numerical sequence.

Subtract approx. 10% on models listed below w/o AccuTrigger (became standard on all centerfire rifles in 2004).

MODEL 10 PREDATOR HUNTER – .204 Ruger, .22-250 Rem., .223 Rem., .243 Win. (new 2008), .260 Rem. (new 2011), 6.5 Creedmoor (new 2011), or 6.5x.285 Norma (left-hand action only, mfg. 2012 only) cal., 22 or 24 in. barrel, laminate stock, Accustock became standard during 2010, 100% Mossy Oak Brush, Snow (mfg. 2009-2011), or RealTree Max 1 (new 2010) patterned camo, no sights, includes scope blocks, detachable box mag., right or left (new 2012) hand action, 7 1/4 lbs. New 2007.

MSR $910	$775	$640	$500	$450	$395	$350	$295	

Add $35 for Model 10XP Predator package, which includes scope (right-hand action only, new 2008).

Add $35 for RealTree Max 1 camo (new 2010).

Add $35 for left-hand action (new 2012).

MODEL 10FCM SCOUT – 7.62x39mm (new 2011), .308 Win. or 7mm-08 Rem. (disc. 2002) cal., 20 in. barrel with removable ghost ring rear sight, one-piece barrel mount (allows long scope eye relief), 4 shot detachable mag., satin blue action with large ball bolt handle, black synthetic dual pillar bedded stock, Accustock became standard 2009, includes swivel set and sling, tripod became standard 2007, 6 1/8 lbs. Mfg. 1999-2003, reintroduced 2007.

MSR $865	$725	$575	$450	$365	$295	$260	$230	

Subtract 15% if w/o Accustock.

MODEL 10FM (SIERRA) – .243 Win., .308 Win., .270 WSM (new 2003), .300 WSM (new 2002), or 7mm-08 Rem. (new 1999) cal., short action, lightweight, features black synthetic stock with dual pillar bedding, button rifling and recessed crown, 20 (Sierra, standard weight, new 1999) or 24 (heavy only, disc. 1998) in. barrel, w/o sights, 6 lbs. Mfg. 1998-2004.

	$435	$360	$290	$245	$210	$175	$160	*$511*

This model was also available in left-hand action (disc.).

GRADING - PPGS™	100%	98%	95%	90%	80%	70%	60%	LAST MSR

MODEL 10FCM (SIERRA) – .243 Win., .270 WSM, .300 WSM, .308 Win., or 7mm-08 Rem cal., 20 in. barrel, synthetic stock, short action, detachable box mag., no sights, 6 1/4 lbs. Mfg. 2005-2006.

	$440	$350	$295	$265	$225	$190	$165	*$540*

MODEL 10 50TH ANNIVERSARY – .300 Savage cal., short action, hinged floorplate with Indian chief engraving and 50th Anniversary markings, 4 shot mag., 22 in. barrel, drilled and tapped, semi-fancy American walnut Monte Carlo stock with shadowline cheekpiece and fleur-de-lis checkering, 24 kt. gold plated double barrel bands, 24 kt. gold plated AccuTrigger, embossed recoil pad, ltd. ed. of 1,000 rifles, approx. 7 lbs. Mfg. 2008 only.

	$1,475	$1,250	$1,050	$875	$750	$650	$595	*$1,724*

MODEL 10 LAW ENFORCEMENT SERIES – .223 Rem., .260 Rem. (mfg. 1999-2001), .308 Win., or 7mm-08 (mfg. 1999-2001) cal., short action, tactical/law enforcement model, checkered black synthetic stock, features 20 (new 2006) or 24 in. heavy barrel w/o sights, AccuTrigger became standard 2003, 8 lbs. Mfg. 1998-2007.

	$505	$395	$320	$275	$230	$190	$165	*$621*

* ***Model 10FP/10FLP*** – .223 Rem. or .308 Win. cal., short action, 20 or 24 in. heavy free floating and button rifled barrel, 4 shot box mag., black McMillan synthetic sporter style stock, drilled and tapped, swivel stud, oversized bolt handle, 6 1/4 lbs. Mfg. 1998-2010.

	$625	$500	$425	$365	$335	$295	$275	*$775*

This model was also available in left-hand action (Model 10FLP, 24 in. barrel only, disc. 2009).

* ***Model 10FP-SR*** – .223 Rem. or .308 Win. cal., short action, 22 in. threaded barrel, 4 shot box mag., Accutrigger, black McMillan synthetic sporter style stock, matte blued finish, no sights, oversized bolt handle. New 2011.

MSR $775	$625	$500	$425	$365	$335	$295	$275	

* ***Model 10FP Duty*** – similar to Model 10FP, except has open iron sights. Mfg. 2002 only.

	$435	$355	$290	$250	$215	$180	$165	*$525*

* ***Model 10FP 20 In. (LE1/LE1A)*** – .223 Rem. (LE1A only, disc. 2007) or .308 Win. cal., similar to Model 10FP, except has 20 in. heavy barrel with no sights, choice of standard (LE1, disc. 2005) or Choate (LE1A) stock (folding only, new 2006). Mfg. 2002-2010.

	$865	$695	$565	$475	$425	$350	$300	*$1,034*

Subtract 20% for standard stock (LE1).

* ***Model 10FP 26 In. (LE2/LE2A)*** – .223 Rem. (LE2A only) or .308 Win. cal., similar to Model 10FP-LE1/LE1A, except has 26 in. heavy barrel and choice of standard (LE2, disc. 2005) or Choate stock (LE2A). Mfg. 2002-2006.

	$625	$500	$400	$360	$330	$300	$275	*$754*

Subtract 20% for standard stock.

* ***Model 10FP McMillan (LE2B)*** – .308 Win. cal., short action, features McMillan tactical fiberglass stock with stippled grip areas, 4 shot mag., 26 in. heavy barrel. Mfg. 2003-2006.

	$860	$725	$625	$525	$425	$325	$265	*$1,033*

* ***Model 10FP H-S Precision*** – .308 Win. cal., 24 in. barrel, features H-S Precision stock. Mfg. 2006 only.

	$720	$585	$475	$425	$350	$300	$275	*$864*

* ***Model 10FPCPXP/10FPXP (LE/LEA)*** – .308 Win. cal. only, short action, features skeletonized synthetic stock, 24 (new 2006) or 26 (disc. 2005) in. barrel w/o sights, H-S Precision stock became standard 2006, LEA has Choate stock, LE has standard stock (disc. 2005), includes Burris (disc.) or Leupold (new 2004) 3.5-10x50mm scope with flip covers and sling, 4 shot internal (FPXP, disc. 2006) or detachable (FPCPXP, new 2007) mag., Harris bipod, aluminum case, 10 1/2 lbs. Mfg. 2002-2009.

	$2,275	$1,850	$1,550	$1,300	$1,100	$900	$750	*$2,715*

Subtract 20% LE standard stock or 10% for Choate stock (Model 10FPXP-LEA package).

GRADING - PPGS™	100%	98%	95%	90%	80%	70%	60%	LAST MSR

* ***Model 10FCP H-S Precision*** – .308 Win. cal., 24 in. barrel, features H-S Precision stock, 4 shot detachable box mag., matte blued finish, oversized bolt handle, no sights, 9.6 lbs. New 2007.

MSR $1,230	$1,075	$895	$750	$650	$550	$475	$400	

» ***Model 10FCPXP H-S Precision Package*** – .308 Win. cal., 24 in. barrel, includes top Picatinny rail, 3-9x40mm scope, and bipod, 9.6 lbs. Mfg. 2010-2011.

	$2,550	$2,250	$1,900	$1,625	$1,275	$1,000	$875	*$2,908*

* ***Model 10FCP Choate*** – .308 Win. cal., 24 in. barrel, features Choate stock, detachable box mag. Mfg. 2007 only.

	$700	$575	$475	$425	$350	$300	$275	*$833*

* ***Model 10FCP McMillan*** – .308 Win. cal., 24 in. barrel, features McMillan stock, 4 shot detachable box mag., no sights, matte blued finish, oversized bolt handle, 10 lbs. New 2007.

MSR $1,485	$1,275	$995	$875	$750	$650	$550	$450	

* ***Model 10 FCP-K/ Model 10 FLCP-K*** – .223 Rem. or .308 Win. cal., short action, 24 in. heavy blue barrel with muzzle brake, 4 shot detachable box mag., drilled and tapped, black synthetic AccuStock with aluminum spine and 3-D bedding cradle, swivel stud for bipod, oversized bolt handle, 8.9 lbs. New 2009.

MSR $975	$850	$725	$595	$475	$425	$350	$300	

This model is also available in left-hand action at no extra charge (Model 10 FLCP-K).

MODEL 10 PRECISION CARBINE – .223 Rem., .308 Win., or .300 AAC Blackout (mfg. 2012 only) cal., 20 in. matte blue free floating button rifled threaded (new 2012) or un-threaded (disc. 2011) barrel, 4 shot detachable box mag., swivel stud, oversized bolt handle, green camo Accustock with aluminum spine and 3-D bedding cradle, 7 lbs. New 2009.

MSR $925	$795	$675	$550	$425	$375	$350	$300	

* ***Model 10FCP-SR*** – .308 Win. cal., short action, 24 in. heavy fluted threaded barrel, 10 shot detachable box mag., matte black metal finish, synthetic tan digital camo stock, Accutrigger, Accustock, one-piece scope rail, 8 3/4 lbs. New 2012.

MSR $1,250	$1,100	$950	$825	$725	$625	$525	$425	

MODEL 10BA/BAS-K – .308 Win. cal., 24 in. barrel with muzzle brake, short action, 10 shot detachable box mag., all aluminum Accustock, Magpul PRS-G3 buttstock, Picatinny rail, no sights, matte blued finish, oversize bolt handle, 13.4 lbs. New 2009.

MSR $2,285	$1,925	$1,575	$1,225	$995	$875	$775	$695	

* ***Model 10BAT/S-K*** – .308 Win. cal., 24 in. barrel with muzzle brake, short action, 10 shot detachable box mag., similar to Model 10BAS-K, except has tactical stock with adj. buttpad. Mfg. 2009-2010.

	$1,750	$1,450	$1,125	$925	$800	$700	$600	*$2,071*

MODEL 10GY – .223 Rem., .243 Win., or .308 Win. cal., ladies/youth model with shorter checkered hardwood stock and 22 in. barrel with open sights. Disc. 2007.

	$455	$360	$295	$240	$200	$175	$160	*$541*

* ***Model 10GYXP3 Package*** – .223 Rem., .243 Win., or .308 Win. (disc. 2009) cal., ladies/youth model with shorter checkered hardwood stock and 22 in. barrel with open sights, includes scope, bipod, and case.

	$515	$410	$315	$250	$200	$175	$160	*$691*

MODEL 10GXP3 PACKAGE – various short action cals., 22 or 24 in. blue free floating and button rifled barrel, 2 or 4 shot mag., checkered Monte Carlo walnut stock, includes 3-9x40mm scope, approx. 7 1/2 lbs. Disc. 2011.

	$525	$415	$325	$250	$200	$175	$160	*$712*

Add $28 for .270 WSM or .300 WSM cal.

This model is also available in left-hand at no charge (Model 10GLXP3, not available in WSM cals., disc. 2011).

GRADING - PPGS™	100%	98%	95%	90%	80%	70%	60%	LAST MSR

MODEL 10 TROPHY HUNTER XP PACKAGE – .22-250 Rem., .223 Rem., .243 Win., or .308 Win. cal., short action, 4 shot detachable box mag., 22 in. barrel, matte black metal finish, satin finished wood stock, Accutrigger, includes 3-9x40 Nikon BDC scope, 8.3 lbs. New 2012.

MSR $745	$650	$575	$500	$450	$400	$365	$325

MODEL 11 HUNTER XP PACKAGE – .22-250 Rem., .223 Rem., .243 Win., or .308 Win. cal., short action, 4 shot detachable box mag., 22 in. barrel, matte black metal finish, black synthetic stock, includes 3-9x40 Bushnell scope, Accutrigger not available on this model, 7 1/4 lbs. New 2012.

MSR $525	$450	$400	$360	$330	$300	$275	$250

MODEL 11 LADY HUNTER – .223 Rem., .22-250 Rem., .243 Win., .308 Win., 6.5 Creedmoor, or 7mm-08 Rem. cal., short action, 20 in. barrel without sights, black matte metal finish, 4 shot mag., Accutrigger, drilled and tapped, satin finished walnut with pressed checkering and forward angled Monte Carlo stock with recoil pad, stock features include shorter LOP, higher front angled comb, slimmer forend and pistol grip, three-position safety, sling swivels, 6 lbs. New mid-2012.

MSR $840	$700	$575	$475	$400	$350	$300	$265

MODEL 11 LIGHTWEIGHT HUNTER – .223 Rem., .243 Win., 6.5 Creedmoor, 7mm-08 Rem., .260 Rem., or .308 Win. cal., short action, 20 in. barrel without sights, AccuTrigger, 4 shot detachable box mag., hinged floorplate, blue finish, uncheckered walnut stock, spiral fluted bolt, 5 1/2 lbs. New 2011.

MSR $925	$795	$675	$575	$450	$395	$350	$300

MODEL 11 HOG HUNTER – .223 Rem. or .308 Win. cal., short action, centerfire, matte black metal finish, 20 in. threaded barrel, 4 shot internal box mag., AccuTrigger, iron sights, OD Green synthetic stock, 7 1/4 lbs., New 2012.

MSR $535	$465	$415	$375	$335	$295	$265	$235

MODEL 11 LONG RANGE HUNTER – .260 Rem. (new 2011), 6.5 Creedmoor (new 2011), .308 Win. or .300 WSM cal., 26 in. fluted carbon steel barrel with muzzle brake, drilled and tapped, Karsten adj. and detachable cheekpiece, matte black synthetic AccuStock and forearm, 2 or 3 shot mag., AccuTrigger, 8.4 lbs. New 2010.

MSR $1,020	$875	$725	$600	$525	$425	$365	$325

Add $40 for .300 WSM cal.

MODEL 11 TROPHY HUNTER XP PACKAGE – .204 Ruger, .22-250 Rem., .223 Rem., .243 Win., .260 Rem., .270 WSM, .300 WSM, .308 Win., 6.5 Creedmoor, or 7mm-08 Rem. cal., short action, 4 shot detachable box mag., 22 or 24 (WSM cals. only) in. barrel, matte black metal finish, synthetic black stock, Accutrigger, includes 3-9x40 Nikon scope, right or left-hand action. 7 1/4 lbs. New 2012.

MSR $675	$595	$525	$450	$415	$375	$335	$295

Add $25 for WSM cals.

MODEL 11 TROPHY HUNTER XP YOUTH PACKAGE – .223 Rem., .243 Win., .308 Win., or 7mm-08 Rem. cal., short action, 20 in. barrel, 4 shot detachable box mag., matte black metal finish, synthetic black stock, Accutrigger, includes 3-9x40 Nikon scope, right or left-hand action. New 2012.

MSR $675	$595	$525	$450	$415	$375	$335	$295

MODEL 11BTH HUNTER – .204 Ruger (disc. 2011), .22-250 Rem., .223 Rem., .243 Win., or .308 Win. cal., short action, 22 in. barrel with no sights, drilled and tapped, hinged floorplate, 4 shot mag, ventilated forend, AccuTrigger, brown laminated thumbhole stock. New 2008.

MSR $890	$775	$675	$550	$450	$400	$350	$300

MODEL 11FNS (11F) HUNTER – .22-250 Rem., .223 Rem., .243 Win., .260 Rem. (mfg. 1999-2000), .270 WSM (mfg. 2003-2008), .308 Win., .300 RSUM (mfg. 2003), .300 WSM (mfg. 2002-2008), 7mm RSUM (mfg. 2003), 7mm WSM (mfg. 2003-2005, reintroduced 2007-2008 in left-hand only), or 7mm-08 Rem. (new 1999) cal., short action, dual pillar bedding,

GRADING - PPGS™	100%	98%	95%	90%	80%	70%	60%	LAST MSR

checkered black synthetic stock, 22 or 24 (WSM cals. only) in. blue barrel with open sights (disc. 2008) or no sights (standard beginning 2009), 6 3/4 lbs. Mfg. 1998-2011.

	$475	$400	$340	$285	$230	$200	$175	*$609*

Add $23 for WSM cals. (left-hand only, disc. 2008).

This model is also available in left-hand action (Model 11FL).

MODEL 11FCNS/FHNS (11FC) – .204 Ruger (new 2008), .22-250 Rem., .223 Rem. (new 2008), .243 Win., .260 Rem. (disc. 2000, reintroduced 2011), 7.62x39mm (mfg. 2011 only), .270 WSM (new 2005), .308 Win., .300 WSM (new 2005), 7mm WSM (mfg. 2005-2008, FHNS only 2008-2009), or 7mm-08 Rem. cal., 22 or 24 in. barrel without sights, blue finish, short action, fixed (disc. 2004), detachable box mag. (new 2005, Model FCNS), or hinged floorplate (new 2006, Model FHNS), AccuTrigger, dual pillar bedded black synthetic stock, AccuStock became standard 2009, 6 3/8 lbs. Mfg. 1999-2001, reintroduced 2003.

MSR $715	$595	$475	$375	$325	$295	$260	$230	

Add $30 for WSM cals.

This model is also available in left-hand action (Model 11FLC, disc. 2001).

The Model FHNS is not available in WSM cals.

MODEL 11FYXP3 PACKAGE – .223 Rem. (new 2003), .243 Win., 7mm-08 Rem. (new 2003) or .308 Win. (new 2009) cal., similar to 11F Hunter, except is Youth Model with 12 1/2 LOP, 22 in. barrel, AccuTrigger, includes 3-9x40mm scope, 6 1/2 lbs. Mfg. 2002-2011.

	$525	$450	$380	$310	$240	$210	$185	*$678*

This model is also available in left hand action in all calibers beginning 2009.

MODEL 11FYCXP3 YOUTH PACKAGE – .243 Win. cal., short action, detachable 4 shot box mag., Youth model w/shorter dimensions, 22 in. barrel, AccuTrigger not available, includes scope, 6 1/2 lbs. Mfg. 2006-2011.

	$425	$350	$300	$275	$225	$200	$175	*$525*

MODEL 11FCXP3 PACKAGE – .243 Win. or .308 Win. cal., detachable box mag., 22 in. barrel, AccuTrigger not available, black synthetic stock, includes scope. Disc. 2011.

	$425	$350	$300	$275	$225	$200	$175	*$525*

MODEL 11FYCAK – .243 Win., 7mm-08 Rem., or .308 Win. cal., 22 in. barrel, detachable box mag., Youth Model with shortened LOP. Mfg. 2006-2010.

	$585	$435	$355	$300	$270	$235	$200	*$712*

MODEL 11FXP3 – see listing later in this category, combined with Model 111FXP3 package.

MODEL 11GNS/GCNS (11G) HUNTER – similar to 11F Hunter, except has wood stock with pressed fleur-de-lis checkering, 22 in. barrel, AccuTrigger, no sights (Model 11GNS), also available with detachable box mag (new 2005, Model 11GCNS, standard beginning 2011). Mfg. 1998-2011.

	$500	$415	$325	$250	$200	$175	$160	*$699*

Add $25 for .270 WSM or .300 WSM cals. (11GCNS Model only, disc.).
Subtract $10 if w/o sights (Model 11GNS, disc. 2004).

This model was also available in left-hand action (Model 11GL or Model 11GLNS). This model's nomenclature changed from 11G to 11GNS during 2009 (no sights).

MODEL 11GC – .22-250 Rem., .243 Win., .260 Rem. (disc. 2000), .308 Win. or 7mm-08 Rem. cal., detachable mag., hardwood stock, open sights, 22 in. barrel, blue finish, 6 3/8 lbs. Mfg. 1999-2001.

	$375	$310	$270	$230	$200	$175	$160	*$441*

This model is also available in left-hand action (Model 11GLC).

MODEL 12 LONG RANGE PRECISION – .243 Win., .260 Rem., or 6.5 Creedmoor cal., short action, 26 in. barrel, Target AccuTrigger, H-S Precision fiberglass stock, 4 shot detachable box mag., no sights, oversized bolt handle, 11 lbs. New 2011.

MSR $1,170	$995	$875	$750	$650	$550	$475	$400	

GRADING - PPGS™	100%	98%	95%	90%	80%	70%	60%	LAST MSR

MODEL 12 VARMINTER LOW PROFILE – .204 Ruger (new 2005), .22-250 Rem., .223 Rem., .243 Win. (new 2007), .300 WSM (new 2007), or .308 Win. (new 2007) cal., choice of repeater or single shot (.204 Ruger, .22-250 Rem., or .223 Rem. cals. only, disc. 2009), right-hand bolt, smaller ejection port on left side of receiver, 2 or 4 shot detachable box mag., 26 in. fluted stainless heavy barrel and action, AccuTrigger standard, low profile brown laminated stock with extra wide beavertail forend, no sights, short action, 10 lbs. New 2004.

MSR $1,080	$925	$750	$650	$525	$450	$400	$350	

Add $50 for .300 WSM cal.

Subtract $40 for single shot (disc. 2009).

During 2005, this model became available in left-hand action at no extra charge in select cals.

MODEL 12 LONG RANGE PRECISION VARMINTER – .204 Ruger, .22-250 Rem., .223 Rem., or 6mm Norma BR (new 2008) cal., single shot, right-hand bolt, left port ejection or dual port with left load and right eject (became standard 2011), stainless short action, 26 in. X-Tra heavy fluted free floating barrel, black synthetic H-S Precision varmint stock with molded alloy bedding system, no sights, drilled and tapped, target AccuTrigger, oversized bolt handle, swivel studs, 12 lbs. New 2005.

MSR $1,395	$1,175	$995	$875	$775	$675	$575	$450	

During 2005-2006, this model was available in left-hand action at no extra charge.

MODEL 12 LONG RANGE PRECISION VARMINTER REPEATER – .204 Ruger, .22-250 Rem., .223 Rem., or 6mm Norma BR cal., 26 in. barrel, short action, detachable box mag., target AccuTrigger. Mfg. 2008-2010.

	$1,085	$925	$825	$725	$625	$525	$450	*$1,319*

MODEL 12BTCSS VARMINTER THUMBHOLE – .204 Ruger, .22-250 Rem., or .223 Rem. cal., 26 in. heavy fluted barrel, stainless short action, 4 shot detachable box mag., laminated thumbhole stock, AccuTrigger, no sights, drilled and tapped, 10 lbs. New 2008.

MSR $1,175	$1,025	$895	$750	$650	$550	$450	$375	

MODEL 12BVSS – .204 Ruger (mfg. 2009-2010), .22-250 Rem., .223 Rem., .243 Win. (mfg. 2002-2006), .300 WSM (mfg. 2003-2006), or .308 Win. (disc. 1999, reintroduced 2001-2006, again in 2009) cal., short action, right bolt, left port ejection, 26 in. heavy fluted stainless barrel w/o sights, dual pillar bedding, brown laminated wood stock with flat beavertail forend, AccuTrigger became standard 2003, 9 lbs. New 1998.

MSR $1,040	$900	$775	$650	$550	$450	$400	$350	

This model was also available in left-hand action in cals. .22-250 Rem. and .223 Rem. at no extra charge (mfg. 2004, Model 12BLVSS).

* ***Model 12BVSS-S*** – .220 Swift (new 2004), .22-250 Rem., .223 Rem., or .308 Win. cal., similar to Model 12BVSS, except is single shot, AccuTrigger became standard 2003. Mfg. 1998-2001, mfg. 2002-2005.

	$600	$490	$395	$335	$290	$245	$215	*$721*

* ***Model 12BVSS-SXP*** – similar to Model 12BVSS, except not available in .243 Win. cal., target style heavy prone laminate stock with Wundhammer palm swell and black forend cap, 26 in. fluted stainless barrel w/o sights, includes 6-18x37mm scope and black aluminum hard case, 12 lbs. Mfg. 2002-2004.

	$1,050	$895	$775	$665	$560	$465	$410	*$1,225*

MODEL 12FVSS – .22-250 Rem., .223 Rem., .270 WSM (mfg. 2003-2008), .300 WSM (mfg. 2003-2008), or .308 Win. cal., short action, right-hand bolt, left ejection port, features 26 in. fluted heavy stainless free floating barrel w/o sights, black checkered synthetic stock with dual pillar bedding, drilled and tapped, AccuTrigger became standard 2003, 9 lbs. Mfg. 1998-2012.

	$800	$700	$600	$525	$450	$375	$300	*$895*

Add $30 for WSM cals. (disc. 2009).

This model was also available in left-hand action (Model 12FLVSS, not available in WSM cals., disc. 2004).

GRADING - PPGS™	100%	98%	95%	90%	80%	70%	60%	LAST MSR

* ***Model 12FVSS-S*** – similar to Model 12FVSS, except is single shot and not available in .308 Win. cal. Mfg. 1998-2001.

	$480	$405	$335	$275	$235	$200	$175	*$549*

* ***Model 12VSS/12VSS-S*** – .22-250 Rem., .223 Rem., or .308 Win. cal., available in long (12VSS) or short (12VSS-S, mfg. 2003-2004, not available in .308 Win. cal.) action, semi-skeletonized Choate adj. black synthetic stock with cheekpiece, 24 (disc. 2004) or 26 in. fluted stainless barrel, blue stainless steel receiver, 4 shot mag., drilled and tapped receiver, AccuTrigger became standard 2003, 11 1/4 lbs. Mfg. 2000-2006.

	$700	$595	$495	$425	$375	$315	$270	*$865*

MODEL 12FV/FVY – .204 Ruger (new 2005), .22-250 Rem., .223 Rem., .243 Win. (mfg. 2002-2009), or .308 Win. (mfg. 1999-2008) cal., short action, right bolt, left ejection port, features 26 in. regular barrel with low luster bluing, black synthetic stock with dual pillar bedding, 5 shot top loading mag., drilled and tapped, AccuTrigger became standard 2003, right or left-hand action, 9 lbs. New 1998.

MSR $710	$595	$475	$415	$365	$335	$300	$275

This model was also available as a Youth Model (Model 12FVY, available in .22-250 Rem. and .223 Rem. cal. only, mfg. 2003-2004). This model is also available in left-hand action (Model 12FLV, disc. 2001, reintroduced during 2004, not available in .243 Win. or .308 Win. cal.).

MODEL 12 F/TR TARGET – .223 Rem. (new 2010) or .308 Win. cal., short action, single shot, 30 in. stainless steel barrel, target features, target AccuTrigger, oversize bolt handle, no sights, 12 1/2 lbs. New 2007.

MSR $1,425	$1,225	$1,050	$900	$800	$700	$600	$475

MODEL 12FCV – .204 Ruger, .22-250 Rem., or 223 Rem. cal., 4 shot detachable box mag., 26 in. barrel, AccuTrigger, checkered pistol grip matte black Accustock, no sights, blued finish, 9 lbs. New 2010.

MSR $870	$775	$665	$575	$495	$425	$350	$295

MODEL 12 F CLASS – 6.5x284mm Norma or 6mm Norma BR (new 2008) cal., short action, single shot, 30 in. stainless steel barrel, target features, target AccuTrigger, ergonomic grey laminate stock, oversize bolt handle, no sights, 13 lbs. New 2007.

MSR $1,525	$1,325	$1,150	$1,000	$875	$725	$600	$500

MODEL 12LRPV – .204 Ruger, .223 Rem., .22-250 Rem., or 6mm Norma BR cal., right hand action, left port, 26 in. fluted barrel w/o sights, black synthetic stock, 11 lbs. New 2013.

MSR $1,395	$1,150	$975	$850	$725	$600	$500	$425

MODEL 12 BENCHREST – 6.5x284mm Norma, 6mm Norma BR, or .308 Win. cal., short dual port action featuring left load with right eject, 29 in. heavy barrel, stainless steel action and barrel, target AccuTrigger, heavy laminate stock with vented wide forend, 12 3/4 lbs. New 2009.

MSR $1,550	$1,345	$1,150	$1,000	$850	$725	$600	$500

MODEL 12 PALMA – .308 Win. cal., short action, 30 in. heavy stainless steel barrel, laminated stock with adj. comb and buttplate, vent forend, target AccuTrigger, 11 1/2 lbs. New 2009.

MSR $1,985	$1,750	$1,550	$1,300	$1,050	$900	$775	$675

MODEL 14 CLASSIC/AMERICAN CLASSIC – .204 Ruger (mfg. 2008-2011), .22-250 Rem. (disc. 2012), .223 Rem. (mfg. 2008-2012), .243 Win. (also avail. w/stainless steel barrel), .250 Savage (new 2009), 7mm-08 Rem. (new 2011), .270 WSM (left-hand only, disc.2012), .300 WSM (left hand only, disc. 2012), .300 Savage (mfg. 2009-2011), .325 WSM (mfg. 2007-2008), .308 Win. (also avail. w/stainless steel barrel), or 7mm-08 Rem. cal., 22 or 24 (Mag. cals. only) in. steel or stainless steel (new 2011) barrel, detachable box mag. (American Classic, right or left (new 2008) hand action) or hinged floorplate (Classic, mfg. 2006-2011), no sights, checkered walnut stock and black forend tip, high polish blue, AccuTrigger standard, 7 or 7 1/2 lbs. New 2005.

MSR $885	$765	$650	$550	$475	$400	$350	$295

Add $34 for WSM cals. (disc. 2012).

Subtract $35 for stainless steel (.243 Win. or .308 Win. cal. only, new 2011).

GRADING - PPGS™	100%	98%	95%	90%	80%	70%	60%	LAST MSR

MODEL 14 EURO CLASSIC – .22-250 Rem. (disc. 2009), .243 Win., or .308 Win. cal., 22 in. barrel, detachable box mag., AccuTrigger standard, open sights with adj. rear sight on barrel, checkered walnut stock with cheekpiece, 7 1/2 lbs. Mfg. 2006-2010.

	$750	$595	$525	$445	$375	$325	$275	*$909*

MODEL 16 BEAR HUNTER – .300 WSM or .325 WSM cal., 2 shot mag., 23 in. barrel, hinged floorplated, adj. muzzlebrake, AccuStock, AccuTrigger, checkered synthetic (disc.) or Mossy Oak Break-Up Infinity camo stock, 7 1/2 lbs. New 2011.

MSR $1,030	$895	$750	$650	$550	$500	$400	$325	

MODEL 16FXP3 PACKAGE – .204 Ruger (new 2005), .22-250 Rem. (new 2003), .223 Rem., .243 Win., .270 WSM (new 2003), .300 RSUM (mfg. 2003), .308 Win., .300 WSM, .325 WSM (mfg. 2007-2008), 7mm-08 Rem. (new 2010), 7mm WSM (mfg. 2003-2008), or 7mm RSUM (mfg. 2003) cal., short action, stainless action and 22 or 24 in. stainless barrel w/o sights, checkered black synthetic stock, includes nickel finished 3-9x40mm scope and mounts, supplied with sling, approx. 6 1/2 lbs. Mfg. 2002-2011.

	$625	$495	$425	$360	$315	$270	$225	*$782*

Add $31 for WSM cals.

MODEL 16 TROPHY HUNTER XP PACKAGE – .204 Ruger, .22-250 Rem., .223 Rem., .243 Win., .260 Rem., .270 WSM, .300 WSM, .308 Win., 6.5 Creedmoor, or 7mm-08 Rem. cal., short action, 22 or 24 (WSM cals. only) in. stainless barrel, 4 shot detachable box mag., black synthetic stock, Accutrigger, includes 3-9x40 Nikon BDC scope, 7 1/4 lbs. New 2012.

MSR $795	$685	$595	$515	$465	$415	$365	$325	

Add $30 for WSM cals.

MODEL 16BSS WEATHER WARRIOR – .270 WSM (new 2003), .300 WSM, .300 RSUM (disc. 2002), 7mm WSM (new 2003), or 7mm RSUM (disc. 2002) cal., 24 in. barrel w/o sights, 2 or 3 shot mag., brown laminated stock with cut checkering, stainless action and barrel, 7 3/4 lbs. Mfg. 2002-2003.

	$560	$460	$355	$290	$250	$215	$185	*$668*

MODEL 16FCSS WEATHER WARRIOR – .243 Win., .260 Rem. (disc. 2000), .308 Win., or 7mm-08 Rem. cal., stainless steel barreled action with 22 in. barrel, detachable mag., dual pillar bedded black synthetic stock, 6 3/4 lbs. Mfg. 1999-2001.

	$460	$395	$325	$265	$230	$195	$170	*$532*

This model was also available in left-hand action at no additional charge (Model 16FLCSS).

MODEL 16FCSAK WEATHER WARRIOR – .243 Win., .270 WSM, .300 WSM, .308 Win., 7mm-08 Rem., or 7mm WSM cal., short action, 22 or 24 in. fluted barrel with adj. muzzle brake, detachable box mag., no sights. Mfg. 2005 only.

	$560	$495	$415	$350	$315	$275	$245	*$661*

MODEL 16FSS – .204 Ruger (new 2005), .22-250 Rem. (new 2003), .223 Rem., .243 Win., .260 Rem. (mfg. 1999-2000), .270 WSM (disc. 2009), .308 Win., .300 WSM (mfg. 2002-2009), .300 RSUM (mfg. 2002-2003), 7mm WSM (mfg. 2003-2007), 7mm RSUM (mfg. 2002-2003), or 7mm-08 Rem. (mfg. 1999-2009) cal., short action, stainless steel 22 or 24 (WSM and RSUM cals only) in. barreled action w/o sights, checkered black synthetic stock with dual pillar bedding, 6 3/4 lbs. Mfg. 1998-2011.

	$575	$475	$415	$330	$285	$240	$210	*$720*

Add $27 for WSM cals.

Also available in left-hand action at no additional charge (Model 16FLSS, not available in WSM or .204 Ruger cals.).

* ***Model 16FCSS*** – .204 Ruger, .22-250 Rem., .223 Rem., .243 Win., .260 Rem. (new 2011), .270 WSM, .300 WSM, .308 Win., 6.5 Creedmoor (new 2011), or 7mm-08 Rem. cal., short action, stainless steel, 22 or 24 in. barrel, AccuTrigger, 2 or 4 shot detachable box mag., AccuStock standard beginning 2009, no sights, 7 lbs. New 2005.

MSR $850	$725	$625	$525	$450	$400	$350	$275	

Add $35 for WSM cals.

GRADING - PPGS™	100%	98%	95%	90%	80%	70%	60%	LAST MSR

* ***Model 16FHSS*** – .22-250 Rem., .223 Rem., .243 Win., .250 Savage, .270 WSM, .300 WSM, .308 Win., 7mm-08 Rem. (left hand only) cal., short action, stainless steel, 22 or 24 in. barrel, AccuTrigger, 2 or 4 shot mag., hinged floorplate, AccuStock became standard 2009, right or left hand action, no sights. New 2006.

MSR $850	$725	$625	$525	$450	$400	$350	$275	

Add $35 for WSM cals.

This model is also available in left-hand action at no additional charge (Model 16FLHSS, new 2007, not available in Savage cals.).

* ***Model 16FHSAK*** – .243 Win. (disc. 2009), .270 WSM, .300 WSM, or .308 Win. cal., 22 or 24 in. barrel, similar to Model 16FHSS, except has adj. muzzle brake, AccuStock became standard 2009. Mfg. 2006-2010.

	$715	$540	$465	$410	$350	$300	$250	*$864*

MODEL 25 LIGHTWEIGHT VARMINTER – .17 Hornet (new 2012), .22 Hornet, .204 Ruger or .223 Rem. cal., 22 (Classic, disc. 2010) or 24 in. barrel, short action, 4 shot detachable box mag., AccuTrigger, brown laminated stock or Classic walnut stock with checkering and black forend tip (disc. 2010), 3 lug bolt with 60 degree throw, Weaver style base, triple pillar bedding, 7 lbs. New 2008.

MSR $730	$625	$550	$450	$400	$350	$300	$250	

Add $25 for 22 in. barrel (Model 25 Classic, disc. 2010).

* ***Model 25 Lightweight Varminter-T*** – .17 Hornet (new 2012), .22 Hornet (new 2011), .222 Rem. (new 2011), .223 Rem., .204 Ruger, or 5.7x28 (mfg. 2011 only) cal., 24 in. barrel, short action, 4 shot detachable box mag., satin finished laminated thumbhole stock and vent. forend, AccuTrigger, includes Weaver scope bases, 8 1/4 lbs. New 2008.

MSR $775	$675	$575	$475	$425	$375	$325	$275	

MODEL 25 WALKING VARMINTER – .17 Hornet (new 2012), .22 Hornet, .204 Ruger, .222 Rem., .223 Rem., or 5.7x28mm (mfg. 2011 only) cal., short action, 22 in. barrel, black synthetic or Realtree Extra camo (not avail. in .204 Ruger cal., new 2013) stock, AccuTrigger, 4 shot detachable box mag., 7.1 lbs. New 2011.

MSR $567	$485	$400	$330	$285	$235	$200	$175	

Add $50 for Realtree Extra camo stock (new 2013).

MODEL 40 VARMINT HUNTER SINGLE SHOT – .22 Hornet or .223 Rem. (disc. 2004) cal., single shot action, varmint configuration featuring 24 in. heavy contour barrel and brown laminate stock with full beavertail forend, AccuTrigger became standard 2003, 7 3/4 lbs.

	$465	$360	$310	$265	$220	$190	$170	*$582*

MODEL 110 PREDATOR HUNTER – 6.5x284 Norma cal., right or left (new 2012) hand action, 24 in. barrel, RealTree Max 1 patterned camo AccuStock, AccuTrigger, no sights, includes scope blocks, 4 shot detachable box mag., 7 1/4 lbs. New 2011.

MSR $915	$815	$700	$575	$475	$425	$375	$325	

MODEL 110 SPORTER BOLT ACTION – .243 Win., .270 Win., .308 Win., or .30 - 06 cal., 22 in. barrel, open sight, 4 shot, checkered pistol grip stock. Mfg. 1958-63.

	$375	$325	$275	$250	$225	$200	$185	

MODEL 110-MC – similar to Model 110, with Monte Carlo stock. Mfg. 1959-69.

	$385	$325	$275	$250	$225	$200	$185	

MODEL 110-M – similar to Model 110MC, except 7mm Rem. Mag., .264 Win. Mag., .300 Win. Mag., or .338 Win. Mag. cal., recoil pad. Mfg. 1963-69.

	$395	$335	$285	$250	$225	$200	$185	

MODEL 110-C/CL – various cals., push-button detachable mag., walnut stock. Mfg. 1966-85.

	$425	$365	$325	$295	$275	$250	$225	

MODEL 110-D – .22-250 Rem. (disc.), .223 Rem., .243 Win., .25-06 Rem. (disc.), .270 Win., .308 Win. (disc.), .30-06, 7mm Rem. Mag., .300 Win. Mag. (disc.), or .338 Win. Mag.

GRADING - PPGS™	100%	98%	95%	90%	80%	70%	60%	LAST MSR

cal., similar to Model 110B, hinged floorplate (1972-75 only), checkered walnut stock, removable and adj. rear sight, 7 1/2 lbs. Mfg. 1966-88.

$350	$300	$275	$250	$225	$190	$170	*$409*

Add $80 for left-hand version.

MODEL 110-E – .22-250 Rem., .223 Rem., .243 Win., .270 Win., 7mm Rem. Mag., .308 Win., or .30-06 cal., 22 or 24 (Mag. only) in. barrel, open sights, uncheckered hardwood Monte Carlo stock, blind internal magazine with floorplate, 7 lbs. Mfg. 1963-1988.

$350	$300	$275	$250	$225	$190	$170	*$325*

Subtract $16 without sights.

MODEL 110-F – .22-250 Rem., .223 Rem., .243 Win., .250 Sav. (new 1993), .25-06 Rem. (new 1993), .308 Win., .30-06, .270 Win., 7mm-08 Rem. (new 1993), 7mm Rem. Mag., .300 Sav. (new 1993), .300 Win. Mag., or .338 Win. Mag. (new 1991) cal., 22 or 24 (Magnum) in. barrel, black DuPont Rynite stock with swivel studs and recoil pad, adj. rear sight, drilled and tapped for scope mounts, 4 or 5 shot mag., 6 3/4 lbs. Mfg. 1989-1993.

$335	$300	$265	$235	$210	$195	$180

* ***Model 110-FNS*** – similar to Model 110-F, except has no sights. Mfg. 1991-93.

$325	$285	$250	$225	$200	$190	$175

* ***Model 110-FXP3*** – .22-250 Rem. (new 1992), .223 Rem. (new 1992), .243 Win., .270 Win., .30-06, .308 Win. (new 1992), 7mm Rem. Mag., or .300 Win. Mag. cal., similar to Model 110-F except is without sights and has integral Weaver type scope bases. Mfg. 1989-93.

$415	$370	$325	$285	$250	$225	$195

MODEL 110-GY – .223 Rem. (Mfg. 1993-99), .243 Win. (disc. 1999), .270 Win. (new 1994), .300 Sav. (disc. 1995), or .308 Win. (mfg. 1994-99) cal., 22 in. barrel, youth/ladies variation with shortened classic stock, open sights, 6 1/2 lbs. Mfg. 1991-2000.

$350	$300	$260	$220	$195	$175	$160	*$395*

MODEL 110-WLE – .250-3000 Sav., .300 Sav., or 7x57mm Mauser cal. Mfg. 1991-93.

$425	$390	$360	$320	$280	$250	$225

Approx. 1,000 of each cal. were mfg. in this model.

* ***Model 110-WLE 1 of 1,000*** – 7x57mm Mauser cal., features select walnut stock with Monte Carlo cheekpiece, high luster blue finish with laser etched Savage logo on bolt body, drilled and tapped, 1,000 mfg. beginning 1992, 7 3/4 lbs. Mfg. 1992-93 only.

$415	$370	$325	$285	$250	$225	$195

MODEL 110-FM SIERRA ULTRA LIGHT – .243 Win. (disc. 1998), .270 Win., .30 - 06, or .308 Win. (disc. 1998) cal., features 20 in. high gloss barrel w/o sights, black graphite/fiberglass-filled stock with non-glare finish, drilled and tapped, 6 1/4 lbs. Mfg. 1996-2000.

$380	$325	$270	$230	$205	$175	$160	*$449*

MODEL 110-FP LAW ENFORCEMENT (TACTICAL POLICE) – .223 Rem. (disc. 1998), .25-06 Rem. (new 1995), .300 Win. Mag. (new 1995), .30-06 (mfg. 1996-2006), .308 Win. (disc. 1998), or 7mm Rem. Mag. (mfg. 1995-2007) cal., long action, 24 in. heavy barrel pillar bedded tactical rifle, all metal parts are non-reflective, 4 shot internal mag., black Dupont Rynite stock, right or left-hand (mfg. 1996-2001) action, drilled and tapped for scope mounts, AccuTrigger became standard 2003, 8 1/2 lbs. Mfg. 1990-2001, reintroduced 2003-2008.

$575	$465	$360	$310	$265	$240	$210	*$678*

Also available in left-hand action at no additional charge (mfg. 1996-2001, Model 110-FLP).

* ***Model 110FCP*** – .25-06 Rem. or .300 Win. Mag. cal., 24 in. heavy barrel with Savage muzzle brake, 4 shot detachable box mag., black synthetic AccuStock with aluminum spine and 3-D bedding cradle, drilled and tapped, swivel stud for bipod, oversized bolt handle, 9 lbs. Mfg. 2009.

$725	$600	$500	$425	$375	$350	$300	*$866*

GRADING - PPGS™	100%	98%	95%	90%	80%	70%	60%	LAST MSR

MODEL 110-G – .22-250 Rem., .223 Rem., .243 Win., .250 Sav. (new 1992), .25-06 Rem. (new 1992), .300 Sav. (new 1993), .308 Win., .30-06, .270 Win., 7mm-08 Rem. (new 1992), 7mm Rem. Mag., or .300 Win. Mag. cal., top loading internal box mag., 22 or 24 in. barrel, adj. iron sights, checkered hardwood stock, approx. 7 lbs. Mfg. 1989-93.

	$325	$285	$250	$225	$200	$190	$175	

Subtract $10-$20 if without sights (Model 110-GNS).

* ***Model 110-GC*** – .270 Win., .30-06, 7mm Rem. Mag., or .300 Win. Mag. cal., features detachable 3 or 4 shot mag., 22 or 24 in. barrel, checkered hardwood stock, adj. sights, 6 3/4 lbs. Mfg. 1992-93.

	$410	$325	$275	$240	$210	$180	$165	

Add $20 for Mag. cals.

* ***Model 10GXP3/110-GXP3 Package*** – .22-250 Rem., .223 Rem., .243 Win., .250 Savage (disc. 1995), .25-06 Rem., .270 Win., .270 WSM (new 2003), .300 Sav. (disc. 1995), .30-06, .300 RSUM (mfg. 2002-2003), .308 Win., 7mm-08 Rem. (disc. 1995, reintroduced 1999), 7mm WSM (mfg. 2003-2007), 7mm Rem. Mag., 7mm RSUM (mfg. 2003), .300 WSM (new 2005), .300 Rem. Ultra Mag. (mfg. 2002-2006), or .300 Win. Mag. cal., short (10GXP3) or long (110-GXP3) action, similar to Model 110-G, except has no sights, includes 3-9x32 scope, rings, bases, QD swivels, and deluxe rifle sling, includes integral Weaver type scope bases. Mfg. 1989-2011.

	$525	$415	$325	$250	$200	$175	$160	*$712*

Add $29 for WSM cals. (Model 10GXP3 only).

Also available in left-hand action at no additional charge (Model 10GLXP3/110-GLXP3).

* ***Model 110-GCXP3 Package*** – .270 Win., .30-06, .300 Win. Mag., or 7mm Rem. Mag. cal., 22 or 24 in. barrel, checkered hardwood stock, detachable box mag., package includes 3-9x32 scope, rings, bases, QD swivels, and deluxe rifle sling, 7 1/4 lbs. Disc. 2001.

	$445	$375	$315	$275	$235	$190	$175	*$524*

Was also available in left-hand action at no additional charge (Model 110-GLCXP3 - disc. 2000).

MODEL 110 TROPHY HUNTER XP PACKAGE – .270 Win., .30-06, .300 Win. Mag. (new 2013), or 7mm Rem. Mag. (new 2013) cal., long action, 4 shot detachable box mag., 22 in. barrel, matte black metal finish, satin finished wood stock, Accutrigger, includes 3-9x40 Nikon BDC scope, 8.3 lbs. New 2012.

MSR $745	$635	$565	$500	$450	$400	$365	$335	

* ***Model 110-GL*** – .30-06, .270 Win., or 7mm Rem. Mag. cal., left-hand variation of the Model 110-G. Mfg. 1989-93.

	$325	$265	$225	$200	$180	$165	$150	

* ***Model 110-GLNS*** – similar to Model 110-GL, except has no sights. Mfg. 1991-1993.

	$320	$260	$220	$200	$180	$165	$150	

MODEL 110-K – .243 Win., .270 Win., or .30-06 cal., laminated camouflage stock. Mfg. 1986-88.

	$335	$280	$240	$185	$155	$135	$115	*$399*

MODEL 110-S – .308 Win., 7mm-08 Rem. (mfg. 1981-1983) cals., silhouette model, 22 in. heavy barrel, Wundhammer swell pistol grip with stippling, no sights, 4 shot mag., 8 lbs. 10 oz. Disc. 1985.

	$340	$290	$255	$225	$205	$190	$175	*$385*

Add 75% for 7mm-08 Rem. cal.

MODEL 110-V – .22-250 Rem. or .223 Rem. cal. only, varmint model, 26 in. heavy barrel, no sights, 5 shot mag., stippled walnut Wundhammer pistol grip stock, 9 1/4 lbs. Disc. 1989.

	$370	$315	$265	$230	$205	$190	$175	*$439*

MODEL 110-GV – .22-250 Rem. or .223 Rem. cal., varmint variation, 24 in. medium barrel, no sights, checkered hardwood stock with rubber recoil pad, drilled and tapped for scope, 8 1/4 lbs. Mfg. 1989-1993.

	$380	$285	$250	$225	$200	$190	$175	

GRADING - PPGS™	100%	98%	95%	90%	80%	70%	60%	LAST MSR

MODEL 110-B – similar to Model 110E, except available in .243 Win., .270 Win. or .30-06 cal., select stock and pistol grip cap, features blind mag., walnut Monte Carlo stock. Reintroduced 1989 with laminate stock (Model 110-B Laminate). Mfg. 1978-1979.

	$360	$300	$265	$235	$205	$190	$175	

This model was also available in left-hand action (Model 110-BL).

MODEL 110-B LAMINATE – similar to Model 110-B, except is available in .300 Win. Mag. or .338 Win. Mag. cal. also, has brown laminate hardwood stock with iron sights, approx. 7 1/2 lbs. Mfg. 1989-91.

	$385	$310	$250	$225	$200	$190	$180	*$477*

MODEL 110BA/BAS – .300 Win. Mag. or .338 Lapua cal., right or left (new 2013) hand action, 26 in. fluted carbon steel barrel with muzzle brake, 5 or 6 shot detachable box mag., drilled and tapped, open sights, includes Picatinny top rail, matte black aluminum tactical AccuStock with handguard, AccuTrigger, 15 3/4 lbs. New 2010.

MSR $2,465	$2,100	$1,850	$1,600	$1,350	$1,100	$900	$775	

MODEL 110FCP HS PRECISION – .300 Win. Mag. or .338 Lapua cal., short or long action, 24 in. carbon steel barrel, matte black metal finish, 4 shot detachable box mag., black fiberglass stock, drilled and tapped, AccuTrigger, 9 lbs. New 2012.

MSR $1,230	$1,095	$950	$825	$700	$600	$500	$400	

Add $380 for .338 Lapua cal.

MODEL 110-P PREMIER GRADE – similar to Model 110B, with select French walnut stock, skip checkered, rosewood forend and pistol grip cap, sling swivels, 7mm Mag. has recoil pad. Mfg. 1964-70.

	$440	$330	$310	$275	$250	$220	$195	
7mm Mag. cal.	$460	$350	$330	$305	$275	$240	$220	

MODEL 110-PE PRESENTATION GRADE – similar to Model 110P, with engraved receiver, floorplate and trigger guard. Mfg. 1968-70.

	$660	$550	$525	$470	$440	$415	$385	
7mm Mag. cal.	$690	$580	$550	$495	$470	$440	$415	

MODEL 111B HUNTER .25 06 Rem., .270 Win. or .30-06 cal., long action, 22 in. barrel with no sights, hinged floorplate. Ltd. mfg. 2008.

	$625	$525	$460	$400	$350	$300	$250	*$735*

MODEL 111BTH HUNTER – .25-06 Rem., .270 Win., or 30-06 cal., 4 shot mag., 22 in. barrel with no sights, drilled and tapped, hinged floorplate, ventilated forend, Accutrigger, brown laminated thumbhole stock, 7 lbs. New 2010.

MSR $890	$775	$665	$550	$450	$400	$350	$300	

MODEL 111 CHIEFTAIN ACTION – .243 Win., .270 Win., 7x57mm, 7mm Mag., or .30-06 cal., 22 or 24 (Mag. cals.) in. barrel, leaf sight, 4 shot detachable mag., checkered walnut Monte Carlo stock, pistol grip cap, sling swivels. Mfg. 1974-78.

	$375	$350	$300	$250	$225	$200	$175	
Mag. cals.	$395	$375	$325	$295	$275	$225	$195	

MODEL 111 HUNTER XP PACKAGE – .270 Win., .300 Win. Mag., .30-06, or 7mm Rem. Mag. cal., long action, 4 shot detachable box mag., 22 or 24 in. barrel, matte black metal finish, black synthetic stock, includes 3-9x40 Bushnell scope, AccuTrigger is not available on this model, 7 1/4 lbs. New 2012.

MSR $525	$465	$400	$360	$330	$300	$275	$250	

MODEL 111 LADY HUNTER – .270 Win. or .30-06 cal., long action, 20 in. barrel without sights, black matte metal finish, 4 shot mag., drilled and tapped, satin finished walnut with pressed checkering and forward angled Monte Carlo stock with recoil pad, stock features include shorter LOP, higher front angled comb, slimmer forend and pistol grip, three-position safety, sling swivels, 6 lbs. New mid-2012.

MSR $840	$695	$575	$450	$400	$350	$300	$265	

GRADING - PPGS™	100%	98%	95%	90%	80%	70%	60%	LAST MSR

MODEL 111 HOG HUNTER – .338 Win. Mag. cal., long action, 4 shot internal box mag., 20 in. threaded barrel with iron sights, matte black metal finish, AccuTrigger, OD Green synthetic stock, 8 lbs. New 2012.

MSR $535	$465	$400	$365	$335	$295	$265	$235	

MODEL 111 LIGHTWEIGHT HUNTER – .270 Win., .30-06, or 6.5x284 Norma cal., long action, 20 in. barrel, AccuTrigger, 4 shot detachable box mag., hinged floorplate, no sights, blued finish, walnut stained stock, 6 lbs. New 2011.

MSR $925	$795	$675	$550	$450	$395	$350	$300	

MODEL 111 LONG RANGE HUNTER – .25-06 Rem., 6.5x284 Norma, 7mm Rem. Mag., .300 Win. Mag., or .338 Lapua (new 2012) cal., 3 or 5 (.338 Lapua cal. only) shot mag., 26 in. fluted carbon steel barrel with adj. muzzle brake, drilled and tapped, AccuTrigger, Karsten adj. and detachable cheekpiece, matte black synthetic AccuStock and forearm, no sights, hinged floorplate, 8.65 lbs. New 2010.

MSR $1,020	$875	$725	$600	$500	$425	$365	$325	

Add $270 for .338 Lapua cal. (new 2012).

MODEL 111 TROPHY HUNTER XP PACKAGE – .25-06 Rem., .270 Win., .30-06, .300 Win. Mag., 6.5x284 Norma (right hand only), or 7mm Rem. cal., long action, 4 shot detachable box mag., 22 or 24 in. barrel, matte black metal finish, synthetic black stock, Accutrigger, includes 3-9x40 Nikon scope, right or left-hand action, 7 1/4 lbs. New 2012.

MSR $675	$595	%525	$450	$415	$375	$335	$295	

MODEL 111FNS (111-F) – similar to Model 111-G, except has black graphite/fiberglass stock (with non-glare finish) and was also available in .338 Win. Mag. (disc. 2005) cal., long action, 22, 24, or 26 (disc. 2003) in. barrel, solid recoil pad, no sights (reintroduced 2009 as the Model 111FNS), 6 1/2 lbs. Mfg. 1994-2011.

	$475	$400	$340	$285	$230	$200	$175	*$609*

This model's nomenclature changed during 2009 to the Model 111FNS. This model was previously discontinued in 2002, and was not available in .300 Rem. Ultra Mag. or 7mm Rem. Ultra Mag. cals.

This model is also available in left-hand (Model 111-FL. disc. 2008, or Model 111FLNS (no sights, new 2009).

* ***Model 111-FC*** – .270 Win., .30-06, .300 Win. Mag., or 7mm Rem. Mag. cal., 22 or 24 in. barrel, detachable box mag., black graphite/fiberglass stock, 6 1/2 lbs. Mfg. 1994-2003.

	$400	$340	$285	$230	$195	$175	$160	*$468*

This model was also available with left-hand action (Model 111-FLC).

* ***Model 111-FCNS*** – .25-06 Rem., .270 Win., .30-06, .300 Win. Mag., .338 Win. Mag. (disc.), .375 Ruger (new 2012), or 7mm Rem. Mag. cal., features detachable box mag., 22 or 24 in. barrel, no sights, AccuStock became standard 2009, AccuTrigger, approx. 6 1/2 lbs. New 2005.

MSR $715	$595	$500	$425	$365	$325	$275	$225	

* ***Model 111-FHNS*** – .25-06 Rem., .270 Win., or 30-06 cal., long action, 4 shot mag., 22 in. barrel, AccuTrigger, no sights, hinged floorplate, synthetic AccuStock (became standard 2009), blued finish, 7 1/4 lbs. Mfg. 2006-2012.

	$575	$495	$425	$365	$325	$275	$225	*$696*

MODEL 111FYCAK – .270 Win.or .30-06 cal., 22 in. barrel with adj. muzzle brake, detachable box mag., long action, Youth Model with shortened LOP. Mfg. 2006-2009.

	$525	$400	$340	$300	$270	$235	$200	*$652*

MODEL 111-FAK EXPRESS – .270 Win., .30-06, .300 Win. Mag., .338 Win. Mag., or 7mm Rem. Mag. cal., 22 in. barrel with adj. muzzle brake, black or black matte graphite/fiberglass-filled stock, w/o sights, 6 3/4 lbs. Mfg. 1996-98.

	$390	$340	$285	$240	$200	$180	$165	*$450*

GRADING - PPGS™	100%	98%	95%	90%	80%	70%	60%	LAST MSR

MODEL 11/111-FCXP3 PACKAGE – .243 Win. (Model 11FCXP3), .270 Win., .30-06, .300 Win. Mag. (disc. 2001, reintroduced 2005), 7mm-08 Rem. (mfg. 2009), or 7mm Rem. Mag. (disc. 2001, reintroduced 2005) cal., 4 shot detachable box mag., checkered black synthetic stock, 22 or 24 in. barrel, package includes bore sighted 3-9x32mm scope, rings, bases, QD swivels, and deluxe rifle sling, not available w/AccuTrigger, 6 1/2 lbs. Mfg. 1994-2011.

$425 $350 $300 $275 $225 $200 $175 *$525*

This model was also available with left-hand action (Model 111-FLCXP3 - disc. 2000).

MODELS 11FXP3 & 111-FXP3 PACKAGES – .204 Ruger (new 2005), .22-250 Rem., .223 Rem., .243 Win., .250 Savage (disc. 1996), .25-06 Rem., .270 WSM (new 2003), .270 Win., .300 Sav. (disc. 1996), .30-06, .308 Win., .300 Rem. Ultra Mag. (mfg. 2003-2004), .300 Win. Mag., .300 WSM (new 2002), .338 Win. Mag., 7mm WSM (mfg. 2003-2007), 7mm RSUM (mfg. 2003), 7mm Rem. Mag., 7mm Rem. Ultra Mag. (mfg. 2002-2003), or 7mm-08 Rem. (disc. 1996, reintroduced 1999-2001, again in 2009) cal., short (11FXP3) or long (111-FXP3) action, 22 or 24 in. barrel, black graphite/fiberglass composite stock, non-glare finish, package consists of bore sighted 3-9x32 scope, rings, bases, QD swivels, and deluxe rifle sling, approx. 7 1/4 lbs. Mfg. 1994-2011.

$525 $450 $380 $310 $240 $210 $185 *$678*

Add $27 for WSM cals. (Model 11FXP3 only).

This model was also available with left-hand action (Model 11FLXP3/111-FLXP3, disc. 2002).

MODEL 111GNS (111-G) – .22-250 Rem. (disc. 1998), .223 Rem. (disc. 1998), .243 Win. (disc. 1998), .250 Savage (disc. 1996), .25-06 Rem., .270 Win., .300 Sav. (disc. 1996), .30-06, .308 Win. (disc. 1998), .300 Win. Mag. (disc. 2007), .300 Rem. Ultra Mag. (mfg. 2002-2003), .338 Win. Mag. (disc. 1993 - not available with wood stock), 7mm-08 Rem. (disc. 1996), 7mm Rem. Ultra Mag. (mfg. 2002-2003), or 7mm Rem. Mag. (disc. 2007) cal., long action, walnut finished hardwood stock with cut checkering and vent. recoil pad, open sights, top tang safety with red dot indicator, 22, 24, or 26 (disc. 2005) in. barrel, drilled and tapped, no sights, 6 3/8 or 7 lbs. Mfg. 1994-2010.

$515 $465 $410 $350 $300 $250 $200 *$635*

This model's nomenclature changed in 2009 to the Model 111-GNS, which was originally disc. in 2004 and not available in .300 Rem. Ultra Mag. or 7mm Rem. Ultra Mag. cals.

This model is also available in left-hand (Model 111-GL, not available in 7mm Rem. Ultra Mag.).

* ***Model 111-GC*** – .270 Win., .30-06, .300 Win. Mag., or 7mm Rem. Mag. cal., 22 or 24 in. barrel, detachable box mag., walnut finished hardwood stock with cut checkering and vent. recoil pad. Mfg. 1994-2001.

$385 $325 $275 $240 $210 $175 $160 *$441*

This model was also available with left-hand action (Model 111-GLC - disc. 2000).

* ***Model 111-GCNS*** – .25-06 Rem., .270 Win., .30-06, .300 Win. Mag. (disc. 2008), or 7mm Rem. Mag. (disc. 2008) cal., features detachable box mag., no sights, 22 or 24 in. barrel, approx. 7 lbs. Mfg. 2005-2012.

$500 $415 $325 $250 $200 $175 $160 *$699*

MODEL 112V VARMINT RIFLE – .220 Swift, .222 Rem., .223 Rem. (new 1976), .22-250 Rem., .243 Win., or .25-06 Rem. cal., single shot, bolt action, 26 in. heavy barrel, no sights, heavy select walnut stock, checkered, swivels. Mfg. 1975-78.

$350 $325 $300 $275 $250 $235 $225

MODEL 112 VARMINTER LOW PROFILE – .25-06 Rem. or .300 Win. Mag. cal., stainless long action, right-hand bolt, smaller ejection port on left side of receiver, 26 in. heavy fluted free floating barrel, low profile laminated stock with extra-wide beavertail forend, drilled and tapped, AccuTrigger, oversized bolt handle, 4 shot internal box mag., swivel studs, 10 lbs. Mfg. 2006 only.

$665 $545 $435 $370 $325 $260 $225 *$806*

MODEL 112 R – .22-250 Rem., .25-06 Rem., or .243 Win. cal., similar to Model 112V, except has 4 shot mag. Disc. 1980.

$340 $305 $275 $250 $230 $210 $175

GRADING - PPGS™	100%	98%	95%	90%	80%	70%	60%	LAST MSR

MODEL 112-BV – .22-250 Rem. or .223 Rem. cal., alloy steel construction, 26 in. barrel with recessed muzzle, 4 shot mag., brown laminate stock with ambidextrous Wundhammer style pistol grip, 9 1/2 lbs. Mfg. 1993 only.

	$475	$430	$365	$315	$285	$250	$215	

MODEL 112-BVSS LONG RANGE – .22-250 Rem. (disc. 1998), .223 Rem. (disc. 1998), .25-06 Rem. (new 1996), .30-06 (new 1996), .308 Win. (mfg. 1996-98), .300 Win. Mag. (new 1996), or 7mm Rem. Mag. (new 1996) cal., 4 shot, pillar bedded laminate wood stock with Wundhammer palm swell, right-hand bolt, smaller ejection port on left side of receiver, 26 in. stainless steel fluted barrel, bolt handle and trigger guard, recessed muzzle, AccuTrigger became standard 2003, 10 1/2 lbs. Mfg. 1994-2005.

	$595	$470	$390	$325	$280	$235	$200	*$721*

* ***Model 112-BVSS-S Long Range*** – .220 Swift, .223 Rem. (disc. 1998), .22-250 Rem. (disc. 1998), or .300 Win. Mag. (new 1996) cal., single shot, 26 in. stainless steel fluted barrel, with target features, 10 1/2 lbs. Mfg. 1994-2001.

	$510	$420	$360	$295	$255	$220	$190	*$595*

MODEL 112-BT COMPETITION GRADE – .223 Rem. or .308 Win. cal., laminated pillar bedded wood stock with adj. cheek rest and Wundhammer palm swell, vent. forend, 5 shot internal mag., alloy steel receiver with 26 in. matte black finished heavy stainless steel barrel w/o sights, drilled and tapped receiver, approx. 10 7/8 lbs. Mfg. 1994-2001.

	$930	$810	$705	$625	$550	$495	$400	*$1,049*

* ***Model 112-BT-S Competition Grade*** – .300 Win. Mag. cal., single shot, otherwise similar to Model 112 - BT Competition Grade. Mfg. 1995-2001.

	$930	$810	$705	$625	$550	$495	$400	*$1,049*

MODEL 112-FV – .22-250 Rem. or .223 Rem. cal., varmint variation with 26 in. heavy barrel, with or w/o iron sights, 4 shot mag., black Rynite synthetic stock with recoil pad, 8 7/8 lbs. Mfg. 1991-98.

	$360	$300	$260	$235	$200	$175	$160	*$410*

* ***Model 112-FVS*** – similar to Model 112-FV, except is single shot with solid bottom receiver and is available in .220 Swift (new 1993) cal. Mfg. 1992-93 only.

	$375	$340	$295	$265	$235	$210	$195	

* ***Model 112-FVSS (Long Range)*** – .22-250 Rem. (disc. 1998), .223 Rem. (disc. 1998), .25-06 Rem. (new 1995), .30-06 (new 1996), .308 Win. (mfg. 1996-98), .300 Win. Mag. (new 1995), or 7mm Rem. Mag. (new 1995) cal., alloy receiver with 26 in. fluted stainless steel barrel, 4 shot mag., black synthetic pillar bedded sporter stock w/o sights, 8 7/8 lbs. Mfg. 1993-2002.

	$495	$425	$360	$295	$255	$220	$190	*$569*

This model was also available with left-hand action (Model 112-FLVSS, mfg. 1996-2002, not available in .30-06 cal.).

* ***Model 112-FVSS-S*** – .220 Swift, .22-250 Rem. (disc. 1998), .223 Rem. (disc. 1998), or .300 Win. Mag. (new 1996) cal., single shot variation, pillar bedded stock, 8 7/8 lbs. Mfg. 1994-2001.

	$480	$415	$355	$300	$270	$230	$200	*$549*

MODEL 114 AMERICAN CLASSIC/CLASSIC – .270 Win., .30-06, .300 Win. Mag., or 7mm Rem. Mag. cal., features detachable box mag. (American Classic) or hinged floorplate (Classic, mfg. 2006-2011), 22 or 24 in. steel barrel, AccuTrigger, long action, drilled and tapped, satin lacquer American walnut with ebony forend and wraparound checkering, right or left (new 2008) action, no sights, 7 or 7 1/2 lbs. New 2005.

MSR $885	$775	$675	$575	$500	$425	$350	$295	

Add $50 for Classic Model (disc. 2011).

The American Classic Model is also available in left-hand at no extra charge.

GRADING - PPGS™	100%	98%	95%	90%	80%	70%	60%	LAST MSR

* ***Model 114 American Classic Stainless*** – .270 Win., .30-06, .300 Win. Mag., or 7mm Rem. Mag. cal., 22 or 24 in. stainless steel barrel, oil finished American walnut stock, right hand action, otherwise similar to American Classic model, 7 1/2 lbs. New 2011.

MSR $995	$875	$750	$650	$575	$500	$425	$350	

MODEL 114 EURO CLASSIC – .270 Win. or .30-06 cal., 22 in. barrel, detachable box mag., AccuTrigger standard, checkered oil finished Monte Carlo walnut stock with cheekpiece, high polished blued action/barrel, open sights, 7 3/4 lbs. Mfg. 2006-2010.

	$750	$595	$525	$445	$375	$325	$275	*$909*

MODEL 114-C (CLASSIC) 114-CU (CLASSIC ULTRA) – .270 Win., .30-06, .300 Win. Mag., or 7mm Rem. Mag. cal., 22 or 24 in. barrel, features high gloss classic American black walnut stock with cut checkering, fitted grip cap, and recoil pad, removable 3 or 4 shot staggered box mag., available with deluxe adj. sights (Model 114-CU, disc. 1995) or w/o sights (Model 114-C, new 1996), approx. 7 1/8 lbs. Mfg. 1991-2000.

	$485	$410	$355	$300	$270	$230	$200	*$556*

MODEL 114-U – similar to Model 114-C, except is also available in 7mm STW (disc. 2002) cal., 3 shot internal mag, no sights, approx. 7 lbs. Mfg. 1999-2004.

	$490	$415	$350	$285	$250	$230	$200	*$569*

MODEL 114-CE (CLASSIC EUROPEAN) – same cals. as the Model 114-C, except also available in 7x64mm Brenneke cal., features oil finished stock with Schnabel forend and skip-line checkering, high luster bluing, 22 or 24 in. barrel with adj. rear sight, 7 1/8 lbs. Mfg. 1996-2001.

	$480	$400	$350	$285	$260	$235	$200	*$554*

MODEL 116 ALASKAN BRUSH HUNTER – .338 Win. Mag. or .375 Ruger cal., satin stainless steel action with 20 in. barrel with iron sights, large bolt handle knob, AccuTrigger, black synthetic stock, blind magazine, 7.6 lbs. New 2012.

MSR $705	$595	$495	$450	$395	$325	$300	$275	

MODEL 116 BEAR HUNTER – .300 Win Mag., .338 Win. Mag., or .375 Ruger (new 2012) cal., 23 in. barrel, hinged floorplated, adj. muzzlebrake, 3 shot mag., AccuTrigger, checkered synthetic Accustock, 7 3/4 lbs. New 2011.

MSR $995	$850	$725	$625	$525	$425	$375	$325	

MODEL 116-BSS WEATHER WARRIOR – .270 Win., .30-06, .300 Win. Mag., .300 Rem. Ultra Mag., or 7mm Rem. Mag. cal., long action, brown wood laminate stock with cut checkering, stainless steel action and tapered barrel, 2-4 shot internal mag., 24 or 26 in. barrel, 7-7 3/4 lbs. Mfg. 2001-2002.

	$560	$480	$410	$345	$295	$250	$220	*$644*

MODEL 116-FSS – .22-250 Rem. (mfg. 1992 only), .223 Rem. (mfg. 1992-98), .243 Win. (mfg. 1993-98), .270 Win., .30-06, .308 Win. (disc. 1998), 7mm Rem. Mag., 7mm STW (mfg. 2001-2002), 7mm Rem. Ultra Mag. (mfg. 2002-2003), .300 Win. Mag., .300 Rem. Ultra Mag. (mfg. 2001-2006), .338 Win. Mag., or .375 H&H (mfg. 2002, reintroduced 2007-2008) cal., short (disc.) or long (new 2001) action, features black Dupont Rynite synthetic stock, stainless steel metal parts, drilled and tapped for scope mounting, 22, 24, or 26 (disc. 2005) in. barrel, 3 or 4 shot mag., 6 3/4 lbs. Mfg. 1991-2011.

	$575	$475	$415	$330	$285	$240	$210	*$720*

Add $145 for .375 H&H cal. (iron sights only).

This model is also available with left-hand action (Model 116-FLSS, not available in .375 H&H).

* ***Model 116-FCSS*** – .25-06 Rem. (new 2009), .270 Win., .30-06, 6.5x284 Norma (new 2011), 7mm Rem. Mag., .300 Win. Mag., .338 Win. Mag. (new 2005), or .375 Ruger (new 2012) cal., otherwise similar to Model 116-FSS, except has detachable 3 or 4 shot box mag. with recessed push-button release, 22 or 24 in. barrel, AccuStock became standard 2009, 6 1/2 lbs. Mfg. 1992-2001, reintroduced 2005.

MSR $850	$725	$625	$525	$450	$400	$350	$275	

Subtract $21 for left-hand action (Model 116-FLCSS, disc. 2005).

GRADING - PPGS™	100%	98%	95%	90%	80%	70%	60%	LAST MSR

* ***Model 116-FHSS/116FHSAK*** – .270 Win., .30-06, .300 Win. Mag., .338 Win. Mag., or 7mm Rem. Mag. cal., 22 or 24 in. free floating barrel with muzzle brake (Model FHSAK only), drilled and tapped stainless action, hinged floorplate, AccuTrigger, 3 or 4 shot mag., black synthetic stock, AccuStock became standard 2009, 6 1/2 - 7 1/2 lbs. New 2006.

MSR $850	$725	$625	$525	$450	$400	$350	$275	

Add $86 for Model FHSAK with muzzle brake (disc. 2010).

This model is also available in left-hand action (Model 116-FLHSS, new 2007).

* ***Model 116-FSK (Kodiak)*** – similar cals. as Model 116-FCSS, except also available in .338 Win Mag. cal., stainless steel construction, 22 in. barrel with recoil arrester, cocking indicator, 3 shot mag., black synthetic sporter stock, no sights, 6 1/2 lbs. Mfg. 1993-2000.

	$495	$430	$370	$325	$290	$260	$230	$569

This model was also available with left-hand action (Model 116-FLSK).

MODEL 116-US (ULTRA STAINLESS) – .270 Win., .30-06, 7mm Rem. Mag., or .300 Win. Mag. cal., 24 in. stainless steel barrel, checkered walnut stock and forearm with ebony tip, no sights, 7 1/8 lbs. Mfg. 1995-98.

	$625	$550	$500	$450	$400	$360	$330	$700

MODEL 116-SE (SAFARI EXPRESS) – .300 Win. Mag. (disc. 2002), .300 Rem. Ultra Mag. (mfg. 2002), .338 Win. Mag. (disc. 2001), .375 H&H (mfg. 2000-2002), .425 Express (mfg. 1995 only), or .458 Win. Mag. cal., stainless steel receiver and 24 in. barrel with adj. muzzle brake, controlled round feeding, select grade checkered walnut stock with solid recoil pad and ebony forend, 3-leaf express sights, 8 1/2 lbs. Mfg. 1994-2004.

	$895	$775	$685	$625	$575	$535	$475	$1,045

MODEL 116-FSAK – .270 Win., .30-06, .300 Win. Mag., .300 Rem. Ultra Mag. (new 2001), .338 Win. Mag., .375 H&H (mfg. 2002 only), 7mm STW (mfg. 2001-2002), 7mm Rem. Ultra Mag. (mfg. 2002 only), or 7mm Rem. Mag. cal., short (disc.) or long (new 2001) action, features 22 in. fluted stainless steel barrel with adj. muzzle brake, 6 1/2 lbs. Mfg. 1994-2004.

	$530	$465	$390	$340	$295	$265	$235	$619

This model was also available with left-hand action (Model 116-FLSAK, not available in 7mm STW, 7mm Rem. Ultra Mag., or .375 H&H cals.).

MODEL 116-FCSAK – .270 Win., .30-06, .300 Win. Mag., .338 Win. Mag. (new 2005), or 7mm Rem. Mag. cal., features push-button activated detachable box mag., 22 or 24 (new 2005) in. fluted barrel with adj. muzzle brake, 6 1/2 lbs. Mfg. 1994-2000, reintroduced 2005.

	$560	$495	$415	$350	$315	$275	$245	$661

This model was also available with left-hand action (Model 116-FLCSAK).

MODEL 116FXP3 PACKAGE – .270 Win., .30-06, .300 Rem. Ultra Mag. (disc. 2003), .300 Win. Mag., .338 Win. Mag. (disc. 2010), 7mm STW (disc. 2002), 7mm Rem. Mag., or 7mm Rem. Ultra Mag. (disc. 2003) cal., stainless long action, 22, 24, or 26 (disc. 2010) in. stainless barrel w/o sights, checkered black synthetic stock, includes nickel finished 3-9x40 scope and mounts, supplied with sling, AccuTrigger, approx. 6 1/2 - 7 lbs. Mfg. 2002-2011.

	$625	$495	$425	$360	$315	$270	$225	$782

MODEL 170 PUMP RIFLE – .30-30 Win. or .35 Rem. (rare) cal., 22 in. barrel, folding leaf sight, 3 shot tube mag., checkered pistol grip stock. Mfg. 1970-81.

	$225	$195	$165	$145	$110	$90	$65	

Add 20% for .35 Rem. cal.

This model was mfg. by Emhart.

MODEL 116 TROPHY HUNTER XP PACKAGE – .25-06 Rem., .270 Win., .30-06, .300 Win Mag., .338 Win., .375 Ruger, 6.5x284 Norma, or 7mm Rem. Mag. cal., long action, stainless action with 22 or 24 in. stainless barrel, 4 shot detachable box mag., black synthetic stock, Accutrigger, includes 3-9x40 Nikon BDC scope, 7 1/4 lbs. New 2012.

MSR $795	$695	$595	$515	$465	$415	$365	$325	

GRADING - PPGS™	100%	98%	95%	90%	80%	70%	60%	LAST MSR

MODEL 170C – .30-30 Win. cal. only, similar to 170, 18 1/2 in. barrel. Mfg. 1974-81.

	100%	98%	95%	90%	80%	70%	60%	LAST MSR
	$250	$225	$195	$175	$160	$140	$120	

EDGE BOLT ACTION – .223 Rem., .22-250 Rem., .243 WIn., 7mm-08 Rem., .308 Win., .25-06 Rem., .270 Win., or .30-06 cal., 22 in. barrel, drilled and tapped, carbine steel construction, synthetic stock, 4 shot detachable box mag., matte black or camo finish, not available with AccuTrigger, approx. 6 1/2 lbs. Mfg. mid-2010-2011.

	100%	98%	95%	90%	80%	70%	60%	LAST MSR
	$285	$265	$245	$225	$200	$185	$170	*$329*

Add $50 for camo.

* ***Edge XP Bolt Action*** – .223 Rem., .22-250 Rem., .243 WIn., 7mm-08 Rem., .308 Win., .25-06 Rem., .270 Win., or .30-06 cal., similar to Edge, except has matte blued 3-9x40 scope, mounted and bore sighted, matte black or camo finish, approx. 6 1/2 lbs. Mfg. mid-2010-2011.

	100%	98%	95%	90%	80%	70%	60%	LAST MSR
	$335	$295	$265	$245	$215	$195	$180	*$379*

AXIS – .223 Rem., .22-250 Rem., .243 Win., .25-06 Rem., .270 Win., .30-06, .308 Win., or 7mm-08 Rem. cal., short or long action, 22 in. carbon steel barrel without sights, matte black finish, 4 shot detachable box mag., right or left (new 2012, not avail. on camo model) hand action, matte black synthetic or Mossy Oak Breakup camo stock, drilled and tapped for scope mounts, AccuTrigger not available on this model, 6 1/2 lbs. New 2011.

	100%	98%	95%	90%	80%	70%	60%	LAST MSR
MSR $375	$335	$285	$260	$240	$220	$200	$185	

Add $50 for Mossy Oak Breakup camo stock.

* ***AXIS Stainless*** – .223 Rem., .22-250 Rem., .243 Win., .25-06 Rem., .270 Win., .30-06, .308 Win., or 7mm-08 Rem. cal., stainless action with 22 in. stainless steel barrel, right hand action, matte black synthetic stock, no sights, AccuTrigger not available on this model, otherwise similar to AXIS model, 6 1/2 lbs. New 2011.

	100%	98%	95%	90%	80%	70%	60%	LAST MSR
MSR $425	$360	$325	$295	$275	$250	$225	$200	

* ***AXIS Youth Model*** – .223 Rem. (new 2012), .243 WIn., or 7mm-08 Rem. cal., 20 in. carbon steel barrel, right or left hand action, 4 shot detachable mag., matte black synthetic stock, otherwise similar to AXIS Model, except has shorter LOP, 6.2 lbs. New 2011.

	100%	98%	95%	90%	80%	70%	60%	LAST MSR
MSR $375	$335	$285	$260	$240	$220	$200	$185	

AXIS SR – .223 Rem. or .308 Win. cal., 20 in. carbon steel threaded barrel, matte black finish, 4 shot detachable box mag., matte black synthetic stock, no sights, pillar bedding, drilled and tapped for scope mounts, AccuTrigger not available on this model, 6 1/2 lbs. New 2012.

	100%	98%	95%	90%	80%	70%	60%	LAST MSR
MSR $395	$345	$300	$265	$245	$225	$200	$185	

AXIS XP PACKAGE – .223 Rem., .22-250 Rem., .243 Win., .25-06 Rem., .270 Win., .30-06, .308 Win., or 7mm-08 Rem. cal., 22 in. carbon steel barrel, matte black finish, 4 shot detachable box mag., right hand action, matte black synthetic or Mossy Oak Breakup camo stock, AccuTrigger not available on this model, includes mounted and bore sighted 3-9x40 scope, 6 1/2 lbs. New 2011.

	100%	98%	95%	90%	80%	70%	60%	LAST MSR
MSR $415	$365	$335	$300	$275	$250	$225	$200	

Add $60 for Mossy Oak Breakup camo stock.

* ***AXIS XP Stainless Package*** – .223 Rem., .22-250 Rem., .243 Win., .25-06 Rem., .270 Win., .30-06, .308 Win., or 7mm-08 Rem. cal., 22 in. stainless steel barrel, right hand action, includes mounted and bore sighted 3-9x40 scope, otherwise similar to AXIS XP model, 7 lbs. New 2011.

	100%	98%	95%	90%	80%	70%	60%	LAST MSR
MSR $500	$440	$375	$335	$300	$275	$250	$225	

* ***AXIS XP Youth Package*** – .223 Rem. (new 2012), .243 Win., or 7mm-08 Rem. cal., 20 in. carbon steel barrel, otherwise similar to AXIS XP Model, 6.8 lbs. New 2011.

	100%	98%	95%	90%	80%	70%	60%	LAST MSR
MSR $415	$365	$335	$300	$275	$250	$225	$200	

GRADING - PPGS™	100%	98%	95%	90%	80%	70%	60%	LAST MSR

AXIS XP CAMO YOUTH – .223 Rem., .243 Win., or 7mm-08 Rem. cal., 20 in. barrel, matte blued finish, 4 shot detachable box mag., Realtree Extra or Muddy Girl camo stock, AccuTrigger not available on this model, includes mounted and bore sighted 3-9x40 scope, 6.2 lbs. New 2013.

MSR $475	$415	$360	$325	$295	$275	$250	$225	

SHOTGUNS: DISC.

Most Savage shotguns (except the Model 312 Series) fall under the domain of Savage Industries, Inc. Savage made a wide variety of inexpensive, utilitarian shotguns that, to date, have attracted mostly shooting interest, but little collector interest. A listing of these models may be found in the back of this text under "Serialization."

The models listed are grouped by configuration, and are not in numerical sequence.

MODEL 420 O/U – 12, 16, or 20 ga., 26-30 in. barrel, various chokes, boxlock, double trigger, extractors, plain pistol grip stock. Mfg. 1937-43.

	$385	$305	$275	$250	$210	$195	$155	
Single trigger	$440	$360	$330	$305	$265	$220	$195	

MODEL 430 O/U – similar to Model 420, with checkered stock and solid rib, recoil pad.

	$440	$360	$305	$275	$240	$220	$195	
Single trigger	$495	$415	$360	$320	$285	$265	$220	

MODEL 220 SINGLE BARREL – 12, 16, 20, 28 ga., or .410 bore, 26-32 in. barrel, various chokes, hammerless, plain pistol grip stock. Mfg. 1938-65.

	$125	$100	$85	$75	$65	$50	$40	

MODEL 220P – similar to Model 220, with poly choke, not made in .410 bore.

	$90	$65	$55	$45	$35	$30	$30	

MODEL 220 AC – similar to Model 220, with Savage adj. choke.

	$100	$85	$65	$55	$45	$35	$30	

MODEL 220L – similar to Model 220, with sidelever. Mfg. 1965-72.

	$90	$65	$55	$45	$35	$30	$30	

MODEL 720 AUTOLOADER STANDARD – 12 or 16 ga., Browning A-5 style semi-auto action, 26-32 in. barrels, various chokes, checkered pistol grip stock. Mfg. 1930-49.

	$225	$180	$165	$155	$140	$120	$110	

MODEL 720 RIOT – see the "Trench/Riot Shotgun" category in the T section for more information and prices.

MODEL 726 SEMI-AUTO UPLAND SPORTER – similar to Model 720, except 2 shell mag. Mfg. 1931-49.

	$275	$195	$165	$155	$140	$120	$110	

MODEL 740C SKEET GUN – similar to Model 726, with Cutts Compensator and skeet stock, 24 1/2 in. barrel. Mfg. 1936-49.

	$305	$230	$200	$175	$155	$140	$120	

MODEL 745 LIGHTWEIGHT – similar to Model 720, with alloy receiver, 12 ga. only, 28 in. barrel. Mfg. 1940-49.

	$275	$195	$165	$155	$140	$120	$110	

MODEL 755 STANDARD SEMI-AUTO – 12 or 16 ga., 26, 28, or 30 in. barrel, various chokes, rounded-off receiver, checkered pistol grip stock. Mfg. 1949-58.

	$265	$180	$160	$150	$140	$120	$110	

MODEL 755SC – similar to Model 755, with Savage Super Choke.

	$275	$195	$165	$155	$140	$120	$110	

MODEL 775 LIGHTWEIGHT SEMI-AUTO – similar to Model 755, with alloy receiver. Mfg. 1950-65.

	$275	$195	$180	$165	$150	$140	$120	

GRADING - PPGS™	100%	98%	95%	90%	80%	70%	60%	LAST MSR

MODEL 775SC – similar to Model 775, with Savage Super Choke.

	$285	$205	$195	$175	$160	$150	$130	

MODEL 750 SEMI-AUTO – 12 ga., Browning patterned semi-auto, 26 or 28 in. barrels, various chokes, checkered pistol grip stock. Mfg. 1960-69.

	$275	$195	$165	$155	$140	$120	$110	

MODEL 750SC – similar to Model 750, with Savage Super Choke.

	$285	$205	$175	$165	$150	$130	$120	

MODEL 750AC – similar to Model 750, with poly choke.

	$285	$205	$175	$165	$150	$130	$120	

MODEL 21 SLIDE ACTION – similar to Model 28, except stock has no checkering. Mfg. 1920-28.

	$300	$265	$235	$190	$165	$150	$130	

MODEL 28 SLIDE ACTION – 12, 16, or 20 ga., patterned after the Winchester Model 12. Mfg. 1927-34.

	$300	$265	$235	$190	$165	$150	$130	

This model was available in either standard configuration (Models 28A and 28B), Riot (28C), Trap (28D), or Special (28S).

MODEL 30 SLIDE ACTION – 12, 16, 20 ga., or .410 bore, 26, 28, or 30 in. barrels, various chokes, VR, plain pistol grip stock. Mfg. 1958-70.

	$220	$175	$155	$140	$120	$100	$85	
Checkered Late Model	$230	$185	$165	$150	$130	$110	$95	

MODEL 30AC – similar to Model 30, with adj. choke, checkered wood, 12 ga. only. Mfg. 1959-70.

	$240	$200	$175	$160	$145	$120	$100	

MODEL 30T TRAP AND DUCK GUN – similar to Model 30, with 30 in. full barrel, 12 ga. only, Monte Carlo stock and pad. Mfg. 1963-70.

	$230	$185	$165	$150	$130	$110	$90	

MODEL 30FG TAKEDOWN ACTION – 12, 20 ga., or .410 bore, 26, 28, or 30 in. barrel, various chokes, checkered pistol grip stock. Mfg. 1970-75.

	$175	$155	$130	$110	$95	$85	$70	

MODEL 30T TAKEDOWN TRAP – 12 ga. only, 30 in. full barrel, Monte Carlo stock with pad. Mfg. 1970-73.

	$195	$175	$155	$140	$110	$100	$85	

MODEL 30AC TAKEDOWN – similar to Model 30FG, with adj. choke, 12 or 20 ga., 26 in. barrel. Mfg. 1971-72.

	$200	$180	$165	$150	$120	$110	$90	

MODEL 30 TAKEDOWN SLUG GUN – similar to Model 30FG, with 32 in. cylinder bore barrel, rifle sights. Mfg. 1971-disc.

	$195	$175	$160	$140	$110	$100	$85	

MODEL 30D TAKEDOWN – similar to Model 30FG, with VR, engraved receiver and pad. Mfg. 1971-disc.

	$200	$180	$165	$150	$120	$110	$90	

MODEL 67 SLIDE ACTION – see listing under Stevens Section.

FOX MODELS B, B-SE – see listings under Fox Sections.

SAVAGE/FOX MODEL FA-1 – 12 ga., 2 3/4 in. chamber, semi-auto, gas operated, walnut stock and forend, cut checkering, 28 or 30 in. vent. rib barrel. Mfg. 1981-82 in Japan.

	$250	$215	$185	$160	$140	$120	$100	

GRADING - PPGS™	100%	98%	95%	90%	80%	70%	60%	LAST MSR

SAVAGE/FOX MODEL FP-1 – 12 ga., similar to Model FA-1, except is slide action. Mfg. 1981-82 in Japan.

	$175	$150	$125	$100	$85	$70	$60	

MODEL 242 O/U – .410 bore, single exposed hammer, single trigger, barrel selector lever, full chokes. Mfg. 1977-81.

	$425	$350	$285	$230	$200	$175	$150	

MODEL 440/440B O/U – 12 or 20 ga., 26, 28, or 30 in. barrels, various chokes, boxlock, ST (Model 440) or SST (Model 440B), extractors, checkered pistol grip stock, VR. Imported from Italy 1968-72.

	$495	$440	$415	$385	$330	$305	$250	

MODEL 440T – similar to Model 440, 12 ga., 30 in. barrel only, imp mod. or full choke, wide VR, trap style stock, pad. Mfg. 1969-72.

	$550	$470	$440	$415	$385	$360	$330	

MODEL 444 DELUXE – similar to Model 440, with auto ejectors, select walnut. Mfg. 1969-72.

	$550	$470	$440	$415	$385	$360	$330	

MODEL 550 SxS – 12 or 20 ga., 26, 28, or 30 in. barrels (made by Valmet - rare), various chokes, boxlock, auto ejectors, single trigger, checkered pistol grip stock. Mfg. 1971-73.

	$275	$220	$195	$165	$150	$130	$110	

KIMEL KAMPER SINGLE SHOT – 20 ga. or .410 bore, 3 in. chamber, 18 1/2 in. barrel, pistol grip hardwood stock and forearm, butt trap holds 3 shells, bottom opening, exposed hammer. Mfg. 1979-c.1981

	$175	$150	$135	$120	$105	$90	$75	

MODEL STEVENS 311 – please refer to Stevens section.

MODEL 312 SERIES O/U – 12 ga. only, boxlock action, 3 in. chambers, vent. barrels, satin chrome finished receiver, checkered walnut stock and forearm, SST, choke tubes, approx. 7 lbs. Mfg. 1990-93.

The Model 312 Series falls under the domain of Savage Arms, Inc.

* ***Model 312 Series O/U Field*** – 26 or 28 in. VR barrels with choke tubes.

	$585	$520	$485	$435	$395	$360	$330	

* ***Model 312 Series O/U Trap*** – 30 in. barrels only, Monte Carlo stock with recoil pad.

	$615	$550	$500	$460	$415	$375	$330	

* ***Model 312 Series O/U Sporting Clays*** – 28 in. barrels only with 7 choke tubes provided, recoil pad.

	$595	$530	$485	$435	$395	$360	$320	

MODEL 330 O/U – 12 or 20 ga., 26, 28, or 30 in. barrels, various chokes, boxlock, SST, extractors, checkered pistol grip stock. Mfg. by Valmet 1969-1980.

	$495	$440	$385	$335	$275	$250	$220	

Add 25% for extra set of barrels.

MODEL 333T – similar to Model 330, with 30 in. VR barrels bored imp. mod. and full choke, trap stock with pad. Mfg. by Valmet 1972-1980.

	$550	$470	$415	$385	$360	$305	$275	

MODEL 333 O/U – 12 or 20 (rare) ga., 26, 28, or 30 in. VR barrels, various chokes, boxlock, SST, auto ejectors, checkered pistol grip stock. Mfg. by Valmet 1973-1980.

	$650	$575	$500	$450	$400	$375	$330	

Add 25% for extra set of barrels.

Add 30% for 20 ga.

SHOTGUNS: RECENT MFG.

Currently manufactured Stevens shotguns can be found in the Stevens section.

GRADING - PPGS™	100%	98%	95%	90%	80%	70%	60%	LAST MSR

MODEL 210F SLUG WARRIOR BOLT ACTION (MASTER SHOT) – 12 ga. only, 3 in. chamber, built on Model 100 action with controlled round feeding, 24 in. rifled barrel (1:35 twist), 2 shot detachable mag., 60 degree bolt lift, Realtree camo finished (new 2003) or black synthetic stock with checkering and recoil pad, top tang safety, no sights, 7 1/2 lbs. Mfg. 1997-2009.

	$500	$400	$350	$300	$260	$230	$200	*$634*

Add $42 for camo finish (Model 210F Camo).

Add $41 for Turkey configuration with 24 in. barrel and camo coverage (Model 210FT Camo, mfg. 2005-2006).

* ***Model 210FT Slug Warrior Bolt Action*** – similar to Model 210F, except has Advantage camo stock and mag., 24 in. smooth bore barrel accepts Win. style choke tubes. Mfg. 1997-2000.

	$410	$350	$305	$265	$235	$215	$195	*$466*

MODEL 212 SLUG GUN – 12 ga., 22 in. barrel, 2 shot detachable box mag., black synthetic or 100% Realtree Hardwoods (mfg. 2011 only), or Mossy Oak Breakup Infinity (new 2012) camo coverage stock, AccuTrigger, approx. 7 1/2 lbs. New 2011.

MSR $645	$525	$450	$385	$340	$295	$275	$250

Add $55 for camo.

MODEL 220 SLUG GUN – 20 ga., 22 in. carbon steel barrel, matte black or camo synthetic stock, 2 shot detachable box mag., matte blue finish, cut checkering, oversized bolt handle, drilled and tapped, AccuTrigger, available in right or left (new 2012) hand action, 7 lbs. New 2010.

MSR $565	$485	$435	$365	$325	$275	$225	$200

Add $65 for camo stock.

* ***Model 220 Slug Gun Stainless*** – 20 ga., 22 in. stainless steel barrel, camo stock, 2 shot detachable box mag., AccuTrigger, oversized bolt handle, Mossy Oak Break-Up Infinity camo stock, no sights, 7 lbs. New 2012.

MSR $725	$600	$500	$425	$375	$325	$295	$275

* ***Model 220 Slug Gun Youth*** – 20 ga., 22 in. barrel, similar to Model 220 Slug Gun, except has youth dimensions, 7 lbs. New 2010.

MSR $565	$485	$435	$365	$325	$275	$225	$200

MILANO O/U – 12, 20, 28 ga., or .410 bore, ejectors, 28 in. chrome lined vent. rib barrels, satin nickel finished boxlock action, satin finished Turkish walnut stock and forearm with laser engraved checkering, rubber recoil pad, Schnabel forend, SST, fiber optic front sight, includes three choke tubes (except for .410 bore), elongated forcing cones, 6 1/4 - 7 1/2 lbs., imported from Italy. Mfg. mid-2006-2008.

	$1,475	$1,250	$995	$900	$800	$700	$600	*$1,714*

SAVIN, J.C.

Previous manufacturer located in St. Etienne, France. J.C. Savin manufactured only best quality shotguns and rifles per custom order. Annual production was approx. 25 long guns. Each gun should be individually appraised and evaluated based on configuration and options.

RIFLES: DOUBLE, CUSTOM

Guns were available in either O/U or SxS sidelock or Anson & Deeley boxlock, in various cals. (.30 - .577 NE), 24 or 26 in. barrels.

SHOTGUNS: DOUBLE, CUSTOM

Guns were available in either O/U or SxS sidelock configuration, 12 or 20 ga., DT or ST, premier quality. A SxS round action Dixon model with trigger plate was also available in 12 or 20 ga.

GRADING - PPGS™	100%	98%	95%	90%	80%	70%	60%	LAST MSR

SAXONIA

Previous manufacturer located in Schwarzenberg, Germany.

Saxonia manufactured good quality semi-auto pistols, security/combat shotguns, and bolt action sniper rifles in various configurations. These guns had very little or no importation in the U.S.

SCATTERGUN TECHNOLOGIES INC. (S.G.T.)

Current manufacturer located in Berryville, AR since 1999. Previously located in Nashville, TN 1991-1999. Distributor, dealer, and consumer sales.

During 1999, Wilson Combat purchased Scattergun Technologies. S.G.T. manufactures practical defense, tactical, and hunting shotguns in 12 ga. only, utilizing Remington Models 870 and 11-87 (disc.) actions in various configurations as listed. All shotguns feature 3 in. chamber capacity and parkerized finish.

SHOTGUNS: SEMI-AUTO

Add $15 for short stock on models listed.
Add $125 for Armor-Tuff finish on models listed.

K-9 MODEL – 12 ga., 18 in. barrel, adj. ghost ring sight, 7 shot mag., side saddle, synthetic buttstock and forearm. Disc. 2003.

$1,100	$875	$775	$665	$560	$465	$410	*$1,325*

SWAT MODEL – 12 ga., similar to K-9 Model, except has 14 in. barrel and forearm with 11,000 CP flashlight. Disc. 2003.

$1,400	$1,150	$895	$785	$655	$550	$465	*$1,750*

This model was available for military and law enforcement only.

URBAN SNIPER MODEL – 12 ga., 18 in. rifled barrel, scout optics, 7 shot mag., side saddle, synthetic buttstock, forearm and bipod. Disc. 1999.

$1,225	$1,075	$950	$835	$685	$585	$485	*$1,390*

SHOTGUNS: SLIDE ACTION

On the following models, Armor-Tuff finish became standard during 2003.
Add $15 for short stock on models listed.
Subtract approx. $100 if w/o Armor Tuff finish.

STANDARD MODEL – 12 or 20 (disc. 2011) ga., 18 1/2 in. barrel, adj. ghost ring sight, 7 shot mag., side saddle, synthetic buttstock and forearm with 11,000 CP flashlight.

MSR $1,540	$1,395	$1,150	$975	$875	$650	$550	$450

Add $15 for short stock.

PROFESSIONAL MODEL – 12 ga., similar to Standard Model, except has 14 1/2 in. barrel and 6 shot mag.

This model is NFA and available for military and law enforcement only.

EXPERT MODEL – 12 ga., 18 in. barrel with mod. choke, nickel/Teflon finished receiver, adj. ghost ring sight, forearm incorporates 11,000 CP flashlight. Mfg. 1997-2000.

$1,200	$995	$775	$665	$560	$465	$410	*$1,350*

ENTRY MODEL – 12 ga., 12 1/2 in. barrel with mod. choke, adj. ghost ring sights, 5 shot mag., side saddle, synthetic buttstock with 5,000 CP flashlight and nylon loop strap. Disc.

$995	$800	$600	$495	$430	$365	$315	*$1,125*

This model was available for military and law enforcement only.

COMPACT MODEL – 12 1/2 in. barrel with mod. choke, adj. ghost ring sight, 5 shot mag., synthetic buttstock and forearm. Mfg. 1994-99.

$575	$510	$420	$360	$315	$260	$225	*$635*

This model was available for military and law enforcement only.

GRADING - PPGS™	100%	98%	95%	90%	80%	70%	60%	LAST MSR

PRACTICAL TURKEY MODEL – 20 in. barrel with extra full choke, adj. ghost ring sight, 5 shot mag. for 3 in. shells, synthetic buttstock and forearm. Mfg. 1995-99.

	$545	$500	$465	$405	$350	$290	$250	*$595*

LOUIS AWERBUCK SIGNATURE MODEL – 18 in. barrel with fixed choke, adj. ghost ring sight, 5 shot mag., side saddle, wood buttstock with recoil reducer and forearm. Mfg. 1994-99.

	$625	$490	$385	$325	$275	$230	$200	*$705*

F.B.I. MODEL – similar to Standard Model, except has 5 shot mag. Disc. 1999.

	$715	$625	$490	$420	$370	$305	$265	*$770*

MILITARY MODEL – 18 in. barrel with vent. handguard and M-9 bayonet lug, adj. ghost ring rear sight, 7 shot mag., synthetic stock and grooved corncob forearm. Mfg. 1997-98.

	$625	$490	$385	$325	$275	$230	$200	*$690*

PATROL MODEL – 18 in. barrel, adj. ghost ring sight, 5 shot mag., synthetic buttstock and forearm. Disc. 1999.

	$545	$500	$465	$405	$350	$290	$250	*$595*

BORDER PATROL (MODEL 20) – 12 or 20 (disc. 2011) ga., 18 1/2 or 20 (disc. 2011) in. barrel, similar to Patrol Model, except has 7 shot mag., black synthetic stock and forearm.

MSR $1,135	$995	$875	$775	$675	$575	$475	$395	

Add $15 for short stock.
Add $35 for 20 ga. (disc. 2011).

BORDER PATROL (MODEL 21) – similar to Border Patrol Model 20, except has 14 in. barrel and 6 shot mag.

This model is NFA and available for military and law enforcement only.

CONCEALMENT 00, 01, 02, 03, & BREACHING MODELS – 12 ga., short 12 1/2 in. barrel, various configurations, mfg. for military and law enforcement only. Disc. 1998.

	$490	$395	$280	$230	$200	$170	$145	

Last MSRs range from $500-$625

SCHALL

Previous manufacturer located in Hartford, CT.

Schall provided parts and repair service for Fiala pistols, and produced additional repeating pistols with the Schall name between 1930-1936.

PISTOLS

REPEATING HANDGUN – .22 LR cal., 10 round mag. fed manual repeating action, tapered 7 1/2 in. barrel with fixed sights and blue finish, walnut ribbed grips, usually marked "Schall & Co./New Haven, Conn. USA", some have no markings. Most Schalls appear to fall at the end of the serial number range for Fialas and Schalls between ser. no. 5567 and 7398 with those between 5638 and 5794 having no makers markings.

	$550	$525	$475	$425	$375	$315	$280	

Subtract 50% if not in working order.

SCHEIRING GmbH

Current custom rifle manufacturer located in Ferlach, Austria.

H. Scheiring manufactures best quality rifles (including O/U, SxS, and Stalking variations) per individual customer special order. Scheiring was a member of the Ferlach Guild until it was dissolved in 2004. The factory should be contacted directly for more information regarding current models and domestic availability (see Trademark Index).

SCHELLER SPEZIALWAFFEN

Previous manufacturer located in Suhl, Germany that specialized in bolt action rifles.

SCHERZ, MICHAEL

Please refer to Gila River Gun Works in the G section.

GRADING - PPGS™	100%	98%	95%	90%	80%	70%	60%	LAST MSR

SCHILLING, FA. ALFRED

Current rifle manufacturer and gunsmith established in 1898, and located in Zella-Mehlis, Germany. Special order guns are currently being imported exclusively by Sundog Firearms, located in Kimberly, OR.

RIFLES: CUSTOM

Current owner Jorg Schilling manufactures high quality hunting and target rifles in many configurations, in addition to providing gunsmithing services, including traditional case color hardening, bluing, restoration of damascus barrels and engravings, plus a line of unique accessories. All guns are custom order and include the standard Schilling bolt action rifle ($17,245-$22,995), the single shot rifle ($20,125), the Hagn falling block rifle ($15,530-$21,275), the breech block rifle ($22,425), the varmint rifle ($10,920), and the Aydt target model ($17,245). Please contact the importer for more information, including an individual price quotation, delivery time and availability (see Trademark Index).

SCHMIDT-RUBIN RIFLES

Please refer to the Swiss Military listing in this section.

SCHMITT FRERES

Previous manufacturer located in Saint Etienne, France.

This manufacturer produced copies of 1894 patent Darne R model guns until 1956. While higher grades do exist, they do not command the prices given for the later patent (1909) Darne-produced guns. Lower grade guns will be priced in the same range as Soleihac and lower grade Darne R models.

SCHUERMAN ARMS., LTD.

Current bolt action rifle manufacturer located in Desert Hills, AZ. Previously located in Scottsdale, AZ. Consumer direct sales.

RIFLES: BOLT ACTION

MODEL SA40 - various cals., including WSMs (disc.), WSSMs (disc.), and Rem. Ultra Mags., right or left-hand action (four sizes) features three rotating locking lugs in short throw bolt, 70 degree bolt lift, 20-26 in. matte stainless steel barrel and ultra smooth action, trigger safety, controlled round feeding, fully enclosed case head, three-position safety, choice of detachable mag., hinged floorplate, or blind box mag., laminated fiberglass sporter style stock made in-house, integral scope base and muzzle brake became standard 2008. New 2001.

MSR $6,850	$6,850	$5,750	$5,100	$4,250	$3,600	$3,000	$2,225

SCHUETZEN PISTOL WORKS

Schuetzen Pistol Works is the in-house custom shop of Olympic Arms. Schuetzen Pistol Works has been customizing Safari Arms and Olympic Arms 1911 style pistols since 1997. For currently manufactured pistols, please refer to the Olympic Arms listing. For discontinued models, please refer to the Safari Arms listing.

SCHUETZEN RIFLES

A Schuetzen Rifle is a special single-shot target rifle. During the time span 1875-1945 this target configuration rifle was very popular with competition shooters, especially in Europe. Many of these guns had elaborate locking systems, top quality sights, double-set triggers, heavy barrels, palm and thumbrests, sculptured cheekpiece, Swiss style buttplate, etc. Rather than list all the various domestic and European makers (there are hundreds), it should be noted that, since there are so many combinations of options for this configuration, most guns have to be examined and appraised individually. Most non-major trademarks sell in the $900 - $6,500 range, depending on features and condition. A famous trademark specimen (Ballard, Stevens, Winchester, etc.) in a rare model with elaborate factory engraving, and superior original condition can bring over $25,000. Schuetzen Rifles are a field in themselves and a knowledgeable dealer/collector should be consulted before buying or selling one of these guns.

GRADING - PPGS™	100%	98%	95%	90%	80%	70%	60%	LAST MSR

SCHULTZ & LARSEN

Current rifle manufacturer located in Rask Molle, Denmark since 1994. Previously manufactured in Otterup, Denmark circa 1889-1994. The company also manufactures barrels, scope mounts, and other components, in addition to having a custom shop. No current U.S. importation.

RIFLES: BOLT ACTION

NO. 47 MATCH RIFLE – .22 LR cal., single shot, 28 in. heavy barrel, target sights, set trigger, free rifle stock.

$660	$550	$495	$440	$385	$360	$330

M61 MATCH RIFLE – .22 LR cal., single shot, 28 in. heavy barrel, target sights, set trigger, free rifle stock, palm rest.

$895	$825	$740	$680	$600	$550	$500

M62 MATCH RIFLE – various cals., single shot, 28 in. heavy barrel, target sights, set trigger, free rifle stock, palm rest.

$995	$875	$780	$700	$620	$550	$500

MODEL 54 FREE RIFLE – any American centerfire standard caliber, plus 6.5x55mm, 27 in. heavy barrel, target sights, free rifle stock.

$825	$745	$690	$605	$550	$495	$440

MODEL 54J SPORTING RIFLE – .244 Rem., .270 Win., .30-06, 6.5x55mm, or 7x61 Sharpe and Hart cal., 3 shot, 24 in. barrel, checkered Monte Carlo stock, no sights. Mfg. 1954-1957.

$650	$550	$470	$415	$360	$330	$300

MODEL 60 – 7x61 S&H cal. only, improved Model 54J, mfg. 1957-1960.

$675	$575	$475	$425	$375	$330	$300

MODEL 65 – .308 Norma Mag., .358 Win. Mag., or 7x61 S&H cal., improved Model 60, replaced by the Model 68DL, mfg. 1960-1967.

$675	$575	$475	$425	$375	$330	$300

MODEL 68 DL – .22 250 Rem., .243 Win., 6mm Rem., .264 Win. Mag., .270 Win., .30-06, .308 Win., 7x61 S&H, 7mm Rem. Mag., 8x57JS, .300 Win. Mag., .308 Norma Mag., .338 Win. Mag., .358 Norma Mag., or .458 Win. Mag. cal., 24 in. barrel, Bofors Steel receiver, bolt has 4 rear locking lugs, select French walnut stock, adj. trigger, no sights except for .458 Mag. Mfg. 1967-mid-1980s.

$725	$650	$575	$525	$495	$460	$430

MODEL 97-DL – various cals., configurations include Target, Takedown, and Sporter variations. No current U.S. importation.

Please contact the company directly for more information regarding pricing and availability on this model.

SHOTGUNS: O/U

Schultz & Larsen also manufactured a very limited quantity of O/U shotguns, including a 20 ga. boxlock. Values reflect shooting value more than collectibility.

SCHWABEN ARMS GMBH

Current manufacturer located in Rottweil, Germany. No current U.S. importation.

Schwaben Arms GmbH manufactures 600-800 guns annually. Production includes an extensive lineup of quality tactical rifles and carbines, primarily patterned after H&K models and other historically significant military rifles/carbines, including a .308 Win. cal. semi-auto MP5. Both commercial and military/law enforcement models are available. Please contact the factory directly for U.S. availability and pricing (see Trademark Index).

GRADING - PPGS™	100%	98%	95%	90%	80%	70%	60%	LAST MSR

SCOTT, W.C., LTD.

Previous manufacturer established during 1834 and located in Birmingham, England. All operations ceased during 1991.

Established in 1834 by William Scott, located in Birmingham, England, and remained in the family until 1897. Scott then merged with P. Webley & Son to form Webley & Scott Revolver and Arms Co., Ltd. (later changed to Webley & Scott Ltd.). Even though Scott family members were no longer associated with this new company, the Scott product line was continued with the trademark intact until 1935. Thereafter, only a few guns were marked Scott. In 1979, Webley & Scott ceased manufacture of all firearms. A new company, W. & C. Scott, was formed in 1980 utilizing mostly employees of Webley & Scott. W. & C. Scott remained part of its parent company, Harris & Sheldon (also had controlling interest in Hardy and Churchill trademarks), until 1985 when Scott was purchased by Holland & Holland. Manufacture of Scott guns decreased substantially after the merger, and in September 1991, W. & C. Scott ceased operation altogether. During its 157 years of production, Scott and Webley & Scott produced approximately, 150,000 double guns, 10,000 rifles (either double or bolt-action) and thousands of single guns and single rifles.

SHOTGUNS: SxS

All W.C. Scott Shotguns were discontinued in 1990. W.C. Scott also manufactured many hammer guns that vary in price from $250-$2,500, depending on grade and original condition.

KINMOUNT – 12, 16, 20, or 28 ga., boxlock action, ejectors, deluxe checkered walnut, scroll engraving.

	100%	98%	95%	90%	80%	70%	60%	LAST MSR
	$6,500	$5,750	$5,000	$4,500	$4,000	$3,000	$2,500	*$11,000*

Add 20% for 28 ga. or .410 bore.
Add 10% for SNT.

BOWOOD – 12, 16, 20, or 28 ga., boxlock action, ejectors, deluxe checkered walnut, extensive scroll engraving.

	100%	98%	95%	90%	80%	70%	60%	LAST MSR
	$7,500	$6,500	$5,750	$5,000	$4,500	$4,000	$3,500	*$12,500*

Add 20% for 28 ga. or .410 bore.
Add 10% for SNT.

CHATSWORTH – 12, 16, 20, or 28 ga., top-of-the-line boxlock action, ejectors, deluxe checkered walnut, extensive scroll engraving.

	100%	98%	95%	90%	80%	70%	60%	LAST MSR
	$8,750	$7,500	$6,500	$5,750	$5,000	$4,500	$4,000	*$14,000*

Add 20% for 28 ga. or .410 bore.
Add 10% for SNT.

BLENHEIM – 12 bore only, upgraded models, custom-made to individual specifications, originally priced per individual order.

Specimen rarity precludes percentage grading pricing.
Individual appraisals have to be secured on this model.

SEARCY, B. & CO.

Current custom rifle manufacturer established in 1975 and located in Boron, CA.

RIFLES: CUSTOM

B. Searcy & Co. manufactures a unique stainless steel double rifle in a variety of calibers. Current models include: Classic ($18,000 - MSR), Deluxe Grade ($21,500 - MSR), Back Action Sidelock ($30,000 - MSR), .600 NE Sidelock (MSR - $55,000), .577 NE Boxlock (MSR - $35,000), .577 NE Sidelock ($35,000 - MSR), .600 NE Boxlock ($55,000 - MSR), .700 NE Boxlock ($85,000 - MSR). Previous models included the Deluxe Grade double rifle (disc. 2011, $21,500 last MSR), PH Boxlock Model w/ejectors (disc. 2008, $12,000 last MSR), Under Lever Model (disc. 2008, $19,500 - last MSR), and the .700 NE Sidelock (last MSR was $50,000).

Beginning in 2010, B. Searcy & Co. makes a Rigby Bisell patterned rising bite sidelock in .450 NE caliber. Each gun is built per order and prices begin at $45,000.

B. Searcy also manufactures a bolt action rifle - starting price is $15,000, and many options are

GRADING - PPGS™	100%	98%	95%	90%	80%	70%	60%	LAST MSR

available. Additionally, a stalking rifle is available in cals. .22 Centerfire-.500 Nitro - base price is $8,500 or $14,500 for takedown model. Please contact the company directly (see Trademark Index) for current model information, availability, pricing for options, and delivery time.

SEARS, ROEBUCK AND CO.

Catalog merchandiser that, in addition to selling major trademark firearms, also private labeled many configurations of firearms (mostly longarms) under a variety of trademarks and logos (i.e., J.C. Higgins, Ted Williams, Ranger, etc.). Sears discontinued the sale of all firearms circa 1980, and the Ted Williams trademark was stopped circa 1978.

A general guideline for Sears Roebuck and related labels (most are marked "Sears, Roebuck and Co." on left side of barrel) is that values are generally lower than those of the major factory models from which they were derived. Remember, 99% of Sears Roebuck and related label guns get priced by their shootability factor in today's competitive marketplace, not collectibility. An extensive crossover listing (see Storebrand Cross-Over List) has been provided in the back of this text for linking up the various Sears Roebuck models to the original manufacturer with respective "crossover" model numbers.

SECURITY INDUSTRIES

Previous manufacturer located in Little Ferry, NJ.

REVOLVERS

MODEL PSS 38 DOUBLE ACTION – .38 Spl. cal., 5 shot cylinder, 2 in. barrel, stainless steel, fixed sights, wood grips. Mfg. 1973-78.

$175	**$150**	**$140**	**$130**	**$125**	**$110**	**$100**	

MODEL PM357 – .357 Mag. cal., similar to Model PSS 38, 2 1/2 in. barrel. Mfg. 1975-disc.

$225	**$175**	**$165**	**$150**	**$140**	**$125**	**$110**	

MODEL PPM 357 – .357 Mag. cal., 5 shot, 2 in. barrel, spurless hammer until 1977, new models have spur. Mfg. 1965-disc.

$225	**$175**	**$165**	**$150**	**$140**	**$125**	**$110**	

SEDCO INDUSTRIES, INC.

Previous manufacturer located in Lake Elsinore, CA until 1991.

PISTOLS: SEMI-AUTO

MODEL SP-22 – .22 LR cal., single action, 2 1/2 in. barrel, rotary safety, serrated slide, nickel, satin nickel (new 1990), or black metal finish, simulated pearl grips in white, blue, grey, or pink, 11 oz. Mfg. 1989-90 only.

$60	**$55**	**$50**	**$45**	**$40**	**$35**	**$35**	***$69***

SEDGLEY, R.F., INC.

Previous manufacturer located in Philadelphia, PA.

RIFLES: BOLT ACTION

SPRINGFIELD SPORTING RIFLE – .218 Bee, .220 Swift, .22-3000, .22-4000, .22 Hornet, .25-35 WCF, .250-3000 Sav., .257 Roberts, .270 Win., 7x57mm Mauser, or .30-06 cal., '03 Springfield bolt action, 24 in. barrel, Lyman receiver sight, checkered pistol grip stock, pre-WWII.

$1,250	**$1,125**	**$995**	**$875**	**$750**	**$625**	**$495**	

SPRINGFIELD CARBINE SPORTER – similar to Rifle, with 20 in. barrel, and full length stock.

$1,450	**$1,250**	**$1,125**	**$995**	**$875**	**$750**	**$625**	

SEECAMP, L.W. CO., INC.

Current handgun manufacturer located in Milford, CT. Dealer direct sales only.

Ludwig (Louis) Wilhelm Seecamp (1901-1989), after whom the company was named, was trained as a master gunsmith in the technical academy system of pre-WW II Germany. Having survived the Eastern Front in an elite Gebirgsjaeger (Mountain Troops)

GRADING - PPGS™	100%	98%	95%	90%	80%	70%	60%	LAST MSR

unit, he brought his family to the United States in 1959 by way of Canada. From 1959 until his retirement in 1971, he was the gun designer for O.F. Mossberg.

L.W. Seecamp Co, Inc. was founded in 1973 as a family business specializing in Ludwig's patented double action conversion of the venerable 1911 semi-auto pistol (Colt .45). This conversion, done during a period when the single-action versus double-action controversy was at its peak, resulted in the first commercially available DA .45 autoloaders anywhere in the world. Nearly 2000 such DA conversions were done from the early 70s to the early 80s.

PISTOLS: SEMI-AUTO

All Seecamp pistols are hand machined and fitted from stainless steel. Manufacture has always emphasized quality over quantity - this explains why values can exceed the company's retail pricing.

LWS .25 ACP MODEL – .25 ACP cal., double action, 2 in. barrel, 7 shot mag., stainless steel, matte finish, no sights, 12 oz. Approx. 4,000 mfg. 1981-85.

	100%	98%	95%	90%	80%	70%	60%	LAST MSR
	$400	$325	$275	$225	$195	$165	$140	$275

LWS 32 MODEL – .32 ACP cal., (mfg. recommends .32 ACP Win. Silvertip ammo only), double action, 2.06 in. barrel, stainless steel, 6 shot mag., no sights, 11 1/2 oz. Mfg. began Jan. 1985.

	100%	98%	95%	90%	80%	70%	60%	LAST MSR
MSR $446	$425	$375	$350	$285	$250	$215	$185	

Add $81 for California edition (with trigger mounted safety).

This model is available in either a matte or polished finish. The polished finish carries a slight premium.

MATCHED PAIR – includes both .25 ACP and .32 ACP pistols with the same serial number, approx. 200 sets were mfg. before the BATFE stopped this practice.

	100%	98%	95%	90%	80%	70%	60%	LAST MSR
	$1,200	$1,000	$850	$740	$620	$515	$440	

This set contained a matte finished .25 ACP and a polished .32 ACP.

LWS-380 MODEL – .380 ACP cal. (mfg. recommends .380 ACP Win. Silvertip ammo only), identical in appearance to the LWS 32 Model, 2.06 in. barrel, double action only, delayed blowback mechanism, polished stainless steel, checkered black glass filled nylon grips, no sights, 11 1/2 oz. Very limited production beginning 2000.

	100%	98%	95%	90%	80%	70%	60%	LAST MSR
MSR $795	$795	$725	$650	$540	$465	$385	$335	

SEITZ

Previous manufacturer located in Portland, OR circa mid-1980s-1993.

SHOTGUNS: SINGLE BARREL TRAP

SINGLE BARREL TRAP GUN – 12 ga. only, single barrel, various barrel lengths, pull or release trigger, only 45 guns mfg.

	100%	98%	95%	90%	80%	70%	60%	LAST MSR
	$18,500	$16,000	$13,000	$10,000	$8,500	$7,700	$6,950	

SEMMERLING

Current trademark owned by American Derringer Corp., located in Waco, TX. Previously manufactured by Semmerling Corporation, located in Boston, MA from 1978-1982.

Less than 600 LM-4 pistols were originally mfg. by the Semmerling Corporation.

PISTOLS: SLIDE ACTION

LM-4 PISTOL – .45 ACP cal., 2 in. barrel, blue, smallest .45 ACP repeater available, slide is worked manually with thumb on serrated slide-top, extremely high quality, hand fitted and choice of finishes include chrome, electroless nickel, or high polish blue.

	100%	98%	95%	90%	80%	70%	60%	LAST MSR
Chrome	$2,950	$2,600	$2,300	$2,100	$1,950	$1,725	$1,600	
Electroless nickel	$3,200	$2,950	$2,600	$2,300	$2,100	$1,950	$1,725	
High polish blue	$4,950	$4,500	$4,000	$3,600	$3,200	$2,800	$2,500	

The original U.S. Army contract pistol mfg. by Semmerling in Boston had an MSR for $5,000. Earlier mfg. by Lichtman will also command a premium over values listed.

GRADING - PPGS™	100%	98%	95%	90%	80%	70%	60%	LAST MSR

*** *LM-4 Pistol (Current Mfg.)***

Please refer to the American Derringer section.

SENNI ARMS CO.

Current manufacturer located in Queensland, Australia. No current U.S. importation.

Senni Arms manufactures a complete line of 1911-style semi-auto pistols, including the Stinger, 2010, Black Snake, Lawson, Silhouette, Razorback, and the Trooper. Senni Arms also manufactures the Siege semi-auto tactical shotgun and the Elysium M4 semi-auto tactical carbine. Please contact the company directly for more information, including pricing and domestic availability (see Trademark Index).

SENTINEL ARMS

Previous importer of Arsenal Bulgaria pistols and rifles.

SERBU FIREARMS, INC.

Current manufacturer located in Tampa, FL.

Serbu Firearms also manufactures a Super-Shorty short barreled slide action shotgun based on the Remington 870 or Mossberg 500. These shotguns are classified NFA only.

RIFLES: BOLT ACTION

BFG-50 RIFLE/CARBINE – .50 BMG cal., single shot bolt action, 22 (carbine), 29 1/2 (rifle), or 36 (alloy or stainless, new 2011) in. match grade barrel with muzzle brake, AR-15 style trigger and safety, Picatinny rail, parkerized finish, 17-22 lbs. New 1999.

MSR $2,195	$2,195	$1,850	$1,650	$1,450	$1,250	$1,175	$975

Add $75 for "Have a Nice Day" engraving on Shark muzzle brake.
Add $150 for bi-pod.
Add $400 for 36 in. barrel (alloy or stainless), new 2011.

BFG-50A – .50 BMG cal., gas operated, 26 in. barrel with 8 port Shark Brake muzzle brake, 10 shot mag., 3-lug bolt, sliding plate extrator, dual plunger ejectors, removeable barrel extension and handguard, 23 lbs. New 2008.

MSR $6,700	$6,250	$5,500	$4,950	$4,000	$3,650	$3,350	$2,995

SERENGETI RIFLES, INC.

Previous custom rifle manufacturer and stock maker located in Kalispell, MT until 2010.

Serengeti was famous for its stealth lamination stocks, originally called the Acra-Bond laminate. Stealth lamination technology provides greater stock stability, while preserving the full beauty, figure, and feel of a traditional walnut stock.

Please refer to the Kilimanjaro Rifles listings in the K section for more information on the new Serengeti rifle.

RIFLES: BOLT ACTION, CUSTOM

Serengeti Rifles Inc. manufactured a complete line of high-quality, custom-order bolt action rifles, including the Standard African ($7,369 last MSR), Dangerous Game African ($8,249 last MSR), Montanan ($6,269 last MSR), Red Mist ($6,269 last MSR), TigerCat ($6,869 last MSR), and the Walkabout ($6,269 last MSR). A number of options were available. Additionally, Serengeti Rifles manufactured its own line of proprietary actions and high quality walnut stocks.

SERO LTD.

Current rifle manufacturer located in Budapest, Hungary. No domestic importation.

RIFLES: SEMI-AUTO

GEPARD GM6 LYNX – 14.5x114mm Soviet or .50 BMG cal., bullpup configuration, 28 3/4 in. barrel with muzzle brake, 100% desert camo coverage, 5 shot mag. is located in back of the pistol grip, full Picatinny rail, 25.3 lbs. New 2012.

As this edition went to press, values on this model could not be determined.

GRADING - PPGS™	100%	98%	95%	90%	80%	70%	60%	LAST MSR

C. SHARPS ARMS CO. INC.

Current manufacturer located in Big Timber, MT.

C. Sharps Arms Co. Inc. currently distributes smokeless powder replicas of C. Sharps rifles/carbines and the Winchester Model 1885 single shot. They are able to shoot both smokeless and black powder loads. Most models are available in the following cals.: .38-55, .40-50, .40-65, .40-70, .40-90, .45-70, .45-90, .45-100, .45-110, .45-120, .50-70, .50-90, .50-100, and .50-140. All models are authentically reproduced and high quality.

RIFLES: REPRODUCTIONS, SHARPS BLACK POWDER

Because each rifle is a special order, there are many options available which would be added to the base price shown. Please contact the company directly for availability (see Trademark Index).

NEW MODEL 1874 BRIDGEPORT SPORTING RIFLE – 26, 28, or 30 in. tapered octagon barrel, DT, drilled and tapped, straight grip walnut stock with Schnabel forend, checkered steel buttplate, color case hardened receiver, approx. 10 1/2 lbs.

	100%	98%	95%	90%	80%	70%	60%	LAST MSR
MSR $1,895	$1,895	$1,625	$1,450	$1,400	$1,350	$1,300	$1,200	

In addition to the 1874 Sporting Model, a custom long range target rifle or Schuetzen short range target rifle is available in this model.

NEW MODEL 1874 HARTFORD SPORTING RIFLE – 26, 28, or 30 in. tapered octagon barrel, DT, drilled and tapped, Hartford semi-crescent military and sporting smooth steel buttplate and silver nose cap, straight grain American walnut stock with oil finish, color case hardened receiver, approx. 10 1/2 lbs.

	100%	98%	95%	90%	80%	70%	60%	LAST MSR
MSR $2,095	$2,095	$1,700	$1,575	$1,475	$1,400	$1,350	$1,300	

NEW MODEL 1874 CARBINE HUNTER – 22, 24, or 26 in. tapered round barrel with buckhorn and silver blade front sights, semi-crescent military style buttstock, slender forend, color case hardened receiver, DT, drilled and tapped.

	100%	98%	95%	90%	80%	70%	60%	LAST MSR
MSR $1,825	$1,825	$1,550	$1,395	$1,300	$1,250	$1,200	$1,150	

CUSTOM NEW MODEL 1874 BOSS GUN – features 34 in. No. 1 heavy tapered octagon barrel, vernier tang sight, straight grip stock with cheekrest, shotgun buttstock and steel buttplate.

This gun is custom order only. Please contact the factory to obtain a quotation on this model.

NEW MODEL 1875 SPORTING RIFLE – similar to New Model 1875 Classic, except has receiver with round crown.

	100%	98%	95%	90%	80%	70%	60%	LAST MSR
MSR $1,370	$1,370	$1,250	$1,125	$975	$900	$825	$750	

Add $300 for 1875 Classic Sporting Rifle.

NEW MODEL 1875 TARGET SPORTING RIFLE – .38-55, .40-65, .40-70 Sharps Straight, .45-70 Govt., or .45-90 cal., 30 in. heavy tapered round barrel American walnut stock with pistol grip, black buttplate, color case receiver, drilled and tapped, single trigger, 11 lbs. Limited mfg. 2004, 2011-current.

	100%	98%	95%	90%	80%	70%	60%	LAST MSR
MSR $1,325	$1,325	$1,225	$1,100	$975	$900	$825	$750	

NEW MODEL 1875 CLASSIC HARTFORD – receiver with octagon top, 26, 28, or 30 in. tapered full octagon barrel, straight grip stock with steel toe plate, 9 1/2 lbs. New 1992.

	100%	98%	95%	90%	80%	70%	60%	LAST MSR
MSR $2,495	$2,495	$1,950	$1,775	$1,575	$1,375	$1,175	$1,000	

NEW MODEL 1875 CARBINE – features 24 in. tapered round barrel. Mfg. 1996-98.

	100%	98%	95%	90%	80%	70%	60%	LAST MSR
	$875	$750	$675	$600	$500	$450	$375	*$810*

NEW MODEL 1875 SADDLE RIFLE – receiver with octagon top, 26 in. barrel only. Disc. 1998.

	100%	98%	95%	90%	80%	70%	60%	LAST MSR
	$925	$850	$775	$700	$625	$550	$460	*$910*

NEW MODEL 1875 BUSINESS RIFLE – receiver with round top, 28 in. heavy tapered round barrel. Disc. 1998.

	100%	98%	95%	90%	80%	70%	60%	LAST MSR
	$875	$775	$700	$625	$550	$500	$450	*$810*

Add $50 for barrel sights.

GRADING - PPGS™	100%	98%	95%	90%	80%	70%	60%	LAST MSR

CUSTOM NEW MODEL 1877 – .44-90, .45-70 Govt., .45-90, or .45-100 cal., 32 or 34 in. tapered round barrel, presentation grade American or English walnut stock, checkered pistol grip and forend, ebony forend tip, classic long range sights, 10 lbs. Limited production 2004 only.

	100%	98%	95%	90%	80%	70%	60%	LAST MSR
	$5,250	$4,750	$4,450	$4,100	$3,750	$3,450	$3,100	*$5,500*

NEW MODEL 1885 HIGHWALL – .22 LR, .22 Hornet, .219 Zipper, .30-40 Krag, .32-40, .348 Win., .38-55 WCF, .40-65, .405 Win., .444 Marlin, or .45-70 cal., patterned after the Winchester Model 1885 single shot, falling block action, case colored receiver and small parts, 26-30 in. octagon barrel. Mfg. 1992-2008, reintroduced 2011.

	100%	98%	95%	90%	80%	70%	60%
MSR $1,750	$1,750	$1,500	$1,250	$1,000	$875	$750	$625

Add $200 for New Model 1885 Highwall Classic rifle (crescent buttplate and satin grey receiver finish, disc.).

SHARPS, CHRISTIAN

Previously manufactured by Sharps Rifle Manufacturing Company circa 1851-1855 and located in Windsor, VT. Also manufactured in Hartford, CT under same name between 1855-1874. Reorganized as Sharps Rifle Company in 1876 with production resuming in Hartford (1876 only) and Bridgeport, CT from 1877-1881.

100%	98%	95%	90%	80%	70%	60%	50%	40%	30%	20%	10%

HANDGUNS

SHARPS BREECH-LOADING SINGLE SHOT PISTOL – 5 in. round barrel, dropping block, lever action single shot percussion, patent 1848 style carbine action of reduced size, all iron mountings, walnut grips. Made mid-1850s in Philadelphia, about 850 total of two types produced.

* ***Type I*** – .31-.34 cal., "SHARPS PATENT/ARMS MFrd FAIRMOUNT/PHILA. PA" stamped within a oval panel on left side of frame, serial numbered from 1 to approx. 500.

100%	98%	95%	90%	80%	70%	60%	50%	40%	30%	20%	10%
N/A	N/A	$12,000	$10,000	$9,500	$8,000	$7,000	$6,500	$5,000	$4,500	$4,000	$3,000

* ***Type 2*** – .36 cal., 6 1/2 in. round barrel, "C. SHARPS & CO./PHILA.PA." or "C. SHARPS & CO'S RIFLE WORKS/PHILA. PA." stamped on right frame, "C. SHARPS/PATENT/1848" stamped on left side of frame. Approx. serial numbers between 470 to 950. Approx. 350 mfg.

100%	98%	95%	90%	80%	70%	60%	50%	40%	30%	20%	10%
N/A	N/A	$12,500	$10,500	$9,500	$8,500	$7,500	$7,000	$6,000	$5,000	$4,500	$4,000

SHARPS PISTOL RIFLE – .31 and .38 cal., lever action single shot percussion, using the single shot pistol action with the additions of a longer barrel and a rifle pistol grip buttstock, various barrel lengths with 28 in. being most common, early rifles have German silver buttplate, forend cap and escutcheon plates on forend which is held on by a wedge, standard production uses iron mountings, dropping block. Made mid-1850s in Philadelphia. About 650 total of two types produced.

* ***Type I*** – pistol action with a ramrod mounted under the barrel and German silver mountings, "C. SHARPS PATENT 1848-52" marked on left side of frame. Approx. only 50 made.

100%	98%	95%	90%	80%	70%	60%	50%	40%	30%	20%	10%
N/A	N/A	$15,000	$12,500	$9,500	$9,000	$8,000	$7,000	$6,500	$6,000	$5,000	$4,500

* ***Type 2*** – standard model, has iron mountings, no ramrod, "C. SHARPS & CO. PHILADA. PA" marked on left side of frame. Approx. only 600 made.

100%	98%	95%	90%	80%	70%	60%	50%	40%	30%	20%	10%
N/A	N/A	$15,000	$12,500	$9,500	$9,000	$8,000	$7,000	$6,500	$6,000	$5,000	$4,500

REVOLVER, PERCUSSION – made 1850s in Philadelphia, production about 2000, 3 in. octagonal tip-up barrel with rib, .25 caliber, 6 shot.

100%	98%	95%	90%	80%	70%	60%	50%	40%	30%	20%	10%
N/A	N/A	$5,000	$4,500	$4,000	$3,700	$3,500	$3,200	$2,800	$2,500	$2,300	$1,750

PEPPERBOX PISTOL – also marked Sharps and Hankins, shot breech-loading, .32, .30, or .22 rimfire cal., firing pin rotates, brass frame with silver plating, or case-hardening on iron frame.

100%	98%	95%	90%	80%	70%	60%	50%	40%	30%	20%	10%

* ***Pepperbox Pistol First Model*** – 5 variations, 2 1/2 in. barrel. Scarcer variations can be worth up to 150% more.

N/A	N/A	$1,100	$1,000	$850	$800	$750	$700	$650	$600	$550	$450

* ***Pepperbox Pistol Second Model*** – 5 variations, 3 in. barrel. Scarcer variations can be worth up to 150% more.

N/A	N/A	$1,100	$1,000	$875	$850	$800	$750	$700	$600	$500	$400

* ***Pepperbox Pistol Third Model*** – Sharps and Hankins markings, .32 rimfire short, 4 variations, 3 1/2 in. barrel. Premium for scarcer variations.

N/A	N/A	$1,250	$1,100	$1,000	$925	$850	$775	$725	$625	$525	$425

* ***Pepperbox Pistol Fourth Model*** – 4 variations, 2 1/2, 3, or 3 1/2 in. barrel, bird's head grip, .32 rimfire long. Premium for scarcer variations.

N/A	N/A	$2,000	$1,800	$1,700	$1,500	$1,400	$1,200	$1,000	$900	$800	$600

RIFLES: BREECH LOADING

The earliest Sharps rifles and carbines were made for Christian Sharps by A.S. Nippes, in Mill Creek, PA circa 1850, and a year later by Robbins and Lawrence Co. of Windsor, VT. Not until 1856 did the Sharps Rifle Co. of Hartford, CT begin to manufacture its own guns.

MODEL 1849 RIFLE – .36 or .44 cal., percussion breechloader, 30 in. barrels and brass patchboxes were standard, serial numbered 1 and up, very few examples exist, less than 100 mfg. These are the first of all Sharps long guns, there is no fixed value range. Depending on condition, they could range from $5,000 to $50,000+.

MODEL 1850 RIFLE – .36 or .44 cal., incorporated the Maynard tape primer on the right side of the breech, features similar to Model 1849, approx. 150 mfg. by A.S. Nippes, very rare. Values only slightly less than Model 1849.

MODEL 1851 CARBINE – .52 cal. percussion, 21 5/8 barrel, hammer mounted inside frame, Maynard tape primer. Approx. 1,800 mfg. by Robbins and Lawrence, 200 went to U.S. Government - these will bring a premium.

N/A	N/A	$17,000	$15,000	$11,000	$10,000	$9,500	$9,000	$8,500	$8,000	$6,000	$5,000

MODEL 1852 CARBINE – this design became standard for all the Sharps for the next two decades, first to be called "slant breech," established Christian Sharps as a major gun manufacturer. Approx. 5,000 mfg. by Robbins and Lawrence, U.S. military markings will command a premium.

N/A	N/A	$10,000	$9,000	$8,000	$7,000	$6,500	$6,000	$5,500	$5,000	$4,000	$3,000

MODEL 1853 CARBINE – .52 cal., very similar to Model 1852, with walnut stock and brass patchbox, Sharps patented pellet primer feed, ser. no. range 9,000-19,000.

N/A	N/A	$10,000	$9,000	$8,000	$7,000	$6,500	$6,000	$5,500	$5,000	$4,000	$3,000

Approx. 10,000 mfg. by Robbins and Lawrence 1854-1858, an additional 3,000 rifles mfg. - subtract 25%.

MODEL 1855 CARBINE – .52 cal., U.S. military model, all with Maynard tape primer, this was the period during which Robbins and Lawrence failed, and Sharps Rifle Co. took over production. 800 mfg.

N/A	N/A	$16,000	$15,500	$15,000	$14,000	$13,000	$12,000	$11,000	$10,000	$8,000	$7,000

Sharps "New Model"

Manufactured in Hartford, CT by Sharps Rifle Manufacturing Co. circa 1859-1866. Visibly different from earlier models because of straight breech and pellet priming feature built into lock plate. Approx. 115,000 were built, all in .52 cal. breechloading paper cartridge. Carbines had 22 in. barrels, rifles came standard with 30 in. round barrels. After ser. nos. reached 100,000, a "C" prefix was used in the number - i.e. C500 represents ser. no. 100,500.

MODEL 1859 CARBINE – standard with all-iron furniture and patchbox, first 3,000 had brass instead of iron, ser. no. range 30,000-75,000. Approx. 33,000 mfg.

N/A	N/A	$12,000	$10,500	$9,500	$7,500	$7,000	$6,500	$6,000	$5,000	$4,000	$3,500

100%	98%	95%	90%	80%	70%	60%	50%	40%	30%	20%	10%

MODEL 1863 CARBINE – made with and w/o iron patchbox, ser. no. range 75,000 - 140,000. Approx. 65,000 mfg. - those with patchbox will bring a premium.

N/A	N/A	$9,000	$8,000	$7,000	$6,500	$6,000	$5,500	$5,000	$4,500	$4,000	$3,500

MODEL 1865 CARBINE – made w/o patchbox, ser. no. range 140,000-145,000. Only 5,000 mfg.

N/A	N/A	$9,000	$8,500	$7,500	$6,500	$6,000	$5,500	$5,000	$4,500	$4,000	$3,500

MODEL 1859 RIFLE – iron patchbox only, long forearm fastened with three barrel bands, approx. 4,300 mfg. in carbine ser. range with lug on barrel for attachment of saber bayonet. Approx. 600 were mfg. with 36 in. long barrel - these will command a premium.

N/A	N/A	$9,000	$8,500	$8,000	$7,000	$6,500	$6,000	$5,500	$4,500	$4,000	$3,500

COFFEE MILL MODEL – experimental variation buttstock with a grinding device and detachable handle that was fitted to several Model 1859 & 1863 Carbines. Designed to provide a quick and easy method for cavalry troops in the field to process coffee beans or corn for meals. Field trials are believed to have been in Trenton, NJ circa 1863. Very few originals known - no official records indicating government acceptance. Originals are extremely rare and values could range from $10,000-$50,000.

Buyer beware! Many fakes exist.

MODEL 1863 RIFLE – adapted for socket bayonet, shared ser. range with carbine. Approx. 6,000 mfg.

N/A	N/A	$9,500	$9,000	$8,000	$7,000	$6,000	$5,500	$5,000	$4,000	$3,500	$3,000

MODEL 1865 RIFLE – only 1,000 mfg. in carbine ser. range.

N/A	N/A	$11,500	$10,500	$8,600	$7,500	$6,000	$5,500	$5,000	$4,500	$4,000	$3,500

Sharps Cartridge Conversions

In 1867, the U.S. government decided to convert their percussion Sharps carbines and rifles to the new .50/70 metallic cartridge. Approx. 31,000 carbines and 1,000 rifles were converted by the Sharps Co. Any original, six groove barrels that were worn beyond specification had a groove liner installed. Those barrels meeting specs. remained unaltered. All buttstocks were stamped on the left side with "D.F.C." in a ribbon cartouche, the initials for the principal sub-inspector, David F. Clark. Damaged buttstocks were all replaced with the plain (no patchbox) Model 1865 buttstock, regardless of the model of the carbine; however, many of the old style buttplates with notches for patchboxes were retained.

.50/70 CARBINES – most had relined three groove barrels, approx. 31,000 remodeled. Those found with original six groove barrels will command a slight premium, as will those Model 1859s & Model 1863s with original patchbox buttstocks.

N/A	N/A	$7,000	$6,500	$6,000	$5,500	$5,000	$4,500	$4,000	$3,500	$3,000	$2,500

.50/70 RIFLES – all had three groove relined barrels, approx. 1,000 converted in 1867. More rare, but do not command any higher prices than their carbine counterparts.

SPRINGFIELD/SHARPS MODEL 1870-1871 – approx. 1,000 rifles and 300 carbines altered by Springfield Armory to fire .50/70 metallic cartridge, in addition to those done by Sharps Co., rifle barrels 35 1/2 in., carbine barrels 22 in., receivers color case hardened, all other metal parts bright finish, own ser. range, and numbered on receiver tang and left side of barrel.

* ***Springfield/Sharps Model 1870-1871 Rifles***

N/A	N/A	$6,500	$6,000	$5,500	$5,200	$5,000	$4,750	$4,500	$4,000	$3,500	$3,000

* ***Springfield/Sharps Model 1870-1871 Carbines***

N/A	N/A	$8,000	$7,850	$7,500	$7,250	$7,000	$6,500	$6,250	$6,000	$5,500	$5,000

Sharps Metallic Cartridge Models

MODEL 1874 – mfg. in several configurations and a variety of calibers, designed to fire metallic cartridges and was not a conversion from percussion parts, made famous for its deadly accuracy at long distances and became known as the "Buffalo Rifle" of its day. Mfg. in Hartford, CT circa 1874-76, and in Bridgeport, CT circa 1881.

100%	98%	95%	90%	80%	70%	60%	50%	40%	30%	20%	10%

* ***Model 1874 Sporting Model*** – .40, .44, .45 or .50 cal., variety of barrel lengths and weights, many special order features. Approx. 6,500 mfg.

N/A	N/A	$15,000	$11,000	$9,500	$8,500	$8,250	$8,000	$7,750	$7,500	$7,200	$7,000

* ***Model 1874 Business Rifle*** – no frills version of the 1874 Sporting, with shorter, round barrel and open sights.

N/A	N/A	$9,500	$8,500	$7,500	$7,000	$6,500	$6,000	$5,500	$5,000	$4,500	$4,250

* ***Model 1874 Military Rifle*** – .45/70 or .50/70 cal., long forearm and three barrel bands. Approx. 1,700 mfg.

N/A	N/A	$8,000	$7,750	$7,500	$7,000	$6,500	$6,000	$5,500	$5,000	$4,500	$4,250

* ***Model 1874 Military Carbine*** – most in .50/70 cal., very similar to previous Sharps carbines. Less than 500 mfg.

N/A	N/A	$9,000	$8,500	$8,000	$7,750	$7,500	$7,000	$6,000	$5,500	$5,000	$4,500

* ***Model 1874 Meachan Type Conversion*** – most in .45/70 cal., very similar to Business Rifle, with both round and octagon barrels, mfg. from Civil War Sharps carbine actions and surplus, as well as new parts by several commercial firms in the 1880s after Sharps Rifle Co. closed. Sharps Co. assembled several hundred of these from 1879-1881 from existing parts on hand.

N/A	N/A	$7,500	$6,800	$6,000	$5,250	$5,175	$5,000	$4,750	$4,500	$4,250	$4,000

While of lesser quality than the Model 1874, these rifles were widely used on the Western frontier and have become very desirable to today's firearms collectors.

MODEL 1878 SHARPS-BORCHARDT – many cals. and barrel lengths, single trigger, hammerless action designed by Hugo Borchardt, carbines, military, sporting, and target rifles were all mfg., but sales suffered from a bolt and lever action market glut. Less than 9,000 mfg. by Sharps Rifle Co. in Bridgeport, CT c. 1878-81.

N/A	N/A	$7,000	$6,000	$5,500	$5,250	$5,175	$5,000	$4,750	$4,500	$4,250	$4,000

Special order or deluxe models with other than standard features will command a premium.

GRADING - PPGS™	100%	98%	95%	90%	80%	70%	60%	LAST MSR

SHARPS-LEE – material for 1,300 rifles was purchased in 1879 but little work was done on the U.S. Navy order for 300 rifles before Sharps ceased operations Oct. 18, 1880. Only a few hand-made tool room models for demonstration purposes were completed.

	N/A	$10,000	$8,000	$6,000	$5,500	$5,000	$4,000	

Add 50% for carbine or factory sporting rifle.

SHARPS MILSPEC

Previous trademark and division of Sharps Rifle Company, located in Chamberlain, SD 2011 only.

RIFLES: SEMI-AUTO

SHARPS 2010 CARBINE – 5.56 NATO cal., AR-15 style with gas piston operation, 16 in. 5 groove rifling barrel with muzzle brake, redesigned charging handle, aluminum free floating quad Picatinny rail, Magpul ACS buttstock and MIAD pistol grip, supplied with two 30 shot mags. Limited mfg. 2011 only.

	$2,425	$2,100	$1,800	$1,500	$1,250	$1,000	$850	*$2,695*

SHARPS RIFLE COMPANY

Previous parent company of A-Square Rifles & Ammunition, Hermann H. Heiser Manufacturing and Co., Merwin Hulbert & Co., and Sharps MilSpec, and manufacturing facility was located in Glenrock, WY. Previous corporate headquarters located in Chamberlain, SD until 2011. Please check individual listings for current information and pricing.

SHERIDAN PRODUCTS INCORPORATED

Previous manufacturer located in Racine, WI.

GRADING - PPGS™	100%	98%	95%	90%	80%	70%	60%	LAST MSR

PISTOLS: SINGLE SHOT

KNOCKABOUT – .22 S-L-LR cal., 5 in. barrel, checkered plastic grips, fixed sights. Mfg. 1953-60.

$275	$225	$200	$150	$110	$100	$85	

SHILEN RIFLES, INCORPORATED

Previous manufacturer located in Enis, TX circa 1975-mid 1980s.

RIFLES: BOLT ACTION

Older Shilen rifles have become very desirable for target shooters and other accuracy enthusiasts. Because of their small quantities of manufacture (approx. 3,350 mfg.) and new-found demand, prices have gone up considerably on this trademark. Originally, the Sporters retailed in the $600-$700 range, but at the end, prices were in the $3,500 range.

DGA SPORTER – .17 Rem., .223 Rem., .22-250 Rem., .220 Swift, 6mm Rem., .243 Win., .250 Savage, .257 Roberts, .284 Win., .308 Win., or .358 Win. cal., 3 shot mag., 24 in. barrel, no sights, claro walnut stock.

$1,475	$1,175	$950	$800	$675	$575	$495	

DGA VARMINTER – similar to Sporter, except 25 in. medium heavy barrel.

$1,395	$1,100	$900	$775	$650	$575	$495	

DGA SILHOUETTE RIFLE – similar to Varminter, .308 Win. cal. only.

$1,395	$1,100	$900	$775	$650	$575	$495	

DGA BENCHREST RIFLE – single shot, choice of cals., 26 in. heavy or medium barrel, no sights, choice of fiberglass or walnut stock, thumbhole available.

$1,450	$1,200	$950	$800	$650	$575	$495	

Actions for this model are currently selling in the $450 - $550 range.

SHILOH SHARPS RIFLE MANUFACTURING COMPANY

Current manufacturer located in Big Timber, MT since 1976. Previously manufactured by Shiloh Products, a division of Drovel Tool Company of Farmingdale, NY, 1976-1983. Dealer or consumer direct sales.

For more information on Shiloh's lineup of black powder reproductions and replicas, please refer to the *Blue Book of Modern Black Powder Arms* by John Allen (also online).

RIFLES: REPRODUCTIONS

The Shiloh Rifle Mfg. Co. is currently manufacturing quality replicas of Sharps rifles and carbines. Models include: 1874 #2 Creedmor Silhouette Rifle ($2,825 MSR), 1874 Military Carbine ($1,854 MSR), 1874 Business Rifle ($1,854 MSR), 1874 Creedmoor Target Rifle ($2,825 MSR), 1874 Quigley Buffalo Rifle ($3,396 MSR), 1874 Long Range Express ($1,959 MSR), 1874 Sporter #3 ($1,854 MSR), 1874 Sporter #1 ($1,959 MSR), 1874 Montana Roughrider ($1,959 MSR), 1874 Saddle Rifle ($1,907 MSR), 1874 Hartford Model ($2,082 MSR), and the 1874 Military Rifle ($2,154 MSR). Please contact Shiloh Rifle Mfg. Co. directly regarding availability and the current waiting period (see Trademark Index.)

SHOOTERS ARMS MANUFACTURING INCORPORATED

Current manufacturer established in 1992, and located in Cebu, the Philippines. Currently imported by Century International Arms, located in Delray Beach, FL. Previously imported by Pacific Arms Corp. in Modesto, CA.

Shooter Arms Manufacturing Inc. makes semi-auto pistols, including the Elite, Commodore, Military, GI, Desert Storm, Seahawk, 1911A1, Eagle, Hawk, and the Trojan. Previous models have included the React, React-2, Military Enhanced, GI Enhanced, Elite Sport, Chief, Scout, Falcon, Raven, Omega, and Alpha. Shooters Arms Manufacuring Inc. also manufactures a revolver, the Protector, and a 12 ga. shotgun called the SAS 12. Please contact the importer directly for more information, including pricing and U.S. availability (see Trademark Index).

GRADING - PPGS™	100%	98%	95%	90%	80%	70%	60%	LAST MSR

SIDEWINDER

Previous trademark manufactured by D-Max, Inc. located in Bagley, MN circa 1993-96. Dealer or consumer sales.

REVOLVERS

SIDEWINDER – .45 LC or 2 1/2/3 in. .410 bore shotshells/slugs, 6 shot, stainless steel construction, 6 1/2 or 7 1/2 in. bull barrel (muzzle end bored for removable choke), Pachmayr grips, transfer bar safety, adj. rear sight, unique design permits one cylinder to shoot above listed loads, cased with choke tube, 3.8 lbs. Mfg. 1993-1996.

$695	$575	$475	$415	$360	$300	$255	*$775*

SIG ARMS AG

Current Swiss company (SIG) established during 1860 in Neuhausen, Switzerland. P 210 pistols are currently imported and distributed by Sig Sauer (formerly SIG Arms, Inc.), established in 1985, located in Exeter, NH. Previously located in Herndon, VA and Tysons Corner, VA.

In late 2000, SIG Arms AG, the firearms portion of SIG, was purchased by two Germans named Michael Lüke and Thomas Ortmeier, who have a background in textiles. Today the Lüke & Ortmeier group includes independently operational companies such as Blaser Jadgwaffen GmbH, Mauser Jagdwaffen GmbH, J.P. Sauer & Sohn GmbH, SIG-Sauer Inc., SIG-Sauer GmbH and SAN Swiss Arms AG. Please refer to individual listings.

PISTOLS: SEMI-AUTO

SIG Custom Shop variations of the P 210 were also available in three configurations - United We Stand ($8,990 last MSR) and two variations of the 50 Year Jubilee ($4,995 or $5,999 last MSR).

Add $1,473 for .22 LR conversion kit on the following models (not available on the P 210-8).

TRAILSIDE/TRAILSIDE COMPETITION – please refer to the Hämmerli section for more information and current pricing on these models.

P 210 & VARIATIONS – 9mm Para. or 7.65mm Para. (disc.) cal., single action, 4 3/4 in. barrel, 8 shot mag., standard weapon of the Swiss Army, 2 lbs.

Originally mfg. in 1947, this pistol was first designated the SP 47/8 and became the standard military pistol of the Swiss Army in 1949. Later designated the P 210, this handgun has been mfg. continuously for over 55 years.

* ***P 210 Danish Army M49*** – Danish Army version of the Model P 210, approx. 25,000 mfg.

$3,000	$2,500	$2,000	$1,750	$1,500	$1,250	$1,000

* ***P 210-1*** – polished finish, walnut grips, special hammer, fixed sights. Importation disc. 1986.

$2,500	$2,000	$1,500	$1,250	$1,000	$900	$750	*$1,861*

* ***P 210-2*** – matte finish, field or combat (recent mfg.) sights, plastic (disc.) or wood grips. Limited importation 1987-2002.

$1,800	$1,500	$1,200	$900	$750	$625	$550

Last MSR $1,680

Add 25% for high polish Swiss Army pistols with "A" prefix.

Add 50% for West German Police Contract models with unique loaded chamber indicator on slide. Approx. 5,000 mfg. in "D" prefix serial range.

* ***P 210-5*** – matte finish, heavy frame, micrometer target sights, 150mm or 180mm (disc.) extended barrel, hard rubber (disc.) or wood (current mfg.) grips, bottom (EU) or push-button side mounted (U.S.) mag. release, very limited mfg. Limited importation 1997-2007.

$2,250	$2,150	$1,675	$1,350	$1,125	$1,000	$895

Add 15% for side mounted mag. release.

Add 50% for early mfg. guns.

GRADING - PPGS™	100%	98%	95%	90%	80%	70%	60%	LAST MSR

* ***P 210-6*** – matte blue finish, fixed (recent importation) or micrometer sights, 120mm barrel, checkered walnut grips, bottom (EU) or push-button side mounted (U.S.) mag. release.

	$1,850	$1,700	$1,500	$1,300	$1,125	$1,000	$895	

* ***P 210-7*** – .22 LR or 9mm Para. cal., regular or target long barrel, limited importation. Disc.

	$3,500	$3,000	$2,700	$2,350	$2,000	$1,750	$1,500	

* ***P 210-8*** – features heavy frame, target sights, and wood grips. Special order only. Limited importation 2001-2003.

	$3,750	$3,250	$2,650	$2,300	$1,950	$1,600	$1,275	*$4,289*

* ***P 210 Deluxe Models*** – various models differ in the amount of engraving, gold inlays, carved wood grips, presentation cases, and other special order features available from the factory.

These models were available by special order only, and should be appraised individually. Values generally fall in the $4,500 - $6,500 range.

* ***P 210 Legend*** – please refer to listing in the Sig Sauer section, new mfg.

RIFLES: BOLT ACTION

SHR 970 – .25-06 Rem., .270 Win., .280 Rem., .30-06, .308 Win., .300 Win. Mag., or 7mm Rem. Mag. cal., steel receiver, standard model featuring easy take-down (requires single tool) and quick change 22 or 24 (Mag. cals. only) in. barrel, detachable 3 or 4 shot mag., 65 degree short throw bolt, 3 position safety, standard medium gloss walnut stock with checkering, ultra-fast lock time, nitrided bore, no sights, includes hard carry case, approx. 7.3 lbs. Mfg. 1998-2002.

	$475	$395	$350	$325	$295	$275	$250	*$550*

Add $395 for extra barrel.

* ***SHR 970 Synthetic*** – similar to SHR 970, except has checkered black synthetic stock with stippled grip. Mfg. 1999-2002.

	$445	$375	$325	$295	$275	$250	$230	*$499*

STR 970 LONG RANGE – .308 Win. or .300 Win. Mag. cal., inlcudes stippled black McMillan composite stock with precision bedding blocks, 24 in. fluted heavy barrel with integral muzzle brake and non-reflective Ilaflon metal coating, cased, 11.6 lbs. Mfg. 2000-2002.

	$875	$795	$675	$575	$525	$475	$425	*$899*

RIFLES: SEMI-AUTO

MODEL 1908 MONDRAGON – 7.5mm cal. and others, serial number is stamped externally in four locations, unique operating mechanism, first semi-auto military contract rifle, approx. 500 rifles Mexican contract.

	$22,500	$19,000	$16,000	$12,500	$9,750	$7,500	$6,500	

PE-57 – 7.5 Swiss cal. only, semi-auto version of the Swiss military rifle, 24 in. barrel, includes 24 shot mag., leather sling, bipod and maintenance kit. Importation disc. 1988.

	$7,500	$6,000	$4,500	$4,000	$3,500	$3,000	$2,500	*$1,745*

The PE-57 was previously distributed in limited quantities by Osborne's located in Cheboygan, MI.

SIG-AMT RIFLE – .308 Win. cal., semi-auto version of SG510-4 auto paramilitary design rifle, roller delayed blowback action, 5, 10, or 20 shot mag., 18 3/4 in. barrel, wood stock, folding bipod. Mfg. 1960-1988.

	$5,500	$4,500	$3,750	$3,250	$2,750	$2,250	$1,750	*$1,795*

SG 550/551 – .223 Rem. cal. with heavier bullet, Swiss Army's semi-auto version of newest paramilitary design rifle (SIG 90), 20.8 (SG 550) or 16 in. (SG 551 Carbine) barrel, some synthetics used to save weight, 20 shot mag., diopter night sights, built-in folding bipod, 7.7 or 9 lbs.

Sig 550 (Rifle)	$8,500	$7,750	$7,000	$6,250	$5,500	$4,950	$4,500	
Sig 551 (Carbine)	$9,500	$9,000	$8,500	$8,000	$7,250	$6,500	$5,600	*$1,950*

This model had very limited domestic importation before 1989 Federal legislation banned its configuration.

GRADING - PPGS™	100%	98%	95%	90%	80%	70%	60%	LAST MSR

SIG 556 – Please refer to the Sig Sauer section.

SIG-HÄMMERLI

Previously manufactured by Hämmerli Ltd. in Lenzburg, Switzerland.

PISTOLS: SEMI-AUTO

P240 TARGET PISTOL – .32 S&W Long Wadcutter or .38 Mid-range (disc.) cal., single action, 5 shot mag., 5.9 in. barrel, blue finish, thumbrest walnut grips, adj. sights and trigger, 3 lbs. Importation mostly disc. 1986.

	100%	98%	95%	90%	80%	70%	60%	LAST MSR
	$1,475	$1,225	$1,000	$875	$775	$700	$660	*$1,350*

Add $100 for Morini adj. grips.

.38 Mid-range cal. is very desirable in this model - healthy (and inconsistent) premiums are being asked.

	100%	98%	95%	90%	80%	70%	60%	LAST MSR
* ***P240 Target Pistol .22 Conversion Unit***	$550	$495	$400	$335	$290	$245	$215	*$595*

SIG SAUER

Current firearms trademark manufactured by SIG Arms AG (Schweizerische Industrie-Gesellschaft) located in Neuhausen, Switzerland. Most models are currently manufactured in the U.S., and some models continue to be imported from Switzerland. Sig Sauer, Inc. was established in 2007, and is located in Exeter, NH. Previously imported and distributed from 1985-2006 by Sigarms, Inc. located in Exeter, NH. Previously located in Herndon, VA and Tysons Corner, VA.

In late 2000, SIG Arms AG, the firearms portion of SIG, was purchased by two Germans named Michael Lüke and Thomas Ortmeier, who have a background in textiles. Today the Lüke & Ortmeier group includes independently operational companies such as Blaser Jadgwaffen GmbH, Mauser Jagdwaffen GmbH, J.P. Sauer & Sohn GmbH, SIG-Sauer Inc., SIG-Sauer GmbH and SAN Swiss Arms AG. Please refer to individual listings.

On Oct. 1, 2007, SIG Arms changed its corporate name to Sig Sauer.

PISTOLS: SEMI-AUTO

Beginning 2001, SIG started manufacturing variations which are compliant by state. They include CA (10 shot mag. max only), MA (requires a loaded chamber indicator), and NY (must include empty shell casing) are priced slightly higher than the standard models available for the rest of the states.

The Sigarms Custom Shop, located in Exeter, NH, has recently been established, and offers a wide variety of custom shop services, including action enhancement, full servicing, DA/SA conversions, trigger and hammer modifications, barrel replacement, and many refinishing options. Please contact Sigarms Custom Shop directly for more information and current pricing on these services.

During 2005, the Sigarms Custom Shop produced 12 limited editions, including the P229 Rail (January), P245 w/nickel accents and Meprolight night sights (February), P220 .45 ACP Rail (March), P239 Satin Nickel w/Hogue rubber grips (April), GSR 1911 Reverse Two-Tone (May), P229 Satin Nickel Reverse Two-Tone (June), P232 Rainbow Titanium (July), P226 Rail (August), P220 Sport Stock (September), P239 w/extra .357 SIG cal. barrel (October), P228 Two-Tone (November), and the P226 package w/Oakley glasses (December).

Early SIG Sauer pistols can be marked either with the Herndon or Tysons Corner, VA barrel address, and can also be marked "W. Germany" or "Germany". Earlier mfg. had three proofmarks on the bottom front of the slide, with a fourth on the frame in front of the serial number. Early guns with these barrel markings will command a slight premium over prices listed below, if condition is 98%+. Current mfg. has Exeter, NH barrel address.

Add $285-$356 for caliber X-Change kit on current models.

P 210 LEGEND – 9mm Para. cal., SA only, 4 3/4 in. barrel with fixed 2-dot or adj. target sights, black nitron finish, side release mag., 8 shot mag., checkered wood grips, improved

GRADING - PPGS™	100%	98%	95%	90%	80%	70%	60%	LAST MSR

and extended beavertail, grooved grip straps, nickel plated safety, hammer, trigger, and slide release. Importation began 2011.

MSR $2,199	$2,000	$1,800	$1,600	$1,400	$1,200	$1,000	$850	

Add $200 for adj. target sights.

For pre-2011 manufacture, please refer to listings in the Sig Arms AG section.

MOSQUITO – .22 LR cal., compact design similar to P226, 3.98 in. barrel, polymer frame, 10 shot mag., SA/DA, decocker, ambidextrous manual safety, Picatinny rail on bottom of frame, internal locking device, adj. rear sight, molded composite grips, black, nickel (mfg. 2007-2008), blue (disc. 2012), two-tone, pink (new 2009), desert digital camo (mfg. 2009-2012), reverse two-tone (new 2007), carbon fiber (mfg. 2012 only), flat dark earth (FDE) frame (new 2012), multi-cam (mfg. 2012 only), OD frame (new 2012), or deep purple (new 2012) frame finish, 24.6 oz. New 2005.

MSR $398	$345	$300	$260	$220	$190	$170	$155	

Add $7 for two-tone finish. Add $14 for reverse two-tone finish.
Add $28 for hot pink frame, flat dark earth frame (new 2012), OD frame finish, or deep purple frame finish.
Add $44 for threaded barrel.
Add $15 for nickel (disc. 2008) finish. Add $79 for carbon fiber or multi-cam (mfg. 2012 only).
Add $112 for desert digital camo frame with threaded barrel, disc. 2012.
Add $142 for camo finish, threaded barrel, and tactical trainer package (disc. 2009).
Add $75 for long slide with barrel weight (black finish only, new 2007, Sporter model). Disc. 2012.

MODEL P220 – .22 LR (disc.), .38 Super (disc.), 7.65mm (disc.), 9mm Para. (disc 1991), or .45 ACP cal., 7 (.45 ACP, disc.) or 8 shot mag., full size, SAO option, regular double action or double action only (.45 ACP cal. only), 4.4 in. barrel, decocking lever, choice of matte blue (disc. 2006), black nitron (new 2007), stainless steel (mfg. 2001-2007), K-Kote (disc. 1999), electroless nickel (disc. 1991), two-tone with nickel finished slide, or Ilaflon (mfg. 2000 only) finish, lightweight alloy frame, black plastic grips, optional DAK trigger system (DAO with 6 1/2 lb. trigger pull) available during 2005 only, tactical rail became standard 2004 at no extra charge (blue or stainless only), approx. 30.4 or 41.8 (stainless steel) oz. New 1976.

MSR $993	$885	$730	$625	$525	$450	$400	$350	

Add $92 for Siglite night sights, available in either DA/SA or SA only with Ambi safety (new 2012).
Add $149 for black stainless with Hogue rubber grips and Siglite night sights (new 2012).
Add $40 for DAK trigger system (limited mfg. 2005).
Add $103 for two-tone (nickel slide) finish (disc. 2011).
Add $100 for P220 SAO Model (single action only, disc. 2009).
Add $306 for Crimson Trace laser grips w/night sights (disc. 2009).
Add $95 for stainless steel frame & slide (mfg. 2001-2007).
Add $40 for Ilaflon finish (disc. 2000).
Add $45 for factory K-Kote finish (disc. 1999).
Add $70 for electroless nickel finish (disc. 1991).
Add $285 for .22 LR conversion kit (current mfg.) or $680 for older mfg. .22 LR conversion kit.
Subtract 10% for "European" Model (bottom mag. release - includes 9mm Para. and .38 Super cals.).

Values are for .45 ACP cal. and assume American side mag. release (standard 1986).

This model was also available as a Custom Shop Limited Edition during July, 2004 (MSR was $800 and November, 2004 (MSR was $861).

* ***Model P220 Combat*** – .45 ACP cal., features flat Dark Earth finish, alloy frame, Nitron stainless slide, corrosion resistant parts, 8 shot mag., M1913 Picatinny rail, Siglite night sights, with (Combat TB) or w/o (Combat) threaded barrel. Mfg. 2007-2012.

	$1,065	$935	$825	$725	$625	$525	$425	*$1,228*

Add $61 for Combat TB Model w/threaded barrel.

GRADING - PPGS™	100%	98%	95%	90%	80%	70%	60%	LAST MSR

* ***Model P220 Elite*** – .45 ACP cal., similar to P220, except has short reset trigger, DA/SA or SAO, two-tone (limited mfg.), black Nitron finish, or stainless steel, 8 shot mag., ergonomic beavertail, Picatinny rail, front cocking serrations, custom shop wood grips, black aluminum (Dark Elite), or checkered aluminum (platinum Elite- disc. 2011) grips. New 2007.

MSR $1,228 $1,065 $935 $825 $725 $625 $525 $425

Add $140 for stainless steel.
Add $61 for Elite Dark with threaded barrel (disc.2012).
Add $72 for platinum Elite with aluminum grips (stainless only), disc. 2011.

* ***Model P220 Carry Elite*** – .45 ACP cal., similar to P220 Elite, except is compact model, stainless or black Nitron (mfg. 2009-2012) finish. New 2007.

MSR $1,368 $1,175 $1,025 $895 $750 $650 $550 $450

Subtract $140 for black nitron finish (disc. 2012).

* ***Model P220 Carry*** – .45 ACP cal., compact model w/full size frame, 3.9 in. barrel, 8 shot single stack mag., DA/SA, DAK, or SAO, black Nitron, two-tone (only available in Carry SAS mfg. 2010 only), or reverse two-tone with Hogue rubber grips (new 2012) finish, Siglite night sights, Picatinny rail, black polymer or custom shop brown (Carry SAS) wood grips. New 2007.

MSR $993 $895 $735 $625 $525 $450 $400 $350

Add $92 for Siglite night sights or SA only with Ambi safety (new 2012).
Add $132 for two-tone finish (Carry SAS only), disc. 2011.
Add $100 for SAO trigger (disc. 2008).
Add $149 for stainless reverse two-tone with Hogue rubber grips (new 2012).
Add $132 for P220 Carry SAS model (Generation II features became standard 2008).

* ***Model P220 Carry Equinox*** – similar to P220 Carry, except has two-tone accented slide with nitron finish, Truglo TFO front sight, Siglite rear sight, black wood grips w/custom shop logo. New 2007.

MSR $1,218 $1,050 $925 $825 $725 $625 $525 $425

* ***Model P220 Compact*** – .45 ACP cal., compact beavertail frame, 3.9 in. barrel, 6 shot mag., DA/SA or SAO, black Nitron or two-tone finish, Siglite night sights, black polymer or custom shop wood (Compact SAS) grips. New 2007.

MSR $1,085 $940 $815 $700 $600 $500 $400 $350

Add $75 for two-tone finish (disc. 2010).
Add $58 for Siglite night sights only (disc. 2011).
Add $57 for P220 Compact SAS model (Generation II features became standard 2009), disc. 2012.

* ***Model P220 Equinox*** – .45 ACP cal., similar to P220, except has two-tone accented slide with nitron finish, Truglo TFO front sight, Siglite rear sight, black wood grips w/custom shop logo. New 2007.

MSR $1,228 $1,065 $935 $825 $725 $625 $525 $425

* ***Model P220 Extreme*** – .45 ACP cal., black nitron finish with stainless reverse two-tone, 4 in. barrel, forward slide serrations, Siglite night sights, and Hogue G-10 grips, approx. 30 oz. New 2012.

MSR $1,213 $1,050 $935 $825 $725 $625 $525 $425

* ***Model P220 Match*** – .45 ACP cal., similar to P220, except has 5 in. cold hammer forged barrel, DA/SA or SAO, ambidextrous safety, two-tone or stainless (Match Elite) finish, adj. sights, black polymer or custom shop wood (Super Match) grips, Elite Match became standard during 2010. Mfg. 2007-2012.

$1,175 $975 $850 $725 $625 $550 $450 *$1,368*

Add $7 for Super Match model.
Subtract approx. $200 for Match (disc. 2009, last MSR was $1,170).

GRADING - PPGS™	100%	98%	95%	90%	80%	70%	60%	LAST MSR

* ***Model P220 NRALE*** – .45 ACP cal., features NRA Law Enforcement logo and the words "NRA Law Enforcement" engraved in 24Kt. gold, cocobolo grips with NRA medallions, gold trigger and appointments. Limited production of 1,000, including P226 NRALE 2002-2003.

	$850	$650	$495	N/A	N/A	N/A	N/A	*$911*

* ***Model P220 Scorpion Elite*** – .45 ACP cal., features flat dark earth (FDE) metal finish, beavertail, stainless reverse two-tone, Siglite night sights and Hogue Extreme G-10 grips. New 2012.

MSR $1,285	$1,150	$975	$850	$750	$650	$550	$450	

Add $71 for threaded barrel (disc. 2012).

* ***Model P220 Sport*** – .45 ACP cal., features 4.8 in. heavy compensated barrel, stainless steel frame and slide, 10 shot mag., target sights, improved trigger pull, single or double action, 46.1 oz. Imported 1999-2000, reintroduced 2003-2005.

	$1,375	$975	$800	$695	$585	$485	$415	*$1,600*

* ***Model P220R*** – .22 LR cal., 4.4 in. barrel, 10 shot mag., DA/SA, matte black anodized finish, adj. sights, otherwise similar to standard P220. Mfg. 2009-2012.

	$565	$500	$450	$395	$350	$300	$275	*$642*

* ***Model P220 TacPac*** – .45 ACP cal., features black nitron finish, Siglite sights, one-piece enhanced E2 grip, STL 900L, includes holster. New 2013.

MSR $1,212	$1,050	$925	$825	$725	$625	$525	$425	

MODEL P224 – 9mm Para., 357 Sig., or .40 S&W cal., 3 1/2 in. barrel, DA/SA or DAK trigger, alloy frame with stainless steel slide, 10 or 12 (9mm Para. only) shot mag., satin nickel slide and controls, Siglite night sights, wood grips, 25.4 oz. New 2012.

MSR $1,085	$950	$825	$725	$625	$525	$425	$400	

* ***Model P224 SAS Gen. 2*** – similar to P224, except has black nitron finish, dehorned metal parts, stainless reverse two-tone, Siglite night sights, and one-piece enhanced E2 grip. New 2012.

MSR $1,125	$975	$850	$750	$650	$550	$450	$400	

* ***Model P224 Extreme*** – 9mm Para. or .40 S&W cal., similar to Model P224 SAS Gen. 2, except has Hogue Extreme G-10 grips. New 2012.

MSR $1,146	$995	$850	$750	$650	$550	$450	$400	

* ***Model P224 Equinox*** – .40 S&W cal. only, two-tone polished nitron finish, Truglo front sight with Siglite rear night sight, black wood grips. New 2012.

MSR $1,218	$1,050	$900	$875	$675	$575	$475	$400	

MODEL P225 – 9mm Para. cal., regular double action or double action only, similar to P220, shorter dimensions, 3.85 in. barrel, 8 shot, thumb actuated button release mag., fully adj. sights, 28.8 oz. Disc. 1998.

	$595	$525	$450	$425	$395	$350	$310	*$725*

Add $45 for factory K-Kote finish.
Add $105 for Siglite night sights.
Add $45 for nickel finished slide (new 1992).
Add $70 for electroless nickel finish (disc. 1991).

This model was also available as a Custom Shop Limited Edition during March, 2004. MSR was $803.

MODEL P226 – .357 SIG (new 1995), 9mm Para. (disc. 1997, reintroduced 1999), or .40 S&W (new 1998) cal., full size, choice of double action or double action only (new 1992) operation, 10 (C/B 1994), 12 (new mid-2005, .357 SIG or .40 S&W cal.) or 15* (9mm Para. cal. only) shot mag., 4.4 in. barrel, alloy frame, currently available in blackened stainless steel (Nitron finish became standard 2000), two-tone (disc. 2011), reverse two-tone (.40 S&W cal. only - mfg. 2012 only), or nickel (disc. 2002) finish (stainless slide only), tactical rail became standard 2004, choice of traditional DA or DAK trigger system

GRADING - PPGS™	100%	98%	95%	90%	80%	70%	60%	LAST MSR

(DAO with 6 1/2 lb. trigger pull, not available in all stainless) available beginning 2005, E2 grips became standard 2011, high contrast sights, automatic firing pin block safety, 31.7 or 34 oz. New 1983.

MSR $993	**$885**	**$730**	**$625**	**$525**	**$450**	**$400**	**$350**	

Add $92 for Siglite night sights.
Add $285 for .22 LR cal. conversion kit.
Add $92 for .357 SIG cal. (includes night sights, black Nitron finish only).
Add $149 for reverse two-tone finish - all stainless with Siglite night sights and Hogue rubber grips (mfg. 2012 only).
Add $306 for Crimson Trace laser grips w/Siglite night sights (mfg. 2007).
Add $95 for stainless steel frame and slide (mfg. 2004-2005).
Add $103 for two-tone finish (nickel finished stainless steel slide) w/night sights, (disc. 2011).
Add $45 for K-Kote (Polymer) finish (mfg. 1992-97, 9mm Para. only).
Add $70 for electroless nickel finish (disc. 1991).

This model is also available in double action only (all finishes) at no extra charge.

This model was also available as a Custom Shop Limited Edition during Feb., 2004 (MSR was $1,085). A limited edition P226 America with blue titanium and gold finishes was also available from SIG's Custom Shop (MSR was $7,995).

This model is also available as the P226R Tactical, sold exclusively by Ellett Bros distributors - no pricing information is available.

* ***Model P226 Combat*** – 9mm Para. cal., DA/SA, 4.4 in. barrel, 10 or 15 shot mag., Siglite night sights, flat dark earth frame and grips, black Nitron slide, Picatinny rail, 34 oz. Mfg. 2008-2012.

	$1,050	**$925**	**$825**	**$725**	**$625**	**$525**	**$425**	***$1,218***

Add $71 for TB model with threaded barrel.

* ***Model P226 Elite*** – 9mm (new 2011), .357 SIG (mfg. 2011-2012), .40 S&W (new 2011), or .45 ACP (disc. 2011) cal., similar to P226, except has short reset trigger, DA/SA or SAO, two-tone (disc.), black Nitron finish (Dark Elite), or stainless steel, 8 shot mag., ergonomic beavertail, Picatinny rail, front cocking serrations, custom shop wood grips. New 2007.

MSR $1,218	**$1,050**	**$925**	**$825**	**$725**	**$625**	**$525**	**$425**	

Add $150 for stainless steel (not available in .357 SIG cal.).
Add $72 for platinum Elite with aluminum grips (disc. 2011).
Add $71 for TB Model with threaded barrel (9mm Para. only), disc. 2012.

* ***Model P226 Enhanced Elite*** – 9mm Para., .357 SIG, or .40 S&W cal., includes lower Picatinny rail in front of trigger guard, black nitron finish, beavertail, stainless reverse two-tone, E2 polymer grips and night sights. Mfg. 2011-2012.

	$1,025	**$900**	**$800**	**$700**	**$600**	**$500**	**$400**	***$1,175***

* ***Model P226 Equinox*** – .40 S&W cal., 4.4 in. barrel, two-tone Nitron stainless steel slide, lightweight black anodized alloy frame, nickel accents, 10 or 12 shot mag., Truglo tritium front sight, rear Siglite night sight, Picatinny rail, grey laminated wood grips, 34 oz., mfg. by the Custom Shop. Mfg. 2006-2012.

	$1,050	**$925**	**$825**	**$725**	**$625**	**$525**	**$425**	***$1,218***

* ***Model P226 Extreme*** – 9mm Para. or .40 S&W cal., similar to Model P226 Enhanced Elite, except has Hogue Extreme Series G10 grips. New 2011.

MSR $1,213	**$1,050**	**$925**	**$800**	**$700**	**$600**	**$550**	**$450**	

* ***Model P226 E2*** – 9mm Para. cal., 15 shot mag., black Nitron finish, ergonomic slim profile one piece grips, Siglite night sights, short reset trigger, integral accessory rail, includes three mags. New 2010 only.

	$1,000	**$895**	**$775**	**$675**	**$575**	**$525**	**$450**	***$1,149***

GRADING - PPGS™	100%	98%	95%	90%	80%	70%	60%	LAST MSR

*** *Model P226 Jubilee*** – 9mm Para. cal., limited edition commemorating SIG's 125th anniversary, features gold-plated small parts, carved select walnut grips, special slide markings, cased. Mfg. 1985 only.

	$1,495	$1,175	$950	$835	$685	$585	$485	*$2,000*

*** *Model P226 MK25*** – 9mm Para. cal., 4.4 in. barrel, black Nitron finish with phosphated small components, features anchor engraving, three 15 shot mags., Picatinny rail, UID label on right side of slide, Siglite night sight, otherwise similar to Model P226. New 2012.

MSR $1,142	$995	$825	$750	$600	$500	$450	$400	

*** *Model P226 NRALE*** – .40 S&W cal., features NRA Law Enforcement logo and the words "NRA Law Enforcement" engraved in 24Kt. gold, cocobolo grips with NRA medallions, gold trigger and appointments. Limited production of 1,000, including P220 NRALE, 2002-2003.

	$850	$650	$495	N/A	N/A	N/A	N/A	*$911*

*** *Model P226R*** – .22 LR cal., Nitron finish, adj. sights, DA/SA or SAO, 10 shot mag., with or w/o beavertail grips and stainless reverse two-tone. Mfg. 2009-2012.

	$585	$515	$465	$400	$350	$300	$275	*$656*

Add $33 for beavertail and stainless reverse two-tone.

*** *Model P226 Scorpion Elite*** – 9mm Para. cal. only, features flat dark earth (FDE) finish, beavertail, stainless reverse two-tone, Siglite night sights, and Hogue Extreme G-10 grips. Mfg. 2012 only.

	$1,150	$975	$850	$750	$650	$550	$450	*$1,285*

Add $71 for threaded barrel.

*** *Model P226 Special Editions*** – 9mm Para. or .40 S&W (Cops Commemorative only, disc. 2008) cal., engraved, variations include Navy (black Nitron finish, phosphate components and anchor engraving), Cops Commemorative (Siglite night sights and wood grips, disc. 2008). Series disc. 2011.

	$895	$775	$675	$575	$475	$400	$350	*$1,020*

*** *Model P226 Sport*** – 9mm Para. cal., features 5.6 in. match or heavy compensated barrel, stainless steel frame and slide, 10 shot mag., target sights, improved trigger pull, single or double action, rubber grips, 48.8 oz. Mfg. 2003-2005.

	$1,375	$975	$800	$695	$585	$485	$415	*$1,600*

*** *Model P226 ST*** – 9mm Para., .40 S&W, or .357 Mag. cal., 4.4 in. barrel, white stainless slide and frame, blue barrel, Picatinny rail, 10 shot mag., 38.8 oz.

While advertised during 2006, this model never went into production - prototypes only.

*** *Model P226 Super Cap Tactical*** – .40 S&W cal., similar to P226 Tactical, black Nitron finish, TruGlo front sight, Siglite rear sight, includes four 15 shot mags. Mfg. 2009-2010.

	$1,025	$925	$825	$725	$625	$525	$425	*$1,156*

*** *Model P226 TACOPS*** – 9mm Para., .357 SIG (mfg. 2012 only), or .40 S&W cal., features Truglo tradium fiber optic front sight and Siglite rear night sight, beavertail, stainless reverse two-tone, Magwell grips, black nitron finish, 34 oz. New 2011.

MSR $1,289	$1,150	$975	$850	$750	$650	$550	$450	

Add $13 for 9mm Para. cal.

*** *Model P226 TacPac*** – .45 ACP cal., features black nitron finish, Siglite sights, one-piece enhanced E2 grip, STL 900L, includes holster. New 2013.

MSR $1,212	$1,050	$925	$825	$725	$625	$525	$425	

*** *Model P226 Tactical/Blackwater Tactical*** – similar to P226, black Nitron finish, Picatinny rail, threaded barrel, post and dot contrast Siglite night sights, available in standard (disc. 2009) and Blackwater configuration (black Nitron finish, Siglite night sights, and wood grips). Mfg. 2007-2010.

	$1,150	$975	$850	$750	$650	$550	$450	*$1,300*

Subtract approx. $50 for standard tactical - (disc. 2009, last MSR was $1,245).

GRADING - PPGS™	100%	98%	95%	90%	80%	70%	60%	LAST MSR

* ***Model P226 USPSA*** – 9mm Para. cal., short reset trigger, 4.4 in. barrel, 15 shot mag., Dawson fiber optic front sight, Warren rear sight, polymer grips, aluminum frame with stainless steel slide, black Nitron finish, USPSA engraving, includes three mags. Mfg. 2009-2010.

  $1,095 $950 $825 $725 $625 $525 $400 *$1,246*

MODEL P226 X-FIVE – 9mm Para. or .40 S&W cal., SA, adj. trigger, 5 in. stainless steel barrel and slide, ambidextrous thumb safety, all stainless construction with magwell, low profile adj. sights, 14 (.40 S&W) or 19 (9mm Para.) shot mag., available in blue, two-tone, stainless or black Nitron finish, checkered walnut grips, includes 25 meter test target, checkered front grip strap, 47.2 oz. Mfg. mid-2005-2012.

$2,400 $2,050 $1,700 $1,400 $1,225 $1,000 $850 *$2,747*

* ***Model P226 X-Five Competition*** – 9mm Para. or .40 S&W cal., similar to X-Five, except has black polymer grips. Mfg. 2007-2012.

  $1,725 $1,475 $1,250 $1,050 $875 $700 $650 *$1,976*

* ***Model P226 X-Five All Around*** – 9mm Para. or .40 S&W cal., adj. sights, ergonomic beavertail grip, DA/SA, stainless slide and frame, black polymer grips. Mfg. 2007-2012.

  $1,425 $1,200 $975 $850 $750 $650 $550 *$1,696*

* ***Model P226 X-Five Tactical*** – 9mm Para. cal., black Nitron finish, contrast sights, lightweight alloy frame, Picatinny rail, single action trigger, ergonomic beavertail grips. Mfg. 2007-2012.

  $1,425 $1,200 $975 $850 $750 $650 $550 *$1,696*

MODEL P227 – .45 ACP cal., DA/SA, 4.4 in. stainless steel barrel, 10 shot mag., black nitron finish, contrast sights, lower Picatinny rail, 32 oz. New 2013.

MSR $993 $885 $730 $625 $525 $450 $400 $350

Add $92 for Siglite night sights.

* ***Model P227 Carry*** – .45 ACP cal., DA/SA, 3.9 in. stainless steel barrel, 10 shot mag., black nitron finish, Siglite night sights, lower Picatinny rail, 30 1/2 oz. New 2013.

MSR $1,085 $950 $825 $725 $600 $500 $400 $350

* ***Model P227 Carry SAS*** – .45 ACP cal., Gen. 2, 3.9 in. stainless steel barrel, black nitron finish, Dehorning, SRT, contrast or Siglite night sights, Sig anti-snag treatment on slide and frame with no rail, one piece ergonomic grips, 30 1/2 oz. New 2013.

MSR $1,125 $975 $850 $750 $625 $525 $425 $375

MODEL P228 (OLD MFG.) – 9mm Para., choice of double action or double action only (new 1992) operation, compact design, 3.86 in. (compact) barrel, 10 (C/B 1994) or 13* (reintroduced 2004) shot mag., automatic firing pin block safety, high contrast sights, alloy frame, choice of blue, Nitron (new 2004), nickel (mfg. 1991-97), or stainless steel (new 2004) slide, or K-Kote (disc. 1997) finish, 29.3 oz. Mfg. 1990-97, reintroduced 2004-2006.

$700 $600 $500 $450 $400 $350 $310 *$840*

Add $50 for Siglite night sights.
Add $376 for .22 LR cal. conversion kit.
Add $45 for K-Kote (Polymer) finish (disc. 1997).
Add $45 for nickel finished slide (1991-97).
Add $70 for electroless nickel finish (disc. 1991).

This model was also available in double action only (all finishes) at no extra charge.

This model was also available as a Custom Shop Limited Edition during April, 2004 (MSR was $800).

MODEL P228 (NEW MFG.) – 9mm Para. cal., SA/DA, Siglite night sights, includes two 15 shot mags., choice of black nitron or stainless reverse two-tone (SRT) finish. New 2013.

MSR $1,125 $995 $875 $750 $625 $525 $475 $$25

MODEL P229 – .357 SIG (new 1995), 9mm Para. (mfg. 1994-96, reintroduced 1999), or .40 S&W cal., compact size, 3.9 in. barrel, similar to Model P228, except has blackened Nitron or satin nickel (disc.) finished stainless steel slide with aluminum alloy frame, 10

GRADING - PPGS™	100%	98%	95%	90%	80%	70%	60%	LAST MSR

(C/B 1994), 12* (.357 SIG or .40 S&W cal. only), or 13 (9mm Para. cal. only, new 2005) shot mag., choice of traditional DA or DAK trigger system (DAO with 6 1/2 lb. trigger pull) available beginning 2005, E2 (enhanced ergonomics) grips became standard 2011, tactical rail became standard in 2004 (Nitron finish only), includes lockable carrying case, 31.1 or 32.4 oz. New 1991.

MSR $993 $885 $730 $625 $525 $450 $400 $350

Add $92 for .357 SIG cal. - includes Siglite night sights.

Add $92 for Siglite night sights.

Add $306 for Crimson Trace laser grips w/Siglite night sights (mfg. 2007-2008).

Add $180 for black Nitron finish with TruGlo TFO front and Siglite rear sights with four hi-cap mags. (Super Cap Tactical model, not available in .357 SIG cal.), disc. 2010.

Add $103 for two-tone finish (nickel finished stainless steel slide) with night sights (disc. 2011).

Add $285 for .22 LR cal. conversion kit.

This model was also available in double action only at no extra charge.

This model was also available as a Custom Shop Limited Edition during June, 2004 (MSR was $873), during August, 2004 (MSR was $916) and during Dec. 2004 (MSR was $844).

* ***Model P229 Elite*** – .45 ACP cal., similar to P229, except has short reset trigger, DA/SA or SAO, two-tone (disc.), dark (Elite Dark, new 2009) or black Nitron (disc. 2011) finish, 8 shot mag., ergonomic beavertail, Picatinny rail, front cocking serrations, custom shop wood or aluminum grips. Mfg. 2007-2012.

$1,050 $925 $825 $725 $625 $525 $425 *$1,218*

Add $71 for TB model with threaded barrel.

Add $72 for platinum Elite with aluminum grips (disc. 2011).

* ***Model P229 Elite Stainless*** – 9mm Para. or .40 S&W cal., SA/DA, stainless steel slide with SRT finish, 10, 12 (.40 S&W only), or 15 (9mm Para.) shot mag., ergonomic beavertail, Picatinny rail, front cocking serrations, custom shop wood grips only. New 2007.

MSR $1,368 $1,225 $1,025 $875 $775 $675 $575 $450

* ***Model P229 Enhanced Elite*** – 9mm Para.(disc. 2012), .40 S&W (disc. 2012), or .357 SIG cal., includes lower Picatinny rail in front of trigger guard, black nitron finish, beavertail, stainless reverse two-tone, E2 polymer grips and Siglite night sights. New 2011.

MSR $1,175 $1,000 $900 $800 $700 $600 $500 $400

* ***Model P229 Scorpion Elite*** – 9mm Para. or .40 S&W cal., features flat dark earth (FDE) finish, beavertail, stainless reverse two-tone, Siglite night sights, and Hogue Extreme G-10 grips. New 2012.

MSR $1,285 $1,150 $975 $850 $750 $650 $550 $450

Add $71 for threaded barrel (9mm Para. only), disc. 2012.

* ***Model P229 Equinox*** – .40 S&W cal., 4.4 in. barrel, two-tone Nitron stainless steel slide, lightweight black anodized alloy frame, nickel accents, 10 or 12 shot mag., Truglo tritium front sight, rear Siglite night sight, Picatinny rail, grey laminated wood grips, 34 oz., mfg. by the Custom Shop. Mfg. 2007-2012.

$1,050 $925 $825 $725 $625 $525 $425 *$1,218*

* ***Model P229 Extreme*** – 9mm Para. cal., features black nitron finish, stainless reverse two-tone, front slide serrations, Siglite night sights, and Hogue Extreme Series G10 grips. Mfg. 2012 only.

$1,050 $925 $800 $700 $600 $550 $450 *$1,213*

* ***Model P229 Sport*** – .357 SIG or .40 S&W (new 2003) cal., features 4.8 in. match or heavy (disc. 2000) compensated barrel, stainless steel frame and slide, target sights, improved trigger pull, single or double action, 43.6 oz. Mfg. 1998-2000, reintroduced 2003-2005.

$1,375 $975 $800 $695 $585 $485 $415 *$1,600*

GRADING - PPGS™	100%	98%	95%	90%	80%	70%	60%	LAST MSR

* ***Model P229 SAS*** – 9mm Para., .357 SIG, or .40 S&W cal., 3.86 in. barrel, 12 shot mag., DAK trigger, smooth dehorned stainless steel slide, two-tone (disc.), or black Nitron (new 2009) finish, Siglite night sights, contrast rear sight, light-weight black hard anodized frame, rounded trigger guard, checkered wood grips, designed for snag-free profile for concealed carry, Generation II features became standard 2009, 32 oz. Mfg. by Custom Shop. Mfg. 2005-2012.

	100%	98%	95%	90%	80%	70%	60%	LAST MSR
	$995	$875	$750	$625	$525	$475	$425	$1,125

Add $30 for two-tone finish (disc. 2010).

* ***Model P229 E2*** – 9mm Para. cal., 15 shot mag., black Nitron finish, ergonomic slim profile one piece grips, Siglite night sights, short reset trigger, integral accessory rail, includes three mags. Mfg. 2010 only.

	100%	98%	95%	90%	80%	70%	60%	LAST MSR
	$1,000	$895	$775	$675	$575	$525	$450	$1,149

* ***Model P229 TacPac*** – 9mm Para. or .40 S&W cal., features black nitron finish, Siglite sights, one-piece enhanced E2 grip, STL 900L, includes holster. New 2013.

	100%	98%	95%	90%	80%	70%	60%	LAST MSR
MSR $1,212	$1,050	$925	$825	$725	$625	$525	$425	

* ***Model P229 HF (Heritage Fund)*** – .40 S&W cal., 10 shot, 3.9 in. barrel, slide marked "10th Anniversary P229", frame marked "1992-2002", gold engraving and accents, brushed stainless steel, gold trigger, cocobolo Hogue grips with NSSF Heritage Fund medallion, includes wood display case. Limited mfg. late 2001-2004.

	100%	98%	95%	90%	80%	70%	60%	LAST MSR
	$1,195	$750	$600	N/A	N/A	N/A	N/A	$1,299

* ***Model P229R .22 LR*** – .22 LR cal., 4.4 in. barrel, 10 shot mag., DA/SA, matte black anodized finish, adj. sights, E2 polymer grip, otherwise similar to standard P229. Mfg. 2009-2012.

	100%	98%	95%	90%	80%	70%	60%	LAST MSR
	$585	$515	$465	$400	$350	$300	$275	$656

MODEL P230 – .22 LR (disc.).32 ACP, .380 ACP, or 9mm Ultra (disc.) cal., 7, 8, or 10 shot, 3.6 in. barrel, regular double action or double action only, blue, composite grips, 17.6 oz. Mfg. 1976-1996.

	100%	98%	95%	90%	80%	70%	60%	LAST MSR
	$425	$375	$300	$270	$240	$215	$190	$510

Add $35 for stainless slide (.380 ACP only).

* ***Model P230 SL Stainless*** – similar to Model P230, except stainless steel construction, 22.4 oz. Disc. 1996.

	100%	98%	95%	90%	80%	70%	60%	LAST MSR
	$480	$400	$375	$315	$270	$230	$200	$595

MODEL P232 – .380 ACP cal., choice of double action or double action only, 3.6 in. barrel, 7 shot mag., aluminum alloy frame, compact personal size, blue (disc.), black nitron or two-tone stainless (disc. 2012) slide, automatic firing pin block safety, composite (disc.) or Hogue rubber grips, Siglite night sights (became standard 2010), 17.6 oz. New 1997.

	100%	98%	95%	90%	80%	70%	60%	LAST MSR
MSR $720	$640	$575	$495	$410	$360	$310	$260	

Add $29 for two-tone finish (mfg. 2007-2012).
Subtract $71 if w/o Siglite night sights (became standard 2010).

* ***Model P232 Stainless*** – .380 ACP cal., similar to Model P232, except stainless steel construction, natural finish, 22.4 oz. New 1997.

	100%	98%	95%	90%	80%	70%	60%	LAST MSR
MSR $799	$725	$600	$500	$425	$350	$300	$275	

Subtract approx. $75 if w/o Siglite night sights and Hogue grips (standard beginning 2007).

MODEL P238 – 9mm Para. (mfg. 2012 only), or .380 ACP cal., lightweight aluminum frame, 2.7 in. barrel, stainless steel slide, SAO trigger, thumb safety, black Nitron or two-tone finish, fixed or Siglite night sights, fluted grips (new 2012), 15.2 oz. New 2009.

	100%	98%	95%	90%	80%	70%	60%	LAST MSR
MSR $679	$550	$475	$450	$375	$340	$300	$275	

Add $14 for two-tone finish.
Subtract $40 if w/o Siglite night sights (standard beginning 2010).

* ***Model P238 Blackwood*** – .380 ACP cal., similar to Model P238, except has two-tone finish and blackwood grips. New 2010.

	100%	98%	95%	90%	80%	70%	60%	LAST MSR
MSR $738	$650	$575	$475	$425	$385	$325	$275	

Add $28 for Ambi safety (mfg. 2012 only).

GRADING - PPGS™	100%	98%	95%	90%	80%	70%	60%	LAST MSR

* ***Model P238 Desert*** – .380 ACP cal., similar to Model P238, except has Desert tan finish, Siglite night sights, Hogue one-piece FDE rubber grip, Ambi safety (mfg. 2012 only), and X-Grip 7 shot mag. New 2012.

MSR $752	$650	$575	$475	$425	$375	$325	$275

Add $28 Ambi safety (mfg. 2012 only).

* ***Model P238 Diamond Plate*** – .380 ACP cal., similar to Model P238, except has two-tone finish or black nitron (mfg. 2012 only), "Diamond Plate" engraving, and black G10 grips. New 2011.

MSR $752	$650	$575	$475	$425	$375	$325	$275

Add $28 for Ambi safety (mfg. 2012 only).

* ***Model P238 Equinox*** – .380 ACP cal., similar to Model P238, except has two-tone nitron finish, TruGlo TFO front sight, Siglite rear sight, black wood grips, approx. 16 oz. New 2010.

MSR $752	$650	$575	$475	$425	$385	$325	$275

Add $28 for Ambi safety (mfg. 2012 only).

* ***Model P238 Extreme*** – .380 ACP cal., similar to Model P238, except has black nitron finish, Siglite night sights, Hogue Extreme G10 grips, X-Grip 7 shot mag. New 2012.

MSR $752	$650	$575	$475	$425	$385	$325	$275

* ***Model P238 Lady*** – .380 ACP cal., similar to Model P238, except built on red Cerakote alloy frame with "rose and scroll" 24K gold engraving, and rosewood grips. New 2011.

MSR $752	$650	$575	$475	$425	$375	$325	$275

* ***Model P238 Rainbow*** – .380 ACP cal., similar to Model P238, except has Rainbow titanium slide and accents, and rosewood grips. New 2010.

MSR $752	$650	$575	$475	$425	$385	$325	$275

* ***Model P238 Rosewood*** – similar to Model P238, except has rosewood grips, black nitron finish only. New 2010.

MSR $723	$650	$575	$475	$425	$385	$325	$275

Add $29 for Ambi safety (mfg. 2012 only).

* ***Model P238 Scorpion*** – .380 ACP cal., similar to Model P238, except has flat dark earth (FDE) finish, Siglite night sights, Ambi safety, and Hogue G-10 grips. New 2012.

MSR $795	$695	$600	$525	$475	$400	$350	$295

* ***Model P238 Stainless*** – .380 ACP cal., similar to P238, except has stainless steel frame and slide, Siglite night sights, G10 or rosewood (disc. 2012) grips, approx. 20 oz. New 2010.

MSR $786	$695	$600	$525	$475	$400	$350	$295

* ***Model P238 SAS*** – .380 ACP cal., features two-tone finish with Siglite night sights, Custom Shop (disc.) or Brown Goncalo checkered wood grips and logo engraved on slide, dehorned frame and slide. New 2011.

MSR $766	$665	$615	$525	$475	$425	$375	$325

Add $29 for Ambi safety (mfg. 2012 only).

* ***Model P238 Tactical Laser*** – similar to Model P238, except has two-tone finish, black checkered aluminum grips, Ambi safety (new 2012), Ambi laser module. Mfg. 2010-2012.

	$725	$625	$525	$475	$425	$375	$325	*$829*

MODEL P239 – .357 SIG, 9mm Para., or .40 S&W (new 1998) cal., compact personal size, DA or DAO, black Nitron or two-tone stainless steel slide and aluminum alloy frame, firing pin block safety, 3.6 in. barrel, 7 or 8 (9mm Para. only) shot mag., fixed sights, approx. 29 oz. New 1996.

MSR $942	$795	$675	$575	$475	$395	$350	$325

Add $143 for Siglite night sights.
Add $143 for .357 SIG cal. with night sights.
Add $305 for Crimson Trace laser grips and night sights (mfg. 2007).
Add $135 for two-tone stainless slide with night sights (disc. 2009).

This model was also available as a Custom Shop Limited Edition during May, 2004 (MSR was $673).

GRADING - PPGS™	100%	98%	95%	90%	80%	70%	60%	LAST MSR

* ***Model P239 Rainbow*** – .40 S&W cal., otherwise similar to Model P239, Rainbow titanium finish, Siglite night sights. Mfg. 2012 only.

	$925	$825	$725	$625	$525	$450	$350	*$1,000*

* ***Model P239 SAS*** – 9mm Para. (new 2008), .357 SIG (disc. 2012), or .40 S&W cal., 3.6 in. barrel, 7 or 8 shot mag., DAK trigger, smooth dehorned stainless steel slide, Siglite night sights, contrast rear sight, light-weight black hard anodized frame, black Nitron or two-tone finish, rounded trigger guard, checkered/carved wood grips, designed for snag-free profile for concealed carry, Generation II features became standard 2009, 29 1/2 oz. Mfg. by Custom Shop beginning June, 2005.

MSR $1,125	$950	$825	$700	$600	$500	$450	$395

Add $14 for two-tone finish.

* ***Model P239 Tactical*** – 9mm Para. cal., otherwise similar to Model P239, except has threaded barrel, front cocking serrations, stainless reverse two-tone, Siglite night sights. Mfg. 2010-2012.

	$925	$825	$700	$600	$500	$400	$350	*$1,058*

MODEL P245 – .45 ACP cal., compact model featuring 3.9 in. barrel, traditional double action, includes 6 and 8 shot mag., blue, two-tone (disc. 2005), Ilaflon (mfg. 2000 only), or K-Kote (disc. 1999) finish, approx. 30 oz. Mfg. 1999-2006.

	$695	$585	$495	$440	$400	$350	$310	*$840*

Add $75 for Siglite night sights.
Add $56 for two-tone or K-Kote finish (disc.).
Add $50 for Ilaflon finish (mfg. 2000 only).

MODEL P250 – 9mm Para., .357 SIG (disc. 2010), .380 ACP (new 2012), .40 S&W, or .45 ACP cal., DAO, choice of 4.7 (full size), 3.9 (Compact), or 3.1 (Subcompact) in. barrel, steel frame with black polymer grip shell (three different sizes), features modular synthetic frame with removable fire control assembly, 10 (.45 ACP), 17 (.357 SIG or .40 S&W) or 20 (9mm Para.) shot mag., ambidextrous slide release lever, black Nitron or two-tone finish, contrast or Siglite night sights, integrated Picatinny rail, converts into various calibers by changing slides, grip modules, and magazine, 27.6 oz. New mid-2008.

MSR $570	$475	$415	$365	$325	$285	$260	$230

Add $72 for Siglite night sights.
Add $15 for two-tone finish (not available in .45 ACP cal.), disc. 2010.
Add $243 for 2 SUM package, includes sub-compact caliber exchange kit (not available in .357 SIG or .45 ACP cal.).

* ***Model P250 Compact*** – similar to P250 Full Size, except has 3.9 in. barrel, 9 (.45 ACP), 13 (.357 SIG or .40 S&W) or 15 (9mm Para.) shot mag., 24.6 oz. New mid-2008.

MSR $570	$475	$415	$365	$325	$285	$260	$230

Add $72 for Siglite night sights.
Add $94 for Ambidextrous manual safety (9mm Para. cal. only), mfg. 2012 only.
Add $141 for threaded barrel and Siglite night sights (9mm Para. cal. only), mfg. 2012 only.
Add $15 for two-tone finish (disc. 2010).
Add $215 for desert digital camo finish (9mm Para. cal. only), includes Siglite night sights, medium grips, and DAO (mfg. 2009-2010).

* ***Model P250 Compact Diamond*** – similar to P250 Compact, except has black nitron or two-tone finish with "Diamond Plate" engraving, Siglite night sights. Mfg. 2012 only.

	$495	$425	$375	$325	$275	$250	$225	*$582*

Add $15 for two-tone finish (disc. 2010).
Add $215 for desert digital camo finish (9mm Para. cal. only), includes Siglite night sights, medium grips, and DAO (mfg. 2009-2010).

* ***Model P250 Subcompact*** – similar to P250 Compact, except is also available in .380 ACP cal. (new 2012), and has 3.1 in. barrel, 6 (.45 ACP), 10 (.357 SIG - disc. 2010 or .40 S&W) or 12 (9mm Para.) shot mag., 22.6 oz. New mid-2008.

MSR $570	$475	$415	$365	$325	$285	$260	$230

GRADING - PPGS™	100%	98%	95%	90%	80%	70%	60%	LAST MSR

Add $72 for Siglite night sights.
Add $72 for .380 ACP (new 2012, or .45 ACP cal. with Siglite night sights (new 2012).
Add $15 for two-tone finish (9mm Para. or .40 S&W cal.), disc. 2010.
Add $375 for desert digital camo finish (9mm Para. cal. only), includes Siglite night sights, medium grips, and DAO (mfg. 2009-2010).

MODEL P290 – 9mm Para. cal., DAO, sub-compact design utilizing light polymer frame, 2.9 in. barrel, 6 or 8 (new 2012) shot mag., Re-strike firing pin (became standard in 2012), black polymer grips are standard, Siglite night sights, options include integrated laser module and personalized grip inserts, black nitron or two-tone finish, 20 oz. New 2011.

MSR $570	$495	$450	$395	$360	$330	$295	$260	

Add $43 for two-tone finish.
Add $71 for integrated laser module (disc. 2012).
Add $24 for Diamond Plate engraving (mfg. 2012 only).

MODEL P516 – 5.56 NATO cal., short stroke pushrod gas operating system with adj. gas valve, 7 or 10 (new 2012) in. barrel with muzzle brake, Magpul MOE grip, flip up adj. iron sights, 30 shot mag., aluminum quad rail, black finish. Mfg. 2011-2012.

	$1,475	$1,275	$1,075	$925	$775	$650	$550	*$1,666*

MODEL P522 – .22 LR cal., blowback action, 10.6 in. barrel, aluminum flat-top upper receiver, choice of polymer or quad rail (P522 SWAT) forend, flash suppressor, 10 or 25 shot polymer mag., ambidextrous safety selector, sling attachments, approx. 6 1/2 lbs. Mfg. 2010 only.

	$525	$465	$415	$365	$335	$300	$275	*$572*

Add $71 for P522 SWAT model with quad rail forend.

MODEL P556 – 5.56 NATO cal., gas piston operating mechanism similar to SIG 556 carbine, 10 in. cold hammer forged barrel with A2 type flash suppressor, Picatinny top rail, pistol grip only, ribbed and vented black polymer forearm, black Nitron finish, mini red dot front sight, aluminum alloy two-stage trigger, ambidextrous safety, 30 shot mag (accepts standard AR-15 style mags.), 6.3 lbs. Mfg. 2009-2010.

	$1,825	$1,650	$1,450	$1,300	$1,200	$1,100	$1,000	*$1,876*

Add $147 for P556 SWAT model with quad rail forend.

* ***Model P556 Lightweight*** – similar to Model P556, except has lightweight polymer lower unit and forend. New 2010.

MSR $1,207	$1,075	$950	$825	$725	$625	$525	$425	

Add $133 for quad rail forend (SWAT Model).

MODEL P938 – 9mm Para. cal., SAO, 3 in. barrel, lightweight aluminum frame, stainless steel slide, thumb safety, black nitron or two-tone finish, 6 shot, Siglite night sights, Ambi safety, rosewood or blackwood grips, 16 oz. New 2012.

* ***Model P938 Aluminum*** – 9mm Para. cal., 3 in. barrel, 6 shot mag., black nitron finish, Siglite night sights, Ambi safety, black aluminum grips. New 2013.

MSR $836	$725	$575	$475	$425	$395	$350	$295	

* ***Model P938 Black Rubber*** – 9mm Para. cal., 3 in. barrel, 6 shot mag., black nitron finish, Siglite night sights, Ambi safety, black rubber grips. New 2013.

MSR $836	$725	$575	$475	$425	$395	$350	$295	

* ***Model P938 Blackwood*** – 9mm Para. cal., 3 in. barrel, 6 shot mag., black nitron finish, Siglite night sights, Ambi safety, blackwood grips. New 2012.

MSR $819	$700	$575	$475	$425	$395	$350	$295	

* ***Model P938 Equinox*** – 9mm Para. cal., 3 in. barrel, features two-tone polished nitron finish, TruGlo front and Siglite rear sights, Ambi safety, Hogue black diamondwood grips. New 2012.

MSR $833	$725	$575	$475	$425	$395	$350	$295	

GRADING - PPGS™	100%	98%	95%	90%	80%	70%	60%	LAST MSR

* ***Model P938 Extreme*** – 9mm Para. cal., features black nitron finish, Siglite night sights, Hogue Extreme G10 grips, Ambi safety, X-Grip 7 shot mag., otherwise similar to Model P938. New 2012.

MSR $833	$725	$575	$475	$425	$395	$350	$295	

* ***Model P938 Nightmare*** – 9mm Para. cal., 3 in. barrel, 6 shot mag., black nitron finish, Siglite night sights, Ambi safety, custom blackwood grips. New 2013.

MSR $836	$725	$575	$475	$425	$395	$350	$295	

* ***Model P938 Rosewood*** – 9mm Para. cal., 3 in. barrel, 6 shot mag., black nitron finish, Siglite night sights, Ambi safety, rosewood grips. New 2012.

MSR $805	$685	$550	$475	$425	$375	$325	$275	

* ***Model P938 SAS*** – 9mm Para. cal., features two-tone finish, dehorning, Siglite night sights, Brown Goncalo checkered wood grips, Ambi safety. New 2012.

MSR $848	$735	$575	$475	$425	$385	$325	$275	

MODEL 1911 FULL SIZE (GSR REVOLUTION) – .45 ACP cal., single action, 5 in. match grade barrel, choice of white (disc.), standard blue (disc.), two-tone, reverse two-tone (mfg. 2007-2010), XO Black (new 2007) or black Nitron finish, includes two 8 shot mags., with or w/o (disc. 2012) under frame Picatinny rail, firing pin safety, front and rear strap checkering, Novak (disc.) or low profile sights, checkered wood (all stainless), rosewood, aluminum, or synthetic (blued stainless) grips, approx. 41 oz. Mfg. in Exeter, NH. New 2004.

MSR $1,142	$995	$875	$750	$650	$550	$450	$375	

Subtract $43 if without M-1913 Picatinny rail (disc. 2012).
Add $100 for platinum Elite with two-tone finish, adj. combat night sights and aluminum grips (mfg. 2008-2011).
Add $120 for Blackwater model (mfg. 2009-2010).
Subtract $40 for reverse two-tone finish (disc. 2010).
The abbreviation GSR on this model stands for Granite Series Revolution.

* ***Model 1911 Desert*** – .45 ACP cal., features desert tan finish, contrast sights, Ergo XT OD Green grips, otherwise similar to the 1911. Mfg. 2012 only.

	$950	$825	$725	$625	$525	$450	$375	*$1,070*

* ***Model 1911 Extreme*** – .45 ACP cal., black nitron finish, Hogue Extreme G-10 grips, Ambi safety, low profile night sights, Magwell housing, flat trigger, otherwise similar to the 1911. Mfg. 2012 only.

	$1,075	$950	$825	$725	$625	$525	$425	*$1,213*

* ***Model 1911 Fastback*** – .45 ACP, Fastback rounded frame, black nitron finish, low profile night sights, two 8 shot mags., and rosewood grips, otherwise similar to the 1911. Mfg. 2012 only.

	$1,025	$875	$750	$625	$525	$450	$375	*$1,170*

* ***Model 1911 Max*** – .45 ACP cal., Custom Competition, features reverse two-tone finsh, fiber optic front and adj. rear sights, ICE Magwell, Wilson Mag. G-10 grips, and Max logo, otherwise similar to the 1911. Mfg. 2012 only.

	$1,500	$1,250	$1,100	$925	$800	$700	$600	*$1,713*

* ***Model 1911 Molon Labe*** – .45 ACP cal., features custom engraved nitron finish, Spartan helmet grips, and low profile sights, otherwise similar to the 1911. Mfg. 2012 only.

	$1,100	$975	$850	$750	$650	$550	$450	*$1,356*

* ***Model 1911 POW-MIA*** – .45 ACP cal., features custom engraved nitron finish, and custom Hogue POW-MIA grips, otherwise similar to the 1911. Mfg. 2012 only.

	$1,100	$975	$850	$750	$650	$550	$450	*$1,356*

Add $143 for custom engraved stainless, engraved KaBar knife, and Pelican case.

* ***Model 1911 Nightmare*** – .45 ACP cal., black nitron finish, stainless controls and black G-10 grips. New 2012.

MSR $1,242	$1,075	$975	$850	$750	$650	$550	$425	

GRADING - PPGS™	100%	98%	95%	90%	80%	70%	60%	LAST MSR

* ***Model 1911 Railed Tacpac*** – .45 ACP cal., features 1911 XO with lower Picatinny rail, includes holster with attached mag. pouch and two magazines, laser module. New 2013.

MSR $1,142	$995	$875	$750	$650	$550	$450	$375	

* ***Model 1911 Scorpion*** – .45 ACP cal., features flat dark earth (FDE) finish, low profile night sights, Ambi safety, Magwell housing, and Hogue Extreme Series G10 grips, otherwise similar to 1911. New 2011.

MSR $1,213	$1,075	$950	$825	$725	$625	$525	$425	

Add $72 for threaded barrel (mfg. 2012 only).

* ***Model 1911 Stainless*** – .45 ACP cal., features stainless finish and blackwood grips, otherwise similar to the 1911.

MSR $1,156	$995	$875	$750	$650	$550	$450	$425	

Subtract $43 if without M-1913 Picatinny rail (disc. 2012).

* ***Model 1911 STX*** – .45 ACP cal., features two-tone finish, flat top, adj. combat night sights and wood grips, Ambi safety, Magwell, otherwise similar to the 1911.

MSR $1,213	$1,075	$950	$825	$725	$625	$525	$425	

* ***Model 1911 TTT*** – .45 ACP cal., features two-tone finish, black controls, adj. combat night sights and wood grips, otherwise similar to the 1911. Disc. 2012.

	$1,025	$875	$750	$650	$550	$450	$375	*$1,170*

* ***Model 1911 Tacops*** – .45 ACP cal., features black nitron finish, integral accessory rail, Ambi thumb safety, Magwell Ergo XT grips, 4 magazines, otherwise similar to 1911. New 2011.

MSR $1,213	$1,075	$950	$825	$725	$625	$525	$425	

Add $72 for threaded barrel.

* ***Model 1911 Tacpac*** – .45 ACP cal., features 1911 XO, holster with attached mag. pouch, Mag loader, and 3 magazines, otherwise similar to the 1911. New 2012.

MSR $1,070	$950	$825	$725	$625	$525	$450	$375	

Add $72 for the Railed Tacpac Model, includes M-1913 rail, laser module, and 2 magazines.

* ***Model 1911 Target*** – .45 ACP cal., features black nitron or stainless finish, adj. target sights, and rosewood or blackwood grips. Mfg. 2011-2012.

	$975	$850	$725	$625	$525	4450	$400	*$1,113*

Add $29 for stainless finish with blackwood grips.

* ***Model 1911 XO*** – .45 ACP cal., features black nitron or stainless (disc. 2012) finish, low profile contrast sights, and Ergo XT grips, otherwise similar to the 1911.

MSR $1,028	$900	$775	$675	$575	$475	$425	$350	

Add $28 for stainless finish (disc. 2012).

MODEL 1911 TRADITIONAL FULL SIZE – .45 ACP cal., SA only, 5 in. barrel, rounded top slide, front cocking serrations, stainless frame with matte black nitron slide and small parts, 3 hole speed trigger, Hogue custom black wood grips, low profile Siglite night sights, two 8 shot mags., reverse two-tone finish, approx. 41 oz. Mfg. 2011-2012.

	$995	$850	$725	$625	$525	$450	$400	*$1,142*

* ***Model 1911 Traditional Compact*** – .45 ACP cal., SA only, compact slide with 3.9 in. barrel, rounded top slide, stainless frame, 3 hole speed trigger, Hogue custom black wood grips, low profile Siglite night sights, two 7 shot mags., stainless finish, approx. 35 oz. Mfg. 2011-2012.

	$995	$850	$725	$625	$525	$450	$400	*$1,142*

* ***Model 1911 Traditional Tacops*** – .45 ACP cal., alloy frame, features black nitron finish, M1913 rail, Ambi thumb safety, Magwell Ergo XT grips, and 4 magazines, flared magwell, lower Picatinny rail, otherwise similar to 1911 Traditional. New 2012.

MSR $1,213	$1,075	$950	$825	$725	$625	$525	$425	

GRADING - PPGS™	100%	98%	95%	90%	80%	70%	60%	LAST MSR

MODEL 1911 MATCH ELITE – 9mm Para., .40 S&W, or .45 ACP cal., round top, 5 in. barrel, double slide serrations on frame, adj. target sights, 3 hole trigger, Hogue custom wood grips, choice of stainless or two-tone (.45 ACP cal. only) finish. Mfg. 2011-2012.

	$925	$875	$750	$650	$550	$450	$400	*$1,170*

MODEL 1911 CARRY (REVOLUTION) – similar to Model 1911 GSR, except is carry configuration with short stainless slide, 4 in. barrel, stainless steel frame or black Nitron finish, Novak (disc. 2010) or low profile night sights, 8 shot mag., rosewood grips became standard with black nitron finish during 2011, black wood grips became standard on stainless finish during 2011. Mfg. 2007-2012.

	$975	4850	$725	$625	$525	$450	$375	*$1,128*

Add $14 for stainless finish with blackwood grips.

* ***Model 1911 Carry Fastback*** – .45 ACP, Fastback rounded frame, black nitron finish, low profile night sights, two 8 shot mags., and rosewood grips, otherwise similar to the 1911 Carry. Mfg. 2012 only.

	$1,025	$875	$750	$650	$550	$450	$375	*$1,170*

* ***Model 1911 Carry Nightmare*** – .45 ACP cal., black nitron finish, stainless controls and black G-10 grips. New 2012.

MSR $1,242	$1,075	$975	$850	$750	$650	$550	$425

* ***Model 1911 Carry Scorpion*** – .45 ACP cal., features Flat Dark Earth (FDE) finish, low profile night sights, Ambi safety, Magwell housing, and Hogue Extreme Series G-10 grips, otherwise similar to 1911 Carry. New 2012.

MSR $1,213	$1,075	$950	$825	$725	$625	$525	$425

Add $72 for threaded barrel (mfg. 2012 only).

* ***Model 1911 Carry Tacops*** – .45 ACP cal., features black nitron finish, M-1913 rail, Ambi thumb safety, Magwell Ergo XT grips, and 4 magazines, otherwise similar to 1911 Carry. Mfg. 2012 only.

	$1,075	$950	$825	$725	$625	$525	$425	*$1,213*

Add $72 for threaded barrel.

MODEL 1911 COMPACT (REVOLUTION) – .45 ACP cal., short slide and compact frame, 6 shot, stainless or black Nitron finish, 4 in. barrel, night sights. Mfg. 2007-2009.

	$975	$850	$725	$625	$525	$450	$400	*$1,170*

* ***Model 1911 Compact C3*** – .45 ACP cal., black hard coat anodized alloy frame, stainless slide, two-tone finish, 4 in. barrel, SAO, 7 shot, low profile contrast sights, slim profile custom wood grips, otherwise similar to 1911 Compact. New 2011.

MSR $1,042	$925	$825	$725	$625	$525	$450	$400

Add $214 for Magwell and black CTC laser grips (mfg. 2012 only) or add $243 for Magwell and wood grain CTC laser grips (mfg. 2012 only).

* ***Model 1911 Compact RCS*** – .45 ACP cal., dehorning and anti-snag treatment, black Nitron or two-tone finish, 7 shot, low profile night sights, custom wood grips, otherwise similar to 1911 Compact. Disc. 2012.

	$975	$850	$725	$625	$525	$450	$400	*$1,170*

Add $15 for two-tone finish.

Model 1911 ULTRA COMPACT – .45 ACP cal., 3.3 in. barrel, 3 hole trigger, aluminum frame, slip profile custom wood rosewood or blackwood grips, low profile night sights, two 7 shot mags., nitron or two-tone finish, 28 oz. New 2011.

MSR $1,142	$1,000	$875	$750	$650	$550	$450	$400

Add $14 for two-tone finish.

MODEL 1911-22 – .22 LR cal., SA only, black frame and slide finish, 5 in. barrel, low profile 3-dot contrast sights, 3 hole trigger, bobbed hammer, beavertail, Hogue custom rosewood grips, one 10 shot mag., black, camo (new 2013), Flat Dark Earth (new 2012), or OD Green (new 2012) finish, 34 oz. New 2011.

MSR $460	$395	$350	$315	$275	$260	$240	$200

Add $51 for Flat Dark Earth, OD Green (new 2012), or camo (new 2013) finish.

GRADING - PPGS™	100%	98%	95%	90%	80%	70%	60%	LAST MSR

MODEL SIG PRO SP2009 – 9mm Para. cal., otherwise identical to SP2340, 28 oz. Mfg. 1999-2005.

	$510	$450	$355	$290	$260	$220	$195	*$640*

Add $60 for Siglite night sights.
Add $31 for two-tone finish.

MODEL SIG PRO SP2022 – 9mm Para., .357 SIG, or .40 S&W cal., 10, 12 or 15 (9mm Para. cal. only) shot mag., 3.85 in. barrel, polymer frame, Picatinny rail, Nitron, blue, or two-tone (disc. 2005) stainless steel slide, black Nitron finish, convertible DA/SA to DAO, optional interchangeable grips, 26.8 (9mm Para.) or 30 oz. Mfg. 2004-2007.

	$495	$440	$355	$290	$260	$220	$195	*$613*

Subtract 10% if w/o Siglite night sights (became standard 2007).

MODEL SIG PRO SP2340 – .357 SIG, or .40 S&W cal., features polymer frame and one-piece Nitron finished stainless steel or two-tone (new 2001) finished slide, 3.86 in. barrel, includes two interchangeable grips, 10 shot mag., approx. 30.2 oz. Mfg. 1999-2005.

	$510	$450	$355	$290	$260	$220	$195	*$640*

Add $60 for Siglite night sights.
Add $31 for two-tone finish.

MODEL SP2022 – 9mm Para. or .40 S&W cal., SA/DA operation, 3.9 in. barrel, polymer frame with integraded lower Picatinny rail, choice of black nitron or natural stainless slide, modular fire control unit, interchangeable grip assemblies, 10 (disc.) 12, or 15 (9mm Para. cal. only) shot mag., contrast (standard) or Siglite night sights, black nitron finish, 29 oz. New 2011.

MSR $570	$495	$435	$375	$325	$300	$275	$250	

Add $72 for Siglite night sights.
Add $161 for threaded barrel (mfg. 2012 only).

* ***Model SP2022 Diamond*** – similar to Model SP2022, except has two-tone or black nitron finish with "Diamond Plate" engraving, and Siglite night sights. Mfg. 2012 only.

	$550	$475	$400	$350	$300	$250	$225	*$626*

* ***Model SP2022 TacPac*** – 9mm Para. or .40 S&W cal., 15 shot mag., features black nitron finish, Siglite sights, one-piece enhanced E2 grip, STL 900L, includes holster. New 2013.

MSR $710	$625	$550	$500	$450	$400	$365	$335	

RIFLES: BOLT ACTION

TACTICAL 2 – .223 Rem. (mfg. 2010-2012), .308 Win., .300 Win. Mag., or .338 Lapua cal., left or right hand straight pull action, 24.7 (.308 Win. cal. only), 25.6 (.300 Win. cal. only), or 27 (.338 Lapua cal. only) in. fluted barrel with muzzle brake, aluminum receiver, black hard coat anodized finish, adj. single stage trigger, 4 or 5 shot polymer box mag., ambidextrous Blaser adj. composite pistol grip stock with adj. buttplate and cheekpiece, Picatinny rail, optional Harris bipod, 12 - 12 1/2 lbs. New 2007.

MSR $4,171	$3,700	$3,300	$2,900	$2,400	$1,900	$1,750	$1,500	

Add $303 for .338 Lapua cal.
Add $141 for left-hand action accept for .223 Rem. cal.
Add $299 per individual bolt head.
Add $1,688 per interchangeable barrel.

SIG 50 – .50 BMG cal., 29 in. barrel, 5 shot detachable mag., detachable butt stock, includes bipod. Mfg. 2011-2012.

	$8,700	$7,500	$6,100	$5,000	$4,750	$3,850	$3,000	*$9,325*

SSG 3000 PRECISION TACTICAL RIFLE – .308 Win. cal., modular design, ambidextrous McMillan tactical stock with adj. comb, 23.4 in. barrel with muzzle brake, folding aluminum chassis (new 2012), 5 shot detachable mag., supplied in 3 different levels, Level I does not have bipod or scope, cased, 12 lbs. Mfg. 2000-2012.

	$2,400	$2,100	$1,700	$1,500	$1,250	$1,000	$875	*$2,799*

Add $933 for folding aluminum chassis (new 2012).
Add $1,500 for Level II (includes Leupold Vari-X III 3.5-10x40mm duplex reticle scope and

GRADING - PPGS™	100%	98%	95%	90%	80%	70%	60%	LAST MSR

Harris bipod, disc.).
Add $2,300 for Level III (includes Leupold Mark 4 M1 10x40mm Mil-Dot reticle scope and Harris bipod, disc.).
Add $1,500 for .22 LR cal. conversion kit (disc.).

* ***SSG 3000 Patrol*** – .308 Win. cal., 18 or 23 1/2 in. barrel, Patrol stock with integral aluminum bedding. New 2012.

MSR $1,499	$1,325	$1,100	$950	$825	$700	$575	$495	

RIFLES: SEMI-AUTO

State compliant rifles on some of the currently manufactured models listed within this section include CA, HA, MA, MD, NJ, and NY. Compliance features will vary from state to state, and typically, these compliant state MSR's are slightly higher than the standard models available from the rest of the states.

IMPORTANT NOTE: On model(s) where *N/A has replaced the normal 100% value, it indicates current market conditions are too unstable to accurately ascertain 100%-60% values. Factory retail prices (MSRs) reflect most recent updates. For more up-to-date information on current pricing trends and additional useful information, please visit www.bluebookofgunvalues.com, select "Information & Services" from the menu, and click on "Additional Book Information".

SIG 516 – 5.56 NATO cal., features short stroke pushrod gas operating system, 3 or 4 position system gas valve, various configurations. New 2011.

* ***SIG 516 Basic Patrol*** – 5.56 NATO cal., features polymer handguard and 2 Picatinny rails - one on top of receiver and the other in front of handguard, 16 in. free floating barrel with muzzle brake, Magpul stock and pistol grip, 30 shot mag. Mfg. 2011 only.

	*N/A	$950	$800	$700	$600	$500	$425	*$1,252*

* ***SIG 516 Patrol*** – 5.56 NATO or 7.62x39mm (new 2012) cal., features Magpul MOE adj. stock and MOE grip, rear charging handle, free floating quad Picatinny rail, 3 position gas valve, 16 in. free floating barrel with muzzle brake, 30 shot mag., ladder rail covers (new 2012), Pmag (new 2012), black, Flat Dark Earth (FDE, new 2012) or OD (new 2012) finish. New 2011.

MSR $1,666	*N/A	$1,175	$1,000	$875	$750	$625	$525	

Add $40 for Flat Dark Earth finish (new 2012).

The SIG Model 516 is also available in CQB configuration with 10 in. barrel and PDW (Personal Defense Weapon) configuration with 7 1/2 in. barrel for military/law enforcement only.

* ***SIG 516 Sport Configuration Model (SCM)*** – features fixed stock, A2 pistol grip, 10 shot mag. Mfg. 2011-2012.

	*N/A	$1,150	$1,000	$875	$750	$625	$525	*$1,599*

* ***SIG 516 Precision Marksman*** – features 18 in. free floating match barrel w/o muzzle brake, free floating quad Picatinny rail, 2 stage trigger, Magpul PRS stock, MIAD grip, 30 shot mag. New 2011.

MSR $2,399	*N/A	$1,800	$1,650	$1,425	$1,200	$1,000	$875	

SIG 522 – .22 LR cal., 16 in. barrel, blowback action, 10 or 25 shot mag., black polymer frame, folding/telescopic or non-folding Swiss style (disc.) stock, Picatinny rail, polymer or flash suppressor, approx. 6 1/2 lbs. New 2009.

Add $199 for mini red dot sight (disc. 2012).
Add $53 for non-folding stock (disc.).
Add $222 for rotary front sight (disc. 2009).
Add $210 for Harris bipod (disc. 2010).
Add $66 (Variable Power) or $106 (Prismatic Scope) with polymer handguards and telescopic stock (mfg. 2011 only).

* ***SIG 522 Classic*** – .22 LR cal., 16 in. barrel, features folding/telescopic stock, polymer handguards, rail kit, 10 or 25 shot mag.

MSR $520	$450	$415	$365	$335	$300	$275	$250	

GRADING - PPGS™	100%	98%	95%	90%	80%	70%	60%	LAST MSR

* ***SIG 522 Classic SWAT*** – .22 LR cal., features folding/telescopic stock, aluminum quad rail, 10 or 25 shot mag. Disc. 2012.

	$550	$475	$425	$375	$325	$275	$225	*$640*

* ***SIG 522 Commando*** – .22 LR cal., 16 in. barrel, polymer handguard, folding/telescopic stock, tactical training suppressor, rail kit. New 2011.

MSR $574	$495	$450	$400	$350	$300	$275	$250

* ***SIG 522 Commando SWAT*** – .22 LR cal., quad rail handguards, folding/telescopic stock, tactical training suppressor. Mfg. 2012 only.

	$625	$550	$475	$400	$350	$300	$275	*$707*

* ***SIG 522 Field*** – .22 LR cal., 20 in. barrel, folding/telescopic stock, polymer handguard, rail kit, 10 shot mag. New 2012.

MSR $534	$465	$415	$365	$335	$300	$275	$250

* ***SIG 522 Target*** – .22 LR cal., 20 in. barrel, Hogue free floating forend, folding/telescopic stock, variable power scope, 10 shot mag. New 2012.

MSR $794	$695	$600	$500	$425	$375	$325	$295

SIG 556 CLASSIC – 5.56 NATO cal., gas operated w/rotary bolt, paramilitary design, 16 in. barrel with muzzle brake, polymer forearm, alloy trigger housing, choice of SIG quad-rail (SWAT Model) or tri-rail, integrated Picatinny rails, two-stage trigger, collapsible or collapsible/folding tube stock, Magpul CTR Carbine stock type (SWAT) or M4 style stock (556ER or 556 Holo), 30 shot AR-15 type mag., 7.8-8.7 lbs. New 2007.

MSR $1,266	*N/A	$1,025	$900	$800	$700	$600	$500

Add $133 for quad-rail system (Classic SWAT Model).
Add $45 for Holo model with holographic sight (disc. 2009).
Add $150 for collapsible stock with GLR and Stoplite (disc. 2009).
Add $306 for Classic 16 with adj. folding stock and red dot sight (disc. 2009).
Add $456 for Classic 17 with adj. folding stock and rotary sight (disc. 2009).
Add $300 for 16 in. barrel with GLR and Stoplite (disc. 2009).
Subtract $200 if w/o iron sights (became standard 2008).

* ***SIG 556R*** – 7.62x39mm cal., 16 in. barrel, polymer handguards or aluminum quad rail (mfg. 2012 only), folding/telescopic (mfg. 2011 only), or Swiss style (new 2012) stock, mini red dot sight, 5 (Hunting Model, mfg. 2012 only) or 30 shot AK type mag. New 2011.

MSR $1,332	*N/A	$1,050	$900	$800	$700	$600	$500

Add $34 for Hunting Model (mfg. 2012 only).
Add $133 for aluminum quad rail (mfg. 2012 only).

* ***SIG 556 DMR*** – 5.56 NATO cal., similar to Model 556, except has 18 in. heavy barrel w/o sights, adj. Magpul PRS stock, vented synthetic forearm, Picatinny rail on bottom of forearm and top of receiver, includes tactical bipod, 12 lbs. New 2008.

MSR $1,732	*N/A	$1,350	$1,100	$975	$850	$750	$650

* ***SIG 556 Patrol*** – similar to SIG 556, 16 in. barrel, 30 shot mag., steel upper receiver, choice of polymer (Patrol) or alloy quad rail (Patrol SWAT) forend, black anodized finish, A2 flash suppressor, folding collapsible Swiss style stock, rotary diopter sight, 7 1/2 lbs. New 2010.

MSR $1,266	*N/A	$1,000	$875	$750	$650	$550	$450

Add $133 for SWAT model with quad rail forend.

* ***SIG 556 xi Patrol Swat*** – 5.56mm NATO cal., 16 in. barrel, steel receiver with M1913 rail, flip-up front and rear sights, M1913 quad rail, removable barrel, Ambi safety, Ambi mag. release, Swiss style stock. Mfg. 2012 only.

	*N/A	$1,125	$1,000	$875	$750	$625	$475	*$1,424*

GRADING - PPGS™	100%	98%	95%	90%	80%	70%	60%	LAST MSR

SIG 556/P226 MATCHED PAIR – 5.56 NATO/9mm Para. cals., includes matched set of Desert Digital Special Editions of SIG 556 ER folding stock and P226 pistol. Both rifle and pistol have unique matching serial numers, includes pelican hard carry case in Flat Dark Earth, certificate of authenticity. Limited production run of 1,500 sets. Mfg. 2012.

Retail pricing was not established on this set.

SIG 716 PATROL – 7.62 NATO cal., 16 in. barrel, 20 shot mag., MagPul ACS stock and MIAD grip, quad rail, black, Flat Dark Earth, or OD finish. New 2011.

MSR $2,132	*N/A	$1,575	$1,325	$1,100	$900	$750	$675	

Add $40 for Flat Dark Earth finish (new 2012).

SIG 551A1 – 5.56 NATO cal., 16 in. barrel, gas piston operated, rotary bolt, utilizes original Swiss 550-style 20 or 30 shot translucent mags., black polymer folding skeletonized stock and forearm that surrounds barrel, gray finish, post front sights, adj. rotary diopter drum rear sight, two-stage trigger, top accessory rail, 7 lbs. New 2012.

MSR $1,599	*N/A	$1,300	$1,100	$925	$800	$675	$550	*$1,599*

* ***SIG 716 Precision Marksman*** – 7.62 NATO cal., 18 in. barrel, 20 shot mag., Magpul UBR stock and MIAD grip, 2-stage match trigger, 11 lbs. New 2011.

MSR $2,666	*N/A	$1,900	$1,575	$1,300	$1,100	$950	$875	

SIG M400 – 5.56 NATO cal., direct impingement gas system, 16 in. barrel, A2 grip, M4 buttstock, 600 meter adj. and removable rear sight, 30 shot mag., includes hard case. New 2012.

MSR $1,054	*N/A	$950	$850	$675	$600	$550	$495	

Add $146 for M4 handguards or $240 for quad rail (new 2013).
Add $40 for lightweight steady ready platform (mfg. 2012 only).
Add $104 for Classic Model with removable carrying handle (mfg. 2012 only).

* ***SIG M400 Enhanced Carbine*** – 5.56 NATO cal., features 16 in. barrel, MOE handguards, MOE grip, MOE stock, and flip up rear sights, available in black, OD Green, or Flat Dark Earth (FDE) finish, otherwise similar to SIG M400. New 2012.

MSR $1,234	*N/A	$995	$875	$775	$675	$600	$550	

Add $26 for Flat Dark Earth finish.

* ***SIG M400 Hunting*** – 5.56 NATO cal., features 20 in. barrel, 1:8 twist, MOE handguard, MOE grip, optic ready, black or Mix Pine2 finish, otherwise similar to SIG M400. Mfg. 2012 only.

	*N/A	$875	$775	$675	$600	$550	$495	*$1,099*

Add $90 for Mix Pine2 finish.

* ***SIG M400 SWAT*** – 5.56 NATO cal., features 16 in. barrel, and quad rail, otherwise similar to SIG M400. Mfg. 2012 only.

	*N/A	$925	$800	$700	$625	$550	$495	*$1,199*

SIG SCM – 5.56 NATO cal., 16 in. barrel, 10 shot mag., steel upper receiver, polymer forend with lower accessory rail, Holo sight, aluminum lower, target crowned muzzle, A2 fixed stock, Picatinny top rail, approx. 8 lbs. Mfg. 2010-2011.

	*N/A	$950	$825	$725	$625	$525	$425	*$1,191*

SIG SCM 22 – .22 LR cal., 18 in. barrel, choice of polymer handguard, or aluminum quad rail, blow-back operating system, adj. iron sights, fixed stock, 10 shot mag. Mfg. 2011 only.

	*N/A	$450	$395	$350	$300	$275	$250	*$587*

Add $103 for aluminum quad rail.

SHOTGUNS: O/U

The following Aurora shotguns were mfg. by Battista Rizzini, located in Marcheno, Italy.

L.L. BEAN NEW ENGLANDER SERIES – 12, 20, 28 ga., or .410 bore. Imported 2001-2004.

	$1,895	$1,575	$1,325	$1,100	$950	$800	$675	

AURORA TR20 FIELD (APOLLO) – 12, 20, 28 ga., or .410 bore, 3 in. chambers except for 28 ga., 26 or 28 in. VR barrels with choke tubes, satin finished low profile boxlock receiver,

GRADING - PPGS™	100%	98%	95%	90%	80%	70%	60%	LAST MSR

monobloc construction, removable hinge pins, gold SST, ejectors, deluxe checkered round pistol grip walnut stock and forearm, 6-7 lbs. Mfg. 2000-2005.

$1,995 $1,750 $1,475 $1,265 $1,050 $925 $800 *$2,250*

* ***Aurora TR20U Field (Apollo)*** – similar to Apollo/Aurora TR20 Field, except has straight English stock (Upland Model) and color case hardened receiver. Mfg. 2000-2005.

$1,995 $1,750 $1,475 $1,265 $1,050 $925 $800 *$2,250*

AURORA TR30 FIELD (APOLLO) – similar to Apollo/Aurora TR20 Field, except has color case hardened receiver with sideplates. Mfg. 2000-2005.

$2,275 $1,900 $1,675 $1,375 $1,150 $975 $850 *$2,650*

AURORA TR40 GOLD/SILVER (APOLLO) – similar to Apollo/Aurora TR30 Field, except receiver and sideplates are engraved and have multiple gold bird inlays, choice of color case hardened (Gold Series) or silver receiver (Silver Series) finish, deluxe checkered walnut stock and forearm. Mfg. 2000-2005.

$2,575 $2,125 $1,850 $1,575 $1,350 $1,100 $950 *$3,050*

* ***Aurora TR40U Gold/Silver (Apollo)*** – similar to Apollo/Aurora TR40 Gold/Silver, except has straight English grip stock and silver finished receiver only. Imported 2000 only.

$2,250 $1,950 $1,725 $1,500 $1,300 $1,000 $825 *$2,595*

AURORA TT25 COMPETITION (APOLLO) – 12 or 20 ga., 3 in. chambers, features include polished 5 in. forcing cones and American stock dimensions with palm swell and Schnabel forearm, oil finished checkered walnut stock and forearm, matte finished 28, 30, or 32 (12 ga. only) in. VR barrels, 6 3/4 or 7 1/4 lbs. Mfg. 2000-2005.

$2,475 $2,000 $1,750 $1,500 $1,300 $1,075 $950 *$2,950*

AURORA TT45 COMPETITION – 12 or 20 ga., 28, 30, or 32 (12 ga. only) in. VR barrels. Imported 2001-2005.

$2,745 $2,250 $1,925 $1,700 $1,500 $1,300 $1,100 *$3,350*

SA 3 – 12 or 20 (new 1998) ga., 3 in. chambers, scalloped coin finished monobloc boxlock action with game scene engraving, field or Sporting Clays (new 1998) configuration, 26, 28, or 30 (Sporting Clays only) in. separated barrels with VR and choke tubes, ejectors, SST, checkered walnut stock and forearm, approx. 7 lbs. Mfg. 1997-98 only.

$1,175 $925 $775 $650 $550 $475 $400 *$1,335*

SA 5 – 12 or 20 ga., 3 in. chambers, features coin finished boxlock action with hand engraved detachable side plates, ejectors, SST, select checkered walnut stock and forearm, field or Sporting Clays (new 1998) configuration, 26 1/2, 28, or 30 (Sporting Clays only) in. barrels with VR and choke tubes, supplied with lockable case, 6 or 7 lbs. Mfg. 1997-99.

$2,175 $1,775 $1,450 $1,225 $1,075 $900 $775 *$2,670*

Add $130 for Sporting Clays Model (12 ga. only, 28 or 30 in. barrels).

SILE DISTRIBUTORS

Previous distributor, importer, and previous manufacturer located in New York, NY.

In addition to distributing a wide variety of firearms and related accessories (including the mfg. of stocks and grips), Sile Distributors also had some firearms "private labeled" to their specifications.

SILMA SPORTING GUNS

Current manufacturer established during 1949 and located in Brescia, Italy. No current U.S. importation.

Previously distributed and imported beginning 2000 on a limited basis by Legacy Sports, International, LLC, located in Alexandria, VA (Model 70 EJ variations only). All Silma shotguns, double rifles, and combination models are high quality and utilize premium materials in their manufacture.

Please contact the factory directly (see Trademark Index) for current domestic model availability and pricing.

GRADING - PPGS™	100%	98%	95%	90%	80%	70%	60%	LAST MSR

RIFLES

Currently, Silma offers one O/U double rifle, the Model 70 Express N in 7x65R, 8x57JRS, and 9.3x74R cal. Please contact the company directly for U.S. availability and pricing (see Trademark Index).

SHOTGUNS

In addition to the models listed, Silma also manufactures the Model 80 O/U Series in Trap, Skeet, and Sporting Clays configurations. Competition models, including Cobra M1, M2, or M3 are also available for trap, skeet, or sporting clays events. Two side-by-side models, the AS/70 N and the AS/70 EJ, and the M70 Combination rifle/shotgun are also available. Please contact the company directly for current pricing and U.S. availability (see Trademark Index).

MODEL 70 SERIES O/U – 12 or 20 ga., various configurations, including M70 N, M70 EJ, M70 Ergal, M70 Cartelle, M70 Canardier, M70 Becassier, and the M70 Slug. N refers to extractors, EJ refers to ejectors.

Please contact the company directly for U.S availability and current pricing on these models.

SILVER EAGLE

Current trademark of shotguns manufactured by Huglu in Turkey and imported by TR Imports, located in Keller, TX. Please refer to TR Imports listing for information.

SILVER SEITZ

Current trademark of high grade shotguns manufactured by AIM, Inc., located in Parkton, MD. Consumer direct sales.

SHOTGUNS: CUSTOM, TRAP

SILVER SEITZ – stainless steel receiver, choice of 33, 34, or 35 in. adj. rib barrels, top of the line, made to order, custom trap shotgun per customer's specifications, large number of options available, including choke tubes, quality of wood, and custom fit.

Base price for this model starts at $12,400 for adj. comb model and goes up accordingly depending on options. Please contact the company directly for a list of available options (see Trademark Index).

SIMILLION, GENE

Current custom rifle maker located in Gunnison, CO. Consumer direct sales.

RIFLES: BOLT ACTION, CUSTOM

CLASSIC HUNTER RIFLE – various cals., new Winchester Model 70 Classic action, options include LOP, caliber, and barrel length, deluxe walnut, custom made to individual customer specifications. Disc. 2004.

$6,950 $5,750 $5,150 $4,500 $3,750 $3,000 $2,500 *$7,500*

Add $1,000 for Mag. cals. up to .375 H&H.
Add $1,500 for heavy Mag. cals. .375 H&H. and larger.

EXTREME HUNTER RIFLE – various cals., customer supplied Winchester Model 70 Classic action, match grade barrel, McMillan fiberglass stock, 8 1/2-10 lbs. New 2003.

MSR $7,800 $7,350 $6,450 $5,400 $4,500 $3,650 $3,150 $2,625

Add $800 for Mag. cals through .338.
Add $1,100 for heavy Mags. cals. .375 H&H and greater.

PREMIER MODEL 70 RIFLE – various cals., mostly Winchester new Model 70 action (others available), custom made to individual customer specifications, finest materials and workmanship, individually tested.

MSR $14,000 $13,500 $11,500 $9,250 $8,250 $7,250 $6,250 $5,250

Add $1,000 for Mag. cals. up to .375 H&H.
Add $1,700 for heavy Mag. cals. .375 H&H and larger.

PREMIER MODEL 98 RIFLE – various cals., Granite Mountain Arms Model 98 short or long action, custom made to individual customer specifications, exhibition grade walnut, ebony forend tip, swivel bases, solid steel grip cap, wide variety of custom options. New 2005.

MSR $14,800 $13,750 $9,950 $8,700 $7,600 $6,500 $5,500 $4,950

GRADING - PPGS™	100%	98%	95%	90%	80%	70%	60%	LAST MSR

Add $300 for standard length action, or $2,000 for long Magnum action.
Add $4,900 for scope sighted rifle with long Mag. action.

SIMSEK

Previous shotgun manufacturer located in Turkey.

Simsek manufactured shotguns in O/U, SxS, and semi-auto configurations. They had very limited importation into the U.S.

SIMSON

Previous firearms and airgun manufacturer established in 1856 and located in Suhl, Germany.

Simson & Co. began building guns and gun barrels circa 1856, and continued its enterprise until 1936, when Hitler's dictatorship forced the Simson family to flee the country. The factory continued to build firearms, bicycles, and cars until 1945, when the Soviets took over and the factory was integrated into a Russian state motorcycle company. In 1952, the USSR returned the control of the factory to the GDR. Production of sporting arms, prams, and bicycles slowly resumed, with the main focus on motorcycle manufacture. The company struggled during the 1980s to modernize the production and the facility, but the company finally ceased operations in late 2002, and bankruptcy was declared in Feb., 2003. Collectibility for Simson firearms is mostly for pre-1936 mfg.

Simson made a wide variety of rifles and shotguns, including some private labels. A comprehensive listing of everything Simson made would be nearly impossible, as most of its guns were not imported in the U.S. on a regular basis, and much of the company's history was destroyed after the Russians occupied Suhl after WWII. A general rule for evaluating Simson firearms is to determine the overall desirability of the configuration which takes into consideration the following - action type (boxlock or sidelock), caliber/gauge, ejectors or extractors, plain or engraved frame, special features, cocking indicators, overall eye appeal, and of course, original condition. Each Simson's unique mix of these factors determines the value, and as a result, each gun must be appraised individually. A good pricing guideline is to compare a Simson with other major European trademarks such as Krieghoff and Merkel, determine the value on those, and use them as a comparison.

SIRKIS INDUSTRIES, LTD.

Previous manufacturer located in Ramat-Gan, Israel. Previously imported and distributed by Armscorp of America, Inc. located in Baltimore, MD.

PISTOLS: SEMI-AUTO

S.D. 9 – 9mm Para. cal., double action mechanism, frame is constructed mostly of heavy gauge sheet metal stampings, 3.07 in. barrel, parkerized finish, loaded chamber indicator, 7 shot mag., plastic grips, 24 1/2 oz. Imported under the Sirkis and Sardius trademarks between 1986-90.

100%	98%	95%	90%	80%	70%	60%	LAST MSR
$375	$295	$250	$200	$190	$180	$170	*$350*

RIFLES

MODEL 35 MATCH RIFLE – .22 LR cal. only, single shot bolt action, 26 in. full floating barrel, select walnut, match trigger, micrometer sights. Disc. 1985.

100%	98%	95%	90%	80%	70%	60%	LAST MSR
$650	$625	$595	$550	$510	$460	$420	*$690*

MODEL 36 SNIPER RIFLE – .308 Win. cal. only, gas operated action, carbon fiber stock, 22 in. barrel, flash suppressor, free range sights. Disc. 1985.

100%	98%	95%	90%	80%	70%	60%	LAST MSR
$670	$580	$520	$475	$430	$390	$350	*$760*

SJOGREN

Previous trademark of semi-auto shotguns invented by Carl Axel Theodor Sjögren in Sweden, and manufactured in Copenhagen, Denmark circa early 1900s.

GRADING - PPGS™	100%	98%	95%	90%	80%	70%	60%	LAST MSR

SHOTGUNS: SEMI-AUTO

SJORGEN – 12 ga., unusual inertia operating system features fixed barrel and fully locked breech block, marked "AUTOMAT SYSTEM SJÖGREN PATENT" on three lines on frame above trigger guard. Approx. 5,000 mfg. 1907-1909.

	N/A	$1,450	$1,250	$975	$800	$675	$525	

SKORPION

Current semi-auto or select-fire pistol model manufactured in the Czech Republic. Currently imported by Czechpoint, Inc. located in Knoxville, TN beginning 2010. Previously imported by CZ USA 2009-2010.

PISTOLS: SEMI-AUTO

SA VZ. 61 SKORPION – .32 ACP cal., semi-auto copy of VZ 61 Skorpion submachine gun, SA, forward charging knob, steel frame, 4.52 in. barrel, 20 shot mag., hardwood grips, flip up rear sight, lanyard rings, 41 oz.

MSR $520	$475	$425	$375	$325	$275	$250	$225	

Above values represent base model with blue or nickel finish.

SMITH-CORONA

Previous WWII subcontractor of 1903 Springfield rifles located in Syracuse, NY.

Please refer to the Springfield Armory listing for more information.

SMITH, L.C.

Previously, L.C. Smith shotguns were manufactured 1878-1888 by W.H. Baker & Co and L.C. Smith Maker located in Syracuse, NY, 1890-1946 by Hunter Arms Company, 1946-1950 by L.C. Smith Gun Co. in Fulton, NY, and 1968-1971 by Marlin Firearms Company, in North Haven, CT. L.C. Smith trademarked shotguns were also manufactured in Italy and imported by Marlin Firearms Company, located in North Haven, CT between 2004-2009.

The L.C. Smith sidelock shotgun with its famous rotary locking bolt is considered an "American Best" and is recognized as one of America's most prestigious and collectible shotguns. Recently released records indicate that L.C. Smith sold more medium to high grade models than Parker Bros., and collector interest has been very high. The *Blue Book of Gun Values* strongly recommends an expert appraisal when contemplating a purchase of a higher grade L.C. Smith, particularly in 90%+ original condition. L.C. Smith shotguns with a second set of barrels and forend serial numbered to the gun (1 and 2) with matching serial numbers and forends are valued at 60% more if they were made at the factory when the shotgun was built. A second set of barrels will add 40% to the value if the shotgun was sent back to the factory to be fitted with the second set. Guns that are mechanically factory original, but have been expertly restored (barrels, receivers, and wood) are of less interest to collectors. Therefore, these expertly restored guns should be valued at 80% of the highest value listed for a particular grade in this section, assuming the restored gun exhibits little, if any wear. Values of upgraded shotguns are dependent upon grade and craftsmanship and are not included in these suggested values.

The L.C. Smith Collectors Association offers a variety of services as well as a quarterly collector's journal. Readers may reach the organization through the website: www.lcsmith.org. The L.C. Smith Collectors Association has records and can provide research letters for the following L.C. Smith and Hunter Arms Co. shotguns: Hunter Arms Company factory records 1890-1918, production and shipping records 1918-1946 (including Ranger, Fulton and Hunter shotguns), L.C. Smith Gun Co. records 1946-1950 ("FWS" prefix), and Marlin records 1968-1971 (Field Grade and Deluxe Model). The price guide in this book is based on the remaining percentage of original case color finish. However, due to the sheer age of most of these guns, the original finish, especially case colors, have faded over time. Therefore, most Smith collectors generally make the following adjustments when converting to NRA Modern Standards.

100%	98%	95%	90%	80%	70%	60%	50%	40%	30%	20%	10%

CONVERTING PPGS TO NRA CONDITION STANDARDS
EXC = 95% barrel rust blue and wood finish/condition plus 66% case color coverage.
VG = 90% barrel rust blue and wood finish/condition plus 50% case color coverage.
Good = 80% barrel rust blue and wood finish/condition plus 33% case color coverage.
Fair = 40% barrel rust blue and wood finish/condition plus 0% case color coverage.
Original bold vivid case colors will command a substantial premium on most models.

SHOTGUN-RIFLES: BAKER 3-BARREL, HAMMER-DAMASCUS, SYRACUSE MFG. 1878-1888

The ser. no. range is 1-1,600, and estimated total shotguns produced is 1,186.

QUALITY NO. 1												
	N/A	N/A	N/A	N/A	$4,000	$3,500	$3,000	$2,500	$2,000	$1,500	$1,200	$1,000
QUALITY NO. 2												
	N/A	N/A	N/A	N/A	$5,000	$4,500	$4,000	$3,500	$3,000	$2,500	$2,000	$1,500
QUALITY NO. 3												
	N/A	N/A	N/A	N/A	$6,000	$5,500	$5,000	$4,500	$4,000	$3,500	$3,000	$2,500
QUALITY NO. 4												
	N/A	N/A	N/A	N/A	$6,500	$6,000	$5,500	$5,000	$4,500	$4,000	$3,500	$3,000
QUALITY NO. 5												
	N/A	N/A	N/A	N/A	$7,000	$6,500	$6,000	$5,500	$5,000	$4,500	$4,000	$3,500

SHOTGUNS: SXS, BAKER HAMMER-DAMASCUS, SYRACUSE MFG. 1878-1884

The ser. no. range is 50-10,000, and estimated total shotguns produced is 8,305.

QUALITY A												
	N/A	N/A	N/A	N/A	$625	$550	$475	$400	$350	$300	$250	$200
QUALITY B												
	N/A	N/A	N/A	N/A	$800	$700	$600	$500	$425	$375	$325	$250
QUALITY C												
	N/A	N/A	N/A	N/A	$1,000	$800	$700	$600	$500	$425	$375	$300
QUALITY D												
	N/A	N/A	N/A	N/A	$1,200	$1,000	$800	$700	$600	$500	$425	$375
QUALITY E												
	N/A	N/A	N/A	N/A	$1,500	$1,200	$1,000	$800	$700	$600	$500	$425
QUALITY F												
	N/A	N/A	N/A	N/A	$2,100	$1,600	$1,300	$1,000	$800	$700	$600	$500

QUALITY AA

Extreme rarity precludes accurate pricing on this model.

SHOTGUNS: SxS, L.C. SMITH SIDELOCK, HAMMER-DAMASCUS & FLUID STEEL, MFG. 1884-1932

L.C. Smith hammer guns have become very popular with collectors and shooters and this popularity has coincided with the availability of commercially manufactured black powder loads. The vast majority of these shotguns had twist steel or damascus barrels. Collectors' interest in damascus barrels has increased in recent years. The values shown are based on damascus-barreled shotguns in 90% original condition, without pitting, reboring or polishing out. Royal fluid steel was available 1901-1932. All damascus barreled guns should be examined by an expert gunsmith before being shot.

Serial number ranges for bar action Syracuse guns: 10,000-72,900 and Fulton guns: 26,000, 50,000-59,000

Serial number range for back action (1899-1932) Fulton guns: 73,000-180,925.

Quality	100%	98%	95%	90%	80%	70%	60%	50%	40%	30%	20%	10%
QUALITY F – three different Quality/Grade F shotgun barrel steels were used, (damascus, English stub twist, and Royal fluid steel).	N/A	N/A	N/A	$1,850	$1,550	$1,375	$1,100	$900	$700	$550	$400	$300
QUALITY E	N/A	N/A	N/A	$2,400	$2,000	$1,700	$1,450	$1,150	$975	$800	$650	$525
QUALITY D	N/A	N/A	N/A	$3,000	$2,500	$1,850	$1,500	$1,000	$795	$625	$475	$350
QUALITY C	N/A	N/A	N/A	$3,800	$3,300	$2,500	$1,850	$1,100	$850	$675	$525	$375
QUALITY B	N/A	N/A	N/A	$5,000	$4,000	$2,750	$2,100	$1,250	$1,050	$800	$650	$450
QUALITY A – approx. 104 mfg.	N/A	N/A	N/A	$10,000	$7,500	$5,500	$3,500	$2,500	$2,000	$1,500	$1,250	$1,000
QUALITY AA – approx. 50 mfg., 1888 and earlier.	N/A	N/A	N/A	$18,000	$14,000	$11,000	$9,000	$7,000	$5,000	$3,000	$2,500	$2,000

SHOTGUNS: SxS, L.C. SMITH SIDELOCK, HAMMERLESS-DAMASCUS, MFG. 1886-1895

The L.C. Smith "Syracuse style" hammerless guns in both 10 and 12 gauge have become extremely popular with serious collectors. All of the shotguns manufactured in Syracuse had damascus barrels. The values shown are based on damascus barrels in 90% original condition, without pitting, reboring or polishing out. The Syracuse style guns are all over 100 years old and should be graded pursuant to NRA Antique Conditions.

Serial number range for Syracuse guns: 16,000-16,999, 18,000-20,999, 22,000-23,500. Serial number range for Fulton guns: 30,000-40,334 and 500-1,683 (ejector).

Add $500 for HunterOne-Trigger on all grades valued at $1,500+.

Add $500 for automatic ejectors on all grades valued at $1,500+, or 33% for values less than $1,500.

Add $500 for a factory second set of barrels on all grades valued at $1,500+.

Add $500 for a gold dog on the trigger guard or $1,000 for gold dogs on the lockplates.

Quality	100%	98%	95%	90%	80%	70%	60%	50%	40%	30%	20%	10%
QUALITY 2	N/A	N/A	N/A	$3,000	$2,200	$1,850	$1,500	$1,150	$900	$750	$600	$450
QUALITY 3	N/A	N/A	N/A	$4,000	$2,700	$2,100	$1,800	$1,300	$1,100	$825	$650	$475
QUALITY 4 – approx. 330 mfg.	N/A	N/A	N/A	$5,000	$3,500	$2,600	$2,050	$1,400	$1,100	$850	$675	$500
QUALITY 5 – approx. 138 mfg.	N/A	N/A	N/A	$6,500	$5,000	$4,000	$3,000	$2,500	$2,000	$1,150	$900	$700
QUALITY 6 – approx. 47 mfg., disc. 1892.	N/A	N/A	N/A	$16,500	$13,000	$10,000	$8,000	$6,500	$5,500	$4,500	$3,500	$2,000
QUALITY 7 – approx. 35 mfg.	N/A	N/A	N/A	$22,000	$17,000	$13,000	$10,000	$8,500	$7,500	$6,500	$5,500	$3,500

SHOTGUNS: SxS, L.C. SMITH/HUNTER ARMS, SIDELOCK, HAMMERLESS, FLUID STEEL BARRELS, MFG. 1892-1913

Pre-1913 guns - individual grades were designated as Quality from 1892 to 1895 and as Grade from 1896 to 1913. All values listed are for hammerless 10 and 12 ga. guns with fluid steel barrels (except the A-1 Grade). Guns were manufactured in the following gauges on regular weight frames in 8 ga. and 10 ga., and regular and light frames in 12, 16, and 20 ga. Guns with damascus barrels are of almost equal value if the damascus barrels are in 90% original condition, without pitting, reboring or polished out. L.C. Smith shotguns are rare and were all made to exacting standards. Collector interest can be high, and guns in 90%+ original condition are very hard to evaluate and the values shown are meant as a guide only. It is important to note that 16 ga. guns are almost as rare as 20 ga., and that collector interest and values for these gauges are approaching parity.

Add 75% for 20 ga. on all grades.
Add 50% for 16 ga. on all grades.
Add 1,000% for 8 ga. on all grades (approx. 41 mfg.)
Add $500 for auto ejectors on all grades with values of $1,500+, or 33% for values less than $1,500.
Add $500 for Hunter One-Trigger on all grades with values of $1,500+, or 33% for values less than $1,500.

100%	98%	95%	90%	80%	70%	60%	50%	40%	30%	20%	10%
NO. 00 - approx. 58,000 mfg.											
N/A	N/A	N/A	$1,600	$1,200	$1,000	$800	$650	$600	$550	$500	$450
NO. 0 - approx. 30,000 mfg.											
N/A	N/A	N/A	$1,750	$1,300	$1,100	$900	$800	$700	$600	$550	$500
NO. 1 - approx. 10,000 mfg.											
N/A	N/A	N/A	$2,150	$1,700	$1,450	$1,200	$1,000	$800	$700	$600	$550
NO. 2 - approx. 13,000 mfg.											
N/A	N/A	N/A	$2,750	$2,200	$1,700	$1,400	$1,300	$1,200	$1,100	$1,000	$900
NO. 3 - approx. 4,000 mfg.											
N/A	N/A	N/A	$3,850	$3,150	$2,700	$2,300	$1,950	$1,750	$1,550	$1,450	$1,350
PIGEON GUN - approx. 1,395 mfg.											
N/A	N/A	N/A	$6,500	$4,300	$3,700	$3,200	$2,750	$2,200	$1,950	$1,750	$1,650
NO. 4 - 496 mfg.											
N/A	N/A	N/A	$7,500	$6,300	$5,600	$5,000	$4,400	$3,800	$3,200	$2,800	$2,400
A-1 - Syracuse style frames, damascus barrels only, approx. 740 mfg.											
N/A	N/A	N/A	$6,500	$5,200	$4,500	$3,800	$3,200	$2,800	$2,600	$2,400	$2,200
NO. 5 - 523 mfg.											
N/A	N/A	N/A	$8,500	$7,300	$6,600	$6,000	$5,400	$4,800	$4,200	$3,800	$3,400
MONOGRAM - 152 mfg.											
N/A	N/A	N/A	$14,000	$10,500	$8,800	$7,700	$6,600	$6,000	$5,500	$4,800	$4,400
A-2 - approx. 210 mfg.											
N/A	N/A	N/A	$20,000	$16,500	$14,500	$13,000	$12,500	$11,500	$10,000	$9,000	$8,000
A-3 - approx. 17 mfg.											
N/A	N/A	N/A	$50,000	$37,500	$30,000	$25,000	$22,500	$20,000	$18,000	$17,000	$15,000

SHOTGUNS: SxS, L.C. SMITH/HUNTER ARMS, SIDELOCK, HAMMERLESS, FLUID STEEL BARRELS, MFG. 1913-1950

Post 1913 guns - Values shown are for hammerless 12 ga. guns with fluid steel barrels. Guns were manufactured in 12, 16, 20 ga. and .410 bore on either regular or featherweight frames. Shotguns with damascus barrels are of almost equal value if the damascus barrels are in 90%+ original condition, without pitting, reboring or polished out. L.C. Smith shotguns are rare and were all made to exacting standards. Collector interest can be high, and guns in 90%+ original condition are very hard to evaluate and the values shown are meant as a guide only.

Add 33% for 20 ga. with 32-inch barrels.
Add 25% for 10 ga. Field and Ideal Grades; 40% for Trap and Specialty Grades; and 75% for Eagle, Crown, and Monogram Grades.
Add 65% for 20 ga. on all grades.
Add 50% for 16 ga. on all grades.
Add 500% for .410 bore on Field Grades.
Add 750% for .410 bore on Ideal and higher grades.
Add 25% for Long Range and Wild Fowl models.
Add $500 for automatic ejectors on all grades with values of $1,500+, or 33% for values less than $1,500.

100%	98%	95%	90%	80%	70%	60%	50%	40%	30%	20%	10%

Add $500 for selective or nonselective Hunter One-Trigger on all grades with values of $1,500+, or 33% for values less than $1,500.

Add $500 for ventilated rib. on all grades with values of $1,500+, or 33% for values less than $1,500.

FIELD - approx. 195,000 mfg.

N/A	N/A	$2,000	$1,500	$1,200	$1,000	$800	$650	$600	$550	$500	$450

IDEAL - approx. 26,000 mfg.

N/A	N/A	$3,300	$2,700	$2,000	$1,700	$1,400	$1,100	$900	$800	$700	$600

SKEET SPECIAL - 666 mfg. (includes automatic ejectors, Hunter One-Trigger, and beavertail forend).

N/A	N/A	$4,400	$3,800	$3,300	$3,000	$2,700	$2,400	$2,100	$1,900	$1,700	$1,600

OLYMPIC - 26 mfg.

N/A	N/A	$16,000	$14,000	$12,000	$11,000	$10,000	$9,000	$8,000	$7,000	$6,000	$5,000

PREMIER SKEET - 515 mfg., (includes automatic ejectors, Hunter One-Trigger, and beavertail forend).

N/A	N/A	$5,500	$4,000	$3,000	$2,500	$2,250	$2,000	$1,800	$1,700	$1,600	$1,500

TRAP - approx. 3,209 mfg.

N/A	N/A	4,000	$3,400	$2,500	$2,000	$1,500	$1,300	$1,100	$900	$750	$600

SPECIALTY - approx. 6,675 mfg.

N/A	N/A	$4,500	$3,750	$2,950	$2,700	$2,450	$2,250	$2,000	$1,800	$1,650	$1,500

EAGLE - 539 mfg.

N/A	N/A	$8,500	$7,200	$6,000	$4,900	$4,400	$3,900	$3,400	$3,000	$2,600	$2,200

CROWN - 846 mfg.

N/A	N/A	$12,000	$10,000	$8,000	$6,000	$5,000	$4,500	$4,000	$3,600	$3,300	$3,200

MONOGRAM - approx. 154 mfg.

N/A	N/A	$17,000	$14,000	$11,000	$9,000	$7,700	$6,600	$6,000	$5,400	$4,800	$4,400

PREMIER - 28 mfg.

N/A	N/A	$50,000	$42,500	$33,000	$25,000	$22,500	$20,000	$18,000	$16,500	$15,000	$14,000

DELUXE - 30 mfg.

N/A	N/A	$100,000	$80,000	$60,000	$50,000	$40,000	$30,000	$27,500	$25,000	$22,500	$20,000

SHOTGUNS: SINGLE BARREL TRAP, BOXLOCK, HAMMERLESS, MFG. 1917-1950

The L.C. Smith Single Barrel Trap (SBT) is considered one of America's best made guns, and awards for both the guns and shooters are legendary, including Olympic medals and world titles. Collector interest can be high, and an expert appraisal is recommended on guns in 80%+ condition. Single barrel trap models were made in 12 ga. only, with 30, 32, or 34 in. ventilated rib barrel, boxlock, auto ejector, checkered pistol grip stock, recoil pad, and beavertail forend. A total of 2,219 were mfg. between 1917-1951. In addition to the grades listed, SBTs were made in the following grades and quantities: Trap (1), Ideal (5), Field (1), and Whippet (12), and extreme rarity excludes accurate pricing on these grades.

OLYMPIC - 596 mfg.

N/A	$3,400	$2,700	$2,200	$1,800	$1,400	$1,200	$1,000	$900	$800	$700	$600

SPECIALITY - 1,409 mfg.

N/A	$5,000	$4,000	$3,000	$2,400	$1,900	$1,500	$1,250	$1,000	$900	$800	$700

EAGLE - 90 mfg.

N/A	$7,000	$5,800	$4,800	$3,900	$3,100	$2,400	$1,900	$1,600	$1,400	$1,300	$1,200

CROWN - 86 mfg.

N/A	$9,600	$8,000	$6,800	$5,700	$4,700	$3,900	$3,200	$2,700	$2,300	$2,100	$2,000

MONOGRAM - 15 mfg.

N/A	$16,500	$12,600	$10,900	$9,400	$8,000	$6,900	$5,900	$5,000	$4,300	$3,700	$3,200

100%	98%	95%	90%	80%	70%	60%	50%	40%	30%	20%	10%

PREMIER – 2 mfg.

Extreme rarity precludes accurate pricing on this model.

DELUXE – 3 mfg.

Extreme rarity precludes accurate pricing on this model.

SHOTGUNS: SxS, HUNTER ARMS, FULTON BOXLOCK, HAMMERLESS, FLUID STEEL, MFG. 1915-1945

These models have been unduly maligned over the years, being referred to as cheap boxlocks, and are not to be confused with actual L.C. Smith sidelock shotguns. In reality, these models are high quality, less expensive boxlocks built with quality similar to Field Grade L.C. Smiths. The receiver, forend iron, trigger guard and triggers were all machined (not stamped) from forgings. These models have excellent durability and collector interest is increasing.

Manufactured in 12, 16, 20 ga. and .410 bore with 26, 28, 30, or 32 in. barrels.

Add 75% for 20 ga.
Add 50% for 16 ga.
Add 500% for .410 bore.
Add $300 for non-selective Hunter One-Trigger.

FULTON – plain checkered stock with half pistol grip.

100%	98%	95%	90%	80%	70%	60%	50%	40%	30%	20%	10%
N/A	N/A	$900	$700	$575	$500	$400	$350	$325	$300	$275	$250

FULTON SPECIAL – checkered stock with full pistol grip, engraved (roll stamped) frame.

100%	98%	95%	90%	80%	70%	60%	50%	40%	30%	20%	10%
N/A	N/A	$1,000	$800	$675	$600	$500	$450	$400	$375	$350	$325

HUNTER SPECIAL – similar to Fulton Special, except has L.C. Smith rotary locking bolt system.

100%	98%	95%	90%	80%	70%	60%	50%	40%	30%	20%	10%
N/A	N/A	$1,050	$900	$800	$725	$650	$575	$525	$475	$450	$425

RANGER – 8,237 mfg. (similar to Fulton, made for Sears Roebuck).

100%	98%	95%	90%	80%	70%	60%	50%	40%	30%	20%	10%
N/A	N/A	$700	$600	$550	$475	$375	$300	$275	$250	$200	$200

GLADIATOR FIELD – 166 mfg. (similar to Fulton, made for Sears Roebuck).

100%	98%	95%	90%	80%	70%	60%	50%	40%	30%	20%	10%
N/A	N/A	N/A	$600	$550	$475	$375	$300	$275	$250	$200	$200

GLADIATOR TOURNAMENT – 61 mfg. (similar to Fulton, made for Sears Roebuck).

100%	98%	95%	90%	80%	70%	60%	50%	40%	30%	20%	10%
N/A	N/A	N/A	$625	$575	$500	$400	$325	$300	$275	$225	$200

GLADIATOR DIAMOND – 53 mfg. (similar to Fulton, made for Sears Roebuck).

100%	98%	95%	90%	80%	70%	60%	50%	40%	30%	20%	10%
N/A	N/A	N/A	$650	$600	$525	$425	$350	$325	$300	$250	$225

SHOTGUNS: SxS, L.C. SMITH/MARLIN, SIDELOCK, HAMMERLESS, FLUID STEEL, MFG. 1968-1971

The Marlin Firearms Company reintroduced the L.C. Smith trademark in 1968. These models are considered real L.C. Smiths, not copies, and collector interest is increasing. The following Marlin-manufactured shotguns with an "FWM" prefix.

FIELD – 12 ga., 28 in. barrels, aluminum ventilated rib, F/M chokes, extractors, double triggers, checkered pistol grip stock. 2,351 mfg.

100%	98%	95%	90%	80%	70%	60%	50%	40%	30%	20%	10%
N/A	$1,800	$1,500	$1,200	$1,000	$900	$850	$800	$750	$700	$675	$650

DELUXE – 12 ga., 28 in. barrels, Simmons floating ventilated rib, F/M chokes, extractors, double triggers, select walnut pistol grip stock, beavertail forearm. 188 mfg.

100%	98%	95%	90%	80%	70%	60%	50%	40%	30%	20%	10%
N/A	$2,300	$1,900	$1,400	$1,300	$1,150	$1,075	$1,025	$975	$875	$825	$775

SHOTGUNS: O/U, L.C. SMITH/MARLIN, MFG. 2005-2009

MODEL LC12 – 12 ga., 28 in. vent. rib barrels with choke tubes, SST, ejectors, fleur-de-lis checkered walnut pistol grip stock with fluted comb, recoil pad, bead front sight, approx. 7 1/4 lbs. Mfg. for Marlin in Italy and Spain 2005-2009.

GRADING - PPGS™	100%	98%	95%	90%	80%	70%	60%	LAST MSR
	$850	$750	$675	$575	$650	$350	$250	$1,385

GRADING - PPGS™	100%	98%	95%	90%	80%	70%	60%	LAST MSR

MODEL LC20 – 20 ga., 26 in. vent. rib barrels with choke tubes, otherwise similar to LC12, approx. 6 3/4 lbs. Mfg. for Marlin in Italy and Spain 2005-2009.

	$1,000	$875	$775	$675	$575	$500	$450	*$1,385*

SHOTGUNS: SxS, L.C. SMITH/MARLIN, MFG. 2005-2009

MODEL LC12-DB – 12 ga., boxlock action patterned after the first generation L.C. Smith action, 28 in. vent. rib barrels with choke tubes, single trigger, ejectors, detachable sideplates, semi-beavertail forearm, fleur-de-lis checkered walnut pistol grip stock with fluted comb, recoil pad, bead front sight, approx. 7 1/2 lbs. Mfg. for Marlin in Italy and Spain 2005-2009.

	$1,400	$1,275	$1,150	$1,000	$900	$700	$550	*$2,167*

MODEL LC20-DB – 20 ga., 26 in. vent. rib barrels with choke tubes, otherwise similar to Model LC12-DB, approx. 6 1/2 lbs. Mfg. for Marlin in Italy and Spain 2005-2009.

	$1,600	$1,475	$1,350	$1,200	$1,075	$900	$750	*$2,167*

MODEL LC28-DB/LC410-DB – 28 ga. or .410 bore, 26 in. vent. rib barrels with three choke tubes, scaled down version of the Model LC20-DB, gold game scenes on sides and bottom of receiver, approx. 6 1/4 - 6 1/2 lbs. Mfg. for Marlin in Italy and Spain 2007-2009.

	$1,900	$1,700	$1,650	$1,400	$1,300	$1,200	$1,100	*$1,639*

SMITH & WESSON

Current manufacturer located in Springfield, MA, 1857 to date. Partnership with H. Smith & D.B. Wesson 1856-1874. Family owned by Wesson 1874-1965. S&W became a subsidiary of Bangor-Punta from 1965-1983. Between 1983-1987, Smith & Wesson was owned by the Lear Siegler Co. On May 22, 1987, Smith & Wesson was sold to Tomkins, an English holding company. During 2001, Tomkins sold Smith & Wesson to Saf-T-Hammer, an Arizona-based safety and security company. Smith & Wesson was the primary distributor for most Walther firearms and accessories in the United States from 2002-2012. During 2012, Carl Walther GmbH Sportwaffen and Umarex announced the formation of Walther Arms, Inc. to import, sell, and market all Walther products in the U.S. beginning Jan. 1, 2013, except the P22 and PK380 models.

Smith&Wesson

Smith & Wessons have been classified under the following category names - PISTOLS: LEVER ACTION, ANTIQUE, TIP-UPS, TOP-BREAKS, SINGLE SHOTS, EARLY HAND EJECTORS (Named Models), NUMBERED MODEL REVOLVERS (Modern Hand Ejectors), SEMI-AUTOS, RIFLES, and SHOTGUNS.

Each category is fairly self-explanatory. Among the early revolvers, Tip-ups have barrels that tip up so the cylinder can be removed for loading or unloading, whereas Top-breaks have barrels & cylinders that tip down with automatic ejection.

Hand Ejectors are the modern type revolvers with swing out cylinders. In 1958, S&W began a system of numbering all models they made. Accordingly, the Hand Ejectors have been divided into two sections - the Early Hand Ejectors include the named models introduced prior to 1958. The Numbered Model Revolvers are the models introduced or continued after that date, and are easily identified by the model number stamped on the side of the frame, visible when the cylinder is open. The author wishes to express his thanks to Mr. Sal Raimondi, Jim Supica, Rick Nahas, and Roy Jinks, the S&W Historian, for their updates and valuable contributions.

Factory special orders, such as ivory or pearl grips, special finishes, engraving, and other production rarities will add premiums to the values listed. After 1893, all ivory and pearl grips had the metal S&W logo medallions inserted on top.

FACTORY LETTER OF AUTHENTICITY - S&W charges $50 for a formal letter of authenticity. A form is available for downloading on their website: www.smith-wesson.com for this service. Turnaround time is usually 8-12 weeks.

For more information and current pricing on both new and used Smith & Wesson airguns, please refer to the *Blue Book of Airguns* by Dr. Robert Beeman & John Allen (also online).

	Above Average	Average	Below Average

PISTOLS: LEVER ACTION, ANTIQUE

Pistols were produced in Norwich CT in 1853-1855 using the 1854 patent of Horace Smith and Daniel B. Wesson. The pistol fired a projectile that was chambered in the pistol using a newly designed lever action mechanism. The pistol was loaded by inserting the ammunition into a integral tube located below the barrel when the follower was moved forward and rotated, exposing the loading tube. The barrel assembly contained a steel spring and follower that aided in the loading of the ammunition into the receiver. This design was later perfected in the Henry rifle. The pistol was produced in two different models.

NO. 1 (SMALL FRAME) – .31 cal., 4 in. half-round barrel, steel frame, moderate rose and scroll engraving, varnished walnut (bag style shape standard), or ivory grips, blue frame with brown barrel assembly, approx. 1,200-1,300 mfg.

Above Average	Average	Below Average
$35,000-$40,000	$15,000-$20,000	$7,500-$10,000

Add 20% for ivory grips.

Barrels are marked: "SMITH WESSON, NORWICH, CT, CAST STEEL" and "FEB. 14, 1854 PATENT" marked on the barrel flats. Stamping variations are common as to placement, depth, off-center to barrel flats, and even slight double stamps have been observed. "CAST STEEL" is even observed upside down on some guns. Serial numbered from 1-100 initially and then 1-100 again for each letter prefix A-F on the frame and inside the grips for a total of 700 guns. The last 500-600 guns were assembled by the New Haven Arms company using letter prefixes G,H,I. Specimens usually exhibit pitting and or lack of finish.

NO. 2 (LARGE FRAME) – .41 cal., 6 or 8 in. half-round barrel, steel frame, moderate rose and scroll engraving, flared type flat bottom design varnished walnut grips, blue frame with brown barrel assembly, approx. 500 mfg.

Above Average	Average	Below Average
$40,000-$45,000	$20,000-$25,000	$10,500-$12,500

Add 30% for 6 in. barrel.

Barrels are marked: "SMITH WESSON, NORWICH, CT, CAST STEEL" and "FEB. 14, 1854 PATENT" marked on the barrel flats. Stamping variations are common as to placement, depth, off-center to barrel flats, and even slight double stamps have been observed. Serial numbered from 1-500 (est.) on the inside of the grips and on small parts such as the rear sight. Specimens usually exhibit pitting and or lack of finish.

TIP-UPS

Spur-trigger rimfires, these include the earliest S&W revolvers, made 1857-1881. A latch at the bottom front of the frame allows the hinged barrel to be tipped up and the cylinder removed for loading and unloading. These pistols are listed in order of model number (1, 1 1/2, 2).

MODEL NO. 1 FIRST ISSUE TIP-UP – .22 Short cal., single action, 7 shot non-fluted cylinder, 3 3/16 in. octagon barrel, bottom break, spur trigger, silver-plated brass frame, blue barrel and cylinder, square rosewood grips, circular sideplate, cross-section of frame is oval with rounded frame sides. Approx. 11,500 mfg. 1857-60.

* ***Model No. 1 First Issue Tip-Up First Type*** – serial range approx. 1-213.

Extreme rarity factor of this model precludes accurate pricing - a nice condition model can easily exceed $10,000.

* ***Model No. 1 First Issue Tip-Up Second Type*** – serial range approx. 214-1130.

Extreme rarity factor of this model precludes accurate pricing - a nice condition model can easily exceed $10,000.

* ***Model No. 1 First Issue Tip-Up Third Type*** – has spring loaded barrel catch, serial range approx. 1131-3000.

100%	98%	95%	90%	80%	70%	60%	50%	40%	30%	20%	10%
N/A	N/A	$8,000	$7,000	$5,500	$5,000	$4,500	$3,000	$2,500	$2,000	$1,500	$1,000

* ***Model No. 1 First Issue Tip-Up Fourth Type*** – diameter of recoil plates is reduced, serial range approx. 3000-4200.

100%	98%	95%	90%	80%	70%	60%	50%	40%	30%	20%	10%
N/A	$3,500	$3,000	$2,000	$1,800	$1,650	$1,600	$1,500	$1,350	$1,200	$1,000	$900

100%	98%	95%	90%	80%	70%	60%	50%	40%	30%	20%	10%

* ***Model No. 1 First Issue Tip-Up Fifth Type*** – rifling changed from three left hand to five right hand, serial range approx. 4200-5500.

N/A	$3,500	$3,000	$2,000	$1,800	$1,650	$1,600	$1,500	$1,350	$1,200	$1,000	$900

* ***Model No. 1 First Issue Tip-Up Sixth Type*** – eliminate rotating plate, serial range approx. 5,500-11,500.

N/A	$2,000	$1,900	$1,800	$1,600	$1,500	$1,400	$1,300	$1,100	$900	$800	$750

MODEL NO. 1 SECOND ISSUE TIP-UP – similar to First Issue, except flat-sided frame and irregular-shaped sideplate. 114,900 mfg. 1860-1868. Serial range approx. 11,500 - approx. 126,000.

$1,500	$1,000	$700	$650	$600	$575	$550	$500	$450	$400	$350	$300

An early sideplate variation with 2 patent dates on cylinder occurred in the serial range 11,500-12,100. The second sideplate variation with 2 patent dates occurred in the serial range 12,100-20,000.

* ***Model No. 1 Second Issue Tip-Up Second Quality***

Extreme rarity precludes accurate pricing on this model. May bring double or triple values over the Model No. 1 Second Issue Tip-Up. Beware of fakes!

MODEL NO. 1 THIRD ISSUE TIP-UP – similar to Second Issue, except fluted cylinder, round barrel, and birdshead grip. This model has its own serial range no. 1-131,163. Mfg. 1868-1882.

* ***Model No. 1 Third Issue Tip-Up 3 3/16 in. Barrel Model.*** – will have markings on top of barrel.

$1,500	$1,000	$600	$500	$425	$375	$350	$300	$250	$225	$200	$175

* ***Model No. 1 Third Issue Tip-Up Short Barrels 2 11/16 - 2 3/4 in.*** – will have markings on side of barrel.

$900	$850	$775	$720	$680	$640	$600	$560	$520	$480	$440	$400

MODEL NO. 1 1/2 OLD MODEL (MODEL 1 1/2 FIRST ISSUE) – .32 rimfire, single action, 3 1/2 or 4 (rare) in. octagon barrel, 5 shot non-fluted cylinder, bottom break, spur trigger, blue or nickel, rosewood grips, square butt. 26,300 mfg. 1865-68. Serial range 1-approx. 26,300.

$1,200	$800	$600	$500	$425	$350	$275	$250	$225	$210	$195	$185

Early production had 2 patent dates with the barrel markings (approx. serial range 1-15,500). Later production had 3 patent dates (approx. serial range 15,501-26,300).

* ***Model No. 1 1/2 Old Model 4 in. Barrel***

Extreme rarity precludes accurate pricing on this model

May bring double or triple values over the Model No. 1 1/2 Old Model. Watch for fakes (i.e. stretched barrels).

* ***Model 1 1/2 Old Model Transitional*** – octagon barrel with birdshead grips, serial range 27,200-28,800, rare.

$3,000	$2,500	$1,800	$1,500	$1,350	$1,275	$1,200	$1,125	$1,075	$1,000	$950	$900

MODEL NO. 1 1/2 NEW MODEL (MODEL 1 1/2 SECOND ISSUE) – similar to First Issue, with birdshead grips and round barrel, fluted cylinder. 100,800 mfg. 1868-75. Serial range 26,301-127,100.

* ***Model No. 1 1/2 New Model Short Barrel Model*** – barrel markings on side, length varies from 2 1/2-2 3/4 in. (scarce).

Extreme rarity precludes accurate pricing on this model. May bring double or triple values over the Model No. 1 1/2 New Model. Beware of fakes!

* ***Model No. 1 1/2 New Model 3 1/2 in. Barrel Model***

$900	$750	$500	$400	$350	$300	$225	$200	$180	$165	$150	$135

MODEL NO. 2 ARMY TIP-UP – .32 rimfire long, similar in appearance to No. 1 1/2 First Issue, except 6 shot cylinder, different barrel lengths, used as a sidearm during Civil War. 77,155 mfg. 1861-74. Serial number range 1-77,155.

100%	98%	95%	90%	80%	70%	60%	50%	40%	30%	20%	10%

* ***Model No. 2 Army Tip-Up 5 or 6 in. Standard Model***

$3,000	$2,500	$1,500	$1,000	$900	$800	$700	$625	$525	$450	$400	$375

Premiums exist for early 2 pin models under ser. no. 3,000. Large premiums will be asked for 4 in. barrel - beware of fakes!

TOP-BREAKS

These revolvers have a latch just in front of the hammer, which locks the barrel to the frame. When the action is opened, the barrel & cylinder tip down, with an automatic extractor ejecting the shells. Mfg. 1870-1940, they include single action (spur-trigger or trigger guard), double action, and safety hammerless designs. They are listed in order of frame size. Model 1 1/2 is the smallest or .32 cal. pocket sized frame; Model 2 is the medium or .38 cal. belt sized frame; Model 3 is the large holster or .44 cal. frame. Within each frame size, they are listed by action type - SA, DA, or Hammerless, as applicable.

Changes from one Top-Break model type to another are not necessarily definitive at a specific serial number. Therefore, an overlap of serial numbers from one model to another may be observed.

.32 SINGLE ACTION (MODEL 1 1/2 CENTERFIRE) – .32 S&W cal., spur trigger, top break, rebounding hammer, auto extraction, 3, 3 1/2, 6 (rare), 8 (rare) or 10 (rare) in. barrel, w/o external strain screw. 97,599 mfg. 1878-1892. Serial range 1-97,599.

* ***.32 Single Action Later Model*** – with external strain screw, remainder of serial range.

$750	$500	$400	$350	$300	$275	$250	$225	$210	$200	$190	$150

Add 10%-15% for early models under ser. no. 6,000 w/o strain screw.

Add 50%-100% for factory original 6, 8, or 10 in. barrel, depending on the original condition factor.

.32 DOUBLE ACTION FIRST MODEL – .32 S&W cal., 5 shot fluted cylinder, 3 in. round barrel, square edged side plate, blue or nickel finish, black rubber grips, one of the rarest of all S&Ws. Only 30 mfg. 1880. Serial range 1-30.

Extreme rarity precludes accurate pricing on this model.

.32 DOUBLE ACTION SECOND MODEL – similar to First Model, except irregular shaped sideplate, 3, 3 1/4, 4, 5, or 6 in. barrel, 22,142 mfg. 1880-82. Serial range 31-22,172.

$475	$425	$380	$340	$300	$260	$220	$180	$150	$120	$100	$90

.32 DOUBLE ACTION THIRD MODEL – similar to Second Model, except without groove around cylinder. 22,232 mfg. 1882-83. Serial range 22,173-43,405.

$475	$425	$380	$340	$300	$260	$220	$180	$150	$120	$100	$90

.32 DOUBLE ACTION FOURTH MODEL – similar to Third Model, except rounded trigger guard, pinned front sight. 239,600 mfg. 1883-1909. Serial range 43,406-approx. 282,999. Approx. 239,600 mfg.

$345	$305	$270	$240	$210	$185	$160	$135	$115	$100	$90	$85

An 8 or 10 in. barrel on this model will command a premium.

.32 DOUBLE ACTION FIFTH MODEL – similar to Fourth Model, except integral front sight. 44,641 mfg. 1909-19. Serial range approx. 282,300-327,641.

$375	$335	$300	$270	$240	$215	$190	$165	$135	$120	$105	$90

.32 SAFETY HAMMERLESS FIRST MODEL (LEMON SQUEEZER) – .32 S&W cal., double action only, 5 shot fluted cylinder, 2, 3 (most common), 3 1/4, 3 1/2, or 6 (rare) in. round barrel, blue or nickel, black rubber grips. This model was officially called the New Departure. 91,417 mfg. 1888-1902. Serial range 1-91,417.

Short 2 in. barrel versions known as "Bicycle model" will bring 25% to 50% premium on all Safety Hammerless models. Six inch barrels will bring a premium as well.

* ***.32 Safety Hammerless First Model Standard*** – 2, 3, 3 1/4, or 3 1/2 in. barrel.

$500	$475	$450	$425	$400	$375	$350	$325	$275	$235	$185	$150

100%	98%	95%	90%	80%	70%	60%	50%	40%	30%	20%	10%

.32 SAFETY HAMMERLESS SECOND MODEL – 2, 3, 3 1/4, 3 1/2, or 6 in. barrel, similar to First Model with pinned front sight and T-shaped latch. 78,500 mfg. 1902-09. Serial range 91,418-170,000.

$450	$425	$400	$375	$350	$325	$300	$275	$235	$200	$165	$130

.32 SAFETY HAMMERLESS THIRD MODEL – 2, 3, 3 1/4, 3 1/2, or 6 in. barrel, usually has forged front sight. 73,000 mfg. 1909-37. Serial range 163,082-242,981 (with some overlap from the Second Model).

$450	$425	$400	$375	$350	$325	$300	$275	$235	$200	$165	$130

.38 SINGLE ACTION FIRST MODEL (BABY RUSSIAN) WITH SPUR TRIGGER – .38 S&W cal., 5 shot fluted cylinder, 3 1/4, 4, 5, or 6 in. barrel, blue with wood grips, nickel with "S&W" monogram hard black or red rubber grips. 25,548 mfg. 1876-77. Serial range 1-25,548.

* ***.38 Single Action First Model Standard***

$1,750	$700	$600	$500	$400	$350	$325	$300	$275	$250	$225	$200

Substantial premiums will be asked for "Aldritch" safety models (first 50-100 guns). Add a slight premium for ser. nos. under 1,500 with filler screws on right side of frame.

.38 SINGLE ACTION SECOND MODEL – similar to above, except very short ejector housing under barrel, cal. and cylinder same as above, 3 1/4, 4, 5, 6, 8, or 10 in. barrel, grips same as above. 108,225 mfg. 1877-1891. Serial range 1-108,255.

* ***.38 Single Action Second Model Standard***

$700	$500	$375	$285	$250	$225	$210	$200	$190	$185	$180	$150

* ***.38 Single Action Second Model 8 or 10 in. Barrel***

Extreme rarity precludes accurate pricing on this model.

.38 SINGLE ACTION THIRD MODEL (MODEL OF 1891) – similar to above, except has trigger guard, cal. and cylinder same as above, 3 1/4, 4, 5, or 6 in. barrel (also accepts the single shot barrel), blue or nickel finish with "S&W" monogram, hard black rubber grips. 26,850 mfg. 1891-1911. Serial range 1-28,107 which also includes the serial number range of the Single Action First Model in .22 LR, .32 S&W, or .38 S&W cal. and the .38 S.A. Mexican Model described below. Barrel marked "Model of 1891".

$2,600	$2,300	$1,800	$1,525	$1,275	$1,075	$950	$850	$775	$700	$625	$550

Add 50%-75% for single shot barrel with matching serial number.

.38 SINGLE ACTION MEXICAN MODEL – essentially same as above, except has inserted spur trigger, .38 S&W cal., 5 shot fluted cylinder, 3 1/4, 4, 5, or 6 in. barrel, blue or nickel finish, "S&W" monogram checkered hard rubber or walnut grips. Features unique to this model are flat sided hammer, half cock notch, and "inserted" spur trigger assembly (not integral with frame). This model would also accept the single shot barrel, limited mfg. 1891-1911. Approx. 2,000 mfg. in ser. no. range 1-28107. Watch out for fakes (and conversions)!

N/A	$4,000	$3,500	$2,750	$2,000	$1,650	$1,400	$1,250	$1,150	$1,050	$975	$950

Add 50%-75% for single shot barrel with matching serial number.

.38 DOUBLE ACTION FIRST MODEL – .38 S&W cal., 5 shot fluted cylinder, 3 1/4 or 4 in. barrel, blue or nickel finish, "S&W" monogram checkered hard rubber grips. 4,000 mfg. 1880. Serial range 1-4,000.

$900	$850	$750	$650	$550	$475	$400	$325	$250	$200	$175	$150

.38 DOUBLE ACTION SECOND MODEL – .38 S&W cal., cylinder same as above, 3 1/4, 4, 5, or 6 in. barrel, blue or nickel finish, "S&W" monogram checkered hard rubber grips in black or red. 115,000 mfg. 1880-84. Serial range approx. 4,001-approx. 119,000.

$500	$350	$250	$225	$200	$185	$170	$165	$160	$145	$135	$125

.38 DOUBLE ACTION THIRD MODEL – .38 S&W cal., cylinder same as above, 2 (rare), 3 1/4, 4, 5, 6, 8, or 10 in. barrel, blue or nickel finish, "S&W" monogram hard rubber grips. 203,700 mfg. 1884-95. Serial range approx. 119,001-322,700.

$500	$350	$225	$200	$190	$175	$160	$155	$150	$140	$125	$115

Add 175%-300% for 2 in. barrel depending on condition.

100%	98%	95%	90%	80%	70%	60%	50%	40%	30%	20%	10%

* ***.38 Double Action Third Model 8 or 10 in. Barrel***

Extreme rarity precludes accurate pricing on this model.

.38 DOUBLE ACTION FOURTH MODEL – .38 S&W cal., cylinder same as above, 2 (rare), 3 1/4, 4, 5, or 6 in. barrel, blue or nickel finish, "S&W" monogram checkered hard rubber grips, also offered in an extended square butt target style. 216,300 mfg. 1895-1909. Serial range 322,701-539,000.

$450	$300	$230	$200	$185	$170	$155	$150	$145	$135	$120	$110

Add 175%-300% for 2 in. barrel depending on condition.

.38 DOUBLE ACTION FIFTH MODEL – .38 S&W cal., cylinder, barrel, and grip specifications same as above with the additional availability of an extended square butt target style walnut grip as an accessory. 15,000 mfg. 1909-11. Serial range approx. 539,001-554,077.

$500	$465	$425	$375	$325	$285	$250	$225	$200	$180	$150	$125

Add 175%-300% for 2 in. barrel depending on condition.

.38 DOUBLE ACTION PERFECTED MODEL – .38 S&W cal., 2 (extremely rare - watch for fakes), 3 1/4, 4, 5, or 6 in. barrel, cylinder change in frame incorporates rolled I frame revolver and lockwork, trigger guard is integral part of frame, and side plate is on right side, not left side. The last of the S&W break open revolvers. 59,400 mfg. 1909-20. Serial range 1-59,400. Identified by having both top latch and side latch.

$875	$550	$475	$425	$360	$315	$275	$250	$225	$200	$170	$150

* ***.38 Double Action Perfected Model Top Latch Only*** – as above, except no side latch thumbpiece - rare.

Add a substantial premium for trigger guard with integral frame.

Extreme rarity precludes accurate pricing on this model.

.38 SAFETY HAMMERLESS FIRST MODEL (.38 NEW DEPARTURE) – .38 S&W cal., 5 shot fluted cylinder, 3 1/4, 4, 5, or 6 in. barrel, blue or nickel finish, "S&W" monogram checkered hard rubber grips, features "Z-Bar" latch. Approx. 5,000 mfg. in 1887. Serial range 1-5,250.

$1,325	$875	$775	$600	$525	$475	$415	$360	$315	$275	$250	$175

Add 25% for blue finish.

* ***.38 Safety Hammerless First Model 6 in. Barrel***

Extreme rarity precludes accurate pricing on this model.

.38 SAFETY HAMMERLESS SECOND MODEL – .38 S&W cal., cylinder same as above, 3 1/4, 4, 5, or 6 in. barrel, finish and grips same as above. 37,350 mfg. 1887-1890. Serial range approx. 5,251-42,483.

$600	$465	$425	$375	$325	$285	$250	$225	$200	$180	$150	$125

U.S. MARTIALLY MARKED – 100 purchased by Govt. in 1890, serial range 41,333 - 41,470, serial numbers in Second Model range, but are true Third Models.

Extreme rarity precludes accurate pricing on this model. Beware of fakes!

.38 SAFETY HAMMERLESS THIRD MODEL – .38 S&W cal., cylinder same as above, 3 1/4, 4, 5, or 6 in. barrel, finish and grips same as above. 73,500 mfg. 1890-1898. Serial range 42,484-116,002.

$500	$375	$330	$300	$275	$250	$225	$200	$175	$150	$135	$110

.38 SAFETY HAMMERLESS FOURTH MODEL – .38 S&W cal., cylinder, barrel lengths, finishes and grips same as above. 104,000 mfg. 1898-1907. Serial range 116,003 to approx. 220,000.

$375	$280	$240	$205	$190	$165	$155	$145	$135	$125	$115	$100

A 2 in. barrel in this variation is rare (Bicycle Model).

.38 SAFETY HAMMERLESS FIFTH MODEL – .38 S&W cal., cylinder same as above, 2, 3 1/4, 4, 5, or 6 in. barrel, blue or nickel finish, "S&W" monogram checkered hard rubber or checkered walnut grips. 41,500 mfg. 1907-40. Serial range 220,000-261,493.

$450	$350	$240	$205	$190	$165	$155	$145	$135	$125	$115	$100

100%	98%	95%	90%	80%	70%	60%	50%	40%	30%	20%	10%

* ***.38 Safety Hammerless Fifth Model 2 in. Barrel***

Extreme rarity precludes accurate pricing on this model - will bring a premium.

MODEL 3 AMERICAN FIRST MODEL (SINGLE ACTION) – .44 S&W American or .44 rimfire Henry cal., single action, 6 shot fluted cylinder, 6, 7, or 8 in. round barrel, blue or nickel finish, walnut grips. 8,000 mfg. 1870-72. Serial range 1-approx. 8,000. Serial number overlaps on the variations below are known to exist.

Slight premiums will be asked for models with vent. hole in bottom rear barrel (approx. first 1,500). Original barrel lengths other than 8 in. are worth a premium - beware of cut barrels.

* ***Model 3 American First Model Standard*** – without hole in extractor.

N/A	$8,000	$4,500	$3,500	$3,000	$2,500	$2,150	$1,850	$1,650	$1,450	$1,250	$1,100

* ***Model 3 American First Model Transitional*** – includes locking notch on hammer, with small trigger pin, serial range 6,700-8,000.

N/A	$8,000	$4,600	$3,600	$3,100	$2,650	$2,250	$2,150	$1,850	$1,650	$1,450	$1,200

* ***Model 3 American First Model .44 Rimfire Henry*** – limited mfg. Watch for fakes!

N/A	$8,250	$7,000	$6,000	$5,000	$4,000	$3,750	$3,500	$3,250	$3,000	$2,750	$2,500

* ***Model 3 American First Model U.S. Marked*** – approx. 1,000 mfg., 800 in blue, and 200 in nickel finish, most nickel plated revolvers are serial numbered above 1,950 - watch for fakes. Serial range 125 - 2,199.

N/A	$15,000	$10,750	$9,100	$8,100	$7,250	$6,500	$5,900	$5,375	$4,850	$4,450	$4,000

* ***Model 3 American First Model Nashville Police*** – very rare, only 32 manufactured, marked "Nashville Police" on backstrap. Scarcity precludes accurate pricing - beware of fakes.

MODEL 3 AMERICAN SECOND MODEL – .44 S&W American or .44 rimfire Henry cal., single action, 6 shot fluted cylinder, mechanism allows the hammer to lock the barrel latch in place, larger trigger pin, 5 1/2, 6, 6 1/2, 7, or 8 in. barrel, blue or nickel, walnut grips. 19,635 mfg. 1872-1874, serial range approx. 8,000-32,800 which includes commercial version of Model 3 Russian First Model.

* ***Model 3 American Second Model Standard*** – .44 S&W American cal., 8 in. barrel.

N/A	$7,000	$3,750	$3,250	$2,750	$2,250	$2,150	$1,850	$1,650	$1,450	$1,250	$1,100

Add 35% for 5 1/2, 6, 6 1/2, or 7 in. barrel.
Add 50% if factory cut for stock or 100% if accompanied with original Factory shoulder stock.
Smith & Wesson Historian Verification of Factory Cut for Stock required for premium value.
Add 20% if professionally retrofitted with NON-Factory Stock if accompanied with Stock.
608 were factory cut for shoulder stock.

* ***Model 3 American Second Model Standard .44 Rimfire Henry*** – 6, 7, or 8 in. barrel, non-locking hammer below approx. serial number 25,000. 3,014 mfg.

N/A	$8,000	$4,750	$3,750	$3,525	$3,050	$2,650	$2,250	$2,150	$1,850	$1,650	$1,450

MODEL 3 FIRST MODEL RUSSIAN (OLD OLD MODEL RUSSIAN) – .44 S&W Russian, 5 1/2, 6, 7, or 8 in. barrel, Russian contract revolvers had 8 in. barrels, blue finish, and Cyrillic barrel markings, commerical mfg. had blue or nickel finish, walnut grips, looks similar to First and Second Model American. 5,165 mfg. 1871-1874 for commercial sale and 20,014 for Russian Contract (separate ser. no. range). Serial range 6,000-32,800, see Model 3 Second Model American.

* ***Model 3 First Model Russian Commercial Version*** – 4,665 mfg.

N/A	$5,000	$4,000	$3,250	$2,750	$2,250	$2,150	$1,850	$1,650	$1,450	$1,250	$1,100

* ***Model 3 First Model Russian Reject Russian Contract*** – approx. 500 mfg., can be determined by the barrel, latch, and cylinder having a full serial number, rather than assembly numbers.

N/A	$5,000	$4,000	$3,250	$2,750	$2,250	$2,150	$1,850	$1,650	$1,450	$1,250	$1,100

* ***Model 3 First Model Russian Russian Contract*** – 20,014 mfg., rare, most sent to Russia, Cyrillic marked. Serial range 1-approx. 20,014.

N/A	N/A	$6,750	$5,975	$5,125	$4,450	$3,800	$3,350	$2,950	$2,600	$2,250	$2,000

100%	98%	95%	90%	80%	70%	60%	50%	40%	30%	20%	10%

MODEL 3 SECOND MODEL RUSSIAN (OLD MODEL RUSSIAN) – 2nd and 3rd Model Russians have an extreme knuckle at the top of backstrap and trigger guard spur, 85,200 mfg. in all variations between 1873-78, 7 in. barrel, small screw in top-strap of frame, features longer ejector housing and "Russian Model" marking on top of barrel. Ser. nos. started at 32,800.

* ***Model 3 Second Model Russian Commercial Version*** – 6,200 mfg.

100%	98%	95%	90%	80%	70%	60%	50%	40%	30%	20%	10%
N/A	$3,750	$3,000	$2,375	$2,000	$1,750	$1,500	$1,300	$1,100	$995	$895	$795

* ***Model 3 Second Model Russian .44 Rimfire Henry*** – approx. 500 mfg.

100%	98%	95%	90%	80%	70%	60%	50%	40%	30%	20%	10%
N/A	$5,500	$5,000	$4,500	$4,000	$3,525	$3,050	$2,650	$2,250	$2,150	$1,850	$1,650

* ***Model 3 Second Model Russian Contract*** – approx. 70,000 mfg. for Russian Military contract, Cyrillic marked, rare in U.S.

100%	98%	95%	90%	80%	70%	60%	50%	40%	30%	20%	10%
N/A	N/A	$3,150	$2,850	$2,525	$2,275	$2,100	$1,950	$1,800	$1,650	$1,500	$1,350

* ***Model 3 Second Model Turkish Model*** – 1,000 mfg. in their own serial number range in .44 Rimfire, features rimfire hammer, but the cylinder is chambered for .44 Russian. This is probably the rarest and most valuable variation.

100%	98%	95%	90%	80%	70%	60%	50%	40%	30%	20%	10%
N/A	N/A	$5,750	$5,100	$4,650	$4,150	$3,650	$3,250	$2,900	$2,675	$2,475	$2,250

This model was converted to rimfire from .44 S&W Russian cal.

* ***Model 3 Second Model Japanese Contract*** – may be marked with an anchor.

100%	98%	95%	90%	80%	70%	60%	50%	40%	30%	20%	10%
N/A	N/A	$3,200	$2,600	$2,300	$2,050	$1,825	$1,650	$1,500	$1,375	$1,250	$1,175

MODEL 3 THIRD MODEL RUSSIAN – commonly called the "New Model Russian" and is similar to old model, except has shorter extractor housing, 6 1/2 in. barrel, front sight is forged as an integral part of barrel instead of an interchangeable part, large knurled screw in top-strap of frame, shorter ejector housing, butt is usually marked with "1874" in a square, approx. 60,600 mfg. 1874-78. Values are similar to old model for comparable variations. In addition, the Tula Arsenal in Russia also mfg. 300,000-400,000 pistols for domestic use and Ludwig & Loewe in Germany mfg. 100,000.

* ***Model 3 Third Model Russian Commercial Version*** – approx. 13,500 mfg.

100%	98%	95%	90%	80%	70%	60%	50%	40%	30%	20%	10%
N/A	$3,750	$3,000	$2,375	$2,000	$1,750	$1,500	$1,300	$1,100	$995	$895	$795

* ***Model 3 Third Model Russian .44 Rimfire Henry***

100%	98%	95%	90%	80%	70%	60%	50%	40%	30%	20%	10%
N/A	$5,000	$4,500	$4,000	$3,525	$3,050	$2,650	$2,250	$2,150	$1,850	$1,650	$1,500

* ***Model 3 Third Model Russian Contract*** – 41,138 mfg. Cyrillic markings.

100%	98%	95%	90%	80%	70%	60%	50%	40%	30%	20%	10%
N/A	$3,500	$3,200	$2,900	$2,650	$2,400	$2,200	$2,000	$1,775	$1,575	$1,325	$1,100

* ***Model 3 Third Model Russian Ludwig & Loewe, & Tula Copies*** – these copies were manufactured by private Foreign Arsenals, as contracted by the Russian Government to circumvent paying contractual obligations to Smith & Wesson. These are not Smith & Wesson manufacture; however, the quality is impeccable and in some aspects, not only meet but exceed the quality and craftsmanship of those manufactured by Smith & Wesson.

100%	98%	95%	90%	80%	70%	60%	50%	40%	30%	20%	10%
N/A	$2,800	$2,500	$2,250	$2,000	$1,800	$1,625	$1,475	$1,350	$1,225	$1,100	$950

Add 40% for Tula copies.

* ***Model 3 Third Model Turkish Contract*** – 5,000 mfg., utilizes .44 Russian cylinder - chambered for .44 Rimfire.

100%	98%	95%	90%	80%	70%	60%	50%	40%	30%	20%	10%
N/A	$4,000	$3,700	$3,425	$3,100	$2,850	$2,575	$2,325	$2,025	$1,700	$1,425	$1,200

* ***Model 3 Third Model Japanese Contract*** – 1,000 made.

100%	98%	95%	90%	80%	70%	60%	50%	40%	30%	20%	10%
N/A	$3,800	$3,150	$2,300	$2,000	$1,750	$1,500	$1,300	$1,225	$1,100	$950	$800

MODEL 3 SCHOFIELD FIRST MODEL – .45 S&W cal., single action, 7 in. barrel, 6 shot fluted cylinder, blue finish only, walnut grips, ser. no. range 1-3035. 3,035 mfg. 1875.

* ***Model 3 Schofield First U.S. Issue*** – 3,000 mfg., "U.S." marked.

100%	98%	95%	90%	80%	70%	60%	50%	40%	30%	20%	10%
N/A	$15,000	$9,000	$6,000	$4,500	$4,000	$3,600	$3,400	$3,200	$3,000	$2,600	$2,250

100%	98%	95%	90%	80%	70%	60%	50%	40%	30%	20%	10%

* ***Model 3 Schofield First Commercial Model (not U.S. marked)*** – 35 were produced without U.S. markings, very rare - beware of fakes - there could be more phony ones than real ones.

Extreme rarity factor of this model precludes accurate pricing.

* ***Model 3 Schofield First Wells Fargo and Company*** – barrel cut to approx. 5 in. with Wells Fargo markings.

N/A	N/A	N/A	N/A	$7,000	$5,100	$4,550	$4,175	$3,750	$3,350	$3,050	$2,750

Warning - Beware of fakes! There may be more fake Wells Fargo Schofields than authentic ones. While most fakes are usually poor quality, others may be quite impressive.

Many Schofields are found with cut 5 in. barrels and no Wells Fargo marking - these will bring approx. 66% of uncut values, or if they have fake WF markings, then their value is 1/2 of the uncut values.

MODEL 3 SCHOFIELD SECOND MODEL – ser. no. range 3036-8969. Mfg. 1876-1877.

* ***Model 3 Schofield Second Standard Model*** – "U.S." on butt.

N/A	$14,000	$8,000	$5,500	$4,500	$4,000	$3,600	$3,400	$3,200	$3,000	$2,600	$2,250

* ***Model 3 Schofield Second Commercial Model*** – blue or nickel finish, 650 mfg.

N/A	$9,500	$7,000	$5,000	$4,500	$4,000	$3,600	$3,400	$3,200	$3,000	$2,600	$2,250

* ***Model 3 Schofield Second Wells Fargo and Company*** – barrel cut to 5 in. with Wells Fargo markings.

N/A	N/A	N/A	N/A	$7,000	$5,100	$4,550	$4,175	$3,750	$3,350	$3,050	$2,750

Warning - Beware of fakes! There may be more fake Wells Fargo Schofields than authentic ones. While most fakes are usually poor quality, others may be quite impressive. Many Schofields are found with cut 5 in. barrels and no Wells Fargo marking - these will bring approx. 66% of uncut values, or if they have fake WF markings, then their value is 1/2 of the uncut values.

NEW MODEL NO. 3 – features very short extractor housing under the barrel, knuckle on backstrap is less pronounced than Russian Models, single action, round butt. 35,796 mfg. between 1878-1912.

Slight premiums will be asked for cut shoulder stock ($750-$1,250), target sights (standard non-target models only).

Add a premium for barrel lengths other than 6 1/2 in. (beware of .44 DA barrels!), and for calibers other than .44 Russian, .32-44, or .38-44.

Add a premium for .44 Target variation if all numbers match (usually found in the 25,000 - 35,796 ser. no. range).

Substantial Premium for FACTORY Verified Target Models in calibers other than .44 Russian, .32-44 and .38-44 , if all numbers match.

NOTE: Numbers on frame, cylinder, barrel, and LATCH must match. There are also numbers on the ejector star/rod and the front sight (when removed). As the front Target sights were easily damaged and often replaced, deduct slightly if front sight replaced with correct, original sight.

Early production had rack and gear extractor (serial number range 1-13,500), and will bring a slight premium over the later mfg. Also, premiums do exist for all but 6 and 6 1/2 in. barrel lengths; premiums for unusual chamberings.

* ***New Model No. 3 Commercial Version***

$8,500	$5,000	$2,850	$2,000	$1,800	$1,625	$1,475	$1,325	$1,175	$995	$795	$695

* ***New Model No. 3 Japanese Navy Model*** – Japan purchased approx. 1/3 of total production.

Add 50% for Japanese characters on ejector housing. Japanese anchor brings only a small premium, if any.

* ***New Model No. 3 Australian Model*** – 7 in. barrel, detachable stock, for Australian Colonial Police, broad arrow marking on both pistol and stock, stocks were originally numbered to the matching pistol, but are seldom seen with matching numbers today, approx. 250 mfg., usually found in the low 12,000-low 13,000 ser. no. range.

Add a substantial premium if with shoulder stock.

Original holsters for this model are extremely scarce. Holster is a double flap type which will

100%	98%	95%	90%	80%	70%	60%	50%	40%	30%	20%	10%

holster the gun with or w/o shoulder stock attached. There is also a separate holster for shoulder stock when it is not attached to the gun. All types are scarce, and have Broad Arrow stamp.

* ***New Model No. 3 Argentine Model*** – unknown total production, marked "Ejercito Argentina" (very rare).

Add a premium over the Commercial Version.

* ***New Model No. 3 State of Maryland Model*** – "U.S." marked, serial number range 7,126-7,405.

Add a premium over the Commercial Version.

Add a premium for Revenue Cutter Service (Coast Guard) model, identifiable only by ser. no.

NEW MODEL NO. 3 FRONTIER – .44-40 WCF cal., single action, 4, 5, or 6 1/2 in. barrel, blue or nickel finish, walnut or hard rubber grips, ser. no. range 1-2072. 2,072 mfg. 1885-1908.

* ***New Model No. 3 Frontier Japanese Purchase*** – 786 converted to .44 Russian cal., cylinder should measure 1 9/16 in., in the Frontier serial range of 1-2,072.

N/A $5,000 $3,000 $2,250 $1,800 $1,625 $1,475 $1,325 $1,175 $995 $795 $695

* ***New Model No. 3 Frontier Standard Model*** – .44-40 WCF cal.

$9,000 $6,000 $3,500 $3,000 $2,500 $2,250 $2,000 $1,850 $1,600 $1,400 $1,250 $1,100

NEW MODEL NO. 3 - .38-40 WCF – separate ser. range, only 74 mfg., ser. no. 1-74. Mfg. 1900-1907.

Extreme rarity factor of this model precludes accurate pricing.

NEW MODEL NO. 3 TARGET MODEL – .32-44 S&W or .38-44 S&W cal., target sights, ser. no. range 1-4333. 4,333 mfg. between 1887-1910.

$6,500 $3,250 $2,500 $2,250 $1,925 $1,700 $1,500 $1,350 $1,100 $950 $800 $700

NEW MODEL NO. 3 TURKISH – .44 rimfire cal., 5,461 mfg. 1879-1888, in separate serial number series, 1 - 5,461.

N/A $7,000 $4,675 $4,350 $4,050 $3,750 $3,450 $3,150 $2,850 $2,550 $2,275 $1,950

.44 CAL. DOUBLE ACTION FIRST MODEL – .32-44 (rare), .38-44 (rare), .38 Military (rare), .44 S&W Russian (most common), and .455 (rare) cal., caliber markings on later production for .44 S&W Russian is ".44 Smith & Wesson", 6 shot fluted cylinder, 4, 5, 6, or 6 1/2 in. barrel, blue or nickel finish, "S&W" monogram checkered hard rubber or walnut grips. Walnut grips with "S&W" inlays will be found after 1900. 53,590 mfg. 1881-1913. Serial range 1-54,668.

Add 100% for cals. other than .44 S&W Russian with target sights on sub-models listed.

* ***.44 Cal. Double Action First Model Standard***

$4,500 $1,900 $1,500 $1,275 $1,000 $925 $825 $695 $650 $575 $475 $375

* ***.44 Cal. Double Action First Model Wesson Favorite*** – similar to Standard Model, but in 5 in. barrel only with special front sight, blue or nickel finish, patent markings are on the cylinder rather than on the barrel, grooved barrel rib, external and internal lightening cuts to reduce weight. Approx. 1,000 mfg. 1882-1883. Serial numbers within the .44 Double Action First Model range, approx. 8,900 - 10,100.

N/A $10,000 $8,000 $7,000 $5,500 $4,500 $3,600 $3,200 $2,825 $2,500 $2,275 $2,000

Add 30-40% for blue finish.

.38 WIN. DOUBLE ACTION – .38-40 WCF cal., 4, 5, 6, or 6 1/2 in. barrel, only 276 mfg. in separate ser. range 1-276. Mfg. 1900-1910.

N/A $6,000 $5,000 $4,000 $3,000 $2,500 $2,000 $1,750 $1,500 $1,300 $1,225 $1,125

.44 DOUBLE ACTION FRONTIER – .44-40 WCF cal., 4, 5, 6, or 6 1/2 in. barrel, only 15,340 mfg. in separate ser. range 1-15,340. Mfg. 1886-1913.

$4,500 $1,900 $1,500 $1,275 $1,000 $925 $825 $695 $650 $575 $475 $375

Add 100% for factory target sights.

.44 DOUBLE ACTION WESSON FAVORITE – .44 S&W Russian cal., ser. no. range 8900-10100. Approx. 1,000 mfg. 1882-1883.

N/A N/A $10,000 $8,200 $7,500 $6,500 $6,000 $5,000 $4,000 $2,500 $2,000 $1,500

100%	98%	95%	90%	80%	70%	60%	50%	40%	30%	20%	10%

SINGLE SHOTS

FIRST MODEL (SINGLE SHOT MODEL OF 1891) – .22 LR (862 mfg.), .32 S&W (229 mfg.), or .38 S&W (160 mfg.) cal., 6, 8, or 10 in. barrel marked "Model of 1891", blue or nickel, hard rubber extension grips, single action trigger. 1,251 mfg. 1893-1905, ser. range (same as Third Model 38 Single Action) 1-28,107. Serial number is located on the front strap.

* ***First Model .22 LR*** – approx. 862 mfg.

N/A	$2,700	$2,475	$2,100	$1,900	$1,575	$1,325	$1,075	$875	$625	$500	$375

Add a premium for .32 S&W or .38 S&W cals.

SECOND MODEL .22 LR – similar to First Model, but will not accommodate a revolver cylinder, flatsided frame (does not have recoil shield) 6 (rare) or 10 in. barrel, single action trigger, black hard rubber extension grips, 4,617 mfg. 1905-09. Ser. range 1-4,617 (ser. no. located on front gripstrap).

N/A	$2,200	$2,000	$1,825	$1,575	$1,375	$1,200	$975	$775	$550	$450	$350

THIRD MODEL .22 (PERFECTED MODEL) – similar to Second Model, except is built on "I" solid frame with integral trigger guard, side plate on right side, will fire in both single or double action, checkered walnut extension grips. 6,949 mfg. 1909-1923. Serial range 4,618-11,641 (ser. no. located on front gripstrap).

N/A	$2,200	$2,000	$1,825	$1,575	$1,375	$1,200	$975	$775	$550	$450	$350

Add 30% for Olympic Model in extra short .22 LR rifle chamber.

FOURTH MODEL STRAIGHT LINE TARGET SINGLE SHOT – .22 LR cal., single shot, 10 in. barrel, sideswing barrel, blue, target sights, smooth walnut grips, shaped like an autoloader. 1,870 mfg. 1925-36. Ser. range 1-1,870. Values below assume steel case and accessories.

N/A	$3,250	$2,750	$2,175	$1,975	$1,675	$1,400	$1,125	$900	$650	$525	$400

Subtract 30% w/o case and accessories.

EARLY HAND EJECTORS (NAMED MODELS)

Named Models. 1896-1958. Listed in order by caliber, except where newer mfg. might also include model number. These will NOT have any model number stamped on the frame. Several were continued after 1958 as Numbered Models, so be sure to check that section as well.

MODEL .22 HAND EJECTOR (LADYSMITH) – originally chambered for .22 S&W (same as .22 Long) cal., 7 shot fluted cylinder, small frame, available in blue or nickel finish, nicknamed "Ladysmith" due to its small size, Tiny "M" frame. Over 26,000 mfg. between 1902-1921.

* ***Model .22 Hand Ejector First Model*** – .22 L cal., 3, or 3 1/2 in. barrel, serial numbered 1-4,575, checkered hard rubber grips, round butt. 4,575 mfg. 1902-1906. Serial range 1-4,575. Identifiable by small frame mounted cylinder release button.

N/A	$2,500	$2,000	$1,500	$1,250	$975	$800	$650	$550	$475	$435	$390

* ***Model .22 Hand Ejector Second Model*** – .22 L cal., 3, or 3 1/2 in. barrel, distinguishable from first model in that cylinder locking device was placed on barrel bottom, locking both ends. 9,400 mfg. 1906-1910. Serial range 4,576-13,950.

N/A	$2,500	$2,000	$1,500	$1,250	$975	$800	$650	$550	$475	$435	$390

* ***Model .22 Hand Ejector Third Model*** – .22 L cal., 2 1/2, 3, 3 1/2, or 6 in. barrel, smooth walnut grips with "S&W" medallion inlays, square butt. 12,200 mfg. 1910-21. Serial range 13,951-26,154.

N/A	$2,500	$2,000	$1,500	$1,250	$975	$800	$650	$550	$475	$435	$390

Add 85% for 6 in. barrel with target sights.

Add 95% for 6 in. barrel with plain sights.

.22/.32 HAND EJECTOR (ALSO KNOWN AS .22/32 BEKEART MODEL) – .22 LR cal., 6 shot fluted cylinder, 6 in. barrel, blue, checkered walnut grips with "S&W" medallions, extension style square butt, there were several hundred thousand of the standard .22/.32 Hand Ejector mfg. The first 3,000 mfg. will be found with a separate ser. no. (1-3,000) stamped into the bottom of the wood grips. This model was cataloged as the .22/.32 heavy frame target unit in 1931. Mfg. 1911-1941.

100%	98%	95%	90%	80%	70%	60%	50%	40%	30%	20%	10%

* ***.22/.32 Hand Ejector Bekeart Model*** – will be found with separate identification number on bottom of its wooden grip. Serial numbers for early Bekeart models start at 138,226.

N/A	$1,575	$1,325	$1,075	$875	$750	$650	$550	$450	$350	$275	$200

Add 50% premium for ser. no. 1-1,000 ("True Bekearts").

Add 20% over the values listed for early production in lower ser. no. range 1,001-3,000.

This model was specifically mfg. for a San Francisco retailer, Philip Bekeart. Originally, Mr. Bekeart ordered 1,000 guns to his specifications, S&W mfg. 5,000. While the first 1,000 revolvers in ser. no. range 138226 to 139275 with grip numbered 1-1,000 are accepted as "True Bekearts", only 292 were actually delivered to Philip Bekeart.

* ***.22/.32 Hand Ejector Standard Model*** – mfg. approx. 1913-53, in a serial range of 101 to 135465, continued as the Model 35.

$1,150	$950	$750	$575	$400	$325	$275	$225	$175	$135	$115	$100

.22/.32 KIT GUN – similar to Standard .22/32 Hand Ejector Model, except has 2 or 4 in. barrels, round or square butt. Mfg. 1935-53, serial number overlaps occur within this model, continued as the Model 34.

$850	$750	$575	$425	$350	$300	$250	$200	$175	$160	$150	$125

Pre-war kit guns in ser. no. range approx. 525,670 to 536,684 will bring a 400%-500% premium over above values, if in 95%+ condition. Mfg. 1935-1941.

Early post-war kit guns in ser. no. range approx. 536,685 to 590,000 will bring a 350% premium over above values, if in 95%+ condition. Mfg. 1946-1952.

* ***.22/.32 Kit Gun 1953-1957 "Pre-Model 34" Production*** – improved I or J frame, continued in 1957 as the Model 34.

$800	$725	$600	$475	$375	$300	$250	$200	$175	$160	$140	$120

Early alloy frame "Airweight" (not "Airweight Marked) kit guns (pre-Model 43), will bring values similar to the steel frame pre-Model 34.

K-22 OUTDOORSMAN - K-22 1st MODEL – .22 LR cal., 6 shot, 6 in. round barrel, K-frame, blue, adj. target sights, walnut grips, serial numbers in the 600,000 range with the .38 M&P 1905 4th change. Approx. 19,500 mfg. 1931-1940.

$2,500	$2,050	$1,850	$1,625	$1,375	$1,100	$875	$625	$425	$300	$250	$200

PRE-WAR K-22 MASTERPIECE – similar to K-22 Outdoorsman, but has micro click rear sight, short action, round barrel w/o rib. 1,067 mfg. in 1940 in the .38 Hand Ejector range, ser. no. range 682,420-696,952.

$5,000	$4,650	$4,350	$3,800	$3,200	$2,650	$2,000	$1,400	$1,100	$775	$500	$350

POST-WAR K-22 MASTERPIECE – similar to pre-war K-22, serrated ribbed barrel, ser. no. started with "K" prefix, pre-Model 17, mfg. 1946-1957, then continued as the Model 17.

$850	$775	$725	$650	$575	$500	$425	$325	$250	$200	$175	$150

Add 10% for early serial numbers with large ejector rod.

THE K-22 COMBAT MASTERPIECE – .22 LR cal., double action revolver built on the square butt K target frame with 5 screws, similar to K-22 masterpiece except with 4 inch pinned barrel, blue finish, (nickel scarce) combat style 1/8 in. Baughman Quick Draw on plain ramp base front sight, micrometer click adjustable rear sight, short action. Mfg. circa 1949-1957, continued there after as the Model 18.

$750	$650	$550	$400	$300	$275	$250	$225	$200	$175	$150	$125

Add 100% for nickel guns that letter as factory.

THE .22 MILITARY AND POLICE (POST OFFICE MODEL) – .22 LR cal., double action revolver built on the square butt K frame with 5 screws, designated as a training gun for the U.S. Postal Service, the only K frame produced in .22 LR with fixed sights, blue finish, 6 shot with 4 inch round barrel, not cataloged by S&W. Mfg. circa 1948-1957 and continued as the Model 45.

N/A	$1,750	$1,425	$1,150	$850	$775	$650	$525	$400	$300	$250	$200

MODEL K-.256 WINCHESTER TEST REVOLVER – .256 Win. cal., DA, K target (and also N target) frame, made as a test gun in the trials between the .22 Centerfire Magnum (Jet) cartridge and the standard .256 Winchester cartridge, essentially a K-22 frame

100%	98%	95%	90%	80%	70%	60%	50%	40%	30%	20%	10%

with a cylinder chambered for this cartridge, built on a 4 screw K frame, 6 were built as prototypes circa 1960. No K frame sales have been reported.

Extreme rarity precludes accurate pricing.

.22 HORNET CALIBER EXPERIMENTAL REVOLVER – .22 cal. Hornet, DA, aluminum alloy N target frame, barrel marking is "S&W .22 Magnum" fitted with a target hammer and trigger, a pinned Patridge front sight, micrometer click rear sight. Also see the 38/44 Alloy N frame.

Extreme rarity precludes accurate pricing - Last known selling price was $30,000.

9MM CALIBER TEST REVOLVER – 9mm, double action revolver built on the N frame. A small number of test revolvers were built on a prewar N frame. Serial #3 and possibly serials #6 and #9 were made on a test basis for the Chinese government in June of 1945. Originally requested to be in 8mm Nambu, S&W did not have an 8mm reamer, but instead supplied a sample chambered in 9mm. This rare 1940s vintage prototype should not be confused with the production 9mm revolvers which were regular cataloged items in later decades. You will find those listed in the Numbered Model Revolver section at Models 547 and 940. No sales reported.

Extreme rarity precludes accurate pricing.

.30 CALIBER CARBINE TEST REVOLVER – .30 M1 Carbine cal., double action revolver built on N target frame. S&W produced several revolvers with fixed and target sights, chambered in .30 Carbine, which were built on a five screw N frame on a test basis. Some of these were submitted to the Army for evaluation and tested on Jan. 17, 1944 at APG . These revolvers passed an endurance test with no breakages, but shooters objected to the severe muzzle blast, and the Army did not see a military requirement for further purchase. The military report also states that the shooters did not wear hearing protection. In this case it is apparent that muzzle blast would be excessive. At least three examples are known to still exist in private collections. Serial number 4 is of a prewar target configuration with a cylinder length of 1.6 in. using half moon clips when needed. It has a 5 in. barrel with a Patridge front sight and prewar features with post war grips on a frame with a 6 groove backstrap and forestrap. In October 2003, serial number 2 was auctioned by James D. Julia and is the revolver in the 1944 test by APG. Reports are that this and two others were ordered by General "Hap" Arnold, further accurate details are unknown. Records in the National Archives about this revolver are scarce, but research is still on-going by Charles Pate.

Any of these revolvers are extremely rare among collectors, and would probably bring in the low five figures.

.32 HAND EJECTOR FIRST MODEL (MODEL OF 1896) – .32 S&W Long cal., 6 shot fluted cylinder, 3 1/4, 4 1/4, or 6 in. barrel, blue or nickel, black rubber grips, round butt, cylinder stop is mounted in frame top-strap, patent markings are on cylinder, rather than on barrel. 19,712 mfg. 1896-1903. Serial range 1-19,712.

$1,000	$775	$650	$600	$550	$525	$475	$425	$400	$375	$335	$300

Add 10% for short hammer variation.

.32 HAND EJECTOR SECOND MODEL (MODEL OF 1903) – .32 S&W Long cal., 6 shot fluted cylinder, 3 1/4, 4 1/4, or 6 in. barrel, blue or nickel, black rubber grips. 19,425 mfg. 1903-1904. Serial range 1-19,425.

N/A	$1,575	$1,325	$1,075	$875	$750	$650	$550	$450	$350	$275	$200

* ***.32 Hand Ejector Second Model (Model of 1903 - 1st Change)*** – rubber grips. 31,700 mfg. 1904-1906. Serial range 19,426-51,126.

N/A	$1,850	$1,625	$1,375	$1,100	$875	$625	$425	$300	$250	$200	$175

* ***.32 Hand Ejector Second Model (Model of 1903 - 2nd Change)*** – rubber grips. 44,373 mfg. 1906-1910. Serial range 51,127-95,500.

N/A	$650	$575	$475	$375	$300	$275	$250	$225	$200	$175	$150

* ***.32 Hand Ejector Second Model (Model of 1903 - 3rd Change)*** – rubber grips. 624 mfg. 1909-10. Serial range 95,501-96,125.

N/A	$650	$575	$475	$375	$300	$275	$250	$225	$200	$175	$150

* ***.32 Hand Ejector Second Model (Model of 1903 - 4th Change)*** – rubber grips. 6,374 mfg. 1910. Serial range 96,126-102,500.

N/A	$650	$575	$475	$375	$300	$275	$250	$225	$200	$175	$150

100%	98%	95%	90%	80%	70%	60%	50%	40%	30%	20%	10%

* ***.32 Hand Ejector Second Model (Model of 1903 - 5th Change)*** – rubber grips. Serial range 102501-to approx 263000. Approx. 160,499 mfg. 1910-1917.

N/A	$650	$575	$475	$375	$300	$275	$250	$225	$200	$175	$150

.32 HAND EJECTOR THIRD MODEL – .32 S&W Long cal., 6 shot fluted cylinder, 3 1/4, 4 1/4, or 6 in. barrel, blue or nickel finish, grips of checkered hard rubber with "S&W" monogram, round butt. 271,531 mfg. 1917-1942. Serial range approx. 263,001-534,532.

N/A	$650	$575	$475	$375	$300	$275	$250	$225	$200	$175	$150

Add 50% for pre-war mfg.

.32 HAND EJECTOR POST WWII (PRE-MODEL 30) – .32 S&W Long cal., 6 shot, 2, 3, 4, or 6 in. barrel, blue or nickel, fixed sights, walnut or rubber grips. Serial range 536685 -712953 as an "I" frame mfg. 1946-1960.

N/A	$600	$500	$400	$300	$275	$250	$225	$200	$175	$150	$125

This model was designated Model 30 after 1958.

.32 REGULATION POLICE – .32 S&W cal., 6 shot, 2, 3, 4, or 6 in. barrel, square butt, walnut grips, fixed sights, blue or nickel, wide serial range of 260000 to 536000 s/n on front tang Mfg. 1917-1957.

N/A	$650	$575	$475	$375	$300	$275	$250	$225	$200	$175	$150

Add 300% for Regulation Police Target (6 in. barrel only, blue).
Subtract 25% for post-war manufacture.

K-32 HAND EJECTOR FIRST MODEL (K-32 TARGET) – .32 S&W Long cal., double action revolver built on the square butt K target 5 screw frame, 6 in. round and pinned barrel, 6 shot fluted cylinder with a nominal length of 1.56 in., blue finish, 1/8 or 1/10 in. Patridge front sights were cataloged, with gold bead available, adjustable rear sight for windage and elevation, both magna and standard walnut grips with a diamond around the screw escutcheon were available, 34oz. Built on the Model 1905 .38 M&P 4th Change frame in serial number range 653388 to 682207. About 94 mfg. circa 1936-1941.

N/A	$18,500	$15,000	$12,500	$10,500	$9,000	$7,000	$5,000	$3,750	$2,500	$1,250	$800

K-32 HAND EJECTOR (POSTWAR) K-32 MASTERPIECE – .32 S&W Long cal., double action revolver built on the square butt K target 5 screw frame, short cocking action, anti-backlash trigger, 6 groove tangs and serrated trigger, 1/8 or 1/10 in. Patridge front sights were cataloged, micrometer click rear sight, narrow ribbed 6 in. barrel, checkered walnut stocks with S&W monograms. A large S&W trademark is found on the sideplate. Quite a scarce gun, with serial number ranges hard to pin down. Known serial numbers include all of K 58921 through K-58970 and K-67601 67670; and K-68470 68530 ranges along with some of the guns in K-767574 767599. All of these have the narrow rib. In 1950, the wide rib was introduced, and some K-32s from 1956 will be found in the K-271792 to K-271836 serial number range. Additional known serial number ranges listed under Model 16. Weight 38.5 oz. Mfg. circa 1946-1957, K-32 Masterpiece continued as the Model 16.

N/A	$3,250	$2,800	$2,500	$2,000	$1,500	$1,250	$1,050	$850	$650	$450	$250

.32 MILITARY & POLICE – .32 S&W Long cal., double action revolver built on the square butt K 5 screw frame, 2 and 4 in. barrel lengths are found and approximately 910 with a 5 in. barrel are reported, a small group of revolvers were chambered for .32 Long rather than the .38 and built on the larger .38 M&P K frame., fixed sights with round blade front and square notch rear. 6 shot cylinder with a nominal length of 1.56 in. "Smith & Wesson 32 Long CTG" on the barrel's left side, with the right side blank. "Made in U.S.A." on the frame next to the trigger guard. Large S&W Monogram on the sideplate. .240 in. serrated trigger and checkered hammer spur. Serial prefixes of S and C are found mixed in the 38 M&P series with 4,813 mfg. circa 1948-1950.

N/A	$2,800	$2,500	$2,200	$1,850	$1,500	$1,250	$1,000	$750	$500	$425	$350

.32-20 WCF HAND EJECTOR FIRST MODEL – .32-20 WCF cal., 6 shot fluted cylinder, 4, 5, 6, or 6 1/2 in. barrel, blue or nickel, case hardened trigger and hammer, hard rubber with "S&W" monogram or non-monogrammed walnut grips, round butt style, serial range 1-5311. Mfg. 1899-1902.

N/A	$2,800	$2,450	$2,100	$1,850	$1,500	$1,200	$950	$750	$550	$350	$250

100%	98%	95%	90%	80%	70%	60%	50%	40%	30%	20%	10%

.32-20 WCF HAND EJECTOR SECOND MODEL (MODEL OF 1902) – .32-20 WCF cal., 6 shot fluted cylinder, 4, 5, or 6 1/2 in. barrel, blue or nickel, hard rubber with "S&W" monogram or walnut round butt style grips. 4,499 mfg. 1902-1905. Serial number range 5,312-9,811.

N/A	$1,850	$1,625	$1,375	$1,100	$875	$625	$425	$300	$250	$200	$175

* ***.32-20 WCF Hand Ejector Second Model (Model of 1902 - 1st Change)*** – grip also available in checkered walnut. 8,313 mfg. 1903-1905. Serial number range 9,812-18,125.

N/A	$1,850	$1,625	$1,375	$1,100	$875	$625	$425	$300	$250	$200	$175

.32-20 WCF HAND EJECTOR (MODEL OF 1905) – .32-20 WCF cal., (revolvers manufactured until approx. 1916 were marked .32 Winchester, .32 WCF between 1916-1928, and late production was marked .32/20), cylinder and barrel specifications same as above, with round or square butt grip. 4,300 mfg. 1905-1906. Serial number range 18,126-22,426.

N/A	$1,850	$1,625	$1,375	$1,100	$875	$625	$425	$300	$250	$200	$175

Add 75% for Target Models.

* ***.32-20 WCF Hand Ejector (Model of 1905 - 1st Change)*** – 4, 5, 6, or 6 1/2 barrel, blue or nickel, grips same as above, round or square butt. 11,073 mfg. 1906-1907. Serial number range 22,427 to approx. 33,500.

N/A	$1,850	$1,625	$1,375	$1,100	$875	$625	$425	$300	$250	$200	$175

* ***.32-20 WCF Hand Ejector (Model of 1905 - 2nd Change)*** – caliber, cylinder, barrel and grip specifications same as above, serial number range 33501-45200. 11,699 mfg. 1906-1909 with overlap to the 1905 1st change.

N/A	$1,850	$1,625	$1,375	$1,100	$875	$625	$425	$300	$250	$200	$175

* ***.32-20 WCF Hand Ejector (Model of 1905 - 3rd Change)*** – caliber and cylinder same as above, 4 or 6 in. barrel, finish and grips same as above. 20,499 mfg. 1909-1915. Serial number range approx. 45,201-65,700.

N/A	$1,850	$1,625	$1,375	$1,100	$875	$625	$425	$300	$250	$200	$175

* ***.32-20 WCF Hand Ejector (Model of 1905 - 4th Change)*** – caliber and cylinder same as above, 4, 5, or 6 in. barrel, finish and grips same as above, serial number range 65,701-144,684. 78,983 mfg. 1915-1940.

N/A	$1,850	$1,625	$1,375	$1,100	$875	$625	$425	$300	$250	$200	$175

.38 MILITARY & POLICE FIRST MODEL (MODEL OF 1899) – .38 S&W Special cal., early Army & Navy models were marked "S&W .38 MIL.", civilian guns and standard models are 2-line barrel marked ".38 S&W SPECIAL & U.S. SERVICE CTG'S" with the "Maltese Cross" emblem stamped both before and after the caliber, these models are also referred to as .38 Hand Ejectors, 6 shot fluted cylinder, 4, 5, or 6 1/2 in. barrel, blue or nickel finish, "S&W" monogram checkered hard rubber or checkered walnut grips with walnut grips exhibiting an impressed circle at top, left plain for civilian issue, marked with inspector's initials for military issue. 20,975 mfg. 1899-1902. Serial number range 1-20,975.

On these models, barrel markings are somewhat confusing, generally marked .38 S&W Spl. & U.S. Service cartridge, Military Issue is typically marked .38 Military. Fixed sights are referred to as Military & Police Models while target sights are referred to as .38 Hand Ejectors.

* ***.38 Military & Police First Model Standard*** – Civilian Issue

N/A	$1,850	$1,625	$1,375	$1,100	$875	$625	$425	$300	$250	$200	$175

Add 100%-200% for target sights, depending on condition.

* ***.38 Military & Police First Model U.S. Navy*** – 1,000 revolvers in .38 S&W Spl. cal. with 6 in. barrel, blue, checkered walnut grips, delivered in 1900. Stamped on butt "U.S.N." with an anchor and inspector's initials. All in S&W serial range 5,001-6,000. U.S. Navy serial number range 1-1,000.

N/A	$3,600	$3,300	$2,875	$2,500	$1,975	$1,550	$1,100	$825	$685	$550	$425

* ***.38 Military & Police First Model U.S. Army*** – 1,000 revolvers in .38 Military cal. with 6 in. barrel, blue, checkered walnut grips, inspector's initials "K.S.M." on right grip panel with "J.T.T.1901" on left grip panel. Stamped on butt "U.S. ARMY/MODEL 1899", lanyard ring. S&W serial number range 13,001-14,000.

N/A	$3,600	$3,300	$2,875	$2,500	$1,975	$1,550	$1,100	$825	$685	$550	$425

100%	98%	95%	90%	80%	70%	60%	50%	40%	30%	20%	10%

.38 MILITARY & POLICE SECOND MODEL (MODEL OF 1902) – .38 S&W Special and .38 Military cal., civilian and standard models barrels have a 2-line marking ".38 S&W SPECIAL & U.S. SERVICE CTG'S" with the "Maltese Cross" emblem stamped both before and after the caliber, 6 shot, fluted cylinder, 4, 5, 6, and 6 1/2 in. barrels, blue or nickel, "S&W" monogram checkered hard rubber or checkered walnut grips. 12,827 mfg. 1902-1903. Serial number range 20,976-33,803.

* ***.38 Military & Police Second Model Standard*** – civilian issue, all in .38 S&W Special cal.

N/A	$1,475	$1,275	$1,150	$900	$775	$650	$525	$400	$300	$250	$200

Add 100%-200% for target sights, depending on condition.

* ***.38 Military & Police Second Model U.S. Navy*** – 1,000 revolvers in .38 United States Service caliber with 6 in. barrel, delivered in 1902, "U.S.N." with "J.A.B.", anchor, and arrow through horizontal "S" and "No." (Naval Ser. No. designation) stamped on butt, Navy ser. no. range is 1001 - 2000. S&W serial range 25001 to 26000 on the front tang.

N/A	$4,425	$4,100	$3,600	$3,200	$2,750	$2,150	$1,650	$1,300	$1,000	$800	$600

.38 MILITARY & POLICE SECOND MODEL OF 1902 - 1ST CHANGE – .38 S&W Special cal., 6 shot fluted cylinder, 4, 5, or 6 1/2 in. barrel, blue or nickel, "S&W" monogram checkered hard rubber or checkered walnut grips, rounded butt style. 28,645 mfg. 1903-1904. Serial number range 33,804-62,449.

Add 100%-200% for target sights, depending on condition.

* ***.38 Military & Police Second Model 1st Change Standard Round Butt*** – hard rubber grips, round butt.

N/A	$1,475	$1,275	$1,150	$900	$775	$650	$525	$400	$300	$250	$200

* ***.38 Military & Police Second Model 1st Change Standard Square Butt*** – checkered walnut grips or square butt to frame style. All will have serial numbers over the 58,000 range.

N/A	$1,275	$1,150	$900	$775	$650	$525	$400	$300	$250	$200	$175

.38 MILITARY & POLICE (MODEL OF 1905) – .38 S&W Special cal., 6 shot fluted cylinder, 4, 5, or 6 1/2 in. barrel, blue or nickel finish, "S&W" monogram checkered hard rubber (round butt) or checkered walnut (square butt) grips. 10,800 mfg. 1905-1906. Serial number range 62,450-73,250.

N/A	$1,400	$1,225	$1,050	$850	$775	$650	$525	$400	$300	$250	$200

Add 50% for Target Model.

* ***.38 Military & Police (Model of 1905 - 1st Change)*** – .38 S&W Special cal., 6 shot fluted cylinder, 4, 5, 6, or 6 1/2 in. barrel, blue or nickel finish, grips same as above. 73,648 mfg. (including Model 1905 2nd change), exact quantity of both models has not been determined. The first change mfg. in 1906-1909. Serial number range 73251 - 146899 overlapping with the 1904 2nd model change.

N/A	$1,400	$1,225	$1,050	$850	$775	$650	$525	$400	$300	$250	$200

Add 50% for Target Model.

* ***.38 Military & Police (Model of 1905 - 2nd Change)*** – .38 S&W Special cal., cylinder barrel lengths, finishes and grip styles same as above. 73,648 (including Model 1905 1st change) mfg. Exact quantity unknown. The second change mfg. in 1906-1909 overlapping the 1905 1st change in a serial number range 73251 to 146899.

N/A	$1,400	$1,225	$1,050	$850	$775	$650	$525	$400	$300	$250	$200

Add 50% for Target Model.

* ***.38 Military & Police (Model of 1905 - 3rd Change)*** – .38 S&W Special cal., 6 shot fluted cylinder, 4, 5, or 6 in. barrel, finishes and grip styles same as above. 94,803 mfg. 1909-1915. Serial number range 146,900-241,703.

N/A	$1,400	$1,225	$1,050	$850	$775	$650	$525	$400	$300	$250	$200

Add 50% for Target Model.

* ***.38 Military & Police (Model of 1905 - 4th Change)*** – .38 S&W Special cal., 6 shot fluted cylinder, 2, 4, 5, or 6 in. barrel, finishes and grip styles same as above. 758,296 mfg. 1915-1942. Serial number range 241704-approx. 1000000.

N/A	$1,125	$900	$850	$700	$600	$500	$400	$325	$250	$225	$175

Add 50% for Target Model.

100%	98%	95%	90%	80%	70%	60%	50%	40%	30%	20%	10%

.38/200 BRITISH SERVICE REVOLVER – . 38 S&W cal. 200 grain bullet, approx 110, 379 sold to British with black Magic finish at around serial number 680000 and continues in the 1905 4th model series in a wide range of 700000 to 1000000. And again numbered within the Victory Model series from V1-V769000.

N/A	$750	$625	$500	$425	$375	$340	$300	$265	$225	$160	$90

GRADING - PPGS™	100%	98%	95%	90%	80%	70%	60%	LAST MSR

VICTORY MODEL – .38 Spl. (post-WWII commercial sales only), .38 S&W Spl. (U.S. government sales only), or .38 S&W (Lend-Lease arms to Allied Forces only) cal., 2 (rare) or 4 in. barrel, mfg. in accordance with British/American Lend-Lease agreement of WWII, parkerized finish, most with "V" prefix, approx. 240,000 mfg. 1942-1945.

U.S. Govt. Models	$750	$655	$565	$510	$415	$340	$265
Lend-lease mfg.	$700	$615	$525	$475	$385	$315	$245
Post WWII Commercial	$700	$615	$525	$475	$385	$315	$245

Post-WWII Victory models sold commercially went through the Defense Supply Commission, and had no U.S. markings. These models will bring a premium. Be careful of fake markings.

100%	98%	95%	90%	80%	70%	60%	50%	40%	30%	20%	10%

.38 MILITARY & POLICE (POSTWAR) "PRE-MODEL 10" – .38 S&W Special cal., double action revolver built on the square butt K 5 screw frame. Mfg. circa 1946-1957

N/A	$500	$400	$300	$285	$265	$250	$235	$210	$185	$140	$95

This model is a continuation of the previous model without the V serial prefix or the lanyard ring. S prefix postwar guns began as early as Dec. 27, 1944 at around s/n S769000. Postwar production frames will also have the four address lines of "Made In U.S.A., Marcas Registradas, Smith & Wesson Springfield, Mass." on the right side. C prefix began on March 22, 1948 starting over at C-1, and was also numbered concurrently with the M&P Airweights and the M&P .22 or pre-Model 45. Available in 2, 4, 5, or 6 in. round pinned barrel lengths with a 1/10 inch fixed round blade front sight and a square notch rear sight (later changed to 1/8 in.). Available in blue or nickel finish. Serial numbers are found on the butt, cylinder face, barrel flat, yoke face (viewed thru a charge hole), the rear of the star extractor, and on the right grip panel. The round butt frame variation became available in late 1947. The 2 in. variation will have Smith & Wesson and the caliber marking on the left side of the barrel. Weight is 29.5 oz for a 4 in. version. Became the Model 10 in 1957.

THE K-38 TARGET MASTERPIECE "PRE- MODEL 14" –.38 S&W Special cal., double action revolver built on the square butt K target 5 screw frame, this original postwar Model has a 6 in. barrel with a narrow rib, 1/8 or 1/10 in. Patridge front sight with the new micrometer click rear sight, blue finish. Companion gun to the K-32 and K-17. Became the Model 14 in 1957. 38.5 oz. Introduced at serial K 1661. Mfg. circa 1946-1957.

N/A	$750	$650	$500	$400	$350	$300	$275	$225	$185	$135	$100

The major distinction between the K-38 Target Masterpiece and the K-38 Combat Masterpiece is the barrel length and front sight.

THE K-38 COMBAT MASTERPIECE "PRE- MODEL 15" – .38 S&W Special cal., double action revolver built on the square butt K Target 5 screw frame, 4 in. pinned and ribbed barrel with markings of "38 S&W Special CTG" on the right side, available in blue or nickel finish, 1/8 in. Baughman Quick Draw plain ramp base front sight with Micrometer click adjustable rear sight, square butt frame with diamond walnut grips, original K serial prefix. Mfg. circa 1949-1957, K-38 Combat Masterpiece continued as the Model 15.

N/A	$725	$600	$475	$375	$315	$290	$265	$220	$175	$135	$100

.38 MILITARY AND POLICE AIRWEIGHT "PRE- MODEL 12" – .38 S&W Special cal., double action revolver built on the round or square butt KA 5 screw aluminum alloy service frame, similar to the Model 10 but made with an alloy frame and originally an alloy cylinder, which was later changed to steel due to problems with cylinders cracking, numbered with the Model 10, 11, 45 and Aircrewman revolvers in production. This alloy frame is slightly

100%	98%	95%	90%	80%	70%	60%	50%	40%	30%	20%	10%

thinner than a standard K frame by .080 in. and has a smooth backstrap and forestrap. Mfg. circa 1951-1957, then continued as the Model 12.

N/A	$950	$775	$600	$475	$385	$335	$285	$260	$235	$170	$110

USAF M-13 (THE AIRCREWMAN) – .38 Special cal., double action revolver originally built on the round butt alloy K frame, blue anodized finish, 2 in. pinned barrel, diamond insert walnut grips, 1/10 in. serrated ramp front sight w/square notch rear, similar to the Model 12, has "Revolver, Lightweight, M13" stamped on the topstrap, "Property of U.S. Air Force" stamped on the backstrap, most were destroyed by the government, C serial prefix in a range of C 247000 to C 405363. Numbered concurrently with Model 10, 11, 12, and 45.

Extreme rarity precludes accurate pricing.

A production run of 605 early versions (6 Shot) were serial numbered with an A.F.NO prefix (serial Range A.F.NO.1190 A.F.NO.1794). These are a 5 screw variation with "Aircrewman" on the barrel, but with no topstrap markings and will have Air Force medallions in the grip circles with a smooth backstrap. A "P" inspectors stamp is found on the left side of the frame above the trigger guard. These early Genuine Aircrewman's have all matching serial numbers on the frame, cylinder face, grips, and barrel. Many were repaired by military armorer's who interchanged parts, especially cylinders with non matching numbers.

THE AIRCREWMAN (BABY AIRCREWMAN) – .38 S&W Special cal., double action revolver built on the alloy J 4 screw frame, 5 shot alloy cylinder, fixed sight, 605 Aircrewman versions, serial numbers "A.F.NO. 1795 A.F.NO. 2399", were shipped to the U.S. Air Force in 1953. Four others went to The Springfield Amory. Marked with "AIRCREWMAN" on the barrel and "PROPERTY OF U.S. AIR FORCE" on the smooth backstrap, P proof mark over the trigger-guard with air force medallions in the grip circles. Most of these guns were destroyed and very few authentic examples exist. It is estimated that 10 to 15 have survived, so beware of many counterfeit examples. Weight 10.5 oz. Mfg. circa 1952.

N/A	$5,200	$4,600	$4,075	$3,600	$2,950	$2,300	$1,600	$1,450	$1,300	$1,200	$1,100

.38 CHIEFS SPECIAL "PRE-MODEL 36" – .38 Spl. cal., round or square butt steel J frame, coiled mainspring, 5 shot, fluted cylinder, 2 in. round pinned or 3 in. barrel, blue or nickel finish, early production had round blade front sight on five screw round butt frame with standard thumbpiece, smooth backstrap and rounded trigger guard, can be found with five, four, or three screw frames with ramp front sight, checkered walnut grips, later production had longer trigger guard with serrated ramped front sight, ser. no. range 1-786544. Mfg. began 1950, by 1957, this model became known as the Model 36.

N/A	$595	$500	$400	$300	$275	$250	$225	$200	$175	$150	$125

THE .38 CHIEFS SPECIAL AIRWEIGHT " PRE- MODEL 37" – .38 S&W Special cal., double action revolver built on the round or square butt alloy J 4 screw frame, 5 shot, later built with a steel cylinder due to cracks in the alloy cylinders, 2 in. barrel with round or square butt or 3 in. barrel with square butt only, available in blue or nickel finish, earliest production frames were a 5 screw alloy frame with a rounded trigger guard and a shorter grip and grip frame, examples of this frame are extremely rare. Continued as the Model 37.

N/A	$650	$525	$425	$375	$325	$300	$275	$250	$225	$150	$90

About 3,777 were manufactured with an alloy cylinder. Original serial number range approximately 13000 to 786544 numbered in the Chiefs Special series.

THE BODYGUARD AIRWEIGHT "PRE-MODEL 38" – .38 S&W Special cal., double action revolver built on the round butt alloy 4 screw J frame, with the obvious distinguishing characteristic of having the frame built up at the top rear to form an integral shroud for the hammer, 2 in. pinned barrel with some production of 3 in. barrels (very rare), blued or nickel aluminum finish, walnut diamond grips, Airweight stamped on the barrel, also found in combinations of nickel cylinder with blue frame and barrel (scarce), serrated ramp front sight, .240 in. shrouded service hammer, .312 in. smooth trigger. Serial range 66000 to 786544 in the Chiefs Special series. 14oz. Mfg. circa 1955-1957.

N/A	$675	$550	$450	$400	$350	$315	$285	$240	$200	$145	$90

THE CENTENNIAL "PRE-MODEL 40" – .38 S&W Special cal., double-action-only revolver built on the round butt steel J 4 screw frame, distinctive features of "hammerless" design (actually concealed hammer), and lemon-squeezer style grip safety on grip frame

100%	98%	95%	90%	80%	70%	60%	50%	40%	30%	20%	10%

backstrap, 5 shot, blue or nickel finish, 2 in. pinned barrel, fully concealed hammer, numbered concurrently with the Model 42. 19 oz. Serial number range in an original series 1 to 30160 mfg. circa 1952-1957.

N/A	$650	$525	$425	$375	$325	$305	$285	$240	$200	$145	$90

THE CENTENNIAL AIRWEIGHT "PRE-MODEL 42" - .38 S&W Special cal., double-action-only revolver built on the round butt alloy J 4 screw frame, a lightweight version of the Centennial Model, 5 shot, steel cylinder (37 manufactured with an alloy cylinder), blue or nickel finish, 2 in. pinned barrel, numbered concurrently with Model 40. Very early production may have a small lock screw on the upper sideplate screw. Ramped front sight with serrations and notch cut rear sight. Serial range of 1 to 30160 in an original series. Mfg. circa 1952-1957.

N/A	$750	$625	$500	$425	$375	$340	$300	$265	$225	$160	$90

THE .38/44 HEAVY DUTY (PREWAR) - .38 S&W Special or .38/44 S&W Special cal., introduced April 1930, double action revolver built on the larger square butt N 5 screw frame, 6 shot, blue or nickel finish. Standard barrel length was a 5 in. round pinned barrel, with limited production of 4 or 6-1/2 in. length barrels, Twelve are documented to be chambered in .45 Colt, some of which were shipped in 1937, 1938 and 1939 to law enforcement. Originally intended for a high powered .38 Special round, at times called the .38 Super Police (predecessor of the .357 Magnum). Serial number range 35037 to 62335 in the .44 Hand Ejector 3rd Model series. Guns manufactured from 1930-35 shipped in maroon boxes and from 1935 to 1940 in Blue Picture Boxes. 41 oz., 11,111 manufactured circa 1930-1941.

N/A	$1,900	$1,250	$750	$625	$500	$425	$350	$300	$250	$200	$150

THE .38/44 HEAVY DUTY TRANSITION (POSTWAR TRANSITIONAL) - .38 S&W Special cal., reintroduced in June of 1946, double action revolver built on the square butt N 5 screw frame, 4 or 5 in. barrels (6-1/2 in. rare). Reintroduced postwar with an S serial prefix beginning at approximately S62496, incorporating a new slide action hammer block. A short throw hammer was introduced in 1948 at approximately serial number S72300. This postwar model has the "Made in U.S.A." marking in early models and will be found with the Four Line address as it is produced closer to 1950. Serial number range is approximately S62496 to S75206 with about 2500 mfg. circa 1946-1950. Guns were shipped in either maroon or gold boxes.

N/A	$1,500	$1,175	$850	$700	$550	$450	$385	$315	$250	$180	$125

THE .38/44 HEAVY DUTY MODEL OF 1950 "PRE-MODEL 20" - .38 S&W Special cal., introduced in September of 1950, double action revolver built on the square butt N 5 screw frame, having 4 or 5 in. barrels (6-1/2 in. rare), the 1950 Model became the Model 20 in 1957. Serial number range is spread over a wide range from approximately S75000 to S256133 with 9,493 mfg. circa 1950-1966.

N/A	$1,200	$975	$650	$550	$450	$375	$325	$275	$225	$175	$125

THE .38/44 OUTDOORSMAN (PREWAR) - .38 S&W Special or .38/44 S&W Special cal., introduced in November of 1931, double action revolver built on the square butt N target 5 screw frame. Target version of the Heavy Duty, Patridge front sight, the adjustable rear sight leaf is rounded and contoured to the frame, serial number range 38939 to 62077 in the .44 Hand Ejector 3rd Model series. Another source reports the last pre-war Outdoorsman as s/n 62023 on 1/3/1941. Total approx. 4,761 mfg. circa 1931-1941.

N/A	$2,500	$1,950	$1,400	$1,125	$850	$650	$450	$375	$300	$225	$175

THE .38/44 OUTDOORSMAN TRANSITION (POSTWAR-TRANSITIONAL) - .38 S&W special cal., reintroduced August 1946, double action revolver built on the square butt N 5 screw target frame, reintroduced with a new sliding hammer block and an S serial prefix beginning at approximately S62940. Similar to the prewar model with postwar improvements. 6 1/2 in. pinned barrel with a shrouded extractor, (4 in. rare, with a small production run of 5 in. barrels produced and estimated at 50-100). 1/8 or 1/10 in., early postwar guns are known with Prewar Magnum barrels with checked ribs. Serrated backstrap and forestrap with 6 grooves, Approximate serial number range S62940 to S75000. Approximately 2,326 mfg. circa 1946-1949.

N/A	$1,800	$1,525	$1,250	$975	$600	$475	$385	$335	$285	$215	$150

100%	98%	95%	90%	80%	70%	60%	50%	40%	30%	20%	10%

THE .38/44 OUTDOORSMAN MODEL OF 1950 "PRE-MODEL 23" – .38 S&W Special cal., introduced September 1950, double action revolver built on the square butt N 5 screw Target frame, introduced with a raised ribbed barrel and a micrometer click rear sight and short throw hammer and trigger, blue finish is now a polished blue or nickel finish, the S&W trademark is now found on the sideplate, checkered Magna diamond walnut grips. Approximate serial number range S75000 to S261999 in the N frame S series with a total of 6,039 mfg. circa 1950-1957.

100%	98%	95%	90%	80%	70%	60%	50%	40%	30%	20%	10%
N/A	$900	$775	$600	$475	$385	$335	$285	$260	$235	$170	$110

THE .38/44 HEAVY DUTY/OUTDOORSMAN ALLOY FRAME – .38 S&W Special cal., double action Revolver built on the square butt alloy N 5 screw frame. A small group (about 12) of aluminum alloy N frame handguns were made in various calibers and configurations as specials in 1955. Several of these were of a 38/44 configuration with a steel cylinder, with both 4 and 5 in. barrels being made. S serial prefix and "X" serial prefixes have been observed. It was verified that both target and fixed sight models were made in blue and nickel finish, alloy frames are 6 ounces lighter than their steel counterparts. Five are known in private collections. See also .22 Hornet caliber.

Last known traded price was $14,000 in 1996.

GRADING - PPGS™	100%	98%	95%	90%	80%	70%	60%	LAST MSR

.38 CHIEFS SPECIAL TARGET "PRE-MODEL 50" – satin blue original finish (military post-war type), early production (1955-1956), found sporadically in the 55,000 - 57,000 ser. no. range, polished blue finish from 1957-1959 (in approx. 149,000 - 150,000 ser. no. range).

	100%	98%	95%	90%	80%	70%	60%	LAST MSR
	$850	$745	$640	$580	$470	$385	$300	

.38 REGULATION POLICE – .38 S&W cal., 5 shot, 2, 3, 4, or 6 in. barrel, square butt, walnut grips, fixed sights, blue or nickel. Mfg. 1917-57.

	100%	98%	95%	90%	80%	70%	60%	LAST MSR
Pre-war	$750	$655	$565	$510	$415	$340	$265	
Post-war								
Pre-Model 33	$475	$415	$355	$325	$260	$215	$165	

Add 300% for Regulation Police Target (6 in. barrel only, blue).

.357 REGISTERED MAGNUM – .357 Mag. cal., this model could be custom ordered with any barrel length from 3 1/2 - 8 3/4 inches in 1/4 in. increments (23 barrel lengths in all), adj. sights, blue (most common), or nickel (only 174 mfg.) finish, two hammer styles, checkered walnut grips, hand fitted and registered to the buyer by a number found on the inside of the yoke, ser. no. with "REG" prefix. This practice was disc. 1939 (approx. 5,500 were mfg.) due to the tremendous demand for the .357 Mag. revolver. Mfg. 1935-1939.

	100%	98%	95%	90%	80%	70%	60%	LAST MSR
	$8,000	$7,000	$6,000	$5,440	$4,400	$3,600	$2,800	

Add $1,300 for rare registration certificate.

Add 20% for non-standard barrel lengths.

Common barrel lengths were 3 1/2, 4, 5, 6 1/2, and 8 3/4 in. Production totals by barrel length are as follows: 4 1/2 in. (108 mfg.), 5 1/2 in. (140 mfg.), 5 in. (869 mfg.), 6 1/2 in. (1,518 mfg.), 6 in. (839), 7 1/2 in. (79 mfg.), and 8 3/4 in. (735 mfg.). Rest of production was divided between the other barrel lengths.

Be wary of fakes - it is highly recommended to get a factory letter when buying, selling, or trading this model. This is perhaps S&W most collectible revolver currently, and prices have risen significantly in the past several years.

.357 MAGNUM PRE-WAR NON-REGISTERED – similar to above, but not registered. 1,142 mfg. 1938-1941.

	100%	98%	95%	90%	80%	70%	60%	LAST MSR
	$6,500	$5,690	$4,875	$4,420	$3,575	$2,925	$2,275	

.357 MAGNUM POST-WAR (PRE-MODEL 27) – ser. no. had "S" prefix, 3 1/2, 5, 6, 6 1/2, or 8 3/8 in. barrel. Mfg. 1950-1957.

	100%	98%	95%	90%	80%	70%	60%	LAST MSR
	$1,975	$1,730	$1,480	$1,345	$1,085	$890	$690	

Add 10% for 8 3/8 in. barrel.

THE HIGHWAY PATROLMAN "PRE-MODEL 28" – .357 Magnum/.38 Special cal., introduced in April 15, 1954, double action revolver built on the square butt N target 5 screw frame, a

GRADING - PPGS™	100%	98%	95%	90%	80%	70%	60%	LAST MSR

utility version of the pre-Model 27 with a satin blue finish, this model is the only "N" frame with an adjustable rear sight leaf that is non serrated as well as no serrations on the barrel rib, 4 or 6 in. pinned and ribbed barrel without serrations, Magna style or target walnut grips with S&W medallions and diamond around the screw escutcheon. This model has a 6 groove serrated backstrap and forestrap. Has "Highway Patrol" stamped on the barrel, 1/8 in. Baughman Quick Draw front sight with adjustable micrometer click rear sight, shrouded extractor rod, .400 in. semi target hammer, .265 in. serrated or .400 in. smooth trigger, original test production marked "PATROLMAN", 8,427 manufactured in the first year of production. Mfg. circa 1954-1957, continued as the Model 28.

N/A	$1,000	$875	$790	$630	$520	$400

THE .357 COMBAT MAGNUM "PRE-MODEL 19" – .357 Magnum cal., double action revolver built on the square butt K target 4 screw frame that is slightly larger than a standard K frame in the yoke area. Available in blue or nickel finish and originally available in 4 in. barrel length only with a 1/8 in. Baughman Quick Draw on plain ramp base front sight with an adjustable micrometer click rear sight. 6 shot fluted and counter-bored cylinder with a nominal length of 1.67 in. Mfg. circa 1955-1957, the .357 Combat Magnum continued as the Model 19 until 1999.

N/A	$1,250	$1,095	$990	$790	$650	$500

100%	98%	95%	90%	80%	70%	60%	50%	40%	30%	20%	10%

.44 HAND EJECTOR FIRST MODEL (.44 HAND EJECTOR NEW CENTURY OR .44 TRIPLE LOCK) – .38-40 WCF, .44 S&W Special (standard), .44-40 WCF, .44 S&W Russian, .45 LC, or .455 Mark II cal., 4, 5, 6 1/2, or 7 1/2 in. barrel, non-monogrammed checkered walnut grips and square butt on early production, gold monogram inlay on later production. 15,375 mfg. 1908-1917. Serial range 1-15,375 (overlapping occurs between the 1st and 2nd models, and there is some ser. no. duplication with the .455 Mark II).

* ***.44 Hand Ejector First Model Special Caliber*** – .38-40 WCF, .44 Russian, .44-40 WCF, .45 LC (marking, only 21 mfg.), or .455 Mark II (commercial) cal.

Due to the rarity of these calibers, prices could be 200% or more above Standard Model values.

* ***.44 Hand Ejector First Model Conversion*** – .455 Mark II cal.

N/A	$4,650	$4,250	$3,700	$3,250	$2,750	$2,150	$1,500	$995	$750	$500	$325

Only 808 factory conversions of .44 Special to .455 cal. were mfg. and sold to the British government.

* ***.44 Hand Ejector First Model Standard*** – .44 S&W Special cal.

$2,750	$1,525	$1,325	$1,100	$1,000	$900	$800	$715	$630	$545	$460	$400
w/Factory Target Sights											
$5,500	$5,000	$4,500	$3,750	$3,300	$2,975	$2,650	$2,300	$1,850	$1,450	$1,200	$995

* ***.44 Hand Ejector First Model British Target Triple Lock*** – .455 cal., 6 1/2 or 7 1/2 in. barrel, with drift adj. sights (not screw operated) for shooting at Bisley, England, typically unmarked for cal., very few mfg.

$3,200	$2,950	$2,675	$2,350	$1,875	$1,650	$1,450	$1,275	$1,130	$985	$840	$695

.44 HAND EJECTOR 2ND MODEL – .44 S&W Special cal. as standard, .38-40 WCF, .44-40 WCF, or .45 LC cal., 4, 5, 6, or 6 1/2 in. barrel, blue or nickel finish, checkered walnut square butt grips, with or w/o "S&W" monogram inlays. 17,510 mfg. circa 1915-1940. Ser. range 15376-approx. 60000.

* ***.44 Hand Ejector 2nd Model Standard Caliber*** – .44 S&W Special cal., mfg. 1915-1940

N/A	$2,375	$2,050	$1,850	$1,500	$1,200	$900	$625	$475	$350	$250	$200

Add 50% for factory target sights.

* ***.44 Hand Ejector 2nd Model Special Calibers*** – .38-40 WCF, .44-40 WCF, or .45 LC cal.

Due to the rarity of these calibers, prices could be 200% or more above Standard Model values.

.44 HAND EJECTOR THIRD MODEL (MODEL 1926 HAND EJECTOR THIRD MODEL) – .44 S&W Special cal., very rare in .44-40 WCF or .45 LC cal., 6 shot fluted cylinder, 4, 5, or 6

100%	98%	95%	90%	80%	70%	60%	50%	40%	30%	20%	10%

1/2 in. barrel, finishes and grips same as above, same ser. range as the Second Model .44 Hand Ejectors, approx. 4,976 mfg. pre-war. Ser. range 28358-61412. Mfg. 1926-1941.

* ***.44 Hand Ejector Third Model Standard*** – .44 S&W Special cal.

N/A	$3,675	$3,300	$2,950	$2,600	$2,200	$1,750	$1,250	$850	$575	$450	$300

There is also a post-war variation of this model mfg. 1946-49 in ser. range S62,490-S74,000 (approx. 1,432 mfg. 1946-49). These transitional guns have hammer block safeties but long actions. The values are about 2/3 of the pre-war models.

* ***.44 Hand Ejector Third Model 1926 Target*** – pre-war, target sights, blue only, otherwise same as above. Mfg. 1926-1941.

N/A	$9,500	$8,550	$7,250	$6,500	$5,500	$4,500	$3,500	$3,000	$2,200	$1,500	$1,100

There is also a post-war variation of this model mfg. 1946-49 in ser. range S62,490-S74,000. These transitional guns have hammer block safeties but long actions. The post-war Target Model has a barrel rib and 1950s style micrometer rear sight. The values are similar to those listed.

GRADING - PPGS™	100%	98%	95%	90%	80%	70%	60%	LAST MSR

.44 MAGNUM PRE-MODEL 29 (5 SCREW) – .44 Mag. cal., 5 screw, can be discerned by 3 visible screws on right sideplate, 1 hidden under the grip, and 1 in front of the trigger guard, 4 (scarce), 5 (only 2 mfg.), or 6 1/2 in. barrel. Approx. 6,500 mfg. during 1956-1958, mfg. began with ser. no. S130,927.

Bright blue finish	$3,750	$3,000	$2,500	$2,040	$1,650	$1,350	$1,050	
Nickel (approx. 10 mfg.)	$10,500	$8,500	$7,500	$6,500	$5,500	$4,500	$3,500	

.44 MAGNUM PRE-MODEL 29 (4 SCREW) – similar to 5 screw model, except has four screws total, the top sideplate screw was eliminated, serialization began at approx. S167,600. Mfg. 1957-1958.

	$2,350	$2,050	$1,700	$1,475	$1,200	$1,000	$875	
5 in. barrel, blue	$4,500	$4,150	$3,600	$3,150	$2,500	$2,000	$1,500	
5 in. bbl., nickel, 10 mfg.	$9,500	$8,550	$7,250	$6,500	$5,500	$4,500	$3,500	

Add 40% for nickel finish.

Approx. 400 .44 Magnums with a 5 in. barrel were manufactured between the Pre-Model 29 with a 4 screw frame, and the Model 29-2 with a 3 screw frame. Most models were primarely shipped from 1958-1963.

.45 HAND EJECTOR (MODEL OF 1917) – .45 Auto Rim, or .45 ACP (in half moon clip) cal., 6 shot, 5 1/2 in. barrel, fixed sights, satin blue on military - high gloss blue on commercial, smooth walnut on military, checkered walnut on commercial models. Early military revolvers have concentric groove cut on the sides of the hammer (approx. serial range 1-15,000), 210,866 mfg. 1917-1948, ser. no. range 1-210,866.

* ***.45 Hand Ejector Military*** – approx. 175,000 mfg., 1917-1919.

	$1,850	$1,620	$1,390	$1,260	$1,020	$835	$650	

Add 25% for early military mfg. with concentric groove cut on the sides of the hammer.

Military overruns (unissued guns) were sold to the civilian market. Be sure to properly identify.

* ***.45 Hand Ejector Commercial*** – mfg. 1920-1948.

	$2,450	$2,145	$1,840	$1,665	$1,350	$1,105	$860	

There was also a "1917 Army" commercial mfg. May 14, 1946-July 25, 1947 (approx. 991 mfg.). At approx. ser. no. 210,321, from October 1947, guns were mfg. with a hammer block safety and ser. nos. had an "S" prefix.

* ***.45 Hand Ejector Brazilian Contract of 1937*** – Brazilian shield and 1937 contract date stamped on sideplate, 25,000 originally sold to Brazil, 14,000 were imported.Serial numbered throughout the 1-210,000 range.

	$1,450	$1,270	$1,090	$985	$800	$655	$510	
Older "non-import"	$2,900	$2,540	$2,175	$1,970	$1,595	$1,305	$1,015	

100%	98%	95%	90%	80%	70%	60%	50%	40%	30%	20%	10%

.455 HAND EJECTOR FIRST MODEL – .455 Mark II cal., ser. range 1-5,000 in its own range, English or Canadian proofmarks.

N/A	$1,750	$1,550	$1,325	$1,150	$975	$885	$765	$675	$600	$540	$480

Add 25% for commercially sold revolvers.
Subtract 20%-40% for conversion to American caliber.

.455 HAND EJECTOR SECOND MODEL – ser. range 5,001-74,755, generally British or Canadian proofmarks.

N/A	$1,350	$1,175	$1,000	$875	$750	$650	$550	$450	$350	$250	$200

Add 25% for commerically sold revolvers.
Subtract 20%-40% for conversion to American caliber.

THE .45 HAND EJECTOR MODEL OF 1950, MILITARY (1950 ARMY) "PRE-MODEL 22" – .45 ACP cal., introduced November 1951, double action revolver built on the square butt N 5 screw frame, similar to the 1917 Model with a new shorter throw hammer and trigger with a new slide action hammer block as indicated with an S serial prefix, 5 1/2 inch round barrel, the lanyard ring was now discontinued, 6 shot fluted cylinder with a nominal length of 1.53 in. Magna style walnut grips, 1/10 in. forged round blade front sight with square notch rear sights, 203 were reported chambered in .45 Colt at serial S103000, but only one has been found. This model can be marked "45 CAL MODEL 1950" or "S&W D.A. 45" on the barrels right side. Became the Model 22 in 1957. The four standard address lines now appear on the frame's right side, with a large S&W trademark on the sideplate. Serial number range S85000 to S236000 in the N frame series and possibly as high as S263000. One collector reports a serial number in the S2558xx serial area. 3,976 reported mfg. circa 1951-1966.

N/A	$1,800	$1,400	$1,000	$850	$700	$600	$500	$425	$375	$325	$275

THE 1950 .45 TARGET MODEL (LIGHT BARREL) "PRE MODEL 26" – .45 ACP (standard), or .45 Colt (scarce) cal. available, introduced February 1950, double action revolver built on the square butt N Target 5 screw frame having a 6-1/2 in. ribbed and pinned barrel. 6 shot fluted cylinder with a nominal length of 1.55 in. when chambered in .45 ACP, and with nominal cylinder length of 1.67 in. when chambered in .45 Colt, blue finish, Patridge front sight with a micrometer click rear sight, .400 in. semi-target hammer, .265 in. grooved trigger standard with .500 in. target trigger optional, shrouded extractor rod with uniform diameter. Barrel marked ".45 CAL MODEL 1950". 200 were chambered in .45 Colt spread over several years of production. Checked magna type diamond walnut stocks, or smooth rosewood target stocks on a square butt frame, S serial prefix. .45 ACP caliber with the tapered barrel became the Model 26. Earliest production may lack caliber marking on the side of barrel. Serial number range S76212 to S211000 with 2,768 reported mfg. circa 1950-1961.

N/A	$1,400	$1,100	$800	$675	$550	$475	$425	$385	$350	$300	$250

GRADING - PPGS™	100%	98%	95%	90%	80%	70%	60%	LAST MSR

THE 1955 .45 TARGET MODEL (HEAVY BARREL) "PRE-MODEL 25" – .45 ACP cal., introduced March 1955, double action revolver built on the square butt N target frame with 5 screws having a 6 1/2 in. pinned barrel. Heavy barrel version of the 1950 Target Model, with .500 in. target hammer and .500 in. target trigger, target stocks, shrouded barrel marked "45 CAL. MODEL 1955" , supplied with half moon clips, Patridge front sight with Micrometer click rear sight, S serial prefix, designated the Model 25 in 1957. Serial number range is S143XXX to S333454, and continued with the N serial prefix in 1969. Approximately 1000 units had barrels marked ".45 Caliber Model of 1950" and occurred during 1976. Mfg. circa 1955-1992.

N/A	$1,100	$965	$870	$695	$570	$440	

NUMBERED MODEL/RECENT MFG. REVOLVERS (MODERN HAND EJECTORS)

Smith & Wesson handguns manufactured after 1958 are stamped with a model number on the frame under the cylinder yoke. The number is visible when the cylinder is open. All revolvers manufactured by S&W from 1946-1958 were produced without model numbers.

To locate a particular revolver in the following section, simply swing the cylinder out to the loading

GRADING - PPGS™	100%	98%	95%	90%	80%	70%	60%	LAST MSR

position and read the model number inside the yoke. The designation Mod. and a two- or three-digit number followed by a dash and another number designates which engineering change was underway when the gun was manufactured. Hence, a Mod. 15-7 is a Model 15 in its 7th engineering change (and should be indicated as such when ordering parts). Usually, earlier variations are the most desirable to collectors unless a particular improvement is rare. The same rule applies to semi-auto pistols, and the model designation is usually marked on the outside of the gun.

Beginning 1994, S&W started providing synthetic grips and a drilled/tapped receiver for scope mounting on certain models.

S&W revolvers are generally categorized by frame size. Frame sizes are as follows: J-frame (small), K-frame (medium), L-frame (medium), N-frame (large), and X-frame (extra large). All currently manufactured S&W revolvers chambered for .38 S&W Spl. cal. will also accept +P rated ammunition.

Current S&W abbreviations for revolver feature codes used on its price sheets and literature are as follows: Grips: CTG - Crimson Trace laser grips, RG - rubber grips, WG - wood grips. Sights: ADJ - adjustable, BB - black blade front, DWD - dovetail white dot, INTCH - interchangeable front, FIX - fixed, FO - fiber optic, GB - gold bead front, INTEG - integral front, PAT - Patridge front, NS - night sight, RR - red ramp front, WB - white bead, and WO - white outline. Frame Material: AL - alloy, SS - stainless, CS - carbon. Frame Sizes: SM - Small/Compact, MD - Medium, LG - Large, XL - Extra Large. Older finish abbreviations include: ZB - Blue/Black, ZC - Clear Cote, ZG - Grey, ZM - Matte, ZS - Satin. Cylinder: CA - alloy, CC - carbon, CS - stainless, CT - titanium. Barrel: BF - full lug, BO - one piece, BP - PowerPort, BT - traditional, B2 - two piece. Action: DAO - double action only, SA/DA - single action/double action. Older finish abbreviations include: ZB - Blue/Black, ZC - Clear Cote, ZG - Grey, ZM - Matte, ZS - Satin. Cylinder: CA - alloy, CC - carbon, CS - stainless, CT - titanium.

Pre-2010 S&W abbreviations for revolver feature codes used on its price sheets and literature are as follows: Grips: GC - Crimson Trace laser grips, GR - rubber grips, GW wood grips, GF - finger groove grips. Sights: SA - adj., SB - black blade front, SC - interchangeable front, SF - fixed, SG - gold bead front, SH - Hi-Viz, SI - integral front, SP - Patridge front, SN - front night, SR - red ramp front, SW - white outline adj. rear. Frame Material: FA alloy, FS stainless, FC - carbon.

During 2009, S&W started manufacture of a Classic Firearms series of revolvers. These guns incorporate many features of S&W's older and most famous/collectible revolvers, but have also been enhanced with modern engineering changes. This series is referred to as Classics in the model nomenclature, as opposed to Classic which indicates standard production S&W models and nomenclature.

Add 10%-15% for those models listed that are pinned and recessed (pre-1981 mfg.), if in 90% or better condition.

Earlier mfg. on the following models with lower engineering change numbered suffixes are more desirable than later mfg. (i.e., a Model 10-1 is more desirable than a Model 10-14).

Factory error stamped revolvers generally bring a small premium (5%-10%, if in 95%+ original condition) over a non-error gun, if the right collector is found.

BODYGUARD 38 – .38 Spl. + P cal., 5 shot, DAO, 1.9 in barrel, small J-frame, internal hammer, aluminum alloy upper frame, steel reinforced polymer lower frame, stainless steel cylinder, ambidextrous cylinder release, fixed sights with laser module next to cylinder latch behind the recoil shield, and activated with thumb, round butt with integrated black polymer grips, matte black finish, 14.3 oz. New late 2010.

MSR $509	$425	$385	$350	$315	$280	$260	$240

GOVERNOR – .45 LC/.410 shotshell or .45 ACP/.410 shotshell, 2 1/2 in. shotshell, N-frame, 2 3/4 in. barrel, 6 shot, SA/DA, tritium night front sight, fixed rear sight, Scandium alloy frame with stainless steel cylinder, matte black finish, black synthetic finger groove or Crimson Trace Laser grips, 29.6 oz. New 2011.

MSR $769	$625	$550	$450	$395	$350	$300	$275

Add $250 for Crimson Trace laser grips.

GRADING - PPGS™	100%	98%	95%	90%	80%	70%	60%	LAST MSR

MODEL 10 (.38 M&P POST-WWII) – .38 Spl. +P cal., 6 shot, K-frame, round or square butt (4 in. barrel only starting 1992), fixed sights, 2 (disc. 1996), 3 (disc.), 4 (standard - disc. or heavy), 5 (disc.), or 6 (disc.) in. barrels, current mfg. utilizes Uncle Mike's combat grips, 36 oz. Disc. 2010.

	$595	$400	$295	$235	$165	$135	$120	*$814*

Add $12 for nickel finish (disc. 1991, 4 in. barrel only).

The Model 10 is currently available in 4 in. heavy barrel only (a 4 in. heavy barrel nickel square butt variation was disc. in 1992).

To date, there have been 14 engineering changes in this model.

MODEL 10 CLASSICS – .38 S&W Spl. + P cal., 4 in. barrel, 6 shot, carbon steel frame/cylinder, checkered wood grips, fixed sights, blue finish, approx. 36 oz. New 2010.

MSR $719	$535	$395	$295	$235	$165	$135	$120	

MODEL 11 (.38/200 M&P) – .38 S&W cal. only, similar to Model 10, limited production. Mfg. 1938-1965.

	$1,250	$1,050	$900	$700	$550	$400	$200	

Add 100% for 6 in. barrel.

There were 4 engineering changes in this model.

MODEL 12 (.38 M&P AIRWEIGHT) – similar to Model 10, except alloy frame, 2 or 4 in. barrel. Disc. 1986.

	$500	$400	$350	$275	$225	$200	$180	*$320*

Add $40 for nickel finish (disc.).

There were 4 engineering changes in this model.

MODEL 13 (.357 MAG. M&P) – .357 Mag. cal., K-frame, 6 shot, fixed sights, 3 (round butt, disc. 1996) or 4 (square butt) in. heavy barrel. Disc. 1998.

	$500	$425	$375	$250	$185	$175	$165	*$411*

Add $20 for nickel finish (disc. 1986).

There were 5 engineering changes in this model.

* ***Model 13 M & P - N.Y. State Police*** – .357 Mag. cal., K-frame, 4 in. barrel, blue, fixed sights, 1,200 were mfg. for the N.Y. State Police and are marked 10-6. All 1,200 were recalled by S&W and exchanged for Model 28s.

	$550	$500	$375	$300	$250	$175	$150	

MODEL 14 (K-38 TARGET MASTERPIECE) – .38 Spl. cal., K-frame, 6 or 8 3/8 (new 1959) in. barrel, target model, blue only. Mfg. 1947-1981.

	$650	$525	$450	$350	$245	$220	$195	

Add $100 for single action.

There were 4 engineering changes on this model.

MODEL 14 K-38 FULL-LUG – .38 Spl. cal., 6 in. full lug barrel, K-frame, adj. rear sight, combat style Morado wood square butt grips, blue finish, 47 oz. Mfg. 1991-1999.

	$600	$500	$425	$350	$275	$250	$195	*$498*

There were 3 engineering changes on this model.

MODEL 14 CLASSICS (RECENT MFG.) – .38 S&W Spl.+P cal., blue or nickel (disc. 2010) finish, 6 in. barrel, 6 shot, SA/DA, medium frame, wood grips, adj. rear sight, Patridge front sight. Mfg. 2009-2011.

	$695	$550	$450	$375	$335	$295	$250	*$909*

Add $79 for nickel finish (disc. 2010).

MODEL 15 (K-38 COMBAT MASTERPIECE) – .38 Spl. cal., adj. sights, K-frame, 6 shot, square butt, 2 (disc.), 4, 6 (mfg. 1986-91), or 8 3/8 (new 1986, disc.) in. barrel. Disc. 1999.

	$575	$475	$400	$350	$300	$275	$195	*$450*

Add $31 for TT or TH (disc. 1991).
Add $11 for 8 3/8 in. barrel (disc.).

GRADING - PPGS™	100%	98%	95%	90%	80%	70%	60%	LAST MSR

Add $20 for nickel finish (disc. 1987).
Add 300% for USAF marked (mfg. 1965).

There were 9 engineering changes on this model.

MODEL 15 CLASSICS (RECENT MFG.) – .38 S&W Spl.+P cal., blue finish, 4 in. barrel, 6 shot, SA/DA, medium carbon frame, wood grips, adj. rear sight, Patridge front sight. Mfg. 2010-2011.

	$780	$560	$350	$300	$265	$240	$220	*$919*

MODEL 16 (K-32 MASTERPIECE) – .32 S&W Long cal., K-frame, 6 shot, 6 in. barrel, adj. sights, checkered walnut grips, blue finish. Only 3,630 mfg. 1947-1974.

	$1,650	$1,250	$995	$875	$750	$625	$525	

There were 3 engineering changes to this model.

* ***Model 16 Post-War K-32 (Pre-Model 16)*** – mfg. 1946-1957.

	$3,500	$3,200	$2,800	$2,100	$1,800	$1,500	$1,325	

* ***Model 16 Post-War*** – mfg. 1957-1974.

	$2,500	$2,250	$1,950	$1,700	$1,500	$1,250	$1,000	

MODEL 16-4 MASTERPIECE (FULL LUG) – .32 H&R Mag. cal., K-frame, 6 shot, 4 (mfg. 1990-91 only), 6, or 8 3/8 (disc. 1991) in. barrel, square butt, blue finish only, TH and TT. Mfg. 1990-92.

	$1,250	$950	$800	$650	$500	$375	$300	*$419*

Add 5%-10% for 8 3/8 in. barrel.

MODEL 17 (K-22 MASTERPIECE) – .22 LR cal., K-frame, blue only, 6 shot, 4 (mfg. 1986-93), 6 (current mfg.), or 8 3/8 (disc. 1992) in. barrel. Disc. 1993, reintroduced 1996, disc. 1998.

	$750	$625	$550	$450	$375	$300	$200	*$508*

There were 5 engineering changes in this model.

MODEL 17 FULL LUG – .22 LR cal., 6 (mfg. 1990-95) or 10 (mfg. 1996-99) shot, 4, 6, or 8 3/8 in. full lug barrel, steel (6 shot) or alloy (10 shot) cylinder.

	$800	$725	$600	$475	$375	$300	$280	

Add $39 for full lug 6 in. barrel (w/TT & TH, disc.).
Add $50 for full lug 8 3/8 in. barrel (w/TT & TH, disc. 1992).

There were 3 engineering changes in this model.

MODEL 17-2 PROTOTYPE MERCOX DART PROJECTILE GUN – .530 Dart Projectile, .22 Ramset blank gas generator, 12 in. barrel, blue finish only, 25 prototype units mfg. 1966 only.

	$5,000	$4,500	$3,500	N/A	N/A	N/A	N/A	

Add $500 for handmade Safariland holster.
Add $100-$500 depending on variation of projectile (six known).

MODEL 17 CLASSICS (CURRENT MFG.) – .22 LR cal., blue finish, 6 in. barrel, 6 shot, SA/DA, medium frame, wood grips, adj. rear sight, part of S&W's Classic Firearms Series, 40 oz. New 2009.

MSR $959	$725	$625	$535	$465	$415	$375	$325	

MODEL 18 (.22 COMBAT MASTERPIECE) – .22 LR cal., adj. rear sight, 4 in. barrel, blue only. Disc. 1985.

	$750	$650	$550	$475	$400	$375	$325	*$352*

Add $30 for TT and TH. Add $100 for 5 screw frame.

There were 4 engineering changes to this model.

MODEL 18 CLASSICS (RECENT MFG.) – .22 LR cal., blue finish, 4 in. barrel, otherwise similar to Model 18, part of S&W's Classic Firearms Series, 37.6 oz. Mfg. 2009-2011.

	$695	$550	$465	$395	$350	$300	$260	*$919*

GRADING - PPGS™	100%	98%	95%	90%	80%	70%	60%	LAST MSR

COMBAT MAGNUM (PRE-MODEL 19) – .357 Mag. cal., 4 screw frame, bright blue or nickel (scarce) finish.

	100%	98%	95%	90%	80%	70%	60%	LAST MSR
Bright blue finish	$1,850	$1,600	$1,375	$1,050	$875	$675	$550	
Nickel finish (scarce)	$2,750	$2,400	$2,000	$1,600	$1,200	$850	$575	

MODEL 19 – .357 Mag. cal., 4 in. barrel, 4 screw frame, bright blue or nickel finish.

	100%	98%	95%	90%	80%	70%	60%	LAST MSR
Bright blue finish	$1,250	$1,100	$950	$825	$700	$575	$450	
Nickel finish	$1,850	$1,600	$1,375	$1,050	$875	$675	$550	

MODEL 19-1 – .357 Mag. cal., 4 in. barrel, 4 screw frame, stamped "MOD. 19-1" in the yoke cut, bright blue or nickel finish.

	100%	98%	95%	90%	80%	70%	60%	LAST MSR
	$1,850	$1,600	$1,375	$1,050	$875	$675	$550	

MODEL 19-2 – .357 Mag. cal., 2 1/2, 4, or 6 in. barrel, bright blue or nickel finish.

	100%	98%	95%	90%	80%	70%	60%	LAST MSR
	$550	$395	$325	$275	$245	$220	$195	
3 or 5 in. barrel (rare)	$4,500	$4,000	$3,400	$2,800	$2,200	$1,600	$1,000	

MODEL 19-3 (.357 COMBAT MAGNUM) – .357 Mag. cal. (some variations found in .38 Spl.), K-frame, adj. rear sight, 2 1/2 (round butt, disc. 1998), 4 (square butt), or 6 (square butt, disc. 1996) in. barrel, bright blue or nickel (disc. 1992) finish, drilled/tapped receiver and synthetic grips became standard 1994. Disc. 1999.

	100%	98%	95%	90%	80%	70%	60%	LAST MSR
	$550	$395	$325	$275	$245	$220	$195	*$457*

Add $9 for 4 in. or $14 for 6 in. (disc. 1996) barrel.

Add $35 for white outline rear sight (disc. 1994).

Add $20 for nickel finish - disc. 1991.

Add $60 for TS, TT, TH, RR, and WO - disc. 1991 (6 in. barrel only).

This model was supplied with a round butt on 2 1/2 in. barrel. The 2 1/2 and 6 in. barrels (blue finish) were disc. in 1991 along with the 4 and 6 in. nickel variations.

There were 8 engineering changes to this model.

MODEL 20 HEAVY DUTY (.38/44 HEAVY DUTY) – .38 Spl. cal., 6 shot, 4, 5, or 6 1/2 in. barrel lengths, N frame, fixed sights, walnut grips, blue or nickel, walnut grips. Mfg. 1930-1941 and re-introduced 1946 (with "S" prefix starting at serial 62,930), became the Model 20 in 1957.

	100%	98%	95%	90%	80%	70%	60%	LAST MSR
.38/44 H.D. Pre-war	$1,950	$1,750	$1,500	$1,300	$1,075	$875	$700	
Pre-Model 20 (1950-57 mfg.)	$1,125	$975	$825	$700	$575	$500	$425	
Post-war (1958-1966 mfg.)	$2,250	$1,875	$1,600	$1,350	$1,100	$900	$750	

Add 40% for 6 1/2 in. barrel.

Early post-war models had pre-war long action (ser. range S62,489-approx. S74,000).

There were two engineering changes in this model.

MODEL 21 (.44 HAND EJECTOR FOURTH MODEL - MODEL OF 1950 MILITARY) – .44 S&W cal., 6 shot, 4, 5, or 6 1/2 in. barrel, large frame, blue or nickel finish, features short action and redesigned hammer block, walnut grips, fixed sights, 1,200 mfg. scattered throughout serial range S75,000-S263,000. Mfg. 1950-1966.

	100%	98%	95%	90%	80%	70%	60%	LAST MSR
	$2,950	$2,500	$2,000	$1,200	$950	$750	$600	

Add 50% for 6 1/2 in. (rare).

There were 3 engineering changes for this model.

MODEL 21-4 "THUNDER RANCH SPECIAL" – .44 Spl. cal., 4 in. barrel, 24Kt. gold plated Thunder Ranch insignia, blue, nickel, or case colored finish. Mfg. 2004-2006.

	100%	98%	95%	90%	80%	70%	60%	LAST MSR
	$750	$675	$600	$525	$450	$375	$300	*$958*

MODEL 22 (.45 HAND EJECTOR MODEL OF 1950 MILITARY) – .45 Auto Rim (disc. 1966) or .45 ACP cal., same specifications as 1917 Army, except redesigned hammer block, short action, fixed sights. Approx. 1,200 mfg. 1950-1966.

	100%	98%	95%	90%	80%	70%	60%	LAST MSR
	$2,000	$1,750	$1,500	$1,100	$900	$800	$700	

There were 2 engineering changes for this model from 1950-1966.

GRADING - PPGS™	100%	98%	95%	90%	80%	70%	60%	LAST MSR

MODEL 22 CLASSICS – .45 ACP cal., 6 shot, N-frame, 4 or 5 1/2 in. barrel, case colored frame, blue or nickel finish, pinned half-moon service front sight, Altamont wood grips, lanyard ring, carbon steel frame and cylinder, 37.2 oz. Mfg. 2008-2010.

	$850	$650	$525	$465	$415	$375	$325	*$1,090*

Add $87 for nickel finish.
Add $182 for case colored frame.

MODEL 22 CLASSICS, MODEL OF 1917 – .45 ACP cal., 6 shot, 5 1/2 in. barrel, blue finish only, Altamont checkered wood grips, lanyard ring, 37.2 oz. New 2008.

MSR $999	$775	$650	$525	$465	$415	$375	$325

PRE-MODEL 23 – please refer to .38/44 Outdoorsman Model of 1950 in the Early Hand Ejectors section.

MODEL 23 (.38-44 OUTDOORSMAN) – .38 Spl. cal., similar to Model 20 in .38 Spl., except with rear adj. sight, blue only, featured ribbed 6 1/2 in. barrel standard. Mfg. 1930-1967.

Pre-war	$2,500	$2,250	$1,950	$1,700	$1,500	$1,250	$1,000
Post-war (1946-49)	$1,750	$1,550	$1,350	$1,150	$950	$775	$625
Numbered Mod. 23	$2,500	$2,250	$1,950	$1,700	$1,500	$1,250	$1,000

Early post-war models had long action with barrel rib and micrometer sights (ser. range S62,489-approx. S74,000). There were 4,761 pre-war revolvers, 2,036 post-war transitional, and 6,039 styled after the 1950 model.

The "44" in this model's name refers to the size frame, not the caliber. This variation was designated the Model 23 after 1958.

There were 2 engineering changes for this model.

MODEL 24 (.44 HAND EJECTOR FOURTH MODEL - 1950 TARGET) – .44 Spl. cal., redesigned hammer, short action, 6 1/2 in. ribbed barrel standard, satin blue (standard), bright blue (optional), or nickel (optional) finish, micrometer rear sight, ser. no. range S75,000 - S263,000. 5,050 mfg. 1950-1966.

	$2,750	$2,300	$1,650	$1,400	$1,175	$800	$600

Add 20% for bright blue.
Add 50% for 4 in. barrel.
Add 100% for 5 in. barrel.

There were 2 engineering changes for this model.

MODEL 24 – .44 Spl. cal., 4, 5, 5 1/2 (rare), or 6 1/2 in. barrel, bright blue only, checkered Goncalo Alves target grips (without speedloader cutout), barrel and frame not pinned, 7,500 mfg. 1983 only.

* ***Model 24 4 in. barrel.*** – 2,625 mfg.

	$750	$650	$550	$475	$400	$375	$325	

* ***Model 24 6 1/2 in. barrel.*** – 4,875 mfg.

	$725	$650	$550	$500	$450	$375	$300	*$359*

This model's serialization is triple alpha - 4 numeric (i.e. ABC0123).

* ***Model 24 Lew Horton Special*** – .44 Spl. cal., 3 in. barrel, round butt, adj. rear sight, blue finish, includes special fitted holster.

	$850	$750	$625	$525	$475	$375	$300

Subtract 10% without holster.

MODEL 24 CLASSICS (RECENT MFG.) – .44 Spl. cal., N-frame, 3 (Lew Horton only) or 6 1/2 in. barrel, choice of blue or nickel (disc. 2009) finish, carbon steel frame and cylinder, square butt wood grips, 43 oz. Mfg. 2008-2012.

	$765	$640	$525	$465	$415	$375	$325	*$979*

Add $56 for nickel finish (6 1/2 in. barrel only, disc. 2009).

There have been three additional engineering changes in this model.

GRADING - PPGS™	100%	98%	95%	90%	80%	70%	60%	LAST MSR

MODEL 25 (1955 TARGET MODEL) – .45 ACP, .45 Auto Rim, or .45 LC (earlier mfg.) cal., N-frame, blue finish only, target grips, 6 (later mfg.) or 6 1/2 (earlier mfg.) in. barrel. Disc. approx. 1985.

	$700	$600	$500	$400	$350	$300	$235	
.45 LC cal.	$4,200	$3,675	$3,150	$2,855	$2,310	$1,890	$1,470	*$347*

Add $150 for 6 1/2 in. barrel (with pinned barrel, mfg. until 1979).

After 1961, the Model 25 in .45 ACP cal was designated Model 25-2, with trigger guard screw eliminated.

There were 13 engineering changes to this model.

* ***Model 25 Lew Horton Special*** – .45 ACP cal., 3 in. barrel, adj. rear sight, blue finish, 100 mfg.

	$500	$450	$375	$300	$260	$230	$200

MODEL 25 – .45 LC cal., 4, 6, or 8 3/8 in. barrel, blue or nickel finish (no extra charge - disc. 1987). This model was originally marked "45 Cal Model of 1989". Disc. 1991.

	$550	$375	$275	$225	$200	$190	$180	*$429*

Add 5%-10% for 8 3/8 in. barrel.

MODEL 25 CLASSICS (CURRENT MFG.) – .45 ACP cal., 6 shot, N-frame, 3 (Lew Horton) or 6 1/2 in. barrel, blue or nickel (disc. 2010) finish, square butt wood grips, carbon steel frame and cylinder, red ramp front sight, 45 oz. New 2008.

MSR $979	$765	$640	$525	$465	$415	$375	$325

Add $55 for nickel finish (6 1/2 in. barrel only), disc. 2010.

MODEL 26 (.45 HAND EJECTOR MODEL OF 1950 TARGET) – .45 ACP, or .45 LC cal., adj. rear sight, thin ribbed barrel, 2,768 mfg. 1950-1960.

	$4,500	$4,000	$3,500	$2,750	$2,000	$1,500	$1,000

MODEL 27 – .357 Mag. cal., N-frame, 3 1/2 (disc. 1977), 4 (disc. 1991), 5 (disc. 1977), 6, 6 1/2, or 8 3/ 8 (disc. 1991) in. barrel, blue or nickel (disc. 1987) finish. Disc. 1994.

4 screw	$850	$775	$700	$575	$450	$325	$225	
3 screw	$700	$600	$475	$325	$250	$200	$175	*$486*

Add 20% for 3 1/2 or 5 in. barrel.
Add $28 for white outline rear sight - (disc. 1991).
Add $8 for 8 3/8 in. barrel - (disc. 1991).

There were 7 engineering changes to this model.

* ***Model 27 3 1/2 and 5 in. barrel*** – disc.

	$1,200	$1,050	$900	$815	$650	$540	$425

MODEL 27 CLASSICS (CURRENT MFG.) – .357 Mag. cal., N-frame, 4 or 6 1/2 in. barrel, blue or nickel (disc. 2010) finish. New 2008.

MSR $989	$775	$640	$525	$465	$415	$375	$325

Add $40 for 6 1/2 in. barrel.
Add approx. $65 for nickel finish (disc. 2010).

MODEL 28 HIGHWAY PATROLMAN – .357 Mag. cal., "Highway Patrol" utility model, dull blue or brushed nickel (very rare) finish, adj. rear sight, standard grips, blue only, 4 or 6 in. barrel. Mfg. 1954-1986.

1954-1957 mfg.	$850	$775	$700	$575	$450	$325	$225	
1957-1986 mfg.	$495	$400	$350	$300	$275	$250	$225	*$306*

Add $20 for TS.
Add 30% for 5 screw variation (pre-Model 28).
Add 300% for brushed nickel finish (beware of fakes).

There were 3 engineering changes to this model.

MODEL 29 .44 MAGNUM (5 SCREW) – please refer to listing under Early Hand Ejectors, Named Models.

GRADING - PPGS™	100%	98%	95%	90%	80%	70%	60%	LAST MSR

MODEL 29 .44 MAGNUM (4 SCREW) – .44 Mag. cal., 4 screw, can be discerned by 2 exposed screws on lower right sideplate (one is concealed by the right grip, and one in front of the trigger guard). Mfg. began 1957 after approx. ser. no. S172,250 and was disc. 1961.

	$2,100	$1,850	$1,550	$1,250	$1,000	$875	$775	
5 in. barrel (scarce)	$4,500	$3,850	$3,400	$2,950	$2,500	$2,000	$1,500	
5 in. barrel, nickel	$9,500	$8,500	$7,500	$6,500	$5,500	$4,500	$3,500	
5 1/2 in. bbl. (13 known)	$11,500	$10,000	$8,500	$7,000	$5,000	$4,000	$3,000	

Approx. 230 .44 Magnums with a 5 in. barrel were manufactured between the Pre-Model 29 with a 4 screw frame, and the Model 29-2 with a 3 screw frame. Most models were primarely shipped from 1958-1963.

MODEL 29-1 & LATER VARIATIONS (3 SCREW) – .44 Mag. cal., 4, 6 1/2, or 8 3/8 in. barrel, eliminated top screw on sideplate and screw in front of trigger guard. Disc. 1999.

Older .44 Magnum Pre-Model 29 mfg. (4 & 5 screw variations) will appear under the previous subheading: "EARLY HAND EJECTORS (NAMED MODELS)."

* ***Model 29-1*** – stamped "MOD. 29-1" in the yoke cut.

	$3,750	$3,100	$2,650	$2,200	$1,700	$1,400	$1,100	

Rare variations of this model include a 4 screw frame (only 2 known to exist with nickel finish), and a 5 in. barrel (3 known to exist). Values range from $7,500-$9,500, if original condition is better than 95%.

* ***Model 29-2*** – 3 screw frame, 4, 6 1/2, or 8 3/8 in. barrel, bright blue or nickel finish.

S prefix ser. no. (1962-1969)	$1,400	$1,250	$950	$850	$750	$650	$550	
N prefix ser. no. (1970-1983)	$950	$850	$750	$625	$475	$425	$400	
5 in. barrel	$4,200	$3,850	$3,400	$2,950	$2,500	$2,000	$1,500	

Add 10%-20% premium for 4 in. barrels.

The "S" serial number prefix was used on this model until 1968, at which time the law required a new numbering system, and the serial number prefix was changed to "N". The "S" prefix originally designated the additional hammer block safety.

There were 9 engineering changes to this model.

Approx. 230 .44 Magnums with a 5 in. barrel were manufactured between the Pre-Model 29 with a 4 screw frame, and the Model 29-2 with a 3 screw frame. Most models were primarely shipped from 1958-1963.

* ***Model 29-3 & Higher Prefixes***

	$850	$725	$650	$500	$465	$435	$400	*$574*

Add $25-$50 for 4 in. barrel.
Add $50% for 3 in. barrel.
Add $25 for nickel finish (disc. 1991).
Add $1,005 for combat grips with scope mount - disc. 1991 (8 3/8 in. barrel only).

MODEL 29 CLASSICS (MFG. 1990-1994) – .44 Mag. cal., 5, 6 1/2, or 8 3/8 in. full lug barrel, blue only, round butt with Hogue conversion square butt grips, interchangeable front sights with white outline rear sight, frame is drilled and tapped to accept scope mounts, blue finish only. Mfg. 1990-94.

	$695	$600	$500	$425	$350	$325	$300	*$591*

Add $25 for 8 3/8 in. barrel.
Add $100 for 5 in. barrel.

* ***Model 29 Classic DX (Mfg. 1991-1992)*** – similar to Model 29 Classic, except supplied with 2 sets of grips, 6 1/2 or 8 3/8 in. barrel, 5 interchangeable front sights, numbered test target, 51-54 oz. Mfg. 1991-92.

	$1,250	$950	$750	$650	$550	$475	$425	

Add $150 for 5 in. barrel.

GRADING - PPGS™	100%	98%	95%	90%	80%	70%	60%	LAST MSR

MODEL 29 SILHOUETTE – .44 Mag. cal., 10 5/8 in. barrel, adj. front and rear sights, bright blue only, Goncalo Alves target stocks. Mfg. 1983-91.

	$850	$750	$650	$550	$450	$425	$360	*$536*

Add $50 for N prefix serial number.
Add $100 for original presentation case.

MODEL 29 MAGNACLASSIC – .44 Mag. cal., 7 1/2 in. full lug, ported barrel, high polish bright bluing, round butt, interchangeable front sight, supplied with cherry wood display case mfg. in England, 1,200 mfg. in 1990 only.

	$1,150	$900	$800	$625	$500	$450	$395	*$999*

MODEL 29 CLASSIC HUNTER – .44 Mag. cal., 6 in. barrel with full length barrel lug, non-fluted cylinder, Hogue grips, four position adj. front sight. Mfg. late 1980s.

	$850	$695	$550	$450	$400	$350	$300	

MODEL 29 50TH ANNIVERSARY – .44 Mag. cal., N-frame, blue finish, 6 1/2 in. barrel, 6 shot, 24Kt. gold anniversary logo medallion on rear frame signifying 50th anniversary, checkered African cocobolo grips, red ramp front sight, adj. white outline rear sight, includes mahogany presentation case. Limited mfg. 2006.

	$1,075	$950	$825	N/A	N/A	N/A	N/A	*$1,129*

Add 400% for the first 50 with Class A engraving.

MODEL 29 STATE QUARTER LIMITED EDITION COLLECTORS SERIES – .44 Mag. cal., N-frame, 6 1/2 in. barrel, gold bead front sight, Altamont bonded ivory grips, Class "A" engraving, 24 Kt. gold cylinder bands and barrel bands, image of state quarter inlayed in 24 Kt. gold on side plate, includes black walnut glass top presentation case, state coin collector's quarter, a roll of uncirculated state quarters and letter of authenticity.

S&W released these guns through Ellett Brothers circa 2006. While a series of 100 revolvers (2 per state) were planned, only 14 were actually completed. Each gun should be evaluated individually when determining value.

MODEL 29 CLASSICS (CURRENT MFG.) – .44 Mag. or .44 Spl. cal., N-frame, 6 shot, 3 (Lew Horton), 4 (Talo exclusive first year, blue finish only), or 6 1/2 in. barrel, Altamont walnut (6 1/2 in. only), square butt wood (3 in. only), or custom Hogue monogrip (4 in. only), adj. white outline rear sight, black or red ramp front sight, blue or nickel (disc. 2012) finish, 39.3 - 48 1/2 oz. New 2008.

MSR $969	$775	$650	$525	$465	$415	$375	$325	

Add $160 for 6 1/2 in. barrel.
Add $160 for machine engraving and case (new 2010).

MODEL 30 – .32 S&W Long cal., improved I-frame and J-frame, 6 shot, 2, 3, 4, or 6 in. barrel, square butt, walnut grips, fixed sights, blue or nickel finish. Mfg. 1948-1976.

	$495	$350	$250	$220	$195	$175	$165	

There was one engineering change to this model.

MODEL 31 – .32 S&W Long cal., improved I-frame and J-frame, fixed sights, 2, 3 or 4 (disc.) in. barrel, blue or nickel only. Disc. 1991.

	$495	$350	$250	$220	$195	$175	$165	*$365*

Add 25% for early flatlatch models.
There were 3 engineering changes to this model.

MODEL 32 (.38 TERRIER) – .38 S&W cal., 5 shot, 2 in. barrel, walnut or rubber grips, blue or nickel, fixed sights, built on .32 cal. frame. Mfg. 1936-1974.

	$450	$375	$275	$175	$150	$135	$125	

Add $100 for 5 screw frame.

There was one engineering change to this model.

MODEL 032 – .32 Mag. cal., 6 shot, alloy J-frame, blue, scarce, mfg. 1992 only.

	$525	$450	$325	$250	$200	$150	$75	

GRADING - PPGS™	100%	98%	95%	90%	80%	70%	60%	LAST MSR

MODEL 33 (.38 REGULATION POLICE) – .38 S&W cal., 5 shot, 2, 3, or 4 in. barrel, square butt, walnut grips, fixed sights, blue or nickel finish, improved I-frame and J-frame. Mfg. 1958-1974.

	100%	98%	95%	90%	80%	70%	60%	LAST MSR
	$400	$325	$250	$200	$160	$135	$125	

There was one engineering change to this model.

MODEL 34 – .22 LR cal., adj. sights in J-frame, improved I-frame and J-frame, 6 shot, 2 or 4 in. barrel, round or square butt, blue or nickel (disc. 1986) finish, this model was reissued for 2-3 years. Disc. 1991.

	100%	98%	95%	90%	80%	70%	60%	LAST MSR
	$750	$650	$500	$450	$350	$300	$275	$366

Add $25 for nickel finish.
Add 25% for early flatlatch models.

There were 2 engineering changes to this model.

MODEL 35 (.22/32 TARGET MODEL OF 1953) – similar to Standard .22/.32 Hand Ejector Model, except micrometer rear sight, 6 in. barrel, improved I and J-frame, target grips. Mfg. 1953-1974.

	100%	98%	95%	90%	80%	70%	60%	LAST MSR
	$1,150	$950	$800	$700	$500	$450	$400	

There was one engineering change to this model.

MODEL 36 CLASSICS (.38 CHIEFS SPECIAL) – .38 Spl. cal., 5 shot, J-frame, round or square (disc. 1991) butt, 1 7/8 in. regular or 3 in. (heavy only, disc. 1994, reintroduced 2008-2009) barrel, case colored frame (mfg. 2008-2009), blue or nickel (disc. 1992, reintroduced 2008-2012) finish, 19 1/2 oz. Disc. 1999, reintroduced 2008 as part of S&W's Classic Firearms series.

	100%	98%	95%	90%	80%	70%	60%	LAST MSR
MSR $729	$535	$425	$360	$300	$265	$215	$190	

Add $20 for nickel finish (disc. 2012).
Add $20 for 3 in. barrel (disc. 2010).
Add $158 for case colored frame (mfg. 2008-2009).
Add 25% for early small trigger guard and grips (below ser. no. 2,500).

Note: 1st models with high polish blue and diamond grips will bring premiums when mint in original box.

There were 10 engineering changes to this model through 2007.

MODEL 36 TARGET – similar to Model 50, 2 in. barrel, square butt, usually marked 36-1 with target sights, mfg. started 1955.

	100%	98%	95%	90%	80%	70%	60%	LAST MSR
	$850	$725	$650	$575	$500	$400	$350	

MODEL 36 LADYSMITH (36LS) – .38 Spl. +P cal., 5 shot, J-frame, 1 7/8 in. standard or 3 (disc. 1991) in. standard or heavy barrel, blue finish only, Combat Dymondwood grips are anatomically designed for women (round butt on 1 7/8 in., wood combat grips on 3 in.), fixed sights, redesigned double action, 20-23 oz., Morocco grained (disc. 1991) or soft side jewelry case. Mfg. 1990-2008.

	100%	98%	95%	90%	80%	70%	60%	LAST MSR
	$475	$350	$285	$225	$185	$180	$175	$672

MODEL 37 CHIEFS SPECIAL AIRWEIGHT – similar to Model 36 Chiefs Special, except alloy frame and 1 7/8 or 3 (disc. 1988) in. barrel, J-frame, blue or nickel (disc. 1995) finish, barrels are marked "Airweight", no internal lock, 15 oz.

	100%	98%	95%	90%	80%	70%	60%	LAST MSR
	$450	$350	$250	$210	$190	$180	$175	$602

Add $16 for nickel finish (disc.).

There were 3 engineering changes to this model.

MODEL 38 BODYGUARD AIRWEIGHT – .38 S&W Spl. cal., 5 shot, alloy frame, round butt, shrouded hammer, 2 in. barrel, blue or nickel (disc. 1996) finish. Disc. 1998.

	100%	98%	95%	90%	80%	70%	60%	LAST MSR
	$450	$350	$300	$250	$200	$185	$175	$462

Add $15 for nickel finish (disc. 1996).

There were 3 engineering changes for this model.

GRADING - PPGS™	100%	98%	95%	90%	80%	70%	60%	LAST MSR

MODEL 40 CENTENNIAL/CENTENNIAL CLASSICS – .38 S&W Spl. cal., 1 7/8 (new 2008) or 2 (disc. 1974) in. barrel, double action only, fully concealed hammer, grip safety, smooth walnut grips, case colored frame, blue or nickel finish. Mfg. 1952-1974 (non-Classic), reintroduced 2008-2010.

	$645	$535	$425	$350	$315	$275	$235	$877

Add $32 for nickel finish.
Add $174 for case colored frame (disc. 2009).

This model commands a premium for the first series with no letter prefix. After 1968, "L" prefix series began.

MODEL 42 CENTENNIAL AIRWEIGHT – .38 S&W Spl. cal., aluminum variation of Model 40 Centennial, mfg. 1953-1974.

Blue	$595	$500	$425	$395	$325	$300	$265	
Nickel	$1,250	$1,100	$950	$875	$775	$675	$550	

MODEL 42 CLASSICS (CURRENT MFG.) – .38 Spl.+ P cal., 5 shot, aluminum alloy J frame, 1 7/8 in. barrel, blue finish, grip safety lever, DAO, integral black ramp front sight, fixed rear sight, walnut grips, 14.4 oz. New mid-2009-2010.

	$635	$500	$425	$350	$325	$295	$250	$861

MODEL 042 – .38 Spl. cal., 5 shot, blue finish, alloy frame. Mfg. 1992 only.

	$450	$350	$300	$275	$225	$175	$100	

MODEL 43 (.22/32 KIT GUN AIRWEIGHT) – .22 LR cal., 3 1/2 in. barrel, round or square butt, adj. sights, aluminum frame and cylinder, mfg. 1955-74.

	$750	$650	$500	$450	$350	$250	$200	

Add 50% for nickel finish.

MODEL 43C CENTENNIAL – .22 LR cal., 1 7/8 in. barrel, alloy J-frame, blue finish, 8 shot, internal hammer, DAO, rubber grips, fixed rear sight, white bead front sight, 11 oz. New 2010.

MSR $689	$525	$385	$275	$220	$160	$130	$110	

MODEL 45 (.22 MILITARY & POLICE) – .22 LR cal. only, originally mfg. as training gun, not cataloged. Mfg. 1948-1978.

	$2,200	$1,900	$1,650	$1,350	$1,000	$800	$600	

There were 3 engineering changes to this model.

MODEL 48 (K-22 MRF MASTERPIECE) – .22 WMR cal., 4, 6 or 8 3/8 in. barrel, blue only. Disc. 1986.

	$750	$650	$550	$500	$450	$400	$375	$320

Add $25 for 8 3/8 in. barrel.
Add $50 for TT, TH, and TS (disc.).
Add $100 for 4 screw frame.

There were 5 engineering changes to this model.

MODEL 48 CLASSICS (CURRENT MFG.) – .22 WMR cal., 4 or 6 in. barrel, blue finish, wood grips, adj. rear sight, Patridge front sight, carbon steel frame/cylinder, approx. 38 oz. New 2010.

MSR $919	$750	$625	$575	$450	$375	$300	$260	

Add $40 for 6 in. barrel.

MODEL 49 BODYGUARD – similar to Model 38, only steel frame, 2 in. barrel, blue or nickel (disc.) finish. Disc. 1996.

	$450	$350	$300	$250	$225	$200	$175	$409

Add $25 for nickel finish (disc.).
There were 3 engineering changes to this model.

GRADING - PPGS™	100%	98%	95%	90%	80%	70%	60%	LAST MSR

MODEL 50 (.38 CHIEFS SPECIAL TARGET) – .38 S&W Spl. cal., Chiefs Special Target, mfg. from 1955 in 2 in. (see Model 36 Target listing and .38 Chiefs Special Target under Early Hand Ejectors) or 3 (211 mfg. beginning 1973) in. barrels, target sights, most were unmarked for model number, approx. 1,100 mfg. The other variation was designated Model 36 Target.

	$950	$850	$750	$650	$500	$400	$350	

The Model 50 designation was not used until 1970.

MODEL 51 – .22 WMR cal. only, variant of the .22/32 kit gun, 3 1/2 in. barrel, 6 shot, adj. rear sight, blue or nickel, square or round (rare) butt, walnut stocks. Disc. 1974.

	$750	$650	$550	$475	$375	$350	$300	

Add 50% for nickel.
Add 200%-300% for round butt.
Add $150 for extra .22 LR cylinder.

MODEL 53 .22 REM. JET – .22 Jet cal. with S, L, or LR rimfire inserts, 6 shot, 4, 6, or 8 3/8 in. barrel, blue, walnut grips, adj. rear sight. Mfg. 1960-1974.

4 screw	$1,450	$1,250	$975	$850	$675	$575	$500	
3 screw	$1,250	$1,000	$850	$750	$600	$525	$475	

Add 10% for 8 3/8 in. barrel.
Add 15% for 4 in. barrel.
Add $200 for extra matching .22 LR cylinder.
There was one engineering change to this model.

MODEL 56 "USAF" – .38 Spl. cal., 2 in. barrel marked "U.S." on backstrap. 15,205 mfg. 1963 only.

	$7,500	$5,750	$5,000	$4,500	$3,500	$2,900	$2,200	

MODEL 57 – .41 Mag. cal., N-Target frame, 6 shot, 4 (disc. 1991), 5 (1 known, nickel finish), 6, or 8 3/8 (disc. 1991) in. barrel, blue or nickel finish, micrometer rear sight, special oversize Goncalo Alves grips, shrouded extractor rod, "S" ser. no. prefix 1964-68, changed to "N" prefix during 1969, 44-52 oz. Mfg. 1964-1993.

N prefix ser. no.	$850	$750	$650	$550	$400	$350	$300	
S prefix ser. no.	$1,800	$1,600	$1,375	$1,100	$800	$600	$450	*$466*

Add 10-20% for "S" prefix serialization.
Add 10% for nickel finish if NIB.
Add 5% for 8 3/8 in. barrel.
Add 10% for pinned barrel and recessed cylinder.
Current value for the 5 in. barrel model is approx. $12,000.

There were 6 engineering changes to this model.

MODEL 57 CLASSICS (CURRENT MFG.) – .41 Mag. cal., N-frame, 4 (disc. 2010) or 6 in. barrel, blue or nickel (disc. 2010) finish, 6 shot, single action/double action, wood grips, 48.1 oz. New 2009.

MSR $979	$775	$650	$525	$465	$415	$375	$325	

Add approx. $55 for nickel finish (disc. 2010).

MODEL 58 – .41 Mag cal., M&P, fixed sights, 4 in. barrel, blue or nickel finish. Mfg. 1964-1977.

	$850	$775	$650	$575	$500	$400	$300	

Add 10% for nickel finish or "S" serial number prefix.

MODEL 58 CLASSICS (RECENT MFG.) – .41 Mag. cal., 6 shot, SA/DA, bright blue or nickel (disc. 2010) finish, integral ramp front sight, fixed rear sight, wood grips, carbon steel frame/cylinder, 40.8 oz. Mfg. mid-2009-2011.

	$775	$650	$525	$465	$415	$375	$325	*$969*

Add $56 for nickel finish (disc. 2010).

GRADING - PPGS™	100%	98%	95%	90%	80%	70%	60%	LAST MSR

MODEL 60 .38 SPL. CHIEFS SPECIAL – .38 S&W Spl. cal., stainless version of Chiefs Special, 2 or 3 in. standard or full lug barrel. Disc. 1996.

	$450	$350	$300	$250	$200	$150	$120	*$458*

Subtract $25 for 2 in. barrel.

Add 30% for early Model 60s without letter prefix and bright satin finish.

The full lug barrel option began in 1990 with limited mfg. It had been tested for +P ammo and features an adj. rear sight - 24 1/2 oz.

There were 18 engineering changes to the base model in two calibers.

MODEL 60 .357 MAG. CHIEFS SPECIAL – .357 Mag. cal., 2 1/8, 3 (new 1997), or 5 (mfg. 2005-2008) in. barrel, round butt, satin stainless steel, J-frame, Uncle Mike's Combat or wood (5 in. barrel only) grips, 22 1/2 - 30 oz. New 1996.

MSR $729	$525	$400	$325	$265	$220	$180	$160	

Add $30 for 3 in. full lug barrel with adj. rear sight - new 1997, choice of Hi-Viz (disc.) or black blade front sight.

Add $71 for 5 in. barrel (mfg. 2005-2008).

MODEL 60LS (LADYSMITH) – .38 S&W Spl. +P or .357 Mag. cal., 5 shot, 2 in. regular (disc. 1996), 2 1/8 (new 1997), or 3 in. heavy (disc. 1991) barrel, J-frame, frosted stainless steel finish, Combat Dymondwood grips are anatomically designed for women (round butt on 2 in., wood combat grips on 3 in.), fixed sights, redesigned double action, 20-23 oz, Morocco grained (disc. 1991) or soft side jewelry case. New 1990.

MSR $759	$550	$425	$330	$265	$220	$180	$160	

MODEL 60 PRO SERIES – .357 Mag. or .38 S&W Spl. cal., 3 in. barrel, SA/DA, 5 shot, J-frame, adj. rear sight, matte stainless finish, stainless steel frame and cylinder, Pro Series features include chamfered charge holes, front pinned ramp night sight and ergonomic high hand hold oversized laminate grip, 23.4 oz. New mid-2007.

MSR $779	$595	$500	$425	$355	$325	$295	$250	

MODEL 63 .22/32 KIT GUN – .22 LR cal., J-frame, stainless steel kit gun, 2 or 4 in. barrel, 19 oz. Disc. 1998.

	$750	$650	$525	$475	$425	$350	$325	*$476*

Add 25% for 2 in. barrel.

There were 4 engineering changes to this model.

MODEL 63 (CURRENT MFG.) – .22 LR cal., 8 shot, J-frame, stainless steel frame and cylinder, SA/DA, 3 or 5 (disc. 2009) in. barrel, adj. black blade rear sight, black ramp (disc. 2009) or fiber optic (new 2010) front sight, black rubber grips with finger grooves, 28.8 oz. New 2008.

MSR $769	$525	$425	$350	$300	$250	$225	$195	

MODEL 64 M & P – .38 Spl. +P cal., K-frame, satin stainless Model 10, 6 shot, 2 (disc. 2005), 3 (square butt, disc. 1992) or 4 in. (square butt only) barrels are heavy, current production uses Uncle Mike's combat grips, 30 1/2 - 36 oz.

MSR $689	$515	$375	$275	$220	$150	$125	$100	

There have been 8 engineering changes to this model.

MODEL 65 – .357 Mag. cal., stainless version of Model 13, K-frame, has 3 (round butt, disc. 2000) or 4 (square butt) in. heavy barrels, satin stainless steel, current production uses Uncle Mike's grips, fixed sights, 35 oz. Disc. 2004.

	$400	$350	$300	$250	$200	$175	$150	*$563*

There have been 7 engineering changes to this model.

MODEL 65 LADYSMITH – .357 Mag. cal., K-frame, 3 in. barrel with round butt, glass beaded stainless finish, soft side jewelry case, smooth Dymondwood combat grips, 32 oz. Mfg. 1992-2004.

	$400	$325	$230	$180	$145	$125	$105	*$618*

GRADING - PPGS™	100%	98%	95%	90%	80%	70%	60%	LAST MSR

MODEL 66 COMBAT MAGNUM – .357 Mag. cal., K-frame, satin stainless version of Model 19, has 2 1/2, 3 (disc., only 2,500 mfg.), 4, or 6 (disc.) in. barrel, recent production used Uncle Mike's Combat grips, 32-39 oz. Disc. 2004.

	$675	$595	$500	$460	$375	$300	$235	*$614*

Add 10% for 2 1/2 in. barrel.
Add $29 for 6 in. barrel (disc.).
Add $48 for TH and TT with 4 (disc. 1991) or 6 in. barrel only (disc. 1999).

Note: Several models of the Model 66 were made - such features as an all-stainless steel rear sight and a recessed cylinder will bring a slight premium if NIB. There were 6 engineering changes to this model.

MODEL 67 COMBAT MASTERPIECE – .38 S&W Spl.+P cal., K-frame, stainless version of Model 15, has 4 in. barrel, current production uses Uncle Mike's Combat grips, 36 oz. Disc. 1988, reintroduced 1991.

MSR $749	$495	$425	$275	$225	$115	$125	$110	

1991 mfg. included square butt and red ramp front sight insert.

There have been 6 engineering changes to this model.

MODEL 68 – .38 S&W Spl. cal., similar in appearance to the Model 66, except is in .38 Spl. cal., 6 in. barrel, approx. 7,500 mfg.

	$750	$625	$495	$425	$375	$315	$270	

Add 10% for CHP markings.

This model was originally ordered by CA Highway Patrol (usually has "OHB" overstamp).

MODEL 73 – .38 Spl. cal., built on C-frame, 6 shot.

A general price range for this model is $2,250-$5,000.

Most copies of this model were destroyed by S&W in 1973. Few examples have survived.

MODEL 242 AIRLITE Ti CENTENNIAL – .38 Spl.+P cal., L-frame, 7 shot, similar to Model 296. Mfg. 1990 only.

	$500	$400	$300	$240	$210	$180	$155	

MODEL 296 AIRLITE Ti CENTENNIAL – .44 S&W Spl. cal., L-frame, 5 shot, 2 1/2 in. barrel, similar to Model 242 in construction materials, alloy frame and titanium cylinder, Uncle Mike's Boot grips, 18.9 oz. Mfg. 1999-2002.

	$650	$525	$400	$300	$250	$215	$185	*$754*

MODEL 310 NIGHTGUARD – 10mm or .40 S&W (mfg. 2009) cal., 2 3/4 (mfg. 2009) or 2 1/2 (new 2010) in. barrel, matte black finish, large Scandium alloy frame with stainless steel cylinder, 6 shot, SA/DA, XS 24/7 standard dot tritium (mfg. 2009) or night (new 2010) front sight, fixed rear sight, Pachmayr grips, 28 oz. Mfg. 2009-2010.

	$895	$685	$530	$425	$350	$300	$275	*$1,185*

MODEL 315 NIGHTGUARD – .38 Spl. + P cal., 2 1/2 in. barrel, K-frame, blue/black finish, 6 shot, rubber grips, front night sight, fixed rear sight, alloy frame with stainless cylinder. Mfg. 2009 only.

	$740	$550	$460	$385	$335	$295	$250	*$995*

MODEL 317 AIRLITE/KIT GUN – .22 LR cal., J-frame, 8 shot, 1 7/8 (disc. 2012), or 3 (new 1998, Hi-Viz sights became standard in 2001, Model 317 Kit Gun) in. barrel, combination of aluminum alloy or stainless steel (disc.) construction, brushed aluminum (disc.) clear coat (1 7/8 in.) or matte silver (3 in.) finish, round (Kit gun) or square butt, choice of synthetic or Dymondwood Boot (disc. 1998) grips, fixed sights, approx. 10 1/2 oz. New 1997.

MSR $759	$575	$425	$325	$295	$250	$200	$150	

Add $33 for Dymondwood Boot grips (disc.).

There have been three engineering changes to this model.

* ***Model 317 Airlite LadySmith*** – .22 LR cal., 1 7/8 in. barrel only, includes Dymondwood Boot grips, 9.9 oz. Mfg. 1998-2002.

	$445	$320	$220	$170	$135	$120	$100	*$596*

GRADING - PPGS™	100%	98%	95%	90%	80%	70%	60%	LAST MSR

MODEL 325 PD-AIRLITE Sc – .45 ACP cal., 2 1/2 (disc. 2006) or 4 in. barrel, otherwise similar to Model 329 PD, approx. 21 1/2 - 25 oz. Mfg. 2004-2007.

	$800	$625	$485	$400	$335	$300	$275	$1,067

MODEL 325 NIGHTGUARD – .45 ACP cal., two-piece 2 1/2 in. barrel, alloy frame with stainless steel cylinder, black alloy finish, 6 shot, N-frame, SA/DA, rubber grips, fixed rear sight with front night sight, 28 oz. Mfg. 2008-2012.

	$825	$650	$525	$425	$350	$300	$275	$1,049

MODEL 327 PD-AIRLITE Sc – .357 Mag. cal., 8 shot, N-frame, 4 in. two-piece barrel, wood grips, Scandium frame with titanium cylinder, matte black finish, 26 1/2 oz. Mfg. 2008-2009.

	$950	$725	$550	$450	$350	$315	$285	$1,264

MODEL 327 NIGHTGUARD – .357 Mag. cal., two-piece 2 1/2 in. barrel, alloy frame with stainless steel cylinder, black alloy finish, 8 shot, N-frame, SA/DA, rubber grips, fixed rear sight with front night sight, 27.6 oz. Mfg. 2008-2012.

	$825	$650	$525	$425	$350	$300	$275	$1,049

MODEL 329 PD-AIRLITE Sc – .44 Mag. cal., 4 in. barrel, N-frame, 6 shot, Scandium frame and titanium cylinder with matte black metal finish, wood Ahrends grips with finger grooves, and Hogue rubber monogrip, Hi-Viz front sight, approx. 26 oz. New 2003.

MSR $1,159	$915	$715	$550	$450	$375	$325	$300	

MODEL 329 XL HUNTER AIRLITE Sc – .44 Mag. or .44 Spl. cal., N-frame, SA/DA, 6 1/2 in. barrel, blue finish, rubber grips, fixed rear sight, fiber optic front sight. Mfg. 2010 only.

	$860	$675	$525	$425	$350	$300	$275	$1,138

MODEL 329 NIGHTGUARD – .44 Mag. cal., two-piece 2 1/2 in. barrel, alloy frame with stainless steel cylinder, black alloy finish, 6 shot, N-frame, SA/DA, rubber grips, fixed rear sight with front night sight, 29.3 oz. Mfg. 2008-2012.

	$825	$650	$525	$425	$350	$300	$275	$1,049

MODEL 331 AIRLITE Ti CHIEFS SPECIAL – .32 H&R Mag. cal., J-frame, 6 shot, 1 7/8 in. barrel with stainless steel liner, features titanium cylinder and aluminum alloy frame, barrel shroud, and yoke, fixed sights, Uncle Mike's or Dymondwood Boot (disc.) wood grips, two-tone matte stainless/grey finish approx. 12 oz. Mfg. 1999-2003.

	$575	$450	$375	$335	$300	$275	$250	$716

Add $24 for Dymondwood Boot grips (mfg. 1999 only).

MODEL 332 AIRLITE Ti CENTENNIAL – .32 H&R Mag. cal., J-frame, similar to Model 331 Airlite Ti, except is hammerless and double action only, recent production used Uncle Mike's Boot grips, 12 oz. Mfg. 1999-2003.

	$575	$455	$390	$345	$310	$280	$250	$734

Add $24 for Dymondwood Boot grips (mfg. 1999 only).

MODEL 332 AIRWEIGHT CENTENNIAL – .32 H&R Mag. cal., J-frame, 6 shot, blue finish. Approx. 380 mfg., most exported during 1994 only.

	$495	$450	$375	$325	$250	$215	$185	

MODEL 337 AIRLITE Ti CHIEFS SPECIAL – .38 S&W Spl.+P cal., J-frame, 5 shot, 1 7/8 in. barrel, similar design as the Model 331, 11.9 oz. Mfg. 1999-2003.

	$565	$435	$375	$335	$310	$280	$250	$716

Add $24 for Dymondwood Boot grips (mfg. 1999 only).

MODEL 337 AIRLITE Ti KIT GUN – .38 S&W Spl.+P cal., J-frame, 5 shot, 3 1/8 in. barrel with Hi-Viz front sight (new 2001), choice of Dymondwood or Uncle Mike's combat grips, approx. 13 oz. Mfg. 2000-2003.

	$600	$460	$385	$345	$315	$285	$250	$779

MODEL 337 PD AIRLITE Ti CHIEFS SPECIAL – .38 S&W Spl.+P cal., J-frame, 5 shot, 1 7/8 in. barrel, black/grey finish, black Hogue Bantam grips, 10.7 oz. Mfg. 2000-2003.

	$580	$450	$385	$340	$310	$280	$250	$740

GRADING - PPGS™	100%	98%	95%	90%	80%	70%	60%	LAST MSR

MODEL 340 AIRLITE Sc CENTENNIAL – .357 Mag. cal., J-frame, 5 shot, 1 7/8 in. barrel only, Scandium alloy frame, barrel shroud, and yoke, titanium cylinder, two-tone matte stainless/grey finish, hammerless, Hogue Bantam grips, 12 oz. Mfg. 2001-2008.

	$775	$575	$475	$400	$340	$295	$250	*$1,019*

MODEL 340 PD AIRLITE Sc (CENTENNIAL) – similar to Model 340 Airlite Sc, except has black/grey finish, Hi-Viz sight became standard 2009, also available with no internal lock (new 2011), 12 oz. New 2000.

MSR $1,019	$795	$625	$500	$400	$340	$295	$250	

MODEL 340 M & P (CENTENNIAL) – .357 Mag. cal., 5 shot, J-frame, DAO, concealed hammer, 1 7/8 in. barrel, includes XS sights (24/7 tritium night and integral U-notch), Scandium alloy frame with stainless steel cylinder, also available with no internal lock (new 2011), matte black finish, synthetic or Crimson Trace laser grips, 13.3 oz. New 2007.

MSR $869	$600	$500	$395	$325	$275	$250	$225	

Add $260 for Crimson Trace laser grips.

MODEL 342 AIRLITE Ti CENTENNIAL – .38 S&W Spl.+P cal., similar to Model 337, except is hammerless and double action only, matte stainless/grey finish, Uncle Mike's Boot grips, 12 oz. Mfg. 1999-2003.

	$575	$445	$390	$345	$310	$280	$250	*$734*

Add $24 for Dymondwood Boot grips (mfg. 1999 only).

MODEL 342 PD AIRLITE Ti CENTENNIAL – .38 S&W Spl.+P cal., J-frame, 5 shot, double action only, aluminum alloy frame with titanium cylinder and stainless steel 1 7/8 in. barrel, hammerless, black/grey finish, Hogue Bantam grips, 10.8 oz. Mfg. 2000-2003.

	$595	$460	$390	$340	$310	$280	$250	*$758*

MODEL 351 PD AIRLITE Sc (CHIEFS SPECIAL, CENTENNIAL) – .22 WMR cal., J-frame, 1 7/8 in. barrel, 7 shot, black finish, aluminum (new 2007) or Scandium (disc. 2006) alloy frame and cylinder, wood grips, 10.6 oz. New 2004.

MSR $759	$575	$495	$400	$310	$255	$220	$200	

MODEL 351C AIRLITE (CENTENNIAL) – .22 WMR cal., Centennial style J-frame, 1 7/8 in. barrel, 7 shot, internal hammer, DAO, white dot sights, matte black metal finish, alloy frame and cylinder, synthetic grips, 11 oz. New 2010.

MSR $689	$540	$475	$375	$275	$225	$200	$180	

MODEL 357 PD – .41 Rem. Mag. cal., 6 shot, 4 in. barrel, N frame, Scandium alloy frame with titanium cylinder, matte black finish, uncheckered wood grips with finger grooves, Hi-Viz front sight, adj. V-notch rear sight, 27 1/2 oz. Mfg. mid-2005-2007.

	$815	$575	$475	$400	$340	$300	$275	*$1,067*

MODEL 357 NIGHTGUARD – .41 Mag. cal., 2 1/2 in. barrel, N-frame, matte black metal finish, 6 shot, black synthetic grips, alloy frame with stainless steel cylinder, fixed rear sight, front night sight, 29.7 oz. Mfg. 2010 only.

	$895	$685	$530	$425	$350	$300	$275	*$1,185*

MODEL 360 AIRLITE Sc CHIEFS SPECIAL – .357 Mag. cal., J-frame, 5 shot, 1 7/8 in. barrel, Scandium alloy frame with titanium cylinder, matte stainless/grey finish, Hogue Bantam grips, fixed sights, 12 oz. Mfg. 2001-2007.

	$775	$575	$475	$400	$340	$295	$250	*$1,019*

MODEL 360 PD AIRLITE Sc (CHIEFS SPECIAL) – .357 Mag. or .38 Spl. + P cal., similar to Model 360 Airlite Sc Chiefs Special, except has matte stainless/grey finish, Hi-Viz sight became standard 2009, 12 oz. New 2002.

MSR $1,019	$850	$675	$525	$400	$340	$295	$250	

MODEL 360 AIRLITE Sc KIT GUN – .357 Mag. cal., J-frame, 5 shot, 3 1/8 in. barrel with Hi-Viz front sight, Scandium alloy frame with titanium cylinder, matte stainless/grey finish, Uncle Mike's Combat grips, 14 1/2 oz. Mfg. 2001-2007.

	$775	$650	$525	$435	$365	$325	$280	*$940*

GRADING - PPGS™	100%	98%	95%	90%	80%	70%	60%	LAST MSR

MODEL 360 M & P (CHIEFS SPECIAL) – .357 Mag. cal., 5 shot, J-frame, SA/DA, 1 7/8 in. barrel, includes XS sights (24/7 tritium night and integral U-notch), Scandium alloy frame with stainless steel cylinder, matte black finish, synthetic grips, 13.3 oz. Mfg. 2007-2012.

$725	$600	$475	$350	$300	$250	$225	*$869*

MODEL 386 AIRLITE Sc MOUNTAIN LITE – .357 Mag. cal., L-frame, 7 shot, 2 1/2 (new 2007) or 3 1/8 (disc. 2006) in. stainless steel barrel with Hi-Viz front sight, Scandium alloy frame with titanium cylinder, two-tone matte stainless/grey finish, Hogue Bantam grips, 18 1/2 oz. Mfg. 2001-2007.

$650	$510	$420	$365	$325	$295	$265	*$869*

MODEL 386 PD AIRLITE Sc – .357 Mag. cal., L-frame, 7 shot, 2 1/2 in. stainless barrel with adj. black rear sight, Scandium alloy frame with titanium cylinder, black/grey finish, Hogue Bantam grips, 17 1/2 oz. Mfg. 2001-2005.

$665	$500	$415	$355	$315	$285	$250	*$872*

Add $22 for Hi-Viz front sight (disc. 2005).

MODEL 386 Sc/S – .357 Mag. cal., L-frame, 7 shot, 2 1/2 in. barrel, synthetic finger groove grips, matte black finish, Scandium alloy frame with stainless steel cylinder, red ramp front sight, adj. rear sight, 21.2 oz. Mfg. mid-2007-2008.

$775	$600	$475	$385	$335	$295	$265	*$948*

MODEL 386 NIGHTGUARD – .357 Mag. cal., two-piece 2 1/2 in. barrel, alloy frame with stainless cylinder, black alloy finish, 7 shot, L-frame, SA/DA, rubber grips, fixed rear sight with front night sight, 24 1/2 oz. Mfg. 2008-2012.

$750	$595	$500	$450	$400	$350	$325	*$979*

MODEL 386 XL HUNTER (AIRLITE Sc) – .357 Mag. or .38 Spl. + P cal., 7 shot, L-frame, SA/DA, 6 in. barrel, black synthetic grips, adj. rear sight, Hi-Viz fiber optic front sight, alloy frame with stainless steel cylinder, matte black finish, 30 oz. Mfg. 2010-2012.

$695	$550	$450	$425	$375	$325	$300	*$899*

MODEL 396 AIRLITE Ti MOUNTAIN LITE – .44 S&W Spl. cal., L-frame, 5 shot, 3 1/8 in. barrel with stainless liner and Hi-Viz front sight, aluminum alloy frame with titanium cylinder, matte stainless/grey finish, Hogue Bantam grips, 18 oz. Mfg. 2001-2004.

$625	$475	$400	$355	$315	$285	$250	*$812*

There has been one engineering change to this model.

MODEL 396 NIGHTGUARD – .44 Spl. cal., two-piece 2 1/2 in. barrel, alloy frame with stainless steel cylinder, black alloy finish, 5 shot, L-frame, SA/DA, rubber grips, fixed sight with front night sight, 24.2 oz. Mfg. 2008-2009.

$825	$650	$550	$475	$425	$375	$335	*$1,074*

MODEL 431 CENTENNIAL AIRWEIGHT – .32 H&R Mag cal., J-frame, 6 shot, 2 in. barrel, blue finish. New mid-2004-2005.

$425	$375	$300	$260	$230	$200	$180	*$450*

MODEL 432 CENTENNIAL AIRWEIGHT – .32 H&R Mag cal., J-frame, DAO, 6 shot, 2 in. barrel, blue finish. New mid-2004-2005.

$450	$365	$310	$265	$235	$200	$180	*$469*

Add $263 for Crimson Trace laser grips (new 2005).

MODEL 437 CHIEFS SPECIAL AIRWEIGHT – .38 Spl. +P cal., blue finish with stainless cylinder, barrel and small parts, special edition - not cataloged. Limited mfg. 2010.

$495	$450	$375	$325	$250	$215	$185

MODEL 438 AIRWEIGHT (BODYGUARD) – .38 Spl.+P cal., 1 7/8 in. barrel, shrouded hammer, matte black metal finish, J-frame, 5 shot, black synthetic grips, SA/DA, fixed rear sight, black blade front sight, alloy frame with stainless steel cylinder, approx. 15 oz. Mfg. 2009-2012.

$350	$315	$260	$225	$180	$150	$125	*$449*

GRADING - PPGS™	100%	98%	95%	90%	80%	70%	60%	LAST MSR

MODEL 442 AIRWEIGHT (CENTENNIAL) – .38 S&W Spl.+P cal., J-frame, 5 shot, DAO, 1 7/8 in. barrel only with fixed sights, hammerless, aluminum alloy/steel frame, blue (disc.), matte black (current mfg.) or nickel (disc. 1995) finish, round butt, optional Pro Series version with full moon clip (new 2010), synthetic, Uncle Mike's Boot (disc.), or pink (new 2012) grips, no lock became an option during 2011, 15 oz. New 1993.

MSR $459	$350	$315	$250	$215	$170	$150	$125	

Add $20 for pink grips (new 2012).
Add $20 for Pro Series version (new 2010).
Add $15 for nickel finish (disc.).
Add $270 for machine engraving and case (new 2010).
There have been two engineering changes to this model.

MODEL 460 V/XVR – .460 S&W Mag. cal., 5 shot, X-frame, SA/DA, 5 (V, disc. 2010, reintroduced 2013) or 8 1/2 (XVR) in. barrel with Hi-Viz sights, stainless steel frame with matte finish (approx. 16 mfg. in blue/black finish), similar in design to the Model 500, many variations and barrel lengths, approx. 70 oz. New 2005.

MSR $1,319	$1,075	$940	$785	$675	$575	$475	$425	

Product Codes: 163460 and 163465

MODEL 500 – .500 S&W Mag. cal., X-frame, 5 shot, DA, two-piece 4 (new 2004), 6 1/2 (new 2009), or 8 3/8 in. ported barrel with full shroud, stainless steel, recoil compensator, new Sorbathane Hogue wraparound rubber finger groove grips, micrometer click adj. rear sight, red ramp (4 in. barrel) or interchangeable front sight blades (8 3/8 in. barrel only), frame is drilled and tapped, many variations and barrel lengths, 56 or 72 1/2 oz. (with 8 3/8 in. barrel), satin finish. New 2003.

MSR $1,249	$975	$825	$725	$625	$550	$450	$395	

Add $70 for 4 in. barrel.
Add $70 for Hi-Viz sights (8 3/8 in. barrel only, new 2005).

* ***Model 500 SCI "Big 5" Master's Edition*** – features hand engraving by S&W master engraver Wayne D'Angelo, with 24Kt. gold inlays of the African Big 5 animals, ivory grips, includes presentation case, serial numbered SCI001-SCI005. Limited mfg. 2004.

	$10,000	$8,000	$6,000	N/A	N/A	N/A	N/A	*$10,000*

* ***Model 500 SCI "Big 5" Limited Edition*** – features roll engraving, with 24Kt. gold inlays of the African Big 5 animals, ivory grips, includes presentation case, serial numbered SCI0006-SCI0300. Limited mfg. 2004.

	$3,000	$2,250	$1,500	N/A	N/A	N/A	N/A	*$3,000*

MODEL 520 (1980 MFG.) – .357 Mag. cal., 4 in. barrel, fixed sights, N-frame, originally ordered for N.Y. State Police but never purchased. Approx. 3,000 mfg. with box during 1980 only.

	$925	$800	$700	$575	$450	$350	$275	

MODEL 520 (RECENT MFG.) – .357 Mag. cal., L-frame, two-piece, semi-lug 4 in. barrel, 7 shot, adj. rear sight, wood grips with finger grooves, matte black finish, carbon steel frame with titanium cylinder, Hi-Viz front sight, 37.9 oz. Mfg. mid-2005-2006.

	$495	$425	$375	$330	$295	$265	$235	*$731*

MODEL 544 – please refer to the Commemorative section.

MODEL 547 M & P – 9mm Para. cal., 3 or 4 in. heavy barrel, 6 shot, round (3 in. barrel) or square (4 in. barrel) butt, blue only, 32 oz. Disc. 1985.

	$1,000	$675	$575	$450	$350	$275	$225	*$317*

Add 10% for 3 in. model.

MODEL 581 (DISTINGUISHED SERVICE MAGNUM) – .357 Mag. cal., L-Frame, fixed sights, 4 in. barrel, 6 shot, blue or nickel finish, 38 oz. Disc. 1992.

	$600	$525	$450	$375	$300	$250	$200	*$335*

Add $20 for nickel (mfg. 1980-88).

GRADING - PPGS™	100%	98%	95%	90%	80%	70%	60%	LAST MSR

MODEL 586 (DISTINGUISHED COMBAT MAGNUM) – .357 Mag. cal., L-Frame, 4, 6, or 8 3/8 (disc. 1991) in. barrel, adj. rear sight, blue or nickel (disc. 1991) finish. Disc. 1999.

$650 $550 $450 $375 $300 $250 $200 *$494*

Add 5%-10% for nickel finish (disc.).
Add $4 for white outline rear sight (disc. 1994).
Add $5 for 6 in. barrel.
Add $22 for 8 3/8 in. barrel (disc. 1991).
Add $35 for adj. front sight - disc. 1991 (6 in. barrel only, new 1986).

There have been 7 engineering changes to this model.

MODEL 586 CLASSICS DISTINGUISHED COMBAT MAGNUM – .38 S&W Spl.+P cal., N-frame, 6 shot, 4 or 6 in. barrel, blue finish, wood grips. New 2012.

MSR $809 $595 $475 $350 $250 $210 $185 $165

MODEL 610 CLASSIC – 10mm Norma or .40 S&W cal., N-frame, 6 shot, 4 (new 2001), 5 (disc. 2000), or 6 1/2 (disc. 2000) in. full lug barrel, stainless steel construction, fluted or unfluted (4 or 6 1/2 in. barrel only) cylinder, round butt, adj. rear sight, current production uses Hogue rubber grips, target hammer optional, 50 oz., approx. 5,000 mfg. 1990 only, reintroduced 1998-2004.

$650 $525 $425 $350 $295 $245 $215 *$833*

There have been three engineering changes to this model.

MODEL 610 (RECENT MFG.) – 10mm or .40 S&W cal., 3 7/8 or 6 in. barrel, stainless N-frame, satin finish, 6 shot, SA/DA, rubber grips, black blade front sight, adj. rear sight. Mfg. 2009.

$725 $600 $525 $400 $350 $300 $250 *$1,043*

MODEL 617 K-22 MASTERPIECE STAINLESS – .22 LR cal., K-frame, stainless steel variation of the Model 17 (K-22 Masterpiece), 4, 6, or 8 3/8 (disc. 2002) in. full lug barrel, 6 (6 in. full lug barrel only mfg. 1999-2009) or 10 (new 1997, current mfg.) shot, satin stainless finish, combat trigger and Hogue rubber grips are standard on current production, semi-target, 41-52 1/2 oz. New 1990.

MSR $829 $750 $650 $525 $475 $400 $380 $325

Add $54 for 8 3/8 in. barrel (disc. 2002).
Subtract 5% for 6 shot cylinder.

In 2000, this model included target hammer with 8 3/8 in. barrel. 4 and 6 in. barrels were standard during a limited production period in 1991.

MODEL 619 – .357 Mag. cal., L-frame, 7 shot, two-piece 5 in. barrel, stainless steel with satin finish, rubber grips, fixed sights, 37 1/2 oz. Mfg. 2005-2006.

$450 $375 $275 $225 $185 $150 $125 *$646*

MODEL 620 – .357 Mag. cal., 4 in. barrel, similar to Model 619, except has white outline rear sight and red ramp front sight, 38 oz. Mfg. 2005-2009.

$585 $465 $385 $325 $270 $225 $195 *$893*

MODEL 624 .44 TARGET – .44 S&W Spl. cal., 6 shot, 4 or 6 1/2 in. barrel, 42 oz. Mfg. 1986-1987 only.

$675 $595 $525 $450 $395 $365 $340 *$449*

Add $14 for 6 1/2 in. barrel.

MODEL 625 (MODEL OF 1988/MODEL OF 1989) – .45 ACP or .45 LC cal., DA, round butt N target frame with three screws, 6 shot, fluted cylinder, 3, 4, or 5 in. full lug barrel, Pachmayr or Hogue grips, non-glare glass bedded matte finish, smooth combat trigger, adj. rear sight, first introduction of this model is actually Model 625-2, early variations can be marked "Model of 1988" or "Model of 1989". Mfg. 1989-disc.

$625 $500 $425 $350 $325 $295 $250

MODEL 625 JM – .45 ACP or .45 Colt (disc.) cal., N-frame, stainless variation of the Model 25-2, 6 shot, 3 (disc. 1991), 4 (disc. 1991, reintroduced 2002), or 5 (disc. 2010) in. barrel, round butt, choice of matte (mfg. 2005-2007) or satin stainless finish, ramp front

GRADING - PPGS™	100%	98%	95%	90%	80%	70%	60%	LAST MSR

(3 or 4 in. barrel) or Patridge front (5 in. barrel) sight, full lug barrel, Pachmayr (disc.), Jerry Miculek wood, or Hogue rubber combat (disc. 2008) grips, 45 oz. New 1988.

MSR $979	$795	$650	$550	$475	$425	$375	$335	

Subtract approx. 5% if w/o Jerry Miculek initialled wood grips, which became standard during 2009 (originally introduced during 2007).

Approx. 1,500 of the 5 in. barrel models had the frame stamped "625-2", roll engraved barrel with "45 Cal Model of 1989" barrel inscription, and a ramp front sight. Laser engraving replaced roll engraving in 1989.

There have been 10 engineering changes for this model.

MODEL 627 (OLDER MFG.) – .357 Mag. cal., originally marked "357 Magnum Model of 1989" (stamped on barrel), N-frame, smooth combat grips, S&W medallion logo, round butt, unfluted cylinder, full underlug 5 1/2 in. barrel. Disc.

	$700	$600	$500	$425	$325	$265	$230	

This model evolved into a Performance Center model.

MODEL 627 (RECENT MFG.) – .357 Mag. cal., 8 shot, SA/DA, 4 in. barrel, N-frame, adj. rear sight, red ramp front sight, stainless steel frame, rubber finger groove grips, 42 oz. Mfg. 2008-2009.

	$750	$600	$425	$350	$300	$275	$250	*$1,003*

MODEL 627 PRO SERIES – .357 Mag. or .38 Spl.+P cal., similar to Model 627 (recent mfg.), except has Pro Series features, including custom barrel with recessed precision crown, chamfered charge holes, and bossed main spring, 41.2 oz. New 2008.

MSR $969	$750	$625	$525	$475	$425	$375	$325	

MODEL 629 PINNED BARREL – .44 Mag. cal., 4, 6, or 8 3/8 in. barrel, features pin barrel and counter bored charge holes in cylinder. Disc.

	$950	$850	$725	$675	$600	$525	$450	
4 in. barrel	$1,050	$900	$775	$650	$525	$450	$350	
Pre-production	$3,500	$3,050	$2,625	$2,375	$1,925	$1,575	$1,225	

During 1978, 100 pre-production revolvers were made with pinned barrels and recessed cylinders, serial range is N629,062-N629,200, includes wood box. Values for these prototype Model 29 revolvers range from $1,500-$3,000 depending on original condition.

MODEL 629 – .44 Mag./.44 S&W Spl. cal., N-frame, 6 shot, similar to Model 29 mfg. 1990-1994, available with 4, 5 (disc.), 6, or 8 3/8 (disc. 2002) in. barrel, satin stainless, current production uses Hogue rubber combat grips, 41 1/2 - 49 1/2 oz. New 1979.

MSR $949	$725	$600	$525	$425	$350	$300	$250	

Add $47 for fully shrouded 5 in. barrel (disc.) or $39 for 8 3/8 in. barrel (disc.).

Add $52 for combat grips and barrel scope mount (cut across barrel rib) - disc. 1991 (8 3/8 in. barrel only).

Add $198 for Model 629 ES (Emergency Survival) kit with blankets, knife, compass, whistle, signal mirror, fire starter, tinder, chain saw, "Bear Attacks of the Century" book and waterproof storm case (disc.)

* ***Model 629 Backpacker*** – similar to Model 629, except 3 in. barrel, Hogue rubber grips, red ramp front sight, white outline rear sight, 40 oz. Introduced 1994.

	$795	$700	$650	$600	$525	$475	$375	

MODEL 629 CLASSIC – .44 Mag./.44 S&W Spl. cal., satin stainless steel variation of the Model 29 Classic, 5, 6 1/2 (with or w/o PowerPort), or 8 3/8 (disc. 2010) in. barrel, current production uses Hogue rubber combat grips, 49 1/2 - 53 1/2 oz. New 1990.

MSR $989	$750	$625	$540	$450	$375	$325	$300	

Add $16 for Powerport (disc. 2008).

Add $27 for 6 1/2 in. barrel with white outline rear sight (disc.).

Add $54 for Hi-Viz front sight, 6 1/2 in. barrel only (disc.).

Add $245 for Crimson Trace laser grips (Model 629CT, mfg. 2006).

GRADING - PPGS™	100%	98%	95%	90%	80%	70%	60%	LAST MSR

* ***Model 629 Classic DX*** – similar to Classic, except is supplied with 2 sets of grips (Hogue combat square and Morado wood round buttstocks), 6 1/2 or 8 3/8 in. barrel, satin stainless finish, 5 interchangeable front sights, numbered test target, 51-54 oz. Mfg. 1992-2002.

	$875	$750	$700	$650	$575	$520	$475	*$986*

Add $32 for 8 3/8 in. barrel.

* ***Model 629 Magna Classic*** – .44 Mag. cal., similar to Model 29, 1,800 mfg. during 1990 only.

	$975	$875	$800	$700	$650	$550	$490	*$999*

MODEL 631 – .32 H&R Mag. cal., 6 shot, 2 (fixed sight) or 4 (adj. sight) in. barrel, combat stocks, round butt only, stainless steel J-frame, approx. 5,500 mfg. 1990-1992.

	$795	$700	$650	$575	$500	$450	$425	*$386*

MODEL 631 LADYSMITH – .32 H&R Mag. cal., 2 in. barrel only, rosewood stocks, LadySmith marked.

	$400	$350	$300	$250	$195	$150	$125	*$400*

MODEL 632 CENTENNIAL – .32 H&R Mag. cal., 2 or 3 (mfg. 1991 only) in. barrel, stainless/alloy construction, fully concealed hammer, J-frame, Santoprene combat grips, fixed sights, 15 1/2 oz. Mfg. 1991-1992.

	$500	$450	$350	$250	$195	$165	$140	*$410*

Add 20% for 3 in. barrel.

MODEL 632 PRO SERIES – .327 Mag. cal., 2 1/8 (new 2010) or 3 (disc.) in. black PowerPort barrel, blue/black finish, 6 shot, stainless small frame and cylinder, rubber grips, SA/DA, adj. sight, night sights (new 2010), approx. 23 oz. Mfg. 2009-2012.

	$600	$475	$350	$275	$225	$195	$165	*$809*

Add $90 for 3 in. PowerPort barrel and blue/black metal finish with SA/DA action.

MODEL 637 AIRWEIGHT (CHIEFS SPECIAL) – .38 S&W Spl.+P cal., J-frame, 5 shot, matte finish, alloy frame with 1 7/8 (current mfg.), 2 1/8 (PowerPort only, disc.), or 2 1/2 (mfg. 2010 only) in. satin stainless steel barrel and cylinder, current production uses Uncle Mike's Boot, Crimson Trace Laser (new 2005), or pink (new 2012) grips, 15 oz., 560 mfg. during 1991, reintroduced 1996.

MSR $459	$350	$315	$275	$225	$190	$170	$150	

Add $20 for pink grips (new 2012).
Add $16 for Carry Combo configuration (mfg. 2004-2008).
Add $230 for Crimson Trace laser grips (new 2005).
Add $24 for 2 1/2 in. barrel (mfg. 2010 only).
Add $142 for 2 1/8 in. barrel with PowerPort (Pro Series, mfg. 2009-2010).

MODEL 638 AIRWEIGHT (BODYGUARD) – .38 S&W Spl.+P cal., J-frame, 5 shot, alloy frame, 1 7/8 or 2 1/2 (mfg. 2010 only) in. stainless steel barrel and cylinder, shrouded hammer, round butt, Uncle Mike's Boot, Crimson Trace Laser, or pink (new 2012) grips, 15 oz. 1,200 mfg. during 1990 only, reintroduced 1998.

MSR $459	$350	$315	$275	$225	$190	$170	$150	

Add $20 for pink grips (new 2012).
Add $24 for 2 1/2 in. barrel (disc. 2010).
Add $230 for Crimson Trace laser grips (new 2010).

MODEL 640 (CENTENNIAL) – .357 Mag./.38 Spl.+P or .38 S&W Spl. (disc.) cal., J-frame, 5 shot, double action only, 1 7/8 (mfg. 1998-2001), 2 1/8 (new 1991), or 3 (disc. 1992) in. barrel, hammerless, current production uses Uncle Mike's Combat grips, satin stainless, round butt, Pro Series version with full moon clips became optional 2010, 23 oz. New 1991.

MSR $729	$525	$450	$375	$315	$265	$215	$190	

Add $190 for machine engraving and case (new 2009).
Add $80 for Pro Series features with full moon clips (new 2010).

GRADING - PPGS™	100%	98%	95%	90%	80%	70%	60%	LAST MSR

MODEL 642 AIRWEIGHT (CENTENNIAL) – .38 S&W Spl.+P cal., J-frame, 5 shot, 1 7/8, 2 (disc. 1997), 2 1/8 (PowerPort, mfg. 2009-2010), 2 1/2 (mfg. 2010 only), or 3 (disc. 1991) in. barrel, alloy frame with stainless steel cylinder and barrel, combat or pink (new 2012) grips, hammerless, satin stainless finish, fixed rear sight, no internal lock became an option during 2011, 15 oz. Mfg. 1990-1992, reintroduced 1996.

MSR $459	$350	$315	$275	$225	$190	$170	$150	

Add $10 for pink grips (new 2012).
Add $20 for Pro Series features and full moon clips (new 2010).
Add $142 for 2 1/8 in. barrel with PowerPort (mfg. 2009-2010).
Add $24 for 2 1/2 in. barrel (mfg. 2010 only).

* ***Model 642 CT Airweight (Centennial)*** – similar to Model 642 Centennial Airweight, except has Crimson Trace laser grips, no internal lock became an option during 2011. New 2004.

MSR $689	$500	$430	$365	$315	$285	$260	$220	

MODEL 642 LADYSMITH (AIRWEIGHT) – .38 Spl.+ P cal., J-frame, 5 shot, 1 7/8 in. barrel, stainless steel/alloy construction, smooth wood grips, satin stainless finish, includes soft side carry or jewelry case, 14 1/2 oz. New 1996.

MSR $489	$375	$325	$280	$230	$190	$170	$150	

MODEL 646 – .40 S&W cal., 4 in. barrel, stainless steel, L-frame, 6 shot, titanium cylinder. Limited mfg. during 2000 and 2003.

	$795	$695	$565	$510	$465	$425	$400	

MODEL 647 – .17 HMR cal., K-frame, 6 shot, stainless steel, 8 3/8 in. barrel with full lug, Hogue rubber grips with finger grooves, Patridge front and adj. rear sight, 52 oz. Mfg. 2003-2004.

	$795	$675	$575	$515	$470	$425	$400	*$697*

MODEL 648 – .22 WMR cal., K-frame, 6 in. full lug barrel, combat grips, square butt, combat trigger, semi-target hammer. Mfg. 1989-1996.

	$695	$625	$550	$495	$465	$440	$375	*$464*

* ***Model 648-2*** – .22 WMR cal., K-frame, 6 shot, stainless steel, 6 in. barrel with full lug, Hogue rubber grips with finger grooves, Patridge front and adj. rear sight, 45 oz. Mfg. 2003-2005.

	$650	$550	$495	$400	$360	$335	$315	*$703*

MODEL 649 (BODYGUARD) – .357 Mag./.38 S&W Spl.+P or .38 S&W Spl. (disc.) cal., J-frame, otherwise similar to Model 49 Bodyguard, except is satin stainless steel, 1 7/8 (mfg. 1998 only), 2 (disc. 1997), or 2 1/8 (new 1998) in. barrel, shrouded hammer, current production uses Uncle Mike's Combat grips, 23 oz. New 1986.

MSR $729	$585	$410	$300	$235	$165	$135	$120	

There have been five engineering changes to this model.

MODEL 650 KIT GUN – .22 WMR cal., service kit gun, stainless steel, 3 in. heavy barrel, J-frame, fixed sights. Mfg. 1983-1987.

	$850	$795	$675	$600	$550	$500	$450	*$305*

Add $150 for extra .22 LR cylinder.

MODEL 651 KIT GUN – .22 WMR cal., target kit gun, stainless steel, 4 in. barrel, J-frame, adj. rear sight. Mfg. 1983-87, re-released in late 1990, disc. 1998.

	$750	$695	$575	$500	$450	$400	$375	*$478*

Add 25% for 2 in. barrel.

This model could be ordered with a factory fitted optional .22 LR cylinder until 1987 (last mfg. sug. retail was $295 for the cylinder alone). This variation with the extra cylinder is very desirable.

MODEL 657 – .41 Mag. cal., N-frame, 4 (disc.), 6 (disc. 2000), 7 1/2 (new 2001), or 8 3/8 (disc. 1992) in. barrel, satin stainless steel, recent production uses Hogue rubber combat grips, approx. 53 oz. Mfg. 1986-2008.

	$650	$575	$500	$450	$415	$385	$365	*$869*

There have been 5 engineering changes to this model.

GRADING - PPGS™	100%	98%	95%	90%	80%	70%	60%	LAST MSR

MODEL 681 DISTINGUISHED SERVICE MAGNUM – .357 Mag. cal., stainless steel, 4 in. barrel, L-Frame. Mfg. 1980-1992.

	$425	$350	$275	$225	$175	$140	$125	*$412*

1991 mfg. includes square butt.

MODEL 686 DISTINGUISHED COMBAT MAGNUM – .357 Mag./.38 Spl.+ P cal., L-Frame, 6 shot, similar to Model 586, except has 2 1/2 (new 1990), 4, 6 (with (disc.) or w/o PowerPort), or 8 3/8 (disc. 2002) in. barrel, fixed (disc.) or adj. sights, blue, stainless, Midnight Black (ltd. ed. 1989 only, 2,876 mfg. in 6 in. barrel, and 1,559 mfg. in 4 in. barrel) finish, current production uses Hogue rubber grips, 35-51 oz. New 1980.

MSR $829	$600	$475	$350	$300	$250	$225	$200	

* ***Model 686 Distinguished Combat Magnum Plus*** – .357 Mag./.38 Spl.+ P cal., L-frame, 7 shot, 2 1/2, 3 (new 2007), 4, or 6 in. barrel, synthetic or Hogue rubber grips, stainless steel, round (2 1/2 in. barrel only) or square butt, white outline rear sight on 4 or 6 in. barrel, 34 1/2 - 43 oz. New 1996.

MSR $849	$615	$485	$350	$300	$250	$225	$200	

MODEL 686/686SSR PRO SERIES – .357 Mag./.38 Spl. + P cal., 6 shot, L-frame, 4 (Model 686SSR) or 5 (Model 686 with full moon clips, new 2010) in. barrel, SA/DA, interchangeable front sight, adj. rear sight, satin stainless (Model 686SSR) or bead (Model 686) finish, checkered wood grips, stainless steel frame and cylinder, forged hammer and trigger, custom barrel with recessed Precision crown, Bossed mainspring, and tuned action, 38.3 oz. New 2007.

MSR $969	$725	$600	$500	$400	$350	$325	$275	

Subtract $30 for full moon clips (Model 686, new 2010).

MODEL 696 – .44 S&W Spl. cal., L-frame, 5 shot, 3 in. barrel with full shroud, Hogue rubber (disc. 2000) or Uncle Mike's Combat grips, satin stainless steel, adj. rear sight, 36 oz. Mfg. 1997-2002.

	$485	$315	$250	$195	$165	$140	$120	*$620*

MODEL 940 CENTENNIAL – 9mm Para. cal., fully concealed hammer, 2 or 3 (disc. 1992) in. barrel, fixed rear sight, Santoprene combat grips, 23-25 oz. Mfg. 1991-1998.

	$875	$725	$575	$425	$325	$225	$175	*$493*

PISTOLS: SEMI-AUTO, CENTERFIRE

Listed in order of model number (except .32 and .35 Automatic Pistols). Alphabetical models will appear at the end of this section.

To understand S&W 3rd generation model nomenclature, the following rules apply. The first two digits (of the four digit model number) specify caliber. Numbers 39, 59, and 69 refer to 9mm Para. cal. The third digit refers to the model type. 0 means standard model, 1 is for compact, 2 is for standard model with decocking lever, 3 is for compact variation with decocking lever, 4 is for standard with double action only, 5 designates a compact model in double action only, 6 indicates a non-standard barrel length, 7 is a non-standard barrel length with decocking lever, and 8 refers to non-standard barrel length in double action only. The fourth digit refers to the material(s) used in the fabrication of the pistol. 3 refers to an aluminum alloy frame with stainless steel slide, 4 designates an aluminum alloy frame with carbon steel slide, 5 is for carbon steel frame and slide, 6 is a stainless steel frame and slide, and 7 refers to a stainless steel frame and carbon steel slide. Hence, a Model 4053 refers to a pistol in .40 S&W cal. configured in compact version with double action only and fabricated with an aluminum alloy frame and stainless steel slide. This model nomenclature does not apply to 2 or 3 digit model numbers (i.e., Rimfire Models and the Model 52).

Current S&W abbreviations for pistol feature codes used on its price sheets and literature are as follows: Grips: CTG - Crimson Trace laser grips, PG - plastic grips, RG - rubber grips, WG - wood grips. Sights: ADJ - adjustable, ADJFO - adj. fiber optic, FIXEDB - fixed black, LMC - low mount carry, WD - white dot, BB - black blade, BP - black post, FO - fiber optic, GB - gold bead - INTCH - interchangeable, NS - night sights, PAT - Patridge, RR - red ramp, WB - white bead, WD - white dot.

100%	98%	95%	90%	80%	70%	60%	50%	40%	30%	20%	10%

Frames: AL - alloy, SS - stainless steel, CS - carbon steel, SM - stainless melonite, POLY - polymer. Safeties: AMBI - ambidextrous, MS - magazine safety, NMS - no magazine safety, IL - internal lock. Action: DA - double action only, SA - single action only, SA/DA - single action/double action, SF - striker fire.

Pre-2010 S&W abbreviations are as follows: Grips: GC - Crimson Trace laser grips, GR - rubber grips, GW - wood grips, GF - finger groove grips, GP - plastic grips. Sights: SA - adj., SB - black blade front, SC - interchangeable front, SD - dot front, SF - fixed, SG - gold bead front, SH - Hi-Viz, SL - Lo Mount Carry, SP - Patridge front, SR - red ramp front, SV - black post, S1 - front night. Frame Material: FA - alloy, FS - stainless, FC - carbon, FM - stainless Melonite, FP - polymer. Frame Sizes: SM - Small/Compact, MD - Medium, LG - Large, XL - Extra Large. Finishes: ZB - Blue/Black, ZC - Clear Cote, ZG - Grey, ZL - Melonite, ZM - Matte, ZS - Satin Stainless, ZT - Two-Tone, ZW - Camo. Barrel: BC - carbon, BL - light, BO - one piece, BS - stainless, BT - traditional, BX - heavy, B2 - two piece. Action: AD - double action only, AF - striker fire, AS - single action only, AT - traditional double action. Slide: DS - stainless steel, DC - carbon, DM - stainless Melonite.

When applicable, early variations of some of the older semi-auto models listed in this category will be more desirable than later mfg.

.32 AUTOMATIC PISTOL – .32 ACP cal., 7 shot mag., 3 1/2 in. barrel, blue with "S&W" monogram inlaid plain walnut grip. 957 mfg. 1924-1936. Serial range starting with S/N 1.

100%	98%	95%	90%	80%	70%	60%	50%	40%	30%	20%	10%
N/A	$2,500	$2,000	$1,750	$1,500	$1,250	$1,000	$800	$700	$600	$500	$400

.35 AUTOMATIC PISTOL (MODEL 1913) – .35 S&W Auto cal., 7 shot mag., 3 1/2 in. barrel, blue or nickel w/"S&W" monogram inlaid in plain walnut grips. 8,350 mfg. 1913-1921. Serial range starting with no. 1.

100%	98%	95%	90%	80%	70%	60%	50%	40%	30%	20%	10%
N/A	$875	$775	$625	$525	$450	$375	$325	$275	$235	$200	$185

A slight premium might exist for the first model (up to ser. no. 3,125).

GRADING - PPGS™	100%	98%	95%	90%	80%	70%	60%	LAST MSR

MODEL 39 STEEL FRAME – 9mm Para. cal., 8 shot, 4 in. barrel, long ejector, walnut stocks, blue, adj. rear windage only sight, double action, walnut grips, 927 mfg. during 1966 only in 3 ser. no. ranges.

GRADING - PPGS™	100%	98%	95%	90%	80%	70%	60%	LAST MSR
	$1,800	$1,600	$1,400	$1,000	$850	$735	$650	

MODEL 39 ALLOY FRAME – 9mm Para. cal., alloy frame, this model was unmarked up to ser. no. approx. 2,600, early guns had a short safety lever, checkered walnut grips, blue or nickel finish. Mfg. started 1954.

GRADING - PPGS™	100%	98%	95%	90%	80%	70%	60%	LAST MSR
	$600	$375	$325	$260	$210	$175	$140	

Add $200 for nickel finish.

S&W completed one lot of 200 guns mfg. with nickel finish. Additionally, there were special orders for nickel finish. The model change from the Model 39 to the Model 39-2 took place with the change from the long extractor to the new short type. Collectors report an approx. ser. no. range 1,001-120,000 with long extractor. This model was the first commercially mfg. 9mm Para. double action semi-auto in the U.S.

Models 39 Alloy Frame & Model 39 Alloy Frame Early Mfg. (Pre-39) are intermixed, as is the production of the two variations. There is no positive serial number that can be established when the Model number was added, however it occurred between serial number 2500 and 5000, with the production changes taking place some what randomly over the same serial range. It must be remembered that Smith & Wesson did not make pistols in order of serial number. There is no first group of 298 produced for military inspection. Also the serial numbers are intermixed with the Model 41 pistols and there are more Model 41s produced than Model 39s. The guns that were submitted for military testing went to the Springfield Armory, and had X prefix serial numbers. The first shipments of Model 39s was in Dec. 1954, the model numbers were assigned in 1957.

GRADING - PPGS™	100%	98%	95%	90%	80%	70%	60%	LAST MSR

MODEL 39 ALLOY FRAME EARLY MFG. (PRE-39) – short safety, approx. ser. no. range 1,001-2,600. Mfg. 1954-1957.

	$1,800	$1,600	$1,400	$1,000	$800	$700	$600	

Add 200% for early manufacture original military trial guns. Factory letter/military documentation.

The distinguishing features of the Pre-39 compared to the Model 39 are as follows: short safety, short tang, a unique frame back strap insert and hammer stirrup, a unique left grip (no safety relief), no trigger play spring, no model number on frame, no patent pending on early slides (Late Pre-39 slides have the patent pending; however, slides were fitted without regard for serial numbers. For example, serial number 1069, which was shipped from the factory on Oct. 4, 1955, has the patent pending marking, while 1,150 that shipped on July 7, 1955 does not), two types of early flat magazine followers were used before standardizing on a third type, supplied with an instruction booklet (only the Pre-39s and early Model 39s to about serial number 7,000 were supplied with the instruction booklet).

MODEL 39-2 ALLOY FRAME (LATER PRODUCTION) – 7.65mm (.30 Luger) or 9mm Para. cal., double action, 8 shot mag., 4 in. barrel, checkered walnut grips, adj. sight, alloy frame, approx. 1971, the 39-2 was introduced as an improved version. Mfg. 1970-82.

9mm Para. cal.	$550	$375	$325	$260	$240	$225	$200	
7.65mm cal.	$1,375	$1,250	$1,100	$950	$825	$700	$625	

Add 15% for nickel finish.

The .30 Luger cal. (7.65mm) was mfg. for the European marketplace only. Very hard to find in the U.S.

In 1971 approximately 500 Model 39-2s were shipped to West Germany without barrels. The pistols were fitted with 7.65mm barrels in West Germany and were then proofed and shipped to an Italian distributor for commercial sales in that country. The slides, barrels, and frames of these guns all have the West German 1971 Ulm Proof House Marks. Three of these guns were imported by Sarco in 1995, serial numbers A129,214,A129,498, and one with an unknown serial number. There is one other 7.65mm Model 39 known. The gun (serial number A166,311) had smooth grips with a nickel finish and is without the German Proof Marks.

MODEL 44 – 9mm Para. cal., single action design, S&W's rarest semi-auto pistol, 10 mfg.

Original examples are typically seen in the $15K-$20K range, depending on condition.

MODEL 52-A – .38 AMU cal., same action as Model 39, 4 in. barrel. Originally mfg. for U.S. Army Marksman Training Unit, 87 mfg.

	$3,750	$3,250	$2,750	$2,250	$1,950	$1,600	$1,300	

MODEL 52 – .38 S&W Spl. Wadcutter cal. only, similar action to Model 39, except incorporates a set screw locking out the double action, 5 in. barrel, 5 shot mag. Approx. 3,500 mfg. 1961-63.

	$1,100	$875	$775	$675	$575	$475	$395	

MODELS 52-1 & 52-2 – .38 Spl. Mid-Range Wadcutter cal. only, single action semi-auto, 5 in. barrel, adj. sights, checkered walnut grips, blue only, 5 shot mag.

	$950	$850	$775	$675	$575	$475	$395	*$908*

The Model 52-1 was mfg. 1963-1971, and the Model 52-2 was mfg. 1971-93.

MODEL 59 – similar to Model 39, except has 14 shot mag., black nylon grips, total production approx. 231,841. Disc. 1981.

	$550	$400	$350	$275	$250	$225	$215	

Add $50 for nickel finish.
Add $150 for smooth front (ungrooved) grip frame.
Add 200% for smooth front and rear grip straps (20 mfg.).

MODEL 147-A – 9mm Para. cal., 14 shot, steel frame, 4 in. barrel, black plastic grips, adj. sights for windage only, similar to Model 59, except has steel frame, 112 mfg. 1979 only.

	$2,000	$1,500	$1,050	$800	$750	$450	$400	

This model was originally marked Model 47 for export, prefix and suffix were added. Ser. nos. were stamped, and are crude by today's standard.

GRADING - PPGS™	100%	98%	95%	90%	80%	70%	60%	LAST MSR

MODEL 410 – .40 S&W cal., traditional double action, steel slide with alloy frame, blue finish, 4 in. barrel, 10 or 11 shot mag., single side safety, 3-dot sights, straight backstrap with synthetic grips, 28 1/2 oz. Mfg. 1996-2007.

	$525	$370	$275	$230	$195	$175	$165	*$687*

Add $21 for Hi-Viz front sight (disc. 2003).

* ***Model 410S*** – similar to Model 410, except has stainless steel slide with alloy frame, 28 1/2 oz. Mfg. 2003-2007.

	$545	$375	$275	$245	$205	$175	$165	*$711*

Add $237 for Crimson Trace laser grips (new 2005).

MODEL 411 – .40 S&W cal., 4 in. barrel, 11 shot mag., fixed sights, blue finish, aluminum alloy frame, manual safety. Mfg. 1993-95.

	$475	$400	$350	$325	$295	$280	$265	*$525*

MODEL 439 – 9mm Para. cal., double action, 4 in. barrel, blue or nickel finish, alloy frame, 8 shot mag., checkered walnut grips, 30 oz. Disc. 1988.

	$475	$35	$325	$275	$240	$225	$210	*$472*

Add $50 for nickel finish (disc. 1986).
Add $26 for adj. sights.

MODEL 457 COMPACT – .45 ACP cal., traditional double action, alloy frame and steel slide, 3 3/4 in. barrel, single side safety, 3-dot sights, 7 shot mag., straight backstrap, blue finish only, black synthetic grips, 29 oz. Mfg. 1996-2006.

	$525	$365	$270	$225	$195	$175	$165	*$681*

* ***Model 457S Compact*** – similar to Model 457, except has stainless steel slide with alloy frame, 29 oz. Mfg. 2003-2006.

	$545	$390	$280	$245	$200	$175	$165	*$710*

MODEL 459 – 9mm Para. cal., 14 shot version of Model 439, checkered nylon stocks, limited mfg. with squared-off trigger guard with serrations. Disc. 1988.

	$450	$400	$350	$300	$275	$255	$240	*$501*

Add $26 for adj. sights.
Add $44 for nickel finish (disc. 1986).
Add 30% for Model 4590 (Transitional 5903).

* ***Model 459 Brushed Finish*** – 9mm Para. cal., 14 shot, 4 in. barrel, dull finish, fixed sights, special grips made to F.B.I. or police specs., 803 mfg.

	$750	$625	$550	$440	$385	$330	$300	

Add 100%-200% for F.B.I. guns, very few released. Values assume proper F.B.I. documentation (be wary).

MODEL 469 "MINI" – 9mm Para. cal., double action, alloy frame, 12 shot finger extension mag., short frame, bobbed hammer, 3 1/2 in. barrel, sandblast blue or satin nickel finish, ambidextrous safety standard (1986), molded Delrin black grips, 26 oz. Disc. 1988.

	$475	$35	$325	$275	$240	$225	$210	*$478*

MODEL 539 – 9mm Para. cal., double action, steel frame, steel slide, 8 shot, 4 in. barrel, blue or nickel. Approx. 8,300 mfg. Disc. 1983.

	$550	$475	$415	$375	$350	$325	$300	

Add $50 for nickel finish.
Add $30 for fixed rear sight.

MODEL 559 – 9mm Para. cal., double action, steel frame, 14 shot mag., 4 in. barrel, blue or nickel. Approx. 1,700 mfg. Disc. 1983.

	$600	$525	$450	$375	$275	$250	$225	

Add $50 for nickel finish.
Add $30 for fixed rear sight.

GRADING - PPGS™	100%	98%	95%	90%	80%	70%	60%	LAST MSR

MODEL 639 STAINLESS – 9mm Para. cal., similar to Model 439, only stainless steel, 8 shot mag., ambidextrous safety became standard 1986, 36 oz. Disc. 1988.

$475	$400	$350	$300	$250	$200	$165	*$523*

Add $27 for adj. sights.

MODEL 645 STAINLESS – .45 ACP cal. only, 5 in. barrel, 8 shot mag., squared-off trigger guard, black molded nylon grips, ambidextrous safety, fixed sights, 37 1/2 oz. New 1986. Disc. 1988.

$550	$475	$400	$350	$300	$250	$200	*$622*

Add approx. 25% for the approx. 479 Model 645 "Interim" pistols were mfg. in 1988 only.
Add $27 for adj. sight.

MODEL 659 STAINLESS – 9mm Para. cal., similar to Model 459, only stainless steel, 14 shot mag., ambidextrous safety became standard 1986, 39 1/2 oz. Disc. 1988.

$475	$400	$350	$300	$250	$215	$180	*$553*

Add approx. 30% for the approx. 150 Model 659 "Interim" pistols were mfg. in 1988 only.
Add $27 for adj. sights.

MODEL 669 STAINLESS – 9mm Para. cal., smaller version of Model 659 with 12 shot finger extension mag., 3 1/2 in. barrel, fixed sights, molded Delrin grips, ambidextrous safety standard, 26 oz. Mfg. 1986-88 only.

$475	$375	$300	$250	$195	$165	$140	*$522*

Add approx. 30% for the approx. 150 Model 669 "Interim" pistols were mfg. in 1988 only.

MODEL 745 IPSC – .45 ACP cal., single action, 5 in. barrel, stainless steel frame with steel slide, hammer, and trigger, checkered walnut stocks, Novak adj. competition rear sight, 38 3/4 oz. Mfg. 1987-1990.

$750	$600	$500	$350	$275	$235	$200	*$699*

Early guns had optional "IPSC" markings. Later, these markings became standard. A total of approx. 9,704 units were produced through 1990. In 1990, a special limited production run of approx. 100 pistols fitted with adj. sights was mfg.

MODEL 908 COMPACT – 9mm Para. cal., compact variation of the Model 909/910, 3 1/2 in. barrel, 3-dot sights, 8 shot mag., straight backstrap, 24 oz. Mfg. 1996-2007.

$495	$355	$275	$230	$195	$175	$165	*$648*

* ***Model 908S Compact*** – similar to Model 908, except has stainless steel slide with alloy frame, 24 oz. Mfg. 2003-2007.

$495	$355	$275	$230	$195	$175	$165	*$648*

Add $24 for carry combo variation (includes Kydex carry holster, new 2004).

MODEL 909 – 9mm Para. cal., 4 in. barrel, traditional double action, large frame, 9 shot mag., fixed sights, single side safety, alloy frame and steel slide, curved backstrap with black synthetic grips, 27 oz. Mfg. 1994-96.

$450	$375	$300	$250	$210	$190	$175	*$443*

MODEL 910 – similar to Model 909, except has 10 or 15 shot mag., 28 oz. Mfg. 1994-2007.

$455	$345	$270	$230	$195	$175	$165	*$616*

Add $22 for Hi-Viz front sight (disc. 2003).

* ***Model 910S*** – similar to Model 910, except has stainless steel slide with alloy frame, 28 oz. Mfg. 2003-2007.

$460	$345	$270	$225	$195	$175	$165	*$624*

MODEL 915 – 9mm Para. cal., 4 in. barrel, fixed sights, 10 (C/B 1994) or 15* shot mag., manual safety, aluminum alloy frame, blue finish. Mfg. 1993-94.

$425	$350	$275	$225	$205	$190	$175	*$467*

MODEL 1006 STAINLESS – 10mm cal., double action semi-auto, stainless steel construction, 5 in. barrel, exposed hammer, 9 shot mag., fixed or adj. sights, ambidextrous safety, 26,979 units produced 1990-93.

$675	$575	$425	$350	$300	$245	$215	*$769*

Add $27 for adj. rear sight.

GRADING - PPGS™	100%	98%	95%	90%	80%	70%	60%	LAST MSR

Product Codes: 104800, 105004, 108234, 108237.

MODEL 1026 STAINLESS – 10mm cal., 5 in. barrel, traditional double action, features frame mounted decocking lever, 9 shot mag., straight backstrap, 3,135 units produced 1990-91 only.

	$850	$675	$550	$425	$325	$245	$215	*$755*

Product Codes: 105006, 105021, 108239.

MODEL 1046 STAINLESS – 10mm cal., 5 in. barrel, fixed sights, double action only, 9 shot mag., straight backstrap, 151 units produced 1991 only.

	$1,000	$800	$675	$500	$400	$300	$250	*$747*

Product Codes: 104602, 108233.

MODEL 1066 STAINLESS – 10mm cal., 4 1/4 in. barrel, 9 shot mag., straight backstrap, ambidextrous safety, traditional double action, fixed sights, 5,067 units produced 1990-1992.

	$750	$625	$500	$400	$325	$250	$225	*$730*

Add $75 for Tritium night sights - disc. 1991 (Model 1066-NS).

Product Codes: 105500, 108270.

Only 1,000 Model 1066-NSs were manufactured.

MODEL 1076 STAINLESS – similar to Model 1026 Stainless, except has 4 1/4 in. barrel, 13,805 units produced 1990-93.

	$700	$625	$550	$450	$350	$300	$245	*$778*

Product Codes: 10506, 105021, 108239.

* ***Model 1076 Stainless FBI Contract Gun*** – needs to be verified by S&W semi-auto pistol expert.

	$2,800	$2,500	$2,200	$1,800	$1,400	$1,200	$975	

MODEL 1086 STAINLESS – similar to Model 1066 Stainless, except is double action only, 1,660 units produced 1990-1992.

	$900	$700	$525	$400	$325	$250	$210	*$730*

Product Codes: 106004, 108251.

MODEL SW1911 – .45 ACP cal., patterned after the Colt M1911, large frame, SA, 5 in. barrel, 8 shot single stack mag., alloy (disc. 2006), steel or stainless steel frame, steel slide, matte, blue/black (new 2005) or Clear Coat finish, patented S&W firing pin safety release activated by the grip safety, pinned-in external extractor, Wolff springs throughout, Texas Armament match trigger, Hogue rubber (standard) or wood (new 2004) grips, McCormick hammer and thumb safety, Briley barrel bushing, two Wilson magazines, full-length heavy guide rod, high profile Wilson beavertail safety, adj. rear black blade, or Novak Lo-Mount Carry sights, 39 oz. Mfg. 2003-2011.

	$875	$675	$525	$425	$375	$335	$300	*$1,039*

Add $60 for rear adj. sight.

Add $270 or Doug Koenig Model w/two-tone finish and adj. rear sight.

* ***Model SW1911 Stainless*** – features stainless steel frame and slide, checkered wood or black synthetic grips, 39.4 oz.

MSR $1,019	$865	$675	$525	$425	$395	$350	$325	

Add $110 for wood grips and adj. rear sight.

Add $93 for matte finish with black blade front sight (disc. 2006).

Add $72 for tactical lower frame rail w/wood grips (mfg. 2006-2010).

Add $301 for Crimson Trace laser grips (mfg. 2005-2010).

* ***Model SW1911 w/no firing pin block*** – similar to SW1911, except does not have firing pin block, Melonite finish. Mfg. 2009-2011.

	$925	$750	$525	$450	$400	$375	$350	*$1,099*

GRADING - PPGS™	100%	98%	95%	90%	80%	70%	60%	LAST MSR

MODEL SW1911 E SERIES – .45 ACP cal., 4 1/4 (disc. 2012) or 5 (new 2011) in. barrel, features front and rear scalloped slide serrations, 7 or 8 shot, white dot sights, alloy or stainless steel (new 2011) frame, blue/black (alloy frame), GI Bead (stainless) or Melonite (stainless) finish, wood or Crimson Trace Laser grips, approx. 40 oz. New 2009.

MSR $919	$775	$650	$525	$450	$400	$350	$300	

Add $220 for 4 1/4 in. barrel with alloy frame (disc. 2012).
Add $170 for Crimson Trace Laser grips.
Add $400 for tactical rail (5 in. barrel only, stainless steel, new 2011).

* ***Model SW1911 E Series Scandium*** – .45 ACP cal., 4 1/4 in. barrel, 8 shot mag., features Scandium alloy frame with choice of two-tone or Melonite finish, wood grips, night sights, 29.6 oz. New 2011.

MSR $1,369	$1,095	$950	$800	$700	$600	$500	$450	

MODEL SW1911 PD (Sc) – similar to Model SW1911, except has 4 1/4 or 5 (new 2007) in. barrel with small Scandium alloy frame, 8 shot, black finish, and wood grips. Mfg. 2004-2011.

	$950	$725	$550	$475	$425	$375	$325	*$1,109*

Add $240 for Crimson Trace laser grips.
Add $120 for Gunsite model with gold bead front sight.
Add $30 for tactical lower rail.

SW1911 PRO SERIES – .45 ACP or 9mm Para. (new 2009) cal., SA, 5 in. barrel, 8 (.45 ACP) or 10 (9mm Para.) shot mag., 3-dot (9mm Para. cal. only), Novak fiber optic front and rear or Black Dovetail rear adj. sights, checkered wood grips, stainless steel frame and slide, satin stainless finish, Pro Series features include 300 LPI front strap checkering, hand polished barrel feed ramp, crisp 4 1/2 lb. trigger pull, full length guide rod, oversized external extractor, ambidextrous frame safety, precision crowned muzzle, 41 oz. New mid-2007.

MSR $1,379	$1,100	$875	$750	$650	$550	$450	$400	

Add $110 for 9mm Para. cal. (new 2009).
Add $140 for adj. Black Dovetail rear sight (new late 2011).

* ***SW1911 Pro Series Subcompact*** – similar to SW1911 Pro Series, except has 3 in. barrel, 7 shot mag., and subcompact frame, 26 1/2 oz. New 2009.

MSR $1,159	$895	$775	$650	$550	$450	$400	$350	

MODEL 3904 – 9mm Para. cal., double action semi-auto, aluminum alloy frame, 4 in. barrel with fixed bushing, 8 shot mag., Delrin one piece wraparound grips, exposed hammer, ambidextrous safety, beveled magazine well, extended squared-off trigger guard, adj. or fixed rear sight, 3-dot sighting system, 28 oz. Mfg. 1989-91.

	$475	$385	$350	$325	$300	$280	$265	*$541*

Add $25 for adj. rear sight.

MODEL 3906 STAINLESS – stainless steel variation of the Model 3904, 35 1/2 oz. Mfg. 1989-91.

	$510	$435	$375	$315	$270	$230	$200	*$604*

Add $28 for adj. rear sight.

MODEL 3913 COMPACT STAINLESS – stainless steel variation of the Model 3914, 25 oz. Mfg. 1990-99.

	$535	$440	$365	$305	$260	$220	$190	*$662*

* ***Model 3913NL Compact Stainless*** – similar to Model 3913 Ladysmith, except does not have Ladysmith on the slide. Disc. 1994.

	$550	$475	$395	$350	$295	$250	$220	*$622*

* ***Model 3913 LS Compact Stainless (Ladysmith)*** – similar to Model 3913 Stainless, except is matte stainless with white Delrin grips and mag. does not have finger extension, includes case, 25 oz. Mfg. 1990-2006.

	$710	$525	$400	$335	$290	$245	$215	*$901*

GRADING - PPGS™	100%	98%	95%	90%	80%	70%	60%	LAST MSR

MODEL 3913TSW TACTICAL – 9mm Para. cal., traditional double action, compact frame, 3 1/2 in. barrel, 8 shot mag., Novak Lo-Mount 2-dot sights, stainless steel slide, aluminum alloy frame, matte stainless finish, straight black backstrap synthetic grips, 24.8 oz. Mfg. 1998-2006.

	$690	$520	$400	$335	$290	$245	$215	*$876*

MODEL 3914 COMPACT – 9mm Para. cal., double action semi-auto, aluminum alloy frame, 3 1/2 in. barrel, hammerless, 8 shot finger extension mag., fixed sights only, ambidextrous safety, blue finish, straight backstrap grip, 25 oz. Mfg. 1990-95.

	$495	$425	$350	$325	$295	$280	$265	*$562*

This model was also available with a single side manual safety at no extra charge - disc. 1991 (Model 3914NL).

* ***Model 3914 Compact LadySmith*** – similar to Model 3914, except has Delrin grips, 25 oz. Mfg. 1990-91 only.

	$485	$415	$365	$305	$260	$220	$190	*$568*

* ***Model 3914 TSW*** – similar to Model 3914, except slide is marked "9 Tactical", blue finish, 8 shot mag. 1,060 mfg. 1990 only.

	$800	$650	$475	$395	$345	$280	$235	

MODEL 3953 COMPACT STAINLESS – 9mm Para. cal., double action only, aluminum alloy frame with stainless steel slide, compact model with 3 1/2 in. barrel, 8 shot mag. Mfg. 1990-99.

	$535	$440	$365	$305	$260	$220	$190	*$662*

MODEL 3953TSW – similar to Model 3913TSW, except is double action only, 24.8 oz. Mfg. 1998-2002.

	$615	$475	$380	$320	$275	$230	$200	*$760*

MODEL 3954 – similar to Model 3953, except has blue steel slide. Mfg. 1990-92.

	$475	$395	$350	$325	$295	$280	$265	*$528*

MODEL 4003 STAINLESS – .40 S&W cal., traditional double action, 4 in. barrel, 11 shot mag., white dot fixed sights, ambidextrous safety, aluminum alloy frame with stainless steel slide, one piece Xenoy wraparound grips, straight gripstrap, 28 oz. Mfg. 1991-93.

	$575	$495	$395	$330	$285	$240	$215	*$698*

* ***Model 4003TSW Stainless*** – similar to Model 4003 Stainless, but has aluminum alloy frame, 10 shot mag., stainless steel slide, S&W tactical features, including equipment rail and Novak Lo-Mount Carry sights, traditional double action only, satin stainless finish, 28 1/2 oz. Mfg. 2000-2004.

	$700	$600	$500	$450	$400	$360	$330	*$940*

MODEL 4004 – .40 S&W cal., similar to Model 4003, except has aluminum alloy frame with blue carbon steel slide. Mfg. 1991-92.

	$540	$460	$375	$325	$295	$280	$265	*$643*

MODEL 4006 STAINLESS – .40 S&W cal., 3 1/2 (Shorty Forty) or 4 in. barrel, 10 (C/B 1994) or 11* shot mag., satin stainless finish, exposed hammer, Delrin one piece wraparound grips, 3-dot sights, 38 1/2 oz. Mfg. 1990-99.

	$655	$545	$400	$335	$290	$245	$215	*$791*

Add $31 for adj. rear sight.
Add $115 for fixed Tritium night sights (new 1992).

The bobbed hammer option on this model was disc. in 1991.

* ***Model 4006TSW Stainless*** – similar to Model 4006 Stainless, except has stainless steel frame and slide, S&W tactical features, including equipment rail, traditional double action only, 37.8 oz. Mfg. 2000-2004.

	$700	$600	$500	$450	$400	$360	$330	*$963*

Add $38 if w/o Novak Lo-Mount Carry (NLC) sights.
Add $133 for night sights (disc.).

GRADING - PPGS™	100%	98%	95%	90%	80%	70%	60%	LAST MSR

MODEL 4013 COMPACT STAINLESS – .40 S&W cal., semi-auto, standard double action, 3 1/2 in. barrel, 8 shot mag., fixed sights, ambidextrous safety, alloy frame. Mfg. 1991-96.

$595	$485	$385	$330	$295	$280	$265	$722

MODEL 4013TSW TACTICAL – .40 S&W cal., semi-auto, standard double action, 3 1/2 in. barrel, 9 shot mag. with reversible mag. catch, aluminum alloy frame with stainless steel slide, satin stainless finish, black synthetic grips, fixed 3-dot Novak Lo-Mount Carry sights, ambidextrous safety, 26.8 oz. Mfg. 1997-2006.

$825	$630	$450	$385	$335	$280	$235	$1,021

MODEL 4014 COMPACT – similar to Model 4013, except is steel with blue finish. Mfg. 1991-93.

$550	$475	$425	$375	$330	$300	$275	$635

MODEL 4026 STAINLESS – .40 S&W cal., traditional double action with frame mounted decocking lever, 10 (C/B 1994) or 11* shot mag., fixed sights, curved backstrap, 36 oz. Mfg. 1991-93.

$625	$525	$400	$335	$290	$245	$215	$731

MODEL 4040 PD – .40 S&W cal., compact frame using Scandium, 3 1/2 in. barrel, Hogue rubber grips, Novak Lo-Mount Carry 3-dot sights, matte black finish, 25.6 oz. Mfg. 2003-2005.

$625	$525	$400	$335	$290	$245	$215	$840

MODEL 4043 STAINLESS – .40 S&W cal., double action only, aluminum alloy frame with stainless steel slide, 4 in. barrel, 10 (C/B 1994) or 11* shot mag., one piece Xenoy wraparound grips, straight backstrap, white-dot fixed sights, 30 oz. Mfg. 1991-99.

$635	$510	$390	$325	$280	$240	$210	$772

* ***Model 4043TSW Stainless*** – .40 S&W cal., double action only, similar to Model 4043 Stainless, but has S&W tactical features, including equipment rail, 28 1/2 oz. Mfg. 2000-2002.

$650	$550	$425	$350	$290	$245	$215	$886

MODEL 4044 – .40 S&W cal., similar to Model 4043, except has carbon steel slide. Mfg. 1991-92.

$540	$460	$375	$325	$295	$280	$265	$643

MODEL 4046 STAINLESS – similar to Model 4006 Stainless, except is double action only, 4 in. barrel only. Mfg. 1991-99.

$655	$540	$400	$335	$290	$245	$215	$791

Add $115 for Tritium night sights (new 1992).

* ***Model 4046TSW Stainless*** – double action only, similar to Model 4046 Stainless, but has S&W tactical features, including equipment rail, 37.8 oz. Mfg. 2000-2002.

$700	$625	$500	$455	$400	$360	$330	$907

Add $133 for night sights.

MODEL 4053 COMPACT STAINLESS – .40 S&W cal., double action only variation of the Model 4013. Mfg. 1991-1997.

$625	$525	$400	$335	$290	$245	$215	$734

MODEL 4053TSW (TACTICAL) – .40 S&W cal., double action only, 3 1/2 in. barrel, 9 shot mag. with reversible mag. catch, alloy frame with stainless steel slide, satin stainless finish, black synthetic grips, fixed sights, ambidextrous safety, 26.8 oz. Mfg. 1997-2002.

$730	$580	$425	$360	$315	$260	$225	$886

MODEL 4054 – .40 S&W cal., double action only variation of the Model 4014. Mfg. 1991-92.

$650	$550	$425	$350	$290	$245	$215	$629

MODEL 4056TSW (TACTICAL) – .40 S&W cal., double action only, 3 1/2 in. barrel, 9 shot mag. with reversible mag. catch, stainless steel frame and slide, satin stainless finish, black synthetic grips, fixed sights, ambidextrous safety, 37 1/2 oz. Mfg. 1997 only.

$675	$575	$450	$350	$290	$245	$215	$844

GRADING - PPGS™	100%	98%	95%	90%	80%	70%	60%	LAST MSR

MODEL 4505 – .45 ACP cal., carbon steel variation of the Model 4506, fixed or adj. rear sight. 1,200 mfg. 1991 only.

	$650	$550	$425	$350	$290	$245	$215	*$660*

Add $27 for adj. rear sight.

MODEL 4506 STAINLESS – .45 ACP cal., 5 in. barrel, 8 shot mag., combat trigger guard, exposed hammer, fixed or adj. rear sight, straight backstrap (curved is optional), Delrin one-piece grips, 40 1/2 oz. Mfg. 1990-99.

	$680	$550	$410	$345	$300	$250	$220	*$822*

Add $33 for adj. rear sight.

Approx. 100 Model 4506s left the factory mismarked Model 645 on the frame. In NIB condition they are worth $700.

MODEL 4513TSW – .45 ACP cal., traditional double action, compact frame, 3 3/4 in. barrel, 7 shot mag., 3-dot Novak Lo-Mount Carry sights, stainless steel slide, aluminum alloy frame, satin stainless finish, 28.6 oz. Mfg. 1998-2004.

	$725	$625	$475	$395	$340	$285	$240	*$980*

MODEL 4516 COMPACT STAINLESS – .45 ACP cal., bobbed hammer, compact variation of the Model 4506, 3 3/4 in. barrel, 7 shot mag., ambidextrous safety, fixed rear sight only, 34 oz. Mfg. 1990-1997.

	$650	$525	$400	$335	$290	$245	$215	*$787*

Original model is marked 4516 while later mfg. changed slide legend to read 4516-1. Original mfg. is more collectible and slight premiums are being asked.

MODEL 4526 STAINLESS – similar to Model 4506 Stainless, except has frame mounted decocking lever. Mfg. 1990-91 only.

	$675	$550	$425	$350	$290	$245	$215	*$762*

MODEL 4536 STAINLESS – .45 ACP cal., similar to Model 4516 Compact, except has frame mounted decocking lever only. Mfg. 1990-91 only.

	$675	$550	$425	$350	$290	$245	$215	*$762*

MODEL 4546 STAINLESS – .45 ACP cal., similar to Model 4506 Stainless, except is double action only. Mfg. 1990-91 only.

	$675	$550	$425	$350	$290	$245	$215	*$735*

MODEL 4553TSW – .45 ACP cal., similar to Model 4513TSW, except is double action only. Mfg. 1998-2002.

	$755	$595	$450	$385	$335	$280	$235	*$924*

MODEL 4556 STAINLESS – .45 ACP cal., features double action only, 3 3/4 in. barrel, 7 shot mag., fixed sights. Mfg. 1991 only.

	$675	$550	$425	$350	$290	$245	$215	*$735*

MODEL 4563TSW – .45 ACP cal., traditional double action only, 4 1/4 in. barrel, 8 shot mag., aluminum alloy frame with stainless steel slide, satin stainless finish, includes S&W tactical features, including equipment rail and Novak 3-dot sights, synthetic black straight backstrap grips, 30.6 oz. Mfg. 2000-2004.

	$750	$625	$450	$390	$340	$280	$235	*$977*

MODEL 4566 STAINLESS – .45 ACP cal., traditional double action with ambidextrous safety, 4 1/4 in. barrel, 8 shot mag. Mfg. 1990-99.

	$650	$550	$410	$345	$300	$250	$220	*$822*

* ***Model 4566TSW Stainless*** – similar to Model 4566, except has ambidextrous safety, 39.1 oz. Disc. 2004.

	$725	$600	$450	$390	$340	$280	$235	*$1,000*

MODEL 4567-NS STAINLESS – similar to Model 4566 Stainless, except has Tritium night sights, stainless steel frame and carbon steel slide. 2,500 mfg. in 1991 only.

	$650	$550	$425	$350	$290	$245	$215	*$735*

GRADING - PPGS™	100%	98%	95%	90%	80%	70%	60%	LAST MSR

MODEL 4576 STAINLESS – .45 ACP cal., features 4 1/4 in. barrel, frame mounted decocking lever, fixed sights. Mfg. 1990-92.

	$635	$535	$410	$345	$300	$250	$220	$762

MODEL 4583TSW – similar to Model 4563TSW, except is double action only, 30.6 oz. Mfg. 2000-2002.

	$700	$575	$450	$380	$330	$275	$230	$921

MODEL 4586 STAINLESS – .45 ACP cal., 4 1/4 in. barrel, double action only, 8 shot mag. Mfg. 1990-99.

	$695	$575	$425	$345	$300	$250	$220	$822

* ***Model 4586TSW Stainless*** – similar to Model 4566TSW, except is double action only, 39.1 oz. Mfg. 2000-2002.

	$700	$600	$445	$380	$330	$275	$230	$942

MODEL 5903 – 9mm Para. cal., double action semi-auto, 4 in. barrel, stainless steel slide and alloy frame, exposed hammer, 10 (C/B 1994) or 15* shot mag., adj. (disc. 1993) or fixed rear sight, ambidextrous safety. Mfg. 1990-97.

	$650	$575	$475	$395	$365	$325	$300	$701

Add $30 for adj. rear sight (disc).

Add 20% for Model 5903 SSV, only 1,500 mfg.

* ***Model 5903TSW*** – 9mm Para. cal., traditional double action, aluminum alloy frame with stainless slide, satin stainless finish, includes S&W tactical features, such as equipment rail and Novak Lo-Mount Carry sights, black synthetic grips with curved backstrap, 28.9 oz. Mfg. 2000-2004.

	$725	$580	$430	$385	$330	$275	$250	$892

* ***Model 5903-SSV*** – 9mm Para. cal., similar to Model 5903, except has 3 1/2 in. barrel, bobbed blue hammer, Novak Lo-Mount fixed two-dot rear sight, two-tone finish, straight backstrap with Delrin wraparound grip, 15 shot mag. 1,500 mfg. during 1990 only.

	$750	$595	$430	$385	$330	$275	$250	

MODEL 5904 – 9mm Para. cal., similar to Model 5903, except has steel slide and blue finish, 26 1/2 oz. Mfg. 1989-98.

	$535	$445	$360	$330	$300	$280	$265	$663

Add $30 for adj. rear sight (disc. 1993).

MODEL 5905 – 9mm Para. cal., similar to Model 5904, except has carbon steel frame and slide. Approx. 5,000 mfg. 1990-91 only.

	$650	$575	$500	$440	$375	$335	$300	

MODEL 5906 STAINLESS – 9mm Para. cal., stainless steel variation of the Model 5904, 37 1/2 oz. Mfg. 1989-1999.

	$615	$500	$400	$335	$290	$245	$215	$751

Add $37 for adj. rear sight.

Add $115 for Tritium night sights.

Add 100% for Model 5906M (South American military model with melonite finish).

* ***Model 5906TSW Stainless*** – 9mm Para. cal., traditional double action only, similar to Model 5906 Stainless, but has S&W tactical features, including equipment rail, 38.3 oz. Mfg. 2000-2004.

	$650	$575	$475	$350	$300	$265	$235	$915

Add $44 if w/o Novak Lo Mount Carry sight.

Add $132 for night sights (disc.).

MODEL 5924 – 9mm Para. cal., 4 in. barrel, features frame mounted decocking lever, 15 shot mag., 37 1/2 oz. Mfg. 1990-91 only.

	$625	$550	$475	$375	$335	$300	$280	$635

GRADING - PPGS™	100%	98%	95%	90%	80%	70%	60%	LAST MSR
MODEL 5926 STAINLESS – 9mm Para. cal., stainless variation of the Model 5924. Disc. 1992.								
	$600	$525	$425	$350	$295	$250	$210	*$697*
MODEL 5943 STAINLESS – 9mm Para. cal., double action only, 4 in. barrel, aluminum alloy frame with stainless steel slide, straight backstrap, 15 shot mag. Mfg. 1990-91 only.								
	$550	$465	$390	$325	$280	$235	$205	*$655*
* ***Model 5943-SSV Stainless*** – 9mm Para. cal., similar to Model 5943 Stainless, except has 3 1/2 in. barrel, Tritium night sights. Mfg. 1990-91 only.								
	$625	$550	$475	$395	$330	$285	$240	*$690*
* ***Model 5943TSW Stainless*** – 9mm Para. cal., double action only, aluminum alloy frame with stainless steel slide, includes S&W tactical features, equipment rail, and Novak Lo-Mount Carry sights, 28.9 oz. Mfg. 2000-2002.								
	$650	$575	$450	$375	$325	$280	$265	*$844*
MODEL 5944 – 9mm Para. cal., similar to Model 5943 Stainless, except has blue finish slide. Mfg. 1990-1991 only.								
	$625	$550	$475	$400	$350	$300	$280	*$610*
MODEL 5946 STAINLESS – 9mm Para. cal., double action only, one piece Xenoy wraparound grips, all stainless steel variation of the Model 5943, 39 1/2 oz. Mfg. 1990-99.								
	$615	$500	$400	$335	$290	$245	$215	*$751*
* ***Model 5946TSW Stainless*** – 9mm Para. cal., double action only, includes S&W tactical features, equipment rail, and Novak Lo-Mount Carry sights, 38.3 oz. Mfg. 2000-2002.								
	$725	$600	$450	$375	$315	$260	$225	*$863*
MODEL 6904 COMPACT – 9mm Para. cal., compact variation of the Model 5904, 3 1/2 in. barrel, 10 (C/ B 1994) or 12* shot finger extension mag., fixed rear sight, 26 1/2 oz. Mfg. 1989-97.								
	$550	$475	$400	$350	$325	$300	$280	*$625*
MODEL 6906 COMPACT STAINLESS – 9mm Para. cal., stainless steel variation of the Model 6904, 26 1/2 oz. Mfg. 1989-1999.								
	$585	$470	$380	$320	$275	$235	$200	*$720*
Add $116 for Tritium night sights (new 1992).								
MODEL 6926 STAINLESS – 9mm Para. cal., 3 1/2 in. barrel, standard double action, features frame mounted decocking lever, aluminum alloy frame with stainless slide, 12 shot mag. Mfg. 1990-91 only.								
	$650	$575	$450	$375	$315	$270	$230	*$663*
MODEL 6944 – 9mm Para. cal., double action only, 3 1/2 in. barrel, 12 shot mag., aluminum alloy frame with blue steel slide. Mfg. 1990-1991 only.								
	$600	$525	$450	$375	$325	$300	$280	*$578*
MODEL 6946 STAINLESS – 9mm Para. cal., similar to Model 6944, except has stainless steel slide, semi-bobbed hammer, 26 1/2 oz. Mfg. 1990-1999.								
	$675	$575	$475	$375	$315	$270	$230	*$720*
BODYGUARD 380 – .380 ACP cal., 2 3/4 in. barrel, sub-compact, black polymer frame with integral laser and finger groove grips, stainless steel slide with black melonite finish, 6 shot mag., DAO (hammer fired), adj. sight, 11.85 oz. New mid-2010.								
MSR $419	$365	$325	$285	$265	$245	$225	$200	
MODEL CS9 CHIEFS SPECIAL – 9mm Para. cal., compact design with traditional double action, hammerless, 3 in. barrel, 7 shot mag., alloy frame/stainless slide or stainless steel construction (disc. 2000), Hogue wraparound rubber grips, 3-dot Novak low mount sights, 20.8 oz. Mfg. 1999-2006.								
	$600	$460	$380	$325	$270	$230	$195	*$777*

GRADING - PPGS™	100%	98%	95%	90%	80%	70%	60%	LAST MSR

MODEL CS40 CHIEFS SPECIAL – .40 S&W cal., similar to Model CS9, except has 3 1/4 in. barrel, 24.2 oz. Mfg. 1999-2002.

	$575	$435	$375	$315	$275	$230	$195	*$717*

MODEL CS45 CHIEFS SPECIAL – .45 ACP cal., similar to Model CS40, except has 6 shot mag., matte finished stainless steel slide, 23.9 oz. Mfg. 1999-2006.

	$660	$485	$410	$335	$285	$230	$195	*$826*

SIGMA MODEL SW9F SERIES – 9mm Para. cal., double action only, 4 1/2 in. barrel, fixed sights, polymer frame and steel slide, striker firing system, blue finish only, 10 (C/B 1994) or 17* shot mag., 26 oz. Mfg. 1994-96.

	$475	$400	$350	$325	$295	$280	$265	*$593*

Add $104 for Tritium night sights.

* ***Sigma Model SW9C Series Compact*** – 9mm Para. cal., similar to Sigma Model SW9F, except has 4 in. barrel, 25 oz. Mfg. 1996-1998.

	$450	$355	$325	$295	$280	$265	$240	*$541*

* ***Sigma Model SW9M Series Compact*** – 9mm Para. cal., features 3 1/4 in. barrel, 7 shot mag., fixed channel rear sight, grips integral with frame, satin black finish, 18 oz. Mfg. 1996-1998.

	$300	$270	$240	$220	$195	$175	$160	*$366*

SIGMA MODEL SW9VE/GVE (SW9E/SW9P/SW9G/SW9V) – 9mm Para. cal., DAO, features 4 in. standard or ported (SW9P, mfg. 2001-2003) barrel, 10 or 16 (new late 2004) shot mag., 3-dot sighting system, grips integral with grey (disc. 2000), Nato Green (SW9G, disc. 2003) or black polymer frame, black (SW9E, mfg. 1999-2002) or satin stainless steel (SW9VE) slide, 24.7 oz. New 1997.

MSR $379	$320	$275	$230	$200	$175	$150	$140	

Add $8 for Allied Forces model w/Melonite slide (mfg. 2007-2009).
Add $380 for SW9VE/SW40VE Allied Forces model w/emergency kit, including space blankets, emergency food, first aid kit, crank radio/flashlight, multi-tool, and pocket survival pack, cased (mfg. 2007-2009).
Add $48 for SW9P or SW9G with night sights (disc. 2003).
Add $210 for Tritium night sights (disc. 2000).

The Enhanced Sigma Series Model SW9VE was introduced during 1999, after the SW9V was discontinued.

SIGMA MODEL SW40F SERIES – .40 S&W cal., double action only, 4 1/2 in. barrel, fixed sights, polymer frame, blue finish only, 10 (C/B 1994) or 15* shot mag., 26 oz. Mfg. 1994-98.

	$450	$355	$325	$295	$280	$265	$240	*$541*

Add $104 for Tritium night sights (disc. 1997).

* ***Sigma Model SW40C Series Compact*** – .40 S&W cal., similar to Sigma Model SW40F, except has 4 in. barrel, 26 oz. Mfg. 1996-1998.

	$450	$355	$325	$295	$280	$265	$240	*$541*

SIGMA MODEL SW40VE/SW40P/SW40G/SW40GVE (SW40E/SW40V) – .40 S&W cal., features 4 in. standard or ported (SW40P, mfg. 2001-2005) barrel, 10 or 14 (new mid-2004) shot mag., 3-dot sighting system, grips integral with grey (disc. 2000), Nato green (SW40G) or black polymer frame, black slide with Melonite finish (SW40E, mfg. 1999-2002) or satin stainless steel slide, 24.4 oz. New 1997.

MSR $379	$320	$275	$230	$200	$175	$150	$140	

Add $8 for Allied Forces model w/Melonite slide, (mfg. 2007-2009).
Add $210 for Tritium night sights (disc.).
Add $145 for Model SW40P or SW40G (includes night sights, disc. 2005).
Add $380 for SW9VE/SW40VE Allied Forces model w/emergency kit, including space blankets, emergency food, first aid kit, crank radio/flashlight, multi-tool, and pocket survival pack, cased (mfg. 2007-2009).

The Enhanced Sigma Series Model SW40VE was introduced during 1999, after the SW40V was discontinued.

GRADING - PPGS™	100%	98%	95%	90%	80%	70%	60%	LAST MSR

MODEL SW99 – 9mm Para., .40 S&W, or .45 ACP (new 2003) cal., traditional double action, 9 (.45 ACP cal.) or 10 shot mag., similar to the Walther P99, black polymer frame with black stainless slide and barrel, 4, 4 1/8 (.40 S&W cal. only), or 4.25 (.45 ACP cal. only, new 2003) in. barrel, black finish, ambidextrous mag. release, frame equipment groove, interchangeable backstraps, decocking lever, cocking indicator, adj. 3-dot or night sights, 25.4 (9mm Para cal.) or 28 1/2 oz. Mfg. 2000-2004.

	$565	$485	$430	$380	$340	$300	$275	*$667*

Add $123 for night sights.

Add $41 for .45 ACP cal. (new 2003).

* ***Model SW99 Compact*** – similar to SW99, except is compact version, not available in .45 ACP cal., 3 1/2 in. barrel, 8 (.40 S&W cal.) or 10 (9mm Para cal.) shot mag. with finger extension, approx. 23 oz. Mfg. 2003-2004.

	$565	$485	$430	$380	$340	$300	$275	*$667*

SIGMA MODEL SW357 – .357 SIG cal., 4 in. barrel, 10 shot mag., black finish, stainless steel. Mfg. 1998 only.

	$525	$450	$375	$325	$250	$195	$165	

SIGMA MODEL SW380 – .380 ACP cal., double action only, 3 in. barrel, fixed sights, polymer frame and steel slide, striker firing system, blue finish only, 6 shot mag., shortened grip, 14 oz. Mfg. 1996-2000.

	$285	$245	$210	$190	$180	$170	$160	*$358*

MODEL SW990L – 9mm Para., .40 S&W, or .45 ACP cal., DAO, 9 (.45 ACP cal. only), 10 (all cals. except .45 ACP), 12 (.40 S&W cal.) or 16 (9mm Para.) shot mag., similar to the Walther P99, black polymer frame with black stainless Melonite slide and barrel, 4 (9mm Para. cal. only), 4 1/8 (.40 S&W cal. only), or 4.25 (.45 ACP cal. only) in. barrel, black finish, approx. 25 oz. Mfg. 2005-2006.

	$610	$515	$450	$400	$350	$300	$275	*$729*

Add $44 for .45 ACP cal.

* ***Model SW990L Compact*** – similar to SW990L, except is compact version with small polymer frame, not available in .45 ACP cal., 3 1/2 in. barrel, 8 (.40 S&W cal.) or 10 (9mm Para cal.) shot mag. with finger extension, approx. 23 oz. Mfg. 2005-2006.

	$610	$515	$450	$400	$350	$300	$275	*$729*

MODEL SW SD9 – 9mm Para. cal., DAO, striker fire action, w/o hammer, 4 in. barrel, 10 or 16 shot mag., stainless steel slide/barrel, black polymer frame with Picatinny rail, front and rear slide serrations, Tritium night front sight, two-dot fixed rear sight, black Melanite finish, 22.7 oz. Mfg. 2010-2011.

	$375	$325	$295	$275	$250	$225	$200	*$459*

Add $40 for home defense kit that includes NanoVault lockable case and S&W Micro90 compact pistol light (disc. 2011).

MODEL SW SD40 – .40 S&W cal., DAO, striker fire action, w/o hammer, 4 in. barrel, 10 or 14 shot mag., stainless steel slide/barrel, black polymer frame with Picatinny rail, front and rear slide serrations, Tritium night front sight, two-dot fixed rear sight, black Melanite finish, 22.7 oz. Mfg. 2010-2011.

	$375	$325	$295	$275	$250	$225	$200	*$459*

Add $40 for home defense kit that includes NanoVault lockable case and S&W Micro90 compact pistol light (disc. 2011).

MODEL M&P SERIES – 9mm Para., .40 S&W, .357 SIG (disc. 2010), or .45 ACP (new 2007) cal., black Melonite finished stainless steel barrel and slide with twin scalloped slide serrations, black Zytel polymer frame reinforced with stainless steel, matte black or Dark Earth brown (new 2007) finish, 8, 10, 12, 15, or 17 shot mag., ramp front sights, Novak Lo-Mount Carry rear sight, ambidextrous manual safety became an option during 2009, 6 1/2 lbs. trigger pull, 18 degree grip angle, Picatinny rail in front of trigger guard, three interchangeable grip sizes, 24 1/4-29 1/2 oz. Approx. 25 variations in each caliber. New 2006.

Add $50 for ambidextrous manual safety with lanyard loop on non-compact models.

GRADING - PPGS™	100%	98%	95%	90%	80%	70%	60%	LAST MSR

* ***M&P Shield*** – 9mm Para. or .40 S&W cal., striker fire DAO, 6, 7, or 8 shot mag., 3.1 in. barrel, polymer frame with textured front and back straps, black Melonite finish, white dot front and rear sights, 19 oz. New mid-2012.

MSR $449	$375	$325	$275	$250	$200	$175	$125	

* ***M&P357*** – .357 SIG cal., 4 1/4 in. barrel, 10 or 15 shot mag., similar to M&P9. Disc. 2010.

	$575	$475	$375	$335	$285	$260	$230	*$727*

* ***M&P357 Compact*** – .357 SIG cal., 10 shot mag., 3 1/2 in. barrel, similar to M&P9 Compact, 22 oz. Mfg. 2007-2010.

	$575	$475	$375	$335	$285	$260	$230	*$727*

* ***M&P9*** – 9mm Para. cal., 10 or 17 shot mag., 4 1/4 in. barrel, full size polymer frame, white dot or steel ramp dovetail front sight, steel low profile or Novak Lo-Mount carry rear sight, stainless steel slide and barrel, black Melonite finish, with or w/o thumb safety, black grips with three interchangeable palmswell grip sizes or Crimson Trace Laser grips (new 2008), lower accessory rail, includes two magazines, 24 oz.

MSR $569	$425	$350	$315	$285	$260	$230	$200	

Add $40 for carry and range kit - includes Blade Tech Kydex holster, double magazine pouch, Maglula Uplula speed loader, ear plugs, and extra magazine.
Add $150 for threaded barrel kit.
Add $240 for Crimson Trace Laser grips (new 2008).

» ***M&P9 JG*** – 9mm Para. cal., 17 shot mag., similar to M&P9, except has fiber optic front sight, Warren tactical rear sight, five interchangeable palmswell grip sizes (three black and two pink), breast cancer awareness ribbon engraved on slide, designed in collaboration with champion Julie Goloski-Golob. Disc. 2012.

	$465	$375	$325	$300	$280	$250	$215	*$619*

* ***M&P9L*** – 9mm Para. cal.,17 shot mag., 5 in. barrel, full size polymer frame, white dot or steel ramp dovetail front sight, steel low profile carry rear sight, stainless steel slide and barrel, black Melonite finish, three interchangeable palmswell grip sizes, includes two magazines, 25 oz. Disc. 2011.

	$575	$475	$395	$350	4325	4295	$250	*$758*

* ***M&P9 VTAC (Viking Tactics)*** – 9mm Para. cal., 17 shot mag., 4 1/4 in. barrel, full size polymer frame, VTAC Warrior front and rear sights, durable PVD coated stainless steel slide, Flat Dark Earth finish, 24 oz.

MSR $779	$625	$525	$425	$375	$325	$295	$250	

* ***M&P9 Compact*** – 9mm Para. cal., 12 shot mag., 3 1/2 in. barrel, steel ramp dovetail mount front sight, Novak Lo-Mount carry rear sight, compact Zytel polymer frame with stainless steel slide and barrel, black Melonite finish, with or w/o thumb safety, with or w/o three interchangeable palmswell or Crimson Trace Laser grips, 22 oz. New 2007.

MSR $569	$425	$350	$315	$285	$260	$230	$200	

Add $150 if w/o thumb safety and interchangeable grips (disc. 2011).
Add $240 for Crimson Trace laser grips.

» ***M&P9 Compact XGRIP*** – 9mm Para. cal., 17 shot mag., similar to Model M&P9 Compact, except has XGRIP magazine adapter.

MSR $559	$415	$350	$315	$285	$260	$230	$200	

This model is distributed exclusively by Talo.

* ***M&P40*** – .40 S&W cal., 10 or 15 shot mag., SA or DAO, 4 1/4 in. barrel, similar to Model M&P9, with or w/o thumb safety, 24 1/4 oz.

MSR $569	$425	$350	$315	$285	$260	$230	$200	

Add $40 for carry and range kit - includes Blade Tech Kydex holster, double magazine pouch, Maglula Uplula speed loader, ear plugs, and extra magazine.
Add $240 for Crimson Trace laser grips.

GRADING - PPGS™	100%	98%	95%	90%	80%	70%	60%	LAST MSR

* ***M&P40 VTAC (Viking Tactics)*** – .40 S&W cal., 15 shot mag., 4 1/4 in. barrel, full size polymer frame, VTAC Warrior front and rear sights, durable PVD coated stainless steel slide, Flat Dark Earth finish, 24 oz.

MSR $779	$625	$525	$425	$375	$325	$295	$250	

* ***M&P40 Compact*** – 9mm Para. cal., 10 or 12 shot mag., 3 1/2 in. barrel, steel ramp dovetail mount front sight, Novak Lo-Mount carry rear sight, compact Zytel polymer frame with stainless steel slide and barrel, black Melonite finish, with or w/o thumb safety, with or w/o three interchangeable palmswell or Crimson Trace Laser grips, 22 oz. New 2007.

MSR $569	$425	$350	$315	$285	$260	$230	$200	

Add $240 for Crimson Trace laser grips.

* ***M&P45*** – .45 ACP cal., 10 shot mag., 4 or 4 1/2 in. barrel, full size black polymer frame, Melanite or Dark Earth Brown finish, otherwise similar to M&P9, 29.6 oz.

MSR $599	$450	$375	$325	$295	$260	$230	$200	

Add $90 for night sights (disc. 2012).
Add $20 for Dark Earth Brown finish.
Add $230 for Crimson Trace laser grips (disc. 2012).

* ***M&P45 Compact*** – .45 ACP cal., 8 shot mag., 4 in. barrel, similar to M&P9 Compact, 27 oz. New 2007.

MSR $599	$450	$375	$325	$295	$260	$230	$200	

Add $20 for ambidextrous safety with either melonite or dark brown finish.

MODEL M&P PRO SERIES – 9mm Para. or .40 S&W cal., 4 1/4 or 5 in. barrel, polymer frame, blue/black or satin (9mm Para. cal. only) stainless steel, plastic grips, Lo-Mount Carry, night or fiber optic sights, striker fire action, 26 oz. Disc. 2012.

MSR $669	$575	$475	$400	$350	$300	$265	$235	

Add $60 for optic ready variation (new 2013).

PISTOLS: SEMI-AUTO, RIMFIRE

MODEL 22A SPORT SERIES – .22 LR cal., single action, 10 shot mag., aluminum alloy frame, stainless steel slide, choice of 4 in. standard, 5 1/2 in. standard or bull, or 7 in. standard barrel with raised solid rib, adj. rear and Hi-Viz (5 1/2 in. bull barrel only, new 2001) sights, 2-piece black polymer hard (disc.) or Soft Touch and Dymondwood (5 1/2 bull barrel only) grips, blue/black, two-tone (new 2006, 5 1/2 in. barrel only), or Realtree APG HD camo (new 2004, 5 1/2 in. barrel only) finish, 28-39 oz. New 1997.

MSR $329	$265	$225	$195	$175	$150	$125	$95	

Add $10 for 4 (disc. 2012), 5 1/2 or 7 in. barrel with blue/black finish. Add $40 for 5 1/2 in. bull barrel with Hi-Viz green dot front sight. Add $40 for wood target grips and adj. rear sight (5 1/2 in. barrel only). Add $40 for two-tone frame/slide finish with Hi-Viz green dot front sight. Add $40 for 100% Real Tree APG HD camo finish. Add $127 for 5 1/2 in. bull barrel with camo finish (disc. 2007). Add $114 for 5 1/2 in. bull barrel with Dymondwood target grips (disc. 2005). Add $71 for 5 1/2 in. bull barrel with 2 piece target grips and thumbrest (disc. 2000).

The standard Model 22A has a two-tone finish with Patridge front and adj. rear sights.

MODEL 22S SPORT SERIES – .22 LR cal., single action, 10 shot mag., aluminum alloy frame, stainless steel slide, choice of 5 1/2 standard or bull (disc. 2005) or 7 (disc. 2004) in. standard barrel with raised solid rib, adj. rear and Hi-Viz (5 1/2 in. bull barrel only, new 2001) sights, 2-piece black polymer (hard or soft) or Dymondwood (5 1/2 in. bull barrel only) grips, satin stainless finish, 41-48 oz. Mfg. 1997-2007.

	$325	$255	$210	$170	$140	$125	$110	*$419*

Add $40 for 7 in. standard barrel with thumbrest soft-touch grips (disc. 2004).
Add $83 for 5 1/2 in. bull barrel with Dymondwood target grips (disc. 2004).
Add $102 for 5 1/2 in. bull barrel with Hi-Viz sights (mfg. 2001-2004).
Add $44 for 5 1/2 in. bull barrel with 2 piece target grips and thumbrest (disc. 2000).

MODEL M&P15-22P – .22 LR cal., 6 in. threaded carbon steel barrel with A1 style compensator, 25 shot detachable mag., blow back action similar to M&P 15-22 rifle, quad

GRADING - PPGS™	100%	98%	95%	90%	80%	70%	60%	LAST MSR

rail handguard, adj. sights on top Picatinny rail, polymer lower receiver, matte black finish, black pistol grip, 51 oz. Mfg. mid-2010-2011.

	$425	$385	$360	$330	$295	$275	$250	*$519*

Product Code: 813000.

MODEL M&P 22 – .22 LR cal., 4.1 in. barrel, single action hammerless, 10 or 12 shot mag., plastic grips, fixed backstrap, aluminum alloy slide, adj. rear sight, black blade front sight, ambidextrous safety, blue/black finish, ambidextrous manual safety and slide stop, reversible mag release, lower Picatinny rail, approx. 24 oz. New 2011.

MSR $419	$350	$315	$285	$260	$240	$220	$195	

MODEL 41/41-1 .22 RF – .22 S (disc., Model 41-1) or LR cal., match target pistol, single action, 10 shot mag., adj. rear and Patridge front sights, checkered walnut grips with thumbrest, 5 (disc.), 5 1/2 (heavy), 7 (standard) or 7 3/8 (disc. 2004) in. barrel, blue finish only, 41 oz. New 1957.

MSR $1,369	$1,150	$1,000	$865	$775	$635	$525	$400	

Add $100 for 5 1/2 in. barrel with extended sight (disc.) or add $35 for 7 3/8 in. barrel with muzzle brake (disc.).

Add 125% for .22 Short cal. with counterweight and muzzle brake (disc.).

Add 15%-40% for early variations with cocking indicator (disc. 1978).

Factory engraving Model 41s with cocking indicator in NIB condition are currently selling in the $2,500 range.

There are several disc. barrels on the Model 41, including a 5 in. standard weight with extended sight, 7 3/8 in. with muzzle brake, and 5 1/2 in. heavy barrel with extended sight.

* ***Model 41 50th Anniversary*** – similar to Model 41, except has blue finish with gold line engraving, 500 mfg. to commemorate the 50th year of the Model 41, ser. no. range FYA001-FYA500, 41 oz. Mfg. 2007-2009.

	$1,795	$1,575	$1,350	$1,150	$925	$800	$675	*$2,150*

MODEL 46 – .22 LR cal., 5 (1,000 mfg.), 5 1/2 (500 mfg.), or 7 (2,500 mfg.) in. barrel, blue, nylon grips, adj. sights. Mfg. 4,000, 1957-1966.

	$1,200	$1,000	$750	$550	$450	$400	$350	

Add 50% for 5 1/2 in. heavy barrel.

Add 25% for 5 in. field barrel.

This model is similar to the Model 41, but does not have high polish bluing, and has brown plastic grips.

MODEL 61 ESCORT – .22 LR cal., 5 shot, semi-auto, blue or nickel, 2 1/2 in. barrel, plastic grips. Mfg. 1970-1974.

Blue finish	$350	$250	$225	$175	$150	$140	$110	
Nickel finish	$395	$275	$235	$185	$155	$140	$110	

Four variations of this model were produced - Model 61 serial numbered B1001-B7800 (6,800 mfg.), Model 61-1 serial numbered B001-B0499 and B7801-B9850, Mode 61-2 serial numbered B9851-B40000 and Model 61-3 serial numbered B40001-B65438.

MODEL 422 .22 RF (FIELD) – .22 LR cal., single action, 4 1/2 or 6 in. barrel, aluminum frame with steel slide, 10 shot mag., fixed sights, black plastic or wood grips, matte blue finish, 22 oz. Mfg. 1987-1996.

	$300	$250	$200	$150	$125	$90	$65	*$235*

* ***Model 422 Target*** – .22 LR cal., single action, 4 1/2 or 6 in. barrel, aluminum frame with steel slide, 10 shot mag., adj. rear sight, checkered walnut grips, matte blue finish, 22 oz. Mfg. 1987-1996.

	$350	$300	$250	$200	$150	$100	$70	*$290*

MODEL 622 .22 RF (Field) – .22 LR cal., single action, 4 1/2 or 6 in. barrel, stainless/alloy construction, 10 shot mag., fixed sights, black plastic grips, 21 1/2 or 23 1/2 oz. Mfg. 1990-96.

	$325	$200	$175	$150	$120	$100	$75	*$284*

GRADING - PPGS™	100%	98%	95%	90%	80%	70%	60%	LAST MSR

* ***Model 622 Target*** – .22 LR cal., single action, 4 1/2 or 6 in. barrel (VR was an option in 1996 only), stainless steel construction, 10 shot mag., adj. rear sight, checkered walnut grips, 21 1/2 or 23 1/2 oz. Mfg. 1990-96.

$375	$300	$225	$175	$150	$125	$100	*$337*

MODEL 2206 STAINLESS .22 RF (FIELD) – .22 LR cal., similar to Model 622 Field, except all stainless steel components, black plastic grips, 6 in. barrel with standard (disc. 1995) or adj. rear sight, 35 or 39 oz. Mfg. 1990-96.

$290	$225	$175	$135	$115	$100	$85	*$385*

Subtract $58 if w/o adj. sights.

* ***Model 2206 Stainless Target*** – similar to Model 2206 Stainless, except has adj. target sight, target stocks, and is drilled and tapped. Mfg. 1994-96.

$360	$275	$225	$175	$140	$125	$105	*$433*

MODEL 2213 STAINLESS .22 RF "SPORTSMAN" – .22 LR cal., single action, 3 in. barrel, alloy frame with stainless steel slide, 8 shot mag., 2 dot fixed rear sight, black plastic molded grips, 18 oz., includes holster/carry case. Mfg. 1992-99.

$255	$200	$160	$130	$115	$100	$85	*$340*

MODEL 2214 .22 RF "SPORTSMAN" – .22 LR cal., similar to Model 2213, except has alloy frame with blue carbon steel slide with matte black finish, and no case. Mfg. 1991-99.

$230	$185	$160	$150	$140	$130	$120	*$292*

PRE-2009 ENGRAVING OPTIONS FOR HANDGUNS

The prices listed were for original factory finished guns with no extra engraving.

CLASS "C" ENGRAVING - 1/3 METAL COVERAGE

Pistols - add $1,108.
For J Frame - add $876.
10 5/8 in. N Frame - add $1,343.
2-5 in. K, L, or N Frame - add $1,130.
6-8 3/8 in. K, L, or N Frame - add $1,285.

CLASS "B" ENGRAVING - 2/3 METAL COVERAGE

Pistols - add $1,448.
For J Frame - add $1,430.
10 5/8 in. N Frame - add $1,672.
2-5 in. K, L, or N Frame - add $1,477.
6-8 3/8 in. K, L, or N Frame - add $1,599.

CLASS "A" ENGRAVING - FULL COVERAGE

Pistols - add $1,761.
For J Frame - add $1,501.
10 5/8 in. N Frame - add $2,006.
2-5 in. K, L, or N Frame - add $1,814.
6-8 3/8 in. K, L, or N Frame - add $1,919.

LASERSMITH ENGRAVING – laser etching was available 1989-90 only. This process involved a digitally-controlled laser producing a variety of designs, logos, commemorative messages, or autograph on the metal surface(s). Some of these designs were made exclusively for major firearms distributors. Others were custom designed for clubs or organizations. Retail prices started at just under $18 and went as high as $150+, depending on the amount and complexity of the laser etching. To date, premiums are not being paid for these "rarer" variations.

CURRENT ENGRAVING OPTIONS FOR HANDGUNS

SPECIAL ENGRAVING – Also available with custom artwork: inlays, seals, scenes, lettering - prices quoted on request. Please call 1-800-331-0852, ext. 216 - a free color brochure on custom engraving services is available.

MASTER ENGRAVING – 100% coverage.

J-frame - $3,325
K, L, and N frame (2-5 in. barrel) - $4,015, $4,245 for 6 or 8 3/8 in. barrel, or $4,445 for over 8 3/8 in. barrel.
X-frame (4 in. barrel) - $8,290, $8,450 for over 8 in. barrel.
Pistols - $4,015.

CLASS A ENGRAVING – 75% coverage.

J-frame - $2,310
K, L, and N frame (2-5 in. barrel) - $2,790, $2,950 for 6 or 8 3/8 in. barrel, or $3,090 for over 8 3/8 in. barrel.
X-frame (4 in. barrel) - $5,710, $5,865 for over 8 in. barrel.
Pistols - $2,790.

CLASS B ENGRAVING – 50% coverage.

J-frame - $1,840
K, L, and N frame (2-5 in. barrel) - $1,895, $2,060 for 6 or 8 3/8 in. barrel, or $2,155 for over 8 3/8 in. barrel.
X-frame (4 in. barrel) - $4,285, $4,445 for over 8 in. barrel.
Pistols - $1,895

CLASS C ENGRAVING – 25% coverage.

J-frame - $1,085
K, L, and N frame (2-5 in. barrel) - $1,385, $1,585 for 6 or 8 3/8 in. barrel, or $1,650 for over 8 3/8 in. barrel.
X-frame (4 in. barrel) - $2,865, $3,025 for over 8 in. barrel.
Pistols - $1,425

S&W SPECIAL/LIMITED EDITIONS

During the course of a year, I receive many phone calls and letters on special editions and limited editions that do not appear in this section. Many of these are listed separately under the Davidson's or Lew Horton sections. It should be noted that a commemorative issue is a gun that has been manufactured, marketed, and sold through the auspices of the specific trademark (in this case S&W). During the past several decades, hundreds of limited editions have been ordered through various police agencies, state highway patrol units, and other law enforcement organizations. Many of these variations do not have the special suffix serialization (and may not have had a retail price when issued). Since most of these special editions/commemoratives were made for a specific organization, regional demand has a lot to do with determining values (a Model 27 special edition mfg. for a sheriff's dept. in Arkansas will not bring a premium in California). For this reason, most of these guns will not appear in this section and you should contact the factory to learn more about the provenance of these special editions. Remember - values on these models can vary A LOT from one region to another and an averaged "national" single price is almost impossible. While these guns do have special interest, they do not have the collectibility or desirability of many of the standard models listed. As one anonymous contributing editor states, "Hard to price, no real guidelines, generally seem to be dogs to sell, always cost more but bring less."

GRADING - PPGS™	100%	Issue Price	Qty. Made

S&W FACTORY COMMEMORATIVES

These variations listed represent only factory S&W Commemoratives manufactured to date. Anything else will be a special or limited edition made for a organization, company, or special event.

MODEL 19 TEXAS RANGER – .357 Mag., with or without knife, approx. 8,000 with knife, approx. 2,000 without, cased. Mfg. 1973 only.

	100%	Issue Price	Qty. Made
	$750	$250	10,000

Subtract 15% if without knife.

GRADING - PPGS™	100%	Issue Price	Qty. Made

* ***Model 19 Texas Ranger Deluxe*** – approx. 50 mfg. with a serial numbers divisible by 10, class A engraved, cased.

	$3,000	N/A	50

MODEL 25 125TH ANNIVERSARY COMMEMORATIVE – .45 LC cal., plain variation was called Model 25-3, 10,000 mfg. total in 1977, cased with nickel silver medallion, and Roy Jinks's book, *125th Anniversary of Smith & Wesson*.

	$1,395	$350	10,000

* ***Model 25 125th Anniversary Commemorative Deluxe*** – Model 25-4, approx. 50 mfg. with S&W prefix serial numbers divisible by 10, cased, sterling silver medallion, and a leather-bound *History of Smith & Wesson* book by Roy Jinks.

	N/A	N/A	50

MODEL 26-1 GEORGIA STATE PATROL COMMEMORATIVE – .45 ACP cal. Mfg. 1988.

	$1,425	N/A	800

MODEL 29 ELMER KEITH COMMEMORATIVE – .44 Mag. cal., 4 in. barrel, standard and deluxe editions, approx. 2,500 total mfg.

Standard	$975	N/A	2,500
Deluxe	$2,000	N/A	100

50TH ANNIVERSARY OF THE .357 MAGNUM – Model 27, both standard and deluxe editions. Mfg. 1985.

Standard	$895	N/A	2,500
Deluxe	$1,900	N/A	N/A

MODEL 544 TEXAS WAGON TRAIN COMMEMORATIVE – .44-40 WCF cal. only, 6 shot, 5 in. barrel, bright blue finish, adj. sights, 4,782 mfg. 1986 to commemorate the Texas Sesquicentennial (1836-1986). Special markings on frame and barrel, smooth Goncalo commemorative grips, ser. no. TWT0001-TWT7800 (estimated). Made 1986 only.

	$600	N/A	7,800

S&W PERFORMANCE CENTER FIREARMS

The Performance Center (PC) of Smith & Wesson got its start in 1990 from the efforts of two Master Gunsmiths, Paul Liebenburg and John French. The Performance Center is today managed by Tom Kelly and has grown to about 26 employees, all of which are engaged in the handgun shooting sports, a condition of being in the Center. The Performance Center generally does not take production guns and improve them. These handguns are built from scratch. Using two CNC machines, the Performance Center turns out about 400+ guns a month. There is no inventory of PC products. They are pre-sold before they are made. Once a new design is made and prototyped, it is shown to distributors of specialty guns. The distributor is given an exclusive on a particular model and those handguns are sold through the distributor's network of retailers. Currently, the major distributors ordering PC products include: Lew Horton, RSR Group, Camfour, and Talo Dist. The Performance Center delivers limited production runs, unique design and special feature firearms, and also provides gunsmithing services to existing S&W standard products.

While we have tried to list all the Performance Center guns in this section, it is possible that you may find some models listed with their corresponding numbered model in the Semi-Auto Pistols and Numbered Model Revolvers section in this text. Models are listed in the general order of the model number upon which they are based, with descriptions of each gun. At the end of the model descriptions, you may find a collected listing of variations, changes, and/or product codes for PC guns based on a particular model. In the Serialization section in the back of this text, a listing of all Performance Center guns in order of Product Code number has been provided.

During the past 10 years, all PC guns have been marked with the Performance Center trademark on the frame. The product codes are only on the shipping container or box. The 170XXX Performance Center product code indicates a handgun that has been designed and made from scratch by the Performance Center, while the 178XXX code indicates an exisiting

product/SKU that has been improved/changed.

Pricing of Performance Center Firearms

Whenever possible, original PC model MSRs have been provided. In some cases, the distributor never posted an MSR on a particular PC model. N/As designate that more research is under way to find out more about the original MSRs, if they exist, and will be included in future editions and our online services.

As a general rule, the easiest way to determine values for Performance Center handguns is to look at the current pricing of the models from which they are derived. In other words, on a PC Model 442 Ultralight, check the standard Model 442 pricing in this text, and use the MSR - 100% price range to establish a base price, assuming the condition is NIB. Depending on the desirability of the PC configuration, such as finishes, barrel lengths, styling, special orders/ features (i.e., laser or hand engraving, precious metal inlays, ivory or exotic wood grips, etc.), special sights, and other production variances from the standard model, premiums may exist over the 100% or current MSR values listed for the standard model. If a particular PC model has an original MSR that's significantly higher than the standard model, the buyer and seller are going to have to interpolate a possible premium which both feel comfortable with.

It is important to note that PC models are essentially limited runs of custom guns, which sell out in a relatively short period of time, and only resurface sporadically in the secondary marketplace. Many can be found in NIB or Excellent condition. Also, dealer or retail pricing is very rarely published on these models, making values difficult to determine for the secondary marketplace. PC gun values can form a bell curve, with the peak being around $1,000. Semi-auto pistols generally sell for more than revolvers. Elaborate engraving, custom shop options, and the desirability of the configuration make all the difference when determining the value of an S&W Performance Center handgun. Semi-auto pistols can reach $3,000.

Heritage Series From Lew Horton & Performance Center Handguns

Beginning in 2001, Lew Horton Distributors and the Performance Center manufactured a series of specials from Smith & Wesson called "The Heritage Series." These were produced over a period of 2 years and included case color Models (10 & 24) and other models no longer manufactured but were very popular over the last century. This series included Models 10, 15, 17, 19, 24, 25, 29, and the Model of 1917 in various finishes. Each had a gold color antique style box unique to the Heritage series, with a picture of Horace Smith and Daniel Wesson on the top with blue metal corners and a modern end label. All guns were shipped with a fired case from the gun in a small sealed envelope signed by the shooter, along with a trigger lock or cable lock. Mfg. 2001-2003.

PERFORMANCE CENTER REVOLVER VARIATIONS

SCHOFIELD MODEL OF 2000 - .45 (.45 Schofield) cal., 6 shot, 7 in. barrel, SA, this 3rd Model Schofield is a modern top break, features the design concepts of the original Model 3 Schofield and incorporates the technical and engineering advantages of the last 125 years, modern hammer block safety, case colored hammer, smooth case colored trigger, 1st edition latches, fixed notch rear and pinned half moon post front sights, walnut grips, carbon steel frame w/polished blue finish, 40 oz., 12 1/2 in. overall, Serial prefix of "GWS" for Col. George W. Schofield. Mfg. began in Jan. 2000.

Last MSR was $1,800.

Product Code: 170146.

* ***Schofield Model of 2000 w/Nickel Finish*** - .45 S&W (.45 Schofield) cal., 7 in. barrel, nickel finish, "US" stamped on the butt with ser. no., black pinned round blade front sight with Mod 3 Schofield 1875" on the right side, case colored hammer, latch and trigger guard, shipped in the Heritage Series box. Mfg. began in Nov. 2001.

Last MSR was $1,520.

Product Code: 170209FC.

* ***Schofield Model of 2000 Wells Fargo Editions*** – .45 S&W (.45 Schofield) cal., 5 in. barrel, blue or nickel finish, black pinned round blade front sight, case colored hammer, latch and trigger guard, similar to other editions with "US" on butt with ser. no., marked ".45 S&W" on left side of barrel, and "Schofield Pat. Apr. 22nd 1873" on right side, shipped in Heritage Series box. Mfg. beginning Nov. 2001.

Last MSR was $1,500.

Product Codes: 170207FC (nickel), 170208FC (blue).

LEW HORTON MODEL 10 – .38 S&W Spl. cal., DA, case colored square butt or round butt frame and yoke, blue 4 1/4 in. tapered barrel, blue cylinder and thumb piece, brown laminated magna style wood grips with silver medallions, limited production from Lew Horton Dist. "Heritage Series", serial prefix of CRS0001-CRS0080, model stampings of 10-7 and 10-9 have been observed.

Last MSR was $790.

Product Code: 178006FC.

MODEL PC-13 – .357 Mag. cal., DA, 6 shot, 3 in. Magna ported barrel, fixed rear w/ramp front sight, Eagle Secret Service boot or Uncle Mike's grips on a K-frame, matte blue finish with beveled cylinder latch, trigger, and charge holes, shrouded extractor rod, trigger has an overtravel stop, 400 mfg., distributed by Lew Horton during 1995.

Last MSR was $760.

Product Codes: 170059 (eagle grips) or 170063 (Uncle Mike's grips).

MODEL 14 PPC – .38 Spl. cal., DA, 4 in. full lug barrel, precision crowned muzzle, custom duty action, polished forcing cone, shipped to a law enforcement distributor in Mississippi for the National Police Shooting Championships, received by the MS Highway Patrol and L.A.P.D. pistol teams, accurized by the Performance Center, not for retail trade. Limited production of less than 100 units 1995-96.

Last MSR was N/A.

Product Code: 170154.

LEW HORTON HERITAGE SERIES MODEL 15-8 – .38 Spl. cal., special case colored frame and yoke, 4 in. blue barrel, blue cylinder, ramp on ramp base front sight with micrometer click rear sight, drilled and tapped, smooth trigger with checked hammer spur, round butt frame with wood laminated checkered grips, Performance Center logo under the thumbpiece, ser. no. prefix CSC0164 (example), shipped in a Heritage Series box with metal corners. Mfg. Aug. 2001.

Last MSR was $922.

Product Code: 17009FC.

LEW HORTON HERITAGE SERIES MODEL 15-8 NICKEL – .38 Spl. cal., similar to previous model, except has bright nickel finish, wood laminate grips on round butt 3 screw frame, ser. prefix NSC0170 (example). Mfg. Sept. 2001.

Last MSR was $922.

Product Code: 178008FC.

LEW HORTON HERITAGE SERIES MCGIVERN MODEL 15-9 – .38 Spl. cal., 6 in. barrel, new Model 15-9 round butt frame with integral frame lug, commemorates Ed McGivern's world speed records in 1934, 6 shot with Patridge front sight and McGivern gold bead, micrometer click rear sight, Altamont fancy checkered service grips, color case hardened, nickel or blue finish, McGivern speed record sideplate attached. Mfg. 2001.

Last MSR was $1,059.

Product Codes: 170217FC (nickel), 170216FC (case colored), or 170199FC (blue).

MODEL 17-8 KT22 – .22 LR cal., DA, 6 shot, all blue or case colored frame with blue barrel and cylinder, 4 screw sideplate, blue finish, serial numbers w/LRM prefix on the butt and in two places on the frame under the grips, Performance Center logo under the thumbpiece, shipped in "Heritage Series" box. Distributed by Lew Horton in 2003.

Last MSR was $1,040.

Product Codes: 170198FC (blue) or 170212FC (case colored).

MODEL 19 PERFORMANCE CENTER K COMP – .38 Spl./.357 Mag. cal., DA, blue matte finish, Target K-frame w/round butt, 6 shot fluted cylinder with counterbores, 3 in. full lug ported barrel, blue matte finish, smooth combat trigger, set back tritium night front sight on post, black blade adjustable rear sight, contoured thumbpiece, rubber combat grips, 36 oz. Mfg. 1994 and 2000.

Last MSR was $800.

Product Codes: 170025 (1994 mfg.) and 170163 (2000 mfg.).

LEW HORTON HERITAGE SERIES MODEL 24-5 – .44 Spl. cal., case colored frame, blue 6 1/2 in. barrel, blue cylinder, 4 screw sideplate, round butt frame, ball detent lockup at yoke, traditional thumpiece, diamond checkered walnut grips with S&W monogram, PC trademark under thumbpiece, ser. prefix "CSH". 150 mfg. May 2001.

Last MSR was $1,110.

Product Code: 170185FC.

* ***Lew Horton Heritage Series Model 24-5 Blue Finish*** – similar to previous model except has all blue finish, ser. prefix of BCBxx66. Mfg. Sept. 2001.

Last MSR was $1,050.

Product Code: 170189FC.

MODEL 25-10 "HAND EJECTOR" 2001 – .45 Colt cal., 6 in. tapered barrel with shrouded extractor, pinned gold bead Patridge front sight with black blade micrometer click rear sight, 1955 Hand Ejector features built on the most modern N-frame design, yoke has a ball detent front lockup with the normal extractor rod lock, 4 screw sideplates, chamfered charge holes, wood grips with S&W medallions, bright blue finish, supplied with Certificate signed by the Performance Center manager, shipped with aluminum PC locking gun case, 42 oz., approx. 150 mfg. Distributed by Sports South, Inc. in 2001.

Last MSR was N/A.

Product Code: 170179FC.

MODEL 25-11 – .45 Colt cal., 6 1/2 in. blue barrel, case colored frame, adj. rear sight, 6 shot fluted cylinder, 4 screw frame stamped Model 25-11, ser. prefix "GBP", marked "45 Colt CTG" on right side of barrel, shipped in Heritage Series gold box. 150 mfg. July 2001.

Last MSR was $1,150.

Product Code: 170186FC.

MODEL 25-11 BLUE FINISH – .45 LC cal., 6 1/2 in. barrel, all blue finish, adj. rear sight, 6 shot fluted cylinder, 4 screw frame stamped Model 25-11, ser. prefix "BAK", marked "45 Colt CTG" on right side of barrel, shipped in Heritage Series gold box. Mfg. July 2001.

Last MSR was $1,150.

Product Code: 170196FC.

LEW HORTON HERITAGE SERIES MODEL OF 1917 – .45 ACP cal., 5 1/2 in. barrel, blue finish, fixed rear sight, lanyard ring and half moon clips, 4 screw frame, marked Model 25-12, 6 shot fluted cylinder, marked ".45 ACP" on right side of barrel and "S&W D.A. 45" on left, PC logo under thumbpiece, ser. no. prefix "NCS", shipped in Heritage Series gold box. 150 mfg. Aug. 2001.

Last MSR was $1,050

Product Code: 170197FC.

* ***Lew Horton Heritage Series Model of 1917 Case Colored*** – similar to Lew Horton Heritage Series Model of 1917, except has case colored finish. 150 mfg. Sept. 2001.

Last MSR was $1,050.

Product Code: 170211FC.

* ***Lew Horton Heritage Series Model of 1917 Military*** – similar to Lew Horton Heritage Series Model of 1917, except has dull military-style finish.

Last MSR was $1,050.

Product Code: 170218FC.

MODEL 27-7 – .357 Mag. cal., 8 shot, 100 with 4 in. barrel with black ramp front sight, 100 with 6 1/2 in. barrel with black Patridge front sight, Magna combat grips, 42-45 oz. Distributed by Bangers.

Last MSR was N/A.

Product Codes: 170166 (4 in.) or 170167 (6 1/2 in.).

GRADING - PPGS™	100%	98%	95%	90%	80%	70%	60%	LAST MSR

"CLASSIC SERIES" MODEL 27 – .357 Mag. cal., the last 6 shot Model 27s were mfg. with frame and barrels from 50th Anniversary Commemoratives, and frames recessed cylinders from the "outnumbered" series "AVU" ser. prefix. 14 were mfg. and sold through Lew Horton in June 1999.

Last MSR was N/A.

Product Code: 170151.

MODEL 27-8 "THE REGISTERED MAGNUM" – .357 Mag. cal., 3 1/2 or 5 in. barrel, bright blue or nickel, 8 shot, modern CNC square butt frame with four screws and serrated tangs, two variations were designed with machining which characterizes the famous revolver with top strap checkering and checkering along the barrel rib, shipped containing a Registered Magnum Certificate of a design made in 2007. Introduced during SHOT Show 2007.

	$875	$675	$625	$525	$495	$475	$450	*$1,000*

Product codes: 170271 3-1/5 in. bright blue, 170272 5 in. bright blue, 170308 3-1/2 in. nickel, 170309 5 in. nickel.

MODEL 28 – .357 Mag., red ramp front sight with white outline rear sight, 4 in. barrel with recessed cylinder, during 2000 approx. five Model 28s were stamped with the Performance Center trademark, ser. no. N951647 Model 28-2 is one example.

Extreme rarity precludes accurate pricing on this model.

MODEL 29 "AMERICAN PRIDE" – .44 Mag. cal., first ever carbon steel Performance Center Hunter model, Hi-Viz interchangeable front sight, high polish blue finish, unique barrel design with removable scope base, 4 screw sideplate, unfluted cylinder, checkered wood grips with American Pride logo, internal key lock. 200 mfg. 2005.

Last MSR was N/A.

Product Code: 170253.

MODEL 29-9 HERITAGE SERIES – .44 Mag. cal., 6 1/2 in. barrel, blue finish, adj. rear sight, 6 shot fluted cylinder, 4 screw frame stamped "Model 29-9", extractor shroud, PC logo under thumbpiece, target grips, shipped in Heritage Series gold box. Mfg. 2002.

Last MSR was $1,045.

Product Code: 170213FC.

* ***Heritage Series Model 29-9 Lew Horton*** – similar to Model 29-9 Heritage Series, except has nickel finish, serial prefix is BBR. Mfg. 2002.

Last MSR was $1,045.

Product Code: 170214FC.

MODEL 41 – "Classic 41", approx. 10 mfg.

Last MSR was N/A.

Product Code: 170108.

MODEL 60 ET COMP – .38 Spl.+P cal., 3 in. ported full lug barrel, dovetail front and adj. rear sight, round butt frame, contoured thumbpiece, rosewood laminate or pearl inlaid synthetic grips, blue hard case, approx. 300 mfg. Distributed by Lew Horton, 1993.

Last MSR was $795.

Product Code: 170029.

MODEL 66 F COMP (1993) – .357 Mag. cal., 3 in. full lug barrel w/compensator, dovetailed tritium front night sight, tuned action, round butt w/rubber grips, counterbored cylinder, contoured cylinder latch, "LHF" serial number prefix, approx. 300 mfg. Distributed by Lew Horton, 1993.

Last MSR was N/A.

Product Code: 170024.

MODEL 66 THE SUPER K – .357 Mag. cal., 3 in. specially contoured barrel with 2 port magna porting, white synthetic grip with S&W medallions, Performance Center Tuned action and overtravel trigger stop. Distributed by Lew Horton, 1997.

Last MSR was N/A.

Product Code: 170090.

GRADING - PPGS™	100%	98%	95%	90%	80%	70%	60%	LAST MSR

MODEL 66 F-COMP – .357 Mag. cal., 3 in. full lug ported barrel with drift adj. dovetailed ramp front sight and micrometer click rear sight, 6 shot cylinder with chamfered charge holes, front sight set behind barrel port, glass bead finish, shipped with walnut combat grips and an additional Hogue Bantam monogrip.

Last MSR was $798.

Product Code: 170024FC.

MODEL 67 F-COMP – .38 Spl. cal., 6 shot, SA/DA, 3 in. full lug Power Port barrel, adj. white outline rear and tritium front sights, stainless steel frame, matte black finish, synthetic finger groove grips, 35 oz. Mfg. mid-2007-2009.

	$1,025	$875	$750	$625	$525	$450	$400	*$1,311*

Product Code: 170324.

MODEL 325 THUNDER RANCH – .45 ACP cal., SA/DA, 6 shot, 4 in. barrel, interchangeable front sight, adj. rear sight, Scandium alloy N-frame with stainless steel cylinder, matte black finish, rubber finger groove grips, 31 oz. New 2008.

MSR $1,289	$1,050	$875	$750	$625	$525	$425	$350	

Product code: 170316.

MODEL 327 Sc – .357 Mag. cal., 8 shot, 2 in. barrel with titanium shroud, black finish with natural grey titanium cylinder, Scandium alloy N-frame, teardrop color case hammer and trigger with overtravel stop, Ahrends cocobolo round butt grips with finger grooves, small lanyard pin, PC logo under thumbpiece, fixed or adj. sights, shipped with black PC marked gun rug made by Allen with internal pouch, 2 full moon clips, special ser. no. range. New 2006.

MSR $1,269	$1,040	$875	$750	$625	$525	$425	$350	

Add $16 for 5 in. barrel with adj. sights (disc.).

Product Codes: 170245FC (black) or 170251FC (clear, disc.).

MODEL 327 Sc JERRY MICULEK – similar to Model 327 Sc, 5 in. barrel, 8 shot, unfluted titanium cylinder with adj. rear sights, orange Hi-Viz fiber optic front sight, unique new two-piece barrel design, Jerry Miculek signature grip and extra Hogue rubber grips. Mfg. 2005.

Last MSR was $1,149.

MODEL 327 TRR8 – .357 Mag. cal., 8 shot, 5 in. barrel, large frame, interchangeable front sight, adj. V-notch rear sight, Scandium alloy with titanium alloy cylinder, synthetic finger groove grips, black finish, equipment rail, 35.3 oz. New mid-2007.

MSR $1,289	$1,050	$875	$750	$625	$525	$425	$350	

Product code: 170269.

MODEL 327 M&P R8 – .357 Mag. or .38 Spl. + P cal., 8 shot, SA/DA, 5 in. two-piece barrel, large frame, Scandium alloy frame, stainless steel cylinder, interchangeable dot front sight, adj. V-notch rear sight, accessory rail, 36.3 oz. New mid-2007.

MSR $1,289	$1,050	$875	$750	$625	$525	$425	$350	

Product code: 170292.

MODEL 329-1 AIRLITE PD – .44 Mag. cal. DA, serrated and ported 3 in. barrel, round butt Scandium alloy N-frame, 6 shot titanium cylinder, painted red ramp front sight, adj. black blade front sight, Ahrends cocobolo finger groove wood grips. Mfg. 2003.

Last MSR was $1,100.

Product Codes: 170233 (clear) or 170232FC (matte black).

All Model 329-1 Airlites were recalled by S&W during July, 2004.

MODEL 442 THE ULTRALIGHT – .38 S&W Spl. cal., similar to Model 442 Centennial, it has been reported (and photographed) that a few (approx. 10) with an alloy cylinder were made for the U.S. Secret Service as prototypes but were never sold or released to the general public. These prototypes have no markings on the sideplate, and have a matte blue finish. One observed Ser. no. prefix is "BSS". Mfg. 1997.

Last MSR was N/A.

This model was never offered for commercial sale.

Product Code: 170023.

GRADING - PPGS™	100%	98%	95%	90%	80%	70%	60%	LAST MSR

MODEL 460 XVR – .460 S&W Mag. cal., capable of shooting both the .45 Colt and .454 Casull cartridges, 5 shot, similar to Model 500, stainless frame, cylinder, and one-piece 3 1/2 (disc.), 6 1/2 (disc. 2008), 7 1/2 (disc. 2008), 10 1/2 or 12 (new 2008) in. stainless steel barrel with interchangeable green Hi-Viz front sight, integral Weaver style scope mount, Hogue dual density monogrip with S&W monogram, barrel mounted recoil reducer, glass bead finish, Uncle Mike's detachable sling and swivels, 82 1/2 oz. New 2006.

MSR $1,519	$1,295	$1,095	$975	$800	$700	$625	$550	

Add $100 for 12 in. barrel.

Product Codes: 170262 or 170280 (170299).

Lew Horton ordered a number of 3 1/2 in. models - product code is 170268FC.

The 6 1/2 in. barrel does not have sling mounts.

In late summer 2005, a 7 1/2 in. barrel version was manufactured for Ellett Bros. distributors with black finish, stainless steel cylinder, muzzle brake, and shoulder sling. This model included a Lothar-Walther custom rifled barrel and a special ser. no. (EBD0001-EBD0500).

MODEL 460 HUNTER – .460 S&W Mag. cal., 14 in. fluted barrel with Patridge front sight in back of integral muzzle break, adj. rear sight, upper and lower Picatinny rails on rear of barrel, unfluted cylinder, rubber grips, satin stainless steel, 88 oz. New 2011.

MSR $1,419	$1,150	$975	$875	$775	$675	$575	$475	

Product Code: 170339.

MODEL 460 AIRWEIGHT – .38 S&W Spl. cal., DA only, alloy J-frame w/round butt, 5 shot fluted steel cylinder, fully concealed hammer, 2 in. steel Magna Ported barrel, fixed sight, blue matte finish, Eagle Secret Service grips, smooth trigger, ser. no. prefix "SDE", 15.8 oz. approx. 450 mfg. 1994.

Last MSR was $595.

Product Code: 170055.

MODEL 500 MAGNUM HUNTER – .500 S&W Mag. cal., X-frame, 5 shot, fluted cylinder, 6 1/2 (Compensated Hunter, mfg. 2004 only), 7 1/2, or 10 1/2 in. tapered lug barrel, with recoil compensator and integral Weaver base, Hogue mono-grip, stainless steel, glass bead finish with flash chromed hammer and trigger, adj. white outline rear sight, includes black nylon sling, swivels, and soft case, 82 oz. New 2004.

MSR $1,509	$1,275	$1,050	$925	$825	$725	$650	$550	

Add $10 for 7 1/2 in. barrel.

Product Codes: 170231 (10 1/2 in.), 170246FC (6 1/2 in.), 170299 (7 1/2 in.).

MODEL 500 MAGNUM BONE COLLECTOR – .500 S&W Mag. cal., 10 1/2 in. barrel with Picatinny rail on rear, adj. white outline rear and red ramp front sight, two-tone finish, stainless steel, features animal rack graphics on rear of frame and marked "Bone Collector", barrel engraved "X of 1,000", 82 oz., 1,000 mfg. 2011 only.

	$1,150	$1,025	$900	$800	$700	$600	$500	*$1,389*

MODEL 586 L COMP – .357 Mag. cal., 3 in. full lug ported barrel with tritium dot front and micrometer click rear sight, Altamont Rosewood grips, 7 shot cylinder rebated for moon clips, black or blue finish, shipped with locking aluminum case & Master Gun Lock, first blue finish revolver in 7 shot offered by S&W, 37 1/2 oz. Distributed by Camfour, 2000 and 2004.

Last MSR was N/A.

Product Code: 170170 (2000 mfg.) or 170248FC (2004 mfg.).

MODEL 610 – 10mm cal., 6 1/2 in. barrel.

Last MSR was N/A.

Product Code: 170109.

MODEL 617 – .22 LR cal., new profile barrel for export, only 327 mfg. 1995 and 1999.

Last MSR was N/A.

Product Code: 170122 or 170066 (235 were mfg. in 1995 for export only).

GRADING - PPGS™	100%	98%	95%	90%	80%	70%	60%	LAST MSR

MODEL 625 – .45 ACP cal., 4 in. barrel with full shroud, SA/DA, satin stainless steel, 6 shot, round butt with smooth Hogue Combat red, white, and blue laminated wood grips, adj. rear sight, gold bead front sight, 42 oz. New 2010.

MSR $1,049	$895	$700	$550	$450	$400	$350	$300	

Product Code: 170161.

MODEL 625-5 JERRY MICULEK DESIGN – .45 ACP cal., 5 1/4 in. barrel, Patridge front w/ gold bead and adj. black blade rear sight, reduced cylinder freebore, 6 shot fluted cylinder w/chamfered charge holes, deep cut broached rifling, hand honed bore, satin stainless finish, "Jerry Miculek" Hogue Laminate combat grips, lockable aluminum case, 42 oz. Distributed by Camfour, 2001.

Last MSR was $899.

Product Code: 170176.

MODEL 625-6 FLUTED HUNTER – .45 Colt cal., 6 in. ported barrel, chamfered cylinder, red ramp dovetailed front sight, round butt frame, serrated backstrap & forestrap, will accept Weaver style scope mount on the integral rail system, removable weights and spacers internal to the barrel with a small allen wrench, ser. no. prefix "LHD", most were sent to Germany with about 50 remaining in the U.S. Distributed by Lew Horton, 1997.

Last MSR was N/A.

Product Code: 170081.

MODEL 625-6 HUNTER – .45 Colt cal., 6 in. ported slabside barrel, non-fluted cylinder, marked "45 Colt CTG". Mfg. 1997.

Last MSR was N/A.

Product Code: 170085.

MODEL 625-6 "V COMP" – .45 ACP cal., 4 in. slabside barrel with a removable compensator or a replacement muzzle to protect the crown, 6 shot non-fluted cylinder has a ball-detent lockup in the yoke, Millett dovetailed red ramp front and micrometer click rear sight, Hogue Combat wood grips, semi-target hammer, smooth combat trigger w/overtravel stop, shipped w/double combo lock aluminum carry case, 43 oz. Distributed by RSR, 1999.

Last MSR was $925.

Product Code: 170136.

MODEL 625-7 LIGHT HUNTER – .45 Colt cal., 6 in. ported match grade barrel with integral Weaver style base rail, ball detent lockup, fluted cylinder w/chamfered charge holes, Millett dovetail front sight, forged and flash chromed trigger and hammer, satin stainless finish, Hogue wood combat grips, shipped with aluminum PC carry case, 43 oz. Distributed by RSR, 1999.

Last MSR was N/A.

Product Code: 170132.

MODEL 625-8 – 45 ACP cal., 4 in. barrel with interchangeable Patridge front sight with gold bead, adj. black blade rear sight, black tear drop hammer, black trigger with stop and black thumbpiece, reduced cylinder freebore, 6 shot fluted cylinder with chamfered charge holes, deep cut broached rifling, and hand honed bores, stainless steel material with satin stainless finish, "Jerry Miculek" Hogue red and blue laminate combat grip, 42 oz. Mfg. 2010.

	$1,050	$875	$750	$625	$500	$450	$400	*$1,266*

Product code: 170161.

MODEL 625-10 – .45 ACP cal., 6 shot, 2 in. barrel, Scandium N-frame, fixed V-notch rear sight with serrated and dovetailed ramp front sight, Eagle wood and Hogue rubber grips, stainless steel cylinder, glass bead finish, barrel marked ".45 ACP", includes PC locking case, 24 oz. Distributed by Lew Horton Sept. 2003.

Last MSR was $925.

Product Code: 170252FC (black).

MODEL 625-11 – .45 Colt cal., 1 1/8 in. barrel, 6 shot, aluminum/Scandium N frame, fixed sight, V-notch rear sight, serrated and dovetailed black ramp front sight with white dot,

GRADING - PPGS™	100%	98%	95%	90%	80%	70%	60%	LAST MSR

Eagle wood grip, includes extra Hogue rubber grip, stainless steel cylinder, chamfered charge holes, smooth trigger and checkered teardrop hammer, Performance Center locking case, 25 oz. 103 mfg. for Lew Horton 2005.

Last MSR was $1025.

Product Code: 170266FC.

MODEL 627-2 STAINLESS – .357 Mag./.38 Spl. cal., DA, stainless steel version of the Model 27, 8 shot cylinder, 5 in. tapered barrel, interchangeable front sights, drilled & tapped for scope mount, chamfered charge holes, flash chrome teardrop hammer, Hogue hardwood combat grips, new thumbpiece, engraved ".357 Magnum 8 Times" on barrel, floating firing pin, RJM serial prefix, 44 oz. Distributed by Lew Horton, 1997-1998.

Last MSR was $1,000.

Product Code: 170089.

MODEL 627 1998 LEW HORTON SPECIAL "HUNTER STYLE" – .357 Mag. cal., 6 1/2 in. magna ported slabside barrel, fluted cylinder w/beveled edges, contoured thumb latch, integral scope mount and weight system, adj. sights, rosewood grips.

Last MSR was $1,025.

Product Code: 170102.

MODEL 627PC 1998 LEW HORTON SPECIAL – .357 Mag. cal., 8 shot, 6 in. barrel. ser. no. prefix "LHV", unfluted cylinder, engraved ".357 Magnum 8 Times" with floating firing pin.

Last MSR was N/A.

Product Code: 170095.

MODEL 627-3 "V-COMP JERRY MICULEK SPECIAL" – 8 shot cylinder, 5 in. barrel, removable compensator, removable/interchangeable cap to protect the rifling, smooth combat trigger w/overtravel stop pin, TH, drift adj. red ramp front sight, micrometer click rear sight. "Jerry Miculek" design Hogue wooden grips, locking aluminum case, 47 oz. Distributed by RSR in 2000.

Last MSR was N/A.

Product Code: 170142.

On July 24th 1999, Jerry Miculek set a world record for firing a S&W 8 shot revolver. The results were: 8 Shots on 1 target in 1.00 seconds and 8 Shots on 2 targets in 1.06 seconds. Both records were set using a Model 627 from the Performance Center.

MODEL 627-PC – .357 Mag. cal., 8 shot, 2 5/8 in. barrel, Millett red ramp drift adj. front sight with micrometer click white outline rear sight, Eagle wood boot grips, flash chromed custom teardrop hammer, smooth combat trigger, full length extractor, stainless steel with glass bead finish, shipped with aluminum double lock carrying case, 37.6 oz. Approx. 302 mfg. 1999-2000.

Last MSR was $1,025.

Product Code: 170133.

MODEL 627-4 – .38 Super cal., 8 shot, black non-fluted cylinder, 5 1/2 in. barrel, angled cut removable compensator and cap, red/white/blue Jerry Miculek designed grip, Patridge front sight with adj. black outline rear sight, chrome teardrop hammer and chrome trigger with overtravel stop, stainless steel, glass bead finish, drilled and tapped. Mfg. for Banger's 2002.

Last MSR was N/A.

Product Code: 170205.

MODEL 627-5 – .357 Mag. cal., 2 5/8 (new 2010) or 5 in. tapered and countoured barrel with fluted or unfluted cylinder, 8 shot, floating firing pin, interchangeable front sight with black blade rear sight, wood grips, trigger overtravel stop, internal lock system, new frame design, shipped with black PC marked gun rug, 37.6 or 44 oz.

MSR $1,049	$895	$700	$550	$450	$400	$350	$300

Add $200 for 5 in. barrel.

Product Codes: 170210 and 170133.

GRADING - PPGS™	100%	98%	95%	90%	80%	70%	60%	LAST MSR

* ***Model 627-5 (Disc.)*** – .357 Mag. cal., 8 shot, 5 in. full lug barrel, removable cap and crown, wood grips with extra Hogue grip, fluted cylinder, black drift adj. front sight, black rear sight, marked ".357 Magnum-V8" on left side of barrel and "Performance Center" on right, floating firing pin, internal lock system, new frame design, ser. no. prefix "VCM". Limited mfg. 2004.

	100%	98%	95%	90%	80%	70%	60%	LAST MSR
	$875	$600	$525	$475	$425	$375	$335	$1,106

Product Code: 170237FC.

MODEL 627 V-COMP – .357 Mag. cal., 8 shot, 5 in. barrel, SA/DA, adj. front and rear sights, stainless steel/alloy frame with two-tone matte or satin stainless (disc. 2011) finish, synthetic rubber or wood laminate (disc. 2011) finger groove grips, chrome tear drop hammer, 47 oz. New 2008.

	100%	98%	95%	90%	80%	70%	60%
MSR $1,509	$1,225	$1,100	$975	$850	$725	$600	$525

Product code: 170296.

MODEL 629 CARRY COMP – .44 Mag. cal., 6 shot, 3 in. barrel, adj. orange dovetail front sight, stainless steel frame and cylinder, matte stainless finish, fixed notch rear sight, large frame, wood combat grips with finger grooves, 38 oz. Mfg. mid-2007-2009.

	100%	98%	95%	90%	80%	70%	60%	LAST MSR
	$1,025	$875	$750	$625	$525	$450	$400	$1,311

Product code: 170279.

MODEL 629 STEALTH HUNTER – .44 Mag. cal., 6 shot, 7 1/2 in. barrel, stainless steel frame and cylinder, matte black finish, adj. front and rear sight, synthetic finger groove grips, 56 oz. New mid-2007.

	100%	98%	95%	90%	80%	70%	60%
MSR $1,579	$1,275	$1,025	$975	$850	$725	$600	$525

Product code: 170323.

MODEL 629-3 CARRY COMP STAINLESS – .44 Mag. cal., 3 in. barrel, integral compensator, dovetailed interchangeable red ramp front sight, fixed rear sight, beveled cylinder, semi-target hammer, smooth combat trigger, N-frame, round butt, Goncalo Alves grips w/finger grooves, contoured thumbpiece, 42 oz. Distributed by Lew Horton, 1992.

Last MSR was $1,000.

Product Code: 170012.

MODEL 629-3 THE CLASSIC HUNTER I – .44 Mag. cal., fluted cyl. Distributed by Lew Horton, 1992.

Last MSR was $1,234.

Product Code: 170008.

MODEL 629-3 CARRY COMP II – .44 Mag. cal., 3 in. barrel, adj. rear sight, compensator system, unfluted Classic Hunter style cylinder, hard case, approx. 100 mfg. Distributed by Lew Horton, 1993.

Last MSR was $1,000.

Product code: 170026.

MODEL 629-4 .44 MAGNUM LIGHT HUNTER – .44 Mag. cal., 6 in. Magna ported slabside barrel, non-fluted cylinder, round butt frame, scope broaching, recessed crown, radiused smooth trigger w/overtravel stop, serial number range RSR3500-RSR4000, 500 mfg. Distributed by RSR.

Last MSR was N/A.

May 1995. Two additional variations were also made for Lew Horton Dist.

Product Code: 170056.

MODEL 629-4 THE CLASSIC HUNTER II – .44 Mag. cal., 6 in. slab side barrel, integral variable weight system, Weaver scope mount rail system, Magna ported, non fluted chamfered cylinder, red ramp dovetail front sight, ser. no. prefix "LHK". Distributed by Lew Horton, 1996.

Last MSR was $1,234.

Product Code: 170046.

GRADING - PPGS™	100%	98%	95%	90%	80%	70%	60%	LAST MSR

MODEL 629 "THE AVENGER" – .44 Mag. cal., 3 in. Dual Magna-port barrel, unfluted cylinder, 26 Mfg.

Last MSR was N/A.

Product code: 170058.

MODEL 629 MAGNUM HUNTER PLUS – .44 Mag. cal., 7 1/2 in. slabside barrel, Magna ported, integral Weaver Scope Rail, unfluted cylinder. Distributed by RSR, 1996.

Last MSR was N/A.

Product Code: 170065.

MODEL 629-4 TROPHY WHITE TAIL – .44 Mag. cal., 6 1/2 in. ported barrel, dovetailed front sight, adj. rear sight, target hammer, smooth trigger with stop, chambered cylinder, contoured thumbpiece, Hogue Grips with S&W trademark, two deer scene laser etched on the sideplate, with "Trophy Whitetail" etched on the barrel's right side, drilled and tapped for scope mount, Performance Center logo on the frame, ser. no. range is ZAN0001-ZAN0200. 200 mfg. Distributed by Zanders Sports, 1997.

Last MSR was N/A.

Product Code: 170050.

MODEL 629-4 "SCOPE ONLY" MASTER HUNTER – .44 Mag. cal., 7 1/2 in. barrel, non-fluted cylinder, drilled and tapped for scope mount only w/rear cutout for a standard rear sight, smooth barrel without a rib, satin stainless finish, Performance Center logo, ser. no. prefix "MHS". Mfg. 1997.

Last MSR was N/A.

Product Code: 170087.

MODEL 629-4 "COMPED HUNTER" – .44 Mag. cal., 6 in. barrel, Weaver integral base, fully adj. micrometer click rear sight, dovetailed Millett red ramp front sight, removable 4 port compensator, w/replacement muzzle, glass bead finish, stainless steel, N-frame, round butt, Altamont wood grips, unfluted cylinder with chamfered charge holes, ball detent lock up, flash chromed and radiused hammer, smooth combat trigger with overtravel stop, "CMH" ser. no. prefix, 58.9 oz. Distributed by RSR, 1998.

Last MSR was $1,080.

Product Code: 170100.

MODEL 629-4 COMP & CAP – .44 Mag. cal., 6 1/2 in. barrel, removable muzzle brake with replaceable end cap, rosewood grips. Distributed by Lew Horton, 1998.

Last MSR was N/A.

Product code: 170124.

MODEL 629-5 V-COMP – .44 Mag. cal., 4 in. slabside barrel with removable compensator, muzzle cap, non-fluted cylinder, ball-detent lockup in the yoke, flash chromed semi-target hammer, smooth combat trigger w/overtravel stop, dovetail red ramp front sight, micrometer click rear sight, Hogue wood combat grips w/S&W Monogram, aluminum carry case, 43 oz. Distributed by RSR in 1999, reintroduced in 2009.

MSR $1,509	$1,225	$1,100	$975	$850	$725	$600	$525

Product code: 170137.

MODEL 629-5 DEFENSIVE REVOLVER – .44 Mag. cal., 2 5/8 in. barrel, ball detent lockup system in the yoke, 6 shot non-fluted cylinder, flash chromed teardrop hammer and smooth combat trigger, Millett dovetailed red ramp front sight, micrometer click rear sight, Hogue wood combat grips, glass bead stainless steel finish, aluminum carry case with the Performance Center logo, 39.6 oz. Distributed by Lew Horton, 1999-2000.

Last MSR was $1,026.

Product code: 170135.

MODEL 629-5 "THE EXTREME HUNTER" – .44 Mag./.44 S&W Special cal., 12 in. barrel, 6 shot fluted cylinder, Wilson rubber combat grips, round butt frame, Uncle Mike's swivels and sling, long under extension to support the long barrel and front swivel mount, dovetailed Patridge front sight, Wilson Silhouette rear sight, glass bead stainless steel finish, modern

GRADING - PPGS™	100%	98%	95%	90%	80%	70%	60%	LAST MSR

frame with floating firing pin and MIM hammer and trigger, Waller 21 in. gun rug, ser. no. prefix "AMH", 65 oz. Distributed by Lew Horton, 2000.

Last MSR was $1,201.

Product code: 170157.

MODEL 629-5 "STEALTH HUNTER" – .44 Mag. cal., 7 1/2 in. Magna ported Hunter style barrel, 6 shot unfluted flat black cylinder with ball detent lockup and chamfered charge holes, integral Weaver style rib and counterbored muzzle, adj. Millett red ramp drift front sight, white outline micrometer adj. rear sight, Hogue black rubber monogrip with the S&W trademark, black smooth trigger with a rubber stop, black tapered hammer spur, NATO green stainless steel frame and barrel, black contrasting screws, grip, cylinder, thumbpiece, hammer, and trigger, Performance Center aluminum case, ser. no. prefix "FBS", approx. 50 oz. Distributed by Camfour, 2000-2001.

Last MSR was $1,200.

Product code: 170171.

MODEL 629-5 "COMPENSATED HUNTER" – .44 Mag. cal., 7 1/2 in. ported barrel, glass bead finish, stainless steel, fixed compensator, 6 shot fluted cylinder w/chamfered charge holes, ball detent lock-up, adj. front sight w/orange ramp insert, adj. micrometer black blade rear sight, removable stainless steel scope mount, rosewood laminate grips, extra Hogue monogrip, round butt frame, lockable Performance Center aluminum case, 52.2 oz. Distributed by Talo, 2001.

Last MSR was $1,104.

Product code: 170181.

MODEL 629-5 "LIGHT HUNTER PLUS" – .44 Mag. cal., 7 1/2 in. barrel, all black Birdsong finish, barrel is cut for scope mount with Weaver rail, unfluted cylinder, gold bead front sight, Hogue monogrip, ser. no. prefix "DEL". Mfg. 2002.

Last MSR was N/A.

Product code: 170194.

MODEL 629 (LIGHT HUNTER) – .44 Mag. cal., large frame, 6 shot, 2 5/8 (new 2010) or 7 1/2 in. barrel with integral muzzle brake, stainless steel, tapered ejector rod housing, wood combat grips, includes scope rail, 49.7 oz. New 2003.

MSR $1,049	$895	$700	$550	$450	$400	$350	$300

Add $230 for 7 1/2 in. barrel.

Product codes: 170181 and 170135.

MODEL 629 HUNTER – .44 Mag. cal., 7 1/2 in. barrel with extended muzzle break, 6 shot, two-tone finish with black frame and satin finished cylinder and barrel sides, Picatinny rail, Red Ramp adj. rear sight, black synthetic grips with finger grooves, 57 1/2 oz. New 2011.

MSR $1,329	$1,125	$1,000	$875	$750	$650	$550	$475

Product Code: 170318.

MODEL 629-7 "HUNTER PLUS" – .44 Mag. cal., black finish, 7-1/2 in. polished slabside barrel with compensator, 6 shot unfluted polished cylinder, ".44 MAGNUM HUNTER PLUS" on the barrels right side. Mfg. 2007.

Last MSR was N/A.

Product Code: 170295FC.

MODEL 632-1 – .327 Mag. Federal cal., 3 in. ported barrel, ramp front sight with adjustable rear sight, black overall finish with Uncle Mike's combat grips, stainless steel frame and cylinder and steel internal parts. Mfg. 2009.

Last MSR was N/A.

Product code: 170329.

This model is the first production handgun in this caliber made by S&W.

MODEL 637-2 POWER PORT – .38 Spl. cal., 2 1/8 in. ported barrel, frame # 38219, black finish, Uncle Mike's combat grips, white dot front sight, U notch cut rear sight, does not have the Performance Center trademark, with internal lock. Mfg. 2008.

Last MSR was N/A.

Product code: 170327.

GRADING - PPGS™	100%	98%	95%	90%	80%	70%	60%	LAST MSR

MODEL 640 CARRY COMP – .38 Spl.+P cal., 2 in. ported barrel, adj. front sight, fixed rear sight, radiused hammer and trigger, 150 mfg. w/rosewood grips, 150 mfg. w/Bader mother-of-pearl inlaid fingergroove grips, blue plastic case w/Performance Center logo, 23 oz. Distributed by Lew Horton. Mfg. 1993.

Last MSR was $750.

Product code: 170042.

MODEL 640 "PAXTON QUIGLEY" – .38 Spl. cal., 2 5/8 in. barrel, integral compensator, dovetailed adj. front sight, tuned by the S&W Performance Center, laminated wood grips w/ mother-of-pearl inlaid heart, Boyt tapestry case and letter of authenticity from Paxton Quigley, author of *Armed & Female.* Distributed by Lew Horton, 1994. Limited production of 250.

Last MSR was $725.

Product codes: 170014 (3 in.) or 170043 (2 in.).

MODEL 640 RSR SPECIAL – .357 Mag. cal., 2 1/8 in. Magna-Ported barrel, 5 shot non-fluted cylinder, glass bead stainless steel finish, concealed hammer, J-frame, round butt, Heritage walnut grips, chrome smooth combat trigger, pinned black ramp front sight, square notch rear sight, 25 oz. Mfg. 1996.

Last MSR was N/A.

Product code: 170073.

MODEL 640 LEW HORTON – .357 Mag. cal., 5 shot, 2 1/8 in. ported barrel, dovetail front sight with tritium insert on black post, matte stainless finish, Performance Center tuned action, Pachmayr Decelerator grips, chrome smooth combat trigger. Mfg. 1996.

Last MSR was $839.

Product code: 170068.

At least one Model 640 is known to have been chambered in .38 Super caliber for test purposes by the Performance Center.

MODEL 640 "LEW HORTON .357 MAGNUM" – .357 Mag. cal., 2 1/8 in. Quad Port barrel, glass bead finish. Mfg. 1999.

Last MSR was $851.

Product code: 170078.

MODEL 642-2 POWER PORT – .38 Spl. cal., satin black finish, 2 1/8 in. ported barrel, Uncle Mike's grips, white dot front sight, no Performance Center trademark, internal lock. Mfg. 2008.

Product code: 170328.

MODEL 646 – .40 S&W cal., 4 in. ribbed slabside barrel, SA/DA, 6 shot fluted titanium cylinder, drift adj. Patridge front sight, micrometer adj. rear sight, drilled and tapped for scope mount, smooth combat trigger, round butt, L-target frame, "Performance Center" on the left side and "40 S&W" on the right side of barrel, frosted glass bead stainless finish, Altamont wood combat grips, 2 sets of half moon clips and extraction tool, ser. no. prefix "RDA", 36 oz. Mfg. 2000.

Last MSR was $845.

Product code: 170165.

MODEL 647-1 VARMINTER – .17 HMR cal., stainless steel K-frame, 12 in. Walther barrel, Weaver scope rail, includes bipod adapter, black Patridge front sight with adj. black blade rear sight, glass bead satin stainless finish, wood target square butt grips, internal trigger lock system, black Allen soft zipper case, distributed by Camfour and Hill Country.

Last MSR was $1,200.

Product code: 170229FC.

MODEL 647 – .17 HMR cal., 12 in. partially fluted barrel with raised black front sight, 6 shot, satin stainless steel, upper and lower Picatinny rails on back of barrel, red dot/green dot fixed sights, also includes optical sight and bipod, checkered wood grained brown synthetic grips, 54 oz. New 2011.

MSR $1,299	$1,075	$900	$775	$650	$550	$450	$350

Product Code: 170229.

GRADING - PPGS™	100%	98%	95%	90%	80%	70%	60%	LAST MSR

MODEL 657 – .41 Mag. cal., 2 5/8 in. full shroud barrel, 6 shot, unfluted cylinder, glass bead stainless steel, wood grips with finger grooves, adj. rear sight, red ramp front sight, 39.6 oz. Mfg. 2010-2011.

$895	$700	$550	$450	$400	$350	$300	*$1,049*

Product Code: 170134.

MODEL 657 DEFENSIVE REVOLVER – .41 Mag. cal., 2 5/8 in. barrel, 6 shot non-fluted cylinder, ball detent lockup, full length extractor, round butt, N-frame, adj. Millett red ramp front sight, micrometer adj. white outline rear sight, flash chromed teardrop hammer, chromed trigger with travel overstop, Hogue combat grips, glass bead stainless steel finish, aluminum carry case, 39.6 oz. Distributed by Lew Horton, 1999.

Last MSR was $1,001.

Product code: 170134.

MODEL 657 HUNTER – .41 Mag. cal., 6 in. Magna-Ported barrel, integral Weaver base, N-frame, round butt, 6 shot unfluted cylinder, ball detent lockup, adj. Millett red ramp front sight, adj. rear sight, 48 oz. Distributed by RSR, 1995-1999.

Last MSR was N/A.

Product code: 170062.

MODEL 681-4 LEW HORTON SPECIAL – .357 Mag. cal., 3 in. Quadra-port barrel, 7 shot chamfered cylinder, trigger overtravel stop, fixed sight, ser. no. prefix "LHB", 300 mfg. Distributed by Lew Horton, 1996.

Last MSR was $700.

Product code: 170080.

MODEL 681-5 SPECIAL FOR CAMFOUR – .357 Mag. cal., 3 or 4 in. full lug barrel, 7 shot fluted cylinder, adj. black ramp front sight, Quad Porting, glass bead stainless steel finish, laminate checkered wood and Hogue Bantam Monogrip, 7 shot moon clips, chamfered cylinder charge holes, Performance Center case. Distributed by Camfour, 2001.

Last MSR was N/A.

Product codes: 170172 (4 in.) or 170178 (3 in.).

MODEL 686 MAG COMP – .357 Mag. cal., 3 in. barrel, integral compensator, adj. front red ramp sight, white outline rear sight, radiused full lug barrel, radiused hammer, radiused combat trigger w/overtravel stop, Uncle Mike's grips, Performance Center logo, contoured thumbpiece, full-length extractor rod, 350 mfg. Distributed by Lew Horton, 1992.

Last MSR was $1,000.

Product code: 170010.

MODEL 686 CARRY COMP 4 IN. – .357 Mag. cal., 4 in. barrel, integral compensator, dovetailed front sight w/interchangeable post or red ramp, white outline rear sight, Uncle Mike's grips. Distributed by Lew Horton.

Last MSR was $1,000.

Product code: 170016.

MODEL 686 PPC REVOLVER – .357 Mag. cal., 6 in. barrel, custom underlug, integral barrel port.

Last MSR was N/A.

MODEL 686 CARRY COMP 6 IN. – .357 Mag. cal., 6 in. barrel, integral port, replaceable front sight, Hogue grips, semi-target hammer, smooth combat trigger, full underlug contour. Mfg. 1994.

Last MSR was $1,099.

Product code: 170009.

MODEL 686 "THE COMPETITOR" – .357 Mag. cal., 6 in. barrel, fluted cylinder w/radiused charge holes, integral scope base, 6 ounce variable underweight, dovetailed front post, black blade rear sight, Hogue grips, semi-target hammer, smooth combat trigger, 52-58 oz. Distributed by Lew Horton.

Last MSR was $1,100.

Product code: 170015.

GRADING - PPGS™	100%	98%	95%	90%	80%	70%	60%	LAST MSR

MODEL 686 ACTION REVOLVER – .357 Mag. cal., 6 in. match grade barrel, barrel compensator.

Last MSR was N/A.

MODEL 686 "THE HUNTER" – .357 Mag. cal., similar to the Model 657 Hunter, except has wood grips. 200 mfg.

Last MSR was $1,153.

Product code: 170021.

MODEL 686 PLUS – .357 Mag. cal., 6 in. tapered barrel, 7 shot fluted cylinder, machined for full moon clips w/chamfered charge holes, L-frame drilled and tapped for scope mount, round butt, Altamont wood grips, flash chromed semi-target hammer and smooth combat trigger, gold bead Patridge front sight, micrometer adj. white outline rear sight, satin stainless steel finish, 44 oz. Distributed by Lew Horton, 1998.

Last MSR was $929.

Product code: 170103.

MODEL 686-4 WITH ADJUSTABLE SIGHTS – .357 Mag. cal., 2 1/2 in. barrel, Magna Port, 7 shot cylinder, wood grips. Mfg. 1998.

Last MSR was N/A.

Product code: 170077.

MODEL 686 – .38 Super cal., 4 in. tapered lug barrel, interchangeable red ramp front sight, adj. black rear sight, Ahrends cocobolo finger groove grips, stainless steel, glass bead finish, 6 shot, unfluted cylinder, L-frame, internal key lock system, accepts full moon clips, includes PC aluminum carry case, 37 oz. Distributed by Banger's 2003.

Last MSR was N/A

Product code: 170225.

MODEL 686-6 LIGHT RAIL – 5 in. barrel with small rail under the full lug for accessories, 6 shot cylinder, green Hi-Viz front sight, white outline rear sight, synthetic rubber grip, internal lock. Mfg. 2007.

Product Code: 170322.

MODEL 940 SPECIAL – .356 TSW cal., ported barrel, dovetail front sight, barrel markings are ".356 TSW" on the right and "Smith & Wesson" on the left side. S/N prefix "APC". Limited Production of 300. Distributed by Lew Horton, 1994.

Last MSR was $575.

Product code: 170047.

This model has also been referred to as the "Pocket Rocket."

MODEL 942 AIRWEIGHT 9MM CENTENNIAL – 9mm cal., 2 in. ported barrel, one was made as a prototype using a Model 642-1 alloy frame, stainless steel cylinder, S/N CAN1706. Built as a T&E prototype, it was shipped to firearms journalist Wiley Clapp in 1999 for test and evaluation.

Last MSR was N/A.

MODEL M&P R8 – .357 Mag. or .38 Spl.+P cal., 8 shot, SA/DA, 5 in. two-piece barrel, large frame, Scandium alloy frame, stainless steel cylinder, interchangeable dot front sight, adj. V-notch rear sight, accessory rail, matte black finish, black synthetic grips with finger grooves, 36.3 oz. New mid-2007.

MSR	100%	98%	95%	90%	80%	70%	60%
MSR $1,289	$1,050	$875	$750	$625	$525	$425	$350

Product Code: 170292.

PERFORMANCE CENTER RIFLE VARIATIONS

M&P RIFLE – 5.56 NATO cal., 10 shot mag., 20 in. stainless steel barrel, Hogue synthetic stock with pistol grip, free-floating anodized forend, two-stage match trigger, billet aluminum receiver with Picatinny rail, no sights, hard coat black or camo anodized finish, includes rifle case, 8 lbs. 2 oz. New 2008.

MSR	100%	98%	95%	90%	80%	70%	60%
MSR $1,509	$1,275	$1,050	$925	$825	$725	$625	$525

Add $30 for camo finish.

Product codes: 178016 (black) or 178015 (camo).

GRADING - PPGS™	100%	98%	95%	90%	80%	70%	60%	LAST MSR

M&P 15-22 PC TB – .22 LR cal., 18 in. fluted barrel, 10 shot detachable mag., fixed (compliant) or 6-position VLTOR adj. buttstock, polymer receiver with modular rail forend, adj. A2 post front sight and adj. dual aperture rear sight, black finish, 5.6 lbs. New 2011.

MSR $769	$650	$575	$500	$450	$425	$400	$395	

Product Codes: 170335 or 170337 (compliant).

M&P 15PC LIMITED EDITION – 5.56 NATO cal., 20 in. barrel, 10 shot mag., Wylde Chamber, skeletonized full length buttstock, integral Picatinny style rail system, black matte finish, anodized streamlined free floating forend, black rubber pistol grip, swivel stud for sling or bipod attachment, PC marked soft carry case, master trigger lock and manual, marked "M&P 15PC" laser engraved on the right side, no forward assist on the upper. Mfg. 2006.

	$1,675	$1,425	$1,150	$925	$825	$725	$625	*$1,999*

Product Code: 170293.

PERFORMANCE CENTER SEMI-AUTO PISTOL VARIATIONS

MODEL 845 LIMITED – .45 ACP cal., full target version of the Model 745, Bo-Mar low-profile sights, extended beavertail, checkered front strap, fitted barrel bushing, Hi-Impact plastic grips, 8-round magazine, extra recoil spring, S/N prefix "MPC" (1995) "SDN" (1998). Distributed by Lew Horton.

Last MSR was $1,496.

Product code: 170064.

MODEL 945 PERFORMANCE CENTER .45 MATCH PISTOL – .45 ACP cal., 5 in. barrel, titanium coated spherical barrel bushing, 8 round mag., Performance Center markings, post front sight, adj. Bo-Mar rear sight, checkered two-piece laminated wood grips, bead blast stainless steel finish, ambidextrous frame mounted thumb safety, grip safety as part of the short beavertail, Master trigger lock, "Performance Center" marked foam-filled aluminum case starting in 1999, 43.5 oz. (1998) 42 oz. (1999 and later mfg.) Mfg. 1998-2000.

* ***Model 945 Performance Center .45 Match Pistol 170104*** – 5 in. barrel, stainless steel, 8 shot, 43.5 oz. Mfg. 1998.

Last MSR was $1,618.

* ***Model 945 Performance Center .45 Match Pistol 170147*** – 5 in. barrel, two-tone or blue finish, lightened trigger, grip safety, Bo-Mar rear sight, post front sight, stainless steel, ambidextrous frame mounted safety, 42 oz. Distributed by RSR. Mfg. 1998-2000.

Last MSR was N/A.

* ***Model 945 Performance Center .45 Match Pistol 170152*** – 4 in. barrel, black finish, 8 shot mag., post front and Novak 2 Dot Lo- Mount Carry rear sight, frame mounted safety, titanium coated spherical bushing, 20 LPI checkering front and back strap, extended magazine catch, checkered two-piece wood grips, stainless steel, grip safety, S/N prefix "PCZ", 36 oz. Distributed by Camfour, 2000.

Last MSR was N/A.

* ***Model 945 Performance Center .45 Match Pistol 170153*** – 4 in. barrel, post front and Novak 2 Dot Lo-Mount carry rear sight, grip safety, checkered two piece wood grips, lightened trigger, bead blast stainless steel finish, frame mounted safety, S/N prefix "PCZ", 36 oz. Distributed by RSR, 2000.

Last MSR was N/A.

* ***Model 945 Performance Center .45 Match Pistol 170169*** – 3 3/4 in. barrel, white dot dovetail front and Novak 2 Dot Lo-Mount Carry rear sight, grip and single side frame mounted safety, 7 round mag., checkered laminate wood grips, lightened trigger, black finish alloy frame, stainless steel slide, S/N Prefix "CMF", 28 oz. Distributed by Camfour, 2000.

Last MSR was N/A.

* ***Model 945 Performance Center .45 Match Pistol 170177*** – 3 1/4 in. barrel, white dot dovetail front and Novak 2 Dot Lo-Mount Carry rear sight, beavertail grip and single-side frame mounted safety, 6 round mag., checkered Hogue laminated wood grips, alloy frame with clear glass bead stainless steel slide, Performance Center carry case, 2 mags., 24.5 oz. Distributed by Camfour, 2001.

Last MSR was N/A.

GRADING - PPGS™	100%	98%	95%	90%	80%	70%	60%	LAST MSR

* ***Model 945 Performance Center .45 Match Pistol 170180*** – .40 S&W cal., 3 3/4 in. barrel, white dot dovetail front and Novak 2 Dot Lo-Mount Carry rear sight, beavertail grip and single-side frame mounted safety, 7 round mag., checkered Hogue laminated wood grips, alloy frame w/glass bead finish stainless steel slide, Performance Center carry case, 2 mags., 25.7 oz. Distributed by Sports South, 2001.

Last MSR was N/A.

* ***Model 945 Performance Center .45 Match Pistol 170184*** – 3 1/4 in. glass bead black barrel, white dovetail front and Novak 2 Dot Lo-Mount Carry rear sight, grip and single side frame mounted safety, 6 round mag., checkered Hogue laminated wood grips, alloy frame with stainless steel slide, lightened trigger, S/N prefix "PCZ", 24 oz. Distributed by RSR, 2001.

Last MSR was N/A.

MODEL 945-1 – .45 ACP cal., 8 shot mag., SA, 5 in. barrel, features scalloped slide serrations, black (disc.) or two-tone finish, checkered front and rear gripstrap, checkered wood panel grips, stainless steel, adj. rear sight, target trigger and bobbed hammer, 40 1/2 oz., released during 2003, reintroduced 2005-2010.

	100%	98%	95%	90%	80%	70%	60%	LAST MSR
	$1,925	$1,650	$1,425	$1,225	$1,000	$900	$800	*$2,410*

Product codes: 170173 (stainless) and 170300 (two-tone).

MODEL 952 – 9mm Para. cal., 5 in. match grade black finish stainless steel barrel, titanium coated spherical barrel bushing, 9 round mag., loaded chamber indicator, dovetail post front and adj. Wilson rear sight, carbon steel frame and slide, two-piece wood grip panels w/alloy backstrap, slide mounted decocking lever, marked "Performance Center 952" with small "mm" in the curl of the 9, Performance Center case, 200 mfg., 41 oz. Distributed by Bangers, 2000.

Last MSR was N/A.

Product code: 170168.

MODEL 952-1 – 9mm Para. cal., 5 in. barrel, 9 shot mag., SA, checkered wood panel grips, black finish, steel frame with stainless steel barrel, released during 2003.

Last MSR was $1,515.

Product code: 170220.

MODEL 952-2 – 9mm Para. cal., 5 or 6 (mfg. 2004, reintroduced 2007) in. barrel, blue finish, 9 shot mag., checkered wood grips, stainless steel frame, wide spur hammer, firing pin block safety, wide smooth trigger with frame stop, adj. dovetailed black post front sight and Wilson adj. black rear sight, 39.2 oz., released during 2004.

	100%	98%	95%	90%	80%	70%	60%	LAST MSR
MSR $2,129	$1,825	$1,625	$1,400	$1,150	$1,000	$875	$750	

Add $480 for 6 in. barrel.

Product codes: 170244 (5 in.) or 170274 (6 in.).

MODEL 1911 – .38 Super (mfg. 2005-2010) or .45 ACP cal., 5 in. barrel, single action, black finish, 8 or 10 (.38 Super cal.) shot mag., dovetailed black front sight with adj. micro-click black rear sight, checkered laminate wood grips, stainless steel or stainless Melonite (new 2005) frame/barrel, glass bead finish, full length guide rod, ambidextrous frame mounted safety, 30 LPI front strap checkering, hand lapped and polished fitted barrel, frame and slide, unique front and rear serrations, includes two magazines, 41 oz., released during 2004.

	100%	98%	95%	90%	80%	70%	60%	LAST MSR
MSR $2,209	$1,795	$1,575	$1,325	$1,150	$1,000	$875	$750	

Add $160 Melonite finish.

Product codes: 170243, 170261 and 170257.

* ***Model 1911 (2005)*** – .45 ACP cal., two additional variations of this model were produced during 2005, stainless steel with glass bead satin finish, 8 shot mag., 5 in. barrel, Doug Koenig speed hammer, lightweight match trigger with over travel stop, black dovetail front sight with black micro adj. rear sight, laminate fully checkered grips, oversized external extractor, full length guide rod and oversized mag. well extension, custom front and rear slide serrations, ambidextrous frame mounted safety, shipped with two 8 shot mags, other variation had high polished flats on the slide and barrel.

Last MSR was N/A.

Product codes: 170258 and 170261.

* ***Model 1911 .38 Super cal. (2005)*** – .38 Super cal., another variation of the original 2004 model, part of Doug Koenig Professional Series, 5 in. barrel, satin stainless steel finish, 10 shot mag., Doug Koenig speed hammer, competition match trigger with overtravel stop, black dovetail front sight, Doug Koenig logo on smooth black Micarta grips, oversized external extractor, full length guide rod, competition mag. well, 30 LPI front strap checkering. Mfg. 2005.

Last MSR was N/A.

Product code: 170257.

MODEL 3566 – .356 TSW (9x21.5 mm) cal., 3 1/2 (approx. 200 mfg. Compact), 4 1/4 (Tactical), or 5 in. (.356 TSW Limited) match grade barrel, titanium barrel bushing, stainless frame, matte blue and hand rubbed stainless finish, oversize frame rails, 12 shot (Compact) or 15 shot (Limited) mag., adj. trigger, fitted slide and barrel, adj. Bo-Mar sights, checkered front strap, extended mag. well, Hogue rubber grips w/S&W logo or plastic panel grips, Performance Center trademark on the right side of the slide, S/N prefix "TSW". Distributed by Lew Horton, 1993.

Last MSR was $1,000-$1,350.

Product codes: 170027 (3 1/2 in., 12 shot Compact), 170032 (5 in., 15 shot Limited), 170037/39 (exported models), or 170052(4 1/4 in., 12 shot Tactical).

THE SHORTY 9 MKIII – 9mm cal., match grade barrel w/hand fitted titanium bushing, oversize slide rails, ambidextrous safety, Performance Center action tuning job, adj. Novak Lo-Mount sights, included Zippo lighter with Performance Center logo. Distributed by Lew Horton, 1997.

Last MSR was $1,024.

9 RECON – 9mm cal., 3 1/2 in. match grade barrel, titanium coated spherical barrel bushing, double stack 12 + 1 mag., white dot front and Novak 2 Dot Lo-Mount rear sight, traditional DA trigger, hand lapped oversize rails, ambidextrous spring loaded decocker, 20 LPI checkering on the front strap, Hogue wraparound rubber grips, compact frame, two-tone finish with a clear anodized alloy frame and a carbon steel blue slide, aluminum carry case, 27.2 oz. Distributed by RSR, 1999-2000.

Last MSR was N/A.

Product code: 170140.

S&W 4006 SHORTY FORTY – .40 S&W cal., 3 1/2 in. Bar-Sto barrel, spherical bushing, bobbed hammer, Novak Lo-Mount carry sights, 9-round single stack magazine, alloy frame, grips and frame stamped with Performance Center logo, beveled trigger, adj. front dovetail sight, oversize slide rails, 500 mfg., 27 oz. Distributed by Lew Horton, 1992, 1993, and 1995.

Last MSR was $1,500.

* ***S&W 4006 Shorty Forty Tactical*** – .40 S&W cal., full size companion to Shorty Forty, 5 in. barrel. Distributed by Lew Horton, limited production 1993.

Last MSR was $1,500.

Product code: 170020.

* ***S&W 4006 Shorty Forty Compensated*** – .40 S&W cal., compensator mounted on ported barrel. Distributed by Lew Horton.

Last MSR was $1,700.

* ***S&W 4006 Shorty Forty MK III*** – third variation S/N prefix "PCW". Mfg. 1995.

Last MSR was $949.

Product code: 170011.

* ***S&W 4006 Shorty Forty MKIII 1997*** – ambidextrous safety, low mount adj. sights, hand fitted titanium barrel bushing, precision checkered front strap, hand honed double action S/N prefix "KPC". Distributed by Lew Horton.

Last MSR was $1,025.

Product code: 170061.

* ***S&W 4006 Shorty Forty Performance Center .40 S&W Tactical*** – .40 S&W cal., 5 in. match grade barrel, fixed tritium night front and Novak 2-dot rear sight, stainless steel frame w/carbon steel slide materials, tactical black matte slide w/satin stainless frame finish, 10 round mag., box cut frame and slide rails for 100% contact, balanced slide, ambidextrous decocker, 41.6 oz. Distributed by RSR, 1997.

Last MSR was $1,146.

Product code: 170091.

* ***S&W 4006 Shorty Forty Performance Center Compact*** – .40 S&W cal., 4 1/4 in. barrel. Mfg. August, 1994.

Last MSR was N/A.

Product code: 170054.

MODEL 4006 SHORTY FORTY Y2000 – .40 S&W cal., 3 1/2 in. barrel, white dovetail front sight, Novak Lo-Mount Carry 2 Dot rear sight, aluminum frame with stainless slide, 9 round mag., two-tone black finish, Performance Center aluminum case. Distributed by Camfour 2000.

Last MSR was N/A.

Product code: 170164.

PERFORMANCE CENTER 40 RECON – .40 S&W cal., 4 1/4 in. match grade barrel w/ compensator, titanium coated spherical barrel bushing, white dot post front and all black Novak Lo-Mount rear sight, 7 round magazine, ambidextrous spring loaded decocker, Hogue wraparound rubber grip, stainless steel material with matte black finish, laser etched with "40 RECON Performance Center" on the left side. Distributed by RSR, 1998.

Last MSR was N/A.

Product code: 170099.

PERFORMANCE CENTER 45 RECON – .45 ACP cal., 4 1/4 in. match grade ported barrel, titanium coated spherical barrel bushing, white dot post front and black Novak Lo-Mount rear sight, ambidextrous spring loaded decocker, Hogue wraparound rubber grip, 7 round magazine, stainless steel construction, stainless or matte black finish, laser etched "45 RECON Performance Center" on the left side, aluminum carry case, S/N prefix "SFF", 27.8 oz. Distributed by RSR, 1998.

Last MSR was $1022.

Product code: 170098 (matte black), 170141 (stainless finish), or 170128 (includes Recon SWAT knife).

PERFORMANCE CENTER 45 CQB PISTOLS (CLOSE QUARTERS BATTLE) – .45 ACP cal., 4 in. match grade barrel, two variations offered in 1998, Novak Lo-Mount Dot front and Novak Lo-Mount 2 Dot rear sight, 7 round mag., straight backstrap grip, stainless steel slide, titanium coated spherical barrel bushing, alloy frame with a matte black finish (Model CQB-AL) or stainless steel frame with a matte stainless (Model CQB-SS) finish, ".45 C.Q.B. Performance Center" laser etched on the slide's left side. Distributed by Lew Horton, 1998-1999.

Last MSR was $1,235.

Product code: 170106 (alloy) or 170105 (stainless).

THE SHORTY .45 – .45 ACP cal., match grade barrel, ambidextrous safety, adj. sights, hand fitted titanium barrel bushing, oversize frame and slide rails, precision checkered front strap, hand honed double action. Mfg. 1997.

Last MSR was $1,146.

Product code: 170075.

THE .45 LIMITED – 45 ACP cal., match grade barrel, SA trigger, oversize precision cut frame and slide rails, hand fitted titanium barrel bushing and slide lock, adj. sights, oversize mag. well, tuned action, Zippo lighter with Perf. Center logo. Distributed by Lew Horton, 1997.

Last MSR was $1,470.

MODEL 5906 PC-9 – 9mm cal., 3 1/2 in. titanium spherical barrel bushing, 15 shot mag., blue slide with satin stainless frame, smooth trigger, bobbed hammer, dovetail front and Novak Lo-Mount fixed rear sight, 27 oz. Distributed by Lew Horton in 1993.

Last MSR was N/A.

Product code: 170030.

100%	98%	95%	90%	80%	70%	60%	50%	40%	30%	20%	10%

RIFLES

Rifles: Revolving

MODEL 320 REVOLVING RIFLE – .320 S&W cal., 6 shot cylinder, 16, 18, or 20 in. round barrel, hard rubber grips, detachable shoulder stock, blue or nickel (rare, add a premium) finish. 977 mfg. 1879-87.

* ***Model 320 Revolving Rifle 16 or 20 in. barrel*** – 239 mfg. with 16 in., and 224 with 20 in. barrel.

100%	98%	95%	90%	80%	70%	60%	50%	40%	30%	20%	10%
N/A	$15,000	$12,000	$10,000	$8,700	$8,100	$7,675	$7,000	$6,375	$5,600	$4,800	$3,850

* ***Model 320 Revolving Rifle 18 in. barrel*** – 514 mfg.

100%	98%	95%	90%	80%	70%	60%	50%	40%	30%	20%	10%
N/A	$13,500	$11,000	$9,750	$9,350	$8,700	$8,100	$7,675	$7,000	$6,375	$5,600	$4,800

GRADING - PPGS™	100%	98%	95%	90%	80%	70%	60%	LAST MSR

MODEL 1940 LIGHT RIFLE MARK I/II – 9mm Para. cal., 20 shot mag., fires from open bolt, black tenonite stock. Mfg. for the British goverment during 1940.

100%	98%	95%	90%	80%	70%	60%
N/A	N/A	$6,750	$6,000	$5,250	$4,750	$3,950

This model was done at the British Government's request in 1939 to Smith & Wesson for a 9mm assault rifle. Smith & Wesson designed, built and sent a group of these production Mark I rifles to the British Government for testing in 1940. The Mark I failed the 5000 round test due to the rifle being made to shoot the 9mm American manufacture ammunition not the 'hotter" European manufacture. After this discovery, at the request of the British Government, the British wanted S&W to do further engineering on this rifle. Improvements were done and group of the Mark II rifles were sent for addition testing. By this time, the British had lost interest in the rifle. In spite of its failure in testing, it was a very well made rifle with lots of steel and machining required in its manufacturing, unlike the Sten gun.

A total of 1227 known 9mm Light Rifles were built, of which 200 were of the Mark II variation. 1010 were sold to the British Government. More frames were made than guns built; therefore serial numbers range between 1-2200.

At the end of WWII all of the Light rifles in possession of the British government were supposedly cut in half and dumped in the English Channel, except for five that are in a British Military Museum.

A very interesting note: In 1974 S&W discovered some crated and unfired 1940 Light rifles in their facility. In 1975 they were then sold as a curio and relic to a distributor. These had a 9 3/4 inch barrel, blue finish and black tenonite stock.

Also noted: Any of the 1940 9mm Light Rifles should not be loaded with or fired with any modern manufactured 9mm ammunition.

Rifles: Bolt Action

In 1984 S&W discontinued importation of all Howa manufactured rifles. Mossberg continued importation utilizing leftover S&W parts in addition to fabricating their own.

MODEL A – .22-250 Rem., .243 Win., .270 Win., .308 Win., .30 - 06, 7mm Mag., or .300 Win. Mag. cal., 23 3/4 in. barrel, folding leaf sight, checkered Monte Carlo stock with rosewood forend tip and pistol grip cap. Mfg. by Husqvarna in Sweden 1969-1972.

100%	98%	95%	90%	80%	70%	60%
$425	$375	$325	$300	$275	$220	$195

MODEL B – .243 Win., .270 Win., or .30-06 cal., similar to Model A, except has 20 3/4 in. barrel, Monte Carlo stock with Schnabel forend.

100%	98%	95%	90%	80%	70%	60%
$475	$425	$305	$275	$250	$195	$165

MODEL C – similar to Model B, with sporting stock.

100%	98%	95%	90%	80%	70%	60%
$475	$425	$300	$275	$250	$195	$165

MODEL D – similar to Model C, with full length two-piece Mannlicher style stock.

100%	98%	95%	90%	80%	70%	60%
$725	$650	$575	$495	$425	$350	$300

MODEL E – similar to Model D, with cheekpiece.

100%	98%	95%	90%	80%	70%	60%
$725	$650	$575	$495	$425	$350	$300

GRADING - PPGS™	100%	98%	95%	90%	80%	70%	60%	*LAST MSR*

MODEL 1500 MOUNTAINEER – .222 Rem., .22-250 Rem., .223 Rem, .243 Win, .25-06 Rem, .270 Win, .30-06, or .308 Win. cal., bolt action, 22 in. barrel, 5 or 6 shot mag., no sights, walnut stock, approx. 7 lbs. 10 oz. Imported 1983-1984.

$400 $350 $300 $250 $245 $210 $185

Add $27 for sights.

* ***Model 1500 Mountaineer Magnum*** – 7mm Rem. Mag. or .300 Win. Mag. cal.

$425 $375 $325 $275 $260 $225 $200

MODEL 1500 DELUXE – same cals. as standard 1500, Monte Carlo stock, skip-line checkering, select walnut, no sights. Imported 1983-1984.

$450 $400 $350 $300 $260 $220 $200

Add 10% for 7mm Mag. and .300 Win. Mag.

MODEL 1500 DELUXE VARMINT – .222 Rem, .22-250 Rem., or .223 Rem. cal., heavy 24 in. barrel, skip-line checkering, no sights. Imported 1983-1984.

$475 $425 $375 $325 $275 $225 $200

MODEL 1700 LS "CLASSIC HUNTER" – .243 Win, .270 Win, or .30-06 cal., 22 in. barrel, removable 5 shot mag., solid recoil pad, no sights, Schnabel forend, finely checkered. Imported 1983-1984.

$495 $450 $400 $350 $315 $265 $240

I-BOLT RIFLE – .25-06, .270 Win., .30-06, 7mm Rem. Mag. (disc. 2008), or .300 Win. Mag. (disc. 2008), cal. short or long action, 4 shot mag., 23 or 25 (disc. 2008) in. barrel, black synthetic, Realtree camo synthetic, or Monte Carlo walnut (mfg. 2008) stock, blue carbon steel or stainless steel (disc. 2008) action and barrel, Picatinny rail integral with receiver, approx. 7 lbs. Mfg. mid-2007-2009.

$475 $425 $375 $325 $295 $275 $250 ***$553***

Add $84 for camo.

Add approx. 10%-15% for walnut stock and stainless barrel (disc. 2008).

* ***I-Bolt Rifle w/Weathershield*** – .25-06, .270 Win., .30-06, 7mm Rem. Mag., or .300 Win. Mag. cal., short or long action, 23 in. barrel, similar to I-Bolt model, except has Weathershield coated black or camo synthetic stock. Mfg. 2009.

$495 $435 $380 $330 $300 $275 $250 ***$588***

Add $70 for camo.

Rifles: Semi-Auto

The following is a listing of abbreviations with related feature codes of both centerfire and rimfire semi-auto rifles: Stock: S/6 ADJ - 6 position adj., S/BLK - black synthetic, S/CAM - camo synthetic, S/SF - solid fixed, S/W - wood stock. Pistol Grip: PG - plastic grip, RG - rubber grip, WG - wood grip, NA - no grip. Rear Sight: R/ADJ - adjustable, R/FS - folding stock, R/FSADJ - folding adjustable, NA - no rear sight. Front Sight: F/BB - Black Blade, F/BP - Black Post, F/FO - fiber optic, F/FS - folding sight, F/FSADJ - folding adjustable, F/GB - Gold Bead, F/WBF - white bead front sight, NA - no front sight. Forend: CFF - custom free float, MR - modular rail, STD - standard, NA - no forend (one piece stock). Receiver Material: AL - alloy, CA - carbon, SS - Stainless steel, POLY - polymer. Action: BA - bolt action, FA - fixed action, SAT - semi-auto.

IMPORTANT NOTE: On model(s) where *N/A has replaced the normal 100% value, it indicates current market conditions are too unstable to accurately ascertain 100%-60% values. Factory retail prices (MSRs) reflect most recent updates. For more up-to-date information on current pricing trends and additional useful information, please visit www.bluebookofgunvalues.com, select "Information & Services " from the menu, and click on "Additional Book Information".

MODEL M&P15 CENTERFIRE SEMI-AUTO SERIES – .223 Rem./5.56 NATO or 5.45x39mm cal., gas operated, AR-15 style design with 16 in. or longer chrome lined barrel with muzzle brake, aluminum upper and lower receiver, 10 or 30 shot mag. (most are mil-spec), one piece, fixed position, skeletonized, or six position CAR collapsible stock, hard coat black anodized finish, features detachable carrying handle, A2 post front sight, adj.

GRADING - PPGS™	100%	98%	95%	90%	80%	70%	60%	LAST MSR

dual aperture rear sight, and thinned handguard, M&P15T features extended Picatinny rail on receiver and barrel, in addition to RAS on both sides and bottom of barrel, adj. front and rear folding battle sights, supplied with hard carry case, approx. 6 1/2 lbs. New 2006.

The lowest serial number encountered to date is SW00200.

* ***Model M&P15*** – 5.56 NATO cal., 16 in. carbon steel barrel, 30 shot mag., alloy receiver, black alloy finish, six-position adj. pistol grip stock, adj. rear sight, black post front sight.

MSR $1,249	*N/A	$875	$775	$675	$575	$500	$450	

Product Code: 811000.

* ***Model M&P15A*** – 5.56 NATO cal., gas operated semi-auto, AR-15 style design, 16 in. barrel, 30 shot mag., similar to Model M&P15, except features a receiver Picatinny rail and adj. rear folding battle sight with ribbed handguard, 6 1/2 lbs. Mfg. 2006-2012.

	*N/A	$875	$775	$675	$575	$500	$450	*$1,289*

Product Code: 811002.

* ***Model M&P15T*** – 5.56 NATO cal., gas operated semi-auto, AR-15 style design, fixed 10 (CA compliant) or detachable 30 shot mag., 16 in. barrel, similar to Model M&P15A, except features folding (disc. 2010) or fixed Black Post front sight (new 2011), fixed (new 2011) or folding adj. rear sight (disc. 2010), modular rail (disc. 2010) or custom free float forend (new 2011), 6.85 lbs.

MSR $1,159	*N/A	$875	$775	$650	$550	$500	$450	

Product Codes: 811001 (disc. 2010), or 811041 (new 2011).

* ***Model M&P15FT*** – 5.56 NATO cal., gas operated semi-auto, AR-15 style design, 16 in. barrel, 10 shot mag. (compliant for CT, MA, MD, NJ, and NY), one-piece pistol grip fixed stock, custom free float forend (new 2012), folding adj. (new 2012) front and rear sights, modular rail (disc. 2011), alloy receiver. Mfg. 2008-2011.

MSR $1,159	*N/A	$875	$775	$650	$550	$500	$450	

Last MSR for product code 811004 was $1,709 in 2011

Product Code: 811004 (disc. 2011), 811048 (new 2012).

* ***Model M&P15OR*** – 5.56 NATO cal., 16 in. carbon steel barrel with flat top Picatinny rail and gas block, 30 shot mag., optics ready alloy receiver, black alloy finish, six-position adj. stock, no rear sight. New 2008

MSR $1,069	*N/A	$800	$700	$600	$500	$400	$350	

Product Code: 811003.

* ***Model M&P15ORC*** – 5.56 NATO cal., gas operated semi-auto, AR-15 style design, 16 in. barrel, 10 shot mag. (compliant CT, MA, MD, NJ and NY), black alloy finish, pistol grip stock, alloy receiver, optics ready. New mid-2008.

MSR $1,039	$875	$795	$695	$600	$500	$400	$350	

Product Code: 811013.

* ***Model M&P15X*** – 5.56 NATO cal., gas operated semi-auto, AR-15 style design, 16 in. barrel, 30 shot mag., black alloy finish, six-position adj. pistol grip stock, folding rear and black post front sights, modular rail, alloy receiver. New 2008.

MSR $1,379	*N/A	$935	$825	$725	$625	$525	$475	

Product Code: 811008.

* ***Model M&P15I*** – .223 Rem. cal., gas operated semi-auto, AR-15 style design, 17 in. barrel, 10 shot mag. (compliant CT, MA, MD, NJ, and NY), black alloy finish, pistol grip stock, adj. rear sight, black post front sight, alloy receiver, 7 lbs. Mfg. mid-2008-2011.

	*N/A	$875	$775	$675	$575	$500	$450	*$1,259*

Product Code: 811010.

GRADING - PPGS™	100%	98%	95%	90%	80%	70%	60%	LAST MSR

* ***Model M&P15R*** – 5.45x39mm cal., gas operated semi-auto, AR-15 style design, 16 in. barrel, 30 shot mag., black alloy finish, pistol grip stock, adj. rear and black post front sight, alloy receiver, Picatinny rail, 6 1/2 lbs. Mfg. 2008-2011.

	*N/A	$800	$700	$600	$500	$400	$350	*$1,089*

Product Code: 811011.

* ***Model M&P15VTAC*** – 5.56 NATO cal., gas operated semi-auto, AR-15 style design, Viking Tactics Model, 16 in. barrel, 30 shot mag., black alloy finish, pistol grip stock, modular rail, alloy receiver. Mfg. mid-2008-2011.

	*N/A	$1,450	$1,225	$995	$875	$725	$600	*$1,989*

Product Code: 811012.

* ***Model M&P15VTAC II*** – 5.56 NATO cal., similar to M&P 15VTAC, except features mid-length system for lower recoil, enhanced flash hider, 13 in. TRX Extreme handguard and other VLTOR 6-position collapsible stock. New 2012.

MSR $1,949	*N/A	$1,450	$1,225	$995	$875	$725	$600	

Product Code: 811025.

* ***Model M&P15MOE*** – 5.56 NATO cal., gas operated semi-auto, AR-15 style design, 16 in. barrel, 30 shot mag., black alloy finish, six position adj. stock, alloy receiver, post front sight, folding rear sight. Mfg. 2010-2011.

	*N/A	$875	$775	$675	$575	$500	$450	*$1,249*

Product Codes: 811020 and 811021.

MODEL M&P MOE MID – 5.56 NATO cal., 16 in. barrel, features Magpul hardware, 30 shot, alloy receiver, 6-position adj. stock, black post front sight and folding adj. rear sight, black or Flat Dark Earth finish. New 2012.

MSR $1,259	*N/A	$875	$775	$675	$575	$500	$450	

Product Codes: 811053 and 811054.

* ***Model M&P15PS*** – 5.56 NATO cal., gas operated semi-auto, AR-15 style design, 16 in. barrel, fixed 10 (CA compliant) or 30 shot mag., black alloy finish, six position adj. stock with standard forend, alloy receiver, solid hand guard, Picatinny rail above gas block, no sights, flattop upper, chrome lined bore, gas key, and bolt carrier, adj. gas plug with three settings. New 2010.

MSR $1,359	*N/A	$925	$825	$725	$625	$525	$475	

Product Code: 811022.

* ***Model M&P15PSX*** – 5.56 NATO cal., gas operated semi-auto, AR-15 style design, 16 in. barrel, 30 shot mag., black alloy finish, six position adj. stock with standard forend and tactical rail, alloy receiver. New 2010.

MSR $1,499	*N/A	$975	$875	$775	$650	$550	$500	

Product Code: 811023.

* ***Model M&P15 Sport*** – 5.56 NATO cal., 16 in. melonite treated barrel, fixed (CA compliant) or detachable 10 (compliant CT, MA, MD, NJ, and NY), or 30 shot mag., single stage trigger, hard coat black anodized upper and lower receiver, polymer handguard, chrome lined gas key and bolt carrier, adj. A2 post front sight, adj. dual aperture rear sight, six-position telescoping buttstock, A2 flash suppressor. New 2011.

MSR $839	*N/A	$725	$600	$565	$535	$495	$465	

Product Codes: 811036 and 811037 (compliant).

* ***Model M&P15 TS*** – 5.56 NATO cal., gas operated semi-auto, AR-15 style design, 16 in. barrel with flash hider, 30 shot mag., Magpul folding front and rear sights, Magpul MOE stock and mag., full Troy TRX free floating quad rail, 6 1/2 lbs. New 2011.

MSR $1,569	*N/A	$1,025	$900	$800	$700	$550	$500	

Product Code: 811024.

GRADING - PPGS™	100%	98%	95%	90%	80%	70%	60%	LAST MSR

MODEL M&P15 300 WHISPER – .300 Whisper cal., 16 in. barrel with or without sound suppressor, 10 shot mag., low recoil and muzzle blast, Realtree APG camo on all surfaces except barrel. New 2012.

MSR $1,119	*N/A	$900	$775	$675	$550	$450	$400

Product Code: 811300.

MODEL M&P15-22 RIMFIRE SEMI-AUTO – .22 LR cal., gas operated semi-auto, blowback action, AR-15 style design, 16 1/2 in. barrel with or w/o threading, 10 (disc. 2011) or 25 shot mag., matte black or 100% Realtree APG HD camo finish, A2 post front sight and dual aperture rear sight, fixed or six position CAR adj. stock, quad rail handguard, 5 1/2 lbs. New 2009.

MSR $499	$425	$385	$350	$325	$300	$280	$260

Add $20 for threaded barrel.
Add $50 for 100% Realtree APG HD camo finish with threaded barrel (new 2011).

Product Code: 811030 for base model.

* ***Model M&P15-22 MOE Rimfire Semi-Auto*** – .22 LR cal., similar to Model M&P15-22, except has 16 in. barrel, folding front and rear sight and skeletonized MagPul MOE stock, flat black or Flat Dark Earth (new 2012) finish, approx. 5 1/2 lbs. New 2011.

MSR $609	$525	$450	$395	$365	$335	$300	$275

Product Codes: 811034 and 811035.

* ***Model M&P15-22 PC TB***

Please see listing under Performance Center rifles.

SHOTGUNS

In 1984 S&W discontinued importation of all Howa manufactured shotguns. Mossberg continued importation utilizing leftover S&W parts in addition to fabricating their own.

MODEL 916 SLIDE ACTION SHOTGUN – 12, 16, or 20 ga., 20, 26, 28, or 30 in. barrels, various chokes, plain pistol grip stock, solid frame. Mfg. by S&W in Springfield, MA. 1972-disc.

	$175	$150	$140	$130	$120	$110	$100

* ***Model 916 Slide Action Shotgun Vent. rib and pad***

	$200	$175	$155	$145	$135	$130	$120

MODEL 916T SLIDE ACTION – similar to 916, except barrels can be interchanged.

	$195	$170	$155	$145	$135	$130	$125

* ***Model 916T Slide Action Vent. rib and pad***

	$225	$200	$180	$170	$155	$145	$135

MODEL 96 SLIDE ACTION – various gauges, disc.

	$125	$110	$100	$90	$75	$70	$65

MODEL 1000 P SLIDE ACTION – 12 ga., various barrel lengths, chokes, VR.

	$350	$305	$270	$230	$210	$190	$170

This model is the same as the Model 3000.

MODEL 1000 AUTOLOADER – 12 or 20 ga., 22-30 in. barrels, various chokes, gas operated, vent rib, engraved alloy receiver, checkered pistol grip stock. Mfg. 1972-1984.

	$350	$325	$295	$260	$240	$220	$200

Add $30 for multi-choke tubes.
Add approx. $125 for slug barrel.

* ***Model 1000 Autoloader Waterfowler*** – 3 in. chamber, parkerized finish, Magnum 28 or 30 in. barrel, multi-chokes, steel receiver, "M" suffix, camo sling and swivels.

	$500	$450	$375	$340	$310	$275	$255

GRADING - PPGS™	100%	98%	95%	90%	80%	70%	60%	LAST MSR

* ***Model 1000 Autoloader Super 12*** – handles all loads interchangeably, top-of-the-line model during its time.

	$500	$450	$400	$360	$330	$300	$280	

Add $50 for multi-choke.

* ***Model 1000 Autoloader Target*** – 12 or 20 ga., skeet, super skeet, and trap models available. Super skeet has 15 barrel muzzle vents to reduce recoil. Trap model has multi-choke tubes, Monte Carlo select walnut stock and forend. Both alloy and steel receivers available in Skeet model, Trap is steel only.

Skeet/Super Skeet	$400	$390	$335	$260	$235	$215	$190	
Trap (Model 1000T)	$595	$525	$450	$375	$325	$285	$235	

Note: Shotguns made for S&W by Howa Machinery, Ltd., Japan. This line was picked up by Mossberg after S&W discontinued them - these models may be more desirable.

MODEL 1012 SEMI-AUTO – 12 ga., 3 in. chamber, 24, 26, 28, or 30 in. barrel with vent. rib and 5 flush choke tubes, micro coated twin piston gas operated, checkered satin walnut, black synthetic, or synthetic stock with 100% Max-4 or APG camo treatment, includes four-piece shim kit, approx. 6 1/2 lbs., mfg. in Turkey. Imported 2007-2009.

	$525	$475	$425	$395	$350	$300	$275	*$644*

Add $35 for satin finished walnut stock and forearm.
Add $91 for 100% camo coverage.

* ***Model 1012 Super Semi-Auto*** – similar to Model 1012, except has 3 1/2 in. chamber, not available with walnut stock and forearm, approx. 7.3 lbs. Imported 2007-2009.

	$650	$575	$525	$475	$425	$395	$360	*$784*

Add $98 for full camo coverage.

MODEL 1020 SEMI-AUTO – 20 ga., 3 in. chamber, otherwise similar to Model 1012, single piston gas operation, approx. 6 lbs.

	$525	$475	$425	$395	$350	$300	$275	*$644*

Add $35 for satin finished walnut stock and forearm.
Add $91 for 100% camo coverage.
Subtract $21 for Model 1020SS w/short stock and 24 in. barrel.

MODEL 3000 SLIDE ACTION – 12 or 20 ga., 3 in. chambers, 22-30 in. barrels, walnut stock and forend, 6 1/4-7 1/2 lbs.

	$350	$305	$270	$230	$210	$190	$170	

Add $30 for multi-choke tubes.
Subtract $40 for slug gun (rifle sights on 22 in. barrel).

This model was also available in a "Waterfowler" variation - values are approx. the same as listed.

MODEL 3000 POLICE – 12 ga. only, 18 or 20 in. barrel, blue or parkerized finish, many combinations of finishes, stock types, and other combat accessories were available for this model.

	$325	$255	$215	$185	$170	$155	$140	

Add $125 for folding stock.

ELITE GOLD GRADE I SxS – 20 ga., 3 in. chamber, scalloped boxlock action, 26 or 28 in. barrels with fixed chokes, ejectors, ST or DT, Grade III checkered walnut straight grip English or pistol grip stock, color case hardened frame with light scroll engraving, 6.5-6.7 lbs., mfg. in Turkey and imported 2007-2010.

	$1,975	$1,750	$1,525	$1,350	$1,150	$950	$775	*$2,380*

ELITE SILVER GRADE I O/U – 12 ga., scalloped boxlock action, 26, 28, or 30 in. VR barrels with 5 flush choke tubes, ST, ejectors, color case hardened frame with light scroll engraving, Grade III checkered walnut pistol grip stock, solid recoil pad, engine turned internal barrel parts, 7.6-7.8 lbs., mfg. in Turkey and imported 2007-2010.

MSR $2,380	$1,975	$1,750	$1,525	$1,350	$1,150	$950	$775	

GRADING - PPGS™	100%	98%	95%	90%	80%	70%	60%	LAST MSR

SMITHSON, J.P.

Current custom long arm manufacturer located in Provo, UT.

J.P. Smithson specializes in custom long arms, including bolt action and single shot rifles, as well as shotguns. J.P. Smithson also specializes in fiberglass and carbon stocked rifles, as well as wood stocks, custom metal work, and his own design of quick detachable scope mounts. Many options for long guns are available. Since each gun is built per customer specifications, please contact him directly for more information, including availability, delivery time, and pricing (see Trademark Index).

SNAKE CHARMER

Previously manufactured by Verney-Carron USA, Inc. located in Clay Center, KS a joint venture of Verney-Carron SA located in Saint-Etienne, France (please refer to the separate Verney-Carron listing) and Y.B.E., Inc. located in Clay Center, KS (distributor of Hastings barrels and choke tubes). Distributor sales only.

SHOTGUNS: SINGLE SHOT

SNAKE CHARMER II – .410 bore only, stainless steel, break open single shot, black molded plastic stock and forend, shell holder in stock, also available as Night Charmer (disc. 1988) and Sea Charmer (disc. 1988), 3 1/2 lbs. Disc. 2009.

$180	$160	$145	$130	$115	$100	$90	*$216*

Add $10 for Night Charmer (disc. 1988).
Add $18 for Sea Charmer (disc. 1988).
Subtract $18 for black carbon steel barrel (New Generation Model).

SOCIETA SIDERURGICA GLISENTI

Previous manufacturer located in Brescia, Italy. Also see the Italian Military Arms listing.

PISTOLS: SEMI-AUTO

GLISENTI MODEL 1910 – 9mm Glisenti cal., 7 shot, 4 in. barrel, fixed sights, blue, checkered wood, rubber or plastic grips, Italian service pistol. Mfg. 1910-WWII.

$750	$625	$450	$325	$275	$225	$200

Warning: While some Glisentis may chamber and fire the 9mm Para. cartridge, it is extremely dangerous to do so.

SODIA, FRANZ

Current manufacturer established during 1871, and located in Salzburg, Austria since 1961. Previously located in Ferlach, Austria.

LONG GUNS: CUSTOM

Older Sodia arms are very high quality and are often excellently engraved and inlaid. Sodia is famous for its high quality long arms in many configurations. Current models include: Model 557 Mountain Carbine O/U combination gun, Model 557 Super De Luxe O/U combination gun, Model 270 AD Drilling, Model 30 Drilling, Model 160 EJ Safari SxS double rifle, Model 260 EJ SxS double rifle, Model 158 AN Drilling, Model 360 EJ SxS double rifle, Model 560 EJ Safari SxS double rifle, Model 150 HH single barrel rifle, in addition to a bolt action model in many calibers. Please contact the company for more information, including U.S. availability, delivery time, and a custom quotation (see Trademark Index).

To determine current values on older Franz Sodia rifles and shotguns, it is very important to consider the overall desirability of the gun's configuration (i.e. boxlock or sidelock action, caliber/gauge, special features, amount and quality of engraving (including gold inlays), type and quality of wood, checkering/carving, eye appeal, and original condition factor). All Franz Sodia guns are hand crafted, and need to be evaluated individually to determine value and shootability.

SOKOLOVSKY CORPORATION SPORT ARMS (SCSA)

Previous manufacturer until 1990 located in Sunnyvale, CA.

GRADING - PPGS™	100%	98%	95%	90%	80%	70%	60%	LAST MSR

PISTOLS: SEMI-AUTO

SOKOLOVSKY .45 AUTOMASTER – .45 ACP cal. only, stainless steel, single action, 6 in. barrel, 6 shot mag., adj. Millet sights, unique action, is free of external devices, 55 oz. Mfg. 1984-90.

	$2,700	$2,200	$1,850	$1,620	$1,335	$1,115	$930	*$3,300*

Total production on this model is 50 pistols.

SOG ARMORY

Current rifle manufacturer located in Houston, TX.

SOG Armory also makes a wide variety of components and accessories for both AR-10 and AR-15/M16 carbines and rifles.

CARBINES/RIFLES: SEMI-AUTO

All AR-15 style rifles come standard with one 10 or 30 shot magazine, manual, sling, and hard case.

SOG CRUSADER – .223 Rem. cal., 16 in. chrome lined steel barrel, 30 shot mag., Mil Spec hard coat anodized upper and lower, black, tan, or OD green phosphate finish, enhanced mag well and trigger guard, M16 bolt and carrier, flash hider, ERGO pistol grip, M4 six position tactical stock, M4 stock pad, charging handle, SOG/Troy four rail handguard, SOG/Troy rear flip up sight.

MSR $1,700	$1,500	$1,250	$1,025	$875	$750	$725	$675

SOG DEFENDER – .223 Rem. cal., 16 in. chrome lined steel barrel, 30 shot mag., Mil Spec hard coat anodized upper and lower, black, tan, or OD green phosphate finish, enhanced mag well and trigger guard, M16 bolt and carrier, flash hider, ERGO pistol grip, M4 six position tactical stock, M4 stock pad, charging handle, SOG/Troy four rail handguard, detachable carry handle.

MSR $1,600	$1,425	$1,175	$1,000	$850	$725	$650	$550

SOG ENFORCER – .223 Rem. cal., 16 in. chrome lined steel barrel, 30 shot mag., Mil Spec hard coat anodized upper and lower, black phosphate finish, enhanced mag well and trigger guard, M16 bolt and carrier, flash hider, ERGO pistol grip, M4 six position tactical stock, M4 stock pad, charging handle, CAR M4 handguard with double heat shield, SOG/Troy rear slip up sight.

MSR $1,500	$1,350	$1,125	$975	$825	$700	$600	$495

SOG GUARDIAN – .223 Rem. cal., 16 in. chrome lined steel barrel, 30 shot mag., Mil Spec hard coat anodized upper and lower, black phosphate finish, enhanced mag well and trigger guard, M16 bolt and carrier, flash hider, ERGO pistol grip, M4 six position tactical stock, M4 stock pad, charging handle, CAR M4 handguard with double heat shield and detachable carry handle.

MSR $1,400	$1,275	$1,075	$925	$800	$700	$600	$495

SOG OPERATOR – .223 Rem. cal., 16 in. chrome lined steel barrel, 30 shot mag., Mil Spec hard coat anodized upper and lower, black, tan, or OD green phosphate finish, enhanced mag well, M16 bolt and carrier, flash hider, ERGO pistol grip, six position tactical stock, M4 stock pad, charging handle, SOG/Troy four rail handguard, SOG/Troy flip up sight, Magpul Winter trigger guard, Wolf Eye's 260 Lumens tactical light, SOG mount, graphite vertical grip.

MSR $2,300	$2,075	$1,825	$1,675	$1,450	$1,200	$825	$750

SOG PREDATOR – .223 Rem. cal., 20 in. Lothar Walther fully fluted barrel with muzzle brake, SOG Extreme vent. handguard with upper and lower Picatinny rails, SOG sights, low profile gas block, Magpul trigger guard and PRS stock, 8.3 lbs. New 2011.

MSR $2,000	$1,800	$1,550	$1,275	$1,050	$850	$750	$675

SOG WARRIOR – .223 Rem. cal., 16 in. chrome lined steel barrel, 30 shot mag., Mil Spec hard coat anodized upper and lower, black or tan phosphate finish, enhanced mag well and trigger guard, M16 bolt and carrier, flash hider, ERGO pistol grip, VLTOR EMOD stock, M4

GRADING - PPGS™	100%	98%	95%	90%	80%	70%	60%	LAST MSR

stock pad, charging handle, SOG/Troy Extreme free float handguard with rails, SOG/Troy flip front and rear sights.

MSR $1,800	$1,600	$1,375	$1,150	$1,000	$875	$725	$600	

SOLEIHAC ARMURIER

Previous manufacturer located in Saint Etienne, France.

This manufacturer produced copies of 1894 patent Darne R model guns until 1950. The guns produced were generally simple and less expensive than other manufacturers' sliding breech guns. Most unmarked sliding breech guns were probably manufactured by Soleihac Armurier. Quality and pricing will be similar to low grade (Halifax and RIO model) Darne guns in average condition.

SOMMER + OCKENFUSS GmbH

Previous manufacturer located in Baiersbronn, Germany until 2002. Previously imported by Lothar Walther Precision Tool, located in Cumming, GA. Previously imported by Intertex Carousels Corporation during 1998-2000, and located in Pineville, NC.

Sommer + Ockenfuss also produced a bolt adapter to convert the Remington 700 bolt action into a straight pull repeater, enabling the addition of a firing pin safety and firing chamber lock.

PISTOLS: SEMI-AUTO

P21 – .224 HV, 9mm Para., or .40 S&W cal., 3.11 (Combat) or 3.55 (Police) in. rotating barrel, SA/DA operation, release grip safety uncocks the hammer, keyed slide lock blocks firing pin and slide, 10 shot mag., approx. 24 oz. Mfg. 2001.

	$550	$495	$450	$415	$375	$340	$310	*$608*

Add approx. $320 for conversion slide assemblies.

RIFLES: SLIDE ACTION

SHORTY – most popular cals., unique slide action rifle in bullpup configuration featuring a straight line design with a grip safety pistol grip which also works the slide assembly, stainless or black coated barrel, compact 6-lug bolt with a locking surface of 0.263 sq. in., with or w/o sideplates inlet into walnut or black synthetic (new 1999) stock. Imported 1998-2002.

* ***Shorty Wilderness Rifle*** – match trigger, polymer stock, and stainless steel barrel.

	$1,495	$1,275	$1,100	$995	$925	$850	$750	*$1,660*

Add $310 for .375 H&H or .416 Rem. Mag. cal. (Shorty Safari).
Add $200 for walnut stock (Shorty American Hunter).
Add $210 for sight mounts.
Add $88 for recoil brake.

* ***Shorty Marksman Rifle*** – similar to Wilderness Rifle, except has choice of black coated or fluted heavy match barrel and recoil brake.

	$1,875	$1,675	$1,450	$1,275	$1,100	$995	$850	*$2,020*

Add $80 for .308 Win. or .300 Win. Mag. (fluted barrel), $420 for .338 Lapua Mag. with black coated barrel, or $710 for .338 Lapua Mag. with fluted stainless barrel.
Add $80 for stainless barrel.
Add $210 for sight mount, $168 for bipod, $210 for Spigot stock cap.

There were also deluxe variations, limited editions, and Marksman's packages ($4,100-$4,860 MSR) available in this model.

SOROKA RIFLE COMPANY

Current rifle manufacturer located in New Zealand. Exclusively distributed by New England Custom Gun Service Ltd. located in Claremont, NH.

RIFLES: SINGLE SHOT

MODEL 07 – various standard magnum and dangerous calibers, features the Gibbs Farquharson action, engraved cased colored receiver, 24 or 26 in. barrel with quarter rib,

GRADING - PPGS™	100%	98%	95%	90%	80%	70%	60%	LAST MSR

barrel band, and integral Talley base, checkered deluxe walnut stock and forearm with ebony tip, solid rubber pad, top tang safety.

This model has a current MSR of $16,500.

SPARTAN GUN WORKS

Previous trademark of Remington Arms Company, Inc. for long arms imported from Russia (mostly Baikal) from 2004-2009.

Remington referred to these firearms as part of its ISP (International Sourced Product) line.

COMBINATION GUNS

SPR94 – choice of 12 ga. over .223 Rem., .30-06 (disc. 2006) or .308 Win. (disc. 2006) cal., or .410 bore over .17 HMR (disc. 2006), .22 LR or .22 WMR cal., .22 cal., 3 in. chamber, DT, boxlock action, 24 in. barrels with rifle sights, extractors, checkered walnut stock and forearm with recoil pad, sling swivels, separated barrels grooved for scope mount, approx. 7 1/2 lbs. Imported 2006-2009.

Model	100%	98%	95%	90%	80%	70%	60%	LAST MSR
* ***SPR94 .410 Bore/Rimfire***	$330	$275	$235	$210	$180	$170	$160	*$392*
* ***SPR94 12 ga./Centerfire***	$525	$465	$410	$360	$315	$280	$260	*$661*

RIFLES

SPR18 SINGLE SHOT – .223 Rem., .243 Win., .270 Win., .30-06, .308 Win. or 7.62x39mm cal., break open single shot with opening lever on rear of trigger guard, 23 1/2 in. spiral cut fluted barrel, choice of blue or nickel finished frame, adj. sights and scope rail, walnut stock with recoil pad and forearm, 6 3/4 lbs. Imported 2006-2009.

$225	$190	$165	$140	$125	$110	$100	*$277*

Add $28 for scope and case (blue finish only, disc. 2006).
Add $49 for nickel finish.

SPR22 SxS – .30-06 or .45-70 Govt. cal., boxlock action, blue metal finish, sling swivels, 23 1/2 in. monobloc barrels with iron sights, DT, extractors, top opening lever, checkered walnut stock and forearm with recoil pad, 7 1/2 lbs. Limited importation 2006 only.

$585	$535	$475	$425	$385	$350	$325	*$699*

SHOTGUNS

SPR100 SINGLE SHOT – 12, 20 ga., or .410 bore, 3 in. chamber, 24 (Youth only), 26 (20 ga.) or 28 (12 ga.) in. barrel with or w/o VR and fixed choke, trigger guard opening lever, blue or nickel plated steel action with selectable ejector or extractor, cocking indicator, crossbolt safety, hardwood stock and forearm, 5.8-6 lbs. Imported 2004-2009.

$90	$80	$65	$55	$45	$40	$35	*$118*

Add $9 for standard Youth model (.410 bore or 20 ga.).
Add $86 for SPR100 Max with nickel plated receiver (also available in Youth Model).

* ***SPR100 Single Shot Sporting*** – 12 or 20 ga., nickel receiver, includes choke tubes and recoil pad, Monte Carlo walnut stock and forearm. Imported 2006-2009.

$235	$190	$160	$140	$120	$100	$90	*$300*

SPR210 SxS – 12, 16 (disc. 2007), 20, 28 ga., or .410 bore, 3 in. chambers except for 16 and 28 ga., boxlock action, SST, ejectors, 26 or 28 in. barrels with choke tubes (N/A on 28 ga. or .410 bore), tang safety, blued or nickel frame, VR, checkered walnut stock and forearm with recoil pad, 6.8-7 lbs. Imported 2004-2009.

$390	$330	$280	$250	$225	$200	$185	*$479*

Add $82 for 28 ga. or .410 bore (fixed chokes only).
Add $52 for nickel plated frame (12 or 20 ga. only).
Add $8 for hammerless cowboy gun in 12 or 20 ga. only with 20 in. barrels (disc. 2007).

GRADING - PPGS™	100%	98%	95%	90%	80%	70%	60%	LAST MSR

SPR220 SxS – 12 or 20 ga., 3 in. chambers, boxlock action, DT, extractors, 20 (cowboy only), 26, or 28 in. barrels with choke tubes, tang safety, blue or nickel frame, checkered walnut stock and forearm, 6.8-7 lbs. Imported 2004-2009.

	$325	$275	$240	$210	$185	$140	$120	*$392*

Add $169 for hammers.
Subtract $50 for cowboy gun with hardwood stock and forearm, 12 ga. only and fixed cylinder chokes.
Add $29 for hammerless cowboy gun with nickel finished frame, 12 or 20 ga. with choke tubes.
Subtract $20 for 2 3/4 in. chambers on cowboy gun.

SPR310 O/U – 12, 16, 20, 28 ga., or .410 bore, 3 in. chamber except for 28 ga., boxlock action with monobloc barrels, SST, ejectors, 26 or 28 in. VR barrels with choke tubes (N/A on 28 ga. or .410 bore), tang safety, blue or nickel plated receiver, checkered walnut stock and forearm with rubber recoil pad, 7.3-7.4 lbs. Imported 2004-2009.

	$485	$415	$365	$320	$295	$250	$225	*$598*

Add $88 for 28 ga. or .410 bore.
Add $54 for nickel plated receiver.
Add $70 for nickel plated receiver with bird scene engraving.
Add $172 for nickel Sporting Model (12 or 20 ga. only, new 2006).

SPR320 O/U – 12, 16, 20, 28 ga., or .410 bore, 3 in. chamber except for 16 and 28 ga., boxlock action with monobloc barrels, DT, extractors, 26 or 28 in. VR barrels with choke tubes (N/A on 28 ga. or .410 bore), tang safety, blued finish, checkered walnut stock and forearm with rubber recoil pad, 7.3-7.4 lbs. Limited importation 2004-2005.

	$350	$295	$250	$215	$185	$165	$145	*$419*

SPR453 SEMI-AUTO – 12 ga. only, 3 1/2 in. chamber, gas operated, choice of matte black or new Mossy Oak Break-Up (disc.) camo finish, black synthetic or camo stock and forearm, 24, 26, or 28 in. VR barrel with four extended choke tubes, dual extractors on bolt face, approx. 8 1/8 lbs. Imported 2006-2009.

	$400	$350	$300	$265	$230	$200	$185	*$497*

Add $56 for 100% new Mossy Oak Break-Up camo finish (disc. 2006).

SPECIAL WEAPONS LLC

Previous paramilitary rifle manufacturer 1999-2002, and located in Mesa, AZ. Previously located in Tempe, AZ.

Special Weapons LLC closed its doors on Dec. 31, 2002. Another company, Special Weapons, Inc., is handling the warranty repairs on Special Weapons LLC firearms (see Trademark Index).

CARBINES: SEMI-AUTO

OMEGA 760 – 9mm Para. cal., reproduction of the S&W Model 76, 16 1/4 in. partially shrouded barrel, fixed wire stock, 30 shot mag., 7 1/2 lbs. Limited mfg. 2002.

	$495	$450	$425	$395	$375	$350	$325	*$575*

SW-5 CARBINE – 9mm Para. cal., paramilitary configuration styled after the HK-94 (parts interchangeable), stainless steel receiver, plastic lower housing, 16 1/4 in. stainless steel barrel, A2 style black synthetic stock with wide forearm, 10 shot mag. (accepts high capacity HK-94/MP-5 mags also), approx. 6 3/4 lbs. Mfg. 2000-2002.

	$1,475	$1,225	$1,025	$875	$800	$750	$695	*$1,600*

SW-45 CARBINE – .45 ACP cal., otherwise similar to SW-5 Carbine. Mfg. 2000-2002.

	$1,550	$1,275	$1,050	$895	$825	$775	$725	*$1,700*

RIFLES: SEMI-AUTO

SW-3 – .308 Win. cal., paramilitary configuration styled after the HK-91 (parts interchangeable), tooled receiver, metal steel lower trigger housing, 17.71 stainless steel barrel, A2 style stock, approx. 10 lbs. Mfg. 2000-2002.

	$1,425	$1,175	$995	$850	$800	$750	$695	*$1,550*

GRADING - PPGS™	100%	98%	95%	90%	80%	70%	60%	LAST MSR

* ***SW-3 SP*** – similar to SW-3, except has PSG-1 style trigger assembly, 22 in. custom target barrel and Weaver rail welded to top. Mfg. 2000-2002.

$2,250	$1,975	$1,700	$1,500	$1,250	$1,050	$895	*$2,500*

SPENCER CARBINES/RIFLES - CURRENT MFG.

Currently manufactured by Armi Sport di Chiappa Silvia & C., located in Brescia, Italy. Current reproductions are imported by Cimarron, Dixie Gun Works, and Taylor's & Co. Please refer to individual sections for listings.

SPENCER REPEATING RIFLES CO.

Previous manufacturer located in Boston, MA between 1860-1868. Spencer manufactured approximately 144,000 rimfire rifles and carbines, of which approximately 107,000 were contracted to the United States Government during the Civil War.

The brainchild of young Christopher Miner Spencer, more than 13,500 Spencer M1860 Army rifles, 800 M1860 Navy rifles, and 48,000 M1860 Army carbines saw action during the Civil War.

In late 1864, the Chief of Ordnance directed modifications, including reducing the bore from .52 to .50 caliber, and shortening the barrel from 22 inches to 20 inches. The new carbine was designated the Spencer M1865 carbine. Nearly 19,000 were produced by the Spencer Repeating Rifle Company, and another 30,500 by the Burnside Rifle Company, although all were delivered too late to see action in the Civil War. Model 1865 carbines and refurbished M1860 carbines became the mainstay of America's troops on the Western Frontier until replaced by "Trap-Door" Springfield carbines after 1873.

The author wishes to express thanks to Roy Marcot, author of *Spencer Repeating Rifles*, for providing most of the information listed here.

100%	98%	95%	90%	80%	70%	60%	50%	40%	30%	20%	10%

RIFLES: LEVER ACTION

SMALL-FRAME MILITARY CARBINES AND SPORTING RIFLES – less than four dozen prototype small-frame .38 rimfire cal. sporting rifles and .44 rimfire cal. military carbines were made by Christopher Spencer in Hartford between 1860 and 1861. They are exceedingly rare, and only a few are in private hands.

N/A	$16,500	$15,500	$13,500	$11,500	$9,500	$9,000	$8,000	$7,000	$6,000	$5,000	$4,500

MODEL 1860 NAVY RIFLES – the rarest of production Spencer firearms, 803 Spencer Model 1860 Navy rifles with sword-type bayonets were produced for the U.S. Navy Bureau of Ordnance between 1862 and 1863.

N/A	$15,000	$13,500	$12,000	$11,000	$9,000	$8,500	$7,500	$7,000	$6,000	$5,500	$5,000

Add $1,250 for correct Collins produced sword-type bayonet. Add $250 for the correct scabbard in at least very good condition.

Beware: a Collins-produced sword-type bayonet for the Sharps M1859 rifle can be made to fit the Spencer Navy rifle, but it is not a true Spencer Navy bayonet.

MODEL 1860 ARMY RIFLES – between 1863 and 1864, the Spencer factory in Boston produced 11,471 Spencer M1860 Army rifles for the Federal Ordnance Department, another 200 for the U.S. Navy, and approximately 2,000 for private purchase. All were issued with a style of Pattern M1855 angular bayonets which fit only these rifles.

N/A	$12,000	$11,000	$10,000	$8,000	$6,500	$5,000	$4,000	$3,000	$2,500	$2,000	$1,800

Add $600 for correct angular bayonet and scabbard.

MODEL 1860 CARBINES – beginning in October 1863, the Spencer factory began delivering the first of 45,733 Spencer M1860 carbines to the Ordnance Department for use by Federal cavalrymen. As many as 3,000 additional M1860 carbines went to private purchasers, and also saw action in the war. Because Spencer carbines were so important to the Federal war effort, nearly all saw hard use during the last 18 months of fighting. This resulted in

100%	98%	95%	90%	80%	70%	60%	50%	40%	30%	20%	10%

very few weapons available today in excellent condition, and fewer yet with case colors remaining on the receiver.

N/A	$12,000	$11,000	$10,000	$7,500	$6,000	$4,500	$3,750	$2,750	$2,000	$1,800	$1,500

Subtract 25% for Springfield Armory reconditioned Spencer Model 1860 carbines (modified after the war).

MODEL 1865 CARBINES – in 1865 and 1866, the Spencer factory delivered 18,959 Spencer M1865 carbines to the Federal Ordnance Department. Concurrently, the Burnside Rifle Company of Providence, Rhode Island manufactured and delivered 30,502 Spencer M1865 carbines to the Ordnance Department.

N/A	$7,000	$6,000	$5,000	$3,000	$2,750	$2,500	$2,000	$1,750	$1,500	$1,200	$1,000

MODEL 1865 ARMY RIFLES – as many as 3,000 Spencer M1865 Army rifles were made by the Spencer factory in 1865. While none were ordered by the U.S. Army Ordnance Department, 2,000 went to the Commonwealth of Massachusetts National Guard, and another 1,000 went to Canadian troops and to private purchasers.

N/A	$6,000	$5,000	$4,000	$3,000	$2,750	$2,500	$2,000	$1,750	$1,500	$1,200	$1,000

SPRINGFIELD ARMORY RIFLE MUSKET CONVERSION OF SPENCER CARBINES – in 1871, General Dyer, Chief of Ordnance, directed that 1,109 Spencer M1865 carbines be converted to two-band muskets. Each was fitted with Springfield .50 caliber barrels which held the standard M1855 pattern bayonet. The conversion work was done at Springfield Armory.

N/A	$6,000	$5,000	$4,000	$3,000	$2,750	$2,500	$2,000	$1,750	$1,500	$1,200	$1,000

Note: There is no record that these rifles were ever issued to U.S. troops. This is the reason why so many examples are known in 80% or better condition.

MODEL 1867 ARMY RIFLES AND CARBINES – in 1867, the Spencer factory produced approx. 1,000 M1867 Army rifles and 12,000 carbines. All were intended for private domestic or foreign military sales.

N/A	$4,500	$3,500	$2,500	$2,000	$1,900	$1,750	$1,500	$1,400	$1,200	$1,000	$900

NEW MODEL ARMY RIFLES AND CARBINES – in their final year of production, 1868, the Spencer Repeating Rifle Company produced approx. 1,000 Army rifles and 5,000 carbines. These too, were intended for private domestic or foreign military sales.

N/A	$4,500	$3,500	$2,500	$2,000	$1,900	$1,750	$1,500	$1,400	$1,200	$1,000	$900

SPORTING RIFLES – between 1864-68, the Spencer factory produced approximately 2,000 sporting rifles for the civilian trade. The initial 200 or so were made from surplus military M1860 Army rifle receivers. Thereafter, approximately 1,800 sporting rifles were made expressly as such. The majority chambered the Spencer 56-46 bottleneck rimfire cartridge, but a small number were produced in .50 caliber, chambering 56-50 and the 56-52 cartridges. Spencer sporting rifles missing the rear tang sight are worth approximately 25% less than those listed, as factory tang sights are near-impossible to find. Most Spencer sporting rifles had 26-inch long round barrels, but more desirable versions with octagon barrels command a substantial premium.

Only a relatively few Factory engraved, Spencer sporting rifles are known, and will command a substantial premium. Over the past few years such rifles sold at auction from $15,000 to $45,000, depending on condition.

* ***Round Barrel Sporting Rifles***

N/A	$7,000	$6,500	$5,000	$3,500	$2,500	$2,250	$2,000	$1,750	$1,500	$1,300	$1,200

* ***Octagon Barrel Sporting Rifles***

N/A	$8,500	$8,000	$7,000	$5,000	$3,750	$3,000	$2,750	$2,250	$1,750	$1,500	$1,250

SPHINX SYSTEMS LTD.

Current manufacturer established in 1876, and presently located in Matten b. Interlaken, Switzerland. Currently imported by Kriss Arms USA, beginning 2011 and located in Virginia Beach, VA. In late 2010, Kriss Arms acquired Sphinx Systems Ltd., including the Sphinx trademark. Previously distributed until 2009 by Sabre Defence Industries, LLC, located in Nashville, TN. Previously imported by Rocky Mountain Armoury, located in Silverthorne, CO. Previously manufactured by Sphinx

GRADING - PPGS™	100%	98%	95%	90%	80%	70%	60%	LAST MSR

Engineering S.A. located in Porrentruy, Switzerland, and by Sphinx U.S.A., located in Meriden, CT until 1996. Previously imported by Sile Distributors located in New York, NY.

PISTOLS: SEMI-AUTO

Please contact the importer directly for current U.S. availability and pricing on the following current models.

MODEL AT-380 – .380 ACP cal., semi-auto double action only, 3.27 in. barrel, stainless steel frame, two-tone finish, 10 shot mag. with finger extension, checkered walnut grips. Disc. 1996.

$435	$375	$350	$325	$295	$275	$250	*$494*

Add $20 for black finish.
Add $71 for N/Pall finish.

MODEL 2000S STANDARD – 9mm Para. or .40 S&W (new 1993) cal., semi-auto in standard double action or double action only, 4.53 in. barrel, stainless steel fabrication, 10 (C/B 1994), 15* (9mm Para.), or 11* (.40 S&W) shot mag., checkered walnut grips, fixed sights, 35 oz. Importation disc. 2002.

$965	$750	$625	$525	$450	$410	$375

Add $117 for .40 S&W cal.

* ***Model 2000PS Standard Police Special*** – similar to Model 2000S, except has compact slide and 3.66 in. barrel.

$850	$625	$525	$450	$410	$380	$350

Add $40 for .40 S&W cal.
Add $87 for N/Pall finish.

* ***Model 2000P Standard Compact*** – similar to Model 2000 Standard, except has 3.66 in. barrel and 13 shot mag., 31 oz.

$850	$625	$525	$450	$410	$380	$350

Add $40 for .40 S&W cal.
Add $87 for N/Pall finish.

* ***Model 2000H Standard Sub-Compact*** – similar to Model 2000 Compact, except has 3.31 in. barrel and 10 shot mag., 26 oz. Disc. 1996.

$850	$625	$525	$450	$410	$380	$350	*$940*

Add $40 for .40 S&W cal.
Add $87 for N/Pall finish.

MODEL 2000 MASTER – 9mm Para., 9x21mm, or .40 S&W cal., single action only, two-tone finish only, designed for Master's stock class competition.

$1,795	$1,350	$1,100	$995	$895	$775	$650	*$2,035*

MODEL AT-2000 (NEW MODEL) – 9mm Para. or .40 S&W cal., 4.53 in. barrel, 10 shot mag., machined slide with electro deposited finish, decocking mechanism. Limited mfg. 2004-2005.

$1,825	$1,675	$1,450	$1,225	$1,000	$800	$675	*$1,995*

MODEL AT-2000CS COMPETITOR – 9mm Para., 9x21mm, or .40 S&W cal., single or double action, competition model featuring many shooting improvements including 5.3 in. compensated barrel, 10 (C/B 1994), 11* (.40 S&W), or 15* shot mag., Bo-Mar adj. sights, two-tone finish. Imported 1993-96.

$1,725	$1,275	$1,050	$950	$850	$750	$675	*$1,902*

Add $287 for Model AT-2000C (includes Sphinx scope mount).
Add $1,538 for AT-2000K conversion kit (new 1995).
Add $1,490 for Model AT-2000CKS (competition kit to convert AT-2000 to comp. pistol, disc. 1994).

GRADING - PPGS™	100%	98%	95%	90%	80%	70%	60%	LAST MSR

MODEL 2000 COMPETITION – similar to Model 2000 Master, except is SA only and includes more advanced competitive shooting features, Bo-Mar sights, top-of-the-line competition model. Imported 1993-96.

	$2,475	$1,925	$1,725	$1,500	$1,250	$1,050	$895	*$2,894*

Add $78 for Model AT-2000GM (includes Sphinx scope mount).

MODEL 3000 SERIES – 9mm Para., 9x21mm (disc.), .40 S&W, or .45 ACP cal., SA/DA, available in standard (4.53 in. barrel), tactical (3 3/4 in. barrel), or competition (4.53 in. barrel, adj. sights), configuration, choice of manual safety or decocker, titanium upper/lower frame with stainless slide, stainless steel slide with titanium lower frame or stainless steel frame/slide, front/rear gripstrap stipling or grooved, two-tone finish, approx. 40 oz. New 2001.

MSR N/A	$2,525	$2,275	$2,000	$1,800	$1,575	$1,375	$1,150

Add $350 for titanium frame with stainless steel slide.

Add $800 for stainless steel slide with titanium upper/lower frame (disc.).

Add $75 for tactical model.

Add $350 for competition model.

SPHINX COMPETITION MODELS – currently available in either an Open (extended barrel with 3 port compensator and Aimpoint scope), Modified (2 port compensator and rear sight optics), or Standard.

Please contact the company directly for more information on these models, including U.S. availability and pricing.

SPHINX .45 ACP – .45 ACP cal., SA/DA, steel construction, 3 3/4 in. barrel, double slide serrations, blue finish, 10 shot mag., fixed Trijicon night sights, black polymer grips, decocker mechanism, approx. 43 oz. New 2007.

MSR N/A	$2,850	$2,500	$2,150	$1,850	$1,500	$1,250	$1,000

SDP SERIES – 9mm Para. cal., 3 1/8 (Sub-Compact), 3.7 (Compact), 4 1/2 (Standard) in. barrel, aluminum frame and slide, full length guide rails, 13, 15, or 17 shot mag., match grade trigger, six integrated safeties including loaded chamber indicator, notched Picatinny rail avail. on compact and standard models, twin slide serrations, various sight combinations available per individual model, interchangeable aluminum/rubber grip system, 21-31 3/4 oz. New 2012.

As this edition went to press, no pricing information was available on this series.

SPIDER FIREARMS

Current rifle manufacturer located in St. Cloud, FL.

RIFLES: SINGLE SHOT

FERRET 50 – .50 BMG cal., single shot bolt action, A2 style buttstock and pistol grip, Picatinny rail, choice of 18, 29, or 36 in. barrel, matte black finish, perforated handguard with bipod, includes muzzle brake. New 2003.

MSR $3,011	$2,850	$2,575	$2,375	$2,100	$1,800	$1,600	$1,400

Add $250 for stainless steel barrel (SS Sportsman)

Add $500 for stainless super match barrel (SM Sportsman).

SUPERCOMP FERRET – similar to Ferret 50, except also available in .408 CheyTac and .338 Lapua cal., features solid steel construction, fixed scope rails, 29 or 36 in. Lothar Walther stainless Supermatch barrels, adj. 1 lb. competition style trigger, two-axis cheekrest, and detachable rear monopod. New 2004.

MSR $3,190	$2,850	$2,600	$2,300	$2,000	$1,750	$1,600	$1,450

Add $250 for stainless steel barrel.

Add $500 for stainless steel super match barrel.

SPIKE'S TACTICAL LLC

Current manufacturer located in Apopka, FL.

CARBINES/RIFLES: SEMI-AUTO

Spike's Tactical manufactures a complete line of AR-15 style tactical semi-auto rifles and carbines for both the civilian and law enforcement/military marketplace. A wide variety of

GRADING - PPGS™	100%	98%	95%	90%	80%	70%	60%	LAST MSR

calibers, options and configurations is available. Please contact the company directly for more information, including pricing, options, and availability (see Trademark Index).

SPIRIT GUN MANUFACTURING COMPANY LLC

Previous manufacturer located in West Palm Beach, FL until 2011.

PISTOLS: SEMI-AUTO

SGM9P – 5.56 NATO cal., 7 1/2 in. stainless steel barrel with KX3 compensator, 30 shot mag., black, green, or tan finish, pistol length tuned direct gas impingement system, SGM9 lower with integral three position sling mount and swivel, VLTOR custom CASV hand guard, flip up front sight, VLTOR MUR upper receiver, National Match phosphate and chromed custom bolt carrier. Limited mfg. Disc. 2011.

	100%	98%	95%	90%	80%	70%	60%	LAST MSR
	$2,200	$1,950	$1,725	$1,500	$1,300	$1,100	$825	*$2,495*

RIFLES/CARBINES: SEMI-AUTO

Spirit Gun Manufacturing offered a complete line of AR-15 style rifles and carbines in law enforcement/military and civilian configurations. Current models included (last MSRs reflect 2011 pricing): SGM-15, SGM-16, and SGM 17 ($2,495 MSR), SGM-A39, SGM-40, and SGM-41 ($2,495 MSR), SGM-A19 ($2,695 MSR), SGM-A43 ($2,695 MSR), SGM-A23 ($2,795 MSR), SGM-A47 ($2,795 MSR), SGM-A24 ($2,895 MSR), and the SGM-A48 ($2,895 MSR). A variety of options and accessories were available.

SPITFIRE

See listing under JSL (Hereford) in the J section.

SPORTCO/SPORTING ARMS CO.

Previous rifle manufacturer located in Adelaide, Australia circa 1947-mid 1960s.

Sportco was founded by Jack Warne (later the founder of Kimber) in 1947 to manufacture barrels for the Army surplus .303s. The company is best known for its production of the single shot .22 LR cal. Huntsman that started in 1951. After its introduction, various other rimfire and centerfire rifles were manufactured as well.

RIFLES

Sportco .22 cal. rimfire rifles are currently priced in the $125-$500 range depending on the configuration and condition. Centerfire rifles are priced in the $350-$1,000 range depending on configuration and condition.

SPORT-SYSTEME DITTRICH

Current manufacturer established in 2003 and located in Kulmbach, Germany. Limited importation in North America by Wolverine Supplies, located in Manitoba, Canada. Previously imported by Marstar Canada, located in Ontario, Canada.

Sport-Systeme Dittrich manufactures high quality semi-auto reproductions of famous military guns, including the MP38 (BD 38), Sturmgewehr 44 (BD 44) and the Gerät Neumünster (BD 3008). Its latest model is a reproduction of the Fallschirmjägergewehr FG42 as the BD42 I. Please contact the importer or the company directly for more information, including pricing and U.S. availability (see Trademark Index).

SPORTING ARMS COMPANY

Previous manufacturer established circa mid-1950s and located in Adelaide, Australia until circa mid-1980s.

Known to sporting shooters in Australia and overseas as "Sportco", this Adelaide based company produced sporting firearms for over 35 years for the Australian market and export to Great Britain, Rhodesia, Borneo, South Africa, Canada, New Zealand and the U.S. For more information on this company's history, please visit www.sportco.org.au.

Sportco's firearms were of good quality utilitarian manufacture, and to date, there has been little collector interest. Sportco manufactured the Winchester Model 310 and 320 actions before they were shipped to the U.S. for completion. Values for Sportco firearms must be based on their shooting value only in today's competitive marketplace involving new firearms.

GRADING - PPGS™	100%	98%	95%	90%	80%	70%	60%	LAST MSR

SPRINGER'S ERBEN, JOHANN

Current manufacturer, retailer, and auction house established in 1836, and located in Vienna, Austria.

Joh. Springer's Erben is one of the leading retailers for hunting and sporting guns and rifles, shooting supplies, security equipment, and related accessories in Austria. Additionally, Springer's manufactures custom made long guns in a variety of configurations on a limited basis. Two of Austria's oldest and most respected gunmakers/trademarks, Johann Springer and Franz Sodia, have joined forces in Johann Springer's Erben, an upscale store and gun room located in the first district in Vienna, Austria. This newest generation of family members includes Christian Johann Springer, whose great-great grandfather started the family business during 1836 in Vienna, and Werner Sodia, whose great-grandfather began making guns in Ferlach in 1871.

Johann Springer's Erben also has two auctions annually, which include a wide variety of sporting firearms, especially older European trademarks and configurations.

Please contact the company directly for more information, including U.S. availability and an individualized price quotation based on the configuration (see Trademark Index).

SPRINGFIELD ARMORY

America's first federal armory located in Springfield, MA. Production began in 1795 and an Act of Congress made it an official federal arsenal in 1872. Not associated with the private firm of the same name located in Geneseo, IL.

In recent years, collectors have realized that military specimens in 90%-100% original condition are very rare and desirable. Since the supply of these guns is limited, values listed for these condition factors may actually be a little under current market values, especially auction pricing. On Springfields and other U.S. military long arms, the importance of the wood being original, unsanded, and with crisp, clear cartouches cannot be overstated.

CARBINES/RIFLES, SINGLE SHOT

MODEL 1870 ROLLING-BLOCK RIFLE, U.S.N. – .50 cal. centerfire, 32 5/8 in. barrel, not serial numbered, 22,013 mfg.

100%	98%	95%	90%	80%	70%	60%
N/A	$2,500	$2,200	$1,950	$1,500	$1,100	$900

MODEL 1871 ROLLING-BLOCK RIFLE, U.S.A. – .50 cal. centerfire, 36 in. barrel, not serial numbered, 10,001 mfg.

100%	98%	95%	90%	80%	70%	60%
N/A	$2,150	$1,750	$1,350	$1,000	$900	$750

MODEL 1873 RIFLE "TRAPDOOR" – .45-70 Govt. cal., 32 5/8 in. barrel, 2 bands. Approx. 73,000 mfg. between 1873-77.

100%	98%	95%	90%	80%	70%	60%
$2,500	$2,200	$1,800	$1,500	$1,150	$775	$650

Subtract 40% if stock cartouche faint or absent.

MODEL 1884 RIFLE "TRAPDOOR" – .45-70 Govt. cal., 32 5/8 in. barrel, 2 bands. Approx. 232,000 mfg. between 1885-1890.

100%	98%	95%	90%	80%	70%	60%
$2,250	$1,850	$1,450	$975	$725	$625	$525

Subtract 40% if stock cartouche faint or absent.

MODEL 1884 CARBINE "TRAPDOOR" – .45-70 Govt. cal., similar to Model 1879 Carbine with 22 in. barrel, half stock, single barrel band, Buffington rear sight, barrel band grooved on top to allowing for sight leaf to rest, approx. ser. no. range 325,000 - 480,000. Approx. 20,000 mfg. 1886-1889.

100%	98%	95%	90%	80%	70%	60%
N/A	$3,500	$2,850	$2,300	$1,950	$1,500	$1,000

MODEL 1873 CARBINE – 22 in. barrel, half stock, single barrel band/stacking swivel, 20,000 made, but semi-scarce.

100%	98%	95%	90%	80%	70%	60%
N/A	$6,000	$5,250	$4,250	$3,250	$2,750	$2,250

Add up to 50% for Pre-Custer serial numbers below 43,700 (pre-1876 mfg.).
Subtract 50% for faint or no stock cartouche.

GRADING - PPGS™	100%	98%	95%	90%	80%	70%	60%	LAST MSR

MODEL 1873 CADET RIFLE – .45-70 Govt. cal., 29 1/2 in. barrel, stacking swivel, no sling swivels.

	$2,500	$2,000	$1,475	$1,100	$925	$775	$650	

Subtract $100 for variation with sling-swivels.

Subtract 25-35% if restocked with buttplate and hole drilled for cleaning tools.

MODEL 1875 OFFICER'S RIFLE FIRST TYPE – .45-70 Govt. cal., 477 mfg. between 1875 and 1886, 26 in. barrel, single barrel band. Not serial numbered, some dated, three different types, with First Type being the most desirable (approx. 125 mfg. 1875-1877), Second Type had approx. 250 mfg. 1877-1881, and Third Type has approx. 100 mfg. during 1885 only, not issued by U.S. government, but sold to Army officers for sporting use.

	N/A	$39,000	$34,000	$27,000	$23,000	$17,500	$15,000	

Approx. 25 rifles were mfg. prior to the standardization of this model.

MODEL 1875 SPRINGFIELD LEE VERTICAL ACTION – 32 1/2 in. barrel, 143 rifles in .45-70 US Govt cal. were manufactured at Springfield Armory in 1875, as per 1874 Congressional appropriation of $10,000. Rifles were issued to companies of the 1st and 20th Infantry Regiments for field trials. Rifles were withdrawn, declared surplus and purchased by Bannerman's who later sold them in his catalog for $36.

	N/A	$15,000	$12,000	$10,000	$8,000	$6,000	$4,000	

MODEL 1877 RIFLE – .45-70 Govt. cal., mfg. 3,943.

	N/A	$3,000	$2,650	$2,250	$1,875	$1,625	$1,325	

MODEL 1877 CARBINE – .45-70 Govt. cal., 22 in. barrel, "C" rear sight to 1,200 yards. Mfg. 2,946.

	N/A	$4,750	$4,250	$3,850	$3,300	$2,850	$2,450	

MODEL 1877 CADET RIFLE – .45-70 Govt. cal., 29 1/2 in. barrel. 1,050 mfg.

	N/A	$2,000	$1,400	$1,100	$950	$900	$800	

MODEL 1879 RIFLE – .45-70 Govt. cal., approx. 140,000 mfg.

	$1,800	$1,400	$1,150	$950	$850	$700	$650	

MODEL 1879 CARBINE – .45-70 Govt. cal., no stacking swivel. Approx. 15,000 mfg.

	N/A	$3,500	$2,850	$2,300	$1,950	$1,500	$1,000	

MODEL 1879 CADET RIFLE – .45-70 Govt. cal., stacking swivel but no sling swivels. 5,000 mfg.

	$2,000	$1,600	$1,150	$950	$775	$650	$600	

MODEL 1880 – .45-70 Govt. cal., combination triangular, sliding type, bayonet-ramrod. 1,001 mfg.

	N/A	$2,800	$2,200	$1,950	$1,650	$1,325	$1,050	

PISTOLS: SEMI-AUTO

M1911 MILITARY MFG. SPRINGFIELD ARMORY – approx. 30,000 mfg. 1914-1915, blue finish.

	N/A	$5,950	$4,600	$3,500	$3,000	$2,500	$2,000	

Serialization is 72,751-83,855, 102,597-107,596, 113,497-120,566, and 125,567-133,186.

Most mint/100% specimens encountered in this model have been refinished - be careful.

RIFLES: BOLT ACTION, KRAG-JORGENSEN

Please refer to Krag-Jorgensen section for models and pricing.

RIFLES: BOLT ACTION, MODEL 1903 & VARIATIONS

On Springfields and other U.S. military long arms, the importance of the wood being original, unsanded, and with crisp, clear cartouches cannot be overstated.

Values listed for Model 1903s assume 100% original guns. Values listed for Model 1922s assume 100% original blued guns.

GRADING - PPGS™	100%	98%	95%	90%	80%	70%	60%	LAST MSR

U.S. MODEL 1903 SPRINGFIELD – .30-06 cal., bolt action, mfg. by Springfield Armory and Rock Island Arsenal, 24 in. barrel. Mfg. 1903-1930.

* ***U.S. Model 1903 Springfield Pre-WWI Mfg.*** – values below represent original rifles.

	$7,500	$6,500	$5,000	$4,000	$3,000	$2,250	$1,850

Subtract 80% if reworked.

* ***U.S. Model 1903 Springfield Serialized 800,000 - 1,275,767*** – double heat treated receiver.

	$4,950	$4,000	$3,300	$2,750	$2,500	$2,100	$1,650

* ***U.S. Model 1903 Springfield Serialized 1,275,768 +*** – nickel steel receiver.

	$4,950	$4,000	$3,300	$2,750	$2,500	$2,100	$1,650

MODEL 1903 MARK I – .30-06 cal., similar to U.S. Model 1903 Springfield, except altered for the Pedersen device, a slot is milled into the left side of receiver to act as an ejection port for use of the semi-auto bolt insert.

	$4,950	$4,000	$3,500	$1,800	$1,200	$1,000	$850

Values listed are w/o the Pedersen device.

* ***Model 1903 Mark I w/Pedersen*** – includes Pedersen device.

Current pricing for this model range from $20,000-$40,000, depending on original condition.
Complete Pedersen devices in 98%+ original condition have sold for $35,000.

Be aware - inspect carefully for originality!

1903-A1 – .30-06 cal., similar to U.S. Model 1903 Springfield, except type C pistol grip stock. Mfg. 1930-39. In 1941 Remington mfg. approx. 350,000.

	$4,500	$4,000	$3,500	$1,800	$1,200	$1,000	$850

* ***1903-A1 Remington produced***

	$4,500	$4,000	$3,500	$1,800	$1,200	$1,000	$850

1903-A1 NATIONAL MATCH

	$5,000	$4,500	$3,500	$2,000	$1,200	$1,000	$850

1903-A3 – .30-06 cal., similar to 1903, with production modifications, aperture rear sight, no finger groove in forestock, lower quality finish, stamped floorplate and barrel band. Mfg. WWII by Remington and Smith Corona.

	$1,250	$800	$700	$500	$400	$330	$300

Add 25% for Smith Corona mfg.

1903-A3 NATIONAL MATCH – 200 mfg., known as the "unmatched" match rifle.

	$3,700	$3,350	$3,000	$2,600	$2,200	$1,875	$1,625

1903-A4 SNIPER – .30-06 cal., with M73B1 or M84 scope in Redfield mount, no front sight.

	$5,000	$4,500	$3,800	$2,500	$1,800	$1,000	$700

Subtract 30% if reworked with parkerized small parts.

1903 MARINE SNIPER – .30-06 cal., includes 8X Unertl scope.

	$20,000	$18,000	$12,000	$8,000	$5,000	$3,000	$2,000

Original condition is key for values listed above. Be very careful and get an evaluation from a dealer/collector who knows the difference before buying/selling.

1903 NRA NATIONAL MATCH – .30-06 cal., similar to 1903, with hand selected and custom fit parts, produced for target shooting. "NRA" and flaming bomb proofed on trigger guard. 1915 date.

	$5,000	$4,500	$3,500	$2,400	$1,500	$995	$850

1903 SPORTER – .30-06 cal., similar to National Match, with sporter stock and Lyman sight.

	$6,000	$4,800	$3,500	$1,800	$1,200	$925	$825

1903 MATCH STYLE T – .30-06 cal., similar to Sporter, with heavy barrel, globe sight, target bases, 26, 28, or 30 in. barrel.

Excellent original condition specimens have been seen with asking prices in the $8,500-$10,000+ range.

GRADING - PPGS™	100%	98%	95%	90%	80%	70%	60%	LAST MSR

1903 FREE RIFLE TYPE A – .30-06 cal., similar to Style T, with 28 in. barrel, and Swiss hook butt.

Excellent original condition specimens have been seen with asking prices in the $8,500-$10,000+ range.

1903 FREE RIFLE TYPE B – .30-06 cal., similar to Type A, with double-set triggers, cheekpiece stock, modified firing pin.

Excellent original condition specimens have been seen with asking prices in the $8,500-$10,000+ range.

MODEL 1922-M1 – .22 LR cal., Target Rifle, 5 shot mag., 24 in. barrel, modified 1903, Lyman receiver sight, sporter stock, issued 1927.

Blue finish	$3,500	$3,000	$2,000	$1,500	$1,000	$625	$550	

MODEL 1922 NRA VARIATION – not tapped for scope, without forend grooves, blue finish.

	$3,500	$3,000	$2,250	$1,925	$1,725	$1,500	$1,250	

M2 .22 TARGET RIFLE – similar to 1922 M1, except improved lock time, adj. head space bolt design.

	$1,800	$1,500	$1,200	$1,000	$700	$600	$550	

RIFLES: SEMI-AUTO

Please refer to the U.S. Military section for more information on previously manufactured military and commercial M1 carbines and Garands.

SHOTGUNS: SINGLE SHOT

MODEL 1881 FORAGER – 20 ga., 1,376 mfg. 1881-1885. Be cautious when purchasing.

	N/A	$3,000	$2,500	$1,800	$1,500	$1,300	$1,150	

SPRINGFIELD ARMORY (MFG. BY SPRINGFIELD INC.)

Current trademark manufactured by Springfield Inc., located in Geneseo, IL. Springfield Inc. has also imported a variety of models. This company was named Springfield Armory, Geneseo, IL until 1992.

Springfield Inc. manufactures commercial pistols and rifles, including reproductions of older military handguns and rifles.

COMBINATION GUNS

M6 SCOUT RIFLE – .22 LR, .22 WMR (disc.), or .22 Hornet cal. over smoothbore .410 bore w/3 in. chamber, O/U Survival Gun, 14 (legal transfer needed) or 18 1/4 in. barrels, parkerized or stainless steel (new 1995), approx. 4 lbs. Disc. 2004.

.22 LR/.22 Win. Mag. cal.	$425	$375	$325	$275	$250	$225	$195	
.22 Hornet cal.	$775	$725	$650	$550	$475	$400	$325	*$215*

Add approx. 10% for stainless steel.

Add 10% for lockable Marine flotation plastic carrying case.

Early mfg. does not incorporate a trigger guard while late production had a trigger guard.

M6 SCOUT PISTOL/CARBINE – .22 LR or .22 Hornet cal. over .45 LC/.410 bore, 16 in. barrels, parkerized or stainless steel. Mfg. 2002-2004.

.22 LR cal.	$425	$375	$325	$275	$250	$225	$195	
.22 Hornet cal.	$775	$725	$650	$550	$475	$400	$325	*$223*

Add 10% for stainless steel.

Add approx. $200 per interchangeable 10 in. pistol barrel assembly.

Add 15% for detachable stock.

This model was also available with an optional detachable stock ($49-$59 MSR, not legal with a rifled barrel less than 16 in. or smoothbore less than 18 in.).

GRADING - PPGS™	100%	98%	95%	90%	80%	70%	60%	LAST MSR

M6 SCOUT PISTOL – .22 LR or .22 Hornet cal. over .45 LC/.410 bore, 10 in. barrels, parkerized or stainless steel. Mfg. 2002-2004.

.22 LR cal.	$425	$375	$325	$275	$250	$225	$195	
.22 Hornet cal.	$775	$725	$650	$550	$475	$400	$325	*$199*

Add approx. 10% for stainless steel.
Add approx. $200 per interchangeable 16 in. carbine barrel.

PISTOLS: SEMI-AUTO

OMEGA PISTOL – .38 Super, 10mm Norma, or .45 ACP cal., single action, ported slide, 5 or 6 in. interchangeable ported or unported barrel with Polygon rifling, special lockup system eliminates normal barrel link and bushing, Pachmayr grips, dual extractors, adj. rear sight. Mfg. 1987-90.

	$775	$650	$575	$495	$425	$360	$295	*$849*

Add $663 for interchangeable conversion units.
Add $336 for interchangeable 5 or 6 in. barrel (including factory installation).

Each conversion unit includes an entire slide assembly, one mag., 5 or 6 in barrel, recoil spring guide mechanism assembly, and factory fitting.

OMEGA MATCH – same cals. as Omega, except has low profile combat sights, 8 shot mag., and beveled mag. well. Mfg. 1991-92 only.

	$925	$775	$660	$535	$460	$420	$385	*$1,103*

Pistols: Semi-Auto - P9 Series

MODEL P9 – 9mm Para., 9x21mm (new 1991) .40 S&W (new 1991), or .45 ACP cal., patterned after the Czech CZ-75, selective double action design, blue (standard beginning 1993), parkerized (standard until 1992), or duotone finish, various barrel lengths, checkered walnut grips. Mfg. in U.S. starting 1990.

* ***Model P9 Standard*** – 4.72 in. barrel, 15 shot (9mm Para.), 11 shot (.40 S&W), or 10 shot (.45 ACP) mag., parkerized finish standard until 1992 - blue finish beginning 1993, 32.16 oz. Disc. 1993.

	$430	$375	$335	$295	$275	$240	$215	*$518*

Add $61 for .45 ACP cal.
Add $182 for duotone finish (disc. 1992).
Subtract $40 for parkerized finish.

In 1992, Springfield added a redesigned stainless steel trigger, patented sear safety which disengages the trigger from the double action mechanism when the safety is on, lengthened the beavertail grip area offering less "pinch," and added a two-piece slide stop design.

* ***Model P9 Stainless*** – similar to P9 Standard, except is constructed from stainless steel, 35.3 oz. Mfg. 1991-93.

	$475	$425	$350	$285	$250	$215	$185	*$589*

Add $50 for .45 ACP cal.

* ***Model P9 Compact*** – 9mm Para. or .40 S&W cal., 3.66 in. barrel, 13 shot (9mm Para.) or 10 shot (.40 S&W) mag., shorter slide and frame, rounded trigger guard, 30 1/2 oz. Disc. 1992.

	$395	$350	$300	$275	$250	$225	$200	*$499*

Add $20 for .40 S&W cal.
Add $20-$30 for blue finish depending on cal.
Add $78 for duotone finish.

* ***Model P9 Sub-Compact*** – 9mm Para. or .40 S&W cal., smaller frame than the P9 Compact, 3.66 in. barrel, 12 shot (9mm Para.) or 9 shot (.40 S&W) finger extension mag., squared-off trigger guard, 30.1 oz. Disc. 1992.

	$395	$350	$300	$275	$250	$225	$200	*$499*

Add $20 for .40 S&W cal.
Add $20-$30 for blue finish depending on cal.

GRADING - PPGS™	100%	98%	95%	90%	80%	70%	60%	LAST MSR

* ***Model P9 Factory Comp*** – 9mm Para., .40 S&W, or .45 ACP cal., 5 1/2 in. barrel (with compensator attached), extended sear safety and mag. release, adj. rear sight, slim competition checkered wood grips, choice of all stainless (disc. 1992) or stainless bi-tone (matte black slide), dual port compensated, 15 shot (9mm Para.), 11 shot (.40 S&W), or 10 shot (.45 ACP) mag., 33.9 oz. Mfg. 1992-93.

$595	$525	$450	$420	$390	$360	$330	*$699*

Add $36 for .45 ACP cal.
Add $75-$100 for all stainless finish.

* ***Model P9 Ultra IPSC (LSP)*** – competition model with 5.03 in. barrel (long slide ported), adj. rear sight, choice of parkerized (standard finish until 1992 when disc.), blue (disc. 1992), bi-tone (became standard 1993), or stainless steel (disc. 1992) finish, extended thumb safety, and rubberized competition (9mm Para. and .40 S&W cals. only) or checkered walnut (.45 ACP cal. only) grips, 15 shot (9mm Para.), 11 shot (.40 S&W), or 10 shot (.45 ACP) mag., 34.6 oz. Disc. 1993.

$555	$475	$415	$350	$300	$275	$250	*$694*

Add $30 for .45 ACP cal.

* ***Model P9 Ultra LSP Stainless*** – stainless steel variation of the P9 Ultra LSP. Mfg. 1991-92.

$675	$525	$425	$360	$315	$260	$225	*$769*

Add $30 for .40 S&W cal.
Add $90 for .45 ACP cal.

* ***Model P9 World Cup*** – see listing under 1911-A1 Custom Models heading.

Pistols: Semi-Auto - R-Series

PANTHER MODEL – 9mm Para., .40 S&W, or .45 ACP cal., semi-auto single or double action, 3.8 in. barrel, hammer drop or firing pin safety, 15 shot (9mm Para.), 11 shot (.40 S&W), or 9 shot (.45 ACP) mag., Commander hammer, frame mounted slide stop, narrow profile, non-glare blue finish only, walnut grips, squared-off trigger guard, 29 oz. Mfg. 1992 only.

$600	$500	$400	$350	$300	$275	$250	*$609*

FIRECAT MODEL – 9mm Para. or .40 S&W cal., single action, 3 1/2 in. barrel, 3-dot low profile sights, all steel mfg., firing pin block and frame mounted ambidextrous safety, 8 shot (9mm Para.) or 7 shot (.40 S&W) mag., checkered combat style trigger guard and front/rear gripstraps, non-glare blue finish, 35 3/4 oz. Mfg. 1992-93.

$550	$450	$400	$350	$300	$275	$250	*$569*

BOBCAT MODEL – while advertised in 1992, this model was never mfg.

LINX MODEL – while advertised in 1992, this model was never mfg.

Pistols: Semi-Auto - Disc. 1911-A1 Models

MODEL 1911-A1 STANDARD MODEL – .38 Super, 9mm Para., 10mm (new 1990), or .45 ACP cal., patterned after the Colt M1911-A1, 5.04 (Standard) or 4.025 (Commander or Compact Model) in. barrel, 7 shot (Compact), 8 shot (.45 ACP), 9 shot (10mm), or 10 shot (9mm Para. and .38 Super) mag., walnut grips, parkerized, blue, or duotone finish. Mfg. 1985-90.

$400	$360	$330	$300	$280	$260	$240	*$454*

Add $35 for blue finish.
Add $80 for duotone finish.

This model was also available with a .45 ACP to 9mm Para. conversion kit for $170 in parkerized finish, or $175 in blue finish.

* ***Model 1911-A1 Standard Defender Model*** – .45 ACP cal. only, similar to Standard 1911-A1 Model, except has fixed combat sights, beveled mag. well, extended thumb safety, bobbed hammer, flared ejection port, walnut grips, factory serrated front strap and two stainless steel magazines, parkerized or blue finish. Mfg. 1988-90.

$485	$435	$375	$340	$300	$280	$260	*$567*

Add $35 for blue finish.

GRADING - PPGS™	100%	98%	95%	90%	80%	70%	60%	LAST MSR

* ***Model 1911-A1 Standard Commander Model*** – .45 ACP cal. only, similar to Standard 1911-A1 Model, except has 3.63 in. barrel, shortened slide, Commander hammer, low profile 3-dot sights, walnut grips, parkerized, blue, or duotone finish. Mfg. in 1990 only.

	$450	$415	$350	$325	$285	$260	$245	*$514*

Add $30 for blue finish.
Add $80 for duotone finish.

* ***Model 1911-A1 Standard Combat Commander Model*** – .45 ACP cal. only, 4 1/4 in. barrel, bobbed hammer, walnut grips. Mfg. 1988-89.

	$435	$385	$325	$295	$275	$250	$230	

Add $20 for blue finish.

* ***Model 1911-A1 Standard Compact Model*** – .45 ACP cal. only, compact variation featuring shortened Commander barrel and slide, reduced M1911 straight gripstrap frame, checkered walnut grips, low profile 3-dot sights, extended slide stop, combat hammer, parkerized, blue, or duotone finish. Mfg. 1990 only.

	$450	$415	$350	$325	$285	$260	$245	*$514*

Add $30 for blue finish.
Add $80 for duotone finish.

* ***Model 1911-A1 Standard Custom Carry Gun*** – .38 Super (special order only), 9mm Para., 10mm (new 1990), or .45 ACP cal., similar to Defender Model, except has tuned trigger pull, heavy recoil spring, extended thumb safety, and other features. Mfg. 1988-disc.

	$860	$725	$660	$535	$460	$420	$385	*$969*

Add $130 for .38 Super Ramped, 10mm was POR.

* ***Model 1911-A1 Standard National Match Hardball Model*** – .38 Super (disc.), 9mm Para. (disc.), or .45 ACP cal., National Match barrel and bushing, specially fitted frame and slide, Bo-Mar adj. rear sight, Herrett walnut grips, plastic cased. Mfg. 1988-90.

	$780	$650	$565	$515	$460	$415	$385	*$897*

This model was made specifically for DCM competition shooting.

* ***Model 1911-A1 Standard Bullseye Wadcutter Model*** – .45 ACP cal. only, designed for wadcutter loads only, 5 or 6 (ported or unported) in. barrel, Bo-Mar rib mounted on slide, checkered gripstraps, match trigger, beavertail grip safety, polished feed ramp and throated barrel. Mfg. 1989-disc.

	$1,415	$1,200	$1,025	$925	$825	$750	$675	*$1,599*

Add $25 for 6 in. barrel.
Add $80 for 6 in. ported barrel.

* ***Model 1911-A1 Standard Trophy Master Competition Pistol*** – .38 Super, 9mm Para. (disc.), 10mm (new 1990), or .45 ACP cal., competition model which includes low profile combat sights, ambidextrous safety, long match trigger, bobbed hammer, Pachmayr wraparound grips. Mfg. 1988-90.

	$1,300	$1,100	$950	$875	$800	$730	$660	*$1,443*

Add $130 for .38 Super with supported chamber, 10mm was POR.

* ***Model 1911-A1 Standard Trophy Master Competition Expert Model*** – .38 Super, 9mm Para. (disc.), 10mm (new 1990), or .45 ACP cal., mfg. for IPSC competition shooting, dual chamber compensator system on match barrel, blue finish, ambidextrous thumb safety, beveled and polished mag. well, lowered and flared ejection port, wraparound Pachmayr grips, shock buffer, includes 2 mags. and plastic carrying case. Mfg. 1988-90.

	$1,664	$1,450	$1,225	$1,025	$950	$890	$850	*$1,664*

Add $130 for .38 Super with supported chamber, 10mm was POR.

This model was an improved variation of the Master Grade Competition Pistol "A."

* ***Model 1911-A1 Standard Trophy Master Competition Distinguished Model*** – similar to Expert Model, except has brushed hard chrome finish, checkered gripstraps and trigger guard, top-of-the-line competition model. Mfg. 1988-1990.

	$2,000	$1,675	$1,450	$1,225	$1,025	$950	$875	*$2,275*

GRADING - PPGS™	100%	98%	95%	90%	80%	70%	60%	LAST MSR

Add $130 for .38 Super with supported chamber, 10mm was POR.
Subtract $130 for "B" Model.

This model was an improved variation of the Master Grade Competition Pistol "B-1."

Pistols: Semi-Auto - 1911-A1 (90s Series)

The initials "PDP" refer to Springfield's Personal Defense Pistol series.

Beginning in 2000, Springfield Armory started offering a Loaded Promotion package on their 1911-A1 pistol line. Many of these features and options are found on the FBI's Hostage Rescue Teams (HRT) pistol contract with Springfield Armory. Standard features of this Loaded Promotion package are hammer forged premium air-gauged barrel, front and rear cocking serrations, Novak patented low profile sights or Bo-Mar type adj. sights, extended thumb safety, tactical beavertail, flat mainspring housing, Cocobolo grips, High Hand grip, lightweight match trigger, full length guide rod, and machine beveled mag. well. This promotion includes all pistols except the Mil-Spec Model 1911 A1.

In 2001, Springfield's Custom Loaded 1911-A1 Series pistols came equipped standard with Springfield's integral locking system, carry bevel, hammer forged premium air-gauged barrel, front and rear cocking serrations, Novak patented low profile sights (some models come equipped with Tritium sights or Bo-Mar type adj. sights), extended thumb safety, tactical beavertail, flat mainspring housing, cocobolo grips, high hand grip, lightweight adj. match trigger, full length guide rod, machine beveled magwell, and a "loaded" coupon ($600 consumer savings). These Custom Loaded features will vary by model. All models with less than a 5 in. and all alloy pistols supplied with ramped, fully supported barrels.

Beginning 2002, every Springfield pistol is equipped with a patented integral locking system (I.L.S., keyed in the rear gripstrap) at no extra charge.

Beginning 2007, most models were shipped with an 11 gear system, including one (GI models only) or two mags., belt holster, magazine pouch, and bore brush supplied in a lockable blue plastic case.

PDP DEFENDER MODEL – .40 S&W (disc. 1992) or .45 ACP cal., standard pistol with slide and barrel shortened to Champion length (4 in.), tapered cone dual port compensator system, fully adj. sights, Videcki speed trigger, rubber grips, Commander style hammer, serrated front strap, parkerized (disc. 1992), duotone/bi-tone, or blue (disc. 1993) finish. Mfg. 1991-1998.

$850	$745	$635	$580	$465	$380	$295	*$992*

* ***PDP Defender Model Factory Comp*** – .38 Super (disc.) or .45 ACP cal. only, entry level IPSC gun, featuring 5 5/8 in. barrel with compensator attached, adj. rear sight, Videki speed trigger, checkered walnut grips, beveled mag. well, 10 shot (.38 Super) or 8 shot (.45 ACP) mag., blue finish only, 40 oz. Mfg. 1991-2000.

$900	$785	$675	$610	$495	$400	$315	*$1,049*

* ***PDP Defender Model High Capacity Factory Compensated*** – .38 Super (disc.) or .45 ACP cal. only, blue finish. Mfg. 1995-2000.

$955	$835	$715	$650	$525	$430	$335	*$1,109*

1911-A1 90s EDITION (CUSTOM LOADED) – .38 Super, 9mm Para., 10mm (disc. 1991), .40 S&W, or .45 ACP cal., patterned after the Colt M1911-A1, except has linkless operating system, 5.04 (Standard) or 4 (Champion or Compact Model) in. barrel, 7 shot (Compact), 8 shot (.40 S&W or .45 ACP Standard), 9 shot (9mm Para., 10mm, or .38 Super), or 10 shot (.38 Super) mag., checkered walnut grips, parkerized (.38 Super beginning 1994 or .45 ACP beginning 1993), blue or duotone (disc. 1992) finish. New 1991.

* ***1911-A1 90s Edition Mil-Spec*** – .38 Super (disc. 2011) or .45 ACP cal., blue (disc.), 5 in. stainless steel barrel, parkerized, bi-tone (mfg. 2004 only), or OD Green (mfg. 2004 only) finish, 3-dot Hi-Viz fixed combat sights, standard loaded features include belt holster, double mag. pouch and extra set of grips (Mil-Spec Package), 39 oz.

MSR $775	$650	$550	$475	$400	$325	$285	$245

GRADING - PPGS™	100%	98%	95%	90%	80%	70%	60%	LAST MSR

Add $17 for blue finish (disc. 2001).
Add $21 for OD Green or bi-tone finish (mfg. 2004 only).
Subtract approx. $70 if without Mil-Spec package (became standard in 2012, includes belt holster, double mag. pouch and extra set of grips, introduced 2009).
Add $631 for .38 Super cal. in High Polish Nickel (Acusport exclusive 2004-2007).

» ***1911-A1 90s Edition Mil-Spec Stainless Steel*** – similar to Mil-Spec Model, except is .45 ACP cal. only and stainless steel, includes belt holster, double mag. pouch and extra set of grips (Mil-Spec package). New 2003.

MSR $851	$755	$650	$550	$495	$400	$325	$255	

* ***1911-A1 90s Edition Mil-Spec Operator*** – .45 ACP cal. only, similar to Mil-Spec 1911-A1, except has Picatinny light mounting system forged into lower front of frame, parkerized finish only. Disc. 2002.

	$615	$540	$460	$420	$340	$275	$215	*$756*

* ***1911-A1 90s Edition Loaded Operator*** – .45 ACP cal. only, similar to full size service model, except has Picatinny light mounting platform forged into lower front of frame, checkered hardwood (disc. 2003) or plastic grips, OD Green with black bi-tone Armory Kote finish, Novak low mount tritium (disc.) or Trijicon night sights. New 2002.

MSR $1,387	$1,175	$1,025	$875	$775	$635	$515	$400	

* ***1911-A1 90s Edition Lightweight Operator*** – .45 ACP cal. only, 5 in. stainless steel barrel, blue finish, 7 shot mag., fixed low profile combat rear sight, dovetail front sight, cocobolo grips, 34 oz. New 2006.

MSR $1,305	$1,125	$975	$825	$750	$600	$495	$385	

* ***1911-A1 90s Edition Standard or Lightweight Model*** – .45 ACP cal. (current mfg.), Standard model has parkerized, blue, or OD Green with Armory Kote (new 2002) finish, Custom Loaded features became standard in 2001, Lightweight Model was mfg. 1995-2012 with either matte (disc. 2002), bi-tone (mfg. 2003-2012) or blue (mfg. 1993-disc.) finish, current mfg. is w/either Novak low mount or Trijicon night sights, 28.6 or 35.6 oz.

MSR $1,003	$875	$750	$650	$575	$475	$375	$295	

Add $52 for Lightweight Model (with Trijicon night sights), disc. 2012.
Subtract approx. 10%-25% if w/o Custom Loaded features (new 2001), depending on condition.

* ***1911-A1 90s Edition Stainless Standard Model*** – 9mm Para. (mfg. 1994-2012), .38 Super (disc.), .40 S&W (mfg. 2001-2002), or .45 ACP cal., 7 (.45 ACP cal.), 8 (.40 S&W), or 9 (9mm Para.) shot mag., Custom Loaded features became standard in 2001, wraparound rubber (disc.) or checkered hardwood grips, 11 Gear system holster became standard 2009, Novak Lo-Mount (disc.), Bo-Mar type (mfg. 1996-2001), or combat 3 dot sights, beveled mag. well, 39.2 oz. New 1991.

MSR $1,039	$915	$800	$675	$595	$480	$395	$325	

Add $62 for 9mm Para. cal., or $32 for .40 S&W cal. (disc.).
Add $230 for Tactical Combat Model with combat features and black stainless steel (new 2005).
Add $50 for Bo-Mar type sights (disc. 2001).
Add $202 for long slide variation in .45 Super cal. with V16 porting and Bo-Mar sights (disc.).

* ***1911-A1 90s Edition Stainless Super Tuned Standard*** – .45 ACP cal. only, super tuned by the Custom Shop, 7 shot mag., 5 in. barrel, Novak fixed Lo-Mount sights, 39.2 oz. Mfg. 1997-99.

	$875	$765	$655	$595	$480	$395	$305	*$995*

* ***1911-A1 90s Edition Target Model*** – 9mm Para. or .45 ACP cal., includes Custom Loaded features, stainless steel or black stainless steel (mfg. 2003-2012), with (.45 ACP cal. only) or w/o V12 ported barrel, adj. sights, 38 oz. New 2001.

MSR $1,103	$965	$850	$700	$630	$510	$415	$325	

Add $166 for black stainless steel with adj. Trijicon sights (.45 ACP cal. only). Disc. 2012.
Subtract approx. $15 for non-ported V12 barrel.

GRADING - PPGS™	100%	98%	95%	90%	80%	70%	60%	LAST MSR

* ***1911-A1 90s Edition Trophy Match*** – .40 S&W (mfg. 2001-2005) or .45 ACP cal. only, top-of-the-line pistol featuring improved trigger pull, adj. rear sight, 5 in. match grade barrel and bushing, Custom Loaded features became standard in 2001, choice of Armory Kote (.40 S&W cal. only, new 2001), stainless steel, bi-tone (disc.), or blue (disc.) finish, 35.6 oz. New 1994.

MSR $1,605	$1,375	$1,195	$1,025	$920	$740	$605	$470	

Add $10 for bi-tone finish (disc.).
Add $8 for High Capacity Trophy Match (disc.).
Subtract $100 for blue finish (disc.).

* ***1911-A1 90s Edition Standard High Capacity*** – 9mm Para. (disc.) or .45 ACP cal., 5 in. barrel, blue (disc. 2001) or matte parkerized (new 1996) finish with plastic grips, 3-dot fixed combat sights, 10 shot (except for law enforcement) mag. Mfg. 1995-2003.

	$635	$555	$475	$430	$350	$285	$220	*$756*

Add $50 for blue finish (disc.).

* ***1911-A1 90s Edition Stainless High Capacity*** – similar to Standard High Capacity, except is stainless steel. Mfg. 1996-2000.

	$675	$590	$505	$460	$370	$305	$235	*$819*

* ***1911-A1 90s Edition XM4 High Capacity Model*** – 9mm Para. or 45 ACP cal., features widened frame for high capacity mag., blue (mfg. 1993 only) or stainless finish only. Mfg. 1993-94.

	$595	$520	$445	$405	$325	$270	$210	*$689*

1911-A1 TRP (TACTICAL RESPONSE PISTOL) OPERATOR – .45 ACP cal., 5 in. standard or bull barrel, 7 shot mag., fixed combat 3-dot tritium or adj. Trijicon sights, black Armory Kote or stainless steel, checkered front strap, available in Standard, Stainless, and Operator configurations, 4 1/2 - 5 lbs. New mid-2008.

MSR $1,867	$1,615	$1,400	$1,200	$1,075	$875	$750	$625	

1911-A1 LONG SLIDE CUSTOM LOADED STAINLESS – .45 ACP or .45 Super (mfg. 2001 only) cal., 6 in. ported (disc. 2004) or unported barrel, 7 shot mag., checkered wood grips, adj. sights, 41 oz. Mfg. 2001-2012.

	$1,095	$950	$825	$725	$575	$475	$365	*$1,237*

Add $72 for ported barrel (V16, disc. 2004).
Add $403 for Trophy Match Model (disc. 2004).

MODEL 1911-A1 GI – .45 ACP cal., 5 in. barrel, parkerized, OD Green Armory Kote finish or stainless steel, 7 (standard) or 13 (high capacity) shot mag., low profile military sights, diamond checkered walnut grips with U.S. initials, includes 5.11 Gear belt holster, 36 oz. Mfg. 2004-2011.

	$565	$485	$415	$375	$300	$245	$190	*$656*

Add $52 for stainless steel.
Add $61 for high capacity magazine (parkerized finish, new 2005).

1911-A1 RANGE OFFICER (RO) – .45 ACP cal., 5 in. stainless match grade barrel with fully adj. target rear sight, blue frame/slide, beavertail grip safety, Delta hammer, speed trigger, beveled mag. well, lowered and flared ejection port includes two 7 shot mags., diamond checkered walnut grips with Springfield Armory logo, includes case and holsters, 40 oz. New 2011.

MSR $977	$850	$725	$625	$565	$455	$385	$315	

1911-A1 TACTICAL RESPONSE (TRP SERIES) – .45 ACP only, 5 in. standard or bull (Operator Model only) barrel, 7 shot mag., matte Armory Kote finish or stainless steel, checkered rosewood grips, Trijicon (new 2006), Novak or Hi-Viz (disc., Operator Model only) 3-dot Tritium (disc. 2001) sights, 36 oz. New 1999.

MSR $1,777	$1,525	$1,325	$1,125	$1,025	$825	$675	$525	

GRADING - PPGS™	100%	98%	95%	90%	80%	70%	60%	LAST MSR

1911-A1 COMMANDER MODEL – .45 ACP cal. only, similar to Standard 1911-A1 Model, except has 3.63 in. barrel, shortened slide, Commander hammer, low profile 3-dot sights, walnut grips, parkerized, blue, or duotone finish. Mfg. 1991-92.

	$425	$370	$320	$290	$235	$190	$150	

* ***1911-A1 Commander Model Combat*** – .45 ACP cal. only, 4 1/4 in. barrel, bobbed hammer, walnut grips. Mfg. 1991 only.

	$425	$370	$320	$290	$235	$190	$150	

1911-A1 CHAMPION MODEL – .380 ACP (Model MD-1, mfg. 1995 only) or .45 ACP cal., similar to Standard Model, except has 4 in. barrel and shortened slide, blue (disc. 2000) or parkerized (Mil-Spec Champion, new 1994) finish, Commander hammer, checkered walnut grips, 3-dot sights (Novak night sights became standard 2001), 7 shot mag., 33 1/2 oz. Mfg. 1992-2002.

	$695	$610	$520	$470	$380	$315	$245	*$856*

Add $30 for Ultra Compact slide (mfg. 1997-98).
Add $79 for ported Champion V10 with Ultra Compact slide (disc.).
Subtract approx. 10%-25% if w/o Custom Loaded features (new 2001), depending on condition.
Subtract approx. $150 for .380 ACP cal. (Model MD-1, disc.).

* ***1911-A1 Champion Model (Custom Loaded)*** – .45 ACP cal. only, stainless steel or Lightweight bi-tone with OD Green with Black Armory Kote finish (new 2004), Trijicon night sights. Mfg. 1992-2012.

	$900	$800	$675	$615	$500	$400	$315	*$1,031*

Add $42 for stainless steel.
Add $119 for Ultra Compact slide (mfg. 1997-98).
Add $52 for ported Champion V10 with Ultra Compact slide (disc. 2000).
Subtract approx. 10%-25% if w/o Custom Loaded features (new 2001), depending on condition.

* ***1911-A1 Champion Model Lightweight Operator*** – .45 ACP cal., 4 in. stainless steel barrel, blue finish, 7 shot mag., fixed low profile combat rear sight, dovetail front sight, cocobolo grips, 34 oz. Mfg. 2006-2012.

	$940	$825	$700	$630	$510	$415	$325	*$1,076*

* ***1911-A1 Champion Model GI*** – .45 ACP cal., parkerized or blued slide with black anodized frame (Lightweight Model, new 2005), low profile military sights, diamond checkered wood grips with U.S. initials, includes belt holster, 34 oz. Mfg. 2004-2012.

	$560	$485	$410	$375	$300	$245	$190	*$656*

* ***1911-A1 Champion Model TRP*** – .45 ACP cal., 4 in. barrel, otherwise similar to TRP Tactical Response. Mfg. 1999-2001.

	$1,045	$915	$785	$710	$575	$470	$365	*$1,249*

* ***1911-A1 Champion Model Lightweight*** – .45 ACP cal., aluminum frame, matte metal finish, night sights became standard during 2001. New 1999.

	$700	$610	$525	$475	$385	$315	$245	*$867*

Subtract approx. 10%-25% if w/o Custom Loaded features (new 2001), depending on condition.

* ***1911-A1 Champion Model Comp PDP*** – .45 ACP cal. only, compensated version of the Champion Model, blue. Mfg. 1993-98.

	$780	$680	$585	$530	$430	$350	$275	*$869*

* ***1911-A1 Champion Model Super Tuned*** – .45 ACP cal., super tuned by the Custom Shop, 7 shot mag., 4 in. barrel, blue or parkerized finish, Novak fixed Lo-Mount sights, 36.3 oz. Mfg. 1997-99.

	$850	$745	$635	$580	$465	$380	$295	*$959*

Add $30 for blue finish.

* ***1911-A1 Champion Model XM4 High Capacity*** – 9mm Para. or .45 ACP cal., high capacity variation. Mfg. 1994 only.

	$615	$540	$460	$420	$340	$275	$215	*$699*

GRADING - PPGS™	100%	98%	95%	90%	80%	70%	60%	LAST MSR

1911-A1 COMPACT MODEL – .45 ACP cal. only, compact variation featuring shortened 4 in. barrel and slide, reduced M1911-A1 curved gripstrap frame, checkered walnut grips, low profile 3-dot sights, 6 or 7 shot mag., extended slide stop, standard or lightweight alloy (new 1994) frame, combat hammer, parkerized, blue, or duotone (disc. 1992) finish, standard or lightweight (new 1995) configuration, 27 or 32 oz. Mfg. 1991-96.

$415	$365	$310	$280	$230	$185	$145	*$476*

Add $66 for blue finish.
Add $67 for Compact Lightweight Model (matte finish only).

* ***1911-A1 Compact Model Stainless*** – stainless steel variation of the Compact Model. Mfg. 1991-96.

$495	$435	$370	$335	$270	$225	$175	*$582*

* ***1911-A1 Compact Model Lightweight*** – .45 ACP cal., forged alloy frame, matte metal finish, 6 shot mag., Novak night sights became standard 2001. Mfg. 1999-2003.

$585	$510	$440	$395	$320	$265	$205	*$733*

Subtract approx. 10%-25% if w/o Custom Loaded features (new 2001), depending on condition.

» **1911-A1 Compact Model Lightweight Stainless** – similar to Compact Lightweight, except is stainless steel. Disc. 2001.

$725	$635	$545	$495	$400	$325	$255	*$900*

Subtract approx. 10%-25% if w/o Custom Loaded features (new 2001), depending on condition.

* ***1911-A1 Compact Model Comp Lightweight*** – compensated version of the Compact Model, bi-tone or matte finish, regular or lightweight alloy (new 1994) frame. Mfg. 1993-98.

$775	$680	$580	$525	$425	$350	$270	*$869*

* ***1911-A1 Compact Model High Capacity*** – blue or stainless steel, 3-dot fixed combat sights, black plastic grips, 10 shot (except for law enforcement) mag. Mfg. 1995-96 only.

$550	$475	$400	$365	$295	$245	$190	*$609*

Add $39 for stainless steel.

* ***1911-A1 Compact Model High Capacity PDP Comp*** – .45 ACP cal. only, features compensated 3 1/2 in. barrel, 10 shot (except law enforcement) mag., blue finish only. Mfg. 1995-96 only.

$830	$725	$620	$565	$455	$375	$290	*$964*

1911 A-1 ULTRA COMPACT (CUSTOM LOADED) – .380 ACP (lightweight only, mfg. 1995 only), 9mm Para. (new 1998, lightweight stainless only), or .45 ACP cal., 3 1/2 in. barrel, bi-tone (.45 ACP only, disc.), matte (.380 ACP, MD-1), or parkerized (Mil-Spec Ultra Compact) finish, 6, 7 (.380 ACP cal.) or 8 (9mm Para. cal.) shot mag., Custom Loaded features and night sights became standard in 2001, 24 or 30 oz. Mfg. 1995-2003.

$680	$595	$510	$460	$375	$305	$240	*$837*

Add $12 for V10 porting.
Add $12 for Novak Tritium sights (not available on 9mm Para cal.).
Add $110 for bi-tone finish (disc.).
Subtract $50 for MD-1 variation (.380 ACP only).
Subtract approx. 10%-25% if w/o Custom Loaded features (new 2001), depending on condition.

* ***1911 A-1 Ultra Compact Mil-Spec*** – .45 ACP cal., parkerized (disc.) or blued (new 2004) finish, similar to full size Mil-Spec Model, 6 shot mag., checkered grips, 3-dot fixed Hi-Viz combat sights. Mfg. 2001-2002, reintroduced 2004 only.

$550	$480	$410	$375	$300	$245	$190	*$641*

Subtract approx. 10%-25% if w/o Custom Loaded features (new 2001), depending on condition.

* ***1911 A-1 Ultra Compact Stainless Custom Loaded*** – 9mm Para. (disc. 2004) or .45 ACP cal., stainless steel, Novak (disc.) or Fixed Combat Trijicon (current mfg.) night sights became standard 2001. Mfg. 1998-2012.

$925	$800	$675	$615	$490	$400	$315	*$1,073*

Add $17 for 9mm Para cal. (lightweight, disc. 2004).
Subtract approx. 10%-25% if w/o Custom Loaded features (new 2001), depending on condition.

GRADING - PPGS™	100%	98%	95%	90%	80%	70%	60%	LAST MSR

* ***1911 A-1 Ultra Compact Lightweight*** – .45 ACP cal., aluminum frame, matte metal finish, night sights became standard 2001. Mfg. 1999-2001.

$695	$610	$520	$470	$380	$315	$245	$867

Subtract approx. 10%-25% if w/o Custom Loaded features (new 2001), depending on condition.

* ***1911 A-1 Ultra Compact V10 Lightweight Ported*** – .45 ACP cal., bi-tone finish. Mfg. 1999-2001.

$750	$655	$560	$510	$410	$335	$260	$737

» **1911 A-1 Ultra Compact V10 Lightweight Stainless** – 9mm Para. or .45 ACP (exclusive) cal., similar to Ultra Compact Lightweight, except is stainless steel, Novak Lo-Mount sights. Mfg. 1999-2002.

$725	$635	$545	$495	$400	$325	$255	$870

Add $31 for night sights (.45 ACP cal. only).
Subtract approx. 10%-25% if w/o Custom Loaded features (new 2001), depending on condition.

* ***1911 A-1 Ultra Compact High Capacity*** – 9mm Para. (disc.) or .45 ACP cal., parkerized (Mil-Spec) or blue (disc.) finish, and stainless steel (disc.) construction, 10 shot mag., 3-dot fixed combat (disc.) or Novak Lo-Mount (new 2002) sights, black plastic grips. Mfg. 1996-2002.

$735	$645	$550	$500	$405	$330	$255	$909

Add $98 for stainless steel.
Add $145 for stainless steel with V10 ported barrel (disc.).
Subtract approx. 10%-25% if w/o Custom Loaded features (new 2001), depending on condition.

* ***1911 A-1 Ultra Compact V10 Ported*** – .45 ACP cal. only, 3 1/2 in. specially compensated barrel/slide, blue (disc.), bi-tone, or parkerized (Mil-Spec Ultra Compact) finish, Novak Lo-Mount or 3-dot combat sights, 30 oz. Mfg. 1995-2002.

$690	$605	$515	$470	$380	$310	$240	$853

Subtract approx. 10%-25% if w/o Custom Loaded features (new 2001), depending on condition.

* ***1911 A-1 Ultra Compact V10 Super Tuned Ported*** – .45 ACP cal. only, super tuned by the Custom Shop, 3 1/2 in. ported barrel, bi-tone finish or stainless steel (exclusive), Novak fixed Lo-Mount sights, 32.9 oz. Mfg. 1997-99.

$925	$810	$695	$630	$510	$415	$325	$1,049

Add $70 for stainless steel (exclusive).

1911-A1 MICRO COMPACT – .45 ACP cal. only, 3 in. tapered barrel w/o bushing, matte finish, checkered grips, 6 shot mag., Novak Lo-Mount night sights. Mfg. 2002 only.

$625	$545	$470	$425	$345	$280	$220	$749

* ***1911 A-1 Micro Compact Lightweight Custom Loaded*** – similar to Micro Compact 1911 A-1, except also available in .40 S&W (disc.) cal., bi-tone, OD Green (mfg. 2003 only), or black Armory Kote (mfg. 2003-2004) finish with forged steel slide (grey) and aluminum alloy frame (blue), checkered cocobolo grips, Trijicon night sights, 24 oz. Mfg. 2002-2012.

$1,195	$995	$875	$750	$625	$525	$425	$1,377

Add $71 for Operator Model with XML X-treme mini light (disc. 2011).

* ***1911 A-1 Micro Compact Lightweight Stainless Custom Loaded*** – .45 ACP cal. only, similar to Micro Compact 1911 A-1 Custom Loaded, except is stainless or black stainless steel slide. Mfg. 2003.

$825	$720	$620	$560	$455	$370	$290	$993

* ***1911 A-1 Micro Compact GI*** – .45 ACP cal., parkerized finish, checkered diamond walnut grips with U.S. initials, includes belt holster, 32 oz. Mfg. 2004-2011.

$615	$535	$465	$400	$325	$270	$210	$708

1911-A1 EMP (ENHANCED MICRO PISTOL) – 9mm Para. or .40 S&W cal., bi-tone finish, 9 shot mag., 3 in. stainless steel bull barrel, polished stainless slide with blue frame, tritium

GRADING - PPGS™	100%	98%	95%	90%	80%	70%	60%	LAST MSR

3-dot sights, available in Standard or Lightweight configuration, reduced dimensions result in narrower profile, cocobolo or G10 grips, 27 (Lightweight) or 33 oz. New 2007.

MSR $1,345	$1,175	$1,025	$875	$785	$635	$515	$400	

Add $79 for G10 grips (new 2008).

GULF VICTORY SPECIAL EDITION - .45 ACP cal., special edition featuring presentation grade blue finish, gold etching on slide and other gold-plated small parts, includes specially padded and embroidered storage case with jacket patch, window decal, and cloisonne medallion honoring all U.S. Armed Forces. Mfg. 1991-92.

	$750	$655	$560	$510	$410	$335	$260	*$869*

Pistols: Semi-Auto - 1911-A1 Custom Models

In addition to the models listed, Springfield also custom builds other configurations of Race Guns that are available through Springfield dealers. Prices range from $2,245-$2,990.

Add $100 for all cals. other than .45 ACP.

CUSTOM CARRY GUN - .45 ACP (other cals. available upon request) cal., similar to Defender Model, except has tuned trigger pull, 7 shot mag., heavy recoil spring, extended thumb safety, available in blue or phosphate (disc.) finish. New 1991.

MSR $2,119	$1,775	$1,450	$1,150	$950	$800	$700	$600	

CUSTOM OPERATOR - .45 ACP cal. New 2001.

MSR $2,810	$2,495	$2,225	$1,775	$1,400	$1,100	$950	$850	

BASIC COMPETITION - .45 ACP (other cals. available upon request) cal., Bo-Mar adj. rear sight, blue finish, checkered walnut grips. New 1994.

MSR $2,199	$1,825	$1,475	$1,175	$975	$825	$725	$625	

PROFESSIONAL MODEL - .45 ACP cal., FBI contract model, black finish, custom fitted National Match barrel and bushing, many other custom shop features, low mount Novak rear sight, checkered cocobolo grips, with or w/o integral light rail on lower frame. New 1999.

MSR $2,700	$2,395	$2,150	$1,700	$1,325	$1,025	$925	$825	

PPC 1500

MSR $2,550	$2,200	$1,775	$1,400	$1,100	$950	$850	$750	

PPC TROPHY MATCH - 9mm Para. cal. Mfg. 2004-2006.

	$1,200	$1,000	$825	$700	$625	$525	$450	*$1,395*

NRA PPC DISTINGUISHED - .45 ACP (other cals. available upon request) cal., designed to comply with NRA PPC competitive rules/regulations, factory test target, custom carrying case. New 1995.

MSR $2,195	$1,875	$1,525	$1,175	$975	$825	$750	$675	

1911-A1 CUSTOM COMPACT - .45 ACP cal. only, carry or lady's model with shortened slide and frame, compensated, fixed 3-dot sights, Commander style hammer, Herrett walnut grips, other custom features, blue only.

	$1,615	$1,325	$1,100	$950	$850	$750	$675	*$1,815*

1911-A1 CUSTOM CHAMPION - similar to Custom Compact, except is based on Champion model with full size frame and shortened slide.

	$1,615	$1,325	$1,100	$950	$850	$750	$675	*$1,815*

NATIONAL MATCH HARDBALL - .45 ACP cal. only, National Match barrel and bushing, specially fitted frame and slide, blue only, Bo-Mar adj. rear sight, Herrett walnut grips, plastic cased.

MSR $1,980	$1,750	$1,400	$1,100	$925	$800	$700	$600	

This model is made specifically for DCM competition shooting.

BULLSEYE WADCUTTER - .45 ACP (other cals. available upon request) cal., specifically designed for wadcutter loads, Bo-Mar rib mounted on slide top, 5 or 6 in. barrel.

MSR $2,145	$1,800	$1,475	$1,150	$950	$800	$700	$600	

GRADING - PPGS™	100%	98%	95%	90%	80%	70%	60%	LAST MSR

ENTRY LEVEL WADCUTTER – .38 Super, .40 S&W, 10mm, or .45 ACP cal., 5 in. barrel, standard competition features.

	100%	98%	95%	90%	80%	70%	60%	LAST MSR
	$925	$800	$700	$600	$550	$475	$425	$1,049

Add $200 for .38 Super cal.
Add $391 for 10mm or .40 S&W cal.

This model featured supported chambers in all cals. except .45 ACP.

TROPHY MASTER "COMPETITION" – .45 ACP (other cals. available upon request) cal., competition model which includes low profile combat sights, ambidextrous safety, long match trigger, bobbed hammer, Pachmayr wraparound grips. Disc. 1996.

	100%	98%	95%	90%	80%	70%	60%	LAST MSR
	$1,420	$1,125	$950	$875	$800	$725	$650	$1,598

EXPERT LIMITED – .45 ACP (other cals. available upon request) cal., mfg. for IPSC competition shooting, dual chamber compensator system on match barrel, duotone finish.

	100%	98%	95%	90%	80%	70%	60%	LAST MSR
MSR $2,270	$1,875	$1,525	$1,175	$975	$825	$725	$625	

Add $175 for Expert Model.

This model is an improved variation of the Trophy Master Competition Model.

DISTINGUISHED LIMITED – similar to Expert Model, except has brushed hard chrome finish, checkered gripstraps and trigger guard, top-of-the-line competition model.

	100%	98%	95%	90%	80%	70%	60%	LAST MSR
MSR $3,340	$2,995	$2,600	$2,150	$1,750	$1,350	$1,050	$875	

Add $330 for Distinguished Model.

DISTINGUISHED BIANCHI/COMPETITION STEEL – .38 Super cal. New 2004.

	100%	98%	95%	90%	80%	70%	60%	LAST MSR
MSR $3,670	$3,295	$2,850	$2,450	$2,050	$1,775	$1,500	$1,250	

CUSTOM HIGH CAPACITY LTD – .40 S&W cal. Mfg. 2004-2011.

	100%	98%	95%	90%	80%	70%	60%	LAST MSR
	$2,200	$1,775	$1,425	$1,125	$975	$875	$775	$2,650

OPERATOR LIGHTWEIGHT – .45 ACP cal., 3 in. barrel, bi-tone finish, XML mini-light, includes Novak Trijicon night sights. Limited mfg. 2005.

	100%	98%	95%	90%	80%	70%	60%	LAST MSR
	$1,050	$925	$800	$700	$600	$500	$400	$1,247

OPERATOR TACTICAL RESPONSE – .45 ACP cal., 5 in. barrel, black Armory Kote finish, adj. Trijicon night sights. Limited mfg. 2005.

	100%	98%	95%	90%	80%	70%	60%	LAST MSR
	$1,395	$1,075	$900	$775	$675	$575	$475	$1,639

LOADED OPERATOR – .45 ACP cal., 5 in. barrel, OD Green or black Armory Kote finish and slide, Novak or Trijicon night sights. Limited mfg. 2005.

	100%	98%	95%	90%	80%	70%	60%	LAST MSR
	$1,025	$900	$800	$700	$600	$500	$400	$1,218

LEATHAM TROPHY MATCH – .40 S&W cal., 5 in. barrel, high capacity model, Armory Kote finish. Mfg. 2005-2007.

This model was POR.

LEATHAM LEGEND SERIES CUSTOM 1 – Disc. 2011.

	100%	98%	95%	90%	80%	70%	60%	LAST MSR
	$2,875	$2,475	$2,050	$1,775	$1,500	$1,250	$995	$3,367

These models were available exclusively through Davidson's until 2010.

FULL HOUSE RACE GUN – .45 ACP cal., high capacity frame, chrome finish only. Mfg. 1998-2011.

	100%	98%	95%	90%	80%	70%	60%	LAST MSR
	$2,925	$2,475	$2,100	$1,800	$1,550	$1,350	$1,150	$3,395

Add $150 for STI/SV style frame (disc.).

P9 WORLD CUP – 9mmx21 or .40 S&W cal., state-of-the-art competition pistol, based on factory P9 Race gun, hard chrome finish only.

	100%	98%	95%	90%	80%	70%	60%	LAST MSR
	$2,550	$2,100	$1,775	$1,500	$1,250	$975	$795	$2,935

TGO1

	100%	98%	95%	90%	80%	70%	60%	LAST MSR
MSR $3,367	$2,995	$2,650	$2,350	$2,025	$1,700	$1,475	$1,125	

GRADING - PPGS™	100%	98%	95%	90%	80%	70%	60%	LAST MSR

Pistols: Semi-Auto - XD Series

All XD pistols are manufactured in Croatia. All XD pistols were originally shipped with two magazines. Beginning 2005, high capacity magazines are legal for civilian sales in those states that permit high cap. mags. During 2006, all XD pistols are shipped with the XD Gear System, consisting of belt holster, double magazine pouch, magazine loader, two magazines and cable lock.

In 2013, Springfield Armory USA released its XD-S Series in .45 ACP cal. with many compact features.

XD 5 IN. TACTICAL (X-TREME DUTY) – 9mm Para., .357 SIG, .40 S&W, .45 ACP (new 2006), or .45 GAP (mfg. 2005-2007) cal., cold hammer forged 5 in. barrel, 9 (.45 GAP), 10, 12 (.40 S&W or .357 SIG), or 15 (9mm Para.) shot mag., lightweight polymer frame, matte black, bi-tone (.45 ACP only), Dark Earth (mfg. 2007-2012) or OD Green finish, steel slide, single action striker fired with U.S.A. trigger system, firing pin and loaded chamber indicators, dual recoil spring system, integral accessory rails standard on frame, ambidextrous mag. release, grip safety, front and rear slide serrations, external thumb safety became separate model in 2008, approx. 29 (9mm Para. cal.) or 33 oz. New 2002.

MSR $599	$535	$450	$400	$350	$300	$265	$235	

Add $30 for thumb safety (black or bi-tone finish only).
Add $30 for .45 ACP cal. (new 2006), or $80 for bi-tone finish (.45 ACP cal. only).
Add $92 for Trijicon sights or approx. $90 for Heinie (disc.) tritium Slant Pro sights.
Subtract $7 for .45 GAP cal. black tactical (disc. 2007).

* ***XD Tactical Pro*** – limited mfg. 2003 only.

	$875	$775	$675	$575	$475	$400	$350	*$1,099*

XD 4 IN. SERVICE (X-TREME DUTY) – 9mm Para., .357 SIG, .40 S&W, .45 ACP (new 2006), or .45 GAP (mfg. 2005-2007) cal., cold hammer forged 4 in. ported or unported barrel, 9 (.45 GAP), 10 (.45 ACP), 12 (.40 S&W or .357 SIG), or 15 (9mm Para.) shot mag., lightweight polymer frame, matte black (only finish available on .357 SIG cal.), bi-tone (new 2003), Dark Earth (mfg. 2007-2012) or OD Green finish, steel slide, single action striker fired with U.S.A. trigger system, firing pin and loaded chamber indicators, dual recoil spring system, integral accessory rails standard on frame, ambidextrous mag. release, grip safety, front and rear slide serrations, thumb safety became separate model during 2008, approx. 28 (9mm Para.) or 30 oz. New 2002.

MSR $578	$515	$435	$365	$310	$275	$235	$200	

Add $29 for .45 ACP cal.
Add $35 for V10 ported barrel (black or OD Green finish, not available in .45 ACP or .45 GAP cal.).
Add $67 for bi-tone finish.
Add $100 for stainless steel slide (.45 ACP cal. only), disc.
Add $29 for thumb safety in .45 ACP cal.
Add $96 for Trijicon or Heinie tritium Slant Pro night sights (not available on .45 GAP cal.).
Subtract $7 for .45 GAP cal. (disc. 2007).

XD 3 IN. SUB-COMPACT (X-TREME DUTY) – 9mm Para. or .40 S&W (new 2004) cal., cold hammer forged 3 in. barrel, 9 (.40 S&W), 10 (9mm Para.), or 13 (9mm Para.) shot mag., lightweight polymer frame, bi-tone (new 2004), matte black or OD Green finish, steel slide, single action striker fired with U.S.A. trigger system, firing pin and loaded chamber indicators, dual recoil spring system, integral accessory rails standard on frame, ambidextrous mag. release, grip safety, front and rear slide serrations, 26 oz. New 2003.

MSR $549	$490	$425	$365	$310	$275	$235	$200	

Add $67 for bi-tone finish.
Add $96 for Trijicon or Heinie tritium Slant Pro night sights.
Add $100 for X-treme mini light (disc. 2011).

This model is not available with a thumb safety.

GRADING - PPGS™	100%	98%	95%	90%	80%	70%	60%	LAST MSR

XD COMPACT SERIES – 9mm Para. (mfg. 2007 only), .40 S&W (mfg. 2007 only), or .45 ACP cal., 4 or 5 in. barrel, shortened grip frame, black, OD Green (disc.2012), bi-tone (new 2008), or Dark Earth (disc. 2011) finish, stainless steel slide (OD Green (disc.2012) or Dark Earth (disc. 2011) only, mfg. 2008-2012), 10 or extended 13 shot mag., 29 or 32 oz. New 2007.

MSR $600	$525	$440	$400	$350	$315	$280	$245

Add $46 for 5 in. barrel.
Add $66 for bi-tone finish or stainless steel slide (4 in. barrel only, disc. 2012).
Add $94 for Trijicon night sights (disc. 2011).
Subtract $30 for 9mm or .40 S&W cal. (4 in. barrel only), w/o night sights (disc. 2007).

XD CUSTOM SERIES – the Springfield custom shop makes three variations of the XD pistol, including the XD Carry, XD Production, and XD Custom Competition. Most calibers and sizes are available.

Current MSRs on this series are as follows - XD Carry is $795, XD Production is $1,200, and XD Custom Competition is $1,460.

XD(M) SERIES – 9mm Para., .40 S&W, or .45 ACP (new mid-2010) cal., 3.8 (available in 9mm Para. or .40 S&W only, new 2010) or 4 1/2 in. match grade barrel, 10 (.45 ACP only, new 2012), 13, 16 or 19 shot mag., polymer frame with lower Picatinny rail, minimal reset trigger, contoured frame is slightly modified from XD model, black, bi-tone, or OD Green Melonite oxide finish, deepened and diagonal slide serrations, black or stainless steel slide, interchangeable back straps, includes 3 interchangeable grip straps, includes XD Gear holster and black plastic carrying case, 28-31 oz. New mid-2008.

MSR $697	$615	$540	$465	$410	$360	$310	$265

Add $12 for .45 ACP cal. (new 2011).
Add approx. $66 for bi-tone finish or for OD Green w/stainless slide (not available in .45 ACP cal.).
Add $118 for night sights (Tritium or Trijicon).

XD(M) COMPACT SERIES – 9mm Para., .40 S&W, or .45 ACP (new 2012) cal., 3.8 in. barrel, 9 (flush, disc. 2012) or 13 shot mag., black or bi-tone polymer frame with lower Picatinny rail, Melonite metal finish, low profile dovetail front and rear 3 dot sights, includes the XD(M) Gear System, 26 oz. New 2011.

MSR $705	$620	$550	$465	$410	$360	$310	$265

Add $27 for .45 ACP cal. (new 2012).
Add $64 for bi-tone finish.
Subtract $112 for flush magazines (disc. 2012).

This model is also available with an extended 16 (.40 S&W cal.) or 19 (9mm Para. cal.) shot mag. in states where legal.

XD(M) COMPETITION SERIES – 9mm Para., .40 S&W, or .45 ACP cal., 5 1/4 in. match grade select fit barrel, Melonite fully supported ramp, 13 (.45 ACP), 16 (.40 S&W), or 19 (9mm Para.) shot mag., black polymer frame, red fiber optic front and fully adj. target rear sight, forged steel slide, black or bi-tone finish, 29-32 oz. New late 2011.

MSR $795	$725	$650	$550	$475	$400	$350	$300

Add $40 for .45 ACP cal.
Add $70 for bi-tone finish.

XD(M) CUSTOM SERIES – the Springfield custom shop makes three variations of the XD(M) pistol, including the XD(M) Carry, XD(M) Production, and XD(M) Custom Competition. Most calibers and sizes are available.

Current MSRs on this series are as follows - XD(M) Carry is $910, XD(M) Production is $1,295, and XD(M) Custom Competition is $1,525.

XD-S – 9mm Para. or .45 ACP cal., hammerless striker ignition system, 3.3 in. steel barrel, 5 shot mag., polymer frame with textured grip panels, fiber optic front and low profile dovetail rear sights, black or bi-tone melonite finish, loaded chamber indicator, single position

GRADING - PPGS™	100%	98%	95%	90%	80%	70%	60%	LAST MSR

Picatinny rail system, short reset trigger, rear grip safety, includes XD-S Gear System (paddle holster, double magazine pouch, 2 mags., and cable lock), 21 1/2 oz. New 2013.

MSR $599	**$525**	**$465**	**$425**	**$385**	**$350**	**$325**	**$295**	

Add $70 for bi-tone finish.

PISTOLS: SINGLE SHOT, 1911-A2 SASS SERIES

1911-A2 SASS – various cals., single shot break open action featuring interchangeable barrels, Pachmayr grips, adj. front and rear sights, blue finish only, 61-66 oz. Mfg. 1990-1992.

* ***1911-A2 SASS 10 3/4 in. barrel*** – .22 LR, 7mm BR, .243 Win., .357 Mag., or .44 Mag. cal.

	$650	**$560**	**$495**	**$450**	**$420**	**$390**	**$360**	***$749***

Add $399 per interchangeable conversion unit (includes barrel).

* ***1911-A2 SASS 15 in. barrel*** – .22 LR, .223 Rem., .243 Win. (new 1991), 7mm BR, 7mm-08 Rem., .308 Win., or .358 Win. cal.

	$650	**$560**	**$495**	**$450**	**$420**	**$390**	**$360**	***$749***

Add $399 per interchangeable conversion unit (includes barrel).

RIFLES: BOLT ACTION

MAUSER M98 – 7x57mm Mauser cal., surplus rifles with standard military dimensions and features. Importation disc. 1989.

* ***Mauser M98 Hunting/Utility Grade***

	$70	**$50**	**$45**	**$45**	**$40**	**$40**	**$35**	***$75***

* ***Mauser M98 Collector Grade***

	$105	**$90**	**$80**	**$70**	**$60**	**$50**	**$40**	***$116***

* ***Mauser M98 Premium Grade***

	$170	**$150**	**$130**	**$115**	**$100**	**$90**	**$80**	***$194***

CZ 98 HUNTER CLASSIC – .243 Win., .270 Win., .30-06, .308 Win., 6.5x55mm, 7x57 Mauser, 7x64mm, 7.29x57mm, .300 Win. Mag., or 7mm Rem. Mag. cal., features Mauser 98 Large Ring action, mfg. by CZ in the Czech Republic and Springfield Armory, controlled feeding, 24 in. hammer forged barrel, adj. trigger, choice of walnut or synthetic stock, 7.7 lbs. Limited mfg. 1995 only.

	$345	**$315**	**$285**	**$260**	**$240**	**$220**	**$195**	***$411***

Add $38 for walnut stock.

RIFLES: SEMI-AUTO, MILITARY DESIGN

Many models listed are CA legal, since they do not have a muzzle brake. MSRs are typically the same as those guns available with a muzzle brake. Pricing on CA legal firearms is not included within the scope of this listing - please contact the factory directly for this information (see Trademark Index).

M1 CARBINE – .30 Carbine cal., features new receiver on older military M1 GI stocks. Disc.

	$495	**$435**	**$370**	**$335**	**$270**	**$225**	**$175**	

M1 GARAND AND VARIATIONS – .30-06, .270 Win. (disc. 1987), or .308 Win. cal., semi-auto, 24 in. barrel, gas operated, 8 shot mag., adj. sights, 9 1/2 lbs.

* ***M1 Garand Rifle*** – .30-06 or .308 Win. cal., mfg. with original U.S. government issue parts, with new walnut stock, 8 shot mag., 24 in. barrel, 9 1/2 lbs. Limited mfg. 2002-2007.

	$1,175	**$1,030**	**$880**	**$800**	**$645**	**$530**	**$410**	***$1,439***

Add $30 for .308 Win. cal.

* ***M1 Garand Standard Model*** – supplied standard with camo GI fiberglass stock.

	$725	**$635**	**$545**	**$495**	**$400**	**$325**	**$255**	***$761***

Subtract $65 if with GI stock.

GRADING - PPGS™	100%	98%	95%	90%	80%	70%	60%	LAST MSR

* ***M1 Garand National Match*** – walnut stock, match barrel and sights.

	$850	$745	$635	$580	$465	$380	$295	*$897*

Add $240 for Kevlar stock.

* ***M1 Garand Ultra Match*** – match barrel and sights, glass bedded stock, walnut stock standard.

	$950	$830	$710	$645	$520	$425	$330	*$1,033*

Add $240 for Kevlar stock.

* ***M1-D Sniper Rifle*** – .30-06 or .308 Win. cal., limited quantities, with original M84 scope, prong type flash suppressor, leather cheek pad and slings.

	$1,100	$960	$825	$750	$605	$495	$385	*$1,033*

* ***M1 Garand Tanker Rifle*** – similar to T-26 authorized by Gen. MacArthur at the end of WWII, 18 1/4 in. barrel, .30-06 or .308 Win. cal., GI stock standard.

	$850	$745	$635	$580	$465	$380	$295	*$797*

Add $23 for walnut full stock.

* ***D-Day M1 Garand Rifle*** – .30-06 cal., 24 in. barrel, gas operated, military square post front sights, engraved stock, two 8 shot mags., leather sling, cleaning kit, includes wooden crate and limited edition lithograph print, 9 1/2 lbs. 1,944 mfg. 2004-2005.

	$1,375	$1,205	$1,030	$935	$755	$620	$480	*$1,490*

BM 59 – .308 Win. cal., mfg. in Italy and machined and assembled in the Springfield Armory factory, 19.32 in. barrel, 20 shot box mag., 9 1/2 lbs.

* ***BM 59 Standard Italian Rifle*** – with grenade launcher, winter trigger, tri-compensator, and bipod.

	$1,750	$1,530	$1,310	$1,190	$960	$785	$610	*$1,950*

* ***BM 59 Alpine Rifle*** – with Beretta pistol grip type stock.

	$2,025	$1,770	$1,520	$1,375	$1,115	$910	$710	*$2,275*

This model was also available in a Paratrooper configuration with folding stock at no extra charge.

* ***BM 59 Nigerian Rifle*** – similar to BM 59, except has Beretta pistol grip type stock.

	$2,075	$1,815	$1,555	$1,410	$1,140	$935	$725	*$2,340*

* ***BM 59 E Model Rifle***

	$1,975	$1,730	$1,480	$1,345	$1,085	$890	$690	*$2,210*

M1A RIFLES – .243 Win. (disc.), .308 Win., or 7mm-08 Rem. (1991 mfg. only) cal., patterned after the original Springfield M14 - except semi-auto, walnut or fiberglass stock, 22 in. steel or stainless steel barrel, fiberglass handguard, "New Loaded" option (see separate listing) beginning 2001 includes NM air gauged barrel, trigger group, front and rear sights, and flash suppressor or Springfield proprietary muzzle brake, 9 lbs.

* ***M1A Standard/Basic Model*** – 7.62mm, above specifications, choice of Collector (original GI stock, disc. 2001), birch (disc. 2003), walnut (M1A Standard Model beginning 1993), Mossy Oak camo finished (new 2003), Green composite (new 2011), black fiberglass (M1A Basic Model), camo fiberglass (disc.), GI wood (disc. 1992), and brown (disc.) or black laminated (M1A Standard Model mfg. 1996-2000) stock, regular or National Match (disc.) barrel.

MSR $1,640	$1,425	$1,250	$1,050	$950	$765	$630	$490

Add $9 for Green composite stock (new 2011).
Add $99 for new walnut stock.
Add $44 for Mossy Oak camo finished stock.
Add $59 for birch stock (disc. 2003).
Add $44 for stainless steel barrel (disc.), $74 for bipod and stabilizer (disc.) or $159 for brown laminated stock (disc.), $59 for National Match barrel (disc.), $155 for National Match barrel and sights (disc.), $200 for folding stock (disc. 1994).
Subtract $58 for camo fiberglass stock (disc.).

Standard (entry level model) stock configuration for 1996 was black or camo fiberglass.

GRADING - PPGS™	100%	98%	95%	90%	80%	70%	60%	LAST MSR

* ***M1A E-2*** – standard stock is birch. Disc.

	$975	$855	$730	$665	$535	$440	$340	*$842*

Add $30 for walnut stock.
Add $120 for Shaw stock with Harris bipod.

* ***M1A Bush Rifle*** – .308 Win. cal., 18 in. shrouded barrel, 8 lbs. 12 oz., collector GI, walnut, Mossy Oak camo finished (new 2003), black fiberglass folding (disc. 1994 per C/B), and black fiberglass (disc.) or laminated black (disc.) stock. Disc. 1999, reintroduced 2003 only.

	$1,300	$1,135	$975	$885	$715	$585	$455	*$1,529*

Add $29 for walnut stock (disc.), $15 for black fiberglass stock (disc.), $86 for black laminated stock (disc.), $235 for National Match variation (disc.), and $525 for Super Match variation (disc.)

* ***M1A National Match*** – .308 Win. cal., 22 in. steel or stainless steel (new 1999) barrel, National Match sights, mainspring guide, flash suppressor, and gas cylinder, special glass bedded oil finished match stock, tuned trigger, walnut stock became standard in 1991, 9 lbs.

MSR $2,318	$2,000	$1,750	$1,500	$1,350	$1,085	$890	$690	

Add $55 for stainless steel barrel.
Add $155 for heavy composition stock (disc.).
Add $250 for either fiberglass or fancy burl wood stock (disc.).

.243 Win. and 7mm-08 Rem. cals. were also available at extra charge until discontinued.

* ***M1A Super Match*** – .308 Win. cal., similar to National Match, except has air-gauged Douglas or Hart (disc.) heavy barrel, oversized walnut, black fiberglass, or Marine Corp Green Camo fiberglass super match stock, modified operating rod guide, rear lugged receiver beginning 1991, approx. 11 1/2 lbs.

MSR $2,905	$2,550	$2,200	$1,875	$1,685	$1,360	$1,115	$865	

Add $230 for stainless steel Douglas barrel.
Add $738 for McMillan black or Marine Corps camo fiberglass stock.
Add $250 for Krieger or Hart barrel (disc.).
Add $200 for fancy burl walnut (disc.) stock.

.243 Win. and 7mm-08 Rem. cals. were also available at extra charge until discontinued.

M1A LOADED STANDARD – .308 Win. cal., 22 in. National Match steel or stainless steel barrel, features shooting upgrades such as National Match trigger assembly, front and rear sights, and National Match flash suppressor, 10 shot mag., black or green fiberglass, Collector GI walnut (disc. 2000), or new walnut stock, approx. 9 1/2 lbs. New 1999.

MSR $1,794	$1,650	$1,425	$1,225	$1,075	$875	$725	$575	

Add $114 for new walnut stock.
Add $16 for green stock.
Add $211 for stainless steel barrel and walnut stock.
Add $99 for stainless steel barrel.
Add $525 for extended cluster rail with black fiberglass stock and National Match stainless steel barrel (mfg. 2006-2011).
Add $100 for Collector GI walnut (disc. 2000).

M1A "GOLD SERIES" – .308 Win. cal., heavy walnut competition stock, gold medal grade heavy Douglas barrel. Mfg. 1987 only.

	$1,944	$1,700	$1,460	$1,320	$1,070	$875	$680	*$1,944*

Add $126 for Kevlar stock, add $390 for special Hart stainless steel barrel, add $516 for Hart stainless steel barrel with Kevlar stock.

M1A SCOUT SQUAD – .308 Win. cal., 18 in. barrel, choice of GI Collector (disc. 1998), new walnut, green (disc. 2011) or black fiberglass, Mossy Oak camo finished, or black laminated (disc. 1998) stock, muzzle stabilizer standard, supplied with Scout mount and handguard, approx. 9 lbs. New 1997.

MSR $1,761	$1,550	$1,350	$1,150	$1,050	$840	$685	$535	

Add $132 for walnut stock.

GRADING - PPGS™	100%	98%	95%	90%	80%	70%	60%	LAST MSR

Add $87 for Mossy Oak camo finish.
Add $14 for green stock (disc. 2011).

M1A SOCOM 16/SOCOM II – .308 Win. cal., 16 1/4 in. barrel with muzzle brake, black or green fiberglass stock with steel buttplate, black or urban camo (disc. 2011) finish, upper handguard has been cut out for sight rail, 10 shot box mag., tritium front sight with ghost ring aperture rear sight, two-stage military trigger, 8.9 lbs. New 2004.

MSR $1,893	$1,725	$1,495	$1,275	$1,150	$925	$750	$585	

Add $12 for green composite stock.
Add $315 for urban camo stock with cluster rail (Socom II, mfg. 2005-2011).
Add $283 for Generation II black fiberglass stock with cluster rail (Socom II, new 2005) or $393 for extended cluster rail (Socom II, new 2007).

M1A/M21 TACTICAL – .308 Win. cal., Garand action, 22 in. barrel, tactical variation of the Super Match mfg. with match grade parts giving superior accuracy, adj. walnut cheekpiece stock, choice of Douglas carbon steel or stainless Krieger barrel, 11.6 lbs. New 1990.

MSR $3,555	$3,150	$2,800	$2,325	$2,075	$1,675	$1,350	$1,075	

Add $420 for Krieger stainless barrrel.

M25 "WHITE FEATHER" TACTICAL – .308 Win. cal., Garand action, includes black fiberglass M3A McMillan stock, 22 in. Kreiger heavy carbon barrel standard, Rader trigger, White Feather logo and Carlos Hathcock II signature, 10 shot box mag., includes Harris bipod, 12 3/4 lbs. Mfg. 2001-2009.

	$4,750	$4,155	$3,560	$3,230	$2,610	$2,135	$1,660	*$5,278*

SAR-3 – .308 Win. cal., licensed copy of the pre-import ban HK-91, predecessor to the SAR-8, mfg. in Greece.

	$995	$870	$745	$675	$545	$450	$350	

SAR-8 – .308 Win. cal., patterned after the H & K Model 91, roller locking delayed blowback action, fluted chamber, rotary adj. rear aperture sight, 18 in. barrel, recent mfg. incorporated a cast aluminum receiver with integrated Weaver rail, pistol grip, slim forearm, and green furniture (for law enforcement only), supplied with walnut (disc. 1994) or black fiberglass thumbhole sporter stock, 10 (C/B 1994) or 20 (disc. 1994) shot detachable mag., 8.7 lbs. Mfg. in U.S. starting 1990, disc. 1998.

	$1,015	$890	$760	$690	$560	$455	$355	*$1,204*

SAR-8 parts are interchangeable with both SAR-3 and HK-91 parts.

* ***SAR-8 Tactical Counter Sniper Rifle*** – .308 Win. cal., tactical sniper variation of the SAR-8. Mfg. 1996-98.

	$1,325	$1,160	$995	$900	$730	$595	$465	*$1,610*

SAR-48 MODEL – .308 Win. cal., authentic model of the Belgian semi-auto FAL/LAR rifle, 21 in. barrel, adj. gas piston operation, 20 shot mag., walnut or synthetic stock, adj. sights, sling, and mag. loader. Mfg. 1985-89.

	$1,675	$1,465	$1,255	$1,140	$920	$755	$585	

Add approx. 20% for Israeli configuration with heavy barrel, bipod, flash hider, and flip-up buttplate.

The SAR-48 was disc. in 1989 and reintroduced as the Model SAR-4800 in 1990.

* ***SAR-48 Bush Rifle*** – similar to SAR-48 model, except has 18 in. barrel.

	$1,750	$1,530	$1,310	$1,190	$960	$785	$610	

* ***SAR-48 .22 Cal.*** – .22 LR cal., variation of the Sporter Model. Disc. 1989.

	$725	$635	$545	$495	$400	$325	$255	*$760*

SAR-4800 SPORTER MODEL – .223 Rem. (new 1997) or .308 Win. cal., authentic model of the Belgian semi-auto FAL/LAR rifle, 18 (.223 Rem. cal. only) or 21 in. barrel, adj. gas piston operation, 10 (C/B 1994) or 20 (disc.) shot mag., walnut (disc.) or black fiberglass thumbhole sporter stock, adj. sights, sling, and mag. loader. Mfg. 1990-98.

	$1,080	$945	$810	$735	$595	$485	$380	

GRADING - PPGS™	100%	98%	95%	90%	80%	70%	60%	LAST MSR

All SAR - 4800 parts are interchangeable with both SAR-48 and FN/FAL parts. This model is an updated variation of the pre-WWII FN Model 49.

* ***SAR-4800 Bush Rifle Sporter Model*** – similar to standard model, except has 18 in. barrel.

	$1,085	$950	$815	$735	$595	$490	$380	*$1,216*

DR-200 SPORTER RIFLE – while advertised, this model never went into production. ($687 was planned MSR).

SPRINGFIELD ARMS CO.

Previous assumed business name of Stevens Arms during the Savage era. Many long arm variations were marked with this company listing even though Savage manufactured the guns. Most were average quality utilitarian firearms and most have a current value in the $75-$300 range depending on configuration and condition.

STAG ARMS

Current rifle manufacturer located in New Britain, CT.

RIFLES: SEMI-AUTO

All AR-15 style carbines/rifles are available in post-ban configuration for restricted states, and include one mag., instruction manual, plastic rifle case, and lifetime warranty.

IMPORTANT NOTE: On model(s) where *N/A has replaced the normal 100% value, it indicates current market conditions are too unstable to accurately ascertain 100%-60% values. Factory retail prices (MSRs) reflect most recent updates. For more up-to-date information on current pricing trends and additional useful information, please visit www.bluebookofgunvalues.com, select "Information & Services " from the menu, and click on "Additional Book Information".

MODEL 1 CARBINE – .223 Rem. cal., 16 in. chrome lined barrel, A3 forged aluminum upper, standard safety, black anodized finish, six position collapsible stock, removable carry handle, standard GI carbine design, available in right or left (Model 1L) hand, 7.1 lbs.

MSR $949	*N/A	$750	$645	$585	$475	$385	$300

Add $40 for Model 1L.

MODEL 2 CARBINE – .223 Rem. cal., 16 in. chrome lined barrel, A3 forged aluminum upper, standard safety, black anodized finish, six position collapsible stock, flip up rear sight, tactical top rail, available in right or left (Model 2L) hand, 6.4 lbs.

MSR $940	*N/A	$745	$635	$580	$465	$380	$295

Add $24 for Model 2L.

* ***Model 2T Carbine*** – .223 Rem. cal., 16 in. chrome lined barrel, A3 forged aluminum upper, ambidextrous (left hand only) or standard safety, six position collapsible stock, flip up rear sight, tactical rail, pistol grip, available in right or left hand, approx. 6.6 lbs.

MSR $1,130	*N/A	$895	$765	$695	$565	$450	$350

Add $25 for left hand (Model 2T-L).

MODEL 3 CARBINE – .223 Rem. cal., 16 in. chrome lined barrel, A3 forged aluminum upper, standard safety, black anodized finish, six position collapsible stock, tactical top rail, available in right or left (Model 3L) hand, V-RS modular rail platform became standard 2011, 6.1 lbs.

MSR $895	*N/A	$700	$600	$550	$450	$360	$275

Add $25 for Model 3L.

MODEL 3G RIFLE – 5.56mm cal., 18 in. stainless steel heavy fluted barrel, matte black finish, Samson Evolution handguard, Geissle Super 3-Gun trigger, Magpul ACS buttstock and MOE pistol grip. New 2012.

MSR $1,149	*N/A	$1,095	$925	$850	$675	$550	$425

Add $20 for left hand.

GRADING - PPGS™	100%	98%	95%	90%	80%	70%	60%	LAST MSR

MODEL 4 RIFLE – .223 Rem. cal., 20 in. heavy barrel, A3 forged aluminum upper, standard safety, black anodized finish, A2 fixed stock, removable carry handle, available in right or left (Model 4L) hand, 7 1/2 lbs.

MSR $1,015	*N/A	$815	$695	$625	$515	$415	$325

Add $80 for Model 4L.

MODEL 5 CARBINE – 6.8 SPC cal., 16 in. chrome lined barrel, A3 forged aluminum upper, standard or ambidextrous (left hand only) safety, black anodized finish, six position collapsible stock, available in right or left (Model 5L) hand, 7.1 lbs.

MSR $1,045	*N/A	$825	$700	$635	$515	$415	$325

Add $50 for left hand (Model 5L).

MODEL 6 RIFLE – .223 Rem. cal., 24 1/8 in. stainless steel heavy barrel, A3 forged aluminum upper, standard or ambidextrous (left hand only) safety, fixed A2 buttstock, black anodized finish, tactical top rail, no sights, pistol grip, approx. 10 lbs.

MSR $1,055	*N/A	$830	$710	$645	$520	$425	$330

Add $40 for left hand (Model 6L).

STAG 7 HUNTER – 6.8 SPC cal., 20.8 in. stainless steel barrel, A3 forged aluminum upper, standard or ambidextrous (left hand only) safety, fixed A2 buttstock, black anodized finish, no sights, tactical top rail, two-stage match trigger, Hogue pistol grip, available in right or left hand, approx. 10 lbs.

MSR $1,055	*N/A	$830	$710	$645	$520	$425	$330

Add $40 for left hand (Model 7L).

MODEL 8 CARBINE – .223 Rem. cal., 16 in. chrome lined barrel, A3 forged aluminum upper, ambidextrous (left hand only) or standard safety, six position collapsible stock, flip up rear sight. New 2011.

MSR $1,145	*N/A	$900	$775	$695	$565	$450	$350

Add $30 for left hand (Model 8L).

* ***Model 8H Carbine*** – .223 Rem. cal., 16 in. chrome lined barrel, A3 forged aluminum upper, right or left hand safety, six position collapsible stock, flip up rear sight. New 2011.

MSR $869	*N/A	$650	$600	$550	$450	$360	$275

Add $20 for left hand (Model 8HL).

STAGGS-BILT

Previous manufacturer located in Phoenix, AZ circa 1970.

Staggs-Bilt manufactured a lever action combination gun, in addition to other firearms for Hunter Arms and several other gun companies. Approx. 2,000 combination lever action guns were manufactured with the Staggs-Bilt name, mostly in 20 ga./.30-30 Win. cal., with uncheckered straight grip walnut stock with recoil pad, DT, and iron sights.

Current values on this gun are in the $500-$750 range, depending on condition.

STALLARD ARMS

Current manufacturer of 9mm Para. pistols located in Mansfield, OH since 1991. Distributed by MKS Supply, Inc. located in Dayton, OH.

Please refer to the Hi-Point listing in the H section.

STANDARD ARMS & STANDARD ARMS MFG. CO.

Previous manufacturer that started production in Wilmington, DE, in Sept., 1909, and closed in 1912. The company was restarted in 1913 as Standard Arms Mfg. Co., and closed in April, 1914.

Nearly 5,000 rifles were manufactured at the actual factory. At the time the plant closed, approx. 2,200 rifles were in various stages of production, and a supply of parts remained. These were primarily purchased by Numrich Arms, made into complete rifles, and sold. Total production (Standard Arms, Standard Arms Mfg. Co. & those assembled by Numrich Arms) reached approx. 7,000 rifles. The highest known serial number is

GRADING - PPGS™	100%	98%	95%	90%	80%	70%	60%	LAST MSR

9012. Within serialization, large blocks of numbers were abandoned, and this is thought to be due to changes and improvements made during production. In addition, as the factory closed with a large number of rifles in partial stages of production, it is often not possible to determine which rifles were actually made and completed at the factory, and which were completed outside the factory at a later date.

Many special order options were available, such as checkering, pistol grip, deluxe grades of woods, special sights, etc. Several grades of engraving were available, including Rocky Mountain, Adirondack, Sierra, and Selkirk. Lower priced "etched" models were also available and less frequently encountered than engraved models. A .50 caliber "Camp Carbine" was offered in smooth bore, slide action only. Approx. 25-30 were manufactured and utilized a special cartridge similar to the .50-70 shot cartridge. These are rarely encountered, although they are known to exist in collections.

RIFLES: SEMI-AUTO

MODEL G AUTOLOADER – .25 Rem., .30 Rem., .32 Rem. (scarce), or .35 Rem. cal., bottom loading box mag., 22 in. barrel, open sight, straight stock. This was the first gas operated rifle in the U.S.A. Gas port can be closed and gun will function as a slide action. Approx. 7,000 mfg. 1910.

	$2,000	$1,800	$1,500	$1,250	$1,000	$800	$650	

Add substantial premiums for higher grade examples.
Subtract 10% for slide action only (Model M).

STANDARD ARMS OF NEVADA, INC.

Previous manufacturer 1999-2000, and located in Reno, NV.

PISTOLS: SEMI-AUTO

SA-9 – 9mm Para. cal., double action only, sub-compact design, 10 shot mag., 3.1 in. barrel, black polymer frame with matte black steel slide, 14 oz. Mfg. 1999-2000.

	$220	$190	$175	$165	$150	$140	$130	*$249*

STANDARD 380 – while advertised, this model never went into production. MSR was $176.

STANDARD MANUFACTURING CO. LLC

Current manufacturer located in Newington, CT. Dealer and consumer direct sales through FFL dealer.

RIFLES: SEMI-AUTO

MODEL M1927 .22 CAL. – .22 LR cal., semi-auto, half scale replica patterned after the Thompson Model 1927, thin barrel, 10 shot (standard) or optional aluminum drum magazine, high gloss blue, deluxe walnut stock, pistol grip, and forearm, 5 1/2 lbs. New 2012.

MSR $1,299	$1,195	$1,050	$900	$825	$750	$675	$595	

STANDARD PRODUCTS CO.

Previous WWII subcontractor of M1 carbines located in Port Clinton, OH.

Please refer to US Military carbines/rifles listing for more information.

STAR, BONIFACIO ECHEVERRIA S.A.

Previous manufacturer located in Eibar, Spain. Star, Bonifacio Echeverria S.A. closed its doors on July 28th, 1997, due to the intense financial pressure the Spanish arms industry experienced during the late 1990s. Previously imported by Interarms, located in Alexandria, VA.

PISTOLS: SEMI-AUTO

MODEL H – similar to Model HN, except 7.65mm, 7 shot.

	$350	$305	$265	$240	$195	$160	$125	

GRADING - PPGS™	100%	98%	95%	90%	80%	70%	60%	LAST MSR

MODEL HN – .380 ACP cal., 6 shot, 2 3/4 in. barrel, blue, fixed sights, plastic grips. Mfg. 1934-41.

	$375	$330	$280	$255	$205	$170	$130

MODEL I – .32 ACP cal., 9 shot, 4 3/4 in. barrel, blue, fixed sights, plastic grips. Mfg. 1934-36.

	$350	$305	$265	$240	$195	$160	$125

MODEL IN – similar to Model I, except .380 ACP, 8 shot, 4 3/4 in. barrel, blue.

	$395	$345	$295	$270	$215	$180	$140

MODEL 1920 – 9mm Bergmann Bayard or .38 Super cal., easily identified by unusual safety located on left rear slide. Issued to Spanish Guardia Civil.

	$650	$570	$490	$440	$360	$295	$230

MODEL 1921 – 9mm Bergmann Bayard cal., this model was fitted with a grip safety that was later dropped when standardizing the Model A production. Issued to Spanish Guardia Civil.

	$700	$615	$525	$475	$385	$315	$245

MODEL 1922 – designation for the early Model A. Issued to Spanish Guardia Civil.

	$550	$480	$415	$375	$305	$250	$195

MODEL A – .38 Super cal., modified Government Colt, 5 in. barrel, no grip safety, blue, checkered wood grips. Mfg. 1934-disc.

	$350	$300	$250	$225	$200	$180	$160

Add 50% for Spanish Air Force issue if in original box.

MODEL A CARBINE – usually 7.63mm cal., unusual variation, slotted with tangent rear sight and extended barrel.

	$3,500	$3,000	$2,500	$2,250	$2,000	$1,750	$1,500

Add $500 for original stock (different from MB and MMS stock).

MODEL B – similar to Model A, but 9mm Para. cal. Mfg. 1934-1975.

	$475	$395	$340	$305	$250	$205	$160

Add 50% for post-war German police if with 2 matching magazines.
Add 200% if Waffenamt proofed (WaA251).

MODEL BS – 9mm Para. cal., similar to Model B. 83,129 mfg. 1968-1994.

	$350	$305	$265	$240	$200	$180	$160

MODEL M – similar to Model A, except has large frame, available in 9mm Bergmann Bayard, 9mm Para., 8 shot, and .45 ACP, 7 shot, 5 in. barrel, blue, fixed sights, checkered wood or plastic grips.

	$400	$350	$300	$250	$225	$200	$175

Add 100% for early variation with ser. no. under 4,835.

MODEL P – .45 ACP cal. only, similar to Model A, except has large frame, 7 shot mag. Mfg. 1934-1975.

	$450	$400	$325	$295	$225	$200	$175

Add 100% for early variation with ser. no. under 5,112.

MODELS SUPER A (9mm Largo), M (9mm Largo), & P (.45 ACP) – similar to Models A, M, & P, except has loaded chamber indicator, mag. safety, and easier takedown feature. Mfg. 1946-89.

	$395	$345	$295	$270	$215	$180	$140	
Super M	$850	$750	$700	$600	$550	$450	$350	
Super P	$1,000	$850	$750	$650	$550	$450	$350	*$340*

The Super A was a Spanish Service pistol. Recent imports in 80% condition were available in the $150 range.

GRADING - PPGS™	100%	98%	95%	90%	80%	70%	60%	LAST MSR

MODEL SUPER B – 9mm Para. cal., similar to Model B, except has loaded chamber indicator, mag. safety and easier takedown feature, choice of blue or Starvel finish on Model B, late production models are poorly polished and have parkerized small parts. Importation disc. in 1990.

	$350	$305	$265	$240	$200	$180	$160	*$330*

Add $30 for Starvel finish.
Add 100% for Early guns.

SUPER TARGET MODEL – similar to Star Super, but target sights, extended trigger guard, modified trigger. Rare.

	$1,750	$1,500	$1,250	$1,100	$950	$850	$750

MODEL MB – 9mm Para. cal., late production Model M cut for shoulder stock, mag. safety.

	$2,500	$2,250	$1,950	$1,725	$1,500	$1,200	$900

Add $450 for shoulder stock.
Add 20% to rig if matching stock.

MODEL MMS – 7.63mm cal., late production Model M cut for shoulder stock, mag. safety.

	$2,250	$1,950	$1,725	$1,500	$1,200	$900	$600

Add $450 for shoulder stock.
Add 20% to rig for matching stock.

MODEL SI – .32 ACP cal., 8 shot, 4 in. barrel, blue, without grip safety, small version of Government .45 in appearance, plastic grips. Mfg. 1941-1965.

	$300	$265	$225	$205	$165	$135	$105

MODEL S – similar to Model SI, except .380 ACP cal., 9 shot, mfg. 1941-1965. Importation of these Police contract models was disc. 1991.

	$300	$260	$225	$195	$160	$135	$100	*$237*

Add $30 for Starvel finish.
Add 100% for guns issued to the Spanish Air Force with original box and 2 matching mags.
Add $3,000 for gold damascene finish, if in 98%+ condition.

In 1989, Interarms imported factory reconditioned used Spanish Police Contract Model S pistols - these guns were available in either blue or Starvel finish and were supplied with a plastic box with accessories.

MODELS SUPER SI AND S – similar to Model S, with Super Star improvements. Mfg. 1946-1972.

	$275	$240	$205	$185	$150	$125	$95

MODEL SUPER SM – similar to Model Super S, except adjustable sight and wood grips. Mfg. 1973-81.

	$375	$325	$275	$240	$195	$160	$125

MODEL CO POCKET – .25 Auto cal., 2 3/4 in. barrel, blue, fixed sights, plastic grips. Mfg. 1929-56.

	$300	$250	$200	$185	$150	$125	$95

MODEL CU STARLET – .25 Auto cal., 2 3/8 in. barrel, alloy frame, fixed sights, plastic grips, blue, or chrome slide, frame anodized in black, blue, green, grey, or gold. Mfg. 1957-72.

	$250	$220	$190	$170	$140	$115	$90

Minor changes prompted a model redesignation as CK during 1973.

MODEL D – .380 ACP cal., small steel frame version of the Model A with several minor variations, 40,416 mfg. 1922-47.

	$550	$475	$400	$350	$300	$250	$200

MODEL DK (STARFIRE) – .380 ACP cal., 3 1/8 in. barrel, fixed sights, plastic stocks, finished in same color availability as Model CU. Mfg. 1957-1972, U.S. import ceased as of 1968 due to Federal GCA legislation.

	$400	$350	$295	$255	$225	$180	$155

Add 30% for unusual alloy colors.

Minor changes prompted a redesignation as DKL (.380 ACP) 1972 and DKI (.32 ACP) 1972.

GRADING - PPGS™	100%	98%	95%	90%	80%	70%	60%	LAST MSR

MODEL HK LANCER – similar to Model Starfire, except .22 LR cal. Mfg. 1955-68.

	$275	$240	$205	$185	$150	$125	$95	

MODEL F – .22 LR cal., 10 shot, 4 in. barrel, fixed sights, blue, plastic grips. Mfg. 1942-67.

	$325	$285	$245	$220	$180	$145	$115	

MODEL FS – similar to Model F, except 6 in. barrel, adj. sights. Mfg. 1942-67.

	$325	$285	$245	$220	$180	$145	$115	

MODEL F OLYMPIC RAPID FIRE – .22 Short cal., 9 shot, 7 in. barrel, adj. sight, aluminum slide, barrel weights and muzzle brake, blue, plastic grips. Mfg. 1942-67.

	$650	$550	$450	$400	$350	$300	$250	

MODEL FR – restyled Model F, with "squared" barrel, adj. sight and slide stop. Mfg. 1967-72.

	$325	$285	$245	$220	$180	$145	$115	

Add 15% for chrome finish.

MODELS FR SPORT AND MODEL FR TARGET – similar to Model FR, except FR Sport has 150mm barrel, and the Model FR Target has 180mm barrel, 65,534 mfg. 1967-83.

	$350	$305	$265	$240	$195	$160	$125	

Add 15% for chrome finish.

MODEL FM – similar to Model FR, except heavier frame, web ahead of trigger guard, 4 1/2 in. barrel. 8,799 mfg. 1972-83.

	$325	$285	$245	$220	$180	$145	$115	

MODEL BKS STARLIGHT – 9mm Para. cal., 8 shot, 4 1/4 in. barrel, plastic grips. Mfg. 1970-1981.

Blue	$350	$305	$265	$240	$195	$160	$125	

Add 10% for chrome finish.

MODEL BM – 9mm Para. cal., single action, 8 shot mag., 4 in. barrel, steel frame, Colt 1911 action, blue, chrome (disc. 1989), or Starvel (new 1990) finish, plastic grips, 35 oz. Importation disc. 1991.

	$325	$285	$245	$220	$180	$145	$115	*$415*

Add $30 for Starvel or chrome (disc. 1990) finish.
Add 150% for Navy issue with escutcheon grips.

MODEL BKM – identical to Model BM, except lightweight duraluminum frame, blue finish only, 26 oz. Importation disc. 1991.

	$350	$305	$265	$240	$195	$160	$125	*$415*

MODEL PD – .45 ACP cal., 6 shot mag., single action, 4 in. barrel, adj. rear sight, blue or Starvel (new 1990) finish only, walnut grips, alloy frame, 25 oz. Mfg. 1975-importation disc. 1991.

	$400	$350	$300	$250	$225	$200	$175	*$475*

Add $20 for Starvel finish (new 1990).
Add 20% for late variation with 30M rear sight.

MODEL 28 – 9mm Para. cal., double action, 15 shot mag., 4 1/4 in. barrel, blue finish only, advanced design, 40 oz. Mfg. 1983 and 1984 only.

	$450	$400	$350	$300	$250	$200	$150	

Note: Model 28 is interesting since no screws were used in its manufacture. Hammer assembly (including spring, cocking lever, sear, disconnector and ejector) is housed under removable backstrap.

MODEL 30M – 9mm Para. cal. only, successor to the Model 28, double action, 4.33 in. barrel, 15 shot mag., blue finish only, adj. rear sight, checkered wraparound plastic grips, steel frame, 40 oz. New 1985. Importation disc. 1991.

	$400	$350	$300	$250	$200	$175	$150	*$495*

GRADING - PPGS™	100%	98%	95%	90%	80%	70%	60%	LAST MSR

MODEL 30 PK DURAL FRAME – similar to Model 30M, except slightly shorter duraluminum frame, 3.86 in. barrel, 30 oz. Disc. 1989.

$425	$375	$325	$275	$225	$175	$150	*$580*

MODEL 31P (STEEL FRAME)/31PK (DURAL FRAME) – 9mm Para. (disc. 1993) or .40 S&W (new 1990) cal., compact variation utilizing double action, features Acculine barrel (3.86 in.), 14 shot mag., ambidextrous safety with decocking lever, blue or Starvel finish, all steel construction, 39.4 oz. Imported 1990-94.

$400	$350	$300	$250	$200	$175	$150	*$398*

Add $30 for Starvel finish (disc. 1993).

Prices are the same for Model 31PK Dural Frame (imported 1990-93).

MODEL M40 FIRESTAR – .40 S&W cal., single action, 6 shot mag., 3.39 in. Acculine barrel, checkered rubber grips, compact design utilizing all steel construction, 3-dot sighting system with adjustable rear sight, blue, Starvel, or nickel (new 1997) finish, 30.35 oz. Mfg. 1990-disc.

$325	$285	$245	$220	$180	$145	$115	*$306*

Add $17 for nickel finish.
Add $20 for Starvel finish.

* ***Model M40 Firestar Plus*** – similar to M40 Firestar, except incorporates alloy frame, new grip design, ambidextrous easy-view safety, and fast button release 10 shot mag. Advertised initially during 1995.

This model was never released for commercial sale.

MODEL M43 FIRESTAR – 9mm Para. cal., 7 shot mag., otherwise similar to Model M40 Firestar. Disc.

$325	$285	$245	$220	$180	$145	$115	*$296*

Add $17 for nickel finish.
Add $20 for Starvel finish.

* ***Model M43 Firestar Plus*** – similar to M43 Firestar, except incorporates alloy frame, new grip design, ambidextrous easy-view safety, and fast button release 10 shot double stack mag. Mfg. 1995-97.

$325	$285	$245	$220	$180	$145	$115	*$351*

Add $12 for nickel finish.
Add $25 for Starvel finish.

MODEL M45 FIRESTAR – .45 ACP cal., single action, ultra compact design featuring 4 barrel lugs, steel frame and slide, 3.6 in. reverse taper Acculine barrel, 6 shot mag., black synthetic grips, blue or Starvel finish, 35 oz. Mfg. 1992-97.

$350	$305	$265	$240	$195	$160	$125	*$351*

Add $12 for nickel finish.
Add $20 for Starvel finish.

* ***Model M45 Firestar Plus*** – similar to M45 Firestar, except incorporates alloy frame, new grip design, ambidextrous easy-view safety, and fast button release 10 shot mag. Advertised during 1995.

This model was never released for commercial sale.

MEGASTAR – 10mm or .45 ACP cal., larger variation of the Firestar featuring 4.6 in. barrel and 12 (.45 ACP) or 14 (10mm) shot mag., 47.6 oz. Imported 1992-94.

$450	$395	$340	$305	$250	$205	$160	*$653*

Add $29 for Starvel finish.

ULTRASTAR – 9mm Para. or .40 S&W (new 1996) cal., compact double action design, 3.57 in. barrel, 9 shot mag., blue steel metal, triple dot sights, steel internal mechanism, polymer exterior construction, 26 oz. Mfg. 1994-97.

$350	$300	$250	$225	$180	$145	$115	*$296*

GRADING - PPGS™	100%	98%	95%	90%	80%	70%	60%	LAST MSR

STEEL CITY ARMS, INC.

Previous manufacturer located in Pittsburgh, PA until 1990. In 1991, the name was changed to Desert Industries, Inc. and manufacture was moved to Las Vegas, NV. Very few guns exist with Steel City markings.

PISTOLS: SEMI-AUTO

DOUBLE DEUCE – .22 LR cal. only, double action, matte finish stainless steel, 2 1/2 in. barrel, 7 shot mag., uncheckered rosewood grips, 18 oz. Mfg. 1984-90.

	100%	98%	95%	90%	80%	70%	60%	LAST MSR
	$265	$230	$200	N/A	N/A	N/A	N/A	*$290*

Various select hardwood stocks were also available at extra cost ($20-100).

STEINKAMP MASCHINENBAU GmbH & Co. KG

Current long gun manufacturer located in Espelkamp, Germany. No current U.S. importation.

LONG GUNS

STEINKAMP SW1 – various cals./gauges, configurations include: standard double rifle version in 8x57R cal., also available as a combination gun with either 20 ga. or .410 bore with 3 in. chamber and rifle calibers, including 5.6x50R Mag., 7x65R, 8x57R, or 9.3x74R, or an O/U shotgun, 24 in. barrels, bullpup with pistol grip styling, choice of plastic or wood, hinged buttplate opened by trigger guard mechanism allows access to chambers, falling block action, extractor or ejector, non-selective single trigger, manual cocking, Picatinny rail, designed by A. Görzen, overall length of 26 3/4 in., 7 1/2 lbs. New 2007.

Base price on this model is €3,495.

STEERING GEAR (GRAND RAPIDS & SAGINAW LOCATIONS)

Previous WWII subcontractor of M1 carbines located in Saginaw and Grand Rapids, MI. Saginaw Steering Gear was a division of General Motors Corp.

Please refer to US Military carbines/rifles listing for more information.

STERLING

Previous manufacturer located in Gasport and Lockport (1978-1986), NY until 1986.

PISTOLS

Rather than list individual models, the following generalizations will help in ascertaining values for this trademark. Models 300, 302 and 402 will average between $75 and $150 if in 70%+ condition, Models 283, 284, 285 (Husky), and 286 (Trapper) are semi-auto .22 cal. pistols with various barrel lengths - values will range between $90-$150. Models 400 (.380 ACP), PPL (.380 ACP short barrel), and 450 (.45 ACP, prototype only - no mfg.) usually range between $150-$275.

STERLING ARMAMENT, LTD.

Previous manufacturer established c. 1900, and located in Dagenham, Essex, England. Previously imported and distributed by Cassi Inc. located in Colorado Springs, CO until 1990.

CARBINES: SEMI-AUTO

AR-180 – please refer to Armalite section for more information and pricing on this model.

STERLING MK 6 – 9mm Para. cal., blowback semi-auto with floating firing pin, shrouded 16.1 in. barrel, side mounted mag., folding stock, 7 1/2 lbs. Disc. 1989.

	100%	98%	95%	90%	80%	70%	60%	LAST MSR
	N/A	$1,750	$1,500	$1,400	$1,200	$1,000	$795	*$650*

PISTOLS: SEMI-AUTO

PARAPISTOL MK 7 C4 – 9mm Para. cal., 4 in. barrel, semi-auto paramilitary design pistol, crinkle finish, same action as MK. 6 Carbine, fires from closed bolt, 10, 15, 20, 30, 34 or 68 shot mag., 5 lbs. Disc. 1989.

	100%	98%	95%	90%	80%	70%	60%	LAST MSR
	N/A	$1,500	$1,400	$1,200	$1,000	$800	$700	*$600*

Add $50 per 30 or 34 shot mag., $125 for 68 shot mag.

GRADING - PPGS™	100%	98%	95%	90%	80%	70%	60%	LAST MSR

PARAPISTOL MK 7 C8 – 9mm Para. cal., similar to C4, except has 7.8 in. barrel, 5 1/4 lbs. Disc. 1989.

	N/A	$1,500	$1,400	$1,250	$1,050	$900	$750	*$620*

Add $50 per 30 or 34 shot mag., $125 for 68 shot mag.

STEVENS, J., ARMS COMPANY

Current trademark of long arms produced by Savage Arms, Inc. Beginning in 1999, Savage Arms, Inc. began manufacturing/importing Stevens trademarked guns again, including rifles and shotguns. J. Stevens Arms Company was founded in 1864 at Chicopee Falls, MA as J. Stevens & Co. In 1886 the name was changed to J. Stevens Arms and Tool Co. In 1916, the plant became New England Westinghouse, and tooled up for Mosin-Nagant Rifles. In 1920, the plant was sold to the Savage Arms Corp. and manufactured guns were marked "J. Stevens Arms Co." This designation was dropped in the late 1940s, and only the name "Stevens" has been used up to 1990.

Depending on the remaining Stevens factory data, a factory letter authenticating the configuration of a particular specimen may be obtained by contacting Mr. John Callahan (see Trademark Index for listings and address). The charge for this service is $25.00 per gun - please allow 8 weeks for an adequate response.

For more Stevens model information, please refer to the Serialization section in the back of this text.

COMBINATION GUNS

MODEL 22-410 – .22 LR cal. over .410 bore, selector on right side of frame, Tenite stock. Introduced mid-1939-disc.

$425	$375	$300	$250	$200	$165	$140

PISTOLS

NO. 10 TARGET SINGLE SHOT – .22 LR cal., 8 in. barrel, blue, adj. sights, rubber grips, squared-off like an automatic pistol, tip up action. Mfg. 1919-39.

$220	$200	$185	$165	$140	$120	$100

NO. 35 TARGET SINGLE SHOT – .22 LR or .25 Rimfire cal., 6, 8, 10, or 12 1/4 in. barrel, blue, walnut grips. Mfg. 1907-39.

$350	$300	$265	$220	$200	$185	$165

NO. 35 "OFF-HAND" SHOTGUN – .410 smoothbore cal., 8 or 12 1/4 in. barrel. Mfg. 1923-35.

$350	$300	$250	$225	$200	$150	$125

If this model is not currently registered with the BATFE, it cannot be legally owned, and is subject to seizure.

NO. 35 "OFF-HAND" AUTOSHOT – similar to Off-Hand Shotgun. Mfg. 1929-34.

$300	$250	$225	$200	$150	$125	$100

RIFLES

Stevens made a wide variety of inexpensive, utilitarian rifles that, to date, have attracted mostly shooting interest, but little collector interest. A listing of these models may be found in the back of this text under "Serialization."

TIP-UP RIFLES – .22 S, .22 LR, .25 Stevens, .32, .38, or .44 Long RF or CF, variations No. 1 - No. 15 feature various weights, wood styles, sights, and other differences, later series has full loop at rear trigger guard, circa 1870s-1895.

* ***Tip-Up Rifle Basic Model No. 1 without forearm***

$500	$475	$425	$375	$300	$250	$200

* ***Tip-Up Rifle Model 101*** – .44 shot cartridge, built on the No. 12 Marksman action, lever action opening, straight grip stock, 26 in. barrel. Mfg. 1914-20.

$250	$225	$195	$175	$150	$125	$100

GRADING - PPGS™	100%	98%	95%	90%	80%	70%	60%	LAST MSR

NO. 12 MARKSMAN – .22 LR, .25 Long or .32 rimfire cal., boys type single shot with traditional Stevens profile, operated with underlever that allows barrel to tip up for loading, 22 in. round tapered barrel, walnut stock and forend, silver blade front sight and "V" block rear sight, knurled thumbscrew for take-down. Mfg. 1912-1933.

	$425	$350	$275	$240	$215	$185	$160	

NO. 14 1/2 LITTLE SCOUT – .22 RF cal., 18 or 20 in. barrel, rolling breech block action, iron sights. Mfg. 1909-36.

	$425	$350	$275	$240	$215	$185	$160	

STEVENS/SPRINGFIELD MODEL 15/120 – .22 S, L, or LR, bolt action single shot, one piece integral barrel and receiver, manually operated cocking piece at rear of bolt, birch hardwood stock, open rear and bead front sight, thousands mfg. for companies such as Sears, Montgomery Wards, J.C. Penny, Cotter & Co., etc. Mfg. 1936-1971.

	$200	$185	$165	$135	$115	$95	$80	

POCKET RIFLES – detachable serially numbered nickel-plated stock, variations found within each frame size.

* ***Pocket Rifle Small Frame*** – .22 cal. (various issues).

	$450	$400	$350	$300	$275	$235	$200	

* ***Pocket Rifle Small Frame Without Stock***

	$300	$250	$200	$150	$125	$100	$80	

* ***Pocket Rifle Medium Frame*** – .22, .32, .38, .44 cals. (various issues).

	$500	$450	$400	$350	$300	$250	$200	

* ***Pocket Rifle Medium Frame Without Stock***

	$300	$250	$200	$150	$125	$100	$75	

* ***Pocket Rifle Large Frame*** – .22 to .44 cals.

	$600	$550	$500	$450	$400	$350	$300	

* ***Pocket Rifle Large Frame Without Stock***

	$425	$375	$325	$275	$225	$200	$175	

MODEL 44 IDEAL SINGLE SHOT – .22 LR through .44-40 WCF cals., rolling block, lever action, takedown, 24 or 26 in. barrels, straight grip stock and forearm. Mfg. 1894-1932.

	$650	$600	$550	$500	$425	$325	$300	

Subtract 20% for Rimfire cals.

MODEL 44 1/2 IDEAL SINGLE SHOT – similar to Model 44, except .22 LR through .44-40 WCF cals., falling block, lever action, takedown, 24 or 26 in. barrels, straight grip stock and forearm, action redesigned 1903. Mfg. 1903-16.

	$950	$850	$750	$625	$500	$425	$350	

Subtract 10% for rimfire cals.

MODELS 45-54 SINGLE SHOTS – .22 LR through .44-40 WCF cals., rolling and falling block receivers, lever action, takedown, deluxe versions of the Models 44 and 44 1/2, many special order features, including double-set triggers, types of finish, engraving, length and weight of barrels, stock configuration could be special ordered. Mfg. 1896-1916.

The higher grade Schuetzens and Stevens-Pope are very collectible. These models have to be appraised individually when determining value.

MODEL 200 BOLT ACTION – .22-250 Rem., .223 Rem., .243 Win., .25-06 Rem. (disc. 2011), .270 Win., .30-06, .308 Win., .300 Win. Mag., 7mm-08 Rem. (disc. 2011) or 7mm Rem. Mag. cal., short or long action, no sights, 3 or 4 shot internal mag., AccuTrigger not available on this model, 22 or 24 in. barrel, checkered synthetic stock and forend with pillar bedding, with or w/o camo (select cals. only, disc. 2011), Stevens laser etched on bolt, 6 1/2 lbs. New 2005.

MSR $420	$365	$325	$280	$240	$210	$190	$170	

Add $42 for camo (disc. 2011).
Add $50 for scope package that includes 3-9x40mm scope (mfg. 2010-2011).

GRADING - PPGS™	100%	98%	95%	90%	80%	70%	60%	LAST MSR

MODEL 300 BOLT ACTION – .22 LR cal., 20 3/4 in. barrel, AccuTrigger not available, 10 shot detachable mag., grey checkered synthetic stock, adj. rear sight, swivel studs, approx. 5 lbs. New 2006.

MSR $205	$175	$155	$130	$110	$90	$80	$70	

Add $11 for 4x15mm scope (disc. 2012).

MODEL 305 BOLT ACTION – .22 WMR cal., similar to Model 300 bolt action, except has 5 shot detachable box mag. New 2006.

MSR $230	$190	$165	$135	$115	$95	$85	$75	

MODEL 310 BOLT ACTION – .17 HMR cal., similar to Model 305 bolt action, except has 21 in. standard or heavy barrel w/o sights. New 2006.

MSR $245	$200	$175	$140	$120	$95	$85	$75	

Add $31 for heavy barrel (disc. 2008).

MODEL 315 BOLT ACTION YOUTH – .22 LR cal., single shot, uncheckered hardwood stock, shortened Youth dimensions, 19 in. barrel, 5 lbs. Mfg. 2006-2011.

	$175	$135	$100	$85	$75	$55	$45	*$218*

CADET BOLT ACTION – .22 LR cal., does not have AccuTrigger, single shot mini-Youth Model with 16 in. barrel, shortened hardwood stock, fixed sights w/rear aperture sight, 4 1/2 lbs. Mfg. 2006-2011.

	$165	$135	$100	$85	$75	$65	$60	*$211*

MODEL 322 BOLT ACTION (INCLUDING A, B, C, & S) – .22 Hornet cal., otherwise similar to Model 325. Mfg. 1947-50.

	$450	$395	$335	$275	$225	$185	$150	

The Model 322S had an aperture sight.

MODEL 325 BOLT ACTION (INCLUDING A, B, C) – .30-30 Win. cal., 4 shot detachable mag. Introduced 1947. Disc. 1950.

	$375	$335	$275	$225	$185	$150	$135	

NO. 414 ARMORY MODEL – .22 LR or .22 Short cal. only, lever action, 26 in. barrel, single shot, Lyman aperture sight. Mfg. 1912-32.

	$450	$400	$375	$330	$290	$250	$220	

MODEL 416 – .22 LR cal., bolt action, 25 in. medium barrel, 5 shot mag. Disc.

	$140	$120	$110	$100	$90	$80	$70	

This model was also mfg. as a U.S. military training rifle. Can be denoted by "U.S. Property" on rear of bolt housing. Healthy premiums exist for this variation. Originally, 10,000 were mfg. at a cost of $22.42 each.

NO. 417 WALNUT HILL MODEL – .22 LR, .22 Short, and .22 Hornet cal., lever action, 28 or 29 in. extra heavy barrel, target stock with full pistol grip, beavertail forend, made in 0-3 suffix variations (different sights). Mfg. 1932-47.

	$875	$675	$525	$475	$440	$395	$360	

NO. 417 1/2 WALNUT HILL MODEL – similar to No. 417, except available in .25 rimfire also. Mfg. 1932-40.

	$875	$675	$525	$475	$440	$395	$360	

NO. 418 WALNUT HILL MODEL – .22 LR or .22 Short only, 26 in. barrel, pistol grip stock, semi beavertail forearm. Mfg. 1932-40.

	$950	$825	$700	$600	$500	$400	$360	

NO. 425 HIGH POWER LEVER ACTION RIFLE – .25, .30, .32, or .35 Rem. cals., 22 in. round barrel with 2/3 length mag. tube, side ejection, blue only, plain walnut stock and forearm, originally designed by John Redfield. Approx. 26,000 mfg. 1910-17.

	$1,850	$1,700	$1,500	$1,250	$1,000	$850	$700	

Variations of the No. 425 included the No. 430 (deluxe checkered stock and forearm), No. 435 (extra fancy checkered stock and forearm with engraved designs on receiver borders

GRADING - PPGS™	100%	98%	95%	90%	80%	70%	60%	LAST MSR

and lever), or No. 440 (best quality checkered walnut with fully engraved game scenes, and engraved forearm tip and lever). Values range respectively from $450-$950, $650-$1,400, and $1,000-$2,950.

NO. 430 HIGH POWER LEVER ACTION RIFLE – upgraded variation of the No. 425, deluxe checkered stock and forearm.

	100%	98%	95%	90%	80%	70%	60%	LAST MSR
	$4,000	$3,500	$3,000	$2,500	$2,000	$1,700	$1,400	

NO. 435 HIGH POWER LEVER ACTION RIFLE – upgraded variation of the No. 425, extra fancy checkered stock and forearm, with engraved designs on receiver border and lever.

	100%	98%	95%	90%	80%	70%	60%	LAST MSR
	$8,000	$6,500	$5,500	$4,500	$3,500	$3,000	$2,500	

NO. 440 HIGH POWER LEVER ACTION RIFLE – upgraded variation of the No. 425, best quality checkered walnut stock and forearm, with fully engraved game scenes and engraved forearm tip.

	100%	98%	95%	90%	80%	70%	60%	LAST MSR
	$10,000	$8,500	$7,000	$6,000	$5,000	$4,500	$4,000	

STEVENS FAVORITE NO.'S 17-29 – .22 LR, .25 RF or .32 RF cal., 24 in. barrel most common, other lengths available, Rocky Mountain front sight, straight grip stock, small tapered forearm. Mfg. 1894-1935.

	100%	98%	95%	90%	80%	70%	60%	LAST MSR
	$450	$395	$300	$195	$165	$145	$125	

Add 35% for octagon barrels.

MODEL 1915 FAVORITE – .22 LR, .22 WRF (special order option), .25, or .32 cal., redesign of original Steven's Favorite, action slightly heavier and stronger, blue takedown frame, walnut stock and forearm, other internal changes, similar outward appearance, marked "SVG" after 1920, offered as the No. 27 with full octagon barrel, the No. 17 with round barrel, and the No. 20 with smooth bore barrel, 4 1/2 lbs. Mfg. 1915-1940.

	100%	98%	95%	90%	80%	70%	60%	LAST MSR
	$450	$395	$300	$195	$165	$145	$125	

STEVENS FAVORITE MODEL 30 (RECENT MFG.) – .17 HMR (Model 30R17, mfg. 2004-2005), .22 LR (Model 30G), or .22 WMR (Model GM, mfg. 2002-2005) cal., choice of solid or takedown (new 2004) action, lever action falling block with inertia firing pin, 20 in. round or 21 (disc.) in. half octagon (Model 30G) or full octagon (Model GM) barrel, uncheckered wood stock and forearm, open sights, 4 1/4 lbs. New mfg. began in late 1998 by Savage Arms, Inc., limited availability 2007-2012.

	100%	98%	95%	90%	80%	70%	60%	LAST MSR
	$315	$245	$220	$195	$170	$155	$130	*$379*

Add $38 for .22 WMR cal. (mfg. 2002-2005).
Add $64 for .17 HMR cal. (mfg. 2004-2005).
Add $17 for takedown action (.22 LR or .17 HMR cal. only, TD Model).

STEVENS MODEL 65 – .22 LR cal., bolt action, 20 in. barrel, open sights, 5 shot mag., checkered walnut stock. Mfg. 1969-disc.

	100%	98%	95%	90%	80%	70%	60%	LAST MSR
	$90	$70	$55	$45	$35	$30	$30	

NO. 70 "VISIBLE LOADING" SLIDE ACTION RIFLE – .22 S, L, or LR cal., exposed hammer, 22 in. barrel, open sights, straight grip stock, tube mag., grooved slide handle. Other variations with different barrel lengths and sights will command slight premiums.

	100%	98%	95%	90%	80%	70%	60%	LAST MSR
	$550	$475	$400	$350	$300	$250	$200	

MODEL 71 "STEVENS FAVORITE" COMMEMORATIVE – .22 LR cal., replica of original, 22 in. octagon barrel, plain straight stock, medallion inlaid, crescent butt. 1,000 mfg. in 1971.

	100%	98%	95%	90%	80%	70%	60%	LAST MSR
	$250	$195	$150	N/A	N/A	N/A	N/A	*$75*

SIDE LEVER CRACKSHOT – .22 RF or .32 RF cal., boys type single shot rifle, breech block is operated by a small lever on the side of the frame, side lever opening, 20 in. round barrel with fixed sights. Mfg. 1900-1913.

	100%	98%	95%	90%	80%	70%	60%	LAST MSR
	$295	$235	$195	$150	$100	$60	$50	

NO. 20 FAVORITE – .22 RF or .32 RF smooth bore, 24 in. barrel, smooth bore variation of the No. 17 rifle.

	100%	98%	95%	90%	80%	70%	60%	LAST MSR
	$250	$225	$200	$165	$125	$95	$75	

GRADING - PPGS™	100%	98%	95%	90%	80%	70%	60%	LAST MSR

NO. 26 CRACKSHOT – .22 RF or .32 RF cal., boys type single shot rifle, under lever opening, 18 in. round barrel, hardwood straight grip stock and forend, open sights. Mfg. 1913-41.

	$295	$235	$195	$150	$100	$60	$50	

NO. 26 1/2 CRACKSHOT – .22 RF or .32 RF shotshell, smooth bore variation of the No. 26 rifle.

	$225	$200	$175	$135	$110	$85	$65	

MODEL 72 CRACKSHOT – .22 LR cal., single shot falling block action, 22 in. octagon barrel, open sights, color case hardened frame, straight stock. Mfg. 1972-89.

	$145	$125	$110	$100	$90	$80	$70	*$165*

MODEL 74 – similar to Model 72 Crackshot, except has round barrel. Mfg. 1972-89.

	$140	$120	$110	$100	$90	$80	$70	*$165*

MODEL 987 – .22 LR cal. only, semi-auto, 15 shot tube mag., 20 in. barrel, hardwood Monte Carlo stock, adj. rear sight, 6 lbs. Disc. 1989.

	$95	$80	$70	$60	$50	$40	$45	*$119*

MODEL 83/083 BOLT ACTION – .22 S, L, LR, .22 WMR, or .25 Stevens rimfire cal., 24 in. round barrel, chrome bolt and trigger, walnut pistol grip stock, single shot, gold bead front and open rear sights (Model 83) or hooded front with interchangeable inserts and #105 rear aperture and folding middle sight (Model 083), 5 lbs. Mfg. 1935-1942.

	$175	$150	$125	$100	$85	$70	$60	

Add 15% for .22 WMR, or 30% for .25 Stevens cal.

MODEL 87 SEMI-AUTO – .22 LR cal., tube mag., round tapered barrel, over 1.8 million made in numerous variations, including the Model 6, 76, 87, 187, 188, 60, 90, 88, 388, 887 and many others under brand names for Sears, Montgomery Ward, Western Auto, CIL, Coast to Coast, etc., model numbers include letter suffix added as changes were made. Introduced in 1938, and continued through the early 1980s.

	$150	$130	$110	$90	$70	$60	$50	

MODEL 89 LEVER ACTION – .22 LR cal., single shot, 18 1/2 in. barrel, Martini type action, Western style lever, straight stock. Mfg. 1976-disc.

	$85	$65	$60	$50	$45	$40	$35	

SHOTGUNS

Stevens made a wide variety of inexpensive, utilitarian shotguns that, to date, have attracted mostly shooting interest, but little collector interest. A listing of these models may be found in the back of this text under "Serialization."

MODEL 67 SLIDE ACTION – 12, 20 ga., or .410 bore, 3 in. chamber, steel receiver, 5 shot, upper receiver safety, 6 1/4-7 1/2 lbs. Recent mfg. by Stevens. Disc. 1989.

	$200	$180	$170	$155	$145	$135	$125	*$229*

Add $30 for choke tubes (with VR).
Add $10 for VR only.

* ***Model 67 Slide Action VTR-K Camo*** – 12 or 20 ga., 28 in. VR barrel with choke tubes, laminated camo stock. Mfg. 1986-88.

	$250	$220	$190	$170	$155	$145	$135	*$295*

* ***Model 67 Slide Action Slug Model*** – 12 ga. only, 21 in. barrel, rifle sights. Disc. 1989.

	$200	$165	$140	$110	$100	$90	$80	*$245*

* ***Model 67 Slide Action VRT-Y*** – 20 ga. only, 22 in. VR barrel with choke tubes, youth model with smaller stock dimensions. Mfg. 1987-88.

	$205	$170	$140	$110	$100	$90	$80	*$259*

MODEL 69-RXL SLIDE ACTION – 12 ga. only, law enforcement version of the Model 67, 18 1/4 in. cylinder bore barrel with recoil pad, 6 1/2 lbs. Disc. 1989.

	$200	$165	$140	$110	$100	$90	$80	*$245*

GRADING - PPGS™	100%	98%	95%	90%	80%	70%	60%	LAST MSR

MODEL 77 SLIDE ACTION W/J, K, M, OR SC SUFFIX – 12 ("J" suffix), 16 ("K" suffix), or 20 ("M" suffix) ga. or .410 bore, "SC" designates Super Choke. Mfg. 1955-1971.

	$175	$160	$140	$120	$100	$80	$60	

MODEL 94 – 12, 16, 20, 28 ga., or .410 bore, single shot breakopen, hammer, 6 1/4 lbs. Mfg. 1929-disc.

	$95	$85	$75	$60	$50	$45	$40	*$92*

MODEL 124 BOLT ACTION – 12 ga. only, straight pull action, 28 in. barrel, 3 shot, Tenite buttstock and forearm, circa 1950.

	$215	$190	$175	$155	$145	$135	$125	

NO. 200 SLIDE ACTION – 20 ga., 3 in. chamber, tube mag., 26, 28, 30, or 32 in. barrel, take-down, 5 shot, 6 1/2 lbs., c. 1910.

	$225	$190	$180	$150	$125	$95	$85	

MODEL 240 O/U – .410 bore, split hammers, double trigger.

	$350	$300	$250	$220	$190	$170	$155	

MODEL 311 SxS – 12, 16, 20 ga., or .410 bore, 3 in. chambers, double triggers, extractors, VR. Disc. 1989.

	$275	$235	$200	$175	$160	$145	$130	*$309*

Add 30% for .410 bore.
Add 20% for 16 or 20 ga.
Add 200% for early models in .410 bore w/walnut stocks and case colors.

* ***Model 311-R SxS*** – 12 or 20 ga., similar to Model 311, except has 18 1/4 in. cylinder bore barrels for law enforcement use, 3 in. chambers, 6 3/4 lbs. Disc. 1989.

	$245	$205	$185	$150	$140	$125	$115	*$309*

MODEL 315 SxS – 12, 16, 20 ga., or .410 bore, DT, extractors, hammerless, case colored frame, walnut stock and forearm, model identification is on top lever, this model also was mfg. under various trade names, including Riverside and Springfield.

	$225	$185	$150	$140	$125	$115	$100	

MODEL 320 SLIDE ACTION FIELD – 12 ga., 3 in. chamber, side ejection, 28 in. VR barrel with fixed modified choke, matte black metal finish, black synthetic stock and forearm, approx. 7 1/2 lbs. New 2012.

MSR $265	$225	$195	$175	$155	$140	$120	$110	

Add $30 for combo model with extra 18 1/2 in. cyl. bore barrel.

MODEL 320 SLIDE ACTION SECURITY – 12 ga., 3 in. chamber, 18 1/2 in. cyl. bore barrel, side ejection, with or w/o pistol grip, bead, ghost ring, or rifle (mfg. 2012 only) sights, avail. with one piece rail and heat shield, matte black metal finish, black synthetic stock and forearm, approx. 7 lbs. New 2012.

MSR $245	$200	$175	$155	$135	$120	$110	$100	

Add $25 for ghost ring or rifle (mfg. 2012 only) sights.
Add $35 for one piece rail with heat shield.

MODEL 350 SLIDE ACTION FIELD – 12 ga., 28 in. barrel, 5 shot tube mag., bottom ejection, matte black synthetic stock, vent. rib, bead sights, 8.2 lbs. Mfg. mid-2010-2011.

	$250	$200	$175	$150	$135	$125	$115	*$294*

MODEL 350 SLIDE ACTION SECURITY – 12 ga., 18 1/4 in. barrel, 5 shot tube mag., bottom ejection, matte black synthetic pistol grip stock, bead (disc. 2012), ghost ring, or rifle (disc. 2012) sights, 7.6 lbs. New mid-2010.

MSR $285	$230	$195	$170	$150	$135	$125	$115	

* ***Model 350 Slide Action Security/Field Combo*** – 12 ga., includes both 18 1/4 and 28 in. barrels. Mfg. mid-2010-2011.

	$275	$235	$200	$185	$170	$160	$150	*$339*

GRADING - PPGS™	100%	98%	95%	90%	80%	70%	60%	LAST MSR

MODEL 411 SxS – 12, 20 ga. (disc. 2004) or .410 bore (disc. 2004), 28 in. monobloc barrels with choke tubes, boxlock action with laser engraved sideplates, SST, checkered walnut stock and splinter forearm, approx. 6 1/4 lbs., mfg. in Russia. Imported 2004-2005.

	$380	$330	$280	$235	$200	$180	$160	*$438*

MODEL 512 GOLD WING O/U – 12, 20, 28 ga., or .410 bore, boxlock action, 2 3/4 (28 ga.) or 3 in. chambers, 24 (Youth Model, 20 ga.), 26 or 28 in. VR barrels, choke tubes (except for .410 bore), ST, extractors, Turkish walnut pistol grip stock, Schnabel forearm, fleur-de-lis checkering, blue receiver with light relief engraving and gold pheasant inlays. Mfg. in Turkey. New 2007.

MSR $690	$575	$475	$425	$375	$340	$300	$265	

MODEL 520 SLIDE ACTION – this model was designed by John M. Browning, slight humpback in receiver.

	$190	$180	$150	$125	$95	$85	$75	

MODEL 520-30 TRENCH/RIOT MILITARY SHOTGUNS – see the "Trench/Riot Shotgun" category in the T section for more information and prices.

MODEL 530A SxS – 12, 16, 20 ga. or .410 bore, 2 3/4 in. chambers, boxlock action similar to Model 311, DT, extractors, 28 in. barrels, F/Mod. chokes, handcut checkered walnut stock, splinter forearm, case colored hardened finish, light engraving with dog, no ser. no.

	$275	$235	$200	$175	$160	$145	$130	

Add 30% for .410 bore.
Add 20% for 16 or 20 ga.

MODEL 612 GOLD WING SxS – 12, 20, 28 ga., or .410 bore, boxlock action, 2 3/4 (28 ga.) or 3 in. chambers, 26 or 28 in. VR barrels, choke tubes (except for .410 bore), ST, extractors, Turkish walnut pistol grip stock, fleur-de-lis checkering, lightweight alloy receiver with light relief engraving and gold pheasant inlays. Mfg. 2010-2011.

	$625	$525	$450	$375	$340	$300	$265	*$799*

MODEL 612 SxS TRAIL GUN – 12 or 20 ga., 20 in. barrels, 3 in. chambers, checkered walnut stock and forearm, blue receiver. Mfg. 2010-2011.

	$625	$525	$450	$375	$340	$300	$265	*$799*

MODEL 620 SLIDE ACTION – an improved version of the Model 520 with streamlined receiver.

	$275	$240	$215	$180	$160	$135	$100	

MODEL 620 TRENCH/RIOT MILITARY SHOTGUNS – see the "Trench/Riot Shotgun" category in the T section for more information and prices.

MODEL 675 SLIDE ACTION – 12 ga. only, 24 in. VR multi-choked barrel with iron sights (including removable rear ramp), hardwood stock with recoil pad, 6 1/2 lbs. Mfg. 1987-88.

	$250	$220	$190	$170	$155	$145	$135	*$295*

MODEL 9478 – 10, 12, 20 ga., or .410 bore, single shot break open, inertia firing pin, external hammer. Mfg. 1978-85.

	$95	$85	$75	$60	$50	$45	$40	

FOX/STEVENS MODEL B SxS – please refer to this listing in the A.H. Fox section.

FOX/STEVENS MODEL B-SE SxS – please refer to this listing in the A.H. Fox section.

STEYR AUSTRIAN MILITARY

Previously manufactured for the Austrian military in Steyr, Austria.

RIFLES: BOLT ACTION

MODEL 95 RIFLE – 8x56R Mannlicher cal., straight pull bolt action, 30 in. barrel, adj. sights, military full stock.

	$295	$265	$225	$195	$170	$135	$100	

These rifles were converted (rechambered) from 8x50R caliber, which was the original round during WWI until 1930. The chamber is marked with a large "S" for S-Patrone (round). Conversion began in 1930.

GRADING - PPGS™	100%	98%	95%	90%	80%	70%	60%	LAST MSR

MODEL 95 CARBINE – similar to Model 95 Rifle, except has 19 1/2 in. barrel.

	$395	$360	$315	$275	$225	$175	$125	

STEYR DAIMLER PUCH A.G.

Previous manufacturer located in Steyr, Austria 1911 to circa 1960.

PISTOLS

POCKET AUTO (MODEL 1909) – 6.35mm or 7.63mm cal., tip-down barrel, mag. fed., N. Pieper patent. Mfg. 1909-1914 and 1921-1939.

	$400	$300	$250	$200	$175	$150	$125	

Add 10% for 7.63mm cal.

ROTH STEYR MODEL 1907 (ROTH/KRNKA M.7) – 8mm Steyr cal., 10 shot, 5 1/8 in. barrel, fixed magazine top loaded by stripper clip. Total production in Steyr and Budapest is approx. 100,000.

	$1,750	$1,350	$1,100	$950	$800	$700	$600	

Add 30% for "Budapest" markings.

STEYR-HAHN MODEL AUTOMATIC – 9mm Steyr cal., 8 shot, 5.1 in. barrel, fixed magazine top loaded by stripper clip, blue, checkered wood grips, may be encountered with mixed numbers on parts, Chile adopted in 1911 (Model 1911), Romania adopted in 1912 (Model 1912), and Austro-Hungary in 1914 with the beginning of WWI (most common). Mfg. 1911-1919, with total production reaching nearly 300,000. In 1938, the Germans confiscated and converted a quantity of these to 9mm Para., "08" was stamped on the left side of these guns.

	$950	$750	$600	$500	$450	$400	$350	

Add 100% if marked "08" or with Romanian or Chilean Crest, if intact.

MODEL SP (SICHERHEITSPISTOLE) – .32 ACP cal., semi-auto, DAO, trigger cocking mechanism, very rare. Mfg. in 1959 only, total production was 912.

	$875	$750	$650	$550	$500	$450	$400	

Sicherheitspistole means "security pistol".

STEYR ARMS (STEYR MANNLICHER)

Currently manufactured by Steyr-Mannlicher AG & Co. KG in Austria. Founded in Steyr, Austria by Joseph Werndl circa 1864. Currently imported beginning mid-2005 by Steyr Arms, Inc., located in Trussville, AL. Previously located in Cumming, GA. Previously imported 2004-mid-2005 by Steyr USA, located in West Point, MS. Previously imported 2002-2003 by Dynamit Nobel, located in Closter, NJ. Previously imported and distributed until 2002 by Gun South, Inc. (GSI) located in Trussville, AL.

2008-Current

Pre-2008

In 2007, the firm of Steyr-Mannlicher was sold to new owners and the factory was relocated to Kleinraming, approx. 12 miles from the original site in Steyr, Austria. The new firm, Steyr Arms, was purchased by Dr. Ernst Reichmayr and his friend and partner, Gerhard Unterganschnigg.

Note: also see Mannlicher Schoenauer in the M section for pre-WWII models.

For more information and current pricing on both new and used Steyr airguns, please refer to the *Blue Book of Airguns* by Dr. Robert Beeman & John Allen (also online).

PISTOLS: SEMI-AUTO

MODEL GB – 9mm Para. cal., double action, 18 shot mag., gas delayed blowback action, non-glare checkered plastic grips, 5 1/4 in. barrel with Polygon rifling, matte finish, steel construction, 2 lbs. 6 oz. Importation disc. 1988.

Commercial	$675	$600	$525	$450	$400	$350	$300	
Military	$795	$725	$650	$600	$525	$450	$400	*$514*

In 1987, Steyr mfg. a military variation of the Model GB featuring a phosphate finish - only 937

GRADING - PPGS™	100%	98%	95%	90%	80%	70%	60%	LAST MSR

were imported into the U.S.

MODEL SPP – 9mm Para. cal., single action semi-auto, delayed blow back system with rotating 5.9 in. barrel, 15 or 30 shot mag., utilizes synthetic materials and advanced ergonomics, adj. sights, grooved receiver for scope mounting, matte black finish, 44 oz. Limited importation 1992-93.

	$800	$675	$600	$550	$495	$450	$400	*$895*

MODEL M SERIES – 9mm Para., .357 SIG, or .40 S&W cal., features first integrated limited access key lock safety in a semi-auto pistol, 3 different safety conditions, black synthetic frame, 10 shot mag., matte black finish, loaded chamber indicator, triangle/trapezoid sights, 28 oz. Limited importation 1999-2002.

	$500	$450	$400	$350	$300	$275	$250	*$610*

Add $65 for night sights.

M-A1 SERIES – .357 SIG (M357 A-1), 9mm Para. (M9 A-1), or .40 S&W (M40 A-1) cal., DAO, updated Model M with Picatinny rail on lower front of frame, redesigned grip frame, trigger safety and lockable safety system, black polymer frame with matte black finished slide, 3 1/2 (not available in .357 SIG cal.) or 4 in. barrel, 10, 12 (.40 S&W or .357 SIG) or 15 (9mm Para.) shot mag., white outlined triangular sights, approx. 27 oz. Imported 2004-2009, reintroduced late 2010.

MSR $560	$495	$450	$395	$350	$300	$275	$250	

Add $23 for right angle sights with Trilux (disc.)
Add $40 for night sights.

S-A1 SERIES – 9mm Para. (S9 A-1), or .40 S&W (S40 A-1) cal., similar to M-A1 Series, 10 shot mag., smaller compact frame.

MSR $560	$495	$450	$395	$350	$300	$275	$250	

C-A1 SERIES – 9mm Para. (C9 A-1), or .40 S&W (C40 A-1, importation disc. 2011) cal., similar to M-A1 Series, 12 or 17 shot mag., compact frame.

MSR $560	$495	$450	$395	$350	$300	$275	$250	

MODEL S – similar to Model M, except has 3 1/2 in. barrel and shorter grip frame, 10 shot mag., 22 1/2 oz. Limited importation 2000-2002.

	$475	$435	$385	$350	$325	$300	$280	*$610*

RIFLES: BOLT ACTION, RECENT PRODUCTION

The Steyr-Mannlicher models were in production 1968-1996.

Current production guns are now called Steyr-Mannlicher models. For models manufactured 1903 - 1971, please refer to the Mannlicher Schoenauer Sporting Rifles section in this text. All known calibers are listed for each model. Caliber offerings varied often throughout the 28 year run of the Steyr-Mannlicher, stock designs evolved, and sights and magazine styles changed. The only truly rare caliber is the 6mm Rem., which was always special order. Next in North American rarity is the .25-06. Certain additional European calibers are rare in the USA because they were not imported due to lack of popularity - 5.6x57mm, 6.5x57mm, 6x62mm Freres, 6.5x65mm, and 9.3x62mm.

All four action lengths, SL, L, M, S, were offered in numerous deluxe variations with engraving and stock carving on special order blued metal and highly polished engraved actions. Stock carving is heavy and elegant. The "twisted appearance" of the hammer rifles barrels on all firearms of this group lends a unique and unmistakable look to these rifles.

A major irritant for hardcore Steyr-Mannlicher collectors is the continued misidentification of Luxus models by online sellers. First, a standard USA version Luxus has the word "Luxus" engraved on the left side of the receiver. A Luxus also has a steel box magazine instead of a rotary plastic one and a rotary shotgun style safety, although some apparently early Luxus models exist with the sliding side safety.

Pricing shows the result of continued cost increases at Steyr, which finally caused the end of

GRADING - PPGS™	100%	98%	95%	90%	80%	70%	60%	LAST MSR

the production run and redesign to the SBS-96 model to save costs, regain competition, and take advantage of improved safety features.

ZEPHYR 22 – .22 LR cal., features full length Mannlicher stock, single or double-set triggers, open sights, checkered walnut stock with metallic cap or half stock and no checkering (Standard model), sling swivels, sights, trigger guard and forend cap are original Mannlicher Schoenauer parts. Mfg. 1953-late 1970, with total production of 3,913 rifles.

	$1,350	$1,200	$1,000	$850	$725	$600	$525	

MODEL ML-79 – various U.S. and metric cals., apparently the European predecessor of the Luxus, factory literature shows both L and M actions with various calibers, extremely rare in the USA, marked on the receiver as ML-79, set trigger, adj. sights, has the detachable magazine and stock (full or half-stock) design of the Luxus with the sliding side safety of the standard Steyr-Mannlicher Sporter. Mfg. 1977-1979.

Extreme rarity factor precludes accurate pricing on this model.

PROFESSIONAL RIFLE – 6.5x55mm, .270 Win., 7x57mm, 7x64mm, .30-06, 7.5x55mm Swiss, 8x57mm, or 9.3x62mm cal., brown (disc. 1970) or green (new 1970) synthetic half stock, double set trigger, sights optional. Mfg. 1968-1993.

	$1,000	$800	$700	$600	$550	$500	$400	*$995*

The 6.5x55mm cal. Professionals were totally unknown in the U.S.A. until a small lot was imported by GunSouth in the mid-1990s.

JAGDMATCH – .222 Rem., .243 Win., or .308 Win. cal., match rifle for European sports competition, special Steyr SSG match type receiver, laminated half stock only, 23.6 in. barrel, 5 shot rotary mag., single or double set trigger, 8 1/2 lbs.

	$1,600	$1,200	$1,000	$800	$725	$625	$550	*$2,450*

MODEL S – 6.5x68mm, .257 Wby., .264 Win. Mag., 7mm Rem. Mag., .300 H&H, .300 Win. Mag., 8x68mm, .338 Win. Mag., 9.3x64mm, or .375 H&H cal., 25.6 in. barrel with half stock, 4 shot rotary mag., double set or single trigger, optional with reserve magazine in butt-stock, 8.4 lbs. Mfg. 1968-1996.

	$1,600	$1,200	$1,000	$800	$725	$625	$550	*$2,745*

* ***Model S/T (Tropical Model)*** – 9.3x64mm, .375 H&H, .458 Win. Mag. cal., 25.6 in. barrel with half stock, 4 shot rotary mag., reserve magazine in buttstock, double set or single trigger, 9.02 lbs. Mfg. 1968-1996.

	$1,750	$1300	$1,000	$800	$700	$600	$550	*$2,850*

* ***Model S Luxus*** – same calibers as S, stock design, magazine, and safety are different from other Steyr-Mannlichers, full or half stock with better checkering, rotary thumb safety, single set trigger, in-line, non-rotary, 3 shot steel mag., open sights, 8 lbs. Mfg. 1980-1996.

	$1,950	$1,700	$1,500	$1,400	$1,200	$1,000	$800	*$3,250*

MANNLICHER CL LUXUS – .243 Win., .270 Win., .30-06, 6.5x55mm, 7x64R, 7mm-08 Rem., .308 Win., 9.3x62mm, .270 WSM, .300 WSM, 8x68mm, or .375 H&H cal., 23 1/2 or 25.6 in. barrel, open sights, Picatinny rail, Luxus wood stock.

MSR $3,299	$2,900	$2,575	$2,175	$1,800	$1,500	$1,275	$1,075	

MANNLICHER (STEYR) ULTRA LIGHT – .222 Rem., .223 Rem., .243 Win., .308 Win., or 7mm-08 Rem. cal., bolt has 4 locking lugs and a 70 degree bolt throw, 3-position roller tang safety, 19 in. fluted barrel, Weaver rail, 4 shot detachable mag., checkered European walnut stock with rosewood pistol grip and forend caps, approx. 6 lbs. Importation began 2004.

MSR $2,799	$2,400	$2,100	$1,825	$1,475	$1,200	$1,050	$925	

MANNLICHER/STEYR SCOUT – .223 Rem. (new 2000), .243 Win. (mfg. 2000 only, reintroduced 2005), .308 Win., 7mm-08 Rem. (new 2000), or .376 Steyr (mfg. 1999-2000, reintroduced 2005) cal., designed by Jeff Cooper, features grey, black synthetic Zytel or camo (.308 Win. cal. only beginning 2005) stock, 19 1/4 in. fluted barrel, Picatinny optic

GRADING - PPGS™	100%	98%	95%	90%	80%	70%	60%	LAST MSR

rail, integral bipod, Package includes Steyr or Leupold (disc. 2005) M8 2.5x28 IER scope with factory Steyr mounts, and luggage case. New 1998.

MSR $2,099	$1,850	$1,575	$1,375	$1,125	$900	$750	$650	

Add $100 for camo.

Add $600 for Steyr Scout Package with Steyr or Leupold (disc. 2004) scope, mounts and luggage case.

* ***Steyr Scout Jeff Cooper*** – .223 Rem., .308 Win. or .376 Steyr (disc. 2000, reintroduced 2005) cal., grey synthetic Zytel stock with Jeff Cooper logo and integral bipod, certificate of authenticity with test target, Package (disc. 2004) included Leupold M8 2.5x28 IER scope with factory Steyr mounts, and luggage case. Mfg. 1999-2009.

	$2,375	$2,050	$1,750	$1,425	$1,175	$1,050	$900	*$2,699*

Add approx. 15% for Steyr Scout Package with Leupold scope, mounts and luggage case (disc. 2004).

» **Steyr Scout Jeff Cooper Limited Edition** – 308 Win. cal., 20 in. fluted barrel, 10 shot polymer double stack detachable box mag., flip up iron sights, intergral top rail, gray Mannox finish, Scout stock with intergrated bipod and UIT rail, "JC" crest of arms, special ser. no., single stage trigger, three position safety, two removable sling swivels, includes Leupold 2.5X28mm Scout Scope, Galco Ching Sling, Boyt hard and soft case, Steyr scope mounts, extra magazine, and copy of Cooper's book *Art of the Rifle*, approx. 8 lbs., limited mfg. of 300. New mid-2010.

MSR $2,975	$2,625	$2,250	$1,875	$1,550	$1,275	$1,050	$925	

* ***Steyr Scout*** – .243 Win. cal., similar to Jeff Cooper Package, except does not include scope, mounts, or case. Mfg. 1999-2002.

	$1,525	$1,350	$1,200	$1,050	$900	$750	$625	*$1,969*

Add $100 for .376 Steyr cal. (black stock only, disc. 2000).

Add $100 for Jeff Cooper grey stock.

* ***Steyr Scout Tactical*** – .223 Rem. (new 2000) or .308 Win. cal., similar to Steyr Scout, except has black synthetic stock with removable spacers, oversized bolt handle, and emergency ghost ring sights. Mfg. 1999-2002.

	$1,600	$1,400	$1,250	$1,050	$900	$750	$625	*$2,069*

» **Steyr Scout Tactical Stainless** – similar to Steyr Scout Tactical, except has stainless steel barrel. Mfg. 2000-2002.

	$1,650	$1,425	$1,150	$1,025	$830	$710	$590	*$2,159*

MANNLICHER/SBS PROHUNTER MODEL – .222 Rem. (new 2004), .223 Rem. (new 2004), .243 Win., .25-06 Rem., .260 Rem. (mfg. 2000-2004), .270 Win., .280 Rem. (new 2000), .30-06, .308 Win., 7mm-08 Rem., 6.5x55mm, 6.5x57mm (disc. 1999), 7x64mm (disc. 1999), or 9.3x62mm (disc. 1999) cal., features safe bolt system (SBS), detachable mag., black synthetic or camo (new 2000) stock, matte blue finish, 23.6 in. barrel without sights. New 1996.

MSR $1,150	$1,000	$895	$775	$650	$525	$465	$400	

Add $75 for camo stock (new 2000).

Add $152 for heavy barrel (.308 Win. cal. only, disc. 2005).

SBS stands for Steyr Bolt Safe, which indicates the use of a relatively complicated bolt action designed with hunter safety in mind.

* ***SBS ProHunter Model Magnum*** – .270 WSM (new 2004), .300 WSM (new 2004), .300 Win. Mag., 7mm WSM (new 2004), 7mm Rem. Mag., 6.5x68mm (disc. 1999), or 8x68S (disc. 1999) cal., similar to SBS ProHunter Model, except has 23.6 in. or 25.6 (disc.) in. barrel. New 1997.

MSR $1,150	$1,000	$895	$775	$650	$525	$465	$400	

Add $75 for camo stock (new 2000).

Add $152 for heavy barrel (.300 Win. Mag. only, disc.).

Add $150 for metric cals (disc.).

GRADING - PPGS™	100%	98%	95%	90%	80%	70%	60%	LAST MSR

* ***SBS ProHunter Model SS*** – similar to SBS ProHunter, except has stainless steel barrel with matte finish. New 2000.

MSR $1,250	$1,100	$975	$850	$725	$625	$525	$425	

Add $129 for camo stock (.270 Win. or .30-06 cal.).

» **SBS ProHunter Model SS Magnum** – similar to SBS ProHunter Magnum, except has stainless steel barrel with matte finish. New 2000.

MSR $1,250	$1,100	$975	$850	$725	$625	$525	$425	

Add $75 for camo stock (.300 Win. Mag. or 7mm Rem. Mag. cal. only).
Add $165 for black finish (7mm Rem. Mag. cal. only, mfg. 2005).

* ***SBS ProHunter Model .376 Steyr*** – .376 Steyr cal. only, 20 in. barrel with iron sights, black synthetic or camo (new 2000) stock, matte blue finish. Mfg. 1999-2004.

	$695	$600	$500	$450	$395	$350	$300	*$799*

Add $60 for camo.

* ***SBS ProHunter Model Compact (Youth/Ladies) Rifle*** – .243 Win., .260 Rem. (new 2000) 7mm-08 Rem., or .308 Win. cal., shortened stock with 2 butt spacers for adj. length, 20 in. barrel with iron sights, matte blue finish. Mfg. 1999-2002.

	$710	$640	$570	$500	$450	$395	$350	*$819*

* ***SBS ProHunter Model Compact (Youth/Ladies) SS*** – similar to ProHunter Compact, except has stainless steel barrel with matte finish. Mfg. 2000-2002.

	$780	$675	$600	$495	$430	$365	$315	*$909*

* ***SBS ProHunter Model Mountain Rifle*** – .243 Win., .25-06 Rem., .260 Rem. (new 2000), .270 Win., .270 WSM (mfg. 2004), .30-06, .300 WSM (mfg. 2004), .308 Win., .376 Steyr (new 2005), 7mm-08 Rem., 7mm WSM (mfg. 2004), or 6.5x55mm (new 2000) cal., 20 in. barrel, no sights, matte blue finish, black or camo (mfg. 2000-2002) synthetic stock, detachable mag. Mfg. 1999-2008.

	$895	$775	$650	$525	$465	$400	$350	*$991*

* ***SBS ProHunter Model Mountain Rifle SS*** – similar to ProHunter Mountain Rifle, except has stainless steel barrel with matte finish. Mfg. 2000-2008.

	$1,050	$850	$700	$600	$495	$430	$375	*$1,195*

Add $129 for camo stock (.243 Win., .270 Win. or .30-06 cal. only).

* ***SBS ProHunter Model Tactical*** – .308 Win. cal., features 20 in. barrel and 10 shot mag. Limited mfg. 2005.

	$850	$700	$575	$500	$450	$400	$350	*$983*

MANNLICHER PRO VARMINT – .223 Rem. cal., 23.6 in. heavy fluted barrel, black synthetic or camo vented stock, includes tactical rail. New 2009.

MSR $1,799	$1,600	$1,450	$1,275	$1,075	$900	$775	$650	

Add $200 for camo.

PRO ALASKAN – .30-06, .338 RCM, or .375 Ruger cal., 23.6 in. barrel, stainless steel action, set trigger, 4 shot detachable mag., open sights, soft touch camo stock. New 2009.

MSR $1,999	$1,795	$1,525	$1,350	$1,100	$925	$800	$675	

PRO AFRICAN – .30-06, 9.3x62mm, .338 RCM, or .375 Ruger cal., black soft touch synthetic stock, 4 shot detachable box mag., two-piece Weaver style scope bases, tactical bolt, black finish. New 2009.

MSR $2,099	$1,875	$1,575	$1,375	$1,100	$925	$800	$675	

SBS FORESTER MODEL – similar to SBS Pro Hunter Model, except has wood stock and standard blue finish. Mfg. 1997-2002, reintroduced 2005.

	$925	$800	$700	$600	$525	$425	$350	*$1,051*

* ***SBS Forester Model Mountain Rifle*** – .243 Win. (disc. 2002), .25-06 Rem., .260 Rem. (new 2000), .270 Win. (disc. 2002, reintroduced 2005), .30-06 (disc. 2002), .308 Win. (disc. 2002), 7mm-08 Rem., 6.5x55mm (mfg. 2000-2002) cal., 20 in. barrel, no

GRADING - PPGS™	100%	98%	95%	90%	80%	70%	60%	LAST MSR

sights, matte blue finish, checkered walnut stock, detachable mag. Mfg. 1999-2002, reimported 2004-2005.

	$925	$800	$700	$600	$525	$425	$350	*$1,051*

* ***SBS Forester Model Magnum*** – .300 Win. Mag., 7mm Rem. Mag., 6.5x68mm (disc. 1999), or 8x68S (disc. 1999) cal., similar to SBS Forester Model, except has 25.6 in. barrel. Mfg. 1997-2002.

	$720	$635	$565	$510	$450	$395	$350	*$829*

CLASSIC MANNLICHER (SBS) HALF STOCK (AMERICAN) – .222 Rem., .223 Rem., .243 Win., .25-06 Rem., .260 Rem. (disc. 2002), .270 Win., .280 Rem. (disc. 2002), .30-06, .308 Win., 7mm-08 Rem., 6.5x55mm, 6.5x57mm, 6.5x58mm, 7x64mm, or 8x57JRS cal., features deluxe checkered walnut stock with full pistol grip and forend cap, deep blue finish, 23.6 in. barrel with exterior hammer forged swirls, with or w/o sights. New 2000.

MSR $2,799	$2,450	$2,100	$1,825	$1,475	$1,200	$1,050	$925	

Add $1,000 for case colors.

* ***SBS Classic Mannlicher Half Stock Magnum*** – .270 WSM (new 2004), .300 WSM (new 2004), .300 Win. Mag., 7mm WSM (new 2004) or 7mm Rem. Mag. cal., 25.6 in. barrel. New 2000.

MSR $2,799	$2,400	$2,100	$1,825	$1,475	$1,200	$1,050	$925	

Add $1,000 for case colors.

* ***SBS Classic Mannlicher Half Stock Mountain*** – similar cals. as SBS Classic Mannlicher Full Stock, features 20 in. barrel with open sights. Mfg. 2006-2008.

	$2,050	$1,625	$1,250	$1,025	$875	$750	$650	*$2,269*

SBS CLASSIC MANNLICHER FULL STOCK – various cals., similar to SBS Classic Mannlicher Half Stock, except has deluxe full length stock and 20 in. barrel with sights. New 2000.

MSR $2,999	$2,600	$2,275	$1,925	$1,550	$1,250	$1,075	$950	

Add $1,200 for case colors.

* ***SBS Classic Mannlicher Goiserer*** – .270 Win., .30-06, or .308 Win. cal., similar to Classic Mannlicher Half Stock, except has iron sights and 20 in. barrel, 4 shot mag. Mfg. 2003-2005.

	$1,725	$1,325	$1,100	$950	$775	$675	$575	*$2,014*

CLASSIC MANNLICHER ANTIQUE – various cals., 20 or 23 in. barrel with open sights, choice of half-stock or Mannlicher full stock, case colored receiver, barrel, and bolt. New 2006.

MSR $4,899	$4,400	$3,850	$3,400	$2,900	$2,450	$2,000	$1,650	

Add $300 for Mannlicher full stock.

MANNLICHER CLASSIC LIGHT – .270 Win., .30-06 or 7x64R cal., half-stock, 20 in. fluted barrel, set trigger, open sights.

MSR $2,799	$2,450	$2,100	$1,750	$1,500	$1,275	$1,050	$925	

SBS TACTICAL – .308 Win. cal. only, 20 in. barrel w/o sights, features oversized bolt handle and high capacity 10 shot mag. with adapter, matte blue finish. Mfg. 1999-2002.

	$840	$735	$625	$550	$500	$450	$395	*$969*

* ***SBS Tactical Heavy Barrel*** – .300 Win. Mag. (new 2000) or .308 Win. cal., features 20 (carbine, new 2000, .308 Win. only) or 26 in. heavy barrel w/o sights and oversized bolt handle, matte blue finish or stainless steel (carbine only, new 2000). Mfg. 1999-2002.

	$865	$745	$635	$550	$500	$450	$395	*$1,019*

Add $30 for .300 Win. Mag. cal.
Add $40 for stainless steel.

* ***SBS Tactical McMillan*** – similar to SBS Tactical Heavy Barrel, except has custom McMillan A - 3 stock with adj. cheekpiece and oversized bolt handle, matte blue finish. Mfg. 1999-2002.

	$1,465	$1,245	$1,035	$850	$725	$600	$550	*$1,699*

Add $30 for .300 Win. Mag. cal.

GRADING - PPGS™	100%	98%	95%	90%	80%	70%	60%	LAST MSR

* ***SBS Tactical CISM*** – .308 Win. cal., 20 in. heavy barrel w/o sights, laminated wood stock with black lacquer finish, adj. cheekpiece and buttplate, 10 shot detachable mag., vent. forend. Mfg. 2000-2002.

	$3,050	$2,650	$2,300	$1,950	$1,600	$1,300	$1,150	$3,499

Subtract approx. 35% for Swiss contract CISM Match in 7.5x55mm cal. with match diopter sights and 23 1/2 in. barrel. (Only 100 were imported.)

MANNLICHER BIG BORE – .450 Marlin cal., 22 in. barrel, open sights, black synthetic stock, 3 shot mag.

MSR $1,799	$1,600	$1,450	$1,275	$1,075	$900	$775	$650	

STEYR ELITE (SBS TACTICAL) – .223 Rem. (disc. 2008) or .308 Win. cal., 20 (carbine, disc.), 22.4 (new 2006) or 26 (disc. 2005) in. barrel with full length Picatinny spec. mounting rail, oversize bolt handle, two 5 shot detachable mags. (with spare buttstock storage), adj. black synthetic stock, matte blue finish or stainless steel. New 2000.

MSR $2,299	$1,950	$1,725	$1,500	$1,275	$1,050	$875	$775	

* ***Steyr Elite 08*** – .308 Win. cal., 23.6 in. blue or stainless steel barrel, Dural aluminum folding stock, 10 shot high capacity box mag., extra long Picatinny rail. New 2009.

MSR $5,999	$5,325	$4,650	$4,325	$3,750	$3,250	$2,600	$1,995	

150TH YEAR FERDINAND RITTER VON MANNLICHER COMMEMORATIVE – 6.5x54mm Mannlicher Schoenauer cal. only, checkered high grade full stock carbine or half stock rifle, polished blue metal, gold filled engraving, open sights, SST, euro-style trigger guard, originally specified production was announced to be six units, then 150 units, and finally 250 units. Mfg. 1999.

	$3,500	$3,150	$2,700	$2,250	$1,850	$1,500	$1,250	$3,500

MANNLICHER SBS EUROPEAN MODEL – .243 Win., .25-06 Rem., .270 Win., .30-06 (disc. 1998), .308 Win., 7mm-08 Rem., 6.5x55mm, 6.5x57mm, 7x64mm, 7.5x55mm, or 9.3x62mm cal., features safe bolt system (SBS), 23.6 in. barrel with sights, checkered walnut stock and forearm. Mfg. 1997-99.

	$2,300	$1,850	$1,600	$1,325	$1,100	$925	$850	$2,795

* ***Mannlicher SBS European Model Magnum*** – .300 Win. Mag., 7mm Rem. Mag., 6.5x68mm, or 8x68S cal., 25.6 in. barrel with sights, checkered walnut stock and forearm. Mfg. 1997-99.

	$2,375	$1,900	$1,625	$1,350	$1,100	$925	$850	$2,895

* ***Mannlicher SBS European Model "Goiserer"*** – similar to Mannlicher SBS European Model, except has 20 in. barrel. Mfg. 1997-99.

	$2,500	$2,000	$1,650	$1,350	$1,100	$925	$850	$2,995

* ***Mannlicher SBS European Model Full Stock*** – similar to Mannlicher SBS European Model, except has full-length Mannlicher stock. Mfg. 1997-99.

	$2,500	$2,000	$1,650	$1,350	$1,100	$925	$850	$2,995

MODEL SSG – .243 Win. (disc., PII Sniper only) or .308 Win cal., for competition or law-enforcement use. Marksman has regular sights, detachable rotary mag., teflon coated bolt with heavy duty locking lugs, synthetic stock has removable spacers, parkerized finish. Match version has heavier target barrel and "match" bolt carrier, can be used as single shot. Extremely accurate.

* ***Model SSG 69 Sport (PI Rifle)*** – .243 Win. or .308 Win. cal., 26 in. barrel with iron sights, 3 shot mag., black or green ABS Cycolac synthetic stock.

	$1,775	$1,500	$1,225	$1,000	$850	$725	$650	$1,989

Add 15% for walnut stock (disc. 1992, retail was $448).

* ***Model SSG PII/PIIK Sniper Rifle*** – .22-250 Rem. (new 2004), .243 Win. (disc.) or .308 Win. cal., 20 in. heavy (Model PIIK) or 26 in. heavy barrel, no sights, green or black synthetic Cycolac or McMillan black fiberglass stock, modified bolt handle, choice of single or set triggers.

MSR $1,899	$1,695	$1,500	$1,300	$1,050	$875	$750	$625	

Add 15% for walnut stock (disc. 1992, retail was $448).

GRADING - PPGS™	100%	98%	95%	90%	80%	70%	60%	LAST MSR

* ***Model SSG PIII Rifle*** – .308 Win. cal., 26 in. heavy barrel with diopter match sight bases, H-S Precision Pro-Series stock in black only. Importation 1991-93.

	$2,300	$1,875	$1,425	$1,050	$825	$700	$600	$3,162

* ***Model SSG PIV (Urban Rifle)*** – .308 Win. cal., carbine variation with 16 1/2 in. heavy barrel and flash hider (disc.), ABS Cycolac synthetic stock in green or black. Imported 1991-2002, reimported beginning 2004.

MSR $1,899	$1,695	$1,500	$1,300	$1,050	$875	$750	$625	

* ***Model SSG Jagd Match*** – .222 Rem., .243 Win., or .308 Win. cal., checkered wood laminate stock, 23.6 in. barrel, Mannlicher sights, DT, supplied with test target. Mfg. 1991-1992.

	$1,550	$1,050	$950	$800	$675	$600	$540	$1,550

* ***Model SSG Match Rifle*** – .308 Win. only, 26 in. heavy barrel, brown ABS Cycolac stock, Walther Diopter sights, 8.6 lbs. Mfg. disc. 1992.

	$2,000	$1,500	$1,225	$925	$800	$700	$600	$2,306

Add $437 for walnut stock.

* ***Model SPG-T*** – .308 Win. cal., Target model. Mfg. 1993-98.

	$3,225	$2,850	$2,550	$2,200	$1,850	$1,500	$1,200	$3,695

* ***Model SPG-CISM*** – .308 Win. cal., 20 in. heavy barrel, laminated wood stock with adj. cheekpiece and black lacquer finish. Mfg. 1993-99.

	$2,995	$2,600	$2,300	$1,950	$1,700	$1,450	$1,200	$3,295

* ***Model SSG Match UIT*** – .308 Win. cal. only, 10 shot steel mag., special single set trigger, free floating barrel, Diopter sights, raked bolt handle, 10.8 lbs. Disc. 1998.

	$3,000	$2,500	$2,000	$1,800	$1,500	$1,200	$1,000	$3,995

UIT stands for Union Internationale de Tir.

* ***Model SSG 04*** – .308 Win. or .300 Win. Mag. cal., 20 (disc. 2005) or 23.6 heavy hammer forged barrel with muzzle brake, two-stage trigger, matte finished metal, black synthetic stock, adj. bipod, 8 (.300 Win. Mag.) or 10 (.308 Win.) shot mag., Picatinny rail, adj. buttstock, 10.1 lbs. Importation began 2004.

MSR $2,299	$1,950	$1,725	$1,500	$1,275	$1,050	$875	$775	

Add $200 for 16.1 in. barrel.
Add $1,300 for A1 model (new 2009).

* ***Model SSG 08*** – .308 Win. cal., 23.6 in. barrel, folding stock.

MSR $5,899	$5,250	$4,800	$4,300	$3,750	$3,250	$2,600	$1,995	

HS-50 – .460 Steyr or .50 BMG cal., bolt action, 33 in. barrel with muzzle brake, includes Picatinny rail and bipod. Importation began 2004.

MSR $5,299	$4,850	$4,350	$3,900	$3,500	$3,150	$2,850	$2,500	

Rifles: Bolt Action, Model 72 Series (Mannlicher Schonauer M 72)

There is no model designation on the Model 72 Series. Only the caliber is stamped on the left-hand side of the barrel in front of the rear sight. There are two different action lengths - L/M (light and middle) and S/T (heavy and tropics). Production started on May 4, 1972 with ser. no. 1500 in .30-06 cal., and was exported to America, the last rifle in the series was ser. no. 10026, and was in .243 Win. cal. Total production was 8,526.

MODEL M72 (MODEL M) – 5.6x57mm, .243 Win., .270 Win., 7x57mm, 7x64mm, .30-06, or 308 Win. cal., available in rifle and full stock carbine versions, single and double set triggers, 5 shot rotary mag., this is a hybrid design resembling the original Mannlicher-Schoenauer with features from the new (1968) Steyr-Mannlicher Sporter to reduce costs. Mfg. 1973-circa 1980.

	$875	$795	$725	$650	$575	$500	$460	$525

GRADING - PPGS™	100%	98%	95%	90%	80%	70%	60%	LAST MSR

* ***Model 72 (Model S & S/T Mag.)*** – 6.5x68mm, 8x68mm, 9.3x64mm, 7mm Rem. Mag., .300 Win. Mag., .375 H&H, or .458 Win. Mag., 4 shot rotary mag., half stock, 25.6 in. barrel, DT or optional ST, S/T Model has heavy tropical barrel, which was also optional in 23.6 inches, and only offered in 9.3x64mm, .375 H&H, or .458 Win. Mag. Mfg. 1973-1975.

$1,750 $1,600 $1,450 $1,300 $1,150 $1,000 $900

Note: some rare catalogs show these S and S/T Magnum action versions, though none appear to have been imported into the U.S.A. by U.S. importers.

MODEL SL – .222 Rem., .222 Rem. Mag., .223 Rem, .22-250 Rem, or 5.6x50mm cal., available in carbine (20 in. barrel); rifle (23.6 in. barrel); and heavy barrel (25.6 in. barrel) with double set or single trigger and 5 shot rotary mag., 6.27 lbs. Mfg. 1968-1996.

$1,400 $1,100 $900 $700 $600 $495 $450 *$2,540*

* ***Model SL Carbine Model*** – same calibers as SL rifle, 20 in. barrel with full stock, early models possess slimmer stock design, 38 1/2 inches overall, 6.16 lbs. (some list 5.95 lbs.)

$1,600 $1,200 $1,000 $900 $700 $650 $500 *$2,450*

* ***Model SL Varmint Rifle*** – same calibers as SL rifle, 25.6 in. barrel, two heavy barrel varmint versions with either traditional heavy stock and heavy barrel or square forearm vented stock, double set or single trigger, no sights, 7.92 lbs.

$1,625 $1,325 $900 $800 $650 $550 $500 *$2,450*

MODEL L – 5.6x50mm, 5.6x57mm, .22-250, .243 WCF, 6mm Rem., or .308 Win. cal., available in carbine (20 in. barrel), rifle (23.6 in. barrel), and heavy barrel (25.6 in. barrel) varmint rifle, double set and single trigger, 5 shot rotary mag., 6.38 lbs. Mfg. 1968-1996.

$1,500 $1,300 $900 $750 $675 $600 $540 *$2,250*

This model is most often seen in .243 Win. and .308 Win. - special order calibers included 6mm Rem. and .22-250 Rem.

* ***Model L Carbine Model*** – same calibers as L rifle, 20 in. barrel with full stock, early models possess a slimmer stock design, 38 1/2 inches overall, approx. 6.2 lbs.

$1,600 $1,300 $995 $825 $700 $600 $540 *$2,450*

* ***Model L Varmint Rifle*** – same calibers as L rifle, 25.6 in. barrel, two heavy barrel varmint versions with either traditional stock and heavy barrel square forearm vented stock, double set or single trigger, no sights, 7.92 lbs.

$1,600 $1,325 $875 $800 $650 $550 $500 *$2,450*

* ***Model L Luxus*** – same calibers as L, stock design, magazine, and safety are different from other Steyr-Mannlichers, full or half stock with better checkering, rotary thumb safety, single set trigger, and in-line, non-rotary 3 shot steel magazine, open sights, available in full stock and half-stock versions. Mfg. 1980-1996.

$1,700 $1,450 $1,100 $950 $800 $700 $650

Last MSR was $2,950 or $3,150.

* ***Model L Luxus Carbine (Full Stock)*** – similar to L Luxus rifle, except has full stock and 20 in. barrel. Disc. 1996.

$1,800 $1,500 $1,200 $1,000 $800 $700 $650 *$3,150*

MODEL M – 6x62mm Freres, .25-06 Rem., 6.5x55mm, 6.5x57mm, 6.5x65mm, .270 Win., 7x57mm, 7x64mm, .30-06, 7.5x55mm Swiss, 8x57mm, or 9.3x62mm cal., available in carbine (20 in. barrel), and rifle (23.6 in. barrel), double set and single trigger, 5 shot rotary mag. Mfg. 1968-1996.

$1,500 $1,300 $900 $700 $650 $600 $540 *$2,250*

Add $400 for left-hand action.

Special order and unlisted calibers varied and included .25-06, 6.5x55mm, and 7.5x55mm.

* ***Model M Carbine Model*** – 6.5x55mm, 6.5x57mm, .270 Win., .30-06, 8x57mm, or 9.3x62mm cal., full stock, 20 in. barrel, 7.26 lbs.

$1,600 $1,400 $900 $825 $700 $600 $540 *$2,450*

GRADING - PPGS™	100%	98%	95%	90%	80%	70%	60%	LAST MSR

* ***Model M Luxus*** – same calibers as Model M, stock design, magazine, and safety are different from other Steyr-Mannlichers, full or half stock with better checkering, rotary thumb safety, single set trigger, and in-line, non-rotary, 3 shot steel mag., open sights, 7.7 lbs. Mfg. 1980-1996.

	$1,750	$1,500	$1,200	$900	$800	$700	$650	*$2,950*

* ***Model M Luxus Carbine (Full Stock)*** – similar to Model M Luxus, except with full stock and 20 in. barrel. Disc. 1996.

	$1,900	$1,650	$1,300	$950	$825	$700	$650	*$3,150*

* ***Model M "1000 Year City of Steyr Commemorative" Luxus Carbine*** – .30-06 cal., deluxe full stock, gold inlayed on receiver and trigger guard, single set trigger, in-line, non-rotary, 3 shot steel mag., open sights, approx 7.7 lbs. Mfg. 1980-1983.

	$3,650	$2,850	$2,400	N/A	N/A	N/A	N/A	*$4,200*

RIFLES: SEMI-AUTO

AUG S.A. – .223 Rem. cal., gas operated paramilitary design rifle, design incorporates use of advanced plastics, short stroke piston, integral Swarovski scope or Picatinny rail (24 in. heavy barrel only), 16, 20, 21, or 24 in. barrel, green composite stock (original bullpup configuration), rotating breech bolt, later mfg. was black or desert tan stock , 10, 30 or 42 shot mag., 7.9 lbs. Importation resumed mid-2006.

MSR $2,295	$2,150	$1,875	$1,600	$1,475	$1,350	$1,100	$995

Add approx. 10% for 24 in. heavy barrel with Picatinny rail and bipod (disc.).
Add $48 for 42 shot mag.

* ***AUG S.A. Commercial*** – similar to AUG S.A., grey (3,000 mfg. circa 1997), green, or black finish.

SP receiver (Stanag metal)	$2,950	$2,750	$2,450	$2,150	$1,750	$1,575	$1,400
Grey finish	$3,150	$2,875	$2,600	$2,250	$1,825	$1,625	$1,450
Green finish (last finish)	$3,400	$2,975	$2,700	$2,300	$1,875	$1,675	$1,500
Black finish	$4,125	$3,750	$3,300	$2,950	$2,750	$2,500	$2,250

Last MSR was $1,362 (1989) for Green finish.

STEYR USR (UNIVERSAL SPORTING RIFLE) – .223 Rem. cal., unthreaded barrel, USR thumbhole stock, AUG barrels are not interchangeable with this model. Approx. 3,000 imported circa 1996 before the sporting arms ban began.

	$1,650	$1,450	$1,250	$1,050	$900	$775	$650

MODEL MAADI AKM – 7.62x39mm cal., copy of Soviet AKM paramilitary design rifle, 30 shot mag., open sights.

	$2,250	$2,000	$1,800	$1,600	$1,450	$1,250	$1,125

SHOTGUNS

MODEL 300 SxS – boxlock, cocking indicators, DT, pistol grip stock with cheekpiece, 28 in. barrels, selector switch to change from extractors to ejectors, sling swivels, light scroll engraving. Mfg. circa mid 1920s - late 1930s, scarce.

	N/A	N/A	$1,500	$1,300	$1,100	$925	$700

STINGER MANUFACTURING CORP.

Previous company located in Sault Sainte Marie, MI circa 2002-2004.

PISTOLS: PEN DESIGN

STINGER – .22 LR cal. (most common), pen pistol design, originally marketed by R. J. Braverman Corp. located in Meredith, NH, manufactured by Remcon North Corp. from Meredith, NH, in 2002 a new company called Stinger Manufacturing Corp. revived this pen pistol design and went back into production until early 2004.

	$550	$475	$425	$375	$350	$325	$300

GRADING - PPGS™	100%	98%	95%	90%	80%	70%	60%	LAST MSR

STOCK, FRANZ

Previous manufacturer located in Berlin, Germany.

PISTOLS: SEMI-AUTO

.22 LR PISTOL – .22 LR cal. Mfg. in Germany 1920-40.

	100%	98%	95%	90%	80%	70%	60%	LAST MSR
	$295	$250	$225	$175	$125	$100	$75	

.25 ACP PISTOL – .25 ACP or .32 ACP cal. Mfg. in Germany 1920-40.

	100%	98%	95%	90%	80%	70%	60%	LAST MSR
	$295	$225	$175	$150	$100	$90	$80	

STOCKWORKS

Please refer to Robert Hisserich Co. section.

STOEGER INDUSTRIES, INC.

Current importer/trademark established in 1924, and currently located in Accokeek, MD. Previously located in Wayne, NJ, until 2000. Stoeger Industries, Inc. was purchased by Beretta Holding of Italy in 2000, and is now a division of Benelli USA. Please refer to the IGA listing for currently imported Stoeger shotgun models.

Stoeger has imported a wide variety of firearms during the past seven decades. Most of these guns were good quality and came from known makers in Europe (some were private labeled). Stoeger carried an extensive firearms inventory of both house brand and famous European trademarks - many of which were finely made with beautiful engraving, stock work, and other popular special order features. As a general rule, values for Stoeger rifles and shotguns may be ascertained by comparing them with a known trademark of equal quality and cal./ga. Certain configurations will be more desirable than others (i.e. a Stoeger .22 caliber Mannlicher with double-set triggers and detachable mag. will be worth considerably more than a single shot target rifle).

Perhaps the best reference works available on these older Stoeger firearms (not to mention the other trademarks of that time) are the older Stoeger catalogs themselves - quite collectible in their own right. You are advised to purchase these older catalogs (some reprints are also available) if more information is needed on not only older Stoeger models, but also the other firearms being sold at that time.

PISTOLS: SEMI-AUTO

Stoeger Lugers can be found in the Luger section.

PRO SERIES 95 – .22 LR cal., target pistol with choice of either 5 1/2 or 7 1/4 in. VR, fluted, or bull barrel, adj. rear sight, adj. trigger, push-button takedown, Pachmayr rubber grips, gold accents, 10 shot mag., 45-47 oz. Mfg. 1995-96.

	100%	98%	95%	90%	80%	70%	60%	LAST MSR
5 1/2 in. bull barrel	$440	$375	$335	$300	$275	$250	$225	
5 1/2 in. VR barrel	$515	$425	$365	$325	$285	$255	$225	
7 1/4 in. fluted barrel	$455	$385	$340	$300	$275	$250	$225	

Last MSR's were $495 for 5 1/2 in. bull barrel, $595 for 5 1/2 in. VR barrel, and $525 for 7 1/4 in. fluted barrel.

COUGAR – 9mm Para., .40 S&W, or .45 ACP (new 2010) cal., SA/DA operation, copy of Beretta, 3.6 in. barrel, matte black finish, 8 (.45 ACP), 11 (.40 S&W), 13 (compact version 9mm, new 2011) or 15 (9mm Para.) shot mag., ambidextrous safety, 3-dot sights, Bruniton black, silver or two-tone matte finish, checkered plastic grips, blowback action with rotating bolt, removable front sight, mfg. in Turkey. Importation began 2007.

	100%	98%	95%	90%	80%	70%	60%	LAST MSR
MSR $469	$375	$335	$290	$255	$225	$200	$180	

Add $40 for .45 ACP cal. in black finish with accessory rail.
Add $30 for silver or two-tone finish.

GRADING - PPGS™	100%	98%	95%	90%	80%	70%	60%	LAST MSR

SHOTGUNS: O/U

CLASSIC MODEL – 12 ga., 3 1/2 in. chambers, engraved boxlock action, 26, 28, or 30 in. vent. barrels with VR and 3 choke tubes, gold SST, AE, checkered walnut stock and forearm, approx. 7 1/2 lbs.

While advertised for $919 by Stoeger Industries during 2000, this model was never imported by Stoeger Industries. However, it has had limited importation to date from domestic distributors.

CONDOR I SINGLE TRIGGER – 12, 16 (new 2006), 20 ga. 28 (new 2012) or .410 bore (new 2005), 3 in. chambers, boxlock action, deluxe checkered walnut, extractors, 24 (28 ga. only, new 2012), 26 or 28 in. VR separated barrels with choke tubes on 12 and 20 ga. (standard beginning 1992), 7.7 lbs.

MSR $449	$375	$335	$275	$240	$215	$195	$180	

Add $170 for Condor combo, including set of 12 ga. and 20 ga. barrels (new 2004).

This model is also available in a Youth model with 22 in. barrels and 13 in. LOP stock in 20 ga. or .410 bore.

CONDOR I SPECIAL – similar to Condor I, except features matte stainless steel receiver, oil finished hardwood stock and forearm. Imported 2002-2006.

	$365	$325	$275	$235	$215	$195	$180	*$415*

Add $135 for Condor combo, including set of 12 ga. and 20 ga. barrels (new 2004).

CONDOR SUPREME DELUXE – 12 or 20 ga., 3 in. chambers, 24 (20 ga. only, disc. 2010), 26, 28, or 30 (disc. 2001) in. VR barrels with choke tubes, high polish blue, gold SST, AE, checkered AA grade high gloss American walnut stock and forearm, approx. 7.7 lbs. Importation began 2000.

MSR $599	$525	$440	$385	$345	$300	$285	$265	

Add $190 for Condor combo, including set of 12 ga. and 20 ga. barrels (new 2004).

CONDOR OUTBACK – 12 or 20 ga., 3 in. chambers, 20 in. barrels with screw-in chokes, ST, extractors, choice of checkered walnut or black painted walnut stock and forearm, rifle sights, separated barrels, blue or polished nickel finish, 6 1/2 - 7 lbs. New 2007.

MSR $449	$375	$335	$275	$240	$215	$195	$180	

Add $50 for black finished walnut and polished nickel metal.

CONDOR COMPETITION – 12 or 20 ga., 3 in. chambers, 30 in. ported barrels with choke tubes, SST, AE, checkered AA grade select walnut stock (with or w/o adj. comb, LH or RH) and forearm. New 2005.

MSR $669	$575	$495	$440	$385	$350	$325	$295	

Add $230 for Condor combo with 12 and 20 ga. barrels (new 2007, available in right or left hand).

DOUBLE DEFENSE – 12 or 20 ga., 3 in. chambers, 20 in. barrels with fixed IC chokes, black finished walnut.

MSR $479	$415	$350	$275	$225	$180	$150	$130	

LONGFOWLER – 12 ga., 3 in. chambers, 30 in. vented barrels with VR and two extended choke tubes, single trigger, extractors, checkered walnut stock and semi-beavertail forearm, top tang safety. New 2013.

MSR $449	$395	$360	$325	$295	$275	$250	$225	

SHOTGUNS: SxS

UPLANDER MODEL – 12, 16 (new 1996), 20, 28 ga., or .410 bore, 3 in. chambers, 24 (English style stock only, disc.), 26, or 28 in. barrels with extractors, DT, underlug lockup, checkered satin finished grade A pistol grip or straight English (20 ga. or .410 bore only) stock.

MSR $449	$375	$335	$275	$240	$215	$195	$180	

Subtract approx. 10% if w/o choke tubes.

This model is also available in a Youth variation in 20 ga. or .410 bore with 22 in. barrels and shortened LOP.

GRADING - PPGS™	100%	98%	95%	90%	80%	70%	60%	LAST MSR

UPLANDER SPECIAL – 12, 20, or 28 ga., 3 in. chambers (not available in 28 ga.), 24 or 26 in. barrels, fixed chokes on 28 ga., features straight grip Brazilian hardwood checkered English stock and forearm, DT, approx. 7.3 lbs. Mfg. 2002-2005.

	$340	$300	$260	$230	$200	$165	$125	*$375*

UPLANDER SUPREME – 12 or 20 ga., 3 in. chambers, 24 (20 ga. only, disc. 2010), 26, or 28 in. barrels with choke tubes, extractors, gold ST, high gloss AA grade checkered walnut stock and forearm. Importation began 2000.

MSR $539	$465	$395	$350	$300	$250	$215	$195	

Add $140 for combo package (includes 12 and 20 ga. or 20 and 28 ga. barrels, new 2005).

LONGFOWLER – 12 ga., 3 in. chambers, 30 in. barrels with two extended choke tubes, single trigger, extractors, checkered walnut stock and semi-beavertail forearm, top tang safety. New 2013.

MSR $449	$395	$360	$325	$295	$275	$250	$225	

COACH GUN MODEL – 12, 20 ga., or .410 (new 1991) bore, hammerless, choice of blue, polished nickel, or matte nickel (new 1996) finish, 20 in. barrels with choke tubes (disc.) or fixed IC/M chokes, choice of dark (nickel finish only) or light hardwood stock, ST or DT, 6 1/2 lbs.

MSR $449	$375	$335	$275	$240	$215	$195	$180	

Add $50 for black finished walnut and polished matte nickel finish.
Add $64 for carved stagecoach scene on stock (mfg. 1996-99).

* ***Coach Gun Model Deluxe*** – similar to Coach Gun Model, includes deluxe checkered walnut stock and forearm, fixed (IC/M) or choke tubes (new 1998), gold triggers. Mfg. 1997-99.

	$385	$325	$290	$260	$230	$195	$170	*$499*

COACH GUN SILVERADO – similar to Coach Gun, except features a matte nickel metal finish and oil finished hardwood pistol grip or straight English (not available in .410 bore) stock and forearm. Imported 2002-2004.

	$320	$270	$215	$180	$150	$130	$110	*$375*

COACH GUN SUPREME – 12, 20 ga. or .410 bore (disc. 2005), blue, hammerless, polished nickel, or stainless steel receiver, blue or polished nickel, 20 or 24 (disc. 2005) in. barrels with choke tubes (except for .410 bore), checkered AA grade walnut stock with recoil pad and beavertail forearm, ST or DT, extractors. Importation began 2004.

MSR $499	$435	$350	$275	$225	$180	$150	$130	

DOUBLE DEFENSE – 12 or 20 ga., 3 in. chambers, hammerless, matte blue finish, 20 in. ported barrels, fixed IC chokes, single trigger, non-reflective matte black hardwood stock, fiber optic front sight, top and bottom Picatinny rails, 6 1/2 lbs. New mid-2009.

MSR $499	$435	$350	$275	$225	$180	$150	$130	

SHOTGUNS: SEMI-AUTO

ULTRA-LIGHT MODEL – 12 ga. only, 3 in. chamber, gas operated, 26 or 28 in. VR barrel with 3 choke tubes, checkered walnut stock and forearm, approx. 6 1/2 lbs.

	$295	$260	$230	$210	$195	$180	$165	

While advertised by Stoeger Industries during 2000, this model was never imported by Stoeger Industries. However, it has had limited importation to date from domestic distributors.

MODEL 2000 – 12 ga. only, 3 in. chamber, Benelli licensed inertia recoil operating system, 18 1/2 (new 2012), 24 (new 2010), 26, 28, or 30 in. VR barrel with 5 choke tubes, checkered walnut or black synthetic (new 2002) stock and forearm, matte metal, 100% Advantage Timber HD (mfg. 2002-2010), Realtree APG HD (new 2007), or Advantage Max-4 camo (new 2004) finish, approx. 7.1 lbs. Mfg. by Vursan Manufacturing located in Istanbul, Turkey, with importation beginning 2001.

MSR $509	$435	$365	$315	$265	$230	$195	$175	

Add $60 for 100% camo coverage.
Add $90 for Turkey configuration with Timber HD steady grip and 24 in. barrel.

GRADING - PPGS™	100%	98%	95%	90%	80%	70%	60%	LAST MSR

Add $59 (11 oz.) or $89 (13 oz.) for recoil reducer.

Add $121 for Model 2000 Deluxe with upgraded wood and floral etched receiver trim (disc. 2003).

Add $146 for synthetic combo package which includes a smoothbore slug barrel with screw-in IC choke and rifle sights, $226 if with camo, or $81 if with walnut (disc. 2002).

* ***Model 2000 Slug*** – 12 ga. only, 3 in. chamber, available with walnut or synthetic with 100% Advantage Timber HD finish, 24 in. smoothbore barrel with adj. rifle sights, 6.7 lbs. Imported 2003-2004.

	$365	$320	$285	$250	$225	$195	$175	*$430*

Add $15 for walnut stock and forearm.

Add $75 for 100% camo coverage.

MODEL 3500 – 12 ga. only, 3 1/2 in. chamber, Benelli licensed inertia recoil operating system, 24, 26, or 28 in. barrel with 5 choke tubes, black synthetic, 100% Realtree APG, or Realtree Max-4 100% camo coverage. New 2011.

MSR $629	$550	$475	$425	$375	$325	$275	$250

Add $90 for 100% camo coverage.

Add $49 for recoil reducer (new 2012).

SHOTGUNS: SLIDE ACTION

MODEL P350 – 12 ga. only, 3 1/2 in. chamber, 18 1/2 (Home Security, cyl. fixed choke), 24, 26, or 28 in. barrel, includes 5 screw-in chokes, choice of black synthetic, Timber HD (disc. 2008), Realtree APG HD or Realtree Max-4 HD camo coverage, approx. 6.9 lbs. New 2005.

MSR $349	$285	$240	$200	$170	$150	$125	$110

Add $30 for pistol grip (18 1/2 in. barrel only).

Add $100 for 100% camo coverage.

Add $63 for 13 oz. recoil reducer (disc. 2010).

Add $130 for Turkey configuration with camo, steady grip and 24 in barrel.

STONER RIFLE

Please refer to the Knight's Manufacturing Company listing in the K section.

STRANK, ANDREAS

Current long gun manufacturer established in 1995 and located in Baesweiler, Germany. No current U.S. importation.

Andreas Strank manufactures high quality shotguns and bolt action rifles per individual special order. Please contact the company directly for more information and current pricing (see Trademark Index).

STRASSER

Current trademark of bolt action rifles manufactured by HMS GmbH, located in Eugendorf, Austria. Please refer to the H section.

STRATEGIC ARMORY CORPS, LLC

Current manufacturer located Phoenix, AZ.

Strategic Armory Corps, LLC was formed in August of 2011 and is the parent company of AWC Systems Technology LLC, which manufactures sound supressors, AWC Ammo, and Surgeon Rifles. Please refer to Surgeon Rifles listing for current firearms manufacture.

STRAYER TRIPP INTERNATIONAL

Please refer to the STI International listing in this section.

STRAYER-VOIGT, INC.

Current manufacturer of Infinity pistols located in Grand Prairie, TX. See the Infinity listing for more information.

GRADING - PPGS™	100%	98%	95%	90%	80%	70%	60%	LAST MSR

STREET SWEEPER

Previously manufactured by Sales of Georgia, Inc. located in Atlanta, GA.

SHOTGUNS

STREET SWEEPER – 12 ga. only, 12 shot rotary mag., paramilitary configuration with 18 in. barrel, double action, folding stock, 9 3/4 lbs. Restricted sales following the ATF classification as a "destructive device." Mfg. 1989-approx. 1995.

$1,495	$1,350	$1,100	$995	$895	$795	$695	

Unless this model was registered with the ATF before May 1st, 2001, it is subject to seizure with a possible fine/imprisonment.

STURM, RUGER & CO., INC.

Current manufacturer with production facilities located in Newport, NH and Prescott, AZ. Previously manufactured in Southport, CT 1949-1991 (corporate and administrative offices remain at this location). A second factory was opened in Newport, NH in 1963, and still produces single action revolvers, rifles and shotguns.

Sturm, Ruger & Co. was founded in 1949 by Alexander Sturm and William B. Ruger to manufacture .22 cal. semi-auto pistols. The original factory was in a wooden structure located across from the train depot in Southport, CT. By 1959, the company moved into a larger modern factory not too far from the original buildings. The product line quickly expanded to a Target Model, single action revolvers, rifles, DA revolvers and shotguns.

From four separate factories, Ruger has manufactured and shipped over 25 million guns. The two Southport, CT facilities are no longer utilized. Guns are manufactured at the two large modern facilities located in Newport, NH and Prescott, AZ. Ruger is America's third largest small arms maker, and offers a complete line of firearms for sportsmen, law enforcement, and military.

Mr. Alex Sturm passed away in November 1951. On July 6, 2002, the legendary William B. Ruger, Sr. passed away in his home in Prescott, AZ.

Beginning 1996, all handguns are supplied with a case and lock. Beginning late 2000, a spent cartridge case was supplied with all handguns.

Please refer to the *Blue Book of Modern Black Powder Arms* by John Allen (also online) for more information and prices on Sturm Ruger black powder models.

Black Powder Revolvers - Reproductions & Replicas and *Black Powder Long Arms & Pistols - Reproductions & Replicas* by Dennis Adler are also invaluable sources for most black powder reproductions and replicas, and include hundreds of color images on most popular makes/models, provide manufacturer/trademark histories, and up-to-date information on related items/accessories for black powder shooting - www.bluebookofgunvalues.com

The publisher would like to thank Bill Hamm, Richard Machniak, John Dougan, and Chad Hiddleson for their contributions in this and previous editions.

RUGER COLLECTIBILITY OVERVIEW

For the past three decades Ruger collecting has become very popular and as a result, many of the early pistols, revolvers and rifles are actively sought after. Some models and sub-models were produced in such small quantities that they were not cataloged. The engraving project in the mid-1950s produced 275 ornamented guns which are regarded as the holy grail of Ruger collecting.

Ruger firearms fall into three categories identified by the time frames they were produced; 1949-1963, 1963-1973 and those made from 1973 to date. In most instances the earliest time frame encompasses the rarest and most collectable specimens; certain of these guns command the highest prices.

All Ruger firearms produced in 1976 were marked MADE IN THE 200th YEAR OF AMERICAN LIBERTY, collectors refer to them as "Liberty Models". Most guns that fall into this category will sell for a slight premium if in NIB condition.

GRADING - PPGS™	100%	98%	95%	90%	80%	70%	60%	LAST MSR

Some guns of all models can have special markings, "S" denoting sold as seconds, "D" duplicate numbered, "U" used, "US" on guns shipped to the military. A star designates a single cylinder. Foreign proof marks and ATF marked guns appear occasionally. A premium will be added to specimens featuring any of the markings. The premium will sometimes equal the amount of the basic price of the gun.

From 2004 to 2007 the Ruger Studio of Art & Decoration offered factory engraving on any current Ruger models. This engraving could range from presentation inscriptions to bas-relief and extensively gold inlaid masterpieces, and ranging in price from up to $50,000 or more.

The 100% condition factor in this section assumes the gun is new or in mint original condition. Guns that are in their original factory packaging with all their paperwork require an individual evaluation and/or appraisal due to the wide varying values that such packaging and paperwork add to individual pieces.

PISTOLS: SEMI-AUTO, RIMFIRE

Many distributors and customizers have produced special/limited editions of this popular series of .22 cal. pistols; these editions are not listed in the *Blue Book of Gun Values*. After 1999, all .22 cal. pistols were fitted with Ruger logo medallions with a red background.

"RED EAGLE" STANDARD & TARGET MODEL – Ruger's first offerings, popular designation with red grip medallions, changed to black medallions in memory of Alexander Sturm in 1952, ser. no. range 0001-33000. Approx. 30,000 mfg. 1949-1952.

Standard Model	$650	$550	$450	$350	$265	$235	$175
Standard Model w/ "salt cod" box	$3,750	$2,850	$1,900	$1,400	$900	$700	$600
Target w/ 6 7/8 in. barrel	$725	$595	$525	$425	$375	$350	$300

Produced until early 1952. Serialized approx. 0001 - 25,300 and 30001 to 35000 with Mark I Auto occupying blocks from 15,000-16,999 and 25,000-25,300.

"BLACK OR SILVER EAGLE" STANDARD MODEL – .22 LR cal., 9 shot, 4 3/4 in. or 6 in. barrel, blue, fixed sights, checkered walnut or hard rubber grips, some minor parts variants, most common configuration, ser. no. above 33,000. Mfg. 1952-1982.

Standard	$425	$375	$350	$275	$225	$175	$100
"HENCHO EN MEXICO" marked (250 mfg.)	$1,775	$1,400	$1,000	$800	$700	$625	$550
Stainless 1 of 5000 Signature Series w/box	$475	$375	$325	N/A	N/A	N/A	N/A

» **"Black or Silver Eagle" Standard Model (Post Red Eagle) Stainless Steel 1 of 5,000 w/California Freedom Inscription** – engraved "CAL. FREEDOM '82" on chamber, donated by Ruger to the California Citizens Against the Gun Initiative in 1982, and raffled to NRA members and CA gun owners, known ser. no. range is 17-03379 to 17-04792. 26 mfg., including one prototype.

$1,000	$750	$625	N/A	N/A	N/A	N/A

"BLACK OR SILVER EAGLE" MARK I TARGET – similar to Standard, except has 5 1/2 in. heavy, 5 1/4 in. tapered (scarce, mfg. 1952 - 1955 only) barrel, or 6 7/8 in. heavy tapered barrel, adj. target sights, some minor part variants, ser. no. starts at approx. 33000. Mfg. 1952-1982.

5 1/4 in. bbl.	$850	$750	$650	$475	$325	$250	$200
5 1/2 in. bull bbl.	$425	$350	$300	$250	$200	$175	$150
6 7/8 in. bbl.	$425	$350	$300	$250	$175	$150	$135
6 7/8 in. U.S. marked	N/A	$850	$650	$475	$325	$250	$200

Add $125 for Ruger marked muzzle brake.

GRADING - PPGS™	100%	98%	95%	90%	80%	70%	60%	LAST MSR

MARK II STANDARD – .22 LR cal., 4 3/4 or 6 in. barrel, checkered black Delrin synthetic grips, blue finish, 10 shot mag., approx. 2 1/4 lbs., ser. nos. start at 18-00001. Mfg. 1982-2004.

	$225	$175	$135	$115	$110	$100	$95	*$299*

* ***Mark II Standard Stainless Steel*** – variation of the Mark II Standard. Disc. 2004.

	$295	$215	$175	$135	$115	$100	$85	*$390*

Serial numbers start approx. at 211-00001 and thereafter are intermixed with the blue model.

MARK II STANDARD 50TH ANNIVERSARY – .22 LR cal., features blue receiver machined to same contour as original production, stainless steel bolt with Ruger medallion on rear, 50th Anniversary Ruger crest on top of frame in front of ejection port, black grips with Ruger medallion in red background, lockable red case. Approx. 35,000 mfg. 1999 only.

	$345	$300	$225	$175	$125	$110	$100	*$287*

After 1999, all Ruger .22 pistols were fitted with Ruger logo medallions having a red background.

MARK II TARGET – .22 LR cal., blued steel, 4 (mfg. 1996-99) bull, 5 1/4 (disc. 1994), 5 1/2 bull, 6 7/8 standard, 6 7/8 bull, 8 bull, or 10 in. bull barrel, 2 5/8 - 3 1/4 lbs. depending on barrel. Disc. 2004.

	$375	$325	$250	$175	$150	$120	$110	*$365*

Add $16 for 4 in. bull barrel.
Add $15 for 10 in. bull barrel.
Add $75 for 8 in. bull barrel.

* ***Mark II Target Stainless Steel*** – stainless variation of the Mark II Target, includes choice of 5 1/4 (disc. 1994), 5 1/2 bull, 6 7/8 standard, 6 7/8 bull, or 10 in. bull barrel. Disc. 2004.

	$425	$325	$250	$200	$150	$115	$95	*$460*

Add $10 for 10 in. bull barrel.

MARK II MODEL 22/45 – .22 LR cal. only, Zytel frame is patterned after the Model 1911 .45 ACP Govt, 4, 4 3/4, 5 1/4 (Target, disc.), or 5 1/2 in. bull barrel, 10 shot mag. (push-button release), fixed (4 3/4 in. barrel only) or adj. sights, 28-35 oz. Mfg. 1993-2004.

* ***Mark II Model 22/45 Blue Finish*** – 4 in. regular barrel with adj. sights (Model P4, new 1997) or 5 1/2 in. bull barrel with adj. sights (Model P512). Mfg. 1994-2004.

	$225	$190	$165	$135	$125	$115	$100	*$290*

* ***Mark II Model 22/45 Stainless*** – 4 3/4 in. regular barrel with fixed sights (Model KP4, new 1997), 5 1/4 in. tapered barrel (Model KP514 disc. 1994) or 5 1/2 in. bull barrel with adj. sights (Model KP512). Disc. 2004.

	$250	$210	$190	$165	$135	$125	$115	*$315*

Add $65 for adj. sights (5 1/2 in. bull barrel only).

GOVERNMENT TARGET MODEL (MK678G) – commercial variation of the government training model without "U.S." markings, 6 7/8 in. bull barrel, adj. rear sight, blue finish, black plastic grips, 46 oz., first 30,000 were individually test targeted. Mfg. 1987-2004.

	$375	$325	$250	$200	$165	$150	$125	*$445*

* ***Government Target Model (MK678G) Military "U.S." Marked*** – adj. sights, 6 7/8 in. bull barrel, U.S. marking on chamber, issued to U.S. military personnel for training purposes, must be factory verified, ser. no. range 210-00001 - 210-18500, approx. 25 believed to be in civilian hands. Disc. 1999.

	$1,100	$975	$700	$425	$360	$330	$300	*$600*

* ***Government Target Model (KMK678G) Stainless Steel*** – .22 LR cal., stainless steel, black polymer grips, 6 7/8 in. barrel, adj. rear sight, fixed front sight, 46 oz.

	$450	$375	$325	$225	$175	$125	$100	*$509*

* ***Government Target Model (KMK678GC) Competition Slabside*** – .22 LR cal., stainless steel, black polymer grips, 6 7/8 in. slabside barrel, adj. sights, drilled and tapped, includes two magazines. Mfg. 1992-2004.

	$450	$350	$300	$200	$175	$125	$100	*$555*

GRADING - PPGS™	100%	98%	95%	90%	80%	70%	60%	*LAST MSR*

* ***Government Target Model (MK678G) Stainless Foreign Military Contract*** – .22 LR cal., stainless steel, black phosphate finish, black polymer grips, with blackened Ruger medallion, 5 1/2 in. bull barrel (KMK512B) with narrow aperture rear sight and thin front sight blade, contract overrun of 84 pistols sold to domestic market, ser. no. range 212-89651 - 213-52645.

	$750	$600	$500	$450	$400	$350	$300	

MARK III STANDARD – .22 LR cal., 4 3/4 or 6 in. barrel with fixed sights, the Mark III action is an evolution of the Mark II design, featuring a relocated mag. release button on the left side of the grip, behind the trigger guard, recontoured ejection port and tapered bolt ears, blue finish, loaded chamber indicator, internal lock, 10 shot mag., magazine disconnector safety, checkered composition grip panels, 35-37 oz. New 2005.

MSR $389	$300	$240	$180	$135	$110	$100	$95	

MARK III TARGET – .22 LR cal., 5 1/2 in. bull or 6 7/8 (disc.) in. tapered barrel, adj. rear sight, operating mechanism is the same as the Mark III Standard, blue finish, checkered composition grip panels, laminate target grips (new 2013), approx. 42 oz. New 2005.

MSR $459	$355	$290	$230	$200	$175	$140	$125	

Add $50 for laminate target grips (new 2013).

* ***Mark III Target (KMKIII) Stainless*** – similar to Mark III Target, except has stainless steel construction, 5 1/2 in. bull barrel, 42 oz. New 2005.

MSR $569	$445	$355	$285	$225	$185	$165	$140	

* ***Mark III Target Government Competition*** – features 6 7/8 in. slab sided bull barrel and brown laminated cocobolo grip panels with thumb rest, adj. rear sight, 45 oz. New 2005.

MSR $659	$530	$435	$360	$280	$245	$215	$195	

MARK III HUNTER – .22 LR cal., stainless steel construction, 4 1/2 (new 2008) or 6 7/8 in. target crowned fluted barrel, checkered cocobolo, laminate target (new 2013) or Crimson Trace (mfg. 2008-2010) grips, V-notch rear sight blade, Hi-Viz/Fiber optic front sights with interchangeable LitePipes, adj. rear sight, drilled and tapped, 41 oz. New 2005.

MSR $679	$550	$450	$385	$330	$275	$230	$195	

Add $50 for laminate target grips (new 2013).

Add $173 for Crimson Trace laser grips (4 1/2 in. barrel only, disc. 2010).

MARK III 22/45 – .22 LR cal., Zytel frame is patterned after the Model 1911 .45 ACP Gov't, push button mag. release, 4 in. slab-sided bull (2,000 mfg., disc. 2005), 4 in. bull, 4 1/2 slab-sided bull (disc. 2010) or 5 1/2 in. bull barrel, fixed dot or adj. sights, blue finish, tapered bolt ears, approx. 31 oz. New 2005.

MSR $359	$265	$215	$170	$140	$130	$115	$100	

Add $40 for 5 1/2 in. bull barrel, or $160 for 5 1/2 in. slab sided bull barrel (disc. 2011).

* ***Mark III 22/45 Threaded Barrel*** – .22 LR cal., 10 shot mag., similar to Mark III 22/45, except has 4 1/2 in. threaded bull barrel, fixed sights or Picatinny rail, blue finish, 32 oz. New 2011.

MSR $449	$360	$285	$225	$200	$175	$140	$125	

* ***Mark III 22/45 Stainless*** – .22 LR cal., similar to Mark III 22/45, except is stainless steel, 5 1/2 in. bull barrel only with adj. rear sight, 35 oz. Mfg. 2005-2011.

	$335	$265	$200	$170	$150	$130	$125	*$448*

* ***Mark III 22/45 Hunter*** – .22 LR cal., similar to Model 22/45, except has 5 1/2 or 6.8 in. stainless steel fluted barrel, fiber optic front adj. rear sight, 32-34 oz. Mfg. 2011 only.

	$450	$350	$275	$215	$175	$160	$140	*$593*

* ***Mark III 22/45 Hunter Stainless*** – .22 LR cal., stainless with 4 1/2 or 6 7/8 in. fluted barrel, green case, scope base adapter, six interchangeable Litepipes and lock. Mfg. 2005-2010.

	$435	$350	$260	$210	$165	$140	$120	*$548*

GRADING - PPGS™	100%	98%	95%	90%	80%	70%	60%	LAST MSR

* ***Mark III 22/45 Target*** – .22 LR cal., 4 (new 2012) or 5 1/2 in. barrel, 10 shot mag., fixed front and adj. rear sight, Zytel polymer grips or replaceable brown or black (new 2013) laminate grip panels (5 1/2 in. bbl. only), approx. 32 oz.

MSR $359	$275	$220	$170	$140	$130	$115	$100	

Add $40 for replaceable brown or black (new 2013) laminate grip panels.

22 CHARGER – .22 LR cal., features 10/22 action with 10 in. barrel and 10 shot rotary mag. with mag. release in front of trigger guard, black/grey laminated or black Axiom (new 2009) one-piece ergonomic pistol grip stock and forend, scope rail and bipod included, matte black metal finish, 3 1/2 lbs. Mfg. 2008-2012.

	$325	$265	$230	$195	$175	$150	$125	*$389*

22/45 LITE – .22 LR cal., 10 shot mag., 4.4 in. stainless steel threaded barrel, black anodized finish, upper receiver with fluted barrel shroud, fixed front and adj. rear sights, Zytel polymer replaceable Black laminate 1911-style grip panels, push button mag. release on left side of frame, marked "RUGER 22/45 LITE" in front of ejection port, loaded chamber indicator, includes two magazines, internal lock key and soft case, 23 oz. New 2013.

MSR $499	$425	$365	$330	$300	$275	$250	$225	

SR-22 – .22 LR cal., SA/DA operation with external hammer, 3 1/2 in. stainless steel or threaded (new 2013) barrel, 10 shot mag., aluminum/black or aluminum/silver (new 2013) anodized slide with front and rear serrations, polymer frame and two interchangeable black rubberized grips, adj. 3-dot sights with fully adj. rear, Picatinny rail in front of triggerguard, ambidextrous manual thumb safety/decocking lever and magazine release, includes two 10 shot mags in soft case, 17 1/2 oz. New 2012.

MSR $399	$350	$300	$275	$250	$225	$200	$180	

Add $20 for threaded barrel (new 2013).
Add $30 for aluminum/silver anodized finish (new 2013).

"FRIENDS OF NRA" MK6 – .22 LR cal., high polish blue finish, NRA logo, faux ivory grips, "NATIONAL RIFLE ASSOCIATION" in gold on left side of barrel, ser. no. range 221-78058 to 221-89364, 650 mfg. for NRA auction events in the U.S. during 1997.

	$525	$450	$400	N/A	N/A	N/A	N/A	

"FRIENDS OF NRA" KMK6 – .22 LR cal., stainless steel with black enamel type ornamentation highlights, two-line "Limited Edition" appearing on one side of the barrel, two-line "NATIONAL RIFLE ASSOCIATION" on other side of barrel with NRA logo on rear of bolt, ser. no. range 223-76165 to 224-33634, 750 mfg. for NRA auction events in the U.S. during 2001.

	$525	$450	$400	N/A	N/A	N/A	N/A	

KMK4 "ONE OF ONE THOUSAND" – .22 LR cal., stainless steel, produced as a commemoration of the last 1,000 Mark II pistols mfg. before the introduction of the Mark III series, ser. no. range 226-17150 to 226-18143.

	$350	$300	$250	N/A	N/A	N/A	N/A	

PISTOLS: SEMI-AUTO, CENTERFIRE

LCP (LIGHTWEIGHT COMPACT PISTOL) – .380 ACP cal., DAO, hammerless, black glass filled nylon frame with molded checkering, blued steel slide, 2 3/4 in. barrel, 6 shot mag., .82 in. frame width, fixed sights, black Ruger logos inset in grip panels, includes external locking device, Crimson trace laser grips and pocket holster (mfg. 2011 only), Lasermax Centerfire laser (new 2012), 9.4 oz. New 2008.

MSR $379	$315	$270	$225	$180	$160	$150	$140	

Add $70 for Lasermax Centerfire laser (new 2012).
Add $180 for Crimson trace laser grips and pocket holster (mfg. 2011 only).

LC9 – 9mm Para. cal., hammerless DA only, 3.12 in. barrel, alloy steel slide, blue finish, black glass filled nylon grip frame, 7 shot mag., 3-dot fixed front and adj. rear sights, 1 inch smaller than the LCP, finger grip extension, includes soft case, and Lasermax Centerfire laser (new 2012) or Crimson trace laser grips, loaded chamber indicator, 17.10 oz. New 2011.

GRADING - PPGS™	100%	98%	95%	90%	80%	70%	60%	LAST MSR
MSR $449	$350	$295	$250	$195	$165	$140	$120	

Add $80 for Lasermax Centerfire laser (new 2012).
Add $180 for Crimson trace laser grips.

LC380 – .380 ACP cal., alloy steel slide and barrel, blued finish, 3.12 in. barrel, 7 shot mag., black glass-filled checkered nylon grips, adj. 3-dot sights, includes loaded chamber indicator and soft case, 17.2 oz. New 2013.

MSR $449	$360	$285	$230	$200	$175	$150	$130	

P85 – 9mm Para. cal., double action, 4 1/2 in. barrel, aluminum frame with steel slide, 3-dot fixed sights, 15 shot mag., oversized trigger, polymer grips, matte black finish, 2 lbs. Mfg. 1987-1990.

	$350	$295	$265	$235	$215	$200	$185	*$410*

Subtract $30 if without case and extra mag.

Any P85 models without the "MKIIR" stamp on either the left or right side of the safety must be returned to the factory for a free safety modification.

* ***KP85*** – stainless variation of the P85. Mfg. 1990 only.

	$375	$315	$280	$230	$200	$165	$140	*$452*

Subtract $30 if without case and extra mag.

Variants included a decocking or double action only version at no extra charge.

P85 MARK II – 9mm Para. cal., double action, 4 1/2 in. barrel, aluminum frame with steel slide, 3-dot fixed sights, 15 shot mag., ambidextrous safety beginning in 1991, oversized trigger, polymer grips, matte black finish, 2 lbs. Mfg. 1990-1992.

	$350	$295	$265	$235	$215	$200	$185	*$410*

Subtract $30 if without case and extra mag.

Decocker and DAO models were not available in the Mark II series.

* ***KP85 Mark II*** – stainless variation of the P85. Mfg. 1990-1992.

	$375	$315	$280	$230	$200	$165	$140	*$452*

Subtract $30 if without case and extra mag.

P89 – 9mm Para. cal., improved variation of the P85 Mark II, 10 (C/B 1994) or 15 (new late 2005) shot mag., ambidextrous safety or decocker (Model P89D), blue finish, 32 oz. Mfg. 1992-2007.

	$380	$330	$280	$250	$215	$200	$185	*$475*

Variants were available in a decocking (P89DC) or double action only (P-89DAO, disc. 2004) version at no extra charge.

KP89 STAINLESS – stainless variation of the P89, also available in double action only (disc.). Mfg. 1992-2009.

	$425	$360	$305	$250	$215	$200	$185	*$525*

Add $45 for convertible 7.65mm Luger cal. barrel (Model KP89X, approx. 5,750 mfg. during 1994 only).

P90 – .45 ACP cal., similar to KP90 Stainless, except has blue finish, 8 shot mag., 33 1/2 oz. Disc. 2010.

	$475	$395	$335	$265	$215	$200	$185	*$591*

Add $50 for tritium night sights (disc. 2006).

P90 models were produced in a variety of models for law enforcement or government contracts and will be found with any combination of safety model, decocker or double action only with fingergroove tactical rubber grip and/or tritium night sights.

KP90 STAINLESS – .45 ACP cal., double action, 4 1/2 in. barrel, oversized trigger, aluminum frame with stainless steel slide, 8 shot single column mag., ambidextrous safety (KP90) or decocking (KP90D), polymer grips, 3-dot fixed sights, ambidextrous safety began approx ser. no. 660-12800. Mfg. 1991-2010.

	$495	$415	$360	$295	$250	$225	$200	*$636*

GRADING - PPGS™	100%	98%	95%	90%	80%	70%	60%	LAST MSR

Add $50 for tritium night sights (disc. 2006).

KP90 models were produced in a variety of models for law enforcement or government contracts and will be found with any combination of safety model, decocker or double action only with fingergroove tactical rubber grip and/or tritium night sights.

KP91 STAINLESS – .40 S&W cal., similar to Model KP90 Stainless, except is not available with external safety and has 11 shot double column mag. Mfg. 1991-1994.

	$385	$335	$295	$240	$210	$180	$155	*$489*

This model was available in a decocking variation (KP91D) or double action only (KP91DAO). Approx. 39,600 of all models were mfg. before being discontinued in favor of the tapered slide KP944 model.

P93D BLUE – similar to KP93 Stainless, except has blue finish, compact model, ambidextrous decocker, 31 oz. Mfg. 1998-2004.

	$395	$330	$285	$240	$215	$200	$185	*$495*

Add $50 for tritium night sights.

P93 models were produced in a variety of models for law enforcement or government contracts and will be found with any combination of decocker model or double action only with fingergroove tactical rubber grip and/or tritium night sights.

P93 CHICAGO POLICE SPECIAL CONTRACT – produced in the late 1990s for a Chicago Police Department contract, this blued stainless P93 was ordered with a special P89M rollmark on the slide so that those who were concerned about having a "compact" pistol would not be alerted to the fact that it was indeed a P93. Extremely rare in civilian hands.

Extreme rarity precludes accurate pricing on this model, and should be examined for authenticity. NIB specimens have been noted at $550.

KP93 STAINLESS – 9mm Para. cal., compact variation with 3 9/10 in. tilting barrel - link actuated, matte blue or REM (new 1996) finish, 3-dot sights, 10 (C/B 1994) or 15* shot mag., available with DA/SA ambidextrous decocker action or double action only, 31 oz. Mfg. 1994-2004.

	$450	$370	$315	$260	$220	$200	$185	*$575*

Add $50 for tritium night sights.

KP93 models were produced in a variety of models for law enforcement or government contracts and will be found with any combination of decocker model or double action only with fingergroove tactical rubber grip and/or tritium night sights.

P94 BLUE – similar to KP94 Stainless, except has blue finish. Mfg. 1998-2004.

	$395	$330	$285	$240	$215	$200	$185	*$495*

Add $50 for tritium night sights.

P94 models have been produced in a variety of models for law enforcement or government contracts and will be found with any combination of safety model, decocker or double action only with fingergroove tactical rubber grip and/or tritium night sights.

KP94 STAINLESS – 9mm Para. or .40 S&W cal., available with ambidextrous safety, matte blue or REM (new 1996) finish, DA/SA ambidextrous decocker action or double action only, 10 (C/B 1994), or 15* (9mm Para.) shot mag., 33 oz. Mfg. 1994-2004.

	$450	$370	$315	$260	$220	$200	$185	*$575*

Add $50 for tritium night sights.

KP94 models have been produced in a variety of models for law enforcement or government contracts and will be found with any combination of safety model, decocker or double action only with fingergroove tactical rubber grip and/or tritium night sights.

P95PR – 9mm Para. cal., available in ambidextrous decocker (D/DPR suffix), ambidextrous safety (new 2001) or double action only configuration (DAO suffix, disc.), polymer frame, 3.9 in. barrel, fixed sights, blue finish, 10 or 15 (new late 2005) shot mag., lower Picatinny rail became standard in 2006, 27 oz. New 1997.

MSR $399	$320	$275	$235	$195	$165	$150	$135	

Add $50 for tritium night sights (disc. 2006).

GRADING - PPGS™	100%	98%	95%	90%	80%	70%	60%	LAST MSR

During 2006, this model's nomenclature changed from P95 to P95PR to reflect the Picatinny style rail.

P95 models have been produced in a variety of models for law enforcement or government contracts and will be found with any combination of safety model, decocker or double action only with fingergroove tactical rubber grip and/or tritium night sights. The P95DAO double action only model was disc. 2004.

KP95PR STAINLESS – stainless variation of Model P95PR. New 1997.

MSR $439	$355	$310	$250	$200	$175	$140	$120	

During 2006, this model's nomenclature changed from KP95 to KP95PR to reflect the Picatinny style rail.

P97D – .45 ACP cal., ambidextrous decocker, 8 shot mag., blue finish, 30 1/2 oz. Mfg. 2002-2004.

	$370	$315	$275	$235	$215	$200	$185	*$460*

Add $50 for tritium night sights.

KP97 STAINLESS – .45 ACP cal., similar to KP95 Stainless, except has 8 shot mag., 27 oz. Mfg. 1999-2004.

	$395	$315	$265	$235	$215	$200	$185	*$495*

Add $50 for tritium night sights.

P345 – .45 ACP cal., ambidextrous safety or decocker (P345DPR), black polymer frame with matte stainless or blue stainless steel slide, 4.2 in. barrel, fixed sights, polyurethane grips, slimmer profile frame, 8 shot single column mag., with or w/o (disc. 2008) Picatinny rail, loaded chamber indicator, 29 oz. Mfg. 2005-2012.

	$485	$425	$335	$275	$225	$210	$195	*$599*

KP345 – .45 ACP cal., decocker (KP345DPR), similar to P345, except has stainless steel slide, Picatinny rail became standard 2009 (KP345PR), 29 oz. Mfg. 2005-2012.

	$515	$440	$345	$280	$230	$210	$195	*$639*

P944 – .40 S&W cal., similar to P94, ambidextrous safety, blue finish, 34 oz. Mfg. 1999-2010.

	$445	$360	$300	$245	$215	$200	$185	*$557*

Add $50 for tritium night sights (disc. 2006).

This model has been produced in many versions for law enforcement or government contracts and will be found with any combination of safety type, decocker, or double action only, fingergroove tactical rubber grip, and/or tritium night sights.

KP944 STAINLESS – similar to P944, except is stainless steel, also available as decocker (KP944D). Mfg. 1999-2010.

	$500	$400	$345	$275	$230	$195	$170	*$647*

Add $50 for tritum night sights (disc. 2006).

This model has been produced in many versions for law enforcement or government contracts and will be found with any combination of safety type, decocker, or double action only, fingergroove tactical rubber grip, and/or tritium night sights. The KP944DAO double action only model was disc. 2004.

SR9 – 9mm Para. cal., striker fired ignition, semi-double action trigger pull, 4 1/8 in. barrel, 10 or 17 shot mag., reversible backstrap, low profile 3-dot sights, glass filled nylon frame, choice of black stainless, brushed stainless steel, alloy steel/Nitridox Pro Black (SR9B Model), or OD Green (mfg. 2009-2010) stainless steel slide, Picatinny rail, ambidextrous safety, 26 1/2 oz. New late 2007.

MSR $529	$450	$400	$350	$315	$275	$240	$210	

Add $40 for OD Green finish (disc. 2010).

Note that all SR9 models serial numbered 330-29999 and earlier are subject to a factory recall at no charge. If your pistol has not yet had the new parts installed, please contact Sturm, Ruger

GRADING - PPGS™	100%	98%	95%	90%	80%	70%	60%	LAST MSR

& Company at 1-800-784-3701 or email SR9Recall@ruger.com and they will provide you with shipping instructions.

* ***SR9C*** – 9mm Para. cal., similar to the Model SR9, except has compact frame and 3 1/2 in. barrel, 23.4 oz. New mid-2010.

MSR $529	$450	$400	$350	$315	$275	$240	$210

SR40 – .40 S&W cal., hammerless striker fired ignition, 10 or 15 shot mag., 4.14 in. barrel, alloy or stainless steel slide with brushed stainless or Nitridox Pro Black finish, adj. 3-dot sights, black glass filled nylon grips, reversible backstrap, integral mounting rail, ambidextrous thumb safety, loaded chamber indicator, includes two mags., 27 1/4 oz. New 2011.

MSR $529	$450	$400	$350	$315	$275	$240	$210

* ***SR40c*** – .40 S&W cal., similar to SR40, except has compact frame, 3 1/2 in. barrel, brushed stainless or Nitridox Pro Black finish, 9 or 15 shot mag., adj. 3-dot sights, 23.4 oz. New mid-2011.

MSR $529	$450	$400	$350	$315	$275	$240	$210

SR45 – .45 ACP cal., similar to SR40, except has 4 1/2 in. barrel, 10 shot mag. only, choice of brushed stainless slide or alloy steel with black nitride finish, 30.15 oz. New 2013.

MSR $529	$450	$400	$350	$315	$275	$240	$210

SR-1911 – .45 ACP cal., SA, patterned after the Colt M1911 Series 70, 5 in. barrel, supplied with one 7 and one 8 shot stainless steel mags., matte stainless steel frame and slide, diamond checkered cocobolo grips with black Ruger medallion inserts, skeletonized trigger and bobbed hammer, Novak 3-dot adj. sights, approx. 40 oz. New mid-2011.

MSR $829	$715	$565	$465	$385	$325	$275	$250

* ***SR-1911CMD*** – .45 ACP cal., similar to SR-1911, except has 4 1/4 in. barrel, 7 shot mag., 36.4 oz. New 2013.

MSR $829	$715	$565	$465	$385	$325	$275	$250

REVOLVERS: SINGLE ACTION, OLD MODELS

These vintage revolvers were manufactured between 1953 and 1973, and are chambered in .22 RF and several popular centerfire calibers. There are models and sub-models with variants in the Single-Six, Bearcat, Blackhawk & Super Blackhawk families. The single-shot Hawkeye is considered as part of the Old Model classification. The Old Model or Three Screw Single-Six, Blackhawk and Super Blackhawk models are visually identified apart from the New Model by the presence of three screws on the side of the cylinder frame - the New Model features two pins at the same location.

Ruger offers a free conversion kit that will upgrade the lock work, similar to the New Model, thereby offering the best of both technologies. Ruger will fit these parts-sets at their Service Dept. at no charge and return the original parts to the customer (see Trademark Index).

SINGLE SIX – .22 LR cal., 4 5/8, 5 1/2, or 9 1/2 in. barrel, fixed sights, rubber grips, blue finish. Mfg. 1953-1973.

Add $650 for Factory stag XR3 grips on models that apply.

Add $1,200 for Factory ivory XR3 grips on models that apply.

A negotiated premium can be added for examples with S (seconds) or D (duplicate) marking.

After 1962, only the 5 1/2 gun was available as an LR only model (RSS5W). Walnut grips became standard equipment in 1961 and from 1961 to 1962 hard rubber grips were available only as an option on this model. Genuine stag and ivory grips were also available as an accessory for the XR3 grip frame and due to their rarity, authentication by an expert is necessary. Varnished walnut grips appear at ser. no. 160000. XR3 grip frame changed to XR3-RED in 1963, and was standard with oilded walnut grip panels and fitted with anodized aluminum ejector rod housing.

* ***Single Six Flat loading gate*** – 5 1/2 in. barrel only, approx. 60,000 mfg. from 1953-1957. Four variations with ser. no. range 1-60000.

GRADING - PPGS™	100%	98%	95%	90%	80%	70%	60%	LAST MSR
	$850	$650	$500	$350	$300	$250	$200	

Add 100% for those serial numbered under 2000 with a non-serrated front sight.

* ***Single Six Round loading gate*** – with round loading gate, serial numbered up to approximately 195000.

4 5/8 in. bbl. (1953-1963 mfg.)	**$1,000**	**$750**	**$550**	**$325**	**$250**	**$225**	**$200**
4 5/8 in. bbl. (1963-1973 mfg.)	**$650**	**$525**	**$425**	**$300**	**$225**	**$200**	**$175**
5 1/2 in. bbl. (1953-1973 mfg.)	**$525**	**$450**	**$350**	**$250**	**$195**	**$145**	**$125**
6 1/2 in. bbl. (1963-1973 mfg.)	**$475**	**$375**	**$300**	**$225**	**$195**	**$145**	**$125**
9 1/2 in. bbl. (1953-1963 mfg.)	**$850**	**$650**	**$500**	**$375**	**$275**	**$200**	**$175**
9 1/2 in. bbl. (1963-1973 mfg.)	**$650**	**$525**	**$450**	**$300**	**$250**	**$200**	**$175**

Add $75 for extra .22 WMR cylinder w (4 5/8 in. bbl., mfg. 1961-1962, ser. no. range 173000 to 189000) or (9 1/2 in. bbl., mfg. 1961-1962, ser. no. range 164000 to 193700).

1953-1963 mfg. ser. no. range for the 5 1/2 in. barrel is 60,000-195,000. 4 5/8 in. barrel ser. no. range is 128,500-195,000. 9 1/2 in. barrel ser. no. range is 139,070-195,000.

1963-1973 mfg. ser. no. range for the 4 5/8 in. barrel is 195000-196940, 342450-399999, 400000-499999, 8000000-833350, 20-00000-20-99999, and 21-0000-21-56100.

1963-1973 mfg. ser. no. range for the 5 1/2 in. barrel is 195000-196940, 244020-244320, 342450-399999, 400000-499999, 8000000-833350, 20-0000 0-20-99999, and 21-0000 - 21-56100.

1963-1973 mfg. ser. no. range for the 6 1/2 in. barrel is 342450-399999, 400000-499999, 8000000-833350, 20-00000-20-99999, and 21-0000-21-56100.

1963-1973 mfg. ser. no. range for the 9 1/2 in. barrel is 195000-196940, 342450-399999, 400000-499999, 8000000-833350, 20-00000-20-99999, and 21-0000-21-56100.

* ***Single Six Factory Engraved Models*** – factory cased with varnished walnut grip panels, several groups of engraving patterns, each commanding a separate valuation, considered the most desirable of entire SA line, except for 22 guns engraved in Spain, all others engraved by Charles H. Jerred, limited to only 260 examples. Mfg. 1954-1958.

Subtract $1,000 if w/o presentation case.
Add a premium for consecutively numbered pairs that are verified as being shipped together.

» **Spanish Engraved** – ser. nos. 7 and 8, 5,100-5,119.

$20,000	**$16,000**	**$12,000**	**N/A**	**N/A**	**N/A**	**N/A**

» **All Blue Engraved** – ser. no. range 135XX-243XXX, 28 mfg.

$15,000	**$12,000**	**$10,000**	**N/A**	**N/A**	**N/A**	**N/A**

» **Standard Pattern** – ser. no. ranges 308XX, 355XX, 449XXX, 50XXX, and 74XXX, 210 mfg.

$9,500	**$8,000**	**$6,500**	**N/A**	**N/A**	**N/A**	**N/A**

SINGLE SIX .22 MAGNUM – 6 1/2 in. barrel only, serial numbered between 300000-342500, left side of frame rollmarked in two lines with "RUGER SINGLE-SIX WIN..22RF MAG.CAL.". The last few thousand of this variety were fitted with XR3-RED grip frame. Approx. 42,450 mfg. 1959-1962.

$525	**$425**	**$350**	**$275**	**$195**	**$145**	**$125**

GRADING - PPGS™	100%	98%	95%	90%	80%	70%	60%	LAST MSR

Add $75 if revolver was originally shipped as a convertible with extra .22 LR cylinder.
A very few Mag. only Single-Sixes (not magnum marked) were produced after 340200. These are very rare and authentication through factory letter (as RSSMW) is necessary - add $75.

SINGLE SIX CONVERTIBLE – similar to Single Six, except .22 LR and .22 WMR interchangeable cylinders, redesigned grip frame (XR-3 red), wood grips, 4 5/8, 5 1/2, 6 1/2, or 9 1/2 in. barrel with 4 5/8 in. being the rarest. Mfg. 1962-1972.

Add $30-$35 for auxilary .22 LR/.22 WMR cylinder.

* ***Single Six Convertible 5 1/2, 6 1/2 in. barrel***

	$450	$400	$300	$195	$150	$110	$100

Ser. no. range for 5 1/2 in. barrel begins about 194000.
Ser. no. range for 6 1/2 in. barrel begins about 340200.

* ***Single Six Convertible 4 5/8 or 9 1/2 in. barrel***

	$650	$575	$500	$375	$275	$175	$150

Ser. no. range for 4 5/8 in. barrel begins about 428000.
Ser. no. range for 9 1/2 in. barrel begins about 360000.

LIGHTWEIGHT SINGLE SIX – similar to Single Six, except aluminum alloy frame, XR3 grip frame, 4 5/8 in. barrel, 200,000-212,000 serial range, alloy or steel cylinder, black hard rubber grips, steel ejector rod housing. Three variations, 12,530 mfg. 1956-1959.

* ***Lightweight Single Six Tri-color*** – silver colored aluminum cylinder frame, ser. no. range 200,000-205,500.

	$1,200	$850	$675	$550	$425	$300	$225

* ***Lightweight Single Six Tri-color w/S Marking*** – "S" (seconds) marked (verified), ser. nos. are random, 226 mfg.

	$1,600	$1,250	$975	$875	$750	$500	$375

* ***Lightweight Single Six Blue Alloy*** – all blue with black anodized aluminum cylinder frame, alloy cylinder, ser. no. range 205500-206000.

	$1,100	$950	$875	$750	$500	$375	$275

* ***Lightweight Single Six Blue Steel*** – steel cylinder, with black anodized aluminum cylinder frame, ser. no. range 20000-212530.

	$950	$650	$525	$475	$350	$275	$200

SUPER SINGLE SIX CONVERTIBLE – similar to Single Six Convertible, except adj. sights. 5 1/2 or 6 1/2 barrel lengths std. 183,170 mfg. 1964-1972.

4 5/8 in. bbl.	$1,800	$1,500	$1,200	$1,000	$750	$450	$300
5 1/2 in. bbl.	$475	$450	$325	$250	$200	$175	$150
6 1/2 in. bbl.	$475	$450	$325	$250	$200	$175	$150
Chrome plated	$2,450	$2,200	$1,800	$1,400	$1,000	$850	$500

A negotiated premium can be added for examples with S (seconds) or D (duplicate) marking.

BLACKHAWK "FLATTOP" – .357 Mag. cal., 6 shot, 4 5/8 (39,690 mfg.), 6 1/2 (2,500 mfg.), or 10 (500 mfg.) in. barrel, flat-top cylinder strap, adj. sight, blue, black rubber or varnished walnut grip panels (became standard at approx. ser. no. 30000). Approx. 42,690 mfg. between 1955-1962 in ser. no. range 1-42,690.

4 5/8 in. bbl.	$1,200	$850	$600	$500	$350	$250	$200
6 1/2 in. bbl.	$1,000	$800	$600	$500	$350	$250	$200
10 in. bbl.	$2,500	$2,000	$1,600	$1,000	$700	$600	$500

Add $650 for Factory stag grips.
Add $1,200 for Factory ivory grips.
A negotiated premium can be added for examples with S (seconds) or D (duplicate) marking.

BLACKHAWK – .30 Carbine, .357 Mag., .41 Mag., or .45 LC cal., this model is the 1962 variation with protected rear sight, ramp front sight, and 4 5/8 (.357 Mag., .41 Mag. or .45

GRADING - PPGS™	100%	98%	95%	90%	80%	70%	60%	LAST MSR

Colt), 6 1/2 (.357 Mag. or .41 Mag.), or 7 1/2 (.30 Carbine or .45 LC) in. barrel.

.30 Carbine cal.	$500	$450	$400	$350	$300	$250	$200	
.357 Mag. cal.	$500	$425	$400	$350	$300	$250	$200	
.357 Mag. cal. w/brass frame (570 mfg.)	$1,500	$1,200	$850	$700	$475	$400	$300	
.41 Mag. cal.	$750	$650	$575	$500	$425	$350	$225	
.41 Mag. cal. w/brass frame (230 mfg.)	$2,850	$2,250	$1,650	$1,200	$950	$650	$500	
.45 Colt cal.	$875	$700	$500	$400	$325	$275	$225	
.45 Colt cal. w/brass frame (620 mfg.)	$1,850	$1,675	$1,400	$1,000	$750	$500	$425	

A negotiated premium can be added for examples with S (seconds) or D (duplicate) marking.

Note that the values listed above for revolvers with brass grip frames must be for guns that have been factory authenticated.

Total production was 32,985 for .30 carbine (mfg. 1967-1973), 245,059 for .357 Mag. (mfg. 1962-1973), 40,371 for .41 Mag. (mfg. 1962-1973), and 23,030 for .45 LC (mfg. 1970-1973).

BLACKHAWK CONVERTIBLE – similar to Blackhawk, with extra cylinder, .357 Mag. and 9mm Para., or .45 LC and .45 ACP cals.

.357 Mag./9mm Para. cal.	$750	$650	$500	$300	$225	$195	$175	
.45 LC/.45 ACP cal.	$1,200	$875	$650	$550	$475	$400	$300	

Add $350 for .357/9mm Para with non-prefix serial number (103000 to 141000). Factory authentication necessary.

This model did not feature a brass grip frame.

BLACKHAWK FLATTOP .44 MAGNUM – similar to .357 Mag. cal. Blackhawk Flat-top, except heavier frame and cylinder, .44 Mag., 6 1/2 (27,610 mfg.), 7 1/2 (750 mfg.), or 10 in. (1,500 mfg.) barrel. 28,806 guns mfg. between 1956-1963 in ser. no. range 1-29860.

6 1/2 in. bbl.	$1,250	$1,050	$850	$725	$475	$325	$250	
7 1/2 in. bbl.	$2,500	$1,750	$1,100	$900	$750	$600	$400	
10 in. bbl.	$3,000	$2,000	$1,400	$1,000	$850	$650	$475	

Add $650 for Factory stag grips.

Add $1,200 for Factory ivory grips.

A negotiated premium can be added for examples with S (seconds) or D (duplicate) marking.

Distinguishable from Super Blackhawk by fluted cylinder and rounded trigger guard.

SUPER BLACKHAWK – .44 Mag. cal., 6 1/2 (rare) or 7 1/2 in. barrel, larger grip frame and square back trigger guard, unfluted cylinder, adj. sights, walnut grips. Mfg. 1959-72.

7 1/2 in. barrel	$750	$625	$500	$350	$200	$185	$175	

*** *Super Blackhawk Early Variations***

Mahogany cased	$1,250	$1,100	$950	$800	$700	$500	$400	
Long frame cased	$2,600	$1,850	$1,650	$1,400	$1,100	$850	$700	
White box cased	$2,600	$1,850	$1,650	$1,400	$1,100	$850	$700	
Non-cased	$750	$600	$500	$450	$400	$350	$225	
6 1/2 in. bbl.	$1,500	$1,250	$1,150	$1,000	$800	$550	$400	
Brass frame, Prefix S/N	$1,850	$1,550	$1,100	$850	$600	$450	$375	

A negotiated premium can be added for examples with S (seconds) or D (duplicate) marking.

Production totals are as follows: mahogany cased (approx. 3,850), long frame cased (approx. 300), white box cased (approx. 7,350, few surviving cases), non-cased (94,360), 6 1/2 in. bbl. (approx. 600), and brass frame (approx. 1,660).

OLD MODEL BEARCAT – .22 LR cal., 6 shot, 4 in. barrel, black anodized alloy frame, blue

GRADING - PPGS™	100%	98%	95%	90%	80%	70%	60%	LAST MSR

(73,200-76,400 ser. no. range) or brass anodized trigger guard, epoxy resin rosewood grips w/o medallion on early models, models mfg. after 1963 had oil filled walnut with insert eagle medallion and anodized aluminum housing, gold tone trigger guard and steel ejector rod housing until 1964, early guns were marked with a letter of the alphabet before the ser. no., 17 oz. Mfg. 1958-1970.

Early Mfg.	$550	$450	$400	$325	$250	$180	$175
w/ alphabetical prefix	$600	$550	$475	$375	$250	$225	$200
Later Mfg.	$450	$400	$350	$300	$250	$180	$175

A negotiated premium can be added for examples with S (seconds) or D (duplicate) marking.

Numerous variations exist within this model incorporating production changes.

Total production was 143,195 guns.

OLD MODEL SUPER BEARCAT - similar to Bearcat, except steel frame, made with brass anodized aluminum trigger guard (early model), or blue steel guard, 25 oz. Mfg. 1971-74.

$500	$425	$350	$250	$200	$180	$165

A negotiated premium can be added for examples with S (seconds) or D (duplicate) marking.

Total production was 64,420 guns.

HAWKEYE SINGLE SHOT - .256 Mag. cal., XR3-RED grip frame, round cylinder replaced by rectangular rotating breech block, 8 1/2 in. barrel, blue, oiled walnut grips, adj. sight, one inch scope base, very rare, 45 oz. 3,037 mfg. Mfg. 1963 only.

$2,500	$2,200	$1,850	$1,500	$1,200	$1,000	$900

A negotiated premium can be added for examples with S (seconds) or D (duplicate) marking.

REVOLVERS: SINGLE ACTION, NEW MODELS

The following single actions are known as "New Models." They have 2 pins through the frame and cock without the clicks associated with Ruger's Old Model mechanism. The changeover occurred as a result of incorporating safety features. The "New Models" have a transfer bar similar to those found on modern double action revolvers and do not accidentally discharge if dropped. Manufacture started 1973. During certain years of manufacture, Ruger's changes in production on certain models (cals., barrel markings, barrel lengths, etc.) have created rare variations that are now considered premium niches. These areas of low manufacture will add premiums to the values listed on standard models. Beginning 1996, Ruger started supplying all New Model revolvers with a case and lock.

SUPER SINGLE SIX "STAR" MODEL - .22 LR cal., so named because of star stamped on bottom of frame, blue or stainless, single cylinder (not convertible). Mfg. 1974-75 only.

Blue 5 1/2 or 6 1/2 in. bbl.	$495	$450	$350	$295	$275	$250	$225
Blue 9 1/2 in. bbl. (rare)	$695	$595	$500	$425	$350	$300	$250
Blue 4 5/8 in. bbl. (very rare)	$1,000	$800	$750	$700	$625	$550	$475
Stainless 5 1/2 or 6 1/2 in. bbl.	$495	$300	$250	$195	$165	$140	$120
Stainless 9 1/2 in. bbl.	$675	$550	$500	$430	$375	$315	$270
Stainless 4 5/8 in. bbl. (rare)	$675	$550	$500	$430	$375	$315	$270

* ***Super Single Six "Arrow" Model*** - similar to Star Model, except produced with an arrow stamp (also looks to be in the shape of a house) on bottom of frame. Blue models only. Models SSR4, SSR5, SSR6, and SSR9. Mfg. 1986 only.

$525	$450	$400	$325	$265	$235	$200

Add $200 for 4 5/8 in. or 9 1/2 in. barrel.

SUPER SINGLE SIX HIGH GLOSS STAINLESS - 5 1/2 (disc. 1996) or 6 1/2 in. barrel,

GRADING - PPGS™	100%	98%	95%	90%	80%	70%	60%	LAST MSR

features high gloss stainless steel finish, simulated ivory grips became standard 1997. Mfg. 1994-97.

	$450	$350	$275	$150	$120	$110	$95	*$425*

A model with simulated ivory grips (GKNR6-I) was also offered in 1996 for one year only. Last MSR was $425. Add 8% to pricing shown above.

COLORADO CENTENNIAL SUPER SINGLE SIX – 15,000 mfg. 1975 only, includes walnut case with medallion insert, stainless steel grip frame, 6 1/2 in. barrel, issue price was $250.

	$500	$350	$250	$225	$195	N/A	N/A

Although a single example has yet to be uncovered, rumors persist of a few of this model having the "MADE IN THE 200th YEAR OF AMERICAN LIBERTY" rollmark on the barrel in addition to the standard Colorado Centennial/US Bicentennial rollmark and the Sturm, Ruger & Co., Inc. rollmark.

SINGLE SIX .17 HMR (SUPER SINGLE SIX .17 HMR) – .17 HMR cal., 6 shot, 6 1/2 in. barrel with special crown, blue finish, adj. rear sight, smooth rosewood (disc. 2010) or black checkered grips, 35 oz. New 2003.

MSR $569	$455	$365	$315	$250	$215	$185	$160

* ***Super Single Six Stainless Steel Hunter*** – .22 LR or .22 WMR cal., similar to Super Single Six, except stainless steel, 7 1/2 in. barrel, black laminate grips, includes Ruger scope rings, 45 oz. Mfg. 2004-2006.

	$625	$550	$475	$385	$330	$275	$225	*$617*

SINGLE SIX CONVERTIBLE (SUPER SINGLE SIX CONVERTIBLE) – .22 LR cal., includes interchangeable .22 WMR cylinder, 4 5/8, 5 1/2, 6 1/2, or 9 1/2 in. barrel, 6 shot, similar to old Super Single Six, except has new interlocking safety mechanism previously described, fixed or adj. rear sight, black checkered grips, 33 oz (w/5 1/2 in. barrel). New 1973.

MSR $569	$465	$385	$330	$265	$215	$185	$160
4 5/8 in. barrel	$525	$450	$400	$375	$300	$250	$200
9 1/2 in. barrel or adj. rear sight	$495	$415	$365	4295	$245	$200	$175

* ***Super Single Six Convertible Stainless Steel*** – similar to Super Single Six, except stainless steel construction, 4 5/8 (disc. 1976), 5 1/2, 6 1/2, or 9 1/2 (disc. 1975-rare) in. barrel, hardwood grips, adj. rear sight.

MSR $639	$510	$435	$365	$325	$265	$225	$200
4 5/8 or 9 1/2 in. bbl	$595	$550	$500	$450	$400	$325	$250

Add 5% for "Friends of NRA" model KNR6-NRA issue of 750 produced in 2000.

Only 300 Stainless 4 5/8 in. barrels were rollmarked "Liberty".

* ***Single Six Convertible 50th Anniversary*** – similar to Single Six Convertible, 4 5/8 in. barrel only, cocobolo wood grips special high polish, and "50th Anniversary 1953-2003" Ruger logo, includes red plastic case. Mfg. 2003 only.

	$450	$350	$300	$200	$150	$140	$125	*$425*

* ***Super Single Six Convertible Stainless Steel Hunter*** – similar to Super Single Six Stainless Steel, except has 7 1/2 in. barrel, black laminate grips, integral scope mounts with one inch rings, 45 oz. New 2004.

MSR $799	$650	$575	$495	$400	$350	$295	$250

* ***Super Single Six Convertible Hunter 17 HMR/17 Mach 2 Stainless*** – includes .17 HMR and .17 Mach 2 cylinders, 6 shot, stainless steel, 7 1/2 in. barrel, black laminated wood grips, integral scope mounts with one inch rings, 45 oz. Mfg. 2005-2006.

	$750	$650	$550	$400	$300	$250	$200	*$695*

NEW MODEL SUPER SINGLE SIX SSM – similar to original Super Single-Six except .32 H&R Mag. cal., 4 5/8, 5 1/2, 6 1/2 or 9 1/2 in. barrel, blue frame, 6 shot, adj. sights, wood grips, 32-35 oz. Mfg. 1984-1994.

	$650	$550	$500	$450	$400	$350	$300

GRADING - PPGS™	100%	98%	95%	90%	80%	70%	60%	LAST MSR

Add 20% if frame is marked "SSM" (5-1/2 in. and 6-1/2 in. most common although only one in 4 5/8" with this marking believed to have been produced).
Add $50 for 4 5/8 and 9 1/2 in. barrel.

NEW MODEL .32 H&R MAG. (SUPER SINGLE SIX SSM) – .32 H&R Mag. cal., 4 5/8 or 5 1/2 in. barrel, case colored frame or high gloss stainless steel (new 2001), 6 shot, fixed sights, choice of steel XR3-RED grip frame (later shortened) with faux ivory, bird's head with black Micarta grips (new 2002) or regular grips (simulated ivory became standard 2001), 32-35 oz. Mfg. 2001-2004, reintroduced 2006.

	100%	98%	95%	90%	80%	70%	60%	LAST MSR
	$550	$475	$425	$375	$200	$175	$150	*$535*

Add $50 for Early XR3-Red grip frame.
Add $50 for stainless steel or bird's head grip frame.
Add $40 for faux ivory or black micarta grips.

SINGLE NINE – .22 LR cal., 6 1/2 in. barrel, 9 shot, stainless steel finish, Williams adj. fiber optic sights, hardwood Gunfighter grips, 39 oz. New 2013.

	100%	98%	95%	90%	80%	70%	60%
MSR $639	$515	$435	$370	$330	$270	$230	$200

SINGLE TEN – .22 LR cal., 5.5 in. barrel, 10 shot, stainless steel slide with satin stainless finish, hardwood Gunfighter grips, Williams adj. fiber optic sights, 38 oz. New 2012.

	100%	98%	95%	90%	80%	70%	60%
MSR $639	$500	$430	$375	$325	$275	$225	$200

NEW MODEL BLACKHAWK – .30 Carbine (disc. 1996, reintroduced 1998), .357 Mag., .41 Mag. (disc. 1996, reintroduced 1999), .44 S&W Spl. (new 2010, Flattop only), or .45 LC cal., similar to old Model Blackhawk, with new interlocking safety mechanism, alloy frame, choice of round or flattop (new 2010), 6 shot, 4 5/8, 5 1/2 (Flattop only), 6 1/2, or 7 1/2 in. (.30 Carbine and .45 LC only) barrel, current mfg. has black checkered grips, adj. sight, 40-44 oz. New 1973.

	100%	98%	95%	90%	80%	70%	60%
MSR $609	$470	$400	$325	$250	$200	$165	$140

New Model .357 Mag. Blackhawks are serial numbered 32-00001 on up. New Model .45 LC Blackhawks are serial numbered 46-00001 on up. New Model .30 Carbine Blackhawks are serial numbered 51-00001 on up and the earliest .41 Blackhawks were serial numbered 41-00001 on up only to be included within the 46- prefix beginning in 1980.

* ***New Model Blackhawk Bisley*** – .44 Mag. or .45 LC cal., 7 1/2 in. barrel, 6 shot mag., alloy frame, blued finish, hardwood grips, ramp front and adj. rear sights, 48-50 oz. New 2012.

	100%	98%	95%	90%	80%	70%	60%
MSR $799	$675	$550	$425	$375	$325	$300	$275

* ***New Model Blackhawk Buckeye Special*** – 10mm Auto/.38-40 Win. cal., 6 1/2 in. barrel. Mfg. 1989.

	100%	98%	95%	90%	80%	70%	60%
	$750	$600	$450	$250	$220	$200	$180

Add 10% for limited edition Buckeye Special in .32/.32-20 cal. (mfg. for Buckeye Sports in 1990).

* ***New Model Blackhawk Stainless Steel*** – .327 Fed. Mag. (mfg. 2011-2012), .357 Mag. or .45 LC (mfg. 1993-2009) cal., 4 5/8, 5 1/2 (.45 LC only, disc.), 6 1/2 (.357 Mag. only) or 7 1/2 (.45 LC only, disc. 2009) in. barrel, 6 shot, 46-48 oz.

	100%	98%	95%	90%	80%	70%	60%
MSR $729	$600	$425	$325	$275	$250	$200	$180

Add approx. 75% for .357 Mag./9mm Para. convertible pistols (300 were made in this model).

The 5 1/2 in. .45 LC is very scarce in stainless.

* ***New Model Blackhawk High Gloss Stainless Steel*** – .357 Mag. or .45 LC cal., 4 5/8, 6 1/2 (.357 Mag. only), or 7 1/2 (.45 LC only) in. barrel, features high gloss stainless steel finish. Mfg. 1994-96.

	100%	98%	95%	90%	80%	70%	60%	LAST MSR
	$575	$425	$350	$250	$240	$200	$180	*$443*

All models are considered rare.

* ***New Model Blackhawk Arizona Ranger Commemorative*** – .45 Colt cal., 4 5/8 in. barrel,

GRADING - PPGS™	100%	98%	95%	90%	80%	70%	60%	LAST MSR

stainless steel grip frame. 304 produced in 46-44228 to 46-44550 serial range for the Arizona Rangers in 1979.

	$875	$750	$625	N/A	N/A	N/A	N/A	

NEW MODEL BLACKHAWK 50th ANNIVERSARY MATCHED SET – includes one .44 Mag. and one .357 Mag. revolver, 4 5/8 (.357 Mag.) and 6 1/2 in. barrel, gold rollmark "50 Years of Blackhawk 1955-2005", and "50 Years of .44 Magnum 1955-2005", black checkered grips with medallions, matched serial numbers, collector's wood case. Mfg. 2007-2008.

	$1,000	$875	$825	N/A	N/A	N/A	N/A	*$1,350*

These models were also available individually - MSR was approx. $600.

NEW MODEL BLACKHAWK 50th ANNIVERSARY – .357 Mag. or .44 Mag. cal., 4 5/8 (mfg. 2005 only) or 6 1/2 (new 2006) in. barrel, flat-top frame, smaller, pre-1962 XR-3 grip frame with checkered hard rubber grips with black Ruger medallions, cylinder indexing aligns loading gate cutout with cylinder borings, unobtrusive internal lock, "50th YEAR BLACKHAWK 1955-2005" gold rollmark, supplied with red case. Mfg. 2005-2006.

	$500	$365	$320	$280	$260	$240	$220	*$605*

* ***50 Years of .44 Magnum Blackhawk*** – similar to 50th Anniversary Blackhawk, except has "50 YEARS OF .44 MAGNUM 1956-2006" rollmarked on barrel, hard rubber style grips with black medallions. Mfg. 2006.

	$550	$485	$440	$400	$360	$330	$295	*$605*

NEW MODEL BLACKHAWK CONVERTIBLE – similar to New Model Blackhawk, except interchangeable cylinders, .357 Mag./9mm Para., .44 Mag./.44-40 WCF (disc.), or .45 LC/.45 ACP (disc. 1985, reintroduced 1999) cal., 4 5/8, 5 1/2 (.45 Colt/.45 ACP only), or 6 1/2 in. barrel, 46 oz.

MSR $679	$550	$475	$400	$325	$250	$200	$175	

Add 50% for .44 Mag./.44-40 WCF cal., disc.

BLACKHAWK-SRM .357 REM. MAXIMUM – similar to New Model Blackhawk, except is chambered for .357 Rem. Maximum, 7 1/2 or 10 1/2 in. barrels available, target sights, 53 oz., 11,500 mfg. 1982-84; production suspended due to unresolvable engineering problems.

	$750	$650	$500	$400	$325	$300	$250	

NEW MODEL SUPER BLACKHAWK – .44 Mag. cal., 4 5/8 (new 1994), 5 1/2 (new 1987), 7 1/2 or 10 1/2 (bull/target) in. barrel, 6 shot, blue finish, fluted (5 1/2 in. barrel only) or unfluted cylinder, walnut, rosewood (disc.), or brown laminate (disc.) grips, square back trigger guard (avail. on 7 1/2 or 10 1/2 in. barrel models only, new 2012), similar to old model in appearance, but has new action, steel ejector housing was introduced in 2000, 45-55 oz. New 1973.

MSR $739	$565	$475	$375	$300	$220	$185	$160	

Add approx. 75% for Tomahawk version mfg. circa 1980 (Mag-na-port converted a limited run of 4 5/8 in. barrels) if in 95%-NIB condition.

The new model started with serial number 81-00001.

* ***New Model Super Blackhawk Stainless Steel*** – stainless variation of the Super Blackhawk.

MSR $739	$565	$475	$375	$300	$220	$185	$160	

Add $30 for 10 1/2 in. bull/target barrel.

* ***New Model Super Blackhawk High Gloss Stainless Steel*** – high gloss stainless steel finish, not available in 10 1/2 in. bull barrel. Mfg. 1994-96.

	$575	$500	$400	$325	$200	$185	$160	*$450*

* ***New Model Super Blackhawk Stainless Hunter*** – .44 Mag. cal., 6 shot, 7 1/2 in. ribbed barrel only, black laminated wood grips, includes scope rings and integral scope mounts (new 2002), 52 oz. Mfg. 1992-95, reintroduced 2002.

MSR $859	$750	$595	$435	$365	$295	$245	$215	

A special edition of this model with wood grain laminated grips and lockable plastic case was available through Davidson's - retail was $639.

GRADING - PPGS™	100%	98%	95%	90%	80%	70%	60%	LAST MSR

* ***New Model Super Blackhawk Bisley Stainless Hunter*** – .44 Mag. cal., 7 1/2 in. barrel with scope mounts built into solid rib, stainless steel, 6 shot, black laminate grips, adj. rear sight, 52 oz. New 2009.

MSR $859	**$750**	**$575**	**$475**	**$400**	**$335**	**$275**	**$225**	

NEW MODEL SUPER BLACKHAWK 50TH ANNIVERSARY – .44 Mag. cal., 6 shot, 7 1/2 in. barrel, blue gloss finish, gold anniversary trim and rollmarked "50TH ANNIVERSARY" in gold, commemorates 50th anniversary of the Super Blackhawk, gold band at front and rear of cylinder, smooth cocobolo grips with black eagle medallions, included special white cardboard packaging with Ruger logo carrying case. 1,500 mfg. 2009 only.

	$750	**$625**	**$550**	**$475**	**$425**	**$375**	**$325**	***$880***

VAQUERO – .357 Mag. (new 1997), .44-40 WCF (new 1994), .44 Mag. (new 1994), or .45 LC cal., 6 shot, 4 5/8, 5 1/2, or 7 1/2 (not available in .357 Mag.) in. barrel, color case hardened frame, blue steel frame, barrel, and cylinder, steel ejector housing became standard in 2000, transfer bar hammer safety, smooth rosewood, smooth bird's head (mfg. 2001 only) or black Micarta bird's head, (.45 LC cal. only, 4 3/4 in. barrel, new 2002), or simulated ivory (new 1996) grips, patterned after the Colt SAA, fixed sights, 39-41 oz. Mfg. 1993-2004.

	$550	**$500**	**$400**	**$325**	**$200**	**$170**	**$160**	***$555***

Add $40 for simulated ivory grips (new 1996).

Add approx. $150 for simulated ivory grips and engraved cylinder (mfg. 1998-99).

* ***Vaquero High Gloss Stainless Steel*** – high gloss stainless steel finish, black Micarta bird's head grips became optional 2002. Mfg. 1994-2004.

	$575	**$525**	**$400**	**$300**	**$200**	**$170**	**$160**	***$555***

Add $40 for simulated ivory grips (new 1996).

* ***Vaquero Bird's Head*** – .357 Mag. or .45 Colt cal., 3 3/4 (.357 Mag.) or 4 5/8 (.45 Colt) in. barrel, color case hardened frame or high polish stainless steel bird's head frame, choice of black Micarta or simulated ivory (new 2003) grips. Disc. 2004.

	$650	**$500**	**$400**	**$325**	**$225**	**$195**	**$165**	***$595***

NEW VAQUERO – .357 Mag. or .45 LC cal., 4 5/8, 5 1/2, or 7 1/2 (.45 LC cal. only, disc.) in. barrel, 6 shot, redesigned using a slimmer pre-1962 XR-3 style grip frame, color case hardened frame with blued gripstraps, barrel, and cylinder, recontoured hammer, new hammer spring, beveled cylinder, checkered hard rubber grips, crescent-shaped ejector rod head, 37-41 oz. New 2005.

MSR $739	**$585**	**$440**	**$350**	**$295**	**$240**	**$210**	**$180**	

Add $445 for standard Grade 1 engraving (mfg. 2006-2011) or $1,395 for consecutive pair with standard Grade 1 engraving (mfg. 2006-2011).

* ***New Vaquero High Gloss Stainless*** – similar to New Vaquero, except is stainless steel. New 2005.

MSR $739	**$585**	**$440**	**$350**	**$295**	**$240**	**$210**	**$180**	

Add $445 for standard Grade 1 engraving (mfg. 2006-2011) or $1,395 for consecutive pair with standard Grade 1 engraving (mfg. 2006-2011).

NEW VAQUERO COWBOY PAIR – .45 LC cal., 5 1/2 in. barrel, includes two consecutively numbered and engraved revolvers with presentation case, 500 sets mfg. 2007.

	$3,450	**$3,150**	**$2,850**	**N/A**	**N/A**	**N/A**	**N/A**	***$3,863***

NEW VAQUERO SASS PAIR – .357 Mag. or .45 LC cal., 4 5/8 (.357 Mag. only), or 5 1/2 (.45 LC only) in. barrel, 6 shot, fixed sights, black checkered grips with SASS logo grip medallions, high gloss stainless steel, lower and wider Montado-style hammer, only available in set of two with consecutive SASS prefix serial numbers, includes commemorative red case, 43-45 oz. New 2010.

MSR $1,618	**$1,450**	**$1,225**	**$1,050**	**$925**	**$850**	**$775**	**$725**	

BISLEY VAQUERO – .357 Mag. (new 1999, 5 1/2 in. barrel only), .44 Mag. or .45 LC cal., 4 5/8 (new 1999) or 5 1/2 in. barrel, case colored frame with blue steel grips, barrel, and

GRADING - PPGS™	100%	98%	95%	90%	80%	70%	60%	LAST MSR

cylinder, steel ejector housing became standard in 2000, fixed sights, approx. 40 oz. Mfg. 1998-2004.

	$575	$525	$450	$325	$225	$180	$160	$555

Add $40 for simulated ivory grips.

* ***Bisley Vaquero Stainless*** – similar to Bisley Vaquero, except is stainless steel. Disc. 2004.

	$575	$525	$450	$325	$225	$180	$160	$575

Add $40 for simulated ivory grips.

* ***Bisley Vaquero High Gloss Stainless*** – .357 Mag. or .45 LC cal., 5 1/2 in. barrel only, high gloss stainless steel, simulated ivory grips, fixed sights, 6 shot, 41-45 oz. New 2009.

MSR $809	$675	$550	$435	$350	$300	$250	$225	

BISLEY MODEL – .22 LR (disc.), .32 H&R Mag. (disc. 1996), .357 Mag. (disc. 2007), .41 Mag. (disc. 1996), .44 Mag., or .45 LC cal., 6 shot, incorporates Bisley features (flat-top frame, raked hammer, longer grip frame), 6 1/2 (.22 LR or .32 H&R Mag. only) or 7 1/2 in. barrel, fixed (disc. 1992, except for .32 H&R Mag.) or adj. sights, available with fluted/unfluted or roll-marked/unmarked (disc.) cylinders, satin blue finish only, Goncalo Alves smooth grips. Mfg. 1986-2011.

* ***Bisley Model .22 LR or .32 H&R Mag.***

	$450	$325	$250	$210	$180	$160	$150	$475

Add $200 for .32 H&R Mag. (disc. 1996).

* ***Bisley Model .357 Mag., .41 Mag., .44 Mag., or .45 LC*** – .357 Mag. and .41 Mag. cals. disc. 2012.

	$575	$445	$335	$265	$215	$180	$160	$729

Add 15% for .41 Mag. cal.

* ***Bisley Model Shootist*** – .22 LR cal., special limited edition, stainless steel, 4 5/8 in. barrel, adj. sights, marked "In Memory of Our Friend, Tom Ruger, The Shootist", inscribed with the name of the recipient on backstrap, only 52 mfg. 1994.

	$2,000	$1,650	$1,200	$1,000	$850	$650	$500	

NEW BEARCAT – .22 LR cal., frame slightly longer than old Bearcat, engraved non-fluted cylinder, 4.2 in. barrel, 6 shot, transfer bar hammer block safety, blue finish, smooth rosewood grips, fixed sights, 24 oz. New 1994.

MSR $569	$450	$337	$295	$225	$175	$155	$130	

Add $110 for LR cylinder without firing pin groove (disc. 2010).

* ***New Bearcat Stainless Steel*** – similar to New Bearcat, except is matte stainless steel. New 2002.

MSR $619	$515	$365	$280	$235	$200	$180	$160	

Add $110 for LR cylinder without firing pin groove (disc. 2010).

* ***New Bearcat Convertible*** – similar to New Bearcat, except has convertible interchangeable .22 WMR cyl., early production, recalled by the factory.

	$1,200	$1,000	$900	$785	$655	$550	$465	

The .22 WMR cylinder was recalled to the factory in 1994. It is estimated that at least 60% of the 1,000 New Bearcat Convertibles produced had their .22 WMR cylinders returned to the factory due to the recall.

NEW BEARCAT 50th ANNIVERSARY – .22 LR cal. only, gold plated trigger guard, cylinder with two gold bands and "RUGER BEARCAT" in gold, gold filled "50TH ANNIVERSARY BEARCAT - 2008" rollmark on barrel, smooth cocobolo grip panels without medallions (reminiscent of original 1958 to 1961 production plastic impregnated rosewood Bearcat panels), "SBC" prefix serial number and special white cardboard packaging with Ruger logo carrying case. Mfg. 2008 only. Only 2,539 produced.

	$695	$625	$575	N/A	N/A	N/A	N/A	$758

REVOLVERS: DOUBLE ACTION

During certain years of manufacture, Ruger's changes in production on certain models (cals.,

GRADING - PPGS™	100%	98%	95%	90%	80%	70%	60%	LAST MSR

barrel markings, barrel lengths, etc.) have created rare variations that are now considered premium niches. These areas of low manufacture will add premiums to the values listed on standard models.

SPEED SIX (MODELS 207, 208 and 209) – .38 Spl., .357 Mag., or 9mm Para. cal., 2 3/4, 3 (U.S. Marshal and Postal Inspector contracts), or 4 in. barrel, fixed sights, checkered walnut grips, round butt, blue finish, some guns have factory speed hammer (no hammer spur). Mfg. 1973-88. Model 207 and 208 disc. 1988.

$400	$350	$275	$170	$160	$150	$140	*$292*

Add $250 for 9mm Para. (Model 209 disc. 1984).

* ***Speed Six Models 737 and 738*** – stainless steel versions of Models 207 and 208, .357 Mag and .38 Spl. cals., 2 3/4 or 4 in. barrel. Disc. 1988.

$425	$350	$300	$175	$140	$125	$105	*$320*

* ***Speed Six Model 739*** – stainless steel, 9mm Para. Disc. 1984.

$650	$550	$500	$400	$275	$195	$175

SECURITY SIX (MODEL 117) – .357 Mag. cal., 6 shot, 2 3/4, 3 (late production only), 4, 4 (heavy), or 6 in. barrel, adj. sights, checkered walnut grips, square butt. Mfg. 1970-1985.

$400	$350	$275	$200	$160	$150	$140	*$309*

Add $15 for target grips.

Note that beginning late in the 150- serial number prefix, the grip frame was changed to have a more outward "highback" shape. Revolvers with the earlier "lowback" grip frame are generally considered more collectible. All revolvers having fixed sights and square butt grip frame with "lowback" shape to the backstrap were also marked "SECURITY-SIX". Only when the new highback gripframe came out were the fixed sight and square butt revolvers marked "SERVICE-SIX".

500 of this model were mfg. for the California Highway Patrol during 1983 (.38 Spl. cal.) in stainless steel only. They are distinguishable by a C.H.P. marking. Other Security Six Model 117 special editions have been made for various police organizations - premiums might exist in certain regions for these variations.

* ***Security Six Model 717*** – stainless steel version of Model 117. Disc. 1985.

$400	$350	$300	$225	$180	$145	$125	*$338*

POLICE SERVICE SIX – .357 Mag, .38 Spl., or 9mm Para. cal., blue finish only, square butt, fixed sights, checkered walnut grips.

* ***Police Service Six Model 107*** – .357 Mag. cal., 2 3/4 or 4 in. barrel, fixed sights. Disc. 1988.

$400	$300	$250	$190	$180	$170	$165	*$287*

* ***Police Service Six Model 108*** – .38 Spl. cal., 4 in. barrel, fixed sights. Disc. 1988.

$350	$275	$225	$190	$180	$170	$165	*$287*

* ***Police Service Six Model 109*** – 9mm Para. cal., 4 in. barrel, fixed sights. Disc. 1984.

$650	$550	$500	$400	$275	$195	$175

POLICE SERVICE SIX STAINLESS STEEL – stainless construction, 4 in. barrel only, fixed sights, checkered walnut grips.

* ***Police Service Six Stainless Steel Model 707*** – .357 Mag. cal., square butt. Disc. 1988.

$425	$325	$250	$190	$180	$170	$165	*$310*

* ***Police Service Six Stainless Steel Model 708*** – .38 Spl. cal., square butt. Disc. 1988.

$350	$275	$225	$190	$180	$170	$155	*$310*

GP-100 – .357 Mag./.38 Spl. cal., 3 (new 1990, fixed sights, .357 Mag. only), 4.2, or 6 (.357 Mag. only) in. standard or heavy barrel, 6 shot, strengthened design intended for constant use with all .357 Mag. ammunition, rubber cushioned grip panels with polished Goncalo Alves wood inserts, fixed (mfg. 1989-2006) or adj. sights (standard beginning

GRADING - PPGS™	100%	98%	95%	90%	80%	70%	60%	LAST MSR

2007) with white outlined rear and interchangeable front, 35-46 oz. depending on barrel configuration. New 1986.

MSR $699	$550	$400	$340	$275	$220	$195	$175	

* ***GP-100 Stainless Steel*** – similar to GP-100, .327 Fed. Mag. (new 2009) or .357 Mag. cal., 6 or 7 shot (.327 Fed. Mag. only), stainless steel. New 1987.

MSR $729	$575	$425	$330	$265	$210	$170	$140	

Add $30 for adj. sights.

* ***GP-100 High Gloss Stainless Steel*** – .357 Mag. cal. only, high gloss stainless steel finish, adj. sights, 3 or 4 in. heavy barrel. Mfg. 1996 only.

	$485	$375	$295	$250	$195	$165	$140	*$457*

Fixed sights were cataloged but not known to have been produced in this model.

SP-101 STAINLESS STEEL – .22 LR (6 shot - mfg. 1990-2004, re-introduced 2012), .32 H&R (6 shot - mfg. 1991-2012), .327 Federal (6 shot - mfg. 2007-2011), .38 Spl.+P (5 shot), 9mm Para. (5 shot - mfg. 1991-2000), or .357 Mag. (5 shot - new 1991) cal., 2 1/4, 3 1/16, 4 (mfg. 1990-2007), or 4.2 (new 2012) in. barrel, small frame variation of the GP-100 Stainless, fiber optic (new 2012) or Black Ramp front sight, fixed or adj. rear (new 1996) sights, cushioned rubber/black plastic or engraved hardwood insert (new 2012) grips, 25-34 oz. New 1989.

MSR $659	$530	$400	$315	$240	$180	$145	$120	

Add $40 for fiber optic sights (new 2012, 4.2 in. barrel only).
Add $170 for Crimson Trace laser grips (mfg. 2008-2011).
Add $100 for .357 Mag. models with "125 GR. BULLET" rollmarked on barrel lug (disc. 2010).
Add $175 for 9mm Para. caliber (disc. 2000).
Add $150 for .22 LR caliber (disc. 2004).

The .327 Federal caliber configuration will also shoot .32 H&R Mag., .32 S&W, and .32 S&W Long cartridges.

The first few thousand SP-101s in .38 Special had green grip inserts. Also, approximately 3,000 total of the earliest KSP-321 and KSP-331 .357 Mag. models were rollmarked with "125 GR. BULLET" on the barrel under the caliber designation (serial range 570-59359 to 570-67976).

Ruger introduced adj. sights in 1996 available in .22 LR or .32 H&R cal. only.

Ruger introduced a .357 Mag./2 1/4 in. (new 1993) or .38 Spl./2 1/4 (new 1994) in. configuration featuring a spurless hammer, double action only.

SP-101 barrel lengths are as follows: .22 cal. is available in 2 1/4 or 4 in. standard or heavy barrel, .32 H&R is available in 3 1/16 or 4 (new 1994) in. heavy barrel, .38 Spl. is available in 2 1/4 or 3 1/16 in. length only, 9mm Para. is available in 2 1/4 (new 1992) or 3 1/16 in. length only, and .357 Mag. is available in 2 1/4 or 3 1/16 in. length only.

* ***SP101 Stainless Steel .22 LR*** – .22 LR cal., 4 in. barrel, 8 shot, satin stainless steel, black rubber grips with checkered wood panel inserts, adj. rear sight, fiber optic front sight, 30 oz. New late 2011.

MSR $699	$550	$400	$330	$275	$210	$190	$175	

* ***SP-101 Stainless Steel High Gloss*** – .38 Spl. (disc. 1996), 9mm Para. (disc. 1996), or .357 Mag. cal., similar to SP-101 Stainless Steel, except has high gloss stainless steel finish. Mfg. 1996-1997.

	$550	$475	$350	$275	$225	$195	$150	*$443*

Add $175 for 9mm Para. cal.

Estimated 100 produced in .38 Spl, 1,500 produced in .357 Mag. and an unknown quantity in 9mm (very rare). Serial range 571-81675 to 572-44777.

Ruger introduced adj. sights in 1996 available in .22 LR or .32 H&R cal. only.

REDHAWK – .357 Mag. (disc. 1985), .41 Mag. (mfg. 1984-1991), or .44 Mag. cal., 6 shot fluted cylinder, redesigned large frame, 5 1/2 and 7 1/2 (disc. 2005) in. barrel, blue finish, square butt, smooth hardwood grips, 49-54 oz. Disc. 2009.

	$615	$460	$375	$285	$225	$180	$165	*$789*

GRADING - PPGS™	100%	98%	95%	90%	80%	70%	60%	LAST MSR

Add $40 for scope rings (disc. 2005).

.357 Mag. and .41 Mag. cals. will bring collector premiums if NIB.

* ***Redhawk Stainless Steel*** – .357 Mag. (mfg. 1984-1991), .41 Mag. (mfg. 1984-1991), .44 Mag or .45 LC (mfg. 1998-2005, reintroduced 2008, 4 in. barrel only) cal., stainless steel construction, 4.2 (new 2007), 5 1/2, or 7 1/2 in. barrel, choice of regular or Hogue (4 in. barrel only) grips, 6 shot, adj. sights, 49-54 oz.

MSR $989	$785	$600	$475	$375	$300	$250	$225

Add $60 for scope rings (Hunter model, .44 Mag. only in 7 1/2 in. barrel).

This model was also available as a KRH-35, and is marked both "Redhawk" and ".357 Magnum". Mfg. was circa 1984-1991.

The 7 1/2 in. barrel was available with or w/o integral scope mounting system.

SUPER REDHAWK STAINLESS – .44 Mag., .454 Casull, or .480 Ruger (mfg. 2001-2007, reintroduced 2013) cal., 6 shot, 7 1/2 or 9 1/2 in. barrel, fluted (.44 Mag. cal. only, disc.) or non-fluted cylinder, choice of regular or high gloss (mfg. 1997-2004) stainless steel, adj. rear sight, cushioned grip panels (GP-100 style), stainless steel scope rings, 53-58 oz. New late 1987.

MSR $1,049	$795	$700	$575	$475	$400	$350	$325

Add $30 for .454 Casull or .480 Ruger cal.

Add $75 for early .44 Mag. with "SUPER REDHAWK" rollmarked on both sides of cylinder frame extension, serial range 550-00500 to at least 550-00659.

.44 Mag. cal. has stainless steel satin finish and calibers .454 Casull and .480 Ruger have stainless steel Target Grey finish.

* ***Super Redhawk Stainless Alaskan*** – .44 Mag. (new 2008), .454 Casull, or .480 Ruger (disc. 2007, reintroduced 2013) cal., 6 shot, 2 1/2 in. barrel, includes Hogue monogrips and unfluted cylinder, 42 oz. New 2005.

MSR $1,079	$875	$750	$625	$450	$400	$325	$265

LCR – .22 LR (new 2012), .22 WMR (new 2013), .38 Spl.+P or .357 Mag. cal., 5 (.38 Spl. or .357 Mag.), 6 (.22 WMR only, new 2013), or 8 (.22 LR only, new 2012) shot, DAO, hammerless, 1 7/8 in. barrel, monolithic aluminum frame, stainless steel cylinder, polymer fire control housing, matte black or blackened stainless (.357 Mag. only) finish, Hogue Tamer or Crimson Trace finger groove grips, integral rear sight with pinned ramp front sight, 13 1/2-16 1/2 oz. New 2010.

MSR $529	$450	$400	$365	$335	$300	$275	$250

Add $70 for .357 Mag. cal.

Add $50 for XS standard dot tritium front sight (.38 Spl.+P cal. only) and U-notch integral rear sight (new 2011).

Add $270 for Crimson Trace laser grips.

RIFLES: BOLT ACTION, RIMFIRE

MODEL 77/17 – .17 Mach 2 (disc. 2006) or .17 HMR cal., 22 in. barrel, blue finish, 9 shot rotary mag., checkered walnut or black laminate (mfg. 2003-2012, .17 HMR cal. only) stock, 6 1/2 lbs. New 2002.

MSR $899	$675	$525	$425	$335	$285	$250	$225

* ***Model 77/17 Stainless*** – .17 HMR or .17 Hornet (new 2013) cal., similar to Model 77/17, except has stainless steel action/barel and target grey (disc.), or matte stainless finish, 22 (disc. 2005) or 24 in. barrel (new 2006), 6 (.17 Hornet), 9 (HMR) or 10 (disc.) shot mag., black laminate (became standard 2006) or Green Mountain (new 2013) stock, 7 1/2 lbs. New 2002.

MSR $969	$750	$550	$395	$300	$250	$215	$185

MODEL 77/22-R/RS – .22 LR cal. only, 10 shot rotary mag., 20 in. barrel, all steel construction, 3 position safety, checkered walnut stock, blue finish, non-adj. trigger, available with either optional iron sights (RS suffix, disc. 2004) or plain barrel (no sights) with scope rings (included), 2.7 millisecond lock time on trigger, 6 lbs. 2 oz. New 1984.

MSR $899	$675	$525	$400	$300	$250	$225	$195

GRADING - PPGS™	100%	98%	95%	90%	80%	70%	60%	LAST MSR

Add $25 for iron sights (disc. 2004).

Add 125% if w/o 77/22 roll mark or with green laminated stock.

* ***Model 77/22-RP/RSP All-Weather Stainless*** – .22 LR cal., similar to Model 77/22, except has brushed stainless steel finish, metal with matte black DuPont Zytel or Next G1 Vista camo (mfg. 2011 only) synthetic stock, no sights, 6 lbs. New 1989.

MSR $899 $675 $525 $400 $325 $275 $225 $195

Add $25 for iron sights (disc. 2004). Add $26 for camo (disc. 2011).

* ***Model 77/22-VBZ Varmint Stainless Laminated*** – .22 LR cal., similar to Model 77/22, except stainless steel (target grey finish became standard 2005), 24 in. heavy stainless barrel, laminated brown hardwood stock, no sights, 7 1/2 lbs. New 1995.

MSR $969 $755 $540 $385 $300 $250 $215 $185

MODEL 77/22-RM/RSM MAG. – .22 WMR cal., similar to Model 77/22-R/RS, except has 20 in. barrel, 9 shot rotary mag., blue finish, checkered walnut stock, iron (RSM suffix, disc. 2004) or no sights, 6 1/2 lbs. New 1990.

MSR $899 $675 $525 $400 $300 $250 $225 $195

Add $25 for iron sights (disc. 2004, RSM suffix).

* ***Model 77/22-RMP/RSMP Mag. All-Weather Stainless*** – .22 WMR cal., 20 in. barrel, similar to Model 77/22-RM/RSM Mag., except has brushed stainless steel metal with matte black Dupont Zytel synthetic stock, 6 lbs. New 1990.

MSR $899 $675 $525 $400 $300 $250 $225 $195

Add $25 for iron sights (disc. 2005).

* ***Model 77/22-VMBZ Mag. Varmint Stainless Laminated*** – .22 WMR cal., similar to Model 77/22 RM/RSM MAG., except stainless steel (target grey finish became standard 2005), 24 in. heavy stainless barrel, laminated brown hardwood stock, 7 1/2 lbs. New 1993.

MSR $969 $750 $550 $395 $300 $250 $215 $185

RIFLES: BOLT ACTION, CENTERFIRE

During certain years of manufacture, Ruger's changes in production on certain models (cals., barrel markings, barrel lengths, etc.) have created rare variations that are now considered premium niches. These areas of low manufacture will add premiums to the values listed on standard models.

Earlier mfg. had flat-bolt handle or hollow round bolt, and will bring $150+ premium, depending on configuration.

Early (pre-1972) mfg. with flat-bolt handle are desirable in the rarer cals. and will command a 100% premium if in 98%+ original condition.

MODEL 77/22-RH/RSH HORNET – .22 Hornet cal., features lengthened receiver, detachable 6 shot rotary mag. (not interchangeable with other 77/22 mags.), 20 in. blue barrel, checkered American walnut stock, includes scope rings, 6 1/2 lbs. New 1994.

MSR $899 $675 $525 $400 $315 $265 $225 $195

Add $20 for iron sights (RSH suffix, disc. 2002).

* ***Model 77/22-VHZ Hornet Varmint Stainless Laminated*** – similar to Model 77/22 Hornet, stainless steel action, 24 in. heavy stainless barrel (target grey finish became standard 2005), no sights, laminated brown hardwood (disc. 2011), or Green Mountain (new 2012) stock, 7 1/2 lbs. New 1995.

MSR $969 $760 $550 $400 $315 $265 $225 $195

MODEL 77/357 – .357 Mag. cal., 18 1/2 in. barrel, 5 shot mag., stainless steel finish, black synthetic stock, bead front and adj. rear sights, 5 1/2 lbs. New 2012.

MSR $969 $760 $550 $400 $315 $265 $225 $195

MODEL 77/44 – .44 Mag. cal., 18 1/2 in. barrel, 4 shot rotary mag., plain birch (disc.), checkered walnut (disc.), or black synthetic stock, brushed stainless or Next G1 Vista Camo (new 2011) metal finish, stainless action and barrel (new 2009), open sights, 6 lbs. Mfg. 1998-2004, reintroduced 2009.

GRADING - PPGS™	100%	98%	95%	90%	80%	70%	60%	LAST MSR
MSR $899	$675	$525	$400	$315	$265	$225	$195	

Add $70 for black synthetic stock.

* ***Model 77/44 Stainless*** – .44 Mag. cal., black synthetic stock, stainless steel construction, open sights. Mfg. 1999-2004.

	$510	$380	$310	$270	$245	$200	$175	*$635*

MODEL 77R – .22-250 Rem., .220 Swift, 6mm Rem. (disc.), .243 Win. (disc.), .250 Savage (disc.), .257 Roberts, .25-06 Rem., .270 Win., 7x57mm, 7mm-08 (disc.), 6.5mm Rem. Mag. (scarce), 7mm Rem. Mag., .280 Rem., .284 Win., .308 Win. (disc.), .30-06, .300 Win. Mag., .338 Win Mag., .350 Rem. Mag., or .358 Win. cal., long or short action, blue finish, 5 shot mag., 3 shot in Mag. cals., 22 or 24 in. barrel, available with integral bases or round top, some models supplied with sights, stock is checkered walnut with red rubber buttplate, approx. 7 lbs. Mfg. 1968-92.

	$450	$395	$325	$265	$245	$200	$200	
.250 Savage cal.	$515	$450	$385	$350	$285	$230	$180	
.284 Win. or .350 Rem. cal.	$900	$790	$675	$610	$495	$405	$315	*$558*

* ***Model 77 RL*** – .22-250 Rem. (disc.), .243 Win., .250 Sav., .257 Roberts, .270 Win., .30-06, or .308 Win. cal., ultra light variation weighing 6 lbs., black forearm tip. Disc. 1992.

	$500	$450	$375	$325	$270	$250	$225	*$592*

Add 75% for .250 Sav. cal.

* ***Model 77 RS*** – .243 Win., .250 Sav., 6mm Rem., 6.5mm Rem. Mag., 7x57mm, .25-06 Rem. (disc.), 270 Win., .280 Rem., .284 Win., .30-06, .308 Win., 7mm Rem. Mag., 300 Win. Mag., .338 Win. Mag, .35 Whelen, .350 Rem. Mag., or .358 Win. cal., similar to Model 77R, except has open sights. Disc. 1992.

	$500	$425	$350	$300	$265	$230	$210	
.250 Savage cal.	$575	$505	$430	$390	$315	$260	$200	*$616*

» ***Model 77 RS Premium Calibers*** – .284 Win., .35 Whelen, .350 Rem. Mag. or .358 Win. cal.

	$1,000	$875	$750	$680	$550	$450	$350

* ***Model 77PL*** – .25-06 Rem., .270 Win., .30-06, .300 Win., .338 Win. Mag., 7mm Rem. Mag., or 7x57mm cal., differs from R Model in that it has a round top, drilled to take Redfield scope mounts, w/o sights.

	$500	$450	$375	$300	$245	$200	$200

* ***Model 77ST*** – .25-06 Rem., .257 Roberts, 7x57mm, .300 Win. Mag., .338 Win. Mag., 7mm Rem. Mag., .30-06, or .270 Win. cal., differs from RS Model in that is has round top drilled to take Redfield scope mounts with iron sights on barrel.

	$550	$500	$375	$325	$265	$230	$210

* ***Model 77V Varmint*** – .22-250 Rem., .220 Swift, .243 Win. (disc.), 6mm Rem. (disc.), .25-06 Rem., .280 Rem., .308 Win., or .30-06 cal., 24 in. heavy barrel (26 in. on .220 Swift), drilled and tapped for target bases, approx. 9 lbs. Mfg. 1968-92.

	$500	$450	$395	$325	$265	$245	$210	*$574*

* ***Model 77 RS African*** – similar to Model 77R, except in .458 Win. Mag. cal. Disc. 1991.

	$600	$500	$400	$365	$335	$315	$300	*$680*

This model was supplied standard with a steel trigger guard and steel floor plate.

* ***Model 77 RSC*** – similar to Model 77 RS African, except has Circassian walnut stock (C suffix). Mfg. 1976-78.

	$800	$650	$500	$450	$400	$365	$335

GRADING - PPGS™	100%	98%	95%	90%	80%	70%	60%	LAST MSR

* ***Model 77 RLS*** – .243 Win. (disc. 1989), .270 Win., .30-06, or .308 Win. cal. (disc. 1989), ultra light, 18 1/2 in. barrel, open sights, 6 lbs. Mfg. 1987-93.

$445	**$395**	**$310**	**$280**	**$260**	**$230**	**$210**	***$592***

* ***Model 77 RSI*** – .22-250 Rem. (disc. 1991), .243 Win. .250-3000 Sav. (reintroduced 1990), .270 Win., .30-06, .308 Win. (disc. 1991), 7x57mm (rare), or 7mm-08 Rem. cal., International Mannlicher (full length stock) with 18 1/2 in. barrel and open sights (includes scope rings), approx. 7 lbs. Disc. 1993.

$575	**$450**	**$375**	**$300**	**$265**	**$230**	**$210**	***$623***

Add 50% for 7mm-08, .250-3000 Sav., or 7x57mm cal.

MODEL 77R MARK II SERIES – various cals. as listed in the submodels below, evolutionary design of the Ruger Model 77R featuring slenderized proportioning, 3 position swing-back safety, new trigger, trigger guard and floor plate latch, stainless steel bolt with Mauser extractor design, various barrel lengths, receiver with integral scope bases, hand checkered American walnut stock, includes scope rings, various weights. New 1989.

The Hawkeye Model was introduced during 2007, and please refer separate model listings.

* ***Model 77R Mark II*** – .204 Ruger (new 2004), .220 Swift (new 1995), .22-250 Rem. (new 1993), .223 Rem. (new 1992), .243 Win., .25-06 Rem. (new 1993), .257 Roberts (new 1993), .260 Rem. (new 1999), .270 Win. (new 1993), .270 WSM (new 2004), .280 Rem. (new 1993), 6mm Rem., 6.5x55mm Swedish (new 1993), 7x57mm (new 1993), .30-06 (new 1993), .308 Win., 7mm WSM (new 2004), 7mm Rem. Mag. (new 1993), 7mm RSUM (new 2002), .300 Win. Mag. (new 1993), .300 WSM (new 2004), .300 RSUM (new 2002), .338 Win. Mag. (new 1993). or .350 Rem. Mag. (new 2004) cal., checkered walnut stock is standard, 22 or 24 in. barrel, standard model of the new Mark II Series, approx. 7 lbs. Disc. 2006.

$480	**$395**	**$325**	**$285**	**$245**	**$200**	**$200**	***$695***

* ***Model 77LR Mark II*** – .25-06 Rem., .270 Win., .30-06, .300 Win. Mag., or 7mm Rem. Mag. cal., left-hand variation of the Model 77R. Mfg. 1991-2007.

$515	**$415**	**$335**	**$295**	**$245**	**$200**	**$200**	***$749***

* ***Model 77RL Mark II*** – .223 Rem., .243 Win., .257 Roberts (new 1993), .270 Win. (new 1993), .30-06 (mfg. 1993-2004, reintroduced 2006), or .308 Win. cal., 20 in. barrel, black forend tip, ultra light variation weighing approx. 6 lbs. Mfg. 1990-2008.

$640	**$475**	**$370**	**$280**	**$245**	**$210**	**$180**	***$837***

* ***Model 77RLFP Mark II Stainless*** – .204 Ruger, .223 Rem. (new 2005), .243 Win., .270 Win., or .30-06 cal., 20 in. barrel, black synthetic stock, ultralight variation of the Model 77, w/o sights, 6 1/2 lbs. Mfg. 1999-2008.

$540	**$435**	**$345**	**$295**	**$245**	**$200**	**$200**	***$779***

* ***Model 77RS Mark II*** – 6mm Rem., .243 Win., .25-06 Rem. (new 1993), .270 Win. (new 1993), .30-06 (new 1993), .308 Win., 7mm Rem. Mag. (new 1993), .300 Win. Mag. (new 1993), .338 Win Mag. (new 1993), or .458 Win. Mag. (mfg. 1994-98) cal., 22 or 24 in. barrel, similar to Model 77R, except has open sights. Mfg. 1990-2004.

$555	**$435**	**$355**	**$310**	**$270**	**$230**	**$210**	***$780***

* ***Model 77CR Mark II Compact*** – .223 Rem., .243 Win., .260 Rem., .308 Win., or 7mm-08 Rem. cal., features 16 1/2 in. barrel, checkered walnut stock, includes scope rings, no sights, approx. 5 3/4 lbs. Mfg. 2002-2008.

$540	**$435**	**$345**	**$295**	**$245**	**$200**	**$200**	***$779***

» **Model 77CRBBZ Mark II Compact Stainless** – stainless variation of the Model 77CR Compact, black laminate stock. Mfg. 2002-2008.

$575	**$465**	**$350**	**$295**	**$255**	**$225**	**$205**	***$837***

* ***Model 77FRBBZ Mark II Frontier*** – .243 Win., .308 Win., .300 WSM (disc. 2006), or 7mm-08 Rem. cal., compact design features 16 1/2 in. barrel, and shortened grey laminate stock, barrel cantilever base allows scope to be mounted over barrel in front

GRADING - PPGS™	100%	98%	95%	90%	80%	70%	60%	LAST MSR

of action, blue finish, includes scope rings and Weaver style scope base adapter. Mfg. 2005-2008.

	$595	$460	$365	$315	$275	$230	$210	$831

» **Model 77FRTG Mark II Frontier Stainless** – .338 Federal (new 2007), .358 Win. (new 2008), .325 WSM (disc. 2007), or other cals. similar to Frontier model disc. 2007, stainless variation of the Model 77 FRBBZ Frontier, target grey finish stainless steel barrel/action. Mfg. 2006-2008.

	$725	$625	$525	$400	$335	$290	$245	$936

* **Model 77RSI Mark II** – .243 Win., .270 Win., .30-06, or .308 Win. cal., International Mannlicher (full length stock) with 18 1/2 in. barrel and open sights (includes scope rings), approx. 7 lbs. Mfg. 1993-2008.

	$715	$625	$525	$400	$335	$290	$245	$911

* **Model 77RLS Mark II** – .243 Win. or .308 Win. cal., ultra light, 18 1/2 in. barrel, open sights. Mfg. 1990 only.

	$460	$375	$310	$280	$260	$230	$210	$564

* **Model K77RFP Mark II All-Weather Stainless** – .204 Ruger (new 2005), .22-250 (new 1996), .223 Rem., .243 Win., .25-06 Rem. (new 1999), .260 Rem. (new 1999), .270 Win., .270 WSM (new 2004), .280 Rem. (new 1993), 7.62x39mm (disc. 2000), .30-06, .308 Win., .325 WSM (New 2006), .350 Rem. Mag. (new 2006), 7mm-08 Rem. (new 2005), 7mm Rem. Mag., 7mm WSM (new 2004), 7mm RSUM (new 2002), .300 Win. Mag., .300 WSM (new 2004), .300 RSUM (new 2002), or .338 Win. Mag. (new 1992) cal., 22 or 24 in. barrel, similar to Model 77R Mark II except has stainless steel metal with matte black DuPont Zytel synthetic stock, no sights. Mfg. 1990-2006.

	$480	$395	$325	$285	$245	$200	$185	$695

* **Model K77RSFP Mark II All-Weather Stainless** – .223 Rem. (new 2002), .243 Win., .270 Win., .30-06, 7mm Rem. Mag., .300 Win. Mag., or .338 Win. Mag. cal., otherwise similar to Model K77RFP All-Weather Stainless, except has open sights. Disc. 2004.

	$525	$425	$355	$285	$250	$215	$185	$780

* **Model K77RBZ Mark II Satin Stainless** – .22-250 Rem. (new 1999), .223 Rem., .243 Win., .270 Win., .280 Rem. (disc. 2006), .30-06, .308 Win., 7mm Rem. Mag., .300 Win. Mag., .338 Win. Mag., or .350 Rem. Mag. (disc. 2005) cal., features brown wood laminate stock with sling swivels, 22 or 24 in. barrel without sights, approx. 7 5/16 lbs. Mfg. 1997-2008.

	$575	$465	$350	$295	$255	$225	$205	$837

* **Model K77RSBZ Mark II** – .243 Win., .270 Win., .30-06, .300 Win. Mag., .338 Win. Mag., or 7mm Rem. Mag. cal., 22 or 24 in. barrel, laminated stock, open sights, includes scope rings, approx. 7 3/8 lbs. Disc. 2004.

	$515	$470	$355	$285	$250	$215	$185	$825

* **Model K77RVT (VBZ) Mark II** – .22 PPC (disc. 1996), .204 Ruger (new 2004), .220 Swift (disc. 2006), .22-250 Rem., .223 Rem., .243 Win., .25-06 Rem., .308 Win., 6.5 Creedmor (new 2009), or 6mm PPC (disc. 1996) cal., 26 or 28 (new 2009, 6.5 Creedmor cal. only) in. heavy barrel, features stainless steel construction, target grey finish was standard 2005-2009, brown (new 2009) laminated stock, approx. 9 3/4 lbs. Mfg. 1993-2012.

	$750	$640	$535	$400	$335	$290	$245	$963

This model's nomenclature changed from VBZ to VT during 1994.

* **Model KM77VTBBZ Mark II Target** – .204 Ruger, .22-250 Rem., .223 Rem., .243 Win. (disc. 2012), .25-06 Rem. (disc. 2012), 6.5 Creedmoor, or .308 Win. cal., 26 or 28 (6.5 Creedmoor only) in. stainless steel barrel, black laminate stock, 4 or 5 shot mag., no sights, 9 1/2 - 9 3/4 lbs.

MSR $1,029	$795	$700	$575	$450	$345	$295	$245	

* **Model 77RLRBBZ Mark II Stainless** – .25-06 Rem. (new 2004), .270 Win., .30-06, 7mm

GRADING - PPGS™	100%	98%	95%	90%	80%	70%	60%	LAST MSR

Rem. Mag., or .300 Win. Mag. cal., left-hand action, 22 in. barrel, uncheckered grey laminated stock, includes scope rings. Mfg. 1999-2008.

	$575	$465	$350	$295	$255	$225	$205	$837

MODEL 77 COMPACT MAGNUM – .300 RCM, .308 Win. Mag. (new 2011) or .338 RCM cal., 20 in. barrel, matte finish, American walnut stock, U-type notch rear sight with elevated brass bead front sight, 3 or 4 shot mag., left hand became available in 2010, 7 1/4 lbs. Mfg. mid-2008-2012.

	$765	$625	$500	$425	$375	$325	$275	$929

* ***Model 77 Compact Magnum Stainless*** – .300 RCM or .338 RCM cal., 20 in. barrel, matte stainless finish, black synthetic stock, U-type notch rear sight with elevated brass bead front sight, 3 shot mag., 6 3/4 lbs. New mid-2008-2011.

	$750	$615	$500	$425	$375	$325	$275	$914

MODEL 77-GS GUNSITE SCOUT – .308 Win. cal., 16 1/2 in. barrel with flash suppressor, 10 shot box mag., alloy steel receiver, matte black finish, forward mounted Picatinny rail, checkered grey laminate stock, recoil pad, sling swivels, protected front sight and adj. ghost ring rear sight, Gunsite engraved logo grip cap, non-rotating Mauser type controlled round feed extractor, right or left hand (new 2012) action, approx. 7 lbs. New 2011.

MSR $1,039	$800	$700	$600	$475	$400	$325	$295	

* ***Model 77-GS Gunsite Scout Stainless*** – .308 Win. cal., 16 1/2 in. barrel with flash suppressor, 10 shot box mag., alloy steel receiver, matte black finish, forward mounted Picatinny rail, checkered grey laminate stock, recoil pad, sling swivels, protected front sight and adj. ghost ring rear sight, Gunsite engraved logo grip cap, non-rotating Mauser type controlled round feed extractor, right or left hand (new 2012) action, approx. 7 lbs. New 2011.

MSR $1,039	$775	$675	$575	$450	$375	$300	$265	

MODEL 77 RSM – .375 H&H, .416 Rigby, or .458 Lott (new 2002) cal., 23 or 24 (.375 H&H cal.) in. barrel, 3 or 4 (.375 H&H cal.) shot mag., premium grade Circassian walnut with hand cut checkering and ebony forend tip, integral barrel and sighting quarter rib with two folding sights, approx. 9 1/2 lbs. Mfg. 1990-2010.

	$1,950	$1,425	$1,100	$975	$850	$725	$675	$2,404

MODEL 77 RS EXPRESS – .270 Win., .30-06, 7mm Rem. Mag., .300 Win. Mag., or .338 Win. Mag. (new 1994) cal., 22 or 24 in. barrel, 3 or 4 shot mag., similar construction to Model 77RSM with premium grade wood and other materials, 7 1/2 lbs. Mfg. 1991-2002.

	$1,250	$875	$815	$750	$700	$675	$595	$1,625

MODEL HM77R HAWKEYE SERIES – various cals., newest variation of the M77, featuring one-piece stainless bolt, new LC6 trigger, rotating Mauser type controlled round extractor, slimmer profile, checkered American walnut stock with solid red recoil pad, matte bluing on barrel and action, redesigned steel floorplate and latch, left-hand available in certain cals. beginning 2008, includes scope rings, various weights. New 2007.

* ***Model HM77R Hawkeye*** – .204 Ruger, .22-250 Rem., .223 Rem., .243 Win., .25-06 Rem., .257 Roberts, .270 Win., .280 Rem. (mfg. 2008-disc.), .30-06, .308 Win., 7mm Rem. Mag., 7mm-08 Rem., .300 Win. Mag., .300 RCM (disc. 2012), .338 Win. Mag., .338 RCM (mfg. 2011-2012), .338 Federal (mfg. 2008-2010), 6.5 Creedmoor (new 2010), or .358 Win. (mfg. 2008-2009) cal., newest variation of the M77, featuring one-piece stainless bolt, alloy steel became standard 2011, 3, 4, or 5 shot mag., 22 or 24 in. barrel, rotating Mauser type controlled round extractor, slimmer profile, checkered American walnut stock with solid red recoil pad, matte bluing on barrel and action, new LC6 trigger, redesigned steel floorplate and latch, no sights, includes scope rings, 7 - 8 1/4 lbs. New 2007.

MSR $899	$675	$525	$400	$315	$265	$225	$195	

This model is available in left-hand action in most cals. at no extra charge.

* ***Model HM77RFP Hawkeye All-Weather Stainless*** – same cals. as Model HM77R Hawkeye, except not available in .257 Roberts, 22 or 24 in. barrel, matte finish stainless steel,

GRADING - PPGS™	100%	98%	95%	90%	80%	70%	60%	LAST MSR

black checkered synthetic stock, no sights, similar Hawkeye features as the HM77R. New 2007.

MSR $899	$675	$525	$400	$315	$265	$225	$195	

* ***Model HM77R Hawkeye Laminated Stainless*** – .25-06 Rem., .270 Win., .30-06, 7mm Rem. Mag., or .300 Win. Mag. cal., left-hand action, 22 in. barrel, black laminated stock, includes scope rings. Mfg. mid-2008-2010.

	$675	$575	$450	$400	$350	$300	$250	*$862*

* ***Model HM77RBH*** – .30-06 cal., 22 in. blue or stainless steel barrel, brown Hogue overmolded stock. Limited mfg. 2008.

	$575	$450	$365	$315	$275	$230	$210	*$821*

* ***Model HM77RGH*** – .270 Win. cal., 22 in. blue or stainless steel barrel, green Hogue overmolded stock. Limited mfg. 2008.

	$575	$450	$365	$315	$275	$230	$210	*$821*

* ***Model HM77R Hawkeye Alaskan*** – .375 Ruger or .416 Ruger (new 2010) cal., 20 in. stainless steel (disc. 2010) or alloy steel (new 2011) barrel with choice of Diamondblack corrosion resistant coating or stainless Hawkeye matte finish, express sights with adj. V-notch rear sight, black Hogue overmolded stock with recoil pad, 8 lbs. Mfg. 2007-2012.

	$950	$825	$735	$650	$575	$525	$475	*$1,099*

* ***Model HM77RS Hawkeye African*** – .223 Rem. (new 2011), 9.3x62mm (mfg. 2011-2012), .375 Ruger (disc. 2012), .300 Win. Mag. (mfg. 2010-2012), or .338 Win. Mag. (mfg. 2010-2012) cal., matte blue finish, 23 in. alloy steel barrel, checkered American walnut stock and forearm, 3 (disc. 2012) or 5 shot mag., 7 3/4 lbs. New 2007.

MSR $1,199	$1,025	$875	$750	$650	$575	$525	$475	

This model was also available in left-hand action at no extra charge in .375 Ruger cal. only.

* ***Model HM77RSB Hawkeye African with Muzzle Brake*** – .300 Win. Mag., .338 Win. Mag., .375 Ruger, or .416 Ruger cal., 3 shot mag., 23 in. barrel with removable radial port muzzle brake and barrel band, satin blue finish, American walnut stock with ebony forend cap, LC6 trigger, Express style bead front and adj. rear sights, round feed extractor, fixed blade-type ejector, hinged steel floorplate with engraved Ruger logo, three position safety, integral scope mounts, 8 lbs. New 2013.

MSR $1,199	$1,025	$900	$800	$700	$600	$500	$400	

* ***Model HM77-CR Hawkeye Compact*** – .223 Rem., .243 Win., .260 Rem. (mfg. 2009-disc.), 7mm-08 Rem., 7.62x39mm (disc. 2012), .308 Win., or 6.8mm SPC (disc. 2011) cal., 16 1/2 in. barrel w/o sights, blue finish, 12 1/2 LOP American walnut stock, alloy steel became standard 2011, approx. 6 lbs. New 2009.

MSR $899	$675	$525	$400	$315	$265	$225	$195	

* ***Model HKM77-CRBBZ Hawkeye Compact Laminate Stainless*** – .223 Rem., .243 Win., .260 Rem. (disc. 2011), 7mm-08 Rem., .308 Win., 6.8mm SPC (mfg. 2009-disc.), or .300 RCM (mfg. 2009-disc.) cal., 16 1/2 in. barrel, stainless steel matte finish, black laminate stock, no sights, 6-6 1/2 lbs. New 2009.

MSR $969	$760	$550	$400	$315	$265	$225	$195	

* ***Model HM77R Hawkeye Ultra Light*** – .223 Rem., .243 Win., .257 Roberts, .270 Win., .30-06, or .308 Win. cal., 20 in. barrel w/o sights, matte blue metal finish, checkered walnut stock with black forend cap, approx. 6 1/2 lbs. Mfg. 2009-2010.

	$695	$585	$460	$410	$350	$300	$250	*$888*

» ***Model HM77R Hawkeye All-Weather Ultra Light*** – .204 Ruger, .223 Rem., .243 Win., .270 Win., or .30-06 cal., similar to Ultra Light, except has stainless steel action with matte finish and black synthetic stock, approx. 6 1/2 lbs. Mfg. 2009.

	$575	$450	$375	$325	$275	$250	$220	*$803*

* ***Model HKM77-RBBZ Hawkeye Sporter*** – .22-250 Rem. (disc. 2011), .223 Rem. (disc. 2011), .243 Win., .270 Win., .280 Rem. (new 2012), .30-06, .308 Win., .300 Win.

GRADING - PPGS™	100%	98%	95%	90%	80%	70%	60%	LAST MSR

Mag., .338 Win. Mag., or 7mm Rem. Mag. cal., features matte finished stainless steel action with 22 or 24 in. barrel w/o sights, brown (disc.) or black (new 2010) laminate stock, 7 1/2 - 8 1/2 lbs. New 2009.

MSR $959	$760	$550	$400	$315	$265	$225	$195	

* ***Model HM77R Hawkeye International*** – .243 Win., .270 Win., .30-06, or .308 Win. cal., 18 1/2 in. barrel with adj. rear express sight and blade front sight, matte blued metal finish, checkered Mannlicher walnut stock with sling swivels, 6 1/4 - 7 lbs. Mfg. 2009-2010.

	$750	$650	$550	$425	$350	$315	$275	*$967*

* ***Model HKM77-MH Hawkeye Magnum Hunter*** – .300 Win. Mag. cal., 3 shot mag., stainless steel receiver and 24 in. barrel with removable radial-port muzzle brake, Green Hogue overmolded stock, no sights, 8 lbs. New 2013.

MSR $1,099	$875	$775	$650	$525	$450	$350	$295	

* ***Model HKM77R-Z Hawkeye Predator*** – .204 Ruger, .22-250 Rem., .223 Rem., .308 Win. (new 2013), or 6.5 Creedmoor (new 2013) cal., matte finished stainless steel action with adj. two-stage target trigger, 22 or 24 in. heavy barrel, Green Mountain or brown laminate (disc.) stock, approx. 8 lbs. New 2009.

MSR $1,029	$815	$665	$550	$425	$350	$315	$275	

* ***Model HM77-VLEHFS Hawkeye Tactical*** – .223 Rem., .243 Win. (disc. 2010), or .308 Win. cal., 4 or 5 shot mag., matte finished blued action and 20 in. bull barrel with flash suppressor, no sights, adj. two-stage target trigger, black Hogue overmolded stock with Harris bipod, 8 3/4 lbs. New 2009.

MSR $1,199	$1,050	$900	$765	$650	$575	$525	$475	

AMERICAN RIFLE – .22-250 Rem., .243 Win., .270 Win., .30-06, .308 Win. Mag., or 7mm-08 Rem. cal., 18 (new 2013) or 22 in. hammer forged barrel, flush fitting 4 shot rotary mag., black composite stock, matte black finish, soft rubber recoil pad, w/o sights, Power Bedding allows free floating barrel, 3-5 lb. Marksman adj. trigger, tang safety, three lug 70 degree bolt, approx. 6 1/4 lbs. New 2012.

MSR $449	$375	$335	$300	$275	$250	$225	$200	

GUIDE GUN – .300 RCM, .300 Win. Mag., .338 RCM, .338 Win. Mag., .375, or .30-06 cal., 3 or 4 shot mag., 20 in. stainless steel barrel with removable radial-port muzzle, round feed extractor, fixed blade-type ejector, Hawkeye matte finish, Green Mountain laminate stock, soft rubber recoil pad with buttpad spacers, Express style bead front and adj. rear sights, right or left (.375 Ruger cal. only) hand action, LC6 trigger, three position safety, hinged steel floorplate with engraved Ruger logo, integral scope mounts, 8.1 lbs. New 2013.

MSR $1,199	$1,050	$925	$800	$700	$600	$500	$400	

RIFLES: LEVER ACTION

MODEL 96 CARBINE – .17 HMR (new 2002), .22 LR (disc. 2003), .22 WMR, or .44 Mag. (disc. 2007) cal., 18 1/2 in. barrel with single barrel band, uncheckered hardwood stock with curved buttplate, 10 (.17 HMR or .22 LR), 9 (.22 WMR), or 4 (.44 Mag.) shot detachable rotary mag., crossbolt safety on trigger guard, adj. rear sight, .44 Mag. has case hardened lever, rimfire receivers are drilled and tapped while the .44 Mag. has a receiver with integral bases, scope rings (became standard 1997), approx. 5 1/4 - 6 lbs. Mfg. 1996-2008.

	$400	$350	$275	$200	$150	$135	$125	*$451*

Add $174 for .44 Mag. cal. with scope rings (disc. 2007).

RIFLES: SEMI-AUTO, RIMFIRE

During certain years of manufacture, Ruger's changes in production on certain models (cals., barrel markings, barrel lengths, etc.) have created rare variations that are now considered premium niches. These areas of low manufacture will add premiums to the values listed on standard models. The Model 10/22 has been mfg. in a variety of limited production models including a multi-colored or green laminate wood stock variation (1986), a brown laminate stock (1988), a Kittery Trading Post Commemorative (1988), a smoke or tree bark laminate stock (1989), a Chief AJ Model, Wal-Mart (stainless with black laminated hardwood stock - 1990), etc.

GRADING - PPGS™	100%	98%	95%	90%	80%	70%	60%	LAST MSR

These limited editions will command premiums over the standard models listed, depending on the desirability of the special edition.

Note: All Ruger Rifles, except Stainless Mini-14, all Mini-30s, and Model 77-22s were made during 1976 in a "Liberty" version. Add $50-$75 when in 100% in the original box condition.

10/17 CARBINE – .17 HMR cal., steel receiver, birch stock only, 18 1/2 in. barrel, otherwise similar to 10/22 Standard Carbine. Limited mfg. 2004 only.

$475 $400 $350 $300 $225 $165 $150 *$510*

While advertised, very few of this model were manufactured.

10/22 COMPACT – .22 LR cal., similar to 10/22 Standard Carbine, except has 16 1/2 in. barrel with hardwood stock, 10 shot mag., fiber optic front sight and adj. rear sight, 12 3/4 LOP, 4 1/2 lbs.

MSR $329 $260 $185 $140 $105 $80 $60 $55

10/22 STANDARD CARBINE – .22 LR cal., 10 shot rotary mag., 18 1/2 in. barrel with barrel band, birch (disc. 2008), uncheckered hardwood stock, blued (disc.) or satin black finish, adj. folding rear and gold bead front sights, 5 lbs. New 1964.

MSR $279 $225 $190 $130 $100 $80 $60 $55

10/22 Standard Carbine Synthetic – .22 LR cal., 10 shot rotary mag., 18 1/2 in. barrel with barrel band, black synthetic stock, satin black finish, folding adj. rear and gold bead front, or LaserMax laser (new 2013) sights integrated into forend, 5 lbs. New 1999.

MSR $279 $225 $190 $130 $100 $80 $60 $55

Add $120 for Lasermax laser sights (new 2013).

* ***10/22 Standard Carbine Stainless*** – similar to 10/22 Standard Carbine, except has stainless steel barrel and action, choice of birch (disc. 2008) or black synthetic (new 1997) stock, 5 lbs. New 1992.

MSR $309 $250 $200 $160 $120 $100 $85 $65

* ***10/22 Standard Carbine 40th Anniversary*** – similar to 10/22 Standard Carbine, except includes 40th Ruger anniversary medallion. Mfg. 2004 only.

$225 $165 $125 $100 $85 $65 $55 *$279*

10/22 STANDARD SPORTER – .22 LR cal., 10 shot rotary mag., 18.88 in. barrel, deluxe hand checkered walnut stock, blued (disc.) or satin black finish, adj. rear and gold bead front sights, 5 3/4 lbs. New 1964.

MSR $379 $295 $265 $230 $210 $175 $150 $125

Add 10% for uncheckered walnut stock (mfg. 1964-1980 and 1987-1989).

10/22 RIFLE – similar to 10/22 Standard Carbine, except has 20 in. barrel with hardwood stock. Mfg. 2004-2006.

$220 $165 $125 $105 $80 $60 $55 *$275*

10/22 TAKEDOWN TD – .22 LR cal., 10 shot rotary mag., 18 1/2 in. barrel, takedown action with recessed locking lever, black synthetic stock, polymer trigger housing, adj. rear sight, gold bead front sight, includes black synthetic backpack style bag, 4 2/3 lbs. New mid-2012.

MSR $399 $335 $290 $260 $240 $220 $200 $185

* ***10/22 Takedown TDT*** – .22 LR cal., similar to 10/22 Takedown TD, except has 16.62 in. threaded barrel with Mini-14 style flash suppressor, satin black finish, 4 2/3 lbs. New 2013.

MSR $419 $340 $295 $256 $245 $225 $200 $185

10/22 FS TACTICAL – .22 LR cal., 10 shot rotary mag., alloy steel receiver, 16 1/8 in. barrel with SR-556/Mini 14 style flash suppressor and barrel band, black synthetic stock, Picatinny rail on top of receiver, satin black finish, 4.3 lbs. New late-2010.

MSR $329 $255 $210 $175 $140 $115 $90 $75

GRADING - PPGS™	100%	98%	95%	90%	80%	70%	60%	LAST MSR

10/22 TACTICAL w/HEAVY BARREL – .22 LR cal., 10 shot rotary mag., alloy steel receiver, 16 1/8 in. heavy hammer forged barrel w/o sights and spiraled exterior, black Hogue overmolded stock, target trigger, adj. bipod, 6.8 lbs. New late-2010.

MSR $579	$450	$375	$315	$275	$240	$215	$175	

10/22-T TARGET MODEL – .22 LR cal., features brown laminated American hardwood stock, 20 in. blue hammer-forged spiral finish heavy barrel, target trigger, w/o sights, 10 shot mag., 7 1/2 lbs. New 1996.

MSR $529	$425	$340	$265	$210	$175	$150	$125	

* ***K10/22-T Target Model Stainless*** – similar to 10/22T-Target Model, except is stainless steel, and has black laminate stock. Mfg. 1998-2008, reintroduced 2010.

MSR $569	$445	$350	$275	$225	$185	$160	$140	

* ***K10/22-TNZ Target Model Stainless*** – features 20 in. barrel w/o sights, stainless steel action and barrel, laminated thumbhole stock with slanted forend, 7 lbs. Mfg. 2001-2002.

	$450	$375	$300	$240	$210	$180	$155	*$649*

* ***K10/22-T Target Tactical*** – similar to 10/22-T Target Model, except available in black matte finish, black Hogue overmolded stock, receiver with Picatinny style rail, 16.1 in. barrel with no sights, includes precision adj. bipod, 6.9 lbs. Mfg. 2010 only.

	$435	$345	$275	$225	$185	$160	$140	*$555*

10/22 FINGERGROOVE SPORTER – similar to 10/22 Standard, except Monte Carlo stock and beavertail forearm. Mfg. 1966-1971.

	$625	$550	$475	$350	$300	$225	$200	
w/checkered stock	$1,200	$950	$800	$650	$550	$450	$400	

10/22 INTERNATIONAL (OLD PRODUCTION) – similar to 10/22 Standard, except walnut full stock Mannlicher style. Mfg. 1966-69.

	$675	$575	$500	$450	$375	$350	$325	

Add 50% for checkered stock.

10/22RBI INTERNATIONAL (NEW PRODUCTION) – features Mannlicher style international birch full stock. Mfg. 1994-2003.

	$220	$180	$135	$105	$95	$80	$65	*$279*

* ***K10/22RBI International (New Production) Stainless*** – stainless variation of the 10/22RBI International. Disc. 2003.

	$325	$250	$175	$110	$100	$80	$75	*$299*

10/22 CANADIAN CENTENNIAL – 2,000 mfg. in 1967.

	$450	$400	$350	N/A	N/A	N/A	N/A	*$100*

10/22 MAGNUM – .22 WMR cal., steel receiver, longer and heavier bolt, 10 shot rotary mag., 18 1/2 in. barrel, uncheckered birch stock, blue metal, folding rear sight, 6 1/2 lbs. Mfg. 1999-2006.

	$900	$750	$625	$450	$300	$225	$200	*$536*

RUGER/REMINGTON CANADIAN CENTENNIAL MATCHED NO. 3 SET – includes a Remington Model 742 in .308 Win. cal. and a Ruger 10/22 Sporter with special commemorative appointments, cased. 1,000 sets mfg. 1967 only.

	$750	$575	$500	N/A	N/A	N/A	N/A	

* ***Ruger/Remington Canadian Centennial Matched No. 2 Set*** – 70 sets mfg. 1967 only.

	$950	$775	$550	N/A	N/A	N/A	N/A	

* ***Ruger/Remington Canadian Centennial Matched No. 1 Special Deluxe Set*** – 30 sets mfg. 1967 only.

	$1,150	$895	$675	N/A	N/A	N/A	N/A	

SR-22 – .22 LR cal., 16.1 in. barrel with Mini-14 flash suppressor, 10 shot rotary mag.,

GRADING - PPGS™	100%	98%	95%	90%	80%	70%	60%	LAST MSR

Hogue monogrip pistol grip, six position telescoping buttstock, integrated Picatinny rail on top of receiver, mid-length vented circular handguard with Picatinny rail, Ruger Rapid Deploy sights, 6 1/2 lbs. New 2013.

MSR $649	$550	$475	$425	$375	$325	$275	$250	

RIFLES: SEMI-AUTO, CENTERFIRE

IMPORTANT NOTE: On model(s) where *N/A has replaced the normal 100% value, it indicates current market conditions are too unstable to accurately ascertain 100%-60% values. Factory retail prices (MSRs) reflect most recent updates. For more up-to-date information on current pricing trends and additional useful information, please visit www.bluebookofgunvalues.com, select "Information & Services" from the menu, and click on "Additional Book Information".

MODEL 44 STANDARD CARBINE – .44 Mag. cal., 4 shot mag., 18 1/2 in. barrel, blowback action, folding sight, curved butt. Mfg. 1961-85.

	$600	$500	$450	$375	$300	$250	$225	*$332*

* ***Model 44 Standard Carbine Deerstalker*** – approx. 3,750 mfg. with "Deerstalker" marked on rifle until Ithaca lawsuit disc. manufacture (1962).

	$925	$850	$725	$600	$550	$475	$400	

* ***Model 44 Standard Carbine 25th Year Anniversary*** – mfg. 1985 only, limited production, has medallion in stock.

	$675	$575	$450	N/A	N/A	N/A	N/A	*$495*

MODEL 44RS – similar to 44 Standard Carbine, but has aperture sight and swivels.

	$675	$600	$525	$450	$400	$350	$300	

MODEL 44 FINGERGROOVE SPORTER – Monte Carlo stocked version of 44 Standard. Mfg. until 1971.

	$850	$650	$550	$500	$450	$400	$350	
w/factory checkered stock	$1,500	$1,315	$1,125	$1,020	$825	$675	$525	

MODEL 44 INTERNATIONAL – similar to Model 44 Standard Carbine, except full length Mannlicher style stock. Mfg. until 1971.

	$900	$750	$650	$550	$475	$400	$350	

Add 50% for factory checkered stock.

MODEL 99/44 DEERFIELD CARBINE – .44 Mag. cal., 4 shot rotary mag., 18 1/2 in. barrel with folding aperture rear sight, rotating bolt with dual front locking lugs, blue finish only, uncheckered hardwood stock, includes integral scope mounts and rings, 6 1/4 lbs. Mfg. 2000-2006.

	$650	$550	$450	$400	$335	$300	$260	*$702*

RUGER CARBINE – 9mm Para. (PC9) or .40 S&W (PC4) cal., 16 1/4 in. barrel, 10 (PC4) or 15 (PC9) shot detachable mag., black synthetic stock, matte metal finish, with or w/o sights, with fully adj. rear sight or rear receiver sight, crossbolt safety, 6 lbs. Mfg. 1998-2006.

	$575	$475	$375	$310	$265	$240	$215	*$623*

Add $24 for adj. rear receiver sight.

Beginning 2005, this model came standard with an adjustable ghost ring aperture rear sight and protected blade front sight.

MINI-14 – .223 Rem. or .222 Rem. (disc.) cal., 5 (standard mag. starting in 1989), 10 (disc.), or 20* shot detachable mag., 18 1/2 in. barrel, gas operated, blue finish, aperture rear sight, military style stock, approx. 6 3/4 lbs. Mfg. 1974-2004.

	*N/A	$445	$365	$320	$275	$240	$215	*$655*

Add 20% for .222 Rem. cal.
Add $300 for folding stock (disc. 1989).
Add 25% for Southport Model with gold bead front sight.
Add 100% for Mini-14 GB (primarily used for law enforcement) with a flash hider and bayonet lug (blue or stainless) if in 95%+ original condition.

GRADING - PPGS™	100%	98%	95%	90%	80%	70%	60%	LAST MSR

* ***Mini-14 Stainless*** – mini stainless steel version, choice of wood or black synthetic (new 1999) stock. Disc. 2004.

	*N/A	$445	$380	$320	$275	$230	$200	*$715*

Add 20% for .222 Rem. cal.
Add $300 for folding stock (disc. 1990).

MINI-14 RANCH RIFLE – .223 Rem. cal., 5 (standard mag. starting in 1989), 10 (disc.), or 20 shot detachable mag., blued finish, 18 1/2 in. barrel, choice of black synthetic or hardwood stock, receiver cut for factory rings, similar to Mini-14, supplied with scope rings, folding (disc.) or adj. ghost ring aperture rear sight, protected front sight, and flat style recoil pad (became standard 2005), 7 lbs. New 1982.

MSR $909	*N/A	$565	$475	$425	$365	$315	$275

Add $10 for black synthetic stock.
Add $50 for 20 shot mag. (2008).
Add $260 for Mini 14 NRA-ILA Limited Edition with 16 1/8 in. barrel and black Hogue overmolded stock (ltd. mfg. 2008-2009).

Due to 1989 Federal legislation and public sentiment at the time, the Mini-14 Ranch Rifle was shipped with a 5 shot detachable mag., 1989-2008.

* ***Mini-14 Stainless Ranch Rifle*** – 5.56 NATO (current mfg.) or .223 Rem. (older mfg.) or 6.8mm SPC (mfg. 2007-2011) cal., stainless steel construction, choice of wood (disc.) or black synthetic (new 1999) stock, 5 or 20 shot mag., adj. rear sight, 6 3/4 lbs. New 1986.

MSR $979	*N/A	$665	$535	$450	$400	$350	$300

Add $60 for 20 shot mag. (not available in 6.8mm SPC cal.).
Add $300 for folding stock (disc. 1990).

MINI-14 TARGET RIFLE w/THUMBHOLE STOCK – .223 Rem. cal., 22 in. stainless steel heavy barrel with adj. harmonic tuner, no sights, ergonomic black or grey (disc.) laminated thumbhole stock, stainless scope rings, 5 shot mag., 3 position rubber recoil pad with adj. LOP, 9 1/2 lbs. New 2007.

MSR $1,149	*N/A	$795	$675	$550	$475	$425	$375

Add $16 for 20 shot mag. (mfg. 2009-disc.).

MINI-14 TARGET RIFLE w/BLACK SYNTHETIC STOCK – .223 Rem. cal., 22 in. stainless steel heavy barrel with adj. harmonic tuner, black Hogue overmolded stock, stainless scope rings, 5 shot mag., 8 1/2 lbs. New 2007.

MSR $1,149	*N/A	$795	$675	$550	$475	$425	$375

Add $16 for 20 shot mag. (mfg. 2009-disc.).

MINI-14 TACTICAL RIFLE FIXED STOCK – 5.56 NATO cal., blued steel or stainless steel action and barrel, compact 16 1/8 in. blue barrel with flash suppressor, 5 or 20 shot mag., fixed black synthetic stock with vents on upper forend, blade front and adj. rear sights, 6 3/4 lbs. New 2009.

MSR $989	*N/A	$675	$550	$475	$425	$375	$325

Add $80 for stainless steel action and barrel.

MINI-14 TACTICAL RIFLE w/COLLAPSIBLE STOCK – 5.56 NATO cal., compact 16 1/8 in. blue barrel with flash suppressor, 5 or 20 shot mag., six position ATI folding/collapsible stock, includes quad Picatinny accessory rails on forend, blade front and adj. rear sights, 7 1/4 lbs. New 2009.

MSR $989	*N/A	$675	$550	$475	$425	$375	$325

MINI-THIRTY – 7.62x39mm Russian cal., 18 1/2 in. barrel, 5 shot detachable mag., hardwood stock, includes scope rings, 7 lbs. 3 oz. Mfg. 1987-2004.

	*N/A	$450	$405	$375	$335	$300	$260	*$695*

* ***Mini-Thirty Stainless*** – 7.62x39mm cal., 18 1/2 in. barrel, stainless steel variation of the Mini-Thirty, black synthetic stock, adj. ghost ring aperture rear sight and protected front sight became standard 2005, 5 or 20 shot mag., integral sling swivels, 6 3/4 lbs. New 1990.

MSR $979	*N/A	$665	$525	$450	$400	$350	$325

Add $60 for 20 shot mag.

GRADING - PPGS™	100%	98%	95%	90%	80%	70%	60%	LAST MSR

* ***Mini-Thirty Tactical*** – 7.62x39mm cal., similar to Mini-Thirty Stainless, except has 16 1/8 in. barrel with flash suppressor, 20 shot mag., adj. ghost ring aperture rear sight and non-glare post front sight, Ruger scope bases, black synthetic stock, approx. 6 3/4 lbs. New late 2010.

MSR $989	*N/A	$650	$535	$450	$400	$350	$325

SR-556/SR-556 CARBINE – 5.56 NATO or 6.8mm SPC (mfg. mid-2010-2011) cal., gas piston operation, 10, 25 (6.8mm SPC only, disc. 2011), or 30 shot mag., 16.1 in. barrel with muzzle brake, matte black finish, four position chrome plated gas regulator, quad rail handguard, with or without Troy folding sights, fixed (556SC) or six position telescoping M4 style buttstock, Hogue monogrip pistol grip with finger grooves, upper receiver has integrated Picatinny rail, chrome plated bolt, bolt carrier, and extractor, includes rail covers, soft sided carry case and three magazines, 7.4 (Carbine) or 7.9 lbs. New mid-2009.

MSR $1,995	$1,795	$1,575	$1,075	$900	$775	$650	$575

* ***SR-556E*** – 5.56 NATO cal., gas piston operation (two-stage with regulator), 10 (SR-556ESC) or 30 shot mag., 16.1 in. cold hammer forged barrel with flash suppressor, Ruger Rapid Deploy folding sights, A2 style pistol grip, 6-position telescoping M4 style buttstock, vented aluminum handguard with full length Picatinny rail, upper receiver has integrated Picatinny rail, 7.35 lbs. New mid-2011.

MSR $1,375	$1,175	$1,025	$900	$775	$650	$550	$495

SR-556VT – 5.56 NATO cal., gas piston operation, 5 shot mag., 20 in. hammer forged stainless steel barrel, round, lightweight adaptable vented handguard with Picatinny rail on top, fixed A2-style buttstock, Magpul MOE grip, two-stage trigger, charging handle with tactical latch, 8 1/2 lbs. New 2013.

MSR $1,995	$1,795	$1,575	$1,075	$900	$775	$650	$575

XGI – while advertised, this model was never shipped commercially because it could not maintain Ruger accuracy standards.

MSR was originally targeted at $425.

RIFLES: SINGLE SHOT

During certain years of manufacture, Ruger's changes in production on certain models (cals., barrel markings, barrel lengths, etc.) have created rare variations that are now considered premium niches. These areas of low manufacture will add premiums to the values listed on standard models.

Non-prefix rifles are known in .222, .22-250, .243, 6mm, .25-06, .270, .280, 7mm Rem. Mag., 7x57, .300 Win. Mag., .30-06, .308, .375 H&H., 45-70 and .458 cal.

Calibers 6.5mm Rem., .264 Win. Mag., 7x65R, .300 H&H and .338 were also rumored or cataloged during the 1966-1968 time period but are not known to have been produced.

One rifle chambered in .225 Win. is known to be in the factory collection.

In addition to the calibers listed above, the Number 1 during this time period could be ordered with nearly any combination of barrel length and weight (22" light weight or 26" medium weight barrel). The .375 H&H and .458 were available with a 24" heavy weight barrel and most in .45-70 were produced with a 22" medium weight barrel.

For all but the .375 H&H, .45-70 and .458, the 1966-1968 period rifles could also be ordered with any combination of no sights/open sights/target blocks or either Alex Henry or Semi-Beavertail forearm.

Pre-1969, non-prefix rifles will command a 30%-50% premium (ser. no. 1-8XXX).

NO. 1-A LIGHT SPORTER – similar to No. 1-B Standard, .204 Ruger (mfg. 2005-2006), .22 Hornet (disc., 355 mfg.), .222 Rem. (new 2013), .223 Rem. (rare), .243 Win. (disc. 2012), .270 Win. (disc. 2012), 7mm-08 (rare), 7x57mm (disc. 2009), .30-06 (disc. 2012), .300 RCM (mfg. 2009-2012), .303 British (mfg. 2011-2012), .308 Win. (mfg. 2011-2012), or 6.5 Creedmoor (mfg. 2011-2012) cal., 22 in. barrel, folding sight on quarter rib, ramp front sight, no rings, American walnut stock, Alexander Henry forearm, front swivel in barrel band, 7 1/4 lbs. New 1966.

MSR $1,349	$1,025	$795	$650	$475	$375	$300	$275

The "A" suffix designates an Alexander Henry classic forearm with light barrel.

GRADING - PPGS™	100%	98%	95%	90%	80%	70%	60%	LAST MSR

NO. 1-AB – various cals., .204 Ruger (new 2006) or .223 Rem. (new 2009) cal., 22 in. barrel, checkered walnut stock and forearm. Mfg. 1967-1968, 1982-1983, 2006, resumed 2009.

	$895	$650	$525	$400	$325	$275	$250	*$1,147*

NO. 1-B STANDARD – falling block action with curved Farquharson lever, popular cals. include .204 Ruger (new 2004), .218 Bee (disc. 2006), .22 Hornet (mfg. 1988-2006), .22-250 Rem. (disc. 2006), .220 Swift (disc. 2006), .223 Rem. (disc. 2009), .257 Roberts (disc. 2003), .243 Win. (disc. 2006), 6.5 Creedmoor (new 2010), 6mm Rem (disc. 2003), .25-06 Rem., .270 Win. (disc. 2009), .280 Rem. (disc. 2003), .30-06, .308 Win. (mfg. 2002-2008), 6.5mm Rem. Mag. (disc.), 7x57 (disc.), 7mm Rem. Mag. (disc. 2009), .270 Wby. Mag. (mfg. 1990-2006), .300 Wby. Mag. (mfg. 1990-2006), .300 Win. Mag., or .338 Win. Mag. (disc. 2006) cal., 22 or 26 in. barrel, quarter rib with integral scope bases, supplied with rings and no sights, checkered stock and semi-beavertail forearm, approx. 8 1/4 lbs. Mfg. 1966-2010.

	$925	$675	$550	$425	$350	$300	$275	*$1,182*

Add 50% for 6.5mm Rem. Mag. or 30% for 7x57 cal.

The "B" suffix designates semi-beavertail forearm with medium barrel and is available in all cals. under .375 H&H.

NO. 1-H TROPICAL RIFLE – similar to Medium Sporter, except .45-70 Govt. (rare, mfg. 1976), .375 H&H, .404 Jeffery (rare, mfg. 1993-95), .416 Rem. (mfg. 1993-2003), .416 Rigby (mfg. 1991-2009), .416 Ruger (mfg. 2009-2011), .450/400 NE (mfg. 2007-2012), .458 Lott (disc. 2012), .458 Win. Mag. (disc. 2008), or .405 Win. (mfg. 2004-2008) cal., 24 in. heavy barrel, blued finish, walnut stock, open sights, 7 3/4-9 1/4 lbs.

MSR $1,349	$1,025	$795	$650	$475	$375	$325	$295
.404 Jeffrey cal.	$1,850	$1,620	$1,390	$1,260	$1,020	$835	$650
.45-70 Govt. cal.	$3,700	$3,240	$2,775	$2,515	$2,035	$1,665	$1,295

NO. 1-RSI INTERNATIONAL – .243 Win. (disc. 2006), .270 Win. (disc. 2012), 7x57mm, .300 RCM (mfg. 2011 only), or .30-06 (disc. 2012) cal., features 20 in. lightweight barrel with full length walnut Mannlicher stock, includes swivels and open sights, 7 lbs.

MSR $1,399	$1,075	$835	$650	$500	$400	$350	$295

NO. 1-S MEDIUM SPORTER – .218 Bee (disc. 2003), 7mm Rem. Mag. (disc. 2003), 9.3x74R (mfg. 2007-2011), .45-70 Govt., .300 Win. Mag. (disc. 2003, reintroduced 2011-2012), .300 H&H (mfg. 2010-2012), .338 RCM (mfg. 2009-2011), .338 Win. Mag. (disc. 2003), .375 Ruger (mfg. 2009-2011), .38-55 Win. (mfg. 1989), .460 S&W Mag. (mfg. 2009-2012), or .475 Linebaugh/.480 Ruger (mfg. 2009-2012) cal., similar to Light Sporter, 22 or 26 (.300 H&H cal. only) in. medium barrel, open sights, 7 1/4-8 lbs.

MSR $1,349	$1,025	$795	$650	$475	$375	$325	$295

* ***No. 1-S Medium Sporter 50th Anniversary*** – .45-70 Govt. cal. only, engraved action with gold inlays, including the Ruger logo and 50 years, William B. Ruger signature on receiver bottom, checkered Circassian walnut stock and forearm. 1,500 mfg. 1999 only.

	$1,950	$1,500	$1,300	$1,100	$995	$850	$700	*$1,950*

NO. 1-V VARMINTER – similar to No. 1-B Standard, except .22 PPC (mfg. 1993-96), .22-250 Rem., .220 Swift (disc.), .223 Rem. (disc. 2012), .243 Win. (disc.), .25-06 Rem. (disc. 2012), 6mm Rem. (disc. 2005), 6mm PPC (mfg. 1993-96), 6.5 Creedmoor (mfg. 2011-2012), 6.5-284 Norma (new 2013), 7mm Rem. (disc.), .280 Rem. (disc.), or .300 Win. Mag. (disc.) cal., 24 or 26 (disc., was .220 Swift only) in. heavy barrel, without rib, w/o sights, checkered walnut stock and forearm, target scope blocks, approx. 8 3/4 lbs. New 1970.

MSR $1,349	$1,025	$795	$650	$475	$375	$325	$295

Add 20% for .22 PPC cal.

NO. 1 K1-B-BBZ STAINLESS – various cals. and configurations, satin stainless steel action and barrel, grey laminate hardwood stock with black recoil pad, drilled and tapped rear quarter rib w/o sights. Mfg. 2001-2010.

GRADING - PPGS™	100%	98%	95%	90%	80%	70%	60%	LAST MSR

* ***No. 1 K1-B-BBZ Stainless Standard*** – .243 Win. (disc. 2009), .25-06 Rem. (disc. 2009), .270 Win. (new 2004), .30-06 (disc. 2009), .308 Win. (mfg. 2002-2006), .300 Win. Mag., 7mm STW (disc. 2004), or 7mm Rem. Mag. (disc. 2009) cal., 26 in. barrel, 8 lbs.

	$975	$725	$575	$475	$400	$350	$300	*$1,222*

* ***No. 1 K1-H-BBZ Stainless Tropical*** – .375 H&H, .416 Rigby (mfg. 2002-2006), .405 Win. (mfg. 2004, reintroduced 2006-2008), .416 Ruger (new 2009), .458 Win. (mfg. 2005-2006), or .458 Lott (mfg. 2002-2004, reintroduced 2007) cal., 24 in. barrel, 9 lbs. Mfg. 2001-2009.

	$925	$675	$550	$425	$350	$300	$250	*$1,186*

* ***No. 1 K1-S-BBZ Stainless Sporter*** – .45-70 Govt. or .375 Ruger (mfg. 2008-2009) cal., 22 in. barrel with iron sights, black laminated stock, 7 1/4 lbs.

	$975	$725	$575	$475	$400	$350	$300	*$1,222*

* ***No. 1 K1-V-BBZ Stainless Varminter*** – .204 Ruger (new 2004), or .22-250 Rem. cal. only, 24 in. bull barrel, black laminate stock, 9 lbs. Mfg. 2001-2009.

	$925	$675	$550	$425	$350	$300	$250	*$1,186*

NO. 3 CARBINE – same basic action as No. 1, except simpler lever design, uncheckered stock, available in .22 Hornet, .30-40 Krag, .45-70 Govt. (only cal. available 1986), .223 Rem., .44 Mag., or .375 Win. cal., 22 in. barrel, folding sight. Mfg. 1972-87.

	$750	$650	$525	$400	$300	$225	$150	*$284*

Add 20% for .44 Mag. or .375 Win. cal.

RUGER/LYMAN 1878 CENTENNIAL RIFLE – .45-70 Govt. cal., 101 sets mfg. in Grade I and 1,000 in Grade II. Grade I has hand engraving, custom stock, 28 in. D weight barrel, tubular 4X Lyman Century scope, ser. nos. L-001-1878 to L-101-1978. Grade II had photo engraved frame, ser. nos. L-78-0001 to L-78-1000. Mfg. 1978 only.

Grade I	$2,500	$2,000	$1,200	$900	$800	$700	$600	
Grade II	$1,750	$1,425	$1,050	$850	$725	$600	$525	

One William Lyman commemorative cased rifle was also mfg., preceeding Grades I & II. This model was auctioned off at the 1978 NRA Show.

SHOTGUNS: O/U

RED LABEL – 12, 20, or 28 (new 1994) ga., 3 in. chambers (except 28 ga.), various barrel lengths and choke (including skeet) combinations, boxlock, SST, 26 or 28 in. VR barrels, auto ejectors, choice of checkered pistol grip or English straight grip (new 1992, Red Label English Field) stock, stainless steel frame became standard on 12 ga. 1985 (not available in 20 ga.), choke tubes became optional in 1988, standard 1990, 6-7 3/4 lbs. New 1977.

* ***Red Label Standard Grade*** – Disc. 2011.

	$1,550	$1,175	$900	$775	$650	$550	$475	*$2,015*

Add $622 for .410 bore Briley conversion tube set for 28 ga. only (disc. 2005).
Subtract 15%-20% without choke tubes.

During late 1994, some 12 and 20 ga. Red Label boxes were marked "EZ", indicating the new easy-opening feature (this is not mechanically spring-assisted, but rather works on tight machining tolerances). All Red Label shotguns have the "EZ" opening feature beginning 1995.

Earlier all-steel 12 ga. models (approx. 500 mfg.) with short field tubes could command 10%-15% premiums over values listed from collectors interested in acquiring this variation. 20 ga. models w/o choke tubes are blue only.

* ***Red Label All Weather Stainless*** – 12 ga. only, stainless steel (disc.) or target grey stainless steel (new 2003) receiver and barrels, checkered black synthetic stock and forearm, 26, 28, or 30 in. VR barrels with choke tubes, 7 1/2 lbs. Mfg. 1999-2006.

	$1,275	$975	$800	$700	$600	$500	$450	*$1,702*

* ***Red Label Sporting Clays*** – 12 or 20 (mfg. 1994-2007) ga., features 30 in. separated barrels, choice of walnut or synthetic (12 ga. only) stock, Briley choke tubes with forcing cones back bored to .744 in., 3/8 in. VR with middle bead, sporting clays recoil pad, approx. 7 1/2 lbs. Mfg. 1992-2011.

	$1,550	$1,175	$900	$775	$650	$550	$475	*$2,015*

GRADING - PPGS™	100%	98%	95%	90%	80%	70%	60%	LAST MSR

» **Red Label Sporting Clays Engraved** – available in 12 ga. only with 1/3 engraving pattern. Mfg. 1997.

	$2,500	$2,200	$1,900	$1,650	$1,300	$1,000	$850	$3,068

* ***Red Label English Field*** – 12, 20, or 28 (new 1995) ga., similar to Red Label, except has English style straight grip stock. Mfg. 1992-2000.

	$965	$775	$685	$600	$550	$500	$450	$1,276

* ***Red Label Engraved (2001-2011 Mfg.)*** – 12, 20, or 28 ga., 26, 28, or 30 (disc. 2004) in. barrels, 4 different gold inlay options depending on ga., with receiver scroll engraving, pheasant standard on 12 ga., grouse on 20 ga., and woodcock on 28 ga., available in Standard Model, All Weather Stainless (disc. 2004), and Sporting Clays (disc. 2004, reintroduced 2009) configurations. Mfg. 2001-2011.

	$1,750	$1,375	$1,000	$825	$700	$600	$500	$2,245

* ***Red Label Hand Engraved (1997-2000 Mfg.)*** – available in 12 (167 or 168 made), 20 (55 or 56 made), or 28 (73 to 75 made) ga., available in 2/3 "C" coverage, 1/3 "B" coverage or dit-dot border "A" pattern coverage (standard). Only the earliest hand engraved guns had circassian walnut buttstock and forearm. Later guns were produced with circassian walnut buttstock and black walnut forearm or black walnut for both pieces. The contracted engravers of this series were John J. Adams, Sr., John J. Adams, Jr., Carmine Lombardy, Alvin White, Andrew Bourbon, and Jon Ashford. Mfg. 1997-2000.

	$2,200	$1,900	$1,650	$1,300	$1,000	$850	$725	$2,552

Add $190 for 1/3 engraving coverage.
Add $532 for 2/3 engraving coverage (12 ga. only, disc.).

28 ga production quantities: KRL-2826A (27); KRL-2827A (24); KRL-2826B (19); KRL-2827B (1 or 2); KRL-2826C (1); KRL-2827C (1 or 2).

20 ga. production quantities: KRL-2029B (40); KRL-2030B (11); KRL-2029C (3 or 4); KRL-2030C (1).

12 ga. production quantities: KRL-1227A (18); KRL-1226B (44); KRL-1227B (88 or 89); KRL-1236B (1); KRL-1226C (10) and KRL-1227C (6)

In all, only 295 to 299 Red Label special hand engraved models were produced.

* ***Red Label 50th Anniversary Engraved*** – 12, 20, or 28 ga., 26 or 28 in. barrels, receiver scroll engraving, 3 different gold inlay options (depending on ga.) on right side of receiver and Ruger 50th Anniversary logo on left side of receiver. Mfg. 1999 only. Probably not more than 1,500 of each model produced.

	$1,350	$1,125	$850	N/A	N/A	N/A	N/A	

RED LABEL "WOODSIDE" – 12 ga. only, 3 in. chambers, 26, 28, or 30 (Sporting Clays Model only with special chokes, new 1996) in. barrels, straight or pistol grip stock, features premium checkered walnut, satin nickel finish, unique stock design permitting wood to fill-in where frame boxlock action would normally be, hand-engraving available at extra cost, 7 1/2-8 lbs. Mfg. 1995-2002.

	$1,525	$1,250	$1,000	$800	$625	$550	$500	$1,889

* ***Red Label "Woodside" Engraved*** – available in 2/3 "C" coverage, 1/3 "B" coverage or dit-dot border "A" pattern coverage (standard) with pistol grip and 26 or 28 in. barrels. Only the earliest hand engraved guns had circassian walnut buttstock and forearm. Later guns were produced with circassian walnut buttstock and black walnut forearm or black walnut for both pieces. The contracted engravers of this series were John J. Adams, Sr., John J. Adams, Jr., Carmine Lombardy, Alvin White, Andrew Bourbon, and Jon Ashford. Mfg. 1997-2000.

	$2,200	$2,050	$1,725	$1,350	$1,050	$875	$750	$2,805

Add $190 for 1/3 engraving coverage.
Add $532 for 2/3 engraving coverage.

Production quantities: KWS-1226A (44); KWS-1227A (17); KWS-1226B (8); KWS-1227B (6); KWS-1226C (1) and KWS-1227C (5).

GRADING - PPGS™	100%	98%	95%	90%	80%	70%	60%	LAST MSR

WILDLIFE FOREVER SPECIAL EDITION – 12 ga. only, limited edition to celebrate the 50th anniversary of Wildlife Forever, features Baron & Son engraving with gold pheasant and mallard inlays on receiver sides, 300 mfg. 1993 only.

	$1,595	$900	$775	N/A	N/A	N/A	N/A	$1,595

Add $125 for hard case.

SHOTGUNS: SxS

GOLD LABEL SxS – 12 ga. only, 3 in. chambers, 28 in. barrels with solid rib and choke tubes, rounded stainless boxlock action, SST, blue barrel finish, ejectors, choice of deluxe 22 LPI checkered English straight grip or pistol grip stock and splinter forearm, approx. 6 1/2 lbs. Mfg. late 2002-2008.

	$3,650	$2,850	$2,200	$1,725	$1,250	$1,050	$925	$3,226

SHOTGUNS: SINGLE BARREL

TRAP MODEL – 12 ga., 34 in. stainless barrel with straight grooves and 2 choke tubes, fully adj. high post rib, engraved stainless receiver with gold Ruger name, adj. deluxe checkered walnut stock, beavertail forearm, adj. trigger, 9 lbs. Approx. 300 mfg. 2000-2003.

	$3,850	$3,200	$2,500	$2,000	$1,500	$1,300	$1,200	$2,850

SUHLER JAGDGEWEHR MANUFAKTUR GmbH

Previous manufacturer and firearms restorer located in Suhl, Germany.

Suhler Jagdgewehr manufactured a variety of SxS shotguns, in addition to restoring both antique and historical guns.

SUNDANCE INDUSTRIES, INC.

Previous manufacturer located in Valencia, CA.

DERRINGERS

POINT BLANK DERRINGER – .22 LR cal., O/U design, double action, 3 in. barrels, black matte finish, 8 oz. Mfg. mid-1994-2002.

	$80	$60	$50	$45	$40	$35	$30	$99

PISTOLS: SEMI-AUTO

MODEL A-25 – .25 ACP cal., single action design, 2 7/16 in. barrel, 7 shot mag., rotary safety, lower grip push button mag. release, satin nickel (disc.), bright chrome, or black teflon finish, choice of simulated pearl with different colors or grooved black grips, serrated slide. Mfg. 1989-2002.

	$65	$55	$45	$40	$35	$30	$25	$79

LADY LASER/LASER 25 – .25 ACP cal., similar to Model A-25, except has factory installed and sighted 5mW Laser sight with no exposed wiring or switch, polished chrome or black finish (Laser 25 only), dual safety switch. Mfg. 1995-2002.

	$195	$160	$135	$115	$95	$80	$70	$220

The Laser Lady was disc. during 1998.

MODEL BOA – similar to Model A-25, except has patented squeeze grip safety. Mfg. 1990-2002.

	$75	$60	$50	$45	$40	$35	$30	$95

SUPER SIX LIMITED

Previous manufacturer located in Brookfield, WI until 1992.

REVOLVERS

GOLDEN BISON SERIES – .45-70 Govt. cal., 6 shot revolver, 8 or 10 1/2 in. octagon barrel, large size (overall length 15-17 1/2 in.), manganese bronze frame, crossbolt manual safety, smooth hardwood grips, approx. 6 lbs. 177 total mfg. (including special/limited editions). Disc. approx. 1992.

	$1,675	$1,475	$1,275	$1,000	$875	$775	$675	$1,895

Low serialization specimens (ser. nos. 1-15) have asking prices of $2,250-$2,950.

GRADING - PPGS™	100%	98%	95%	90%	80%	70%	60%	LAST MSR

* ***Golden Bison Series Centennial Limited Edition*** – features special engraving and case. 20 total mfg.

	$2,950	$2,275	$1,675	N/A	N/A	N/A	N/A	*$3,995*

SUPER SIX LLC

Previous manufacturer located in Milwaukee, WI from 1999-2004.

During late 1998, Super Six LLC purchased the previous trademark of Super Six Limited. This trademark had very limited manufacture.

SUPER SIX CLASSIC, LLC

Current trademark manufactured by Defense Supply & Manufacturing, located in Fort Atkinson, WI. Distributed exclusively by Zanders Sporting Goods.

REVOLVERS

Please contact Zanders directly for more information, including prices for available options and delivery time (see Trademark Index).

BISON BULL – .45-70 Govt. cal., 10 in. octagon custom Badger barrel, manganese bronze frame, chrome-moly steel cylinder, 6 shot, manual cross bolt safety, adj. Millett rear sight, ramp blade front sight, integral scope mount, deluxe custom hardwood grips, 6 lbs.

MSR $1,495	$1,375	$1,200	$995	$875	$750	$675	$600	

SUPERIOR AMMUNITION

Previous custom rifle and current ammunition manufacturer located in Sturgis, SD. Consumer direct sales only.

RIFLES: BOLT ACTION

SUPERIOR CLASSIC LIGHTWEIGHT – various cals. up to .375 H&H, Rem. Mod. 700, Win. Mod. 70 Classic, or Dakota Mod. 76 action, blind box mag. or hinged floorplate, approx. 5 3/4 lbs.

	$1,850	$1,650	$1,350	$1,100	$900	$750	$625	*$2,000*

SUPERIOR VARMINT MODEL – various smaller cals., Rem. Mod. 700, Dakota Varmint, or Searcy action, stainless match grade barrel, heavy or light variations.

	$1,900	$1,725	$1,400	$1,125	$900	$750	$625	*$2,100*

SUPERIOR PROFESSIONAL MODEL – various large cals. up to .470 Capstick, only available in Win. Mod. 70 Classic or Dakota Mod. 76 action, blind box mag. (optional) or hinged floorplate.

	$2,350	$2,050	$1,850	$1,600	$1,350	$1,150	$900	*$2,500*

SUPERIOR ARMS

Current manufacturer established in 2004 and located in Wapello, IA.

PISTOLS: SEMI-AUTO

Superior Arms manufactured complete AR-style semi-auto pistols, with either an A4 flattop or A2 carry handle, and 10 1/2 or 11 1/2 in. barrel.

RIFLES: SEMI-AUTO

Please contact the company directly for more information on options, delivery, and availability on the following AR-15 style carbines/rifles (see Trademark Index).

IMPORTANT NOTE: On model(s) where *N/A has replaced the normal 100% value, it indicates current market conditions are too unstable to accurately ascertain 100%-60% values. Factory retail prices (MSRs) reflect most recent updates. For more up-to-date information on current pricing trends and additional useful information, please visit www.bluebookofgunvalues.com, select "Information & Services" from the menu, and click on "Additional Book Information".

Add $55 for detachable A2 carry handle.

GRADING - PPGS™	100%	98%	95%	90%	80%	70%	60%	LAST MSR

S-15 M4 CARBINE – .223 Rem. cal., A4 flattop receiver with integral rail, 16 in. chrome-moly barrel, A2 flash hider, M4 handguard, six position telescoping stock, A2 pistol grip, front sling swivel.

MSR $905	*N/A	$750	$650	$595	$550	$500	$450	

S-15 CARBINE – .223 Rem. cal., A4 flattop receiver with integral rail, 16 in. chrome-moly barrel, A2 flash hider, M4 handguard, bayonet lug, six position telescoping stock, A2 pistol grip, front sling swivel.

MSR $905	*N/A	$750	$650	$595	$550	$500	$450	

S-15 MID-LENGTH CARBINE – .223 Rem. cal., A4 flattop receiver with integral rail, 16 in. chrome-moly barrel, A2 flash hider, mid-length handguard, bayonet lug, six position telescoping stock, A2 pistol grip, front sling swivel.

MSR $925	*N/A	$775	$675	$600	$525	$450	$395	

S-15 H-BAR RIFLE – .223 Rem. cal., A4 flattop receiver with integral rail, 20 in. chrome-moly barrel, A2 flash hider, A2 buttstock, bayonet lug, A2 pistol grip, front sling swivel.

MSR $985	*N/A	$800	$700	$625	$550	$500	$495	

S-15 VARMINT RIFLE – .223 Rem. cal., A4 flattop receiver with integral rail, 20 in. stainless steel bull contour barrel, Picatinny rail gas block, aluminum free floating handguard with sling swivel stud, A2 buttstock, bayonet lug, A2 pistol grip.

MSR $1,075	*N/A	$850	$775	$675	$600	$550	$495	

SURGEON RIFLES, INC.

Current custom rifle manufacturer located in Prague, OK.

Surgeon Rifles manufactures a variety of bolt action rifles, including tactical and long range configurations. Models include the short action Scalpel ($4,255 MSR), the long action Scalpel ($4,380 MSR), and the Remedy ($5,400 MSR). Many options and accessories are available. Please contact the company directly for more information, including delivery time and availability (see Trademark Index).

SURVIVAL ARMS, INC.

Previous manufacturer established in 1990 located in Orange, CT. Previously located in Cocoa, FL, until 1995.

In 1990, Survival Arms, Inc. took over the manufacture of AR-7 Explorer rifles from Charter Arms located in Stratford, CT.

RIFLES: SEMI-AUTO

AR-7 EXPLORER RIFLE – .22 LR cal., takedown or normal wood stock, takedown barreled action stores in Cycolac synthetic stock, 8 shot mag., adj. sights, 16 in. barrel, black matte finish on AR-7, silvertone on AR-7S, camouflage finish on AR-7C, 2 1/2 lbs. Disc.

	$150	$125	$100	$85	$75	$65	$55	*$150*

Add 20% for takedown action.

AR-20 SPORTER – similar to AR-22, except has shrouded barrel, tubular stock with pistol grip, 10 or 20 shot mag. Mfg. 1996-98.

	$195	$165	$140	$120	$105	$95	$80	*$200*

AR-22/AR-25 – .22 LR cal., 16 in. barrel, black rifle features pistol grip with choice of wood or metal folding* stock, includes 20 (1995 only) or 25 (disc. 1994) shot mag. Disc. 1995.

	$175	$150	$125	$100	$80	$70	$60	*$200*

Subtract $50 for wood stock model.

SVENDSEN, ERL, F.A. MFG. CO.

Previous manufacturer located in Itasca, IL.

DERRINGERS

LITTLE ACE – .22 S cal., patterned after the Ethan Allen "HIDE-A-WAY", bronze frame, blue steel barrel with case hardened hammer and spur trigger.

	$85	$75	$70	$65	$60	$55	$50	

GRADING - PPGS™	100%	98%	95%	90%	80%	70%	60%	LAST MSR

4-ACES – .22 S cal., 4 barrel derringer with rotating firing pin and spur trigger, bronze frame with blue rifled steel barrels and case hardened parts.

	$175	$150	$135	$120	$105	$90	$75	

SWING

Previously manufactured by Schutzen Bohme GmbH located in Rintein, Germany.

RIFLES: BOLT ACTION

SWING BOLT ACTION – .308 Win. cal., target bolt action rifle with thumbhole stock and vented forearm, target sights, 30 in. barrel, 12.1 lbs. Mfg. 1994.

	$850	$750	$650	$575	$500	$450	$395	

SWISS MILITARY

Previously manufactured Swiss military rifles.

RIFLES: BOLT ACTION

The models were manufactured by Schmidt-Rubin, unless otherwise indicated.

MODEL 1889 – usually encountered between 85%-95% condition.

	$995	$870	$745	$675	$545	$450	$350	

MODEL 1911 – available in either carbine or rifle configuration.

	$750	$655	$565	$510	$415	$340	$265	
Carbine	$1,695	$1,485	$1,270	$1,155	$930	$765	$595	

MODEL 1931

	$850	$775	$650	$575	$475	$375	$275	
Sniper model	$5,000	$4,375	$3,750	$3,400	$2,750	$2,250	$1,750	

Subtract 30% if import marked.

VETTERLI – .41 Swiss or 10.4mm Swiss cal., not mfg. by Schmidt Rubin.

	$750	$675	$600	$525	$450	$375	$295	

SYMES & WRIGHT LTD.

Previous manufacturer located in London, England.

Symes & Wright Ltd. manufactured approx. 25 best quality shotguns and double rifles annually. Values must be determined after evaluating each firearm individually.

SZECSEI & FUCHS FINE GUNS GmbH

Current long gun manufacturer established in 1986, and located in Innsbruck, Austria. Currently imported into North America by Beale's Guns located in Windsor, Canada.

Szecsei & Fuchs manufactures extremely high quality and unique long guns, including combination guns, drillings, bolt action and double rifles, and SxS shotguns. The company is well known for its unique magazine fed SxS double rifle, which utilizes a single bolt to load/unload both chambers. Many options are available, including a titanium bolt and trigger system. Please contact the North American office directly for more information on their current models (virtually anything is possible), including pricing, availability, delivery time, and U.S. pricing.

RIFLES: BOLT ACTION

DOUBLE BARREL REPEATER – various cals., unique action allows single bolt to chamber both barrels from one twin column detachable titanium mag., titanium bolt face, right or left hand action, various engraving and wood options available. Base weight is approx. 13 lbs.

Please contact the company directly for a price quotation.

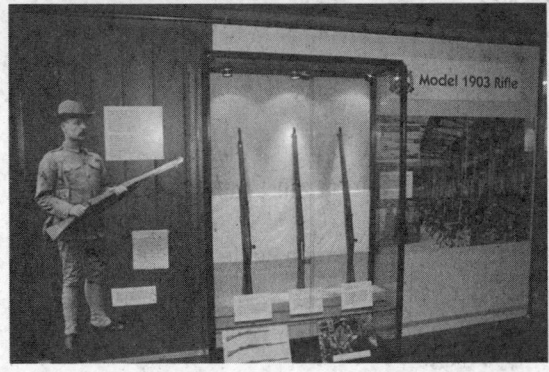

T SECTION

TG INTERNATIONAL

Current importer located in Knoxville, TN.

TG International imports a wide variety of firearms in various configurations. Since inventory can change daily, it is recommended that you contact the company directly for current offerings and pricing (see Trademark Index).

TNW, INC.

Current rifle manufacturer located in Vernonia, OR. Consumer direct sales.

RIFLES: SEMI-AUTO

TNW makes a belt-fed semi-auto variation of the original Browning M2HB machine gun in .50 BMG cal. Prices were $7,500 - $8,500 until 2009, and are now POR. To commemorate its 10th Anniversary, TNW is offering a limited edition M3HB for $6,995-$7,399. TNW also makes a semi-auto Model 1919 A4 .30 cal., prices range from $2,000 - $2,200, as well as a M230 conversion for $699, and a M37 semi-auto .30 cal. for $3,995. TNW also manufactures a variation of the German MG-34 semi-auto (POR). Please contact the company directly for more information regarding these semi-auto working replicas (see Trademark Index).

TR IMPORTS

Current importer located in Fort Worth, TX, Previously located in Keller, TX.

SHOTGUNS

The Silver Eagle shotguns are manufactured by Huglu in Turkey.

Current Silver Eagle O/U models include the Fieldmaster ($994 MSR), Fieldmaster Deluxe ($1,050 MSR), Kofs Cavalry ($759 MSR), and the Custom Grade ($1,852 MSR). SxS models include the Model 200A Grouse ($994-$1,173 MSR), and the Model 200AC Ptarmigan ($1,050-$1,297 MSR). Semi-Auto models include: the Sporter Series ($449-$549 MSR), SE121 ($449 MSR), SE122 ($449 MSR) and the SE202 Series ($449 MSR). Previously imported O/U models included the Model 101B Competition Trap, Model 101SE Competiton Skeet, Model 101BE Competition Trap, Skeet, Sporting Clays, Model 103C Patagonian, Model 103DE Rangemaster, Model 103FE Rangemaster Deluxe, Model 104A Sharptail, and the Model 105A Eagle Ultra-Light. Previously imported Custom Grade Models included: SGR Series SGR1-SGR20. Previously imported SxS models included: Model 201A Hungarian, and the Model 202B Chukar. Previously imported semi-auto models included: the Model 901GB Excellence, Model 601GM Canadian, Model 701GB Widgeon, Model SE12B Silver Eagle and the Model SE12 Silver Eagle Combo.

Please contact the company directly for current options and availability (see the Trademark Index).

TS FINE GUNS

Current custom rifle and shotgun manufacturer located in Grobmaischeid, Germany. No current U.S. importation.

Thomas Spohr specializes in custom made rifles and drillings. Since each gun is made per customer specifications, please contact him directly for more information including pricing, availability, and various options (see Trademark Index).

TACONIC FIREARMS, LTD.

Previous rifle manufacturer located in Cambridge, NY until 2003.

GRADING - PPGS™	100%	98%	95%	90%	80%	70%	60%	LAST MSR

RIFLES: BOLT ACTION, CUSTOM

TACONIC 98 ULTIMATE MOUNTAIN HUNTER – various cals., features double square bridge, titanium alloy M-98 action, XXX Grade English or Circassian walnut, stainless or chrome moly barrel, matte finished metal, available with a variety of options, base prices are listed below.

	100%	98%	95%	90%	80%	70%	60%	LAST MSR
	$5,750	$5,100	$4,500	$4,000	$3,500	$3,000	$2,500	*$5,995*

GRADING - PPGS™ 100% 98% 95% 90% 80% 70% 60% *LAST MSR*

TACTICAL RIFLES

Current rifle manufacturer located in Zephyrhills, FL. Previously located in Dade City, FL until 2010.

RIFLES

Tactical Rifles makes a complete lineup of bolt action and semi-auto tactical rifles in various configurations. Current bolt action offerings include: the Tactical M40, Tactical M40 Magnum, Tactical Chimera Hunter, Tactical Classic Sporter, Tactical Long Range, Tactical Long Range Magnum, and Tactical Paratrooper. Current custom rifles include: Tactical M40-A4, M40A1-3, M40-A4, Tactical M21 (disc.) and Tactical M40. Semi-auto AR-15 style models include: Tactical SPG, Tactical SVR (Special Varmint Rifle), Dow Custom AR 10 (disc. 2004, last MSR was $2,695), Dow FAL 15 (disc. 2007, last MSR was $1,895), and the Tactical M4C. Please contact the company directly for more information, availability, and current pricing (see Trademark Index).

Tactical Rifles has partnered with Coonan Inc. for a rifle and pistol package consisting of a special limited edition 1 of 100 rifle and Coonan pistol. Package price is $7,889.

TACTICAL SOLUTIONS

Current rifle and components manufacturer located in Boise, ID. Dealer sales.

RIFLES

Tactical Solutions makes a Pac-Lite barrel assembly for the Ruger Mark and .22/.45 Series pistol frame and conversion units for both pistols and AR-15 style rifles. Please contact the manufacturer directly for additional information, availability, and current pricing (see Trademark Index).

X-RING SEMI-AUTO RIFLE – .22 LR cal., 16 1/2 in. standard or threaded barrel, 10 shot mag., choice of black, OD Green, Ghillie Green or Ghillie Tan Hogue overmolded or Slate, Forest, Crimson or Royal Vantage laminate stock, extended mag. release, Ruger trigger group, 4.3 - 5.1 lbs.

MSR $850 $725 $625 $550 $495 $400 $325 $250

Add $45 for threaded barrel or $120 for Vantage stock.

TACTICAL WEAPONS

Current law enforcement/military division of FNH USA, located in McLean, VA.

Tactical Weapons currently manufactures machine guns only for law enforcement/ military.

TALO DISTRIBUTORS, INC.

Current wholesale buying cooperative established in 1965 and located in Framingham, MA.

Over the years, Talo Distributors, Inc. has released a wide variety of both special and limited editions for many major firearms companies. More research is underway to compile a listing of all special/limited editions made to date. Please contact the company directly for more information on both its current and older special/limited editions (see Trademark Index).

TALON INDUSTRIES, INC.

Previous pistol manufacturer located in Ennis, MT until 2001.

PISTOLS: SEMI-AUTO

T100 – .380 ACP cal., double action only, 3.3 in. barrel, black polymer frame with choice of black (T100B) or satin (T100S) slide finish, or alloy frame and slide, 10 shot mag., failsafe loaded chamber indicator positioned on top of slide in back of breech bolt, 3-dot sights, 20 1/2 oz. Mfg. 2000-2001.

$115 $95 $85 $75 $65 $55 $50 *$135*

T200 – 9mm Para. cal., otherwise similar to Model T100. Mfg. 2000-2001.

$145 $125 $100 $90 $75 $65 $55 *$170*

GRADING - PPGS™	100%	98%	95%	90%	80%	70%	60%	LAST MSR

TANFOGLIO, FRATELLI, S.r.l.

Current pistol, rifle, and parts manufacturer located in Gardone, Italy. Currently imported on a limited basis by the Italian Firearms Group (IFG) beginning 2011 and located in Rockledge, FL and European American Armory located in Sharps, FL. Previously imported by K.B.I., located in Harrisburg, PA, and also by Excam, F.I.E., and others.

Tanfoglio manufactures a wide variety of high quality semi-auto pistols, including the Witness Series, and the Appeal semi-auto rifle which is currently imported by European American Armory Corp. (please refer to EAA in the E section). Tanfoglio also manufactures a proprietary line of pistols, including competition models and the Raptor single shot, which has been mostly distributed in Europe.

TANNER, ANDRÉ

Previous manufacturer located in Switzerland. Previously imported and distributed by Mandall Shooting Supplies, Inc. located in Scottsdale, AZ, and by Osborne's located in Cheboygan, MI.

Tanner rifles are noted for their superior accuracy and limited production - less than 150 were mfg. annually.

RIFLES: BOLT ACTION

300 METER MATCH RIFLE – 7.5 Swiss (special order) or 7.62mm cal. only, single shot, top-of-the-line 300 meter match rifle incorporating all match shooting features including deluxe palm rest, aperture sights. Importation disc.

	100%	98%	95%	90%	80%	70%	60%	LAST MSR
	$4,650	$3,995	$3,400	$2,775	$2,250	$1,900	$1,600	*$4,900*

Add $100 for adj. cheekpiece.
Subtract $190 for repeating model with similar features.

* ***300 Meter Match Rifle UIT Standard*** – similar to Model 300, except is without palm rest and adj. Swiss buttplate, 10 shot mag., aperture sights. Importation disc.

	100%	98%	95%	90%	80%	70%	60%	LAST MSR
	$4,450	$3,850	$3,350	$2,750	$2,225	$1,925	$1,600	*$4,700*

Add $100 for adj. cheekpiece.

SUPERMATCH MODEL 50 M – .22 LR cal. only, 50 meter free rifle, deluxe palm rest, adj. buttplate, thumbhole stock. Importation disc.

	100%	98%	95%	90%	80%	70%	60%	LAST MSR
	$3,600	$3,200	$2,850	$2,450	$2,050	$1,800	$1,600	*$3,900*

Add $100 for adj. cheekpiece.

TAR-HUNT CUSTOM RIFLES, INC.

Current custom rifled shotgun manufacturer established in 1990, and located in Bloomsburg, PA. Dealer and consumer direct sales.

SHOTGUNS: BOLT ACTION

Add $110 for left-hand action on all current models.

DSG (DESIGNATED SLUG GUN) – 12 or 16 ga., based on Rem. 870, non-removable custom fit Shaw 23 in. rifled slug barrel with muzzle brake, includes Leupold two-piece windage bases which accept any standard rings, available in Express Mag., Wingmaster Mag., or Express Super Mag. configurations.

	100%	98%	95%	90%	80%	70%	60%	LAST MSR
	$795	$725	$650	$550	$475	$400	$350	*$840*

Add $356 for Wingmaster Mag.
Add $69 for left hand.

PROFESSIONAL MODEL RSG-12 – 12 ga., 2 3/4 or 3 (new 2003) in. chamber, bolt action slug gun featuring 21 1/2 or 23 (new 2003) in. Shaw barrel and 2 lug bolt, 1 shot mag. (new 1998), matte black finish, McMillan fiberglass stock with Pachmayr Decelerator rifle pad, receiver drilled and tapped for standard Leupold windage bases (included, new 1997), muzzle brake became standard 1994, various finish options, 7 3/4 lbs. New 1991.

	100%	98%	95%	90%	80%	70%	60%	LAST MSR
MSR $2,850	$2,575	$2,275	$1,925	$1,550	$1,275	$1,050	$900	

* ***Professional Model RSG-12 Combo Slug Gun*** – includes standard Professional RSG-12 Slug Gun and a second benchrest McMillan heavy weight stock. Mfg. 1994-2004.

	100%	98%	95%	90%	80%	70%	60%	LAST MSR
	$2,250	$1,900	$1,575	$1,250	$1,000	$850	$750	*$2,175*

GRADING - PPGS™	100%	98%	95%	90%	80%	70%	60%	LAST MSR

* ***Professional Model RSG-12/RSG-20 10th Anniversary*** – 12 or 20 ga., hand selected actions and barrels, Jewell custom adj. trigger, NP-3 nickel/Teflon metal finish, black McMillan stock with Pachmayr Decelerator pad. Only 25 mfg. during 2000 only, reintroduced 2005-disc.

$2,150 $1,875 $1,525 $1,275 $1,050 $900 $800 ***$2,395***

MATCHLESS MODEL RSG-12 – upgraded variation featuring 400 grit polished gloss metal finish and the McMillan regular or "Fiber" grain stock (wood grain finish, disc. 2000). Mfg. 1995-2004. Re-introduced 2010.

MSR $3,000 $2,750 $2,500 $2,150 $1,800 $1,475 $1,225 $1,000

PEERLESS MODEL RSG-12 – upgraded variation featuring NP-3 (nickel/Teflon) metal finish by Robar of Phoenix, AZ, McMillan regular or "Fiber" grain stock (wood grain finish, disc. 2000). Mfg. 1995-2004. Re-introduced 2010.

MSR $3,500 $3,150 $2,600 $2,200 $1,750 $1,450 $1,250 $1,100

ELITE MODEL RSG-16 – 12 ga., 2 3/4 in. chamber, 23 in. Shaw rifled barrel, and 2 lug bolt, 1 shot mag., matte black finish, black McMillan fiberglass stock with Pachmayr decelerator pad, drilled and tapped for Rem. 700 long action style bases. Mfg. 2003-2004. Re-introduced 2010.

MSR $2,835 $2,575 $2,275 $1,925 $1,550 $1,275 $1,050 $900

MOUNTAINEER MODEL RSG-20 – 20 ga., 2 3/4 in. chamber, features 21 in. Shaw rifled barrel and 2 lug bolt, one shot mag., matte black finish only, McMillan fiberglass stock with Pachmayr Decelerator pad, receiver drilled and tapped for Rem. Mod. 700 long action style bases, muzzle brake standard, 6 1/2 lbs. Mfg. 1997-2004. Reintroduced 2010.

MSR $2,850 $2,575 $2,275 $1,925 $1,550 $1,275 $1,050 $900

RSG-TACTICAL (SNIPER) MODEL – 12 ga. only, similar to RSG-12, except has M-86 McMillan fiberglass black tactical stock with Pachmayr Decelerator pad and heavy barrel. Mfg. 1992-98.

$1,495 $1,250 $995 $875 $750 $700 $650 ***$1,595***

Add $150 for Bipod.

BLOCK CARD MODEL – 12 ga., 2 3/4 in. chamber, various barrel lengths, cartage type chokes, special McMillan fiberglass stock, Pachmayr Decelerator pad, fluted barrels optional, special chambers, weighted stocks optional, single shot actions. Disc.

$1,625 $1,425 $1,125 $900 $800 $750 $700 ***$1,775***

TASK FIREARMS

Current importer located in Miami, FL. Dealer sales.

Task Firearms currently imports the Fatih model semi-auto pistol manufactured by Trabzon Gun Industry Corp. located in Ankara, Turkey, and a line of Diamond Doubles shotguns. Please contact the company directly for more information on current models, availability, and pricing (see Trademark Index).

TATE GUNMAKERS LLC

Previous shotgun manufacturer 1995-2010 and located in Ione, CA.

SHOTGUNS: CUSTOM

Dale Tate, formerly of J. Purdey & Sons, made custom order shotguns per individual customer specifications in 12, 16, 20, or 28 ga. until mid-2010. All models were POR. Tate Gunmakers also specialized in gun repair and restoration. An individual expert appraisal is recommended before buying or selling a Tate shotgun.

TAURUS INTERNATIONAL MFG., INC.

Currently manufactured by Taurus Forjas S.A., located in Porto Alegre, Brazil. Currently imported by Taurus International Mfg., Inc. located in Miami, FL since 1982. Beginning 2007, Taurus Tactical, a separate entity, was created for law enforcement/military sales and service. Distributor sales only.

During late 2012, Taurus Holdings purchased an exclusive global distribution agreement

GRADING - PPGS™	100%	98%	95%	90%	80%	70%	60%	LAST MSR

with Diamondback Firearms, LLC. Taurus will assume all sales and marketing efforts of the Diamondback branded products from its Miami office.

All Taurus products are known for their innovative design, quality construction, and proven value, and are backed by a lifetime repair policy.

Taurus order number nomenclature is as follows: the first digit followed by a dash refers to type (1 = pistol, 2 = revolvers, 3 = longuns, 4 = Magazines/Accessories, 5 = grips, and 10 = scope mount bases), the next 2 or 3 digits refer to model number, the next digit refers to type of hammer (0 = exposed, 1 = concealed), the next digit refers to barrel length (w/o fractions), the last digit refers to finish (1 = blue, 9 = stainless), and the suffix at the end refers to special features (T = total titanium, H = case hardened, M = matte finish, PLY = polymer, UL = Ultra-Lite, C = ported (compensation), G = gold accent, PRL = mother-of-pearl grips, R = rosewood grips, NS = night sights, MG = magnesium, and FO = fiber optic). Hence, 2-454089M refers to a Model 454 Raging Bull revolver in .454 Casull cal. with an exposed hammer and a 8 3/8 in. barrel in matte stainless finish.

PISTOLS: SEMI-AUTO

From 1990-92, certain models became available with a Laser Aim LA1 sighting system that included mounts, rings (in matching finish), a 110 volt AC recharging unit, a 9 volt DC field charger, and a high impact custom case.

Taurus incorporated their keyed Taurus security system on most models during 2000, except the PT-22 and PT-25, and this is now available with all models. When the security system is engaged (via a keyed button on the bottom of rear grip strap), the pistol cannot be fired, cocked, or disassembled, and the gun's manual safety cannot be disengaged. This security key also works for the revolvers.

Recent variations that are CA approved are not broken out separately, as pricing is usually the same as the standard model.

Add approx. $30 for the Deluxe Shooter's Pack option (includes extra mag. and custom case) on the 92, 99, 100, and 101 Series (disc. 2000).

22 PLY – .22 LR cal., DAO, 2.33 in. tip up barrel, polymer frame with steel inserts, fixed sights, matte black or stainless steel slide with fish scale serrations, 8 shot mag., polymer grips, blow back action, 10.8 oz. New 2012.

While advertised during 2012, this model never went into production.

25 PLY – .25 ACP cal., otherwise similar to 22 Ply. New 2012.

While advertised during 2012, this model never went into production.

PT-22 – .22 LR cal., double action only, tip-up design, 2 3/4 in. barrel, 8 shot mag., fixed sights, polymer (new 2011) or steel frame, stainless (new 2011) or steel slide, blue, nickel (new 1995), blue/nickel (mfg. 1997-2000), Duo-tone (new 2000), or deluxe blue/gold (new 1997) finish, wood (new 1999), mother-of-pearl (mfg. 2000-2011, deluxe blue/gold finish only), black pearl (mfg. 2006-2011), rosewood, checkered wood, or black synthetic (new 2012) grips, 12.3 oz. New 1992.

MSR $282	$215	$185	$160	$135	$110	$90	$70	

Add $22 for blue/gold or nickel/gold finish with rosewood or $38 for blue/gold or nickel/gold finish with black pearl (mfg. 2006-2011) or mother-of-pearl grips (disc. 2011).

Add $22 for pink pearl grips with blue or nickel finish (disc. 2011) or $38 for pink pearl grips with blue/nickel and gold finish (Model PP-22), disc. 2011.

Add $16 for polymer frame with stainless steel slide (new 2011).

Subtract $8 for black synthetic grips (new 2012).

PT-24/7 – 9mm Para., .40 S&W, or .45 ACP (new 2005) cal., DAO, large black polymer frame with blued steel or satin stainless steel slide, 4 in. barrel with 3-dot sights, grips have Ribber grip overlays, 10, 12 (.45 ACP cal.), 15 (.40 S&W cal.), or 17 (9mm Para. cal.) shot mag., built-in Picatinny rail system on bottom of frame, includes 3 safeties, 27 1/2 oz. Mfg. late 2004-2005.

	$450	$400	$350	$310	$250	$200	$180	*$578*

Add $16 for stainless steel.

GRADING - PPGS™	100%	98%	95%	90%	80%	70%	60%	LAST MSR

PT-24/7 PRO FULL SIZE – 9mm Para., .40 S&W, or .45 ACP cal., SA first shot, and follows continually in SA model, large black polymer frame with blued steel, Duo Tone (new 2009), titanium (9mm Para. cal. only), or satin stainless steel slide, 4 in. barrel with Heinie front and Slant Pro rear sight, Ribber grips (.45 ACP cal.) or Ribber overmold grips (grip inlays), 10, 12 (.45 ACP cal.), 15 (.40 S&W cal.), or 17 (9mm Para. cal.) shot mag., built-in Picatinny rail system on bottom of frame, includes 3 safeties, 27.2 oz. Mfg. 2006-2010.

	$415	$365	$310	$275	$220	$180	$140	*$498*

Add $16 for stainless steel or $188 for titanium.

This model uses a SA trigger mechanism. However, if a cartridge does not fire, a DA feature allows the shooter a second firing pin strike via the DA trigger pull. If the cartridge still does not fire, then extraction by slide operation will insert a fresh round while reverting to the SA model automatically.

* ***PT-24/7 Pro Long Slide*** – similar to Full Size 24/7-Pro, except has 5.2 in. barrel, also available in .38 Super cal. (new 2010), similar mag. capacities, Tenifer finish new 2010, 29.1 oz. Mfg. 2006-2010.

	$445	$390	$335	$305	$245	$200	$155	*$530*

Add $15 for stainless steel. Add $31 for Tenifer finish (new 2010). Add $197 for Tenifer finish with night sights (.40 S&W cal. only, new 2010).

* ***PT-24/7 Pro Compact*** – similar to Full Size 24/7-Pro, except has 3 1/3 in. barrel, similar mag. capacities. Mfg. 2006-2010.

	$415	$365	$310	$275	$220	$180	$140	*$498*

Add $16 for stainless steel or $188 for titanium.

PT-24/7 G2 – 9mm Para., .40 S&W, or .45 ACP cal., advanced DA/SA trigger system, 4.2 in. barrel, large black polymer frame, horizontally grooved grips with metallic inserts and 3 interchangeable backstraps, ambidextrous thumb rests, matte blue or stainless steel slide, Strike Two trigger with safety, ambidextrous manual decocker latch and safety, fixed front and low-profile adj. rear sight, vertical loaded chamber indicator, built-in Picatinny rail system on bottom of frame, 10, 12 (.45 ACP cal. only), 15 (.40 S&W cal. only) or 17 (9mm Para. only) shot mag., 28 oz. New 2011.

MSR $539	$435	$380	$320	$280	$225	$180	$140	

Add $16 for stainless steel.

* ***PT-24/7 G2 Compact*** – similar to PT-24/7 G2, except has 3 1/2 in. barrel, 27 oz. New 2011.

MSR $539	$435	$380	$315	$280	$225	$180	$140	

Add $16 for stainless steel.

PT-24/7 OSS – 9mm Para., .40 S&W, or .45 ACP cal., similar operating system as PT-24/7 Pro Full Size, including SA/DA trigger system, choice of tan or black frame, 5 1/4 in. match grade barrel, Novak sights, lower frame Picatinny rail, 10, 12, 15, or 17 shot mag., ambidextrous decocking safety, black Tenifer steel or stainless (new 2009) slide with front and rear serrations, approx. 32 oz. Mfg. 2007-2010.

	$475	$425	$365	$325	$260	$215	$190	*$623*

Add $63 for Novak Lo-Mount night sights.
Add $18 for matte finished stainless steel slide (new 2009).

PT-25 – .25 ACP cal., similar to PT-22, except has 9 shot mag., 12.3 oz. New 1992.

MSR $282	$215	$180	$155	$135	$110	$90	$70	

Add $22 for blue/gold or nickel/gold finish with rosewood or $38 for blue/gold or nickel/gold finish with mother-of-pearl grips (disc. 2011).
Add $22 for pink pearl grips with blue or nickel finish (disc. 2011) or $38 for pink pearl grips with blue/nickel and gold finish (Model PP-25), disc. 2011.
Add $16 for polymer frame with stainless steel slide (new 2011).

PT-38S – .38 Super cal., 4 1/4 in. barrel, DA/SA utilizes Model PT-945 alloy frame, choice of blue, stainless steel, or stainless/gold finishes, 3-dot fixed sights, 10 shot mag., checkered rubber (standard) or smooth faux mother-of-pearl grips, 30 oz. Mfg. 2005-2010.

	$525	$450	$385	$335	$270	$225	$195	*$695*

Add $16 for stainless steel slide.
Add $48 for stainless steel slide, gold accents, and faux mother-of-pearl grips.

GRADING - PPGS™	100%	98%	95%	90%	80%	70%	60%	LAST MSR

PT-58 – .380 ACP cal., similar to PT-99AF, except in .380 ACP cal., 4 in. barrel, 10 (C/B 1994) or 12* shot mag. Mfg. 1988-96.

$325 $285 $245 $220 $180 $145 $115 *$429*

Add $32 for satin nickel finish (disc. 1994).

Beginning 1993, the PT-58 utilized the Taurus Tri-Position safety system which features hammer-drop or "cocked-and-locked" options.

* ***PT-58SS (Stainless Steel)*** – similar to PT-58, except is stainless steel. Mfg. 1992- 96.

$385 $345 $295 $250 $215 $170 $150 *$470*

PT-58 HC PLUS – .380 ACP cal., medium frame, similar to PT-58, except has 19 shot mag., ambidextrous safety, fixed sights, 18.7 oz. Mfg. 2006-2010.

$495 $435 $360 $315 $250 $200 $180 *$664*

Add $16 for stainless steel slide.

PT-91AF – .41 Action Express cal., action similar to PT-92AF, except is in .41 AE cal., 10 shot mag., 34 oz. Imported 1990 only.

$365 $320 $275 $230 $195 $160 $140 *$446*

Add $36 for satin nickel finish.

Add $25 for shooter's pack (includes custom case and extra mag.).

PT-92(AF) – 9mm Para. cal., semi-auto double action, design similar to Beretta Model 92 SB-F, exposed hammer, ambidextrous safety, 5 in. barrel, current mfg. has frame accessory rail in front of trigger guard, 10 (C/B 1994), 15*, or 17 (new late 2004) shot mag., smooth Brazilian walnut (disc.) or checkered rubber (new 1999) grips, blue, nickel (disc.), or stainless steel finish, fixed or night (mfg. 2000-2004) sights, 34 oz.

MSR $660 $510 $435 $365 $320 $260 $210 $155

Add $40 for satin nickel finish (disc. 1994).

Add $415 for Laser Aim Sight (disc. 1991).

Add $78 for night sights (disc. 2004).

Add $266 for blue or stainless conversion kit to convert 9mm Para. to .22 LR (mfg. 1999-2004).

* ***PT-92SS (Stainless Steel)*** – similar to PT-92AF, except is combat matte (new 2006, high cap. mag. only) or regular stainless steel. New 1992.

MSR $668 $515 $435 $365 $315 $260 $210 $155

Add $78 for night sights (disc. 2004).

* ***PT-92 Deluxe*** – choice of blue/gold (disc. 2004) or stainless steel with gold finish, rosewood, or mother-of-pearl (new 2000) grips. Mfg. 1999-2011.

$515 $450 $380 $345 $280 $230 $180 *$655*

Add $25 for faux mother-of-pearl grips.

Add $40 for stainless gold finish with rosewood grips (new 2011).

Subtract approx. $15 for blue/gold finish (disc. 2004).

* ***PT-92AFC*** – compact variation of the Model PT-92AF, 4 in. barrel, 10 (C/B 1994) or 13* shot mag., fixed sights. Disc. 1996.

$335 $295 $250 $225 $185 $150 $115 *$449*

Add $38 for satin nickel finish (disc. 1993).

* ***PT-92AFC (Stainless Steel)*** – similar to PT-92AFC, except stainless steel. Mfg. 1993-96.

$400 $350 $300 $270 $220 $180 $140 *$493*

PT-99 (AF) – 9mm Para. cal., similar to Model PT-92AF, except has adj. rear sight, 10 or 17 shot mag., 34 oz. Disc. 2011.

$495 $435 $370 $335 $270 $225 $175 *$617*

Add $45 for satin nickel finish (disc. 1994).

Add $266 for blue or stainless conversion kit to convert 9mm Para. to .22 LR (mfg. 1999-2004) or .40 S&W (mfg. 2000-2004).

This action is similar to the Beretta Model 92SB-F.

GRADING - PPGS™	100%	98%	95%	90%	80%	70%	60%	LAST MSR

* ***PT-99SS (Stainless Steel)*** – similar to PT-99, except is fabricated from stainless steel. Mfg. 1992-2011.

	$495	$425	$355	$325	$260	$215	$165	*$633*

PT-100 – .40 S&W cal., standard double action, 5 in. barrel, 10 (C/B 1994), 11* (reintroduced late 2004) shot mag., safeties include ambidextrous manual, hammer drop, inertia firing pin, and chamber loaded indicator, choice of blue, satin nickel (disc. 1994), or stainless steel finish, accessory rail, smooth Brazilian hard wood (disc.) or rubber grips, 34 oz. Mfg. 1992-97, reintroduced 2000. Disc. 2012.

	$495	$425	$360	$315	$260	$210	$155	*$641*

Add $40 for satin nickel finish (disc. 1994).
Add $78 for night sights (mfg. 2000-2004).
Add $266 for blue or stainless conversion kit to convert .40 S&W to .22 LR cal. (disc. 2004).

* ***PT-100SS (Stainless Steel)*** – .40 S&W cal., similar to PT-100, except is fabricated from stainless steel, and 16 shot mag. Mfg. 1992-96, reintroduced 2000.

MSR $668	$515	$435	$365	$315	$260	$210	$155	

Add $78 for night sights (disc. 2005).

* ***PT-100 Deluxe*** – choice of blue/gold (disc. 2004) finish or stainless steel with gold, rosewood, or mother-of-pearl grips. Mfg. 2000-2011.

	$525	$450	$380	$345	$280	$230	$180	*$670*

Add $25 for faux mother-of-pearl grips.
Subtract approx. $15 for blue/gold finish (disc. 2004).

PT-101 – .40 S&W cal., similar to PT-100, except has adj. rear sight., 10 or 11 shot mag., 34 oz. Mfg. 1992-96, reintroduced 2000-2011.

	$495	$435	$370	$335	$270	$225	$175	*$617*

Add $266 for blue or stainless conversion kit to convert .40 S&W to .22 LR cal. (disc. 2004).
Add $45 for satin nickel finish (disc. 1994).

* ***PT-101SS (Stainless Steel)*** – similar to PT-101, except is stainless steel. Mfg. 1992-96, reintroduced 2000-2011.

	$495	$425	$355	$325	$260	$215	$165	*$633*

PT-111 MILLENNIUM – 9mm Para. cal., double action only, 3 1/4 in. barrel with fixed 3-dot sights, black polymer frame with steel slide, striker fired, 10 shot mag. with push-button release, 18.7 oz. Mfg. 1998-2004.

	$355	$310	$265	$225	$190	$155	$135	*$422*

Add $78 for night sights (new 2000).
Add $47 for pearl or burl walnut grips (limited mfg. 2003).

* ***PT-111 Millennium Stainless*** – similar to Model PT-111, except has stainless steel slide. Mfg. 1998-2004.

	$360	$315	$270	$245	$200	$160	$125	*$438*

Add $78 for night sights (new 2000).
Add $46 for pearl or burl walnut grips (limited mfg. 2003).

* ***PT-111 Millennium Titanium*** – similar to Model PT-111, except has titanium slide and night or 3-dot (new 2004) sights. Mfg. 2000-2004.

	$415	$365	$320	$275	$225	$185	$165	*$508*

Add $78 for night sights.

PT-111 MILLENNIUM PRO – 9mm Para. cal., SA/DA trigger, 10 or 12 (new late 2004) shot mag., blue steel frame, current mfg. has Heinie Straight 8 sights, improved ergonomics, Posi-Traction slide serrations, recessed magazine release, manual safety lever, trigger block mechanism, firing pin block, and lightweight frame, 18.7 oz. Mfg. 2003-2012.

	$375	$325	$270	$245	$200	$160	$125	*$467*

Add $78 for night sights (disc. 2004).

GRADING - PPGS™	100%	98%	95%	90%	80%	70%	60%	LAST MSR

* ***PT-111 Millennium Pro Stainless*** – similar to Model PT-111 Millennium Pro, except has stainless steel slide. Mfg. 2003-2012.

	$395	$330	$285	$260	$210	$170	$135	*$483*

Add $78 for night sights (mfg. 2004).

* ***PT-111 Ti Millennium Pro Titanium*** – similar to Model PT-111 Millennium Pro, except has titanium slide and 3 dot sights, 16 oz. Mfg. 2005-2011.

	$525	$460	$395	$355	$290	$235	$185	*$655*

PT-132 MILLENNIUM – .32 ACP cal., double action only, 3 1/4 in. barrel, black polymer frame, manual safety, 10 shot mag., fixed 3-dot (disc. 2002) or adj. (new 2003) sights, blue steel slide, 18.7 oz. Mfg. 2001-2004.

	$355	$315	$265	$225	$190	$155	$135	*$422*

* ***Model PT-132 Millennium Stainless*** – similar to Model PT-132, except has stainless steel slide. Mfg. 2001-2004.

	$360	$315	$270	$245	$200	$160	$125	*$438*

PT-132 MILLENNIUM PRO – .32 ACP cal., similar to Model PT-132 Millennium, SA/DA trigger, current mfg. has Heinie Straight 8 sights, improved ergonomics, Posi-Traction slide serrations, recessed magazine release, manual safety lever, trigger block mechanism, firing pin block, adj. rear sight, and lightweight frame, 19.9 oz. Mfg. 2003, reintroduced 2005-2011.

	$375	$325	$270	$245	$200	$160	$125	*$467*

* ***PT-132 Millennium Pro Stainless*** – similar to Model PT-132 Millennium Pro, except has stainless steel slide. Mfg. 2003, reintroduced 2005-2011.

	$395	$330	$285	$260	$210	$170	$135	*$483*

PT-138 MILLENNIUM – .380 ACP cal., double action only, 3 1/4 in. barrel, black polymer frame, manual safety, 10 shot mag., fixed 3-dot sights, blue steel slide, 18.7 oz. Mfg. 1999-2004.

	$355	$310	$265	$240	$195	$160	$125	*$422*

Add $78 for night sights (mfg. 2000-2003).

* ***Model PT-138 Millennium Stainless*** – similar to Model PT-138, except has stainless steel slide. New 1999.

	$360	$315	$270	$245	$200	$160	$125	

Add $78 for night sights (mfg. 2000-2003).

PT-138 MILLENNIUM PRO – .380 ACP cal., similar to Model PT-138 Millennium, 10 or 12 shot (new 2005) mag., SA/DA trigger, current mfg. has Heinie Straight 8 sights, improved ergonomics, Posi-Traction slide serrations, recessed magazine release, manual safety lever, trigger block mechanism, firing pin block, and lightweight frame, 18.7 oz. Mfg. 2003, reintroduced 2005-2011.

	$375	$325	$270	$245	$200	$160	$125	*$467*

Add $78 for night sights (disc. 2003).

* ***PT-138 Millennium Pro Stainless*** – similar to Model PT-138 Millennium Pro, except has stainless steel slide. Mfg. 2003, reintroduced 2005-2011.

	$395	$330	$285	$260	$210	$170	$135	*$483*

PT-140 MILLENNIUM – .40 S&W cal., double action only, 3 1/4 in. barrel, black polymer frame, manual safety, 10 shot mag., fixed 3-dot sights, blue steel slide, 18.7 oz. Mfg. 1999-2004.

	$375	$335	$280	$240	$200	$165	$150	*$461*

Add $78 for night sights (new 2000).
Add $47 for pearl or burl walnut grips (mfg. 2003).

* ***PT-140 Millennium Stainless*** – similar to Model PT-140, except has stainless steel slide. Mfg. 1999-2004.

	$380	$340	$285	$240	$200	$165	$150	*$476*

Add $78 for night sights (new 2000).
Add $46 for pearl or burl walnut grips (mfg. 2003).

GRADING - PPGS™	100%	98%	95%	90%	80%	70%	60%	LAST MSR

PT-140 MILLENNIUM PRO – .40 S&W cal., similar to Model PT-140 Millennium, except has SA/DA trigger, current mfg. has Heinie Straight 8 sights, improved ergonomics, Posi-Traction slide serrations, recessed magazine release, manual safety lever, trigger block mechanism, firing pin block, and lightweight frame, 23 1/2 oz. Mfg. 2003-2012.

	$395	$330	$285	$260	$210	$170	$135	*$483*

Add $78 for night sights (disc. 2004).

* ***PT-140 Millennium Pro Stainless*** – similar to Model PT-140 Millennium Pro, except has stainless steel slide. Mfg. 2003-2012.

	$415	$345	$295	$270	$215	$180	$140	*$498*

Add $78 for night sights (disc. 2004).

PT-145 MILLENNIUM – .45 ACP cal., otherwise similar to Model PT-140 Millennium, 23 oz. Mfg. 2000-2003.

	$400	$350	$300	$260	$215	$175	$155	*$484*

Add $79 for night sights (new 2000).

* ***PT-145 Millennium Stainless*** – similar to Model PT-140, except has stainless steel slide. Mfg. 1999-2003.

	$400	$350	$300	$260	$200	$165	$150	*$500*

Add $78 for night sights (new 2000).

PT-145 MILLENNIUM PRO – .45 ACP cal., similar to Model PT-145 Millennium, except has SA/DA trigger, current mfg. has Heinie Straight 8 sights, improved ergonomics, Posi-Traction slide serrations, recessed magazine release, manual safety lever, trigger block mechanism, firing pin block, and lightweight frame, 22.2 oz. Mfg. 2003-2012.

	$395	$330	$285	$260	$210	$170	$135	*$483*

Add $78 for night sights (disc. 2004).

* ***PT-145 Millennium Pro Stainless*** – similar to Model PT-145 Millennium Pro, except has stainless steel slide. New 2003.

MSR $498	$415	$345	$295	$270	$215	$180	$140	

Add $78 for night sights (mfg. 2000-2004).

PT-400 – .400 Cor-Bon cal., similar to Model PT-940, except has 4 1/4 in. ported barrel and 8 shot mag., 29 1/2 oz. Mfg. 1999 only.

	$415	$365	$320	$275	$225	$185	$165	*$523*

* ***PT-400 Stainless*** – similar to Model PT-400, except has stainless steel slide. Mfg. 1999 only.

	$415	$365	$320	$275	$225	$185	$165	*$539*

PT-609/609TI-PRO – 9mm Para. cal., DA/SA, 3 1/4 in. barrel with titanium slide, fixed sights, black polymer grips, lower rail on frame, 13 shot mag., 19.7 oz. Mfg. 2007-2010.

	$535	$470	$400	$365	$295	$240	$185	*$670*

PT-638 PRO COMPACT – .380 ACP cal., SA target style trigger with trigger safety, 3.2 in. barrel, low mount sights with adj. rear, 15 shot mag., ambidextrous manual safety, loaded chamber indicator, blue or matte stainless slide, black polymer frame with Memory Pad, 28 oz. Mfg. 2011 only.

	$395	$330	$285	$260	$210	$170	$135	*$483*

Add $15 for matte stainless steel slide.

PT-709 SLIM – 9mm Para. cal., SA (disc.) or SA/DA trigger (current mfg.), 3 in. barrel, 7 shot mag., blue finish, black polymer frame with grip texturing, compact frame, 3 dot sights, 19 oz. Mfg. late 2008-2012.

	$425	$365	$325	$280	$240	$210	$165	*$498*

Add $14 for Bulldog Case (mfg. 2010-2011).

* ***PT-709 Slim Stainless*** – similar to Model 709, except has matte finished stainless steel slide, 19 oz. New late 2008.

MSR $513	$425	$350	$295	$270	$215	$180	$140	

Add $15 for Bulldog Case (new 2010).

GRADING - PPGS™	100%	98%	95%	90%	80%	70%	60%	LAST MSR

* ***PT-709 Slim Titanium*** – similar to Model 709 Slim, except has titanium slide, 17 oz. Disc. 2010.

	$515	$425	$370	$325	$260	$210	$180	*$623*

Add $15 for Bulldog Case (new 2010).

PT-709 G2 SLIM – 9mm Para. cal., sub-compact frame, 7 or 9 (extended) shot mag., 3.2 in. barrel with low profile adj. rear sights, loaded chamber indicator, black polymer frame and blue or matte stainless slide, 19.4 oz. Limited mfg. 2011 only.

	$395	$345	$295	$270	$215	$180	$140	*$483*

* ***PT-709 G2 Slim Stainless*** – similar to PT-709 G2 Slim, except has matte finished stainless steel slide. Limited mfg. 2011 only.

	$415	$365	$310	$275	$220	$180	$140	*$498*

PT-732 TCP (TAURUS COMPACT PISTOL) – .32 ACP cal., 3.3 in. barrel, DAO, 6 shot mag., blue or matte stainless steel slide, low profile fixed sights, loaded chamber indicator, checkered black or pink polymer frame, 10.2 oz. Mfg. 2011-2012.

	$295	$250	$220	$185	$160	$140	$120	*$352*

PT-738 TCP (TAURUS COMPACT PISTOL) – .380 ACP cal., 3.3 in. barrel, DAO, choice of Barbie pink or black polymer frame, blue (disc. 2011), matte stainless, black stainless (new 2011), or titanium (disc. 2011) slide, 6 shot mag., fixed front sight, checkered polymer grips, 9 or 10.2 oz. New mid-2009.

MSR $362	$300	$255	$220	$195	$155	$130	$100	

Add $110 for titanium slide (disc. 2011).

MODEL 738FS – .380 ACP cal., DAO trigger, 3.3 in. barrel, blue slide, polymer frame, loaded chamber indicator, low profile fixed sights, hammerless, 10.2 oz. New 2013.

MSR $199	$175	$160	$150	$140	$130	$120	$110	

PT-740 SLIM – .40 S&W cal., similar to PT-709 Slim, except has 6 shot mag., 19 oz. Mfg. 2011-2012.

	$395	$330	$285	$260	$210	$170	$135	*$483*

* ***PT-740 Slim Stainless*** – similar to PT-740 Slim, except is matte stainless steel slide.

MSR $513	$425	$370	$310	$275	$220	$180	$140	

PT-740 G2 SLIM – While advertised during 2010 this model never went into production.

PT-745 COMPACT MILLENNIUM PRO – .45 ACP cal., SA/DA, compact variation of Millennium Pro with 3 1/4 in. barrel, Heinie Straight 8 sights, 6 shot mag. with finger extension, matte blue steel slide, loaded chamber indicator, black polymer grip frame, Desert Tan grips were added 2006 (disc.), 20.8 oz. Mfg. 2005-2012.

	$395	$330	$285	$260	$210	$170	$135	*$483*

* ***PT-745 Compact Millenium Pro Stainless*** – similar to PT-745 Compact Millennium Pro, except has stainless steel slide. Mfg. 2005-2012.

	$415	$345	$295	$270	$215	$180	$140	*$498*

PT-809 – 9mm Para. cal., similar design to the PT-24/7 OSS, 4 in. barrel, SA/DA with Strike Two capability, Novak sights, 17 shot mag., blue or stainless (disc. 2012), front and rear slide serrations, lower Picatinny rail, 30.2 oz. New 2007.

MSR $497	$410	$340	$290	$260	$210	$170	$135	

Add $15 for stainless steel slide (disc. 2012).
Add $188 for .22 LR conversion kit (10 shot mag., mfg. 2011 only).

* ***PT-809 Compact*** – 9mm Para. cal., similar to PT-809, except has 3.5 in. barrel, 3 dot fixed sights, polymer grips with metallic inserts, 24.7 oz. New 2011.

MSR $497	$410	$340	$290	$260	$210	$170	$135	

Add $15 for stainless steel slide (disc. 2012).

GRADING - PPGS™	100%	98%	95%	90%	80%	70%	60%	LAST MSR

PT-840 – .40 S&W cal., similar design to the PT-24/7 OSS, 4 in. barrel, SA/DA with Strike Two capability, Novak sights, 15 shot mag., matte blue or matte stainless slide (disc. 2012), front and rear slide serrations, lower frame Picatinny rail, approx. 30 oz. New 2008.

MSR $497	$410	$340	$285	$260	$210	$170	$135	

Add $15 for stainless steel slide (disc. 2012).
Add $188 for .22 LR conversion kit (10 shot mag., mfg. 2011 only).

* ***PT-840 Compact*** – .40 S&W cal., similar to PT-840, except has 3.5 in. barrel, 3 dot sights, polymer grips with metallic inserts, 24.7 oz. New 2011.

MSR $497	$410	$340	$285	$260	$210	$170	$135	

Add $16 for stainless steel slide (disc. 2012).

PT-845 – .45 ACP cal., similar design to the PT-24/7 OSS, 4 in. barrel, SA/DA with Strike Two capability, Novak sights, 12 shot mag., blue or stainless, front and rear slide serrations, lower frame Picatinny rail, approx. 30 oz. New 2008.

MSR $497	$410	$340	$285	$260	$210	$170	$135	

Add $15 for stainless steel slide (disc. 2012).
Add $188 for .22 LR conversion kit (10 shot mag., mfg. 2011 only).

PT-908 – 9mm Para. cal., compact version of the PT-92 with 3.8 in. barrel and 8 shot mag., fixed sights, blue or nickel finish. Mfg. 1993-97.

	$330	$290	$250	$210	$180	$150	$130	*$435*

* ***PT-908D SS (Stainless Steel)*** – similar to Model PT-908, except is stainless steel. Mfg. 1993-97.

	$385	$345	$295	$250	$215	$170	$150	*$473*

PT-909 – 9mm Para. cal., DA/SA, 4 in. barrel, lower frame Picatinny rail, 10 or 17 shot mag., blue finish, fixed rear sight, alloy medium frame with steel slide, checkered rubber grips, 28.2 oz. Mfg. 2006-2010.

	$500	$415	$360	$315	$250	$200	$180	*$648*

Add $16 for stainless steel slide.

PT-911 COMPACT – 9mm Para. cal., single or double action, 4 in. barrel, 10 or 15 (new late 2004) shot mag., checkered rubber grips, fixed sights, 28.2 oz. Mfg. 1997-2010.

	$500	$415	$360	$315	$250	$200	$180	*$648*

Add $79 for night sights (disc. 2004).

* ***PT-911 Compact SS (Stainless Steel)*** – stainless variation of the PT-911 Compact. Disc. 2010.

	$530	$445	$380	$345	$280	$230	$180	*$664*

Add $78 for night sights (disc. 2004).

* ***PT-911 Compact Deluxe*** – choice of blue/gold finish or stainless steel with gold, rosewood, or mother-of-pearl grips. Mfg. 2000-2010.

	$550	$455	$390	$355	$285	$235	$180	*$702*

Add $15 for stainless steel with gold or faux mother-of-pearl grips.

PT-917 COMPACT PLUS – 9mm Para. cal., DA/SA, 4 in. barrel with fixed sights, rubber grips, 19 shot mag., medium frame, blue finish or stainless steel, 31.8 oz. Mfg. 2007-2010.

	$500	$415	$360	$315	$250	$200	$180	*$609*

Add $18 for stainless steel.

PT-922 – .22 LR cal., sport model with 10 shot mag., 6 in. tapered barrel, adj. sights, medium frame, blue finish, angled synthetic grip frame with Taurus medallions on bottom, 25 oz. Limited mfg. 2004.

	$285	$250	$215	$195	$155	$130	$100	*$370*

PT-938 COMPACT – .380 ACP cal., DA/SA, 3 3/4 in. barrel, ambidextrous safety, 10 or 15 (new late 2004) shot mag., blue finish with alloy frame and steel slide, rubber grips, fixed sights, 34 oz. Mfg. 1997-2005.

	$410	$360	$315	$270	$220	$180	$160	*$516*

GRADING - PPGS™	100%	98%	95%	90%	80%	70%	60%	LAST MSR

* ***PT-938 Compact SS (Stainless Steel)*** – stainless slide variation of the PT-938 Compact with matte stainless finish.

	$420	$370	$320	$275	$225	$185	$165	*$531*

PT-940 – .40 S&W cal., compact version of the PT-100 with 3 5/8 in. barrel and 10 shot mag., fixed sights, 28.2 oz. Mfg. 1996-2010.

	$500	$415	$360	$315	$250	$200	$180	*$648*

Add $79 for night sights (disc. 2004).

* ***PT-940 SS (Stainless Steel)*** – similar to PT-940, except is stainless steel. Mfg. 1996-2010.

	$530	$445	$380	$345	$280	$230	$180	*$664*

Add $80 for night sights (disc. 2009).

* ***PT-940 Deluxe*** – choice of blue/gold or stainless steel with gold finish, rosewood, or mother-of-pearl grips. Mfg. 2000-2010.

	$545	$455	$390	$355	$285	$235	$180	*$702*

Add $15 for stainless steel with gold with rosewood grips or for mother-of-pearl grips.

PT-945 – .45 ACP cal., DA/SA, 4 1/4 in. ported (mfg. 1997-2003) or unported barrel, 8 shot single stack mag., ambidextrous 3 position safety, chamber loaded indicator, 3-dot sights, 29 1/2 oz. Mfg. 1995-2010.

	$560	$470	$400	$365	$295	$240	$185	*$695*

Add $78 for night sights (disc. 2004).
Add $39 for ported barrel (disc. 2003).

* ***PT-945 SS (Stainless Steel)*** – stainless steel variation of the PT-945. Mfg. 1995-2010.

	$575	$475	$410	$370	$300	$245	$190	*$711*

Add $78 for night sights (disc. 2004).
Add $39 for ported barrel (disc. 2003).

* ***PT-945 Deluxe*** – choice of blue/gold (disc. 2004) or stainless steel finish, mother-of-pearl (new 2000), or rosewood grips. Mfg. 1999-2010.

	$615	$540	$460	$420	$340	$275	$215	*$764*

Add $16 for mother-of-pearl grips.
Subtract approx. $15 for blue/gold finish.

PT-957 – .357 SIG cal., compact model with 3 5/8 in. ported (available only with night sights or in 957 Deluxe beginning 2002) or non-ported (new 2002) barrel and slide, 10 shot mag., ambidextrous 3-position safety, blue finish, checkered rubber grips, fixed sights, 28 oz. Mfg. 1999-2003.

	$425	$375	$325	$275	$225	$185	$165	*$523*

Add $90 for night sights.
Add $40 for ported barrel (disc. 2002).

* ***PT-957 SS (Stainless Steel)*** – stainless steel variation of the PT-957. Mfg. 1999-2003.

	$430	$380	$330	$275	$225	$185	$165	*$539*

Add $40 for ported (disc. 2001) barrel, or $130 for ported barrel and night sights (disc. 2003).

* ***PT-957 Deluxe*** – choice of blue/gold or stainless steel with gold finish, rosewood, or mother-of-pearl grips. Mfg. 2000-2002.

	$475	$425	$365	$325	$265	$215	$190	*$610*

Add $15 for stainless steel.
Add $15 for mother-of-pearl grips.

PT-1911 – .38 Super (mfg. 2006-2011), 9mm Para. (new 2006), .40 S&W (mfg. 2006-2010) or .45 ACP cal., SA, 5 in. barrel, choice of Heinie front and rear sights or Picatinny rail, 8 (.40 S&W or .45 ACP) or 9 (.38 Super or 9mm Para.) shot mag., blue or Duo-tone (new 2008) finish, choice of steel or aluminum (new 2008) frame with steel slide, checkered diamond pattern or bull's head wood grips, bobbed hammer, front and rear serrations on slide, accurized hand tuned action, 32 oz. New mid-2005.

MSR $853	$660	$560	$475	$415	$350	$300	$265	

GRADING - PPGS™	100%	98%	95%	90%	80%	70%	60%	LAST MSR

Subtract $34 if without Picatinny rail (.45 ACP cal. only).
Add $53 for Duo-tone finish (.45 ACP cal. only).
Add $13 for bull's head grips (.45 ACP cal. only).
Subtract $120 for 9mm Para cal. (not available with Picatinny rail).
Add approx. $75 for aluminum frame (disc. 2011).

* ***PT-1911 Compact*** – .45 ACP cal., only, similar to PT-1911, except has 4 1/4 in. barrel, 6 shot mag. Mfg. 2006 only.

	$490	$430	$365	$335	$270	$220	$170	*$599*

Add $20 for stainless steel slide.

* ***PT-1911 Stainless*** – similar to PT-1911, except has stainless steel frame and slide (mirror finished beginning 2008).

MSR $927	$765	$660	$555	$500	$400	$325	$255

Add $39 for lower frame Picatinny rail.
Add $48 for bull's head grips.
Subtract $84 for 9mm Para cal.

PT-1911B SERIES – .38 Super (1911B-38, disc.), 9mm Para. (1911B-9), or .45 ACP (1911BHC-12) cal., 5 in. barrel, blue, stainless, 9, 11, or 12 shot mag., with or w/o Novak night sights (disc. 2010), Heinie sights became standard 2011, 38-40 oz. Mfg. mid-2009-2011.

	$535	$470	$400	$365	$295	$240	$185	*$677*

Add $103 for stainless steel. Add $17 for 11 shot mag. Add $79 for .45 ACP with 12 shot mag. Add $63 for Novak night sights. Add $93 for Hi-Polish with bull's head walnut grips. Add $16 for pearl grips.

MODEL 1911FS – .45 ACP cal., 5 in. barrel, blued steel slide and frame, skeletonized trigger, double slide serrations, fixed sights, double diamond black synthetic grips, 7 shot mag., 38 oz. New 2013.

MSR $499	$450	$400	$375	$350	$325	$300	$275

PT-2011 DT INTEGRAL – .380 ACP or 9mm Para cal., SA/DA with trigger safety, 3.2 in. barrel, 11 (.380 ACP), 13 or 15 (.380 ACP) shot mag., aluminum frame with black polymer grips, loaded chamber indicator, matte black metal finish, removable back straps, adj. rear sight, 21 or 24 oz. Mfg. 2012 only.

	$475	$415	$360	$320	$285	$260	$240	*$572*

* ***PT-2011 DT Integral Stainless*** – similar to PT-2011 DT Integral, except has stainless steel slide. Mfg. 2012 only.

	$485	$420	$360	$320	$285	$260	$240	*$588*

PT-2011 DT HYBRID – 9mm Para or .40 S&W cal., SA/DA with trigger safety, 3.2 in. barrel, 11 (.40 S&W) or 13 (9mm Para) shot mag., black polymer lower frame with steel upper frame and slide, loaded chamber indicator, matte black metal finish, removable back straps, adj. rear sight, 24 oz. New 2012.

MSR $589	$490	$425	$365	$320	$285	$260	$240

* ***PT-2011 DT Hybrid Stainless*** – similar to PT-2011 DT Hybrid, except has stainless upper frame and slide. New 2012.

MSR $605	$500	$425	$365	$320	$285	$260	$240

PT-2045 – .45 ACP cal., 4.2 in. barrel, blue or stainless, 12 shot mag., checkered polymer grips, with or w/o Novak night sights, approx. 32 oz. Limited mfg. 2009 only.

	$450	$395	$340	$305	$250	$205	$160	*$561*

Add $16 for stainless steel. Add $62 for night sights.

REVOLVERS: RECENT PRODUCTION

From 1990-1992, certain models became available with a Laser Aim LA1 sighting system that included mounts, rings (in matching finish), a 110 volt AC recharging unit, a 9 volt DC field charger, and a high impact custom case.

GRADING - PPGS™	100%	98%	95%	90%	80%	70%	60%	LAST MSR

The following Taurus revolvers have been listed in numerical order. All currently manufactured revolvers listed are rated for +P ammunition.

Tracker model nomenclature refers to a heavy contoured barrel with full shroud, porting, and with or w/o VR.

All currently manufactured Taurus revolvers are equipped with the patented Taurus Security System, introduced in 1998, which utilizes an integral key lock on the back of the hammer, locking the action.

Add approx. $45 for scope base mount on currently produced models that offer this option.
Add $31 for carrying case on Raging Bull & Raging Hornet Models listed (disc. 2006).

MODEL GAUCHO SA – .357 Mag. (new 2006), .44-40 WCF (mfg. 2006), or .45 LC cal., SA Western style revolver, large frame, 4 3/4 (new 2006), 5 1/2, 7 1/2 (new 2006), or 12 (mfg. 2006) in. barrel, fixed sights, four click action, choice of all blue, blue/color case hardened, matte stainless, or polished stainless steel, 36.7 oz (5 1/2 in. barrel). Mfg. 2005-2007.

	$425	$375	$325	$275	$225	$185	$165	*$520*

Add $16 for stainless steel or blue/color case hardened finish.
Add $26 for 12 in. barrel (mfg. 2006).

MODEL 17C – .17 HMR or .17 Mach 2 (mfg. 2004-2006) cal., small frame, 8 shot, 2, 4, or 5 in. barrel, blue only, adj. sights, full underlug on 4 and 5 in. barrels, soft rubber grips, 24-27 1/2 oz. Mfg. 2003-2007.

	$295	$260	$220	$200	$160	$135	$105	*$391*

* ***Model 17C Ultra-Lite*** – ultra light hammer forged frame, 2 in. barrel, available in matte blue (disc. 2004, reintroduced 2006) or bright stainless steel, 18 1/2 oz. Mfg. 2003-2006.

	$340	$300	$260	$220	$185	$155	$135	*$453*

Subtract $47 for matte blue finish.

* ***Model 17CSS (Stainless Steel)*** – similar to Model 17C, except is polished (disc.) or matte stainless steel, 5 in. barrel disc. 2006. Mfg. 2003-2007.

	$330	$290	$250	$210	$180	$150	$130	*$439*

MODEL 17-IB (INSTANT BACKUP) – .17 HMR or .17 Mach 2 cal., small steel frame, 1 3/4 in. barrel, concealed hammer, blue finish, 8 (.17 HMR) or 9 (.17 Mach 2) shot, DA/SA, checkered rubber grips, adj. rear sight, transfer bar safety, 22.2 oz. Mfg. 2005-2007.

	$295	$260	$220	$200	$160	$135	$105	*$391*

* ***Model 17 Instant Backup Stainless*** – .17 HMR or .17 Mach 2 cal., similar to Model 17 Instant Backup, except is matte stainless steel. Mfg. 2005-2007.

	$330	$290	$250	$210	$180	$150	$130	*$439*

MODEL 17 TRACKER – .17 HMR cal., compact frame, 7 shot, adj. sights, 4 (mfg. 2012 only), 6 1/2 or 8 3/8 (mfg. 2004 only) in. Tracker VR barrel, blue (mfg. 2004-2005, reintroduced 2007), duo-tone (mfg. 2004 only, 6 1/2 in. barrel only) finish or matte stainless steel, ribber grip, 41 or 45 oz. New 2003.

MSR $491	$355	$300	$260	$240	$200	$165	$130

Add $48 for matte stainless steel.
Subtract approx. 10% for blue finish (disc. 2007).

MODEL 17-12 SILHOUETTE – .17 HMR cal., compact frame, features 12 in. barrel, adj. sights, includes scope mount. Mfg. 2003-2004.

	$320	$280	$240	$215	$175	$145	$110	*$430*

MODEL 21T TRACKER – .218 Bee cal., compact frame, 7 shot, 6 1/2 in. Tracker barrel with VR, matte stainless steel, adj. sights. Mfg. 2003-2004.

	$325	$285	$245	$210	$180	$150	$130	*$438*

MODEL 22H SS RAGING HORNET – .22 Hornet cal., large frame, 8 shot, stainless steel construction, 10 in. VR barrel with full shroud, fully adj. sights, scope mount bases included, contoured rubber grips, 50 oz. Mfg. 1999-2004.

	$795	$695	$600	$525	$465	$390	$295	*$898*

GRADING - PPGS™	100%	98%	95%	90%	80%	70%	60%	LAST MSR

MODEL 30C SS RAGING THIRTY HUNTER – .30 Carbine cal., large frame, 8 shot, 10 in. heavy VR barrel with full shroud and adj. sights, matte stainless steel, includes scope mounts and full moon clips, 50 oz. Mfg. 2003-2004.

$795 $695 $600 $525 $465 $390 $295 *$898*

MODEL 30S SILHOUETTE/HUNTER – .30 Carbine cal., large frame, 8 shot, double action, 12 in. VR barrel with partial shroud, matte stainless steel, adj. hammer tension, trigger overtravel stop, includes scope mounts, 50 oz. Mfg. 2003-2004.

$625 $545 $470 $425 $345 $280 $220 *$743*

MODEL 44 – .44 Mag. cal., 6 shot, large frame, integral porting compensator, exposed or concealed (3 in. barrel only, mfg. 1997-98) hammer, bright blue finish, adj. sights, rubber grips, 3 (mfg. 1997-98), 4, 6 1/2 (VR), or 8 3/8 (VR) in. ported or non-ported (disc. 2002) barrel, 45-57 oz. Mfg. 1994-2004.

$400 $350 $300 $260 $215 $175 $155 *$500*

Add $23 for 6 1/2 or 8 3/8 in. ported barrel.
Subtract approx. 10% for non-ported barrel.

* ***Model 44SS (Stainless Steel)*** – .44 Mag. cal., similar to Model 44, except has matte finished stainless steel. New 1994.

MSR $742 $600 $500 $435 $385 $310 $250 $195

Add $16 for 6 1/2 or 8 3/8 in. ported barrel.
Add $46 for 3 in. ported barrel with fixed sights and round butt grips (mfg. 1996-1997).

* ***Model 44 Silhouette*** – similar to Model 44, except has 12 in. VR non-ported barrel, adj. hammer tension and trigger overtravel stop, includes scope base mounts. Mfg. 2003-2004.

$485 $425 $365 $330 $265 $220 $170 *$602*

MODEL 44C TRACKER – .44 Mag. cal., 5 shot, blue or matte stainless steel, 4 in. ported barrel, adj. rear sight, Ribber grips, 34 oz. New 2005.

MSR $660 $540 $460 $390 $345 $280 $230 $175

Add $48 for matte stainless steel.

MODEL 45-410 "THE JUDGE" (44-TEN TRACKER) – .45 LC/.410 shotshell cal., 2 1/2 or 3 (new 2008) in. chamber, SA/DA, 5 shot, 2 1/2 (disc.), 3 (new 2007), or 6 /12 (not available in 3 in. chamber) in. barrel, blue or stainless, fiber optic front sight, Ribber grips, compact frame, 29 or 32 oz. New 2006.

MSR $620 $515 $460 $390 $325 $285 $225 $175

Add $48 for 3 or 6 1/2 (new 2013) in. cylinder. Add $39 for 2 1/2 in. cylinder with ported barrel and accessory rail (mfg. 2010-2012).
Add $156 for Crimson Trace laser grips (mfg. 2010-2012).
During late 2007, this model's nomenclature changed to the Model 45-410 Judge.

* ***Model 45-410 The Judge Stainless (44-Ten Tracker Stainless)*** – similar to Model 45-410, except is matte stainless steel, 29, 32, or 36.8 (3 in. chamber) oz. New 2006.

MSR $668 $560 $495 $430 $380 $310 $250 $195

Add $48 for 3 in. cylinder. Add $31 for 2 1/2 in. cylinder with ported barrel and accessory rail (mfg. 2010-2012).
Add $157 for Crimson Trace laser grips (mfg. 2010-2012).

* ***Model 45-410 The Judge Ultra-Lite*** – similar to Model 45-410 Judge, 2 1/2 in. barrel, except has alloy frame, choice of blued steel or stainless steel cylinder, not available in 3 in. cylinder, 22.4 oz. Mfg. 2008-2011.

$575 $505 $430 $390 $315 $260 $200 *$648*

Add $32 for stainless steel barrel and cylinder. Add $313 for Crimson Trace laser grips (new 2010).

MODEL 45-410 "THE JUDGE" PUBLIC DEFENDER – .45/.410 shotshell, 2 in. barrel, similar to original Judge, except only available with 2 1/2 in. chamber, blue or matte stainless, steel or titanium cylinder, reduced profile hammer, Ribber grips, 28.2 oz. New mid-2009.

MSR $620 $515 $460 $390 $315 $285 $225 $175

GRADING - PPGS™	100%	98%	95%	90%	80%	70%	60%	LAST MSR

Add $48 for stainless steel cylinder or $78 for titanium cylinder (disc. 2011).
Add $47 for pink Ribber grips (mfg. 2010-2011) or $82 for pink Ribber grips and Bulldog Case (mfg. 2010-2011).

* ***Model 45-410 "The Judge" Public Defender Ultra-Lite*** – similar to Model 45-410 The Judge Public Defender, except has ultra-lite aluminum frame and choice of blue steel or stainless, 2 1/2 in. cylinder, 20.7 oz. Mfg. 2011 only.

	$575	$505	$430	$390	$315	$260	$200	*$648*

Add $32 for stainless steel barrel and cylinder.

* ***Model 45-410 "The Judge" Public Defender Polymer*** – similar to Model 45-410 The Judge Public Defender, except has black light-weight polymer frame, choice of 2 1/2 in. blue (disc. 2011) or stainless cylinder, 27 oz. New 2011.

MSR $668	$560	$495	$430	$380	$310	$250	$195	

Subtract approx. 10% for blue cylinder (disc. 2011).

* ***Model 45-410FS Polymer*** – .45 LC/.410 bore, features polymer frame with blued steel cylinder, 2 1/2 in. chamber, 23 oz. New 2013.

MSR $399	$350	$315	$285	$260	$240	$220	$200	

MODEL 45 RAGING BULL – .45 LC cal., 6 shot, 6 1/2 or 8 3/8 in. VR ported barrel, adj. sights, soft rubber grips, 53 or 63 oz. Mfg. 1999-2001.

	$475	$425	$365	$325	$265	$215	$190	*$575*

* ***Model 45 .45 LC Raging Bull Stainless*** – similar to Model 45 Raging Bull, except is stainless steel. Disc. 2001.

	$530	$465	$395	$360	$290	$240	$185	*$630*

MODEL 65 – .357 Mag./.38 Spl. cal., medium frame, SA/DA, 6 shot, fixed sights, 2 1/2 (mfg. 1993-97), 3 (disc. 1992) or 4 in. full underlug barrel, blue finish, checkered walnut (disc.) or rubber (new 1999) grips, 38 oz. Disc. 1997, reintroduced 1999.

MSR $499	$390	$335	$285	$250	$200	$165	$130	

Add $15 for satin nickel finish (disc.).

* ***Model 65SS (Stainless Steel)*** – similar to Model 65, except is matte finished stainless steel. Mfg. 1993-97, reintroduced 1999.

MSR $547	$425	$345	$290	$255	$205	$170	$130	

MODEL 66 – .357 Mag./.38 Spl. cal., medium frame, SA/DA, 6 (disc. 2001) or 7 (new 1999) shot, 2 1/2 (mfg. 1993-97), 3 (disc. 1992), 4 or 6 in. barrel, checkered walnut (disc. 1999) or rubber (new 2000) grips, blue finish, adj. sights, 38-40 oz. Disc. 1997, reintroduced 1999.

MSR $555	$425	$345	$290	$255	$215	$170	$130	

Add $15 for satin nickel finish (disc.).
Add $10 for 4 or 6 in. compensated (66CP) barrel (mfg. 1993-94).

* ***Model 66SS (Stainless Steel)*** – similar to Model 66, but in stainless steel. Mfg. 1987-97, reintroduced 1999.

MSR $604	$495	$425	$365	$315	$255	$205	$160	

Add $10 for 4 or 6 in. compensated (66CP) barrel (mfg. 1993-94).

* ***Model 66 Silhouette/Hunter*** – .357 Mag./.38 Spl. cal., 7 shot, 12 in. barrel with adj. sights, rubber grips, adj. hammer tension and trigger overtravel stop became standard 2003, includes scope mount. Mfg. 2001-2004.

	$330	$290	$250	$210	$180	$150	$130	*$430*

* ***Model 66 Silhouette/Hunter SS (Stainless Steel)*** – similar to Model 66 Silhouette/Hunter, except is matte finished stainless steel. Mfg. 2001-2004.

	$380	$340	$290	$245	$210	$170	$150	*$477*

MODEL 73 – .32 Long cal. only, double action, 6 shot, 3 in. heavy barrel only, checkered walnut grips, 20 oz. Disc. 1992.

	$190	$165	$140	$130	$105	$85	$65	*$223*

Add $20 for satin nickel finish.

GRADING - PPGS™	100%	98%	95%	90%	80%	70%	60%	LAST MSR

MODEL 76 – .32 H&R Mag. cal., double action, 6 shot, 6 in. heavy barrel with solid rib, fully adj. rear sight, transfer bar safety, checkered hard wood grips, blue only, 34 oz. Mfg. 1991-94.

	$240	$210	$180	$165	$130	$110	$85	*$308*

MODEL 80 – .38 Spl. cal. only, double action, 6 shot, 3 or 4 in. barrel, checkered walnut grips, fixed sights, 30 oz. Disc. 1996.

	$190	$165	$140	$130	$105	$85	$65	*$252*

Add $15 for satin nickel finish (disc. 1992).

* ***Model 80SS (Stainless Steel)*** – similar to Model 80, except stainless steel. Mfg. 1993-97.

	$245	$215	$185	$165	$135	$110	$85	*$313*

MODEL 82 SECURITY – .38 Spl. cal. only, medium frame, SA/DA, 6 shot, 3 (disc. 1998) or 4 in. heavy barrel, checkered walnut (disc.) or rubber (new 1999) grips, full underlug, fixed sights, blue finish, 36.5 oz.

MSR $481	$370	$315	$265	$235	$190	$155	$120	

Add $15 for satin nickel finish (disc.).

* ***Model 82SS (Stainless Steel) Security*** – similar to Model 82, except is polished stainless steel. New 1993.

MSR $514	$400	$345	$295	$260	$210	$175	$135	

MODEL 83 – .38 Spl. cal. only, double action, 6 shot, 4 in. heavy barrel, checkered walnut grips, adj. sights, 34 1/2 oz. Disc. 1998.

	$220	$190	$165	$150	$120	$100	$75	*$278*

Add $13 for satin nickel finish.

* ***Model 83SS (Stainless Steel)*** – similar to Model 83, except stainless steel. Mfg. 1993-98.

	$250	$210	$190	$165	$145	$120	$100	*$324*

MODEL 85 – .38 Spl.+P cal. only, small frame, SA/DA, 5 shot, 2 or 3 (disc. 2001, reintroduced 2006) in. heavy ported (new 1997) or unported barrel, hammer forged frame, bobbed (mfg. 2011 only) or exposed hammer, checkered walnut (disc. 2000) or soft rubber boot grips, fixed sights, 21-24 1/2 oz. Disc. 2012.

	$345	$300	$260	$235	$190	$155	$120	*$445*

Add $53 for pink pearl grips (disc. 2011).
Add $16 for bobbed hammer (mfg. 2011 only) or ported barrel (disc. 2003).
Add $20 for satin nickel finish (3 in. barrel only, disc. 1992).
Subtract $15 for Hy-Lite magnesium grey finish (disc.).

* ***Model 85SS (Stainless Steel)*** – stainless version of Model 85. Disc. 2012.

	$385	$335	$290	$260	$210	$175	$135	*$492*

Add $53 for pink pearl grips (disc. 2011).
Add $47 for gold accents and rosewood grips (disc. 2011).
Add $16 for ported barrel (mfg. 1997-2003).

* ***Model 85CH (Blue or Stainless)*** – similar to Model 85, except has Brazilian hardwood combat (disc. 2000) or soft rubber grips and spurless concealed hammer that fits flush with the frame, 2 in. barrel, double action only, 21 oz. Mfg. 1992-2004.

	$285	$250	$215	$195	$155	$130	$100	*$375*

Add $16 for ported barrel (disc. 2003).
Add $47 for polished stainless steel.

* ***Model 85 Titanium Ultra-Lightweight*** – features titanium barrel and cylinder and choice of matte aluminum or stainless steel (disc. 2001) small frame, fixed sight, rubber grips, choice of hammer or concealed hammer (Police Model 85), 17 oz. Mfg. 1999-2010.

	$535	$470	$400	$365	$295	$240	$185	*$648*

Add $94 for Crimson Trace laser grips (disc. 2008).

GRADING - PPGS™	100%	98%	95%	90%	80%	70%	60%	LAST MSR

* ***Model 85PLYB2/Protector Ply*** – .38 Spl.+P cal., small frame, 5 shot, features lightweight polymer frame and checkered wood colored polymer grips, blued or stainless cylinder assembly, ambidextrous thumb safety, 1 1/4 or 1 3/4 in. barrel with VR in high vis. fiber optic front sight, 16.5 oz. Mfg. 2011-2012.

	$355	$300	$260	$235	$190	$155	$120	*$461*

* ***Model 85T*** – similar to Model 85, except 100% titanium construction, 2 in. ported barrel only, choice of bright spectrum blue, matte spectrum blue, matte spectrum gold, stealth grey (mfg. 2000 only), or shadow grey (new 2000) finish, 15.4 oz. Mfg. 1999-2006.

	$530	$465	$395	$360	$290	$240	$185	*$625*

Add $39 for blue and gold titanium finish and mother-of-pearl grips (disc. 2004, reintroduced 2006).

* ***Model 85 Special Edition/Deluxe*** – features blue finish with gold trim or stainless/gold trim, ported 2 in. barrel, rosewood or mother-of-pearl grips, includes integral key lock. Mfg. 1998-2011.

	$380	$335	$285	$260	$210	$170	$135	*$492*

Add $47 for stainless/gold trim with rosewood grips.
Add $16 for blue/gold trim with faux mother-of-pearl grips.
Add $57 for stainless/gold trim with faux mother-of-pearl grips.

* ***Model 85 Ultra-Lite*** – ultra-lightweight version of Model 85 using an alloy frame, choice of blue or gray finish, 17 oz. Disc. 2012.

	$335	$295	$250	$230	$185	$150	$115	*$430*

Add $53 for pink pearl grips (disc. 2011).
Add $177 for LG185 (new 2012) or $312 (disc. 2011) for Crimson Trace laser grips (new 2009).

» **Model 85SSUL Ultra-Lite Stainless** – matte stainless variation of the Model 85 Ultra-Lite, 17 oz. Disc. 2012.

	$360	$315	$270	$245	$200	$160	$125	*$461*

Add $125 for LG-185 (new 2012) or $312 (disc. 2011) for Crimson Trace grips.
Add $53 for pink pearl grips (mfg. 2010-2011).

» **Model 85 Ultra-Lite Deluxe** – ported barrel, choice of blue/gold or stainless/gold, mother-of-pearl (new 2000) or rosewood grips, 17 oz. Mfg. 1999-2011.

	$400	$350	$285	$260	$210	$170	$130	*$530*

Add $9 for matte stainless/gold and rosewood grips.
Add $31 for matte stainless/gold finish with faux mother-of-pearl grips.

MODEL 85FS SERIES – .38 Spl.+P cal., 2 in. barrel, 6 shot, SA/DA, textured rubber grips with finger grooves, blue finish, 21 oz. New 2013.

MSR $299	$250	$225	$195	$175	$150	$135	$120	

* ***Model 85FS Stainless*** – .38 Spl.+P cal., similar to Model 85FS, except is stainless steel, 22 1/2 oz. New 2013.

MSR $319	$265	$235	$200	$175	$150	$135	$120	

* ***Model 85FS Polymer*** – .38 Spl.+P cal., similar to Model 85FS, except features polymer frame and steel cylinder, 16 1/2 oz. New 2013.

MSR $299	$250	$225	$195	$175	$150	$135	$120	

» **Model 85FS Polymer Stainless** – .38 Spl.+P cal., similar to Model 85FS Polymer, except features polymer frame and stainless steel cylinder, 16 1/2 oz. New 2013.

MSR $319	$265	$235	$200	$175	$150	$135	$120	

* ***Model 85FS Ultra-Lite*** – .38 Spl.+ P cal., similar to Model 85FS, except features aluminum frame, 17 oz. New 2013.

MSR $309	$255	$230	$195	$175	$150	$135	$120	

» **Model 85FS Stainless Ultra-Lite** – .38 Spl.+ P cal., similar to Model 85FS Ultra-Lite, except features aluminum frame and stainless steel cylinder, 17 oz. New 2013.

MSR $329	$275	$240	$200	$180	$150	$135	$120	

GRADING - PPGS™	100%	98%	95%	90%	80%	70%	60%	LAST MSR

MODEL 86 CUSTOM TARGET – .38 Spl. cal. only, double action target model, 6 shot, 6 in. barrel, specially contoured smooth walnut grips, adj. rear sight, blue only, 34 oz. Disc. 1994.

	$270	$235	$200	$185	$150	$120	$95	*$352*

This model was available in either single or double action with adj. counterweight and interchangeable front sight inserts.

MODEL 94 – .22 LR cal., small frame, SA/DA, 9 shot, 2 (new 1997), 3 (mfg. 1991-98), 4 or 5 (new 1996) in. barrel, full underlug on 4 or 5 in. barrel, blue finish, adj. rear sight, target features, 25 oz. New 1989.

MSR $438	$340	$290	$240	$215	$175	$140	$110	

* ***Model 94 Ultra-Lite*** – .22 LR cal., ultra light hammer forged frame, 2 in. barrel, available in matte blue or bright stainless steel, 18 oz. New 1999.

MSR $481	$370	$300	$250	$220	$180	$145	$115	

Add $32 for matte stainless steel construction.

* ***Model 94SS (Stainless Steel)*** – .22 LR cal., stainless version of Model 94. New 1990.

MSR $486	$375	$320	$270	$240	$195	$160	$125	

MODEL 96 TARGET SCOUT – .22 LR cal. only, double action, 6 shot, 6 in. barrel, checkered walnut grips, same features as Model 86, 34 oz. Disc. 1998.

	$275	$235	$205	$175	$150	$125	$110	*$376*

MODEL 218 RAGING BEE – .218 Bee cal., large frame, 8 shot, 10 in. heavy VR barrel with full shroud and adj. sights, matte stainless steel, includes scope mounts, 50 oz. Mfg. 2003-2004.

	$795	$695	$600	$525	$465	$390	$295	*$898*

MODEL 218 SILHOUETTE/HUNTER – .218 Bee cal., large frame, 7 shot, double action, 12 in. VR barrel with partial shroud, matte stainless steel, rubber boot grips, adj. hammer tension and trigger overtravel stop, includes scope mounts, 49.8 oz. Mfg. 2003-2004.

	$400	$350	$300	$260	$215	$175	$155	*$461*

MODEL 327 – .327 Federal cal., small frame, 2 in. barrel, blue or matte stainless, with or w/o concealed hammer, 6 shot, fixed sights, rubber grips. Mfg. mid-2009-2010.

	$360	$315	$270	$245	$200	$160	$125	*$467*

Add $47 for stainless steel. Add $10 for blue frame with concealed hammer. Add $63 for stainless steel frame with concealed hammer.

MODEL 380 IB – .380 ACP cal., 5 shot, 1 3/4 in. barrel, adj. rear sight, textured rubber grips, blue finish, marked "Taurus Ultra-Lite" on left side of frame, bobbed hammer, DAO, 15 1/2 oz. New 2012.

MSR $443	$340	$290	$240	$215	$175	$140	$110	

* ***Model 380 IB Stainless*** – .380 ACP cal., similar to Model 308, except is matte stainless steel. New 2012.

MSR $475	$375	$320	$270	$240	$195	$160	$125	

MODEL 405 – .40 S&W cal., medium frame, 5 shot mag., SA/DA, fixed sights, blue finish, Ribber grips, 29 oz. Mfg. 2011-2012.

	$365	$315	$270	$240	$195	$160	$125	*$477*

* ***Model 405SS (Stainless Steel)*** – similar to Model 405, except has stainless steel finish. Mfg. 2011-2012.

MSR $523	$400	$340	$295	$260	$210	$175	$135	

MODEL 415SS – .41 Mag. cal., compact frame, 5 shot, similar to Model 415T, except has matte stainless steel construction, Ribber grips, 30 oz. Mfg. 1999-disc.

	$435	$385	$335	$285	$235	$190	$170	*$508*

MODEL 415T – .41 Mag. cal., compact frame, 5 shot, all titanium construction, 2 1/2 in. ported barrel with fixed sights, choice of bright spectrum blue (disc. 2001), matte spectrum blue (disc. 2001), matte gold (mfg. 1999 only), stealth grey (mfg. 2000 only), or shadow grey (new 2000) finish, Ribber grips. Mfg. 1999-2003.

	$500	$435	$375	$340	$275	$225	$175	*$602*

GRADING - PPGS™	100%	98%	95%	90%	80%	70%	60%	LAST MSR

MODEL 415SS TRACKER – .41 Mag. cal., medium frame, 5 shot, 2 1/2 in. barrel, stainless steel, fixed sights, Ribber grips, 30 oz. Mfg. 2006-2011.

	$500	$430	$375	$330	$265	$210	$185	*$623*

MODEL 416 SS RAGING BULL – .41 Mag. cal., large frame, 6 shot, 6 1/2 or 8 3/8 in. ported heavy barrel with VR, adj. sights, matte stainless steel, rubber grips with cushion inserts, 53 or 63 oz. Mfg. 2003-2011.

	$650	$570	$490	$440	$360	$295	$230	*$780*

MODEL 425 SS TRACKER – .41 Mag. cal., medium frame, 5 shot, similar to Model 415T, 4 in. ported barrel with full shroud, adj. sights with red inserts, Ribber grips, stainless steel with matte finish, 34.8 oz. Mfg. 2000-2012.

	$515	$440	$380	$330	$265	$210	$185	*$655*

MODEL 425T TRACKER – similar to Model 425 Tracker, except is all titanium construction, choice of stealth grey (mfg. 2000 only) or matte shadow grey finish, 4 or 6 in. barrel, adj. sights, 24.3 oz. Mfg. 2000-2006.

	$625	$545	$470	$425	$345	$280	$220	*$766*

MODEL 431 – .44 Spl. cal., 5 shot, 2 (new 1995), 3, or 4 in. barrel, blue only, fixed sights. Mfg. 1993-97.

	$220	$190	$165	$150	$120	$100	$75	*$286*

* ***Model 431SS (Stainless Steel)*** – similar to Model 431, except stainless steel. Mfg. 1993-97.

	$285	$250	$215	$195	$155	$130	$100	*$368*

MODEL 441 – similar to Model 431, except has 3, 4, or 6 in. barrel, adj. sights. Mfg. 1993-97.

	$240	$210	$180	$165	$130	$110	$85	*$313*

* ***Model 441SS (Stainless Steel)*** – similar to Model 441, except is stainless steel. Mfg. 1993-97.

	$350	$310	$265	$225	$190	$155	$135	*$468*

MODEL 444 RAGING BULL – .44 Mag. cal., large frame, 6 shot, 6 1/2 or 8 3/8 in. VR ported barrel with full shroud and adj. sights, soft rubber grips with cushion inserts, 53 or 63 oz. New 1999.

MSR $769	$630	$535	$455	$400	$320	$265	$205	

* ***Model 444 Raging Bull Stainless*** – .44 Mag. cal., similar to Model 444, except is matte stainless steel. New 1999.

MSR $818	$665	$575	$480	$430	$345	$280	$220	

* ***Model 444 Raging Bull Ultra-Lite Multi*** – .44 Mag. cal., 6 shot, 2 1/2 or 4 in. barrel, blue alloy or stainless steel Raging Bull style frame with titanium cylinder, rubber grips with finger grooves and insert cushion, fiber optic front sight, 28.3 oz. New 2005.

MSR $810	$670	$545	$455	$400	$320	$260	$200	

Add $48 for matte stainless steel frame.

Add $15 for 4 in. barrel with adj. rear sight (disc. 2011).

MODEL 445 – .44 Spl. cal., compact frame, 5 shot, 2 in. ported (new 1999) or standard barrel, fixed sights, blue or stainless, Ribber or rubber grips, 28 oz. Mfg. 1997-2003.

	$280	$245	$210	$190	$155	$125	$100	*$359*

Add $16 for ported barrel (new 1999).

* ***Model 445 Concealed Hammer*** – similar to Model 445, except w/o hammer, ported or unported barrel. Mfg. 1999-2003.

	$280	$245	$210	$190	$155	$125	$100	*$359*

Add $16 for ported barrel.

GRADING - PPGS™	100%	98%	95%	90%	80%	70%	60%	LAST MSR

* ***Model 445 Concealed Hammer Stainless*** – similar to Model 445 Concealed Hammer, except is stainless steel. Mfg. 1999-2003.

	$310	$270	$230	$210	$170	$140	$110	*$406*

Add $16 for ported barrel.

* ***Model 445 SS (Stainless Steel)*** – stainless variation of the Model 445. Mfg. 1997-2003.

	$310	$270	$230	$210	$170	$140	$110	*$406*

Add $16 for ported barrel.

* ***Model 445 Ultra-Lite*** – .44 Spl. cal., features ported (disc. 2002) or unported (new 2012) 2 in. barrel, blue or matte stainless steel, 22 oz., Ribber grips on new mfg. Mfg. 1999-2002, re-introduced 2012 only.

	$395	$340	$295	$260	$210	$175	$135	*$508*

Add $31 for matte stainless steel.

* ***Model 445 Ultra-lite Concealed Carry*** – features stainless steel or titanium frame, ported 2 in. barrel, walnut combat grips. Mfg. 2002 only.

	$370	$325	$275	$250	$205	$165	$130	*$500*

Add $100 for titanium construction.

MODEL 445T – .44 Spl. cal., 5 shot, all titanium construction, 2 in. ported barrel with fixed sights, choice of bright spectrum blue, matte spectrum blue, matte gold (mfg. 1999 only), stealth grey (new 2000), or shadow grey (new 2000) finish, Ribber grips. Mfg. 1999-2002.

	$500	$435	$375	$340	$275	$225	$175	*$600*

MODEL 450 – .45 LC cal., 5 shot, compact frame, similar to Model 450T, except is matte stainless steel, also available in Ultra-Lite variation, Ribber grips, 20 (Ultra Lite) or 28 oz. Mfg. 1999-2005.

	$425	$375	$325	$275	$225	$185	$165	*$492*

Add $31 for Ultra-Lite Model.

MODEL 450T – .45 LC cal., 5 shot, all titanium construction, 2 in. ported barrel with fixed sights, choice of bright spectrum blue, matte spectrum blue, matte gold (mfg. 1999 only), stealth grey (new 2000), or shadow grey (new 2000) finish, Ribber grips. Mfg. 1999-2002.

	$500	$435	$375	$340	$275	$225	$175	*$600*

MODEL 454 RAGING BULL – .454 Casull cal., large frame, SA/DA, 5 shot, front and rear cylinder locks, bright blue or case colored (new 1999) finish, 2 1/4 (mfg. 2005-2006), 5 (case colored, disc. 2000), 6 1/2 or 8 3/8 in. full lug ported barrel with integral VR, soft black rubber grips with recoil absorbing insert, micrometer adj. rear sight, transfer bar safety, integral key lock, 53-63 oz. Mfg. 1998-2012.

	$850	$735	$625	$560	$460	$365	$285	*$1,016*

Add $96 for case colored frame (disc. 2000).
Subtract $53 for 2 1/4 in. ported barrel (disc.).

* ***Model 454 Casull Raging Bull Stainless*** – .454 Casull cal., similar to Model 454 Casull Raging Bull, except is stainless steel, 2 1/2 (new 2007), 5, 6 1/2 or 8 3/8 in. barrel, satin (6 1/2 in. barrel only, disc. 2000) or matte (new 1999) stainless finish. New 1998.

MSR $1,078	$900	$775	$650	$595	$475	$385	$300	

Add $16 for 5, 6 1/2, or 8 3/8 in. barrel.

* ***Model 454 Casull Raging Bull Silhouette*** – similar to Model 454 Casull Raging Bull Stainless, except has 12 in. non-ported barrel with adj. sights, adj. hammer tension and trigger overtravel stop. Mfg. 2003-2004.

	$725	$640	$565	$485	$425	$360	$280	*$859*

MODEL 455 TRACKER – .45 ACP cal., compact frame, 5 shot, 2, 4 or 6 in. ported barrel, adj. rear sight, matte stainless steel, includes 5 Stellar full moon clips, Ribber grips. Mfg. 2002-2004.

	$450	$400	$350	$310	$250	$200	$180	*$523*

GRADING - PPGS™	100%	98%	95%	90%	80%	70%	60%	LAST MSR

* ***Model 455 Tracker Titanium*** – similar to Model 455 Tracker, except has titanium construction with shadow gray finish. Mfg. 2004 only.

	$525	$460	$395	$355	$290	$235	$185	*$625*

MODEL 460 TRACKER – .45 LC cal., compact frame, 5 shot, 4 or 6 1/2 in. VR ported barrel, adj. sights, matte stainless steel. Mfg. 2003-2004.

	$445	$395	$345	$295	$240	$195	$175	*$516*

* ***Model 460T Tracker*** – similar to Model 460 Tracker, except has titanium construction, 4 VR or non-VR 6 1/2 in. barrel. Mfg. 2003-2004.

	$565	$495	$425	$385	$310	$255	$200	*$688*

MODEL 465 RAGING BULL – .460 S&W Mag. cal., large frame, 2 1/2, 4, 6 1/2, or 10 in. ported barrel, matte stainless steel construction, fixed or adj. sights, soft rubber grips. Mfg. 2006.

	$750	$650	$575	$500	$440	$375	$290	*$880*

MODEL 480 RUGER RAGING BULL – .480 Ruger cal., large frame, 5 shot, 5 (limited mfg.), 6 1/2, or 8 3/8 in. VR barrel, matte stainless finish only, otherwise similar to Model 454 Casull, 51-63 oz. Mfg. 2001-2005.

	$525	$460	$395	$355	$290	$235	$185	*$641*

MODEL 500 – .500 S&W Mag. cal., 5 shot, 2 1/2 (fixed sights only, new 2006), 4 (new 2006), 6 1/2 (new 2006), or 10 in. ported barrel, adj. rear sight, soft rubber cushioned grips, stainless steel only, 68-72 oz. Mfg. mid-2005-2007.

	$775	$665	$585	$515	$450	$385	$290	*$934*

Subtract $17 for 2 1/2 in. barrel.

MODEL 513 RAGING JUDGE MAGNUM – interchangeably shoots .454 Casull, .45 LC, or .410 ga., 3 in. non-fluted cylinder, large frame, 6 shot, SA/DA, 3 (non-ported) or 6 1/2 (VR) in. barrel with Hi-Viz fiber optic front sight, rubber grips with cushion inserts and red "Raging Bull" backstrap, blue or matte stainless finish, 60.6 or 72.7 oz. New 2011.

MSR $1,012	$850	$740	$660	$595	$550	$495	$450

* ***Model 513 Raging Judge Magnum SS*** – similar to Model 513 Raging Judge Magnum, except is matte stainless steel.

MSR $1,061	$910	$810	$720	$630	$550	$495	$450

MODEL 513 RAGING JUDGE MAGNUM ULTRA-LITE – .45 LC cal./.410 bore with 3 in. cylinder, SA/DA, 7 shot, 3 or 6 1/2 in. barrel with high vis. fiber optic front sights, features Ultra-Lite frame, blue finish, rubber grips with cushion inserts, 41.4 or 47.2 oz. Mfg. 2011-2012.

	$825	$725	$650	$595	$550	$495	$450	*$983*

* ***Model 513 Raging Judge Magnum Ultra-Lite SS*** – similar to Model 513 Raging Judge Magnum Ultra-Lite, except is matte stainless steel. Mfg. 2011-2012.

	$885	$795	$715	$630	$550	$495	$450	*$1,030*

MODEL 528 RAGING JUDGE – 28 ga., large frame, 5 shot, SA/DA, 6 1/2 in. VR rifled barrel with high vis. fiber optic front sight, unfluted cylinder, blue or matte stainless finish, black rubber grips with cushion inserts and red "Raging Bull" backstrap, 67 oz. Advertised 2011.

While advertised during 2011, this model never went into production.

MODEL 590 TRACKER – 5mm Rem. Rimfire Mag. cal., medium frame, SA/DA, 9 shot, 6 1/2 in. barrel, blue finish, adj. sights, Ribber grips, 43.7 oz. Mfg. late 2008-2011.

	$360	$315	$270	$245	$200	$160	$125	*$467*

* ***Model 590 Tracker SS*** – similar to Model 590 Tracker, except is matte stainless steel. Mfg. late 2008-2011.

	$400	$330	$280	$255	$205	$170	$130	*$514*

MODEL 605 – .357 Mag. cal., small frame, 5 shot, 2 in. unported (new 2002), 2 1/4 (disc. 2005), or 3 (mfg. 1996-98, reintroduced 2006) in. barrel, blue steel, 4 port compensated barrel (2 1/4 in. only) with fixed sights, exposed or concealed (Model 605CH, mfg. 1997-

GRADING - PPGS™	100%	98%	95%	90%	80%	70%	60%	LAST MSR

2005, 2 1/4 in. barrel) hammer, full barrel shroud, oversized finger grooved rubber grips, 24 1/2 oz. New 1995.

MSR $459	$350	$310	$260	$230	$185	$155	$120	

Add $16 for ported barrel (disc. 2003).
Add $303 for Crimson Trace laser grips (disc. 2011).

* ***Model 605 SS (Stainless Steel)*** – stainless variation of the Model 605.

MSR $507	$385	$330	$280	$250	$200	$165	$130	

Add $16 for ported barrel (disc. 2003).
Add $303 for Crimson Trace laser grips (mfg. 2008-2011).

* ***Model 605T Titanium*** – similar to Model 605, except is titanium with shadow grey finish. Mfg. 2005-2006.

	$535	$470	$400	$365	$295	$240	$185	*$625*

* ***Model 605PLYB2/Protector Ply*** – .357 Mag. cal., small frame, 5 shot, features lightweight polymer frame, Ribber grips, blued or stainless cylinder assembly, ambidextrous thumb safety, 1 or 2 in. barrel with VR in high vis. fiber optic front sight, 19 3/4 oz. New 2011.

MSR $459	$350	$310	$260	$230	$185	$155	$120	

Add $16 for stainless steel cylinder (new 2012).

MODEL 606 – .357 Mag. cal., 6 shot, 2 or 2 1/4 in. uncompensated or compensated barrel, exposed or concealed hammer, fixed sights. Mfg. 1997-98.

	$235	$205	$175	$160	$130	$105	$80	*$296*

Add $19 for ported barrel (2 in. only).

* ***Model 606 SS (Stainless Steel)*** – stainless variation of the Model 606. Disc. 1998.

	$260	$225	$195	$175	$145	$115	$90	*$344*

Add $20 for ported barrel (2 in. only).

MODEL 607 – .357 Mag. cal., 7 shot, 4 or 6 1/2 (VR) in. compensated barrel, adj. rear sight, Santoprene synthetic grips, 44 oz. Mfg. 1995-97.

	$335	$295	$250	$215	$185	$150	$130	*$447*

Add $18 for 6 1/2 in. VR barrel.

* ***Model 607SS (Stainless Steel)*** – stainless variation of the Model 607. Mfg. 1995-97.

	$375	$335	$285	$240	$200	$165	$150	*$508*

Add $20 for 6 1/2 in. VR barrel.

MODEL 608 – .357 Mag. cal., large frame, 8 shot, 3 (mfg. 1997-98), 4, 6 1/2 (VR), or 8 3/8 (VR, new 1997) in. barrel with integral compensator, rubber finger grooves, exposed or concealed (mfg. 1997-2010, 3 in. barrel) hammer, adj. sights, 44-56 oz. Mfg. 1996-2004.

	$355	$315	$270	$225	$190	$155	$135	*$469*

Add $15 for 6.5 or 8 3/8 in. VR ported barrel.

* ***Model 608SS (Stainless Steel)*** – .357 Mag. cal., matte stainless variation of the Model 608, 3 (disc.), 4, 6 1/2, or 8 3/8 (disc. 2012) in. barrel, 51 or 56 oz. New 1996.

MSR $702	$540	$460	$380	$335	$270	$225	$175	

Add $22 for 6 1/2 or 8 3/8 (disc. 2012) in. VR barrel.

MODEL 617 – .357 Mag. cal., medium frame, 7 shot, double action, 2 in. regular or ported (disc.) barrel, fixed sights, exposed or concealed (Model 617CH, disc. 2005) hammer, rubber (disc. 2006) or Ribber (new 2007) grips, 28.3 oz. Mfg. 1998-2012.

	$415	$360	$300	$270	$215	$180	$140	*$508*

Add $15 for ported barrel (disc. 2003).

* ***Model 617SS (Stainless Steel)*** – .357 Mag. cal., similar to Model 617, except is polished (disc. 2007) or matte stainless steel. New 1998.

MSR $571	$455	$390	$330	$290	$235	$190	$150	

Add $15 for ported barrel (disc. 2003).

GRADING - PPGS™	100%	98%	95%	90%	80%	70%	60%	LAST MSR

* ***Model 617 ULT*** – similar to Model 617, except is 5 shot, aluminum alloy receiver and titanium cylinder, matte stainless finish, 2 in. regular or ported barrel, soft rubber grips. Mfg. 2001-2002.

	$455	$400	$340	$310	$250	$205	$160	*$530*

Add $15 for ported barrel.

* ***Model 617T*** – .357 Mag. cal., compact frame, 7 shot, all titanium construction, 2 in. ported barrel with fixed sights, choice of bright spectrum blue, matte spectrum blue (disc. 2001), matte gold (mfg. 1999 only), stealth grey (mfg. 2000 only), or shadow grey (new 2000) finish, Ribber grips, 19.9 oz. Mfg. 1999-2006.

	$550	$480	$410	$375	$300	$245	$190	*$680*

MODEL 627 SS TRACKER – .357 Mag. cal., medium frame, 7 shot, 4 or 6 1/2 (new 2001, VR) in. ported barrel, adj. sights, heavy full underlug, stainless steel with matte finish, Ribber grips, 28.8 or 40 oz. New 2000.

MSR $684	$530	$455	$380	$335	$270	$225	$175	

* ***Model 627T Tracker*** – .357 Mag. cal., 7 shot, all titanium construction, 4 or 6 1/2 (new 2001, non-VR) in. ported barrel, adj. sights, choice of stealth grey (disc. 2001) or shadow grey finish, Ribber grips, 24.3 or 28 oz. Mfg. 2000-2006.

	$610	$535	$455	$415	$335	$275	$215	*$766*

MODEL 650 CIA – .357 Mag. cal., small frame, 5 shot, DAO, hammerless, 2 in. barrel, fixed sights, soft rubber boot grips, blue finish, 24.2 oz. New 2001.

MSR $523	$395	$340	$285	$250	$200	$165	$130	

* ***Model 650 CIA SS (Stainless Steel)*** – similar to Model 650 CIA, except is matte stainless steel. Mfg. 2001-2012.

	$415	$340	$285	$255	$205	$170	$130	*$555*

MODEL 651 PROTECTOR (CIA) – .357 Mag. cal., small frame, 5 shot, 2 in. barrel, SA/DA, shrouded zero profile hammer, soft rubber boot grips, 25 oz. Mfg. 2003-2012.

	$365	$315	$270	$240	$195	$160	$125	*$477*

* ***Model 651T Protector*** – similar to Model 651 CIA Protector, except is shadow grey titanium construction, 17.3 oz. Mfg. 2004-2006.

	$510	$445	$380	$345	$280	$230	$180	*$625*

* ***Model 651 Protector SS (CIA)*** – similar to Model 651 Protector, except has matte stainless steel. Mfg. 2003-2012.

	$400	$340	$295	$260	$210	$175	$135	*$523*

MODEL 669 – similar to Model 66 except has fully shrouded 4 or 6 in. barrel, blue finish, 37 oz. Disc. 1998.

	$260	$225	$195	$175	$145	$115	$90	*$344*

Add $10 for VR barrel (mfg. 1989-1992).
Add $400 for Laser Aim Sight (offered 1990-1992).
Add $19 for compensated (669CP) barrel (new 1993).

* ***Model 669SS (Stainless Steel)*** – similar to Model 669, but in stainless steel. Disc. 1998.

	$325	$285	$245	$220	$180	$145	$115	*$421*

Add $21 for compensated (669CP) barrel (new 1993).

MODEL 689 – similar to Model 669, except has VR. Disc. 1998.

	$265	$230	$200	$180	$145	$120	$95	*$358*

Add $390 for Laser Aim Sight (mfg. 1990-91 only).

* ***Model 689SS (Stainless Steel)*** – similar to Model 669, but in stainless steel. Disc. 1999.

	$340	$300	$260	$220	$185	$155	$135	*$435*

MODEL 709FS – 9mm Para. cal., 3 in. barrel, blue finish, checkered polymer grip, 19 oz. New 2013.

MSR $299	$250	$225	$200	$185	$170	$160	$150	

GRADING - PPGS™	100%	98%	95%	90%	80%	70%	60%	LAST MSR

MODEL 731 SS ULTRA-LITE – .32 H&R Mag. cal., small frame, SA/DA, 6 shot, aluminum frame with matte stainless steel cylinder, 2 in. ported barrel, fixed sights, rubber boot grips, 17 oz. Mfg. 1998-2011.

	$390	$330	$280	$255	$205	$170	$130	*$514*

* ***Model 731T*** – .32 H&R Mag. cal., small frame, 6 shot, all titanium construction, 2 in. ported barrel with fixed sights, bright blue (disc. 1999), matte blue, shadow grey (new 2003) or matte gold (disc. 1999) finish, rubber grips. Mfg. 1999, reintroduced 2003-2004.

	$455	$400	$340	$310	$250	$205	$160	*$531*

Subtract $64 for matte blue finish.

MODEL 740FS – .40 S&W cal., 3 in. barrel, blue finish, checkered polymer grip, 19 oz. New 2013.

MSR $299	$250	$225	$200	$185	$170	$160	$150	

MODEL 741 – .32 H&R Mag. cal., 6 shot, 3 or 4 in. barrel, blue only, adj. sights. Mfg. 1993-94.

	$210	$185	$155	$140	$115	$95	$75	*$254*

* ***Model 741SS (Stainless Steel)*** – similar to Model 741, except is stainless steel. Mfg. 1993-94.

	$275	$235	$200	$175	$150	$125	$110	*$342*

MODEL 761 – .32 H&R Mag. cal., 6 shot, 6 in. barrel, blue only, adj. sights. Mfg. 1993-94.

	$250	$210	$190	$165	$145	$120	$100	*$326*

MODEL 817 ULTRA-LITE – .38 Spl.+P cal., medium frame, 7 shot, 2 in. ported (disc. 2002) or unported solid rib barrel, soft rubber (disc. 2006) or Ribber (new 2007) grips, bright blue finish, 21 oz. Mfg. 1999-2012.

	$400	$345	$295	$260	$210	$175	$135	*$508*

Add $20 for ported barrel (disc. 2002).

* ***Model 817 Ultra-Lite Stainless*** – similar to Model 817 Ultra-Lite, except is matte stainless steel. Mfg. 1999-2012.

	$425	$360	$300	$275	$215	$180	$140	*$555*

Add $20 for ported barrel (disc. 2003).

MODEL 827 – .38 Spl.+P cal., 7 shot, 4 in. heavy solid rib barrel, fixed sights, rubber grips, 36 1/2 oz. Mfg. 1999 only.

	$240	$210	$180	$165	$130	$110	$85	*$317*

* ***Model 827 Stainless*** – similar to Model 827, except is stainless steel. Mfg. 1999 only.

	$280	$245	$210	$190	$155	$125	$100	*$364*

MODEL 850 CIA – .38 Spl.+P cal., small frame, 5 shot, hammerless, DAO, 2 in. barrel with fixed sights, rubber boot grips, blue finish, approx. 23 oz. Mfg. 2001-2010.

	$350	$305	$265	$240	$195	$160	$125	*$452*

* ***Model 850 CIA SS (Stainless Steel)*** – similar to Model 850 CIA, except is matte stainless steel. Mfg. 2001-2010.

	$380	$315	$270	$245	$200	$160	$125	*$498*

* ***Model 850 CIA Ultra Lite*** – .38 Spl.+P cal., similar to Model 850 CIA, except is ultralight variation with adj. sight. Mfg. 2005, reintroduced 2008.

MSR $481	$375	$325	$275	$245	$200	$160	$125	

Add $47 for aluminum frame and matte stainless cylinder (disc. 2012).

* ***Model 850T CIA*** – .38 Spl. cal., similar to Model 850 CIA, except has shadow grey finish and all titanium construction, spectrum blue/titanium gold finish and mother-of-pearl grips optional 2005. Mfg. 2001-2009.

	$560	$485	$425	$370	$320	$250	$220	*$701*

Add $47 for blue and gold finish with mother-of-pearl grips (disc. 2006).

GRADING - PPGS™	100%	98%	95%	90%	80%	70%	60%	LAST MSR

MODEL 851 PROTECTOR (CIA) – .38 Spl.+P cal., small frame, 5 shot, 2 in. full underlug barrel, DAO, shrouded hammer, rubber boot grips, 25 oz. Mfg. 2003-2010.

	$350	$305	$265	$240	$195	$160	$125	*$452*

* ***Model 851 Protector SS (Stainless Steel)*** – similar to Model 851 Protector, except is matte stainless steel. Mfg. 2003-2010.

	$380	$315	$270	$245	$200	$160	$125	*$498*

* ***Model 851 Protector Ultra-Lite*** – similar to Model 851 Protector, except is Ultra-Lite model with blue finish and adj. sight. Mfg. 2003-2012.

	$385	$335	$290	$260	$210	$175	$135	*$492*

* ***Model 851 Protector Ultra-Lite Aluminum/Titanium*** – similar to Model 851 Protector Ultra-Lite, except is aluminum/stainless steel or aluminum/titanium. Mfg. 2003-2012.

	$430	$375	$325	$290	$235	$195	$150	*$530*

Add $118 for aluminum/titanium construction (disc. 2010).

* ***Model 851 Protector Titanium*** – similar to Model 851 Protector, except is shadow grey titanium. Mfg. 2003-2004, reintroduced 2006.

	$525	$460	$395	$355	$290	$235	$185	*$625*

Add $39 for spectrum blue/titanium gold finish and mother-of-pearl grips (disc. 2004).

MODEL 856 – .38 Spl.+P cal., compact frame, 6 shot, 2 in. barrel, fixed sights, rubber boot grips, SA/DA, blue finish, 22.2 oz. Mfg. late 2008-2012.

	$350	$295	$250	$225	$185	$150	$115	*$461*

* ***Model 856SS*** – similar to Model 856, except is matte stainless steel. Mfg. late 2008-2012.

	$395	$330	$280	$255	$205	$170	$130	*$508*

Add $8 for adj. sight (disc. 2010).

MODEL 905 – 9mm Para. cal., small frame, 5 shot, 2 in. barrel, rubber boot grips, exposed or concealed (CH Model, disc. 2005) hammer, fixed sights, includes 5 Stellar full moon clips, 21 oz. New 2003.

MSR $491	$375	$300	$255	$220	$180	$145	$115

* ***Model 905SS (Stainless Steel)*** – similar to Model 905, except is stainless steel. New 2003.

MSR $539	$415	$335	$280	$245	$200	$160	$125

* ***Model 905 Ultra-Lite*** – ultra light frame, blue finish. Mfg. 2003-2004.

	$310	$270	$230	$210	$170	$140	$110	*$414*

» **Model 905 Ultra-Lite Stainless** – matte stainless variation of the Model 905 Ultra-Lite. Mfg. 2003-2004.

	$380	$340	$290	$245	$210	$170	$150	*$461*

MODEL 941 – .22 WMR cal., small frame, 8 shot, 2 (new 1997), 3 (disc. 1998), 4, or 5 (disc. 2012) in. barrel, blue only, adj. sights, full underlug on 4 and 5 in. barrels, soft rubber or wood (disc. 2000, 5 in. barrel only) grips, 24-27 1/2 oz. New 1993.

MSR $465	$355	$310	$260	$225	$180	$150	$115

* ***Model 941 Ultra-Lite*** – ultra light hammer forged frame, available in matte blue or bright stainless steel, 2 in. barrel standard beginning 2007, 18 1/2 oz. New 1999.

MSR $499	$380	$320	$260	$225	$185	$150	$115

Add $32 for matte stainless steel construction (2 in. barrel only).

* ***Model 941SS (Stainless Steel)*** – similar to Model 941, except is polished (disc.) or matte stainless steel. New 1993.

MSR $513	$400	$350	$290	$255	$205	$170	$130

GRADING - PPGS™	100%	98%	95%	90%	80%	70%	60%	LAST MSR

MODEL 970 TRACKER – .22 LR cal., medium frame, double action, 7 shot, 6 1/2 in. heavy VR barrel, adj. rear sight, Ribber grips, matte stainless steel or blue finish (new 2007), 45.6 oz. Mfg. 2001-2010.

	$335	$295	$250	$230	$185	$150	$115	*$445*

Add $47 for matte stainless steel.

MODEL 971 TRACKER SS (STAINLESS STEEL) – .22 WMR cal., otherwise similar to Model 970 Tracker, 45.2 oz. Mfg. 2001-2004, and 2006-2010.

	$365	$320	$275	$250	$200	$165	$130	*$498*

MODEL 980 SILHOUETTE/HUNTER SS (STAINLESS STEEL) – .22 LR cal., compact frame, 7 shot, double action, 12 in. heavy barrel, adj. rear sight, Ribber grips, adj. trigger tension and trigger stop, includes scope mount, 56.8 oz. Mfg. 2001-2004.

	$335	$295	$250	$225	$185	$150	$115	*$414*

MODEL 981 SILHOUETTE/HUNTER SS (STAINLESS STEEL) – .22 WMR cal., otherwise similar to Model 980 Silhouette SS, 56.2 oz. Mfg. 2001-2004.

	$350	$310	$265	$225	$190	$155	$135	*$430*

MODEL 990 TRACKER – .22 LR cal., medium frame, 9 shot, 4 or 6 1/2 in. VR barrel with low mount adj. sights, blue finish, rubber boot (disc.) or Ribber grips, 44 oz. Mfg. late 2008-2012.

	$370	$310	$260	$230	$185	$150	$115	*$492*

* ***Model 990 Tracker SS*** – .22 LR cal., similar to Model 990 Tracker, except is matte stainless steel. New late 2008.

MSR $555	$430	$350	$290	$255	$205	$170	$130	

MODEL 991 TRACKER – .22 WMR cal., medium frame, 9 shot, 4 or 6 1/2 in. VR barrel with low mount adj. sights, blue finish, rubber boot (disc.) or Ribber grips, 38 or 44 oz. Mfg. late 2008-2012.

	$370	$310	$260	$230	$185	$150	$115	*$492*

* ***Model 991 Tracker SS*** – similar to Model 991 Tracker, except is matte stainless steel. New late 2008.

MSR $555	$430	$350	$290	$255	$205	$170	$130	

MODEL 992 TRACKER – includes interchangeable 9 shot .22 LR and .22 WMR cylinders, SA/DA, 6 1/2 in. VR barrel with low profile adj. rear sights, blue finish, Ribber grips, 55 oz. New 2011.

MSR $589	$490	$435	$355	$295	$250	$225	$195	

* ***Model 992 Tracker SS*** – similar to Model 992 Tracker, except is matte stainless steel. New 2011.

MSR $637	$560	$525	$400	$350	$315	$275	$230	

RIFLES: LEVER ACTION

MODEL 62 LA RIFLE/CARBINE – .22 LR cal., blue finish, 16 1/2 (mfg. 2006 only) or 23 in. barrel, uncheckered walnut hardwood stock, adj. rear sight, 11 or 12 shot tube mag., 4 1/2 lbs. Mfg. 2006-2007.

	$280	$240	$210	$175	$155	$140	$125	*$329*

* ***Model 62 Rifle/Carbine Stainless*** – similar to Model 62 Rifle/Carbine, except is polished stainless steel, 4 1/2 lbs. Mfg. 2006-2007.

	$295	$250	$210	$175	$155	$140	$125	*$349*

RIFLES: REVOLVING

CIRCUIT JUDGE – .410 bore/.45 LC cal., 18 1/2 in. barrel, shotgun/rifle crossover, SA/DA revolver action based on the original "Judge" with fluted cylinder, 5 shot, bright blue finish, fiber optic sights, Brazilian hardwood Monte Carlo stock with vent. recoil pad, available as smoothbore shotgun or back bored rifle barrel, 4 lbs. Mfg. mid-2010-2011.

	$550	$475	$415	$365	$325	$295	$275	*$618*

GRADING - PPGS™	100%	98%	95%	90%	80%	70%	60%	LAST MSR

RIFLES: SEMI-AUTO

MODEL 63 – .22 LR cal., patterned after the Winchester Model 63, 10 shot tube mag., blue finish, takedown design, 23 in. round barrel, adj. rear sight, 4 1/2 lbs. Imported 2003-2007.

	100%	98%	95%	90%	80%	70%	60%	LAST MSR
	$285	$240	$210	$185	$155	$140	$125	$329

Add $33 for tang sight (mfg. 2005-2006).
Add $30 for scope mount (new 2007).

* ***Model 63 Stainless*** – similar to Model 63, except is stainless steel. Mfg. 2003-2007.

	100%	98%	95%	90%	80%	70%	60%	LAST MSR
	$295	$250	$210	$185	$155	$140	$125	$349

Add $33 for tang sight (mfg. 2005-2006).

MODEL 73 – .22 WMR cal., similar to Model 63, except mag. has less capacity. Imported late 2003-2004.

	100%	98%	95%	90%	80%	70%	60%	LAST MSR
	$270	$235	$200	$175	$155	$140	$125	$311

* ***Model 73 Stainless*** – similar to Model 73, except is stainless steel. Imported 2003-2004.

	100%	98%	95%	90%	80%	70%	60%	LAST MSR
	$290	$250	$210	$185	$160	$145	$130	$342

MODEL 173 – .17 HMR cal., similar to Model 73. Imported late 2003-2004.

	100%	98%	95%	90%	80%	70%	60%	LAST MSR
	$290	$250	$210	$185	$160	$145	$130	$342

* ***Model 173 Stainless*** – similar to Model 173, except is stainless steel. Imported 2003-2004.

	100%	98%	95%	90%	80%	70%	60%	LAST MSR
	$300	$260	$210	$185	$160	$145	$130	$358

CARBINE CT G2 SERIES – 9mm Para. (Model CT9G2L), .40 S&W (Model CT40G2M), or .45 ACP (Model GT45G2M) cal., tactical design featuring hybrid aluminum/polymer frame with steel reinforcement, 10 (.45 ACP cal), 15 (.40 S&W cal.), or 34 (9mm Para. cal) shot mag., 16 in. barrel, fixed black polymer pistol grip skeletonized stock, ribbed polymer forearm with lower Picatinny rail, flat-top aluminum upper receiver with built-in full length Picatinny rail, fixed front and adj. rear sights, 9 1/4 lbs. Mfg. 2011.

Retail pricing was not established on this model.

RIFLES: SLIDE ACTION

Add $30 for Weaver style scope base mount.
Add $14 for Taurus Rimfire Recharger (2 pack w/o ammo, new 2002).

MODEL 62 RIFLE/CARBINE – .22 LR or .22 WMR (disc. 2000) cal., patterned after the Win. Model 62, 16 1/2 (carbine) or 23 (rifle) in. barrel, open adj. sights, 11 or 12 shot tube mag., includes switchable manual firing pin block safety on top of receiver and integral Taurus Security System lock on hammer, uncheckered hardwood stock and grooved forearm, blue or case colored receiver, approx. 4 1/2 lbs. Imported 1999-2007.

	100%	98%	95%	90%	80%	70%	60%	LAST MSR
	$265	$230	$195	$170	$160	$140	$125	$299

Add $34 for rear tang sight (new 2002).

* ***Model 62 Rifle/Carbine Stainless*** – similar to Model 62 Rifle/Carbine, except is stainless steel. Mfg. 2000-2007.

	100%	98%	95%	90%	80%	70%	60%	LAST MSR
	$275	$240	$200	$150	$125	$110	$95	$319

Add $78 for rear tang sight (mfg. 2002-2004).

* ***Model 62 Rifle/Carbine "Upstart" Youth/Adult Combo*** – similar to Model 62 Rifle/Carbine, except is available with both youth (shortened LOP), and adult stocks. Imported 2002-2004.

	100%	98%	95%	90%	80%	70%	60%	LAST MSR
	$270	$235	$200	$150	$125	$110	$95	$311

Add $16 for stainless steel.

MODEL 72 RIFLE/CARBINE – .22 WMR cal., 10 or 11 shot tube mag., blue or case colored receiver, similar to Model 62 Rifle/Carbine, 4 1/2 lbs. Imported 2001-2007.

	100%	98%	95%	90%	80%	70%	60%	LAST MSR
	$285	$240	$210	$185	$155	$140	$125	$329

Add $34 for rear tang sight (new 2002).
Add $20 for case colored receiver.

Beginning 2001, this model's nomenclature changed from Model 62 to Model 72 (.22 WMR cal. only).

GRADING - PPGS™	100%	98%	95%	90%	80%	70%	60%	LAST MSR

* ***Model 72 Rifle/Carbine Stainless*** – similar to Model 72 Rifle/Carbine, except is stainless steel, 80 oz. Imported 2001-2007.

$295	$250	$210	$185	$155	$140	$125	*$349*

Add $34 for rear tang sight (new 2002).

MODEL 172 RIFLE/CARBINE – .17 HMR cal., 16 1/2 (carbine, disc. 2005) or 23 (rifle) in. barrel, adj. sights, 4 1/2 oz. Imported 2003-2006.

$280	$240	$200	$175	$155	$140	$125	*$327*

* ***Model 172 Rifle/Carbine Stainless*** – similar to Model 172 Rifle/Carbine, except is stainless steel. Imported 2003-2006.

$290	$245	$205	$180	$160	$140	$125	*$342*

THUNDERBOLT RIFLE/CARBINE – .357 Mag./.38 Spl. or .45 LC cal., 20 (carbine) or 26 in. (rifle) round barrel with full mag., patterned after the Colt Lightning rifle, 11 (carbine) or 13 (rifle) shot tube mag., choice of case colored or blue finish, short stroke action, uncheckered hardwood stock and forearm, hammer drop release button hidden in the hammer, solid metal curved crescent buttplate, long horn adj. rear sight, 8 lbs. Mfg. 2006-2009.

$515	$400	$325	$260	$225	$195	$180	*$705*

Add $43 for case colors.

* ***Thunderbolt Rifle/Carbine Stainless*** – similar to Thunderbolt Rifle/Carbine, except is polished stainless steel. Mfg. 2006-2009.

$675	$575	$515	$435	$350	$300	$250	*$813*

TAYLOR, F.C. FUR CO.

Previous company which marketed animal trap guns circa 1921-1941.

PISTOLS: SINGLE SHOT

.22 CAL. TAYLOR FUR GETTER – .22 LR cal., designed to shoot animal at close range once trigger mechanism has been activated (usually with bait attached to a lever). Mfg. by O.F. Mossberg for Taylor, ser. range 1-3,100.

N/A	$1,800	$1,650	$1,500	$1,300	$1,000	$750

Add 15% for very early serial number with stake made from two pieces and capable of swiveling, usually found in the 1-300 serial number range.
Subtract $150 if w/o stake.

.38 CAL. TAYLOR FUR GETTER – .38 cal., believed to have been mfg. by Hopkins & Allen, markings cast in top of frame (brass) with iron barrel - all bearing the 1914 patent date.

N/A	$850	$775	$700	$625	$550	$475

Add 10%-15% premium for alloy frame with top plate attached with two screws and uncracked frame.

This model was mfg. on the April 1914 patent of C.D. Lovelace, who worked mainly in the San Angelo, TX area and manufactured two variations of this gun in .38 cal. The first variation was marked "Texas Gun Co." around the cocking rod. The second variation has "The Texas Gun Co, San Angelo, TX" cast into the top of the action. The Lovelace patent was issued in 1914 and an arrangment was made with F.C. Taylor Fur Co. to market these guns under the name of SureShot, with the F.C. Taylor logo and 1914 patent date cast into the top of two variations of the gun, a rounded top brass frame and a flattop brass frame. An alloy or pot metal frame version had two screws attaching the top frame cover. Most of this variation will be found badly damaged, with cracked frames (rarely seen). From 1914-1921, three variations of the Taylor .38 cal. were marketed in this seven-year period, which indicates the rarity of the .38 cal. It took from 1921 to 1939 for F.C. Taylor to sell just over 3,100 .22 cal. guns. A fourth variation .38 cal. will be found with the Taylor logo ground off the round top frame variation, with the 1914 patent date. These guns were sold to and marketed by Biggs Fur Co. of Kansas City.

TAYLOR'S & CO., INC.

Current importer and distributor established during 1988, and located in Winchester, VA.

Taylor's & Co. is an Uberti importer and distributor of both black powder and firearms reproductions, in addition to being the exclusive U.S. distributor for Armi Sport, located in

GRADING - PPGS™	100%	98%	95%	90%	80%	70%	60%	LAST MSR

Brescia, Italy. Taylor's is also a distributor for Bond Arms - please refer to the Bond Arms section.

For more information and up-to-date pricing regarding current Taylor's & Co., Inc. black powder models, please refer to the *Blue Book of Modern Black Powder Arms* by John Allen. This book features information, complete pricing, and reference guides.

Black Powder Revolvers - Reproductions & Replicas and *Black Powder Long Arms & Pistols - Reproductions & Replicas* by Dennis Adler are also invaluable sources for most black powder reproductions and replicas, and include hundreds of color images on most popular makes/models, provide manufacturer/trademark histories, and up-to-date information on related items/accessories for black powder shooting - www.bluebookofgunvalues.com.

DERRINGERS: REPRODUCTIONS

DEADWOOD DOUBLE DERRINGER – .22 LR or .22 WMR cal., coal black, antique black, bright nickel, or gold plated finish, 3 in. barrels. Mfg. 2009-2010.

	$130	$110	$100	$90	$80	$70	$60	*$149*

PISTOLS: SEMI-AUTO

1911-A1 MODEL – .45 ACP cal., 5 in. barrel, straight mainspring housing or arched checkered "grain" mainspring housing, 8 shot single stack mag., smooth or checkered walnut, cocobolo, olive diamond, or walnut diamond grips, blue finish, with or w/o lanyard ring, includes black carrying case and two mags. New 2011.

MSR $519	$450	$395	$340	$300	$250	$200	$160	

Add $20 for lanyard ring.
Add $31 for checkered walnut diamond grips, $36 for olive diamond checkered grips, or $49 for cocobolo diamond checkered grips (all new 2013).
A Combat model with adj. sights is also available - retail is POR.

1911 TACTICAL – .45 ACP cal., 3 5/8 (Compact Carry) or 5 in. barrel, 7 or 8 shot mag., combat hammer, skeletonized trigger, ambidextrous safety, extended beavertail, Picatinny underrail, parkerized finish, checkered walnut grips. Importation began 2013.

MSR $570	$475	$415	$350	$325	$260	$215	$165	

Add $15 for Compact Carry.

1911 .22 – .22 LR cal., 5 in. barrel, black frame with black or olive green slide, checkered wood grips, 10 shot mag., mfg. by Chiappa. New 2011.

MSR $300	$250	$225	$195	$175	$140	$115	$90	

Add $79 for black slide (disc. 2012).
Add $65 for target model (disc. 2012).

M4 TACTICAL SERIES – .22 LR cal., 6 in. solid steel barrel, 10 or 28 shot mag., fire control group, dust cover, adj. sights, pseudo flash hider, bayonet lug, forward assist, and bolt release, quad rail capable forearm, includes two mags. Imported 2011-2012.

	$350	$315	$275	$235	$200	$180	$165	*$419*

REVOLVERS: REPRODUCTIONS, CONVERSIONS

1858 REMINGTON CONVERSION – .32-20 WCF (mfg. 2009), .38 Spl., .38-40 WCF (mfg. 2009), .44-40 WCF, or .45 LC cal., 5 1/2, 7 3/8, or 8 in. barrel, steel frame and backstrap, brass trigger guard, smooth walnut grips, blue finish, case colored hammer. New 2009.

MSR $571	$485	$425	$365	$325	$265	$225	$175	

Add $7 for .44-40 WCF with 8 in. barrel.

MODEL 1871-1872 OPEN TOP – .38 Spl., .38 LC (disc. 2011), .44 Colt (disc. 2011), .44 Spl. (disc. 2011), .45 Schofield (disc. 2011), or .45 LC cal., 4 3/4, 5 1/2, or 7 1/2 in. barrel, choice of Early (1851 Navy size grips) or Late (1860 Army grips, 7 1/2 in. barrel only) Model frame, steel or nickel finish, brass backstrap and trigger guard. New 2007.

MSR $518	$440	$385	$325	$300	$240	$200	$150	

Add $29 for Late Model frame with 1860 Army size grips.
Add $104 for nickel finish.

GRADING - PPGS™	100%	98%	95%	90%	80%	70%	60%	LAST MSR

MODEL 1871 C. MASON – .38 Spl., .38 LC (disc. 2011), .44 Colt (disc. 2011), .44 Spl. (disc. 2011), .45 LC, or .45 Schofield (disc. 2011), 4 3/4, 5 1/2, 7 1/2, or 8 in. barrel, choice of 1851 Navy or 1860 Army frame, steel backstrap and trigger guard. New 2007.

MSR $553	$475	$415	$350	$325	$260	$215	$165	

Add $32 for 1860 Army frame.
Add $109 for nickel finish.

REVOLVERS: REPRODUCTIONS, SAA

CATTLEMAN VARIATIONS – available in .32-20 WCF, .357 Mag., .38-40 WCF, .44 Spl., .44-40 WCF, .45 ACP (new 2003), or .45 LC cal., 4 3/4, 5 1/2, and 7 1/2 in. barrel lengths, brass (New Model frame) or steel (Old Model frame) backstrap and trigger guard, mfg. by Uberti. New 2002.

* ***Cattleman Variations Steel backstrap and trigger guard*** – choice of new or old model frame, old model frame not available in .357 Mag. cal.

MSR $540	$450	$395	$340	$300	$250	$200	$160	

Add $5 for .44-40 WCF cal.
Add $98 for .45 LC/.45 ACP cal.
Add $10 for .38-40 WCF or .44 Spl. cal.
Add $21 for .32-20 WCF cal.
Add $49 for non-fluted cylinder or $99 for non-fluted cylinder with 7 1/2 in. barrel (new 2011).
Add $76 for charcoal blue finish.
Add $120 for Antique finish.
Add $105 for nickel finish or $300 for nickel finish and polymer pearl, black buffalo, or polymer ivory grips.
Add $60 for in-the-white finish.
Add $86 for convertible cylinder (.45 LC/.45 ACP in 5 1/2 in. barrel only).

* ***Cattleman Variations Brass backstrap and trigger guard*** – .357 Mag. (disc. 2008, reintroduced 2011), or .45 LC cal. Disc. 2011.

	$390	$330	$285	$250	$215	$175	$150	*$456*

* ***Cattleman Variations Millenium*** – .45 LC cal., 4 3/4 in. barrel, brass backstrap and trigger guard. Mfg. 2000-2008.

	$300	$265	$225	$200	$175	$155	$125	*$365*

* ***Cattleman Variations Engraved*** – .357 Mag. or .45 LC cal., 4 3/4 or 5 1/2 in. barrel, features unique photo engraving on frame, cylinder, and barrel (Taylor's exclusive), choice of blue (new 2006), colored case hardened, or white heat treated finish with charcoal blue screws. New 2003.

MSR $904	$765	$675	$575	$525	$425	$350	$275	

Add $38 for white finish (disc. 2011).

* ***Cattleman Variations "TR" Presidential*** – .45 LC cal. only, 5 1/2 in. barrel, features unique photo engraving on frame, cylinder, and barrel (Taylor's exclusive), white heat treated finish with charcoal blue screws, simulated ivory, wood, or black hard rubber grips. Mfg. 2005-2006.

	$565	$450	$375	$315	$275	$240	$215	*$685*

Add $30 for black grips, or $100 for simulated ivory grips.

* ***Cattleman Carbine*** – .357 Mag., .44-40 WCF, or .45 LC cal., 18 in. barrel with shoulder stock. New 2009.

MSR $800	$675	$595	$500	$450	$375	$300	$225	

Add $6 for .44-40 WCF cal.

CATTLEMAN QUICK DRAW – .357 Mag. or .45 LC cal., 4, 4 3/4, 5 1/2, or 7 1/2 in. barrel, choice of Old or New (disc. 2008) Model frame. New 2006.

MSR $547	$465	$400	$350	$315	$250	$210	$165	

GRADING - PPGS™	100%	98%	95%	90%	80%	70%	60%	LAST MSR

CATTLEMAN ISLAND GIRL QUICK DRAW – .38 Spl., 4 3/4 in. barrel, nickel finish with one-piece white checkered polymer grips, fire blued screws, beveled cylinder, Ruger style coil spring. Mfg. 2006-2008.

	$595	$525	$465	$400	$345	$275	$240	*$710*

CATTLEMAN SHERIFF BIRDSHEAD – .357 Mag. or .45 LC cal., 3 1/2 or 4 3/4 in. barrel, patterned after the Colt 1877 Thunderer, choice of Old or New Model frame, case colored frame, smooth walnut birdshead grips. New 1997.

MSR $547	$465	$400	$350	$315	$250	$210	$165

Add $188 for polymer ivory grips (mfg. 2011 only).
Add $79 for nickel finish (.357 Mag. cal. only, with 4 3/4 in. barrel, disc. 2008).

GUNFIGHTER CATTLEMAN – .357 Mag. or .45 LC cal., 5 1/2 in. barrel, Army grips. Importation began 2011.

MSR $553	$475	$415	$350	$325	$260	$215	$165

CATTLEMAN BISLEY – .357 Mag. (disc. 2008, reintroduced 2011), .38-40 WCF (disc. 2008) or .45 LC cal., patterned after the Colt Bisley Model, 4 3/4, 5 1/2, or 7 1/2 in. barrel, case colored New Model frame, wood grips. Mfg. 1997-2008, reintroduced 2010.

MSR $591	$500	$440	$375	$340	$275	$225	$175

STALLION 1873 POCKET – .22 LR (new 2008) or .38 Spl. cal., 3 1/2, 4 3/4, or 5 1/2 in. barrel, scaled down SAA with small frame, standard or birdshead smooth grips, steel backstrap and trigger guard. Mfg. 1999-2004, reintroduced 2006.

MSR $480	$400	$350	$300	$275	$225	$175	$140

Add $16 for birdshead grips.
Add $32 for .38 Spl. cal.
Add $41 for .22 LR/.22 WMR convertible cylinder.
Add $8 for brass backstrap and trigger guard.

1873 CATTLEMAN STAINLESS (OUTFITTER) – .357 Mag. (disc. 2008) or .45 LC cal., all stainless construction with two-piece walnut grips, 4 3/4, 5 1/2, or 7 1/2 in. barrel. New 2003.

MSR $696	$595	$525	$450	$400	$325	$275	$210

NEW VAUQUERO "HANDLEBAR DOC SIGNATURE SERIES" – .357 Mag. or .45 LC cal., color case hardened blue or stainless steel frame, 4 5/8, 5 1/2, or 7 1/2 in. barrel, checkered black grips with white "HD" medallions, "Handlebar Doc Series" etched on barrel, Taylor's exclusive. Mfg. 2005-2009.

	$595	$525	$450	$395	$340	$275	$240

NEW MODEL BLACKHAWK – .357 Mag. cal., 4 5/8 in. barrel, flattop frame with adj. rear sight and pre-1962 XR3 grip frame, choice of blue or stainless, hard rubber grips with Handlebar Doc white medallions. Mfg. 2006-2008.

	$575	$500	$450	$395	$340	$275	$240	*$675*

SMOKE WAGON – .38 Spl (disc. 2011)., .357 Mag., .44-40 WCF, or .45 LC cal., 4 3/4 or 5 1/2 in. barrel, blue finish with case color hardened frame, checkered wood grips, low profile hammer, wider style sights. New 2008.

MSR $540	$450	$395	$340	$300	$250	$200	$160

Add $110 for deluxe edition, which features custom tuned action.

RUNNIN' IRON – .357 Mag. or .45 LC cal., 3 1/2, 4 3/4, or 5 1/2 in. barrel, blue or stainless, checkered black polymer or walnut grips, designed by Deke Rivers for cowboy action shooting, low and wide hammer spur, crescent style ejector rod. New 2010.

MSR $555	$475	$415	$350	$325	$260	$215	$165

Add $155 for stainless.
Add $148 for Deluxe Edition.
Add $44 for checkered polymer grips (disc. 2011).

GRADING - PPGS™	100%	98%	95%	90%	80%	70%	60%	LAST MSR

RUNNIN' REVOLVING CARBINE – .44-40 WCF or .45 LC cal., similar to Runnin' Iron, 18 in. revolving carbine barrel, straight grip walnut stock with brass buttplate, deluxe tuned action. Importation began 2012.

MSR $772	$650	$575	$495	$440	$360	$295	$225

1875 ARMY OUTLAW – .357 Mag., .44-40 WCF, .45 LC, or .45 ACP cal., 5 1/2 or 7 1/2 in. barrel, case hardened frame with blue or white finish, smooth walnut grips, steel backstrap. New 2011.

MSR $578	$495	$425	$375	$325	$275	$225	$175

Add $7 for .44-40 WCF or .45 ACP cal., or $101 for .45 LC/.45 ACP cylinder.

1890 ARMY POLICE – .357 Mag., .44-40 WCF, .45 LC, or .45 ACP cal., 5 1/2 in. barrel, blue finish, lanyard ring, two-piece smooth walnut grips. New 2011.

MSR $589	$500	$440	$375	$340	$275	$225	$175

Add $7 for .44-40 WCF or .45 ACP cal., or $101 for .45 LC/.45 ACP cal. cylinder.

CATTLEMAN TAYLOR GAMBLER – .357 Mag. or .45 LC cal., 5 1/2 in. barrel, fancy checkered walnut or white PVC grips, blue finish, case hardened frame. Importation began 2012.

MSR $585	$500	$440	$375	$340	$275	$225	$175

CATTLEMAN TAYLOR MARSHALL – .45 LC cal., 5 1/2 in. barrel, fancy checkered white PVC ivory grips, blue finish, case hardened frame. Importation began 2012.

MSR $672	$575	$500	$425	$395	$315	$260	$200

THE RANCH HAND – .357 Mag. or .45 LC cal., 4 (.45 LC cal. only), 4 3/4, 5 1/2, or 7 1/2 in. barrel, brass backstrap and trigger guard. Importation began 2012.

MSR $516	$425	$375	$325	$295	$235	$195	$150

UBERTI SINGLE ACTION – .22 LR cal., 4 3/4 or 5 1/2 in. barrel, 6 or 12 shot, brass or steel backstrap and trigger guard, case colored frame, smooth walnut grips. New 2013.

MSR $502	$425	$375	$325	$295	$235	$195	$150

Add $27 for steel backstrap or $51 for 12 shot.

CHIAPPA SINGLE ACTION – .22 LR cal., 4 3/4 in. barrel, 6 shot, blue finish, black plastic checkered or wood grips. New 2013.

MSR $179	$150	$125	$115	$100	$85	$70	$55

Add $16 for wood grips.

REVOLVERS: REPRODUCTIONS, SCHOFIELD

1875 NO. 3 NEW MODEL RUSSIAN – .38 Spl. (disc. 2011), .44 Russian, .44-40 WCF (disc. 2011), or .45 LC cal., 6 shot, top-break action, 3 1/2 (disc. 2008), 5 (disc. 2008), or 6 1/2 (with lanyard ring and trigger guard spur, special order only until 2008 with case colored trigger guard), or 7 (disc. 2008) in. barrel with solid rib, automatic extraction, blue finish with smooth walnut grips. New 2007.

MSR $1,112	$945	$825	$710	$645	$525	$425	$325

Add $15 for .44 Russian cal.
Subtract approx. 5% for 3 1/2, 5, or 7 in. barrel.

NO. 3 SECOND MODEL – .38 Spl., .44-40 WCF, .44 Russian, or .45 LC cal., 3 1/2, 5, or 7 in. barrel with solid rib, case colored trigger guard, opening top break lever and hammer, smooth walnut grips, blued finish. New 2009.

MSR $1,083	$925	$810	$695	$625	$510	$415	$325

Add $13 for .44-40 WCF cal.

NEW MODEL NO. 3 FRONTIER – .45 LC cal., 5 or 6 1/2 in. barrel, blue, charcoal blue, white, antique, or nickel finish, checkered wood grips, blade rear sight. New mid-2009.

MSR $1,112	$945	$825	$710	$645	$525	$425	$325

Add $84 for charcoal blue finish.
Add $115 for antique finish.
Add $185 for nickel finish.
Add $75 for white finish.

GRADING - PPGS™	100%	98%	95%	90%	80%	70%	60%	LAST MSR

RIFLES: REPRODUCTIONS, LEVER ACTION

HENRY RIFLE – .44-40 WCF or .45 LC cal., brass or steel frame, 24 1/2 in. barrel, 13 shot mag., available in brass, case colored, or in-the-white finish, with or w/o sling swivels.

MSR $1,475	$1,250	$1,095	$940	$850	$695	$565	$440	

Add $202 for charcoal blue barrel finish.
Add $52 for steel frame.
Add $111 for in-the-white finish.
Add $83 for sling swivels.
Add $120 for transition model with hinged loading port (mfg. 2006-2008).
Add $315 for laser engraving with hand chasing.

1866 YELLOWBOY RIFLE/CARBINE – .32-20 WCF (disc. 2011), .38 Spl., .44-40 WCF, or .45 LC cal., 18 (Trapper), 19 (carbine), 20 (rifle), or 24 1/4 (rifle) in. round or octagonal barrel, pistol grip or straight stock. New 2002.

MSR $1,238	$1,050	$925	$795	$715	$575	$475	$375	

Add $11 for carbine.
Add $324 for transition model (mfg. 2009-2012).

1873 CARBINE – .32-20 WCF, .38-40 WCF, .357 Mag., .44 Spl. (disc. 2011), .44 Mag. (new 2012), or .45 LC cal., steel receiver, 16 1/8 (Ladies/Youth, new 2011), 18 1/2 in. octagon (Trapper, not available in .32-20 WCF cal.) or 19 in. round barrel, blued steel receiver w/o saddle ring. New 2002.

MSR $1,305	$1,100	$965	$825	$750	$600	$495	$385	

Add $71 for 19 in. carbine w/o sling swivels (mfg. 2011-2012), or $155 for Ladies/Youth Model with 16 1/8 in. barrel (new 2011).
Add $67 for rubber stock pad.
Add $50 for Trapper model with full octagon barrel.
Add $58 for case colored frame (.357 Mag. cal. only).

1873 SPORTING RIFLE – .32-20 WCF (disc. 2004, reintroduced 2007), .357 Mag., .38-40 WCF (disc. 2004, reintroduced 2007), .44-40 WCF, .44 Spl., or .45 LC cal., case hardened receiver, 18 in. half-octagon (Short Rifle), 20 in. half-octagon, 24 1/4 in. octagon, or 30 (Deluxe) in. octagon barrel. New 2002.

MSR $1,339	$1,125	$985	$850	$765	$625	$500	$395	

Add $30 for .38-40 WCF cal.
Add $31 for half octagon barrel or $95 for Special Sporting Rifle with pistol grip stock.
Add $75 for Deluxe Special Sporting Model with checkered pistol grip.
Add $122 for Special Sporting Rifle with half-round barrel and pistol grip stock.
Add $188 for Antique finish (new 2011) or $192 for in-the-white finish (new 2012).
Add $26 for 24 1/4 in. full octagon or $35 for .30 in. (disc. 2010) octagon barrel.
Add $33 for Sporting Rifle with octagon barrel and checkered straight grip stock (new 2012).

1873 MAVERICK – .357 Mag. or .45 LC cal., 18 or 20 in. octagon barrel, choice of straight or pistol grip checkered stock, custom tuned by Cody Conager. Imported 2009 only.

	$1,475	$1,275	$1,050	$895	$750	$625	$525	*$1,600*

Add $105 for checkered pistol grip stock.

1873 COMANCHERO – .357 Mag. or .45 LC cal., 18 or 20 in. octagon barrel, blue finish, uncheckered or checkered (new 2013) straight grip or checkered pistol grip stock, custom tuning by Cody Conagher, buckskin lever covering and laced buckskin butt stock cover. New 2010.

MSR $1,770	$1,575	$1,300	$995	$800	$650	$525	$450	

Add $125 for pistol grip checkered stock.
Add $61 for half-round, half-octagon barrel.

1873 RUNNIN' COMMANCHERO CARBINE – .44-40 WCF or .45 LC cal., similar to Commanchero, except has 16 1/8 in. round barrel. New 2012.

MSR $1,650	$1,475	$1,200	$900	$725	$575	$475	$425	

GRADING - PPGS™	100%	98%	95%	90%	80%	70%	60%	LAST MSR

1876 CENTENNIAL RIFLE (SPORTING) – .40-60 (disc. 2011), .45-60, .45-75 (disc. 2011), or .50-95 cal., 22 or 28 in. round or octagon barrel, case colored frame. New 2006.

MSR $1,676	$1,425	$1,250	$1,075	$975	$785	$640	$500	

Add $45 for .50-95 cal. or $90 for round barrel.

1883 BURGESS CARBINE/RIFLE – .44-40 WCF or .45 LC cal., 20 or 25 1/2 round or octagon barrel, uncheckered straight grip walnut stock, blue, charcoal blue, white, or antique finish. New 2009.

MSR $1,551	$1,315	$1,150	$985	$895	$725	$595	$460	

Add $22 for 25 1/2 in. round barrel, or $45 for octagon barrel.

1886 RIFLE/CARBINE – .444 Marlin or .45-70 Govt. cal., case colored frame with blue barrel and mag. tube, 22 in. round barrel with saddle ring or 26 in. octagon barrel. New 2008.

MSR $1,416	$1,175	$1,025	$875	$800	$650	$525	$410	

Add $362 for Wildbuster model (new 2013), or $539 for Premium or Boarbuster model (new 2013, Pedersoli mfg.).

.444 Marlin cal. and the Carbine is POR on this model.

1892 CARBINE/RIFLE – .32-20 WCF (disc. 2006), .32 H&R Mag. (disc. 2006), .38-40 WCF (disc. 2011), .38 Spl. (disc. 2011), .357 Mag., .44 S&W (disc. 2006), .44-40 WCF, or .45 LC cal., choice of 20 or 24 1/2 round (new 2005) or octagon barrel, solid (.32-20 WCF, .38-30 WCF, or .44 S&W cal. only) frame or takedown action.

MSR $1,062	$900	$795	$675	$610	$495	$400	$315	

Add $20 for .38 Spl., .38-40, or .44-40 cal.

Add $104 for takedown action (disc. 2008).

Add $34 for Rio Bravo carbine with large loop lever (new 2007, select cals.).

1892 ALASKAN TAKEDOWN CARBINE/RIFLE – .44 Mag. cal., 16 or 20 in. barrel, 7 or 10 shot, large loop lever, matte chrome finish, overmolded black rubber coated wood stock, recoil pad, Skinner Express rear sight, drilled and tapped, takedown action, "Alaskan" engraved on receiver. New 2013.

MSR $1,324	$1,125	$985	$850	$765	$625	$500	$395	

UBERTI SCOUT RIFLE – .22 LR cal., 19 in. blue barrel, chrome plated alloy receiver, 15 shot, straight grip walnut finished hardwood stock, 5.8 lbs. New 2013.

MSR $599	$500	$440	$375	$340	$275	$225	$175	

RIFLES: REPRODUCTIONS, SINGLE SHOT

1865 SPENCER CARBINE/RIFLE (160 SERIES) – .44 Russian (limited mfg., disc. 2006), .44-40 WCF (new 2005), .45 Schofield (disc. 2011), .45 LC (new 2012) or .56-50 (rifle only) cal., reproduction of the Civil War Spencer carbine, case colored receiver, lock, and hammer, 20 or 30 (rifle, new 2005) in. barrel, 7-9 shot mag., walnut stock and forearm, includes slings, mfg. by Armi-Sport. Imported 2002-2012.

	$1,325	$1,175	$995	$850	$725	$595	$425	*$1,566*

Add $227 for rifle.

1874 SHARPS SPORTING RIFLE – .40-65 (disc. 2006), .45-70 Govt., .45-90, or .45-120 cal., 30, 32, or 34 in. barrel, single or double set triggers, case colored or white finished frame, with or w/o pewter accents, double set triggers with Schnabel forend became standard 2011.

MSR $1,256	$1,050	$925	$795	$715	$575	$475	$375	

Add $90 for Hartford style pewter forearm tip, or $221 for checkered pistol grip and patchbox.

Add $304 for in-the-white finish (new 2012).

Add $225 for pistol grip stock with buckhorn sight (disc. 2009) or $295 for pistol grip stock and heavy barrel (disc. 2006).

Taylor's also imported engraved models of the 1874 Sporting Rifle in either .45-70 Govt. or .45-120 cal., including standard engraving ($2,040 last MSR) and hand engraving with gold medallions ($2,975 last MSR).

GRADING - PPGS™	100%	98%	95%	90%	80%	70%	60%	LAST MSR

1874 SHARPS QUIGLEY – .45-70 Govt. or .45-120 cal., 32 or 34 in. octagon barrel, exact reproduction of rifle used in the "*Quigley Down Under*" movie, with patchbox, includes Hartford style pewter forearm tip.

	$1,095	$950	$825	$725	$575	$475	$400	*$1,310*

Add $35 for steel buttplate.

1874 SHARPS QUIGLEY SPORT – .45-70 Govt. cal., 34 in. barrel with German silver forearm cap and checkered walnut stock with patchbox, case colored frame and patchbox, ladder rear sight, mfg. by Pedersoli. New 2008.

MSR $2,524	$2,150	$1,875	$1,615	$1,460	$1,185	$975	$750	

1874 SHARPS CAVALRY CARBINE – .45-70 Govt. or .50-70 (mfg. 2005-2006) cal., patterned after Sharps Cavalry carbine, 22 in. barrel, color case hardened frame.

	$875	$825	$725	$625	$525	$425	$325	*$1,090*

Add approx. 10% for .50-70 cal.

1874 SHARPS INFANTRY/BERDAN MODEL – .45-70 Govt. cal., 30 in. barrel, musket configuration with 3 barrel bands and patchbox. Disc. 2006.

	$925	$775	$625	$500	$425	$375	$350	*$1,045*

Add $45 for Berdan model with DT.

1885 LOW/HIGH WALL – .17 HMR (mfg. 2005-2008), .17 Mach 2 (mfg. 2005-2008), .22 LR, .32-20 WCF, .38-40 WCF, .38-55 WCF, .45 LC, or .45-70 Govt. (High Wall only) cal., 30 or 32 (High Wall only) in. octagon barrel, case colored receiver, straight (High Wall) or checkered pistol grip (Low Wall) walnut stock and forearm. New 1999.

MSR $1,149	$975	$850	$725	$665	$535	$440	$340	

Add $77 for octagon barrel.
Add $21 for .32-20 WCF, $52 for .45-70 Govt. or .38-55 WCF cal.
Add $209 for double set triggers.
Add $78 for 32 in. barrel.
Add $170 for High Wall with checkered pistol grip stock.
Add $98 for Low Wall.

LITTLE SHARPS/HALF PINT SHARPS – .17 HMR, .22 LR, .22 WMR, .22 Hornet, .218 Bee, .30-30 Win., .38-55 WCF, .44 Win., or .45 LC cal., 20% smaller version of the original Sharps rifle, 24, 26, or 32 in. octagon barrel, double set triggers, rear tang aperture sight, case colored or chrome plated alloy (new 2013) frame, 5.9 lbs, mfg. by Armi-Sport. New 2008.

MSR $1,191	$1,000	$875	$750	$675	$550	$450	$350	

The chrome plated alloy frame is only available in .22 LR cal. and is POR.

SPRINGFIELD TRAPDOOR CARBINE – .45-70 Govt., cal., 22 in. round barrel with barrel band, uncheckered straight grip walnut stock, blue finish with case colored trapdoor, ladder rear sight, mfg. by Pedersoli. New 2008.

MSR $1,377	$1,175	$1,025	$875	$800	$650	$525	$400	

ROLLING BLOCK BABY CARBINE – .22 LR (new 2012), .22 WMR (new 2012), .357 Mag., .44-40 WCF (disc. 2011), or .45 LC (disc. 2011) cal., 20 in. round barrel, case hardened frame, uncheckered straight grip walnut stock. New mid-2009.

MSR $730	$625	$550	$450	$325	$250	$200	$175	

Add $16 for .357 Mag.

ROLLING BLOCK JOHN BODINE – .45-70 Govt. or .45-90 cal., 30 or 34 in. blue octagon barrel, double set trigger, uncheckered pistol grip walnut stock and forend, inlet German silver cap. New mid-2009.

MSR $2,260	$1,925	$1,675	$1,450	$1,300	$1,050	$865	$675	

Add $49 for .45-90 cal.

ROLLING BLOCK CREEDMORE NO. 2 – .45-70 Govt. cal., 30 in. round blue barrel, coin finished frame, double set trigger, checkered walnut pistol grip stock and forend. New mid-2009.

MSR $2,134	$1,800	$1,575	$1,350	$1,225	$995	$810	$625	

GRADING - PPGS™	100%	98%	95%	90%	80%	70%	60%	LAST MSR

RIFLES: REPRODUCTIONS, SLIDE ACTION

LIGHTNING SLIDE ACTION – .357 Mag. (disc. 2011), .44-40 WCF (disc. 2011), or .45 LC cal., 20 in. round, 24 1/4 (rifle only), or 26 in. octagon barrel, case colored frame, straight grip walnut stock with checkered forearm. New 2007.

MSR $1,205	$1,025	$895	$775	$695	$565	$460	$360	

Add $40 for 26 in. round barrel.
Add $71 for 20 in. octagon barrel or $100 for 24 1/4 in. octagon barrel.

RIFLES: SEMI-AUTO

M4 22 – .22 LR cal., 16 in. solid steel barrel, 10 or 28 shot mag., fire control group, dust cover, adj. sights, pseudo flash hider, bayonet lug, forward assist, and bolt release, quad rail capable forearm, includes two mags, 5 1/2 lbs. Mfg. 2011-2012.

	$350	$295	$260	$230	$200	$180	$165	*$419*

SHOTGUNS: REPRODUCTIONS

1878 COACH GUN – 12 ga., 20 in. barrel, blue frame, steel buttplate, uncheckered (disc.) or checkered (new 2011) walnut pistol grip stock, double triggers, 6.7 lbs. Mfg. by CZ, new mid-2009.

MSR $905	$800	$750	$695	$595	$400	$295	$175	

1887 LEVER ACTION STANDARD MODEL – 12 ga., 22 or 28 in. barrel, chrome or color case hardened frame, uncheckered pistol grip American walnut stock, 6.6 lbs. New mid-2009.

MSR $1,226	$1,050	$925	$795	$715	$575	$475	$375	

Add $23 for color case hardening w/o fastload.
Add $68 for 28 in. barrel.
Add $214 for chrome.

* ***1887 Lever Action 18 1/2 in.*** – 12 ga., 18 1/2 in. barrel, 5 shot, available in Bootleg with matte black or case colored receiver and uncheckered wood stock, T-Model with matte black finish and overmolded black rubber coated stock, or Zombie Blaster with matte black finish and Zombie Blaster logo, 7.9 lbs. New 2013.

MSR $995	$845	$740	$635	$575	$465	$380	$295	

Add $195 for extended full stock attachment.

SxS MODEL – 12 ga., 28 9/16 in. barrels with chokes, approx. 7 lbs. Mfg. by Pedersoli.

	$925	$800	$750	$695	$595	$400	$295	*$1,122*

WYATT EARP MODEL – 12 ga., 20 in. chrome bored barrels, checkered pistol grip walnut stock, color case hardened frame with or w/o (new 2013) Wyatt Earp stamp, fast shell loading, approx. 7 lbs. Mfg. by Pedersoli, new 2011.

MSR $1,737	$1,475	$1,295	$1,100	$1,000	$810	$665	$515	

TECHNO ARMS (PTY) LIMITED

Previous manufacturer located in Johannesburg, S. Africa circa 1994-1996. Previously imported by Vulcans Forge, Inc. located in Foxboro, MA.

SHOTGUNS: SLIDE ACTION

MAG-7 SLIDE ACTION SHOTGUN – 12 ga. (60mm chamber length), 5 shot detachable mag. (in pistol grip), 14, 16, 18, or 20 in. barrel, straight grip or pistol grip stock, matte finish, 8 lbs. Imported 1995-96.

	$795	$675	$625	$550	$500	$450	$400	*$875*

TELO, RENATO

Current manufacturer located in Brescia, Italy. Currently imported by Kevin's Fine Outdoor Gear & Apparel, located in Thomasville, GA.

Renato Telo manufactures best quality O/U long guns with and without sideplates, with prices starting at $15,000. Please contact the importer directly for more information, including models, availability, delivery time and U.S. pricing (see Trademark Index).

GRADING - PPGS™	100%	98%	95%	90%	80%	70%	60%	LAST MSR

TERRIER ONE

Previous trademark distributed by Serrifile located in Lancaster, CA.

REVOLVERS

TERRIER ONE – .32 S&W cal., double action, 2 1/4 in. barrel, 5 shot, nickel-plated, 17 oz. Mfg. 1984-87.

	$45	$35	$30	$25	$25	$25	$25	*$55*

TESRO SPORTWAFFEN GMBH & CO. KG

Current manufacturer located in Bächingen, Germany. Previously located in Niederstotzingen, Germany. No current U.S. importation.

Tesro also manufactures high quality air pistols and air rifles. Please contact the company directly for more information regarding U.S. availability and pricing (see Trademark Index).

PISTOLS: SEMI-AUTO

TS 22-3 – .22 LR cal., 4.45 in. barrel, target model with ergonomic wood grips, 5 shot mag., black finish, adj. rear sight, 2 1/4 lbs.

Current MSRs are €1,510 for the TS 22-3, and €1,660 for the TS 22-3 Pro.

TS 32-3 – .32 Wadcutter cal., 4.45 in. barrel, target model with ergonomic wood grips, 5 shot mag., black finish, adj. rear sight, 2 1/4 lbs.

Current MSRs are €1,680 for the TS 32-3, and €1,830 for the TS 32-3 Pro.

TEXAS ARMS

Previous manufacturer located in Waco, TX, until circa 1999.

DERRINGERS: O/U

DEFENDER – .357 Mag., .38 Spl., 9mm Para., .44 Mag., .45 ACP, or .45 LC cal./.410 bore shotshell, features stainless steel 3 in. interchangeable octagon barrels, spur trigger, shell ejector for rimmed cartridges, rebounding hammer and retracting firing pins, crossbolt safety, bead blasted grey finish, 16-21 oz. Mfg. 1993-circa 1999.

	$275	$235	$200	$175	$160	$145	$130	*$310*

Add $100 per interchangeable set of barrels.

TEXAS GUNFIGHTERS

Previous importer located in Irving, TX circa 1988-1990.

REVOLVERS: SINGLE ACTION

SHOOTIST EDITION – .45 LC cal., patterned after the Colt SAA, 4 3/4 in. barrel, nickel-plated black powder frame, one piece walnut grips, mfg. by A. Uberti of Italy. New 1988.

* ***Shootist Edition Standard Model*** – 1,000 total mfg., cased.

	$625	$525	$440	N/A	N/A	N/A	N/A	*$649*

* ***Shootist Edition 1 of 100*** – 100 total mfg., fully engraved, genuine mother-of-pearl one-piece grips, cased.

	$1,275	$1,050	$775	N/A	N/A	N/A	N/A	*$1,395*

This model was also supplied with an extra set of walnut grips.

TEXAS LONGHORN ARMS, INC.

Previous manufacturer located in Richmond, TX circa 1988-1997.

REVOLVERS

SINGLE-ACTION – various cals., patterned after Colt's SAA, except the loading gate and ejector rod have been moved to left side of frame enabling left-hand loading, mfg. from 4140 steel, 1-piece grip, adj. trigger, case-hardened and blue finish, entirely handmade, supplied with lifetime warranty. Models included the Texas Border Special (last MSR was $1,595), South Texas Army (last MSR was $1,595), West Texas Flat-Top Targer (last MSR was $1,595), Grover's Northpaw (last MSR was $685), and Grover's Improved Number Five (last MSR was $1,195). Special editions and sets were also advertised (ranging from $1,500 MSR - $7,650 MSR), but very few were actually built. Mint examples are currently in the $1,350-$1,500

GRADING - PPGS™	100%	98%	95%	90%	80%	70%	60%	LAST MSR

range, except for Grover's Northpaw, which is in the $650 range. While production plans called for 1,000 of each model to be manufactured, very few pistols were actually made.

THOMAS

Previous trademark manufactured by Alexander James Ordnance, Inc. located in Covina, CA.

Please refer to listing under A.J. Ordnance in this text.

THOMPSON & CAMPBELL

Current rifle manufacturer located in Cromarty, the Black Isle, Scotland. No current U.S. importation. Consumer direct sales.

RIFLES: BOLT ACTION

Thompson & Campbell manufactures high quality bolt action rifles featuring the patented Inver action, which utilizes a rear extension plate and reinforcement rod that is inletted into the stock for additional strength. Individual models include the Inver, Cromie, the Islay, and Jura (Mannlicher configuration). Thompson & Campbell manufactures approx. 20-24 rifles annually. Please contact the factory directly for more information, current pricing, and delivery times (see Trademark Index).

THOMPSON

Current trademark of pistols and carbines manufactured by Auto Ordnance located in Worcester, MA, and corporate offices in Blauvelt, NY. Auto Ordnance became a division of Kahr Arms in 1999. Dealer and distributor sales.

Auto-Ordnance Corporation

Auto-Ordnance Corp. manufactures an exact reproduction of the original 1927 Thompson sub-machine gun. They are currently available from Kahr Arms in semi-auto only since production ceased on fully automatic variations (Model 1928 and M1) in 1986 (mfg. 1975-1986 including 609 M1s). All current models utilize the Thompson trademark, are manufactured in the U.S., and come with a lifetime warranty.

CARBINES: SEMI-AUTO

The Auto-Ordnance Thompson replicas listed below are currently supplied with a 15, 20, or 30 shot stick mag. Tommy Guns are not currently legal in CA or CT.

Add the following for currently manufactured Thompson 1921 A-1 models:
Add $70 for 20 or 30 shot stick mag.
Add $68 for 10 shot stick mag.
Add $193 for 10 shot drum mag. (they resemble the older 50 shot L-type drum) - new 1994.
Add $299 for 50* shot drum mag. or $577 for 100* shot drum mag. (mfg. 1990-93, reintroduced 2006).
Add $221 for factory violin case or $204 for hard case.

1927 A3 - .22 CAL. – .22 LR cal., 16 or 18 in. finned barrel with compensator, alloy frame and receiver, fixed or detachable walnut stock, pistol grip, and forearm pistol grip, 7 lbs. Disc. 1994.

	100%	98%	95%	90%	80%	70%	60%	LAST MSR
	$995	$875	$750	$650	$550	$500	$450	*$510*

1927 A5 PISTOL/CARBINE – .45 ACP cal., 13 in. finned barrel, alloy construction, overall length 26 in., 10 (C/B 1994) shot mag., 7 lbs. Disc. 1994.

	100%	98%	95%	90%	80%	70%	60%	LAST MSR
	$1,050	$925	$825	$750	$650	$600	$500	*$765*

THOMPSON M1 CARBINE (.45 ACP CAL.) – .45 ACP cal., combat model, 16 1/2 in. smooth barrel w/o compensator, 30 shot original surplus mag., side-cocking lever, matte black finish, walnut stock, pistol grip, and grooved horizontal forearm, current mfg. will not accept drum mags., 11 1/2 lbs. New 1986.

	100%	98%	95%	90%	80%	70%	60%
MSR $1,334	$1,050	$850	$625	$525	$425	$375	$325

* ***Thompson M1-C Lightweight*** – similar to M1 Carbine, except receiver is made of a lightweight alloy, current mfg. accepts drum mags., 9 1/2 lbs. Mfg. 2001-2002, reintroduced 2005.

	100%	98%	95%	90%	80%	70%	60%
MSR $1,206	$1,075	$925	$825	$725	$625	$525	$425

During 2006, this model incorporated a large machined radius on the bottom of the receiver to improve magazine insertion.

GRADING - PPGS™	100%	98%	95%	90%	80%	70%	60%	LAST MSR

THOMPSON 1927 A-1 DELUXE CARBINE – 10mm (mfg. 1991-93) or .45 ACP cal., 16 1/2 in. finned barrel with compensator, includes one 30 shot original surplus mag., current mfg. accepts drum mags., solid steel construction, matte black finish, adj. rear sight, walnut stock, pistol grip, and finger grooved forearm grip, 13 lbs.

MSR $1,420	$1,100	$975	$800	$675	$550	$495	$450	

Add $433 for detachable buttstock and horizontal foregrip (new 2007).

During 2006, design changes included a more authentic spherical cocking knob, improved frame to receiver fit, and a large machined radius at the bottom of the receiver to help with magazine insertion.

* ***Thompson 1927 A-1C Lightweight Deluxe*** – .45 ACP cal., similar to 1927 A-1 Deluxe, except receiver made of a lightweight alloy, currently shipped with 30 shot stick mag. (where legal), current mfg. accepts drum mags., 9 1/2 lbs. New 1984.

MSR $1,286	$1,075	$950	$800	$700	$600	$500	$425	

Add $413 for 100 shot drum mag.

* ***Thompson 1927 A-1 Presentation Walnut Carbine*** – .45 ACP cal., similar to 1927 A-1 Deluxe, except has presentation grade walnut buttstock, pistol grip, and foregrip, supplied with plastic case. Limited mfg. 2003.

	$850	$675	$525	$425	$350	$325	$295	*$1,121*

* ***Thompson 1927 A-1 Deluxe .22 LR Cal.*** – .22 LR cal., very limited mfg., 30 shot mag. standard.

	$1,100	$995	$925	$800	$700	$650	$575	

THOMPSON 1927 A-1 COMMANDO – .45 ACP cal., 16 1/2 in. finned barrel with compensator, 30 shot mag., black finished stock and forearm, parkerized metal, black nylon sling, 13 lbs. New 1997.

MSR $1,393	$1,095	$975	$800	$675	$550	$495	$450	

During 2006, this model incorporated a spherical cocking knob.

THOMPSON SBR – .45 ACP cal., 10 1/2 in. finned barrel, closed bolt, blue metal finish, pistol grip forearm, 30 shot mag., 12 lbs. New 2004.

MSR $2,053	$1,825	$1,600	$1,375	$1,150	$975	$850	$725	

Add $501 for detachable buttstock and horizontal foregrip (new 2007).

This carbine model may only be shipped from the factory to an NFA Class II manufacturer or NFA Class III dealer.

THOMPSON M1 SBR – .45 ACP cal., 10 1/2 in. barrel, closed bolt, blue metal finish, regular forearm, 30 shot mag., 12 lbs. New 2004.

MSR $1,970	$1,750	$1,500	$1,300	$1,125	$925	$800	$700	

This carbine model may only be shipped from the factory to an NFA Class II manufacturer or NFA Class III dealer.

PISTOLS: SEMI-AUTO

1911 THOMPSON CUSTOM – .45 ACP cal., stainless steel or aluminum (Lightweight model, mfg. 2005-2007) construction, Series 80 design, 5 in. barrel, Thompson bullet logo on left side of double serrated slide, 7 shot mag., grip safety, checkered laminate grips with medallion, skeletonized trigger, combat hammer, low profile sights, 31 1/2 (Lightweight) or 39 oz. New 2004.

MSR $813	$695	$575	$485	$415	$350	$300	$275	

THOMPSON 1927 A-1 DELUXE – .45 ACP cal., single action, blow back design, 10 1/2 in. finned barrel, grooved walnut forearm with sling swivel, blade front sight, adj. rear sight, 10 or 30 shot mag., also accepts 50 shot drum, 30 shot stick, 10 shot stick, and 100 shot drum magazines, approx. 6 lbs. New 2008.

MSR $1,284	$1,050	$875	$775	$675	$575	$475	$425	

Add $93 for 50 shot mag. or $259 for 100 shot drum mag.

This model is marked "Model of 1927A-1" and "Thompson Semi-Automatic Carbine" on the left side and Auto-Ordnance Corporation on the right side.

GRADING - PPGS™	100%	98%	95%	90%	80%	70%	60%	LAST MSR

THOMPSON/CENTER ARMS CO., INC.

Current manufacturer established during 1967, and located in Springfield, MA. Previously located in Rochester, NH. Distributor and dealer sales.

On Dec. 18, 2006 Smith & Wesson holding corp. announced that it purchased Thompson Center Arms Co., Inc. During late 2010, Smith & Wesson moved their production to its Springfield, MA facility.

Thompson/Center also has created a custom shop to enable customers to create custom pistols, rifles, shotguns, and muzzleloaders. Please contact the factory for availability and an individualized quotation.

Please refer to the *Blue Book of Modern Black Powder Arms* by John Allen (also online) for more information and prices on Thompson/Center's lineup of modern black powder models.

Black Powder Revolvers - Reproductions & Replicas and *Black Powder Long Arms & Pistols - Reproductions & Replicas* by Dennis Adler are also invaluable sources for most black powder reproductions and replicas, and include hundreds of color images on most popular makes/models, provide manufacturer/trademark histories, and up-to-date information on related items/accessories for black powder shooting - www.bluebookofgunvalues.com.

PISTOLS: SINGLE SHOT

Caution: older and newer TC components do not interchange safely. Although parts will fit, they may not function properly. Special ordering of barrels, frames, and calibers started in 1988. Values listed are for complete guns - including frame and barrel.

PRO-HUNTER – various cals., 15 in. fluted stainless steel barrel, adj. sights, hardwood (disc. 2007) or rubber grips. Mfg. 2006-2012.

	100%	98%	95%	90%	80%	70%	60%	LAST MSR
	$650	$550	$475	$425	$350	$300	$250	*$779*

Add $30 for hardwood grips (disc. 2007).
Add $413-$450 per extra barrel, depending on caliber.

G2 CONTENDER – various rimfire and centerfire cals., 12 or 14 (disc.) in. barrel, adj. sights, blued finish, walnut finger groove grip and forearm, replacement for the Contender model, will accept older Contender barrels w/o frame alteration, automatic hammer block safety with built-in interlock, hammer recocking w/o breaking open the gun, opening has been made easier, approx. 3 1/2 lbs. Mfg. late 2002-2012.

	100%	98%	95%	90%	80%	70%	60%	LAST MSR
	$650	$550	$450	$395	$350	$300	$250	*$729*

Add approx. $10 for 14 in. barrel (disc.).
Add approx. 5% for .17 HMR or 17 Mach 2 cal.
Add $333-$458 per additional barrel, depending on length and caliber.

* ***G2 Contender Stainless*** – various cals., similar to G2 Contender, except is stainless steel with black rubber grips, 14 in. barrel only. Mfg. 2006-2011.

	100%	98%	95%	90%	80%	70%	60%	LAST MSR
	$695	$550	$475	$425	$350	$300	$265	*$809*

CONTENDER – .22 LR, .22 Rem., 5mm Rem., .218 Bee, .22 Hornet, .22 Jet, .221 Fireball, .222 Rem., .25-35 WCF, .256 Mag., .30 Carbine, .30-30 Win., .38 Spl., .357 Mag., .17 Ackley Bee, .17 Bumblebee, .17 Hornet, .17K Hornet, .17 Rem., .300 Whisper (new 1994), .30 Herrett, .357 Herrett, .357-44 B&D, 7x30 Waters, .32 H&R Mag., .32-20 WCF, 6mm TCU, 6.5mm TCU, or 9mm Para. cal., barrels are interchangeable, 8 3/4 (disc.), 10, or 14 in. barrel, hinged break open action, trigger guard action lever, blue, .44, .357 Mag., and .45 Colt available with detachable choke for hot shot cartridges, VR, 10 in. barrel available, 10 in. bull barrel, adj. sights, checkered walnut grip and forearm. Mfg. 1967-2000.

The Contender action was made in 3 variations, and a wide variety of changes were made to grips, stocks, sights, etc. during 1967-2000. These production variances do not necessarily add premiums to values listed.

* ***Contender Bull Barrel*** – available in 13 cals. between .17 Rem. and .45 Win. Mag., 10 in. round barrel only.

	100%	98%	95%	90%	80%	70%	60%	LAST MSR
	$380	$295	$220	$190	$170	$160	$150	*$510*

GRADING - PPGS™	100%	98%	95%	90%	80%	70%	60%	LAST MSR

Add $22 for .45 Colt/.410 bore with internal chokes.
Add $11 for .22 LR match grade chamber (new 1996).
Add approx. $230-$267 per additional barrel.

* ***Contender Armour Alloy II Bull Barrel*** – 7 cals. between .22 LR and .30-30 Win., similar to regular Bull Barrel, except has Armour Alloy II satin finish which is harder than stainless steel. Mfg. 1986-89.

$320	$285	$230	$180	$170	$155	$130	*$415*

Add $5 for .45 Colt/.410 bore internal choke.

* ***Contender Vent. Rib*** – .357 Mag. (disc.), .44 Mag. (disc.) or .45 Colt/.410 bore cal., 10 in. VR barrel only, adj. front and flip-up rear sight, internal choke became standard in 1985.

$400	$300	$225	$185	$170	$160	$150	*$533*

* ***Contender Armour Alloy Vent. Rib*** – .45/.410 bore cal., internal choke, has Armour Alloy II satin finish which is harder than stainless steel. Mfg. 1986-disc.

$350	$295	$230	$180	$170	$155	$130	*$435*

* ***Contender Stainless Steel*** – various cals., 10 in. bull barrel. Mfg. 1993-2000.

$435	$315	$220	$190	$170	$160	$150	*$578*

Add approx. $240 per additional barrel.
Add $5 for .45/.410 bore with adj. sights.
Add $20 for .45/.410 bore with VR.

* ***Contender Octagon Barrel*** – .22 LR, .22 WMR (disc.), .22 Hornet (disc.), .22K Hornet (disc.), .222 Rem. (disc.), or .357 Mag. (disc.) cal., 10 in. barrel. Disc. 1998.

$355	$260	$200	$180	$170	$160	$150	*$474*

* ***Contender Match Grade Barrel*** – .22 LR cal. only, choice of 10 or 14 in. match barrel. Mfg. 1992-98.

$350	$265	$200	$180	$170	$160	$150	*$460*

Add $10 for 14 in. barrel.

CONTENDER SHOOTERS PACKAGE – .22 LR Match, .223 Rem., .30-30 Win., or 7-30 Waters cal., includes blue frame and 14 in. barrel w/o sights, 2.5-7X scope, composite grips and forend, Weaver style base and rings, pistol case. Mfg. 1998-2000.

$650	$575	$550	$450	$400	$360	$330	*$754*

CONTENDER SUPER (14 & 16 IN.) – 13 cals. available from .17 Rem. - .45 Win. Mag. (disc.), 14 or 16 in. bull barrel only, special grips, beavertail forearm, adj. sight, 3 1/2 lbs. Disc. 1997.

$360	$265	$200	$180	$170	$160	$150	*$474*

Add $5 for 16 in. barrel.
Add $31 for .17 Rem. cal. (new 1992).
Add $10 for .45-70 Govt. cal. in 16 in. barrel only with muzzle brake (new 1992).
Add approx. $224 per additional barrel.
Add $31 for VR barrel (.45 LC/.410 bore only).
Thompson Center also made special order guns in cals. other than those listed above. If factory work, these pistols will be worth a premium.

* ***Contender Super Stainless*** – various cals., choice of 14 or 16 in. barrel. Mfg. 1993-97.

$385	$275	$215	$165	$130	$120	$100	*$505*

Add $5 for 16 in. barrel.
Add $25 for .45-70 Govt. bull barrel with muzzle tamer.
Add $30-$35 for .45 LC/.410 bore with internal choke.
Add approx. $240 per additional barrel.

* ***Contender Super Armour Alloy II*** – 5 cals. between .22 LR and 7mm Rem. Mag., similar to regular Super Contender, except has Armour Alloy II satin finish which is harder than stainless steel. Mfg. 1986-89.

$355	$295	$240	$185	$160	$135	$115	*$425*

GRADING - PPGS™	100%	98%	95%	90%	80%	70%	60%	LAST MSR

SUPER CONTENDER (14 & 16 IN.) – various cals. between .22 LR - .45-70 Govt., wood grips with rear stipling, configurations include 14 or 16 in. bull (with or w/o VR) barrel, adj. sights, blue finish only. Mfg. 1999-2000.

	$410	$345	$285	$255	$220	$195	$170	$520

Add $35 for 14 in. VR barrel.
Add $5 for 16 in. tapered barrel.

* ***Super Contender Stainless*** – similar to Super Contender, except only available in 14 in. barrel. Mfg. 1999-2000.

	$430	$320	$215	$165	$135	$120	$100	$578

Add $35 for VR barrel.
Add $22 for .45/.410 ga. barrel.

CONTENDER HUNTER PACKAGE – .223 Rem., .7-30 Waters, .30-30 Win., .35 Rem., .357 Rem. Max. (disc. 1994), .375 Win. Mag. (new 1992), .44 Mag., or .45-70 Govt. cal., special 12 (disc.) or 14 (new 1992) in. barrel with muzzle brake, 2.5 power scope with lighted reticle, walnut grip has nonslip rubber insert to cushion recoil, includes studs, swivels, sling, and deluxe carrying case, approx. 4 lbs. Mfg. 1990-97.

	$695	$575	$495	$430	$365	$315	$275	$798

CONTENDER 25TH ANNIVERSARY – .22 LR cal. only, 10 in. octagon barrel, laser etched anniversary logo on receiver sides and barrel, checkered stock and forearm, limited mfg. in 1992 only.

	$610	$535	$465	$410	$360	$315	$275	$700

* ***Contender 25th Anniversary Cased Set*** – cased set with 5 barrels including .22 LR, .22 WMR, .22 Jet, .22 Hornet, and .38 Spl. cal., 50 sets mfg. 1992 only.

	$1,850	$1,550	$1,225	$1,050	$900	$775	$650	$1,975

ENCORE – various cals. between .22 LR and .480 Ruger (new 2002), walnut grip with finger grooves and forend, blue finish, 10 (disc. 1999), 12 (new 1999), or 15 in. barrel with adj. sights, VR barrel on .45 LC/.410 bore, hammer block safety with bolt interlock, 4-4 1/2 lbs. Mfg. 1998-2012.

	$575	$485	$415	$335	$285	$250	$225	$679

Add $228 for extra 10 in. (disc.), approx. $313 for extra 12 in. barrel, or $318 for extra 15 in. barrel, depending on caliber.
Add $40 for .45 LC/.410 bore barrel, depending on barrel length.
Values are for base caliber - most calibers will add approx. 5% to base price.
Encore pistol barrels ARE NOT interchangeable with Contender pistol barrels.

* ***Encore Stainless*** – .22-250 Rem., .223 Rem., .243 Win., .30-06, .308 Win., 7mm-08 Rem., .44 Mag., .45 LC/.410 bore, or .480 Ruger (mfg. 2003) cal., black synthetic finger groove grips and forearm, 12 (disc.) or 15 in. barrel. Mfg. 1999-2012.

	$625	$525	$475	$425	$350	$300	$265	$729

Add $23 for .480 Ruger cal. (mfg. 2003).
Add $40 for .45LC/.410 bore.

* ***Encore Hunter Package*** – .22-250 Rem., .270 Win., or .308 Win. cal., features 15 in. barrel w/o sights and 2.5-7X scope, Weaver base and rings, composite grip and forend, includes case. Mfg. 1998-2005, reintroduced 2010-2012.

	$875	$750	$650	$550	$450	$375	$325	$969

RIFLES: BOLT ACTION

A recall has been issued for all Venture rifles manufactured prior to October 28, 2011. To determine if your rifle is affected, please visit Smith & Wesson's website: www.smith-wesson.com or call 1-800-713-0356.

ICON – .22-250 Rem., .243 Win., .270 Win., .280 Rem., .30-06, .300 Win. Mag., .338 Win. Mag., .308 Win., .30 TC (disc. 2011), 6.5 Creedmoor (new 2010), or 7mm Rem. Mag. cal., medium or long action, black synthetic (medium action), Realtree camo (medium action), checkered American walnut (long action only), Classic Sporter style walnut (Icon

GRADING - PPGS™	100%	98%	95%	90%	80%	70%	60%	LAST MSR

Classic, new 2008), or choice of Ultra Wood pistol grip stock and forearm, 24 in. barrel, hinged floor plate on long action, cocking indicator, adj. trigger, detachable 3 shot mag. on medium action, interlocked bedding system, butterknife jeweled bolt handle, 60 degree bolt lift, Weaver style base, guaranteed to shoot 1 in. or less at 100 yards, approx. 7 1/2 lbs. Mfg. 2007-2012.

	$795	$650	$550	$475	$400	$350	$295	*$889*

Subtract $80 for synthetic stock with Weathershield dull nickel finish (medium action only).
Add $10 for camo stock.
Subtract $10 for Ultrawood stock (.22-250 Rem., .243 Win., .30 TC, or .308 Win. cal.).

ICON PRECISION HUNTER – .204 Ruger, .223 Rem., .22-250 Rem., .243 Win., 6.5 Creedmoor (mfg. 2010-2011), or .308 Win. cal., 22 in. heavy fluted barrel with 5R button rifling, fat bolt design with tactical style handle, classic varminter style brown synthetic stock with cheekpiece and beavertail forend, detachable 3 shot mag. with single shot adapter, Picatinny rail, adj. trigger, two position safety, sling swivel studs, 8 lbs. Mfg. 2009-2012.

	$900	$775	$675	$575	$475	$425	$350	*$1,019*

ICON WARLORD – .308 Win. or .338 Lapua cal., 5 or 10 shot mag., hand lapped stainless steel fluted barrel, carbon fiber tactical style stock with adj. cheekpiece, available in OD Green, Flat Black, or Desert Sand, Weather Shield finish on all metal, adj. trigger, Picatinny rail, tactical bolt handle, 12 3/4 - 13 3/4 lbs. Mfg. 2010-2011.

	$3,000	$2,600	$2,200	$1,800	$1,500	$1,250	$1,125	*$3,499*

VENTURE – .204 Ruger, .223 Rem., .22-250 Rem., .243 Win., .25-06, .270 Win., .280 Rem., .30-06, 7mm-08 Rem., 7mm Rem. Mag., .270 WSM, .308 Win. , .30 TC, .300 Win. Mag., or .338 Win. Mag. cal., 22 or 24 in. match grade tapered barrel with 5R button rifling, fat bolt design, classic sporter black synthetic stock, detachable 3 shot mag., Weaver style base, adj. trigger, two position safety, textured grip, 7 1/2 lbs. New 2009.

MSR $537	$450	$395	$340	$300	$250	$200	$160

Add $41 for Weathershield composite stock.

* ***Venture Compact*** – .22-250 Rem., .243 Win., 7mm-08 Rem., or .308 Win. cal., similar to Venture, except has 20 in. barrel, one inch spacer, and short (12 1/2 to 13 1/2 in.) LOP, drilled and tapped, 6 3/4 lbs. New 2012.

MSR $537	$450	$395	$340	$300	$250	$200	$160

VENTURE PREDATOR – .204 Ruger, .223 Rem., .22-250 Rem., or .308 Win. cal., 22 in. fluted barrel, adj. trigger, 3 shot mag., composite stock with 100% Realtree Max-1 or AP Snow (new 2012) camo coverage, Hogue panels, Weather Shield bolt handle, 6 3/4 lbs. New 2010.

MSR $638	$540	$475	$400	$365	$295	$245	$190

DIMENSION – various cals., short or long action, 22 or 24 in. 5R rifled barrel, matte blue finish, 3 shot detachable box mag., drilled and tapped, textured grip black synthetic stock with competition cheekpiece and removable stock spacers, 3-lug fluted bolt, left or right hand action, adj. trigger, 7 lbs. New 2012.

MSR $689	$595	$525	$450	$375	$300	$250	$225

RIFLES: SEMI-AUTO

SILVER LYNX – .22 LR cal., 20 in. match grade barrel with adj. fiber optic open sights, 5 shot mag., stainless steel action and barrel, black composite stock with Monte Carlo cheekpiece, 5 1/2 lbs. Mfg. 2004-2005.

	$340	$295	$240	$200	$165	$145	$120	*$423*

MODEL R-55 CLASSIC – .17 Mach 2 (mfg. 2006-2007) or .22 LR cal., blowback action, all steel construction, 5 (new 2003) or 8 (disc. 2002) shot mag., 22 in. match grade barrel with muzzle crown, adj. rear sight, blue finish, uncheckered Monte Carlo walnut stock, 5 1/2 lbs. Mfg. 2000-2009.

	$475	$400	$335	$285	$240	$195	$160	*$586*

GRADING - PPGS™	100%	98%	95%	90%	80%	70%	60%	LAST MSR

MODEL R-55 CLASSIC BENCHMARK TARGET – same action as Classic, 18 in. heavy target barrel, brown laminated hardwood Monte Carlo target stock, matte blue finish, 10 shot mag., no sights, receiver is drilled and tapped, 6.8 lbs. Mfg. 2003-2009.

	$475	$400	$335	$285	$240	$195	$160	*$586*

MODEL R-55 SPORTER – .17 Mach 2 (disc.) or .22 LR cal., blue steel, 20 in. barrel, brown laminate or black composite stock, fiber optic sights, 6 1/4 - 7 1/4 lbs. Mfg. 2005-2011.

	$460	$400	$335	$285	$240	$215	$180	*$545*

Add $92 for brown laminate stock.

* ***Model R-55 Sporter Stainless*** – .22 LR cal., similar to Sporter, except with All Weather stainless steel and black composite stock, 7 1/4 lbs. Disc. 2011.

	$625	$550	$495	$450	$400	$325	$250	*$705*

RIFLES: SINGLE SHOT

ENCORE RIFLE – available in many rimfire and centerfire cals. between .17 Mach 2 (mfg. 2005-2009) and .45-70 Govt., interchangeable standard 24 or heavy 26 in. barrel, automatic hammer block safety, trigger guard opening lever, choice of black synthetic (new 1999), Realtree camo (new 2005), Realtree Hardwoods HD camo, or American walnut uncheckered forearm and Monte Carlo stock with pistol grip, adj. rear sight, approx. 7 lbs. Mfg. 1997-2012.

	$575	$475	$375	$325	$275	$250	$225	*$689*

Add $50 for walnut.
Add $50 for camo.
Add $35 for .17 Mach 2 cal. (disc.).
Add $352 per extra blue finish barrel.
Add $173 for thumbhole stock (disc.).

Encore rifle barrels ARE NOT interchangeable with Contender Carbine barrels.

* ***Encore Rifle Stainless*** – similar to Encore Rifle, except has black synthetic stock and forearm or Realtree/Realtree Hardwoods HD (new 2005) camo treatment, and is stainless steel. Mfg. 1999-2012.

	$650	$525	$425	$350	$300	$265	$235	*$769*

Add $399 per extra barrel.
Add $70 for camo.
Add $265 for thumbhole stock (camo only, disc.).

* ***Encore Rifle Katahdin Carbine*** – .444 Marlin (disc. 2003), .450 Marlin, or .45-70 Govt. cal., 18 in. barrel with muzzle tamer, blue steel, black composite stock and forearm, fiber optic sights, drilled and tapped, 6 lbs., 10 oz. Mfg. 2002-2005.

	$490	$370	$255	$235	$195	$180	$170	*$617*

Add $292 for extra barrel.

* ***Encore Rifle Hunter Package*** – .300 Win. Mag., or .308 Win. cal., includes 3-9x40mm scope, Weaver style base and rings, and hard case. Mfg. 2002-2005.

	$770	$640	$585	$475	$400	$360	$330	*$905*

PRO HUNTER RIFLE – various cals., 28 in. fluted barrel only w/o sights, drilled and tapped, stainless steel, features recoil reducing Flex Tech stock and choice of black, Hardwoods camo, with or w/o thumbhole, 7 3/4 lbs. Mfg. 2006-2012.

	$725	$575	$475	$400	$350	$315	$275	*$839*

Add $70 for camo.
Add $99 for .416 Rigby cal. (disc. 2011).
Add $333 per extra barrel.

* ***Pro Hunter Katahdin*** – .45-70 Govt., .460 S&W, or .500 S&W cal., similar to Pro Hunter, except 20 in. stainless steel barrel with sights, 7 lbs. New 2010.

MSR $852	$725	$635	$545	$495	$400	$325	$250	

GRADING - PPGS™	100%	98%	95%	90%	80%	70%	60%	LAST MSR

ENCORE PRO HUNTER PREDATOR – .204 Ruger, .223 Rem., .22-250 Rem., or .308 Win. cal., 28 in. fluted barrel, synthetic Flextech stock with 100% Realtree Max-1 camo coverage, scope base, recoil pad, 7 3/4 lbs. New 2010.

MSR $882	$750	$650	$565	$510	$415	$340	$265	

CONTENDER CARBINE – available in 15 cals. between .17 Rem. and .44 Rem. Mag., also .410 bore (3 in.), Contender action with pistol grip full stock and forearm, 21 in. interchangeable barrel, drilled for scope mounts, iron sights standard. Mfg. 1986-2000.

	$415	$315	$255	$215	$190	$175	$160	$540

Add $31 for .17 Rem. cal. (disc. 1997).
Add $21 for .410 bore barrel. (disc. 1997).
Add approx. $244 per extra barrel.
Add $11 for match grade .22 LR barrel.
Subtract $36 for Youth Model (16 1/4 in. barrel w/o VR - disc. 1998).
Add $175 for Survival Carbine System (disc. - includes Rynite stock, 16 1/4 in. .223 Rem. barrel, extra .45 Colt/.410 bore barrel, and soft camo cordura case).

* ***Contender Carbine Rynite*** – similar to Contender Carbine, except has Rynite stock and forend. Mfg. 1990-93.

	$335	$270	$220	$195	$180	$165	$155	$425

Add $30 for .17 Rem. cal.
Add $10 for match grade barrel.
Add $25 for 21 in. VR smooth bore .410 bore barrel.

* ***Contender Carbine Stainless*** – various cals., 21 in. barrel, choice of walnut (disc. 1993) or Rynite synthetic stock. Mfg. 1993-2000.

	$415	$310	$230	$200	$185	$165	$155	$546

Add $35 for walnut stock (disc.).
Add $11 for .22 LR match barrel (new 1995).
Add $26 for .410 bore smooth bore barrel with screw-in full choke (disc.).

This model was also available in a Youth Model with walnut stock at no extra charge (disc. 1993).

HUNTER RIFLE MODEL – single shot, top lever break open action w/interchangeable barrels, .22 Hornet, .223 Rem., .22-250 Rem., .243 Win., .270 Win., 7x57mm, .30-06, .308 Win., .375 H&H (new 1992), or .416 Rem. Mag. (new 1992) cal., 23 in. barrel, 6 lbs. 14 oz., checkered walnut stock, choice of medium or light sporter weight barrel. New 1983 and improved in 1987. Available in left hand at no extra charge. Disc. 1992.

	$500	$415	$350	$295	$265	$240	$220	$595

Add $20 for .375 H&H or .416 Rem. Mag. cal. Add approx. $275 per extra rifle barrel.

* ***Hunter Rifle Model Deluxe*** – similar to Hunter Model, except features double triggers and upgraded walnut stock and forearm. Mfg. 1992 only.

	$550	$450	$375	$325	$285	$250	$225	$675

Add $20 for .375 H&H or .416 Rem. Mag. cal.

* ***Hunter Rifle Model Shotgun*** – same action as Hunter Rifle, except is supplied with 12 ga. barrel (field choke with 3 1/2 in. chamber or slug barrel with 3 in. chamber and iron sights) or 10 ga. barrel (3 1/2 in. chamber). Disc. 1992.

	$500	$415	$350	$295	$265	$240	$220	$595

Add $275 per additional shotgun barrel.

TCR '83 ARISTOCRAT – similar to Hunter Model, except stock has cheekpiece and forearm is checkered, stainless steel, double set triggers. Disc. 1986.

	$550	$450	$375	$325	$285	$250	$225	$475

Add $175 for each additional barrel(s) (including 12 ga. slug).

HOTSHOT – .22 LR cal., 19 in. barrel, synthetic stock with black, Realtree AP camo, or AP Pink camo, short LOP, designed for Youth, automatic safety, drilled and tapped, 3 lbs. Mfg. 2010-2012.

	$175	$150	$130	$110	$95	$80	$70	$219

Add $30 for camo finish.

GRADING - PPGS™	100%	98%	95%	90%	80%	70%	60%	LAST MSR

G2 CONTENDER – various rimfire and centerfire cals., 23 in. blue or stainless steel barrel, compact design, uncheckered hardwood walnut (blue finish only) or black composite stock, drilled and tapped. Mfg. 2009-2012.

	$650	$525	$425	$350	$300	$265	$235	$759

Add $20 for .17 HMR cal. Add $10 for walnut.

SHOTGUNS: SINGLE SHOT

ENCORE SHOTGUN – 12 (new 2004) or 20 ga., 3 in. chamber, action based on Encore pistol with trigger guard for barrel opening, 26 in. VR barrel with three choke tubes (Field model only, N/A in Slug or Turkey model), recoil pad. Mfg. 1998-2009.

	$725	$600	$500	$400	$325	$250	$200	$876

Add approx. $408 per additional shotgun VR barrel with choke tubes.
Subtract $23 for 20 ga.

* ***Encore Shotgun Slug Gun*** – 12 or 20 ga. only, 3 in. chamber, 24 or 26 (20 ga. only) in. rifled barrel with fiber optic sights, walnut stock and forearm. Mfg. 2000-2005, reintroduced 2008-2009.

	$750	$625	$515	$400	$325	$250	$200	$895

Subtract approx. $25 for 20 ga. Add $20 for fluted barrel.

* ***Encore Shotgun Turkey Gun*** – 12 (disc. 2005) or 20 ga., 3 in. chamber, 24 in. smoothbore barrel with screw-in turkey choke tube, 100% Realtree Hardwoods (new 2003) or Advantage Timber (mfg. 2002 only) camo coverage, and fiber optic sights. Mfg. 2002-2011.

	$825	$725	$625	$525	$450	$400	$325	$978

Add $71 for muzzleloading barrel (disc. 2003).
Subtract $21 if w/o camo coverage.

* ***Encore Shotgun Katahdin Turkey Gun*** – 12 ga., 3 in. chamber, 20 in. barrel with turkey choke tube, composite stock with Realtree Hardwoods HD camo pattern, fiber optic sights. Limited mfg. 2005.

	$590	$510	$410	$325	$275	$225	$200	$748

PRO HUNTER TURKEY GUN – 12 or 20 ga., 24 or 26 in. rifled bore barrel, Flextech synthetic stock with 100% Realtree AP camo coverage, adj. fiber optic sights, extra full turkey choke tube, 6 1/2 lbs. New 2010.

MSR $892	$750	$650	$565	$510	$415	$340	$265

Add $20 for 12 ga. Slug gun with 28 in. rifled bore barrel.

THOR

Current trademark manufactured by Thor Global Defense Group, located in Van Buren, AR. Distributed by Knesek Guns, located in Van Buren, AR.

PISTOLS: SEMI-AUTO

THOR 1911 SERIES – .45 ACP cal., 4 1/4 (Carry) or 5 in. (Tactical) barrel, carbon steel frame, matte black finish, GI night sights, mfg. in partnership with Guncrafter Industries.

MSR $3,250	$2,750	$2,400	$2,065	$1,875	$1,515	$1,240	$965

Add $205 for Carry Model.

RIFLES: BOLT ACTION

THOR M408 – .408 Cheytac cal., 29 in. fluted barrel, 7 shot mag., no sights, fully adj. aluminum modular stock, M-1913 Picatinny rail, integral bipod, muzzle brake, polymer pistol grip, advanced long range interdiction system, 27 lbs.

MSR $11,495	$9,775	$8,550	$7,325	$6,650	$5,375	$4,400	$3,425

THOR XM408 – .408 Cheytac cal., 30 in. fluted match grade barrel with removable muzzle brake, 5 or 7 shot detachable box mag., 10 in. Mil-Std 1913 upper rail, CNC machined receiver and bolt, adj. hardened aluminum stock with sliding mechanism, adj. mono-pod, black or camo finish, optional advanced shroud assembly, approx. 26 lbs.

MSR $5,999	$5,850	$5,300	$4,850	$4,350	$3,900	$3,250	$2,650

Add $6,000 for advanced shroud assembly.

GRADING - PPGS™	100%	98%	95%	90%	80%	70%	60%	LAST MSR

THOR TR408 – .408 Cheytac cal., 29 in. fluted stainless steel barrel, fluted bolt with tactical bolt knob, Huber Concepts trigger, Harris HBRS bipod, McMillan A5 stock, 7 shot mag., beavertail forearm.

MSR $5,999	$5,850	$5,300	$4,850	$4,350	$3,900	$3,250	$2,650	

THOR TRSA SERIES – .300 Blackout or .308 Win. cal., 16 1/2 (.300 Blackout cal. only), 20 or 24 in. threaded or unthreaded barrel, lightweight aluminum chassis with folding stock, Surefire SOCOM muzzle brake, Huber Concepts trigger, Harris HBRS bipod.

MSR $5,199	$4,400	$3,850	$3,300	$2,995	$2,425	$1,975	$1,550	

Add $200 for .300 Blackout cal.

RIFLES: SEMI-AUTO

IMPORTANT NOTE: On model(s) where *N/A has replaced the normal 100% value, it indicates current market conditions are too unstable to accurately ascertain 100%-60% values. Factory retail prices (MSRs) reflect most recent updates. For more up-to-date information on current pricing trends and additional useful information, please visit www.bluebookofgunvalues.com, select "Information & Services" from the menu, and click on "Additional Book Information".

THOR TR-15 – 5.56 NATO cal., 16.1 in. barrel, 30 shot mag., detachable carry handle, M4 handguard, variety of Cerakote custom finishes available, with or w/o flash hider and muzzle brake, collapsible Mil-spec stock, F marked front sight post, flattop upper receiver, optional THOR rail system.

MSR $1,450	*N/A	$1,125	$950	$825	$700	$600	$500	

Add $250 for THOR rail system.

THUNDER-FIVE

Previous trademark manufactured by MIL Inc., located in Piney Flats, TN. Previous company name was Holston Enterprises, Inc. Previously manufactured by Mil, Inc. located in Piney Flats, TN. Previously distributed by C.L. Reedy & Associates, Inc. located in Jonesborough, TN.

While previously advertised as the Spectre Five (not mfg.), this firearm was re-named the Thunder-Five.

REVOLVERS

THUNDER-FIVE – .45 LC cal./.410 bore with 3 in. chamber or .45-70 Govt. cal. (mfg. 1994-98), single or double action, unique 5 shot revolver design permits shooting .45 LC or .410 bore shotshells interchangeably, 2 in. rifled barrel, phosphate finish, external ambidextrous hammer block safety, internal transfer bar safety, combat sights, hammer, trigger, and trigger guard, Pachmayr grips, padded plastic carrying case, 48 oz., serialization started at 1,101. Mfg. 1992-circa 2007.

	$495	$450	$400	$375	$350	$325	$300	*$545*

Sub-caliber sleeve inserts were available until 1998 for 9mm Para., .357 Mag./.38 Spl., and .38 Super cals.

THUREON DEFENSE

Current manufacturer located in New Holstein, WI.

PISTOLS: SEMI-AUTO

THUREON SA PISTOL – 9mm Para. or .45 ACP cal., same operating as the SA Carbine. New 2012.

MSR $959	$815	$715	$610	$550	$450	$365	$285	

THUREON GA PISTOL – 9mm Para., 357 SIG, .40 S&W, 10mm Auto, or .45 ACP cal., similar to Thureon SA pistol. New 2012.

MSR $959	$815	$715	$610	$550	$450	$365	$285	

RIFLES: SEMI-AUTO

IMPORTANT NOTE: On model(s) where *N/A has replaced the normal 100% value, it indicates current market conditions are too unstable to accurately ascertain 100%-60% values. Factory retail prices (MSRs) reflect most recent updates. For more up-to-date information on

GRADING - PPGS™	100%	98%	95%	90%	80%	70%	60%	LAST MSR

current pricing trends and additional useful information, please visit www.bluebookofgunvalues.com, select "Information & Services" from the menu, and click on "Additional Book Information".

Add $15 for M4 telescoping buttstock.
Add $35 for laser/tactical light mount.
Add $75 for open sights nested in sight rail.

THUREON SA CARBINE – 9mm Para. or .45 ACP cal., blowback action, 32 shot mag. (modified Uzi or Colt SMG mag.), AR-15 trigger components, integral Picatinny rail, closed bolt, aluminum upper and lower receivers, adj. buttstock, black finish, approx. 6 1/2 lbs.

MSR $959	*N/A	$715	$610	$550	$450	$365	$285	

THUREON GA CARBINE – 9mm Para., .357 SIG, .40 S&W, 10mm Auto, or .45 ACP cal., similar to Thureon SA Carbine, except uses Glock magazines. New 2012.

MSR $959	*N/A	$715	$610	$550	$450	$365	$285	

Add $40 for 10mm or .357 SIG cal.

TIKKA

Current trademark imported by Beretta U.S.A. Corp., located in Accokeek, MD. Previously imported until 2000 by Stoeger Industries, located in Wayne, NJ. Tikka rifles are currently manufactured by Sako, Ltd. located in Riihimäki, Finland. Previously manufactured by Oy Tikkakoski Ab, of Tikkakoski, Finland (pre-1989).

During 2000, Tikka was purchased by Beretta Holding of Italy. All currently produced Tikkas are imported by Beretta U.S.A. Corp., located in Accokeek, MD.

Also see listings under Ithaca combination guns and bolt action rifles for older models.

COMBINATIONS GUNS: O/U

Previously manufactured in Jyvaskyla, Finland. In 1989, under a joint venture agreement, the 412 O/U shooting system was manufactured in Italy. Older models may be found in the Valmet trademark section of this text.

During 1993, the new models of the 512S series replaced the older 412S series. Separate listings have not been provided, since they are almost identical in most respects.

Add $745-$765 for extra shotgun barrels (includes screw-in chokes), $810 for extra shotgun/rifle combo, and $1,040 for double rifle barrels.

MODEL 512S/412S SHOOTING SYSTEM – interchangeable barrel assemblies permit a double rifle, shotgun/rifle, and O/U shotgun configuration, user installed interchangeable barrels, monobloc locking, rifle barrel positioning by adjustment, SST, extractors or ejectors, checkered walnut stock and forend, cocking indicators, blue finish.

* ***Model 512S Field Grade*** – 12 ga. only, 3 in. chambers, auto ejectors, screw-in choke tubes (includes 5), 26 or 28 in. barrels, matte nickel finish. New 1986-importation disc. 1997, reintroduced 2000 only.

	$1,050	$750	$595	$550	$475	$440	$400	*$1,134*

Subtract 10% if w/o choke tubes.
Add $45 for Sporting Clays Model (new 2000).

The Premium Grade became standard issue beginning 1995. This model was reintroduced in 2000 only, and new features included back boring and ported barrels (Sporting Clays Model only).

* ***Model 412ST Trap*** – 12 ga., Monte Carlo stock, 30 in. barrels, screw-in chokes standard.

	$1,125	$925	$725	$650	$580	$540	$475	*$1,325*

This variation was made by Valmet in Finland.

* ***Model 412ST Premium Grade Trap*** – similar to Model 412ST Trap, except better walnut and checkering.

	$1,425	$1,000	$875	$750	$625	$580	$515	*$1,665*

This variation was made by Valmet in Finland.

GRADING - PPGS™	100%	98%	95%	90%	80%	70%	60%	LAST MSR

* ***Model 512S Sporting Clays*** – 12 ga. only, sporting clays configuration with 28 or 30 (new 1994) in. VR barrels and choke tubes. Imported 1992-97.

	$1,160	$950	$735	$650	$580	$540	$475	*$1,360*

* ***Model 512S Combination Gun*** – combination rifle/shotgun, 12 ga, 3 in. chambers, 24 in. barrels, under rifle barrel in .222 Rem., .30-06, or .308 Win. cal., extractors. Importation disc. 1997.

	$1,425	$1,025	$775	$675	$600	$525	$475	*$1,770*

* ***Model 512S Double Rifle*** – .30-06 (new 1994), .308 Win. (new 1994), 9.3x74R cal., 24 in. barrels, extractors. Importation disc. 1997.

	$1,525	$1,125	$825	$750	$625	$550	$500	*$1,890*

RIFLES: BOLT ACTION

About 3,000 rifles sold under the Tikka name have been recalled following catastrophic failures, but a small number of guns sold in the American market remain in the hands of consumers who have apparently not heard about the recall. A weakness in the stainless steel used to manufacture rifles during 2003-2004 has led to ruptured barrels. Consumers are urged to contact the Tikka Recall Center at 800-503-8869 with their rifle's serial number to find out if their firearm is affected.

NEW GENERATION RIFLE (MODELS 595/695) – .22-250 Rem., .223 Rem., .243 Win., .270 Win., .30-06, .308 Win., 7mm Rem. Mag, .300 Win. Mag., or .338 Win Mag. cal., 22 1/2 (non-Mag.) or 24 1/2 (Mag. cals.) in. barrel, detachable 3 (standard) or 5 (optional) shot mag., forged and milled action in two lengths, checkered walnut stock, 7-7 1/2 lbs. Sako mfg. 1989-94.

	$725	$600	$550	$500	$450	$400	$360	*$835*

Add $25 for Mag. cals.

Cals. .22-250 Rem., .308 Win., and .300 Win. Mag. were introduced in late 1989.

This model's nomenclature also included the Models 595 (short actions with cals. up to .308 Win. cal.) and 695 (long action, including Mag. cals.).

PREMIUM GRADE MODEL – same cals. as New Generation Rifle, select walnut stock with rollover cheek-piece and rosewood pistol grip cap and forend tip, high polished barrel blue. Imported 1989-94.

	$860	$715	$600	$550	$500	$450	$400	*$1,030*

Add $40 for Mag. cals.

VARMINT MODEL – .22-250 Rem., .223 Rem., .243 Win., or .308 Win. cal., 24 1/2 in. heavy barrel, no sights. Mfg. 1991-94.

	$895	$750	$625	$550	$500	$450	$400	*$1,090*

T3 HUNTER – .22-250 Rem. (disc. 2009), .223 Rem. (disc. 2009), .243 Win., .25-06 Rem. (disc. 2009), .270 Win., .270 WSM (disc. 2012), .30-06, .308 Win., 6.5x55mm (disc. 2009), 7mm-08 Rem. (mfg. 2006-2009), 7mm Rem. Mag. (disc. 2009, reintroduced 2013), .300 WSM (disc. 2012), .300 Win. Mag., .338 Federal (disc. 2008), or .338 Win. Mag. (disc. 2009) cal., cold hammer forged 22 7/16-24 3/8 in. barrel, similar action as the Whitetail Hunter, choice of checkered walnut or black synthetic stock (disc. 2003), 3-4 shot detachable mag., 2 position rear safety, designed by Giugiaro of Italy, approx. 6 3/4 lbs. Importation began mid-2003.

MSR $745	$640	$550	$475	$415	$365	$315	$285	

Subtract 10% for synthetic stock.

* ***T3 Deluxe*** – similar cals. as T3 Hunter, oil finished deluxe Tripartiti checkered walnut stock with rosewood forend tip and pistol grip cap. Mfg. 2006-2007.

	$895	$725	$600	$550	$500	$450	$400	*$1,075*

* ***T3 Lite*** – various cals., similar to T3 Hunter, except has TrueBody glass fiber reinforced polymer black stock, adj. buttplate, approx. 6 1/4 lbs. Importation began 2004.

MSR $625	$535	$465	$410	$360	$310	$275	$250	

Add $35 for WSM cals.

GRADING - PPGS™	100%	98%	95%	90%	80%	70%	60%	LAST MSR

* ***T3 Lite Stainless*** – various cals., similar to T3, except has stainless action and barrel, available with black synthetic stock only. Importation began mid-2003.

MSR $750	$625	$525	$450	$385	$325	$285	$250	

Add $50 for WSM cals.
Add $75 for left-hand action (available in most right-hand cals.).

* ***T3 Camo Stainless*** – similar to T3 Lite Stainless, except has Realtree HD Hardwoods camo stock finish. Mfg. 2006-2007.

	$650	$575	$495	$425	$350	$300	$260	*$795*

* ***T3 Laminated Stainless*** – .243 Win., .25-06 Rem., .270 Win., .270 WSM, .30-06, .300 WSM, .300 Win. Mag., .308 Win., 7mm Rem. Mag., or .338 Win. Mag., similar to T3 Stainless, available with grey matte laminated hardwood stock, approx. 6 3/4 lbs. Imported 2004-2008.

	$725	$625	$525	$450	$400	$350	$300	*$850*

Add $25 for WSM cals.

* ***T3 Scout CTR*** – .223 Rem. or .308 Win. cal., 20 in. heavy barrel w/o sights, black synthetic stock with built in Monte Carlo cheekpiece, 5 or 6 shot mag., Picatinny rail on receiver. Mfg. 2010-2012.

	$825	$725	$625	$525	$425	$365	$330	*$950*

* ***T3 Big Boar Synthetic*** – .30-06, .308 Win. or .300 WSM cal., black synthetic stock, 19 in. barrel, features Giugiaro design, 6.1 lbs. Imported 2005-2007.

	$585	$515	$460	$400	$350	$300	$275	*$695*

* ***T3 Varmint*** – .22-250 Rem., .223 Rem., or .308 Win. (disc. 2009) cal., choice of steel or stainless steel action/barrel, 23 3/8 in. heavy barrel, reinforced copolymer polypropylene adj. stock, 3-6 shot detachable mag., 8 lbs. Imported 2004-2011.

	$825	$725	$625	$500	$400	$365	$330	*$940*

* ***T3 Super Varmint*** – .22-250 Rem., .223 Rem., or .308 Win. cal., 23 3/8 in. heavy stainless barrel, 3 or 4 shot mag., laminated synthetic stock with adj. comb, Picatinny rail, extra swivel stud, adj. trigger. Imported 2005-2007.

	$1,250	$1,000	$800	$695	$585	$485	$415	*$1,425*

* ***T3 Tactical*** – .223 Rem. or .308 Win. cal., T3 action, 20 or 24 (disc. 2007) in. free floating match grade barrel with protected threaded muzzle, 5 shot mag., black synthetic stock with adj. comb, wide forearm, Picatinny rail, 7 1/4 lbs. Importation began 2004.

MSR $1,700	$1,495	$1,200	$1,025	$850	$750	$650	$550	

WHITETAIL HUNTER/SYNTHETIC (BATTUE) – .22-250 Rem. (new 1995), .223 Rem. (new 1995), .243 Win. (new 1995), .25-06 Rem.(new 1995), .270 Win., .30-06, .308 Win. (not available in synthetic), 6.5x55mm Swedish (new 2002), 7mm Rem. Mag., 7mm-08 Rem. (new 1999), .300 Win. Mag., or .338 Win. Mag. cal., 20 1/2 (disc. 1994), 22 1/2 (new 1995), or 24 1/2 (new 1995, Mag. cals. only), in. barrel, 3 or 5 (optional) shot detachable mag., choice of wood or black synthetic (new 1996) stock, no sights (Hunter Model), or open sights on raised rib (disc., Battue Model), approx. 7 1/4 lbs. Mfg. 1991-2002.

	$525	$450	$390	$350	$325	$300	$275	*$615*

Add $30 for Mag. cals.
Add $60 for carved elk or deer game scene stock (mfg. 1996-97).

* ***Whitetail Hunter/Synthetic Left Hand*** – similar cals. as Whitetail Hunter, left-hand action. Importation disc. 2003.

	$590	$530	$460	$395	$360	$325	$295	*$680*

Add $30 for Mag. cals.

* ***Whitetail Hunter/Synthetic/Battue Stainless*** – similar cals. as Whitetail Hunter, except not available in 6.5x55mm Swedish cal., black synthetic stock only and satin finished stainless steel, 7 1/4 lbs. Mfg. 1997-2002.

	$590	$530	$460	$395	$360	$325	$295	*$680*

Add $30 for Mag. cals.

GRADING - PPGS™	100%	98%	95%	90%	80%	70%	60%	LAST MSR

* ***Whitetail Hunter/Synthetic Stainless Laminate*** – .25-06 Rem., .270 Win., .30-06, .300 Win. Mag., or 7mm Rem. Mag. cal., similar to Whitetail Hunter Stainless, except has grey laminate wood stock and forend with checkering, satin finished stainless steel, 3 shot detachable mag., 7 1/4 lbs. Imported 2002-2003.

	$650	$565	$500	$430	$375	$315	$270	*$745*

Add $30 for Mag. cals.

* ***Whitetail Hunter/Synthetic Deluxe*** – similar cals. as Whitetail Hunter, gloss finished deluxe checkered walnut stock and forearm with rollover cheekpiece. Imported 1999-2003.

	$650	$565	$500	$460	$400	$360	$330	*$745*

Add $30 for Mag. cals.

CONTINENTAL VARMINT MODEL – .17 Rem. (mfg. 2000-2002), .22-250 Rem., .223 Rem., or .308 Win. cal., heavy 26 in. barrel w/o sights, adj. trigger, quick release 3 shot detachable mag., integral scope mount rails, checkered walnut stock with beavertail forend, recoil pad spacer system, 8 1/8 lbs. Mfg. 1996-2003.

	$615	$520	$460	$400	$350	$325	$300	*$720*

CONTINENTAL LONG RANGE HUNTER – .25-06 Rem. (disc. 2002), .270 Win. (disc. 2002), 7mm Rem. Mag., or .300 Win. Mag. cal., heavy 26 in. barrel w/o sights, checkered walnut stock and forend, 8 3/8 lbs. Mfg. 1996-2003.

	$640	$540	$475	$415	$365	$325	$300	*$750*

Subtract 5% for non-Mag. cals. (disc. 2002).

TARGET (SPORTER) MODEL – .22-250 Rem., .223 Rem., .308 Win., 7mm-08 Rem. (new 2002), or 6.5x55mm Swedish (new 2003) cal., 23 3/8 in. barrel w/o sights, competition style stock with adj. buttplate and cheekpiece, detachable 5 shot mag., stippled pistol grip and forend, 9 lbs. Mfg. 1998-2003.

	$845	$765	$660	$580	$515	$450	$395	*$950*

This model was designated the Tikka Sporter until 2003.

TIMBERWOLF

Previous trademark manufactured by I.M.I. (Israel Military Industries) located in Israel. Previously imported and distributed by Action Arms located in Philadelphia, PA until 1994.

RIFLES: SLIDE ACTION

TIMBERWOLF – .357 Mag. or .44 Mag. (disc.) cal., slide action, straight grip shotgun style stock with adj. drop, blue or satin chrome finish, takedown, 18 1/2 in. barrel, 10 shot tube mag., sear locking and firing pin safeties, integral scope base, approx. 5 1/2 lbs. Imported 1989-93.

.357 Mag. cal.	$850	$775	$700	$625	$525	$425	$350	
.44 Mag. cal. (blue only)	$1,100	$1,000	$875	$725	$625	$525	$425	*$299*

Add $80 for satin chrome finish.

This model was designed by Evan Whilden, and imported/distributed by Action Arms Ltd. Springfield Armory imported 1,000 .44 Mag. Timberwolf models during 1990-91.

TIME PRECISION ARMS

Current custom riflemaker located in New Milford, CT. Previously located in Bethel, CT, and Brookfield, CT. Consumer direct sales.

RIFLES: BOLT ACTION

Time Precision rifles feature SLV/ALV actions and are available in over 30 different types, in cals. from .22 LR - .416 Rigby, prices range from $1,980-$2,332 depending on options. All guns are made per individual custom order, but are basically available in 3 different configurations - Hunting, Benchrest, and Target rifles. Please contact the company directly for availability, pricing, options and delivery time (see Trademark Index).

GRADING - PPGS™	100%	98%	95%	90%	80%	70%	60%	LAST MSR

TIPPMAN ARMS CO.

Previous manufacturer located in Fort Wayne, IN.

Tippman Arms manufactured 1/2 scale semi-auto working models of famous machine guns. All models were available with an optional hardwood case, extra ammo cans, and other accessories. Mfg. 1986-1987 only.

RIFLES: REPRODUCTIONS, SEMI-AUTO

MODEL 1919 A-4 – .22 LR cal. only, copy of Browning 1919 A-4 Model, belt fed, closed bolt operation, 11 in. barrel, tripod, 10 lbs.

	100%	98%	95%	90%	80%	70%	60%	LAST MSR
	$4,750	$4,300	$3,950	$3,600	$3,250	$2,850	$2,350	*$1,325*

MODEL 1917 – .22 LR cal. only, copy of Browning M1917, watercooled, belt fed, closed bolt operation, 11 in. barrel, tripod, 10 lbs.

	100%	98%	95%	90%	80%	70%	60%	LAST MSR
	$6,375	$6,000	$5,500	$5,000	$4,350	$3,750	$3,250	*$1,830*

MODEL .50 HB – .22 WMR cal. only, copy of Browning .50 cal. machine gun, belt fed, closed bolt operation, 18 1/4 in. barrel, tripod, 13 lbs.

	100%	98%	95%	90%	80%	70%	60%	LAST MSR
	$6,625	$6,400	$5,950	$5,400	$4,950	$4,500	$4,000	*$1,929*

TISAS

Current trademark of semi-auto pistols established in 1993 and manufactured by Trabzon Gun Industry Corp., located in Ankara, Turkey. Currently imported by American Tactical Imports, located in Rochester, NY beginning 2008, and by Umarex USA Inc. beginning late 2011. Previously imported briefly by Interstate Arms located in Billerica, MA.

PISTOLS: SEMI-AUTO

Trabzon manufactures good quality semi-auto pistols with white and black chrome slides in .380 ACP, 7.65mm, 9mm Para., and .45 ACP cal. Please refer to the American Tactical Imports section for current information and pricing. The Regent trademark is imported by Umarex USA, and please refer to the Umarex section for current models and values. Additionally, Task Firearms imports the Tisas Fatih model - please refer to the Task Firearms listing for more information.

TOKAREV

See Russian Service Pistols and Rifles section.

TOLLEY, J & W

Current trademark owned by F.J. Wiseman & Co., Ltd., located in Staffordshire, England.

J & W Tolley was renowned for big bore wildfowl guns, as well as express and big game rifles. Current double rifles are built to order. Please contact the company directly for a price quotation, available options, and delivery time (see Trademark Index).

RIFLES: SxS

Please contact the company directly for prices on these models.

J & W TOLLEY BOXLOCK – various cals. and options, custom made to order.

J & W TOLLEY SIDELOCK – various cals. between .375 H&H - .600 NE, true H&H style action, custom made to order, approx. 12-18 months delivery time.

TOMAHAWK

Current trademark of shotguns manufactured by M&U, located in Konya, Turkey. No current U.S. importation.

M&U manufactures a complete line of hunting and tactical style shotguns under the Tomahawk trademark, including semi-auto, slide action, O/U, SxS, and single barrel configurations. Currently, these guns have had little or no importation into the U.S. Please contact the company directly for more information, including pricing and domestic availability (see Trademark Index).

GRADING - PPGS™	100%	98%	95%	90%	80%	70%	60%	LAST MSR

TOMPKINS

Previous pistol trademark manufactured under license by Varsity Manufacturing Co., located in Springfield, MA circa 1947-1953. Also manufactured by Walter Woodman in limited quantities after 1953.

PISTOLS: SINGLE SHOT

TOMPKINS PRECISION PISTOL – .22 LR cal., single shot pistol utilizing flexible sear mechanism and trap door style breech block, checkered walnut grips with full length forend, adj. sights, approx. 200 mfg. through 1953, late mfg. will be marked WE Woodman (approx. 2 dozen) on receiver top, instead of AH Tompkins.

	100%	98%	95%	90%	80%	70%	60%	LAST MSR
	$1,100	$900	$750	$600	$500	$400	$350	

TORNADO

Currently manufactured by AseTekno located in Helsinki, Finland.

RIFLES: BOLT ACTION

TORNADO MODEL – .338 Lapua Mag. cal., unique straight line design with free floating barrel, 5 shot mag., pistol grip assembly is part of frame, limited importation into the U.S.

The factory should be contacted directy regarding domestic availability and pricing (see Trademark Index).

TORUNARMS

Current manufacturer located in Konya, Turkey. No current U.S. importation.

Torunarms manufactures a complete line of good quality O/U, SxS, semi-auto, slide action, and single shot shotguns. The company also manufactures air rifles. Currently, these models are not imported into the U.S. Please contact the company directly for more information, including pricing and domestic availability (see Trademark Index).

TOZ

Current manufacturer established in 1712, and located in Tula, Russia. Limited U.S. pistol importation by Larry's Guns, located in Portland, ME. Previously imported by Tula Firearms, located in San Diego, CA. TOZ is an abbreviation for Tulsky Oruzheiny Zavod. Dealer sales.

TOZ manufactures a wide variety of quality O/U, SxS, single shot, and semi-auto shotguns, in addition to pistols, rifles and combination guns. TOZ also provides a complete line of custom services, including elaborate inlays (gold, silver, and platinum) and wood carving. Please contact the importer directly for more information on the TOZ pistol. For more information on TOZ long guns, please refer to the Tula Arms Plant section.

PISTOLS: SINGLE SHOT

TOZ-35 FREE PISTOL – .22 LR cal., employs virtually every shooting refinement possible in a single shot target pistol, fully adj. target grips (with or w/o Rink laminate grip and forestock), limited mfg.

	100%	98%	95%	90%	80%	70%	60%	LAST MSR
No MSR	$1,367	$1,299	$1,050	$900	$800	$725	$650	

TRACKINGPOINT

Current bolt action rifle manufacturer located in Austin, TX.

RIFLES: BOLT ACTION

XS1 – .338 Lapua cal., 27 in. Krieger barrel with AAC Blackout 90T muzzle brake, matte black finish, Surgeon Rifles XL action, Accuracy International AX chassis system with detachable rails, Harris bipod with LaRue quick detach mount.

	100%	98%	95%	90%	80%	70%	60%	LAST MSR
MSR $22,500	$19,125	$16,725	$14,350	$13,000	$10,525	$8,600	$6,695	

XS2 – .300 Win. Mag. cal., 24 in. Krieger barrel with AAC Blackout 90T muzzle brake, matte black finish, Surgeon Rifles XL long action, Accuracy International AX chassis system with detachable rails, Harris bipod with LaRue quick detach mount.

	100%	98%	95%	90%	80%	70%	60%	LAST MSR
MSR $20,000	$17,000	$14,875	$12,750	$11,550	$9,350	$7,650	$5,950	

GRADING - PPGS™	100%	98%	95%	90%	80%	70%	60%	LAST MSR

XS3 – .300 Win. Mag. cal., 22 in. Krieger threaded barrel with thread protector, matte black finish, Surgeon Rifles XL long action, McMillan A5 stock, Harris bipod with LaRue quick detach mount.

MSR $17,500 $14,875 $13,000 $11,150 $10,125 $8,175 $6,695 $5,200

TRADEWINDS

Previous importer located in Tacoma, WA.

RIFLES

HUSKY MODEL 5000 – .22-250 Rem., .243 Win., .270 Win., .308 Win., or .30-06 cal., bolt action, 23 3/4 in. barrel, adj. sight, removable mag., hand-checkered walnut stock.

$325 $310 $290 $250 $225 $200 $175

NORAHAMMER 900 SERIES – .270 Win., .308 Win., or .30-06 cal., similar to Husky Model, 20 1/2 in. barrel, 6 lbs. 8 oz.

$325 $310 $290 $250 $225 $200 $175

MODEL 311-A – .22 LR cal., bolt action, 5 shot, 22 1/2 in. barrel, folding leaf rear sight, walnut checkered stock.

$180 $170 $150 $130 $120 $100 $85

MODEL 260-A – .22 LR cal., semi-auto, 5 shot, 22 1/2 in. barrel, 3 leaf folding sight, checkered walnut stock.

$200 $190 $175 $150 $130 $120 $100

SHOTGUNS: SEMI-AUTO

MODEL H-170 – 12 ga., 2 3/4 in. chamber, 26 in. mod. or 28 in. full choked barrel, recoil action, alloy receiver, 5 shot tube mag., VR, checkered walnut stock.

$275 $265 $250 $225 $200 $180 $150

TRADITIONS PERFORMANCE FIREARMS

Current black powder replicas and muzzleloading importer located in Old Saybrook, CT. Distributor and dealer sales.

During 2011, Traditions discontinued all importation of modern firearms, and now offers a complete line of black powder replicas and muzzleloading shotguns and rifles, as well as a line of black powder shooting accessories. Until 2010, the company offered two proprietary single shot rifles, the Outfitter and Tip-Up models, in addition to select single shot (Pedersoli mfg.) rifles and accessories. Traditions previously imported a wide variety of Stefano Fausti shotguns until 2007, Emilio Rizzini shotguns from Italy, a semi-auto shotgun, and a line of Uberti mfg. black powder models. Please contact the company directly for more information (see Trademark Index).

Please refer to the *Blue Book of Modern Black Powder Arms* by John Allen (also online) for more information and prices on Traditions' extensive lineup of modern black powder models.

Black Powder Revolvers - Reproductions & Replicas and *Black Powder Long Arms & Pistols - Reproductions & Replicas* by Dennis Adler are also invaluable sources for most black powder reproductions and replicas, and include hundreds of color images on most popular makes/models, provide manufacturer/trademark histories, and up-to-date information on related items/accessories for black powder shooting - online at www.bluebookofgunvalues.com.

RIFLES

Traditions previously imported the Pedersoli 1874 Sharps rifle, Remington rolling block sporting rifle, and a Springfield Trapdoor carbine. Traditions also imported Uberti black powder guns until 2002, including the Henry, Model 1866, and Model 1873.

OUTFITTER – .243 Win., .270 Win., .30-06, .308 Win., or .444 Marlin (disc.) cal., 24 in. Wilson rifled barrel, drilled and tapped, black synthetic Soft-Touch (with or w/o thumbhole), or Mossy Oak Treestand camo stock, sling swivels, tip-up action, opening lever in front of trigger guard, fiber optic front sight, single shot, recoil pad, dual safety system, 7 1/4 lbs. Mfg. 2008-2010.

$475 $415 $350 $295 $245 $210 $185 *$543*

GRADING - PPGS™	100%	98%	95%	90%	80%	70%	60%	LAST MSR

Add $56 for camo.
Add $22 for thumbhole stock.
Add $192 for Outfitter centerfire/muzzleloader combo which includes extra .50 cal. 28 in. barrel using a 209 primer for ignition.

TIP-UP – .45-70 Govt. cal., 24 in. nickel or blue Wilson barrel, steel frame, fiber optic front sight, adj. rear sight on barrel, crossbolt sear block safety in trigger group, transfer bar safety, black synthetic (with or w/o thumbhole) or Mossy Oak Treestand camo stock, drilled and tapped, 7 1/4 lbs. Mfg. 2008-2010.

$425	$365	$315	$275	$230	$200	$175	$484

Add $15 for nickel finish.
Add $56 for camo.
Add $20 for thumbhole stock.

SHOTGUNS: O/U

CLASSIC FIELD SERIES – 12, 16 (disc. 2002), 20, 28 ga., or .410 bore, boxlock action, vent. barrels, vent. recoil pad, various configurations. Mfg. by Fausti, imported 2000-2006.

* ***Classic Field Series Hunter*** – 12 or 20 ga., 3 in. chambers, 26 or 28 in. VR barrels with 3 choke tubes included, blue (disc.) or matte silver finished frame, SST, extractors, checkered walnut stock and forearm, blue finish, 6 lbs. 7 oz. - 7 lbs. 4 oz.

$795	$675	$575	$500	$450	$400	$375	$899

Subtract 5% for blue finish.

* ***Classic Field Series I*** – 12, 20, 28 ga., or .410 bore, 3 in. chambers (except for 28 ga.), 26 or 28 in. VR barrels with fixed chokes, gold SST, extractors, coin finished frame with etched engraving, checkered walnut stock and forearm, blue finish, 6 lbs. 5 oz. - 7 lbs. 4 oz.

$750	$625	$535	$500	$450	$395	$375	$849

Add $50 for 28 ga. or .410 bore.

* ***Classic Field Series II*** – 12, 16 (mfg. 2001 only), 20, 28 ga., or .410 bore, 3 in. chambers (12 and 20 ga. only), 26 or 28 in. VR barrels with 3 choke tubes (except 28 ga. and .410 bore), coin finished frame with etched engraving, gold SST, ejectors, checkered walnut stock and forearm, blue finish, 6 lbs. 5 oz. - 7 lbs. 4 oz.

$895	$775	$675	$575	$525	$475	$425	$1,039

Add $10 for 28 ga. or .410 bore.

* ***Classic Field Series II Combo*** – 20 ga. frame, includes 20 ga. and .410 bore 26 in. barrels with extra forearm, cased. Mfg. 2004-2007.

$1,395	$1,175	$995	$900	$825	$750	$675	$1,649

* ***Classic Field Series III Gold*** – 12 or 20 (new 2003) ga., 3 in. chambers, 26 or 28 in. VR blue finish barrels with 3 choke tubes included, gold SST, ejectors, coin finished frame with 3 gold engraved pheasants, deluxe checkered walnut stock and forearm, protective gun sock and molded hard gun case became standard 2002, approx. 7 lbs. 5 oz.

$1,125	$925	$825	$700	$600	$550	$495	$1,299

Add $100 for 20 ga.

CLASSIC UPLAND SERIES – 12 or 20 ga., boxlock action, gold SST, vent. recoil pad, various configurations. Mfg. by Fausti, protective gun sock and molded hard gun case became standard 2002. Imported 2000-2004.

* ***Classic Upland Series II*** – 3 in. chambers, 24 or 26 in. VR barrels with 3 choke tubes included, blue engraved frame, straight English grip walnut stock with Schnabel forearm, 6 lbs. 3 oz. - 7 lbs. 3 oz.

$995	$850	$725	$650	$575	$500	$425	$1,119

* ***Classic Upland Series III*** – 3 in. chambers, 26 in. VR barrels with 3 choke tubes, blue engraved frame with gold pheasant inlays, checkered pistol grip walnut stock with Schnabel forearm, 7 lbs. 3 oz.

$1,300	$1,075	$950	$825	$725	$625	$525	$1,519

GRADING - PPGS™	100%	98%	95%	90%	80%	70%	60%	LAST MSR

CLASSIC SERIES SPORTING CLAYS II – 12 ga. only, 28, 30 or 32 (new 2005) in. wide VR ported barrels with 4 extended choke tubes, SST, ejectors, coin finished frame with perimeter engraving, checkered walnut stock with Schnabel forearm, approx. 8 lbs.

$1,115	$915	$800	$700	$600	$500	$400	*$1,299*

* ***Classic Series Sporting Clays III*** – 12 or 20 ga., 28 or 30 in. wide VR ported barrels, SST, ejectors, extended choke tubes, hand finished silver engraved frame with gold inlays, premium checkered walnut stock with Schnabel forearm, protective gun sock and molded hard gun case, approx. 7 1/2 -8 lbs. Imported 2002-2007.

$1,400	$1,175	$1,025	$900	$775	$675	$575	*$1,649*

Add $50 for 20 ga.

REAL 16 SERIES – 16 ga., features proportioned 16 ga. receiver, 26 in. VR barrels with choke tubes, gold SST, silver engraved frame with or w/o gold snipes on sides, ejectors, checkered semi-gloss walnut stock and forearm, shock absorbing recoil pad, 6 3/4 lbs. Mfg. by Fausti. Imported 2004-2007.

$1,150	$900	$800	$700	$600	$500	$425	*$1,249*

Add $250 for gold receiver inlays and hardshell case.

MAG. HUNTER (350 SERIES) – 12 ga. only, 3 1/2 in. chambers, SST, ejectors, vent. recoil pad, various configurations.

* ***Mag. 350 Series Hunter II*** – 28 in. vent. barrels with VR, matte black metal finish, matte finished checkered walnut stock and forearm, 3 choke tubes, sling swivels, 7 lbs. 2 oz. Importation disc. 2002.

$700	$630	$575	$530	$480	$425	$400	*$799*

* ***Mag. Hunter II Field*** – 12 ga., 28 in. barrels, checkered walnut stock and forearm with sling swivels, matte finished engraved black frame, SST, ejectors. Imported 2005-2007.

$895	$800	$700	$600	$525	$475	$425	*$1,039*

* ***Mag. Hunter II Waterfowl*** – 12 ga., 28 in. vent. barrels with VR, engraved matte black frame with Realtree Max-4 (new 2006) or Advantage Wetlands (disc. 2005) wood and barrel coverage, 3 choke tubes, sling swivels, 7 1/4 lbs.

$1,050	$900	$750	$650	$550	$475	$400	*$1,199*

* ***Mag. Hunter II Turkey*** – 12 ga., 24 or 26 in. vent. barrels with VR, engraved matte black frame with Mossy Oak Breakup wood and barrel coverage, 3 choke tubes, sling swivels, approx. 7 lbs.

$1,050	$900	$750	$650	$550	$475	$400	*$1,199*

GOLD WING SERIES – 12 ga. only, boxlock action with patented 4 lock system, 28 in. barrels with choke tubes, choice of case colored or silver finished frame, checkered oil finished pistol grip stock and forearm, recoil pad, ST, approx. 7 1/2 lbs. Mfg. by E. Rizzini. Imported 2004 only.

* ***Gold Wing Series II Silver*** – silver finished frame with engraving.

$1,575	$1,350	$1,025	$900	$800	$700	$600	*$1,759*

* ***Gold Wing Series III Silver*** – similar to Gold Wing II Silver, except has gold snipes inlaid on frame, upgraded walnut stock and forearm.

$1,925	$1,650	$1,350	$1,025	$925	$825	$725	*$2,289*

Add $220 for engraved silver finished sideplates (Gold Wing SL III Silver) with gold bird inlays.
Add $250 for engraved silver finished sideplates (Gold Wing SL III) case colored frame with gold inlays.

SHOTGUNS: SxS

ELITE SERIES – 12, 20, 28 ga., or .410 bore, boxlock action, 3 in. chambers (except 28 ga.), fixed or multichoke tubes. Mfg. by Fausti, importation began 2000.

GRADING - PPGS™	100%	98%	95%	90%	80%	70%	60%	LAST MSR

* ***Elite Field Hunter*** – 12 or 20 ga. only, 26 in. barrels with 4 choke tubes, gold SST, blue finish with etched engraving, checkered walnut stock and forearm, approx. 6 or 6 1/2 lbs. Importation disc. 2002.

	$890	$785	$700	$575	$525	$475	$425	*$999*

* ***Elite Hunter*** – 12 or 20 ga. only, 26 or 28 in. barrels with 3 screw-in chokes, ST, extractors, coin finished frame with engraving, checkered walnut stock and forearm. Imported 2003-2007.

	$1,185	$975	$850	$750	$650	$550	$450	*$1,399*

* ***Elite Field I*** – 12, 20, 28 ga. or .410 bore, 26 in. barrels with fixed chokes, DT or ST, extractors, coin finished frame with etched engraving, checkered walnut stock and forearm, 5 lbs. 12 oz.-6 lbs. 8 oz.

	$950	$800	$700	$600	$550	$500	$425	*$1,099*

Add $150 (DT) or $200 (ST) for 28 ga. or .410 bore.
Add $150 for ST.

* ***Elite Field III*** – 28 ga. or .410 bore only, 26 in. barrels with fixed chokes, DT or gold SST, ejectors, coin finished frame with multiple gold inlays, deluxe checkered straight grip walnut stock and forearm, approx. 6 1/4 lbs. Importation disc. 2002.

	$1,825	$1,550	$1,275	$1,000	$875	$750	$625	*$2,099*

Subtract approx. $100 for DT.

UPLANDER SERIES – 12 or 20 ga., 26 or 28 in. barrels with choke tubes, boxlock action with or w/o sideplates and engraving, DT or ST, checkered oil finished straight grip English stock and splinter forearm. Mfg. by E. Rizzini. Imported 2004 only.

* ***Uplander Series II Silver*** – silver finished frame with engraving, 6 3/4 lbs.

	$1,825	$1,575	$1,225	$975	$875	$775	$700	*$2,129*

* ***Uplander Series III Silver*** – similar to Uplander II Silver, except has gold snipes inlayed on engraved frame, upgraded walnut stock and forearm, includes long trigger guard.

	$2,400	$1,975	$1,675	$1,375	$1,100	$975	$875	*$2,889*

* ***Uplander Series IV Silver*** – similar to Uplander III Silver, except has gold game birds on engraved sideplates, includes long trigger guard.

	$2,995	$2,500	$2,150	$1,775	$1,500	$1,275	$1,100	*$3,439*

SHOTGUNS: SEMI-AUTO

AL 2100 SERIES – 12 or 20 ga., 3 in. chamber, various VR barrel lengths, lightweight alloy receiver, gas operation, choke tubes in most models. Imported from Europe 2000-2004.

* ***AL 2100 Series ALS Field Model*** – checkered walnut stock and forearm, blue metal, multichokes, also available in Youth Model, 5 lbs. 10 oz. - 6 lbs. 5 oz.

	$295	$265	$235	$200	$185	$170	$155	*$349*

* ***AL 2100 Series ALS Hunter Model*** – similar to ALS Field Model, except has black synthetic stock and forearm, not available in Youth Model, approx. 6 1/4 lbs.

	$275	$245	$215	$185	$170	$155	$140	*$319*

* ***AL 2100 Series ALS Hunter Combo*** – includes 26 or 28 in. VR barrel and choice of 24 in. rifled slug barrel and walnut or synthetic stock and forearm. Importation began 2002.

	$435	$385	$340	$305	$275	$250	$225	*$499*

Add $30 for cantilever scope mount.
Add $30 for walnut stock and forearm.

* ***AL 2100 Series ALS Slug Hunter Model*** – similar to ALS Hunter Model, except is 12 ga. only, 24 in. rifled barrel with choice of rifle sights or cantilever scope mount, Turkish walnut or black synthetic stock and forearm. Importation began 2002.

	$300	$270	$235	$200	$185	$170	$155	*$359*

Add $30 for cantilever scope mount or walnut stock and forearm.

GRADING - PPGS™	100%	98%	95%	90%	80%	70%	60%	LAST MSR

* ***AL 2100 Series ALS Turkey/Waterfowl Hunter Model*** – 21 (Turkey Model with Mossy Oak Breakup, disc. 2001), 26 (Turkey), or 28 (Waterfowl Model with Advantage Wetlands) in. barrel, 100% camo coverage.

	$315	$280	$240	$200	$185	$170	$155	*$379*

* ***AL 2100 Series ALS Home Security Model*** – 12 ga. only, 20 in. barrel bored IC, black synthetic stock and forearm, bead sights, 6 lbs. Importation began 2002.

	$275	$245	$215	$185	$170	$155	$140	*$319*

TRANSFORMATIONAL DEFENSE INDUSTRIES, INC.

Previous name of a manufacturer of civilian and law enforcement firearms 2008-late 2010 and located in Virginia Beach, VA.

Transformational Defense Industries, Inc. was part of the Gamma Applied Visions Group SA. On Sept. 1, 2010, the company name was changed to Kriss USA. Please refer to the Kriss listing for current information.

TRAVOR

Current trademark manufactured by IWI US, Inc., located in Harrisburg, PA.

RIFLES: SEMI-AUTO

TRAVOR SAR – 5.56 NATO cal., bullpup design, 16 1/2 or 18 in. barrel chrome lined barrel, non-lubricated long stroke gas piston system, matte black or Flat Dark Earth finish, flattop with full Picatinny rail, optional bayonet lug, 30 shot mag., accepts AR-15/M16 style magazines, approx. 8 lbs.

MSR $1,999	$1,700	$1,495	$1,275	$1,150	$935	$765	$595	

Add $600 for SAR IDF Model with Mepro-21 reflex sight affixed to barrel.

TRENCH/RIOT SHOTGUNS

The following is a chronological listing beginning with WWI of the various U.S. commercial Riot and military Trench and Riot shotguns mfg. to date.

The publisher wishes to express thanks to the late Pat Redmond and Rick Crosier for the information in this section.

Some 100% values have been intentionally omitted in this section as they are seldom seen or sold.

Values listed below are for original, unmodified shotguns with proper parts makers, and unsanded wood with crisp stock cartouches.

All Trench/Riot shotguns listed are in 12 ga. only.

SHOTGUNS: MILITARY TRENCH, WWI

WINCHESTER MODEL 1897 MILITARY TRENCH GUN – high-polish commercial blue finish, solid frame with 6 row ventilated handguard for bayonet attachment, walnut high comb stock with hard rubber buttplate (no cartouches in stock). Guns used by the U.S. Army for trench warfare in WWI, originally did not have military markings. A "U.S." and ordnance bomb were hand stamped on the right side of the receiver on trench guns kept in the Army's inventory after the war. Military markings were added in the 1920s to about 10% of the total production. Serial range 650,000-695,000.

Trench Gun	N/A	$4,800	$3,500	$1,400	$1,000	$800	$700	
Trench Gun w/military markings	N/A	$6,500	$4,800	$3,000	$1,800	$1,500	$1,250	

REMINGTON MODEL 10 MILITARY TRENCH GUN – high polish commercial blue finish with wood handguard on top of barrel, separate bayonet adaptor attaches to front of barrel for bayonet attachment. "U.S." and ordnance bomb marked on left side receiver, stock is unmarked. Extremely rare and hard to find complete and in original condition. Trench gun barrel length is 22 in. as compared to 20 in. Riot gun. Prices quoted only for complete guns with wood handguard and bayonet adaptor. Serial range 160,000-165,000.

Trench Gun	N/A	$14,000	$12,500	$4,800	$3,500	$2,000	$1,800	
Riot Gun	N/A	$5,000	$3,000	$1,200	$650	$500	$400	

GRADING - PPGS™	100%	98%	95%	90%	80%	70%	60%	LAST MSR

SHOTGUNS: MILITARY RIOT/TRENCH, WWII

ITHACA MODEL 37 MILITARY SHOTGUNS – rarest of all Trench shotguns, high polish commercial blue finish, "RLB" and ordnance bomb on left side of receiver, ordnance bomb on barrel, stocks not proofed, blue vent. handguard for bayonet attachment, only 1,420 Trench guns were ordered in 1941. Ithaca supplied mostly long barrel martially marked shotguns. Serial range 49,000-62,000.

Trench Gun	N/A	$15,000	$12,500	$7,500	$4,000	$3,250	$2,350	
Riot Gun	N/A	$5,000	$3,500	$2,000	$1,000	$750	$600	
Long Barrel	N/A	$1,850	$1,500	$1,000	$750	$600	$500	

REMINGTON MODEL 31 MILITARY SHOTGUNS – commercial blue finish (high polish and flat blue finishes noted). Can be marked "U.S. Property" on receiver and/or barrel. Some examples noted with only ordnance mark on stock. Serial range 39,500-60,500.

Riot Gun	N/A	$2,800	$1,800	$1,000	$750	$650	$500	
Long Barrel	N/A	$1,200	$1,000	$650	$500	$400	$300	
Trainer w/ comp.	N/A	$1,300	$1,100	$750	$600	$500	$400	

REMINGTON MODEL 11 MILITARY SHOTGUNS – this is the most commonly found military shotgun. Examples of 5 shot and 3 shot Sportsman Model. Examples with plain or engraved receivers and plain or fancy checkered wood. Military marked with "U.S." and ordnance bomb on receiver and barrel. Later models are marked "Military Finish". These shotguns all have highly polished commercial blue finish and ordnance marked stocks. Serial range 450,000-500,000 and 700,000-711,000.

Riot Guns	N/A	$1,000	$650	$450	$400	$350	$300	
Long Barrel	N/A	$850	$500	$350	$300	$250	$200	
Aerial Trainer w/machine gun mount	N/A	$4,500	$4,000	$3,350	$2,500	$2,000	$1,750	

* ***Remington Model 11 Military Shotgun Riot*** – this configuration was sold by the government as surplus as late as the 1970s and can occasionally be found NIB with packing materials and instruction manual. Mint in factory box - $2,800.

SAVAGE MODEL 720 MILITARY SHOTGUNS – appears identical to Remington Model 11. This was mfg. by Stevens/Savage in very limited quantities, plain and engraved receivers noted with high quality commercial blue finish. Stocks are unmarked and must have ramp sights to be original. Watch for altered guns made into Riots. Serial range 69,000-90,000.

Riot Gun	N/A	$2,500	$1,850	$1,250	$925	$750	$600	
Long Barrel	N/A	$1,000	$800	$750	$500	$350	$300	

STEVENS MODEL 620 MILITARY SHOTGUNS – this was the current model being sold by Stevens and has a commercial blue finish, but not of the same quality as the other companies. Trench guns are equipped with handguards that have a definite purple/reddish color to the front and dark blue vent. shroud. Model 620s are much rarer than 520s and have "U.S." and ordnance bomb on receiver, ordnance bomb on barrel and unmarked stock. Serial range 1,000-30,000.

Trench Gun	N/A	$4,000	$2,800	$1,700	$1,200	$800	$600	
Riot Gun	N/A	$1,800	$750	$450	$400	$350	$250	
Long Barrels	N/A	$600	$400	$250	$200	$175	$150	

STEVENS 520-30 MILITARY SHOTGUNS – this model was resurrected due to available machinery and is the most commonly found Trench gun. Riot guns in mint condition are hard to find. Same finish as Model 620, "U.S." and ordnance bomb on receiver, ordnance bomb on barrel and no proofing on stocks, except for reworks. Trench gun has same style handguard as Model 620. Serial range 30,000-70,000.

Trench Gun	N/A	$3,000	$2,000	$1,500	$800	$600	$500	
Riot Gun	N/A	$1,000	$750	$350	$300	$250	$200	
Long Barrels	N/A	$500	$400	$225	$175	$150	$125	

GRADING - PPGS™	100%	98%	95%	90%	80%	70%	60%	LAST MSR

STEVENS SINGLE & DOUBLE BARREL MILITARY SHOTGUNS – these guns were procured by the government from distributors and gun dealers. "U.S." and oversized flaming bomb hand stamped on left side receiver.

Single Barrel	N/A	$750	$600	$400	$350	$300	$250
Double Barrel	N/A	$950	$800	$600	$400	$350	$300

WINCHESTER MODEL 97 MILITARY SHOTGUNS – takedown model, high polish commercial blue finish, finger groove walnut stock with hard rubber buttplate. All early riot and trench guns have "WB" and crossed cannons cartouches on the left side of stock, left side of receiver is machined marked "U.S." with or w/o ordnance bomb. All "WB" trenchguns have a 6 row ventilated handguard. All 97s will have ordnance bomb on top of barrel. Around serial range 950,000, receivers were all marked on left side with a machined "U.S." and ordnance bomb proofs, ventilated handguard was changed to a 4 row, "GHD" and ordnance bomb cartouches on left side of stock. During this transition, a very few examples with 6 row handguards were mfg. Serial range 920,000-960,000.

Riot Gun w/ WB	N/A	$2,000	$1,700	$800	$600	$500	$400
Trench Gun w/ WB	N/A	$6,500	$4,500	$2,850	$1,500	$1,200	$1,000
Trench Gun w/ GHD	N/A	$6,200	$4,500	$2,700	$1,800	$1,200	$1,000
Long Barrel	N/A	$1,500	$1,200	$800	$650	$500	$400

WINCHESTER MODEL 12 MILITARY SHOTGUNS – takedown model with improved hammerless receiver. These were made to supplement Model 97 production. Riot guns and Trench guns share same serial range. Finished in high polished commercial blue, except for some Trench guns (only) which were the only WWII shotguns to have factory parkerized finishes. All Model 12s have "U.S." and ordnance bomb on right side of receiver, ordnance bomb on barrel and cross cannons ordnance mark and inspector initials on left side of stock. Trench guns have 4 row vent. handguards.

* ***Winchester Model 12 Military Shotgun Blue finish*** – serial range 926,000-1,030,000.

Trench Gun	N/A	$6,000	$5,500	$2,200	$1,600	$1,400	$1,000
Riot Gun	N/A	$1,850	$1,500	$750	$650	$500	$400
Long Barrel	N/A	$1,200	$1,000	$750	$600	$450	$350

* ***Winchester Model 12 Military Shotgun Parkerized finish*** – serial range 1,030,000-1,040,000.

Trench Gun	N/A	$5,500	$3,800	$3,000	$2,000	$1,500	$1,200

WINCHESTER MODEL 37 MILITARY SHOTGUNS – high polish, commercial blue, single barrel, procured from Winchester. "U.S." and ordnance bomb proofmarks were applied to left side of receiver. Winchester records show shipment of 5,410 guns to the military - very few examples of this model have ever been found.

Single Barrel	N/A	$2,500	$1,500	$1,200	$1,000	$750	$500

SHOTGUNS: MILITARY RIOT/TRENCH, VIETNAM

ITHACA MODEL 37 – parkerized finish with "U.S." marks on right side of receiver. Receiver and barrel are also marked "P". Serial range, applied on gun upside-down, is from S1,000-S23,500. Used in the Vietnam era. A very few original Trench guns with parkerized handguards have been noted.

Riot Gun	N/A	$2,500	$1,800	$800	$600	$500	$400
Trench Gun	N/A	$6,000	$4,000	$2,500	$2,000	$1,800	$1,200

SAVAGE 77E – parkerized finish with sling swivels and red rubber buttpad. "U.S." marked on right side of receiver and military "P" proofmark on receiver and barrel. Hard to find in excellent condition.

Riot Gun	N/A	$1,200	$800	$400	$300	$250	$225

WINCHESTER MODEL 1200 – parkerized barrel, mag. tube, and bayonet adapter with U.S. marking on barrel. Aluminum receiver with black or matte type finish, "U.S." is marked under serial number. Very rare as few examples have been released by the government due to its continued use by military forces.

Trench Gun	N/A	$4,000	$3,000	$1,375	$850	$600	$500

GRADING - PPGS™	100%	98%	95%	90%	80%	70%	60%	LAST MSR

SHOTGUNS: RIOT/TRENCH GUN, COMMERCIAL SALES

WINCHESTER MODEL 12 RIOT – thousands mfg. late 1930s-1960s.

	N/A	$550	$450	$395	$350	$295	$240

WINCHESTER MODEL 97 – commercial high polish blue, changed from solid frame to takedown in 1935. Trench guns made through 1945 and Riot gun mfg. continued until 1960s.

* ***Winchester Model 97 Solid Frame*** – Serial range 700,000+.

Trench Gun	N/A	$3,500	$2,800	$1,500	$1,200	$1,000	$750
Riot Gun	N/A	$1,500	$1,000	$750	$600	$500	$300

* ***Winchester Model 97 Takedown*** – Serial range 800,000+.

Trench Gun	N/A	$3,000	$2,500	$1,300	$1,100	$900	$600
Riot Gun	N/A	$1,500	$800	$600	$500	$400	$300

REMINGTON MODEL 10 – commercial high polish blue, sold in the 1920s to various government and banking agencies.

Riot Gun	N/A	$800	$600	$300	$275	$250	$200

REMINGTON MODEL 11 – made in 1930s for law enforcement use.

Riot Gun	N/A	$400	$350	$300	$275	$250	$200

MODEL 31R RIOT GUN – similar to 31A, with 20 in. barrel.

	N/A	$300	$200	$175	$150	$130	$110

ITHACA MODEL 37 – parkerized models made in 1960s for police agencies and commercial sales.

Trench Gun	N/A	$1,600	$900	$700	$600	$500	$400
Riot Gun	N/A	$375	$250	$225	$175	$150	$125

U.S. MILITARY SHOTGUN ACCESSORIES

WWI BAYONETS – military acceptance proofs, leather scabbards, and two variations of attachments to belt, two-toned blue handle and parkerized blade.

* ***WWI Bayonet Winchester 1917 date***

Prices range from $150-$400, depending on original condition.

* ***WWI Bayonet Remington 1917-1918 dates***

Prices range from $125-$300, depending on original condition.

LEATHER SLING – WWI dates, w/brass hardware.

Prices range from $75-$300, depending on original condition. Mint condition will bring $400.

SHOTGUN SHELL POUCHES

* ***Shotgun Shell Pouch 32 round with sling***

Prices range approx. $500, depending on original condition. Mint condition prices are approx. $1,200.

* ***Shotgun Shell Pouch 12 round dated 1921-1922***

Prices range approx. $400, depending on original condition. Mint condition will bring $1,200.

WWII BAYONETS – same as from WWI, but have plastic scabbard w/large ordnance bomb, or original WWI leather scabbard.

Prices range approx. $125-$650, depending on original condition.

LEATHER SLING – WWII dates, w/steel hardware.

Prices range from $50-$300, depending on original condition. Mint condition will bring $400.

SHOTGUN SHELL POUCHES – 12 round pouches with contract dates from 1960s-1990s.

Prices range from $50-$125.

SHOTGUN SHELL POUCHES – 12 round pouches dated 1942-45, various manufacturers, watch for recent 1943 JQMD fake pouches - they have extreme two-tone colors.

Prices range approx. $350, depending on original condition.

GRADING - PPGS™	100%	98%	95%	90%	80%	70%	60%	LAST MSR

VIETNAM BAYONETS – new contracts to supplement large quantities of shotguns being sent to Vietnam, black plastic handles, green plastic scabbards, marked "M-1917".

Gen. Cut - mfg. by General Cutlery prices range from $150-$250.

CA-mfg. by Canadian Arsenal prices range from $150-$300.

TRIPLE ACTION LLC

Previous gun design firm located in Logan, UT.

PISTOLS: SINGLE SHOT

Triple Action LLC planned to manufacture a .50 BMG single shot pistol with 13.2 in. barrel, with muzzle brake and nitrogen recoil controller. Only a few prototypes were manufactured. Construction materials included titanium and aircraft grade aluminum, and the weight was 10 or 12 lbs.

TRISTAR SPORTING ARMS, LTD.

Current importer established in 1994, and located in N. Kansas City, MO. Distributor and dealer sales.

PISTOLS: SEMI-AUTO

The following semi-auto pistol variations are manufactured by Canik55 in Turkey.

C-100 – 9mm Para. and .40 S&W cal., SA/DA, 12 (.40 S&W) or 15 (9mm Para.) shot mag., 3.9 in. barrel, steel slide, rear snag-free dovetail sights and fixed blade front sight, black polycoat or chrome finish, black polymer checkered grips, includes two magazines and hard plastic case, 1.53-1.63 lbs. New 2013.

MSR $429	$365	$330	$300	$275	$250	$225	$200	

Add $10 for chrome finish.

T-100 – 9mm Para. cal., SA/DA, 15 shot mag., 3.7 in. barrel, blued or chrome finish, 1.64 lbs. New 2013.

MSR $429	$365	$330	$300	$275	$250	$225	$200	

Add $10 for chrome finish.

L-120 – 9mm Para. cal., SA/DA, 4.7 in. barrel, blued or chrome finish, 17 shot mag., 1.75 lbs. New 2013.

MSR $429	$365	$330	$300	$275	$250	$225	$200	

Add $10 for chrome finish.

P-120 – 9mm Para. cal., SA/DA, 17 shot mag., 4.7 in. barrel, blued or chrome finish, 1.87 lbs. New 2013.

MSR $429	$365	$330	$300	$275	$250	$225	$200	

Add $10 for chrome finish.

S-120 – 9mm Para. cal., SA/DA, 17 shot mag., 4.7 in. barrel, blued or chrome finish, 2.26 lbs. New 2013.

MSR $429	$365	$330	$300	$275	$250	$225	$200	

Add $10 for chrome finish.

T-120 – 9mm Para. cal., SA/DA, 17 shot mag., 4.7 in. barrel, blued or chrome finish, 1.88 lbs. New 2013.

MSR $439	$375	$335	$300	$275	$250	$225	$200	

Add $20 for chrome finish.

TP-9C – 9mm Para. cal., SA/DA, 10 shot mag., 3 1/2 in. barrel, polymer, 1.39 lbs. New 2013.

MSR $469	$395	$350	$315	$285	$260	$230	$210	

REPRODUCTIONS: REVOLVERS, SAA

REGULATOR – .357 Mag. (disc. 2005) or .45 LC cal., 4 3/4 or 5 1/2 in. barrel, choice of brass or steel backstrap/trigger guard, two-piece smooth walnut grips. Mfg. by Uberti.

	$385	$335	$295	$260	$225	$200	$180	*$455*

Add $34 for Regulator DLX with steel backstrap/trigger guard (.45 LC only).

GRADING - PPGS™	100%	98%	95%	90%	80%	70%	60%	LAST MSR

STALLION – .17 HMR/.17 Mach 2 cal., 5 1/2, 7 1/2 (mfg. 2005 only), or 9 (mfg. 2005 only) in. barrel. Mfg. by Uberti. Imported 2005-2006.

$395	$350	$300	$265	$235	$200	$180	*$459*

Add $94 for Stallion DLX with steel backstrap/trigger guard (mfg. 2005 only).

REPRODUCTIONS: RIFLES

HENRY LEVER ACTION – .44-40 WCF (disc 2005) or .45 LC cal., brass frame only, 18 1/2 (Trapper, disc. 2005) or 24 1/4 (rifle) in. barrel, 9.4 lbs. Mfg. by Uberti.

$1,125	$875	$750	$625	$525	$425	$325	*$1,359*

MODEL 1866 LEVER ACTION – .38 Spl. (disc. 2005), .44-40 WCF (disc. 2005) or .45 LC cal., 19 (Yellowboy), 20 (disc. 2005), or 24 1/4 in. barrel, 7.2 (Yellowboy) or 8.4 (rifle) lbs. Mfg. by Uberti.

$840	$700	$600	$500	$450	$400	$350	*$999*

Add $110 for Sport configuration (20 or 24 1/4 in. barrel).

MODEL 1873 SPORT LEVER ACTION – .44-40 WCF (disc. 2005) or .45 LC cal., 24 1/4 or 30 (disc. 2005) in. barrel, 8.4 lbs. Mfg. by Uberti.

$1,075	$800	$675	$575	$500	$425	$325	*$1,259*

Add $45 for 30 in. barrel (disc. 2005).

MODEL 1885 SINGLE SHOT HIGH WALL – .45-70 Govt. cal., 28 in. barrel. Mfg. by Uberti, importation disc. 2005.

$725	$595	$535	$475	$400	$325	$250	*$852*

MODEL 1874 SHARPS – .45-70 Govt. cal., 28, 32, or 34 (disc. 2006) in. barrel, double set triggers, adj. rear sight, case hardened frame, approx. 10 lbs. Mfg. by Pedersoli. Importation disc. 2004, resumed 2006-2009.

$950	$850	$750	$650	$550	$450	$350	*$1,099*

Add $60 for Bridgeport Model with higher sideplate (disc. 2006).

RIFLES: BOLT ACTION

PEE-WEE .22 – .22 LR cal., single shot, manual cocking bolt, 16 1/2 in. barrel, steel construction, blue finish, adj. rear leaf sight, 12 in. LOP, uncheckered walnut Monte Carlo stock, 2 3/4 lbs. Limited mfg. 1998 only.

$170	$140	$130	$120	$110	$100	$90	*$189*

SHOTGUNS: LEVER ACTION

MODEL 1887 – 12 ga. only, patterned after the Winchester Model 1887, "WRA Co." logo on left side of receiver, 30 in. barrel, 5 shot tube mag., blue finish, 2-piece walnut forearm and rounded pistol grip stock, 8 lbs. Limited importation 1997-98.

$535	$475	$435	$400	$360	$330	$295	*$599*

SHOTGUNS: O/U

MODEL 300 – 12 ga. only, 3 in. chambers, under-lug action, double triggers, extractors, etched engraving, standard checkered Turkish walnut stock and forearm, 26 or 28. in. VR barrels with fixed chokes. Imported 1994-98 from Turkey.

$375	$330	$300	$275	$250	$225	$200	*$429*

MODEL 333 FIELD GRADE – 12 or 20 ga., 3 in. chambers, engraved boxlock frame with satin finish, SST, ejectors, fancy grade Turkish walnut with hand-cut checkering, 26 (12 ga. only), 28, or 30 in. VR barrels, supplied with 5 choke tubes, approx. 7 1/2 lbs. Imported from Turkey 1994-98.

$735	$625	$550	$500	$450	$400	$360	*$800*

* ***Model 333 Field Grade Sporting Clays*** – similar to Model 333 Field Grade, except has sporting recoil pad, elongated forcing cones, 28 or 30 in. ported barrels with extended stainless steel choke tubes, 7 3/4 lbs. Imported from Turkey 1994-97.

$825	$725	$625	$550	$500	$450	$400	*$900*

GRADING - PPGS™	100%	98%	95%	90%	80%	70%	60%	LAST MSR

* ***Model 333SCL Ladies Sporting Clays*** – similar to Model 333 Sporting Clays, except is fitted with special ladies stock, 28 in. barrels only with four choke tubes. Imported from Turkey. Disc. 1997.

	$825	$725	$625	$550	$500	$450	$400	*$900*

MODEL 330 – 12 or 20 ga., 3 in. chambers, etched satin finished frame, SST, extractors, fixed chokes, checkered standard Turkish walnut stock and forearm, approx. 7 1/2 lbs. Imported from Turkey 1994-99.

	$475	$415	$375	$325	$295	$280	$265	*$549*

* ***Model 330D*** – similar to Model 330, except has ejectors and three choke tubes. Imported from Turkey 1994-99.

	$615	$525	$495	$450	$400	$360	$330	*$689*

SILVER HUNTER – 12 or 20 ga., 3 in. chambers, under-lug action, SST, extractors, silver receiver with etched engraving, standard checkered Turkish walnut stock and forearm, 26 or 28. in. VR barrels with choke tubes, 7 lbs. Imported from Spain 2002-2004.

	$615	$500	$450	$400	$365	$335	$300	*$737*

SILVER II – 12, 16, or 20 ga., similar to Silver Hunter, except has ejectors, approx. 7.4 lbs. Imported from Spain 2002-2006.

	$740	$550	$480	$420	$365	$335	$300	*$915*

SILVER CLASSIC – 12 or 20 (new 2002) ga., similar to Silver II, except has case colored receiver and long forcing cones. Imported from Spain 2002-2004.

	$750	$625	$525	$465	$415	$365	$315	*$899*

SILVER SPORTING – 12 ga., similar to Silver II, except has 3 in. chambers and 28 or 30 in. ported barrels with broadway VR, 7 lbs., 6 oz. Imported from Spain 2002-2004.

	$750	$625	$525	$465	$415	$365	$315	*$899*

WS/OU MAGNUM – 12 ga., 3 1/2 in. chambers, ejectors, SST, 28 in. VR barrels with choke tubes, 100% Skyline Excel camo (new 2003) coverage (except frame) or matte black metal and checkered black finished walnut stock and forearm. 7 lbs. 2 oz. Imported 2002-2004.

	$650	$550	$475	$425	$395	$375	$350	*$779*

Add $84 for Skyline Excel camo coverage.

HUNTER – 12 or 20 ga., 3 in. chambers, 26 or 28 in. VR barrels with choke tubes, blued boxlock action, SST, extractors, checkered walnut stock and forearm, 6-7 1/4 lbs. Imported 2006-2007.

	$425	$365	$325	$275	$235	$200	$180	*$499*

* ***Field Hunter*** – similar to Hunter, 12 or 20 (disc. 2010) ga., has auto ejectors and vent. recoil pad, 6-7 1/4 lbs. Importation began 2007.

MSR $729	$625	$525	$450	$400	$350	$295	$250	

* ***Hunter Lite*** – similar to Hunter, except has lightweight construction with silver alloy frame, 5 1/2 or 6 lbs. Imported 2006-2007.

	$440	$380	$325	$285	$240	$200	$180	*$529*

* ***Hunter Gold Combo*** – 12/20 or 20/28 ga. two barrel sets, extractors, ST, 28 in. barrels with Beretta style choke tubes, distinquishable by gold pheasants on receiver and styling grooves next to checkering, 7.4 lbs. Imported 2009 only.

	$875	$750	$675	$600	$525	$475	$425	*$999*

HUNTER EX – 12, 16 (new 2011), 20, 28 ga., or .410 bore, 3 in. chambers, 26 or 28 in. VR barrels, extractors, blued steel, choke tubes, SST, checkered walnut, black synthetic (mfg. 2010 only) or camo (mfg. 2011 only) pistol grip stock and forearm, 4.8 - 7.2 lbs. Importation began 2008.

MSR $609	$550	$485	$425	$375	$325	$295	$280	

Add $50 for 28 ga. or .410 bore (28 in. barrels).

Subtract $55 for black synthetic stock and forearm (mfg. 2010 only) or camo stock/forearm and fiber optic night sight (mfg. 2011 only).

GRADING - PPGS™	100%	98%	95%	90%	80%	70%	60%	LAST MSR

HUNTER EX LT – 12 or 20 ga., 3 in. chamber, 26 or 28 in. barrel, five chokes, walnut stock, 5.4-6.8 lbs. New 2013.

MSR $659	$575	$500	$450	$395	$350	$325	$295	

HUNTER MAG. CAMO 3-1/2 IN. – 12 ga., 3 1/2 in. chambers, 26 or 28 in. barrels with 5 choke tubes, fiber optic front sight, 100% Mossy Oak Duck Blind or Mossy Oak Break-Up camo coverage, 7.6 lbs. New 2009.

MSR $709	$625	$525	$450	$400	$350	$295	$250	

* ***Hunter Mag. Black 3-1/2 In.*** – similar to Hunter Mag. Camo, except has 100% matte black finish on wood and metal, 7.6 lbs. New 2012.

MSR $609	$550	$495	$450	$415	$375	$350	$325	

SETTER MODEL – 12 ga., 3 in. chambers, boxlock action, 28 in. VR barrels with 3 Beretta style chokes, extractors, DT, silver finished steele receiver with laser etching, checkered walnut stock and forearm, brass bead front sight, 7.4 lbs. Limited importation 2011 only.

	$375	$325	$285	$250	$225	$200	$175	*$444*

SETTER MODEL (CURRENT MFG.) – 12 or 20 ga., 3 in. chamber, 26 or 28 in. barrel with 3 Beretta style choke tubes, fiber optic front sight, high gloss walnut stock, vent. rib, SST, extractors, 6.3-7.2 lbs. New 2013.

MSR $534	$465	$425	$385	$340	$300	$260	$230	

SPORTING MODEL – 12 ga., 3 in. chambers, 28 (disc. 2010) or 30 in. chrome lined ported barrels, checkered walnut pistol grip stock, semi-beavertail forend, coin finished steel frame, self-adj. locking bolts, SST, ejectors, choke tubes, gold trigger, approx. 7 1/2 lbs. Importation began 2008.

MSR $789	$695	$595	$525	$450	$395	$350	$295	

SHOTGUNS: SxS

MODEL 311 – 12 or 20 ga., 3 in. chambers, Greener boxlock action, 26 or 28 in. barrels, standard checkered Turkish walnut stock and forearm, DTs, supplied with five choke tubes, white chrome frame finish, extractors. Imported 1994-97 from Turkey.

	$535	$475	$435	$400	$360	$330	$295	*$599*

* ***Model 311R*** – 12 or 20 ga., 20 in. cylinder bore barrels designed for cowboy re-enactment shooting or home defense, other features similar to Model 311. Imported from Turkey. Disc. 1997.

	$375	$325	$300	$275	$250	$225	$200	*$429*

MODEL 411 – 12, 16 (mfg. 1999-2004), 20 (disc. 2004), 28 (disc. 2004) ga., or .410 bore (disc. 2004), 3 in. chambers (except 28 ga.), 26 or 28 (12 ga. only) in. barrels with (12 and 20 ga.) or w/o (28 ga. or .410 bore) choke tubes, boxlock action, DT, extractors, steel shot compatible, case colored frame, checkered walnut stock and forearm, recoil pad, 6 1/2-7 1/4 lbs, mfg. by Luciano Rota (R.F.M.). Imported 1998-2005.

	$710	$650	$575	$525	$450	$400	$350	*$849*

* ***Model 411D*** – similar to Model 411, except not available in 16 ga., features engraved case colored frame, single trigger, ejectors, and English style stock, 6 1/2-7 1/4 lbs. Imported 1999 - 2005.

	$915	$800	$700	$600	$500	$400	$325	*$1,110*

* ***Model 411F*** – 12, 20 (disc. 2004), 28 (disc. 2004) ga., or .410 bore (disc. 2004), 3 in. chambers (except 28 ga.), silver engraved sideplates, gold SST, English straight stock with cut checkering, ejectors, choke tubes (except for 28 ga. and .410 bore), 6 1/2-7 1/4 lbs. Imported 2000-2005.

	$1,425	$1,200	$995	$850	$725	$650	$575	*$1,608*

* ***Model 411R Coach Gun*** – 12 or 20 ga., 3 in. chambers, hammerless, 20 in. fixed choke (C/C) barrels, case colored frame, DT, extractors, 6-6 1/2 lbs. Imported 1999-2003.

	$650	$575	$525	$475	$425	$375	$325	*$745*

This model was designed for both cowboy competition shooting and quail hunting.

GRADING - PPGS™	100%	98%	95%	90%	80%	70%	60%	LAST MSR

GENTRY – 12, 16, 20, 28 ga., or .410 bore, 3 in. chambers, engraved coin finished boxlock action with sideplates, SST, extractors, 20 (Gentry Coach Model, 12 or 20 ga. only), 26, or 28 in. barrels with matted rib and three choke tubes (fixed chokes on 16, 20 ga. and .410 bore) checkered pistol grip stock and semi-beavertail forearm, approx. 6 1/2 lbs. Imported 2003-2006.

	$775	$600	$500	$440	$380	$325	$275	*$929*

Add $16 for 28 ga. or .410 bore.
Subtract $14 for Gentry Coach Model (hammerless, disc. 2003).

BRITTANY – 12, 16 (new 2006), 20, 28 (new 2006) ga., or .410 bore (disc. 2006), 3 in. chambers, boxlock action, case colored frame, SST, ejectors, 26 in. barrels with matted rib and three choke tubes, checkered straight grip stock and semi-beavertail forearm, 6.2 - 7.4 lbs. Imported 2003-2007.

	$950	$775	$650	$525	$450	$400	$350	*$1,150*

Add $30 for 28 ga. or .410 bore.

* ***Brittany Classic*** – 12, 16, 20, 28 ga., or .410 bore, similar to Brittany, except has 27 in. barrels, upgraded features, including fancy checkered pistol grip walnut stock and forearm with oil finish, engraved frame, 6.3 - 6.7 lbs. Imported 2007-2008.

	$1,185	$1,025	$875	$745	$630	$525	$425	*$1,419*

Add $40 for 28 ga. or .410 bore.

BRITTANY SPORTING – 12 or 20 ga., 3 in. chambers, boxlock action with sideplates, engraved case colored frame, SST, ejectors, 28 in. barrels with matted rib and three choke tubes, checkered pistol grip stock and semi-beavertail forearm, approx. 6 3/4 lbs. Imported 2003-2005.

	$875	$725	$625	$525	$475	$425	$375	*$1,049*

DERBY CLASSIC – 12 or 20 ga., 3 in. chambers, true sidelock case colored action, DT, ejectors, checkered straight grip stock and splinter forearm, 7 3/4 lbs. Mfg. by Zabala Hermanos in Spain 2002-2005.

	$1,300	$1,075	$900	$775	$675	$600	$525	*$1,550*

YORK – 12 or 20 ga., boxlock action, 26 or 28 in. barrels with choke tubes, approx. 7 lbs. Imported during 2006.

	$525	$450	$400	$350	$300	$260	$230	*$609*

PHOENIX – 12, 20, or 28 ga., 3 in. chambers, boxlock action, 28 in. barrels with Beretta style choke tubes, SST, top tang safety, checkered pistol grip walnut stock, engraved blue frame with engraved gold pheasant, 6.8 lbs. Mfg. 2009-2010.

	$925	$800	$675	$575	$475	$400	$325	*$1,049*

* ***Phoenix Combo*** – includes 12/20 or 20/28 ga., 28 in. barrels. Mfg. 2009-2010.

	$1,225	$1,075	$900	$775	$675	$575	$475	*$1,359*

SHOTGUNS: SEMI-AUTO

Shim kits and fiber optic sights became standard on all hunting models (except Setter) beginning 2011.

PHANTOM SERIES – 12 ga. only, 3 or 3 1/2 (Phantom Field/Synthetic Mag. only) in. chamber, various VR (except Phantom HP) barrel lengths with choke tubes, available in Field (blue metal finish, gold accents, and checkered walnut stock and forearm), Synthetic (black non-glare matte metal and flat black synthetic stock and forearm), or HP (home security with open sights, matte finished metal, and synthetic stock and forearm), 6 lbs. 13 oz.-7 lbs. 6 oz. Italian mfg., limited importation 2001-2002.

	$385	$350	$315	$285	$265	$245	$225	*$425*

Subtract $44 for Phantom Synthetic.
Add $74 for 3 1/2 in. Mag. (Field).
Add $44 for Mag. Synthetic.

TSA SERIES (DIANA SERIES) – 12, 20, or 28 (disc. 2003) ga., 3 or 3 1/2 in. chamber, various VR barrel lengths with choke tubes, available in Marine (19 in. barrel), Field (blue metal finish, gold accents, and checkered walnut stock and forearm), Synthetic (black non-glare

GRADING - PPGS™	100%	98%	95%	90%	80%	70%	60%	LAST MSR

matte metal and flat black synthetic stock and forearm), Slug (24 in. rifled barrel with iron sights), or camo model (100% camo coverage), 6 3/4 - 7 1/2 lbs. Imported 2003-2007.

	$340	$310	$285	$255	$225	$200	$185	*$399*

Add $30 for Field Grade.
Add $30 for 20 ga. (disc.) or Youth Model with synthetic stock, or $60 for Youth with walnut stock.
Add $200 for Synthetic Model with 3 1/2 in. chamber.
Add $200 for camo model with 3 1/2 in. chamber.
Add $100 for camo model with 3 in. chamber.
Add $25 for Slug Model (24 in. rifled barrel, disc. 2004).
Add $34 for Marine Model with 19 in. barrel and choke tubes (mfg. 2004).

This model was designed by CD Europe of Italy and manufactured in Turkey.

* ***TSA Camo 3-1/2 In.*** – 12 ga., 3 (disc.) or 3 1/2 in. chamber, twin gas piston operation, 24, 26, or 28 in. chrome lined barrel, fiber optic front sight, vent. rib with matted sight plane, 5 shot, 100% Realtree Advantage Timber (24 in. barrel only), 100% Mossy Oak Obsession (disc., 24 in. barrel only), Duck Blind (disc.), or Realtree Max-4 camo coverage, 7.2 - 7.6 lbs. Importation began 2008.

MSR $729	$650	$575	$500	$450	$395	$350	$295

Subtract 10% for 3 in. chambers.

* ***TSA Black 3-1/2 In.*** – similar to TSA Camo 3-1/2 in., except 26 or 28 in. barrel, metal is flat black and black finished stock and forearm, 7.4 lbs. New 2012.

MSR $639	$550	$495	$450	$400	$350	$325	$295

VIPER G2 SERIES – 12, 20, or 28 (wood stock or silver only) ga., 2 3/4 or 3 in. chamber, 26 or 28 in. barrel, 5 shot mag., G2 action became standard 2010, configurations include wood, synthetic, and silver, brass bead front sight, mag. cut off, vent. rib with matted sight plane, choice of wood, black synthetic or carbon fiber pistol grip (disc. 2009) stock, gas operated, choke tubes, approx. 6.2 - 6.8 lbs. Importation began 2007.

MSR $499	$440	$385	$335	$265	$225	$195	$170

Add $50 for checkered walnut stock and forearm (Viper G2 Wood).
Add $50 for left-hand action on Viper G2 Synthetic model only.
Add $110 for silver alloy receiver (Viper G2 Silver, new 2010), or $170 for 28 ga. on Viper G2 Silver.
Add $120 for carbon fiber stock (disc. 2009).

Soft touch finish became standard on synthetic models beginning 2011.

* ***Viper G2 Camo*** – 12 or 20 ga., 3 in. chamber, features 100% Realtree Advantage Timber (24 & 26 in. only) or Realtree Max-4 (28 in. only) camo finish, 24, 26, or 28 in. VR barrel with 3 choke tubes, 6.2-6.9 lbs. New 2012.

MSR $599	$500	$440	$365	$310	$275	$240	$195

Add $30 for left-hand action (28 in. barrel only).

VIPER G2 YOUTH – 12 or 20 ga., 24 in. barrel, 5 shot mag., black synthetic stock and forearm with soft touch finish, 5.7 - 6 1/2 lbs.

MSR $499	$440	$385	$335	$265	$225	$195	$170

Add $50 for 2 stock combo (includes both youth and adult stocks, 20 ga. only).
Add $80 for checkered walnut stock and forearm (20 ga. only).

* ***Viper G2 Camo Youth*** – 12 (disc.) or 20 ga., 3 in. chamber, 24, 26 (disc) or 28 (disc.) in. barrel, G2 action became standard during 2010, similar to Viper Series, except has 100% Mossy Oak Duck Blind (disc.), 100% Realtree Advantage Timber camo coverage, soft touch stock/forearm finish became standard 2011, 5.7 lbs. New 2008.

MSR $589	$485	$430	$360	$310	$275	$235	$185

Add $16 for Viper G2 TW (Turkey/Waterfowl) Model with 12 or 20 ga., 24 or 28 in. barrel.

VIPER G2 SPORTING – 12 or 28 (new 2013) ga., 3 in. chamber, 30 in. ported barrel, extended Beretta style choke tubes, vent. rib, Tristar checkered walnut stock with adj. comb, fiber optic front sight, 7.4 lbs. New 2010.

MSR $759	$675	$595	$540	$465	$395	$350	$295

Subtract $30 for 28 ga.

GRADING - PPGS™	100%	98%	95%	90%	80%	70%	60%	LAST MSR

VIPER G2 TURKEY – 12 ga., 3 in. chamber, similar to the Viper Series, except has 24 in. barrel with extended Turkey choke, fixed black soft rubber pistol grip stock, fiber optic front sight, Picatinny rail, 100% Realtree Advantage Timber camo finish, 6.8 lbs. Importation began 2011.

MSR $609 $515 $450 $365 $315 $275 $235 $185

VIPER G2 TACTICAL – 12 ga., 20 in. barrel, matte black finish, blade front sight, 5 shot mag., cylinder choke, swivel studs, 6 1/2 lbs. Mfg. 2010-2012.

$395 $350 $300 $265 $235 $200 $175 *$444*

RAPTOR – 12 or 20 ga., 3 in. chamber, 26 or 28 in. barrel, three choke tubes, matte black synthetic stock, 6.4-6.8 lbs. New 2013.

MSR $389 $335 $295 $275 $250 $225 $200 $185

* ***Raptor Youth*** – similar to Raptor, except 20 ga. and has 24 in. barrel, 6.1 lbs. New 2013.

MSR $389 $335 $295 $275 $250 $225 $200 $185

RAPTOR A-TAC – 12 ga., 3 in. chamber, gas operated, 20 in. barrel with extended choke, fixed pistol grip synthetic stock, Picatinny rail, swivel studs, tactical style operating handle, bridge front sight with fiber optic bead, 7 lbs. New 2013.

MSR $419 $365 $325 $295 $265 $235 $200 $185

TEC12 – 12 ga., 3 in. chamber, capable of operating in pump or semi-auto mode by the turn of a dial, inertia rotary bolt action, 20 or 28 in. barrel with choke tubes, external ported cyl. choke, black synthetic stock with rubber fixed pistol grip plus one set of military sling swivels and swivel studs, matte black finish, Picatinny rail, ghost ring sight and raised front bridge sight with fiber optic bead, 7 lbs. New 2013.

MSR $599 $525 $465 $435 $395 $365 $335 $295

Add $90 for 20 in. barrel with fixed pistol grip and external ported cyl. choke.

SHOTGUNS: SINGLE BARREL

TT-09 TRAP – 12 ga., 2 3/4 in. chamber, 34 in. ported VR barrel with extended choke tubes, ejector, select Monte Carlo walnut stock (drilled for recoil reducer), fiber optic front and brass mid-rib bead sight, acid etched alloy receiver, rubber buttpad, 8 1/2 lbs. Mfg. 2009-2012.

$750 $675 $600 $525 $475 $425 $375 *$899*

SHOTGUNS: SLIDE ACTION

DIANA SERIES – 12 or 20 ga., 3 or 3 1/2 in. chamber, choice of Field, camo Mag., or black synthetic configuration, dual slide rails, 20, 24, or 28 (VR) in. barrel with choke tubes, 5 shot mag., crossbolt safety behind trigger, 6-7 lbs. Imported 2004 only.

$160 $140 $120 $100 $90 $80 $70 *$188*

Add $51 for Field or synthetic Mag.

Add $31 for synthetic stock/forearm.

Add $147 for Mag. camo in 12 ga., or $94 for Mag. w/o camo.

COBRA SERIES – 12 ga. only, 3 in. chamber, various barrel lengths, includes 1-3 choke tubes. Importation began 2007.

COBRA FIELD BLACK – 12 ga., 3 in. chamber, 24 (Turkey configuration with fixed pistol grip stock), 26, or 28 in. barrel, 3 choke tubes, fiber optic front sight, extended forearm, swivel studs, matte black finish, 6 1/2 lbs.

MSR $329 $275 $250 $225 $200 $185 $175 $165

Add $50 for 24 in. barrel with fixed pistol grip stock (Turkey configuration).

* ***Cobra Field Camo*** – 12 ga., 3 in. chamber, 24 (Turkey configuration with fixed pistol grip stock), 26, or 28 in. barrel, 3 choke tubes, fiber optic front sight, extended forearm, swivel studs, camo finish, 6.5-6.9 lbs. New 2012.

MSR $409 $350 $315 $275 $250 $225 $200 $185

Add $60 for 24 in. barrel with fixed pistol grip stock (Turkey configuration).

GRADING - PPGS™	100%	98%	95%	90%	80%	70%	60%	LAST MSR

COBRA FORCE – 12 ga. only, 3 in. chamber, 20 in. barrel, fixed pistol grip stock with soft rubber grip, 2 choke tubes, Picatinny rail on top of receiver, fiber optic bridge front sight, rear sight, swivel studs, matte black finish, 6.6 lbs.

MSR $379	$325	$295	$260	$240	$220	$200	$185	

COBRA TACTICAL – 12 ga., 3 in. chamber, 20 in. barrel, spring-loaded forearm, faux extended mag tube, 1 choke tube, blade front sight, swivel studs, 6.3 lbs.

MSR $309	$265	$235	$215	$190	$175	$160	$150	

TROMIX CORPORATION

Previous firearms manufacturer established in 1999, and located in Inola, OK. Previously located in Broken Arrow, OK.

Tromix currently offers conversions for Saiga shotguns, as well as accessories and modifications. Please contact the company directly for its current services and conversion pricing (see Trademark Index).

RIFLES: SEMI-AUTO

Tromix manufactured AR-15 style rifles until 2008. Tromix lower receivers bear no caliber designation. Serialization was TR-0001-0405.

The models listed were also available with many custom options.

TR-15 SLEDGEHAMMER – .44 Rem. Mag. (disc. 2001), .440 Cor-Bon Mag., .458 SOCOM, .475 Tremor, or .50 AE cal., 16 3/4 in. barrel, other lengths and weights available by custom order. Mfg. 1999-2006.

	$1,175	$975	$850	$775	$700	$650	$600	*$1,350*

TR-15 TACKHAMMER – various cals., 24 in. bull barrel, other lengths and weights were available by custom order. Mfg. 1999-2006.

	$1,175	$975	$850	$775	$700	$650	$600	*$1,350*

SHOTGUNS

Tromix manufactures Class II short barrel shotguns based on the Saiga model. Please contact the company directly for more information (see Trademark Index).

TROY DEFENSE

Current firearms manufacturer located in West Springfield, MA.

Troy Defense, created in 2012, is the firearms division of Troy Industries. Troy is well-known for its high quality accessories, including sights and rails. Troy Defense offers a complete line of AR-15 style rifles for military and law enforcement, as well as some models for the civilian marketplace. A wide variety of options and accessories are available. Please contact the company directly for more information, including pricing and availability (see Trademark Index).

TRUVELO ARMOURY

Current manufacturer located in Midrand, South Africa. Truvelo Armoury is a division of Truvelo Manufacturers (Pty) Ltd. No current U.S. importation.

Truvelo Armoury manufactures a variety of barrels (.22 to 40mm cal.) and firearms, including the 12 ga. Neostead shotgun, the BXP 9mmP Tactical pistol, custom built hunting and sporting rifles, and military sniper rifles in 7.62x51 NATO, .338 Lapua, 12.7x99mm, 14.5x114mm, 20x82mm, and 20x110mm cals. Truvelo also manufactures the Raptor Infantry rifle and carbine in 5.56 NATO cal. Please contact the factory directly for more information, including delivery time and availability (see Trademark Index).

TULA ARMS PLANT

Current manufacturer established during 1712, and located in Tula, Russia. Previously imported by SSME Deutsche Waffen, Inc., located in Plant City, FL until 2010. Previously distributed by Tulsky Souvenir, LLC, located in San Diego, CA.

Currently, Tula is increasing exportation of sporting arms to western countries, but has no importation into the U.S. currently.

GRADING - PPGS™	100%	98%	95%	90%	80%	70%	60%	LAST MSR

TULA HISTORY

The Tula Arms Plant is one of the world's oldest and largest gun manufacturing facilities. Plant construction began on Feb. 15, 1712, under the decree of Peter the Great. By 1720, this new plant had supplied the Russian Army with 22,000 flintlock pistols and light infantry/dragoon shotguns. By 1749, Tula was engaged in the production of cold steel used for knives, sabres, swords, etc.

Many great names and inventors have been associated with the famous Tula Arms Plant, including Ivan Pushkin, Ivan Lyalin, Ivan Polin, Sergei Ivanovich Mosin, I. Nagant, F.V. Tokarev, etc. Many famous designs and models have originated from the Tula plant over the years, including the Model 1891 Mosin-Nagant rifle, Model 1910 Maxim-type machine gun, many TOZ sporting rifles, SVT-38 WWII semi-auto rifle, Nagant revolver, SKS rifles and many different styles and variations of commercial firearms, and military machine guns.

RIFLES

TOZ-78 BOLT ACTION – .22 LR cal., full floating barrel, detachable 5 or 10 shot mag., checkered hardwood stock and forend, flip adj. rear sight, adj. post front sight, sling swivels, adj. trigger. Imported 2002-2010.

$250	$220	$185	$170	$135	$110	$85	*$299*

Add $125 for factory supplied scope and mount with rifle receiver cross machined for scope lock.
Add 20% for TOZ 78-05.
Add 40% for TOZ 78-04L luxury model, with deluxe stock, cheekpiece and Schnabel forend.

The basic variations in models are TOZ 78-01 standard model, TOZ-78-02 included optical sight, TOZ 78-04 included threaded muzzle, TOZ 78-05 heavy barrel, no sights. L designation after model number indicates luxury model.

TOZ-99 SEMI-AUTO – .22 LR, full floating barrel, detachable 5 or 10 shot mag., checkered hard wood stock and forend, flip adj. rear sight, front adj. post sight, sling swivels, includes two 5 and two 10 round mags. Imported 2004-2010.

$350	$295	$265	$235	$200	$165	$135	*$390*

Add $125 for factory supplied scope and mount with rifle receiver cross machined for scope lock.
Add 40% for TOZ 99-04L luxury model, with deluxe stock, cheekpiece and Schnabel forend.

The basic variations in models are TOZ 99-01 standard model and the TOZ 99-4 which has a threaded muzzle. L designation after model number indicates luxury model.

TOZ-122-11 BOLT ACTION – .223 Rem., .30-06, 9.32x62mm, or 308 Win. cal., turn down bolt, full floating barrel, 3 shot detachable mag, two included, drilled and tapped for included Picatinny scope rail, two position rear sight, chrome lined barrel, checkered hardwood stock, rubber recoil pad, sling swivels. Imported 2006-2010.

$495	$435	$370	$335	$270	$225	$175	*$599*

SHOTGUNS

TOZ 34 O/U – 12 ga., 2 3/4 or 3 in. chambers, 28 or 30 in. chrome lined VR barrels, fixed or screw in chokes, SST, selectable ejectors, checkered walnut Monte Carlo stock and forearm, sling swivels, rubber recoil pad, blue or nickel frame, 7.4 lbs. Imported 2004-2010.

$475	$425	$375	$325	$275	$225	$175	*$550*

Add 20% for gold triggers.
Add $30 for nickel finish.

V or B designation after model number indicates interchangeable choke tubes.

M designation after model number indicates 3 in. chamber.

E designation after model number indicates ejectors.

TOZ 120 O/U – 12 ga., 2 3/4 or 3 in. chambers, 28 or 30 in. chrome lined VR barrels, fixed or screw in chokes, SST, selectable ejectors, checkered walnut Monte Carlo stock and forearm, sling swivels, rubber recoil pad, blue or nickel frame, 7.8 lbs. Imported 2004-2010.

$625	$545	$470	$425	$345	$280	$220	*$695*

Add 20% for gold triggers.
Add $30 for nickel finish.

GRADING - PPGS™	100%	98%	95%	90%	80%	70%	60%	LAST MSR

V or B designation after model number indicates interchangeable choke tubes.

M designation after model number indicates 3 in. chamber.

E designation after model number indicates ejectors.

TOZ 200 O/U – 12 ga., 2 3/4 or 3 in. chambers, 28 in. chrome lined ventilated rib barrels, extractors, fixed or screw in chokes, DT, decocking mechanism, loaded chamber indicators, checkered walnut stock and forend, sling swivels, 7.7 lbs. Limited importation 2006-2010.

	100%	98%	95%	90%	80%	70%	60%	LAST MSR
	$625	$545	$470	$425	$345	$280	$220	$695

Add 20% for gold triggers.

Add $30 for nickel finish.

V or B designation after model number indicates interchangeable choke tubes.

M designation after model number indicates 3 in. chamber.

TOZ 87 SEMI-AUTO – 12 ga., 2 3/4 or 3 in. chambers, 21 in. barrel, external threaded IC, M, or F choke tubes, 4 or 7 shot mag., sling swivels, tool kit for cleaning and replacing chokes and sizing of shot shells, 7 lbs. Imported 2002.

	100%	98%	95%	90%	80%	70%	60%	LAST MSR
	$440	$385	$330	$300	$240	$200	$155	$525

M designation after model number indicates 3 in. chamber.

Guns were supplied with a 21 in. barrel for externally threaded chokes. When the 8 in. external choke was threaded to the barrel, overall length was 28-30 in.

TURKISH FIREARMS CORPORATION

Please refer to the Huglu section in this text.

TURNBULL MANUFACTURING CO.

Current firearms restoration and manufacturing company established circa 1990 and located in Bloomfield, NY, which specializes in the accurate recreation of historic metal finishes on period firearms, from initial polishing to final finishing. These finishes include bone charcoal color case hardening, charcoal bluing, rust bluing, and Nitre bluing.

Turnbull Manufacturing, previously known as Doug Turnbull Restoration, has performed extensive restoration work on Colt 1911s, A.H. Foxes, Parkers, L.C. Smiths, and lever action Winchesters (including upgrades and antique finishes to duplicate natural aging). These guns have been provided with documentation.

Please contact the company directly for more information and pricing on the wide variety of services available (see Trademark Index).

PISTOLS: SEMI-AUTO

TURNBULL 1911 – .45 ACP cal., exact replica of the Colt M1911 with early 1913 patent markings, hand polished, period correct carbonia charoal bluing on all parts, variations include the 1911 U.S. Army, U.S. Navy, and for the the Marines, U.S. Marine Corp., double diamond checkered walnut grips, Turnbull logo on left side of rear slide, correct repro magazine, mfg. to commemorate the 100th Anniversary of the Colt M1911 Government Model, Turnbull Mfg. Co. worked in conjunction with by Cylinder & Slide located in Fremont, NE on this project. 20 mfg. New 2011.

Current MSR on this model is $5,000.

REVOLVERS: SAA

Turnbull Restoration has reworked current Colt SAAs to look like a pre-1920 SAA. These guns have special factory assigned serial numbers beginning with 000DT. The retail price is $2,200, not including many options. Additionally, the company produced a special run of Colt SAAs in .45 LC, 5 1/2 in. barrel configuration, which are serial numbered EHBM01-EHBM50. These guns have color case hardened frames with charcoal bluing, long flutes (1st Generation), beveled cylinder, and ejector housing. Retail price was $2,150.

A portion of the proceeds from many of the guns listed in this section benefit the Doug Turnbull Firearms Conservation Laboratory at the National Firearms Museum.

GRADING - PPGS™	100%	98%	95%	90%	80%	70%	60%	LAST MSR

GEORGE PATTON SERIES COLT SAA – .45 LC cal., patterned after Patton's original factory engraved SAA, 4 3/4 in. barrel, Helfricht style engraving by John Adams & Son, ivory grips with carved eagle on left and "GSP" monogram on right, silver plated finish, ser. nos. GP01-GP10. 10 mfg. 2003 - sold out early 2004.

	100%	98%	95%	90%	80%	70%	60%	LAST MSR
	$5,500	$4,250	$2,995	N/A	N/A	N/A	N/A	$5,500

CATTLE BRAND COLT SAA – .45 LC cal., 5 1/2 in. barrel, two-piece ivory grips with blind screw hole, 3/4 engraving coverage by John Adams & Son, bone charcoal color case hardening and charcoal blue (ser. nos. CB01B-CB10B) or silver plated (ser. nos. CB01S-CB10S) finish, guns sold in sets of two, owner's personal cattle brand or initials can be scrimshawed on one side of grips, includes fitted hardwood case. Mfg. 2003-2004.

MSR on this model was $7,995.

THEODORE ROOSEVELT COLT SAA – .44-40 WCF cal., 7 1/2 in. barrel, one-piece ivory grips with carved "TR" monogram on right grip and buffalo on left grip, black powder style frame, Nimschke style pattern engraving by John Adams & Son, gold-plated hammer, cylinder, and ejector rod housing, rest of gun silver plated, ser. nos. TR01-TR25, includes French style fitted monogrammed case and factory letter. 25 mfg. 2003.

MSR on this model was $7,500.

COWBOY CLASSIC SAA – .45 LC cal. standard, other cals. available, 4 3/4, 5 1/2, or 7 1/2 in. barrel, hard rubber grips standard with many options available, bone charcoal color case hardening and carbona bluing, barrel address is from U.S. Firearms Mfg. Co., ser. no. range 001DT-999DT. Mfg. 2004-2008.

Last MSR was $1,250

OPEN RANGE SAA – .45 LC cal., 4 3/4 or 5 1/2 in. barrel, additional calibers and barrel lengths available by special request, one-piece hand fitted and shaped walnut grips standard, ivory, stag, and fancy wood optional, hand assembled and polished, barrel address is "Turnbull Mfg. Co.". New 2009.

Current MSR on this model is $1,450. Sheriff's configuration is $2,200.

CUSTOM OPEN RANGE SAA – .45 LC cal., features genuine pre-banned elephant ivory grips and B coverage engraving, 24Kt. gold borders, metal finishes include color case hardening, charcoal bluing, and nitre blue, 4 3/4 or 5 1/2 in. barrel. New 2011.

Current MSR on this model starts at $4,250.

CAVALRY SAA – .45 LC cal., metal finishes include color case hardening, charcoal blue, and nitre blue, 7 1/2 in. barrel, includes inspector markings, customer can choose ser. no., only 5 mfg. beginning 2011.

Current MSR on this model is $1,575.

BUNTLINE SAA – .44 Spl. or .45 Colt cal., color case hardened frame and hammer, charcoal blue finish, unique ladder sight, choice of barrel length up to 16 inches, engraved initials on backstrap. Limited mfg. of 10 beginning late 2011.

Base price on this model is $1,650.

RIFLES

Turnbull Restoration also announced the introduction of its Big Bore Classics line during late 2003, utilizing either new or original Winchester and Browning Model 1886 receivers. Chambering includes: .45-70, .45-90, .450 Alaskan (new 2005), .50-110 (.50 Express), and .50 Alaskan. Many metal options and wood choices are available - please contact the company directly for more information on these custom rifles.

Turnbull Restoration introduced its own .475 Turnbull proprietary rifle cartridge during 2007. This caliber can be used in the company's modified Winchester Model 1886 or Model 71.

Turnbull Restoration introduced a proprietary rifle cartridge during 2008. The .470 Turnbull is designed specifically for use in the Marlin 1895 action, and can be used in the company's modified Marlin 1895 rifles.

During 2009, Turnbull Restoration introduced the .475 Turnbull, designed for the Winchester Model 1886.

GRADING - PPGS™	100%	98%	95%	90%	80%	70%	60%	LAST MSR

THEODORE ROOSEVELT WINCHESTER MODEL 1876 – exact duplicate of the rifle ordered in 1883 from Winchester and carried by Roosevelt, copied from the original model, historically accurate, including measurements, dimensions, and specifications, 25 mfg. beginning 2006. Roosevelt's 1876 is one of the most elaborate and certainly the most historic Model 1876 ever built. Five North American big game animals are represented on this piece including antelope, buffalo, bear and deer scenes.

Current MSR is $28,000, and price includes display case.

This model is for sale exclusively through the NRA Foundation. A portion of the proceeds will benefit the Doug Turnbull Firearms Conservation Laboratory at the National Firearms Museum. The purchaser of this rifle may qualify for a $6,000 charitable contribution itemized Federal Tax deduction.

NEW BIG MEDICINE MODEL 1886 – .475 Turnbull cal., take down action, copy of Roosevelt's original "Big Medicine", 22 in. octagon barrel, 2X fancy wood, bone case color finish. New 2009.

Base price on this model is $4,995.

Please contact the company directly for more information and other options on this model.

TURNBULL MODEL 1886 – 45-70, 45-90 standard cal., 26 in. full octagon barrel. This is a true reproduction of an original Model 1886 with 100% interchangeable parts. Features Turnbull's period correct finishes - color case hardening, charcoal bluing and rust bluing; hand-rubbed oil walnut stock and forend. Many options are available including fancy and extra fancy wood, checkering, and new barrel (.475, 50-110, etc).

Base price on this model is $2,650.
Add $800 for .475 Turnbull cal.

Many upgrades are available on this model - please contact the company for a list and pricing (see Trademark Index).

USRAC/WINCHESTER MODEL 1892 TAKE-DOWN – available in several calibers including 44-40 WCF, 45 Colt, and 44 Special. Turnbull Manufacturing has reworked these modern rifles taking them back to the way it was originally designed by removing the factory tang safety and bringing it back to a half-cock safety notch. Turnbull Mfg. Co. then finished the rifle with the period correct finishes that they are famous for.

Base price on this model is $1,950.

RUGER NO. 1 1-H TROPICAL – .475 Turnbull cal., color case hardened receiver, lever, rings, and quarter rib, refinished woo, slow rust blued barrel. New 2011.

Base price on this model is $1,750.

TAR-10 SEMI-AUTO – .308 Win. cal., scaled down AR-15 style, 16 1/2 in. fluted chromemoly barrel with screw on muzzle brake, carbine gas system, color case hardened steel lower and flattop upper with high Picatinny rail, MOE triggerguard, premium American walnut forend, pistol grip, 4 or 10 shot mag., includes lockable hard case, approx. 13 lbs. New mid-2012.

MSR	100%	98%	95%	90%	80%	70%	60%
MSR $4,995	$4,250	$3,715	$3,185	$2,885	$2,335	$1,910	$1,485

TURNER RICHARDS GUNMAKERS

Previous gunmaker located in Bromsgrove, U.K.

Robert Turner grew up in Birmingham and was trained by Westley Richards craftsmen while still a teenager. While only a handful of longuns have been manufactured under his own name, his craftsmanship can be found in guns bearing some of Britain's best names, including Boss & Co., Churchill, Atkin, Grant & Lang, Dickson & MacNaughton, William Evans, Holland & Holland, P.V. Nelson, William Powell, and Westley Richards.

While Turner no longer makes guns for the gun trade, he is currently one of the fifteen elected Guardians of the Birmingham Proof House.

It is highly recommended that an expert individual appraisal be done on any Turner long gun in order to determine current value before buying or selling.

Information appears courtesy of Vic Venters and Shooting Sportsman *magazine.*

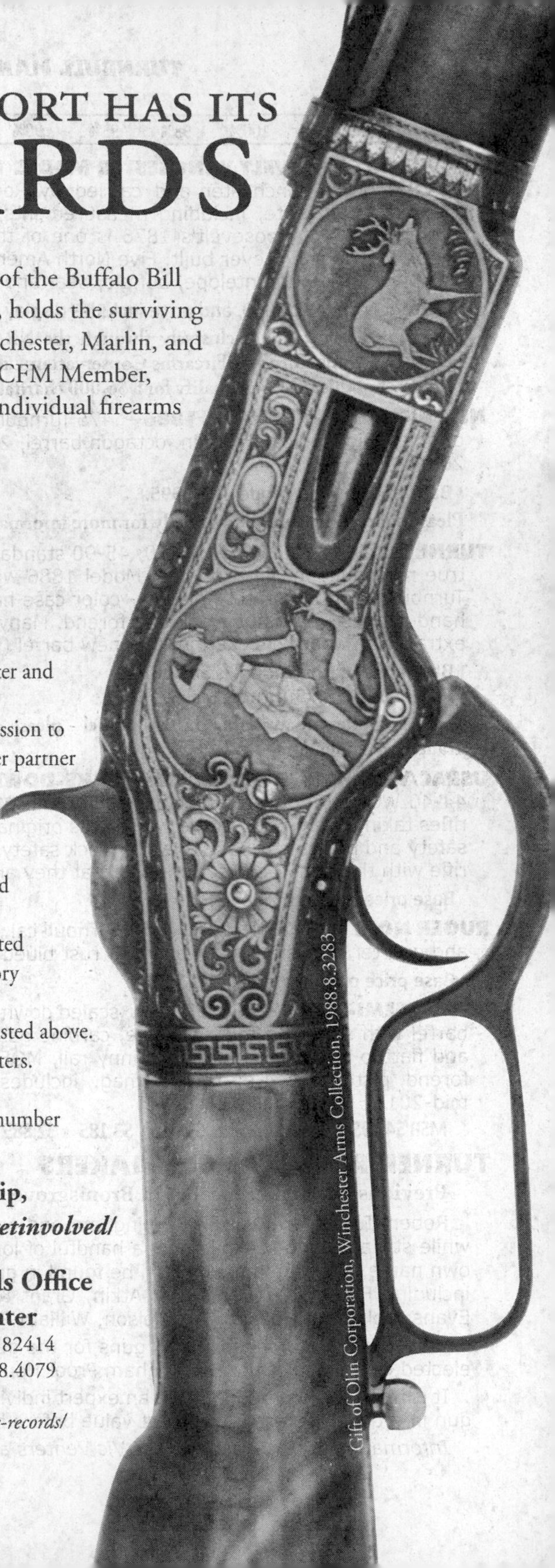

Gift of Olin Corporation, Winchester Arms Collection, 1988.8.3283

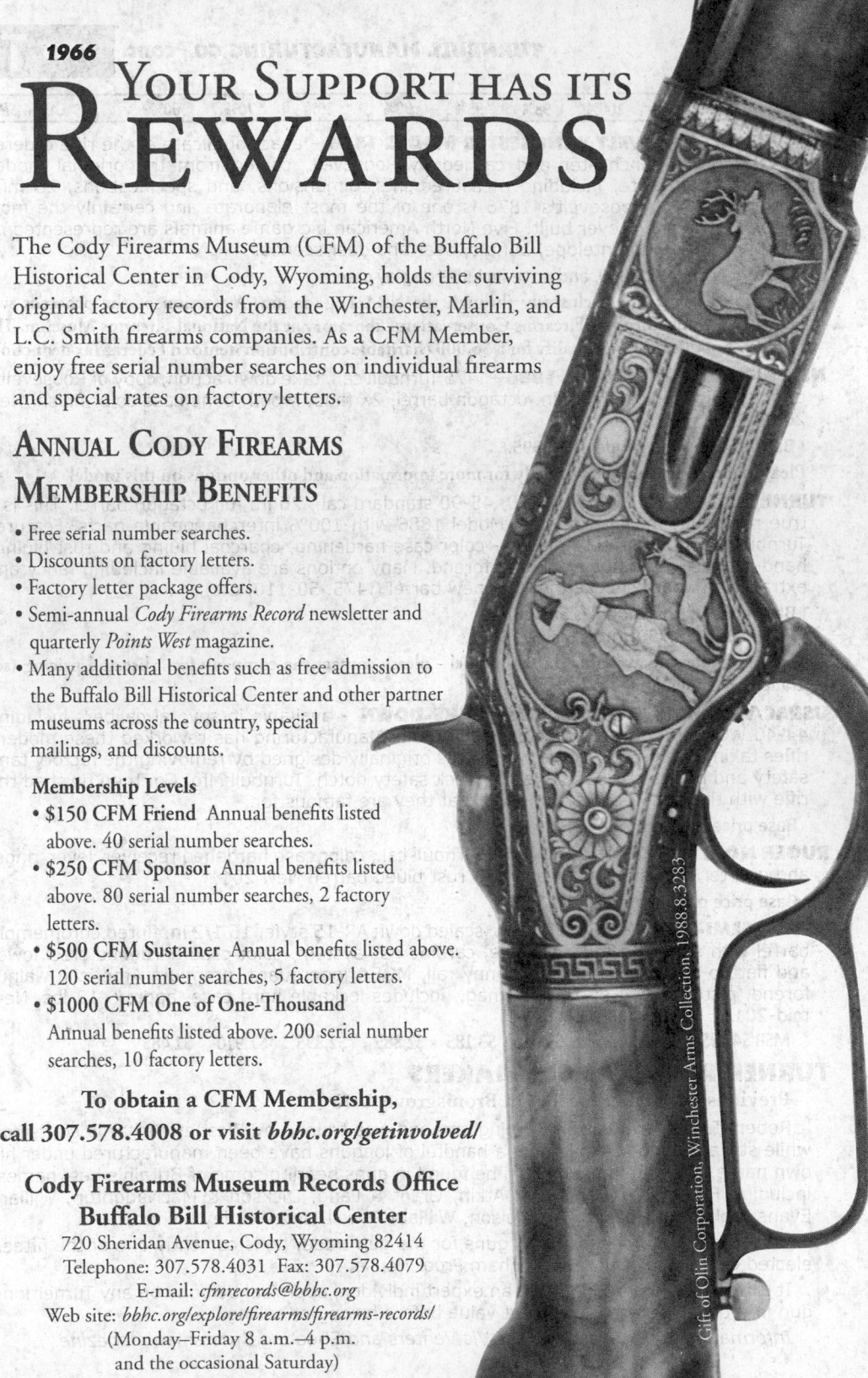

U SECTION

U.S. ARMAMENT CORP.

Current manufacturer located in Ephrata, PA.

U.S. Armament Corp. manufactures full size replicas of the 1877 Bulldog Gatling Gun. Prices start at $36,500. Please contact the company directly for more information, including options, pricing, and availability (see Trademark Index).

U.S. ARMS COMPANY

Previous manufacturer located in Riverhead, NY.

GRADING - PPGS™	100%	98%	95%	90%	80%	70%	60%	LAST MSR

REVOLVERS: SINGLE ACTION

ABILENE .357 MAG. – 6 shot, 4 5/8, 5 1/2, or 6 1/2 in. barrel, adj. sights, transfer bar ignition, smooth walnut grips, blue finish only. Mfg. 1976-83.

	100%	98%	95%	90%	80%	70%	60%	LAST MSR
	$325	$275	$240	$200	$185	$170	$155	

* ***Abilene .357 Mag. Stainless Steel*** – similar to Abilene, only in stainless steel.

	100%	98%	95%	90%	80%	70%	60%	LAST MSR
	$350	$285	$240	$200	$185	$170	$155	

ABILENE .44 MAG. – 7 1/2 and 8 1/2 in. barrel, unfluted cylinder blue finish only, otherwise similar to .357 Mag.

	100%	98%	95%	90%	80%	70%	60%	LAST MSR
	$325	$265	$240	$220	$200	$165	$150	

* ***Abilene .44 Mag. Stainless Steel*** – similar to Abilene .44 Mag., only stainless steel.

	100%	98%	95%	90%	80%	70%	60%	LAST MSR
	$375	$330	$290	$235	$210	$180	$155	

U.S. GENERAL TECHNOLOGIES, INC.

Previous manufacturer located in S. San Francisco, CA circa 1994-96.

RIFLES: SEMI-AUTO

P-50 SEMI-AUTO – .50 BMG cal., includes 10 shot detachable mag., folding bipod, muzzle brake, matte black finish. Mfg. 1995-96.

	100%	98%	95%	90%	80%	70%	60%	LAST MSR
	$5,600	$4,950	$4,475	$3,975	$3,500	$3,050	$2,600	*$5,995*

U.S. HISTORICAL SOCIETY

Previous organization which marketed historically significant firearms reproductions until April, 1994. Located in Richmond, VA. Most firearms were manufactured by the Williamsburg Firearms Manufactory and the Virginia Firearms Manufactory.

On April 1, 1994, the Antique Arms Divison of the U.S. Historical Society was acquired by America Remembers located in Mechanicsville, VA. America Remembers affiliates include the Armed Forces Commemorative Society, American Heroes & Legends, and the United States Society of Arms and Armor. Issues that were not fully subscribed are now available through America Remembers (please refer to listing in A section).

The information listed below represents current information up until America Remembers acquired the Antique Arms Division of the U.S. Historical Society.

Please refer to the *Blue Book of Modern Black Powder Arms* by John Allen (also online) for more information and prices on U.S. Historical Society's modern black powder models.

Manufacturer/Model	Quantity	Year	Issue Price
HANDGUNS: SPECIAL EDITIONS			
UBERTI Secret Service Museum Edition	500	1988	$2,750
UBERTI Secret Service Investigator's Edition	1,000	1988	$1,250
UBERTI George Jones SAA	950	1993	$1,675
UBERTI Richard Petty Silver Edition SAA	1,000	1992	$1,675
COLT King Richard Hand Engraved .45 SAA	100	1993	$4,500
UBERTI Charlton Heston SAA	500	1993	$1,850

Manufacturer/Model	Quantity	Year	Issue Price
UBERTI Hopalong Cassidy Cowboy Edition SAA	950	1993	$1,675
COLT Hopalong Cassidy Premier Edition	100	1993	$4,500
COLT Mel Torme SAA	100	1992	$4,500
UBERTI Roy Rogers Cowboy Edition SAA	2,500	1990	$1,350
COLT Roy Rogers Premier Edition SAA	250	1990	$4,500
ARMI SAN MARCO U.S. Marshals Wyatt Earp SAA	2,500	1991	$1,250
UBERTI National Cowboy Hall of Fame SAA	1,000	1992	$1,600
COLT Interpol SAA	154	1991	$4,500
SPRINGFIELD Eisenhower .45 Auto	1,000	1992	$1,675
COLT "Don't Give Up the Ship" Model .45 Auto	1,997	1993	$1,485
COLT American Eagle .45 Auto	2,500	1993	$1,950
REVOLVERS: MINIATURE SPECIAL EDITIONS			
UBERTI SA Army Presidential Edition	1,500	1988	$1,550
UBERTI SA Army Classic Edition	1,500	1988	$575
SHOTGUNS: SPECIAL EDITIONS			
BERTUZZI Chuck Yeager Tribute	100	1989	$12,500
RENATO TELO Arnold Palmer Tribute	100	1990	$9,750
ANTONIO ZOLI Christopher Columbus Tribute	200	1991	$12,500

U.S. MILITARY HANDGUNS

Please refer to listings in the Colt (includes subcontracted variations of the M1911 and M1911A1) and Smith & Wesson sections.

U.S. MILITARY LONG ARMS

Also see listings under Colt, Enfield, Krag-Jorgensen, Springfield Armory, and Winchester. U.S. Military Trench and Riot guns may be found under the "Trench/Riot Shotguns" category in the T section.

GRADING - PPGS™	100%	98%	95%	90%	80%	70%	60%

CARBINES: SEMI-AUTO

Values are for original unmodified carbines, with proper parts makers, unsanded wood, and crisp stock cartouches.

U.S. M1 CARBINE (MILITARY & COMMERCIAL) – .30 Carbine cal., 18 in. barrel, 15 or 30 shot box mag., wood stocked, two or four position aperture rear, blade front sight with protective ears, with or without bayonet lug. This weapon was designed by Winchester for the U.S. government, over 6 million were produced by 12 different companies. Plainfield mfg. after WWII was for civilian sales. It is a gas operated lightweight carbine which was also used by other countries' armed forces. Makers and values as follows. Some variations have the type III barrel band.

* ***Carbines: Semi-Auto, Reworks & Commercial Mfg.*** – includes carbines that have been factory reworked at U.S. arsenals.

Underwood	$850	$675	$495	$400	$350	$300	$275
S.G. Saginaw	$825	$650	$475	$400	$350	$300	$275
Quality Hardware	$850	$675	$495	$415	$370	$325	$295
Nat'l Postal Meter	$950	$775	$525	$425	$375	$325	$295
IBM	$950	$775	$525	$425	$370	$325	$295
Standard Products	$800	$650	$495	$415	$370	$325	$295
Inland	$850	$675	$495	$415	$370	$325	$295
SG Grand Rapids	$950	$775	$525	$425	$375	$325	$295
Winchester	$1,150	$850	$750	$550	$425	$350	$325
Irwin Pedersen	$1,700	$1,400	$995	$850	$775	$675	$580
Rockola	$995	$925	$700	$525	$425	$350	$325

GRADING - PPGS™	100%	98%	95%	90%	80%	70%	60%	LAST MSR
Plainfield	$395	$360	$330	$295	$260	$230	$195	
Commercial Mfg. (43 mfgs.)	$350	$300	$265	$235	$200	$185	$170	

An Inland presentation carbine with white stock was also mfg. in limited quantities for military service organizations (i.e. V.F.W., American Legion, etc.). Values for original guns are currently in the $1,750-$2,000 range.

Recent imports can usually be denoted by visible import markings and/or alterations to original finish.

* ***Carbines: Semi-Auto, Original Type I*** – includes original carbines with flip rear sight and no bayonet lug.

Underwood	$2,125	$1,675	$1,250	$1,000	$875	$750	$675
S.G. Saginaw	$2,050	$1,600	$1,200	$950	$825	$700	$650
Quality Hardware	$2,125	$1,675	$1,250	$1,000	$875	$750	$675
Nat'l Postal Meter	$2,375	$1,950	$1,325	$1,050	$950	$800	$750
IBM	$2,375	$1,950	$1,325	$1,050	$950	$800	$750
Standard Products	$2,000	$1,625	$1,250	$1,050	$925	$800	$750
Inland	$2,125	$1,675	$1,250	$1,000	$875	$750	$675
SG Grand Rapids	$2,375	$1,950	$1,325	$1,050	$950	$800	$750
Winchester	$2,875	$2,200	$1,875	$1,375	$1,075	$875	$800
Irwin Pedersen	$4,250	$3,500	$2,500	$2,125	$1,925	$1,675	$1,425
Rockola	$2,500	$2,275	$1,750	$1,300	$1,050	$875	$800

Subtract 30% for original finish guns that have been changed back to the original configuration by switching parts.

* ***Carbines: Semi-Auto, Original Type II*** – includes original carbines with adj. rear sight and no bayonet lug.

S.G. Saginaw	$1,825	$1,450	$1,050	$875	$775	$650	$600
Quality Hardware	$1,875	$1,650	$1,075	$875	$775	$650	$600
IBM	$2,100	$1,700	$1,150	$925	$825	$715	$650
Standard Products	$1,750	$1,425	$1,050	$875	$775	$650	$600
Inland	$1,875	$1,475	$1,075	$875	$775	$650	$600
SG Grand Rapids	$2,100	$1,700	$1,150	$925	$825	$715	$650
Winchester	$2,525	$1,875	$1,650	$1,200	$925	$775	$700
Irwin Pedersen	$3,750	$3,050	$2,175	$1,875	$1,700	$1,475	$1,275
Rockola	$2,175	$2,025	$1,550	$1,150	$925	$775	$700

Subtract 30% for original finish guns that have been changed back to the original configuration by switching parts.

* ***Carbines: Semi-Auto, Original Type III*** – includes original carbines with adj. rear sight and bayonet lug.

Inland	$1,700	$1,350	$1,000	$800	$700	$600	$550
Winchester	$2,300	$1,700	$1,500	$1,100	$850	$700	$650

Subtract 30% for original finish guns that have been changed back to the original configuration by switching parts.

Subtract 50% for modified guns with adj. sight and bayonet lug.

M1 A1 PARATROOPER CARBINE – .30 Carbine cal., mfg. by Inland - WWII production, folding stock, crossed cannon proofed on bottom, 140,000 mfg. 1942-1945. Overall length 26 1/2 in. with stock folded.

Beware of after-market fakes.

* ***M1 A1 Paratrooper Carbine Type I*** – values assume original guns with flip rear sight and no bayonet lug.

$5,500	$5,000	$3,250	$2,500	$2,150	$1,750	$1,450

GRADING - PPGS™	100%	98%	95%	90%	80%	70%	60%	LAST MSR

* ***M1 A1 Paratrooper Carbine Type II*** – values assume original guns with adj. rear sight and no bayonet lug.

	$5,500	$5,000	$2,700	$2,100	$1,750	$1,450	$1,150	

* ***M1 A1 Paratrooper Carbine Type III*** – values assume original guns with adj. rear sight and bayonet lug.

	$3,200	$2,800	$2,150	$1,750	$1,500	$1,250	$1,000	

RIFLES: BOLT ACTION

For U.S. Military Enfields, please refer to the Enfield section.

RIFLES: SEMI-AUTO

On original (non-reworked) variations listed, it is absolutely critical that rifles have not been rebuilt and must have original cartouche stock.

Values are for original unmodified rifles, with proper parts makers, unsanded wood, and crisp stock cartouches. Without original wood and non-original parts, values drop to rework prices. Beware of fake stock cartouches.

M1 GARAND – .30-06 cal., semi-auto, 8 shot en bloc clip fed, gas operated, adj. aperture sight, wooden stock. Made 1937-57 by Springfield, Winchester, H&R, and International Harvester.

* ***M1 Garand Reworks*** – includes rifles reworked at U.S. Arsenals.

	$1,250	$1,050	$900	$800	$700	$600	$500	

* ***M1 Garand Early Type I*** – identified by gas trap barrel up to ser. no. 50,000, all were mfg. by Springfield.

	$1,875	$1,575	$1,350	$1,200	$1,050	$900	$750	

Some early original gas trap Type I guns with rare features are bringing up to $40,000.

* ***M1 Garand Type II*** – identified by gas port barrel and ser. no. over 50,000.

	$1,450	$1,200	$1,035	$925	$800	$695	$575	

* ***M1 Garand Pre-WWII Winchester Mfg.***

	$3,750	$3,150	$2,700	$2,400	$2,100	$1,800	$1,500	

* ***M1 Garand Pre-WWII Springfield Mfg.***

	$3,750	$3,150	$2,700	$2,400	$2,100	$1,800	$1,500	

* ***M1 Garand WWII Mfg.*** – serialization starts at approx. 400,000.

	$5,000	$4,200	$3,600	$3,200	$2,800	$2,400	$2,000	

* ***M1-C or M1-D Garand Sniper*** – with scope and mounts (beware of fakes and rewelds with boxes and papers). M1-D values assume paperwork for values listed.

M1-D	$4,500	$3,400	$2,800	$2,200	$1,725	$1,350	$1,150	
M1-C	N/A	N/A	$3,650	$3,250	$2,850	$2,500	$2,150	

Top values require original DCM shipping box, paperwork, and all listed accessories.

M1 GARAND NATIONAL MATCH – target version of the Garand, using National Match barrel and sights, glass bedding, etc. Must have serialized N.M. paperwork for prices listed below.

	$2,800	$2,500	$1,800	$1,400	$1,000	$800	$650	

U.S. ORDNANCE

Current manufacturer and distributor located in Reno, NV. Commercial sales through Desert Ordnance, located in Sparks, NV.

U.S. Ordnance is licensed by Saco Defense to be the exclusive manufacturer and distributor for the M60 Series machine gun and spare parts.

RIFLES: SEMI-AUTO

U.S. Ordnance manufactures semi-auto reproductions (BATFE approved) of the M-60/M-60E3 (MSR is POR), M60E4/Mk43 (MSR POR, new 2004). Previous models included the .303 Vickers (MSR was $4,500 w/o tripod), Browning M-1919 (last MSR was $1,995), and the M-1919A4 (last MSR was $2,095). These belt-fed variations are machined to military specifications, and have a 5 year warranty. Please contact the distributor directly for more information, including pricing and availability (see Trademark Index).

GRADING - PPGS™	100%	98%	95%	90%	80%	70%	60%	LAST MSR

USAS 12

Previous trademark manufactured by International Ordnance Corporation located in Nashville, TN circa 1992-95. Previously manufactured (1990-91) by Ramo Mfg., Inc. located in Nashville, TN. Previously distributed by Kiesler's Wholesale located in Jeffersonville, IN until 1994. Originally designed and previously distributed in the U.S. by Gilbert Equipment Co., Inc. located in Mobile, AL. Previously manufactured under license by Daewoo Precision Industries, Ltd. located in South Korea.

SHOTGUNS: SEMI-AUTO

USAS 12 – 12 ga. only, gas operated action available in either semi or fully auto versions, 18 1/4 in. cylinder bore barrel, closed bolt, synthetic stock, pistol grip, and forearm, carrying handle, 10 round box or 20 round drum mag., 2 3/4 in. chamber only, parkerized finish, 12 lbs. Mfg. 1987-1995.

	100%	98%	95%	90%	80%	70%	60%	LAST MSR
	$1,500	$1,250	$1,050	$925	$850	$750	$650	*$995*

Add $300-$500 for extra 20 shot drum magazine (banned by the BATFE).

Values above are for a semi-auto model. This model is currently classified as a destructive device and necessary federal NFA Class III transfer paperwork must accompany a sale.

U.S.R.A.

Previous organization (United States Revolver Association) that established certain rules for target pistol shooting. Target pistols were manufactured by Harrington & Richardson - please refer to the Handgun section under Harrington & Richardson.

Readers interested in obtaining more information about specific U.S.R.A. pistols, or with information to share, are encouraged to contact Mr. L. Richard Littlefield (see Trademark Index).

USSG/U.S. SPORTING GOODS INC.

Current importer located in Rockledge, FL.

U.S. Sporting Goods Inc. is the importer for select firearms from Baikal, Izhmash (Saiga), Sabatti, Sarsilmaz (Sar Arms), Tanfoglio and Zastava. Please refer to these individual listings for more infomation and current values.

UBERTI, A. S.r.l.

Current firearms, black powder, replica firearms, and accessories manufacturer established in 1959 and located in Serezzo, Italy. Currently imported and distributed by Stoeger Industries (beginning 2003), located in Accokeek, MD, Taylor's & Co, located in Winchester, VA, Cimarron F.A. Co, located in Fredricksburg, TX, E.M.F., located in Santa Ana, CA, Navy Arms, located in Martinsburg, WV, Cabela's (certain models only), located in Sidney, NE, and Dixie Gun Works, located in Union City, TN. Previously imported by Tristar Sporting Arms, located in N. Kansas City, MO, and until Dec. 31st, 2002 by Uberti USA, Inc., located in Lakeville, CT.

A. Uberti. HISTORY REPEATS ITSELF

In late 1999, Beretta purchased Aldo Uberti & Co. S.r.l.

The current importers listed above import Uberti guns with their own importer stamp. However, all guns will also have the Uberti name listed as the manufacturer. Please refer to the individual importers for additional information on Uberti firearms.

For more information and up-to-date pricing regarding current Aldo Uberti black powder models, please refer to the *Blue Book of Modern Black Powder Arms* by John Allen.

Black Powder Revolvers - Reproductions & Replicas and *Black Powder Long Arms & Pistols - Reproductions & Replicas* by Dennis Adler are also invaluable sources for most black powder reproductions and replicas, and include hundreds of color images on most popular makes/models, provide manufacturer/trademark histories, and up-to-date information on related items/accessories for black powder shooting - www.bluebookofgunvalues.com.

PISTOLS: REPRODUCTIONS, SINGLE SHOT

1871 ROLLING BLOCK TARGET PISTOL – available in .22 LR, .22 WMR, .22 Hornet (disc.

GRADING - PPGS™	100%	98%	95%	90%	80%	70%	60%	LAST MSR

2004), .357 Mag. (disc. 2002), or .45 LC (Navy Model with open sights only, mfg. 1992-95) cal., 9 1/2 in. half-round, half-octagon barrel, case colored frame and backstrap, brass trigger guard. Imported 2002-2006.

	$385	$300	$250	$210	$175	$155	$135	*$480*

REVOLVERS: DOUBLE ACTION

INSPECTOR MODEL – .32 S&W or .38 Spl. cal., 3, 4, or 6 in. barrels, double action, blue or chrome finish. Imported 1985-89.

	$390	$295	$245	$210	$170	$145	$125	*$406*

Add $35 for target sights.
Add $25 for chrome plating.

REVOLVERS: REPRODUCTIONS, SA/SAA & VARIATIONS

Factory engraving and other embellishments or finishes (including antique charcoal blue, in-the-white steel, nickel, etc.) may be special ordered by contacting the importer(s) directly.

Add $85 for antique patina finish (disc.), $45 for antique charcoal blue finish (disc.) on all Cattleman variations, $130 for silver plating (disc.), $40 for in-the-white finish (disc.), $85 for nickel plating (not available on Schofield, disc.), $85 for select grade walnut one-piece fitted grips (disc.), $49 for walnut grip, $250 or $575 (solid silver) for Army/Navy Tiffany grips (disc.), $45 for checkered grips (disc.), $50 for stag horn grips (disc.), $69 for gunfighter grip, $189 for faux ivory, $189 for black bison horn grips, $189 for faux pearl, $350 for mother-of-pearl grips (disc.), or $650-$1,450 for Cattleman engraving, depending on amount, and if with gold inlays (disc.).

COLT 1851 NAVY CONVERSION – .38 Spl. cal. only, 4 3/4, 5 1/2, or 7 1/2 in. barrel, patterned after original 1851 Navy, brass backstrap and trigger guard, 2.6 lbs. Importation began 2007.

MSR $529	$440	$375	$315	$270	$230	$200	$170

REMINGTON 1858 NEW ARMY CONVERSION – .45 LC cal., 8 in. barrel, brass backstrap and trigger guard, case hardened frame, one-piece walnut grips, 2.6 lbs. Importation began 2007.

MSR $539	$445	$375	$315	$270	$230	$200	$170

COLT 1860 ARMY CONVERSION – .38 Spl. or .45 LC cal., 4 3/4 (.38 Spl. cal. only), 5 1/2, 7 1/2 (disc.), or 8 in. barrel, patterned after original 1860 Army, blued steel backstrap and trigger guard, 2.6 lbs. Importation began 2007.

MSR $559	$460	$390	$330	$280	$250	$220	$180

COLT 1871 RICHARDS/MASON CONVERSION – .38 Spl., .38 LC, .44 Colt (8 in. barrel only), or .45 Schofield cal., choice of brass (New Model) or steel BS/TG (Old Model), 5 1/2, 7 1/2, or 8 in. round or octagon barrel, one-piece walnut grips, approx. 2.6 lbs. Imported 2002 only.

	$385	$350	$315	$275	$250	$225	$200	*$450*

COLT 1871-1872 OPEN TOP EARLY/LATE MODEL – .38 Spl., .38 LC (disc. 2002), .44 Russian (disc. 2002), .44 Colt (disc. 2002), .44 LC (disc. 2002), .44 Spl. (disc. 2002), .45 Schofield (disc. 2002), or .45 LC cal., open top frame, 4 3/4 (Early Model only), 5 1/2 (Early Model only), or 7 1/2 in. octagon barrel, Army (Late Model) or Navy (Early Model) size grips. Imported 2002, reintroduced 2007.

MSR $532	$440	$375	$315	$270	$230	$200	$170

Subtract $20 for Early Model Navy with brass backstrap and trigger guard.

BUCKHORN SAA – .44 Mag., .44 Spl. (disc.), or .44-40 WCF (disc.) cal., 4 3/4, 5 1/2 (new 2002), 6 (disc.), or 7 1/2 in. barrel, brass or steel backstrap. Importation disc. 2002.

* ***Buckhorn New Model Frame SAA*** – steel or brass backstrap and trigger guard.

	$345	$265	$210	$175	$160	$150	$135	*$410*

Add $69 for convertible cylinder.
Add $40 for Target Model (disc.).
Subtract $51 for New Model frame (brass BS & TG).

GRADING - PPGS™	100%	98%	95%	90%	80%	70%	60%	LAST MSR

* ***Buckhorn Buntline SAA*** – .44-40 WCF (disc.) or .44 Mag. cal., 18 in. barrel, includes non-detachable shoulder stock with brass hardware and lanyard ring. Importation disc. 1989, resumed 2001-2002.

	$375	$310	$240	$195	$175	$160	$150	*$455*

Add $40 for target sights.
Add $40 for extra .44-40 WCF cylinder combo (disc.).
Add $122 for detachable shoulder stock (disc.).
Subtract $45 for New Model frame (BB & TG).

1873 CATTLEMAN FLAT-TOP SAA ("FIRST ISSUE") – .357 Mag. (mfg. 2001-2002), .38-40 WCF (disc. 2002), .44-40 WCF, or .45 LC cal., 4 3/4, 5 1/2, or 7 1/2 in. barrel, choice of regular (disc. 2002) or flat-top receiver. Imported 1997-2004.

	$365	$310	$240	$195	$175	$160	$150	*$430*

1873 CATTLEMAN SAA & VARIATIONS – available in .22 LR (disc. 1990), .22 WMR (disc. 1990), .32-20 WCF (mfg. 2001-2003), .357 Mag., .38 Spl. (disc. 2003), .38-40 WCF (mfg. 1989-2003), .44 Spl. (disc. 2003), .44-40 WCF, or .45 LC cal., 3 3/4 (.45 LC only, disc.), 4 (.45 LC only, disc.), 4 3/4, 5 1/2, or 7 1/2 in. barrel, brass or steel backstrap and trigger guard, Old Model (with cylinder pin retainer) or New Model (with plunger) frame, 2.3 lbs. (with 5 1/2 in. barrel). New 2002.

* ***1873 Cattleman SAA with Steel Grip Strap and Trigger Guard*** – choice of New or Old Model frame, case colored or nickel finished, charcoal blue barrel/cylinder also available on Old Model.

MSR $509	$425	$365	$310	$265	$230	$200	$170	

Add $110 for nickel finish (New Model, .45 LC cal. only).
Add $120 for Old Model with Old West (distressed) finish (not available in .44-40 WCF cal.).
Add $280 for Cattleman Cody Model with nickel finish and faux ivory grips (new 2005 .45 LC cal. only).
Add $270 for Cattleman Frisco model with charcoal blue finish with pearl grips (new 2005, .45 LC cal. only).
Add $35 for walnut grips or $50 for Gunfighter grips.
Add $110 for charcoal blue finish or $140 for charcoal blue finish and martially marked grips (.45 LC cal. only).
Add $175 for faux ivory, black buffalo horn, or faux pearl grips (new 2006).
Add $60 for charcoal blue barrel, cylinder, and grip frame/trigger guard (.45 LC cal. only).
Add $75 for convertible cylinder (.45 LC/.45 ACP, .22 LR/.22 WMR in 5 1/2 in. barrel only, disc. 2002).

* ***1873 Cattleman SAA with Brass Grip Strap and Trigger Guard*** – .357 Mag., .38-40 WCF (mfg. 2001-2002), .44 Mag. (mfg. 2001-2002), .44 Spl. (mfg. 2001-2002), .44-40 WCF, or .45 LC cal., 3 3/4 (.45 LC only, disc.), 4 (.45 LC only, disc.), 4 3/4, 5 1/2, or 7 1/2 in. barrel.

MSR $489	$395	$335	$285	$225	$185	$160	$150	

Add $51 for convertible cylinder (.45 LC/.45 ACP, disc. 2002).

* ***1873 Cattleman SAA Stainless Steel*** – .45 LC cal., similar to 1873 Cattleman SAA with New Model frame, 4 3/4, 5 1/2, or 7 1/2 in. barrel, stainless steel.

MSR $669	$550	$450	$375	$300	$250	$210	$180	

» **1873 Cattleman Stainless Engraved** – .45 LC cal., 4 3/4 or 5 1/2 in. barrel, engraved frame, faux pearl grips. New 2011.

MSR $1,199	$1,050	$925	$825	$750	$650	$550	$450	

* ***1873 Cattleman SAA Matched Set*** – .45 LC or .357 Mag. (new 2011) cal., 4 3/4 (disc. 2010) or 5 1/2 in. barrel, New Model frame, choice of blue/case colored, nickel/faux ivory grips (disc. 2010), or matte blue (disc. 2010) with walnut grips. New mid-2008.

MSR $1,069	$975	$875	$775	$700	$625	$550	$495	

Add $550 for nickel finish with faux ivory grips (disc. 2010).
Add $40 for matte blue finish with walnut grips (disc. 2010).

GRADING - PPGS™	100%	98%	95%	90%	80%	70%	60%	LAST MSR

* ***1873 Cattleman SAA Engraved*** – .45 LC cal. only, 4 3/4 or 5 1/2 in. barrel, engraved action, New Model frame, choice of white finish/AAA walnut grips, blue coin finish/bison horn grips, or silver plated finish/faux pearl grips. Mfg. mid-2008-2010.

	$950	$850	$750	$650	$550	$450	$375	*$1,069*

Add $40 for blue coin finish with buffalo horn grips.
Add $110 for silver plated finish and faux pearl grips.

* ***1873 Cattleman SAA Target Model*** – similar to standard Cattleman Model, only fully adj. rear blade sight, brass backstrap. Importation disc. 1990.

	$315	$245	$200	$185	$170	$150	$135	*$335*

Add $25 for steel backstrap and trigger guard.
Add $60 for stainless steel construction (disc.).

1873 CATTLEMAN U.S. SAA CAVALRY – .45 LC cal. only, 7 1/2 in. barrel, Old Model frame, charcoal blue finish, steel backstrap and trigger guard, one piece walnut grips, 2.3 lbs. Disc. 2009.

	$540	$450	$375	$310	$250	$215	$190	*$629*

1873 CATTLEMAN ARTILLERY SAA – .45 LC cal. only, 5 1/2 in. barrel, Old Model frame, charcoal blue finish, steel backstrap and trigger guard, one piece walnut grips, 2.3 lbs. Disc. 2009.

	$540	$450	$375	$310	$250	$215	$190	*$629*

1873 CATTLEMAN MILLENIUM SAA – .357 Mag. or .45 LC cal., 4 3/4 in. barrel, matte finished metal, brass backstrap and trigger guard, New Model frame only. Imported 2000-2006.

	$260	$215	$190	$165	$150	$130	$120	*$300*

1873 CATTLEMAN HOMBRE SAA – .357 Mag. or .45 LC cal., New Model frame, 4 3/4 in. barrel, brass grip strap and trigger guard, matte blue metal finish with case colored hammer, smooth walnut grips, 2.3 lbs. Importation began 2007.

MSR $429	$340	$285	$250	$225	$200	$180	$160	

1873 CATTLEMAN GUNFIGHTER SAA – .45 LC cal., 4 3/4, 5 1/2, or 7 1/2 in. barrel, steel backstrap and trigger guard, matte metal finish, black checkered synthetic grips, New Model frame, 2.3 lbs. Mfg. 2005-2009.

	$400	$350	$300	$260	$230	$210	$180	*$479*

1873 CATTLEMAN CHISHOLM SAA – .45 LC cal. only, New Model frame, 4 3/4, 5 1/2, or 7 1/2 (disc. 2010) in. barrel, matte metal finish with case colored hammer and checkered walnut grips, 2.3 lbs. Importation began 2006.

MSR $529	$450	$400	$330	$280	$240	$210	$180	

1873 CATTLEMAN DESPERADO SAA – .45 LC cal. only, New Model frame, choice of 4 3/4, 5 1/2, or 7 1/2 (disc. 2010) in. barrel, nickel finish and black buffalo horn grips. Importation began 2006.

MSR $789	$660	$550	$425	$350	$300	$270	$250	

1873 CATTLEMAN EL PATRON SAA – .357 Mag. or .45 LC cal., New Model frame, 4 3/4 or 5 1/2 in. barrel, blue or stainless, checkered walnut grips. New 2009.

MSR $589	$495	$425	$350	$285	$240	$210	$180	

Add $140 for stainless steel (.45 LC cal.).

* ***1873 Cattleman El Patron Cowboy Mounted Shooter (CMS) SAA*** – .357 Mag. or .45 LC cal., New Model frame, 3 1/2 or 4 in. barrel, blue or stainless, checkered walnut grips. New 2011.

MSR $609	$495	$425	$350	$285	$240	$210	$180	

Add $120 for stainless steel (3 1/2 in. barrel only).

1873 CATTLEMAN CALLAHAN SAA – .44 Mag. cal., New Model frame, 4 3/4, 6, or 7 1/2 in. (Target only) barrel, 100% blue finish, smooth walnut grips. New 2010.

MSR $589	$485	$420	$350	$300	$260	$220	$180	

Add $40 for Target Model (includes ramped front sight and adj. rear sight).

GRADING - PPGS™	100%	98%	95%	90%	80%	70%	60%	LAST MSR

1873 CATTLEMAN SHERIFF'S MODEL SAA – .44-40 WCF or .45 LC cal., choice of steel or brass grip strap and trigger guard, 3 or 4 in. barrel. Importation disc. 2002.

	$345	$265	$210	$175	$160	$150	$135	*$410*

Subtract approx. 10% with brass grip strap and trigger guard.

1873 CATTLEMAN BIRD'S HEAD SAA – .357 Mag. (new 2001), .44 Spl. (disc. 2002), .44-40 WCF (disc. 2004), or .45 LC cal., 3 (Sheriff's Model, .44-40 WCF or .45 LC cal. only, disc.), 3 1/2 (OM Frame only) 4, 4 3/4, or 5 1/2 in. barrel, choice of Old or New Model frame, patterned after the Colt 1877 Thunderer, case colored frame, checkered (disc.) or smooth walnut bird's head grips, 2.3 lbs. New 1997.

MSR $549	$465	$410	$335	$280	$240	$210	$180	

1873 CATTLEMAN BISLEY SAA – .357 Mag., .38-40 WCF (disc. 2002), .44 Spl. (disc. 2002), .44-40 WCF (disc. 2004), or .45 LC cal., New Model frame, patterned after the Colt Bisley Model, 4 3/4, 5 1/2, or 7 1/2 in. barrel, case colored frame, wood grips. New 1997.

MSR $579	$490	$425	$355	$310	$260	$220	$180	

* ***1873 Cattleman Bisley Flat-top SAA*** – similar to Cattleman Bisley, except has flat-top frame with fixed or target (.44-40 WCF - disc. or .45 LC cal., 7 1/2 in. barrel only) sights. Importation disc. 2004.

	$365	$310	$240	$195	$175	$160	$150	*$435*

Add $25 for target sights (disc.).

1873 CATTLEMAN BUNTLINE SAA – .22 LR/.22 WMR combo (disc. 2000), .357 Mag., .44-40 WCF (disc. 2010), .44 Mag. (mfg. 2001-2002), or .45 LC cal., 12 (mfg. 2001-2002, .45 LC only) or 18 in. barrel, New Model frame with steel or brass (disc. 2002) backstrap cut for shoulder stock, choice of field sights with round frame or target sights on flat-top frame. Importation disc. 1989, re-introduced 1993.

MSR $589	$495	$425	$365	$300	$260	$220	$180	

Add $50 for Target Model with extended ramp front and adj. rear blade sight.
Subtract $56 for brass backstrap and trigger guard (disc. 2002).

* ***1873 Cattleman Buntline Carbine SAA*** – similar to Cattleman Buntline, 18 in. barrel, detachable or non-detachable shoulder stock with brass hardware and lanyard ring. Importation disc. 1989, re-introduced 1993-95.

	$390	$310	$245	$200	$175	$160	$150	*$475*

Add $34 for target sights.
Add $34 for .22 LR/.22 WMR combo. (disc. 1989).
Add $175 for detachable shoulder stock.

1873 CATTLEMAN SAA REVOLVER CARBINE – .357 Mag. (disc. 2002), .44-40 WCF (disc. 2002), or .45 LC cal., New Model frame, 18 (new 2004) or 19 (disc. 2003) in. barrel, fixed stock with brass rifle buttplate, finger rest extension on trigger guard, choice of quick detachable mounts or target sights, 4.4 lbs. New 1997.

MSR $729	$625	$560	$430	$355	$300	$260	$240	

Add $70 for target sights on flat-top frame.

1873 STALLION COLT SAA – .22 LR/.22 WMR cal. combo only, 4 3/4, 5 1/2, or 6 1/2 in. barrel, case hardened frame, 1-piece walnut grip, 2.4 lbs. Importation disc. 1989.

	$300	$210	$195	$170	$155	$140	$120	*$325*

Add $27 for steel backstrap and trigger guard.
Add $26 for Target Model.

* ***1873 Stainless Colt Stallion SAA*** – similar to standard Stallion, except is stainless steel. Importation disc. 1989.

	$370	$275	$225	$175	$140	$125	$105	*$425*

1873 STALLION STEEL GRIP STRAP/TG SAA – .22 LR (new 2000) or .38 Spl. cal., 3 1/2 (disc. 2002), 4 3/4, or 5 1/2 in. barrel, smaller, scaled-down SAA case colored New Model frame, approx. 32 oz. New 1999.

MSR $449	$390	$330	$285	$250	$225	$195	$165	

Add $30 for .38 Spl. cal.

GRADING - PPGS™	100%	98%	95%	90%	80%	70%	60%	LAST MSR

Add $60 for target sights.
Add $39 for Target Model (38 Spl. cal. only, not available with 3 1/2 in. barrel, disc. 2002).
Add $55 for .22 LR/.22 WMR combo (disc. 2002).

* ***1873 Stallion Brass Grip Strap/TG SAA*** – .22 LR cal., 4 3/4 (new 2011) or 5 1/2 in. barrel, 6 or 10 (new 2010) shot mag.

MSR $419	$365	$310	$260	$220	$185	$165	$140	

Add $70 for target sights.
Add $60 for 10 shot variation (new 2010).
Add $39 for dual cylinder (.22 LR/.22 WMR, disc. 2002).
Add $120 for Target Model (10 shot only).
Add $90 for Target Model with dual cylinder (disc.).

* ***1873 Stallion Bird's Head SAA OWD*** – .38 Spl. cal. only, New Model frame, 3 1/2 in. barrel, checkered walnut grips, Old West Defense (OWD) features. New 2011.

MSR $559	$460	$410	$335	$280	$240	$210	$180	

* ***1873 Stallion Conversion SAA*** – .22 LR/.22 WMR cal. includes .22 LR and .22 WMR cylinders, 4 3/4 (previously available w/o extra .22 WMR cylinder), 5 1/2, or 6 1/2 in. barrel, choice of blue/case colored frame or brass grip strap and trigger guard with case colored frame, one piece smooth walnut grips, 24 oz. New mid-2009.

MSR $509	$425	$365	$315	$285	$250	$225	$200	

Add $30 for steel grip strap.
Add $50 Target Model.
Subtract approx. $70 if without .22 WMR cylinder (disc. 2010).

1875 REMINGTON ARMY/FRONTIER SA – .357 Mag. (disc. 2002), .44-40 WCF (disc. 2002), .45 ACP (mfg. 1992-2002, extra cylinder only), or .45 LC cal., 5 1/2 (Frontier configuration, disc. 1995, resumed 2001) or 7 1/2 (Outlaw configuration) in. barrel, brass (disc.) or steel (new 1993) trigger guard, blue/case colored frame or nickel (new 2006) finish, two-piece walnut grips, approx. 2.6 lbs. Imported 2002, reimported beginning 2005.

MSR $539	$455	$400	$340	$285	$240	$210	$180	

Add $42 for convertible cylinder (.45 LC/.45 ACP, disc.).
Add $90 for nickel finish and walnut grips in Outlaw configuration only (new 2006).

* ***1875 Remington SA Carbine*** – .357 Mag. .44-40 WCF, or .45 LC cal., 18 in. barrel, includes non-detachable shoulder stock with brass hardware and lanyard ring. Importation disc. 1989.

	$425	$285	$230	$200	$185	$180	$175	*$440*

Add $110 for nickel plating.

1890 REMINGTON POLICE SA – .357 Mag., .44-40 WCF (disc. 2002), .45 ACP (mfg. 1993-2002, dual cylinder only), or .45 LC cal., 5 1/2, or 7 1/2 (disc. 1995) in. barrel, blue finish with lanyard ring, brass (disc. 2002) or steel (new 1993) trigger guard, two-piece walnut grips, 2.6 lbs. Imported 2002, reimported beginning 2005.

MSR $559	$460	$410	$340	$285	$240	$210	$180	

Add $42 for dual cylinder (disc.).

PHANTOM MODEL SAA – .357 or .44 Mag. cal. only, 10 1/2 in. barrel for silhouette use. Imported 1985-89.

	$475	$395	$325	$290	$260	$230	$215	*$509*

1874 SCHOFIELD RUSSIAN SA – .44 Russian cal., 6 shot, break open, 6 (disc.), 6 1/2 (new 2002) or 7 (new 2002) in. barrel. Imported 2000-2002.

	$675	$585	$475	$425	$365	$300	$275	*$800*

1875 SCHOFIELD SA – .44-40 WCF or .45 LC cal., 3, 5, or 7 in. barrel. Imported 2000-2002.

	$635	$550	$465	$400	$350	$300	$275	*$750*

RUSSIAN NEW MODEL NO. 3 SA – .44 Russian or .45 LC (new 2006) cal., 6 1/2 in. barrel, features trigger guard finger extension, steel frame, break open, 6 shot with automatic

GRADING - PPGS™	100%	98%	95%	90%	80%	70%	60%	LAST MSR

extraction, Cyrillic barrel stamping, case colored opening mechanism and trigger guard, 2.7 lbs. Importation began 2005.

MSR $1,019	$850	$750	$625	$550	$475	$425	$350	

Add $330 for nickel finish with faux ivory grips (.45 LC cal. only).

1875 NO. 3 SECOND MODEL TOP BREAK SA – .38 Spl. (new 2006), .44-40 WCF or .45 LC cal., patterned after the Schofield break open action, 3 1/2, 5, or 7 in. barrel, 6 shot, blue or nickel (new 2005) finish, walnut or pearl (new 2006) grips, case colored opening lever and trigger guard, available in First or Second Model (disc.), approx. 2 1/2 lbs. Importation began 2005.

MSR $1,009	$850	$725	$625	$525	$425	$350	$300	

Add $340 for nickel finish with pearl grips (not available in .44-40 WCF cal.).

Add $2,000-$2,140 for nickel finish engraved model with pearl/wood grips (.45 LC cal. only, mfg. 2010-2011).

* ***1875 No. 3 Second Model Top Break Premium*** – .45 LC cal. only, 6 shot, faux pearl or walnut grips, blue or nickel finish, extensive scroll engraving with blue screws (nickel) or gold-lined border (blue), available from World Class dealers only. Imported 2007-2011.

	$2,550	$2,100	$1,800	$1,500	$1,200	$900	$700	*$2,999*

Add $140 for blue finish with faux pearl grips.

RIFLES: REPRODUCTIONS, LEVER ACTION

Add $140 for antique patina finish, $80 for charcoal blue finish, $75 for in-the-white finish, $235 for silver plating, $210 for nickel plating, $90 for checkered wood, $210 for select wood, or $475 for deluxe wood.

Add $850-$3,500 for hand-engraving options, depending on the amount of engraving and gold inlays.

All special order options, including wood upgrades and engraving were discontinued in 2011.

SILVERBOY RIFLE – .22 LR cal., 19 in. round barrel, 15 shot mag., chrome plated alloy receiver, straight grip uncheckered walnut stock, controlled round feed, 5.8 lbs. New 2012.

MSR $589	$525	$465	$435	$400	$375	$325	$275	

1860 HENRY RIFLE/CARBINE – .44-40 WCF or .45 LC (rifle only) cal., iron (disc. 2010), brass, or steel frame, 10 or 13 shot mag., 24 1/4 in. barrel on rifle, 22 1/2 in. barrel on carbine (disc. 2002), metal finishes include case colored frame/blue barrel, charcoal blue (disc.), white (disc.), or chrome (disc.) finish, approx. 9 lbs.

MSR $1,349	$1,125	$925	$725	$625	$525	$475	$425	

Add $20 for steel or iron (disc.) frame.

The carbine was disc. in 1989, re-introduced 1992-2002.

* ***1860 Henry Carbine Trapper*** – similar to above, except has 16 1/2 (disc. 2002) or 18 1/2 in. barrel. New 1990.

MSR $1,349	$1,125	$925	$725	$625	$525	$475	$425	

* ***1860 Henry Rifle/Carbine 1 of 1,000*** – disc.

	$1,450	$1,150	$975	$850	$700	$575	$425	

1866 YELLOWBOY CARBINE – .22 LR (disc. 1989), .22 WMR (disc. 1989), .38 Spl., .44-40 WCF, or .45 LC cal., brass receiver, 10 shot mag., 19 in. round barrel, 7.4 lbs. Importation disc. 1995, resumed 2002.

MSR $1,049	$895	$775	$625	$525	$450	$400	$350	

* ***1866 Yellowboy Carbine Trapper*** – .22 LR, .38 Spl., or .44-40 WCF cal., 16 in. barrel. Importation disc. 1989.

	$650	$475	$395	$340	$285	$260	$235	*$686*

* ***1866 Yellowboy Carbine Indian*** – .22 LR, .22 WMR, .32-20 WCF (new 2002), .38 Spl., .44-40 WCF, or .45 LC (new 1996) cal., 19 in. barrel. Imported 2002 only.

	$670	$535	$430	$360	$310	$275	$240	*$760*

Subtract $50 without brass tacks (disc.).

GRADING - PPGS™	100%	98%	95%	90%	80%	70%	60%	LAST MSR

* ***1866 Yellowboy Carbine Red Cloud Commemorative*** – same cals., special engraving and brass tacks in forearm and stock. Importation officially disc. 1989.

	$720	$600	$475	$400	$350	$330	$300	*$850*

1866 SPORTING RIFLE – .22 LR (mfg. 2001-2002), .22 WMR (mfg. 2001-2002), .32-20 WCF (mfg. 2002-2011), .38 Spl., .38-40 WCF (mfg. 2002-2011), .44-40 WCF, or .45 LC (new 1996) cal., brass receiver, 10 or 13 shot mag., 20 (short rifle, new 2001) round (new 1993, carbine only) or 24 1/4 in. octagon barrel, 8.2 lbs.

MSR $1,099	$925	$795	$650	$550	$450	$400	$350	

* ***1866 Sporting Rifle Deluxe Uberti Model*** – .44-40 WCF cal., features high polished receiver with fire blue small parts, ladder rear sight. Imported 1995.

	$895	$675	$525	N/A	N/A	N/A	N/A	*$895*

This model was sold exclusively by Cherry's, located in Greensboro, NC.

* ***1866 Sporting Rifle "L.D. Nimschke" Special Edition*** – .44-40 WCF cal., receiver, buttplate, and forend cap feature recreations of Nimschke scroll engraving by Giovanelli of Italy, silver plated, deluxe walnut, optional 2nd Edition of Nimschke pattern book by R.L. Wilson ($100), only 300 mfg. beginning 1995. Disc.

	$1,650	$1,150	$800	N/A	N/A	N/A	N/A	*$1,495*

This model was sold exclusively by Cherry's, located in Greensboro, NC.

* ***1866 Sporting Rifle Yellowboy Indian Rifle*** – .22 LR (disc. 1989), .22 WMR (disc. 1989), .38 Spl., or .44-40 WCF cal., 24 1/4 in. barrel. Importation disc. 1989, reintroduced 1993-95.

	$700	$560	$475	$385	$300	$260	$235	*$800*

1866 MUSKET – .44-40 WCF or .45 LC cal., features 27 in. barrel with barrel bands. Imported 1999-2002.

	$810	$600	$500	$425	$360	$320	$280	*$910*

1873 CARBINE – .22 LR (disc. 1991), .22 WMR (disc. 1991), .32-20 WCF (mfg. 2001-2005), .357 Mag., .38 Spl. (disc. 1991) .38-40 (mfg. 2002-2011), .44 Mag., .44-40 WCF, or .45 LC (new 1992) cal., 10 shot mag., steel receiver, 19 in. round barrel with forearm barrel bands, 7.4 lbs.

MSR $1,169	$975	$825	$700	$575	$475	$425	$375	

Add $90 for .44 Mag. cal.
Add $35 for case colored frame (disc.).

* ***1873 Carbine Trapper*** – .357 Mag., .44-40 WCF, or .45 LC cal. only, 16 1/8 in. barrel. Importation disc. 1990.

	$750	$600	$500	$425	$360	$320	$280	*$750*

1873 TRAPPER RIFLE – .357 Mag. or .45 LC cal., 16 1/8 in. barrel, otherwise similar to 1873 Sporting Rifle. New 2010.

MSR $1,209	$995	$775	$725	$575	$475	$400	$350	

1873 SPORTING RIFLE – .32-20 WCF (mfg. 2001-2002), .357 Mag. (new 1995), .38-40 WCF (mfg. 2002-2011), .44-40 WCF (new 1995), or .45 LC cal., case hardened receiver, 10 or 13 shot mag., 20 in. octagon (new 1990, Short Rifle), 24 1/4 in. octagon, half-round/half-octagon, or 30 (mfg. 1990-2002) in. octagon barrel, can be drilled and tapped for Uberti rear tang aperture sight (new 1993), 8.2 lbs.

MSR $1,209	$995	$850	$725	$600	$500	$450	$400	

Add $50 for half-round/half-octagon barrel.
Add approx. $100 for Deluxe model with hand checkered pistol grip stock and forearm (disc.).
Add $140 for Special Sporting/Deluxe Model with hand-checkered pistol grip stock/forearm and 24 1/2 in. half-round, half-octagon barrel.
Add $17 for 30 in. barrel (.44-40 WCF or .45 LC cal. only, disc. 2002).
Add $77 for Deluxe Model with 30 in. barrel (disc. 2002).

GRADING - PPGS™	100%	98%	95%	90%	80%	70%	60%	LAST MSR

MODEL 1873 125th ANNIVERSARY – .44-40 WCF cal., special anniversary offering featuring engraved gold plated metal with fire blue receiver and small parts, long rifle configuration with deluxe pistol grip and forearm. 125 mfg. 1998 only, marketed exclusively by Cherry's.

	$3,250	$2,500	$1,750	N/A	N/A	N/A	N/A	*$3,500*

1873 MUSKET – .44-40 WCF or .45 LC cal., features 30 in. round barrel with barrel bands. Imported 1999-2002.

	$875	$700	$575	$450	$375	$325	$300	*$999*

1876 CENTENNIAL RIFLE – .40-60 WCF (disc. 2010), .45-60 WCF, .45-75 WCF, or .50-95 WCF cal., 28 in. octagon barrel, blue finish and case hardened frame, full mag., iron sights, walnut stock and forearm, 10 lbs. Importation began 2008.

MSR $1,549	$1,325	$1,150	$925	$775	$675	$575	$500	

1883 BURGESS LEVER ACTION RIFLE/CARBINE – .45 LC cal., case colored frame with blued barrel and mag. tube, 20 (carbine) or 25 1/2 (rifle) in. barrel. New 2010.

MSR $1,439	$1,175	$975	$800	$700	$600	$500	$450	

RIFLES: REPRODUCTIONS, SINGLE SHOT

1871 ROLLING BLOCK TARGET CARBINE/RIFLE – available in .22 LR, .22 WMR, .22 Hornet (disc. 2004), or .357 Mag. (disc.) cal., 22 in. round (carbine) or 26 in. octagon barrel, color case hardened receiver and hammer, brass trigger guard, open sights, approx. 5 lbs. Disc. 2007.

	$440	$350	$295	$240	$200	$175	$155	*$535*

Add $65 for rifle model.

1871 ROLLING BLOCK HUNTER CARBINE – .30-30 Win., .38-55 WCF, or .45-70 Govt. cal., 22 in. barrel, otherwise similar to Rolling Block Target. New 2010.

MSR $769	$695	$625	$575	$500	$425	$350	$295	

1871 ROLLING BLOCK HUNTER CARBINE RIMFIRE – .17 HMR, .22 LR, or .22 WMR cal., 22 in. barrel, otherwise similar to Rolling Block Hunter Carbine. New 2011.

MSR $689	$625	$525	$475	$400	$325	$275	$225	

1874 SHARPS RIFLE/CARBINE – .45-70 Govt. cal., patterned after the original 1874 Sharps action, 22 in. (carbine, new 2007) or 32-34 in. octagon barrel, available in standard (disc. 2011), special, deluxe, Down Under, Adobe Walls (disc.), Buffalo Hunter, or Long Range (disc. 2011) configuration. Importation began 2006.

MSR $1,639	$1,425	$1,200	$975	$800	$700	$600	$500	

Add $200 for Special Model with 32 in. barrel and pistol grip stock and flat buttplate.

Add $110 for Cavalry carbine with 22 in. barrel and barrel band (disc. 2009).

Add $1,200 for Deluxe Model with 34 in. barrel, AA grade walnut, and gold inlaid bison head on receiver.

Add $670 for Buffalo Hunter Model.

Add $670 for Down Under or $820 for Long Range (34 in. half-round, half-octagon barrel, disc. 2009) model.

Add $550 for Adobe Walls configuration (disc.).

* ***1874 Sharps Extra Deluxe Rifle*** – .45-70 Govt. cal., 32 in. barrel, AAA grade walnut stock, elaborate scroll engraving with gold buffalo inlays. Importation began 2007.

MSR $4,569	$3,875	$3,150	$2,825	$2,375	$1,975	$1,725	$1,425	

SPRINGFIELD TRAPDOOR CARBINE/RIFLE – .45-70 Govt. cal., choice of 22 (carbine) or 32 1/2 (rifle) in. round barrel, case colored receiver, uncheckered walnut stock and forearm. Importation began 2006.

MSR $1,509	$1,300	$1,100	$900	$750	$675	$575	$495	

Add $260 for rifle configuration.

1885 WINCHESTER HIGH WALL CARBINE/RIFLE – .22 Hornet (mfg. 2004-2011), .30-30 Win. (disc. 2004), .38-55 WCF (disc. 2002), .40-65 WCF (disc. 2002), .44 Mag. (mfg. 2004-2011), .44-40 WCF (disc. 2002), .45 LC (disc. 2004), .45-70 Govt., .45-90 WCF

GRADING - PPGS™	100%	98%	95%	90%	80%	70%	60%	LAST MSR

(disc. 2002, reintroduced 2005), or .45-120 (disc. 2002, reintroduced 2005) cal., Low Wall (disc. 2004) or High Wall, 28 (carbine, High Wall only, .45-70 Govt. cal. only) round, 30 (rifle), or 32 in. octagon barrel, case colored receiver, straight grip walnut stock and forearm, 7.7 or 9.9 lbs. New 1999.

MSR $1,029	$895	$750	$650	$550	$450	$400	$350	

Add $120-$170 for Special Sporting (Deluxe) Model with checkered pistol grip and aperture sights, depending on barrel length.
Add $60 for 32 in. barrel (.45-90 cal. only).
Subtract $70 for 28 in. carbine barrel.

RIFLES: REPRODUCTIONS, SLIDE ACTION

COLT LIGHTNING CARBINE/RIFLE – .357 Mag. or .45 LC cal., patterned after the Colt Lightning carbine/rifle, 20 (carbine (disc. 2011) or short rifle) or 24 1/4 (rifle) in. barrel, blue (disc. 2010) or case colored frame finish, uncheckered walnut stock and forearm, 6.2-6 1/2 lbs. Importation began 2006.

MSR $1,219	$1,025	$825	$700	$550	$475	$425	$375	

Subtract approx. $100 for blue metal finish on rifle (disc. 2010).
Subtract approx. $50 for carbine variation (disc. 2011).

SHOTGUNS: SxS

DOUBLE BARREL – 12 ga. only, 2 3/4, 3, or 3 1/2 in. chambers, 20, 21 1/2 , 24, or 26 in. barrels, exposed hammers, checkered walnut pistol grip stock and forearm. Imported 1999-2001.

	$875	$700	$575	$450	$375	$325	$300	*$999*

UGARTECHEA, ARMAS

Current manufacturer located in Eibar, Spain. Currently being imported by Aspen Outfitting Co., located in Aspen, CO, and by Lion Country Supply, located in Port Matilda, PA.

Currently, Aspen Outfitting Co. exclusively imports Models 116, 119, 1000, 1030, 1042, and the AOC/SG boxlock. Lion Country Supply exclusively imports Models 30, 40, 40 NEX, 75, 75EX, 110, 257, 357, and 2000.

SHOTGUNS: SxS, BOXLOCK

MODEL AOC/SG – 12, 16, 20, 28 ga., or .410 bore, 2 3/4 in. chambers, Anson & Deeley boxlock action with extra polishing and fitting of parts, scalloped action shaping, 28 in. chopper lump barrels, IC/M choke, front bead sight, concave rib, DT w/articulating front trigger, Southgate auto ejectors, auto safety, free floating firing pins, engraved receiver with border scroll, upgraded European straight grip walnut stock and splinter forend with plunger release, inlaid forend screw escutcheon, hand-checkered buttstock, initial shield, case hardened action finish, long tang trigger guard with comfort roll, upgraded wood finish. Importation began in 1999.

MSR $3,500	$3,225	$2,750	$2,350	$1,950	$1,750	$1,575	$1,425	

Add $350 for 28 ga. or $650 for .410 bore.

This model is imported exclusively by Aspen Outfitting Company.

UPLAND CLASSIC GRADE I (MODEL 30) – 12, 16, 20, 28 ga., or .410 bore, Anson & Deeley boxlock action, DT, concave rib, extractors, case colored receiver, hand-checkered straight grip walnut stock and splinter forend.

MSR $1,695	$1,595	$1,275	$1,100	$875	$700	$600	$500	

Add $300 for 28 ga.
Add $400 for .410 bore.

This model is imported exclusively by Lion Country Supply.

UPLAND CLASSIC GRADE II (MODEL 40) – 12, 16, 20, 28 ga., or .410 bore, Anson & Deeley boxlock action, extractors, DT, coin finished and engraved receiver, hand-checkered straight grip walnut stock and splinter forend.

MSR $1,995	$1,895	$1,595	$1,475	$1,275	$1,025	$825	$700	

GRADING - PPGS™	100%	98%	95%	90%	80%	70%	60%	LAST MSR

Add $300 for 28 ga.

This model is imported exclusively by Lion Country Supply.

UPLAND CLASSIC GRADE III (MODEL 40 NEX) – 12, 16, 20, 28 ga. or .410 bore, Anson & Deeley boxlock action, ejectors, DT or NSST, case colored and engraved receiver, hand-checkered straight grip walnut stock and splinter forend.

MSR $2,695	$2,595	$2,195	$1,895	$1,500	$1,200	$975	$800	

Add $300 for 28 ga. or $500 for .410 bore.

This model is imported exclusively by Lion Country Supply.

BILL HANUS BIRDGUN – 16, 20, 28 ga., or .410 bore (6 mfg.), boxlock action, 26 in. barrels bored SK1/SK2, Churchill raised rib, SNT, ejectors, lightly engraved case colored receiver, tang and lever, checkered straight grip walnut oil finished stock and semi-beavertail forearm, lifetime operational warranty, 5 1/4-6 1/2 lbs. Approx. 200 mfg. Imported 1989-circa 1992.

	$1,425	$1,250	$1,050	$880	$750	$635	$540	*$1,695*

Add $100 for 28 ga.
Add $150 for .410 bore.
Add 15% for optional fitted luggage case.

BILL HANUS BIRDGUN CLASSIC – 20, 28 ga., or .410 bore (4 mfg.), similar to Birdgun Model, except has double triggers with hinged front trigger, 27 in. barrels, splinter forearm and English leather handguard. Imported 1989-circa 1992.

	$1,355	$1,220	$1,035	$880	$750	$635	$540	*$1,595*

Add 15% for optional fitted luggage case.
Add $100 for 28 ga.
Add $200 for .410 bore.

SHOTGUNS: SxS, SIDELOCK

Ugartechea sidelocks are best quality guns. Currently, Lion Country Supply stocks the Upland Classic Series. Additionally, custom orders are available through Aspen Outfitting and Lion Country Supply.

UPLAND CLASSIC GRADE IV (MODEL 75 EX) – 12, 16, 20, or 28 (new 2009) ga., best quality true sidelock with intercepting sears, DT or NSST with hinged front trigger, case colored or coin finished receiver with English style scroll engraving, ejectors, available with upgraded wood with hand rubbed oil finish.

MSR $3,195	$2,995	$2,700	$2,350	$2,000	$1,750	$1,500	$1,250	

Add $300 for 28 ga.
Add $800 for wood upgrades.

This model is imported exclusively by Lion Country Supply, and is also available on a custom order basis.

UPLAND CLASSIC GRADE V (MODEL 110) – 12, 16, 20, 28 ga., or .410 bore, best quality round body game gun, true sidelock with intercepting sears, DT or NSST with hinged front trigger, case colored or coin finished receiver with English style scroll engraving, auto ejectors, upgraded wood with hand rubbed oil finish.

MSR $4,195	$3,795	$3,275	$2,725	$2,300	$1,950	$1,575	$1,325	

Add $300 for 28 ga. or $400 for .410 bore.

This model is imported exclusively by Lion Country Supply, and is also available on a custom order basis.

CUSTOM GRADE 257 – 12, 16, or 20 ga., intercepting sears, DT, hinged front trigger, case colored or coin finished receiver with classic very deep relief floral hand engraving, concave rib, automatic Southgate ejectors, gas escape valves, chopper lump system barrels and a nicely finished walnut stock. New 2009.

MSR $4,295	$3,595	$3,200	$2,800	$2,400	$2,000	$1,650	$1,200	

The 257 is a special order only gun and many options are available, from upgraded wood and wood finish to barrel lengths from 26 to 30 inches as well as custom stock dimensions.

GRADING - PPGS™	100%	98%	95%	90%	80%	70%	60%	LAST MSR

CUSTOM GRADE 357 – 12, 16 or 20 ga, intercepting sears, single or double triggers, hinged front trigger, case colored or coin finished receiver with fine scroll engraving, concave rib, automatic Southgate ejectors, gas escape valves, chopper lump system barrels. New 2009.

MSR $4,595	$4,295	$3,850	$2,950	$2,325	$1,950	$1,575	$1,325

The 357 is a special order only gun and gives you the flexibility of options from upgraded wood and wood finish to barrel lengths from 26 to 30 inches as well as custom stock dimensions.

CUSTOM GRADE 2000 – 12, 16 or 20 ga., intercepting sears, DT, hinged front trigger, case colored or coin finished receiver with very fine wildlife hand engraving with ducks on the right, quail on the left and pheasant on the bottom of the receiver, concave rib, automatic Southgate ejectors, gas escape valves, chopper lump system barrels and upgraded walnut stock with hand rubbed oil finish. New 2009.

MSR $5,295	$5,295	$4,250	$3,500	$2,850	$2,400	$2,000	$1,625

The 2000 is a special order only gun with a variety of options from upgraded wood and wood finish to barrel lengths from 26 to 30 inches as well as custom stock dimensions.

MODEL 116 – 12, 16, 20, 28 ga., or .410 bore, sidelock action, antique silver finish with elaborate floral engraving, deluxe oil finished walnut stock and forearm.

MSR $7,250	$6,800	$5,900	$4,500	$3,875	$3,250	$2,600	$2,000

Add $525 for 28 ga. or $750 for .410 bore.

This model is imported exclusively by Aspen Outfitting Company.

MODEL 119 – 12, 16, 20, 28 ga., or .410 bore, sidelock action with coin finish or case hardened frame, Purdey style engraving, deluxe oil finished walnut stock and forearm.

MSR $7,550	$7,125	$6,150	$4,650	$3,950	$3,350	$2,650	$2,000

Add $600 for 28 ga. or $900 for .410 bore.

This model is imported exclusively by Aspen Outfitting Company.

MODEL 1000 – 12, 16, 20, or 28 ga., sidelock action with coin finish or case hardened frame, Churchill style deep relief engraving, deluxe oil finished walnut stock and forearm.

MSR $9,350	$8,750	$7,950	$6,250	$5,250	$4,500	$3,750	$3,000

Add $450 for 28 ga.

This model is imported exclusively by Aspen Outfitting Company.

MODEL 1030 – 12, 16, or 20 ga., coin finished or case hardened frame, Woodward style scalloped fences and engraving. Importation began 1994.

MSR $9,675	$9,000	$8,150	$6,400	$5,350	$4,500	$3,750	$3,000

This model is imported exclusively by Aspen Outfitting Company.

MODEL 1042 – 12, 16, or 20 ga., sidelock action, coin finished or case hardened frame, exquisite full coverage fine scroll engraving, deluxe oil finished walnut stock and forearm.

MSR $11,500	$10,750	$8,750	$7,500	$6,500	$5,500	$4,500	$3,750

This model is imported exclusively by Aspen Outfitting Company.

SPECIAL MODELS – available in all gauges with game scene engraving and/or gold inlays to customer specifications. POR only. Please contact Aspen Outfitting Company (see Trademark Index).

UGARTECHEA, IGNACIO

Previous manufacturer located in Eibar, Spain. Previously imported exclusively by Aspen Outfitting Company, located in Aspen, CO.

Ignacio Ugartechea was founded in 1922 and was the oldest maker of side-by-side sidelock and boxlock shotguns in Spain (please refer to Armas Ugartechea for current information). From 1970 until the Parker-Hale name was sold in 1990 to Navy Arms, Ugartechea manufactured the popular line of Anson & Deeley boxlocks imported by Precision Sports in Cortland, NY. Precision Sports continued to import these guns under the Classic "600" name until 1994. Previously imported by Precision Sports, Inc. located in Cortland, NY until 1994, by Exel Arms in Gardener, MA until 1987 as the Exel Model 200 series, and by Jana, located in Denver, CO, dates unknown.

GRADING - PPGS™	100%	98%	95%	90%	80%	70%	60%	LAST MSR

The importation of Parker-Hale shotguns was disc. in 1993. Please contact Apsen Outfitting Company for more information on older Ignacio Ugartechea models.

SHOTGUNS: SxS, BOXLOCK

Included in this section are older Exel Series 200 shotguns (disc. 1986-87) in addition to the Parker-Hale 600 Series. The importation of Parker-Hale shotguns was disc. in 1993.

EXEL 200 SERIES – these side-by-sides were available in 12 or 20 ga. (3 in.) only. Model 201 is basic gun with 213 being the highest grade. - top-of-the-line model, best quality engraving and walnut. Special order only.

* ***Exel 200 Series Model 201, 202, and 203*** – double triggers, extractors, straight grip, matted rib, various chokes and barrel lengths.

$375	$325	$260	$240	$215	$180	$165	*$429*

Previously designated Model 30.

* ***Exel 200 Series Model 281*** – similar to 201 series, except 28 ga.

$420	$325	$275	$250	$235	$210	$195	*$472*

Previously designated Model 30.

* ***Exel 200 Series Model 240*** – similar to 201 series, except .410 bore.

$450	$355	$295	$270	$250	$235	$210	*$472*

Previously designated Model 30.

* ***Exel 200 Series Models 204, 205, and 206*** – single trigger optional, ejectors, straight grip, silver finish, various chokes and barrel lengths. Importation disc. 1986.

$550	$470	$415	$370	$340	$315	$280	*$627*

* ***Exel 200 Series Models 207 and 207A*** – 12 ga. only, sidelock, case hardened action. 207A is deluxe model with ejectors. Model 201 disc. 1986.

$725	$650	$580	$515	$465	$400	$345	*$836*

Subtract 33% without ejectors (Model 207).

This model was previously designated the Milano EX.

* ***Exel 200 Series Models 208 and 208A*** – similar to 207/207A, only engraved coin finished receiver. 208A is deluxe model with ejectors. Model 208 disc. 1986.

$775	$695	$625	$550	$485	$420	$360	*$925*

Subtract 33% without ejectors (Model 208).

This model was previously designated the Model 75 EX.

* ***Exel 200 Series Models 209 and 210*** – better engraving and walnut than 207/207A. Model 210 is 20 ga. Importation disc. 1986.

$580	$505	$450	$415	$375	$340	$310	*$672*

* ***Exel 200 Series Models 211, 212, and 213***

$2,350	$2,000	$1,780	$1,475	$1,200	$1,000	$850	*$3,100*

Previously designated Model 110.

MODEL 251 – .410-3 in. bore, folding design, 26 in. barrels only, DTs, extractors, walnut stock and forearm. Imported 1987 only.

$185	$165	$140	$120	$105	$95	$85	*$215*

MODEL 630 – 12 ga. only, 3 in. chambers, boxlock action with color case hardening, extractors, DTs, 26 or 28 in. barrels with fixed chokes, checkered English grip stock and forearm, includes deluxe shotgun case. Imported 1993 only.

$625	$525	$450	$400	$365	$330	$295	*$699*

MODEL 640E (ENGLISH) – 12, 16, 20, 28 ga., or .410 bore, boxlock action, double triggers, straight grip stock, splinter forearm, concave rib, extractors, silver finished receiver. Imported 1986-1993.

$750	$595	$540	$475	$415	$350	$295	*$850*

Add $90 for 28 ga. or $120 for .410 bore.

The "E" suffix in this model designates English configuration.

GRADING - PPGS™	100%	98%	95%	90%	80%	70%	60%	LAST MSR

* ***Model 640A (American)*** – same ga.'s as Model 640E, except has non-selective single trigger, pistol grip, beavertail forearm, and raised matted rib. Imported 1986-1993.

	$840	$700	$630	$560	$475	$400	$350	*$970*

Add $110 for 28 ga. or $130 for .410 bore.

The "A" suffix in this model designates American configuration (pistol grip stock and single trigger).

MODEL 640M (MAGNUM) – 10 ga., 3 1/2 in. chambers, 26, 30, or 32 in. barrels bored full and full, DTs, recoil pad. Imported 1989-1993.

	$860	$725	$650	$575	$495	$415	$365	*$1,000*

In this model, the 26 in. barrels were referred to as the Turkey Gun, the 30 in. as Big Ten, and the 32 in. as the Goose Gun.

MODEL 640 SLUG GUN – 12 ga. only, 25 in. barrels bored IC/IC. Imported 1991-93.

	$995	$850	$725	$650	$575	$495	$415	*$1,120*

MODEL 645E (ENGLISH) – 12, 16, 20, 28 ga., or .410 bore, boxlock action, double triggers, straight grip stock, moderate engraving, splinter forearm, concave rib, ejectors, silver finished receiver. Imported 1986-1993.

	$940	$775	$675	$595	$500	$415	$365	*$1,090*

Add $60 for 28 ga. or $110 for .410 bore.

* ***Model 645E-XXV*** – available in all ga.'s, 25 in. barrels only, ejectors, Churchill rib, moderately engraved, silver finished receiver. Imported 1986-1993.

	$940	$775	$675	$595	$500	$415	$365	*$1,100*

Add $100 for 28 ga. or $130 for .410 bore.

* ***Model 645E Bi-Gauge*** – 2 barrel set available in either 20/28 ga. or 28 ga./.410 bore combination. Mfg. 1988-1992.

	$1,475	$1,175	$950	$800	$700	$600	$550	*$1,620*

Add $150 for 28 ga./.410 bore combo. (disc. 1991).

MODEL 645A (AMERICAN) – same ga.'s as 645E, except has non-selective single trigger, pistol grip, beavertail forearm, and raised matted rib. Imported 1986-1993.

	$1,025	$825	$700	$615	$515	$440	$400	*$1,200*

Add $110 for 28 ga. or $150 for .410 bore.

* ***Model 645A Bi-Gauge*** – 2 barrel set available in either 20/28 ga. or 28 ga./.410 bore combination. Mfg. 1988-92.

	$1,600	$1,325	$995	$850	$750	$625	$575	*$1,750*

Add $150 for 28 ga./.410 bore combo. (disc. 1991).

MODEL 650 ENGLISH OR AMERICAN – 12 ga. only, 28 in. barrels with IC/M choke tubes, extractors, choice of English (DT and straight grip stock) or American (SNT, pistol grip stock, and beavertail forearm), silver frame finish. Imported 1992-93.

	$825	$700	$630	$560	$475	$400	$350	*$920*

Add $120 for Model 650 American option.

MODEL 655 ENGLISH OR AMERICAN – 12 ga. only, 28 in. barrels with IC/M choke tubes, ejectors, choice of English (DT and straight grip stock) or American (SNT, pistol grip stock, and beavertail forearm), silver frame finish. Imported 1992-93.

	$925	$825	$700	$630	$560	$475	$400	*$1,150*

Add $110 for Model 655 American option.

MODEL 670E (ENGLISH) – 12, 16, or 20 ga., sidelock action, 26, 27, or 28 in. barrels, ejectors, engraved silver finished receiver, double triggers, straight grip. Imported 1986-91.

	$3,700	$2,975	$2,450	$1,850	$1,550	$1,375	$1,200	*$4,270*

Add $770 for 28 ga. or .410 bore.

This model was available by custom order only.

GRADING - PPGS™	100%	98%	95%	90%	80%	70%	60%	LAST MSR

MODEL 680E-XXV (ENGLISH) – similar to Model 670E, except has color case hardened sideplates and 25 in. barrels only. Imported 1986-91.

	$3,500	$2,800	$2,300	$1,700	$1,475	$1,300	$1,175	*$4,070*

Add $400 for 28 ga. or .410 bore.

This model was available by custom order only.

BILL HANUS BIRDGUN – 16, 20, or 28 ga., boxlock action, 26 in. barrels bored SK1/SK2, Churchill raised rib, SNT, ejectors, case colored receiver, checkered straight grip walnut stock and semi-beavertail forearm, oil finish, lifetime warranty, 5 1/4-6 1/2 lbs. Imported 1989-93.

	$1,100	$835	$700	$615	$515	$440	$400	*$1,270*

Add $130 for 28 ga.

Add $325 with hard case and accessories.

ULTIMATE

Please refer to Camex-Blaser USA in the C section.

ULTRA LIGHT ARMS, INC.

Previous manufacturer located in Granville, WV. Ultra Light Arms, Inc. was purchased by C.F. Holding Corp. in 1999.

PISTOLS: BOLT-ACTION

MODEL 20 HUNTERS PISTOL – various cals., 14 in. Douglas heavy barrel, 5 shot mag., Kevlar graphite reinforced stock in choice of 4 colors, Timney trigger, left or right-hand bolt, approx. 4 lbs. Mfg. 1987-89.

	$1,295	$1,150	$975	$850	$700	$640	$575	*$1,600*

MODEL 20 REB – popular cals. from .22-250 Rem. through .308 Win. (other cals. on request), 14 in. Douglas #3 barrel, 5 shot mag., composite Kevlar graphite reinforced stock, green, brown, black, or camo Dupont Imron paint, Timney adj. trigger, includes hard case, 4 lbs. Mfg. 1994-95, reintroduced 1998 only.

	$1,475	$1,200	$1,000	$875	$750	$625	$500	*$1,600*

RIFLES: BOLT ACTION

ULTRA LIGHT RIFLE – caliber to customer specs., various actions, 2-position 3-function safety in top of stock, Timney trigger, Douglas 22 or 24 in. barrel, no sights, graphite reinforced stock with recoil pad, matte finish standard, other finishes at extra cost. Many special order features and services were available on these models, 4 3/4-5 3/4 lbs. Mfg. 1985-1999.

MODEL 20 – many cals. available between .17 Rem. and .358 Win., short action, Kevlar stock.

	$2,225	$1,675	$1,225	$950	$800	$700	$640	*$2,500*

Add $100 for left-hand action.

* ***Model 20 RF*** – .22 LR cal., convertible from repeater to single shot, 22 in. Douglas premium barrel, DuPont composite stock with Imron paint (some color options available), no sights, drilled and tapped, 5 1/4 lbs. Mfg. 1983-1999.

	$750	$650	$550	$475	$400	$350	$300	*$800*

Add $50 for repeater action.

The first 100 pre-production rifles in this model were marked "1-of-100" consecutively, with owner's initials.

MODEL 24 – .25-06 Rem., .270 Win., .280 Rem. (mfg. 1992 only), .30-06, or 7mm Exp. cal., long action, Kevlar stock, 5 1/4 lbs. Disc. 1999.

	$2,325	$1,775	$1,300	$995	$825	$700	$640	*$2,600*

Add $100 for left-hand action.

MODEL 28 MAGNUM – .264 Win. Mag., .300 Win. Mag., .338 Win. Mag., 7mm Rem. Mag., or .416 Rigby (mfg. 1992 only) cal., Kevlar stock, 5 3/4 lbs. Disc. 1999.

	$2,625	$1,975	$1,550	$1,225	$950	$700	$600	*$2,900*

Add $100 for left-hand action.

GRADING - PPGS™	100%	98%	95%	90%	80%	70%	60%	LAST MSR

MODEL 40 MAGNUM – .300 Wby. Mag. or .416 Rigby cal., otherwise similar to Model 28 Series. Mfg. 1993-99.

	$2,625	$1,975	$1,550	$1,225	$950	$700	$600	*$2,900*

Add $100 for left-hand action.

ULTRAMATIC

Previous trademark with manufacture located in Enzesfeld, Austria. Ultramatic Productions, GmbH, changed its name to Wolf Sporting Pistols in 1997.

PISTOLS: SEMI-AUTO

ULTRAMATIC PISTOL – 9mm Para. cal., double action semi-auto, various barrel lengths, competition model with muzzle brake. Disc. approx. 1996.

	$1,150	$975	$850	$700	$640	$575	$500	

Add 20% for early mfg.

UMAREX SPORTWAFFEN GmbH & Co. KG.

Current firearms, airguns, air soft, and signal pistol manufacturer established in 1972 as Uma Mayer Ussfeller GmbH, with headquarters located in Arnsberg, Germany.

Initially, the company manufactured tear gas and signal pistols for eastern bloc countries, and then started producing air rifles. After acquiring Reck Sportwaffen Fabrick Karl Arndt, the company was reorganized under the Umarex name.

Umarex purchased Walther during 1993, and also manufactures ammunition, optics, and accessories. During 2006, Umarex purchased Hämmerli, and production equipment was moved from Lenzburg, Switzerland to Ulm, Germany. During mid-2006, Umarex purchased RUAG Ammotec USA INc., and moved the company to Fort Smith, Arkansas, and the company's name was changed to Umarex USA. During 2008, Colt Industries licensed Umarex to manufacture the Colt AR-15 in .22 LR cal. During 2009, H&K licensed Umarex to manufacture replicas in .22 LR cal. During 2011, Colt Industries licensed Umarex to manufacture a Govt. 1911-A1 Model in .22 LR cal. In late 2011, IWI licensed Umarex to manufacture a .22 LR copy of the UZI carbine and pistol. These guns are being imported exclusively by Umarex USA located in Fort Smith, AR. During late 2012, Umarex and Carl Walther GmbH Sportwaffen announced the formation of Walther Arms, Inc. to import, sell, and market all Walther products in the U.S. beginning Jan. 1, 2013, except the P22 and PK380 models.

Please refer to the Colt, H&K, Hämmerli, Regent (trademark only), UZI, and Walther listings for information and values on currently imported firearms. For more information on currently manufactured (beginning circa 1984) Umarex airguns, including many major U.S. trademark mfg. under license, please refer to the *Blue Book of Airguns* by Dr. Robert Beeman & John Allen (also online).

UNDERWOOD-ELLIOT-FISHER CORP.

Previous WWII subcontractor of M1 carbines located in Chicago, IL.

Please refer to U.S. Military rifles/carbines section.

UNERTL ORDNANCE COMPANY, INC.

Previous manufacturer circa 2004-2006 and located in Las Vegas, NV.

Unertl Ordnance Company manufactured a .45 ACP cal. semi-auto pistol in various configurations, including MEU (SOC) $2,795 last MSR, UCCP $2,195 last MSR, and the DLX $2,195 last MSR. The company also manufactured the UPR bolt action sniper rifle in .308 Win. cal. Last MSR was $5,900.

UNIQUE

Previous manufacturer 1923-2006 located in Patin, France. Previously located in Hendaye, France until 2001. Previously imported by Nygord Precision Products located in Prescott, AZ.

FMR owns the rights to the Unique trademark. Please refer to the FMR listing for current information.

GRADING - PPGS™	100%	98%	95%	90%	80%	70%	60%	LAST MSR

PISTOLS: SEMI-AUTO

Unique pistols were supplied with leatherette case, weights were an optional accessory.

KRIEGSMODELL L – 7.65mm cal., 9 shot, 3.2 in. barrel, blue, plastic grips, fixed sights. Mfg. 1940-45, during German occupation of France, has German acceptance marks.

$325	$250	$220	$200	$180	$160	$140	

MODEL RR – .22 LR or 7.65mm cal., post-war commercial version of Kriegsmodell, higher quality finish. Mfg. 1951-disc.

$180	$170	$155	$130	$120	$110	$90	

Add 15% for .22 LR.

MODEL B/CF – 7.65mm cal., 9 shot, or .380 auto cal., 8 shot, 4 in. barrel, blue, plastic thumbrest grips. Mfg. 1954-disc.

$205	$195	$175	$155	$145	$130	$110	

MODEL D6 – .22 LR cal., 10 shot, 6 in. barrel, adj. sights, blue, plastic grips. Mfg. 1954-disc.

$300	$250	$200	$160	$145	$135	$120	

MODEL D2 – similar to D6, except 4 1/2 in. barrel.

$300	$250	$200	$160	$145	$135	$120	

MODEL L – .22 LR cal., 10 shot, 7.65mm cal., 7 shot, and .380 ACP cal., 6 shot, 3.3 in. barrel, fixed sights, steel and alloy frame offered, plastic grips. Mfg. 1955-disc.

$300	$250	$175	$150	$125	$100	$90	

Add $500 for .22 LR cal. pistol-rifle combination.

MODEL MIKROS POCKET – .22 Short or .25 ACP cal., 6 shot, fixed sights, blue, plastic grips, steel or alloy frame. Mfg. 1957-disc.

$200	$155	$140	$120	$100	$90	$75	

MODEL DES/32U – .32 S&W Wadcutter cal., 5.9 in. barrel, dry firing device, ergonomically designed French walnut grips with adj. hand rest, 5 or 6 shot mag., 40.2 oz.

$1,350	$1,225	$1,025	$900	$775	$625	$500	

MODEL DES/69 MATCH – .22 LR cal. target pistol, wraparound grips, adj. features. Imported 1986-1988.

$995	$850	$725	$625	$550	$490	$445	*$1,198*

Add $62 for left-hand model.

MODEL DES/69U STANDARD MATCH – .22 LR cal., 5 shot mag., 5.9 in. barrel, adj. rear sight, adj. target stippled stocks, blue finish only. Imported 1969-1999.

$1,150	$995	$875	$750	$625	$500	$450	*$1,250*

Add $30 for left-hand model.

MODEL DES/96U – .22 LR cal., replacement for the Model DES/69U, top loading model, thinner grips, features gold-plated slide. Mfg. 1996-2002.

$1,350	$1,225	$1,025	$900	$775	$625	$500	

MODEL DES/823-U RAPID FIRE MATCH – .22 Short cal., 5 shot, 6 in. barrel, adj. sight, adj. trigger, adj. walnut target grips, squared barrel assembly, dry fire mechanism. Imported 1974-1988.

$1,100	$850	$725	$625	$550	$490	$445	*$1,300*

Add $60 for left-hand model.

MODEL 2000-U – .22 Short cal. only, specifically designed for rapid fire U.I.T. competition, 5.9 in. barrel, ergonomic styled grips with adj. hand rest, 5 shot mag. (inserted in top), 43.4 oz. Importation disc. 1995.

$1,300	$1,050	$925	$775	$625	$500	$450	*$1,450*

Add $30 for left-hand model.

GRADING - PPGS™	100%	98%	95%	90%	80%	70%	60%	LAST MSR

RIFLES: BOLT ACTION

T66 MATCH RIFLE – .22 LR cal., single shot, bolt action, 25 1/2 in. barrel, micro rear and globe front sight, full target stock. Mfg. 1966-disc.

$425	$410	$390	$350	$300	$280	$250	

MODEL F 11 – .22 LR cal., military trainer, adj. sights, target walnut stock. Limited importation.

$560	$435	$350	$285	$260	$240	$220	$695

MODEL T DIOPTRA – .22 LR or .22 WMR cal., bolt action Sporter with 23.6 in. barrel and adj. rear sight, 5 (.22 WMR only) or 10 shot mag., grooved receiver for scope, checkered French walnut Monte Carlo stock, approx. 6.4 lbs. Importation disc. 1995.

$795	$700	$600	$525	$450	$375	$300	$890

MODEL T/SM – .22 LR or .22 WMR cal., bolt action Target variation with 20 1/2 in. barrel, no sights, 5 (.22 WMR only) or 10 shot mag., stippled pistol grip stock and forearm, right or left-hand action, 6.6 lbs. Importation disc. 1995.

$850	$735	$625	$525	$450	$375	$300	$960

Add $50 for left-hand action.

MODEL T/STANDARD UIT – .22 LR cal., designed for UIT competition, single shot, aperture sights, adj. cheekpiece and buttplate on stippled walnut stock, right or left-hand action, 10.8 lbs. Importation disc. 1995.

$1,350	$1,125	$975	$850	$725	$625	$525	$1,450

Add $50 for left-hand action.

MODEL 2000 FREE RIFLE – .22 LR cal., Free Rifle variation of the Model T/Standard UIT.

$2,600	$2,250	$1,875	$1,500	$1,250	$1,000	$850	

UNIQUE-ALPINE

Current manufacturer established in 2002 and located in Bavaria, Germany, with manufacturing sites in Germany and Switzerland. No current U.S. importation.

RIFLES: BOLT ACTION

TPG-1/TPG-2/TPG-3 A1/A4 (TACTICAL PRECISION GEWEHR) – various cals. (TPG-1/TPG-2), TPG3 -A1 is chambered in .308 Win., .300 Win. Mag., or .338 Lapua Mag. cal., 20, 24, or 26 in. match grade free floating fluted barrel with muzzle brake, 8 or 10 shot mag., full length Picatinny rail, modular interchangeable rifle system allows for transfer from single shot to magazine fed rifle, tactical adj. and detachable (TPG3-A1 or TPG3-A4) stock available in right hand or Universal configuration and a variety of colors and camo, adj. palm rest, accessory rails. 15 lbs. (TPG-3 A1).

A wide variety of options are available on these models. Please contact the company directly for more information, including options, pricing, and U.S. availability (see Trademark Index).

UNITED SPORTING ARMS, INC.

Previous manufacturer located in Tombstone and Tucson, AZ and Post Falls, ID.

UNITED SPORTING ARMS HISTORY

The Seville and El Dorado line of single actions began life in 1972 as the "Abilene". It was during that year that Sig Himmelman built the prototype and formed United States Arms of Riverhead, NY. In 1976, the company became two separate entities, with Sig and Forrest Smith reorganizing as United Sporting Arms of Hauppauge, NY, manufacturing the blue model Seville and the stainless El Dorado. The El Dorado was an important model, because it was the first time that an all stainless .44 Mag. was available to the general public. United States Arms continued to produce the Abilene in Riverhead until Mossberg acquired the line in 1979. Production was moved to New Haven, CT and ceased in 1983.

In 1979, United Sporting Arms of Hauppage established a second facility in Tombstone, AZ. Sevilles weren't manufactured in Tombstone, but were assembled from parts shipped from Hauppage. Only a few hundred models were produced before the New York operations were

GRADING - PPGS™	100%	98%	95%	90%	80%	70%	60%	LAST MSR

moved to Bisbee, AZ. While most models were blue, the Silver Seville was a Tombstone variant, with stainless backstrap and high blue finish.

The Bisbee operation was short lived too, and during mid-1979, Sig Himmelman relocated the western operations of United Sporting Arms to Tucson. By 1980, the company had split again into El Dorado Arms of Hauppauge and Sporting Arms Inc. of Tucson. These were separate companies with their own lines of revolvers. Stainless El Dorados were produced in NY and the blue/stainless Sevilles came from Arizona.

While El Dorado Arms (NY) primarily built .44 Mags., Sporting Arms Inc. (AZ) expanded the line with many new chamberings. In 1982, the company unveiled the stretch-frame Seville in .357 Maximum. A couple of .375 Super Mags were also produced before the company was sold and the name changed to United Sporting Arms in 1983. That same year, El Dorado Arms closed shop.

The Tucson facility closed in late 1985. Many unique variants were produced between 1983-1985, including .454 Mag., .375 SuperMag, Sheriff's models, and silhouette guns.

During 1986, United Sporting Arms, Inc. was reformed in Post Falls, ID, but operations could not be sustained. Only 200 (approx.) guns were produced in this location, and quality was sub par compared to earlier Seville models.

By 1988, Forrest Smith and Russell Wood resurrected El Dorado Arms, basing production in Chimney Rock, NC. During 1988-1998, the company manufactured hand fitted and tuned single actions. Both standard frame and stretch platforms were offered, as well as a rimfire model. Production was low, but quality was very high.

The publisher would like to thank Mr. Rick Maples for providing the above information.

REVOLVERS: SINGLE ACTION

SEVILLE – .357 Mag., .41 Mag., .44 Mag., or .45 LC cal., single action revolver, 4 5/8, 5 1/2, 6 1/2, or 7 1/2 in. barrels, adj. sights, smooth walnut grips.

$395	$350	$315	$280	$260	$240	$220	*$435*

* ***Seville Stainless steel*** – all stainless version of the Seville.

$395	$350	$315	$280	$260	$240	$220	*$435*

* ***Seville Silver*** – similar to Seville, except has blue barrel, and high polish stainless steel grip frame.

$425	$370	$330	$290	$270	$245	$225	*$460*

* ***Seville Stainless .357 Maxi*** – available in 5 1/2 or 7 1/2 in. barrel only.

$575	$475	$395	$335	$290	$245	$215	*$465*

* ***Seville Stainless .375 USA*** – only in 7 1/2 in. barrel.

$625	$525	$425	$360	$315	$260	$225	*$490*

* ***Seville Stainless .454 Mag.*** – only in 7 1/2 in. barrel, 5 shot.

$700	$600	$500	$430	$375	$315	$270	*$595*

Note: In late 1986, some .454 Mags. were made up from parts purchased from the manufacturer. Unfortunately, while the exterior appearance might seem normal, they were not involved with any type of factory quality control program. As a result, shooting these non-factory revolvers could be dangerous, and careful inspection should be made before purchasing/shooting this particular specimen.

* ***Seville Eldorado Stainless*** – .44 Mag., 4 5/8, 5 1/2, 6 1/2, 7 1/2, or 10 1/2 in. barrel, adj. sights.

$700	$600	$500	$430	$375	$315	$270	

SILVER SEVILLE SILHOUETTE – .357 Mag., .41 Mag., or .44 Mag. cal., single action revolver, 10 1/2 in. barrel, adj. sights, Pachmayr grips, blue barrel finish with stainless grip frame.

$445	$370	$330	$295	$270	$250	$230	*$485*

* ***Silver Seville Silhouette Stainless steel*** – stainless version of the Silver Seville Silhouette.

$425	$370	$330	$290	$270	$245	$225	*$460*

GRADING - PPGS™	100%	98%	95%	90%	80%	70%	60%	LAST MSR

* ***Silver Seville Silhouette Stainless .357 Maxi*** – available in 10 1/2 in. barrel only.

	$575	$475	$395	$335	$290	$245	$215	*$480*

* ***Silver Seville Silhouette Stainless .375 USA*** – available in 10 1/2 in. barrel only.

	$625	$525	$425	$360	$315	$260	$225	*$515*

* ***Silver Seville Silhouette Stainless .454 Mag.*** – available in 10 1/2 in. barrel only, 5 shot.

	$700	$600	$500	$430	$375	$315	$270	*$620*

SHERIFF MODEL – .357 Mag., .38 Spl., .44 Spl., .44 Mag., or .45 LC cal., single action revolver, 3 1/2 in. barrel, adj. sights, smooth walnut grips.

	$395	$350	$315	$280	$260	$240	$220	*$435*

* ***Sheriff Model Stainless steel*** – stainless version of the Sheriff Model.

	$395	$350	$315	$280	$260	$240	$220	*$435*

UNITED STATES FIRE ARMS MFG. CO., INC./USFA

Previous manufacturer located in Hartford, CT 1995-2012. Previously located at Colt's original old armory in Hartford, CT. Previous company name was United States Patent Firearms Manufacturing Company until 1997. Distributed exclusively beginning 2008 by Acusport.

PISTOLS: SEMI-AUTO

1910 COMMERCIAL MODEL – .45 ACP cal., 5 in. barrel, high polish Armory Blue, hand checkered fancy walnut grips, 7 shot mag., fire blue appointments, 1905 patent dates, grip safety, checkered thumb safety, round 1905 fire blue hammer with hand cut checkering, original Colt 1910 rollmarks on both sides of slide. Mfg. 2006-2009.

	$1,650	$1,425	$1,275	$1,075	$925	$800	$700	*$1,895*

1911 MILITARY MODEL – .45 ACP cal., 5 in. barrel, military polish Armory Blue, hand checkered standard walnut grips, 7 shot mag., fire blue appointments, 1905 patent dates, grip safety, small contoured checkered thumb safety, spur hammer with hand cut checkering, original Colt 1911 military rollmarks on both sides of slide, including choice on right side of U.S. Navy or U.S. Army. Limited mfg. 2006-2009.

	$1,650	$1,425	$1,275	$1,075	$925	$800	$700	*$1,895*

1911 SUPER 38 – .38 Super cal., features original 1911 Super 38 metal finishes and blue appointments, 1905 patent dates, grip safety, small thumb safety and spur hammer. Limited mfg. 2007-2009.

	$1,650	$1,425	$1,275	$1,075	$925	$800	$700	*$1,895*

REVOLVERS

SHOOTING MASTER – .357 Mag. cal., 7 1/2 in. barrel, 6 shot, full blue finish, adj. rear sight, U.S. hard rubber grips, large heavy frame, knurled take-down pin, large loop trigger guard. Limited mfg. 2011-2012 only.

	$1,350	$1,200	$995	$825	$700	$600	$450	*$1,495*

SPARROWHAWK – .327 Federal cal., 7 1/2 in. barrel, 8 shot, full blue finish, adj. rear sight, U.S. hard rubber grips, scaled down frame, knurled takedown pin, large loop trigger guard. Limited mfg. 2011-2012.

	$1,350	$1,200	$995	$825	$700	$600	$450	*$1,495*

REVOLVERS: SAA

USFA also had a custom shop offering the following levels of engraving: Armory Grade A ($830 MSR), Armory Grade B ($1,135 MSR), Armory Grade C ($1,395 MSR), Armory Grade D ($1,650 MSR), Master Grade A ($1,260 MSR), Master Grade B ($2,615 MSR), Master Grade C ($3,725 MSR) or Master Grade D ($5,045 MSR).

Add $725 for elephant ivory grips, $495 for stag, $275 Tru-Ivory two-piece Natural White, Slightly Aged, or Antique Ultra Aged, $75 for ivory, $330 for standard American one-piece walnut, $250 for two-piece American walnut, $400 for smooth fancy European one-piece walnut, $330 for fancy grade European two-piece walnut, or $175 for diamond checkered grips.

GRADING - PPGS™	100%	98%	95%	90%	80%	70%	60%	LAST MSR

COLT 1851 RICHARDS NAVY CONVERSION – .38 Spl. cal. only, 7 1/2 in. barrel with ejector, Old Armory Bone Case finish frame, gate, hammer, and conversion ring, Dome Blue barrel, cylinder, and ejector housing, smooth walnut grips.

$1,175 $950 $825 $700 $600 $500 $400 ***$1,300***

THE SINGLE ACTION – .32-20 WCF, .44-40 WCF, .44 Spl., .38-40 WCF, .38 Spl., or .45 LC cal., 4 3/4, 5 1/2, or 7 1/2 in. barrel, Bone Case and Dome Blue finish, or nickel, white sided hammer, U.S. hard rubber grips. Mfg. 2009-2012.

$1,050 $925 $850 $725 $550 $475 $350 ***$1,150***

Add $275 for nickel finish.

SINGLE ACTION ARMY PREMIUM GRADE – .22 LR (mfg. 1996-2001), .22 WMR (mfg. 1996-2001), .32-20 (new 1998), .357 Mag. (disc. 1998), .38 Spl. (new 2004), .38-40 WCF, .41 Colt (mfg. 1999-2003), .44 Spl. (new 2004), .44-40 WCF, .45 ACP (disc. 2006), or .45 LC cal., 3 (no ejector), 4 (no ejector), 4 3/4, 5 1/2, 7 1/2, or 10 (new 1997) in. barrel, original screw cylinder release, white sided hammer standard beginning 2005, choice of Dome Blue, Dome Blue/Old Armory Bone Case, or nickel finish, checkered U.S. hard rubber grips.

$895 $775 $650 $525 $450 $375 $325 ***$975***

Add $205 for nickel finish.

The barrel marking for this revolver is "U.S.F.A. MFG. Co. HARTFORD CT. U.S.A."

* ***SAA Flat-top Target*** – similar to SAA, except has flat-top receiver with target sights, full Dome Blue finish is standard. Mfg. 1997-2002, reintroduced 2004-2012.

$1,500 $1,325 $1,165 $975 $800 $700 $600 ***$1,695***

Add $195 for full Armory Blue or nickel finish.
Add $195 for case colored frame and hammer.
Add $55 for Dome Blue/Old Armory Bone Case finish (disc.).
Add $179 for Armory Blue/Old Armory Bone Case finish (disc.).

* ***SAA U.S. Pre-War*** – similar cals. as the SAA Premium, except also available in .41 Colt, most historically correct and accurate pre-war SAA reproduction available. Mfg. 2000-2012.

$1,350 $1,200 $995 $825 $700 $600 $450 ***$1,495***

* ***SAA New Buntline Special*** – .45 LC cal. only, 16 in. barrel, includes correct skeleton shoulder stock, ser. numbered 28,8xx and up. Mfg. 2000-2002.

$1,850 $1,675 $1,500 $1,250 $1,000 $900 $800 ***$2,199***

Add $396 for nickel finish.

CUSTER BATTLEFIELD GUN – .45 LC cal., 7 1/2 in. barrel, has Orville W. Ainsworth inspector cartouche on one-piece walnut grips, antique patina finish, script barrel legend with slanted cross at each end, ser. range 200-14,343. Mfg. 2006-2012.

$1,550 $1,350 $1,200 $975 $775 $700 $600 ***$1,725***

PATRIOT SERIES – .30 Carbine or .45 ACP cal., 5 1/2 (.45 ACP) or 7 1/2 (.30 Carbine) in. barrel with lanyard loop, Old Armory Bone case colored frame, Dome Blue (.30 Carbine) or Armory Blue (.45 ACP) finish, "AUTOMATIC 45" rollmark. Mfg. 2005-2008.

$1,125 $925 $800 $650 $525 $450 $400 ***$1,280***

Add $210 for .45 ACP cal.

GOVERNMENT INSPECTOR SERIES – .45 LC cal., exact recreations of guns inspected by government inspectors, including Henry Nettleton, Orville Ainsworth, David Clark, and Rinaldo Carr, exact cartouche stampings and hand-stamped markings, 5 1/2 or 7 1/2 in. barrel, historically correct, one-piece walnut grips, Old Armory Bone case color hardened frame, Armory Blue, antique, or nickel finish. Mfg. 2005-2012.

$1,500 $1,325 $1,165 $975 $800 $700 $600 ***$1,695***

Add $40 for antique finish.
Add $134 for nickel finish (disc. 2007).

GRADING - PPGS™	100%	98%	95%	90%	80%	70%	60%	LAST MSR

BISLEY MODEL SAA – same cals. as SAA, 4 3/4, 5 1/2, 7 1/2, or 10 (disc.) in. barrel, patterned after the Colt Bisley Model, smooth walnut grips, standard or target configuration, choice of Bone Case/Dome Blue, Bone Case/Armory Blue, or nickel finish. Disc. 1998, reintroduced 2000-2002, again 2004-2012.

$1,550	$1,350	$1,200	$975	$775	$700	$600	*$1,725*

Add $225 for Armory Blue/Old Armory Bone Case finish.
Add $225 for nickel finish.
Add $200 for Bisley Target variation.

BIRDSHEAD MODEL SAA – same cals. as SAA, patterned after the Colt Model 1877 Thunderer, 3 1/2, 4, or 4 3/4 in. barrel with ejector, case colored frame. Mfg. 1997-2002.

$975	$825	$725	$625	$525	$425	$325	*$1,150*

Add $149 for nickel finish.

CHINA CAMP – various cals., designed for competition shooting, silver steel competition finish with two-piece hard rubber grips. Mfg. 2000-2003.

$975	$850	$725	$625	$525	$425	$325	*$1,200*

SHERIFF'S MODEL – similar cals. as the SAA, 2 1/2, 3, 3 1/2, or 4 in. barrel w/o ejector rod housing, U.S. hard rubber grips, choice of bone case/blue or nickel finish. Mfg. 2004-2012.

$1,050	$925	$850	$725	$550	$475	$350	*$1,150*

Add $370 for nickel finish. Add $200 for birdshead grip (new 2010).

RODEO – .32-20 WCF (mfg. 2005-2006), .38 Spl., .38-40 WCF (mfg. 2005-2006), .44-40 WCF (disc. 2006), .44 Spl. (mfg. 2005-2006), or .45 LC, 4 3/4, 5 1/2, or 7 1/2 (new 2004) in. barrel, matte blue finish, fixed firing pin, square notch rear sight, hard rubber or Tru-Ivory grips, white sided hammer became standard 2005, entry level cowboy action shooting model. Mfg. 2002-2012.

$675	$595	$475	$425	$375	$325	$295	*$760*

Add $131 for Rodeo Heritage Model with Tru-Ivory grips (disc. 2005).
Add $358 for Rodeo Race Groove (limited mfg. 2006).

* ***Rodeo II*** – .38 Spl. or .45 LC cal., 4 3/4 or 5 1/2 in. barrel, similar to Rodeo, except has satin nickel finish with U.S. burlwood grips. Mfg. 2008-2012.

$750	$650	$550	$475	$365	$335	$295	*$825*

COWBOY – .38 Spl. or .45 LC cal., 4 3/4, 5 1/2, or 7 1/2 in. barrel, full Dome Blue metal finish, U.S. brown hard rubber grips, cross pin frame, square notch rear and square front blade sights. Mfg. 2007-2008.

$725	$650	$575	$500	$425	$375	$325	*$790*

GUNSLINGER – .32-20 WCF, .38-40 WCF, .38 Spl., .44-40 WCF, .44 Spl., or .45 LC cal., 4 3/4, 5 1/2, or 7 1/2 in. barrel, cross-pin frame, cowboy action aged bluing, hard rubber grips, antique finish, square notch rear and front blade sights. Mfg. 2005-2012.

$1,250	$1,025	$995	$850	$625	$475	$375	*$1,375*

Add $70 for black powder frame (disc. 2006).

DOUBLE EAGLE – .44-40 WCF, .44 Spl., or .45 LC cal., 3, 3 1/2, or 4 in. barrel with ejector, blue finish with bone color case hardening or nickel finish, US hard rubber grips, large loop trigger guard, birdshead hammer. Mfg. 2010-2012.

$1,225	$1,000	$975	$850	$625	$475	$375	*$1,350*

Add $250 for nickel finish.

OLD ARMORY ORIGINAL – .32-20 WCF, .38 WCF, .38 Spl., .44-40 WCF, .45 LC, or .455 Eley cal., historically correct 1st Generation Colt frame or blackpowder frame, 4 3/4, 5 1/2, or 7 1/2 in. barrel, U.S. hard rubber grips, color case hammer, bone case and Armory blue finish, available in standard original, correct 1890 British proofed (.455 Eley cal. only), or ejectorless model (7 1/2 in. barrel, blackpowder frame, .45 LC cal. only). Mfg. 2011-2012.

$1,895	$1,750	$1,625	$1,500	$1,250	$995	$750	*$2,095*

GRADING - PPGS™	100%	98%	95%	90%	80%	70%	60%	LAST MSR

OMNI-POTENT SIX SHOOTER – various cals., 4 3/4, 5 1/2, or 7 1/2 in. barrel, choice of case colored, Old Armory Bone Case or Armory Blue finish, checkered Bisley style walnut grips with round butt and lanyard loop. Mfg. 2000-2002, reintroduced 2004-2009.

$1,450 $1,275 $1,050 $900 $750 $650 $525 *$1,625*

Add approx. $200 for nickel finish.
Add $270 for Omni-Target Model with raised adj. sights.

OMNI-POTENT SNUBNOSE – various cals., 2, 3, or 4 in. barrel, full Armory Blue or nickel finish, checkered Bisley style walnut grips with round butt and lanyard loop. Mfg. 2000-2002, reintroduced 2004-2009.

$1,300 $1,100 $900 $750 $625 $500 $450 *$1,475*

Add $200 for nickel finish.

PLINKER – .22 LR or .22 WMR cal., 4 3/4, 5 1/2, or 7 1/2 in. barrel, Old Armory Bone Case/Dome Blue finish, U.S. hard rubber grips, square notch rear and square front blade sights, includes extra .22 WMR cylinder. Mfg. 2004-2012.

$1,050 $925 $850 $725 $550 $475 $350 *$1,150*

Add $545 for Target Model with adj. sights and Dome Blue finish.
Add $245 for nickel.

USFA 12/22 – .22 LR cal., Dome Blue or nickel finish, 4 3/4, 5 1/2, or 7 1/2 in. barrel, U.S. hard rubber grips. Mfg. 2009-2012.

$950 $825 $725 $650 $525 $450 $400 *$1,095*

Add $330 for nickel finish.

HUNTER – .17 HMR cal., 7 1/2 in. barrel, matte blue finish, adj. rear sight, replaceable front blade sight, drilled and tapped, U.S. hard rubber grips, 3 1/2 lbs. Limited mfg. 2004-2005.

$750 $650 $550 $475 $400 $325 $275 *$839*

JOHN WAYNE CENTENNIAL LTD. ED. – .45 LC cal., 5 1/2 in. barrel, nickel or Color Case and Armory Blue finish, cross pin frame, ser. nos. begin at JW-1, 25 sets and 50 singles mfg. 2007 2010.

$4,500 $4,000 $3,500 $3,000 $2,500 $2,000 $1,750 *$4,999*

JOHN WAYNE RED RIVER D CLASSIC – .45 LC cal., 4 3/4 or 5 1/2 in. black powder style cross pin frame, faux ivory grips, V-notch rear sight, "Duke's Movie Gun Blue" finish, could be ordered as a pair with holster and belt.

$1,725 $1,550 $1,325 $1,150 $995 $875 $675 *$1,899*

SHOT PISTOL – .45 LC/.410 bore, 2 1/2 in. chambers, 2 in. standard barrel with front bead sight, or with M4 muzzle brake (M4-410), 6 shot, blue finish, larger open trigger guard, black checkered grips with USFA markings. New late 2011.

While advertised during 2011, this model never went into production.

RIFLES: REPRODUCTIONS, LEVER ACTION

STANDARD LIGHTNING MAGAZINE RIFLE – .38-40 WCF, .44-40 WCF, or .45 LC cal., patterned after the Colt Lightning rifle, 26 in. round, half-round or octagon barrel, 15 shot mag., straight grip uncheckered walnut stock and small checkered forearm. Disc. 2009.

$1,325 $1,150 $950 $825 $700 $600 $500 *$1,480*

Add $270 for octagon barrel.
Add $245 for half-round/half-octagon barrel.
Nickel finish was POR.

* ***Standard Lightning Deluxe Rifle*** – similar to Standard, except has deluxe checkered semi-pistol grip stock and forearm, choice of 26 in. octagon, round or half-round, half-octagon barrel with half mag. Disc. 2009.

$2,225 $1,950 $1,750 $1,500 $1,250 $1,000 $875 *$2,559*

Add $100 for half-round, half-octagon barrel.

GRADING - PPGS™	100%	98%	95%	90%	80%	70%	60%	LAST MSR

STANDARD LIGHTNING MAGAZINE CARBINE – similar to Lightning Rifle, except has 16 (Trapper) or 20 in. round barrel and 8 (Trapper, new 2006) or 12 shot mag. Disc. 2009.

	$1,325	$1,150	$950	$825	$700	$600	$500	*$1,480*

Add $515 for Lightweight Baby Carbine with 20 in. special tapered barrel and lightweight forearm with special checkering.
Add $675 for Trapper Model with 16 in. special taper barrel and checkering.
Add $270 for checkered stock and forearm.

STANDARD LIGHTNING COWBOY RIFLE/CARBINE – .38-40 WCF, .44-40 WCF, or .45 LC cal., 20 in. (carbine) or 26 (rifle) in. round barrel with ladder (carbine) or buckhorn rear sight, matte blue metal and matte wood finish. Disc. 2006.

	$1,175	$1,025	$900	$800	$700	$600	$500	*$1,345*

UNIVERSAL FIREARMS

Previous manufacturer 1958-1987 and located in Hialeah, FL. Previous company name was Bullseye Gunworks, located in Miami, FL. The company moved to Hialeah, FL in 1958 and began as Universal Firearms.

Universal Firearms M1 carbines were manufactured and assembled at the company's facility in Hialeah starting in the late 1950s. The carbines of the 1960s were mfg. with available surplus GI parts on a receiver subcontracted to Repp Steel Co. of Buffalo, NY. The carbines of the 1970s were mfg. with commercially manufactured parts due to a shortage of GI surplus. In 1983, the company was purchased by Iver Johnson Arms of Jacksonville, AR, but remained a separate division as Universal Firearms in Hialeah until closed and liquidated by Iver Johnson Arms in 1987.

PISTOLS: SEMI-AUTO

MODEL 3000 ENFORCER PISTOL – .30 Carbine cal., walnut stock, 11 1/4 in. barrel, 17 3/4 in. overall, 15 and 30 shot. Mfg. 1964-83. Also see listing under Iver Johnson.

Blue finish	$450	$375	$325	$275	$235	$200	$185	
Nickel-plated	$500	$425	$350	$295	$250	$235	$220	
Gold-plated	$500	$425	$350	$275	$250	$225	$200	
Stainless	$600	$550	$450	$350	$275	$225	$195	

Add $50 for Teflon-S finish.

RIFLES: SEMI-AUTO, CARBINES

1000 MILITARY – .30 Carbine cal., "G.I." copy, 18 in. barrel, satin blue finish, birch stock. Disc.

	$375	$325	$275	$235	$200	$180	$170	

MODEL 1003 – 16, 18, or 20 in. barrel, .30 M1 copy, blue finish, adj. sight, birch stock, 5 1/2 lbs. Also see listing under Iver Johnson.

	$375	$325	$275	$235	$200	$180	$170	*$203*

* ***Model 1010*** – nickel finish, disc.

	$425	$375	$325	$275	$235	$200	$180	

* ***Model 1015*** – gold electroplated, disc.

	$425	$375	$325	$275	$235	$200	$180	

Add $45 for 4X scope.

1005 DELUXE – .30 Carbine cal., custom Monte Carlo walnut stock, high polish blue, oil finish on wood.

	$425	$365	$325	$275	$235	$200	$180	

1006 STAINLESS – .30 Carbine cal., stainless steel construction, birch stock, 18 in. barrel, 6 lbs.

	$475	$425	$375	$325	$275	$235	$200	*$234*

GRADING - PPGS™	100%	98%	95%	90%	80%	70%	60%	LAST MSR

1020 TEFLON – .30 Carbine cal., Dupont Teflon-S finish on metal parts, black or grey color, Monte Carlo stock.

$425	$375	$325	$275	$235	$200	$180	

1025 FERRET A – .256 Win. Mag. cal., M1 Action, 18 in. barrel, satin blue finish, birch stock, 5 1/2 lbs.

$400	$350	$300	$265	$235	$200	$175	*$219*

2200 LEATHERNECK – .22 LR cal., blowback action, 18 in. barrel, birch stock, satin blue finish, 5 1/2 lbs.

$350	$300	$250	$215	$185	$170	$160	

5000 PARATROOPER – .30 Carbine cal., metal folding extension or walnut stock, 16 or 18 in. barrel.

$550	$475	$400	$350	$295	$250	$225	*$234*

5006 PARATROOPER STAINLESS – similar to 5000, only stainless with 18 in. barrel only.

$650	$575	$500	$425	$350	$285	$250	*$281*

1981 COMMEMORATIVE CARBINE – .30 Carbine cal., "G.I Military" model, cased with accessories. Mfg. for 40th Anniversary 1941-1981.

$700	$525	$425	N/A	N/A	N/A	N/A	

RIFLES: SLIDE ACTION

MODEL 440 VULCAN – .44 Mag. cal., slide action, 18 1/4 in. barrel with adj. rear and front ramp sight, 5 shot detachable mag.

$400	$350	$300	$250	$215	$185	$165	

SHOTGUNS

All Universal shotguns were disc. after 1982.

MODEL 7312 O/U – 12 ga., 30 in. full and mod., VR barrel, boxlock, vent. barrel spacer, SST, auto ejectors, barrels ported to reduce recoil, engraved, color case hardened receiver, trap or skeet style, checkered select stock.

$1,650	$1,540	$1,485	$1,430	$1,320	$1,210	$1,045	

MODEL 7412 O/U – similar to 7312, without ejectors, blue and silver receiver.

$1,430	$1,210	$1,155	$1,100	$9,900	$880	$825	

MODEL 7712 O/U – 12 ga., 26 or 28 in. barrel, VR, non-selective single trigger, extractors, light engraving, checkered pistol grip stock.

$440	$415	$385	$360	$330	$275	$220	

MODEL 7812 O/U – similar to 7712, with auto ejectors and more engraving.

$605	$580	$550	$525	$470	$415	$385	

MODEL 7912 O/U – similar to 7812, with selective single trigger and gold damascene engraving.

$1,210	$1,155	$1,100	$1,045	$965	$880	$825	

MODEL 7112 SxS – 12 ga., 26 or 28 in. barrels, various chokes, boxlock, extractors, engraved case hardened frame, checkered pistol grip stock.

$330	$305	$275	$250	$195	$165	$140	

DOUBLE WING SxS – 10, 12, 20 ga., or .410 bore, 26, 28, or 30 in. barrels, various chokes, double triggers, boxlock, extractors, checkered pistol grip stock.

	$330	$305	$275	$250	$195	$165	$140	
10 gauge	$385	$360	$330	$305	$250	$220	$165	

MODEL 7212 SINGLE BARREL TRAP – 12 ga., 30 in. full, Simmons type VR, engraved case colored frame, ported barrel to reduce recoil, boxlock, auto ejector, select checkered trap style stock.

$1,100	$990	$935	$880	$770	$715	$605	

USELTON ARMS INC

Current manufacturer located in Franklin, TN. Previously located in Madison, TN.

PISTOLS: SEMI-AUTO

Uselton Arms Inc. manufactures M1911-style semi-auto pistols. Models include the Mil-Spec ($2,499 MSR), Compact Classic Stainless ($2,799 MSR), Compact Classic Black with stainless slide ($2,899 MSR), Compact Classic Bobtail Black w/stainless slide or all stainless ($2,799 MSR), Compact Classic Officer (last MSR in 2011 was $3,150), Carry Classic ($2,699 MSR), Classic National Match with Uselton Armor/Ceramic coat ($2,899 MSR), Tactical (last MSR in 2011 was $2,770), Tac-Rail (MSR $2,8799 stainless, $2,899 MSR with Ceramic Coat), Match Classic Bobtail Government Model stainless ($2,899 MSR), Integrate Aluminum Commander IAC Model "The Uselton 1911" in aluminum, stainless or Uselton Armor ($3,699 MSR), Integrated Aluminum Government - IAG Model "The Uselton 1911" ($3,799 MSR), Integrated Aluminum Officer's - IAO Model "The Uselton 1911" in aluminum, stainless, or Uselton Armor ($3,699 MSR), Integrated Aluminum "1911 Recon Tac" Commander Model ($3,699 MSR), Integrated Aluminum Uselton 1911 Tac Government Model ($3,599 MSR), Uselton 1911 Recon Tac Commander Model ($2,899 MSR), and the Double Stack Race Gun (last MSR in 2011 was $3,200).

Limited editions, including the Eagle National Match (last MSR in 2011 was $4,500) are also available. The 2nd Amendment (MSR is POR), Match Classic Bobtail with damascus slide, trigger, and hammer is $6,900 MSR, 1911 Limited Edition High Polish stainless with American flag and stag grips ($3,885 MSR), 1911 100th Anniversary Government Model is $4,200 MSR, and the 100th Anniversary Officer's Model ($3,699 MSR). The Classic National Match with damascus slide and burl wood grips is $6,900 MSR and $3,500 MSR with mammoth ivory grips (non-damascus). The Stainless USA/Germany model (last MSR in 2011 was $3,700), Puma Stainless (last MSR in 2011 was $3,700), and the 1911 Aluminum Frame is POR.

RIFLES: BOLT ACTION

Uselton offers a Warbird Mountain Lite bolt action rifle in 7.82 Warbird cal., with stainless steel long action and choice of Kevlar or laminate thumbhole stock. Prices begin at $3,899 MSR. Additionally, the Warbird is offered in a Tactical configuration with lightweight stock - prices begin at $5,400 MSR. Other configurations include the Stalker, Stealth, Predator, Raptor, and Warrior prices begin at $3,899 MSR. A variety of options are available. Please contact the company directly for more information, including pricing and delivery time (see Trademark Index).

RIFLES: SEMI-AUTO

Uselton offers a Black Widow AR in 5.56 NATO and 7.62 NATO cal., 16 in. barrel with Magpul CTR 6-position stock, adj. rear sights, quad rail, patented piston system, 6.1-7.2 lbs. $2,199 MSR.

UTAS

Current shotgun manufacturer located in Antalya, Turkey. Currently imported by UTAS-USA, located in Des Plaines, IL.

SHOTGUNS: SLIDE ACTION

UTAS manufactures the UTS 15 line of tactical style slide action 12 ga. shotguns. All shotguns are 7 shot with polymer receivers and integrated top mounted Picatinny rails. The UTS 15 has a matte black non-glare finish. The UTS 15 Hunting has a camo finish. The UTS 15 Marine has a blue camo patterned finish. Please contact the importer directly for more information, including pricing and available options (see Trademark Index).

UZI

Current trademark manufactured by Israel Weapon Industries (IWI, previously called Israel Military Industries) and Umarex Sportwaffen GmbH (.22 cal. pistols/rifles only). Semi-auto pistols are currently imported begining 2013 by IWI US, Inc., located in Harrisburg, PA. .22 cal. Uzi pistols and rifles are currently imported by Umarex USA, located in Fort Smith, AR. Uzi America, a partnership between IMI and Mossberg, is

GRADING - PPGS™	100%	98%	95%	90%	80%	70%	60%	LAST MSR

currently importing a 9mm Para. and .40 S&W cal. submachine gun carbine built on the mini-Uzi receiver for the law enforcement market. During 1996-1998, Mossberg imported the Uzi Eagle pistols. These models were imported by UZI America, Inc., subsidiary of O.F. Mossberg & Sons, Inc. Previously imported by Action Arms, Ltd., located in Philadelphia, PA until 1994.

Serial number prefixes used on Uzi Firearms are as follows: "SA" on all 9mm Para. semi-auto carbines Models A and B; "45 SA" on all .45 ACP Model B carbines; "41 SA" on all .41 AE Model B carbines; "MC" on all 9mm Para. (only cal. made) semi-auto mini-carbines; "UP" on 9mm Para. semi-auto Uzi pistols, except Eagle Series pistols; and "45 UP" on all .45 semi-auto Uzi pistols (disc. 1989). There are also prototypes or experimental Uzis with either "AA" or "AAL" prefixes - these are rare and will command premiums over values listed below.

CARBINES/RIFLES: SEMI-AUTO

CARBINE MODEL A – 9mm Para. cal., semi-auto, 16.1 in. barrel, parkerized finish, 25 shot mag., mfg. by IMI 1980-1983 and ser. range is SA01,001-SA037,000.

	$1,650	$1,475	$1,325	$1,125	$975	$875	$750	

Approx. 100 Model As were mfg. with a nickel finish. These are rare and command considerable premiums over values listed above.

CARBINE MODEL B – 9mm Para., .41 Action Express (new 1987), or .45 ACP (new 1987) cal., semi-auto carbine, 16.1 in. barrel, baked enamel black finish over phosphated (parkerized) base finish, 16 (.45 ACP), 20 (.41 AE) or 25 (9mm Para.) shot mag., metal folding stock, includes molded case and carrying sling, 8.4 lbs. Mfg. 1983 - until Federal legislation disc. importation 1989 and ser. range is SA037,001-SA073,544.

	$1,500	$1,325	$1,200	$1,000	$950	$850	$750	*$698*

Subtract approx. $150 for .41 AE or .45 ACP cal.
Add $150 for .22 LR cal. conversion kit (new 1987).
Add $215 for .45 ACP to 9mm Para./.41 AE conversion kit.
Add $150 for 9mm Para. to .41 AE (or vice-versa) conversion kit.
Add $215 for 9mm Para. to .45 ACP conversion kit.

MINI CARBINE – 9mm Para. cal., similar to Carbine except has 19 3/4 in. barrel, 20 shot mag., swing-away metal stock, scaled down version of the regular carbine, 7.2 lbs. New 1987. Federal legislation disc. importation 1989.

	$2,375	$2,175	$1,850	$1,600	$1,350	$1,150	$995	*$698*

UZI RIFLE – .22 LR cal., patterned after the Uzi Carbine Model B, 17.9 in. barrel with faux suppressor, blowback semi-auto action, features metal receiver, folding stock, traditional Uzi handguard, hidden Picatinny rail, adj. front and rear sights, grip safety, 10 or 20 shot mag., black finish, 7.7 lbs. Importation began 2012.

MSR $600	$510	$450	$385	$350	$275	$225	$180	

PISTOLS: SEMI-AUTO

UZI PISTOL – 9mm Para. or .45 ACP cal. (disc.), 4 1/2 in. barrel, parkerized finish, 10 (.45 ACP) or 20 (9mm Para.) shot mag., supplied with molded carrying case, sight adj. key and mag. loading tool, 3.8 lbs. Importation disc. 1993.

	$1,000	$875	$795	$750	$700	$650	$600	*$695*

Add $285 for .45 ACP to 9mm Para./.41 AE conversion kit.
Add $100 for 9mm Para. to .41 AE conversion kit.
Add approx. 30%-40% for two-line slide marking "45 ACP Model 45".

UZI .22 CAL. PISTOL – .22 LR cal., patterned after the Uzi centerfire pistol, blowback semi-auto action, 5 in. barrel with muzzle brake slots on top, black metal receiver, lower Picatinny rail, adj. sights, grip safety, 20 shot mag., 3.9 lbs. Importation began 2012.

MSR $480	$425	$375	$335	$300	$275	$250	$225	

GRADING - PPGS™	100%	98%	95%	90%	80%	70%	60%	LAST MSR

UZI EAGLE SERIES – 9mm Para., .40 S&W, or .45 ACP cal., semi-auto double action, various configurations, matte finish with black synthetic grips, 10 shot mag. Mfg. 1997-1998.

* ***Uzi Eagle Series Full-Size*** – 9mm Para. or .40 S&W cal., 4.4 in. barrel, steel construction, decocking feature, tritium night sights, polygonal rifling. Imported 1997-98.

	$485	$440	$400	$365	$335	$330	$275	*$535*

* ***Uzi Eagle Series Short Slide*** – 9mm Para., .40 S&W, or .45 ACP cal., similar to Full-Size Eagle, except has 3.7 in. barrel. Imported 1997-98.

	$485	$440	$400	$365	$335	$330	$275	*$535*

Add $31 for .45 ACP cal.

* ***Uzi Eagle Series Compact*** – 9mm Para. or .40 S&W cal., available in double action with decocking or double action only, 3 1/2 in. barrel. Imported 1997-98.

	$485	$440	$400	$365	$335	$330	$275	*$535*

* ***Uzi Eagle Series Polymer Compact*** – similar to Compact Eagle, except has compact polymer frame. Imported 1997-98.

	$485	$440	$400	$365	$335	$330	$275	*$535*

UZI PRO PISTOL – 9mm Para cal., blowback action, closed bolt, 4 1/2 in. mil-spec cold hammer forged CrMoV barrel, matte black finish, includes 20 and 25 shot mag., polymer pistol grip lower, firing pin block, thumb operated manual safety, approx. 3 2/3 lbs. Importation began 2013.

MSR $1,099	$950	$825	$700	$600	$500	$400	$375	

NOTES

V SECTION

VM HY-TECH LLC

Previous rifle manufacturer located in Phoenix, AZ.

GRADING - PPGS™	100%	98%	95%	90%	80%	70%	60%	LAST MSR

RIFLES

VM15 – .223 Rem. or 9mm Para. cal., AR-15 style, semi-auto, unique side charging on left side of receiver operated by folding lever allowing easy replacement of scopes, 16, 20, or 24 in. fluted and ported Wilson barrel, aluminum free-floating hand guard, forged lower receiver, A-2 style buttstock with pistol grip, black finish. Mfg. 2002-2009.

	100%	98%	95%	90%	80%	70%	60%	LAST MSR
	$800	$750	$675	$600	$550	$500	$400	*$865*

Add $34 for side-charging loading (new 2005).
Add $310 for 9mm Para. cal.

VM-50 – .50 BMG cal., single shot, 18, 22, 30, or 36 in. Lothar Walther barrel with muzzle brake, aluminum stock, includes bipod, black finish, 22-29 lbs. Mfg. 2004-2009.

	100%	98%	95%	90%	80%	70%	60%	LAST MSR
	$2,299	$2,000	$1,775	$1,600	$1,475	$1,350	$1,225	*$2,299*

Add $40 - $120 for 22-36 in. barrel.

VO VAPEN AB

Current rifle manufacturer established in 1977 and located in Fjalkinge, Sweden. No current U.S. importation.

VO Vapen AB is a small family company founded by Master Gunsmith Viggo Olsson that manufactures hand made hunting rifles utilizing a patented takedown system allowing interchangeable barrels. Please contact the company directly for more information, U.S. availability, and current pricing (see Trademark Index).

VAIL, ROY

Previous custom shotgun and rifle maker located in Warwick, NY circa 1950s - early 1970s.

Roy Vail was a top quality custom gunmaker who manufactured approx. 150 custom shotguns and 200 custom rifles. Francotte actions were typically used on his SxSs, and he would add the wood, engraving inlays, and checkering. Secondary values are difficult to establish, and each gun must be evaluated individually for its overall desirability factor, which includes configuration, condition, embellishments, and quality of wood and checkering.

VALKYRIE ARMS LTD.

Current manufacturer located in Olympia, WA. Dealer sales.

Valkyrie Arms Ltd. manufactures semi-auto copies of the M3A1 and DeLisle Commando Carbine. Models include: M3-A1 SA Grease Gun, Delisle Commando Carbine, DeLisle 2000, and the Sten MKII/MKIII pistol and carbine. Custom suppressors are made to order. Currently, Valkyrie Arms is only accepting orders for the Delisle Commando Carbine.

Previously, Valkyrie Arms manufactured the Browning M1919-SA and the DeLisle Sporter Carbine. For more information, including availability and pricing, please contact the company directly (see Trademark Index).

VALMET

Previous trademark manufactured in Finland. Previously imported 2004-2005 by Tristar, located in N. Kansas City, MO.

VALMET, INC.

Previous manufacturer located in Jyvaskyla, Finland. Previously imported by Stoeger Industries, Inc. located in South Hackensack, NJ.

The Valmet line was discontinued in 1989 and replaced by Tikka (please refer to the Tikka section in this text) in 1990.

GRADING - PPGS™	100%	98%	95%	90%	80%	70%	60%	LAST MSR

RIFLES: SEMI-AUTO

Magazines for the following models are a major consideration when purchasing a Valmet semi-auto rifle, and prices can run anywhere from $85 (.223 Rem.) up to $250 (.308 Win.). Model 76 .308 mags. will function in a Model 78, but not vice versa.

HUNTER MODEL – .223 Rem., .243 Win., .30-06 (scarce) or .308 Win. cal., gas operated semi-auto, Kalashnikov action, 20 1/2 in. barrel, checkered walnut stock and forearm, matte finished metal, 5, 9, or 20 shot mag., 8 lbs. New 1986, Federal legislation disc. importation 1989.

	100%	98%	95%	90%	80%	70%	60%	LAST MSR
	$895	$795	$700	$625	$550	$500	$450	*$795*

M-62S TACTICAL DESIGN RIFLE – 7.62x39 Russian, semi-auto version of Finnish M-62, 15 or 30 shot mag., 16 5/8 in. barrel, gas operated, rotary bolt, adj. rear sight, tube steel or wood stock. Mfg. 1962-disc.

	100%	98%	95%	90%	80%	70%	60%	LAST MSR
	$2,500	$2,250	$1,750	$1,500	$1,250	$1,000	$900	

Add approx. $200 for tube stock.

M-71S – similar to M-62S, except .223 Rem. cal., stamped metal receiver, reinforced resin or wood stock.

	100%	98%	95%	90%	80%	70%	60%	LAST MSR
	$1,650	$1,450	$1,325	$1,175	$975	$875	$775	

MODEL 76 – .223 Rem., 7.62x39mm, or .308 Win. cal., gas operated semi-auto tactical design rifle, 16 3/4 in. or 20 1/2 (.308 only) in. barrel, 15 or 30 (7.62x39mm only) shot mag., parkerized finish. Federal legislation disc. importation 1989.

	100%	98%	95%	90%	80%	70%	60%	LAST MSR
Plastic Stock	$1,500	$1,250	$1,100	$900	$800	$700	$600	
Wood Stock	$1,700	$1,300	$1,100	$900	$800	$700	$600	*$740*

Add approx. 10% for folding stock.
Add 100% for 7.62x39mm cal. with wood stock.
Add 20% for wood stock in .308 Win. cal.

MODEL 78 – .223 Rem., 7.62x39mm, or .308 Win. cal., similar to Model 76, except has 24 1/2 in. barrel, wood stock and forearm, and barrel bipod, 11 lbs. New 1987. Federal legislation disc. importation 1989.

	100%	98%	95%	90%	80%	70%	60%	LAST MSR
	$1,750	$1,525	$1,375	$1,175	$950	$825	$700	*$1,060*

Add 10% for 7.62x39mm cal.

MODEL 82 BULLPUP – .223 Rem. cal., limited importation.

	100%	98%	95%	90%	80%	70%	60%	LAST MSR
	$1,675	$1,425	$1,200	$995	$775	$650	$525	

SHOTGUNS/RIFLES: O/U

LION MODEL – 12 ga., 26, 28, or 30 in. barrels, various chokes, boxlock, SST, checkered stock. Mfg. 1947-68.

	100%	98%	95%	90%	80%	70%	60%	LAST MSR
	$415	$370	$340	$320	$305	$275	$240	

MODEL 412 O/U SHOOTING SYSTEM – interchangeable barrel assemblies permit a double rifle, shotgun/rifle, and O/U shotgun configuration, user-installed interchangeable barrels, monobloc locking, rifle barrel positioning by adjustment, SST, extractors or ejectors, checkered walnut stock and forend, cocking indicators, blue finish. Importation on all models was disc. 1989.

Add $100 for synthetic stock on all 412 models.

* ***Model 412S O/U Shooting System Field Grade*** – 12 ga. was standard, auto ejectors, screw-in choke tubes, matte nickel finish. Imported 1986-89.

	100%	98%	95%	90%	80%	70%	60%	LAST MSR
	$855	$670	$580	$540	$475	$440	$400	*$999*

Add 15% for 20 ga.

* ***Model 412S O/U Shooting System Field and Target*** – 12 ga. only, 2 3/4 and 3 in. chambers, ejectors. Disc. 1988.

	100%	98%	95%	90%	80%	70%	60%	LAST MSR
	$775	$660	$580	$540	$475	$440	$400	*$874*

GRADING - PPGS™	100%	98%	95%	90%	80%	70%	60%	LAST MSR

* ***Model 412ST O/U Shooting System Trap and Skeet*** – 12 ga., Monte Carlo stock on Trap model, 28 in. barrels on Skeet model, screw-in chokes standard.

	$1,040	$875	$695	$650	$580	$540	$475	*$1,215*

* ***Model 412ST O/U Shooting System Premium Grade Target*** – similar to Model 412ST Trap and Skeet, except has better walnut and checkering. Imported 1987-89.

	$1,355	$1,050	$865	$750	$640	$580	$515	*$1,550*

* ***Model 412S O/U Shooting System Combination Gun*** – combination, 12 ga, 3 in. chamber over choice of .222 Rem., .223 Rem., .243 Win., .30-06, or .308 Win. cal., extractors.

	$1,025	$850	$675	$600	$550	$475	$440	*$1,615*

* ***Model 412S O/U Shooting System Double Rifle*** – .243 Win. (disc. 1987), .30-06, .308 Win. (disc. 1987), .375 H&H Mag. (disc. 1987), or 9.3x73R cal., extractors, 24 in. barrels.

	$1,060	$895	$725	$650	$580	$540	$475	*$1,275*

Add $100 for 9.3x74R cal. or .375 H&H Mag. cal.

This model in .30-06 cal. has extractors only while in 9.3x74R cal. ejectors are standard.

* ***Model 412K O/U Shooting System Double Rifle*** – .30-06 or .308 Win. cal. only, 24 in. separated barrels, extractors. Importation disc. 1986.

	$800	$660	$580	$540	$475	$440	$400	*$899*

* ***Model 412 O/U Shooting System Engraved*** – satin finish, receiver extensively bank note engraved in choice of 4 patterns, select Triple-X wood hand-checkered - choice of field or target, available in any Valmet model.

This model had limited availability and prices were on request from the manufacturer.

* ***Model 412 O/U Shooting System Extra Barrel Assemblies*** – $505-$605 each for shotgun (includes screw-in chokes), $579 each for shotgun/rifle combo, $660 each for double rifle (add $100 for ejectors).

VALOR ARMS

Current rifle manufacturer located in Akron, OH circa 1997.

CARBINES: SEMI-AUTO

OVR-16 – various cals. including 5.56 NATO and 6.5 Grendel, AR-15 style, 16.1 in. barrel, 30 shot mag., black Valorite coated stainless steel, single stage match trigger, six or eight (includes ambi-sling adapter) position adj. stock, rifle length forearm, free floating quad rail standard, flat top receiver with Picatinny rail continuing into quad rail, ergonomic soft rubber grip with battery storage, with or w/o sight package, approx. 8 lbs.

Base price on this model starts at $2,350.

Add $200 for iron sight package.

Add $300 for .264 LBC-AR cal.

Add $700 for Designated Marksmen Rifle (DMR).

VALTRO

Current trademark established during 1988 manufactured by Italian Arms and located in Collebeato, Brescia, Italy. Currenly imported by Valtro USA, located in Hayward, CA. Previously located in San Rafael, CA.

Valtro manufactures both excellent quality slide action and semi-auto shotguns, in addition to a very high quality semi-auto pistol, and a variety of signal pistols. Currently Valtro USA is importing only semi-auto pistols. Please contact them directly for more information and availability (see Trademark Index listing).

PISTOLS: SEMI-AUTO

1998 A1 .45 ACP – .45 ACP cal., forged National Match frame and slide, 5 in. barrel, deluxe wood grips, 8 shot mag., ambidextrous safety, blue finish, flat checkered mainspring housing, front and rear slide serrations, beveled mag. well, speed trigger, 40 oz., lifetime guarantee. Very limited importation.

	$5,500	$5,200	$4,950	$4,650	$4,250	$3,850	$3,500	

GRADING - PPGS™	100%	98%	95%	90%	80%	70%	60%	LAST MSR

SHOTGUNS: SLIDE ACTION

TACTICAL 98 SHOTGUN – 12 ga. only, 18 1/2 or 20 in. barrel featuring MMC ghost ring sights and integral muzzle brake, 5 shot mag., internal chokes, receiver sidesaddle holds 6 exposed rounds, pistol grip or standard stock, matte black finish, lightweight. Imported 1998 - disc.

	$790	$630	$525	$475	$425	$400	$360	

PM5 – 12 ga., 20 in. barrel, 7 shot mag., black synthetic stock with matte black finish, available with or w/o ghost ring sights, optional folding stock. Limited importation.

	$995	$900	$800	$725	$650	$575	$500	

VAN DYKE RIFLE DESIGNS

Current rifle manufacturer located in Plainville, KS.

RIFLES: BOLT ACTION

Van Dyke Rifle Designs manufactures bolt action rifles in a variety of configurations, with many options available. Prices listed represent base rifles w/o optics or available options. Please contact the company directly for more information on the variety of available options for each rifle, as well as custom made rifles (see Trademark Index).

DECISION MAKER – .308 Win. cal., 25 in. Shilen stainless steel match grade barrel, teflon coated Earth Tan desert camo finish, A-4 McMillan tactical stock with saddle cheekpiece, three baffle muzzle brake.

MSR $3,425	$3,085	$2,700	$2,315	$2,095	$1,695	$1,395	$1,075

TACTICAL ELIMINATOR SUPER MAGNUM – .338 Lapua cal., Shilen match grade barrel, advanced muzzle brake, designed for extreme distance, wide variety of options available.

Base price on this model is POR.

M24 SUPER MAGNUM – .338 Lapua cal., 28 1/2 or 30 in. Shilen stainless steel free floating barrel, custom chamber dimension, aluminum bedding block, many options available, including rail systems, optics, muzzle brakes, trigger types and stock.

Base price on this model is POR.

REAPER CUSTOM SNIPER – various cals., Shilen stainless steel barrel, Reaper stock design includes aluminum bedding block, three-way adj. buttpad, adj. cheekpiece, long or short action, various options available.

MSR $3,495	$3,150	$2,750	$2,350	$2,150	$1,725	$1,425	$1,100

AI TACTICAL ELIMINATOR I/II – .308 Win. cal., Rem. 700 short action, 22 (Eliminator I) or 24 (Eliminator II) in. Shilen stainless steel match barrel, black matte Teflon finish, multibaffled muzzle brake, Accuracy International stock with adj. cheekpiece and adj. LOP, 5 or 10 shot mag., five sling attachments.

MSR $3,725	$3,360	$2,950	$2,525	$2,285	$1,850	$1,525	$1,175

Subtract $30 for Eliminator II.

* ***AI Tactical Eliminator III*** – similar to Eliminator I & II, except has Rem. long action, Magnum calibers, longer barrel length.

MSR $3,775	$3,400	$2,975	$2,550	$2,325	$1,875	$1,525	$1,195

DISTANCE DOMINATOR I/II – various cals., Rem. 700 long action, 26 in. Shilen stainless steel barrel (I) or match grade barrel with heavy varmint benchrest contour (II), muzzle brake, H-S Precision heavy Kevlar tactical stock, adj. LOP, variety of options, including floorplate, detachable box mag., and optics.

MSR $3,580	$3,225	$2,820	$2,425	$2,200	$1,775	$1,450	$1,125

Subtract $90 for Distance Dominator II.

RANGEMASTER SERIES – various cals., designed for long range target shooting.

* ***Rangemaster I*** – M70 short action, controlled round push feed, Shilen stainless steel match grade free floating barrel, glass pillar bedded A4 McMillan tactical stock, adj. cheekpiece, adj. spacer system, sling swivels, deep forend, various finishes.

MSR $3,450	$3,100	$2,710	$2,325	$2,125	$1,700	$1,400	$1,075

GRADING - PPGS™	100%	98%	95%	90%	80%	70%	60%	LAST MSR

* ***Rangemaster II*** – M70 short action, controlled round push feed, 24 in. Shilen stainless steel match grade heavy varmint barrel, stainless bead blast natural texture finish, muzzle brake, A2 McMillan tactical stock, vertical pistol grip, extra high comb, tapered forend, adj. cheekpiece, various finish and available optics.

MSR $3,475 $3,125 $2,735 $2,350 $2,125 $1,725 $1,400 $1,100

* ***Rangemaster III*** – Rem. 700 long action, 26 in. Shilen stainless steel match grade light varmint benchrest contour barrel, triple baffle muzzle brake, bead blast natural stainless color with Teflon silver matte finish, box mag., A3 McMillan lightweight tactical stock, adj. cheekpiece, adj. spacer system, vertical pistol grip, various options available.

MSR $3,375 $3,050 $2,675 $2,285 $2,075 $1,675 $1,375 $1,075

* ***Rangemaster IV*** – similar to Rangemaster III, 30 in. Shilen stainless steel barrel, A5 McMillan tactical stock, wider beavertail forend, adj. cheekpiece, Teflon OD green finish, double baffle semi-box muzzle brake, box mag., various options available.

MSR $3,575 $3,225 $2,825 $2,425 $2,200 $1,775 $1,450 $1,125

AMERICAN HUNTER – various cals., Rem. 700 short action, Shilen stainless steel match grade barrel, glass pillar bedding, custom Gel Coat McMillan stock, beavertail forend, three attachment studs, blind box mag., various options, including optics.

MSR $3,115 $2,800 $2,450 $2,100 $1,900 $1,550 $1,250 $980

CRITTER GITTER – .22-250 Rem. cal., Rem. 700 short action, 24 in. Shilen stainless steel light varmint benchrest barrel, based on the Anschütz Silhouette design, green and tan camo finish, aluminum bedding block H-S Precision stock, Pachmayr Decelerator pad, blind box mag., various optic options available.

MSR $2,850 $2,565 $2,250 $1,925 $1,750 $1,425 $1,150 $900

DISINTEGRATOR – various varmint cals., Rem. 700 short action, based on the Anschütz Silhouette design, 26 in. stainless steel light varmint match grade barrel, Teflon black matte finish, H-S Precision black/grey web stock, double baffle muzzle brake, blind mag., two sling swivels, various options and optics available.

MSR $2,795 $2,525 $2,225 $1,900 $1,725 $1,395 $1,125 $885

SAFARI EXPRESS – dangerous game cals., custom designed, Pachmayr Decelerator pad, engraving, various options available.

MSR $3,450 $3,100 $2,725 $2,325 $2,125 $1,700 $1,400 $1,085

LONG RANGE HUNTER – various cals., Rem. 700 long action, 26 in. Shilen stainless steel sporter weight barrel, McMillan BDL style stock, Magna Port muzzle brake, bolt sleeved, glass pillar bedded, various optical options.

MSR $3,095 $2,785 $2,435 $2,100 $1,895 $1,525 $1,250 $975

VARMINT VINDICATOR – various cals., Rem. 700 short action, single shot, heavy fill solid glass McMillan stock, 26 in. Shilen benchrest barrel, various options.

MSR $3,095 $2,785 $2,435 $2,100 $1,895 $1,525 $1,250 $975

VARBERGER

Previous rifle manufacturer located in Varberg, Sweden. Previously imported by Hill Country Wholesale, Inc. located in Austin, TX, and distributed by Paul & Associates, located in Wellsville, KS until late 1995.

VARBERGER PRECISION PRODUCTS AB

RIFLES: BOLT ACTION

MODEL 711 GRADE 1 – available in 19 cals. between .22 PPC and .358 Norma, bolt action design featuring specially designed and manufactured receiver, rotary mag., 6 lug engine-turned bolt, and stock featuring metal retainer plate, individually test-fired. Imported 1994-98.

$950 $850 $750 $650 $550 $450 $375 ***$1,080***

GRADING - PPGS™	100%	98%	95%	90%	80%	70%	60%	LAST MSR

MODEL 717 GRADE 1 MAGNUM – available in 11 Mag. cals. between .257 Wby. Mag. and .375 H&H. Imported 1994-98.

$980	$875	$765	$650	$550	$450	$375	*$1,130*

MODEL 757 GRADE 2 DELUXE – deluxe variation of the Model 711. Imported 1994-98.

$1,775	$1,500	$1,250	$995	$895	$795	$695	*$2,035*

Add $45 for Mag. cals.

MODEL 77 GRADE 3 PREMIER – top-of-the-line model. Imported 1994-98.

$1,995	$1,675	$1,350	$1,050	$925	$795	$695	*$2,375*

Add $65 for Mag. cals.

VARNER SPORTING ARMS, INC.

Previous manufacturer located in Marietta, GA circa 1988-1989.

RIFLES: SINGLE SHOT

VARNER FAVORITE HUNTER – .22 LR cal., patterned after J. Stevens Favorite Model, 1/2 round - 1/2 octagon 21 1/2 in. takedown barrel, blue frame, walnut stock and forearm, aperture rear sight, 5 lbs. Mfg. 1988-89.

$325	$270	$220	$185	$150	$130	$110	*$369*

* ***Varner Favorite Hunter Deluxe*** – similar to Favorite Hunter, except has case colored frame and lever, and deluxe walnut stock and forearm. Mfg. 1988-89.

$450	$375	$285	$225	$175	$150	$135	*$500*

* ***Varner Favorite Hunter Presentation Grade*** – includes target hammer and trigger, AAA quality checkered stock and forearm, includes takedown case. Mfg. 1988-1989.

$480	$400	$310	$250	$195	$170	$155	*$569*

PRESENTATION ENGRAVED – previously available in a No. 1 Grade for $649, a No. 2 for $779, or a No. 3 for $1,099.

VATAN HUNTING FIREARMS COMPANY

Previous manufacturer from 1965-circa 2012 and located in Konya, Turkey.

Vatan manufactured good quality O/U, SxS, semi-auto, slide action, and single barrel rifles under their trademark name Egemen. Additionally, Vatan manufactured a line of blank pistols and airguns. These guns were not imported into the U.S. in any sizeable quantity.

VECTOR ARMS, INC.

Current tactical rifle, pistol, and parts manufacturer located in N. Salt Lake, UT.

PISTOLS: SEMI-AUTO

Currently, Vector Arms is offering Uzi pistols with stainless, painted, or parkerized finish in .22 LR, 9mm Para. or .45 ACP cal., along with a 5 year warranty. Please contact the company directly for more information on these pistols, including availability and options (see Trademark Index).

RIFLES: SEMI-AUTO

Currently, Vector is offering AK-47 style and Uzi SBR rifles, including a wide variety of parts, accessories and ammunition. Please contact the company directly for more information on these rifles, including availability and options (see Trademark Index).

Until 2009, Vector Arms offered the following semi-auto tactical style rifles: V-53 (semi-auto version of the HK53 - $1,350 last MSR), V51 (semi-auto version of the HK-91, $1,024 last MSR). Vector also offered the V-93 (semi-auto version of the HK33 - $1,104 last MSR), Uzi full size post-ban ($595 last MSR), and the RPD (drum or belt fed - $1,999 last MSR).

VEGA

Current rifle and shotgun manufacturer located in Istanbul, Turkey. Shotguns are currently imported by Task Firearms, located in Miami, FL. Previously imported by Adco Sales, located in Woburn, MA.

GRADING - PPGS™	100%	98%	95%	90%	80%	70%	60%	LAST MSR

Vega manufactures private label Diamond shotguns that are currently imported into the U.S. Additionally, Vega offers a complete line of SxS shotguns (current models include the H12, H14, H16, H410, and the Coach Gun), O/U shotguns (current models include: De Luxe, S10, S20, S30, S40, S50, S28, S410), as well as semi-auto shotguns (current models include: D-2170, D-2171, Camo, FD-2170, D-1371, D-1171, S-Camo, F-1010, and the FF-1010), and slide action shotguns (current models include: PW-1001, PS-1001, and the FP-1001).

Vega also manufactures bolt action and single barrel rifles. Current models include: BA-1002, SB-1003, SB-1004, and the SB-410.

These models have had little or no recent importation into the U.S.

Please contact the importer directly for more information, including current models, pricing and availability (see Trademark Index).

VEKTOR

Current trademark established during 1953 as part of LEW (Lyttelton Engineering Work). In 1995, Vektor became a separate division of Denel of South Africa.

Vektor has manufactured a wide variety of firearms configurations, including semi-auto pistols, bolt action and slide action rifles, as well as military arms for South African law enforcement for quite some time. Currently, the company does not make any civilian small arms.

PISTOLS: SEMI-AUTO

All Vektor pistols feature polygonal rifling, excluding the Z88.

MODEL CP1 – 9mm Para. cal., 4 in. barrel, compact model with unique aesthetics and ergonomic design allowing no buttons or levers on exterior surfaces, hammerless, striker firing system, black or nickel finished slide, 10 shot mag., approx. 25 1/2 oz. Imported 1999-2000.

$440	$400	$360	$330	$300	$280	$260	*$480*

Add $20 for nickel slide finish.

This model was recalled due to design problems.

MODEL Z88 – 9mm Para. cal., double action, patterned after the M92 Beretta, 5 in. barrel, steel construction, black synthetic grips, 10 shot mag., 35 oz. Importation began 1999.

$550	$495	$450	$400	$360	$330	$295	*$620*

MODEL SP1 – 9mm Para. cal., double action, 5 in. barrel with polygonal rifling, wraparound checkered synthetic grips, matte blue or normal black finish, 2.2. lbs. Importation began 1999.

$535	$485	$445	$395	$360	$330	$295	*$600*

Add $30 for natural anodized or nickel finish.
Add $230 for Sport Pistol with compensated barrel.

* ***Model SP1 Compact (General's Model)*** – similar to Model SP1, except is compact variation with 4 in. barrel, 25.4 oz. Importation began 1999.

$575	$510	$460	$410	$360	$330	$295	*$650*

* ***Model SP1 Sport Pistol/Tuned*** – similar to Model SP1, except is available with tuned action or target pistol features. Importation began 1999.

$1,050	$900	$775	$650	$525	$400	$350	*$1,200*

Add $100 for Target Pistol with dual color finish.

MODEL SP2 – .40 S&W cal., otherwise similar to Model SP1. Importation began in 1999.

$575	$510	$460	$410	$360	$330	$295	*$650*

Add $190 for 9mm Para. conversion kit.

* ***Model SP2 Compact (General's Model)*** – similar to Model SP2, except is compact variation. Importation began 1999.

$575	$510	$460	$410	$360	$330	$295	*$650*

GRADING - PPGS™	100%	98%	95%	90%	80%	70%	60%	LAST MSR

* ***Model SP2 Competition*** – competition variation of the Model SP2 featuring 5 7/8 in. barrel, additional magazine guide, enlarged safety levers and mag. catch, and straight trigger, 35 oz. Importation began 2000.

	$850	$775	$675	$575	$510	$460	$395	*$1,000*

STOCK GUN – 9mm Para. cal., normal black finish. Importation began 2000.

	$850	$775	$675	$575	$510	$460	$395	*$1,000*

ULTRA MODEL – 9mm Para. or .40 S&W (new 2000) cal., top-of-the-line double action with most performance features, optional Lynx (disc. 1999) or Tasco (new 2000) scope. Importation began 1999.

	$1,950	$1,700	$1,500	$1,300	$1,100	$900	$700	*$2,150*

Subtract $150 if w/o Tasco scope.

RIFLES: BOLT-ACTION

K98 – standard cals are .243 Win., .270 Win., .30-06, .308 Win., 7x57mm Mauser, 7x64 Bren., Mag. cals. include .300 Win. Mag., .300 H&H, .416 Rigby, .470 Capstick, .458 Win. Mag., or 9.3x62mm, 5 shot staggered mag., non-rotating long extractor, positive bolt stop, checkered walnut stock, hammer forged barrel, iron sights on Mag. cals. only. Imported 2000-disc.

	$995	$850	$775	$675	$575	$510	$460	*$1,149*

Add $100 for Mag. cals.

RIFLES: SLIDE ACTION

H5 – .223 Rem. cal., 18 or 22 in. barrel, rotating bolt, uncheckered forearm and thumb-hole stock with pad, includes 4X scope with long eye relief, 9 lbs., 7 oz.-10 1/4 lbs. Imported 2000-disc.

	$775	$650	$575	$510	$460	$410	$350	*$850*

VEPR

Current trademark manufactured by Molot JSC (Vyatskie Polyany Machine Building Factory) located in Russia. Currently imported by ZDF Import/Export, Inc., located in Salt Lake City, UT. Previously imported during 2004 by European American Armory, located in Sharps, FL.

RIFLES: SEMI-AUTO

VEPR HUNTER (VEPR II) CARBINE/RIFLE – .223 Rem., .270 Win. (new 2004), .30-06 (new 2004), .308 Win., or 7.62x39mm (new 2001) cal., features Vepr.'s semi-auto action, 16 (.223 Rem. or 7.62x39mm cal.), 20 1/2 (carbine, .308 Win. only, disc.), 21.6 or 23 1/4 (disc.) in. barrel with adj. rear sight, scope mount rail built into receiver top, standard or optional thumbhole checkered walnut stock with recoil pad and forend, paddle mag. release, 5 or 10 shot mag., approx 8.6 lbs.

MSR $550	$550	$495	$440	$395	$365	$335	$300	

SUPER VEPR – .308 Win. cal., thumbhole stock. Limited importation 2001-2007.

	$950	$850	$750	$650	$550	$475	$400	

SHOTGUNS: SEMI-AUTO

VEPR 12 – 12 ga., AK-47 design, various configurations and barrel lengths, two lever safety, folding tube stock with recoil pad, pistol grip, 8 shot mag, approx. 8 1/2 lbs. New 2011.

As this edition went to press, U.S. pricing had yet to be established on this model.

VERNEY-CARRON

Current manufacturer of shotguns and rifles established during 1820, and located in St. Etienne, France. Currently imported by Kebco LLC, located in Hanover, PA. Previously imported until 2008 by Verney-Carron USA, Inc., located in Clay Center, KS. Previously distributed until 2002 by the Graystone Group, located in Chicago, IL. Previously imported by Yellow Brick Enterprises, located in Clay Center, KS during 1998 only.

VERNEY-CARRON HISTORY

The company was established during 1820 by Claude Verney-Carron, whose ancestors were "Faiseur de fusils" - gunmakers since at least 1650. Verney-Carron is proud to reflect on six generations of family ownership, and is the largest French manufacturer of hunting shotguns and rifles. Please contact the manufacturer directly for more information, including current model availability and domestic pricing regarding these fine firearms (see Trademark Index).

In 2000, Verney-Carron SA and Y.B.E., Inc. located in Clay Center, KS (distributor of Hastings barrels & choke tubes) established a joint venture, Verney-Carron USA, Inc., located in Clay Center, KS. This joint venture purchased Sporting Arms Manufacturing, Inc., the manufacturer of the Snake Charmer II shotgun. During 2001, Sporting Arms Manufacturing was dissolved, and the Snake Charmer II is now manufactured by Verney-Carron USA, Inc. Please refer to the separate Snake Charmer listing.

In 2002, Verney-Carron SA and Club Interchasse SAS established another joint venture, Ligne Verney-Carron SAS, located in Bourges, France to develop and sell hunting clothes and accessories.

In 2004, Verney-Carron SA purchased 100% of Ets. Demas SAS (please refer to the seperate Demas listing) maker of fine handcrafted shotguns and double rifles (SxS or O/U).

During December, 2008, Verney-Carron legally absorbed its subsidiary and moved its facility to the Verney-Carron factory. The custom workshop is now known as L'Atelier Verney-Carron.

RIFLES

All values listed are base MSRs only, and do not take into consideration any special orders, features, or additional engraving. Recent models include the Azur XA SxS double rifle ($9,400), Azur XB SxS double rifle ($12,360), Azur XC SxS double rifle ($15,600), Azur Eloge SxS double rifle ($20,870), Azur Eloge FC SxS double rifle ($23,625), Azur Damascus SxS double rifle ($27,040), Azur Legend SxS double rifle ($41,560), Azur Legend Single Shot rifle ($39,990), Azur PH SxS Safari double rifle with round body ($13,135), Azur PH SxS Safari double rifle with ejectors ($14,445), Azur Imperial SxS Safari double rifle ($23,640), Azur STD SxS Safari double rifle ($12,669), Azur Luxe SxS Safari double rifle ($18,030), Azur Elog SxS Safari double rifle ($27,840), SX O/U double rifle ($9,250), SX Passion O/U double rifle ($9,890), SX Prodige O/U double rifle ($13,080), SX Eloge FC O/U double rifle ($21,800), SX Eloge Elogance ($23,640), Sagittaire O/U (with or w/o sideplates, not imported), the Impact Plus bolt action with vent. quarter rib, front and rear sight ($2,100 last MSR), Impact Plus take-down ($2,700 last MSR), AD110 combination gun (20 ga./.300 Win. mag., $7,650 last MSR), as well as the semi-auto Impact NT Rifle (approx. $1,600 last MSR). All of these rifles are currently equipped for the easy mounting of an Optimum Infallible sight system.

SHOTGUNS

Verney-Carron makes a wide variety of shotgun models and configurations. All values listed are base MSRs only, and do not take into consideration any special orders, features, or additional engraving. Current SxS models include: Azur Legend double shotgun ($40,170), Azur AD210 shotgun ($9,575), Azur AD230 ($11,960), Azur Absolu ($14,410), Azur Eloge ($20,200), and the Azur Eloge FC ($23,875). O/U models include SL 1040 ($8,520), SL 1050 ($12,175), SL Eloge ($20,805), and the SL 1060 ($23,640). Recent models have included the "Sagittaire Model" (last MSR $3,400), Azur Eloge (.410 bore, base price starts around $9,000), Super 9 O/U (with or w/o sideplates, many options are available, base price was $3,300), Sagittaire O/U ($1,235 last MSR), V12 semi-auto (not imported), 1050 Atelier ($8,576 last MSR), Sagittaire Polynox O/U 12 ga. Mag. ($1,935 last MSR), Sagittaire Hastings 20 ga. O/U ($1,700 last MSR), and the J.E.T. SxS (not imported).

VERONA

Previous trademark of shotguns manufactured by F.A.I.R., Fausti, and Pietta, located in Brescia, Italy. Previously imported 2009-2011 by Legacy Sports International, located in Reno, NV. Previously imported until late 2005 by B.C. Outdoors, located in Boulder City, NV.

GRADING - PPGS™	100%	98%	95%	90%	80%	70%	60%	LAST MSR

COMBINATION GUNS

LX1001 EXPRESS COMBO – .223 Rem., .243 Win., .270 Win., .30-06. or .308 Win. over 20 ga., 2 3/4 in. chambers, 26 in. barrels, vent. rib, ejectors, sling swivel, checkered oil finished walnut stock with Bavarian cheekpiece, includes screw chokes, leather canvas hard case, approx. 6 lbs.

	$2,250	$1,900	$1,500	$1,200	$975	$875	$800	$2,583

SHOTGUNS: O/U

501 SERIES (LX501 HUNTING MODEL) – 12, 20, 28 ga. or .410 bore, 2 3/4 (28 ga.) or 3 in. chambers, 28 in. barrels with five choke tubes, gold plated SST, ejectors, blue steel (disc. 2005) or nickel receiver with light engraving and gold inlays, checkered oil finished pistol grip walnut stock, fiber optic front sight, vent. black rubber recoil pad, 6-7 lbs. Mfg. by F.A.I.R. Importation disc. 2010.

	$1,125	$950	$775	$675	$575	$475	$400	$1,299

* ***501 Series Two Barrel Set*** – includes 20 and 28 ga., 28 in. monobloc barrels with choke tubes, standard nickel receiver with light engraving and gold bird inlays, gold SST, oil finished checkered pistol grip stock and rounded forend, bottom locking bolt system, lengthened forcing cones, mfg. by Fausti. Importation began 2009.

MSR $3,242	$2,950	$2,750	$2,500	$1,995	$1,500	$995	$750	

* ***LX501 Hunting Model Two Barrel Set*** – includes choice of 20 and 28 ga., or 28 ga. and .410 bore, 28 in. barrels. Imported 2002-2005.

	$1,200	$1,050	$900	$815	$660	$540	$420	$1,379

LX680 SERIES – 12 or 20 ga., 2 3/4 or 3 in. chambers, available in Sporting or Trap configuration, 29, 30, 32, or 34 in. ported or unported barrels, Interchokes, available in Sporting Clays, Skeet, or Competition Trap configurations, gold SST, silver alloy receiver with light engraving, vent. rib, adj. comb, 6 1/4-8 lbs.

	$925	$810	$695	$630	$510	$415	$325	$1,043

Add $468 for Gold Trap configuration.
Add $1,222 for Gold Trap combo.

LX692 SERIES – 12, 20, 28 ga. or .410 bore, 2 3/4 (28 ga.) or 3 in. chambers, available in Skeet, Sporting, or Trap configuration, 28 in. barrels, gold plated SST, ejectors, steel receiver with engraved sideplates and gold bird inlays, oil finished hand-checkered walnut stock and Schnabel forend, black rubber recoil pad, 6-7 lbs.

	$925	$810	$695	$630	$510	$415	$325	$1,043

Add $468 for Gold Trap configuration.
Add $1,222 for Gold Trap combo.

702 SERIES (LX702) – 12, 20, 28 ga., or .410 bore, 3 in. chambers, 28 in. barrels with 5 choke tubes, hand-rubbed Turkish (disc.) or oil finished checkered (new 2009) walnut stock and forend, color case hardened (disc.) or nickel finish receiver, engraving with gold inlaid bird hunting scenes, vent. rubber recoil pad, fiber optic front sight, gold ST, 6-7 lbs. Mfg. by F.A.I.R. Importation disc. 2010.

	$1,200	$1,000	$800	$675	$575	$475	$400	$1,399

LX980 SERIES – 12 ga., 2 3/4 in. chambers, available in Trap, Skeet or Sporting configuration, 30 or 32 in. ported barrels, oil finished Montecarlo Turkish walnut stock and forend with adj. comb, color case hardened receiver, wide competition rib, removable competition trigger assembly, includes deluxe case, 7 1/2 lbs.

	$3,150	$2,700	$2,325	$2,000	$1,650	$1,325	$1,175	$3,527

Add $249 for Gold Competition Skeet or Trap configuration.

SHOTGUNS: SxS

662 SERIES – 12, 20, or 28 ga., 2 3/4 (28 ga.) or 3 in. chambers, 26 (28 ga. only) or 28 in. barrels, boxlock action, color case hardened receiver with long profile laser engraved sideplates, ejectors, oil finished straight grip walnut stock with semi-beavertail forend,

GRADING - PPGS™	100%	98%	95%	90%	80%	70%	60%	LAST MSR

gold ST, mfg. by Fausti. Imported 2009-2011.

	$2,750	$2,500	$2,000	$1,750	$1,500	$1,250	$1,000	*$2,826*

Add $748 for 28 ga.

SHOTGUNS: SEMI-AUTO

Beginning 2009, semi-auto shotguns are manufactured by Pietta.

401 SERIES (SX401) – 12 or 20 (new 2009) ga., 3 in. chamber, inertia operated action, 26 (new 2009) or 28 in. barrel, 4 (new 2009) or 5 (disc.) shot mag., oil finished walnut stock, lightweight aluminum aircraft alloy receiver in blue, nickel, or pewter finish, sling swivels (disc. 2005), black nylon recoil pad, patented locking forend, approx. 6 3/4 lbs. Disc. 2011.

	$1,050	$920	$785	$715	$575	$470	$365	*$1,199*

Add $51 for nickel finish.
Add $100 for pewter finish.

405 SERIES (SX405) – 12 or 20 (new 2009) ga., 3 in. chamber, 22 (disc. 2005), 24 (disc. 2005), 26 (disc. 2005), or 28 in. barrel, 4 (new 2009) or 5 (disc. 2005) shot mag., black synthetic, Realtree Wetland (disc. 2005) or Hardwood camo finished (disc. 2005) stock, lightweight aluminum aircraft alloy blue receiver, sling swivels (disc. 2005), black nylon recoil pad, approx. 6 1/2 lbs. Disc. 2011.

	$975	$895	$750	$675	$575	$475	$375	*$1,099*

* ***SX405 Hunting Series Combo*** – includes 22 in. slug and 26 in. barrels.

	$450	$395	$335	$305	$245	$200	$155	*$503*

406 SERIES – 12 ga. only, 28 in. barrel, blue steel receiver, black synthetic stock, patented locking forend, inertia operated action, black nylon recoil pad. Imported 2009-2011.

	$1,050	$920	$785	$715	$575	$470	$365	*$1,199*

SX801 SERIES – 12 ga. only, 2 3/4 in. chamber, 28 or 30 in. ported barrel, available in Sporting or Gold Sporting configuration, vent. rib, Hi-Viz front sight, black anodized receiver, gold trigger, includes four extended Trulock chokes, oil finished Turkish Monte Carlo stock, approx. 6 3/4 lbs.

	$775	$680	$580	$525	$425	$350	$270	*$868*

Add $197 for Gold Sporting model with adj. comb.

VICKERS LIMITED

Previous manufacturer located in Crayford/Kent, England.

RIFLES: SINGLE SHOT, TARGET

JUBILEE SINGLE SHOT TARGET RIFLE – Martini type action, .22 LR cal., 28 in. heavy barrel, target sights, one-piece pistol grip, target stock, pre-WWII.

	$440	$330	$305	$275	$250	$220	$165

EMPIRE MODEL – similar to Jubilee, with 27 or 30 in. barrel, straight grip stock.

	$415	$310	$285	$260	$220	$195	$150

VICTOR ARMS CORPORATION

Previous manufacturer located in Houston, TX.

Victor Arms Corporation manufactured limited quantities of a .22 LR upper unit for the AR-15. The V22 and its .22 LR cal. magazine replaced the standard .223 upper assembly/magazine. Additionally, a complete protoype gun was also manufactured.

VICTORY ARMS CO. LIMITED

Previously manufactured in prototype format only by Modern Manufacturing Company located in Phoenix, AZ.

PISTOL: SEMI-AUTO

MODEL MC5 – while a few prototypes were mfg. for trade shows (circa 1991-92), this model was never commercially manufactured. Last advertised retail was $465.

GRADING - PPGS™	100%	98%	95%	90%	80%	70%	60%	LAST MSR

VIERLINGS

The German word Vierling denotes a four barrel long arm configuration mostly manufactured in Germany and Austria.

This configuration of long arm has four barrels, usually a mixture of centerfire/rimfire caliber barrel(s) and shotgun barrel(s). Some Vierlings may also have all-shotgun barrels or all-rifle barrels (rare). Vierlings typically have two triggers, both single-set. Barrel selectors are usually on the top tang. In order to reduce weight, quite a few have actions made from high grade aluminum with steel reinforcements in critical areas. This unusuai configuration is mostly of German mfg., although there are a few Austrian specimens also (the gunmakers of Ferlach still custom-make this model). All Vierlings are mfg. one at a time, with fabrication being very complicated, lengthy, and expensive. Perhaps the most rare Vierling configuration is a gun with four shotgun barrels. As a result, every Vierling must be appraised individually - most older manufactured specimens, however, are priced in the $4,500-$10,000 range, depending on the desirability of the configuration, and overall condition. Recently and currently manufactured special order Vierlings are priced from $8,500-$40,000 range, depending on features, engraving, and other options.

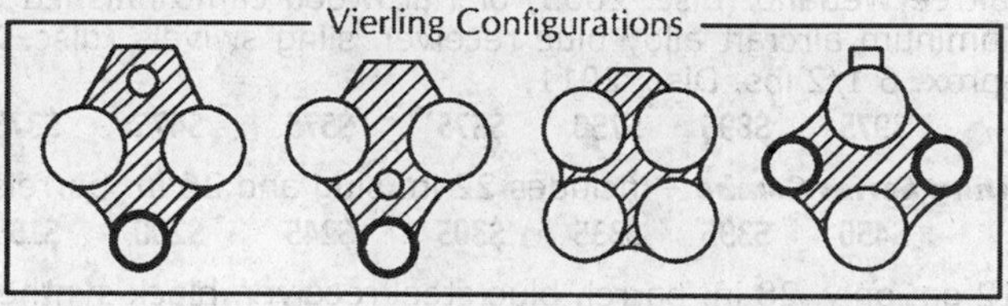

VIGILANCE RIFLES

Current rifle manufacturer located in Chino Valley, AZ beginning 2012. Previously located in Banning, and Redlands, CA.

RIFLES: SEMI-AUTO

VR1 – .338 Lapua, .375 Cheytac, .408 Cheytac, or .505 Gibbs (disc. 2012) cal., gas operated, stainless steel upper receiver, bull barrel, titanium muzzle brake, premium wood stock in a variety of colors or synthetic tactical stock, two-stage trigger, detachable 5 shot mag., many options available, weights vary according to configuration.

MSR $10,000 $8,500 $7,450 $6,375 $5,775 $4,675 $3,825 $2,975

VI-MA SNC.

Current rifle and shotguns manufacturer located in Brescia, Italy. No current U.S. importation.

Vi-Ma manufactures a high quality single shot boxlock rifle with unique sliding breech, available in various cals between .222 Rem. - .375 H&H. Six variations are available and include the Pegaso, Pegaso SL, Pegaso XL, Pegaso XLO, Pegaso OXL, and Pegaso Black Gold. The standard Pegaso has a current MSR of €3,510. Vi-Ma also manufactures SxS hammer shotguns. Please contact the company directly for more information, including pricing, delivery time, and U.S. availability (see Trademark Index).

VINTAGE ORDNANCE COMPANY, LLC

Current single shot pistol manufacturer located in Elizabethtown, KY. Dealer sales.

PISTOLS: SINGLE SHOT

FP-45 REPRODUCTION LIBERATOR PISTOL – .45 ACP cal., patterned after the original WWII Liberator pistol, rifled barrel, stamped construction, serial number marked in front of the grip frame with additional company information, packaging kit also available. New 2011.

MSR $600 $550 $495 $450 $400 $350 $300 $250

Add $100 for pistol packaging set.

GRADING - PPGS™	100%	98%	95%	90%	80%	70%	60%	LAST MSR

VIPER

Current trademark imported by Tristar, located in North Kansas City, MO. Please refer to the Tristar section.

VIRGIN VALLEY CUSTOM GUNS

Previous manufacturer of custom bolt action rifles located in Hurricane, UT until 2005.

RIFLES: BOLT ACTION

Virgin Valley offered custom barrels, stocks, wildcat chamberings, many other options and riflesmithing services.

SAFARI RIFLE – various big game cals., choice of Dakota Mod. 76, Mauser, or Win. Mod. 70 action, individually custom ordered.

This model was POR.

VIRGINIAN

This trademark can be located under the Interarms section in this text.

VIS

Currently manufactured by the F.B. Radom arsenal in Radom, Poland. Please refer to the Radom section in this text.

VLTOR WEAPON SYSTEMS

Current manufacturer of AR-15 style rifles, receivers, parts, and related accessories located in Tucson, AZ.

CARBINES: SEMI-AUTO

TS3 CARBINE – 5.56 NATO cal., AR-15 style, 16 1/4 in. barrel with muzzle brake, flat top Vltor receiver with full length Picatinny rail, 30 shot mag., Geissele high speed National Match trigger, flip up combat sights, collapsible stock, quad rail, black finish, approx. 7 1/2 lbs. New 2011.

MSR	100%	98%	95%	90%	80%	70%	60%
MSR $2,495	$2,275	$2,000	$1,800	$1,600	$1,400	$1,200	$995

VOERE (AUSTRIA)

Current manufacturer established during 1965, and located in Kufstein, Austria. No current U.S. importation.

Voere of Austria is not associated with Voere (Germany), which was absorbed by Mauser-Werke subsequent to the Voere (Germany) bankruptcy. Voere manufactures a complete line of quality rimfire semi-auto and centerfire bolt-action/semi-auto rifles. Their caseless ammunition released in 1991 was a unique step in the development of ammunition. More information on this trademark, including current models, U.S. availability, and U.S. pricing, can be obtained by contacting the company directly (see Trademark Index for information).

RIFLES

Values listed are in euros, w/o tax.

MODEL K98 VOERE-KESSLER BOLT ACTION – various cals., Mauser 98 action, wing type 3 position safety, 21 1/2 in. barrel, select hand-checkered walnut stock with bavarian cheekpiece, rosewood pistol grip cap. Mfg. 2004-2008.

The last European MSR on this model was €2,780.

MODEL VEC 91 BOLT ACTION – 5.7 UCC or 6mm UCC caseless ammo, unique ignition system requires electrical impulse to activate semi-conducting primer that ignites propellant (2 small batteries are housed in the pistol grip capable of igniting 5,000 shots), 5 shot detachable mag., 20 in. free floating barrel, twin forward locking lugs, 2-stage electrical trigger adj. from 1/2 oz. to 7 lbs, 55 grain bullet achieves 3,300 fps with no loss in accuracy, 6 lbs. Mfg. 1992 - circa 2008.

The last European MSR on this model was €2,388.

GRADING - PPGS™	100%	98%	95%	90%	80%	70%	60%	LAST MSR

Unfortunately, BATFE import certificates have made it very expensive to bring UCC caseless ammunition in small quantities into this country. This model was distributed in Europe and other countries.

MODEL TIROLERIN BOLT ACTION – various cals., set trigger, 3 shot mag., checkered pistol grip walnut stock, take down, scope base.

The current European MSR on this model is €2,599.
Add €430 for interchangeable barrel set.

MODEL 20-02 XXL BOLT ACTION – various dangerous game cals., Magnum action, two locking lugs, checkered high grade walnut stock, iron sights, approx. 8 lbs. New 2003.

The current European MSR on this model is €6,384 for the base model.

MODEL 20-03 LBW BOLT ACTION – various cals., interchangeable barrels, three lug fluted bolt, uncocking safety, walnut or rubber coated stock, 6 1/2 lbs. New 2003.

The current European MSR on this model is €1,208 for the base model.

A Luxus and Deluxe Takedown variations are also available on this model.

MODEL 2155 BOLT ACTION – various cals., K-98 Mauser action, 20 in. barrel, tang safety, no sights.

The current European MSR on this model is €850 for the base model.
Add €60 for Mag. cals. (7mm Rem. Mag. or .300 Win. Mag.).

MODEL 2165 BOLT ACTION DELUXE – same cals. as Model 2155, European traditional style K-98 Mauser bolt action, 22 in. barrel, detachable 5 shot mag., hand-checkered deluxe walnut.

The current European MSR on this model is €1,299.
Add €60 for Mag. cals. (24 in. barrel).

MODEL 2185 SERIES MATCH/SPORTER SEMI-AUTO – .30-06, .308 Win., or 7x64mm cal., gas operated, free-floating barrel, 3 or 5 shot detachable mag., manual safety, iron sights, laminate wood, 11 lbs.

The current European MSR on this model is €3,569.
Add $1,500 for position style rifle (includes adj. cheekpiece, buttplate, and bottom sling rail, and Voere special scope base, disc.).

Other calibers are available on special order only. Sporter model has adj. aperture rear sight with post front sight.

MODEL 2185 SEMI-AUTO HUNTING RIFLE – 9.3x62mm, other cals. available upon special request, checkered stock and forend, iron sights.

The current European MSR on this model is €1,969.
Add €68 for Mannlicher full stock with 20 in. carbine barrel.
Add €87 for Europe model with hinged bottom plate.

AMERICAN CUSTOM CLASSIC BOLT ACTION – .22-250 Rem., .243 Win., .270 Win., 7x57mm, 7x64mm, .30-06, or .308 Win. cal., K-98 Mauser action, 3 position safety, hinged floorplate, deluxe walnut with hand-rubbed oil finish and checkering. Mfg. 1996 only.

$1,575	$1,450	$1,300	$1,150	$995	$850	$675	*$1,795*

Add $50 for Mag. cals. (.300 Win. Mag., .338 Win. Mag., 7mm Rem. Mag., or 9.3x64mm).
Add $100 for .375 H&H or .458 Win. Mag. cal.

.22 SEMI-AUTO – .22 LR cal., open (disc.) or closed bolt design, 10 shot mag., checkered hardwood stock, adj. rear sight and trigger. Limited importation.

$585	$535	$460	$400	$350	$300	$250	*$645*

Add $50 for Deluxe Model.

VOERE (GERMAN)

Previous manufacturer located in Vohrenvach, Germany. Voere was absorbed by Mauser-Werke circa 1986, and most of the company machinery was moved to Oberndorf during that time. Voere of Germany should not be confused with the current Austrian firm of the same name.

Voere of Germany manufactured a wide variety of rifles in many configurations, including both bolt action and semi-auto (closed and open bolt) .22 cal. rifles. Bolt

	Above Average	Average	Below Average

action centerfire rifles were also produced in many styles and calibers, including some private label contracts with such firms as Shikar, Frankonia, Akah, and others. While not considered as highly collectible today, most German Voere rifles were noted for their quality craftsmanship and above-average accuracy. Secondary values today depend on the desirability of the rifle configuration (stock design, finish, caliber, etc.) and original condition, but most .22 cal. rifles sell in the $150 - $350 range, while centerfire rifles are typically priced in the $425 - $725 range, if complete with magazines.

VOLCANIC

Previous trademark manufactured 1855-1860 by the Volcanic Repeating Arms Company, and New Haven Firearms Company, located in New Haven, CT.

The author and publisher would like to express his thanks to Mr. Casey Nanz for providing the following information.

HISTORY OF VOLCANIC REPEATING ARMS COMPANY

In 1855 Smith & Wesson changed their name to the Volcanic Repeating Arms Company and began adding additional investors. One of the new investors was a successful shirt maker with an interest in firearms named Oliver F. Winchester. Over the next year, Winchester increased his ownership in the company until he eventually purchased the company from Smith and Wesson and became the president and largest shareholder. The company was still using .41 caliber ammunition and had expanded to offer different models of firearms. By this time, all of the guns being produced were designed with a new style, corrosion resistant brass frame in hopes of securing Navy contracts. Blued steel barrels were now standard with the same rotating barrel assembly for loading the weapon. Early guns were engraved in the floral type scroll pattern sometimes called a grapevine pattern and will command an extra premium. The barrel address had been changed to: "THE VOLCANIC REPEATING ARMS CO. NEW HAVEN CONN. PATENTED FEB.14 1854." Serial numbers began with 1 and ran throughout the estimated production of 3500 guns.

By mid 1857, Winchester had reorganized the Volcanic Repeating Arms Company into the New Haven Arms Company. The company would remain in business until 1860 when Winchester introduced the Henry Rifle based on the Volcanic's lever action design. The main way to distinguish a "Volcanic" from a "New Haven" is the change in the barrel address with the omission of "Volcanic" and the addition of "New Haven" in the address. The New Haven Arms company began producing guns in .31 and .41 caliber like Smith & Wesson had done years before. The guns are serial numbers begin with one and ascend throughout the end of production of an estimated 3,500 guns.

CARBINES

NAVY CARBINE – .41 cal., lever action carbine with 16 in. barrel, perch belly walnut stock with piano type varnish, brass crescent buttplate, produced with excess barrels from the Navy No. 3 pistol production, approx. 500 mfg.

$20,000 - $25,000 $15,000 - $20,000 $12,500 - $15,000

NEW HAVEN PISTOL CARBINE – .41 cal., lever action, 16 in. barrel with attachable shoulder stock and crescent brass buttplate, this is the rarest variation of the New Haven guns and production numbers are unknown but estimated to be less than 100.

$40,000 - $50,000 $30,000 - $40,000 $17,500 - $30,000

Prices are for original matching shoulder stock, if missing subtract 20%-35%.

This model is almost impossible to obtain in excellent condition with few known specimens. It is highly recommended to seek a competent appraisal before selling/purchasing.

NEW HAVEN CARBINES – .41 cal., lever action, 16, 21, or 25 in. barrel, engraved or plain brass frame with piano finish, walnut perch belly stock, standard barrel markings and serial numbered on the frame and internal parts, resembles a miniature Henry rifle at a glance. Approx. 1,000 mfg.

Add a premium for 21 or 25 in. barrel.

	Above Average	Average	Below Average
*** 16 in. Model**	$25,000-$35,000	$20,000-$25,000	$15,000-$20,000
*** 21 in. Model**	$30,000 - $40,000	$22,500 - $30,000	$17,500 - $12,500
*** 25 in. Model**	$30,000 - $40,000	$25,000 - $30,000	$20,000 - $25,000

PISTOLS

These models are rarely seen and desirable in almost any condition. Higher condition guns are seldom seen and pricing escalates quickly for better condition.

NAVY PISTOL NO. 1 – .41 cal., lever action, 6 in. barrel, approx. 1,200 mfg.

$15,000 - $25,000+ $8,000 - $15,000 $6,000 - $8,000

NAVY PISTOL NO. 2 – .41 cal., lever action, 8 in. barrel, approx. 1,500 mfg.

$15,000 - $20,000+ $7,000 - $15,000 $5,000 - $7,000

NAVY PISTOL NO. 3 – .41 cal., lever action, 16 in. barrel, attachable shoulder stock, approx. 300 mfg.

$40,000 - $50,000+ $30,000 - $40,000 $20,000 - $25,000

Subtract 20% for mismatched shoulder stock or 35% if w/o shoulder stock.

This model is that rarest variation, and an individual appraisal is highly recommended before buying or selling.

NEW HAVEN NO. 1 3 1/2 IN. – .31 caliber, lever action, 3 1/2 in. barrel, brass frame, some of which were engraved and gold or silver washed, varnished walnut grips (some examples of ivory have been encountered), most common model produced and encountered. Approx. 1,000 mfg.

$10,000 - $15,000 $6,000 - $10,000 $4,000 - $6,000

Any special features will command an extra premium if original.

Rock Island Auction sold a mint specimen still in the cardboard box during December 2007 for $143,750.

NEW HAVEN NO. 1 6 IN. – .31 caliber, lever action, 6 in. barrel, brass frame, some of which were engraved and gold or silver washed, varnished walnut grips (some examples of ivory have been encountered), rare example. Approx. 250 mfg.

$12,000 - $16,000 $8,000 - $12,000 $6,000 - $8,000

Any special features will command an extra premium if original.

This model is rarely found in higher condition factors.

NEW HAVEN NO. 2 – .41 caliber, lever action, 6 (rare) or 8 in. barrel, brass frame, some of which were engraved and gold or silver washed, varnished walnut grips (some examples of ivory have been encountered). Approx. 1,250 mfg.

$12,500 - $15,000 $10,000 - $12,500 $7,000 - $9,000

Any special features will command an extra premium if original.

This model is rarely found in higher condition factors.

VOLKMANN PRECISION, LLC

Current pistol manufacturer established in 2007 and located in Littleton, CO. Previously located in Lakewood, CO until 2011.

Volkmann Precision LLC was founded by Luke Volkmann, formerly a pistolsmith for Ed Brown Products. In 2011, the company name changed from Volkmann Custom Inc. to Volkmann Precision, LLC.

PISTOLS: SEMI-AUTO

All pistols are hand built, and a variety of options are available. Please contact the company directly (see Trademark Index).

Add $100 for ambidextrous safety. Add $250 for custom finish. Add $300 for engraving. Add $250 for custom serial number.

GRADING - PPGS™	100%	98%	95%	90%	80%	70%	60%	LAST MSR

COMBAT CUSTOM – .45 ACP cal., 5 in. barrel, full size frame, 7 or 8 shot mag., black Rockote or blue finish, fixed tritium night sights, 25 LPI checkering.

MSR $2,995	$2,995	$2,550	$2,150	$1,850	$1,500	$1,250	$995	

COMBAT CARRY – .45 ACP cal., 4 1/4 in. barrel, 7 or 8 shot mag., Commander size frame and slide with Ed Brown Bobtail mainspring housing, Rockote black, OD green, titanium blue, or desert tan finish, fixed tritium night sights, 25 LPI checkering.

MSR $3,095	$3,095	$2,625	$2,200	$1,875	$1,500	$1,250	$995	

CLINT SMITH COMBAT SPECIAL – .45 ACP cal., Clint Smith inspired and designed 1911 style, 7 or 8 shot mag., carbon or stainless steel frame, Rockote finish, Heine Ledge combat sights, gold dot front post sights, tactical accessory rail, lanyard loop mainspring, short match trigger and safety, 34-38 oz. New 2012.

MSR $3,595	$3,595	$3,150	$2,625	$2,175	$1,725	$1,400	$1,200	

CENTENNIAL MODEL – .45 ACP cal., anniversary edition of the 1911, hand polished slide with custom scroll engraving and gold or platinum inlay work, color case hardened frame, custom sights, grips, and wood presentation box. New 2011.

MSR $7,495	$6,995	$5,750	$4,500	N/A	N/A	N/A	N/A	

SIGNATURE SERIES – .45 ACP cal., 5 in. barrel, 7 or 8 shot mag., full size frame and mirror polished slide, blue, hard chrome, or stainless steel, adj. tritium night sights, 25 LPI checkering, front slide serrations.

MSR $3,495	$3,495	$3,000	$2,500	$2,100	$1,650	$1,375	$1,125	

VOLQUARTSEN CUSTOM (LTD.)

Current pistol/rifle customizer and manufacturer established in 1974 and located in Carroll, IA. Dealer sales.

PISTOLS: SEMI-AUTO

Volquartsen manufactures a wide variety of custom pistols based on the Ruger Mark II & III action. Prices range from $800 - $1,395, depending on the configuration. Please contact the company directly for more information on these conversions.

CHEETAH – .17 HMR, .17 Mach 2 (disc. 2005), .22 LR, or .22 WMR cal., titanium 7 in. (.22 LR cal. only) or 10 in. barrel, 9 or 10 shot mag., synthetic finger groove stock with ambidextrous grip, CNC aluminum frame, Weaver style scope mount, available with black, blue, red, green, or silver stock, 46 oz. Mfg. 2003-2006.

	$875	$775	$700	$625	$575	$525	$475	*$972*

PREDATOR – .17 HMR or .22 WMR cal., choice of brown laminate wood grips (disc. 2006) or black McMillan grips, 12 in. stainless steel bull barrel, wedge locking block system, includes scope mount. Mfg. 2005-2009.

	$1,175	$950	$850	$750	$675	$625	$550	*$1,353*

Add $220 for barrel only.

Subtract approx. $300 if w/o black McMillan grips (became standard 2007).

V-10X – 22 LR cal., aluminum frame, ergonomic finger groove laminated wood panel grips, target trigger, blue receiver and barrel, TL rear adj. target sight, optional Picatinny rail, drilled and tapped, hard anodized finish in choice of black, silver, red, green, blue, or purple finish. New mid-2009.

MSR $1,199	$1,075	$950	$825	$725	$625	$525	$425	

Add $150 for comp. model.

SCORPION – .22 LR cal., 4 1/2 or 6 in. stainless steel barrel with muzzle threads and thread protector, lightweight target frame, competition bolt, optional target sights, available in silver, blue, red, black, or OD green finish, Volthane Target grips, laminated wood target grips, or Hogue monogrips, 28 oz. New 2012.

MSR $1,055	$895	$785	$675	$615	$495	$400	$315	

Beginning in mid-2013, this model can also be ordered in a 1911 style grip frame.

GRADING - PPGS™	100%	98%	95%	90%	80%	70%	60%	LAST MSR

RIFLES: SEMI-AUTO

Current Volquartsen stock configurations include: brown synthetic, grey synthetic, Hogue, McMillan Sporter, McMillan thumbhole, or laminated stocks in Brown, Blue, Gray, Green, Yellow, Orange, Pink, Yellow, Red, or Brown/Grey. Base values listed represent standard Hogue synthetic stock.

Add approx. $190 for grey/brown synthetic or laminated stock on models listed below.
Add approx. $415 for McMillan Sporter or McMillan Thumbhole stock on most models listed below.
Add $305 for laminated thumbhole stock on most models listed below.

STANDARD 17 HMR – .17 HMR cal., similar to Standard 22 LR, similar configurations as the .22 WMR model, 18 1/2 (standard) or 20 in. fluted and compensated stainless steel bull barrel, approx. 9 lbs.

MSR $1,487	$1,350	$1,125	$900	$775	$675	$575	$500	

Add $112 for Deluxe model.
Subtract $32 for Lightweight model with Hogue stock.
Subtract $55 for Super Lightweight model with Hogue stock.
Subtract $187 for snake flute, radial flute, or I flute.
Add $385 for VX5000 Lightweight (disc. 2012).

STANDARD 17 MACH 2 – .17 Mach 2 cal., otherwise similar to Standard 17 HMR, approx. 8 lbs. Mfg. 2006-2012.

	$1,200	$1,075	$925	$775	$650	$550	$450	*$1,334*

Add $112 for Deluxe model.
Subtract $32 for Lightweight model with Hogue stock.
Subtract $55 for Super Lightweight model with Hogue stock.
Add $187 for snake flute, radial flute, or I flute. Add $109 for Deluxe model.
Add $375 for VX5000 Lightweight.

STANDARD 22 LR – .22 LR cal., similar to .22 WMR, 18 1/2 in. stainless steel bull barrel, stainless steel receiver, available in same configurations as .22 WMR, except not available in VG-1 or radial flute versions, approx. 8.2 lbs.

MSR $1,288	$1,150	$975	$850	$725	$650	$550	$450	

Add $112 for Deluxe model.
Subtract $32 for Lightweight model with Hogue stock.
Subtract $55 for Super Lightweight model with Hogue stock.
Subtract $187 for snake flute, radial flute, or I flute.
Add $385 for VX5000 Lightweight (disc. 2012).

STANDARD 22 MAG. – .22 WMR cal., Ruger 10/22 type blowback action in stainless steel or hard anodized alloy (Superlight), CNC machined bolt with round titanium firing pin and heavy duty extractor, Weaver style mount machined intergral to receiver, Picatinny rail became option in 2010, Ruger style 9 or 10 shot rotary style mag., choice of standard (18 1/2 in. stainless steel), deluxe (20 in. fluted), or lightweight (16 1/2 in. aluminum) barrel, Monte Carlo laminated wood or Hogue Overmolded composite stock, available in Standard, Lightweight, Snake, radial flute, Deluxe, Signature Series (top-of-the-line), VG-1, and VX5000 models. approx. 9 lbs.

MSR $1,487	$1,350	$1,125	$925	$800	$700	$600	$500	

Add $112 for Deluxe model.
Subtract $32 for Lightweight model with Hogue stock.
Subtract $55 for Super Lightweight model with Hogue stock.
Subtract $187 for snake flute, radial flute, or I flute.
Add $385 for VX5000 Lightweight (disc. 2012).

SIGNATURE SERIES – .17 HMR, .22 LR, or .22 WMR cal., top-of-the-line model, 20 1/2 in. stainless steel Snake Fluted and compensated barrel, features hand cut engraving on the receiver, trigger guard and Nova scope rings, includes Zeiss Conqest 4.5x14 scope, walnut stock, many options are available.

MSR $3,995	$3,600	$3,225	$2,850	$2,550	$2,275	$1,900	$1,675	

Add $199 for .17 HMR or .22 WMR cal.

GRADING - PPGS™	100%	98%	95%	90%	80%	70%	60%	LAST MSR

TF SERIES – .17 HMR (TF-17) or .22 WMR (TF-22) cal., similar to Standard Series, except has machined counterweight system attached to CNC machined bolt, matte black stainless steel bull barrel, birch stock, 14 in. LOP, 9 shot mag., Picatinny rail, approx. 8 1/2 lbs. New 2011.

MSR $1,086	$1,025	$900	$775	$675	$550	$450	$350	

FUSION TAKE DOWN MODEL – .17 HMR, .17 Mach 2 (disc. 2012), .22 LR, or .22 WMR cal., features interchangeable barrels from .17 HMR to .22 WMR cals., black finished alloy receiver, 18 3/8 in. barrel with muzzle brake, Picatinny rails on top of receiver and bottom of barrel shroud, 9 shot rotary mag., 6 1/2 lbs. Limited mfg. 2004, reintroduced 2006.

MSR $1,870	$1,725	$1,450	$1,275	$975	$825	$675	$550	

Add $309 for barrel only.
Subtract $250 for .17 Mach 2 or .22 LR cal.

EVOLUTION MODEL – .204 Ruger or .223 Rem. cal., gas operated, stainless steel receiver, trigger guard, and bolt, integral machined Picatinny rail on receiver top, brown laminate stock with extended Monte Carlo cheekpiece, 20 or 24 (.204 Ruger only) in. standard barrel, 10 shot AR-15 style mag., 11 1/2 lbs. New 2005.

MSR $2,433	$2,000	$1,950	$1,700	$1,475	$1,225	$1,000	$850	

Add $226 for camo (now avail. only as part of camo package w/scope), disc. 2011.
Add $1,321 for green camo package with scope.

INFERNO – .17 HMR (disc. 2010) .17 Mach 2, .22 LR, or .22 WMR (disc. 2010) cal., Superlite aluminum receiver with Weaver style scope mount and carbon fiber THM tension barrel threaded into the receiver, barreled action fits into specially designed CNC machined aluminum stock with adj. LOP and adj. cheekpiece, black, blue, red, purple, silver (new 2012), or OD Green (new 2012) stock, TG2000 trigger group, EDM extractor, Inferno muzzle compensator. New 2010.

MSR $1,924	$1,750	$1,475	$1,250	$975	$825	$725	$625	

Add $46 for .17 Mach 2 or .17 HMR (disc. 2010) cal.
Add $100 for blue, red, purple, silver (new 2012), or OD Green (new 2012) stock.

VG-1 – .17 HMR, .17 Mach 2, .22 LR, or .22 WMR cal., 20 in. stainless steel fluted and compensated barrel, matte black epoxy coated action, military green McMillan fiberglass sporter stock, NOVA rings.

MSR $1,975	$1,750	$1,495	$1,225	$1,000	$850	$725	$650	

Add $56 for .17 Mach 2, $195 for .17 HMR, or $199 for .22 WMR cal.

ULTRALITE – .22 LR, .22 WMR, or .17 HMR cal., Ultralite barrel, hard anodized alloy receiver, integral Picatinny rail, lightweight thumbhole laminated stock, 2 lbs., 6 oz. New 2013.

MSR $1,485	$1,350	$1,125	$900	$775	$675	$575	$500	

VOLTRAN

Current trademark manufactured by Ücyilidiz Arms Ind. Co. Ltd., located in Istanbul, Turkey.

Voltran is one of several trademarks manufactured by Ücyidiz Arms Ind. Co. Ltd. - others include Akdal and Blow. Please refer to these sections for more information.

VOLUNTEER ENTERPRISES

Previous manufacturer located in Knoxville, TN.

Volunteer Enterprises became Commando Arms after 1978.

CARBINES

COMMANDO MARK III CARBINE – .45 ACP cal., semi-auto, blowback action, 16 1/2 in. barrel, aperture sight, stock styled after the Auto-Ordnance "Tommy Gun." Mfg. 1969-1976.

	$750	$675	$625	$565	$525	$475	$425	

Add 10% for vertical grip.

COMMANDO MARK 9 – similar to Mark III in 9mm Para. cal.

	$675	$625	$565	$525	$475	$425	$375	

Add 10% for vertical grip.

GRADING - PPGS™	100%	98%	95%	90%	80%	70%	60%	LAST MSR

VOUZELAUD

Previous manufacturer located in France. Previously imported by Waverly Arms Co. located in Suffolk, VA.

SHOTGUNS: SxS

MODEL 315 E – 12, 16 or 20 ga., boxlock, 28 in. barrels, auto ejectors, straight grip French walnut stock, double triggers, case colored receiver, light engraving. Importation disc. 1987.

Values generally range between $1,350-$2,000 for this model.

MODEL 315 EL – similar to Model 315 E, except has satin finish receiver engraved with bouquets of fine English scrollwork, trigger guard and forearm also engraved. Importation disc. 1987.

Values generally range between $1,475-$2,250 for this model.
Add $600 for 28 ga. or .410 bore (Model 315 EL-S, special order only).

MODEL 315 EG – 12, 16 or 20 ga., sidelock, 28 in. barrels, selective ejectors, double triggers, extensive scroll engraving on coin finish receiver, English style stock of extra fancy French walnut. Importation disc. 1987.

Values generally range between $1,750-$2,750 for this model.

MODEL 315 EGL-S – same general features as the Model 315 EGL, except monobloc barrel construction, extensive game scene engraving, and grand deluxe walnut stock and forearm with extra fine hand-checkering. Importation disc. 1987.

Last MSR was $5,895.

Values generally range between $1,950-$2,950 for this model.

VULCAN ARMAMENT, INC.

Current rifle manufacturer established in 2003 and located in South St. Paul, MN.

CARBINES/RIFLES: SEMI-AUTO

Vulcan Armament makes a wide variety of AR-15 styled semi-auto carbines and rifles, including configurations for military and law enforcement. Please contact the factory directly for more information about options and availability (see Trademark Index).

All rifles include sling, manual, cleaning kit, Vulcan knife, and hard case.

Add $20-$25 for removable carry handle.

V15 9MM CARBINE SERIES – 9mm Para. cal., 16 in. chrome-moly vanadium steel barrel with threaded muzzle, A2 front sight bases with bayonet lug, all parts manganese phosphate finished, M4 contour, M4 length handguard, full heat shield, A2 upper receiver or A3 flat-top receiver, carry handle, adj. sights, Picatinny rail, black anodized hard coat finish, forward assist, hinged ejection port cover, six position adj. buttstock, removable flash hider, accepts Sten magazines, 6 1/2 lbs.

MSR $860	$775	$685	$585	$525	$425	$350	$275

V15 DISPATCHER SERIES – .223 Rem. cal., 16 in. chrome-moly vanadium steel barrel with threaded muzzle, gas block mounted under the handguard, A2 flash hider, A2 front sight bases, bayonet lug, fixed A2 stock, A2 or A3 flat-top upper receiver, black hard coat anodized finish, 6 1/2 lbs.

MSR $860	$775	$685	$585	$525	$425	$350	$275

V15 M4 CARBINE SERIES – .223 Rem. cal., 16 in. chrome-moly vanadium steel button rifled barrel with threaded muzzle, A2 flash hider, A2 front sight bases, bayonet lug, A2 or A3 flat-top upper reciever, black hard coat anodized finish, M4 length handguard with full heat shields, six position M4 buttstock, 6.4lbs.

MSR $860	$775	$685	$585	$525	$425	$350	$275

V15 POLYMER SERIES – .223 Rem. cal., 16 or 20 in. chrome-moly vanadium steel button rifled H-Bar barrel with threaded muzzle, all parts manganese phosphate finished, A2 flash hider, A2 sight bases, bayonet lug, six position M4 buttstock, Picatinny rail, A2 or A3 polymer receiver, forward assist, hinged ejection port cover.

MSR $700	$625	$550	$475	$425	$350	$280	$225

GRADING - PPGS™	100%	98%	95%	90%	80%	70%	60%	LAST MSR

V15 TARGET RIFLE – .223 Rem. cal., 20 in. chrome-moly vanadium steel threaded button rifled heavy barrel, A2 flash hider, all parts manganese phosphate finished, rifle length handguard, full heat shield, A2 or A3 flat-top upper receiver, Picatinny rail, black hard coat anodized finish, fixed A2 buttstock, removable flash hider, aluminum spacer, trap door buttplate.

MSR $860	$775	$685	$585	$525	$425	$350	$275	

Add $25 for A2 carrying handle.

V15 VARMINATOR SERIES – .223 Rem. cal., 20 or 24 in. stainless steel bull barrel, full length aluminum handguard, hard coat anodized finish, aluminum gas block, four Picatinny rails, forged A3 upper receiver, forward assist, hinged ejection port cover, fixed A2 buttstock, aluminum spacer, trap door buttplate, 9.2 lbs.

MSR $950	$850	$750	$635	$580	$465	$380	$295	

V15 200 SERIES – 7.62x39mm cal., 16 in. chrome-moly vanadium steel threaded barrel, A2 flash hider, A2 front sight bases, bayonet lug, all parts manganese phosphate finished, M4 length handguard, full heat shields, forged A2 or A3 flat-top upper receiver, forward assist, hinged ejection port, six position buttstock, 6.4 lbs.

MSR $900	$815	$715	$615	$555	$450	$365	$285	

* ***V15 200 Piston Series*** – .223 Rem. cal., similar to V15 200 Series, except has proprietary short stroke gas piston operation.

MSR $950	$860	$750	$650	$585	$475	$385	$300	

V15 202 MODULAR CARBINE – .223 Rem. cal., 16 in. chrome-moly vanadium steel threaded barrel, A2 flash hider, all parts manganese phosphate finished, A3 flat-top upper receiver, four Picatinny rails, black hard coat anodized finish, forward assist, hinged ejection port cover, modular handguard, low profile aircraft aluminum gas block, six position buttstock, 6 1/2 lbs.

MSR $925	$835	$730	$625	$565	$460	$375	$295	

V18 SERIES – .223 Rem. cal., 16 1/2 or 20 in. chrome lined barrel, copy of the AR-180, machined gas block, front sight base, Picatinny rail, FAL style handguard, short stroke gas piston, ambidextrous charging handle, carbon fiber lower, AR pistol grip, polymer FAL stock, rubber buttpad, aluminum recoil plate, last round hold open, 6.8 lbs.

MSR $689	$625	$545	$475	$425	$345	$280	$220	

V73 SERIES – 7.62x39mm, 223 Rem., or .308 Win. cal., copy of Israeli Galil, 100% part interchangeability, including mags. and accessories, machined monoblock receiver, skeletonized black tactical stock, available in AR, ARM, SAR, and Micro configurations.

MSR $1,550	$1,395	$1,220	$1,050	$950	$765	$630	$495	

Add $300 for .308 Win. cal.
Add $100 for ARM model with top carry handle.
Add $449 for SAR or Micro configuration.

RIFLES: BOLT ACTION

All rifles include manual, bipod, removable muzzle brake, gun lock, Vulcan knife, cleaning rod and brush, and scope rail.

V50 SERIES – .50 BMG cal., single shot, 60 degree bolt throw, capable of hits at ranges exceeding one mile, scope mounting rail, standard Mauser pattern trigger, thick recoil pad, "Shark Fin" muzzle brake, available in SS-100 (30 in. barrel, brown laminated thumbhole wood stock), SS-200 (36 in. barrel, grey laminated thumbhole wood stock), SS-300 (30 in. barrel, retractable black tactical stock) or the SS-400 Bullpup (30 in. barrel, bullpup stock).

MSR $1,900	$1,725	$1,525	$1,295	$1,175	$950	$775	$600	

The SS-400 Bullpup model is POR.
Add $300 for SS-200.

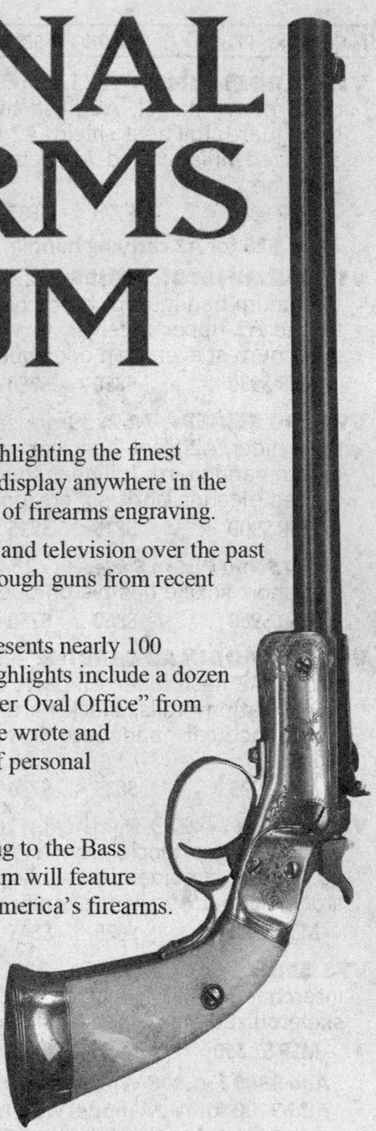

W SECTION

W. SCHASCHL-OUTSCHAR GmbH

Current long arm manufacturer established during 1864 and located in Ferlach, Austria.

W. Schaschl-Outschar has been making high quality long arms in Ferlach since 1864. Many rifle and shotgun configurations are possible - please contact the manufacturer directly for more information, U.S. availability, and pricing (see Trademark Index).

WAFFEN GLATZ

Previous manufacturer located in Erlendorf, Austria.

Johann Glatz manufactured high quality rifles, including a stalking rifle, a bolt action, and a drilling. All guns were custom ordered, and must be appraised individually for value.

WAFFEN HIENDLMAYER

Current manufacturer located in Eggenfelden, Germany. No current U.S. importation.

Klaus Hiendlmayer specializes in custom guns and engraving, and manufactures a version of the SIG 550 sniper rifle and prices range from €1,999-€2,750. Please contact the company directly for more information, including domestic availability (see Trademark Index).

WAFFEN JUNG GMBH

Current rifle manufacturer located in Lohmar, Germany. No current U.S. importation.

Waffen Jung GmbH manufactures a high quality Stutzen style Rominten edition bolt action rifle, in addition to a takedown model, Mauser sporter, Mauser Magnum sporter, and a Jagen Weltweit (synthetic stock) bolt action rifles. All guns are custom order. Please contact the company directly for more information, including U.S. availability (see Trademark Index).

WAFFEN KESSLER

Current rifle manufacturer located in Deggendorf, Germany. No current U.S. importation.

Waffen Kessler builds high quality bolt action rifles in a variety of configurations, including a Mannlicher. Many options are available. Please contact the company directly for more information, including pricing and U.S. availability (see Trademark Index).

WAFFENFABRIK HEIN

Previous bolt action rifle manufacturer located in Tekoa, WA until 2009.

RIFLES

Hein was known for its N-Series rifle action. Recent bolt action rifles include Palouse Custom Trophy ($2,900 last MSR) and the Palouse Custom Classic ($4,700 last MSR). A single shot rifle, the Model C-97 was POR.

WAFFENSTUBE GUGGI

Current long gun manufacturer and custom order stock carver established during 1978, and located in Graz, Austria. No current U.S. importation.

Waffenstube Guggi manufactures custom order sidelock combination guns, single barrel and SxS rifles, bolt action rifles, and shotguns. They also perform outstanding stock carving and checkering services. Please contact the company directly for more information and an individual price quotation (see Trademark Index).

WAFFEN, PRECHTL

Current rifle manufacturer specializing in Mauser actions located in Birkenau, Germany. Currently imported by New England Custom Gun, located in Claremont, NH, and by Mitchell's Mausers, located in Fountain Valley, CA.

Waffen Prechtl specializes in manufacturing a Mauser 98 short, standard, or Magnum length bolt action rifle patterned after the Mauser drawings from the 1930s. A wide variety of calibers and options are available. Please contact the importer for more information, including pricing and U.S. importation (see Trademark Index).

GRADING - PPGS™	100%	98%	95%	90%	80%	70%	60%	LAST MSR

WAFFEN VERATSCHNIG

Previous manufacturer located in Ferlach, Austria.

Waffen Veratschnig manufactured a variety of high grade, made to individual special order rifles, shotguns, combination guns, drillings, and vierlings. A wide variety of engraving scenes, wood carvings, and other special features were available at extra cost. Very few models were actually imported into the U.S.

WALTHER

Current manufacturer established in 1886, and currently located in Ulm, Germany 1953 to date. Most models, except the P22 and PK380, are imported by Walther Arms, Inc. located in Fort Smith, AR. Previously imported and distributed by Smith & Wesson circa 2002-2012, and located in Springfield, MA. Walther target pistols and target rifles are distributed by Champions Choice located in La Vergne, TN. All target, competition and service pistols are also currently imported, distributed, and factory serviced by Earl's Repair Service, Inc., located in Tewksbury, MA since 1984. Previously imported and distributed 1998-2001 by Walther USA LLC, located in Springfield, MA, and by Interarms located in Alexandria, VA circa 1962-1999. Previously manufactured in Zella-Mehlis, Germany 1886 to 1945. Walther was sold to Umarex Sportwaffen GmbH circa 1994, and company headquarters are located in Arnsberg, Germany. Smith & Wesson was the primary distributor for most Walther firearms and accessories in the United States from 2002-2012. During 2012, Carl Walther GmbH Sportwaffen and Umarex announced the formation of Walther Arms, Inc. located in Fort Smith, AR to import, sell, and market all Walther products in the U.S. beginning Jan. 1, 2013.

The calibers listed in the Walther Pistol sections are listed in American caliber designations. The German metric conversion is as follows: .22 LR - 5.6mm, .25 ACP - 6.35mm, .32 ACP - 7.65mm, and .380 ACP - 9mm kurz. The metric caliber designations in most cases will be indicated on the left slide legend for German mfg. pistols listed in the Walther section.

For more information and current pricing on both new and used Walther airguns, please refer to the *Blue Book of Airguns* by Dr. Robert Beeman & John Allen (also online).

PISTOLS: SEMI-AUTO, PRE-WAR

MODEL 1 – .25 ACP cal., 2.1 in. barrel, fixed sights, blue, checkered hard rubber grips, pre-WWI, 13.1 oz. Mfg. 1908-1909.

$895 $775 $650 $550 $450 $350 $250

MODEL 2 – .25 ACP cal., 2.1 in. barrel, blue finish, hard rubber grips, pop-up rear sight on early models, fixed on late models, 9 3/4 oz. Mfg. 1902-1909.

$650 $525 $400 $275 $185 $135 $125

This model can usually be distinguished by its knurled barrel ring.

* ***Model 2 Early*** – differentiated by its pop-up rear sight.

$1,900 $1,600 $1,300 $1,000 $750 $675 $550

Beware of fakes!

MODEL 3 – .32 ACP cal., 2.6 in. barrel, blue, fixed sights, hard rubber grips, ejection port on left side, 16 1/2 oz. Mfg. 1910-1913.

$4,000 $3,250 $2,500 $2,000 $1,500 $1,000 $750

MODEL 4 – .32 ACP cal., 8 shot, 3 1/2 in. barrel, blue, hard rubber grips, ejection port on left side, 19.4 oz. Mfg. 1910-28.

$550 $425 $325 $250 $200 $150 $100

Add 10% for WWI "Eagle" proofs.

MODEL 5 – better quality version of Model 2, fixed rear sight, 9.71 oz. Mfg. 1913-1915.

$600 $500 $400 $275 $145 $135 $125

GRADING - PPGS™	100%	98%	95%	90%	80%	70%	60%	LAST MSR

MODEL 6 – 9mm Para. cal., 4 7/8 in. barrel, blue, hard rubber grips, ejection port on right side, 34 oz. Approx. 1,000 mfg. 1915-17. Some are Imperial proofed.

	$9,500	$7,250	$5,750	$4,250	$3,000	$2,500	$2,000

MODEL 7 – .25 ACP cal., 3 in. barrel, blue, fixed sights, hard rubber grips, ejection port on right side, 12 oz. Mfg. 1917-18.

	$750	$675	$550	$465	$385	$285	$200

MODEL 8 – .25 ACP cal., 2 7/8 in. barrel, blue or nickel finish, fixed sights, black checkered plastic grips with round medallions, 12.7 oz. Mfg. 1920-43.

	$750	$600	$475	$325	$240	$150	$125

Add 25% for nickel.
Add 25% for engraved slide.

MODEL 9 VEST POCKET – .25 ACP cal., engineering revision of Model 1, 2 in. barrel, blue finish standard, upward ejection, 6 shot bottom release mag., fixed sights, black checkered plastic grips with round medallions, safety lever on left frame side behind trigger, 9 oz. Mfg. 1921-45.

	$750	$650	$575	$495	$395	$285	$160

Add 100% for engraved slide.
Add 20% for nickel.
Add 10% for "Eagle N" proofing.

MODEL PP DOUBLE ACTION – .22 LR, .25 ACP, .32 ACP, or .380 ACP cal., PP designates "Polizei Pistole," 3 7/8 in. barrel, blue, fixed sights, plastic grips. Mfg. 1929-1945. "Crown N" proof until 1939, "Eagle N" Nazi commercial proof until 1945. Approx. serialization 750,000 (1929) - 1,000,000 (combined with PPK, late 1930s), then PP was assigned its own ser. no. range beginning at 100,000P, and by 1945, serialization had reached approx. 396,000P.

.22 LR cal.	$1,500	$1,250	$995	$825	$675	$550	$450
.25 ACP cal.	$8,500	$7,500	$6,500	$5,250	$4,000	$3,000	$2,000
.32 ACP cal.	$850	$725	$600	$475	$375	$275	$225
.380 ACP cal.	$2,000	$1,750	$1,500	$1,200	$1,050	$875	$650

Add 15% for alloy frame.
Values assume original guns without import markings. Recently imported WWII/surplus police used guns are stamped on the frame or receiver, indicating the current importer and address - subtract 20%-30% from values listed for these recent imports.

Original nickel finished Model PPs are very rare; this precludes accurate price evaluation.

* ***Model PP .32 ACP Bottom Release Magazine*** – safety rotates 90 degrees.

	$1,500	$1,200	$800	$650	$550	$425	$395

* ***Model PP .380 ACP Bottom Release Magazine*** – safety rotates 90 degrees.

	$2,750	$2,325	$1,950	$1,650	$1,250	$900	$700

* ***Model PP Pre-War Persian Proofed*** – 9mm kurz cal., BMR proof.

	$2,500	$2,150	$1,825	$1,600	$1,450	$1,250	$995

Subtract 75% for recent imports which have been relisted.

* ***Model PP Pre-War Verchromt .32 or .380 ACP cal.***

	$3,500	$3,000	$2,500	$1,850	$1,400	$1,200	$800

Add 50% for .380 ACP cal.

* ***Model PP Pre-War Stoeger*** – .32 ACP cal. only.

	$2,500	$2,125	$1,650	$1,400	$1,050	$800	$625

* ***Model PP Aluminum Frame*** – safety rotates 90 degrees.

	$1,200	$995	$825	$700	$550	$400	$275

GRADING - PPGS™	100%	98%	95%	90%	80%	70%	60%	LAST MSR

MODEL PP WARTIME PRODUCTION – mfg. 1940-1945, "Eagle N" Proof (Nazi commercial nitro proof after April 1940) or "Crown N" proof (German commercial proofmark used until April, 1940) found on pre-WWII military production. Variations are listed either by proofmarks or frame/slide markings.

* ***Model PP "Waffenamt" Proofed*** – .32 ACP or .380 ACP cal., "Eagle N" military acceptance marking.

.32 ACP cal.								
Milled finish	$1,000	$800	$650	$475	$375	$275	$225	
.380 ACP cal.	$3,500	$3,000	$2,500	$2,000	$1,000	$700	$600	

Add 25%-50% if Waffenamt proofed, depending on condition (late war PPs are sometimes encountered with Walther marked beechwood grips).

* ***Model PP "Eagle N" Proofed*** – .22 LR or .32 ACP cal., with lanyard loop.

.32 ACP cal.	$900	$775	$650	$550	$425	$350	$250	
.22 LR cal.	$1,200	$1,000	$850	$700	$650	$495	$450	

Add 50% to .32 ACP cal., Waffenamt proofed PPs that are hi-gloss finish (all .380s are hi-gloss).
Subtract 25% for post-WWII French added lanyard to the left side of the grip.

In most cases, the .380 ACP cal. has the bottom mag. release.

* ***Model PP "Eagle C & F" Marked (Nazi Police)*** – .32 ACP cal., "Eagle F" or "Eagle C" proofed on left side of frame.

	$1,800	$1,550	$1,200	$875	$725	$650	$525	

Add 25% if Eagle C marked. All hi-gloss are early productions.

* ***Model PP RFV Marked*** – .32 ACP cal., "Crown N". Mfg. for "Reichsfinanzverwaltung" Reich Finance Administration.

	$2,000	$1,650	$1,300	$1,000	$800	$500	$400	

* ***Model PP RJ Marked*** – .32 ACP cal., "Crown N". Mfg. for "Reichsjustizministerium" Reich Justice Ministry.

	$1,700	$1,550	$1,275	$1,000	$800	$500	$450	

* ***Model PP SA Marked*** – .22 LR or .32 ACP cal., "Crown N". Mfg. for SA (Sturm Abteilung - group leaders) of the Nazi party.

	$3,250	$2,650	$2,100	$1,675	$1,250	$925	$600	

Add 20% for .22 LR.
Rare SA markings may bring as much as 50% more over values listed.

There were 28 SA groups.

* ***Model PP NSKK Marked*** – .32 ACP cal., "Crown N" or "Eagle N" proofed. Mfg. for "National- sozialistischer Kraftfahrkorps" Nazi Party Transport Corps, rare.

	$3,500	$2,650	$2,150	$1,700	$1,300	$950	$650	

* ***Model PP RRZ Proofed*** – .32 ACP cal., mfg. for "Reichsrundfunkzentrale" Reich Radio Broadcasting - only 3 known.

Extreme rarity precludes accurate pricing.

* ***Model PP PDM Marked*** – .32 ACP cal., "Crown N" for "Polizeidirektion München" Munich Police Department, all have bottom mag. release.

	$2,750	$2,325	$1,775	$1,450	$1,075	$750	$550	

* ***Model PP AC Marked*** – .32 ACP cal., replaced Walther Banner during 1945, "Eagle N".

	$800	$675	$525	$400	$300	$250	$200	

Some are mismatched (assembled at factory by GIs after the factory was captured). Subtract 20% if mismatched.

* ***Model PP Czech. Contract*** – stamped with "Rampant Lion" design.

	$1,125	$900	$800	$700	$600	$500	$400	

GRADING - PPGS™	100%	98%	95%	90%	80%	70%	60%	LAST MSR
* ***Model PP Panagraph Slide***								
	$2,000	$1,675	$1,425	$1,150	$875	$675	$475	
* ***Model PP Danish Rplt.***								
	$1,200	$1,050	$925	$825	$775	$700	$625	

MODEL PP LIGHTWEIGHT – aluminum alloy frame version.

Add 20% to Standard Model prices.
Add 20%-40% for original nickel finish (very rare).
Add 25% for early hi-gloss finish.

MODEL PPK PRE-WAR PRODUCTION – .22 LR, .25 ACP, .32 ACP, or .380 ACP cal., PPK designates "Polizei Pistole Kriminal" 3 1/4 in. barrel, blue, gold, nickel, or chrome silver, fixed sights, plastic grips. Mfg. circa 1930-1940.

.22 LR cal.	$2,500	$1,550	$1,025	$775	$650	$525	$400
.25 ACP cal.	$10,000	$8,750	$7,500	$4,550	$3,800	$3,400	$2,800
.32 ACP cal.	$1,500	$1,250	$950	$700	$575	$450	$325
.380 ACP cal.	$4,500	$2,500	$1,750	$1,500	$900	$700	$500

Add 60% for bottom release mag (.32 ACP cal.).

MODEL PPK WARTIME PRODUCTION – mfg. 1940-1945, "Eagle N" proofed after April 1940, "Crown N" proofs appear on pre-1940 production with frame/slide markings. Variations are listed either by proof-marks, frame/slide markings, configuration, or type of finish.

* ***Model PPK Commercial "Eagle N" Proofed*** – .22 LR, .32 ACP, or .380 ACP cal., Nazi Eagle over N (standard Nazi commercial acceptance proof).

.22 LR cal.	$2,500	$1,850	$1,350	$900	$750	$525	$460
.32 ACP cal.	$1,500	$1,225	$950	$725	$450	$350	$300
.380 ACP cal.	$3,750	$2,900	$2,200	$1,500	$1,000	$750	$550

This variation is normally encountered with semi-polished, exterior metal showing milling marks to various degrees.

* ***Model PPK Waffenamt Proofed With High Polish Finish***

$2,800 | $2,150 | $1,500 | $1,200 | $700 | $500 | $400

* ***Model PPK "Eagle C" Marked*** – .32 ACP cal., "Crown N" "Eagle C", mfg. for Nazi Police.

$1,850 | $1,400 | $1,000 | $850 | $600 | $500 | $400

Add 25% for high polish finish.

* ***Model PPK "Eagle F" Marked*** – .32 ACP cal., "Crown N" "Eagle F", Nazi Police, all have the light weight aluminum frame.

$2,500 | $2,100 | $1,650 | $1,200 | $900 | $650 | $500

* ***Model PPK RZM Marked*** – .32 ACP cal., "Crown N" proof-marking for "Reichszeugmeisterei" Reich Party Purchasing Office.

$3,250 | $2,750 | $2,250 | $1,750 | $1,250 | $1,000 | $750

* ***Model PPK Party Leader*** – .32 ACP cal., named because grips (brown or black plastic) have the German eagle holding a Swastika, "Crown N" or "Eagle N" proofed, honor weapon awarded 3rd Reich political leaders, rare. Beware of fake grips (especially black color), as reproductions have been made recently. Unfortunately, the grips on a Party Leader (mfg. 1936-41) are the only distinguishing feature on this very desirable configuration.

$8,500 | $6,800 | $5,250 | $3,650 | $3,000 | $2,500 | $2,000

* ***Model PPK RFV Marked*** – .32 ACP cal., "Crown N", mfg. for "Reichsfinanzverwaltung" Reich Finance Administration.

$3,000 | $2,500 | $1,875 | $1,500 | $1,150 | $800 | $700

GRADING - PPGS™	100%	98%	95%	90%	80%	70%	60%	LAST MSR

* ***Model PPK PDM Marked*** – .32 ACP cal., "Crown N", mfg. for "Polizeidirektion München" Police Dept. Munich, all have the bottom mag. release.

	$3,500	$3,000	$2,350	$1,625	$1,100	$800	$600	

* ***Model PPK DRP Marked*** – .32 ACP cal., "Crown N", mfg. for "Deutsche Reichspost" German Postal Service.

	$3,250	$2,850	$2,275	$1,700	$1,050	$800	$600	

* ***Model PPK Panagraph Slide***

	$2,250	$1,825	$1,500	$1,250	$1,025	$875	$750	

* ***Model PPK Verchromt*** – .32 ACP or .380 ACP cal., differentiated by dull silver satin type finish.

	$4,500	$3,850	$3,100	$2,550	$2,000	$1,500	$1,000	

Add 50% for .380 ACP cal.

* ***Model PPK "K" Suffix*** – "K" beneath ser. no., with numbered slide.

	$3,000	$2,500	$1,875	$1,500	$1,150	$800	$700	

Add 10% for matching mag.

* ***Model PPK "W" Suffix*** – .32 ACP cal., "Crown N" proofed, "W" suffix ser. no.

	$1,500	$1,250	$1,000	$850	$650	$475	$375	

* ***Model PPK Early 90 Degree Safety***

	$2,250	$1,825	$1,500	$1,250	$1,025	$875	$750	

* ***Model PPK Early Bottom Release Mag.***

	$3,750	$3,100	$2,500	$2,000	$1,500	$1,250	$1,000	

* ***Model PPK 7-Digit Ser. No.***

	$1,800	$1,500	$1,200	$1,000	$850	$600	$550	

* ***Model PPK Dural Frame*** – .22 LR, .32 ACP, or .380 ACP cal., chrome finish (very rare), "Eagle N".

.32 ACP cal.	$2,250	$1,600	$1,250	$950	$700	$600	$500	
.380 ACP cal.	$6,000	$4,800	$3,800	$2,800	$2,400	$2,000	$1,600	
.22 LR cal.	$3,500	$3,000	$2,400	$1,900	$1,400	$1,200	$1,000	

Add 100% for early production with high-gloss finish (brown cast and green cast).

* ***Model PPK Czech Contract*** – stamped "Rampant Lion" design.

	$2,000	$1,575	$1,250	$1,000	$750	$625	$550	

* ***Model PPK Danish Rplt.***

	$1,750	$1,400	$1,025	$850	$625	$550	$425	

MODEL PPK LIGHTWEIGHT – aluminum alloy frame version.

Add 20% to .32 cal. commercial price listing.

SPORT MODEL 1926 – .22 S or LR cal. (known as Standard Model in Germany).

	$2,500	$2,000	$1,500	$1,200	$1,000	$725	$600	

1932 OLYMPIA MODEL – .22 S or LR cal., 10 shot, 6 or 9 in. barrel, target sights, one-piece grip, introduced in 1928 and used in 1932 Olympics. Marketed by Stoeger and Chas. Heyer-Nairobi.

	$2,500	$1,850	$1,300	$1,000	$800	$700	$600	

Add 20% for longer barrel.

OLYMPIA SPORT MODEL – .22 LR cal., 7.4 in. barrel, adj. target sights, blue, wood grips, 4 barrel weights available. Mfg. 1936-40.

	$2,000	$1,625	$1,275	$1,050	$900	$800	$700	

Add 20% for weight set.

GRADING - PPGS™	100%	98%	95%	90%	80%	70%	60%	LAST MSR

1936 OLYMPIA "JÄGERSCHAFTS" HUNTING MODEL – similar to Sport, with 4 in. barrel. Mfg. 1936-40. Also seen with "Eagle N" proofs.

$2,750	$2,250	$1,650	$1,250	$1,000	$800	$700	

OLYMPIA RAPID FIRE MODEL – .22 Short cal. only, 7.4 in. barrel, blue, adj. sight, wood grip, has alloy slide. Mfg. 1936-40.

$2,500	$2,100	$1,600	$1,200	$995	$600	$525	

1936 OLYMPIA FÜNFKAMPF MODEL – .22 Short or LR cal., 9 1/4 in. barrel, blue, adj. sight, wood grips, barrel weights, circa 1936.

$3,250	$2,750	$2,250	$1,750	$1,500	$1,200	$900	

MODEL HP COMMERCIAL DOUBLE ACTION – 9mm Para. cal., pre-war version of P-38, 5 in. barrel, fixed sight, blue, wood or plastic grips. Mfg. 1937-1944. Many variations, including several different finishes.

See P.38 WWII Military Pistols section for values on this model.

PISTOLS: SEMI-AUTO, POST-WAR

Smith & Wesson has placed a recall on all Walther PPK and PPK/S pistols manufactured by Smith & Wesson from March 21, 2002-Feb. 3, 2009. Ser. no. ranges subject to this recall are as follows: 0010BAB-9999BAB, 0000BAC-9999BAC, 0000BAD-9999BAD, 0000BAE-999BAE, 0000BAF-9999BAF, 0000BAH-9999BAH, 00000BAJ-9999BAJ, 0000BAK-9999BAK, 0000BAL-5313BAL, 0000BAM-1320BAM, 0000LTD-0499LTD, 0001PPK-1500PPK, 0026REP-0219REP, and 0001WLE-0459WLE. Smith & Wesson has advised all owners to discontinue usage and return the pistol to S&W for free repair. Please contact S&W directly for more information (see Trademark Index).

MODEL PP & VARIATIONS – .22 LR, .32 ACP, or .380 ACP cal., double action, specifications similar to pre-war PP, 3 7/8 in. barrel. Imported 1963-2000. German manufacture.

* ***Model PP .380 ACP cal.*** – 7 shot mag.

$750	$600	$450	$350	$300	$275	$250	*$999*

* ***Model PP .32 ACP cal.*** – 8 shot mag.

$650	$500	$395	$295	$275	$250	$225	*$999*

* ***Model PP .22 LR cal.*** – 10 shot mag., disc. 1984.

$800	$650	$425	$375	$325	$300	$275	*$783*

* ***Model PP Blue Engraved*** – .22 LR (disc.) or .380 ACP cal. Disc. 1984.

$1,425	$1,125	$950	$835	$685	$585	$485	*$1,650*

Add 5% for .22 LR cal.

* ***Model PP Chrome Engraved*** – .22 LR or .380 ACP cal. Disc. 1984.

$1,450	$1,125	$900	$785	$655	$550	$465	*$1,600*

Add $50 for .22 LR cal.

* ***Model PP Silver Engraved*** – .22 LR (disc.) or .380 ACP cal. Disc. 1984.

$1,750	$1,200	$1,000	$885	$715	$610	$515	*$1,948*

* ***Model PP Gold Engraved*** – .22 LR (disc.) or .380 ACP cal. Disc. 1984.

$1,950	$1,500	$1,150	$1,025	$830	$710	$590	*$2,053*

* ***Model PP Manurhin*** – .22 LR, .32 ACP, or .380 ACP cal. Disc. 1984.

$525	$440	$350	$225	$180	$165	$150	

Add 10% for .380 ACP cal.

* ***Model PP 50th Anniversary Commemorative*** – .22 LR., .32 ACP, or .380 ACP cal., gold-plated parts, hand-carved grips, presentation case. 500 imported to U.S. 1979. 800 mfg.

$1,625	$1,175	$650	N/A	N/A	N/A	N/A	*$1,700*

GRADING - PPGS™	100%	98%	95%	90%	80%	70%	60%	LAST MSR

* ***Model PP "100 Jahre" 1886-1986*** – 7.65mm cal., 100th anniversary PP edition, primarily made for the German marketplace, inscription marked on right side of slide.

Plastic Grips	$1,050	$750	$625	N/A	N/A	N/A	N/A
Extended Wood Grips	$1,150	$850	$675	N/A	N/A	N/A	N/A

* ***Model PP Last Edition*** – supplied with fitted hard case, certificate, and video of Walther history, 400 mfg. in .32 ACP cal., 100 mfg. in .380 ACP cal., 500 total mfg. in Germany 1999 only.

	$1,350	$1,050	$900	N/A	N/A	N/A	N/A

Add $100 for .380 ACP cal.

This model was the last of the PP, PPK, PPK/S models to be manufactured when Germany stopped production in 1999.

PP SPORT – double action, thumbrest grips, round hammer with spur, adj. rear sight, 6.1 or 8.1 in. barrel, 25.6 or 27.2 oz. Mfg. 1953-70.

Manurhin Mfg.	$900	$750	$625	$550	$495	$425	$350
Mark II (1955-1957)	$1,000	$775	$650	$600	$545	$500	$450
Walther Mfg.	$1,250	$1,000	$750	$625	$575	$525	$450

Subtract 10% if not marked.

Add $75 for barrel weight, $100 for factory case, 20% for factory nickel, 5% for single action.

* ***PP Sport "C" Model C*** – mfg. for competition shooting, single action, 7 5/8 in. barrel, spur hammer.

	$1,250	$1,000	$750	$675	$575	$525	$450

MODEL PP SUPER – .380 ACP cal., 3.6 in. barrel, 7 shot, fixed sights, plastic grips, blue, 1,000 mfg. in .380 ACP cal., 26.8 oz. Mfg. 1973-79.

	$975	$750	$550	$395	$285	$250	$235

* ***Model PP Super Ultra/Police*** – 9x18mm Ultra (aka 9x18mm Police) cal., recently imported West German police trade-ins, approx. 4,000 mfg.

	$475	$400	$350	$300	$275	$250	$225

* ***Model PP Super Super-Cutaway***

	$795	$650	$550	N/A	N/A	N/A	N/A

MODEL PPK – similar to pre-war PPK, .22 LR, .32 ACP, or .380 ACP cal., 3.31 in. barrel. Mfg. post-war-1999, U.S. import stopped by GCA 68 on W. German and French production.

.32 ACP Cal.	$775	$550	$425	$350	$325	$295	$275
.22 LR Cal.	$1,075	$750	$600	$525	$450	$375	$325
.380 ACP Cal.	$1,075	$750	$600	$475	$425	$350	$300
Blue Engraved	$1,675	$1,300	$950	$835	$685	$585	$485
Silver Engraved	$1,950	$1,400	$1,000	$885	$715	$610	$515
Gold Engraved	$2,275	$1,675	$1,250	$1,100	$895	$785	$630

100% column assumes NIB condition - subtract 15% if not boxed.

MODEL PPK LAST EDITION – similar to PP Last Edition, but was never imported into the U.S. because of the GCA of 1968.

MODEL PPK LIGHTWEIGHT – similar to Standard, with dural frame, .22 LR or .32 ACP cal.

	$995	$725	$500	$375	$325	$295	$275

Add 20% for .22 LR cal.

MODEL PPK-1986 U.S. PRODUCTION – .380 ACP cal. only, 3.35 in. barrel, similar specifications as previous W. German and French manufacture, blue or bright nickel (new

GRADING - PPGS™	100%	98%	95%	90%	80%	70%	60%	LAST MSR

1997) finish, 7 shot finger extension mag., black plastic grips, 21 oz. Made in the U.S. Mfg. 1986-2001.

	$450	$365	$320	$295	$270	$250	$225	$543

Manufacture in the U.S. was under an exclusive licensing agreement with Walther of Germany.

* ***Model PPK 1996 U.S. Production Stainless*** – .32 ACP (new 1998) or .380 ACP cal., stainless steel construction. Mfg. 1986-2001.

	$450	$365	$320	$295	$270	$250	$225	$543

MODEL PPK (CURRENT MFG.) – .32 ACP (stainless only beginning 2008) or .380 ACP cal., 3.35 in. barrel, choice of blue or stainless steel, 6 (.380 ACP cal.) or 7 shot mag., 20.8 oz.

MSR $630	$515	$440	$375	$330	$295	$265	$225

Add $230 for Crimson Trace laser grips (disc. 2009).
Add $270 for machine engraving and case (mfg. 2011-2012).

* ***Model PPK 75th Anniversary*** – .380 ACP cal. only, blue finish scroll engraving on frame and slide, "75th Anniversary" script on frame, gold Walther banner and PPK on left side, smooth wood grips, includes wooden presentation case, 1,500 mfg. 2006.

	$875	$750	$675	N/A	N/A	N/A	N/A	$996

MODEL PPK/E – .380 ACP cal., 3.4 in. barrel., high polish blue, 7 (.380 ACP) or 8 (.32 ACP) shot mag., 23 oz.

	$525	$465	$435	$395	$360	$330	$295

While advertised in America during 2000 with a MSR of $294, this model was distributed in Europe only until circa 2008, and was produced with the cooperation of F.E.G., located in Hungary.

Century Arms International began importing used guns circa 2009.

MODEL PPK/S & VARIATIONS – .22 LR, .32 ACP, or .380 ACP cal., similar to PPK, except has larger PP frame to meet import requirements of 1968, 3 1/4 in. barrel, production in W. Germany, Manurhin of France (disc. 1986), and in the U.S. (mfg. under license from Walther by Interarms), 10 (.22 LR) or 8 (.32 ACP and .380 ACP) shot, double action, fixed sights.

* ***American Model PPK/S*** – .380 ACP cal. only, blue or two-tone (.380 ACP cal. only) finish, 8 shot, one finger extension and one flat bottom mag., approx. 26 oz. Disc. 2001, reintroduced 2007.

MSR $630	$515	$440	$375	$330	$295	$265	$225

Add $170 for machine engraving and case (mfg. 2010-2012).

* ***Model PPK/S Stainless*** – .32 ACP (new 1998) or .380 ACP cal., American manufacture, introduced July of 1983.

MSR $629	$510	$435	$375	$330	$295	$265	$225

Add $230 for Crimson Trace laser grips (.380 ACP cal. only, new 2008).

* ***Model PPK/S .22 LR*** – .22 LR cal., 3.3 in. barrel, choice of black finish or stainless steel, checkered black synthetic grips, 10 shot mag. with finger extension, fixed sights, 24 oz. Manufactured in Ulm, Germany. New 2013.

MSR $400	$350	$300	$275	$250	$225	$200	$185

Add $30 for stainless steel.

* ***West German Model PPK/S*** – .22 LR (disc. 1984), .32 ACP (disc. 1999), or .380 ACP (disc. 1999) cal.

.22 LR cal.	$850	$725	$595	$450	$375	$325	$300
.32 ACP cal.	$600	$525	$450	$400	$325	$295	$275
.380 ACP cal.	$750	$675	$550	$400	$325	$295	$275

* ***American Model PPK/S Blue Engraved*** – blue engraved. Disc. 1985.

	$875	$850	$800	$695	$585	$485	$415	$990

GRADING - PPGS™	100%	98%	95%	90%	80%	70%	60%	LAST MSR

* ***American Model PPK/S Gold-Engraved Commemorative*** – 500 total mfg. Disc. 1987.

	$1,000	$875	$700	N/A	N/A	N/A	N/A	*$1,200*

* ***American Model PPK/S Gold-Engraved*** – disc. 1985.

	$975	$850	$700	$585	$500	$415	$365	*$1,070*

* ***West German Model PPK/S Blue Engraved*** – inventory depleted 1990.

	$1,475	$1,050	$850	$740	$620	$515	$440	*$1,550*

* ***West German Model PPK/S Chrome Engraved*** – importation disc. 1991.

	$1,525	$1,075	$950	$835	$685	$585	$485	*$1,700*

* ***West German Model PPK/S Silver Engraved*** – disc. 1988.

	$1,675	$1,150	$975	$860	$700	$600	$500	*$1,700*

* ***West German Model PPK/S Gold Engraved*** – disc. 1985.

	$1,950	$1,250	$1,000	$885	$715	$610	$515	*$1,800*

MANURHIN PPK/S – see listings under Manurhin section.

MODEL PPS – 9mm Para. or .40 S&W cal., 3.2 in. barrel, 5 (.40 S&W cal. only), 6, 7, or 8 (9mm Para. cal. only) shot single stack mag., black polymer frame, matte black metal finish, fixed sights, thinner profile than the PPK (1.04 in.), ambidextrous safety, interchangeable back straps, pre-cocked striker ignition, magazine extension, 6.1 lbs. trigger pull, 21 oz. Importation began 2008.

MSR $600	$525	$450	$415	$365	$325	$295	$275

Add $153 for night sight kit (mfg. 2010-2012).

A first edition was also available in this model in anthracite finish. First edition marking appears on left side of slide. This edition sold out during late 2008.

MODEL PPQ – 9mm Para. or .40 S&W cal., striker fire action, synthetic frame with steel slide, 4 (.40 S&W cal. only), or 4.1 (threaded barrel available on first edition only) in. barrel, 12 (.40 S&W cal. only), 15, or 17 shot mag., black finish, textured synthetic grips, night sights (first edition only) or adj. front and rear sights, Quick Defense Trigger, 24 1/2 oz. Mfg. 2011-2012.

	$525	$450	$415	$365	$325	$295	$275	*$600*

Add $300 for first edition model.

MODEL PPQ M2 – 9mm Para. or .40 S&W cal., appearance and most features similar to Model PPQ, except 4 (9mm Para. only), 4.1 (.40 S&W cal.), 4.6 (threaded, 9mm Para.), or 5 in. barrel, 11, 15, or 17 shot mag., ambidextrous mag. release button, low profile combat sights, 24 oz. New 2013.

MSR $600	$525	$450	$415	$365	$325	$295	$275

Add $100 for 5 in. barrel.

Add $100 for PPQ M2 Navy SD variation with 4.6 in. threaded barrel.

MODEL PPX M1 – 9mm Para. or .40 S&W cal., hammer fired action, DAO, 4 or 4.6 (PPX SD) in. barrel, low profile 3 dot sights, lower Picatinny rail, checkered trigger guard, ergonomic textured synthetic grips, ambidextrous slide stop, bobbed hammer, polymer frame with steel or stainless steel slide, 14 or 16 shot mag., 27.2 oz. Manufactured in Ulm, Germany. New 2013.

MSR $450	$395	$350	$315	$285	$260	$240	$220

Add $50 for stainless steel slide.

MODEL TP – .22 LR or .25 ACP cal., updated version of Model 9, 6 shot, 2.6 in. barrel, concealed hammer, 12 oz. Mfg. 1961-1971.

.22 LR cal.	$950	$750	$550	$350	$300	$260	$225
.25 ACP cal.	$750	$600	$500	$300	$275	$250	$200

GRADING - PPGS™	100%	98%	95%	90%	80%	70%	60%	LAST MSR

MODEL TPH – .22 LR or .25 ACP cal., double action, 2.8 in. barrel, 6 shot, alloy frame, blue, fixed sights, plastic grips, 11 1/2 oz. Mfg. 1968-98 in W. Germany, U.S. import stopped by GCA of 1968.

.22 LR cal.	$1,000	$800	$550	$475	$350	$300	$250	
.25 ACP cal.	$1,100	$850	$600	$500	$400	$325	$275	

Subtract 10% on the 100% values if not boxed with all accessories.

TPH cutaways were also mfg. in small quantities for instructional use. Current pricing for a mint specimen is approx. $1,500.

100% price assumes NIB condition.

AMERICAN MODEL TPH – .22 LR or .25 ACP (new 1992) cal., blue finish or stainless steel, double action, black plastic grips, 6 shot mag., 2 1/4 in. barrel, 14 oz. Mfg. 1987-2000.

	$425	$350	$280	$250	$225	$200	$185	*$460*

* ***American Model TPH Stainless*** – stainless steel fabrication. Disc. 2000.

	$440	$350	$280	$250	$225	$200	$185	*$460*

MODEL P.38 & VARIATIONS – Please refer to listings under the P.38 entries in the P section. Only the currently imported Walther P.38 appears in this section.

* ***Model P.38 (Current Importation)*** – .22 LR, 7.65mm Luger, or 9mm Para. cal., currently imported by Earl's Repair Service.

Current MSR on a 9mm Para. alloy frame is $995, $1,995 for steel frame.

MODELS P1 & P4 – Please refer to listings under the P.38 entries in the P section.

MODEL P5 – 7.65mm Luger, 9mm Para., or 9x21mm cal., double action, alloy frame, ejection port on left side, frame mounted decocking lever, 3 1/2 in. barrel, adj. rear sight, blue finish only, 8 shot mag., auto safeties, 28 oz. New 1977-currently imported by Earl's Repair Service.

No MSR	$1,595	$1,200	$950	$725	$575	$450	$395	

P-5 cutaways were also mfg. in small quantities for instructional use. Current pricing for a mint specimen is approx. $2,000.

* ***Model P5 Compact*** – compact variation of P-5 with 3.1 in. barrel, 26 1/2 oz. Limited importation beginning 1987.

No MSR	$1,695	$1,275	$995	$750	$575	$450	$395	

* ***Model P5 Long*** – special edition, 5.3 in. barrel, wood grips, 29.6 oz. 50 mfg. 1988 only.

	$3,750	$2,750	$2,000	N/A	N/A	N/A	N/A	

* ***Model P5 100th Year Commemorative*** – marked "1886-1986 100 Jahre" with Walther banner, elaborate grip carving, presentation walnut case. Imported 1986-91.

	$2,650	$1,750	$1,100	N/A	N/A	N/A	N/A	*$2,890*

P22 – .22 LR cal., 3/4 scale of the P99, 3.42 in. barrel, hammer fired, black polymer frame with grooved and stippled grip, SA or DA, matte black finish, military green frame or nickel slide, or brushed chrome slide and anthracite frame finish (disc. 2010), internal trigger lock with loaded chamber indicator and mag. disconnect, 10 shot mag., firing pin drop safety, safety key lock on right side of frame, interchangable backstrap, adj. rear (disc.) or 3-dot sights, 15.2 oz. New 2001.

MSR $380	$325	$275	$235	$200	$175	$160	$140	

Add $70 for nickel finish.

Add $71 for brushed chrome slide and anthracite frame finish (mfg. 2007-2010).

Add $100 for laser sight (black finish only).

Add $257 for red dot sight (mfg. 2006-2007).

Walther offered a limited P22 first edition which included two barrels, stabilizer assembly/frame extension for 5 in. barrel, and a blue plastic case. These were marked "Limited Edition P22" and 1,000 were mfg. Current value for a mint gun with all accessories is in the $400-$450 range.

GRADING - PPGS™	100%	98%	95%	90%	80%	70%	60%	LAST MSR

A special edition two barrel set of this model was available exclusively through Davidson's during 2006 - MSR was $370.

* ***P22 Target*** – .22 LR cal., similar to P22, except has 5 in. barrel, and frame extension that slides over barrel, available in black frame with nickel slide or black slide and OD Green frame, 18 1/2 oz. w/o mag. New 2001.

MSR $480	**$430**	**$375**	**$325**	**$275**	**$225**	**$200**	**$175**	

Add $60 for nickel finish.

* ***P22 Military*** – .22 LR cal., similar to P22, except has light brown graphite frame, 17.6 oz. New 2013.

MSR $380	**$325**	**$275**	**$235**	**$200**	**$175**	**$160**	**$140**	

SP22-M1 – .22 LR cal., 4 in. barrel, 10 shot, SA, polymer frame, stainless steel slide, target trigger, wide variety of options, including accessory rails, grips, and optics, 27 oz. Mfg. 2008-2010.

	$325	**$265**	**$225**	**$200**	**$180**	**$160**	**$140**	***$399***

Add $173 for red dot sight, $132 for laser sight, $317 for adj. match grips, $22 for Picatinny rail, and $59 for Truglo fiber optic sights.

* ***SP22-M2*** – .22 LR cal., similar to SP22-M1, except has 6 in. barrel, vertical cutouts under barrel in front of frame assembly. Mfg. 2008-2010.

	$350	**$300**	**$250**	**$225**	**$195**	**$175**	**$150**	***$421***

* ***SP22-M3 Target*** – .22 LR cal., similar to SP22-M2, except has upper and lower accessory rails. Mfg. 2008-2010.

	$425	**$350**	**$300**	**$260**	**$240**	**$220**	**$200**	***$485***

* ***SP22-M4 Match Sport*** – .22 LR cal., 6 in. match grade barrel, ergonomic black stippled wood target grips, 10 shot mag., SA, match trigger, 32 1/2 oz. Mfg. 2008-2010.

	$675	**$600**	**$525**	**$450**	**$400**	**$350**	**$295**	***$784***

MODEL P88 & VARIATIONS – 9mm Para. or 9x21mm cal., double action, alloy frame, 4 in. barrel, 15 shot button release mag., fully ambidextrous, decocking lever, matte finish, adj. rear sight, internal safeties, plastic grips, 31 1/2 oz. Mfg. 1987-93.

	$1,100	**$925**	**$750**	**$600**	**$500**	**$450**	**$400**	***$1,129***

P88 cutaways were also mfg. in small quantities for instructional use. Current pricing for a mint specimen is approx. $2,000.

* ***Model P88 Compact*** – 9mm Para. or 9x21mm cal., 3.93 in. barrel, 14* (disc.) or 10 (C/B 1994) shot mag., 29 oz. Imported 1993-2003.

	$975	**$800**	**$650**	**$550**	**$500**	**$475**	**$450**	***$900***

Add 25% for 14 shot mag.

* ***Model P88 Champion*** – 9mm Para. only, 6 in. barrel, SA only, 14* shot mag., 30.9 oz. Very limited mfg. 1992-disc.

	$2,800	**$1,850**	**$1,500**	**$1,250**	**$995**	**$775**	**$625**	

* ***Model P88 Competition*** – similar to P88 Champion, except has 4 in. barrel, SA only, 14* shot mag., 28.2 oz. Very limited mfg. 1992-disc.

	$2,200	**$1,500**	**$1,250**	**$995**	**$775**	**$625**	**$550**	

* ***Model P88 Sport*** – .22 LR cal. only, 6 in. barrel, SA only, 10 shot mag. Very limited mfg. 1995-disc.

	$2,450	**$1,900**	**$1,550**	**$1,250**	**$995**	**$775**	**$625**	

P99 & VARIATIONS – 9mm Para., 9x21mm (limited importation 1996), or .40 S&W (new 1999) cal., 4 (9mm Para.) or 4.1 (.40 S&W) in. barrel, polymer frame, 10, 12 (.40 S&W cal. only), 15, or 16 (9mm Para. cal. only, disc. 2006) shot mag., standard, anti-stress (traditional double action, AS Model, new 2004), or quick action (QA, allowing consistent

GRADING - PPGS™	100%	98%	95%	90%	80%	70%	60%	LAST MSR

SA trigger performance) trigger, decocking, and internal striker safeties, cocking and loaded chamber indicators, choice of matte black, QPQ (mfg. 1999-2003) finished (silver colored) slide, or titanium coated (mfg. 2003-2006) finish, ambidextrous mag. release, ergonomic black, desert tan (disc. 2008), or green (Military model, new 1999) synthetic grip with interchangeable backstrap, adj. rear sight, 25 oz. Importation began 1995.

MSR $600	$525	$475	$425	$365	$315	$275	$250	

Add $140 for tritium sight set with green 3-dot system (.40 S&W only), or $109 for white 3-dot metal sights (disc. 2011).

Add $260 for night sight kit (mfg. 2010-2011).

Add $31 for titanium finish (disc. 2006).

Add $125 for 9x21mm cal. (disc.).

Engraved P99s were also available in the following configurations in 9mm Para. cal. only - Grade I Arabesque ($3,700 last MSR), Grade II Goldline ($4,200 last MSR), Grade III Arabesque w/gold ($4,660 last MSR).

* ***P99 Compact*** – 9mm Para. or .40 S&W cal., 3 1/2 in. barrel, 8 (.40 S&W cal.) or 10 shot mag. with finger extension, available in QA, AS, or DAO (disc. 2006), Weaver rail, compact frame, blue finish only, 20 oz. New 2004.

MSR $600	$525	$475	$425	$365	$315	$275	$250	

* ***P99 QSA*** – 9mm Para. or .40 S&W cal., first introduced before the QA, slide marked with QSA inscription, large decocking plate. Very few mfg.

	$900	$750	$525	N/A	N/A	N/A	N/A	

* ***P99 2000 Commemorative*** – 9mm Para. or .40 S&W cal., features high polish blue slide with laser inscription "Commemorative for the Year 2000". Limited mfg. 1,000 (only 500 for the U.S.) of each cal. in 2000 only, cased with Walther videotape.

	$850	$650	$495	N/A	N/A	N/A	N/A	*$840*

* ***P99 La Chasse DU Engraved*** – 9mm Para. or .40 S&W cal., similar to Model P-99 Military, except has laser engraved slide, wooden backstrap and green lanyard, luminescent sights, special case. Mfg. 1998-2000.

	$950	$800	$725	N/A	N/A	N/A	N/A	*$1,078*

* ***P99 La Chasse Engraved*** – features choice of elaborate oak leaf, arabesque, or English style hand scroll engraving on polished slide. Mfg. 1998-2000.

	$1,995	$1,600	$1,400	N/A	N/A	N/A	N/A	*$2,126*

* ***P99 Canada Edition*** – 9mm Para. cal. only, 105mm barrel, black finish only, scarce in the U.S., includes two 16 shot mags.

	$1,000	$750	$600	N/A	N/A	N/A	N/A	

* ***P99 Malta Arms Act Special Edition*** – special edition commemorating the Malta Arms Act of 2005, 99 mfg. 2005 only.

	$950	$725	$550	N/A	N/A	N/A	N/A	

MODEL L102A1 – mfg. for the British Special Air Service (SAS), 20-30 imported.

	$1,500	$1,275	$1,050	$900	$750	$600	$495	

MODEL PK380 – .380 ACP cal., 3.6 in. barrel, SA/DA, patterned after the P22, 8 shot mag., choice of black or nickel finish, steel frame, lightweight ergonomic polymer grip, ambidextrous manual safety, 3 dot steel sights, Picatinny bottom rail, approx. 21 oz. New 2009.

MSR $390	$345	$315	$280	$250	$225	$200	$185	

Add $70 for nickel finish.

Add $100 for laser sight (black finish only).

Add 10% for First Edition model (limited mfg. 2009 only).

GRADING - PPGS™	100%	98%	95%	90%	80%	70%	60%	LAST MSR

P990 – similar to P99, except is double action only, features Walther's constant pull trigger system, black, QPQ slide finish, or Military Model (green), 25 oz. Mfg. 1998-2003.

	$550	$475	$425	$385	$350	$325	$295	*$644*

PISTOLS: SEMI-AUTO, TARGET

Walther target pistols are imported by Champions Choice located in La Vergne, TN. Previously imported by Interarms until 1993, Nygord Precision Products until 1996, and by Earl's Repair Service, located in Tewksbury, MA.

Add 10% to the values listed for left-hand stocks (available on most models).

MODEL GSP TARGET STANDARD – .22 LR cal., 4 1/2 in. barrel, single action, 5 shot mag. standard, 8 or 10 shot mag. optional, adj. sights, nickel, two-tone, or blue finish, walnut target grips, 2-stage trigger became optional in 1995, optional carrying case, 42.3 oz. Mfg. 1969-2001.

	$1,425	$1,225	$995	$650	$550	$475	$425	*$1,450*

This model was also available as a complete international package, including a GSP with .22 Short and .32 S&W Wadcutter conversion units, including triggers. MSR was approx. $3,100.

* ***Model GSP Target Junior*** – similar to GSP Target, except has slimmer 4 1/4 in. barrel design, smaller walnut grips, 40.1 oz. Importation disc. 1992.

	$1,450	$1,350	$995	$775	$600	$500	$425	*$1,810*

* ***Model GSP-C Target*** – similar to Model GSP Target, except in .32 S&W Wadcutter, and 4 1/4 in. barrel, 49.4 oz. Mfg. 1971-2001.

	$1,475	$1,025	$800	$650	$550	$475	$425	*$1,595*

Add $1,095 for OSP-2000 .22 Short conversion unit.
Add $995 for GSP .22 LR cal. conversion unit.
Add $1,195 for GSP-C .32 S&W Wadcutter conversion unit.

* ***Model GSP Target Expert*** – .22 LR cal. only, similar to GSP Standard, except for recoil compensation system located in barrel weight, sight radius has been changed, and sights are located further to the rear of the gun, modified frame (cut on an angle) behind the trigger area, stippled blonde/blue ergonomic laminated wood grips, 42.3 oz. New 2001.

MSR $1,795	$1,675	$1,425	$1,250	$1,050	$850	$700	$575	

* ***Model GSPC Target Expert*** – similar to Model GSP Expert, except available in .32 S&W Wadcutter cal., 45.1 oz. Mfg. 2001-2005.

	$2,275	$1,695	$1,100	$850	$675	$575	$495	*$1,695*

* ***Model GSP Target Atlanta*** – .22 LR cal., "Special Edition for the 1996 Olympic Games, Atlanta" inscribed on right side of bolt housing, black laminate grips, titanium plated bolt, otherwise same as GSP Target Standard.

	$1,800	$1,450	$1,000	N/A	N/A	N/A	N/A	

* ***Model GSP Target 25th Year Commemorative Special Limited Edition*** – .22 LR cal., aluminum carrying case, options included two-tone finish, laminated Canadian black birch grip, titanium plated bolt, special 70 g. barrel weight with "25 Jahre GSP" engraved, adj. front sight, two-stage trigger, 3 lbs. 1,000 mfg. 1994.

	$2,500	$2,150	$1,850	N/A	N/A	N/A	N/A	

This model was only available from Earl's Repair Service.

* ***Model GSP-C Target 25th Year Commemorative Special Limited Edition*** – similar to GSP 25th Year Commemorative, except in .32 S&W Wadcutter, engraved 65 g. barrel weight, 1,000 mfg. as complete pistols or conversion units. Mfg. 1996 only.

	$1,995	$1,600	$1,250	N/A	N/A	N/A	N/A	

GRADING - PPGS™	100%	98%	95%	90%	80%	70%	60%	LAST MSR

* ***Model GSP Target Special Anniversary Pistol/Rifle Combination*** – only 50 sets mfg. for 2000, includes scope, pistol, and rifle conversion kit, includes carry case. Disc.

	$5,000	$3,750	$2,750	N/A	N/A	N/A	N/A	*$5,500*

This combo was only available from Earl's Repair Service.

* ***Model GSP Target Rifle Conversion Kit*** – .22 LR cal., unique conversion allows inserting a GSP action in a rifle stock, includes 16 3/4 in. (18 1/4 with GSP compensator) stainless barrel, black, brown, camo, or Walther blue, laminate stock, right or left-hand, 5, 8, or 10 shot mag. New 1996.

MSR $995	$995	$850	$725	$610	$515	$425	$375	

Add $155 with Super Match stock.
Add $300 for Super Match Kit.
Add $75 for left-hand stock.

This rifle conversion kit is only available from Earl's Repair Service, Inc.

MODEL KSP 200 – .22 LR cal., adj. laminated ergonomic grips, target trigger and sights, two-tone slide finish, mfg. in cooperation with Baikal. Mfg. 2000-2004.

	$500	$450	$415	$385	$350	$325	$295	*$575*

MODEL OSP – similar to GSP, in .22 Short cal. Mfg. 1961-1994 for international competition (meets ISU and NRA regs.), 3.35 (new 1994, current model is OSP 2000) or 4 1/4 in. barrel, 44.4 oz.

MSR $1,795	$1,675	$1,425	$1,200	$975	$850	$725	$600	

MODEL SSP EXPERT – .22 LR cal., 6 in. barrel, lightweight construction, black synthetic ergonomic grips in three different sizes, pneumatic buffer, cocking indicator, extended rear sight, 5 shot mag., 34 oz. Importation began 2006.

MSR $2,095	$1,950	$1,775	$1,550	$1,350	$1,150	$875	$700	

FREE PISTOL – .22 LR cal., single shot, electronic trigger, 11.8 in. heavy barrel, advanced target design with fully adj. grips and sights, 49.4 oz. Mfg. 1977-91.

	$1,450	$1,200	$1,000	$850	$675	$575	$500	*$2,140*

HÄMMERLI-WALTHER – see Hämmerli.

REVOLVERS

MODEL R99 – .357 Mag. cal., 6 shot, double action, 3 in. barrel, adj. rear sight, blue or stainless steel, unique Duo-grip allows for different hand sizes (2 grips included), 28 1/2 oz. Mfg. by Smith & Wesson 1999 only for the European market with no U.S. importation.

This model was basically a variation of the S&W Models 19 (blue) or 66 (stainless).

RIFLES: DISC.

MODEL B – .30-06 cal., bolt action, post-war mfg., 22 in. barrel. Disc.

	$775	$625	$500	$400	$300	$250	$200	

Add 20% for double-set triggers.

MODEL 1 AUTOLOADING – .22 LR cal., Carbine model, autoloading, 20 1/2 in. barrel, 5 or 9 (optional) shot detachable mag., could be used as bolt action or semi-auto, checkered pistol grip, walnut sporter stock, 5 1/2 lbs.

	$895	$800	$700	$600	$500	$400	$300	

MODEL 2 AUTOLOADING – .22 LR cal., similar to Model 1, except has 24 1/2 in. barrel, finger grooved forearm, tangent sight, adj. trigger, checkered sporter stock, pre-war, 7 lbs.

	$995	$875	$775	$625	$500	$400	$300	

MODEL V CHAMPION – micrometer adj. sight and checkered pistol grip stock.

	$775	$625	$500	$400	$300	$250	$200	

GRADING - PPGS™	100%	98%	95%	90%	80%	70%	60%	LAST MSR

MODEL DSM 34 – .22 LR cal., single shot, military stock, tangent sight. Pre-war and wartime mfg.

	$1,000	$650	$550	$500	$450	$375	$300	

Add 50% for stamp in stock.
Add 20% for AS stamp in stock.

MODEL KKM INTERNATIONAL MATCH – .22 LR cal., single shot bolt action, 28 in. heavy barrel, adj. aperture sight, adj. hook butt, thumbhole stock, accessory rail, post-war mfg.

	$880	$770	$715	$660	$550	$495	$440	

MODEL KKM-S – similar to KKM, with adj. cheekpiece.

	$935	$825	$770	$715	$605	$550	$495	

MODEL KKJ SPORTER – .22 LR cal., bolt action, 5 shot, 22 1/2 in. barrel, open sight, checkered sporter stock, post-war.

	$1,250	$995	$650	$550	$450	$385	$330	

Add 20% for double-set triggers.

MODEL KKJ-MA – .22 WMR cal.

	$1,250	$1,100	$775	$650	$550	$450	$385	

MODEL KKJ-HO – .22 Hornet cal., repeater or single shot (Model KKJ-E).

	$1,450	$1,225	$825	$700	$575	$450	$385	

Add 20% for double-set triggers.

MODEL KKW – .22 LR cal., single shot, military stock, tangent sight, pre-war and wartime mfg.

	$750	$600	$420	$300	$260	$220	$195	

Add 50% for SA stamp on stock.

MODEL SSV VARMINT – .22 LR cal., single shot bolt action, 25 1/2 in. barrel, no sights, Monte Carlo pistol grip stock, post-war mfg.

	$700	$600	$525	$495	$415	$360	$330	
.22 Hornet cal.	$825	$725	$600	$550	$475	$415	$385	

MODEL UIT BV UNIVERSAL – .22 LR cal., single shot bolt action, 25.6 in. heavy barrel, adj. aperture sight, target stock with palm rest, adj. butt, meets ISU regs., 11 lbs. Disc. 1990.

	$1,325	$1,050	$850	$700	$635	$580	$530	*$1,700*

This model was previously known as the Model UIT Special.

MODEL UIT MATCH – .22 LR cal., similar to Model UIT, except with improved stock design which includes fully stippled lower forearm and pistol grip, 25.6 in. barrel, 8.6 lbs. Importation disc. 1993.

	$1,125	$925	$800	$660	$610	$555	$510	*$1,400*

* ***Model UIT-E Match*** – electronic trigger, 25.6 in. barrel, 10.4 lbs. Disc. 1986.

	$1,350	$940	$860	$770	$670	$630	$560	*$1,250*

GX-1 – .22 LR cal., similar to Model UIT Match, 25 in. barrel with fully adj. free rifle stock, all accessories included, 16 1/2 lbs. Importation disc. 1991.

	$1,895	$1,375	$1,125	$985	$860	$775	$680	*$2,350*

MODEL PRONE 400 – similar to UIT Match, with Prone style competition stock and no sights. Disc.

	$750	$635	$580	$525	$415	$360	$305	

MODEL KK/MS SILHOUETTE – .22 LR cal. only, designed for silhouette shooting, no sights, thumbhole stock with adj. butt, fully stippled forend and stock grip, front barrel weight, 23.6 in. barrel, 16.3 lbs. Imported 1984-91.

	$975	$795	$625	$560	$495	$435	$395	*$1,175*

GRADING - PPGS™	100%	98%	95%	90%	80%	70%	60%	LAST MSR

RUNNING BOAR MODEL 500 – similar to KK/MS Silhouette, no sights, thumbhole stock with adj. wood buttplate and cheekpiece, 23.6 in. barrel, 8.4 lbs. Disc. 1990.

$1,195 $900 $675 $575 $500 $435 $395 *$1,300*

MODEL WA-2000 – .300 Win. Mag. (55 mfg., standard) or .308 Win. (92 mfg., optional) cal., ultra-deluxe semi-auto, 25.6 in. barrel, 5 or 6 shot mag., optional extras include aluminum case, spare mags., integral bipod, adj. tools and leather sling, regular or night vision scope, special order only, 16 3/4 lbs. Disc. 1988.

$36,000 $32,000 $29,000 $27,000 $25,000 $22,500 $20,000

A 7.5 Swiss cal. conversion kit was also optional on this model.

RIFLES: CURRENT/RECENT MFG.

Except for the G22 and GSP rifles, the following models are available from Champion's Choice.

MODEL G22 SEMI-AUTO – .22 LR cal., bullpup design, 20 in. barrel, 10 shot mag., fire control and mag. integrated in rear of stock, black synthetic, carbon fiber, or camo (disc. 2006) thumbhole stock, adj. sliding sights, right or left-hand controls and ejection, blue or military green finish, Weaver style rails on rear sight/carry handle, lower forearm, and on front right mount, approx. 6 lbs. Mfg. 2004-2011.

$435 $380 $330 $290 $250 $225 $195 *$509*

Add $39 for scope or $67 for laser or $102 for red-dot sights (disc. 2009).

Add $56 for carbon fiber stock (disc. 2007) or $50 for camo stock (disc. 2006).

MODEL KK200 – .22 LR cal., available in standard rifle laminated stock, power match, and sport configurations, top-of-the-line competition model, 19.7 in. barrel, 11.57 lbs.

MSR N/A $1,995 $1,675 $1,375 $1,050 $850 $725 $600

Add approx. $1,000 for machined KK200 Power Match Model with nickel plated stippled stock and forend, 25 1/2 in. barrel, 13 lbs. (limited mfg. 1995).

Add approx. $500 for KK200 S (sport configuration).

Add $265 for electronic trigger on Power Match or Sport Models.

MODEL KK300 – similar to Model KK200, except has target or adj. aluminum competition stock. Importation began 2006.

MSR N/A $2,625 $2,350 1,900 $1,600 $1,300 $995 $750

Add $1,200 for adj. aluminum competition stock.

MODEL KK CLUB SPORT RIFLE – .22 LR cal. New 2000.

MSR N/A $525 $450 $400 $350 $275 $260 $230

MODEL GSP RIFLE – .22 LR cal., utilizes GSP sport pistol action, 16 3/4 in. stainless fluted barrel, through engraved compensator, laminated "silhouette style" thumbhole stock, 5 shot standard, 8 or 10 shot optional, optics or scope optional, 8.55 lbs. Imported 1996-2007.

$2,400 $2,100 $1,800 $1,500 $1,250 $1,125 $1,000 *$2,590*

This model was only available from Earl's Repair Service.

SHOTGUNS: SxS

MODEL WSF – 12 or 16 ga., checkered walnut stock, double triggers, boxlock, sling swivels, 28.4 in. barrel. Introduced 1932-disc.

$725 $575 $425 $325 $275 $240 $200

MODEL WSFD – 12 or 16 ga., cheekpiece, checkered walnut stock, double triggers, boxlock, sling swivels, 6.3 (16 ga.) or 6.6 (12 ga.) lbs. Introduced 1932-disc.

$925 $725 $575 $450 $400 $350 $300

SHOTGUNS: SEMI-AUTO

WALTHER SEMI-AUTO – 12 ga. only, 2 3/4 in. chamber, 25 1/2 in. barrel, crossbolt safety, checkered walnut stock and forearm. Mfg. in Zella-Mehlis 1921-1931.

$975 $895 $795 $675 $550 $450 $375

GRADING - PPGS™	100%	98%	95%	90%	80%	70%	60%	LAST MSR

WALTHER, FRENCH-MADE BY MANURHIN

Previously manufactured in Mulhouse, France. Previously imported 1984-86 by Matra-Manurhin International, Inc. located in Alexandria, VA.

PISTOLS: SEMI-AUTO

Manufacture of these Walther PP type pistols commenced in Mulhouse, France in 1951. They were marked "MANURHIN" on the slide until 1954. Since then they were designated Walther MKII. They were imported into the USA by Interarms up to 1983.

In 1984, following a disagreement regarding the use of the Walther trademark, a few pistols were manufactured using the standard Walther slide legend, w/o the "under license of" above the legend. Additionally, the Manurhin name, logo, and the words "Made in France" were stamped on the heel of the gun in very small letters. Following this French production, pistols were made in Germany and marked Walther, or made in France and marked Manurhin. Manurhin briefly set up an office in New York to do its own importation, and later moved to Florida.

In 1984, Manurhin was imported directly with no Interarms logo or Walther trademark appearing on Models PP and PPK/S. Importation was discontinued 1986, when all production resumed in Ulm, Germany.

MODEL PP – .22 LR, .32 ACP, or .380 ACP cal., 3 7/8 in. barrel, 10 shot mag. (.22 LR), 8 shot mag. (.32 ACP), 7 shot mag. (.380 ACP), blue only, all steel construction, double action with positive hammer block safety, 24 oz.

$450 $350 $300 $230 $205 $185 $170 *$419*

Add 20% for .22 LR or .380 ACP cal.
Add $46 for Durgarde finish.

* ***Model PP Collector*** – blue finish, special engraving. Imported 1986 only.

$465 $415 $350 $285 $250 $215 $185 *$529*

* ***Model PP Presentation*** – blue finish, special ornamentation. Imported 1986 only.

$720 $650 $500 $430 $375 $315 $270 *$819*

* ***Model PP Interarms Import***

$395 $325 $285 $235 $200 $170 $145

This model was also available with various engraving options in either blue, nickel, or gold finish - prices ranged from $222 - $540.

PP SPORT – .22 LR cal. only, double action, 6.1 or 8.1 in. barrel, blue finish only, precision adj. sights, contoured plastic grips with thumbrest, 25 oz. New Manurhin design beginning 1985-disc.

$545 $485 $430 $385 $325 $290 $270 *$635*

* ***PP Sport-C*** – similar to PP Sport, except is single action.

$540 $475 $415 $370 $310 $280 $260 *$635*

MODEL PPK – .22 LR, .32 ACP, or .380 ACP cal., 3 1/4 in. barrel, 7 (.380 ACP), 8 (.32 ACP), or 10 (.22 LR) shot mag., blue only, all steel construction, double action with positive hammer block safety, 23 oz.

$550 $475 $425 $375 $350 $325 $300

Add 20% for .22 LR or .380 ACP cal.

MODEL PPK/S – .22 LR, .32 ACP, or .380 ACP cal., 3 1/4 in. barrel, 7 (.380 ACP), 8 (.32 ACP), or 10 (.22 LR) shot mag., blue only, all steel construction, double action with positive hammer block safety, 23 oz.

$400 $350 $300 $230 $205 $185 $170 *$419*

Add 20% for .22 LR cal.

GRADING - PPGS™	100%	98%	95%	90%	80%	70%	60%	LAST MSR

* ***Model PPK/S Durgarde*** – similar to Model PPK/S, only with bonded brushed chrome finish.

	$450	$400	$350	$300	$275	$250	$240	*$465*

Add 20% for .22 LR cal.

* ***Model PPK/S Collector*** – blue finish, special engraving. Imported 1986 only.

	$465	$415	$350	$300	$275	$250	$225	*$529*

* ***Model PPK/S Presentation*** – blue finish, special ornamentation. Imported 1986 only.

	$720	$650	$500	$430	$375	$315	$270	*$819*

* ***Model PPK/S Interarms Import***

	$395	$340	$300	$230	$205	$185	$170	

This model was also available with various engraving options in either blue, nickel, or gold finish - prices ranged from $222-$540.

WAMO MFG.

Previous manufacturer located in San Gabriel, CA.

In addition to making air guns, Wamo also manufactured the .22 LR Powermaster pistol, the Hamilton pirate pistol, and the Tommygun. Pistol values are currently in the $150-$350 range, while the Tommygun ranges from $195-$350 (must be original and complete).

WARNER ARMS CORPORATION

Previous manufacturer located in Norwich, CT.

PISTOLS: SEMI-AUTO

INFALLIBLE POCKET AUTO PISTOL – .32 ACP cal., 7 shot, 3 in. barrel, fixed sights, rubber grips. Mfg. 1917-19.

	$450	$350	$250	$150	$125	$100	$90	

WASATCH PRECISION ARMS

Previous custom bolt action rifle manufacturer located in Ogden, UT until 2011.

RIFLES: BOLT ACTION

Wasatch Precision Arms manufactured custom bolt action rifles based on the Rem. 700 action with synthetic and carbon fiber stocks. Models included: Wasatch Summit (last MSR in 2011 was $3,995), Wasatch Summit Carbon (last MSR in 2011 was $3,995), Open Country (last MSR in 2011 was $2,295), Open Country Carbon (last MSR in 2011 was $2,495), Ridge Top Carbon (last MSR in 2011 was $1,895), and the Flat Lander (last MSR in 2011 was $1,695).

WATSON BROS.

Current long gun manufacturer established in 1885, and located in London, England.

Watson Bros. manufactures distinct round body actions with self-opening locks in both SxS and O/U shotgun configurations. Back action sidelock double rifles are also available. All guns are built to custom order. Please contact the factory directly (see Trademark Index) for more information including current pricing.

WEATHERBY

Current trademark manufactured and imported by Weatherby located Paso Robles, CA since 2006. Previously located in Atascadero, CA 1995-2006, and in South Gate, CA, 1945-1995. Weatherby began manufacturing rifles in the U.S. during early 1995. Dealer and distributor sales.

Weatherby is an importer and manufacturer of long arms. Earlier production was from Germany and Italy, and German mfg. is usually what is collectible. Rifles are currently produced in the U.S., while O/U shotguns are made in Italy and semi-autos are mfg. in Turkey.

GRADING - PPGS™	100%	98%	95%	90%	80%	70%	60%	LAST MSR

Weatherby is well-known for their high-velocity proprietary rifle calibers.

Weatherby offers a research authentication service for Weatherby firearms. The cost is $50 per serial number ($75 for custom rifles, $100 for special editions and commemoratives), and includes a certificate signed by Roy Weatherby Jr. and company historian Dean Rumbaugh. Please contact the company directly for more information regarding this service (see Trademark Index).

Early Weatherby rifles used a Mathieu Arms action in the 1950s - primarily since it was available in left-hand action. Right-handed actions were normally mfg. from the FN Mauser type.

DRILLINGS

WEATHERBY DRILLING – mfg. by J. P. Sauer during the late 1960s-early 1970s for Weatherby importation (marked "Weatherby" on right barrel), identical to Sauer Model 3000, except was not available in all metric cals. Disc.

	100%	98%	95%	90%	80%	70%	60%	LAST MSR
	$2,850	**$2,450**	**$2,100**	**$1,800**	**$1,500**	**$1,250**	**$1,000**	

PISTOLS: BOLT ACTION

SILHOUETTE PISTOL – .22-250 Rem. or .308 Win. cal., mfg. in Japan during late 1970s, 14 1/2 in. barrel, Lyman or Williams sights, fitted case. Only 50 were mfg. in .22-250 Rem. and 150 in .308 Win. cal. Disc. 1981.

	100%	98%	95%	90%	80%	70%	60%	LAST MSR
	$3,750	**$3,300**	**$2,750**	**$2,450**	**$2,100**	**$1,850**	**$1,650**	

MARK V CFP (CENTERFIRE PISTOLS) – .22-250 Rem., .223 Rem. (new 2000), .243 Win., 7mm-08 Rem., or .308 Win. cal., features 15 in. fluted stainless steel barrel with recessed crown, ambidextrous designed multi-layer brown laminate stock with finger grooves and swivel studs, blue Mark V lightweight action, no sights, 3 shot internal mag., 5 1/4 lbs. Mfg. 1997-2000.

	100%	98%	95%	90%	80%	70%	60%	LAST MSR
	$935	**$815**	**$735**	**$650**	**$600**	**$550**	**$500**	***$1,099***

* ***Mark V CFP Accumark*** – same cals. as Mark V CFP, features specially designed synthetic stock with Kevlar and other fibers, matte black finish with grey spider web pattern, 5 lbs. Limited mfg. 2000 only.

	100%	98%	95%	90%	80%	70%	60%	LAST MSR
	$935	**$815**	**$735**	**$650**	**$600**	**$550**	**$500**	***$1,099***

MARK V CFP (COMPACT FIRING PLATFORM) – .22-250 Rem., .223 Rem., .243 Win., or 7mm-08 Rem. cal., 16 in. unfluted matte blue barrel w/o sights, matte blue action, right hand Mark V one-piece bolt with 54 degree lift, tan Fibermark composite stock with black spider webbing and ambidextrous grip, 5 shot internal mag., Talley rings and bases became standard 2007, 5 1/4 lbs. Mfg. 2006-2010.

	100%	98%	95%	90%	80%	70%	60%	LAST MSR
	$1,425	**$1,150**	**$875**	**$750**	**$625**	**$525**	**$475**	***$1,689***

RIFLES: RIMFIRE

ACCUMARK CLASSIC & DELUXE BOLT ACTION – while these models were advertised in 1990 ($635 retail), they never went into production.

MARK XXII CLIP MAG OR TUBE FEED SEMI-AUTO – .22 LR cal., mag. feed, skip-line checkered walnut stock with or without rosewood forend and pistol grip cap, clip models have 5 or 10 shot detachable mag., 24 in. barrel, open V rear fold down sight, grooved alloy receiver, all XXIIs had a right side lever that allowed changing from semi-auto to single shot, tube feed model weighs approx. 6 lbs., 10 oz., clip model weighs 5 lbs., 13 oz. Approx. 100,000 mfg. 1964-1989.

	100%	98%	95%	90%	80%	70%	60%	LAST MSR
Italian/ Japanese mfg.	**$775**	**$695**	**$650**	**$500**	**$400**	**$325**	**$275**	***$454***

Subtract 15% if trigger guard and floor plate is discolored (should be dark black like the receiver NOT turning gray), beware of refinished trigger guard/floor plates.

Subtract 5% without original sling swivels.

Subtract 5-10% for stocks with knots (usually JC or JT serial number prefix guns) and also stocks lacking figuring.

GRADING - PPGS™	100%	98%	95%	90%	80%	70%	60%	LAST MSR

Tube feed models are the most common, but more clip fed models were made.

There were three different Japanese manufacturers between 1967-1989 (not domestically imported after 1989). During this time, the type and quality of the wood and finish, safety lever, rear sight, trigger, floorplate design and magazines were just some of the many changes that occurred during this manufacturing period. Because of this, prices could fluctuate approx. 10%-20%, depending on what features have become more desirable today. A slight premium may be asked for U.S. mfg. Weatherby Mark XXII.

A Weatherby Mark XXII 4x50 scope was also marketed with these .22 cal rifles. The scope was made in Japan. It is a 4x28mm and not 4x50mm. The 4x was the magnification power. The 50 was a measure of the relative brightness or light gathering capabilities and not the diameter of the objective lens. If new in original box with papers the value is approx. $175.00. If used in good condition with original box, the value is approx. $140.00. If used without box, the value is approx. $45.00 to $100.00 (depending upon condition).

This model was originally mfg. in Italy by Beretta (there were no tube feed models made in Italy), followed by two different Japanese manufacturers, then production went to the U.S. briefly (Mossberg mfg.) and ended up back in Japan. This rifle was marketed for a stylish appearance and most buyers took good care of these guns and as a result, it is common to find these guns in 95% condition or better. Buyers beware, in recent years, there has been a wide difference between the "advertised prices" and the "actual selling prices". Also many Italian XXIIs have been appearing which have been refinished. Blonde wood is quite common on guns made after 1980, and often lack wood grain figuring.

MARK XXII BOLT ACTION – .17 HMR or .22 LR cal., features Anschutz action/barrel, 23 in. target grade barrel w/o sights, blue finish, deluxe checkered gloss finished Monte Carlo full pistol grip stock and forearm with rosewood caps, target type bolt handle with special cam cocking, 4 or 5 shot mag., adj. single stage trigger, supplied w/test target, approx. 6 1/2 lbs. Mfg. 2007-2011.

$950	$895	$795	$675	$500	$425	$325	*$999*

Add $100 for .17 HMR cal.

RIFLES: BOLT ACTION, MARK V SERIES

Pre-Mark V production started in 1945 and ended in 1961. Initially, rifles were customized from customer supplied guns, and this ended circa 1949. Between 1949-1963, Weatherby manufactured rifles in Southgate from FN Mauser actions in various cals., including the .257, .270, 7mm, .300, and .375 Wby. Mag. cals. From 1955-1959, Southgate also manufactured guns using the Mathieu left-hand action. Additionally, Schultz & Larson from Denmark was subcontracted to make rifles in .378 Wby. Mag. circa 1955-1962. Between 1956-1962, Southgate manufactured a .460 Wby. Mag. cal. using the Brevex Magnum action. Sako of Finland was also subcontracted circa 1957-1961 to produce rifles using a FN Mauser action. Initial Mark V production began in Southgate circa 1958-1959. During 1959-1973, J.P. Sauer of W. Germany was subcontracted to make the Mark V in a variety of calibers up to .460 Wby. Mag. These earlier pre-Mark V rifles will have a 20%-30% premium, depending on original condition and caliber.

In 1992, 24 in. barrels were disc. on most calibers of .300 or greater (including Models Mark V Deluxe, Fibermark, Lazermark, and Euromark). The Mark V action has also been manufactured in Japan.

All recently manufactured Weatherby Magnums in .30-378, .338-378, .378, .416, and .460 cal. are equipped with an Accubrake.

MARK V DELUXE – .22-250 Rem. (mfg. 1999-2004), .240 Wby. Mag. (disc. 1996, reintroduced 1999-2004, 2007-2011), .243 Win. (mfg. 1999-2004, reintroduced 2007-2011), .25-06 Rem. (mfg. 1999-2004), .257 Wby. Mag., .270 Win. (mfg. 1999-2004, reintroduced 2007-2011), .270 Wby. Mag., .280 Rem. (mfg. 1999-2004), 7mm Wby. Mag., 7mm-08 Rem. (mfg. 1999-2004, reintroduced 2007), .30-06 (disc. 1996, reintroduced 1999-2004, again beginning 2007), .308 Win. (mfg. 1999-2004, reintroduced 2007), .300 Wby. Mag., .340 Wby. Mag., .375 H&H (mfg. 1993 only), .378 Wby. Mag., .416 Wby. Mag., or .460 Wby. Mag. cal., bolt action, 3-5 shot mag., 24 (short action cals.) or 26 (Wby. Mag. cals) in. barrel, current mfg. has 9 locking lugs (Mag. cals.) or 6 locking lugs (standard cals. and

GRADING - PPGS™	100%	98%	95%	90%	80%	70%	60%	LAST MSR

.240 Wby. Mag.), deluxe skip line checkered (disc.) or fineline checkered pistol grip walnut stock with rosewood tipped forearm and pistol grip, current production includes Pachmayr Decelerator pad, no sights, 8 lbs. Left-hand actions (.270 Wby. Mag. and .300 Wby. Mag.) were available at no extra charge through 1997. Mfg. began 1957.

Add 15%-25% for German manufacture (J.P. Sauer) in calibers under .35 if condition is 95% or better.

* ***Mark V Deluxe Short Action Cals.*** – .22-250 Rem. (disc.), .243 Win. (disc. 2011), .240 Wby. Mag. (disc. 2010, reintroduced 2013), .25-06 Rem. (disc.), .270 Win., .280 Rem. (disc.), .30-06, .308 Win., or 7mm-08 Rem. (disc. 2010) short action cals. Mfg. 1999-2004, reintroduced 2007.

MSR $2,400	$1,850	$1,600	$1,350	$1,175	$975	$800	$625

* ***Mark V Deluxe Wby. Mag. Cals.*** – includes cals. between .257 Wby. Mag. - .375 H&H, 8 1/2 lbs.

MSR $2,400	$1,850	$1,600	$1,350	$1,175	$975	$800	$625

Add approx. $200 for .375 H&H cal. (disc. 1993).

* ***Mark V Deluxe .30-378 or .378 Wby. Mag. Cals.*** – .30-378 Wby. Mag. (mfg. 2006), .378 Wby. Mag. cal., 26 (disc.) or 28 (with muzzle brake) in. barrel, 8 1/2 lbs.

MSR $2,800	$2,225	$1,900	$1,650	$1,495	$1,195	$980	$760

* ***Mark V Deluxe .416 Wby. Mag. Cal.*** – first new caliber (introduced 1989) since the .240 Mag. was released 1965, 26 (disc.) or 28 in. barrel, includes muzzle brake, 9 lbs.

MSR $2,800	$2,225	$1,900	$1,650	$1,495	$1,195	$980	$760

* ***Mark V Deluxe .460 Wby. Mag. Cal.*** – 24 (disc.), 26 (disc.) or 28 (new 2004) in. barrel, includes custom stock, integral muzzle brake, 10 lbs.

MSR $3,300	$2,625	$2,300	$1,950	$1,750	$1,400	$1,175	$900

This model is available in left-hand at no charge.

ACCUMARK (MAG. CALS.) – .240 Wby. Mag., .257 Wby. Mag., .270 Wby. Mag., .300 Win. Mag., .300 Wby. Mag., .30-378 Wby. Mag. (new 1997), .338-378 Wby Mag. (new 1998), 7mm STW (mfg. 1998-2004), 7mm Rem. Mag., 7mm Wby. Mag.,.338 Lapua (new 2012) or .340 Wby. Mag. cal., features Bell & Carlson hand laminated fiberglass (disc.) or raised comb Monte Carlo composite stock with matte gel coat finish and spiderweb accents, Pachmayr Decelerator pad, 2 or 3 shot mag., 26 or 28 (.30-378 or .338-378 Wby. Mag. cals. only) in. stainless steel fluted barrel, aluminum bedding plate, fully adj. trigger, approx. 8 3/4 lbs. New 1996.

MSR $2,100	$1,650	$1,425	$1,200	$1,050	$875	$725	$550

Add $200 for .338 Lapua (new 2012). Add $300 for .30-378 Wby. Mag., or .338-378 Wby. Mag. cals. with Accubrake barrel.

Add $100 for left-hand action (current mfg. is .257 Wby., .300 Wby. Mag., or .30-378 Wby. Mag. (disc. 2012) cals. only, other cals. available 1999-2004, reintroduced 2006).

Subtract $70 for .240 Wby. Mag. cal. (disc. 2010).

* ***Accumark (Reg. Cals.)*** – .22-250 Rem. (disc.), .223 Rem. (mfg. 2000-2004), .243 Win. (disc. 2011), .25-06 Rem. (disc. 2010), .270 Win., .280 Rem. (disc.), 7mm-08 Rem. (disc.), .30-06 (disc. 2009, reintroduced 2013), or .308 Win. cal., 5 shot mag., features hand laminated fiberglass stock (disc.) or raised comb Monte Carlo composite stock with matte gel coat finish and spiderweb accents, Pachmayr Decelerator pad, 24 in. fluted stainless barrel w/o sights, 7 1/4 lbs. Mfg. 1998-2004, reintroduced 2007.

MSR $2,100	$1,650	$1,425	$1,200	$1,050	$875	$725	$550

ACCUMARK RC (MAG. CALS.) – .240 Wby. Mag., .257 Wby. Mag., .270 Wby. Mag., .300 Win. Mag., .300 Wby. Mag., .340 Wby. Mag., .338 Lapua, .30-378 Wby. Mag., .338-378 Wby. Mag., 7mm Wby. Mag., or 7mm Rem. Mag. cal., 2, 3, or 5 (.240 Wby. Mag. only) shot mag., 24, 26, or 28 in free floating stainless steel fluted barrel, hand laminated raised

GRADING - PPGS™	100%	98%	95%	90%	80%	70%	60%	LAST MSR

comb Monte Carlo composite stock with matte gel coat finish and spiderweb accents, Pachmayr Decelerator pad, fully adj. trigger, Special RC engraved floorplate, 7 1/4-9 lbs. New 2013.

MSR $2,400 $1,850 $1,600 $1,550 41,175 $975 $800 $625

Add $300 for .30-378 Wby. Mag., .338-378 Wby. Mag., or .338 Lapua cals.

ACCUMARK RC (REG. CALS.) – .270 Win., .30-06, or .308 Win. cal., 5 shot mag., 24 in free floating stainless steel fluted barrel, hand laminated raised comb Monte Carlo composite stock with matte gel coat finish and spiderweb accents, Pachmayr Decelerator pad, fully adj. trigger, Special RC engraved floorplate, 7 1/4 lbs. New 2013.

MSR $2,400 $1,850 $1,600 $1,550 41,175 $975 $800 $625

CLASSICMARK I – available in 9 Wby. Mag. cals. in addition to .270 Win., 7mm Rem. Mag., .30-06, or .375 H&H cal., oil finished American claro walnut stock with no cheekpiece and ebony forend cap, 1 in. solid recoil pad, panel point checkering. Mfg. 1992-1993.

$1,075 $940 $805 $730 $590 $485 $375 *$1,295*

Add $15 for 26 in. barrel.
Add $130 for .375 H&H cal.

* ***Classicmark I .300 or .340 Wby. Mag. Cals.*** – 26 in. barrel only, right or left-hand action, 8 1/2 lbs.

$1,095 $960 $820 $745 $600 $495 $385 *$1,323*

* ***Classicmark I .378 Wby. Mag. Cal.*** – 26 in. barrel only, right or left-hand action, 8 1/2 lbs.

$1,125 $985 $845 $765 $620 $505 $395 *$1,356*

* ***Classicmark I .416 Wby. Mag. Cal.*** – 26 in. barrel only, right or left-hand action, integral muzzle brake.

$1,150 $1,005 $865 $780 $635 $520 $405 *$1,411*

* ***Classicmark I .460 Wby. Mag. Cal.*** – 26 in. barrel only, includes custom stock, integral muzzle brake, 10 lbs. No extra charge for left-hand.

$1,250 $1,095 $940 $850 $690 $565 $440 *$1,573*

CLASSICMARK II – available in 9 Wby. Mag. cals. in addition to .270 Win., 7mm Rem. Mag., or .30-06, similar to Classicmark I, except has deluxe American walnut with 22 LPI multiple point checkering, steel grip cap, satin finished wood and metal, guaranteed 1 1/2 in. or less 3 shot grouping at 100 yards, right-hand action only. Mfg. 1992 only.

$1,525 $1,335 $1,145 $1,035 $840 $685 $535 *$1,775*

Add $28 for 26 in. barrel.

* ***Classicmark II .300 or .340 Wby. Mag. Cals.*** – 26 in. barrel only.

$1,550 $1,355 $1,165 $1,055 $855 $700 $545 *$1,803*

* ***Classicmark II .378 Wby. Mag. Cal.*** – 26 in. barrel only.

$1,700 $1,490 $1,275 $1,155 $935 $765 $595 *$1,976*

* ***Classicmark II .416 Wby. Mag. Cal.*** – 26 in. barrel only, integral muzzle brake.

$1,875 $1,640 $1,405 $1,275 $1,030 $845 $655 *$2,128*

* ***Classicmark II .460 Wby. Mag. Cal.*** – 26 in. barrel only, includes custom stock, integral muzzle brake, 10 lbs.

$1,925 $1,685 $1,445 $1,310 $1,060 $865 $675 *$2,207*

* ***Classicmark II Safari Classic*** – .375 H&H cal., 24 in. barrel only, right-hand action, limited edition featuring custom action, quarter rib express and front ramp sights, barrel band swivel and engraved floor plate, stock similar to Classicmark II. Mfg. 1992 only.

$2,300 $2,015 $1,725 $1,565 $1,265 $1,035 $805 *$2,693*

GRADING - PPGS™	100%	98%	95%	90%	80%	70%	60%	*LAST MSR*

EUROMARK – .257 Wby. Mag., .270 Wby. Mag., .300 Win. Mag., .300 Wby. Mag., .340 Wby. Mag., .375 H&H Mag., .375 Wby. Mag., .416 Wby. Mag., 7mm Rem. Mag., or 7mm Wby. Mag., 2 (.416 Wby. Mag. only) or 3 shot mag., 24, 26, or 28 (.416 Wby. Mag. only) in. barrel, oil finished, hand checkered, deluxe American claro (disc.) or Monte Carlo select walnut stock with ebony pistol grip cap and forend tip, diamond point checkering, low luster bluing, and solid black (disc.) or Pachmayr Decelerator recoil pad, 8-9 lbs. Mfg. 1986-92, re-introduced 1995-2002, again in 2010.

MSR $2,400 $1,825 $1,500 $1,275 $1,100 $975 $800 $625

Last MSR in 2002 was $1,819.

Add $100 for .375 Wby. Mag. or $400 for .416 Wby. Mag. cal.

Add approx 10% for .378 Wby. Mag. (disc. 2011).

* ***Euromark .460 Wby. Mag. Cal.*** – 24 or 26 in. barrel, includes custom stock, internal muzzle brake, no extra charge for left-hand. Disc. 1992.

$1,450 $1,270 $1,090 $985 $800 $655 $510 *$1,708*

FIBERMARK – available in .240 Wby. Mag., .257 Wby. Mag., .270 Wby. Mag., .30-06, 7mm Wby. Mag., .300 Wby. Mag., or .340 Wby. Mag. cal., black non-glare fiberglass with wrinkle finish stock, metal has non-glare matte finish, 24 or 26 in. barrel, available in right (disc. 1991) or left-hand action, 7 1/4 lbs. Mfg. 1983-92.

$1,195 $1,045 $895 $815 $655 $540 $420 *$1,376*

Add $118 for .300 or .340 Mag. cal.

This model was available in left-hand action (22 in. barrel) in .270 Win. or .30-06 cal. only.

FIBERMARK (CURRENT MFG.) – available in many cals. between .22-250 Rem. - .375 H&H, Mag. cals. only beginning 2005, 2 (.30-378 Wby. Mag. only), 3, or 5 shot internal mag., pillar bedded black composite Monte Carlo stock of Aramid cross-directional fibers, Pachmayr Decelerator pad, matte blue metal, 24, 26 (Mag. cals. only), or 28 (.30-378 Wby. Mag. cal. only) in. steel barrel, 6 3/4-8 1/2 lbs. New 2001.

MSR $1,500 $1,200 $1,050 $875 $775 $650 $525 $450

Add $300 for .30-378 Wby. Mag. cal.

* ***Fibermark Mark V Stainless*** – similar to Mark V Fibermark, except has stainless steel action and barrel with matte finish. Mfg. 2001-2004.

$1,075 $940 $805 $730 $590 $485 $375 *$1,334*

Add $98 for Mag. cals.

Add $301 for .30-378 Wby. Mag. cal.

LAZERMARK – various cals., 3 shot mag., 24 (disc.) or 26 in. barrel, raised comb Monte Carlo stock with laser carved oak leaf pattern, maplewood spacers and rosewood forend and grip cap, Pachmayr Decelerator pad, high lustre finish, 8 1/2 lbs. New 1985.

MSR $2,600 $2,100 $1,775 $1,525 $1,350 $1,125 $900 $725

* ***Lazermark .378 Wby. Mag. or .416 Wby. Mag. Cals.*** – first new caliber (introduced 1989) since the .240 Mag. was released 1965, includes muzzle brake. Disc. 2002.

$1,850 $1,620 $1,390 $1,260 $1,020 $835 $650 *$2,266*

* ***Lazermark .460 Wby. Mag. Cal.*** – 24 (disc. 2000), 26 (disc. 2000), or 28 in. barrel, includes custom stock, internal muzzle brake, no extra charge for left-hand. Disc. 2002.

$2,150 $1,880 $1,615 $1,460 $1,185 $970 $755 *$2,661*

* ***Lazermark Varmintmaster*** – .22-250 Rem. or .224 Varmintmaster cal., 24 or 26 in. barrel. Disc. 1991.

$1,085 $950 $815 $740 $595 $490 $380 *$675*

Add $25 for 26 in. barrel.

Not available in left-hand action.

GRADING - PPGS™	100%	98%	95%	90%	80%	70%	60%	LAST MSR

ULTRAMARK (OLDER MFG.) – .240 Wby. Mag., .257 Wby. Mag., .270 Wby. Mag., .30-06, 7mm Wby. Mag., .300 Wby. Mag., .378 Wby. Mag. (mfg. 1989 only), or .416 Wby. Mag. (mfg. 1989 only) cal., fancy American walnut, individually hand-bedded, high luster finish, customized action, 24 or 26 in. barrel, basket weave checkering (including pistol grip). Imported 1989-90 only.

	$1,125	$985	$845	$765	$620	$505	$395	*$1,315*

Add $25 for 26 in. barrel.
Add $220 for .378 Wby. Mag. cal. (26 in. barrel only).
Add $325 for .416 Wby. Mag. cal. (26 in. barrel only).

ULTRAMARK (NEW MFG.) – .257 Wby. Mag. or .300 Wby. Mag. cal., 3 shot mag., 26 in. barrel, fancy checkered American walnut stock with rosewood forend and pistol grip caps with maplewood/ebony spacers, Pachmayr Decelerator pad, fully adj. trigger, individually hand-bedded, high gloss finish, customized blue action, 8 1/2 lbs. New 2007.

MSR $3,200	$2,675	$2,200	$1,850	$1,575	$1,325	$1,100	$900	

WEATHERMARK – available in various Wby. Mag. cals. from .240 (disc. 1996) to .340 and .257 Roberts (disc. 1994), .270 Win., 7mm Rem. Mag., .300 Win. Mag., .30-06, .338 Win. Mag., or .375 H&H (disc.) cal., design is similar to Classicmark II, except is fitted with black checkered composite stock, satin finish black metal, 22 (disc. 1995, .270 Win. or .30-06 only), 24, or 26 in. barrel, right-hand only, 7 1/2 lbs. Mfg. 1992-94.

	$685	$600	$515	$465	$375	$310	$240	*$799*

SYNTHETIC (MAG. CALS.) – .240 Wby. Mag (disc. 2010), .257 Wby. Mag., .270 Wby. Mag., .300 Wby. Mag., .30-378 Wby. Mag. (new 1998), .300 Win. Mag., .338 Win. Mag. (disc. 2004), .338-378 Wby. Mag. (new 2001), .340 Wby. Mag., 7mm Wby. Mag., 7mm Rem. Mag., 7mm STW (mfg. 2001-2004), or .375 H&H cal., 24, 26, or 28 in. barrel, 2 or 3 shot mag., features lightweight black synthetic stock, bead blasted matte metal finish, approx. 8 lbs. Mfg.1997-2012.

	$1,075	$925	$775	$700	$600	$500	$425	*$1,300*

Add $300 for .30-378 Wby. Mag. or .338-378 Wby. Mag. cal. (28 in. barrel only).

* ***Synthetic (Standard Cals.)*** – .22-250 Rem. (disc. 2009), .243 Win., .25-06 Rem., .270 Win., .280 Rem., .30-06, .308 Win., or 7mm-08 Rem. cal., 4 or 5 shot mag., features raised comb, matte black injection mold synthetic stock, no sights, 20 (carbine, .243 Win., .308 Win., or 7mm-08 Rem., disc. 2002) or 24 in. barrel, approx. 6 1/2 lbs. Mfg. 1997-2011.

	$1,050	$925	$775	$700	$600	$500	$425	*$1,235*

* ***Synthetic Fluted*** – .257 Wby. Mag., .270 Wby. Mag., .300 Wby. Mag., .300 Win. Mag., 7mm Wby. Mag., or 7mm Rem. Mag. cal., features 24 or 26 in. fluted barrel, black synthetic stock with Monte Carlo cheekpiece, approx. 7 1/2 lbs. Mfg. 1997-98.

	$785	$685	$590	$535	$430	$355	$275	*$949*

* ***Synthetic Weathermark Alaskan Model*** – same cals. as Weathermark, similar to Weathermark, except has non-glare electroless nickel-plated metal parts, right or left-hand (mfg. 1992 only) action. Mfg. 1992-94.

	$750	$655	$565	$510	$415	$340	$265	*$875*

Add $37 for Wby. Mag. cals.
Add $164 for .375 H&H cal.
Add $375 for left-hand action (disc.).

SYNTHETIC STAINLESS MODEL (MAG. CALS.) – same cals. as Synthetic, except not available in .338-.378 Wby. Mag. or 7mm STW, features bead blasted matte stainless construction, synthetic Monte Carlo stock. Mfg. 1995-2004.

	$1,075	$940	$805	$730	$590	$485	$375	*$1,282*

Add $200 for .30-378 Wby. Mag. (28 in. barrel only).

GRADING - PPGS™	100%	98%	95%	90%	80%	70%	60%	LAST MSR

* ***Synthetic Stainless (Standard Cals.)*** – .22-250 Rem., .243 Win., .240 Wby. Mag., .25-06 Rem., .270 Win., .280 Rem., .30-06, .308 Win., or 7mm-08 Rem. cal., features raised comb, matte black injection molded synthetic stock, no sights, 20 (carbine, .243 Win., .308 Win., or 7mm-08 Rem. cal.) or 24 in. stainless barrel and action, approx. 6 1/2 lbs. Mfg. 1997-2004.

	$975	$855	$730	$665	$535	$440	$340	$1,166

* ***Synthetic Fluted Stainless*** – .257 Wby. Mag., .270 Wby. Mag., .300 Wby. Mag., .300 Win. Mag., 7mm Wby. Mag., or 7mm Rem. Mag., features 24 or 26 in. fluted stainless barrel and action, black synthetic stock with Monte Carlo cheekpiece, approx. 7 1/2 lbs. Mfg. 1997-98.

	$1,025	$895	$770	$695	$565	$460	$360	$1,149

EUROSPORT – various cals., features hand-rubbed satin oil finished American claro walnut stock with low luster blue metal work. Mfg. 1995-2002.

	$915	$800	$685	$620	$505	$410	$320	$1,143

MARK V SLS (STAINLESS LAMINATE SPORTER) – .257 Wby. Mag., .270 Wby. Mag., .300 Wby. Mag., .300 Win. Mag., .338 Win. Mag., .340 Wby. Mag., 7mm Wby. Mag., or 7mm Rem. Mag. cal., 24 or 26 (Wby. Mag. cals. only) in. barrel, features grey laminate stock with recoil pad, stainless steel with matte blue finish, approx. 8 1/2 lbs. Mfg. 1997-2002.

	$1,125	$985	$845	$765	$620	$505	$395	$1,393

SPORTER (LONG ACTION) – .240 Wby. Mag. (mfg. 1996 only), .257 Wby. Mag., .270 Wby. Mag., 7mm Wby. Mag., 7mm Rem. Mag., .270 Win. (mfg. 1996 only), .30-06 (disc. 1996), .300 Wby. Mag., .300 Win. Mag., .338 Win. Mag. (disc. 2004), .340 Wby. Mag., or .375 H&H (disc. 2002) cal., 3 shot mag., 24 or 26 in. barrel, checkered walnut stock without forearm or pistol grip caps (disc.) or raised comb Monte Carlo walnut stock with satin finish and fineline diamond checkering and rosewood forend and grip cap, low luster metalwork, vent. recoil pad (disc.) or Pachmayr Decelerator pad, no sights, approx. 8 lbs. New 1993.

MSR $1,600	$1,295	$1,075	$925	$825	$725	$625	$525	

* ***Sporter Standard Action*** – .22-250 Rem., .243 Win., .240 Wby. Mag., .25-06 Rem., .270 Win., .280 Rem., .30-06, .308 Win., or 7mm-08 Rem. cal., features raised comb, checkered walnut stock, 54 degree bolt lift, no sights, 24 in. barrel, approx. 6 3/4 lbs. Mfg. 1997-2004.

	$1,000	$875	$750	$680	$550	$450	$350	$1,249

ULTRA LIGHTWEIGHT – .243 Win. (disc. 2011), .240 Wby. Mag., .257 Wby. Mag. (new 1999), .25-06 Rem. (disc. 2011), .270 Win., .270 Wby. Mag. (new 1999), .280 Rem. (disc. 2010), .300 Wby. Mag. (new 1999), .300 Win. Mag. (new 1999), 7mm-08 Rem. (disc. 2012), 7mm Rem. Mag. (new 1999), 7mm Wby. Mag. (new 1999), .30-06, .308 Win., or .338-06 A-Square (mfg. 2001-2003) cal., 3 or 5 shot mag., 24 or 26 in. blackened stainless steel barrel and lightweight synthetic stock, Pachmayr Decelerator pad, 5 3/4 or 6 3/4 lbs. New 1998.

MSR $2,100	$1,750	$1,450	$1,250	$1,075	$900	$750	$650	

Add $200 for left-hand action (.257 Wby. Mag., .270 Wby. Mag. (disc.), .300 Wby. Mag., .300 Win. Mag. (disc.), 7mm Rem. Mag. (disc.), or 7mm Wby. Mag. (disc.).

WHITETAIL – .257 Sav. cal., limited edition features deluxe high grade American claro walnut, hand checkered bolt knob and engraved floorplate, 22 in. #1 contoured barrel, 6 lbs. Mfg. 1993 only.

	$1,150	$1,005	$865	$780	$635	$520	$405	$1,366

SVR (SPECIAL VARMINT RIFLE) – .22-250 Rem. or .223 Rem. cal., features 22 in. free-floating Kreiger barrel, 4 or 5 shot mag., black Monte Carlo composite stock with grey spider webbing, aluminum bedding block, Pachmayr Decelerator pad, 7 1/4 lbs. Mfg. 2003-2005.

	$925	$810	$695	$630	$510	$415	$325	$1,176

GRADING - PPGS™	100%	98%	95%	90%	80%	70%	60%	LAST MSR

SPM (SUPER PREDATORMASTER) – .22-250 Rem., .223 Rem., .243 Win., .308 Win., or 7mm-08 Rem. cal., features 24 in. Criterion button rifled barrel with flutes, black spider webbing on tan Accumark type stock with slim forend and CNC aluminum bedding block, Pachmayr Decelerator pad, 6 1/2 lbs. Mfg. 2001-2004.

	$1,375	$1,205	$1,030	$935	$755	$620	$480	*$1,670*

SVM (SUPER VARMINTMASTER) – .220 Swift (single shot only, disc., reintroduced 2005 only), .22-250 Rem., .223 Rem., .243 Win., .308 Win. (disc. 2004), or 7mm-08 Rem. (disc. 2004) cal., features 26 in. Criterion button rifled fluted barrel with crown, 4 or 5 shot mag., available as repeater or single shot, black spider webbing on tan Accumark type stock with beavertail forend and CNC aluminum bedding block, Pachmayr Decelerator pad, approx. 8 1/2 lbs. Mfg. 2000-2009.

	$1,600	$1,400	$1,200	$1,090	$880	$720	$560	*$1,959*

MARK V SVR (SPECIAL VARMINT RIFLE) – .22-250 Rem. or .223 (new 2008) cal., similar to Super Varmintmaster, except has 22 in. barrel. Mfg. 2007-2009.

	$1,025	$895	$770	$695	$565	$460	$360	*$1,259*

SBGM (SUPER BIG GAME MASTER) – various cals. between .240 Wby. Mag. - .338-06 A-Square (disc.), 24 or 26 (Mag. cals. only) in. Criterion hand-lapped fluted Krieger barrel, barreled action is bedded to a specially-designed, hand-laminated, raised comb, Monte Carlo composite stock (a combination of Aramid, graphite and unidirectional fibers, and fiberglass) with black spiderweb patterning, Pachmayr Decelerator pad, 6 3/4 lbs. New 2002.

	$1,375	$1,205	$1,030	$935	$755	$620	$480	*$1,670*

Add $66 for Mag. cals.

TRR (THREAT RESPONSE RIFLE) – .223 Rem., .308 Win., .300 Win. Mag. (disc. 2002), .300 Wby. Mag. (disc. 2002), .30-378 Wby. Mag. (disc. 2002), or .338-.378 Wby. Mag. (disc. 2002) cal., 22 in. barrel, 5 shot mag., Mark V action with black finished metal and black hybrid composite stock, various barrel lengths, optional Picatinny style ring and base system, 8 1/2-10 1/2 lbs. Mfg. 2002-2005.

	$1,400	$1,225	$1,050	$950	$770	$630	$490	*$1,737*

Add $52 for .300 Win. Mag. or .300 Wby. Mag. cals. (disc. 2002).
Add $208 for .30-378 Wby. Mag. or .338-378 Wby. Mag. cals. (disc. 2002).

TRR RC (RANGE CERTIFIED) – .300 Win. Mag., .300 Wby. Mag., .30-378 Wby. Mag., .338 Lapua Mag. (new 2012), or .338-378 Wby. Mag. cal., 26 in. Kreiger barrel with Accubrake, adj. trigger, 2 shot mag., laminated stock with T-6 aluminum bedding system with three position buttstock, includes Leupold 4.5-14x50 LRT M1 scope (disc. 2012), Talley ring rail, bipod, and hard case, 9 1/4 lbs. New 2010.

MSR $4,200	$3,575	43,050	$2,575	$2,250	$1,900	$1,650	$1,375

Add approx. $1,700 for TRR Package including Leupold scope, ring rail, bipod, and hard case (disc. 2012).

VARMINTMASTER – .22-250 Rem. or .224 Varmintmaster (disc. 1994) cal., 24 (disc. 1991) or 26 in. barrel, 6 1/2 lbs. Disc. 1995.

	$1,075	$940	$805	$730	$590	$485	$375	*$1,297*

Not available in left-hand action.

1976 BICENTENNIAL MARK V – .257 Wby. Mag., .270 Wby. Mag., 7mm Wby. Mag., or .300 Wby Mag. cal., 1,000 mfg. in 1976 only.

	$1,495	$1,310	$1,120	$1,015	$820	$675	$525	*$2,000*

1984 MARK V OLYMPIC COMMEMORATIVE – .257 Wby. Mag., .270 Wby. Mag., 7mm Wby. Mag., or .300 Wby. Mag. cal., special gold accenting, extra-fancy walnut stock with burnished brass oval depicting the Olympic "Star In Motion" emblem inlay. Mfg. 1984, only 1,000 mfg. at $2,000 retail.

	$1,000	$875	$750	N/A	N/A	N/A	N/A

GRADING - PPGS™	100%	98%	95%	90%	80%	70%	60%	LAST MSR

MARK V 35TH ANNIVERSARY COMMEMORATIVE – .257 Wby. Mag., .270 Wby. Mag., 7mm Wby. Mag., or .300 Wby. Mag. cal., limited mfg. 1980, 1,000 produced total.

	$1,000	$875	$750	N/A	N/A	N/A	N/A	

MARK V 40TH ANNIVERSARY COMMEMORATIVE – .257 Wby. Mag. (35 mfg.), .270 Wby. Mag. (35 mfg.), 7mm Wby. Mag. (35 mfg.), or .300 Wby. Mag. (95 mfg.) cal. Limited mfg. 1985, 200 produced total.

	$1,000	$875	$750	N/A	N/A	N/A	N/A	

MARK V 50TH ANNIVERSARY COMMEMORATIVE – .300 Wby. Mag. cal., 26 in. barrel, checkered high grade Claro Monte Carlo walnut stock with cheekpiece and brass Weatherby anniversary logo plaque, gold trigger, rosewood pistol grip cap, engraved floorplate, 9 lbs. Limited mfg. 1995.

	$2,000	$1,650	$1,350	N/A	N/A	N/A	N/A	

RIFLES: BOLT ACTION, CUSTOM SHOP

OUTFITTER CUSTOM – various cals. between .243 Win. - .338-06 A-Square (disc.), ultra lightweight bolt action, 5 shot mag., 24 or 26 in. stainless steel fluted barrel with titanium nitride hardcoating (disc.) or black Teflon coating, raised comb, Monte Carlo composite Kevlar stock in Desert Camo, 5 3/4 lbs. New 2001.

MSR $3,000	$2,650	$2,050	$1,725	$1,500	$1,250	$1,050	$850	

OUTFITTER KREIGER CUSTOM – same cals. as Outfitter Custom, ultra lightweight action, 24 or 26 in. Kreiger ultra lightweight contoured barrel with cut rifling, trued receiver and bolt face, lapped locking lugs, titanium nitride coating, desert camo stock. Mfg. 2001-2002.

	$2,995	$2,620	$2,245	$2,035	$1,645	$1,350	$1,050	*$3,499*

Add $50 for Mag. cals.

DGR (DANGEROUS GAME RIFLE) CUSTOM – .300 Win. Mag. (mfg. 2002-2004, reintroduced 2013), .300 Wby. Mag. (new 2002), .338 Win. Mag. (mfg. 2002-2004, reintroduced 2013), .340 Wby. Mag. (new 2002), .375 H&H, .375 Wby. Mag., .378 Wby. Mag., .416 Rem. Mag., .416 Wby. Mag., .458 Win. Mag., .458 Lott (new 2005), or .460 Wby. Mag. cal., 24 or 26 in. button rifled chrome moly barrel with express sights (rear is adj.), black fiberglass stock (disc.) with CNC machined aluminum bedding block and Pachmayr Decelerator pad (disc.) or Monte Carlo tan stock with black spiderweb accents, black oxide metal finish, 8 3/4 or 9 1/2 (.460 Wby. Mag.) lbs. New 2001.

MSR $3,400	$2,900	$2,450	$2,075	$1,850	$1,550	$1,225	$995	

Add $399 for snow or desert camo stock with titanium nitride coating (disc.).

CUSTOM GRADE – various cals. from .240 Wby. Mag. to .340 Wby. Mag., 24 or 26 in. barrel, super fancy walnut stock featuring No. 7 style inlays, floorplate is engraved "Weatherby Custom", 6-8 months delivery time. Disc. 2001.

	$4,250	$3,720	$3,190	$2,890	$2,340	$1,915	$1,490	*$5,099*

TRCM (THREAT RESPONSE CUSTOM MAGNUM) – .300 Win. Mag., .300 Wby. Mag., .30-378 Wby. Mag., or .338-.378 Wby. Mag. cal., Mark V action with ergonomic, fully adjustable composite stock, black finished metal, various barrel lengths, optional Picatinny style ring and base system. Mfg. 2002-2009.

	$2,325	$2,035	$1,745	$1,580	$1,280	$1,045	$815	*$2,899*

Add $270 for .30-378 Wby. Mag. or .338-378 Wby. Mag. cals.
Add $499 for desert camo stock and titanium nitride coating.

TRR CUSTOM MAGNUM – .300 Win. Mag., .300 Wby. Mag., .30-378 Wby. Mag., .338 Lapua Mag. (new 2012), or .338-378 Wby. Mag. cals., 26 or 28 in. barrel with Accubrake, fully adj. black tactical stock, adj. trigger, w/o sights, approx. 9 lbs. New 2011.

MSR $2,800	$2,375	$2,000	$1,700	$1,475	$1,275	$1,100	$900	*$2,700*

Add $200 for .30-378 Wby. Mag., .338 Lapua Mag. (new 2012) or .338-378 Wby. Mag. with 28 in. barrel and Accubrake.

GRADING - PPGS™	100%	98%	95%	90%	80%	70%	60%	LAST MSR

SAFARI GRADE CUSTOM – .257 Wby. Mag. (new 2000), .270 Wby. Mag. (new 2000), .300 Wby. Mag., .340 Wby. Mag., .375 H&H (new 2000), .375 Wby. Mag. (disc. 2006), .378 Wby. Mag., .416 Wby Mag., .416 Rem. Mag. (new 2007), .458 Lott (new 2007), .458 Win. Mag., .460 Wby. Mag., or 7mm Wby. Mag. (mfg. 2000-2012) cal., 2 shot mag., 28 in. barrel, fancy French walnut Monte Carlo stock with satin oil finish, ebony forend and pistol grip cap with fleur-de-lis checkering, damascened bolt and follower with engraved floorplate "Safari Custom", adj. express ramp rear and hooded front sights, 8 3/4 lbs. 6-8 month delivery.

MSR $6,700	$5,900	$5,100	$4,275	$3,625	$3,000	$2,550	$1,950	

Left-hand action became available during 2013 at no extra charge.

ROYAL ULTRAMARK CUSTOM – .257 Wby. Mag., .270 Wby. Mag., .300 Wby. Mag., .340 Wby. Mag., or 7mm Wby. Mag. cal., 26 in. barrel, features high grade fancy American claro checkered walnut stock with rosewood pistol grip cap and forend, damascened bolt and follower, engraved receiver and floorplate, select 24Kt. gold and nickel plating, custom order only. New 2002.

MSR $5,600	$4,950	$4,300	$3,700	$3,175	$2,550	$2,100	$1,675	

CROWN CUSTOM MODEL – .257 Wby. Mag., .270 Wby. Mag., .300 Wby. Mag., .340 Wby. Mag., or 7mm Wby. Mag. cal., custom order only, engraved barrel, receiver, and scope mount, top-of-the-line model. Disc. 2010.

	$8,250	$7,225	$6,200	$5,625	$4,550	$3,725	$2,900	*$9,699*

RIFLES: BOLT ACTION, VANGUARD SERIES 1

The Vanguard Series 1 rifles were discontinued in 2011. All guns were shipped with a factory three shot target, guaranteeing 1.5 in. accuracy at 100 yards.

VANGUARD – .243 Win., .25-06 Rem., .270 Win., .30-06, .308 Win., 7mm Rem. Mag., .264 Win. Mag., or .300 Win. Mag. cal., mfg. circa late 1960s-early 1970s.

	$435	$380	$325	$295	$240	$195	$150	

Add 10% for .264 Win. Mag. cal.

VANGUARD SYNTHETIC (RECENT MFG.) – .22-250 Rem., .223 Rem., .243 Win., .25-06 Rem. (new 2007), .257 Wby. Mag., .270 Win., .270 WSM (new 2005), .30-06, .308 Win., .300 WSM, .300 Win. Mag., .300 Wby. Mag., .338 Win. Mag., 7mm-08 Rem. (new 2008), or 7mm Rem. Mag. cal., choice of matte black metal or satin stainless steel action/barrel, black synthetic stock, includes many Mark V features, including one-piece fluted bolt with 3 gas ports, 2 locking lugs, and 90-degree bolt lift, 3 or 5 shot mag., 24 in. barrel, adj. trigger, each gun supplied with 3 shot factory target, approx. 7 1/2 lbs. Domestic mfg. 1997-2011.

	$450	$395	$340	$305	$250	$205	$160	*$523*

Add $20 for WSM cals.
Add $76 for detachable box magazine (Synthetic DBM, new 2010).
Add $106 for Vanguard Combo with Simmons 3.5-10x40mm scope and Leupold rings/bases (new 2011).
Add $206 for Vanguard package (includes Bushnell Banner 3-9x40mm scope mounted and bore sighted, Uncle Mike's nylon sling, and Plano molded case, new 2005).
Add $210 for stainless steel action/barrel (disc. 2009).
Add $263 for Vanguard stainless package (disc. 2006).

* ***Vanguard Synthetic HB-ST*** – .223 Rem. or .308 Win. cal., 22 in. matte blue barrel, 5 shot mag., adj. trigger, features black synthetic injection molded stock with textured Silent-Tek sure grip finish, recessed target crown, low density recoil pad, 8 lbs. Mfg. 2010-2011.

	$560	$485	$450	$375	$325	$270	$230	*$642*

GRADING - PPGS™	100%	98%	95%	90%	80%	70%	60%	LAST MSR

VANGUARD SPORTER – same cals. as Vanguard Synthetic, features checkered walnut stock with rosewood forend tip, satin finish and checkering, matte blue metal, 24 in. barrel, 3 or 5 shot mag., 7 3/4 lbs. Mfg. 2005-2011.

$595	$520	$445	$400	$325	$270	$210	*$754*

Add $55 for detachable box magazine (Sporter DBM, new 2010).
Add $200 for matte stainless steel action/barrel (Sporter SS, disc. 2009).
Add $30 for WSM cals.

VANGUARD DELUXE – .257 Wby. Mag., .270 Win., .30-06, .300 Win. Mag. (new 2007), .300 Wby. Mag., or 7mm Rem. Mag. (new 2007) cal., 24 in. barrel w/o sights, features high gloss walnut Monte Carlo stock with rosewood forend tip and pistol grip cap, high gloss bluing, 3 or 5 shot mag., 7 3/4 lbs. Mfg. 2006-2009.

$835	$730	$625	$570	$460	$375	$290	*$989*

Add $133 for matte stainless steel action/barrel (Deluxe SS, disc. 2006).

VANGUARD BACK COUNTRY CUSTOM – .257 Wby. Mag., .270 Win., .30-06, .300 Win. Mag., or .300 Wby. Mag., features stainless steel action and 24 in. fluted barrel, Ultralight composite stock with spider webbing and Pachmayr Decelerator pad, 6 3/4 lbs. Mfg. 2008-2009.

$900	$790	$675	$610	$495	$405	$315	*$1,119*

VANGUARD SAGE COUNTRY CUSTOM – available in various cals. between .22-250 Rem. - .338 Win. Mag., injection molded stock with desert camo, 24 in. barrel, low density recoil pad. Mfg. 2008-2009.

$575	$505	$430	$390	$315	$260	$200	*$659*

Add $30 for .270 WSM or .300 WSM cals.

VANGUARD VARMINT SPECIAL – .204 Ruger (new 2007), .22-250 Rem., .223 Rem., or .308 Win. cal., features checkered hand laminated tan Monte Carlo composite stock with aluminum bedding plate, 22 in. barrel w/o sights, 5 shot mag., 8 1/4 lbs. Mfg. 2006-2008, reintroduced 2010-2011.

$600	$525	$450	$400	$340	$295	$250	*$713*

Add $61 for .204 Ruger (new 2007).

VANGUARD PREDATOR – .22-250 Rem., .223 Rem., or .308 Win. cal., 22 in. contoured barrel, injection molded composite stock with 100% Natural Gear camo coverage (including barrel and action), adj. trigger, low density recoil pad, 8 lbs. Mfg. 2009-2011.

$735	$640	$550	$495	$400	$325	$255	*$866*

VANGUARD COMPACT – .22-250 Rem., .223 Rem. (new 2008), .243 Win., .308 Win. or 7mm-08 Rem. (new 2006) cal., 20 in. barrel, shortened 12 1/2 LOP, 5 shot mag., matte black hardwood stock, 6 3/4 lbs. Mfg. 2005-2009.

$575	$505	$430	$390	$315	$260	$200	*$649*

VANGUARD YOUTH – .22-250 Rem., .223 Rem., .243 Win., 7mm-08 Rem., or .308 Win. cal., 5 shot mag., 20 in. contoured barrel, lighter Vanguard action, adj. trigger, black synthetic stock with removable elongated spacer to adj. length of pull, low density recoil pad, approx. 6 1/2 lbs. Mfg. 2010-2011.

$450	$395	$340	$300	$250	$200	$160	*$523*

VANGUARD CARBINE – .22-250 Rem., .223 Rem., .243 Win., 7mm-08 Rem., .308 Win. cal., 20 in. contoured barrel, matte black metal finish, adj. trigger, composite stock, 6 3/4 lbs. Mfg. 2009-2011.

$440	$385	$330	$300	$240	$200	$155	*$523*

VANGUARD SUB-MOA – same cals. as Vanguard Synthetic, matte finished steel or stainless steel action and 24 in. barrel, choice of light tan or charcoal Monte Carlo Fiberguard stock with Pachmayr Decelerator pad, no sights, guaranteed to shoot a three shot .99 in. group at 100 yards, 3 or 5 shot mag., 7 3/4 lbs. Mfg. 2005-2011.

$865	$750	$650	$580	$475	$385	$300	*$1,019*

GRADING - PPGS™	100%	98%	95%	90%	80%	70%	60%	LAST MSR

Add $31 for WSM cals.
Add $150 for stainless steel action/barrel (disc. 2009).

* ***Vanguard Sub-MOA TR*** – .223 Rem. or .308 Win. cal., 22 in. contoured barrel with recessed target crown, 5 shot mag., laminated Monte Carlo composite stock with beavertail forearm and Pachmayr Decelerator pad, three swivel studs, adj. trigger, guaranteed to shoot 3-shoot group of .99 in. or less with factory or premium ammo, 8 3/4 lbs. Mfg. 2010-2011.

$875	$750	$640	$580	$470	$385	$300	*$1,016*

* ***Vanguard Sub-MOA TRR Package*** – .300 Win. Mag., .300 Wby. Mag., .30-378 Wby. Mag., or .338-378 Wby. Mag. cal., 28 in. barrel with Accubrake, adj. trigger, laminated stock with T-6 aluminum bedding system with three position buttstock, includes Leupold 4.5-14x50 LRT M1 scope, Talley ring rail, bipod, and hard case. Mfg. 2010 only.

$3,350	$2,975	$2,550	$2,200	$1,875	$1,550	$1,300	*$3,999*

VANGUARD SUB-MOA VARMINT – .204 Ruger (mfg. 2007-2010), .22-250 Rem., .223 Rem., or .308 Win. cal., features hand laminated composite stock with oversized vented forend and CNC machined aluminum bedding plate, Pachmayr decelerator pad, three sling swivels, 22 in. barrel, 5 shot mag., 8 1/4 lbs. Mfg. 2006-2011.

$925	$800	$700	$600	$500	$425	$375	*$1,101*

Add $59 for .204 Ruger cal. (disc. 2010).

VANGUARD CLASSIC I – .223 Rem., .243 Win., .270 Win., 7mm-08 Rem., 7mm Rem. Mag., .30-06, or .308 Win. cal., checkered walnut stock with satin finish, black buttpad, 24 in. barrel, 3 (7mm Rem. Mag.) or 5 shot mag., No. 1 barrel contour, approx. 7 lbs. 5 oz. Mfg. 1989-93.

$480	$420	$360	$325	$265	$215	$170	*$549*

This model was the replacement for the Vanguard VGS and VGL.

VANGUARD CLASSIC II – .22-250 Rem., .243 Win., .270 Wby. Mag., .270 Win., 7mm Rem. Mag., .30-06, .300 Win. Mag., .300 Wby. Mag., or .338 Win. Mag. cal., 24 in. No. 2 barrel contour, 3 or 5 shot mag., custom checkered deluxe walnut stock with pistol grip cap and black forend cap, solid black recoil pad, matte finished metal, approx. 7 3/4 lbs. Mfg. 1989-92.

$675	$590	$505	$460	$370	$305	$235	*$750*

This model was also available in a No. 3 barrel contour in .22-250 Rem. cal. only.

VANGUARD VGD – .22-250 Rem., .243 Win., .25-06 Rem., .270 Win., 7mm Rem. Mag., .30-06, or .300 Win. Mag. cal., bolt action, checkered deluxe walnut stock with rosewood tip forearm and pistol grip, 24 in. barrel, no sights, 5 shot mag. (except 3 shot for .300 Win. Mag.), high luster bluing, about 8 lbs. Disc. 1988.

$525	$460	$395	$355	$290	$235	$185	*$600*

Not available in left-hand action.

VANGUARD VGX DELUXE – .22-250 Rem., .243 Win., .270 Win., .270 Wby. Mag., .300 Win. Mag., .300 Wby. Mag., .30-06, .338 Win. Mag., or 7mm Rem. Mag. cal., 24 in. barrel, Monte Carlo stock with skipline checkering, high gloss wood and metal, rosewood grip cap and forend tip. Mfg. 1989-1993.

$625	$545	$470	$425	$345	$280	$220	*$699*

VANGUARD VGS – same cals. as Vanguard VGX, bolt action, checkered satin finished walnut stock, 24 in. barrel, no sights, approx. 8 lbs. Disc. 1988.

$415	$365	$310	$280	$230	$185	$145	*$467*

Not available in left-hand action.

VANGUARD VGL – .223 Rem., .243 Win., .270 Win., 7mm Rem. Mag., .30-06, or .308 Win. cal., lightweight bolt action, checkered walnut stock, 5 shot mag. (6 on .223 Rem.), 20 in. barrel, no sights, 6 1/2 lbs. Disc. 1988.

$415	$365	$310	$280	$230	$185	$145	*$467*

Not available in left-hand action.

GRADING - PPGS™	100%	98%	95%	90%	80%	70%	60%	LAST MSR

VANGUARD WEATHERGUARD – same cals. as Classic I, replacement for Fiberguard, wrinkle black finished synthetic stock, entry level Weatherby, similar specs. as Classic I, approx. 8 lbs. Mfg. 1989-1993.

	$440	$385	$330	$300	$240	$200	$155	$499

VANGUARD ALASKAN – same cals. as Classic I, features electroless nickel metal plating, no sights. Mfg. 1993-1994.

	$625	$545	$470	$425	$345	$280	$220	$699

VANGUARD FIBERGUARD – .223 Rem., .243 Win., .270 Win., 7mm Rem. Mag., .30-06, or .308 Win. cal., 20 in. barrel, green fiberglass stock, 3 to 6 shot mags., no sights, blue metal parts, approx. 6 1/2 lbs. Disc. 1988.

	$500	$440	$375	$340	$275	$225	$175	$560

Not available in left-hand action.

VANGUARD THUMBHOLE LAMINATE – .204 Ruger (disc. 2009), .22-250 Rem. (disc. 2009), .223 Rem., .25-06 Rem. (new 2010), .257 Wby. Mag. (new 2010), , 270 Win. (new 2010), 7mm Rem. Mag. (new 2010), .30-06 (new 2010), .300 Win. Mag. (new 2010), or .300 Wby. Mag. (new 2010) cal., 24 in. hammer forged barrel, nutmeg laminate stock with thumbhole and barrel vents, Pachmayr Decelerator pad, adj. trigger. Mfg. 2009-2010.

	$725	$635	$545	$495	$400	$325	$255	$799

Add $60 for .204 Ruger cal. (disc. 2009).

VANGUARD AXIOM BIG GAME – .25-06 Rem., .270 Win., .30-06, .257 Wby. Mag., 7mm Rem. Mag., .300 Win. Mag., or .300 Wby Mag., 24 in. blue barrel, patented Knoxx adj. stock with pistol grip, black finish. Limited mfg. 2009.

	$875	$775	$675	$575	$475	$375	$325	$969

VANGUARD AXIOM VARMINT – .22-250 Rem., .223 Rem., or .308 Win. cal., similar to Axiom Big Game, except has 22 in. barrel, 8 3/4 lbs. Limited mfg. 2009.

	$775	$680	$580	$525	$425	$350	$270	$879

RIFLES: BOLT ACTION, VANGUARD SERIES 2

Weatherby discontinued its Vanguard Series 1 in 2011, and released the Vanguard Series 2 in 2012. Differences on the Series 2 include a creep-free, match quality, two-stage trigger, 3-position safety, and Griptonite synthetic stock with special inserts and palm swell (select models). All Series 2 Vanguards come with a Sub-MOA accuracy guarantee.

VANGUARD SERIES 2 CARBINE – .22-250 Rem., .223 Rem., .243 Win., 7mm-08 Rem., or .308 Win. cal., 20 in. contoured barrel, 5 shot mag., matte blue finish, lightweight composite Monte Carlo Griptonite stock features pistol grip and forend inserts, right side palm swell, 7 lbs. New 2012.

MSR $649	$525	$450	$375	$325	$295	$260	$230

VANGUARD SERIES 2 DELUXE – .257 Wby. Mag., .270 Win., .30-06, .300 Win. Mag., or .300 Wby. Mag. cal., 24 in. barrel, raised comb, features Monte Carlo claro walnut stock in high gloss finish, Rosewood forend and grip cap with maplewood spacers, fineline checkering, high gloss bluing, 3 or 5 shot mag., 7 lbs. New 2012.

MSR $1,149	$995	$850	$725	$625	$500	$400	$325

VANGUARD SERIES 2 RC – .22-250 Rem., .223 Rem., .243 Win., .25-06 Rem., .240 Wby. Mag. (new 2013), .257 Wby. Mag., .270 Win., .30-06, .300 Wby. Mag., .300 Win. Mag., .308 Win., .338 Win. Mag., 7mm-08 Rem., or 7mm Rem. Mag. cal., 24 in. forged barrel with matte blue finish, pillar-bedded composite stock with Monte Carlo raised cheekpiece and non-slip black spiderwebbing, 3 or 5 shot mag., Special RC engraved floorplate, approx. 7 1/2 lbs. New 2012.

MSR $1,199	$1,025	$875	$750	$625	$525	$425	$350

GRADING - PPGS™	100%	98%	95%	90%	80%	70%	60%	LAST MSR

VANGUARD SERIES 2 RC VARMINT – .223 Rem., .22-250 Rem., or .308 Win. cal., 22 in. free-floated barrel with recessed target crown and matte blue finish, hand laminated Monte Carlo composite stock with beavertail forend, Pachmayr Decelerator pad, aluminum bedding plate, 5 shot mag., Special RC engraved floorplate, 8 3/4 lbs. New 2012.

MSR $1,199	$1,025	$875	$750	$625	$525	$425	$350

VANGUARD SERIES 2 SPORTER – .22-250 Rem., .223 Rem., .243 Win., .25-06 Rem., .257 Wby. Mag., .270 Win., .270 WSM (disc. 2012), .30-06, .300 Wby. Mag., .300 Win. Mag., .300 WSM (disc. 2012), .308 Win., .338 Win. Mag., 7mm-08 Rem., or 7mm Rem. Mag. cal., 24 in. barrel, 3 or 5 shot mag., features raised comb, Monte Carlo Turkish walnut stock with satin urethane finish, rosewood forend and fineline diamond point checkering, matte blue finish, approx. 7 1/2 lbs. New 2012.

MSR $849	$695	$595	$475	$400	$350	$300	$275

Add $50 for detachable box magazine (Vanguard Series 2 Sporter DBM, .25-06 Rem., .270 Win., or .30-06 cal. only).

VANGUARD SERIES 2 SYNTHETIC – .22-250 Rem., .223 Rem., .240 Wby. Mag., .243 Win., .25-06 Rem., .257 Wby. Mag., .270 Win., .270 WSM (disc. 2012), .30-06, .308 Win., .300 WSM (disc. 2012), .300 Win. Mag., .300 Wby. Mag., .338 Win. Mag., 7mm Rem. Mag., or 7mm-08 Rem. cal., 3 or 5 shot mag., 24 in. barrel, lightweight composite Monte Carlo Griptonite stock with pistol grip and forend inserts, matte blue or stainless finish, 7 1/2 lbs. New 2012.

MSR $649	$525	$465	$400	$360	$330	$295	$260

Add $100 for detachable box magazine (Vanguard Series 2 Synthetic DBM .25-06 Rem., .270 Win., or .30-06 cal. only).

Add $150 for stainless finish (Stainless Synthetic, not available in .22-250 Rem., .240 Wby., .25-06, .300 Win. Mag., .338 Win. Mag., or 7mm-08 Mag. cals.).

Add $100 for Series 2 Synthetic Combo (includes Simmons 3.5-10x40mm Truplex Reticle scope, and Leupold Rifleman rings and bases), mfg. 2012 only.

Add $200 for Series 2 Synthetic Package (includes Simmons 3.5-10x40mm Truplex Reticle scope, Leupold Rifleman rings and bases, adj. nylon sling, and injection-molded scoped rifle case), mfg. 2012 only.

Add $350 for Series 2 Synthetic Package (includes 3-9x42mm Redfield Revenge riflescope with matte finish and 4-plex reticle, mounted and boresighted, Talley-designed Weatherby Vanguard mounts, adj. nylon sling, injection-molded scoped rifle case), new 2013.

VANGUARD SERIES 2 SYNTHETIC YOUTH – .22-250 Rem., .223 Rem., .243 Win., 7mm-08 Rem., or .308 Win. cal., 5 shot mag., 20 in. contoured barrel, injection molded composite stock with removable elongated spacer to adj. length of pull, matte blued finish, 6 1/2 lbs. New 2012.

MSR $599	$495	$435	$385	$325	$275	$225	$195

VANGUARD SERIES 2 BACK COUNTRY – .240 Wby. Mag., .257 Wby. Mag., .270 Win., .300 Wby. Mag., .30-06, or .300 Win. Mag. cal., pillar bedded action, fluted 24 in. barrel w/o sights, blue metal finish, Cerakote treated Tactical Grey finished Monte Carlo composite stock with spiderweb accents, Pachmayr Decelerator pad, approx. 6 3/4 lbs. New 2013.

MSR $1,399	$1,195	$1,025	$900	$800	$700	$600	$500

VANGUARD SERIES 2 TRR RC – .223 Rem., or .308 Win. cal., 22 in. barrel with recessed target crown, hand laminated Monte Carlo composite stock with aluminum bedding plate, beavertail forend, Pachmayr Decelerator recoil pad, includes factory-shot target certified and signed by Ed Weatherby and special RC engraved floorplate, 8 3/4 lbs. New 2012.

MSR $1,199	$1,025	$875	$750	$625	$525	$425	$350

VANGUARD SERIES 2 VARMINT SPECIAL – .22-250 Rem., .223 Rem., or .308 Win. cal., 22 in. contoured barrel with recessed target crown, 5 shot mag., matte blue finish, lightweight composite Monte Carlo Griptonite stock with pistol grip and forend inserts, 8 3/4 lbs. New 2012.

MSR $849	$725	$650	$575	$475	$425	$375	$325

GRADING - PPGS™	100%	98%	95%	90%	80%	70%	60%	LAST MSR

SHOTGUNS: O/U

Recent Weatherby O/U shotguns were previously manufactured by Fausti of Italy until 2011. Previous manufacture was by SKB of Japan, and by Nikko Firearms of Japan from May 1972 to 1981.

Japanese manufacture utilized the IMC choke system (integral multi-choke), which allows interchangeability with Briley choke tubes.

REGENCY FIELD GRADE – 20 ga. (new 1968) or 12 ga., checkered stock, VR, engraved side plates, SST, early importation beginning in 1967 was from Italy, later mfg. was switched to Japan.

$1,395 $1,250 $1,095 $940 $850 $690 $565

Add 10-15% for early Italian mfg. (note proofmarks).

REGENCY TRAP GRADE – 12 ga., checkered trap stock, engraved, VR, SST. Imported from Italy.

$1,200 $1,050 $850 $725 $650 4550 $450

OLYMPIAN STANDARD – 12 and 20 ga., lightly engraved sideplates. Disc. 1980.

$850 $745 $640 $580 $470 $385 $300

OLYMPIAN SKEET – 26 or 28 in. barrel.

$885 $775 $665 $600 $485 $400 $310

OLYMPIAN TRAP – 30 or 32 in. barrel, VR.

$850 $745 $640 $580 $470 $385 $300

ATHENA GRADE III CLASSIC FIELD – 12, 20, or 28 (new 2001) ga., 2 3/4 (28 ga. only) or 3 in. chambers, 26 or 28 in. barrels, features oil finished American claro walnut stock with rounded pistol grip and slender forearm, gold SST (push button on trigger), silver grey nitride sideplates with rose and scroll engraved gold pheasant and quail hunting scenes, gold "W" on opening lever, 6 1/2-8 lbs. Mfg. 1999-2007.

$2,125 $1,860 $1,595 $1,445 $1,170 $955 $745 *$2,510*

ATHENA D'ITALIA III – 12 or 20 ga., 3 in. chambers, vented 26 or 28 in. VR barrels with choke tubes, ejectors, four-lock boxlock action with chrome plated sideplates with gold game bird scenes, SST (tang operated), checkered oil finished walnut stock and forearm, pierced top lever, trigger guard features Weatherby flying "W", 6 1/2 - 8 lbs. Mfg. by Fausti 2008-2011.

$2,200 $1,925 $1,650 $1,495 $1,210 $990 $770 *$2,599*

ATHENA GRADE IV FIELD – 12, 20, 28 (mfg. 1989-1993) ga., or .410 (mfg. 1989-1993) bore, 3 in. chambers, 26 or 28 in. VR barrels with or without choke tubes, boxlock with Greener Crossbolt, SST, ejectors, high luster finish on hand checkered claro walnut stock (full pistol grip with rosewood cap) and forearm, recoil pad, engraved sideplates with satin nickel finish, vent. barrels and rib, multi-chokes became standard (except .410 bore) 1986 and 1992 (28 ga.), 6 1/2-8 lbs. Mfg. 1982-2002.

$2,085 $1,825 $1,565 $1,420 $1,145 $940 $730 *$2,549*

Subtract 10% if without choke tubes.

This model was redesignated the Grade IV in 1989.

* ***Athena Grade IV Field Skeet & Trap Models*** – 12 (Trap only) or 20 ga., special stock dimensions, target sights. Disc. 1992.

$1,675 $1,465 $1,255 $1,140 $920 $755 $585 *$1,965*

Skeet models were available in fixed choke only.

* ***Athena Grade IV Field Single Trap Model*** – 12 ga., 32 or 34 in. barrel with multi-choke feature. Disc. 1992.

$1,675 $1,465 $1,255 $1,140 $920 $755 $585 *$1,975*

GRADING - PPGS™	100%	98%	95%	90%	80%	70%	60%	LAST MSR

* ***Athena Grade IV Field Trap Combo*** – 12 ga., includes a set of O/U barrels and oversingle barrel with multi-choke feature. Disc. 1992.

$2,300	$2,015	$1,725	$1,565	$1,265	$1,035	$805	*$2,616*

* ***Athena Grade IV Field Master Skeet Set*** – 12 ga., includes 6 fitted full length Briley tubes with integral extractors (20, 28 ga., and .410 bore), cased. Imported 1988-91.

$3,100	$2,715	$2,325	$2,110	$1,705	$1,395	$1,085

ATHENA D'ITALIA IV – similar to Athena D'Italia III, except also available in 28 ga. Mfg. 2008-2010 by Fausti.

$2,500	$2,190	$1,875	$1,700	$1,375	$1,125	$875	*$2,799*

Add $300 for 28 ga.

ATHENA GRADE V CLASSIC FIELD – 12 or 20 ga., 3 in. chambers, similar to Grade IV, except has more elaborate engraving w/o gold inlays, gold SST, and better walnut, 6 1/2 - 8 lbs. Mfg. by SKB 1989-2007.

$2,375	$2,080	$1,780	$1,615	$1,305	$1,070	$830	*$2,773*

In 1993, Weatherby changed the styling of this gun to incorporate European shooting features including an oil finished, round knob stock and slim forearm, tight rose-and-scroll engraving, and matted VR.

ATHENA D'ITALIA V – 12 or 20 ga., vented 26 or 28 in. VR barrels with choke tubes, ejectors, four-lock boxlock action with chrome plates sideplates featuring intricate rose and scroll engraving, raised and engraved hingepin, extra select checkered oil finished walnut stock and forearm, 7 1/2 - 8 lbs. Mfg. by Fausti 2008-2011.

$3,350	$2,930	$2,515	$2,280	$1,845	$1,510	$1,175	*$3,999*

ORION UPLAND CLASSIC FIELD – 12 or 20 ga., 3 in. chambers, features high luster checkered Claro walnut stock and forearm, blue frame, gold SST, gold Weatherby flying "W" on trigger guard, rounded checkered pistol grip stock and slender forearm, ejectors, 26 or 28 in. VR barrels with choke tubes, 6 1/2 - 8 lbs. Mfg. 1999-2007.

$1,225	$1,070	$920	$835	$675	$550	$430	*$1,500*

ORION I FIELD – 12 or 20 ga., 3 in. chambers, 26, 28, or 30 (12 ga. only) in. VR barrels with multi-chokes, SST, ejectors, checkered walnut full pistol grip stock and forearm, recoil pad, blue receiver with engraved upland and waterfowl scenes, 6 1/2-8 lbs. Mfg. 1989-2002.

$1,240	$1,085	$930	$845	$680	$560	$435	*$1,539*

* ***Orion I Field Ducks Unlimited*** – 12 ga. (sponsor gun in 1986) or 20 ga. (sponsor gun in 1987), deluxe walnut with gold duck scenes, blue frame, multi-chokes, includes presentation case.

$1,395	$1,220	$1,045	$950	$765	$630	$490

ORION D'ITALIA I – 12 or 20 ga., 3 in. chambers, vented 26 or 28 in. VR barrels, ejectors, high lustre checkered walnut stock and forearm, blue boxlock action with game and floral engraving, engraved forearm iron and hinge pin, trigger guard has Weatherby flying "W" engraved in gold, 6 1/2 - 8 lbs. Mfg. by Fausti 2008-2011.

$1,425	$1,245	$1,070	$970	$785	$640	$500	*$1,699*

ORION II FIELD – 12, 20, 28 ga., or .410 bore, 3 in. chambers (except 28 ga.), boxlock with Greener Crossbolt, SST, ejectors, walnut with high-gloss finish, silver nitride receiver with light engraving. Multi-chokes became standard 1986. Field Grade disc. 1993.

$1,075	$940	$805	$730	$590	$485	$375	*$1,207*

Subtract 10% without choke tubes on older models.

Subtract $14 for Skeet grade (12 and 20 ga., fixed chokes only).

This model was redesignated Grade II in 1989. In 1993, the Standard Field Models in this variation were discontinued (Classic Grade took its place) - only Field and Sporting Clays variations were available.

GRADING - PPGS™	100%	98%	95%	90%	80%	70%	60%	LAST MSR

* ***Orion II Field Classic*** – 12, 20, or 28 ga., multi-choked barrels with matted VR, features rounded pistol grip stock and oil finished Claro walnut stock and forearm, gold SST, ejectors, waterfowl and upland game scenes on silver grey nitride finish, 6 1/2 - 8 lbs. Mfg. 1993-2007.

$1,500	$1,315	$1,125	$1,020	$825	$675	$525	*$1,873*

ORION II FIELD/CLASSIC SPORTING – 12 ga. only, Sporting Clays configuration, early mfg. was blue finish, recent mfg. had silver nitride finish, choice of Field Sporting (with rosewood pistol grip cap and grooved upper forearm) or Classic Field Sporting (rounded pistol grip and smaller forearm), acid etched engraving, rounded recoil pad, matte finish VR, lengthened forcing cones. Mfg. 1991-2002.

$1,400	$1,225	$1,050	$950	$770	$630	$490	*$1,753*

ORION D'ITALIA II – 12, 20, or 28 ga., vented 26, 28, or 30 (12 ga. only) in. VR barrel, ejectors, fancy grade checkered walnut stock and forearm, hard chrome receiver with game and floral engraving, engraved forearm iron and hinge pin, trigger guard has Weatherby flying "W" engraved in gold, 6 1/2 - 8 lbs. Mfg. 2008-2010 by Fausti.

$1,600	$1,400	$1,200	$1,090	$880	$720	$560	*$1,899*

Add $80 for 28 ga.

SUPER SPORTING CLAYS (SSC) – 12 ga. only, 3 in. chambers, 28, 30, or 32 in. vented barrels with 12mm target VR and gas ports, choke tubes, fully adj. trigger, satin oil finished sporter style pistol grip stock with Schnabel forearm, Pachmayr Decelerator pad, approx. 8 lbs. Mfg. 1999-2007.

$1,875	$1,640	$1,405	$1,275	$1,030	$845	$655	*$2,378*

ORION D'ITALIA SC (SPORTING CLAYS) – 12 ga., 28, 30, or 32 in. ported barrels, ejectors, four-lock boxlock action, satin oil finished checkered walnut stock with adj. comb, pistol grip, and Schnabel forend, chrome plated receiver with engraved Weatherby logo, trigger guard has gold engraved flying "W", 8 lbs. Mfg. by Fausti 2008-2009.

$2,250	$1,970	$1,690	$1,530	$1,240	$1,015	$790	*$2,599*

ORION III FIELD – 12 or 20 ga. only, similar to Grade II, except has silver grey receiver with custom engraving including mallard and pheasant game scenes, multi-chokes standard. Mfg. 1989-2002.

$1,545	$1,350	$1,160	$1,050	$850	$695	$540	*$1,917*

* ***Orion III Field Classic*** – 12 or 20 ga., multi-choked 26 or 28 in. VR barrels, features rounded pistol grip stock and oil finished Claro walnut stock and forearm, extensive engraving on silver grey nitride finish with gold game scene inlays, matted VR, 7 1/4-8 lbs. Mfg. 1993-2007.

$1,800	$1,575	$1,350	$1,225	$990	$810	$630	*$2,258*

* ***Orion III Field English*** – 12 or 20 ga., 3 in. chambers, features straight grip stock and silver grey nitride receiver with engraving and gold inlays, approx. 6 1/2 lbs. Mfg. 1997-2002.

$1,595	$1,395	$1,195	$1,085	$875	$720	$560	*$1,998*

ORION D'ITALIA III – similar to Orion D'Italia II, except has better walnut and gold inlays. Mfg. 2008-2010 by Fausti.

$1,850	$1,620	$1,390	$1,260	$1,020	$835	$650	*$2,199*

SHOTGUNS: SxS

Recent SxS manufacture was by Fausti of Italy until 2011. SxS manufacture utilizes the IMC choke system (integral multi-choke), which allows interchangeability with Briley choke tubes. Importation was disc. during 2003, and reintroduced during 2005.

ORION – 12, 20, 28 ga. or .410 bore, 3 in. chambers standard except for 28 ga., ejectors, case colored boxlock action, gold SST, 18 LPI checkered half-round pistol grip Turkish

GRADING - PPGS™	100%	98%	95%	90%	80%	70%	60%	LAST MSR

walnut stock and semi-beavertail forearm, 26 or 28 in. barrels, solid pad, 6 3/4-7 lbs., approx. 400 mfg. (including Athena) in Spain by Abolla 2002-2003.

	$960	$840	$720	$655	$530	$430	$335	*$1,149*

ORION D'ITALIA SBS – 12 or 20 ga., 3 in. chambers, SST, 26 (20 ga. only) or 28 (12 ga. only) in. back bored barrels with choke tubes, coin finished boxlock action, gloss finished checkered pistol grip stock and beavertail forearm, Weatherby flying "W" in gold on trigger guard, 6 3/4 - 7 1/4 lbs. Mfg. by Fausti 2008-2011.

	$1,875	$1,650	$1,425	$1,250	$1,025	$875	$725	*$2,199*

ATHENA – 12 or 20 ga., 3 in. chambers, ejectors, case colored engraved boxlock action with sideplates, gold SST, 22 LPI checkered straight grip select Turkish walnut stock and splinter forearm, 26 or 28 in. barrels with IMC choke system (interchangeable with Briley), solid pad, 6 3/4-7 lbs., approx. 400 (including Orion) mfg. in Spain by Abolla 2002-2003.

	$1,285	$1,125	$965	$875	$705	$580	$450	*$1,599*

ATHENA D'ITALIA – 12, 20, or 28 ga., 2 3/4 (28 ga. only) or 3 in. chambers, engraved coin finished Anson & Deeley boxlock action with sideplates, double locking system, monobloc barrels with ejectors and stainless steel choke tubes, DT, oil finished English straight grip select walnut stock and slim forearm with new Scottish checkering, gold "W" on trigger guard, supplied with hardshell takedown case, 6 3/4 - 7 1/4 lbs. Mfg. by Fausti of Italy 2005-2011.

	$2,725	$2,385	$2,045	$1,855	$1,500	$1,225	$955	*$3,129*

Add $140 for 28 ga.

* ***Athena D'Italia PG*** – 12, 20, or 28 ga., similar boxlock action, except has more engraving, gold SST, deluxe checkered walnut rounded pistol grip stock and semi-beavertail forearm, 6 3/4 - 7 1/4 lbs. Mfg. by Fausti of Italy. Mfg. 2006-2010.

	$3,250	$2,845	$2,450	$2,210	$1,790	$1,465	$1,150	*$3,799*

Add $130 for 28 ga.

* ***Athena D'Italia Deluxe*** – 12, 20, or 28 ga., coin finished boxlock action with sideplates featuring Bulino style game scene engraving and gold inlays by A. Posilini (hand signed), relief engraved shoulders, AAA straight grip 24 LPI checkered Turkish walnut stock with wood buttplate and splinter forearm, gold SST, ejectors, 6 3/4 - 7 1/4 lbs. Mfg. by Fausti of Italy. Mfg. 2006-2008.

	$6,900	$6,040	$5,175	$4,690	$3,795	$3,105	$2,415	*$7,625*

Add $164 for 28 ga.

SHOTGUNS: SEMI-AUTO

Beginning 2008, all semi-autos are manufactured in Turkey. Previous manufacture was by ITI of Italy until 2007, and utilized the IMC choke system (integral multi-choke), which allows interchangeability with Briley choke tubes.

Add $359 for interchangeable SAS rifled 22 in. slug barrel (mfg. 2004-2007).

CENTURION FIELD GRADE – 12 ga.,gas operation, VR, full pistol grip checkered walnut stock. Mfg. 1972-1981.

	$300	$265	$225	$205	$165	$135	$105	

CENTURION TRAP GRADE – 12 ga., checkered stock, VR.

	$335	$295	$250	$230	$185	$150	$115	

CENTURION DE LUXE – 12 ga., VR, checkered stock, lightly engraved.

	$375	$330	$280	$255	$205	$170	$130	

Add 20% for deluxe wood.

* ***Centurion De Luxe DU*** – mfg. 1980 for DU chapters.

	$550	$480	$415	$375	$305	$250	$195	

GRADING - PPGS™	100%	98%	95%	90%	80%	70%	60%	LAST MSR

MODEL 82 – 12 ga. only, 2 3/4 or 3 in. chamber, gas operation, alloy receiver, VR, deluxe walnut, multi-chokes became standard in 1985, Trap Grade was disc. 1984. Mfg. 1983-89.

	$395	$345	$295	$270	$215	$180	$140	*$500*

Subtract $30 without multi-chokes.
Subtract $35 for Trap Grade (disc. 1984).

* ***Model 82 Buckmaster*** – 22 in. barrel choked skeet, rifle sights, 7 1/2 lbs. Disc. 1989.

	$395	$345	$295	$270	$215	$180	$140	*$500*

MODEL SAS FIELD – 12 ga., 3 in. chamber, self-compensating gas operated mechanism, high grade satin oil finished checkered American claro walnut stock and forearm, includes stock shim system, "Weatherby" outlined in gold on right side of receiver, 26, 28 (disc. 2001, reintroduced 2005), or 30 (12 ga. only. disc. 2001) in. VR barrel with Briley choke tubes, 6 3/4-7 3/4 lbs., mfg. in Italy. Mfg. 1999-2007.

	$775	$680	$580	$525	$425	$350	$270	*$926*

* ***Model SAS Field Sporting Clays*** – similar to SAS Field, except has choice of 26 (disc. 2004), 28, or 30 (new 2005) in. ported VR barrel with extended choke tubes, includes molded plastic case, 7 - 7 3/4 lbs. Mfg. 2002-2005.

	$850	$745	$640	$580	$470	$385	$300	*$999*

* ***Model SAS Field Synthetic*** – similar to Model SAS Field, except has black synthetic stock and forearm. Mfg. late 2000-2007.

	$745	$650	$560	$505	$410	$335	$260	*$879*

* ***Model SAS Field Camo*** – 12 ga. only, 24 (Mossy Oak Breakup only, new 2001) 26, or 28 (Shadow Grass only) in. VR barrel with 5 extended Briley choke tubes, HiViz front sight, 100% camo coverage in either Mossy Oak Breakup (disc. 2006), Shadow Grass (disc. 2006), Skyline Fall Flight (new 2007), or Skyline Apparition Excel (new 2007), 7 1/4 - 7 3/4 lbs. Mfg. late 2000-2007.

	$810	$710	$610	$550	$445	$365	$285	*$977*

* ***Model SAS Field Slug Gun*** – 12 ga. only, 3 in. chamber, 22 in. rifled barrel w/o sights, includes cantilever base, checkered Monte Carlo walnut stock and forearm with sling swivels, 7 3/4 lbs. Mfg. 2003-2007.

	$825	$720	$620	$560	$455	$370	$290	*$987*

SA-08 DELUXE – 12 or 20 ga., 3 in. chamber, 26 or 28 in. VR barrel with choke tubes, matte black receiver with "Weatherby" in gold on right side, oil finished checkered walnut stock and forearm with high gloss finish, dual valve system, 6 - 6 3/4 lbs. New 2010.

MSR $799	$675	$575	$495	$440	$375	$325	$275	

SA-08 ENTRE RIOS – 28 ga. only, scaled down frame, 26 or 28 in. VR barrel with 3 choke tubes, checkered walnut stock and forearm, 5 1/4 lbs. Mfg. 2011 only.

	$625	$550	$475	$425	$375	$325	$275	*$749*

SA-08 UPLAND – 12 or 20 ga., 3 in. chamber, gas action with dual valves for light or heavy loads, 26 or 28 in. VR barrel with choke tubes, matte black receiver with "Weatherby" in gold on right side, oil finished checkered walnut stock and forearm with satin finish, 6-6 3/4 lbs., mfg. in Turkey. New 2008.

MSR $799	$675	$575	$495	$440	$375	$325	$275	

This model was also available as a SA-08 Youth in 20 ga. with 12 1/2 LOP at no extra charge (disc. 2011).

SA-08 SYNTHETIC – 12 or 20 ga., 26 or 28 in. barrel, otherwise similar to SA-08 Upland, except has black synthetic stock. New 2009.

MSR $599	$495	$435	$365	$325	$275	$235	$185	

This model is also available as a SA-08 Synthetic Youth in 20 ga. with 12 1/2 in. LOP and 24 in. barrel at no extra charge (new 2010).

GRADING - PPGS™	100%	98%	95%	90%	80%	70%	60%	LAST MSR

SA-08 WATERFOWLER – 12 ga. only, 3 in. chamber, 26 or 28 in. barrel with choke tubes, similar to Synthetic model, except has 100% Mothwing Marsh Mimicry camo coverage, special dipping process adheres camo to all exterior stock and metalwork, 6 1/2 lbs. New 2010.

MSR $749	$650	$575	$500	$400	$335	$295	$240	

SA-459 TR – 12 or 20 ga., 3 in. chamber, 18 1/2 in. ported barrel, 5 shot mag., tactical configuration with black synthetic pistol grip stock and forearm, includes ghost ring rear sight on Picatinny receiver rail, M-16 front sight, oversized bolt handle, approx. 7 lbs. New 2011.

MSR $699	$625	$550	$495	$425	$350	$295	$250	

SA-459 TURKEY – 12 or 20 ga., 3 in. chamber, 21-1/4 in. barrel with removeable extended choke tube, gas operated action, fiber optic front and ghost ring rear sights, features Mothwing Spring Mimicry camo finish, oversized hourglass bolt handle, 6-6 1/2 lbs. New 2012.

MSR $699	$625	$550	$495	$425	$350	$295	$250	

SHOTGUNS: SLIDE ACTION

PATRICIAN FIELD GRADE – 12 ga., checkered stock, VR. Mfg. 1972-81.

	$275	$240	$205	$185	$150	$125	$95	

PATRICIAN TRAP GRADE – 12 ga., checkered stock, VR.

	$295	$260	$220	$200	$160	$135	$105	

PATRICIAN DE LUXE – 12 ga., checkered stock, lightly engraved, fancy wood, VR.

	$325	$285	$245	$220	$180	$145	$115	

MODEL 92 – 12 ga. only, 2 3/4 and 3 in. chambers, ultra-short slide action w/twin rails, 26-30 in. VR barrels, engraved black alloy receiver, checkered pistol grip walnut stock and forearm. Mfg. 1982-89.

	$325	$285	$245	$220	$180	$145	$115	*$400*

Subtract 10% for Trap grade (disc. 1984).

Subtract 10% if fixed choke (multi-chokes became standard 1985) barrel.

* ***Model 92 Buckmaster*** – 22 in. skeet bore barrel, rifle sights, 7 1/2 lbs. Disc. 1987.

	$345	$300	$260	$235	$190	$155	$120	*$400*

PA-08 KNOXX STRUTTER X – 12 ga., 24 in. VR barrel with choke tubes, features adj. Knoxx recoil reduction system stock with pistol grip, fiber optic sights, drop out trigger system, choice of matte black metal finish and black synthetic stock and forearm or 100% Apparition Excel camo coverage, 7 lbs., mfg. in Turkey. Mfg. 2008.

	$425	$370	$320	$290	$235	$190	$150	*$499*

Add $80 for 100% camo coverage.

PA-08 KNOXX HD – 12 ga., 3 in. chamber, 18 in. barrel with fixed IC choke, features black synthetic Knoxx SpecOps adj. stock with pistol grip, extended mag. (5 shot capacity), 7 lbs., mfg. in Turkey. Mfg. 2008.

	$425	$370	$320	$290	$235	$190	$150	*$499*

PA-08 UPLAND – 12 or 20 ga., 3 in. chamber, 26 or 28 in. VR ribbed barrel with choke tubes, dual slide bar action, brass bead front sight, matte black metal, checkered low lustre walnut stock and forearm, 6 1/2 lbs. New 2008.

MSR $449	$365	$335	$285	$250	$225	$200	$185	

This model is also available as a PA-08 Upland Youth in 20 ga. with 12 1/2 LOP and 22 in. barrel at no extra charge (new 2012).

GRADING - PPGS™	100%	98%	95%	90%	80%	70%	60%	LAST MSR

PA-08 UPLAND SLUG GUN COMBO – 12 ga., 3 in. chamber, 24 in. rifled barrel with cantilever scope mount in matte black, 28 in. field barrel with IMC chokes, brass bead front sight, and has gloss black finish, Walnut stock with gloss finish, 7 1/4 lbs. New 2012.

MSR $649 $550 $475 $395 $340 $300 $265 $240

PA-08 SYNTHETIC – 12 or 20 (new 2013) ga., 3 in. chamber, 26 or 28 in. chrome lined VR ribbed barrel with choke tubes, dual slide bar action, brass bead front sight, matte black metal, lightweight black injection-molded synthetic stock and forearm, 6 1/2 lbs. New 2010.

MSR $399 $350 $310 $270 $240 $210 $180 $160

Add $150 for Synthetic Slug Gun Combo (12 ga. only, includes 24 in. rifled barrel with cantilever mount, and 28 in. field barrel with chokes), new 2012.

PA-08 SYNTHETIC WATERFOWLER – 12 ga., 3 in. chamber, 26 or 28 in. barrel, lightweight and durable injection-molded synthetic stock with Mothwing Marsh Mimicry camo pattern, special dipping process adheres camo directly to all stock components, brass bead front sight, 7 1/4 lbs. New 2012.

MSR $399 $350 $310 $270 $240 $210 $180 $160

PA-08 TR – 12 or 20 (new 2013) ga., 3 in. chamber, 19 in. barrel with fixed cylinder choke and bladed white dot front sight, matte black finish, black synthetic stock and forearm, crossbolt trigger guard safety, 5 shot mag., dual action slide bars, 6 3/4 lbs. New 2011.

MSR $399 $350 $310 $270 $240 $210 $180 $160

Add $20 for TR accessory rail that attaches to screw-on magazine end cap.

PA-08 TURKEY – 12 ga., 3 in. chamber, 22 in. barrel with removeable full choke tube, white dot blade front sight, dual action bar system, 5 shot mag., features Mothwing Spring Mimicry camo finish, 7 lbs. New 2012.

MSR $399 $350 $310 $270 $240 $210 $180 $160

PA-459 HOME DEFENSE – 12 ga. only, 3 in. chamber, 19 in. barrel, black synthetic stock and forearm. Mfg. 2010 only.

$350 $305 $265 $240 $195 $160 $125 ***$469***

PA-459 TR – 12 or 20 (new 2013) ga. only, 3 in. chamber, 19 in. ported removeable cylinder choke tube, M-16 style fiber optic front sight, black synthetic grooved pistol grip stock and forearm, alloy receiver with integral Picatinny rail and adj. ghost ring sight, 13 1/2 in. LOP, 5 shot mag., matte black metalwork, 6 1/2 lbs. New 2011.

MSR $499 $425 $375 $335 $295 $265 $235 $210

* ***PA-459 Digital TR*** – 12 ga. only, otherwise similar to PA-459 TR, except has green/tan digital camo pattern on stock (not pistol grip) and forearm. New 2011.

MSR $549 $450 $395 $350 $295 $265 $235 $210

PA-459 TURKEY – 12 ga., 3 in. chamber, 21-1/4 in. barrel with removeable extended ported choke tube, 13-1/2 in. LOP, 5 shot mag., fiber optic front and ghost ring rear sight, ergonomic pistol grip buttstock with rubber texturized grip, Picatinny accessory rail, features Mothwing Spring Mimicry camo finish, 7 1/4 lbs. New 2012.

MSR $549 $450 $385 $340 $295 $265 $235 $210

WEAVER ARMS CORPORATION

Previous manufacturer located in Escondido, CA circa 1984-1990.

CARBINES

NIGHTHAWK CARBINE – 9mm Para. cal., semi-auto paramilitary design carbine, fires from closed bolt, 16.1 in. barrel, retractable shoulder stock, 25, 32, 40, or 50 shot mag. (interchangeable with Uzi), ambidextrous safety, parkerized finish, 6 1/2 lbs. Mfg. 1987-90.

$675 $600 $525 $450 $375 $325 $300 ***$575***

GRADING - PPGS™	100%	98%	95%	90%	80%	70%	60%	LAST MSR

PISTOLS: SEMI-AUTO

NIGHTHAWK PISTOL – 9mm Para. cal., closed bolt semi-auto, 10 or 12 in. barrel, alloy upper receiver, ambidextrous safety, black finish, 5 lbs. Mfg. 1987-90.

	$800	$700	$625	$550	$475	$425	$350	*$475*

WEBLEY & SCOTT AG (LIMITED)

Current trademark of sub-contracted firearms and airgun manufacturer with headquarters located in Luzern, Switzerland beginning 2010. Currently imported beginning mid-2011 by Webley & Scott USA, located in Reno, NV. Previously located in West Midlands, England, with history dating back to 1790, and Birmingham, England. SxS shotguns were previously imported and distributed late 2007-2008 by Legacy Sports International, located in Reno, NV.

Webley & Scott is one the oldest names in the UK gun industry, being able to trace its origins back to 1790 when William Davies started making bullet moulds in his small factory in Birmingham, England. In this early period Birmingham flourished as the greatest manufacturing centre of firearms in the world. Yet the only official proof house was in London, then in 1813 the world famous Birmingham Proof House was established by an Act of Parliament.

For more information and current pricing on both new and used Webley & Scott airguns, please refer to the *Blue Book of Airguns* by Dr. Robert Beeman & John Allen (also online).

HISTORY OF WEBLEY & SCOTT

In 1827, 14 year old Philip Webley was apprenticed to Benjamin Watson, a gun lock filer. Having completed his apprenticeship, he joined up with his brother in 1835 and formed Webley Brothers - Percussioners, Gun Lock & c. makers in Weaman Street, next door to William Davis. Philip began courting Caroline Davis, who following the death of her father three years earlier was running the family business alongside her mother. When the pair married in 1838 the two firms amalgamated. Over the next sixty years P. Webley and Sons prospered and grew, sons Thomas and Henry joining the company.

During the 1850s the company began manufacturing percussion cap and ball revolvers. This was a time of unrest across the globe with the Crimea War, Indian Mutiny and the American Civil War and it created great demand for Webley's products. The last quarter of the 19th century witnessed the rise of muzzle loaders, the breech loading rifle and the conversion from black powder to smokeless powder. In 1887 the company took over the well known firm of Tipping & Lawden of Constitution Hill, Birmingham, England and in the same year saw the award of the first of many Government contracts for the supply of revolvers from its new, modern and automated factory. Philip Webley died in 1888 aged 76 leaving the firm in the hands of his sons. In 1896 they built a second factory in Weaman Street for the production of rifles, notably the Martini-Henry Target Rifle.

W & C Scott was founded in 1832 by the brothers William and Charles Scott, who had moved to Birmingham from their native Suffolk and by the mid 1840s were gaining a reputation for the production of high quality double guns. Two of William's sons, William Middleditch and James Charles, joined the company and it was renamed as W & C Scott & Sons, and in 1855 moved to larger premises at 94-95 Bath Street, Birmingham. In 1864 the continued success of the company necessitated a move to larger premises and the building of the world famous Premier Gun Works on Lancaster Street, Birmingham.

The Scott brothers were innovators with many patents to their name, some of them truly historic. One of the earliest was the Scott spindle in connection with the top lever, this is still used today by makers of high grade breech loaders. They introduced the block safety catch for hammerless guns and later still the double catch hammerless lock which is still in use today.

William Middleditch was a brilliant engineer, having his first patent filed in 1865 and in 1878 he became the first man to design and patent a successful sidelock shotgun. This shotgun was manufactured under royalty arrangements by a number of firms, including Holland and Holland.

GRADING - PPGS™	100%	98%	95%	90%	80%	70%	60%	LAST MSR

He retired from the firm in 1894 and James became head of the company until he too retired at the time of the amalgamation of the three companies in 1897.

The amalgamation in 1897 of the three companies created a new public company registered under the name Webley and Scott Revolver and Arms Co Ltd, with a total capital of £335,000. Thomas Webley became Managing Director. Martin Scott, Richard Ellis, William Henry Ellis and Albert Ellis became departmental managers. Webley revolvers and Scott shotguns were popular and the new company prospered.

Over the 20th century, many forces came to bear on the company such as the 1920 Firearms Act that virtually barred individuals from owning handguns, the compulsory purchase of the Weaman Street factory for a road widening scheme and a general increase in competition from abroad. The company changed hands several times and in 1965 the company took over the gunmakers W.W. Greener who had moved to Birmingham in 1844.

The company diversified, producing parts for cars, airguns and general engineering components. At the end of the 1970s the production of shotguns was terminated at Webley and Scott and a separate company was formed, W&C Scott (Gunmakers) Limited. In January 1985, this entire business was sold to the world famous shotgun makers Holland and Holland. Holland and Holland had been one of the companies which originally bought firearms "in-the-white" from Webley and Scott. Shortly after being acquired by Holland & Holland, firearms manufacture was discontinued while airgun production resumed.

In 2006 Webley & Scott was purchased by AGS, and once again began making shotguns under the name Webley & Scott.

To list all the types and models of guns and rifles produced by the company over the centuries would fill a separate book, but some of the more famous are the Webley falling block rifles, the Scott Imperial Premier Sidelock Hammerless shotgun and the Model 700 Boxlock Hammerless Sporting Shotgun.

Historical information courtesy of Webley & Scott.

PISTOLS: SEMI-AUTO

MODEL 1903 – .38 cal., experimental model.

Extreme rarity precludes accurate pricing on this model.

MODEL 1904 – .455 Webley Auto cal., limited production, 10-15 mfg.

Extreme rarity precludes accurate pricing on this model.

MODEL 1905 – 7.65mm/.32 ACP cal., ser. no. range 1-22,309, approx. 13,000+ mfg. from 1906-1909.

100%	98%	95%	90%	80%	70%	60%
$1,500	$1,300	$1,100	$750	$600	$400	$300

MODEL 1906 – .45 cal., never reached serial production.

Extreme rarity precludes accurate pricing on this model.

MODEL 1907 – 6.35mm/.25 ACP cal., hammer model, ser. no. range 7,060-163,109, approx. 50,000 mfg. from 1906-1939.

100%	98%	95%	90%	80%	70%	60%
$1,000	$900	$800	$700	$600	$500	$400

MODEL 1908 – .32 ACP cal., ser. no. range 22,310-163,709, approx. 90,000 mfg. from 1909-1940.

100%	98%	95%	90%	80%	70%	60%
$750	$650	$550	$450	$350	$250	$200

MODEL 1909 – 9mm Browning Long cal., ser. no. range 16,000-116,8873, approx. 1,700 mfg. from 1909-1915.

100%	98%	95%	90%	80%	70%	60%
$2,000	$1,900	$1,800	$1,700	$1,600	$1,500	$1,400

MODEL 1910 – .380 ACP cal., ser. no. range 55,047-156,175, less than 2,000 mfg. from 1910-1932.

100%	98%	95%	90%	80%	70%	60%
$2,000	$1,900	$1,800	$1,700	$1,600	$1,500	$1,400

GRADING - PPGS™	100%	98%	95%	90%	80%	70%	60%	LAST MSR

MODEL 1910 – .380 ACP cal., ser. no. range 40,000-66,664, less than 1,000 mfg. from 1909-1911.

	$3,500	$3,000	$2,500	$2,000	$1,750	$1,500	$1,400	

METROPOLITAN POLICE MODEL – .32 ACP cal., ser. no. range 57,000-163,382, approx. 15,000 mfg. from 1911-1940.

	$1,500	$1,400	$1,300	$1,000	$750	$500	$400	

MODEL 1911 – .22 LR cal., single shot target pistol, 4 1/2 or 9 in. barrel, ser. no. range 58,536-156,398, less than 1,400 mfg. from 1911-1932.

	$2,000	$1,900	$1,800	$1,700	$1,600	$1,500	$1,400	

Add 100%-200% for shoulder stock or sets with both barrel lengths.

MODEL 1912 – 6.35mm/.25 ACP cal. hammerless version of the Model 1907, ser. no. range 41,000-161,859, approx. 15,000 mfg. from 1909-1938.

	$1,500	$1,400	$1,300	$1,000	$750	$500	$400	

NAVY MODEL .455 MKI – .455 Webley Auto cal. version of the Model 1913, government contract, ser. no. range 1-8,000, approx. 500 were Australian contract, commercial production probably never reached 1,000 with number 158919 being finished in Dec. 1933. Mfg. 1913-1919.

	$2,500	$2,200	$1,900	$1,750	$1,600	$1,500	$1,400	

ROYAL HORSE ARTILLERY MODEL .455 MKI – .455 Webley Auto cal., ser. no. range 2,501-8,050, less than 500 mfg. 1913-1919.

	$8,500	$7,000	$5,500	$4,500	$4,000	$3,700	$3,600	

Add 100%-200% for shoulder stock.

MODEL 1921 – .32 ACP cal., Improved Model, Webley's final attempt at modernizing the .32 ACP, ser. no. range 106,000-160,000, less than 4,500 mfg. from 1921-1940.

	$3,500	$3,300	$3,000	$2,500	$2,000	$1,800	$1,700	

MODEL 1922 – 9mm cal., also known as the New Military & Police Model, the African Model, and the Romanian Model, ser. no. range 130,000-160,000, less than 1,900 mfg. from 1920-1932.

	$4,500	$4,000	$3,500	$3,000	$2,500	$2,000	$1,900	

"HUMANE KILLER" MODEL – .32 ACP cal., single shot variation based on the .32 ACP cal. models, designed specifically for the humane put-down of livestock, used by vets, the Royal Society for the Prevention of Cruelty to Animals, and the Ministry of Agriculture and Fisheries, ser. no. range 100,000-200,000, less than 1,000 mfg. 1920-1940.

	$1,000	$900	$800	$700	$550	$450	$350	

PISTOLS: SINGLE SHOT

SINGLE SHOT MODELS – usually found in .22 LR cal., tip-up 10 3/8 in. barrel, target model, checkered walnut grips, early model grip terminates with steel weight to provide balance, also provides a means to attach a shoulder stock on some models, original model is improved with thumbrest as part of the wood grip, by the 1950s, thumbrest was enlarged and made of plastic with a compartment for steel weight at the bottom.

	$1,500	$1,400	$1,300	$1,200	$1,100	$1,000	$900	

Add 200%-300% for special order .32 S&W or .38 S&W cals.

M1911 TARGET MODEL – .22 LR cal., developed as companion piece for the Metropolitan Police .32 cal. service semi-auto, interchangeable 4 1/2 or 9 in. barrel, shoulder stock, could be ordered with both barrels, ser. no. range 58536 - 156398. Approx. 1,400 mfg. 1911-1932.

	$2,000	$1,900	$1,800	$1,700	$1,600	$1,500	$1,400	

Add 150% - 200% four shoulder stock or sets with both barrel lengths.

GRADING - PPGS™	100%	98%	95%	90%	80%	70%	60%	LAST MSR

WEBLEY PERCUSSION MODELS

The first patents for the Webley revolver were issued to brothers James and Phillip Webley in February and March of 1853. Prior to 1853 and up to 1867, Webley revolvers went through a period of development, including the percussion system, the pinfire, rimfire, and finally, the more common centerfire system. Webley made the early Webley pistols, while other makers in England and on the continent made pistols to the Webley design.

The early percussion revolvers were of the open frame design similar to the Colt 1851 or 1860. Of particular note are the three single action Longspur models. The Longspur was easily identified by its overly long hammer spur, and made in a pocket, holster or belt model, with barrel lengths from 3 1/2 to 7 inches, and in calibers from 48 ga. to 120 ga.

FIRST MODEL LONGSPUR – barrel hinged to frame, sides of frame obscure hammer except for spur, and no attached rammer, ser. no. range 131-388. Mfg. 1853-1855.

Extreme rarity preclues accurate pricing on this model.

SECOND MODEL LONGSPUR – barrel still hinged to frame, hammer more visible, also featured rammer attached to frame, ser. no. range 199-969. Mfg. 1855-1857.

Extreme rarity precludes accurate pricing on this model.

THIRD MODEL LONGSPUR – barrel not hinged to frame but attached via barrel over cylinder pin and is secured with thumb screw to frame with screw through cylinder pin, compound rammer is attached to barrel side, ser. no. range 985-1602. Mfg. 1857-1867.

Extreme rarity precludes accurate pricing on this model.

WEDGE FRAME MODELS – between 1857 and 1859, Webley developed the "wedge frame" as a transition between the "open frame" of the Longspur and the final "solid frame" percussion pistol which would develop into the solid frame cartridge pistols that became a hallmark of the Webley brand. This model met with great success with numerous guns being produced during a short time, most were made with attached ram under barrel or side barrel, five or six shot cylinder, numerous calibers and barrel lengths. Few examples have survived. Mfg. 1857-1859.

Extreme rarity precludes accurate pricing on this model.

SOLID FRAME MODELS – the development of the solid frame percussion revolver offered a rigidity in frame design that would last into the modern revolver, few of the percussion revolvers with the solid frame were produced by Webley because of the development of more modern cartridge systems. Final development of the Webley solid frame revolver culminates with the arrival in 1867 of Webely's RIC No. 1, the model officially adopted by the Royal Irish Constabulary in Jan. 1868, presented to George A. Custer in 1869, and the model produced by Webley until the 1930s in one form or another.

Extreme rarity factor of solid frame percussion, pinfire, and rimfire models precludes accurate pricing.

REVOLVERS

WEBLEY-FOSBERY AUTOMATIC MODELS – .455 cal., 6 shot, hinged frame, 4, 6, or 7 1/2 in. barrel, blue or nickel finish, walnut or hard rubber grips, ser. nos. less than 5,000. Mfg. 1901-1924.

* ***Webley-Fosbery Automatic Model First 1901*** – ser. nos. under 300, production prior to Dec. 1901.

$12,500	$10,000	$8,500	$7,500	$6,500	$5,500	$4,500	

* ***Webley-Fosbery Automatic Model 1902*** – .38 Webley auto cal., 8 shot, ser. no. range mid 200-mid 1,300, extremely rare, less than 800 mfg. 1902-1903.

This model is extremely rare, and values may exceed 200% - 400% of values for the Model 1901 or the Model 1903.

* ***Webley-Fosbery Automatic Model First 1903*** – .455 cal., 6 shot, large and small frame, ser. nos. between 100 and 4930.

$10,000	$8,500	$7,500	$6,500	$5,500	$4,500	$3,500	

GRADING - PPGS™	100%	98%	95%	90%	80%	70%	60%	LAST MSR

R.I.C. MODELS – .320, .380, .442, .450, .455, .476, .44 Win., .45 Colt, or .45 ACP cal., adopted by the Royal Irish Constabulary in Jan., 1868, recognized worldwide and produced in one variation or another from 1867-1939.

* ***R.I.C. Model No. 1*** – .442 or .455 cal., first of the series was offered in .442 cal. with 4 1/2 barrel, later No. 1 New Model was offered in .455 cal., ser. nos. exceeded 60,300 by Oct., 1884.

	$1,000	$900	$800	$700	$600	$500	$400

* ***R.I.C. Model No. 2*** – .320, .380, .442, or .450 cal., 2 to 4 in. barrels, ser. nos. reached 100139 by 1914.

	$1,000	$900	$800	$700	$600	$500	$400

* ***R.I.C. Model No. 3*** – typically found in .442 cal., 2 to 4 in. barrels, ser. nos. range from single digits to 15,000, 16,000, 30,000, and 70,000, 4 in. barrel variation was chosen as the official police weapon of the Queensland Govt., Australia.

	$1,000	$900	$800	$700	$600	$500	$400

* ***R.I.C. Model 83*** – .320, .380, .450, or .455 cal., 2 1/4, 2 1/2, 3, or 3 1/2 in. barrel, ser. no. 102,634. Mfg. until 1939.

	$900	$800	$700	$600	$500	$400	$300

* ***M. P. Model*** – .450 cal., introduced after the R.I.C. New Model No. 1, 6 shot, adopted by the London Metropolitan Police in 1883 and remained in service until 1911.

	$900	$800	$700	$600	$500	$400	$300

WEBLEY NO. 1 1/2 MODEL – .442 or .450 cal., 4 1/4 in. octagon barrel, limited examples of ser. nos. 28,000 and 60,000 have been observed.

	$1,000	$900	$800	$700	$600	$500	$400

WEBLEY NO. 2 BRITISH BULL DOG PATTERN – .320, .380, .442, .450 centerfire, or .44 Short rimfire cal., short (2 1/2 in.) barrel, designed and manufactured by Webley as pocket models for civilians, with model names such as British Bulldog, The Pug, The Ulster Bulldog, or The Tower Bulldog, serial numbers vary by model.

	$900	$800	$700	$600	$500	$400	$300

WEBLEY NO. 5 EXPRESS MODEL – .360, .380, .450, .455, or .476 cal., include the large caliber military version and the small caliber civilian version, early military versions were based on the R.I.C. No. 1 frame with 6 in. barrel and came in .450 or .455 cal., New Model Express had new birdshead grip frame, .455 cal., and 5 1/2 in. barrel, military versions also included a single action in .476 cal., with 5 1/2 in. barrel issued to the Cape Mounted Rifles in 1881, civilian version offered in .360 or .380 cal., with a 2 1/2 - 4 1/2 in. barrel being the most common, ser. nos. range from the low 1,000 to excess of 10,000,000.

Large Cals. (Military)	$2,000	$1,900	$1,800	$1,700	$1,200	$900	$600
Small Cals. (Civilian)	$1,000	$900	$800	$700	$600	$500	$400

Cased, engraved, or unusual examples will command a premium.

REVOLVERS: HINGED FRAME, CENTERFIRE

WOODS PATTERN – .450 cal., 6 shot, double action, 5 in. barrel, mfg. circa 1870.

Extreme rarity precludes accurate pricing on this model.

WEBLEY NO. 4 PRYSE PATTERN – .32, .38, .44, .450, .455, .476, or .577 cal., double action, 3 to 5 3/4 in. barrel, numerous makers produced this model from the mid 1870s, Webley production covered a ser. no. range from 364 to 81,035.

	$2,500	$2,000	$1,500	$1,000	$800	$700	$600

Webley-marked models may command premiums over other makers. Cased, engraved, or inscribed examples will also command a premium.

WEBLEY IMPROVED GOVT. – .455 cal., 5 3/4 in. barrel, 6 shot, birdshead grips, blue or nickel finish, identified as the "Kaufmann" pattern. Mfg. circa early 1880s.

GRADING - PPGS™	100%	98%	95%	90%	80%	70%	60%	LAST MSR

* ***Webley Improved Govt. First Pattern*** – Kaufmann serial numbers 33-121.

$3,750 $3,500 $3,000 $2,500 $2,000 $1,700 $1,500

* ***Webley Improved Govt. Second Pattern*** – Kaufmann serial numbers 165-1,228.

$3,750 $3,500 $3,000 $2,500 $2,000 $1,700 $1,500

* ***Webley Improved Govt. Third Pattern*** – Kaufmann serial numbers 1,245-1,316.

$3,750 $3,500 $3,000 $2,500 $2,000 $1,700 $1,500

WEBLEY IMPROVED GOVT. MODEL 1886 – .455 or .476 cal., 6 shot "church steeple" cylinder, 6 in. barrel, birdshead grips, ser. no. range 1,467-1,876. Mfg. circa mid-1880s.

$2,500 $2,000 $1,500 $1,000 $800 $700 $600

WEBLEY GOVT. MODEL 1889 – .455 or .476 cal., 6 shot "church steeple" cylinder, 6 in. barrel, flared or birdshead grips, ser. no. range 1,982-3,933. Mfg. late 1880s.

$2,500 $2,000 $1,500 $1,000 $800 $700 $600

WEBLEY GOVT. MODEL 1891 – .450 or .476 cal., 6 shot "church steeple" cylinder, 7 1/2 in. barrel, flared grips, ser. no. range 4,100-4,200. Approx. 200 mfg. early 1890s.

$3,500 $3,000 $2,500 $2,000 $1,500 $1,400 $1,300

WEBLEY GOVT. MODEL 1892 – .450, .455, or .476 cal., 6 shot "church steeple" cylinder, 7 1/2 in. barrel, flared grips, blue or nickel finish, ser. no. range 4197-6499. Mfg. circa early 1890s.

$3,000 $2,500 $2,000 $1,500 $1,400 $1,300 $1,200

WEBLEY GOVT. MODEL 1893 – .450 or .455 cal., 6 shot "church steeple" cylinder, 7 1/2 in. barrel, flared grips, ser. no. range 5,000-6,000. Mfg. early 1890s.

$3,300 $2,800 $2,300 $1,800 $1,700 $1,600 $1,500

WEBLEY GOVT. MODEL 1894 – .450 or .455 cal., 6 shot fluted cylinder, 6 or 7 1/2 (Target Model) in. barrel, birdshead or flared grips, ser. no. range 6,000-10,000. Mfg. early-mid 1890s.

$2,500 $2,000 $1,500 $1,000 $800 $700 $600

Target models command 10-20% premium.

WEBLEY GOVT. ARMY (TARGET) MODEL 1896 – .450, .455, or .476 cal., 6 (Army) or 7 1/2 (Target) in. barrel, birdshead (Army) or flared (Target) grips, ser. no. range 10,000-23,000. Mfg. late 1890s.

$2,500 $2,000 $1,500 $1,000 $800 $700 $600

Target models command a 10-20% premium.

Cased, engraved, or inscribed examples will command additional premium.

WEBLEY W.S. NEW MODEL ARMY – .455 cal., 4, 6, or 7 1/2 (Target) in. barrel, ser. no. range 88,056-454,229. Mfg. early 1900s to 1935.

$1,800 $1,400 $1,000 $900 $800 $700 $600

Cased Target Model w/accessories $3,600 $2,800 $2,000 $1,800 $1,600 $1,400 $1,200

WEBLEY WILKINSON MODELS – .450/.455, or .455/.476 cal., during production of the Webley No. 4 Model, Webley produced the Wilkinson Models, well-made and finished, which Henry Wilkinson sold through his retail business, barrels were typically 5 3/4 or 6 in., with Target models in 7 1/2 in. Mfg. 1884-1914.

* ***Webley Wilkinson Model First 1884 Small Hinge Pattern*** – Wilkinson serial numbers 7,896-8,301.

$3,500 $3,000 $2,500 $2,000 $1,800 $1,600 $1,500

* ***Webley Wilkinson Model Second 1888 Large Hinge Pattern*** – Wilkinson serial numbers 8,357-8,741.

$3,500 $3,000 $2,500 $2,000 $1,800 $1,600 $1,500

GRADING - PPGS™	100%	98%	95%	90%	80%	70%	60%	LAST MSR

* ***Webley Wilkinson Model 1892*** – Wilkinson serial numbers 8,788-9,385.

	$3,500	$3,000	$2,500	$2,000	$1,800	$1,600	$1,500

* ***Webley Wilkinson Model 1900*** – Wilkinson serial numbers W467-W967.

	$3,500	$3,000	$2,500	$2,000	$1,800	$1,600	$1,500

* ***Webley Wilkinson Model 1905*** – Wilkinson serial numbers W1102-W2977.

	$3,000	$2,500	$2,000	$1,500	$1,300	$1,100	$1,000

* ***Webley Wilkinson Model 1910*** – transitional model, Wilkinson serial numbers around 3,000. Mfg. between 1905-1911.

	$4,500	$4,000	$3,500	$3,000	$2,500	$2,000	$1,500

* ***Webley Wilkinson Model 1911*** – Wilkinson serial numbers 3,104-4,400.

	$3,000	$2,500	$2,000	$1,500	$1,300	$1,100	$1,000

WEBLEY MARK II POCKET MODEL – .380 cal., 3 or 4 in. barrel, 6 shot, blue or nickel finish, folding trigger, ser. no. range 1-808. Mfg. circa early 1890s.

	$1,000	$900	$800	$700	$600	$500	$400

WEBLEY MARK III POCKET MODEL – .380 cal., 3, 4, 6 (Target), or 10 (Target) in. barrel, 6 shot, blue or nickel finish, ser. no. range 1,656-55,627. Mfg. mid-1890s.

	$1,000	$900	$800	$700	$600	$500	$400

WEBLEY MARK III POCKET MODEL – .320 cal., 3 in. barrel, 6 shot, blue or nickel finish, ser. no. range 10,000-22,000. Mfg. early 1900s.

	$1,000	$900	$800	$700	$600	$500	$400

WEBLEY W.P. – .32 S&W or .320 cal., 2 or 3 in. barrel, 6 shot, hammerless or hammer type, blue or nickel finish, ser. no. range 1000-8527. Mfg. circa early 1900s to mid-1930s.

	$1,000	$900	$800	$700	$600	$500	$400

WEBLEY MARK IV – .22 LR (scarce), .32 (scarce), .38 S&W, or .380 cal., 3, 4, 5, or 6 (Target) in. barrel, 6 shot, wartime production exceeded 125,000, commerical production approx. 50,000. Mfg. early 1920s to late 1970s.

	$450	$400	$350	$300	$250	$200	$150

Add 75%-100% for .22 LR or .32 cal.

REVOLVERS: SERVICE MODELS

Mark I-V Service Models were very similar, but some were made with longer barrels.

Many service Webleys were modified to use .45 ACP cal. ammo - this will decrease their value by 50% or more.

Cased, engraved, or inscribed examples have also been seen (usually in the commercial/non-military variation), and will bring a premium over values listed.

Mark III variations which include flared butt and half-cock models may bring a 200%-300% premium, if in 90% or better condition.

MARK I SERVICE – .455 cal., single/double action, 4 in. barrel, fixed sights, blue finish, top break 6 shot, service and commercial ser. no. range 4-39,436. Mfg. 1894-1897.

	$800	$750	$700	$625	$500	$400	$300

MARK II SERVICE – .455 cal., single/double action, 4 in. barrel, fixed sights, blue finish, top break 6 shot, service and commercial ser. no. range 41,675-63,584. Mfg. 1894-1897.

	$850	$800	$750	$675	$550	$450	$350

MARK III SERVICE – .455 cal., single/double action, 4 in. barrel, fixed sights, blue finish, top break 6 shot, ser. no. range 12-10,808 and 75,966-79,256. Mfg. 1894-1897.

	$900	$850	$800	$725	$600	$500	$400

GRADING - PPGS™	100%	98%	95%	90%	80%	70%	60%	LAST MSR

MARK IV SERVICE – .455 cal., single/double action, 4 in. barrel, fixed sights, blue finish, top break 6 shot, "Boer War" model, ser. no. range 79,462-129,185. Mfg. 1899-1914.

$750	$700	$650	$575	$500	$400	$300

MARK V SERVICE – .455 cal., single/double action, 4 in. barrel, fixed sights, blue finish, top break 6 shot, ser. no. range 129,942-159,724 and 173,015-193,025. Mfg. 1914-1915.

$750	$700	$650	$575	$500	$400	$300

MARK VI SERVICE – .455 cal., single/double action, 6 in. barrel, fixed sights, blue finish, top break 6 shot, ser. no. range 214,000-445,999. Mfg. 1915-1919.

$600	$550	$500	$425	$350	$250	$200

Add approx. 300% - 400% for rare shoulder stock and bayonet.

MARK VI SERVICE (LATER MFG.) – .455 cal., single/double action, 6 in. barrel, fixed sights, blue finish, top break 6 shot, ser. no. range 450,000-454,000. Mfg. by Enfield circa 1922-1935.

$900	$800	$700	$600	$500	$300	$250

MARK VI TARGET – .22 cal., otherwise similar to Mark VI Service.

$1,200	$1,000	$900	$800	$700	$600	$500

SHOTGUNS: CURRENT MFG.

Currently, Webley & Scott has a line of private label shotguns manufactured for them in Turkey by Komando Av Sa. Tic. Ltd. Sti. Current models include the Model 900K Sporter (12 and 20 ga., 26 or 28 in. barrel) - MSR $1,200 - $1,300, Premium 2000 Game 12 ga. O/U - MSR $2,500, and the 3000 Series sidelock O/U - MSR $6,000. The SxS line includes the 2000 Series boxlock ($2,500 MSR), and the Premium 3000 Series sidelock (MSR $6,000). Please contact Webley & Scott, USA for more information and availability on these models currently being imported (see Trademark Index).

SHOTGUNS: SxS, DISC.

MODEL 700 – 12 or 20 ga., boxlock, case hardened receiver, minimum engraving, single trigger. Mfg. 1949-80.

$3,000	$2,600	$2,200	$1,850	$1,550	$1,200	$995

Subtract $50 for double trigger.

MODEL 701 – similar to Model 700 but fanciest walnut, most engraving. Mfg. 1949-80.

$3,500	$3,150	$2,600	$2,300	$1,995	$1,675	$1,350

This model is hard to differentiate from the Model 702.

MODEL 702 – similar to Model 700 but middle grade. Mfg. 1949-80.

$3,250	$2,800	$2,400	$2,200	$1,700	$1,425	$1,175

Subtract $75 for double trigger.

MODEL 712 – 12 ga., specifically designed for the American market.

$2,500	$2,250	$1,875	$1,600	$1,350	$1,100	$895

MODEL 720 – 20 ga.

$4,500	$3,995	$3,500	$3,100	$2,600	$2,150	$1,625

MODEL 728 – same action as the Model 700, except is 28 ga. and designed specifically for the American market, only 40 were mfg. 1966-68.

$5,000	$4,500	$4,000	$3,500	$2,800	$2,350	$1,800

SHOTGUNS: SxS, RECENT MFG.

During 2007-2008, Webley & Scott imported a line of boxlock 700 Series SxS shotguns that were manufactured in Turkey. Models imported into the U.S. by Legacy Sports included the 712 (last MSR $3,477, 12 ga.), 720 (last MSR $3,477, 20 ga.), and the 728 (last MSR $3,644, 28 ga.).

GRADING - PPGS™	100%	98%	95%	90%	80%	70%	60%	LAST MSR

SHOTGUNS: SEMI-AUTO

During 2007-2008, Webley & Scott had a line of private label, gas operated semi-auto shotguns manufactured in Turkey. Models included: the 812 (12 ga.), 820 (20 ga.) and 828 (28 ga.). These guns were not imported into the U.S.

WEIHRAUCH & WEIHRAUCH SPORT GmbH & CO. KG SPORTWAFFENFABRIK

Current manufacturer of rifles, airguns, and blank pistols located in Mellrichstadt, Germany.

Weihrauch manufactures air rifles, air pistols, and small bore repeating rifles under the name Weihrauch Sport GmbH & Co. KG. Please contact the company directly for more information, including model availability and pricing (see Trademark Index).

For more information and current pricing on both new and used Weihrauch airguns, please refer to the *Blue Book of Airguns* by Dr. Robert Beeman & John Allen (also online).

RIFLES: BOLT ACTION

MODEL HW 60 TARGET – .22 LR cal., target rifle featuring adj. sights, 26 3/4 in. barrel, single shot, match walnut stock and other match features, aperture sights, 10.8 lbs. Importation disc. 1995.

$625	$550	$450	$395	$350	$295	$275	*$705*

Add $220 for left-hand action.

MODEL HW 60J – .22 LR or .222 Rem. cal., sporter model with checkered walnut stock. Importation disc. 1992.

$525	$475	$425	$395	$345	$300	$250	*$585*

Add $300 for .222 Rem. cal.

MODEL HW 66 – .22 Hornet or .222 Rem. cal., match grade. Imported 1989-1990.

$575	$495	$395	$325	$285	$250	$215	*$688*

Add $80 for double set triggers. Add $50 for stainless steel barrel in .22 Hornet cal.

MODEL HW 660 MATCH – 22 LR cal., match rifle variation featuring adj. comb, vent. forend, with or w/o aperture sights, 10.8 lbs. Imported 1991-2005.

$850	$725	$600	$500	$400	$350	$300	*$999*

Add $150 for laminate stock (new 1998). Subtract $150 if w/o Anschütz aperture sights.

WEIHRAUCH, HERMANN REVOLVER GmbH

Current revolver manufacturer located in Mellrichstadt, Germany. Some models are currently imported exclusively by E.A.A. Corp., located in Sharpes, FL.

REVOLVERS

The Windicator and Bounty Hunter private label models are currently imported by EAA Corp. Please refer to the separate listing in the E section for more information. Recently manufactured Weihrauch revolvers with no U.S. importation are not individually listed, including the Arminius Series. There are, however, many models, including combat, sport, and target variations. Calibers include .22 LR, .22 WMR, .32 S&W Wadcutter, .357 Mag., and .38 Spl. Please contact the company directly for pricing and availability on these currently manufactured revolvers (see Trademark Index).

WELLS

Previous custom rifle manufacturer located in Prescott, AZ.

RIFLES: BOLT ACTION

Wells manufactured a custom rifle based on a Mauser double square bridge action, using the finest materials available. Action prices started at $5,500, and stocks were priced from $5,500 on up. Many custom features and options were available, including engraving by Rachel Wells. Delivery time was approx. 24 months. Additionally, Wells also had a complete barrel manufacturing facility, specializing in cut rifle barrels in almost every caliber.

100%	98%	95%	90%	80%	70%	60%	50%	40%	30%	20%	10%

WERNER BARTOLOT

Current custom gun manufacturer established in 1986 and located in Hermagor, Austria. Consumer direct sales only.

Werner Bartolot manufactures very high quality SxS and O/U double rifles, drillings, and single shot rifles. Please contact the company for more information, including availability and an individual price quotation (see Trademark Index).

WESSON, FRANK

Previous manufacturer located in Worcester, MA 1854 to 1865, and Springfield, MA circa 1865-1875.

PISTOLS: SINGLE SHOT

SMALL FRAME FIRST MODEL – .22 cal., tip up action, 3 1/2 in. 1/2 octagon barrel, brass frame, spur trigger, rosewood grips, round frame, irregular sideplate. 2,500 mfg. 1859-1862.

$605 $550 $495 $440 $385 $330 $275 $220 $195 $165 $140 $110

SMALL FRAME SECOND MODEL – similar to First Model, with flat sided frame and circular sideplate. 12,000 mfg. 1862-1880.

$550 $495 $440 $385 $330 $305 $250 $195 $165 $110 $105 $85

MEDIUM FRAME FIRST MODEL – .30 S-L or .32 S rimfire cal., 4 in. 1/2 octagon barrel, iron frame, same as Small Frame in other respects, narrow hinge and short trigger. 1,000 mfg. 1859-1862.

$525 $470 $415 $360 $305 $275 $220 $195 $165 $110 $105 $85

MEDIUM FRAME SECOND MODEL – similar to First Model Medium Frame, with wider hinge and longer trigger. 1,000 mfg. 1862-1870.

$495 $440 $385 $330 $275 $250 $220 $195 $165 $110 $105 $85

RIFLES: SINGLE SHOT

NO. 1 LONG RANGE – .44-100 or .45-100 standard cal., side hammer, falling block lever actuated, 34 in. octagon barrel, aperture rear sight on upper tang, select checkered pistol grip stock. Less than 50 mfg., circa 1870-1880.

$4,950 $4,675 $4,400 $3,850 $3,575 $3,080 $2,860 $2,475 $2,200 $2,035 $1,760 $1,540

NO. 2 HUNTING RIFLE – similar to No. 1, with finger loop lever. Less than 100 mfg.

$4,400 $4,180 $3,850 $3,520 $3,025 $2,750 $2,420 $2,255 $2,035 $1,925 $1,760 $1,540

NO. 1 SPORTING RIFLE – .38-100, .40-100, .45-100 standard cal., similar to No. 2, with center hammer, less than 25 mfg.

$4,400 $4,180 $3,850 $3,520 $3,025 $2,750 $2,420 $2,255 $2,035 $1,925 $1,760 $1,540

MODEL 1870 SMALL FRAME FIRST TYPE – similar to Small Frame Tip Up, except barrel rotates on its axis to load, detachable stock. Approx. 3,000 mfg., 1870-90.

$550 $495 $470 $440 $415 $385 $360 $305 $275 $220 $195 $165

If without stock-subtract 25%.

MODEL 1870 SMALL FRAME SECOND TYPE – full octagon barrel.

$525 $470 $440 $415 $385 $360 $330 $275 $250 $195 $165 $140

MODEL 1870 SMALL FRAME THIRD TYPE – iron frame, push-button half cock.

$495 $440 $415 $385 $360 $330 $305 $250 $220 $165 $140 $110

MODEL 1870 MEDIUM FRAME FIRST TYPE – similar to Small Frame, except in size and availability of .32 cal. Approx. 5,000 mfg., 1870-93.

$525 $495 $470 $440 $415 $385 $360 $305 $275 $250 $195 $165

Subtract 25% if without stock.

MODEL 1870 MEDIUM FRAME SECOND TYPE – external push-button half cock and iron frame.

$440 $415 $385 $330 $305 $275 $220 $195 $165 $140 $110 $90

Subtract 25% if without stock.

100%	98%	95%	90%	80%	70%	60%	50%	40%	30%	20%	10%

MODEL 1870 MEDIUM FRAME THIRD TYPE – has three screws in iron frame.

$440	$415	$385	$330	$305	$275	$220	$195	$165	$140	$110	$90

Subtract 25% if without stock.

MODEL 1870 LARGE FRAME FIRST TYPE – .32, .38, .42, or .44 rimfire cal., 15-24 in. barrels, similar to smaller frame models, auto extractor. Approx. 500 mfg., 1870-80.

$825	$770	$715	$660	$605	$550	$525	$495	$440	$385	$305	$275

Subtract 25% if without stock.

MODEL 1870 LARGE FRAME SECOND TYPE – similar to First Type, with standard sliding extractor.

$825	$770	$715	$660	$605	$550	$525	$495	$440	$385	$305	$275

Subtract 25% if without stock.

RIFLES: SINGLE SHOT, TIP UP

SMALL FRAME TIP UP – .22 Rimfire cal., 6 in. 1/2 octagon barrel, brass frame, spur trigger, rosewood grips. Approx. 500 mfg., 1865-75.

$605	$550	$525	$495	$470	$440	$415	$360	$330	$275	$220	$165

If without stock-subtract 25%.

MEDIUM FRAME TIP UP – .22, .30, or .32 rimfire cals, 10 or 12 in. barrel, same as small frame, with exceptions noted and larger frame. Approx. 1,000 mfg., 1862-70.

$605	$550	$525	$495	$470	$440	$415	$360	$330	$275	$220	$165

If without stock-subtract 25%.

WESSON & HARRINGTON

Previous trademark of special/limited editions manufactured by H&R 1871, LLC 1995-2001. During 2000, Marlin Firearms Co. purchased the assets of H&R 1871, Inc., and the name was changed to H&R 1871, LLC. Factory Wesson & Harrington products were manufactured in Gardner, MA.

RIFLES: SINGLE SHOT

Please refer to the H & R 1871 section for earlier Wesson & Harrington Buffalo Classic & Target Models.

GRADING - PPGS™	100%	98%	95%	90%	80%	70%	60%	LAST MSR

SHOTGUNS: SINGLE SHOT

WESSON & HARRINGTON NWTF LONG TOM CLASSIC – 12 ga., top lever break open action, 32 in. FC barrel, case hardened frame, checkered straight grip walnut stock and forearm, 7 1/2 lbs. Mfg. 1995-2001.

$300	$240	$195	$150	$125	$110	$95	*$350*

DAN WESSON FIREARMS

Please refer to Dan Wesson Firearms listing in the D section.

WESSON FIREARMS CO. INC.

Previous manufacturer located in Palmer, MA 1992-95. Previously located in Monson, MA until 1992. In late 1990, ownership of Dan Wesson Arms changed (within the family), and the new company was renamed Wesson Firearms Co., Inc.

REVOLVERS: DOUBLE ACTION

As a guideline, the following information is provided on Wesson Firearms frames. The smallest frames are Models 738P and 38P. Small frame models include 22, 722, 22M, 722M, 32, 732, 322, 7322, 8-2, 708, 9-2, 709, 14-2, 714, 15-2, and 715-2. Large frames include 41, 741, 44, 744, 45, and 745. SuperMag frame models include 40, 740, 375 (disc.), 414 (new 1995), 7414 (new 1995), 445, and 7445. Small frames are sideplate design, while large frames are solid frame construction. Dan Wesson revolvers were mfg. with solid rib barrels as standard equipment.

GRADING - PPGS™	100%	98%	95%	90%	80%	70%	60%	LAST MSR

MODEL 11 – .357 Mag. cal., 6 shot, 2 1/2, 4, or 6 in. interchangeable barrels, fixed sights, blue, interchangeable grips, exposed barrel nut. Mfg. 1970-71 only.

$200 $175 $160 $150 $140 $130 $120

Add $60 per extra barrel.

MODEL 12 – similar to Model 11, with adj. sights. Mfg. 1970-71 only.

$245 $200 $175 $160 $150 $140 $130

MODEL 14 (1970s Mfg.) – similar to Model 11, with recessed barrel nut. Mfg. 1971-75.

$225 $185 $170 $160 $150 $140 $130

MODEL 8 – similar to Model 14, except .38 Spl. cal.

$200 $170 $155 $145 $135 $125 $115

MODEL 15 (1970s Mfg.) – similar to Model 14, with adj. sights. Mfg. 1971-75.

$245 $200 $155 $145 $135 $125 $115

MODEL 9 (1970s Mfg.) – similar to Model 15, except .38 Spl. cal. Mfg. 1971-75.

$245 $200 $155 $145 $135 $125 $115

MODEL 22 – .22 LR cal., double action, 6 shot, adj. sights, 2 1/2, 4, 6, 8, or 10 in. (disc. 1987) barrel, disc. 1995.

$285 $225 $200 $190 $180 $170 $160 *$357*

Add approx. $9 for each additional barrel length, $21 for VR, $57 for vent. heavy rib shroud.

* ***Model 22 Pistol Pac*** – includes 2 1/2, 4, 6, and 8 in. barrel assemblies, extra grip, 4 additional front sight blades, and aluminum case. Disc. 1995.

$520 $400 $360 $330 $300 $275 $260 *$653*

Add $103 for full shroud VR barrels.
Add $227 for heavy full shroud VR barrels.

* ***Model 22 Silhouette*** – .22 LR cal., choice of 10 in. vent. or heavy vent. barrel, single action only, combat style grip, narrow rear sight blade and Patridge front. Mfg. 1992-95.

$395 $325 $295 $275 $260 $245 $230 *$474*

Add $18 for vent. heavy barrel.

MODEL 22M – .22 WMR cal., otherwise similar to Model 22. Disc. 1994.

$290 $230 $200 $190 $180 $170 $160 *$349*

* ***Model 22M Pistol Pac*** – includes 2 1/2, 4, 6, and 8 in. barrel assemblies, extra grip, 4 additional front sight blades, and aluminum case. Disc. 1994.

$500 $400 $360 $330 $300 $275 $260 *$637*

Add $101 for full shroud VR barrels.
Add $191 for heavy full shroud VR barrels.

MODEL 32 – .32 H&R Mag. cal., 2 1/2, 4, 6, or 8 in. barrel, adj. rear sight, interchangeable colored front sight blades, blue finish, checkered target grips. Mfg. 1986-95.

$285 $225 $200 $190 $180 $170 $160 *$357*

Add $21 for VR barrel shroud (Model 32-V), $57 for VR heavy barrel shroud (Model 32-VH), approx. $9 for each additional barrel length over 2 1/2 in.

* ***Model 32 Pistol Pac*** – includes 2 1/2, 4, 6, and 8 in. barrel assemblies, extra grip, 4 additional front sight blades, and aluminum case. Disc. 1995.

$520 $400 $360 $330 $300 $275 $260 *$653*

Add $103 for full shroud VR barrels.
Add $227 for heavy full shroud VR barrels.

MODEL 38P – .38+P cal., 5 shot, 6 1/2 in. barrel, fixed sights, wood or rubber grips, 24.6 oz. Mfg. 1992-93.

$230 $190 $170 $150 $135 $120 $110 *$285*

GRADING - PPGS™	100%	98%	95%	90%	80%	70%	60%	LAST MSR

MODEL 322 – .32-20 WCF cal., 2 1/2, 4, 6, or 8 in. barrel, adj. rear sight, interchangeable colored front sight blades, blue finish, checkered target grips. Mfg. 1991-95.

	$285	$225	$200	$190	$180	$170	$160	*$357*

Add $21 for VR barrel shroud (Model 322-V), $57 for VR heavy barrel shroud (Model 322-VH), approx. $9-$30 for each additional barrel length over 2 1/2 in.

* ***Model 322 Pistol Pac*** – includes 2 1/2, 4, 6, and 8 in. barrel assemblies, extra grip, 4 additional front sight blades, and aluminum case. Disc. 1995.

	$520	$400	$360	$330	$300	$275	$260	*$653*

Add $103 for full shroud VR barrels.
Add $227 for heavy full shroud VR barrels.

MODEL 14 – .357 Mag. cal., 2 1/2, 4, 6, or 8 (disc. 1994) in. interchangeable barrels, fixed sights, blue. Mfg. 1975-95.

	$215	$170	$150	$140	$130	$120	$110	*$274*

Add approx. $7 for each additional barrel length.

* ***Model 14 Fixed Barrel*** – .357 Mag. cal., 2 1/2 or 4 in. (fixed sight Service Model) barrel, satin blue finish. Mfg. 1993-95.

	$225	$175	$150	$140	$130	$120	$110	*$289*

Add $7 for 4 in. barrel.

* ***Model 14 PPC*** – .357 Mag. cal., extra heavy shrouded 6 in. bull barrel with removable underweight, Hogue Gripper grips, Aristocrat sights. Mfg. 1992 only.

	$675	$550	$450	$375	$330	$300	$275	*$780*

* ***Model 14 Pistol Pac*** – includes 2 1/2, 4, and 6 in. barrel assemblies, extra grip and aluminum case. Disc. 1994.

	$390	$325	$300	$275	$260	$245	$230	*$463*

MODEL 8 – similar to Model 14, except .38 Spl. cal. Disc. 1995.

	$220	$170	$150	$140	$130	$120	$110	*$274*

Add approx. $6 for each additional barrel length.

* ***Model 8 PPC*** – .38 Spl. cal., extra heavy shrouded 6 in. bull barrel with removable underweight, Hogue Gripper grips, Aristocrat sights. Mfg. 1992 only.

	$675	$550	$450	$375	$330	$300	$275	*$780*

MODEL 15 – similar to Model 14, except adj. sights, available with 2, 4, 6, 8, 10, 12, or 15 in. barrels. Disc. 1995.

* ***Model 15 2 in. barrel***

	$285	$225	$200	$190	$180	$170	$160	*$346*

Add approx. $8-$13 for each additional barrel length over 2 inches, $22 for VR barrel (Model 15V), or $60 for VR heavy barrel shroud (Model 15HV).

* ***Model 15 Target Fixed Barrel*** – .357 Mag. cal., 3, 4, 5, or 6 in. barrel, high bright blue finish. Mfg. 1993-95.

	$270	$220	$190	$175	$150	$125	$110	*$322*

Add approx. $9 for each barrel length over 3 in.
Add approx. $80 for compensated barrel (4, 5, or 6 in. - new 1994).

MODEL 15 GOLD SERIES – .357 Mag. cal., 6 or 8 in. VR heavy slotted barrel, "Gold" stamped shroud with Dan Wesson signature, smoother action (8 lb. double action pull), 18kt. gold-plated trigger, white triangle rear sight with orange-dot Patridge front sight, exotic hardwood grips. Mfg. 1989-94.

	$425	$380	$340	$300	$260	$225	$185	*$544*

GRADING - PPGS™	100%	98%	95%	90%	80%	70%	60%	*LAST MSR*

* ***Model 15 Pistol Pac*** – includes 2 1/2, 4, 6, and 8 in. barrel assemblies, extra grip, 4 additional front sight blades, and aluminum case. Disc. 1995.

	$500	$395	$360	$330	$300	$275	$260	*$629*

Add $104 for full shroud VR barrels.
Add $214 for heavy full shroud VR barrels.

MODEL 9 – similar to Model 15, except .38 Spl. cal. Use same add-ons as in Model 15. Disc. 1995.

	$346	$285	$225	$200	$190	$180	$170	*$346*

This model was also available in a Pistol Pac - same specifications and values as the Model 15 Pistol Pac.

MODEL 375 SUPERMAG – .375 Super Mag. cal., 4, 6, 8, or 10 in. VR barrel, adj. rear sight, interchangeable front and rear sight blades, bright blue finish, smooth target grips. Mfg. 1986-94.

	$650	$575	$500	$450	$400	$365	$335	*$498*

Add approx. $15 for each barrel length after 6 in., $39 for slotted shroud (Model 375-V8S, 8 in. barrel only), $10-$12 for VR heavy shroud (Model 375-VH).

MODEL 40 (.357 SUPERMAG) – .357 Super Mag. cal. (.357 Max.), double action, 6 shot, 4, 6, 8, or 10 in. barrel VR. Disc. 1995.

	$650	$575	$500	$450	$400	$365	$335	*$502*

Add $87 for slotted barrel shroud (8 in. barrel only), $22-$129 for heavy VR barrel, approx. $33 for each additional barrel length.

MODEL 41 – .41 Mag. cal., double action, 6 shot, 4, 6, 8, or 10 in. barrel VR. Disc. 1995.

	$375	$305	$265	$250	$230	$215	$200	*$447*

Add approx. $20 for heavy barrel shroud, approx. $15 for each additional barrel length.

* ***Model 41 Pistol Pac*** – includes 6 and 8 in. VR barrel assemblies, extra grip, 2 additional front sight blades, and aluminum case. Disc. 1995.

	$555	$430	$380	$330	$300	$275	$260	*$678*

Add $53 for full shroud VR barrels.

MODEL 414 SUPERMAG – .414 Super Mag. cal., 4, 6, 8, or 10 in. VR barrel, adj. rear sight, interchangeable front and rear sight blades (optional), bright blue finish, smooth target grips. Mfg. 1995 only.

	$650	$575	$500	$450	$400	$365	$335	*$519*

Add approx. $14 for each barrel length after 4 in., $58 for slotted shroud (Model 414-V8S, 8 in. barrel only), approx. $23 for VR heavy rib shroud.

MODEL 44 – .44 Mag. cal., double action, similar to Model 41, adj. sights. Disc. 1995.

	$375	$305	$265	$250	$230	$215	$200	*$447*

Add approx. $20 for heavy barrel shroud, approx. $15 for each additional barrel length.

* ***Model 44 Target Fixed Barrel*** – .44 Mag. cal., 4, 5, 6, or 8 in. barrel, high bright blue finish. Mfg. 1994-95.

	$375	$305	$265	$250	$230	$215	$200	*$447*

Add approx. $4 for each barrel length over 3 in.

* ***Model 44 Pistol Pac*** – includes 6 and 8 in. VR barrel assemblies, extra grip, 4 additional front sight blades, and aluminum case. Disc. 1995.

	$555	$430	$380	$330	$300	$275	$260	*$678*

Add $53 for full shroud VR barrels.

MODEL 45 – .45 LC cal., 4, 6, 8, or 10 in. VR barrel, same frame as Model 44V, blue finish. Mfg. 1988-95.

	$375	$305	$265	$250	$230	$215	$200	*$447*

Add $20 for VR heavy barrel shroud, approx. $15 for each additional barrel length.

GRADING - PPGS™	100%	98%	95%	90%	80%	70%	60%	LAST MSR

* ***Model 45 Pistol Pac*** – includes 6 and 8 in. VR barrel assemblies, extra grip, 2 additional front sight blades, and aluminum case. Disc. 1995.

	$555	$430	$380	$330	$300	$275	$260	*$678*

Add $53 for full shroud VR barrels.

MODEL 45 PIN GUN – .45 ACP cal., competition pin gun model with 5 in. vent. or heavy vent. barrel configuration, blue steel, two stage Taylor forcing cone, 54 oz. Mfg. 1993-95.

	$575	$495	$440	$395	$350	$300	$250	*$654*

Add $9 for VR heavy shroud barrel.

MODEL 445 SUPERMAG – .445 Super Mag. cal., 4, 6, 8, or 10 in. VR barrel, adj. rear sight, interchangeable front and rear sight blades (optional), bright blue finish, smooth target grips. Mfg. 1991-95.

	$650	$575	$500	$450	$400	$365	$335	*$519*

Add approx. $14 for each barrel length after 4 in., $58 for slotted shroud (Model 445-V8S, 8 in. barrel only), approx. $23 for VR heavy rib shroud.

HUNTER SERIES – .357 Super Mag., .41 Mag., .44 Mag., or .445 Super Mag. cal., 7 1/2 in. barrel with heavy shroud, Hogue rubber finger grooved and wood presentation grips, choice of Gunworks iron sights or w/o sights with Burris base and rings, non-fluted cylinder, with or w/o compensator, approx. 4 lbs. Mfg. 1994-95.

	$750	$575	$475	$400	$360	$330	$300	*$805*

Add $32 for compensated barrel.
Add $33 for scope mounts (w/o sights).

REVOLVERS: STAINLESS STEEL

Models 722, 722M, 709, 715, 732, 7322, 741V, 744V, and 745V were available in a pistol pack including 2 1/2, 4, 6, and 8 in. solid rib barrel assemblies, extra grip, 4 additional sight blades, and fitted carrying case. Last published retail prices were $712 and $785 for the standard and stainless steel models, respectively. VR or full shroud barrels were optional and were approx. priced $103 and $210, respectively.

MODEL 722 – stainless version of Model 22, use same add-ons for various barrel options. Disc. 1995.

	$335	$255	$205	$150	$125	$110	$95	*$400*

* ***Model 722 Silhouette*** – .22 LR cal., choice of 10 in. vent. or heavy vent. barrel, single action only, combat style grip, narrow rear sight blade and Patridge front. Mfg. 1992-95.

	$410	$340	$295	$240	$210	$180	$155	*$504*

Add $28 for heavy vent. barrel.

MODEL 722M – .22 WMR cal., otherwise similar to Model 722, use same add-ons for various barrel options. Disc. 1994.

	$320	$270	$230	$175	$140	$125	$105	*$391*

MODEL 708 – .38 Spl. cal., similar to Model 8. Add approx. $6 for each additional barrel length. Disc. 1995.

	$265	$200	$170	$135	$115	$100	$85	*$319*

* ***Model 708 Action Cup/PPC*** – .38 Spl. cal., extra heavy shrouded 6 in. bull barrel with removable underweight, Hogue Gripper grips, mounted Tasco Pro Point II on Action Cup, Aristocrat sights on PPC. Mfg. 1992 only.

	$725	$650	$550	$460	$395	$335	$285	*$857*

Add $56 for Action Cup Model with Tasco Scope.

MODEL 709 – .38 Spl. cal., target revolver, adj. sights. Also available in special order 10, 12 (disc.), or 15 (disc.) in. barrel lengths. Disc. 1995.

	$310	$255	$205	$150	$125	$110	$95	*$376*

Add approx. $10 for each additional longer barrel length, approx. $19 for VR, approx. $56 for heavy VR.

GRADING - PPGS™	100%	98%	95%	90%	80%	70%	60%	LAST MSR

MODEL 714 (INTERCHANGEABLE OR FIXED) – .357 Mag. cal., fixed sight Service Model with 2 1/2, 4, or 6 in. barrel, brushed stainless steel. Mfg. 1993-95.

	$260	$200	$160	$125	$110	$95	$85	*$319*

Add approx. $6 for 4 or 6 in. barrel.
Subtract $6 for fixed barrel (2 1/2 or 4 in. barrel only).

* ***Model 714 Action Cup/PPC*** – .357 Mag. cal., extra heavy shrouded 6 in. bull barrel with removable underweight, Hogue Gripper grips, mounted Tasco Pro Point II on Action Cup, Aristocrat sights on PPC. Mfg. 1992 only.

	$725	$650	$550	$460	$395	$335	$285	*$857*

Add $56 for Action Cup Model with Tasco Scope.

MODEL 715 INTERCHANGEABLE – .357 Mag. cal., 2 1/2, 4, 6, 8, or 10 in. barrel with adj. rear sight, brushed stainless steel. Mfg. 1993-95.

	$310	$255	$205	$150	$125	$110	$95	*$376*

Add approx. $10 for each additional longer barrel length, approx. $19 for VR, approx. $56 for heavy VR.

* ***Model 715 Fixed Target*** – .357 Mag. cal., 3, 4, 5, or 6 in. fixed barrel, adj. rear sight. Mfg. 1993-95.

	$280	$210	$170	$135	$115	$100	$85	*$345*

Add approx. $70 for compensated barrel (4, 5, or 6 in. - new 1994).

MODEL 732 – .32 H&R Mag. cal., similar to Model 32, except is stainless steel. Mfg. 1986-95.

	$335	$255	$205	$150	$125	$110	$95	*$400*

Add $22 for VR barrel shroud (Model 732-V), $53 for VR heavy barrel shroud (Model 732-VH), approx. $9 for each additional barrel length over 2 1/2 in.

MODEL 738P – .38 +P cal., 5 shot, 6 1/2 in. barrel, fixed sights, wood or rubber grips, 24.6 oz. Mfg. 1992-95.

	$275	$210	$175	$135	$115	$100	$85	*$340*

MODEL 7322 – .32-20 WCF cal., similar to Model 322, except is stainless steel. Mfg. 1991-95.

	$335	$255	$205	$150	$125	$110	$95	*$400*

Add $22 for VR barrel shroud (Model 7322-V), $53 for VR heavy barrel shroud (Model 7322-VH), approx. $9 for each additional barrel length over 2 1/2 in.

MODEL 740V - .357 SUPERMAG – .357 Max. cal., 4, 6, 8, or 10 in. barrel, adj. rear sight with interchangeable front and rear blades, high polished finish, smooth target grips. Mfg. 1986-95.

	$650	$575	$500	$450	$400	$365	$335	*$567*

Add approx. $20 for each additional barrel length after 4 in., $78 with vent. slotted shroud (only avail. with 8 in. barrel), $20 for VR heavy barrel shroud (Model 740-VH).

MODEL 741V – .41 Mag. cal., similar to Model 41V. Disc. 1995.

	$420	$325	$270	$225	$195	$165	$140	*$524*

Add approx. $20 for heavy VR, approx. $13 for each barrel length over 4 in.

MODEL 744V – .44 Mag. cal., similar to Model 44V. Disc. 1995. - limited mfg.

	$430	$345	$285	$235	$200	$170	$145	*$524*

Add approx. $20 for heavy VR, $13 for each barrel length over 4 in.

* ***Model 744V Target Fixed Barrel*** – .44 Mag. cal., 4, 5, 6, or 8 in. barrel, brushed stainless steel. Mfg. 1994-95.

	$395	$315	$265	$215	$185	$155	$130	*$493*

Add approx. $4 for each barrel length over 3 in.

GRADING - PPGS™	100%	98%	95%	90%	80%	70%	60%	LAST MSR

*** *Model 744 Commemorative***

	$595	$475	$325	N/A	N/A	N/A	N/A	

MODEL 745V – .45 LC cal., similar to Model 45, except in stainless steel. Disc. 1995.

	$430	$345	$285	$235	$200	$170	$145	*$524*

Add $20 for heavy full shroud VR barrels, $13 for each additional barrel length.

MODEL .45 PIN GUN – .45 ACP cal., similar to Model 45 Pin Gun, except is stainless steel. Mfg. 1993-95.

	$625	$525	$425	$360	$315	$260	$225	*$713*

Add $49 for VR heavy rib shroud.

MODEL 7414 SUPERMAG – .414 Super Mag. cal., 4, 6, 8, or 10 in. VR barrel, adj. rear sight, interchangeable front and rear sight blades (optional), bright blue finish, smooth target grips. Mfg. 1995 only.

	$650	$575	$500	$450	$400	$365	$335	*$596*

Add approx. $14 for each barrel length after 4 in., $74 for slotted shroud (Model 7414-V8S, 8 in. barrel only), approx. $25 for VR heavy rib shroud.

MODEL 7445 SUPERMAG – .445 Super Mag. cal., 4, 6, 8, or 10 in. VR barrel, adj. rear sight, interchangeable front and rear sight blades (optional), high polished finish, smooth target grips. Mfg. 1991-95.

	$650	$575	$500	$450	$400	$365	$335	*$596*

Add approx. $17 for each barrel length after 6 in., $74 for slotted shroud (Model 7445-VH8S, 8 in. barrel only), approx. $25 for VR heavy rib shroud, approx. $40 for VR heavy shroud and interchangeable sights (Model 7445-VH).

SUPER RAM SILHOUETTE – .357 Max., .414 Super Mag., or .44 Mag. cal., silhouette variation featuring modified Iron Sight Gun Works rear sight, Allen Taylor throated barrel, factory trigger job, 4 lbs. Mfg. 1995 only.

	$775	$650	$550	$375	$315	$270	$230	*$807*

Add $43 for .414 Super Mag. cal.

HUNTER SERIES – .357 Super Mag., .41 Mag., .44 Mag., or .445 Super Mag. cal., 7 1/2 in. barrel with heavy shroud, Hogue rubber finger grooved and wood presentation grips, choice of Gunworks iron sights or w/o sights with Burris base and rings, non-fluted cylinder, with or w/o compensator, approx. 4 lbs. Mfg. 1994-95.

	$795	$675	$500	$445	$385	$350	$300	*$849*

Add $32 for compensated barrel.
Add $32 for scope mounts (w/o sights).

WESTERN ARMS COMPANY

Previous manufacturer located in Ithaca, NY.

SHOTGUNS: SxS

WESTERN LONG RANGE – 12, 16, 20 ga., or .410 bore, 26-32 in. barrels, mod. and full choke, boxlock, extractors, double or single trigger, plain pistol grip stock, Western Arms Co. was a division of Ithaca Gun. Mfg. 1929-46.

	$275	$225	$200	$175	$150	$125	$100	

*** *Western Long Range Single Trigger***

	$325	$275	$250	$225	$200	$150	$125	

WESTERN FIELD

Previous trademark used on Montgomery Ward rifles and shotguns.

The Western Field trademark has appeared literally on hundreds of various models (shotguns and rifles) sold through the Montgomery Ward retail network. Most of these models were manufactured through subcontracts with both domestic and international

GRADING - PPGS™	100%	98%	95%	90%	80%	70%	60%	LAST MSR

firearms manufacturers. Typically, they were "spec." guns made to sell at a specific price to undersell the competition. Most of these models were derivatives of existing factory models with less expensive wood and perhaps missing the features found on those models from which they were derived. To date, there has been very little interest in collecting Western Field guns, regardless of rarity. Rather than list Western Field models, a general guideline is that values generally are under those of their "1st generation relatives." As a result, prices are ascertained by the shooting value of the gun, rather than its collector value. See Store Brand Crossover List located in the back of this text.

WESTLEY RICHARDS & CO. LTD.

Current manufacturer located in Birmingham, England 1812 to date. In 1995, Westley Richards opened its own agency in the U.S. currently located in Bozeman, MT. Previously located in Springfield, MO. Originally William Westley Richards was located in Birmingham, England.

Note: Westley Richards guns are essentially custom ordered - only 40-45 guns are made annually. They make many guns that are impossible to list and evaluate, except on an individual basis. Professional appraisal is necessary upon purchase or sale.

To obtain a quotation for a new Westley Richards shotgun or rifle, an inquiry should be submitted to the manufacturer or importer (see Trademark Index).

WESTLEY RICHARDS & CO. HISTORY

There seems to be a lot of confusion regarding W. Richards, W. R. Richards, William Richards, and other generic derivatives of the famous English gunmaker, Westley Richards. Part of the problem is that there are seventeen registered firms in England, including several in London, who have made guns by the name of Richards. A genuine Westley Richards gun never has the first name abbreviated, and the London address is usually found on the rib panel. Further compounding the problem, a previous Belgian gunmaker, identifiable by W. Richards on the locks or rib, had many shotguns exported into the United States, which are commonly confused with the real London maker. These Belgian guns are commonly hammer guns with damascus twist barrels most frequently encountered in either 10, 12, or 16 ga. The easiest way to determine this maker is to recognize the Liege proofmarks on the barrel flats and chamber length given in millimeters. Most of these Belgian guns sell in the $375-$750 range, depending on condition and configuration.

RIFLES

MSR values for currently manufactured rifles are listed in English pounds. On older rifles, a knowledgeable appraisal/evaluation should be procurred before buying.

FIXED LOCK (BOXLOCK) DOUBLE RIFLE - .470 NE or .500 NE cal., standard features include type 'C' doll's head, disc set strikers, two triggers, automatic ejectors, chopper lump barrels, quarter rib, express sights, ramp foresight, standard walnut stock, and traditional scroll engraving.

* ***Fixed Lock Double Rifle Current Mfg.***

Current MSR for the base model is £29,250.
Add £3,000 for .577 NE cal.
Add £4,500 for traditional scroll engraving.

The values listed represent the standard model without additional options (of which there are a wide array).

* ***Fixed Lock Double Rifle Older & Recent Mfg.***

100%	98%	95%	90%	80%	70%	60%
N/A	$29,500	$25,000	$22,000	$20,000	$18,000	$16,000

HAND DETACHABLE LOCK (DROPLOCK) DOUBLE RIFLE - nearly all calibers available; standard features include type 'C' doll's head, disc set strikers, hand detachable locks, two triggers, automatic ejectors, manual or automatic safety, chopper lump barrels, quarter rib, express sight.

GRADING - PPGS™	100%	98%	95%	90%	80%	70%	60%	LAST MSR

* ***Hand Detachable Lock Double Rifle Current Mfg.***

Current MSR for the base model is £43,500.
Add £3,000 for .577 NE or .600 NE cal.
Add £1,550 for sideplates.
Engraving is POR.

The values listed represent the standard model without additional options (of which there are a wide array).

* ***Hand Detachable Lock Double Rifle Older & Recent Mfg.***

	N/A	$40,000	$34,000	$29,000	$25,000	$21,500	$16,750	

Add 20% for Mag. cals. .460 NE or higher.

SIDELOCK DOUBLE RIFLE – nearly all calibers available, standard features include type 'C' doll's head, disc set strikers, two triggers, automatic ejectors, scroll engraving standard, manual or automatic safety, chopper lump barrels, quarter rib, express sight.

Current MSR for the base model is £57,500.
Add £2,000 for .577 NE or .600 NE cal.
Engraving is POR.

The values listed represent the standard model without additional options (of which there are a wide array).

BOLT ACTION MAGAZINE RIFLE – nearly all calibers available; choice of standard, magnum, or short action, adjustable trigger, Model 70 style 3-position safety, express sight, ramp foresight.

* ***Bolt Action Magazine Rifle Current Mfg.***

Current MSR for the base model is £12,250.
Add £2,500 for traditional scroll engraving.

The values listed represent the standard model without additional options (of which there are a wide array).

* ***Bolt Action Magazine Rifle Older & Recent Mfg.***

	N/A	$11,000	$9,000	$7,750	$6,750	$5,750	$4,750	

SHOTGUNS: PRE-WWII MFG.

Add 50% for 20 ga.
Add 100% for 28 ga.
Add $1,500 for cased extra set of locks.

OVUNDO O/U – detachable lock boxlock, optional sideplates. Disc.

	$18,000	$15,000	$12,500	$9,750	$8,500	$7,250	$6,000	

MODELE DE GRANDE LUXE - SxS – scalloped receiver, detachable locks, profuse scroll & game scene engraving. Disc.

	$15,000	$13,000	$11,000	$9,750	$8,500	$7,250	$6,000	

MODEL DE LUXE - SxS – scalloped receiver, detachable locks, fine scroll & game scene engraving. Disc.

	$11,000	$9,500	$8,500	$7,500	$6,000	$5,500	$5,000	

HAMMERLESS EJECTOR PLAIN QUALITY - SxS – scalloped receiver, Anson & Deeley fixed locks.

	$6,000	$5,000	$4,000	$3,500	$3,000	$2,500	$2,000	

"B" QUALITY EJECTOR - SxS – boxlock with plain (unscalloped) receiver, light scroll engraving. Disc.

	$5,000	$4,000	$3,500	$3,000	$2,500	$2,250	$2,000	

GRADING - PPGS™	100%	98%	95%	90%	80%	70%	60%	LAST MSR

SHOTGUNS: O/U, RECENT MFG.

BEST QUALITY O/U – 16 or 20 ga. only. 2 1/2 or 2 3/4 in. chambers, standard features include Westley Richards top lever, automatic ejectors, automatic safety, two triggers or Westley Richards patent single trigger, hand detachable locks, hinged coverplate, sideplates with inspection port, chopper lump barrels.

Current MSR on the base model is £43,500.

The values listed represent the standard model without additional options (of which there are a wide array).

SHOTGUNS: SxS, RECENT MFG.

MSR values for currently manufactured rifles are listed in English pounds. For used values, an appraisal/evaluation should be procured before buying.

CONNAUGHT MODEL – 12, 20, or 28 ga., Anson & Deeley scalloped boxlock action, scroll engraving, 26 or 28 in. barrels, ejectors, about 6 1/2 lbs. Disc.

	100%	98%	95%	90%	80%	70%	60%	LAST MSR
	$9,250	$8,000	$6,600	$5,600	$4,800	$4,000	$3,400	*$10,900*

HAND DETACHABLE LOCK (DROPLOCK) – available in 8, 10, 12, 16, 20, 28 ga., or .410 bore, 2 3/4 in. or 3 in. chambers, standard features include model 'C' doll's head, Westley Richards top lever, automatic ejectors, automatic safety, two triggers, hand detachable locks, hinged coverplate, chopper lump barrels.

* ***Hand Detachable Lock (Droplock) Current Mfg.***

Current MSR for the base model is £29,500.
Add £3,000 for 28 ga. or .410 bore, or £14,000 for 8 or 10 ga.
Add £3,850 for SST.
Add £3,250 for spare detachable locks.
Engraving is POR.

The values listed represent the standard model without engraving and additional options (of which there are a wide array).

* ***Hand Detachable Lock (Droplock) Older & Recent Mfg.***

	100%	98%	95%	90%	80%	70%	60%
	N/A	$21,000	$17,500	$14,250	$11,000	$9,500	$7,750

Add 50% for 20 ga.
Add 100% for .410 bore or for 28 ga.
Only six .410 best quality boxlocks have been mfg. to date.

BEST QUALITY SIDELOCK – 12, 16, 20, 28 ga., or .410 bore, 2 3/4 in. or 3 in. chambers, standard features include Best London sidelock action, assisted opening system, automatic ejectors, automatic safety, two triggers, chopper lump barrels, scroll engraving standard.

* ***Best Quality Sidelock Current Mfg.***

Current MSR for the base model is £38,750.
Add £2,000 for 28 ga. or .410 bore.
Add £3,250 for SNT.
Engraving is POR.

The values listed represent the standard model without engraving and additional options (of which there are a wide array).

* ***Best Quality Sidelock Older & Recent Mfg.***

	100%	98%	95%	90%	80%	70%	60%
	N/A	$27,500	$24,000	$21,500	$17,500	$13,750	$9,950

Add 50% for 20 ga.
Add 100% for 28 ga. or for .410 bore.
Add $1,000 for SST.
Most specimens in this model were custom ordered, so each gun should be evaluated individually.

100%	98%	95%	90%	80%	70%	60%	50%	40%	30%	20%	10%

WHITNEY ARMS COMPANY

Previous manufacturer located in New Haven, CT, 1798-1886.

Whitney Arms Company began firearms production in 1798. Eli Whitney Sr. & Eli Whitney Jr. were prominent figures and prolific producers in the arms manufacturing world for a great many years, and their production plant in New Haven is credited as being the first major manufacturer of commercial firearms in America. The Whitneys produced a tremendous variety of firearms under family ownership for approximately 90 years before selling the company to Winchester in 1888. Numerous long arms, starting with the Whitney 1798 U.S. Contract Musket, and moving forward through various other flintlock, percussion, rimfire, and centerfire rifles, handguns, and shotguns, contributed to the vast broadness of the Whitney line. Whitney collaborated with Burgess, Kennedy, Morse, Tiesing, Howard, Cochran, Scharf, and many others. Many of the early Whitney rifles, such as the historic 1798 Flintlock muskets, are rare and highly collectible, commanding substantial premiums when found in original configuration, and not converted to percussion. The Whitney lever action repeaters are also quite popular among collectors. A fair number remain in circulation.

The author wishes to express his thanks to Mr. Steve Engleson for providing the following information on Whitney Arms Company.

RIFLES: LEVER ACTION

WHITNEY-KENNEDY LEVER ACTION MAGAZINE RIFLES – a repeating rifle with loading port on right side, top ejection, approx. 15,000 mfg. between 1879-1886, barrels are typically marked "Whitney Arms Co." or "Whitneyville Armory" with some variations having the Kennedy name included, often referred to as the Kennedy rifle, two basic frame styles, large and small caliber, frame sizes were the same, but internal parts and configuration had several differences, both frame styles also available in carbines and muskets, two other basic variations were the standard loop lever, a serpentine or "S" shaped finger lever, ser. nos. were sequential from 1-5,000, and from there a letter prefix was added, these appeared from "A" through "S", with numbers 1-999 following.

* ***Whitney-Kennedy Lever Action Magazine Rifles Large Caliber*** – .40-60 WCF, .45-60 WCF, .45-75 WCF, or .50-95 Express cal., 26 or 28 in. round or octagon barrels, walnut stocks, crescent steel buttplate, full magazine capacity of 9 rounds in standard rifle.

N/A	**N/A**	**$4,500**	**$4,000**	**$3,600**	**$3,300**	**$3,000**	**$2,700**	**$2,500**	**$2,100**	**$1,950**	**$1,500**

Add 300% for .50-95 Express cal. (extremely rare).
Add 10% for .45-75 cal. (rare).
Add 50% for carbine or musket.
Add 100% for half-round, half-octagon barrel.
Add 20% for nonprefix (early) serial numbers.
Add 10% for serpentine lever.

* ***Whitney-Kennedy Lever Action Magazine Rifles Small Caliber*** – .44-40 WCF, .38-40 WCF, or .32-20 WCF cal., 24 in. round or octagon barrel, walnut stock and crescent buttplate, full magazine capacity of 13 rounds in standard rifle.

N/A	**N/A**	**$3,500**	**$2,900**	**$2,700**	**$2,500**	**$2,200**	**$2,000**	**$1,800**	**$1,600**	**$1,300**	**$1,100**

Add 50% for carbine or musket (extremely rare).
Add 100% for half-round, half-octagon barrel.
Add 20% for half-magazine.
Add 20% for 26 or 28 in. barrel.
Add 20% for .38-40 WCF and .32-20 WCF cals.

1878 BURGESS REPEATING RIFLE – .45-70 Govt. cal., standard sporting rifle, 28 in. octagon or round barrel, loading port on right side, serpentine shaped lever, walnut stock, blue receiver and full magazine capacity of 9 rounds, typically w/o Whitney markings, barrels marked "G.W. Morse Patented Oct. 28th 1856", and tangs are marked "A. Burgess Patented Jan. 7th 1873", several variations, including the first, second, and third models, as well as military carbines and muskets.

N/A	**N/A**	**$6,500**	**$5,500**	**$4,000**	**$3,500**	**$3,000**	**$2,700**	**$2,500**	**$2,300**	**$2,100**	**$1,950**

GRADING - PPGS™	100%	98%	95%	90%	80%	70%	60%	LAST MSR

Add 300% for the first model top loader (few made and most converted by the factory to sideloader).
Add 100% for military carbine or musket (certain variations will command a higher premium).
Add 30% for first or second model.

Values shown are for the most typically encountered variation, the third model sporting rifle.

This model was also known as the Whitney-Burgess-Morse lever action repeating rifle, mfg. through a license agreement with Andrew Burgess, total production of approx. 2,000 were made between 1878-82.

WHITNEY FIREARMS COMPANY

Previous manufacturer from 1956-1959 located in Hartford, CT.

PISTOLS: SEMI-AUTO

WOLVERINE OR LIGHTNING – .22 LR cal., unique futuristic sci-fi appearance, 10 shot, 4 5/8 in. barrel, plastic grips, aluminum alloy frame and barrel shroud, blue model is more common (approx. 13,000 mfg.), nickel is rare (approx. 900 mfg.). Mfg. 1955-1962.

	100%	98%	95%	90%	80%	70%	60%	LAST MSR
Blue finish	$675	$625	$575	$495	$425	$350	$300	
Nickel finish	$1,325	$1,200	$1,075	$950	$850	$600	$500	

WHITWORTH

This trademark can be found in the Interarms section of this text.

WICHITA ARMS, INC.

Previous manufacturer located in Wichita, KS.

PISTOLS

WICHITA INTERNATIONAL PISTOL (WIP) – available in 8 cals. between .22 LR and .357 Mag., single shot, break open action, stainless steel, adj. sights, 10 or 14 in. barrel, adj. sights or scope mounts, smooth walnut stocks and forearm. Disc. 1994.

100%	98%	95%	90%	80%	70%	60%	LAST MSR
$680	$465	$350	$285	$250	$215	$185	*$775*

Add $100 for 14 in. barrel.

WICHITA CLASSIC PISTOL – assorted cals. to .308 Win., 11 1/4 in. barrel, action has left-hand bolt for shooting with right hand, deluxe walnut, custom made, 3 lbs. 15 oz. Disc. 1997.

100%	98%	95%	90%	80%	70%	60%	LAST MSR
$3,280	$2,550	$2,150	$1,865	$1,715	$1,295	$1,075	*$3,495*

* ***Wichita Classic Pistol Engraved*** – similar to Wichita Classic, except is extensively engraved.

100%	98%	95%	90%	80%	70%	60%	LAST MSR
$5,250	$3,750	$2,750	N/A	N/A	N/A	N/A	*$5,250*

WICHITA SILHOUETTE PISTOL (WSP) – .308 Win. or 7mm/IHMSA cal., adj. trigger and sights, 14 15/16 in. barrel, center grip walnut stock, rear grip, 4 1/2 lbs. Left-hand action for shooting with right hand. Disc. 1994.

100%	98%	95%	90%	80%	70%	60%	LAST MSR
$1,520	$1,050	$850	$740	$620	$515	$440	*$1,800*

WICHITA MAGAZINE PISTOL – .308 Win. or 7mm/IHMSA cal., fiberthane (disc. 1987) or walnut (new 1988) stock, choice of MK-40, Silhouette, or Classic configuration, 13 in. barrel, adj. trigger, multi-range sights, 4 1/2 lbs. Disc. 1994.

100%	98%	95%	90%	80%	70%	60%	LAST MSR
$1,250	$875	$700	$585	$500	$415	$365	*$1,550*

* ***Wichita Magazine Pistol Classic*** – features 11 1/4 in. octagon barrel, AAA walnut stock, 3 lbs. 15 oz. Disc. 1994.

100%	98%	95%	90%	80%	70%	60%	LAST MSR
$2,975	$2,450	$2,000	$1,740	$1,495	$1,215	$1,000	*$3,400*

WICHITA BENCH PISTOL – .222 Rem., 6 PPC, or .22 Cheetah cal., uses WBR 1200 action, rear grip, 18 in. stainless steel Douglas barrel. Mfg. 1994-98.

100%	98%	95%	90%	80%	70%	60%	LAST MSR
$1,875	$1,500	$1,250	$1,100	$895	$785	$630	*$1,875*

GRADING - PPGS™	100%	98%	95%	90%	80%	70%	60%	LAST MSR

RIFLES: BOLT ACTION

WICHITA CLASSIC RIFLE (WCR) – .17-222, .17-222 Mag., .222 Rem., .222 Mag., 223 Rem., 6x47mm, and other cals. up to and including .308 Win. cal., bolt action, single shot, select walnut, 21 in. octagon barrel, Canjar trigger, no sights, 7 lbs.

	$3,275	$2,500	$2,150	$1,865	$1,715	$1,295	$1,075	*$3,495*

Add $175 for left-hand action.

* ***Wichita Classic Rifle Varmint (WVR)*** – similar to WCR, except available only in Varmint cals. (up to and including .308 Win.) and round barrel. Disc. 1997.

	$2,500	$1,795	$1,375	$1,215	$985	$855	$685	*$2,695*

Add $175 for left-hand action.

* ***Wichita Classic Rifle Silhouette (WSR)*** – available in most cals., grey fiberthane stock, 24 in. match grade barrel, 2 oz. Canjar trigger, no sights, 9 lbs. Disc. 1995.

	$2,475	$1,775	$1,375	$1,215	$985	$855	$685	*$2,650*

Add $175 for left-hand action.

* ***Wichita Classic Rifle Magnum*** – Mag. cals., stainless steel only. Disc. 1984.

	$1,725	$1,300	$1,175	$1,040	$845	$735	$600	

WICKLIFFE RIFLES

Previously manufactured by Triple S Development located in Wickliffe, OH.

RIFLES: SINGLE SHOT

MODEL 76 STANDARD – falling block action, most popular cals., 22 or 26 in. barrel, no sights, select walnut pistol grip, 2 piece stock. Mfg. 1976-disc.

	$395	$350	$325	$300	$275	$250	$225	

MODEL 76 DELUXE GRADE – similar to Standard, in .30-06 cal. only, 22 in. barrel, fancy wood, silver pistol grip cap.

	$460	$415	$385	$360	$320	$290	$250	

MODEL 76 COMMEMORATIVE – similar to Deluxe, except etched receiver, U.S. silver dollar inlaid in stock, presentation case. 100 mfg. 1976.

	$1,100	$825	$550	$495	$440	$330	$305	

STINGER – similar to Model 76 Standard, in .22 Hornet or .223 Rem. cal., lightweight 22 in. barrel.

	$395	$350	$325	$300	$275	$250	$225	

STINGER DELUXE – similar to 76 Deluxe, in .22 Hornet or .223 Rem. cal., lightweight 22 in. barrel.

	$460	$415	$385	$360	$325	$290	$250	

TRADITIONALIST – similar to Standard 76, in .30-06 or .45-70 Govt. cal., 24 in. barrel.

	$395	$350	$325	$300	$275	$250	$225	

KODIAK COMMEMORATIVE – similar to Model 76 Deluxe, .338 Win. Mag. cal., 26 in. barrel, etched receiver.

	$650	$550	$475	$425	$375	$325	$275	

WIDFORSS

Please refer to Mauritz Widforss AB.

WIENER WAFFENFABRIK

Previous manufacturer located in Vienna, Austria.

PISTOLS: SEMI-AUTO

LITTLE TOM – 6.35mm (.25 ACP) or 7.65mm (.32 ACP) cal., 2 1/2 (.25 ACP) or 3 1/2 (.32 ACP) in. barrel, DA, designed by Alois Tomiska, small quantities mfg. in Czechoslovakia

GRADING - PPGS™	100%	98%	95%	90%	80%	70%	60%	LAST MSR

circa 1908-1918, later production in Austria circa 1919-1925.

.25 ACP cal.	$500	$450	$400	$350	$300	$250	$200	
.32 ACP cal.	$600	$550	$500	$450	$400	$350	$300	

Values assume Austrian production. Czech production will bring a premium. The .32 ACP cal. model is more scarce.

WIFRA

Please refer to W.R. Saleri listing in the S section.

WILD WEST GUNS

Current custom gunsmith and manufacturer established in 1992 and located in Anchorage, AK and in Las Vegas, NV beginning 2013. Dealer and consumer direct sales.

PISTOLS: SEMI-AUTO

Wild West Guns builds custom 1911 style handguns per customer order. Please contact the company directly for pricing and available options (see Trademark Index). Wild West Guns previously manufactured a customized M1911 style semi-auto model called the ShadowLite package - 1997 retail was $2,495.

REVOLVERS

Wild West Guns custom builds the .454 Wolverine revolver in a variety of calibers. Many custom options are available. Please contact the company directly for more information (see Trademark Index).

RIFLES: BOLT ACTION

SUMMITLITE – various short action cals., Rem. action, fluted match grade barrel, lightweight configuration with scaled down synthetic stock, parkerized or matte blue finish, 4 1/2 lbs.

MSR $3,495	$3,125	$2,750	$2,400	$2,100	$1,800	$1,600	$1,200	

Add $175 for stainless steel, or $110 for thumbhole stock.
Left-hand action is POR.

PROGUIDE – .375 H&H, .416 Rem., .458 Win., or .458 Lott cal., Win. controlled feed action, slab side barrel with muzzle brake and quarter rib, parkerized finish, camo or black synthetic stock with Pachmayr decelerator pad.

MSR $3,995	$3,650	$3,250	$2,850	$2,500	$2,200	$1,800	$1,600	

Add $175 for stainless steel.
Left-hand action is POR.

RIFLES: LEVER ACTION

ALASKAN COPILOT RIFLE – .30-30 Win. (disc. 1999, reintroduced 2011), .35 Rem. (new 2011), .357 Mag. (disc. 1999, reintroduced 2011), .44 Mag. (disc. 1999, reintroduced 2011), .444 Marlin (disc. 1999), .45 LC)new 2011), .45-70 Govt., .457 Mag. (new 2000), or .50 Alaskan (new 2000) cal., 16 1/2, 18 1/2, or 20 in. barrel with ghost ring rear sight, features customized Marlin lever action with takedown conversion, various finishes, ported barrel, matte blue or parkerized finish, includes soft case. New 1996.

MSR $2,249	$1,900	$1,665	$1,425	$1,295	$1,050	$850	$665	

Add $19 for .30-30 Win., .35 Rem., .44 Mag., .357 Mag., or .45 LC cal.
Add $250 for .50 Alaskan cal. conversion package.
Add $200 for Marlin 1895 XLR Model in stainless.
Subtract approx. 20% for older disc. cals.

* ***Alaskan CoPilot Rifle Limited*** – .457 Mag. or .45-70 Govt. cal., takedown action, features most of Wild West Guns custom shop options, includes hard case. Only 150 to be mfg. beginning 2001 with custom ser. nos.

	$2,995	$2,650	$2,150	$1,750	$1,500	$1,300	$1,100	*$2,995*

GRADING - PPGS™	100%	98%	95%	90%	80%	70%	60%	LAST MSR

ALASKAN GUIDE – .457 Mag. or .50 Alaskan cal., similar to Alaskan CoPilot, except is non-takedown, has 18 1/2 in. ported barrel with fiberoptic front sight, ghost ring rear sight, parkerized finish, straight style stock and recoil control porting. New 1997.

MSR $1,749	$1,475	$1,295	$1,100	$1,000	$815	$665	$515	

Add $250 for .50 Alaskan cal. conversion package.
Add $125 for stainless steel.
Add $200 for Marlin 1895 XLR Model in stainless.

MASTER GUIDE – .457 Mag., .45-70 Govt., or .50 Alaskan cal., takedown action.

MSR $2,399	$2,025	$1,775	$1,525	$1,375	$1,115	$910	$710	

Add $250 for .50 Alaskan cal. conversion package.
Add $125 for stainless steel.

MODEL 04 – .454 Casull or .500 S&W cal., stainless steel CNC machined frame, takedown or solid rifle, 16 1/2, 18 1/2, or 20 in. barrel, walnut, laminate or synthetic stock, ghost ring sights, Pachmayr decelerator pad. Limited mfg. 2005.

	$1,350	$1,150	$975	$860	$700	$600	$500	*$1,499*

Add $300 for synthetic stock.
Add $400 for takedown.

RIFLE – various cals., big loop lever, bear proof ejector, ghost ring rear sight, fiber optic front sight with cut hood, straight grip walnut stock, hand fitted max recoil pad, stainless steel. New 2013.

MSR $1,899	$1,615	$1,415	$1,215	$1,100	$895	$725	$565	

WILDEY, INC.

Previous manufacturer located in Warren, CT 2000-circa 2011. Previously located in New Milford, CT until 1999.

Originally, the company was named Wildey Firearms Co., Inc. located in Cheshire, CT. At that time, serialization of pistols was 45-0000. When Wildey, Inc. bought the company out of bankruptcy from the old shareholders, there had been approximately 800 pistols mfg. To distinguish the old company from the present company, the serial range was changed to 09-0000 (only 633 pistols with the 09 prefix were produced). These guns had the Cheshire, CT address. Pistols produced by Wildey, Inc., New Milford, CT are serial numbered with 4 digits (no numerical prefix).

CARBINES: SEMI-AUTO

WILDEY CARBINE – .44 Auto Mag., .45 Wildey Mag., .45 Win. Mag., or .475 Wildey Mag. cal., features 18 in. barrel with forearm and detachable skeleton walnut stock, polished or matte stainless steel. Mfg. 2003-2011.

	$2,700	$2,225	$1,750	$1,500	$1,235	$1,030	$855	*$3,110*

Add $237 for matte stainless steel finish.

PISTOLS: SEMI-AUTO

Add $585-$1,950 per interchangeable barrel assembly, depending on barrel length and finish.

WILDEY AUTO PISTOL – .45 Win. Mag., .45 Wildey Mag., or .475 Wildey Mag., gas operated, 5, 6, 7, 8, 10, or 14 in. VR barrel, selective single shot or semi-auto, 3 lug rotary bolt, fixed barrel (interchangeable), polished stainless steel construction, 7 shot, double action, adj. sights, smooth or checkered wood grips, designed to fire proprietary new cartridges specifically for this gun including the .45 Win. Mag. cal., 64 oz. with 5 in. barrel.

Add $560-$1,148 per interchangeable barrel.

* ***Wildey Survivor Model*** – .357 Mag., .44 Auto Mag. (new 2003), .45 Win. Mag., 45 Wildey Mag., or .475 Wildey Mag. cal., 5, 6, 7, 8, 10, 12, 14 (new 2000), or 18 (new 2003) in. VR barrel, polished stainless steel finish. Mfg. 1990-2011.

	$1,375	$1,025	$800	$665	$560	$465	$410	*$1,571*

Add $26 - $125 for 5 in. - 12 in. barrel, depending on length, and $1,206 for 18 in. silhouette model.

GRADING - PPGS™	100%	98%	95%	90%	80%	70%	60%	LAST MSR

Add $26 for .45 Wildey Mag. or .475 Wildey Mag. cal.

The .475 Wildey cal. is derived from a factory cartridge.

* ***Wildey Survivor Guardsman*** – similar to Survivor Model, except has squared-off trigger guard, same options apply to this model as for the Survivor model. Mfg. 1990-2011.

	100%	98%	95%	90%	80%	70%	60%	LAST MSR
	$1,375	$1,025	$800	$665	$560	$465	$410	*$1,571*

* ***Wildey Hunter Model*** – .45 Win. Mag., .45 Wildey Mag., or .475 Wildey Mag. cal., 5, 6, 7, 8, 10, 12, 14 (new 2000) or 18 (new 2003) in. VR barrel, matte finish on all metal parts, adj. sights. Mfg. 1990-2011.

	100%	98%	95%	90%	80%	70%	60%	LAST MSR
	$1,575	$1,225	$950	$810	$670	$565	$475	*$1,829*

Add $15 - $582 for 8 in. - 14 in. barrel, depending on length, or $1,210 for 18 in. silhouette model.
Add $25 for .45 Wildey Mag. or .475 Wildey Mag. cal.

.475 Wildey Mag. was available in 8, 10, or 12 in. barrel only.

* ***Wildey Hunter Guardsman*** – similar to Hunter Model, except has squared-off trigger guard, same options apply to this model as for the Hunter model. Mfg. 1990-2011.

	100%	98%	95%	90%	80%	70%	60%	LAST MSR
	$1,575	$1,225	$950	$810	$670	$565	$475	*$1,829*

Add $100 for 12 in. barrel.
Add $625 for 14 in. barrel.
Add $1,175 for 18 in. silhouette barrel.

* ***Wildey Presentation Model*** – same specifications as Hunter Guardsman model, except is engraved with hand-checkered or smooth stocks.

	100%	98%	95%	90%	80%	70%	60%	LAST MSR
	$2,500	$2,000	$1,600	$1,410	$1,160	$980	$800	*$2,000*

WILDEY AUTO PISTOL OLDER MFG. – .475 Wildey Mag. cal. was available in 8 or 10 in. barrel only.

* ***Older Wildey Serial Nos. 1-200.***

	100%	98%	95%	90%	80%	70%	60%	LAST MSR
	$1,900	$1,700	$1,550	$1,365	$1,125	$950	$775	*$2,180*

Add $20 for 8 or 10 in. barrel.

* ***Older Wildey Serial Nos. 201-400.***

	100%	98%	95%	90%	80%	70%	60%	LAST MSR
	$1,750	$1,550	$1,400	$1,235	$1,000	$870	$700	*$1,980*

Add $20 for 8 or 10 in. barrel.

* ***Older Wildey Serial Nos. 401-600.***

	100%	98%	95%	90%	80%	70%	60%	LAST MSR
	$1,650	$1,375	$1,250	$1,100	$895	$785	$630	*$1,780*

Add $20 for 8 or 10 in. barrel.

* ***Older Wildey Serial Nos. 601-800.***

	100%	98%	95%	90%	80%	70%	60%	LAST MSR
	$1,450	$1,200	$1,000	$885	$715	$610	$515	*$1,580*

Add $20 for 8 or 10 in. barrel.

* ***Older Wildey Serial Nos. 801-1,000.***

	100%	98%	95%	90%	80%	70%	60%	LAST MSR
	$1,100	$925	$800	$695	$585	$485	$415	*$1,275*

Add $25 for 8 or 10 in. barrel.

* ***Older Wildey Serial Nos. 1,001-2,489.***

	100%	98%	95%	90%	80%	70%	60%	LAST MSR
	$1,025	$850	$750	$640	$535	$450	$390	*$1,175*

Add $20 for 8 or 10 in. barrel.

WILKES, JOHN GUNMAKERS LTD.

Current manufacturer established circa 1833, and located in Arundel, West Sussex, U.K. Previously imported and distributed 2004-2007 by John Wilkes Gunmakers Ltd., located in Colorado Springs, CO, and from 2001-2004 by First National Gun Banque, located in Colorado Springs, CO.

GRADING - PPGS™	100%	98%	95%	90%	80%	70%	60%	LAST MSR

All current guns are built per individual custom order. Please contact the manufacturer directly for more information, U.S. availability, and pricing (see Trademark Index).

RIFLES

SOLID BOLT ACTION – various cals., bolt action, made of one piece of steel (action and barrel), 30 degree bolt lift.

Base price for this model was $10,500.
A Signature Model limited edition (20 mfg.) was available for $22,500.

SHOTGUNS: O/U, SIDELOCK

O/U SIDELOCK BEST MODEL CLASSIC – 20 ga., unique sideplate locks w/o "V" springs (plungers instead), ST or DT, best quality wood and worksmanship, Brazier "solid solid," mono solid (new 2004), monobloc, or chopper lump barrels, lifetime warranty, special order only. Imported 2001-2007.

	100%	98%	95%	90%	80%	70%	60%	LAST MSR
	$22,500	$17,750	$14,500	$12,250	$11,000	$10,000	$9,250	*$22,500*

Add $3,000 for "solid solid" barrels.
Add $2,500 per pair of additional locks.

*** *O/U Sidelock Best Model Classic Special Series***

Prices for the Special Series started at $32,950 with "solid solid" barrels.

WILKINSON ARMS

Previous trademark established circa 1996 and manufactured by Ray Wilkinson circa 1996-1998 (limited production), and by Northwest Arms located in Parma, ID circa 2000-2005.

CARBINES

LINDA CARBINE – 9mm Para. cal., 16 3/16 in. barrel, aluminum receiver, pre-ban configuration (limited supplies), fixed tubular stock with wood pad, vent. barrel shroud, aperture rear sight, small wooden forearm, 18 or 31 shot mag., beginning 2002, this model came standard with many accessories, 7 lbs. Mfg. circa 1996-2005.

	100%	98%	95%	90%	80%	70%	60%	LAST MSR
	$1,295	$1,075	$850	$725	$600	$500	$425	*$1,800*

Only 2,200 Linda Carbines were marked "Luger Carbine" on the receiver. The last 1,500 distributed by Northwest Arms include a longer stock, and matched bolt and barrel (Rockwell 57).

*** *Linda Carbine L2 Limited Edition*** – mfg. from the last 600 of the original 2,200 pre-ban Linda Carbines, includes many upgrades and accessories. Mfg. 2002-2005.

Last MSR was $4,800.

There isn't enough activity in the secondary marketplace to accurately predict values on this limited ed. Linda carbine.

TERRY CARBINE – 9mm Para. cal., blowback semi-auto action, 31 shot mag., 16 3/16 in. barrel, closed breech, adj. sights, 7 lbs. Disc.

	100%	98%	95%	90%	80%	70%	60%
With black P.V.C. stock	$475	$395	$325	$295	$260	$230	$200
With maple stock	$625	$525	$400	$350	$340	$325	$300

PISTOLS: SEMI-AUTO

DIANE MODEL – .25 ACP cal., 6 shot, 2 1/8 in. barrel, fixed sight, matte blue, plastic grips. Disc.

	100%	98%	95%	90%	80%	70%	60%
	$150	$125	$95	$80	$65	$55	$50

LINDA MODEL – 9mm Para. cal., blowback action firing from closed bolt, 8.3 in. barrel, 31 shot mag., PVC pistol grip, maple forearm, Williams adj. rear sight. Disc.

	100%	98%	95%	90%	80%	70%	60%
	$675	$625	$550	$475	$425	$350	$295

GRADING - PPGS™	100%	98%	95%	90%	80%	70%	60%	LAST MSR

SHERRY MODEL – .22 LR cal., 2 1/2 in. barrel, aluminum frame, fully machined steel slide, trigger group, and bolt insert, available in various colors, 9 1/4 oz. Mfg. 2000-2005.

$245	$200	$160	$140	$125	$110	$100	*$280*

Add $25 for gold anodized frame.
Add $20 for collector's edition.
Add $100 for Robar coating.

WILLIAM & SON

Current firearms manufacturer and luxury retailer established in 1999, and located in London, England. Previous company name was William R. Asprey. William R. Asprey is the 7th generation of the renowned Asprey family who established their first business in 1781. William & Son continues the family tradition of building best quality English guns.

A competent appraisal is highly suggested for used Asprey and William & Son rifles and shotguns, as all guns have been built to custom order, and older guns need to be appraised individually based on condition, gauge, engraving, and possible accessories.

Deluxe game scene engraving is available by quotation only.

Prices do not include English VAT.

RIFLES: BOLT ACTION

BOLT ACTION MAGAZINE RIFLE – standard cals. include .243 Win., .270 Win., .308 Win., or .375 H&H, Mauser or Mannlicher action, 3/4 rib with standard and two-folding leaf rear sight, best quality pistol grip walnut stock with traditional cheekpiece, custom order only, Magnum or short action and scopes are priced upon individual quotation only.

This model's MSR starts at £15,000, depending on caliber.

RIFLES: SxS, SIDELOCK

SxS DOUBLE RIFLE – various cals. up to .700, sidelock ejector with engraved reinforced action, pinless lockplates, best quality walnut, folding leaf rear sight on 3/4 rib, custom order only - prices below reflect base models, and include leather case with accessories. Limited mfg.

This model's MSR starts at £80,000, depending on caliber..
Add £3,400 for detachable scope mounts.

SHOTGUNS: O/U, SIDELOCK

SIDELOCK MODEL – 12, 16 (disc. 2011), or 20 ga., best quality sidelock ejector model, DTs, scroll engraving standard, best quality checkered walnut, custom order only.

This model's MSR starts at £58,500.

SHOTGUNS: SxS, SIDELOCK

SIDELOCK MODEL – available in 12 ga. - .410 bore, best quality sidelock ejector model, scroll engraving standard, DTs, best quality checkered walnut, custom order only.

This model's MSR starts at £43,500.

WILLIAM DOUGLAS & SONS

Previous manufacturer located in Staffordshire, England. Limited U.S. importation by Cape Outfitters located in Cape Girardeau, MO until circa 2004.

RIFLES: SxS

EXPRESS RIFLE – .375 H&H cal., H&H type back action sidelock with bolster fences, DTs, ejectors, 24 in. regulated barrels, folding leaf rear sight, oil finished European walnut stock with 20 LPI checkering, light engraving, case hardened action.

$19,750	$15,250	$11,000	$8,750	$7,400	$6,200	$5,300

BOXLOCK EXPRESS RIFLE – .470 NE or .500 NE (new 1998) cal., Anson & Deeley action with DT (front trigger is articulated), case colored action with deep blue small parts, 24

GRADING - PPGS™	100%	98%	95%	90%	80%	70%	60%	LAST MSR

in. regulated barrels, checkered European walnut stock and forearm with oil finish, light border engraving.

	$12,975	$9,950	$9,000	$8,250	$7,500	$6,750	$6,000	

Add $1,000 for .500 NE cal.

* ***Boxlock Express Rifle Deluxe*** – includes better walnut and fully engraved receiver.

	$15,650	$12,750	$10,750	$9,500	$8,750	$7,500	$6,750	

SHOTGUNS: SxS

WILLIAM DOUGLAS BOXLOCK – 16, 20, or 28 ga., 2 3/4 in. chambers, case colored receiver, chopper lump barrels, DT, 26 or 28 in. barrels.

	$4,650	$4,200	$3,750	$3,250	$2,750	$2,250	$1,750	

Add $800 for ST.

WILLIAM EVANS LIMITED

Current manufacturer of long arms established during 1883, and located in London, England.

William Evans Limited, Gun & Rifle Makers, have been manufacturing high quality shotguns and rifles for over 100 years. Most William Evans shotguns and double rifles must be appraised individually since they were all custom ordered initially. All new guns must be ordered from the factory directly. All prices are FOB England, less VAT. Please contact William Evans (refer to the Trademark Index) for more information, including any special orders.

RIFLES

MSR values for currently manufactured rifles are listed in English pounds, and used prices are not listed, since these models are only infrequently encountered in today's marketplace.

BEST QUALITY SIDELOCK DOUBLE RIFLE – various cals., traditional bold scroll-engraved sidelock action, many options available, custom order only.

* ***Best Quality Sidelock Double Rifle Current Mfg.***

Current MSR on this model is £75,000.
Add £15,000 for .500 NE-.577 NE cals.
Cals. .600 NE and above are POR.

BOLT ACTION MAGAZINE RIFLE – various cals., Mauser standard or Magnum action, many options available, custom order only.

* ***Bolt Action Magazine Rifle Current Mfg.***

Current MSR on this model is £11,500.
Add £6,000 for Mauser Magnum action.

SHOTGUNS: O/U & SxS

Delivery time on custom guns ranges from 24-30 months.

BEST QUALITY O/U SIDELOCK – 12, 16, 20, 28 ga., or .410 bore, best quality sidelock gun with DT, bold scroll engraving standard, custom order only.

* ***Best Quality O/U Sidelock Current Mfg.***

Current MSR on this model is £65,000.
Add £10,000 for 28 ga. or .410 bore.

BEST QUALITY SxS SIDELOCK – 12, 16, 20, 28 ga., or .410 bore, best quality sidelock gun with DT, bold scroll engraving standard, custom order only.

* ***Best Quality SxS Sidelock Current Mfg.***

Current MSR on this model is £40,000.
Add £5,000 for 28 ga. or .410 bore.

GRADING - PPGS™	100%	98%	95%	90%	80%	70%	60%	LAST MSR

PALL MALL SxS – 12 or 20 ga., 2 3/4 in. chambers, 28 or 30 in. barrels, fixed chokes, DT, choice of straight or pistol grip walnut stock with splinter forend, Anson style pushrod, hand engraved with traditional rose and scroll, produced in collaboration with Grulla Armas, 6 -7 lbs. New 2011.

Current MSR on this model is £15,000.

Delivery time on this model is approx. 4 months.

WILLIAM LARKIN MOORE

Current importer and dealer established in 1973, and located in Scottsdale, AZ. Previously located in Agoura, CA, and Westlake Village, CA.

William Larkin Moore imports a variety of high grade quality shotguns and double rifles. Currently, the company imports Arrieta, Pedro Arrizabalaga, Armas Garbi, Chapuis Armes, B. Rizzini, and is the exclusive U.S. importer for F.lli Piotti. Please refer to the individual listings for information on current models and pricing (see Trademark Index).

WILLIAM POWELL & SON (GUNMAKERS) LTD.

Current manufacturer established in 1802, and located in Oxfordshire, England. Previously located in Birmingham, England until 2008. The company was controlled by the descendants of William Powell I until 2008. No current U.S. importation. Previously imported 1999-2002 by John Higgins, located in Richmond Hill, GA, and by Bells Legendary Countrywear located in New York, NY, until 1999. The Heritage Series was introduced into the U.S. in 1984.

William Powell & Sons celebrated their 200th anniversary during 2002, and are one of England's oldest premier gunmakers. The company was sold to Mark and Christine Osborne in January 2008. The Osbornes had, with Sir Edward Dashwood, started West Wycombe Shooting Ground in 1991 and subsequently acquired and successfully revived the previously dormant E. J. Churchill Firm of Gunmakers.

Please contact the factory directly for more information. They have a fine catalog, which includes a lineup of accessories and clothing.

SHOTGUNS: SxS

Current MSRs are shown in pounds (£), and do not include VAT.

Add 10% for 16, 20, 28 ga. or .410 bore on models listed.

NO. 1 SIDELOCK EJECTOR – 12, 16, 20 ga., or .410 (disc.) bore, chopper lump barrels, extra choice French walnut, DTs, many special orders available. Gold inlays, deep relief carved action fences, can be obtained in self opener.

* ***No. 1 Sidelock Ejector Current Mfg.***

Current MSR on this model is £42,688.

Add £4,005 for assisted opening action.

Add £3,327 for SNT.

* ***No. 1 Sidelock Ejector Recent & Older Mfg.***

100%	98%	95%	90%	80%	70%	60%
N/A	$39,500	$34,000	$28,750	$23,250	$17,500	$14,750

NO. 3 BOXLOCK EJECTOR – 12, 16, 20 ga., or .410 (disc.) bore, chopper lump barrels, scalloped boxlock action, extra choice French walnut, many special orders available.

* ***No. 3 Boxlock Ejector Current Mfg.***

Current MSR on this model is £23,168.

* ***No. 3 Boxlock Ejector Recent & Older Mfg.***

100%	98%	95%	90%	80%	70%	60%
N/A	$27,000	$21,000	$16,000	$9,900	$7,500	$6,250

MODEL NO. 4 BOXLOCK EJECTOR – similar to Number 3, but has dovetail lump barrels and less engraving.

Current MSR on this model is £20,155.

Add £2,131 for SNT.

GRADING - PPGS™	100%	98%	95%	90%	80%	70%	60%	LAST MSR

*** *Model No. 4 Boxlock Ejector Older Mfg.***

	N/A	$23,000	$16,500	$10,250	$7,950	$6,600	$5,400	

MODEL 6 BOXLOCK EJECTOR – disc. 1988.

	$2,750	$2,450	$2,050	$1,700	$1,400	$1,150	$900	

HERITAGE NO. 1 SIDELOCK EJECTOR MKII – 12 or 20 ga., 2 3/4 in. chambers, chopper lump barrels, choice of game scene or bouquet and scroll engraving, DTs. Mfg. 1984-2000.

	$8,710	$12,750	$10,750	$9,000	$7,800	$6,700	$5,500	*$8,710*

HERITAGE NO. 2 SIDELOCK MARK 11 – similar to Heritage No. 1, except has less engraving and lesser grade walnut, easy opening action.

*** *Heritage No. 2 Sidelock Mark 11 Current Mfg.***

Current MSR on this model is £4,775.

Add £1,495 for traditional scroll engraving.

*** *Heritage No. 2 Sidelock Mark 11 Recent & Older Mfg.***

	N/A	$5,900	$5,200	$4,750	$4,375	$3,675	$3,100	

HERITAGE "CONSORT" SIDELOCK EJECTOR – 12, 20, or 28 ga., 2 3/4 in. chambers chopper lump barrels, round body action, full bouquet and scroll engraving. New 1998.

*** *Heritage "Consort" Sidelock Ejector Current Mfg.***

Current MSR on this model is £7,895.

*** *Heritage "Consort" Sidelock Ejector Recent & Older Mfg.***

	N/A	$8,200	$6,850	$6,000	$5,000	$4,250	$3,500	

HERITAGE DE LUXE BOXLOCK DETACHABLE LOCK – features detachable locks, choice of traditional scroll or game scene engraving, ejectors. Disc. 1999.

	$21,485	$16,750	$13,750	$11,000	$8,500	$7,250	$5,950	*$21,485*

HERITAGE ROUND ACTION EJECTOR – features unscalloped, rounded boxlock action with fine English scrollwork throughout, DTs. Disc. 1999.

	$15,785	$12,000	$9,600	$7,800	$6,600	$5,400	$4,500	*$15,785*

WILSON COMBAT

Current firearms manufacturer, customizer, and supplier of custom firearms parts and accessories established in 1978, and located in Berryville, AR.

PISTOLS

Prices reflect .45 ACP cal. base model w/o upgrades. A wide variety of options are available - contact the company directly for pricing.

Add $110 for 9mm Para, .38 Super, or .40 S&W cal. or $225 for 10mm cal. on most models.

CONTEMPORARY CLASSIC CENTENNIAL – .45 ACP cal., 100th anniversary of the 1911, full size carbon steel frame and slide, 5 in. carbon match grade barrel and bushing, 8 shot mag., Turnbull charcoal blue finish, French walnut double diamond grips, beavertail grip safety, contoured mag well, lanyard loop mainspring housing, 30 LPI high cut checkered front gripstrap, "1911-2011" engraving, battlesight with gold bead front sight, tactical thumb safety, top and rear slide serrations, special serial numbers (JMB001-JMB100) includes walnut presentation box, 45 oz. Limited edition of 100 mfg. during 2011.

	$3,550	$3,150	$2,725	$2,350	$1,950	$1,650	$1,350	*$3,995*

CLASSIC SUPERGRADE – 9mm Para., 10mm, .38 Super, .40 S&W, or .45 ACP cal., full size stainless steel frame, 5 in. stainless match grade barrel and bushing, carbon steel slide, blue finish, 30 LPI high cut checkered front strap, top and rear slide serrations, Lo-Mount adj. rear sight, improved ramp front sight, ambidextrous safety, Speed-Chute mag well, cocobolo double diamond grips, beavertail grip safety, full length guide rod, each gun hand built. Limited mfg.

MSR $5,195	$4,675	$4,225	$3,750	$3,150	$2,650	$2,200	$1,700	

GRADING - PPGS™	100%	98%	95%	90%	80%	70%	60%	LAST MSR

TACTICAL SUPERGRADE - 9mm Para., 10mm (disc. 2011), .38 Super, .40 S&W (disc. 2011), or .45 ACP cal., full size stainless steel frame, 5 in. stainless match grade barrel and bushing, carbon steel slide, blue finish, 30 LPI high cut checkered front strap, top and rear slide serrations, ambidextrous safety, Speed-Chute mag well, G10 starburst grips, beavertail grip safety, battlesight with white outline tritium front sight.

MSR $5,045	$4,550	$4,125	$3,700	$3,100	$2,600	$2,100	$1,650

Add $105 for .38 Super or 9mm Para. cal.

* ***Tactical Supergrade Professional*** - 9mm Para., .38 Super, or .45 ACP cal., carbon steel frame, 4 in. stainless match grade cone barrel, carbon steel slide, 8 shot mag., blue finish, 30 LPI high cut checkered front strap, top and rear slide serrations, ambidextrous thumb safety, Speed-Chute mag well, G10 starburst grips, beavertail grip safety, battlesight with white outline tritium front sight, full length guide rod and reverse plug, 44.8 oz. New 2010.

MSR $5,045	$4,550	$4,125	$3,700	$3,100	$2,600	$2,100	$1,650

Add $105 for .38 Super or 9mm Para. cal.

* ***Tactical Supergrade Compact*** - 9mm Para., .38 Super, or .45 ACP cal., compact carbon steel frame, 4 in. stainless match grade cone barrel, carbon steel slide, blue finish, 30 LPI high cut checkered front strap, top and rear slide serrations, ambidextrous thumb safety, Speed-Chute mag well, G10 starburst grips, beavertail grip safety, battlesight with white outline tritium front sight, full length guide rod and reverse plug.

MSR $5,045	$4,550	$4,125	$3,700	$3,100	$2,600	$2,100	$1,650

ULTRALIGHT CARRY - 9mm Para., .38 Super, or .45 ACP cal., full size aluminum round butt frame, 5 in. stainless match grade barrel and bushing, flush cut and crowned, carbon steel slide, blue finish, 30 LPI high cut checkered front strap, top and rear slide serrations, tactical thumb safety, contoured mag well, G10 starburst grips, beavertail grip safety and hammer, battlesight with fiber optic front sight, countersunk slide stop.

MSR $3,650	$3,350	$2,950	$2,550	$2,150	$1,825	$1,525	$1,225

* ***Ultralight Carry Compact*** - 9mm Para., .38 Super, or .45 ACP cal., similar to Ultralight Carry, except has compact frame and 4 in. fluted barrel.

MSR $3,650	$3,350	$2,950	$2,550	$2,150	$1,825	$1,525	$1,225

* ***Ultralight Carry Sentinel*** - 9mm Para. cal., Sentinel aluminum round butt frame, 3 1/2 in. stainless match grade cone fluted barrel, 8 shot mag., carbon steel slide, blue finish, 30 LPI high cut checkered front strap, top and rear slide serrations, tactical thumb safety, contoured mag well, G10 starburst grips, beavertail grip safety and hammer, battlesight with fiber optic front sight, shortened rounded mag. release, countersunk slide stop, approx. 31 oz.

MSR $3,875	$3,500	$3,100	$2,650	$2,225	$1,875	$1,575	$1,275

CARRY COMP COMPACT - 9mm Para. (disc. 2011), .38 Super, or .45 ACP cal., full size stainless steel, lightweight aluminum, or carbon steel frame, 4 1/2 in. compensated match grade barrel, green, black, tan, or grey Amor-Tuff finish, high ride beavertail grip safety, Diamondwood grips, combat tactical sight system 30 LPI front strap checkering, skeletonized ultra light hammer.

MSR $3,765	$3,425	$3,025	$2,600	$2,175	$1,850	$1,550	$1,250

Add $165 for Carry Comp Compact Lightweight.

* ***Carry Comp Professional*** - 9mm Para. (disc. 2011), .38 Super, or .45 ACP cal., similar to Carry Comp, except has compact frame that is 1/2 in. shorter.

MSR $3,765	$3,425	$3,025	$2,600	$2,175	$1,850	$1,550	$1,250

Add $165 for Carry Comp Professional Lightweight.

X-TAC - .45 ACP cal., full size carbon steel frame, 8 shot mag., 5 in. stainless match grade barrel and bushing, carbon steel slide, parkerized finish, X-Tact front strap/mainspring housing, X-Tac rear cocking serrations, tactical thumb safety, contoured mag well, G10

GRADING - PPGS™	100%	98%	95%	90%	80%	70%	60%	LAST MSR

starburst grips, beavertail grip safety, battlesight with fiber optic front sight, 46.2 oz.

MSR $2,760	$2,495	$2,100	$1,800	$1,550	$1,225	$1,050	$925

Add $25 for X-Tac Compact with smaller frame.

CQB – 9mm Para., .38 Super, .40 S&W (new 2012), 10mm (new 2012), or .45 ACP cal., full size aluminum round butt frame, 5 in. stainless match grade barrel and bushing, flush cut and crowned, carbon steel slide, blue finish, 30 LPI high cut checkered front strap, top and rear slide serrations, tactical thumb safety, contoured mag well, G10 starburst grips, beavertail grip safety and hammer, battlesight with fiber optic front sight, countersunk slide stop.

MSR $2,865	$2,575	$2,150	$1,825	$1,550	$1,225	$1,050	$925

* ***CQB Elite*** – 9mm Para., 10mm, .38 Super, .40 S&W, or .45 ACP cal., full size carbon steel frame, 5 in. stainless match grade barrel and bushing, carbon steel slide, blue finish, 30 LPI high cut checkered front strap, top and rear slide serrations, tactical thumb safety, Speed-Chute mag well with lanyard loop, G10 diagonal flat bottom grips, beavertail grip safety, battlesight with fiber optic front sight.

MSR $3,425	$3,100	$2,700	$2,400	$2,000	$1,700	$1,400	$1,150

* ***CQB Tactical LE Light-Rail*** – 9mm Para., 10mm, .38 Super, .40 S&W, or .45 ACP cal., full size carbon steel frame, 5 in. stainless match grade bull barrel, carbon steel slide, blue finish, integral light rail, 30 LPI high cut checkered front strap, top and rear slide serrations, tactical thumb safety, Speed-Chute mag well with lanyard loop, G10 diagonal flat bottom grips, beavertail grip safety, battlesight with fiber optic front sight.

MSR $3,115	$2,700	$2,300	$2,000	$1,750	$1,450	$1,200	$1,050

* ***CQB Light-Rail*** – 9mm Para., 10mm, .38 Super, .40 S&W, or .45 ACP cal., full size aluminum frame, 5 in. stainless match grade barrel and bushing, carbon steel slide, blue finish, integral light rail, 30 LPI high cut checkered front strap, top and rear slide serrations, tactical thumb safety, contoured mag well, G10 starburst grips, beavertail grip safety, battlesight with fiber optic front sight.

MSR $3,005	$2,625	$2,225	$1,950	$1,700	$1,400	$1,175	$1,025

* ***CQB Lightweight/Light-Rail Lightweight*** – 9mm Para., 10mm, .38 Super, .40 S&W, or .45 ACP cal., full size aluminum frame, 5 in. stainless match grade barrel and bushing, carbon steel slide, blue finish, with or w/o integral light rail, 30 LPI high cut checkered front strap, top and rear slide serrations, tactical thumb safety, contoured mag well, G10 starburst grips, beavertail grip safety, battlesight with fiber optic front sight, weighs 14% less than steel model.

MSR $3,030	$2,650	$2,225	$1,950	$1,700	$1,400	$1,175	$1,125

Add $115 for light rail.

» **CQB Light-Rail Lightweight Professional** – 9mm Para., .38 Super or .45 ACP cal., similar to CQB Light-Rail Lightweight, except has professional size aluminum frame and 4 in. stainless match grade cone barrel.

MSR $3,205	$2,775	$2,350	$2,025	$1,775	$1,475	$1,225	$1,075

» **CQB Light-Rail Lightweight Compact** – 9mm Para., .38 Super (disc. 2011) or .45 ACP cal., compact aluminum round butt frame, 4 in. stainless match grade cone barrel, carbon steel slide, blue finish, integral light rail, 30 LPI high cut checkered front strap, top and rear slide serrations, tactical thumb safety, contoured mag well, G10 starburst grips, high ride beavertail grip safety, battlesight with fiber optic front sight, weighs 14% less than steel model.

MSR $3,280	$2,825	$2,375	$2,050	$1,800	$1,500	$1,200	$1,125

* ***CQB Compact*** – 9mm Para., .38 Super or .45 ACP cal., compact carbon steel frame, 4 in. stainless match grade cone barrel, carbon steel slide, blue finish, 30 LPI high cut checkered front strap, top and rear slide serrations, tactical thumb safety, contoured

GRADING - PPGS™	100%	98%	95%	90%	80%	70%	60%	LAST MSR

mag well, G10 starburst grips, high ride beavertail grip safety, battlesight with fiber optic front sight.

MSR $2,890	$2,575	$2,150	$1,850	$1,575	$1,250	$1,075	$950	

Add $205 for CQB Compact Lightweight.

PROFESSIONAL – 9mm Para., .38 Super, 40 S&W (disc. 2011), or .45 ACP cal., professional size carbon steel frame, 4 in. stainless match grade cone barrel, carbon steel slide, blue finish, 30 LPI high cut checkered front strap, top and rear slide serrations, tactical thumb safety, contoured mag well, G10 starburst grips, high ride beavertail grip safety, battlesight with fiber optic front sight.

MSR $2,920	$2,600	$2,150	$1,850	$1,575	$1,250	$1,075	$950	

* ***Professional Lightweight*** – 9mm Para., .38 Super or .45 ACP cal., similar to Professional, except has lightweight aluminum frame.

MSR $3,090	$2,725	$2,250	$1,925	$1,625	$1,275	$1,100	$1,000	

CLASSIC – 9mm Para., 10mm, .38 Super, 40 S&W, or .45 ACP cal., full size carbon steel frame, 5 in. stainless match grade barrel and bushing, carbon steel slide, two-tone finish, 30 LPI high cut checkered front strap, rear slide serrations, tactical thumb safety, contoured mag well, cocobolo double diamond grips, high ride beavertail grip safety, Lo-Mount adj. rear sight with improved ramp front sight.

MSR $3,030	$2,250	$1,950	$1,750	$1,425	$1,175	$1,000	$900	

PROTECTOR – 9mm Para., 10mm, .38 Super, 40 S&W, or .45 ACP cal., full size carbon steel frame, 5 in. stainless match grade barrel and bushing, carbon steel slide, two-tone finish, 30 LPI high cut checkered front strap, front and rear slide serrations, tactical thumb safety, contoured mag well, G10 starburst grips, high ride beavertail grip safety, battlesight with fiber optic front sight.

MSR $2,920	$2,275	$1,975	$1,675	$1,375	$1,150	$1,025	$875	

TACTICAL ELITE – 9mm Para., 10mm, .38 Super, 40 S&W, or .45 ACP cal., full size carbon steel frame, 5 in. stainless match grade heavy flanged cone barrel, carbon steel slide, blue finish, 30 LPI high cut checkered front strap, front and rear slide serrations, ambidextrous thumb safety, Speed-Chute mag well, G10 starburst grips, high ride beavertail grip safety, battlesight with fiber optic front sight.

MSR $3,650	$3,350	$2,950	$2,550	$2,150	$1,825	$1,525	$1,225	

Add $165 for Tactical Elite Lightweight.

ELITE PROFESSIONAL – 9mm Para., .38 Super or .45 ACP cal., professional size carbon steel frame, 4 in. stainless match grade heavy flanged cone barrel, carbon steel slide, blue finish, 30 LPI high cut checkered front strap, rear slide serrations, ambidextrous thumb safety, Speed-Chute mag well, G10 diagonal flat bottom grips, high ride beavertail grip safety, battlesight with fiber optic front sight.

MSR $3,650	$3,350	$2,950	$2,550	$2,150	$1,825	$1,525	$1,225	

Add $165 for Elite Professional Lightweight.

STEALTH (S.D.S.) – 9mm Para., .38 Super, .40 S&W (disc. 2011) or .45 ACP cal., compact carbon steel frame, 4 in. stainless match grade heavy flanged cone barrel, carbon steel slide, blue finish, 30 LPI high cut checkered front strap, rear slide serrations, ambidextrous thumb safety, contoured mag well, G10 starburst grips, high ride beavertail grip safety, battlesight with fiber optic front sight, full length guide rod with reverse plug.

MSR $3,535	$3,225	$2,875	$2,500	$2,100	$1,775	$1,475	$1,175	

Add $280 for Stealth Lightweight.

SENTINEL – 9mm Para. cal., carbon steel frame that is 1/2 in. shorter than compact, 3 1/2 in. stainless match grade cone barrel, 8 shot mag., carbon steel slide, blue finish, 30 LPI high cut checkered front strap, rear slide serrations, tactical thumb safety, contoured mag well, G10 slimline grips, high ride beavertail grip safety, battlesight with fiber optic front sight, full length guide rod with reverse plug, approx. 32 oz.

MSR $3,310	$2,850	$2,375	$2,050	$1,800	$1,500	$1,225	$1,125	

GRADING - PPGS™	100%	98%	95%	90%	80%	70%	60%	LAST MSR

Add $115 for Sentinel Lightweight.

* ***Sentinel Compact*** – 9mm Para. cal., similar to Sentinel, except has carbon steel compact frame. New 2012.

MSR $3,255	$2,800	$2,375	$2,050	$1,800	$1,500	$1,250	$1,075	

Add $170 for Sentinel Compact Lightweight.

* ***Sentinel Professional*** – 9mm Para. cal., similar to Sentinel, except has professional size carbon steel frame. New 2012.

MSR $3,310	$2,850	$2,375	$2,050	$1,800	$1,500	$1,225	$1,125	

Add $115 for Sentinel Professional Lightweight.

MS. SENTINEL – 9mm Para. cal., aluminum frame that is 1/2 in. shorter than compact, 3 1/2 in. stainless match grade cone fluted barrel, 8 shot mag., carbon steel slide, blue finish, 30 LPI high cut checkered front strap, rear slide serrations, tactical thumb safety, contoured mag well, cocobolo starburst grips, concealment Bullet Proof beavertail grip safety and hammer, Bullet Proof shortened/rounded mag. release, battlesight with fiber optic front sight, countersunk slide stop, heavy machine chamfer on bottom of slide, full length guide rod with reverse plug, approx. 31 oz.

MSR $3,875	$3,500	$3,100	$2,650	$2,225	$1,875	$1,575	$1,275	

BILL WILSON CARRY PISTOL – 45 ACP cal., compact carbon steel round butt frame, 4 in. stainless match grade cone barrel, 7 shot mag., carbon steel slide, blue finish, 30 LPI high cut checkered front strap, rear slide serrations, tactical thumb safety, contoured mag well, G10 starburst grips, high ride beavertail grip safety, battlesight with fiber optic front sight, countersunk slide stop, full length guide rod with reverse plug, approx. 39 oz.

MSR $3,205	$2,775	$2,350	$2,025	$1,775	$1,475	$1,275	$1,075	

SPEC-OPS 9 – 9mm Para. cal., 4 1/4 in. stainless steel match grade barrel, mid-size polymer frame with fully machined stainless steel rail insert, 16 shot mag., blue finish, 20 LPI checkered frontstap, concealment Bullet Proof beavertail grip safety and Spec-Ops ultralight hammer, tactical thumb safety, starburst grip pattern with textured grip radiuses, countersunk slide stop, contoured mag well, 30 LPI slide top serrations, Spec-Ops Lo-Profile rear sight, inline dovetail improved ramp fiber optic front sight, 37 oz.

MSR $2,285	$2,000	$1,750	$1,525	$1,300	$1,100	$900	$775	

HUNTER – 10mm or .460 Rowland cal., 5 1/2 single port compensated barrel with fully supported chamber, full size carbon steel frame with carbon steel slide, 30 LPI high cut checkered frontstrap, high ride beavertail grip safety, tactical thumb safety, contoured mag well, high ride beavertail grip safety, Crimson Trace laser grips, countersunk slide stop, full length guide rod with reverse plug, approx. 40 oz.

MSR $4,100	$3,650	$3,150	$2,750	$2,350	$1,875	$1,550	$1,350	

RIFLES

All rifles come standard with nylon tactical case.

A variety of accessories are available for additional cost - please contact the company directly for more information on available options (see Trademark Index).

IMPORTANT NOTE: On model(s) where *N/A has replaced the normal 100% value, it indicates current market conditions are too unstable to accurately ascertain 100%-60% values. Factory retail prices (MSRs) reflect most recent updates. For more up-to-date information on current pricing trends and additional useful information, please visit www.bluebookofgunvalues.com, select "Information & Services " from the menu, and click on "Additional Book Information".

UT-15 URBAN TACTICAL CARBINE – .223 Rem. cal., 16 1/4 in. fluted match grade barrel with muzzle brake, aluminum flattop upper and lower receiver, quad rail free float aluminum handguard, black, green, tan or gray anodized finish, 20 shot mag., single stage trigger, ERGO pistol grip, six position collapsible stock, 6.9 lbs. Disc. 2011.

	*N/A	$1,625	$1,450	$1,250	$1,050	$875	$675	*$2,025*

GRADING - PPGS™	100%	98%	95%	90%	80%	70%	60%	LAST MSR

M4 TACTICAL CARBINE – .223 Rem. cal., 16 1/4 in. fluted match grade barrel with muzzle brake, aluminum flattop upper and lower receiver, quad rail free float aluminum handguard, black, green, tan or gray anodized finish, 20 shot mag., single stage trigger, ERGO pistol grip, six position collapsible stock, 6.9 lbs. Disc. 2011.

	100%	98%	95%	90%	80%	70%	60%	LAST MSR
	*N/A	$1,625	$1,450	$1,250	$1,050	$875	$675	*$2,000*

SPR SPECIAL PURPOSE RIFLE – 5.56 NATO cal., 18 in. barrel, rifle length gas system with lo-profile gas block, forged flattop upper and lower receiver, quad rail free float aluminum handguard, black, green, tan or gray anodized finish, 20 shot mag., single stage trigger, ERGO pistol grip, A2 fixed buttstock, 6.9 lbs.

	100%	98%	95%	90%	80%	70%	60%
MSR $2,450	*N/A	$1,850	$1,625	$1,450	$1,250	$1,050	$875

SS-15 SUPER SNIPER RIFLE – .223 Rem. (disc. 2011) or .223 Wylde (new 2012) cal., 20 in. fluted heavy match grade stainless steel barrel with muzzle brake, aluminum flattop upper and lower receiver, aluminum free float handguard, black, green, tan or gray anodized finish, 20 shot mag., single stage trigger, ERGO pistol grip, fixed A2 stock, 8.7 lbs.

	100%	98%	95%	90%	80%	70%	60%
MSR $2,225	*N/A	$1,625	$1,450	$1,250	$1,050	$875	$675

RECON TACTICAL – 5.56 NATO, .300 Blackout, 6.8SPC, or 7.62x40 WT cal., 16, 18, or 20 (7.62x40 WT cal. only) in. medium weight stainless steel barrel, mid-length gas system with lo-profile gas block, quad rail, flash hider, 15 shot mag., Magpul CTR buttstock with MOE pistol grip and tactical trigger guard, black, green, tan, or grey finish, single stage trigger, 7 1/2 lbs.

	100%	98%	95%	90%	80%	70%	60%
MSR $2,250	*N/A	$1,775	$1,550	$1,225	$1,050	$925	$750

Add $50 for fluted barrel.

Add $300 for 6.8 SPC or 7.62x40 WT cal.

TACTICAL HUNTER LIGHTWEIGHT – 5.56 NATO, 6.8 SPCII, or 7.62x40 WT cal., 16.2, 18 (7.62x40 WT cal. only), or 20 (7.62x40 WT cal. only) in. match grade barrel, mid-length gas system with lo-profile gas block, Picatinny rail, ERGO pistol grip, tactical trigger guard, two-stage trigger, black Armor-Tuff finish, 20 shot mag., adj. black synthetic Rogers/Wilson Super-Stoc buttstock. New 2012.

	100%	98%	95%	90%	80%	70%	60%
MSR $2,250	*N/A	$1,775	$1,550	$1,225	$1,050	$925	$750

Add $300 for 6.8SPCII cal.

SHOTGUNS

Please refer to Scattergun Technologies for complete listing of shotguns and accessories.

WINCHESTER

Current trademark established in 1866 in New Haven, CT. Currently manufactured by Miroku of Japan since circa 1992, Herstal, Belgium (O/U shotguns since 2004), and in Columbia, SC (Model 70 only beginning 2008). Previously manufactured in New Haven, CT, 1866-2006, and by U.S. Repeating Arms from 1981-2006 through a licensing agreement from Olin Corp. to manufacture shotguns and rifles domestically using the Winchester Trademark. Corporate offices are located in Morgan, UT. Olin Corp. previously manufactured shotguns and rifles bearing the Winchester Hallmark at the Olin Kodensha Plant (closed 1989) located in Tochigi, Japan, Cobourg, Ontario, Canada, and also in European countries. In 1992, U.S. Repeating Arms was acquired by GIAT located in France. In late 1997, the Walloon region of Belgium acquired controlling interest of both Browning and U.S. Repeating Arms.

For more information and current pricing on both new and used Winchester airguns and current black powder models, please refer to the *Blue Book of Airguns* by Dr. Robert D. Beeman & John B. Allen, and the *Blue Book of Modern Black Powder Arms* by John Allen (also online).

In addition to the models listed within this section, Winchester also offered various models/variations that were available only at the annual SHOT SHOW beginning 2004. More research is underway to identify these models, in addition to their original MSRs (if listed).

WINCHESTER OVERVIEW

Note: Winchester Rifles are a field in themselves. Models Henry, 1866, 1873, 1876, 1885, 1886, 1892, 1894, and 1895 all were produced with a multitude of special order options. Special orders included front and rear special sights, half or 2/3 magazines, takedown, various barrel lengths (barrel lengths from 14 to 36 inches could be special ordered for many models), configurations, and weights, special metal finishes, deluxe wood (either checkered or carved) in a variety of finishes, an impressive range of engraving options, different butt plates, etc. All of these special orders act independently and interdependently to determine the correct value of a particular Winchester. Some of the finest rifles ever made are special order Winchesters engraved by the Ulrichs, G. Young, L.D. Nimschke, and others. For these reasons, a Model 1886 Winchester can range in price from $1,000 to over $500,000 - quite a price range for one model alone! When contemplating a purchase on the higher dollar range, qualified and professional opinions should be secured, preferably from at least 2 sources. Unfortunately many fakes and upgraded (non-original) guns have surfaced in the last 10 years with the sudden increase in prices. Winchesters shown in this section are priced assuming a standard model with no special orders. Any special orders will further add to the prices shown. Caliber rarities must also be considered. Many of the early Winchesters are broken down by year of manufacture. Refer to the "Model Serialization" section in this book.

A factory letter specifying original shipping information by serial number will certainly help solidify values shown on older out of production Winchester rifles and shotguns. A listing has been provided by model number with serialization range which can be historically researched by the Winchester Museum now located in Cody, WY. To use this outstanding service, make sure the model and its serial number fall within the ranges listed. Simply mail in your informational request with serial number, model, and caliber to the Cody Firearms Museum, 720 Sheridan Ave. in Cody, WY, 82414. There is a $70 charge for lever action models, and $85 for Model 21 SxS shotguns. Research results will include (if available) specimen caliber, barrel length, any special orders or finishes, return(s) to the factory, as well as any additional provenance contained by interpolating existing factory shipping ledgers. I would recommend a trip to the Buffalo Bill Historical Center as it contains the most comprehensive collection of projectile arms (including Chinese specimens that date back 2,000 years) and Americana housed under one roof in this country.

With the recent price appreciation of most upper condition Winchester rifles, excellent original condition has become so expensive that the many special order features Winchester offered do not cost that much more. However, on lesser condition guns that are much less expensive, these same special order features will cost more percentage-wise since the condition factor does not cost a premium.

Model 1866 Lever Action Rifle - ser. no. range 125,000-170,101.

Approx. 33 specimens have been researched outside of this ser. no. range.

Model 1873 Lever Action Rifle - ser. no. range 1-720,496.

Approx. 160 specimens have been researched outside of this ser. no. range.

Model 1876 Lever Action Rifle - ser. no. range 1-63,871.

Model 1883 Bolt Action Rifle (Hotchkiss Repeater) - ser. no. range 1-84,555.

May be referred to as Model 1879, 1880, or 1883.

Model 1885 Single Shot Rifle or Shotgun - ser. no. range 1-109,999.

Not available in ser. nos. 74,459-74,556. Also known as High and Low Wall.

Model 1886 Lever Action Rifle - ser. no. range 1-156,599.

Not available in ser. nos. 135,125-135,144 and 146,000-150,799.

Model 1887 & 1901 Lever Action Shotguns - ser. no. range 1-72,999.

Model 1890 Slide Action Rifle - ser. no. range 1-329,999.

Not available in ser. nos. 10,809-10,884, 20,000-29,999, 32,629-32,698, 37,599-37,627, 234,061-234,140, and 234,142-234,160.

Model 1892 Lever Action Rifle - ser. no. range 1-379,999.
Not available in ser. nos. 374,851-376,100.
Model 1893 Slide Action Shotgun - ser. no. range 1-34,050.
Model 1894 Lever Action Rifle - ser. no. range 1-353,999.
Model 1895 Lever Action Rifle - ser. no. range 1-59,999.
Model "Lee" Bolt Action Rifle - ser. no. range 1-19,999.
Model 1897 Slide Action Shotgun - ser. no. range 34,051-377,999.
Model 1903 Semi-Auto .22 Cal. Rifle - ser. no. range 1-39,999.
Model 1905 Semi-Auto Rifle - ser. no. range 1-29,078.
Model 1906 Slide Action Rifle - ser. no. range 1-79,999.
Model 1907 Semi-Auto Rifle - ser. no. range 1-9,999.

Winchester factory data on models produced between approx. 1907-1961 is almost non-existent (except Custom Shop mfg.) since there was a fire at the Winchester factory in 1961.

A NOTE ON WINCHESTER FINISHES: It is very important to understand that there is a big value difference between a Model 1873 with 90% bright blue as opposed to a gun that has patina finish (turning brown). A bright blue specimen might bring several times more, because it is closer to the way it originally left the factory - with bright bluing. "Brown" guns are simply not as desirable as guns that show little or no use and retain bright blue finish.

GRADING EXPLANATION FOR WINCHESTER LEVER ACTIONS

A combination of grading systems is being used exclusively for Winchester Models 1873 and 1876 in this section to assist the reader in ascertaining the value of a particular specimen more accurately. They work as follows - the top pricing line contains three value ranges (Above Average, Average, or Below Average) which have been created to encompass most of the specimens commonly encountered within these models.

Since there is a drastic value difference between 95%-50% bright blue and 30% dull patina/fading finish on older Winchesters, a traditional grading/value line has been included to give you examples of values from 100% down to 10% providing you a better perspective of the top end of the marketplace.

The three value groupings include "Below Average," "Average," and "Above Average" condition factors. These value ranges indicate the following conditions:

BELOW AVERAGE VALUE RANGE - a specimen with no finish remaining, perhaps some parts have been replaced, deteriorated metal may be lightly pitted with faint barrel/frame markings, rounded edges of wood and metal, wood showing much wear with possible repairs or cracks, must be in working order.

AVERAGE VALUE RANGE - a specimen with all original parts, exhibits gun metal patina finish, metal mostly smooth (perhaps lightly pitted), principal lettering and markings legible throughout, wood showing honest wear with little finish remaining (may have small cracks and other imperfections), good working order.

ABOVE AVERAGE VALUE RANGE - a specimen featuring unpolished brass (on Henrys and Model 1866s) or plum brown patina with traces of bluing in protected areas (on all steel frame models), sharp corners, crisp barrel markings, traces of original finish remaining, metal should exhibit nice patina or older flaking finish, wood should have some original stock varnish remaining and minor handling marks and dings, good bore, perfect working order with no replacement parts.

VALUES FOR 10%-100% CONDITION FACTORS - this includes the entire range of condition factors from 10% - 100% in many cases. N/As indicate that the condition factor is so infrequently encountered, it does not have a value. Normally, below average value ranges will approximately correspond to the 0%-10% pricing line values, average value range represents 10%-20%, and above average can range from 20%-40%, depending on the model. Typically, over 50% refers to a rifle which exhibits over 30% bright bluing/case colors or unpolished brass on the frame.
See PPGS for precentage grading examples.

PISTOLS: SINGLE SHOT

SINGLE SHOT PISTOL – .22 LR cal., bolt action, walnut, brass, or pot metal grips, 9 in. barrel with open sights, no two are exactly alike, and quality can run from very good to

Above Average	Average	Below Average

crude, ser. nos. under 20.

Prices on this model typically range from $3,750 - $4,950, depending on original condition.

RIFLES: LEVER ACTIONS - 1860-1964

Values by percentages are not listed on the Models Henry and 1866, as original condition over 30% is seldom encountered.

Volcanic pistols and carbines may be found under the Volcanic listing.

For the following lever action rifles, multiple special order features that add value are not cumulative (i.e., do not add 30% for an octagon barrel to the premium for a Deluxe rifle). Also, as a general rule, premiums for calibers, options, and special order features become less important on the following lever action models in under 90% original condition (i.e., do not add a 50% premium for .44-40 WCF on a Model 1892 rifle if original condition is under 90%).

Subtract 20%-40% on the following models if metal is pitted or poorly refinished (i.e., rounded edges on metal because of over buffing, and/or wood has been excessively sanded).

HENRY RIFLE – .44 Henry Flat (rimfire) cal., 15 shot, 24 in. barrel with integral slotted tube mag. and loading lever, blue barrel, brass or iron frame. Approx. 13,000 total production, mfg. 1860-1866.

Because almost all Henrys have little or no original finish remaining, values are in ranges rather than listed by separate condition factors.

* ***Henry Rifle Iron Frame Model*** – frame made of iron, round type buttplate, without lever latch, adj. sporting type rear leaf sight, serial numbers are in three digits only. Total production is believed to be less than 300.

$75,000 - $150,000 $50,000 - $75,000 $25,000 - $50,000

* ***Henry Rifle First Model*** – approx. 3,500 mfg., generally serialized below 3,500, with or without lever latch, perch belly stock and slotted receiver for rear sight.

$50,000 - $100,000 $25,000 - $50,000 $12,000 - $25,000

* ***Henry Rifle Martial Marked*** – contracted by U.S. military for Civil War use, denoted by "C.G.C." inspector markings on upper barrel breech and stock, approx. 1,900 with serialization scattered.

$60,000 - $120,000 $35,000 - $60,000 $20,000 - $35,000

This rifle was the most revolutionary shoulder weapon introduced in the Civil War.

* ***Henry Rifle Late Model*** – similar to first model, except buttplate heel has pointed profile, lever latch became standard and receiver is not slotted for rear sight, serial numbers over approx. 3,500, most commonly encountered Henry with approx. 8,000 mfg.

$40,000 - $75,000 $20,000 - $40,000 $10,000 - $20,000

MODEL 1866 – .44 rimfire or centerfire (4th Model only), 24 in. barrel, blue barrel with brass frame, differs from Henry in that it has a wood forearm, frame cartridge loading port, and separate tube mag. Total production reached 170,101 for all models, mfg. 1866-98.

Because almost all Model 1866s have little or no original finish remaining, values are in ranges rather than listed by separate condition factors.

* ***Model 1866 First Model Rifle*** – "Improved Henry" action, .44 cal. rimfire, without forend cap, serialization is concealed on lower tang inside buttstock, serial range is from mid-12,000 to mid-15,000 (in Henry serial range sequence).

$40,000 - $85,000 $20,000 - $40,000 $7,500 - $20,000

Buyer beware - watch for fakes!

* ***Model 1866 Carbine First Model*** – same action as Rifle, only with 20 in. barrel, 2 barrel bands and saddle ring.

$25,000 - $40,000 $10,000 - $25,000 $4,000 - $10,000

* ***Model 1866 Rifle Second Model*** – "New Model" with redesigned frame, with Henry barrel markings, serial number inside on the earlier guns after ser. no. 19,000, outside lower tang beneath lever (approx. after ser. no. 20,000).

$25,000 - $45,000 $12,500 - $25,000 $5,000 - $12,500

	Above Average	Average	Below Average

* ***Model 1866 Carbine Second Model*** – frame and other changes similar to Second Model Rifle.

	$20,000 - $35,000	$8,000 - $20,000	$3,000 - $8,000

* ***Model 1866 Rifle Third Model*** – block style serial numbers usually located behind trigger, improved frame. Serial numbered approx. 25,000-149,000.

	$20,000 - $35,000	$8,000 - $20,000	$3,000 - $8,000

* ***Model 1866 Carbine Third Model*** – same changes as Model 1866 Third Model Rifle, 20 in. barrel with 2 bands.

	$20,000 - $35,000	$8,000 - $20,000	$3,000 - $8,000

* ***Model 1866 Musket Third Model*** – 27 in. round barrel, 24 in. magazine, 3 barrel bands.

	$20,000 - $35,000	$8,000 - $20,000	$3,000 - $8,000

* ***Model 1866 Rifle/Carbine/Musket Fourth Model*** – .44 cal., twin rimfire and centerfire, script style serial number on lower tang near lever latch, improved frame, serial range approx. 149,000-170,101.

	$20,000 - $35,000	$8,000 - $20,000	$3,000 - $8,000

Subtract 20% for steel buttplate and forend cap on rifle.

This rifle is usually found with steel buttplate and forend cap.

100%	98%	95%	90%	80%	70%	60%	50%	40%	30%	20%	10%

MODEL 1873 – .32-20 WCF, .38-40 WCF, or .44-40 WCF cal., iron frame with sideplates, frame loading port, 20 or 24 in. round or octagon barrel, rifles have forearm caps and carbines have forearm bands, tube mag., blue finish with case hardened parts, oil finished stock, serial numbered on lower tang, 720,610 mfg. between 1873-1919.

Since early Model 1873s were only made in .44 cal., no caliber markings are present. With the introduction of additional calibers, barrels (just in front of the receiver) and the brass elevator were stamped with the caliber.

Model 1873s are serial numbered sequentially on the lower tang. On guns serial numbered 80,000 to 170,000, an "A" followed the number. From 170,000 to 190,000, either "A" or "B" may be found, while after 200,000, usually "B" was used. The letter does not seem to have any definite meaning. The earliest guns had no marking on the upper tang, but were marked "Model 1873" on the lower tang next to the ser. no. up to number 350, after which "Model 1873" is marked on the upper tang, where it remained through the model run.

* ***Model 1873 First Model Rifle*** – serial numbers approx. 1-30,000, sliding thumbprint dust cover on 2 guides which are an integral part of upper frame, absence of any cal. marking.

N/A	N/A	$22,000	$18,000	$16,000	$12,000	$10,000	$6,000	$4,000	$2,500	$1,500	$1,000

A below average Model 1873 First Model Rifle is currently valued in the $900-$1,650 range.

An average Model 1873 First Model Rifle is currently valued in the $1,650-$2,500 range.

An above average Model 1873 First Model Rifle is currently valued in the $2,500-$4,950 range.

Percentage values listed above are for original guns with corresponding percentages of bright blue finish remaining (refer to PPGS for accurate grading).

* ***Model 1873 Carbine First Model*** – 20 in. round barrel with carbine style forearm band. Distinctive curved buttplate, with saddle ring.

N/A	N/A	$28,000	$23,000	$18,000	$14,000	$10,000	$7,000	$5,500	$4,000	$2,500	$1,500

A below average Model 1873 Carbine First Model is currently valued in the $1,100-$2,100 range.

An average Model 1873 Carbine First Model is currently valued in the $2,100-$3,350 range.

An above average Model 1873 Carbine First Model is currently valued in the $3,350-$4,650 range.

Percentage values listed above are for original guns with corresponding percentages of bright blue finish remaining (refer to PPGS for accurate grading).

* ***Model 1873 Musket First Model*** – 30 in. round barrel, 27 in. mag. with 3 barrel bands, approx. 500 mfg.

N/A	N/A	$17,000	$15,000	$13,000	$11,000	$9,000	$7,000	$5,500	$3,600	$2,200	$1,500

100%	98%	95%	90%	80%	70%	60%	50%	40%	30%	20%	10%

A below average Model 1873 Musket First Model is currently valued in the $1,100-$2,150 range.
An average Model 1873 Musket First Model is currently valued in the $2,150-$2,650 range.
An above average Model 1873 Musket First Model is currently valued in the $2,650-$3,750 range.

Percentage values listed above are for original guns with corresponding percentages of bright blue finish remaining (refer to PPGS for accurate grading).

* ***Model 1873 Rifle Second Model*** – improved dust cover which slides on center rail on rear section of frame top which is held in place by two screws, serial range 31,000-90,000.

N/A	N/A	$12,000	$11,000	$9,000	$8,700	$6,600	$4,500	$3,300	$2,250	$1,300	$800

A below average Model 1873 Rifle Second Model is currently valued in the $675-$1,325 range.
An average Model 1873 Rifle Second Model is currently valued in the $1,325-$1,825 range.
An above average Model 1873 Rifle Second Model is currently valued in the $1,825-$2,750 range.

Percentage values listed above are for original guns with corresponding percentages of bright blue finish remaining (refer to PPGS for accurate grading).

* ***Model 1873 Carbine Second Model*** – changes similar to 1873 Second Model Rifle, with 20 in. round barrel and 2 barrel bands.

N/A	N/A	$20,500	$17,750	$15,750	$13,000	$11,000	$9,000	$6,800	$4,500	$2,500	$1,200

A below average Model 1873 Carbine Second Model is currently valued in the $875-$1,550 range.
An average Model 1873 Carbine Second Model is currently valued in the $1,550-$2,425 range.
An above average Model 1873 Carbine Second Model is currently valued in the $2,425-$3,300 range.

Percentage values listed above are for original guns with corresponding percentages of bright blue finish remaining (refer to PPGS for accurate grading).

* ***Model 1873 Musket Second Model*** – changes similar to 1873 Second Model Rifle, with 30 in. barrel and 3 barrel bands.

N/A	N/A	$6,250	$5,600	$5,000	$4,200	$3,500	$3,000	$2,500	$1,800	$1,400	$1,200

A below average Model 1873 Musket Second Model is currently valued in the $1,000-$1,400 range.
An average Model 1873 Musket Second Model is currently valued in the $1,400-$1,800 range.
An above average Model 1873 Musket Second Model is currently valued in the $1,800-$2,500 range.

Percentage values listed above are for original guns with corresponding percentages of bright blue finish remaining (refer to PPGS for accurate grading).

* ***Model 1873 Rifle Third Model*** – dust cover rail integral with frame, serial 90,000-end of production.

N/A	N/A	$7,500	$6,300	$5,500	$4,500	$3,750	$3,250	$3,000	$1,700	$1,500	$800

Add 20% for .44-40 WCF cal.
Add 30% for octagon barrel for .44-40 WCF cal. only.
A below average Model 1873 Rifle Third Model is currently valued in the $750-$1,000 range.
An average Model 1873 Rifle Third Model is currently valued in the $1,000-$1,650 range.
An above average Model 1873 Rifle Third Model is currently valued in the $1,650-$2,300 range.

Percentage values listed above are for original guns with corresponding percentages of bright blue finish remaining (refer to PPGS for accurate grading).

* ***Model 1873 Carbine Third Model*** – changes similar to 1873 Rifle Third Model, with 20 in. barrel and 2 barrel bands.

N/A	N/A	$15,000	$14,000	$12,000	$11,000	$10,000	$7,500	$5,600	$3,400	$2,300	$1,200

Add 10% for .32-20 WCF cal.
A below average Model 1873 Carbine Third Model is currently valued in the $800-$1,300 range.
An average Model 1873 Carbine Third Model is currently valued in the $1,300-$2,000 range.
An above average Model 1873 Carbine Third Model is currently valued in the $2,000-$3,000 range.

Percentage values listed above are for original guns with corresponding percentages of bright blue finish remaining (refer to PPGS for accurate grading).

100%	98%	95%	90%	80%	70%	60%	50%	40%	30%	20%	10%

* ***Model 1873 Musket Third Model*** – 30 in. round barrel and 3 barrel bands.

100%	98%	95%	90%	80%	70%	60%	50%	40%	30%	20%	10%
N/A	N/A	$5,100	$4,500	$4,000	$3,400	$2,900	$2,400	$1,850	$1,300	$1,000	$850

A below average Model 1873 Musket Third Model is currently valued in the $800-$1,200 range.
An average Model 1873 Musket Third Model is currently valued in the $1,200-$1,500 range.
An above average Model 1873 Musket Third Model is currently valued in the $1,500-$2,000 range.

Percentage values listed above are for original guns with corresponding percentages of bright blue finish remaining (refer to PPGS for accurate grading).

* ***Model 1873 .22 Rimfire Rifle*** – .22 S, L, or Extra L (very rare) cal., 24 in. barrel, no loading gate, the first .22 caliber repeater, 19,552 produced, mfg. 1884-1904. Made in rifle configuration only.

100%	98%	95%	90%	80%	70%	60%	50%	40%	30%	20%	10%
N/A	N/A	$10,250	$8,750	$7,750	$7,000	$5,800	$4,750	$3,600	$2,400	$1,200	$800

Add 30% for takedown model.
A below average Model 1873 .22 Rimfire Rifle is currently valued in the $725-$1,375 range.
An average Model 1873 .22 Rimfire Rifle is currently valued in the $1,375-$1,875 range.
An above average Model 1873 .22 Rimfire Rifle is currently valued in the $1,875-$2,500 range.

The takedown mechanism is unique in that a pin is driven out of the receiver, and is very prone to wear.

Percentage values listed above are for original guns with corresponding percentages of bright blue finish remaining (refer to PPGS for accurate grading).

* ***Model 1873 Deluxe Rifle*** – distinguishable by color case hardened frame and deluxe checkered stock and forearm, this model was special order only with many features and options available at an extra cost.

100%	98%	95%	90%	80%	70%	60%	50%	40%	30%	20%	10%
N/A	N/A	N/A	$55,000	$47,500	$40,000	$32,500	$25,000	$17,500	$10,000	$7,500	$5,000

A below average Model 1873 Deluxe Rifle is currently valued in the $2,750-$4,500 range.
An average Model 1873 Deluxe Rifle is currently valued in the $4,500-$7,500 range.
An above average Model 1873 Deluxe Rifle is currently valued in the $7,500-$10,000 range.

Values are for standard deluxe gun, w/o any special orders.

Percentage values listed above are for original guns with corresponding percentages of bright blue finish remaining (refer to PPGS for accurate grading).

* ***Model 1873 Trapper's Carbine*** – all features similar to .22 rimfire model, except available with 14, 15, or 16 in. barrel.

100%	98%	95%	90%	80%	70%	60%	50%	40%	30%	20%	10%
N/A	N/A	$34,000	$31,500	$27,000	$23,000	$20,500	$17,000	$12,250	$8,500	$6,500	$4,000

A below average Model 1873 Trapper's Carbine is currently valued in the $2,250-$3,500 range.
An average Model 1873 Trapper's Carbine is currently valued in the $3,500-$4,500 range.
An above average Model 1873 Trapper's Carbine is currently valued in the $4,500-$6,000 range.

Other barrel lengths were also available on this model, but are much rarer.

Percentage values listed above are for original guns with corresponding percentages of bright blue finish remaining (refer to PPGS for accurate grading).

* ***Model 1873 "One of One Thousand "*** – special care taken during assembly and testing to guarantee better accuracy, markings on top of breech designate model, deluxe walnut, extremely rare, barrel marked "One of One Thousand" in most cases, 136 mfg. Original cost was $100.

Values can range from $75,000 - $500,000, depending on condition.

A factory letter is a must for any "One of One Thousand" Winchester. Watch for fake letters. Note: Rarity of the "One of One Thousand" and the "One of One Hundred" models has made unethical upgrading of this model fairly common. Use extreme caution in purchasing.

* ***Model 1873 "One of One Hundred "*** – similar to "One of One Thousand" only rarer, 8 known. Sold new for $20 over the list price of a similarly equipped Model 1873.

Values can range from $75,000 - $500,000, depending on condition.

A factory letter is a must for any "One of One Hundred" Winchester. Watch for fake letters.

MODEL 1876 – .40-60 WCF, .45-60 WCF, .45-75 WCF (first caliber offered), or .50-95 Express cal., 22, 26, or 28 in. round or octagon barrel, similar but larger frame than Model

1873, tube mag., rifles have forearm caps while carbines and muskets have forearm bands and caps, crescent butt, blue finish, straight grip stock, 63,871 mfg. between 1876-1897.

The Model 1876 was also called the Centennial Model since its introduction coincided with the U.S. Centennial Exposition held in Philadelphia, PA in 1876. Popularity for this model decreased ten years later when the more powerful and advanced Model 1886 was introduced.

1876 Deluxe Models with 90%+ original case colors are extremely rare.

* ***Model 1876 Rifle First Model*** – serial numbered approx. 1-5,000, distinguishable by no dust cover on frame top.

N/A	N/A	$21,250	$19,125	$17,000	$14,875	$12,750	$10,625	$8,400	$6,200	$3,950	$2,700

A below average Model 1876 Rifle First Model is currently valued in the $1,875-$2,525 range.
An average Model 1876 First Model is currently valued in the $2,525-$3,600 range.
An above average Model 1876 First Model is currently valued in the $3,600-$4,400 range.

Percentage values listed above are for original guns with corresponding percentages of bright blue finish remaining (refer to PPGS for accurate grading).

* ***Model 1876 Carbine First Model*** – 22 in. round barrel, one barrel band, saddle ring, full-length forearm giving a musket appearance.

N/A	N/A	$20,000	$18,000	$16,000	$14,000	$12,000	$10,000	$7,900	$5,800	$3,800	$2,500

A below average Model 1876 Carbine First Model is currently valued in the $2,000-$2,500 range.
An average Model 1876 Carbine First Model is currently valued in the $2,500-$3,250 range.
An above average Model 1876 Carbine First Model is currently valued in the $3,250-$4,500 range.

Percentage values listed above are for original guns with corresponding percentages of bright blue finish remaining (refer to PPGS for accurate grading).

* ***Model 1876 Musket First Model*** – 32 in. round barrel with 1 band, scarce model because no foreign military contracts.

N/A	N/A	$30,000	$25,250	$21,350	$19,250	$16,450	$12,600	$9,800	$6,800	$4,600	$3,300

A below average Model 1876 Musket First Model is currently valued in the $2,500-$3,750 range.
An average Model 1876 Musket First Model is currently valued in the $3,750-$5,500 range.
An above average Model 1876 Musket First Model is currently valued in the $5,500-$6,200 range.

Percentage values listed above are for original guns with corresponding percentages of bright blue finish remaining (refer to PPGS for accurate grading).

* ***Model 1876 Rifle Second Model*** – "Thumbprint" dust cover rail held on by screw, serial range 5,000-30,000.

N/A	N/A	$15,000	$12,750	$10,875	$9,000	$7,750	$6,000	$4,750	$3,750	$2,250	$1,500

Add 35% for .50-95 WCF cal.
A below average Model 1876 Rifle Second Model is currently valued in the $1,000-$1,600 range.
An average Model 1876 Rifle Second Model is currently valued in the $1,750-$2,500 range.
An above average Model 1876 Rifle Second Model is currently valued in the $2,750-$3,7500 range.

Percentage values listed above are for original guns with corresponding percentages of bright blue finish remaining (refer to PPGS for accurate grading).

* ***Model 1876 Carbine Second Model*** – changes similar to Model 1876 Rifle Early Second Model, with 22 in. round barrel and full length forearm giving a musket appearance.

N/A	N/A	$22,500	$18,000	$13,000	$10,500	$8,500	$6,750	$5,000	$3,250	$2,400	$1,650

A below average Model 1876 Carbine Second Model is currently valued in the $1,200-$1,500 range.
An average Model 1876 Carbine Second Model is currently valued in the $1,500-$2,500 range.
An above average Model 1876 Carbine Second Model is currently valued in the $2,500-3,500 range.

Percentage values listed above are for original guns with corresponding percentages of bright blue finish remaining (refer to PPGS for accurate grading).

* ***Model 1876 Musket Second Model*** – changes similar to Model 1876 Rifle Early Second Model, with 32 in. round barrel and carbine forend tip.

N/A	N/A	$19,500	$17,500	$14,000	$12,750	$11,250	$10,500	$8,500	$5,750	$3,250	$2,000

A below average Model 1876 Musket Second Model is currently valued in the $1,200-$2,500 range.

100%	98%	95%	90%	80%	70%	60%	50%	40%	30%	20%	10%

An average Model 1876 Musket Second Model is currently valued in the $2,500-$3,750 range.
An above average Model 1876 Musket Second Model is currently valued in the $3,750-$5,000 range.

Percentage values listed above are for original guns with corresponding percentages of bright blue finish remaining (refer to PPGS for accurate grading).

* ***Model 1876 Rifle Third Model*** – dust cover rail integral with frame, serial range 30,000-end of production.

N/A	N/A	$15,000	$12,750	$10,750	$9,000	$7,500	$6,000	$4,750	$3,750	$2,250	$1,500

Add 25% for .50-95 WCF cal.
A below average Model 1876 Rifle Third Model is currently valued in the $1,000-$1,600 range.
An average Model 1876 Rifle Third Model is currently valued in the $1,600-$2,500 range.
An above average Model 1876 Rifle Third Model is currently valued in the $2,750-$3,750 range.

Percentage values listed above are for original guns with corresponding percentages of bright blue finish remaining (refer to PPGS for accurate grading).

* ***Model 1876 Carbine Third Model*** – frame similar to Model 1876 Rifle Third Model, with 22 in. round barrel and full-length forearm giving a musket appearance.

N/A	N/A	$22,500	$18,000	$13,000	$10,500	$8,500	$6,750	$5,000	$3,250	$2,400	$1,650

A below average Model 1876 Carbine Third Model is currently valued in the $1,200-$1,500 range.
An average Model 1876 Carbine Third Model is currently valued in the $1,500-$2,500 range.
An above average Model 1876 Carbine Third Model is currently valued in the $2,500-$3,500 range.

Percentage values listed above are for original guns with corresponding percentages of bright blue finish remaining (refer to PPGS for accurate grading).

* ***Model 1876 Musket Third Model*** – frame similar to Model 1876 Rifle Third Model, with 32 in. round barrel.

N/A	N/A	$17,000	$15,000	$13,000	$11,000	$9,500	$8,250	$6,500	$4,500	$3,000	$2,000

A below average Model 1876 Musket Third Model is currently valued in the $1,500-$2,000 range.
An average Model 1876 Musket Third Model is currently valued in the $2,000-$3,000 range.
An above average Model 1876 Musket Third Model is currently valued in the $3,000-$4,500 range.

Percentage values listed above are for original guns with corresponding percentages of bright blue finish remaining (refer to PPGS for accurate grading).

* ***Model 1876 Deluxe Rifle*** – distinguishable by color case hardened frame and deluxe checkered stock and forearm, this model was special order only with many features and options available at extra cost.

N/A	N/A	N/A	$80,000	$72,500	$65,000	$55,000	$45,000	$35,000	$25,000	$17,500	$10,500

Values are for standard deluxe gun.
A below average Model 1876 Deluxe Rifle is currently valued in the $4,400-$11,000 range.
An average Model 1876 Deluxe Rifle is currently valued in the $11,000-$16,500 range.
An above average Model 1876 Deluxe Rifle is currently valued in the $16,500-$30,000 range.

Percentage values listed above are for original guns with corresponding percentages of bright blue finish remaining (refer to PPGS for accurate grading).

* ***Model 1876 "One of One Thousand"*** – special care taken in manufacture to guarantee better accuracy, markings on top of breech designate model, deluxe walnut, extremely rare, 54 mfg. Original cost was $100.

Values can range from $75,000 - $500,000, depending on condition.

A factory letter is a must for any "One of One Thousand" Winchester. Watch for fake letters. Values are not listed because too few original specimens are bought or sold to accurately establish pricing. A factory letter is a must for any "One of One Thousand" Winchester.

Note: Rarity of the "One of One Thousand" and the "One of One Hundred" models has made unethical upgrading of this model fairly common. Use extreme caution in purchasing.

* ***Model 1876 "One of One Hundred"*** – similar to "One of One Thousand" only rarer, 8 mfg. Sold new for $20 over the list price of a similarly equipped Model 1876.

100%	98%	95%	90%	80%	70%	60%	50%	40%	30%	20%	10%

Values can range from $75,000 - $500,000, depending on condition.

A factory letter is a must for any "One of One Hundred" Winchester. Believe it or not, watch for fake letters. Values are not listed because too few original specimens are bought or sold to accurately establish pricing. A factory letter is a must for any "One of One Hundred" Winchester.

* ***Model 1876 Northwest Mounted Police Carbine*** – .45-75 WCF cal. only, 22 in. barrel, "NWMP" or "MP" marking may appear on stock (with wear, this cartouche may not be visible - the majority were not marked) approx. 1,600 mfg., factory records can only verify 150.

N/A	N/A	$16,500	$13,750	$11,000	$9,000	$7,750	$6,250	$5,250	$4,250	$3,500	$2,750

A below average Model 1876 Northwest Mounted Police Carbine is currently valued in the $2,500-$4,150 range.

An average Model 1876 Northwest Mounted Police Carbine is currently valued in the $4,150-$5,250 range.

An above average Model 1876 Northwest Mounted Police Carbine is currently valued in the $5,250-$6,500 range.

Above average specimens in this model should have traces of blue. Be very wary of the stock cartouche since these buttstocks were sold as surplus back in the 1920s. A letter of authenticity is a good idea on this model.

Percentage values listed above are for original guns with corresponding percentages of bright blue finish remaining (refer to PPGS for accurate grading).

MODEL 1886 – .33 WCF, .38-56 WCF, .38-70 WCF (830 mfg.), .40-65 WCF, .40-70 WCF (629 mfg.), .40-82 WCF, .45-70 Govt., .45-90, .50-110 Express, or .50-100-450 (234 mfg.) cal. available, Browning's first high power lever action design distinguishable by vertical locking bars, .45-70 Govt. most popular cal., 26 in. round or octagon barrel, tube mag., steel forend cap, straight grip stock. Case colored receiver was standard finish until 1901, then blue became the standard finish. Approx. 159,990 mfg. between 1886-1935.

On the following Model 1886 variations add the percentages non-cumulative for special order features and/or configuration.

Add 20% for octagon barrel.

Add 30% for octagon barrel with takedown (not on Lightweight).

Add 25% for .45-70 Govt. or .45-90 cal.

Add 100% for .50-110 or 200% for .50-100-450 cal.

Add 100%-150% for case colored receivers on standard guns only (pre-1902 mfg.), depending on original condition.

* ***Model 1886 Standard Rifle*** – various cals., color case hardening was standard on the frame, buttplate, and forend cap until 1901 (approx. 122,000 ser. no. range), when the standard finish became blue.

N/A	N/A	$8,525	$7,700	$6,600	$5,950	$5,125	$4,000	$2,975	$2,000	$1,625	$1,250

* ***Model 1886 Carbine*** – same general specifications as Rifle, except 22 in. round barrel and saddle ring, solid frame only.

N/A	N/A	$20,000	$17,000	$14,500	$12,000	$10,000	$8,250	$6,300	$5,000	$3,600	$2,400

Add 40% for full stock carbine (very rare).

.33 WCF cal. is the rarest caliber in this model.

* ***Model 1886 Musket*** – almost all are chambered in .45-70 Govt. cal., 30 in. round barrel, full-length military style forearm, military sights, only 350 mfg., very rare.

N/A	N/A	$20,000	$17,000	$14,500	$12,000	$10,000	$8,250	$6,300	$5,000	$3,600	$2,400

Most specimens encountered in this variation are in very good condition. A pitted musket is almost never encountered.

* ***Model 1886 Deluxe Rifle*** – distinguishable by deluxe checkered pistol grip walnut stock and forearm, color case hardened frame, this model was special order only with many features and options available at extra cost.

N/A	N/A	N/A	$39,500	$34,500	$29,500	$25,000	$20,000	$15,500	$11,500	$7,500	$4,000

Values are for standard deluxe gun, w/o any special orders.

* ***Model 1886 Lightweight Rifle*** – .45-70 Govt. or .33 WCF cal. only, 22 (.45-70 Govt. cal.) or 24 (.33 WCF cal.) in. round nickel steel tapered barrel, half mag., rubber shotgun buttplate.

» **Model 1886 Lightweight .33 cal.**

100%	98%	95%	90%	80%	70%	60%	50%	40%	30%	20%	10%
N/A	N/A	$4,500	$4,000	$3,200	$2,600	$2,200	$1,800	$1,500	$1,250	$1,000	$600

» **Model 1886 Lightweight .45-70 Govt. cal.**

100%	98%	95%	90%	80%	70%	60%	50%	40%	30%	20%	10%
N/A	N/A	$6,500	$5,750	$5,000	$4,200	$3,625	$3,150	$2,725	$2,000	$1,650	$1,200

Since lightweight rifles were fairly late production, all specimens are blue and in very good condition usually.

* ***Model 1886 Deluxe Lightweight Rifle*** – distinguishable by fancy checkered wood stock.

100%	98%	95%	90%	80%	70%	60%	50%	40%	30%	20%	10%
N/A	N/A	$19,500	$16,700	$13,250	$11,000	$9,500	$7,100	$5,600	$4,500	$3,300	$2,500

Since lightweight rifles were fairly late production, all specimens are blue and in very good condition usually.

MODEL 1892 RIFLE – .25-20 WCF, .32-20 WCF, .38-40 WCF, or .44-40 WCF cal., 24 in. round or octagon barrel, blue, tube mag., forend cap, crescent butt. Approx. 1,000,000 mfg. between 1892-1941.

100%	98%	95%	90%	80%	70%	60%	50%	40%	30%	20%	10%
N/A	N/A	$3,400	$2,800	$2,175	$1,725	$1,275	$1,100	$900	$750	$600	$500

Add 75% for .44-40 WCF cal.
Add 25% for .38-40 WCF cal.
Add 25% for Takedown Model.

A short rifle configuration was available in this model with special order barrels under 16 inches, 12 in. being the rarest. These guns are very rare (most went to South America) and prices typically range $2,750-$8,000, depending on original condition.

* ***Model 1892 Rifle Antique*** – .25-20 WCF, .32-20 WCF, .38-40 WCF, or .44-40 WCF cal., 24 in. round or octagon barrel, blue, tube mag., forend cap, crescent butt, ser. no. range under 168,000. Mfg. 1892-1898.

100%	98%	95%	90%	80%	70%	60%	50%	40%	30%	20%	10%
N/A	N/A	$4,900	$3,550	$2,850	$2,450	$1,850	$1,650	$1,400	$1,125	$950	$750

Add 100% for .44-40 WCF cal.
Add 25% for .38-40 WCF cal.
Add 25% for Takedown Model.

* ***Model 1892 Deluxe Rifle*** – distinguishable by fancy pistol grip checkered wood. Mfg. 1892-1941.

100%	98%	95%	90%	80%	70%	60%	50%	40%	30%	20%	10%
N/A	N/A	$15,250	$13,500	$11,500	$9,500	$8,250	$6,850	$5,350	$3,850	$2,600	$1,875

MODEL 1892 CARBINE – 20 in. round barrel, 2 barrel bands, and saddle ring, except one barrel band and one rifle style mag. tube retainer on cals. .25-20 WCF and .32-20 WCF.

100%	98%	95%	90%	80%	70%	60%	50%	40%	30%	20%	10%
N/A	N/A	$5,400	$4,475	$3,450	$2,650	$2,175	$1,575	$1,150	$1,000	$825	$725

Add 50% for .44-40 WCF cal. or 25% for .38-40 WCF cal.

MODEL 1892 TRAPPER'S CARBINE – all features similar to standard SRC, except has a 12, 14, 15, 16, or 18 in. barrel, so called Trapper's Model because it was handy for trappers who had to carry a powerful but lightweight repeating rifle.

100%	98%	95%	90%	80%	70%	60%	50%	40%	30%	20%	10%
N/A	N/A	$14,250	$11,750	$8,950	$7,400	$6,350	$4,225	$3,350	$2,400	$1,875	$1,250

Most 1892 Trapper's Carbines are in the 15 in., .44-40 WCF cal. configuration. Most of the 1892 Trapper's Carbine were shipped to South America or Australia. This variation is almost never encountered over 30% condition - most are brown guns. Check federal laws regarding 12, 14 and 15 inch barrels.

MODEL 1892 MUSKET – most are chambered in .44-40 WCF cal., 30 in. round, full length military style forearm with military style rear sight.

100%	98%	95%	90%	80%	70%	60%	50%	40%	30%	20%	10%
N/A	N/A	$21,750	$18,150	$14,575	$12,000	$9,600	$7,700	$5,950	$4,675	$3,700	$2,850

Add $1,500 - $2,000 for correct bayonet.

100%	98%	95%	90%	80%	70%	60%	50%	40%	30%	20%	10%

MODEL 1894 RIFLE – .25-35 WCF, .30-30 Win. (.30 WCF), .32-40 WCF, .32 Spl., or .38-55 WCF cal., most common (and popular) is .30-30 Win. cal., tube mag., 24 or 26 in. round or octagon barrel was standard, blue, straight grip stock, Model 1894 barrel marking changed just before ser. no. 500,000 circa 1908, tang marking changed after ser. no. 500,000, "18" was removed around ser. no. 1,000,000 circa 1927. Over 5,000,000, mfg. 1894-2006.

Newer Model 94 mfg. may be found in the RIFLES: MODEL 94 LEVER ACTION - POST 1964 PRODUCTION section. The Model 1894 rifle configuration (forearm stock with forearm cap) was discontinued circa 1929 at approx. ser. no. 1,070,000. The Model 1894 rifle was replaced by the Model 55 (mfg. 1924-1932), and the Model 64 (mfg. 1933-1957 and 1972-1973).

* ***Model 1894 Rifle 1894-1898 Mfg.*** – antique mfg., pre-148,000 ser. no.

100%	98%	95%	90%	80%	70%	60%	50%	40%	30%	20%	10%
N/A	$6,400	$5,400	$4,650	$3,725	$3,125	$2,150	$1,650	$1,275	$1,100	$900	$750

Add 20% for takedown variation.

Add approx. 25% for cals. other than .30-30 Win. or .32 Spl.

The Model 1894 Winchester has the distinction of being the world's most popular rifle.

* ***Model 1894 Rifle 1899-1929 Mfg.*** – Model 94s built 1899-1929.

100%	98%	95%	90%	80%	70%	60%	50%	40%	30%	20%	10%
N/A	$4,150	$3,675	$2,950	$2,350	$1,850	$1,300	$975	$800	$675	$550	$475

Add 25% for takedown variation.

Add approx. 50% for cals. other than .30-30 Win. or .32 Spl.

The Model 1894 Winchester has the distinction of being the world's most popular rifle.

* ***Model 1894 Deluxe Rifle*** – distinguishable by fancy pistol grip checkered wood. Mfg. 1894-1929.

100%	98%	95%	90%	80%	70%	60%	50%	40%	30%	20%	10%
N/A	N/A	$12,500	$11,000	$9,500	$8,000	$7,500	$6,000	$4,500	$3,000	$2,250	$1,250

MODEL 1894 TRAPPER'S CARBINE – all features similar to the standard SRC, except with a 14, 15, or 16 in. barrel.

100%	98%	95%	90%	80%	70%	60%	50%	40%	30%	20%	10%
N/A	N/A	$7,100	$6,150	$5,000	$4,250	$3,550	$2,850	$2,200	$1,650	$1,350	$1,000

The large majority of this variation are encountered in .30-30 Win. cal. with 15 in. barrel. Any other caliber or barrel length will create a premium. Most of these carbines are brown and rusty. Rarely, if ever, encountered with very much finish remaining.

Note: Check federal laws on legality of 14 and 15 in. barrels.

MODEL 1894 SADDLE RING CARBINE – 20 in. round barrel.

100%	98%	95%	90%	80%	70%	60%	50%	40%	30%	20%	10%
N/A	N/A	$2,800	$2,350	$1,875	$1,450	$1,075	$925	$775	$625	$500	$450

Add 40% for any cal. other than .30-30 Win. or .32 Spl.

Carbines with special order features such as pistol grip, deluxe wood, checkering, etc. can bring even greater premiums than the rifle.

* ***Model 1894 Saddle Ring Carbine Antique*** – 20 in. round barrel, antique mfg., pre-148,000 ser. no.

100%	98%	95%	90%	80%	70%	60%	50%	40%	30%	20%	10%
N/A	N/A	$4,600	$3,950	$3,300	$2,550	$1,700	$1,550	$1,300	$1,000	$825	$750

Add 40% for any cal. other than .30-30 Win. or .32 Spl.

Carbines with special order features such as pistol grip, deluxe wood, checkering, etc. can bring even greater premiums than the rifle.

* ***Model 1894 Saddle Ring Carbine Eastern*** – features long forearm, early stock design, early style carbine post or hooded ramp (later mfg.) front sight, and without saddle ring, mfg. late 1920s-early 1930s.

100%	98%	95%	90%	80%	70%	60%	50%	40%	30%	20%	10%
N/A	N/A	$2,000	$1,875	$1,650	$1,475	$1,300	$1,100	$925	$775	$650	$495

MODEL 1894 1940-1964 PRODUCTION CARBINE – 1940-1964 mfg. without saddle ring, barrel is marked Model 94.

100%	98%	95%	90%	80%	70%	60%	50%	40%	30%	20%	10%
$825	$725	$600	$500	$450	$400	$350	$300	$275	$250	$225	$200

Add 100% for .25-35 WCF cal.

Some WWII carbines with special U.S. markings will bring a premium over prices listed.

100%	98%	95%	90%	80%	70%	60%	50%	40%	30%	20%	10%

MODEL 1895 RIFLE FLATSIDE – .30 US (most common), .38-72, or .40-72 cal., early model, distinguishable in that frame does not have fluting or ridge contouring, serial range approx. 1-5000. Mfg. 1895-1896.

N/A	N/A	$8,500	$7,650	$6,350	$5,750	$3,875	$3,150	$2,700	$2,200	$1,600	$1,100

Add 30% for octagon barrel on cals. .38-72 or .40-72.

MODEL 1895 RIFLE – .30-03, .30-06, .30-40 Krag, .303 Brit., .35 Win., .38-72, .40- 72, .405 Win., or 7.62mm Russian cal., 24-28 in. barrel, blue action, box mag., straight grip stock, 425,881 mfg. from 1896-1931.

N/A	N/A	$4,900	$4,300	$3,750	$3,250	$2,825	$2,350	$1,925	$1,450	$1,000	$750

Add 25% for octagon barrel.
Add 75% for .405 Win. cal.
Add 20% for takedown model.

The Model 1895 was a Browning design incorporating the first box type mag. in a lever action repeating rifle. .30 US is the most commonly encountered cal. in this model. A large Russian military contract was secured in 1915 with chambering for the 7.62mm Russian cartridge (over 293,000 mfg. or over 66% of total production).

* ***Model 1895 Deluxe Rifle*** – distinguishable by fancy pistol grip checkered wood. Mfg. 1894-1929.

N/A	N/A	$11,500	$10,000	$8,750	$7,500	$6,250	$5,000	$4,250	$3,300	$2,200	$1,150

MODEL 1895 CARBINE – .30 US (.30-40 Krag Army - most common cal.), .30-03, .30-06, or .303 Brit. cal., 22 in. round barrel, military style top handguard wood and military sights, with or without saddle ring.

N/A	N/A	$4,625	$4,175	$3,650	$3,175	$2,800	$2,300	$1,850	$1,375	$1,000	$825

Add 20% for caliber other than .30 U.S.
Add 50% for U.S. government marked.

MODEL 1895 FLATSIDE MUSKET – early models have serial range under 5,000, no flutes on frame, .30-40 Krag only.

Rarity on this model means only a few specimens in several museums.

MODEL 1895 MUSKET – .30-03, .30-06, or .30-40 Krag cal., 28 in. round barrel with hand guard over barrel, military sights.

N/A	N/A	$6,000	$5,250	$4,750	$4,200	$3,600	$3,150	$2,650	$2,125	$1,600	$1,100

Add 10%-15% if U.S. Govt. marked.

MODEL 1895 NRA MUSKET – .30-03, .30-06, or .30-40 Krag cal., similar to Standard Musket grade with 24 or 30 in. barrel, 1901 Krag style rear sight. NRA approved for official NRA competition.

N/A	N/A	$5,275	$4,725	$4,125	$3,475	$2,975	$2,375	$2,000	$1,550	$1,100	$825

Add 30% if U.S. government marked.

MODEL 1895 RUSSIAN MUSKET – 7.62mm Russian cal., over 293,000 mfg. for Imperial Russian Govt., mfg. 1915-16, various Russian Ordnance stamps should be present.

N/A	N/A	$4,400	$3,950	$3,475	$3,000	$2,575	$2,100	$1,700	$1,400	$1,150	$950

MODEL 53 RIFLE – .25-20 WCF, .32-20 WCF, or .44-40 WCF cal., 22 in. round barrel, 1/2 tube mag. holding 6 cartridges, solid frame or takedown, blue finish, pistol grip or straight grip stock, serial numbered both separately and within the Model 92 range. Mfg. 24,916 between 1924-32.

N/A	N/A	$2,100	$1,875	$1,625	$1,350	$1,175	$900	$725	$600	$500	$375

Add 75% for .44-40 WCF cal.
Add 25% for Takedown Model.

* ***Model 53 Deluxe Rifle*** – distinguishable by fancy pistol grip checkered wood.

N/A	N/A	$4,000	$3,650	$3,350	$3,000	$2,600	$2,300	$1,950	$1,650	$1,350	$995

MODEL 55 RIFLE – .25-35 WCF (rare), .30-30 Win. (takedown only), or .32 Win. Spl. cal., lever action design, solid frame (less common) and takedown (more common), 24 in. round barrel, shotgun style buttstock with serrated steel buttplate, tube mag., holds

100%	98%	95%	90%	80%	70%	60%	50%	40%	30%	20%	10%

3 cartridges. Approx. 20,500 mfg. between 1924-1932. Serial numbered independently to approx. 2,865, then serialized with Model 1894 production on underside of receiver. Simply could not compete with the Model 1894.

* ***Model 55 Rifle Standard Cals.*** – .30-30 Win. or .32 Win. Spl. cal.

100%	98%	95%	90%	80%	70%	60%	50%	40%	30%	20%	10%
N/A	$2,425	$2,150	$1,775	$1,425	$1,175	$995	$825	$725	$600	$475	$375

Add 20% for solid frame model.

* ***Model 55 Rifle .25-35 WCF Cal.***

100%	98%	95%	90%	80%	70%	60%	50%	40%	30%	20%	10%
N/A	$6,000	$5,375	$4,350	$3,575	$2,950	$2,500	$2,100	$1,825	$1,500	$1,200	$950

MODEL 64 RIFLE – .219 Zipper (very rare), .25-35 WCF (rare), .30-30 Win., or .32 Win. Spl. cal., 20 (may be referred to as carbine) or 24 in. round barrel, with standard 26 in. on the .219 Zipper, blue metal, pistol grip stock, revamped Model 55 action with increased mag. capacity, 66,783 mfg. between 1933-1957 and 1972-73 (over 8,250 mfg. in .30-30 Win. cal. only - these last two years with minor changes).

100%	98%	95%	90%	80%	70%	60%	50%	40%	30%	20%	10%
N/A	$1,200	$1,050	$900	$800	$725	$650	$600	$550	$500	$450	$400

Add 150% for 20 in. barrel (sometimes referred to as Carbine).
Add 300% for .25-35 WCF cal. (rare).
Add 500% for .219 Zipper cal. (very rare).

Many of this variation now have extra holes drilled on the top of the receiver to accept scope mounts - subtract 50% for this alteration. The Model 64 is usually found in excellent condition.

Model 64 1972-73 mfg. may be found in the post-'64 section.

* ***Model 64 Deluxe Rifle*** – distinguishable by fancy checkered wood stock with pistol grip.

100%	98%	95%	90%	80%	70%	60%	50%	40%	30%	20%	10%
N/A	N/A	$2,750	$2,375	$2,100	$1,875	$1,700	$1,475	$1,275	$1,050	$900	$800

MODEL 65 RIFLE – .218 Bee (introduced 1939), .25-20 WCF, or .32-20 WCF cal., 22 in. round barrel (except .218 Bee - 24 in.), 1/2 tube mag. holding 7 cartridges, blue with pistol grip stock. Mfg. 5,704 between 1933-1947.

100%	98%	95%	90%	80%	70%	60%	50%	40%	30%	20%	10%
N/A	$5,450	$4,650	$4,000	$3,450	$2,950	$2,425	$2,100	$1,750	$1,425	$1,125	$950

While the .25-20 WCF cal. is the rarest, the .218 Bee has the most demand.

The Model 65 was a design evolved from the Model 53. The Model 65 was not tapped on receiver side for scope mounts. As a rule, most specimens are in either pretty nice or refinished condition.

* ***Model 65 Deluxe Rifle*** – distinguishable by fancy pistol grip checkered wood.

100%	98%	95%	90%	80%	70%	60%	50%	40%	30%	20%	10%
N/A	$8,750	$7,750	$6,850	$6,000	$5,000	$4,275	$3,750	$3,200	$2,500	$2,000	$1,500

MODEL 71 RIFLE – .348 Win. cal., 2/3 tube mag. holding 4 cartridges, improved Model 1886 frame, blue metal with pistol grip stock, 20 or 24 in. barrel, short or long tang. Mfg. 47,254 between 1935-1957.

100%	98%	95%	90%	80%	70%	60%	50%	40%	30%	20%	10%
N/A	$2,000	$1,800	$1,675	$1,500	$1,300	$1,100	$975	$875	$800	$725	$650

Add 30%-40% for early variation long tang, depending on condition.
Add 150% for short rifle with 20 in. barrel.
Add $250 for bolt peep sight.

* ***Model 71 Deluxe Rifle*** – distinguishable by fancy pistol grip checkered wood.

100%	98%	95%	90%	80%	70%	60%	50%	40%	30%	20%	10%
N/A	$4,000	$3,650	$3,350	$3,000	$2,600	$2,300	$1,950	$1,650	$1,350	$995	$800

Add 20% for long tang.

MODEL 88 RIFLE – pre-'64 version with diamond cut checkering, no barrel band, 22 in. barrel. Mfg. 1955-63. Total production for all varieties of the Model 88 Lever Action was approx. 284,000 units. Mfg. 1955-1963.

GRADING - PPGS™	100%	98%	95%	90%	80%	70%	60%	LAST MSR
.308 Win. (1955-1963)	$995	$875	$650	$495	$400	$350	$300	
.243 Win. (1956-1963)	$1,395	$1,250	$1,100	$950	$825	$750	$550	
.358 Win. (1956-1962)	$3,750	$3,350	$2,750	$2,100	$1,800	$1,400	$1,100	
.284 Win. (Intro-1963)	$2,850	$2,550	$2,300	$2,100	$1,650	$1,150	$850	

100%	98%	95%	90%	80%	70%	60%	50%	40%	30%	20%	10%

RIFLES: SINGLE SHOT

MODEL 1885 – available in most popular rimfire and centerfire cals. between .22 S-L-LR and .50, falling block trigger guard activated action, John Browning's first high power single shot rifle design, many variations were made and we will list the standard types. Over 139,725 mfg. between 1885-1920.

This design was originally mfg. as the Model 1878 by the Browning Brothers in Ogden, UT, in the early 1880s. Fewer than 600 were mfg. - see the Browning section for values.

* ***Model 1885 Sporting Rifle Low Wall*** – 24 or 26 in. round or octagon barrel was standard, open sights, solid frame, standard trigger.

N/A	N/A	$1,500	$1,350	$1,200	$1,100	$975	$825	$700	$550	$400	$300

Add 30% for centerfire cal.
Add 50% for case colored frame, if in 95%+ original condition.

* ***Model 1885 Sporting Rifle High Wall*** – 30 in. barrel, standard trigger, open sights, solid frame. Available in various size and weight barrels numbered (in front of forearm) from lightest to heaviest: 1, 2, 3, 3 1/2 (introduced 1910), 4, and 5. Case hardened frames standard until 1901 when bluing became standard, three different frames depending on caliber. Heavier barrels in rare calibers will bring a premium.

N/A	N/A	$5,000	$3,500	$2,800	$2,500	$2,000	$1,725	$1,500	$1,325	$1,100	$875

Add 30% for 20 ga. shotgun.
Add 30% for Takedown Model.
Add 25% for No. 5 barrel.
Add 10% for set trigger.
Add 30% for .405, .45, and .50 caliber.

* ***Model 1885 Schuetzen Rifle*** – high wall, 30 in. octagon barrel, double-set triggers, spur lever, aperture sight, Schuetzen style stock, adj. palm rest and buttplate.

N/A	N/A	$9,000	$6,500	$5,000	$4,250	$3,650	$3,200	$2,850	$2,500	$2,250	$1,875

Add 30% for Takedown frame.
Add 50% for case colored frame, if in 95%+ original condition.

Prices are for factory original guns only. Since this model had many shooting alterations performed by various aftermarket suppliers of its time, perhaps only 10% of remaining specimens are unaltered (or 100% factory).

* ***Model 1885 Deluxe Sporting Rifle*** – various cals., available in Low Wall, High Wall, or Schuetzen configuration, distinguishable by case colored receiver and fancy pistol grip checkered wood.

N/A	N/A	$7,000	$5,500	$4,550	$3,750	$3,300	$2,975	$2,650	$2,300	$1,850	$1,450

Add 50%-100% for Deluxe Schuetzen Model with fancy pistol grip checkered wood and case colored receiver, depending on original condition.

* ***Model 1885 High Wall Musket*** – usually found in .22 LR cal.

N/A	N/A	$1,400	$1,275	$1,100	$975	$850	$750	$650	$550	$475	$400

Add 100% for .45-70 Govt. or .45-90 cal.

* ***Model 1885 Low Wall Musket (Winder Musket)*** – low wall, 3rd model, .22 Short or LR (most common) cal., 28 in. barrel, standard trigger and lever, military style stock and sights, grooved forearm, one barrel band.

N/A	N/A	$1,425	$1,225	$1,050	$925	$800	$700	$600	$500	$400	$300

MODEL 1885 (RECENT MFG.) – please refer to the RIFLES: SINGLE SHOT, POST 1964 MFG. section for these listings.

MODEL 1900 SINGLE SHOT – .22 S and L cal., bolt action, 18 in. round barrel, blue metal, open sights, one-piece straight grip gumwood stock without fitted buttplate, takedown, not serial numbered. Approx. 105,000 mfg. between 1899-1902.

N/A	N/A	$1,000	$825	$625	$400	$300	$200	$165	$145	$125	$110

Add 100% for later models marked M1900 on barrel, and Win. stamped butt.

100%	98%	95%	90%	80%	70%	60%	50%	40%	30%	20%	10%

This model is usually encountered with flaked frames.

MODEL 1902 SINGLE SHOT – similar to 1900, bolt action, with minor improvements. Distinguishable by specially shaped extended trigger guard. Not serial numbered. Approx. 640,299 mfg. between 1902-1931.

100%	98%	95%	90%	80%	70%	60%	50%	40%	30%	20%	10%
N/A	$500	$400	$300	$200	$150	$125	$100	$90	$80	$70	$60

Chambering included .22 cal. Extra Long cal. in 1914 (interchangeable with S&L).

THUMB TRIGGER MODEL 99 – similar to 1902, with button behind cocking piece used to fire with thumb instead of trigger, not serial numbered. Approx. 75,433 were mfg. between 1904-1923.

100%	98%	95%	90%	80%	70%	60%	50%	40%	30%	20%	10%
N/A	$2,250	$2,000	$1,750	$1,500	$1,200	$1,000	$800	$700	$600	$400	$350

MODEL 1904 SINGLE SHOT – improved version of 1902, 21 in. round barrel, chambering included .22 Extra Long in 1914, not serial numbered. Approx. 302,859 mfg. between 1904-31.

100%	98%	95%	90%	80%	70%	60%	50%	40%	30%	20%	10%
N/A	$450	$400	$350	$300	$200	$175	$160	$150	$125	$100	$90

* ***Model 1904-A Single Shot*** – introduced 1927 with new sear bar and chambered for .22 LR.

100%	98%	95%	90%	80%	70%	60%	50%	40%	30%	20%	10%
N/A	$450	$350	$300	$250	$200	$175	$150	$125	$100	$90	$80

MODEL 47 – .22 S, L, or LR cal., single shot bolt action, 25 in. round barrel, unique bolt design, uncheckered walnut stock, 5 1/4 lbs., approx. 43,000 (not serial numbered) mfg. during 1948-54.

100%	98%	95%	90%	80%	70%	60%	50%	40%	30%	20%	10%
$350	$300	$250	$200	$180	$150	$140	$130	$125	$120	$115	$110

MODEL 52 – please refer to listings in the Rifles: Bolt Action section.

MODEL 55 – .22 cal. only, top loading single shot, bottom ejection, 22 in. round barrel, open sporting sights, not serial numbered. Over 45,000 mfg. between 1958-61.

100%	98%	95%	90%	80%	70%	60%	50%	40%	30%	20%	10%
$200	$175	$160	$130	$115	$100	$85	$85	$75	$70	$65	$60

GRADING - PPGS™	100%	98%	95%	90%	80%	70%	60%	LAST MSR

MODEL 58 SINGLE SHOT – similar to Models 1902 and 1904, .22 LR cal., 18 in. round barrel, open sights, takedown. Approx. 38,992 mfg. between 1928-31.

GRADING - PPGS™	100%	98%	95%	90%	80%	70%	60%	LAST MSR
	$1,000	$875	$750	$680	$550	$450	$350	

MODEL 59 SINGLE SHOT – improved Model 58 with 23 in. round barrel and pistol grip stock with buttplate. Approx. 9,200 mfg. between 1930-31.

GRADING - PPGS™	100%	98%	95%	90%	80%	70%	60%	LAST MSR
	$1,200	$1,000	$900	$800	$600	$500	$350	

This model was disc. due to lack of sales.

MODEL 60 – .22 S, L, or LR cal., improved Model 59, 23 in. round barrel increased to 27 in. 1933. Approx. 160,754 mfg. between 1930-34.

GRADING - PPGS™	100%	98%	95%	90%	80%	70%	60%	LAST MSR
	$425	$375	$325	$275	$195	$160	$125	

Add 20% for 23 in. barrel.

MODEL 60A SPORTER – .22 S, L, or LR cal., sporter variation of Model 60, pistol grip walnut stock. Disc.

GRADING - PPGS™	100%	98%	95%	90%	80%	70%	60%	LAST MSR
	$550	$475	$425	$375	$325	$250	$225	

MODEL 60A TARGET – similar to Model 60 with Lyman 55W aperture rear sight, heavier target stock, and 27 in. round tapered barrel. Approx. 6,118 mfg. between 1932-39.

GRADING - PPGS™	100%	98%	95%	90%	80%	70%	60%	LAST MSR
	$675	$595	$525	$475	$425	$350	$295	

MODEL 67/67A – .22 S, L, LR or .22 WRF (introduced 1935) cal., 20 in. (Boys Rifle), 24 (miniature target boring), and 27 in. (sporting or smooth bore) round barrels, same basic action as the Model 60, not serial numbered. Approx. 383,000 mfg. between 1934-1963.

GRADING - PPGS™	100%	98%	95%	90%	80%	70%	60%	LAST MSR
	$300	$250	$225	$175	$125	$100	$75	
.22 WRF cal.	$685	$600	$500	$465	$375	$310	$240	

GRADING - PPGS™	100%	98%	95%	90%	80%	70%	60%	LAST MSR

Add 30% for Boys rifle.

Add 100%-150% for smooth bore, depending on condition.

MODEL 677 – same basic specifications as Model 67, except no iron sights or sight cuts in barrel, not serial numbered, supplied with Win. 5-A scope, .22 WRF is scarce. Approx. 2,240 mfg. between 1937-39.

	$2,300	$2,015	$1,725	$1,565	$1,265	$1,035	$805

MODEL 68 – .22 LR or .22 WRF cal., bolt action single shot, similar to Model 67, walnut stock, supplied with aperture sight (no rear sight), not serial numbered. Approx. 100,000 mfg. between 1934-46.

.22 LR cal.	$300	$265	$225	$200	$165	$135	$100
.22 WRF cal.	$1,200	$1,050	$900	$800	$650	$525	$400

MODEL 121 SINGLE SHOT RIFLE – .22 LR cal., bolt action, 20 3/4 in. barrel, open sights, plain pistol grip stock. Mfg. 1967-73.

	$115	$100	$85	$80	$65	$50	$40

MODEL 121Y SINGLE SHOT RIFLE – similar to 121, with shorter stock.

	$115	$100	$85	$80	$65	$50	$40

MODEL 121 DELUXE – similar to 121, with ramp front sight and sling swivels.

	$125	$110	$95	$85	$70	$55	$45

MODEL 310 SINGLE SHOT – .22 LR cal., bolt action, 22 in. barrel, open sights, checkered pistol grip stock, swivels. 13,544 mfg. 1972-1975.

	$200	$175	$150	$135	$110	$90	$70

WINGO "ICE PALACE" RIFLE – 5mm shot cartridge, 22 in. round barrel with vent. rib, modified lever action Martini type single shot, walnut Monte Carlo stock and forearm, marked "WINGO" on both sides of receiver, mfg. in England for Winchester "Ice Palace" shooting center, electrical cord extends from the magazine connecting to a target throwing device which threw black clay mini-pigeons, approx. 20 mfg.

	$2,750	$2,405	$2,065	$1,870	$1,515	$1,240	$965

Add approx. 33% if with electric cables, operating trap mechanism, and at least 50 rounds of 5mm ammo and mini-pigeons.

100%	98%	95%	90%	80%	70%	60%	50%	40%	30%	20%	10%

RIFLES: BOLT ACTION

On Models 52, 54, 56, 57, 58, 59, 60, 60A, 67, 677, 68, 69, 69A, 697, and 70 values in 50% or less original condition have been omitted since values in those conditions will approximate the 60% price. This reflects the fact that while these lower condition specimens are not as desirable to collectors, they are still sought after as shooters.

MODEL 1883 (HOTCHKISS REPEATER) – .45-70 Govt. cal., designed by Benjamin D. Hotchkiss, unique tube mag. located in buttstock attached to receiver, up-turn/pull-back bolt action, 26 in. round or octagon barrel standard on rifle. Over 84,000 mfg. between 1879-1889. Carbine extremely rare in Third Model (20 in. barrel).

Subtract 25% for carbine configuration (24 in. round barrel with one band), or musket (32 in. round barrel with cleaning rod and two barrel bands).

Add 25% for Deluxe Model with fancy pistol grip checkered wood.

* ***Model 1883 First Style*** – approx. 6,419 mfg. with magazine cut off and safety control incorporated into one unit.

N/A	N/A	$2,500	$2,150	$1,800	$1,500	$1,350	$1,200	$1,050	$900	$850	$800

* ***Model 1883 Second Style*** – approx. 16,102 mfg., magazine cut off on right receiver top, safety on left side.

N/A	N/A	$2,500	$2,150	$1,800	$1,500	$1,350	$1,200	$1,050	$900	$850	$800

100%	98%	95%	90%	80%	70%	60%	50%	40%	30%	20%	10%

* ***Model 1883 Third Style*** – most commonly encountered Hotchkiss, 2-piece stock, approx. 62,034 mfg. 1883-1899.

N/A	N/A	$2,150	$1,800	$1,500	$1,350	$1,200	$1,050	$900	$850	$750	$650

The Model 1883 Hotchkiss was the first bolt action designed for the U.S. military .45-70 Govt. cartridge. On the First and Second models, inspect wood directly below bolt and left frame side for cracks, breaks, or older repairs as it is frequently encountered on these early models with thin wrists.

LEE STRAIGHT PULL RIFLE – 6mm Lee (.236 U.S.N. cal.), 5 shot non-detachable box mag., 24 (Sporting Rifle) or 28 (Musket) in. barrel, folding leaf sight, blue metal, military style full stock, mfg. 1897-1902, Navy Issue Model is the Musket with "236 U.S.N." on barrels. Approx. 20,000 mfg. (including 15,000 Muskets for the U.S. Navy military contract) between 1895-1902 with parts clean up occurring in 1916.

* ***Lee Straight Pull Rifle U.S.N. Military Musket***

N/A	$2,750	$2,350	$2,000	$1,750	$1,500	$1,250	$1,100	$1,000	$875	$750	$625

* ***Lee Straight Pull Rifle Sporting*** – similar to Musket, with 24 in, barrel, sporter style stock. Approx. 1,700 mfg. 1897-1902.

N/A	$3,000	$2,650	$2,300	$2,000	$1,750	$1,500	$1,250	$1,050	$975	$875	$800

This design was originally patented by James Paris Lee and assigned to the Lee Arms Company. Winchester obtained manufacturing rights to produce this model for the U.S Navy military contract 1895-1902.

MODEL 43 – .218 Bee, .22 Hornet, .25-20 WCF, or .32-20 WCF cal., dubbed "Poor Man's Model 70," 24 in. round tapered barrel, box type mag. Approx. 62,617 mfg. between 1949-1957.

$800	$675	$575	$500	$425	$375	$325	$275	$225	$175	$150	$125

Add 100% for Deluxe Model with fancy checkered wood.
Add 100% for .32-20 WCF and .25-20 WCF cal.
Add 20% for .218 Bee cal.
Subtract 60% if non-factory drilled and tapped (early models).

GRADING - PPGS™	100%	98%	95%	90%	80%	70%	60%	LAST MSR

MODEL 52 TARGET – .22 S (rare) or LR cal., 5 shot mag., 28 in. standard or heavy barrel (1st cataloged 1933), target sights and target style stock, speedlock trigger feature was introduced in 1929. Approx. 125,233 Model 52s in all variations were mfg. between 1919-79.

	$825	$750	$650	$550	$500	$450	$400	
With speedlock	$700	$625	$575	$525	$475	$425	$350	

Barrel drilling and tapping for scope blocks was not standard until ser. no. 5200.

A few Model 52 Target models with stainless steel barrels have been encountered. Values range from $1,500-$2,100, depending on condition.

* ***Model 52A Target*** – similar to Model 52, except all "A" suffix Model 52s have a speedlock trigger. Values are similar to Model 52 Target with speedlock trigger. In terms of rarity, it seems the "E" suffix is probably the scarcest (also the most poorly mfg.), followed by the "A" suffix variation.

MODEL 52A HEAVY BARREL – similar to Standard Target, with heavy barrel.

	$1,050	$900	$775	$675	$550	$450	$400	

MODEL 52-B TARGET – extensively redesigned action, improved stock design, offered with a variety of sights. Approx. mfg. 1940-47.

	$1,225	$1,100	$1,000	$900	$750	$650	$550	

MODEL 52-B HEAVY BARREL – similar to 52-B, with heavy barrel, with adj. sling swivel as to position of front swivel, and single shot adapter became available.

	$1,325	$1,200	$1,100	$1,000	$900	$800	$700	

GRADING - PPGS™	100%	98%	95%	90%	80%	70%	60%	LAST MSR

MODEL 52-B BULL GUN – extra heavy weight barrel.

	$1,650	$1,500	$1,300	$1,000	$900	$800	$650	

MODEL 52 SPORTER (SPORTING RIFLE) – 24 in. round lightweight barrel with front sight cover, sporting type select walnut stock with cheekpiece, hard rubber pistol grip cap, black plastic tipped forearm, checkered steel buttplate, 5 shot mag. is standard, about 7 1/4 lbs. Mfg. 1934-1958. There is some controversy as to whether any of the Model 52 Sporters were drilled and tapped per factory worksmanship. Be cautious of "factory" drilled and tapped receivers on all model 52s, as there are many "gunsmith" Sporters that have been made with turned down, shortened target barrels.

* ***Model 52 Sporter*** – advertised approx. 1936.

	$4,500	$3,750	$2,750	$2,250	$1,650	$1,400	$1,100	

* ***Model 52A Sporter*** – introduced approx. 1937, receiver and locking lug were strengthened.

	$4,250	$3,700	$3,250	$2,500	$2,250	$2,000	$1,500	

* ***Model 52B Sporter*** – introduced approx. 1940.

	$4,500	$3,600	$2,750	$2,250	$1,650	$1,400	$1,100	

* ***Model 52B (1993 Re-issue) Sporter*** – .22 LR cal., patterned after the original Model 52B and includes steel buttplate, 24 in. barrel w/o sights, Micro Motion trigger with adjustment screw on bottom plate, high-polish blue, 5 shot mag., checkered 52B style stock with ebony forend tip, 7 lbs. Mfg. by Miroku in Japan 1993-2002.

	$600	$525	$450	$400	$360	$330	$300	*$662*

* ***Model 52C Sporter*** – introduced 1947 with adj. Micro Motion trigger, approx. 500-1,000 mfg., 2 screws in trigger guard.

	$5,000	$4,500	$3,750	$2,850	$2,250	$1,650	$1,400	

A few Model 52 Sporters & Targets were mfg. with stainless steel barrels (17,XXX-27,XXX serial range) - these guns will command a premium over values shown. Stainless steel barrels were also offered by Winchester as after market parts.

MODEL 52-C STANDARD TARGET – "Micro Motion" trigger and "Marksman" stock, single shot adaptor, 5 or 10 shot mag. was avail., standard barrel, otherwise similar to 52-B. Mfg. 1947-61.

	$1,300	$1,200	$1,100	$1,000	$800	$600	$500	

MODEL 52-C HEAVY TARGET – similar to Standard Target, with heavy barrel.

	$1,350	$1,250	$1,100	$1,000	$800	$700	$650	

MODEL 52-C BULL TARGET – extra heavy (bull) barrel model of Heavy Target 52-C. Mfg. approx. 1947-1961.

	$1,800	$1,500	$1,300	$1,200	$1,100	$1,000	$900	

MODEL 52-D TARGET – improved version of 52-C with free-floating standard or heavy barrel and adj. bedding device, all 52-Ds were single shot. Fewer than 750 rifles were shipped.

	$1,300	$1,150	$1,000	$900	$800	$700	$600	

MODEL 52-D INTERNATIONAL MATCH – similar to 52-D, with free rifle stock, accessory rail. Mfg. 1969-1975.

	$1,500	$1,300	$1,075	$900	$775	$650	$525	

Previous Model 52s had ser. no. suffixes - either A, B, C, or D" After approx. 1975, rifles started appearing with an "E" serial prefix. Both Model 52 International and Prone could have factory stocks that were not Winchester mfg.

MODEL 52-D PRONE – similar to International Match, with prone style stock. Mfg. 1960-75.

	$1,400	$1,250	$1,075	$850	$725	$600	$550	

GRADING - PPGS™	100%	98%	95%	90%	80%	70%	60%	LAST MSR

MODEL 52-E TARGET – similar to Model 52-D Target, approx. 652 mfg. 1975-1980.

$1,750 $1,500 $1,250 $1,000 $875 $750 $650

MODEL 52-E INTERNATIONAL PRONE – similar to 52-D, with lighter colored wood stock, removable roll over cheekpiece. Approx. 37 mfg. 1975-1980.

$1,400 $1,250 $1,075 $900 $775 $650 $525

MODEL 52-E INTERNATIONAL MATCH – heavy match barrel, lower accessory rail, uncheckered light colored walnut thumbhole stock with adj. buttplate and beavertail forend, no sights, scattered in ser. no. range E-123,000 - E125,000. Approx. 44 mfg. 1975-1980.

$2,000 $1,750 $1,500 $1,300 $1,075 $900 $775

MODEL 54 HIGH POWER SPORTER – .270 Win., 7x57mm, 7.65x57mm Mauser (rare), .30-30 Win., .30-06, 9x57mm Mauser (rare) cal., 5 shot mag., 24 in. barrel, open sights, checkered pistol grip stock. Mfg. 1925-30. Approx. 50,145 Model 54s were mfg. in all variations between 1925-36.

$1,150 $1,000 $900 $800 $700 $600 $500

Rare cals. will add premiums to the values listed. This model was also mfg. with a stainless steel barrel during the late 1920s-early '30s with premiums also being asked.

MODEL 54 CARBINE – introduced 1927, similar to Rifle, with 20 in. barrel, plain stock.

$1,500 $1,200 $1,000 $900 $800 $650 $500

MODEL 54 IMPROVED SPORTER – .22 Hornet, .220 Swift, .250-3000, .257 Robts., .270, 7x57mm, or .30-06 cal., 5 shot mag., 24 or 26 in. barrel, one piece firing pin, checkered pistol grip stock. Mfg. 1930-36.

$1,375 $1,200 $1,000 $900 $800 $700 $600

Rare cals. will add premiums to the values listed.

MODEL 54 CARBINE IMPROVED – similar to Rifle, with 20 in. barrel.

$1,750 $1,500 $1,250 $1,000 $875 $750 $650

MODEL 54 SUPER GRADE – introduced 1934, similar to Sporter, with better wood and black forend tip and pistol grip cap.

$3,000 $2,650 $2,250 $1,775 $1,525 $1,375 $1,200

Rare calibers will command considerable premiums (i.e. this variation in 7x57mm cal. will sell for $2,500 in mint condition).

MODEL 54 SPORTING SNIPER'S RIFLE – introduced 1929, similar to Sporter, with 26 in. heavy barrel, .30-06 only, aperture sight.

$2,400 $1,850 $1,500 $1,300 $1,100 $1,000 $900

MODEL 54 NATIONAL MATCH – introduced 1935, similar to Standard, with Lyman sights and Marksman stock.

$1,650 $1,350 $1,100 $1,000 $850 $725 $600

MODEL 56 SPORTER – .22 S or LR cal., 5 or 10 shot box mag., 22 in. round barrel, open sights, plain pistol grip stock. Approx. 8,297 mfg. between 1926-29.

$1,650 $1,350 $1,100 $1,000 $850 $725 $600

Approx. 1,000 mfg. in .22 Short cal.

MODEL 57 TARGET – .22 S (disc. 1930) or LR cal., 22 in. barrel with barrel band, open sights, stock cutaway for aperture sight on left side, drilled and tapped receiver, heavy target uncheckered pistol grip walnut stock, 5 (standard) or 10 shot mag., left side push-button mag. release, checkered steel buttplate approx. 5 lbs. Approx. 18,600 were mfg. between 1927-1936.

$775 $700 $625 $525 $475 $425 $375

GRADING - PPGS™	100%	98%	95%	90%	80%	70%	60%	LAST MSR

MODEL 69 & 69A – .22 S, L, or LR cal., 5 or 10 shot repeater, 25 in. barrel, aperture or open rear sight, not serial numbered. Approx. 355,000 mfg. between 1935-63.

$425	$365	$300	$235	$150	$100	$85	

Add 40% for Target Model.
Add 20% for grooved receiver (Model 69A only).
Add 5% for chrome plated bolt handle and trigger guard.

The Model 69 was cocked by the closing motion of the bolt and had a non-swept back bolt handle, whereas the 69A was cocked by the opening motion of the bolt and had a swept back bolt handle. Number 97B rear aperture sight and 80A hooded front target sights and standard open sights were offered on both the Model 69 and 69A.

MODEL 72/72A – .22 LR and Gallery Model (.22 short only), tube mag., bolt action, 25 in. round, tapered barrel, aperture or open rear sight, not serial numbered. Over 161,000 mfg. between 1938-59.

$450	$375	$300	$250	$115	$100	$85	

Add 30% for Target Model.
Add 100% for Gallery Model (mfg. 1939-1942) - rare.
Add 20% for grooved receiver (Model 72A only).
Add 5% for chrome plated bolt handle and trigger guard.

The Model 72 and 72A both cocked on opening. The Model 72A has a swept back bolt handle and some minor internal mechanical improvements. Same open sight options as Models 69/69A.

MODEL 75 TARGET – .22 LR cal., 5 or 10 shot mag., 28 in. barrel, target sights, slight variation used by Government in WWII. Approx. 88,715 Model 75 Target and Model 75 Sporter rifles were mfg. between 1938-1958.

$550	$475	$425	$350	$300	$275	$250	

Add 25% for Olympic sights.
Add 20% for original Winchester leather sling.

MODEL 75 SPORTER – similar to Target, except 24 in. tapered barrel, detachable mag., non-target sights and select checkered walnut.

$1,375	$1,100	$875	$725	$650	$600	$500	

Add 20%-25% for "grooved" receiver allowing "tip-off" scope mounts.

MODEL 131 – .22 S, L, and LR cal., 7 shot mag.

$225	$200	$175	$150	$125	$95	$75	

MODEL 141 – .22 S, L, and LR cal., butt loading tube mag.

$225	$200	$175	$150	$125	$95	$75	

MODEL 320 RIFLE – .22 LR cal., similar to Single Shot Model 310, with 5 shot mag. Mfg. 1972-74.

$325	$325	$300	$265	$235	$185	$150	

MODEL 325 RIFLE – .22 WMR cal., otherwise similar to Model 320, limited mfg. 1972-74.

$375	$350	$325	$300	$250	$200	$100	

MODEL 670 RIFLE – another economy version of the Model 70, .225 Win., .243 Win., .270 Win, .308 Win., or .30-06 cal., 22 in. barrel, open sights, no hinged floorplate, pistol grip stock. Mfg. 1967-73.

$300	$250	$220	$195	$175	$165	$140	

MODEL 670 CARBINE – similar to 670, with 19 in. barrel, not available in .308 Win. Mfg. 1967-70.

$300	$250	$220	$195	$175	$165	$140	

MODEL 670 MAGNUM – similar to 670, with reinforced stock, .264 Mag., 7mm Mag., or .300 Win. Mag. cal. Mfg. 1967-70.

$330	$275	$255	$220	$205	$195	$165	

GRADING - PPGS™	100%	98%	95%	90%	80%	70%	60%	LAST MSR

MODEL 697 – .22 WRF cal., same general specifications as the Model 69, except no iron sights or sight cuts in barrel and no ramp or sight cover. Telescope bases attached to barrel were standard.

	100%	98%	95%	90%	80%	70%	60%	LAST MSR
	$2,200	$1,975	$1,650	$1,375	$1,100	$875	$725	

MODEL 770 – .22-250 Rem., .222 Rem., .243 Win., .270 Win., .30-06, or .308 Win. cal., 22 in. barrel, open sights, no floorplate or forend tip. Mfg. 1969-71.

	100%	98%	95%	90%	80%	70%	60%	LAST MSR
	$375	$335	$300	$275	$250	$225	$200	

MODEL 770 MAGNUM – similar to Standard, in .264 Mag., 7mm Mag., or .300 Win. Mag. cal., recoil pad. Mfg. 1969-71.

	100%	98%	95%	90%	80%	70%	60%	LAST MSR
	$395	$350	$315	$285	$260	$240	$220	

MODEL 777 – .30-06 cal., bolt action, 4 shot mag., mfg. by Nikko in Japan during 1979-80 for sale to Winchester subsidiaries in Australia, Germany, Italy, and Scandinavia, only 3 were shipped to the U.S., checkered Monte Carlo stock with Wundhammer swell grip, lightweight barrel, engraved action, "Winchester" is cast on the left side of the receiver near the top, approx. 1,000 mfg. with 250 in .30-06 cal. - 750 mfg. in different cal. and sold elsewhere, 8 1/2 lbs.

	100%	98%	95%	90%	80%	70%	60%	LAST MSR
	$1,850	$1,675	$1,500	$1,350	$1,200	$1,100	$1,00	

WILDCAT – .22 LR cal., 21 in. regular or heavy (Target/Varmint model) barrel with (Sporter) or w/o (Target/Varmint) sights, detachable 5 or 10 shot mag., checkered hardwood stock and forend (Target or Sporter configuration), sling swivels, fold down rear sight, includes one 5 and three 10 shot mags., two-stage trigger, two-position safety on trigger guard, 4 1/2 or 5 1/2 (Target/Varmint) lbs. Importation from Russia 2007-2009.

	100%	98%	95%	90%	80%	70%	60%	LAST MSR
	$215	$185	$150	$130	$110	$90	$80	*$259*

Add $50 for Wildcat Target/Varmint variation with heavy barrel and beavertail forend (no sights).

100%	98%	95%	90%	80%	70%	60%	50%	40%	30%	20%	10%

RIFLES: SEMI-AUTO

MODEL 1903 – .22 Win. Auto rimfire cal., 10 shot tube mag., 20 in. round barrel, open sights, straight grip stock cut out for partial magazine filling. Approx. 126,000 mfg. between 1903-1932.

100%	98%	95%	90%	80%	70%	60%	50%	40%	30%	20%	10%
N/A	$1,500	$1,325	$1,025	$900	$775	$650	$550	$475	$400	$325	$250

Add 100% for deluxe checkered model.

First U.S. semi-auto rifle designed for a special .22 cal. rimfire cartridge. Regular .22 cal. rimfire will not function or chamber properly in this model. The earliest models up to around ser. no. 5,000 were mfg. w/o a safety. Watch for fake boxes.

MODEL 1905 – .32 Win. or .35 Win. cal., 5 or 10 shot box mag., 22 in. round barrel, open sights, straight or plain pistol grip stock. Approx. 29,113 mfg. between 1905-20.

100%	98%	95%	90%	80%	70%	60%	50%	40%	30%	20%	10%
N/A	$725	$650	$575	$525	$465	$400	$365	$330	$300	$275	$250

MODEL 1907 – .351 Win. cal., 5 or 10 shot box mag., 20 in. round barrel, open sights, plain pistol grip stock, an improved version of the Model 1905. Approx. 58,490 mfg. between 1907-57.

100%	98%	95%	90%	80%	70%	60%	50%	40%	30%	20%	10%
N/A	$675	$595	$525	$450	$375	$325	$295	$265	$230	$195	$175

MODEL 1910 – .401 Win. cal., 4 shot box mag., 20 in. barrel, open sight, plain pistol grip stock. Mfg. 20,786 between 1910-36.

100%	98%	95%	90%	80%	70%	60%	50%	40%	30%	20%	10%
N/A	$850	$750	$625	$550	$500	$450	$400	$365	$330	$300	$275

Add 50% for Fancy Sporting Rifle (special checkered walnut).

MODEL 55 – please refer to listing in Rifles: Single Shot.

MODEL 63 – .22 LR cal., styling similar to Model 1903, takedown, 10 shot tube mag., 20 (disc. 1936) or 23 in. barrel, open sights, plain pistol grip stock. Approx. 174,692 mfg. between 1933-1958.

100%	98%	95%	90%	80%	70%	60%	50%	40%	30%	20%	10%
$1,275	$1,100	$975	$850	$750	$675	$550	$425	$350	$300	$265	$235

100%	98%	95%	90%	80%	70%	60%	50%	40%	30%	20%	10%

Add 100%-150% for 20 in. barrel (carbine) depending on condition.

The Model 63 was introduced to take advantage of the new .22 LR cartridge, which the older Model 1903 couldn't chamber.

Watch for fake boxes and hanging tags on this model, especially with rifles in over 95%+ original condition.

* ***Model 63 w/Grooved Receiver*** – with grooved receiver.

100%	98%	95%	90%	80%	70%	60%	50%	40%	30%	20%	10%
$2,000	$1,825	$1,500	$1,300	$1,000	$800	$700	$600	$500	$400	$300	$250

GRADING - PPGS™	100%	98%	95%	90%	80%	70%	60%	LAST MSR

MODEL 63 GRADE I - RECENT PRODUCTION – .22 LR cal., similar to original Model 63, 10 shot mag., 23 in. barrel, checkered walnut stock and forearm, blue finish with engraved receiver, 6 1/4 lbs. Mfg. 1997-98.

	100%	98%	95%	90%	80%	70%	60%	LAST MSR
	$675	$600	$550	$500	$430	$375	$315	*$678*

* ***Model 63 High Grade - Recent Mfg.*** – .22 LR cal., similar to original Model 63, 10 shot mag., deluxe checkered walnut stock and forearm, blue finish with engraved gold animals and accents on receiver, 6 1/4 lbs. 1,000 mfg. 1997 only.

	100%	98%	95%	90%	80%	70%	60%	LAST MSR
	$1,050	$875	$750	N/A	N/A	N/A	N/A	*$1,083*

MODEL 74 – .22 S or LR (introduced in 1940) cal., tubular mag. in stock, pop-out bolt assembly. Approx. 406,574 mfg. between 1939-1955. Distinguishable by squared-off rear receiver.

	100%	98%	95%	90%	80%	70%	60%
	$295	$250	$215	$175	$150	$125	$70

Add 25% for .22 Short cal. (mfg. 1939-1952).
Add 25% for pre-WWII mfg.

MODEL 77 – .22 LR cal., detachable box mag. or tubular mag. under barrel. Over 217,000 mfg. between 1955-62.

	100%	98%	95%	90%	80%	70%	60%
	$250	$225	$200	$175	$110	$100	$70

Add $50 for tube mag.

MODEL 100 RIFLE – .243 Win., .284 Win., or .308 Win. cal., 4 shot detachable mag., 22 in. round barrel with open sights, gas operated, basket weave checkering impressed on stock, pistol grip cap. Over 262,000 mfg. 1961-73 with some production occurring in Japan.

	100%	98%	95%	90%	80%	70%	60%
	$550	$500	$450	$400	$300	$250	$230

The pre-1964 .284 Win. cal. with cut checkering was made for less than one year (WFF, ser. range 72,XXX with no letter suffix or prefix).

* ***Model 100 Rifle Pre-1964 Mfg.***

	100%	98%	95%	90%	80%	70%	60%
	$650	$575	$500	$450	$400	$300	$250

Add $50 for .243 Win. cal.
Add $250 for .284 Win. cal.

MODEL 100 CARBINE – similar to rifle, with 19 in. barrel, plain pistol grip stock, barrel band. Mfg. 1967-1973.

	100%	98%	95%	90%	80%	70%	60%
	$725	$600	$500	$425	$375	$300	$250

Add $50 for .243 Win. cal.
Add $300 for .284 Win. cal.

MODEL 190 RIFLE – .22 S, L, or LR cal., semi-auto, 15 shot LR tube mag., alloy receiver, uncheckered walnut finished hardwood stock, 20 1/2 (Carbine Model) or 24 (Rifle Model) in. barrel, approx. 2,150,000 (including the Model 290 listed also) during 1967-1980.

	100%	98%	95%	90%	80%	70%	60%
	$175	$150	$125	$100	$85	$75	$65

MODEL 290 DELUXE RIFLE – similar to 190, with select Monte Carlo stock. Mfg. 1965-1973.

	100%	98%	95%	90%	80%	70%	60%
	$225	$200	$175	$150	$115	$100	$90

GRADING - PPGS™	100%	98%	95%	90%	80%	70%	60%	LAST MSR

MODEL 490 RIFLE – .22 LR cal., 5 shot mag., 22 in. barrel, folding sight, checkered one piece stock. Mfg. 1975-1980.

	100%	98%	95%	90%	80%	70%	60%	LAST MSR
	$295	$250	$225	$185	$155	$145	$130	

SUPER X RIFLE GRADE I (SXR) – .30-06, .270 WSM, .300 WSM, or .300 Win. Mag. cal., gas operated action with multi-lug rotating bolt locking system, blued alloy receiver, 22 (.30-06 cal.) or 24 in. blue barrel w/o sights, hinged floorplate with 3 or 4 shot detachable box mag., enlarged trigger guard with cross bolt safety, walnut stock and raked forearm featuring unique circle pattern checkering on stock and forearm for grip, removable trigger assembly, approx. 7 1/4 lbs. Mfg. 2006-2009.

	100%	98%	95%	90%	80%	70%	60%	LAST MSR
	$785	$700	$600	$500	$450	$375	$325	*$949*

Add $30 for Mag. cals.

SUPER X RIFLE GRADE II (SXR) – similar to Super X Grade I, except also available in .325 WSM cal., deluxe wood ergonomic stock with adj. LOP and recoil reduction system, with or w/o TruGlo fiber optic sight system, 7 1/2 lbs. Mfg. 2007 only.

	100%	98%	95%	90%	80%	70%	60%	LAST MSR
	$725	$650	$575	$500	$425	$375	$325	*$864*

Add $28 for Mag. cals.

Add $68 for adj. LPA Sights with TruGlo fiber optic elements (.300 Win. Mag. or .325 WSM cal. only).

MODEL SX-AB – .308 Win. cal., 20 in. heavy barrel w/o sights, fully adj. stock with textured pistol grip and forearm, includes three interchangeable cheekpieces, 10 shot detachable mag., Picatinny bottom rail on forearm, 100% Mossy Oak Brush camo coverage, 10 lbs. Approx. 2,000 mfg. during 2009 only.

	100%	98%	95%	90%	80%	70%	60%	LAST MSR
	$1,150	$1,000	$900	$800	$700	$600	$550	*$1,379*

100%	98%	95%	90%	80%	70%	60%	50%	40%	30%	20%	10%

RIFLES: SLIDE ACTION, DISC.

MODEL 1890 – .22 S, L, LR, or WRF rimfire, cals. are non-interchangeable (don't shoot a .22 S in a gun chambered for .22 L) and the barrel is marked for single cal. only, visible hammer, solid-frame (first 15,000) or takedown, 24 in. octagonal barrel, case hardened receivers until 1901, model nomenclature changed to Model 90 circa 1919 at approx. ser. no. range 640,000. Approx. 849,000 mfg. between 1890-1932.

* ***Model 1890 First Model Solid Frame*** – color case hardened receiver, mfg. 1890-1892.

100%	98%	95%	90%	80%	70%	60%	50%	40%	30%	20%	10%
N/A	$15,000	$12,000	$10,000	$8,500	$6,500	$5,000	$4,750	$4,000	$3,500	$2,750	$2,250

Add 20% for .22 L or WRF cal.

* ***Model 1890 Second Model Takedown*** – color case hardened or blue receiver, takedown feature was added in 1892 after over 15,000 solid frames had been made, approx. ser. no. range 15,500-326,000. Mfg. 1892-1907.

» **Model 1890 Second Model Takedown w/Case Colored Receiver**

100%	98%	95%	90%	80%	70%	60%	50%	40%	30%	20%	10%
N/A	$8,000	$7,250	$6,500	$6,000	$5,000	$4,275	$3,750	$3,200	$2,500	$2,000	$1,500

» **Model 1890 Second Model Takedown w/Blue Finish**

100%	98%	95%	90%	80%	70%	60%	50%	40%	30%	20%	10%
N/A	$2,875	$2,550	$2,050	$1,750	$1,425	$1,100	$900	$750	$575	$500	$450

* ***Model 1890 Third Model Takedown w/Blue Finish*** – most commonly encountered Model 1890, post-1901 manufacture.

100%	98%	95%	90%	80%	70%	60%	50%	40%	30%	20%	10%
N/A	$3,000	$2,000	$1,250	$825	$650	$550	$450	$385	$335	$300	$250

Add 50% for .22 LR cal. (mfg circa 1919-1932, starting at ser. no. approx. 610,000).

.22 LR cal. accounted for approx. 10% of the total production on this model.

Deluxe model will bring premiums over values listed. There were also a limited amount of guns mfg. with stainless steel barrels which will add to values of post-1901 mfg.

The Model 1890 was Winchester's first slide action repeating rifle. It replaced the Model 1873 .22 cal. It was an excellent and inexpensive .22 rifle that rapidly became the universal firearm used in

shooting galleries. Even though production reached approx. 849,000 units, most guns were heavily used and specimens existing today in 98%+ condition are rare. Check carefully for rebarreling (notice proofmarks on barrel).

MODEL 1906 – .22 S, L, or LR, 20 in. round barrel, tube mag., visible hammer, open sights, straight stock with shotgun buttplate. Approx. 848,000 mfg. between 1906-1932.

100%	98%	95%	90%	80%	70%	60%	50%	40%	30%	20%	10%
N/A	N/A	$2,000	$1,500	$900	$550	$450	$350	$275	$250	$200	$175

Add 20% for non-grooved forearm.
Add 20% for .22 S cal. only.
This model is seldom encountered in over 90% original condition - original mint specimens can top $2,000.

Model nomenclature was changed to the Model 06 circa 1918.

* ***Model 1906 Expert*** – similar to Model 1906, except has a pistol grip stock and different shaped slide handle, finish choices included blue, nickel trimmed receiver, guard, and bolt, or full nickel trimmed, .22 S cal. only until approx. 70,000, mfg. 1917-1925.

100%	98%	95%	90%	80%	70%	60%	50%	40%	30%	20%	10%
N/A	N/A	$2,500	$2,000	$1,300	$900	$750	$600	$475	$350	$275	$225

MODEL 61 HAMMERLESS – .22 S, L, LR, WRF or Mag. cal., 24 in. round or octagon barrel (disc. 1947), with rifling or smooth bore (either small bore or Routledge), tube mag., open sights, plain grip stock. Approx. 350,000 mfg. between 1932-1963.

100%	98%	95%	90%	80%	70%	60%	50%	40%	30%	20%	10%
$1,325	$1,200	$1,050	$875	$725	$550	$475	$375	$325	$275	$225	$200

Add up to 150% for single cal. barrel marking (S or LR, Short is very rare).
Add $400 for pre-war mfg. w/small forearm.
Add 20% for grooved receiver.
Add 20% for pre-WWII rust blue metal finish.
Mint original pre-war Model 61s in the proper picture box are selling in the $3,800-$4,500 range. Post-war boxed Model 61s (Kraft box) are selling in the $2,800-$3,200 range. Smooth bore small diameter shot variations are selling in the $3,000-$4,000 range, while the Routledge shot variation with .410 diameter bore are selling in the $8,500-$10,000 range.

Pre-war manufacture has small forearm. "WRF" marked round barrel is rare - front of receiver must be marked "W.R.F."

Watch for fake boxes and hanging tags on this model, especially with rifles in over 95%+ original condition.

* ***Model 61 WRF*** – .22 WRF cal. only, front of the receiver, bottom side, must be stamped "WRF", octagon barrel mfg. 1932-1946, and round barrel mfg. 1947-1950.

100%	98%	95%	90%	80%	70%	60%	50%	40%	30%	20%	10%
$2,600	$2,475	$2,350	$2,000	$1,750	$1,250	$1,000	$750	$575	$475	$400	$250

Add 20% for round barrel.
Mint original pre-war WRF Model 61s in the proper picture box are selling in the $3,500-$3,800 range. Post-war boxed WRF Model 61s (Kraft box) are selling in the $3,800-$4,500 range.

* ***Model 61 Octagon .22 LR*** – .22 LR cal., octagon barrel variation of the Model 61. Disc. approx. 1947.

100%	98%	95%	90%	80%	70%	60%	50%	40%	30%	20%	10%
$3,500	$3,250	$2,875	$2,550	$2,100	$1,750	$1,425	$1,100	$900	$750	$575	$500

* ***Model 61 Octagon .22 WRF*** – .22 WRF cal. octagon barrel variation of the Model 61. Disc. approx. 1947.

100%	98%	95%	90%	80%	70%	60%	50%	40%	30%	20%	10%
$3,750	$3,450	$3,150	$2,750	$2,200	$1,850	$1,525	$1,250	$1,000	$750	$500	$400

* ***Model 61 Magnum*** – similar to Standard 61, but chambered for .22 WMR, three variations include two barrel marking differences and the third has an additional letter "A" stamped on the bottom of the trigger guard assembly, indicating a factory update. Mfg. 1959-1961.

100%	98%	95%	90%	80%	70%	60%	50%	40%	30%	20%	10%
$2,425	$2,200	$1,975	$1,575	$1,325	$1,050	$875	$750	$600	$500	$450	$375

Add $600-$1,000 for rare "WMRF" barrel marking.
Mint original rifles in the proper Kraft box are currently selling for approx. in the $3,000-$3,500 range.

100%	98%	95%	90%	80%	70%	60%	50%	40%	30%	20%	10%

* ***Model 61 Octagon .22 Short*** – .22 Short cal., octagon barrel variation of the Model 61. Disc. approx. 1947.

$4,000	$3,800	$3,500	$3,150	$2,750	$2,200	$1,850	$1,525	$1,250	$1,000	$750	$500

* ***Model 61 Smoothbore*** – .22 cal. shot cartridge only, 24 in. round smoothbore barrel, three variations include the Routledge bore with 3/8 in. muzzle bore diameter and matted frame top (approx. 75 mfg. in the 45,000-47,000 ser. range), second variation is referred to as the Winchester Counter Bore (bore is slightly larger than a .22 cartridge), third variation is the Straight Smoothbore with bore diameter the same as the .22 cartridge.

$3,850	$3,500	$3,150	$2,750	$2,200	$1,850	$1,525	$1,250	$1,000	$750	$500	$400

Add 100% for Routledge bore.

Mint original boxed guns are currently selling for $4,500-$6,000 for the Winchester Counter Bore and Straight Smoothbore, and $8,000-$10,000 for the Routledge Bore.

MODEL 62/62A VISIBLE HAMMER – modern version of 1890, will shoot calibers interchangeably, 23 in. round tapered or octagon barrel. Over 409,000 mfg. between 1932-1958.

$1,500	$950	$675	$475	$375	$300	$250	$200	$185	$170	$155	$130

Add 50% for Gallery model (Gallery style loading port).

Add 30% for pre-WWII mfg.

Pre-war Model is 62, distinguishable by small forearm. The Model 62-A was introduced 1940 at approx. serial number 99,200 with minor changes. Model 62A single cal. barrel markings do not add premiums. .22 Short only models without the Winchester roll die receiver marking are more scarce than the so-called "Gallery Rifle" - mint specimens without the roll die marking are approx. $2,000. Also watch for fake roll die markings. Gallery variations of these models will also command sizable premium. Watch for fake boxes and hanging tags on this model, especially with rifles in over 95%+ original condition.

GRADING - PPGS™	100%	98%	95%	90%	80%	70%	60%	LAST MSR
MODEL 270 – .22 LR cal., tube mag., 20 1/2 in. barrel, checkered walnut pistol grip stock. Mfg. 1963-73.	$175	$150	$135	$120	$100	$80	$70	
* ***Model 270 Plastic Forearm Variation***	$150	$135	$120	$100	$80	$70	$60	
* ***Model 270 Deluxe*** – similar to 270, with select wood, Monte Carlo stock. Mfg. 1965-73.	$250	$200	$150	$110	$80	$70	$60	
MODEL 275 – similar to 270, in .22 WMR cal.	$200	$175	$150	$135	$100	$80	$70	
* ***Model 275 Deluxe*** – similar to 270 Deluxe, in .22 WMR cal.	$350	$295	$250	$200	$150	$125	$90	

RIFLES: LEVER ACTION - POST 1964 PRODUCTION

MODEL 64 1972-1974 MODEL – .30-30 Win. cal., lever action, 5 shot, 2/3 tube mag., 24 in. barrel, open sight, plain pistol grip stock. Mfg. 1972-74.	$450	$400	$350	$300	$250	$200	$150	
MODEL 71 STANDARD – .348 Win. cal., 24 in. round tapered barrel with buckhorn rear and hooded ramp front sight, top tang safety, 4 shot half mag., uncheckered walnut stock with steel buttplate and forearm, approx. 8 lbs. Mfg. by Miroku 2012 only.	$1,275	$1,125	$900	$800	$700	$600	$500	*$1,470*
MODEL 71 DELUXE – .348 Win. cal., similar to Model 71 Standard, except has deluxe checkered walnut stock and forearm. Mfg. 2012 only.	$1,475	$1,275	$1,075	$950	$825	$700	$575	*$1,660*

GRADING - PPGS™	100%	98%	95%	90%	80%	70%	60%	LAST MSR

MODEL 88 RIFLE (1955-1963 MFG.) – Please see listing under Rifles: Lever Action - 1860-1964.

MODEL 88 RIFLE (1964-1973 MFG.) – .243 Win., .284 Win., or .308 Win. cal., 1964 model with impressed basket weave checkering, no barrel band, 22 in. barrel. Mfg. 1964-1973.

	100%	98%	95%	90%	80%	70%	60%	LAST MSR
.308 Win. cal.	$850	$650	$475	$400	$350	$275	$225	
.243 Win. cal.	$1,100	$800	$550	$500	$450	$400	$300	
.284 Win. cal.	$2,000	$1,700	$1,500	$1,200	$1,000	$750	$600	

MODEL 88 CARBINE – introduced 1968, no checkering, one-piece stock, barrel band, 19 in. barrel. Mfg. 1968-1973.

	100%	98%	95%	90%	80%	70%	60%	LAST MSR
.308 Win. cal. (1968-1973)	$1,225	$1,100	$850	$725	$525	$450	$395	
.243 Win. cal.	$1,650	$1,350	$1,200	$1,025	$925	$800	$650	
.284 Win. cal.	$3,000	$2,600	$2,250	$2,000	$1,600	$1,300	$1,000	

MODEL 150 – .22 LR, 20 1/2 in. barrel, tube mag., hammerless, uncheckered hardwood stock and forearm, sling swivels, approx. 47,400 mfg. 1967-74.

	100%	98%	95%	90%	80%	70%	60%	LAST MSR
	$125	$110	$95	$70	$60	$50	$40	

MODEL 250 – .22 LR, 20 1/2 in. barrel, tube mag., hammerless, checkered pistol grip stock. Mfg. 1963-73.

	100%	98%	95%	90%	80%	70%	60%	LAST MSR
	$175	$150	$125	$110	$95	$70	$60	

* ***Model 250 Deluxe*** – similar to Model 250, with select wood and sling swivels. Mfg. 1965-71.

	100%	98%	95%	90%	80%	70%	60%	LAST MSR
	$250	$200	$160	$115	$95	$70	$60	

MODEL 255 – .22 WMR, otherwise similar to Model 250. Mfg. 1964-70.

	100%	98%	95%	90%	80%	70%	60%	LAST MSR
	$235	$200	$175	$150	$135	$110	$85	

* ***Model 255 Deluxe*** – .22 WMR cal., with select wood and swivels. Mfg. 1965-73.

	100%	98%	95%	90%	80%	70%	60%	LAST MSR
	$300	$260	$215	$165	$150	$135	$100	

MODEL 1873 SHORT RIFLE – .357 Mag./.38 Spl. cal., 10 or 11 shot full mag., 20 in. barrel with semi-buckhorn rear sight and Marbles gold bead front sight, straight grip satin oil finished walnut stock and forearm, crescent buttplate, blue finish, features firing pin/striker block safety, rear tang is drilled and tapped, brass carrier block, 7 1/4 lbs. New 2013.

	100%	98%	95%	90%	80%	70%	60%	LAST MSR
MSR $1,300	$1,150	$995	$850	$725	$625	$525	$425	

MODEL 1886 GRADE I – .45-70 Govt. cal., 26 in. octagon barrel. Mfg. 1997-98.

	100%	98%	95%	90%	80%	70%	60%	LAST MSR
	$995	$900	$850	$750	$650	$600	$500	*$996*

* ***Model 1886 High Grade*** – .45-70 Govt. cal., features gold-line receiver engraving with multiple gold animals, polished blue, deluxe checkered walnut stock and forearm with metal cap, 1,000 mfg. 1997 only.

	100%	98%	95%	90%	80%	70%	60%	LAST MSR
	$1,625	$1,325	$1,050	N/A	N/A	N/A	N/A	*$1,588*

MODEL 1886 TAKEDOWN – .45-70 Govt. cal., features original takedown action design, uncheckered semi-pistol grip walnut stock with crescent buttplate, 26 in. octagon barrel with buckhorn rear sight, forend has ebony cap, 9 1/4 lbs. Mfg. 1999 only.

	100%	98%	95%	90%	80%	70%	60%	LAST MSR
	$1,200	$1,050	$900	$775	$700	$600	$500	*$1,140*

MODEL 1886 EXTRA LIGHT GRADE I – .45-70 Govt. cal., 22 in. round tapered barrel, shotgun buttplate, half magazine, high polish receiver and barrel bluing, open sights, uncheckered walnut stock and forearm, 7 1/4 lbs. 3,500 mfg. 2000-2001, and 2010-2012.

	100%	98%	95%	90%	80%	70%	60%	LAST MSR
	$1,175	$950	$800	$725	$650	$575	$495	*$1,270*

* ***Model 1886 Extra Light High Grade*** – similar to Model 1886 Extra Light Grade I, except features engraved elk and whitetail deer and game scenes on blue receiver, extra fancy checkered walnut stock and forearm, 7 1/4 lbs. 1,000 mfg. 2000-2001.

	100%	98%	95%	90%	80%	70%	60%	LAST MSR
	$1,500	$1,100	$950	N/A	N/A	N/A	N/A	*$1,440*

GRADING - PPGS™	100%	98%	95%	90%	80%	70%	60%	LAST MSR

MODEL 1886 SHORT RIFLE – .45-70 Govt. cal., 24 in. round barrel with full length mag. tube, adj. buckhorn rear sight and gold bead Marble's front sight, 8 shot mag., blued metal finish, uncheckered satin finished walnut stock and forearm, crescent steel buttplate, approx. 8 3/8 lbs. New 2011.

MSR $1,340	$1,175	$925	$825	$700	$600	$500	$425	

MODEL 1892 GRADE I – .357 Mag. (new 1998), .44-40 WCF (new 1998), or .45 LC cal., similar to original Model 1892 Winchester, 24 in. round barrel, top tang mounted manual hammer stop, blue finish with etched receiver engraving, gold trigger, satin finished walnut straight grip stock and forend with metal cap, 6 1/4 lbs. Mfg. 1997-99.

	$725	$600	$475	$400	$350	$295	$250	*$744*

* ***Model 1892 Grade I Short Rifle*** – .44 Mag. cal., features 20 in. round barrel with full mag., uncheckered staight grip walnut stock with crescent buttplate, buckhorn rear sight, high polish blue finish only, 6 lbs. Mfg. 1999-2000.

	$750	$625	$500	$425	$375	$325	$275	*$752*

* ***Model 1892 Grade I Short Rifle (2009-2012 Mfg.)*** – .44 Rem. Mag. or .357 Mag. cal., 20 in. round gloss blue barrel, steel receiver, tube mag., oil finished Grade I straight grip walnut stock with crescent buttplate, short forearm with steel cap, Marble's gold bead front sight, buckhorn style rear sight, tang safety, 6 lbs., 8 oz. Mfg. 2009-2012.

	$925	$800	$725	$625	$550	$500	$450	*$1,069*

* ***Model 1892 Trapper*** – .44-40 WCF, .44 Rem. Mag., .357 Mag., or .45 LC cal., 16 in. round gloss blue barrel, high polish blue steel receiver, tube mag., oil finished Grade I straight grip walnut stock with plastic shotgun style buttplate, Marble's gold bead front sight, buckhorn style rear sight, tang safety, 5 lbs. 14 oz. Mfg. mid-2011-2012.

	$925	$800	$725	$625	$550	$500	$450	*$1,069*

* ***Model 1892 Trapper Takedown*** – .44-40 WCF, .44 Rem. Mag., .357 Mag., or .45 LC cal., 16 in. octagon gloss blue barrel, takedown action, high polish blue steel receiver, tube mag., oil finished Grade I pistol grip checkered walnut stock with polished crescent buttplate, rifle forearm, Marble's gold bead front sight, buckhorn style rear sight, tang safety, 6 lbs. 4 oz. Mfg. mid-2011-2012.

	$1,395	$1,100	$950	$850	$750	$650	$550	*$1,549*

* ***Model 1892 Case Hardened Sporter*** – .44-40 WCF, .44 Rem. Mag., .357 Mag., or .45 LC cal., 24 in. octagon gloss blue barrel, case colored steel receiver, tube mag., oil finished Grade I straight grip uncheckered walnut stock with case colored crescent buttplate, rifle forearm, with case colored forearm cap, Marble's gold bead front sight, buckhorn style rear sight, tang safety, 7 lbs., 4 oz. Mfg. mid-2011-2012.

	$1,125	$900	$800	$700	$600	$500	$425	*$1,269*

* ***Model 1892 High Grade*** – .45 LC cal., features gold accents and receiver game scene, 1,000 mfg. 1997 only.

	$1,250	$1,050	$795	N/A	N/A	N/A	N/A	*$1,285*

MODEL 1892 CARBINE – .357 Mag., .44 Rem. Mag., .44-40 Win., or .45 LC cal., top tang safety, 20 in. round barrel with barrel band and full length mag., blade front and semi-buckhorn rear sight, satin finish, uncheckered straight grip walnut stock and forearm, steel crescent buttplate, 10 shot mag., approx. 6 lbs. Mfg. by Miroku in Japan. New 2011.

MSR $1,160	$995	$850	$725	$625	$500	$400	$300	

* ***Model 1892 Large Loop Carbine*** – .357 Mag., .44 Rem. Mag., .44-40 Win., or .45 LC cal., similar to Model 1892 Carbine, except has large loop lever and carbine ladder rear sight, 5 lbs. 12 oz. Mfg. 2011-2012.

	$1,075	$925	$800	$675	$550	$425	$300	*$1,260*

GRADING - PPGS™	100%	98%	95%	90%	80%	70%	60%	LAST MSR

MODEL 1892 JOHN WAYNE HIGH GRADE – .44-40 WCF cal., 18 1/2 in. barrel, 9 shot, silver nickel nitride receiver with engraved John Wayne portrait, initials, and flowing banner with "Courage, Strength, Grit" on right side, two portraits and banner with "John Wayne American 1907-2007" on left side, blue loading gate and action screws, ladder style adj. rear sight, saddle ring, blue hammer and trigger, large loop lever, uncheckered walnut stock, limited mfg. of 4,000, first 1,000 offered as match set with Custom Grade. Disc. 2009.

	$1,895	$1,750	$1,500	N/A	N/A	N/A	N/A	*$1,999*

MODEL 1892 JOHN WAYNE CUSTOM GRADE – .44-40 WCF cal., 18 1/2 in. barrel with gold signature, 9 shot, blue receiver with engraved John Wayne portrait, initials, and flowing banner with "Courage, Strength, Grit" on right side, two portraits and banner with "John Wayne American 1907-2007" on left side, blue loading gate and action screws, ladder style adj. rear sight, saddle ring, blue hammer and trigger, large loop lever, checkered Grade 5/6 satin walnut stock and forearm, limited mfg. of 1,000. Disc. 2009.

	$3,250	$2,750	$2,325	N/A	N/A	N/A	N/A	*$3,499*

MODEL 1895 GRADE I – .270 Win. (disc. 1999), .30-06 (mfg. 1998-1999, reintroduced 2010), .30-40 Krag (new 2010), or .405 Win. (mfg. 2000-2004, reintroduced 2010) cal., similar to original Model 1895 Winchester, checkered straight grip stock and Schnabel forearm, 24 in. round barrel, with buckhorn rear sight, 4 shot mag., top tang safety, blue finish, 8 lbs. Mfg. 1997-2004, and limited production 2010.

	$1,050	$900	$775	$675	$575	$525	$475	*$1,179*

MODEL 1895 LIMITED EDITION – .30-06, similar to original Model 1895 Winchester, blue receiver, 24 in. round barrel, 4 shot mag. (box mag.), uncheckered woodstock and forearm, rear buckhorn sight, 2 piece cocking lever, 8 lbs. 4,000 mfg. 1995-97.

	$975	$700	$550	N/A	N/A	N/A	N/A	*$853*

* ***Model 1895 Limited Edition High Grade*** – .30-06 (mfg. 1995-99) or .405 Win. (mfg. 2000-2002) cal., same general specifications as the Model 1895 Limited Edition, features older No. 3 engraving pattern with double scenes, gold borders with multiple gold inlays, deluxe checkered walnut stock and forearm. 4,000 mfg. 1995-2002.

	$1,750	$1,275	$1,000	N/A	N/A	N/A	N/A	*$1,532*

Add 20% for .405 Win. cal.

MODEL 1895 THEODORE ROOSEVELT 150TH ANNIVERSARY CUSTOM GRADE – .405 Win. cal., high polish blue receiver engraved with North American big game scenes, extensive gold plating, gold "Theodore Roosevelt" signature on receiver, top of barrel is matted, deluxe high grade walnut stock, includes commemorative brochure. 500 mfg. in sets with High Grade matching serial numbers 2008.

	$2,750	$2,350	$1,875	$1,525	$1,200	$995	$795	*$3,299*

MODEL 1895 THEODORE ROOSEVELT 150TH ANNIVERSARY HIGH GRADE – .405 Win. cal., nitride finished receiver engraved with North American big game scenes, gold accents, gold "Theodore Roosevelt" signature on receiver, top of barrel is matted, deluxe high grade walnut stock, includes commemorative brochure. 1,000 mfg. 2008.

	$1,500	$1,275	$1,050	$900	$775	$650	$525	*$1,599*

MODEL 1895 THEODORE ROOSEVELT SAFARI HIGH GRADE – .405 Win. cal., 4 shot mag., 24 in. blue barrel, checkered Grade II/III walnut stock and forearm, silver nitride receiver with deep engraving, gold African big game inlays and embellishments, matte blue finish, TR "Safari Centennial 1909-2009" medallion on stock, gold signature on trigger guard, buckhorn rear sight, Marbles front sight, drilled and tapped, special matching ser. nos., includes full color box sleeve, special edition hang tag, owner's manual, and hardcover copy of Roosevelt's book, *African Game Trails,* and deluxe double gun case, 8 lbs. Ltd. mfg. of 1,500, the first 1,000 sold as a set with the Custom Grade, remaining 500 sold individually. Mfg. 2009.

	$1,575	$1,350	$1,100	N/A	N/A	N/A	N/A	*$1,749*

GRADING - PPGS™	100%	98%	95%	90%	80%	70%	60%	LAST MSR

MODEL 1895 THEODORE ROOSEVELT SAFARI CUSTOM GRADE TWO GUN SET – .405 Win. cal., 4 shot mag., 24 in. blue barrel, checkered Grade III/IV walnut stock and forearm, blue receiver with deep engraving, gold African big game inlays and embellishments, matte blue finish, TR "Safari Centennial 1909-2009" medallion on stock, jeweled hammer, special matching ser. nos., patterned after Roosevelt's 1895 rifle featured in Cody Firearms Museum, includes full color box sleeve, special edition hang tag, owner's manual, and hardcover copy of Roosevelt's book, *African Game Trails,* and deluxe double gun case, 8 lbs. Ltd. mfg. of 1,000 two gun sets, sold only with Model 1895 Safari High Grade. Mfg. 2009.

	$3,350	**$2,950**	**$2,450**	**N/A**	**N/A**	**N/A**	**N/A**	***$3,649***

RIFLES: LEVER ACTION - MODEL 94, 1964-2006 MFG.

Due to engineering changes in 1992, all Model 94s and variations (not including the 9422 models) had a crossbolt safety in the upper rear of the receiver which prevents the hammer from contacting the firing pin.

100th Anniversary Model 1894s (mfg. 1994) are marked "1894-1994" on the receiver. During 2003, Winchester discontinued the crossbolt receiver safety, and introduced the new top tang safety.

U.S. Repeating Arms closed its New Haven, CT manufacturing facility on March 31, 2006, and an auction was held on Sept. 27-28, 2006, selling the production equipment and related assets.

AE suffix on the following models indicates angle eject.

The Model 94s listed below w/crossbolt safety (1992-2006 mfg.) are not as desirable as those models w/o the crossbolt safety manufactured pre-1992, unless a rare variation, configuration and/or caliber is involved.

MODEL 94 STANDARD MODEL – .30-30 Win., .32 Win. Spl. (disc. 1973, reintroduced 1992), 7-30 Waters (new 1989), .44 Mag. (mfg. circa late 1960s-1970s), .44 Spl. (mfg. 1984), .444 Marlin (mfg. 1984), or .45 LC (mfg. 1984) cal., lever action, 6 or 7 (24 in. barrel only) shot tube mag., 20 or 24 (mfg. 1987-88 only) in. round barrel, open sights, straight walnut stock, two barrel bands on forearm, Angle Eject became standard 1984, 6 1/2 lbs. Mfg. 1964-1997.

	$425	**$350**	**$295**	**$250**	**$200**	**$175**	**$150**	***$363***

Add 25% for 7-30 Waters cal.

MODEL 94 TRADITIONAL (DELUXE WALNUT) – .30-30 Win., .44 Mag. (new 1999), or .480 Ruger Big Bore (mfg. 2002-2003) cal., similar to Standard Rifle, except has plain (new 1998, not available in .44 Mag. cal.) or checkered walnut stock and forearm, 6 (.30-30 Win. cal.) 10 (.480 Ruger cal.), or 11 (.44 Mag. cal.) shot mag., 6 1/4 lbs. Mfg. 1988-2004.

	$495	**$375**	**$325**	**$275**	**$225**	**$200**	**$175**	***$436***

Add $34 for Traditional-CW Model (w/checkered stock and forearm).
Add $57 for .44 Mag. cal. (Traditional-CW Model with checkered stock, mfg. 1999-2004).
Add for .480 Ruger Big Bore cal. (mfg. 2002-2003) - $43 (Traditional) or $105 (Traditional-CW).
Add $55 for 1.5 - 4.5X scope with low mounts (disc.).

MODEL 94 LEGACY ROUND – .30-30 Win., .357 Mag. (new 1997), .44 Mag. (new 1997), or .45 LC (new 1997) cal., 7 (.30-30 Win. cal. only) or 12 shot mag., features pistol grip checkered walnut stock and forearm, 20 (disc. 1999) or 24 (new 1997) in. round barrel, 6 3/4 lbs. Mfg. 1995-2006.

	$550	**$400**	**$350**	**$275**	**$225**	**$200**	**$175**	***$497***

Subtract $15 for 20 in. barrel.

* ***Model 94 Legacy Round 26 In.*** – .30-30 Win. or .38-55 Win. cal., 7 shot mag., adj. Marble's rear tang sight, similar to Model 94 Legacy Round, except features blue or color case hardened receiver and 26 in. round barrel, 7 lbs. Mfg. 2004-2006.

	$725	**$575**	**$425**	**$350**	**$300**	**$250**	**$200**	***$783***

Add 15% for case colored receiver.
Add a slight premium for .38-55 WCF cal.

GRADING - PPGS™	100%	98%	95%	90%	80%	70%	60%	LAST MSR

MODEL 94 LEGACY OCTAGON – .30-30 Win. or .38-55 Win. cal., 7 shot mag., adj. Marble's rear tang sight, features crescent buttplate, blue or color case hardened receiver and 26 in. octagon barrel, 7 1/4 lbs. Mfg. 2004-2006.

$750	$600	$450	$375	$325	$300	$275	$882

Add 20% for case colored receiver.

Add a slight premium for .38-55 WCF cal.

MODEL 94 RANGER – .30-30 Win. cal. only, 20 in. barrel, uncheckered hardwood stock and forearm, 6 shot mag., 6 1/4 lbs. Mfg. 1985-2006.

$395	$325	$275	$225	$200	$175	$150	$386

Add approx. 15% for 4x32 scope with see-through mounts (disc. 1999).

* ***Model 94 Ranger Compact*** – .30-30 Win. or .357 Mag. cal., 16 in. barrel, uncheckered hardwood stock with 12 1/2 LOP with recoil pad, post-style front sight, 5 (.30-30 Win. cal.) or 9 shot mag., 5 7/8 lbs. Mfg. 1998-2004.

$525	$425	$300	$200	$175	$150	$125	$402

MODEL 94 TRAILS END – .357 Mag., .44-40 WCF (mfg. 1998-99), .44 Mag., or .45 LC cal., similar to standard rifle, except has 11 shot tube mag., 20 in. barrel, choice of standard or large loop lever (disc. 1998), crossbolt safety, 6 1/2 lbs. Mfg. 1997-2006.

$700	$575	$475	$300	$225	$175	$150	$480

Add approx. $20 for large loop lever (disc. 1998).

* ***Model 94 Trails End Takedown*** – similar to Model 94 Trails End, except has takedown action. Limited mfg. 2006.

$750	$600	$450	$375	$325	$300	$275	$559

* ***Model 94 Trails End Octagon*** – similar to Model 94 Trails End, except has octagon barrel, choice of blue or case colored receiver finish, 6 3/4 lbs. Mfg. 2004-2006.

$825	$700	$575	$425	$300	$250	$200	$757

Add 15% for case colored receiver.

MODEL 94 TRAILS END HUNTER ROUND – .25-35 Win., .30-30 Win., or .38-55 Win. cal., 20 in. round barrel, 6 shot mag., uncheckered walnut stock and forearm, shotgun buttplate, 6 1/2 lbs. Mfg. 2005-2006.

$695	$575	$450	$325	$250	$175	$150	$480

Add a premium for .25-35 WCF or .38-55 WCF cal.

* ***Model 94 Trails End Hunter Round Takedown*** – similar to Model 94 Trails End Hunter Round, except has takedown action. Limited mfg. 2006.

$775	$600	$475	$350	$275	$225	$200	$559

* ***Model 94 Trails End Hunter Octagon*** – similar to Model 94 Trails End Hunter, except has blued (new 2006) or case colored receiver and octagon barrel, crescent buttplate. Mfg. 2005-2006.

$825	$700	$550	$425	$325	$275	$250	$757

Add 15% for case colored receiver.

Add a premium for .25-35 WCF or .38-55 WCF cal.

MODEL 94 SHORT HUNTER TAKEDOWN – .30-30 Win., .44 Mag., or .450 Marlin cal., takedown action, 18 in. barrel, 6 or 10 (.44 Mag. only) shot mag., uncheckered walnut stock, XS ghost ring sight, 6 lbs. Limited mfg. 2006.

$775	$600	$475	$350	$275	$225	$200	$587

MODEL 94 PACK RIFLE – .30-30 Win. or .44 Mag. cal., 18 in. barrel, 4 or 5 shot 3/4 mag., over-dimension walnut stock and forearm cap w/o checkering, removable hood sight, 6 1/4 lbs. Mfg. 2000-2001.

$450	$375	$325	$250	$200	$175	$140	$496

GRADING - PPGS™	100%	98%	95%	90%	80%	70%	60%	LAST MSR

MODEL 94 TIMBER CARBINE – .444 Marlin (disc. 2001) or .450 Marlin (new 2004) cal., 18 in. ported barrel with 4 (.450 Marlin cal. only) or 5 (disc. 2001) shot 2/3 mag., top tang safety, checkered semi-pistol grip stock and forearm, blue finish only, adj. XS ghost ring rear sight (new 2004), hooded front sight (disc. 2001) or ramp style front sight, 6 lbs. Mfg. 1999-2001, reintroduced 2004-2006.

	$825	$675	$550	$400	$300	$250	$200	*$623*

* ***Model 94 Timber Carbine Scout*** – .30-30 Win. or .44 Mag. cal., similar to Model 94 Timber Carbine, 18 in. non-ported barrel with rail base, 4 (.30-30 Win.) or 8 (.44 Mag.) shot mag., XS ghost ring sights, uncheckered walnut stock and forearm, 6 lbs. Mfg. 2005-2006.

	$675	$550	$425	$325	$250	$175	$150	*$623*

* ***Model 94 Timber Carbine Scout Takedown*** – similar to Model 94 Timber Scout, except has takedown action and Pachmayr recoil pad. Limited mfg. 2006.

	$750	$600	$450	$375	$325	$300	$275	*$699*

MODEL 94 WIN-TUFF RIFLE – .30-30 Win. cal., similar to Model 94 Rifle, except has laminated hardwood stock and forearm with checkering. Drilled and tapped for scope mounts. Mfg. 1987-disc.

	$375	$300	$250	$200	$180	$160	$140	*$404*

MODEL 94 BLACK SHADOW – .30-30 Win. or .44 Mag./.44 Spl. cal., 20 or 24 (.30- 30 Win. cal. only) in. barrel, 4 or 5 shot mag., non-glare finish, features black composite synthetic stock with recoil pad and Fuller forearm, approx. 6 1/4 lbs. Mfg. 1998-2000.

	$575	$450	$325	$225	$175	$150	$135	*$381*

* ***Model 94 Black Shadow Big Bore*** – .444 Marlin cal., 20 in. barrel only, otherwise similar to Model 94 Black Shadow, 6 1/2 lbs. Mfg. 1998-2000.

	$550	$425	$325	$250	$200	$150	$135	*$394*

MODEL 94 TRAPPER – .30-30 Win., .357 Mag. (mfg. beginning 1992), .44 Mag./.44 Spl. (new 1985), or .45 LC (new 1985) cal., 16 In. barrel, side ejection, walnut stock, 5 (.30-30 Win. cal.) or 9 shot tube mag., blue finish, dovetailed front sight, 6 lbs. Disc. 2006.

	$675	$550	$425	$325	$250	$175	$150	*$470*

* ***Model 94 Trapper Compact*** – .357 Mag. cal., similar to Model 94 Trapper, except has 12 1/2 in. LOP stock. Limited mfg. 2006.

	$775	$600	$450	$375	$325	$300	$275	*$486*

MODEL 94 BIG BORE – .307 Win. (disc. 1998), .356 Win. (disc. 1998), or .375 Win. (disc. 1987), or .444 Marlin (new 1998) cal., angled ejection port provides scope mounting, checkered walnut Monte Carlo stock with recoil pad, 20 in. barrel, 6 shot mag., sling swivels, 6 1/2 lbs. New 1983.

	$775	$600	$450	$375	$325	$300	$275	*$465*

Add 25% for .356 Win. or .375 Win. cal.

Also mfg. in a top eject (pre-USRA). This model had an "XTR" suffix until 1989.

MODEL 94 HERITAGE CUSTOM 1 OF 100 – .38-55 WCF cal., special edition for the NSSF Heritage Fund, features Winchester's historic No. 2 pattern hand engraved with 24Kt. gold inlays and individually signed by the engraver, deluxe spade checkered straight grip stock and forearm with metal cap, 1/2 round, 1/2 octagon 26 in. barrel, 6 3/4 lbs. Mfg. by the custom shop 2002-2003.

	$4,750	$3,150	$1,600	N/A	N/A	N/A	N/A	*$5,200*

MODEL 94 HERITAGE HIGH GRADE 1 OF 1000 – .38-55 WCF cal., special edition for the NSSF Heritage Fund, features Winchester's historic No. 3 engraving pattern with 24Kt. gold inlays, deluxe checkered straight grip stock and forearm with metal cap, 1/2 round, 1/2 octagon 26 in. barrel, signed by engraver with factory letter, ser. no. prefix HER, 6 3/4 lbs. Mfg. 2002 only. While 1,000 rifles were scheduled to be manufactured, only 255 were mfg.

	$2,250	$1,850	$1,450	N/A	N/A	N/A	N/A	*$1,883*

GRADING - PPGS™	100%	98%	95%	90%	80%	70%	60%	LAST MSR

MODEL 94 CUSTOM LIMITED EDITION – .44-40 WCF (mfg. 2000 only) or .38-55 WCF (new 2001) cal., features case colored receiver and 24 in. octagon match (.44-40 WCF cal. only) or 1/2 round, 1/2 octagon (.38-55 WCF cal. only) barrel with satin bluing, full (.44-40 WCF only) or 3/4 mag. tube, spade checkered straight grip walnut stock and forearm with metal cap, 7 1/4 (.38-55 WCF cal.) or 7 3/4 lbs. Only 75 mfg. in .44-40 WCF cal. 2000-2002.

	100%	98%	95%	90%	80%	70%	60%	LAST MSR
	$2,400	**$1,875**	**$1,700**	**N/A**	**N/A**	**N/A**	**N/A**	***$2,393***

MODEL 94 NEW GENERATION CUSTOM – .30-30 Win. cal., fancy pistol grip stock and long forearm with spade checkering, high lustre bluing with custom scroll engraving and hand engraved gold moose on right side of frame and gold doe/buck on left, new tang safety, 20 in. barrel. Limited mfg. 2003-2004.

	100%	98%	95%	90%	80%	70%	60%	LAST MSR
	$2,750	**$2,275**	**$1,900**	**N/A**	**N/A**	**N/A**	**N/A**	***$2,995***

MODEL 94 LIMITED EDITION CENTENNIAL – .30-30 Win. cal., crossbolt safety, manufactured to commemorate the 100th anniversary of the Model 94 in 1994.

* ***Model 94 Limited Edition Centennial Grade I*** – features No. 9 style Winchester engraving pattern (rolled) on both sides of receiver, 26 in. half-round half-octagonal barrel, pistol grip stock and forearm with cut checkering, half mag., open sights, crescent buttplate, 12,000 mfg. 1994.

	100%	98%	95%	90%	80%	70%	60%	LAST MSR
	$995	**$800**	**$650**	**N/A**	**N/A**	**N/A**	**N/A**	***$811***

* ***Model 94 Limited Edition Centennial High Grade*** – features No. 6 style Winchester engraving pattern (rolled) on both sides of receiver with gold outlines and 2 gold animals (mountain sheep and deer), Lyman No. 2 tang mounted rear sight, F-style checkering and carving, deluxe walnut, 26 in. half-round half-octagonal barrel, half-mag., crescent buttplate, 3,000 mfg. 1994.

	100%	98%	95%	90%	80%	70%	60%	LAST MSR
	$1,995	**$1,575**	**$1,200**	**N/A**	**N/A**	**N/A**	**N/A**	***$1,272***

* ***Model 94 Limited Edition Centennial Custom High Grade*** – .30 WCF cal., features No. 5 style Winchester engraving pattern (hand-executed) on both sides of greyed receiver, etched by Baron Technology, gold outline panel scenes featuring caribou and pronghorns, Lyman No. 2 upper tang sight, F-style checkering and carving, 26 in. half-round half-octagonal barrel, half-mag., crescent buttplate, 94 mfg. in 1994.

	100%	98%	95%	90%	80%	70%	60%	LAST MSR
	$5,500	**$4,500**	**$3,750**	**N/A**	**N/A**	**N/A**	**N/A**	***$4,684***

MODEL 94 XTR – .30-30 Win. or 7-30 Waters (new 1985) cal., 20 or 24 (7-30 Waters only) in. barrel, checkered select walnut, hooded front sight (except 7-30 Waters which has dovetailed front blade), 6 1/2 lbs. Disc. 1988.

	100%	98%	95%	90%	80%	70%	60%	LAST MSR
	$650	**$550**	**$425**	**$325**	**$250**	**$175**	**$150**	***$285***

Add $100 for 7-30 Waters cal. rifle.

The XTR nomenclature was disc. 1988.

* ***Model 94 XTR Deluxe*** – .30-30 Win. cal. only, deluxe American walnut stock and lengthened forearm with fancy checkering, 20 in. barrel with deluxe script, rubber buttpad. Mfg. 1987-88 only.

	100%	98%	95%	90%	80%	70%	60%	LAST MSR
	$675	**$575**	**$450**	**$325**	**$250**	**$175**	**$150**	***$426***

MODEL 94 .44 MAG. S.R.C. – .44 Mag. cal., top eject, 20 in. barrel, SRC. Mfg. 1967-1972.

	100%	98%	95%	90%	80%	70%	60%
	$600	**$475**	**$300**	**$225**	**$175**	**$150**	**$135**

MODEL 94 CLASSIC SERIES – .30-30 Win. cal., 20 or 26 in. octagon barrel. Approx. 47,000 mfg. 1967-1970.

	100%	98%	95%	90%	80%	70%	60%
	$575	**$425**	**$275**	**$225**	**$175**	**$150**	**$135**

MODEL 94 ANTIQUE CARBINE – similar to Standard, with case hardened scroll engraved receiver, gold-plated saddle ring. Mfg. 1964-1983.

	100%	98%	95%	90%	80%	70%	60%
	$550	**$425**	**$325**	**$250**	**$225**	**$195**	**$175**

GRADING - PPGS™	100%	98%	95%	90%	80%	70%	60%	LAST MSR

MODEL 94 CARBINE – .30-30 Win. cal., features uncheckered walnut stock and hooded front sight, w/o saddle ring. Manufactured circa 1976.

$550	$425	$325	$275	$225	$200	$175	

MODEL 94 WRANGLER – .32 Win. Special, top ejection, saddle ring, 16 in. barrel, oversized loop lever, western scene roll engraved on receiver, "Wrangler" logo on barrel, 5 shot mag. Only 7,947 mfg. 1983-1984.

$575	$450	$350	$275	$250	$225	$200	

MODEL 94 WRANGLER IA – .30-30 Win. cal., top ejection, 18 in. barrel, small loop lever, western scene roll engraved on receiver, "Wrangler IA" logo on barrel. Limited mfg. 1983 only.

$625	$550	$450	$375	$325	$275	$225	

MODEL 94 WRANGLER II – .32 Win. Special (disc. 1984) or .38-55 WCF cal., angle ejection, 16 in. barrel, saddle ring, oversized loop-shaped lever, western scene roll-engraved receiver, 5 shot mag., uncheckered stock and forearm, "Wrangler II" logo on barrel, 6 1/8 lbs. Made 1983-85 only.

$575	$475	$375	$300	$250	$225	$200	*$275*

MODEL 94 WRANGLER LARGE LOOP – .30-30 Win., .44 Mag., or .45 LC (new 1999) cal., 16 in. barrel, has large loop lever, uncheckered walnut stock and forearm, blue finish, open sights, 6 lbs. Mfg. 1992-99.

$425	$350	$275	$200	$175	$150	$140	*$400*

MODEL 94 DU – .30-30 Win. cal., approx. 2,800 rifles were mfg. in the U.S. during 1986. Serial numbered DU-860001-DU-8628000.

$995	$875	$750	$625	$500	$375	$225	

MODEL 94 DU GOLD – .30-30 Win. cal., gold plated receiver, 300 mfg.1986. Serial numbered DU-863000-DU-863299.

$1,395	$1,200	$1,000	$775	$625	$450	$250	

MODEL 9417 TRADITIONAL – .17 HMR cal., 11 shot mag., 20 1/2 in. barrel, checkered straight grip stock and forearm, full mag., 6 lbs. Limited mfg. 2003-2004.

$775	$675	$550	$375	$225	$175	$150	*$515*

MODEL 9417 LEGACY – .17 HMR cal., 11 shot mag., 22 1/2 in. barrel, checkered pistol grip grip stock and longer forearm, 6 lbs. Limited mfg. 2003-2004.

$925	$850	$750	$600	$500	$400	$300	*$551*

MODEL 9422 XTR TRADITIONAL (STANDARD WALNUT) – .22 LR or .22 WMR cal., takedown, 20 1/2 in. round barrel, 15 shot (LR) or 11 shot (Mag. cal.) mag., grooved forged steel receiver, uncheckered (early mfg.) or checkered straight grip, uncheckered or checkered high gloss (disc.) or satin weather resistant finish (new 1988) walnut stock and forearm, regular or large loop (mfg. 1998-99) lever, sights, 6 lbs. Mfg. 1972-2004.

$675	$550	$350	$275	$225	$175	$150	*$479*

Add 25% for early pre-XTR mfg. with uncheckered straight grip stock.
Add $25 for large loop lever (disc. 1999).
Add approx. 15% for .22 WMR cal.

This model had an "XTR" suffix until 1989. Earlier mfg., including pre-XTR and early XTR rifles, had no checkering.

MODEL 9422 XTR CLASSIC – same general specifications as Model 9422 XTR Standard, except has 22 1/2 in. barrel and non-checkered, satin finished, pistol grip walnut stock and extended forearm, stock also has fluted comb with crescent steel buttplate, curved finger lever, 6 1/2 lbs. Mfg. 1985-1987.

$800	$725	$575	$475	$375	$300	$250	*$301*

GRADING - PPGS™	100%	98%	95%	90%	80%	70%	60%	LAST MSR

MODEL 9422 LEGACY – .22 LR or .22 WMR (new 1999) cal., features 22 1/2 in. barrel with deluxe checkered semi-pistol grip stock, 11 (.22 WMR) or 15 shot non-full length mag., 6 lbs. Mfg. 1998-2004.

	$800	$675	$575	$425	$325	$250	$200	*$512*

Add 15% for .22 WMR cal.

MODEL 9422 SPECIAL EDITION TRADITIONAL TRIBUTE – .22 LR or .22 WMR cal., 20 1/2 in. round barrel, features a Winchester horse and rider engraved on right side of receiver, and Model 9422 Tribute banner on left, checkered straight grip walnut stock and forearm, 6 lbs. While 9,422 were scheduled to be mfg. 2005-2006, this production total was not achieved.

	$725	$575	$450	$350	$275	$225	$195	*$516*

Add 10% for .22 WMR cal.

MODEL 9422 SPECIAL EDITION LEGACY TRIBUTE – .22 LR or .22 WMR cal., similar to Model 9422 Special Edition Traditional, except has 22 1/2 in. barrel and pistol grip stock with crescent recoil pad, although 9,422 were scheduled to be mfg. 2005-2006, production total was not achieved.

	$925	$725	$550	$425	$325	$265	$235	*$551*

Add 10% for .22 WMR cal.

MODEL 9422 HIGH GRADE TRADITIONAL TRIBUTE – .22 LR or .22 WMR cal., 20 1/2 in. round barrel, features silver banner with Model 9422 Tribute on left receiver side and horse and rider on right side, etched engraving on blued receiver, checkered straight grip walnut stock and forearm, 6 lbs. Although 9,422 were scheduled to be mfg. 2005-2006, production total was not achieved.

	$1,325	$1,125	$1,000	$800	$675	$550	$450	*$1,050*

Add 10% for .22 WMR cal.

MODEL 9422 HIGH GRADE LEGACY TRIBUTE – .22 LR or .22 WMR cal., similar to High Grade Traditional Tribute, except has 22 1/2 in. barrel and crescent recoil pad, pistol grip stock, 6 lbs. Although 9,422 were scheduled to be mfg. 2005-2006, production total was not achieved.

	$1,400	$1,250	$1,000	$800	$675	$550	$450	*$1,085*

Add 5% for .22 WMR cal.

MODEL 9422 CUSTOM TRIBUTE – .22 LR cal., 20 1/2 in. barrel, features engraved silver plated receiver with gold inlaid Model 9422 Tribute banner on left side of receiver and gold horse and rider on right, engine turned bolt and extractor, gold plated trigger, select walnut with fleur-de-lis checkering on straight grip stock and forearm, 6 lbs. 222 mfg. by the Custom Shop 2005.

	$2,800	$2,200	$1,600	N/A	N/A	N/A	N/A	*$2,313*

MODEL 9422 TRAPPER – .22 S, L, LR, or .22 WMR (new 1998), 16 1/2 in. barrel, checkered walnut stock and forearm, 11 (.22 LR), 8 (.22 WMR), 15 (.22 S), or 12 (.22 L) shot tube mag., 5 3/4 lbs. Mfg. 1996-2001.

	$875	$775	$600	$350	$250	$175	$150	*$437*

Add $150 for .22 WMR cal.

500 Trapper special edition models were made for W.A.C.A. with engraving and silver and gold wash. Current estimated value is $1,300 for NIB condition. C.D.N.N. Sports Inc. in Abilene, TX ordered 1,002 Trapper models (501 in .22 WMR and 501 in .22 S, L, LR cal.) with case colored receivers and special serial numbers. Current estimated value is $1,200 for NIB condition.

Some barrel markings on this model may not have the "S" for .22 Short cal.

MODEL 9422 WIN-CAM – .22 WMR cal. only, similar to 9422 XTR Standard, except has checkered greenish laminated hardwood stock and forearm. Mfg. 1987-1997.

	$700	$550	$400	$275	$175	$150	$135	*$424*

GRADING - PPGS™	100%	98%	95%	90%	80%	70%	60%	LAST MSR

MODEL 9422 WINTUFF – .22 LR or .22 WMR cal., 20 1/2 in. barrel, checkered laminated brown hardwood stock and forearm, 6 1/4 lbs. Mfg. 1988-1999.

	$575	$450	$325	$225	$190	$175	$160	*$423*

Add 10% for .22 WMR cal.

MODEL 9422 HIGH-GRADE – .22 LR cal., features engraved receiver with raccoon and coonhound, deluxe checkered walnut stock and forearm. Mfg. 1995-96 only.

	$725	$575	$450	$350	$265	$220	$190	*$489*

MODEL 9422 HIGH GRADE SERIES II – .22 LR cal., 20 1/2 in. barrel, features high grade walnut stock and forearm with cut checkering, engraved receiver includes dog and squirrels, 6 lbs. Mfg. 1998-99.

	$750	$575	$500	$400	$300	$200	$165	*$504*

MODEL 9422 25TH ANNIVERSARY GRADE I – .22 LR cal., features deluxe checkered walnut stock and forearm, engraved receiver with Winchester Horse and Rider, 2,500 mfg. 1997 only, inventory remained through 1999.

	$850	$625	$425	N/A	N/A	N/A	N/A	*$606*

MODEL 9422 25TH ANNIVERSARY HIGH GRADE – .22 LR cal., features extra deluxe checkered walnut stock and forearm, high gloss blue and engraved receiver with Winchester Horse and Rider, featuring silver borders and lever accents, 250 mfg. 1997 only.

	$1,625	$1,350	$1,025	N/A	N/A	N/A	N/A	*$1,348*

RIFLES: LEVER ACTION - MODELS 94 AND 1894, 2010-CURRENT

The following models in this category are manufactured in Miroku, Japan beginning 2010.

MODEL 1894 OLIVER WINCHESTER 200TH ANNIVERSARY CUSTOM GRADE – .30-30 Win. cal., 24 in. half-round, half-octagon barrel, top tang safety, buckhorn rear sight, Marble's front sight, checkered Grade IV/V walnut stock with high gloss finish, 8 shot mag., blue receiver with deep scroll engraving, left side has Winchester Repeating Arms crest, and right has "Two Hundred Years, Oliver F. Winchester" and "1810-2010" in gold, Oliver F. Winchester signature in gold on top of bolt, approx. 8 lbs. 500 mfg. in sets with High Grade during 2010 only.

	$1,875	$1,625	$1,375	N/A	N/A	N/A	N/A	*$1,959*

MODEL 1894 OLIVER WINCHESTER 200TH ANNIVERSARY HIGH GRADE – .30-30 Win. cal., 24 in. half-round, half-octagon barrel, top tang safety, buckhorn rear sight, Marble's front sight, checkered Grade II/III walnut stock with high gloss finish, 8 shot mag., silver nitride receiver with delicate scroll engraving, left side has Winchester Repeating Arms crest, and right has "Two Hundred Years, Oliver F. Winchester" and "1810-2010" in gold, Oliver F. Winchester signature in gold on top of bolt, approx. 8 lbs. 500 mfg. in sets with Custom Grade during 2010 only, remaining quantities were sold individually.

	$1,395	$1,050	$900	N/A	N/A	N/A	N/A	*$1,469*

MODEL 94 SPORTER – .30-30 Win. or .38-55 Win. cal., top tang safety, all steel construction, blue finish, articulated cartridge stop, rebounding hammer, 24 in. half-round, half-octagon barrel with Marble's front sight and semi-buckhorn rear sight, 8 shot full length mag., checkered satin finished walnut stock and forearm with crescent buttplate, includes knurled hammer spur, approx. 7 1/2 lbs. New 2011.

MSR $1,400	$1,275	$1,075	$950	$825	$675	$550	$425	

MODEL 94 SHORT RIFLE – .30-30 Win. or .38-55 Win. (new 2012) cal., top tang safety, similar to Model 94 Sporter, except has 20 in. round barrel and unchecked satin finished walnut stock and forearm, 7 shot mag., black synthetic buttplate, approx. 6 3/4 lbs. New 2011.

MSR $1,230	$1,075	$950	$825	$700	$600	$500	$400	

MODEL 94 TRAILS END TAKEDOWN – .30-30 Win. or .450 Marlin cal., top tang safety, features 20 in. ported round barrel with Marble's front sight and semi buckhorn rear sight,

GRADING - PPGS™	100%	98%	95%	90%	80%	70%	60%	LAST MSR

satin finished plain walnut stock and forearm, .450 Marlin cal. has Pachmayr decelerator recoil pad, 6 shot mag., approx. 6-3/4 lbs. New 2012.

MSR $1,460	$1,275	$1,025	$900	$775	$650	$525	$400

MODEL 94 CARBINE – .30-30 Win. or .38-55 Win. cal., 7 shot tube mag., 20 in. barrel with barrel band, semi-buckhorn rear sight and Marbles blade front sight, uncheckered satin finished plain walnut stock and forearm, blue metal finish, top tang safety, drilled and tapped, 6 1/2 lbs. New 2013.

MSR $1,200	$1,050	$925	$825	$700	$600	$500	$400

RIFLES: BOLT ACTION - PRE-1964 MODEL 70

The Pre-'64 Model 70 Bolt Action Rifle (advertised by Winchester throughout much of its production history as "The Rifleman's Rifle") was produced from 1936 through 1963. Collectors recognize three major manufacturing periods: "Pre-War" (1936-1941); "Transition" (1946-1948); and "Latter" (1949-1963). There were only eighteen (18) original chamberings, these are: .22 Hornet, .220 Swift, .243 Win., .250 Savage (.250-3000), .257 Roberts, .264 Win. Mag., .270 Win., 7x57mm Mauser, .300 Savage, .300 H&H, .300 Win. Mag., .30-06 (.30 Govt. '06 Springfield - approx. 80% of total mfg. by cal.), .308 Win. (standard in Featherweight Style only), .338 Win. Mag., .35 Rem., .358 Win. (in Featherweight Style only), .375 H&H, and .458 Win. Mag. (in Super Grade AFRICAN Style only). It is important to note that every caliber was not available during each manufacturing period. Any other caliber encountered (including 7.65mm Argentine and 9x57mm Mauser) may be regarded as either special ordered or non-original. Magazine capacities are as follows: "Standard Calibers" (including .22 Hornet) five (5) rounds; "H&H Magnums" (.300 & .375) four (4) rounds; and "Winchester Short Magnums" (.264, .300, .338, .458) three (3) rounds. The rifle was produced in a myriad of styles and variations - most of which are covered individually. Unfortunately, a veritable "cottage industry" has developed involving the alteration, "upgrading," and/or outright faking of these guns. Be careful when contemplating a purchase of any rare Model 70 (and get a receipt describing the purchase accurately).

MODEL 70 PRE-WWII PRODUCTION STANDARD GRADE – 12 standard cals., 5 shot mag., 4 shot mag. on Magnums, 24, 25, or 26 in. barrel, open sights, checkered walnut pistol grip stock, approx. ser. range is 1-41,750. Mfg. 1937-1941.

Standard Cals.	$2,100	$1,875	$1,675	$1,150	$875	$725	$525
.22 Hornet	$3,350	$3,000	$2,550	$1,925	$1,525	$1,200	$950
.220 Swift	$2,350	$2,175	$1,800	$1,150	$975	$800	$650
.257 Roberts	$4,000	$3,500	$2,925	$1,825	$1,450	$1,050	$775
.270 Win.	$2,400	$2,225	$1,925	$1,250	$975	$800	$650
.300 H&H	$3,500	$3,100	$2,525	$1,850	$1,425	$1,100	$825
.375 H&H	$4,650	$3,900	$3,450	$2,450	$1,975	$1,600	$1,200
7x57mm Mauser	$6,000	$5,400	$4,500	$3,800	$3,100	$2,625	$2,100
.250-3000 Savage	$5,250	$4,800	$4,500	$3,800	$3,100	$2,625	$2,100

Add approx. 100% for Super Grades in common cals.

Values listed assume original, unaltered specimens - modifications/alterations to either the metal or wood surfaces can reduce prices by large amounts. All pre-war Model 70s have only 2 holes drilled in the front of the receiver (none in the back). An extra set of "holes" can decrease value as much as 50%. Some pre-WWII Model 70s have a "D" suffix indicating a doubled up serial number - this variation will command a premium because of its rarity. The Model 70 is one gun for which caliber ranks before condition in terms of desirability. Specimens encountered in under 60% condition will not decrease in price substantially since almost any shooter is worth $500-$600.

There are more fakes than legitimate specimens in cals. 7x57mm and .250-3000 Savage!

Rare cals. such as the .300 Savage, .35 Rem., 7.65mm, and 9x57mm Mauser are seldom encountered,

GRADING - PPGS™	100%	98%	95%	90%	80%	70%	60%	LAST MSR

and their scarcity precludes accurate price evaluation. Cals. 7.65mm and 9x57mm Mauser were special order only and were made up from leftover Model 54 barrels. Also, the original factory box, papers, and hanging tag will add 25%-30% to the values listed. Believe it or not, there are getting to be a lot of fake Model 70 boxes that have been intentionally aged. Carefully screen NIB (watch the hanging tag also) specimens in this model for possible expert refinishing.

MODEL 70 CARBINE (MFG. 1936-1946) – available in most cals. during its period, 20 in. barrel, short rifle variation of the Pre-'64 Model 70 (Winchester never officially used the "Carbine" terminology). If original, front sight base will be an integral part of the barrel. All carbines were disc. shortly after WWII. Beware of fakes.

Add 50%-100% for carbine variations mfg. 1936-1946 with 20 in. barrel in .22 Hornet (watch for fakes with cut off barrels, rechambered "K" models, and examine the front sight carefully), .250-3000 Savage, .257 Roberts, .270 Win., 7mm, or .30-06 (most common) cal.

MODEL 70 TRANSITION (MFG. 1946-1948) – several of the post-war Model 70s mfg. between 1946-48 exhibit the pre-war receiver characteristics and have a transition safety. This variation is more rare than normal models, ser. no. range is 60,000-100,000.

Add 10%-20% above values for post-Transitional models.

On this Transitional Model, the receiver bridge may or may not be factory drilled.

MODEL 70 STANDARD GRADE (1946-1963 PRODUCTION) – 18 standard cals. including .22 Hornet, .220 Swift, .243 Win., .250 Savage (.250-3000), .257 Roberts, .264 Win. Mag., .270 Win., 7x57mm Mauser, .300 Savage, .300 H&H, .300 Win. Mag., .30-06, .308 Win., .338 Win. Mag., .35 Rem., .358 Win., and .375 H&H, 5 shot mag., 4 shot mag. on Magnums, 24, 25, or 26 in. barrel, open sights, checkered walnut pistol grip stock, ser. range is 52,549-581,471. Mfg. 1946-1963.

Standard cals.	$1,450	$1,200	$1,100	$900	$650	$550	$500
.22 Hornet	$3,150	$2,950	$2,400	$2,175	$1,575	$1,225	$1,050
.220 Swift	$2,450	$1,975	$1,800	$1,125	$825	$625	$550
.243 Win.	$1,975	$1,700	$1,475	$1,050	$900	$775	$700
.257 Roberts	$3,250	$2,500	$2,075	$1,650	$1,150	$800	$625
.264 Mag. (Westerner)	$2,200	$1,900	$1,750	$1,125	$850	$650	$550
.270 Win.	$1,600	$1,325	$1,100	$750	$625	$575	$550
.300 H&H	$2,650	$2,300	$1,775	$1,175	$975	$750	$625
.300 Win. Mag.	$3,850	$3,400	$2,900	$2,375	$1,800	$1,325	$1,050
.338 Win. Mag.	$3,100	$2,575	$2,375	$1,650	$1,250	$1,000	$825
.375 H&H	$4,000	$3,500	$3,150	$2,375	$2,150	$1,850	$1,500

Add 10% for .300 H&H or .375 H&H if rear receiver is not drilled and tapped.

Add 30% for stainless steel barrel in .300 H&H or .270 Win. cal.

Values listed assume original, unaltered specimens - modifications/alterations to either the metal or wood surfaces can reduce prices by large amounts. Most post-war Model 70s are drilled on top of the receiver (2 holes in front and 2 holes in back) to accept scope mounts (except early .300 and .375 H&H cals.). Pre-1962 mfg. Model 70s are desirable since Winchester implemented manufacturing techniques that lowered the quality beginning in 1964.

Rare cals. such as the .250-3000, .300 Savage, .308 Win. (extremely rare, so watch for fakes), .35 Rem., and 7x57mm Mauser are seldomly seen or sold. Premiums depend on the rarity of the caliber and original condition.

Believe it or not, there are getting to be a lot of fake Model 70 boxes that have been intentionally aged. Carefully screen NIB (watch the hanging tag also) specimens in this model.

MODEL 70 SUPER GRADE – similar to Standard Model, except has deluxe wood, black pistol grip cap and forend tip, all Super Grades have a raised cheekpiece with deluxe wraparound

GRADING - PPGS™	100%	98%	95%	90%	80%	70%	60%	LAST MSR

checkering, and Super Grade marked floorplate. Disc. 1960.

.375 H&H	$7,000	$6,150	$5,250	$4,600	$4,000	$3,500	$3,000

A general rule for Super Grades is that if you add 100% to the standard grade in similar cals., values should be rather close. For .375 H&H cal., values are listed.

Later Model 70 Super Grades have jeweled action components and rust blued barrels.

MODEL 70 SUPER GRADE AFRICAN – .458 Win. Mag. cal. only, front swivel base relocated and attached to bottom of barrel, nearly all possess one or two visible stock crossbolts (usually covered with Bakelite). Most have all action components (bolt body, extractor, extractor ring and magazine follower) jeweled (i.e., engine turned), rust blued barrel. 1,226 mfg. 1956-63.

	$8,000	$7,500	$7,000	$6,500	$5,500	$4,500	$4,000

While other Super Grades were disc. approx. 1960, the "AFRICAN" continued in that style until the end of all production. Normal attrition and collectors owning more than one contribute to extreme rarity. Retains considerable "shooter" value in lesser external conditions. Watch for cracked and/or repaired stocks.

MODEL 70 FEATHERWEIGHT – lightened version of Standard, .243 Win., .264 Win. Mag. (Westerner, mfg. 1962-1963), .270 Win., .308 Win., .30-06, or .358 Win. cal., 22 (standard) or 26 (Westerner only) in. barrel, aluminum trigger guard and floorplate, ser. range is 206,626-581,471. Mfg. 1952-1963.

.243 Win.	$1,475	$1,150	$900	$700	$600	$550	$475
.264 Mag. (Westerner)	$2,600	$2,200	$1,875	$1,550	$1,250	$1,000	$850
.270 Win.	$1,625	$1,450	$1,275	$1,050	$900	$775	$650
.30-06	$900	$675	$550	$525	$475	$425	$395
.308 Win.	$1,150	$995	$875	$775	$600	$550	$475
.358 Win. Alum. butt only	$4,350	$3,750	$2,950	$2,450	$1,950	$1,600	$1,250

Add 10% for .30-06, .308 Win., .243 Win., or .270 Win. cal. models with aluminum buttplate.

The .358 Win. cal. is rare because Winchester had problems with this cal. Many of them were exchanged for other calibers, and the result is that original guns are rare in this cal. The .264 Mag. Westerner was only mfg. with a Win. recoil pad.

MODEL 70 SUPER GRADE FEATHERWEIGHT – .243 Win., .270 Win., .30-06, or .308 Win. cal. only, because of inconsistencies of Super Grade action component jeweling (i.e., engine turning), a simple stock and hinged floorplate change can create an "instant" Super Grade Featherweight (check stock carefully for wood filling near area of Standard Super Grade rear sight "boss" in barrel channel), all Super Grade Featherweights have a raised cheekpiece with wraparound "fish tail" checkering, all have rust blued barrels, less than 1,000 mfg.

	$6,600	$6,000	$5,500	$4,350	$3,500	$2,950	$2,750

This is perhaps the rarest variation of the Pre-'64 Model 70 - beware of fakes.

MODEL 70 NATIONAL MATCH – similar to Standard, with target stock and scope bases, .30-06 only. Disc. 1960.

	$3,200	$3,000	$2,500	$2,200	$2,000	$1,700	$1,500

MODEL 70 TARGET – similar to Model 70 Standard, in .243 Win. or .30-06 cal. (mfg. 1955-1963), earlier pre-'51 Target guns were available in virtually any cal. (i.e., .22 Hornet, .220 Swift, etc.), 24 in. medium weight barrel and target stock. Disc. 1963.

Add 50%-75% over standard values if condition is over 90%. 60% condition will be priced the same.

MODEL 70 BULL GUN – similar to Standard Model 70, with 28 in. heavy barrel, .300 H&H or .30-06 cal. only, .30-06 cal is much rarer.

.300 H&H cal.	$4,500	$4,000	$3,750	$3,500	$3,000	$2,500	$2,250
.30-06	$4,950	$4,250	$3,875	$3,600	$3,100	$2,800	$2,400

GRADING - PPGS™	100%	98%	95%	90%	80%	70%	60%	LAST MSR

MODEL 70 VARMINT – similar to Standard Model 70, in .220 Swift or .243 Win. cal., 26 in. heavy barrel, scope bases, varmint style stock. Mfg. 1956-63.

	$2,300	$1,925	$1,625	$1,325	$1,050	$800	$700

Add 40% for .220 Swift cal. Add 10% for steel buttplate.

Less than 900 were mfg. in .220 Swift cal. Stainless steel barrels are also encountered in this model with 3 different types of finishes.

MODEL 70 ALASKAN – similar to Standard Model 70, in .300 Win. Mag. (mfg. 1963 only with 25 in. barrel - known as Alaskan), .338 Win. Mag., or .375 H&H cal., 24 (Westerner Alaskan) or 25 in. barrel, recoil pad. Mfg. 1960-63.

.375 H&H	$3,750	$3,200	$2,650	$2,100	$1,500	$1,300	$1,200
.300 or .338 Win. Mag.	$3,500	$3,150	$2,900	$2,650	$2,250	$1,800	$1,500

RIFLES: BOLT ACTION - MODEL 70, 1964-2006 MFG.

Beginning 1994, Winchester began using the Classic nomenclature to indicate those models featuring a pre-1964 style action with controlled round feeding.

U.S. Repeating Arms closed its New Haven, CT manufacturing facility on March 31, 2006, and an auction was held on Sept. 27-28, 2006, selling the production equipment and related assets.

WSM cals. will bring an approx. 10% premium, and WSSM cals. will bring an approx. 15% premiums on most of the following models, if in 95%+ condition.

MODEL 70 STANDARD – .22-250 Rem., .222 Rem., .225 Win. (mfg. 1964-1972), .243 Win., .25-06 Rem., .270 Win., .308 Win., or .30-06 cal., 5 shot, 22 or 24 in. heavy barrel, open sights, Monte Carlo stock with sling swivels. Mfg. 1964-1980.

	$600	$475	$400	$350	$300	$250	$200
.225 Win. cal.	$1,200	$950	$800	$700	$600	$500	$400

MODEL 70 WESTERNER – .22-250 Rem. (new 1983), .223 Rem. (new 1983), .243 Win., .270 Win., .30-06, .300 Win. Mag., or 7mm Rem. Mag. cal., 22 or 24 (Mag. cals. only) in. barrel, checkered satin finished straight comb stock with recoil pad, folding rear sight in middle of barrel, polished blue barrel with satin finished receiver, no forend tip or sling swivels. Mfg. 1982-1985.

	$650	$550	$475	$425	$375	$325	$275

MODEL 70 MAGNUM – .264 Win. Mag., 7mm Rem. Mag., .300 H&H Mag., .300 Win. Mag., .338 Win. Mag., .375 H&H, or .458 Win. Mag. cal., 24 in. barrel.

	$650	$550	$475	$425	$375	$325	$275

Add 25%-35% for .375 H&H or .458 Win. Mag. (African Model) cal.

MODEL 70 SUPER GRADE – various cals., deluxe wood with ebony forend cap, Super Grade appears on the floorplate. Disc.

	$875	$725	$625	$525	$475	$450	$425

MODEL 70 DELUXE – .243 Win., .270 Win., .30-06, or .300 Win. Mag. cal., 22 in. barrel, open sight, hand-checkered, black forend tip. Mfg. 1964-71.

	$700	$575	$500	$425	$375	$275	$225

The Model 70 Deluxe was redesignated the Standard Model 70 in 1972.

MODEL 70 TARGET RIFLE 1964-1971 – .308 Win. or .30-06 cal., 24 in. heavy barrel, no sights, target bases, heavy target style stock with hand stop. Disc. 1971.

	$775	$650	$600	$525	$425	$400	$325

MODEL 70 INTERNATIONAL ARMY MATCH 1971 – .308 Win. cal., 5 shot, 24 in. heavy barrel, no sights, adj. trigger, ISU stock with forearm, accessory rail, adj. butt. Disc. 1971.

	$975	$875	$800	$700	$600	$525	$450

MODEL 70 MANNLICHER 1969-1971 – .243 Win., .270 Win., .30-06, or .308 Win. cal., 19 in. barrel, open sight, full-length Monte Carlo stock with steel forend cap. Disc. 1971.

	$925	$825	$750	$675	$575	$500	$425

GRADING - PPGS™	100%	98%	95%	90%	80%	70%	60%	LAST MSR

MODEL 70A – economy version of 1972 type Model 70, same cals., no hinged floorplate or forend tip. Mfg. 1972-78.

$450 $375 $325 $275 $240 $200 $165

MODEL 70A MAGNUM – similar to Model 70A, except in Mag. cals. but not .375 H&H or .458. Mfg. 1972-78.

$475 $400 $350 $300 $250 $210 $170

MODEL 70 FEATHERWEIGHT – .22-250 Rem., .223 Rem., .243 Win., .25-06 Rem. (disc. 1993), .257 Roberts (disc.), .270 Win., .280 Rem., 6.5x55mm Swedish (new 1991), 7x57mm Mauser (disc.), .30-06, .308 Win., 7mm-08 Rem. (new 1992), 7mm Rem. Mag. (mfg. 1991-92 only), or .300 Win. Mag. (mfg. 1991-92 only) cal., bolt action, both short and medium action, 5 shot mag., 22 in. barrel (24 in. with .300 Win. Mag.), checkered walnut stock, with or w/o sights, approx. 6 1/2 lbs. Mfg. 1981-94.

$675 $600 $450 $375 $325 $275 $250 *$562*

In 1981, during U.S.R.A. takeover transition, guns were distinguishable by the U.S.R.A. trademark on the recoil pad. Some collectors will pay a premium for Win. marked pads. Cals. .257 Roberts and 7x57mm Mauser were disc. 1985.

This model had an "XTR" suffix until 1989.

MODEL 70 CLASSIC FEATHERWEIGHT – .22-250 Rem. (new 1994), .223 Rem. (mfg. 1994 only), .243 Win. (new 1994), .270 Win., .280 Rem. (disc. 2000), .30-06, .308 Win. (new 1994), 6mm Rem. (limited mfg. circa 1995), 6.5x55mm Swedish (new 1997), or 7mm-08 Rem. (new 1994) cal., 22 in. barrel, 5 shot mag., blue action, features claw-controlled round feeding action bedded into standard grade walnut stock, jewelled bolt, knurled bolt handle, includes rings and bases, approx. 7 lbs. Mfg. 1992-2006.

$675 $600 $450 $375 $325 $275 $250 *$762*

* ***Model 70 Classic Featherweight WSM*** – .270 WSM (new 2002), .300 WSM, .325 WSM (new 2005) or 7mm WSM (new 2002) cal., controlled round feeding, 24 in. round barrel, 3 shot internal mag., approx. 7 1/4 lbs. Mfg. 2001-2006.

$750 $650 $500 $425 $350 $300 $260 *$792*

Add $39 for left-hand action (new late 2003, not available in .325 WSM cal.).

* ***Model 70 Classic Featherweight Super Short WSSM*** – similar to Model 70 Classic Featherweight, except available in .223 WSSM, .243 WSSM, and .25 WSSM (new 2004) cals., 22 in. barrel, 3 shot mag., 6 lbs. Mfg. 2003-2006.

$750 $650 $500 $425 $350 $300 $260 *$814*

* ***Model 70 Classic Featherweight BOSS*** – similar to Model 70 Classic Featherweight, except has 22 in. barrel with BOSS. Mfg. 1996 only.

$725 $625 $475 $400 $325 $275 $250 *$735*

* ***Model 70 Classic Featherweight Stainless (Recent Mfg.)*** – .223 WSSM, .243 WSSM, .25 WSSM, .270 WSM, .300 WSM, .325 WSM, or 7mm WSM cal., 22 or 24 in. stainless barrel and action, no sights, three position safety, controlled round feed, Pachmayr Decelerator pad on WSM models, 3 shot mag., cut checkering with Schnabel forend, 6-7 1/4 lbs. Mfg. 2005-2006.

$775 $700 $525 $425 $350 $300 $260 *$806*

* ***Model 70 Classic Featherweight Stainless*** – .22-250 Rem., .243 Win., .270 Win., .30-06, .308 Win., .300 Win. Mag. (disc. 1998), or 7mm Rem. Mag. cal., 22 or 24 (Mag. cals. only) in. stainless barrel, checkered walnut stock, 3 or 5 shot mag., approx. 7-7 1/2 lbs. Mfg. 1997-99.

$675 $600 $450 $375 $325 $275 $250 *$746*

* ***Model 70 Classic Featherweight All-Terrain*** – .270 Win., .30-06, .300 Win. Mag., or 7mm Rem. Mag. cal., 22 or 24 in. matte finish stainless steel barrel/receiver, black

GRADING - PPGS™	100%	98%	95%	90%	80%	70%	60%	LAST MSR

fiberglass/graphite stock with checkering, with (1996-1997 only) or without BOSS, 3 or 5 shot mag., 7 1/4 lbs. Mfg. 1996-98.

	$675	$600	$450	$375	$325	$275	$250	$672

Add 20% for BOSS (disc. 1997).

* ***Model 70 Classic Featherweight Win-Tuff Rifle*** – .22-250 Rem., .223 Rem., .243 Win., .270 Win., .30-06, or .308 Win. cal., features brown laminated checkered stock with Schnabel forend, includes base and rings, pistol grip cap, 7 lbs. Mfg. 1988-90. Reintroduced 1992-93.

	$525	$475	$425	$375	$325	$275	$250	$572

* ***Model 70 Classic Featherweight Special*** – .243 Win. cal., features custom fitted stock, hand-honed action, barrel, and bolt/follower, custom shop proof stamp, select American walnut with rounded pistol grips, no sights. Only 50 mfg.

	$795	$725	$600	$500	$425	$380	$340	

This model is distinguishable by the Super Grade floorplate marking.

MODEL 70 XTR EUROPEAN FEATHERWEIGHT – 6.5x55 Swedish Mauser cal., 22 in. barrel, 5 shot mag., rifle sights, 6 3/4 lbs. Made 1986 only.

	$500	$425	$375	$330	$305	$280	$260	$460

MODEL 70 LIGHTWEIGHT RIFLE – .22-250 Rem. (disc. 1992), .223 Rem., .243 Win., .270 Win., .280 Rem. (mfg. 1988-92), .30-06, or .308 Win. cal., 22 in. barrel, checkered walnut stock, no sights, 6 1/2 lbs. Mfg. 1987-1995.

	$550	$450	$400	$350	$300	$250	$225	$513

* ***Model 70 Lightweight Rifle Win-Tuff*** – .22-250 Rem. (mfg. 1988-89), .223 Rem. (new 1989), .243 Win. (new 1988), .270 Win. .30-06 or .308 Win. (new 1989) cal., similar to Model 70 Lightweight Rifle, except has laminated brown hardwood stock with checkering. Mfg. 1987-92.

	$500	$425	$375	$325	$275	$235	$190	$471

* ***Model 70 Lightweight Rifle Win-Cam*** – .270 Win. or .30-06 cal., greenish laminated hardwood stock with checkering, 22 in. barrel. Mfg. 1987-disc.

	$500	$425	$375	$325	$275	$235	$190	$471

This model was previously designated Featherweight before 1989.

MODEL 70 LIGHTWEIGHT CARBINE – .22-250 Rem., .222 Rem. (scarce), .223 Rem., .243 Win., .250 Savage (new 1986), .308 Win., .270 Win., or .30-06 cal., bolt action, 5 shot mag., both short and medium action, 20 in. barrel, checkered walnut stock, no sights, approx. 6 lbs. Mfg. 1984-87.

	$550	$450	$400	$350	$300	$250	$225	$395

Add $15 for open sights.

MODEL 70 SPORTER – .22-250 Rem. (mfg. 1989-1993), .223 Rem. (mfg. 1989-93), .243 Win. (mfg. 1989-93), .25-06 Rem. (mfg. 1985-87 and reintroduced 1990), .264 Win. Mag., .270 Win., .270 Wby. Mag. (new 1988), .30-06, .300 Win. Mag., .300 Wby. Mag. (new 1989), .300 H&H (mfg. 1989- 1992), .308 Win. (mfg. 1986-89), .338 Win. Mag., or 7mm Rem. Mag. cal., 24 in. barrel, 3 or 5 shot mag., custom Sporter styling, Monte Carlo cheek piece, detachable sling swivels, 7 3/4 lbs. Disc. 1994.

	$650	$550	$425	$350	$300	$275	$250	$556

Add approx. 5% for iron sights (.270 Win., .30-06, .300 Win. Mag., or 7mm Rem. Mag. only).

This model had an "XTR" suffix until 1989.

* ***Model 70 Sporter Win-Tuff*** – .270 Win., .30-06, 7mm Rem. Mag., .300 Win. Mag., .300 Wby. Mag., or .338 Win. Mag. cal., similar to Model 70 Sporter, except has checkered brown laminate stock with sling swivels, solid recoil pad, 24 in. barrel, approx. 7 3/4 lbs. Mfg. 1992 only.

	$550	$450	$400	$350	$300	$250	$225	$572

GRADING - PPGS™	100%	98%	95%	90%	80%	70%	60%	LAST MSR

MODEL 70 CLASSIC SPORTER III (LT) – .25-06 Rem., .264 Win. Mag. (disc. 2000), .270 Win., .270 Wby. Mag. (disc. 1998), .270 WSM (new 2004), .30-06, .300 Win. Mag., .300 WSM (new 2004), .300 Wby. Mag. (disc. 2000), .325 WSM (new 2005), .338 Win. Mag., 7mm STW (mfg. 1997-2002), 7mm WSM (new 2004), or 7mm Rem. Mag. (disc. 2005) cal., similar to Model 70 Sporter, except features controlled round feeding, 3 (Mag. cals. only) or 5 shot internal mag., 24 or 26 in. barrel, checkered walnut stock, blue finish, stock was redesigned by David Miller in 1999 (denoted by "LT" Model suffix), approx. 7 3/4-8 lbs. Mfg. 1994-2006.

$700	$600	$450	$375	$325	$275	$250	*$742*

Add 10% for Mag. cals.
Add 10% for left-hand action (new 1997).
Add 10% for iron sights - disc. 1998 (available in .270 Win., .30-06, .300 Win. Mag., .338 Win. Mag., or 7mm Rem. Mag.).

This model's nomenclature was changed from Model 70 Classic Sporter LT to Model 70 Classic Sporter III during 2005. Sporter III improvements include a trimmer forend and stock, Pachmayr Decelerator pad, and a more open pistol grip.

* ***Model 70 Classic Sporter Stainless*** – .270 Win., .30-06, .300 Win. Mag., .338 Win. Mag., or 7mm Rem. Mag. cal., 24 or 26 in. barrel with (1997 only) or without BOSS, checkered walnut stock, controlled round feeding, 3 or 5 shot mag., right or left-hand action, approx. 7 3/4 lbs. Mfg. 1997-98.

$775	$650	$500	$425	$350	$300	$275	*$716*

Add 10% for BOSS.
Add 5% for left-hand action.

* ***Model 70 Classic Sporter BOSS*** – .25-06 Rem. (disc. 1996), .270 Win., .30-06, .264 Win. Mag. (disc. 1996), 7mm STW (new 1997), 7mm Rem. Mag., .270 Wby. Mag. (mfg. 1996 only), .300 Win. Mag., .300 Wby Mag. (mfg. 1996 only), or .338 Win. Mag. cal., 24 or 26 in. barrel with BOSS, 3 or 5 shot mag., checkered walnut stock, approx. 7 3/4 lbs. Mfg. 1995-98.

$700	$600	$450	$375	$325	$275	$250	*$728*

Add approx. 10% for left-hand action (new 1997).

* ***Model 70 Classic Sporter Laredo*** – .300 Win Mag., 7mm STW (mfg. 1997-98), or 7mm Rem. Mag. cal., features claw extraction and controlled round feeding, 26 in. round or fluted (new 1998) barrel with (.300 Win. Mag. and 7mm Rem. Mag. disc. 1997) or without BOSS. Mfg. 1996-99.

$825	$700	$550	$450	$375	$325	$290	*$794*

Add approx. 20% for BOSS (disc. 1998).
Add approx. $130 for fluted barrel.

* ***Model 70 Classic Sporter Safari Express*** – .375 H&H, .416 Rem. Mag., or .458 Win. Mag. cal., features Express style rear sight with standing blade, redesigned stock with negative drop and Pachmayr decelerator recoil pad, trigger guard and floorplate are one assembly, 3 shot mag., controlled round feed, 24 in. barrel with barrel band swivel attachment, checkered walnut stock and forearm, 8 1/2 lbs. Mfg. 1999-2006.

$1,395	$1,200	$850	$700	$575	$500	$450	*$1,149*

* ***Model 70 Classic Sporter Super Express Mag.*** – .375 H&H, .416 Rem. Mag. (new 1994), or .458 Win. Mag. cal., 3 shot mag., claw extractor controlled round feeding (new 1993), open sights, 22 or 24 in. (.375 H&H or .416 Rem. Mag.) barrel, 8 1/2 lbs. Disc. 1998.

$1,250	$1,100	$850	$700	$575	$500	$450	*$865*

This model had an "XTR" suffix until 1989.

MODEL 70 CLASSIC LAMINATED WSM – .270 WSM, .300 WSM, .325 WSM (new 2005) or 7mm WSM cals., claw extractor controlled round feed, brown laminate stock, 24 in. barrel w/o sights, one inch deluxe recoil pad, blued receiver and barrel, 3 shot mag., 7 3/4 lbs. Mfg. 2003-2005.

$650	$550	$450	$400	$350	$300	$275	*$810*

GRADING - PPGS™	100%	98%	95%	90%	80%	70%	60%	LAST MSR

MODEL 70 DBM (DETACHABLE BOX MAGAZINE) – .22-250 Rem. (mfg. 1993 only), .223 Rem. (mfg. 1993 only), .243 Win. (new 1993), .270 Win., .30-06, .308 Win. (mfg. 1993 only), 7mm Rem. Mag., or .300 Win. Mag. cal., checkered walnut stock and forend, features 3 shot detachable box mag., 24 or 26 in. barrel with or without sights, includes bases and rings or iron sights (new 1993, optional) in .30-06, .300 Win. Mag., or 7mm Rem. Mag., 7 3/4 lbs. Mfg. 1992-94.

	$650	**$550**	**$450**	**$400**	**$350**	**$300**	**$275**	***$598***

Add $35 for iron sights.

MODEL 70 CLASSIC DBM – .22-250 Rem., .243 Win., .270 Win., .284 Win., .30-06, .308 Win., .300 Win. Mag., or 7mm Rem. Mag. cal., similar to Model 70 DBM, except has controlled round feeding, 24 or 26 in. barrel. Mfg. 1994 only.

Most cals.	**$650**	**$550**	**$450**	**$400**	**$350**	**$300**	**$275**	
.284 Win. (less than 200 mfg.)	**$900**	**$800**	**$675**	**$575**	**$450**	**$375**	**$325**	***$619***

Add $50 for iron sights (.270 Win., .30-06, .300 Win. Mag., or 7mm Rem. Mag.).

* ***Model 70 Classic DBM-S*** – .270 Win., .30-06, .300 Win. Mag., or 7mm Rem. Mag. cal., similar to Model 70 DBM, except has black synthetic stock, this model became a Classic series in 1994 (featuring controlled round feeding). Mfg. 1993-94.

	$650	**$550**	**$450**	**$400**	**$350**	**$300**	**$275**	***$619***

MODEL 70 STAINLESS – .270 Win., .30-06, 7mm Rem. Mag., .300 Win. Mag., or .338 Win. Mag. cal., features matte finished stainless steel receiver, barrel, and bolt, black synthetic composite stock, 22 (.270 Win. or .30-06 only, disc. 1992) or 24 in. barrel, approx. 6 3/4 lbs. Mfg. 1992-94.

	$600	**$500**	**$450**	**$400**	**$350**	**$300**	**$250**	***$616***

MODEL 70 CLASSIC STAINLESS – .22-250 Rem. (disc. 1999), .223 Rem. (disc. 1994), .243 Win. (disc. 1998), .270 Win., .270 WSM (mfg. 2002), .30-06, .308 Win. (disc. 1998), .270 Wby. Mag. (mfg. 1997 only), .300 Win. Mag., .300 Wby. Mag. (disc. 2000), .300 Rem. Ultra Mag. (disc. 2002), .300 WSM (mfg. 2001-2003), .338 Win. Mag., .375 H&H, 7mm STW (mfg. 2001-2002), 7mm WSM (mfg. 2002), or 7mm Rem. Mag. (disc. 2003, reintroduced 2004) cal., features controlled round feeding, 22 (disc. 2001), 24, or 26 in. barrel, black synthetic composite stock, 3, 5, or 6 shot mag., without sights except for .375 H&H cal., 6 3/4-7 1/2 lbs. Mfg. 1994-2005.

	$775	**$675**	**$525**	**$425**	**$325**	**$275**	**$225**	***$817***

Add $30 for Mag. cals., or $125 for .375 H&H cal.

* ***Model 70 Classic Stainless BOSS*** – .22-250 Rem. (disc. 1996), .243 Win. (disc. 1996), .270 Win., .30-06, .308 Win. (disc. 1996), .270 Wby. Mag. (mfg. 1997 only), .300 Win. Mag., .300 Wby. Mag. (mfg. 1996-97), .338 Win. Mag., or 7mm Rem. Mag. cal., 22, 24, or 26 in. barrel with BOSS, black synthetic stock, 6 3/4-7 1/2 lbs. Mfg. 1995-98.

	$800	**$700**	**$550**	**$450**	**$350**	**$300**	**$250**	***$788***

MODEL 70 CLASSIC LAMINATED STAINLESS – .270 Win., .30-06, .300 Win. Mag., .338 Win. Mag., or 7mm Rem. Mag. cal., 24 or 26 (Mag. cals. only) in. barrel without sights, checkered grey/black laminate stock with sporter style dimensions, stainless action and barrel, 3 or 5 shot mag., approx. 8 lbs. Mfg. 1998-99.

	$800	**$700**	**$550**	**$450**	**$350**	**$300**	**$250**	***$753***

* ***Model 70 Classic Laminated Stainless Camo*** – similiar to Model 70 Classic Stainless, except has Mossy Oak Treestand finish composite stock, not available in .338 Win. Mag. cal. approx. 7 1/4 lbs. Mfg. 1998 only.

	$800	**$700**	**$550**	**$450**	**$350**	**$300**	**$250**	***$745***

MODEL 70 COYOTE STAINLESS LAMINATED – various standard, WSSM, or WSM cals., push feed (non-WSM/WSSM cals.) or controlled round feed (WSM/WSSM cals. only) action, 24 in. medium heavy stainless steel sporter barrel, uncheckered brown or grey (new 2006)

GRADING - PPGS™	100%	98%	95%	90%	80%	70%	60%	LAST MSR

laminate stock with reverse taper on forend, 3 (WSM cals. only), 5, or 6 (.223 Rem. or .204 Ruger only) shot mag., 8 3/4 lbs. Mfg. 2000-2006.

$675	$600	$450	$375	$325	$275	$250	$689

Add 10% for WSM cals.
Add 15% for WSSM cals.

MODEL 70 COYOTE LAMINATED BLUE – .223 Rem., .270 WSM, .300 WSM, .325 WSM, 7mm WSM, .223 WSSM, .243 WSSM, or .25 WSSM cal., similar to Model 70 Coyote Laminated Stainless, except has blued barrel/receiver finish. Mfg. 2005 only.

$725	$650	$500	$400	$350	$300	$260	$689

Add 10% for WSM cals.
Add 15% for WSSM cals.

MODEL 70 COYOTE OUTBACK STAINLESS LAMINATED – various standard, Mag., or WSM cals., grey laminate stock with three oval holes in buttstock and four in forend, matte finished stainless receiver and 24 in. fluted barrel w/o sights, 3-6 shot mag., controlled round push feeding, approx. 7 3/4 lbs. Limited mfg. 2006.

$1,200	$1,000	$800	$650	$525	$425	$350	$1,016

Add 10% for WSM and standard Mag. cals.

MODEL 70 COYOTE LITE – similar cals. as Model 70 Coyote Laminated Blue, except also available in .22-250 Rem., .243 Win., and .308 Win. (new 2006) cal., features 24 in. blued steel (WSSM cals. only) or stainless steel fluted barrel/action, controlled round feed action, floorplate, carbon fiber/fiberglass composite Bell & Carlson stock with vented forend, Pachmayr Decelerator pad, 7 1/2 lbs. Mfg. 2005-2006.

$825	$725	$550	$425	$375	$325	$275	$889

Add 10% for WSM cals.

MODEL 70 CLASSIC SM (SYNTHETIC MATTE) – .22-250 Rem. (mfg. 1993 only), .223 Rem. (mfg. 1993 only), .243 Win. (mfg. 1993 only), .270 Win., .30-06, .308 Win. (mfg. 1993 only), 7mm Rem. Mag., .300 Win. Mag., .338 Win. Mag., or .375 H&H (new 1993) cal., features black composite stock with checkering and sling swivels, 22 (.22-250 Rem., .223 Rem., .243 Win., or .308 Win. - mfg. 1993 only), 24, or 26 in. barrel with matte metal finish, 3 or 5 shot, approx. 7 1/2 lbs. Mfg. 1992-96.

$675	$600	$500	$400	$350	$300	$275	$620

Add 10% for Mag. cals.

Until 1993, this model was called the Model 70 SSM. In 1994, this model became the Model 70 Classic SM featuring controlled round feeding.

MODEL 70 CLASSIC SM BOSS – .270 Win., .30-06, 7mm Rem. Mag., .300 Win. Mag., or .338 Win. Mag. cal., 24 or 26 in. barrel with BOSS, 3 or 5 shot, approx. 7 1/4 lbs. Mfg. 1995-96 only.

$775	$600	$500	$400	$350	$300	$275	$735

MODEL 70 CLASSIC COMPACT – .243 Win., .308 Win. (disc. 2003), or 7mm-08 Rem. cal., features 12 1/2 in. LOP, 20 in. barrel and shallow profile, pre-64 type action, 4 shot mag., checkered walnut stock and forearm, blue action and barrel, 6-6 1/2 lbs. Mfg. 1998-2006.

$775	$600	$450	$375	$300	$275	$250	$762

MODEL 70 VARMINT – same general specifications as standard Sporter, .22-250 Rem., .223 Rem., .225 Win., .243 Win., or .308 Win. cal., 26 in. cold hammer forged heavy barrel, counter-sunk muzzle, no sights, 5 shot mag., target scope bases, 7 3/4 lbs. Mfg. 1964-1993.

$625	$500	$450	$400	$350	$300	$250	$720

Add 50% for .225 Win. cal.

This model had an "XTR" suffix 1978-89.

GRADING - PPGS™	100%	98%	95%	90%	80%	70%	60%	LAST MSR

* ***Model 70 Varmint Heavy (HBV)*** – .220 Swift (mfg. 1994-98), .22-250 Rem., .222 Rem. (mfg. 1997-98), .223 Rem., .243 Win., or .308 Win. cal., push-feed action, 26 in. heavy stainless fluted (new 1997) or plain barrel (countersunk muzzle) without sights, features black synthetic beavertail H-S Precision stock with aluminum bedding block, 10 3/4 lbs. Mfg. 1993-1999.

$750	$600	$500	$450	$400	$350	$300	*$795*

Add approx. $125 for fluted barrel.

MODEL 70 SHB (SYNTHETIC HEAVY BARREL) – .308 Win. cal., features checkered black composite stock, 26 in. barrel with matte metal finish, jeweled bolt, 9 lbs. Mfg. 1992 only.

$600	$500	$450	$400	$350	$300	$250	*$563*

MODEL 70 WINLIGHT – .25-06 Rem., .270 Win., .280 Rem. (new 1987), .30-06, 7mm Rem. Mag., .300 Win. Mag., .300 Wby. Mag., or .338 Win. Mag. cal., McMillan fiberglass stock, thermoplastic receiver bedding, blue metal parts, 22 or 24 (Mag. cals. only) in. barrel, 3 or 4 shot mag., no sights, approx. 6 1/2 lbs. Mfg. 1986-90.

$750	$650	$600	$550	$500	$450	$400	*$637*

MODEL 70 RANGER RIFLE – .22-250 Rem. (new 1999), .223 Rem. (new 1992), .243 Win. (new 1991), .270 Win., .30-06, or 7mm Rem. Mag. cal., push-feed action, 22 or 24 in. barrel, 3 (7mm Rem. Mag.), 5, or 6 shot mag., plain hardwood stock without checkering, open sights, approx. 7 lbs. Disc. 1999.

$475	$400	$350	$300	$250	$200	$175	*$503*

* ***Model 70 Ranger Rifle Compact (Ladies/Youth)*** – .22-250 Rem. (mfg. 1999 only), .223 Rem. (disc. 1989, reintroduced 1997, disc. 1998), .243 Win., .308 Win. (new 1991), or 7mm-08 Rem. (mfg. 1997-98, reintroduced 2000) cal., push-feed action, 20 (disc. 1992) or 22 (new 1993) in. barrel, 5 or 6 shot mag., shorter hardwood stock dimensions, open sights, 6 1/2 lbs. Disc. 2000.

$525	$450	$350	$300	$250	$225	$200	*$528*

MODEL 70 STEALTH – .22-250 Rem., .223 Rem., .308 Win. cal., push-feed action, 26 in. heavy barrel w/o sights, non-glare matte metal finish, Accu-Block black synthetic stock with full length aluminum bedding block, 5 or 6 shot mag., 10 3/4 lbs. Mfg. 1999-2003.

$850	$700	$650	$600	$550	$500	$450	*$800*

MODEL 70 STEALTH II – .22-250 Rem., .223 WSSM, .243 WSSM, .25 WSSM, or .308 Win. cal., push-feed action, 26 in. heavy barrel w/o sights, matte blue finish, redesigned black synthetic stock with aluminum pillar bedding, 3 or 5 shot mag., 10 lbs. Mfg. 2004-2006.

$750	$600	$500	$425	$375	$325	$300	*$886*

Add 10% for WSSM cals.

MODEL 70 BLACK SHADOW – .270 Win., .30-06, .300 Win. Mag., or 7mm Rem. Mag cal., push-feed action, 3 (Mag. cals.) or 5 shot internal mag., 24 or 26 (Mag. cals.) in. barrel w/o sights, matte receiver and barrel finish, black composite stock with conventional floorplate mag., 7 1/4 lbs. Mfg. 1998-2003.

$475	$350	$300	$275	$250	$225	$200	*$523*

Add approx. 10% for Mag. cals.

MODEL 70 CLASSIC/CAMO ULTIMATE SHADOW – .223 WSSM (new 2004), .243 WSSM (new 2004), .25 WSSM (new 2004), .270 WSM, .300 WSM, .325 WSM (new 2005) or 7mm WSM cal., features controlled round feed, black or Dura-Touch armor coated Mossy Oak New Break-Up camo finished molded synthetic stock with rubber grip inserts and new recoil pad, matte black metal, 3 shot mag., 24 in. blued steel or stainless steel barrel, 6 3/4 lbs. Mfg. 2003-2005.

$700	$600	$500	$450	$375	$335	$300	*$817*

Add 10% for WSM cals. or 15% for WSSM cals.
Add 10% for stainless steel action.
Add approx. $100 Mossy Oak New Break-Up camo finish.

GRADING - PPGS™	100%	98%	95%	90%	80%	70%	60%	LAST MSR

MODEL 70 SUPER SHADOW – various cals., similar to Classic Ultimate Shadow, except has oval dot textured gripping surfaces on pistol grip and forearm, blue finish, controlled round push feed action, available in either short or super short action, blind mag., 22 (.223 WSSM, .243 WSSM, or .25 WSSM cal.) or 24 in. barrel w/o sights, 6 (WSSM cals.) or 6 3/4 lbs. Mfg. 2003-2006.

	$475	$375	$300	$250	$200	$180	$165	*$525*

Add 10% for WSM and Mag. cals. or 15% for WSSM cals.

MODEL 70 SHADOW ELITE STAINLESS – various standard, WSM, and Mag. cals., short or long action, lightweight black synthetic stock with rubberized overmolded gripping surfaces on pistol grip and forearm, and Dura-Touch Armor coating, WinSorb recoil pad, 24 or 26 in. stainless fluted barrel, no sights, except .375 H&H cal., controlled round feed action, 3 or 5 shot mag., 6 3/4 - 7 3/4 lbs. Limited mfg. 2006.

	$650	$525	$400	$325	$275	$235	$200	*$739*

Add 10% for WSM and standard Mag. cals.
Add approx. $125 for .375 H&H cal.

* ***Model 70 Shadow Elite Stainless Camo*** – similar to Model 70 Shadow Elite Stainless, except available in Mossy Oak Break-Up camo. Limited mfg. 2006.

	$725	$550	$475	$400	$350	$300	$250	*$808*

Add 10% for standard Mag. and WSM cals.
Add $200 for .375 H&H cal.

MODEL 70 PRO SHADOW – various standard, WSM, and Mag. cals., short or long action, 22 or 24 in. blue barrel, black synthetic stock with Dura-Touch Armor coating and oval-dot gripping surfaces, controlled round push feed, 3 or 5 shot mag., 6 1/2 - 7 lbs. Limited mfg. 2006.

	$625	$500	$450	$400	$350	$300	$250	*$594*

Add 10% for standard Mag. and WSM cals.

* ***Model 70 Pro Shadow Stainless*** – similar to Model 70 Pro Shadow, except has stainless barrel/action. Limited mfg. 2006.

	$675	$550	$500	$450	$400	$350	$300	*$638*

Add 10% for standard Mag. and WSM cals.
Add $125 for .375 H&H cal.

MODEL 70 CLASSIC SUPER GRADE III – .25-06 Win. (new 2001), .270 Win. (mfg. 1991-2003), .270 WSM (new 2004), .30-06 (new 1991), 7mm STW (230 mfg. 1999 only), 7mm WSM (new 2004), 7mm Rem. Mag. (disc. 1998, reintroduced 2000-2003), .264 Win. Mag. (limited mfg. 2000 only), .300 WSM (new 2004), .300 Win. Mag. (disc. 2003, reintroduced 2005), .325 WSM (new 2005), or .338 Win. Mag. cal., 24 or 26 in. barrel, 3 (Mag. cals.) or 5 shot mag., jewelled bolt, stainless steel extractor for true claw controlled round feeding and ejecting, three-position safety, checkered satin finish walnut stock with wood cheekpiece, black forend tip, bases and rings included, approx. 7 3/4 - 8 lbs. Mfg. 1990-2006.

	$1,250	$1,000	$900	$800	$700	$600	$500	*$1,036*

Add 10% for WSM and Mag. cals.

This model was designated the Model 70 Super Grade until 1995. During 1999, this model was redesigned to include a new Express style rear sight with standing blade, negative stock drop, Pachmayr Decelerator pad, one-piece floorplate and full barrel band swivel attachment. This model was on its third generation of design improvements (now called the Super Grade III) with trimmer sporter style stock, steel stock crossbolt, and inlaid swivel studs.

* ***Model 70 Classic Super Grade III RMEF*** – .300 WSM or .325 WSM (new 2005) cal., similar to Model 70 Classic Super Grade, except is Rocky Mountain Elk Foundation special edition, includes Super Grade Stock with ebony forend and Pachmayr decelerator pad, special RMEF emblem on grip cap, 26 in. barrel, 8 lbs. Limited mfg. 2003-2006.

	$1,375	$1,100	$1,000	$900	$800	$700	$500	*$1,183*

This model was redesignated the Super Grade III RMEF in 2005.

GRADING - PPGS™	100%	98%	95%	90%	80%	70%	60%	LAST MSR

* ***Model 70 Classic Super Grade III BOSS*** – similar to Model 70 Classic Super Grade, except has BOSS. Mfg. 1995-97.

	$895	$725	$600	$475	$400	$350	$300	*$956*

MODEL 70 SUPER GRADE CENTENNIAL – .30-06 cal., deluxe checkered walnut stock, black forend cap, controlled round feed with engraved "1906-2006 - 100 Years of .30-06 Springfield" on bolt face, 24 in. blue steel barrel, 3 shot mag., polished engraved floorplate with special gold and nickel accents, 8 lbs. 306 mfg. 2005-2006.

	$1,400	$1,250	$1,150	N/A	N/A	N/A	N/A	*$1,259*

MODEL 70 50TH ANNIVERSARY MODEL – .300 Win. Mag. cal., 24 in. barrel, deluxe walnut stock, engraving and special motifs on metal surfaces, serial numbered 50 ANV 1 - 50 ANV 500, 7 3/4 lbs. 500 mfg. 1987 only.

	$1,600	$1,400	$1,200	N/A	N/A	N/A	N/A	*$939*

RIFLES: BOLT ACTION - POST 1964 MODEL 70 CUSTOM GRADES

MODEL 70 CUSTOM GRADE – various cals., old style Model 70 action, semi-fancy American walnut checkered stock, engine turned bolt and follower, hand honed internal parts. Mfg. 1988-89 only.

	$1,700	$1,450	$1,100	$925	$800	$700	$600	*$1,172*

MODEL 70 XTR FEATHERWEIGHT ULTRA GRADE "1 OF 1,000" – .270 Win. cal., extensively engraved, finely checkered deluxe French walnut stock, with mahogany presentation case.

	$3,000	$2,500	$2,000	N/A	N/A	N/A	N/A	*$5,000*

MODEL 70 CLASSIC CUSTOM GRADE – .264 Win. Mag. (new 1994), .270 Win., .30-06, 7mm Rem. Mag., .300 Win. Mag., .300 Wby. Mag. (new 1994) or .338 Win. Mag. cal., 24 or 26 in. barrel, similar to Model 70 Super Grade, but had to be special ordered through the Custom Gun Shop, and with many custom features including semi-fancy walnut with satin finish and hand-honed internal parts. Mfg. 1990-1994.

	$2,000	$1,800	$1,400	$1,100	$1,000	$800	$700	*$1,757*

A Model 70 Collector Grade was also a variant of this model which was mfg. in the Custom Gun Shop - this model was priced on request only.

* ***Model 70 Classic Custom Grade Featherweight*** – .22-250 Rem. (new 1994), .223 Rem. (new 1994), .243 Win. (new 1994), .270 Win., .280 Rem., .30-06, .308 Win. (new 1994), 7mm-08 Rem. (new 1994) cal., 22 in. barrel, Featherweight features, controlled round feeding, higher grade wood. Mfg. 1992-1994.

	$2,000	$1,800	$1,400	$1,100	$1,000	$800	$700	*$1,757*

* ***Model 70 Classic Custom Grade Sharpshooter I/II*** – .22-250 Rem. (new 1993), .223 Rem. (mfg. 1993-94), .30-06, .308 Win., or .300 Win. Mag. cal., specially designed McMillan A-2 (disc. 1995) or H-S Precision heavy target stock, Schneider (disc. 1995) or H-S Precision (new 1996) 24 (.308 Win. cal. only) or 26 in. stainless steel barrel, choice of blue or grey finish starting 1996. Mfg. 1992-1998.

	$1,950	$1,500	$1,050	$900	$850	$750	$675	*$1,994*

Subtract $100 if without stainless barrel (pre-1995).

This model was designated the Sharpshooter II in 1996 (features H-S Precision stock and stainless steel barrel).

This model was also available in left-hand action beginning 1998 (.30-06 and .330 Win. Mag. cals. only).

* ***Model 70 Classic Custom Grade Sporting Sharpshooter I/II*** – .270 Win. (disc. 1994), 7mm STW, or .300 Win. Mag. cal., 1/2-minute of angle sporting version of the Custom Sharpshooter, custom shop only, Sharpshooter II became standard in 1996. Mfg. 1993-98.

	$1,875	$1,425	$1,000	$875	$825	$750	$675	*$1,875*

This model was also available in left-hand action in 1998.

GRADING - PPGS™	100%	98%	95%	90%	80%	70%	60%	LAST MSR

* ***Model 70 Classic Custom Grade Sporting Sharpshooter*** – .220 Swift cal., 26 in. Schneider barrel, controlled round feeding, available with either McMillan A-2 or Sporting synthetic (disc. 1994) stock. Mfg. 1994-95 only.

$1,950	$1,525	$1,200	$975	$850	$750	$650	*$1,814*

* ***Model 70 Classic Custom Grade Express*** – .300 Petersen (mfg. 1995 only), .375 H&H, .375 JRS (mfg. 1992-96), 7mm STW (mfg. 1993-94), .416 Rem. Mag., .458 Win. Mag., or .470 Capstick (disc. 1995) cal., 24 in. (22 in. on .458 Win. Mag.) barrel, claw controlled round feeding, deluxe walnut with satin finish and checkering, 3-leaf express (disc. 1995) or pre-64 style adj. rear sight (new 1996), high luster metal finish, bolt and follower are engine turned, available by special order through the custom gun shop only. Mfg. 1990-1998.

$2,750	$2,200	$1,800	$1,500	$1,200	$1,050	$900	*$2,512*

Subtract $200 for 7mm STW cal.

In 1994, the model nomenclature was changed from Model 70 Custom Grade Express, and in 1996 it was changed from Model 70 Classic Express.

MODEL 70 CUSTOM ULTIMATE CLASSIC – .25-06 Rem., 6.5x55mm Swedish (new 2001), .270 Win., .280 Rem. (mfg. 1996, reintroduced 1999), .30-06, 7mm STW (disc. 2006), .264 Win. Mag. (disc. 2006), .270 Wby. Mag. (disc. 1996), .35 Whelen (new 1998), 7mm Rem. Mag., 7mm Rem. Ultra Mag., .300 Win. Mag., .300 Wby. Mag., .300 H&H (mfg. 1996-99), .300 Rem. Ultra Mag. (new 2000), .338 Win. Mag., .338-06 (mfg. 1999-2001), .338 Rem. Ultra Mag. (new 2001), .340 Wby. Mag. (mfg. 1998), .375 H&H (1995 only), .416 Rem. Mag. (1995 only), or .458 Win. Mag. (1995 only) cal., controlled round feeding, engine turned bolt, checkered fancy walnut stock, choice of 22 (.458 Win. Mag. only), 24 or 26 in. tapered round full-fluted, 1/2 round, 1/2 octagonal, or full octagonal tapered stainless barrel, one inch black decelerator recoil pad, choice of blue or stainless barreled action, 3 or 5 shot mag., includes bases/rings except on some Mag. cals., approx. 7 3/4 lbs., except for large disc. cals., included hard case. Mfg. 1995-2006.

$3,000	$2,750	$2,500	$2,200	$1,800	$1,500	$1,000	*$3,060*

Add $100 for stainless steel barrel, $110 for fluted round barrel, or $235 for full or half octagon barrel.

Add approx. 15% for .375 H&H and larger Mag. cals (disc. 1995).

This model was previously designated the Model 70 Ultimate Classic until 2000, and was changed to the Model 70 Custom Ultimate Classic.

Left-hand action (new 1997) was available in all recent cals.

MODEL 70 CLASSIC CUSTOM SHORT ACTION – .243 Win. (disc. 2000, reintroduced 2002 only), .257 Roberts, .260 Rem. (disc. 2006), .270 WSM (new 2002), .284 Win. (new 2006), .308 Win., .358 Win., .300 WSM (new 2001), .325 WSM (new 2005), 7mm-08 Rem., 7mm WSM (new 2002), or .450 Marlin (mfg. 2001-2004) cal., 22 (disc. 2002) or 24 (new 2003) in. match grade tapered stainless or chrome-moly barrel with cut rifling, controlled round feed, no sights, deluxe high gloss checkered walnut stock and forend, one inch black decelerator recoil pad, satin matte blue finished action and barrel, 3-5 shot mag., approx. 7 1/2 lbs. Mfg. 2000-2006.

$2,650	$2,050	$1,650	$1,350	$1,125	$950	$800	*$2,866*

Left-hand action was available on this model.

MODEL 70 CLASSIC CUSTOM FEATHERWEIGHT – .223 WSSM (mfg. 2004), .243 WSSM (mfg. 2004), .25 WSSM (mfg. 2004), .243 Win. (new 2006), .25-06 Rem. (new 2006), .270 Win., .280 Rem. (new 2004), .284 Win. (new 2006), .30-06, .308 Win. (new 2006), 6.5x55mm Swedish (new 2006), or 7mm-08 Rem. (mfg. 2003) cal., 5 shot mag., Featherweight stock with Schnabel forend, match grade 22 in. barrel w/o sights, matte blue or stainless action/barrel, 7 1/4 lbs. Mfg. 2003-2006.

$2,650	$2,050	$1,650	$1,350	$1,125	$950	$800	*$2,866*

GRADING - PPGS™	100%	98%	95%	90%	80%	70%	60%	LAST MSR

MODEL 70 CLASSIC CUSTOM CARBON – .25-06 Rem., .270 WSM, .300 WSM, .338 Win. Mag., or 7mm WSM cal., satin stainless action, features 24 or 26 in. carbon fiber barrel with Shilen stainless barrel liner, controlled round feed, reinforced black composite stock, 6 1/2 - 7 lbs. Mfg. 2003-2004.

	$3,050	$2,350	$1,825	$1,400	$1,150	$975	$825	$3,233

MODEL 70 CLASSIC CUSTOM EXTREME WEATHER – .25-06 Rem. (disc. 2001), .270 Win. (disc. 2000), .270 WSM (new 2004), .30-06, .300 Win. Mag., .300 Rem. Ultra Mag. (new 2001), .300 WSM (new 2004), .308 Win. (new 2004), .325 WSM (new 2005), .338 Win. Mag., 7mm WSM (new 2004), 7mm Rem. Mag., or .375 H&H (new 2001) cal., controlled round feed, matte finished stainless action and match grade 22 lightweight (.375 H&H only), 24, or 26 in. fluted stainless barrel w/o sights, black McMillan fiberglass stock with cheekpiece and 1 in. Pachmayr Decelerator pad, 3 or 5 shot mag., available in either right or left-hand action, approx. 7 1/2 lbs. Mfg. 2000-2005.

	$2,350	$1,900	$1,575	$1,375	$1,150	$950	$750	$2,576

MODEL 70 CUSTOM EXTREME LIGHTWEIGHT WEATHER II – various standard, WSM, and Mag. cals., 22, 24, or 26 in. fluted Krieger barrel w/o sights, black lightweight McMillan Hunter's Edge fiberglass stock with Pachmayr Decelerator recoil pad, 3 or 5 shot mag., matte finished stainless steel action/barrel, 6 1/4 - 7 lbs. Limited mfg. 2006.

	$2,600	$2,025	$1,650	$1,400	$1,175	$975	$775	$2,800

This model was also available with left-hand action, except in WSM cals.

MODEL 70 CUSTOM STAINLESS LAMINATE – .270 WSM, .300 WSM, .325 WSM, or 7mm WSM cal., choice of brown or black/grey featherweight stock with Pachmayr Decelerator recoil pad, controlled round feed, 24 in. stainless sporter barrel w/o sights, engine turned bolt, 8 lbs. Limited mfg. 2006.

	$2,150	$1,850	$1,450	$1,200	$1,050	$900	$725	$2,332

MODEL 70 CLASSIC CUSTOM MANNLICHER – .260 Rem., .308 Win., or 7mm-08 Rem. cal., features full length checkered walnut stock, smooth tapered barrel and blue action, 19 in. barrel w/o sights (sights optional), 4 shot internal mag., approx. 6 3/4 lbs. Mfg. 1999-2000.

	$2,475	$1,975	$1,550	$1,275	$1,000	$850	$750	$2,595

This model was designated the Model 70 Custom Mannlicher until 2000.

MODEL 70 CUSTOM MAPLE – .270 Win., .284 Win., .30-06, or .308 Win. cal., features gloss finished checkered hand-made fiddleback curly maple stock with black forend cap, custom shop pistol grip cap, right or left hand blue or stainless steel action, 24 in. sporter barrel w/o sights, 7 3/4 lbs. Limited mfg. 2006.

	$4,100	$3,475	$3,025	$2,425	$1,950	$1,575	$1,325	$4,355

MODEL 70 CUSTOM CONTINENTAL HUNTER – .270 Win., .284 Win., .30-06, or .308 Win. cal., features gloss finished Claro walnut stock with round pistol grip and Schnabel forend, Niedner style steel buttplate, controlled round feed, 22 in. Krieger stainless or blue sporter barrel w/o sights, right or left hand action, 4 or 5 shot mag., 6 3/4 lbs. Limited mfg. 2006.

	$4,900	$4,350	$3,850	$3,150	$2,625	$2,100	$1,625	$5,226

MODEL 70 CLASSIC CUSTOM SAFARI EXPRESS – .340 Wby. Mag. (disc. 1999), .358 STA (disc. 2000), .375 H&H, .375 Rem. Ultra Mag. (new 2001), .404 Jeffery (mfg. 2004), .416 Rem. Mag., .416 Rigby (mfg. 2001), .458 Win. Mag., .458 Lott, or .470 Capstick (new 2002) cal., features honed internal parts, engine turned bolt and follower, adj. Dietrich Apel Express rear and front sights, deluxe checkered walnut stock and forend, 22 (.458 Win. Mag. & .458 Lott) or 24 in. barrel with sling stud, 3 shot mag., approx. 9 1/4 lbs. Mfg. 1999-2006.

	$3,050	$2,375	$1,775	$1,375	$1,025	$875	$775	$3,252

Add $490 for .416 Rigby cal. (mfg. 2001 only).

Beginning in 2000, this model was available in left-hand action in all cals. except .470 Capstick.

This model was designated the Model 70 Custom Safari Express until 2000.

GRADING - PPGS™	100%	98%	95%	90%	80%	70%	60%	LAST MSR

MODEL 70 WSM CUSTOM NORTH AMERICAN BIG GAME SERIES – .270 WSM, .300 WSM, or 7mm WSM cal., controlled round feed, checkered XXX American walnut stock with Schnabel forend, Pachmayr Decelerator recoil pad, engraved receiver, trigger guard, and floorplate, high lustre bluing. Only 125 of each edition (Whitetail Deer - .270 WSM, Elk - .300 WSM, and Antelope - 7mm WSM) mfg. 2004-2005 with matching serial numbers.

	100%	98%	95%	90%	80%	70%	60%	LAST MSR
	$2,875	$2,375	$1,775	$1,375	$1,025	$875	$775	*$3,030*

This model was sold in sets only (all 3 calibers.)

MODEL 70 CLASSIC CUSTOM AFRICAN EXPRESS – .340 Wby. Mag. (disc. 1999), .358 STA (disc. 2000), .375 H&H, .416 Rem. Mag., .416 Rigby (mfg. 2001 only), .458 Win. Mag., .458 Lott, or .470 Capstick (mfg. 2001 only) cal., features drop down floorplate, increasing mag. capacity to 4, checkered fancy English walnut stock with black Pachmayr Decelerator pad and ebony pistol grip and forend caps, adj. Dietrich Apel Express rear and front sights, 22 (.458 Win. Mag. only) or 24 in. barrel with sling stud, approx. 9 1/2 lbs. Mfg. 1999-2006.

	100%	98%	95%	90%	80%	70%	60%	LAST MSR
	$4,575	$3,700	$3,150	$2,525	$1,975	$1,525	$1,325	*$4,867*

Add $437 for .416 Rigby cal. (disc. 2001).

Beginning in 2000, this model was available in left-hand action in all cals. except .458.

This model was designated the Model 70 Custom African Express until 2000.

MODEL 70 CLASSIC CUSTOM TAKE-DOWN – .300 Rem. Rem. Ultra Mag., .300 Win. Mag. (new 2002), .375 H&H, .416 Rem. Mag., or 7mm Rem. Mag. cal., all stainless construction with blue Teflon finish, take-down receiver/barrel assembly, brown synthetic stock and forearm, .75 MOA guaranteed for take-down action assembly/reassembly, 24 (.375 H&H or .416 Rem. Mag. cal. only) or 26 (fluted only) in. barrel, 3 shot internal mag., 8 1/2 - 9 lbs. Limited mfg. 2001-2006.

	100%	98%	95%	90%	80%	70%	60%	LAST MSR
	$3,475	$2,950	$2,550	$2,150	$1,800	$1,550	$1,250	

While advertised beginning in 1998 with a MSR of $2,495, this model was finally produced during 2001. This model was only available from the Bass Pro Shops.

MODEL 70 ULTRA GRADE – .270 Win. cal., gold line engraved, includes wood display case, 500 mfg.

	100%	98%	95%	90%	80%	70%	60%	LAST MSR
	$3,000	$2,500	$2,000	$1,800	$1,500	$1,200	$1,000	*$5,000*

MODEL 70 CUSTOM 100TH ANNIVERSARY .30-06 – 30-06 cal., 22 in. blue sporter barrel with "100th Anniversary Custom 1 of 100" engraved in gold, 5 shot mag., semi-fancy checkered American walnut stock with recoil pad, single steel crossbolt, controlled round feed action, gold and nickel engraved floorplate with WWI Allied soldiers and sport hunter with whitetail deer, 7 1/4 lbs. 100 mfg. 2006.

	100%	98%	95%	90%	80%	70%	60%	LAST MSR
	$2,500	$1,950	$1,650	N/A	N/A	N/A	N/A	*$2,660*

MODEL 70 CUSTOM SPECIAL "70 YEARS OF THE MODEL 70" – .270 Win., .30-06, or .300 Win. Mag. cal., 24 or 26 (.300 Win. Mag. only) in. blue barrel with "One of Seventy" engraved in gold, semi-fancy checkered walnut stock with inletted sling swivel bases, controlled round feed action, each caliber has special engraved floorplate, 7 1/2 - 7 3/4 lbs. 70 of each caliber mfg. 2006.

	100%	98%	95%	90%	80%	70%	60%	LAST MSR
	$2,400	$1,900	$1,575	N/A	N/A	N/A	N/A	*$2,547*

MODEL 70 COLLECTOR GRADE – various cals., this variation was a special order through the Winchester Custom Shop and values will vary per individual gun.

MODEL 70 CUSTOM BUILT – various cals., this variation was a special order through the Winchester Custom Shop and values will vary per individual gun.

MODEL 70 EXHIBITION GRADE – various cals., fancy checkered American walnut stock with hardwood forend tip. Mfg. 1988-89 only.

	100%	98%	95%	90%	80%	70%	60%	LAST MSR
	$2,050	$1,625	$1,075	N/A	N/A	N/A	N/A	*$2,192*

GRADING - PPGS™	100%	98%	95%	90%	80%	70%	60%	LAST MSR

RIFLES: BOLT ACTION - MODEL 70, 2007-CURRENT MFG.

In late 2007, Olin announced that its famous Winchester Model 70 would be reintroduced with a new M.O.A. trigger system, and manufactured by FN Manufacturing located in Columbia, SC. Winchester continues to introduce more variations of the new Model 70.

MODEL 70 FEATHERWEIGHT (DELUXE) – various short action, long action, and WSM cals., pre-64 style controlled round feeding, new M.O.A. trigger system adj. from 3-5 lbs., blade type ejector, 3 or 5 shot mag., 22 or 24 in. hammer forged blue barrel w/o sights, one-piece trigger guard and hinged mag. floorplate, satin finished Grade II fleur-de-lis checkered walnut stock with Schnabel forend, jeweled bolt, knurled bolt handle, 3-position safety, Pachmayr Decelerator recoil pad, 6 1/2 - 7 lbs. New 2008.

MSR $880	$775	$675	$600	$525	$450	$375	$325	

Add $40 for regular Mag. and WSM cals.

During the first year of manufacture (2008), this model featured an engraved custom one-piece floor plate marked "2008 Model 70 Limited Edition".

* ***Model 70 Featherweight Compact*** – .22-250 Rem., .243 Win., .308 Win., or 7mm-08 Rem. cal., similar to Model 70 Featherweight except has 20 in. barrel and 13 in. LOP, approx. 6 1/2 lbs. New 2011.

MSR $880	$775	$675	$600	$525	$450	$375	$325	

MODEL 70 SPORTER (DELUXE) – various cals., similar to Featherweight Deluxe, 3 or 5 shot mag., 24 or 26 (.300 Win. Mag. only) in. barrel, satin finished Grade II walnut stock with cheekpiece and cut checkering, Pachmayr Decelerator recoil pad, 7 1/2 - 7 3/4 lbs. New 2008.

MSR $880	$775	$675	$600	$525	$450	$375	$325	

Add $40 for Mag. cals.

During the first year of manufacture (2008), this model featured an engraved custom one-piece floor plate marked "2008 Model 70 Limited Edition".

MODEL 70 SUPER GRADE – .270 Win. (new 2009), .30-06, .300 Win. Mag., 270 WSM (new 2009), .300 WSM (new 2009), .338 Win. Mag. (new 2010), or 7mm Rem. Mag. (new 2012) cal., similar to Model 70 Sporter Deluxe, except has fancy grade checkered walnut stock and forearm with cheekpiece and rosewood forend tip, no sights, one-piece steel trigger guard, and flush mounted hinged mag. floorplate, approx. 8 lbs. New 2008.

MSR $1,300	$1,125	$950	$725	$625	$550	$475	$425	

Add $40 for Mag. cals.

During the first year of manufacture (2008), this model featured an engraved custom one-piece floor plate marked "2008 Model 70 Limited Edition".

MODEL 70 75TH ANNIVERSARY SUPER GRADE – .30-06 cal., 24 in. barrel w/o sights, features grade IV/V fancy walnut stock with cut checkering and shadowline cheekpiece, floorplate features "75th Anniversary Model 70" with scroll engraving, right side of upper receiver has engraved banner "The Rifleman's Rifle", engraved steel grip cap, 8-1/4 lbs. Mfg. 2012 only.

	$1,775	$1,600	$1,400	$1,200	$1,000	$875	$750	*$2,000*

MODEL 70 SAFARI EXPRESS – .375 H&H, .416 Rem. Mag., or .458 Win. Mag. cal., 24 in. blue barrel with hooded blade front sight, express rear barrel sight, 3 shot mag., pre-'64 type claw extractor, dual recoil lugs, reinforced crossbolts, checkered satin finished walnut stock with cheekpiece, one piece steel trigger guard, flush mount hinged magazine floorplate, barrel band front swivel base, Pachmayr Decelerator recoil pad, 9 lbs. New 2010.

MSR $1,420	$1,200	$925	$825	$725	$650	$575	$500	

MODEL 70 ALASKAN – .30-06, .300 Win. Mag., .338 Win. Mag., or .375 H&H cal., 25 in. barrel with folding adj. rear sight and hooded gold bead front sight, satin finished Monte Carlo walnut stock and forearm with cut checkering, MOA trigger system, Pachmayr

GRADING - PPGS™	100%	98%	95%	90%	80%	70%	60%	LAST MSR

Decelerator recoil pad, Pre-64 style controlled round feed with claw extractor, 8-1/2 lbs. New 2012.

MSR $1,270	$1,100	$950	$725	$625	$550	$475	$425	

MODEL 70 EXTREME WEATHER SS – various standard and Mag. cals., 3 or 5 shot mag., stainless steel action, 22, 24, or 26 in. free floating, stainless steel fluted barrel, black Bell & Carlson synthetic stock with alloy skeletal bedding block and cheekpiece, M.O.A. trigger system, one-piece trigger guard and mag. frame, no sights, 7 - 7 1/4 lbs. New 2008.

MSR $1,200	$995	$765	$625	$550	$475	$425	$375	

Add $40 for Mag. cals.

During the first year of manufacture (2008), this model featured an engraved custom one-piece floor plate marked "2008 Model 70 Limited Edition".

MODEL 70 COYOTE LIGHT – various cals. in standard short action, including WSM, 22 (disc. 2010) or 24 in. heavy stainless fluted free floating barrel, 3 or 5 shot mag., black lightweight carbon fiber/fiberglass Bell & Carlson composite stock with diagonally vented forend, matte blue receiver, Pachmayr Decelerator recoil pad, 7 1/2 lbs. New 2009.

MSR $1,100	$950	$775	$675	$575	$475	$425	$375	

Add $50 for Mag. cals.

MODEL 70 ULTIMATE SHADOW – various cals., 3 or 5 shot mag., 22, 24, or 26 in. blue barrel, black pistol grip composite stock with oval dot gripping surfaces, controlled round feed action, hinged mag. floorplate, external claw extractor, Winsorb recoil pad, no sights, approx. 6 1/2 - 7 lbs. New 2009.

MSR $760	$650	$595	$525	$450	$400	$365	$335	

Add $40 for Mag. cals.

* ***Model 70 Ultimate Shadow SS*** – various cals., similar to Model 70 Ultimate Shadow, except has matte stainless steel action and barrel, 6-3/4-7/14 lbs. New 2012.

MSR $930	$795	$695	$615	$540	$465	$385	$335	

Add $40 for Mag. cals.

MODEL 70 ULTIMATE SHADOW HUNTER – various standard and Mag. cals., Pre-64 style controlled round feed with claw extractor, 3 or 5 shot mag., 22, 24, or 26 in.Sporter free floating barrel, lightweight synthetic Mossy Oak Break-Up Infinity camo, gray overmolded rubberized gripping surfaces, satin blued metal finish, three position safety, recessed target crown, M.O.A. trigger system, blade type ejector, Winsorb technology recoil pad, no sights, approx. 6 3/4 - 7 1/4 lbs. New 2013.

MSR $830	$725	$650	$575	$500	$450	$400	$350	

Add $40 for Mag. cals.

* ***Model 70 Ultimate Shadow Hunter SS*** – various cals., similar to Model 70 Ultimate Shadow Hunter, except has matte stainless steel action and barrel, 6-3/4-7/14 lbs. New 2013.

MSR $1,040	$895	$800	$725	$650	$575	$500	$425	

Add $40 for Mag. cals.

COMBINATION GUNS

SHOTGUN/RIFLE COMBINATION – combination 12 ga. and .222 Rem., .223 Rem., .243 Win., .270 Win., .30-06, .308 Win., .300 Win. Mag., 5.6x57R, 6.5x55mm, 7x65R, 7x57 Mauser, or 9.3x74R cal. rifle, O/U, 25 in. barrels, top barrel is WinChoked, Grand European engraving and finish, 8 1/2 lbs. Mfg. 1983-85.

	$2,795	$2,475	$2,100	$1,875	$1,650	$1,550	$1,425	$2,550

Add 50% for .300 Win. Mag. or 6.5x55mm cal.

This model was advertised in .222 Rem., .223 Rem., 6.5x55mm, or .300 Win. Mag. cal., but very few 6.5x55mm or .300 Win. Mag. cals. have been encountered to date.

GRADING - PPGS™	100%	98%	95%	90%	80%	70%	60%	LAST MSR

RIFLES: O/U

DOUBLE XPRESS RIFLE – .30-06, .257 Roberts, .270 Win., 7x57M, 7x57R, 7x65R, or 9.3x74R cal., 23 1/2 in. O/U barrels, iron sights with claw scope mounts, ejectors, fully engraved satin finish receiver with game scene engraving, walnut specially hand checkered, sling swivels, 8 1/2 lbs. Mfg. 1984-85 only.

$4,950	$4,500	$3,000	$2,500	$2,250	$2,000	$1,750	*$2,995*

In 1984, Aero Marine located in Birmingham, AL special ordered 200 deluxe double rifles in 7x57mm Mauser cal. They featured better engraving and game scenes with bottom of receiver marked Jaeger. Of the 200, 100 were rifles with 90 being standard grade and 10 being deluxe. The other 100 were supplied with an extra set of O/U shotgun barrels. Sales were slow on these special guns and eventually they were liquidated to another wholesaler. Recently, prices are in the $3,250-$3,750 range for the rifle alone and $4,500-$5,000 for the Combo, depending on condition.

RIFLES: SINGLE SHOT, POST 1964 MFG.

MODEL 1885 LOW WALL GRADE I .22 LR CAL. – .22 LR cal., features 24 1/2 in. half-round, half-octagon barrel with buckhorn rear sights, uncheckered straight grip walnut stock and forearm, crescent buttplate, blue finish only, 8 lbs. 2,400 mfg. late 1999-2001.

$735	$625	$525	$450	$400	$350	$300	*$828*

* ***Model 1885 Low Wall High Grade*** – similar to Model 1885 Low Wall Grade I, except features frame engraving, 24Kt. squirrel/cottontail scenes, fancy walnut stock and forearm with cut checkering. 1,100 mfg. late 1999-2001.

$1,050	$875	$750	$650	$550	$450	$350	*$1,180*

MODEL 1885 LOW WALL – .17 HMR (disc. 2006), .17 Mach 2 (new 2005), .22 Hornet, .223 Rem., .22-250 Rem., or .243 Win. cal., 24 in. octagon barrel, checkered straight grip or pistol grip walnut stock and Schnabel forearm, open sights, sling swivels, drilled and tapped, 8 lbs. Mfg. 2003-2006.

$875	$700	$575	$500	$450	$400	$350	*$1,069*

MODEL 1885 HIGH WALL – .22-250 Rem. (new 2006), .223 Rem. (new 2006), .270 WSM, .300 WSM, .325 WSM (new 2006), or 7mm WSM cal., 28 in. full octagon barrel without sights, checkered walnut stock, Schnabel forearm, adj. trigger, Pachmayr Decelerator pad, blued receiver, 8 1/2 lbs. Mfg. 2005-2006.

$1,000	$800	$675	$575	$500	$425	$375	*$1,085*

MODEL 1885 BPCR – .45-70 Govt. cal., 30 in. half round, half octagon barrel, case colored receiver, lever, buttplate, and pistol grip cap, drilled and tapped, oil finished Grade III/IV walnut Creedmor style stock with Schnabel forearm, 10 lbs., 8 oz.

$1,450	$1,275	$1,075	$925	$800	$700	$600	*$1,779*

MODEL 1885 HIGH WALL CENTENNIAL HUNTER – .30-06 cal., features gold embellished .30-06 seal on right side of engraved receiver, special barrel inscription, 28 in. octagon barrel, 8 1/2 lbs. Limited mfg. 2006.

$1,525	$1,275	$975	N/A	N/A	N/A	N/A	*$1,617*

SHOTGUNS: 1879-1963

BREECH LOADING SxS – 10 or 12 ga., imported from England for sales through the Winchester New York City office only, exposed hammers, available in 5 grades ranging from Class D - Class A and Match gun (lowest to highest). Higher grades were mfg. by W.C. Scott & Sons, C.G. Bonehill, W.C. McEntree, Richard Redmond, and H. & E. Hammond Gun Mfg.'s. Approx. 10,000 were imported between 1879-84.

Prices vary greatly due to condition and grade. Prices can range from $350 (poor condition Class D) to over $5,500 (95%+ condition specimen in Class A or Match gun).

This side by side model was the first shotgun bearing the Winchester name sold in the U.S. Identifiable by "Winchester Repeating Arms Co., New Haven, Connecticut, USA" marking on barrel rib top.

100%	98%	95%	90%	80%	70%	60%	50%	40%	30%	20%	10%

MODEL 1887 LEVER ACTION – 10 or 12 ga., 4 shot tube mag., 30 or 32 in. full choke fluid steel barrels, plain pistol grip stock, first Browning patent shotgun mfg. by Winchester, first lever action repeating shotgun mfg. domestically. Mfg. 1887-1901. Approx. 64,855 mfg.

N/A	$3,850	$3,300	$2,975	$2,650	$2,200	$1,875	$1,325	$1,100	$900	$775	$675

Standard frame finish on this model was color case hardening. Premiums exist for original bright case colored specimens. 10 ga. began production with serial number 22148. Also mfg. in Riot configuration (20 in. cylinder bore barrel). Gauges were chambered for 2 5/8 in. (12 ga.) and 2 7/8 in. (10 ga.). A very small amount was also made up in .70-150 cal. - add a significant premium.

* ***Model 1887 Lever Action Deluxe*** – damascus barrel, checkered stock, and other special order features.

N/A	$8,250	$6,600	$5,500	$4,500	$3,100	$2,450	$1,975	$1,650	$1,325	$1,100	$900

MODEL 1893 SLIDE ACTION – 12 ga., 30 (standard) and 32 in. barrel, black powder only. First Winchester shotgun with sliding forearm action, first Browning slide action patent, disc. 1897 after run of some 34,050. Note: chambered for 2 5/8 shells only, damascus barrels were available at extra cost, as were fancy stocks.

N/A	$1,050	$925	$825	$725	$625	$550	$500	$450	$400	$350	$300

This gun had limited sales because mechanical weaknesses developed when shooting smokeless powder. Winchester offered a brand new shotgun of the customer's choice when they returned their Model 1893.

MODEL 1897 SLIDE ACTION – 12 or 16 ga. (introduced 1900), improved Model 1893 action, 26-32 in. barrels, visible hammer, various chokes, takedown or solid frame, plain pistol grip stock. Over 1,024,700 mfg. between 1897-1957.

$1,000	$825	$650	$550	$500	$400	$300	$250	$225	$200	$175	$150

Add 50% for 16 ga.

Early 16 ga. Model 1897s were chambered for 2 9/16 in. shotshells, and are not as valuable because of the 2 3/4 in. shell length currently manufactured. This model was marked "Model 1897" on the slide action rails until circa 1912 (approx. ser. no. 500,000). After approx. ser. no. 500,000, the marking was moved to the barrel and changed to Model 97. The Model 1897 was the first Winchester shotgun chambered for 2 3/4 in. smokeless ammunition. This model was also manufactured with a damascus barrel for a short period of time, and is rare.

MODEL 1897 RIOT GUNS – see the "Trench/Riot Shotgun" category in the T section for more information and prices.

MODEL 1897 TRENCH GUNS – see the "Trench/Riot Shotgun" category in the T section for more information and prices.

This model changed its stock configuration after WWI.

MODEL 1897 TRAP – higher grade version of Standard, checkered stock, could have black diamond inlay in stock until 1919 (Black Diamond Trap), breech block marked "Trap" until approx. 1926. Mfg. 1897-1931.

N/A	$2,500	$2,200	$1,975	$1,750	$1,450	$1,100	$825	$675	$500	$450	$400

* ***Model 1897 Trap Black Diamond Trap*** – distinguishable by diamond ebony inlays in stock pistol grip.

N/A	$2,500	$2,200	$1,975	$1,750	$1,450	$1,100	$825	$675	$500	$450	$400

MODEL 1897 PIGEON – higher grade version of Standard 97, should have engraved pigeon behind hammer on frame, breech block marked "Pigeon", most exhibit black diamond stock inlays until 1919. Mfg. 1897-1939.

N/A	$11,000	$9,350	$8,250	$6,600	$4,950	$3,850	$3,300	$2,200	$1,650	$1,100	$900

MODEL 1901 – 10 ga. only, strengthened Model 1887 action to accept smokeless powder, lever action, standard barrel 32 in., blue barrel and frame, 5 shot mag., barrel address on upper tang. 13,500 mfg. between 1901-1920, starting with serial number 64,856.

N/A	$3,850	$3,500	$3,300	$2,750	$2,200	$1,975	$1,650	$1,375	$900	$775	$550

100%	98%	95%	90%	80%	70%	60%	50%	40%	30%	20%	10%

Add 50% for Deluxe Grade (checkered wood).

This shotgun was chambered for 2 7/8 in. smokeless powder ammunition.

MODEL 1911 SL AUTOLOADER – 12 ga., recoil operated, 26 or 28 in. barrel, various chokes, pistol grip laminated birch stock. Mfg. 1911-1921, with some production occuring between 1921-1928, 103,246 produced, action had design problems, nicknamed "Head Buster."

$675	$600	$550	$500	$450	$350	$275	$200	$150	$140	$130	$120

Values assume original wood without splitting, repair, or replacement. The Model 1911 was Winchester's first semi-auto shotgun. It did not prove to be satisfactory partly because the design had to avoid infringing the patents for Browning's famous A-5 model. Interestingly enough, this was a design which Winchester originally had helped Browning patent.

GRADING - PPGS™	100%	98%	95%	90%	80%	70%	60%	LAST MSR

MODEL 12 SLIDE ACTION – 12 (introduced 1914), 16 (introduced 1914), 20 (initial ga., mfg. 1912, 2 1/2 in. chamber mfg. until 1927), or 28 (introduced 1937) ga., 25 (20 ga. only, mfg. 1912-14), 26, 28, 30, or 32 in. standard, nickel, or stainless steel (scarce) barrel with or without rib (matted, solid, or VR), 2 9/16 (early 16 or 20 ga., until 1927, at ser. no. 464,565), 2 3/4 (became standard 1927) or 3 in. chamber, 6 shot, blue metal, various chokes, hammerless, plain pistol grip or straight walnut stock and forearm, marked Model 1912 from 1912-1919, approx. ser. no. 172,000. 14 in. LOP was original standard, then changed to 14 1/2 in. circa 1930. Mfg. 1912-1976.

12 ga. (28 or 30 in. FC bbl.)	$725	$600	$500	$425	$325	$295	$250
16 ga.	$825	$700	$600	$475	$375	$300	$275
20 ga.	$1,100	$900	$700	$625	$525	$475	$425
28 ga.	$6,000	$5,000	$4,500	$4,100	$3,500	$2,900	$2,500

Subtract 50% if with non-factory Cutts compensator (has choke marked on barrel).
Add 50% for factory installed Cutts compensator (no choke marking on barrel).
Add 20% for 32 in. barrel.
Add 50% for original box with papers.
The following add-ons DO NOT apply to 28 ga. values.
Add 20%-40% for Win. solid rib, depending on original condition.
Add 50%-60% for Win. milled VR.
Add 25%-50% for "Deluxe Field Grade" with fancy checkered wood, depending on condition.
Add 10% for pre-WWII mfg.
Add 60% for each extra barrel(s).
Add 40%-50% for Win. special VR (offset barrel proofmark).

"Y" prefix appears on Model 12s built 1964-1980 - see listing under Post-64 Models.

Nickel steel barrel Model 12s (mfg. 1912-1931) have become very popular in recent years, and some collectors are actually specializing on nickel steel Model 12s only. Winchester proofed steel barrels were introduced in 1931.

Stainless steel barrel Model 12s were introduced during 1926 as a special order only, and discontinued in 1931 (65X,XXX serial range). Values typically range between $1,450 - $3,500, and are very rare in over 95% original condition, as the bluing easily wore off the stainless steel barrel since it was a "Japaned" finish, not regular bluing.

Original gauge can be determined by removing the buttstock and observing the gauge marking on the stock screw boss.

"Donut" post Winchester VRs are more desirable than the rectangular post.

13-15 in. LOPs could be special ordered on Model 12s until 1964.

Special order features on field guns have captured much collector interest in recent years. Combinations of these features can add a considerable percentage to the base values listed. Rare special orders on rare variations are very desirable and prices can double and more if the combination is right. As is the

GRADING - PPGS™	100%	98%	95%	90%	80%	70%	60%	LAST MSR

case with most other collectible shotguns at this time, Model 12s with open choked barrels in shorter lengths are A LOT more desirable (and expensive) than a specimen with a 30 in. full choke barrel (most common). Values listed are for standard configuration (28 or 30 in. full choke barrel with no rib). For most Model 12s, values for condition factors less than 60% will approximate the 60% price, because of shooter demand. Premiums must be added for the rarer open choked barrels in shorter length on all gauges.

Recently, some non-original, re-stamped 28 ga. barrels have been added to 16 or 20 ga. frames "creating" a more desirable (and expensive) gun to unsuspecting buyers. Roll die markings are getting better and better so be very cautious when considering a non-Cutts 28 ga. (as in get a receipt specifying originality). 28 ga. ser. no. range is approx. 720,138 to 1,857,XXX. 28 ga. Model 12s were available with both 2 3/4 (common) or 2 7/8 (infrequent) in. chamber. The 28 ga. has a magazine tube which is crimped, swaged, and necked at the rear and is visible with barrel assembly off and slide pulled back, enabling mag tube to protrude slightly at the rear of receiver extension. Believe it or not, there are getting to be a lot of fake Model 12 boxes that have been intentionally aged. Carefully screen NIB (watch the hanging tag also) specimens in this model.

Editor's Note: The Model 12 Winchester was produced continuously from 1912-1980. Over 2,027,500 were produced both in standard and deluxe (Pigeon) grades. Pigeon grades were first listed in 1914 and disc. during the war (1941). Reintroduced in 1948, they were disc. permanently in 1964, after which the Super Pigeon Grade became available only on a custom-order basis from Winchester's Custom Gun Shop. These guns are worth 50%-300% premiums depending on gauge, barrel lengths, stock options, engraving patterns, etc.

With an attrition rate of approximately 33%, Model 12s with rare features produced 50 years ago will only be much rarer today (and expensive). 28 ga. guns were built between 1937 and 1960. Gauge rarity in increasing order is 12 ga. (approx. 360,000 mfg. 1925-1943), 16 ga. (approx. 190,000 mfg. 1925-1943), 20 ga. (approx. 71,000 mfg. 1925-1943), .410 bore (Model 42), and 28 ga. (approx. 2,600 mfg. 1925-1943). Serialization breakdown by year of manufacture is provided under the "Model Serialization" section of this book. When collecting Model 12s, ser. nos. on the underside of receiver (forward end), should match ser. no. on bottom rear of Mag. tube.

MODEL 12 FEATHERWEIGHT – similar to Standard, except with alloy guard and different takedown system. Mfg. 1959-62. "F" suffix after ser. no.

	100%	98%	95%	90%	80%	70%	60%
	$700	$650	$550	$450	$375	$300	$250

MODEL 12 RIOT GUNS – see the "Trench/Riot Shotgun" category in the T section for more information and prices.

MODEL 12 MILITARY TRENCH GUNS – see the "Trench/Riot Shotgun" category in the T section for more information and prices.

MODEL 12 HEAVY DUCK GUN – 12 ga., 3 in. chamber, 30 or 32 in. barrel, solid rubber recoil pad, 1/2 in. shorter pull than regular Model 12 (13 5/8 in LOP.). Mfg. 1935-1963.

	100%	98%	95%	90%	80%	70%	60%
	$1,250	$1,100	$1,000	$900	$800	$600	$500

Add 60% for solid rib.
Add 50% for 32 in. barrel.

* ***Model 12 Heavy Duck Gun Vent. rib*** – factory Winchester or 2 different rib styles mfg. by Simmons, notice barrel proof marking - rare.

	100%	98%	95%	90%	80%	70%	60%
	$3,000	$2,850	$2,500	$2,250	$1,800	$1,500	$1,400

Add 25%-50% for "Deluxe Field Grade" with fancy checkered wood, depending on condition.

MODEL 12 SKEET GUN – 12, 16, 20, or 28 ga., 26 in. barrel, skeet choke, checkered pistol grip stock, 14 in. LOP standard on pre-war guns. Mfg. 1933-1976.

	100%	98%	95%	90%	80%	70%	60%
	$2,250	$1,750	$1,300	$1,100	$900	$750	$650

16 gauge - rarity will command a premium.
Add 30% for solid rib.
Add 75% for Win. Special VR.
Add 100% for Win. milled VR.

GRADING - PPGS™	100%	98%	95%	90%	80%	70%	60%	LAST MSR

Subtract 50% for non-Factory-Cutts compensator.
Add 150-200% for 20 ga.
Add 400% for 28 ga.
Add approx. 20%-25% for brown plastic Hydrocoil stock, 12 ga. only.
Add approx. 40%-50% for white plastic Hydrocoil stock (approx. 50 mfg, 12 ga. only).

Another variation of the Model 12 Skeet was called the "Lady and Junior Model", with a factory LOP of 13 in., supplied with an original Mershon recoil pad - the configuration could also be special order during later years.

MODEL 12 TRAP GUN – various gauges, full choke barrel, deluxe straight or pistol grip stock, solid recoil pad, 14 3/8 in. LOP standard on pre-war guns. Mfg. 1938-1964.

	100%	98%	95%	90%	80%	70%	60%	LAST MSR
	$2,100	$1,600	$1,400	$1,200	$950	$800	$700	

Add 20% for milled VR.
Add approx. 20% for brown plastic Hydrocoil stock.
Add approx. 50% for white plastic Hydrocoil stock (approx. 50 mfg).

While plain barreled variation is rare, it is not as desirable.

MODEL 12 SUPER FIELD GRADE – 12, 16, or 20 ga., features 26, 28, or 30 in. matted rib barrel, deluxe walnut with checkered pistol grip stock and forearm, mfg. 1955-59.

	100%	98%	95%	90%	80%	70%	60%	LAST MSR
	$2,100	$1,900	$1,700	$1,500	$1,300	$1,000	$850	

Add 60% for 20 ga.
Add 50% for 16 ga.

MODEL 12 "BLACK DIAMOND" TRAP GRADE – various configurations, straight or pistol grip stock, features a small ebony diamond inlaid on each side of the pistol grip, 30 or 32 in. barrel with solid rib.

	100%	98%	95%	90%	80%	70%	60%	LAST MSR
	$3,500	$3,250	$2,750	$2,500	$1,800	$1,650	$1,400	

Add 50% for milled VR.

MODEL 12 TOURNAMENT GRADE – 12 ga. only, straight grip stock, small checkered forearm, usually stamped "Tourn" in wood on buttstock under buttplate. Mfg. 1914-1930.

	100%	98%	95%	90%	80%	70%	60%	LAST MSR
	$3,250	$2,750	$2,500	$2,250	$1,800	$1,500	$1,300	

MODEL 12 PIGEON GRADE – finer and more deluxe version of Model 12, many variations. Mfg. 1914-41 and 1948-64, engine turned breech block and shell follower, usually with engraved pigeon on bottom rear of mag. tube.

	100%	98%	95%	90%	80%	70%	60%	LAST MSR
	$4,000	$3,750	$3,100	$2,600	$2,100	$1,650	$1,400	
28 ga.	$9,000	$7,250	$6,500	$5,500	$4,750	$4,000	$3,600	

Add 25% for VR.
Add 100% for 20 ga.

Beware of potential fakes (i.e., inspect the engraved pigeon carefully if engraved on gun, and also note the quality and finish of the extra grade wood).

MODEL 20 – .410 bore, single shot, hammer, boxlock, 26 in. full choke (a few guns have been observed with cylinder choking), 6 lbs. 23,616 mfg. between 1919-1924.

	100%	98%	95%	90%	80%	70%	60%	LAST MSR
	$1,200	$950	$800	$650	$500	$350	$300	

While most Model 20s have 2 1/2 in. chambers, late parts cleanup guns could be chambered for 3 in. also.

* ***Model 20 Winchester Junior Trap Shooting Outfit*** – includes shotgun, midget hand trap, 150 .410 bore shells, 100 clay targets and accessories, cased.

	100%	98%	95%	90%	80%	70%	60%	LAST MSR
	$4,625	$4,200	$3,750	$3,450	$3,050	$2,750	$2,400	

Prices for this model assume all accessories are included - if not, subtract substantially. Just the shotshell boxes and accessories from this outfit are worth $2,500+ in nice condition.

MODEL 21 – 12, 16, 20, 28 ga., or .410 bore, boxlock action, after years in the design stage, production began in 1929 with guns being shipped to the warehouse in 1930 and first offered in Winchester's 1931 price list. Regular production continued for thirty years,

GRADING - PPGS™	100%	98%	95%	90%	80%	70%	60%	LAST MSR

through 1959. Approx. 32,500 mfg. 1931-1988. Approx. 1,100 were mfg. by the Custom Shop (including Custom, Pigeon, and Grand American Grades) during 1960-1982. Factory records for these models (early mfg. is sketchy) are available by contacting the Cody Firearms Museum located in Cody, WY. The following retail prices are for a standard field gun with average wood, beavertail forearm, ejectors, and single selective trigger with no alterations.

12 ga.	**$7,250**	**$6,450**	**$5,500**	**$4,950**	**$4,500**	**$4,000**	**$3,750**
16 ga.	**$9,000**	**$8,000**	**$7,000**	**$6,500**	**$6,000**	**$5,500**	**$5,000**
20 ga.	**$10,000**	**$8,750**	**$7,500**	**$7,000**	**$6,500**	**$6,000**	**$5,500**

Add 15%-25% for VR depending on condition.
Add 15%-30% per extra barrel assembly, depending on original condition.
Add 25% for 3 in. chambers (Duck Gun, 12 ga. only).
Add 20% for "Deluxe" marked guns, depending on original condition.
Subtract approx. 20% for double triggers w/extractors.
Subtract 10% for double triggers with ejectors (normally encountered with splinter forearm).

The early guns were plain, standard 12 gauge models with double triggers and extractors. Later in 1931, 16 and 20 gauge chamberings became available, as did selective single trigger and automatic ejectors.

By the end of 1933 the Model 21 skeet gun had been introduced as well as Tournament, Trap, and Custom Built grades. By about this time options included fancier wood, beavertail or semi-beavertail forends, checkered butts (standard on skeet guns) or skeleton steel buttplates, recoil pads and almost any variation the customers might desire. Metal finishes on a Model 21 are unusual in that they have salt blue frames and rust blue barrels - this explains the difference in coloration between these metal surfaces.

The Tournament Grade was dropped in 1936 and the Trap Grade in 1940. A Standard Grade Trap Gun was added in 1941. The early Custom Built Grade was dropped in 1942 and the Deluxe Grade was added. This grade included as standard many of the previously available extra cost options.

Relatively few guns were produced in chamberings smaller than 20 gauge. 28 gauge first appeared in the 1936 catalog, although a few were probably produced before that. Winchester records are unclear as to the total but it is generally believed that fewer than 100 original factory guns were made. In addition, a number of original 20 gauge guns have been modified at the factory or elsewhere with factory 28 gauge barrels. These latter guns are just as valuable if the conversion was done at the Winchester Custom Gun Shop. Authenticity of the original guns should be established by factory letter.

.410 bore guns were first listed in 1955 but, again, some had been produced earlier, one having been built for John Olin in 1950. Throughout Winchester history all the rules seem to have had exceptions and nowhere is this more apparent than with respect to the Model 21 which, after all, has been pretty much a custom gun from the very beginning. Factory records and tallies among dealers indicate the existence of 40 to 50 original factory guns. As in the case of the 28 gauge, extra barrels were available and at least some of those have been added to original 20 gauge guns.

The 3 inch Magnum 12 gauge Duck gun (stamped "Duck" on floor plate) was offered in Winchester catalogs from 1940 through 1952. Selective single triggers and automatic ejectors were standard as were the solid red Winchester recoil pads and 30 in. or 32 in. barrels. Some cases of non-factory upgrading of 2 3/4 or 3 inch Magnum guns have been reported. If authenticity is important to the buyer, a factory letter should be requested available from the Cody Firearms Museum at $85 per gun. With respect to such letters, in cases where records may be missing or incomplete, the resultant letters may be less conclusive than desired. In some instances, consultation with, or a written appraisal from an authoritative collector arms dealer might be helpful. As can be seen, values are partly based on a certain interdependence between options. Higher grade guns, of course, will bring somewhat higher prices, although much of their increased value results from the many "options" being included as standard features.

Buyers or sellers with limited experience should always seek expert advice or appraisals in dealing with a Model 21. This is especially true with regard to higher grade guns and those with extra ornamentation.

Refinishing or Restoration: There is disagreement as to the effects of refinishing a Model 21. Many

GRADING - PPGS™	100%	98%	95%	90%	80%	70%	60%	LAST MSR

shooters and at least some collectors prefer a professionally refinished gun to a badly worn one. Higher grade guns restored by a master craftsman may approach factory original guns in value.

Six standard patterns of engraving and several stock checkering and carving styles evolved during the production years. Values added by these and other embellishments such as precious metal inlays are beyond the scope of this work.

* ***Model 21 Skeet Gun*** – available in Standard, Tournament, and Trap grades. Introduced 1933.

Add 10% to standard Model 21 values. Larger premiums exist for special order grades.

* ***Model 21 Trap Gun*** – introduced 1940, Trap Grade disc. same year.

Add 10-25% to standard Model 21 values (be wary of non-factory modifications, especially to the stock).

* ***Model 21 3 Inch Duck Gun*** – 12 ga. only, 30 or 32 in. barrels, introduced in 1940, must be so stamped (observe the 3 in. and Duck markings very carefully).

	100%	98%	95%	90%	80%	70%	60%	LAST MSR
	$9,000	$8,000	$7,000	$6,500	$6,000	$5,500	$5,000	

Add 10% for 32 in. barrels.

* ***Model 21 .410 Bore*** – retail prices for original guns may be expected to range between $37,500 and $50,000 for mechanically sound guns depending on quality of finish. Non-original guns with add-on factory barrels would probably be reduced by one-third.

* ***Model 21 28 Ga.*** – factory original guns will probably bring from $25,000 to $30,000 and, as with the .410 bore guns, 20 gauge guns modified to 28 gauge with factory barrels would be worth approx. the same if done at the factory.

MODEL 21: RECENT PRODUCTION – refer to listing under SHOTGUNS: RECENT PRODUCTION SxS.

MODEL 24 SxS – 12, 16, or 20 ga., boxlock, hammerless, double triggers. Introduced 1940, disc. 1957 after approx. 116,280 mfg.

	100%	98%	95%	90%	80%	70%	60%	LAST MSR
12 ga.	$825	$725	$625	$475	$350	$275	$225	
16 ga.	$950	$775	$675	$525	$400	$325	$275	
20 ga.	$1,000	$900	$800	$675	$550	$425	$350	

MODEL 25 SLIDE ACTION – 12 ga. only, non-takedown version of the Model 12, 26 or 28 in. barrel. 87,937 mfg. between 1949-1954.

	100%	98%	95%	90%	80%	70%	60%	LAST MSR
	$550	$475	$400	$350	$300	$250	$200	

MODEL 36 SINGLE SHOT – 9mm Rimfire cal., long shot, short shot, and ball, 18 in. round barrel, single shot bolt action, guns were not serial numbered, one-piece plain stock and forearm, special shaped trigger guard, 2 3/4 lbs. Approx. 20,000 mfg. between 1920-27.

	100%	98%	95%	90%	80%	70%	60%	LAST MSR
	N/A	$1,700	$1,500	$1,300	$1,050	$895	$750	

MODEL 37 SINGLE SHOT – 12, 16, 20, 28 ga., or .410 bore, top-lever break-open action, all barrels are full choke. Note on pricing that there is a big difference between a 100% gun without a box and NIB condition. Not serial-numbered. Over 1,015,000 mfg. between 1936-63.

	100%	98%	95%	90%	80%	70%	60%	LAST MSR
12 gauge	$450	$325	$250	$200	$125	$100	$90	
16 gauge	$450	$325	$250	$200	$125	$100	$90	
20 gauge	$495	$395	$325	$250	$150	$110	$90	
28 gauge	$2,500	$1,825	$1,325	$995	$725	$575	$450	
.410 bore	$650	$500	$450	$375	$325	$200	$150	

If models are truly NIB, add $125-$175 to 100% condition values only, depending on gauge.

Add 20% for "Red Letter" models.

Add 15% for 32 in. barrel (12, 16, or 20 ga. only).

Most 28 ga. Model 37s have the "Red Letter."

GRADING - PPGS™	100%	98%	95%	90%	80%	70%	60%	LAST MSR

* ***Model 37 Single Shot Youth/Boys/Red Dot*** – 20 ga. only, 26 in. barrel marked Mod. Choke on barrel, solid red factory pad, identifiable by red dot inset into metal that is visible when hammer is cocked.

	N/A	$500	$400	$325	$250	$195	$150	

MODEL 40 SEMI-AUTO – 12 ga. only, long recoil action, 28 or 30 in. barrel, walnut stock, skeet model also, poorly designed, many recalled by Winchester. Approx. 12,000 mfg. 1940-41.

	$825	$675	$550	$450	$400	$300	$225	

MODEL 41 BOLT ACTION – .410 bore, 2 1/2 in. chamber until 1933 when it changed to 3 in., bolt action, single shot, 24 in. round barrel bored F, one-piece plain walnut stock and forearm, not serialized, approx. 22,145 were mfg. 1920-34.

	$725	$650	$550	$500	$425	$350	$300	

Add 15% for 3 in. chamber.

This model is rarely encountered with over 80% original condition.

MODEL 42 SLIDE ACTION – first pump specifically designed for the .410 bore, hammerless, 2 1/2 (introduced 1935) or 3 in. chamber, 26 or 28 in. barrel, plain walnut pistol grip stock with circular grooved forearm (modified 1947), invented by William Roemer, approx. 6 1/2 - 7 lbs. Approx. 164,800 mfg. in 4 grades between 1933-1963.

Add 40% to any Model 42 chambered for 2 1/2 in. shells.
Add 25% for factory installed Cutts compensator (no choke marking on barrel).
Add 25% for pre-war guns.
Subtract 50% for non-factory installed Cutts compensator (choke marked on barrel).

Special order features on field guns have captured much collector interest in recent years. Combinations of these features can add a considerable percentage to the base values listed. Special orders on rare variations are very desirable, and prices can double, or more than double, if the combination is right.

A note on Model 42 Vent. Ribs:

Early Model 42 vent. ribs were designed "Winchester Special Ventilated Rib" circa 1954 in the 125,000 ser. no. range. This rib had a wavy line matting on top of the rib, no stamping on the side, is known as the "Doughnut" post rib, and were in production until the end of 1957 with approx. ser. no. 149,000. The second variation Model 42 rib appears on guns in the approx. ser. no. range 141,000-149,000. This rib was made with both solid and hollow round posts. All parts for the vent. rib were made at the Winchester plant. A third variation was introduced at the end of 1957, when Winchester decided to send its Model 42 barrels to the Simmons Gun Specialty Co. in Kansas City for installation of the vent. ribs. In-the-white barrels were proofed in New Haven and marked on the left side so that the rib would not cover up the proofmark before shipment to Simmons. The ser. no. was not stamped on the receiver extension until the gun was completely assembled. This last variation, or oval post, appears on Model 42s starting at approx. ser. no. 150,000. This third variation is marked either "SIMMONS PATENTED" or "SIMMONS GUN SPECIALTY CO., KANSAS CITY, MO". The longer Simmons marking was stamped on the rib until the end of production.

* ***Model 42 Slide Action Standard Grade*** – 26 or 28 in. plain, solid rib or vent. rib (after market) barrel, plain walnut straight or pistol grip stock, walnut grooved forearm. Mfg. 1933-1963.

Plain barrel	$2,250	$2,000	$1,775	$1,450	$1,350	$1,250	$1,075	
Solid rib	$3,375	$3,000	$2,600	$2,150	$2,000	$1,900	$1,625	

A factory vent rib on this model is very rare and desirable, as only a very few have been encountered.

* ***Model 42 Slide Action Skeet Grade*** – 26 or 28 in. plain, solid rib or vent. rib barrel, select checkered walnut straight grip or pistol grip stock and checkered forearm extension, 4 different chokes (full, modified, skeet, or cylinder) during pre-war (approx. ser. no. 1-52,000), post-war (approx. ser. no. 52,000-164,000) had same chokes available

GRADING - PPGS™	100%	98%	95%	90%	80%	70%	60%	LAST MSR

through 1953, when cylinder choke was dropped, and improved cylinder was added.

Plain barrel	$4,500	$4,000	$3,725	$3,225	$2,850	$2,550	$2,200
Solid rib	$5,850	$5,400	$4,950	$4,275	$3,825	$3,375	$2,925
Vent rib	$6,750	$6,250	$5,700	$4,950	$4,375	$3,875	$3,375

* ***Model 42 Slide Action Trap Grade/Trap Grade Skeet*** – first variation had small checkered forearm with one diamond in center, field choke (full, modified, or cylinder), second variation has large checkered forearm with 2 diamonds in center, both variations had 26 or 28 in. plain or solid rib barrel, select checkered walnut straight grip (one closed diamond on underside of grip) or pistol grip (one closed diamond on each side of grip) stock, usually choked skeet, stamped "TRAP" at bottom of receiver under the ser. no. Only 231 mfg.

$15,000 $13,000 $11,750 $9,500 $8,000 $6,500 $5,000

Add 10% for small slide handle.

* ***Model 42 Slide Action Deluxe Grade*** – same configurations as Trap Grade, 20 LPI checkering, most are fitted with special vent. rib after 1954 in 3 styles: round post-donut base, round post, and rectangle post, pre-1954 mfg. had plain or solid rib barrel, 1946-1950 mfg. may have "DELUXE" stamp under ser. no. on receiver. Mfg. 1946-63.

» **Model 42 Slide Action Deluxe Grade Solid Rib**

$13,000 $12,500 $11,500 $11,000 $10,500 $8,000 $7,500

» **Model 42 Slide Action Deluxe Grade Vent. Rib (factory)**

$14,000 $13,000 $12,500 $11,500 $11,000 $8,500 $8,000

* ***Model 42 Slide Action Pigeon Grade*** – same configurations as Deluxe Grade, except has pigeon engraved on underside of mag. tube, most were factory engraved, very few mfg.

Must be appraised individually. Before purchasing any factory engraved Model 42, it is advised that a reputable dealer/collector be consulted.

MODEL 50 SEMI-AUTO – 12 or 20 ga., 3 shot, recoil-operated (non-recoiling barrel), 26-30 in. barrels, VR optional, steel frame or Feather Weight Model (aluminum receiver, FTW) introduced 1958. Over 196,000 mfg. between 1954-61, starting with serial number 1,000.

Standard Model	$650	$525	$450	$400	$350	$300	$250
Trap or Skeet Model	$1,300	$1,050	$950	$800	$700	$600	$500

Add $100 for VR (Simmons installed).
Add $50 for Feather Weight Model (denoted by "A" suffix in ser. no.).
Add $150 for 20 ga.

* ***Model 50 Semi-Auto Pigeon Grade*** – can be denoted by PIGEON stamped above the serial number on the barrel assembly, deluxe wood.

$2,300 $2,100 $1,850 $1,625 $1,400 $1,200 $995

MODEL 59 SEMI-AUTO – 12 ga. only, 3 shot, short recoil operation, Win-lite (steel and fiberglass) ribless barrels, 26-30 in. barrel lengths, alloy receiver inscribed with hunting scenes, Versalite (first interchangeable choke tubes) option introduced 1961, 6 1/2 lbs. 82,085 mfg. between 1960-65.

$750 $625 $500 $400 $300 $250 $200

Add 30% for barrel with all three choke tubes.

Inspect carefully for either cracked receiver (by bolt handle cutout and over serial numbers), or separating fiberglass on end of barrel. Winchester also mfg. 20 and 14 gauges experimentally in this model, which are extremely rare and expensive.

* ***Model 59 Semi-Auto Pigeon Grade*** – mfg. 1962-1965.

$3,000 $2,500 $2,000 $1,600 $1,200 $1,000 $800

SHOTGUNS: POST-1964

Winchester introduced WinChokes in 1969.

Shotguns: Post-1964, Lever Action

MODEL 9410 TRADITIONAL – .410 bore, 2 1/2 in. chamber, lever action based on the Model 94 rifle, 24 in. round barrel with cylinder bore or standard Invector chokes (new 2003), 9 shot tube mag., iron sights with TruGlo front and modified V adj. rear, checkered straight grip walnut stock and forearm, top tang safety became standard in 2003, approx. 6 3/4 lbs. Mfg. 2001-2006.

	100%	98%	95%	90%	80%	70%	60%	LAST MSR
	$850	$725	$600	$475	$400	$325	$250	*$626*

Subtract approx. $50 if w/o Invector chokes.

* ***Model 9410 Traditional Semi-Fancy*** – similar to Model 9410 Traditional, except has checkered semi-fancy walnut stock and standard Invector choke system. Mfg. 2004.

	100%	98%	95%	90%	80%	70%	60%	LAST MSR
	$1,150	$975	$800	$700	$550	$425	$325	*$789*

* ***Model 9410 Traditional Packer*** – cylinder bored or standard Invector chokes (new 2003, includes 3 chokes), 20 in. barrel, 5 shot, 2/3 mag., open sights, checkered semi-pistol grip walnut stock and forearm with sling swivel studs, also available in Packer Compact Model (12 1/2 in. LOP, new 2003), 6 1/4 - 6 1/2 lbs. Mfg. 2002-2006.

	100%	98%	95%	90%	80%	70%	60%	LAST MSR
	$850	$725	$600	$475	$400	$325	$250	*$647*

Subtract approx. $50 if w/o standard Invector chokes (includes 3).

* ***Model 9410 Traditional Ranger*** – similar to Model 9410 Traditional, except has uncheckered hardwood stock and forearm, 24 in. barrel with fixed cylinder bore barrel, 6 3/4 lbs. Mfg. 2003-2006.

	100%	98%	95%	90%	80%	70%	60%	LAST MSR
	$700	$575	$475	$400	$325	$250	$200	*$532*

* ***Model 9410 Traditional TS Custom Case Colored*** – similar to Model 9410 Traditional, features case colored receiver, lever, crescent buttplate, lower tang, and barrel bands, deluxe straight grip checkered walnut stock and extended forearm, matte bluing, 24 in. round barrel, gold trigger, top safety, 7 lbs. Mfg. 2005 only.

	100%	98%	95%	90%	80%	70%	60%	LAST MSR
	$2,000	$1,600	$1,325	$1,150	$950	$800	$600	*$1,418*

Shotguns: Post-1964, Semi-Auto

Winchester introduced WinChokes in 1969.

MODEL 140 RANGER SEMI-AUTO – 12, 16, or 20 ga., entry level model. Disc.

	100%	98%	95%	90%	80%	70%	60%	LAST MSR
	$275	$250	$220	$200	$175	$155	$140	

MODEL 1400 SEMI-AUTO – 12, 16, or 20 ga., 26, 28, or 30 in. barrel, 2 3/4 in. chamber, alloy receiver, various chokes, gas operated, 2 shot mag., checkered pistol grip stock. Mfg. 1964-1981.

	100%	98%	95%	90%	80%	70%	60%	LAST MSR
	$275	$250	$220	$200	$175	$155	$140	
Vent. rib	$315	$265	$240	$220	$195	$165	$150	

Add 33% for Winchester recoil reduction system (mfg. 1964-1970).

Note: In 1968 the model 1400 series was modified. The action release was improved and the checkering redesigned. From 1968-72, they were designated MKII, which was then dropped. The values for the later guns mfg. from 1968-73 may run approx. 10% higher - values shown are for guns mfg. from 1965-1968. A left-hand version was also available, and was disc. in 1973.

NEW MODEL 1400 WALNUT – 12 or 20 ga., 2 3/4 in. chamber, 22 (disc.), 26 (mfg. 1991-93), or 28 in. VR barrel, checkered walnut stock and forearm, WinChokes standard, 3 shot mag., rotary bolt system, 7-7 1/2 lbs. Mfg. 1989-94.

	100%	98%	95%	90%	80%	70%	60%	LAST MSR
	$350	$290	$260	$240	$220	$190	$165	*$419*

Add $15 for limited mfg. 1993 Quail Unlimited Model (2,500 mfg. 1993).

GRADING - PPGS™	100%	98%	95%	90%	80%	70%	60%	LAST MSR

MODEL 1400 CUSTOM HIGH GRADE – 12 ga. only, 28 in. VR WinChoke barrel, special order only through the Custom Gun Shop, features deluxe hand checkered walnut and special engraving. Mfg. 1991-92.

	$1,295	$995	$750	N/A	N/A	N/A	N/A	*$1,695*

MODEL 1400 SKEET GRADE – similar to 1400, 12 or 20 ga., with 26 in. VR barrel, skeet bore, select skeet style stock. Mfg. 1965-73.

	$425	$350	$300	$275	$220	$195	$165	

MODEL 1400 TRAP GRADE – similar to 1400, with 30 in. full choke VR barrel, select trap style stock. Mfg. 1965-73.

	$360	$330	$305	$275	$220	$195	$165	

MODEL 1400 DEER GUN – similar to 1400, with 22 in. barrel, rifle sights, 12 ga. only. Mfg. 1965-74.

	$265	$240	$220	$200	$175	$165	$140	

MODEL 1400 SLUG HUNTER – 12 ga. only, 22 in. smooth bore cyl. or rifled Sabot choke-tubed barrel, drilled and tapped for scope, includes bases or iron sights, 7 1/4 lbs. Mfg. 1990-92.

	$355	$310	$270	$250	$225	$195	$165	*$420*

MODEL 1400 RANGER – 12 or 20 ga., gas operation, alloy receiver, 22 cyl. deer, 26 (mfg. 1991-93), or 28 in. WinChoke barrel, checkered walnut finished hardwood stock and forearm, VR became standard 1985, 7 1/4 lbs. Disc. 1994.

	$285	$235	$200	$180	$160	$140	$120	*$377*

Add $53 for deer combo. (includes extra 22 in. cyl. bore barrel).

Subtract $40 without VR.

MODEL 1500 XTR – 12 or 20 ga., 2 3/4 inch only, 28 inch barrel, plain or VR, WinChoke tubes, gas operation. Mfg. 1978-82.

	$300	$260	$240	$220	$200	$180	$160	

SUPER X MODEL 1 – 12 ga., 26, 28, or 30 in. VR barrel, various chokes, steel receiver, self compensating gas operation, checkered pistol grip stock and forearm. Mfg. 1974-1981.

	$500	$450	$400	$350	$300	$250	$225	

SUPER X MODEL 1 SKEET – 12 ga., similar to Standard, with 26 in. skeet bore barrel, select skeet style stock. Mfg. 1974-1981.

	$695	$595	$500	$475	$450	$425	$400	

Add 20% if NIB condition.

SUPER X MODEL 1 TRAP – 12 ga., similar to Standard, with 30 in. barrel, imp. mod. or full choke, select trap style stock.

	$595	$550	$475	$425	$415	$395	$350	

Add 20% if NIB condition.

SUPER X MODEL 1 CUSTOM TRAP OR SKEET – 12 ga. only, limited production from the Custom Shop, deluxe checkered walnut stock and forearm, extensive scroll engraving on receiver, built to custom order. Limited mfg. 1987-92.

	$1,295	$925	$725	N/A	N/A	N/A	N/A	

* ***Super X Model 1 Custom Trap or Skeet Engraved*** – 12 ga., features number 5 engraving pattern with 7 gold inlays. Disc.

	$2,395	$1,900	$1,350	N/A	N/A	N/A	N/A	*$1,295*

Add $700 for factory gold inlays (8 flying ducks).

SUPER X2 3 IN. MAGNUM FIELD – 12 ga. only, 3 in. chamber, self-adjusting gas operation, 26 or 28 in. VR back-bored barrel with Invector chokes, 5 shot mag., choice of checkered walnut or black synthetic stock and forearm with recoil pad, high gloss blue or matte metal finish, approx. 7 1/4 - 8 lbs. Mfg. 1999-2004.

	$750	$650	$575	$525	$465	$400	$325	*$874*

GRADING - PPGS™	100%	98%	95%	90%	80%	70%	60%	LAST MSR

* ***Super X2 3 in. Magnum Field Light*** – 12 ga., 26 or 28 in. VR back-bored barrel with Invector Plus chokes, alloy receiver, checkered pistol grip walnut stock and forearm, 6 1/2 - 6 3/4 lbs. Mfg. 2005-2006.

$835	**$710**	**$600**	**$560**	**$500**	**$450**	**$375**	***$945***

* ***Super X2 3 in. Magnum Field Sporting Clays*** – 12 ga., 28 or 30 in. VR back-bored barrel with Invector chokes, adj. stock using spacers, includes 2 gas pistons, checkered walnut or Signature Red Dura-Touch finished (new 2003) hardwood stock and forearm, approx. 8 lbs. Mfg. 2001-2007.

$875	**$730**	**$610**	**$560**	**$500**	**$450**	**$375**	***$999***

Add $16 for Signature Red Dura-Touch finish on stock and forearm.

* ***Super X2 3 in. Magnum Field Sporting Clays Signature II*** – 12 ga., features red anodized alloy receiver and forearm cap, two gas pistons provided, 28, 30 or 32 (mfg. 2005 only) in. barrel, black metallic paint on stock and forearm, adj. stock spacers provided, approx. 8 lbs. Mfg. 2005-2006.

$885	**$735**	**$625**	**$575**	**$500**	**$450**	**$375**	***$1,015***

* ***Super X2 3 in. Magnum Field Composite*** – 12 ga., 26 or 28 in. VR barrels with three Invector chokes, black composite stock and forearm with Dura-Touch armor coating, matte metal finish, includes sling swivel studs, approx. 7 3/4 lbs. Mfg. 2004-2005.

$775	**$665**	**$585**	**$525**	**$465**	**$400**	**$325**	***$908***

* ***Super X2 3 in. Magnum Field Rifled Deer*** – 12 ga., 22 in. rifled barrel with cantilever scope base and Tru-Glo sights (rear sight folds down), black synthetic stock and forearm, 7 1/4 lbs. Mfg. 2002-2005.

$800	**$675**	**$585**	**$530**	**$455**	**$395**	**$325**	***$957***

* ***Super X2 2 3/4 in. Magnum Field Practical MK I*** – 12 ga., similar to Super X2 Practical MKII, except is 2 3/4 in. chamber, has regular TruGlo iron sights, and does not have Dura-Touch, cylinder bore Invector choke standard, 8 lbs. Mfg. 2003-2007.

$960	**$800**	**$675**	**$575**	**$500**	**$465**	**$435**	***$1,116***

* ***Super X2 3 in. Magnum Field Practical MK II*** – 12 ga., home defense configuration featuring black composite stock and forearm, black metal finish, 22 in. barrel with Invector choke system and removable LPA ghost ring sights, 8 shot extended mag., includes sling swivels, Dura-Touch armor coated composite finish became standard during 2003, 8 lbs. Mfg. 2002-2006.

$1,075	**$885**	**$715**	**$635**	**$550**	**$495**	**$440**	***$1,287***

Subtract 10% if w/o Dura-Touch finished stock and forearm.

SUPER X2 3 1/2 IN. MAG. COMPOSITE – 12 ga. only, 3 1/2 in. chamber, similar to Super X2, black synthetic stock and forearm with vent. recoil pad, Dura-Touch armor coated stock/forearm treatment became standard during 2003 for all models, 24 (disc. 2000), 26, or 28 in. VR back-bored barrel with Invector chokes, 7 1/2-8 lbs. Mfg. 1999-2005.

$885	**$725**	**$625**	**$565**	**$500**	**$450**	**$375**	***$1,027***

* ***Super X2 3 1/2 In. Mag. Composite Universal Hunter*** – 12 ga., similar to Super X2 3 1/2 In. Mag., except has full coverage Mossy Oak Break-Up camo composite stock and forearm, 26 in. VR barrel with 3 Invector Plus chokes, including optional extended extra full (standard beginning 2006), TruGlo sights, 7 3/4 lbs. Mfg. 2002-2007.

$1,050	**$875**	**$700**	**$600**	**$515**	**$455**	**$375**	***$1,252***

Subtract approx. 5% for standard Invector Plus chokes.

* ***Super X2 3 1/2 In. Mag. Composite Greenhead*** – 12 ga., similar to Super X2 3 1/2 In. Mag., except has green Dura-Touch stock and forearm for enhanced durability and non-slip hold during cold/wet conditions, 28 in. VR barrel, matte metal finish, 8 lbs. Mfg. 2002-2005.

$900	**$740**	**$620**	**$565**	**$500**	**$450**	**$375**	***$1,036***

GRADING - PPGS™	100%	98%	95%	90%	80%	70%	60%	LAST MSR

* ***Super X2 3 1/2 In. Mag. Composite Turkey*** – 12 ga., similar to Super X2 3 1/2 In. Mag., except has 24 in. VR barrel with TruGlo sights and extra full turkey choke tube, matte finish only, 7 1/2 lbs. Mfg. 1999-2002.

	$880	$730	$615	$555	$495	$450	$375	$1,018

During 2001-2002, this model incorporated a "Team NWTF" logo on the stock.

* ***Super X2 3 1/2 In. Mag. Composite Camo Turkey (NWTF)*** – 12 ga., similar configuration as regular Turkey, except has 100% Mossy Oak Break-Up camo treatment and TruGlo sights, 7 1/2 lbs. Mfg. 2000-2007.

	$1,035	$850	$700	$550	$495	$425	$375	$1,236

Beginning in 2001, this model incorporates a "Team NWTF" logo on the stock.

* ***Super X2 3 1/2 In. Mag. Composite Camo Waterfowl*** – 12 ga., similar to Super X2 3 1/2 In. Mag., except has 100% Mossy Oak Shadow Grass treatment, 28 in. VR back-bored barrel with Invector chokes, 8 lbs. Mfg. 1999-2005.

	$1,000	$840	$685	$565	$495	$425	$375	$1,185

SX3 (SUPER X3) 3 IN. MAGNUM WALNUT FIELD – 12 or 20 (new 2009) ga., 3 in. chamber, self-adjusting Active Valve gas operation, 26 or 28 in. VR barrel with Invector Plus chokes, variable checkered walnut stock with second generation Pachmayr Decelerator pad, adj. LOP, alloy receiver and 4 shot mag. tube, grey Perma-Cote Ultra Tough or Dura-Touch Armor coating (current) surface finish, 6 3/8 - 7 lbs. Mfg. 2006-2011.

	$1,025	$875	$750	$650	$575	$500	$450	$1,220

This model is also known as the SX3 (Super X3).

* ***SX3 (Super X3) Compact Field*** – 12 or 20 ga., similar to Super X3 3 in. Magnum Walnut Field, except has shortened 13 in. LOP. Mfg. 2011 only.

	$1,025	$875	$750	$650	$575	$500	$450	$1,220

* ***SX3 (Super X3) 3 in. Magnum Classic Field*** – 12 or 20 ga., similar to 3 in. Walnut Field, except has traditional diamond pattern checkering and non-adj. Decelerator recoil pad. Mfg. 2008-2009.

	$975	$850	$750	$650	$575	$500	$450	$1,159

* ***SX3 (Super X3) 3 in. Flanigun Exhibition/Sporting*** – 12 or 20 ga., features black composite stock and forearm with Dura-Touch armor coating and red annodized frame and forearm cap, 28 or 30 (new 2010) in. VR barrel with Invector Plus chokes, designed for Winchester exhibition shooter Patrick Flanigan, 7 1/4 lbs. Mfg. 2008-2010.

	$1,195	$995	$850	$725	$625	$550	$475	$1,479

* ***SX3 (Super X3) 3 in. Magnum Field Composite*** – 12 or 20 (new 2011) ga., similar to 3 in. Mag. Walnut Field, features black composite stock and forearm, alloy receiver, 26 or 28 in. barrel with Invector Plus chokes, approx. 6 3/4 lbs. Mfg. 2006-2011.

	$975	$850	$725	$625	$525	$475	$425	$1,140

Add $10 for 12 ga.

* ***SX3 (Super X3) 3 in. Magnum Field Cantilever Deer*** – 12 or 20 (new 2011) ga., 22 in. rifled barrel with Weaver style cantilever scope base and Tru-Glo sights, alloy receiver, black synthetic stock and forearm, approx. 7 1/2 lbs. Mfg. 2006-2011.

	$1,025	$895	$775	$650	$575	$500	$450	$1,200

Add $20 for 12 ga.

SX3 BLACK FIELD – 12 or 20 ga., 3 in. chamber, 26 or 28 in. VR back bored barrel with three invector plus chokes, matte black aluminum alloy receiver with red accents, active valve system, satin finished walnut stock and forearm with cut checkering, Pachmayr Decelerator recoil pad, ambidextrous safety, drop out trigger, approx. 6-3/4 lbs. New 2012.

MSR $1,070	$950	$850	$750	$650	$575	$500	$425	

GRADING - PPGS™	100%	98%	95%	90%	80%	70%	60%	LAST MSR

* ***SX3 Black Field Compact*** – similar to SX3 Black Field, except has 13 in. LOP stock, approx. 6 -1/2 lbs. New 2012.

MSR $1,070	$950	$850	$750	$650	$575	$500	$425	

SX3 BLACK SHADOW – 12 or 20 ga., 3 in. chamber, 26 or 28 in. VR back bored barrel with three invector plus choke tubes, features matte black synthetic stock with textured gripping surface and matching forearm, Inflex technology recoil pad, matte black receiver with red accents, ambidextrous safety, 6-3/4 - 7-1/4 lbs. New 2012.

MSR $1,000	$875	$775	$675	$600	$525	$425	$375	

SX3 CANTILEVER BUCK – 12 or 20 ga., 3 in. chamber, features 22 in. rifled barrel with Truglo front sight and rear Weaver style cantilever, matte black synthetic stock with textured gripping surface and Inflex technology recoil pad, approx. 7-1/2 lbs. New 2012.

MSR $1,150	$995	$875	$750	$650	$575	$500	$425	

SX3 WATERFOWL HUNTER – 12 or 20 ga., 3 in. chamber, 26 or 28 in. VR back bored barrel with three invector plus choke tubes, 100% Mossy Oak Duck Blind camo, Truglo fiber optic front sight, Inflex technology recoil pad, active valve system, ambidextrous safety, drop out trigger, approx. 6-5/8 - 7 lbs. New 2012.

MSR $1,140	$995	$875	$750	$650	$575	$500	$425	

SX3 UNIVERSAL HUNTER – similar to SX3 Waterfowl Hunter, except features 100% Mossy Oak Break-Up Infinity camo coverage. New 2012.

MSR $1,160	$995	$875	$750	$650	$575	$500	$425	

SX3 (SUPER X3) SPORTING – 12 ga. only, 2 3/4 in. chamber, 28, 30, or 32 in. ported VR barrel with 5 extended choke tubes and TruGlo front sight, checkered adj. comb walnut stock and forearm, Active Valve gas system, gun metal grey receiver finish, Pachmayr Decelerator recoil pad, approx. 7 1/2 lbs., includes red ABS hard case with Winchester logo. New 2011.

MSR $1,700	$1,450	$1,175	$1,000	$875	$750	$625	$550	

SX3 (SUPER X3) 3 1/2 IN. MAGNUM COMPOSITE – 12 ga. only, 3 1/2 in. chamber, features black composite stock and forearm, alloy receiver, grey Perma-Cote Ultra Tough (disc.) or Dura-Touch Armor coating (current) surface finish, 26 or 28 in. VR barrel with Invector Plus chokes, 4 shot mag., approx. 7 1/4 lbs. Mfg. 2006-2011.

	$1,050	$925	$800	$675	$575	$525	$475	*$1,280*

* ***SX3 (Super X3) 3 1/2 In. Magnum Composite Waterfowl*** – 12 or 20 (new 2011, 3 in. chamber) ga., similar to Super X3 3 1/2 In. Mag., except has 100% Mossy Oak New Shadow Grass (disc.) or Mossy Oak New Duck Blind (new 2007) treatment, 26 or 28 in. VR barrel with 3 choke tubes, approx. 6 1/2 (20 ga.) or 7 lbs. Mfg. 2006-2011.

	$1,225	$975	$825	$725	$625	$525	$450	*$1,480*

Subtract $140 for 20 ga. (new 2011).

* ***SX3 (Super X3) 3 1/2 In. Magnum Composite All Purpose Field*** – 12 or 20 (new 2011, 3 in. chamber), similar to Super X3 3 1/2 In. Mag., except has 100% Mossy Oak New Break-Up (disc. 2009) or Mossy Oak Infinity (new 2010) camo treatment, 26 or 28 in. VR barrel with 3 choke tubes, approx. 6 1/2 (20 ga.) or 7 lbs. Mfg. 2006-2011.

	$1,225	$975	$825	$725	$625	$525	$450	*$1,480*

* ***SX3 (Super X3) 3 1/2 in. Mag. NWTF Cantilever Extreme Turkey*** – 12 ga., 24 in. cantilever barrel with extra-full extended turkey choke tube, composite stock with full Mossy Oak New Break-Up camo treatment and Dura-Touch Armor coating, Active Valve system, Pachmayr Decelerator recoil pad, steel sling swivels, includes TruGlo deluxe red dot scope and Weaver style mount, includes hardshell case, approx. 7 1/2 lbs. Mfg. 2008-2010.

	$1,225	$1,000	$850	$725	$600	$525	$450	*$1,539*

GRADING - PPGS™	100%	98%	95%	90%	80%	70%	60%	LAST MSR

* ***SX3 (Super X3) 3 1/2 In. Mag. Gray Shadow*** – 12 ga., 3 1/2 in. chamber, gray Perma-Cote UT surface finish, 26 or 28 in. barrel, gray composite stock with Dura-Touch Armor coating, Active Valve System, three Invector-Plus chokes, sling swivel studs, red "W" embedded in stock, 7 - 7 1/4 lbs. Mfg. 2009.

	100%	98%	95%	90%	80%	70%	60%	LAST MSR
	$1,050	$900	$800	$700	$625	$550	$475	$1,299

SX3 BLACK SHADOW 3-1/2 IN. MAG. – 12 ga., 3-1/2 in. chamber, otherwise similar to the SX3 3 in. Black Shadow, 7-7/14 lbs. New 2012.

	100%	98%	95%	90%	80%	70%	60%
MSR $1,070	$925	$800	$700	$600	$500	$400	$350

SX3 WATERFOWL HUNTER 3-1/2 IN. MAG. – 12 ga., 3-1/2 in. chamber, otherwise similar to SX3 3 in. Waterfowl Hunter, approx. 7-1/8 lbs. New 2012.

	100%	98%	95%	90%	80%	70%	60%
MSR $1,200	$1,050	$900	$775	$675	$575	$500	$425

SX3 UNIVERSAL HUNTER 3-1/2 IN. MAG. – 12 ga., 3-1/2 in. chamber, otherwise similar to SX3 Universal Hunter 3 in., 7-71/8 lbs. New 2012.

	100%	98%	95%	90%	80%	70%	60%
MSR $1,230	$1,025	$875	$750	$650	$575	$500	$425

SX3 (SUPER X3) NWTF CANTILEVER (EXTREME) TURKEY – 12 (3 1/2 in.) or 20 (3 in.) ga., 24 in. cantilever barrel with extra-full extended turkey choke tube and TruGlo front sight, composite stock with full Mossy Oak New Break-Up Infinity camo treatment and Dura-Touch Armor coating, Active Valve system, Inflex technology recoil pad, steel sling swivels, approx. 7 1/2 lbs. New 2011.

	100%	98%	95%	90%	80%	70%	60%
MSR $1,140	$975	$850	$725	$625	$550	$475	$395

Add $60 for 12 ga.

Shotguns: Single Barrel

MODEL 370 – 12, 16, 20, 28 ga., or .410 bore, 28-32 in. full choke plain barrel, replaced the Model 37, top lever break open, exposed hammer, plain pistol grip stock. Approx. 221,578 mfg. between 1968-73.

100%	98%	95%	90%	80%	70%	60%
$150	$125	$100	$90	$85	$80	$75

Add 20%-75% for 28 ga. and .410 bore, depending on original condition.

The Model 370 was mfg. in Winchester's Canadian plant in Cobourg, Ontario.

MODEL 370 YOUTH – similar to 370, with 26 in. barrel, 12 1/2 in. stock, with recoil pad.

100%	98%	95%	90%	80%	70%	60%
$145	$110	$95	$85	$80	$75	$70

MODEL 37A – replaced the Model 370, roll engraved receiver, gold trigger. Approx. 391,168 mfg. between 1973-80 in the Winchester plant in Cobourg, Ontario.

100%	98%	95%	90%	80%	70%	60%
$140	$110	$95	$85	$75	$65	$55

Add 10% for 36 in. goose barrel.

Add 50% for 28 ga. and 75% for .410 bore.

MODEL 37A YOUTH – similar to 37A, except 20 ga. or .410 bore with 12 1/2 in. LOP stock.

100%	98%	95%	90%	80%	70%	60%
$145	$110	$95	$85	$80	$75	$70

MODEL 840 – various gauges, mfg. in Canada until 1980.

100%	98%	95%	90%	80%	70%	60%
$140	$110	$95	$85	$75	$65	$55

MODEL 1370 SLAGBLASTER – 12 ga., 26 in. heavy barrel, shoots special Winchester/Western CE8Z industrial ammunition with extended 3 oz. zinc slug (rare), industrial sales only - used to clean slag from steel kilns, 9 lbs. Mfg. in Canada, disc.

100%	98%	95%	90%	80%	70%	60%
$750	$700	$650	$575	$525	$450	$400

SHOTGUNS: SLIDE ACTION, 1964-CURRENT

Winchester introduced WinChokes in 1969.

U.S. Repeating Arms closed its New Haven, CT manufacturing facility on March 31, 2006. There may be some speculation on recently manufactured Model 1300 shotguns. All Model 1300 last MSRs listed are from the Winchester 2006 price sheet.

GRADING - PPGS™	100%	98%	95%	90%	80%	70%	60%	LAST MSR

MODEL 12 SUPER PIGEON GRADE – 12 ga., slide action, 26, 28, or 30 in. barrel, VR, any choke, hand honed action, engine turned breech block and loading flap, "B" checkering and No. 5 engraving, custom order grade walnut stock. Limited production between 1964-72.

	$3,750	$3,275	$2,650	$2,275	$1,995	$1,650	$1,400	

Subtract 20% for Super Pigeon Grades mfg. 1984-85 (480 total).

MODEL 12 FIELD GRADE – 12 ga., slide action, 26, 28, or 30 in. VR barrel, various chokes, jeweled bolt, hand checkered, checkered select walnut stock. Mfg. 1972-75, "Y" ser. no. prefix.

	$750	$650	$600	$550	$500	$450	$400	

In 1984, Y series Model 12s were once again available through a private contract with U.S.R.A. Co. which included engraving on Grades 1A-1C and 2-5. These guns were available in either Field, Trap, or Skeet configurations. Since there was no manufacturer's suggested retail, Model 12 values shown are established by analyzing the sales of the two private contractors - no more of these variations are available.

* ***Model 12 Field Grades 1-A, 1-B, & 1-C*** – light engraving depicting dogs or ducks. Disc.

	$1,425	$1,250	$1,025	$875	$785	$695	$600	*$1,375*

* ***Model 12 Field Grades 2 & 3*** – engraving features large duck and dog game scenes on receiver flats. Disc.

	$1,875	$1,650	$1,500	$1,300	$1,150	$900	$800	*$1,695*

* ***Model 12 Field Grade 4*** – more elaborate game scene engraving than Grades 2 & 3. Disc.

	$2,200	$1,875	$1,600	$1,400	$1,200	$1,050	$950	*$1,995*

* ***Model 12 Field Grade 5*** – elaborate game scene engraving with style B checkering. Disc.

	$2,750	$2,300	$1,900	$1,600	$1,350	$1,200	$995	*$2,450*

Also available with gold inlays - add $1,000 to values.

* ***Model 12 Field Grade 3 Barrel Set*** – grade 5 engraving with gold inlays and two extra barrels. Disc.

	$5,995	$5,495	$4,795	$4,295	$3,995	$3,495	$2,795	*$6,000*

MODEL 12 SKEET GRADE – similar to Field Grade, with 26 in. VR skeet bore barrel, skeet style stock, with recoil pad. Mfg. 1972-75.

	$1,195	$995	$895	$750	$650	$550	$500	

See listings under Model 12 Field Grade for engraved values.

MODEL 12 TRAP GRADE – similar to Field grade, with 30 in. VR full choke barrel, trap style stock, straight or Monte Carlo, recoil pad. Mfg. 1972-80.

	$1,095	$950	$850	$750	$650	$500	$450	

See listings under Model 12 Field Grade for engraved values.

MODEL 12 DU – 800 mfg. during 1975 for auction at Ducks Unlimited chapter banquets. Please refer to Ducks Unlimited section.

MODEL 12 LIMITED EDITION

* ***Model 12 Limited Edition Grade I 20 Ga.*** – 20 ga. only, 2 3/4 in. chamber only, reproduction of the famous Winchester Model 12 with slight design improvements, 26 in. VR barrel bored modified, 5 shot mag., high post floating rib, walnut stock and forearm with semi-gloss finish, takedown, 7 lbs. 4,000 mfg. by Miroku 1993-95.

	$995	$825	$650	N/A	N/A	N/A	N/A	*$879*

* ***Model 12 Limited Edition Grade IV 20 Ga.*** – similar specifications to Grade I, except has select walnut checkered 22 lines per inch with high gloss finish, extensive game scene engraving including multiple gold inlays. 1,000 mfg. 1993-95.

	$1,500	$1,250	$995	N/A	N/A	N/A	N/A	*$1,431*

GRADING - PPGS™	100%	98%	95%	90%	80%	70%	60%	LAST MSR

MODEL 42 HIGH GRADE LIMITED EDITION – .410 bore, 26 in. full choke VR barrel, features Grade V-VI wood with special scroll and gold border engraving, 850 mfg. 1993 only.

	$1,850	$1,425	$1,100	N/A	N/A	N/A	N/A	*$1,617*

MODEL 120 RANGER – 12, 16, or 20 ga., entry level model, VR and WinChokes. Disc.

	$200	$180	$165	$140	$110	$100	$90

MODEL 1200 FIELD GRADE – 12, 16, or 20 ga., 26, 28, or 30 in. barrel, alloy receiver, various chokes, checkered pistol grip stock, pad. Mfg. 1964-1981.

	$200	$180	$165	$140	$110	$100	$90
Vent. rib	$220	$205	$195	$165	$140	$110	$100
WinChoke	$240	$215	$200	$190	$180	$160	$140

Add 33% for Winchester recoil reduction system (mfg. 1966-1970).

MODEL 1200 MAGNUM – similar to 1200, chambered for 12 or 20 ga., 3 in. magnum shells. Mfg. 1964-80.

	$210	$190	$175	$165	$140	$110	$100
Vent. rib	$240	$215	$200	$185	$150	$140	$110

MODEL 1200 SKEET GUN – similar to 1200, 12 or 20 ga., 26 in. VR barrel, skeet bore, 2 shot mag. and select style stock. Mfg. 1965-74.

	$325	$275	$235	$200	$165	$140	$120

MODEL 1200 TRAP GUN – similar to 1200, with 12 ga., VR, 30 in. full choke barrel, select trap style stock. Mfg. 1965-74.

	$295	$275	$300	$195	$165	$140	$120
WinChoke	$330	$305	$275	$250	$220	$165	$140

MODEL 1200 DEER GUN – similar to 1200, with 22 in. barrel, rifle sights, 12 ga. only. Mfg. 1965-74.

	$250	$200	$165	$110	$100	$85	$75

MODEL 1200 POLICE STAINLESS – 12 ga. only, 18 in. barrel, 7 shot mag. Disc.

	$250	$195	$165	$125	$105	$90	$75

MODEL 1200 DEFENDER – 12 ga. only, 18 in. cylinder bore barrel, 7 shot mag., 6 lbs. Disc.

	$250	$200	$180	$155	$140	$125	$110

MODEL 1300 FEATHERWEIGHT – 12 or 20 ga., 3 in. chamber, takedown, 26 (new 1991) or 28 in. barrel, 5 shot, plain or VR (became standard 1990), WinChoke tubes, checkered walnut stock and grooved forearm, alloy frame, recoil pad, 6 3/4 - 7 1/8 lbs. Mfg. 1978-93.

	$300	$260	$230	$195	$175	$160	$145	*$374*

Subtract $30 without VR.

This model had an "XTR" suffix until 1989. Older Model 1300 Featherweights had roll-engraving but no premiums are being asked at this time.

MODEL 1300 WALNUT FIELD – 12 or 20 (disc. 1994) ga., 3 in. chamber, 26 or 28 in. VR barrel with WinChokes (includes 3), checkered satin (disc. 2003) or gloss finished (new 2004) walnut stock and forearm, approx. 7 1/4 - 7 1/2 lbs. Mfg. 1994-2006.

	$350	$250	$200	$160	$140	$120	$110	*$444*

Beginning 2003, Winchester started engraving "Speed Pump" on receiver on all Model 1300 variations.

* ***Model 1300 Walnut Black Shadow Field*** – 12 or 20 (new 1996) ga., 3 in. chamber, 26 or 28 in. (12 ga. only) VR WinChoke barrel, black composite stock and forearm, 6 3/4 - 7 1/4 lbs. Mfg. 1995-2006.

	$275	$210	$170	$135	$120	$110	$95	*$357*

GRADING - PPGS™	100%	98%	95%	90%	80%	70%	60%	LAST MSR

* ***Model 1300 Walnut Field Sporting*** – 12 ga., 3 in. chamber, 24 (compact) or 28 in. VR barrel with 5 WinChokes, satin finished checkered walnut full length or compact (13 in. LOP) stock and forearm with radiused recoil pad, Tru-Glo front sight, matte metal finish, 6 3/4 or 7 1/2 lbs. Mfg. 2002-2006.

$350	$255	$205	$165	$135	$120	$110	$444

* ***Model 1300 Walnut Field Advantage Camo*** – 12 ga. only, 28 in. barrel with choke tubes, full coverage. Advantage Camo. Mfg. 1997.

$340	$265	$235	$195	$165	$145	$125	$432

* ***Model 1300 Walnut Field New Shadow Grass*** – 12 ga. only, 26 or 28 in. VR barrel with 3 WinChokes, features 100% Mossy Oak New Shadow Grass camo coverage, approx. 7 lbs. Mfg. 2004-2006.

$365	$275	$215	$180	$150	$130	$115	$472

MODEL 1300 UPLAND SPECIAL FIELD – 12 or 20 (new 2000) ga., 3 in. chamber, features gloss finished (new 2004) or satin finished (disc. 2003) checkered straight grip walnut stock and forearm, solid recoil pad, 24 in. VR barrel with choke tube, blue only, 6 3/4 lbs. Mfg. 1999-2006.

$350	$255	$205	$165	$135	$120	$110	$444

MODEL 1300 CUSTOM HIGH GRADE – while advertised, this model never went into production. Advertised retail was $1,395.

MODEL 1300 WATERFOWL – 12 ga. only, 3 in. chamber, 28 or 30 (disc.) in. VR barrel, matte finished metal, choice of low luster walnut finish or brown Win-Tuff wood stock, recoil pad, camo sling, and swivels, WinChokes standard, 7 lbs. Mfg. 1984-1991.

$295	$260	$235	$200	$180	$165	$150	$367

MODEL 1300 TURKEY GUN – 12 ga. only, 3 in. chamber, 22 in. VR barrel, WinChoked, walnut stock and forearm with low luster finish, metal surfaces have matte finish, supplied with camouflaged fabric sling, 6 3/8 lbs. Mfg. 1985-88.

$290	$265	$235	$200	$180	$165	$150	$348

* ***Model 1300 Turkey Gun Win-Cam*** – similar to Model 1300 Turkey Gun, except has greenish laminated hardwood stock and forearm. Mfg. 1987-93.

$350	$295	$250	$200	$180	$165	$150	$435

* ***Model 1300 Turkey Gun Win-Cam Combo Pack*** – 12 ga., supplied with 22 and 30 in. VR non-glare finished barrels, greenish laminated hardwood stock and forearm, camo sling, matte finished metal. Mfg. 1987-88 only.

$375	$330	$290	$260	$230	$200	$185	$425

* ***Model 1300 Turkey Gun Ladies-Youth Win-Cam Turkey Gun*** – 20 ga. only, 3 in. chamber, 22 in. VR barrel, green camo laminate shortened stock and forearm, includes sling and National Wild Turkey Federation engraving, 6 lbs. Mfg. 1992 only.

$340	$295	$250	$200	$180	$165	$150	$411

* ***Model 1300 Turkey Gun Win-Cam NWTF Series I-IV*** – 12 or 20 ga., Series I was released 1989 (12 ga. only) and included special receiver engraving featuring National Wild Turkey Federation motifs, Series II was released 1990 with a choice of either 12 (disc.) or 20 ga. Ladies/Youth model, Series III was released 1991-92, Series IV was released 1993. Disc. 1994.

$365	$300	$250	$200	$180	$165	$150	$458

MODEL 1300 TURKEY - SYNTHETIC STOCK – 12 or 20 (mfg. 1996-99, Black Shadow only) ga., 3 in. chamber, 22 in. VR barrel with choke tube, choice of 2 color Realtree camo patterns on synthetic stock and forearm, full camo coverage available in Realtree or Advantage (new 1996), or non-glare black (Black Shadow) finish on all surfaces, approx. 6 3/4 lbs. Mfg. 1994-2000.

GRADING - PPGS™	100%	98%	95%	90%	80%	70%	60%	LAST MSR

* ***Model 1300 Turkey Synthetic Stock Black Shadow Finish*** – disc. 2000.

	$260	$195	$160	$135	$120	$110	$95	*$328*

* ***Model 1300 Turkey Synthetic Stock Mossy Oak Break-Up*** – 12 ga. only, 3 in. chamber, 22 in. VR barrel with TruGlo sights, high density X-full turkey choke tube, 100% Mossy Oak coverage on wood and metal, 6 3/4 lbs. Mfg. 2000 only.

	$375	$295	$260	$225	$200	$185	$170	*$459*

This model was also available with iron sights and rifled sabot choke tube for deer hunting - add approx. $30.

* ***Model 1300 Turkey Synthetic Stock RealTree/Advantage Camo Finish*** – RealTree covered synthetic stock and forearm or full coverage camo. Disc. 1998.

	$290	$240	$180	$150	$130	$115	$100	*$370*

Add $62 for full coverage camo.
Add $40 for full coverage without sling (disc. 1997).
Add $40 for smoothbore barrel (Advantage full camo only).

MODEL 1300 UNIVERSAL HUNTER/TURKEY – 12 ga. only, 3 in. chamber, 26 in. VR barrel with 3 WinChokes, full coverage standard or New Mossy Oak Break-Up (new 2003) camo, with or w/o Tru-Glo 3-dot sights, composite stock and forearm, 7 lbs. Mfg. 2002-2006.

	$400	$350	$300	$255	$200	$165	$140	*$517*

Subtract 5% if w/o TruGlo sights (Hunter Model).

MODEL 1300 NWTF TURKEY MODELS – 12 ga. only, 3 in. chamber, 18 (Short Turkey, new 2002) or 22 in. barrel, choice of Black Shadow (black synthetic stock and forearm with non-glare metal finish and extra full choke tube, mfg. 2001 only), Turkey Superflauge with full coverage TreBark Superflauge (mfg. 2001) or Mossy Oak Break-Up camo with TruGlo sights, Buck & Tom Superflauge with full coverage TreBark Superflauge (mfg. 2001) or Mossy Oak Break-Up (new 2002) camo with 2 choke tubes including rifled sabot, or Short Turkey (18 in. barrel with rifled sights and full coverage Mossy Oak Break-Up camo) configurations, "Team NWTF" logo printed on stock, 6 3/4 lbs. Mfg. 2001-2006.

	$425	$360	$260	$225	$175	$150	$125	*$514*

Subtract approx. $160 for Black Shadow configuration.
Add $42 for Buck & Tom Superflauge configuration.

MODEL 1300 LADIES-YOUTH – 20 ga. only, 3 in. chamber, 22 in. VR barrel, shortened stock dimensions, walnut stock with recoil pad and rearward positioned, grooved forearm, 6 1/4 lbs. Mfg. 1992 only.

	$315	$260	$220	$180	$165	$150	$135	*$355*

MODEL 1300 SLUG HUNTER – 12 ga. only, 3 in. chamber, 22 in. rifled or smooth bore barrel with iron sights, checkered stock and forearm, satin walnut finish or brown laminate stock (Win-Tuff). Supplied with camo fabric sling and rings and bases. Mfg. 1988-disc.

	$360	$300	$250	$200	$180	$165	$150	*$445*

Add $10 for smooth bore barrel with Sabot rifled tubes (disc. 1992).
Add $4 for "Whitetails Unlimited" Model (new 1991).

MODEL 1300 WALNUT DEER – 12 ga. only, 3 in. chamber, 22 in. rifled barrel, non-glare metal surfaces, rifle sights, checkered walnut stock with recoil pad and forearm, 7 1/4 lbs. Mfg. 1994-1999.

	$350	$285	$255	$225	$200	$185	$170	*$429*

* ***Model 1300 Walnut Deer Black Shadow*** – 12 or 20 (mfg. 1996-97, reintroduced 2000) ga., 3 in. chamber, 22 in. smoothbore (12 ga. only, disc. 2003) or rifled (new 1996) barrel with IC WinChoke, matte black stock, forearm, and metal parts, rifle sights, drilled and tapped receiver, approx. 6 3/4 lbs. Mfg. 1994-2006.

	$300	$225	$175	$150	$125	$115	$95	*$382*

Add $44 for Cantilever scope mount, available in 12 ga. only (new 2000).
Add $77 for deer combo package that includes 22 in. cyl. bore (disc. 1998) or rifled (new 2000)

GRADING - PPGS™	100%	98%	95%	90%	80%	70%	60%	LAST MSR

barrel and 28 in. VR WinChoke barrels.

Subtract approx. $25 for smoothbore barrel (disc. 2003).

* ***Model 1300 Walnut Deer Ranger*** – 12 or 20 (Ranger regular or compact) ga., 3 in. chamber, 22 in. rifled barrel with rifle or TruGlo sights, smaller dimensions on 20 ga. Deer Ranger Compact (13 in. LOP, disc. 2005), brown composite stock and forearm, non-glare finish, 6 3/4 lbs. Mfg. 2000-2006.

	$305	$230	$170	$145	$125	$110	$100	$396

* ***Model 1300 Walnut Deer Full Advantage Camo*** – 12 ga. only, 3 in. chamber, choice of 22 in. rifled or smoothbore barrel, entire gun is in Full Advantage camo pattern, drilled and tapped receiver, iron sights, 7 lbs. Mfg. 1995-98.

	$350	$295	$260	$225	$200	$185	$170	$432

Subtract $22 for smoothbore barrel.

MODEL 1300 RANGER – 12 or 20 ga., 3 in. chamber, 22 cyl. or rifled (deer only, disc.), 24 1/8 cyl. (disc. deer barrel), 26 (mfg. 1991-98), 28, or 30 (disc. 1992) in. plain or VR barrel, walnut finished hardwood stock, alloy receiver, approx. 7 1/4 lbs. Mfg. 1983-2004.

	$285	$215	$170	$135	$120	$110	$95	$367

Subtract $40 without VR or WinChokes.

This model was also available in a deer combination package which included either a 22 in. rifled or smoothbore deer barrel and a 28 in. VR WinChoke barrel in either 12 or 20 ga. (disc.). - add approx. 25% to values listed.

* ***Model 1300 Ranger Gloss*** – 12 or 20 ga., 3 in. chamber, 26 or 28 in. VR barrel, gloss finished checkered hardwood stock and forearm, 7 1/4 - 7 1/2 lbs. Limited mfg. 2006.

	$300	$225	$180	$140	$125	$110	$95	$391

» ***Model 1300 Ranger Gloss Compact*** – similar to Model 1300 Ranger Gloss, except has 22 or 24 in. barrel and 13 in. LOP. Limited mfg. 2006.

	$285	$215	$170	$135	$120	$110	$95	$366

* ***Model 1300 Ranger Ladies/Youth Model*** – 20 ga. only, 3 in. chamber, 22 in. VR barrel, shorter stock dimensions - 13 in. LOP and rearward positioned forearm. Disc. 1998.

	$285	$235	$200	$170	$150	$125	$110	$309

Subtract $40 if without WinChoke and VR.

* ***Model 1300 Ranger Compact*** – 12 or 20 ga., 3 in. chamber, features shorter dimensions (13 LOP), 22 (20 ga. only) or 24 (12 ga. only) in. VR barrel with WinChoke and TruGlo sights, uncheckered hardwood stock and grooved forearm, blue only, approx. 6 3/4 lbs. Mfg. 1999-2005.

	$300	$225	$175	$140	$120	$110	$95	$391

MODEL 1300 CAMP DEFENDER – 12 ga. only, 3 in. chamber, 8 shot mag., 22 in. barrel with rifle sights and WinChoke, choice of black synthetic (disc. 2000) or hardwood (new 2001) stock and forearm, matte metal finish, 6 7/8 lbs. Mfg. 1999-2004.

	$300	$230	$180	$150	$125	$110	$100	$392

MODEL 1300 DEFENDER – 12 or 20 (disc. 1996, reintroduced 2001) ga., 3 in. chamber, available in Police (disc. 1989), Practical (new 2005), Marine, and Defender variations, 18 or 24 (mfg. 1994-98) in. cyl. bore barrel, 5 (disc. 1998), 7 (disc. 1998), or 8 shot mag., matte metal finish, choice of hardwood (disc. 2001), composite (matte finish), or pistol grip (matte finish, 12 ga. only) stock, TruGlo sights became standard 1999, 5 3/4 - 7 lbs. Disc. 2006.

	$270	$210	$160	$130	$110	$95	$85	$341

Add $13 for short pistol grip and full length stocks.

Add approx. $100 for Combo Package (includes extra 28 in. VR barrel - disc. 1998).

GRADING - PPGS™	100%	98%	95%	90%	80%	70%	60%	LAST MSR

* ***Model 1300 Defender NRA*** – 12 or 20 ga., 18 in. barrel with removable TruGlo fiber optic front sight, composite stock, 8 shot mag., features NRA medallion on pistol grip, also available in 12 ga. combo with pistol grip stock, 6 1/4 - 6 1/2 lbs. Limited mfg. 2006.

	$285	$215	$175	$140	$120	$110	$95	*$364*

Add $13 for combo with pistol grip and full length stock.

* ***Model 1300 Defender Practical*** – 12 ga. only, 3 in. chamber, 8 shot mag., 22 in. barrel with TruGlo adj. open sights, designed for practical shooting events, black synthetic stock and forearm. Mfg. 2005.

	$300	$230	$170	$145	$125	$110	$100	*$392*

» **Model 1300 Defender Practical NRA** – 12 ga. only, 3 in. chamber, 8 shot mag., 22 in. barrel with TruGlo sights, black synthetic stock and forearm, Winchoke system, adj. open sights, NRA logo grip cap, 6 1/2 lbs. Limited mfg. 2006.

	$315	$240	$180	$150	$130	$110	$100	*$414*

* ***Model 1300 Defender Stainless Coastal Marine*** – 12 ga. only, 18 in. cyl. bore stainless steel barrel and mag. tube, a Sandstrom 9A phosphate coating was released late 1989 to give long lasting corrosion protection to all receiver and internal working parts, Dura-Touch armor coating stock treatment added 2004, 6 shot mag., synthetic pistol grip (disc. 2001) or full black stock configuration, approx. 6 3/8 lbs. Mfg. 2002-2005.

	$465	$380	$275	$225	$195	$165	$140	*$575*

» **Model 1300 Defender Stainless Coastal Marine NRA** – 12 ga. only, 18 in. nickel plated stainless steel barrel, anodized aluminum alloy receiver and plated parts for corrosion resistance, Dura-Touch Armor coating on composite stock, 7 shot mag., sling swivel studs, removable TruGlo fiber optic front sight, 6 1/2 lbs. Limited mfg. 2006.

	$480	$390	$280	$230	$200	$165	$140	*$598*

* ***Model 1300 Lady Defender*** – 20 ga. only, 3 in. chamber, choice of synthetic regular or pistol grip stock, 4 (disc. 1996) or 7 shot mag., 18 in. cyl. bore barrel (new 1996), 5 3/8 lbs. Disc. 1998.

	$235	$190	$150	$120	$105	$90	$80	*$290*

SPEED PUMP FIELD – 12 ga., 3 in. chamber, side ejection, four lug rotary bolt, 26 or 28 in. VR barrel with Invector Plus chokes, choice of gloss finished checkered walnut or black synthetic stock and forearm, approx. 7 1/4 lbs. Mfg. by Miroku during 2008.

	$295	$250	$215	$200	$185	$170	$155	*$349*

Add $50 for checkered walnut stock and forearm.

SPEED PUMP DEFENDER – 12 ga., 3 in. chamber, side ejection, 5 shot mag., features 18 in. plain barrel with fixed cylinder choke, black composite stock with non-glare finish and ribbed forearm. Mfg. by Miroku during 2008.

	$240	$210	$190	$170	$150	$135	$120	*$299*

SXP (SUPER X PUMP) BLACK SHADOW FIELD – 12 ga., 3 or 3-1/2 (new 2012) in. chamber, 26 or 28 in. VR barrel with 3 Invector Plus choke tubes, rotary bolt with dual steel action slide bars, black pistol grip composite stock, non-glare matte metal finish with red accents, crossbolt trigger guard safety, styling similar to Super X3 semi-auto, Inflex recoil pad, approx. 6-3/4 -7 lbs. New 2009.

MSR $380	$325	$275	$240	$215	$185	$170	$150

Add $50 for 3-1/2 in. chamber (new 2012).

SXP (SUPER X PUMP) DEFENDER – 12 ga., 3 in. chamber, 18 in. fixed cylinder bore barrel, non-glare metal finish, 5 shot mag., deep groove forearm, black composite pistol grip stock, 6 1/4 lbs. New 2009.

MSR $350	$295	$265	$230	$200	$175	$150	$125

GRADING - PPGS™	100%	98%	95%	90%	80%	70%	60%	LAST MSR

SXP (SUPER X PUMP) WATERFOWL HUNTER – 12 ga., 3 or 3-1/2 (new 2012) in. chamber, 100% Mossy Oak Duck Blind (disc. 2012) or non-glare Mossy Oak Shadow Grass Blades (new 2013) camo coverage, 26 or 28 in. VR barrel with 3 Invector-Plus choke tubes, speed-plug 3 shot adaptor, Inflex recoil pad, approx. 6 3/4-7 lbs. New 2011.

MSR $460	$395	$350	$300	$250	$200	$175	$150

Add $40 for 3-1/2 in. chamber (new 2012).

SXP TURKEY HUNTER – 12 ga., 3-1/2 in. chamber, 4 shot mag., features 24 in. VR barrel with TruGlo sights, 100% Mossy Oak Break-Up Infinity camo coverage, Inflex technology recoil pad, 6-5/8 lbs. New 2012.

MSR $520	$450	$400	$365	$335	$300	$265	$235

SXP (SUPER X PUMP) FIELD – 12 ga., 3 in. chamber, 4 shot mag., 26 or 28 in. barrel, full, mod., or IC Invector plus choke tubes, checkered satin finished stock and forearm with premium recoil pad, brass bead front sight, drop out trigger, crossbolt safety, 6 3/4 lbs. New 2013.

MSR $400	$350	$315	$285	$250	$220	$195	$175

SXP (SUPER X PUMP) BLACK SHADOW DEER – 12 ga., 3 in. chamber, 4 shot mag., 22 in. fully rifled barrel, black synthetic stock with textured gripping surfaces, Inflex technology recoil pad, TruGlo fiber optic front and adj. rear sights, receiver mounted Picatinny rail, rotary bolt, drop out trigger, crossbolt safety, 6 7/8 lbs. New 2013.

MSR $520	$450	$400	$350	$300	$265	$235	$195

SXP (SUPER X PUMP) MARINE DEFENDER – 12 ga., 3 in. chamber, 18 in. barrel with Invector Plus cylinder choke tube, black synthetic stock with textured gripping surfaces, Inflex technology recoil pad, non-glare matte black alloy drilled and tapped receiver with hard chrome barrel and mag. tube, tactical ribbed forearm, includes both brass bead and TruGlo fiber optic front sights, drop out trigger, crossbolt safety, 4-lug rotary bolt, 6 1/4 lbs. New 2013.

MSR $400	$350	$315	$285	$250	$220	$195	$175

SHOTGUNS: O/U - RECENT PRODUCTION

Model 101 dates of manufacture and serialization data can be found in the SERIALIZATION section in the back of this text.

In November of 1987 Olin/Winchester disc. the Model 101. Classic Doubles (listed separately in this text) imported this model under their own trademark until approx. 1990. With the discontinuance of the Model 101 and its many variations, both dealers and collectors have created a lot more demand for this model recently. As a result, prices have escalated and the scramble is on to try and pick off those rare and desirable variations. Since there have been a lot of limited editions and production changes in the 101 O/U series, it could very well be that this model might become very collectible in upcoming years (as happened to the Model 12).

Note: Model 101 and Model 96 Xpert guns were made by Olin Kodensha located in Tochigi, Japan.

Add 10% for the following discontinued Model 101s listed in this section if in NIB condition only.

MODEL 91 – 12 ga. only, mfg. by Laurona in Spain for international sales including Europe, SST, ejectors optional, VR, distinguishable by black chrome finish on metal parts. Disc.

Prices are difficult to evaluate because of limited importation domestically. In some regions they are bought as medium priced field guns ($550-$650), while in others they are sold as a rare Winchester O&U ($900-$1,100).

MODEL 96 XPERT FIELD GRADE – 12 or 20 ga., similar action to Model 101, 3 in. chambers, auto ejectors, SST, various barrel lengths and chokes, action similar to 101, no engraving, checkered pistol grip stock and forearm. Mfg. 1976-82.

	$875	$775	$650	$550	$475	$425	$375

Add 10% for 20 ga.

This model has become known as the "Poor Man's 101".

GRADING - PPGS™	100%	98%	95%	90%	80%	70%	60%	LAST MSR

MODEL 96 XPERT SKEET GRADE – 2 3/4 in. chambers, similar to Field Grade, with 27 in. skeet barrels, skeet style stock. Mfg. 1976-82.

	$925	$850	$725	$600	$500	$450	$410	

Add 10% for 20 ga.

MODEL 96 XPERT TRAP GRADE – 12 ga. only, 2 3/4 in. chambers, similar to Field, 30 in. imp. mod./full or full/full choke, trap style stock. Mfg. 1976-82.

	$875	$775	$650	$550	$475	$425	$375	

MODEL 99 – 12 ga., DT, no engraving. Disc.

	$700	$575	$525	$470	$430	$395	$360	

MODEL 101 FIELD VARIATION – 12, 20 ga., or .410 bore, 26, 28, or 30 in. barrels, various chokes, boxlock, auto ejectors, SST, engraved receiver, checkered American walnut pistol grip stock. Mfg. 1963-87.

Values assume WinChokes (standard since 1983) - subtract $60 if without.

* ***Model 101 Field Variation Older Production*** – checkered walnut stock and forearm, ejectors, SST, blue metal with light engraving on receiver, various barrel lengths, w/o choke tubes.

	$995	$850	$725	$625	$585	$550	$500	

Add 50% for 28 ga. or .410 bore.
Add 20% for 20 ga.

* ***Model 101 Field Variation 25th Anniversary Model*** – 12 ga., 32 in. F/M barrels, 2 3/4 in. chambers, engraved "1 of 101" with silver inlays, cased. Mfg. 1988.

	$5,000	$4,500	$4,000	$3,500	$3,000	$2,000	$1,500	*$3,500*

* ***Model 101 Field Variation Special*** – 12 ga., 3 in. chambers, VR, 27 in. barrels with WinChokes, blue receiver with scroll engraving, ejectors, 7 lbs. Disc. 1987.

	$1,350	$1,225	$995	$875	$775	$695	$600	*$1,185*

* ***Model 101 Field Variation Lightweight*** – 12 or 20 ga., similar to regular Field Grade, except has coin finished receiver, vent. barrels, and solid rubber recoil pad, w/o WinChokes, 6 1/2 - 7 lbs. Disc. 1987.

	$1,200	$1,100	$1,000	$900	$800	$600	$500	*$1,425*

Add 20% for 20 ga.

* ***Model 101 Field Variation Waterfowl Model*** – 12 ga. only, 3 in. chambers, 30 or 32 (disc.) in. WinChoked barrels, VR, matte blue receiver with moderate engraving, low gloss walnut stock with vent. recoil pad, 7 3/4 lbs. Disc. 1987.

	$1,895	$1,700	$1,500	$1,250	$1,050	$800	$700	*$1,570*

* ***Model 101 Field Variation Grade 2 Barrel Hunting Set*** – 12 or 20 ga. barrels, both with WinChokes, 26 in. barrels - 20 ga., 28 in. barrels - 12 ga., scroll engraved, blue receiver with game scene engraving and borders, cased. Mfg. 1984-87.

	$3,300	$2,800	$2,600	$2,400	$2,200	$2,000	$1,800	*$2,345*

* ***Model 101 Field Variation Quail Special*** – 12, 20 (disc.1984), 28 (new 1987) ga., or .410 bore (new 1987), 25 1/2 in. WinChoke barrels, straight grip stock, vent. barrels and rib, coin finished receiver with game scene engraving, 6 3/4 lbs, 500 of each ga. were mfg. Imported 1984-86.

12 ga.	$2,900	$2,495	$2,250	$1,995	$1,750	$1,550	$1,450	
20 ga.	$3,500	$3,100	$2,650	$2,200	$1,850	$1,750	$1,650	
28 ga.	$5,250	$4,500	$3,950	$3,600	$3,200	$2,700	$2,500	
.410 bore	$4,500	$3,850	$3,250	$2,800	$2,350	$1,900	$1,800	*$1,950*

All 28 ga. models are baby frames.

GRADING - PPGS™	100%	98%	95%	90%	80%	70%	60%	LAST MSR

* ***Model 101 Field Variation National Wild Turkey Federation Commemorative*** – features golden turkeys on receiver sides, 27 in. VR barrels with choke tubes, only 300 mfg.

$3,000	**$2,400**	**$1,900**	**$1,700**	**$1,500**	**$1,300**	**$1,000**	

Original issue price was $1,950.

* ***Model 101 Field Variation American Flyer Live Bird*** – 12 ga. only, 28 or 29 1/2 (new 1988) in. separated barrels with special competition VR, blue frame with gold wire borders and pigeon inlay, 8 - 8 1/2 lbs. Imported 1987 only.

$2,595	**$2,275**	**$1,950**	**$1,775**	**$1,600**	**$1,425**	**$1,300**	***$2,910***

Add $925 for Combo Model (with extra set of 28 & 29 1/2 in. barrels with WinChokes - 45 mfg.).
Add $265 for 29 1/2 in. barrel with WT4 choke tubes.

Approx. 200 of this model were mfg.

MODEL 101 MAGNUM – similar to 101 Field, 12 or 20 ga., 3 in. Mag. chambering, recoil pad, 30 in. barrels, full and mod., or full and full choke. Mfg. 1966-81.

$1,300	**$1,100**	**$1,000**	**$800**	**$700**	**$600**	**$500**

Add 20% for 20 ga.

MODEL 101 SKEET VARIATION – similar to 101 Field, with 26 1/2 (12 or 20 ga.) or 28 (28 ga. or .410 bore) in. skeet bored barrels, skeet style stock. Mfg. 1966-84.

$1,200	**$1,000**	**$825**	**$770**	**$700**	**$650**	**$595**

Add 50% for 28 ga. or .410 bore.
Add 30% for 20 ga.

MODEL 101 THREE GAUGE SKEET SET – similar to Skeet 101, with 20, 28 ga., and .410 bore barrels, cased. Mfg. 1974-84.

$3,800	**$3,475**	**$3,150**	**$2,850**	**$2,600**	**$2,250**	**$1,900**

MODEL 101 TRAP VARIATION – 12 ga. only, 30 or 32 in. barrels with normal or wide VR, imp. mod. and full or full and full chokes, trap style stock. Mfg. 1966-84.

$1,320	**$1,100**	**$935**	**$825**	**$715**	**$660**	**$605**

MODEL 101 SINGLE BARREL TRAP – similar to O/U Trap, with 32 or 34 in. F or IM choke barrel, Monte Carlo trap style stock. Mfg. 1967-71.

$880	**$660**	**$550**	**$495**	**$385**	**$360**	**$330**

Add 100% for an extra O/U barrel (Trap Set).

MODEL 101 PIGEON GRADE (XTR) – 12, 20, 28 ga. or .410 bore (disc. 1986), vent. O/U barrels, deluxe engraved silver receiver version of 101, select checkered wood. Mfg. 1974-87.

* ***Model 101 Pigeon Grade Lightweight Field Model*** – lightweight variation, WinChokes standard, 28 ga. baby frame has 27 in. barrels, 6 1/2 - 7 lbs. Disc. 1987.

12 ga.	**$2,195**	**$2,000**	**$1,800**	**$1,450**	**$1,350**	**$1,250**	**$1,150**	
20 ga.	**$2,700**	**$2,350**	**$2,000**	**$1,800**	**$1,700**	**$1,600**	**$1,500**	
28 ga. standard	**$3,750**	**$3,300**	**$2,900**	**$2,500**	**$2,200**	**$2,100**	**$1,700**	
28 ga. baby frame	**$5,000**	**$4,650**	**$4,250**	**$3,800**	**$3,350**	**$2,750**	**$2,500**	
.410 bore	**$3,500**	**$3,250**	**$2,925**	**$2,500**	**$2,200**	**$2,100**	**$1,700**	***$1,950***

Subtract 5% if without WinChokes (available in all gauges).

* ***Model 101 Pigeon Grade Lightweight recent mfg.*** – 20 ga. only, 27 in. barrels only with WinChokes, previously manufactured guns that have been photo-chemically engraved and gold plated, 101 (total mfg.) shotguns were sold by Guns Unlimited Inc. located in Omaha, NE 1995-96.

$2,495	**$2,200**	**$2,000**	**$1,800**	**$1,600**	**$1,500**	**$1,300**	***$1,795***

* ***Model 101 Pigeon Grade Lightweight two barrel set*** – includes either 12/20 ga. with WinChokes (28 in. barrels on 12 ga. and 27 in. on 20 ga.) or 28 ga./.410 bore (27 in.

GRADING - PPGS™	100%	98%	95%	90%	80%	70%	60%	LAST MSR

barrels, 28 ga. has WinChokes; .410 bore has fixed M/F chokes), 250 sets mfg. serial numbered HS1-HS250. Disc. 1986.

	$3,595	$3,350	$2,950	$2,750	$2,300	$2,150	$1,900	*$2,500*

Add 30% for 28 ga./.410 bore combo.

* ***Model 101 Pigeon Grade 3 barrel set*** – coin finished Pigeon Grade frame, approx. 250 mfg.

	$4,750	$4,350	$3,900	$3,400	$2,750	$2,450	$2,250	

* ***Model 101 Pigeon Grade Featherweight*** – 12 or 20 ga., English straight stock, 25 1/2 in. barrels bored IC/IM, 6 1/2 - 6 3/4 lbs. Disc. 1987.

	$1,950	$1,750	$1,450	$1,275	$950	$850	$750	*$1,580*

Add 20% for 20 ga.
Add 20% for WinChokes.

* ***Model 101 Pigeon Grade Skeet*** – 12, 20, 28 ga., or .410 bore.

	$1,850	$1,650	$1,450	$1,225	$1,100	$875	$775	

Add 25% for 20 ga.
Add 50% for 28 ga. or .410 bore.

* ***Model 101 Pigeon Grade Trap (Disc.)*** – 12 ga. only, vent. barrels and rib, coin finish receiver with fine scroll engraving, engraved pigeon on floorplate, WinChoke standard, 8 1/4 lbs. Disc. 1985.

	$1,550	$1,350	$1,100	$925	$825	$725	$650	*$1,475*

Subtract 15% if w/o WinChokes.

* ***Model 101 Pigeon Grade Super*** – 12 ga. only, blue receiver with elaborate engraving including multiple gold inlays, extra select walnut with fleur-de-lis checkering on stock and forearm, WinChoke standard, 7 1/2 lbs. Imported 1985-87 only.

	$5,000	$4,800	$4,500	$3,800	$3,000	$2,750	$2,200	*$4,590*

MODEL 101 PIGEON GRADE TRAP (CURRENT) – 12 ga., 2 3/4 in. chambers, engraved nickel finished action, choice of 30 or 32 in. 10mm VR ported barrels with Invector Plus choking and TruGlo interchangeable fiber optic front sights, checkered Grade III/IV walnut with adj. comb, adj. trigger shoe, approx. 7 1/2 lbs., includes ABS hard case. Mfg. in Belgium. New 2008.

MSR $2,470	$2,125	$1,800	$1,575	$1,350	$1,075	$900	$750

Add $160 for adj. comb.

MODEL 101 PIGEON SPORTING – 12 ga., 30 or 32 in. ported barrels, 2 3/4 in. chambers, 10mm rib, gloss finished checkered Grade II/III walnut stock with adj. comb, five choke tubes, adj. trigger, silver nitride receiver with light scroll engraving, Tru-Glo front sight, includes hard case, 7 - 7 1/4 lbs. Mfg. 2009-2010.

	$2,275	$1,850	$1,625	$1,375	$1,100	$900	$825	*$2,619*

MODEL 101 DIAMOND GRADE – Trap or Skeet O/U, 12 (Trap only), 20, 28 ga., or .410 bore, vent. barrels and rib, WinChoke standard on Trap - add $75 on Skeet model (disc.1986), select hand checkered walnut, engraved satin-finish receiver. Trap model has extra high VR. Skeet model has raised rib and muzzle vents.

* ***Model 101 Diamond Grade Standard Trap*** – 12 ga. only, 30 or 32 in. vent. barrels, 8 3/4 - 9 lbs. Disc. 1987.

	$1,700	$1,500	$1,275	$1,100	$900	$780	$640	*$1,860*

* ***Model 101 Diamond Grade Unsingle Trap*** – 12 ga. only, lower single barrel, 32 or 34 in. barrel, extended rib. Disc. 1986.

	$1,900	$1,675	$1,425	$1,200	$1,000	$800	$600	*$1,760*

Add $60 for WinChoke.

GRADING - PPGS™	100%	98%	95%	90%	80%	70%	60%	LAST MSR

* ***Model 101 Diamond Grade Oversingle Trap*** – 12 ga. only, WinChokes, 34 in. upper barrel only, 8 1/2 lbs. Imported 1986-87 only.

	$2,100	$1,795	$1,600	$1,425	$1,200	$995	$895	*$2,145*

* ***Model 101 Diamond Grade Oversingle Combo*** – includes one set of O/U barrels and an oversingle barrel, cased. Imported 1987 only.

	$2,950	$2,725	$2,500	$2,250	$2,000	$1,800	$1,600	*$3,550*

Add $275 for ATA Trap set.

* ***Model 101 Diamond Grade Trap Combo*** – 12 ga. only, includes a set of 30 or 32 in. vent. O/U barrels and a 32 or 34 in. high ribbed unsingle (lower) barrel, standard or Monte Carlo stock, approx. 9 lbs. Disc. 1987.

	$2,950	$2,600	$2,325	$1,975	$1,800	$1,600	$1,400	*$2,940*

* ***Model 101 Diamond Grade Standard Skeet*** – 12, 20, 28 ga., or .410 bore, 27 1/2 in. vent. barrels and competition rib, 6 1/2 - 7 1/4 lbs. Disc. 1987.

	$1,725	$1,525	$1,300	$1,125	$950	$850	$700	*$1,950*

Add 30% for 28 ga. or .410 bore.
Add 20% for 20 ga.

Certain design features may increase/decrease the values of this model.

* ***Model 101 Diamond Grade Four Gauge Skeet Set*** – includes 12, 20, 28 ga., and .410 bore 27 1/2 in. separated barrel assemblies, cased. Imported 1985-87 only.

	$4,500	$4,000	$3,500	$3,000	$2,800	$2,500	$2,000	*$5,025*

* ***Model 101 Diamond Grade Sporting Clay*** – 12 ga. only, marked Diamond Sporter, 28 in. barrels with WinChokes, designed for Sporting Clay competition. Disc. 1987.

	$2,250	$1,875	$1,550	$1,225	$1,025	$875	$725	*$1,965*

MODEL 101 SPORTING - CURRENT MFG. (SELECT) – 12 ga., 28, 30, or 32 in. lightweight ported barrels, 2 3/4 in. chambers, ejectors, Invector-Plus chokes with 5 Signature extended choke tubes, traditional 101 styling with low profile blue engraved receiver, high-gloss Grade II/III walnut stock and forearm, adj. SST, Pachmayr Decelerator pad, 10mm broadway rib, white mid-bead and TruGlo front sight, 7 1/4 - 7 1/2 lbs. Mfg. by FN in Belgium. New 2007.

MSR $2,320	$2,025	$1,750	$1,495	$1,225	$995	$875	$800	

Select was dropped from this model's nomenclature beginning 2008.

MODEL 101 FIELD - CURRENT MFG. (SELECT) – 12 ga., 26 or 28 in. lightweight barrels, 3 in. chambers, ejectors, Invector-Plus flush chokes with three choke tubes, blue receiver with deep relief engraving, high-gloss Grade II/III walnut stock and forearm, adj. SST, vented Pachmayr Decelerator pad, 10mm broadway rib, brass bead front sight, 7 1/4 - 7 1/2 lbs. Mfg. by FN in Belgium. New 2007.

MSR $1,870	$1,650	$1,350	$1,150	$995	$875	$775	$675	

Select was dropped from this model's nomenclature beginning 2008.

MODEL 101 DELUXE FIELD (SELECT) – 12 ga. only, 3 in. chambers, 26, 28, or 30 in. barrels, ejectors, oil finished Grade II checkered walnut stock and forearm, Pachmayr Decelerator pad, adj. SST, Invector-Plus chokes and three Signature flush choke tubes, silver nitride receiver with engraving, includes hard case, 7 - 7 1/2 lbs. Mfg. by FN in Belgium. Mfg. 2007-2010.

	$1,395	$1,150	$950	$850	$750	$650	$575	*$1,679*

Select was dropped from this model's nomenclature beginning 2009.

MODEL 101 LIGHT – 12 ga., 3 in. chambers, 26 or 28 in. barrels, Grade II/III checkered gloss finished walnut stock and forearm, engraved aluminum alloy receiver with quail and pheasants, springer spaniel on bottom, Pachmayr Decelerator pad, three Invector-Plus choke tubes, 6 - 6 1/4 lbs. Mfg. 2009-2010.

	$1,725	$1,475	$1,250	$1,050	$925	$800	$675	*$2,039*

GRADING - PPGS™	100%	98%	95%	90%	80%	70%	60%	LAST MSR

501 GRAND EUROPEAN – Trap or Skeet, 12 or 20 (Skeet only) ga., 27, 30, or 32 in. vent. barrels and rib, extra select hand checkered walnut with oil finish, Schnabel forearm, extensive scroll engraving on satin-finished receiver. Mfg. 1981-1986.

$2,300	$2,100	$2,000	$1,800	$1,600	$1,400	$1,200	*$1,720*

Add 20% for 20 ga. Skeet.

* ***501 Grand European Featherweight*** – 20 ga. only, straight grip stock, 25 1/2 in. VR barrels, 5 3/4 lbs. Disc. 1986.

$3,150	$2,750	$2,500	$2,175	$1,900	$1,700	$1,500	*$1,720*

PRESENTATION GRADE – 12 ga. only, available in both Trap and Skeet models, blue action extensively engraved with gold inlays, special crotch walnut, 27 (Skeet) or 30 in. vent. barrels, hand checkered, silver wire borders on perimeter of receiver. Imported 1984-87 only.

$3,950	$3,395	$3,075	$2,400	$2,000	$1,800	$1,600	*$3,840*

Subtract 10% for Trap Model.

MODEL 1001 FIELD GRADE – 12 ga. only, 3 in. chambers, boxlock action, 28 in. VR (8mm) barrel with WinPlus chokes, blue metal featuring 40% engraving coverage, Grade I stock and forearm, high luster finish, mfg. in Italy by Marocchi 1993, disc. 1998.

$975	$795	$725	$650	$595	$550	$495	*$1,099*

* ***Model 1001 Field Grade Sporting Clays*** – 12 ga. only, 2 3/4 in. chambers, 28 or 30 in. VR (10mm) vent. barrels with WinPlus chokes, full engraving (includes scroll and flying W with clay bird), silver nitride receiver with remaining parts blue, Grade II-III stock and forearm, satin finish, mfg. in Italy by Marocchi 1993, disc. 1998.

$1,075	$925	$795	$725	$650	$595	$550	*$1,253*

* ***Model 1001 Field Grade Sporting Clays Lite*** – 12 ga. only, 3 in. chambers, blue finish, 28 in. VR barrels with WinPlus chokes, checkered walnut stock and forearm, gold SST, 7 lbs. Mfg. 1995-98.

$1,000	$795	$725	$650	$595	$550	$495	*$1,153*

MODEL G5500 SPORTER – 12 ga. only, marked Sporter, 28 or 30 in. barrels with fixed chokes (bored IC/M, IM/F, or XF/F) or WinChokes.

$1,795	$1,475	$1,275	$1,075	$900	$780	$640	

Add 20% for WinChokes.

MODEL G6500 SPORTER – 12 ga. only, marked Sporter, barrels and chokes same as G5500.

$2,295	$1,925	$1,625	$1,400	$1,225	$1,050	$900	

Add 20% for WinChokes.

SELECT FIELD (SUPREME) – 12 ga. only, 3 in. chambers, low profile boxlock action with dual tapered locking lugs positioned between the barrels, SST, ejectors, game scene engraved receiver, 26 (new 2001) or 28 in. 6mm VR back-bored barrels with Invector Plus choking (high polish barrels became standard in 2005), redesigned barrels in 2003, checkered walnut stock and forearm, blue action and barrels, barrel selector on safety switch, approx. 7 lbs. Mfg. 2000-2005.

$1,265	$1,025	$900	$800	$700	$600	$500	*$1,498*

During 2004, this model's nomenclature was changed from Supreme Select Field to Select Field.

SELECT WHITE FIELD TRADITIONAL/EXTREME – 12 ga. only, 3 in. chambers, 26 or 28 in. barrels, engraved low profile silver nitride receiver, walnut stock with oval (Extreme) or standard (Traditional) checkering, Invector-Plus choke system, 7 - 7 1/4 lbs., mfg. by Miroku. Limited mfg. 2006.

$1,295	$1,050	$900	$800	$700	$600	$500	*$1,533*

SELECT ELEGANCE (SUPREME) – 12 ga. only, 3 in. chambers, grey game scene engraved low profile receiver with dual locking pin design, choice of regular checkered (Traditional Elegance) or oval checkered (Extreme Elegance, new 2004) Grade III walnut stock and Schnabel forearm, 26 or 28 in. non-ported barrels with Invector Plus choke system (high polish barrels became standard in 2005), includes red hardshell case, approx. 7 lbs., mfg.

GRADING - PPGS™	100%	98%	95%	90%	80%	70%	60%	LAST MSR

by FN Belgium. Mfg. 2003-2006.

	$1,950	$1,625	$1,275	$995	$875	$775	$675	$2,320

SELECT MIDNIGHT – 12 ga. only, 3 in. chambers, 26 or 28 in. barrels, high gloss blued receiver with gold bird accents on both sides and bottom, satin finished Grade II/II walnut stock with oval checkering pattern, deluxe recoil pad, approx. 7 lbs., limited mfg. by Miroku 2006 only.

	$1,995	$1,650	$1,300	$1,025	$900	$800	$700	$2,380

SUPREME SELECT SPORTING – 12 ga. only, 2 3/4 in. chambers, features satin finished bi-tone receiver w/o engraving, 28 or 30 in. 10mm VR back-bored barrels with porting, redesigned barrels in 2003, SST with adj. trigger shoe system, sharply checkered walnut stock and Schnabel style forearm, approx. 7 1/2 lbs. Mfg. 2000-2003.

	$1,200	$995	$900	$800	$700	$600	$500	$1,406

SELECT ENERGY SPORTING – 12 ga. only, 2 3/4 in. chambers, 28, 30, or 32 in. ported and vented side rib high polish barrels with Invector Plus chokes (high polish barrels became standard in 2005), marked "Select Energy Sporting" on contrasting chrome finished receiver, 10mm VR, select American walnut stock with oval checkering and palm swell, with or w/o adj. cheekpiece, adj. trigger shoe, TruGlo front sight, approx. 7 1/2 lbs., mfg. by Miroku 2004-2006.

	$1,635	$1,425	$1,125	$965	$855	$750	$650	$1,950

Add $165 for adj. comb stock.

SELECT ENERGY TRAP – 12 ga. only, 2 3/4 in. chambers, 30 or 32 in. VR barrels with Invector Plus chokes (high polish barrels became standard in 2005), similar features as the Select Energy Sporting, features oval checkering on stock and forearm, palm swell, TruGlo front sight, Monte Carlo or adj. comb stock with solid recoil pad, approx. 7 1/2 lbs., made by FN in Belgium. Mfg. 2004-2007.

	$1,635	$1,425	$1,125	$965	$855	$750	$650	$1,948

Add $164 for adj. comb stock.

SELECT PLATINUM SPORTING – 12 ga. only, 2 3/4 in. chambers, 28, 30, or 32 in. ported barrels, ejectors, oil finished Grade II/III checkered walnut stock and forearm, Invector-Plus chokes and five Signature extended choke tubes, silver nitride receiver with light game scene engraving, adj. SST system, 10mm broadway rib, mid-bead and TruGlo competition front sight, includes hard case, approx. 7 - 7 1/2 lbs. Mfg. by FN in Belgium. Mfg. 2007-2008.

	$2,200	$1,925	$1,650	$1,400	$1,200	$1,000	$875	$2,625

SELECT PLATINUM FIELD – 12 ga. only, 3 in. chambers, 26 or 28 in. barrels, ejectors, oil finished Grade II/III checkered walnut stock and Schnabel forearm, Invector-Plus chokes and three Signature extended choke tubes, adj. SST, silver nitride receiver with deep relief engraving, includes hard case, 7 - 7 1/2 lbs. Mfg. by FN in Belgium. Mfg. 2007-2008.

	$1,975	$1,650	$1,300	$1,025	$900	$800	$700	$2,359

SHOTGUNS: RECENT PRODUCTION SxS

Values for recently manufactured side-by-sides assume NIB condition - subtract 10%-15% if without box, warranty card, and original shipping container (with packing materials).

MODEL 21: RECENT/CURRENT MFG. – between 1960-1987, Model 21 production was limited to high grades, built to special order only, and 1987 was the last year Winchester carried Model 21 pricing in its catalog. On custom shop guns mfg. 1960-1969, there is no Winchester name on the barrels, but the Winchester proofmark is on the water table, along with a designation "Model 21" or "New Haven, CT" plus the ser. no. On Model 21s produced from 1969-1988, the water tables are stamped as already noted, and the designation "Model 21 - Winchester" is stamped on the top of the left barrel adjacent to the rib, next to the receiver. Connecticut Shotgun Manufacturing Company is currently manufacturing Model 21 shotguns (marked "Model 21" only), including Grades 21-1, 21-5, 21-6, Grand American, and the Royal Exhibition. These guns are not marked "Winchester", and will not letter

GRADING - PPGS™	100%	98%	95%	90%	80%	70%	60%	LAST MSR

from the Cody Firearms Museum. Please refer to the Connecticut Shotgun Manufacturing Company listing for more information regarding these newer custom Model 21s. Also refer to previously mfg. Winchester Model 21 listings under SHOTGUNS: 1879-1963.

Add 25% for 16 or 20 ga.
Add $1,500 for vent. rib.

* ***Model 21 Custom Built*** – standard model with no engraving.

	$8,000	$7,000	$5,000	N/A	N/A	N/A	N/A	*$8,100*

* ***Model 21 Custom Grade*** – includes No. 6 engraved receiver and VR.

	$12,500	$10,500	$9,000	N/A	N/A	N/A	N/A	*$11,080*

* ***Model 21 Pigeon Grade*** – single set of barrels, No. 6 engraved, w/o gold inlays, 37 mfg. total in 12, 16, and 20 ga.

	$21,000	$19,000	$16,000	N/A	N/A	N/A	N/A	

* ***Model 21 Grand American Grade*** – includes 2 sets of barrels with forearms, No. 6 engraved with gold inlays, cased. Must letter from CFM.

	$28,500	$23,000	$19,500	N/A	N/A	N/A	N/A	*$22,745*

* ***Model 21 Grand American Small Gauge*** – 28 ga. or .410 bore. Must letter from CFM.

	$39,000	$31,000	$24,500	N/A	N/A	N/A	N/A	*$34,460*

Add 25% for 28 ga./.410 bore combo.

* ***Model 21 Grand American ("1 of 8" set)*** – includes 20, 28 ga., and .410 bore VR barrels. Only 4 of 8 sets actually mfg. Must letter from CFM.

	N/A	$65,000	$45,000	N/A	N/A	N/A	N/A	*$55,000*

* ***Model 21 Grand Royal (2 barrel set)*** – the highest grade of Model 21s ever produced, originally made in a .410 bore 2 barrel set for John Olin, only 4 others were ever manufactured, and all were 2 barrel sets.

Extreme rarity precludes accurate pricing on this model.

MODEL 22 – 12 ga. only, subcontracted by Winchester and manufactured in Spain by Laurona circa 1975 for international sales including Europe, field configuration only with 28 in. barrels, DT, oil finished checkered walnut stock and semi-beavertail forearm, matted rib, black-chrome finish on metal parts, hand engraved receiver, limited mfg.

	$1,200	$995	$825	$700	$600	$525	$475	

MODEL 23 XTR – 12 or 20 ga., 3 in. chambers, 25 1/2, 26, 28, or 30 in. barrels, various chokes, single trigger, VR, auto ejectors, scroll engraved, silver grey satin finish, blue barrel, checkered select walnut stock and forearm, first commercial gun to employ interchangeable chokes. Mfg. 1978-disc.

* ***Model 23 Grade 1***

	$1,900	$1,750	$1,600	$1,350	$1,100	$950	$800	

Add 20% for 20 ga.
Subtract 10% for fixed chokes.

* ***Model 23 XTR Pigeon Grade*** – standard weight model, 6 1/2 - 7 lbs, coin finished receiver with scroll engraving. WinChoke option became standard in 1986. Disc. 1986.

	$2,300	$2,100	$1,850	$1,600	$1,300	$1,100	$900	*$1,460*

Add 20% for 20 ga.
Subtract 10% if w/o WinChokes.

* ***Model 23 XTR Pigeon Grade Lightweight*** – 25 1/2 in. barrels only bored IM/IC (12 ga.) or IC/M (20 ga.) or with WinChokes, 6 1/4 - 6 3/4 lbs., coin finished receiver with bird scene engraving, English stock. Disc. 1986.

	$2,495	$2,150	$1,925	$1,750	$1,250	$1,000	$800	*$1,420*

Add 15% for 20 ga.
Subtract 10% if w/o WinChokes.

GRADING - PPGS™	100%	98%	95%	90%	80%	70%	60%	LAST MSR

MODEL 23 PIGEON GRADE DUCKS UNLIMITED – 12 or 20 ga., 500 mfg. in 1981 (12 ga.), and 500 mfg. in 1983 (20 ga.), 1981 12 ga. serialization is 81-DU-XXX, 1983 20 ga. serialization is 83-DU-XXX, cased.

	$2,500	$2,300	$2,200	$2,000	$1,800	$1,500	$1,200	

Add 20 % for 20 ga. (1983 mfg.).

MODEL 23 GOLDEN QUAIL SERIES – 12 ga. (1986), 20 ga. (1984), 28 ga. (1985), or .410 bore (1987), 25 1/2 in. solid rib barrels bored IC/M, mono-blocks are marked "IC/M" but the barrels are marked "Q1/Q2", coin finished receiver with one gold inlay on floorplate, beavertail forearm, straight grip English stock with recoil pad. Only 500 mfg. each year per gauge. Disc. 1987.

12 ga.	$2,995	$2,775	$2,500	$2,150	$1,850	$1,475	$1,325	
20 ga.	$3,400	$3,100	$2,700	$2,300	$1,975	$1,750	$1,475	
28 ga. (20 ga. frame)	$4,750	$4,350	$3,950	$3,650	$3,300	$2,900	$2,450	
410 bore (small frame)	$4,750	$4,350	$3,950	$3,650	$3,300	$2,900	$2,450	*$1,950*

MODEL 23 LIGHT DUCK – 20 ga., blue receiver and 28 in. barrels F/F, select walnut, 8 1/2 lbs. Limited edition, 500 mfg., introduced 1985.

	$2,895	$2,400	$2,075	$1,775	$1,350	$1,100	$975	*$1,660*

MODEL 23 HEAVY DUCK – 12 ga., 30 in. barrels, F/F, blue receiver, select walnut, 8 1/2 lbs. Limited edition, 500 mfg. 1984 only.

	$2,995	$2,895	$2,695	$2,495	$2,195	$1,895	$1,595	

MODEL 23 CUSTOM 2 BARREL SET – interchangeable 20 and 28 ga. 26 in. barrels, blue engraved receiver with gold inlays, "B" checkering on stock and forearm, leather cased with accessories, only 500 sets mfg. 1986. Disc. 1987.

	$5,975	$5,325	$4,975	$4,075	$3,525	$3,375	$3,075	*$4,625*

MODEL 23 GRANDE CANADIAN – 12 or 20 ga., 25 1/2 in. barrels with fixed chokes, coin finished receiver with oak leaf engraving and one gold leaf inlay on receiver bottom, English AAA select walnut stock with beavertail forearm, 51 mfg. in 12 ga., 450 mfg. in 20 ga., approx. 50 two-gun sets were also offered with cases (approx. ser. nos. 1-51).

	$2,850	$2,400	$1,950	$1,700	$1,500	$1,250	$1,125	
Cased set	$6,750	$6,050	$5,150	$4,450	$4,000	$3,450	$3,000	

Add 20% for 20 ga.

MODEL 23 CUSTOM – 12 ga. only, 27 in. WinChoke barrels, high luster bluing, no engraving, SST, ejectors, solid red rubber recoil pad, 7 lbs. Imported 1987 only.

	$2,800	$2,600	$2,400	$2,200	$1,900	$1,600	$1,200	*$1,975*

MODEL 23 CLASSIC SERIES – 12, 20, 28 ga., or .410 bore, 26 in. VR barrels, single trigger, deluxe hand-checkered walnut stock and beavertail forearm, solid recoil pad, brass nameplate, gold inlay on bottom of receiver, ebony inlay in forearm, 5 3/4 - 7 lbs. Imported 1986-1987 only.

12 ga.	$2,650	$2,375	$2,100	$1,825	$1,400	$1,250	$1,150	
20 ga.	$2,950	$2,550	$2,225	$1,900	$1,675	$1,395	$1,295	
28 ga. (small frame)	$5,400	$5,000	$4,000	$3,500	$3,000	$2,500	$2,250	
.410 bore (small frame)	$4,495	$4,100	$3,600	$3,350	$3,100	$2,750	$2,400	*$1,975*

100% values assume NIB for this model.

The 28 ga. on this model features a smaller frame, and was the only 28 ga. small frame produced in the Model 23 Series.

FACTORY WINCHESTER COMMEMORATIVES: U.S. PRODUCTION

During the course of a year, we receive many phone calls, emails, and letters on Winchester non-factory special editions and limited editions which do not appear in this section. It should be noted that a factory commemorative issue is a gun that has been manufactured, marketed, factory cataloged, and sold through the auspices of the specific trademark. There have literally been hundreds of non-factory special and limited editions which, although mostly made by Winchester (some were subcontracted), were not marketed or retailed by Winchester. These guns are NOT considered Winchester factory commemoratives in this publication, and for the most part, do not have the desirability factor that the factory commemoratives have. Non-factory cataloged special/limited editions are not listed in this text, because there are literally hundreds of them and collector interest is not as great as for the factory commemoratives. Remember, the least your special/limited edition can be worth is a little more than the standard edition value. Do not concentrate on the rarity or you will be disappointed.

Typically, special and limited editions are made for distributors and typically manufactured by sub-contract for an organization, state, special event, personality, etc. and are typically sold and marketed through a distributor to dealers, or a company/individual to those people who want to purchase them. These special editions may or may not have a retail price and many times, the demand may be regional with values decreasing rapidly in other areas of the country. Also, most special/limited editions do not have alphabetical prefixes/suffixes within their serial ranges. Desirability is the key to determining values on these editions.

As a reminder on commemoratives, especially for the beginning collector, here are a few facts applicable to all manufacturers of commemoratives. Commemoratives were guns specifically designed as a reproduction of an historically famous gun model, or as a tie-in with historically famous persons or events. They are generally of very excellent quality and often embellished with select woods and finishes such as silver, nickel, or gold plating. Obviously, they are manufactured to be instant collectibles and to be pleasing to the eye. As with firearms in general, not all commemorative models have achieved collector status, although most enjoy an active market. Consecutive-numbered pairs as well as collections based on the same serial number will bring a premium. Remember that handguns usually are in some type of wood presentation case, and that rifles may be cased or in packaging with graphics styled to the particular theme of the collectible.

The original factory packaging and papers should always accompany the firearm as they are necessary to realize full value. All commemorative firearms should be absolutely new, unfired, and as issued since any obvious use or wear removes it from collector status and lowers its value significantly. Many owners have allowed their commemoratives to sit in their boxes and plastic bags (could be serious if there is moisture where storage occurs) for years without inspecting them for corrosion or oxidation damage. Periodic inspection should be implemented to ensure no damage occurs - this is important, since even light "freckling" created from touching the metal surfaces can reduce values significantly. A fired gun with obvious wear or without its original packaging can lose as much as 50% of its normal value - many used commemoratives get sold as "fancy shooters" with little, if any, premiums being asked.

The values listed reflect actual prices paid recently through dealer offerings, at gun shows, and both online and brick and mortar auctions. In some regions it may be possible to purchase a Winchester 94 commemorative made in substantial quantity for a slight premium over a standard production Winchester 94. Because of this, prices could fluctuate over 25% depending on the geographic location of purchase or sale.

A final note on factory commemoratives: One of the characteristics of commemoratives/special editions is that over the years of ownership, most of the original amount manufactured stays in the same NIB condition. Thus, if supply always is constant and in one condition, demand has to increase before price appreciation can occur. Many commemorative dealers have told me that recent changes in overseas currency rates have made domestic guns less expensive to own - for Europeans especially. For this reason, more commemoratives are being sold overseas resulting in less supply for the domestic market. After almost 50 years of factory commemoratives and non-factory commemorative/special editions, the performance of these older guns can now

GRADING - PPGS™	100%	Issue Price	Qty. Made

be accurately analyzed and the appreciation (or depreciation) can be compared against other purchases of equal vintage. A definitive series of articles has been written on Commemoratives and how they have performed as investments against other traditional economic items - please visit www.bluebookofgunvalues.com click on the Blogs tab - S.P. Fjestad's Lethal Blogging - Archived Articles - then click on Commemorative Firearms - Beauty or the Beast Parts 1-4. You be the judge.

U.S. Repeating Arms announced in 1990 that they would once again resume the production of factory commemorative firearms.

There are no factory records available on Winchester Commemoratives from the Buffalo Bill Historical Center, and as a result, no factory letters are available.

1964 WYOMING DIAMOND JUBILEE 94 CARBINE – ser. no. range WJ1- WJ1500.

	$1,200	$100	1,501

1966 CENTENNIAL '66 RIFLE – no ser. no. prefix or suffix.

	$695	$125	N/A

1966 CENTENNIAL '66 CARBINE – total mfg. of both the rifle and carbine was 102,309, no ser. no. prefix or suffix.

	$695	$125	102,309

Add $50-$75 over individual prices for consecutively serial numbered rifle and carbine set.

1966 NEBRASKA CENTENNIAL 94 RIFLE – ser. no. range NC1- NC2500.

	$1,200	$100	2,500

1967 CANADIAN '67 CENTENNIAL RIFLE – no ser. no. prefix or suffix.

	$650	$125	N/A

1967 CANADIAN '67 CENTENNIAL CARBINE – total mfg. of both the rifle and carbine was 90,301, no ser. no. prefix or suffix.

	$650	$125	90,301

Add $50-$75 over individual prices for consecutively serial numbered rifle and carbine set.

1967 ALASKAN PURCHASE CENTENNIAL CARBINE – ser. no. range AP1- AP1500, w/rack.

	$1,395	$125	1,501

1968 ILLINOIS SESQUICENTENNIAL 94 CARBINE – ser. no. range IS1- IS37468.

	$595	$110	37,468

1968 BUFFALO BILL RIFLE "1 OF 300" PRES. – ser. no. range WCF1- WCF300.

	$3,995	$1,000	300

1968 BUFFALO BILL RIFLE – ser. no. range WC1- WC112923.

	$695	$130	N/A

1968 BUFFALO BILL CARBINE – total mfg. of both the rifle and carbine was 112,923, ser. no. range WC1- WC112923.

	$695	$130	112,923

Add $50-$75 over individual prices for consecutively serial numbered rifle and carbine set.

1969 GOLDEN SPIKE CARBINE – ser. no. range GS1- GS69996.

	$700	$120	69,996

1969 THEO. ROOSEVELT RIFLE – ser. no. range TR1- TR52386.

	$695	$135	N/A

1969 THEO. ROOSEVELT CARBINE – total mfg. of both the rifle and carbine was 52,386, ser. no. range TR1- TR52386.

	$695	$135	52,386

1970 COWBOY COMMEMORATIVE CARBINE – ser. no. range CB1- CB27549.

	$750	$125	27,549

GRADING - PPGS™	100%	Issue Price	Qty. Made

1970 COWBOY CARBINE "1 OF 300" – ser. no. range NCHF1- NCHF300.

	$3,995	$1,000	300

1970 LONE STAR RIFLE – ser. no. range LS1- LS38385.

	$695	$140	N/A

1970 LONE STAR CARBINE – total mfg. of both the rifle and carbine was 38,385, ser. no. range LS1- LS38385.

	$695	$140	38,385

1971 NRA CENTENNIAL MUSKET – ser. no. range NRA1- NRA47380, not all shipped.

	$695	$150	23,400

1971 NRA CENTENNIAL RIFLE – ser. no. range NRA1- NRA47380, not all shipped.

	$695	$150	21,000

1974 TEXAS RANGER CARBINE – ser. no. range RA151- RA5000.

	$795	$135	4,850

1974 TEXAS RANGER PRESENTATION – ser. no. range RA1- RA150.

	$3,995	$1,000	150

1976 U.S. BICENTENNIAL CARBINE – ser. no. range USA1- USA19999.

	$795	$325	19,999

1977 WELLS FARGO – ser. no. range WFC1- WFC19999.

	$795	$350	19,999

1977 "LIMITED EDITION I" – ser. no. range 77L1- 77L1500.

	$1,595	$1,500	1,500

1977 LEGENDARY LAWMEN – ser. no. range LL1- LL19999.

	$895	$375	19,999

1978 ANTLERED GAME CARBINE – ser. no. range AG1- AG19999.

	$895	$375	19,999

1979 LEGENDARY FRONTIERSMAN RIFLE – ser. no. range LF1- LF19999.

	$895	$425	19,999

1979 "LIMITED EDITION II" – ser. no. range 78L1- 78L1500.

	$1,595	$1,750	1,500

1979 MATCHED SET ONE OF ONE THOUSAND – ser. no. range MC1- MC1000 and MR1- MR1000.

	$3,000	$3,000	1,000

1980 "OLIVER WINCHESTER" – ser. no. range OFW1- OFW1999.

	$895	$375	19,999

1981 U.S. BORDER PATROL - MEMBERS MODEL – ser. no. range USBP1- USBP800.

	$995	$695	800

1981 JOHN WAYNE – ser. no. range JW1- JW49000.

	$1,595	$600	49,000

Optional accessories were also available for this model: the gun rack with leather insert is currently selling for approx. $395 and the leather scabbard is trading for $395.

1981 "DUKE" – ser. no. range DUKE1- DUKE1000.

	$3,750	$2,250	1,000

1981 JOHN WAYNE "1 OF 300" SET – ser. no. range JWM1- JWM300 and JWMD1-JWMD300.

	$7,500	$10,000	300

1982 ANNIE OAKLEY – ser. no. range AOK1- AOK6000.

	$1,395	$699	6,000

GRADING - PPGS™	100%	Issue Price	Qty. Made

1982 OKLAHOMA DIAMOND JUBILEE – ser. no. range ODJ-1 - ODJ-1001.

	$1,750	$2,250	1,001

1982 AMERICAN BALD EAGLE - SILVER – ser. no. range ABE1984- ABE4784.

	$795	$895	2,800

1982 AMERICAN BALD EAGLE - GOLD – ser. no. range ABE1782- ABE1983.

	$4,000	$2,950	200

1983 CHIEF CRAZY HORSE – ser. no. range CCH1- CCH19999.

	$895	$600	19,999

1984 WINCHESTER-COLT COMMEMORATIVE SET – 1 each of the Model 1894 Carbine and Colt Peacemaker, serial numbered 1 WC-4440 WC., .44-40 WCF cal., elaborate gold etching, cased.

	$3,000	$3,995	2,300

Approx. 2,300 sets were actually put together in this combination. Some sets were split up with individual prices being discounted. Colt SAAs have been selling individually in the $1,350-$1,495 range.

1985 BOY SCOUTS 75TH ANNIVERSARY – Model 9422 action, .22 cal., rifle configuration, 6 1/4 lbs.

* ***1985 Boy Scouts 75th Anniversary*** – 15,000 mfg., serial numbered BSA 1 - BSA 15,000, roll engraved, antique pewter receiver, hooded front sight.

	$1,100	$495	15,000

* ***1985 Eagle Scouts 75th Anniversary*** – 1,000 mfg., serial numbered EAGLE 1 - EAGLE 1,000, receiver has triple level gold etching, select American walnut stock and forearm, gold-plated lever, hammer, and forearm cap.

	$6,000	$1,710	1,000

1985 MODEL 94 TEXAS SESQUICENTENNIAL – .38-55 WCF cal., available in carbine or rifle.

* ***1985 Model 94 Texas Sesquicentennial Rifle*** – 24 in. round barrel, elaborate gold etching, includes Bowie knife, oak cased, 586 mfg, ser. no. range TSR1- TSR586.

	$2,995	$2,995	586

* ***1985 Model 94 Texas Sesquicentennial Carbine*** – 18 1/2 in. round barrel, gold finished receiver and barrel bands, roll engraved receiver, 2,600 mfg., serial numbered TEX1 -TEX2600.

	$995	$695	2,600

* ***1985 Model 94 Texas Sesquicentennial Rifle/Carbine Set*** – includes one each of the Model 94 rifle and carbine, Bowie knife, 150 mfg., ser. no. range Carbine: TEXM1- TEXM150 and Rifle: TSRM1- TSRM150.

	$6,500	$7,995	150

1986 120TH ANNIVERSARY MODEL 94 CARBINE – .44-40 WCF cal. only, 20 in. barrel, large loop type finger lever, crescent buttplate, deluxe checkered walnut stock and forearm, extensive gold etching on barrel and framesides, 1,000 mfg. ser. no. WRA001-WRA1000.

	$995	$995	1,000

1986 STATUE OF LIBERTY MODEL 94 – Model 94 rifle in .30-30 Win. cal. with octagon barrel, extensive C. Giovanelli scroll engraving with multiple 22Kt. gold inlays, deluxe walnut with fine checkering, also includes 29 in. hand-carved wooden statue of the Statue of Liberty, serial numbers can range from SL001-SL100, while 100 were scheduled to be produced, only 62 were mfg. on a special order basis only, and the customer could pick out the serial number. This model is a USRAC factory commemorative.

	$10,000	$6,500	62

Must have matching carved statue.

GRADING - PPGS™	100%	Issue Price	Qty. Made

1987 U.S. CONSTITUTION 200th ANNIVERSARY – .44-40 WCF cal., 20 in. octagon barrel, deluxe checkered walnut, crescent buttplate, full coverage master engraving, No more than 50 guns were to be mfg., the serial number is the name of the state and is done in gold on the top of the tang, cased in a leather luggage style case.

	$17,500	**$12,000**	**19**

This model was distributed exclusively by Cherry's, located in Greensboro, NC.

1990 WYOMING CENTENNIAL – .30-30 Win. cal., 20 in. round barrel, deluxe checkered walnut, engraved by Bottega C. Giovanelli, coin finished receiver. Originally advertised as an issue of 999 guns, the Winchester strike caused the edition to be reduced in size to only 500 pieces. Serial numbered WYC001-WYC500.

	$1,750	**$895**	**500**

This model was distributed exclusively by Cherry's, located in Greensboro, NC.

1991 125th ANNIVERSARY – .44-40 WCF cal., 24 in. octagon barrel, deluxe checkered walnut, crescent style buttplate, engraving by Bottega C. Giovnaelli utilizing some of Winchester's most historic engraving patterns, includes walnut display case. Serial numbered from WRAC001-WRAC125. Serial numbers were made to order.

	$6,500	**$4,995**	**61**

This model was distributed exclusively by Cherry's, located in Greensboro, NC.

1992 KENTUCKY BICENTENNIAL – .30-30 Win. cal., lever action, 20 in. round barrel, receiver, lever and hammer casehardened and lacquered by Doug Turnbull, semi-fancy checkered American walnut stock, optional display case. Serial numbered KY001-KY500.

	$1,750	**$995**	**500**

This model was distributed exclusively by Cherry's, located in Greensboro, NC.

1992 ARAPAHO – .30-30 Win. cal., 20 in. round barrel, checkered walnut stock, lever, receiver and barrel bands gold plated, etched receiver scenes by Baron technology, optional display case. Originally advertised as uncheckered, Winchester made the mistake of checkering all the wood when it was on the production line. The advertisement showed the gun as uncheckered but all guns were delivered as checkered. Serial number ARAP001-ARAP500.

	$1,750	**$895**	**500**

This model was distributed exclusively by Cherry's, located in Greensboro, NC.

1993 NEZ PERCE MODEL 94 CARBINE – .30-30 Win. cal., 20 in. round barrel, receiver, lever, and barrel bands nickel plated, etched receiver scenes done by Baron Technology, includes suede leather soft case with trim and a branded head and shoulders image of Chief Joseph. Serial numbered NEZ001-NEZ600.

	$1,750	**$950**	**600**

This model was distributed exclusively by Cherry's, located in Greensboro, NC.

1995 FLORIDA SESQUICENTENNIAL 94 CARBINE – .30-30 Win. cal., 20 in. round barrel, brushed gold plate on the receiver, lever and barrel bands, scenes are roll dyed with hand touch up by Bottega C. Giovanelli. All 500 receivers were mfg., but not all of these receivers were used to make the Florida guns. Other special issue receivers were used that bear this serial number as the reception to this commemorative was poor, optional presentation case. Serial numbered FL001-FL500.

	$1,750	**$1,195**	**350**

This model was distributed exclusively by Cherry's, located in Greensboro, NC.

1996 WILD BILL HICKOK RIFLE – .45 LC cal., 20 in. round barrel, "John Wayne" style lever loop, receiver, lever, and bands are brushed nickel, left side of the receiver features a full coverage engraving pattern, right side of the receiver has his famous engraved 1851 Navy Colts, surrounded by scrollwork, a banner with his birth and date of death along with his famous "Dead Man's Hand" (Aces & Eights), deluxe uncheckered walnut. Serial numbered WBH001-WBH350.

	$1,750	**$1,195**	**350**

This model was distributed exclusively by Cherry's, located in Greensboro, NC.

GRADING - PPGS™	100%	Issue Price	Qty. Made

WINCHESTER COMMEMORATIVES: NON-DOMESTIC - 1970 TO DATE

Between 1970-1982, Winchester Model 94 Commemoratives were made by Cooey, located in Cobourg, Ontario, Canada.

1970 NORTHWEST TERRITORIES (CANADIAN) – ser. no. range NWT501- NWT3106.

	$1,150	$150	2,500

1970 NORTHWEST TERRITORIES DELUXE (CANADIAN) – ser. no. range NWT1- NWT500.

	$1,500	$250	500

1973 YELLOW BOY (SOLD IN EUROPE ONLY) – ser. no. range YB1- YB4903.

	$1,395	$150	4,903

1973 M.P.X. (MADE ESPECIALLY FOR A MOVIE) – ser. no. range MPX1- MPX32.

	$7,500	$78	32

1973 R.C.M.P. (CANADIAN) – ser. no. range RCMP1- RCMP10442, not all shipped.

	$895	$190	9,500

1973 R.C.M.P. MEMBERS ISSUE (CANADIAN) – ser. no. range MP1- MP5100, not all shipped.

	$995	$190	4,850

1973 R.C.M.P. PRESENTATION - (CANADIAN) – ser. no. range RCMP1P- RCMP10P.

	$11,500	N/A	10

1974 APACHE (CANADIAN) – ser. no. range AC1- AC10200, not all shipped.

	$895	$150	8,600

1975 KLONDIKE GOLD RUSH (CANADIAN) – ser. no. range KGR1- KGR10200.

	$895	$230	10,200

1975 K.G.R. (DAWSON CITY ISSUE) - (CANADIAN) – ser. no. range D1KGR- D25KGR.

	$8,500	N/A	25

1975 COMANCHE (CANADIAN) – ser. no. range CC1- CC11511.

	$895	$230	11,511

1976 SIOUX (CANADIAN) – ser. no. range SU1- SU12000, not all shipped.

	$895	$280	10,000

1976 LITTLE BIG HORN (CANADIAN) – ser. no. range LBH1- LBH11000.

	$995	$230	11,000

1977 CHEYENNE .44-40 WCF CAL. (CANADIAN) – .44-40 WCF Cal., ser. no. range CH1- CH13000, not all shipped.

	$895	$300	11,225

1977 CHEYENNE .22 LR CAL. (CANADIAN) – .22 LR Cal., ser. no. range CHF1- CHF8221, not all shipped.

	$1,250	$320	5,000

1978 CHEROKEE .30-30 WIN. CAL. (CANADIAN) – .30-30 Win. Cal., ser. no. range CK1- CK9000.

	$895	$385	9,000

1978 CHEROKEE .22 LR CAL. (CANADIAN) – .22 LR cal., ser. no. range CHF1- CHF4286, not all shipped.

	$1,250	$385	3,950

1978 ONE OF ONE THOUSAND (SOLD IN EUROPE ONLY) – no ser. no. prefix or suffix.

	$9,995	$5,000	250

This model was not advertised in the U.S.

1980 BAT MASTERSON CARBINE – ser. no. range BM1-BM8000.

	$895	$650	8,000

GRADING - PPGS™	100%	Issue Price	Qty. Made

1980 ALBERTA DIAMOND JUBILEE (CANADIAN) – ser. no. range ADJ301- ADJ3000.

	$995	$650	2,700

1980 A.D.J. DELUXE PRESENTATION (CANADIAN) – ser. no. range ADJ1- ADJ300.

	$1,795	$1,900	300

1980 SASKATCHEWAN DIAMOND JUBILEE (CANADIAN) – ser. no. range SDJ301-SDJ3000.

	$995	$695	2,700

1980 S.D.J. DELUXE PRESENTATION (CANADIAN) – ser. no. range SDJ1- SDJ300.

	$1,795	$1,995	300

1981 U.S. BORDER PATROL – ser. no. range BP1- BP1000.

	$995	$1,195	1,000

1981 CALGARY STAMPEDE (CANADIAN) – ser. no. range CS1- CS1000.

	$1,795	$2,200	1,000

1981 CANADIAN PACIFIC CENTENNIAL (CANADIAN) – ser. no. range CPC301- CPC3000.

	$895	$800	2,700

1981 CANADIAN PACIFIC CENTENNIAL PRESENTATION (CANADIAN) – ser. no. range CPC1- CPC300.

	$1,795	$2,200	300

1981 CANADIAN PACIFIC (EMPL.) - (CANADIAN) – ser. no. range CP1- CP2000.

	$895	$800	2,000

1981 JOHN WAYNE (CANADIAN) – ser. no. range CJW1- CJW1000.

	$1,595	$995	1,000

1982 GREAT WESTERN ARTIST I – no ser. no. prefix or suffix.

	$1,595	$2,200	999

1982 GREAT WESTERN ARTIST II – no ser. no. prefix or suffix.

	$1,595	$2,200	999

1986 SECOND SERIES EUROPEAN 1 OF 1,000 – mfg. for European sales only 1986, ser. no. range N/A.

	$9,995	$6,000	150

1992 ONTARIO CONSERVATION – this model was marketed in Canada only, ser. no. range 001CO - 400CO.

	$1,595	$1,195	400

WINDHAM WEAPONRY

Current rifle manufacturer established in 2011, and located in Windham, ME.

Windham Weaponry is located in the former Bushmaster Manufacturing plant in Windham, ME.

CARBINES/RIFLES: SEMI-AUTO

Windham Weaponry also makes several variations of the SBR (Short Barreled Rifle) for military/law enforcement. All Windham rifles and carbines carry a lifetime transferable warranty.

IMPORTANT NOTE: On model(s) where *N/A has replaced the normal 100% value, it indicates current market conditions are too unstable to accurately ascertain 100%-60% values. Factory retail prices (MSRs) reflect most recent updates. For more up-to-date information on current pricing trends and additional useful information, please visit www.bluebookofgunvalues.com, select "Information & Services " from the menu, and click on "Additional Book Information".

CDI CARBINE – .223 Rem. cal., 16 in. M4 chrome lined barrel with Vortex flash suppressor, 30 shot mag., flattop upper receiver, aluminum forged lower receiver, hardcoat black anodized finish, steel bolt, Magpul MOE six position telescoping buttstock with pistol grip, Diamondhead free float forend, Magpul AFG angled foregrip, machined aluminum trigger

GRADING - PPGS™	100%	98%	95%	90%	80%	70%	60%	LAST MSR

guard, Diamondhead flip up front and rear sights, manual safety, includes black sling and hard plastic case, 7 lbs.

MSR $1,680	*N/A	$1,250	$1,075	$975	$785	$650	$500

MPC CARBINE – .223 Rem. cal., 16 in. M4 chrome lined barrel with A2 flash suppressor, 30 shot mag., M4A4 flattop upper receiver with detachable carry handle, aluminum forged lower receiver, hardcoat black anodized finish, steel bolt, six position telescoping buttstock with A2 pistol grip, M4 double heat shield handguards, machined aluminum trigger guard, adj. dual aperture rear sight, adj. square post front sight, manual safety, includes black sling and hard plastic case, 6.9 lbs.

MSR $1,086	*N/A	$815	$695	$625	$515	$415	$325

SRC CARBINE – .223 Rem. cal., 16 in. M4 chrome lined barrel with A2 flash suppressor, 30 shot mag., M4A4 flattop upper receiver with Picatinny rail, aluminum forged lower receiver, hardcoat black anodized finish, steel bolt, six position telescoping buttstock with A2 pistol grip, M4 double heat shield handguards, machined aluminum trigger guard, no sights, manual safety, includes black sling and hard plastic case, 6.3 lbs.

MSR $1,040	*N/A	$775	$665	$600	$485	$400	$310

HBC CARBINE – .223 Rem. cal., 16 in. heavy profile chrome lined barrel with A2 flash suppressor, 30 shot mag., M4A4 flattop upper receiver with detachable carry handle, aluminum forged lower receiver, hardcoat black anodized finish, steel bolt, six position telescoping buttstock with A2 pistol grip, M4 double heat shield handguards, machined aluminum trigger guard, adj. dual aperture rear sight, adj. square post front sight, manual safety, includes black sling and hard plastic case, 7 1/2 lbs.

MSR $1,096	*N/A	$815	$695	$625	$515	$415	$325

VEX-SS RIFLE – .223 Rem. cal., 20 in. matte finished fluted stainless steel, 5 shot mag., M4A4 flattop upper receiver, optics riser blocks, aluminum forged lower receiver, hardcoat black or Snow Camo anodized finish, steel bolt, skeleton stock with Hogue rubber pistol grip, knurled vented aluminum free floating forend with sling swivel, machined aluminum trigger guard, no sights, manual safety, includes black sling and hard plastic case, 8.2 lbs.

MSR $1,295	*N/A	$965	$825	$750	$600	$495	$385

Add $175 for Snow Camo finish.

CARBON FIBER CARBINE – .223 Rem. cal., 16 in. M4 profile chrome lined barrel with A2 flash suppressor, 30 shot mag., M4A4 flattop upper receiver with molded Picatinny rail, molded carbon fiber composite receiver, matte black finish, steel bolt, six position telescoping buttstock with A2 pistol grip, M4 double heat shield handguards, integral molded carbon fiber trigger guard, no sights, manual safety, includes black sling and hard plastic case, 5.6 lbs.

MSR $958	*N/A	$715	$615	$550	$450	$365	$285

WINSLOW ARMS COMPANY

Previous manufacturer located in Camden, SC.

RIFLES: BOLT ACTION

WINSLOW SPORTING RIFLE – offered with various actions, FN Supreme, Mark X Mauser, Rem. 700 and 788, Sako, and Win. 70, offered in all popular calibers from .17 Rem. to .458 Mag., standard calibers have 24 in. barrels and 3 shot magazines, magnum calibers have 26 in. barrels and 2 shot magazines, two style stocks, "Bushmaster Conventional", slender pistol grip and beavertail forearm, "Plainsmaster", full curl, hooked pistol grip and flat wide forearm, both are Monte Carlo with cheekpieces, recoil pads and swivels, walnut, maple, and myrtle are used with rosewood forend tip and pistol grip cap, rifle comes in 8 basic grades, custom embellishments can increase values greatly, discretion must be used, values are for basic models.

* ***Commander Grade***

	$1,750	$1,500	$1,275	$1,025	$850	$725	$600

GRADING - PPGS™	100%	98%	95%	90%	80%	70%	60%	LAST MSR
* **Regal Grade**								
	$1,875	$1,625	$1,300	$1,050	$875	$750	$625	
* **Regent Grade**								
	$1,995	$1,675	$1,350	$1,100	$925	$800	$675	
* **Regimental Grade**								
	$2,750	$2,350	$2,050	$1,750	$1,500	$1,250	$1,000	
* **Crown Grade**								
	$3,000	$2,500	$2,175	$1,850	$1,575	$1,325	$1,100	
* **Royal Grade**								
	$3,450	$2,950	$2,500	$2,150	$1,750	$1,500	$1,250	
* **Imperial Grade**								
	$3,850	$3,500	$3,050	$2,700	$2,375	$2,000	$1,750	
* **Emperor Grade**								
	$6,200	$5,650	$5,000	$4,400	$3,700	$3,000	$2,350	

WISCHO JAGD-UND SPORTWAFFEN GmbH & CO. KG

Current division of Frankonia Handels GmbH & Co.KG, a European firearms and airgun importer located in Rottendorf, Germany. Previously located in Erlangen, Germany.

Wischo has a complete line of shotguns, rifles, pistols, and revolvers. No current U.S. importation. Please contact the factory directly for more information regarding model lineup, availability, and pricing (see Trademark Index).

WISEMAN, BILL AND CO.

Current custom rifle and action manufacturer established in 1980 and located in College Station, TX.

Bill Wiseman also manufactures top quality actions and test barrels used throughout the firearms industry. Additionally, Wiseman/McMillan manufactures rifle barrels and custom stocks. He also performs many gunsmithing services to customer supplied rifles. Please contact the company directly for more information on these products (see Trademark Index).

PISTOLS

SILHOUETTE PISTOL – various cals., Sako action, 14 in. Wiseman/McMillan fluted stainless barrel, 5 or 7 shot magazine, laminate or fiberglass (new 1999) pistol grip stock, no sights, 4 1/2-5 1/2 lbs. Limited mfg. 1989-2002.

	100%	98%	95%	90%	80%	70%	60%	LAST MSR
	$1,295	$1,000	$900	$800	$750	$700	$650	*$1,295*

Subtract $200 for fiberglass stock.

RIFLES: BOLT ACTION

Add 11% excise tax to prices shown for new manufacture. Some models listed have very limited production.

HUNTER MODEL – available in various cals., Sako action, similar to TSR2, stainless steel barrel by Wiseman/McMillan, laminate stock, teflon finished metal parts, Pachmayr Decelerator pad, sling swivels.

	100%	98%	95%	90%	80%	70%	60%	LAST MSR
MSR $4,395	$4,395	$3,650	$3,150	$2,500	$2,200	$1,850	$1,500	

HUNTER DELUXE – similar to Hunter Model except has TSR1 action and custom checkering.

	100%	98%	95%	90%	80%	70%	60%	LAST MSR
MSR $6,995	$6,995	$6,000	$5,250	$4,500	$3,750	$3,000	$2,500	

Add $500 for detachable mag.

MAVERICK – similar to Hunter but with black fiberglass stock. Disc. 2003.

	100%	98%	95%	90%	80%	70%	60%	LAST MSR
	$1,995	$1,575	$1,200	$1,050	$900	$775	$675	*$1,995*

GRADING - PPGS™	100%	98%	95%	90%	80%	70%	60%	LAST MSR

RAMPAGE – .300 WSM cal. only, 24 in. barrel w/o sights and with or w/o muzzle brake, Certa metal coating, pillar bedded Hogue composite stock, hinged floorplate, guaranteed 1/2 MOA accuracy. New 2011.

MSR $1,999	$1,999	$1,775	$1,550	$1,350	$1,150	$875	$675	

VARMENTER – similar to Hunter but with thumbhole stock. Disc. 2003.

	$2,395	$1,925	$1,500	$1,250	$1,025	$875	$775	*$2,395*

TEXAS SAFARI RIFLE (TSR) SERIES – various cals., choice of hidden mag. (no floorplate), standard floorplate, or 4 shot detachable mag., regular or 2-3 position tang safety, stainless steel fluted or non-fluted barrel with or w/o integral muzzle brake, synthetic stock. New 1996.

Add $375 for extra magazine concealed in stock.
Add $195 for 2 or 3 position tang safety.
Add $225 for fluted barrel or muzzle brake.
Add $175 for extra straight in-line feed magazine.
TSR actions are available separately - the short action has an MSR of $2,000, and the long action has an MSR of $2,250.

* ***TSR I*** – various cals., 4 shot inline feed detachable mag.

MSR $2,995	$2,995	$2,750	$2,200	$1,950	$1,750	$1,500	$1,200	

* ***TSR II*** – various cals., features standard floorplate.

MSR $2,595	$2,595	$2,300	$2,000	$1,700	$1,500	$1,250	$950	

* ***TSR III*** – various cals., features hidden magazine (no floorplate).

MSR $2,295	$2,295	$1,850	$1,575	$1,225	$1,025	$875	$750	

TSR TACTICAL (OLDER MFG.) – .300 Win. Mag., .308 Win., or .338 Lapua Mag. cal., 5 shot detachable mag., or standard floorplate, synthetic stock with adj. cheekpiece, stainless steel fluted barrel with integral muzzle brake, guaranteed 1/2 MOA accuracy. Mfg. 1996-2003.

	$2,795	$2,200	$1,700	$1,500	$1,235	$1,030	$855	*$2,795*

Add $195 for fluted barrel.
Add $195 for muzzle brake.
Add $150 for 3 position safety.

TSR TACTICAL (NEW MFG.) – various cals., various barrel lengths with or w/o muzzle brake, receiver features integral Picatinny rail, Certa metal coating, adj. black composite Hogue stock (2 options available), detachable mag., guaranteed 1/4 MOA accuracy. New 2011.

The base MSR on this model is $3,850.
Tactical actions are available separately - the short action has an MSR of $850, and the long action has an MSR of $1,925.

WOLF SPORTING PISTOLS

Previous trademark of pistols manufactured in Vienna, Austria. Previously imported and distributed by J R Distributing, located in Moorpark, CA until 1999.

Wolf pistols were noted for their features, quality construction, and were based on the M 1911 type action.

WOODWARD, JAMES AND SONS

Previously mfg. in London, England. Acquired by James Purdey & Sons in January 1949. In 1996, James Purdey & Sons once again started manufacturing a best quality Woodward shotgun.

SHOTGUNS: DOUBLE AND SINGLE BARREL

Woodward made one of the world's finest shotguns. They were formally acquired by J. Purdey and Sons on January 1, 1949. Most of the long guns they made were custom built and grading and pricing should be done individually. It is strongly recommended to obtain competent professional appraisals when contemplating a Woodward purchase or sale.

All new prices do not include VAT.

GRADING - PPGS™	100%	98%	95%	90%	80%	70%	60%	LAST MSR

BEST QUALITY SxS SHOTGUN – custom-built in all gauges, barrel lengths and chokes, sidelock, auto ejectors, stocked to specifications, pre-WWII and new mfg. circa 1996-2003.

12 ga.	$29,950	$26,205	$22,465	$20,365	$16,475	$13,480	$10,485	
20 ga.	$44,925	$39,310	$33,695	$30,550	$24,710	$20,215	$15,725	
28 ga.	$60,000	$52,500	$45,000	$40,800	$33,000	$27,000	$21,000	
.410 bore	$74,875	$65,515	$56,150	$50,915	$41,180	$33,695	$26,200	

Last MSR was £40,100 (20 ga. only)

Add $1,000 for SST

BEST QUALITY O/U SHOTGUN – custom-built in all gauges, barrel lengths, and chokes, VR, sidelock, auto ejectors, stocked to customer specifications, pre-WWII and new mfg. by special order only beginning 1996.

*** Best Quality O/U Shotgun - 1996-Current Mfg.*** – 12, 16, 20, 28 ga., or .410 bore.

This model is POR. The last posted MSR was £55,000.

*** Best Quality O/U Shotgun - Pre-WWII Mfg.***

12 ga.	N/A	$42,750	$37,405	$33,775	$26,935	$22,230	$17,100	
20 ga.	N/A	$61,250	$53,595	$48,390	$38,590	$31,850	$24,500	
28 ga.	N/A	$140,000	$122,500	$110,600	$88,200	$72,800	$56,000	

.410 bore - 2 mfg., too rare to accurately predict.
Add $1,000 for ST.

BEST QUALITY SINGLE BARREL TRAP GUN – 12 ga. only, limited mfg. pre-WWII only.

	$12,750	$11,155	$9,565	$8,670	$7,015	$5,740	$4,465	

WYOMING ARMORY

Current owner of Pentheny de Pentheny rifle trademark beginning 2009, located in Cody, WY.

Currently, Wyoming Armory is not producing rifles under the Pentheny de Pentheny name, but specializes in gunsmithing and firearms restoration. Please contact the company directly for further information (see Trademark Index).

WYOMING ARMS MFG. CORP.

Previous manufacturer located in Thermopolis, WY. Very small quantities of Parker pistols were mfg.

PARKER PISTOLS: STAINLESS STEEL

STANDARD PISTOL – 9mm Para., 10mm, .40 S&W, or .45 ACP cal., 3 3/8, 5, or 7 in. barrel, 7 (.45 ACP), 8 (10mm & .40 S&W), or 9 (9mm Para.) shot mag., Millett adj. sights, grooved synthetic grips, 29-39 oz. Disc. 1992.

	$350	$300	$250	$195	$165	$140	$120	*$399*

Add $50 for 7 in. barrel.
Add 50%-75% for 9mm Para. cal., only approx. 12 produced.

.357 MAG. – .357 Mag. cal., single action semi-auto, 7 in. barrel, adj. sights, 8 shot mag., lifetime warranty, 44 oz. Disc. 1992.

	$425	$350	$300	$240	$210	$180	$155	*$479*

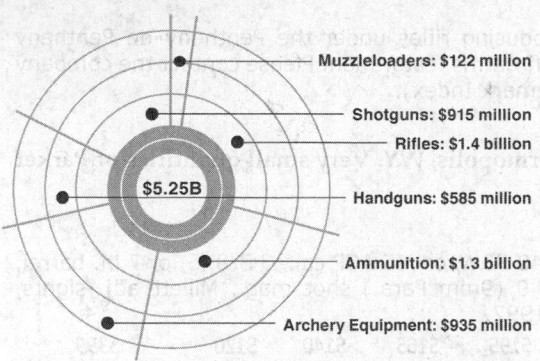

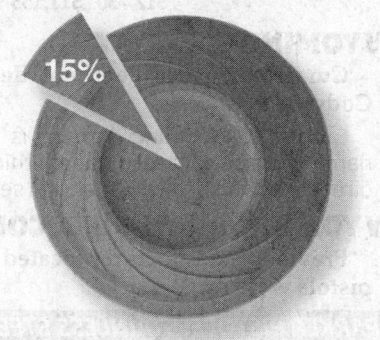

X-Y-Z SECTIONS

XTREME MACHINING

Current rifle manufacturer located in Grassflat, PA. Previously distributed until 2012 by American Tactical Imports, located in Rochester, NY.

GRADING - PPGS™	100%	98%	95%	90%	80%	70%	60%	LAST MSR

RIFLES: BOLT ACTION

.338 XTREME – .338 Xtreme cal., single shot (black or tan only) or repeater (5 or 7 shot detachable mag.) action, choice of laminated wood target, aluminum tactical, or McMillan A-5 stock, stainless steel receiver and 30 in. fluted barrel with 42-port muzzle brake, Picatinny rails, black, tan, or green finish, approx. 15 1/2 lbs.

MSR $4,678	$4,150	$3,850	$3,500	$3,000	$2,750	$2,250	$1,750

Add $414 for repeater.

.338 XTREME M100 SERIES – .338 Xtreme cal., 26 (black finish only) or 30 in. fluted barrel, M100 side folding custom stock, full length Weaver rail, 7 shot detachable box mag., avilable in black, tan, desert mirage, or AM tiger stripe finish. New 2011.

MSR $6,199	$5,750	$4,995	$4,300	$3,850	$3,150	$2,600	$2,000

YANKEE HILL MACHINE CO., INC. (YHM)

Current rifle manufacturer established in 1951, and located in Florence, MA. Consumer direct and dealer sales.

CARBINES/RIFLES: SEMI-AUTO

YHM manufactures a complete line of AR-15 style tactical rifles and carbines, as well as upper receivers and a wide variety of accessories. Please contact the company directly for more information about available options and dealer listings (see Trademark Index).

IMPORTANT NOTE: On model(s) where *N/A has replaced the normal 100% value, it indicates current market conditions are too unstable to accurately ascertain 100%-60% values. Factory retail prices (MSRs) reflect most recent updates. For more up-to-date information on current pricing trends and additional useful information, please visit www.bluebookofgunvalues.com, select "Information & Services " from the menu, and click on "Additional Book Information".

BLACK DIAMOND CARBINE – 5.56 NATO, 7.62x39mm (new 2011), or 6.8 SPC (new 2010) cal., 16 in. chrome moly vanadium steel barrel, black anodized finish, aluminum lower and flat-top upper receiver, mil spec bolt carrier assembly, forward assist, Phantom flash hider, carbine length Diamond handguard, flip up tower front and rear sights, adj. carbine stock, 6.7 lbs.

MSR $1,472	*N/A	$1,095	$940	$850	$695	$565	$440

Add $80 for 6.8 SPC or 7.62x39mm cal.

BLACK DIAMOND SPECTER CARBINE – 5.56 NATO, 7.62x39mm (new 2011), or 6.8 SPC (new 2010) cal., 16 in. chrome moly vanadium steel barrel, black anodized finish, aluminum lower and flat-top upper receiver, mil spec bolt carrier assembly, forward assist, Phantom flash hider, Specter length Diamond handguard, low profile gas block, flip up front and rear sights, adj. carbine stock, approx. 7 lbs.

MSR $1,498	*N/A	$1,115	$950	$865	$700	$575	$450

Add $81 for 6.8 SPC or 7.62x39mm cal.

BLACK DIAMOND SPECTER XL CARBINE – 5.56 NATO, 7.62x39mm (new 2011), or 6.8 SPC (new 2010) cal., similar to Black Diamond Specter Carbine, except has Specter XL length Diamond handguard, approx. 7 lbs.

MSR $1,525	*N/A	$1,135	$975	$880	$710	$585	$450

Add $54 for 6.8 SPC or 7.62x39mm cal.

GRADING - PPGS™	100%	98%	95%	90%	80%	70%	60%	LAST MSR

BLACK DIAMOND RIFLE – 5.56 NATO, 7.62x39mm (new 2011), or 6.8 SPC cal., 20 in. chrome-moly vanadium steel barrel, black anodized finish, aluminum lower and flat-top upper receiver, mil spec bolt carrier assembly, forward assist, rifle length Diamond handguard, A2 fixed stock, single rail gas block, two mini-risers, 8 lbs.

MSR $1,445	*N/A	$1,075	$925	$835	$675	$550	$425

Add $53 for 6.8 SPC or 7.62x39mm cal.

ENTRY LEVEL CARBINE – 5.56 NATO, 7.62x39mm (new 2011), or 6.8 SPC (new 2010) cal., 16 in. chrome-moly vanadium steel barrel, black anodized finish, aluminum lower and flat-top upper receiver, mil spec bolt carrier assembly, forward assist, Phantom flash hider, carbine length handguard, adj. carbine stock, single rail gas block, 6.4 lbs.

MSR $1,284	*N/A	$960	$825	$745	$600	$495	$385

Add $54 for 6.8 SPC or 7.62x39mm cal.

LIGHTWEIGHT CARBINE – 5.56 NATO, 7.62x39mm (new 2011), or 6.8 SPC (new 2010) cal., 16 in. chrome moly vanadium steel barrel, black anodized finish, aluminum lower and flattop upper receiver, mil spec bolt carrier assembly, forward assist, Phantom flash hider, carbine length lightweight handguard, adj. carbine stock, forearm endcap, flip up tower front sight, flip up rear sight, 6.7 lbs.

MSR $1,445	*N/A	$1,075	$925	$835	$675	$550	$425

Add $80 for 6.8 SPC or 7.62x39mm cal.

SPECTER LIGHTWEIGHT CARBINE – 5.56 NATO, 7.62x39mm (new 2011), or 6.8 SPC (new 2010) cal., 16 in. chrome moly vanadium steel barrel, black anodized finish, aluminum lower and flattop upper receiver, mil spec bolt carrier assembly, forward assist, Phantom flash hider, Specter length lightweight handguard, adj. carbine stock, forearm endcap, flip up front and rear sights, low profile gas block, 6.9 lbs.

MSR $1,498	*N/A	$1,115	$950	$865	$700	$575	$450

Add $54 for 6.8 SPC or 7.62x39mm cal.

SPECTER XL LIGHTWEIGHT CARBINE – 5.56 NATO, 7.62x39mm (new 2011), or 6.8 SPC (new 2010) cal., similar to Specter Lightweight Carbine, except has XL length lightweight handguard, 7.1 lbs.

MSR $1,525	*N/A	$1,135	$975	$880	$710	$585	$450

Add $54 for 6.8 SPC or 7.62x39mm cal.

SMOOTH CARBINE – 5.56 NATO, 7.62x39mm (new 2011), or 6.8 SPC (new 2010) cal., 16 in. chrome moly vanadium steel barrel, black anodized finish, aluminum lower and flat-top upper receiver, mil spec bolt carrier assembly, forward assist, Phantom flash hider, carbine length smooth handguard, adj. carbine stock, flip up front tower sight and flip up rear sight, 6.8 lbs.

MSR $1,472	*N/A	$1,095	$940	$850	$695	$565	$440

Add $53 for 6.8 SPC or 7.62x39mm cal.

CUSTOMIZABLE CARBINE – 5.56 NATO, 7.62x39mm (new 2011), or 6.8 SPC (new 2010) cal., 16 in. chrome moly vanadium steel barrel, black anodized finish, aluminum lower and flat-top upper receiver, mil spec bolt carrier assembly, forward assist, Phantom flash hider, carbine length customizable handguard, adj. carbine stock, flip up front tower sight and flip up rear sight, 6.3 lbs.

MSR $1,472	*N/A	$1,095	$940	$850	$695	$565	$440

Add $54 for 6.8 SPC or 7.62x39mm cal.

CUSTOMIZABLE RIFLE – 5.56 NATO, 7.62x39mm (new 2011), or 6.8 SPC (new 2011) cal., 20 in. chrome-moly vanadium steel barrel, black anodized finish, aluminum lower and flat-top upper receiver, mil spec bolt carrier assembly, forward assist, rifle length customizable handguard, 12 in. Co-Witness rail, fixed A2 stock, single rail gas block, two mini-risers, 8 lbs.

MSR $1,445	*N/A	$1,075	$925	$835	$675	$550	$425

Add $53 for 6.8 SPC or 7.62x39mm cal.

GRADING - PPGS™	100%	98%	95%	90%	80%	70%	60%	LAST MSR

ENTRY LEVEL RIFLE – 5.56 NATO, 7.62x39mm (new 2011), or 6.8 SPC (new 2011) cal., 20 in. chrome-moly vanadium steel non-fluted barrel, black anodized finish, aluminum lower and flat-top upper receiver, mil spec bolt carrier assembly, forward assist, rifle length tube handguard, fixed A2 stock, single rail gas block, two mini-risers, 8 lbs.

MSR $1,311	*N/A	$975	$835	$760	$615	$500	$395

Add $43 for 6.8 SPC or 7.62x39mm cal.

LIGHTWEIGHT RIFLE – 5.56 NATO, 7.62x39mm (new 2011), or 6.8 SPC (new 2011) cal., 20 in. chrome-moly vanadium steel barrel, black anodized finish, aluminum lower and flattop upper receiver, mil spec bolt carrier assembly, forward assist, rifle length lightweight handguard, fixed A2 stock, single rail gas block, two mini-risers, 8 lbs.

MSR $1,445	*N/A	$1,075	$925	$835	$675	$550	$425

Add $53 for 6.8 SPC or 7.62x39mm cal.

SMOOTH RIFLE – 5.56 NATO, 7.62x39mm (new 2011), or 6.8 SPC (new 2011) cal., 20 in. chrome-moly vanadium steel barrel, black anodized finish, aluminum lower and flat-top upper receiver, mil spec bolt carrier assembly, forward assist, rifle length smooth handguard, fixed A2 stock, single rail gas block, forearm endcap, two mini-risers, 8 lbs.

MSR $1,445	*N/A	$1,075	$925	$835	$675	$550	$425

Add $54 for 6.8 SPC or 7.62x39mm cal.

HUNT READY SERIES – 5.56 NATO, 7.62x39mm, or 6.8 SPC cal., 16 (carbine) or 20 (rifle) in. free floating steel barrel, diamond fluting, forged aluminum flat-top upper and lower receiver, low profile gas block, 5 shot mag., vented round customizable forearm, bolt carrier assembly, forward assist, matte black or 100% Realtree APG camo finish, includes Bushnell Banner 3-9x40mm camo scope zeroed in at 100 yards, Grovetec deluxe padded camo sling. New 2012.

MSR $1,531	*N/A	$1,140	$975	$885	$715	$585	$450

Add $53 for 6.8 SPC or 7.62x39mm cal.
Add $32 for rifle configuration with 20 in. barrel.

SPORTSMAN SERIES – 5.56 NATO, 7.62x39mm, or 6.8 SPC cal., 16 (carbine, includes Phantom 5C2 flash hider) or 20 (rifle) in. free floating chrome-moly vanadium steel barrel, diamond fluting, aluminum lower and flat-top upper receiver with Picatinny rail, 100% Realtree AP camo coverage, mil spec bolt carrier assembly, forward assist, low profile gas block, A2 trapdoor buttstock (rifle only) or adj. commercial stock (carbine), includes two 3 in. modular rails, rifle length customizable handguard, forearm endcap. New 2011.

MSR $1,391	*N/A	$1,035	$895	$800	$650	$535	$415

Add $54 for 6.8 SPC or 7.62x39mm cal. or for rifle configuration with 20 in. barrel.

YILDIZ SILAH SANAYI

Current shotgun manufacturer located in Burdur, Turkey. Currently imported exclusively by Academy Sports (multiple locations).

SHOTGUNS

Yildiz Silah Sanayi manufactures good quality O/U, SxS, semi-auto, slide action, and single barrel shotguns, using a wide variety of wood, engraving, and configurations. Prices range from $130-$1,600 MSR, depending on configuration. Please contact the importer directly for more information on options and U.S. availability (see Trademark Index).

Z-B RIFLE

Previous trademark of rifles manufactured by Brno & Uhersky Brod, located in Czechoslovakia.

RIFLES: BOLT ACTION

Z-B MAUSER VARMINT RIFLE – .22 Hornet cal., short Mauser bolt action, 23 in. barrel, double set triggers, 3 leaf sight, checkered pistol grip stock (also known as Brno Hornet).

$825	$745	$690	$605	$550	$470	$415

GRADING - PPGS™	100%	98%	95%	90%	80%	70%	60%	LAST MSR

ZDF IMPORT EXPORT INC.

Current importer located in Salt Lake City, UT, since 1995.

Please refer to Robinson Armament and Vepr listings.

Z-HAT CUSTOM

Previous custom rifle manufacturer and current custom gunsmithing shop located in Casper, WY.

RIFLES: CUSTOM

Z-Hat Custom manufactured four basic bolt action rifles, with a variety of options and special features, based on a customer supplied action. Current models included the Hunter, Pro Stalker, Varmint Hunter, and the Mountaineer. Base price for all models was $1,000.

Z-M WEAPONS

Current rifle manufacturer and pistol components maker located in Richmond, VT. Previously located in Bernardston, MA. Dealer and consumer direct sales.

PISTOLS: SEMI-AUTO

STRIKE PISTOL – .38 Super, .40 S&W, or .45 ACP cal., several configurations available, with or without compensator. Limited mfg. 1997-2000.

	100%	98%	95%	90%	80%	70%	60%	LAST MSR
	$2,375	$1,825	$1,700	$1,400	$1,150	$995	$750	*$2,695*

RIFLES: SEMI-AUTO

LR 300 & VARIATIONS – .223 Rem. cal., modified gas system using AR-15 style action, features pivoting skeletal metal stock, 16 1/4 in. barrel, flat-top receiver, matte finish, aluminum or Nylatron handguard, 7.2 lbs. New 1997.

	100%	98%	95%	90%	80%	70%	60%	LAST MSR
MSR $2,208	$2,100	$1,800	$1,550	$1,300	$1,100	$900	$750	

Add $23 for Nylatron handguard.
Add $50 for Military/Law Enforcement model.
Add $75 for Military/Law Enforcement model with Nylatron handguard.

ZVI

Current manufacturer located in Prague, Czech Republic. No current U.S. importation.

ZVI manufactures the Kevin line of small frame .380 ACP cal. semi-auto pistols. ZVI also manufactures the Falcon, a .50 BMG bolt bolt action repeater (2 shot mag.). Currently, these guns do not have any U.S. importation. Please contact the company directly for more information, including pricing and U.S. availability (see Trademark Index).

ZABALA HERMANOS, S.A.

Previous manufacturer circa 1932-2010 and located in Eibar, Spain. Zabala Hermanos was acquired by Norica during 2010, and is currently offering a line of shotguns under the Laurona Zabala trademark. Z. Hermanos built private label shotguns for Tristar, located in N. Kansas City. The company also built private labeled shotguns for KBI, Inc. (Charles Daly SxSs only) until early 2010. Previously imported and distributed by American Arms located in Kansas City, MO, until 2000, and by Galef Shotguns.

SHOTGUNS

Zabala Hermanos manufactured good quality boxlock SxS shotguns (Models 213 €370 - €430 last MSR, Kestrel €370 last MSR, Berri €380 - €510 last MSR, Vencedor Magnum (sideplates) €550 - €590 last MSR, Sporting Magnum €535 last MSR, and the Anthea Magnum €560 - €600 last MSR, O/U shotguns (XL 90 Series €445 - €690 last MSR, Suprema Magnum €510 last MSR, and Century Classic Magnum €530 last MSR) and sidelock SxS shotguns (Vencedor Model €720 - €758 last MSR). The company produced over 600,000 long guns, and was family owned.

ZANARDINI

Current manufacturer established in 1946, and located in Brescia, Italy. Currently imported by Kevin's Fine Outdoor Gear & Apparel, located in Thomasville, GA.

GRADING - PPGS™	100%	98%	95%	90%	80%	70%	60%	LAST MSR

Previously imported by S.O.G. Arms, located in Hacienda Heights, CA. Several U.S. firms have stocked a few Zanardini models in the past, but not the complete line.

All rifles and shotguns are custom-built. For current information and up-to-date pricing, please contact the importer directly (see Trademark Index).

The values listed represent older importation.

COMBINATION GUNS: O/U

Zanardini is currently offering the Model 2000 Deluxe Super Light (with or w/o new loading system).

402 STRAUSS – top-of-the-line combination gun with best quality engraving and wood.

	100%	98%	95%	90%	80%	70%	60%	LAST MSR
402 Strauss	$18,000	$16,000	$14,000	$12,000	$10,000	$8,000	$6,000	

BOXER MODEL – H&H styled sidelocks, top-quality engraving.

	100%	98%	95%	90%	80%	70%	60%	LAST MSR
Boxer Model	$11,000	$9,250	$8,000	$7,000	$6,000	$5,000	$4,150	$12,500

BOXER 4-LOCKS MODEL

	100%	98%	95%	90%	80%	70%	60%	LAST MSR
Boxer 4-Locks Model	$8,200	$7,300	$6,400	$5,500	$4,600	$3,750	$3,000	$9,200

PRINCESS – super light variation.

	100%	98%	95%	90%	80%	70%	60%	LAST MSR
Princess	$4,400	$3,850	$3,300	$2,800	$2,400	$2,000	$1,600	$5,085

RIFLES

FUCHS – various cals., case colored frame, double lock system, DT, available in takedown or folding configuration, adj. sights, bead front sight, select oil finished walnut stock with knurled forend, Bavarian style cheekpiece, vent. rubber recoil pad.

Prices start at €2,500.

Add €500 to €1,000 for Lusso model with better wood and coin finished receiver.

PRINZ 401 DE LUXE SINGLE SHOT – various cals., frame with dovetailed 3-locks system, rib welded and milled barrels, fixed rear sight and bead front sight, hard carved stock, hunting scene engraving.

Prices start at €3,000.

	100%	98%	95%	90%	80%	70%	60%	LAST MSR
* *Prinz B 401 Super Deluxe Single Shot*	$18,000	$15,500	$13,000	$10,750	$8,750	$6,400	$4,400	$21,000
* *Prinz C 401 Super Deluxe Single Shot Standard*	$6,400	$5,600	$4,800	$4,200	$3,700	$3,250	$2,800	$7,200

KAISER PRINZ – various cals., external hammer sidelock, octagonal Lothar Walther barrel, Luxus oil finished stock, separated rib, scope mounts, extensive engraving with gold inlays, DT, four locks.

Prices start at €25,000.

403 OXFORD SxS – 9.3x74R and smaller cals.

	100%	98%	95%	90%	80%	70%	60%	LAST MSR
403 Oxford SxS	$6,800	$6,000	$5,400	$4,900	$4,300	$3,750	$3,150	$7,700

* ***403 Oxford SxS Larger cals.*** – .375 H&H Mag. (disc.), .416 Rigby, .458 Win. Mag., .470 NE, or .500 NE cal., case colored or old silver frame, English style frame, European walnut stock with cheekpiece, DT, ejectors.

Prices start at €18,000.

EXPRESS RIFLE SxS – .470 NE cal., boxlock action, ST, checkered walnut stock (with cheekpiece), express sights. Other cals. were available upon special order.

	100%	98%	95%	90%	80%	70%	60%	LAST MSR
Express Rifle SxS	$16,500	$14,000	$12,000	$10,000	$8,750	$7,500	$6,250	$18,000

409 BRISTOL SxS – various cals., H & H style sidelock, ejectors, ST or DT, extensive game scene engraving, oil finished checkered walnunt stock with cheekpiece.

Prices start at €6,000.

GRADING - PPGS™	100%	98%	95%	90%	80%	70%	60%	LAST MSR

407 OXFORD SL SxS – Anson & Deeley scalloped reinforced boxlock action, ejectors, ST or DT.

	$26,000	$22,000	$18,250	$16,000	$14,000	$12,000	$10,000	*$29,900*

KONIG SIDELOCK O/U – 7.65R or 9.3x74R cal., H&H style sidelock, ejectors.

	$46,000	$40,000	$34,000	$27,000	$22,000	$19,000	$17,000	*$54,000*

KONIG BOXLOCK O/U – Anson & Deely boxlock.

	$27,000	$22,000	$18,000	$15,000	$12,500	$10,000	$8,000	*$30,000*

SHOTGUNS: SxS

Models listed are available in 12, 16, 20, 28 ga., or .410 bore, magnum chambers in 20 and 12 ga.

DONAU SIDELOCK SxS – H&H style sidelock action.

Prices on this model ranged from $34,000 - $36,000, depending on engraving.

DONAU STANDARD MODEL SxS – 12, 20, 28 ga., or .410 bore, boxlock action, chopper lump barrels, ejectors, customer choice of engraving and walnut.

Prices start at €30,000.

HAMMER LONDON MODEL SxS – features external hammers.

	$18,250	$16,250	$14,250	$12,250	$10,250	$8,750	$7,250	*$21,500*

HAMMERLESS LONDON MODEL SxS – 12, 20, 28 ga. or .410 bore, ejectors, single trigger or double set trigger, chopper lump barrels, extensive game scene relief engraving, checkered straight grip walnut stock and forearm.

Prices start at €10,000.

HASE CACCIA MONTECATINI SxS – boxlock action, double set triggers, extractors.

	$1,850	$1,600	$1,400	$1,200	$1,050	$900	$700	*$2,100*

Add 30% for ejectors.

HORN MODEL SxS – boxlock action, double set triggers, extractors.

	$1,950	$1,700	$1,500	$1,250	$1,100	$950	$775	*$2,250*

Add 40% for ejectors.

PRESTIGE TRAP AND SKEET SxS

	$4,750	$4,000	$3,400	$2,800	$2,400	$2,000	$1,600	*$5,200*

ZANOTTI

Previous manufacturer located in Bologna, Italy. Previous company names were Zanotti 1625 and Fabio Zanotti. Previously imported and distributed by New England Arms Corp. located in Kittery Point, ME until 1999. Zanotti became part of the Renato Gamba Group in 1985.

SHOTGUNS: O/U

MODEL 725 – 28 ga. or .410 bore only, scalloped case hardened shallow frame, DT or ST, ejectors, game scene and scroll engraving, custom built to individual specifications.

	$6,000	$4,500	$3,650	$3,000	$2,450	$2,000	$1,875	*$7,000*

CASSIANO – 12, 20, 28 ga., or .410 bore, Boss style shallow action, best quality gun built to individual specifications. Prices started at $27,500 and went up accordingly.

SHOTGUNS: SxS

Add $500 for ST.
Add $250 for beavertail forearm.
Add $650 for leather case.

GRADING - PPGS™	100%	98%	95%	90%	80%	70%	60%	LAST MSR

MODEL 625 BOXLOCK

	$6,275	$5,500	$4,250	$3,150	$2,500	$2,000	$1,750	

Last MSR was $7,000 (circa 2000).

MODEL 626 BOXLOCK – scroll, game scene, or combination engraving.

	$7,000	$6,000	$4,450	$3,375	$2,750	$2,175	$1,900	

Last MSR was $7,995 (circa 2000).

MODEL GIACINTO – hammer gun.

	$5,875	$5,300	$4,000	$2,950	$2,400	$1,900	$1,650	

Last MSR was $6,500 (circa 2000).

MODEL MAXIM SIDELOCK

	$10,750	$8,600	$7,450	$6,200	$5,200	$4,600	$3,850	

Last MSR was $12,000 (circa 2000).

MODEL EDWARD SIDELOCK

	$13,000	$9,900	$8,700	$7,000	$5,875	$5,000	$4,000	

Last MSR was $15,000 (circa 2000).

MODEL CASSIANO I SIDELOCK

	$15,500	$13,250	$9,900	$8,700	$7,000	$5,875	$5,000	

Last MSR was $17,500 (circa 2000).

MODEL CASSIANO II

	$17,750	$15,500	$13,250	$9,900	$8,700	$7,000	$5,875	

Last MSR was $20,000 (circa 2000).

CASSIANO EXECUTIVE – prices varied per individual order, top-of-the-line model. Prices started at $20,000.

ZANOTTI, R.

Current manufacturer established during 1625, and located in Bologna, Italy. No current U.S. importation. Previously imported circa 2008-2010 by Zanotti USA, located in Houston, TX.

ZANOTTI FAMILY & COMPANY HISTORY

Cassiano Zanotti began in 1625 producing some of Italy's finest handmade firearms. Giacinto Zanotti opened a shop in Bologna around 1861 and soon become the most famous in the family. Maria and Stefano Zanotti continued the manufacture of guns in 1871. Production was briefly halted during World War I and in 1932 Stefano's nephew, Tomaso, re-opened the shop and Fabio Zanotti soon followed. After Fabio left Bologna, Renato, the last of the Zanotti branch in Bologna continued production. Renato died in 1975, and at his death, his legacy would be destined for oblivion if not for the efforts of the youngest of his shop boys of the time, Giorgio Simoni. Giorgio decided to give it a try, took over the shop, and now with his son Andrea, is continuing production as a Master Armorer using the very same techniques used by the Zanotti family.

RIFLES: SxS

Express SxS rifles are also available, built based on Zanotti's shotgun design, up to .300 H&H caliber. Please contact the company directly for a price quotation and delivery time (see Trademark Index).

SHOTGUNS: SxS

Renato Zanotti shotguns are completely handmade one at a time by master craftsmen and have many innovative trademark features available only in Zanotti firearms. Today Zanotti Armoria continues in that tradition by producing world class handcrafted SxS shotguns.

These fine handmade guns require from 12 to 18 months from time of order to delivery because each one is custom built to the buyer's specifications. The price is the same no matter the gauge of the shotgun. A 50% down payment is required before fabrication can begin.

GRADING - PPGS™	100%	98%	95%	90%	80%	70%	60%	LAST MSR

SxS shotgun base price is €30,988.
Exposed hammers SxS base price is €32,933.
Matched pair SxS base price is €68,860.
Add €5,000 to €30,000 for engraving, depending on complexity, the engraver, and buyer's requirements.

ZASTAVA ARMS

Current manufacturer established in 1853, and located in Serbia. Currently, certain models are imported by Century International Arms, located in Fairfax, VT. Please refer to C section. Some models were imported by EAA, located in Rockledge, FL, and please refer to EAA in the E section. Remington previously imported certain models until 2009, as well as KBI until 2005. Previously distributed by Advanced Weapons Technologies, located in Athens, Greece, and by Nationwide Sports Distributors, located in Southampton, PA. Previously imported by T.D. Arms, followed by Brno U.S.A., circa 1990.

Zastava Arms makes a wide variety of quality pistols, rifles, and sporting shotguns. Zastava Arms was subcontracted by Remington Arms Co. to make certain bolt action rifle models.

HANDGUNS: SEMI-AUTO

MODEL CZ99 – 9mm Para. or .40 S&W cal., double action, 15 shot, 4 1/4 in. barrel, short recoil, choice of various finishes, SIG locking system, hammer drop safety, ambidextrous controls, 3-dot Tritium sighting system, alloy frame, firing pin block, loaded chamber indicator, squared-off trigger guard, checkered dark grey polymer grips, 32 oz.

$550	**$400**	**$375**	**$330**	**$300**	**$285**	**$265**	***$495***

While a latter Z9 was advertised, it was never commercially imported. All guns were CZ99 or CZ40.

Zastava CZ99 configurations (with finishes) included matte blue with synthetic grips (500 imported), commercial blue with synthetic grips (750 imported), military "painted finish" with synthetic grips (1,000 imported), matte blue finish with checkered wood grips (115 imported), high polish blue with checkered grips (115 imported), and military "painted finish" with wood grips (2 prototypes only).

MODEL CZ999 SCORPION – 9mm Para. cal., similar to CZ99, except has indicator for the last three rounds in the magazine, fire selector for pistol and revolver mode.

Please refer to the Skorpion listing in the S section for current information on this model. This pistol was imported by K.B.I. as the ZDA model.

MODEL CZ40 – .40 S&W cal., 55 prototypes were imported for testing, but most had a feeding problem due to improper magazine design, mag. design changes were planned, but were cancelled due to the Serbian/Croatian war.

Suggested retail was $495.

MODEL CZ70 – 9mm Para. cal., Tokarev style, no slide safety, blue finish, limited importation.

$1,000	**$850**	**$775**	**$675**	**$575**	**$510**	**$460**

MODEL M88 – 9mm Para. or .40 S&W cal., SA, 6 or 8 shot mag., 3.6 in. barrel, blue finish, compact frame, military version, not recent import, 28 oz.

$600	**$525**	**$465**	**$415**	**$360**	**$330**	**$295**

RIFLES: BOLT ACTION

Since 1881, Zastava Arms has remained loyal to the Mauser bolt action system while incorporating all the innovations which followed. Zastava Arms produces sporting rifles, based on Mauser system, in many calibers. Barrels for sporting rifles are made of high quality chrome-vanadium steel, by cold forging. Options for Zastava Arms rifles provide a choice of three types of triggering mechanism, three types of stock, various optical sights, and engraving styles.

MODEL CZ22 – .22 LR, .22 WMR or .22 Hornet cal., 35 of each cal. imported circa 1990. Suggested retail was $275.

$225	**$195**	**$175**	**$150**	**$135**	**$120**	**$110**

Add 15% for .22 WMR or .22 Hornet cal.

GRADING - PPGS™	100%	98%	95%	90%	80%	70%	60%	LAST MSR

MODEL CZ99 PRECISION – .22 LR or .22 WMR cal., rotating bolt.

Please refer to the Remington Model Five listing in the Remington section.

MODEL LK M70 – .22-250 Rem., 6mm Rem., 6.5x57mm, 7x57mm, 8x57mm, .270 Win., 7x64mm, .30-06, .25-06 Rem., 6.5x55mm, 9.3x62mm, .243 Win., .308 Win., .264 Win. Mag., 7mm Rem. Mag., .300 Win.Mag., .375 H&H, or .458 Win.Mag. cal., sporting rifle, Mauser action. Previously imported by Interarms, American Arms, Remington, and K.B.I.

Please refer to the Remington Model 798 listing in the Remington section.

MODEL LK M85 – .22 Hornet, .222 Rem., .222 Rem. Mag., .22-250 Rem., .223 Rem., or 7.62x39mm cal., sporting rifle with mini-Mauser system. Previously imported by Interarms, American Arms, Remington, and K.B.I.

Please refer to the Remington Model 799 listing in the Remington section.

RIFLES: SEMI-AUTO

The PAP 762 semi-auto rifle carbine is currently imported by EAA Corp. Please refer to the EAA listing in the E section for current information and pricing.

ZBROJOVKA BRNO

Current manufacturer located in Brno, Czech Republic. This company remains part of CZ Uhersky Brod. It is important not to confuse this new Zbrojovka Brno (formerly Brno Rifles), with the original Zbrojovka Brno which closed its doors in 2006.

ZELENY SPORT s.r.o.

Current manufacturer located in the Czech Republic. No current U.S. importation.

RIFLES: SEMI-AUTO

Zeleny Sport manufactures a AK-47 design Model 96 Beryl semi-auto in .223 Rem. cal., the company also makes a Works 11 Series with fixed wood, fixed synthetic, or folding stock. Please contact the company directly for possible U.S. importation, availability, and pricing (see Trademark Index).

ZEPHYR

Previous Stoeger trademark of guns manufactured in Spain, and imported by Stoegers circa 1930s-1972.

RIFLES

Stoeger has imported a wide variety of bolt action rifles during the past 60 years. Rather than list the many models individually, each Zephyr rifle should be compared to a gun of equal caliber, quality, and features to ascertain an approximate value range.

SHOTGUNS: SxS

WOODLANDER II – 12 or 20 ga., various chokes, boxlock, double triggers, extractors, engraved, checkered pistol grip stock.

$495	$440	$385	$360	$305	$275	$250

UPLANDER (4E) – 12, 16, 20, 28 ga., or .410 bore, sidelock action, double triggers, ejectors, engraved.

$775	$695	$640	$585	$570	$480	$440

STERLINGWORTH II – similar to Woodlander, with sidelock action.

$825	$725	$660	$605	$580	$525	$495

VICTOR SPECIAL – 12 ga., 25, 28, or 30 in. barrels, various chokes, double triggers, extractors, checkered pistol grip stock.

$440	$385	$330	$305	$250	$220	$195

UPLAND KING – 12 or 16 ga., sidelock, single trigger, VR, ejectors, fully engraved.

$1,000	$900	$800	$725	$650	$600	$550

GRADING - PPGS™	100%	98%	95%	90%	80%	70%	60%	LAST MSR

THUNDERBIRD – 10 ga. Mag, 32 in. barrels, double triggers, French walnut, engraved.

	100%	98%	95%	90%	80%	70%	60%	LAST MSR
	$850	$750	$625	$550	$510	$490	$475	

Add $175 for ejectors.

SHOTGUNS: SINGLE SHOT

HONKER – 10 ga. Mag., 36 in. VR barrel, lightly engraved.

	100%	98%	95%	90%	80%	70%	60%	LAST MSR
	$500	$460	$420	$350	$310	$290	$270	

VANDALIA TRAP – 12 ga. Trap Model, 32 in. barrel, engraved.

	100%	98%	95%	90%	80%	70%	60%	LAST MSR
	$700	$620	$575	$525	$475	$425	$390	

ZIEGENHAHN & SOHN OHG

Current custom gun manufacturer established in 1928, and located in Zella-Mehlis, Germany. Currently imported by New England Custom Gun Service, Ltd., located in Plainfield, NH, and by Heirloom Armes, located in Howard Lake, MN.

Ziegenhahn & Sohn manufactures high quality, classic Anson & Deeley boxlock "Big Five" double rifles with Holland & Holland pattern sidelocks and ejectors, and sidelocks in calibers up to .500 NE., with larger calibers also available upon request. Base price starts at $9,250 for small caliber sidelocks, and $13,450 for small caliber sidelocks. Ziegenhahn & Sohn also manufactures high quality shotguns, drillings, and combination guns with a variety of custom order options, including traditional bone charcoal color case hardening. Each gun is individually built per customer's specifications. Please contact the importer directly for current pricing, availability, and delivery time (see Trademark Index).

Ziegenhahn currently is building the Krieghoff Essencia SxS with back action - please refer to the Krieghoff section for more information.

ZOLI, ANGELO

Previous manufacturer located in Brescia, Italy. Previously imported and distributed exclusively by Angelo Zoli USA located in Addison, IL. Mfg. 1985-87.

Angelo Zoli went out of business in December, 1987 and was taken over by the Italian Bank of Brescia in 1989. Many people tend to confuse the shotguns of Angelo and Antonio Zoli (it is hard to determine which manufacturer made a gun marked "A. Zoli").

There is no model/name correlation between these companies/trademarks and Antonio Zoli DOES NOT have parts for these earlier Angelo Zoli long arms. Even though both trademarks may indicate "A. ZOLI" for a barrel address, the mfr. of a gun so marked may be determined by referring to the model name listings under both headings in this section.

COMBINATION GUNS

AIRONE – 12 ga./.30-06 or .308 Win. cal., boxlock with false sideplates, double triggers, checkered walnut stock and forearm, swivels. Disc. 1987.

	100%	98%	95%	90%	80%	70%	60%	LAST MSR
	$1,450	$1,275	$1,050	$900	$800	$700	$600	

CONDOR – similar to Airone, except does not have false sideplates. Disc. 1987.

	100%	98%	95%	90%	80%	70%	60%	LAST MSR
	$1,295	$1,050	$725	$675	$525	$400	$300	

RIFLES: SxS

LEOPARD EXPRESS – .30-06, .308 Win., .375 H&H Mag., or 7x65R cal., boxlock action, double triggers, checkered walnut stock and forearm. Disc. 1987.

	100%	98%	95%	90%	80%	70%	60%	LAST MSR
	$1,325	$1,150	$975	$725	$600	$425	$300	*$1,529*

SHOTGUNS: O/U

SNIPE – .410 bore, 3 in. chambers, 26 or 28 in. barrels, single trigger. Disc. 1987.

	100%	98%	95%	90%	80%	70%	60%	LAST MSR
	$230	$200	$185	$170	$155	$145	$135	*$265*

GRADING - PPGS™	100%	98%	95%	90%	80%	70%	60%	LAST MSR

TEXAS – all gauges, 26 or 28 in. barrels, double triggers, folding design, lever action. Disc. 1987.

	$250	$220	$200	$185	$170	$155	$145	$291

DOVE – .410 bore only, 3 in. chambers, 26 or 28 in. barrels, single trigger. Disc. 1987.

	$260	$230	$200	$185	$170	$155	$145	$306

FIELD SPECIAL – 12, 20, or 28 ga., 3 in. chambers, various barrel lengths and chokings, single trigger. Disc. 1987.

	$450	$400	$360	$330	$300	$270	$240	$699

PIGEON MODEL – 12 or 20 ga., 3 in. chambers, various barrel lengths, single trigger. Disc. 1987.

	$350	$295	$270	$250	$220	$195	$175	$394

Add $60 for 20 ga.

STANDARD MODEL – 12 or 20 ga., 3 in. chambers, various barrel lengths and chokings, single trigger. Disc. 1987.

	$395	$345	$320	$300	$280	$260	$245	$459

SILVER SNIPE – 12 or 20 ga., 3 in. chambers on the 20 ga., single trigger, ejectors, light engraving. Disc. 1987.

	$675	$585	$530	$485	$440	$400	$375	$739

Add $50 for multi-chokes (12 ga. only).

This model was distributed by Euroarms of America, Inc.

CONDOR MODEL – 12 ga. skeet model, 28 in. barrels, SST, ejectors, wide VR, engraved silver finished receiver, recoil pad. Disc. 1987.

	$795	$700	$640	$585	$530	$485	$440	$895

This model was distributed by Mandall Shooting Supplies, Inc.

TARGET MODEL 208 – 12 ga. only, available in either Trap, Skeet, or Monotrap configuration. Disc. 1987.

	$895	$775	$550	$475	$300	$275	$200	$996

Add $494 for Monotrap II 208 Model.

TARGET MODEL 308 – 12 ga. only, available in either Trap, Skeet, or Monotrap configuration. Disc. 1987.

	$1,375	$1,125	$800	$725	$650	$525	$475	$1,581

Add $76 for multi-chokes.
Add $824 for Monotrap II 308 Model.

SPECIAL MODEL – 12 ga. only, 3 in. chambers, various barrel lengths and chokings, SST. Disc. 1987.

	$465	$395	$355	$325	$290	$270	$250	$528

Add $120 for multi-chokes.

DELUXE MODEL – similar to Special Model, except better wood and engraving. Disc. 1987.

	$645	$550	$495	$450	$400	$360	$320	$730

Add $80 for multi-chokes.

PRESENTATION MODEL – 12 ga. only, includes sideplates. Disc. 1987.

	$740	$630	$575	$495	$450	$395	$350	$842

Add $42 for multi-chokes.

ANGEL MODEL – 12 ga. only, field grade, SST, ejectors, wide VR, engraved receiver, recoil pad. Disc. 1987.

	$850	$775	$450	$400	$325	$275	$200	

This model was distributed by Mandall Shooting Supplies, Inc.

GRADING - PPGS™	100%	98%	95%	90%	80%	70%	60%	LAST MSR

ST. GEORGE'S TARGET – 12 ga. only, trap or skeet gun, SST, fixed choke. Disc. 1987.

	100%	98%	95%	90%	80%	70%	60%	LAST MSR
	$900	$725	$525	$425	$350	$250	$200	$1,024

* ***St. George's Competition*** – 12 ga. only, includes 30 in. O/U barrels and single barrel multi-choke. Disc. 1987.

	100%	98%	95%	90%	80%	70%	60%	LAST MSR
	$1,995	$1,750	$1,000	$900	$800	$650	$550	$1,627

PATRICIA MODEL – .410 bore only, 3 in. chambers, 28 in. barrels, SST. Disc. 1987.

	100%	98%	95%	90%	80%	70%	60%	LAST MSR
	$1,175	$1,010	$675	$600	$525	$450	$375	$1,345

Add $121 for case.

SHOTGUNS: SxS

QUAIL SPECIAL – .410 bore, 3 in. chambers, single trigger, 28 in. barrels. Disc. 1987.

	100%	98%	95%	90%	80%	70%	60%	LAST MSR
	$205	$185	$170	$150	$125	$110	$100	$243

FALCON II – .410 bore, 3 in. chambers, 26 or 28 in. barrels, double triggers. Disc. 1987.

	100%	98%	95%	90%	80%	70%	60%	LAST MSR
	$205	$185	$170	$150	$125	$110	$100	$246

SILVER HAWK – 12 or 20 ga., double trigger, engraved.

	100%	98%	95%	90%	80%	70%	60%	LAST MSR
	$420	$395	$360	$330	$300	$280	$260	

SILVER SNIPE – 12 or 20 ga., various barrel lengths, VR, single trigger, engraved.

	100%	98%	95%	90%	80%	70%	60%	LAST MSR
	$485	$440	$400	$360	$330	$300	$280	

PHEASANT – 12 ga. only, 3 in. chambers, 28 in. barrels only, single trigger. Disc. 1987.

	100%	98%	95%	90%	80%	70%	60%	LAST MSR
	$370	$320	$300	$280	$260	$240	$220	$428

ALLEY CLEANER – 12 or 20 ga., 3 in. chambers, 20 in. barrels, riot configuration, SST. Disc. 1987.

	100%	98%	95%	90%	80%	70%	60%	LAST MSR
	$575	$495	$460	$420	$390	$350	$310	$649

Add $65 for multi-chokes.

CLASSIC – 12 or 20 ga., 3 in. chambers, 26-30 in. barrels, ST. Disc. 1989.

	100%	98%	95%	90%	80%	70%	60%	LAST MSR
	$995	$875	$750	$650	$550	$475	$400	$706

Add $80 for multi-chokes.

SHOTGUNS: LEVER ACTION

APACHE – 12 ga. only, 3 in. chambers, 20 in. barrel, SST. Disc. 1987.

	100%	98%	95%	90%	80%	70%	60%	LAST MSR
	$410	$355	$275	$225	$175	$125	$100	$473

Add $80 for multi-chokes.

SHOTGUNS: SINGLE BARREL

DIANO I – 12, 20 ga., or .410 bore, 3 in. chambers, top lever single barrel action, folding configuration, VR. Disc. 1987.

	100%	98%	95%	90%	80%	70%	60%	LAST MSR
	$115	$95	$85	$80	$75	$70	$65	$129

DIANO II – similar to Diano I, except has bottom lever opening. Disc. 1987.

	100%	98%	95%	90%	80%	70%	60%	LAST MSR
	$115	$95	$85	$80	$75	$70	$65	$129

LONER I – similar to Diano I. Disc. 1987.

	100%	98%	95%	90%	80%	70%	60%	LAST MSR
	$95	$80	$75	$65	$55	$45	$35	$109

LONER II – similar to Diano II. Disc. 1987.

	100%	98%	95%	90%	80%	70%	60%	LAST MSR
	$95	$80	$75	$65	$55	$45	$35	$109

SHOTGUNS: SLIDE ACTION

PUMP ACTION – 12 ga. only, available in riot, field, or deer (slug) barrel configurations, 3 in. chamber, hunter model has multi-chokes standard. Disc. 1987.

	100%	98%	95%	90%	80%	70%	60%	LAST MSR
	$290	$245	$205	$185	$170	$150	$125	$329

GRADING - PPGS™	100%	98%	95%	90%	80%	70%	60%	LAST MSR

ZOLI, ANTONIO

Historic gun making family dating back to the late 1860s. Current manufacturing established at the end of WWII in 1945 when the factory was re-started, and located in Brescia, Italy. Currently imported by and distributed beginning 2006 by Antonio Zoli America, located in Canandaigua, NY. Previously located in Weston, FL. O/U rifles were previously imported by Cape Outfitters, located in Cape Girardeau, MO. Previously imported and distributed (1990-91 only) by European American Armory Corp. located in Hialeah, FL. Prior to 1990, A. Zoli was imported and distributed exclusively by Antonio Zoli U.S.A., Inc. located in Fort Wayne, IN.

These guns all bear the Zoli Bow and Arrow logo.

Antonio Zoli firearms are totally unrelated to guns produced by Angelo Zoli (guns marked "A. Zoli" make it hard to determine the correct manufacturer). Parts are not interchangeable and warranties from Antonio Zoli firearms DO NOT apply to Angelo Zoli guns.

COMBINATION GUNS

Zoli currently makes a Corona O/U combination gun with set trigger. This model is imported into the U.S. on a limited basis - please contact the importer directly (see Trademark Index).

COMBINATO – 12 or 20 ga. over .243 Win. or .222 Rem. cal., boxlock action, game scene engraved frame with silver finish, double triggers, folding rear sight, skipline checkering, with sling swivels. Importation disc. 1993.

$1,750 $1,500 $1,300 $1,100 $950 $775 $600 ***$1,995***

* ***Combinato Set*** – includes one set of either 20 or 12 ga. barrels and an additional rifle/shotgun barrel set, same cals. as Combinato, cased. Importation disc. 1993.

$2,400 $2,150 $1,850 $1,600 $1,400 $1,200 $995 ***$2,700***

SAFARI DELUXE – similar to Combinato, except has sideplates with elaborate game scene engraving. Importation disc. 1993.

$4,850 $4,400 $3,950 $2,100 $2,675 $2,400 $2,225 ***$5,200***

Add approx. 50% for Safari Deluxe 2 (includes 2 sets of shotgun barrels).

EXPRESS ELE3 SET – includes one set of .30-06 cal. O/U barrels, one set of 20 ga./.243 Win. cal. barrels, one set of 20 ga./20 ga. barrels, special order, elaborate game scene engraving, includes German claw mount 4X scope and case. Disc.

$7,950 $7,250 $6,500 $5,750 $5,000 $4,500 $3,950

DRILLINGS

Zoli manufactures a MG92 (boxlock) and MG92 EL (boxlock with sideplates and skipline checkering) Drilling in 12 ga. and various U.S. and metric cals. These models do not currently have U.S. importation.

RIFLES: BOLT ACTION

Antonio Zoli was contract manufacturer of the Karl Gustav 1900 design for Husqvarna. Over 55,000 produced.

The AZ 1900 Series has many variations, and the models listed are for U.S. import only. Please contact the factory directly for more information and availability on its other bolt action models.

AZ 1900C - .243 Win., .270 Win., 6.5x55mm, .30-06, .308 Win., 7mm Rem. Mag., or .300 Win. Mag. cal., 21 or 24 (Mag. cals.) in. barrel, checkered walnut stock with weatherproof stock finish, sling swivels, iron sights, 7.4 lbs. Importation disc. 1993.

$1,100 $850 $740 $660 $585 $500 $450 ***$1,295***

Add approx. 10% for AZ 1900 Deluxe (better walnut).
Add 60% for AZ 1900 Super Deluxe (select walnut and moderate engraving).
Add approx. 10% for Model AZ 1900 DL (photo engraved receiver and floorplate).

GRADING - PPGS™	100%	98%	95%	90%	80%	70%	60%	LAST MSR

MODEL AZ 1900M – .243 Win., 6.5x55mm, .270 Win., .30-06, or .308 Win. cal., 21 in. barrel, fiberglass, Kevlar, and graphite composite stock with baked on walnut wood grain finish with checkering, drilled and tapped receiver. Imported 1991 only.

	$725	$625	$550	$495	$450	$415	$375	*$840*

Add approx. 10% for Model AZ 1900M DL (photo engraved receiver and floorplate).

AZ 1900 SERIES – .243 Win., .270 Win. .30-06, .308 Win., .270 Wby. Mag., 7x64R, 7mm Rem. Mag., .300 Win. Mag., or .338 Win. Mag. cal., Gustav action, checkered walnut pistol grip Monte Carlo stock with cheekpiece, blue barrel, available in Pro, Pro Lux, or Pro CL configuration. Importation began 2009.

This model is POR.
Add $195 for AZ 1900 Pro CL Model.
Add $455 for AZ 1900 Pro Lux Model.

RIFLES: O/U

EXPRESS – 7x65R, 7x57mm, .30-06, .308 Win., or 9.3x74R cal., 25.6 in. barrels, hand checkered walnut stock with cheekpiece, set trigger for bottom barrel, extractors. Importation disc. 1993.

	$3,875	$3,250	$2,900	$2,600	$2,200	$1,950	$1,650	*$4,400*

Add $600 for E Model (with ejectors).

EXPRESS EM – 7x65R, .30-06, .308 Win., or 9.3x74R cal., mechanical single trigger, ejectors. Importation disc. 1990, reintroduced 1992 only.

	$4,850	$3,975	$3,300	$2,900	$2,600	$2,200	$1,900	*$5,300*

Add $2,395 for De Luxe Model (disc.).
Add $7,200 for E3 De Luxe Model (disc.).

The Express E3 De Luxe Model includes 2 extra sets of barrels - 1 set is shotgun (20 ga. - 2 3/4 or 3 in. chambers).

Z EXPRESS – 9.3x74R, .30-06, or 8x57mm cal., 22 in. barrel with open sights, standard features include Boss locking system, ejectors, monolithic forged frame, hand detachable mechanical trigger, express rib with folding sights, oil finished Turkish walnut stock, scope mount and rings, includes aluminum case. Importation began 2008.

MSR $6,240	$5,725	$5,100	$4,550	$4,000	$3,500	$3,000	$2,500

Add $2,600 for interchangeable 20 or 28 ga. shotgun barrels.

Z EXPRESS SAFARI (AFRICAN) – .450/400 NE 3 in. Nitro cal., otherwise similar to Z Express Model.

MSR $10,500	$9,750	$8,500	$7,250	$6,000	$5,000	$4,000	$3,350

Z EXPRESS AMBASSADOR EL – similar to Z Express Model, except has better quality wood and more engraving. Importation began 2008.

MSR $11,050	$10,025	$8,750	$7,500	$6,250	$5,250	$4,250	$3,500

Add $2,600 for interchangeable 20 or 28 ga. barrels.

Z SAFARI AMBASSADOR SL (AFRICAN) – similar to Z Express African Model, except has extra select walnut and more elaborate engraving. Importation began 2008.

MSR $18,200	$17,000	$14,500	$12,500	$10,500	$8,750	$7,500	$6,250

Add $2,600 for interchangeable 20 or 28 ga. barrels.

Z CUSTOM GRADE – Zoli's top-of-the-line double rifle, custom order only.

Base price on this model is POR.

RIFLES: SxS

SAVANA E – 7x65R, .30-06, .308 Win., or 9.3x74R cal., boxlock action, ejectors. Importation disc. 1990.

	$5,850	$4,850	$3,975	$3,300	$2,800	$2,350	$2,000	*$6,600*

Add $400 for Savana EM Model (single trigger).

GRADING - PPGS™	100%	98%	95%	90%	80%	70%	60%	LAST MSR

* ***Savana E Deluxe*** – similar to Savana E, except has elaborate game scene engraving. Importation disc. 1990.

	$7,750	$7,100	$6,500	$6,000	$5,500	$5,000	$4,600	*$8,295*

SHOTGUNS: O/U, RECENT PRODUCTION

Designed by Marini (ex-Perazzi employee). All newer manufactured Z guns from Antonio Zoli feature a Boss locking system with fitted recoil shoulders, detachable posi-lock trigger system, and ultra high quality barrels.

Please contact the importer directly for pricing on available options for currently manufactured shotguns (see Trademark Index).

GOLDEN SNIPE – 12 or 20 ga, various barrel lengths, VR, single trigger, ejectors, engraved.

	$560	$520	$475	$430	$395	$360	$330	

DELFINO – 12 or 20 ga., 3 in. chambers, 26 or 28 in. barrels, ejectors, VR, single non-selective trigger, blue frame with delicate engraving, walnut pistol grip stock and forearm. Disc.

	$500	$425	$375	$325	$295	$280	$265	

RITMO HUNTING – 12 ga. only, 3 in. chambers, 26 or 28 in. vent. rib barrels, SST, ejectors, select checkered walnut, blue frame and barrels with moderate engraving, recoil pad, 7 1/4 lbs. Disc.

	$575	$510	$465	$410	$370	$350	$335	

RITMO PIGEON GRADE IV – 12 ga. only, live pigeon gun, 28 in. VR barrels, SST, ejectors, superbly engraved silver finished receiver, extra fine checkering on deluxe walnut, cased, 7 1/2 lbs. Disc.

	$1,250	$1,100	$950	$800	$675	$600	$550	

M85 RITMO TRAP OR SKEET – 12 ga. only, 28 in. (Skeet only), 30, or 32 in. barrels, ejectors, SST, special stock dimensions, engraved blue receiver, select checkered walnut stock and forearm, cased, 7 3/4 lbs. Disc.

	$595	$500	$465	$440	$415	$395	$370	

This model was also available in a single barrel trap model at no extra charge.

* ***M85 Ritmo Trap Combination*** – 12 ga. only, supplied with O/U and single barrel sets, various barrel lengths, cased. Disc.

	$995	$895	$800	$700	$620	$575	$500	

SILVER FALCON – 12 or 20 ga., 3 in. chambers, boxlock action, SST, ejectors, 26 or 28 in. barrels with multi-chokes, coin finished receiver with engraving, checkered Turkish walnut stock and forearm with weatherproof finish. Importation disc. 1991.

	$1,050	$600	$500	$400	$350	$300	$250	*$1,695*

WOODSMAN – 12 ga. only, 3 in. chambers, 23 in. VR barrels are designed to shoot rifle slugs at 55 yards and to accept 5 interchangeable choke tubes, SST, ejectors, quarter rib on barrels with pop-up rifle sights, checkered Circassian walnut stock and forearm with swivels (waterproof finish).

	$1,200	$1,000	$875	$750	$650	$550	$400	*$1,895*

* ***Woodsman Combo*** – includes 2 sets of barrels (3 in. chambers) with Zoli interchangeable choke system.

	$1,800	$1,550	$1,400	$1,200	$1,050	$925	$800	*$2,320*

MODEL Z-90 TARGET MODEL – 12 ga. only, boxlock action, adj. SST, black competition receiver, deluxe checkered Turkish walnut stock with recoil pad and forearm, vent. barrels and rib, SST, ejectors.

* ***Model Z-90 Target Model Trap Gun*** – 29 1/2 or 32 in. barrels with screw-in chokes and raised VR, Monte Carlo stock, blue finish. Importation disc. 1993.

	$1,700	$1,450	$1,050	$825	$775	$625	$500	*$2,495*

GRADING - PPGS™	100%	98%	95%	90%	80%	70%	60%	LAST MSR

* ***Model Z-90 Target Model Mono Trap Gun*** – 32 or 34 in. barrel with screw-in chokes and raised VR, Monte Carlo stock. Importation disc. 1993.

	$1,650	$1,450	$1,125	$850	$775	$625	$500	*$2,495*

* ***Model Z-90 Target Model Combo Trap Set*** – includes O/U trap barrels as well as Mono trap barrel on same receiver, available as 30/32 in. sets or 32/34 in. sets. Imported 1991-92.

	$1,800	$1,750	$1,650	$925	$825	$750	$500	*$2,700*

* ***Model Z-90 Target Model Skeet Gun*** – 28 in. barrels only with screw-in chokes. Importation disc. 1993.

	$1,800	$1,300	$1,200	$995	$850	$700	$600	*$2,495*

* ***Model Z-90 Target Model Sporting Clays Gun*** – 28 in. barrels with screw-in chokes, coin finished receiver with engraved sideplates, separated barrels, Schnabel forend, solid recoil pad. Importation disc. 1990.

	$1,700	$1,450	$1,200	$995	$850	$700	$600	*$2,495*

KRONOS SPORT/COMPETITION – 12, 20, or 28 ga., competition model with detachable trigger group and best quality Zoli barrels, titanium flush or extended choke tubes, deluxe checkered walnut stock and forearm, cased. Importation began 2009.

MSR $4,750	$4,275	$3,650	$3,100	$2,600	$2,200	$2,000	$1,675

Add $1,995 for 20/28 ga. combination set.

KRONOS SKEET – 12 ga. only, similar to Kronos Sport, but is designed for Skeet shooting. Importation began 2009.

MSR $5,000	$4,500	$4,100	$3,400	$2,950	$2,425	$2,150	$1,750

KRONOS DOUBLE TRAP – 12 ga., 29 1/2 or 32 in. barrels, otherwise similar to Kronos Sport. Importation began 2009.

MSR $4,750	$4,275	$3,650	$3,100	$2,600	$2,200	$2,000	$1,675

KRONOS TOP SINGLE TRAP – 12 ga., 34 in. barrel only. Importation began 2009.

MSR $4,750	$4,275	$3,650	$3,100	$2,600	$2,200	$2,000	$1,675

Add $1,495 for Trap Combo with extra O/U barrels.

EXPEDITION – 12, 20, or 28 ga., coin finished boxlock action, SST, ejectors, detachable trigger group, Boss locking system, deluxe checkered Prince of Wales grip walnut stock and forearm with checkered wood buttplate. Importation began 2009.

MSR $4,000	$3,600	$3,125	$2,700	$2,250	$2,000	$1,500	$1,250

Add $1,900 for 20/28 ga. combo.

EXPEDITION EL – 12, 20, or 28 ga., 28, 29 1/2 or 32 in. barrels, coin finished boxlock action, SST, ejectors, detachable trigger group, Boss locking system, deluxe checkered walnut stock and forearm with checkered wood buttplate, scroll engraved receiver with gold bird inlays. New 2011.

MSR $5,000	$4,500	$4,100	$3,400	$2,950	$2,425	$2,150	$1,750

Add $500 for CCH model or $2,100 for 20/28 ga. combo.

Z SPORT – 12 or 20 (new 2008) ga., various barrel lengths to 32 in., 3 choke tubes, choice of blue or French grey receiver finish, border engraved with gold logo, fancy oil finished checkered Turkish walnut stock, detachable posi-lock trigger system, includes hard case with tools. Importation began 2007.

MSR $5,350	$4,900	$4,400	$3,500	$3,000	$2,650	$2,150	$1,750

Add $400 for adj. stock.

Add $1,645 for 20/28 ga. combination set.

GRADING - PPGS™	100%	98%	95%	90%	80%	70%	60%	LAST MSR

* ***Z Sport Extra*** – similar to Z Sport, except has 80% engraving coverage in bold English scroll and checkered extra fancy Turkish walnut. Importation began 2007.

MSR $6,900	$6,500	$5,900	$5,175	$4,500	$3,750	$3,000	$2,300	

Add $400 for adj. stock.

Add $2,200 for 20/28 ga. combination set.

» **Z Sport Extra Bilanx** – 12, 20, or 28 ga., 28, 29 1/2, or 32 in. barrels, similar to Z Sport, except has Zoli BHB balancing system (barrel weight and stock grip). New 2011.

MSR $6,900	$6,500	$5,900	$5,175	$4,500	$3,750	$3,000	$2,300	

Add $2,590 for Combo in 20 and 28 ga.

* ***Z Sport Bilanx*** – 12, 20, or 28 ga., 28, 29 1/2, or 32 in. barrels, similar to Z Sport, except has Zoli BHB balancing system (barrel weight and stock grip), fine nickel or deep blue finish. New 2011.

MSR $5,495	$5,000	$4,500	$3,600	$3,050	$2,700	$2,150	$1,800	

Add $2,105 for Combo in 20 and 28 ga.

Z AMBASSADOR ROUND BODY SPORTING – 12 or 20 ga., 28, 30, or 32 in. barrels with 6 choke tubes, Boss coin finished action, hand engraved with deep floral scroll and 24Kt. gold shield logo, exhibition grade oil finished Turkish walnut stock with hand checkering, includes leather hard case. Limited importation 2007.

	$7,500	$6,500	$5,500	$4,750	$4,000	$3,300	$2,750	*$8,690*

Z AMBASSADOR EL SPORTING – similar to Round Body Sporting, except has 100% deep scroll engraving and three Bulino style game scenes, hand carved oil finished exhibition grade Turkish walnut stock with hand-cut checkering, includes leather hard case, tools, parts kits, and snap caps. Importation began 2007.

MSR $10,500	$9,950	$9,250	$8,250	$7,250	$6,250	$5,250	$4,250	

Add $1,950 for 20/28 ga. combination set (new 2008).

Z AMBASSADOR BILANX EL – 12, 20, or 28 ga., 28, 29 1/2, or 32 in. barrels, similar to Z Ambassador EL, except has Zoli BHB balancing system (barrel weight and stock grip). New 2011.

MSR $10,500	$9,950	$9,250	$8,250	$7,250	$6,250	$5,250	$4,250	

Add $2,200 for Combo in 20 and 28 ga.

Z AMBASSADOR EL HUNTING – similar to Z Expedition EL, except has better wood and engraving with gold inlays. Importation began 2009.

MSR $10,500	$9,950	$9,250	$8,250	$7,250	$6,250	$5,250	$4,250	

Z AMBASSADOR SL HUNTING – top-of-the-line model with round action and extensive scroll engraving on coin finished frame, supplied with aluminum motor case. Imported 2009-2010.

	$11,750	$10,000	$8,500	$7,000	$5,500	$4,500	$4,000	*$13,000*

Add $2,600 for 20/28 ga. combo.

SUPER LUXUS BILANX – 12, 20, or 28 ga., 28, 29 1/2, or 32 in. barrels, Zoli BHB balancing system (barrel weight and stock grip), hand rounded receiver, hand carved fences, deep scroll hand engraving (with or w/o game scenes), oil finished exhibition grade Turkish walnut stock, detachable trigger mechanism, SST or DT, 6.2 - 7 lbs. New 2011.

MSR $13,000	$11,750	$10,000	$8,500	$7,000	$5,500	$4,500	$4,000	

Add $2,600 for Combo in 20 and 28 ga.

SHOTGUNS: SxS, RECENT PRODUCTION

UPLANDER – 12 or 20 ga., 3 in. chambers, 25 in. barrels with fixed chokes (IC/M), ST, ejectors, color case hardened receiver, English style checkered Circassian walnut stock and forearm with oil or polyurethane finish. Importation disc. 1990.

	$750	$625	$560	$520	$485	$450	$425	*$1,295*

GRADING - PPGS™	100%	98%	95%	90%	80%	70%	60%	LAST MSR

SILVER FOX – 12 or 20 ga., 3 in. chambers, 26 or 28 (12 ga. only) in. barrels with fixed chokes, ST, ejectors, hand engraved silver finished receiver with "AZ" in gold, straight grip checkered Circassian walnut stock and forearm. Importation disc. 1990.

	100%	98%	95%	90%	80%	70%	60%	LAST MSR
	$1,400	$1,300	$1,200	$995	$875	$750	$625	*$2,995*

ARIETE M3 – 12 ga. only, 26 or 28 in. barrels, matted rib, single non-selective trigger, ejectors, blue receiver with fine scroll engraving, cased. Disc.

	100%	98%	95%	90%	80%	70%	60%	LAST MSR
	$550	$475	$400	$360	$330	$310	$285	

EMPIRE – 12 or 20 ga. Mag., 27 or 28 in. barrels, moderate engraving, coin finished receiver. Disc.

	100%	98%	95%	90%	80%	70%	60%	LAST MSR
	$1,100	$1,075	$975	$875	$795	$725	$650	

Add $100 for 3 in. Mag. chambers.

This model was distributed by Euroarms of America, Inc.

VOLCANO RECORD – 12 ga. only, 28 in. barrels, H&H type sidelocks, ejectors, SST, treble Purdey locks, silver finished receiver with elaborate engraving, best quality fine checkered walnut, special order only. Disc.

	100%	98%	95%	90%	80%	70%	60%	LAST MSR
	$4,100	$4,000	$3,800	$3,400	$2,950	$2,650	$2,300	

* ***Volcano Record ELM*** – 12 ga. only, built to individual customer specifications, best quality H&H style sidelock. Disc.

	100%	98%	95%	90%	80%	70%	60%	LAST MSR
	$10,750	$9,800	$8,800	$7,100	$6,850	$6,200	$4,400	

This model was distributed by Euroarms of America, Inc.

CUSTOM SERIES – SxS, individual custom order only, every refinement is used in the construction of these extremely rare and expensive shotguns. The Volcano Extra Lusso shotgun is probably the most elaborate Antonio Zoli shotgun.

In 2005, the last MSR for this model was $58,850.

NOTES

TRADEMARK INDEX

by S.P. Fjestad

I can assure you that no single section in the *Blue Book of Gun Values* has had more blood, sweat, tears, and hours put into it than this revised Trademark Index. During the 11th hour of the 10th Anniversary Edition published in 1989, I decided it wouldn't be a bad idea to put together an index of all current firearms manufacturers, importers, and trademarks. Thinking it was going to be a three or four hour job, three days later it was finally determined that this new section would be complete and up-to-date enough to publish. The rest like they say is history. I can guarantee you that no informational source has a more accurate firearms industry trademark index than what you are about to read. Remember, this invaluable section is also available online at no charge, so you can get the most recent contact information any time, any where, with internet access, and is updated quarterly as things change. Why guess when you can be sure?

The following listings of domestic and international firearms manufacturers, trademarks, importers, distributors, auction houses, factory repair centers, and parts companies are the most complete and up-to-date ever published. Even more so than last year, you will note additions and substantial changes regarding website and email listings – this may be your best way of obtaining up-to-date model and pricing information directly from some current manufacturers, importers, and/or distributors who don't post retail pricing. When online with the various company websites, it's not a bad idea to look at the date of the last web update, as this will tell you how current the online information really is.

For a complete listing of companies and contact information for airguns and modern black powder reproduction industries, please refer to the respective Trademark Indexes in the *Blue Book of Modern Black Powder Arms* and the *Blue Book of Airguns*. The *Blue Book of Tactical Firearms* also provides a complete and thorough Trademark Index not only for tactical firearms manufacturers, but is also a source directory for both ammunition and accessories. These Trademark Indexes are available online at no charge (www.bluebookofgunvalues.com).

If parts are needed for older, discontinued makes and models (even though the manufacturer/trademark is current), it is recommended you contact either Numrich Gun Parts Corp. located in West Hurley, NY, or Jack First, Inc. located in Rapid City, SD for domestic availability and prices. For current manufacturers, it is recommended that you contact an authorized warranty repair center or stocking gun shop, unless a company/trademark has an additional service/parts listing. In Canada, please refer to the Bowmac Gunpar Inc. listing.

Hundreds of hours have been spent in this database, and as this edition goes to press, we feel that this information is the most reliable source material available to contact these companies/individuals. However, if you feel that you have something to add or find an error, we would like to know about it. Simply contact us at: cassandraf@bluebookinc.com.

During the course of the year, after each edition is published, the Trademark Index is constantly updated as more information becomes available. Please visit www.bluebookofgunvalues.com for the most current database (available free of charge).

If you should require additional assistance in "tracking" any of the current companies listed in this publication (or perhaps, current companies that are not listed), please contact us and we will try to help you regarding these specific requests. Again, the most up-to-date Trademark Index for the firearms, black powder reproductions, tactical, and airguns industries will be posted on our website: www.bluebookofgunvalues.com. We hope you appreciate this service – no one else in the industry has anything like it.

ADC
Armi Dallera Custom srl
Via G. Rossa No. 4
I-25062 Concesio (BS) ITALY
Phone/Fax No.: 011-39-0308370301
Website: www.adccustom.com
Email: info@adccustom.com

A.M.S.D. (ADVANCED MILITARY SYSTEM DESIGN)
Factory
P.O. Box 487
Vernier/Geneva CH-1214 SWITZERLAND
Fax No.: 011-41-223497691
Website: www.amsd.ch
Email: sales@amsd.ch

AMT
Crusader Gun Company, Inc.
5151 Mitchelldale, Ste. B-11
Houston, TX 77092
Toll Free: 800-272-7816
Fax No.: 713-681-5665
Website: www.highstandard.com
Email: info@highstandard.com

AR57LLC (57 Center LLC)
8525 152nd Ave NE
Redmond, WA 98052
Phone No.: 888-900-5728
Fax No.: 888-900-5728
Website: www.57center.com

AR-7 INDUSTRIES L.L.C.
Please refer to Armalite, Inc. listing.

ATA ARMS
Importer - please refer to Weatherby listing.
Factory - ATA AV Tufekleri San. Ve Tic. Ltd. STI.
Imes Sanayi Sitesi
B Blok 201 Sok. No. 8
Umraniye, Istanbul, TURKEY
Phone No.: 011-90-216-466-4568
Fax No.: 011-90-216-466-4571
Website: www.ataarms.com
Email: info@ataarms.com

AWA USA
2280 W. 80th Street, Ste. 2
Hialeah, FL 33016
Phone No.:305-828-1982
Fax No.: 305-828-1066
Website: www.awaguns.com
Email: info@awaguns.com

AWC SYSTEMS TECHNOLOGY, LLC
23606 N. 19th Ave
Suite 10
Phoenix, AZ 85085
Phone No.: 623-780-1050
Toll Free: 800-401-7269
Fax No.: 623-780-2967
Website: www.awcsilencers.com

AYA
Importer/Distributor - AYA USA
P.O. Box 647
Old Saybrook, CT 06475
Phone No.: 860-388-3989
Email: aya-usa@aya-fineguns.com
Importer/Distributor - please refer to New England Custom Gun Service, Ltd. listing
U.K. Importer/Distributor - A.S.I.
Alliance House, Snape, Saxmundham
Suffolk, U.K. IP17 1SW
Fax No.: 011-44-1728-688950
Email: info@a-s-i.co.uk
Factory - AYA - Aguirre Y Aranzabal, S.A.L.
Avenida Otaol, 25-3 planta
20600 Eibar (Guipuzcoa) SPAIN
Fax No.: 011-34-943200133
Website: www.aya-fineguns.com
Email: aya@aya-fineguns.com

ABBIATICO & SALVINELLI (FAMARS)
Please refer to Famars di Abbiatico & Salvinelli listing.

ACCU-TEK
Factory - Excel Industries, Inc.
4510 Carter Court
Chino, CA 91710
Toll Free Phone No.: 888-442-6096
Phone No.: 909-627-2404
Fax No.: 909-627-7817
Website: www.accu-tekfirearms.com
Email: email@accu-tekfirearms.com

ACCURACY INTERNATIONAL LTD.
U.S. Office
Fredericksburg, VA
Email: aina@accuracyinternational.us
Distributor – Tac Pro Shooting Center
35100 North State Hwy. 108
Mingus, TX 76463-6405
Phone No.: 254-968-3112
Fax No.: 254-968-5857
Website: www.tacproshootingcenter.com
Distributor – Mile High Shooting Accessories
14178 Lexington Circle
Broomfield, CO 80023
Phone No.: 303-255-9999
Fax No.: 303-254-6572
Website: www.milehighshooting.com

Distributor – SRT Supply
4450 60th Ave. N.
St. Petersburg, FL 33714
Phone No.: 727-526-5451
Website: www.srtsupply.com
Factory
P.O. Box 81, Portsmouth
Hampshire, U.K. PO3 5SJ
Fax No.: 011-44-23-9269-1852
Website: www.accuracyinternational.com
Email: ai@accuracyinternational.org

ACCURATE ARMS RIFLE LLC

Phone No.: 205-345-0036
Website: www.accuratearmsinc.com
Email: ricky@accuratearmsinc.com

ADAMS ARMS

612 Florida Ave
Palm Harbor, FL 34683
Phone No.: 727-853-0550
Fax No.: 727-853-0551
Website: www.adamsarms.net
Email: sales@adamsarms.net

ADAMY, GEBR. JADGWAFFEN

Import Agent - please refer to New England Custom Gun Service, Ltd. listing.
Factory - Adamy-Jadgwaffen
Buchsenmacher-Meisterbetrieb
Windeweg 3, Suhl D-98527 GERMANY
Fax No.: 011-49-3681-709076
Website: www.adamy-jagdwaffen.de
Email: info@adamy-jagdwaffen.de

ADCOR DEFENSE

234 South Haven Street
Baltimore, MD 21224
Phone No.: 888-612-3267
Website: www.adcordefense.com

ADEQ FIREARMS COMPANY

4921 W. Cypress Street
Tampa, FL 33607
Phone No.: 813-636-5077
Website: www.adeqfirearms.com

ADVANCED ARMAMENT CORP.

2408 Tech Center Parkway
Suite 150
Lawrenceville, GA 30043
Phone No.: 770-925-9988
Website: www.advanced-armament.com

AERON CZ s.r.o.

Svitavske Nabrezi 27
614 00 Brno, CZECH REPUBLIC
Fax No.: 011-420-545-210-407
Website: www.aeron.cz
Email: info@aeron.cz

AIM SURPLUS

3801 Lefferson Rd.
Middletown, OH 45044
Phone No.: 888-748-5252
Fax No: 513-424-9960
Website: www.aimsurplus.com
Email: sales@aimsurplus.com

AKDAL

Factory - ÜCYILDIZ SILAH SANAYI TIC LTD. STI
Bostanci Cad. Yol Sokak No. 14/A
Y. Dudullu/Ümraniye/Istanbul 34775 TURKEY
Phone No.: 011-90-216-527-6710 (ext. 124)
Fax No.: 011-90-216-527-6705
Website: www.akdalarms.com
Website: www.voltranarms.com
Email: blow@voltranarms.com

AKKAR

Akkar Silah Sanayi Ltd.
Orhanli Merkez Mah.
Gul Sok. 34956
Tuzla, Istanbul TURKEY
Fax: 011-90-216-394-4373
Website: www.akkarsilah.com
Email: akkar@akkar.com.tr

ALEXANDER ARMS LLC

U.S. Army - Radford Arsenal
P.O. Box 1
Radford, VA 24143
Phone No.: 540-639-8356
Fax No.: 540-639-8353
Website: www.alexanderarms.com
Email: support@alexanderarms.com

ALDERFER AUCTION COMPANY

501 Fairgrounds Road
Hatfield, PA 19440
Phone No.: 215-393-3023
Website: www.alderferauction.com

ALFA PROJ. spol. s.r.o.

Importer - Trail Blazin' Innovations
8711 Belle Glen Dr.
Houston, TX 77099-1502
Phone No.: 281-530-3916
Fax No.: 281-530-1275
Website: www.tbicatalog.com
Email: tbifred@aol.com
Factory
Zabrdovicka 11
615 00 Brno CZECH REPUBLIC
Fax No.: 011-420-545-120-622
Website: www.alfa-proj.cz
Email: prodej@alfa-proj.cz

ALMAR
S. Alamanos & Co. O.E.
44 Kyprou Str. 16452 Argiroupolis
Athens GREECE
Fax No.: 011-30-210-9935117
Website: www.alamanosoe.gr

ALPHARMS
Please refer to Leader Arms Technology listing.

AMBUSH FIREARMS
101 War Fighter Way
Black Creek, GA 31308
Phone No.: 855-262-8742
Website: www.ambushfirearms.com

AMERICA REMEMBERS
10226 Timber Ridge Dr.
Ashland, VA 23005
Phone No.: 804-550-9616
Fax No.: 804-550-9603
Website: www.americaremembers.com
Email: america.remembers@comcast.net

AMERICAN CLASSIC
Importer - please refer to Eagle Imports listing.
Website: www.americanclassic1911.com
Email: info@americanclassic1911.com

AMERICAN CUSTOM GUNMAKERS GUILD
22 Vista View Dr.
Cody, WY 82414-9606
Phone/Fax No.: 307-587-4297
Website: www.acgg.org
Email: acgg@acgg.org

AMERICAN DERRINGER CORPORATION
127 N. Lacy Dr.
Waco, TX 76705
Phone No.: 254-799-9111
Fax No.: 254-799-7935
Website: www.ladyderringer.com
Website: www.amderringer.com
Email: amderringer@aol.com

AMERICAN GUN COMPANY, LLC
4051 US Highway 93 S.
Kalispell, MT 59901-8602
Phone No.: 406-755-4907
Fax No.: 406-755-2969
Website: www.americangunllc.com

AMERICAN GUNSMITHING ASSOCIATION
800 Connecticut Ave.
P.O. Box 5656
Norwalk, CT 06856-5656
Phone No.: 800-241-7484

AMERICAN HISTORICAL FOUNDATION
10195 Maple Leaf Court
Ashland, VA 23005
Phone No.: 804-550-7851
Fax No.: 804-550-0923
Website: www.ahffirearms.com
Email: ahffirearms@comcast.net

AMERICAN HUNTING RIFLES, INC.
1711 Mountain View Orchard Road
Corvallis, MT 59828
Phone No.: 406-363-8033
Website: www.hunting-rifles.com
Email: wayne@hunting-rifles.com

AMERICAN LEGACY FIREARMS
P.O. Box 369
Ft. Collins, CO 80522
Phone No.: 877-887-4867
Fax No.: 970-221-0614
Website: www.americanlegacyfirearms.com
Email: info@americanlegacyfirearms.com

AMERICAN PRECISION ARMS
55 Lyle Field Rd.
Jefferson, GA 30549
Phone No.: 706-367-8881
Website: www.americanprecisionarms.com

AMERICAN SPIRIT ARMS
16001 N. Greenway Hayden Loop, Suite B
Scottsdale, AZ 85260
Phone No.: 480-367-9540
Fax No.: 480-367-9541
Website: www.americanspiritarms.com
Email: rifles@americanspiritarms.com

AMERICAN TACTICAL IMPORTS
100 Airpark Drive
Rochester, NY 14624
Phone No.: 800-290-0065
Fax No.: 585-328-4168
Website: www.americantactical.us

AMOSKEAG AUCTION COMPANY, INC.
250 Commercial Street, Unit 3011
Manchester, NH 03101
Phone No.: 603-627-7383
Fax No.: 603-627-7384
Website: www.amoskeagauction.com

ANDERSON MANUFACTURING
1743 Anderson Blvd.
Hebron, KY 41048
Phone No.: 859-689-4085
Fax No.: 859-689-4110
Website: www.andersonrifles.com
Email: sales@ATDMachineshop.com

ANSCHÜTZ

Sporting Rifle Importer & Factory Service
Steyr Arms, Inc.
7661 Commerce Lane
Trussville, AL 35173
Phone No.: 205-655-8299
Fax No.: 205-655-7078
Website: www.steyrarms.com

Importers/Distributors – Match Competition Target Rifles
Please refer to Champion's Choice listing.
Champions Shooter's Supply
P.O. Box 303
New Albany, OH 43054
Phone No.: 800-821-4867
Fax No.: 614-855-1209
Website: www.championshooters.com

Importer & Repair/Warranty/Gunsmithing Services
Altius Handcrafted Firearms
125 Madison Avenue
West Yellowstone, MT 59758
Phone No.: 406-646-9222
Website: www.altiusguns.com
Email: altiusguns@earthlink.net

Factory - ANSCHÜTZ, J.G. GmbH & Co. KG
Postfach 1128
89001 Ulm, GERMANY
Daimlerstrasse 12
89079 Ulm, GERMANY
Fax No.: 011-49-731-4012700
Website: www.anschuetz-sport.com
Email: anschuetz@anschuetz-sport.com

ANZIO IRONWORKS

1905 16th Street North
St. Petersburg, FL 33704
Phone No.: 727-895-2019
Fax No.: 727-827-4728
Website: www.anzioironworks.com
Email: anzioshop@hotmail.com

ARCUS

Importer - please refer to Century International Arms listing.

ARDESA

Camino de Talleri, s/n
E-48170 Zamudio (Viczaya) SPAIN
Fax No.: 011-34-944-521-372
Website: www.ardesa.com
Email: ardesa@ardesa.com

ARES DEFENSE SYSTEMS, INC.

P.O. Box 120789
Melbourne, FL 32912
Phone No.: 321-242-8410
Website: www.aresdefense.com

ARMALITE, INC.

P.O. Box 299
Geneseo, IL 61254
Phone No.: 800-336-0184
Fax No.: 309-944-6949
Website: www.ArmaLite.com
Email: info@armalite.com

Law Enforcement Support Only
P.O. Box 340
Campbellsburg, KY 40011
Phone No.: 502-532-0300
Fax No.: 502-532-0775
Email: emerickc@armalite.com

ARMAMENT TECHNOLOGY

(Repair only - no current mfg.)
3045 Robie St., Suite 113
Halifax, N.S. CANADA B3K 4P6
Phone No.: 902-454-6384
Fax No.: 902-454-4641
Website: www.armament.com

ARMED

Importer – Slide action shotgun only – refer to Iver Johnson Arms

Sales & Export – Izmirlioglu Av Malzemeleri San. Tic. Ltd. Sti.
1456 Sk., No. 83 K:4/ 402 35220 Alsancak
Izmir TURKEY
Phone No.: 011-090-232-464-5640
Fax: 011-090-232-464-5650
Website: www.armedguns.com

Factory - Doruk Silah San. Ltd. St.
Üzümlü Kasabasi Beysehir
Konya, TURKEY
Website: www.doruksilah.com
Email: info@doruksilah.com

LA ARMERIA DE MADRID

Factory
Infanta Maria Teresa, 15
ES-28016 Madrid SPAIN
Fax No.: 011-91-564-6289
Web site: www.armeriademadrid.com
Email: correo@armeriademadrid.com

ARMES MATHELON

Please refer to Mathelon Armes listing.

ARMES PIERRE ARTISAN

8 avenue Paul Doumer B.P. 12
F-42380 Saint Bonnet Le Chateau FRANCE
Fax No.: 011-33-477-507027
Website: www.armes-pierre-artisan.fr
Email: armes.pierre.artisan@wanadoo.fr

ARMI MAGAP

Factory – Armi Magap di Piotti Maurizio Srl
Via Provinciale, 49
I-25060 Marcheno Brescia, ITALY
Fax No.: 011-39-030-861-404
Website: www.armimagap.it
Email: armimagap@libero.it

ARMI SALVINELLI

Factory
via Zanardelli, 210
I-25060 Marcheno, Brescia ITALY
Fax No.: 011-39-030-861-285
Website: www.armisalvinelli.com
Email: info@armisalvinelli.com

ARMI SPORT DI CHIAPPIA SILVIA & C. Snc

Distributor - please refer to Cimarron listing.
Distributor - please refer to Taylor's & Co., Inc. listing.
U.S. Office – please refer to Chiappa Firearms Ltd. listing
Factory
via Milano 2
I-25020 Azzano Mella (BS) ITALY
Fax No.: 011-39-030-9749232
Website: www.armisport.com
Email: info@armisport.com

ARMS ROOM LLC

1372 N. Goldenrod Road #22
Orlando, FL 32807
Phone No.: 407-282-3803
Fax No.: 407-282-1165
Website: www.ArmsRoom.com

ARMS TECH LTD.

5025 N. Central Ave., #459
Phoenix, AZ 85012
Phone No.: 623-936-1510
Fax No.: 623-936-0361
Website: www.armstechltd.com

ARMSAN

Importer - please refer to Mossberg listing.
Factory - Armsan SilahSan. ve Tic.A.S.
Inkilap Mah. Alemdag Cad. Site Yolu Sok. No. 3
34768 Umraniye-Istanbul TURKEY
Fax No.: 011-90-216-630-2288
Website: www.armsan.com
Email: sales@armsan.com

ARMSCOR (ARMS CORPORATION OF THE PHILIPPINES)

Importer & Distributor - Armscor Precision International
150 N. Smart Way
Pahrump, NV 89060
Phone No.: 775-537-1444
Fax No.: 775-537-1446
Website: www.rockislandarmory.com
Email: armscor@armscor.net
Factory office - Arms Corp. of the Philippines
Armscor Avenue, Fortune
Marikina City 1800, PHILIPPINES
Phone No.: 632-941-6243
Fax No.: 632-942-0682
Website: www.armscor.com.ph
Email: info@armscor.com.ph
Executive office - Arms Corp. of the Philippines
6th Floor, Strat 100 Bldg., Emerald Ave.
Ortigas Center, Pasig City, 1600 PHILIPPINES
Fax No.: 632-634-3906
Email: squires@cnl.net

ARRIETA, S.L.

Importer & Distributor - please refer to Quality Arms listing.
Importer - please refer to Griffin & Howe listing.
Importer - please refer to William Larkin Moore listing.
Importer - please refer to Orvis listing.
Importer - please refer to Wingshooting Adventures listing.
Factory - Arrieta, Manufacturas, S.L.
Morkaiko 5
E-20870 Elgoibar (Guipuzcoa) SPAIN
Fax No.: 011-34-943-743154
Website: www.arrietashotguns.com
Email: info@arrietashotguns.com

ARRIZABALAGA, PEDRO

Importer - please refer to Harry Marx Hi-Grade Imports listing.
Importer - please refer to William Larkin Moore listing.
Factory - Arrizabalaga, Pedro, S.A.
Errekatxu, 5
E-20600 Eibar (Gipuzkoa) SPAIN
Fax No.: 011-34-943-201743
Website: www.pedroarrizabalaga.net

ARSENAL, BULGARIA

Importer - please refer to Arsenal Inc. listing.
Factory - Arsenal 2000 JSCo.
100, Rozova Dolina St.
6100 Kazanlack, BULGARIA
Fax No.: 011-359-431-50001
Website: www.arsenal2000-bg.com
Email: marketing@arsenal2000.com

ARSENAL FIREARMS

Gardone, ITALY
Website: www.arsenalfirearms.com

ARSENAL INC.

3395 S. Jones Blvd. #331
Las Vegas, NV 89146
Phone No.: 702-643-2220
Fax No.: 702-643-8860
Website: www.arsenalinc.com
Email: customerservice@arsenalinc.com

ARSENAL USA LLC
Please refer to Armory USA LLC listing.

ART MANIFATTURA ARMI
Please refer to Manifattura Armi Art.

ASHBURY PRECISION ORDNANCE
P.O. Box 8024
Charlottesville, VA 22906-8024
Phone No.: 434-296-8600
Fax No.: 434-296-9260
Website: www.Ashburyintlgroup.com
Email: info@Ashburyintlgroup.com

ASPEN OUTFITTING CO.
315 East Dean St.
Aspen, CO 81611
Phone No.: 800-784-2140
Fax No.: 970-920-3706
Website: www.aspenoutfitting.com
Email: contact@aspenoutfitting.com

ASTRA ARMS S.A.
Case Postale 103
1951 Sion SWITZERLAND
Fax No.: 011-41-027-322-3707
Website: www.astra-arms.ch
Email: astra@astra-arms.ch

ATKIN, GRANT & LANG
Windmill Road, Markyate, St. Albans,
Hertfordshire AL3 8LP U.K.
Phonc No.: 011-44-1582-849382
Fax No.: 011-44-1582-849058
Website: www.atkingrantandlang.com
Email: info@atkingrantandlang.com

ATKIN, HENRY
Factory - please refer to Atkin, Grant & Lang listing.

AUTO-ORDNANCE CORP.
Please refer to the Kahr Arms listing.
Website: www.auto-ordnance.com
Website: www.tommygun.com
Website: www.tommygunshop.com

AXTELL RIFLE COMPANY
Please refer to Shiloh Mfg. Co. listing.

AZTEK ARMS
1641 W. Alvey Drive #1
Mapleton, UT 84664
Phone No.: 801-704-9760
Fax No.: 801-704-9759
Website: www.aztekarms.com
Email: info@aztekarms.com

BCM EUROPEARMS
Via Torino 15/5
10060 Roletto, Torino, ITALY
Website: www.bcmeuropearms.it
Email: info@bcmeuropearms.it

BAER, LES
Please refer to the Les Baer Custom listing.

BWE FIREARMS
Longwood, FL
Phone No.: 407-592-3975
Website: www.bwefirearms.com
Email: Richard@bwefirearms.com

BAIKAL
Importer - please refer to US Sporting Goods listing.
Baikal Factory
Izhevsky Mekhanichesky Zavod
8, Promyshlennaya str.
Izhevsk, 426063 RUSSIA
Fax No.: 011-95-007-341-2665830
Website: www.baikalinc.ru
Email: worldlinks@baikalinc.ru

BALLARD ARMS, INC.
9562 Sand Lake Hwy
Onsted, MI 49265
Phone No.: 866-997-4353
Website: www.ballardarms.com

BANSNER'S ULTIMATE RIFLES L.L.C.
P.O. Box 839
261 East Main Street
Adamstown, PA 19501
Phone No.: 717-484-2370
Fax No.: 717-484-0523
Website: www.bansnersrifle.com
Email: bansner@ptd.net

BARNES PRECISION MACHINE, INC.
1434 Farrington Road
Apex, NC 27523
Phone No.: 919-362-6805
Fax No.: 919-362-5752
Website: www.barnesprecision.com
Email: info@barnesprecision.com

BARRETT FIREARMS MANUFACTURING, INC.
P.O. Box 1077
Murfreesboro, TN 37133
Phone No.: 615-896-2938
Fax No.: 615-896-7313
Website: www.barrett.net
Email: mail@barrett.net

BASERRI
Factory - please refer to Fabarm listing.
U.S. Importer - Baserri USA
116 Oak Dr.
Friendswood, TX 77546
Phone No.: 281-686-3544
Website: www.baserrishotguns.com
Email: baserri.sales@baserrishotguns.com

BATTAGLIA, MAURO
Via Dismano, N. 181 S.
Stefano di Ravenna ITALY
Phone/Fax No.: 011-39-0544-497-879
Website: www.maurobattaglia.com

BATTLE RIFLE COMPANY
4469 Shady Lake Drive
Seabrook, TX 77586
Phone No: 281-777-0316
Fax No.: 866-804-3049
Website: www.battleriflecompany.com
Email: info@battleriflecompany.com

BECAS
Factory - Molot JSC
Vyatskie Polyany Machine Building Plant
135 Lenin St., Vyatski Polyany
RUS-612960 Krov Region, RUSSIA
Fax No.: 011-007-83334-61832
Website: www.molot.biz
Email: molot_ves@list.ru

BEEMAN PRECISION AIRGUNS
5454 Argosy Dr.
Huntington Beach, CA 92649-1039
Toll Free Phone No.: 800-227-2744
Fax No.: 714-890-4808
Website: www.beeman.com

BEEMILLER
Please refer to Hi-Point Firearms listing.

BENELLI
Importer - Benelli USA
17603 Indian Head Highway
Accokeek, MD 20607-2501
Phone No.: 800-264-4962
Fax No.: 301-283-6988
Website: www.benelliusa.com
Pistol/Airgun Importer - please refer to Larry's Guns listing.
Warranty Repair Address - Benelli USA
901 Eighth Street
Pocomoke, MD 21851
Factory - Benelli Armi S.p.A.
Via della Stazione, 50
I-61029 Urbino (PU) ITALY
Fax No.: 011-39-0722-307-207
Website: www.benelli.it

BERETTA, PIETRO
Importer - Beretta U.S.A. Corp
17601 Beretta Drive
Accokeek, MD 20607
Phone No.: 301-283-2191
Fax No.: 301-283-0189
Website: www.berettausa.com
Beretta Premium Grades
Website: www.berettagallery.com
Beretta Gallery
718 Madison Avenue
New York, NY 10021
Phone No.: 212-319-3235
Fax No.: 212-207-8219
Beretta Gallery
41 Highland Park Village
Dallas, TX 75205
Phone No.: 214-559-9800
Fax No.: 214-559-9805
Factory - Fabbrica d'Armi Pietro Beretta S.p.A
Via Pietro Beretta 18
25063 Gardone Val Trompia
Brescia, ITALY
Fax No.: 011-39-30-834-1421
Website: www.beretta.it

WAYNE BERGQUIST CUSTOM PISTOLS
5760 Shirley Street, #21
Naples, FL 34109
Phone No.: 239-594-1573
Fax No.: 239-597-8259
Website: www.naplesflguns.com
Email: wbcustom@aol.com

BERGARA
Importer – please refer to Connecticut Valley Arms listing.
Factory – Dikar, S.Coop.
Urate, 26
E-20570 Bergara, SPAIN
Phone No.: 011-34-943-769893
Website: www.bergararifles.com
Email: info@bergararifles.com

BERNARDELLI, GIULIO
Via Lorenzo Bernini
San Zeno Naviglio
4-25010 Brescia, ITALY
Phone No. 011-39-030-2106959
Fax No.: 011-39-030-2106742
Website: www.bernardelli.it
Email: info@bernardelli.it

BERNARDELLI, VINCENZO
Via Achille Grandi, 10
Torbole Casaglia
I-25030 Brescia, ITALY
Fax No.: 011-39-030-215-0963
Website: www.bernardelli.com
Email: bernardelli@bernardelli.com

BERSA
Importer - please refer to Eagle Imports listing.
Website: www.bersa.com
Email:info@bersa.com
Factory - Bersa S.A.
Castillo 312
(1704) Ramos Mejia, ARGENTINA
Fax No.: 011-54-1-656-2093

BETTINSOLI, TARCISIO Srl

Importer - see Franchi listing (private label models).

European Distributor - Bignami S.p.A.

via Lahn
I-39040 Ora (Bolzano), ITALY
Fax No: 011-39-471-810899
Website: www.bignami.it

Factory

Via I Maggio 116
Sarezzo, Brescia, I-25068 ITALY
Fax No.: 011-39-030-890-0240
Website: www.bettinsoli.it
Email: info@bettinsoli.it

BIG HORN ARMORY, INC.

2301 Lt. Childers Road
Cody, WY 82414
Phone No.: 307-586-3700
Fax No.: 307-586-3701
Website: www.bighornarmory.com
Email: general@bighornarmory.com

BILL HANUS BIRDGUNS LLC

P.O. Box 533
Newport, OR 97365
Phone No.: 541-265-7433
Fax No.: 541-265-7400
Website: www.billhanusbirdguns.com
Email: billhanus@gmail.com

BLACK FORGE

Phone No.: 407-737-7222
Website: www.blackforgeweapons.com

BLACKHEART INTERNATIONAL LLC

RR 3, Box 115
Philippi, WV 26416
Phone No.: 304-457-1280
Fax No.: 304-457-1281
Website: www.bhiarms.com

BLACKOPS TECHNOLOGIES

196 Sunrise Creek Loop
Suite 55
Columbia Falls, MT 59912
Website: www.blackopsprecision.com

BLACK RAIN ORDNANCE, INC.

P.O. Box 1111
Neosho, MO 64850
Phone No.: 417-456-1920
Toll Free: 888-836-2620
Fax No.: 417-451-2811
Website: www.blackrainordnance.com
Email: blackrainordnance@yahoo.com

BLACK RIFLE COMPANY LLC

15140 SE 82nd Drive, Ste. 350
Clackamas, OR 97015
Toll Free: 888-566-1405
Website: www.blackriflecompany.com

BLAND, THOMAS & SONS GUNMAKERS LTD.

Woodcock Hill, Inc.

192 Spencers Road
Benton, PA 17814
Phone No.: 570-864-3242
Fax No.: 570-864-3232
Website: www.woodcockhill.com
Email: bland@epix.net

BLASER

Importer & Distributor - Blaser USA, Inc.

403 East Ramsey, Ste. 301
San Antonio, TX 78216
Phone No.: 210-377-2527
Fax No.: 210-377-2533
Website: www.blaser-usa.com

Factory - Blaser Jagdwaffen GmbH

Ziegelstadel 1
D-88316 Isny im Allgau, GERMANY
Fax No.: 011-49-75-62702-43
Website: www.blaser.de

H. BLEIKER FEINMECHANIK/SPORTWAFFEN

Neufeldstrasse 1
CH - 9606 Bütschwil, SWITZERLAND
Phone No.: 011-41-71-982-8210
Fax No.: 011-41-71-982-8219
Website: www.bleiker.ch
Email: hbleiker@bleiker.ch

BLOW

Please refer to Akdal listing.

Importer - Palco Sports

8555 Revere Lane N.
Maple Grove, MN 55369
Phone No.: 800-882-4656
Fax No.: 763-559-2286
Website: www.palcosports.com
E-Mail: Info@palcosports.com

BLUEGRASS ARMORY

Good Times Outdoors

4600 West Highway 326
Ocala, FL 34482
Phone No.: 352-401-9070
Fax No.: 352-401-9667
Website: www.bluegrassarmory.com
Email: support@bluegrassarmory.com

BOBCAT WEAPONS INC.

Please refer to Red Rock Arms listing.

BOBERG ARMS CORPORATION

1755 Commerce Court
White Bear Lake, MN 55110
Phone No.: 651-209-4812
Fax No: 651-209-4813
Website: www.BobergArms.com

BOLLINGER, JOHN

Please refer to Mountain Riflery listing.

BOND ARMS, INC.
P.O. Box 1296
Granbury, Texas 76048
Phone No.: 817-573-4445
Fax No.: 817-573-5636
Website: www.bondarms.com
Email: info@bondarms.com

BORDEN RIFLES
1325 Sheldon Hill Road
Springville, PA 18844
Phone No.: 570-965-2505
Website: www.bordenrifles.com
Email: info@bordenrifles.com

BOROVNIK, LUDWIG KG
Bahnofstrasse 7
A-9170 Ferlach, AUSTRIA
Fax No.: 011-43-0-4227-4349
Website: www.ludwigborovnik.com
Email: office@ludwigborovnik.com

BOSIS, LUCIANO
Importer – Manchester Arms LLC.
3556 Main St. Ste. 0
Manchester, VT 05254
Phone No.: 585-394-1909
Importer – Larry's Trading Post
7201 Pompano Terrace
Gaithersburg, MD 20879
Phone No.: 301-996-8680
Website: www.larrystradingpost.com
Factory
via G. Marconi 30
I-25039 Travagliato, Brescia, ITALY
Phone/Fax No.: 011-39-030-660-413
Website: www.bosis.com
Email: info@bosis.com

BOSS & CO., LTD.
The Caxton Bldg., 110 Kew Green
Richmond, London U.K. TW9 3AP
Phone No.: 011-44-020-7493-1127
Fax No.: 011-44-020-8605-3684
Website: www.bossguns.com
Email: info@bossguns.com

BOSWELL, CHARLES
Importer - Chris Batha
43 Pinckney Colony Road
Okatie, SC 29902
Phone No.: 866-254-2406
Website: www.chrisbatha.com
Email: chrisbatha@aol.com

BOWEN, BRUCE & COMPANY
3541 Mayer Ave.
Sturgis, SD 57785
Phone No.: 605-347-3133
Website: www.bbgunssturgis.com
Email: Bbowen999@aol.com

BOWMAC GUNPAR INC.
Canadian Parts Supplier
69 Iber Rd., Unit 101
Stittsville, Ontario CANADA K2S 1E7
Phone No.: 800-668-2509
Phone No.: 613-831-8548
Fax No.: 613-831-0530

BOXALL & EDMISTON LTD.
45 Atcham Business Park
Upton Magna
Shrewsbury, Shropshire, U.K. SY4 4UG
Phone No.: 011-44-01743-762352
Website: www.boxallandedmiston.co.uk
Email: info@boxallandedmiston.co.uk

BRAVO COMPANY MFG., INC.
P.O. Box 361
Hartland, WI 53029
Phone No.: 877-272-8626
Fax No.: 262-367-0989
Website: www.bravocompanymfg.com
Email: info@bravocompanyusa.com

BREDA MECCANICA BRESCIANA
Factory
Via Galilei, 6
I-25068 Brescia ITALY
Fax No.: 011-39-030-8900370
Website: www.bredafucili.com
Email: info@bredafucili.com

RYAN BREEDING CUSTOM RIFLES
4573 W. Saddle Ridge Dr.
Nampa, ID 83687
Phone No.: 661-317-2996
Phone No.: 208-230-3081
Website: www.rbbigbores.com
Email: ryan@rbbigbores.com

BREMAC SRL
Via Artigiani, 93
25063 Gardone V.T. (Brescia), ITALY
Phone No.: 011-39-030-8910264
Website: www.renatogamba.it
Email: infocomm@renatogamba.it

BRENZOVICH FIREARMS TRAINING CENTER
22301 Old Texas
Ft. Hancock, TX 79839
Phone/Fax No.: 915-764-2030
Website: www.brenzovich.com
Email: GunChamp@aol.com

BRETTON-GAUCHER
Factory
17 rue Victor Grignard
Z1 de Montreynaud
F-42 026 St. Etienne FRANCE
Fax No.: 011-33-477419572
Website: www.bretton-gaucher.com
Email: info@bretton-gaucher.com

BRIGNOLI, SILVIO
via Alfieri 6
I-25063 Gardone VT, Brescia ITALY
Phone No.: 011-39-030-8912295
Web site: www.brignoliarmi.com
Email: info@brignoliarmi.com

BRILEY MANUFACTURING INC.
1230 Lumpkin Rd.
Houston, TX 77043
Phone No.: 713-932-6995 (Technical)
Phone No.: 800-331-5718 (Orders only)
Fax No.: 713-932-1043
Website: www.briley.com

BRITISH SPORTING ARMS LTD.
3684 Route 44
Millsbrook, NY 12545
Phone No.: 845-677-8303
Fax No.: 845-677-5756
Website: www.bsaltd.com
Email: info@bsaltd.com

BRNO RIFLES
Importer - please refer to CZ USA listing.
Factory - ZBROJOVKA BRNO, a.s.
Lazaretni 7
615 00 Brno, CZECH REPUBLIC
Fax No.: 011-42(0)-545-152-288
website: www.zbrojovkabrno.com

BROCKMAN'S RIFLES
2165 South 1800 East
Gooding, ID 83330
Phone No.: 208-934-5050
Fax No.: 208-934-5284
Website: www.brockmansrifles.com
Email: Brockman@brockmansrifles.com

A.A. BROWN & SONS GUNMAKERS
Snake Lane, Alvechurch
Birmingham, B48 7NT U.K.
Phone No.: 011-44-121445-5395
Fax No.: 011-44-121 445 2113
Website: www.aabrownandsons.com
Email: robin@aabrownandsons.com

DAVID MCKAY BROWN GUNMAKERS, LTD.
U.S. Agent - please refer to Griffin & Howe listing.
Importer - please refer to Wingshooting Adventures listing.
Factory - David Mckay Brown Gunmakers, Ltd.
32 Hamilton Road, Bothwell
Glasgow, SCOTLAND (U.K.) G71 8NA
Fax No.: 011-44-141-1698-854207
Website: www.mckaybrown.com
Email: info@mckaybrown.com

BROWN PRECISION, INC.
P.O. Box 270 W
7786 Molinos Avenue
Los Molinos, CA 96055
Phone No.: 530-384-2506
Fax No.: 530-384-1638
Website: www.brownprecision.com
Email: info@brownprecision.com

BROWNING
Administrative Headquarters
One Browning Place
Morgan, UT 84050-9326
Phone No.: 801-876-2711
Product Service: 800-333-3288
Fax No.: 801-876-3331
Website: www.browning.com
Website: www.browningint.com
Custom Shop U.S. Representative
Mr. Ron McGhie
Email: ronm@browning.com
Browning Parts and Service
3005 Arnold Tenbrook Rd.
Arnold, MO 63010-9406
Phone No.: 800-322-4626
Fax No.: 636-287-9751
Historical Research (Browning Arms Co. marked guns only)
Browning Historian
One Browning Place
Morgan, UT 84050-9326
Fax No.: 801-876-3331
Website: www.browning.com

BRÜGGER & THOMET
Importer - please refer to DSA listing.
Factory
Zelglistrasse 10
CH-3608 Thun, SWITZERLAND
Fax No.: 011-41-33-334-6701
Website: www.bt-ag.ch

BUEHLER CUSTOM SPORTING ARMS
P.O. Box 4096
Medford, OR 97501
Phone No.: 541-664-9109
Website: www.customsportingarms.com
Email: info@customsportingarms.com

BUL LTD.
Importer – M1911 Parts Only
All America Sales, Inc.
8884 Hwy. 62 West
Piggot, AR 72454
Phone No.: 870-544-2809
Fax: 870-544-2695
Factory - Bul Transmark Ltd.
10 Rival Street
Tel-Aviv 67778, ISRAEL
Fax No.: 011-972-3-687-4853
Website: www.bultransmark.com
Email: info@bultransmark.com

BUMAR
Exclusive Distributor – Beryl ASG
Al. Jana Pawla il nr 11,
00-b28 Warszawa, Poland
Phone No.: 011-48-22-311-2512
Fax No.: 011-48-22-311-2642
Website: www.bomar.com
Email: bumar@bumar.com

BUTLER ARMS USA
2355 S 1070 W
Salt Lake City, UT 84119
Phone: 801-886-0188
Website: www.butlerarmsusa.com
Email: info@butlerarmsusa.com

BUTTERFIELD & BUTTERFIELD (AUCTIONS)
Main Gallery & Corporate Office
220 San Bruno Ave.
San Francisco, CA 94103
Phone No.: 415-861-7500
Fax No.: 415-861-8951
Website: www.butterfields.com

BUSHMASTER FIREARMS INTERNATIONAL
Part of Freedom Group - Headquarters
PO Box 556
Madison, NC 27025
Phone No.: 800-883-6229
Fax No.: 207-892-8068
Website: www.bushmaster.com
Email: info@bushmaster.com

BÜYÜK HUGLU
Factory - Büyük Huglu Av Tüfekleri San. Tic. Ltd. Sti.
Huglu-Beysehir, Konya TURKEY
Fax No.: 011-90-332-516-1182
Website: www.buyukhuglu.com
Email: info@buyukhuglu.com

C3 DEFENSE, INC.
110 Thompson Road
Suite 103
Hiram, GA 30141
Phone No.: 888-803-2764
Fax: 678-244-3669
Website: www.c3defenseinc.com

CMMG, INC.
P.O. Box 369
Fayette, MO 65248
Phone No.: 660-248-2293
Fax No.: 660-248-2290
Website: www.cmmginc.com
Email: sales@cmmginc.com

CVA
A division of Blackpowder Products, Inc.
1685 Boggs Road – Suite 300
Duluth, GA 30096
Phone No.: 770-449-4687
Fax No.: 770-242-8546
Website: www.cva.com
Email: sales@cva.com

C Z (CESKA ZBROJOVKA)
Firearms & Airguns Importer - CZ-USA
P.O. Box 171073
Kansas City, KS 66117-0073
Phone No.: 913-321-1811
Toll Free No.: 800-955-4486
Fax No.: 913-321-2251
Website: www.cz-usa.com
Email: info@cz-usa.com
Website: www.safariclassics.com
(custom rifles only)
Administration Offices - Ceska Zbrojovka
Svatopluka Cecha 1283
CZ-68827 Uhersky Brod CZECH REPUBLIC
Fax No.: 011-420-63363-3811
Website: www.czub.cz
Email: info@czub.cz

CZ (STRAKONICE)
Factory - LUVO Prague Ltd.
Rejskova 7
120 00 Praha 2 CZECH REPUBLIC
Fax No.: 011-420-222-562-238
Email: luvo@iol.cz

CBC
(Ammo only, no mfg.)
Av. Humberto de Campos 3220
09426 900 Ribeirao Pires SP BRAZIL
Fax No.: 011-55-11-4822-8323
Website: www.cbc.com.br

CABELAS INC.
One Cabela Dr.
Sidney, NE 69160
Phone No.: 800-237-4444
Fax No.: 800-496-6329
website: www.cabelas.com

CABOT GUN COMPANY LLC
799 N. Pike Road
Cabot, PA 16023
Phone No.: 855-THE-1911
Website: www.cabotguns.com
Email: info@cabotguns.com

CAESAR GUERINI, s.r.l.
Importer - Caesar Guerini USA LLC
700 Lake Street
Cambridge, MD 21613
Phone No.: 410-901-1131
Fax No.: 410-901-1137
Website:www.gueriniusa.com
Email: info@gueriniusa.com
Factory - Caesar Guerini USA LLC
Via Canossi, 18F
I-25060 Marcheno Brescia, ITALY
Fax No.: 011-39-030-896-6147
Website: www.caesarguerini.it
Email: info@caesarguerini.it

CALICO LIGHT WEAPON SYSTEMS
924 N. Freemont Lane
Cornelius, OR 97113
Phone No.: 503-649-3010
Toll free: 888-442-2542
Fax No.: 503-649-3831
Website: www.calicolightweaponsystems.com

CANIK55
Importer - Please refer to Tristar listing.
Factory - Samsub Domestic Defense and Industry Corporation
Organize Sanayi Bölgesi
No: 28 Kutlukent/SAMSUN TURKEY
Fax No.: 011-90-362-266-6671
Website: www.canik55.com
Email: samsun@canik55.com

CARACAL
Importer – Caracal USA
7661 Commerce Lane
Trussville, AL 35173
Phone No.: 205-655-7050
Fax No.: 205-655-7078
Website: www.caracalusa.com
Email: info@caracalusa.com
Distributor (Italy only) – please refer to Fratelli Tanfoglio listing.
Factory
Tawazun Industrial Park
Sweihan
P.O. Box 94499
Abu Dhabi, UNITED ARAB EMIRATES
Tel: 011-971-2-5854441
Fax: 011-971-2-5854445
Website: www.caracal.ae
Email: info@caracal.ae

CASPIAN ARMS, LTD.
75 Cal Foster Dr.
Wolcott, VT 05680
Phone No.: 802-472-6454
Fax No.: 802-472-6709
Website: www.caspianarms.com
Email: info@caspianarms.com

CENTURY INTERNATIONAL ARMS, INC.
430 South Congress Ave., Ste. 1
Delray Beach, FL 33445
Phone No.: 800-527-1252
Phone No.: 561-265-4530
Fax No.: 561-265-4520
Website: www.centuryarms.com
Email: support@centuryarms.com

CHAMPIONS CHOICE, INC.
201 International Blvd.
LaVergne, TN 37086
Phone No.: (Orders Only) 800-345-7179
Phone No.: 615-793-4066
Fax No.: 615-793-4070
Email: sales@champchoice.com

CHAMPLIN FIREARMS, INC.
P.O. Box 3191
Enid, OK 73702
Phone No.: 580-237-7388
Fax No.: 580-242-6922
Website: www.champlinarms.com
Email: info@champlinarms.com

CHAPPARAL ARMS
Factory
via Locchi 6
Brescia, ITALY I-25133
Fax No.: 011-39-030-3387727
Website: www.chaparralarms.com
Email: info@chaparralarms.com

CHAPUIS ARMES
Importer - Please refer to William Larkin Moore listing.
Importer - Please refer to Evolution USA
Importer - Please refer to Heirloom Armes listing.
Factory - Chapuis Armes
Z.I. La Gravoux, BP 15
F-42380 St. Bonnet le Chateau, FRANCE
Fax No.: 011-33-4-77-501070
Website: www.chapuis-armes.com
Email: info@chapuis-armes.com

CHARLES DALY (2011-PRESENT)
Importer – Samco Global Arms, Inc.
6995 Northwest 43rd Street
Miami, FL 33166
Phone No.: 305-593-9782
Fax No.: 305-593-1014
Website: www.charlesdaly.com

CHARTER ARMS, INC.
281 Canal St.
Shelton, CT 06484
Phone No.: 866-769-4867
Fax No.: 203-922-1469
Website: www.charterfirearms.com

CHERRY'S FINE GUNS
3408-N West Wendover Avenue
Greensboro, NC 27407
Phone No.: 336-854-4182
Fax No.: 336-854-4184
Website: www.cherrys.com
Email: fineguns@cherrys.com

CHEYTAC LLC
541 Hazel Ave.
Nashville, GA 31639
Phone No.: 855-243-9822
Website: www.cheytac.com

CHIAPPA FIREARMS LTD.
Factory - please refer to Armi Sport listing.
U.S. Office
P.O. Box 26178
Dayton, OH 45426-0178
Phone No.: 937-835-5000
Website: www.chiappafirearms.com
Email: info@chiappafirearms.com

CHIPMUNK RIFLES
Current trademark imported by Keystone Sporting Arms – please refer to this listing.

CHRISTENSEN ARMS
550 North Cemetery Rd.
Gunnison, UT 84634
Phone No.: 435-528-7999
Fax No.: 435-528-5773
Website: www.christensenarms.com
Email: sales@christensenarms.com

CHRISTIE'S (AUCTIONS)
Rockefeller Center
20 Rockefeller Plaza
New York, NY 10020
Phone No.: 212-636-2000
Fax No.: 212-636-2399
Website: www.christies.com

E.J. CHURCHILL (GUNMAKERS)
U.S. Agent - please refer to Fieldsport listing.
Factory
Park Lane, Lane End, High Wycombe
Buckinghamshire, HP14 3NS U.K.
Phone No.: 011-44-1494-883066
Fax. No.: 011-44-1494-883215
Website: www.ejchurchill.com
Email: info@ejchurchill.com

CIMARRON, F.A. CO., INC.
105 Winding Oaks
Fredericksburg, TX 78624-0906
Phone No.: 830-997-9090
Fax No.: 830-997-0802
Website: www.cimarron-firearms.com
Email: dealersales@cimarron-firearms.com

CITADEL
Please refer to Legacy Sports listing.

CLARK CUSTOM GUNS, INC.
336 Shootout Lane
Princeton, LA 71067
Phone No.: 318-949-9884
Fax No.: 318-949-9829
website: www.clarkcustomguns.com
Email: ccgweb@shreve.net

COBB MANUFACTURING, INC.
Please refer to Bushmaster listing.

COBRA
Please refer to Tristar listing.

COBRA ENTERPRISES OF UTAH, INC.
1960 S. Milestone Drive, Ste. F
Salt Lake City, UT 84104
Phone No.: 801-908-8300
Fax No.: 801-908-8301
Website: www.cobrapistols.net
Email: info@cobrapistols.net

CODY FIREARMS MUSEUM
720 Sheridan Ave.
Cody, WY 82414
Historical Research Phone No.: 307-578-4031
Website: www.bbhc.org

COGSWELL & HARRISON LTD.
Heathcliffe, Parkers Lane
Maidens Green, Bracknell
Berkshire, U.K.
Phone No.: 011-44-1344885091
Fax No.: 011-44-1344890906
Website: www.cogswell.co.uk
Email: cogswellandharrison@barclays.net

COLE GUNSMITHING
21 Bog Hollow Rd.
Harpswell, ME 04079
Phone No.: 207-833-5027
Fax No.: 207-833-5677
Website: www.colegun.com

COLT
Colt's Manufacturing Company LLC
P.O. Box 1868
Hartford, CT 06144-1868
Phone No.: 800-962-COLT
Fax No.: 860-244-1449
Website: www.coltsmfg.com
Colt Defense LLC (Law Enforcement & Rifles)
P.O. Box 118
Hartford, CT 06141
Phone No.: 860-232-4489
Fax No.: 860-244-1442
Website: www.colt.com

AR-15 Rifles, .22 LR cal. only - please refer to Umarex USA listing.

Historical Research - Colt Archive Properties LLC

P.O. Box 1868
Hartford, CT 01644-1868
If mailing in a request, make sure the proper research fee is enclosed (please refer to appropriate Colt section for current fees and related information).

1st and 2nd Generation phone service only

Phone no: 800-962-COLT
(Ask for Historical Dept. Research fees start at $150.)

Colt Cavalry & Artillery Revolver Authentication Service

Mr. John Kopec, Historian
Phone/Fax No.: 530-222-4440
Website: www.johnakopec.com
Email: books@johnakopec.com (book sales only)

COMANCHE

Master Distributor – please refer to Eagle Imports, Inc. listing

Website: www.comanchepistols.com

COMMANDO ARMS

Komando Av San. Tic. Ltd. Sti.

Hisarici Mah. Ahmet Toprak Cad. No. 9
Balikesir, TURKEY
Fax No.: 011-90-266-243-4764
Website: www.commando-arms.com
Email: info@commando-arms.com

COMPETITIVE EDGE GUNWORKS LLC

17154 CR 180
Bogard, MO 64622
Phone No.: 660-731-5124
Fax No.: 660-731-5091
Website: www.competitiveedgegunworks.com

COMPETITOR CORPORATION

26 Knight Street, Unit 3
P.O. Box 352
Jaffrey, NH 03452
Phone No.: 603-532-9483
Fax No.: 603-532-8209
Website: www.competitor-pistol.com
Email: Competitorcorp@aol.com

CONNECTICUT SHOTGUN MANUFACTURING COMPANY

100 Burritt Street
New Britain, CT 06503-4004
Phone No.: 860-225-6581
Fax No.: 860-832-8707
Website: www.connecticutshotgun.com
Email: Galazan@msn.com

CONNECTICUT VALLEY ARMS

1685 Boggs Rd, Ste. 300
Duluth, GA 30096-9096
Phone No.: 770-449-4687
Fax No.: 770-242-8546
Website: www.cva.com
Email: info@cva.com

CONSTITUTION ARMS

12 Hoffman St.
Maplewood, NJ 07040
Phone No.: 973-378-8011
Website: www.constitutionarms.com

COONAN INC.

2033 105th Ave. NE
Blaine, MN 55449
Phone No.: 763-786-1720
Fax No.: 763-205-2564
Website: www.coonaninc.com
Email: info@coonaninc.com

COOPER FIREARMS OF MONTANA, INC.

P.O. Box 114
4004 Hwy. 93 North
Stevensville, MT 59870
Phone No.: 406-777-0373
Fax No.: 406-777-5228
Website: www.cooperfirearms.com
Email: info@cooperfirearms.com

CORE 15

Good Time Outdoors, Inc.

4600 West Highway 326
Ocala, FL 34482
Phone No.: 352-401-9070
Fax No.: 352-401-9667
Website: www.core15rifles.com
Email: sales@core15rifles.com

CORONADO ARMS

450 S. Porter Road
Dixon, CA 95620
Phone No.: 707-678-2864
Fax No.: 707-678-3542
Website: www.coronadoarms.com
Email: sales@coronadoarms.com

COSMI, AMERICO & FIGLIO s.n.c.

Factory

Via Flaminia 307
I-60020 Torrette di Ancona, ITALY
Fax No.: 011-39-071-887-008
Website: www.cosmi.net
Email: cosmi@cosmi.net

COWAN'S AUCTIONS INC.

6270 Este Ave.
Cincinnati, OH 45232
Phone No: 513-871-1670
Fax No.: 513-871-8670
Website: www.cowanauctions.com

CRICKETT RIFLE
New Mfg. - refer to Keystone Sporting Arms listing.

CROSS CANYON ARMS
2020 South Painter Lane
West Haven, UT 84401
Phone No: 801-731-0172
Website: www.crosscanyonarms.com

CYLINDER & SLIDE, INC.
245 East 4th Street
Fremont, NE 68025
Toll Free: 800-448-1713
Fax: 402-721-0263
Website: www.cylinder-slide.com
Email: bill@cylinder-slide.com

CZECHPOINT, INC.
103 Stone Road
Knoxville, TN 37920
Phone No.: 865-247-0184
Fax No.: 865-247-0185
Website: www.czechpoint-usa.com
Email: dan.brown@czechpoint-usa.com

D'ARCY ECHOLS & CO.
P.O. Box 421
Millville, UT 84326
Phone No.: 435-755-6842
Fax No.: 435-753-2367
Website: www.echolsrifles.com
Email: echolslegend@comcast.net

DGS, INC.
404 N. Jackson
Casper, WY 82601
Phone No.: 307-315-6054
Website: www.rgsllc2010.com
Email: rgsllc2010@yahoo.com

DPMS FIREARMS
3312 12th Street SE
St. Cloud, MN 56304
Phone No.: 320-258-4448
Toll Free: 800-578-3767
Fax No.: 320-258-4449
Website: www.dpmsinc.com
Email: dpms@dpmsinc.com

DSA, INC.
P.O. Box 370
Barrington, IL 60011
Phone No.: 847-277-7258
Fax No.: 847-277-7259
Website: www.dsarms.com
Email: customerservice@dsarms.com

D.Z. ARMS
3840 SW 113th
Oklahoma City, OK 73173
Phone No.: 405-691-1215
Fax No.: 405-691 5088
Website: www.hepman.com
Email: dan@hepman.com

DAEWOO
No current commercial importation

DAKOTA ARMS, INC.
1310 Industry Road
Sturgis, SD 57785
Phone No.: 605-347-4686
Fax No.: 605-347-4459
Website: www.dakotaarms.com
Email: info@dakotarms.com

DALVAR OF U.S.A.
Please refer to the Radom listing.

DANIEL DEFENSE
101 Warfighter Way
Black Creek, GA 31308
Phone No.: 866-554-4867
Phone No.: 912-964-4238
Fax No.: 912-851-3248
Website: www.danieldefense.com

DARNE S.A.
Importer - Geoffroy Gournet
820 Paxinosa Ave.
Easton, PA 18042
Phone No.: 610-559-0710
Website: www.darneusa.com
Email: DarneUSA@yahoo.com

DAUDSONS ARMOURY
Industrial Estate, Kohat Road
Peshawar, 25210 PAKISTAN
Fax No.: 011-92-91-276059
Web site: www.daudsons.org
Email: info@daudsons.org

DAVID MILLER CO.
3131 E. Greenlee Rd.
Tucson, AZ 85716
Phone No.: 520-326-3117
Fax No.: 520-327-7672

DAVIDSON'S
6100 Wilkinson Dr.
Prescott, AZ 86301-6162
Phone No.: 800-367-4867
Fax No.: 928-776-0344
Website: www.galleryofguns.com

DEHANN SHOTGUNS LTD.
4660 E. 267 N.
Rigby, ID 83442
Phone No.: 208-538-6744
Website: www.DHshotguns.com
Email: info@DHshotguns.com

DEL-TON, INCORPORATED
330 Aviation Parkway
Elizabethtown, NC 28337
Phone No.: 910-645-2172
Fax No.: 910-645-2244
Website: www.del-ton.com
Email: sales@del-ton.com

DEMAS, Ets
Importer & Sales - please refer to Kebco listing.
Factory - Atelier Demas
11, rue Agricol Perdiguier
F-42000 St. Etienne, FRANCE
Fax No.: 011-33-477-813437
Website: www.demas.fr
Email: demas@demas.fr

DEMYAN
Factory
10 2nd Donskoy Lane
Moscow, 119071 RUSSIA
Fax: 011-7495-984-7629
Website: www.demyan.info
Email: info@demyan.info

DERYA HUNTING ARMS
Konya, Turkey
Phone No.: 011-90-332-524-6034
Fax No.: 011-90-332-524-6214
Website: www.deryasilah.com.tr
Email: deryasilah@hotmail.com

DESENZANI
Distributor - Kennedy Gunmakers
The Old Armoury, Bisley Camp,
Brookwood, Woking,
Surrey, U.K. GU24 0NY
Phone No.: 011-44-1483-486500
Fax No.: 011-44-1483-486580
Website: www.kennedyguns.com
Email: sales@kennedyguns.com

DESERT TACTICAL ARMS
P.O. Box 65816
Salt Lake City, UT 84165
Phone No.: 801-975-7272
Fax No.: 801-908-6425
Website: www.deserttacticalarms.com
Email: marketing@deserttacticalarms.com

DESERT TOYS
P.O. Box 5946
Mesa, AZ 85211-5946
Phone No.: 480.835.6643
Website: www.deserttoys.com

DETONICS
609 South Breese Street
Millstadt, IL 62260
Phone No.: 618-476-3200
Fax No.: 618-476-3226
Website: www.detonics.ws
Email: contactus@detonics.ws

DIAMONDBACK FIREARMS LLC
Marketing/Sales – please refer to Taurus International listing.
Factory
4135 Pine Tree Place
Cocoa, FL 32926
Phone No.: 888-380-2767
Website: www.diamondbackfirearms.com

DICKSON & MACNAUGHTON
21 Frederick Street
Edinburgh, SCOTLAND, U.K. EH2 2NE
Fax No.: 011-44-131-225-3658
Website: www.dicksonandmacnaughton.com

JOHN DICKSON & SON
Please refer to the Dickson & MacNaughton listing.

DIXIE GUN WORKS
P.O. Box 130
Union City, TN 38281
Phone No.: 731-885-0700
Fax No.: 731-885-0400
Website: www.dixiegunworks.com
Email: info@dixiegunworks.com

DLASK ARMS CORP.
16 7167 Vantage Way
British Columbia, V46 1K7 CANADA
Phone No.: 604-952-0837
Website: www.dlaskarms.com

DOLPHIN GUN COMPANY
2 Vine Street, Stamford
Lincolnshire PE9 1QE U.K.
Phone No.: 011-44-01780-481567
Website: www.dolphinguncompany.co.uk

DOUBLESTAR CORPORATION
Box 4671
Winchester, KY 40392
Phone No.: 859-745-1757
Fax No.: 859-745-4638
Website: www.star15.com
Website: www.jtdistributing.com
Email: sales@star15.com

DOUBLETAP DEFENSE LLC
6121 Baumgartner Crossing
St. Louis, MO 63129
Phone No.: 314-280-1411
Website: www.doubletapfirearmsllc.com

DRULOV
Factory – PPK s.r.o.
Dukelska 451
01 Holice, CZECH REPUBLIC
Phone No.:011-420-739-043-139
Website: www.zbrojovkaholice.cz
Email: info@zbrojovkaholice.cz

DUCKS UNLIMITED, INC.
One Waterfowl Way
Memphis, TN 38120-2351
Phone No.: 901-758-3825
Fax No.: 901-758-3850
website: www.ducks.org

DUMOULIN, ERNEST S.P.R.L.
Factory
10 Rue Florent Boclinville
B-4041 Vottem-Herstal, BELGIUM
Fax No.: 011-32-42280545
Website: www.dumoulin-herstal.com
Email: bdumoulin@dumoulin-herstal.com

DUMOULIN, HENRI & FILS
Herstal, BELGIUM

DUMOULIN HERSTAL S.A.
Factory
13 Rue du Tige
B-4040 Herstal, BELGIUM
Fax No.: 011-32-41-228-89-69
Website: www.dumoulin-herstal.com
Email: contact@dumoulin-herstal.be

DYNAMIT NOBEL
Factory - Dynamit Nobel Ammo Tec GmbH
Kronacher Strasse 63
Furth D-90765 GERMANY
Fax No.: 011-49-180-279-7797
Email: RWS@dynamit-nobel.com

E. ARTHUR BROWN COMPANY, INC.
4088 County Road 40 NW
Garfield, MN 56332
Toll Free.: 800-950-9088
Website: www.EABCO.com

E.D.M. ARMS
2410 West 350 North
Hurricane, UT 84737
Phone No.: 435-635-5233
Fax No.: 435-635-5258
Website: www.edmarms.com
Email: sales@edmarms.com

E.M.F. COMPANY
1900 E. Warner Ave., Suite 1-D
Santa Ana, CA 92705
Phone No.: 949-261-6611
Fax No.: 949-756-0133
Website: www.emf-company.com
Email: sales@emf-company.com

E.R. SHAW INC.
5312 Thoms Run Road
Bridgeville, PA 15017
Website: www.ershawbarrels.com

EAGLE ARMS
Please refer to Armalite listing.

EAGLE IMPORTS, INC.
1750 Brielle Ave., Unit B-1
Wanamassa, NJ 07712
Phone No.: 732-493-0302
Fax No.: 732-493-0301
Website: www.eagleimportsinc.com
Email: info@bersa.com

EAST RIDGE GUN COMPANY, INC.
6319 5th Ave.
Bancroft, WI 54921
Phone No.: 715-366-2006
Website: www.statearms.com
Email: eastrdge@uniontel.net

ED BROWN PRODUCTS, INC.
P.O. Box 492
Perry, MO 63462
Phone No.: 573-565-3261
Fax No.: 573-565-2791
Website: www.edbrown.com
Email: edbrown@edbrown.com

EFFEBI SRL di F. BERETTA
Via Bosellino, 43
I-25062 Concesio ITALY
Fax No.: 011-39-030-2180414
Website: www.effebisrl.eu
Email: info@effebisrl.eu

EGEMEN
Please refer to Vatan Hunting Firearms Co. listing.

ENTRÉPRISE ARMS INC.
15509 Arrow Hwy
Irwindale CA 91706-2002
Phone No.: 626-962-8712
Fax No.: 626-962-4692
Websites: www.entreprise.com

ERHARDT, DENNIS
4508 North Montana Ave.
Helena, MT 59602
Phone No.: 406-442-4533

ERN, MAX
Bergische Landstrasse 87
Leverkusen-Schlebusch D-51375 GERMANY
Fax No.: 011-49-0214-505860
Website: www.max-ern.de
Email: Max.Ern@t-online.de

ESCORT

Importer - please refer to Legacy Sports International listing.

Factory - Hatsan Arms Company

Izmir - Ankara Karayolu 28. km. No. 289
Kemalpasa 35170, Izmir - TURKEY
Fax No.: 011-90-232-878-9102-878-9723
Website: www.hatsan.com.tr
Email: info@hatsan.com.tr

ESSEX ARMS

(Parts Only)

P.O. Box 959
Hardwick, VT 05843
Phone No.: 802-472-3215
Fax No.: 802-472-3126
Website: www.essexarms.com
Email: user@essexarms.com

EUROARMS ITALIA s.r.l.

(formerly Armi San Paolo)

via Europa 172/A
I-25062 Concesio, (BS) ITALY
Fax No.: 011-39-30-218-0365
Website: www.euroarms.net
Email: info@euroarms.net

EUROPEAN AMERICAN ARMORY CORP.

P.O. Box 560746
Rockledge, FL 32959
Phone No.: 321-639-4842
Fax No.: 321-639-7006
Website: www.eaacorp.com
Email: eaacorp@eaacorp.com

EVOLUTION USA

P.O. Box 154
White Bird, ID 83554
Phone No.: 208-983-9208
Fax No. 208-983-0944
Website: www.evo-rifles.com
Email: evorifles@wildblue.net

EXCEL INDUSTRIES, INC.

4510 Carter Court
Chino, CA 91710
Phone No.: 909-627-2404
Fax No.: 909-627-7817
Website: www.excelarms.com
Email: excelind@verizon.net

F&D DEFENSE

2405 Lifehaus Industrial Dr. Suite 101
New Braunfels, TX 78130
Phone No.: 512-745-6482
Website: www.fd-defense.com
Email: sales@fd-defense.com

F.A.I.R. S.r.l.

Importer – please refer to Legacy Sports listing.

Importer – please refer to IFG listing.

Factory - Fabbrica Armi Isidoro Rizzini

Via Gitti, 41
I-25060 Marcheno (BS) ITALY
Fax No.: 011-39-030-861-0179
Website: www.fair.it
Email: info@fair.it

F.A.V.S.

Factory - Fabbrica Armi Valle Susa

Via Nazionale Moncenisio 35
10050 Villar Focchiardo (To) ITALY
Fax No.: 011-39-011-9645-496
Website: www.favsarmi.com
Email: info@favsarmi.com

FAS

Importer (Airguns only) – Airguns of Arizona

970 W. Elliot Road, Ste. 109
Gilbert, AZ 85233
Phone No.: 480-461-1113

Factory

P.O. Box 108
Via IV Novembre 54
I-20019 Settimo, Milanese (MI), ITALY
Website: www.fasdomino.com
Email:info@dominoguns.com

FEG

Factory - FEGARMY

1095 Budapest, Soroksari ut 158
Levelcim: H-1440 Budapest Pf. 6 HUNGARY
Fax No.: 011-361-280-6669

FIAS

Please refer to the Sabatti Armi listing.

FMK

Please refer to the American Tactical Imports listing.

FMR

3 rue Michelet
93500 Pantin FRANCE
Website: www.fmr-unique.com
Email: stephane-rolin@orange.fr

FNH USA

P.O. Box 697
McLean, VA 22101
Phone No.: 703-288-1292
Fax No.: 703-288-1730
Website: www.fnhusa.com
Email: info@fnhusa.com

Military Only

P.O. Box 896
McLean, VA 22101
Phone No.: 703-288-3500
Fax No.: 703-288-4505

Factory - F.N. Herstal S.A.

Voie de Liege, 33
Herstal, Belgium B4040
Fax No.: 011-324-240-8679
Website: www.fnherstal.com

FABARM S.p.A.
Importer - Fabarm USA
700 Lake Street
Cambridge, MD 21613
Phone No.: 410-901-1260
Website: www.fabarmusa.com
Factory - Fabbrica Breciana Armi
Via Averolda 31, Zona Industriale
I-25039 Travagliato, Brescia ITALY
Fax No.: 011-39-030-686-3684
Website: www.fabarm.com

FABBRI s.n.c.
Via Don Filippo Bassi 6
Nave (BS) I-25075 ITALY
Fax No.: 011-39-030-271-5031
Website: www.fabbri.it
Email: info@fabbri.it

FABRIQUE NATIONALE
Factory - Browning S.A.
Fabrique Nationale Herstal SA
Parc Industriel des Hauts Sarts
3me Ave. 25
B-4040 Herstal, BELGIUM
Fax No.: 011-32-42-40-5212

FABRYKA BRONI LUCZNIK - RADOM SP. ZO.O.
Ul. 1905 Roku 1/9
26-600 Radom, POLAND
Phone No.: 011-48-48-380-3122
Website: www.fabrykabroni.pl

FALCO, s.r.l.
Importer - Accardi Importer
7924 Timm Road
Vacaville, CA 95688
Phone No.: 707-888-8179
Fax No.: 707-446-7123
Website: www.accardi-importers.com
European distributor - please refer to Effebi listing.
Factory - FALCO, s.r.l.
via A. Gitti, 60
I-25060 Marcheno (Brescia) ITALY
Fax No.: 011-39-30-896-6413
Website: www.falcoarms.com
Email: info@falcoarms.com

FANZOJ, JOHANN
Factory - Fanzoj Jagdwaffen GmbH
Greisgasse 3
9170 Ferlach, AUSTRIA
Fax No.: 011-43-4227-2867
Website: www.fanzoj.com
Email: office@fanzoj.com

FARQUHARSON
Please refer to Ballard Arms listing.

FAUSTI, STEFANO SRL
Distributor & Repair Center - Fausti USA
3509 Shannon Park Dr.
Fredericksburg, VA 22408
Phone No.: 540-371-3287
Fax No.: 540-371-1170
Website: www.faustiusa.com
Email: info@faustiusa.com
Factory
Via Martiri Dell'Indipendenza, 70
I-25060 Marcheno (Brescia) ITALY
Fax No.: 011-39-030-861-0155
Website: www.faustistefanoarms.com
Email: info@faustistefanoarms.com

FEATHER USA
600 Oak Avenue
P.O. Box 247
Eaton, CO 80615
Phone No.: 800-519-0485
Fax No.: 970-206-1958
Website: www.featherusa.com
Email: featherawi@aol.com

FEINWERKBAU
Importer - please refer to Brenzovich listing.
Importer - please refer to Champion's Choice listing.
Importer - Gartland Precision LLC
200 East Bangor Street
Selby, SD 57472
Phone No.: 605-649-1173
Website: www.gartlandprecisionllc.com
Email: gartland.chuck@yahoo.com
Factory - Westinger & Altenburger GmbH
Neckarstrasse 43
D-78727 Oberndorf GERMANY
Fax No.: 011-49-7423-814-223
Website: www.feinwerkbau.de
Email: info@feinwerkbau.de

FERLACHER WAFFEN PRÄZISIONSTECHNIK PRODUCTIONS GmbH & CO. KG.
Maschinenhausgasse 5
A-9170 Ferlach AUSTRIA
Fax No.: 011-43-4227-3714
Website: www.ferlacherpraezision.com
Email: office@ferlacherpraezision.com

FERELL, ROGER
130 White Oak Ct.
Fayetteville, GA 30214-3885
Phone /Fax No.: 770-460-0533
Email: rogersgunworks@yahoo.com

FIELDSPORT
3313 W. South Airport Road
Traverse City, MI 49684
Phone No.: 231-933-0767
Fax No.: 231-933-0768
Website: www.fieldsportltd.com

FINNCLASSIC
Importer - Network Retailing LLC
22700 S Central Point Rd
Canby, OR 97013
Phone No.: 503-263 3787
Website: www.doublegunhq.com

FIREARMS INTERNATIONAL INC.
5200 Mitchelldale, Suite E-17
Houston, TX 77092
Phone No.: 713-462-4200
Fax No.: 713-681-5665
Website: www.highstandard.com
Email: info@highstandard.com

FIRESTORM
Master Distributor - SGS Imports Int'l, Inc.
1750 Brielle Ave., Unit B-1
Wanamassa, NJ 07712
Phone No.: 732-493-0302
Fax No.: 732-493-0301
Website: www.firestorm-sgs.com
Email: firestormsgs@aol.com

FIOCCHI OF AMERICA, INC.
(Ammunition & Components)
5030 Fremont Rd.
Ozark, MO 65721
Phone No.: 417-725-4118
Fax No.: 417-725-1039
Factory - Fiocchi Munizioni S.P.A.
Via Santa Barbara, 4
I-23900 Lecco ITALY
Fax No.: 011-039-0341473-203
Web site: www.fiocchigfl.it
Email: segreteria@fiocchigfl.it

FIVE RIVERS AUCTIONS, INC.
P.O. Box 344
42 South St., Suite #1
Milford, NH 03055
Phone No.: 603-673-7555
Website: www.fiveriversauctions.com
Email : info@fiveriversauctions.com

FLAVIO FARÈ
Cascina Cuccagnino, 23
Vinzaglio, (NO) ITALY
Fax: 011-39-0161-216956

FLODMAN GUNS SWEDEN
Skullman Enterprise AB
S-647 95 Akers Styckebruk
Jarsta SWEDEN
Fax No.: 011-46-159-30061
Website: www.flodman.com
Email: virve@flodman.com

FORBES RIFLE, LLC
600 Country Road
Westbrook, ME 04092
Phone No: 207-899-3254
Fax No.: 207-775-0011
Website: www.forbesriflellc.com

FORT SOE SIA
Factory - Science Industrial Association Fort of the Ministry of Internal Affairs of Ukraine
27, 600-letiya str.
Vinnitsa 21027 UKRAINE
Fax No.: 011-380-432-468-016-461-002
Website: www.fort.vn.ua
Email: siafort@ukr.net

A.H. FOX
Current mfg. only - please refer to Connecticut Shotgun Manufacturing Co. listing.
Older Fox Historical Research
Mr. John Callahan
P.O. Box 82
Southampton, MA 01073

FRANCHI, LUIGI
Importer - please refer to Benelli USA listing.
Website: www.franchiusa.com
Factory - Franchi, Luigi, S.p.A.
via Artigiani 1
I-25063 Gardone, VT (Brescia) ITALY
Fax No.: 011-039-030-8341-899
Website: www.franchi.com
Email: info@franchi.com

FRANCOTTE, AUGUST & CIE. S.A.
Please refer to Connecticut Shotgun Manufacturing listing.
New mfg. only – no service or parts for older mfg.

FRANKLIN ARMORY
305 Vineyard Town Center #220
Morgan Hill, CA 95037
Phone No.: 408-779=7560
Website: www.franklinarmory.com

FRASER, DANL. & CO.
Please refer to the Dickson & MacNaughton listing.

FREEDOM ARMS
P.O. Box 150
314 Hwy. 239
Freedom, WY 83120
Phone No.: 307-883-2468
Fax No.: 307-883-2005
Website: www.freedomarms.com
Email: freedom@freedomarms.com

FULTON ARMORY
8725 Bollman Place Suite #1
Savage, MD 20763
Phone No.: 301-490-9485
Fax No.: 301-490-9547
Website: www.fulton-armory.com

GA PRECISION
1141 Swift Street
N. Kansas City, MO 64116
Phone No.: 816-221-1844
Website: www.gaprecision.net

GWACS ARMORY
907 S. Detroit Ave
6th Floor
Tulsa, OK 74120
Website: www.gwacsarmory.com
Email: sales@gwacsarmory.com

GALAZAN
Please refer to Connecticut Shotgun Manufacturing Co. listing.

GALIL
No current U.S. importation - semi-auto rifle configuration was banned April, 1998.
Israel Weapon Industries Ltd.
P.O Box 63 Ramat Hashron
47100 ISRAEL
Website: www.israel-weapon.com
Email: info@israel-weapon.com

GAMBA, RENATO
Please refer to Bremac SRL listing.

GAMBARMI
Please refer to Renato Gamba listing.

GARBI
Importer - please refer to William Larkin Moore & Co. listing.
Factory - Armas Garbi
Urki, 12-14
E-20600 Eibar, SPAIN
Website: www.armasgarbi.com

GATLING GUN COMPANY
Please also refer to U.S. Armament Corp. listing.
Battery Gun Co.
5500 Pleasant St.
Metamora, MI 48455
Phone No.: 810-678-8060
Fax: 810-678-2054
Website: www.batteryguncompany.com

GAUCHER
Please refer to Bretton-Gaucher listing.

GENTRY CUSTOM LLC
314 N. Hoffman
Belgrade, MT 59714
Phone No.: 406-388-GUNS
Website: www.gentrycustom.com
Email: gentryshop@earthlink.net

GERMAN SPORT GUNS GmbH
Importer - please refer to American Tactical Imports listing.
Oesterweg 21
Ense-Höingen, D-59469 GERMANY
Fax No.: 011-49-2938-97837-130
Website: www.gsg-5.de

GIBBS, GEORGE
The Granary, Brimslade, Marlborough
Wiltshire, U.K. SN8 4NG
Website: www.gibbsgunmakers.com
Email: gibbsltd@btinernet.com

GIBBS RIFLE CO.
Please refer to Navy Arms listing.

GIL, ANTONIO & CO.
Factory
C/Ibargain, 8-2
Eibar (Guipuzcoa), SPAIN 20600
Fax No.: 011-34-943-700699

GILA RIVER GUN WORKS
P.O. Box 6072
Pocatello, ID 83205
Phone No.: 208-241-2718
Website: www.michaelscherz.com
Email: gilagunworks@aol.com

GIRSAN MACHINE & LIGHT WEAPON INDUSTRY COMPANY
Factory
Batlama Deresi Mevkii Sunta Sokak No. 19
Giresun, TURKEY
Fax No.: 011-90-454-215-3928
Website: www.yavuz16.com
Email: satis@yavuz16.com

GLANZIG PRÄZISIONS-UND SPORTWAFFEN JAGDZUBEHÖR
Werkstrasse 9
A-9170 Ferlach, AUSTRIA
Fax No.: 011-43(0)4227-4851

GLOCK, INC.
Importer
6000 Highlands Pkwy.
Smyrna, GA 30082
Fax No.: 770-433-8719
Website: www.glock.com

Factory - Glock Ges.m.b.H.
Nelkengasse 3, POB 9
A-2232 Deutsch-Wagram AUSTRIA
Fax No.: 011-43-2247-90300312

GRAND POWER s.r.o.
Importer - please refer to STI International listing.
Po ovnícka 29
974 01 Banská Bystrica - Šalková
SLOVAKIA
Fax No.: 011-421-48-414-8754
Website: www.grandpower.eu
Email: sales@grandpower.eu

GRANGER, G.
U.S. Agent – please refer to Jean-Jacques Perodeau listing.
Factory
66 Cours Fauriel
F-42100 St. Etienne FRANCE
Website: www.ggranger.com
Email: g.granger2@wanadoo.fr

GRANITE MOUNTAIN ARMS, INC.
P.O. Box 72736
Phoenix, AZ 85050
Phone No.: 602-996-9009
Website: www.granitemountainarms.com
Email: jmbroden@earthlink.net

GRANT, STEPHEN
Factory - please refer to Atkin, Grant & Lang listing.

GREAT WESTERN
Please refer to E.M.F. listing.

GREEN, ROGER
11611 E. Tom Sawyer Road
Evansville, WY 82636
Phone No.: 307-473-1112
Fax No.: 307-473-1516
Website: www.rogermgreen.com
Email: rmgreen@rogermgreen.com

GREENER, W. W.
U.S. Agent - Kirk Merrington
207 Sierra Road
Kerryville, TX 78028
Phone No.: 830-367-2937
Sales/Administration Offices
Poachers Pocket, Stoppers Hill, Brinkworth
Chippenham, Wiltshire, SN15 5AW U.K.
Fax No.: 011-44-1666-510898
Website: www.wwgreener.com
Email: sales@wwgreener.com
Factory
The Mews, Hagley Hall
Hagley DY9 9LG U.K.

GREYBULL PRECISION
4375 Birchwood Drive
Loveland, CO 80538
Phone No.: 888-427-4868
Fax No.: 970-797-4810
Website: www.greybullprecision.com
Email: info@greybullprecision.com

GRIFFIN & HOWE
Store Location (Gunsmithing also)
33 Claremont Road
Bernardsville, NJ 07924
Phone No.: 908-766-2287
Fax No.: 908-766-1068
Website: www.griffinhowe.com
Store Location
340 West Putnam Ave.
Greenwich, CT 06830
Phone No.: 203-618-0270
Fax No.: 203-618-0419
Website: www.griffinhowe.com
Shooting School & Events
270 Stanhope Rd.
Andover, NJ 07821
Phone No.: 973-398-4330

GRULLA ARMAS, S.L.
Importer – please refer to Harry Marx Hi-Grade Imports listing.
Factory - Grulla Armas
P.O. Box 453
Avda. de Otaola, I2
E-20600 Eibar (Guipuzcoa) SPAIN
Fax No.: 011-34-9-43-702133
Website: www.grullaarmas.com
Email: usobiaga@grullaarmas.com

GRUND, KARL
Pfarrhofgasse 2
A-9170 Ferlach, AUSTRIA
Fax No.: 011-43-4227-2256
Website: www.jagdwaffen-juch-grund-ferlach.at

GRÜNIG & ELMIGER AG
U.S. representative - please refer to Gunsmithing, Inc. listing.
U.S. representative - please refer to Brenzovich listing.
U.S. representative - please refer to Champion's Choice listing.
Factory
Industriestr. 22
CH-6102 Malters SWITZERLAND
Fax No.: 011-041-499-9049
Website: www.gruenel.ch
Email: gruenel@gruenel.ch

GSI (GUN SOUTH INC.)
Please refer to Merkel USA listing.

G.U. INC.
Please refer to SKB Shotguns listing.

THE GUN ROOM CO., LLC
Please refer to Noreen Firearms LLC listing.

GUNCRAFTER INDUSTRIES
171 Madison 1510
Huntsville, AR 72740
Phone No.: 479-665-2466
Website: www.guncrafterindustries.com

GUNSMOKE
9690 W. 44th Ave
Wheat Ridge, CO 80033
Phone No.: 303-456-4545
Website: www.gunsmokeguns.com
Email: info@gunsmokeguns.com

GUNSMOKE ENTERPRISES
P.O. Box 2537
Okeechobee, FL 34973
Phone No.: 863-763-1582
Fax No.: 863-357-3737
Website: www.gunsmokeenterprises.net
Email: gsei@comcast.net

GUNWERKS
P.O. Box 2330
Cody, WY 82414
Phone No.: 866-754-7618
Website: www.gunwerks.com
Email: customerservice@gunwerks.com

HHF
Please refer to Huglu listing.

HMS PRÄZISIONSTECHNIK GmbH
Gewebestrasse 11
A-5301 Eugendorf, AUSTRIA
Fax No.: 011-43-06225-8286
Website: www.hms-strasser.at

H & R 1871, LLC
Harrington & Richardson (post-1991 mfg. only)
P.O. Box 1871
Madison, NC 27025
Phone No.: 866-776-9292
Fax No.: 336-548-7801
Website: www.hr1871.com
Email: hr1871@hr1871.com

H-S PRECISION, INC.
1301 Turbine Dr.
Rapid City, SD 57703
Phone No.: 605-341-3006
Fax No.: 605-342-8964
Website: www.hsprecision.com

HABSBURG, LINIE
Griesgasse 3
A-9170 Ferlach Austria
Fax No.: 011-43-4227-533630
Website: www.linie-habsburg.com
Email: ferlach@linie-habsburg.com

HAENEL, C.G. GmbH
Schutzenstrasse 26
98527 Suhl, GERMANY
Phone No.: 011-49-0-3681-854-257
Fax No.: 011-49-0-3681-854-201
Website: www.cg-haenel.de
Email: info@cg-haenel.de

HALO ARMS, LLC
P.O. Box 552
Phoenixville, PA 19460
Phone No.: 484-614-4860
Fax No.: 610-933-0186
Website: www.haloarms.com
Email: mail@haloarms.com

HAMBRUSCH JAGDWAFFEN GmbH
Factory - Hambrusch Jagdwaffen Gesellschaft
Gartengasse 4
A-9170 Ferlach, AUSTRIA
Fax No.: 011-43-4227-4106
Website: www.ferlachguns.com
Email: hambrush@ferlachguns.com

HÄMMERLI AG
Importer - please refer to Umarex USA
Importer, Sales & Service – please refer to Larry's Guns Inc. listing.
Importer - please refer to Champion's Choice listing.
Importer - please refer to Brenzovich Firearms listing.
Repair/Gunsmithing Services - HÄMMERLI AG
10-Ring-Service, Inc.
2227 West Lou Drive
Jacksonville, FL 32216
Phone No.: 904-724-7419
Fax No.: 904-724-7149
Factory - please refer to Walther factory listing.

HARRISON & HUSSEY
Please refer to Cogswell & Harrison listing.

HARRY MARX HI-GRADE IMPORTS
925 I Street
Los Banos, CA 93635
Phone No.: 209-827-1177
Fax No.: 209-826-7222
Website: www.higradeimports.com
Email: Hi-gradeimports@mindspring.com

HARTMANN & WEISS GmbH
Rahlstedter Bahnhofstr. 47
22143 Hamburg, GERMANY
Phone No.: 011-49-40-677-5585
Fax No.: 011-49-40-677-5592
Website: www.hartmannandweiss.com
Email: info@hartmannundweiss.com

HATCHER GUN COMPANY
76650 Road 342
Elsie, NE 69134
Phone No.: 308-228-2454
Fax No.: 308-228-2522
Website: www.hatchergun.com
Email: th@hatchergun.com

HATFIELD GUN COMPANY LLC
1247 Rand Road
Des Plaines, IL 60016
Phone No.: 847-768-1000
Fax No.: 847-768-1001

HATFIELD'S
2028 Frederick Ave.
St. Joseph, MO 64501
Phone No.: 816-233-9106
Email: TLRiver@aol.com

HATSAN ARMS COMPANY
Importer - please refer to Legacy Sports International LLC listing.
Izmir-Ankara Karayolu 28.km. No. 289
Kemalpasa 35170 Izmir TURKEY
Fax No.: 011-90-232-878-9102
website: www.hatsan.com.tr
Email: info@hatsan.com.tr

KARL HAUPTMANN JAGDWAFFEN
Bahnhofstrasse 5
A-9170 Ferlach, AUSTRIA
Fax No.: 011-43-4227-3435
Website: www.hauptmann-rifles.com
Email: office@hauptmann-rifles.com

HASKELL MFG. INC.
Please refer to Hi-Point listing.

HAUSMANN & CO. GmbH
Ressnig 39
A-9 170 Ferlach, AUSTRIA
Phone No.: 011-43-4227-30920
Website: www.hausmann-co-guns.com

HECKLER & KOCH, INC.
Importer - Merkel USA
5675 Transport Blvd.
Columbus, GA 31907
Phone No.: 706-568-1906
Fax No.: 706-568-9151
Website: www.hk-usa.com
Factory - Heckler & Koch GmbH
Alte Steige 7
P.O. Box 1329
D-78722 Oberndorf Neckar GERMANY
Fax No.: 011-49-7423-792350
Website: www.heckler-koch.com

HEAD DOWN PRODUCTS
Distributor – please refer to American Tactical Imports listing.
4031 Fambrough Court, Suite 300
Dallas, GA 30770-485-7015
Phone No.: 404-590-AR15
Fax No.: 770-421-6345
Website: www.headdownproducts.com

N.L. HEINEKE, INC.
201 South Second Street
Laramie, WY 82070
Phone No.: 307-745-8592
Fax No.: 307-745-4198
Website: www.nlheineke.com
Email: nlh@nlheineke.com

HEINIE SPECIALTY PRODUCTS
(Repair and Sights only)
301 Oak Street
Quincy, IL 62301
Phone No.: 217-228-952
Fax No.: 217-228-9502
Website: www.heinie.com
Email: rheinie@heinie.com

HEIRLOOM ARMES
5996 5th St. SW
Howard Lake, MN 55349
Phone No.: 320-963-5551
Web site: www.heirloomarmes.com
Email: dln@lakedalelink.net

HEIZER FIREARMS
St. Louis, MO
Phone/Fax No.: 855-243-4937
Website: www.heizerfirearms.com

HELLIS, CHARLES
Website: www.hellis.com
Email: info@hellis.com

HENRY, ALEX
Please refer to the Dickson & MacNaughton listing.

HENRY REPEATING ARMS COMPANY
59 East 1st Street
Bayonne, NJ 07002
Phone No.: 201-858-4400
Fax No.: 201-858-4435
Website: www.henry-guns.com
Email: info@henryrepeating.com

HERA ARMS
Ziegelhüttenweg 5
Triefenstein D-97855 GERMANY
Fax No.: 011-49-0939-878723
Website: www.hera-arms.com

HERITAGE AUCTION GALLERIES
3500 Maple Ave., 17th Floor
Dallas, TX 75219
Phone No.: 800-872-6467
Website: www.ha.com

HERITAGE MANUFACTURING, INC.
4600 NW 135th St.
Opa Locka, FL 33054
Phone No.: 305-685-5966
Fax No.: 305-687-6721
Website: www.heritagemfg.com
Email: infohmi@heritagemfg.com

HERMANN HISTORICA AUCTIONS
Lindprunstrasse 16
D-80335 München GERMANY
Fax No.: 011-49-089-523-7103
Web site: www.hermann-historica.com
Email: contact@hermann-historica.com

HERO GUNS INC.
521 S. College Street
Winchester, TN 37398
Phone No.: 931-962-4376
Fax No.: 931-962-4348
Website: www.heroguns.com

HEYM AG
Importer - Double Gun Imports LLC
3416 Rosedale
Dallas, TX 75205
Phone No.: 214-606-2566
Website: www.heymusa.com
Email: info@heymusa.com
Factory - Heym Waffenfabrik AG
Am Aschenbach 2
D-98646 Gleichamberg GERMANY
Fax No.: 011-49-368-75-63222
Website: www.heym-waffenfabrik.de
Email: heym-waffenfabrik@t-online.de

HIENDLMAYER, KLAUS
Please refer to Waffen Hiendlmayer listing.

HI-POINT FIREARMS
U.S. Marketer - MKS Supply, Inc.
8611-A North Dixie Drive
Dayton, OH 45414
Phone No.: 877-425-4867
Fax No.: 937-454-0503
Website: www.hi-pointFirearms.com
Email: mkshpoint@aol.com

HIGH STANDARD MANUFACTURING CO.
5751 Mitchelldale, Ste. B-11
Houston, TX 77092
Phone No.: 713-462-4200
Fax No.: 713-681-5665
Website: www.highstandard.com
Email: info@highstandard.com

HIGH TECH CUSTOMS
3109 N. Cascade Ave., Ste. 103
Colorado Springs, CO 80907
Phone No.: 719-667-1090
Fax No.: 719-632-4505
Website: www.htcustoms.com
Email: htcustoms@pcisys.net

HILL COUNTRY RIFLE COMPANY
5726 Safari Dr.
New Braunfels, TX 78132
Phone No.: 830-609-3139
Fax No.: 830-625-4020
Website: www.hillcountryrifles.com
Email: sales@hillcountryrifles.com

GEORGE HOENIG INC.
4357 Frozen Dog Rd.
Emmett, ID 83617
Phone No.: 208-365-7716
Fax No.: 208-365-3472
Email: gnhoenig@msn.com

HOFER-JAGDWAFFEN, PETER
Kirchgasse 24
A-9170 Ferlach, AUSTRIA
Phone No.: 011-43-4227-3683
Fax No.: 011-43-4227-3683-30
Website: www.hoferwaffen.com
Email: peterhofer@hoferwaffen.com

P.L. HOLEHAN, INC.
5758 E. 34th St.
Tucson, AZ 85711
Phone No.: 520-745-0622
Fax No.: 520-745-2248
Website: www.plholehancustomrifles.com
Email: plholehan@theriver.com

HOLLAND & HOLLAND LTD.
H&H - New York
10 East 40th Street, Ste. 1910
New York, NY 10016
Phone No.: 212-752-7755
Fax No.: 212-752-6975
Website: www.hollandandholland.com
Email: gunroomny@hollandandholland.com
Factory
Attn: Customer Service-BB
33 Bruton Street
London, U.K. W1J 6HH
Phone No.: 011-44-(0)20-7499-4411
Fax No.: 011-44-(0)20-7408-7962
Email: gunroomuk@hollandandholland.com

HOLLOWAY & NAUGHTON
Please refer to Premier English Shotguns, Ltd. listing.

HORTON, LEW, DIST. CO.
Please refer to Lew Horton Dist. Co. listing.

HOULDING PRECISION FIREARMS
2980 Falcon Drive
Madera, CA 93637
Phone No.: 559-675-9922
Website: www.houldingfirearms.com

HOWA
Importer - please refer to Legacy Sports listing.

HUGLU
Importer - please refer to CZ-USA listing.
Importer – please refer to TR Imports, Inc. listing.
Factory - Huglu S.S. AV Tufekleri Kooperatifi
Antalya Cad. No. 58
TR-42710 Huglu-Beyashir-Konya TURKEY
Fax No.: 011-90-332-5161031 130
Website: www.huglu.com.tr
Email: sales@huglu.com.tr
Warranty & Service - (Huglu USA guns only) - please refer to DeHann listing.

HULDRA ARMS
512 Laurel Street
P.O. Box 5055
Brainerd, MN 56401
Phone No.: 218-829-3521
Website: www.huldraarms.com
Email: service@huldraarms.com

IFG (ITALIAN FIREARMS GROUP)
P.O. Box 560746
Rockledge, FL 32956
Phone No.: 321-639-4842
Fax No.: 321-639-7006

I.O. INC.
P.O. Box 847
Monroe, NC 28110
Phone No.: 866-882-1479
Fax No.: 704-225-8895
Website: www.ioinc.us
Email: info@ioinc.us

IGA SHOTGUNS
Importer – please refer to Stoeger Industries, Inc. listing.

ISSC HANDELSGESELLSCHAFT
Importer – please refer to Legacy Sports listing.
Factory
Hannesgrub 3
A-4910 Ried/Innkreis AUSTRIA
Fax: 011-43-7752-21271
Website: www.issc.at
Email: issc@inext.at

IBERIA FIREARMS
Please refer to Hi-Point listing.

INFINITY FIREARMS
Distributor - please refer to JP Enterprises listing.
Manufacturer - Strayer Voight, Inc.
3435 Roy Orr Blvd., Ste. 200
Grand Prairie, TX 75050
Phone No.: 972-513-1911
Fax No.: 972-513-0575
Website: www.sviguns.com
Email: info@sviguns.com
Factory - INTERTEX-Maschinenbau GmbH & Co.
Ludwigstrasse 24-28
D-73054 Eislingen GERMANY
Fax no.: 011-49-7161-98-40-5-50
Email: intertex@t-online.de

INNOGUN
AmBlassenpfad 20
D-97776 Obersfeld, GERMANY
Fax No.: 011-49-9350-909063
Website: www.innogun.de
Email: Christian.scherpf@innogun.de

INTERARMS ARSENAL
Please refer to High Standard listing.

INTERSTATE ARMS CORP.
6 Dunham Road
Billerica, MA 01821
Phone No.: 800-243-3006
Phone No.: 978-667-7060
Fax No.: 978-671-0023
Website: www.interstatearms.com

INVESTARM, s.p.a.
Factory - Fabbrica D'Armi
via Zanardelli, 210
I-25060 Marcheno, Brescia ITALY
Fax No.: 011-39-030-861-285
Website: www.investarm.com
Email: info@investarm.com

IRON BRIGADE ARMORY
100 Radcliffe Circle
Jacksonville, NC 28546
Phone No.: 910-455-3834
Fax No.: 910-346-1134
Website: www.deathfromafar.com

ISRAEL WEAPON INDUSTRIES LTD. (I.W.I.)
Importer –IWI US, Inc. (centerfire firearms)
P.O. Box 12607
Harrisburg, PA 17112
Phone No.: 717-695-2081
Website: www.iwi.us
Importer – Please refer to Umarex USA listing.

ITHACA GUN COMPANY LLC
Repair & Service - please refer to Ithaca Guns USA, LLC listing.

ITHACA GUN COMPANY
420 N. Warpole St.
Upper Sandusky, OH 43351
Phone No.: 877-648-4222
Fax No.: 419-294-3230
Web site: www.ithacagun.com

IVER JOHNSON ARMS, INC.
1840 Baldwin Street, Unit 10
Rockledge, FL 32955
Phone No.: 321-636-3377
Fax No.: 321-632-7745
Website: www.iverjohnsonarms.com

IZHMASH
Exclusive importer - see RWC Group LLC listing.
Factory - Izhmash, Concern OJSC
3 Derjabn Pr. Izhevsk
Izhevsk, RUSSIA 426006
Fax No.: 011-73499-249-5326
Website: www.izhmash.ru
Email: itc@izhmash.ru

J.B. CUSTOM INC.
16335 Lima Rd., Bldg. #5
Huntertown, IN 46748
Phone No.: 260-338-1894
Fax No.: 260-338-1585
Website: www.jbcustom.com
Email: jbcjim@gmail.com

J.L.D. ENTERPRISES, INC.
Please refer to PTR 91 Inc. listing.

JP ENTERPRISES, INC.
P.O Box 378
Hugo, MN 55038
Phone No.: 651-426-9196
Fax No.: 651-426-2472
Website: www.jprifles.com
Email: service@jprifles.com

J R CARBINES, LLC
Distributor – please refer to EMF Company listing.

J R DISTRIBUTING
15634 Tierra Rejada Rd.
Moorpark, CA 93021
Fax No.: 805-529-2368

JAGD-UND SPORTWAFFEN SUHL GmbH
Distributor - please refer to Merkel USA listing.
Factory - please refer to Merkel listing.

JACK FIRST, INC.
Gun Parts/Accessories/Service
1201 Turbine Dr.
Rapid City, SD 57703
Phone No.: 605-343-9544
Fax No.: 605-343-9420
Website: www.jackfirstgun.com

JACKSON RIFLES
(Parts only)
Parton, Castle Douglas
Scotland DG7 3NL U.K.
Fax No.: 011-44-1644-470227
Website: www.jacksonrifles.com

JAMES D. JULIA, INC. (AUCTIONS)
P.O. Box 830, Rte. 201
Skowhegan Rd.
Fairfield, ME 04937
Phone No.: 207-453-7125
Fax No.: 207-453-2502
Website: www.juliaauctions.com

JAMES RIVER ARMORY
3601 Commerce Drive
Suite 110
Halethorpe, MD 21227
Phone No.: 410-242-6991
Website: www.jamesriverarmory.com
Email: jamesriverarmory@gmail.com

JANZ GmbH
Factory – JANZ Präzisionstechnik GmbH
Lütjenburger Str. 84
D-23714 Malente/Holstein GERMANY
Fax No.: 011-49-4523-201655
Website: www.jtl.de/english/revolver
Email: info@jtl.de

JARRETT RIFLES, INC.
383 Brown Road
Jackson, SC 29831
Phone No.: 803-471-3616
Fax No.: 803-471-9246
Website: www.jarrettrifles.com

JEAN-MARC STEVAUX, S.P.R.L.
Avenue de la Vecquée, 222
5020 Malonne, BELGIUM
Fax No.: 011-32-8145-0956
Website: www.armurerie-stevaux.be
Email: info@armurerie-stevaux.be

JEFFERY, W.J. & CO., LTD.
Please refer to the J. Roberts & Son listing.

JEFFERY SHARPS
Please refer to Ballard Arms listing.

JIMENEZ ARMS
Distributor - Shining Star Investments LLC
860 Hembry St., Ste. 403
Lewisville, TX 75057
Phone No.: 866-906-7356
Fax No.: 972-906-7356
Website: www.shiningstardist.com
Email: Contact@shiningStarDist.com

JOHANNSEN RIFLES
Importer - please refer to New England Custom Gun Service listing.
Factory - Reimer Johannsen GmbH
Haart 49
D-24534 Neumünster GERMANY
Fax No.: 011-49-4321-29325
Website: www.johannsen-jagd.de
Email: info@johannsen-jagd.de

JOHNSON AUTOMATIC
Restorations only - Miltech Arms
P.O. Box 322
Los Altos, CA 94023
Phone No.: 650-948-3500
Fax No.: 408-255-7144
Website: www.miltecharms.com

JUST, JOSEF
Hauptplatz 18
A-9170, Ferlach, AUSTRIA
Fax No.: 011-43-04227-2273
Website: www.jagdwaffen-just.at
Email: office@jagdwaffen-just.at

JUST RIGHT CARBINES
Distributor – LDB Supply LLC
812 E. Franklin St.
Dayton, OH 45459
Phone No.: 855-LDB-GUNS

JUSTIN CUSTOM GUNS
152 West Sunset Ave.
Toquerville, UT 84774
Phone No.: 435-635-7808
Website: www.justincustomguns.com
Email: justin@justincustomguns.com

K-VAR CORP.
4001 S. Decatur Blvd. #37383
Las Vegas, NV 89103
Phone No.: 702-364-8880
Fax No.: 702-307-2303
Website: www.k-var.com

KDF, INC.
(Gunsmithing, Accessories, & Parts)
2485 Highway 46 North
Seguin, TX 78155
Phone No.: 800-KDF-GUNS
Phone No.: 830-379-8141
Fax No.: 830-379-8144
Website: www.kdfguns.com

KAHR ARMS
130 Goddard Memorial Dr.
Worcester, MA 01603
Phone No.: 508-795-3919
Fax No.: 508-795-7046
Website: www.kahr.com
Website: www.kahrshop.com

KEBCO, LLC
P.O. Box 300
Hanover, PA 17331
Phone No.: 301-460-9563
Fax No.: 717-633-9365
Website: www.kebcollc.com
Email: info@kebcollc.com

KEL-TEC CNC INDUSTRIES, INC.
P.O Box 236009
Cocoa, FL 32923
Phone No.: 321-631-0068
Fax No.: 321-631-1169
Website: www.keltecweapons.com
Email: ktcustserv@kel-tec-cnc.com

KEMEN
Importer - please refer to Fieldsport listing.
Factory - Armas Kemen, S.L.
Ermuraranbide, 14 - Apartado n. 60
20870 Elgoibar (Guipuzcoa), SPAIN
Fax No.: 011-34-43-74-4401
Website: www.sport-kemen.com
Email: kemen@sport-kemen.com

KEPPELER TECHNISCHE ENTWICKLUNG GmbH
Friedrich-Reinhardt Strasse 4
D-74427 Fichtenberg, GERMANY
Fax No.: 011-49-07971-91-1243
Website: www.keppeler-te.de
Email: keppeler.te@t-online.de

KEVIN'S FINE OUTDOOR GEAR & APPAREL
122 Plantation Oaks Drive
Thomasville, GA 31792
Website: www.kevinscatalog.com

KEYSTONE SPORTING ARMS
155 Sodom Road
Milton, PA 17847
Phone No.: 800-742-0455
Fax No.: 570-742-1455
Website: www.crickett.com
Email: info@crickett.com

KHAN
Importer - please refer to Mossberg listing.
Headquarters
Inkilap Mahallesi Alemdag Caddesi
Site Yolu Sok. No: 3 34768
Umraniye/Istanbul, TURKEY
Fax No.: 011-90-216-632-7444
Website: www.khanshotguns.com
Email: info@khanshotguns.com

KILIMANJARO RIFLES
707 Richards Street, Ste. 201
Honolulu, HI 96813
Toll Free: 877-351-4440
Fax No.: 808-537-5955
Website: www.kilimanjarorifles.com
Email: info@kilimanjarorifles.com

KIMAR SRL
Importer - please refer to Traditions listing.
Factory
Via Milano 2
I-25020 Azzano, Mella (BS) ITALY
Fax No.: 011-39-030-974-9232
Website: www.kimar.com
Email: info@kimar.com

KIMBER
Corporate Offices - Kimber Mfg., Inc.
555 Taxter Road, Suite 235
Elmsford, NY 10523
Phone No.: 888-243-4522
Fax No.: 406-758-2223
Website: www.kimberamerica.com
Email: info@kimberamerica.com

KNESEK GUNS INC.
1204 Knesek Lane
Van Buren, AR 72956
Phone No.: 479-474-1680
Fax No.: 479-471-0377
Website: www.knesekguns.com
Email: sales@knesekguns.com

KNIGHT'S ARMAMENT COMPANY
701 Columbia Blvd.
Titusville, FL 32780
Phone No.: 321-607-9900
Website: www.knightarmco.com

KOFS LTD.
Isparta Organize Sanayi Bolgesi
109. Cad. No. 5 Isparta, TURKEY
Phone No.: 011-90-246-5565-486
Fax No.: 011-90-246-5565-487
Website: www.kofs.com.tr
Email: info@kofs.com.tr

KOLAR ARMS
1925 Roosevelt Ave.
Racine, WI 53406
Phone No.: 262-554-0800
Fax No.: 262-554-9093
Website: www.kolararms.com
Email: info@kolararms.com

KORA BRNO
Factory - Kroko a.s.
Hybesova 46
CZ-602 00 Brno, CZECH REPUBLIC
Fax No.: 011-420-5-43244346
Website: www.korabrno.cz
Email: kroko3@korabrno.cz

KORTH
Repair - Earl's Repair Service, Inc.
437 Chandler Street (rear)
Tewksbury, MA 01876
Phone No.: 978-851-2656
Fax No.: 978-851-9462
Website: www.korthusa.com
Factory - Korth Vertriebsgesellschaft GmbH
Justus-Kilian Strasse 3
Lollar, GERMANY D-35457
Fax No.: 011-49-06408300299
Website: www.korthwaffen.de
Email: info@korthwaffen.de

KOSCHAT, JAKOB
12 November-Strasse 3
A-9170 Ferlach, AUSTRIA
Fax No.: 011-43-4227-2278
Website: www.jagdwaffen-ferlach.at
Email: koschat@jagdwaffen-ferlach.at

KRAL AV
Fatih Mahallesi
Üzümlü, Beysehir, Konya, TURKEY
Fax No.: 011-090-332-524-6871
Website: www.kralav.com
Email: export@kralav.com

KRASSNIK, VALENTIN
Maschinenhausgasse 5
Ferlach, A-9170 AUSTRIA
Website: www.ferlacherpraezision.com
Email: v.krassnik@ferlacherpraezision.com

KRICO
European Sales - please refer to Marocchi listing.
Factory - Krico Jagd-und Sportwaffen GmbH
Nurnberger Strasse 6
Pyrbaum, D-90602 GERMANY
Fax No.: 011-49-091-80-2661
Website: www.krico.de
Email: info@krico.de

KRIEGHOFF, H., GUN CO.
Importer - Krieghoff International, Inc.
P.O. Box 549
7528 Easton Rd.
Ottsville, PA 18942
Phone No.: 610-847-5173
Fax No.: 610-847-8691
Website: www.krieghoff.com
Email: info@krieghoff.com
Factory - H. Krieghoff GmbH
Boschstrasse 22
D-89079 Ulm, GERMANY
Fax No.: 011-49-731-40-18270
Website: www.krieghoff.de

KRISS SYSTEMS SA
Importer/US Factory – Kriss USA
P.O. Box 8928
Virginia Beach, VA 23450
Phone No.: 757-821-1089
Fax No.: 757-821-1094
Website: www.kriss-tdi.com
Factory
Ch. De la Vuarpilliere 35 1260 Nyon
SWITZERLAND
Phone No.: 011-41-22-363-7820
Fax No.: 011-41-22-363-7821

KUFSTEINER WAFFENSTUBE
Carl Wagner Strasse 1-2
Kufstein, AUSTRIA A-6330
Fax No.: 011-43-5372-61887
Website: www.reppelinger-waffen.at

L.A.R. MANUFACTURING, INC.
4133 Farm Road
West Jordan, UT 84088 4997
Phone No.: 801-280-3505
Fax No.: 801-280-1972
Website: www.largrizzly.com
Email: guns@largrizzly.com

LRB ARMS
96 Cherry Lane
Floral Park, NY 11001
Phone No.: 516-327-9061
Website: www.lrbarms.com

LWRC INTERNATIONAL, LLC
815 Chesapeake Dr.
Cambridge, MD 21613
Phone No.: 410-901-1348
Fax No.: 410-228-1775
Website: www.lwrci.com

LAKESIDE MACHINE LLC
1213 Industrial Street
Horseshoe Bend, AR 72512
Phone No.: 870-670-4999
Website: www.lakesideguns.com
Email: sales@lakesideguns.com

LANBER ARMAS S.A.
Factory - ComLanber, S.A.
C/Zubiaurre 3
E-48250 Zaldibar (Vizcaya) SPAIN
Fax No.: 011-34-94-6827999
Website: www.lanber.net
Email: lanber@euskalnet.net

LANG, JOSEPH
Please refer to the Atkin, Grant & Lang Ltd. listing.

LARRY'S GUNS INC.
56 West Gray Road
Gray, ME 04039
Phone No: 207-657-4559
Fax No.: 207-657-3429
Website: www.larrysguns.com
Email: info@larrysguns.com

LARUE TACTICAL
850 Country Road 177
Leander, TX 78641
Phone No.: 512-259-1585
Website: www.laruetactical.com

LAUER CUSTOM WEAPONRY
3601 129th Street
Chippewa Falls, WI 54729
Toll-Free: 800-830-6677
Website: www.lauerweaponry.com

LAURONA
Factory - Norica Laurona S.A.L.
vda de Otaola, 25, 4
E-20600 Eibar (Guipuzcoa) SPAIN
Fax No.: 011-34-943-700-6169
Website: www.laurona.com
Email: info@lauronazabala.com

HARRY LAWSON LLC
3328 N. Richey Blvd.
Tucson, AZ 85716
Phone No.: 520-326-1117
Email: hlawsonllc@gmail.com

LAZZERONI ARMS COMPANY
P.O. Box 26696
Tucson, AZ 85726 6696
Phone No.: 888-492-7247
Fax No.: 520-624-4250
Website: www.lazzeroni.com
Email: arms@lazzeroni.com

LEADER ARMS TECHNOLOGY
Izmir 2 Caddesi No: 36/5
Kizilay-Ankara, TURKEY
Phone No.: 011-90-312-425-5526
Fax No.: 011-90-312-425-5522
Website: www.lideravtufek.com.tr
Email: sales@lideravtufek.com.tr

LEBEAU-COURALLY
Importer - please refer to Griffin & Howe listing.
Importer - please refer to Heirloom Armes listing.
Importer – please refer to Wiliam Larkin Moore listing.
Factory - Aug. Lebeau-Courally
386, rue Saint-Gilles
B-4000 Liege, BELGIUM
Fax No.: 011-32-42-52-2008
Website: www.lebeau-courally.com
Email: info@lebeau-courally.com

LECHNER & JUNGLE Ges.m.b.H.
Schlossergasse 2
A-8010, Graz, AUSTRIA
Fax No.: 011-43-316-8326624
Website: www.lechner-jungl.com
Email: office@lechner-jungl.com

LEGACY SPORTS INTERNATIONAL LLC
4750 Longley Lane, Ste. 209
Reno, NV 89502
Phone No.: 800-553-4229
Fax No.: 800-786-6555
Website: www.legacysports.com

LEGEND RIFLES
Please refer to D'Arcy Echols & Co.

LEGION FIREARMS
1901 Ramcon Drive
Temple, TX 76504
Toll Free : 855-453-4466
Website: www.legacysports.com

LEITNER-WISE DEFENSE
Parts and Accessories only
P.O. Box 25097
Alexandria, VA 22313
Phone No.: 703-209-0556
Fax No.: 703-548-1427
Website: www.leitner-wise.com
Email: info@leitner-wise.com

LES BAER CUSTOM, INC.
1804 Iowa Drive
LeClaire, IA 52753
Phone No.: 563-289-2126
Fax No.: 563-289-2132
Website: www.lesbaer.com
Email: info@lesbaer.com

LEW HORTON DISTRIBUTING CO.
Distributor Only
P.O. Box 5023
Westboro, MA 01581
Toll Free: 800-446-7866
Fax No.: 508-366-5332
Website: www.lewhorton.com
Email: questions@lewhorton.com

LEWIS MACHINE & TOOL COMPANY (LMT)
1305 11th Street West
Milan, IL 61264
Phone No.: 309-787-7151
Fax No.: 309-787-7193
Website: www.lmtdefense.com

LIBERTY ARMS INTERNATIONAL LLC
3505C Houston Hwy.
Victoria, TX 77901
Phone No.: 361-788-3147
Website: www.libertyarmsusa.com
Email: depot@libertyarmsusa.com

LIND, AL
P.O. Box 97268
Tacoma, WA 98497
Phone/Fax No.: 253-584-6361
Website: www.allindgunmaker.com
Email: al@allindgunmaker.com

LINEBAUGH, JOHN
P.O. Box 455
Cody, WY 82414
Phone No.: 307-645-3332
Website: www.customsixguns.com

LION COUNTRY SUPPLY
P.O. Box 480
Port Matilda, PA 16870
Phone No.: 800-662-5202
Fax No.: 814-684-5900
Website: www.lcsupply.com

LIPPARD, KARL
P.O. Box 60719
Colorado Springs, CO 80960
Phone/Fax No.: 719-444-0786
Website: www.karllippard.com

LITTLE JOHN'S AUCTION SERVICE
1740 W. LaVeta Ave.
Orange, CA 92868
Phone No.: 714-939-1170
Fax No.: 714-939-7955
Website: www.littlejohnsauctionservice.com
Email: ltljohns@aol.com

LITTLE SHARPS RIFLE MFG.
Mr. Ronald Otto
P.O. Box 336
Big Sandy, MT 59520
Phone No.: 406-378-3855
Website: www.littlesharps.com
Email: otto@itstriangle.com

LJUTIC INDUSTRIES, INC.
P.O. Box 10668
Yakima, WA 98902
Phone No.: 509-248-0476
Fax No.: 509-576-8233
Website: www.ljuticgun.com
Email: ljuticgun@earthlink.net

LOKI WEAPON SYSTEMS
P.O. Box 1613
320 NW Industrial Rd.
Atoka, OK 74525
Phone No.: 580-889-5504
Fax No.: 580-304-7124
Website: www.lokiweaponsystems.com
Email: info@lokiweaponsystems.com

LON PAUL CUSTOM GUNS
28-950 Bonita Vista Rd., 4A
Mountain Center, CA 92561
Phone No.: 951-659-2699
Website: www.lonpaulcustomguns.com
Email: tanglewoodguns@yahoo.com

LONE STAR TACTICAL SUPPLY
21515 Hufsmith-Kohrville Road
Tomball, TX 77375
Phone No.: 832-454-7549
Website: www.lonestartacticalsupply.com

LONGTHORNE GUNMAKERS
221 Moss Lane
Hesketh Bank, Preston
PR4 6AE Lancashire, U.K.
Phone No.: 011-44-1772-811215
Fax No.: 011-44-1772-81138
Website: www.longthorneguns.com
Email: enquiries@longthorneguns.com

LORENZO, CRESS
349 E. 100 S., Box 14
Minersville, UT 84752
Phone No.: 435-386-1428

LOSOK CUSTOM ARMS
314 Willow Run Lane
Delaware, OH 43015
Phone No.: 740-363-8437

SANDRO LUCCHINI
Importer - Springbrook Manufacturing Ltd.
3809 Ninth St. SE
Calgary, Alberta, T2G 3C7 CANADA
Phone No.: 403-243-3308
Fax No.: 403-243-3792
Website: www.springbrook.ca
Email: info@springbrook.ca
Factory - Armi Italia di Lucchini Sandro
via Petrarca 47
I-25068 Sarezzo, Brescia, ITALY
Fax No.: 011-39-030-89-11573

LUSA USA
1575 Hooksett Road, Ste. 3
Hooksett, NH 03106
Phone No.: 902-922-1515
Website: www.lusausa.com

LUXUS ARMS
222 Homan Way
Mt. Orab, OH 45154
Phone No.: 937-444-6500
Website: www.luxusarms.com
Email: luxuswalnut@yahoo.com

LYMAN
475 Smith Street
Middletown, CT 06457
Toll-Free: 800-225-9626
Website: www.lymanproducts.com

LYNX
Factory - Pirkan Ase Ltd.
Ilmarinkatu 37
FI-33500 Tampere, FINLAND
Phone/Fax No.: 011-358-3255-1096
Website: www.lynxrifles.com

M+M, INC.
Colorado Gun Sales
PO Box 639
East Lake, CO 80614
Phone No.: 866-926-5419
Fax No.: 888-236-2619
Website: www.cogunsales.com
Email: website@cogunsales.com

MAG CUSTOM RIFLES
Via Dante, 163
I-25068 Ponte Zanano (BS) ITALY
Fax No.: 011-39-03065-85141
Website: www.mag.it
Email: info@mag.it

MG ARMS, INC.
6030 Treaschwig Road
Spring, TX 77373
Phone No.: 281-821-8282
Fax No.: 281-821-6387
Website: www.mgarmsinc.com
Email: mgarms@swbell.net

MGI
1168 Main Street
P.O. Box 138
Old Town, ME 04468
Phone No.: 207-817-3280
Fax No.: 207-817-3283
Website: www.mgimilitary.com
Email: mgi@mgimilitary.com

MKE
Factory
06330 Tandogan, Ankara TURKEY
Fax No.: 011-90-312-222-2241
Website: www.mkek.gov.tr

MKS SUPPLY, INC.
8611-A North Dixie Drive
Dayton, OH 45414
Phone No.:937-454-0363
Fax No.: 937-454-0503
Website: www.mkssupply.com

M.O.A. CORPORATION
285 Government Valley Road
Sundance, WY 82729
Phone No.: 307-283-3030
Website: www.moaguns.com
Email: moaguns@rangeweb.net

M.R. NEW SYSTEM ARMS
via Mazzini 30
I-13882 Cerrione Magnonevolo ITALY
Fax No.: 011-39-015-671700
Website: www.newsystemarms.com
Email: info@newsystemarms.com

MTs ARMS
Factory - TsKIB SOO
Krasnoarmeyskiy Prospekt 17
R-300041 Tula, RUSSIA
Fax No.: 011-7-04872-31-5959
Website: www.tulatskib.ru
Email: tularms@tula.net

JAMES MacNAUGHTON & SONS
Please refer to the Dickson & MacNaughton listing.

MAGNUM RESEARCH, INC.
Please refer to Kahr Arms listing.
Factory (Except for Baby Eagle Series)
12602 33rd Ave SW
Pillager, MN 56473
Phone No.: 508-635-4273
Fax No.: 508-795-7046
Website: www.magnumresearch.com
Email: info@magnumresearch.com

MAGTECH AMMUNITION CO., INC.
248 Apollo Drive Suite 180
Lino Lakes, MN 55014
Toll Free Phone No.: 6800-466-7191
Fax No.: 763-235-4004
Website: www.magtechammunition.com
Email: sales@magtechammunition.com

MAKAROV
Importer - please refer to Century International Arms listing.

MANIFATTURA ARMI ART
Importer - please refer to William Larkin Moore listing.
Factory
Via Madonnina 89
Gardone, VT, Brescia
I-25063 ITALY
Phone No.: 011-39-030-8174559
Fax No.: 011-39-030-861-0386
Web site: www.armi-art.com
Email: info@armi-art.com

MÄNNEL SPORT SHOOTING GmbH
Haupstrasse 78
Kronstorf, A-4484 AUSTRIA
Fax No.: 011-43-125330334879
Website: www.maennel.at
Email: office@maennel.at

MANU-ARM
43, avenue de la liberation
F-42340, Veauche, FRANCE
Fax No.: 011-33-0477-947936
Website: www.manuarm.fr
Email: manuarm@manuarm.fr

MANUFRANCE
6, Rue de Lodi
F-42000 St. Etienne 1 FRANCE
Fax No.: 011-33-0477-418830
Website: www.manufrance.eu

MANURHIN REVOLVERS
Factory - Manufacture d. Armes de tir Chapuis - M.A.T.C.H.
Z.I. La Gravoux, BP 15
F-42380 St. Bonnet le Chateau, FRANCE
Fax No.: 011-33-4-77-501070
Website: www.chapuis-armes.com
Email: info@chapuis-armes.com

MARBLE ARMS
420 Industrial Park
Gladstone, MI 49837
Phone No.: 906-428-3710
Fax No.: 906-428-3711
Website: www.marblearms.com
Email: info@marblearms.com

MARLIN FIREARMS COMPANY
P.O. Box 1781
Madison, NC 27025
Phone No.: 203-239-5621
Gun Service No.: 800-544-8892
Repairs: 800-544-8892
Website: www.marlinfirearms.com

MAROCCHI SHOTGUNS
Importer - Network Retailing LLC
22700 S Central Point Rd
Canby, OR 97013
Phone No.: 503-263 3787
Fax No: 775-414 0833
Email: russ@vh2q.com
Factory - C.D. Europe SRL
Via Galilei, 6
I-25068 Sarezzo (Brescia) ITALY
Fax No.: 011-39-030-890-0370
Web site: www.marocchiarms.com
Email: info@marocchiarms.com

MARSTAR CANADA
R.R. #1, Vankleek Hill
Ontario, CANADA K0B 1R0
Phone No.: 888-744-0066
Fax No.: 613-678-2359
Website: www.marstar.ca

MARTIN, ALEX
Please refer to the Dickson & MacNaughton listing.

MASTERPIECE ARMS
Distributor – please refer to the American Tactical Imports listing.
105A Kingsbridge Dr.
Carrollton, GA 30117
Phone No.: 770-832-9430
Phone No.: 866-803-0000
Fax No.: 770-832-3495
Website: www.masterpiecearms.com
Email: darah@masterpiecearms.com

MATCHGUNS srl
Distributor - Gehmann GmbH & Co. KG
Karlstrasse 40
Karlsruhe, GERMANY D-76133
Fax No.: 011-49-721-29888
Website: www.gehmann.com
Factory
Via Fornari Giulio, 17
I-43124 Vigatto, Parma ITALY
Fax No: 011-39-0521-631973
Website: www.matchguns.com
Email: info@matchguns.com

MATCH GRADE ARMS & AMMUNITION
Please refer to MG Arms, Inc. listing.

MATEBA
Please refer to AWA USA listing.

MATHELON ARMES
Importer - please refer to Kebco, LLC listing.
Factory
Rue de l'Artisanat
Zone Industrielle Les Granges
F-74150 Rumilly FRANCE
Fax No.: 011-33-4-50-016786
Website: www.mathelon-armes.com
Email: eric@mathelon-armes.com

MAUNZ MATCH RIFLES LLC
P.O. Box 104
Maumee, OH 43537
Phone No.: 419-832-2512
Website: www.maunzmatchrifles.com
Email: maunzmatchrifles@yahoo.com

MAURITZ WIDFORSS AB
Fredsgatan 5
SE-111 52 Stockholm, SWEDEN
Fax No.: 011-46-0821-0514
Website: www.widforss.se
Email: peter.hahn@widforss.se

MAUSER
Importer – Mauser USA
403 East Ramsey, Ste. 301
San Antonio, TX 78216
Phone No.: 210-377-2527
Factory - Mauser Jagdwaffen GmbH
Ziegelstadel 1
D-88316 Isny, GERMANY
Fax No.: 011-490-368-4750794
Website: www.mauser.com
Email: info@mauser.com

MAVERICK ARMS, INC.
Please refer to Mossberg listing.

MAWHINNEY, CHUCK
Factory - Please refer to Riflecraft listing.
2350 Carter Street
Baker City, OR 97814
Website: www.chuckmawhinney.com
Email: cmawhinney@eoni.com

MAXIMUS ARMS, LLC
1226-C Lakeview Drive
Franklin, TN 37067
Phone No.: 615-595-9777
Website: www.maximusarms.com

MCCANN INDUSTRIES LLC
P.O. Box 641
Spanaway, WA 98387
Phone No. 253-537-6919
Fax No. 253-537-6993
Website: www.mccannindustries.com
Email: info@mccannindustries.com

McMILLAN FIREARMS MANUFACTURING, LLC
1638 W. Knudsen Dr. Suite 101
Phoenix, AZ 85027
Phone No.: 623-582-9635
Fax No.: 623-581-3825
Website: www.mcmillanusa.com

MCREES PRECISION
36159 Hwy. 21
Lesterville, MO 63654
Phone No.: 573-637-2000
Fax No.: 573-637-2004
Website: www.mcreesprecision.net
Email: 1000yards@mcreesprecision.net

MEACHAM TOOL & HARDWARE, INC.
3702 Eberhardt Road
Peck, ID 83545
Phone No.: 208-486-7171
Website: www.meachamrifles.com

MERKEL
Importer and Distributor – Steyr Arms, Inc.
P.O. Box 840
Trussville, AL 35173
Phone No.: 205-655-8299
Fax No.: 205-655-7078
Website: www.steyrarms.com

Website: www.merkel-usa.com
Factory - Merkel Jagd-und Sportwaffen GmbH
Schutzenstrasse 26
D-98527 Suhl, GERMANY
Fax No.: 011-49-3681-854-203
Website: www.merkel-waffen.de

METROARMS CORPORATION
Distributor – please refer to Eagle Imports, Inc. listing.
www.metroarms.com

MICOR DEFENSE, INC.
P.O. Box 2175
Decatur, AL 35602
Phone No.: 256-560-0770
Fax No.: 256-341-0002
Website: www.micordefense.com
Email: orders@micordefense.com

MICROTECH SMALL ARMS RESEARCH, INC. (MSAR)
300 Chesnut Street
Bradford, PA 16701
Phone No.: 814-363-9260
Fax No.: 814-362-7068
Website: www.msarinc.com

MILLER ARMS
Please refer to Dakota Arms listing.

MILLER, DAVID
Please refer to David Miller Co. listing.

MIL-SPEC INDUSTRIES CORP.
(Parts only)
10 Mineola Avenue
Roslyn Heights, NY 11577
Phone No.: 516-625-5787
Fax No.: 516-625-0988
Website: www.milspecindustries.com
Email: info@mil-spec-industries.com

MIROKU FIREARMS MFG. CO.
537-1 Shinohara
Nangoku City Kochi-Pref, JAPAN
Fax No.: 011-81-88-863-3317

MITCHELL'S MAUSERS
P.O. Box 9295
Fountain Valley, CA 92728 -9295
Phone No.: 800-274-4124
Fax No.: 714-848-7208
Website: www.mauser.org
Email: customerservice@mauser.org

MOLOT
Please refer to Becas and Vepr. listings.

MONTANA ARMORY, INC.
Please refer to C. Sharps Arms Co. Inc. listing.

MONTANA RIFLE COMPANY
3174 MT Highway 35
Kalispell, MT 59901
Phone No.: 406-756-4867
Fax No.: 406-756-4874
Website: www.montanarifleco.com
Email: jeff@montanarifleco.com

MOORE, W.L. & CO.
Please refer to William Larkin Moore & Co. listing.

MORAVIA
Please refer to Arms Moravia listing.

MORINI
Importer - please refer to Pilkington Competition Equipment LLC listing.
Factory - Morini Competition Arm SA
Casella Postale 92
CH-6930 Bedano SWITZERLAND
Fax No.: 011-41-91-935-2231
Website: www.morini.ch
Email: morini@morini.ch

MORPHY AUCTIONS
2000 N. Reading Road
Denver, PA 17517
Phone No.: 717-335-3435
Fax No.: 717-336-7115
Website: www.morpyauctions.com
Email: morphy@morphyauctions.com

MORTIMER, THOMAS
Please refer to the Dickson & MacNaughton listing.

MOSSBERG
O.F. Mossberg & Sons, Inc.
7 Grasso Ave., P.O. Box 497
North Haven, CT 06473-9844
Phone No.: 203-230-5300
Fax No.: 203-230-5420
Factory Service Center - OFM Service Department
Eagle Pass Industrial Park
Industrial Blvd.
Eagle Pass, TX 78853
Phone No.: 800-989-4867
Website: www.mossberg.com
Email: service@mossberg.com

MOUNTAIN RIFLERY, INC.
1775 North Elk Road
Pocatello, ID 83204
Phone No.: 208-234-7142
Website: www.mountainriflery.com

NATIONAL WILD TURKEY FEDERATION
P.O. Box 530
Edgefield, SC 29824
Phone No.: 803-637-3106
Fax No.: 803-637-0034
Website: www.nwtf.org
Email: info@nwtf.net

NAVY ARMS CO.
219 Lawn St.
Martinsburg, WV 25401
Phone No.: 304-262-9870
Fax No.: 304-262-1658
Website: www.navyarms.com
Email: info@navyarms.com

NEMISIS ARMS
1090 5th Street, Ste. 110
Calimesa, CA 92320
Phone No.: 909-446-1111
Fax No.: 909-446-1109
Website: www.nemisisarms.com
Email: david@nemisisarms.com

NEMO
3582 Hwy 93 S.
Kalispell, MT 59901
Phone No.: 406-752-NEMO
Website: www.nemoarms.com
Email: asonju@nemoarms.com

NESIKA
Please refer to Dakota Arms listing.

NEW ENGLAND CUSTOM GUN SERVICE LTD.
741 Main Street
Claremont, NH 03743
Phone No.: 603-287-4836
Fax No.: 603-287-4834
Website: www.newenglandcustomgun.com
Email: info@necgltd.com

NEW ENGLAND FIREARMS
For parts and service only, please refer to H&R 1871 listing.

NEW ULTRA LIGHT ARMS LLC
P.O. Box 340
214 Price Street
Granville, WV 26534
Phone No.: 304-292-0600
Fax No.: 304-292-9662
Website: www.newultralight.com

NEWTOWN FIREARMS
1374 Broadway
Placerville, CA 95667
Phone No.: 530-626-9945
Fax No.: 530-644-6684
Website: www.newtown-firearms.com

NEXT GENERATION ARMS
Phone No.: 208-714-4220
Fax No.: 888-207-0688
Website: www.nextgenerationarms.com
Email: info@nextgenerationarms.com

NIGHTHAWK CUSTOM
1306 W. Trimble Ave.
Berryville, AR 72616-4632
Phone No.: 877-268-4867
Fax No.: 870-423-4230
Website: www.nighthawkcustom.com
Email: info@nighthawkcustom.com

NOREEN FIREARMS LLC
351 Floss Flats Rd., Ste. A
Belgrade, MT 59714
Phone No.: 406-388-2200
Fax No.: 406-388-6500
Website: www.onlylongrange.com

NORINCO
European Distributor – Norconia GmbH
Zeppelinstrabe 3
D-97228 Rottendorf, GERMANY
Phone No.: 01149-0903-1405
Factory - China North Industries Corporation
12A Guang An Men Nan Jie
Beijing 100053 CHINA
Fax No.: 011-86-10-63540398
Website: www.norinco.com
Email: norinco@norinco.com.cn

NORSMAN SPORTING ARMS & OUTFITTERS LLC
P.O. Box 500
1028 Second Ave., Ste. A
Havre, MT 59501
Phone No.: 406-262-2403
Email: norsmanarms@yahoo.com

NORTH AMERICAN ARMS, INC.
2150 South, 950 East
Provo, UT 84606-6285
Toll Free: 800-821-5783
Fax No.: 801-374-9998
Website: www.NorthAmericanArms.com

NORTHERN COMPETITION
P.O. Box 366
Bristol, WI 53104
Phone No.: 262-857-8762
Website: www.northerncompetition.com
Email: productsales@northerncompetition.com

NOSLER, INC.
107 SW Columbia St.
Bend, OR 97709
Phone No.: 800-285-3701
Fax No.: 800-766-7537
Website: www.nosler.com
Email: catalog@nosler.com

NOWLIN MFG. INC.
Service and components only
20622 4092 Rd., Unit B
Claremore, OK 74019
Phone No.: 918-342-0689
Fax No.: 918-342-0624
Website: www.nowlinguns.com
Email: nowlinguns@msn.com

NUMRICH GUN PARTS CORP.
Parts supplier only
226 Williams Lane
P.O. Box 299
W. Hurley, NY 12491
Phone No.: 866-686-7424
Fax No.: 877-486-7278
Website: www.e-gunparts.com
Email: info@gunpartscorp.com

OBERLAND ARMS
Am Hundert 3
D-82386 Huglfing GERMANY
Fax No.: 011-49-8802914-751
Website: www.oberlandarms.com
Email: info@oberlandarms.com

OHIO ORDNANCE WORKS, INC.
P.O. Box 687
Chardon, OH 44024
Phone No.: 440-285-3481
Fax No.: 440-286-8571
Website: www.ohioordnanceworks.com
Email: oow@oowinc.com

KULL'S OLD TOWN STATION FIREARMS AUCTIONS
P.O. Box 14040
Lenexa, KS 66285
Phone No.: 913-492-3000
Fax No.: 913-492-3022
Website: www.armsbid.com
Email: Dan@armsbid.com

OLLENDORFF, PHILIPP
Eisack 169
A-6108 Scharnitz AUSTRIA
Phone/Fax No.: 011-43-5213-20133
Website: www.jagdwaffen-ollendorff.com
Email: info@jagdwaffen-ollendorff.com

OLYMPIC ARMS, INC.
624 Old Pacific Hwy. SE
Olympia, WA 98513
Phone No.: 800-228-3471
Fax No.: 360-491-3447
Website: www.olyarms.com
Email: info@olyarms.com

OMNI
Please refer to E.D.M. Arms listing.

ONLY LONG RANGE
Please refer to Noreen Firearms LLC listing.

OPTIMA
Please refer to Hatsan Arms Co. listing.

ORVIS
(Custom shotgun information only)
Historic Route 7A
Manchester, VT 05254
Phone No.: 802-362-2580
Fax No.: 802-362-3525
Website: www.orvis.com

OTTOMANGUNS
Yayalar Mahallesi Yayalar Caddesi No. 6
Kat: 6 Pendik Istanbul 34716 TURKEY
Phone No.: 011-90-216-627-0627
Fax No.: 011-90-216-627-0282
Website: www.ottomanguns.com
Email: info@ottomanguns.com

OWEN, KEN
P.O. Box 813
Moscow, TN 38057
Phone No.: 901-877-6853
Fax No.: 901-877-1957
Email: mkenowen@bellsouth.net

PGW DEFENCE TECHNOLOGIES
Importer – Leroy's Big Valley Gun Works
527 2nd Ave. N.
Glasgow, MT 59230
Phone No.: 406-228-4867
Email: leroygun@nemontel.net
Factory
#6-59 Scurfield Blvd.
Winnipeg, Manitoba, CANADA R3Y1V2
Phone No. 204-487-7325
Fax No.: 204-231-8566
Website: www.pgwdti.com

PHSADC
Pakistan Hunting & Sporting Arms Development Company
Ground Floor, State Life Building, The Mall
Peshawar PAKISTAN
Fax No.: 011-92-91-9210186
Website: www.phsadc.org
Email: iquiry@phsadc.org

PPK s.r.o.
Dukelska 451, 534 01
Holice, CZECH REPUBLIC
Phone/Fax: 011-420-466-251-101
Website: www.zbrojovkaholice.cz
Email: info@zbrojovkaholice.cz

PTR 91 INC.
U.S. Representative - Vincent Pestilli & Associates
193 Sam Brown Hill Rd.
Brownfield, ME 04010
Phone No.: 207-935-3603
Fax No.: 207-935-3996
Email: vapame@fairpoint.net
Factory
30 Cross Street
Bristol, CT 06010
Phone No.: 860-676-1776
Fax No.: 860-676-1880
Website: www.PTR91.com

PALM PISTOLS
Please refer to Constitution Arms listing.

PARA USA INC.
10620 Southern Loop Blvd.
Pineville, NC 28134-7381
Phone No.: 704-930-7600
Fax No.: 704-930-7601
Website: www.para-usa.com
Email: contact@para-usa.com

PARDINI, ARMI S.r.l.
Importer – Pardini USA, LLC
P.O. Box 16001
Tampa, FL 33687
Phone No.: 813-748-3378
Fax No.: 813-899-9696
Website: www.pardiniguns.com
Factory
154/A via Italica
I-55041 Lido di Camaiore, (LU) ITALY
Fax No.: 011-39058490122
Website: www.pardini.it
Email: info@pardini.it

PARDUS
Factory – Pardus Silah Ltd. STI
Imes San. Sit. E-Blok, 501 Sk. No: 24
Umraniye, Istanbul, TURKEY
Fax No.: 011-90-216-526-3164
Website: www.pardusarms.com
Email: pardusarms@pardusarms.com

PARKER (NEW MFG.)
Headquarters – please refer to Remington listing.
Factory – please refer to Connecticut Shotgun Manufacturing listing.
Website: www.parkergunmakers.com
Email: Parker@Remington.com

PARKER BROS. MAKERS
P.O. Box 921
Meriden, CT 06450
Phone No.: 203-206-7287
Website: www.parkerbrosmakers.com
Email: sales@parkerbrosmakers.com

PARKER REPRODUCTIONS
Parker Reproduction Div.
115 U.S. Hwy 202
Ringoes, NJ 08551
Phone No.: 908-284-2800
Fax No.: 908-284-2113

PATRIOT ORDNANCE FACTORY (POF)
23011 N. 16th Lane
Phoenix, AZ 85027
Phone No.: 623-561-9572
Fax No.: 623-321-1680
Website: www.pof-usa.com
Email: sales@pof-usa.com

PEDERSOLI, DAVIDE & C. Snc
Distributor - please refer to Cherry's listing.
Distributor - please refer to Dixie Gun Works listing.
Importer/Distributor – I.F.G.
P.O. Box 560746
Rockledge, FL 32956
Phone No.: 321-639-4842
Fax No.: 321-639-7006
Email: eaacorp@eaacorp.com
Distributor - Flintlocks, Etc.
P.O. Box 181
Richmond, VA 01254
Phone No.: 413-698-3822
Fax No.: 413-698-3866
Email: flintetc@berkshire.rr.com
Importer - please refer to E.M.F. listing.
Importer - please refer to Taylor's listing.
Importer - please refer to Cabela's listing.
Importer - please refer to Cimarron, F.A. & Co listing.
Importer - please refer to Navy Arms listing.
Service & Repair - please refer to VTI Gun Parts listing.
Factory
Via Artigiani 57
I-25063 Gardone V.T. (BS), ITALY
Fax No.: 011-39-030-891-1019
Website: www.davide-pedersoli.com
Email: info@davide-pedersoli.com

PEERLESS RIFLE COMPANY
Ray Riganian
324 N. Central Ave., Unit B
Glendale, CA 91203
Phone No.: 818-502-2678
Website: www.peerless-rifles.com
Email: ray@peerless-rifles.com

PERAZZI
Importer - Perazzi USA, Inc.
1010 W. Tenth St.
Azusa, CA 91702
Phone No.: 626-334-1234
Fax No.: 626-334-0344
Email: perazziusa@aol.com

Factory - Armi Perazzi S.p.A.
Via Fontanelle, 1
I-25080 Botticino Mattina Brescia ITALY
Fax No.: 011-39-030-269-2594
Website: www.perazzi.it
Email: info@perazzi.it

PERODEAU, J.J.
Champlin, Inc.
PO Box 3191
Enid, OK 73702
Phone No.: 580-237-7388
Fax No.: 580-242-6922
Website: www.champlinarms.com
Email: info@champlinarms.com

PERUGINI & VISINI
Importer – P&V USA LLC
4330 Maine Ave.
Lakeland, FL 33801
Phone No.: 888-812-6913
Email: info@p-vusa.com
Factory
Via G, Di Vittorio 2/4
Mazzano, Brescia I-25080 ITALY
Fax No.: 011-39-030-689-7821
Website: www.perugini-visini.com
Email: info@perugini-visini.com

PFEIFER-WAFFEN
10-12 Schlossgraben
A-6800 Feldkirch, AUSTRIA
Fax No.: 011-43-5522-77660
website: www.pfeifer-waffen.at
Email: office@pfeifer-waffen.at

PHOENIX ARMS
4231 E. Brickell St.
Ontario, CA 91761
Phone No.: 909-937-6900
Fax No.: 909-937-0060
Website: www.phoenix-arms.com

PIETTA, F.A.P. F.lli e C. Snc.
Various U.S. distributors and importers
Service & Repair - please refer to VTI Gun Parts listing.
European distributor – please refer to Effebi listing.
Factory - PIETTA, F.A.P. F.lli e C. Snc.
Via Mandolossa 102
I-25064 Gussago (Brescia) ITALY
Fax No.: 011-39-030-373-7100
Website: www.pietta.it
Email: info@pietta.it

PILKINGTON COMPETITION EQUIPMENT LLC
P.O. Box 97, #2 Little Tree's Ramble
Monteagle, TN 37356
Phone No.: 931-924-3400
Fax No.: 931-924-3489
Website: www.pilkguns.com
Email: info@pilkguns.com

PIONEER ARMS CORP.
Importer - Pioneer Arms
25 Main Street
North Bennington, VT 05257-0815
Phone No.: 309-226-4226
Fax No.: 800-496-6012
Email: sales@pioneer-pac.com
Factory
1905 Roku 1/9 Street
26-612 Radom, POLAND
Fax No.: 011-48-383-0776
Website: www.pioneer-pac.com
Email: contact@pioneer-pac.com

PIOTTI
Importer - please refer to William Larkin Moore & Co. listing.
Factory - Piotti, F.lli, S.n.c.
Via Cinelli, 10-12
I-25063 Gardone V.T. Brescia, ITALY
Fax No.: 011-39-030-891-6522
Website: www.piotti.com
Email: info@piotti.com

PISTOL DYNAMICS
2510 Kirby Ave. NE
Palm Bay, FL 32905
Phone No: 321-733-1266
Website: www.pistoldynamics.com
Email: info@pistoldynamics.com

POLI, ARMI F.LLI
Importer - Deep River Sporting Clays
3420 Cletus Hall Road
Sanford , NC 27330
Phone No.: 919-774-7080
Fax No.: 919-708-5052
Website: www.deepriver.net
Factory
Casella Postale, 6
via Giacomo Matteotti 163
I-25063 Gardone, VT (BS), ITALY
Fax No.: 011-39-030-834-9413
Website: www.fpafratellipoli.com
Email: info@fpafratellipoli.com

POLI NICOLETTA & C. snc
via Matteotti, 311
I-25063 Gardone VT Brescia ITALY
Fax No.: 011-39-030-8910743
Website: www.polinicoletta.com
Email: info@polinicoletta.com

WAFFEN PRECHTL
Importer - please refer to Mitchell's Mauser's listing.
Importer – please refer to New England Custom Gun listing.
Factory – Golmatic Werkzeugmaschinen und Zubehör G. Preschtl
Auf der Aue 3
Birkenau, GERMANY D-69488
Fax No.: 011-49-6201-182-701
Website: www.golmatic.de

PRECISION FIREARMS
13337 Clopper Road
Hagerstown, MD 21742
Phone No.: 240-217-6875
Website: www.precisionfirearms.com
Email: precars@aol.com

PRECISION SMALL ARMS, INC.
Distributor - please refer to Acusport listing.
Factory
P.O. Box 931
Aspen, CO 81612
Website: www.precisionsmallarms.com
Email: sales@precisionsmallarms.com

PREDATOR TACTICAL LLC
Tempe, AZ
Phone No.: 602-652-2864
Fax No.: 602-492-9987
Website: www.predatortactical.com

PREMIER ENGLISH SHOTGUNS LTD.
Holloway & Naughton Gunmakers
Turner Barn Farm, Kibworth Road
Three Gates, Billesdon
Leicestershire LE7 9EQ U.K.
Phone No.: 011-441-16-259-6592
Fax No.: 011-441-16-259-6574
Website: www.hollowaynaughton.co.uk
Email: afharvison@hollowaynaughton.co.uk

PRIMARY WEAPONS SYSTEMS
800 E. Citation Court, Ste. E
Boise, ID 83716
Phone No.: 208-344-5217
Fax No.: 208-344-5395
Website: www.primaryweapons.com

PROOF RESEARCH
Columbia Falls, MT
Phone No.: 406-756-9290
Website: www.proofresearch.com
Email: proofinfo@proofresearch.com

PUMA RIFLES
Importer - please refer to Legacy Sports International, LLC listing.

PURDEY, JAMES, & SONS, LTD.
Showroom
57-58 South Audley Street
London, W1K 2 ED U.K.
Phone No.: 011-44-20-7499-1801
Fax No.: 011-44-20-7355-3297
Website: www.purdey.com
Email: sales@james-purdey.co.uk

PUSKARSTVO SPENDAL d.o.o.
Gramozna Pot 9
1000 Ljublijana
Slovenija, SLOVAKIA
Phone No.: 011-00386-041-399-307
Website: www.guns-spendal.si
Email: puskarstvo@siol.net

Q.S. ARMI
via S. Agostino, 9
I-23892, Bulcaigo (Lecco) - ITALY
Fax No.: 011-39-31861186
Web site: www.qsarmi.com
Email: info@qsarmi.com

QIQIHAR HAWK INDUSTRIES CO., LTD.
No. 3 Delong Road
Qiqihar New & High Technique Industrial Development District
Heilongjiang, CHINA 161005
Fax No.: 011-0452-2340633
Website: www.hawkindustries.com.cn

QUAIL UNLIMITED, INC.
P.O. Box 70518
308 Third Ave.
Albany, GA 31708
Phone No.: 229-883-3209
Fax No.: 229-883-3979
Website: www.qu.org
Email: National@qu.org

QUALITY ARMS, INC.
P.O. Box 19477
Houston, TX 77224
Phone No.: 281-870-8377
Fax No.: 281-870-8524
Website: www.arrieta.com
Email: Arrieta2@excite.com

QUALITY PARTS CO.
Please refer to Bushmaster Firearms, Inc. listing.

R GUNS
140 N. Western Ave
Carpentersville, IL 60110
Phone No.: 847-428-3569
Website: www.rguns.net

RAAC
677 S. Cardinal Lane
Scottsburg, IN 47170
Phone No.: 877-752-2894
Website: www.raacfirearms.com
Email: info@raacfirearms.com

R.F.M.
Via Patrioti, 26
25068 Sarezzo (Brescia), ITALY
Phone No.: 011-030-800442
Website: rfmarmi.it
Email: info@rmfarmi.it

RGS, LLC
404 N Jackson
Casper, WY 82601
Phone No.: 307-315-6054
Website: www.rgsllc2010.com
Email: rgsllc2010@yahoo.com

RND MANUFACTURING
14399 Mead Street
Longmont, CO 80504
Phone/Fax No.: 970-535-4458
Website: www.rndedge.com
Email: info@rifles.com

RPA INTERNATIONAL LTD.
P.O. Box 441
Tonbridge, Kent, U.K. TN9 9DZ
Fax No.: 011-44-8458803232
Website: www.rpainternational.co.uk
Email: custom@rpainternational.co.uk

RPM PISTOLS
15481 North Twin Lakes Drive
Tucson, AZ 85739
Phone No.: 520-825-1233
Website: www.rpmxl1.com
Email: rpmxl1@msn.com

RWC GROUP LLC
911 William Leigh Drive
Tullytown, PA 19007
Phone No.: 866-611-9576
Fax No.: 215-949-9191
Website: www.rwcgroupllc.com
Email: info@rwcgroupllc.com

RWS
Disc. firearms only - please refer to Dynamit Nobel listing.

RADOM
Please refer to Fabryka Broni Lucznik listing.

RAMIREZ, TODD
7680 N. US Hwy. 69
Alba, TX 75410
Phone No.: 903-768-2948
Website: www.customgun.com
Email: customgun@att.net

RED ROCK ARMS
P.O. Box 21017
Mesa, AZ 85277
Phone No.: 480-832-0844
Fax No.: 206-350-5274
Website: www.redrockarms.com
Email: info@redrockarms.com

REDOLFI F.LLI
Strada Provinciale 688 km. 28,310
I-25025 Manerbio (BS) ITALY
Fax No.: 011-39-0309385348
Website: www.redolfiarmi.com
Email: info@redolfiarmi.com

GARY REEDER CUSTOM GUNS
2601 E. 7th Ave.
Flagstaff, AZ 86004
Phone No.: 928-527-4100
Fax No.: 928-527-0840
Website: www.reedercustomguns.com
Email: gary@reedercustomguns.com

REGENT
Importer - please refer to Umarex USA listing.

REMINGTON ARMS CO., INC.
Consumer Services
870 Remington Drive
P.O. Box 700
Madison, NC 27025-0700
Phone No.: 800-243-9700
Fax No.: 336-548-7801
Website: www.remington.com
Email: info@remington.com
Repairs
14 Hoefler Ave.
Ilion, NY 13357
Phone No.: 800-243-9700
Fax No.: 336-548-7801

RETAY ARMS CORP.
F. Cakmak mah 10728 Sk.
No: 5, 42050 Konya TURKEY
Phone No.: 011-90-332-342-6513
Fax No.: 011-90-332-342-6514
Website: www.retayarms.com
Email: info@retayarms.com

RHINO ARMS
436 Recycle Dr.
Washington, MO 63090
Phone No.: 636-231-3199
Website: www.rhinoarms.com

RIFLES, INC.
3580 Leal Rd.
Pleasanton, TX 78064
Phone No.: 830-569-2055
Fax No.: 830-569-2297
Website: www.riflesinc.com
Email: info@riflesinc.com

RIFLECRAFT LTD.
18G Speedwell Way
Border Valley Industrial Estate
Harleston, Norfolk, IP20 9EH, U.K.
Website: www.riflecraft.co.uk

RIGANIAN, RAY (RIFLEMAKER)
Please refer to the Peerless Rifle Company listing.

RIGBY, JOHN & CO. (GUNMAKERS), INC.
200 Crescent Court, Ste. No. 1450
Dallas, TX 75201
Phone No.: 214-880-9993
Fax No.: 214-880-0082
Website: www.johnrigbyandco.com
Email: info@johnrigbyandco.com

RIZZINI, BATTISTA
Distributor – Fierce Products
240 South 440 East
Gunnison, UT 84634
Phone No.: 435-528-3039
Importer – see William Larkin Moore listing.
Custom Shop
Attn: Ivano Tanfoglio
Factory - Rizzini srl
Via 2 Giugno, 7/7 bis
I-25060 Marcheno (Brescia), ITALY
Fax No.: 011-39-030-861-319
Website: www.rizzini.it
Email: info@rizzini.it

RIZZINI, EMILIO, s.n.c.
Factory - Fausti Stefano srl
Via Martiri Dell'Indipendenza, 70
I-25060 Marcheno (Brescia) ITALY
Fax No.: 011-39-030-861-0155
Website: www.emiliorizzini.com
Email: info@emiliorizzini.com

RIZZINI, F.LLI.
Factory
Via X Giornate N. 9
I-25063, Magno, VT, ITALY
Fax No.: 011-39-030-8911400
Website: www.fllirizzini.it
Email: fllirizzini@fastwebnet.it

ROBAR COMPANIES, INC.
21438 N. 7th Avenue, Ste. B
Phoenix, AZ 85027
Phone No.: 623-581-2648
Fax No.: 623-582-0059
Website: www.robarguns.com
Email: info@robarguns.com

ROBERTS, J. & SON (GUNMAKERS) LTD.
22 Wyvil Road, Vauxhall
London SW8 2TG U.K.
Fax No.: 011-44-0207-627-4442
Website: www.jroberts-gunmakers.co.uk
Email: shop@jroberts-gunmakers.co.uk

ROBERTSON
Please refer to Boss & Co., Ltd. listing.

ROBINSON ARMAMENT CO.
ZDF Import/Export
P.O. Box 16776
Salt Lake City, UT 84116-0776
Phone No.: 801-355-0401
Website: www.robarm.com
Email: sales@robarm.com

ROCHE, CHRISTIAN
12 Lotissement les Eglantiers
42 340 Veauche, FRANCE
Phone No.: 011-33-477-5423-06
Fax No.: 011-33-7794-3533
Email: Rochechristian9046@neuf.fr

ROCK ISLAND AUCTION COMPANY
7819 42nd Street West
Rock Island, IL 61201
Phone No.: 309-797-1500
Fax No.: 309-797-1655
Website: www.rockislandauction.com
Email: info@rockislandauction.com

ROCK ISLAND ARMORY
Please refer to Armscor listing.

ROCK RIVER ARMS, INC.
1042 Cleveland Road
Colona, IL 61241
Phone No.: 309-792-5780
Fax No.: 309-792-5781
Website: www.rockriverarms.com
Email: info@rockriverarms.com

ROCKY MOUNTAIN ARMS, INC.
1813 Sunset Place, Unit D
Longmont, CO 80501
Phone No.: 800-375-0846
Fax No.: 303-678-8766
Website: www.rockymountainarms.us

ROCKY MOUNTAIN ELK FOUNDATION
2291 W. Broadway
Missoula, MT 59802
Phone No.: 406-523-4500
Fax No.: 406-523-4581
Website: www.rmef.org

ROEDALE PRECISION
Jahnstr, 23
49205 Hasbergen, GERMANY
Fax No.: 011-49-5405-606530
Website: www.roedale.de

ROGUE RIVER RIFLEWORKS
Please refer to John Rigby & Co. listing.

ROHRBAUGH FIREARMS CORP.
P.O. Box 785
Bayport, NY 11705
Phone No.: 800-803-2233
Phone No.: 631-242-3175
Fax No.: 631-242-3183
Website: www.rohrbaughfirearms.com

ROOSEVELT AND DRAKE
418 Main Street
Murray, KY 42071
Phone No.: 270-436-5270
Fax No.: 270-436-5257
Website: www.drake.net

ROSSI
Importer - BrazTech International L.C.
16175 N.W. 49th Ave.
Miami, FL 33014
Phone No.: 305-474-0401
Fax No.: 305-623-7506
Website: www.rossiusa.com
Factory - Amadeo Rossi, S.A.
Rua Amadeo Rossi, 143
B-93030-220 Sao Leopoldo-RS BRAZIL
Email: rossi.firearms@pnet.com.br

RÖSSLER WAFFEN GmbH
Prof. Schlosser Strasse 31
A-6330 Kufstein, Austria
Fax No.: 011-43-5372-90811
Website: www.jagd-shop.at
Email: office@jagd-shot.at

ROTTWEIL
Repair - Pylinski Arms
(Models 72, 720 & Paragon service)
967 Anderson Hwy.
Cumberland, VA 23040
Phone No.: 804-492-4082
Email: pylinskifarms@aol.com

RUSSIAN AMERICAN ARMORY COMPANY
Please refer to RAAC listing.

S.I.A.C.E.
Importer - please refer to Cherry's listing.
Importer - please refer to Kebco, LLC listing.
Importer - please refer to Cabela's listing.
Importer - please refer to Briley Mfg. listing.
Importer - please refer to British Sporting Arms Ltd, listing.
Factory
Via Matteotti 125/127
Gardone, VT, Brescia, ITALY I-25063
Fax No.: 011-39-030-891-1518
Website: www.siacearmi.com
Email: siace@siacearmi.com

S.P.S
Importer - please refer to MetroArms Corporation listing.
Magallanes, 8
08291 Ripollet, Barcelona, SPAIN
Fax No.: 011-34-93-592-1258
Website: www.sps-dc.com
Email: online@sps-dc.com

SI DEFENSE
2902 Highway 93 North
Kalispell, MT 59901
Phone No.: 406-752-4253
Fax No.: 406-755-1302
Website: www.si-defense.com
Email: sales@si-defense.com

SKB SHOTGUNS
SKB Shotguns, USA (G.U. Inc.)
4441 S. 134th Street
Omaha, NE 68137
Phone No.: 800-752-2767
Fax No.: 402-330-8040
Website: www.skbshotguns.com
Email: skb@skbshotguns.com

SOG ARMORY
11707 S. Sam Houston Pkwy. W., Unit R
Houston, TX 77031
Phone No.: 281-568-5685
Fax No.: 281-568-9191
Website: www.sogarmory.com
Email: sog@sogarmory.com

SRM ARMS
Exclusive Distributor
GSA Direct LLC
802 W. Bannock St. Ste 700
Boise, ID 83702
Phone No.: 208-424-3141
Fax No.: 208-248-1111
Factory
4375A W. McMillan Rd.
Meridian, ID 83646
Phone No.: 888-269-1885
Website: www.srmarms.com
Email: order@srmarms.com

SSK INDUSTRIES
590 Woodvue Lane
Wintersville, OH 43953
Phone No.: 740-264-0176
Fax No.: 740-264-2257
Website: www.sskindustries.com
Email: info@sskindustries.com

STI INTERNATIONAL
114 Halmar Cove
Georgetown, TX 78628
Phone No.: 800-959-8201
Fax No.: 512-819-0465
Website: www.stiguns.com
Email: sales@stiguns.com

STL
Krahkopfweg 3
69253 Heiligkreuzsteinach, GERMANY
Phone No.: 011-490-6220-30-79-751
Website: www.stl-rifles.com
Email: Manfred@stl-rifles.com

SABATTI s.p.a.
Importer – Italian Firearms Group (IFG)
P.O. Box 560746
Rockledge, FL 32956
Phone No.: 321-639-4842
Fax No.: 321-639-7006
SxS Double Rifles - please refer to US Sporting Goods listing.
Factory - Armi Sabatti s.p.a.
Via Alessandro Volta 90
I-25063 Gardone Valtrompia, (BS) ITALY
Fax No.: 011-39-030-891-2059
Website: www.sabatti.com
Email: info@sabatti.com

SAFARI CLUB INTERNATIONAL
4800 West Gates Pass Road
Tucson, AZ 85745
Phone No.: 888-724-4868
Fax No.: 520-622-1205
Website: www.safariclub.org
Membership email: huntsci@safariclub.org

SAFETY HARBOR FIREARMS, INC.
P.O. Box 563
Safety Harbor, FL 34695-0563
Phone No.: 727-726-2500
Fax No.: 727-797-6134
Website: www.safetyharborfirearms.com
Email: sales@safetyharborfirearms.com

SAIGA
Exclusive Distributor – please refer to RWC Group LLC listing.
Importer – please refer to U.S. Sporting Goods listing.
Importer - please refer to RAAC (Russian American Armory Company) listing.
Importer – please refer to K-VAR Corp. listing.

SAKO LTD.
Importer (USA) - please refer to Beretta USA listing.
Factory - Sako, Limited
P.O. Box 149
FI-11101 Riihimaki, FINLAND
Fax No.: 011-358-19-720446
Website: www.sako.fi
Email: export@sako.fi

SALERI, W.R. di WILLIAM & C. snc
Factory
Via Zanardelli, 231
Marcheno, Brescia ITALY
Fax No.: 011-39-030-8966322
Website: www.wrsaleri.it
Email: info@wsaleri.it

SAMCO GLOBAL ARMS, INC.
6995 N.W. 43rd St.
Miami, FL 33166
Toll Free: 800-554-1618
Phone No.: 305-593-9782
Fax No.: 305-593-1014
Website: www.samcoglobal.com
Email: samco@samcoglobal.com

SAN SWISS ARMS AG
Industrieplatz 1, Postbox 1071
Neuhausen am Rheinfall
CH-8212 SWITZERLAND
Fax No.: 011-41-052-674-6418
Website: www.swissarms.ch
Email: info@swissarms.ch

SARCO INC.
323 Union Street
Stirling, NJ 07980
Phone No.: 908-647-3800
Fax No.: 908-647-9413
Website: www.sarcoinc.com
Email: info@sarcoinc.com
Parts Only
50 Hilton Ste.
Easton, PA 18042
Phone No. 610-250-3960

SARSILMAZ
Importers - please refer to Armalite, Inc. (pistols) or US Sporting Goods Inc. (shotguns)
Factory
Nargileci Sk. Sarsilmaz is Merkezi No.: 4
Mercan 34116, Istanbul, TURKEY
Fax No.: 011-90212-51119-99
Website: www.sarsilmaz.com

SATTERLEE ARMS LLC
21593 Pahkamaa Road
Deadwood, SD 57732
Phone No.: 605-584-2189
Website: www.satterleearms.com
Email: stujac@hills.net

SAUER, J.P. & SOHN
Importer – Sauer USA, Inc.
403 East Ramsey, Ste. 301
San Antonio, TX 78216
Phone No.: 210-377-2527
Fax No.: 210-377-2533
Website: www.sauer-usa.com
Factory - J.P. Sauer & Sohn GmbH
Ziegelstadel 20
88316 Isny im Allgau, GERMANY
Fax No.: 011-49-7562-97554-801
Website: www.sauer-waffen.de
Email: info@sauer.de

SAVAGE ARMS, INC.
Sales & Marketing
118 Mountain Road
Suffield, CT 06078
Phone No.: 855-493-6962
Fax No.: 860-668-2168
Parts & Service
100 Springdale Road
Westfield, MA 01085
Phone No.: 413-568-7001
Fax No.: 413-562-7764
Website: www.savagearms.com
Older Savage Arms Historical Research
Mr. John Callahan
P.O. Box 82
Southampton, MA 01073
$30.00/gun research fee, $25.00 per gun for Models 1895, 1899, and 99 rifles.

SCATTERGUN TECHNOLOGIES INC.
Please refer to Wilson Combat listing.

SCCY INDUSTRIES
1800 Concept Court
Daytona Beach, FL 32114
Phone No.: 866-729-7599
Fax No.: 386-322-6326
Website: www.sccy.com
Email: sales@sccy.com

SCHEIRING GmbH
Klagenfurter Strasse 19
A-9170 Ferlach AUSTRIA
Fax No.: 011-43-4227-287620
Website: www.jagdwaffen-scheiring.at
Email: waffen.scheiring@aon.at

SCHERZ, MICHAEL
Please refer to Gila River Gun Works.

FA. ALFRED SCHILLING
Importer - Sundog Firearms
Star Route 2
Kimberly, OR 97848
Phone No: 541-934-2117
Website: www.sundogfirearms.com
Email: jerry@sundogfirearms.com
Factory
Peter-Haseney Strasse 32
D-98544 Zella-Mehlis, GERMANY
Fax No.: 011-49-03682-486706
Website: www.Alfred-Schilling.de
Email: schilling@alfred-schilling.de

SCHUERMAN ARMS, LTD.
3322 W. Irvine Road
Desert Hills, AZ 85096
Phone No.: 623-465-5260
Fax No.: 623-465-5372
Website: www.schuermanarms.com
Email: info@schuermanarms.com

SCHUETZEN PISTOL WORKS, INC.
Please refer to Olympic Arms listing.

SCHULTZ & LARSEN
Website: www.schultzlarsen.com
Email: info@schultzlarsen.com

SCHWABEN ARMS GmbH
Neckartal 95
D-78628, Rottweil, GERMANY
Fax No.: 011-49-0741-9429218
Website: www.schwabenarmsgmbh.de
Email: schwabenarmsgmbh@web.de

SCOTT, W. C., LTD.
Holland & Holland, Ltd. (Repairs)
33 Bruton St.
London WiJ 6HH U.K.
Phone No.: 011-44-020-7499-4411
Fax No.: 011-44-020-7499-4544
Website: www.hollandandholland.com

SEARCY, B. & CO.
P.O. Box 584
Boron, CA 93516
Phone No.: 760-762-6131
Fax No.: 760-762-0191
Website: www.searcyent.com
Email: searcy@ccis.com

SEECAMP, L.W. CO., INC.
280 Rock Lane
Milford, CT 06460
Phone No.: 203-877-7926
Fax No.: 203-877-3429
Website: www.seecamp.com
Email: info@seecamp.com

SEMMERLING
Please refer to American Derringer Corp. listing.

SENNI ARMS CO.
Ste. 243/15 Albert Ave.
Broadbeach, Queensland, AUSTRALIA 4218
Fax No.: 011-07-5597-3655
Website: www.senniarms.com

SERBU FIREARMS, INC.
6001 Johns Rd., Ste. 144
Tampa, FL 33634
Phone/Fax No.: 813-243-8899
Website: www.serbu.com

C. SHARPS ARMS CO. INC.
100 Centennial Dr.
P.O. Box 885
Big Timber, MT 59011
Phone No.: 406-932-4353
Fax No.: 406-932-4443
Website: www.csharpsarms.com
Email: info@csharpsars.com

SERO LTD.
1106 Feher Str. 10 3/A
Budapest, HUNGARY
Phone No.: 011-36-1433-2181
Fax No.: 011-36-1433-2182
Email: info@sero.hu

SHILOH RIFLE MFG. CO.
P.O. Box 279
201 Centennial Drive
Big Timber, MT 59011
Phone No.: 406-932-4454
Fax No.: 406-932-5627
Website: www.shilohrifle.com

SHOOTERS ARMS MANUFACTURING INCORPORATED
Importer - please refer to Century International Arms listing.
Factory
National Highway, Wireless
Mandaue City, Cebu, PHILIPPINES
Fax No.: 011-6032-346-2331
Website: www.shootersarms.com.ph
Email: rhonedeleon@yahoo.com

SIG SAUER
18 Industrial Park Drive
Exeter, NH 03833
Phone No.: 603-772-2302
Fax No.: 603-772-9082
Customer Service Phone No.: 603-772-2302
Customer Service Fax No.: 603-772-4795
Law Enforcement Phone No.: 603-772-2302
Law Enforcement Fax No.: 603-772-1481
Website: www.sigarms.com
Factory - SIG - Schweizerische Industrie-Gesellschaft
Industrielplatz , CH-8212
Neuhausen am Rheinfall, SWITZERLAND
Fax No.: 011-41-153-216-601

SILMA s.r.l.
Factory
Via I Maggio, 74
I-25068 Zanano di Sarezzo, (BS) ITALY
Fax No.: 011-39-030-890-0712
Website: www.silma.net
Email: info@silma.net

SILVER SEITZ
Aim, Inc.
19200 Middletown Rd.
Parkton, MD 21120
Phone No.: 410-329-6801
Website: www.silverseitz.com
Email: rich@aimmachining.com

GENE SIMILLION GUNMAKER
220 S. Wisconsin
Gunnison, CO 81230
Phone/Fax No.: 970-641-1126
Email: Gsimillion@hotmail.com

SKORPION
Please refer to Czechpoint, Inc. listing.

SMITH, L.C.
Historical Research - please refer to BBHC/Cody Firearms Museum listing.
Research Letters - L.C. Smith Collectors Association
7651 Kenelley Dr.
Lincoln, NE 68516
Website: www.lcsmith.org

SMITH & WESSON
2100 Roosevelt Avenue
P.O. Box 2208
Springfield, MA 01104
Phone No.: 800-331-0852
Website: www.smith-wesson.com
Service email only: qa@smith-wesson.com
Smith & Wesson Research
Attn: Mr. Roy Jinks, S&W Historian
P.O. Box 2208
Springfield, MA 01102-2208
Phone No.: 413-781-8300
Fax No.: 413-731-8980

SMITHSON, J.P.
927 W. 1500 S.
Provo, UT 84601
Phone No.: 801-224-2041
Website: www.smithson-gunmaker.com

SPIKE'S TACTICAL LLC
2036 Apex Ct.
Apopka, FL 32703
Phone No.: 407-928-2666
Fax No.: 866-283-2215
Website: www.spikestactical.com
Email: sales@spikestactical.com

SODIA, FRANZ
Sodia Jagdwafeen & Bekleidungs GesmbH
Vogelweiderstrasse 55
5020 Salzburg AUSTRIA
Fax No.: 011-43-662-872123-20
Website: www.waffen-sodia.at

SOLD USA (AUCTIONS)
1418 Industrial Drive
Matthews, NC 28105
Phone No.: 704-815-1500
Website: www.soldusa.com
Email: support@soldusa.com

SOROKA RIFLE COMPANY
Exclusive Distributor - see New England Custom Gun Service listing.
Phone No.: 011-64-21-308208
Website: www.sorokarifle.com
Email: info@sorokarifle.com

SOTHEBY'S (AUCTIONS)
U.S. Office
1334 York Ave. at 72nd St.
New York, NY 10021
Phone No.: 212-606-7000
Fax No.: 212-606-7107
Website: www.sothebys.com
U.K. Office
34-35 New Bond Street at Bloomfield Place
London, WIA 2AA U.K.
Phone No.: 011-44-20-7293-5000
Fax No.: 011-44-20-7293-5989
Website: www.sothebys.com

SPARTAN GUN WORKS
Please refer to the Remington listing.

SPECIAL WEAPONS INC.
Warranty service & repair for Special Weapons LLC
Website: www.tacticalweapons.com

SPHINX SYSTEMS LTD.
Importer - please refer to Kriss USA listing
Factory
Gsteigstrasse 12
CH-3800 Matten Interlaken SWITZERLAND
Fax No.: 011-41-033-821-1006
Website: www.sphinxarms.com
Email: info@sphinxarms.com

SPIDER FIREARMS
2005-B Murcott Dr.
St. Cloud, FL 34771-5826
Phone No.: 407-957-3617
Fax No.: 407-957-0296
Website: www.ferret50.com
Email: info@ferret50.com

SPORT-SYSTEME DITTRICH
North American Importer - Wolverine Supplies
Box 729 Virden
Rom2Co Manitoba CANADA
Website: www.wolverinesupplies.com
Factory
Burghaiger Weg 20a
D-95326 Kulmbach, GERMANY
Fax No.: 011-49-09221-8213758
Website: www.ssd-weapon.com

SPORTING PRODUCTS LLC
340 Royal Palm Way, Ste. 101
Palm Beach, FL 33480
Phone No.: 561-837-8001
Website: www.sportingproducts.com

SPRINGER'S ERBEN, JOHANN
Weihburggasse 27
A-1010, Vienna AUSTRIA
Fax No.: 011-43-1512-0309
Website: www.springer-vienna.com

SPRINGFIELD ARMORY
Springfield Inc.
420 W. Main St.
Geneseo, IL 61254
Phone No.: 309-944-5631
Phone No.: 800-680-6866
Fax No.: 309-944-3676
Website: www.springfield-armory.com
Email: sales@springfield-armory.com
Custom Shop Email: customshop@springfield-armory.com

STAG ARMS
515 John Downey Dr.
New Britain, CT 06051
Phone No.: 860-229-9994
Fax No.: 860-229-3738
Website: www.stagarms.com
Email: sales@stagarms.com

STALLARD ARMS
Please refer to Hi-Point listing.

STANDARD MANUFACTURING CO. LLC
240 Day Street
Newington, CT 06111
Phone No.: 860-329-3012
Email: info@standardmfgllc.com

STEINKAMP MASCHINENBAU GmbH & Co. KG
Importer - Steinkamp Molding L.P.
3436 Turfway Road
Erlanger, KY 41018
Phone No.: 859-647-1801
Fax No.: 859-647-1682
Website: www.steinkamp-arms.com
Email: contact@steinkampmold.com
Factory
In der Tüetenbecke 14
D-32339 Espelkamp GERMANY
Fax No.: 011-49-05772-911161
Website: www.stkm.de
Email: info@stkm.de

STEVENS, J., ARMS COMPANY
Please refer to Savage Arms listing.
Older Stevens Historical Research
Mr. John Callahan
P.O. Box 82
Southampton, MA 01073
$25.00/gun research fee.

STEYR ARMS (STEYR MANNLICHER)
P.O. Box 840
376 Argo Park Ct., Ste. 100
Trussville, AL 35173
Phone No.: 205-467-6544
Fax No.: 205-467-3015
Website: www.steyrarms.com

Factory - Steyr Mannlicher A.G. & Co. KG
Ramingtal 46
Kleinraming A-4442 AUSTRIA
Fax No.: 01143-7252-78621
Website: www.steyr-mannlicher.com
Email: office@steyr-mannlicher.com

STOEGER INDUSTRIES
17601 Indian Head Hwy.
Accokeek, MD 20607-2501
Phone No.: 301-283-6981
Toll Free: 800-264-4962
Fax No.: 301-283-6988
Website: www.stoegerindustries.com

STONER RIFLE
Factory - please refer to Knight's Manufacturing Co. listing.

STRANK, ANDREAS
Carl-Alexander-Strabe 93
D-52499 Baesweiler, GERMANY
Phone No.: 011-49-02401-53729
Website: www.jagdwaffen-strank.de
Email: info@jagdwaffen-strank.de

STRATEGIC ARMORY CORPS, LLC
Please refer to Surgeon Rifles listing.

STRASSER
Please refer to HMS GmbH listing.

STRAYER TRIPP INTERNATIONAL
Please refer to the STI International listing.

STURM, RUGER & CO., INC.
Headquarters
1 Lacey Place
Southport, CT 06490
Phone No.: 203-259-7843
Fax No.: 203-256-3367
Website: www.ruger.com
Service Center for Pistols, PC4 & PC9 Carbines
200 Ruger Road
Prescott, AZ 86301-6181
Phone No.: 928-778-6555
Fax No.: 928-778-6633
Website: www.ruger-firearms.com
Service Center for Revolvers, Long Guns & Ruger Date of Manufacture
411 Sunapee Street
Newport, NH 03773
Phone No.: 603-865-2442
Fax No.: 603-863-6165

SUPER SIX CLASSIC LLC
Exclusive distributor - Zander's Sporting Goods
801 Bradbury Lane
Sparta, IL 62286
Phone No.: 618-443-2400
Fax No.: 618-443-5736
Website: www.gzanders.com
Email: sales-support@gzanders.com

Defense Supply & Manufacturing
639 Hilltop Trail
W. Fort Atkinson, WI 53539
Phone No.: 920-568-8299
Fax No.: 920-568-8259
Website: www.bisonbull.com

SUPERIOR ARMS
836 Weaver Blvd.
Wapello, IA 52653
Phone No.: 319-523-2016
Fax No.: 319-527-0188
Website: www.superiorarms.com
Email: sales@superiorarms.com

SURGEON RIFLES, INC.
48955 Moccasin Trail Road
Prague, OK 74864
Phone No.: 405-567-0183
Fax No.: 405-567-0250
Website: www.surgeonrifles.com
Email: info@surgeonrifles.com

SZECSEI Et. FUCHS FINE GUNS GmbH
North America Office
305 Charles St.
Windsor, Ontario N8X 5C5 CANADA
Phone No.: 519-966-1234
Fax No.: 519-966-5290
Website: www.szecseidoubleboltrepeater.ca
Email: bealeguns@szecseidoubleboltrepeater.ca
Factory
Bozner Platz 1
corner Wilhelm-Greil-Strasse
A-6020 Innsbruck AUSTRIA
Phone/Fax No.: 011-43-512-5872-67
Website: www.jagdwaffe.com
Email: fuchs@jagdwaffe.com

TG INTERNATIONAL
P.O. Box 787
Louisville, TN 37777
Phone No.: 865-977-9707
Fax No.: 865-977-9728
Website: www.tnguns.com
Email: sales@tnguns.com

TNW INC.
P.O. Box 311
Vernonia, OR 97064
Phone No.: 503-429-5001
Fax No.: 503-429-3505
Website: www.tnwfirearms.com
Email: tnwcorp@aol.com

TR IMPORTS, INC.
9500 Ray White Rd., Ste. 200
Fort Worth, TX 76244
Phone No.: 800-961-7812
Fax No.: 817-581-4222
Website: TRImports.com
Email: info@trimports.com

TS FINE GUNS
Industriegebiet – Robert-Bosch-Strasse 12
D-56276 Grobmaischeid GERMANY
Fax No.: 011-49-02689-958708
Website: www.fineguns.de
Email: sphor@fineguns.de

TACTICAL RIFLES
38439 5th Ave. #186
Zephryhills, FL 33542
Phone No.: 352-999-0599
Website: www.tacticalrifles.net
Email: info@tacticalrifles.net

TACTICAL SOLUTIONS
2181 Commerce Ave
Boise, ID 83705
Phone No.: 866-333-9901
Website: www.tacticalsol.com

TACTICAL WEAPONS
Please refer to FNH USA listing.

TALO DISTRIBUTORS, INC.
120 Pleasant St.
Framingham, MA 01701
Phone No.: 508-872-9242
Website: www.taloinc.com

TANFOGLIO, FRATELLI, S.n.c
Importer – please refer to Italian Firearms Group (IFG) listing.
Importer (Witness Series) - please refer to European American Armory listing.
Factory
Via Valtrompia 39/41
I-25063 Gardone V.T. (BS) ITALY
Fax No.: 011-39-030-891-0183
Website: www.tanfoglio.it
Email: info@tanfoglio.it

TAR-HUNT CUSTOM RIFLES, INC.
101 Dogtown Rd.
Bloomsburg, PA 17815-7544
Phone No.: 570-784-6368
Fax No.: 507-389-9150
Website: www.tarhunt.com
Email: sales@tarhunt.com

TASK FIREARMS LCC
2757 SW 27th Ave.
Miami, FL 33133
Phone No.: 305-860-6996
Fax No.: 305-860-6995
Website: www.taskfirearms.com
Email: info@taskfirearms.com

TAURUS INTERNATIONAL MANUFACTURING INC.
16175 NW 49th Ave.
Miami, FL 33014-6314
Phone No.: 305-624-1115
Fax No.: 305-623-7506
Website: www.taurususa.com

TAYLOR'S & CO.
304 Lenoir Dr.
Winchester, VA 22603
Phone No.: 540-722-2017
Fax No.: 540-722-2018
website: www.taylorsfirearms.com
Email: info@taylorsfirearms.com

TELO, RENATO
Importer – please refer to Kevin's listing.
Via Goldoni, 8
Gardone, VT, Brescia, ITALY I-25063
Fax No.: 011-39-030-831109

TESRO SPORTWAFFEN GmbH & Co. KG
Seehoffstrasse 14/b
D-89431 Bächingen GERMANY
Fax No.: 011-49-7325-919384
Website: www.tesro.de
Email: info@tesro.de

THOMPSON
Please refer to the Kahr Arms listings.
Website: www.tommygun.com
Website: www.tommygunshop.com

THOMPSON & CAMPBELL
Unit 2, White Dykes
Cromarty the Black Isle
Ross-shire IV11 8YP SCOTLAND, U.K.
Fax No.: 011-44-1463-231-602

THOMPSON/CENTER ARMS CO., INC.
400 North Main Street
Rochester, NH 03867
Customer Service Phone No.: 603-332-2333
Repair Only Phone No.: 866-730-1614
Fax No.: 603-30-8614
Website: www.tcarms.com
Email: tca@tcarms.com
Custom Shop - Fox Ridge Outfitters
P.O. Box 1700
Rochester, NH 03866
Phone No.: 800-243-4570

THOR GLOBAL DEFENSE GROUP
1206 Knesek Lane
Van Buren, AR 72956
Phone No.: 479-474-3434
Fax No.: 479-262-6925
Website: www.thorgdg.com

THUREON DEFENSE
2118 Wisconsin Ave.
P.O. Box 173
New Holstein, WI 53061
Phone No.: 920-898-5859
Fax No.: 920-898-5868
Website: www.thureondefense.com
Email: info@thureondefense.com

TIKKA
Importer - please refer to Beretta U.S.A. Corp. listing.
Factory - please refer to Sako listing.
Website: www.tikka.fi

TIME PRECISION ARMS
4 Nicholas Square
New Milford, CT 06776
Phone No.: 860-350-8343
Fax No.: 860-350-6343
Website: www.benchrest.com/timeprecision
Email: timeprecision@aol.com

TISAS
Importer - please refer to American Tactical Imports.
Trabzon Gun Industry Corp.
De Gol Caddesi No. 13/1 Tandogan
Ankara TURKEY
Fax No.: 011-90-312-213-8570
Website: www.trabzonsilah.com
Email: sales@trabzonsilah.com

TOLLEY, J & W
F.J. Wiseman & Co., Ltd.
262 Walsall Road, Bridgtown
Cannock, Staffordshire
WS11 0JL U.K.
Fax No.: 011-44-1543-574806
Email: fjwiseman@lineone.net

TOMAHAWK
Factory – M&U Tomahawk Shotguns
Hamidiye Mh. 525 Sk. No: 19
42700 Beysehir/Konya TURKEY
Fax No.: 011-90-332-512-6597
Website: www.tomahawk.com.tr

TORNADO
Factory - AseTekno OY
Pälkäneentie 18/PL 94
FIN-00511 Helsinki, FINLAND
Fax No.: 011-358-9-753-6463
Website: www.asetekno.fi
Email: jaakko.vottonen@asetekno.fi

TORUNARMS
Üzümlü – Beysehir
Konya, TURKEY
Fax No.: 011-90-332-524-7065
Website: www.torunarms.com
Email: export@torunsilah.com

TOZ
Pistol Importer - please refer to Larry's Guns listing.
Factory
1 a Sovetskaja Str.
RUS-300002 Tula, RUSSIA
Fax No: 011-70872-27-3439
Website: www.tulatoz.ru
Email: tozmarketing@home.tula.net

TRACKINGPOINT
10535 Boyer Blvd., Ste. 300
Austin, TX 78758
Phone No.: 512-222-0500
Website: www.tracking-point.com

TRADITIONS PERFORMANCE FIREARMS
1375 Boston Post Road
P.O. Box 776
Old Saybrook, CT 06475
Phone No.: 860-388-4656
Fax No.: 860-388-4657
Website: www.traditionsfirearms.com
Email: info@traditionsfirearms.com

TRANSFORMATIONAL DEFENSE INDUSTRIES, INC.
Please refer to Kriss USA listing.

TRAVOR
Importer – IWI US, Inc.
P.O. Box 126707
Harrisburg, PA 17112
Website: www.iwi.us
Email: info@iwi.us

TRISTAR SPORTING ARMS LTD.
1816 Linn St.
N. Kansas City, MO 64116
Phone No.: 816-421-1400
Fax No.: 816-421-4182
Website: www.tristarsportingarms.com
Email: tsaservice@tristarsportingarms.com

TROMIX CORPORATION
20039 E. 600 Road
Inola, OK 74036
Phone No.: 918-543-3456
Fax No.: 918-543-2920
Website: www.tromix.com
Email: rumore@tromix.com

TROY DEFENSE
A division of Troy Industries
West Springfield, MA 01089
Phone No.: 866-788-6412
Fax No.: 413-788-4610
Website: www.troyind.com
Website: www.troydefense.com

TRUVELO MANUFACTURERS (PTY) LTD.
Factory - Truvelo Armoury
P.O. Box 14189
Lyttelton 0140 SOUTH AFRICA
Fax No.: 011-27-11-203-1848
Website: www.truvelo.co.za
Email: armoury@truvelo.co.za

TULA ARMS PLANT
Factory
1 a Sovetskaja Str.
RUS-300002 Tula, RUSSIA
Fax No: 011-70872-27-3439
Website: www.tulatoz.ru
Email: tozmarketing@home.tula.net

TURNBULL MANUFACTURING CO.
6680 Rts. 5 & 20
Bloomfield, NY 14469
Phone No.: 585-657-6338
Fax No.: 585-657-7743
Website: www.turnbullrestoration.com
Email: info@turnbullmfg.com

U.S. HISTORICAL SOCIETY
Please refer to America Remembers listing.

U.S.R.A. PISTOLS
(Information Only)
Mr. L. Richard Littlefield
P.O. Box 9
Jaffrey, NH 03452
Phone No.: 603-532-8004

U.S. ARMAMENT CORP.
121 Valley View Drive
Ephrata, PA 17522
Phone No.: 717-721-4570
Fax No.: 717-738-4890
Website: www.usarmamentcorp.com
Email: info@usarmamentcorp.com

U.S. ORDNANCE
Commercial Distributor - Desert Ordnance
300 Sydney Drive
McCarran, NV 89434
Phone No.: 775-343-1330
Fax No.: 775-313-9852
Website: www.desertord.com
Email: questions@desertord.com

U.S. SPORTING GOODS
P.O. Box 560746
Rockledge, FL 32956
Phone No.: 321-639-4842
Fax No.: 321-639-7006
Website: www.ussginc.com
Email: ussg@eaacorp.com

UBERTI, A. & C., S.r.l.
Importer - please refer to Stoeger Industries listing.
Importer - please refer to Taylor's listing.
Importer - please refer to Dixie Gun Works listing.
Importer - please refer to Cabela's listing.
Importer - please refer to Cimarron, F.A. & Co listing.
Importer - please refer to Navy Arms listing.
Service & Repair - please refer to VTI Gun Parts listing.
Factory - A. Uberti & C., S.r.l.
Via Artigiani 1
I-25063 Gardone, VT (BS) ITALY
Fax No.: 011-39-030-834-1801
Website: www.ubertireplicas.it
Email: info@ubertireplicas.it

UGARTECHEA, ARMAS
Importer - please refer to Aspen Outfitting Co. listing.
Importer - please refer to Lion Country Supply listing.
Factory
P.O. Box 21
E-20600, Eibar, SPAIN
Fax No.: 011-3443-121669

UMAREX SPORTWAFFEN GmbH & CO. KG
Importer - Colt AR-15 .22 LR only & Airguns
Umarex USA (Rimfire firearms)
7700 Chad Colley Blvd.
Ft. Smith, AR 72916
Phone No.: 479-646-4210
Fax No.: 479-646-4206
Website: www.umarexusa.com
Factory
Donnerfeld 2
D-59757 Arnsberg GERMANY
Fax No.: 011-49-2932-638224
Website: www.umarex.de

UNIQUE-ALPINE
Postfach 15 55
D-85435 Erding Bavaria GERMANY
Fax No.: 011-49-08122-9797-230
Website: www.unique-alpine.org
Email: info@unique-alpine.com

USELTON ARMS INC.
390 Southwinds Dr.
Franklin, TN 37064
Phone No.: 615-595-2255
Fax No.: 615-595-2254
Website: www.useltonarms.com

UTAS
Importer – UTAS USA
1247 Rand Road
Des Plaines, IL 60016
Phone No.: 847-768-1011
Fax No.: 847-768-1001
Website: www.utas-usa.com

Factory – UTAS Makine, Ltd.
Caglayan Mah., 2020 Sok. Uğur Apt.
No.:9/1 07230, Antalya, TURKEY
Fax No.: 011-90-242-323-6676
Website: www.utasturk.com

UZI
Importer – IWI US, Inc.
P.O. Box 126707
Harrisburg, PA 17112
Website: www.iwi.us
Email: info@iwi.us
Repair & Service - please refer to Vector Arms, Inc. listing.

VO VAPEN AB
Box 29
290 34 Fjalkinge, SWEDEN
Fax No.: 011-46-44-50822
Website: www.vovapen.com
Email: ulf@vovapen.com

VALKYRIE ARMS LTD.
120 State Ave. NE, No. 381
Olympia, WA 98501
Phone/Fax No.: 360-482-4036
Website: www.valkyriearms.com
Email: info@valkyriearms.com

VALMET
Please refer to Finnclassic listing.

VALOR ARMS
2812 Riverview Road
Akron, OH 44313
Phone No.: 330-962-8269
Website: www.valorarms.us
Email: valorarms@gmail.com

VALTRO
Importer – Valtro USA
P.O. Box 56384
Hayward, CA 94545-6384
Phone No.: 510-489-8477
Website: www.valtrousa.com
Factory – Italian Arms Srl
Via de Gasperi 26/C,
25060 Collebeato (BS), ITALY
Fax No.: 39-030-2512545

VAN DYKE RIFLE DESIGNS
2324 17 RD
Plainville, KS 67663
Phone No.: 785-434-7577
Fax No.: 785-434-7517
Website: www.vandykerifles.com
Email: vandyke82@yahoo.com

VECTOR ARMS INC.
270 West 500 North
N. Salt Lake, UT 84054
Phone No.: 801-295-1917
Fax No.: 801-295-9316
Website: www.vectorarms.com
Email: vectorarms@bbscmail.com

VEGA
Importer – please refer to Task Firearms LLC listing.
Tigcilar Sk. No. 2
34116 Mercan-Istanbul TURKEY
Fax No.: 011-90-212-512-0879
Website: www.vegaarms.com
Email: vega@vegarms.com

VEKTOR
Denel
P.O. Box 7710
Pretoria
0001 SOUTH AFRICA
Fax No.: 011-27-12-664-0397
Website: www.denellandsystems.co.za

VEPR. RIFLES
Importer - please refer to Robinson Armament listing.
Factory - MOLOT JSC
Vyatskie Polyany Machine Building Plant
135 Lenin St., Vyatski Polyany
RUS-612960 Kirov Region, RUSSIA
Fax No.: 011-007-83334-61832
Website: www.molot.biz

VERNEY-CARRON
Importer – please refer to Kebco LLC listing.
Factory - Verney-Carron S.A.
54, Boulevard Thiers
Boite Postale 80072
F-42002 St.-Etienne Cedex 1 FRANCE
Phone No.: 011-33-477-791500
Fax No.: 011-33-477-790702
Website: www.verney-carron.com
Email: email@verney-carron.com

VERONA
Parts and Service only - please refer to Legacy Sports listing.

VIGILANCE RIFLES
3795 N. Hwy 89 Ste. E
Chino Valley, AZ 86323
Phone No.: 877-884-4336
Website: www.vigilancerifles.com
Email: affedm@aol.com

VI-MA s.n.c. di VIVENSI m. & C.
via Madonnina, 42
I-25060 Marcheno, VT (Brescia) ITALY
Fax No.: 011-39-030-8913519
Website: www.meccanicavima.it
Email: info@meccanicavima.it

VINTAGE ORDNANCE COMPANY, LLC
PO Box 902
Elizabethtown, KY 42702
Phone No.: 866-983-0006
Website: www.vintageordnance.com

VIPER
Please refer to Tristar listing.

VLTOR WEAPONS SYSTEM
3735 N. Romero Road
Tucson, AZ 85705
Phone No.: 520-408-1944
Fax No.: 520-293-8807
Website: www.vltor.com
Email: sales@vltor.com

VOERE
Factory - Voere Austria
Untere Sparchen 56
A-6330 Kufstein, AUSTRIA
Fax No.: 011-43-5372-65752
Website : www.voere.com
Email: office@voere.at

VOLKMANN PRECISION LLC
11160 S. Deer Creek Rd.
Littleton, CO 80127
Phone No.: 303-884-8654
Website: www.volkmannprecision.com
Email: volkmannprecision @yahoo.com

VOLQUARTSEN CUSTOM
P.O. Box 397
24276 240th St.
Carroll, IA 51401
Phone No.: 712-792-4238
Fax No.: 712-792-2542
Website: www.volquartsen.com
Email: info@volquartsen.com

VOLTRAN
Please refer to Akdal listing.

VTI GUN PARTS
P.O. Box 509
Lakeville, CT 06039
Phone No.: 860-435-8068
Fax No.: 860-435-8146
Website: www.vtigunparts.com

VULCAN ARMAMENT, INC.
P.O. Box 2473
So. South Paul, MN 55076-8473
Phone No.: 651-451-5956
Website: www.vulcanarms.com

W. SCHASCHL-OUTSCHAR GmbH
Josef-Ogris-Gasse 23
9170 Ferlach, Osterreich, AUSTRIA
Fax No.: 011-43-04227-2998
Website: www.outschar.at
Email: info@outschar.at

WAFFEN HIENDLMAYER GmbH
Landshuter Strasse 59
D-84307 Eggenfelden GERMANY
Fax No.: 011-49-8721-6451
website: www.waffen-hiendlmayer.de
Email: mail@waffen-hiendlmayer.de

WAFFEN JUNG GmbH
Am Alten Garten 7
53797 Lohmar, GERMANY
Fax No.: 011-49-0224618491
Website: www.waffenjung.de
Email: info@waffenjung.de

WAFFEN KESSLER
Land – Au 6
D-94469 Deggendorf, GERMANY
Fax No.: 011-49-991-284841
Website: www.kesslerin.info
Email: roland@waffen-kessler.de

WAFFENSTUBE GUGGI
Wienerstrasse 9
A-8020 Graz AUSTRIA
Fax No.: 011-43-316-711878
Website: www.guggi-arms.com
Email: office@guggi-arms.com

WALTHER
Importer – Walther Arms, Inc.
7700 Chad Colley Boulevard
Fort Smith, AR 72916
Phone No.: 479-242-8500
Website: www.waltherams.com
Target pistol & rifle importer - please refer to Champion's Choice Inc. listing.
GSP/rifle conversion kits & factory repair station - Earl's Repair Service, Inc.
437 Chandler Street (rear)
Tewksbury, MA 01876
Phone No.: 978-851-2656
Fax No.: 978-851-9462
Website: www.carlwalther.com
Email: info@carlwalther.com
German Company Headquarters (Umarex)
Carl Walther Sportwaffen GmbH
Donnerfeld 2
D-59757 Arnsberg GERMANY
Fax No.: 011-49-29-32-638149
Website: www.carl-walther.de
Email: sales@carl-walther.de
Factory - Carl Walther, GmbH Sportwaffenfabrik
Postfach 4325
D-89033 Ulm/Donau, GERMANY
Fax No.: 011-49-731-1539170

WATSON BROS.
54 Redchuch Street,
City of London, U.K.
Website: www.watsonbrosgunmakers.com
Email: Michael.Louca@WatsonBrosGunMakers.com

WEATHERBY
1605 Commerce Way
Paso Robles, CA 93446
Technical Support: 805-227-2600
Service/Warranty: 800-227-2023
Fax No.: 805-237-0427
Website: www.weatherby.com

WEBLEY & SCOTT AG
Importer - Webley & Scott, USA
4750 Longley Lane, Ste 208
Reno, NV 89502
Phone: 775-825-9835
Website: www.webleyandscott.com.
Factory
PilitusStrasse 38
Postfach 2621
CH-6002 Luzern, SWITZERLAND
Fax: 011-41-0800-0073-153
Website: www.webley.co.uk
Factory – please refer to Commando Arms listing.

WEIHRAUCH & WEIHRAUCH SPORT GmbH & CO. KG
Industriestase 13
D-97638 Mellrichstadt, GERMANY
Phone No.: 011-49-09776-81220
Website: www.weihrauch-sport.de
Email: info@weihrach-sport.de

WEIHRAUCH, HERMANNREVOLVER GmbH
Revolvers only
Importer (some models) – please refer to EAA Corp. listing.
Factory
Postfach 25
D-97634 Mellrichstadt, GERMANY
Fax No.: 011-49-9776-707679
Website: www.hermann-weirhauch-revolver.de
Email: info@hermann-weihrauch-revolver.de

WERNER BARTOLOT
Egger Strasse 5
A-9620 Hermagor, AUSTRIA
Fax No.: 011-43-0428225205
Website: www.rifles-and-guns.com
Email: office@bartolot.at

DAN WESSON FIREARMS
Distributor - please refer to CZ-USA listing.
Factory
5169 Highway 12 South
Norwich, NY 13815
Phone No.: 607-336-1174
Fax No.: 607-336-2730
Website: www.danwessonfirearms.com

WESTLEY RICHARDS & CO., Ltd.
Importer - Westley Richards Agency USA
3810 Valley Commons Drive, Ste. 2
Bozeman, MT 59718
Phone No.: 406-586-1946
Fax No.: 406-586-3326
Factory
130 Pritchett Street
Birmingham, U.K. B6 4EH
Fax No.: 011-44-121-333-1901
Website: www.westleyrichards.co.uk

WICHITA ARMS, INC.
(Parts Only)
923 E. Gilbert
Wichita, KS 67211
Phone No.: 316-265-0661
Fax No.: 316-265-0760
Website: www.wichitaarms.com
Email: info@wichitaarms.com

WIFRA
Please refer to W.R. Saleri listing.

WILD WEST GUNS, LLC.
7100 Homer Drive
Anchorage, AK 99518
Phone No.: 800-992-4570
Fax No.: 907-344-4005
Nevada Location
5225 Wynn Road
Las Vegas, NV 89118
Phone No.: 702-798-4570
Fax No.: 702-895-9850
Website: www.wildwestguns.com
Email: Alaska@wildwestguns.com
Email: vegas@wildwestguns.com

JOHN WILKES GUNMAKERS LTD.
Factory
10-12 Fitzalan Road
Arundel, West Sussex
BN18 9JS U.K.
Website: www. craigwhitseygunmakers.co.uk
Email: info@craigwhitseygunmakers.co.uk

WILLIAM & SON
14 Mount Street
Mayfair, London, W1K 2RF U.K.
Phone No.: 011-44-020-7493-8385
Fax No.: 011-44-020-7493-8386
Website: www.williamandson.com
Email: info@williamandson.com

WILLIAM LARKIN MOORE & CO.
16622 North 91st. St., #103
Scottsdale, AZ 85260
Phone No.: 480-951-8913
Fax No.: 480-951-3677
Website: www.williamlarkinmoore.com
Email: info@williamlarkinmoore.com

WILLIAM EVANS LIMITED
The Old Armoury
Bisley Camp, Brookwood
Woking, Surrey, GU24 0NY U.K.
Fax No.: 011-44-1483486580
Website: www.williamevans.com
Email: sales@williamevans.com

WILLIAM POWELL & SON (GUNMAKERS), Ltd.
Factory & Store
Carrs House, 1 Tramway, Banbury
Oxfordshire, OX16 5TD, U.K.
Phone No.: 011-4401295-701701
Website: www.william-powell.co.uk
Email: sales@william-powell.co.uk

WILSON COMBAT
2234 CR 719
P.O. Box 578
Berryville, AR 72616-0578
Phone No.: 800-955-4856
Fax No.: 870-545-3310
Website: www.wilsoncombat.com

WINCHESTER - REPEATING ARMS
Administrative Offices
275 Winchester Avenue
Morgan, UT 84050-9333
Customer Service Phone No.: 800-333-3288
Parts & Service Phone No.: 800-945-1392
Fax No.: 801-876-3737
Website: www.winchesterguns.com
Winchester Parts and Service
3005 Arnold Tenbrook Rd.
Arnold, MO 63010-9406
Phone No.: 800-322-4626
Fax No.: 636-287-9751

WINCHESTER/OLIN
Models 101 & 23 only (Disc.)
Attn: Shotgun Customer Service
427 N. Shamrock Street
East Alton, IL 62024
Fax No.: 618-258-3393
Website: www.winchester.com

WINDHAM WEAPONRY
999 Roosevelt Trail
Windham, ME 04062
Phone No.: 855-808-1888
Fax No.: 207-893-1632
Website: www.windhamweaponry.com

WINGSHOOTING ADVENTURES
9516 Taft Street
Coopersville, MI 49404-9418
Phone No.: 616-837-9000
Fax No.: 616-837-9002
Website: www.wingshootingadv.com
Email: jack@wingshootingadv.com

WISCHO JAGD-UND SPORTWAFFEN
Frankonia Handels GmbH & Co. KG
Schießhausstraße 10
97228 Rottendorf GERMANY
Website: www.wischo.com
Email: info@wischo.com

WISEMAN, BILL & CO., Inc.
18456 State Hwy. 6 South
College Station, TX 77845
Phone No.: 979-690-3456
Fax No.: 979-690-0156
Website: www.wisemanballistics.com
Email: w.w.wiseman1942@gmail.com

WOODWARD, JAMES AND SONS
Factory - please refer to Purdey, James, & Sons, Ltd. listing.

WYOMING ARMORY
356 West Yellowstone Ave.
Cody, WY 82414
Phone No.: 307-527-4570
Website: www.wyomingarmory.com

XTREME MACHINING
Distributor -please refer to American Tactical Imports listing.
500 Cooper Ave.
Grassflat, PA 16839
Phone No.: 814-345-6290
Website: www.xtrememachining.biz

YANKEE HILL MACHINE CO., INC.
20 Ladd Ave., Ste. 1
Florence, MA 01062
Phone No.: 877-892-6533
Fax No.: 413-586-1326
Website: www.yhm.net

YILDIZ SILAH SANAYI
Importer - Academy Sports
Multiple store locations in the Southeast
Website: www.academy.com
Factory
Organize Sanayi Bölgesi 40, Sokak No. 13
TR-15100 Burdur TURKEY
Fax No.: 01190-0248-252-9569
Website: www.yildizshotgun.com

ZDF IMPORT EXPORT INC.
Please refer to Robinson Armament listing.

Z-M WEAPONS
1958 Wes White Hill Road
Richmond, VT 05477
Phone No.: 802-777-8964
Fax No.: 802-434-7426
Website: www.zmweapons.com
Email: zm@zmweapons.com

ZVI
MPI Group Ltd.
Holeckova Str. 31
150 95 Prague 5 CZECH REPUBLIC
Fax No.: 044-420-257-325-910
Website: www.zvi.cz
Email: info@zvi.cz

LAURONA – ZABALA
Please refer to Laurona listing.

ZANARDINI
Importer – please refer to Kevin's listing.
Factory - Zanardini, P. & C., S.n.c.
Via C. Goldoni, 34
I-25063 Gardone V.T. (Brescia), ITALY
Fax No.: 011-39-030-837180
Website: www.zanardini.com
Email: info@zanardini.com

ZANOTTI, R.
Factory
via San Donato 78/A
40127 Bologna, ITALY
Website: www.renatozanottiarmi.it

ZANOTTI, STEFANO
Please refer to Renato Gamba listing.

ZASTAVA ARMS
Importer - please refer to Century listing.
Importer - please refer to European American Armory listing.
Importer – please refer to USSG listing.
Factory
Trg Topolivaca 4
34000 Kragujevac, SERBIA
Fax No.: 011-381-034-323683
Website: www.zastava-arms.co.rs

ZBROJOVKA BRNO
Please refer to the CZ USA listing.

ZELENY SPORT s.r.o.
Slatina 116
56601 Vysoke Myto, CZECH REPUBLIC
Website: www.zelenysport.cz

ZIEGENHAHN & SOHN OHG
Importer - please refer to New England Custom Gun Service, Ltd. listing.
Importer - please refer to Heirloom Arms listing.
Factory
Suhler Str. 9 A
D-98544 Zella-Mehlis GERMANY
Fax No.: 011-49-36-82-896-28
Website: www.ziegenhahn.de
Email: info@ ziegenhahn.de

ZOLI, ANTONIO
Not affiliated with Angelo Zoli.
Importer & Distributor - Antonio Zoli America
4385 Recreational Dr.
Canandaigua, NY 14424
Phone No.: 585-394-2171
Fax No.: 585-394-1909
Website: www.zoli-northamerica.com
Email: zguns@rochester.rr.com
Service, Warranty & Custom Shop - please refer to Cole Gunsmithing listing.
Factory - Antonio Zoli S.r.l.
Via Zanardelli, 39
I-25063 Gardone V.T. (BS) ITALY
Fax No.: 011-39-030-891-1165
Website: www.zoli.it
Email: world@zoli.it

GLOSSARY

1989 BUSH BAN

Refers to the U.S. Federal executive branch study and resulting regulations which banned the importation of firearms which did not meet sporting criteria , i.e. certain paramilitary semi-auto only rifles and shotguns. The study was undertaken in response to the Stockton, CA tragedy in which an AK-47 type rifle was criminally used by a so-called mass murderer. The Federal regulation, U.S.C. Title 18, Section 922r, applies to imported firearms and to firearms assembled in the U.S. using imported components. It is important to note that even though the Assault Weapon Ban (which applied to U.S. manufactured firearms, not imports) has expired, Section 922r remains in effect, and has the force of U.S. Federal law, regardless of its executive branch origin as opposed to U.S. Senate and House of Representatives legislation. Also see Section 922r.

5R

Five groove rifling developed in Russia. Instead of conventional six groove rifling with opposing lands and sharp edged transitions between lands and grooves, 5R lands oppose grooves and the sides of lands are cut at a sixty-five degree angle. Claimed benefits are: decreased bullet deformation, less jacket fouling, increased velocity, and greater accuracy.

A1 STYLE

Refers to an AR style rifle in A1 configuration, or A1 specific components (triangular handguard, short fixed buttstock, receiver with integral carry handle, four slot bird cage flash hider, smooth pistol grip, rear flip sight with short and long range apertures, lighter weight 1:14 twist barrel).

A2 STYLE

Refers to an AR style rifle in A2 configuration, or A2 specific components (circular bi-lateral handguard, longer fixed buttstock, receiver with integral carry handle and spent case deflector, five slot bird cage flash hider, finger rib pistol grip, windage and elevation adjustable rear flip sight with small day and large low light apertures, heavier weight 1:7 twist barrel).

A3 STYLE

Refers to an AR style rifle in A3 configuration, or A3 specific components (circular bi-lateral handguard, collapsible buttstock, receiver with flat top Picatinny rail and detachable carry handle, A2 flash hider/pistol grip/rear sight/barrel).

A4 STYLE

Refers to an AR style rifle in A4 configuration, or A4 specific components (same as A2 except for Modular Weapons System handguard).

ACCOUTREMENT

All equipment carried by soldiers on the outside of their uniform, such as buckles, belts, or canteens, but not weapons.

ACTION

An assembly consisting of the receiver or frame and the mechanism by which a firearm is loaded, fired, and unloaded. See ACTION TYPES for the various kinds of actions.

ACTION BAR FLATS

See WATER TABLE.

ACTION TYPES

Actions are broadly classified as either manual or self-loading. Manual actions may be single shot or repeater. Single shot actions include dropping block (tilting, falling, and rolling), break, hinged, and bolt. Repeater actions include revolver, bolt, lever, pump, and dropping block. Self-loading actions may be semiautomatic or automatic. Semi-auto and automatic actions by sub-type are:

a. blowback: simple, lever delayed, roller delayed, gas delayed, toggle delayed, hesitation locked, and chamber-ring delayed.

b. blow-forward.

c. recoil: short, long, and inertia.

d. gas: short stroke piston, long stroke piston, direct impingement, and gas trap.

ADJUSTABLE CHOKE

A device built into the muzzle of a shotgun enabling changes from one choke to another.

ADJUSTABLE FRONT SIGHT
A front sight which can be moved, relative to the barrel's axis, vertically for elevation and/or horizontally for windage adjustments.

ADJUSTABLE REAR SIGHT
A rear sight which can be moved, relative to the barrel's axis, vertically for elevation and/or horizontally for windage adjustments.

ADJUSTABLE SIGHT
A firearm sight which can be adjusted so that the shooter's point of aim and the projectile's point of impact coincide at a desired target distance. On a majority of firearms only the rear sight is adjustable, but front sights may also be adjustable.

AIRGUN
A gun that utilizes compressed air or gas to launch the projectile.

AK/AKM STYLE ACTION
A gas operated rifle action with a long-stroke gas piston, a tilting breechblock locking design, and a heavy milled (early versions) or lighter sheet metal (later versions) receiver. No regulator is used; the overall design, machining, tolerances, ease of maintenance, and component durability assure reliable function in all circumstances.

ANY OTHER WEAPON
Any other firearm which is not an NFA defined machine gun, short barrel rifle, short barrel shotgun, modern shoulder stocked pistol, suppressor (BATFE uses the term "silencer"), or destructive device. An AOW is: a device capable of being concealed on a person from which a shot can be discharged through the energy of an explosive; a smooth bore barrel pistol or revolver designed or redesigned to fire a fixed shotgun shell; a weapon with combination shotgun and rifle barrels twelve inches or more but less than eighteen inches in length, from which only a single discharge can be made from either barrel without manual reloading; and any such weapon which may be readily restored to fire. AOW examples: H&R Handyguns, Ithaca Auto-Burglar guns, cane guns, and guns modified/disguised so as to be unrecognizable as firearms.

APERTURE SIGHT
An iron rear sight which has a hole or aperture in a disc or semi-circular blade instead of a rectangular or "vee" notch of an open sight. May also be a front sight, or adjustable for windage/elevation, or have adjustable/interchangeable apertures.

AR-15 STYLE ACTION
A gas operated rifle action with a direct gas impingement system (i.e. no gas piston, no regulator, no moving parts), a bolt carrier enclosing a multi-lugged rotating bolt locking design, and a two-part light-weight receiver. Propellant gas flows through a gas tube, acts directly upon the bolt carrier to cycle the action, and vents into the receiver. AR-15 style actions have fewer parts, are more adaptable/modifiable, and are significantly lighter than AK, FAL, or HK91 style actions. However, more maintenance, cleaning, and lubrication are absolutely required for reliability, in contrast to other gas operated actions.

ASSAULT RIFLE
Definition usually depends on if you're pro-gun or anti-gun. If you're pro-gun, it generally refers to a military styled, short to immediate range battle rifle capable of selective fire (semi-auto or full auto). If you're anti-gun, it can include almost anything, including sporter rifles from the turn of the 20th century.

ASSAULT SHOTGUN
Refers to a shotgun manufactured by contract for the military or law enforcement with a barrel shorter than 18 inches, usually a semi-auto or slide action configuration.

ASSAULT WEAPONS BAN
Popular title for the Violent Crime Control and Law Enforcement Act of 1994, Public Law 103-322. See VIOLENT CRIME...LAW 103-322.

AUTO LOADING/LOADER
See SEMI-AUTO ACTION.

AUTOMATIC ACTION
An action design which continuously fires and performs all steps in the operating cycle if the trigger remains fully depressed and ammunition is present in the firearm's magazine or feeding system. Also known as full auto or fully automatic. Machine guns utilize automatic actions, which may be recoil, gas, or externally powered.

AUTOMATIC EJECTOR
See SELECTIVE AUTOMATIC EJECTOR.

BACK BORE/BACK-BORED
A shotgun barrel which has been bored to a diameter greater than normal for its gauge, but not greater than SAAMI specs for that gauge. The advantages of this are: higher shot velocity, more uniform and denser patterns and fewer deformed pellets.

BACK UP IRON SIGHTS
Flip up or fixed iron sights which are not the primary sight system. They are used if the primary optical sight system fails and usually co-witness (optic sight picture and back up sight picture share the same zero).

BACKSTRAP
Those parts of the revolver or pistol frame which are exposed at the rear of the grip.

BARREL
The steel tube (may be wrapped in a sleeve of synthetic material) which a projectile travels through. May or may not be rifled.

BARREL BAND
A metal band, either fixed or adjustable, around the forend of a gun that holds the barrel to the stock.

BARREL FLATS
The lower flat surfaces under the chambers of side-by-side shotgun barrels which contact the corresponding flat areas of the shotgun's receiver. Also see WATER TABLE.

BARREL LUG
A projection which extends from a barrel and performs a locating, supporting, or energy transfer function. Lugs may be separate components, or integral to barrels.

BARREL THROAT
At the breech end of a barrel, the segment of the bore which tapers from a non-rifled projectile diameter to a fully rifled dimension. Also known as a forcing cone, leade, lede, or throat.

BATFE 922r COMPLIANT
A semi-auto paramilitary rifle (assembled with U.S. and foreign manufactured parts) which meets the statutory requirements of Section 922r of the United States code. Also refers to U.S. made parts which bring the rifle into compliance.

BATTUE
A ramped fixed rear sight assembly located on the back of the barrel, allowing quick target acquisition.

BEAVERTAIL FOREND
A wider than normal forend.

BENCH REST STOCK
A rifle stock specifically designed for a "bench rest" competition rifle which is fired from a table or bench, but supported only by sandbags or other devices. Optimized for stability, it often has a very wide flat-bottomed forend.

BESPOKE
A British term for a firearm custom-made to the purchaser's specifications. From the verb "bespeak", which means "to give order for it to be made".

BIRD'S HEAD
Refers to curved grip configuration on revolvers which resembles the outline of a bird's head, usually with 3 1/2 - 5 1/2 in. barrel lengths. Patterned after the grips on Colt's 1877 Thunderer revolver.

BLIND MAGAZINE
A box magazine which is completely concealed within the action and stock.

BLOWBACK ACTION
A semi-automatic or automatic firearm operating design which uses expanding propellant gasses to push a heavy unlocked breech bolt open, and which relies upon the inertia of its moving parts to keep the action closed until the bullet has exited the muzzle and pressure has decreased to a safe level.

BLUING

The chemical process of artificial oxidation (rusting) applied to gun parts so that the metal attains a dark blue or nearly black appearance.

BOLT

An assembly which reciprocates along the axis of a firearm's bore; it supports the cartridge case head and locks the action. Also see BOLT ACTION.

BOLT (REVOLVER)

The lug or projection which rises from a revolver's frame in order to immobilize the cylinder and align a charge hole with the bore of the barrel. Also called a cylinder stop.

BOLT ACTION

A manual action with a bolt body (usually including locking, firing pin, extractor, and ejector components) enclosed by and moving within the firearm's receiver.

BORE

Internal dimensions of a barrel (smooth or rifled) that can be measured using the Metric system (i.e. millimeters), English system (i.e. inches), or by the Gauge system (see GAUGE). On a rifled barrel, the bore is measured across the lands. Also, it is a traditional English term used when referring to the diameter of a shotgun muzzle (gauge in U.S. measure).

BOX MAGAZINE

A boxlike feed device for a firearm, which allows cartridges to be stacked one on top of the other. Most box magazines are removable for reloading.

BOXLOCK ACTION

Typified by Parker shotguns in U.S. and Westley Richards in England. Generally considered inferior in strength to the sidelock. Developed by Anson & Deeley, the boxlock is hammerless. It has two disadvantages. First, the hammer pin must be placed directly below knee of action, which is its weakest spot. Second, action walls must be thinned out to receive locks. These are inserted from below into large slots in the action body, which is then closed with a plate. If a correctly made Greener crossbolt is used, many of the boxlock's weaknesses can be negated. Also see CROSSBOLT.

BRADY ACT/BILL

See BRADY HANDGUN VIOLENCE PREVENTION ACT.

BRADY HANDGUN VIOLENCE PREVENTION ACT

1998 Federal legislation which established the National Instant Criminal Background Check System (NICS). Also commonly known as the Brady Bill, or the Brady Act. See NATIONAL INSTANT CRIMINAL BACKGROUND CHECK SYSTEM.

BREAK BARREL ACTION

A type of action where the barrels pivot on a hinge pin, allowing access to the chamber(s) in the breech. Configurations include: single shot, SxS, O/U, combination guns, drillings, and vierlings.

BREAK OPEN ACTION

See BREAK BARREL ACTION

BREECH

The rear end of a barrel where a cartridge is chambered. Also commonly used in reference to the entire chamber, breech, and receiver of long guns.

BREVETTE

French word which, in gun terminology, refers to a European copy (usually English, French, or Belgian) or patterned after a more famous design (i.e., Brevette Remington O/U derringer refers to a copy of the Remington O/U .41 cal. derringer).

BUCKHORN SIGHT

Open metallic rear sight with sides that curl upward and inward.

BULL BARREL

A heavier, thicker than normal barrel with little or no taper.

BULLET BUTTON

A magazine locking device for AR-15 style rifles. It transforms a rifle with a standard manually operable magazine release and detachable magazine functionality into a fixed magazine rifle in order to comply with the State of California's firearm statutes. Depressing the "button" with a tool, e.g. bullet tip, small screwdriver, etc., is the only way to remove the magazine (which cannot hold more than ten rounds).

BUTT SPIKE

A fixed or adjustable monopod mounted near the rear on the bottom of a rifle's buttstock that, when used with forearm support of the rifle, enables the user to observe the target area for extended periods with minimal fatigue.

BUTTPAD

A rubber or synthetic composition part attached to the buttstock's end; intended to absorb recoil energy, prevent damage to the buttstock, and vary length of pull. May be fixed, solid, ventilated, or adjustable (horizontally, vertically, cant).

BUTTPLATE

A protective plate, usually steel, attached to the back of the buttstock.

BUTTSTOCK

The portion of a stock which is positioned against the user's shoulder; also known as the butt. On AR-15/M16 style or similar long guns, the separate component which is attached to the rear of the receiver. Also see STOCK.

CALIBER

The diameter of the bore (measured from land to land), usually measured in either inches or millimeters/centimeters. It does not designate bullet diameter.

CAMO (CAMOUFLAGE)

Refers to a patterned treatment using a variety of different colors/patterns that enables a gun to blend into a particular outdoors environment. In most cases, this involves a film or additional finish applied on top of a gun's wood and/or metal parts (i.e. Mossy Oak Break-Up, Advantage Timber, Realtree Hardwoods, etc.).

CARTOUCHE

Generally refers to a manufacturer's inspector marking impressed into the wood of a military gun, usually in the form of initials inside a circle or oval.

CASE COLORS

See COLOR CASE HARDENING.

CAST OFF

The distance that a buttplate is offset to the right of the line of sight for a right-handed shooter. Especially important in shotgun stocks.

CAST ON

The same as Cast Off, except that the buttplate is offset to the left of the line of sight for a left-handed shooter.

CENTERFIRE

Refers to ammunition with primers centrally positioned in the cartridge case head; or to a firearm which is chambered for centerfire ammunition.

CERAKOTE

A ceramic based firearms coating with improved performance and reliability compared to traditional firearms finishes. Offers abrasion, corrosion, and solvent protection, in many colors and designs.

CHAMBER

Rear part of the barrel which has been reamed out so that it will contain a cartridge. When the breech is closed, the cartridge is supported in the chamber, and the chamber must align the primer with the firing pin, and the bullet with the bore.

CHAMBER THROAT

See BARREL THROAT.

CHARGE HOLE

The hole bored completely through a revolver's cylinder in which cartridges are loaded.

CHARGING HANDLE

A semi-auto firearm component which is manipulated to cycle the action, but which does not fire the cartridge. Also called cocking handle, cocking knob, or operating handle.

CHECKERING

A functional decoration consisting of pointed pyramids cut into the wood or metal surfaces of a firearm. Generally applied to the pistol grip and forend/forearm areas, affording better handling and control.

CHEEKPIECE
An elevated section of the upper buttstock on which the shooter's cheek rests when holding a rifle or shotgun in firing position. It may be integral to the buttstock, or a separate component. Adjustable cheekpieces may be moved in one or more ways: up, down, fore, aft, or side-to-side.

CHOKE
The muzzle constriction on a shotgun which controls the spread of the shot.

CHOKE TUBES
Interchangeable screw-in devices allowing different choke configurations (i.e., cylinder, improved cylinder, improved modified, modified, full). While most choke tubes fit flush with the end of the barrel, some choke tubes now also protrude from the end of the barrel. Most recently made shotguns usually include three to five choke tubes with the shotgun.

CHOPPER LUMP
An underlug, and the barrel fabrication method, traditionally used for higher grade English SxS shotguns. A lump or underlug extending beneath the breech is forged as an integral part of each barrel. When the barrels are joined, the two lumps are carefully fitted on their mating surfaces and brazed solidly together into a single unit, into which locking and other functional recesses are cut. Also known as demi-bloc, demi-block, monobloc, or monoblock.

CLIP
A metal or synthetic material formed/shaped to hold cartridges in readiness to be loaded into a magazine or chamber. A clip is NOT a magazine (i.e., stripper clips for most variations of the Mauser Broomhandle). Also known as a stripper or cartridge clip.

COCKING INDICATOR
Any device for which the act of cocking a gun moves it into a position where it may be seen or felt, in order to notify the shooter that the gun is cocked. Typical examples are the pins found on some high-grade hammerless shotguns, which protrude slightly when they are cocked, and also the exposed cocking knobs on bolt-action rifles. Exposed hammers found on some rifles and pistols are also considered cocking indicators.

COIN FINISH
Older definition referring to a metal finish, typically on a rifle or shotgun, which resembles the finish of an old silver coin. Most coin finishes are based on nickel plating (not chrome) and are generally high polish.

COLLAPSIBLE STOCK
Mostly used in reference to a buttstock which can be shortened or lengthened along its fore to aft axis. Also applies in theory to top-folding, under-folding, and side folding buttstocks; all of which when folded reduce the weapon's length.

COLOR CASE HARDENING
A method of hardening steel and iron while imparting colorful swirls as well as surface figure. Traditional color case hardening using charcoal and bone meal is achieved by putting the desired metal parts in a crucible packed with a mixture of charcoal and finely ground animal bone to temperatures in the 800°C – 900°C range, after which they are slowly cooled. Then they are submerged into cold water, leaving a thin, colorful protective finish. Can also be achieved by treating the necessary metal parts with a cyanide liquid, which helps harden the metal surface, and can be denoted from charcoal color case hardening by a more layered color appearance.

COMB
The portion of the stock on which the shooter's cheek rests.

COMBINATION GUN
Generally, a break-open shotgun-type configuration that is fitted with at least one shotgun barrel and one rifle barrel. Such guns may be encountered with either two or three barrels, and less frequently with as many as four or five, and have been known to chamber as many as four different calibers.

COMPENSATOR
Slots, vents, or ports machined into a firearm's barrel near its muzzle, or a muzzle device, which allow propellant gasses to escape upwards and partially reduce muzzle jump.

CONTROLLED ROUND FEEDING
A bolt action rifle design in which the cartridge is mechanically secured by the extractor and bolt during all parts of the operating cycle.

CRANE
In a modern solid-frame, swing-out cylinder revolver, the U-shaped yoke on which the cylinder rotates, and which holds the cylinder in the frame. The crane/yoke is the weakest part of a revolver's mechanism.

CRIME BILL
Popular title for the Violent Crime Control and Law Enforcement Act of 1994, Public Law 103-322. See VIOLENT CRIME...LAW 103-322.

CRIMP
A turning in of the case mouth to affect a closure or to prevent the projectile(s) from slipping out of the case mouth. Various crimps include: roll, pie, star or folded, rose, stab, and taper.

CROSSBOLT
A transverse locking rod/bar used in many SxS boxlock shotguns and a few rifles, which locks the standing breech and barrels to each other. Originally designed by W.W. Greener, this term is also referred to as the Greener crossbolt. Also a transverse metal bolt which reinforces and prevents damage to the stock from recoil or abusive handling.

CROWNING
The rounding or chamfering normally done to a barrel muzzle to ensure that the mouth of the bore is square with the bore axis and that its edges are countersunk below the surface to protect it from impact damage. Traditionally, crowning was accomplished by spinning an abrasive-coated brass ball against the muzzle while moving it in a figure-eight pattern, until the abrasive had cut away any irregularities and produced a uniform and square mouth.

CRYOGENIC TEMPERING
Computer controlled cooling process that relieves barrel stress by subjecting the barrel to a temperature of -310 degrees Fahrenheit for 22 hours.

CURIO/RELIC
Firearms which are of special interest to collectors by reason of some quality other than that which is normally associated with firearms intended for sporting use or as offensive or defensive weapons. Must be older than 50 years.

CYLINDER
A rotating cartridge holder in a revolver. The cartridges are held in chambers and the cylinder turns, either to the left or the right, depending on the gun maker's design, as the hammer is cocked.

CYLINDER ARM
See CRANE.

DAMASCENE
The decorating of metal with another metal, either by inlaying or attaching in some fashion.

DAMASCUS BARREL
A barrel made by twisting, forming, and welding thin strips of steel around a mandrel.

DE-HORNING
The removal of all sharp edges from a firearm that would cut or pinch the shooter, the shooter's clothing, and/or holster, but still maintains the nice clean lines of the firearm.

DELAYED IMPINGEMENT GAS SYSTEM
A trademarked gas operating system for AR-15 style carbines, designed by Allan Zitta. Similar to a gas piston action in concept, it has instead an operating rod and recoil spring which run through the receiver, over the barrel, and sleeve the gas tube at the gas block. The gas tube does not enter the receiver, and the recoil spring replaces the buffer and spring in the AR-15 buttstock.

DEMI-BLOC/DEMI-BLOCK
See CHOPPER LUMP.

DERRINGER
Usually refers to a small, concealable pistol with one or two short barrels.

DETACHABLE MILITARY STYLE BIPOD
A bipod designed for severe/heavy use and greater durability, with a Picatinny rail or other type of quick attach/detach mounting system.

DIRECT IMPINGEMENT GAS SYSTEM
A gas operating system in which high pressure and temperature propellant gas is routed into the firearm receiver to make contact with and move action components. There are no "moving parts" (e.g. piston, return spring, operating rod, tappet) in a direct impingement gas sytem. A typical direct impingement gas system has a gas block surrounding the barrel and covering the gas port, and a gas tube.

DOUBLE ACTION
The principle in a revolver or auto-loading pistol wherein the hammer can be cocked and dropped by a single pull of the trigger. Most of these actions also provide capability for single action fire. In auto loading pistols, double action normally applies only to the first shot of any series, the hammer being cocked by the slide for subsequent shots.

DOUBLE ACTION ONLY
A firearm action which cannot be operated in single action mode. Many newer DAO firearms are either hammerless, or their hammers and triggers cannot be positioned in a single action status.

DOUBLE UNDERLUGS
The two underlugs on the lower barrel of an over/under double barrel shotgun or rifle.

DOUBLE-BARREL(ED)
A gun which has two barrels joined either side-by-side or one over the other.

DOUBLE-SET TRIGGER
A device that consists of two triggers - one to cock the mechanism that spring-assists the other trigger, substantially lightening the other trigger's pull weight.

DOVETAIL
A flaring machined or hand-cut slot that is also slightly tapered toward one end. Cut into the upper surface of barrels and sometimes actions, the dovetail accepts a corresponding part on which a sight is mounted. Dovetail slot blanks are used to cover the dovetail when the original sight has been removed or lost; this gives the barrel a more pleasing appearance and configuration.

DRILLED & TAPPED
Refers to holes drilled into the top of a receiver/frame and threaded, which allow scope bases, blocks, rings, or other sighting devices to be rigidly attached to the gun.

DRILLING
German for triple, which is their designation for a three-barrel gun, usually two shotgun barrels and one rifle barrel.

EJECTOR
A firearm component which propels an extracted cartridge or fired case out of the receiver or chamber. Ejectors may be fixed or movable, spring loaded or manually activated. Also see SELECTIVE AUTOMATIC EJECTOR.

ELASTOMER
A synthetic elastic polymer, soft and compressible like natural rubber, used for seals, grip and stock inlays, and other molded firearm components.

ELECTROCIBLE
Unique reusable target designed like an aircraft propeller that causes it to spin and go in different directions. In competition, electrocibles come out of one of five boxes located 25 meters from the shooter, who must hit it before it crosses over the ring at 21 meters.

ELECTRO-OPTICAL SIGHT
An optical sight (see definition) with the addition of electronic battery powered components which illuminate a reticle (least complex), or which generate a reticle/optional reticles. Electro-optical sights may be: magnifying, non-magnifying, full-tube convention optical, or reflex types (see REFLEX SIGHT).

ELEVATION
A firearm sight's vertical distance above the barrel's bore axis; also the adjustment of a sight to compensate for the effect of gravity on a projectile's exterior ballistic path.

ENGINE TURNING
Machined circular polishing on metal, creating a unique overlapping pattern.

ENGLISH STOCK
A straight, slender-gripped stock.

ENGRAVING
The art of engraving metal in decorative patterns. Scroll engraving is the most common type of hand engraving encountered. Much of today's factory engraving is rolled on which is done mechanically. Hand engraving requires artistry and knowledge of metals and related materials.

ERGO SUREGRIP
A Falcon Industries Inc. right hand or ambidextrous replacement pistol grip for AR-15/M-16 style rifles. The grip has finger grooves, upper rear extension to support the web of the shooter's hand, is oil and solvent resistant, and a non-slip textured overmolded rubber surface.

ETCHING
A method of decorating metal gun parts, usually done by acid etching or photo engraving.

EXTRACTOR
A device which partially pulls a cartridge or fired hull/case/casing(s) from the chamber, allowing it to be removed manually.

FALLING BLOCK
A single shot action where the breechblock drops straight down when a lever is actuated.

FARQUHARSON ACTION
A single shot hammerless falling block rifle action patented in 1872 by John Farquharson.

FENCES
The hemispherical formations on a side-by-side shotgun's receiver which are adjacent to the barrel breeches. Originally fences were the curving metal flanges surrounding a percussion ignition firearm's nipple, or a flintlock ignition firearm's priming pan, which protected the shooter from sparks, smoke, and escaping gas.

FIBER OPTIC SIGHT
An iron sight with fiber optic light gathering rods or cylinders; the rod ends are perceived as glowing dots and enhance sight visibility and contrast.

FIT AND FINISH
Terms used to describe over-all firearm workmanship.

FIRE CONTROL GROUP
All components necessary to cause a cartridge to be fired; may be a self-contained assembly, easily disassembled or not user-serviceable, detachable, modular/interchangeable, and may or may not include a safety, bolt release, or other parts.

FIRING PIN
That part of a firearm which strikes the cartridge primer, causing detonation.

FLASH SUPPRESSOR/HIDER
A muzzle attachment which mechanically disrupts and reduces muzzle flash. It does not reduce muzzle blast or recoil.

FLAT-TOP UPPER
An AR-15/M16 style or other tactical semi-auto rifle with a literally flat receiver top. The majority of flat-top uppers have an extended Picatinny rail for mounting iron sights, optical sights, and other accessories, which provides much more versatility than the original "carry handle" receiver design.

FLOATING BARREL
A barrel bedded to avoid contact with any point on the stock.

FLOOR PLATE
Usually, a removable/hinged plate at the bottom of the receiver covering the magazine well.

FN FAL STYLE ACTION
A gas operated rifle action with a short-stroke spring-loaded gas piston, a tilting breechblock locking design, and a heavy receiver. A regulator valve allows the user to increase the volume of gas entering the system in order to ensure reliable operation in adverse conditions. Unlike direct gas impingement or delayed blowback operating systems, propellant gas does not vent into the receiver and fire control components.

FOLDING STOCK
Usually a buttstock hinged at or near the receiver so that it can be "folded" towards the muzzle, reducing the firearm's overall length. Not an adjustable stock as defined above, and usually does not prevent operating/firing when in its folded position.

FORCING CONE

The segment of a shotgun barrel immediately forward of the chamber where its internal diameter is reduced from chamber to bore diameter. The forcing cone aids the passage of shot into the barrel. For revolvers, the tapering portion of the barrel bore from the breech to the rifling.

FOREARM

In this text, a separate piece of wood in front of the receiver and under the barrel used for hand placement when shooting.

FOREARM/FOREND CAP

A separate piece attached to the muzzle end of a forearm; often with a colored spacer, and usually in a contrasting color/material.

FOREND/FORE-END

Usually the forward portion of a one-piece rifle or shotgun stock (in this text), but can also refer to a separate piece of wood.

FORWARD BOLT ASSIST

A button, usually found on AR-15 type rifles, which may be pushed or struck to move the bolt carrier fully forward so that the extractor has completely engaged the cartridge rim and the bolt has locked. Mainly used to close/lock the bolt when the rifle's chamber and receiver are excessively fouled or dirty.

FRAME

The part of a firearm to which the action (lock work), barrel, and stock/grip are connected. Most of the time used when referring to a handgun or hinged frame long gun.

FREE FLOATING FOREARM

A forearm which does not contact the barrel at any point, as it attaches and places mechanical stress only on the receiver. An accuracy enhancement for AR-15/M16 style rifles, which by their modular design, are not able to have a conventionally free floated barrel in a one-piece stock.

FREE RIFLE

A rifle designed for international-type target shooting. The only restriction on design is a weight maximum 8 kilograms (17.6 lbs.).

FRONT STRAP

That part of the revolver or pistol grip frame which faces forward and often joins with the trigger guard. In target guns, notably the .45 ACP, the front strap is often stippled to give shooter's hand a slip-proof surface.

FULL AUTO

See AUTOMATIC ACTION

GAS IMPINGEMENT OPERATING SYSTEM

An action in which high pressure propellant gas is diverted from the barrel to supply the energy required to unlock the breech, extract/eject the fired case, load a cartridge, and lock the breech. This type of system generates a large amount of heat and also a considerable amount of fouling directly back into the action.

GAS PISTON OPERATING SYSTEM

A gas operation design in which a piston is used to transfer propellant gas energy to the action components. No gas enters the receiver or makes contact with other action components. Consequently, less heat is absorbed by, and less fouling accumulates in the receiver. This system also has a much different recoil pulse or "feel".

GAS PORT

A small opening in the barrel of a gas operated firearm which allows high pressure gas to flow into the gas system's components. Also an escape vent in a firearm's receiver, a safety feature.

GAUGE/GA.

A unit of measure used to determine a shotgun's bore. Determined by the amount of pure lead balls equaling the bore diameter needed to equal one pound (i.e., a 12 ga. means that 12 lead balls exactly the diameter of the bore weigh one pound). In this text, .410 is referenced as a bore (if it was a gauge, it would be a 68 ga.).

GAUGE VS. BORE DIAMETER

10-Gauge = Bore Diameter of .775 inches or 19.3mm

12-Gauge = Bore Diameter of .729 inches or 18.2mm

16-Gauge = Bore Diameter of .662 inches or 16.8mm

20-Gauge = Bore Diameter of .615 inches or 15.7mm

28-Gauge = Bore Diameter of .550 inches or 13.8mm

68-Gauge = Bore Diameter of .410 inches or 12.6mm

GCA

The Gun Control Act of 1968, 18 USC Chapter 44.

GLACIERGUARDS

AR-15/M-16 carbine length replacement handguard (two-piece) which has fifteen internal heat dispersing fins rather than the standard heat shield. The fins provide greater strength and rigidity; fiber-reinforced polymer shells resist heat and reduce weight. A DPMS product.

GRIP

The handle used to hold a handgun, or the area of a stock directly behind and attached to the frame/receiver of a long gun.

GRIPS

Can be part of the frame or components attached to the frame used to assist in accuracy, handling, control, and safety of a handgun. Many currently manufactured semi-auto handguns have grips that are molded w/checkering as part of the synthetic frame.

GRIPSTRAP(S)

Typically refers to the front and back metal attached to a handgun frame which supports the grips/stocks. Also known as the front strap and back strap.

GROOVES

The spiral depressions of the rifling in a barrel bore; created by cutting, swaging, broaching, hammering, cation action, or other methods. Also see LANDS and RIFLING.

HALF COCK

A position of the hammer in a hammer activated firing mechanism that serves as a manual safety.

HAMMER

A part of a gun's mechanism which applies force to the firing pin or other components, which in turn fires the gun.

HAMMERLESS

Some "hammerless" firearms do in fact have hidden hammers, which are located in the action housing. Truly hammerless guns, such as the Savage M99, have a firing mechanism based on a spring-powered striker.

HANDGUARD

A wooden, synthetic, or ventilated metal part attached above the barrel and ahead of the receiver to protect the shooter's hand from the heat generated during semi-auto rapid firing.

HEEL

Back end of the upper edge of the butt stock at the upper edge of the buttplate or recoil pad.

HK91/G3 STYLE ACTION

A roller locked delayed blowback rifle action. There is no gas system per se; gas pressure in the cartridge case pushes the case against the bolt and bolt carrier. Spring-loaded rollers in the bolt resist unlocking and carrier/bolt movement until chamber pressure has dropped to a safe level. Components are heavier, recoil (actual and perceived) is greater, chambers must be fluted to assure extraction, and cocking effort is much greater than direct gas or gas piston weapons.

ILAFLON

Industrielack AG trademarked ceramic reinforced enamel firearms finish coating; highly resistant to abrasion, corrosion, and chemicals/solvent.

INTEGRAL LOCKING SYSTEM

A North American Arms safety system; a key allows the user to internally lock the hammer in place, which prevents discharging the firearm.

INTRAFUSE

A trademarked system of synthetic stocks and accessories designed for tactical firearms.

IN-THE-WHITE

Refers to a gun's finish w/o bluing, nickel, case colors, gold, etc. Since all metal surfaces are normally polished, the steel appears white, hence, "in-the-white" terminology.

IRON SIGHTS

A generic term for metallic front or rear sights which do not use optical lens (magnifying or non-magnifying) components.

JUXTAPOSED

See SIDE-BY-SIDE.

LAMINATED STOCK

A gunstock made of many layers of wood glued together under pressure. The laminations become very strong, preventing damage from moisture or heat, and warping.

LANDS

Portions of the bore left between the grooves of the rifling in the bore of a firearm. In rifling, the grooves are usually twice the width of the land. Land diameter is measured across the bore, from land to land.

LASER SIGHT

An aiming system which projects a beam of laser light onto the target. Usually mounted so the beam is parallel to the barrel bore but not a "traditional" front or rear sight as the shooter does not look through the laser apparatus.

LENS COATINGS

Metallic coatings on optic surfaces which increase light transmission, image brightness, and color rendition. Also used to improve abrasion resistance and filter out unwanted or harmful light.

LEVER ACTION

A manual repeating action operated by an external lever.

LUMP

An English term for an underlug.

M1913 PICATINNY RAIL

Original designation for a Picatinny rail. Also see PICATINNY RAIL.

M4 STYLE

Refers to an AR style rifle in M4 carbine configuration (A2 configuration but with short handguard, short barrel, and relocated gas block).

MACHINE GUN

National Firearms Act and Gun Control Act of 1968 definition:

Any weapon which shoots, is designed to shoot, or can be readily restored to shoot, automatically more than one shot, without manual reloading, by a single function of the trigger. The term shall also include the frame or receiver of any such weapon, any part designed and intended solely and exclusively, or combination of parts designed and intended, for use in converting a weapon into a machine gun, and any combination of parts from which a machine gun can be assembled if such parts are in the possession or control of a person.

MAGAZINE (MAG.)

The container (may be detachable) which holds cartridges under spring pressure to be fed into the gun's chamber. A clip is NOT a magazine. May be a single or double or multiple column, rotary, helical, drum, or other design. The term "high capacity" denotes a magazine capable of holding more than ten rounds.

MAGNUM (MAG.)/MAGNUM AMMUNITION

A term first used by Holland & Holland in 1912 for their .375 H&H Magnum cartridge. The term has now been applied to rimfire, centerfire, or shotshell cartridges having a larger cartridge case, heavier shot charge, or higher muzzle velocity than standard cartridges or shotshells of a given caliber or gauge. Most Magnum rifle cartridges are belted designs.

MAINSPRING

The spring that delivers energy to the hammer or striker.

MANNLICHER STOCK

A full-length slender stock with slender forend extending to the muzzle (full stock) affording better barrel protection.

MICROMETER SIGHT

A windage and elevation adjustable sight with very precise and small increments of adjustment.

MICRO SLICK
A firearms finish coating which creates a permanently lubricated surface; it impedes galling and seizing of firearm components.

MIL
See MILRADIAN

MIL SPEC
A series of quality control standards used by manufacturers to guarantee machine tolerances ensuring the consistency and interchangeability of parts.

MIL-DOT
A reticle with dots spaced center-to-center one milradian apart; the distance to an object of known dimension may be calculated based upon the number of milradians which are subtended by the target's known dimension.

MILRADIAN
The horizontal angle subtended by one unit of measurement at 1,000 units distance. Also called a "mil".

MINUTE OF ANGLE (MOA)
1/60 of a degree of circular angle; at 100 yards it subtends 1.047 inches. Also commonly used to describe a firearm's accuracy and precision capability, i.e. a rifle which shoots under one minute of angle. Abbreviated MOA.

MODERN SPORTING RIFLE
A National Shooting Sports Foundation term for civilian legal semiautomatic AR-15 style rifles. The NSSF promotes its usage to counter the negative anti-gun connotations, confusion, and misunderstandings which have become associated with the term "AR15". A modern sporting rifle is not an automatic or assault rifle, not a regulated NFA weapon, not a military/law enforcement M16 despite its similar cosmetic appearance, and no more powerful than other traditional configuration sporting/hunting/competition rifles of the same caliber. Sometimes called Sport Utility Rifle or SUR. Note: the letters "AR" stand for Armalite Rifle.

MODULAR WEAPONS SYSTEM
A generic term of military origin for quick attach/detach components/systems which allow flexibility and adaptability for using various sighting, illumination, and other accessories, etc. on a weapon. Also see PICATINNY RAIL.

MONOBLOC/MONOBLOCK
See CHOPPER LUMP.

MONTE CARLO STOCK
A stock with an elevated comb used primarily for scoped rifles.

MUZZLE
The forward end of the barrel where the projectile exits.

MUZZLE BRAKE
A muzzle device (permanent or removable) or barrel modification which reduces muzzle jump and recoil by diverting propellant gasses sideways or to the rear. Not to be confused with a flash hider or a flash suppressor. Also see COMPENSATOR.

NATIONAL INSTANT CRIMINAL BACKGROUND CHECK SYSTEM (NICS)
A U. S. federal government system which an FFL must, with limited exceptions, contact for information on whether receipt of a firearm by a person who is not licensed under 18 U.S.C. 923 would violate Federal or state law.

NEEDLE GUN
Ignition system invented by Johan Nikolas von Dreyse in 1829. This ignition system used a paper cartridge and became obsolete with the invention of the metallic cartridge.

NFA
The National Firearms Act, 26 USC Chapter 53.

NFA FIREARM
A firearm which must be registered in the National Firearm Registration and Transfer Record, as defined in the NFA and 27 CFR, Part 479. Included are: machine guns, frames or receivers of machine guns, any combination of parts designed and intended for use in converting weapons into machine guns, any combination of parts from which a machine gun can be assembled if the parts are in the possession or under control of a person, silencers and any part designed

or intended for fabricating a silencer, short-barreled rifles, short-barreled shotguns, destructive devices, and "any other weapon".

NICS CHECK

See NATIONAL INSTANT CRIMINAL BACKGROUND CHECK SYSTEM.

NIGHT SIGHTS

Iron sights with radioactive tritium gas capsules; the capsules are inserted into recesses in the sight body with their ends facing the shooter. The tritium glow provides sight alignment and aiming references in lowlight/no-light conditions.

NON-DETACHABLE BOX MAGAZINE

A rectangular magazine which is never removed during normal use or maintenance of the firearm. It may extend beyond/below the receiver or stock, may be high capacity, and generally is loaded from its top (single cartridges or stripper clips).

NON-DETACHABLE FOLDING BAYONET

An articulated bayonet which cannot be removed from the firearm by the end user. Normally locked into its fully folded or extended position.

NP3/NP3 PLUS

An electroless plated nickel-phosphorus alloy firearms finish which offers uniform thickness, lubricity, and hardness equivalent to hard chromium plating.

OBJECTIVE LENS

A telescopic sight's front, usually larger lens which may be adjustable to reduce parallax error.

OCULAR LENS

The rear lens of a telescopic sight, normally adjustable by rotation to focus the sight image.

OPEN SIGHT

A simple rear iron sight with a notch – the shooter aims by looking through the notch at the front sight and the target.

OPTICAL SIGHT

A generic term for a sight which has one or more optical lenses through which the weapon is aimed. Optical sights usually magnify the target image, but there are many non- magnifying optical sights.

OVER-UNDER

A double-barrel gun in which the barrels are stacked one on top of the other. Also called superposed.

PARALLAX

Occurs in telescopic sights when the primary image of the objective lens does not coincide with the reticle. In practice, parallax is detected in the scope when, as the viewing eye is moved laterally, the image and the reticle appear to move in relation to each other.

PARAMILITARY

Typically refers to a firearm configured or styled to resemble a military weapon with one or more of the military weapon's configurations or features, EXCEPT FOR automatic or selective fire capability. Paramilitary firearms may be slide action (primarily shotguns), bolt action, or semi-automatic (most handguns and rifles).

PARKERIZING

Matte rust-resistant oxide finish, usually dull gray or black in color, found on military guns.

PEEP SIGHT

A rear sight consisting of a disc or blade with a hole or aperture through which the front sight and target are aligned.

PEPPERBOX

An early form of revolving repeating pistol, in which a number of barrels were bored in a circle in a single piece of metal resembling the cylinder of a modern revolver. Functioning was the same as a revolver, the entire cylinder being revolved to bring successive barrels under the hammer for firing. Though occurring as far back as the 16th century, the pepperbox did not become practical until the advent of the percussion cap in the early 1800s. Pepperboxes were made in a wide variety of sizes and styles, and reached their popularity peak during the percussion period. Few were made after the advent of practical metallic cartridges. Both single and double action pepperboxes were made. Single-barreled revolvers after the 1840s were more accurate and easier to handle and soon displaced the rather clumsy and muzzle-heavy pepperbox.

PERCH BELLY
Refers to a rifle's stock configuration where the bottom portion is curved rather than straight between the buttplate and pistol grip.

PICATINNY RAIL
A serrated flat rail typically located on the top of a frame/slide/receiver, but may also be located on the sides and bottom, allowing different optics/sights/accessories to be used on the gun. Developed at the U.S. Army's Picatinny Arsenal.

PINFIRE
An obsolete ignition system; a pinfire cartridge had an internal primer and a small firing pin protruding from the rear sidewall of its metallic case.

POLYGONAL
Rifling w/o sharp edged lands and grooves. Advantages include a slight increase in muzzle velocity, less bullet deformation, and reduced lead fouling since there are no traditional lands and grooves. See RIFLING.

POPE RIB
A rib integral with the barrel. Designed by Harry M. Pope, famed barrel maker and shooter, the rib made it possible to mount a target scope low over the barrel.

PORTED BARREL
A barrel with multiple holes or slots drilled near the muzzle. See PORTING.

PORTING
Multiple holes or slots drilled into a firearm barrel near the muzzle. Porting reduces felt/perceived recoil, and if located on the upper half of the barrel reduces muzzle jump. Disadvantages are increased muzzle blast and noise.

POST-BAN
See 1989 BUSH BAN, and SECTION 922r.

PRE-BAN
See 1989 BUSH BAN, and SECTION 922r.

PRIMER
A percussion device designed to ignite the propellant charge of a centerfire cartridge or shotshell by generating flame and high temperature expanding gasses.

PRIMER RING
Refers to a visible dark ring around the firing pin hole in a breech or bolt face, created by the impact of centerfire ammunition primer cups when a cartridge is fired.

PROOFMARK
Proofmarks are usually applied to all parts actually tested, but normally appear on the barrel (and possibly frame), usually indicating the country of origin and time-frame of proof (especially on European firearms). In the U.S., there is no federalized or government proof house, only the manufacturer's in-house proofmark indicating that a firearm has passed its manufacturer's quality control standards per government specifications.

PUMP ACTION
See SLIDE ACTION.

QUAD RAIL FOREARM
A rifle forearm with upper, lower, and lateral Picatinny rails which allow attachment of multiple accessories.

RATE OF TWIST
The distance in which rifling makes one complete revolution; normally expressed as one turn in a specific number of inches in millimeters. Also called rifling pitch, or merely twist.

RECEIVER
That part of a rifle or shotgun (excluding hinged frame guns) which houses the bolt, firing pin, mainspring, trigger group, and magazine or ammunition feed system. The barrel is threaded or pressed into the somewhat enlarged forward part of the receiver, called the receiver ring. At the rear of the receiver, the butt or stock is fastened. In semiautomatic pistols, the frame or housing is sometimes referred to as the receiver.

RECOIL

The rearward motion of a firearm when a shot is fired (i.e. the gun recoiled); the term for the energy or force transferred into the firearm as it discharges a projectile.

RECOIL ACTION/OPERATION

A selfloading or automatic action which uses recoil energy to unlock, extract, eject, cock the firing mechanism, and reload the chamber.

RECOIL SPRING GUIDE ROD

A metal or synthetic rod which positions the recoil spring within the firearm's receiver or slide, and prevents binding/dislocation of the spring during its compression or expansion.

RED DOT SIGHT

See REFLEX SIGHT.

REFLEX SIGHT

An optical sight which generates reticle image upon a partially curved objective lens; the reticle appears superimposed in the field of view and focused at infinity. Most reflex sights are non-magnifying and battery powered. Fiber optic light collectors or tritium may also be used to generate the reticle. Reflex sights are adjustable and virtually parallax free. Popularly known as "red dot" sights; they are NOT laser sights.

RELEASE TRIGGER

A trap shooting trigger which fires the gun when the trigger is released.

RELIC

See CURIO/RELIC.

REPEATER/REPEATING ACTION

An manual action with a magazine or cylinder loaded with more than one cartridge; all cartridges may be fired without reloading.

RETICLE

The shapes, lines, marks, etc. which provide an aiming reference when using an optical sight. Reticles may be illuminated electronically, with tritium, or with fiber optics, and are available in a multitude of designs for many differing requirements.

REVOLVER/REVOLVING ACTION

A manual repeating action so named for its multi-chambered cylinder which rotates on an axis parallel to the barrel bore. Primarily a handgun action, but there have been long gun examples (e.g. Colt Model 1855 Revolving Rifle).

RIB

A raised sighting plane affixed to the top of a barrel.

RIFLING

The spirally cut grooves in the bore of a rifle or handgun barrel. The rifling causes the bullet to spin, stabilizing the bullet in flight. Rifling may rotate to the left or the right, the higher parts of the bore being called lands, the cuts or lower parts being called the grooves. Many types exist, such as oval, polygonal, button, Newton, Newton-Pope gain twist, parabolic, Haddan, Enfield, segmental rifling, etc. Most U.S.-made barrels have a right-hand twist, while British gun makers prefer a left-hand twist. In practice, there seems to be little difference in accuracy or barrel longevity.

RIMFIRE

Self contained metallic cartridge where the priming compound is evenly distributed within the cartridge head, but only on the outer circumference of the rim. Detonated by the firing pin(s) striking the outer edge of the case head.

RINGS

See SCOPE RINGS.

ROLLING BLOCK ACTION

A single shot action, designed in the U.S. and widely used in early Remington arms. Also known as the Remington-Rider action, the breechblock, actuated by a lever, rotates down and back from the chamber. The firing pin is contained within the block and is activated by hammer fall.

SAFETY

A mechanism(s) in/on a gun which prevents it from firing. There are many different types and variations.

SAAMI
The Sporting Arms and Ammunition Manufacturers' Institute; a branch of the National Shooting Sports Foundation.

SAW HANDLE
A distinctive squared off pistol grip design which literally is shaped like a saw handle.

SCHNABEL FOREND/FOREARM
The curved/carved flared end of the forend/forearm that resembles the beak of a bird (Schnabel in German). This type of forend is common on Austrian and German guns. It the U.S., the popularity of the Schnabel forend/forearm comes and goes with the seasons. A Schnabel forend is often seen on custom stocks and rifles.

SCOPE RINGS (BLOCKS/BASES)
Metal mounts used to attach a scope to the top of a gun's frame/receiver.

SEAR
The pivoting part in the firing or lock mechanism of a gun. The sear is linked to the trigger, and may engage the cocking piece, striker, or the firing pin.

SECTION 922r
A 1989 Federal regulation which established sporting criteria for centerfire weapons, either imported, or assembled from imported and domestic components. Firearms which do not meet the criteria are "banned", i.e. non-importable as of the regulation's effective date. Also the source of the popular terms "pre-ban" and post-ban". Due to the complexity of this regulation readers are advised to refer to the actual text of the regulation and contact the BATFE. See 1989 BUSH BAN.

SELECTIVE AUTOMATIC EJECTOR
An ejector which propels only fired cases out of a break open action firearm; and only extracts unfired cartridges. Very often found in double barrel shotguns, and also called an automatic ejector.

SELECTIVE FIRE
Describes a firearm which has more than one firing mode; which is controlled, or "selected", by the user. Most often used in reference to firearms which can fire in semi-auto, burst, or full auto mode.

SEMI-AUTO ACTION/SEMI-AUTOMATIC/SELFLOADING/AUTOLOADING
A pistol, rifle, or shotgun that is loaded manually for the first round. Upon pulling the trigger, the gun fires, ejects the fired round, cocks the firing mechanism, and feeds a fresh round from the magazine. The trigger must be released after each shot and pulled again to fire the next round.

SHELL DEFLECTOR
A protrusion of the receiver near the ejection port which is positioned and shaped to deflect an ejected case away from the shooter's body. Especially appreciated by left-handed shooters when firing a semi-auto with right side ejection.

SHORT ACTION
A rifle action designed for short overall length cartridges.

SHORT BARREL RIFLE
Any rifle having one or more barrels less than sixteen inches in length and any weapon made from a rifle (whether by alteration, modification, or otherwise) if such weapon, as modified, has an overall length of less than twenty-six inches.

SHORT BARREL SHOTGUN
Any shotgun, which was originally equipped with a shoulder stock, with a barrel or barrels less than eighteen inches long and any weapon made from a shotgun (whether by alteration, modification, or otherwise) if such weapon as modified has an overall length of less than twenty-six inches.

SHOTSHELL
An assembly consisting of a rimmed metal head, paper or plastic base wad, 209 battery cup primer, and paper or plastic body. A shotshell cartridge is a shotshell loaded with propellant, wad column, and shot charge or a single large diameter slug.

SIDE-BY-SIDE
A two-barrel rifle or shotgun where the barrels are horizontally arranged side-by-side. Also called juxtaposed.

SIDE FOLDING STOCK
A folding stock variation which has its buttstock rotate horizontally, usually to the right side of the firearm's receiver. See FOLDING STOCK.

SIDE LEVER
Refers to opening mechanism lever on either left or right side of receiver/frame.

SIDELOCK
A type of action, usually long gun, where the moving parts are located on the inside of the lock plates, which in turn are inlet in the sides of the stock. Usually found only on better quality shotguns and rifles.

SIDEPLATES
Ornamental metal panels normally attached to a boxlock action to simulate a sidelock.

SIGHT(S)
Any part or device which allows a firearm to be aimed, versus merely pointed, at a target. There are two main systems: "iron" and optical. Iron sights, also known as "open" sights, are now made of other substances than metal and in many variations. Optical sights have a lens, or lenses, which may or may not magnify the target image.

SINGLE ACTION
A firearms design which requires the hammer to be manually cocked for each shot. Also an auto loading pistol design which requires manual cocking of its mechanism for the first shot only.

SINGLE SHOT ACTION
An action which limits storing or loading only a single cartridge, and is manually operated.

SLIDE ACTION
A manual repeating action with a reciprocating forearm. Sliding the forearm towards the receiver opens the action and extracts/ejects the fired case; forward motion chambers a cartridge and locks the action. Also known as a pump action.

SINGLE TRIGGER
One trigger on a double-barrel gun. It fires each barrel individually by successive pulls, or may be selective, i.e., the barrel to be fired first can be selected via a control button or lever.

SLING SWIVELS
Metal loops affixed to the gun to which a carrying strap is attached.

SPECIAL IMPACT MUNITIONS
A class or type of firearm ammunition loaded with one or more projectiles; when fired at a human target the projectiles have a low probability of causing serious injury or death. For example: bean bag, baton, tear gas, and rubber ball rounds. A sub-class of SIMs is known as SPLLAT, or special purpose less lethal anti terrorist munitions.

SPORT UTILITY RIFLE
See MODERN SPORTING RIFLE.

SPUR TRIGGER
A firearm design which housed the trigger in an extension of the frame in some older guns. The trigger projected only slightly from the front of the extension or spur, and there was no trigger guard.

SQUIB LOAD
A cartridge with no propellant, or so little propellant, that when fired in a semi-auto the action does not cycle; and in any type of firearm a squib load most likely results in the projectile remaining in and completely obstructing the barrel's bore.

STAMPED SHEET METAL RECEIVER
A receiver manufactured out of sheet metal which has been cut, stamped into a three-dimensional shape, and welded. An economical alternative to milling a receiver from a solid block of metal.

STOCK
Usually refers to the buttstock of a long gun, or that portion of a rifle or shotgun that comes in contact with the shooter's shoulder, and is attached to the frame/receiver.

STOCKS
Older terminology used to describe handgun grips. See GRIPS.

SUICIDE SPECIAL

A mass-produced inexpensive single action revolver or derringer, usually with a spur trigger. Produced under a variety of trade names, these guns earned their nickname by being almost as dangerous to shoot as to be shot at.

SUPERPOSED

Refers to an O/U barrel configuration.

SUPPRESSOR

A mechanical device, usually cylindrical and detachable, which alters and decreases muzzle blast and noise. Commonly referred to, in error, as a silencer, it acts only on the sound of the firearms discharge. It does not have any effect on the sounds generated by: the firearm's moving parts, a supersonic bullet in flight, or the bullet's impact.

TACTICAL

An imprecise term referring to certain features on handguns, rifles, and shotguns. Before 2000, a tactical gun generally referred to a rifle or carbine designed for military or law enforcement. In today's marketplace, tactical refers to certain features of both handguns and long arms.

TACTICAL REVOLVERS

Tactical revolvers have at least three of the following factory/manufacturer options or features: non-glare finish (generally but there may be exceptions), Mil Std 1913Picatinny or equivalent rail(s), combat style grips (wood or synthetic), fixed or adjustable low profile primary sights (most often night sights), auxiliary aiming/sighting/illumination equipment, compensators or barrel porting, as well as combat triggers and hammers.

TACTICAL RIFLES

Semi-auto, bolt action, or slide action rifles which have at least two of the following factory/manufacturer options or features: magazine capacity over ten rounds, nonglare finish (generally but there may be exceptions), Mil Std 1913 Picatinny or equivalent rail(s), mostly synthetic stocks which may be fixed, folding, collapsible, adjustable, or with/without pistol grip, most have sling attachments for single, traditional two, or three point slings, tritium night sights, and some Assault Weapon Ban characteristics, such as flash suppressors, detachable magazines, bayonet lugs, etc.

TACTICAL SEMI-AUTO PISTOLS

Tactical semi-auto pistols have at least three of the following factory/manufacturer options or features: magazine capacity over ten rounds, non-glare finish (generally but there may be exceptions), Mil Std 1913 Picatinny or equivalent rail(s), combat style grips (wood or synthetic), fixed or adjustable low profile primary sights (most often night sights), auxiliary aiming/sighting/illumination equipment, and compensators or barrel porting.

TACTICAL SHOTGUNS

Semi-auto or slide action shotguns which have at least two of the following factory/manufacturer options or features: higher capacity (than sporting/hunting shotguns) magazines, or magazine extensions, non-glare finish (generally but there may be exceptions), Mil Std 1913 Picatinny or equivalent rail(s), mostly synthetic stocks which may be fixed, folding, collapsible, adjustable, or with/without pistol grip, most have sling attachments for single, traditional two, or three point slings, some Assault Weapon Ban characteristics, such as bayonet lugs, or detachable high capacity magazines, rifle or night or ghost ring sights (usually adjustable), and short (18-20 inches) barrels with fixed cylinder choke.

TAKE DOWN

A gun which can be easily disassembled into two sections for carrying or shipping.

TANG(S)

Usually refers to the extension straps (upper and lower) of a rifle or shotgun receiver/frame to which the stock or grip is attached.

TARGET STOCK

A stock optimized for accuracy, consistency, ergonomics, and reliability; for firearms used primarily in formal known-distance competition shooting. Rifle versions may have many adjustment options (e.g.length of pull, cast, comb/cheek piece, buttplate, palm rest, hand stop, accessory attachment); handgun versions may have thumb or palm rests, spacers, inserts, etc.

THUMBHOLE STOCK (CRIME BILL)
An adaptation of the sporter thumbhole stock design which removed a weapon from semi-auto assault weapon legal status. The thumbhole was/is very large and provides the functionality of a true pistol grip stock.

THUMBHOLE STOCK (SPORTER)
A sporter/hunting stock with an ergonomic hole in the grip; the thumb of the shooter's trigger hand fits into the hole which provides for a steadier hold.

TOP BREAK
See BREAK BARREL ACTION.

TOP BREAK ACTION
See BREAK BARREL ACTION.

TOP FOLDING STOCK
A folding stock variation; the buttstock pivots upwards and over the top of the frame/receiver. See FOLDING STOCK.

TOP LEVER
Refers to the opening lever mechanism on top of the upper frame/tang.

TOP STRAP
The upper part of a revolver frame, which often is either slightly grooved - the groove serving as rear sight - or which carries at its rearward end a sight (which may or may not be adjustable).

TORQUE
The force which causes a rifled firearm to counter-rotate when a projectile travels down its bore.

TRACER
A type of military bullet that emits a colored flame from its base when fired allowing the gunner to adjust his fire onto a target.

TRAJECTORY
The curved flight path of a bullet from muzzle to target; resembling but not a true parabolic arc.

TRAJECTORY TABLE
A numerical table of computed data summarizing the down range trajectory of a projectile.

TRAP STOCK
A shotgun stock with greater length and less comb drop (Monte Carlo, in many cases) used for trap shooting, enabling a built-in height lead when shooting.

TRIGGER
Refers to a release device (mechanical or electrical) in the firing system that starts the ignition process. Usually a curved, grooved, or serrated piece of metal which is pulled rearward by the shooter's finger, and which releases the sear or hammer.

TRIGGER GUARD
Usually a circular or oval band of metal, horn, or plastic that goes around the trigger to provide both protection and safety in shooting circumstances.

TRIGGER SAFETY
A trigger assembly component which must be depressed or otherwise moved before the trigger can be pulled completely through to fire the weapon. Most often a pivoting blade in the center of a trigger which protrudes from the face of the trigger when it is engaged/"on" and automatically resets itself.

TURRETS
Cylinders on an optical sight's main tube which hold adjustment knobs or screws. A turret is dedicated to one of several functions: windage, elevation, parallax, reticle type, reticle illumination, or ranging.

TWIST BARRELS
A process in which a steel rod (called a mandrel) was wrapped with skelps - ribbons of iron. The skelps were then welded in a charcoal fire to form one piece of metal, after which the rod was driven out to be used again. The interior of the resulting tube then had to be laboriously bored out by hand to remove the roughness. Once polished, the outside was smoothed on big grinding wheels, usually turned by waterpower.

TWIST RATE
Refers to the distance required for one complete turn of rifling, usually expressed as a ratio such as 1:12 in. twist, which refers to one complete twist of rifling within 12 inches of barrel. Typically, the heavier the bullet, the faster the twist rate needs to be.

UNDER-LEVER
Action opening lever that is usually located below or in the trigger guard, can also be side pivoting from forearm.

UNDERLUG
On a break open action firearm, the lug on the chamber end of the barrel which locates the barrel in the receiver, and which locks the barrel into battery when intercepted by the bolt/underbolt. Also called a lump.

UNDER FOLDING STOCK
A folding stock variation; the buttstock rotates downwards and underneath the frame/receiver. See FOLDING STOCK.

UNLOAD
To remove all ammunition/cartridges from a firearm or magazine.

UNSERVICEABLE FIREARM
A firearm that is damaged and cannot be made functional in a minimal amount of time.

UPPER ASSEMBLY
For a semi-auto pistol this includes the barrel and slide assembly, for AR style rifles it includes the barrel, bolt and receiver housing.

VARIABLE POWER OPTICAL SIGHT
A optical sight with a multiple magnification levels, most common are 3-9 power general purpose scopes.

VENTILATED
Denotes a component with holes, slots, gaps, or other voids which reduce weight, promote cooling, have a structural purpose, or are decorative.

VENTILATED RIB
A sighting plane affixed along the length of a shotgun barrel with gaps or slots milled for cooling and lightweight handling.

VERNIER
Typically used in reference to a rear aperture (peep) sight. Usually upper tang mounted, and is adj. for elevation by means of a highly accurate finely threaded screw.

VIERLING
A German word designating a four-barrel gun.

VIOLENT CRIME CONTROL AND LAW ENFORCEMENT ACT OF 1994, PUBLIC LAW 103-322
On September 13, 1994, Congress passed the Violent Crime Control and Law Enforcement Act of 1994, Public Law 103-322. Title IX, Subtitle A, Section 110105 of this Act generally made it unlawful to manufacture, transfer, and possess semiautomatic assault weapons (SAWs) and to transfer and possess large capacity ammunition feeding devices (LCAFDs). The law also required importers and manufacturers to place certain markings on SAWs and LCAFDs, designating they were for export or law enforcement/government use. Significantly, the law provided that it would expire 10 years from the date of enactment. Accordingly, effective 12:01 am on September 13, 2004, the provisions of the law ceased to apply and the following provisions of the regulations in Part 478 no longer apply:

- Section 478.11- Definitions of the terms "semiautomatic assault weapon" and "large capacity ammunition feeding device"
- Section 478.40- Entire section
- Section 478.40a- Entire section
- Section 478.57- Paragraphs (b) and (c)
- Section 478.92- Paragraph (a)(3) – [NOTE: Renumbered from paragraph (a)(2) to paragraph (a)(3) by TD ATF – 461 (66 FR 40596) on August 3, 2001]
- Section 478.92- Paragraph (c)

- Section 478.119- Entire section- [NOTE: An import permit is still needed pursuant to the Arms Export Control Act- see 27 CFR 447.41(a)]
- Section 478.132- Entire section
- Section 478.153- Entire section

NOTE: The references to "ammunition feeding device" in section 478.116 are not applicable on or after September 13, 2004.

NOTE: The references to "semiautomatic assault weapons" in section 478.171 are not applicable on or after September 13, 2004.

Information from BATFE Online - Bureau of Alcohol, Tobacco and Firearms, and Explosives an official site of the U.S. Department of Justice.

WAD

A shotshell component in front of the powder charge and has a cup or flat surface that the shot charge rests on. Various types of wads exist with the most common being a column of plastic.

WADCUTTER BULLET

A lead target bullet for revolvers having a flat nose and a sharp outer edge or shoulder which will cut clean holes in paper targets to aid in spotting and scoring.

WATER TABLE

The flat surfaces forward of the standing breech of a side-by-side shotgun. Also called action bar flats or action flats.

WEAVER-STYLE RAIL

A mounting rail system similar in dimensions and use as the Picatinny Rail. Weaver-style grooves are .180 wide and do not always have consistent center-to-center widths. Most Weaver-style accessories will fit the Picatinny system, however Picatinny accessories will not fit the Weaver-style system. Also see PICATINNY RAIL.

WILDCAT CARTRIDGE

An experimental or non-standard cartridge, not commercially manufactured, often using a standard cartridge case which has been significantly modified.

WINDAGE

The deflection of a projectile from its trajectory due to wind. Also, adjustment of a firearm's sight(s) to compensate for the deflection.

WUNDHAMMER GRIP/SWELL

Originally attributed to custom gunsmith Louis Wundhammer, it consists of a bulge on the right side of the pistol grip that ergonomically fills the palm of a right-handed shooter.

YOKE

See CRANE.

YOUTH DIMENSIONS

Usually refers to shorter stock dimensions and/or lighter weight enabling youth/women to shoot and carry a firearm.

ZERO

The procedure of adjusting a firearm's sight(s) so that the point of aim coincides with the bullet's point of impact at a selected range.

ABBREVIATIONS

*****	Banned due to 1994-2004 Crime Bill (may be current again)
5R	Five (groove) Rifling
A	Standard Grade Walnut
A.R.M.S.	Atlantic Research Marketing Systems
A2	AR-15 Style/Configuration w/fixed carry handle
A3	AR-15 Style/Configuration w/detachable carry handle
AA	Extra Grade Walnut
AAA	Best Quality Walnut
ACB	Advanced Combat Bolt (LWRC)
ACP	Automatic Colt Pistol
ACR	Adaptive Combat Rifle
ACS	MAGPUL Adaptable Carbine/Storage (stock)
adj.	Adjustable
AE	Automatic Ejectors or Action Express
AECA	Arms Export Control Act
AFG	MAGPUL Angled Fore Grip
AK	Avtomat Kalashnikova rifle
AMU	Army Marksman Unit
AOW	Any Other Weapon (NFA)
appts.	Appointments
AR	Armalite Rifle
ASAP	MAGPUL Ambi Sling Attachment Point
ATR	All Terrain Rifle (Mossberg)
ATS	All Terrain Shotgun (Mossberg)
AWB	Assault Weapons Ban
AWR	Alaskan/African Wilderness Rifle
B	Blue
BAC	Browning Arms Company
BAD	MAGPUL Battery Assist Device (bolt catch lever)
BAN/CRIME BILL ERA	Mfg. between Nov. 1989 - Sept. 12, 2004
BAR	Browning Automatic Rifle
BASR	Bolt Action Sniper Rifle (H&K)
BB	Brass Backstrap
BBL	Barrel
BLR	Browning Lever Rifle
BMG	Browning Machine Gun
BOSS	Ballistic Optimizing Shooting System
BOSS-CR	BOSS w/o Muzzle Brake
BP	Buttplate or Black Powder
BPE	Black Power Express
BPS	Browning Pump Shotgun
BR	Bench Rest
BT	Beavertail
BT	Browning Trap shotgun
BUIS	Back-Up Iron Sight(s)
c.	Circa
C/B 1994	Introduced Because of 1994 Crime Bill
CAD	Computer Assisted Design
cal.	Caliber
CAR	Colt Automatic Rifle or Carbine
CAWS	Close Assault Weapons System
CB	Crescent Buttplate
CC	Case Colors
CCA	Colt Collectors Association
CF	Centerfire
CFR	Code of Federal Regulations
CH	Cross Hair
CLMR	Colt Lightning Magazine Rifle
CMV	Chrome Moly Vanadium Steel
CNC	Computer Numeric Controlled (machining/machinery)
COMM.	Commemorative
COMP	Compensated/Competition
CQB	Close Quarter Battle
CQC	Close Quarter Combat
C-R	Curio-Relic
CRF	Controlled Round Feed
CRPF	Controlled Round Push Feed
CSAT	Combat Shooting & Tactics (accessories)
CTF	Copper/Tin Frangible (bullet)
CTG/CTGE	Cartridge
CTR	MAGPUL Compact/Type Restricted (stock)
CYL/C	Cylinder
DA	Double Action
DAK	Double Action Kellerman Trigger (SIG)
DAO	Double Action Only
DB	Double Barrel
DBM	Detachable Box Magazine
DCM	Director of Civilian Marksmanship
DI	Direct Impingement Gas System, see Glossary
DIGS	Delayed Impingement Gas System, see Glossary
DISC or disc.	Discontinued
DMR	Designated Marksman Rifle (U.S Army, LWRC)
DPMS	Defense Procurement Manufacturing Services
DSL	Detachable Side Locks
DST	Double Set Triggers
DT	Double Triggers
DWM	DeutscheWaffen and Munitions Fabriken
EGLM	Enhanced Grenade Launcher Module (FNH)
EJT	Ejector or Ejectors
EMAG	MAGPUL Export MAGazine
EMP	Enhanced Micro Pistol (Springfield Inc.)
EXC	Excellent

EXT	Extractor or Extractors
F	Full Choke
F&M	Full & Modified
FA	Forearm
FAL	Fusil Automatique Leger
FBT	Full Beavertail Forearm
FDE	Flat Dark Earth (finish color)
FDL	Fleur-de-lis
FE	Forend/Fore End
FFL	Federal Firearms License
FIRSH	Free Floating Integrated Rail System Handguard
FK	Flat Knob
FKLT	Flat Knob Long Tang
FM	Full Mag
FMJ	Full Metal Jacket
FN CAL	FN Carabine Automatique Leger
FN GP	FN Grande Puissance (pistol)
FN LAR	Fabrique Nationale Light Automatic Rifle
FN	Fabrique Nationale
FNAR	FN Automatic Rifle
FNC	Fabrique Nationale Carabine
FNH USA	Fabrique Nationale Herstal (U.S. sales and marketing)
FNH	Fabrique Nationale Herstal
FPS	Feet Per Second
g.	Gram
ga.	Gauge
GCA	Gun Control Act
G-LAD	Green Laser Aiming Device
GOVT	Government
gr.	Grain
H&H	Holland & Holland
HB	Heavy Barrel
H-BAR	H(eavy)-BARrel, AR-15/M16
HC	Hard Case
HK	Heckler und Koch
HMR	Hornady Magnum Rimfire
HP	High Power (FN/Browning pistol)
HP	Hollow Point
HPJ	High Performance Jacket
I	Improved
IAR	Infantry Automatic Rifle (LWRC)
IC	Improved Cylinder
ILS	Integral Locking System (North American Arms)
IM	Improved Modified
IMI	Israel Military Industries
in.	Inch
intro.	Introduced
IOM	Individual Officer Model (FNH model suffix)
IPSC	International Practical Shooting Confederation
ISSF	International Shooting Sports Federation
ITAR	International Traffic (in) Arms Regulation
IVT	Italian Value-Added Tax
JCP	Joint Combat Pistol
KAC	Knight's Armament Co.
KMC	Knight's Manufacturing Co.
KSG	Kel Tec Shotgun
L	Long
LBA	Lightning Bolt Action (Mossberg)
LBC	Les Baer Custom (Inc.)
lbs.	Pounds
LC	Long Colt
LCW	Lauer Custom Weaponry
LDA	Light Double Action (PARA USA INC.)
LEM	Law Enforcement Model or Modification
LEO	Law Enforcement Only
LMT	Lewis Machine and Tool (Company)
LOP	Length of Pull
LPA	Lightning Pump Action (Mossberg)
LPI	Lines Per Inch
LR	Long Rifle
LT	Long Tang or Light
LTR	Light Tactical Rifle (Rem.)
LTRK	Long Tang Round Knob
LWRC	Land Warfare Resources Corporation
LWRC	Leitner-Wise Rifle Company, Inc.
M (MOD.)	Modified Choke
M&P	Military & Police
M-4	Newer AR-15/M16 Carbine Style/Configuration
Mag.	Magnum Caliber
mag.	Magazine
MARS	Modular Accessory Rail System
MBUS	MAGPUL Back-Up Sight
MC	Monte Carlo
MCS	Modular Combat System (Rem.)
MFG or Mfg.	Manufactured/manufacture
MIAD	MAGPUL Mission Adaptable (grip, other)
mil	see Glossary
mil-dot	See Glossary
MIL SPEC	Mfg. to Military Specifications
MK	Mark
mm	Millimeter
MOA	Minute of Angle
MOE	MAGPUL Original Equipment
MOUT	Military Operations (on) Urbanized Terrain
MR	Matted Rib
MS2	MAGPUL Multi Mission Sling System
MSR	Manufacturer's Suggested Retail
MVG	MAGPUL MOE Vertical Grip
MWS	Modular Weapons System
N	Nickel
N/A	Not Applicable or Not Available
NATO	North Atlantic Treaty Org.

NE	Nitro Express
NFA	National Firearms Act (U.S. 1934)
NIB	New in Box
NM	National Match
no.	Number
NP	New Police
NP3/NP3 Plus	Nickel-Phosphorus (firearm coating)
NSST	Non Selective Single Trigger
NVD	Night Vision Device
O/U	Over and Under
OA	Overall
OAL	Overall Length
OB	Octagon Barrel
OBFM	Octagon Barrel w/full mag.
OBO	Or Best Offer
OCT	Octagon
ODG	Olive Drab Green (finish color)
ORC	Optics Ready Carbine
oz.	Ounce
P	Police (Rem. rifle/shotgun)
P99AS	Pistol 99 Anti Stress (trigger, Walther)
PAD	Personal Anti-recoil Device (Savage)
Para.	Parabellum
PBR	Patrol Bolt Rifle (FNH)
PDA	Personal Defense Assistant (PARA USA INC.)
PFFR	Percantage of factory finish remaining
PG	Pistol Grip
PK	Pistol Kompact (Walther)
PMAG	MAGPUL Polymer MAGazine
POR/P.O.R.	Price on Request
POST-'89	Paramilitary mfg. after Federal legislation in Nov. 1989
POST-BAN	Refers to production after Sept. 12, 2004
PPC	Pindell Palmisano Cartridge
PPD	Post Paid
PPK	Police Pistol Kriminal (Walther 1931 design)
PPKs	Police Pistol Kriminal (Walther 1968 design)
PPQ	Police Pistol Quick (defense trigger, Walther)
PRE-'89	Paramilitary mfg. before Federal legislation in Nov. 1989
PRE-BAN	Mfg. before September 13, 1994 per C/B or before Nov. 1989.
PRS/PRS2	MAGPUL Precision Rifle/Sniper (stock)
PSD	Personal Security Detail rifle (LWRC)
PSG	PrazisionSchutzenGewehr (H&K rifle)
PSR	Precision Shooting Rifle (FNH)
PXT	Power Extractor Technology (PARA USA INC.)
QD	Quick Detachable
RACS	Remington Arms Chassis System
RAS	Rail Adapter System
RB	Round Barrel/Round Butt
RCM	Ruger Compact Magnum
RCMP	Royal Canadian Mounted Police
RDS	Rapid Deployment Stock
REC	Receiver
REM	Remington
REM. MAG.	Remington Magnum
REPR	Rapid Engagement Precision Rifle (LWRC)
RF	Rimfire
RFB	Rifle Forward (ejection) Bullpup
RFM	Rim Fire Magnum
RIS	Rail Interface system
RK	Round Knob
RKLT	Round Knob Long Tang
RKST	Round Knob Short Tang
RMEF	Rocky Mt. Elk. Foundation
RMR	Rimfire Magnum Rifle (Kel Tec)
RPD	Ruchnoy Pulemyot Degtyaryova (machine gun)
RR	Red Ramp
RSA	MAGPUL Rail Sling Attachment
RSUM	Remington Short-Action Ultra Magnum
RUM	Remington Ultra Magnum
RVG	MAGPUL Rail Vertical Grip
S	Short
S&W	Smith & Wesson
S/N	Serial Number
SA	Single Action
SAA	Single Action Army
SAAMI	Sporting Arms and Ammunition Manufacturers' Institute
SABR	Sniper/Assaulter Battle Rifle (LWRC)
SAE	Selective Automatic Ejectors
SAS	SIG Anti Snag (pistol models)
SASS	Single Action Shooting Society or (U.S. Army) Semi Automatic Sniper System
SAUM	Short Action Ultra Magnum
SAW	Semiautomatic Assault Weapon
SAW	Squad Automatic Weapon
SB	Shotgun butt or Steel backstrap
SBR	Short Barrel Rifle
SCAR	Special (Operations Forces) Combat Assault Rifle (FNH)
SCW	Sub Compact Weapon (Colt)
SDT	Super Dynamic Technology (PARA USA INC.)
ser.	serial
SG	Straight Grip
SIG	Schweizerische Industriegesellschaft
SIM	Special Impact Munition
SK	Skeet
SLP	Self Loading Police (FNH shotgun)
SMG	Submachine Gun
SMLE	Short Magazine Lee Enfield Rifle

SNT	Single Non-Selective Trigger
SOCOM	Special Operations Command
SOPMOD	Special Operations Peculiar Modification
SP	Special Purpose
SPC	Special Purpose Cartridge
SPEC	Special
SPEC-OPS	Special Operations
SPG	Semi-Pistol Grip
Spl.	Special
SPLLAT	Special Purpose Low Lethality Anti Terrorist (Munition)
SPR	Special Police Rifle (FNH), Special Purpose Rifle
SPS	Special Purpose Synthetic (Remington)
SPS	Superalloy Piston System (LWRC)
sq.	Square
SR	Solid Rib
SRC	Saddle Ring Carbine
SRT	Short Reset Trigger
SS	Single Shot or Stainless Steel
SSA	Super Short Action
SSR	Sniper Support Rifle (FNH)
SST	Single Selective Trigger
ST	Single Trigger
SUR	Sport Utility Rifle - see Glossary
SWAT	Special Weapons Assault Team
SWAT	Special Weapons and Tactics
SxS	Side by Side
TB	Threaded Barrel
TBA	To be Announced
TBM	Tactical Box Magazine
TD	Take Down
TDR	Target Deployment Rifle (Rem.)
TGT	Target
TH	Target Hammer
TIR	Target Interdiction Rifle (Rem.)
TPS	Tactical Police Shotgun (FNH)
TRP	Tactical Response Pistol (Springfield Inc.)
TRPAFD	Take Red Pen Away From Dave!
TS	Target Stocks
TSOB	Scope Mount Rail Weaver Type
TSR XP USA	Tactical Sport Rifle - Extreme Performance Ultra Short Action (FNH)
TSR XP	Tactical Sport Rifle - Extreme Performance (FNH)
TT	Target Trigger
TTR	Tactical Target Rifle (PARA USA INC.)
TWS	Tactical Weapons System (Rem.)
UBR	MAGPUL Utility/Battle Rifle (stock)
UCIW	Ultra Compact Individual Weapon (LWRC)
UCP	Universal Combat Pistol (H&K)
UIT	Union Internationale de Tir
UMC	Union Metallic Cartridge Co.
UMP	Universal Machine Pistol (H&K)
USA	Ultra Safety Assurance (Springfield Inc.)
USAMU	U.S. Army Marksmanship Unit
USC	Universal Self-Loading Carbine (H&K)
USG	United States Government (FNH model suffix)
USP	Universal Self-Loading Pistol (H&K)
USPSA	United States Practical Shooting Association
USR	Urban Sniper Rifle (Rem.)
USSOCOM	U.S. Special Operations Command
VAT	Value Added Tax
Vent.	Ventilated
VG	Very Good
VR	Ventilated Rib
VTAC	Viking Tactics, Inc. (accessories)
VTR	Varmint Triangular Profile Barrel (Remington)
w/	With
w/o	Without
WBY	Weatherby
WC	Wad Cutter
WCF	Winchester Center Fire
WD	Wood
WFF	Watch For Fakes
WIN	Winchester
WMR	Winchester Magnum Rimfire
WO	White Outline
WRA	Winchester Repeating Arms Co.
WRF	Winchester Rim Fire
WRM	Winchester Rimfire Magnum
WSL	Winchester Self-Loading
WSM	Winchester Short Magnum
WSSM	Winchester Super Short Magnum
WW	World War
X (1X)	1X Wood Upgrade or Extra Full Choke Tube
XD	Extreme Duty (Springfield Inc.)
XDM	Extreme Duty M Factor (Springfield Inc.)
XX (2X)	2X Wood Upgrade or Extra Extra Full Choke Tube
XXX (3x)	3X Wood Upgrade
YHM	Yankee Hill Machine

MUSEUMS

FIREARMS, WESTERN MEMORABILIA, AND RELATED ARTIFACTS

Please visit the individual museum websites for more information and possibly a listing of special exhibits.

Autry National Center of the American West

4700 Western Heritage Way
Los Angeles, CA 90027-1462
www.autrynationalcenter.org

Buffalo Bill Historical Center/ Cody Firearms Museum

720 Sheridan Ave.
Cody, WY 82414
www.bbhc.org
(Check website for special exhibits)

Frazier Arms Museum

829 W. Main St.
Louisville, KY 48202
www.fraziermuseum.org

J.M. Davis Arms and Historical Museum

330 N. J. M. Davis Blvd. (U.S. Route 66)
Claremore, OK 74017
www.thegunmuseum.com

Museum of Connecticut History

231 Capitol Ave.
Hartford, CT 06106
www.museumofcthistory.org

The National Cowboy & Western Heritage Museum

1700 NE 63rd Street
Oklahoma City, OK 73111
www.nationalcowboymuseum.org

The National Firearms Museum (NFM)

National Rifle Association
11250 Waples Mill Road
Fairfax, VA 22030
www.nramuseum.com
(Check website for special exhibits, open 9:30-5 every day except Christmas w/free admission)

The National World War II Museum

945 Magazine Street
New Orleans, LA 70130
Phone: (504)-528-1944
Fax: (504)-527-6088
Website: www.nationalww2museum.org
Email: info@nationalww2museum.org

Ogden Union Station

2501 Wall Ave.
Ogden, UT 84401
www.theunionstation.org

Rock Island Arsenal

1 Rock Island Arsenal
Rock Island, IL 61299-5000
Website: www.ria.army.mil

Smithsonian – National Museum of American History

National Mall, 14th Street and Constitution Avenue, N.W., Washington, D.C.
www.americanhistory.si.edu

FIREARMS/SHOOTING ORGANIZATIONS

Listed below are the names and addresses of various firearms organizations/associations throughout the U.S. You are encouraged to join those organizations which pertain to your region and area of interest. As thorough as we try to be, every year we get quite a bit of mail back from individual firearms associations that is undeliverable. So, if your club does not appear on the following pages or doesn't have a current address, please forward the correct information to us for inclusion in the next edition.

For the past 50 years, the NRA's affiliated Gun Collecting clubs (identified in the following listings with an *) have been a vital part of NRA's educational outreach programs. With over 100 of these clubs, there is one for almost every collecting interest and area. Collector affiliates are leaders in firearms safety programs for gun shows, and they sponsor some of the most popular and successful shows in the country. They participate in the NRA's Annual Meetings and Exhibits with spectacular displays of rare and historically important arms. Affiliates also sponsor the annual National Gun Show and the annual National Gun Collecting Seminar. An annual awards ceremony for collector affiliates is held every year at the NRA's Annual Meetings.

Academics for the Second Amendment (A2A)
Prof. J.E. Olson, President
Hamline University
P.O. Box 131254
St. Paul, MN 55113
Email: jolson@gw.hamline.edu

*** Alabama Gun Collectors Association**
Tom Campbell, Secretary/Treasurer
P.O. Box 242277
Montgomery, AL 36124-2277
Phone: 334-272-1193
Website: www.agcagunshow.com
Email: AGCABham@aol.com
$20 Annual Membership

*** Alamo Arms Collectors' Association**
P.O. Box 680642
San Antonio, TX 78268-0642
James P. Duke, Secretary
Phone: 830-980-4746
George O. Stenzel, Treasurer
Phone: 210-523-5540
Email: aacanews@satx.rr.com
$20 yearly membership, meetings first Tuesday of each month

***Alaska Gun Collectors Association**
P.O. Box 242233
Anchorage, Alaska 99524
Phone: 907-346-1075
Website: www.agca.net

American Custom Gunmakers Guild
Jan Billeb, Executive Director
22 Vista View Lane
Cody, WY 82414-9606
Phone: 307-587-4297
Website: www.acgg.org
Email: acgg@acgg.org
$95 Associate Membership Fee
$45 Gunsmithing Students
$180 Commercial Associate Membership Fee

*** American Single Shot Rifle Association**
Laurie Gapko, Archivist
800 Wisconsin St. Mail Box 68
Eau Claire, WI 54703
Phone: 608-628-0536
Website: www.assra.com
$35 Annual Membership (includes journal)

*** American Society of Arms Collectors**
J. William La Rue, Secretary
P.O. Box 50400
Albuquerque, NM 87181-0400
Phone: 505-299-7950
Website: www.americansocietyofarmscollectors.org
Invitation only
Dues: $200 annual

*** The American Thompson Association**
Tracie Hill
P.O. Box 8710
Newark, OH 43058-8710
Phone: 740-345-9777
Website: www.nfatoys.com/tsmg/ tata
$30 Annual Membership Dues

*** Arkansas Gun & Cartridge Collectors Club**
Joe Burnett
P.O. Box 1015
Little Rock, AR 72203
Phone: 501-753-1970
Email: joehb@comcast.net

*** Ark - La - Tex Gun Collectors**
Thomas L. Baird, President
9601 Blom Blvd.
Shreveport, LA 71118
Phone: 318-686-7101

*** Arms Collectors of Georgia**
Robert Messner
1554 Bubling Creek Rd.
Atlanta, GA 30319
Phone: 770-740-4908
Dues: $45 annual
Meetings 2nd Monday of each month

*** Arms Collectors of Southwest Washington**
James Hoeflein
P.O. Box 2622
Vancouver, WA 98668
Website: www.acsww.org

*** Association of Ohio Longrifle Collectors**
Robin D. (Dan) Smith, Secretary
23003 St., Rt. 339
Beverly, OH 45715
Phone: 740-984-4896
Website: www.aolrc.org/home1
$15 annual dues

*** Browning Collectors Association**
Charles P. Wagner, Secretary
711 Scott Street
Covington, KY 41011
Phone: 859-431-1712
Website: www.browningcollectors.com
Email: bac_wagner@yahoo.com

Buffalo Bill Historical Center
Cody Firearms Museum
720 Sheridan Ave.
Cody, WY 82414
Phone: 307-587-4771
Website: www.bbhc.org

*** C.A.D.A. (Collector Arms Dealer Association)**
P.O. Box 427
Thomson, IL 61285

California Rifle & Pistol Association, Inc.
271 Imperial Highway, Suite #620
Fullerton, CA 92835
Phone: 714-992-2772
Website: www.crpa.org

*** Central States Gun Collectors Association**
Lois Schwade
633-3 Rd. Street SE
Mason City, IA 50401-4104
Phone: 641-424-9234

*** Central Wisconsin Gun Collectors Association**
Bruce D. Cook, President
10971 Clinic Road
Suring, WI 54174
Phone: 920-842-2083
Fax: 920-842-4203
Email: RamCook1@yahoo.com

Colorado Gun Collectors Association
Les Palmer, Show Chairman
3490 E. Orchard Road
Centennial, CO 80121-3051
Phone: 720-482-0167
Fax: 720-200-3123
Email: CGCAShow@CGCA.com
$35 Annual Membership Fee

*** Colt Collectors Association**
Karen Green, Secretary
P.O. Box 2241
Los Gatos, CA 95031
Website: www.coltcollectors.com
Email: secretary@coltcollectors.com
$50 Annual Membership Fee (U.S.)
$60 Annual Membership Fee (Canada)
$100 Annual Membership Fee (Foreign)

Contemporary Longrifle Association
P.O. Box 2247
Stauton, VA 24402
Phone: 540-886-6189
Fax: 540-213-0531
Website: www.longrifle.com
Email: cla@longrifle.com

*** Dakota Territory Gun Collectors Association**
Vicki Sandvig, Executive Secretary
P.O. Box 5053
West Fargo, ND 58078
Phone: 701-484-5010
Website: www.dtgca.net
$15 Annual Membership Fee
$200 Life Membership Fee

*** Delaware Antique Arms Collectors Association**
Robert Howard
P.O. Box 2966
Wilmington, DE 19805

DIVA – Women Outdoors Worldwide
Judy Rhodes, founder
11241 Ferndale Road
Dallas, TX 75238
Phone/Fax No.: 866-TEX-DIVA
Website: www.divawow.org
Email: txd1va@sbcglobal.net
$75 Membership Dues
$1,000 Lifetime Membership

*** Eastern Shores Arms Collectors**
Rodney Schwarm
P.O. Box 1836
Easton, MD 21601
Phone: 410-822-1555

*** Egyptian Collectors Association**
Bob Leckrone
Box 138
Centralia, IL 62801
Phone: 618-495-2572

The Firearms Coalition of Colorado
Steve Schreiner, President
P.O. Box 1454
Englewood, CO 80150-1454
Phone: 303-296-4867
Blog site: COGunIssues@yahoogroups.com
$25 Annual Membership Fee

*** Forks of the Delaware Historical Arms Society, Inc.**
John Lawson
2060 Northampton St. #1
Easton, PA 18042
Phone: 610-438-9006
Website: www.allentownshow.net
$20 Annual Membership Fee

*** Ft. Lee Arms Collectors**
Walter Dubas
50 Second Street
Clifton, NJ 07011
Phone: 914-796-2300

*** Garand Collectors Association**
James Spawn
P.O. Box 7498
N. Kansas City, MO 64116
Phone No.: 816-471-2005
Website: www.thegca.org

Georgia Arms Collectors Association, Inc.
Michael Kindberg
P.O. Box 277
Alpharetta, GA 30009-0277
Phone: 678-388-9879
Email: gaca1957@yahoo.com

German Gun Collectors Association
P.O. Box 429
Mayfield, UT 84643
Phone No.: 435-979-9723
Fax No.: 435-528-7966
Email: sales@germanguns.com
Questions about German Guns -
Email: info@germanguns.com
438 Willow Brook Rd
P.O. Box 385
Meriden, NH 03770
Phone: 603-469-3438
Website: www.germanguns.com
$45 Annual Fee (U.S.
$48 Annual Fee (Canada)
$60 Annual Fee (Foreign)

Gibbs Military Collector's Club
219 Lawn St.
Martinsburg, WV 25406
Phone: 304-262-1651
Fax: 304-262-1658
Website: www.gibbsrifle.com
Email: support@gibbsrifle.com

*** Glock Collectors Association**
45 Freight Street #1-102
Waterbury, CT 06702
Phone: 203-565-4781
Fax: 203-753-9453
Website: www.glockcollectors.com
Email: sjruselowski@gmail.com
$35 Annual Membership Fee, includes 3-4 journals

Golden Eagle Collectors Association
Chris Showler, Secretary
90 Will Sauer Road
Washoe Valley, NV 89704-8594

Great Lakes Military Collectors Association
P.O. Box 401
Maumee, OH 43537

Gun Owners Civil Rights Alliance/ Concealed Carry Reform Now!
Joseph E. Olson, President
P.O. Box 131254
St. Paul, MN 55113
Phone: 651-636-4465
Website: www.mnccrn.org
$30 Annual Membership Fee

Gun Owners of America
Larry Pratt, Executive Director
8001 Forbes Pl.
Springfield, VA 22151
Phone: 703-321-8585
Website: www.gunowners.org
Email: goamail@gunowners.org
$20 Annual Membership Fee

*** Hawaii Historic Arms Association**
Sheldon Tyau
Box 1733
Honolulu, HI 96806
Phone: 808-955-9552

*** High Standard Collectors Association**
John Hanks
P.O. Box 1578
Decatur, IL 62525-1578
Website: www.highstandard.org
Email: H-S-C-A@comcast.net
$25 Annual Dues

*** Houston Gun Collectors Association**
P.O. Box 741429
Houston, TX 77274-1429
Phone: 713-981-6463
Website: www.hgca.org
$70 Annual Dues

Indian Territory Gun Collectors Association
David Shorten, Secretary/Treasurer
3716 East 45th Place
Tulsa, OK 74135
Phone: 918-743-4558
Website: www.indianterritoryguncollector.com
Email: indianterritoryGCA@yahoo.com
$25 Annual Dues

Indianhead Firearms Association
13810 25th Ave.
Chippewa Falls, WI 54729
Phone: 715-723-0860

*** International Ammunition Association**
Robert P. Ruebel, Secretary
37752 880th Ave.
Olivia, MN 56277-2528
Phone: 320-522-0230
Website: www.cartridgecollectors.org
Email: ruebel.bob@gmail.com
Membership includes 60-page journal 6 times per year
$35 Annual Dues (USA)
$40 Annual (Canada/Mexico)
$55 Foreign
$25 Annual Dues (electronic copy of IAA Journal, world-wide)

*** Iroquois Arms Collectors Association**
Kenneth Keller, Secretary
Susann Keller, Show Secretary
214 70th St.
Niagara Falls, NY 14304

Jersey Shore Antique Arms Collectors
Steve Cassidy
P.O. Box 100
Bayville, NJ 08721-0100
$25 Annual Membership Fee

Jews for the Preservation of Firearms Ownership
P.O. Box 270143
Hartford, WI 53027
Phone No.: 262-673-9745
Fax No.: 262-673-9746
Website: www.jpfo.org
Email: jpfoinfo@gmail.com

Kansas Cartridge Collectors Association
Vic Suelter
2185 E. Iron Drive
Lincoln, KS 67455

*** Kentucky Rifle Association**
Attn: Ruth Collis
2319 Sue Ann Dr.
Lancaster, PA, 17602.

*** Lancaster Muzzle Loading Rifle Association**
James H. Frederick, Jr.
700 Prospect Road
Columbia, PA 17512

Lee County Gun Collectors Association of Ft. Myers, FL
P.O. Box 6168
Fort Myers Beach, FL 33932
Phone: 239-463-2840

Lefever Arms Collectors Association
Robert Decker, MD
44-668 Kuono Place
Kaneohe, HI 96744
Phone: 808-236-1129
Website: www.lefevercollectors.com
Email: laca@hawaii.rr.com
$35 Annual Dues

*** Mahoning Valley Gun Collectors Association**
P.O. Box 86
Campbell, OH 44405
$15 annual dues

*** Mannlicher Collectors Association**
P.O. Box 588
Hamilton, TX 76531
$30 Annual Dues
$35 Annual Foreign Dues
Website: www.mannlicher.org

*** Marlin Firearms Collectors Association, Ltd.**
P.O. Box 491
Clay Center, KS 67432-0491
$5 Initiation Fee
$30 Annual Membership Fee
$32 Canadian (U.S. funds)
$39 International (U.S. Funds)
Website: www.marlin-collectors.com

*** Maryland Arms Collectors Association (MACA)**
Del Kuzemchak, Secretary
33 S. Main Street, P.O. Box 206
Loganville, PA 17342-0206
$35 Annual Membership Fee

Maryland Licensed Firearms Dealers Association, Inc.
Steve Schneider, President
P.O. Box 10237
Baltimore, MD 21234-9998
Phone: 410-356-9485
Fax: 410-356-9486

*** Massachusetts Arms Collectors**
P.O. Box 111
Hingham, MA 02043
Phone: 781-749-2889

*** Maumee Valley Gun Collectors Association**
P.O. Box 492
Maumee, OH 43537
Website: www.mvgca.com

Merwin Hulbert Collectors Association
Terry Wagner
7208 Cessna Drive
Greensboro, NC 27409
Phone: 866-466-3287
Website: www.merwinhulbert.com
Email: MerwinMan@triad.rr.com
$10 Annual Dues

*** Michigan Antique Arms Collectors**
Les Scott
12499 Margaret Dr.
Fenton, MI 48430
Phone: 810-629-8024

*** Midwest Gun Traders Inc.**
Tom Daugherty
8716 Ameberly Dr.
New Haven, IN 46774
Phone: 260-749-6509
$15 Membership Fee

*** Miniature Arms Collectors/Makers Society, Ltd.**
Bill Adrian, President
2502 Fresno Ln.
Plainfield, IL 60544-8470
Phone: 815-254-8692

*** Minnesota Weapons Collectors**
Alvin Olson
P.O. Box 605
Waseca, MN 56093
Phone: 507-833-5615
Website: www.mwca.org
Email: cartal@hickorytech.net
$30 Annual Membership

*** Missouri Valley Arms Collectors Association, Inc. (MVACA)**
Membership Secretary
P.O. Box 6013
Leawood, KS 66206
Phone: 913-649-4248
Website: www.mvacagunshow.com
$25 Annual Membership (age 21 and over)
$10 Annual Membership (under 21)

Mohave Arms Collectors Association
Keith Gilbert, VP
Mohave Sportsmans Club
7 Mile Hill Range
3155 W. Oatman Road
Golden Valley, AZ 86413
Phone: 928-681-4476
$20 Annual Individual Membership
$30 Annual Family Membership

*** Nat'l Automatic Pistol Collectors Association (N.A.P.C.A.)**
Thompson D. Knox
Box 15738
St. Louis, MO 63163
Phone: 314-638-6505
Website: www.napca.net
$50 annual dues U.S.
$55 annual dues Canada
$65 Elsewhere

*** National Mossberg Collectors Association**
Victor Havlin
P.O. Box 487
Festus, MO 63028
$12 Annual Membership Fee
$5 Junior Membership Fee
Phone: 636-937-6401
Website: www.mossbergcollectors.org

National Rifle Association (NRA)
11250 Waples Mill Rd.
Fairfax, VA 22030
Phone: 800-NRA-3888
Fax: 703-267-3970
Website: www.nra.org
Email: membership@nrahq.org
$35 Regular Annual Membership Dues
$30 Annual Senior Membership
(65 years of age and older, also disabled vets)
$85 for three years
$1,000 Life Membership Dues
$375 Senior Life Membership (also disabled vets)
$15 Annual Junior Membership (18 years and younger)

National Shooting Sports Foundation (NSSF)
11 Mile Hill Road
Newtown, CT 06470
Phone: 203-426-1320
Fax: 203-426-1245
Website: www.nssf.org

New Eastcoast Arms Collectors Associates, NEACA, Inc.
Cathy Petronis, Secretary
38 N. Main St.
P.O. Box 385
Mechanicville, NY 12118
Phone: 518-664-9743
Website: www.neaca.com
Email: dpetron1@nycap.rr.com
$50 initial dues, $45 renewal
Promoters of Saratoga Springs & other NY Arms Fairs

*** New Mexico Gun Collectors Association**
Mr. Mark Covell, Show Host
P.O. Box 13687
Albuquerque, NM 87912
Phone: 505-262-1350
Website: www.nmgca.net
$25 Annual Dues
4 shows per year - Mar., June, Aug., Oct.

*** North Eastern Arms Collectors Assoc., Inc.**
Thomas J. Mulligan
P.O. Box 306
Island Park, NY 11558
Email: Mulligun@aol.com
$30 Application Fee
$30 Annual Membership Fee

*** Northern Indiana Gun Collectors**
William Best
15237 W. 12th Road
Plymouth, IN 46563
Phone: 219-936-4431

*** Northwest Montana Arms Collectors Association (NWMACA)**
Paul Willis, Treasurer
P.O. Box 653
Kalispell, MT 59903-0653
Phone: 406-755-3980
Email: pswillis@centurytel.net

*** Ohio Gun Collectors Association**
Laura Knotts, Business Manager
P.O. Box 670406
Sagamore Hills, OH 44067-0406
Phone: 330-467-5733
Fax: 330-467-5793
Website: www.ogca.com
Email: ogca@ogca.com
$30.00 Annual Membership Fee
$10.00 Application Fee
Members and guests of members only

*** Oregon Arms Collectors, Inc.**
P.O. Box 13000-A
Portland, OR 97213-0017
Phone: 503-254-5986
Website: members.tripod.com/ ~oregonarmscollectors/ index.html
$20 Annual Membership Fee

*** Palm Beach Historical Arms Association**
Adolph Stuffer
6304 Silver Moon Lane
Greenacres, FL 33463

Parker Gun Collectors Association
Mary Bowes
477 Ocean Ave.
Wells, ME 04090
$40 Annual Membership
$500 Life Membership
Website: www.parkerguns.org

Research Letters
P.O. Box 5772
Virginia Beach, VA 23471-5772

*** Paso Del Norte Gun Collectors**
James Foran
P.O. Box 31613
El Paso, TX 79930
Phone: 915-566-7968

*** Penn Antique Gun Collectors Assn.**
Bob Tuohy
2264 E. Scenic Drive
Bath, PA 18014
Website: www.pagca.com
Email: rjtouhy@hughes.net
$30 Annual Membership Fee

*** Penn Gun Collectors Assn.**
Phil Dasey, President
P.O. Box 246
Glenshaw, PA 15116
Phone: 412-781-2726
Website: www.paguncollectors.org
Email: president.pgca@verizon.net

*** Potomac Arms Collectors Association, Inc.**
P.O. Box 1812
Wheaton, MD 20915
Phone: 301-384-7177
Website: www.paca-club.org
$30 Annual Membership Fee

*** Remington Society of America**
Richard Shepler, President
P.O. Box 269
Duck River, TN 38454-0269
Phone: 931-583-0564
Website: www.remingtonsociety.com
Email: rjs@isdn.net
$45 New Annual Membership
$40 Renewal Membership
Foreign Memberships Available

*** Ruger Collectors Association, Inc.**
P.O. Box 240
Green Farms, CT 06838
Phone: 203-259-9498, Ext. 124
Website: www.rugercollectorsassociation.com
$30 Annual Membership Fee

SAAMI (Sporting Arms & Ammunition Manufacturers' Institute)
1145 19th St. NW, Ste. 700
Washington, DC 20036-3727
Website: www.saami.org

SASS (Single Action Shooting Society)
215 Cowboy Way
Edgewood, NM 87015
Phone: 505-843-1320
Fax: 505-843-1333
Website: www.sassnet.com
Email: SASS@sassnet.com

San Fernando Valley Arms Collectors Association
Tom Barrabee, Secretary
10655 Olive Grove Ave.
Sunland, CA 91040
$20 Annual Membership Fee

San Gabriel Valley Arms Collectors
Gerald C. Knight, Secretary/Treasurer
1140 Daveric Drive
Pasadena, CA 91107-1740
Phone: 818-351-9368
$20 Annual Dues

*** San Luis Obispo Historical Arms Society**
David M. Saks, Treasurer
P.O. Box 81
Morro Bay, CA 93443-0081

*** Santa Barbara Historical Arms Association**
Charlie Bates, President
P.O. Box 6291
Santa Barbara, CA 93160-6291
Phone/Fax: 805-485-8917
$40 Initiation
$25 Annual Membership Fee
Website: www.sbhaa.org

Second Amendment Foundation
James Madison Building
12500 NE Tenth Place
Bellevue, WA 98005
Phone: 425-454-7012
Fax: 425-451-3959
Member Services: 800-426-4302
Website: www.saf.org
Email: info@saf.org
Tax deductible membership dues $15.00
Tax deductible life membership dues $150

Shasta Arms Collectors
Monte Adams, Secretary/Treasurer
2949 Felstet Lane
Redding, CA 96001
Phone: 530-243-6258

*** Smith & Wesson Collectors Association**
Michael G. Speers, Administrator
P.O. Box 357
Larned, KS 67550-0357
Phone: 620-285-6880
Email: swca357@hotmail.com
$60 first year dues
$50 renewal dues

L.C. Smith Collectors Association
Frank Finch, Executive Director
1322 Bay Avenue
Mantoloking, NJ 08738
Phone: 732-899-1498
Website: www.lcsmith.org
Email: FrankFinch@msn.com
$25 Annual Membership
$300 Life Membership

*** South Carolina Arms Collectors Assn.**
Spencer Barker, Show Director
P.O. Box 4308
Irmo, SC 29063
Phone: 803-463-9377
Website: www.scaca.net
Email: scacadirector@aol.com

*** South Jersey Arms Collectors**
Ralph Fairley
6 Georgetown Road
Glassboro, NJ 08028
Phone: 609-881-0637

*** Southeastern Antique Arms Collectors, Inc.**
Donald Armstrong, Secretary
Doug Eberhart, President & Show Chairman
P.O. Box 1104
Alpharetta, GA 30009
One annual show per year the 3rd week in Feb.

*** Southern California Arms Collectors Association, Inc.**
Martin J. Miller, Jr.
P.O. Box 7432
Thousand Oaks, CA 91359-7432
$40 Annual Membership Fee
Phone: 805-373-0683

*** Stark Gun Collectors**
Terry Roan
Phone: 330-833-2483

Swiss Gun Collectors Association
18 Velie Ave
Barre, VT 05641
Phone: 802-479-0044
Fax: 802-479-3308
Website: www.swiss-guncollectors.com
Email: info@swiss-guncollectors.com

*** Tennessee Military Collectors Assn.**
William Price
P.O. Box 1006
Brentwood, TN 37024
$15 annual dues
Phone: 615-661-9379
Website: www.tmcaonline.org
Email: williamprice4@comcast.net

Texas Gun Collectors Association (TGCA)
Carolyn Mims
P.O. Box 701314
San Antonio, TX 78270

Thompson/Center Association
P.O. Box 537
Sanford, ME 04073
$30 annual dues (includes quarterly magazine)
Website: www.thompsoncenterassoc.org
Email: tcaogs@metrocast.net

*** Tri-State Gun Collectors, Inc.**
Manette Sneary, Business Manager
P.O. Box 1201
Lima, OH 45802
Phone: 419-647-0067

*** Tulsa Arms Collectors Association**
Mr. Joe Wanenmacher,
Secretary-Treasurer
P.O. Box 33201
Tulsa, OK 74153-1201
Phone: 918-492-0401
$40 Annual Dues

*** Utah Gun Collectors**
Carrol Cone
P.O. Box 711161
Salt Lake City, UT 84121
Phone: 801-944-9324

*** Virginia Gun Collectors Association, Inc.**
David Litchfield, President
P.O. Box 328
Manassas, VA 20108-0328
Phone: 703-624-8696
Website: www.vgca.org
Email: litchfd@comcast.net
Meetings: 4th Thursday at NRA HQ
$35 Annual Membership Dues
$150.00 Lifetime Membership Fee
Gunshow in Mar & Nov at PWC Fairgrounds
Contact Rick Nahas at 571-215-8761 for tables

*** Wabash Valley Gun Collectors**
Roger Dorsett
2601 Willow Road
Urbana, IL 61801
Phone: 217-367-5452

Washington Arms Collectors
Jennifer Masterjohn, Office Administrator
P.O. Box 389
Renton, WA 98057-0389
Phone: 425-255-8410
Fax: 425-255-8946
Website: www.washingtonarmscollectors.org
Email: office@washingtonarmscollectors.org
$35 Membership Dues
$500 Life Membership Dues

*** Weapons Collectors Society of Montana**
Ed Spragg, Executive Secretary
71713 US Hwy 89
Belt, MT 59412
Phone: 406-277-4485
Website: www.wsofmt.com
Email: emspragg@3rivers.net
$20 Single Membership (NRA)
$25 Couples Membership (NRA)
$30 Single Membership (non-NRA)
$35 Couples Membership (non-NRA)

*** Weatherby Collectors Association, Inc.**
P.O. Box 1217
Washington, MO 63090
Phone: 636-239-0348
Website: www.weatherbycollectors.com
Email: WCAsecretary@aol.com
$30 Membership Fee
$500 Lifetime Membership Fee

Willamette Valley Arms Collectors Association, Inc.
Bill Sheppard, President
P.O. Box 1299
Springfield, OR 97477-0152
Phone: 541-726-1801
Website: www.wvaca.org
$35 Membership Fee

*** Winchester Arms Collectors Association**
Georgia L. Hill Executive Secretary
915 SW Rimrock Way, Ste. 201-401
Redmond, OR 97756
Phone: 541-526-5929
Fax: 971-285-9046
Web site: www.winchestercollector.org
Email: GHill@winchestercollector.org
$40 annual dues U.S.A.
$50 annual dues Canada
$60 annual dues Foreign
$750 lifetime membership fee

Winchester Club of America
Jennifer Gole, Secretary
261 Whaley Road
Penisula, OH 44624
Email: jennifergole@gmail.com
$35 U.S. Annual membership
$50 Foreign membership
$350 Life U.S. membership
$500 Life Foreign membership

*** Wisconsin Gun Collectors Assn., Inc.**
Robert Zellmer
P.O. Box 181
Sussex, WI 53089
Phone: 262-538-1316

*** Wyoming Weapons Collectors**
Pat Aldrich
P.O. Box 1784
Laramie, WY 82073
Phone: 307-742-4630

*** Ye Conn Gun Guild**
Peter Kuck
602 Park Road
W. Hartford, CT 06107

*** Zumbro Valley Arms Collectors, Inc.**
Floyd Baumler
P.O. Box 6621
Rochester, MN 55901
Phone: 507-289-9383

CONSERVATION ORGANIZATIONS

The following are not firearms associations, but are conservation organizations that may or may not have links to hunting/shooting sports. These organizations are dedicated to preserving wildlife and natural habitat. You are encouraged to contact these organizations to learn more.

Ducks Unlimited, Inc.
One Waterfowl Way
Memphis, TN 38120
Phone: 901-758-3825
Fax: 901-758-3850
Website: www.ducks.org

Foundation for North American Wild Sheep
Raymond Lee, President
720 Allen Ave.
Cody, WY 82414-9981
Phone: 307-527-6261
Website: www.fnaws.org
1 Yr. Membership $45; 3 Yrs. $120

Global Sporting & Conservation Alliance
340 West Putnam Avenue
Greenwich, CT 06830
Phone: 203-618-0436
Fax: 203-618-0419

Hunting Heritage Trust
428 Spalding Lake Circle
Aiken, SC 29803
Phone: 803-641-1030
Fax: 803-641-1070
Website: www.huntingheritagetrust.org

The Mule Deer Foundation
1939 S 4130 W, Ste. H
Salt Lake City, UT 84104-4875
Phone: 866-822-DEER
Fax: 801-747-3344
Website: www.muledeer.org
Email: membercoord@muledeer.org
$35 Annual Membership Fee, includes 6 issues of MDF magazine

The National Wild Turkey Federation
P.O. Box 530
Edgefield, SC 29824
Phone: 800-843-6983
Call for membership details.

North American Moose Foundation
Shannon James, Executive Director
P.O. Box 30
610 W. Custer, Ste. B
Mackay, ID 83251
Phone: 208-588-2939
Fax: 208-588-2980
Website: www.moosefoundation.org
Email: moose@atcnet.net
$1,000 Lifetime Membership

North American Pronghorn Foundation
P.O. Box 13813
Rawlins, WY 82301
Phone: 307-324-5238
Website: www.antelope.org

Pheasants Forever
1783 Buerkle Circle
White Bear Lake, MN 55110
Phone: 651-773-2000
Fax: 651-773-5500
Website: www.pheasantsforever.org
Email: contact@pheasantsforever.org
$30 Annual Membership Fee includes five issues of Pheasants Forever magazine

Quail Forever
1783 Buerkle Circle
White Bear Lake, MN 55110
Phone: 866-457-8245
Fax: 651-773-5500
Website: www.quailforever.org
Email: contact@quailforever.org
$30 Annual Membership, includes 4 issues of Quail Forever magazine

Quail Unlimited
P.O. Box 70518
Albany, GA 31708

Office
308 Third Ave
Albany, GA 31701
Phone No.: 229-883-3209
Fax No: 229-883-3979
http://www.qu.org/
$35 Annual Membership, includes full year of Quail Unlimited magazine

The Ruffed Grouse Society
Ronald P. Burkert
451 McCormick Rd.
Coraopolis, PA 15108
Phone: 888-564-6747
Website: www.ruffedgrousesociety.org
Email: rgs@ruffedgrousesociety.org
$25 Annual Membership Fee
$50 Conservation Membership Fee
$100 Sustaining Membership Fee
$250+ Various Sponsor Membership Fee
All memberships include a subscription to Ruffed Grouse Society magazine.

Safari Club International & SCI Foundation
4800 W. Gates Pass Rd.
Tucson, AZ 85745-9490
Phone: 520-620-1220
Website: www.safariclub.org
$55 Annual Membership Fee USA/ CAN/MEX (includes subscription to monthly Safari magazine and bi-monthly Safari Times newsletter)

Whitetails Unlimited
P.O. Box 720
2100 Michigan Street
Sturgeon Bay, WI 54235
Phone: 800-274-5471
Fax: 920-743-4658
Website: www.whitetailsunlimited.com
Email: nh@whitetailsunlimited.com

REFERENCE SOURCES

Adler, Dennis, *Colt Blackpowder Reproductions & Replicas*. Minneapolis, MN: Blue Book Publications, 1998.

Adler, Dennis, *Black Powder Revolvers - Reproductions & Replicas*. Minneapolis, MN: Blue Book Publications, Inc., 2008.

Adler, Dennis, *Black Powder Long Arms & Pistols - Reproductions & Replicas*. Minneapolis, MN: Blue Book Publications, Inc., 2009.

Adler, Dennis, *Colt Single Actions - From Patersons to Peacemakers*. Edison, NJ: Chartwell Books, 2007.

Adler, Dennis, *Metallic Cartridge Conversions*. Iola, WI: Krause Publications, 2002.

Adler, Dennis, *Winchester Shotguns*, Edison, NJ: Chartwell Books, 2006.

Allen, John & Dennis Adler, The 4th Edition *Blue Book of Modern Black Powder Arms*. Minneapolis, MN: Blue Book Publications, Inc. 2004.

Allen, John, The 5th Edition *Blue Book of Modern Black Powder Arms*. Minneapolis, MN: Blue Book Publications, Inc., 2007.

Allen, John, The 6th Edition *Blue Book of Modern Black Powder Arms*. Minneapolis, MN: Blue Book Publications, Inc., 2009.

Allen, John, The 7th Edition *Blue Book of Modern Black Powder Arms*. Minneapolis, MN: Blue Book Publications, Inc., 2011.

Antaris, Leonardo, Dr., *Astra Automatic Pistols*. Sterling, CO: FIRAC Publishing Co., 1988.

Antaris, Leonardo, Dr., *Star Firearms*, Davenport, IA: Firac Publishing, 2002.

Bady, Donald B., *Colt Automatic Pistols*. Los Angeles, CA: Borden Publishing Co., 1973.

Baer, Larry L., *The Parker Book*. North Hollywood, CA: Beinfeld Publishing Co., 1974.

Ball, Robert., Mauser Military Rifles of the World, Iola, WI: Krause Publications, 1996.

Ball, Robert., *Remington Firearms: The Golden Age of Collecting*, WI: Krause Publications, 1995.

Barnes, Frank C., *Cartridges of the World*. Northbrook, IL: DBI Books, Inc., 2009.

Barnes, Frank C., *Cartridges of the World*. Northbrook, IL: DBI Books, Inc., 2012.

Beeman, Robert, Dr. & John Allen, The 7th Edition *Blue Book of Airguns*, Minneapolis, MN: Blue Book Publications, Inc., 2008.

Beeman, Robert, Dr. & John Allen, The 8th Edition *Blue Book of Airguns*, Minneapolis, MN: Blue Book Publications, Inc., 2009.

Beeman, Robert, Dr. & John Allen, The 9th Edition *Blue Book of Airguns*, Minneapolis, MN: Blue Book Publications, Inc., 2011.

Beeman, Robert, Dr. & John Allen, The 10th Edition *Blue Book of Airguns*, Minneapolis, MN: Blue Book Publications, Inc., 2012.

Belford, James N. and Dunlap, Jack, *Mauser Self Loading Pistol*. Alhambia, CA: Borden Publishing Co., 1969.

Bender, Roy G. III, *Mauser*. Houston, TX: Collector's Press, 1971.

Boothroyd, Geoffry & Susan M., *Boothroyd's Directory of British Gunmakers*. Amity, OR: Sand Lake Press, 1994.

Braceras, Saul, *Express Rifle - A Different Weapon*. Madrid, Spain: Valmayor Ediciones, S.L., 2007.

Breathed and Schroeder, *System Mauser*. Chicago, IL: Handgun Press, 1967.

Brophy, William S., *L.C. Smith Shotguns*. North Hollywood, CA: Beinfeld Publishing Co., 1977.

Brophy, William S., *Marlin Firearms*. Harrisburg, PA: Stackpole Books, 1989.

Butzer, David F., *The American Shotgun*. Middlefield, CT: Lyman Publications, 1973.

Bussard, Michael, *The Ammo Encyclopedia*. Minneapolis, MN: Blue Book Publications, Inc., 2008.

Bussard, Michael, *The Ammo Encyclopedia*, 2nd Edition. Minneapolis, MN: Blue Book Publications, Inc., 2010.

Bussard, Michael, *The Ammo Encyclopedia*, 3rd Edition. Minneapolis, MN: Blue Book Publications, Inc., 2011.

Bussard, Michael, *The Ammo Encyclopedia*, 4th Edition. Minneapolis, MN: Blue Book Publications, Inc., 2012.

Buxton, Warren H., *The P-38 Pistol*. Volumes I,II & III. Los Alamos, NM: U.C. Ross Books.

Byron, David, *Gunmarks, Tradenames, Codemarks, and Proofs from 1870 to the Present*. New York, NY: Crown Publishers, 1979.

Carder, Charles, *Side by Sides of the World*. Delphos, OH: AVIL ONZE Publishing.

Carder, Charles, *Side by Sides of the World Y2K*. Delphos, OH: AVIL ONZE Publishing, 2000.

Carpenter, Mel, *An Introduction to MBA Gyrojets And Other Ordnance*, Orange Park, FL, MRC3 Publishing, 2010.
Condry, Ken, & Jones, Larry, *The Colt Commemoratives, 1961-1986.* Dallas, TX: Taylor Publishing Co., 1989.
Costanza, Sam, *World of Lugers. Volume I.* Mayfield Heights, OH: World of Lugers, 1977.
Eastman, Matt, *Browning, Sporting Arms of Distinction.* Fitzgerald, GA: Published by Author, 1994.
Ezell, Edward Clinton, *Handguns of the World.* Harrisburg, PA: Stackpole Books, 1981.
Ezell, Edward Clinton, *Small Arms of the World.* (12th Ed). Harrisburg, PA: Stackpole Books, 1983.
Dance, Tom, *High Standard; A Collector's Guide to the Hamden & Hartford Target Pistols.* Lincoln, RI: Andrew Mobray Publishers, 1991.
Flayderman, Norm, *Flayderman's Guide to Antique American Firearms.* Iola, WI: Gun Digest Books, 2009.
Gardner, Col. Robert, *Small Arms Makers.* New York, NY: Bonanza Books, 1963.
Grant, James. J., *Boys' Single Shot Rifles.* Prescott, AZ: Wolfe Publishing Company, 1991.
Groenewold, John, *Quackenbush Guns.* Mundelein, IL, published by author, 2000.
Gunther, Mullins, Price, and Cote', *The Parker Story. Vol. I.* Knoxville, TN: Parker Story Joint Venture Group, 1998.
Gunther, Mullins, Price, and Cote', *The Parker Story. Vol. II.* Knoxville, TN: Parker Story Joint Venture Group, 2000.
Hogg, Ian V., *Pistols of the World*, 4th Ed.
Houchins, John, *L.C. Smith - The Legend Lives*, Winston-Salem, NC: Published by Author, 2006.
Hill and Anthony, *Confederate Long Arms and Pistols.* Charlotte, NC: Confederate Arms, 1978.
Jinks, Roy G., *History of Smith & Wesson.* North Hollywood, CA: Beinfeld Publishing Co., 1977.
Karr and Karr, Jr., *Remington Handguns.* Stackpole Co., Second Edition, 1951.
Kenyon, Charles Jr., *Lugers at Random.* Chicago, IL: Handgun Press, 1969.
Kersten, Manfred, *Walther: A German Legend*, Long Beach, CA: Safari Press, Inc., 2001.
Kimmel, J., *Savage & Stevens Arms.* Portland, OR: Corey/Stevens Pub., Inc., 1990.
Kopec, Graham, and Moore, *A Study of the Colt Single Action Army Revolver.* Redding, CA: Kopec, Graham, and Moore Publishers, 2006. www.johnakopec.com
Krasne, Jerry A., *Enyclopedia and Reference Catalog for Auto Loading Guns.* San Diego, CA: Triple K Manufacturing, 1989.
Law, Richard D., *Backbone of the Wehrmacht: The German K98k Rifle.* Coburg, Ontario, Canada: Collector Grade Publications, 2006.
Lee, Jerry (Ed.), *Standard Catalog of Firearms*, Iola, WI, Gun Digest Books, 2012.
Leithe, Frederick, *Japanese Handguns.* California: Borden Publishing Co., 1968.
Madis, George, *The Model 12.* Lancaster, TX: Privately published by Author, 1981.
Madis, George, *The Winchester Book.* Lancaster, TX: Privately Published by Author, 1975.
Marcot, Roy, *Remington, America's Oldest Gunmaker.* Peoria, IL: Primedia Special Interest Publications, 1998.
Marcot, Roy & John Gyde, *Remington .22 Rimfire Rifles.* Creswell, OR: Remington Armory Press, 2007.
Marcot, Roy. *Remington Rolling Block Rifles, Carbines & Shotguns.* Tucson, AZ: Northwood Heritage Press, 2009.
Maxwell, Samuel L., Sr., *Lever Action Magazine Rifles.* Published by Author, 1978.
Muderlak, Ed, *Parker Guns, The Old Reliable.* Long Beach, CA: Safari Press, 1997.
Murray, Douglas, *The Ninety-Nine.* Published by Author, 1985.
Nonte, Jr., George C., *Firearms Encyclopedia.* Outdoor Life: New York, NY, 1973.
Ogle, John, *The Book of Colt Paper.* Blue Book Publications, Inc.: Minneapolis, MN, 2011
Olson, Ludwig, *Mauser Bolt Action Rifles.* Montezuma, IA: F. Brownell & Son Publishers, Inc., 1976.
Price, Charlie & Parker Story Joint Venture Group, *Parker Gun Identification & Serialization*, Minneapolis, MN: Blue Book Publications, Inc. 2002.
Rankin, James L., *Walther. Vols. I, II, III.* Coral Gables, FL: Published by Author, 1976.
Rule, Roger C., *The Rifleman's Rifle.* Northridge, CA: Alliance Books, Inc., 1982.
Sellers, Frank, *American Gunsmiths*, 2nd Edition. Minneapolis, MN: Blue Book Publications, Inc., 2008.
Sellers, Frank, *Sharp's Firearms.* North Hollywood, CA: Beinfeld Publishing Co., 1978.
Serven, editor, *The Collecting of Guns.* Bonanza Books, 1964.
Sharpe, Phillip B., *The Rifle in America.* Funk and Wagnalls, 1947.
Shideler, Dan, *Standard Catalog of Remington Firearms*, Iola, WI, Gun Digest Books, 2008.
Shooter's Bible. S. Hackensack, NJ: Published annually by Skyhorse Publishing.

Skennerton, Ian, *British Small Arms of World War II*, Labrador, Australia: self-published, 1988.

Skennerton, Ian, *The Lee Enfield Story,* Labrador, Australia: self-published, 1992.

Skennerton, Ian & Stamps, *.380 Enfield Revolver*, Labrador, Australia: self-published, 1992.

Skennerton, Ian, *Small Arms Identification Series. Vols. 1-17*. Labrador, Australia: self-published, 1993-2003.

Steindler, *Steindler's New Firearms Dictionary*. Phoenix, AZ: Stackpole Books, 1985.

Still, Jan C., *Axis Pistols*. Marceline, MO: Walsworth Publishing Co., 1986.

Still, Jan C., *Imperial Lugers*. Marceline, MO: Walsworth Publishing Co., 1991.

Still, Jan C., *Third Reich Lugers*. Marceline, MO: Walsworth Publishing Co., 1988.

Supica, Jim and Nahas, Richard, *Standard Catalog of Smith & Wesson*. Iola, WI: Krause Publications, 1996.

Supica, Jim, *Standard Catalog of Smith & Wesson. Vol. II*. Iola, WI: Krause Publications, 2001.

Supica, Jim and Nahas, Richard, *Standard Catalog of Smith & Wesson*, 3rd Ed. Iola, WI: Gun Digest Books, 2006.

Tanner, Hans, *Guns of the World*. Bonanza Books, 1972, 1977.

Tinker, Edward & Johnson, Graham, *Simson Lugers, Simson & Co, Suhl - The Weimar Years*. Galesburg, IL: Brad Simpson Publishing, 2007.

Trolard, Tom, *Winchester Commemoratives*, Plano, TX: Commemorative Investments Press, 1985.

Vanderlinden, Anthony, *Belgian Browning Pistols 1889-1949*, Greensboro, NC: Wet Dog Publications, 2001.

Vanderlinden, Anthony, & H.M. Shirley, *Browning Auto-5 Shotgun - The Belgian FN Production,* Greensboro, NC: Wet Dog Publications, 2003.

Vanderlinden, Anthony, *FN Browning Pistols - Side-Arms That Shaped World History,* Greensboro, NC: Wet Dog Publications, 2010.

Vanderlinden, Anthony, *ARS Mechanica - The Ultimate FN Book,* Greensboro, NC: Wet Dog Publications, 2011.

Webster, Donald B. Jr., *Suicide Specials*. Harrisburg, PA: Stackpole, Co., 1958.

West, Bill, *Browning Arms & History*. Santa Fe Springs, CA: Stockton Trade Press, Inc., 1972.

West, Bill, *Marlin and Ballard Firearms & History*. Norwalk, CA: Stockton Trade Press, Inc., 1977.

West, Bill, *Remington Arms & History*. Whittier, CA: Stockton Trade Press, Inc., 1970.

West, Bill, *Savage and Stevens Arms & History*. Whittier, CA: Stockton Trade Press, Inc., 1971.

Whitaker, Dean H., *Model 70 Winchester 1937-1964*. Dallas, TX: Taylor Publishing Co., 1978.

Wilkerson, Don, *Post-War Colt Single Action Army*. Published by Author, 1978.

Wilkerson, Don, *Post-War Colt Single Action Revolver, 1976-1986*. Dallas, TX: Taylor Publishing, 1986.

Wilkerson, Don, *Colt Scouts, Peacemakers, and New Frontiers in .22 Caliber*, Marceline, MO: Walsworth Publishing Co., 1993.

Wilkerson, Don, *Colt Single Action Army Revolver, Pre-War/Post-War Model*, Minneapolis, MN, Broughton Printing Inc., 1991.

Wilson, R.L., *The Colt Engraving Book. Vols. I & II*. New York, NY: Bannerman's Limited Edition, 2001.

Wilson, R.L., 2nd Ed. *The Book of Colt Firearms*. Minneapolis, MN: Blue Book Publications, Inc., 1993.

Wilson, R.L., 3rd Ed. *The Book of Colt Firearms*. Minneapolis, MN: Blue Book Publications, Inc., 2008.

Wilson, R.L., *The Blue Book Pocket Guide for Colt Dates of Manufacture* . Minneapolis, MN: Blue Book Publications, Inc., 2008.

Wilson, R.L., *Colt, An American Legend*. New York, NY: Abbeville Press.

Wilson, R.L., *Colt Commemorative Firearms*. Geneseo, IL: Robert E.P. Cherry Publishing Co., 1973.

Wilson, R.L., *The Colt Heritage*. New York, NY: Simon and Schuster.

Wilson, R.L., *Silk & Steel*, New York: Random House. 2003

Wilson, R.L., *Winchester: An American Legend,* New York: Random House. 1991.

Wilson, R.L., *The World of Beretta: An International Legend,* New York: Random House. 2000.

Wilson, R.L., *Ruger & His Guns*. New York: Simon and Schuster. 1996.

Wirnsberger, Gerhard, *The Standard Directory of Proofmarks*. Jolex, Inc.

Wood, J.B., *Beretta Automatic Pistols, The Collector's & Shooter's Comprehensive Guide*. Harrisburg, PA: Stackpole Books, 1985.

Zhuk, A.B., *The Illustrated Encyclopedia of Handguns*. London: Greenhill Books. 1995.

PERIODICALS

American Firearms Industry - 2620 Alamanda Ct. Ft. Lauderdale, FL, 33301. Phone No.: 954-467-9994. Web site: www.amfire.com. Email: webmaster@amfire.com Membership is $35 per year. Trade publications and related material.

America's First Freedom - Published by the NRA. 11250 Waples Mill Rd., Fairfax, VA 22030. Phone No.: 800-672-3888. Subscription included in price of NRA Membership ($35). Published monthly.

American Cop - Published by FMG. 12345 World Trade Center Drive, San Diego, CA 92128. Phone No.: 858-605-0253. Web site: www.americancopmagazine.com. Published bi-monthly.

American Gunsmith - P.O. Box 540638, Merrit Island, FL 32954. Phone No.: 321-459-1558. Published monthly. Subscription is $60 per year.

American Handgunner - Published by FMG. 12345 World Trade Center Drive, San Diego, CA 92128. Phone No.: 858-605-0253. Web site: www.americanhandgunner.com. Published bi-monthly. Subscription is $19.95 per year.

American Hunter - Published by the NRA. 11250 Waples Mill Rd., Fairfax, VA 22030. Phone No.: 800-672-3888. Subscription included in price of NRA Membership ($35). Published monthly.

American Rifleman - Published by the NRA. 11250 Waples Mill Rd., Fairfax, VA 22030. Phone No.: 800-672-3888. Subscription included in price of NRA Membership ($35). Published monthly.

Armi Magazine - Published by C.A.F.F. srl, via Sabatelli, Milano, Italy, I-20154, Phone No.: 011-39-02-3453-7504, Fax No.: 011-3902-3453-7513, www.armimagazine.it, Published monthly.

Australian Shooter - Published by the Sporting Shooters Association of Australia, Inc., P.O. Box 2520, Unley, SA 5061, AUSTRALIA. Fax No.: 011-61-8-8272-2945. Web site: www.ssaa.org.au. Subscription is $50 per year in Australia, $60 per year elsewhere, published monthly.

Bear Hunting - P.O. Box 457, Becker, MN, 55308. Web site: www.bear-hunting.com. Subscription is $20 for 6 issues.

Big Show Journal - N7450 Aanstad Road, P.O. Box 217, Iola, WI, 54945, Subscription is $14.95 per year, published 6 times per year.

Black's Wing & Clay - Published by the Ehlert Publishing Group. 6420 Sycamore Lane, Maple Grove, MN 55369. Published annually, $14.95.

Boar Hunter - 865 GW Turner Road, Baxley, GA, 31515, Phone No.: 888-297-2627, Fax No.: 912-366-8085, Subscription is $14.97 for 6 issues.

Buckmaster's Whitetail Magazine - P.O. Box 244022, Montgomery, AL, 36124-4022, Phone No.: 334-215-3337, Web site: www.buckmasters.com. Subscription is $26 per year with membership, published 6 times per year.

The Clay Pigeon - P.O. Box 1022, Milford, PA 18337. Phone No.: 570-296-5768, Fax No.: 570-296-9298. Subscription is $18 per year (11 issues).

Combat Handguns - Published by Harris Publications. 1115 Broadway, 8th Floor, New York, NY 10010. Phone No.: 212-807-7100, Fax No.: 212-807-1479. Subscription rate: $28.97 for 1 year (8 issues).

Deer & Deer Hunting - Published by Krause Publications, 700 E. State St., Iola, WI 54990. Phone No.: 715-445-2214. $23.99 for 12 issues per year.

Deutsches Waffen Journal - DWJ Verlags GmbH, Rudolf-Diesel Strasse 46, D-74572, Blaufelden, Germany. Phone No.: 011-49-7953-9787-0, Fax No.: 011-49-7953-9787-881, Website: www.dwj.de, Email: info@dwj.de

Diana Armi - via E. Fermi, 24, Osmannoro, 50019 Sesto Fiorentino, Firenze, Italy, Fax No.: 011-39-055-303228050, www.edolimpia.it, various publications on shooting and shooting sports.

The Double Gun Journal - P.O. Box 550, East Jordan, MI 49727-9636. Phone No.: 231-536-7439, Fax No.: 231-536-7450. Published quarterly.

Ducks Unlimited - One Waterfowl Way, Memphis, TN 38120. Phone No.: 901-758-3825, Fax No.: 901-758-3850. Web site: www.ducks.org. Membership rate: $35 per year, includes 6 issues.

Eastman's Bowhunting Journal - P.O. Box 798, 1201 East 7th Street, Powell, WY, 82435, Subscription is $19.95 per year, published 6 times per year.

Eastman's Hunting Journal - P.O. Box 798, 1201 East 7th Street, Powell, WY, 82435, Subscription is $19.95 per year, published 6 times per year.

Field & Stream Magazine - P.O. Box 420235, Palm Coast, FL 32142. Phone No.: 800-289-0639 or 212-779-5000. Web site: www.fieldandstream.com. Subscription rate $12 annually. Published monthly (12 issues).

Gazette de Armes - Paris, France.

Gray's Sporting Journal - Published by Morris Communications, 735 Broad Street, Augusta, GA 30901. Phone No.: 706-823-3739. Web site: www.grayssportingjournal.com. Subscription is $39.95 for 7 issues.

Gun Digest - Published by F&W Publications, 700 E. State St., Iola, WI 54990. Phone No.: 715-445-2214. Web site: www.gundigest.com. $37.98 per year, published bi-weekly.

Guns and Ammo - Published by Intermedia Outdoors. P.O. Box 420235, Palm Coast, FL, 32142. Web site: www.gunsandammo.com. Phone Subscription is $14.97 per year, published monthly.

Gun Tests -P.O. Box 8535, Big Sandy, TX 75755, Phone No.: 800-829-9084, Web site: www.gun-tests.com. Subscription is $24 for 13 issues.

The Gun Mag.Com- P.O. Box 35, Buffalo, NY 14205. Annual Subscription is $25 for 12 issues. Phone No.: 716-885-6408.

Gun World - Published by Beckett Media LLC, Lockbox 9481, P.O. Box 8500, Philadelphia, PA, 19178. Phone No.: 800-764-6278, Web site: www.beckettmedia.com Subscription is $22.95 for 12 issues.

Guns Magazine - Published by FMG. 12345 World Trade Center Drive, San Diego, CA 92128. Phone No.:858-605-0253. Subscription is $24.95 per year (12 issues).

Guns & Game - The South Pacific Journal of Firearms & Hunting - P.O. Box 270, Nyngan, NSW, 2825 AUSTRALIA. Phone No.: 011-61-26832-2222. Subscriptions are $37 per year (Australia) or $80 per year (other countries). Published quarterly, mostly for Australia & New Zealand. www.gunsgame.com

Gun Hunter - P.O. Box 244022, Montgomery, AL, 36124-4022, Phone No.: 334-215-3337, Web site: www.buckmasters.com. Subscription is $20.95 per year with membership, published 6 times per year.

Handguns Magazine - Published by Intermedia Outdoors. 2 News Plaza, Peoria, IL 61614. Subscription is $12 for 12 issues.

Handloader - Published by Wolfe Publishing Company, 2180 Gulfstream Suite A, Prescott, AZ 86301, Phone No.: 800-899-7810, Web site: www.riflemagazine.com Subscription is $22.97 for 6 issues.

Le Hussard - www.lehussard.fr. Published in Cedex, France.

Man at Arms - 54 East School St, Woonsocket, RI, 02895. Published bimonthly ($32 yearly). Phone No.: 800-999-4697. Web site: www.manatarmsbooks.com.

Mossy Oak's Hunting the Country - Published by Grandview Media, 3535 Grandview Parkway, 5th Floor, Ste. 500, Birmingham, AL, 35243, Phone No.: 888-431-2877, Subscription is $9.95 for 4 issues.

Muzzle Blasts - Published by the National Muzzle Loading Rifle Association. P.O. Box 67, Friendship, IN 47021. Phone No.: 812-667-5131. Web site: www.nmlra.org Subscription is $40 per year, published monthly.

North American Hunter - 12301 Whitewater Dr., Minnetonka, MN 55343. Web site: www.huntingclub.com Published 8 times per year (subscription included in membership).

North American Whitetail - Dept. NAW, P.O. Box 741, Marietta, GA, 30061, Subscription is $14.97 for 8 issues.

Outdoor Guide Magazine - 505 S. Ewing, St. Louis, MO 63103, Phone No.: 314-535-9786. Web site: www.outdoorguidemagazine.com. Subscription is $19 for 6 issues.

Outdoor Life Magazine - Two Park Ave., New York, NY 10016. Phone No.: 800-365-1580 or 212-779-5000. Web site: www.outdoorlife.com. Subscription is $10 for 12 issues.

Petersen's Hunting - Published by Intermedia Outdoors. 2 News Plaza, Peoria, IL 61614. Subscription is $22 for 12 issues. Web site: www.petersenhunting.com

Pheasants Forever - 1783 Buerkle Circle, White Bear Lake, MN 55110. Phone No.: 651-773-2000, Fax No.: 651-773-5500. Membership is $35 per year, includes 5 issues.

Pointing Dog Journal/Retriever Journal - Published by the Village Press, P.O. Box 509, Traverse City, MI 49685. Phone No.: 800-447-7367. Web site: www.pointingdogjournal.com. Subscription is $26.95 for 6 issues.

Predator Extreme Magazine - Published by Grandview Media Group. Phone No: 800-260-7323. Web site: www.grandviewoutdoors.com. Subscription is $9.99 for 6 issues.

Quail Unlimited - P.O. Box 610 Edgefield, SC 29824. Phone No.: 803-637-5731, Fax No.: 803-637-0037. Membership is $25 per year, published bimonthly.

Rack - P.O. Box 244022, Montgomery, AL, 36124-4022, Phone No.: 334-215-3337, Subscription is $18.95 per year with membership, published 6 times per year.

Rifle - Published by Wolfe Publishing Company, 2625 Stearman Rd., Ste. A, Prescott, AZ 86301, Phone No.: 800-899-7810, Subscription is $19.97 per year.

Rifle Shooter - Published by Intermedia Outdoors. 2 News Plaza, Peoria, IL 61614. Subscription is $20 per year, published bimonthly.

Safari Club International - 4800 W. Gates Pass Rd., Tucson, AZ 85745. Web site: www.safariclub.org.

Sendas de Caza - Published by Ediciones Valmayor, C/los Nardos 2, San Lorenzo de El Escorial, ES-28200, Madrid, Spain. Fax No.: 011-34-0918905287

Shooting Illustrated - Published by the NRA. 11250 Waples Mill Rd., Fairfax, VA 22030. Phone No.: 800-672-3888. Web site: www. Shootingsportsman.com. Subscription is $13.95 for 12 issues.

Shooting Industry - Published by FMG. 12345 World Trade Center Drive, San Diego, CA 92128. Phone No.: 858-605-0254. Web site: www.shootingindustry.com

Shooting Sports USA - Published by the NRA. 11250 Waples Mill Rd., Fairfax, VA 22030. Phone No.: 800-672-3888. Subscription included in price of NRA Membership ($35). Published monthly.

Shooting Sportsman - Published by Down East Enterprise, Inc., P.O. Box 1357, Camden, ME, 04843. Phone No.: 207-594-9544, Fax No.: 207-594-5144. Web site: www.shootingsportsman.com. Subscription is $33 for 6 issues.

Shooting Sports Retailer - 130 W. 42nd St., New York, NY 10036. Phone No.: 212-840-0660. Free to retailers. Published 6 times per year.

Shooting Times - Published by Intermedia Outdoors, Inc. 2 News Plaza, Peoria, IL 61614. Phone No.: 800-727-4353. Web site: www.shootingtimes.com. Subscription is $23.98 for 12 issues.

Shotgun News - Published by Intermedia Outdoors, Inc. 2 News Plaza, Peoria, IL 61614. Phone No.: 800-345-6923. Web site: www.shotgunnews.com. Subscription is $34.95 yearly (36 issues).

Shotgun Sports Magazine - P.O. Box 6810, Auburn, CA 95604. Web site: www.shotgunsportsmagazine.com. Phone No.: 800-676-8920, Fax No.: 530-889-2220. Subscription is $32.95 per year (12 issues).

Sporting Classics - P.O. Box 23707, Columbia, SC 29224. Phone No.: 803-736-2424. Web site: www.sportingclassics.com. Subscription is $19.95 for 6 issues.

Sporting Clays Magazine - 317 S. Washington Ave #201, Titusville, FL, 32796. Phone No.: 800-376-2237. Subscription is $29.95 published monthly.

Sports Afield Magazine - 15621 Chemical Lane, Huntington Beach, CA, 92649. Web site: www.sportsafield.com. Phone No.: 714-373-4910, Fax No.: 714-894-4949. Subscription is $34.97 for 6 issues.

Successful Hunter - Published by Wolfe Publishing Company, 2180 Gulfstream Suite A, Prescott, AZ 86301, Phone No.: 800-899-7810, Subscription is $19.97 for 7 issues.

Turkey & Turkey Hunting - Published by Krause Publications, Inc. 700 E. State St., Iola, WI 54990. Phone No.: 715-445-2214. Web site: www.turkeyandturkeyhunting.com Published bimonthly for $15.95 (6 issues).

True West - Published by True West Publishing, Inc., P.O. Box 8008, Cave Creek, AZ, 85327, Phone No.: 888-687-1881. Web site: www.twmag.com. Subscription is $29.95 for 12 issues.

Varmint Hunter Magazine - Published by the Varmint Hunter's Association. P.O. Box 759, Pierre, SD, 57501. Phone No.: 605-224-6665, Fax No.: 605-224-6544, www.varminthunter.org. Subscription is $34 per year (4 issues).

Visier - International Waffen Magazine - Erich-Kastner-Strasse 2, D-56379, Singhofen, GERMANY. Phone No.: 011-49-2604-9780, Fax No.: 011-49-2604-978-703.

Waterfowl Magazine - Published by Waterfowl USA, P.O. Box 50, Edgefield, SC 29824. Phone No.: 803-637-5767. 6 issues per year.

Whitetail Journal - Published by Grandview Media, 200 Croft St. Suite 1, Birmingham, AL, 35242, Phone No.: 888-431-2877. Web site: www.grandviewoutdoors.com Subscription is $9.99 for 5 issues.

Wildfowl - Published by Intermedia Outdoors. 2 In-Fisherman Drive, Brainerd, MN 56425. Phone No.: 800-800-7724. Web site: www.imoutdoorsmedia.com. Subscription is $24.97 for 7 issues. Published bimonthly.

Women & Guns - Published by Second Amendment Foundation, P.O. Box 35, Buffalo, NY, 14205. Web site: www.womenshooters.com. $18 annual subscription. Published bimonthly.

STORE BRAND CROSS-OVER LIST

The following listing is provided as a cross-reference of Store Brands to original manufacturer and model number. Although not exhaustive, this list covers most major stores and chains that have had their name put on guns by other manufacturers. The values for the firearms listed on these pages are approximately 15% – 40% less than the original manufacturers' model(s).

Our thanks goes out to Numrich Gun Parts Corp., West Hurley, NY. They can be reached at (845) 679-4867.

House Brand	Model No.	Orig. Mfgr.	Orig. Model
Aldens	670	Springfield	67
Aldens	670	Savage	67
Belknap	964A	Stevens	87N
Belknap	B63	Springfield	947
Belknap	B63	Savage	947B
Belknap	B63E	Savage	940E
Belknap	B64	Savage	67
Belknap	B65C	Springfield	745
Belknap	865C	Savage	745
Belknap	B68	Savage	94C
Belknap	B68D	Savage	94D
Belknap	B963	Springfield	120
Belknap	B963	Savage	120
Belknap	B964	Savage	87J
Belknap	B967	Savage	87N
Coast to Coast	180	Savage	58
Coast to Coast	1800	Savage	18D
Coast to Coast	182	Savage	18S
Coast to Coast	184	Savage	951
Coast to Coast	267	Savage	77
Coast to Coast	285	Savage	7J
Coast to Coast	286	Savage	46
Coast to Coast	288	Savage	87J
Coast to Coast	320	Savage	120
Coast to Coast	367	Savage	30
Coast to Coast	40	Marlin	99C
Coast to Coast	42	Marlin	70
Coast to Coast	650	Marlin	55
Coast to Coast	779	Mossberg	479
Coast to Coast	843	Savage	340
Coast to Coast	843	Springfield	840
Coast to Coast	843V2DS	Savage	340(.222)
Coast to Coast	843V3DS	Savage	340(.30/30)
Coast to Coast	946	Stevens	940
Coast to Coast	946	Springfield	947
Coast to Coast	946E	Stevens	940E
Coast to Coast	946Y	Stevens	940Y
Cotter & Co	10-40	Glenfield	10
Cotter & Co	10-40	Marlin	101
Cotter & Co	121	Stevens	120-15
Cotter & Co	167	Springfield	67
Cotter & Co	167T	Savage	30
Cotter & Co	168	Savage	30
Cotter & Co	168	Springfield	67VR
Cotter & Co	287	Springfield	87J
Cotter & Co	33	Marlin	336C
Cotter & Co	410	Savage	110E
Cotter & Co	424	Savage	24F
Cotter & Co	434	Savage	34
Cotter & Co	474	Savage	170
Cotter & Co	474	Springfield	174
Cotter & Co	487T	Springfield	187
Cotter & Co	489	Savage	89
Cotter & Co	60-50	Glenfield	60
Cotter & Co	60-50	Marlin	99C
Cotter & Co	645	Savage	745
Cotter & Co	645C	Savage	745C
Cotter & Co	75-46	Marlin	99M1
Cotter & Co	75-45	Glenfield	75
Cotter & Co	842	Springfield	840
Cotter & Co	911	Springfield	511
Cotter & Co	918	Springfield	18
Cotter & Co	948	Stevens	940
Cotter & Co	948E	Savage	948E
Cotter & Co	949	Springfield	944
Cotter & Co	949C	Savage	940
Cotter & Co	949Y	Savage	944Y
C.I.L.	125	Anschutz	184
C.I.L.	212	Savage	7J
C.I.L.	221	Savage	7J
C.I.L.	227	Savage	871
C.I.L.	233	Savage	85N
C.I.L.	266	Savage	187
C.I.L.	470	Anschutz	520/61
C.I.L.	607	Savage	67
C.I.L.	607 TD	Savage	30 FLD GR.
C.I.L.	621	Savage	30
C.I.L.	621 TD	Savage	30D
C.I.L.	710	Savage	311
C.I.L.	725	Savage	FOX BDE
C.I.L.	830	Savage	340
C.I.L.	871	Savage	170
C.I.L.	950C.D	Savage	110C.D
C.I.L.	MKVII	H & R	865
Eastern Arms	101.1	Stevens	94B
Eastern Arms	IOI.23	Savage	416
Foremost See J.C.Penney			
Gamble Skogmo, Hiawatha			
Gamble Skogmo	130	Savage	30
Gamble Skogmo	1300-567 VR	Savage	67-VR
Gamble Skogmo	180N	Savage	87N
Gamble Skogmo	189J	Savage	87J
Gamble Skogmo	189N	Stevens	87N
Gamble Skogmo	521	Savage	120
Gamble Skogmo	567	Savage	67
Gamble Skogmo	S87	Savage	187
Gamble Skogmo	594	Savage	944
Gamble Skogmo	594Y	Savage	944Y
Gamble Skogmo	GU12-5517A	J.C.Higgins	60 & 66
Glenfield	10	Marlin	101
Glenfield	20	Marlin	80
Glenfield	25	Marlin	80 W/swivels
Glenfield	30A	Marlin	336
Glenfield	35	Marlin	336 .35 cal
Glenfield	50	Marlin	55
Glenfield	60	Marlin	5
Glenfield	60	Marlin	99C
Glenfield	65	Marlin	99M1
Glenfield	70	Marlin	989M2
Glenfield	75	Marlin	989MI
Globco	Mohawk	Russian	Tokarev

House Brand	Model No.	Orig. Mfgr.	Orig. Model
Hawthorn See Wards			
Hercules	50	Stevens	5100
Hiawatha See Gambles			
J.C. Higgins See Sears			
J.C. Penney common name, F - Foremost			
J.C.Penney	2025	Marlin	80C
J.C.Penney	2035	Marlin	80
J.C.Penney	2035	Glenfield	20
J.C.Penney	2066	Marlin	49DL
J.C.Penney	2935	Marlin	336
J.C.Penney	3040	Marlin	336
J.C.Penney	3040	Glenfield	30A
J.C.Penney	4011	High Standard	FLIGHT KING
J.C.Penney	6400	Savage	340
J.C.Penney	6610	Savage	120
J.C.Penney	6630	Glenfield	50
J.C.Penney	6630	Marlin	66
J.C.Penney	6647	Savage	944
J.C.Penney	6647	Springfield	944
J.C.Penney	6660	Glenfield	60
J.C.Penney	6660	Marlin	99C
J.C.Penney	6670	Springfield	67H
J.C.Penney	6670	Savage	67
J.C.Penney	6870	Savage	30
J.C.Penney	6870H	Savage	30H
Katz	F-1282	Marlin	989M2
Katz	F-1282	Glenfield	70
Katz	F-1287	Marlin	55
Katz	F-1287	Glenfield	50
Kresge	151	Boito	CBC
K-Mart	151	Boito	CBC
Marlin/new	780	Marlin/old	80
Marlin/new	781	Marlin/old	81
Marlin/new	782	Marlin/old	980
New Haven	220K	Mossberg	320K-A
New Haven	240K	Mossberg	340K
New Haven	246K	Mossberg	346K-A
New Haven	250K	Mossberg	152K
New Haven	250K8	Mossberg	350K-A
New Haven	273	Mossberg	173
New Haven	273A	Mossberg	173A
New Haven	283.D	Mossberg	183D
New Haven	284	Mossberg	173
New Haven	285	Mossberg	185D-C
New Haven	290	Mossberg	190D-A
New Haven	453	Mossberg	353
New Haven	600AT	Mossberg	500A
New Haven	600C	Mossberg	500C
New Haven	600E	Mossberg	500E
New Haven	679	Mossberg	472
New Haven	740	Mossberg	640
Otasco	30	Marlin	336
Otasco	30	Glenfield	30A
Otasco	65	Glenfield	60
Otasco	65	Marlin	99C
Palmetto	11	Stevens	85,89
Premier	Trail Blazer	Stevens	29A

House Brand	Model No.	Orig. Mfgr.	Orig. Model
Revelation, see Western Auto			
Sears. Ranger. J.C. Higgins			
J.C.Higgins	30	High Standard	30
J.C.Higgins	101.1	Savage	94
J.C.Higgins	101.24	Savage	15-120
J.C.Higgins	20	High Standard	200
J.C.Higgins	42 DL	Marlin	80
J.C.Higgins	52	Sako	L46
J.C.Higgins	S4	Browning	FN-300
J.C.Higgins	583.13 to.23	High Standard	10
J.C.Higgins	583.2078-79	High Standard	20ga pump
J.C.Higgins	583.514-730	High Standard	20ga pump
J.C.Higgins	6670H	Stevens	67H
J.C.Higgins	80	High Standard	101
Ranger	101.2	Savage	238
Ranger	101.8	Stevens	83
Ranger	104.7	H&R	120
Ranger	105.20	H&R	120
Ranger	120	Winchester	1200
Ranger	30	Stevens	520A
Ranger	34A	Marlin	80.C,780
Ranger	34A	Marlin	50-50E
Ranger	35A	Stevens	66A
Ranger	36	Marlin	80 Adj. Trigger
Ranger	400	Stevens	311
Sears	101.1	Savage	94
Sears	101.100	Savage	96/96Y
Sears	101.10040	Savage	94
Sears	101.10041	Savage	94
Sears	101.10080	Stevens	940
Sears	101.1120	Savage	51 and 951
Sears	101.12	Stevens	39
Sears	101.13	Stevens	86-7
Sears	101.138	Savage	38A and 58A
Sears	101.138	Springfield	18.410
Sears	101.1380	Springfield	18,18C
Sears	101.1380	Stevens	58,C
Sears	101.1381	Springfield	18,951 E,F
Sears	101.1381	Stevens	58,51, E,F
Sears	101.16	Savage	6,87
Sears	101.1610	Savage	540 DL
Sears	101.1610	Savage	FOX BDL
Sears	101.1610	Fox BST	EC,BD,BE,B-F
Sears	101.1620-1670	Stevens	530,A;311,A,C
Sears	101.1700	Savage	94
Sears	101.1701	Fox BSE	C,D,Ser F,H
Sears	101.1701-C	Savage	BSE
Sears	101.1710	Savage	FOX BDE
Sears	101.1710	Savage	540 BDE
Sears	101.1750	Savage	94
Sears	101.1760	Savage	94
Sears	101.19	Stevens	827-7
Sears	101.20	Stevens	15
Sears	101.22	Stevens	87M(MUSKET)
Sears	101.25	Stevens	39A,59A,BandC
Sears	101.2830	Savage	63-73
Sears	101.2830	Savage	73
Sears	101.3	Stevens	237
Sears	101.3538830	Stevens	89
Sears	101.4	Stevens	38
Sears	101.40	Springfield	947,D,Y
Sears	101.40	Stevens	940,D,Y,DY
Sears	101.451	Marlin	336
Sears	101.5	Stevens	37
Sears	101.51004	Savage	94
Sears	101.510070	Savage	94

House Brand	Model No.	Orig. Mfgr.	Orig. Model
Sears	101.51009	Springfield	944,Yseries A
Sears	101.51013	Springfield	944,Yseries A
Sears	101.51024	Savage	94
Sears	101.510270	Savage	94
Sears	101.51044	Savage	94
Sears	101.510660	Stevens	9478
Sears	101.510660	Springfield	944,Y series A
Sears	101.510670	Stevens	9478
Sears	101.510680	Stevens	9478
Sears	101.512220	Stevens	5100,530,311
Sears	101.512230	Stevens	5100,530,311
Sears	101.51451	Springfield	67
Sears	101.51452	Springfield	67
Sears	101.51454	Springfield	67
Sears	101.51472	Springfield	67 Series B
Sears	101.52701	Stevens	71,74 S/S
Sears	101.52772	Savage	34,65,34M.65M
Sears	101.52773	Savage	34,65,34M,65M
Sears	101.5350	Springfield	18.58
Sears	101.5350-D	Stevens	18D
Sears	101.53521	Savage	340
Sears	101.53527	Savage	340
Sears	101.5380	Savage	18/18AC.58
Sears	101.5380	Springfield	18,12,16,20ga.
Sears	101.5380D	Stevens	18ADC
Sears	101.538840	Savage	34,65,34M,65M
Sears	101.540	FOX	B-BST,BDL
Sears	101.5410	Springfield	18,58
Sears	101.5410D	Savage	18D
Sears	101.5410D	Springfield	18DS
Sears	101.54880	Stevens	80 Series A
Sears	101.54880	Springfield	187 Series A
Seem	101.64881	Marlin	980 DL,987
Sears	101.600	Stevens	39A,59A,B,C
Sears	101.7	Stevens	311
Sears	101.750	SpringField	18.410
Sears	101.750	Savage	38A and 58A
Sears	101.7C	Stevens	311-C
Sears	101.8	Stevens	83
Sears	102	Stevens	240
Sears	102.25	Stevens	520A
Sears	102.35	Savage	M521
Sears	102.35	Savage	M29-D2
Sears	103.13	Marlin	81
Sears	103.16	Marlin	80
Sears	103.18	Marlin	100
Sears	103.181	Marlin	101
Sears	103.1977	Marlin	101
Sears	103.19770	Marlin	101
Sears	103.19771	Marlin	101
Sears	103.19780	Marlin	101
Sears	103.19790	Marlin	80
Sears	103.19791	Marlin	80
Sears	103.19800	Marlin	80
Sears	103.19801	Marlin	80
Sears	103.1981	Marlin	81
Sears	103.19810	Marlin	81
Sears	103.19811	Marlin	81
Sears	103.1982	Marlin	81DL
Sears	103.19820	Marlin	81
Sears	103.19821	Marlin	81
Sears	103.19840	Marlin	56
Sears	103.19880	Marlin	57 LR-MAG.
Sears	103.19881	Marlin	57 LR-MAG.
Sears	103.19890	Marlin	57 LR-MAG.
Sears	103.2	Marlin	80
Sears	103.228	Marlin	80
Sears	103.229	Marlin	81
Sears	103.273	Marlin	782
Sears	103.273	Marlin	980
Sears	103.274	Marlin	122
Sears	103.275	Marlin	122
Sears	103.2751	Marlin	122
Sears	103.2840	Marlin	80
Sears	103.2850	Marlin	81
Sears	103.2870	Marlin	56
Sears	103.350	Marlin	M90
Sears	103.360	Marlin	90
Sears	103.4	Marlin	A1
Sears	103.450	Marlin	336
Sears	103.451	Marlin	336
Sears	103.720	Marlin	59
Sears	103.740	Marlin	59
Sears	103.8	Marlin	100
Sears	10.19790	Marlin	80
Sears	11.2	Stevens	238
Sears	153.512350	Laurona	S/S
Sears	153.512351	Laurona	S/S
Sears	153.512360	Laurona	S/S
Sears	153.512361	Laurona	S/S
Sears	153.512740	Laurona	71 0/U
Sears	18	Mossberg	183K
Sears	18AC	Savage	18C
Sears	2C	Winchester	131
Sears	20	High Standard	200
Sears	200	Winchester	1200
Sears	200	Mossberg	G4
Sears	201	Mossberg	80
Sears	202	Mossberg	80
Sears	203	Mossberg	85
Sears	204	Mossberg	83
Sears	205	Mossberg	73
Sears	206	Mossberg	70
Sears	207	Mossberg	75
Sears	209	Stevens	84-7
Sears	21	High Standard	K2011
Sears	210	Mossberg	85B
Sears	211	Mossberg	83B
Sears	211	Stevens	86-7
Sears	212	Mossberg	73B
Sears	213	Mossberg	75B
Sears	215	Mossberg	85C
Sears	216	Mossberg	83C
Sears	217	Mossberg	75C
Sears	217	Stevens	87M (MUSKET)
Sears	218	Mossberg	73C
Sears	218	Stevens	22/410
Sears	231	Stevens	83
Sears	232	Stevens	87-7
Sears	233	Stevens	87-7
Sears	234	Savage	234
Sears	238	Stevens	827-7
Sears	25	High Standard	A1041 .22 auto
Sears	273.2400	Winchester	190
Sears	273.27S10(2C)	Winchester	131
Sears	273.27520(2M)	Winchester	131
Sears	273.510770	Winchester	37A
Sears	273.510780	Winchester	37A
Sears	273.510790	Winchester	37A
Sears	273.53421	Winchester	100
Sears	277	Stevens	1S
Sears	278.28180	Cooey	64
Sears	281.512650	Antonio Zoli	O/U
Sears	281.512651	Antonio Zoli	O/U
Sears	281.512660	Antonio Zoli	O/U
Sears	281.512661	Antonio Zoli	O/U
Sears	281.512750	Antonio Zoli	O/U
Sears	282.510821	Boito	ERA Single Bbl

House Brand	Model No.	Orig. Mfgr.	Orig. Model	House Brand	Model No.	Orig. Mfgr.	Orig. Model
Sears	282.510831	Boito	ERASingle Bbl	Sears	97	Savage	94
Sears	282.510841	Boito	ERA Single Bbi	Sears	97AC	Savage	94AC
Sears	282.5227740	CBC	122	Sears	98	Stevens	37
Sears	282.527740	FIE	122	Sears	98	Springfield	944
Sears	2C	Winchester	131	Sears	M30	Stevens	M520
Sears	2T	Winchester	121,131,141	Sears	mzm	Savage	34
Sears	2/57	Stevens	66	Sears 100	273.532141	Winchester	NM 94
Sears	2/58	Stevens	66	Sears 200	2732.5320	Winchester	1200
Sears	30	High Standard	22 PUMP	Sears 200	273.2011	Winchester	1200
Sears	300	Winchester	1400	Sears 200	273.21010	Winchester	1200
Sears	31	J.C. Higgins	31	Sears 200	273.2160	Winchester	1200
Sears	33	J.C. Higgins	33	Sears 200	273.2250	Winchester	1200
Sears	34	J.C. Higgins	34	Sears 200	273.2251	Winchester	1200
Sears	340.530430	Ithaca	49SS	Sears 200	273.2280	Winchester	1200
Sears	35A	Stevens	66A	Sears 200	273.4310	Winchester	1200
Sears	36	Marlin	80	Sears 200	273.4320	Winchester	1200
Sears	375	Mossberg	45B	Sears 200	273.4340	Winchester	1200
Sears	377	Mossberg	42C	Sears 200	273,4350	Winchester	1200
Sears	381	Mossberg	46B	Sears 200	273.4410	Winchester	1200
Sears	382	Mossberg	46B	Sears 200	273.4420	Winchester	1200
Sears	384	Mossberg	45A	Sears 200	273.4450	Winchester	1200
Sears	385	Mossberg	45B	Seem 200	273.514010	Winchester	1200
Sears	387	Mossberg	42C	Sears 200	273.614010	Winchester	1200
Sears	388	Mossberg	42C	Sears 200	273.514011	Winchester	1200
Sears	389	Mossberg	42A OR 26C	Sears 200	273.514020	Winchester	1200
Sears	390	Mossberg	26C	Seem 200	273.514040	Winchester	1200
Sears	3T	Winchester	190	Sears 200	273.514050	Winchester	1200
Sears	41	Marlin	101	Sears 200	273.514051	Winchester	1200
Sears	41 DLA	Marlin	122	Sears 200	273.514210	Winchester	1200
Sears	42	Marlin	80	Sears 200	273.514220	Winchester	1200
Sears	42DL	Marlin	80	Sears 200	273,514250	Winchester	1200
Sears	42DLM	Marlin	980	Sears 200	273.514251	Winchester	1200
Sears	43	Marlin	81	Sears 200	273.514810	Winchester	1200
Sears	43DL	Marlin	81	Sears 200	273.614820	Winchester	1200
Sears	44DL	Marlin	57	Sears 200	273.514830	Winchester	1200
Sears	44DLM	Marlin	57M	Sears 200	273.514840	Winchester	1200
Sears	45	Marlin	336C	Sears 200	273.515010	Winchester	1200
Sears	46	Marlin	56	Sears 200	273.515020	Winchester	1200
Sears	46DL	Marlin	56	Sears 200	273.515050	Winchester	1200
Sears	4980	Stevens	94-2 W/PAD	Sears 200	273.515051	Winchester	1200
Sears	49.11830/30	Savage	99 A	Sears 200	273.515080	Winchester	1200
Sears	53	Winchester	70	Sears 200	273.515090	Winchester	1200
Sears	54	Winchester	94	Sears 200	273.515220	Winchester	1200
Sears	583.1	High Standard	N/A	Sears 200	273.515221	Winchester	1200
Sears	583,126	Sako	L46	Sears 200	273.515250	Winchester	1200
Sears	583.13	High Standard	N/A	Sears 200	273.515251	Winchester	1200
Sears	583.14	H & R	120	Sears 200	273.515280	Winchester	1200
Sears	583.15	H&R	121	Sears 200	273.515290	Winchester	1200
Sears	583.16	High Standard	10	Sears 200	273.515410	Winchester	1200
Sears	583.17	High Standard	N/A	Sears 200	273.515420	Winchester	1200
Sears	583.18	H & R	120	Sears 200	273.515470	Winchester	1200
Sears	583.2	H & R	M120	Sears 200	273.515710	Winchester	1200
Sears	583.20	High Standard	Flight King	Sears 200	273.515720	Winchester	1200
Sears	583.2085-87	High Standard	20ga pump	Sears 200	273.515920	Winchester	1200
Sears	583.21	H&R	M120	Sears 200	273.5310	Winchester	1200
Sears	583.25	H&R	M121	Sears 200	273.5350	Winchester	1200
Sears	583.3	H&R	M121	Sears 2T	273.27530	Winchester	141
Sears	583.4	High Standard	10	Sears 300	273.1310	Winchester	1400
Sears	583.7	High Standard	10	Sears 300	273.1320	Winchester	1400
Sears	583.91	H & R	121	Sears 300	273.1350	Winchester	1400
Sears	6C (Canada)	Winchester	Cooy 64,64B	Sears 300	273.21550	Winchester	1400
Sears	6C(American)	Winchester	490	Sears 300	273.2500	Winchester	1400
Sears	66	High Standard	66	Sears 300	273.2540	Winchester	1400
Sears	73	Savage	73	Sears 300	273.32060	Winchester	1400
Sears	870.528140	Voere	Clip .22	Sears 300	273.32070	Winchester	1400
Sears	92	Stevens	39	Sears 300	273.521050	Winchester	1400
Sears	93	Stevens	38	Sears 300	273.521051	Winchester	1400
Sears	94	Stevens	237	Sears 300	273.521080	Winchester	1400
Sears	95	Stevens	238	Sears 300	273.521090	Winchester	1400

House Brand	Model No.	Orig. Mfgr.	Orig. Model
Sears 300	273.521160	Winchester	1400
Sears 300	273.521161	Winchester	1400
Sears 300	273.521250	Winchester	1400
Sears 300	273.521251	Winchester	1400
Sears 300	273.521260	Winchester	1400
Sears 300	273.521280	Winchester	1400
Sears 300	273.521290	Winchester	1400
Sears 300	273.521580	Winchester	1400
Sears 300	273.521680	Winchester	1400
Sears 300	273.521710	Winchester	1400
Sears 300	273.521770	Winchester	1400
Sears 300	273.521780	Winchester	1400
Sears 300	273.523251	Winchester	1400
Sears 300	273.52151	Winchester	1400
Sears 3T-A	273.2390	Winchester	190-290
Sears 3T-A	273.2400	Winchester	190-290
Sears 3T-A	273.528110	Winchester	190-290
Sears 3T-A	273.528111	Winchester	190-290
Sears 4T	273.2360	Winchester	270
Sears 53A	273.532780	Winchester	70A
Sears 54	273.2120	Winchester	NM 94
Sears 54	273.532140	Winchester	NM 94
Sears 54	273.53419	Winchester	NM 94
Sears 54	273.810	Winchester	NM 94
Sears 54	273.811	Winchester	NM 94
Sears 6C	273.28130	Winchester	490
Sears 6C	273.528131	Winchester	490
Sears 6C	273.528132	Winchester	490
Sears MI	273.27010	Winchester	121
Sears M5,M-5T	273.2340	Winchester	150-250
Sears M5,M-5T	273.2341	Winchester	150-250
Sears M5,M-5T	273.2350	Winchester	150-250
Sears M5,M-5T	273.2351	Winchester	150-250
Sears T.W. 73	273.532730	Winchester	670 Mag.
Sears T.W. 73	23.31020	Winchester	New Mod 70
Sears T.W. 73	273.1390	Winchester	MN 30-06
Sears T.W. 73	273.1400	Winchester	MN 70 (.270)
Sears T.W. 73	273.1830	Winchester	New Mod 70
Sears T.W. 73	273.1840	Winchester	New Mod 70
Sears T.W. 73	273.1850	Winchester	New Mod 70
Sears T.W. 73	273.1860	Winchester	New Mod 70
Sears T.W. 73	273.1870	Winchester	New Mod 70
Sears T.W. 73	273.31010	Winchester	New Mod 70
Sears T.W. 73	273.31060	Winchester	New Mod 70
Sears T.W. 73	273.32020	Winchester	New Mod 70
Sears T.W. 73	273.32030	Winchester	New Mod 70
Sears T.W. 73	273.32040	Winchester	New Mod 70
Sears T.W. 73	273.532061	Winchester	New Mod 70
Sears T.W. 73	273.532071	Winchester	New Mod 70
Sears T.W. 73	273.532081	Winchester	New Mod 70
Sears T.W. 73	273.53403	Winchester	New Mod 70
Sears T.W. 73	273.53406	Winchester	New Mod 70
Sears T.W. 73	273.53409	Winchester	New Mod 70
Sears T.W. 73	273.32010	Winchester	Now Mod 70
Ted Williams	340.530430	Ithaca	49SS
Shapleigh's	KING NITRO	Savage	15
Simmons	411	Savage	540DL
Simmons	411	Savage	Fox BDE 20ga
Simmons	411E	Savage	540 BDE
Simmons	411E	Savage	Fox BDE 20ga
Talo	12DL	Stevens	120
Talo	176 VR	Springfield	67 VR
Talo	176DL	Springfield	67
Western Auto, Revelation			
Revelation	300	Savage	30 D,E,F
Revelation	394 Series P	Stevens	94P
Revelation	76	High Standard	Double Nine
Revelation	R310	Mossberg	500AB
Western Auto	100	Mossberg	321
Western Auto	101Y	Savage	73Y
Western Auto	101.1701	Savage	540BS
Western Auto	101.171	Savage	540BD
Western Auto	101.2830	Savage	73
Western Auto	101.52772	Savage	65M
Western Auto	101.535D	Savage	18
Western Auto	101.53500	Savage	18D
Western Auto	101.53521	Savage	340
Western Auto	101.5380	Savage	18AC
Western Auto	101.5380D	Savage	18DAC
Western Auto	101.5410	Savage	18DS,S
Western Auto	103	Savage	89
Western Auto	103.13	Marlin	81
Western Auto	103.16	Marlin	80
Western Auto	103.18	Marlin	80
Western Auto	103.181	Marlin	101
Western Auto	103.19780	Marlin	101
Western Auto	103.19790	Marlin	80
Western Auto	103.19800	Marlin	80
Western Auto	103.1981	Marlin	81
Western Auto	103.1982	Marlin	81DL
Western Auto	103.19820	Marlin	81
Western Auto	103.19840	Marlin	56
Western Auto	103.19880	Marlin	57
Western Auto	103.19890	Marlin	57M
Western Auto	103.1997	Marlin	101
Western Auto	103.2	Marlin	80
Western Auto	103.228	Marlin	80
Western Auto	103.229	Marlin	81
Western Auto	103.273	Marlin	980
Western Auto	103.274	Marlin	122
Western Auto	103.2751	Marlin	122
Western Auto	103.2840	Marlin	80
Western Auto	103.2850	Marlin	81
Western Auto	103.2870	Marlin	56
Western Auto	103.360	Marlin	90
Western Auto	103.450	Marlin	336
Western Auto	103.451	Marlin	336
Western Auto	103.720	Marlin	59
Western Auto	103.740	Marlin	59
Western Auto	105-2060	Marlin	780
Western Auto	105-2060	Marlin	80
Western Auto	107	Mossberg	640K
Western Auto	107A	Mossberg	640
Western Auto	110-2140	Marlin	81
Western Auto	110-2140	Marlin	781
Western Auto	115	Savage	46
Western Auto	115-2277	Marlin	57
Western Auto	116-2276	Marlin	57M
Western Auto	117	Mossberg	402
Western Auto	120-2220	Marlin	99
Western Auto	125	Mossberg	353
Western Auto	135	Savage	187
Western Auto	135	Springfield	187A
Western Auto	150m	Marlin	49
Western Auto	150-2225	Marlin	49
Western Auto	160	Springfield	187A
Western Auto	160	Savage	80
Western Auto	200-2280	Marlin	39A
Western Auto	200-2282	Marlin	39A
Western Auto	200-2550	Marlin	336
Western Auto	200-2554	Marlin	336(.44MAG)
Western Auto	205	Mossberg	472PCA

House Brand	Model No.	Orig. Mfgr.	Orig. Model
Western Auto	210A	Mossberg	810AH
Western Auto	220A	Mossberg	800A
Western Auto	220AD	Mossberg	800AD
Western Auto	220B	Mossberg	800B
Western Auto	220BD	Mossberg	800BD
Western Auto	220C	Mossberg	800C
Western Auto	220CD	Mossberg	800CD
Western Auto	225	Savage	340
Western Auto	2280	Marlin	39A
Western Auto	2282	Marlin	39A Mountie
Western Auto	230	Savage	340
Western Auto	250	Savage	110E
Western Auto	250A	Savage	110D
Western Auto	250D	Savage	110
Western Auto	260	Savage	170
Western Auto	260	Springfield	174
Western Auto	300	Springfield	67
Western Auto	300	Stevens	30
Western Auto	300A	Savage	30AC
Western Auto	300F	Stevens	77C
Western Auto	300H	Savage	30,HAC
Western Auto	300-300AC	Springfield	67
Western Auto	310	Mossberg	500
Western Auto	310A	Mossberg	500A
Western Auto	310AB	Mossberg	500AB
Western Auto	310B	Mossberg	500B
Western Auto	310C	Mossberg	500C
Western Auto	310E	Mossberg	500E
Western Auto	312	Mossberg	395
Western Auto	312AK	Mossberg	395K
Western Auto	312SB	Mossberg	395T
Western Auto	316	Mossberg	390
Western Auto	316BB	Mossberg	390T
Western Auto	316BK	Mossberg	390K
Western Auto	325B	Mossberg	385T
Western Auto	325BK	Mossberg	385K
Western Auto	330	Mossberg	183 & 183K
Western Auto	330B	Mossberg	183T
Western Auto	335-3725	Marlin	59
Western Auto	336	Springfield	951
Western Auto	350	Stevens	94
Western Auto	350A	Savage	94D
Western Auto	350M	Stevens	94
Western Auto	355	Stevens	947
Western Auto	355Y	Savage	94Y
Western Auto	355YE	Springfield	947YE
Western Auto	356Y	Springfield	944Y
Western Auto	360	Savage	540
Western Auto	360	Savage	FOX mod B
Western Auto	360C	Savage	540C
Western Auto	400	Stevens	745
Western Auto	400C	Savage	745C
Western Auto	420	High Standard	Supmatic C-011
Western Auto	425	High Standard	Supmatic C-120
Western Auto	460	Springfield	511
Western Auto	SD52A	Stevens	311
West Point	45	Marlin	60

Wards, Western Field, and Hawthorne

House Brand	Model No.	Orig. Mfgr.	Orig. Model
Hawthorne	110	Unknown	S shot SG
Hawthorne	580 EJN	Colt	Colteer/bolt
Hawthorne	814 EJN	Colt	Colteer/SS
Hawthorne	820B	Mossberg	340
Hawthorne	880	Colt	Colteer/semi
Hawthorne	880 EJN	Colt	Colteer/bolt
Wards	24M 419A	Mossberg	9
Wards	472	Noble	50
Wards	850	Mossberg	353
Wards Triumph	52	Stevens	315
Western Field	04M-489A	Mossberg	50
Western Field	04M-218A	Mossberg	73C
Western Field	04M-2117A	Mossberg	9
Western Field	04M-217A	Mossberg	75C
Western Field	04M-214A	Mossberg	85C
Western Field	04M-216A	Mossberg	83C
Western Field	I	Mossberg	RF-1
Western Field	10-SD247A	Stevens	94B (Tenite)
Western Field	14	Savage	39A
Western Field	14	Savage	59A
Western Field	14M-215A	Mossberg	85
Western Field	14M-497B	Mossberg	M42
Western Field	14M-488A	Mossberg	50
Western Field	15	Mossberg	80
Western Field	150	Mossberg	183K
Western Field	151X	Kessler	N/A
Western Field	155	Mossberg	173
Western Field	15A	Mossberg	83
Western Field	16	Mossberg	85
Western Field	160	Mossberg	385K
Western Field	16A	Mossberg	85
Western Field	17	Mossberg	73
Western Field	170	Mossberg	395K
Western Field	172	Mossberg	395K
Western Field	173	Mosaberg	395
Western Field	175	Mossberg	385K
Western Field	17A	Mossberg	73
Western Field	I8	Mossberg	75
Western Field	20	Mossberg	9R
Western Field	215A	Mossberg	85
Western Field	24M,488A	Mossberg	51
Western Field	30	Stevens	520
Western Field	31A	Mossberg	44
Western Field	31A	Mossberg	40
Western Field	32	Mossberg	21
Western Field	32	Mossberg	20
Western Field	33	Marlin	336
Western Field	35A	Mossberg	30
Western Field	36	Stevens	521
Western Field	36	Mossberg	10
Western Field	36B	Mossberg	25A
Western Field	36B	Mossberg	10
Western Field	36C	Mossberg	25A
Western Field	360	Mossberg	26C
Western Field	37	Mossberg	30
Western Field	39	Mossberg	25
Western Field	390A	Mossberg	26C
Western Field	40,D	Mossberg	44
Western Field	40	Marlin	101
Western Field	40N	Noble	40NA
Western Field	40M-215A	Mossberg	185
Western Field	41	Mossberg	45
Western Field	45	Marlin	989M2
Western Field	45	Mossberg	42
Western Field	45B	Mossberg	26C
Western Field	45C	Mossberg	25A
Western Field	46	Mossberg	42
Western Field	466	Mossberg	RA1
Western Field	469	Mossberg	RA1-Kit
Western Field	46A	Mossberg	42
Western Field	46C	Moseberg	42A
Western Field	46D	Mossberg	42C
Western Field	47	Mossberg	45A
Western Field	472	Noble	50
Western Field	47A,L	Mossberg	45A
Western Field	48	Mossberg	45A
Western Field	488A	Mossberg	51

House Brand	Model No.	Orig. Mfgr.	Orig. Model
Western Field	48A	Mossberg	45B
Western Field	48A	Mossberg	46MLB
Western Field	5-4	Mossberg	8-M4
Western Field	50	Glenfield	60
Western Field	502-26FR	Mossberg	500
Western Field	505	Mossberg	500
Western Field	509	Mossberg	500
Western Field	524	Mossberg	500
Western Field	534	Mossberg	500
Western Field	536	Mossberg	500
Western Field	539	Mossberg	500
Western Field	550A	Mossberg	500A
Western Field	550AS	Mossberg	500AB
Western Field	550B	Mossberg	500B
Western Field	550C	Mossberg	500B
Western Field	550E	Mossberg	500E
Western Field	550E	Mossberg	500E
Western Field	60	Savage	620A
Western Field	600ERI 12 GA	Remington	SPT 58
Western Field	60SB	Savage	620A
Western Field	679	Mossberg	472
Western Field	710	Savage	110
Western Field	72	Noble	50
Western Field	72C	Mossberg	472
Western Field	730	Mossberg	8I0AH
Western Field	732	Mossberg	810AH
Western Field	734	Mossberg	810A
Western Field	740	Marlin	336
Western Field	765	Mossberg	810A
Western Field	766	Mossberg	810B
Western Field	767	Mossberg	800A
Western Field	768	Mossberg	800A
Western Field	771	Mossberg	472BA
Western Field	772	Mossberg	472PCA
Western Field	775	Mossberg	800AD
Western Field	776	Mossberg	800BD
Western Field	778	Mossberg	472BAS
Western Field	780	Mossberg	800A
Western Field	782	Mossberg	800B
Western Field	79	Mossberg	472 PRA
Western Field	50	Savage	29
Western Field	807A ECH	Colt	Colteer S.S.
Western Field	808	Savage	87
Western Field	808C	Savage	87J
Western Field	815	Mossberg	321
Western Field	820B	Mossberg	340
Western Field	822	Mossberg	640K
Western Field	828	Mossberg	353
Western Field	830	Mossberg	340K
Western Field	832	Mossberg	341
Western Field	836	Savage	187N
Western Field	840	Mossberg	640
Western Field	842	Mossberg	346K
Western Field	846	Mossberg	351C
Western Field	850 855	Mossberg	353
Western Field	852	Mossberg	341
Western Field	865	Mossberg	402
Western Field	880	Colt	Colteer Semi.
Western Field	894	Mossberg	430-432
Western Field	895	Mossberg	402
Western Field	9-2 3/4	Mossberg	9-2 1/2
Western Field	93M	Mossberg	26C
Western Field	93M-213A	Mossberg	75B
Western Field	93M-2116A	Mossberg	9
Western Field	93M-212A	Mossberg	738
Western Field	93M-211A	Mossberg	83B
Western Field	93M-210A	Mossberg	85B
Western Field	93M-497A	Mossberg	42C
Western Field	93M-491A	Mossberg	465
Western Field	93M-495A	Mossberg	45B
Western Field	EMN 171	Marlin	50
Western Field	EMN 176	Marlin	55
Western Field	M-SD57	Stevens	M87
Western Field	M025	Savage	520A
Western Field	M040 O/U	Marlin	90
Western Field	M040N	Stevens	820
Western Field	M051	Stevens	515
Western Field	M059	Stevens	M87
Western Field	M060	Stevens	620
Western Field	M080	Savage	29 & 75
Western Field	M087	Stevens	M87
Western Field	M10	Stevens	94 Short tang
Western Field	M150	Mossberg	183T
Western Field	M155	Mosaberg	183D
Western Field	M160	Mossberg	385T
Western Field	M170	Mossberg	395S
Western Field	M172	Mossberg	395K
Western Field	M175	Mossberg	385K
Western Field	M23 NH402A	Stevens	820
Western Field	M35	Savage	520 POLY
Western Field	M36	Savage	521
Western Field	M60	Savage	620 DELUX
Western Field	M61	Savage	621 DELUX
Western Field	M72	Mossberg	472 PRA
Western Field	M734	Mossberg	81 0BH
Western Field	M771	Moseberg	472SBA
Western Field	M772	Mossberg	472PCA
Western Field	M7 75	Mossberg	800AD
Western Field	M776	Mossberg	800BD
Western Field	M778	Mossberg	472BAS
Western Field	M780	Mossberg	800A
Western Field	M782	Mossberg	800B
Western Field	M808.C	Stevens	87,C,J
Western Field	M808N	Stevens	87N
Western Field	M80A	Savage	M29-D1
Western Field	M815	Mossberg	320
Western Field	M822	Mossberg	640K
Western Field	M85	Stevens	85
Western Field	M-SD57	Stevens	87
Western Field	SS 94B	Stevens	94C
Western Field	SB033	Savage	520 W/POLY
Western Field	SB066	Savage	621 DELX POLY
Western Field	SB067	Savage	621 DELX COMP
Western Field	S5112C	Savage	540C
Western Field	SB115	Savage	115
Western Field	SB300,C	Stevens	311,C
Western Field	SB30A	Savage	520
Western Field	SB311C	Savage	311C
Western Field	SB312	Savage	540D
Western Field	SB312	Savage-Fox	BDL
Western Field	SB33	Savage	520 POLY
Western Field	SB60A	Savage	620 DELUX
Western Field	SB61A	Savage	621 DELUX
Western Field	SB620A	Stevens	620A
Western Field	SB66	Savage	621 DELX POLY
Western Field	SB712	Savage	840
Western Field	SB80A	Savage	29-DI
Western Field	SB85TA	Stevens	85
Western Field	SB87,TA	Stevens	M87
Western Field	XNH 175	Marlin	55
Western Field	XNH 565	Noble	60-66
Widgeon	SA 650	Marlin	55 12 GA

SERIALIZATION

This section has once again been expanded to help you identify the year of manufacture on many popular manufacturers and trademarks. To use these tables, compare your serial number(s) to the correct manufacturer and model, and ascertain which bracket it falls into based on the year of manufacture and corresponding serial number. In several cases, caliber rarity can also be determined. Date codes are now also provided on some manufacturers and countries to allow you to determine the year of manufacture by the date code on the barrel or frame/receiver.

The publisher wishes to thank Galazan's and Dixie Gun Works for providing a portion of this serialization information.

AGUIRRE Y ARANZABAL (AYA) SERIALIZATION 1945 to 1994

From 1945 to 1994 AYA had manufactured over 600,000 shotguns of all models and grades with all serial numbers assigned in chronological order. For 1927-1944 year of manufacture date codes, see "Spanish Year Of MFG. Date Codes" in this section.

YEARS	SER. # START	SER. # END
1945-1948	0001	19999
1949-1954	20000	71999
1955-1959	72000	115286
1960-1965	115287	222508
1966-1971	222509	378548
1972-1977	378549	481401
1978-1983	481402	576551
1984-1987	576553	599999
1988-1993	600000	602422
1994	602423	602642

Beginning 1995 the Spanish proof house implemented a new serial number system. The new system consists of four sets of digits separated by a hyphen. The first set is the manufacturers code, the second designates the type of firearm, the third set is the firearms chronological number, the fourth set shows the year of mfg.

AYA 1995-2006

YEAR	SER. # START	SER. # END
1995	16-03-001-95	16-03-800-95
1996	16-03-001-96	16-03-755-96
1997	16-03-001-97	16-03-642-97
1998	16-03-001-98	16-03-677-98
1999	16-03-001-99	16-03-719-99
2000	16-03-001-00	16-03-758-00
2001	16-03-001-01	16-03-645-01
2002	16-03-001-02	16-03-645-02
2003	16-03-001-03	16-03-781-03
2004	16-03-001-04	16-03-703-04
2005	16-03-001-05	16-03-652-05
2006	16-03-001-06	16-03-750-06

BOSS & CO., LTD. SERIALIZATION

YEAR STARTING	SERIAL NUMBER
1830	680
1850	1400
1857	1600
1900	4700
1920	6618
1930	7730
1945	8711
1951	8912
1953	8920

BOSS & CO., LTD. SERIALIZATION, cont.

YEAR STARTING	SERIAL NUMBER
1963	9219
1970	9559

BROWNING SERIALIZATION PRE-1975 SERIALIZATION

Since 1968-1969 was a transition period in Browning serialization, firearms may be serialized with either 1968 or 1969 style markings.

A-5 (AUTOMATIC 5) SHOTGUN -12 ga.

YEAR	SER. # START	SER. # END
1903	1	4121
1904	4122	15300
1905	15301	19920
1906	19921	22320
1907	22321	26970
1908	26971	30446
1909	30447	33431
1910	33432	35630
1911	35631	35925
1912	35926	38988
1913	38989	44250
1914	44251	47298
1915-1918	No Production	
1919	47719	47950
1920	47299	47718
1921	48951	53500
1922	53501	58150
1923	58151	62600
1924	62601	69300
1925	69301	79150
1926	79151	88000
1927	88001	106250
1928	106251	127650
1929	127651	154500
1930	154501	177100
1931	177101	182300
1932	182301	182788
1933	182789	183152
1934	183153	185560
1935	185561	191604
1936	191605	194535
1937	194536	199200
1938	199201	208400
1939	208401	218808
1940	218809	224596
1941-1943	No Production	
1944	Production limited to servicemen	
1945	Production limited to servicemen	
1946	228729	240950

A-5 (AUTOMATIC 5) SHOTGUN -12 ga., cont.

YEAR	SER. # START	SER. # END
1947	240951	256500
1948	256501	274100
1949	274101	288550
1950	288551	316750
1951	316751	352050
1952	352051	387499
1953	387500	437400
1954	437401	447750
1955	447751	454700
1956	454701	459900
1957	459901	463700

In 1953 Browning added an alpha prefix to the serial number to differentiate between Lightweight and Standardweight guns.

YEAR	STD.12	LT.WT. 12
1953	H1-H6600	L1-L4450
1954	H6601-H39700	L4451-L45250
1955	H39701-H83450	L45251-L83600
1956	H83451-H100000	L83601-L99877
1956	M1-M35250	G1-G35450
1957	M35251-M86300	G35451-G85950
1958	M86301-M99999	G85951-G99663

1958-1976 Ser. No. sequence changed to include a one or two digit numeral followed by an alpha character.

YEAR	STD. WT.	LT. WT.	MAGNUM
1958	8M	8G	8V
1959	9M	9G	9V
1960	0M	0G	0V
1961	1M	1G	1V
1962	2M	2G	2V
1963	3M	3G	3V
1965	5M	5G	5V
1966	6M	6G	6V
1964	4M	4G	4V
1967	7M	7G	7V
1968	8M	8G	8V
1969	69M	69G	69V
1970	Disc.	70G	70V
1971	Disc.	71G	71V
1972	Disc.	72G	72V
1973	Disc.	73G	73V
1974	Disc.	74G	74V
1975	Disc.	75G	75V
1976	Disc.	76G	76V

A-5 (AUTOMATIC 5) SHOTGUN -16 ga.

YEAR	SER. # START	SER. # END
1909	1	3200
1910-1912	3201	15000
1913	15001	19000
1914-1918	No Production	
1919	19671	20500
1920	20501	22237
1921	22238	24050
1922	24051	26000
1923	26001	28400
1924	28401	35650
1925	35651	40010
1926	40011	51600
1927	51599	57900
1928	57901	65100
1929	65101	82750
1930	82751	90500
1931	90501	94000

A-5 (AUTOMATIC 5) SHOTGUN -16 ga., cont.

YEAR	SER. # START	SER. # END
1932	94001	96072
1933	96073	96143
1934	96144	99500
1 Year	Ser. # Start	Ser. # End
935	99501	103500
1936	103501	105850
1937	105851	111000
1938	111001	118200
1939	118201	126123
1940	126123	126175
1941-1943	No Production	
1944	Production limited to servicemen	
1945	Production limited to servicemen	
1946	128117	128646
1947	128647	130616
1947	X1001	X13666
1948	X13667	X23501
1949	X23502	X34600
1950	X34601	X43700
1951	X43701	X59400
1952	X59401	X77700
1953	X77701	X99999

In 1953 Browning changed the Ser. No. alphabetic character to differentiate between Lightweight (Sweet 16) & Standard weight guns.

YEAR	STD.16	SWEET 16
1953	R1-R3100	S1-S3700
1954	R3100-R20800	S3701-S24850
1955	R20801-R48750	S24851-S49350
1956	R48751-R74700	S49350-S72300
1957	R74701-R99999	S72301-S99908

1957-58 Prefix "T" for Standardweight and Prefix "A" for Sweet 16 numbers mixed, but range from 1-10900.
1958-1976 Ser. No. sequence changed to include a one or two digit numeral followed by an alpha character.

YEAR	STD.16	SWEET 16
1958	8R	8S
1959	9R	9S
1960	0R	0S
1961	1R	1S
1962	2R	2S
1963	3R	3S
1964	Disc.	4S
1965	Disc.	5S
1966	Disc.	6S
1967	Disc.	7S
1968	Disc.	8S
1969	Disc.	69S
1970	Disc.	70S
1971	Disc.	71S
1972	Disc.	72S
1973	Disc.	73S
1974	Disc.	74S
1975	Disc.	75S
1976	Disc.	Disc.

A-5 SHOTGUN - 20 ga.

YEAR	LT.WT. 20	MAGNUM 20
1958	8Z	Introduced in 1967
1959	9Z	
1960	0Z	
1961	1Z	
1962	2Z	

A-5 SHOTGUN - 20 ga., cont.

YEAR	LT.WT. 20	MAGNUM 20
1963	3Z	
1964	4Z	
1965	5Z	
1966	6Z	
1967	7Z	7X
1968	68Z	68X
1969	69Z	69X
1970	70Z	70X
1971	71Z	71X
1972	72Z	72X
1973	73Z	73X
1974	74Z	74X
1975	75Z	75X
1976	76Z	76X

SUPERPOSED MODEL - O & U - 12 ga.

YEAR	SER. # START	SER. # END
1931	1	2000
1932	2001	4000
1933	4001	6000
1934	6001	8000
1935	8001	10000
1936	10001	12000
1937	12001	14000
1938	14001	16000
1939	16001	17000
1939-1947 NO PRODUCTION		
1948	17001	17200
1949	17201	20000
1950	20001	21000
1951	21001	27000
1952	27001	33000
1953	33001	37000
1954	37001	43000
1955	43001	48000
1956	48001	54000
1957	54001	59000
1958	59001	68500
1959	68501	76500
1960	76501	86500
1961	86501	96500
1962	96501	99999
1962	1	6500

Serial number change to letter and number suffix.

YEAR	SER. # PREFIX CODE
1962	S2 suffix after Ser. No.
1963	S3 suffix after Ser. No.
1964	S4 suffix after Ser. No.
1965	S5 suffix after Ser. No.
1966	S6 suffix after Ser. No.
1967	S7 suffix after Ser. No.
1968	S8 suffix after Ser. No.
1969	S69 suffix after Ser. No.
1970	S70 suffix after Ser. No.
1971	S71 suffix after Ser. No.
1972	S72 suffix after Ser. No.
1973	S73 suffix after Ser. No.
1974	S74 suffix after Ser. No.
1975	S75 suffix after Ser. No.
1976	S76 suffix after Ser. No.
1976 to 1984	"P" or Presentation Models only

SUPERPOSED MODEL - O & U - 20 ga.

YEAR	SER. # START	SER. # END
1949	201	1700
1950	1701	2800
1951	2801	3200
1952	3201	5300
1953	5301	6700

SUPERPOSED MODEL - O & U - 20 ga., cont.

YEAR	SER. # START	SER. # END
1954	6701	8400
1955	8401	9400
1956	9401	10500
1957	10501	11500
1958	11501	14180
1959	14181	17060
1960	17061	20640
1961	20641	23820
1962	23821	27300

Serial number change to letter and number suffix.

YEAR	SER. # PREFIX CODE
1963	V3 suffix after Ser. No.
1964	V4 suffix after Ser. No.
1965	V5 suffix after Ser. No.
1966	V6 suffix after Ser. No.
1967	V7 suffix after Ser. No.
1968	V8 suffix after Ser. No.
1969	V69 suffix after Ser. No.
1970	V70 suffix after Ser. No.
1971	V71 suffix after Ser. No.
1972	V72 suffix after Ser. No.
1973	V73 suffix after Ser. No.
1974	V74 suffix after Ser. No.
1975	V75 suffix after Ser. No.
1976	V76 suffix after Ser. No.

SUPERPOSED MODEL - O & U - 28 ga. & .410 bore

YEAR	28 GA.	.410 BORE
1960-1962	NOT AVAILABLE	
1963	F3	J3
1964	F4	J4
1965	F5	J5
1966	F6	J6
1967	F7	J7
1968	F8	J8
1969	F69	J69
1970	F70	J70
1971	F71	J71
1972	F72	J72
1973	F73	J73
1974	F74	J74
1975	F75	J75
1976	F76	J76

LIEGE O & U - Approximately 10,000 produced

YEAR	SER. # PREFIX CODE
1973	73J prefix before Ser. No.
1974	74J prefix before Ser. No.
1975	75J prefix before Ser. No.

DOUBLE AUTOMATIC SHOTGUN

YEAR	SER. # START	SER. # END
1952 -	N/A	
1959	N/A	
1960 -	N/A	
1971	N/A	

1st or both digits indicate last 2 digits in year of manufacture (i.e. - OA1947 - 1960 mfg., 70A245671 - 1970 mfg.)

HI-POWER (9mm) PISTOL

YEAR	SER. # START	SER. # END
1945-1954 no data for the annual breakdown		
	1	72250
1955	72251	75000
1956	75001	77250
1957	77251	80000
1958	80001	85267
1959	85268	89687
1960	89688	93027
1961	93028	109145
1962	109146	113548
1963	113549	115822
1964	115823	T136538
1965	T136569	T146372
1966	T146373	T173285
1967	T173286	T213999
1968	T214000	T258000
1969	T258001	T261000

During 1969 the Hi-Power pistol Serial Number code was changed to a two digit year and "C" prefix. Serial Numbers for "T" prefix Hi-Power pistols exceeded T300000 and were shipped into 1970.

YEAR	SER. # PREFIX CODE
1969	69C prefix before Ser. No.
1970	70C prefix before Ser. No.
1971	71C prefix before Ser. No.
1972	72C prefix before Ser. No.
1973	73C prefix before Ser. No.
1974	74C prefix before Ser. No.
1975	75C prefix before Ser. No.
1976	76C prefix before Ser. No.
1977 to date	New style serialization

BROWNING .380 ACP CAL.

YEAR	SER. # START	SER. # END
1955 -	N/A	
1964	N/A	
1965	500000	598804
1966	598805	603890
1967	603891	619474
1968	619475	N/A
1969 -	N/A	
1970 Discontinued due to GCA of 1968. New model has longer barrel, adj. rear sight, modified grip.		

YEAR	SER. # PREFIX CODE
1971	71N prefix before Ser. No.
1972	72N prefix before Ser. No.
1973	73N prefix before Ser. No.
1974	74N prefix before Ser. No.
1975	75N prefix before Ser. No.

.25 ACP CAL. BABY BROWNING

YEAR	SER. # START	SER. # END
1955-1958 Records not available		
1959	181000	206349
1960	206350	230999
1961	231000	250999
1962	251000	278999
1963	279000	286099
1964	286100	308499
1965	308500	329999
1966	333000	367443
1967	367444	412999
1968	413000	479000
1969 Discontinued because of GCA of 1968		

.22 CAL. (Nomad-Challenger-Medalist)

YEAR	NOMAD	CHALLENGER	MEDALIST
1959	P9	U9	T9
1960	P0	U0	T0
1961	P1	U1	T1
1962	P2	U2	T2
1963	P3	U3	T3
1964	P4	U4	T4
1965	P5	U5	T5
1966	P6	U6	T6
1967	P7	U7	T7
1968	P8	U8	T8
1969	P69	U69	T69
1970	P70	U70	T70
1971	P71	U71	T71
1972	P72	U72	T72
1973	P73	U73	T73
1974	Disc.	U74	T74
1975	Disc.	Disc.	Disc.

BOLT ACTION RIFLES
(Safari, Medallion, & Olympian Models)

YEAR	SER. # CODE
1959 -	N/A
1962	No prefix (numeral-letter) before Ser. No. (i.e., only digits)
1963	3-single letter prefix or suffix by Ser. No.
1964	4-single letter prefix or suffix by Ser. No.
1965	5-single letter prefix or suffix by Ser. No.
1966	6-single letter prefix or suffix by Ser. No.
1967	7-single letter prefix or suffix by Ser. No.
1968	8-single letter prefix or suffix by Ser. No.
1969	Single letter (Y, Z, or L) followed by last 2 digits of year of mfg. Prefix only.
1970	"Y70" prefix
1971	"L71" prefix
1972	"Z72" prefix
1973	"Y73" prefix
1974	"Z74" prefix
1975	"L75" prefix

B.A.R.

YEAR	SER. # SUFFIX CODE
1967	"M7" suffix after Ser. No.
1968	"M8" suffix after Ser. No.
1969	"M69" suffix after Ser. No.
1970	"M70" suffix after Ser. No.
1971	"M71" suffix after Ser. No.
1972	"M72" suffix after Ser. No.
1973	"M73" suffix after Ser. No.
1974	"M74" suffix after Ser. No.
1975	"M75" suffix after Ser. No.
1976	"M76" suffix after Ser. No.
1976 to date	New sequence with "RT" appearing in middle of Ser. No.

.22 AUTO RIFLE (Grades I, II, and III)

YEAR	SER. # CODE
1956-Mid. 1961 "T" prefix = LR, "A" prefix = short	
Mid. 1961 "A" changed to "E" prefix 5 digits or less.	
1961	"1T" or "1A" or "1E" prefix before Ser. No.
1962	"2T" or "2E" prefix before Ser. No.
1963	"3T" or "3E" prefix before Ser. No.
1964	"4T" or "4E" prefix before Ser. No.
1965	"5T" or "5E" prefix before Ser. No.
1966	"6T" or "6E" prefix before Ser. No.
1967	"7T" or "7E" prefix before Ser. No.

.22 AUTO RIFLE (Grades I, II, and III), cont.

YEAR	SER. # CODE
1968	"8T" or "8E" prefix before Ser. No.
1969	"69T" or "69E" prefix before Ser. No.
1970	"70T" or "70E" prefix before Ser. No.
1971	"71T" or "71E" prefix before Ser. No.
1972	"72T" or "72E" prefix before Ser. No.
1973	Japan production

T-BOLT RIFLE (T1 and T2)

YEAR	SER. # CODE
1965	"X5" suffix after Ser. No.
1966	"X6" suffix after Ser. No.
1967	"X7" suffix after Ser. No.
1968	"X8" suffix after Ser. No.
1969	"X69" suffix after Ser. No.
1970	"X70" suffix after Ser. No.
1971	"X71" suffix after Ser. No.
1972	"X72" suffix after Ser. No.
1973	"X73" suffix after Ser. No.
1974	"X74" suffix after Ser. No.
1975	"X75" suffix after Ser. No.

BROWNING SERIALIZATION 1975 TO CURRENT

In 1975 Browning began using the two (2) letter code system (located in the middle of the serial number) for determining the year of manufacture. For example "PN" would be "89" indicating 1989.

LETTER	NUMBER
Z	1
Y	2
X	3
W	4
V	5
T	6
R	7
P	8
N	9
M	10

BROWNING MODEL CONFIGURATION CODES

Beginning in 1976 Browning started identifying models and its configuration using a three number (or possibly a combination of letters and numbers) code in the serial number.

Shotguns O/U

Superposed Grade I

CONFIGURATION	CODE
12 Ga. Hunting	214
12 Ga. Superlight	204
20 Ga. Hunting	264
20 Ga. Superlight	224

Superposed Pigeon Grade

CONFIGURATION	CODE
12 Ga. Hunting	314
12 Ga. Superlight	304
20 Ga. Hunting	364
20 Ga. Superlight	324

Superposed Pointer Grade

CONFIGURATION	CODE
12 Ga. Hunting	414
12 Ga. Superlight	404
20 Ga. Hunting	464
20 Ga. Superlight	424

Superposed Diana Grade

CONFIGURATION	CODE
12 Ga. Hunting	514
12 Ga. Superlight	504
20 Ga. Hunting	564
20 Ga. Superlight	524

Superposed Midas Grade

CONFIGURATION	CODE
12 Ga. Hunting	614
12 Ga. Superlight	604
20 Ga. Hunting	664
20 Ga. Superlight	624

Citori Grade I

CONFIGURATION	CODE
12 Ga. 3-1/2	103
12 Ga. Trap Monte Carlo Stock	143
12 Ga. Trap Conventional Stock	N43
12 Ga. Skeet	1B3
12 Ga. Hunting	153
12 Ga. Lightning	753
12 Ga. Superlight	A13
12 Ga. Upland	B13
325 20 Ga. Sporting	C33
20 Ga. Skeet	1C3
20 Ga. Hunting	163
20 Ga. Lightning	763
20 Ga. Micro Lightning	H33
20 Ga. Superlight	A33
20 Ga. Upland	B33
28 Ga. Skeet	1E3
28 Ga. Hunting	173
28 Ga. Lightning	773
28 Ga. Superlight	A73
.410 Bore Skeet	1F3
.410 Bore Hunting	183
.410 Bore Lightning	783
.410 Bore Superlight	A83
Three Barrel Set	1K3
Four Barrel Set	1A3

Citori Grade III

CONFIGURATION	CODE
12 Ga. Trap Monte Carlo Stock	343
12 Ga. Trap Conventional Stock	R43
12 Ga. Skeet	3B3
12 Ga. Hunting	353
12 Ga. Lightning	853
12 Ga. Superlight	M13
20 Ga. Skeet	3C3
20 Ga. Hunting	363
20 Ga. Lightning	863
20 Ga. Superlight	M33
28 Ga. Skeet	3E3
28 Ga. Lightning	873
28 Ga. Superlight	M73
.410 Bore Skeet	3F3

Citori Grade III, cont.

CONFIGURATION	CODE
410 Lightning	883
410 Superlight	M83
Three Barrel Set	3K3
Four Barrel Set	3A3

Citori Grade VI

CONFIGURATION	CODE
12 Ga. Trap Monte Carlo Stock	643
12 Ga. Trap Conventional Stock	S43
12 Ga. Skeet	6B3
12 Ga. Hunting	653
12 Ga. Lightning	953
12 Ga. Superlight	F13
20 Ga. Skeet	6C3
20 Ga. Hunting	663
20 Ga. Lightning	963
20 Ga. Superlight	F33
28 Ga. Skeet	6E3
28 Ga. Lightning	973
.410 Bore Skeet	6F3
.410 Bore Lightning	983
.410 Bore Superlight	F83
Citori Grade VI, cont.	
Configuration	Code
Three Barrel Set	6K3
Four Barrel Set	6A3

Citori Golden Clays

CONFIGURATION	CODE
12 Ga. Trap Monte Carlo Stock	143
12 Ga. Trap Conventional Stock	N43
12 Ga. Skeet	1B3
20 Ga. 325 Sporting	C33
20 Ga. Skeet	6C3
28 Ga. Skeet	6E3
.410 Bore Skeet	6F3
GTI Sporting	P13
325 Sporting	C13
Special Sporting	T13
Lightning Sporting	W53
PLUS Trap	J43
PLUS Combo	1P3
Three Barrel Set	6K3
Four Barrel Set	6A3

Citori Gran Lightning

CONFIGURATION	CODE
12 Ga.	253
20 Ga.	263
28 Ga.	273
.410 Bore	283

Shotguns Semi-Auto

Auto 5

CONFIGURATION	CODE
Magnum 12 Ga.	151
Magnum Stalker 12 Ga.	T51
Light 12 Ga.	211
Light 12 Stalker 12 Ga.	T11
Sweet 16 Ga.	221
Magnum 20 Ga.	161
Light 20 Ga.	231

A-500

CONFIGURATION	CODE
12 Ga. Recoil	751
12 Ga. Gas	351
12 Ga. Gas Sporting Clays	S51

Gold

CONFIGURATION	CODE
10 Ga.	R91
12 Ga.	F51
20 Ga.	F61

Shotguns Slide Action

BPS

CONFIGURATION	CODE
10 Ga.	192
10 Ga. Stalker	T92
12 Ga. 3-1/2	102
12 Ga. 3-1/2" Stalker	T02
12 Ga. Pigeon	P52
12 Ga. Game	152
12 Ga. (includes all hunting & Upland Models)	152
12 Ga. Stalker	T52
20 Ga. (includes all hunting & Upland Models)	162
28 Ga.	172

Model 42 Limited Edition 410 Bore

CONFIGURATION	CODE
Grade I	882
High Grade	982

Shotguns Side by Side

B-SS

CONFIGURATION	CODE
Sidelock 12 Ga.	918
Sidelock 20 Ga.	938

Rifles

MODEL	CODE
BAR Grade IV	437
BAR 22 Grade I	146
BAR 22 Grade II	246
A-Bolt 22 Grade I	136
A-Bolt 22 Gold Med.	G36
Trombone 22	337
B-92	167

Pistols 1975-1998

MODEL	CODE
Hi-Power 9mm	245
Hi-Power .40 S&W	2W5
Hi-Power Military	215

Pistols 1999-Current

MODEL	CODE
Hi-Power 9mm	510

E.J. CHURCHILL GUNMAKERS SER.

YEAR	GUN #
1891	156
1892	339
1893	384
1894	480

E.J. CHURCHILL GUNMAKERS SER., cont.

YEAR	GUN #
1895	569
1896	655
1897	761
1898	923
1899	1047
1900	1156
1924	2834
1957	6901

COLT'S FIREARMS SERIALIZATION

For additional Colt serialization on most Colt models through 1998, please refer to Blue Book Pocket Guide for Colt Dates of Manufacture by R.L. Wilson. This publication is available in book-form only. Visit www.bluebookofgunvalues.com to order.

MODEL 1849 POCKET REVOLVER

YEAR	SER. # START	SER. # END
1849	1	11999
1850	12000	15999
1851	16000	24999
1852	25000	54999
1853	55000	84999
1854	85000	99999
1855	100000	109999
1856	110000	129999
1857	130000	139999
1858	140000	149999
1859	150000	159999
1860	160000	183999
1861	184000	196999
1862	197000	222999
1863	223000	249999
1864	250000	269999
1865	270000	279999
1866	280000	289999
1867	290000	299999
1868	300000	309999
1869	310000	319999
1870	320000	324999
1871	325000	329999
1872	330000	330999
1873	331000	340000

MODEL 1849 POCKET REVOLVER - LONDON BARREL ADDRESS

YEAR	SER. # START	SER. # END
1853	1	999
1854	1000	4999
1855	5000	8999
1856	9000	11000

MODEL 1851 NAVY

YEAR	SER. # START	SER. # END
1850	1	2499
1851	2500	9999
1852	10000	19999
1853	20000	34999
1854	35000	39999
1855	40000	44999
1856	45000	64999
1857	65000	84999

MODEL 1851 NAVY, cont.

YEAR	SER. # START	SER. # END
1858	85000	89999
1859	90000	92999
1860	93000	97999
1861	98000	117999
1862	118000	131999
1863	132000	174999
1864	175000	179999
1865	180000	184999
1866	185000	199999
1867	200000	203999
1868	204000	206999
1869	207000	209999
1870	210000	211999
1871	212000	213999
1872	214000	214999
1873	215000	215348

MODEL 1851 NAVY - LONDON BARREL ADDRESS

YEAR	SER. # START	SER. # END
1853	1	3999
1854	4000	14999
1855	15000	40999
1856	41000	42000

MODEL 1860 ARMY

YEAR	SER. # START	SER. # END
1860	1	1999
1861	2000	24999
1862	25000	84999
1863	85000	149999
1864	150000	152999
1865	153000	155999
1866	156000	161999
1867	162000	169999
1868	170000	176999
1869	177000	184999
1870	185000	189999
1871	190000	197999
1872	198000	198999
1873	199000	200500

MODEL 1861 NAVY

YEAR	SER. # START	SER. # END
1861	1	4599
1862	4600	9999
1863	10000	16999
1864	17000	24999
1865	25000	27999
1866	28000	29999
1867	30000	30999
1868	31000	32999
1869	33000	33999
1870	34000	34999
1871	35000	35999
1872	36000	36999
1873	37000	38843

MODEL 1862 POLICE

YEAR	SER. # START	SER. # END
1861	1	8499
1862	8500	14999
1863	15000	25999
1864	26000	28999
1865	29000	31999

MODEL 1862 POLICE, cont.

YEAR	SER. # START	SER. # END
1866	32000	34999
1867	35000	36999
1868	37000	39999
1869	40000	41999
1870	42000	43999
1871	44000	44999
1872	45000	45999
1873	46000	47000

MODEL 1873 - SINGLE ACTION ARMY

(SAA) - PRE-WAR

YEAR	CALIBER	SER. # START
1873	.45 Colt Caliber, Standard	1
1874	.450 Boxer	200
1875	.44 Rimfire series (own serials, 1-1863 made through 1880)	15000
1876	.476 Eley introduced	22000
1877		33000
1878	.44-40 introduced in quantity	41000
1879		49000
1880		53000
1881		62000
1882	Sheriff's model introduced	73000
1883	.22 rimfire introduced	85000
1884	.32-20 and .38-40 introduced	102000
1885	.41 Colt introduced	114000
1886	.38 Colt introduced	117000
1887	.32 Colt and .32 S&W introduced	119000
1888	Flattop Target	125000
	S.A.A. began; no.	126530
1889	.32 rimfire; ,32-44 S&W, .38 S&W; and .44 Russian introduced	128000
1890	.44 Smoothbore; .380 and .450 Eley; and .44 S&W introduced	130000
1891	.38-44 introduced	136000
1892		144000
1893		149000
1894	Beginning of Bisley models	154000
1895		159000
1896	Transverse cylinder latch introduced, screw lock at front of frame dropped	163000
1897		168000
1898		175000
1899		182000
1900		192000
1901		203000
1902		220000
1903		238000
1904	Revolvers built to handle smokeless powder, Intro. VP Proof on trigger guard	250000
1905		261000
1906		273000
1907		288000
1908		304000
1909		308000
1910		312000
1911		316000
1912	Discontinue Bisley model	321000
1913	S&W Special introduced	325000
1914		328000

MODEL 1873 - SINGLE ACTION ARMY

(SAA) - PRE-WAR cont.

YEAR	CALIBER	SER. # START
1915	Long flute cylinders; range no. 330001 to 331480	329500
1916		332000
1917		335000
1918		337000
1919		337200
1920		338000
1921		341000
1922		343000
1923		344500
1924	.45 ACP introduced, requiring special cylinders	346400
1925		347300
1926		348200
1927		349800
1928		351300
1929		352400
1930	.38 Special introduced	353800
1931		354100
1932		354500
1933		354800
1934		355000
1935	.357 Magnum introduced	355200
1936		355300
1937		355400
1938		356100
1939		356600
1940	A few S.A.A. during and just after the war	357000 thru 357859

1ST GENERATION COLT SINGLE ACTION ARMY - CALIBER BREAKDOWN

CALIBER	S.A.A	FLATTOP TARGET	BISLEY	BISLEY TARGET
.22 Rimfire	107	93	0	0
.32 Rimfire	1	0	0	0
.32 Colt	192	24	160	44
.32 S&W	32	30	18	17
.32-44	2	9	14	17
.32-20	29,812	30	13,291	131
.38 Colt (through 1914)	1,011	122	412	96
.38 Colt (post-1922)	1,365	0	0	0
.38 S&W	9	39	10	5
.38 Colt Special	82	7	0	0
.38 S&W Special	25	0	2	0
.38-44	2	11	6	47
.357 Magnum	525	0	0	0
.380 Eley	1	3	0	0
.38-40	38,240	19	12,163	98
41 LC	16,402	91	3,159	24
.44 Smoothbore	15	0	1	0
.44 Rimfire	1,863	0	0	0
.44 German	59	0	0	0
.44 Russian	154	51	90	62
.44 S&W	24	51	29	64
.44 S&W Special	506	1	0	0
.44-40	64,489	21	6,803	78

1ST GENERATION COLT SINGLE ACTION ARMY - CALIBER BREAKDOWN, cont.

CALIBER	S.A.A	FLATTOP TARGET	BISLEY	BISLEY TARGET
.45	150,683	100	8,005	97
.45 Smoothbore	4	0	2	0
.45 ACP	44	0	0	0
.450 Boxer	729	89	0	0
.450 Eley	2,697	84	5	0
.455 Eley	1,150	37	180	196
.476 Eley	161	2	0	0
TOTAL QUANTITIES	310,386	914	44,350	976

COLT SINGLE ACTION ARMY – POST-WAR PRODUCTION

YEAR	SER. # START	SER. # END
"SA" suffix from 1956 to 1978, "SA" prefix 1978 to 1984		
1956	0001SA	8799SA
1957	8800SA	18499SA
1958	18500SA	23399SA
1959	23400SA	28499SA
1960	28500SA	33599SA
1961	33600SA	35649SA
1962	35650SA	37299SA
1963	37300SA	38499SA
1964	38500SA	39999SA
1965	40000SA	41499SA
1966	41500SA	43799SA
1967	43800SA	46299SA
1968	46300SA	48999SA
1969	49000SA	52599SA
1970	52600SA	59399SA
1971	59400SA	61699SA
1972	61700SA	64399SA
1973	64400SA	69399SA
1974	69400SA	73319SA
1975	NONE PRODUCED	
1976 (start of 3rd generation of production)		
	80000SA	82000SA
1977	82001SA	95999SA
1978	96000SA	99999SA
Mid-1978Start of "SA" prefix on front of ser. no.		
1978	SA01000	SA14808
1979	SA14809	SA30254
1980	SA30255	SA46919
1981	SA46920	SA58627
1982	SA58628	SA65255
1983	SA65256	SA66495
1984	SA66496	C.S. PROD.

NEW FRONTIER SINGLE ACTION ARMY

YEAR	SER. # START	SER. # END
1961	3000NF	3005NF
1962	3006NF	3849NF
1963	3850NF	4699NF
1964	4700NF	4974NF
1965	4975NF	5399NF
1966	5400NF	5674NF
1967	5675NF	5699NF
1968	5700NF	5899NF
1969	5900NF	5924NF
1970	5925NF	6874NF
1971	6875NF	7049NF
1972	7050NF	7074NF
1973	7075NF	7174NF
1974	7175NF	7264NF

NEW FRONTIER SINGLE ACTION ARMY, cont.

YEAR	SER. # START	SER. # END
1975	7265NF	7288NF
1978	7501NF	N/A
REINTRODUCED IN SEPTEMBER		
1978	01001NF	04424NF
1979	04425NF	06274NF
1980	06275NF	11374NF
1981	11375NF	16584NF
1982	16584NF	DISC. 1982

MODEL 1911 AND 1911A1 – Commercial production Capital "C" prefix - .45 cal.

YEAR	SER. # START	SER. # END
1912	C1	C1899
1913	C1900	C5399
1914	C5400	C16599
1915	C16600	C27599
1916	C27600	C74999
1917	C75000	C98999
1918	C99000	C105999
1919	C106000	C120999
1920	C121000	C126999
1921	C127000	C128999
1922	C129000	C133999
1923	C134000	C134999
1924	C135000	C139999
1925	C140000	C144999
1926	C145000	C150999
1927	C151000	C151999
1928	C152000	C154999
1929	C155000	C155999
1930	C156000	C158999
1931	C159000	C160999
1932	C161000	C164799
1933	C164800	C174599
1934	C174600	C177999
1935	C178000	C179799
1936	C179800	C183199
1937	C183200	C188699
1938	C188700	C189599
1939	C189600	C198899
1940	C198900	C199299
1941	C199300	C208799
1942	C208800	C215018
1943-1945: Commercial production interrupted by WWII		
1946	C221001	C222000
1947	C222001	C231999
1948	C232000	C238500
1949	C238501	C240000
1950	C240000	247701C
"C" SUFFIX STARTED WITH SER. NO. 240228		
1951	247701C	253179C
1952	253180C	259549C
1953	259550C	266349C
1954	266350C	270549C
1955	270550C	272549C
1956	272550C	276699C
1957	276700C	281999C
1958	282000C	283799C
1959	283800C	285799C
1960	285800C	287999C
1961	288000C	289849C
1962	289850C	291299C
1963	291300C	293799C
1964	293800C	295999C
1965	296000C	300299C
1966	300300C	308499C

MODEL 1911 AND 1911A1 – Commercial production Capital "C" prefix - .45 cal., cont.

YEAR	SER. # START	SER. # END
1967	308500C	315599C
1968	315600C	324499C
1969	324500C	332649C
1970	332650C	336169C
Mid-1970 New	70G01001	70G05550
1971	70G05551	70G18000
1972	70G18001	70G34400
1973	70G34401	70G43000
1974	70G43001	70G73000
1975	70G73001	70G88900
1976	70G88901	70G99999
Mid-1976 New	01001G70	13900G70
1977	13901G70	45199G70
1978	45200G70	N/A

MODEL 1911 AND 1911A1 MILITARY PRODUCTION

YEAR	SER. # START	SER. # END	MFG.
1912	1	500	COLT
	501	1000	COLT USN
	1001	1500	COLT
	1501	2000	COLT USN
	2001	2500	COLT
	2501	3500	COLT USN
	3501	3800	COLT USMC
	3801	4500	COLT
	4501	5500	COLT USN
	5501	6500	COLT
	6501	7500	COLT USN
	7501	8500	COLT
	8501	9500	COLT USN
	9501	10500	COLT
	10501	11500	COLT USN
	11501	12500	COLT
	12501	13500	COLT USN
	13501	17250	COLT USN
1913	17251	36400	COLT
	36401	37650	COLT USMC
	37651	38000	COLT
	38001	44000	COLT USN
	44001	60400	COLT
1914	60401	72570	COLT
	72571	83855	
SPRINGFIELD-(THESE NUMBERS RESERVED FOR SPRINGFIELD)			
	83856	83900	COLT
	83901	84400	COLT USMC
	84401	96000	COLT
	96001	97537	COLT USN
	97538	102596	COLT
	102597	107596	
SPRINGFIELD(RESERVED NO. RANGE)			
1915	107597	109500	COLT
	109501	110000	COLT USN
	110001	113496	COLT
	113497	120566	SPRING-
FIELD- (RESERVED FOR SPRINGFIELD)			
1915	120567	125566	COLT
	125567	133186	
SPRINGFIELD-(RESERVED FOR SPRINGFIELD)			
1916	133187	137400	COLT
1917	137401	151186	COLT
	151187	151986	COLT USMC
	151987	185800	COLT
	185801	186200	COLT USMC
	186201	209586	COLT
	209587	210386	COLT USMC

MODEL 1911 AND 1911A1 MILITARY PRODUCTION, cont.

YEAR	SER. # START	SER. # END	MFG.
1917	210387	215386	COLT
FRAMES(RESERVED FOR RECEIVERS)			
	215387	216186	COLT USMC
	216187	216586	COLT
	216587	216986	COLT USMC
1918	216987	217386	COLT USMC
1918	217387	223952	COLT
	223953	223990	COLT USN
	223991	232000	COLT
	232001	233600	COLT USN
	233601	580600	COLT
	1	13152	REM. UMC
1919	13153	21676	REM. UMC
	580601	629500	COLT
	629501	717386	COLT
1924	700001	710000	COLT
1937	710001	712349	COLT USN
1938	712350	713645	COLT
1939	713646	717281	COLT USN
1940	717282	721977	COLT
1941	721978	756733	COLT
1942	756734	793657	COLT
	793658	797639	COLT USN
	797640	800000	COLT
	S800001	S800500	SINGER
	800501	801000	H&R
	801001	856100	COLT
1943	856101	958100	COLT
	**856101	856404	Replacement No
	**856405	916404	ITHACA
	**916405	1041404	REM. RAND
	1041405	1096404	US&S
	1088726	1208673	COLT
	1208674	1279673	ITHACA
	1279674	1279698	RE NO AA
	1279699	1441430	REM. RAND
	1441431	1471430	ITHACA
	1471431	1609528	REM. RAND
1944	1609529	1743846	COLT
	1743847	1816641	REM. RAND
	1816642	1890503	ITHACA
	1890504	2075103	REM. RAND
1945	2075104	2134403	ITHACA
	2134404	2244803	REM. RAND
	2244804	2380013	COLT
	2380014	2619013	REM. RAND
	2619014	2693613	ITHACA

** Denotes double issue ranges.

COLT SINGLE-ACTION MODEL NUMBERS

The author wishes to express thanks to the late Mr. Don Wilkerson for allowing the edited information published below from his 1986 Post-War Single-Action Revolver, 1976-1986 *publication.*

A working knowledge of model numbers for the various Colt single-action revolvers is a must for even a novice collector. Since the mid - 1970s Colt has placed the model number on the end label of the shipping cartons of virtually all their firearms. Many collectors and publications regularly use the model number to describe or differentiate between revolvers. Using the model number is an accurate and efficient method to delineate a particular variation. Example: .45 caliber revolver with a 4 3/4 in. barrel, blue and casehardened finish and eagle stocks can be described as a simple "P-1840."

Each Colt model is specified by an alphabetical letter and 4 numerical digits. The basic model number as it pertains to single-action revolvers can be broken down as follows:

MODEL P - basic type of frame. The letter "P" is used to delineate the single-action type of frame.

FIRST NUMERAL - "1" is the first model built on a particular type of frame. Numerals 2, 3, 4, etc. indicate later versions. These versions are not always numbered in numerical order and the same number has been used for different models at different times. A "1" denotes the basic standard single-action frame. A "2" denotes the new black powder frame available through the Colt Custom Gun Shop. A "3" has been used at various times to denote a non-standard frame or cylinder. The "4" is used to specify the New Frontier style of frame. Numbers such as "7" and "8" are frequently used to specify commemorative or special editions.

SECOND NUMERAL - specifies caliber. A "4" denotes .32-20, a "6" denotes .357 Magnum, a "7" denotes .44 Special, an "8" denotes .45 caliber, and a "9" specifies .44-40 caliber.*

THIRD NUMERAL - denotes barrel length. "3" is used to denote both a 3 inch and a 4 inch barrel. "4" is 4 3/4 inch or 5 inch, "5" is 5 1/2 inch, "7" is 7 1/2 inch, and "1" is 12 inch.*

FOURTH NUMERAL - is used to denote several different variations of the standard model. Some of the most common examples are: "1," "2," or "6" for nickel finish, "1" for full blue finish in the case of P-1871, and "2," "3," and "4" as used for the Sheriff's Model series to denote blue and casehardened finish, nickel finish, and Royal Blue and casehardened finish, respectively. The fourth numeral can also denote the type of stocks as in P-1673. The fourth numeral in the basic model designation must be used in conjunction with the preceding three numerals to determine its exact meaning. The fourth numeral is kind of a "catch-all" number. Many times this number serves only to differentiate a later model from a similar model assembled years earlier.

*The .32-20 caliber and the 5 inch barrel length are listed in the 1984 Colt Buyer's Guide, but as of this date neither have been produced.

STANDARD MODEL P REVOLVER CODES

The primary model numbers used by Colt for Model P revolvers produced since 1976 are as follows:

P-1640 - .357 Magnum, 4 3/4 in. barrel, blue finish, eagle stocks.
P-1641 - .357 Magnum, 4 3/4 in. barrel, nickel finish, wood stocks.
P-1650 - .357 Magnum, 5 1/2 in. barrel, blue finish, eagle stocks.
P-1656 - .357 Magnum, 5 1/2 in. barrel, nickel finish, wood stocks.
P-1670 - .357 Magnum, 7 1/2 in. barrel, blue finish, eagle stocks.
P-1673 - .357 Magnum, 7 1/2 in. barrel, blue finish, wood stocks.
P-1676 - .357 Magnum, 7 1/2 in. barrel, nickel finish, wood stocks.
P-1740 - .44 Special, 4 3/4 in. barrel, blue finish, eagle stocks.
P-1746 - .44 Special, 4 3/4 in. barrel, nickel finish, wood stocks.
P-1750 - .44 Special, 5 1/2 in. barrel, blue finish, eagle stocks.
P-1756 - .44 Special, 5 1/2 in. barrel, nickel finish, wood stocks.
P-1770 - .44 Special, 7 1/2 in. barrel, blue finish, eagle stocks.
P-1776 - .44 Special, 7 1/2 in. barrel, nickel finish, wood stocks.
P-1716 - .44 Special, 12 in. barrel, nickel finish, wood stocks.
P-1840 - .45 Colt, 4 3/4 in. barrel, blue finish, eagle stocks.
P-1841 - .45 Colt, 4 3/4 in. barrel, nickel finish, wood stocks.
P-1850 - .45 Colt, 5 1/2 in. barrel, blue finish, eagle stocks.
P-1856 - .45 Colt, 5 1/2 in. barrel, nickel finish, wood stocks.
P-1870 - .45 Colt, 7 1/2 in. barrel, blue finish, eagle stocks.
P-1876 - .45 Colt, 7 1/2 in. barrel, nickel finish, wood stocks.
P-1813 - .45 Colt, 12 in. barrel, blue finish, eagle stocks.
P-1816 - .45 Colt, 12 in. barrel, nickel finish, wood stocks.
P-1940 - .44-40 caliber, 4 3/4 in. barrel, blue finish, eagle stocks.
P-1941* - .44-40 caliber, 4 3/4 in. barrel, nickel finish, wood stocks.
P-1950 - .44-40 caliber, 5 1/2 in. barrel, blue finish, eagle stocks.
P-1970 - .44-40 caliber, 7 1/2 in. barrel, blue finish, eagle stocks.
P-1976* - .44-40 caliber, 7 1/2 in. barrel, nickel finish, wood stocks.
P-1911 - .44-40 caliber, 12 in. barrel, nickel finish, wood stocks.

**These model numbers were used primarily for engraved or special ordered revolvers as the two models indicated were never produced as a regular model. "Blue finish" in the above chart denotes the standard blue finish, i.e., blue with case hardened frame.*

NEW FRONTIER MODEL

P-4671 - .357 Magnum, 7 1/2 in. barrel, nickel finish, wood stocks.
P-4750 - .44 Special, 5 1/2 in. barrel, Royal Blue finish, wood stocks.
P-4770 - .44 Special , 7 1/2 in. barrel, Royal Blue finish, wood stocks.
P-4840 - .45 Colt, 4 3/4 in. barrel, Royal Blue finish, wood stocks.
P-4850 - .45 Colt, 5 1/2 in. barrel, Royal Blue finish, wood stocks.
P-4870 - .45 Colt, 7 1/2 in. barrel, Royal Blue finish, wood stocks.
P-4940 - .44-40 caliber, 4 3/4 in. barrel, Royal Blue finish, wood stocks.
P-4970 - .44-40 caliber, 7 1/2 in. barrel, Royal Blue finish, wood stocks.

Note: The term "Royal Blue" in the New Frontier chart denotes a revolver with a casehardened frame and a Royal (high polish) Blue finish on the other major components.

SHERIFF'S MODELS

P-1932 - .44-40 caliber, 3 in. barrel, blue finish, eagle stocks.
P-1933* - .44-40/.44 Special, 3 in. barrel, nickel finish, wood stocks.
P-1934* - .44-40/.44 Special, 3 in. barrel, Royal Blue finish, wood stocks.
*Circa 1984 all Sheriff's Models are listed as single calibers: .44-40 or .45 caliber.

REVOLVERS WITH FULL BLUE FRAMES

Some of the "full blue" models have had more than one model number assigned to the same variation. As a result, a particular model may have been identified by different model numbers at different times. Following the model numbers and descriptions in this chart will be an approximate time frame during which that particular model was in use. No date following the description indicates that only one model number for that particular variation is known to the author (Don Wilkerson).

P-1640 - FB - .357 Magnum, 4 3/4 in. barrel, fluted cylinder, eagle stocks.
P-1650 - FB - .357 Magnum, 5 1/2 in. barrel, fluted cylinder, eagle stocks.
P-1740 - FB - .44 Special, 4 3/4 in. barrel, fluted cylinder, eagle stocks.
P-1750 - FB - .44 Special, 5 1/2 in. barrel, fluted cylinder, eagle stocks.
P-1770 - FB - .44 Special, 7 1/2 in. barrel, fluted cylinder, eagle stocks.
P-1770 - UB - .44 Special, 7 1/2 in. barrel, unfluted cylinder, eagle stocks.
P-3840 - .45 Colt, 4 3/4 in. barrel, both fluted and unfluted cylinders, eagle stocks (early to mid -1982).
P-1840 - FB - .45 Colt, 4 3/4 in. barrel, fluted cylinder, eagle stocks (mid to late 1982 to date).
P-1840 - UB - .45 Colt, 4 3/4 in. barrel, unfluted cylinder, eagle stocks (mid to late 1982 to date).
P-1850 - FB - .45 Colt, 5 1/2 in. barrel, fluted cylinder, eagle stocks.
P-1850 - UB - .45 Colt, 5 1/2 in. barrel, unfluted cylinder, eagle stocks.
P-1871 - .45 Colt, 7 1/2 in. barrel, fluted cylinder, wood stocks (1977 to 1979).
P-1870 - FB - .45 Colt, 7 1/2 in. barrel, fluted cylinder, wood stocks (1982 to date).
P-1870 - UB - .45 Colt, 7 1/2 in. barrel, unfluted cylinder, wood stocks (1982 to date).
P-1871 - FB - .45 Colt, 12 in. barrel, fluted cylinder, eagle stocks.

FULL BLUE NEW FRONTIERS

P-4770 - FB - .44 Special, 7 1/2 in. barrel, fluted cylinder, wood stocks.
P-4870 - FB - .45 Colt, 7 1/2 in. barrel, fluted cylinder, wood stocks.
P-4870 - UB - .45 Colt, 7 1/2 in. barrel, unfluted cylinder, wood stocks.

MISCELLANEOUS MODEL NUMBERS

1750 - AA - .44 Special, 5 1/2 in. barrel, blue finish with nickel cylinder, eagle stocks.
1750 - AB - .44 Special, 5 1/2 in. barrel, blue finish with nickel cylinder with blue flutes, eagle stocks.
1840 - UC - .45 Colt, 4 3/4 in. barrel, blue finish, unfluted cylinder, eagle stocks.
1850 - UC - .45 Colt, 5 1/2 in. barrel, blue finish, unfluted cylinder, eagle stocks.
1870 - UC - .45 Colt, 7 1/2 in. barrel, blue finish, unfluted cylinder, eagle stocks.
Note: The term "blue finish" in this chart is the standard blue finish with a casehardened frame.

BLACK POWDER MODEL P REVOLVERS

P-2830 - .45 Colt, 3 in. barrel, blue finish.
P-2833 - .45 Colt, 3 in. barrel, nickel finish.
P-2834* - .45 Colt, 3 in. barrel, Royal Blue finish.
P-2836 - .45 Colt, 4 in. barrel, Royal Blue finish.
P-2837 - .45 Colt, 4 in. barrel, nickel finish.
P-2840 - .45 Colt, 4 3/4 in. barrel, blue finish.
P-2841 - .45 Colt, 4 3/4 in. barrel, nickel finish.
P-2847* - .45 Colt, 5 in. barrel, nickel finish.
P-2870 - .45 Colt, 7 1/2 in. barrel, blue finish.
P-2871 - .45 Colt, 7 1/2 in. barrel, nickel finish.
P-2940 - .44-40 caliber, 4 3/4 in. barrel, blue finish.
P-2941 - .44-40 caliber, 4 3/4 in. barrel, nickel finish.
P-2970 - .44-40 caliber, 7 1/2 in. barrel, blue finish.
P-2971 - .44-40 caliber, 7 1/2 in. barrel, nickel finish.
P-2437* - .32-20 caliber, 4 in. barrel, nickel finish.
P-2474* - .32-20 caliber, 7 1/2 in. barrel, Royal Blue finish.

**As of this writing these calibers have not been produced. The terms "blue finish" and "Royal" in this chart refer to Colt's standard single-action finish, i.e., casehardened frame with all components finished in either standard blue or Royal Blue.*

MODEL 1877 LIGHTNING & THUNDERER DA

YEAR	SER. # START	SER. # END
1877	1	2900
1878	3000	13499
1879	13500	18999
1880	19000	27999
1881	28000	33999
1882	34000	39999
1883	40000	47999
1884	48000	51499
1885	51500	52999
1886	53000	57499
1887	57500	62699
1888	62700	72499
1889	72500	73499
1890	73500	80499
1891	80500	85399
1892	85400	88999
1893	89000	94999
1894	95000	96999
1895	97000	101699
1896	101700	105199
1897	105200	107499
1898	107500	111499
1899	111500	115499
1900	115500	122699
1901	122700	130299
1902	130300	139999
1903	140000	148499
1904	148500	156199
1905	156200	158999
1906	159000	161999
1907	162000	163999
1908	164000	164999
1909	165000	166849

MODEL 1878 SxS HAMMER SHOTGUN

YEAR	SER. # START	SER. # END
1878	1	99
1879	100	2249
1880	2250	7849
1881	7850	11799
1882	11800	14999
1883	15000	17399
1884	17400	18549

MODEL 1883 SxS HAMMERLESS SHOTGUN

YEAR	SER. # START	SER. # END
1885	18550	20349
1886	20350	21199
1888	22000	22499
1889	22500	22683
1883	1	249
1884	250	849
1885	850	1399
1886	1400	2199
1887	2200	3055
1888	3056	4057
1889	4058	4449
1890	4450	5349
1891	5350	6249
1892	6250	6749
1893	6750	7249
1894	7250	7549
1895	7550	8366

LIGHTNING SLIDE ACTION - SMALL FRAME

YEAR	SER. # START	SER. # END
1887	1	999
1888	1000	7999
1889	8000	11749
1890	11750	14299
1891	14300	14699
1892	14700	15399
1893	15400	16599
1894	16600	19799
1895	19800	22999
1896	23000	25999
1897	26000	29599
1898	29600	35299
1899	35300	42799
1900	42800	52299
1901	52300	63299
1902	63300	73699
1903	73700	81999
1904	82000	89912

LIGHTNING SLIDE ACTION - MEDIUM FRAME

YEAR	SER. # START	SER. # END
1884	1	3074
1885	3075	12649
1886	12650	20499
1887	20500	24999
1888	25000	32999
1889	33000	40999
1890	41000	49999
1891	50000	63199
1892	63200	65999
1893	66000	70999
1894	71000	75999
1895	76000	78999
1896	79000	80499
1897	80500	82499
1898	82500	83999
1899	84000	85799
1900	85800	87799
1901	87800	89299
1902	89300	89777

LIGHTNING SLIDE ACTION - LARGE FRAME

YEAR	SER. # START	SER. # END
1887	1	999
1888	1000	2399
1889	2400	3799
1890	3800	5199
1891	5200	5699
1892	5700	5999
1893	6000	6299
1894	6300	6496

AR-15 - SPORTER MODELS

YEAR	SER. # START	SER. # END
1963	SP00001	SP00023
SP00024-SP00100 Specials		
1964	SP00101	SP02500
1965	SP02501	SP05599
1966	SP05600	SP08249
1967	SP08250	SP10749
1968	SP10750	SP13999
1969	SP14000	SP14653
1970	SP15001	SP15473
1971	SP16001	SP19400
1972	SP19401	SP24200
1973	SP24201	SP32600
1974	SP32601	SP43800
1975	SP43801	SP55300
1976	SP55301	N/A

COLT BLACKPOWDER 2ND GENERATION SERIALIZATION

MODEL NO.	SER. # RANGE	TOTAL	START	END
MODEL1851 NAVY				
C-1121	4201 25100	20900	1971	1978
C-1122				
As above but at higher range of numbers Unk'n - 1978				
MODEL 1851 NAVY, R. E. LEE				
C-9001	251 REL 5000 REL	4750	-	1971
1851 NAVY, U. S. GRANT				
C-9002	251 USG5000 USG	4750	-	1971
MODEL 1851 GRANT-LEE PAIR				
C-9003	01 GLP 250 GLP	250	-	1971
3rd MODEL DRAGOON				
C-1770	20801 20826	25	1974	1978
Prototype	20901 24501	3601		
C-1770MN				
	S/N As Above	20	1984	1984
MODEL 1851 NAVY				
F-1100	24900 29150	4250	5/80	10/81
F-1101				
	S/N As Above	300	10/81	11/81
W/Blank Cylinders				
F-1110	29151 S 29640 S	489	6/82	10/82
Stainless Steel				
MODEL 1860 ARMY				
F-1200	201000212835	7593	11/78	11/82
Rebated Cylinder				

MODEL 1860 ARMY, cont.

MODEL NO.	SER. # RANGE	TOTAL	START	END
F-1200 EBO				
	S/N As Above	500	1979	1979
Butterfield				
F-1200 LNK				
	S/N As Above	Unk'n	Unk'n	Unk'n
Electroless Nickel				
F-1200 MN				
	S/N As Above	12	1984	1984
Nickel/Ivory				
F-1202				
	S/N As Above	500	1979	1979
Limited Edition				
F-1203	207330211250	2670	7/80	10/81
Fluted Cylinder				
F-1210	211263 S 212540 S	1278	1/82	4/82
Stainless Steel				

1861 NAVY

F-1300	40000	43165	3166	9/80	10/81

1862 POCKET NAVY

F-1400	48000	58850	5765	12/79	11/81
	and skip odd no.				
F-1400MN					
S/N As Above	25	1984	1984		
Nickel/Ivory					
F-1401					
S/N As Above	500	1979	1980		
Limited Edition					

1862 POCKET POLICE

F-1500	49000	57300	4801	1/80	9/81
	and skip even no.				
F-1500 MN					
S/N As Above	25	1984	1984		
Nickel/Ivory					
F-1501					
S/N As Above	500	1979	1980		
Limited Edition					

1847 WALKER

F-1600	1200	4120	2573	6/80	4/82
	32256	32500	245	5/81	9/81

1st MODEL DRAGOON

F-1700	25100	34500	3878	1/80	2/82

2nd MODEL DRAGOON

F-172 S/N As Above and Mix at Random for 1st, 2nd & 3rd2676 1/80 2/82

3rd MODEL DRAGOON

F-140	S/N As Above and Mix at Random for				
1st, 2nd & 3rd	2856	1/80	2/82		
	31401	31450	50	10/81	11/81
F-1740EGA	Unk'n	Unk'n200	1982	1982	
(Garabaldi Model<- "GCA" prefix)					

BABY DRAGOON

F-1760	16000	17851	1852	2/81	4/81
F-1761	S/N As Above500		1979	1980	
Limited Edition					

1860 ARMY

MODEL NO.	SER. # RANGE	TOTAL	START	END
F-9005	US 001/001 US to			
	US 3025/3025 US	3025	9/77	1/80
Cavalry Commemorative (Two Gun Set)				

HERITAGE WALKER

F-9006	01	1853	1853	6/80	6/81

JOHN DICKSON & SON SERIALIZATION

YEAR STARTING	SERIAL NUMBER
1812-1854	1-1500
1860	2000
1864	2500
1870	3000
1878	3500
1885	3933
1886	4000
1889	4889
1892	4500
1898	5000
1903	5500

A.H. FOX SERIALIZATION

GRADE A-F 12 GAUGE

YEAR STARTING	SERIAL NUMBER
1907	7500
1908	7600
1909	9900
1910	15000
1911	18700
1912	20000
1913	20700
1914	21500
1915	22000
1916	23200
1917	24300
1918	24700
1919	25000
1920	25900
1921	27000
1922	27900
1923	29000
1924	30000
1925	30900
1926	31600
1927	32000
1928	32900
1929	33850
1930	33900
1931	33999
1932	34100
1933	34200
1934	34300
1935	34400
1936	34500

GRADE A-F 16 GAUGE

YEAR STARTING	SERIAL NUMBER
1937	34750
1938	34900
1939	35150
1940	35280
1912	300075
1913	300200

GRADE A-F 16 GAUGE, cont.

YEAR STARTING	SERIAL NUMBER
1914	300400
1915	300600
1916	300700
1917	300750
1918	300800
1919	300900
1920	301100
1921	301300
1922	301500
1923	301800
1924	302000
1925	302300
1926	302500
1927	302650
1928	302800
1929	303000
1930	303050
1931	303100
1932	303200
1933	303300
1934	303350
1935	303400
1936	303500
1937	303650
1938	303800
1939	303850
1940	303870
Highest no.	303875

GRADE A-F 20 GAUGE

YEAR STARTING	SERIAL NUMBER
1912	200100
1913	200250
1914	200500
1915	200700
1916	200800
1917	200900
1918	201000
1919	201300
1920	201500
1921	201600
1922	201800
1923	202000
1924	202200
1925	202400
1926	202500
1927	202800
1928	202950
1929	203100
1930	203150
1931	203200
1932	203300
1933	203350
1934	203500
1935	203700
1936	203750
1937	203800
1938	203830
1939	203900
1940	203970
Highest no.	203974

STERLINGWORTH 12 GAUGE

YEAR STARTING	SERIAL NUMBER
1910	53800
1911	59000
1912	63500

STERLINGWORTH 12 GAUGE, cont.

YEAR STARTING	SERIAL NUMBER
1913	66500
1914	74200
1915	75600
1916	77500
1917	79000
1918	82000
1919	84500
1920	89500
1921	92300
1922	94500
1923	97500
1924	99000
1925	100600
1926	105500
1927	113500
1928	119000
1929	122600
1930	128500
1931	130000
1932	132000
1933	134000
1934	136000
1935	138000
1936	139000
1937	145000
1938	150000
1939	155000
1940	161500
Highest no.	161556

STERLINGWORTH 16 GA.

YEAR STARTING	SERIAL NUMBER
1913	351000
1914	351600
1915	352300
1916	353000
1917	353700
1918	354200
1919	355000
1920	356500
1921	357000
1922	357800
1923	358500
1924	359500
1925	359900
1926	360300
1927	362000
1928	364500
1929	366400
1930	367500
1931	368000
1932	368600
1933	369200
1934	369900
1935	372000
1936	373500
1937	374200
1938	374800
Highest no.	378481

STERLINGWORTH 20 GAUGE

YEAR STARTING	SERIAL NUMBER
1912	250100
1913	252000
1914	253000
1915	254500
1916	254600

STERLINGWORTH 20 GAUGE, cont.

YEAR STARTING	SERIAL NUMBER
1917	254700
1918	255000
1919	255300
1920	255800
1921	256100
1922	256400
1923	256800
1924	257200
1925	257700
1926	258200
1927	259300
1928	260500
1929	262000
1930	263600
1931	263800
1932	264000
1933	264300
1934	264600
1935	266500
1936	268500
1937	270500
1938	270800
1939	271200
1940	271225
Highest no.	271304

SINGLE BARREL TRAP - GRADE J, K, L, M

Year Starting	Serial Number
1919	400090
1920	400250
1921	400275
1922	400300
1923	400325
1924	400350
1925	400375
1926	400385
1927	400395
1928	400400
1929	400410
1930	400415
1931	400425
1932	400500
1933	400525
1934	400540
1935	400568

GERMAN EARLY DATE CODES

Determining the date of manufacture for early German arms is not as simple as looking up a serial number. If the manufacturer is still in existence, contacting the manufacturer with model and serial number information may result in determining a date of manufacture. There are, however, some numeric stampings on German arms that, when present, indicate a month and year of manufacture. They will appear as three or four digit date codes that may appear with or without punctuation.

Examples

Code	Date
535	May 1935
5.35	May 1935
5/35	May 1935
1163	November 1963
11.63	November 1963
11/63	November 1963

GERMAN MODERN DATE CODES

Determining the year of manufacture for modern German arms is much simpler. The two letter code is found as part of or near the proof marks and can be interpreted using the following chart.

A	B	C	D	E	F	G	H	I	K
0	1	2	3	4	5	6	7	8	9

Examples

Code	Date
KK	99 or 1999
IF	85 or 1985

STEPHEN GRANT SERIALIZATION

YEAR STARTING	SERIAL NUMBER
1867	2480
1870	3000
1875	3900
1880	4750
1885	5450
1890	6100
1895	6700
1896	6857
1900	7300

W. W. GREENER SERIALIZATION

YEAR STARTING	SERIAL NUMBER
1878	19304
1880	22860
1895	38917
1902	50911
1915	58536
1920	62621
1930	68635
1967	79259

HARRINGTON & RICHARDSON SERIALIZATION 1940 - 1982

The following serial numbered prefixes are related to the corresponding year of manufacture:

YEAR STARTING	S.N. PREFIX
1940	A
1941	B
1942	C
1943	D
1944	E
1945	F
1946	G
1947	H
1948	I
1949	J
1950	K
1951	L
1952	M
1953	N
1954	P
1955	R
1956	S
1957	T
1958	U
1959	V

HARRINGTON & RICHARDSON SERIALIZATION 1940 - 1982, cont.

YEAR STARTING	S.N. PREFIX
1960	W
1961	X
1962	Y
1963	Z
1964	AA
1965	AB
1966	AC
1967	AD
1968	AE
1969	AF
1970	AG
1971	AH
1972	AJ
1973	AL
1974	AM
1975	AN
1976	AP
1977	AR
1978	AS
1979	AT
1980	AU
1981	AX
1982	AY

H&R SINGLE BARREL SHOTGUNS

The following is a years of production listing for all Main Line single barrel shotguns produced by Harrington & Richardson with a cross reference to Deluxe and Youth variations.

MODEL	DATES	YEARS MFG.
1900	1901-1916	15 Years
1905 (Small Frame)	1906-1915	10 Years
1908	1909-1930	32 Years
1915 (Small Frame)	1916-1930	15 Years
No. 5	1931-1942	12 Years
No. 8	1931-1942	12 Years
48 (First use of the TOPPER name)	1943-1956	14 Years
188 (Deluxe variant of Model 48)	1943-1956	14 Years
148	1957-1961	5 Years
488 (Deluxe variant of Model 148)	1957-1961	5 Years
480 (Youth variant of Model 148)	1957-1961	5 Years
158	1962-1973	12 Years
198 (Deluxe variant of Model 158)	1962-1973	12 Years
490 (Youth variant of Model 158)	1962-1981	20 Years
058	1974-1981	8 Years
098 (Deluxe variant of Model 058)	1974-1981	8 Years
088 (Economy model)	1979-1986	5 Years
088 JR (Youth variant of Model 088)	1979-1986	5 Years
099 Deluxe	1982-1986	5 Years

HIGH STANDARD SERIALIZATION

The author wishes to express thanks to Mr. John J. Stimson, Jr. for the following information. The serial numbers listed represent the highest serial number shipped for the year. Regular serial numbers began with 5,000 which was shipped October 15, 1932. Although it appears the guns were generally assembled in numerical sequence, the shipments were not and some guns may have remained in inventory for weeks, months, or even years between assembly and shipment.

YEAR	SERIAL NUMBER
1932	5,102
1933	6,567
1934	8,313
1935	11,651
1936	18,751
1937	30,026
1938	39,430
1939	50,619
1940	70,715
1941	91,986
1942	104,520
1943	115,423
1944	135,659
1945	145,817
1946	174,194
1947	233,402
1948	301,349
1949	326,123
1950	335,693
1951	356,899
1952	357,295
1953	442,984
1954	475,186
1955	508,613
1956	652,405
1957	776,129
1958	913,111
1959	1,044,802
1960	1,147,641
1961	1,224,652
1962	1,285,049
1963	1,353,764
1964	1,418,870
1965	1,507,541
1966	1,610,707
1967	1,853,513
1968	2,030,404
1969	2,172,356
1970	2,232,503
1971	2,828,293
1972	2,356,207
1973	2,424,175
1974	2,469,497

1975 is the last year of the regular serial number series (except for Sr. No. 2,500,811 shipped August 28, 1976) and marks the beginning of the letter prefix serialization.

YEAR	SR. NO.	SR. NO.	SR. NO.
1975	2,500,810	G 04,566	ML 06,747
1976		G 13,757	ML 23,065
1977	G 18,298	G 162,590	ML 29,707
1978	G 20,223		ML 41,270
1979			ML 63,483
1980	MLG 20,408		ML 81,629
1981	SH 18,446		ML 90,000
1982	SH 25,964		
1983	SH 31,558		
1984	SH 34,034		

HOLLAND & HOLLAND SERIALIZATION

PARADOX SERIES

YEAR STARTING	SERIAL NUMBER
1885	11500
1886	N/A
1887	N/A
1888	11691
1889	11788
1890	11865
1891	11948
1895	15036
1892	15075
1895	15347
1900	15558
1903	15655
1905	15750
1906	15825
1907	15860
1911	15900
1914	15950
1919	19560
1922	15970
1930	15980
1956	15979

RECORDED DATES

YEAR STARTING	SERIAL NUMBER
March 1856 (First Recorded Date)	565
October 1868	580
February 1857	584
August 1859	700
A gap in records	728-1059
1864	1060
1865	1101
1868	1352
1869	1439
1870	1578
1871	1769
1872	2002
1873	2401
1874	2759
1875	3174
1876	3649
1877	4179
1878	4774
1879	5274
1880	5819
1881	6382
1882	7009
1883	7473
1884	7904
1885	8406
1886	8809
1887	8999
Unused	9000-10000
Missing	10000-10849
Rook Rifles	10850-10999
Normal Series	11000-11499
Paradox Guns	11500-11999
Normal Series	12000-12999
Rook Rifles	13000-13999
Normal Series	14000-14999
Paradox Guns	15000-15999
Normal Series	16000-16999
Normal Series	17000-17399
Rifles and Rook Rifles	17400-17999

RECORDED DATES, cont.

YEAR STARTING	SERIAL NUMBER
Believed Unused	18000-18999
Rifles	19000-19999
Misc. Guns and Rifles	20000-21999
See separate lists	22000+

ROOK RIFLES

YEAR STARTING	SERIAL NUMBER
1887	10850-10999
Assumed 1888 records missing	11000-11499
1889	13106
1890	13465
1891	13566
1892	13674
1893	13885-13999
1894 Rook/other rifles	17401
1899	17999

MAGAZINE RIFLES

YEAR STARTING	SERIAL NUMBER
1910	28000
1911	28100
1913	28199
1913	28300
1919	28399
1920-29	1-581
1930-33	582-880
1920-32	881-1181
1935-49	1182-1782
1949-60	1783-2179
1951-58	2180-2577
1952-62	2578-2977
1958-65	2978-3377
1964-74	3378-3783
1975-80	3784-4000
1981-87	4001-4250
1988-92	4251-4330

PLAIN GUNS

YEAR STARTING	SERIAL NUMBER
1907	26200
1908	26300
1909	26400
1909	26500
1910	26600
1911	26700
1912	26800
1913	26900
1913	26999
1913	28600
1914	28700
1914	28800
1915	28900
1915	28999
1915	29500
1915	29600
1916	29700
1919	29800
1919	29900
1919	30000
1920	30100
1922	30200
1924	30300
1925	30334

PLAIN GUNS, cont.

YEAR STARTING	SERIAL NUMBER
1925	31100
1926	31200
1928	31300
1929	31399
1929	32200
1931	32300
1933	32400
1935	32499
1935	34000
1936	34100
1937	34200
1939	34300
1949	34400
1953	34500
1956	34600
1961	34700
1975	34800

ROYAL GUNS

YEAR STARTING	SERIAL NUMBER
1899	22000
1900	22500
1902	23000
1903	23500
1906	25000
1907	25500
1910	25599
1910	27000
1911	27250
1912	27500
1913	27750
1914	27999
1914	29000
1915	29100
1919	29200
1920	29300
1920	29400
1921	29499
1921	30500
1922	30600
1922	30700
1924	30800
1925	30900
1926	30999
1926	31500
1927	31600
1927	31700
1928	31800
1929	31900
1929	32900
1934	32999
1934	33000
1935	33100
1936	33200
1937	33300
1937	33400
1939	33500
1946	33600
1948	33700
1950	33800
1952	33900
1954	33999
1954	36251
1956	36300
1958	36400
1959	36500
1962	36600
1964	36700

ROYAL GUNS, cont.

YEAR STARTING	SERIAL NUMBER
1965	36800
1970	36900
1970	40006
1972	40100
1974	40200
1979	40300
1980	40400
1981	40500
1982	40530
1983	40560
1984	40590
1985	40650
1986	40770
1987	40820
1988	40880
1989	40920
1990	41000
1991	41075
1992	41150
1993	41210

ROYAL OVER & UNDER GUNS

YEAR STARTING	SERIAL NUMBER
1950	36000
1952	36010
1954	36020
1958	36029
1993	51001

SPORTING OVER & UNDER GUNS

YEAR STARTING	SERIAL NUMBER
1993	50500

CAVALIER GUNS

YEAR STARTING	SERIAL NUMBER
1986	50001
1989	50150
1992	50250

ROYAL DOUBLE RIFLES - .450 & .465

YEAR STARTING	SERIAL NUMBER
1910	28200
1914	28299
1914	28500
1919	28535
1921	30335
1921	30415
1925	31042
1925	31049
1927	32000
1941	32099

ROYAL DOUBLE RIFLES - .375

YEAR STARTING	SERIAL NUMBER
1911	28400
1920	28499
1920	30416
1925	30499
1925	31050
1927	31099
1927	32100
1933	32199

ROYAL DOUBLE RIFLES - .240 & Small Bores Cals.

YEAR STARTING	SERIAL NUMBER
1920	28566
1923	28599
1923	31000
1926	31041
1926	31400
1931	31450
1955	31499

ROYAL DOUBLE RIFLES ALL CALS.

YEAR STARTING	SERIAL NUMBER
1933	35000
1939	35100
1950	35200
1953	35250
1956	35300
1963	35350
1968	35450
1975	35495
1977	35498
1980	35500
1981	35505
1984	35524
1985	35527
1988	35540
1989	35542
1990	35552
1991	35590

ITALIAN YEAR OF MFG. DATE CODES

Additional information regarding Italian Proof marks, and dates of manufacture can be found in THE WORLD OF BERETTA *An International Legend by R. L. Wilson.*

All Dates Prior to 1945 Have Year in Digits.

CODE	YEAR
I	1945
II	1946
III	1947
IV	1948
V	1949
VI	1950
VII	1951
VIII	1952
IX	1953
X	1954
XI	1955
XII	1956
XIII	1957
XIV	1958
XV	1959
XVI	1960
XVII	1961
XVIII	1962
XIX	1963

ITALIAN YEAR OF MFG. DATE CODES, cont.

CODE	YEAR
XX	1964
XXI	1965
XXII	1966
XXIII	1967
XXIV	1968
XXV	1969
XXVI	1970
XX7	1971
XX8	1972
XX9	1973
XXX	1974
AA	1975
AB	1976
AC	1977
AD	1978
AE	1979
AF	1980
AH	1981
AI	1982
AL	1983
AM	1984
AN	1985
AP	1986
AS	1987
AT	1988
AU	1989
AZ	1990
BA	1991
BB	1992
BC	1993
BD	1994
BF	1995
BH	1996
BI	1997
BL	1998
BM	1999
BN	2000
BP	2001
BS	2002
BT	2003
BU	2004
BZ	2005
CA	2006
CB	2007
CC	2008
CD	2009
CF	2010
CH	2011
CI	2012
CL	2013
CE	2010
CF	2011
CH	2012
CI	2013
CL	2014

ITHACA GUN CO. SERIALIZATION

BAKER MODEL ITHACA DOUBLES

YEAR STARTING	SERIAL NUMBER
1880-1885	2447
1886	4104
1887	7003
1888	8787
1889 (Jan.-Aug.)	10534

CRASS MODEL ITHACA DOUBLES

YEAR STARTING	SERIAL NUMBER
1892	17235-21999
1893	25421
1894	25759
1895	27762
1896	28713
1897	30222
1898	33026
1899	38399
1900	46627
1901	61609
1902	76599
1903	94108

FLUES MODEL ITHACA DOUBLE & SINGLE

YEAR STARTING	SERIAL NUMBER
1908	175000-182031
1909	192499
1910	205399
1911	216499
1912	230099
1913	242599
1914	256699
1915	268199
1916	276899
1917	289299
1918	299799
1919	315399
1920	343335
1921	356513
1922	361849
1923	372099
1924	390499
1925	398352
1926	398365

N.I.D. MODEL ITHACA DOUBLE

YEAR STARTING	SERIAL NUMBER
1925	425000-425299
1926	439199
1927	451099
1928	454530
1929	457299
1930	458399
1931	459139
1932	459162
1933	459195
1935	459637
1936	459649
1935	460799
1936	462399
1937	464699
1938	464827
1939	464850
1940	464899
1938	465199
1939	465999
1940	466999
1941	467146
1946	467199
1941	468099
1946	468699
1947	468794
1948	468799
1947	469949
1948	469979
1948	470099

CHARLES LANCASTER SERIALIZATION

YEAR STARTING	SERIAL NUMBER
1826	100
1830	600
1840	1200
1850	2100
1860	3200
1861	3400
1862	3540
1863	3693
1864	3805
1865	3914
1866	3999
1867	4087
1868	4183
1869	4271
1870	4328
1871	4401
1872	4477
1873	4562
1874	4644
1875	4714
1876	4769
1877	4833
1878	4892
1879	4924
1880	4949
1881	4982
1882	5079
1883	5186
1884	5359
1885	5497
1886	5627
1887	5764
1888	5926
1889	6136
1890	6406
1891	6671
1892	6988
1893	7189
1894	7360
1895	7548
1896	7709
1897	7940
1898	8132
1899	8353
1900	8529
1901	8700

JOSEPH LANG SERIALIZATION

YEAR STARTING	SERIAL NUMBER
1858	2085
1860	2332
1865	2970
1870	3916
1875	5180
1880	6000
1885	7031
1890	7546
1895	8150
1900	9100

MARLIN FIREARMS COMPANY SERIALIZATION

Approximate serialization for Marlin rifles from 1883 to 1906 including Models 1881, 1888, 1889, 1891, 1892, 1893, 1894, and 1897. Marlin did not assign

a specific block of Ser. No. to these models. Using this list will place the year of manufacture plus or minus one year.
For a factory authentication letter on an older Marlin firearm, contact the Buffalo Bill Historical center, Cody Firearms Museum, 720 Sheridan Ave., Cody, WY 82414. Web site www.bbhc.org or phone 307-578-4031. There is a $60 fee per serial number search.

Older Rifles Mfg.

YEAR	FROM #	TO #
1883	4001	6700
1884	6701	8850
1885	8851	11300
1886	11301	15000
1887	15001	17800
1888	17801	21500
1889	21501	30000
1890	30001	45000
1891	45001	63250
1892	63251	80250
1893	80251	95750
1894	95751	115000
1895	115001	133000
1896	133001	144400
1897	144401	161200
1898	161201	175500
1899	175501	196000
1900	196001	213000
1901	213001	233300
1902	233301	262500
1903	262501	287300
1904	287301	310500
1905	310501	329000
1906	329001	355300

1948-1968 Mfg.

YEAR	SERIAL NO. PREFIX
1948	E
1949	F
1950	G
1951	H
1952	J
1953	K
1954	L
1955	M
1956	N
1957	P
1957-1958	R
1958-1959	S
1960	T
1960-Aug. 1961	U
1961-Aug. 1962	V
1963	W
1964	Y & Z
1965	AA
1966	AB
1967	AC
1968	AD

MAUSER BROOMHANDLES SERIALIZATION 1896 - late 1930

SER. #	DATE	NATURE OF CHANGES
before	1896	- The cone hammer used in place of spur hammer.

MAUSER BROOMHANDLES
SERIALIZATION 1896 - late 1930, cont.

SER. #	DATE	NATURE OF CHANGES
#25	1896	- "SYSTEM MAUSER" marked on top of the chamber.
before	1897	- The locking system changed from one to two lugs.
#200-		The barrel contour at the chamber is tapered instead of stepped.
#390	1897	- "WAFFENFABRIK MAUSER OBERNDORF A/N" marked on top of the chamber.
#975	1897	- The center section of the rear panel on the left side of the frame is not milled out (this feature appears earlier on a few 20-shot pistols). This area is sometimes used for special markings on contract pieces such as the Turkish and Persian.
#12,200 to #14,999	1898	- The large ring hammer replaces the cone hammer.
#21,000	1899	- There is no panel milling on either side of the frame.
		- A single lug bayonet type mount adopted for retaining the firing pin instead of the dovetail plate.
		- The trigger is mounted directly to the frame by two integral lugs rather than attached to a removable block.
		- The position of the serial number moved from the rear of the frame above the stock slot to the left side of the chamber.
#22,000	1900	- Two integral lugs used to mount the rear sight instead of a pin.
#29,000	1902	- Very shallow panels milled into the frame on both sides.*
#31,200	1903	- "WAFFENFABRIK MAUSER OBERNDORF A NECKAR" added to the right rear frame panel.*
#34,000	1904	- The depth of the frame panel milling increased.*
#35,000	1904	- The barrel extension side rails lengthened about a half inch.*
		- An additional lug for mounting added to the firing pin.*
		- The hammer changed to the small ring pattern.*
		- The safety mechanism altered to require that the lever be pushed up to engage it instead of down.*
		- The center of the safety lever knob is no longer milled out.*
#38,000	1905	- The short extractor with two ribs replaces the long thin extractor.*
#100,000	1910	- The rifling changed from four groove to six groove.
to #130,000	1911	
#270,000	1915	- "NS" (Neues Sicherung or New Safety) appears on the back of the hammer. The hammer must be moved back beyond the cocked position to engage the safety.
#440,000	1921	- The lanyard ring stud is rotated 90 degrees.
#501,000	1923	- The Mauser "banner" appears on the left rear frame panel.

MAUSER BROOMHANDLES
SERIALIZATION 1896 - late 1930, cont.

SER. #	DATE	NATURE OF CHANGES
#800,000	1930	- The Mauser banner is enlarged.
		- A step is added to the barrel contour just ahead of the chamber.
		- The safety is changed to allow the hammer to be dropped from a cocked position, without danger, by pulling the trigger (called Universal Safety).
		- The front of the grip frame widened to equal the rear part where the stock slot is.
#850,000	1932	- "D.R.P.u.A.P." (Deutsches Reich Patenten und Anderes Patenten) added below the inscription on the right rear frame panel.
#860,000	1932	- The lettering in the frame inscription is slanted forward.
#900,000	1934	- The serial number is moved to the rear of the barrel extension behind the sight.
		- The two grooves in each side of the barrel extension side rails are eliminated.

**These nine changes appear out of sequence on three small batches of guns (29,000 to 29,900, 40,000 to 41,000, and 42,600 to 43,900). Most of these pistols are of the "bolo" style, that is they have 3.9 inch barrels, small grips, six or 10-shot magazines and fixed or adjustable rear sights. A few of these pistols show non-standard barrel contours, barrel extension milling and hammer safety devices. Apparently the factory withheld these numbers from the regular production series and reissued them at later dates.*

PARKER BROTHERS SHOTGUNS SERIALIZATION 1866 - 1942

Additional information regarding Parker shotguns is available in PARKER GUN IDENTIFICATION & SERIALIZATION *compiled and edited by Charles E. Price & S.P. Fjestad available on www.bluebookofgunvalues.com.*

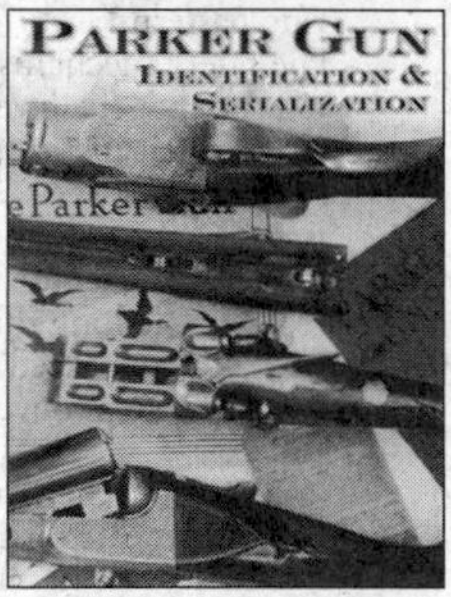

YEAR STARTING	SERIAL NUMBER
1866-1868	0-6,800
1868-1877	9,700
1877-1879	15,700
1880	17,600

PARKER BROTHERS
SHOTGUNS SERIALIZATION 1866 - 1942, cont.

YEAR STARTING	SERIAL NUMBER
1881	22,700
1882	27,300
1883	34,900
1884	36,000
1885	46,450
1886	48,125
1887	56,650
1889	59,500
1890	61,350
1891	66,800
1892	71,600
1893	77,000
1894	80,300
1895	82,400
1896	85,200
1897	86,450
1898	89,350
1899	92,450
1900	97,300
1901	105,750
1902	113,100
1903	121,900
1904	129,200
1905	132,000
1906	138,300
1907	144,250
1908	148,250
1910	153,000
1911	157,050
1912	157,800
first year of Trojan grade	
1913	165,000
1914	168,200
1915	171,500
1916	173,450
1917	175,650
first single barrel trap gun	
1918	180,250
1919	184,900
1920	190,100
1921	195,000
1922	200,500
first Parker single trigger	
1923	205,150
1924	207,150
first beaver tail forend	
1925	214,400
1926	218,050
first ventilated rib, first .410	
1927	222,650
1928	228,200
PH grade dropped	
1929	230,700
1930	234,200
1931	235,950
1932	236,100
1933	236,300
1934	236,650
first skeet guns, takeover of factory by Remington	
1935	237,000
1936	239,900
last regular catalog	
1937	240,300
1938-1942	242,385

PIOTTI SERIALIZATION

YEAR STARTING	SERIAL NUMBER
1962	1
1962	515
1963	1285
1964	1913
1965	2594
1966	2988
1967	3351
1968	3954
1969	4787
1970	5018
1971	5499
1972	5815
1973	6180
1974	6437
1975	6650
1976	6839
1977	7025
1978	7236
1979	7388
1980	7524
1981	7663
1982	7797
1983	7918
1984	8038
1985	8179
1986	8318
1987	8465
1988	8605
1989	8753
1990	8878
1991	8978
1992	9063

JAMES PURDEY & SONS, LTD. SERIALIZATION

YEAR STARTING	SERIAL NUMBER
1814	974
1826	1149
1827	1324
1828	1549
1829	1874
1830	1999
1831	2247
1832	2421
1833	2497
1834	2697
1835	2773
1836	2848
1837	3098
1838	3223
1839	3298
1840	3473
1841	3623
1842	3698
1843	3848
1844	3998
1845	4048
1846	4098
1847	4223
1848	4348
1849	4473
1850	4599
1851	4720
1852	4844
1853	4944
1854	5093
1855	5167

JAMES PURDEY & SONS, LTD. SERIALIZATION, cont.

YEAR STARTING	SERIAL NUMBER
1856	5267
1857	5443
1858	5542
1859	5747
1860	5997
1861	6271
1862	6422
1863	6671
1864	6871
1865	7121
1866	7420
1867	7646
1868	7896
1869	8246
1870	8322
1871	8646
1872	8821
1873	9096
1874	9288
1875	9505
1876	9648
1877	10153
1878	10440
1879	10800
1880	10900
1881	11082
1882	11342
1883	11669
1884	12036
1885	12171
1886	12530
1887	12875
1888	13150
1889	13468
1890	13662
1891	14000
1892	14520
1893	14851
1894	15134
1895	15362
1896	15726
1897	16095
1898	16420
1899	16736
1900	17078
1901	17227
1902	17547
1903	17849
1904	18148
1905	18400
1906	18686
1907	18987
1908	19272
1909	19546
1910	19813
1911	20147
1912	20400
1913	20770
1914	21086
1915	21332
1916	21465
1917	21541
1919	21574
1920	21892
1921	22111
1922	22312
1923	22491
1924	22896
1925	22937

JAMES PURDEY & SONS, LTD. SERIALIZATION, cont.

YEAR STARTING	SERIAL NUMBER
1926	23283
1927	23284
1928	23551
1929	23854
1930	24139
1931	24387
1932	24567
1933	24647
1934	24743
1935	24920
1936	25130
1937	25325
1938	25526
1939	25711
1940	25783
1941	25793
1942	25813
1943	25844
1945	25851
1946	25901
1947	25990
1948	26051
1949	26128
1950	26206
1951	26275
1952	26349
1953	26423
1955	26531
1975	28003
1979	28546
1981	28569

REMINGTON DATE CODE DATA & SxS SHOTGUN SERIALIZATION

Firearms Identification (Code located on barrel, left side of frame) Month of Manufacture (Code letter corresponds to numeral underneath).

The following barrel code information is reliable when used to identify the month and year of manufacture of Remington rifles since Remington seldom replaced barrels. When used to date Remington shotguns, where the barrel is easily changed, make sure the barrel is original to the shotgun.

For example "KP" would be 5 (May) 1923, and "RYY" would be 11 (November) 1952.

B	L	A	C	K	P	O	W	D	E	R	X
1	2	3	4	5	6	7	8	9	10	11	12

YEAR OF MANUFACTURE AND LETTER CODE	
1921	M
1922	N
1923	P
1924	R
1925	S
1926	T
1927	U
1928	W
1929	X
1930	Y
1931	Z
1932	A
1933	B
1934	C
1935	D

REMINGTON DATE CODE DATA & SxS SHOTGUN SERIALIZATION, cont.

YEAR OF MANUFACTURE AND LETTER CODE	
1936	E
1937	F
1938	G
1939	H
1940	J
1941	K
1942	L
1943	MM
1944	NN
1945	PP
1946	RR
1947	SS
1948	TT
1949	UU
1950	WW
1951	XX
1952	YY
1953	ZZ
1954	A
1955	B
1956	C
1957	D
1958	E
1959	F
1960	G
1961	H
1962	J
1963	K
1964	L
1965	M
1966	N
1967	P
1968	R
1969	S
1970	T
1971	U
1972	W
1973	X
1974	Y
1975	Z
1976	I
1977	O
1978	Q
1979	V
1980	A
1981	B
1982	C
1983	D
1984	E
1985	F
1986	G
1987	H
1988	I
1989	J
1990	K
1991	L
1992	M
1993	N
1994	O
1995	P
1996	Q
1997	R
1998	S
1999	T*
2000	U*
2001	V*
2002	W
2003	X

REMINGTON DATE CODE
DATA & SxS SHOTGUN SERIALIZATION, cont.

YEAR OF MANUFACTURE AND LETTER CODE	
2004	Y
2005	Z
2006	A
2007	B
2008	C
2009	D
2010	E
2011	F
2012	G

Additional markings if present will indicate the following.

2	Part order replacement bbl.
3	Service section repair.
4	Returned as received.
5	Employee sale.

** Remington suspended barrel date code stamping circa August 1999 - October 2001, but did continue to mark shipping box end flaps with the date code.*

The author wishes to express thanks to Mr. Charles Semmer for the following Remington SxS shotgun serialization information.

E. REMINGTON & SONS
WHITMORE MODELS

MODEL	YEARS	SER. BLOCK	EST. TOTAL
1873	1873-1878	1-5000	5000
1875	1875-1877	1-3350	3350
1876	1876-1882	3350-5900	2250
1878	1878-1882	1-2400	2400
1879	1879-1888	W/ 1878	N/A

E. REMINGTON & SONS
MODELS 1882, 1883, 1885 AND 1887

MODEL	YEARS	SER. BLOCK	EST. TOTAL
1882	1882-1888	1000-17000	16000
1883	1882-1884	W/ 1882	N/A
1885	1885-1886	16700-20200	3500
1887	1886-1888	20200-23700	3500

REMINGTON ARMS COMPANY
MODEL 1889 TOTAL Mfg. 134200

YEAR STARTING	SERIAL NUMBER
1888	W/ 1887
1889	30000-32199
1890	32200-36949
1891	36950-43012
1892	43013-49844
1893	49845-58879
1894	58880-66016
1895	66017-73571
1896	73572-76980
1897	76981-80389
1898	80390-89123
1899	89124-97714
1900	EST. 97715-105000
1900	EST. 200000-205934
1901	205935-221450
1902	221451-234803
1903	234804-240530

REMINGTON ARMS COMPANY
MODEL 1889 TOTAL Mfg. 134200, cont.

YEAR STARTING	SERIAL NUMBER
1904	240531-247581
1905	247582-251192
1906	251193-254394
1907	254395-257745
1908	257746-259246
1909	N/A
1910	259247-259262

REMINGTON ARMS COMPANY
MODEL 1900 TOTAL Mfg. 98508

YEAR STARTING	SERIAL NUMBER
1900	300000-305000
1901	305001-317502
1902	317503-337038
1903	337039-343893
1904	343894-350207
1905	350208-354620
1906	354621-363060
1907	363061-372117
1908	372118-377925
1909	377926-382072
1910	382073-398507
1911	398508

REMINGTON ARMS COMPANY
MODEL 1894 TOTAL Mfg. 41194

YEAR STARTING	SERIAL NUMBER
1894	100,000-100,660
1895	100,661-103,106
1896	103,107-104,144
1897	104,145-106,916
1898	106,917-110,895
1899	110,896 116,139
1900	116,140-120,932
1901	120,933-123,913
1902	123,914-127,017
1903	127,018-129,349
1904	129,350-131,263
1905	131,264-133,042
1906	133,043-134,627
1907	134,628-136,292
1908	136,293-137,319
1909	137,320-137,988
1910	137,989-141,194

REMINGTON ARMS COMPANY
MODEL 1894 REM. SPCL.

TOTAL Mfg. Approx. 12, W/ 4 recorded

YEAR STARTING	SERIAL NUMBER
1902-1910	400000-400012

SAVAGE/STEVENS PRODUCTION DATA

The information below represents a listing of most Savage/Stevens rifles and shotguns mfg. in the past (some data has been approximated). Rather than list these models separately, they have been provided in this section for quick reference. Values on many of the models listed below typically range between $50-$225, depending on rarity and condition.

SAVAGE ARMS CO.

MODEL	DATES	APPROX.GUNS
1903	1912-20	13,000
1904	1912-32	62,000
1905	1912-15	6,500
1909	1912-15	3,500
1911	1912-15	22,500
1912	1913-15	12,000
1914	1914-26	49,500
19	1933-45	16,000
1920	1920-32	12,000
1922	1922-25	16,000
23A	1924-45	88,000
23B	1924-45	16,500
23C	1924-42	14,500
23D	1932-45	15,000
3	1931-45	121,000
4	1933-45	38,000
5	1936-45	22,000
6	1938-45	45,500
7	1939-45	6,000
40	1928-42	16,000
45	1928-42	6,000
1925	1925-32	36,000
29	1933-45	23,500
CS22	1926-45	87,500
219	1938-45	12,500
220	1937-45	50,000
420	1937-42	13,500
430	1937-42	11,000
1921	1921-32	13,000
1928	1928-32	6,500
721	1930-32	12,000
FOX	1933-45	31,000
FOX B	1940-45	20,000

J. STEVENS ARMS CO.

MODEL	DATES	APPROX.GUNS
No. 12	1912-35	166,500
No. 14-1/2	1912-41	592,500
Fav.	1912-42	462,000
No. 26	1912-45	501,500
No. 44+414	1912-35	23,000
No. 70	1912-31	295,500
No. 71	1930-34	10,000
No. 75	1928-34	19,000
No. 15+425	1912-17	11,500
No. 35	1912-19	12,500
No. 35	1923-42	43,000
No. 41-43	1912-18	18,500
No. 10	1919-34	9,500
No. 85-89	1912-42	38,500
No. 93	1912-19	12,500
No. 97	1912-19	16,000
No. 101	1914-20	5,000
No. 105	1912-45	221,500
No. 107	1912-45	443,500
No. 106-08	1916-35	56,500
No. 115	1912-31	23,000
No. 124	1949-55	N/A
No. 125	1912-23	5,000
No. 180-85	1912-23	16,000
No. 958	1925-33	5,000
No. 116-17	1926-35	5,000
No. 946-48	1928-34	7,000
No. 215	1913-32	61,000
No. 235	1912-32	61,500
No. 315	1914-36	192,000
No. 385	1912-31	67,500
No. 345	1916-31	3,500
No. 311	1926-45	145,500
No. 330	1926-35	33,500
No. 335	1926-35	2,000

J. STEVENS ARMS CO.

MODEL	DATES	APPROX.GUNS
No. 520	1912-32	191,000
No. 521	1930-32	5,000
MODEL	DATES	APPROX.GUNS
No. 60&61	1930-34	6,500
No. 620-21	1926-45	66,500
Mod. 30	1933-34	26,000
Mod. 31	1933-34	2,000
No. 15	1936-45	224,000
No. 11	1923-33	141,500
No. 95	1926-35	55,000
No. 52	1933-37	88,000
No. 55	1935-36	3,500
No. 54	1933-42	23,500
No. 56	1933-45	97,500
No. 57	1939-42	500
No. 58	1933-45	29,500
No. 37	1936-42	29,000
No. 38	1936-45	33,500
No. 39	1938-45	64,000
No. 59	1938-45	21,000
No. 76	1938-45	6,000
No. 65-66	1929-45	174,000
No. 82	1936-37	35,500
No. 83	1936-42	159,000
No. 84	1936-45	99,500
No. 85	1939-43	14,000
No. 86	1936-43	82,500
No. 87	1938-45	200,000
No. 872	1940-42	3,500
No. 89	1926-37	12,000
No. 94	1926-45	934,000
No. 96	1926-33	3,500
No. 416	1937-42	2,000
No. 417	1932-42	1,000
No. 418	1932-42	1,500
No. 419	1932-36	1,000
No. 237	1936-43	16,000
No. 254	1936-42	1,000
No. 238	1936-45	40,000
No. 258	1936-45	11,000
No. 102-04	1936-42	500
No. 116	1936-42	1,000
No. 944	1936-42	1,500
No. 600	1936-42	5,500
No. 900	1936-42	2,000
No. 515	1936-42	500
No. 5151	1936-42	95,000
No. 530	1936-42	8,000
No. 500	1936-42	500
No. 22-410	1939-45	105,000
M.240	1940-45	20,500

SAVAGE MODEL NINETY-NINE SERIALIZATION

SERIAL NUMBERS AT YEAR END:	
10,000	1899
13,400	1900
19,500	1901
25,000	1902
35,000	1903
45,000	1904
53,000	1905
67,500	1906
73,500	1907
81,000	1908
95,000	1909
110,000	1910
119,000	1911
131,000	1912
146,500	1913
162,000	1914
175,500	1915
187,500	1916

SAVAGE MODEL NINETY-NINE SERIALIZATION, cont.

SERIAL NUMBERS AT YEAR END:	
193,000	1917
N/A	1918
212,500	1919
229,000	1920
237,500	1921
244,500	1922
256,000	1923
270,000	1924
280,000	1925
292,500	1926
305,000	1927
317,000	1928
324,500	1929
334,500	1930
338,500	1931
341,000	1932
344,500	1933
345,800	1934
350,800	1935
359,800	1936
N/A	1937
381,351	1938
388,640	1939
398,400	1940
416,000	1941
438,000	1946
464,000	1947
494,000	1948
528,000	1949
566,000	1950

L.C. SMITH SERIALIZATION

Existing L.C. Smith shotgun records include:
Hunter Arms Company factory records circa 1890-1919, Hunter Arms Company shipping records circa 1918-1946, L.C. Smith Gun Company, 1946-1950 (FWS prefix), Marlin Firearms Company, 1969 71 (FWS prefix).
For a factory authentication letter on an older Marlin firearm, contact the Buffalo Bill Historical center, Cody Firearms Museum, 720 Sheridan Ave. Cody, WY 82414. Web site www.bbhc.org or phone 307-578-4031. There is a $75 fee per serial number search.

L.C. Smith (Manufactured by Hunter Arms Co. 1890-1918).

Hammer Shotguns

GAUGE	YEAR	SERIAL NO.
20	1907	5000-5131
20	1908	5379
20	1909	5677
20	1910	6238
20	1911	6593
20	1912	7076
20	1913	7521
20	1914	7828
20	1915	7935
20	1916	8149
20	1917	8250
10, 12, & 16	1894	50000-50867
10, 12, & 16	1895	51735
10, 12, & 16	1896	52602
10, 12, & 16	1897	55301

Hammer Shotguns, cont.

GAUGE	YEAR	SERIAL NO.
10, 12, & 16	1898	58000
10, 12, & 16	1900	79000-84943
10, 12, & 16	1901	89999
10, 12, & 16	1902	125000-129700
10, 12, & 16	1903	133039
10, 12, & 16	1904	137445
10, 12, & 16	1905	144409
10, 12, & 16	1906	150221
10, 12, & 16	1907	156901
10, 12, & 16	1908	159519
10, 12, & 16	1909	163160
10, 12, & 16	1910	166705
10, 12, & 16	1911	168761
10, 12, & 16	1912	171415
10, 12, & 16	1913	173371
10, 12, & 16	1914	175483
10, 12, & 16	1915	176091
10, 12, & 16	1916	176576
10, 12, & 16	1917	178522
10, 12, & 16	1918	179841

Hammerless Shotguns

GAUGE	YEAR	SERIAL NO.
20	1907	1000-1204
20	1908	1329
20	1909	1788
20	1910	2587
20	1911	3615
20	1912	4630
20	1913	4999
20	1913	10000-10786
20	1914	11451
20	1915	11873
20	1916	12361
20	1917	12666
20	1918	12753
10 & 12	1890	30000-32527
10 & 12	1891	34381
10 & 12	1892	36615
10 & 12	1893	37324
10 & 12	1894	38892
10 & 12	1895	40334
8, 10, 12, & 16	1896	40335-42219
8, 10, 12, & 16	1897	44104
8, 10, 12, & 16	1898	45999
16	1895	60000-60144
16	1896	60289
16	1897	60434
16	1898	60579
16	1899	60724
16	1900	60869
16	1901	61014
16	1902	61159
16	1903	61402
16	1904	61685
16	1905	62156
16	1906	62653
16	1907	63698
16	1908	64226
16	1909	65021
16	1910	65861
16	1911	66821
16	1912	67683
16	1913	68704
16	1914	69681
16	1915	69999
16	1915	400000-401758
10 & 12	1899	105210

Hammerless Shotguns, cont.

GAUGE	YEAR	SERIAL NO.
10 & 12	1900	105917
10 & 12	1901	111681
10 & 12	1902	119035
10 & 12	1903	120767
10 & 12	1904	124419
10 & 12	1905	124999
10 & 12	1904	300000-300301
10 & 12	1905	305787
10 & 12	1906	311528
10 & 12	1907	318079
10 & 12	1908	322129
10 & 12	1909	329476
10 & 12	1910	333081
10 & 12	1911	336572
10 & 12	1912	341717
10 & 12	1913	345493
10 & 12	1914	350857
10 & 12	1915	352431
10 & 12	1916	355068
10 & 12	1917	359624
10 & 12	1918	361071
10, 12, & 16	1891	500-559
10, 12, & 16	1898	3173
10, 12, & 16	1901	6959
10, 12, & 16	1902	9000
10, 12, & 16	1902	200000-200025
10, 12, & 16	1903	201758
10, 12, & 16	1904	203272
10, 12, & 16	1905	205098
10, 12, & 16	1906	207093
10, 12, & 16	1907	209368
10, 12, & 16	1908	210579
10, 12, & 16	1909	211885
10, 12, & 16	1910	213084
10, 12, & 16	1911	214246
10, 12, & 16	1912	215615
10, 12, & 16	1913	216939
10, 12, & 16	1914	218260
10, 12, & 16	1915	218829
10, 12, & 16	1916	219603
10, 12, & 16	1917	219750

1918-1950 (These serial numbers include all types of L.C. Smith, Fulton and Hunter Shotguns).

YEAR	SERIAL NO.
1918	101-3850
1919	18252
1920	35228
1921	44566
1922	51985
1923	64187
1924	75897
1925	86695
1926	93841
1927	103900
1928	114817
1929	125347
1930	132827
1931	134242
1932	137779
1933	138371
1934	140146
1935	144296
1936	151123
1937	162670
1938	171179
1939	181701
1940	190280

1918-1950 (These serial numbers include all types of L.C. Smith, Fulton and Hunter Shotguns)., cont.

YEAR	SERIAL NO.
1941	197124
1942	201794
1943	202959
1944	204084
1945	205423
1946	1-8595
1947	25661
1948	41825
1949	55608
1950	56800

SMITH & WESSON PERFORMANCE CENTER PRODUCT CODE INFO.

The following Smith & Wesson Performance Center product code information appears courtesy of Mr. Jim Supica and Mr. Richard Nahas. I would like to thank them for making these product codes available. For additional information on Smith & Wesson firearms, the Standard Catalog of Smith & Wesson by Jim Supica and Richard Nahas is highly recomended. This book is available through www.bluebookofgunvalues.com.

S & W PERFORMANCE CENTER PRODUCT CODES

170 = Designed/made from scratch
178 = Used existing Product / and improved

CODE	CONFIGURATION
170002	M-5906
170008	M-626 HUNTER
170009	M-686 C. C. 6"
170010	M-686 C. C. 3"
170011	SHORTY 40
170012	M-629 3" MAG.COMP.
170014	M-640 3" C. C.
170015	M-686 6" COMPETITOR
170016	M-686 4" C. C.
170020	Tactical Forty
170021	M-686 6" HUNTER
170023	M-442 ULTRALITE
170024	M-66 3" F-COMP.
170025	M-19 3" K-COMP.
170026	M-629 3" UNFLUTED
170027	M-356 COMPACT
170028	S/S SHORTY 40
I70029	M-60 3"FL ET-COMP.
170030	SHORTY 9mm
170032	M-356 LIMITED
170033	M-40 LIMITED
170034	M-686 6" HUNTER (BRAZIL)
170035	M-I9 3" K-COMP (BRAZIL)
170036	M-52 PERF. CTR.
170037	M-356 BRILEY CHASSIS

S & W PERFORMANCE CENTER PRODUCT CODES, cont.

CODE	CONFIGURATION
170038	M-845 WISCHO LIMITED
170039	M-356 PARKER HALE
170040	M-9mm WISCHO LIMITED
170042	M-640 2" Carry Comp.
170043	M-64O 2" Carry Comp.
170044	M-9mm WISCHO LTD. (2TONE)
170046	M-629 6" HUNTER (UNFLUTED)
170047	M-356 2" Carry Comp.
170048	M-629-4 3" Quad Port
170049	M-629 5" Carry Comp
170050	M-629 6.5" Carry Comp.
170052	356 TSW 4 1/4" Stocking Dealer
170053	9mm 4 1/4" Stocking Dealer
170054	40 S&W 4 1/4" Stocking Dealer
170055	M-460 Airweight
170056	M-629 Light Hunter: Duplicate PC
170056	M-625 V Comp 4" : Duplicate PC
170057	M-9mm Horton Limited
170058	M-629 3" DBL Magna Ported
170059	M-13 3" FS DBL Port (Eagle)
170060	Shorty 40 Mark II
170061	Shorty 40 MK III
170062	M-657 .41 Mag Light Hunter
170063	M-13 3" FS Dbl Port (Uncle Mikes)
170064	M-845 HORTON LIMITED
170065	M-629 7.5" HUNTER PLUS
170066	M-617 WISCHO Target
170067	M-9mm Compact
170068	M-640-.357 J-COMP
170069	not active
170070	M-625 5"
170071	not active
170072	M-625 HUNTER (PORTLESS)
170073	M-640-357 2 1/8 FL GB (RSR)
170074	M-686 7SH 3" FL CARRY COMP.
170075	SHORTY 45
170076	SHORTY 40 MARK III-S
170077	M-686 7SH 2.5" FL MAGPORT
170078	M-640.357 2 I/8 FL QUAD GB
170079	M-686 7SH 6" Hunter
170080	M-681 3" Quad Port
170081	M-625 45LC Fluted Hunter
170082	M-686 6" Supertarget
170083	PPC 9mm Limited
170084	M-629 7.5" Hunter
170085	M-625 6" GB Hunter
170086	M-686 7Shot 6" GB Hunter
170087	M-629 7.5" Master Hunter/Scope only
170088	Shorty 45 MKII
170089	M-627 5" 8SH Lew Horton GB
170090	M-66 3" Contour Frame/ bbl
170091	40 S&W Tactical-RSR
170092	M-627 5" 8 Shot Ported
170093	9mm 4" DA/SA FS
170094	M-629 7.5" Master Hunter
170095	M-627 6" 8 Shot Hunter
170096	M-1006 9SH 3 1/2" GB DA SS
170097	M-845 .45 ACP 5" FS MOD '845 OF 1998"
170098	45 RECON 45 ACP
170099	Shorty 4006 RECON 40 S&W
170100	M-629 6" Compensated Hunter
170101	M-745 5" AS SS
170102	M-627 6.5" 8 Shot
170103	M-686 6" 7 Shot Profile Bbl
170104	M-945 5" Stainless
170105	CQB Stainless 45 ACP
170106	CQB Alloy 45 ACP
170107	M-3953 Classic 4" 9mm DA only
170108	M-41 classic 7" 10SH 10 Mfg.

S & W PERFORMANCE CENTER PRODUCT CODES, cont.

CODE	CONFIGURATION
170109	M-610 6 1/2"
170110	Shorty 40 Mark III FS Two Tone (not used)
170111	M-686 6" 6 Shot Profile Bbl
170112	M-4516-7 Sh 3 1/2" GB DA SS
170113	M-586 .357 Mag. GB 4 1/8" FLT
170114	M- 657 4" PBP TH TT "Classic Series" Approx. 25 Mfg.
170115	M-657-6 SH 3" RR SS
170116	M-627 5" 8 Shot unfluted
170117	M-5906 5" 9mm LTD CS Slide (Wischo)
170118	M-4563 CQB Two Tone
170119	M-5906 5" 9mm/356Mag SuperPC
170120	M-629 44 6" 6 shot Competitor
170121	M-686 6" 6 shot Fluted Competitor
170122	M-617 New Profile Barrel
170123	M-627 5" Profile Barrel 6 Shot Fluted
170124	M-629 44 6.5" 6 shot fluted full lug comp & cap
170125	M-657 41 6.5" 6 shot fluted full lug comp & cap
170126	M-629 Compensated Hunter- New Frame/Hammer
170127	M-4566 4" 8SH 45 CQB AS Two-Tone
170128	.45 4515 RECON -RSR w/Knife
170129	M-4587 4.25"
170130	M-629 Classic 7 1/2" Barrel w/ Case
170131	M-29 Classic 7 1/2" Barrel w/Case
170132	M-625 6" .45 Long Colt Light Hunter Fluted GB
170133	M-627 2 5/8" 8 shot Defensive Revolver
170134	M-657 2 5/8" Defensive Revolver
170135	M-629 2 5/8" Defensive Revolver
170136	M-625 Light Hunter 6"
170137	M-629 V Comp 4" -RSR
170138	M-629 7 1/2" Light Hunter RSR
170139	M-4006
170140	9mm M-6906 RECON 3 1/2"
170141	45 RECON Black
170142	M-627-3 V-Comp Jerry Miculek Spcl. 5"
170143	M- 9mm Full Lug
170144	M-332 Never Made
170145	M-632 Never Made
170146	Schofield Model of 2000
170147	M-945 5" Blue 1998
170147	M-945 Two Tone 1999
170148	M-629 5" V-Comp RSR Special
170149	6" 629 Hunter Unfluted
170150	M-627 5 1/2" UnFluted RD
170151	M-27 Classic Series
170152	M-945 4" Black
170153	M-945 4" Stainless-RSR
170154	M-14 4"
170155	M-5906 5" 9mm 10 RDv Mag PPC
170156	M-945 3-3/4" RSR Special
170157	M-629 Extreme Hunter 12"
170158	M-629 12" w/sling
170159	M-629 8.5" Revolver w/sling
170160	M-657 12" Revolver w/sling
170161	M-657 12" Revolver w/sling
170162	M-657 8.5" Revolver w/sling
170163	M-19 K COMP Y2000
170164	M-4006 Shorty Forty -Y2000- Camfour
170165	M-646 4" 40 S&W
170166	M-27-7 8 Shot 4"
170167	M-27-7 8 Shot 6 1/2"
170168	M-952 9mm
170169	M-945 3 3/4" Black -Camfour
170170	M-586 L-Comp 3"
170171	M-629 7 1/2" Stealth Hunter

S & W PERFORMANCE CENTER PRODUCT CODES, cont.

CODE	CONFIGURATION
170172	M-681 4" Quad Port for Camfour
170173	M-945 5" RSR Special
170174	M-945 5" Two Tone RSR Special
170175	M-629 2 5/8" unfluted cyl
170176	M-625 5 1/4" 45 ACP for Camfour
170177	M-945 3 1/4" 45 ACP for Camfour
170178	M-681 3" Quad Port for Camfour
170179	M-25-10 6" for Sports South
170180	M-945 3 3/4" .40 S&W for Sports South
170181	M-629 7 1/2" Compensated Hunter for TALO
170182	M-627 4" w/ Comp RSR Special
170183	M-627 4" w/ Comp RSR Special
170184	M-945 3 1/4" 45ACP for RSR
170185FC	M-24-5 6 1/2" Case Color Frame 44 Spl Heritage
170186FC	FC M-25-11 6 1/2" Case Color Frame 45 Colt Heritage
170187FC	M-25 44-40 6" 6 Sh AS WG Color Case Frame Heritage
170188FC	M-25 38-40 6" 6 Sh AS WG Blue
170189FC	M-24 44 Spl 6.5" AS WG All Blue Finish Heritage
170190FC	M-25 44-40 6" 6Sh AS WG Blue
170191FC	M-25 38-40 6" 6Sh AS WG Blue
170192FC	M-625 FL 5" 45 ACP 6 Sh AS IFS S
170193FC	M-629 7 1/2" Unfluted Green/ Black
170194FC	M-629 7-1/2" Black Unfluted
170195FC	M- 4006 4" SA/DA FS IDPA
170196FC	M-25 Colt 6" Taper Bbl 6 Sh Fluted Blue
170197FC	M-25-12 5 1/2" Fixed Sight Model of 1917 45ACP
170198FC	FC KT-22 6" 6 Sh Fluted Adj Blue Model 17-8 Heritage
170199FC	M-15-9 5" Blue
170200FC	M-681 357 3" FS WG 7 Sh Birdsong
170201FC	M-5906 6" Pistol
170202FC	M-952
170203	Mfg Purposes Only
170204	Mfg Purposes Only
170205FC	M-627 38 Super 8 shot
170206FC	M-586 357 GB 4-1/8"
170207FC	M-3 5" nickel
170208FC	M-3 5" blue
170209FC	M-3 Nickel Schofield 7" 45
170210FC	M-627-5 357 w/Internal Lock
170211FC	M-25-12 Case Colored, 45 ACP
170212FC	M-17-8 6" Heritage Series
170213FC	M-29 Heritage Series Blue
170214FC	M-29 Heritage Series Nickel
170215FC	M-29 Nickel ?
170216FC	M-15-9 Heritage Series 6" Blue (McGivern Model)
170217FC	M-15-9 Heritage Series 6" Nickel (McGivern Model)
170218FC	M-25 45ACP 5-1/2" 1917 w/Military Finish
170219FC	M-629 7 1/2" unflutted Big Rock
170220FC	M-952 5" 9mm Firing Pin Block Safety 2003
170221FC	M-5906 Singapore
170222FC	M-945 Big Rock
170223FC	M-5906 6"
170224FC	M-5906 4" DA SA Mexico
170225FC	M-686-7 .38 Super for Bangers 2003
170226FC	M-625-10 2" .45 ACP Sc Clear/Stainless 2003
170227FC	M-945 5" Big Rock
170228FC	M-629-6 7 1/2" two-tone
170229FC	M-647-1 "Varminter" .17 HMR 12" 2003
170230FC	M-629-6 7 1/2" Unfluted-Birdsong Gn & BI-IL
170231FC	M-500 Magnum Hunter 10 1/2" X Frame 2003
170232FC	M-329-1 Black recalled June 2004 2003

S & W PERFORMANCE CENTER PRODUCT CODES, cont.

CODE	CONFIGURATION
170233FC	M-329-1 Clear recalled June 2004 2003
170234FC	M-629 8 3/8" for Davidson's
170235FC	M-657 8 3/8" for Davidson's
170236FC	M-952-1 6" w/ grip safety
170237FC	M-627-5 5" .357 Mag. V-8
170238FC	M-625 4" Wedge .45 ACP GB Unfluted comp/cap wood
170239FC	M-647 6 1/2" hi-vis Not Mfg.
170240FC	M-627-5 5" .357 Mag. 8 shot blk. Acusport
170241FC	M-629 7 1/2" .44 Mag. scope mount wg.
170242FC	M-647 8 3/8" SS GB black Acusport Not Mfg.
170243FC	M-1911PC 5" SA Stainless
170244FC	M-952-2 5" 9mm Stainless
170245FC	M-327 2" .357 Mag. 8 shot Ti Cyl. Shroud Black
170246FC	M-500 Compensated Hunter 6 1/2" Unfluted
170247FC	M-952-2 6" 9mm Stainless
170248FC	M-856 .357 Mag. 7 shot
170249FC	M-627-5 5" 8 shot black Acusport
170250FC	M-381 2" 7 shot Lew Horton
170251FC	M-327Sc 2" .357 Mag. 8 shot Ti Cyl. Shroud Clear
170252FC	M-625-10 Sc Stainless black Lew Horton 2004
170253FC	M-29 6 1/2" "American Pride" 2005
170254FC	M-327Sc 5" 8 shot Target Sights Ti 2005
170255FC	M-500 Hunter 7 1/2" black finish 2005
170800FC	M-686 6" 7 shot Competitor Unfluted
178001FC	M-686 6" 6 shot Hunter Unfluted
178002FC	M-627 2 5/8" 6 shot .357 Mag.
178003FC	M-657 2 5/8" 6 shot .41 Mag.
178004FC	M-586 3" 7 shot
178005FC	M-29-5 8 3/8 RB TT TH RR WO B Wood Grips
178006FC	M-10 4 1/4" Case Color Frame Square Butt Heritage Series
178007FC	M-19 2 1/2" Nickel
178008FC	M-15-8 4" Nickel
178009FC	M-15-8 4" Heritage Series

S & W ABBREVIATIONS

A2D	Adj. 2-Dot Sight
AA	Aluminum Alloy Frame
AB	Adj. Black Sight
AMSF	Ambidextious Safety
AS	Adj. Rear Sight
ATS	Adj. Target Sight
AV	Adj. V-Notch Sight
AWO	Adj. White Outline Sight
B	Blue
BB	Bead Blast Finish
BBL	Barrel
B/G	Black/Gray Finish
BK	Black Finish
BK/M	Black/Melonite Finish
BP	Black Polymer Grip
BPF	Black Polymer Frame
BULL	Bull Barrel
CB	Curved Backstrap Grip
CC	Clear Cote™ Finish
CS	Carbon Steel
CWG	Checkered Wood Grip
CWP	Checkered Wood Panel
DA	Double Action
DAO	Double Action Only
DBP	Dovetail Black Post
DFS	Dovetail Front Sight
DT	Drilled & Taped
ER	Equipment Rail
F2D	Fixed 2-Dot Sight
FN	Fixed Notch Sight

S & W ABBREVIATIONS, cont.

FNS	Fixed Tritium Night Sight (Fr. & Rr.)
FS	Fixed Sight
FV	Fixed V-Notch Sight
G	NATO Green
GB	Glass Bead Finish
GD	Green Dot
GY	Grey Finish
#SH	Magazine Capacity/Rds
HB	Heavy Barrel
HIVIS®	Light Gathering Sight
HR	Hogue Rubber Grip
HT	Hardwood Target Grip
HV	HIVIS® Front Sight
HWA	Hogue Wrap Around Rubber Grip
I	Integral or Interchangeable Sight
IB	Interchangeable Backstraps
IC	Integral Compensator
IFS	Interchangeable Front Sight
IL	Internal Lock
ISBR	Interchangeable Serrated Black Ramp Sight
LS	LadySmith®
M	Melonite Finish
MCA	Micrometer Click Adj.
MNSF	Manual Safety (Single Side)
MS	Matte Stainless
NG	Nato Green Polymer Grips
NLMC	Novak Lo-Mount Carry 2-Dot Sight
OD	Orange Dot
P	Partridge Sight
PBP	Pinned Black Partridge Sight
PBSR	Pinned Black Serrated Ramp Sight
PF	Polymer Frame
PP	PowerPort™ Ported Barrel
RB	Round Butt
RR	Red Ramp Sight
S	Stainless Finish
SA	Single Action
SB	Black Straight Backstrap Grip
SC	Scandium Alloy Frame
SG	Synthetic Grip
SNS	Satin Stainless Finish
SR	Serrated Ramp Sight
SS	Stainless Steel
STD	Standard Barrel
STG	Soft Touch Grip
T	Tritium
T2D	Tritium 2-Dot Rear Night Sight
TD	Tritium Dot Front Night Sight
TDA	Traditional Double Action
TR	Thumbrest
TS	Target Stock
UC	Unfluted Cylinder
UMB	Uncle Mike's Boot Grip
UMC	Uncle Mike's Combat Grip
UMR	Uncle Mike's Rubber Grip
VR	Vented Rib
WAS	Wilson Adj. Rear Sight
WC	Wood Combat Grip
WD	White Dot Sight
WG	Dymondwood® Grip
WO	White Outline Rear Sight
WT	Wooden Target Grip

SPANISH YEAR OF MFG. DATE CODES

The following Spanish year of manufacture information appears courtesy of Leonardo M. Antaris, M.D., author of *Astra Automatic Pistols*, and *Star Firearms*. For additional information regarding Spanish pistols, particularly Astras and Stars, see www.firac.us.

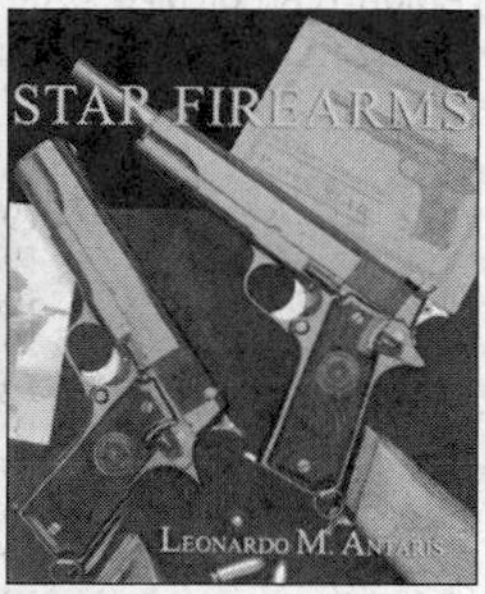

CODE	YEAR
A	1927
B	1928
C	1929
CH	1930
D	1931
E	1932
F	1933
G	1934
H	1935
I	1936
J	1937
K	1938
L	1939
LL	1940
M	1941
N	1942
Ñ	1943
O	1944
P	1945
Q	1946
R	1947
S	1948
T	1949
U	1950
V	1951
X	1952
Y	1953
Z	1954
A1	1955
B1	1956
C1	1957
D1	1958
E1	1959
F1	1960
G1	1961
H1	1962
I1	1963
J1	1964
K1	1965
L1	1966
M1	1967
N1	1968
Ñ1	1969
O1	1970
P1	1971
Q1	1972
R1	1973
S1	1974
T1	1975
U1	1976
V1	1977
X1	1978
Y1	1979
Z1	1980

SPANISH YEAR OF MFG. DATE CODES, cont.

CODE	YEAR
A2	1981
B2	1982
C2	1983
D2	1984
E2	1985
F2	1986
G2	1987
H2	1988
I2	1989
J2	1990
K2	1991
L2	1992
M2	1993
N2	1994
N2	1995
O2	1996
P2	1997
Q2	1998
R2	1999
S2	2000

Beginning in January 1995 the Spanish proof house implemented a new serial number system. Requirements included: 1) all guns would be numbered in a new sequential series starting with the number 1 at the beginning of the year, 2) the serial number was to be followed by the last two digits of the production year, 3) each manufacturer was assigned a code to be stamped on every gun, and 4) weapons were to be marked as to type. The new system consists of four sets of digits separated by a hyphen. The first set is the manufacturer's code, the second set designates the type of weapon, and the third set is the firearms chronological number irrespective of model, the fourth set shows the year of mfg.
The new weapons coding system includes, Carbines 01, Shotguns 03, Pistols 04, Revolvers 05, Rifles 06, Muzzleloaders 13, Short carbines 14, Submachine guns 15; etc.

STURM, RUGER & CO., INC.

Additional information regarding Sturm, Ruger & Co., Inc. firearms (including serialization) can be found in Ruger & His Guns; A History of the Man, the Company and Their Firearms *by R.L. Wilson.*

WINCHESTER RIFLES SERIALIZATION

The following Winchester serial numbers appear courtesy of U.S. Repeating Arms, New Haven, CT. I would like to thank U.S. Repeating Arms and Mr. Pardee for making these production figures available.
Records at the factory indicate the following serial numbers were assigned to guns at the end of the calendar year.
For additional information including factory letters contact the Cody Firearms Museum. Factory letters for Lever Action rifles are $60 and for Model 21 SxS shotguns are $75.

Buffalo Bill Historical Center
Attn: Cody Firearms Museum
720 Sheridan Ave.
Cody, WY 82414

MODEL 1866

YEAR	APPROX. LAST NO.
1866	12476 to 14813
67	15578
68	19768
69	29516
70	52527
71	88184
72	109784
73	118401
74	125038
75	125965
76	131907
77	148207
78	150493
79	152201
80	154379
81	156107
82	159513
1883	162376
84	163649
85	163664
86	165071
87	165912
88	167155
89	167401
90	167702
91	169003
92	NONE
93	169007
94	169011
95	NONE
96	NONE
97	169015
98	170100
99	DISCONTINUED

MODEL 1873

YEAR	APPROX. LAST NO.
1873	1 to 126
74	2726
75	11325
76	23151
77	23628
78	27501
79	41525
80	63537
81	81620
82	109507
83	145503
84	175126
85	196221
86	222937
87	225922
88	284529
89	323220
90	363220
91	405026
92	441625

MODEL 1873, cont.

YEAR	APPROX. LAST NO.
93	466641
94	481826
95	499308
96	507545
97	513421
98	525922
99	541328
1900	554128
01	557236
02	564557
03	573957
04	588953
05	602557
06	613780
07	NONE
08	NONE
09	630385
10	656101
11	669324
12	678527
13	684419
14	686510
15	688431
16	694020
17	698617
18	700734
19	702042
No last # available	
20, 21, 22, 23,	720609

MODEL 1876

YEAR	APPROX. LAST NO.
1876	1 to 1429
77	3579
78	7967
79	8971
80	14700
81	21759
82	32407
83	42410
1884	54666
85	58714
86	60397
87	62420
88	63539
89	NONE
90	NONE
91	NONE
92	63561
93	63670
94	63678
95	NONE
96	63702
97	63869
98	63871

MODEL 1885 SINGLE SHOT

YEAR	APPROX. LAST NO.	POLISHING ROOM SNAS
1885 -	1 to 375	no entry
86 -	6841	8193
87 -	18328	20006
88 -	30571	30132
89 -	45019	37662
90 -	N/A	45109
91 -	53700	54099
92 -	60371	60305
93 -	69534	66163
94 -	N/A	71024
95 -	73771	74649
96 -	78253	77255
97 -	78815	80877
98 -	84700	82492

MODEL 1885 SINGLE SHOT, cont.

YEAR	APPROX. LAST NO.	POLISHING ROOM SNAS
99 -	85086	85257
1900 -	88501	88302
01 -	90424	91733
02 -	92031	94738
03 -	92359	96553
04 -	92785	98953
05 -	93611	102084
06 -	94208	104603
07 -	95743	107063
08 -	96819	108004
09 -	98097	109327
10 -	98506	110870
11 -	99012	112555
12 -	N/A	113267
13 -	100352	114726

No further serial numbers were recorded until the end of 1923. Last No. known was: 139700

MODEL 1886

YEAR	APPROX. LAST NO.	POLISHING ROOM SNAS
1886 -	1 to 3211	3528
87 -	14728	12497
88 -	28577	28609
89 -	38401	38652
90 -	49723	51068
91 -	63601	63738
92 -	73816	74898
93 -	83261	85144
94 -	94543	97034
95 -	103708	107346
96 -	109670	111243
97 -	113997	115106
98 -	119192	118646
99 -	120571	120795
1900 -	122834	No further entries
01 -	125630	
02 -	128942	
03 -	132213	
04 -	135524	
05 -	138838	
06 -	142249	
07 -	145119	
08 -	147322	
09 -	148237	
10 -	150129	
11 -	151622	
12 -	152943	
13 -	152947	
14 -	153859	
15 -	154452	
16 -	154979	
17 -	155387	
18 -	156219	
19 -	156930	
20 -	158716	
21 -	159108	
22 -	159337	

No further serial numbers were recorded until the discontinuance of the Model 1886 which was in 1935 at serial no. 159994.

MODEL 1890

Records on the Model 1890 are somewhat incomplete. Factory records indicate the following serial numbers were assigned to guns at the end of the calendar year beginning with 1908. Actual records on the firearms which were manufactured between 1890 and 1907 will be available from the "Cody Firearms Museum," located at the "Buffalo Bill Historical Center."

MODEL 1890

YEAR	APPROX. LAST NO.	POLISHING ROOM SNAS
1890	N/A	245
91 -	N/A	10884
92 -	N/A	16454
93 -	N/A	25954
94 -	N/A	32554
95 -	N/A	40218
96 -	N/A	46525
97 -	N/A	55855
98 -	N/A	64748
99 -	N/A	80268
1900 -	N/A	100554
01 -	N/A	127181
02 -	N/A	154985
03 -	N/A	186724
04 -	N/A	228104
05 -	N/A	276637
06 -	N/A	302204
07 -	N/A	349947
08 -	NONE	398006
09 -	393427	431483
10 -	423567	450000
11 -	451264	484700
12 -	478595	509100
13 -	506936	527500
14 -	531019	562400
15 -	551290	594300
16 -	570497	608741
17 -	589204	612979
18 -	603438	617978
19 -	630801	649452
20 -	NONE	678928
21 -	634783	679313
22 -	643304	683470
23 -	654837	693040
24 -	664613	701941
25 -	675774	711462
26 -	687049	736246
27 -	698987	767898
28 -	711354	795605
29 -	722125	824623
30 -	729015	837448
31 -	733178	844278
32 -	734454	846022
33 -	N/A	846524
34 -	N/A	848044
35 -	N/A	848584
36 -	N/A	848936
37 -	N/A	No further entries

The Model 1890 was discontinued in 1932, however, a clean up of the production run lasted another 8+ years and included another 14 to 15000 guns. Our figures indicate approximately 849,000 guns were made.

MODEL 1892

YEAR	APPROX. LAST NO.	POLISHING ROOM SNAS
1892 -	1 to 23701	7121
93 -	35987	22804
94 -	73508	38744
95 -	106721	53616
96 -	144935	67853
97 -	159312	85930
98 -	165431	103328
99 -	171820	129983
1900 -	183411	155567
01 -	191787	183683
02 -	208871	209770
03 -	253935	233451
04 -	278546	280321
05 -	315425	324168

MODEL 1892, cont.

YEAR	APPROX. LAST NO.	POLISHING ROOM SNAS
06 -	376496	366950
07 -	437919	413705
08 -	476540	471652
09 -	522162	512627
10 -	586996	581623
11 -	643483	645931
12 -	694752	694420
13 -	742675	747502
14 -	771444	776016
15 -	804622	799690
16 -	830031	811052
17 -	853819	841881
18 -	870942	854878
19 -	903649	881258
20 -	906754	917240
21 -	910476	No further entries
22 -	917300	
23 -	926329	
24 -	938641	
25 -	954997	
26 -	973896	
27 -	990883	
28 -	996517	
29 -	999238	
30 -	999730	
31 -	1000727	
32 -	1001324	

MODEL 1894

Records at the factory, and in some years, estimates, indicate the following serial numbers were assigned to guns at the end of the calendar year.

YEAR	APPROX. LAST NO.	POLISHING ROOM SNAS
1894 -	1 to 14579	1674
95 -	44359	14222
96 -	76464	18571
97 -	111453	33108
98 -	147684	53941
99 -	183371	80148
1900 -	204427	103932
01 -	233975	137058
02 -	273854	168420
03 -	291506	204565
04 -	311363	249782
05 -	337557	291706
06 -	378878	331895
07 -	430985	381524
08 -	474241	429757
09 -	505831	449102
10 -	553062	479073
11 -	599263	534429
12 -	646114	591281
13 -	703701	645304
14 -	756066	722280
15 -	784052	825186
16 -	807741	840846
17 -	821972	873425
18 -	838175	882032
19 -	870762	895365
20 -	880627	926851
21 -	908318	935778
22 -	919583	951501
23 -	938539	964709
24 -	953198	974121
25 -	978523	987148
26 -	997603	997938
27 -	1027571	1012753
28 -	1054465	1038665

MODEL 1894, cont.

YEAR	APPROX. LAST NO.	POLISHING ROOM SNAS
29 -	1077097	1060899
30 -	1081755	1071420
31 -	1084156	1079689
32 -	1087836	1088141
33 -	1089270	1092328
34 -	1091190	1095364
35 -	1099605	1099625
36 -	1100065	1119104
37 -	1100679	1158835
38 -	1100915	1198405
39 -	1101051	1216165
40 -	1142423	1259563
41 -	1191307	1313301
42 -	1221289	1343183
43 -	N/A	no entry
44 -	N/A	1343196
45 -	N/A	1352066
46 -	N/A	No further entries
47 -	N/A	
48 -	1500000	
49 -	1626100	
50 -	1724295	
51 -	1819800	
52 -	1910000	
53 -	2000000	
54 -	2071100	
55 -	2145296	
56 -	2225000	
57 -	2290296	
58 -	2365887	
59 -	2410555	
60 -	2469821	
61 -	2500000	
62 -	2551921	
63 -	2586000	
*1964	2700000 2797428	
65 -	2894428	
66 -	2991927	
67 -	3088458	
68 -	3185691	
69 -	3284570	
70 -	3381299	
71 -	3557385	
72 -	3806499	
73	3929364	
74 -	4111426	
75 -	4277926	
76 -	4463553	
77 -	4565925	
78 -	4662210	
1979 -	4826596	
80 -	4892951	
81 -	5024957	
82 -	5103248	
83-	N/A	
84-	5309432	
85-	5362944	
86-	5409249	
87-	5463790	
88-	5517897	
89-	5574822	
90-	5615397	
91-	6008296	

Model 1894 facts.

** The post-64 Model 94 began with serial number 2,700,000.*

**Serial number 1,000,000 was presented to President Calvin Coolidge in 1927.*

**Serial number 1,500,000 was presented to President Harry S. Truman in 1948.*

**Serial number 2,500,000 and 3,000,000 were presented to the Winchester Gun Museum, now located in Cody, Wyoming.*

**Serial number 3,500,000 was not constructed until 1979 and was sold at auction in Las Vegas, Nevada.*

**Serial number 4,000,000 - whereabouts unknown at this time.*

**Serial number 4,500,000 - shipped to Italy by Olin in 1978. Whereabouts unknown.*

**Serial number 5,000,000 - in New Haven, not constructed as of March 1983.*

MODEL 9422

YEAR	APPROX. LAST NO.
1972 -	F48558
73 -	F121182
74 -	F169044
1975 -	F229666
76 -	F293472
77-	F323197
78-	F367976
79-	F398044
80-	F431532
81-	F489918
82-	F527632
83-	F531722
84-	F539305
85-	F550843
86-	F557835
87-	F571623
88-	F590039
89-	F605281
90-	F617848
91-	F633224
92-	F646000
93-	F658316
94-	F671391

MODEL 1895

YEAR	APPROX. LAST NO.	POLISHING ROOM SNAS
1895 -	1 to 287	56
96 -	5715	2783
97 -	7814	5734
98 -	19871	19567
99 -	26434	24311
1900 -	29817	29808
01 -	31584	34615
02 -	35601	39459
03 -	42514	43963
04 -	47805	48444
05 -	54783	52099
06 -	55011	56688
07 -	57351	62041
08 -	60002	64326
09 -	60951	68094
10 -	63771	72565
11 -	65017	76030
12 -	67331	80423
13 -	70823	84889
14 -	72082	99264
15 -	174233	211410
16 -	377411	400166
17 -	389106	403773
18 -	392731	403791
19 -	397250	405391
20 -	400463	409662
21 -	404075	412928
22 -	407200	416355
23 -	410289	419730

MODEL 1895, cont.

YEAR	APPROX. LAST NO.	POLISHING ROOM SNAS
24 -	413276	420874
25 -	417402	421337
26 -	419533	423100
27 -	421584	423370
28 -	422676	423779
29 -	423680	424651
30 -	424181	424662
31 -	425132	425523
32 -	425825	425825
33 -	N/A	425881

MODEL 1903

YEAR	APPROX. LAST NO.
1903 -	N/A
04 -	6944
05 -	14865
06 -	23097
07 -	31852
08 -	39105
09 -	46496
10 -	54298
11 -	61679
12 -	69586
13 -	76732
14 -	81776
15 -	84563
16 -	87148
17 -	89501
18 -	92617
19 -	96565
20 -	N/A
21 -	97650
22 -	99011
23 -	100452
24 -	101688
25 -	103075
26 -	104230
27 -	105537
28 -	107157
29 -	109414
30 -	111276
31 -	112533
32 -	112992

This model was discontinued in 1932, however, a clean up of parts was used for further production of approximately 2000 guns. Total production was approx. 126000 rifles through 1936.

MODEL 1905

YEAR	APPROX. LAST NO.
1905 -	1 to 5659
06 -	15288
07 -	19194
08 -	20385
09 -	21280
10 -	22423
11 -	23503
12 -	24602
13 -	25559
14 -	26110
15 -	26561
16 -	26910
17 -	27297
18 -	27585
19 -	28287
20 -	29113

MODEL 1906

YEAR	APPROX. LAST NO.	POLISHING ROOM SNAS
1906 -	1 to 52278	55911
07 -	89147	96820
08 -	114138	134258
09 -	165068	187450
10 -	221189	250850
11 -	273355	304600
12 -	327955	355400
13 -	381922	422600
14 -	422734	458300
15 -	453880	497200
16 -	483805	500700
17 -	517743	523127
18 -	535540	538247
19 -	593917	604917
20 -	N/A	652563
21 -	598691	652584
22 -	608011	652780
23 -	622601	663549
24 -	636163	670684
25 -	649952	683119
26 -	665484	685999
1927 -	679892	No further entries
28 -	695915	
29 -	711202	
30 -	720116	
31 -	725978	
32 -	727353	

A clean up of production took place for the next few years (approx. 1932-1937) with a record of production reaching approximately 848000.

MODEL 1907

YEAR	APPROX. LAST NO.
1907 -	1 to 8657
08 -	14486
09 -	19707
10 -	23230
11 -	25523
12 -	27724
13 -	29607
14 -	30872
15 -	32272
16 -	36215
17 -	38235
18 -	39172
19 -	40448
20 -	N/A
21 -	40784
22 -	41289
23 -	41658
24 -	42029
25 -	42360
26 -	42688
27 -	43226
28 -	43685
29 -	44046
30 -	44357
31 -	44572
32 -	44683
33 -	44806
34 -	44990
35 -	45203
36 -	45482
37 -	45920
38 -	46419
39 -	46758
40 -	47296

MODEL 1907, cont.

YEAR	APPROX. LAST NO.
41 -	47957
42 -	48275
43 -	N/A
44 -	N/A
45 -	48281
46 -	48395
47 -	48996
48 -	49684
**49 -	50662
**50 -	51640
**51 -	52618
**52 -	53596
**53 -	54574
**54 -	55552
**55 -	56530
**56 -	57508
**57 -	58486

** Actual records on serial numbers stops in 1948. The serial numbers ending each year from 1948 to 1957 were derived at by taking the last serial number recorded (58486) and the last number from 1948, (49684) and dividing the years of production (9), which relates to 978 guns each year for the nine year period.

MODEL 1910

YEAR	APPROX. LAST NO.
1910 -	1 to 4766
11 -	7695
12 -	9712
13 -	11487
14 -	12311
15 -	13233
16 -	13788
17 -	14255
18 -	14625
19 -	15665
20 -	N/A
21 -	15845
22 -	16347
23 -	16637
24 -	17030
25 -	17281
26 -	17696
27 -	18182
28 -	18469
29 -	18893
30 -	19065
31 -	19172
32 -	19232
33 -	19281
34 -	19338
35 -	19388
36 -	19445

A cleanup of production continued into 1937 when the total of the guns was completed at approximately 20786

MODEL 1911 S.L.

YEAR	APPROX. LAST NO.
1911 -	1 to 3819
12 -	27659
13 -	36677
14 -	40105
15 -	43284
16 -	45391
17 -	49893
18 -	52895
19 -	57337
20 -	60719
21 -	64109

MODEL 1911 S.L., cont.

YEAR	APPROX. LAST NO.
22 -	69132
23 -	73186
24 -	76199
25 -	78611

The Model 1911 was discontinued in 1925. However, guns were produced for three years after that date to clean up production and excess parts. When this practice ceased there were approximately 82774 guns produced.

MODEL 52

YEAR	APPROX. LAST NO.
1920 -	None indicated
21 -	397
22 -	745
23 -	1394
24 -	2361
25 -	3513
26 -	6383
27 -	9436
28 -	12082
29 -	14594
30 -	17253
31 -	21954
32 -	24951
33 -	26725
34 -	29030
35 -	32448
1936 -	36632
37 -	40419
38 -	43632
39 -	45460
40 -	47519
41 -	50317
42 -	52129
43 -	52553
44 -	52560
45 -	52718
46 -	56080
47 -	60158
48 -	64265
49 -	68149
50 -	70766
51 -	73385
52 -	76000
53 -	79500
54 -	80693
55 -	81831
56 -	96869
57 -	97869
58 -	98599
59 -	98899
60 -	102200
61 -	106986
62 -	108718
63 -	113583
64 -	118447
65 -	120992
66 -	123537
67 -	123727
68 -	123917
69 -	E 124107
70 -	E 124297
71 -	E 124489
72 -	E 124574
73 -	E 124659
74 -	E 124744
75 -	E 124828
76 -	E 125019
77 -	E 125211
78 -	E 125315

This Model was discontinued in 1978. A small clean up of production was completed in 1979 with a total of 125419.

MODEL 53

The Model 53 was serial numbered in both its own series (1 to slightly over 15,000) as well as within the Model 1892 series. Early guns predominate the Model 53 serial number series with Model 1892 series serial numbers appearing more frequently mid to late production.
This Model was discontinued in 1932, however, a clean up of production continued for 9 more years.

YEAR	APPROX. LAST NO.	POLISHING ROOM SNAS
1924-	1 to 1488	2458
25-	4350	6086
26-	6882	10302
27-	9180	10874
28-	11139	No further entries
29-	12873	
30-	13794	
31-	14416	
32-	14623	
33-	14727	
34-	14817	
35-	14976	
36-	15047	
37-	15078	
38-	15092	
39-	15099	
1940-	15109	
41-	15118	

Total Production Approximately 24,916.
Records at the factory indicate the following serial numbers were assigned to guns at the end of the calendar year.

MODEL 54

YEAR	APPROX. LAST NO.
1925 -	1 to 3140
26 -	8051
27 -	14176
28 -	19587
29 -	29104
30 -	32499
31 -	36731
32 -	38543
33 -	40722
34 -	43466
35 -	47125
36 -	50145

MODEL 55

YEAR	APPROX. LAST NO.	POLISHING ROOM SNAS
1924 -	1 to 836	1304
25 -	2783	3296
26 -	4957	6748
27 -	8021	11563
28 -	10467	12002
29 -	12258	No further entries
30 -	17393	
31 -	18198	
32 -	19204	
33 -	Clean up 20580	

MODEL 61

YEAR	APPROX. LAST NO.
1932 -	1 to 3532
33	6008
34 -	8554

MODEL 61, cont.

YEAR	APPROX. LAST NO.
35 -	12379
36 -	20615
37 -	30334
38 -	36326
39 -	42610
40 -	49270
41 -	57493
42 -	59871
43 -	59872
44 -	59879
45 -	60512
46 -	71629
47 -	92297
48 -	115281
49 -	125461
50 -	135461
51 -	145821
52 -	156000
53 -	171000
54 -	186000
55 -	200962
56 -	216923
57 -	229457
58 -	242992
59 -	262793
60 -	282594
61	302395
62 -	322196
63 -	342001

This Model was discontinued in 1963. For some unknown reason there are no actual records available from 1949 through 1963. The serial number figures for these years are arrived at by taking the total production figure of 342001, subtracting the last known # of 115281, and dividing the difference equally by the amount of remaining years available (15).

MODEL 62

YEAR	APPROX. LAST NO.
1932 -	1 to 7643
33 -	10695
34 -	14090
35 -	23924
36 -	42759
37 -	66059
38 -	80205
39 -	96534
40 -	116393
41 -	137379
42 -	155152
43 -	155422
44 -	155425
45 -	156073
46 -	183756
47 -	219085
48 -	252298
49 -	262473
50 -	272648
51 -	282823
52 -	293000
53 -	310500
54 -	328000
55 -	342776
56 -	357551
57 -	383513
58 -	409475

MODEL 63

YEAR	APPROX. LAST NO.
1933 -	1 to 2667
34 -	5361
35 -	9830
36 -	16781
37 -	25435
38 -	30934
39 -	36055
40 -	41456
41 -	47708
42 -	51258
43 -	51631
44 -	51656
45 -	53853
46 -	61607
47 -	71714
48 -	80519
49 -	88889
50 -	97259
51 -	105629
52 -	114000
53 -	120500
54 -	127000
55 -	138000
56 -	150000
57 -	162345
58 -	175223

MODEL 70

YEAR	APPROX. LAST NO.
1935 -	1 to 19
36 -	2238
37 -	11573
38 -	17844
39 -	23991
40 -	31675
41 -	41753
42 -	49206
43 -	49983
1944 -	49997
45 -	50921
46 -	58382
47 -	75675
48 -	101680
49 -	131580
50 -	173150
51 -	206625
52 -	238820
53 -	282735
54 -	323530
55 -	361025
56 -	393595
57 -	425283
58 -	440792
59 -	465040
60 -	504257
61 -	545446
62 -	565592
63 -	581471

All post 64 Model 70s began with the serial number 700,000.

YEAR	APPROX. LAST NO.
1964 -	740599
65 -	809177
66 -	833795
67 -	869000
68 -	925908
69 -	G941900
70 -	G957995
71 -	G1018991
72 -	G1099257

MODEL 70, cont.

YEAR	APPROX. LAST NO.
73 -	G1128731
74 -	G1175000
75 -	G1218700
76 -	G1266000
77 -	G1350000
78 -	G1410000
79 -	G1447000
80 -	G1490709
81 -	G1537134
82-	G1632872
83-	G1656883
84-	G1782457
85-	G1783276
86-	G1808838
87-	G1845122
88-	G1893903
89-	G1950701
90-	G1987984
91-	G2037985

The controlled round feed Model 70 was reintroduced in 1990 as the Model 70 Classic at serial number G15000.

MODEL 70 CLASSIC

YEAR	APPROX. LAST NO.
1990-	G16859
1991-	G23072
1992-	G26709

MODEL 71

YEAR	APPROX. LAST NO.
1935 -	1 to 4
36 -	7821
37 -	12988
38 -	14690
39 -	16155
40 -	18267
41 -	20810
42 -	21959
43 -	22048
44 -	22051
45 -	22224
46 -	23534
47 -	25728
48 -	27900
49 -	29675
50 -	31450
51 -	33225
52 -	35000
53 -	37500
54 -	40770
55 -	43306
56 -	45843
57 -	47254

MODEL 74

YEAR	APPROX. LAST NO.
1939 -	1 to 30890
40 -	67085
41 -	114355
42 -	128293
1943 -	NONE
44 -	128295
45 -	128878
46 -	145168
47 -	173524
48 -	223788
49 -	249900
50 -	276012

MODEL 74, cont.

YEAR	APPROX. LAST NO.
51 -	302124
52 -	328236
53 -	354348
54 -	380460
55 -	406574

MODEL 88

YEAR	APPROX. LAST NO.
1955 -	1 to 18378
56 -	36756
57 -	55134
58 -	73512
59 -	91890
60 -	110268
61 -	128651
62 -	139838
63 -	148858
64 -	160307
65 -	162699
66 -	192595
67 -	212416
68 -	230199
69 -	H239899
70 -	H258229
71 -	H266784
72 -	H279014
73 -	H283718

MODEL 100

YEAR	APPROX. LAST NO.
1961 -	1 to 32189
62 -	60760
63 -	78863
64 -	92016
65 -	135388
66 -	145239
67 -	209498
68 -	210053
69 -	A210999
70 -	A229995
71 -	A242999
72 -	A258001
73 -	A262833

WINCHESTER RIFLE AND SHOTGUN SERIAL NUMBER PREFIXES POST-1968

The following serial number prefixes are found on Winchester rifles and shotguns as a result of the Gun Control Act of 1968.

MODEL NO. (S)	S.N. PREFIX
Super X Model 1	M
Super X Model 1 (Ducks Unlimited)	IDU
12	Y
12 (Ducks Unlimited)	DU
21	W
22	WS
23	PWK
52	E
60 (Cooey)	C
40-70A-770-670	G
88	H
91	KS or WS
94	No Prefix used
94 Big Bore	BB
96	K
100	A
101	K
101 Pigeon Grade	PK
Bolt Action Rimfires 121-131 & 141	Z
Rimfire 150-190-250-255-270 275 & 290	B
Rimfire 300-310 & 320	D
370 & 37A	C
490	J
1200	L
1300	LX
1400	N
1500	NX
1500 (European)	NE
9422	F

WINCHESTER SHOTGUNS

Records at the factory indicate the following serial numbers were assigned to guns at the end of the calendar year.

MODEL 1887

YEAR	APPROX. LAST NO.
1887 -	1 to 7431
88 -	22408
89 -	25673
90 -	29105
91 -	38541
92 -	49763
93 -	54367
94 -	56849
95 -	58289
96 -	60175
97 -	63952
98 -	64855

According to these records no guns were produced during the last few years of this model and it was therefore discontinued in 1901.

MODEL 1893 Start

YEAR	APPROX. LAST NO.	POLISHING ROOM SNAS
1893 -	N/A	7958
94 -	N/A	16985
95 -	N/A	24109
96 -	N/A	32908

MODEL 1897 Start

YEAR	APPROX. LAST NO.	POLISHING ROOM SNAS
1897 -	1 to 32335	46190
98 -	64668	63867
99 -	96999	90099
1900 -	129332	121740
01 -	161665	155949
02 -	193998	192780
03 -	226331	232089
04 -	258664	269816
05 -	296037	310112
06 -	334059	352757
07 -	377999	398919
08 -	413618	438586
09 -	446888	474392
1910 -	481062	514224
11 -	512632	544663
12 -	544313	574649
13 -	575213	609337
14 -	592732	621155
15 -	607673	634255

MODEL 1897 Start, cont.

YEAR	APPROX. LAST NO.	POLISHING ROOM SNAS
16 -	624537	645018
17 -	646124	673277
18 -	668383	705627
19 -	691943	713785
20 -	696183	744268
21 -	700428	748404
22 -	715902	760622
23 -	732060	780537
24 -	744942	793623
25 -	757629	806826
26 -	770527	816294
27 -	783574	829515
28 -	796806	845320
29 -	807321	857216
30 -	812729	865591
31 -	830721	875213
32 -	833926	885034
33 -	835637	885040
34 -	837364	885843
35 -	839728	886094
36 -	848684	895261
37 -	856729	901405
38 -	860725	905660
39 -	866938	909925
40 -	875945	918793
41 -	891190	930412
42 -	910072	950579
43 -	912265	965000
44 -	912327	968160
45 -	916472	968160
46 -	926409	975755
47 -	936682	981005
48 -	944085	985270
49 -	953042	989410
50 -	961999	995605
51 -	970956	1001930
52 -	979913	1007515
53 -	988860	1013730
54 -	997827	1017760
55 -	1006784	1021610
56 -	1015741	1024700
57 -	1024700	1024701

Records on this Model are incomplete. The above serial numbers are estimated from 1897 thru 1903 and again from 1949 thru 1957. The actual records are in existence from 1904 through 1949.

MODEL 1897 TRENCH/RIOT SHOTGUN

This information is provided by Mr. Pat Redmond, after many years of research and collecting. Reference a Winchester Repeating Arms Co. Memorandum dated September 1945. Trench, Riot, and Long Barrel Contract Dates 1/31/42 - 3/23/43, Contract Shipments 24829 shotguns.

YEAR	SER. NOS.	TYPE	CONFIGURATION
1937	902117-903762	Mil.	Long Barrel
1939	911788-911813	Mil.	Trench Gun
1940	914087	Com.	Trench Gun
1940	924312	Com.	Trench Gun
1941	920235-956126	Mil.	Trench Gun
1942	930537-956216	Mil.	Trench Gun
1943	956628	Mil.	Trench Gun
1944	965482	Com.	Trench Gun
1944	966144	Com.	Trench Gun
1944	967371	Com.	Riot Gun
1949	993750	Com.	Riot Gun

MODEL 1901

YEAR	APPROX. LAST NO.
1904 -	64,856 to 64,860
05 -	66453
06 -	67486
07 -	68424
08 -	69197
09 -	70009
10 -	70753
11 -	71441
12 -	72167
13 -	72764
14 -	73202
15 -	73509
1916 -	73770
17 -	74027
18 -	74311
19 -	74872
20 -	77000

MODEL 1911

YEAR	APPROX. LAST NO.
1911	1-3819
1912	27659
1913	36677
1914	40105
1915	43284
1916	45391
1917	49843
1918	52895
1919	57337
1920	60719
1921	64109
1922	69132
1923	73186
1924	76199
1925	78611
1926-28 parts clean-up ending at.	82744

MODEL 12

YEAR	APPROX. LAST NO.	POLISHING ROOM SNAS
1912 -	5308	9266
13 -	32418	49344
14 -	79765	110370
15 -	109515	143142
16 -	136412	157861
17 -	159391	191510
18 -	183461	196269
19 -	219457	230343
20 -	247458	281302
21 -	267253	303678
22 -	304314	333678
23 -	346319	379021
24 -	385196	417326
25 -	423056	462132
26 -	464564	498101
27 -	510693	541109
28 -	557850	594589
29 -	600834	637335
30 -	626996	673015
31 -	651255	684476
32 -	660110	698596
33 -	664544	698662
34 -	673994	704074
35 -	686978	723448
36 -	720316	749429
37 -	754250	788635
38 -	779455	813810
39 -	814121	849225
40 -	856499	888006
41 -	907431	903580

MODEL 12

YEAR	APPROX. LAST NO.	POLISHING ROOM SNAS
42 -	958303	1002163
43 -	975640	1034440
44 -	975727	1042155
45 -	990004	1060683
46 -	1029152	1092085
47 -	1102371	1145110
48 -	1176055	1218845
49 -	1214041	1281025
50 -	1252028	1354540
51 -	1290015	1418315
52 -	1328002	1477650
53 -	1399996	1568660
54 -	1471990	1635300
55 -	1541929	1684790
56 -	1611868	1727280
57 -	1651435	1784325
58 -	1690999	1837879
59 -	1795500	1887319
60 -	1800000	1917780
61 -	1930999	1932638
62 -	1956990	1942598
63 -	1962001	1968260
64 -	N/A	1970885
65-	N/A	No further entry
1966 -	1970875	

A clean up of production took place from 1964 through 1966 with the ending serial # 1970875.

MODEL 12 TRENCH/RIOT SHOTGUN

This information is provided by Mr. Pat Redmond after many years of research and collecting. Reference a Winchester Repeating Arms Co. Memorandum dated September 1945. Trench/Riot and long barrel Contract Dates 4/1/42 - 3/21/44, Contract Shipments 61014 shotguns.

Blue Finish

YEAR	SER. NOS.	TYPE	CONFIGURATION
1941	926558--956504	Mil.	Riot & Long Barrel
1942	961934-1001014	Mil.	Trench/Riot/Long
1943	996899-1028856	Mil.	Trench & Riot

Parkerized Finish

YEAR	SER. NOS.	TYPE	CONFIGURATION
1943	1030000-1035214	Mil.	Trench Gun
1944	1035458	Mil.	Trench Gun
1945	1035525	Mil.	Trench Gun
1946	1071586	Com.	Riot Gun
1949	1740610	Com.	Riot Gun

NEW STYLE M/12

YEAR	APPROX. LAST NO.
1972 -	Y200 011-Y2006396
73 -	Y2015662
74 -	Y2022061
75 -	Y2024478
76 -	Y2025482
77 -	Y2025874
78 -	Y2026156
79 -	Y2026399

MODELS 120/1200/1300

YEAR	APPROX. LAST NO.
1972 -	L739617
73-	L828677
74-	L898065
75-	L967242
76-	L1063788
77-	L1163671
78-	L1202123

MODELS 120/1200/1300, cont.

YEAR	APPROX. LAST NO.
79-	L1235083
80-	L1269765
81-	L1320354
82-	L1434776
83-	L1567997
84-	L1755346
85-	L1894542
86-	L1983657
87-	L2075117
88-	L2178816
89-	L2306558
90-	L2386211
91-	L2498813
92-	L2599825

MODEL 24

YEAR	APPROX. LAST NO.
1939 -	1 to 8118
40 -	21382
41 -	27045
42 -	33670
43 -	NONE RECORDED
44 -	33683
45 -	34965
46 -	45250
47 -	58940
48 -	64417

There were no records kept on this model from 1949 until its discontinuance in 1958. The total production was approximately 116280.

MODEL 36

Approximately 20,000 Model 36 single shot 9mm shotguns were manufactured 1920-1927. These shotguns were not serial numbered.

MODEL 37

Approximately 1,000,000 Model 37 single shot shotguns were manufactured 1936-1963. These shotguns were not serial numbered.

MODEL 40

YEAR	APPROX. LAST NO.
1939 -	1 to 2671
1940	10592
1941	13265
1942	18929

MODEL 42

YEAR	APPROX. LAST NO.
1933 -	1 to 9398
34 -	13963
35 -	17728
36 -	24849
37 -	30900
38 -	34659
39 -	38967
40 -	43348
41 -	48203
42 -	50818
43 -	50822
44 -	50828
45 -	51168
46 -	54256
47 -	64853
48 -	75142
49 -	81107
50 -	87071
51 -	93038

MODEL 42

YEAR	APPROX. LAST NO.
52 -	99000
53 -	108201
54 -	117200
55 -	121883
56 -	126566
57 -	131249
58 -	135932
59 -	140615
60 -	145298
61 -	149981
62 -	154664
63 -	159353

MODEL 50

YEAR	APPROX. LAST NO.
1954 -	1 to 24550
55 -	49100
56 -	73650
57 -	98200
58 -	122750
59 -	147300
60 -	171850
61 -	196400

WINCHESTER MODEL 101 SERIALIZATION

12 gauge

SER. NO.	MFG.MO.	YEAR
50,50,000	10	1959
50,500	3	1960
51,000	5	1960
51,500	6	1960
52,000	9	1961
52,500	3	1962
53,000	4	1962
53,500	5	1962
54,000	8	1962
54,500	9	1962
55,000	10	1962
55,500	12	1962
56,000	1	1963
56,500	2	1963
57,000	3	1963
57,500	3	1963
58,000	4	1963
58,500	5	1963
59,000	6	1963
59,500	6	1963
60,000	7	1963
60,500	8	1963
61,000	8	1963
61,500	11	1963
62,000	11	1963
62,500	11	1963
63,000	12	1963
63,500	1	1964
64,000	1	1964
64,500	2	1964
65,000	3	1964
65,500	3	1964
66,500	3	1964
67,000	5	1964
67,500	5	1964
68,000	5	1964
68,500	5	1964
69,000	6	1964
69,500	6	1964
70,000	7	1964

12 gauge, cont.

SER. NO.	MFG.MO.	YEAR
70,500	7	1964
71,000	8	1964
71,500	9	1964
72,000	9	1964
72,500	10	1964
73,000	10	1964
73,500	11	1964
74,000	11	1964
74,500	12	1964
75,000	12	1964
75,500	1	1965
76,000	2	1965
76,500	2	1965
77,000	3	1965
77,500	4	1965
78,000	4	1965
78,500	4	1965
79,000	4	1965
79,500	4	1965
80,000	5	1965
80,500	6	1965
81,000	6	1965
81,500	6	1965
82,000	6	1965
82,500	8	1965
83,000	8	1965
83,500	8	1965
84,000	9	1965
84,500	9	1965
85,000	10	1965
85,500	10	1965
86,000	10	1965
86,500	10	1965
87,000	10	1965
87,500	10	1965
88,000	11	1965
88,500	11	1965
89,000	11	1965
90,000	12	1965
90,500	12	1965
91,000	12	1965
91,500	1	1966
92,000	1	1966
92,500	2	1966
93,000	2	1966
93,500	2	1966
94,000	3	1966
94,500	3	1966
95,000	5	1966
95,500	5	1966
96,000	6	1966
96,500	7	1966
97,000	7	1966
97,500	7	1966
98,000	8	1966
98,500	8	1966
99,000	9	1966
99,500	9	1966
100,000	10	1966
100,500	10	1966
101,000	10	1966
101,500	11	1966
102,000	11	1966
102,500	12	1966
103,000	1	1967
103,500	1	1967
104,000	2	1967
104,500	3	1967
105,000	4	1967
105,500	5	1967
106,000	5	1967
106,500	5	1967
107,000	9	1967
107,500	10	1967

12 gauge, cont.

SER. NO.	MFG.MO.	YEAR
108,000	10	1967
108,500	11	1967
109,000	11	1967
109,500	11	1967
110,000	12	1967
110,500	1	1968
111,000	2	1968
111,500	3	1968
112,000	3	1968
112,500	3	1968
113,000	3	1968
113,500	4	1968
114,000	5	1968
114,500	5	1968
115,000	6	1968
115,500	6	1968
116,000	7	1968
116,500	7	1968
117,000	9	1968
117,500	10	1968
118,000	1	1969
118,500	1	1969
119,000	2	1969
119,500	3	1969
120,000	4	1969
120,500	4	1969
121,000	4	1969
121,500	4	1969
122,000	5	1969
122,500	6	1969
123,000	6	1969
123,500	6	1969
124,000	7	1969
124,500	7	1969
125,000	7	1969
125,500	8	1969
126,000	8	1969
126,500	9	1969
127,000	9	1969
127,500	10	1969
128,000	11	1969
128,500	11	1969
129,000	11	1969
129,500	2	1970
130,000	2	1970
130,500	3	1970
131,000	3	1970
131,500	4	1970
132,000	4	1970
132,500	4	1970
133,000	4	1970
133,500	5	1970
134,000	5	1970
134,500	5	1970
135,000	6	1970
135,500	6	1970
136,000	6	1970
136,500	8	1970
137,000	8	1970
137,500	8	1970
138,000	8	1970
138,500	11	1970
139,000	12	1970
139,500	12	1970
140,000	12	1970
140,500	1	1971
141,000	2	1971
141,500	2	1971
142,000	2	1971
142,500	3	1971
143,000	3	1971
143,500	4	1971
144,000	4	1971
144,500	4	1971

12 gauge, cont.

SER. NO.	MFG.MO.	YEAR
145,000	4	1971
145,500	5	1971

MODEL 101, 20 gauge.

SER. NO.	MFG.MO.	YEAR
200,000	3	1966
200,500	3	1966
201,000	3	1966
201,500	3	1966
202,000	4	1966
202,500	4	1966
203,000	4	1966
203,500	5	1966
204,000	6	1966
204,500	6	1966
205,000	7	1966
205,500	8	1966
206,000	8	1966
206,500	8	1966
207,000	9	1966
207,500	9	1966
208,000	9	1966
208,500	12	1966
209,000	2	1967
209,500	7	1967
210,000	10	1967
210,500	12	1967

MODEL 101, 28 ga. & .410 bore

SER. NO.	MFG.MO.	YEAR
211,000	1	1968
211,500	1	1968
212,000	10	1968
212,500	10	1968
213,000	10	1968
213,500	11	1968
214,000	12	1968
214,500	12	1968
215,000	1	1969
215,500	2	1969
216,000	5	1969
216,500	6	1969
217,000	9	1969
217,500	10	1969
218,500	12	1969
219,000	12	1969
219,500	12	1969
220,000	12	1969
220,500	1	1970
221,000	1	1970
221,500	2	1970
222,000	3	1970
222,500	7	1970
223,000	9	1970
223,500	9	1970
224,000	9	1970
224,500	9	1970
225,000	10	1970
225,500	10	1970
226,000	11	1970
226,500	11	1970
227,000	11	1970
227,500	12	1970
228,000	12	1970
228,500	4	1971
229,000	4	1971
229,500	4	1971

PROOF MARKS

The proof marks shown below will assist in determining nationality of manufacturers when no other markings are evident. Since the U.S. has no proofing houses (as in England, France, Germany and other European countries), most U.S. manufacturers voluntarily proof their firearms with a specifed style of proofmark (i.e. the interlocked ©WPª synonymous with the Winchester trademark can be fired using modern smokeless powder) shells. Pre-1850 European firearms oftentimes do not exhibit any commercial proof marks and, with the exception of an occasional barrel address, they represent the single hardest category of firearms one can research properly. Captured weapons from major wars occasionally show two different nationalities of proof marks. This is acceptable since the gun was proofed in a national proof house after original manufacture and again when the gun was exported to a different country as a military acquisition. Please refer to the References section in this text for proof mark source information.

AUSTRIAN PROOF MARKS

PROOF MARK	CIRCA	PROOF HOUSE	TYPE OF PROOF AND GUN
	since 1891	Vienna	provisional proof for multi barrel guns
	since 1891	Ferlach	provisional proof for multi barrel guns
	1892-1918	Prague	provisional proof for rifles
	1892-1918	Ferlach	black powder proof for rifles
	1892-1918	Prague	black powder proof for rifles
	1892-1918	Weipert	black powder proof for rifles
	1892-1918	Vienna	black powder proof for rifles
	1918-1938	Ferlach	black powder proof for rifles
	1918-1938	Vienna	black powder proof for rifles
	1938-1940	Ferlach	black powder proof for rifles
	1938-1940	Vienna	black powder proof for rifles
	since 1945	Vienna	black powder proof for multi barrel guns
	since 1945	Ferlach	black powder proof for multi barrel guns
 BH	since 1891	Bundesheer	preliminary proof for multi barrel guns

PROOF MARK	CIRCA	PROOF HOUSE	TYPE OF PROOF AND GUN
	1891-1928	Budapest	smokeless powder proof for parabellum pistols
	Since 1981	Ferlach	smokeless powder proof for parabellum pistols
	1891-1931	Ferlach	smokeless powder proof for parabellum pistols
	since 1891	Vienna	smokeless powder proof for parabellum pistols
	1891-1931	Weipert	smokeless powder proof for parabellum pistols

BELGIAN PROOF MARKS

PROOF MARK	CIRCA	PROOF HOUSE	TYPE OF PROOF AND GUN
	since 1852	Liege	provisional black powder proof for breech loading guns and rifled barrels
	-	Liege-	double proof marking for unfurnished barrels
	-	Liege-	triple proof provisional marking for unfurnished barrels
	since 1893	-Liege	definitive black powder proof for breech loading guns, small bore guns and handguns
	since 1853	Liege	View stamp and inspectors mark for firearms "Perron"
	since 1924	-Liege	Nitro proof for rifled barrel and parabellum pistols
	since 1852	-Liege	rifled arms defense for smokeless proof parabellum pistols
	-	-Liege	Superior nitro proof

BRITISH PROOF MARKS

PROOF MARK	CIRCA	PROOF HOUSE	TYPE OF PROOF AND GUN
	since 1856	London	provisional proof for barrels

PROOF MARK	CIRCA	PROOF HOUSE	TYPE OF PROOF AND GUN
	since 1856	Birmingham	provisional proof for barrels
	since 1637	London	definitive black powder proof for shotguns,muzzle loader barrels
	1811-1892	Liege	black powder proof for rifles
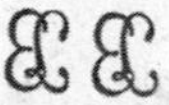	1897-1923	Liege	black powder proof for rifles
	1891-1968	Liege	type EC. smokeless powder proof for rifles
	1898-1968	Liege	type Pt. smokeless powder proof for rifles
	1898-1968	Liege	smokeless powder proof for rifles
	since 1968	Liege	smokeless powder proof for rifles
	since 1904	London	definitive nitro proof for all guns - parabellum pistols
	since 1954	Birmingham	definitive nitro proof for barrel and action
	since 1904	Birmingham	black powder proof only for parabellum pistols
	1868 1925	London	definitive special super power proof for parabellum pistols
	1868-1925	Birmingham	voluntary special black powder proof
	1868-1925	London	reproof marking for black powder rifles
	1868-1925	Birmingham	reproof marking for black powder rifles
	1868-1925	Birmingham	definitive black powder proof for shotguns
	since 1904	Birmingham	definitive nitro proof for all guns
	since 1670	London	view mark
	since 1904	Birmingham	view mark

FRENCH PROOF MARKS

PARIS HOUSE	ST ETIENNE HOUSE	CIRCA	TYPE OF PROOF AND GUN
		since 1897	provisional proof unfinished short barreled guns
		1897	standard proof for finished guns
		1897	double proof finished and joined barrels
	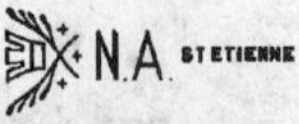	1897	single barrel proof for non-assembled guns
		1897	finished black powder guns
		since 1962	black powder proof for rifles
R		1962-1972	final black powder proof for rifles
		1926-1962	final black powder proof for rifles
		since 1962	final black powder proof for rifles
		since 1900	smokeless powder proof for rifles
☆ PJ		1896-1926	smokeless powder proof for rifles
☆ PS		1896-1926	smokeless powder proof for rifles
☆ PM		1896-1926	smokeless powder proof for rifles
☆ PT		1900-1972	smokeless powder proof for rifles
☆☆ P.T		1926-1972	smokeless powder proof for rifles
☆ PT R		1962-1972	final smokeless powder proof for rifles
		since 1962	final smokeless powder proof for rifles
		since 1982	final smokeless powder proof for rifles

PARIS HOUSE	ST ETIENNE HOUSE	CIRCA	TYPE OF PROOF AND GUN
		1897	special proof for finished guns
		1897	ordinary smokeless powder proof
		1897	superior smokeless powder proo

GERMAN PROOF MARKS

Research continues for the inclusion of Pre-1950 German Proofmarks.

PROOF MARK	CIRCA	PROOF HOUSE	TYPE OF PROOF AND GUN
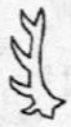	since 1952	Ulm	
	since 1968	Hannover	
	since 1968	Kiel (W. German)	
	since 1968	Munich	
	since 1968	Cologne (W. German)	
	since 1968	Berlin (W. German)	
	since 1952	Ulm	voluntary proof for hand/long guns
	since 1952	Ulm	repair proof for major gun parts
	since 1952	Ulm	provisional black powder for shotgun & multi barreled rifles
	since 1952	Ulm	definitive nitro proof for all guns
	since 1952	Ulm	definitive black powder for smokeless ammo guns
	since 1952	Ulm	Flobert for special purpose guns signal, flare, gas, & stun guns
	since 1945	E. German, Suhl	smokeless powder proof
	since 1950	E. German, Suhl	1st black powder proof for rifled barrels
	since 1950	E. German, Suhl	nitro powder proof

PROOF MARK	CIRCA	PROOF HOUSE	TYPE OF PROOF AND GUN
	since 1950	E. German, Suhl	repair proof
	since 1950	E. German, Suhl	1st black powder proof for smooth bored barrels
	since 1950	E. German, Suhl	inspection mark
	since 1950	E. German, Suhl	choke-bore barrel mark

ITALIAN PROOF MARKS

PROOF MARK	CIRCA	PROOF HOUSE	TYPE OF PROOF AND GUN
	since 1951	Brescia	provisional proof for all guns
	since 1951	Gardone	provisional proof for all guns
	since 1951	Gardone & Brescia	definitive proof for guns with smokeless powder
	since 1951	Gardone & Brescia	finish proof for firearms ready for sale
	since 1951	Gardone & Brescia	1st black powder proof

SPANISH PROOF MARKS

PROOF MARK	CIRCA	PROOF HOUSE	TYPE OF PROOF AND GUN
	since 1910	Eibar	provisional black powder proof for shotguns
	since 1910	Eibar	temporary black powder proof for shotguns
	since 1910	Eibar	final black powder proof for breech loading shotguns
	since 1910	Eibar	final smokeless powder proof for breech loading shotguns
	since 1910	Eibar	reinforced smokeless powder proof for breech loading shotguns
	since 1910	Eibar	provisional proof for shotguns
	since 1910	Eibar	final black powder proof for breech loading shotgun

PROOF MARK	CIRCA	PROOF HOUSE	TYPE OF PROOF AND GUN
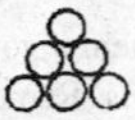	since 1923	Eibar	final and single black powder proof for double barreled muzzle loading shotun
	since 1923	Eibar	final and single black powder proof for single barrel smooth bored breechloading guns
	since 1923	Eibar	final black powder proof for double barreled breechloading rifles
	since 1923	Eibar	final black powder proof for single proof breechloading rifles
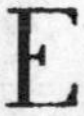	since 1923	Eibar	reinforced voluntary proof for single and double barrel shotguns
	since 1923	Eibar	final proof of military-style rifle
	since 1923	Eibar	single and final proof of non-self loading pistols
	since 1923	Eibar	single and final proof for self loading pistols and revolvers
	since 1929	Eibar	admission proof for guns with old marks
	since 1929	Eibar	proof used in Barcelona for guns with old marks
	since 1929	Eibar	final proof for revolver
	since 1929	Eibar	proof for semiautomatic pistols
	since 1929	Eibar	special manufacturer's mark for guns made for foreign sales
	since 1929	Eibar	smokeless proof for shotgun barrels
	since 1929	Eibar	reinforced smokeless proof for shotgun barrels

BATFE GUIDE

A listing has been provided below of Field Division offices for the BATFE. You are encouraged to contact them if you have any questions regarding the legality of any weapons or their interpretation of existing laws and regulations. Remember, ignorance is no excuse when it involves Federal firearms regulations and laws. Although these various offices may not be able to help you with state, city, county, or local firearms regulations and laws, their job is to assist you on a Federal level.

U.S. Department of Justice
Bureau of Alcohol, Tobacco, Firearms and Explosives:
Website: www.atf.gov

Atlanta Field Division
2600 Century Parkway Suite 300
Atlanta, Georgia 30345
Phone No.: (404) 417-2600
Fax: (404) 417-2601
Email: AtlantaDiv@atf.gov

Baltimore Field Division
31 Hopkins Plaza, 5th Floor
Baltimore, Maryland 21201
Phone No.: (443) 965-2000
Fax: (443) 965-2001
Email: BaltimoreDiv@atf.gov

Boston Field Division
10 Causeway Street, Suite 791
Boston, Massachusetts 02222
Phone No.: (617) 557-1200
Fax: (617) 557-1201
Email: BostonDiv@atf.gov

Charlotte Field Division
6701 Carmel Road, Suite 200
Charlotte, North Carolina 28226
Phone No.: (704) 716-1800
Fax (704) 716-1801
Email: CharlotteDiv@atf.gov

Chicago Field Division
525 West Van Buren Street,
Suite 600
Chicago, Illinois 60607
Phone No.: (312) 846-7200
Fax: (312) 846-7201
Email: ChicagoDiv@atf.gov

Columbus Field Division
230 West Street, Suite 400
Columbus, Ohio 43215
Phone No.: (614) 827-8400
Fax: (614) 827-8401
Email: ColumbusDiv@atf.gov

Dallas Field Division
1114 Commerce Street, Room 303
Dallas, TX 75242
Phone No.: (469) 227-4300
Fax: (469) 227-4330
Email: DallasDiv@atf.gov

Denver Field Division
950 17th Street, Suite 1800
Denver, Colorado 80202 USA
Phone No.: (303) 575-7600
Fax (303) 575-7601
DenverDiv@atf.gov

Detroit Field Division
1155 Brewery Park Boulevard,
Suite 300
Detroit, Michigan 48207
Phone No.: (313) 202-3400
Fax: (313) 202-3445
Email: DetroitDiv@atf.gov

Houston Field Division
5825 N. Sam Houston Pkwy, Suite 300
Houston, Texas 77086 USA
Phone No.: (281) 716-8200
Fax (281) 716-8219
HoustonDiv@atf.gov

Kansas City Field Division
2600 Grand Avenue, Suite 200
Kansas City, Missouri 64108
Phone No.: (816) 559-0700
Fax: (816) 559-0701
Email: KansasCityDiv@atf.gov

Los Angeles Field Division
550 North Brand Avenue
8th Floor
Glendale, California 91203
Phone No.: (818) 265-2500
Fax: (818) 265-2501
Email: LosAngelesDiv@atf.gov

Louisville Field Division
600 Dr. Martin Luther King Jr. Place, Suite 322
Louisville, KY 40202
Phone No.: (502) 753-3400
Fax: (502) 753-3401
Email: LouisDiv@atf.gov

Miami Field Division
11410 NW 20 Street, Suite 201
Miami, FL 33172
Phone No.: (305) 597-4800
Fax: 305-597-4801
Email: MiamiDiv@atf.gov

Nashville Field Division
5300 Maryland Way, Suite 200
Brentwood, Tennessee 37027
Phone No.: (615) 565-1400
Fax: 615-565-1401
Email: NashDiv@atf.gov

Newark Field Division
1 Garret Mountain Plaza Suite 500
Woodland Park, New Jersey 07424
Phone No.: (973) 413-1179
Fax: (973) 413-1190
Email: NJDivision@atf.gov

New Orlearns
One Galleria Boulevard Suite 1700
Metairie, Louisiana 70001
Phone No.: (504) 841-7000
Fax: (504) 841-7039
Email: NewOrleansDiv@atf.gov

New York Field Division
Financial Square
32 Old Slip
Suite 3500
New York, New York 10005 USA
Phone No.: (646) 335-9000
Fax (646) 335-9001
NYDiv@atf.gov

Philadelphia Field Division
The Curtis Center
601 Walnut Street, Suite 1000E
Philadelphia, Pennsylvania 19106
Phone No.: (215) 446-7800
Fax: (215) 446-7811
Email: PhilDiv@atf.gov

Phoenix Field Division
201 E. Washington Street, Suite 940
Phoenix, Arizona 85004
Phone No.: (602) 776-5400
Fax: (602) 776-5429
Email: PhoenixDiv@atf.gov

San Francisco Field Division
5601 Arnold Road, Suite 400
Dublin, California 94568
Phone No.: (925) 557-2800
Fax: (925) 557-2805
Email: SanFranciscoDiv@atf.gov

Seattle Field Division
915 2nd Avenue, Room 790
Seattle, Washington 98174
Phone No.: (206) 389-5800
Fax: (206) 389-5829
Email: SeattleDiv@atf.gov

St. Paul Field Division
30 East Seventh Street , Suite 1900
St. Paul, Minnesota 55101
Phone No.: (651) 726-0200
Fax: (651) 726-0201
Email: StPaulDiv@atf.gov

Tampa Field Division
400 North Tampa Street
Suite 2100
Tampa, Florida 33602
Phone No.: (813) 202-7300
Fax: (813) 202-7301
Email: TampaDiv@atf.gov

Washington Field Division
1401 H. Street NW, Suite 900
Washington, District of Columbia 20226
Phone No.: (202) 648-8010
Fax: (202) 648-8001
Email: WashDiv@atf.gov

BATFE CURIOS OR RELICS LISTINGS

Editor's Note: The following information on Curios or Relics is taken from The Firearms Curios or Relics List, Section II. The Introduction, Section I, Section III, Section IIIA, and Section IV, *have not been included due to space considerations. For more information on these please contact the BATFE at http://www.atf.gov/.*

The Bureau of Alcohol, Tobacco, Firearms, and Explosives (BATFE) has determined that the following firearms are Curios or Relics as defined in 27 CFR 178.11 because they fall within one of the categories specified in the regulations.

Such determination merely classifies the firearms as curios or relics and thereby authorizes licensed collectors to acquire, hold, or dispose of them as curios or relics subject to the provisions of 18 U.S.C. Chapter 44 and the regulations in 27 CFR Part 178. They are still "firearms" as defined in 18 U.S.C. Chapter 44.

What are Curios or Relics?

As set out in the regulations (27 CFR 178.11), curios or relics include firearms which are of special interest to collectors by reason of some quality other than is associated with firearms intended for sporting use or as offensive or defensive weapons. To be recognized as curios or relics, firearms must fall within one of the following categories:

1.) Firearms which were manufactured at least 50 years prior to the current date, but not including replicas thereof;

2.) Firearms which are certified by the curator of a municipal, State, or Federal museum which exhibits firearms to be curios or relics of museum interest; and

3.) Any other firearms which derive a substantial part of their monetary value from the fact that they are novel, rare, bizarre, or because of their association with some historical figure, period, or event. Proof of qualification of a particular firearm under this category may be established by evidence of present value and evidence that like firearms are not available except as collector's items, or that the value of like firearms available in ordinary commercial channels is substantially less.

SECTION II:

Albanian SKS semiautomatic rifles, caliber 7.62 x 39, manufactured in Albania from 1964 to 1978.

Alkartasuna, semiautomatic pistol, caliber .32.

All Original military bolt action and semiautomatic rifles mfd. between 1899 and 1946.

All properly marked and identified semiautomatic pistols and revolvers used by, or mfd. for, any military organization prior to 1946.

All shotguns, properly marked and identified as mfd. for any military organization prior to 1946 and in their original military configuration only.

Argentine D.G.F.M. (FMAP) System Colt Model 1927 pistols, marked "Ejercito Argentino" bearing S/Ns less than 24501.

Argentine D.G.F.M. - (F.M.A.P.) System Colt model 1927, cal. 11.25mm commercial variations.

Armand Gevage, semiautomatic pistols, .32ACP cal. as mfd. in Belgium prior to World War II.

Astra, M 800 Condor model, pistol, caliber 9mm parabellum

Astra, model 1921 (400) semiautomatic pistols having slides marked Esperanzo Y Unceta.

Astra, model 400 pistol, German Army Contract, caliber 9mm Bergmann-Bayard, S/N range 97351-98850.

Astra, model 400 semiautomatic pistol, cal. 9mm Bergmann-Bayard, second German Army Contract, in S/N range 92851 through 97350.

Auto-Mag pistols, calibers .44 AMP and .357 AMP, mfd. and/or assembled by Auto-Mag Corporation, TDE, OMC, High Standard, Lee Jurras, or AMT from 1969 to 1985.

Auto Ordnance, West Hurley, NY, Korean War Commemorative Thompson semiautomatic rifle, caliber .45.

Auto Ordnance, West Hurley, NY, World War II Commemorative Thompson semiautomatic rifle, caliber .45.

Auto Ordnance Thompson, cal. 45 semiautomatic rifle, Vietnam Commemorative, S/Ns V0001- V1500, issued by the American Historical Foundation, Richmond VA.

Baker Gun and Forging Company, all firearms mfd. from 1899 to 1919.

Bannerman model 1937, Springfield rifle, caliber .30-06.

Bayard, model 1923 semiautomatic pistol, cal. 7.65mm or .380, Belgian manufacture.

Beretta, M 1951 pistol Israeli Contract, caliber 9mm parabellum.

Beretta, model 1915 pistols, cal. 6.35mm, 7.65mm, and 9mm Glisenti.

Beretta, model 1915/1919 (1922) pistol (concealed hammer), caliber 7.65mm.

Beretta, model 1919 pistol (without grip safety), caliber 6.35mm.

Beretta, model 1932 pistol, having smooth wooden grips w/"PB" medallion, cal. 9mm.

Beretta, model 1934 pistol, light weight model marked "Tipo Alleggerita" or "All" having transverse ribbed barrel, cal. 9mm.

Beretta, model 1934 pistols, cal. 9mm post war variations bearing Italian Air Force eagle markings.

Beretta, model 1934 pistols, cal. 9mm produced during 1945 or earlier and having S/Ns within the ranges of 500000-999999, F00001-F120000, G0001-G80000, 00001AA-10000AA, 00001BB-10000BB. The classification does not include any post war variations dated subsequent to 1945 or bearing postwar Italian proof marks.

Beretta, model 1935 pistol, Finnish Home Guard Contract, marked "SKY" on the slide, cal. 7.65mm.

Beretta, model 1935 pistol, Rumanian Contract, marked "P. Beretta - cal. 9 Scurt - Mo. 1934 – Brevet." on the slide, cal. 9mm.

Beretta, Model 92SB with detachable folding shoulder stocks, cal. 9mm S/Ns C31509Z through C31538Z.

FN Browning, model 1902 (usually known as the model 1903) semiautomatic pistol, caliber 9mm Browning long.

Browning .22 caliber, semiautomatic rifles, Grade II, mfd. by Fabrique Nationale in Belgium from 1956 to 1976.

Browning FN Medalist Gold Line and "Renaissance" engraved semiautomatic pistols, caliber .22.

Browning FN Model 1910 semiautomatic pistols, calibers .32 and .380, marked "Browning Arms Company."

Browning Superposed Bi-Centennial Ltd. Edition, shotgun.

Browning, "Baby" model pistol, Russian Contract, caliber 6.35mm.

Browning, Centennial model High Power Pistol, cal. 9mm parabellum.

Browning, Centennial model 92 lever action rifle, cal. .44 Magnum.

Browning, model 1906 Pocket Pistol if more than 50 years old.

Browning, model 1922 pistol, cal. 7.65mm or 9mm Kurz, marked "C.P.I.M." denoting issue to the Belgian Political Police.

Browning, model 1922 pistol, cal. 7.65mm, bearing German NSDAP or RFV markings.

Browning, M1935 Hi Power pistol, Canadian, Congolese, Indian and Nationalist Chinese Contracts, cal. 9mm parabellum.

Browning Hi Power, Classic Edition, 9mm caliber pistol, having S/Ns 245BC0001 through 45BC5000.

Browning High Power D-Day Commemorative, 9mm caliber pistol, having S/Ns 245DD0001 through 245DD00150.

Browning High Power, Gold Classic Edition, 9mm caliber pistol, having S/Ns 245GC0001 through 245GC0500.

Browning, Superposed Centennial, consisting of a 20 gauge superposed shotgun, supplied with an extra set of .30-06 cal. superposed barrels.

Budischowsky, model TP70, semiautomatic pistol, cal. .25 ACP, with custom S/N DB1.

Campo-Giro, model 1913 and 1913/16 pistol, cal. 9mm Largo.

Chinese Communist, types 51 and 54 (Tokarev) pistols, cal. 7.62mm.

Chinese, Peoples Republic of China, copy of German Walther PPK .32 ACP cal. w/Chinese proof marks, Type I and II.

Chinese, Peoples Republic of China, copy of Japanese Type Sigiura Shiki semiautomatic pistol, caliber 7.65mm.

Chylewski, semiautomatic pistol mfd. by S.I.G. Switzerland, cal. 6.35mm (.25 ACP).

Clement, pistol, Belgian manufacture, cal. 5mm Clement.

Colt, Model 1911A1, cal. .45, semiautomatic pistols, Famous Generals of WWII, S/Ns WWIIG001 – WWIIG200.

Colt .38 National Match semiautomatic pistol, all S/Ns and in their original configuration.

Colt .38 Special Kit semiautomatic pistols, mfd. from 1964-1970, S/Ns 00100H-00434H.

Colt .45 ACP Kit semiautomatic pistols, mfd. from 1964-1970, S/Ns 001000-011640.

Colt, factory engraved for "Dr. Ramon Grau San Martin," President of Cuba, .45 cal. pistol with 5" barrel and blue steel finish; S/N C231769.

Colt, "Duke," Commemorative, .22 caliber revolver.

Colt, Ace semiautomatic pistol, cal. .22, mfd. by Colt from 1931 to 1947, S/N range from 1 to 10935 including those marked "UNITED STATES PROPERTY" on the right side of the frame.

Colt, Ace Service model semiautomatic pistol, cal. .22, mfd. by Colt from 1935 to 1945, S/N range from SM1 to SM13803 including those marked "UNITED STATES PROPERTY" on the right side of the frame.

Colt, Age of Flight 75th Anniversary semiautomatic pistols, cal. .45.

Colt, Aircrewman revolver produced between 1951 and 1959, cal. .38 Special, marked "Property of U.S. Air Force" on back strap, having Air Force issue numbers of 1 - 1189 and in the S/N range 1902LW – 90470LW.

Colt, Alabama Sesquicentennial, .22.

Colt, Alamo, .22 and .45.

Colt, American Combat Companion Officers model, cal. .45ACP pistol marked "1911 American Combat Companion 1981, 70 Years at America's Side."

Colt, American Combat Companion, Enlisted Man's model, cal. .45ACP pistol marked "1911 American Combat Companion 1981, 70 Years at America's Side."

Colt, American Combat Companion, General Officers model, cal. .45ACP pistol marked "1911 American Combat Companion 1981, 70 Years at America's Side." S/Ns 1 STAR, 2 STAR, 3 STAR, 4 STAR, and 5 STAR.

Colt, Appomattox Court House Centennial, .22 and .45.

Colt AR-15 Sporter "The Viet Nam Tribute Colt Special Edition" .223 cal. semiautomatic rifle, bearing the American Historical Foundation registry numbers of VT0001 through VT1500.

Colt, Argentine model 1927, pistols, cal. .45, commercial variations.

Colt, Arizona Ranger model commemorative, .22 Revolver.

Colt, Arizona Territorial Centennial, .22 and .45.

Colt, Arkansas Territory Sesquicentennial, .22.

Colt, Army Model double action revolver, any cal., mfd. between 1899 and 1907.

Colt Army Special Model revolver, .32-20 cal., having a barrel length of 4'1/2", with factory engraving, S/N 329653.

Colt, ATF Special Edition, Deluxe model automatic pistol, cal. .45 ACP.

Colt, ATF Special Edition, Python Revolver, caliber .357 magnum.

Colt, ATF Special Edition, Standard model automatic pistol, cal. .45 ACP.

Colt, Abilene, .22 (Kansas City-Cow Town).

Colt, Bat Masterson, .22 and .45 (Lawman Series).

Colt, Battle of Gettysburg Centennial, .22.

Colt, Belleau Wood, .45 Pistol, (World War I Series).

Colt, Border Patrol model Revolver, .38 Special Heavy Duty, Police Positive (D) style frame, S/Ns within the range 610000 through 620000.

Colt, Buffalo Bill Historical Center, Winchester Museum, Special Issue, Colt Single Action revolver, cal. .44-40, S/N 21BB.

Colt, Buffalo Bill Wild West Show single action army .45 caliber.

Colt, California Bicentennial, .22.

Colt, California Gold Rush, .22 and .45.

Colt, Camp Perry Single Shot Target Pistols, .22 long rifle or .38 Special caliber.

Colt, Carolina Charter Tercentenary, .22 and .22/.45.

Colt, Chamizal Treaty, .22 and .45.

Colt, Chateau Thierry, .45 Pistol, (World War I Series).

Colt, Cherry's Sporting Goods 35th Anniversary, .22/.45.

Colt, Chisholm Trail, .22 (Kansas Series-Trails).

Colt, Civil War Centennial Single Shot, .22.

Colt, Coffeyville, .22 (Kansas Series-Cow Town).

Colt, Colorado Gold Rush, Colt, Colonel Samuel Colt, Sesquicentennial, .45.

Colt, Colt's 125th Anniversary, .45.

Colt, Columbus (Ohio) Sesquicentennial, .22.

Colt, Custom Gun Shop's "Custom Edition Sheriff's model" Single Action Revolver, cal. .45 Colt, S/Ns 1 to 35.

Colt, DA .38, New Army and Navy Revolver, made from 1899 to 1907.

Colt, Dakota Territory, .22.

Colt, Des Monies, Reconstruction of Old Fort, .22 and .45.

Colt, Detective Special revolver, cal. .38, S/N 418162, owned by Colonel Charles A. Lindbergh.

Colt, Detective Special revolvers, 2" barrels, marked "R.M.S. P.O. DEPT" or "U.S.P.O. DEPT."; S/Ns above 467000.

Colt, Dodge City, .22 (Kansas Series-Cow Town).

Colt, European Theater, .45 Pistol (World War II Series).

Colt, First model, Match Target Woodsman, cal. .22, semiautomatic pistol, mfd. from 1938 to 1944, S/Ns MT1 to MT15,000.

Colt, Florida Territory Sesquicentennial, .22.

Colt, Fort Findlay (Ohio) sesquicentennial, .22.

Colt, Fort Hays, .22 (Kansas Series-Forts).

Colt, Fort Larned, .22 (Kansas Series-Forts).

Colt, Fort McPherson (Nebraska) Centennial Derringer, .22.

Colt, Fort Scott, .22 (Kansas Series-Forts).

Colt, Fort Stephenson (Ohio) sesquicentennial, .22.

Colt, Fourth model Derringer, cal. .22 short rimfire, cased as a set of two pistols in a leather book titled "Colt Derringer, Limited Edition Colt, General George Meade, Pennsylvania, by Colt," on the spine of the book and "A Limited Edition by Colt," on the cover.

Colt, Forty-Niner Miner, .22.

Colt, General George Meade, Pennsylvania Campaign, .22 and .45.

Colt, General Hood, Tennessee Campaign Centennial, .22.

Colt, General John Hunt Morgan, Indiana Raid, .22.

Colt, General Nathan Bedford Forrest, .22.

Colt, Geneseo (Illinois) 125th Anniversary, Derringer, .22.

Colt, Golden Spike Centennial, .22.

Colt, Government model pistols in cal. .45 ACP, BB series.

Colt, H. Cook, "1 to 100," .22/.45.

Colt, Idaho Territorial Centennial, .22.

Colt, Indiana Sesquicentennial, .22.

Colt, J frame, Officers model Match, .38 Special revolver mfd. from 1970-1972, identified by J S/N prefix.

Colt, Joaquin Murrieta, "1 of 100," .22/.45.

Colt, John M. Browning Commemorative, .45 cal., semiautomatic pistol, S/Ns JMB 0001 – JMB 3000, and numbers GAS O JMB, PE CEW JMB, and 0003JMB.

Colt, John Wayne, Commemorative, .45 long Colt caliber revolver.

Colt, Kansas Centennial, .22.

Colt, Lightning model double action revolver, any cal. mfd. between 1899 and 1909.

Colt, Lightning rifles mfd. in 1899 through 1904.

Colt, Lord and Lady Derringer, .22 cal., as mfd. by Colts Patent Firearms Manufacturing Co., Hartford, CT.

Colt, Los Angeles Police Department (L.A.P.D.) Special Edition .45 cal. Government model semiautomatic pistol.

Colt, Maine Sesquicentennial, .22 and .45.

Colt, Mark IV, Government Model, commemorative "Michigan State Police 60th Anniversary, 1917-1977." The left side of slide engraved with scroll pattern and depicts 4 modes of transportation; Horse, Motorcycle, Auto and Helicopter S/Ns 1 to 1608.

Colt, Match Target Woodsman Semiautomatic Pistol, cal. .22LR., S/N 128866S, owned by Ernest Hemingway.

Colt, Meuse Argonne, .45 Pistol, (World War I Series).

Colt, Missouri Sesquicentennial single action army .45 caliber.

Colt, Missouri Sesquicentennial, .22.

Colt, Mk IV Series 70 semiautomatic pistols in all cals., which were incorrectly marked at the factory with both Colt Government model markings and Colt Commander markings.

Colt, model 1873 Peacemaker Centennial 1973, single action revolver, .44/.40 or .45.

Colt, model 1900 semiautomatic pistol, cal. .38, in original configuration.

Colt, model 1902 semiautomatic pistol, military model, cal. .38, in original configuration.

Colt, model 1902 semiautomatic pistol, sporting model, cal. .38, in original configuration.

Colt, model 1903 Pocket (exposed hammer), semiautomatic pistol cal. .38 ACP.

Colt, model 1903 Pocket (hammerless), semiautomatic pistol, cal. .32.

Colt, model 1908 Pocket (hammerless), semiautomatic pistol, cal. .380.

Colt, model 1908, cal. .25 ACP, hammerless semiautomatic pistol, having a grip safety, in S/N range 1 - 409061.

Colt, model 1911, commercial semiautomatic pistols, cal. .45 ACP, S/Ns CI - C130000.

Colt, model 1911-A, commercial model, in cal. .45 and bearing Egyptian inscription meaning police, on the upper forward right-hand side of the trigger guard and having S/Ns within the range of C186000 to C188000.

Colt Model "Courier" double action revolver, .32 caliber, with 3-inch barrel.

Colt Model "Marshal" double action revolver, .38 special caliber, 2-inch and 4-inch barrels.

Colt, 50th Anniversary of the Battle of the Bulge, Model 1911A1, .45 caliber, semiautomatic pistol, having S/Ns between BB001 and BB300.

Colt, Montana Territory Centennial, .22 and .45.

Colt, National Match semiautomatic pistols, all S/Ns, in original configuration.

Colt, Nebraska Centennial, .22.

Colt, Ned Buntline Commemorative, cal. .45 revolver.

Colt, Nevada Centennial "Battle Born," .22 and .45.

Colt, Nevada Centennial, .22. and .45.

Colt, New Frontier .22 LR Revolvers, "Kit Carson" Commemorative, Colt model GB275.

Colt, New Frontier and Single Action Army model revolvers originally ordered & shipped with factory engraving, accompanied by a letter from the manufacturer confirming the authenticity of the engraving.

Colt, New Frontier, .357 magnum cal., single action revolver, barrel length 4-3/4" S/N 4411NF.

Colt, New Frontier, .45 cal., Abercrombie and Fitch, "Trailblazer."

Colt, New Jersey Tercentenary, .22 and .45.

Colt, New Mexico Golden Anniversary, .22.

Colt, New Police revolvers, .32 Colt cal., S/Ns 1 through 49,50.

Colt, New Service revolvers as mfd. between 1899 - 1944, all variations, all calibers.

Colt, NRA Centennial, Gold Cup National Match pistol, in cal. .45.

Colt, NRA Centennial, single action revolver, in cals. .357 Magnum and .45.

Colt, Officers model (1904-1930), .38 cal. revolver.

Colt, Officers model (1930-1949), .22 cal. revolver.

Colt, Officers model Match (1953-1969), .22 and .38 cal. revolvers.

Colt, Officers model Special (1949-1952), .22 and .38 cal. revolvers.

Colt, Officers model Target (1930-1949), .32 and .38 cal revolvers.

Colt, Officer's Model, .38 caliber revolver, S/Ns535472, 585683.

Colt Official Police Model revolver, cal. .32-20, having a barrel length of 5 inches, with factory engraving by Wilbur Glahn, S/N 554399.

Colt Official Police Model revolver, .38 Colt Special cal., having a barrel length of 6 inches, with factory engraving by Wilbur Glahn, S/N 554445.

Colt, Official Police Revolver, cal. .38, Silver Inlaid and Engraved by Wilbur A. Glahn, S/N 583469.

Colt, Oklahoma Territory Diamond Jubilee, .22.

Colt, Oregon Trail, .22 (Kansas Series-Trails).

Colt, Pacific Theater, .45 Pistol (World War II Series).

Colt, Pat Garrett, .22 and .45 (Lawman Series).

Colt, Pawnee Trail, .22 (Kansas Series-Trails).

Colt, Peacemaker Commemorative, .22 and .45 revolver.

Colt, Pocket Positive revolver, .32 cal.

Colt, Pocket Positive revolver, S/N 6164.

Colt, Police Positive .38 cal. revolvers, 2" barrels, marked "R.M.S. P.O. DEPT." or "U.S.P.O. DEPT."; S/Ns above 383000.

Colt, Police Positive revolver (1909); "St. L.P.D. #466" on butt; S/N 24466.

Colt, Pony Express Centennial, .22.

Colt, Pony Express, Russell, Majors and Waddell, Presentation model .45.

Colt, Python Model revolver, .357 cal., having a barrel length of 3 inches, with factory Type A engraving by Denise Thirion, in a presentation case with accessories, S/N T21895.

Colt, Python Revolver, cal. .357 Magnum, engraved and inlaid with the Crest of the United Arab Emirates.

Colt, Revolver, cal. .38, Police Positive, S/N 139212.

Colt, Rock Island Arsenal Centennial Single Shot, .22.

Colt, Santa Fe Trail, .22 (Kansas Series-Trails).

Colt model San Jacinto Special edition single action army revolver, .45 caliber, marked "THE BATTLE OF SAN JACINTO, APRIL 21, 1836" and "REMEMBER GOLIAD," 200 produced.

Colt, Second (2nd) Marne, .45 Pistol (World War I Series).

Colt, Shawnee Trail, .22 (Kansas Series-Trails).

Colt, Sheriffs model revolver, cal. .44 and .45.

Colt, Single Action Army (Bisley, Standard, and target variations), all original, mfd. from 1899 to 1946, S/N range from 182000 to 357869.

Colt, Single Action Army revolver, cal. .45, S/N 85163A, engraved and inlaid with a bust of President Abraham Lincoln.

Colt , Single Action Army (2nd Generation) revolvers, having S/Ns from 0001SA to 82000SA, all calibers, made between 1956 and 1976.

Colt, Single Action Revolvers, cal. .45, engraved & silver inlaid for presentation to Chuck Connors, S/Ns CC1 and CC2.

Colt, St. Augustine Quadricentennial, .22.

Colt, St. Louis Bicentennial, .22 and .45.

Colt Government model Texas Battleship Special Edition, .45 caliber pistols marked "BATTLESHIP EDITION - USS TEXAS," 500 produced.

Colt, Texas Ranger, .45.

Colt, Texas Sesquicentennial Standard and Premier model single action army, .45 cal.

Colt, the Liege Number 1 Colt Single Action Army Revolver, cal. .45, S/N Liege No. 1.

Colt, "The Right to Keep and Bear Arms" commemorative, .22 cal. Peacemaker Buntline, single action revolver having a 7-1/2" barrel with the inscription, "The Right to Keep and Bear Arms" inscribed on the barrel and a S/N range of G0001RB - G3000RB.

Colt, Theodore Roosevelt single action army .44-40 cal.

Colt, United States Bicentennial Commemorative, Python revolver, caliber .357.

Colt, United States Bicentennial Commemorative single action army revolver cal. .45.

Colt, West Virginia Centennial, .22 and .45.

Colt, Wichita, .22 (Kansas Series-Cow Town).

Colt, Wild Bill Hickok, .22 and .45 (Lawman Series).

Colt model Wisconsin State Patrol, 45th Anniversary, Special Edition Commemorative, 70 series, .45 government model pistols, consecutively numbered 1 through 126.

Colt, Woodman, cal. .22, semiautomatic target pistol, mfd. from 1915 to 1943, S/Ns 1 to 157000.

Colt, Woodsman, .22 caliber semiautomatic pistols, all models, all series, all S/Ns, (to include Match Target, Challenger, Huntsmen, and Targetsman), made prior to 1978.

Colt, Woodsman, First Model Match Target, .22 cal. semiautomatic pistols mfd. in or before 1944, and having S/Ns MT1 through MT15100.

Colt, Wyatt Earp, .22 and .45 (Lawman Series).

Colt, Wyatt Earp, Buntline Special, .45 (Lawman Series).

Colt, Wyoming Diamond Jubilee, .22

Colt XIT Special Edition Single Action Army revolver, .45 caliber, barrel chemically etched with a covered wagon scene and "XIT RANCH," and marked "1 of 500."

Colt, 150th Anniversary single action army buntline, .45 cal.

Czechoslovakian, CZ27, 7.65mm semiautomatic pistol with Nazi markings.

Coston Supply Co., Coston Line Throwing Gun, .45-70 cal. S/N 447.

Czechoslovakian, CZ38, pistol cal. .380ACP.

Czechoslovakian, CZ50 pistol, cal. 7.65mm.

Czechoslovakian, CZ52 pistol, cal. 7.62mm.

Czechoslovakian, model 1952 and 1952/57, 7.62 x 45mm and 7.62 x 39mm cal., semiautomatic rifles.

Czechoslovakian, VZ-54 sniper rifle, manufactured from 1954 through 1957, caliber 7.62 x 54R, all S/Ns with scope mount and 2.5 power telescope.

Czechoslovakian, VZ82/CZ82 all calibers, all serial numbers.

* ***Daisy***, Model V/L, .22 caliber caseless rifle, manufactured during 1968-1969.

Danish, M1910/1921 Bayard, pistol, cal. 9mm Bergmann-Bayard.

Davis Warner, Infallible, semiautomatic pistol, cal. .32.

Dreyse, semiautomatic pistols, all calibers.

Egyptian Raschid, semiautomatic rifle, cal. 7.62 x 39mm, original Egyptian military production.

Egyptian, Hakim (Ljungman) 7.92mm semiautomatic rifle as mfd. in Egypt.

Erma-Werke, Model EL 24, cal. .22, rifle, mfd. prior to 1946.

Esser-Barraft, English manufacture, slide action rifle, cal. .303.

Fabrique Nationale 1889-1989 Centenary High Power pistols, cal. 9mm.

Fabrique Nationale, Model 1906, .25 caliber semiautomatic pistol, all S/Ns.

Fabrique Nationale, model SAFN49 semiautomatic rifles, any caliber.

FN F.A.L. G and GL series, semiautomatic rifles, imported by Browning Arms Company, Arnold, MO from 1959 to 1963, with the following S/Ns: G Series: G492, G493, G494, G537-G540, G649-G657, G662-G673, G677-G693, G709-G748, G752-G816, G848-G1017, G1021, G1033, G1035, G1041, G1042, G1174-G1293, G1415-G1524, G1570-Gl784, G1800-Gl979, G1981-G1995, G2247-G2996, G3035-G3134. GL Series: GL749, GL835, GL1095-GL1098, GL1163,GL1164, GL1165, GL2004-GL2009, GL3135-GL3140.

Firepoint International, Ltd. Of England, 7.92x33 cal. S/Ns 08, 10, 11, 12, 14, 15, 16.

French Military Rifle Model 1949/56, in 7.62 x 51mm (NATO) cal. French, model 1949, cal. 7.5mm, semiauto. rifle (Fusil Mle. 1949 (MAS) 7.5mm).

French, model 1949/56 (Fusil Mle (MAS 7.5mm)) semiautomatic rifle.

A.H. Fox, Double barrel shotguns, all gauges, all grades, mfd. By Ansley H. Fox, Philadelphia, PA, and Savage Arms, Utica, NY, from approx. 1907 - 1947.

Geha and Rmo, shotguns made from Mauser rifles after World War I prior to 1946.

German military training rifles, cal. .22, single shot and repeaters, all manufacturers, in their original military configuration, marked "Kleinkaliber Wehersportsgewehr" (KKW), mfd. prior to 1946.

German sporting rifles, cal. .22, sporting rifles, single shot and repeaters, all manufacturers, in original configuration, marked "Deutsche Sportmodell" (DSM), prior to 1946.

German, model 1916 Grenatenwerfer original spigot type mortars.

German, P38 pistols, cal. 9mm parabellum mfd. prior to 1947.

Greener, Martini action, 14 gauge shotgun.

Gustloff, semiautomatic pistol in cal. 7.65mm mfd. by Gustloff Werke, Suhl, Germany.

Hammond or Grant Hammond, pistols, all models, variations or prototypes, made by Grant Hammond Corporation, New Haven, CT.

Hammond/Hi-Standard, semiautomatic pistols, in caliber .45.

Harrington and Richardson "Reising" Model 60 semiautomatic rifles, .45 ACP caliber, manufactured between 1944 and 1946.

Harrington and Richardson (H&R), Abilene Anniversary, .22 revolver.

Harrington and Richardson (H&R) Handy Gun, pistols with original rifled barrel, mfd. At Worcester, MA, all calibers, all barrel lengths, without shoulder stock.

Harrington and Richardson (H&R) Handy guns, mfd. at Worcester, MA, with shoulder stock, having an original smoothbore barrel 18 inches in length or greater, or original rifled barrel 16 inches in length or greater.

Harrington & Richardson Trapdoor Springfield carbine, .45-70 caliber, 100th Anniversary Little Big Horn Commemorative, manufactured between 1973-1981.

H&R, Centennial Officer's model Springfield rifle .45-70 Government.

H&R, Centennial Standard model Springfield rifle .45-70 Government.

H&R, model 999, revolver, cal. 22 Long rifle, barrel 6", 110th year commemorative, S/Ns from 001 to 999.

H&R, self loading semiautomatic pistol, caliber .32.

Hartford Arms and Equipment Company, single shot target pistol, caliber .22LR.

Hartford Arms and Equipment Company, repeating pistol, cal. .22LR.

Hartford Arms and Equipment Company, model 1928 pistol, cal. .22LR.

Hi-Standard, experimental electric free pistol, cal. .22 long rifle.

Hi-Standard, experimental electric free pistol, cal. .38 special.

Hi-Standard, experimental electric free pistol, cal. .38 special.

Hi-Standard, model P 38, semiautomatic pistol, cal. .38 SPL.

Hi-Standard, experimental model T-3 semiautomatic pistol, cal. 9mm Luger.

Hi-Standard, experimental ISU rapid fire semiautomatic pistol, caliber .22 short.

High Standard, Second Model Olympic pistol, cal. .22 short, mfd. between 1951 - 1953, S/Ns 330,000 – 439,999.

High Standard, Crusader Commemorative, Deluxe Pair, .44 Magnum and .45 Colt revolvers.

High Standard, model A pistol, caliber .22LR.

High Standard, model B pistol, caliber .22LR.

High Standard, model C pistol, caliber .22 Short.

High Standard, model D pistol, caliber .22LR.

High Standard, model E pistol, caliber .22LR.

High Standard, model H-A pistol, caliber .22LR.

High Standard, model H-B pistol, first model, caliber .22LR.

High Standard, model H-B pistol, second model, caliber .22LR.

High Standard, model H-D pistol, caliber .22LR.

High Standard, model H-E pistol, caliber .22LR.

High Standard, model USA-HD pistol, caliber .22LR.

High Standard, model HD-Military pistol, caliber .22LR.

High Standard, model G-380 pistol, caliber .380.

High Standard, model G-B pistol, caliber .22LR.

High Standard, model G-D pistol, caliber .22LR.

High Standard, model G-E pistol, caliber .22LR.

High Standard, model G-O (First model Olympic) pistol, caliber .22 Short.

High Standard, Supermatic Trophy model 107, .22 pistol Olympic Commemorative model.

High Standard, 1980 Olympic Commemorative, .22 caliber semiautomatic pistols, S/Ns USA1 - USA1000.

Holland and Holland, Royal Double Barrel Shotgun, .410 Gauge, S/N 36789.

Hopkins and Allen, model 1901, "FOREHAND," caliber .32 S&W long.

Hopkins and Allen, Revolver, .32 cal., S/N G 9545.

Hungarian Model 48 (Mosin Nagant M44 type) carbine, caliber 7.62 x 54R, manufactured in Hungary, and identified by the manufacturer code 02 on the chamber area and marked with the date of manufacture in the 1950's or earlier.

India rifle, cal. 7.62 2A, all variations, originally mfd. At Ishapore Arsenal, India prior to 1965.

Italian, Brixia, M1906, pistol, cal. 9mm Glisenti.

Italian, Glisenti, M1910, pistol, cal. 9mm Glisenti.

* ***Ithaca***, Bicentennial Model 37, pump action shotguns, S/Ns USA0001 to USA1976.

Ithaca, double barrel shotguns actually mfd. in NY by the Ithaca Gun Co. Ithaca, NY. All gauges and all models, having barrels at least 18" in length and an overall length of at least 26", mfd. before 1950.

Ithaca Gun Co., single barrel trap guns, break open all gauges, all models actually mfd. at Ithaca, NY, before 1950.

Ithaca, St. Louis Bicentennial, model 49, .22 rifle.

Iver Johnson Arms, Pistol, cal. .380, U.S. Border Patrol 60th Anniversary commemorative, S/Ns USBP 0001 to USBP 5000.

Iver Johnson Arms, model M 1 Carbine, cal. .30, Korean War commemorative, S/Ns KW0001 to KW2500.

Iver Johnson Arms, model M 1 Carbine, cal. .30, Airborne commemorative, S/Ns KW0001 – KW2500.

Jieffeco, pistol, Belgian manufacture, caliber 7.65mm.

Jieffeco, semiautomatic pistol, cal. .25 ACP, marked "Davis Warner Arms Corp., N.Y."

Kimball, pistols, all models, all calibers.

Kolibri, pistols, cals. 2.7mm and 3mm Kolibri.

L. C. Smith, Shotguns mfd. by Hunter Arms Co. and Marlin Firearms Co. from 1899 to 1971.

Langenhan, semiautomatic pistols, all calibers.

Lahti, L-35 pistol, Finnish manufacture, caliber 9mm parabellum.

Lahti Swedish Model M40 pistols, cal. 9mm, all variations, mfd. prior to 1968.

Lee Enfield, No. 1 Mk III bolt action rifle, cal. .303, mfd. in Ishapore, India between 1946 and 1960. Original military configuration only.

Lee Enfield Rifle, caliber 7.62 2A and 2A1 "India" all variations, originally manufactured at Ishapore Arsenal, India, through 1973.

Lefever, shotguns made from 1899 to 1942.

Luger, Model 1902 Cartridge Counter, Mauser commercial, semiautomatic pistol, cal. 9mm, mfd. 1982.

Luger, pistol, all models and variations mfd. prior to 1946.

Luger, Mauser commercial manufacture, semiautomatic pistol, 70 Jahre, Parabellum-Pistole, Kelsoreich Russiand, commemorative, cal. 9mm.

Luger, Mauser commercial manufacture, semiautomatic pistol, 76 Jahre, Parabellum-Pistole, 1900-1975, commemorative, cal. 7.65mm.

Luger, Mauser commercial manufacture, semiautomatic pistol, 75 Jahre, Parabellum-Pistole, Konigreich Bulgarian, commemorative, caliber 7.65mm.

Luger, Mauser Parabellum, semiautomatic pistol, 7.65mm or 9mm Luger, 4 and 6" barrel, Swiss pattern with grip safety and the American Eagle stamped on the receiver; made from 1970 to 1978.

MAB, model R pistol, caliber 9mm parabellum.

Makarov, pistol, Russian and East German, caliber 9mm Makarov.

Mannlicher, pistol, M1900, M1901, M1903 and M1905, caliber 7.63mm Mannlicher.

Marlin, Model 336 TS carbine, cal. 30-30, Powell Wyoming 75th anniversary commemorative, having PW S/N prefix.

Marlin, 90th Anniversary, model 39-A, .22 rifle.

Marlin, 90th Anniversary, model 39-A, .22 carbine.

Mauser, semiautomatic pistols mfd. prior to 1946, any caliber.

Mauser, Congolese model 1950 rifles marked FP 1952 on the receiver, caliber .30/06.

Mauser Luger, S/N 11.010034, 9mm, special engraving and ivory grips.

Mauser Luger, S/N RG 900/1001, 9mm, special engraving and walnut grips.

Mauser, model 1935 rifle 7 x 57mm cal. with Chilean Police Markings.

Mauser, P 38, pistols caliber 9mm, marked SVW46.

Mauser, rifles, bolt action and semiautomatic any caliber, commercially produced by Waffenfabrik Mauser, Oberndoff, Germany, prior to 1945.

MBA Gyrojet Carbine, S/N B5057.

MBA Gyrojet semiautomatic pistols, cal. 12mm or smaller, all models.

Menz, Liliput, German manufacture caliber 4.25mm.

Menz, PB III, in cal. 7.65mm, mfd. by August Menz, Suhl, Germany.

Menz, PB IIIA, in cal. 7.65mm, mfd. by August Menz, Suhl, Germany.

Menz, PB IV, in cal. 7.65mm, mfd. by August Menz, Suhl, Germany.

Menz, PB IVa, in cal. 7.65mm, mfd. by August Menz, Suhl, Germany.

Menz, Special, in cal. 7.65mm, mfd. by August Menz, Suhl, Germany.

Mexican, Obregon, pistol, caliber .45 ACP.

Mexican Model 1954 bolt action Mauser rifles and carbines, caliber .30-06 (original military configuration only).

Mossberg, Model 40, cal. .22 tubular fed, bolt action rifles mfd. from 1933-1935.

Mossberg, Model 42TR Targo, cal. .22 smoothbore, bolt action rifles, mfd. from 1940-1942.

Mossberg, Model 479RR "Roy Rogers" limited edition, cal. .30-30 lever action rifles, total number mfd. in 1983 only.

Mossberg, Model 25, .22 caliber bolt action rifles.

Mugica, model 120, pistol, caliber 9mm parabellum.

Navy Arms, Oklahoma Diamond Jubilee Commemorative, Yellow Boy Carbine.

Norinco (Chinese) AK47S, 5.56x45mm caliber, S/N 403876.

Norinco (Chinese) AK47S84S-1, 5.5 6x 45mm caliber, S/N 303052.

Norinco (Chinese) AK47S, 7.62 x 39mm caliber, S/N 1620127.

North Korean Type 1964, pistol, caliber 7.62mm Tokarev.

North Korean, Type 68, 7.62 x 25mm caliber semiautomatic pistols.

O.F. Mossberg Model 472SBAS "American Indian Commemorative" .30-30 and .35 Remington caliber lever action rifles, having Indian scenes etched on receiver, manufactured in 1974 only.

Ortgies, semiautomatic, caliber .25, with S/N 10073.

Ortgies, semiautomatic, caliber .32, with S/N 126314. OWA, semiautomatic pistol, caliber .25.

PAF, "Junior" semiautomatic pistol, caliber .25, mfd. by the Pretoria Arms Factory Ltd. of South Africa.

PAF, pistol, marked "BRF," caliber .25, mfd. by the Pretoria Arms Factory Ltd. of South Africa.

Parker-Hale, Model T-4, cal. 7.62mm, bolt action target rifles, mfd. prior to 1975.

Parker, shotguns, all grades, all gauges, produced by Parker Brothers, Meridan, CT, and Remington Arms, Ilion, NY, from 1899 through 1945.

Pedersoli, 120th Anniversary of the Remington Creedmore, .45/70 caliber, single shot rolling block rifle, having S/Ns between CR001 and CR300.

Pedersoli, 125th Anniversary of the Springfield, Model 1873 Trapdoor rifle, .45/70 caliber, having S/Ns between 125th- 001 through 125th-125.

Pedersoli, Sharps Creedmoor, single shot rifles, caliber .45-70, S/Ns SCR001 through SCR300.

* ***Pedersoli***, Springfield Officer's Model trapdoor rifle, .45-70 caliber, having S/Ns 2NFM001 through 2NFM250.

Phoenix, (U.S.A.), pistol, caliber .25 ACP.Polish Mosin Nagant M44 type carbines, caliber 7.62 x 54R, manufactured in Poland, identified by the manufacturer code 11" in an oval on the chamber area, and marked with the actual date of manufacture during the 1950s or earlier.

Poly Tech (Chinese) AK 47S (386), 7.62 x 39mm caliber, S/N P47-11545.

James Purdey, Over & Under shotgun, 12 gauge, S/N 26819, engraved and gold inlaid.

Reising, .22 caliber, semiautomatic pistol.

Remington, No. 1, Mid Range Rolling Block target rifle reproduction, caliber .45-70, S/Ns beginnning with "RB97."

Remington, Model 31, pump action shotguns, 12, 16, and 20 gauge, mfd. 1931 - 1950.

Remington Rolling Block firearms, all models mfd. from 1899 - 1935.

Remington, over/under Derringer, caliber .41 rim fire, Remington Arms Company, Ilion, NY, made between 1898 and 1935.

Remington, Canadian Territorial Centennial, model 742, rifle.

Remington, model 12, rifle, cal. .22 short, long rifle, and .22 Remington Special mfd. by Remington Arms, Union Metallic Cartridge Co., Remington Works, Ilion, NY, from 1909 to 1936.

Remington, model 30 rifles.

Remington, model 720 rifles.

Remington, model 51, semiautomatic pistol, cals. .32 ACP or .380 ACP.

Remington, Montana Territorial Centennial, model 600, rifle.

Remington, 150th Anniversary model Nylon 66 semiautomatic rifle, caliber .22LR.

Remington, 150th Anniversary model 1100SA semiautomatic shotgun, caliber 12 gauge.

Remington, 150th Anniversary model 552A semiautomatic rifle, caliber. 22LR.

Remington, 150th Anniversary model 572A slide action rifle, caliber .22LR.

Remington, 150th Anniversary model 742ADL semiautomatic rifle caliber .30/06.

Remington, 150th Anniversary model 760ADL slide action rifle caliber .30/06.

Remington, 150th Anniversary model 870SA slide action shotgun, caliber 12 gauge.

Rheinmetal, semiautomatic pistols, caliber .32.

Rhode Island Arms Co., Morrone Model 46, shotgun.

* ***Romanian Model 56 semiautomatic carbine (SKS)***, caliber 7.62 x 39mm in original configuration as manufactured at Uzina Mechanica Cugir, Romania, from 1956 through 1962, having original Romanian S/Ns consisting of two letters followed by up to four digits. The right side of the receiver is also marked with the year of production and the manufacturer's trademark consisting of an unfletched arrow within a triangle.

Roth Steyr, 1907, semiautomatic pistol, caliber 8mm.

Romanian AK 47S, 5.45 x 45mm caliber , S/N 3-040053-97.

Ruger, Blackhawk .44 with 6-1/2" barrel, revolver with S/Ns 1 to 29860.

Ruger, Blackhawk .44 with 7-1/2" barrel, revolver with S/Ns 17000 to 29860.

Ruger, Blackhawk .44 with 10" barrel, revolver with S/Ns 18000 to 29860.

Ruger, Blackhawk .357 with 4-5/8" barrel, revolver with S/Ns 1 to 42689.

Ruger, Blackhawk .357 with 6-1/2" barrel, revolver with S/Ns 20000 to 42689.

Ruger, Blackhawk .357 and 9mm stainless steel revolver with S/Ns 32-56000 - 32-59000.

Ruger, Blackhawk .357 magnum with 10" barrel, revolver with S/Ns 20000 - 38000.

Ruger, Canadian Centennial, Matched No. 1 Rifle Sets, Special Deluxe.

Ruger, Canadian Centennial, Matched No. 2 Rifle Sets.

Ruger, Canadian Centennial, Matched No. 3 Rifle Sets.

Ruger, Canadian Centennial, model 10/22, carbine.

Ruger, I0/22 Canadian Centennial, carbine with S/Ns CI to C4500.

Ruger, Falling Block Long Range Creedmore rifle, cal. .45 (Sharps), S/N 130-06888, The Amber Silver Jubilee.

Ruger, flattop, "Blackhawk" revolvers, cals. .44 Magnum and .357 magnum, all barrel lengths, made from 1955 through 1962.

Ruger, flattop, single-six, .22 cal. revolvers with flat side loading gate, all barrel lengths, made from 1953 through 1956.

Ruger, Hawkeye, pistol with S/Ns 1 to 3296.

Ruger, Lightweight Single Six, Revolver with S/Ns 200000 to 212630.

Ruger, Mark I "U.S." stamped medallion, pistol with S/Ns 76000 - 79000.

Ruger, Single Six, engraved revolver with S/Ns 5100 - 75000.

Ruger, Standard Auto with red eagle, pistol with S/Ns 1 - 25000.

Ruger, Super Black Hawk, revolvers having a barrel length of 6½ inches with S/Ns 24000 - 26000.

Ruger, Super Single Six stainless with 4" barrel, revolver with S/Ns 62-07500 - 64-650000.

Ruger, Super Single Six stainless with 9" barrel, revolver with S/Ns 62-07500 - 63-40000.

Ruger, Super Single Six chrome with 4-5/8" barrel, revolver with S/Ns 504000 - 505000.

Ruger, "21 Club" No. 1, rifle with random S/Ns.

Ruger, 44 Deerstalker, carbine with S/Ns 1 to 5000.

Ruger, S47 Code, Model Super Blackhawk, 7 ½ inch barrel, .44 magnum revolvers, in S/N range 196 to 3111, with long grip frame, micro rear sight, and in mahogany wood case, approximately 500 manufactured.

Rumanian Mosin Nagant 1944 type carbines, caliber 7.62 x 54R, manufactured in Romania, and manufactured from 1952 to 1956.

Russian (U.S.S.R.), Nagant revolver, model 1895, cal. 7.62 Nagant and .22 cal. all variations, mfd. by the Tula Arsenal, Tula, Russia, after 1898.

Russian (U.S.S.R.), Tokarev, model TT, 1930, pistol, cal. 7.62, mfd. at the Tula Arsenal, Tula, U.S.S.R., from 1939 through 1956.

Russian (U.S.S.R.), Tokarev, model TT, 1933, pistol, cal. 7.62, mfd. at the Tula Arsenal, Tula, U.S.S.R., from 1933 through 1956.

Russian (U.S.S.R.) Tokarev, model TT R-3, .22 cal., pistol.

Russian (U.S.S.R.) Tokarev, model TT R-4, .22 cal., pistol.

Russian (U.S.S.R.), Tula Korovin, Tk, .25 ACP cal., semiautomatic pistol.

Russian (U.S.S.R.), model 1891, Mosin-Nagant rifles, cal. 7.62 x 54R and .22 cal., all models and all variations, mfd. after 1898 (i.e., M1891/30, M1910, M1938, and M1944).

Russian (U.S.S.R.), Tokarev, semiautomatic rifle, model 1938 (SVT38), cal. 7.62 x 54R, of Soviet manufacture.

Russian (U.S.S.R.), Tokarev, semiautomatic rifle, model 1940 (SVT40), cal. 7.62 x 54R, of Soviet manufacture.

Russian (U.S.S.R.), Tokarev, semiautomatic carbine, model 1932 (nonstandard), cal. 7.62 x 54R, of Soviet manufacture.

Russian (U.S.S.R.), Tokarev, semiautomatic carbine, model 1940 (SVT40), cal. 7.62 x 54R, of Soviet manufacture.

Russian (U.S.S.R.), Simonov, semiautomatic rifle, model SKS, cal. 7.62 x 39, of Soviet manufacture.

Russian (U.S.S.R.), Dragunov, semiautomatic rifle, model SVD, cal. 7.62 x 54R, of Soviet manufacture, Soviet military issue only.

* ***Sako***, Anniversary Model, 7mm Remington magnum caliber, bolt action rifle.

J. P. Sauer & Sohn pistols, mfd. prior to 1946.

Sauer, 38(h), pistol, cal. 7.65mm marked w/Third Reich police acceptance stamps of Eagle C, F, K, or L. Savage Arms, semiautomatic pistols, cal. .45 ACP, all models.

Savage Arms, model 99, lever action, centerfire rifles, mfd. in Utica, NY prior to World War II with S/Ns below 450000.

Savage, Prototype pistols, cal. .25, .32 and .38 made between 1907 and 1927.

Savage model 1907 pistol, caliber .32 and .380.

Savage model 1915 pistol, caliber .32 and .380.

Savage model 1917 pistol, caliber .32 and .380.

Schwarzlose, pocket model 1908 in 7.65mm, pistol mfd. by A.W. Schwarzlose, G.m.b.h., Berlin, Germany, and those assembled or made by Warner Arms.

Smith and Wesson, Model 624 revolver, First Issue, cal. .44 Target, engraved year "1985" over the issue number (1-25) on the right sideplate.

Smith & Wesson Collector's Association, 25th Anniversary Commemorative revolver 1970-1995, Model 29, .44 Magnum caliber, S/Ns SWC 0001 through SWC 0184.

Smith & Wesson, 125th anniversary Commemorative, model 25, revolver, cal. .45, marked "Smith & Wesson 125th Anniversary" and mfd. in 1977.

Smith & Wesson, 150th anniversary Texas Ranger Commemorative model 19 revolver.

Smith & Wesson, 1st model, Ladysmith revolver, cal. .22 rimfire long.

Smith & Wesson, .22/32 Kit Gun, cal. .22LR, S/Ns 525670 - 534636 (no letter).

Smith & Wesson, 2nd model, Ladysmith revolver, cal. .22 rimfire long.

Smith & Wesson, 2nd model, single shot pistol, cals. .22 rimfire, .32 S&W and .38 S&W.

Smith & Wesson, .32 Double Action Top Break, cal. .32 S&W, S/Ns 209302 and higher.

Smith & Wesson, .32 Safety Hammerless Top Break (New Departure), cal. .32 S&W, S/Ns 91401 and higher.

Smith & Wesson, .357 Magnum Hand Ejector, cal. .357 Magnum, S/Ns 45768 to 60000 (no letter).

Smith & Wesson, .38 Double Action Top Break Perfected model, cal. .38 S&W.

Smith & Wesson, .38 Double Action Top Break, cal. .38 S&W, S/Ns 382023 and higher.

Smith & Wesson, .38 Hand Ejector Military and Police, cal. .38, S/Ns 1 to 241703 (no letter).

Smith & Wesson, .38 Safety Hammerless Top Break (New Departure), cal. .38 S&W, S/Ns 19901 and higher.

Smith & Wesson, .38/44 Outdoorsman & Heavy Duty, cal. .38, S/Ns 36500-62023 (no letter).

Smith & Wesson, 3rd model, Ladysmith revolver, cal. .22 rimfire long.

Smith & Wesson, 3rd model, single shot pistol, cals. .22 rimfire, .32 S&W and .38 S&W.

Smith & Wesson, 4 screw side plate revolvers, old style N-frame series, with no model designation stamped in the yoke cut, in cal. .44 magnum, all barrel lengths, falling within the S130000-Sl60350 block of S/Ns, of which a total of 6,500 units were produced from 1956 to 1958.

Smith & Wesson, .44 Hand Ejector, all cal., S/Ns 1-62488 (no letter).

Smith & Wesson, .455 Mark II Hand Ejector, caliber .455.

Smith & Wesson, California Highway Patrol Commemorative model 19 revolver, cal. .357.

Smith & Wesson, City of Los Angeles 200th Anniversary Commemorative model 19 revolver, cal. .357.

Smith & Wesson, K-22 Hand Ejector, cal. .22 LR, S/Ns 632132-696952 (no letter).

Smith & Wesson, K-32 Hand Ejector (K-32 Masterpiece), cal. .32 S&W Long, S/Ns 653388 to 682207 (no letter).

Smith & Wesson, Mercox Dart Gun, cal. .22 rimfire, blank.

Smith & Wesson, Model 16 (K-32 Masterpiece), cal. .32 S&W Long, "K" S/N series.

Smith & Wesson, model 21, .44 Special caliber, also known as the".44 Hand Ejector Fourth Model" and the "1950 Model Military," having S/Ns S75,000 - S263,000.

Smith & Wesson, Model .22/32 Hand Ejector (Bekeart model), cal. .22LR, S/Ns 138220 to 534636 (no letter).

Smith & Wesson, Model 29 "Elmer Keith Commemorative" .44 magnum revolvers, S/N EMK1 – EMK2500.

Smith & Wesson, Model 39, Connecticut State Police 75th Anniversary 1903-1978, pistols, S/Ns CSP001 – CSP704.

Smith & Wesson, Model 39, steel frame pistol, cal. 9mm parabellum.

Smith & Wesson, Model 39-1 (52-A), pistol, cal. 9mm parabellum.

Smith & Wesson, Model 53, Remington Jet Center Fire Magnum, cal. .22.

Smith & Wesson, Model 41-1 .22 short cal. semiautomatic pistols.

Smith & Wesson, Model 42 Centennial Airweight .38 Special 5-shot revolvers, with aluminum alloy frames and cylinders.

Smith & Wesson, Model 45 Military & Police .22LR cal. revolvers.

Smith & Wesson, Model 46 .22LR caliber semiautomatic pistols.

Smith & Wesson, Model 56 U.S. Air Force contract .38 Special 6-shot revolvers, S/N K500001 through K515001.

* ***Smith & Wesson Model 66 Bureau of Alcohol***, Tobacco & Firearms 1933 – 1983 50th Anniversary Commemorative .357 magnum caliber revolvers, having a "BATF" prefix serial number and miniature replica of an agent's badge engraved into the frame.

Smith & Wesson Model 66 Distinguished Combat Magnum, caliber .357 magnum revolver, marked with the Texas Sheriff's Association badge and "TEXAS LAWMAN" on the right side of the frame, commemorating 150 years of law enforcement in Texas 1836-1986.

Smith & Wesson model 66, Dallas Police Department Commemorative Edition 1881-1981.

Smith & Wesson, Model 66, "Naval Investigative Service Commemorative" .357 6-shot revolvers.

Smith & Wesson, Model 147-A, 9mm 14-shot semiautomatic pistols.

Smith & Wesson, Model 544, "Texas Wagon Train Commemorative" .44/40 cal. 6-shot revolvers, S/N TWT001 through TWT7800.

Smith & Wesson, .45 hand ejector model of 1950 Military, .45 caliber, having S/Ns between S76000 and S263000.

Smith & Wesson, Model 1917 revolver, cal. .45 ACP, produced for Brazil.

Smith & Wesson, Model Straight Line, single shot pistol, cal. .22 rimfire long rifle.

Smith & Wesson, pistol, caliber .32 ACP.

Smith & Wesson, pistol, caliber .35, all variations.

Smith & Wesson Registered Model 27 revolvers, cal. .357-magnum, 50 Yr. Commemorative, 5" barrel, S/Ns REG0001 through REG2500, inclusive.

Smith & Wesson U.S. Air Force contract M13 Aircrewman .38 Special 5-shot J frame and 6-shot K frame revolvers.

Smith & Wesson, U.S. Border Patrol 50th Anniversary Commemorative, model 66, stainless steel, cal. .357 Magnum, revolvers.

Sosso, pistols, mfd. by Guilio Sosso, Turin, Italy, or Fabrica Nationale D'Armi, Brescia, Italy, cal. 9mm.

Springfield Armory, Inc., Korean War Commemorative .30 cal., MI Garand Rifle S/Ns from KW0001 to KW1000.

Standard Arms Co., rifle/shotgun combination, U.S., model "Camp," slide action cal. .50.

Standard Arms Co., rifle model G, slide action or gas operated, any caliber.

Standard Arms Co., rifle model M, slide action caliber .25-.35, .30 Rem. and .35 Rem.

* ***Stevens***, Models 425, 430, 435, and 440 High-Power Repeating Rifles in calibers .25 Remington, .30 Remington, .32 Remington, and .35 Remington.

Stevens, Model 77E, 12 gauge, military riot type shotguns, properly marked and identified as mfd. for the U.S. Military, from 1963 to 1969, in original configuration.

Steyr, model 1909, .25 ACP cal. semiautomatic pistol.

Steyr-Hahn, M1912, pistol, cal. 9mm Steyr.

Steyr-Hahn, M1912, pistol, cal. 9mm parabellum marked with Third Reich police acceptance stamps of Eagle C, F, K, or L.

Stock, semiautomatic pistols, all cals. mfd. by Franz Stock.

Swiss Model 1931/55 rifles, cal. 7.5 mm, S/Ns 1001 to 5150.

Swiss Schmidt Rubin, Model 1911, rifle made into a harpoon gun, caliber 12mm.

Swiss self loading rifle, test 1947, cal. 7.5mm, all variations.

Tauler, model military and police pistol.

Thompson/Center 25th Anniversary Contender, cal. .22LR pistol, 10 inch barrel, S/Ns 25 001-25 536.

Thompson Center Contender Pistol, cal. .30 Herrett, Steve Herrett Commemorative, S/Ns SH-001 to SH-500.

Thompson Center Contender Pistol, cal. 7mm TCU, IHMSA 10th anniversary commemorative, S/Ns IHMSA 10-001 to IHMSA 10-200.

Tippman Arms Company Models 1919 A-4, 1917, and .50 HB ½ scale, .22 caliber semi-automatic firearms, manufactured in Fort Wayne, Indiana, from 1986-1987.

Tokagypt 58, pistol, caliber 9mm parabellum.

Trejo, semiautomatic pistols, cal. .22, .32, and .380. mfd. in Mexico, circa 1952 to 1972.

* ***Uberti***, 125th Anniversary of the Winchester, Model 1873 lever action rifle, .44/40 caliber, having S/Ns between A125th001 through A125th125.

Uberti Model 1866 lever action rifles, "An Engraver's Tribute to Gustave Young," .44/40 caliber,S/Ns GY001 through GY300.

Uberti model 1866 L.D. Nimschke, lever action rifles, caliber .44-40, S/Ns LDN001 through LDN300.

Uberti, Single action revolver, cal. .45, General George S. Patton Commemorative, S/Ns P0001 to P2500.

United States Patent Fire Arms Manufacturing Company, Artillery Model single action revolver, 100th anniversary of The Charge Up San Juan Hill, .45 caliber, with a 5 ½ - inch barrel and having S/Ns from NFM001 through NFM500 U.S, model 1911-A-1, .45 cal. pistol, mfd. by Union Switch and Signal Company, prototype model, with S/Ns US&S Exp. 1 to US&S Exp. 100.

U.S., model 1911-A1, semiautomatic, pistol, cal. .45, mfd. by the Singer Manufacturing Company in 1942, S/N range from S800001 to S800500.

U.S., model 1911-A1, semiautomatic pistol, cal. .45, mfd. by Remington Rand, bearing S/N prefix of ERRS.

U.S., model 1911-A1 semiautomatic pistol, cal. .45, produced as original factory cut-a-ways.

U.S., Rifle, cal. .30 M1, original military issue only, produced prior to 1956.

U.S. Rifle, caliber .30, M1, original issue only, produced prior to 1958.

U.S., Rifle, cal. .30, MC-1952, equipped with telescopic sight mount MC, telescopic sight MC1, marked U.S.M.C. or Kollmorgan.

U.S. Repeating Arms, Wyoming Centennial, Winchester Commemorative Model 94 Carbines, cal. .30-30, S/Ns WYC001 through WYC500.

UZI, Model A, semiautomatic carbine, cal. 9mm, having a satin nickel finish applied at the factory, S/Ns SA 0001 to SA 0100.

Walther, bolt action and semiautomatic rifles, all cals., mfd. prior to 1946.

Walther, model PP and PPK semiautomatic pistols, in all cals., mfd. in France and marked "MANURHIN".

Walther, Model PP pistol, 50 Jahre 1929-1959 Commemorative, caliber .22 and .380.

Walther, Model TP and TPH pistols, cal. .22 and .25 ACP, original German manufacture only.

Walther, Olympic bolt action single shot match rifle, in cal. .22 made by Waffenfabrik Walther, Zella-Mehlis (thur.) prior to World War II.

Walther, pistols, mfd. at Zel1a-Mehlis prior to 1946, all models, any caliber.

Walther, rifles, model 182, cal. .22 made by Waffenfabrik Walther, Zelia-Mehlis (thur.) prior to World War II.

Watson Brothers, Lee-Speed type, custom sporting rifle, cal. .303, S/N 7738.

Webley and Scott, model 1910 and 1913 high velocity pistols, cal. .38 ACP.

Webley and Scott, M1913, Navy or Commercial, self loading pistol, cal. .455.

Webley-Fosbury, semiautomatic revolvers, all cals., all models.

Webley, model 1909, pistol, cal. 9mm Browning Long.

Whitney, "Wolverine" and "Lighting" .22 cal. automatic pistols as mfd. by Whitney Firearms Company, Hartford, CT between 1955 - 1962.

Winchester, Model 1894, Florida Sesquicentennial carbine, cal. .30-30, S/Ns FL001-FL500.

Winchester, Apache Commemorative carbine, commemorative edition of model 1894 Winchester with S/N prefix of A.

Winchester, Comanche Commemorative carbine, commemorative edition of model 1894 Winchester with S/N prefix of CC.

Winchester, "Ducks Unlimited" shotgun, model 12, bearing S/Ns DU-001 through DU-800 (Commemorative).

Winchester, Kentucky Bicentennial Model 94 carbines, cal. .30-30, S/N range KY001-KY500.

Winchester, "Matched Set of 1000," a cased pair consisting of a Winchester model 94 rifle, cal. .30-30 and a Winchester model 9422 rifle, cal. .22.

Winchester, Model 12, pump action shotguns, mfd. from 1912 through 1963, S/Ns 1 through 1962017.

Winchester, Model 12, Shotgun, 12 gauge, prototype, for Ducks Unlimited Commemorative, S/N Y2002214.

* **Winchester**, Model 12 Y, pump action shotguns, all variations, manufactured between 1972 and 1979, S/Ns Y2000100 through Y2026399.

Winchester, Model 21, double barrel shotguns, all gauges, all grades, mfd. by Winchester and U.S. Repeating Arms.

Winchester, Model 21, Grand American Double Barrel Shotgun, cal. 20 and 28 gauge, S/N 32984, Engraved Custom Built by Winchester for Philip S. Rane.

Winchester, Model 37, single barrel shotguns, all gauges, manufactured between 1936 and 1963.

Winchester, Model 42, .410 gauge shotguns.

Winchester, Model 52, rifle, bearing S/Ns 1 to 6500.

Winchester, Model 53, all original, mfd. from 1924 to 1947 with 16" or longer barrel, and 26" or longer overall length.

Winchester, Model 54 rifles.

Winchester, Model 54, rifle, speed lock variation, cal. .270.

Winchester, Model 55, .22 caliber, single shot rifle.

Winchester, Model 61, cal. .22 rimfire, slide action repeater, hammerless.

Winchester, Model 62, cal. .22 rimfire, slide action repeater.

Winchester, Model 63, self loading rifles, cal. .22 rimfire.

Winchester, Model 64 and 65, lever action rifles.

* **Winchester**, Model 70, .300 Winchester Magnum, 50th Anniversary bolt action rifle, S/Ns 50 ANV 1 through 50 ANV 500.

Winchester, Model 70, bolt action rifle, all cals., mfd. in or before 1963 having S/Ns less than 581472.

Winchester, Model 70, rifle, cal. .308 rifle, 19" barrel and Mannlicher type stock, made from 1968 to 1971.

Winchester, Model 70, rifles, .308, .270 Winchester, and 30-06 cal., 19" barrel and Mannlicher type stock, made from 1968 to 1971.

Winchester, Model 70, Ultra Match Target Special Grade rifle, cal. .308.

* **Winchester**, Model 70, XTR Featherweight Ultra Grade, .270 caliber, bolt action rifle, 1 of 1,000.

Winchester, Model 71, all original, mfd. from 1936 to 1958 with 16" or longer barrel and 26" or longer overall length.

Winchester, Model 85, (single shot rifle), all original, mfd. from 1899 to 1920, with 16" or longer barrel and 26" or longer overall length.

Winchester, Model 86, all original, mfd. from 1899 to 1935, with 16" or longer barrel and 26" or longer overall length.

Winchester, Model 88, carbine, cal. .243, .284, .308, or .358 mfd. by Winchester Western Division, Olin Corporation, New Haven, CT.

Winchester, Model 88 rifles, all calibers.

Winchester, Model 92, all original, mfd. from 1899 to 1947, with 16" or longer barrel and 26" or longer overall length.

Winchester, Model 94, Alaskan Purchase Centennial, carbine.

Winchester, Model 94, American Bald Eagle Commemorative Carbine.

Winchester, Model 94, Arapaho Commemorative carbines, caliber .30-30, S/Ns ARAPA001 – ARAPA500.

Winchester, Model 94, Bat Masterson commemorative.

Winchester, Model 94, Bicentennial 76, carbine.

Winchester, Model 94, Buffalo Bill, carbine.

Winchester, Model 94, Buffalo Bill, rifle.

Winchester, Model 94, C.M. Russell, Great Western Artist Commemorative Carbine.

Winchester, Model 94, cal. .30-30, Antlered Game Commemorative, carbine.

Winchester, Model 94, cal. .30-30, Legendary Lawman Commemorative, carbine.

Winchester, Model 94, Calgary Stampede Commemorative, carbine, cal. .32 Winchester Special.

Winchester, Model 94, Canadian 1967, Centennial carbine.

Winchester, Model 94, Canadian 1967, Centennial rifle.

Winchester, Model 94, carbine, Canadian Pacific Centennial, cal. .32 Winchester Special.

Winchester, Model 94, carbine, Oklahoma Diamond Jubilee Commemorative.

Winchester, Model 94, carbines, Chevrolet Outdoorsman sets, .30-30 cal., having S/Ns between 5130000 and 5466000.

Winchester, Model 94, "Chief Crazy Horse," commemorative lever action rifle, cal. .38-55, mfd. by U.S. Repeating Arms Co., New Haven, CT.

Winchester, Model 94, Colt Commemorative Set, Winchester Signature model "Oliver F. Winchester" carbine, cal. 44-40, Lever Action, as mfd. by U.S. Repeating Arms Co., New Haven, CT.

Winchester, Model 94, Cowboy Commemorative, carbine.

Winchester, Model 94 rifle, Custom Limited Edition Centennial, .30 WCF cal., S/Ns CNTL 01 through CNTL 94.

Winchester, Model 94, Frederick Remington, Great Western Artist Commemorative Carbine.

Winchester, Model 94, Illinois Sesquicentennial, carbine.

Winchester, Model 94, in cal. .38/55, 1980, Alberta Diamond Jubilee Commemorative, carbine.

Winchester, Model 94, John Wayne Commemorative (Canadian Issue), carbine, cal. .32-40.

Winchester, Model 94, John Wayne commemorative, cal. .32-40, carbine.

Winchester, Model 94, Klondike Gold Rush Commemorative carbine.

Winchester, Model 94, Legendary Frontiersman rifle, cal. .38-55.

Winchester, Model 94, "Limited Edition I."

Winchester, Model 94, "Limited Edition II" rifle, cal. .30-30.

Winchester, Model 94, Limited Edition, carbine, cal. .30-30, S/Ns 77L1 - 77L1500.

Winchester, Model 94, Limited Edition Centennial, .30 WCF rifles, S/Ns CN10,001 - CN10,250, mfd. by the USRAC Custom Gun Shop for the Winchester Arms Collectors Association, having a replica Lyman No. 2 tang sight and with the WACA medallion placed in the buttstock.

Winchester, Model 94, Little Big Horn Centennial, carbine.

Winchester, Model 94, Lone Star Commemorative, carbine.

Winchester, Model 94, Lone Star Commemorative, rifle, .30-30.

Winchester, Model 94, model NRA Centennial, carbine.

Winchester, Model 94, Mounted Police, carbine.

Winchester, Model 94, Nebraska Centennial, carbine.

Winchester, Model 94, NRA Centennial rifle, .30-30.

Winchester, Model 94, One of One Thousand European Rifle commemorative.

Winchester, Model 94, Ontario, Canada Conservation Office, 100th Anniversary Commemorative carbines, caliber 30-30.

Winchester, Model 94, rifles and carbines mfd. prior to January 2, 1964, and having a S/N of less than 2,700,000, provided their barrel length is at least 16" and their overall length at least 26".

Winchester, Model 94, Royal Canadian Mounted Police Centennial carbine.

Winchester, Model 94, Saskatchewan Diamond Jubilee Carbine commemorative.

Winchester, Model 94, Sioux Commemorative carbines, cal. 30-30, with S/Ns beginning with "SU."

Winchester, Model 94, The Oliver F. Winchester commemorative.

Winchester, Model 94, Theodore Roosevelt, Carbine.

Winchester, Model 94, Theodore Roosevelt, Rifle.

Winchester, Model 94 "Trapper," .357 magnum caliber saddle ring carbine, 100th Anniversary Commemorative 1894-1994Winchester, Model 94, United States Border Patrol Commemorative carbine cal. .30-30.

Winchester, Model 94, Wild Bill Hickok Commemorative, Caliber .45, S/Ns WBH001 - WBH350.

Winchester, Model 94, Wells Fargo and Company Commemorative, carbines.

Winchester, Model 94, Wyoming Centennial Commemorative carbines, caliber .30-30, S/Ns WYC001 - WYC500.

Winchester, Model 94, Wyoming Diamond Jubilee, carbine.

Winchester, Model 94, Yellow Boy Indian, carbine.

Winchester, Model 94, 125th Anniversary Commemorative carbines, caliber .30-30, S/Ns WRAC001 - WRAC125.

Winchester, Model 94, 150th Anniversary Texas Ranger Commemorative, carbine.

Winchester, Model 95, all original, mfd. from 1899 to 1938, with 16" or longer barrel and 26" or longer overall length.

Winchester, Model 1866, Centennial, carbine.

Winchester, Model 1866, Centennial, rifle.

Winchester, Model 1873, all original, mfd. from 1899 to 1925, with 16" or longer barrel and 26" or longer overall length.

Winchester Model 1890 rifles.

Winchester, Model 1892 Carbine, .38 WCF cal. with 14. barrel S/N 654311.

Winchester, Model 1894, Golden Spike, carbine.

Winchester, Model 1894 Nez Perce Commemorative carbine, cal. .30-30, mfd. by U.S. Repeating Arms Co., S/Ns NEZ001-NEZ600.

Winchester, Model 1894, Texas Sesquicentennial rifle and carbine, cal. .38-55.

Winchester, Model 1894 Carbine, .30 WCF cal. with 15 1/16. barrel S/N 1040988.

Winchester, Model 1894 Special Carbine .30 WCF cal. S/N 948487.

Winchester, Model 1897, pump action shotguns, all gauges, manufactured between 1899 and 1957, S/Ns 1 through 1,024,700.

Winchester, Model 1897 or 97 riot guns, 12 gauge, 20" barrels with original RIC (Royal Irish Constabulary) markings.

* ***Winchester***, Model 1902, .22 caliber bolt action rifles.

Winchester, Model 1903 .22 cal. semiautomatic rifles.

Winchester, Model 1906 rifles.

Winchester, Model 9422, Annie Oakley Commemorative Carbine .22 cal.

Winchester, Model 9422, Cheyenne Commemorative rifles, .22 cal.

Winchester, Model 9422, "Eagle Scout Commemorative" rifle, .22 cal.

Winchester, Northwest Territories Centennial rifle.

Yugoslavian M1948 (M48) bolt action rifles, 7.92 x 57mm caliber, produced at the Kragujevac Arsenal, original military configuration only.

Yugoslavian manufactured rifles M59 and M59/66, 7.62 x 39 mm caliber, all semiautomatic variations and having a fixed magazine, manufactured from 1947-1992.

Curios or Relics Symbols Abbreviations

1. "*" indicates an entry made since ATF P 5300.11 was last published by way of hardcopy (10-95), supplemental, or Internet posting.
2. "S/N" and "S/Ns" mean "serial number" and "serial numbers".
3. "Cal." and "cals." mean "caliber" and "calibers".
4. "Mfd." means "manufactured".

SHOW TIME 2013-2014

Over the last 35 years, Blue Book Publications, Inc. has attended hundreds of domestic and international industry and consumer shows. This is where much of the new information is gathered, in addition to providing us an opportunity to meet industry leaders, contributing editors, and interested consumers. It's a party! Make sure that you check our website periodically: www.bluebookofgunvalues.com (click on Show Time, located under the Information & Services tab) for the most up-to-date schedule.

Here's a listing of all the related trade shows (both consumer and industry) we'll either be attending or exhibiting at during 2013 and early 2014. If you want to meet with our content providers and the staff while on the show circuit, here's where we'll be. It is highly recommended that you try to attend some of these shows, as these are the best places to acquire up-to-date information on what you like and collect.

In the past, we have had a lot of requests for either appointments or to meet some of our personnel. Keeping this in mind, if you would like to schedule some time to see us at any of these shows, please contact us directly before each show date, so that we can make arrangements.

April 6-7, 2013
Tulsa Gun & Knife Show
(consumer show, exhibiting)
Expo Center - Expo Square
Tulsa Fairgrounds
Sat. 8-7pm, Sun. 8-5pm
Contact: Tulsa Gun Show, Inc.
PO Box 33201
Tulsa, OK 74153-1201
Phone: 918-492-0401
www.tulsaarmshow.com
mail@tulsaarmshow.com

May 3-5, 2013
The 142nd NRA Annual Meetings & Exhibits Show
(consumer show, exhibiting)
George R. Brown Convention Center
Houston, TX
Contact: NRA
Phone: 800-694-9300
www.nraam.org

May 18-19, 2013
Ohio Gun Collectors Association (OGCA) Annual Meeting & Exhibits
(exhibiting, closed to non-members)
Roberts Centre
Wilmington, OH
Contact: OGCA
Phone: 330-467-5733
Website: www.ogca.com

July 26-28, 2013
43rd Annual Kansas City National Summer Arms Show & 13th NRA Gun Collectors Show
(consumer show, exhibiting)
K.C.I. Expo-Center
Kansas City, MO
Contact: MVACA Show Committee
PO Box 6013
Leawood, KS
Phone: 913-631-3942
www.mvaca.org

October 3-6, 2013
Colt Collectors Association Show
(consumer show, exhibiting)
Embassy Suites
Norman, OK
Phone: 866-577-1273
CCA
P.O. Box 2241
Los Gatos, CA 95031-2241
www.coltcollectors.com

November 9-10, 2013
Tulsa Gun & Knife Show
(consumer show, exhibiting)
Expo Center - Expo Square
Tulsa Fairgrounds
Sat. 8-7pm, Sun. 8-5pm
Contact: Tulsa Gun Show, Inc.
PO Box 33201
Tulsa, OK 74153-1201
Phone: 918-492-0401
www.tulsaarmshow.com
mail@tulsaarmshow.com

Jan. 14-17, 2014
SHOT Show (trade only, exhibiting)
Sands Expo & Convention Center
Las Vegas, NV
Contact: Reed Exhibitions
383 Main Avenue
Norwalk, CT 06851
Toll Free: 888-334-8720
Intl: 203-840-5600
Fax: 203-840-9600
Website: www.shotshow.org
Email: inquiry@shot.reedexpo.com

Jan. 17-19, 2014
Las Vegas Antique Arms Show & International Sporting Arms Show (consumer show, exhibiting)
Riviera Hotel & Casino
Las Vegas, NV
Contact: Beinfeld Productions, MB
72 Sunrise Drive
Rancho Mirage, CA 92270
Phone: 760-202-4489
Fax: 760-202-4793
Website: www.antiquearmsshow.com

Feb. 5-8, 2014
SCI (Safari Club International - SCI members only, attending)
Las Vegas, NV
Contact: SCI
4800 West Gates Pass Road
Tucson, Arizona 85745-9490
Main Phone: 520-620-1220
Fax: 520-622-1205
Website: www.safariclub.org

March 14-17, 2014
IWA
(trade show, attending only)
Exhibition Centre Nuremberg (NurnbergMesse)
Nuremberg, Germany
www.iwa.info

INDEX

Title Page 1
Publisher's Note/Copyright 2
Table of Contents 3
Gun Questions/Appraisal Policy 4
Blue Book Publications, Inc.
General Information 5-6
Meet the Staff 7
Acknowledgements 8-9
Fallen Comrades & Cover Credits 9
How to Use This Book 10-13
Anatomy of a Handgun 14
Anatomy of a Rifle 15
Anatomy of a Shotgun 16
Foreword by S.P. Fjestad 17-19
Jessie Duff – A Champion Who's
Winning for Freedom 20-21
Grading Criteria 22
NRA Condition Standards 23
The PPGS – Firearms Grading Made Easy 24
Photo Percentage Grading System™ 25-102
34th Edition Calendar 62-63
Identifying/Buying Older Editions 103-104
Modern Firearms/Antiques
Text & Pricing 105-2,208
NSSF Hunting 456
Autry National Center of the American West 770
NRA Membership Information 830
NRA Stand and Fight 1,370
Rock Island Arsenal Museum 1,890
Buffalo Bill Historical Center
Information/Membership 1,966
National Firearms Museum (NFM) 2,020
Congressional Sportsmen's Foundation 2,190

A

A.A. 105
A.A.A. 105
A.A. ARMS INC. 105
A & B HIGH PERFORMANCE FIREARMS 105
A.R. SALES 105
ADC (ARMI DALLERA CUSTOM) 106
AFC 106
A. J. ORDNANCE 106
AK-47 DESIGN CARBINES, RIFLES, & PISTOLS 106
A M A C 109
A.M.S.D. (ADVANCED MILITARY SYSTEM DESIGN) 109
AMP TECHNICAL SERVICE GmbH 109
A M T 110
AR 57 LLC (57CENTER LLC) 113
AR-7 INDUSTRIES, LLC 114
AR-15 STYLE CARBINES, RIFLES, AND PISTOLS 114
ASAI AG (ADVANCED SMALL ARMS INDUSTRIES) 116
A-SQUARE 116
A T C S A 117
ATA ARMS 117
AWA USA 117
AWC SYSTEMS TECHNOLOGY, LLC 118
AYA (AGUIRRE Y ARANZABAL) 118
ABADIE 122
ABBEY, GEORGE T. 123
ABBEY, F.J. & COMPANY 123
ABBIATICO & SALVINELLI (FAMARS) 123
ACCU-MATCH INTERNATIONAL INC. 123
ACCU-TEK 123
ACCURACY INTERNATIONAL LTD. 125
ACCURATE ARMS RIFLE LLC 126
ACHA 126
ACME 127
ACME ARMS 127
ACME HAMMERLESS 127
ACTION (M.S.) 127
ACTION ARMS LTD. 127
ACTION LEGENDS MFG., INC. 128
ADAMS 128
ADAMS ARMS 128
ADAMS, JOSEPH 129
ADAMY, GEBR. JAGDWAFFEN 129
ADCO ARMS INC. (ADCO SALES INC.) 129
ADCOR DEFENSE 131
ADEQ FIREARMS COMPANY 132
ADIRONDACK ARMS COMPANY 132
ADLER 132
ADVANCED ARMAMENT CORP. 132
ADVANTAGE ARMS USA, INC. 133
AERON CZ s.r.o. 133
AETNA 133
AETNA ARMS COMPANY 133
AGNER 133
AIM SURPLUS 134
AIR MATCH 134

AJAX ARMY 134
AKDAL 134
AKKAR 134
AKRILL, E. 134
ALAMO RANGER 135
ALASKA 135
ALASKAN COMMEMORATIVES 135
ALCHEMY ARMS COMPANY 135
ALDAZABAL 135
ALERT 135
ALESSANDRI, LOU, AND SON 136
ALEXANDER ARMS LLC 136
ALEXIA 138
ALFA 138
ALFA PROJ 139
ALKARTASUNA FABRICA DE ARMAS, S.A. 139
ALLEN & THURBER 139
ALLEN FIREARMS 139
ALMAR 140
ALPHA ARMS INC. 140
ALPHARMS 140
ALPINE INDUSTRIES 140
AMBUSH FIREARMS 140
AMERICA REMEMBERS 141
AMERICAN ARMS 141
AMERICAN ARMS CO. 141
AMERICAN ARMS, INC. 142
AMERICAN BARLOCK WONDER 149
AMERICAN CLASSIC 149
AMERICAN CUSTOM GUNMAKERS GUILD, INC. (ACGG) 149
AMERICAN DERRINGER CORPORATION 149
DERRINGERS: STAINLESS STEEL 150
PISTOLS: PEN DESIGN 152
PISTOLS: SEMI-AUTO 153
PISTOLS: SLIDE-ACTION 153
AMERICAN FIREARMS MANUFACTURING CO., INC. 153
AMERICAN FRONTIER FIREARMS MFG., INC. 153
AMERICAN GUN CO. 154
AMERICAN GUN COMPANY, LLC 155
AMERICAN HISTORICAL FOUNDATION, THE 155
AMERICAN HUNTING RIFLES, INC. (AHR) 155
AMERICAN INDUSTRIES 156
AMERICAN INTERNATIONAL CORP. 156
AMERICAN LEGACY FIREARMS 157
AMERICAN LEGENDS 157
AMERICAN PRECISION ARMS 157
AMERICAN SPIRIT ARMS 157
AMERICAN SPIRIT ARMS CORP. 159
AMERICAN TACTICAL IMPORTS 160
AMERICAN WESTERN ARMS, INC. 163
AMTEC 2000, INC. 164
ANCIENS ETABLISSEMENTS PIEPER 164
ANDERSON MANUFACTURING 165
ANDREAS STRANK BUCHSENMACHERMEISTER 165
ANGEL ARMS INC. 165
ANSCHÜTZ 166
PISTOLS: BOLT ACTION 166
RIFLES: BOLT ACTION, DISC. 167
RIFLES: BOLT ACTION SPORTER, .17 RIMFIRE - RECENT MFG. 169
RIFLES: BOLT ACTION SPORTER, .22 LR - RECENT MFG. 170
RIFLES: BOLT ACTION SPORTER, .22 WMR - RECENT MFG. 173
RIFLES: BOLT ACTION SPORTER, CENTERFIRE - RECENT MFG. 174
RIFLES: BOLT ACTION, SILHOUETTE 176
RIFLES: BOLT ACTION MATCH, RECENT MFG. 177
RIFLES: BOLT ACTION, BIATHLON 179
RIFLES: SEMI-AUTO 179
SHOTGUNS: O/U 180
ANZIO IRONWORKS CORP. 180
APACHE 181
APPLE VALLEY ARMS, cont. 181
ARCUS CO. 181
ARDESA 181
ARES DEFENSE SYSTEMS INC. 181
ARISAKA 182
ARLINGTON ORDNANCE 182
ARMALITE 182
ARMALITE, INC. 183
ARMAMENT TECHNOLOGY 187
ARMAMENT TECHNOLOGY CORP. 188
ARMAS AZOR, S.A. 188
ARMED 189
ARMERIA DE MADRID, LA 189
ARMES DE CHASSE LLC 189
ARMES MATHELON 189
ARMES PIERRE ARTISAN ETS. (P. CHAPUIS) 189
ARMI MAGAP 190
ARMI PERUGINI-VISINI 190
ARMI SALVINELLI 190
ARMI SAN PAOLO 190
ARMI SPORT di CHIAPPA SILVIA & C. Snc 190
ARMINEX LTD. 191
ARMINIUS 191
ARMITAGE INTERNATIONAL, LTD. 192
ARMORY USA L.L.C. 192
ARMS CORPORATION OF THE PHILIPPINES 192
ARMS MORAVIA, LTD. 192
ARMS RESEARCH ASSOCIATES 192
ARMS ROOM LLC 193

ARMS TECH LTD. 193
ARMSAN 193
ARMSCO 193
ARMSCOR 193
ARMSCORP USA, INC. 197
ARM SPORT LLC 199
ARMSPORT, INC. 199
ARMY & NAVY 199
ARNOLD ARMS CO., INC. 199
ARRIETA, S.L. 200
ARRIZABALAGA, PEDRO 202
ARSENAL, BULGARIA 202
ARSENAL FIREARMS 203
ARSENAL INC. 203
ARSENAL USA LLC 206
ART MANIFATTURA ARMI/ART ARMI 206
ASHBURY PRECISION ORDNANCE 206
ASP 207
ASPREY 208
ASTRA 208
ASTRA ARMS S.A. 212
ATKIN, GRANT & LANG LTD. 212
ATKIN, HENRY 212
AUSTRIAN SPORTING ARMS 213
AUSTRALIAN AUTOMATIC ARMS PTY. LTD. 213
AUSTRALIAN INTERNATIONAL ARMS 213
AUTAUGA RIFLES, INC. 214
AUTO MAG 214
AUTO-ORDNANCE CORP. 216
AUTO-POINTER 218
AXTELL RIFLE CO. 218
AZTEK ARMS 218

B

BCM EUROPEARMS 219
BSA GUNS LIMITED 219
BWE FIREARMS 223
B-WEST 223
BAER, LES 223
BAFORD ARMS, INC. 223
BAIKAL 223
BAILONS GUNMAKERS LIMITED 228
BAKER, W.H. & CO. 228
THE BAKER GUN & FORGING CO. 229
BALLARD ARMS, INC. 231
BALLESTER MOLINA/RIGAUD (HAFDASA) 233
BALTIMORE ARMS COMPANY 233
BANSNER'S ULTIMATE RIFLES, L.L.C 233
BARNES PRECISION MACHINE, INC. 235
BARRETT FIREARMS MANUFACTURING, INC. 236
BAR-STO 238
BARTOLOT, WERNER 238
BASERRI 238
BATTAGLIA, MAURO 238
BATTLE RIFLE COMPANY 238
BAUER FIREARMS CORPORATION 239
BAYARD 239
BECAS 240
BEEMAN OUTDOOR SPORTS 240
BEHOLLA PISTOL 241
BENELLI 241
BENSON FIREARMS LTD. 253
BENTON & BROWN FIREARMS, INC. 254
BERETTA, DR. FRANCO 254
BERETTA 256
PISTOLS: SEMI-AUTO, PRE-WWII MFG. 256
PISTOLS: SEMI-AUTO, POST WWII MFG. 257
Pistols: Semi-Auto, Model 92 & Variations - 5.9 in. barrel 263
Pistols: Semi-Auto, Model 92 & Variations - 4.9 in. barrel 263
Pistols: Semi-Auto, Model 92 & Variations - 4.7 in. barrel 267
Pistols: Semi-Auto, Model 92 & Variations - 4.3 in. barrel 267
Pistols: Semi-Auto, Model 96 & Variations, Recent Mfg. 268
REVOLVERS: SINGLE ACTION 270
RIFLES: BOLT ACTION, RECENT MFG. 271
RIFLES: LEVER ACTION 273
RIFLES: SEMI-AUTO, RECENT MFG. 273
RIFLES: O/U, CUSTOM 273
RIFLES: SxS, CUSTOM 274
RIFLES: SLIDE ACTION 274
SHOTGUNS: O/U, DISC. 274
SHOTGUNS: O/U, FIELD - RECENT MFG. 277
SHOTGUNS: O/U, SKEET - RECENT MFG. 282
SHOTGUNS: O/U, SPORTING CLAYS - RECENT MFG. 283
SHOTGUNS: O/U, TRAP - RECENT MFG. 286
SHOTGUNS: O/U, CUSTOM GRADE - RECENT MFG. 288
SHOTGUNS: SxS, RECENT MFG. 290
SHOTGUNS: SxS, CUSTOM GRADE 293
SHOTGUNS: SINGLE BARREL, DISC. 294
SHOTGUNS: SLIDE ACTION, MFG. 1960-1996 295
SHOTGUNS: SEMI-AUTO 295
COMMEMORATIVES 305
BERGARA 305
BERGMANN 305
WAYNE BERGQUIST CUSTOM PISTOLS 307
BERNARDELLI, GIULIO 307
BERNARDELLI, VINCENZO 307
BERSA 315
BERTUZZI, F.LLI 318
BESCHI, MARIO 318
BETTINSOLI, TARCISIO, Srl 319
BIG BEAR ARMS & SPORTING GOODS INC 319

BIG HORN ARMORY INC. 319
BIG HORN ARMS CORP. 320
BIGHORN RIFLE CO. 320
BILL HANUS BIRDGUNS LLC 320
BINGHAM, LTD. 320
BITTNER 320
BLACK FORGE 321
BLACKHEART INTERNATIONAL LLC 321
BLACKOPS TECHNOLOGIES 322
BLACK RAIN ORDNANCE, INC. 322
BLACK RIFLE COMPANY LLC 324
BLAND, THOMAS & SONS GUNMAKERS LTD. 324
BLASER 324
BLEIKER, HEINRICH 331
BLOW 332
BLUEGRASS ARMORY 332
BOBCAT WEAPONS INC 332
BOBERG ARMS CORPORATION 332
BOHICA 332
BOITO 333
BOLLINGER, JOHN 333
BOND ARMS, INC. 333
BORCHARDT 334
BORDEN RIFLES 335
BOROVNIK, LUDWIG KG 335
BOSIS, LUCIANO 335
BOSS & CO., LTD 336
BOSWELL, CHARLES 338
BOWEN, BRUCE & COMPANY 339
BOXALL & EDMISTON LTD. 340
BOY'S RIFLES 340
BRAVO COMPANY MFG. INC. 341
BRAZIER, JOSEPH, LTD 342
BREDA MECCANICA BRESCIANA 343
BREEDING, RYAN 346
BRE-MAC SRL 346
BREN 10 (PREVIOUS MFG.) 346
BREN 10 (RECENT MFG.) 347
BRETTON-GAUCHER 347
BRIGNOLI, SILVIO 348
BRILEY 348
BRITARMS 350
BRNO ARMS (ZBROJOVKA BRNO) 350
BRNO RIFLES 357
BROCKMAN'S RIFLES 357
BROLIN ARMS, INC. 358
BRONCO (PISTOLS) 360
BRONCO (LONG ARMS) 360
A.A. BROWN & SONS 361
DAVID MCKAY BROWN (GUNMAKERS) LTD. 361
ED BROWN CUSTOM, INC. 362
ED BROWN PRODUCTS, INC. 362
BROWN PRECISION, INC. 362
BROWNING 364
BROWNING HISTORY 365
BROWNING FACTS 365
BROWNING VALUES INFORMATION 365
BROWNING SERIALIZATION 366
BROWNING CUSTOM SHOP 366
PISTOLS: SEMI-AUTO, CENTERFIRE, F.N. PRODUCTION UNLESS OTHERWISE NOTED 366
PISTOLS: SEMI-AUTO, .22 CAL. RIMFIRE 372
RIFLES: BOLT ACTION 376
RIFLES: BOLT ACTION, CENTERFIRE A-BOLT I SERIES 378
RIFLES: BOLT ACTION, CENTERFIRE A-BOLT II SERIES 380
RIFLES: BOLT ACTION, CENTERFIRE X-BOLT SERIES 384
RIFLES: BOLT ACTION, RIMFIRE A-BOLT SERIES 385
RIFLES: LEVER ACTION 385
RIFLES: O/U 389
RIFLES: SEMI-AUTO, .22 LR 389
RIFLES: SEMI-AUTO, BAR SERIES 391
RIFLES: SEMI-AUTO, FAL & CAL SERIES 394
RIFLES: SINGLE SHOT 394
RIFLES: SLIDE ACTION 396
SHOTGUNS: BOLT ACTION, A-BOLT SERIES 396
SHOTGUNS: O/U, CYNERGY SERIES 397
SHOTGUNS: O/U, CITORI HUNTING SERIES 398
SHOTGUNS: O/U, CITORI SKEET 404
SHOTGUNS: O/U, CITORI SPORTING CLAYS 406
SHOTGUNS: O/U, CITORI TARGET 410
SHOTGUNS: O/U, CITORI TRAP 410
SHOTGUNS: O/U, SUPERPOSED GENERAL INFO & CHOKE CODES 412
SUPERPOSED: 1931-1940 MFG. (PRE-WWII) 412
SUPERPOSED: 1948-1960 MFG. (POST-WWII) 413
SUPERPOSED: 1960-1976 MFG. 414
SHOTGUNS: O/U, SUPERPOSED HIGH GRADES: 1985-PRESENT 421
Superposed: Custom Shop Current Pricing & Models 422
SHOTGUNS: SxS 423
SHOTGUNS: SEMI-AUTO, A-5 1903-1998, 2012-CURRENT MFG. 424
SHOTGUNS: SEMI-AUTO, DOUBLE AUTO MODELS 428
SHOTGUNS: SEMI-AUTO, MISC. - RECENT MFG. 429
SHOTGUNS: SINGLE BARREL, BT-99 & BT-100 436
SHOTGUNS: SINGLE BARREL, RECOILLESS TRAP 438
SHOTGUNS: SLIDE ACTION 438
SPECIAL EDITIONS, COMMEMORATIVES, & LIMITED MFG. ... 441
BRUCHET 442
BRÜGGER & THOMET 442
BRYCO ARMS 443
BUDISCHOWSKY 443
BUEHLER CUSTOM SPORTING ARMS 444

BULLARD REPEATING ARMS COMPANY.......444
BULLSEYE GUN WORKS.......445
BUL LTD. (TRANSMARK).......445
BUMAR.......447
THE BURGESS GUN CO.......447
BUSHMASTER FIREARMS INTERNATIONAL.......447
BUTLER ARMS USA.......455
BUTLER ASSOC., INC.......455
BÜYÜK HUGLU.......455

C

C3 DEFENSE, INC.......457
CETME.......457
CFS GUNS.......458
CMMG, INC.......458
C.O. ARMS.......458
CVA.......458
C Z (CESKÁ ZBROJOVKA).......458
CZ (STRAKONICE).......477
CABANAS.......478
CABELA'S INC.......478
CABOT GUN COMPANY LLC.......479
CAEM, RENATO.......480
CAESAR GUERINI, s.r.l.......481
CALICO LIGHT WEAPONS SYSTEMS.......485
CAMEX-BLASER USA, INC.......486
CANIK55.......486
CAPRINUS.......487
CARACAL.......487
CARBON 15.......487
CARL GUSTAF.......487
CASARTELLI, CARLO.......488
CASPIAN ARMS, LTD.......489
CASULL ARMS CORPORATION.......489
CAVALRY ARMS CORPORATION.......490
CENTURION ORDNANCE, INC.......490
CENTURY ARMS.......490
CENTURY INTERNATIONAL ARMS, INC.......490
CENTURY MFG., INC.......495
CHAMPLIN FIREARMS, INC.......496
CHAPARRAL ARMS.......496
CHAPUIS ARMES.......497
CHAPUIS, P. ETS.......500
CHARLES DALY.......501
CHARLIN ARMS.......501
CHARTER ARMS.......501
CHARTER ARMS (CURRENT MFG.).......503
CHEYTAC.......505
CHIAPPA FIREARMS LTD.......505
CHIPMUNK RIFLES.......507
CHRISTENSEN ARMS.......508
CHURCHILL.......511
E.J. CHURCHILL GUNMAKERS.......513
CIMARRON F.A. CO.......516
CITADEL.......530
CLARIDGE HI-TEC INC.......531
CLARK CUSTOM GUNS, INC.......531
CLASSIC DOUBLES.......532
CLERKE ARMS, LTD.......533
CLERKE PRODUCTS.......534
CLIFTON ARMS.......534
COACH GUNS.......534
COBB MANUFACTURING, INC.......536
COBRA.......536
COBRA ENTERPRISES OF UTAH, INC.......536
COBRAY INDUSTRIES.......537
COGSWELL & HARRISON (GUNMAKERS), LTD.......537
COLE ARMS INC.......539
COLT'S MANUFACTURING COMPANY, LLC.......539
REVOLVERS: PERCUSSION.......540
Revolvers: Percussion, Paterson Variations.......540
Revolvers: Percussion, Walker Model.......541
Revolvers: Percussion, Dragoon Series.......542
Revolvers: Percussion, Models 1849, 1851, 1855, 1860, 1861, 1862, & 1865.......543
REVOLVERS: PERCUSSION CONVERSIONS.......547
Colt Thuer Conversions.......547
Richards Conversions: All Variations.......547
Richards-Mason Conversions: All Variations.......548
Conversions with Round Cartridge Barrel.......549
REVOLVERS: "OPEN TOP" MODELS.......549
REVOLVERS: PERCUSSION, 2ND & 3RD GENERATION BLACK POWDER SERIES.......549
DERRINGERS.......550
REVOLVERS: POCKET MODELS.......551
REVOLVERS: NEW LINE SERIES & VARIATIONS.......551
REVOLVERS: SAA, 1873-1940 MFG. (SER. NOS. 1-357,000).......552
SAA 1st Generation Civilian/Commercial (Mfg. 1873-1940).......552
SAA 1st Generation Commercial, Non-Standard Mfg.......556
SAA U.S. Military, Mfg. 1873-1903.......559
REVOLVERS: SAA, 2ND GENERATION: 1956-1975 MFG.......562
REVOLVERS: SAA, 3RD GENERATION: 1976-CURRENT MFG.......564
COLT CUSTOM SHOP ENGRAVING, SAA & SEMI-AUTO, 1976-PRESENT.......569
Large Frame Size: Current SAAs and M1911s.......570
Medium Frame Size.......570
Small Frame Size.......570
REVOLVERS: SAA, SCOUT MODEL.......570
PISTOLS: SEMI-AUTO, DISC.......571
PISTOLS: SEMI-AUTO, GOVT. MODEL 1911 COMMERCIAL VARIATIONS.......574
PISTOLS: SEMI-AUTO, GOVT. MODEL 1911 MILITARY VARIATIONS.......574

PISTOLS: SEMI-AUTO, GOVT. MODEL 1911A1 COMMERCIAL VARIATIONS 576
PISTOLS: SEMI-AUTO, GOVT. MODEL 1911A1 MILITARY VARIATIONS 578
PISTOLS: SEMI-AUTO, ACE MODELS, 1931-1947 MFG. 580
PISTOLS: SEMI-AUTO, NATIONAL MATCH MODELS - PRE-WWII 581
PISTOLS: SEMI-AUTO, NATIONAL MATCH MODELS - WWII & POST-WWII 581
PISTOLS: SEMI-AUTO, CUSTOM SHOP ENGRAVING PRICING, PRE-1991 582
PISTOLS: SEMI-AUTO, CURRENT CUSTOM SHOP ENGRAVING PRICING 583
PISTOLS: SEMI-AUTO, SINGLE ACTION, RECENT MFG. 583
PISTOLS: SEMI-AUTO, DOUBLE ACTION - RECENT MFG. 593
PISTOLS: SEMI-AUTO, .22 CAL. - WOODSMAN SERIES & VARIATIONS 594
REVOLVERS: DOUBLE ACTION 597
REVOLVERS: DOUBLE ACTION, SWING OUT CYLINDER 598
RIFLES/CARBINES: PRE-1904 611
RIFLES: BOLT ACTION, CENTERFIRE 614
RIFLES: SINGLE SHOT, CENTERFIRE 615
DRILLINGS 616
RIFLES: SEMI-AUTO, CENTERFIRE, AR-15 & VARIATIONS 616
AR-15, Pre-Ban, 1963-1989 Mfg. w/Green Label Box 616
AR-15, Pre-Ban,1989-Sept. 11,1994 Mfg. w/Blue Label Box 617
AR-15, Post-Ban, Mfg. Sept. 12, 1994-Present 619
RIFLES: SEMI-AUTO, RIMFIRE, AR-15 & VARIATIONS 621
SHOTGUNS: O/U 622
SHOTGUNS: SxS, DISC. 622
SHOTGUNS: SEMI-AUTO 623
SHOTGUNS: SLIDE ACTION 623
FACTORY COMMEMORATIVES & SPECIAL/LIMITED EDITIONS 623
COMANCHE **635**
COMBINATION GUNS **636**
COMMANDO ARMS **636**
COMMANDO ARMS (NEW MFG.) **637**
COMPETITIVE EDGE GUNWORKS LLC **637**
COMPETITOR CORPORATION **637**
CONCO ARMS **637**
CONNECTICUT SHOTGUN MANUFACTURING CO. **638**
CONNECTICUT VALLEY ARMS **641**
CONNECTICUT VALLEY CLASSICS, INC. **642**
CONQUEST **643**
CONSTITUTION ARMS **643**
CONTENTO/VENTURA **643**
CONTINENTAL ARMS CORPORATION **644**
COOEY, H.W., MACHINE & ARMS CO. LTD. **645**
COONAN ARMS **645**
COONAN, INC. **646**
COOPER FIREARMS OF MONTANA, INC. **647**
COP **651**
CORE 15 .... **651**
CORONADO ARMS **652**
CORTONA **652**
COSMI, AMERICO & FIGLIO **653**
COSTER, GEORGE & SON **653**
COUNTY, S.A.L. **654**
CRESCENT FIRE ARMS CO. & CRESCENT-DAVIS ARMS CORP. **654**
CRICKETT RIFLE **655**
CROSS CANYON ARMS **655**
CROSSFIRE LLC **656**
CROWN CITY ARMS **656**
CUMBERLAND MOUNTAIN ARMS, INC. **656**
CUSTOM GUN GUILD **656**
CYLINDER & SLIDE, INC. **656**
CZECHPOINT INC. **656**

D

D'ARCY ECHOLS & CO. **657**
DGS, INC. **657**
DPMS FIREARMS (LLC) **657**
DSA INC. **663**
DWM **667**
D.Z. ARMS **667**
DAEWOO **667**
DAISY **668**
DAIWA **669**
DAKIN GUN CO. **669**
DAKOTA ARMS, INC. **669**
DAKOTA SINGLE ACTION REVOLVERS **673**
DALVAR OF USA **675**
DALY, CHARLES: PRUSSIAN MFG. **675**
DALY, CHARLES: JAPANESE MFG. **677**
DALY, CHARLES: 1976-2010 .... **678**
COMBINATION GUNS 679
HANDGUNS: LEVER ACTION 679
PISTOLS: SEMI-AUTO 679
REVOLVERS: DA 681
REVOLVERS: SA 682
RIFLES: BOLT ACTION 682
RIFLES: LEVER ACTION, REPRODUCTIONS 684
RIFLES: O/U 684
RIFLES/CARBINES: SEMI-AUTO 684
RIFLES: SINGLE SHOT 686
SHOTGUNS: O/U 686
SHOTGUNS: SxS 689
SHOTGUNS: LEVER ACTION 690
SHOTGUNS: SEMI-AUTO 690
SHOTGUNS: SLIDE ACTION 692
DALY, CHARLES: 2011-PRESENT **693**
DAN ARMS OF AMERICA **693**

DAN WESSON....694
DANIEL DEFENSE....697
DARDICK....698
DARNE S.A....698
DAUDSONS ARMOURY....700
DAVID MILLER CO....700
DAVIDSON FIREARMS....701
DAVIDSON'S....701
DAVIS INDUSTRIES....705
DAVIS N.R....705
DEFOURNEY....705
DEHAAN SHOTGUNS LTD....706
DEL-TON INCORPORATED....706
DEMAS, ETS (L'ATELIER VERNEY-CARRON)....707
DEMRO....708
DEMYAN....708
DEPAR....708
DERYA HUNTING ARMS....708
DESENZANI....708
DESERT EAGLE....708
DESERT INDUSTRIES, INC....709
DESERT TACTICAL ARMS....709
DESERT TOYS....709
DETONICS....709
DETONICS FIREARMS INDUSTRIES....709
DETONICS USA....710
DIAMOND SHOTGUNS....710
DIAMONDBACK FIREARMS....710
DIARM S.A....711
DICKSON & MACNAUGHTON....711
JOHN DICKSON & SON, LTD....712
DIXIE GUN WORKS....712
DLASK ARMS CORP....713
DOLPHIN GUN COMPANY....713
DOMINGO, ACHA....713
DOMINION ARMS....713
DOMINO, IGI....714
DOUBLE STAR CORP....714
DOUBLETAP DEFENSE, LLC....717
DOWNSIZER CORPORATION....718
DREYSE....718
DRILLINGS....718
DRULOV....721
DUBIEL ARMS COMPANY....722
DUCKS UNLIMITED, INC....722
DUMOULIN, ERNEST S.P.R.L....724
DUMOULIN, FRANCOIS....728
DUMOULIN, HENRI & FILS....728
DUMOULIN HERSTAL S.A....728

E

84 GUN CO....729
E. ARTHUR BROWN COMPANY INC....729
E.D.M. ARMS....729
E.M.F. CO., INC....730
E.R. SHAW INC....736
EAGLE ARMS, INC....736
EAST RIDGE GUN COMPANY, INC....737
ED BROWN CUSTOM, INC....738
ED BROWN PRODUCTS, INC....738
EFFEBI SRL....741
EGE SPORTING ARMS....741
EGEMEN....742
EGO ARMAS, S.A....742
EKSEN ARMS INDUSTRY AND TRADE CO....742
EMPIRE RIFLE COMPANY LLC....742
ENFIELD AMERICA, INC....743
ENFIELDS....743
ENGLISH SHOTGUNS....749
ENTRÉPRISE ARMS INC....749
ERA....752
ERHARDT, DENNIS....752
ERMA SUHL, GmbH....752
ERMA-WERKE....752
ERN, MAX....754
ESCALADE....754
ESCORT....754
EUROARMS ITALIA Srl....757
EUROARMS OF AMERICA....757
EUROPEAN AMERICAN ARMORY CORP....757
PISTOLS: SEMI-AUTO....757
PISTOLS: SEMI-AUTO, EUROPEAN SERIES....762
PISTOLS: SINGLE SHOT....762
REVOLVERS: DOUBLE ACTION, WINDICATOR SERIES....762
REVOLVERS: SAA, BOUNTY HUNTER SERIES....763
RIFLES....763
SHOTGUNS: O/U....764
SHOTGUNS: SxS....765
SHOTGUNS: SEMI-AUTO....765
SHOTGUNS: SLIDE ACTION....765
EVANS, WILLIAM, GUN & RIFLE MAKERS....765
EVOLUTION USA....765
EXCAM....767
EXCEL ARMS....767
EXEL ARMS OF AMERICA, INC....769

F

F. DARNE FILS AINÉ....771
F&D DEFENSE....773

F.A.I.R. srl 773
F.A.V.S. di FRANCESCO GUGLIELMINOTTI 773
FAS 774
FEG 774
FIAS 776
F.I.E. 776
FMJ 776
FMK FIREARMS 776
FMR 776
FNH USA 777
FTL 780
FABARM, S.p.A. 780
FABBRI s.n.c. 781
FABRIQUE NATIONALE 781
FABRYKA BRONI LUCZNIK - RADOM SP.ZO.O 786
FALCO, srl 786
FALCON FIREARMS 787
FAMARS di ABBIATICO & SALVINELLI SRL 787
FANZOJ, JOHANN 790
FARQUHARSON 791
FAUSTI STEFANO SRL 791
FEATHER INDUSTRIES, INC. 796
FEATHER USA/AWI LLC 797
FEDERAL ENGINEERING CORPORATION 797
FEDERAL ORDNANCE, INC. 797
FEINWERKBAU 799
FELK TRAILERS PTY LTD. 801
FEMARU 801
FERLACH GUNS 801
FERLACHER WAFFEN PRÄZISIONSTECHNIK PRODUCTIONS GmbH & CO. KG. 802
FERLIB 802
FERRELL, ROGER 803
FIALA ARMS AND EQUIPMENT CO. 803
57 CENTER LLC 804
FINNCLASSIC 804
FINNISH LION 804
FIOCCHI OF AMERICA, INC. 805
FIREARMS INTERNATIONAL CORP. (F.I.C.) 805
FIREARMS INTERNATIONAL, INC. 805
FIRESTORM 807
FLAVIO FARÈ 807
FLODMAN GUNS 808
FORBES RIFLE, LLC 808
FORT SOE SIA 808
FORT WORTH FIREARMS 808
FOX, A.H. 809
FOX COMPANY CHRONOLOGY 810
FOX SERIAL NUMBER ASSIGNMENTS 810
FOX MODELS BY YEARS IN MFG. 810
SHOTGUNS: SxS, CURRENT MFG. 810
SHOTGUNS: SxS & SINGLE SHOT, DISC. 811
FOX CARBINE 813
FRANCHI, LUIGI 813
FRANCOTTE, AUGUSTE & CIE. S.A. 822
FRANKLIN ARMORY 824
FRASER, DANL. & CO. 824
FRASER FIREARMS CORP. 825
FREEDOM ARMS 825
FRENCH MILITARY 827
FRIGON GUNS, INC. 828
FROMMER PISTOLS 828
FULTON ARMORY 828
FURR ARMS 829

G

GA PRECISION 831
GALAZAN 831
GALEF SHOTGUNS 831
GALENA INDUSTRIES INC. 831
GALIL 831
GAMBA, RENATO 832
GARBI, ARMAS 833
GARRAY RIFLES LTD. 834
GASTINNE RENETTE 834
GATEWAY PRECISION ARMS 835
GATLING GUNS 835
GAUCHER 835
GAZELLE ARMS 836
GAVAGE 836
GENTRY CUSTOM LLC 836
GERMAN P.38 MILITARY & COMMERCIAL PISTOLS 836
GERMAN SPORT GUNS GmbH 836
GEVARM 837
GIANI, VITTORIO 837
GIB 837
GIBBS, GEORGE 838
GIBBS GUNS, INC. 838
GIBBS RIFLE COMPANY, INC. 838
GIL, ANTONIO & CO. 841
GILA RIVER GUN WORKS 842
GIRSAN MACHINE & LIGHT WEAPON INDUSTRY COMPANY 842
GLANZIG PRÄZISIONS-UND SPORTWAFFEN JAGDZUBEHÖR 842
GLENFIELD 842
GLISENTI 842
GLOCK 842
GOLAN 850

GOLDEN EAGLE....850
GOLDEN STATE ARMS....851
GONCZ ARMAMENT, INC....851
GRAND POWER s.r.o. 851
GRANGER, G....851
GRANITE MOUNTAIN ARMS, INC....852
GRANT, STEPHEN....852
GREAT WESTERN....853
GREAT WESTERN ARMS COMPANY....854
GREEN, ROGER....856
GREENER, W.W., LIMITED....856
GREIFELT AND COMPANY....859
GRENDEL, INC....859
GREYBULL PRECISION....860
GRIFFIN & HOWE....860
GRIFFON....862
GRISEL, H.L....863
GRULLA ARMAS....863
GRUND, KARL....865
GRÜNIG & ELMIGER AG....865
GUERINI, CAESAR....865
GUN 1....865
GUN ROOM CO., LLC....865
GUN WORKS, LTD....865
GUNCRAFTER INDUSTRIES....865
GUNSMOKE....866
GUNSMOKE ENTERPRISES....866
GUNWERKS....866
GUSTAF, CARL....866
GYROJET....866

H

HHF....867
H.J.S. INDUSTRIES, INC....867
HMS PRÄZISIONSTECHNIK GmbH....867
H & R 1871, LLC. (HARRINGTON & RICHARDSON)....867
H-S PRECISION, INC....872
HWP INDUSTRIES....874
HAENEL, C.G. (OLD MFG.)....874
HAENEL, C.G., GmbH (NEW MFG.)....875
HAKIM....875
HALO ARMS, LLC....875
HAMBRUSCH JAGDWAFFEN GmbH....876
HÄMMERLI AG....876
HÄMMERLI-WALTHER....881
HARRINGTON & RICHARDSON, INC....881
HANDGUNS: 1871-1986....882
Single Action Spur Trigger Revolvers: 1871-1883....882
Solid Frame Revolvers: 1880-1952....882
Top Break Revolvers: 1885-1952....886
PISTOLS: SEMI-AUTO....893
PISTOLS: SINGLE SHOT....893
REVOLVERS: RECENT MFG.....894
RIFLES....899
SHOTGUNS: BOLT ACTION....905
SHOTGUNS: DOUBLE....905
SHOTGUNS: SINGLE BARREL, 1900-1942 MFG.....906
SHOTGUNS: SINGLE BARREL, 1943-1986 MFG.....907
SHOTGUNS: SEMI-AUTO....910
SHOTGUNS: SLIDE ACTION....910
COMMEMORATIVES....910
HARRIS GUNWORKS....911
HARRISON & HUSSEY LTD....913
HARTFORD....913
HARTFORD ARMORY....915
HARTFORD ARMS & EQUIPMENT COMPANY....915
HARTMANN & WEISS GmbH....916
HASKELL MANUFACTURING....916
HATCHER GUN COMPANY....917
HATFIELD GUN CO., INC....917
HATFIELD GUN COMPANY LLC....917
HATFIELD'S....917
HATSAN ARMS COMPANY....917
KARL HAUPTMANN JAGDWAFFEN....917
HAUSMANN & CO. GmbH....918
HAWES FIREARMS....918
HEAD DOWN PRODUCTS LLC....918
HECKLER & KOCH....918
N.L. HEINEKE, INC....928
HEINIE SPECIALTY PRODUCTS....928
HEIZER DEFENSE....928
HELLIS, CHARLES....928
HELWAN....928
HENDRY, RAMSAY & WILCOX....928
HENRY, ALEX....928
HENRY REPEATING ARMS COMPANY....929
HENRY RIFLE....931
HERA ARMS....931
HERITAGE MANUFACTURING, INC....932
HEROLD RIFLE....933
HERTERS....933
HESSE ARMS....934
HEYM AG....934
HIENDLMAYER, KLAUS....938
HI-POINT FIREARMS....938
HIGGINS, J.C....940
HIGH STANDARD....941
HIGH STANDARD MANUFACTURING CO....972
HIGH TECH CUSTOM RIFLES....974
HILL COUNTRY RIFLE COMPANY....975

HISPANO ARGENTINO FABRICADE AUTOMOVILES SA (HAFDASA) 975
GEORGE HOENIG, INC. 975
HOFER-JAGDWAFFEN, PETER 975
HOGAN MANUFACTURING LLC 976
P.L. HOLEHAN, INC. 976
HOLLAND & HOLLAND LTD. 976
RIFLES: MODERN 977
SHOTGUNS: O/U 978
SHOTGUNS: SxS 979
SHOTGUNS: SINGLE SHOT 980
HOLLENBECK GUN COMPANY 981
HOLLOWAY & NAUGHTON GUNMAKERS 981
HOLLOWAY ARMS CO. 982
HOLMES FIREARMS 982
HOPKINS & ALLEN ARMS COMPANY, 1902-1914 982
HORTON, LEW, DIST. CO. 986
HOULDING PRECISION FIREARMS 986
HOWA 986
HUG-SAN 989
HUGLU 990
HULDRA ARMS 990
HUNTER ARMS COMPANY 990
HUSQVARNA 990
HY-HUNTER INC. FIREARMS MANUFACTURING CO. 992
HYPER 992

I

I.A.B. srl 993
IAC 993
IAI 993
IAI INC. - AMERICAN LEGEND 993
I A I 993
IAR, Inc. 993
I.F.G. 994
I G A 994
IMI 995
I.O., INC 995
ISSC HANDELSGESELLSCHAFT 995
I.W.I 996
IBERIA FIREARMS 996
IMPALA PRECSION 996
IMPERIAL GUN CO. LTD. 996
INDIAN ARMS 996
INDUSTRIA ARMI GALESI 997
INFALLIBLE 997
INFINITY FIREARMS 997
INGLIS HI-POWERS 997
INGRAM 998
INLAND 998
INNOGUN 999
INTERARMS 999
PISTOLS: SEMI-AUTO, FEG & HELWAN MFG. 999
REVOLVERS: SA, VIRGINIAN SERIES 999
RIFLES: BOLT ACTION, DISC. 1000
RIFLES: BOLT ACTION, HOWA MFG. 1000
RIFLES: BOLT ACTION, MAUSER ACTIONS 1000
RIFLES: SEMI-AUTO 1001
INTERARMS ARSENAL 1001
INTERCONTINENTAL ARMS INC. 1002
INTERDYNAMIC OF AMERICA, INC 1002
INTERNATIONAL BUSINESS MACHINE CORP. (IBM) 1002
INTERNATIONAL HARVESTER CORP. 1002
INTERSTATE ARMS CORP. 1002
INTRAC ARMS INTERNATIONAL INC. 1003
INTRATEC 1003
INTRATEC U.S.A., INC. 1004
INVESTARM, s.p.a. 1005
INVESTMENT ARMS INC. 1005
IRON BRIGADE ARMORY 1005
IRWIN PEDERSON ARMS CO. 1005
IRWINDALE ARMS, INC. (IAI) 1005
ISRAEL ARMS INTERNATIONAL, INC. 1006
ISRAEL ARMS LTD. 1006
ISRAEL MILITARY INDUSTRIES (IMI) 1007
ISRAEL WEAPON INDUSTRIES LTD. (I.W.I.) 1007
ITALIAN MILITARY ARMS 1007
ITHACA CLASSIC DOUBLES 1007
ITHACA GUN COMPANY (NEW MFG.) 1008
ITHACA GUN COMPANY LLC (OLDER MFG.) 1009
IVER JOHNSON ARMS, INC. (NEW MFG.) 1021
IVER JOHNSON ARMS & CYCLE WORKS 1021
IZHMASH 1037

J

J.B. CUSTOM INC. 1039
J.C. HIGGINS 1039
J.L.D. ENTERPRISES, INC. 1039
J.O. ARMS 1039
J. ROBERTS & SON (GUNMAKERS) LTD. 1040
JMC FABRICATION & MACHINE, INC. 1040
JO. LO. AR 1040
JP ENTERPRISES, INC. 1040
J R CARBINES, LLC. 1042
J R DISTRIBUTING 1042
JSL (HEREFORD) 1043
JACKSON HOLE FIREARMS 1043
JACKSON RIFLES 1043

JAEGER, FRANZ 1043
JAGD-UND SPORTWAFFEN SUHL GmbH 1044
JAMES RIVER ARMORY 1044
JANZ GmbH 1044
JAPANESE MILITARY 1044
JARRETT RIFLES, INC. 1045
JEAN-MARC STEVAUX, S.P.R.L. 1048
JEFFERY, W.J. & CO. LTD 1048
JEFFERY SHARPS 1049
JENNINGS FIREARMS 1049
JERICHO 1049
JIMENEZ ARMS 1049
JOHANNSEN RIFLES 1050
JOHNSON AUTOMATICS, INC. 1051
J. JONGMANS ARMS COMPANY PTY. LTD. 1051
JUCH-GRUND JAGDWAFFEN INH. KARL GRUND 1051
JUNG, WAFFEN, GMBH 1051
JURRAS, LEE E. 1051
JUST, JOSEF 1052
JUST RIGHT CARBINES 1052
JUSTIN CUSTOM GUNS 1052

K

K.B.I., INC. 1053
KDF, INC. 1053
K.F.C. 1054
KSN INDUSTRIES LTD. 1054
K-VAR CORP. 1054
KAHR ARMS 1055
KASSNAR IMPORTS, INC. 1059
KEBERST INTERNATIONAL 1059
KEL-TEC CNC INDUSTRIES, INC. 1059
KEMEN 1061
KENDALL INTERNATIONAL 1062
KENTUCKY RIFLES 1062
KEPPELER - TECHNISCHE ENTWICKLUNGEN GmbH 1062
KEPPLINGER, ING. HANNES 1063
KESSLER ARMS CORPORATION 1063
KESSLER, WAFFEN 1063
KEYSTONE SPORTING ARMS 1063
KHAN 1063
KILIMANJARO RIFLES 1064
KIMAR srl 1064
J. KIMBALL ARMS CO. 1064
KIMBER 1064
KIMBER OF OREGON, INC. 1081
KIMEL INDUSTRIES, INC. 1087
KING'S GUN WORKS, INC. 1087
KINTREK, INC. 1087
KLEINGUENTHER FIREARMS CO. 1087
KNIGHT'S ARMAMENT COMPANY 1088
KODIAK CO. 1089
KOFS LTD. 1090
KOLAR ARMS 1090
KOLIBRI 1090
KONGSBERG 1090
KORA BRNO 1091
KORRIPHILA 1091
KORTH 1091
KOSCHAT, JAKOB 1093
KRAG-JORGENSEN (30/40 KRAG) 1093
KRAL AV 1095
KRASSNIK, VALENTIN 1095
KRICO 1095
H. KRIEGHOFF GUN CO. (SHOTGUNS OF ULM) 1096
DRILLINGS 1096
PISTOLS: SEMI-AUTO 1097
RIFLES: O/U & SxS 1097
RIFLES: SINGLE SHOT 1098
RIFLES: SLIDE ACTION 1098
SHOTGUNS: O/U 1098
SHOTGUNS: O/U OR COMBINATION GUNS 1102
SHOTGUNS: SxS 1102
SHOTGUNS: SINGLE BARREL TRAP 1103
KRISS SYSTEMS SA 1104
KUFSTEINER WAFFENSTUBE 1104
KUPEC, PAVEL 1104

L

L.A.R. MANUFACTURING, INC. 1105
L E S INCORPORATED 1107
LMT 1107
LRB ARMS 1107
LWRC INTERNATIONAL, INC. 1107
LA ARMERIA DE MADRID 1109
LABANU INCORPORATED 1109
LAHTI PISTOL 1109
LAKE FIELD ARMS LTD. 1110
LAKELANDER 1110
LAKESIDE MACHINE LLC 1111
LAMBOY, S.R. & CO. INC. 1111
LAMES 1111
LANBER 1111
LANCER SYSTEMS 1111
LANG, JOSEPH 1112
LAPORTE HOLDING 1112
LARUE TACTICAL 1112
LASERAIM ARMS, INC. 1113

LASALLE 1113
LAUER CUSTOM WEAPONRY 1114
LAURONA ZABALA 1114
LAW ENFORCEMENT ORDNANCE CORPORATION 1114
HARRY LAWSON LLC 1114
LAZZERONI ARMS COMPANY 1115
LEADER ARMS TECHNOLOGY 1116
LEBEAU-COURALLY 1117
LECHNER & JUNGL GES.m.b.H. 1118
LEFEVER ARMS COMPANY 1118
LEFEVER, D.M. 1120
LE FORGERON 1121
LE FRANCAIS PISTOLS 1122
LEGACY SPORTS INTERNATIONAL 1122
LEGEND 1122
LEGION FIREARMS 1122
LEGION USA INC. 1122
LEITNER-WISE DEFENSE, INC. 1122
LEITNER-WISE RIFLE CO. INC. 1123
LES BAER CUSTOM, INC. 1123
LEW HORTON DIST. CO. 1128
LEWIS MACHINE & TOOL COMPANY (LMT) 1134
LIBERATOR 1135
LIBERTY 1135
LIBERTY ARMS INTERNATIONAL LLC 1136
LIBERTY ARMS WORKS, INC. 1137
LIEGEOISE D'ARMES 1137
LIGNOSE (BERGMAN) 1137
LILIPUT 1137
LIND, AL 1137
LINDNER GUN COMPANY 1137
LINEBAUGH, JOHN 1138
LIPPARD, KARL 1138
LITTLE SHARPS RIFLE MFG. 1139
LJUNGMAN 1139
LJUTIC LLC 1139
LLAMA - Fabrinor S.A.L. 1141
LOKI WEAPON SYSTEMS, INC. 1144
LON PAUL CUSTOM GUNS 1145
LONE STAR ARMAMENT, INC. 1145
LONE STAR RIFLE CO., INC. 1146
LONE STAR TACTICAL SUPPLY 1147
LONGTHORNE GUNMAKERS 1147
LORCIN ENGINEERING CO., INC. 1147
LORENZO, CRESS 1148
LOSOK CUSTOM ARMS 1148
LUCCHINI, SANDRO 1148
LUGERS WITH VARIATIONS 1149
REFERENCE GUIDE BY TOGGLE MARKING 1149
DWM TOGGLE IDENTIFICATION 1149
DWM COMMERCIAL LUGERS 1150
ERFURT TOGGLE IDENTIFICATION 1150
SIMSON & CO. TOGGLE IDENTIFICATION 1150
SWISS TOGGLE IDENTIFICATION 1150
MAUSER TOGGLE IDENTIFICATION 1151
KRIEGHOFF TOGGLE IDENTIFICATION 1151
VICKERS TOGGLE IDENTIFICATION 1151
LUGERS: MATCHING MAGAZINE(S) & MILITARY HOLSTER ADD ONS 1151
PISTOLS: SEMI-AUTO, LUGERS & VARIATIONS 1151
Lugers: Pre-1900 & 1900 DWM Mfg. 1151
Lugers: 1902-DWM Mfg. 1152
Lugers: 1904-DWM Mfg. 1153
Lugers: 1906-DWM Mfg. 1153
Lugers: 1906-1918 DWM & Erfurt Mfg. 1153
WWI ERFURT MILITARY SERIAL RANGES 1155
WWI DWM MILITARY SERIAL RANGES 1156
Lugers: 1920-1930 DWM 1156
Lugers: Krieghoff Mfg. 1157
Lugers: Mauser Mfg. 1158
Lugers: Reworks 1160
Lugers: Simson Mfg. 1160
Lugers: Swiss Bern 1160
Lugers: KDF, Interarms, Stoeger, & Recent Import 1160
Lugers: Special Interest 1161
LUGERS: ACCESSORIES 1163
Conversion Units - .22 cal. 1163
Detachable Stocks 1163
"Snail" Drum Magazines 1163
SHOTGUNS: O/U 1163
SHOTGUNS: SEMI-AUTO 1163
LU-MAR s.r.l. 1164
LUNA 1164
LUSA USA 1164
LUXUS 1164
LYMAN 1164
LYNX 1164

M

M+M, INC. 1165
MAB 1165
MAC (METROARMS CORP.) 1165
MAC (MILITARY ARMAMENT CORP.) 1165
MAG CUSTOM RIFLES 1165
MAS 1165
MBA ASSOCIATES 1165
MG ARMS INCORPORATED 1166
MGI 1167
M-K SPECIALTIES INC. 1167
MK ARMS INC. 1168
MKE 1168
MKS SUPPLY, INC 1168

M.O.A. CORPORATION **1169**
M.R. NEW SYSTEM ARMS **1169**
MTs ARMS **1169**
JAMES MacNAUGHTON & SONS **1169**
MAADI-GRIFFIN CO. **1170**
MAGNUM RESEARCH, INC. **1170**
MAGTECH **1176**
MAJESTIC ARMS, LTD. **1177**
MAKAROV **1178**
MALIN, F.E. **1178**
MAMBA **1178**
MANCHESTER ARMS INC. **1178**
MANDALL SHOOTING SUPPLIES, INC. **1178**
MANIFATURRA ARMI ART **1178**
MÄNNEL SPORT SHOOTING GmbH **1179**
MANNLICHER PISTOLS **1179**
MANNLICHER SCHOENAUER SPORTING RIFLES **1179**
MANU-ARM **1183**
MANUFRANCE **1183**
MANURHIN **1183**
MARATHON PRODUCTS, INC. **1185**
MARBLE ARMS & MFG. CO. **1185**
MARCEL THYS & SONS **1187**
MARGOLIN **1187**
MARLIN FIREARMS COMPANY **1187**
PISTOLS: DERRINGERS AND REVOLVERS 1187
RIFLES: LEVER ACTION, ANTIQUE & OLDER MFG. 1187
RIFLES: MODERN PRODUCTION INFORMATION 1190
RIFLES: CENTERFIRE 1190
Rifles: Centerfire, Bolt Action 1190
Rifles: Centerfire, Lever Action 1191
Rifles: Centerfire, Miscellaneous 1198
RIFLES: RIMFIRE 1199
Rifles: Rimfire, Bolt Action 1199
Rifles: .22 Cal., Lever Action 1205
Rifles: .22 Cal., Slide Action 1208
Rifles: Rimfire, Semi-Auto 1208
SHOTGUNS: BOLT ACTION 1210
SHOTGUNS: LEVER ACTION 1211
SHOTGUNS: O/U 1212
SHOTGUNS: SxS 1212
SHOTGUNS: SINGLE SHOT 1212
SHOTGUNS: SLIDE ACTION, 1898-1963 PRODUCTION 1212
MAROCCHI **1214**
MARTIN, ALEX **1218**
MARTINI **1218**
MASTERPIECE ARMS **1218**
MASTERPIECE ARMS, INC. **1219**
MASQUELIER S.A. **1219**
MATCHGUNS srl **1220**
MATCH GRADE ARMS & AMMUNITION **1220**
MATEBA **1220**
MATHELON ARMES **1221**
MATRA MANURHIN DEFENSE **1221**
MAUNZ MATCH RIFLES LLC (MAUNZ, KARL) **1221**
MAURITZ WIDFORSS AB **1222**
MAUSER JAGDWAFFEN GmbH **1222**
HANDGUNS: EARLY PRODUCTION 1223
PISTOLS: SEMI-AUTO, DISC. 1223
Mauser Pistols: HSc Models 1224
Mauser Pistols: HSc WWII Military Mfg. 1224
Mauser Pistols: HSc Post-WWII Mfg. 1225
Mauser Pistols: Luger Mfg. 1225
Mauser Pistols: P.38 Mfg. 1225
PISTOLS: SEMI-AUTO, RECENT IMPORTATION 1225
PISTOLS: SEMI-AUTO, MODEL 1896 BROOMHANDLES 1225
Mauser Broomhandles: Conehammer Variations 1226
Mauser Broomhandles: Flatside Variations 1226
Mauser Broomhandles: Post-1900 Variations 1227
Mauser Broomhandles: Post-1930 Variations 1228
Broomhandle Carbines 1229
Broomhandles: Copies from Other Countries 1229
Broomhandles: Spanish Copies 1230
RIFLES: MILITARY PRODUCTION 1230
RIFLES: MILITARY PRODUCTION, K98k (KARBINE) 1240
RIFLES: BOLT ACTION, 1898-1946 COMMERCIAL MFG. 1243
RIFLES: BOLT ACTION, RECENT PRODUCTION 1244
RIFLES: BOLT ACTION, .22 CAL. 1250
RIFLES: SEMI-AUTO, .22 LR 1252
SHOTGUNS 1252
MAVERICK ARMS, INC. **1252**
MAWHINNEY, CHUCK **1253**
MAXIMUS ARMS, LLC **1253**
McCANN INDUSTRIES **1254**
McMILLAN BROS. RIFLE CO. **1254**
McMILLAN FIREARMS MANUFACTURING, LLC **1255**
McMILLAN, G. & CO., INC. **1257**
MCREES PRECISION **1259**
MEACHAM TOOL & HARDWARE, INC. **1259**
MEDWELL & PERRETT LIMITED **1259**
MENZ, AUGUST **1260**
MERCURY (PISTOLS) **1260**
MERCURY (SHOTGUNS) **1260**
MERKEL **1261**
MERKEL HISTORY 1261
COMBINATION GUNS 1261
DRILLINGS 1262
RIFLES: BOLT ACTION 1262
RIFLES: DOUBLE 1263
RIFLES: SEMI-AUTO 1265
RIFLES: SINGLE SHOT 1265
SHOTGUNS: O/U, DISC. 1266
SHOTGUNS: O/U, RECENT PRODUCTION 1267
SHOTGUNS: SxS, PRE-WWII PRODUCTION 1268
SHOTGUNS: SxS, RECENT PRODUCTION 1269
SHOTGUNS: SPORTING CLAYS 1272

MERRILL 1272
MERWIN HULBERT & CO. 1272
MERWIN HULBERT & CO. (NEW MFG.) 1274
METROARMS CORPORATION 1274
MICHIGAN ARMS 1276
MICOR DEFENSE, INC. 1276
MICROTECH SMALL ARMS RESEARCH, INC. (MSAR) 1276
MIDLAND RIFLES 1277
MIIDA 1277
MILLER ARMS 1278
MILLER, DAVID CO. 1278
MIL-SPEC INDUSTRIES CORP. 1278
MILTEX, INC. 1278
MIROKU, B.C. 1278
MITCHELL ARMS, INC. 1279
MITCHELL'S MAUSERS 1284
MODULO MASTERPIECE 1286
MOLL, M.F. 1287
MOLOT 1287
MONTANA ARMORY, INC. 1287
MONTANA RIFLE COMPANY 1287
MONTGOMERY WARD 1287
MORINI COMPETITION ARM SA 1288
MORTIMER, THOMAS 1288
MOSIN-NAGANT 1288
MOSSBERG, O.F. & SONS, INC. 1288
DERRINGERS 1289
RIFLES: DISC. 1289
Mossberg "Targo" Smoothbore Models 1296
RIFLES: BOLT ACTION, CURRENT PRODUCTION 1298
RIFLES: LEVER ACTION 1300
RIFLES: SEMI-AUTO 1300
SHOTGUNS: BOLT ACTION - DISC. 1301
SHOTGUNS: O/U, RECENT PRODUCTION 1302
SHOTGUNS: SxS, RECENT PRODUCTION 1303
SHOTGUNS: SEMI-AUTO & SLIDE ACTION, RECENT PRODUCTION 1303
MOUNTAIN RIFLERY, LLC. 1319
MOUNTAIN RIFLES INC. 1319
MUSGRAVE 1319
MUSKETEER RIFLES 1319

N

NS FIREARMS CORP. 1321
NAMBU PISTOLS 1321
NATIONAL POSTAL METER 1322
NATIONAL WILD TURKEY FEDERATION (NWTF) 1322
NAVY ARMS COMPANY 1323
PISTOLS 1324
REVOLVERS: REPRODUCTIONS 1324
REVOLVERS: REPRODUCTIONS, COLT CARTRIDGE CONVERSIONS 1326
REVOLVERS: PREMIUM BLUE REPRODUCTIONS, CARTRIDGE CONVERSIONS 1326
RIFLES: REPRODUCTIONS 1326
RIFLES: MODERN PRODUCTION 1330
SHOTGUNS: O/U, RECENT IMPORTATION 1331
SHOTGUNS: SxS, RECENT IMPORTATION 1331
SHOTGUNS: SINGLE SHOT 1331
P.V. NELSON GUNMAKERS LTD. 1332
NEMESIS ARMS 1332
NEMO (NEW EVOLUTION MILITARY ORDNANCE) 1332
NESIKA 1332
NEW ADVANTAGE ARMS, INC. 1332
NEW DETONICS MANUFACTURING CORPORATION 1333
NEW ENGLAND ARMS CORP. 1333
NEW ENGLAND CUSTOM GUN SERVICE, LTD. (NECG LTD.) 1333
NEW ENGLAND FIREARMS 1333
NEW ULTRA LIGHT ARMS LLC 1337
NEWTON ARMES 1338
NEWTON ARMS CO. 1338
NEWTOWN FIREARMS 1339
NEXT GENERATION ARMS 1339
NIGHTHAWK CUSTOM 1339
NIKKO FIREARMS CO., LTD. 1343
NOBLE MFG. CO. 1344
NOR-CAL PRECISION 1344
NOREEN FIREARMS LLC 1345
NORICA LAURONA 1345
NORINCO 1345
NORINCO USA 1348
NORSMAN SPORTING ARMS & OUTFITTERS LLC 1348
NORTH AMERICAN ARMS, INC. 1349
NORTH AMERICAN SAFARI EXPRESS 1352
NORTHERN COMPETITION 1352
NORTHWEST ARMS 1352
NOSLER, INC. 1352
NOWLIN MFG., INC. 1354

O

O'BRIEN RIFLE CO. 1355
O.D.I. (OMEGA DEFENSIVE INDUSTRIES) 1355
OBERLAND ARMS 1355
OBREGON 1355
OHIO ORDNANCE WORKS, INC. 1355
OLD-WEST GUN CO. 1356
OLLENDORFF, PHILIPP 1356
OLYMPIC ARMS, INC. 1357

OMEGA 1364
OMEGA FIREARMS 1364
OMEGA PISTOL 1365
OMEGA RIFLES/SHOTGUNS 1365
OMEGA WEAPONS SYSTEMS INC. 1365
OMNI 1366
OMNI (CURRENT MFG.) 1366
ONLY LONG RANGE 1366
OPTIMA 1366
OPUS SPORTING ARMS, INC. 1366
OREGON ARMS 1367
ORTGIES PISTOLS 1367
ORVIS 1367
OTTOMANGUNS 1369
OWEN, KEN 1369

P

P.38 MILITARY & COMMERCIAL PISTOLS 1371
P.A.F. 1376
P.A.W.S., INC. 1376
PGW DEFENCE TECHNOLOGIES, INC. 1376
PHSADC (PAKISTAN HUNTING & SPORTING ARMS DEVELOPMENT COMPANY) 1377
PKP, INC. 1377
POF USA 1377
PPK s.r.o. 1377
P.S.M.G. GUN COMPANY 1378
PTK INTERNATIONAL, INC. 1378
PTR 91, INC. 1378
P.V. NELSON, (GUNMAKERS) 1380
PACIFIC INTERNATIONAL 1380
M. PADRÓNE 1380
PALM PISTOL 1380
PALMETTO ARMS CO. 1380
PARAMOUNT 1380
PARA INC., USA 1381
PARDINI, ARMI S.r.l. 1389
PARDUS 1391
PARKER BROS. MAKERS 1391
PARKER BROTHERS 1391
SHOTGUNS: MISC. FACTS 1391
SHOTGUNS: SxS, DAMASCUS BARRELS & PRICING 1393
SHOTGUNS: SxS, FLUID STEEL BARREL MODELS & PRICING 1393
SHOTGUNS: SINGLE BARREL TRAP 1396
PARKER GUNMAKERS 1396
PARKER PISTOLS 1396
PARKER REPRODUCTIONS 1397
PARKER-HALE LIMITED 1398
PATRIOT ORDNANCE FACTORY (POF) 1399
PASTUSEK INDUSTRIES 1400
PAUZA SPECIALTIES 1401
PEACE RIVER CLASSICS 1401
PEDERSEN CUSTOM GUNS 1401
PEDERSEN DEVICE 1401
PEDERSOLI, DAVIDE & C. Snc. 1401
PEERLESS RIFLE COMPANY 1403
PENTHENY de PENTHENY 1403
PERAZZI 1404
SHOTGUNS 1404
Perazzi Shotguns Information 1404
Perazzi Grades and Descriptions 1404
RIFLES: O/U 1405
SHOTGUNS: O/U, STANDARD MODELS & COMBINATIONS, RECENT MFG 1406
SHOTGUNS: AMERICAN TRAP, SINGLE BARREL & COMBINATIONS 1410
SHOTGUNS: O/U, HIGH GRADE COMBO SETS (TRAP, SKEET, AND SPORTING) 1411
SHOTGUNS: O/U, TRAP, HIGHER GRADES 1411
SHOTGUNS: O/U, SKEET HIGHER GRADES 1412
SHOTGUNS: O/U, 4-GAUGE SKEET SETS 1412
SHOTGUNS: O/U, SPORTING HIGHER GRADES 1412
SHOTGUNS: O/U, PIGEON-ELECTROCIBLES HIGHER GRADE 1412
SHOTGUNS: O/U, GAME/HUNTING - BOXLOCK ACTION 1413
SHOTGUNS: O/U, SIDELOCK MODELS 1413
SHOTGUNS: SxS, HUNTING - SIDELOCK MODELS 1414
SHOTGUNS: SxS GAME SHOTGUNS 1414
PEREGRINE INDUSTRIES, INC. 1415
PERODEAU, J.J. 1415
PERUGINI-VISINI 1415
PETERS STAHL GmbH 1418
PFEIFER-WAFFEN 1418
PHELPS MFG. CO. 1418
PHILLIPS & ROGERS, INC. 1419
PHOENIX ARMS 1419
PHOENIX ARMS CO. 1419
PIETTA, F.LLI 1420
PIONEER ARMS CORP. 1421
PIOTTI 1421
PIRANHA 1422
PISTOL DYNAMICS 1422
PLAINS RIFLE 1422
POINTER 1423
POLI, ARMI F.LLI 1423
POLI NICOLETTA & C. snc 1423
POLY TECHNOLOGIES, INC. 1424
POWELL, WILLIAM & SON (GUNMAKERS) LTD. 1424
PRAIRIE GUN WORKS 1424
PRANDELLI-GASPERINI 1424
PRECHTL, WAFFEN 1424

PRECISION FIREARMS LLC 1424
PRECISION SMALL ARMS, INC. (PSA) 1425
PREDATOR TACTICAL LLC 1426
PREMIER 1426
PRIMARY WEAPONS SYSTEMS 1427
PRINZ 1428
PROFESSIONAL ORDNANCE, INC. 1428
PROOF RESEARCH 1429
PUMA 1429
PURDEY, JAMES & SONS, LTD. 1431
PUSKARSTVO SPENDAL d.o.o. 1432

Q

Q.S. ARMI 1433
QFI (QUALITY FIREARMS INC.) 1433
QIQIHAR HAWK INDUSTRIES CO., LTD. 1434
QUACKENBUSH, H.M. 1434
QUAIL UNLIMITED, INC. 1435
QUALITY PARTS CO./BUSHMASTER 1436

R

R GUNS 1437
RAAC 1437
RAF 1437
RBA 1437
R.F.M. 1437
R.G. INDUSTRIES 1437
RGS LLC 1438
RND MANUFACTURING 1438
RPA INTERNATIONAL LTD. 1438
RPB INDUSTRIES 1439
RPM 1439
RWC (RUSSIAN WEAPON COMPANY) 1439
RWS 1439
RADOM 1440
RAM-LINE, INC. 1442
RAMIREZ, TODD 1442
RAMO DEFENSE SYSTEMS 1442
RANDALL FIREARMS COMPANY 1443
RANGER ARMS INC. 1443
RAPTOR ARMS CO., INC. 1443
RASHEED (RASHID) 1443
RAVELL 1444
RAVEN ARMS 1444
RECORD-MATCH 1444
RED ROCK ARMS 1444
REDOLFI F.LLI S.N.C. 1445
GARY REEDER CUSTOM GUNS 1445
REGENT 1445
REISING ARMS COMPANY 1445
REMINGTON ARMS COMPANY, INC. 1446
REMINGTON TRADEMARKS - 1816-PRESENT 1446
HANDGUNS: 1857-1945 PRODUCTION 1446
HANDGUNS: POST-WWII PRODUCTION 1453
Model XP-100 & Variations 1453
RIFLES: DISC. 1454
RIFLES: CANE VARIATIONS 1460
RIFLES: ROLLING BLOCK, RECENT MFG. 1460
RIFLES: SEMI-AUTO - CENTERFIRE 1461
RIFLES: SLIDE ACTION, CENTERFIRE 1464
RIFLES: RIMFIRE, BOLT ACTION 1468
RIFLES: RIMFIRE, "NYLON SERIES" 1472
RIFLES: RIMFIRE, SEMI-AUTO 1473
RIFLES: RIMFIRE, SLIDE ACTION 1477
RIFLES: BOLT ACTION, CENTERFIRE 1478
RIFLES: BOLT ACTION, MODEL 700 & VARIATIONS 1484
RIFLES: BOLT ACTION, MODEL 40X & VARIATIONS 1496
SHOTGUNS: O/U 1498
SHOTGUNS: SxS 1501
SHOTGUNS: SEMI-AUTO, DISC. 1505
SHOTGUNS: SEMI-AUTO, CURRENT/RECENT PRODUCTION 1507
Shotguns: Semi-Auto, Model 1100 & Variations 1509
Shotguns: Semi-Auto, Model 11-87 & Variations 1513
SHOTGUNS: SINGLE BARREL 1517
SHOTGUNS: SLIDE ACTION, DISC. 1517
SHOTGUNS: SLIDE ACTION, MODEL 870 & RECENT VARIATIONS 1519
RENATO GAMBA 1527
RENETTE, GASTINNE 1527
REPUBLIC ARMS, INC. 1527
REPUBLIC ARMS OF SOUTH AFRICA 1527
RETAY ARMS CORP. 1527
REXIO 1527
RHINO ARMS 1528
RHODE ISLAND ARMS COMPANY 1529
RIB MOUNTAIN ARMS, INC. 1529
RICHLAND ARMS COMPANY 1529
RIEDL RIFLE COMPANY 1530
RIFLES, INC. 1530
RIGANIAN, RAY (RIFLEMAKER) 1531
RIGBY, JOHN & CO. (GUNMAKERS), INC. 1531
RIZZINI & TANFOGLIO srl 1533
RIZZINI, BATTISTA 1534
RIZZINI, EMILIO 1538
RIZZINI, F.LLI 1538
RIZZINI, I. (ISIDORA) 1539
THE ROBAR COMPANIES, INC. 1539
ROBERT HISSERICH COMPANY 1540
ROBERTS, J & SON (GUNMAKERS) LTD. 1540

ROBERTSON 1540
ROBINSON ARMAMENT CO. 1540
ROCHE, CHRISTIAN 1541
ROCK ISLAND ARMORY 1541
ROCK ISLAND ARMORY (CURRENT MFG.) 1541
ROCK-OLA MANUFACTURING CO. 1542
ROCK RIVER ARMS, INC. 1542
ROCKY MOUNTAIN ARMS CORP. 1549
ROCKY MOUNTAIN ARMS, INC. 1549
ROCKY MOUNTAIN ELK FOUNDATION 1551
ROEDALE PRECISION 1551
ROGAK 1551
ROGUE RIVER RIFLEWORKS 1551
RÖHM 1552
ROHRBAUGH FIREARMS CORP. 1552
ROPER 1553
ROSS RIFLE COMPANY 1553
ROSSI 1558
ROSSLER WAFFEN GmbH 1564
ROTA, LUCIANO 1565
ROTTWEIL 1566
ROYAL AMERICAN SHOTGUNS 1567
RUBY 1567
RUGER 1567
RUKO SPORTING GOODS, INC. 1567
RUSSIAN AMERICAN ARMORY COMPANY 1567
RUSSIAN SERVICE PISTOLS AND RIFLES 1567
RUTTEN HERSTAL 1568

S

S.A.C.M. 1569
S.A.M. 1569
S.I.A.C.E. 1569
S.P.S. 1571
S.W.D., INC. 1571
SAE 1571
SCCY INDUSTRIES 1572
SI DEFENSE, INC. 1572
SKB SHOTGUNS 1572
SKS 1586
SRM ARMS 1587
SSK INDUSTRIES 1587
STI INTERNATIONAL 1588
STL 1595
SWS 2000 1595
SABATTI s.p.a. 1595
SABRE 1595
SABRE DEFENCE INDUSTRIES LLC. 1595
SACO DEFENSE INC. 1598
SAFARI ARMS 1598
SAFARI CLUB INTERNATIONAL 1600
SAFETY HARBOR FIREARMS, INC. 1600
SAIGA 1600
SAKO, LTD. 1601
SALERI, W.R. di SALERI WILLIAM & C. snc 1609
SAMCO GLOBAL ARMS, INC. 1609
SAN SWISS ARMS AG 1609
SARASQUETA, FELIX 1609
SAR ARMS 1610
SARASQUETA, J.J. 1610
SARASQUETA, VICTOR 1610
SARCO, INC. 1611
SARDIUS 1611
SARRIUGARTE, FRANCISO S.A. 1611
SARSILMAZ (SAR ARMS) 1611
SATTERLEE ARMS, LLC 1612
SAUER, J.P., & SOHN 1612
DRILLINGS & COMBINATION GUNS 1612
PISTOLS: SEMI-AUTO 1613
REVOLVERS: SA/DA 1613
RIFLES: BOLT ACTION 1613
RIFLES: SEMI-AUTO 1617
RIFLES: SxS 1617
SHOTGUNS 1617
SAVAGE ARMS, INC. 1619
COMBINATION GUNS 1619
PISTOLS: BOLT ACTION 1621
PISTOLS: SEMI-AUTO 1622
PISTOLS: SINGLE SHOT 1622
RIFLES: LEVER ACTION, DISC 1622
RIFLES: DISC., CENTERFIRE & RIMFIRE 1626
RIFLES: RIMFIRE, CURRENT PRODUCTION 1630
RIFLES: CENTERFIRE, CURRENT/RECENT PRODUCTION 1635
SHOTGUNS: DISC. 1654
SHOTGUNS: RECENT MFG. 1656
SAVIN, J.C. 1657
SAXONIA 1658
SCATTERGUN TECHNOLOGIES INC. (S.G.T.) 1658
SCHALL 1659
SCHEIRING GmbH 1659
SCHELLER SPEZIALWAFFEN 1659
SCHERZ, MICHAEL 1659
SCHILLING, FA. ALFRED 1660
SCHMIDT-RUBIN RIFLES 1660
SCHMITT FRERES 1660
SCHUERMAN ARMS., LTD. 1660
SCHUETZEN PISTOL WORKS 1660
SCHUETZEN RIFLES 1660
SCHULTZ & LARSEN 1661
SCHWABEN ARMS GMBH 1661

SCOTT, W.C., LTD. **1662**
SEARCY, B. & CO. **1662**
SEARS, ROEBUCK AND CO. **1663**
SECURITY INDUSTRIES **1663**
SEDCO INDUSTRIES, INC. **1663**
SEDGLEY, R.F., INC. **1663**
SEECAMP, L.W. CO., INC. **1663**
SEITZ **1664**
SEMMERLING **1664**
SENNI ARMS CO. **1665**
SENTINEL ARMS **1665**
SERBU FIREARMS, INC. **1665**
SERENGETI RIFLES, INC. **1665**
SERO LTD. **1665**
C. SHARPS ARMS CO. INC. **1666**
SHARPS, CHRISTIAN **1667**
SHARPS MILSPEC **1670**
SHARPS RIFLE COMPANY **1670**
SHERIDAN PRODUCTS INCORPORATED **1670**
SHILEN RIFLES, INCORPORATED **1671**
SHILOH SHARPS RIFLE MANUFACTURING COMPANY **1671**
SHOOTERS ARMS MANUFACTURING INCORPORATED **1671**
SIDEWINDER **1672**
SIG ARMS AG **1672**
SIG-HÄMMERLI **1674**
SIG SAUER **1674**
SILE DISTRIBUTORS **1693**
SILMA SPORTING GUNS **1693**
SILVER EAGLE **1694**
SILVER SEITZ **1694**
SIMILLION, GENE **1694**
SIMSEK **1695**
SIMSON **1695**
SIRKIS INDUSTRIES, LTD. **1695**
SJOGREN **1695**
SKORPION **1696**
SMITH-CORONA **1696**
SMITH, L.C. **1696**
SHOTGUN-RIFLES: BAKER 3-BARREL, HAMMER-DAMASCUS, ... 1697
SYRACUSE MFG. 1878-1888 1697
SHOTGUNS: SXS, BAKER HAMMER-DAMASCUS, SYRACUSE MFG. 1878-1884 1697
SHOTGUNS: SxS, L.C. SMITH SIDELOCK, HAMMER-DAMASCUS & FLUID STEEL, ... 1697
MFG. 1884-1932 1697
SHOTGUNS: SxS, L.C. SMITH SIDELOCK, HAMMERLESS-DAMASCUS, MFG. 1886-1895 1698
SHOTGUNS: SxS, L.C. SMITH/HUNTER ARMS, SIDELOCK, HAMMERLESS, ... 1698
FLUID STEEL BARRELS, MFG. 1892-1913 1698
SHOTGUNS: SxS, L.C. SMITH/HUNTER ARMS, SIDELOCK, HAMMERLESS, ... 1699
FLUID STEEL BARRELS, MFG. 1913-1950 1699
SHOTGUNS: SINGLE BARREL TRAP, BOXLOCK, HAMMERLESS, MFG. 1917-1950 1700
SHOTGUNS: SxS, HUNTER ARMS, FULTON BOXLOCK, HAMMERLESS, ... 1701
FLUID STEEL, MFG. 1915-1945 1701
SHOTGUNS: SxS, L.C. SMITH/MARLIN, SIDELOCK, HAMMERLESS, FLUID STEEL, ... 1701
MFG. 1968-1971 1701
SHOTGUNS: O/U, L.C. SMITH/MARLIN, MFG. 2005-2009 1701
SHOTGUNS: SxS, L.C. SMITH/MARLIN, MFG. 2005-2009 1702
SMITH & WESSON **1702**
PISTOLS: LEVER ACTION, ANTIQUE 1703
TIP-UPS 1703
TOP-BREAKS 1705
SINGLE SHOTS 1712
EARLY HAND EJECTORS (NAMED MODELS) 1712
NUMBERED MODEL/RECENT MFG. REVOLVERS (MODERN HAND EJECTORS) 1724
PISTOLS: SEMI-AUTO, CENTERFIRE 1746
PISTOLS: SEMI-AUTO, RIMFIRE 1761
PRE-2009 ENGRAVING OPTIONS FOR HANDGUNS 1763
CURRENT ENGRAVING OPTIONS FOR HANDGUNS 1763
S&W SPECIAL/LIMITED EDITIONS 1764
S&W FACTORY COMMEMORATIVES 1764
S&W PERFORMANCE CENTER FIREARMS 1765
Pricing of Performance Center Firearms 1766
Heritage Series From Lew Horton & Performance Center Handguns 1766
PERFORMANCE CENTER REVOLVER VARIATIONS 1766
PERFORMANCE CENTER RIFLE VARIATIONS 1779
PERFORMANCE CENTER SEMI-AUTO PISTOL VARIATIONS 1780
RIFLES 1784
Rifles: Revolving 1784
Rifles: Bolt Action 1784
Rifles: Semi-Auto 1785
SHOTGUNS 1788
SMITHSON, J.P. **1790**
SNAKE CHARMER **1790**
SOCIETA SIDERURGICA GLISENTI **1790**
SODIA, FRANZ **1790**
SOKOLOVSKY CORPORATION SPORT ARMS (SCSA) **1790**
SOG ARMORY **1791**
SOLEIHAC ARMURIER **1792**
SOMMER + OCKENFUSS GmbH **1792**
SOROKA RIFLE COMPANY **1792**
SPARTAN GUN WORKS **1793**
SPECIAL WEAPONS LLC **1794**
SPENCER CARBINES/RIFLES - CURRENT MFG. **1795**
SPENCER REPEATING RIFLES CO. **1795**

SPHINX SYSTEMS LTD. **1796**
SPIDER FIREARMS **1798**
SPIKE'S TACTICAL LLC **1798**
SPIRIT GUN MANUFACTURING COMPANY LLC **1799**
SPITFIRE **1799**
SPORTCO/SPORTING ARMS CO. **1799**
SPORT-SYSTEME DITTRICH **1799**
SPORTING ARMS COMPANY **1799**
SPRINGER'S ERBEN, JOHANN **1800**
SPRINGFIELD ARMORY **1800**
CARBINES/RIFLES, SINGLE SHOT 1800
PISTOLS: SEMI-AUTO 1801
RIFLES: BOLT ACTION, KRAG-JORGENSEN 1801
RIFLES: BOLT ACTION, MODEL 1903 & VARIATIONS 1801
RIFLES: SEMI-AUTO 1803
SHOTGUNS: SINGLE SHOT 1803
SPRINGFIELD ARMORY
(MFG. BY SPRINGFIELD INC.) **1803**
COMBINATION GUNS 1803
PISTOLS: SEMI-AUTO 1804
Pistols: Semi-Auto - P9 Series 1804
Pistols: Semi-Auto - R-Series 1805
Pistols: Semi-Auto - Disc. 1911-A1 Models 1805
Pistols: Semi-Auto - 1911-A1 (90s Series) 1807
Pistols: Semi-Auto - 1911-A1 Custom Models 1813
Pistols: Semi-Auto - XD Series 1815
PISTOLS: SINGLE SHOT, 1911-A2 SASS SERIES 1817
RIFLES: BOLT ACTION 1817
RIFLES: SEMI-AUTO, MILITARY DESIGN 1817
SPRINGFIELD ARMS CO. **1821**
STAG ARMS **1821**
STAGGS-BILT **1822**
STALLARD ARMS **1822**
STANDARD ARMS & STANDARD ARMS MFG. CO. **1822**
STANDARD ARMS OF NEVADA, INC. **1823**
STANDARD MANUFACTURING CO. LLC **1823**
STANDARD PRODUCTS CO. **1823**
STAR, BONIFACIO ECHEVERRIA S.A. **1823**
STEEL CITY ARMS, INC **1828**
STEINKAMP MASCHINENBAU GmbH & Co. KG **1828**
STEERING GEAR
(GRAND RAPIDS & SAGINAW LOCATIONS) **1828**
STERLING **1828**
STERLING ARMAMENT, LTD. **1828**
STEVENS, J., ARMS COMPANY **1829**
STEYR AUSTRIAN MILITARY **1835**
STEYR DAIMLER PUCH A.G. **1836**
STEYR ARMS (STEYR MANNLICHER) **1836**
PISTOLS: SEMI-AUTO 1836
RIFLES: BOLT ACTION, RECENT PRODUCTION 1837
Rifles: Bolt Action, Model 72 Series
(Mannlicher Schonauer M 72) 1843
RIFLES: SEMI-AUTO 1845
SHOTGUNS 1845
STINGER MANUFACTURING CORP. **1845**
STOCK, FRANZ **1846**
STOCKWORKS **1846**
STOEGER INDUSTRIES, INC. **1846**
STONER RIFLE **1849**
STRANK, ANDREAS **1849**
STRASSER **1849**
STRATEGIC ARMORY CORPS, LLC **1849**
STRAYER TRIPP INTERNATIONAL **1849**
STRAYER-VOIGT, INC. **1849**
STREET SWEEPER **1850**
STURM, RUGER & CO., INC. **1850**
RUGER COLLECTIBILITY OVERVIEW 1850
PISTOLS: SEMI-AUTO, RIMFIRE 1851
PISTOLS: SEMI-AUTO, CENTERFIRE 1854
REVOLVERS: SINGLE ACTION, OLD MODELS 1858
REVOLVERS: SINGLE ACTION, NEW MODELS 1862
REVOLVERS: DOUBLE ACTION 1867
RIFLES: BOLT ACTION, RIMFIRE 1870
RIFLES: BOLT ACTION, CENTERFIRE 1871
RIFLES: LEVER ACTION 1877
RIFLES: SEMI-AUTO, RIMFIRE 1877
RIFLES: SEMI-AUTO, CENTERFIRE 1880
RIFLES: SINGLE SHOT 1882
SHOTGUNS: O/U 1884
SHOTGUNS: SxS 1886
SHOTGUNS: SINGLE BARREL 1886
SUHLER JAGDGEWEHR MANUFAKTUR GmbH **1886**
SUNDANCE INDUSTRIES, INC. **1886**
SUPER SIX LIMITED **1886**
SUPER SIX LLC **1887**
SUPER SIX CLASSIC, LLC **1887**
SUPERIOR AMMUNITION **1887**
SUPERIOR ARMS **1887**
SURGEON RIFLES, INC. **1888**
SURVIVAL ARMS, INC. **1888**
SVENDSEN, ERL, F.A. MFG. CO. **1888**
SWING **1889**
SWISS MILITARY **1889**
SYMES & WRIGHT LTD. **1889**
SZECSEI & FUCHS FINE GUNS GmbH **1889**

T

TG INTERNATIONAL **1891**
TNW, INC. **1891**
TR IMPORTS **1891**
TS FINE GUNS **1891**
TACONIC FIREARMS, LTD. **1891**

TACTICAL RIFLES....1892
TACTICAL SOLUTIONS....1892
TACTICAL WEAPONS....1892
TALO DISTRIBUTORS, INC....1892
TALON INDUSTRIES, INC....1892
TANFOGLIO, FRATELLI, S.r.l....1893
TANNER, ANDRÉ....1893
TAR-HUNT CUSTOM RIFLES, INC....1893
TASK FIREARMS....1894
TATE GUNMAKERS LLC....1894
TAURUS INTERNATIONAL MFG., INC....1894
PISTOLS: SEMI-AUTO....1895
REVOLVERS: RECENT PRODUCTION....1904
RIFLES: LEVER ACTION....1918
RIFLES: REVOLVING....1918
RIFLES: SEMI-AUTO....1919
RIFLES: SLIDE ACTION....1919
TAYLOR, F.C. FUR CO....1920
TAYLOR'S & CO., INC....1920
TECHNO ARMS (PTY) LIMITED....1928
TELO, RENATO....1928
TERRIER ONE....1929
TESRO SPORTWAFFEN GMBH & CO. KG....1929
TEXAS ARMS....1929
TEXAS GUNFIGHTERS....1929
TEXAS LONGHORN ARMS, INC....1929
THOMAS....1930
THOMPSON & CAMPBELL....1930
THOMPSON....1930
THOMPSON/CENTER ARMS CO., INC....1932
PISTOLS: SINGLE SHOT....1932
RIFLES: BOLT ACTION....1934
RIFLES: SEMI-AUTO....1935
RIFLES: SINGLE SHOT....1936
SHOTGUNS: SINGLE SHOT....1938
THOR....1938
THUNDER-FIVE....1939
THUREON DEFENSE....1939
TIKKA....1940
TIMBERWOLF....1943
TIME PRECISION ARMS....1943
TIPPMAN ARMS CO....1944
TISAS....1944
TOKAREV....1944
TOLLEY, J & W....1944
TOMAHAWK....1944
TOMPKINS....1945
TORNADO....1945
TORUNARMS....1945
TOZ....1945
TRACKINGPOINT....1945
TRADEWINDS....1946
TRADITIONS PERFORMANCE FIREARMS....1946
TRANSFORMATIONAL DEFENSE INDUSTRIES, INC....1950
TRAVOR....1950
TRENCH/RIOT SHOTGUNS....1950
SHOTGUNS: MILITARY TRENCH, WWI....1950
SHOTGUNS: MILITARY RIOT/TRENCH, WWII....1951
SHOTGUNS: MILITARY RIOT/TRENCH, VIETNAM....1952
SHOTGUNS: RIOT/TRENCH GUN, COMMERCIAL SALES....1953
U.S. MILITARY SHOTGUN ACCESSORIES....1953
TRIPLE ACTION LLC....1954
TRISTAR SPORTING ARMS, LTD....1954
TROMIX CORPORATION....1961
TROY DEFENSE....1961
TRUVELO ARMOURY....1961
TULA ARMS PLANT....1961
TURKISH FIREARMS CORPORATION....1963
TURNBULL MANUFACTURING CO....1963
TURNER RICHARDS GUNMAKERS....1965

U

U.S. ARMAMENT CORP....1967
U.S. ARMS COMPANY....1967
U.S. GENERAL TECHNOLOGIES, INC....1967
U.S. HISTORICAL SOCIETY....1967
U.S. MILITARY HANDGUNS....1968
U.S. MILITARY LONG ARMS....1968
U.S. ORDNANCE....1970
USAS 12....1971
U.S.R.A....1971
USSG/U.S. SPORTING GOODS INC....1971
UBERTI, A. S.r.l....1971
UGARTECHEA, ARMAS....1980
UGARTECHEA, IGNACIO....1982
ULTIMATE....1985
ULTRA LIGHT ARMS, INC....1985
ULTRAMATIC....1986
UMAREX SPORTWAFFEN GmbH & Co. KG....1986
UNDERWOOD-ELLIOT-FISHER CORP....1986
UNERTL ORDNANCE COMPANY, INC....1986
UNIQUE....1986
UNIQUE-ALPINE....1988
UNITED SPORTING ARMS, INC....1988
UNITED STATES FIRE ARMS MFG. CO., INC./USFA...1990
UNIVERSAL FIREARMS....1994
USELTON ARMS INC....1996
UTAS....1996
UZI....1996

V

VM HY-TECH LLC 1999
VO VAPEN AB 1999
VAIL, ROY 1999
VALKYRIE ARMS LTD. 1999
VALMET 1999
VALMET, INC. 1999
VALOR ARMS 2001
VALTRO 2001
VAN DYKE RIFLE DESIGNS 2002
VARBERGER 2003
VARNER SPORTING ARMS, INC. 2004
VATAN HUNTING FIREARMS COMPANY 2004
VECTOR ARMS, INC. 2004
VEGA 2004
VEKTOR 2005
VEPR 2006
VERNEY-CARRON 2006
VERONA 2007
VICKERS LIMITED 2009
VICTOR ARMS CORPORATION 2009
VICTORY ARMS CO. LIMITED 2009
VIERLINGS 2010
VIGILANCE RIFLES 2010
VI-MA SNC. 2010
VINTAGE ORDNANCE COMPANY, LLC 2010
VIPER 2011
VIRGIN VALLEY CUSTOM GUNS 2011
VIRGINIAN 2011
VIS 2011
VLTOR WEAPON SYSTEMS 2011
VOERE (AUSTRIA) 2011
VOERE (GERMAN) 2012
VOLCANIC 2013
VOLKMANN PRECISION, LLC 2014
VOLQUARTSEN CUSTOM (LTD.) 2015
VOLTRAN 2017
VOLUNTEER ENTERPRISES 2017
VOUZELAUD 2018
VULCAN ARMAMENT, INC. 2018

W

W. SCHASCHL-OUTSCHAR GmbH 2021
WAFFEN GLATZ 2021
WAFFEN HIENDLMAYER 2021
WAFFEN JUNG GMBH 2021
WAFFEN KESSLER 2021
WAFFENFABRIK HEIN 2021
WAFFENSTUBE GUGGI 2021
WAFFEN, PRECHTL 2021
WAFFEN VERATSCHNIG 2022
WALTHER 2022
PISTOLS: SEMI-AUTO, PRE-WAR 2022
PISTOLS: SEMI-AUTO, POST-WAR 2027
PISTOLS: SEMI-AUTO, TARGET 2034
REVOLVERS 2035
RIFLES: DISC. 2035
RIFLES: CURRENT/RECENT MFG. 2037
SHOTGUNS: SxS 2037
SHOTGUNS: SEMI-AUTO 2037
WALTHER, FRENCH-MADE BY MANURHIN 2038
WAMO MFG. 2039
WARNER ARMS CORPORATION 2039
WASATCH PRECISION ARMS 2039
WATSON BROS. 2039
WEATHERBY 2039
WEAVER ARMS CORPORATION 2060
WEBLEY & SCOTT AG (LIMITED) 2061
WEIHRAUCH & WEIHRAUCH SPORT GmbH & CO. KG SPORTWAFFENFABRIK 2069
WEIHRAUCH, HERMANN REVOLVER GmbH 2069
WELLS 2069
WERNER BARTOLOT 2070
WESSON, FRANK 2070
WESSON & HARRINGTON 2071
DAN WESSON FIREARMS 2071
WESSON FIREARMS CO. INC. 2071
WESTERN ARMS COMPANY 2077
WESTERN FIELD 2077
WESTLEY RICHARDS & CO. LTD 2078
WHITNEY ARMS COMPANY 2081
WHITNEY FIREARMS COMPANY 2082
WHITWORTH 2082
WICHITA ARMS, INC. 2082
WICKLIFFE RIFLES 2083
WIDFORSS 2083
WIENER WAFFENFABRIK 2083
WIFRA 2084
WILD WEST GUNS 2084
WILDEY, INC. 2085
WILKES, JOHN GUNMAKERS LTD 2086
WILKINSON ARMS 2087
WILLIAM & SON 2088
WILLIAM DOUGLAS & SONS 2088
WILLIAM EVANS LIMITED 2089
WILLIAM LARKIN MOORE 2090
WILLIAM POWELL & SON (GUNMAKERS) LTD. 2090
WILSON COMBAT 2091

WINCHESTER 2096
WINCHESTER OVERVIEW 2097
GRADING EXPLANATION FOR WINCHESTER LEVER ACTIONS 2098
PISTOLS: SINGLE SHOT 2098
RIFLES: LEVER ACTIONS - 1860-1964 2099
RIFLES: SINGLE SHOT 2110
RIFLES: BOLT ACTION 2112
RIFLES: SEMI-AUTO 2117
RIFLES: SLIDE ACTION, DISC. 2119
RIFLES: LEVER ACTION - POST 1964 PRODUCTION 2121
RIFLES: LEVER ACTION - MODEL 94, 1964-2006 MFG. 2125
RIFLES: LEVER ACTION - MODELS 94 AND 1894, 2010-CURRENT 2131
RIFLES: BOLT ACTION - PRE-1964 MODEL 70 2132
RIFLES: BOLT ACTION - MODEL 70, 1964-2006 MFG. 2135
RIFLES: BOLT ACTION - POST 1964 MODEL 70 CUSTOM GRADES 2143
RIFLES: BOLT ACTION - MODEL 70, 2007-CURRENT MFG. ... 2147
COMBINATION GUNS 2148
RIFLES: O/U 2149
RIFLES: SINGLE SHOT, POST 1964 MFG. 2149
SHOTGUNS: 1879-1963 2149
SHOTGUNS: POST-1964 2158
Shotguns: Post-1964, Lever Action 2158
Shotguns: Post-1964, Semi-Auto 2158
Shotguns: Single Barrel 2163
SHOTGUNS: SLIDE ACTION, 1964-CURRENT 2163
SHOTGUNS: O/U - RECENT PRODUCTION 2170
SHOTGUNS: RECENT PRODUCTION SxS 2176
FACTORY WINCHESTER COMMEMORATIVES: U.S. PRODUCTION 2179
WINCHESTER COMMEMORATIVES: NON-DOMESTIC - 1970 TO DATE 2184
WINDHAM WEAPONRY 2185
WINSLOW ARMS COMPANY 2186
WISCHO JAGD-UND SPORTWAFFEN GmbH & CO. KG 2187
WISEMAN, BILL AND CO. 2187
WOLF SPORTING PISTOLS 2188
WOODWARD, JAMES AND SONS 2188
WYOMING ARMORY 2189
WYOMING ARMS MFG. CORP. 2189

X

XTREME MACHINING 2191

Y

YANKEE HILL MACHINE CO., INC. (YHM) 2191
YILDIZ SILAH SANAYI 2193

Z

Z-B RIFLE 2193
ZDF IMPORT EXPORT INC. 2194
Z-HAT CUSTOM 2194
Z-M WEAPONS 2194
ZVI 2194
ZABALA HERMANOS, S.A. 2194
ZANARDINI 2194
ZANOTTI 2196
ZANOTTI, R. 2197
ZASTAVA ARMS 2198
ZBROJOVKA BRNO 2199
ZELENY SPORT s.r.o. 2199
ZEPHYR 2199
ZIEGENHAHN & SOHN OHG 2200
ZOLI, ANGELO 2200
ZOLI, ANTONIO 2203

Trademark Index 2,209-2,265
Glossary 2,266-2,287
Abbreviations 2,288-2,291
Museums 2,292
Firearms/Shooting Organizations 2,293-2,299
Hunting Heritage Trust 2,300
Conservation Organizations 2,301
Reference Sources 2,302-2,304
Periodicals 2,305-2,308
Store Brand Cross-Over Listings 2,309-2,315
Serialization 2,316-2,360
Proof Marks 2,361-2,367
BATFE Guide 2,368
BATFE Curios and Relics Listings 2,369-2,384
Show Time! 2,385
Index 2,386-2,407
P.S. 2,408

P.S. SIG SMART!

Smart guns are back! Even James Bond in the recent *Skyfall* movie uses an extensively modified Walther PPK/S with advanced biometrics in the grips to make sure the bad guys can't use his weapon against him. This smart Sig was manufactured by J.P. Sauer in limited quantities in early 2000.

In early 2000, SIG unveiled the P229 EPLS (Electronic Personal Lock System) in .40 S&W. Based on an M229, the prototype pistols came with a completely redesigned frame whose forward extension housed a battery-powered electronic keypad. Though the shipping box had an English language label, the gun was accompanied by a four-page German language instruction booklet. A separate sheet specified the weapon-specific master code and PIN.

To activate, the user had to punch in his/her PIN and then indicate the operational time slot. Standard settings were reflected by button A (123) .5 hour, button B (456) 2 hours, or button C (789) 8 hours. Button D (0SR) was used for the number "0," "Save," or "Reset." If the PIN number was entered incorrectly three times, as might easily happen in a stressful, off-duty situation, the gun would lockup, pending the input of a master code. Changing the program allowed the active period options to be changed to 1 hour or indefinitely, circumventing the entire concept.

As the keypad was battery driven, there had to be warning lights. So as the code and hour preferences were entered, a light would blink. A green light reflected battery function. Yellow reflected that the gun was on safe or that the code had been entered incorrectly. A red light meant that the pistol was operational or that there was a malfunction. Removing the battery, or a dead battery, kept the gun in its last operational state.

Concerning these prototypes, suffice to say that the engineers who had previously developed the "best of the best" were long retired. It must have taken very little time to determine that the P229 EPLS was a totally impractical answer to the original question. Too bulky, too complicated, and likely needing too many batteries or replacement keypads, the EPLS project was quietly shelved after only 15-20 test guns were manufactured by J.P. Sauer in Germany. Only now, many years later, have a handful of examples come to light.

Information and image courtesy of Leonardo M. Antaris, M.D., noted author and long-time contributing editor to the Blue Book of Gun Values.